THE
DICTIONARY
OF
NEW ZEALAND
ENGLISH

The foundations of the dictionary were laid by these family
members, mentors, and friends to whom much more than
thanks is due

Teresa and William Orsman, Elizabeth Orsman
Professor Philip S. Ardern, Professor Ian A. Gordon
Harry Singh Gajadhar, Ruth Mason

The completion of this dictionary was
made possible by a substantial grant from
THE NEW ZEALAND LOTTERY GRANTS BOARD

THE DICTIONARY OF NEW ZEALAND ENGLISH

A DICTIONARY OF NEW ZEALANDISMS
ON HISTORICAL PRINCIPLES

Edited by H.W. Orsman

Auckland
Oxford University Press
Oxford Melbourne New York

OXFORD UNIVERSITY PRESS NEW ZEALAND
Oxford New York
Athens Auckland Bangkok Bogota Bombay
Buenos Aires Calcutta Cape Town Dar es Salaam
Delhi Florence Hong Kong Istanbul Karachi
Kuala Lumpur Madras Madrid Melbourne
Mexico City Nairobi Paris Port Moresby
Singapore Taipei Tokyo Toronto Warsaw
and associated companies in
Berlin Ibadan

OXFORD is a trade mark of Oxford University Press

Copyright © 1997 H. W. Orsman
First published 1997
Reprinted 1997

All rights reserved. No part of this publication may
be reproduced, stored in a retrieval system or
transmitted, in any form or by any means, without
the prior permission in writing of Oxford University
Press. Within New Zealand, exceptions are allowed
in respect of any fair dealing for the purpose of
research or private study, or criticism or review, as
permitted under the Copyright Act 1994, or, in the
case of reprographic reproduction, in accordance
with the terms of the licences issued by Copyright
Licensing Limited. Enquiries concerning
reproduction outside these terms and in other
countries should be sent to the Rights Department,
Oxford University Press, at the address below.

ISBN 0 19 558347 7 Hardback edition
ISBN 0 19 558380 9 Leather-bound edition

Edited by Simon Cauchi
Typeset by Egan-Reid Ltd, Auckland
Printed through Oxford University Press China
Published by Oxford University Press
540 Great South Road, Greenlane, PO Box 11-149
Auckland, New Zealand

Proprietary names
This dictionary includes some words that are, or are
asserted to be, proprietary names or trade marks.
Their inclusion does not imply that they have
acquired for legal purposes a non-proprietary or
general significance, nor is any other judgment
implied concerning their legal status. In cases where
the editor has some evidence that a word is used as a
proprietary name or trade mark this is indicated, but
no judgment concerning the legal status of such
words is made or implied thereby.

CONTENTS

Editorial staff and benefactors	vi
Introduction	vii
Layout and style of entries	x
General abbreviations	xii
Pronunciation	xv
DICTIONARY	1
List of written sources	933

EDITORIAL STAFF

Executive Editor
    Jean Malcolmson (1989–91)

Advisory Editors
    Desmond E. Hurley (*Supervising Editor*)
    Bernadette Hince (*Consulting Editor*)

    John E. Dowding (*Birds*)
    John P. Egan (*Education*)
    C.M. King (*Mammals*)
    R.M. McDowall (*Freshwater Fish*)
    Elaine C. Murphy (*Birds*)
    Larry J. Paul (*Sea Fish*)
    Wendy Pond (*Insects*)
    Peter Ranby (*Maori Language*)
    Maggy C. Wassilieff (*Plants*)

Editorial Advisers
    J.W. Dawson (*Plants*)
    R.K. Dell (*Shellfish*)
    Robin Elliott (*Small Craft*)

    Alison J. McLeod (*Bibliography*)
    W.H. Oliver (*History*)
    Joseph Romanos (*Sport*)
    Paul Vella (*Geology*)
    A.H. Whitaker (*Reptiles*)

Senior Copy Editors
    Melissa J. Gough
    Maria Verivakis

Computing Assistant
    Alvin M. Jackson

Editorial and Research Assistants
    E.J. Berry, D. Borthwick, E.J. Browning, I.J. Godfrey, J. Hurley, M. Hurley,
    R.J. Kirby, R. Lasenby, C.J. McKay, E.G. Moffitt, M.G. Neazor,
    E.M. Orsman, S.S. Pietkiewicz, J. Pringle, C.L. Simpson, H. Small

Data Entry Assistants
    Thavry Chea, Lynn de Malmanche, Stephanie Diamond, Luisa E. Fruean,
    Mariella Paceco

BENEFACTORS

Mere words cannot express the depth of my thanks to the very many people and institutions whose help of various kinds has improved this dictionary, especially to the New Zealand Lottery Grants Board without whose timely aid it might not have seen the light of day, to the dictionary staff, and to the numerous wellwishers, acknowledged by name in the body of the dictionary, who have over many years provided quotations, commentary, and encouragement.

My particular thanks to the dedicatees who each in their own way gave that primal support and encouragement in exactly those times and places where they were needed; to Jim Cameron, Les Cleveland, Roy Gilberd, George Griffiths, Des Hurley, Bob Lamb, Charles Ransom, and Janet Woolcott for valuable, practical help; to Dr W.S. Ramson, editor of *The Australian National Dictionary*, for friendly, detailed advice arising from a critical appraisal of a draft of the whole dictionary, and to Bruce Moore, his successor as Director of the Australian National Dictionary Centre; to the editorial staff who worked on the dictionary; to those institutions and people who provided research funds—the former University of New Zealand and its successor, the University Grants Committee, for a two-year research fellowship (1951–52) and funds for equipment; the New Zealand Lottery Grants Board (1989) for accepting the dictionary as an official 1990s centenary project and supporting it with a magnificent grant enabling the finalization of the collections; Victoria University of Wellington for various research grants and for colleagues in the English Department (in particular, my fellow medievalists Christine Franzen, Robert Easting, Ian Jamieson and Kathryn Walls) who gave me relief from teaching at the expense of their own time and energy; to the librarians and staff of the Alexander Turnbull Library, General Assembly Library, National Library, Victoria University of Wellington Library (especially to Kathleen Coleridge, Special Materials Librarian, and Lynette Lowe, Periodicals Librarian), the Museum of New Zealand, the (former) New Zealand Oceanographic Institute, the *Evening Post* Library (Wellington) and the Hocken Library (Dunedin), for fundamental help willingly and kindly given; to secondary teachers who administered the slang questionnaire, and those students who completed it; to Oxford University Press in New Zealand and Britain, especially to the New Zealand Publishers Anne French and Linda Cassells and the falcon-eyed proofreader Simon Cauchi; and by no means least, to the following who offered substantial help or who responded to sometimes arcane and often time-consuming requests (I apologize for any omissions): Ruth Ainsworth, John Andrews, James Herries Beattie, Jamie Belich, Bruce Biggs, Sharon Blaikie, David and Motoko Boardman, William Broughton, Goldie Brown, Alistair and Meg Campbell, Peter Chaney, Ross Clark, Mary Cleveland, Frank Climo, Chris Corne, Mary Cresswell, Jack Cummings, Susan Cuthbert, Elliott Dawson, Patrick Downey, Arthur Duncan, Brian Easton, Miles Fairburn (especially for access to copies of the James Cox diaries), Elaine Geering, Russell Grey, Neil Grove, Chris Harfoot, Arthur Helm, Noel Hilliard, Grant Hodgson, Jim Hollyman, Wiremu Kaa, Philip Knight, Mike Leon, Bill Manhire, Bruce Marshall, Peter Newton, James Ng, H.M. Ngata, David Norton, Blaise and Christopher Orsman, Vincent O'Sullivan, Andrew Pawley, Arthur Pomeroy, Bruce Popplewell, Bill Pearson, Dr S.R. Pennycook, Renée, James Ritchie, Chris Robertson, Jeff Sheerin, Jennifer Shennan, David Simmers, Keith Sinclair, Barry Smith, Kendrick Smithyman, Barry Sneddon, John E.P. Thomson, John Mansfield Thomson, George Turner, Pat Walsh, and W.A. Watters. Those who set up and supported the computerization of the dictionary deserve special thanks: Colin Boswell and Frank March, past and present Directors of Victoria University's Information Technology Services and members of their staff, especially Jim Baltaxe, Janet Boutel, Nathan Cottle, Annette Garcia, Jim Gellen, Alex Heatley, Frank Jansen, Margaret King, Ruth Mansford, Michael Newbery, Joy Ng, Andrew Greer, and Murray Robb.

INTRODUCTION

Scope of the Dictionary

The Dictionary of New Zealand English records the history of words and particular senses of words which are in some way distinctively or predominantly, though not always exclusively, 'New Zealand' in meaning or use. It is a regional dictionary of 'New Zealandisms',[1] themselves only a small, but very important, part of any New Zealander's total vocabulary. Included are not only words originating in New Zealand (for example, loans from Maori) but also a large group of words used elsewhere but having in New Zealand a significantly different meaning or application (*station, run*) or a wider or more frequent common or everyday use (for example, original British dialect *skerrick*). This group also includes words having a special significance for our history (*flax-trader*, a whaling and goldmining usage), society (*pioneer*), or physical environment (*fern*), with a further special wide-ranging set of those shared with Australia (*bonzer, Clayton's, wowser*).

Nature of the Dictionary

The principle of arrangement is historical. The subdivisions of each entry are laid out chronologically from earliest to latest, as are the groups of supporting quotations. Such a method is not only a structural convenience; it also allows a clear view both of the components of the New Zealand English lexis and of its development from essentially 19th century origins as a language of an immigrant minority of varied and often far from respectable elements.[2] This situation quickly changed with the arrival of successive waves of European immigrants who soon outnumbered the Maori-speaking majority, to become by the mid-1880s in their turn outnumbered by the non-Maori New Zealand born.[3]

New Zealand English was one result of a human and linguistic hotch-potch. Pioneer immigrants, mainly rural in outlook and intention, were confronted with a vast array of new plants and animals, landscape features, aboriginal forms and artefacts, for which they had to find names. To this descriptive 'Adamizing' they also had to add terms for new experiences in outdoor living—in farming, in coping with the novelty and isolation not of Paradise but of 'the Antipodes' (a common English name applied only to the Australasian colonies)—with 'bush', 'creek' and 'gully' replacing 'woods', 'brook' and 'vale'. But, unlike the original Adam and Eve, they could at least invoke and re-apply 'Home' patterns in different ways, could use and vary the older Australian 'colonial experience' as a local guide, and above all could draw on an established, comprehensive store of Maori names—enabling a parallel use of both Maori and English for the names of plants and animals (and places) which persists to the present.

New Zealanders have developed, too, a lively habit of innovation demonstrated clearly in the processes of compounding (*gumdiggers' soap, Taranaki gate*) and composition (*Maoridom, New Zealandism*). A few elements form a host of compounds (*bush-, Maori, New Zealand, wool-*; or the ubiquitous *-ie* (or *y*) ending used to indicate familiar usage—*cockie, footie, Pommie*). Some elements by their obsolescence illustrate changes in our language and society (*native*, for example, has in many of its uses been replaced by *Maori* or *New Zealand*); and other more recent coinages (some so 'ordinary' as to be not easily recognized as New Zealandisms) illustrate the variety and ongoing nature of such creativity—*bush-clad, chocolate fish, dog-dosing, Instant Kiwi, Peggy square, quarter-acre section, solo mum, tar-seal, wage round*. It is with this kind of everyday innovation added to ongoing bilingual interchange with Maori that the future of a distinctive written and spoken New Zealand English lies.

Origin and Methodology of the Dictionary

The Dictionary of New Zealand English is the product of both 'hard yacker' (in all senses of the word) and the support and encouragement of very many people, especially those named in the dedication. The project began in 1951 as a Ph.D. topic 'The English Language in New Zealand' under the supervision of Professor I.A. Gordon and supported by a research fellowship from the now defunct University of New Zealand (1951–52) and a tutorship in English in 1953. At first I had little idea of what constituted 'New Zealand English'. My main guides were Sidney J. Baker's *New Zealand Slang* and the New Zealand entries in Edward Morris's *Austral-English* and Eric Partridge's *Dictionary of Slang and Unconventional English*. I hit upon the idea of verifying Baker's collection in the sources he quoted, and arranging the results, mainly quotations, in the manner of the *Oxford English Dictionary* and *Austral-English*. I had now empirically if rather shakily in hand the prerequisites of successful historical lexicography: the establishing and defining of sources, and from them building up an evidential body of quotations. Indeed the primal or implicit working definition of 'New Zealand English' was those items or that usage not exactly found outside defined sources. The Baker list led to further sampling of a wide range of books written in or about New Zealand. At this point I was introduced to Dr Hocken's *Bibliography of the Literature Relating to New Zealand*, to the catalogues of the Alexander Turnbull and General Assembly Libraries, and to the kindness and expertise of librarians. I read as my first major newspaper sample the files of the *Evening Post* from the 1860s to 1940, and dipped into various early and later periodicals (discovering by the way the name and nature of the 'A to Js'), before settling down to a long stretch of scanning methodically everything which looked promising in my bibliographies or, as opportunity offered, on library shelves. Before the advent of convenient photocopying, much material had to be copied out by hand. A good deal of this early reading later proved comparatively unproductive and had to be done again because at the time I had no clear idea what I was looking for. My sights were probably then set too directly on the obvious—the 'bush', 'boohai' and 'station' words; or on the unconventional and colloquial, much of which proved to be international rather than regional New Zealand English. I learnt also that I had time only to read for specifics: interesting or peripherally relevant material could only be noted for possible consideration later. Besides headword slips, I developed a topical index of linguistic and other useful references, and a chronological index

---

[1] The language of the keen outdoorsman, for example, illustrates the need for some glossing as in: 'They cooed out, and while he skinned a spiker they found a possie in a bit of a trog and boiled up.' (*Listener* 19 Apr. 1971, p.56).

[2] The American, John B. Williams, writes of Kororareka in 1844: 'From the Police Office to the dealers in liquid fire, "inmates of the abysmal depths of purgatory" where they are not only pugnacious, but deal out blows with sticks, clubs, deadly weapons, gouging out each others eyes, literally tearing their flesh to pieces, perniciously and willfully shouting, "Im a man! Im an Englishman! I'll tear your bloody guts out! I'll drink your hearts blood," pronouncing the most obscene, filthy, blasphemous language, that no words I can express can depict in living colors the most arrant oaths that ever could be uttered by mortal man.' (*The New Zealand Journal of John B. Williams of Salem*, ed. Robert W. Kenny, 1956, p.69). Julius von Haast writes of Westland during the goldrushes c. 1865: 'Everywhere the English language would of course be heard in its principal dialects, as well as German, Italian, Greek, and French, and several other tongues.' (*Geology of the Provinces of Canterbury and Westland*, 1879, p.87).

[3] The English-speaking non-Maori resident population from a base of probably less than a hundred in 1800, and possibly about 2,000 by 1840, had by the 1857–58 Census increased to about 60,000 to outnumber the Maori. At some time between 1881 and 1886 the non-Maori native-born in the total population outnumbered the immigrants; by the 1911 Census the non-Maori urban population (50.4 percent) had exceeded the rural. According to W.D. McIntyre and W.J. Gardner (*Speeches and Documents on New Zealand History*, 1961, p.462) 'There have been six periods of marked increase in the European population of New Zealand from immigration: (i) c. 1846–55: organized settlement by the N.Z. Company and its associates; (ii) the early 1860s: gold rushes in the South Island; (iii) the 1870s: assisted immigration under the 'Vogel' schemes; (iv) c. 1900–14: farming prosperity and some industrial growth; (v) the 1920s: participation in British immigration schemes; (vi) post-1945: industrial expansion. New Zealand's immigrants have been, until recently..overwhelmingly British... There has been significant trans-Tasman exchange of migrants, especially in the 1860s, the period c. 1885–93, and in the 1960s, with two periods of loss to Australia (1885–91 and 1967–8) [and during the 1980s].'

made up of my notes on every substantial item read, arranged in order of date of publication.

Quotations were recorded on paper 'slips' of standard size which included the 'headword' to be illustrated and the date and details of the source. In 1952, with some thousands of the slips collected and sorted, a start could be made on checking each headword and each of its separate senses against those in the main international, regional, slang, technical, etc. dictionaries of English: the *OED*, Joseph Wright's *English Dialect Dictionary*, Eric Partridge's *Dictionary of Slang and Unconventional English*, Milton Mathews's *Dictionary of Americanisms*, and the Craigie and Hulbert *Dictionary of American English*. It was this exercise of lexical comparison which induced a very real appreciation of what New Zealand English (and lexicography) might be and, most importantly, of where the immediate and ultimate sources of its constituents might lie. Much of the headword collection was discarded at this stage as being part of international English, or as non-significant borrowing from other regional Englishes. The method could now be refined to better acknowledge or reflect, for words used elsewhere in English, those often slight shifts in meanings and usage which are at the heart of a New Zealand dialect. The collection and culling process was started again, much more knowledgeably. It has been the operational mode ever since.

By early 1953, there existed a nucleus—a 'ring-binder' dictionary of draft entries with supporting quotations written out on loose-leaf sheets, and a growing supplement of carded quotations and entries—but still no realistic conception of a completed *Dictionary of New Zealand English*. I had also by this time amassed material on New Zealand phonology and pronunciation (an account of which was part of the original intention) from a study of the few existing published sources (for example, the detailed account given by Samuel McBurney, 'Australasian South Eastern—a Comparative Table of Australasian Pronunciation' in A.J. Ellis's *On Early English Pronunciation* (1887) V. 236ff.), from many hours of analysis the 'Boys Overseas' messages sent home by soldiers during WW2, and from forays with a massive 'Sound Mirror' tape recorder around (I hoped) a dialect-ridden countryside.[4] There was as well considerable material on the representation of Maori loanwords in early non-standard transliterations. Later this phonological material was realistically dropped in favour of a purely lexical study.

As the collection grew over the years, so did the difficulty of dealing with it on the usual basis of part-time research among many other competing activities. (The years 1954–58 were spent in the New Zealand Forest Service; 1959 studying for a Diploma of Public Administration; in 1960 I returned to university teaching.) In the early 1970s I prepared a large selection of New Zealand items for what became *The Macquarie Dictionary* (published 1981), and in the late 1970s edited the *Heinemann New Zealand Dictionary* (published 1979, 2edn, 1989)—tasks which further clarified my notions of a New Zealand lexis. And though I had a great deal of help and support, there was no real hope of finalizing a complete *Dictionary of New Zealand English* until computerization was introduced to the project in the early 1980s, an event which coincided with the Government's introduction of the Project Employment Programme (PEP) training scheme for young out-of-work people. This scheme paid for the training and wages of trainee computer operators, who, given basic instruction by Annette Garcia and Janet Boutel of Victoria University's Computing Services Centre, eventually transferred the masses of material to the University's IBM mainframe using a SCRIPT word-processing program. Later, with advances in computer technology, and the decommissioning of the IBM mainframe in 1991, *DNZE* staff, notably Alvin Jackson, devised ways of transferring the original IBM-processed (ASCII) material to desk-top personal computers and a VAX mainframe, allowing the continued use of ASCII text as the editing medium and a Wordperfect processor for printed hard copy.

The 1980s were in other ways fruitful. There was helpful contact with Dr W.S. Ramson, editor of *The Australian National Dictionary* (and a Victoria University graduate), and in 1986 the opportunity to read through drafts of *The Australian National Dictionary* to supply any New Zealand predating of shared headwords. This was a most valuable and reassuring exercise which also allowed Australian first datings of shared entries to be incorporated in the *DNZE*. Early in 1988 an agreement was finalized with New House Publishers of Auckland to edit a selective dictionary (eventually undertaken and completed with Elizabeth Orsman as *The New Zealand Dictionary* (1994)), and later that year Oxford University Press, which had in the 1960s been given access to earlier card entries for inclusion in the supplements to the *Oxford English Dictionary*, renewed, through its New Zealand Publisher Anne French, an interest in the publication of a full New Zealand dictionary on historical principles. Two other major projects were completed during 1986–89: the *Heinemann Dictionary of New Zealand Quotations* (1988) and a fully revised second edition of the *Heinemann New Zealand Dictionary* (1989).

Near the end of the 1980s the dictionary comprised a large number of draft entries, a profusion of unprocessed quotations, and much other material awaiting final verification and editing. Though the Research Fund of Victoria University was as generous as a restricted budget permitted, this massive task was only made possible by the Hon. Michael Bassett's acceptance of the *DNZE* as a 1990 sesquicentenary project enabling a generous grant of $275,000 from the New Zealand Lottery Grants Board. The grant allowed the employment during 1989–91 of highly qualified specialists to check and edit floral, faunal, Maori, and other subject areas, a Science Editor (Dr D.E. Hurley) to coordinate this work (in early consultation with Ms Bernadette Hince, the Science Editor of *The Australian National Dictionary*), and an Executive Editor with linguistic training and administrative experience (Mrs Jean Malcolmson) to oversee the work of a large staff engaged in transferring a large output to disk, accurately and according to a consistent style. This last involved extensive checking and cross-checking against both original and dictionary sources of the basic material collected, proofreading, and a further substantial culling of excess material. I was able to devote almost full time to dictionary work during this busy period by the kindness of English Department staff who took over much of my teaching.

During 1992–93, with the Lottery money almost spent, part-time and freely given help enabled entries to be finalized, quotations to be trimmed or discarded, gaps to be filled, and consistency and accuracy of datelines and general layout to be minutely checked. In this respect, the editorial work of Melissa Gough and the many unpaid hours donated by Dr Hurley in verifying quotations and searching out additional quotations proved invaluable. A 'peer-reading' undertaken by Dr Ramson on behalf of Oxford University Press was also of great value both in its attention to detail and its confirmation of the method and worth of the work as a whole.

The *DNZE* now comprises (approximately) 6,000 main headword entries (700-odd from Maori, and, including sub-entries, some 370 from British dialect use including 60 from Scottish, and some 700 shared with Australian English), with 9,300 separate sub-entries for different senses and uses. Many of these sub-entries themselves comprise groups of the numerous compound words ('combinations' and 'collocations' of *bush* or *Maori* for example, and 'compositions' such as *New Zealandism*) which make up a large part of the New Zealand vocabulary. In addition there are over 1,900 entries for cross-references and spelling variants, making a grand total of nearly 8,000 headword entries of all kinds.

Senses and uses of headwords are supported by some 47,000 quotations (384 from the eighteenth century, 12,500 from the nineteenth, and 34,000 from the twentieth) taken from a reading of some 4,200 written sources (newspapers are not separately listed) as well as oral and questionnaire material. Quotations are an essential part of any historical dictionary method, generating or validating meanings (definitions *must* be read in the context of their quotations), establishing the chronology of a word's use, and providing a guide to usage and register thus reducing the need for labels (*slang, colloq.,* etc.).

The quotations printed are often highly select: only about a quarter to a third of the material collected has been used. The plan at first was to give where possible a quotation for every decade, and to illustrate a full range of early spellings, particularly for adopted Maori words. Exigencies of space forced a modification: for common words whose spelling and meaning has been stable for the last hundred years a few only quotations have been given since say the 1880s. A thousand or so variant spellings have been listed as headwords but not all of them are illustrated by quotation. On the other hand, for many 'informal' New Zealand words and other 'unceremonious' usage from before the Second World War, a single quotation is the only written evidence available and has to suffice, occasionally strengthened by reference to oral sources or editorial recall.

The names of plants and animals are included in the dictionary if their referents breed on, are found on, or are associated with mainland New Zealand or

---

[4] There was also a small regret. I had looked forward to reading a copy of a thesis completed in 1930 by J.W. Shaw, a lecturer in English at Auckland Teachers Training College, entitled 'New Zealand speech: A study in development and tendency' (University of New Zealand registration number 228). His widow told me that it had been rejected as an unsuitable topic by the University of Auckland's Department of Education and then destroyed by its disappointed author.

its offshore islands defined as those between Campbell Island in the south (but for some items including the Australian Macquarie Island), the Kermadec group in the north, and the Chatham group in the east. Some 1,100 species are defined and their common names illustrated. The latest accepted scientific names have been used in the definitions, and synonyms noted. Superseded names which may appear in quotations are often indicated in definitions by 'formerly'. Family names have been given to show broad relationships, otherwise possibly obscured, between New Zealand and non-New Zealand genera.

Entries have been selected and written mindful of the needs of a regional dictionary addressed primarily to New Zealand users. Except for acronyms (which as a rule have been omitted), the policy has been to include rather than exclude, especially in admitting entries for words which, though used elsewhere, have significance for our history or society. This has been done always keeping in mind an implicit larger context of international English supplied pre-eminently by the *OED* and (most recently) the *New Shorter Oxford Dictionary*, but also by the *Merriam-Webster Third International Dictionary*, in a smaller way from a New Zealand point of view, by the *Heinemann New Zealand Dictionary*, and by comprehensive specialist dictionaries such as Partridge's *Dictionary of Slang and Unconventional English*. In particular, etymological material has been limited to that immediately relevant to an entry, often with a reference to a corresponding entry in the *OED* (or elsewhere) when this would supply a larger context of use or history, or an ultimate etymology. At the same time, the special relationship with Australian English is continually recognized by including in the etymological section (usually from W.S. Ramson's *Australian National Dictionary*) comparative datings of shared words and senses, and information about Australian (especially Aboriginal) origins. Loan-words from Maori are treated especially fully. Each is accompanied by early variant spellings, a standard spelling and sense referenced to H.W. Williams's *Dictionary of the Maori Language* (7edn. 1971 (1975)), its pronunciation in Maori, and for some entries the earliest recorded written Maori use. Anglicized pronunciations are given only when clearly evidenced by written forms and/or judged editorially to be (or to have been) frequently or widely used.

LAYOUT AND STYLE OF ENTRIES

An entry may be simple (a single word with a single meaning recorded as one part of speech) or complex, with multiple meanings or with major subdivisions to cover multiple parts of speech (see *Ordering of senses* below), each further subdivided according to its various meanings if it has more than one, thence according to its various uses in compounds, phrases, or derivatives. Compounds, whether spelt as one or two words or hyphenated, make up a very large part of the dictionary, and are usually presented as sequences or groups of *combinations* (noun + noun) or *collocations* (adjective + noun) when their referents are no more than the sum of the parts (for example, **bush-bird** at BUSH C 2 a); or as *special combinations* or *special collocations* when their referents taken together are more than, or independent of, the sum of their parts and indicate that a particular compound is a distinct lexical item (for example, **bush baptist** at BUSH C 3 d). Some of the latter achieve separate headword status (for example, **bush lawyer**).

The Order of an Entry

The parts of an entry (not all of which may be needed in any particular entry) appear in the following order.

Headword and 'preferred' headword. The word which is the subject of the entry appears at its head in **bold roman** type face, as it does in any subordinate entries (*combinations*, etc.) of which it is the main element. It will most often be the 'preferred headword', that is, one which is either (1) the preferred current form or use (for example, **tui** rather than **parson-bird**, **fantail** rather than **flycatcher** or **piwakawaka**) in terms of which synonymous forms indicated by 'See also [...]' will be defined; and/or (2) a standard spelling to which any variant spellings are referred.

Note: • Initial capitals are used only with words which normally take them, e.g. those entries derived from place-names or proper names.
• Superscript numerals distinguish two or more headwords having the same spelling.

Pronunciation. A commonly heard New Zealand English pronunciation, when given, follows the headword. Pronunciations are phonemic, are marked off by slashes, and are presented in International Phonetic Alphabet notation, according to a system devised by the Department of Linguistics, Victoria University of Wellington (see the *Pronunciation* table on page xv). The values, especially that of stress, are those of the words pronounced in isolation. All Maori-derived words have also within the etymology an indication of a standard pronunciation in Maori, but except in some traditional, well-attested cases, no attempt has been made to suggest modern anglicized pronunciations.

Part of speech. If a word is recorded only as a noun, and there is no other noun of the same form, no part of speech is given. Otherwise the part of speech, in abbreviated form and italicized, follows next after the headword or the pronunciation guide. Separate headword entries are given to nominal and verbal forms of the same word, with the noun entry usually preceding the verb unless the logic of the word's history demands otherwise.

Labels. Descriptive labels (designating an occupation, etc.) and restrictive labels such as *Obs.* (obsolete), *Hist.* (now only in an historical context), *SI* (used mainly in the South Island) are printed in italics with an initial capital, except in run-on entries (of special combinations, for example) where those which are not proper names have a lower-case initial.

Variant spellings. A selection of non-standard variant spellings introduced by 'Also (with much variety of form) as [...]' are given in **bold roman** after the preferred headword between the part of speech and the etymology. Such variants, mainly early anglicizations of Maori-derived words, are not always illustrated by quotations; each, however, is given a discrete headword entry cross-referenced to the headword of which it is a variant (for example, **boo-eye**, var. BOOHAI). Variation in the use of hyphens or initial capitals is regarded as non-significant.

Etymology. Etymological information, enclosed in square brackets, aims to establish an immediate source for an entry rather than an ultimate connection which is often more properly explored in dictionaries of wider or of specialist reference.

An etymology which applies to all senses of a word precedes any numbered or lettered subdivision. One which applies to a specific sense follows the enumerator for that sense, or (in the case of grouped special combinations or collocations) the second element of the combination. The primary word which is the basis of the derived word or sense is given in *italics*, unless it is also a headword entry, in which case it is given in SMALL ROMAN CAPITALS. For words derived from Maori the etymology includes a standard Maori pronunciation and spelling and an indication of where its underlying Maori form and sense may be found in H.W. Williams, *Dictionary of the Maori Language* (7edn 1971).

Ordering of senses. General senses within an entry are arranged chronologically. Entries consisting of more than one part of speech are divided into major sections indicated by bold roman capitals (thus **A.** *n.* **1.** etc.; **B.** *a.* **1.** etc.; **C.** *adv.*). The numerous common names for multiple species of plants and animals, usually consisting of *modifier +(headword) noun*, have been treated as belonging primarily with the noun entry, not with the modifier entry. Thus *black cod*, *Cloudy Bay cod*, etc. are defined and illustrated in a consolidated sub-entry of **cod**, with only a cross-reference at **black, Cloudy Bay**. The arrangement for such headwords with distinctive simplex and complex forms will usually be: sub-entry **1.** the simplex form (for example, **cod 1.**) followed by a sub-entry (usually **2.**) presenting the complex forms in alphabetical order of modifier in subdivisions enumerated (1), (2), (3) etc., further subdivided if need be into **a.**, etc.: see the entries **beech**, or **cod** for examples. (The exceptions are **beetle, butterfly, moth, prion, quail**, the simplex forms of which are rarely used distinctively in New Zealand English.)

Definitions. A definition may comprise merely another (synonymous) headword (usually the preferred current name) presented in small capitals often with a specific alpha-numeric reference—thus **piwakawaka** is defined as FANTAIL 1. It may be a sub-entry of a headword presented in italics followed by its headword reference—thus **coal-fish** is defined as *blue cod* (COD 2 (3)); or it may merely comprise the italic sub-entry alone if it, also, is a subordinate item of the same headword—thus under **wool 3** the combination *wool-baron* is defined simply as *wool-king*, an item in the same entry group.

Cross-references. Copious cross-referencing aims to associate often bizarre spelling forms with their originals; and to associate words of like meaning or use. The main entries for compound names of plant and animal species made up of *modifier + noun* are given under their second or noun element (see *Ordering of senses* above). All first elements of such compounds, except the epithets *common* and *wild*, have been separately cross-referenced and the most frequent (for example, **native, New Zealand, red**) are given consolidated sub-entries under a separate headword.

Note: • 'See also [...]' after the definition of a preferred headword introduces a list of its synonyms, the entry for each of which will simply quote the preferred headword as the definition (see, for example, the entry **tui**).
• Occasionally a particular headword is subsumed for the purposes of definition and illustration under a more general entry to which it will be referred using the formula 'see [...]' (for example, **tramperess**: see TRAMPER 1; **treatment-station**: see *milk-treatment station* (MILK)).
• *q.v.* after a headword in an explanatory context refers the user to a related entry containing a fuller discussion of the matter in hand: e.g. 'BUSH q.v.' in entry FOREST[1] refers the reader to a note on the comparative uses of 'bush', 'forest', 'woods'.

Quotations. Select quotations validate the definitions and illustrate the history of a word's use. The principles of selection are: the earliest and latest (or last) dated quotations are essential, as is a reasonable scatter between these. Choice of any quotation takes into account informativeness, relevance, brevity, intrinsic interest, and illustration of early spelling variation. The paucity of written sources, especially for early colloquial language, has meant that single-quotation entries are more frequent than might be ideally wished; occasionally, oral evidence has been noted. For words derived from Maori the earliest known written record is often quoted—within square brackets if the reference is purely to use in Maori.

Note: • A quotation is preceded by a 'dateline' giving the date of (usually)

written, but occasionally of oral publication and a brief reference to the source (volume numbers are in uppercase Roman numerals, issue or part numbers in lower case Roman numerals) which, when used with the *List of Written Sources* (see p.935), will allow any quotation to be verified and a larger context discovered.
- Authors of items from collections or periodicals are not usually named.
- Quotations are given as they appear in the source except that punctuation relative to quotation marks follows modern usage; and, guided by the practice of the *OED*, irrelevant material is omitted in the interests of brevity or elegance, where there is no risk of interfering with the author's intentions. Medial ellipsis is indicated by '..'; or by '...' when it includes a stop. Initial and final ellipses are not indicated: thus, except for a few from glossaries, titles, etc., all quotations, conventionally, begin with an initial capital and end with a stop.
- Non-standard spellings and other oddities are marked with [*sic*] only if they could be taken as errors of transcription. Until the mid-19th century non-standard spellings were very common in holograph journals, logs, etc.
- Following Oxford University Press house style (see *Hart's Rules*, pp. 84–86), editorial matter (which includes the headwords) prefers the spelling **-ize** to **-ise** as a verbal ending in cases where *both* spellings are in use (e.g. *standardize*); similarly **-ization** rather than **-isation**. Quotations of course follow the spelling of their originals.

GENERAL ABBREVIATIONS

Abbreviations are listed in the form in which they most commonly occur; those printed in italics may in some contexts be in roman and vice versa. Abbreviations may similarly be printed with or without an initial capital, as the context requires.

a (before a date)	*ante*, before
AAW	*Aboriginal Australian Words* (Dixon, Ramson, Thomas 1990)
a./adj.	adjective(s)
abbrev.	abbreviation (of), abbreviated (to)
Aborig.	Aboriginal
absol.	absolute(ly)
ad.	adaptation or adoption of
adv.	adverb
adv. phr.	adverbial phrase
Advt	advertisement
AEWS	Army Education Welfare Service
Agric./agric.	Agriculture, agricultural
AJHR	Appendices to the Journals of the House of Representatives
Amer.	American
AND	*Australian National Dictionary*
APL	Auckland Public Library
app.	apparently
Archaeol.	now mainly in an archaeological context
assoc.	association, associated
ATL	Alexander Turnbull Library
ATLTS	Alexander Turnbull Library Typescript source
ATLMS	Alexander Turnbull Library Manuscript source
attrib.	attributive(ly)
AU(C)	Auckland University (College)
Austral.	Australia(n)
Ayto & Simpson	*Oxford Dictionary of Modern Slang* (J. Ayto & J. Simpson, 1992)
bibliogr.	bibliography
Brit.	Britain, British (in derivations broadly = (found in) the English language varieties of Great Britain and Ireland as distinct from any local variety ('Sc., Irish, North. English', etc.) or from overseas varieties ('US', 'Austral.', etc.)
Bull.	*Bulletin*
C.	College
c (before a date)	*circa*, about
c. (as 19th c.)	century
cap./caps.	capital(s)
Century Dict.	*The Century Dictionary* (ed. W.D. Whitney 1900)
cf.	*confer*, compare; refer to
CMS	Church Missionary Society
Coll./coll.	College; (occas.) colloquial
collect.	collective(ly), collected, collection
comb.	combination(s)
compil.	compiled by; compiler(s)
conj.	conjunction
const.	constructed (with)
CU(C)	Canterbury University (College)
d. (after a number)	penny, pence
d.	died
DAE	*Dictionary of American English* (Craigie-Hulbert 1938–44)
DANTE	*The Dictionary of Antarctic English* Bernadette Hince (unpublished draft copy, 1996)
DARE	*Dictionary of American Regional English* (ed. F.G. Cassidy et al.: I–1985, II–1991)
DCan.	*A Dictionary of Canadianisms on Historical Principles* 1967 (1991 repr.)
def. art.	definite article
dept.	department
deriv.	derivation; derived from
derog.	derogatory
DHS	District High School
dial.	dialect(al)
Dict.	Dictionary
Digger Dial.	*Digger Dialects* W.H. Downing 1919 (ed. Arthur & Ramson 1990)
dimin.	diminutive
DNZB	*Dictionary of New Zealand Biography* (I–1990, II–1993, III–1996)
Dom. Mus. Bull.	*Dominion Museum Bulletin*
DOST	*Dictionary of the Older Scottish Tongue*
DSADT	*Dictionary of Street Alcohol and Drug Terms* (2edn. USC 1987)
DSAE	*A Dictionary of South African English* (ed. Jean Bradford, 1980)
Duval	*A Preliminary Dictionary of Maori Gainwords on Historical Principles* T.P. Duval 1995 (Unpublished TS thesis presented for the degree of Doctor of Philosophy, University of Canterbury)
dwt	pennyweight (gold measure)
e./E.	east(ern)
ed(s).	edited by; editor(s); editorial
edn.	edition
EDD	*English Dialect Dictionary* (ed. J. Wright 1898)
e.g.	*exempli gratia*, for example
ellipt.	elliptical(ly)
encycl.	encyclopedia
erron.	erroneous(ly)
esp.	especially
et al.	*et alii*, and others
etc.	*et cetera*, and the rest
et seq.	*et sequentia*, and (the) following (pages, etc.)
etym.	etymology
exc.	except
exclam.	exclamation
f.	formed on; from
f(f). (after number)	and the following (page(s))
F	female(s)
fam.	family
fem.	feminine
fig.	figurative(ly)
Fr.	French
freq.	frequent(ly)
ft.	foot, feet
GAL	General Assembly Library
GBPP	Great Britain Parliamentary Papers
gen.	general
Geogr.	Geography, geographical
Gloss.	Glossary
HDAS	*Random House Historical Dictionary of American Slang* (ed. J.E. Lighter: I–1994)
Hist./hist.	now mainly or only in an historical context
Hist.	historical, history
HNZD	*Heinemann New Zealand Dictionary* (1979, 1989)
H. of R.	House of Representatives

HS	High School	OED	*Oxford English Dictionary* (2edn. 1989)
Ibid./ibid.	*ibidem* (from) the same book, page, passage	OEDAS	*Oxford English Dictionary Additions Series* (ed. J. Simpson & E. Weiner: 2 vols. 1993)
idiom.	idiomatic(ally)		
i.e.	*id est*, that is	*op. cit.*	*opere citato*, from the source already quoted
imit.	imitative	orig.	origin(ally)
imp.	imperative	OU	Otago University
in.	inch(es)	oz.	ounce (28.35g)
incl.	including	p.	page
indef. art.	indefinite article	*pa. ppl.*	past participle
infl.	influenced (by)	Parl.	Parliament(ary)
init.	initial	Partridge	E.H. Partridge, *A Dictionary of Slang and Unconventional English* (with supplements: 1937–83)
int.	interjection		
intens.	intensifier	Partridge 8	8edn. 1984 (ed. Paul Beale)
intr.	intransitive	*pass.*	passive
Ir.	Ireland, Irish	p.c.	personal communication
Is.	Island	PEP	Project Employment Programme
IT	Information Technology	perh.	perhaps
joc.	jocular(ly)	phr.	phrase(s)
JPS	*Journal of the Polynesian Society*	*pl.*	plural
Jrnl(s).	Journal(s)	pop.	popular(ly)
kg	kilogram	poss.	possibly
l	litre(s)	pp.	pages
lb.	pound (453.6g, weight)	*ppl.*	participle
LC	Legislative Council	*ppl. a.*	participial adjective
let(t).	letter(s)	PPN	Proto-Polynesian
loc. cit.	*loco citato*, in the source already cited	prec.	preceding (word or entry)
LU(C)	Lincoln University (College)	predom.	predominantly
m	metre(s)	*prep.*	preposition
M	male(s)	*pres. ppl.*	present participle
Ma.	Maori (language)	prob.	probably
MAF	Ministry of Agriculture and Fisheries	Proc.	Proceedings
Mathews	M.M. Mathews, *A Dictionary of Americanisms on Historical Principles* (1951)	*pron.*	pronoun
		pronunc.	pronunciation
memo.	memorandum	pseud.	pseudonym
mil.	military	pub.	publication, publisher
ml	millilitre	quot(s).	quotation(s)
mm	millimetre	q.v.	*quod vide*, which see
mod.	modern	R	Royal (in names of periodicals, etc.)
Morris	E.E. Morris, *Austral-English* (1898)	Random House (1987)	*Random House Dictionary of the English Language* (2edn. 1987)
MS(S)	manuscript(s)		
MU	Massey University	R. Comm.	Royal Commission
n.	noun	Rec.	Records
n./N.	north(ern)	*redupl.*	reduplicating
N.A.	National Archives	ref.	reference
N. Amer.	North America(n)	*reflex.*	reflexive
naut.	nautical usage	reg(s).	regulation(s)
ne.	northeast(ern)	Rep.	Report(s)
neg.	negative	repr.	reprint(ed)
New SOD	*New Shorter Oxford Dictionary* (1993)	RP	Received Pronunciation ('Southern British Standard')
NI	North Island (of New Zealand)	s. (after a number)	shilling
no.	number	s./S.	south(ern)
NSW	New South Wales	S. Afr.	South Africa(n)
nw.	northwest(ern)	SANZ	Standards Association of New Zealand
NZ	New Zealand	*sb.*	substantive
NZE	New Zealand English	*sc.*	*scilicet*, understand or supply
NZGeogr.	*New Zealand Geographer*	Sc.	Scotland, Scottish
NZGeol.SB (NS)	*New Zealand Geological Survey Bulletin (New Series)*	se.	southeast(ern)
		sect.	section (of a newspaper)
NZGG	*New Zealand Government Gazette*	SI	South Island (of New Zealand)
NZJEcol.	*New Zealand Journal of Ecology*	[*sic*]	thus in the original
NZJAg.	*New Zealand Journal of Agriculture*	*sing.*	singular
NZJH	*New Zealand Journal of History*	SND	*Scottish National Dictionary*
NZJMFR	*NZ Journal of Marine and Freshwater Fish*	SPCK	Society for the Promotion of Christian Knowledge
NZJSc.	*NZ Journal of Science*	*spec.*	specific(ally)
NZJST	*New Zealand Journal of Science and Technology*	sp(p).	species
NZJZ	*New Zealand Journal of Zoology*	subsp.	subspecies
NZ Med. J.	*New Zealand Medical Journal*	Suppl.	supplement
NZNB	*New Zealand National Bibliography* (ed. A.G. Bagnall)	Surfinary	*The Surfin'ary* (A dict. of surfing terms, California 1991)
NZPD	New Zealand Parliamentary Debates		
Obs./obs.	obsolete		
occas.	occasional(ly)	sw.	southwest(ern)

syn.	synonym	Webster (1961)	*Merriam-Webster Third International Dictionary* 1961
trans.	transitive	Webster (1898)	*Merriam-Webster Australasian Supplement* 1898
transf.	transferred (sense or use)	Wentworth & Flexner	H. Wentworth and S.B. Flexner, *A Dictionary of American Slang* (2edn. 1975)
transl.	translated, translator		
TrNZI	*Transactions of the New Zealand Institute*	Wilkes	G.A. Wilkes, *A Dictionary of Australian Colloquialisms* (2edn. 1985)
TrRSNZ	*Transactions of the Royal Society of New Zealand*		
TS	Typescript	Williams	H.W. Williams, *A Dictionary of the Maori Language* (7edn. 1971 (1975 reprint): also 5edn. 1917, 6edn. 1957) (Also with edn. and date shown, William Williams, *A Dictionary of the New Zealand Language* 1edn. 1844, 2edn. 1852, 3edn. 1871, 4edn.1892)
US	United States		
usu.	usual(ly)		
UW	University of Waikato		
v.	verb, verbal		
var.	variant(s) of, variation, various; in scientific nomenclature, variety	WW1	1914–18 war
		WW2	1939–45 war
vbl. n.	verbal noun	yd	yard (0.914m)
vol(s).	volume(s)	( )	often indicates an optional spelling or pronunciation.
VUC	Victoria University College	[ ]	encloses etymological matter; editorial amendment or addition; an illustrative quotation not citing the headword, or citing the headword in a language other than English; occas., phonetic transcription.
VUW	Victoria University of Wellington		
w.	west(ern)		
Walsh & Biggs	D.S. Walsh and Bruce Biggs, *Proto-Polynesian Word List I* (1966)		
		/ /	encloses phonemic transcription.
WDFU	Women's Division of the Farmers Union	* before a word	indicates a hypothetical or reconstructed form.

PRONUNCIATION

1. THE PHONEMES OF NEW ZEALAND ENGLISH (NZE)

(Represented by a system developed by the Department of Linguistics, Victoria University of Wellington.)

Vowels

/ɪ/	bit
/e/	bet
/æ/	bat
/ɒ/	pot
/ʌ/	but
/ʊ/	put
/ə/	salute, pilot
/i/	beat, city (/ˈsɪti/)
/a/	part
/o/	port
/u/	boot
/ɜ/	pert

Diphthongs

/æi/	date
/ai/	bite
/oi/	boy
/æu/	bout
/ʌu/	dote
/iə/	pier
/eə/	lair
/uə/	cure

Consonants

/p/	pat
/b/	bat
/t/	tot
/d/	dark
/k/	cat
/g/	gate
/f/	fern
/v/	vote
/s/	sake
/z/	zoom
/θ/	thorn
/ð/	then
/ʃ/	sharp
/ʒ/	measure
/m/	mark
/n/	net
/ŋ/	sang
/l/	leave
/r/	red (also in Southland 'rolled', and by some Maori speakers 'flapped')
/w/	wine
/j/	yard
/h/	hate
/tʃ/	chap
/dʒ/	judge

Other Symbols

/ɑ/	hah the RP value near that of Maori ā /a:/
/ʔ/	the 'glottal stop'
/ɸ/	Maori wh (a bilabial)
/χ/	Scottish loch
/ˈ/	primary stress, precedes the stressed syllable: e.g. /ˈblæk ˈbɜd/ (black bird)
/ˌ/	secondary stress, precedes the stressed syllable: e.g. /ˈblækˌbɜd/ (blackbird)

2. THE PRONUNCIATION OF LOAN-WORDS FROM MAORI

The standard Maori spelling and the phonemic structure of the Maori original are given in the etymological section of each loan-word. For English speakers, the main perceived differences between English and Maori lie in the vowel phonemes; in certain of the consonants; and in patterns of word-stress which in Maori depend more on the *nature* or weighting of the syllable (long or short or two-vowelled, etc) than on the *force* of enunciation as in English. The rough approximations given below assume that, in general, English speakers (latterly NZE speakers) have since 1769 tried to approach Maori phonetic values in their renderings of individual (often isolated) loan-words—at least as far as their idiolects and perceptions (and structural differences in the two languages) would allow. The resulting wide variety of interpretation given to many Maori phonemes is partly illustrated by the numerous early non-standard spellings included in the dictionary. Attested traditional anglicized pronunciations are occasionally attached to the headword. A fuller and more authoritative guide to the pronunciation of Maori may be found in Bruce Biggs *Let's Learn Maori* (Auckland, 1973, 1986 reprint, pp. 131–3), and, for many individual elements, at the head of each letter entry in the seventh edition of Williams's *Dictionary of the Maori Language*.

Vowels and Diphthongs

The original Maori vowels are presented phonemically by a system which, in differing from that for NZE, assumes that they may be broadly regarded as short or long. The latter are marked in standard spelling by a macron over the vowel (ā) or occasionally in quotations (as in other publications) by doubling the vowel (aa), and in the phonetic transcriptions by a colon (/a:/ long as distinct from /a/ short). NZE speakers have traditionally found it difficult to distinguish length of vowel in Maori, and tend to apply a variety of English rules (*e.g.* Ma. *mana* /mana/ can become NZE /manə/ (rhyming with *garner*), /mʌnə/ or /mʌnʌ/ (rhyming more or less with *gunner*).

In the complex matter of Maori vowel quality and its transliteration into NZE 'equivalents' there is much variety, with perhaps the most noticeable anglicizations (excluding diphthongs) being those of Ma. /o:/ (regularly NZE /ʌu/) and /o/ (regularly NZE /ɒ/, and often /ʌu/ when word final—*Koro* as /ˈkɒrʌu/). A Maori unvoiced final /u/ or /a/ is often not heard by English speakers (*e.g.* /hut/, /ˈwɒkətɪp/ for *he utu*, *Wakatipu*).

Two different vowels occurring together in Maori preserve their distinctiveness and do not usually conform closely to the diphthongs of NZE. NZE speakers will generally try to equate each with its nearest perceived NZE congener, either as heard (*e.g.* /mæuri/ for *Maori*) or as spelt (*e.g.* /kiə/ or less often /keə/ for *kea*), occasionally giving separate (often lengthened) values to individual components (*e.g.* /huwi/ for *hui*).

Consonants

The Maori consonants **h**, **k**, **m**, **n**, **t** and **w** are sounded like their congeners in NZE; **ng**, **p**, **r** and **wh** can be strikingly different from usual NZE values.

Maori **ng** /ŋ/ is like the sound in English *ringer* (never that of *finger*). In the Ngai (or Kai) Tahu South Island dialect it becomes a /k/ (compare **kāinga/kāika**, **Waitangi/Waitaki**).

Maori **p** /p/ is not aspirated as in English, and is only weakly (if at all) plosive. In early transliterations (especially those from the southern South Island) and in some common words it can appear as **b** /b/; as in **bubu** (*pūpū*), **boohai** (*Puhoi*), **bucketeer** (*pukatea*).

Maori **r** (a flapped variety) is quite different from that usually heard in NZE or from rolled or trilled varieties. It approximates and is often perceived as the /l/ of NZE *lip*, and occasionally as some form of NZE /d/: hence **bull-a-bull** for *poroporo*, **biddy-biddy** for *piripiri*, and the various forms **coraddy**, **koladdy**, **claddie**, etc. for *kōrari*. See also Williams *op. cit.* 319.

Maori **wh**, traditionally a bilabial /ɸ/ (approximated by English /hw/), is now usually /f/; it has dialectal variants /h/ (in Hokianga) or /w/ (in Taranaki). **wha-** (and **wa-**) often become /wɒ/- or /wo/-.

Approximate Values of Maori Vowel Sounds

Spelling	Sound	Nearest NZE vowel
a (short a)	/a/	*as in* b<u>u</u>t (/bʌt/)
ā (long a)	/a:/	*as in* p<u>a</u>rt (/pat/—Maori value often nearer to RP /ɑ/)
e (short e)	/e/	*as in* p<u>e</u>t (/pet/)
ē (long e)	/e:/	*as in* p<u>e</u>t or l<u>air</u> (/leə/) but lengthened
i (short i)	/i/	*as in* NZE or Aust. Eng. p<u>i</u>t (/pɪt/); word final -i occas. as NZE /i/ (pip<u>i</u> = /ˈpɪpi/)
ī (long i)	/i:/	*as in* p<u>ea</u>t (/pit/)
o (short o)	/o/	*as in* the noun exp<u>o</u>rts (/ˈeksˌpots/)
ō (long o)	/o:/	*as in* p<u>o</u>rt (/pot/)
u (short u)	/u/	*as in* p<u>u</u>ll (/pʊl/); word final it can tend towards NZE /u/
ū (long u)	/u:/	*as in* p<u>oo</u>l (/pul/)

A

A. & P.: see AGRICULTURAL AND PASTORAL.

Abdul. Mainly *WW1*. [f. a Turkish proper name: AND 1915.] The Turk; a Turk; occas. an Arab. Cf. *Johnny Turk* (Johnny 2 a).

c1915 in Bailey & Roth *Shanties* (1967) 115 Old Abdul under cover was as cunning as a rat; As yet we'd done no shootin'—saw nothin' to shoot at, Till a Turkey popped his head up. **1918** *Chron. NZEF* 30 Aug. 60 The thin, ravenously hungry Abduls complain of the dearth of food in their lines. *Ibid.* 22 Nov. 205 'Jericho Jane', Abdul's only big gun..we found tipped down a gulley. **1938** HYDE *Nor Yrs. Condemn* 168 Fred, remember that big fat Abdul who used to chuck the privates out of Shepherd's [*sic*] [in Cairo, WW1]... All the boys said that Abdul must'a been a eunuch. **1944** *NZEF Times* 18 Aug. 8 'Igri, George'—for every 'Wog' is George or Abdul, just as the private soldier is either George or Johnny to the 'Wogs'. **1982** SHADBOLT *Once on Chunuk Bair* (1990) 21 We're not here just for a blue with the Abduls. **1986** *Dominion* (Wellington) 2 Apr. 10 [In cartoon] Abdul Car Mart. Too much dust and smoke. Abduls are firing.

aboard: see ALL ABOARD!

abolition. *Hist.* Specifically, the abolition of the New Zealand Provinces as a unit of government in 1876. Also *attrib.*

1875 *Richmond-Atkinson Papers* (1960) II. 398 The abolition policy..embodied in the Abolition of Provinces Bill seems quite in the ascendant. **1948** LIPSON *Politics of Equality* 57 [Vogel] found that his program could no longer reconcile the claims of an expanding central government with those of 'a number of miserable little federal republics'. Abolition set the stage for a new conflict.

Hence **abolitionist** *n.*, one supporting the abolition of provincial government. Cf. CENTRALIST.

1949 REED *Story Canterbury* 197 Canterbury..was one of the provinces that favoured abolition, but, says Alan Mulgan, 'the Canterbury abolitionists..counted upon the province being left with its land fund after provincial government had gone.'

aboriginal, *a.* and *n. Hist.*

A. *adj.* Also occas. init. cap.

1. MAORI B 1 a.

1845 INGESTRE *Let.* 5 May in Rutherford *Sel. Documents* (1949) 12 Our system..was..to encourage the settlement of European colonists, and to turn to account the peculiar facilities which the aboriginal race of New Zealand seem to possess for intermixture and amalgamation with the European population. **1848** WAKEFIELD *Handbook NZ* 53 While the two Chiefs were at Cambridge, Professor Lee..reduced the *Maori*, or aboriginal language, into a written one, and composed a grammar and dictionary of it. **1851** SHORTLAND *S. Dist. NZ* 40 The ultimate extinction of the Aboriginal race is now contemplated by many as a matter of certainty.

2. Esp. in the official use, **aboriginal native**, a Maori.

1840 *Charter for Erecting the Colony of NZ* 16 Nov. in Rutherford *Sel. Documents* (1949) 8 Provided always, that nothing in these our letters patent contained shall affect..the rights of any aboriginal natives of the said colony of New Zealand to the actual occupation or enjoyment in their own persons..of any lands..now actually occupied or enjoyed by such natives. **1858** *Memo. by Responsible Advisers on Native Affairs* 29 Sept. in Rutherford *Sel. Documents* (1949) 104.1 The following measures, on subjects specially affecting the aboriginal natives of New Zealand, have passed both Houses:.. The Native Schools Act. **1863** in Gillespie *S. Canterbury* 23 June (1958) 472 [Accommodation House Regulations of Canterbury Provincial Council 14.] The licence to be cancelled..if any spirits shall be supplied..to any Aboriginal Native of New Zealand.

B. *n.* MAORI A 2 a (a).

1844 MONRO *Notes of Journey* in Hocken *Contributions* (1898) 247 Our aboriginals at length consented to proceed with us on being paid for the work they had already done, and we set off. **1879** *Auckland Weekly News* 5 Apr. 21 The aboriginal took the note, departed, but did not deliver it to the sergeant. **1899** *Hawera & Normanby Star* 1 Dec. 2 The well-being of the noble race of aboriginals in our midst demands that the truth should be spoken. **1913** CARR *Country Work* 9 Auckland..will provide work..on account of the large area of unoccupied land, at present mainly held unused by the aboriginals.

aborigine. *Hist.* Also init. cap. Usu. *pl.* [Spec. use of *aborigine* f. an orig. *pl.* form *aborigines*, those inhabiting a country *ab origine* 'from the beginning': AND 1829.] **a.** MAORI A 2, TANGATA WHENUA 2. Cf. PROTECTOR OF ABORIGINES.

1834 MCDONNELL *Extracts Jrnl.* (1979) 14 The aborigines are rapidly emerging from their pristine barbarism. **1848** WAKEFIELD *Handbook NZ* 57 European vices and disease were spread among the diminished native population; and..the numbers of the aborigines visibly decreased. **1858** *NZPD* (1856–58) 18 May 448 I might go on multiplying proofs from the extraordinary correspondence the Native Office carries on with the aborigines. **1866** ANGAS *Polynesia* 55 In New Zealand there exists a frugivorous native rat, called 'kiore maori' by the aborigines. **1874** BAINES *Edward Crewe* 28 There is a pretty general belief that the ancestors of the present aborigines migrated to these islands about 500 years ago. **1881** CAMPBELL *Poenamo* 135 For the influx of Pakehas, consequent upon the colonisation of Maoriodom, killed his monopoly with the aborigines.

b. MORIORI 1 a.

1866 HUNT *Chatham Is.* 29 The aborigines term themselves Moriori, their conquerors still call them *paraiwharas*, or blackfellows.

absentee, *n.* and *attrib. Hist.*

A. *n.* [AND 1872.] A landowner living away from a holding; in early reference, often one living in Britain.

1843 WOOD *Twelve Months in Wellington* 10 We were accompanied by two gentlemen..who had not hitherto seen some town acres belonging to absentees, for which they were agents. **1853** EARP *NZ* 198 The absentees have been induced to buy their lands, in the hope and expectation that the labour which they were thus instrumental in sending out would..shortly return them tenfold for their outlay. **c1871** MASTERS *Autobiography* (ATLMS) 80 The greatest enimies [*sic*] to New Zealand are the absentees... Money drawn from our country and spent in another. **1899** BELL *In Shadow of Bush* 158 The block of bush, which belonged to an absentee, contained two or three hundred acres. **1933** *Press* (Christchurch) (Acland Gloss.) 9 Sept. 15 *Absentee.*—An absentee landowner is one who lives in England, not one who lives elsewhere in New Zealand, or who is on a visit abroad. **1946** SOLJAK *NZ* 117 New Zealanders have coined or adapted many expressions to meet local requirements..*absentee:* applied from 1850 onwards to New Zealand landowners living in England.

B. In *attrib.* use in Comb. [AND 1831.] **absentee boss, owner, proprietor, settler**.

1947 BEATTIE *Early Runholding* 44 The next run..also had an '**absentee boss**', its owner..residing mostly at Woodlands. **1899** BELL *In Shadow of Bush* 21 The [projected] 'town' itself remained a solid block of standing bush, and the **absentee owners**..were only reminded of their possessions by the persistent recurrence of the notices to pay rates. **1938** BURDON *High Country* 150 The land companies and absentee owners came in for the greatest execration. **1959** LAWLOR *Old Wellington Days* 99 [The street] was named after John Haining, 'gentleman of Middlesex, absentee owner'. **1976** BROWN *Difficult Country* 47 Those [sections surveyed in Hampden] sold were bought by residents of Nelson as a spec., and several country blocks had absentee owners. **1986** RICHARDS *Off the Sheep's Back* 100 But the progress of the Kotuku Valley had been hindered by absentee owners. **1843** CHAPMAN *NZ Portfolio* 53 So long indeed as you [*sc.* NZ land proprietors] remain individually isolated and ununited, you are in a false position towards the colonists. They only know you as '**absentee proprietors**'; they will be prone to regard your interest as antagonist [*sic*] to theirs. **1848** WAKEFIELD *Handbook NZ* 175 The number of resident land-owners [in Wellington]..amounts to 300 or 400. The absentee proprietors have generally appointed agents to select, manage, and lease their lands. **1948** IRVINE-SMITH *Streets of My City* 33 Contracts for road-making, attention to sections of **absentee settlers** and the activities of the growing port brought in some welcome cash.

Hence **absenteeism** *n.* land ownership by a non-resident owner.

1849 POWER *Sketches in NZ* 121 [Heading] Evils of Absenteeism..where the *bonâfide* settlers are so much scattered by the intervening lands of speculators. **1938** BURDON *High Country* 150 On both of these [stations] the owners reside permanently, so that the evils of absenteeism are avoided. **1955** *BJ Cameron Collection* (TS July) absenteeism (n) The ownership of land in NZ by people living in England. A source of much complaint in early NZ. (Historical).

A.C.: see ARMED CONSTABULARY.

acacia.

1. *Obs.* [Transf. use of *acacia* (fam. Mimosaceae), poss. from association of the kowhai's profuse yellow flowers with those of the *wattle* (*Acacia*

spp.).] Also as **New Zealand acacia**, KOWHAI 1.
1848 TAYLOR *Leaf from Nat. Hist.* 20 Kowai, *acacia* bearing a yellow flower. (Edwardsia microphylla) **1869** *TrNZI* I. (rev. edn.) 274 The Kowhai, or New Zealand Acacia, (*Sophora*, or *Edwardsia*, *grandiflora*,) is a small tree. **1882** POTTS *Out in Open* 114 Vastly doth it delight in ransacking the sweets yielded by the blossoms of the acacia, fuchsia, tritoma, etc.

2. [Spec. use of *acacia*.] As **prickly acacia**, the deciduous usu. spiny North American tree ('false acacia') *Robinia pseudacacia* (fam. Fabaceae), locally naturalized.
1940 STUDHOLME *Te Waimate* (1954) 271 The Prickly Acacia makes excellent fencing posts, and is a lovely tree. **1946** *NZJST* XXVII. 434 *Robinia pseudoacacia* [*sic*], or prickly acacia, appears to be outstanding in this respect, owing to its being a deciduous leguminous plant that is easily grown from seed. **1951** *Weekly News* (Auckland) 9 May 29 The so-called (by farmers) 'prickly acacia' is a larger growing and far more valuable tree, the true name of which is Robinia pseudo-acacia [*sic*].

Access. *attrib.* [Spec. use of orig. US *access* with reference to broadcasting, special courses, etc., to provide minority groups 'access' to information and training.] Used *attrib.* of a State-supported training and work skills programme for the unemployed introduced in 1987.
1988 *Listener* 9 Apr. 18 The..local Regional Employment Access Council..approves funding of Access schemes. **1990** *Dominion* (Wellington) 20 June 11 Last October he did an Access course for four weeks, got his heavy traffic licence. **1991** *Dominion* (Wellington) 2 Feb. 3 Allan —, Access worker, appeared for sentence in the High Court at Wellington. **1991** *Landfall* 179 Sept. 312 A vestige of an ACCESS scheme is a lone bench beneath a black-necked pohutukawa.

acclimatization.
1. The introduction and establishment of exotic species, esp. game animals and freshwater fish. Also *attrib.*
1880 SENIOR *Travel & Trout* 187 I had strayed into the Domain..and the acclimatization gentlemen of Auckland have the pleasure of knowing that they have provided, in that cool grove a..concert. **1907** *TrNZI* XXXIX. 227 Acclimatisation was commenced in this colony, over forty years ago.

2. In special Comb. (often cap.) **acclimatization garden** *obs.*, an outdoor area devoted to exotic plants and animals; **acclimatization society,** any of several New Zealand regional societies, often with some State financial support, formed to promote the introduction, and regulate the taking, of various game animals, birds, and freshwater fish in its district.
1878 BULLER *Forty Yrs. NZ* 17 In the **acclimatization gardens** our British song-birds..are now finding a home. **1882** POTTS *Out in Open* 122 Sometime [*sic*] ago a very fine specimen could be seen at the Christchurch Acclimatization Gardens. **1866** *Southern Prov. Almanack* in Thomson *Twelve Yrs. in Canterbury* (1867) 20 **Acclimatization Society**. Agricultural and Pastoral Association. **1879** SIMMONS *Old England & NZ* 72 There is an Acclimatisation Society, whose object has been to introduce English birds into the colony. **1898** *TrNZI* XXX. 266 It was only natural in a country like New Zealand..that the settlers should establish acclimatisation societies, and should endeavour to introduce the familiar forms of wild life from their native lands. **1903** *TrNZI* XXXV. 310 During the last whitebait season..[the] secretary of the Westland Acclimatisation Society, obtained a quantity of whitebait. **1922** *Auckland Weekly News* 6 Apr. 45 Witness said he was a ranger for the Auckland Acclimatisation Society. **1958** GILLESPIE *S. Canterbury* 338 The South Canterbury Acclimatisation Society, which began as the Timaru Game Society, was not formed until 1874. **1990** *Motoring Today* July 28 Soon after, the fur seal expert from the Acclimatisation Society arrived.

accommodation-house.
1. a. *Obs.* [AND 1843.] Orig. an often crude rural lodging place or roadside inn, later (see quot. 1926) a more substantial establishment, offering accommodation for travellers (later tourists), and usu. licensed to provide liquor.
[**1853** MACKIE *Traveller under Concern* 19 Mar. (1973) 90 About noon we reached Chas. Gaukrodjer's, another house of accommodation where we halted.] **1857** HARPER *Lett. from NZ* 1 Sept. (1914) 17 There [in the Port Hills] I found what is known as an accommodation house. **1861** *NZ Goldfields 1861* (1976) 24 Our day's journey was now nearly over, and..we reached an 'accommodation house'—that name being the one popularly applied to a description of unlicensed rough public-houses occasionally to be found on the roads here [in Otago]. It was a sort of rendezvous for travellers of all sorts. **1865** BARKER *Station Life* (1870) 24 We reached Leathfield..found a nice inn, or accommodation-house, as roadside inns are called here [in Canterbury]. **1878** ELWELL *Boy Colonists* 126 He went (to use a colonial phrase) 'on the spree', *i.e.* to a public-house..(or accommodation house, as such places were called). **1896** GRACE in Hodgson *Poems* (1896) iv He found himself, at the end of a long and dreary day, located for the night at some desolate, dismal accommodation-house. **1911** MORELAND *Through South Westland* 42 We drove to the little old accommodation-house at the edge of the bush—a punga house, i.e. built of fern logs on end. **1926** COWAN *Travel in NZ* II. 132 [Caption] Glade House, Government Accommodation House, at the head of Lake Te Anau. **1936** *Tararua Tramper* Jan. 5 I drowned it in a hot..bath at the Tapawera Accommodation House. **1973** NEWTON *Big Country SI* (1977) 26 In those early days the Rainbow was famed mainly for its accommodation house. **1985** GOWANS *Heart of High Country* 28 Ceci waited in the cart staring at the newly-made sign 'Curton's Accommodation House, 1871'.

Hence *obs.* **accommodation hut (station, tent** [AND 1861]), a hut, station out-station or tent used as a temporary accommodation house.
1874 KENNAWAY *Crusts* 176 He fears his driver, whom he has left with the dray..is getting drunk at the nearest **accommodation hut** or up-country inn. **1959** MASTERS *Tales of Mails* 62 Rhymers [c1890s] at their own stables and overnight accommodation huts at the foot of the Gentle Annie. **1939** BEATTIE *First White Boy Born Otago* 150 He used to regard our **accommodation station** as a halfway house..and the accommodation house at Hampden as halfway between us and the Waitaki. **1863** WALKER *Jnrl. & Lett.* (ATLTS) 4 Jan. We were fortunately close to an **accom[m]odation tent** [at Dunstan Diggings] so we turned in and enjoyed beds for the night... Tent about 15 feet x 12, stove and all. We had the state bed 6 ft by 2, for two.

b. Special Comb. **accommodation-house keeper,** one who keeps, or is licensee of, an accommodation-house.
1894 NZ *Official Year-book* 268 Table showing the occupations of persons who insured in the Government Insurance Department in 1893... flaxmillers..gum-diggers and sorters... Accommodation house keepers. **1913** *Triad* 10 Sept. 173 I can call to mind several pompous Commissioners..whom I should be quite pleased to see in the clutches of the back-blocks accommodation-housekeeper of New Zealand. **1940** *Tales Pioneer Women* (1988) vii There are stories of the wives of missionaries..farmers, runholders, accommodation-house keepers, and numerous others.

2. An urban boarding-house or guest-house. Cf. PRIVATE HOTEL.
1952 *Evening Post* (Wellington) 30 Aug. 5 A man and his wife were found dead in a room..in an accommodation house in Grafton Road [Auckland] this morning... They were found by the manageress when she entered their single room to collect the rent... They had been at the accommodation house six months. **1960** HILLIARD *Maori Girl* 162 In the evening paper she saw an advertisement for an accommodation house in Hill Street. **1968** *NZ Contemp. Dict. Suppl.* (Collins) 2 *accommodation house n.* boarding house in N.Z.

accommodation paddock. *Obs.* [AND 1843.] A paddock on a stock route for holding animals overnight. See also HOLDING PADDOCK.
1933 *Press* (Christchurch) (Acland Gloss.) 9 Sept. 15 *Accommodation Paddocks.*—Paddocks kept by publicans and others for the use of travelling stock. In my time [c1890–] the charge was 1s a hundred for sheep for a night. They were unknown, of course, until the roads were fenced in the 'seventies. **1947** BRERETON *No Roll of Drums* 143 They [*sc.* cattle] look travel tired; perhaps they have been driven too hard. I know your last accommodation paddock is eaten out! **1952** RICHARDS *Chatham Is.* 131 Delay in unloading stock and lack of suitable accommodation paddocks were a constant cause of complaint in Lyttelton.

accrediting, *vbl. n.* [Spec. use of *accredit* to attribute authorship to someone: see OED 3 a.] The awarding of a pass in an external examination (esp. University Entrance) on an assessment made within the school.
1919 *AJHR* E-6 13 There appears to be a general feeling that the time is ripe for the adoption of some form of accrediting as a means of entrance to the University. **1925** *AJHR* E-7A 29 A step along the road towards 'accrediting' or the recognition of school certificate as a qualification for entrance to the University. **1930** *AJHR* I-8A 99 The [Secondary Schools] Association is in favour of the accrediting system. **1944** *AJHR* E-1 1 The University has adopted, for schools on an approved list, a method of accrediting pupils for entrance to the University. **1960** *Education* II. 35 We see no reason why accrediting for University Entrance by the principals of the post-primary schools should be rejected. **1989** DUDER *Alex in Winter* 14 Well, there's no doubt about her accrediting prospects, provided she keeps up with the homework.

Hence by back-formation **accredit** *v. trans.*, usu. *pass.* **be accredited**, to award or be awarded a pass in an external examination by accrediting.
1966 TURNER *Eng. Lang. Austral. & NZ* 173 [A pupil] may go on to University Entrance, for which he will very likely be *accredited*. **1976** JOHNSTON *New Zealanders* 127 Most schools have the right to accredit pupils with this qualification [*sc.* School Certificate] through internal assessment.

ace. [f. *ace* a playing card with a single spot: AND 1904.] Esp. in the phr. **(up)on one's ace**, alone, on one's own.
1909 *Truth* 29 May 7 And was he on his ace, drinking with the flies, or did he shout for the boys like a toff? **1913** *NZ Bulletin* 8 Feb. 16 Not Understood! Yer meant t' 'elp that neddy by givin' 'im a dose before the race; the stooards cop yer, and yer tale ain't ready; so 'ome yer go upon yer bloomin' ace. **c1926** THE MIXER *Transport Workers' Song Book* 66 When men are

picked around me, And I'm left upon my ace. **1982** NEWBOLD *Big Huey* 244 Ace (n) 2. On your —. Alone, on your own.

acid. [Poss. f. *acid test*, that is, of gold with *aqua fortis*: AND 1906.] In the phr. **to put the acid on** (someone), to make a sharp (or final) demand on, esp. for money or favours.
 1906 *Truth* 24 Feb. 7 *Put the Acid On* [Title of a story, a pun on testing fake jewellery with acid (*aqua fortis*) as part of high-pressure sales tactics towards prospective buyers.] **1910** *Ibid.* 23 July 6 Gibson replied that both Golding and Goram were putting the acid on to a drunk, or a half-drunk, in the bar. **1920** *Quick March* 10 Feb. 31 'Too much acid,' Bill roared, 'I'm telling you, you didn't put the acid on her enough.' **1938** *Press* (Christchurch) (McNab Slang) 2 Apr. 18 To put 'the nips in' and 'the acid on' are clear enough. **1950** CHERRILL *NZ Sheep Farm* 99 But although you had tickets and no mistake on Ju. at the *time* you didn't forget to put the acid on him proper afterwards. **1960** CRUMP *Good Keen Man* 93 A passing fisherman called in for a brew of tea and I put the acid on him for his spare spark plug. **1974** MORRIESON *Predicament* (1981) 73 Instead he puts the acid on the Bramwells and they slung some gold to keep his mouth shut. **1984** *Dominion* (Wellington) 14 Feb. 22 England skipper Bob Willis yesterday put the acid on his batsmen to perform in the remaining two days of the third cricket test.

acre, *n.*[1]

1. *Hist.* town-acre (town 2).
 1841 *Diary* in *William Swainson* 1 July (1992) 85 Papa was very busy making a hedge round the next acre which he now rents. **1842** HEAPHY *NZ* 81 When I left Wellington, the best acres of town land,—those near the beach, were letting rapidly. **1844** *Bradey Papers* (ATLTS) 16 Apr. Planting hedge of quick sets up one side of the Acres.

2. See COUNTRY ACRE; *long acre* (long *a*. 1 a).

acre, *n.*[2] [AND 1965.] A euphemism for ARSE.
 1968 SLATTER *Pagan Game* 103 I haven't got the time to be sitting on me acre or playing games like you lot. **1989** McGILL *Dinkum Kiwi Dict.* 9 *acre* bottom; eg 'Doesn't matter what the situation, even if a home run's hit, Jonesy always slides into the plate on his acre.'

across the way, *adv. phr.* Across the road, street, etc.; opposite, but within sight of, the speaker's location.
 1921 NICOL *Story Two Campaigns* 36 The Turks were equally engrossed with the development of their defences, 'across the way'. **1943** MARSH *Colour Scheme* 175 Just across the way, isn't it? I've never taken a look at these Springs. **1964** HOWE *Stamper Battery* 115 As Bridget lived just across the way, we children were asked to help with the..[wedding] breakfast. **1969** MCINNES *Castle on Run* 72 And how are things across the way [*sc.* across a river valley], at the homestead? Your mum well? **1976** LEE *Soldier* 96 And across the way outside the window I could see swollen buds. **1986** BROWN *Weaver's Apprentice* 116 As they turned out of the driveway..Jimmy saw Matthew Fleming on Nisbet's front porch across the way.

Act. *Ellipt.* for any of several Acts affecting individual liberty: *spec.* the Habitual Criminals and Offenders Act, 6 Edw. VII s2(1)(a) 1906 (see COLLAR 1); also provisions of the Mental Health Act (cf. quot. 1988), esp. in the phr. **under the Act.** Cf. COLLAR 1, KATHLEEN MAVOURNEEN.
 1950 *Here & Now* Nov. 14 Glossary of Technical Terms: The Act or the Collar—The Habitual Criminals Act, under which persons declared habitual criminals can have their sentences increased by the Prisons Board for offences against prison discipline during their incarceration... That's Joe, they said, doing six years and the Act for shooting a copper. **1988** *Dominion Sunday Times* (Wellington) 14 Feb. 19 'They put me under the Act.' He means involuntary committal [to a mental hospital]. 'It took me four years to break that Act.'

Adam: *since Adam was a cowboy*, see SINCE.

adze. *Hist.* Also occas. early **ads.** [Spec. use of *adze* a chipping or shaving tool with a blade at right angles to the handle.] An adze-like stone tool of the early Maori or Chathams Moriori. Cf. AXE 1, TOKI 1. Also *attrib.*
 1773 BAYLY *Journal* 4 June in McNab *Hist. Records* (1914) II. 209 With this [green stone] they make their Togie, or ads of & chissles to carve with. **1830** CRAIK *New Zealanders* 126 [Caption] Adzes, Bread Pounders, and Bottle. **1840** POLACK *Manners & Customs* I. 71 The adze was formed of a blue granite inserted in a handle of the rata or red pine-wood. **1866** HUNT *Chatham Is.* 34 Their [*sc.* Morioris']..axe and adze fashioned from stone, were far more prized than the finest Sheffield hardware. **1881** BATHGATE *Waitaruna* 74 It was really a canoe..and was simply a log of Totara, which had been hollowed out by some patient Maori, assisted by..a stone adze. **1898** CHUDLEIGH *Diary* 10 Feb. (1950) 397 He has ridden 35 miles and carried a kit of Moriori stone adzes on his back. **1903** *TrNZI* XXXV. 241 The axes, adzes..are also made from a hard kind of stone not found on the mainland. **1929** FIRTH *Primitive Econ. NZ Maori* 388 The *pounamu*, the nephrite so much prized for pendants, *mere*, and adzes. **1937** BUICK *Moa-Hunters NZ* 204 Close beside these stone adzes there was a patch of discoloured soil. **1984** HOLMES *Chatham Is.* 90 Adze blades were blocked out roughly, chipped and bruised then rubbed to a smooth surface.

ae, *adv.* Also **ah-e, ai(e).** [Ma. /ˈaːe/: Williams 1 *Āe* (ii) *1.* ad[v]. assenting to an affirmation or affirmative question.] In Maori contexts, indicating assent, 'yes'.
 [**1820** LEE & KENDALL *Gram. & Vocab.* 148 Ai, *ad.* Yes, Ay.] **1832** WILLIAMS *Early Jrnls.* 24 Aug. (1961) 256 *Ae* he said to lift us out... I nodded assent. **1840** *Notes Nopera's speech* in *GBPP House of Commons 1841 (No.311)* Apr. 59 Upon this there was a general exclamation of ai, ai (yes, yes,) and they came forward in an orderly manner, and signed the treaty to the number of sixty. **1860** BUDDLE *Maori King Movement* 13 'When he returned these tribes were asked..'Will you have this man for a King?' The reply was 'Ae'. c**1910** MACDONALD *Reminiscences* (VUWTS) 42 I affirm that from 60 to 70 years ago, the simple 'Ae' of the Maori, was a thing to which a man might, with perfect confidence, trust his life. **1939** GRIEVE *Sketches from Maoriland* (1961) 70 '*Ai*' shouted the class. '*Hankia apopo!*' shouted Rore again..'*Ai*' answered the class. **1949** SARGESON *I Saw in My Dream* (1974) 189 First I have the jerry-riddle, Dave, he said. Ah-e, beer, he said, and he gave a big sigh. **1960** ROGERS *Long White Cloud* 86 Te Rangi's shoulders..drooped. 'Aie. It gets closer.' **1986** IHIMAERA *Matriarch* 38 Yes, and it was that same fullness which..had kept him young. Tired, ae, but still young.

aerial topdressing. The spreading of fertiliser from aircraft, esp. on country not easily accessible to other forms of motorized transport. Also *attrib.*
 1946 *NZJAg.* Sept. LXXIII. 193 The extensive areas of copper-deficient peat land..provided a suitable opportunity to try out aerial topdressing under circumstances reasonably favourable to success. **1951** LEVY *Grasslands NZ* (1970) 74 Aerial topdressing with fertilisers, and over-sowing..since 1949, when the first aerial topdressing trials were made, have altered completely the..carrying capacity of the hills. **1966** *Encycl. NZ* III. 119 In the district there are many landing strips for aerial topdressing aircraft. **1979** *Listener* 24 Nov. 36 The first commercial topdressing flight..in a Tiger Moth in May, 1949, pointed the way to a new industry... Over the next three years, the number of aircraft engaged in aerial topdressing rose by 550 per cent. **1988** WARR *Bush-burn to Butter* 138 Cockayne further recognised that 'Aerial topdressing is increasing at a great rate, an increase from none to 400,000 tons in 5 years'.

 Hence **aerial(l)y topdressed** *a.*; **aerial topdresser** *n.*
 1951 LEVY *Grasslands NZ* (1970) 202 On steep Taranaki hill country, sheep and cattle, efficiently handled on oversown and **aerially topdressed** country, have successfully controlled the return of all forms of secondary growths. **1984** KERSE ed. *Knapdale Run* 138 As we look out over highly productive pastures..the aerial topdressed hills..it is good for us to..reflect where it all began. **1973** WHEELER *Hist. Sheep Stations NI* 59 Within a week we should have the **aerial topdressers** in with super and fresh grass seed.

afghan /ˈæf.gæn/. Occas. init. cap. [Named from its dark colour.] A crunchy cocoa biscuit.
 1936 *Merry Meal Maker Cook. Book* 15 *Afghans*..butter..flour..sugar..cornflakes..cocoa. Place teaspoonfuls on..tray... Ice..and put half walnut on top. **1957** *Cook. Book NZ Women's Inst.* 117 Afghans. Seven ozs butter..cocoa..cornflakes..flour..sugar, essence vanilla... Bake in small quantities (like rock cakes). Ice with chocolate icing. **1961** *Edmonds Sure to Rise Cook. Book* 11 Afghans... Soften butter, add sugar and beat to a cream, add flour, cocoa and lastly cornflakes. Put teaspoonfuls on a greased oven tray and bake... When cold ice with chocolate icing and put walnuts on top. **1972** CURNOW *Four Plays* 143 Afghans, he says. Something oriental. Mona: Oh, dear no, they're just ordinary little cakes. **1984** *NZ Short Stories* 7 You're not to touch those afghans. **1992** *NZ Geographic* 13 Jan.–Mar. 19 The scones, pikelets, Afghans, Anzac biscuits and shortbread with which Sharon filled the biscuit tins on a Saturday had been taught to her by her mum.

aftermatch function. Also *ellipt.* **aftermatch;** *joc.* **aftermatch bash.** An alcoholic get-together usu. after a game or sports event (esp. of rugby football), but also after other events.
 1974 GIFFORD *Loosehead Len's Big Brown Book* 42 Eden Park after-match functions are..just for men. **1985** STEWART *Gumboots & Goalposts* 17 'So we won't be invited to the [rugby] aftermatch function— that's what!' I told him. **1987** *National Bus. Rev.* 20 Mar. 10 The *New Zealand Herald*'s olde-worlde society page carried a picture from the NPA after-match function (sorry, cocktail party). **1990** SMITH *Will the Real Mr NZ Please Stand Up* 197 Women were not allowed to the [rugby union] after-match functions. **1992** *Dominion* (Wellington) 11 Dec. 10 Most at home..with a seven-ounce at an aftermatch, the scribe couldn't resist an invitation to drinks..with the former [rugby] World Cup captain. **1993** *Dominion* (Wellington) 7 May 6 There were no mutton pies to be found at the after-match bash [of the entertainment awards], catered for by some of Wellington's finest restaurants. **1995** *Dominion* (Wellington) 16 Oct. 1 [All Black] Ian Jones apologised to her afterward [*sic*] and..there was a public apology at the aftermatch.

afternoon tea: see TEA 3 b.

afto /ˈaftʌu/. Also **(s)arfto.** [Var. of *after*(noon + -*o*.] In the collocation **this afto,** (this) afternoon. Cf. ARVO.

1964 HELMER *Stag Party* 103 Got another case comin' in..this afto for you, though. 1965 HILLIARD *Power of Joy* 273 Pax says, 'Pace me for the four-forty sarfto?' but he is spent and happy at winning. 1978 HILLIARD *Glory & Dream* 166 'Anybody seen Charlie?' 'In the rubbity this arfto.' 1983 MANTELL *Murder to Burn* 76 Forgot about it till we got your flier this afto.

age, *v. Farming*. [See OED *v.* 5 (of a horse only), 1887.] *trans.* To examine a sheep's teeth to determine its age.
1982 *Agric. Gloss.* (MAF) 49 Hence you can 'mouth' or age a sheep and estimate its age.

agent: see *Government Agent* (Government), *native agent* (NATIVE B 3 b).

Agent-General. *Hist.* From 1871 (Isaac Featherston) to 1905 (William Pember Reeves), the title of the official representative of New Zealand in London, replaced in June 1905 by 'High Commissioner'.
1878 BULLER *Forty Yrs. NZ* [Preface] For the use of many..engravings, I am indebted to the kindness of Sir Julius Vogel, the Agent-General for New Zealand. 1879 *Auckland Weekly News* 26 Apr. 12 If Agents-General are to be at liberty to engage in private speculation for which their position gives them facilities, then these must be considered as 'pickings' and taken into account in fixing the salary. 1894 *Bank of New Zealand Share Guarantee Act 58 Vict.* s13 The Agent-General of New Zealand in London shall in like manner appoint an auditor in respect of the business of the Bank within the United Kingdom. 1940 HOWARD *Rakiura* 247 However..the Agent-General in London had been far from successful in obtaining immigrants. 1968 DALZIEL *Vogel* 32 Agent-General: New Zealand's representative in London who performed similar functions to the Ambassador and Trade Commissioner today.

Agricultural and Pastoral, *attrib.* and *n.*
A. *attrib.* Usu. abbrev. **A. & P.** (in various spellings) esp. in the collocations: **A. & P. Association (Society)**, one of several regional associations founded in the 19th century to promote rural, esp. farming, interests; **A. & P. Show**, a regional, usu. annual, rural fair organized by a local A. & P. Association.
1885 *Wairarapa Daily* 26 Nov. 2 The first annual show under the auspices of the newly formed Masterton **Agricultural and Pastoral Association** was held..yesterday. 1939 *Weekly News* 8 Feb. This 40th annual show of the Wairoa Agricultural and Pastoral Society was held last Wednesday. 1948 SCOTTER *Run Estate & Farm* 25 From the first show of the A. & P. Association in 1863 he was a member of the committee and gained prizes in both merino and long wool classes. 1951 CRESSWELL *Canterbury Tales* 82 Although this report lessened public dissatisfaction, the A. & P. Associations seemed determined to have the school under their management. 1966 *Encycl. NZ* I. 16 The Auckland Agricultural and Pastoral Association, founded in 1843, was the first to be formally organised. 1890 *Cox Diaries 1888–1925* (ATLMS) 7 Nov. I went..this afternoon to the A. & P. Ass. Show, there was a crowd at the show. 1909 *Ibid.* 17 Feb. The second day of the Masterton A. and P. Show, very few Carterton shops closed. 1958 MULGAN *Making of New Zealander* 99 I could see this in the attitude to the annual Agricultural and **Pastoral Show**. 1968 TOMLINSON *Remembered Trails* 33 My cousin Arthur took me to parties [in Gisborne c1909] and the A. & P. Show. 1976 McDERMOTT *Lost & Found NZ* 108 We were just in time to see what we would call a County Fair, the Hawkes Bay Agricultural and Pastoral Show. 1981 KENNEDY *Straight from Shoulder* 33 New Zealand's 100 Agricultural and Pastoral (A&P) shows, beginning with Whakatane in October and ending in Auckland over Easter, have been under increasing pressure. 1989 *Pacific Way* Nov. 63 Agricultural and Pastoral (A&P) Shows have always been meeting places for town and country. There are two kinds of A&P Shows. Ours was a small one serving the local farming community, and there are the large provincial ones, like Canterbury and Hawkes Bay. 1994 LASENBY *Dead Man's Head* 133 They all hooted when Banana Bob drove by because he stole children, nailed them into banana crates, and sold them at the A. and P. Show.

B. *n.* As **the A. & P.**, an A. & P. association or show.
1951 CRESSWELL *Canterbury Tales* 117 The family have long been good supporters of the 'A. & P.' 1987 ELDRED-GRIGG *Oracles & Miracles* 71 I must of looked like something from a sideshow at the A & P.

agricultural college. *Hist.* [Spec. use of *college* a tertiary institution affiliated to a university: see OED 4 e, 1845 quot.] A tertiary institution associated with a university providing specified agricultural and farming courses towards a degree.
1883 *Brett's Colonists' Guide* 74 The Canterbury people have taken the lead in New Zealand by establishing an agricultural college a few miles from Christchurch, where over 30 young men..are trained and educated in the science and practice of agriculture. 1945 *AJHR E-1* 5 The financial and administrative responsibility for the School of Agriculture and its two agricultural colleges was transferred from the Department of Agriculture to the Department of Education. 1956 *Dept. Educ. Circular* 15 Feb. A:56:1 These rulings will assist Registrars of university and agricultural colleges. 1960 SCRYMGEOUR *Memories Maoriland* 56 [Heading] *Canterbury Agricultural College*... Ere long Jim was enrolled as an agricultural student at the Canterbury College at Lincoln. 1990 *North & South* (Auckland) Aug. 78 Massey University, because it started as an agricultural college, retained its agronomic reputation.

agricultural high school. [AND 1905.] A secondary school having its main courses of instruction directed to farming needs.
1933 *NZ Tablet* (Dunedin) 1 Nov. 23 The Principal of the Feilding Agricultural High School gave vent recently to some trenchant criticism of..the rigid prescription of the University Entrance Examination. 1967 ELLIOTT & ADSHEAD *Cowshed to Dog Collar* 20 My principal at the Feilding Agricultural High School was L.J. Wild. 1990 *Evening Post* (Wellington) 8 Sept. 3 Former Feilding Agricultural High School head..has been appointed first principal of Hutt Independent Boys' School.

ah-e, var. AE.

ahuru. Also **ahuruhuru**. [Ma. /'aːhuru/, /aː'huruhuru/: Williams 4 *Āhuru* (ii), *āhuruhuru n. Auchenoceros punctatus*.] Either of two marine fishes, usu. as **ahuru**, *Auchenoceros punctatus* (fam. Moridae), a small, pink morid cod, or *Upeneichthys lineatus* (fam. Mullidae), *red mullet* (MULLET 2 (2)).
1927 PHILLIPPS *Bibliogr. NZ Fishes* (1971) 24 *Auchenoceros punctatus* (Hutton). Ahuru or Ahuruhuru. 1942 *TrRSNZ* 71/241 *Auchenoceros punctatus* (Hutton), Ahuru. 1966 *Encycl. NZ* I. 373 The ahuru (*Auchenoceros punctatus*), a small fish 4–5 in. long superficially similar to the red cod, is frequently found in the stomach contents of southern fish. 1966 ahuruhuru [see MULLET 2 (2)]. 1982 AYLING *Collins Guide* (1984) 142 The ahuru is a small cod with two dorsal fins and a single anal fin. 1982 AYLING *Collins Guide* (1984) 225 *Goatfish Upeneichthys lineatus (Upeneichthys porosus)* (Red mullet, ahuruhuru)... A steeply sloping forehead ends in a small downward facing mouth and beneath the chin are a pair of conspicuous long barbels.

ai(e), varr. AE.

a into g. A euphemism for *arse into gear*, in the phr. **to get one's a into g**, to get started (vigorously); to hurry up, to 'get cracking'.
1979 MITCALFE *Pighunter* 14 Come on, come on, get your A into G. 1984 15-17 F E1 Pakuranga Coll. 6 Get your a into g [F16M9] 1984 14 F E120 Wgton Girls Coll. 6 Get your a into g [F13] 1993 *Listener* 7 Aug. 25 First got their [*sc.* Assemblies of God] A into G in this country in 1927, possibly inspired by crusade of..evangelist Smith Wigglesworth.

air. [f. *air* pertaining to aircraft.] Special Comb. **Air Centre** *obs.*, formerly, the central city passenger reception office of the national airline, handling ticketing, baggsage, and arrival from and departure to the airport; **air hostie**, occas. **hostie** [f. *air host*(ess + -IE; cf. AND *hostie*, 1960], a female flight attendant.
1951 *Telephone Directory* (Wellington) 126 **Air Centre** National Airways Corporation. 1955 *Weekly News* (Auckland) 9 Feb. [Advt] Your N.A.C. Air Centre or Agent will surprise you how near..holiday spots..are by air. 1958 *AJHR H-35* 5 A site for a new 'Aircentre' building at Auckland..was acquired during the year. 1962 *NAC Airline Rev.* III. No.24 6 NAC has established the only point on its network where transport between aircentre and airport serves two cities. 1983 McELDOWNEY *Warm South* 16 Belinda and Richard went with me to the Air Centre to meet her [on 29 December 1962]. 1978 BALLANTYNE *Talkback Man* 53 People get clobbered. **Air hosties**, *girl* librarians, nurses, elderly gentlemen. 1984 *Sunday News* (Auckland) 19 Aug. 2 He walked to the rear of the plane and asked the air hostie (sorry, cabin attendant) if she'd mind if he stood there to ease the agony. 1995 *Dominion* (Wellington) 8 May 16 Judy Potts writes from the rural fastnesses of Havelock North, questioning the diction of hosties who exhort passengers to keep their 'seat bouwts buckoowed'.

aka. Formerly **ake, aki, hoccar** (=he aka); occas. also **akakura**. Plural often *akas*. [Ma. /'akaː/: Williams 6 *Aka* (i)... 2. *Metrosideros* [spp.]. *3. Vine of any climbing plant*.] *rata-vine* (RATA 3 a). Also *attrib*.
1834 MARKHAM *NZ* (1963) 34 One [creeper] is particularly useful. It is like Ivy growing up large Trees, called Hoccar and can be easily found in the Woods. 1843 DIEFFENBACH *Travels in NZ* I. 224 Sometimes the vines, a foot thick, of another creeper, the aki (*Metrosideros buxifolia*), also with scarlet flowers, are seen running up to the highest branches of the rata. 1853 HOOKER *II Flora Novae-Zelandiae I Flowering Plants* 69 *Metrosideros scandens*... Nat. name, 'Aka'... A climbing large shrub or small tree. 1864 CAMPBELL *Martin Tobin* III. 181 Gigantic trees, and festoons of the *aki*, &c., whose deep red blossoms hung like bunches of coral over head. 1867 HOOKER *Handbook* 764 Akakura. *Metrosideros scandens*. a1876 WILLIAMS *East Coast Hist. Records* (1932) 88 The huts were always well constructed..the thatch of toe-toe being securely fastened..with the wire-like stems of the ake or metrosideros scandens. 1889 FEATON *Art Album NZ Flora* 165 The 'Aka' or 'Akakura'..is common in forests throughout both Islands, and at the Lord

Auckland group. **1905** *TrNZI* XXXVII. 116 *Metrosideros scandens. (Aka-kura.)* The sap is used by the Tuhoe tribes for weakness of the eyes (Best). **1910** COCKAYNE *NZ Plants & Their Story* 30 For the different species [of climbing-ratas] the Maoris had the general name 'aka', so scientific names here are alone available. **1926** CROOKES *Plant Life Maoriland* 43 The great tail he took and cast into the forest, and from its long and powerful sinews sprang the akas, the rata vines, whose tough, wiry stems are still as strong as the iron muscles that gave them birth. **c1937** HYDE *Selected Poems* (1984) 37 By bridges slender as the ake ladder Where, Heaphy, climbing, found the Greenstone People. **1981** BROOKER et al. *NZ Medicinal Plants* 74 *Metrosideros fulgens*... Maori names: *Aka, akatawhiwhi, puatawhiwhi, aka vine*... Bushmen quench thirst with the juice of the vine which if cut and the bark left hanging, exudes a large quantity of clear juice tasting somewhat like cider.

akakiore. [Ma. /aka'kiore/: Williams 6 *akakiore..Parsonsia*.] The climbing plant *Parsonsia capsularis* (fam. Apocynaceae), bearing fragrant white to red flowers. See also JASMINE.

1906 CHEESEMAN *Manual NZ Flora* 441 *P[arsonsia] capsularis, R.Br*... Habit of *P. heterophylla* [Kaiku], but smaller and more slender... *Aka-kiore*. **1982** WILSON *Stewart Is. Plants* 44 *Parsonsia capsularis* Native Jasmine..Akakiore..Kaikū... Slender, many-branched climber... Flowers small, clustered, creamy, flushed reddish in bud.

akatea. [Ma. *aka + tea* white. /'aka'tea/: Williams 6 *Akatea..Metrosideros albiflora* and *M. perforata*, climbing plants.] *white rata* (RATA 4).

1904 TREGEAR *Maori Race* 54 The hoop, the frame of which was of forest vine (*akatea*), was about two feet in diameter. **c1910** MACDONALD *Reminiscences* (VUWTS) 9 [The stockyard was] fastened to the rails Maori fashion with Akatea, a very tough species of creeper. **1926** CROOKES *Plant Life Maoriland* 45 The largest of the white ratas is Meterosideros [*sic*] albiflora known to the Mao[ri]s as akatea. **1938** *Auckland Weekly News* 2 Mar. 60 This rata vine called akatea gave his people a proverb which runs, 'Rangitihi's head was bound up with the akatea,' meaning: 'Never say die'. **1981, 1982** [see RATA 4].

ake, var. AKA.

ake: see AKEAKE.

akeake, var. HAKIHAKI.

akeake. /'ʌki,ʌki/, /'æki,æk(i)/. Formerly also **akey akey, ak(k)i, akiaki**. *pl.* often with *-s*. [Ma. /'ake(ake)/: Williams 6 *Ake* (i)... *akeake.. Dodonaea viscosa, Olearia traversii* and other species, trees.]

1. Either of two genera of shrubs or small trees: also **ake,** *Dodonaea viscosa* (fam. Sapindaceae) of New Zealand and elsewhere (see also LIGNUM VITAE); or *Olearia traversii* (fam. Asteraceae or Compositae) of the Chatham Islands and widely planted in New Zealand, and less commonly *O. avicenniaefolia* (see also *bastard sandalwood* (SANDALWOOD 2)). Also *attrib*.

[**1820** LEE & KENDALL *Gram. & Vocab*. 133 A'ke, *s*. Name of a certain tree.] **1835** YATE *NZ* (1970) 47 Aki—called the *Lignum vitae* of New Zealand, from its hardness, weight, and colour: is useless for all common purposes, and is very difficult to work. **1838** POLACK *NZ* II. 398 The *Akki*, (*lignumvitae*,) when young is much used for boat timber. **1841** HODGSKIN *Narr. Eight Months Sojourn NZ* 27 Akey akey is a heavy wood, of a dark colour. **1851** WARD *Journal* 12 June (1951) 193 In shelter of the akiaki shrubbery. **1864** MUELLER *Vegetation Chatham Is*. 19 A very beautiful, not viscid tree, attaining a height of 30–35[ft], called inappropriately by the colonists Bastard Sandalwood-tree and passing under the native name 'Ake-Ake'. **1882** HAY *Brighter Britain* II. 195 The Ake-ake (*Dodonaea viscosa*) gives a handsome wood for cabinet work, which is said to be imperishable. **1890** *Otago Witness* (Dunedin) 6 Nov. 29 He brought from the Chathams..a specimen of akeake, which had been in the ground 30 years, and as good as ever, and which when cut exudes a fragrant aroma. **1928** BAUCKE *White Man Treads* 246 The Chathams grew only one durable timber, the ake-ake which..was seldom without heart-rot, shakes, and other blemishes. **1951** HUNT *Confessions* 137 Amongst the daisies [Pitt Is.] possesses trees which are thirty feet high, and the wood of some of them is so remarkably durable..that the Maoris call them Ake, which means 'for ever' or eternal. **1959** MIDDLETON *The Stone* 9 They leaned their bikes against the ake ake hedge and went up..to the back door. **1983** MATTHEWS *Trees NZ* 74 Ake-ake are easily raised from seed, the purple leaved form coming true.

2. With a modifier: **golden akeake,** AKIRAHO; **mountain akeake,** see quot.

1939 COCKAYNE & TURNER *Trees NZ* 123 *Shawia paniculata*—syn. *Olearia Forsteri* (Compositae). Akiraho, Golden Akeake. **1993** *Dominion* (Wellington) 20 Mar. 11 Golden ake ake is a case in point, for *olieria paniculata* [*sic*] belongs to a different family from the ake ake. **1984** *Hanmer Forest Park* 35 Species prominent in this scrub include..mountain wineberry.. mountain akeake (*Olearia avicenniaefolia*)..and *Celmisia* species.

ake ake (ake) /'akæi 'akæi ('akæi)/. [Ma. /'ake/: Williams 6 *Ake* (ii) *1*. ad[v]. indicating immediate continuation in time: use in English is associated with the King Maori defiance at Orakau (1864) 'Ka whawhai tonu ake! ake! ake!' We shall fight on forever, forever, forever!] For ever and ever.

[**1820** LEE & KENDALL *Gram. & Vocab*. 133 A'ke áke, *paulo post futurum*.] **1868** TAYLOR *Past & Present NZ* 68 He held my hand for a long time in his, saying, 'My father,' and assuring me that he could not give up his faith *ake ake ake*, for ever and ever. **1915** *Evening Post* (Wellington) 20 Sept. (VUW Fildes Clippings 627/20) [Heading: Maori contingent to WW1] 'Ake! Ake! Ake!' Farewell to the Natives. **1943** FINLAYSON *Brown Man's Burden* (1973) 89 The crowd rocked with laughter. 'Ake, ake, ake!' yelled the haka party. **1953** CODY *21 Battalion* 187 Wasn't there something in the school history books about a Maori chief taking on all comers at Orakau... We will fight on forever and ever. Ake Ake Ake. Must ask some Maori in 28 Battalion what it was all about. **1955** *BJ Cameron Collection* (TS July) ake! ake! ake! (excl.) For ever and ever... The words have passed into oratorical speech to convey unyielding resolution.

akekura, var. *akakura* (AKA).

akepirau, akepiri, varr. AKEPIRO.

akepiro. Also **akepirau, akepiri.** [Ma. /ake'piro/: Williams 7 *Akepiro..Olearia furfuracea*.] *Olearia furfuracea* (fam. Asteraceae or Compositae), a shrub or small tree; (rarely) the related *O. paniculata* (akiraho). See also WHARANGIPIRO.

1853 HOOKER *II Flora Novae-Zelandiae I Flowering Plants* 117 Eurybia [=*Olearia*] *furfuracea*, DC... Nat. name, 'Ake piro'. **1870** *TrNZI* II. 123 Olearia Forsteri Akepirau. **1906** CHEESEMAN *Manual NZ Flora* 284 *O[learia] furfuracea, Hook.f*... A much branched shrub or small tree 8–20 ft. high; North Island..*Wharangipiro; Akepiro*. **1916** COWAN *Bush Explorers 'More Reminisc.'* (VUWTS) Here the trees are totara, manuka... The akepiro..is here abundant. **1940** LAING & BLACKWELL *Plants NZ* 444 *Olearia furfuracea* (The Akepiro)... A bush plant. Maori names, *Wharangipiro, Akepiro*. **1961** ALLAN *Flora NZ* I. 665 *O[learia] furfuracea*..Shrub-land, streamsides and forest margins..*Akepiro*.

aki, var. AKA, AKEAKE.

akiraho. [Ma. /aki'raho/: Williams 7 *Akiraho..Olearia paniculata*.] The shrub or small tree *Olearia paniculata* (fam. Asteraceae or Compositae), commonly used as a hedge plant. See also AKEPIRO, *golden akeake* (AKEAKE 2).

1889 KIRK *Forest Flora* 285 Olearia Forsteri... The Akiraho..is a much-branched shrub or small tree, 6ft. to 20 ft. high. **1939** [see AKEAKE 2]. **1940** LAING & BLACKWELL *Plants NZ* 448 *Olearia paniculata* (The Panicled Olearia)... Maori name, *Akiraho*. Usually a seaside plant, much used for hedges. **1965** GILLHAM *Naturalist in NZ* 136 Leatherwood and pepperwood, ngaio and koromiko, tauhinu, and akiraho (*Olearia paniculata*) barred our way. **1978** MOORE & IRWIN *Oxford Book NZ Plants* 130 *Olearia paniculata, akiraho*. A small tree of lowland scrub and forest margins from south Auckland to Nelson and Canterbury, and commonly used as an easily trimmed hedge. **1982** WILSON *Stewart Is. Plants* 98 Akiraho..has yellow-green, wavy-edged, white-backed leaves. **1995** *Dominion* (Wellington) 18 Mar. 19 *Olearia paniculata* (akiraho) also makes a wonderful hedge with its wavy, pale green leaves and slightly scented flowers.

akki, var. AKEAKE.

akoakoa, var. HAKOAKOA.

Albany Surprise. [f. *Albany*, a district near Auckland city, the location of the originating vineyard.] A black table grape used also in red-wine making (see also quot. 1971).

1908 *Department of Agriculture Report* in Thorpy *Wine in NZ* (1971) 52 It is hardly likely the growers of American grapes like the Isabella and Albany Surprise, will obtain such profitable returns as during the past season. **1911** *NZJAg* Aug. III. 131 One of the hardiest and certainly the heaviest-cropping vine..is the Albany Surprise. This grape is claimed to have originated at Albany, in the Auckland District, and was sent out by a firm of nurserymen of Auckland. It is closely akin to the American variety Isabella. **1971** THORPY *Wine in NZ* 46 Albany Surprise..[was] derived from an American hybrid originally developed as a table grape..but now extensively used in making red wine... Albany Surprise is not planted in any vineyard in Europe, Australia, South Africa and Chile. *Ibid*. 56 Albany Surprise was so named by George Pannill of Albany, near Auckland... Some Isabella grapes had been planted there..and one day George Pannill noticed one vine had thrown up three particularly strong canes which bore grapes which were larger and finer than the original ones. In 1897 he was able to offer for sale three cases of grapes which he called Albany Surprise... In the next seven years the vine..spread rapidly through the vineyards of New Zealand.

albatross. With a modifier: **royal albatross,** *Diomedea epomophora* (fam. Diomedeidae), a huge black and white seabird breeding on New Zealand subantarctic islands and elsewhere; **sooty albatross** or **light-mantled sooty albatross** (see also PEE-U), *Phoebetria palpebrata* (fam. Diomedeidae), a small dark albatross with a characteristic white eye-ring breeding on New Zealand subantarctic islands; **wandering albatross**, *Diomedea exulans*, a huge white seabird breeding in the New Zealand subantarctic region and elsewhere. See also TOROA.

1904 HUTTON & DRUMMOND *Animals NZ* 261 **The Royal Albatross**. *Diomedea regia*... These birds sometimes follow a vessel for days together, and are seldom seen to settle on the water except to feed. **1938** *Auckland Weekly News* 21 Sept. 20 The arrival at the heads last year of ten Royal Albatross was regarded as an event of the first importance in local scientific circles. **1955** OLIVER *NZ Birds* 188 *Royal Albatross Diomedea epomophora epomophora*. This magnificent species would be well known to the sealers and whalers who visited Campbell Island during the first third of the nineteenth century. *Ibid*. 192 *Chatham Island Royal Albatross Diomedea epomophora sanfordi*. The Chatham Island Royal Albatross was for a long time not distinguished from the typical subspecies of the Southern Isles. **1990** *Dominion* (Wellington) 23 Nov. 11 Grandma, matria[r]ch of the Royal albatross colony at Taiaroa Head and at over 60, reputedly the oldest known breeding seabird in the world, may have died. **1773** FORSTER *Resolution Jrnl*. 28 Jan. (1982) II. 220 We saw a great Variety of bird this day viz. A white & **sooty Albatross** (*Diomedea exulans & palpebrata*). **1873** BULLER *Birds NZ* 295 Diomedea fuliginosa. (Sooty Albatross.) **1904** HUTTON & DRUMMOND *Animals NZ* 266 *The Sooty Albatross. Phoebetria fuliginosa*. Sooty brown, darkest on the face. **1922** *Auckland Weekly News* 3 Aug. 17 Visitors to the Auckland Islands..usually see sooty albatrosses sitting on their nests, which are in clefts in perpendicular cliff faces, or are on ledges some 30 feet high. **1955** OLIVER *NZ Birds* 165 *Light-mantled Sooty Albatross. Toroa-pango Phoebetria palpebrata* The 'Albatross with white eyebrows' taken during Cook's first voyage in the South Indian Ocean was an example of this species. **1990** *Checklist Birds NZ* 21 *Phoebetria palpebrata* (Forster) *Light-mantled Sooty Albatross*. **1873** BULLER *Birds NZ* 289 *Diomedea exulans*. (**Wandering Albatross**.) **1910** *Proc. in TrNZI* (1911) XLIII. 28 *Diomedea exulans..*(Wandering Albatross.) A good summary of the history of this difficult species is given. It is our Antipodes Island bird, and its only known nesting place is that island. **1955** OLIVER *NZ Birds* 181 *Wandering Albatross. Toroa Diomedea exulans exulans*. On account of its large size and remarkable power of sailing with motionless wings, the Wandering Albatross was well known to early voyagers. **1987** POWELL *Native Animals NZ* 69 The Wandering Albatross has a wing spread of about 3m, and is common off shore throughout New Zealand, especially to the south of the main islands.

alberts: see PRINCE ALBERTS.

alectryon /ə'lektrijən/. The generic name of the TITOKI, *Alectryon excelsum*, orig. used as a poeticism by Domett, and admitted by Morris into *Austral-English* (1898), thence into the Merriam-Webster and other dictionaries.

1872 DOMETT *Ranolf & Amohia* 16 The early season could not yet Have ripened the alectryon's beads of jet, Each on its scarlet strawberry set.

alfonsino /ælfɒn'sinʌu/. [Prob. f. *Alfonsim*, the Portuguese name of northern hemisphere *Beryx* species, or more directly from the Tenerife variant *alfonsino*, poss. from a fancied resemblance of its coloration to that of the royal robes of an Alfonsine King (Alfonso) of Portugal.]

[*Note*] See *Boletim do Museu Municipal do Funchal* No. VII, Art.17 *Beryx splendens* Lowe ALFONSIM DE COSTA ESTREITA [*sc*. 'of the narrow back']; cf. *Memorias de la Real Academia de Ciencias exactas..de Madrid: Serie de Ciencias naturales, Tomo XIV peces fisoclistos, subserie toracicos—Primera Parte Ordenes..por D. Luis Lozano y Rey*, Madrid, 1952 p. 24 *Beryx decadactylus* C... NOMBRES VULGARES.— Palometa roja, besugo [=red gilthead] americano; cardial, imperador, melo (Portugal); alfonsiño (Tenerife). Cf. also letter 20 Feb. 1995 President, *Instituto Português de Investigação Marítima* to L.J. Paul: 'When considering each one of the species we use the following common names: *Beryx decadactylus* — Imperador ['emperor'], Alfonsim.., Cardeal ['priest'], Realista ['related to a king']. *Beryx splendens*— Imperador-de-costa-estreita. Alfonsim-de-costa-estreita... Alfonsino perhaps comes from the name given to a bright golden [15th century] coin... The other Portuguese common names..are due perhaps to the comparison made to the red and silver or gold robes worn by kings..and priests.'

A marine fish of the fam. Berycidae, esp. the brilliant red, widely distributed *Beryx splendens*.

1982 AYLING *Collins Guide* (1984) 178 The alfonsino is a beautifully coloured fish with a brilliant scarlet back, red flanks with a strong tinge of silver, and bright red fins... The flesh is extremely tasty. **1986** PAUL *NZ Fishes* 72 *Alfonsino Beryx splendens*... Brilliant red..on present knowledge is probably common only at certain localities where the seafloor structure and ocean currents are suitable. **1989** *NZ Geographic* IV. 77 We are now exporting these strange-sounding entities (hoki, alfonsino, orange roughy, oreo dory) all around the globe.

alienate /'æiliə,næit/, *v. trans*. [Spec. use of *alienate* to transfer to the ownership of another: see OED *v*. 2.] Of Maori land, to transfer from Maori ownership.

1840 *Treaty of Waitangi* (facsimile 1877, repr. 1976) But the Chiefs..yield to Her Majesty the exclusive right of Preemption over such lands as the proprietors thereof may be disposed to alienate—at such prices as may be agreed. **1854** *Richmond-Atkinson Papers* (1960) I. 145 The natives here after many years' refusal to alienate any further portions of their land have given way at last, and the area of land available for European settlement in this Province [Taranaki] has just been augmented. **1860** SELWYN *Memo*. 8 May in Rutherford *Sel. Documents* (1949) 108d There is reason to think that an independent right to alienate land without the consent of the tribe is unknown in New Zealand. **1946** ZIMMERMAN *Where People Sing* 80 For before the Maori can alienate the land, the consent of all his tribesmen who may have an interest in that land must be obtained. **1951** KOHERE *Autobiog. of a Maori* 54 I don't wonder why a wealthy sheep-farmer a few years ago tried..to persuade the natives to alienate the island to him.

Hence **alienated** *ppl. a*.; **alienation** *n*.

1858 *Memo. by Native Secretary* 13 Oct. in Rutherford *Sel. Documents* (1949) 105.23 The arguments used..appear to be based upon an assumption of a right affecting un**alienated** native territory by virtue of the Crown's right of pre-emption. **1869** *Richmond-Atkinson Papers* (1960) II. 281 I have drafted a letter proposing..a treaty, the basis to be the return of the unsold or alienated lands in Waikato. **1860** BUDDLE *Maori King Movement* 15 The objection..arose from the foolish idea that is entertained by the Maories that opening roads will certainly lead to the **alienation** of their lands. **1935** MAXWELL *Recollections* 116 The only means of alienation of lands recognised under Maori usages was that effected by conquest. **1989** PARKINSON *Travelling Naturalist* 48 The King Country is named after the movement King Tawhiao led last century to resist alienation of Maori land.

alison. [f. *Allison Durbin* a popular New Zealand singer of the 1970s.] Rhyming slang for 'bourbon' (whisky).

1988 *Dominion Sunday Times* (Wellington) 14 Feb. 19 Abbreviated local rhyming slang is also used. 'I'd love an aristotle of alison' means 'I'd love a bottle of bourbon'—bourbon rhyming with Alison [*sic*] Durbin.

all aboard. *Obs*. [Transf. use of a once common coaching cry, with a pun on BOARD *n*.¹, the shearing floor.] A shearers' call; start work! start shearing!

1890 *Otago Witness* (Dunedin) 27 Feb. 20 The first that he knew of anything wrong was when the wool-classer sang out 'All aboard'. **1897** [see WOOL 1]. **1911** KOEBEL *Maoriland Bush* 122 The stentorian cry to commence [shearing] 'all aboard'.

all black /'ɒl,blæk/. Also **all-black**, often with init. cap. or caps.; in early use often within quotation marks. [f. colour of the uniform: poss. orig. an *attrib*. use.]

[*Note*] The theory that *all blacks* was derived from a printer's error for an orig. *all backs* is not supported by evidence. It is concisely stated in the *Encycl. NZ* (1966) I. 32: 'According to the statement (July 1964) of W.J. Wallace..the title was the result of a printer's error. It appears that R.J. Seddon..had arranged with the *Daily Mail* (London) to cover the tour, with the result that a reporter, Buttery, travelled everywhere with the team. After the match against the Hartlepool Clubs on 11 October 1905.., Buttery reported that the whole team, backs and forwards alike, had played with speed and precision as if they were 'all backs'. This comment was repeated after the Northumberland game on 14 October..and the Gloucester City Club match on 19 October... But when the New Zealand team arrived at Taunton to play Somerset County (21 October), they found the whole town placarded with posters welcoming the "All Blacks". Buttery inquired into the matter and reported to the team's management committee that the printer had inserted an "l" in "Backs". The name appealed and henceforth the players were known as All Blacks.' But note that Wallace at 76 years is poss. recollecting an incident described by J.W. Stead in his chapter 'Vice-Captain's Review' on p.169 of G.H. Dixon's *The Triumphant Tour* (1906): 'One prominent football critic struck the right note when he changed the name "All Blacks" to "All Backs".' Buttery himself states in his introduction (p.5): 'The visit of the "All Blacks"—so dubbed because of their sombre football garb—has given a decided fillip to the Rugby game.' Further, Buttery's reports of the Hartlepool (see quot. 1905 below) and other games use 'All Blacks', never 'All Backs'. See also quot. 1907.

1. a. *Pl*. usu. init. caps., the New Zealand representative rugby union team; *sing*., a member or former member of such a team. Often *attrib*., occas. as **black**.

[*Note*] Applied first in England to the 1905 New Zealand rugby union touring team (also then called by the general names (the) COLONIALS', *Maorilanders* (MAORILAND 3 b), or 'the New Zealand (Representative) team', etc., and occas. early *(the) blacks*), prob. orig. by J.A. Buttery, the London *Daily Mail* correspondent in his report of the game v. the Hartlepools played on 11 Oct. 1905. The 1905 British use of the term *All Black(s)* seemed for most of the tour to be confined to the main correspondents of the *Daily Mail*, Buttery and occas. E.J. Vivyan the 'English International'. See esp. the collections of contemporary sports writings in G.H. Dixon *The Triumphant Tour* (1906), and the collection of *Daily Mail* pieces in *Why the 'All Blacks' Triumphed* (1906). New Zealand papers quickly put the term into general New Zealand use.

 [**1905** 16 or 17 Sept. *Daily Mail* (London) in Dixon *Triumphant Tour of the NZ Footballers* 29 [Report of the match v. Devon played 16 Sept.] In the loose, too, the black forwards showed great form.] **1905** *Daily Mail* (London) 12 Oct. 7 The 'All Blacks', as the Colonials are dubbed. *Ibid.* Did Hartlepool expect an 'All Black' to pass, he did nothing of the kind. **1905** *Truth* 9 Dec. 3 [He] states that the expenditure of thousands of pounds would not have given the colonials as fine an advertisement as the tour of the 'all black' football team has done. **1905** *South Wales Echo* 16 Dec. in *The Wales Test 1905* (1983) 19 Suddenly the manscape sways..and at 2.20 the New Zealanders appear—the All Blacks... They wear black jerseys, black pants, black stockings, and black boots. They have, however, white faces and white hands. **1906** *Truth* 6 Jan. 3 The visit of the New Zealand team to Canada will..give an opportunity..of watching their skill against the all-blacks. **1907** Baskerville *Modern Rugby Football* 37 The 'All Blacks' included in their ranks men who were so good at the..art [of passing] that the name was jokingly changed by one writer to 'All Backs'. **1908** Barr *Brit. Rugby Team in Maoriland* 87 The Canterbury man made a good showing on his first experience in an All Black jersey. **1910** Fanning *Players & Slayers* 36 A little bit of hard ground..and farewell the vision of the fern-spangled jersey of the All-Black. **1924** *Otago Witness* (Dunedin) 17 June 4 The matter of an alleged military defaulter being included in the 'All Blacks' team was discussed and a sub-committee was set up to investigate. **1935** Guthrie *Little Country* (1937) 103 Ill-feeling arises to-day only if the North Island gets more men in the All Black rugby football team than the south. **1966** *Encycl. NZ* I. 32 The 1884 New Zealand team to tour Australia, and the first to go overseas, had for its uniform a dark blue jersey with a gold fernleaf over the left breast, dark knickerbockers, and stockings... In April 1893, however, when the New Zealand Rugby Union was established, it was resolved that the New Zealand representative colours should be '..Black Jersey with Silver Fernleaf, [*op. cit.* 33] Black Cap with Silver Monogram, White Knickerbockers and Black Stockings.'.. But by 1901 the New Zealand team to meet New South Wales wore a black jersey (canvas top, no collar), silver fern (now neater and smaller), and black shorts and stockings. The 'All Blacks' had arrived in fact, if not in name. **1986** Davin *Salamander & the Fire* 81 You don't have to be an All Black to know when you're offside. **1990** *Evening Post* (Wellington) 4 July 60 Murray Pierce hopes to be back in New Zealand by the end of the month and wants his All Black jersey back.

b. In later use collocated with **original**, often as **(the) Original All Blacks**, and in modern historical use, *ellipt.* **the Originals**, the 1905 representative touring team.

 1916 *Chron. NZEF* 29 Nov. 155 The first try especially brought back memories of the original and never-to-be-forgotten 'All Blacks'. **1948** Swan *Hist. NZ Rugby Football* I. 146 The [1905] side to Great Britain and Ireland, France and Canada, now known as the 'Original All Blacks', justifying its selection and adding to our prestige. **1992** Palenski *Our National Game* 149 Hart..happily announced his team could now rank with The Originals and The Invincibles—as The Farcicals. **1995** *Dominion* (Wellington) 12 Oct. 22 Just back from the Originals' tour of Britain where the All Blacks had watched a northern union game, [they] set about organising a New Zealand league team to go to England.

c. *transf.* Any rugby representative team composed of New Zealanders.

 1916 *Chron. NZEF* 29 Nov. 153 The 'All Black' team from Sling [Camp] defeated [a] Plymouth team at Plymouth..(11-6).

2. *transf.* in a variety of contexts; see quots.

 1988 *Dominion Sunday Times* (Wellington) 13 Mar. 16 Other well-known [drinking] games are Hokonui Swindle, Bottles, Fluffy Ducks, Bunnies are Hovering, Cardinal Huff, All Blacks, Matches, and The Amazing Grimaldi Brothers. **1990** *Sunday Magazine* 23 Sept. 6 Now he..has plans to launch aerobics Kiwi-style in Japan. Joanna Wayne talks to the All Black of aerobics. **1990** *The Times* (London) 6 Apr. 3 [Heading] MP unearths horror story of All Black worm [He] had tabled questions on the spread of *arthioposthia triangulata*, a New Zealand monster [planarian] worm. **1990** *Dominion* (Wellington) 1 Aug. 13 Writers may be playing for smaller stakes than those who buy their weekly fix of Lotto tickets but many of them regard..book awards as a lottery, a game of chance, a literary All Blacks.

all cock and ribs like a musterer's dog: see musterer 3.

Allen's sweep: see art union 1 b.

alley. Also **ally.** [f. *alabaster*, of which some marbles were orig. made, hence a large or fine marble.] In the phr. **to make one's alley good (with)** [AND *alley* 2, 1924], a var. of *to make one's marble good* (see marble 1), to ingratiate oneself (with); to improve one's prospects.

 1943 Hislop *Pure Gold* 18 He just did not have that little Hollywood way of whispering sweet nothings down Rosie's neck, and he wanted me—to use his own words—to make his ally good and put in a good word for him. **1965** Sargeson *Memoirs of Peon* 40 'Oh, come on in, mate,' he said. 'I don't get the strength of you, but you might be able to make your alley good with mister.' **1970** Slatter *On the Ball* 138 Bob Scott races up and boots the ball into touch. 'Trying to make his alley good,' sniffs Spandau. 'Shouldn't if missed that penalty.' **1989** Newbold *Punish. & Politics* 74 And they were cunning fellows... They knew what they were at. They made their own alley good.

all hands and the cook. [Orig. naut., thence to early rural New Zealand, reinforced by the common use of *hand* station employee.] Everybody.

 1864 Chudleigh *Diary* 20 Oct. (1950) 149 On Tuesday a large bird flew over the [sheep-washing] pen. All hands and the cook took after it. **1889** *Collinson's Col. Mag.* 25 Between eight and nine p.m. 'all hands and the cook' turn in. **1923** Lincoln *Doctor Nye* 118 She told me not to say nothin' about it..'cause a lot more folks would want to come, and 'twouldn't do for Faith to be entertainin' all hands and the cook. **1933** *Press* (Christchurch) (Acland Gloss.) 21 Oct. 15 Everyone employed on a station is a s[tation] h[and] except the manager and cadets, and perhaps the cook. 'All hands' and 'all hands and the cook' are common expressions for 'everybody' among the hands themselves. **1964** Morrieson *Came a Hot Friday* (1981) 78 When Tainuia Junction had its mizzenmast blown away by the discontinuance of the railway, Te Arahau went down with all hands and the cook.

Alliance.

1. Also **New Zealand Alliance**, usu. with **the**. A shortened form of *The New Zealand Alliance for the Abolition of the Liquor Traffic*, occas. informally the **Temperance Alliance**, officially formed in 1886 from decisions taken at a meeting held in Wellington 23–24 Sept. 1885.

 1886 *New Zealand Alliance for the Suppression of the Liquor Traffic* [title: NZNB I. ii. 708, item 3795] **1891** *Evening Post* (Wellington) 11 July 2 A meeting of the New Zealand Alliance was held last night in the Free Methodist School at 8 o'clock..when members of the various societies met to consider Mr. Joyce's Licensing Amendment Bill, and how best to support it. **1917** *Free Lance* (Wellington) 28 Sept. 22 It is Town Talk..that the New Zealand Alliance celebrated the 6 o'clock closing victory in—soda and milk. **1918?** Taylor *To All NZ Voters A Warning*. [unpaged pamphlet: front page] The New Zealand Alliance (professedly) for the Abolition of the Liquor Traffic by the Direct Vote of the People—established in 1886..is now abandoning this Democratic policy. **1925** Burton *Youth versus the Liquor Traffic* 6 The New Zealand Alliance is a federation of religious organisations and temperance bodies with, in addition, individuals who, while belonging to no special organisation, are yet keenly desirous of sweeping away the evils of the Liquor Traffic. ..The Alliance was formed in 1886 under the Presidency of Sir William Fox. **1936?** Murray *The Temperance Problem in New Zealand* 4 During the past fifty years the New Zealand Alliance has sought to secure the abolition of the liquor traffic by the direct vote of the people. **1948** Lipson *Politics of Equality* 174 On many occasions the fight between 'the trade' and 'the Alliance' has been so vigorous that the votes on the liquor referendum have almost equaled the number cast in the political contest. **1972** *New Zealand's Heritage* LII. 1432 [Heading] *The Alliance and 'Local Option'*... In 1886, scattered temperance groups had formed themselves into a national body, 'The New Zealand Alliance for the Abolition of the Liquor Traffic'. With Fox as its President, the Alliance proclaimed its objects as being 1. The abolition of the liquor traffic [etc.]. **1990** *Evening Post* (Wellington) 18 Oct. 1 The Temperance Alliance is campaigning to keep the area dry. Tom Quayle, the recently retired general secretary of the Alliance, says the vote could be a real cliff-hanger.

2. *Hist.* In full the **Alliance of Labour**. A trade union federation of the 1920s. See quot. 1959.

 1924 *Otago Witness* (Dunedin) 9 Sept. 46 [Mr. Atmore's] exposure of the negotiation between the Alliance of Labour and the Post and Telegraph Officers' Association revealed so much that seems to bear a close family resemblance to the Soviet principle..that many hitherto unthinking newspaper readers have experienced an eye opener. **1934** *Fielding Star* 31 Mar. 8 The opinion that there was a general drive..for the restoration of wage cuts was expressed by..[the] president of the New Zealand Alliance of Labour, in addressing the Alliance today. **1959** Sinclair *Hist. NZ* 256 During the twenties a new trade union federation, the Alliance of Labour, had revived the tradition of militant unionism... Now, unemployment forced the Alliance to defend arbitration and to support the Labour Party.

allied shearwater: see shearwater 2 (5).

all on the board: see board *n.*[1] 1 c (b).

allotment. *Hist.* [Spec. use of *allotment* allotted portion of land: see OED 4; AND 1788, 1811.]

1. A surveyed or designated area of land or a section drawn by lot or otherwise allotted to a purchaser.

 1841 Villiers & Lefevre 10 Sept. in *GBPP 1842 (No.569)* 130 The memorial states that certain town lots..had been advertised for sale by auction, but that several allotments, comprising some of the most valuable lands in the township..had been reserved from such sale. **1843** Swainson in Manson *I Take Up My Pen* (1971) 25 The allotments were made to consist of 100 acres each, and these are what we call 'sections'. **1860** Buddle *Maori King Movement* 15 [Ngaruawahia] has been surveyed..and a large Town laid out in one acre allotments..the streets being named after Maori tupunas (ancestors) and living chiefs. **1894** *TrNZI* XXVI. 621 The oak and the elm..are conspicuous in our streets and suburban allotments.

2. *Surveying.* See quot.
1952–53 *NZ Forest Service Gloss.* (TS draft) Allotment A subdivision of a parish under the old land-subdivision for the Auckland Provincial District. Still in use in the North Auckland, Auckland and Gisborne land-districts.

alluvial, *a.* and *n. Goldmining.*

A. *adj.* [Spec. use of *alluvial* pertaining to alluvium ('river silt').] Of gold-bearing alluvium.
1869 *AJHR* D-6 17 Vein mining is a very different operation from alluvial washing. **1896** MACKAY *Narrative of the Opening of the Hauraki Dist.* 17 [I] took my turn at alluvial digging (there was no quartzmining then). **1931** *NZJST* XII. 159 The progress of lode-mining is in some way analogous to that of alluvial digging. **1953** *NZ Geogr.* Apr. 29 Workings..were for the most part alluvial. **1967** MAY *West Coast Gold Rushes* 533 [The book] is a handy summary of the alluvial rushes in Westland and elsewhere. **1987** *National Bus. Rev.* 9 Oct. 1 [The company]..is fast becoming an alluvial producer in addition to its Monowai mine project.

B. *n.* [AND 1871.] Any gold-bearing alluvial soil.
1874 BAINES *Edward Crewe* 265 The latter place..having rich alluvial, or poor men's diggings, was a very bank with an ever-ready balance. **1883** *Brett's Colonists' Guide* 720 In the search for gold..whether it is sought for in the alluvial or in the quartz, the effort..is continued with unabated vigour. **1898** MORRIS *Austral-English* 2 Alluvial, the common term in Australia and New Zealand for gold-bearing alluvial soil. The word is also used adjectivally as in England. **1902** *Settler's Handbook NZ* 2 A distance of half a mile often makes all the difference between rich alluvial and barren pipe-clay. **1914** PFAFF *Diggers' Story* 42 The alluvial only extends a certain distance back from the coast line. **1948** MUNDY *There's Gold* 30 Collingwood is one of the oldest mining fields, but very little alluvial was being worked when we went there.

C. In collocations.
1. alluvial claim [AND 1859], **deposit, digger** [AND 1893], **diggings** [AND 1853], **ground, miner** [AND 1858], **mining** [AND 1867], **washing, workings** [AND 1865].
1862 WEKEY *Otago As It Is* 61 [Otago Goldfields Regs.] Claims shall be classified thus... Ordinary Claims, *i.e.,* **alluvial claims** worked without the aid of sluices or machines. 2. Sluice and machine claims, *i.e.,* alluvial claims worked with the aid of sluices or puddling machines. **1864** *AJHR* C-4 7 [Regulations under Goldfields Act (1862) Otago] Alluvial claims shall mean all claims in alluvial ground. **1871** in Evans *Waikaka Saga* (1962) 14 On December 10, 1871..applied for a licence to build a water race..terminating in an extended alluvial claim. **1894** *NZ Official Year-book* 369 Most of the diggers on prospecting alluvial claims work for themselves. **1903** *TrNZI* XXXV. 403 The old Glengyle and Hit or Miss alluvial claims. **1970** WOOD *Gold Trails Otago* 7 The ordinary alluvial claims were at first 24 ft square, then 30 ft square, but in 1866 the size was increased to 100 ft square. **1892** PYKE *Gold-Miners' Guide* 7 Claims are classified as follows:—**Alluvial deposits**, and river-or creek-beds; Quartz lodes, reefs, and leaders [etc.] **1933** *NZJST* XIV. 272 The alluvial miners thought they were dealing with superficial alluvial deposits. **1974** HEINZ *Bright Fine Gold* 200 *Alluvial deposit*: A deposit formed by material washed down or transported by water. **1869** *AJHR* D-6 3 For the sake of convenience, I shall..observe a distinction between the **alluvial digger**, by whom I understand one who gathers gold from the surface and from later deposits only, and the alluvial miner, that is, one who works the deeper deposits, or deep placer mines as they are called... The **alluvial diggings** which have been discovered..can hardly with any propriety be termed mines. **1889** KNOX *Boy Travellers* 215 Some of the mines are wholly alluvial, or placer, diggings, others are wholly quartz-mines. **1896** HARPER *Pioneer Work* 30 True, there are still many working the **alluvial ground** [on the West Coast], but those making more than 'tucker' are few. **1959** MILLAR *Westland's Golden 'Sixties* 158 Where there was alluvial ground to work, the men thought twice about venturing into country that was even more inhospitable. **1869 alluvial miner** [see *alluvial digger* above]. **1891** *NZJSc.* (NS) I. 60 [He] found the new mineral..in a sample of heavy black sand, reported as saved by alluvial miners in Barn Bay. **1933** alluvial miner [see *alluvial deposit* above]. **1967** MAY *West Coast Gold Rushes* 239 It was..in the variety of methods and contrivances used to seek out and work the auriferous deposits that the skills of the alluvial miner were displayed. **1976** BROWN *Difficult Country* 63 Although work was available in the quartz mines, many preferred the independent life of the alluvial miner. **1863** *AJHR* D-6 17 Mining operations in the Dunstan Goldfield..may be divided into three classes viz.,—River beach workings, ordinary **alluvial mining**, and tunnelling. **1967** MAY *West Coast Gold Rushes* 169 The outcome was a brilliant series of discoveries which added a new facet to alluvial mining. **1879** OLLIVANT *Hine Moa* 63 The miners have long since advanced from the early stage of **alluvial washing** to the crushing process. **1882** HAY *Brighter Britain* II. 274 Here, the mining is all quartz... There is no alluvial washing to enable one to pan out one's dust. **1914** PFAFF *Diggers' Story* 29 These [black sand] leads yielded a richer return..than probably any other **alluvial workings** in New Zealand. **1926** COWAN *Travel in NZ* II. 90 In the sixties there were ten thousand diggers on the alluvial workings here, chiefly on the ocean beach where these heavy dark sands were combed for the gold dust. **1940** HOWARD *Rakiura* 304 The return from alluvial workings was far too slight to meet the cost of lode development. **1976** NOLAN *Hist. Gold Trails Nelson & Marlborough* 72 Up the Blue Creek track today you can still see piles of stones from the old alluvial workings.

2. In special collocations: **alluvial gold** [AND 1851], free gold washed from auriferous material. Also *attrib.*
1852 *Coromandel Gold Field. Provisional Regs.* in SWAINSON *Auckland* (1853) 160 All alluvial or matrix Gold procured without due authority..will be liable to be seized. **1862** LINDSAY *Place & Power Nat. Hist. in Coloniz.* 14 It may exist..where it cannot be collected, as the alluvial gold of Australia and New Zealand is. **1878** BULLER *Forty Yrs. NZ* 116 In 1865, there was another find of alluvial gold. **1890** *TrNZI* XXII. 400 [I will] also dispute the theory that alluvial gold was not derived from reefs. **1902** *Brett's Colonists' Guide* (3edn.) 1030 Alluvial gold has originally been derived from quartz reefs in the adjacent country. **1918** *NZJST* I. 11 Near Deep Creek..miners in search of alluvial gold have sunk through 80 ft. of gravel in the stream bed. **1936** BELSHAW et al. *Agric. Organiz. NZ* 6 The decline in alluvial gold production after 1870 increased the supply of labour available for other industries. **1961** *Evening Post* (Wellington) 1 Dec. 17 Alluvial gold had apparently qualified as a work of art and for some years [the art union] prizes were £4000 in alluvial gold. **1970** WOOD *Gold Trails Otago* 81 The original source of all Otago's alluvial gold is the quartz reefs that cut through the mica schists. Hence **alluvial goldfield** *n.*; **alluvial goldmining** *vbl.n.*
1869 *AJHR* D-6 4 How great is the interval between the digger of alluvial gold and a real miner may be judged by comparing..habits... Of all the **alluvial gold fields**..none have been found permanent. **1873** TINNE *Wonderland of Antipodes* 43 [It] is to be..the great alluvial gold-field of this island. It has not been 'prospected' yet, from the reluctance of the natives to mining encroachments. **1926** COWAN *Travel in NZ* II. viii The chief element of adventure and romance was supplied by the successive 'rushes' to the great alluvial goldfields in Otago and on the West Coast. **1931** *NZJST* XII. 159 Thus Kumara, the best alluvial goldfield on the West Coast, was not discovered till 1876. **1967** MAY *West Coast Gold Rushes* 188 These produced the most imposing mining works on the West Coast and gave Ross a permanence unusual for an alluvial goldfield. **1904** *NZ Illustr. Mag.* May 103 They tell us that in the palmy..days of **alluvial gold-mining**, it was no uncommon sight to see over fifteen hundred miners [there]. **1914** PFAFF *Diggers' Story* 87 For Westland proper, alluvial gold mining has been its main pursuit.

All White /'ol 'wait/. [f. the playing strip of white top and shorts, after the verbal model of *All Black(s).*] As a collective *pl.*, a familiar name for the New Zealand representative soccer team adopted during the run-up to the World Cup games in Spain (1982); a member or former member of such a team.
1982 *Dominion* (Wellington) 13 May 20 [Heading] All Whites struggle to find timing. *Ibid.* 20 May 18 The All Whites could take precious little satisfaction from yesterday's stuttering performance. **1985** *Listener* 27 Apr. 28 To launch an All-White team into another successful World Cup campaign. **1988** *Contact* (Wellington) 22 Jan. 10 The Wellington district has become a happy hunting ground for the New Zealand soccer team, the All Whites. **1990** *Dominion* (Wellington) 31 Mar. 35 All White David Chote will make his first appearance [in] the Air New Zealand soccer league.

ally, var. ALLEY.

alpine. In the names of plants, see: BROOM 1, EYEBRIGHT, FERN 2 (6), (21), *celery pine* (PINE 2 (4) b), RUSH *n.*[1] 2 (1), TOATOA 1 b, TOTARA *n.*[1] 2 (1), TUSSOCK 3 (3) b, TUTU 2 (1).

Alps. *pl.* In New Zealand usu. the **Southern Alps**, a South Island mountain chain; occas. in early writing, the **New Zealand Alps**. See also BACKBONE 1.
1773 FORSTER *Resolution Jrnl.* 18 Apr. (1982) II. 260 We saw the Snow lying on the tops of some of the New-Zeeland Alps, whilst we enjoyed the verdure & mild air below. **1868** DILKE *Greater Britain* I. 340 The Rocky Mountains..are..not less snowy than the New Zealand Alps. **1885** *TrNZI* XVII. 188 In August I measured the ice in one of the lagoons on top of the Alps. **1920** BOLITHO *With the Prince in NZ* 186 The visitors were keenly interested in the country, which looked particularly rich, with endless acres of pasture land..and the back-ground of snow-crowned Alps. **1941** MYERS *Valiant Love* 159 We have the Edelweiss, just like Switzerland. It's a little, flannel-like flower, found on the steep crags of our Alps.

amalgamated claim. *Goldmining.* [AND 1864.] See quot.
1967 MAY *West Coast Gold Rushes* 526 Amalgamated Claim: claims adjoining one another thrown together temporarily or permanently to facilitate working.

amber, *a.* [f. the colour: AND 1906.] Used in collocations designating beer, esp. as **amber fluid, amber liquid**; **amber-and-white**.

1938 Hyde *Nor Yrs. Condemn* (1986) 120 Starkie, looking contentedly through the crisp-beaded amber in his glass, said: 'Oh, you don't want all that skite over again'. **1974** Gifford *Loosehead Len's Big Brown Book* 60 Beer: The pause that refreshes, see also under 'Slops, Turps, Frosty Fluid, The Old Amber Liquid, Suds, Purge, etc, etc.' *Ibid.* 62 *Jar*: Brew of the old amber fluid at the Pot. **1986** Brown *Weaver's Apprentice* 55 They [*sc.* the drinkers] were the ones who shook their heads over the amber-and-white and told the sad tale of how Arthur Fleming had..been lost to them..never again to know the solace of bitter ale and light cheer. **1986** Knight *Geriatrics* 78 McEldowney was left struggling..in the ditch of a French roadside, as he rid himself of some of the worst effects of his Taranaki amber.

amber gambler. One who 'runs' the amber light at a controlled intersection, gambling on getting across safely before red shows.

1979 *Star* (Christchurch) 2 Feb. 6 [Heading] 'Amber gamblers' go scot free. Once again the Mayor of Christchurch..has made a call for a tougher line with traffic light offenders.

Hence **amber gambling** *vbl. n.*

1979 *Star* (Christchurch) 14 May 8 Last October the Ministry of Transport started a campaign to crack down on drivers disobeying traffic lights. Most will share the view of the Mayor..that amber gambling is 'a very serious offence'.

ambrite. [Cf. OED: f. *amber* + the mineral formative *ite*, ad. German *ambrit*, 1861.] A fossil tree resin (probably ancient kauri gum) similar to amber and found in New Zealand Tertiary strata.

1867 Hochstetter *New Zealand* 799 Although originating probably from a coniferous tree related to the Kauri pine, it nevertheless has been erroneously taken for Kauri gum... It is sufficiently characterised to deserve a special name; but it comes so near to real *amber* that it deserves the name of *Ambrite*. **1898** Morris *Austral-English* 2 Ambrite, (generally called *ambrit*)... Mineral, a fossil resin found in masses amidst lignite coals in various parts of New Zealand. Some identify it with the resin of *Dammara australis*, generally called *kauri gum*.

American, *a.*

a. Applied to various things of American origin or having characteristics believed to be American.

1861 *NZ Goldfields 1861* (1976) 31 I subjoin the retail prices of a few articles sold at Tuapeka..common lace-up boots, from £2 to £2 10s. per pair; American pegged boots, £3 10s. **1869** *TrNZI* I. (rev. edn.) 221 [The silvereye] subsists almost entirely on the destructive little *Aphis* known as 'American Blight'. **1936** Lambert *Pioneering Reminisc. Old Wairoa* 111 The first settlers..traded with the Maoris and sold them moleskin trousers, monkey coats, and American shirts. **1972** Sutton-Smith *Folkgames Children* 174 Then there were the terms referring to particular kinds of marbles: for example, agates, aggies, aggotties, American alleys..and woodies.

b. In special collocations: **American stove** *obs.*, a cooking stove with an enclosed firebox; occas. a free-standing 'pot-bellied' stove; **American tank**, a large American sedan; **American wag(g)on** *hist.* [AND 1855], a four-wheeled vehicle, variously a drag, or a kind of stagecoach with seating inside and on top and drawn by four horses.

1861 *Otago Witness* (Dunedin) 16 Feb. 7 [Advt] American Cooking Stoves. Assorted sizes just received of Golden Age, Snow Bird, City Air-tight, Eastern Permium, &c. &c. **1866** Barker *Station Life* (1870) 65 I think the kitchen is the chief glory of the house, boasting a 'Leamington range'—a luxury quite unknown in these parts, where all the cooking is done on an American stove. **c1871** Masters *Autobiography* (ATLMS) 49 I had been to Grey Town, for an American stove. **1989** Duder *Alex in Winter* 126 Several taxis are waiting at a rank, and he propels me towards the first one, a big **American tank**. **1865** Barker *Station Life* (1870) 27 We started in an **American waggon** drawn by a pair of stout cobs. **1869** Lush *Thames Jrnls.* 17 May (1975) 56 After his [the Duke of Edinburgh's] conveyance there was a long drag—or American waggon—drawn by four greys and containing the Governor and some 7 or 8 gentlemen. **1976** Trask *Elizabeth of Lavington* 109 Mr. T['s] transport [c1870]..was a fourwheeler called an 'American waggon'. It had a long body which could take three seats placed crosswise, but if only two or three passengers were aboard just one seat was enough leaving a good deal of spare room behind.

American axe. *Hist.* [AND 1903, for a Plumb broad-bladed axe.] A broad-bladed, typically double-bitted axe of North American manufacture. See also *Yankee axe* (Yankee *a.*).

1842 in Deans *Pioneers Canterbury* (1937) 45 List of outfit... 2 hand saws, 1 cross-cut saw,.. 2 adzes, 6 American felling axes (wedge shape),... 6 American screw augers (assorted). **1853** Earp *NZ* 213 Make a selection of American axes, all others are of no use, handsaws, cross-cut saws. **1857** Hursthouse *NZ* II. 331 The trees are thrown with the x [*sic*] cut saw and American axe. **1864** *AJHR* E-8 8 He answered 'I do consent [to slay my child],' and forthwith took an American axe, and cut off a hand and a foot. **1874** Baines *Edward Crewe* 172 Do not suppose that those ugly dull wedges, sometimes to be seen in a hardware-shop in England, and labelled American axes, though of British manufacture, are equal to the Yankee article. They are no more so than the mis-shapen stick affixed is to an American hickory axe-handle. **1883** *Brett's Colonists' Guide* 17 The best tools for bush-falling are an American axe, about five pounds weight. **1892** Osborn in Richards *Foveaux Whaling Yarns* (1995) 38 Captain Howell set me to chopping down an ironwood tree three and a half feet in diameter, with an English axe that weighed two pounds with the edge beveled on both sides the same as a hatchet is on one side. I told him I could not chop with that axe... He said I could have an American axe... I found one that weighed four and a half pounds. **1910** Fanning *Players & Slayers* 5 If the mangle's mainspring has a fit, don't restore it to consciousness with a tomahawk or the business end of an American axe. **1971** Williams *Dict. Maori Lang.* 289 *Poke* (iv), n. American axe; called also *toki poke*.

American invasion. *Hist.*

a. Used *joc.* to describe the intrusion of American language and ways.

1920 Bolitho *With the Prince in NZ* 175 The American invasion has not spread as far south as this [*sc.* Christchurch].

b. WW2. Also in shortened form, **invasion**. The influx of US servicemen from the Pacific theatre to New Zealand (mainly to Auckland and Wellington) c1942–44.

1946 Simpson *If You'd Care to Know* 75 That happening..which we may now refer to as 'The American Invasion' of 1942. **1958** Mulgan *Making of New Zealander* 144 When the American 'invasion' came, we found this [British] 'yoke' and [imperial] 'exploitation' idea was commonly held [by the Americans]. **1965** Cameron *NZ* 2 The 'invasion' of New Zealand by friendly American troops..obvious signs of a revolution in the making. **1988** *Those Were the Days* 22 It was, however, generally an amicable 'invasion', and the Americans were welcomed into homes wherever they were. **1991** *Evening Post* (Wellington) 12 Nov. 7 The American invasion of New Zealand 50 years ago will be repeated next year.

amoco, amoca, amoko, varr. moko.

amokura /ˌʌmʌuˈkurə/. [Ma. /ˈamokura/: Williams 8 *Amokura*.] *Phaethon rubricauda* (fam. Phaethontidae), a white subtropical seabird having two elongated, red, central tail feathers valued by the Maori as ornaments. See also *red-tailed tropic bird* (tropic bird).

1904 Tregear *Maori Race* 243 The most valued kinds [of feathers] were tail-feathers of the *huia*..and the long red tail-feathers of the *amokura* (Tropic bird: Phaethon rubricauda). **1927** Donne *Maori Past & Present* 29 The heads of the chiefs were adorned with..the long thin red tail feathers of the amokura, 'tropic bird'. **1948** Henderson *Taina* 134 He wore..in his hair plumes of the *amokura*. **1955** Oliver *NZ Birds* 195 *Western Pacific Red-tailed Tropic Bird. Amokura Phaethon rubricauda roseotincta* The breeding range of this tropical and subtropical subspecies includes on its southern boundary the Kermadec Islands. **1966** Falla et al. *Birds NZ* 59 Red-tailed Tropic Bird *Phaethon rubricauda*. *Other names*: Amokura, Strawtail. **1985** *Reader's Digest Book NZ Birds* 108 *Red-tailed Tropic Bird.. Other names*: Bo' sun bird, *amokura*... The Maoris of the North Cape region prized the long tail streamers of the red-tailed tropic bird. After easterly gales it is said they systematically searched the coast for these birds.

anchovy. [Transf. use of *anchovy* the small European fish *Engraulis encrasicholus*.] *Engraulis australis* (fam. Engraulidae), a small silvery marine fish commonly found in shoals.

1872 Hutton & Hector *Fishes NZ* 62 Engraulis encrasicholus... Anchovy. **1886** Sherrin *Handbook Fishes NZ* 9 Anchovy (*Engraulis encrasicholus*)... It was found at the mouth of the River Thames, and called by the Natives there korowhawha. **1927** *TrNZI* LVII. 314 There appear to be three species of fish belonging to the family Clupeidae in New Zealand waters, viz., *Engraulis antipodum*, or anchovy; *Sardinia neopilchardus* or pilchard, and..sprat. **1940** Phillipps *Fishes NZ* 5 The anchovy or korowhawha of the Maori is not well known to many European fishermen. It is very like the European species both in general appearance and in structure. **1956** Graham *Treasury NZ Fishes* 398 Anchovy *Austranchovia australis* (White). (Syn. *Engraulis encrasicholus var. antipodum* Gunther) **1986** Paul *NZ Fishes* 41 The anchovy is not exploited commercially, beyond a few local baitfisheries.

angeange, var. hangehange.

angelfish. As **black angelfish**, *Parma alboscapularis* (fam. Pomacentridae), a small bottom-dwelling marine fish, the adult being black with a white mark above the gill.

1966 Doogue & Moreland *Sea Anglers' Guide* 254 Black Angelfish... Other names: *Parma microlepis*; white-ear (Australia). **1982** Ayling *Collins Guide* (1984) 239 Like many tropical damselfishes the black angelfish is herbivorous, feeding almost exclusively on seaweeds, and is one of only six herbivorous fishes found in New Zealand. **1986** Paul *NZ Fishes* 98 Black angelfish *Parma alboscapularis* Family Pomacentridae. Apparently restricted to New Zealand.

angiangi. [Ma. /'aŋiaŋi/: Williams 11 *angiangi... 3... = taupata.*] A shrub or small tree of the genus *Coprosma* (fam. Rubiaceae). See also TAUPATA. Contrast HANGEHANGE.

1874 *TrNZI* VI. 49 *Coprosma bauleriana*, angeange.—Common on the coast. 1888 BULLER *Birds NZ* II. 151 Around the base..there is a dense growth of stunted angiangi (*Coprosma lucida*) looking very fresh and green. 1930 *NZJST* XI. 152 Where the slopes are broken..the following shrubby trees grow abundantly: Kohepiro.., angiangi (*Coprosma baueri*).

angle-park cowshed: SHED *n.*[1] 4 b.

angle post. *Fencing.* Also **angle.** See quot. 1982.

1952–53 *NZ Forest Service Gloss.* (TS draft) *Angle-post.* A heavy fencepost or light strainer, generally 8in.×5in.×7ft. or if round 6-7in. diam. × 7ft. 1982 *Agric. Gloss.* (MAF) 29 *Angle posts*: Posts placed where the fence changes direction. Need extra support by stays or tie-backs. 1989 RICHARDS *Pioneer's Life* 49 When the line [of the fence] was measured, and the number of strainers, angles, posts and battens calculated, the next job was to saw..the necessary timber.

Anglo-Maori, *n.* and *attrib.*

A. *n.* A person of mixed British and Maori race or descent. Cf. ANGLO-(NEW)ZEALANDER 1.

1850 GREENWOOD *Journey to Taupo* 36 Half-castes..presenting too often the painful picture of an Anglo-Maori, with all the tastes and habits and feelings of the savage. 1882 HAY *Brighter Britain* II. 137 The Anglo-Maori may be said to be divided into two distinct classes—those whose education has been chiefly..English, and those who have 'tumbled up' in the kainga, in all respects like the Maori. 1966 MEAD *Richard Taylor* 169 [Quoting Taylor's diary of Feb. 1851] Wallis's [the Wesleyan missionary's] children were fine specimens of Anglo-Maoris. 1970 MCNEISH *Mackenzie* 12 Wiremu wore a grass skirt over his trousers and a broken panama hat in the style of the Anglo-Maoris of the time.

B. *attrib.*

1. Combining both Maori and European in composition or characteristics.

1868 TAYLOR *Past & Present NZ* 165 Another similar Anglo-Maori force was sent from Wanganui to Opotiki..to punish the murderers. 1885 TREGEAR *Aryan Maori* 95 Such Anglo-Maori words as *paraoa*, flour; *honi*, honey; *karahi*, glass, are easily recognizable. 1979 SORRENSON *Maori Orig. & Migrations* 84 The myth survived with the Maori to bolster pride in the Anglo-Maori achievement. 1986 SORRENSON in *Na To Hoa Aroha* I. 17 By contrast, with his Anglo-Maori ancestry, Buck continued to believe in the amalgamation by miscegenation of the races.

2. *Hist.* In the collocation **Anglo-Maori war(s)**, used by some writers for NEW ZEALAND WAR(S).

1927 DONNE *Maori Past & Present* 122 The sporting nature of the Maori is further illustrated in an incident that occurred at the Bay of Islands during the Anglo-Maori War. 1979 BINNEY et al. *Mihaia* 15 The inland Anglican Station..founded at Te Whaiti in 1847, had been abandoned with the onset of the Anglo-Maori wars. 1984 BOYD *City of the Plains* 6 By peaceful coexistence with settlers, they hoped to avoid the consequences of the Anglo-Maori Wars in Taranaki and the Waikato, namely conquest and land confiscation. 1987 SCOTT *Seven Lives on Salt River* 85 Russell..had escaped active service in the Anglo-Maori wars by selling his commission to become a Hawkes Bay squatter. 1993 SINCLAIR *Halfway Round the Harbour* 157 While serving in the militia during the Anglo-Maori Wars, Tom used to sing to the troops.

Anglo-New Zealand. *Hist.* Also **Anglo-Zealand.**

1. *n.* A name for the combination of English and Maori characteristics found in early 19th century New Zealand society. Also *attrib.*

1836 MARSHALL *Narr. Two Visits* 3 Ware poaka.. [is] a barbarous compound of New Zealand and Anglo-New Zealand; ware signifying poor and poaka, pig, being corrupted from our English word pork.

2. *a.* Of or pertaining to New Zealand inhabitants of non-Maori stock; or to those of mixed British-Maori race (ANGLO-MAORI B 1).

1843 *NZ Jrnl.* IV. 257 We hope that public opinion may..get us back to a helpless and unhelping *laissez faire*, rather than such cruel and foolish legislation as this, of which, in the name of the Anglo New Zealand community, we now complain. 1847 in Wakefield *Handbook NZ* (1848) 250 The young women [British immigrants to Nelson] are all married, and doing their best towards increasing the Anglo-Zealand race. 1849 HURSTHOUSE *New Plymouth* 35 Perhaps, their [*sc.* Maori] entire civilization might be peacefully effected; and their partial amalgamation, following as a consequence, would form an 'Anglo-New-Zealand' race, which physically at least, would vie with any in the world.

Anglo-New Zealander. *Hist.*

1. Also **Anglo-Zealander.** ANGLO-MAORI A 1.

1836 MARSHALL *Narr. Two Visits* 46 Twenty seven infants present, of whom seventeen were native born, and three of these Anglo-New Zealanders. 1838 POLACK *NZ* II. 338 Much as we deplore the original connexion, which notwithstanding its not-to-be defended immorality, has lessened the crime of infanticide..the numerous offspring, or Anglo-Zealanders, are so many perpetual ties, daily presented before their relations and tribes.

2. a. A settler in New Zealand born in Britain.

1842 in *Lett. from Settlers* (1843) 68 During my stay at Port Nicholson with Francis M— that genuine good fellow, and pattern for all Anglo New Zealanders..went to work and cleared his land. 1844 *NZ Jrnl.* IV. 339 We may appeal..to..the opinions of Anglo-New Zealanders both at home and in the colony... We have often said that we have doubts in our own mind as to the faith of the Anglo New Zealander in the resources of New Zealand.

b. A New Zealand-born European residing in Britain.

1944 FULLARTON *Troop Target* 23 Early on he had joined a battery of Anglo-New Zealanders..joining up in the Old Dart.

Anglo-Zealand, var. ANGLO-NEW ZEALAND.

animated straw. *Obs.* Also **animated twig**, occas. **straw insect.** [AND *animated straw* 1805, *-twig* 1839.] A stick insect of fam. Phasmidae. See also JACKSTRAW, *ridgepole rafter* (RIDGEPOLE 1 a), *teatree jack* (TEA-TREE 3 b).

1865 CARTER *Life in NZ* 429 The scrub or bush is covered with a species of Mantidae, called by the settlers animated twigs. 1902 SATCHELL *Land of Lost* (1971) 33 He threw himself down in a thick clump of tea tree, and was soon absorbed in watching a battle between two full-grown 'animated straws'. 1971 SMITHYMAN in Satchell *Land of Lost* (1971) 215 'Animated straws'. Sometimes the Straw or Teatree Straw Insect, usually the New Zealand Stick Insect.

anise /'ænɪs/, /ə'nɪs/. Mainly *SI.* Also **annis(s)**, **Maori (native) anise.** [Transf. use of *anise*, an aromatic plant.] ANISEED.

1844 WAKEFIELD *Let.* 31 Aug. in Hocken *Contributions* (1898) 267 The anise plant, so valuable as pasture for sheep and cattle, abounds over all the land we traversed. 1853 ADAMS *Spring Canterbury Settlement* 64 Thickly spread with the Anis plant of which horses are particularly fond. 1864 BARRINGTON *Diary* 9 Jan. in Taylor *Early Travellers* (1959) 397 Caught a hawk notwithstanding we could have with a little anniss. 1872 BUTLER *Erewhon* ch. iii On the saddle there was coarse grass..very nourishing for the horse; also abundance of anise and sow-thistle, of which they are extravagantly fond. 1922 *NZJST* IV. 282 Sheep & rabbits..have not quite exterminated the native anise.., which I remember seeing growing abundantly in the Molyneux Valley. 1939 BEATTIE *First White Boy Born Otago* 50 Anise grew the thickest I ever saw at Mount Durden. 1940 LAING & BLACKWELL *Plants NZ* 342 *Angelica montana* (*Maori Anise*)... Both islands. 1961 MARTIN *Flora NZ* 288 A third species of Angelica (*A. montana*), the Maori Anise, was at one time an abundant herb... It has a very strong scent of aniseed. 1979 Maori anise [see KOHEPIRO].

aniseed. Mainly *SI.* Also **native aniseed.** [Transf. and extended use of *aniseed* the seed of the ANISE.] *Gingidia montana* (fam. Apiaceae), a highly aromatic herb formerly common but now rare; less commonly (see quot. 1930), a robust native herb of *Anisotome* spp. (fam. Apiaceae). See also ANISE, KOHEPIRO.

1844 TUCKETT *Diary* 24 May in Hocken *Contributions* (1898) 224 Like the narrow plains of the Waikauroa, it grows..no aniseed, perennial groundsel, or milk thistle. 1867 THOMSON *Twelve Yrs. Canterbury* 17 An indigenous aniseed grows in many parts greatly improving the flesh of the animals feeding on it. 1907 LAING & BLACKWELL *Plants NZ* 322 *Angelica Gingidium* (*The Native Aniseed.*).. The whole plant is highly aromatic. It is greedily eaten by sheep, and though originally very abundant, is often almost exterminated in accessible places. The plant is known to shepherds and runholders as *Aniseed*. 1926 CROOKES *Plant Life Maoriland* 154 The family is a very large one, containing among its New Zealand representatives..the Ligusticums..and that highly aromatic plant, the native aniseed. 1930 REISCHEK *Yesterdays in Maoriland* (1933) 281 The vegetation [of Campbell Island] is tussock mixed with cotton-plants, aniseed, veronica, and other plants. 1947–48 BEATTIE *Pioneer Recolls.* (1956) 6 The scent came principally from musk and anise. The latter was usually known as aniseed. 1954 MACFARLANE *Te Raka* 40 The outstanding plant in these preserves and the one that disappeared as the deer came along was aniseed. We do know that it was common everywhere once and gave a bright sheen, when in flower, to the whole of North Canterbury. 1978 JARDINE *Shadows on Hill* 34 Just a hint of dew and the sweet smell of tussock, and a whiff or two of aniseed on the cool air [of the Otago high country].

ankle-biter. [AND 1981.] A small child.

1991 *Sharon Crosbie on Wellington radio 19 Nov.* If we didn't have teachers, we'd have all the anklebiters out on the street. 1992 *Listener* 4 May 87 But does the radio dial offer any more relief for bored ankle-biters, crecheniks and fractious parents today?

Annie: see GENTLE ANNIE.

anniss, var. ANISE.

Anniversary Day. A holiday, celebrated locally, to commemorate the founding of each New Zealand province.

1868 *Marlborough Express* (Blenheim) 7 Nov. 4 Anniversary Day.—Monday [2 November] was kept as a general holiday as being the Anniversary of the Province. **1881** *Let. No.1029: 81/973* 9 Dec. in *Prisons Letterbook* (J 43/2 National Archives) 48 The Minister of Justice directs me to inform you that Canterbury Anniversary Day, 16th inst, is to be prison holiday. **c1910** MacDonald *Reminiscences* (VUWTS) 12 The Chief of our general holidays [c1850s] was Wellington Anniversary Day on 22nd January. **1940** *Tales Pioneer Women* (1988) 104 The anniversary of the landing of the first settlers was celebrated from the very first year, usually with aquatic sports off the Queen's wharf... Climbing the greasy pole was always one of the events on anniversary day. **1958** Miller *Early Victorian NZ* 166 Each settlement had its own Anniversary Day commemorating the landing of the first settlers. It was a time for joyous excitement. **1962** *Public Holidays Amendment Act* s2 Anniversary Day in Chatham Islands..in relation to the Chatham Islands, that reference shall be deemed to be a reference to the thirtieth day of November in each year. **1975** Knight *Poyntzfield* 55 In the evening they chatted about their arrival [in Rangitikei, c1850s] and first experiences, and the first anniversary celebrations, because this was Anniversary Day. **1986** *Pacific Desk Calendar* When Anniversary Day falls on Friday or later, the holiday is observed on the next Monday; if earlier, it is observed on the preceding Monday. In some cases the holiday is taken on the local show day or some other day; in Taranaki it is the second Monday in March to avoid a clash with Easter observance.

Hence **Anniversary weekend**, a 'long' weekend which includes a Monday anniversary day.
1949 *Tararua Tramper* Dec. 3 Anniversary Weekend, January 20–21 – 22–23. **1987** Knox *After Z-Hour* 208 We may have taken Mike's car up the Gold Coast at Anniversary Weekend, and cooled our wine in the rockpools of Pukerua Bay.

anoohe: see aruhe.

Antarctic prion: see prion 1.

ante up, *v. Obs.* Also **anti, anty**. [Transf. use of orig. US *ante up* to put up an *ante* or initial stake in poker: AND 1878.] **a.** *trans.* To produce; to (find and) hand over (something).
1873 Pyke *Wild Will Enderby* (1889, 1974) III. viii 99 Well, now, I guess the plant ain't sprung; though for the matter of that I'd ante up every ounce of gold to have saved poor Harry, I would, Sir. **1905** *Truth* 24 June 5 [They] 'ante up' their silver to support the cute Yankee person.

b. *intr.* To hand over (something), to pay up.
1873 Pyke *Wild Will Enderby* (1889, 1974) III. v 90 Don't suppose they'll ante up to these galoots, so I'll jest take another hand [of cards] myself. **1908** *Truth* 18 Jan. 1 There is a 'tight' in the affairs of man, which taken at the flood leads on the 'rising'—if you haven't 5s to ante-up. **1914** Grace *Tale Timber Town* 114 Where's the key? You young imp, anty up.

Also as a noun, a card game, prob. poker.
1872 *Inangahua Herald* 7 Feb. in Latham *Golden Reefs* (1992) 126 All [hotels] appeared to be doing a thriving trade and their customers appeared all as busy as 'the Devil in a gale of wind'—some were engaged in a little game of 'anti-up'..while a few were in the 'fifteen-two' business.

antipodeal /æntɪpəˈdiəl/, *a. Obs.* [Erron. form of *antipodal* prob. influenced by *antipodean*: AND 1854.]

1859 Thomson *Story NZ* II. 309 The antipodeal colonies, separated by half the globe from England, are tainted with convictism and cannibalism. **1881** Nesfield *Chequered Career* 63 It has often been a matter of regret to me that I could not get hold of a true tale of antipodeal vicissitudes.

antipodean, *a.* and *n.* [Spec. use of *antipodean* of the opposite side of the world.] New Zealand.
A. *adj.*
1. Occas. with init. cap. New Zealand B 2 b (see also 1990 quot.).
1874 Baines *Edward Crewe* 20 Presently on my road to town I fell in with two Maories. I was sitting on a hillside in the [Auckland] Domain when up came my two Antipodean aboriginals. **1881** Campbell *Poenamo* 123 Yet how vivid still the remembrance of that year of grace 1840..on the Antipodean shores of Poenamo. **1934** Ngata *Let.* 25 Mar. in *Na To Hoa Aroha* (1988) III. 145 Some ass has said that it is a delegation of goodwill to lay the position of the poor Antipodean dairyman before his relative and talk to him of the 'Empire' and 'loyalty'! **1944** Marsh *Died in the Wool* 35 His accent was slightly antipodean. **1965** Sinclair *William Pember Reeves* 58 [Reeves] was more than an occasionally irritating but essentially conforming young member of a remote, provincial, antipodean, middle class. **1980** Henderson *New Zealanders* in McLauchlan ed. *Acid Test* (1981) 190 In a way, this [sc. 'she'll be right'] is an Antipodean equivalent of the beloved English: 'Mustn't grumble'. **1990** *Evening Post* (Wellington) 31 July 1 [Caption] Just a friendly Antipodean nip..Dr Rudolph Reinhard..grimaces after being bitten by a rare Antipodes Island Parrot.

2. In the collocation **antipodean gothic**, a scaled-down version of Gothic architecture expressed (most often in wood) in New Zealand ecclesial and public buildings of the 19th century.
1991 Shaw *NZ Architecture* 32 [In chapter 2 headed 'The Birth of Antipodean Gothic'.] Thatcher and Mountfort were the most significant figures in the history of the Gothic Revival to which Ian Lockhead [in Ian Lockhead & Jonathan Mané *W.B. Armion: a colonial architect rediscovered* 1983] has given the title *antipodean gothic*.

B. *n.* With init. cap. A New Zealander.
1875 Cockburn-Hood *Chowbokiana or Notes About the Antipodes & the Antipodeans* [title: *NZNB* I. i. 229, item 1302.] **1987** *Metro* (Auckland) May 59 Some sort of cultural imperative caused the young women to board a ship..and save..for a tour of..the Munich beer festival in the company of other Antipodeans. **1990** *Dominion Sunday Times* (Wellington) 22 Apr. 8 I am not an Enzedder, or a Kiwi, or an Antipodean, or an Anzac... I am a New Zealander, of northern European descent, as it happens.

Antipodes. [Spec. use of *antipodes* places on the Earth directly opposite each other: AND 1833.] Usu. with init. cap., and with *the*. New Zealand regarded as the notional antipodes, geographic, cultural, and seasonal, of Britain.
1832 Earle *NZ* (1966) 74 I could not help thinking..whether this was a way to receive a countryman at the Antipodes. **1850** *Acheron Jrnl.* Apr. in Howard *Rakiura* (1940) 388 She sported a body garment of recent date called 'Polka jacket' by modistes and I believe, not yet quite abandoned by her civilised sisters of the Antipodes. **1863** Butler *First Year* x 145 People do not leave England and go to live at the antipodes to work for the same wages which they had at home. **1871** Money *Knocking About NZ* 4 Except that the hills in the background are not equal in height to those at the Antipodes, one or two of the small towns on the coast of Cornwall..would give a very good impression of the picturesque little town of Lyttelton. **1887** Hopeful *Taken In* 116 The butchers' shops which at home are a grand sight at this time..were quite otherwise at the Antipodes. **1902** *Brett's Colonists' Guide* (3edn.) 10 The following pages will assist in stating matters as they exist at the Antipodes. **1911** Boreham *Selwyn* 89 Very few modern churchmen.. recognise the enormous influence which Bishop Selwyn exerts upon the religious life of our own day as a direct outcome of these early experiments at the Antipodes. **1938** Lancaster *Promenade* 15 At least there will be laxity in the Antipodes, thought Jermyn, seeing himself gathering up Maori wives by the dozen. **1963** Norris *Armed Settlers* 58 To own one's own home was a goal which brought many a craftsman to the Antipodes. **1976** Sargeson *Sunset Village* 34 Then too there was that *word*—and Brixton knew that Antipodes meant opposite feet. **1983** Wilson *Rutherford Simple Genius* 91 [Of Ernest Rutherford.] A rabbit here from the antipodes who burrows mighty deep. **1990** Barber et al. in Majouram *Sergeant, Sinner* 5 On 3 September [1855] the detachment embarked for New Zealand. This time the force had an uneventful voyage to the antipodes.

Antipodes Island In the names of birds, see: parakeet 2 (1), snipe *n.* 2.

anti-shouting law. *Hist.* A regulation to prevent treating ('shouting') in public bars supposing this to lead to drunkenness, introduced in 1916 in the interests of encouraging sobriety among young soldiers.
[**1916** Glover Cartoon in *Truth* 'The Cranks' Chorus' in Grant *Unauthorised Version* (1980) 105 [Two characters captioned 'The Wowser' and 'Jimmy Woodser' hold jointly a song-book with cover respectively showing] 'Six O'C Closing' [and] 'No-shouting'.] **1919** Fanning *Politics and the Public* 68 The so-called 'anti-shouting law' was brought into force on 28th August, 1916, by regulation under the War Regulations Act, amended a month previous to that date... A proposal was..made [21st September, 1917,] to abolish the anti-shouting regulation, but was defeated by 47 votes to 21. **1949** Reed *Story Canterbury* 184 The public-houses, too, were open, and considering that there was no anti-'shouting' law, the conduct of the voters was commendably restrained.

Anzac /ˈænˌzæk/, *n.* and *attrib.* [f. initials of *Australian and New Zealand Army Corps*: AND derives f. the initials orig. used as a code name for the Corps, quoting C.E.W. Bean's *Diary* of 25 Apr. 1915 67, *Col. Knox to Anzac* 'Ammunition required at once.' The NZ military historian, Chris Pugsley (see quot. 1994 A 1 below), places the coining of the term at Birdwood's headquarters in Egypt before the landing at Gallipoli.]
[*Note*] There may have been a proposal to name the Corps the *Australasian Army Corps*: cf. 1915 Williams *New Zealander's Diary* 24 Apr. (c1922) 64, Ourselves (Australasian Army Corps) are to move shortly, and tomorrow, in all probability, all will face the crisis of our lives.

A. *n.* Also formerly **A.N.Z.A.C., A. & N.Z.A.C.**
1. [AND 25 Apr. 1915.] The word ANZAC as an acronym of the Australian and New Zealand Army Corps.
1915 Birdwood 19 Dec. in *Anzac Book* (1916) ix When I took over the command of the Australian and New Zealand Army Corps in Egypt a year ago, I was asked to send a telegraphic code address for my Army

Corps, and then adopted the word 'Anzac.' **1916** *Anzac Book* [title page] *For the benefit of Patriotic Funds connected* with the A. & N.Z.A.C. **1916** *Chron. NZEF* 30 Aug. 10 All colonials, 'big islanders' included..agree with the speaker that in the past there has been too much Anzac; it's about time we heard of the brave and glorious [deeds] accomplished by the British Tommies in France. **1917** *Ibid.* 31 Jan. 243 Discussions are still rampant concerning the origin, meaning and application of the word 'Anzac'. The *Morning Post* has suddenly awoken to the fact that its origin was the Turkish word 'anzak', meaning 'to jump', which, together with the fact that there are kangaroos in Australia and that Australian soldiers jumped ashore at Anzac, finally proves..that code words of initial letters had nothing to do with it. **1919** WAITE *New Zealanders at Gallipoli* 318 *Anzac*.—Formed from the initial letters of Australian and New Zealand Army Corps. First used (written A. and N.Z.A.C.) in Egypt, when the Army Corps was formed. It soon became A.N.Z.A.C., and the new word was so obvious that the full stops were omitted. **1966** *Encycl. NZ* I. 53 Such is the respect with which the term Anzac is held that an Order in Council was promulgated on 31 August 1916 forbidding the use of the word in connection with any trade or business. **1994** PUGSLEY *NZ Defence Quarterly* Autumn 35 The word ANZAC was coined by New Zealand Sergeant K M Little who was working as a clerk in Birdwood's Australia and New Zealand Army Corps Headquarters in Egypt before Gallipoli. It was then adopted as the telegraphic address of the headquarters.

2. *Hist.* As a place-name, esp. with reference to Anzac Cove, thence extended to the Gallipoli Peninsula, and occas. to the Gallipoli campaign as a whole. Fraser & Gibbons *Soldier & Sailor Words* (1925) 8 note: '*Anzac Cove*: The name given to the Anzacs' landing place at Gallipoli to commemorate the heroism displayed on the occasion. Anzac Cove was so named by General Birdwood.' Cf. GALLIPOLI a.
1915 WILLIAMS *New Zealander's Diary* 3 May (c1922) 100 May 3 Anzac was now a position of great strength... May 6 Last evening the New Zealand Brigade..were transported on torpedo-boat destroyers from Anzac to Cape Helles. **1915** *let.* of 5 May to Rev. F.H. Spencer from his son at the Dardanelles in *Wanganui Herald* 4 Aug. 8 Writing again on 5-5-15, he stated that for eleven days, the battle of Anzac Bay (so named from the first letters of 'Australian and New Zealand Army Corp' [*sic*]) has been raging. **1919** WAITE *New Zealanders at Gallipoli* 85 Here at last a stand would be made..picks were laid aside and the indomitable men of Anzac again took up their rifles to face the trials of the day. *Ibid.* 95 A walk along Anzac Cove was full of interest... The Cove became the nerve-centre of Anzac:.. on the beach were the Headquarters of the Army Corps, the hospital..the Ordnance and Supply Depots. **1952** DUFF *Shepherd's Calendar* (1961) 75 It is not that Anzac no longer means anything to me or should now, I feel, be forgotten.

3. a. Orig. a member or former member of the Australian and New Zealand Army Corps. Fraser and Gibbons *Soldier & Sailor Words* (1925) 7 note: 'It had eventually to be officially notified that "Anzac" was restricted to men who had fought at Gallipoli; owing to the loose way people in general used the word often for Australians and New Zealanders who had never been there at all.'
1916 *Chron. NZEF* 30 Aug. 127 If the point I am raising is not already too well-worn..to protest against the tendency of the British Press to confine the word 'Anzac' almost entirely to Australians. **1917** *NZ at the Front* 175 'Well, there are some Anzacs over there—I'll ask them if they can help me.' He called out to one of our boys: 'You're Anzac, aren't you?'..Jack admitted he was a New Zealander. **c1917** Newspaper cutting quoted in Evans *Waikaka Saga* (1962) 148 The funeral..at Waikaka, April 1917, was accorded full military honours... The late A.N.Z.A.C. was a member of the main body of New Zealand Expeditionary Forces and took part in the terrible action on Gallipoli. **1918** MACGILL *An Anzac's Bride* 13 Diamond did fall in love with the big, laughing Anzac... Dick had been through the hell-fire of Gallipoli, and was on seven days' leave. **1922** *Free Lance* (Wellington) 27 Sept. 1 [Caption] The Anzacs' Response. The Two Anzacs (Aussie and En Zed): 'Here we are, Dad. If the Turk wants another scrap we're ready to do our bit.' **1936** HYDE *Passport to Hell* 132 The Anzacs considered the Maltese respectability too much of a good thing.

Hence, **Anzacian**, a New Zealand soldier of WW1.
1916 ROSS *Light & Shade* 181 One Anzacian who had spent a busy morning with his shirt was heard soliloquizing at the mouth of his dug-out.

b. Often *pl.* Any New Zealand soldier (or returned soldier) of WW1, occas. from WW2.
1914–18 FOWLER in Boyack *Behind the Lines* (1989) 130 That is the worst of being a digger, you seem to take on with the girls. Of course who could resist us. Gallant Blue-eyed Anzacs. **1918** *Quick March* 25 Apr. 7 But when we get to Berlin, The Kaiser he will say:—'Hoch! Hoch! Mein Gott What a —— poor lot Are the Anzacs of to-day!' **1935** GUTHRIE *Little Country* (1937) 410 The prose of the English poet who wrote of the Anzacs before the landing on Gallipoli came back to his mind. **1944** FULLARTON *Troop Target* 104 'What's wrong with being an Anzac?' 'Nothing... Except to nine people out of ten Anzac means Australian.' **1953** CODY *21 Battalion* 15 Official news of the Anzacs' arrival [in 1940] was not released until they were safely in camp in the south of England. **1972** MITCHELL *Pavlova Paradise* 182 *Anzac:* In New Zealand a New Zealand soldier. In Australia an Australian soldier. In Britain an enzyme soap powder which is slightly less of a biological miracle than the other two. **1987** KNOX *After Z-Hour* 145 Almost all our officers [*sc.* in WW1] are New Zealanders..Lieutenant Given and our Captain are both Anzacs.

4. As a symbol of unity, often through suffering. Also *attrib.*
1919 WAITE *New Zealanders at Gallipoli* 300 And if Anzac means suffering, a hopeless longing, aching hearts..the gain cannot be measured. **1955** *BJ Cameron Collection* (TS July) Anzac; the spirit of Anzac. The virtue of self-sacrifice in the common good. **1983** HENDERSON *Down from Marble Mountain* 260 Disease, plus the Spirit of Anzac, are thumped into us [soldiers]. **1987** KNOX *After Z-Hour* 71 Anzac no nonsense and suffering in silence. **1990** *Dominion Sunday Times* (Wellington) 22 Apr. 8 Wouldn't it be odd if we were all again touched and driven by the Anzac spirit, by what we've done and what we're still going to do?

B. *attrib.*

1. [AND 1916.] Used attributively in various senses of the noun. Also *transf.* as a trade-name.
1915 HARPER *Let.* 30 Dec. in *Lett. from Gunner 7:516* (1978) 36 We heard, by wireless, the news of the Anzac withdrawal and it caused a deep sensation amongst the 'Anzacs' on board. **1916** *Evening Post* (Wellington) 11 Apr. 9 [Advt] 'ANZAC' Commemoration Jewellery Brooches and Pendants (*Designed, Registered by, and only to be had from W. Littlejohn & Son.*) What better ornament could be worn in honour of our men from under the Southern Cross. **1917** *Wanganui Herald* 21 Apr. [Heading] A Popular War lecture. On 'Anzac' Night. **1917** *NZ at the Front* 103 'Have you not heard of the 'Anzac Cocktail'? That was *my* invention.' *Ibid.* 128 We fought disease, we fought the thirst Of Anzac days—a thing acurst. **1919** WAITE *New Zealanders at Gallipoli* 142 Right along the..front the attacks melted away—nowhere was the Anzac line penetrated. **1936** HYDE *Passport to Hell* 137 This served the Tommies right—for when unpaid they would hang around the Anzac encampments with their tongues out. **1988** SHADBOLT *Voices of Gallipoli* 37 We thought [Cape Helles] was going to be something of a holiday from the Anzac sector.

2. *transf.* Descriptive of things, projects, exercises, etc. involving or affecting both New Zealand and Australia.
1922 *Auckland Weekly News* 9 Nov. 69 The New Zealand Returned Soldiers' Association places on record its disapproval of the suggestion made in Australia that the Tasman Sea be renamed the Anzac Sea. **1923** *Dominion* (Wellington) 23 Feb. (VUW Fildes Clippings 427:103) [Heading of a cable from London] 'ANZAC' or 'TASMAN'. No Sacrilegious Disregard for the Past. The annual report of the [British] Historical Society refers to the intervention of the society in frustrating the effort to change the name of the Tasman Sea to Anzac Sea. The report adds: 'The society yields to none in its admiration of the Anzacs, but we should honour the Anzacs without a sacrilegious disregard for the past.' **1986** MCNEISH *Lovelock* (1987) 51 At these sports an Australian friend..and I had made up an 'Anzac' stable and caused some comment by winning four races between us [at Oxford]. **1991** *Sunday Star* (Auckland) 3 Nov. A7 Now its dependence on the Anzac relationship as its sole active defence backstop means that Wellington must toe Canberra's line. **1994** *Dominion* (Wellington) 11 Aug. 22 Australian-owned Simpson..has also gone for a young kid to hock its merchandise, but the Simpson sales tot boasts a fine Kiwi twang as she carries her buckets of Auckland water to do the washing. Guess the Anzac spirit is alive and well after all.

3. Comb. and special Comb. in the names of foods and drinks: **Anzac biscuit** [poss. orig. a recipe sponsored by 'Oatina'-brand rolled oats: AND 1943], **crispy, hare, nutty, pudding, roll, shandy, wafer** [AND 1918], see quots.
1927 *Terrace Tested Recipes* (Terrace Congreg. Church, Wellington) 110 **Anzac Biscuits**... butter..golden syrup... boiling water..carbonate of soda... coconut..oatina... Place in teaspoon quantities on a cold slide. **1929** *Ideal Cook. Book* 122 Anzac Biscuits..butter..golden syrup..baking soda..boiling water... Oatina..dessicated [*sic*] cocoanut [etc.] chopped walnuts..flour... Put teaspoonfuls on cold tray and bake. **1936** *Cook. Book NZ Women's Inst.* 153 Anzac Biscuits. Melt..butter, 1 tablespoon syrup, add 1 teaspoon soda, dissolve in 2 tablespoons boiling water. Add 1 cup wholemeal, 1 cup dessicated [*sic*] coconut, ³/4 cup flour, 1 cup sugar, 1 cup walnuts. Roll in hands into little balls. Bake ¹/2 hour in slow oven. **1961** *Edmonds Sure to Rise Cook. Book* 12 Anzac Biscuits 1 breakfastcup Oatina [etc.]... Roll into small balls and bake slowly 25–30 mins at 325° F. Leave room for spreading. **1987** *Listener* 20 June 93 I used to run a little cafe opposite Wellington's Cenotaph and appropriately, I thought, had anzac biscuits listed on the blackboard in the window. One morning just before Anzac Day I was visited by a man from the RSA who told me I'd have to call the biscuits something else because it was an offence to use the word Anzac for business purposes. **1932** *St. Andrew's Cook. Book* 170 **Anzac Crispies**.. flaked oatmeal..flour..sugar..melted butter..baking soda..treacle..boiling water..bake in small pieces flattened out. **1982** BURTON *200 Years NZ Cooking* 111 **Anzac hare**. This simple meat loaf bears about as much resemblance to hare as colonial goose does to poultry, but Anzac hare it always has been, and Anzac hare it will remain. **1988** MCGILL *Dict. Kiwi Slang* 10 *Anzac hare* meat loaf looking like no Anzac and no

hare. **1972** NILSON *Penguin Cook. Book* (3edn.) 358 **Anzac Nutties**..sugar..whole-meal flour..white flour..salt..chopped nuts..desiccated coconut..golden syrup..butter..bicarbonate of soda..hot water. Roll into balls..greased tray..moderate oven..20 minutes..cool them on the trays. **1929** MCKAY *Pract. Home Cook.* 146 **Anzac Pudding** flour..sugar..butter..egg..sweet milk..baking powder..raisins or currants..steam. **1936** *Cook.Book NZ Women's Inst.* 135 **Anzac Rolls.** Oatina, sugar, dessicated [*sic*] coconut..flour..golden syrup..butter..soda dissolved in..boiling water. Put small teaspoonfuls on cold slide..hot oven about 8 minutes. Roll while hot and put aside to get cold. **1934** LEE *Children of Poor* (1939) 22 The warm *estaminet* and the **Anzac shandy** seemed to confer on that grubby memory a romantic tinge. **1938** *Press* (Christchurch) (McNab Slang) 2 Apr. 18 [Slang of the N.Z.E.F.] An 'Anzac shandy' contained beer and champagne, while an 'Anzac Wafer' was an army biscuit. **1918** BEATTIE in Boyack *Behind the Lines* (1989) 160 [The strike] took on like wildfire as the men had had a very miserable breakfast—hard biscuits (**Anzac wafers** as they call them). **1920** *Quick March* 10 Apr. 56 [Title] Anzac Wafers and Chestnuts: A dissertation on Hard Tack. Hard! Well I should say so, biscuits (Army) and chestnuts, for I have attempted..masticating both at one meal. **1937** PARTRIDGE *Dict. Slang* 15 *Anzac wafer.* A large (hard) Army biscuit: New Zealand soldiers': 1915–18.

4. Comb. and special Comb.: see quotations below for **Anzac button** [AND 1919], **lily, parade** [AND 1966], **poppy,** an artificial poppy worn as a commemoration, **service, Sunday, weekend,** see quots.
1968 *NZ Contemp. Dict. Suppl.* (Collins) 2 **Anzac button** n. a nail used in place of a trouser button. **1980** Adams *Wild Flowers* 14 The Kaffir lily has been given the local name of **Anzac lily** because it flowers in April... Botanical name: *Schizostylis coccinea*, South Africa. Family: Iridaceae. **1962** LAWLOR *More Wellington Days* 18 Evatt's 'Digger', who used to march with him in the **Anzac parades**, will take a leading part. **1965** STEAD in *Some Other Country* (1984) 138 What did he think he was up to waving a red flag over the Anzac parade. **1987** ELDRED-GRIGG *Oracles & Miracles* 115 Mum had always made us go to the Anzac Parade when we were kids. **1987** *NZ Herald* (Auckland) 29 Apr. quoted in *Listener* 23 May 7 He had worn an **Anzac poppy** last Friday when they met. **1920** BOLITHO *With the Prince in NZ* 24 From the **Anzac service** the prince crossed the harbour to Devonport. **1982** PEAT *Detours* 139 My handbook had an impressive entry for Tinui. The first Anzac service was held there in 1916, a year after the Gallipoli landing. **1920** BOLITHO *With the Prince in NZ* 23 It was **Anzac Sunday**, and a massed church service was held in the Town Hall during the afternoon. **1988** *Salient* (Wellington) 23 May 13 It's **Anzac weekend**, and Small is performing in New Zealand for the second time.

Anzac Day, *n.* and *attrib.* [AND 1916.] April 25 as a public holiday in New Zealand (and Australia) with ceremonies commemorating the Gallipoli landing on 25 April 1915, and New Zealand (orig. WW1) war dead. See also *Gallipoli Day* (GALLIPOLI b).
A. *n.*
1916 *Dannevirke Evening News* 21 Mar. 4 Anzac Day will be on 25th April, and many people, while believing that it should be suitably celebrated, think that the day is too sacred for the holding of a carnival. **1917** BOOTH *Anzac Day* 4 Anzac Day is not a day of mourning only; it is a day for thanksgiving and exultation also. **1918** *Quick March* Apr. 37 Anzac! Fourth Anniversary... Therefore Anzac Day is now a New Zealand Day, a National Day..Anzac Day has tended to become a day of memorial services. **1919** *Chron. NZEF* 10 May 156 [Heading] Anzac Day. The grand day of remembrance passed as the sincerest of Anzacs might wish it. **1920** *Anzac Day Act 11 Geo.V* s1 In commemoration of the part taken by New Zealand troops in the Great War, and in memory of those who gave their lives for the Empire, the twenty-fifth day of April in each year (being the anniversary of the first landing of English, Australian, and New Zealand troops in Gallipoli) shall be known as Anzac Day, and shall be observed throughout New Zealand as a public holiday. **1930** PINFOLD *Fifty Yrs. Maoriland* 133 But we have one day which is special in Maoriland. It is called Anzac Day. **1966** *Anzac Day Act* s2 In commemoration of the part taken by New Zealand servicemen and servicewomen in the First and Second World Wars and in the South African War, and in memory of those who at any time have given their lives for New Zealand and the British Empire or Commonwealth of Nations, the twenty-fifth day of April in each year..shall be known as Anzac Day, and shall be a day of commemoration. **1977** HOLMES *Best of Homespun* 64 Probably it's a confession that we're getting old when we say wistfully that Anzac days are not quite what they were. **1982** MARSHALL *Master Big Jingles* 68 Each year on Anzac Day he emerged to lead the R.S.A. parade and make a dawn address at the lawn cemetery in town.

B. *attrib.* and Comb.
1. *attrib.*
1921 *Anzac Day Amendment Act* s2(a) Section two of the Anzac Day Act, 1920, is hereby amended. **1934** HYDE *Journalese* 22 It's sometimes asked if that lost generation..was really the knightly thing that it has become in the minds of old men who limp along in Anzac Day processions. **1952** *Landfall 23* 216 It may be the New Testament, or Marx, Shakespeare..an Anzac day speech or a verse in an autograph book—they know it's 'all bull-shit'. **1987** HUTCHINS *Tall Half-Backs* 34 As I grew up I came to realise the solemn implications of the Anzac Day ceremonial.

2. Special Comb. **Anzac Day dinner,** ironic for alcoholic liquor or a 'liquid lunch'; **Anzac Day parade** (see also *dawn parade* (DAWN 1), a parade of returned and other servicemen usu. centred on a local war memorial or cenotaph; **Anzac day service,** a commemorative service for war dead.
1938 HYDE *Nor Yrs. Condemn* 160 Starkie thought it [*sc.* moralising] sounded like a lot of **Anzac Day dinner**. He was getting sullen under the mixture of beer and Scotch. Ibid 162 He crawled into bed... Too much Anzac day dinner, and Macnamara made him look silly in the pub. **1939** *Evening Post* (Wellington) 26 Apr. 7 [Caption] The Dawn Parade Large crowds took part yesterday in the **Anzac Day parades** which started at dawn..and terminated at The Retreat. **1963** MORRIESON *Scarecrow* 3 On the strength of his glass eye..Uncle Athol has been known to attend an Anzac Day parade wearing an army overcoat. **1991** *NZ Woman's Weekly* 30 Dec. 61 [Caption] Anzac Day parades have always attracted the crowds and this one, in Thames in 1921, was no exception. **1938** HYDE *Nor Yrs. Condemn* 236 Bede Collins (no longer, unless by courtesy, Sister Collins) was attending **Anzac Day service** in Auckland. There was a church service before the parade and laying of wreaths at the foot of the Cenotaph, which would follow in the Domain grounds. **1984** BOYD *City of the Plains* 312 In 1950 the Borough Council started afternoon teas for ex-servicemen and women after the ANZAC Day service. **1991** *Evening Post* (Wellington) 13 May 6 I took part in two Anzac Day services.

Aotearoa /ˌæɪʌutiəˈrʌuə/, /ˌæɪʌutæɪəˈrʌuə/, /ˌʌʌutæɪəˈroʊ/. [Ma. /ˈaoteaˈroa/ *ao* cloud; daytime; world + *tea* white + *roa* long, tall; or *aotea* bird; or *aoatea* (=*awatea*) with elision of medial /a/, daybreak, dawn.]
[*Note*] Usu. transl. as the LAND OF THE LONG WHITE CLOUD q.v., though 'Land of the Long Day' (or 'Dawn'), or 'Land of the Long Twilight' have more to recommend them.

1. The North Island.
1855 GREY *Polynesian Mythol.* [A translation of 23 of the legends of the Maori text *Ko nga Mahinga a nga Tupuna Maori*.. pub. 1854.] 132 Ngahue went to seek a place where his jasper stones might remain in peace, and he found in the sea this island Aotearoa (the northern island of New Zealand). **1868** TAYLOR *Past & Present NZ* 193 The native name for the North Island is, Te Ika a [M]aui—the fish of Maui..; they have another ancient name for it in their legends, Aotearoa, but it is now never used. **1872** *TrNZI* IV. 56 The first person who undertook the voyage to New Zealand..was Ngahue..'and he found in the sea, the North Island of New Zealand', which he named Aotea-roa, or the long day. **c1930** BEST *Maori Religion* (1982) II. 372 When Maui succeeded in hauling his great fish to the surface, behold, it was Aotearoa, 'the fish of Maui–tikitiki that lies outspread before us'... Having told how Maui hauled this North Island of New Zealand up from the ocean depths the narrator continued. **1933** NGATA *Let.* 22 Mar. in *Na To Hoa Aroha* (1988) III. 72 Dissatisfied younger sons, ambitious women or slighted elders sought redress by force of arms or went into the open spaces of Aotearoa or Tewaipounamu. **1966** *Encycl. NZ* I. 53 Aotearoa is the Maori name for New Zealand, though it seems at first to have been used for the North Island only... The most popular and authoritative meaning usually given is 'long white cloud', and there are two stories current to illustrate this... The other meanings [suggested] are: big glaring light (Hochstetter); continuously clear light, or land of abiding day (Stowell); long white world (Wilson); long bright world, long daylight, long lingering day, or long bright land (Cowan); and long bright day (Tregear).

2. a. New Zealand, esp. as the homeland of the Maori. See also MAORILAND 2 a and b. Also *attrib.*
[*Note*] Quots. 1861 and c1864 could be interpreted as applying to the North Island only.
[**1857** *Ko nga Whakapepeha me nga Whakaahuareka a nga Tupuna o Aotea-roa.—Proverbial and Popular Sayings of the Ancestors of the New Zealand Race.* By Sir George Grey... **1861** *Ko Aotearoa, or the Maori Recorder. Hanuere. January... Akarana.* [Titles]] **c1864** TEMPSKY *Memoranda* (ATLTS) 80 The packet he dropped contained three flags belonging to his tribe, the Ngatihanas; one of the flags was of beautiful red silk worked with great skill—a white cross in the centre—and the word 'Aotearoa'—a watchword of the present crisis in Maori matters. **1878** BULLER *Forty Yrs. NZ* 166 Returning to his own island, [Kupe] gave a glowing account of Aotearoa (long day), as he called New Zealand. **1898** REEVES *The Long White Cloud—Ao Tea Roa* 34 Some centuries ago,.. [the Polynesians] left their isles of reef and palm, and found their way to Ao-tea-roa, as they called New Zealand. **1904** IZETT *Maori Lore* 145 Kupe and his people..landed at many places along the shores of the new land..upon which the name of Ao-tea-roa was bestowed. **1917** *NZ at the Front* 4 May they soon see the red blaze of the blossoms of the *Pohutukawa* on the coasts of *Aotea-roa* in place of the red of the Flanders battlefields. **1922** COWAN *NZ Wars* (1955) I. 2 The inevitable shock of battle between the tribesman of Aotearoa and the white man..is a feature of our history. **c1930** BEST *Maori Religion* (1982) II. 215 Those brothers..at once set to work to prepare their vessel for a sea voyage, that they might return home to Aotearoa (New Zealand). **1938** HYDE *Godwits Fly* (1970) 32 Sometimes the school journal called New Zealand

'Maoriland' or 'Ao-te-aroa'. There, again, you hardly ever saw a Maori, and if you did, it was in town. **c1945** *Sixes & Sevens* (Troopship pub.) 16 'What oh! for old Ao-Tea-Roa and a dirty big feed of lamb and green peas. **1961** MACKAY *Puborama* 42 The average New Zealander's acquaintance with the taverns of Aotearoa cities has always been too casual. **1988** [see NEW ZEALAND A 1]. **1988** *Sunday Star* (Auckland) 17 July A6 After 1870, most Maori referred to the country as Niu Tirani—a result of Pakeha settlers calling the three islands New Zealand. Sir Keith [Sinclair] said that in all the written Maori he had read from last century the word Aotearoa had been used in only one newspaper... *Te Wanaanga*, published in Napier, used Aotearoa in the 1870s. Sir Keith said the literal translation of Aotearoa was 'land of the long twilight'. The name may have come about because the early Polynesians were not used to the long evenings in New Zealand. **1990** *Dominion* (Wellington) 19 Feb. 6 On the azure stage, the intense blue of Aotearoa's sky and sea, is set the furniture of the prosperous bourgeoisie. **1993** EVISON *Te Wai Pounamu* 479 The expression 'The Long White Cloud' was a translation of '*Aotearoa*', which was supposed to be among some northern tribes a name for New Zealand, or some part of it. '*Aotearoa*' was now [c1900] being popularized by Reeves, James Cowan, and other colonial romantics, as the authentic name for New Zealand. *Ibid.* 499 '*Aotearoa*', whatever its provenance, was never a South Island Maori name... The expression in use at Arowhenua in 1905 was 'Niu Tireni' (New Zealand).

b. As **Aotearoa New Zealand**, a symbolic name coined in the 1980s to represent the Maori and Pakeha components of New Zealand society and culture.

[*Note*] In earlier parenthetic uses (as in quot. 1927 below and c1930 in a above) the second element is merely appositional and explanatory.

[**1927** DONNE *Maori Past & Present* 5 Ethnogenic authorities class the 'Maori' New Zealander as of Malayan extraction... When the Malayan reached Aotearoa (New Zealand) he came to his Ultima Thule.] **1988** *Human Rights Comm. Focus* Mar. 1 Statement on the Status of Maori people as Tangata Whenua of Aotearoa New Zealand... The Commission recognises the importance of Maori culture..to all people of Aotearoa New Zealand.

Hence **Aotearoaian, Aotearoan, Aoteroan**, a New Zealander; occas. as an adjective, NEW ZEALAND B 2.

1961 [see 2 a above]. **1988** *Dominion* (Wellington) 1 July 10 All over the world isolated pockets of white and Maori servicemen and women, as well as those in the two divisions, referred to themselves proudly as Kiwis or New Zealanders, not Aotearoaians. **1988** *Dominion* (Wellington) 24 Dec. 8 We have a long and proud history as 'New Zealanders', a concept that would never be carried in a word like 'Aoteroans'. **1993** *Listener* 8 May 7 If all New Zealanders were brought up understanding Maori... Then..we would all be New Zealanders—or should that read Aotearoans?

a over k: see ARSE 2.

aphrodite /ˌæfrʌuˈdaiti/. Rhyming slang for 'nightie'.

c1875 MEREDITH *Adventuring in Maoriland* (1935) 48 It appears that one of them had tucked her feet well inside the hem of her 'aphrodite', and stretched them well down to the bottom of the bed, and in doing so kicked the crab [put there as a practical joke].

apostles: see TWELVE APOSTLES.

appetite like a fantail: see FANTAIL 3 b.

apple.

1. *pl.* [Orig. an abbrev. of *apples and spice* rhyming slang for *nice*: AND 1943.] In the phr. **she'll be** (or **she's**) **apples**, expressing confidence in a happy outcome, reassurance, agreement, etc. See also SHE 2.

1947 in Pearson *Six Stories* (1991) 28 She's apples, Frank! Here's Mama-sa' waiting to turn it on for us!.. You-me, eh? Pompom? **1960** 16C F B4 Wanganui Girls C. 12 She'll be apples **1974** GIFFORD *Loosehead Len's Big Brown Book* 60 Apples, she'll be: Thirty points up with the ref married to the club chairman's daughter. **1963** MORRIESON *Scarecrow* 115 Don't cry, Pru. Yuh go and see old Len Ramsbottom and betcha everything'll be apples. **1989** *Listener* 7 Jan. 13 And it's anybody's guess what Japanese tourists make of such Kiwisms [sic] as 'She's apples 'put the nips in' 'feeling crook' or 'give him some curry'.

2. apple pie, rhyming slang for 'cry'; to whimper.

1905 THOMSON *Bush Boys* 75 His resentment at this taunt killed all thought of apology. No fear, he wasn't going to 'apple pie' to a fellow that cut up rough like that over a little joke.

3. As an abbrev. of *apple tart*, rhyming slang for 'heart'.

1989 *NZ Eng. Newsletter* III. 21 *apple:* Whatever keeps a shearer going, be it his heart, guts or will; e.g. 'He's got a helluvan apple'.

apteryx /ˈæptəˌrɪks/. Also formerly **apterix**. [The bird genus *Apteryx* was named by English naturalist G. Shaw (see quot. 1813) from the Greek ἀ without + πτέρυξ wing, referring to the rudimentary wings of the bird.] KIWI 1.

1813 SHAW *Naturalist's Misc.* XXIV 1058 [OED] The Southern Apteryx. **1838** SYMONDS *Cloudy Bay* (1979) 27 Here also the apteryx abounds and offers capital sport to the hunter, to whom it is valuable for its feathers, which are held in high estimation. **1843** DIEFFENBACH *Travels in NZ* II. 44 As a *fly* [for fishing], a feather of the apterix is highly esteemed. **1859** THOMSON *Story NZ* I. 35 The apteryx, notornis, kakapo, and weka, are only found in New Zealand's solitudes. **1879** HINGSTON *Australian Abroad* 331 It is the apteryx—a little barn-door fowl of a Moa—..and very difficult indeed to be found. **1905** WHITE *My NZ Garden* 68 I suppose the Apteryx (Kiwi) ought to lead the van; for a bird that cannot fly sounds almost as uncommon as a pig that can. **1947** BRERETON *No Roll of Drums* 18 He also saw and heard the kiwi or Apteryx which comes out at night.

araara. Also **arara.** [Ma. (approx.) /ˈaraːra/: Williams 14 *Araara..*, trevally.] TREVALLY 1 a.

[**1820** LEE & KENDALL *Gram. & Vocab.* 136 Arára, s. A certain fish.] **1848** TAYLOR *Leaf from Nat. Hist.* 12 Araara, *a fish* like the Kahawai. **1850** LUSH *Auckland Jrnls.* (1971) 38 Bought for the little girls' dinner two fishes, larger than English mackerel..one called Tamure—the other—Araara. **1872** HUTTON & HECTOR *Fishes NZ* 110 The Arara of the Maoris, or the Trevally or Cavalli of the fishermen (*Caranx georgianus*), is a highly esteemed fish. **1921** *NZJST* IV. 117 *Trevally; Araara*. A school fish taken when trawling from 15 to 20 fathoms. **1947** POWELL *Native Animals NZ* 67 School Trevally.., Araara of the Maoris, is a common school fish in North Auckland waters. **1957** PARROTT *Sea Angler's Fishes* 78 The School Trevally was known to the Maoris as the 'Araara' and to Europeans as the 'Trevally' or 'Cavalli'. **1982** BURTON *Two Hundred Yrs. NZ Food* 81 A handsome fish of iridescent blues, greens and silver, the trevally, or *ara-ara*, occurs in the warmer waters to the north of New Zealand. The early sealers called this fish skipjack.

Arabic volute. *Alcithoe arabica* (fam. Volutidae), an elongate knobbly univalve found from low tide levels downwards into deep water.

1947 POWELL *Native Animals NZ* 28 Arabic Volute (*Alcithoe arabica*). Grows to about 6 inches in height, is distinguished by the spiral folds on the pillar or axis of the shell, strong tubercles on the shoulder and bold pattern of reddish-brown stripes and blotches. **1966** *Encycl. NZ* I. 54 *Arabic Volute* (*Alcithoe arabica*). This handsome shellfish lives, half buried in sand, from low water to a considerable depth... The Maori name is pupu rore. **1970** PENNIKET *NZ Seashells in Colour* 64 Arabic Volute (*Alcithoe arabica*)... Characteristically this shell is patterned with wavy chocolate to brown lines, although considerable local variation exists. **1983** GUNSON *Collins Guide to Seashore* 96 Of the more than 20 species of volute shells living in our waters only two could be regarded as common; the Arabic volute *Alcithoe arabica*, and Swainson's volute, *A. swainsoni*, both growing up to 150 mm.

arakeke, var. HARAKEKE.

arara, var. ARAARA.

Arbitration. *Hist.* [Spec. use of *arbitration settlement*, with reference to industrial relations.] Formerly as **Arbitration Court** (**Court of Arbitration**), a court set up to settle labour disputes and prescribe industrial wages and conditions of work; since c1973, after various changes of name and function, replaced in modern use by *Employment Court* as the name of the institution dealing generally with such matters. See also AWARD.

1894 *Industrial Conciliation and Arbitration Act 58 Vict.* s47 There shall be one Court of Arbitration for the whole colony for the settlement of industrial disputes pursuant to this Act. **1904** *Awards, etc.* 2 [North Auckland Timber-Workers' Award] In the Court of Arbitration of New Zealand, Northern Industrial District. **1910** *Truth* 11 June 4 If the Arbitration Court awards were ignored there would be a danger of upsetting the Conciliation and Arbitration Act, which had done so much good for the workers. **1926** DEVANNY *Butcher Shop* (1981) 66 The Arbitration Court fixes a uniform rate of pay for the whole country and we pay it. **1946** SOLJAK *NZ* 54 The powerful waterside workers' and coal miners' unions chose to remain outside the scope of the Arbitration Court, which was established under the Act to draw up awards or agreements between employer and employee and settle disputes in industry. **1959** SINCLAIR *Hist. NZ* 180 If the decision of a [Conciliation] Board proved unsatisfactory, either party could appeal to the Arbitration Court, which consisted of a Supreme Court judge and two assessors elected by the employers' associations and the unions. An award of this court had legal force.

Arbor Day. [Orig. US (Nebraska) 1872, Austral. 1902 (see OED).] A day set aside each year for the planting of trees.

1891 BATHGATE *A plea for the establishment of Arbor Day* [Dn, ptd..1891.] [title: *NZNB* II. 100, item B377]. **1892** *Auckland Weekly News* 4 June 30 Why should not New Zealand have an Arbor Day?... Who knows with what melody those millions of trees, planted on each succeeding Arbor Day, might be vocal to 'the unborn millions' of our young nation's children. **1894** *NZ Official Year-book* 294 *Arbor Day*. The Government, recognising the importance of tree-planting, and in view of the marvellous results which have been achieved by the setting aside in the United States of America of one day in the year to be called Arbor Day, proclaimed the 4th of August last year as a

ARBOR VITAE

general holiday to be devoted to tree-planting. **1904** *NZ Observer* 23 July 3 Arbour [*sic*] Day in this colony owes its existence to the fact that on that day some years ago Ministers and their friends repaired to Thorndon Esplanade..and planted two or three dozen trees, which..were blown out of the ground by the wind within the next fortnight. **1913** CARR *Country Work* 51 Making tree planting compulsory..in addition to our Arbour [*sic*] Day, [would] make a vast change in the landscape. **1938** HYDE *Godwits Fly* (1970) 32 [He] gave them long lectures about the duty of preserving their heritage of native bush... His favourite day in the year was Arbor Day. **1951** HUNT *Confessions* 136 On August 1, 1934, Arbor Day, I sat in the Memorial Hall..to hear the Governor-General. **1967** *Listener* 28 July In New Zealand,.. Arbor Day is celebrated on the first Wednesday in August. **1994** *Dominion* (Wellington) 2 June 3 Mary-Lee Joyce..lends a helping hand in yesterday's Arbor Day celebrations at Te Marua Bush.

arbor vitae. *Obs.* Also **New Zealand arbor vitae**. [A spec. use of *arbor vitae*, a popular name for plants of the *Libocedrus* genus: see OED.] KAWAKA.

1867 HOOKER *Handbook* 764 Arbor vitae. *Libocedrus Doniana*. **1872** [see KAWAKA]. **1889** KIRK *Forest Flora* 157 Mr. Colenso informs me that this fine tree is termed kawaka and kaikawaka by the Maoris... It is often termed 'the New Zealand arbor-vitae' by the settlers. **1906** CHEESEMAN *Manual NZ Flora* 647 L[*ibocedrus*] *Doniana, Endl*... North Island: *Kawaka*; New Zealand *Arbor-vitae*. **1916** COWAN *Bush Explorers* '*More Reminisc.*' (VUWTS) Here the trees are totara, manuka, and a kind of cypress, or arbor vitae, no kareao.

arch: see NOR'WEST ARCH.

Archey's trevally: see TREVALLY 2.

area school. [AND 1940.] A rural state school which provides both primary and secondary education, the latter also for pupils from other primary schools within its area.

1945 MASON *Educ. Today & Tomorrow* 31 I am inclined to think there will have to be evolved a special type of rural intermediate school resembling in some ways perhaps the 'area schools' of Tasmania. **1969** *AJHR E-1* 38 Also in 1969 the first area school (Primers to Form VI) was set up at Ranfurly. **1974** *Educ. Devel. Conf. Rep. by Working Party Organiz. & Admin.* 27 The area school (or reorganised district high school) is in effect a unified primary and secondary school which draws from other local primary schools at the form I level. **1982** PEAT *Detours* 47 He was pushing for the introduction of carving classes..at the Te Kao Area School where..the secondary roll numbered about thirty. **1986** *Educ. Regulations, Interpretation* (Area Schools) 'Area School' means a school that provides secondary education, and primary education at all levels from the Infant Department to Form II. **1993** *National Education Weekly* 28 June 10 Tolaga Bay Area School... Second teacher for Te Reo, total immersion unit.

Are you there? /ˌaˈjuˈðeə/. In telephone usage: 'Is the line working? Can you hear me?'

1904 MCMURRAN *New York to NZ* 144 In ringing up a telephone, instead of 'Hello, central,' people here ask, 'Are you there' or 'Is that exchange'—then give the number as in London. **1954** WINKS *These New Zealanders* (1956) 58 I called New Zealanders on the phone, was greeted with the superfluous inquiry, 'Are you there?' 'Of course I'm here,' I replied. That didn't go well, but neither did the question. **1972** MITCHELL *Pavlova Paradise* 182 '*Are you there*': Expression of incredulity that the telephone service..has allowed you to reach someone. Avoid any temptation to reply, 'Where the hell do you think I am'.

arfto, var. AFTO.

arikeki, var. HARAKEKE.

ariki /ˈʌrɪki/. Also formerly **Aree**, **Earee** (poss. infl. by Polynesian dial. [ariʔi]); **Arekee**, **Areekee**, **Eareete** (=e areete). [Proto-Polynesian */ʔ/ariki*. Ma. /ˈariki/: Williams 15 *Ariki*: in Maori use, a spiritual or temporal leader, male or female.] A principal or paramount chief as a spiritual or temporal leader. Occas. transf. to a European (see quot. 1777). Also **Te Ariki**, the Lord, Christ.

1769 MONKHOUSE *Jrnl*. 12 Oct. in Cook *Journals* (1955) I. 575 Our three friends informed us that the master of this Canoe was an Earee or Chief. **1777** BAYLY *Journal* 15 Feb. in McNab *Hist. Records* (1914) II. 220 He said that he then killed them all but kept the Aree, or officer, till the last of all. **1820** MARSDEN *Lett. & Jrnls*. (1932) 255 On a point of high land where the two streams meet, and by which it is surrounded, stands the hippah of the head chief or areekee as the natives call him. **1839** MAUNSELL 2 Nov. in WILY & MAUNSELL *Robert Maunsell* (1938) 64 As being connected with the eldest branch, he is considered the Ariki, or Lord of the Tribe, and is therefore peculiarly sacred, and in all religious ceremonies the chief management would fall upon him. **1847** JOHNSON *Notes from Jrnl*. 7 Jan. in Taylor *Early Travellers (1959)* 163 Our hostess was an *ariki* or chieftainess of the tribe. **1879** *Auckland Weekly News* 26 Apr. 14 [Te Whiti] again repeated the words, 'Mackay, submit yourself to my authority as your *ariki*.' **1882** HAY *Brighter Britain* II. 175 Accompanied by a score or so of the rangatira of his hapu, the ariki rode over to the young settler's place. **1904** TREGEAR *Maori Race* 123 The highest title in practical use was that of 'Lord' (*Ariki*), if we allow a spiritual as well as a temporal potency to the rank. He was the Priest-Chief. **1930** GUTHRIE *NZ Memories* 75 Such was the man who was the most..powerful of all the Maori chiefs, their 'Ariki' (chief of chiefs). **1940** COWAN *Sir Donald Maclean* 15 This was Te Heuheu Tukino, the *Ariki* of the Taupo country, head of the Ngati-Tuwharetoa tribe. **1959** SINCLAIR *Hist. NZ* 20 At the head of the tribe there was a paramount chief, the *ariki*. **1972** BAXTER *Autumn Testament* 46 Te Ariki tells us – 'What sorrow is like my sorrow?' **1985** KING *Being Pakeha* 87 A granddaughter took Nga back to Waahi Pa, old home of Mahuta, the ariki and king who had called on her help most often.

Hence **arikiship** *n*., the powers, rights, etc. pertaining to an ariki.

1933 NGATA *Let*. 22 Mar. in *Na To Hoa Aroha* (1988) III. 72 Our Courts recognised the arikiship in the award of shares in land.

aristotle. [AND 1897.] Rhyming slang for 'bottle'.

1988 *Dominion Sunday Times* (Wellington) 14 Feb. 19 Abbreviated local rhyming slang is also used. 'I'd love an aristotle of alison' means 'I'd love a bottle of bourbon'—bourbon rhyming with Alison Durbin. **1989** *NZ Eng. Newsletter* III. 21 *ari, aristotle:* Rhyming slang for a bottle of beer (at dinner time).

Armed Constabulary. *Hist.* Also **A.C.** (esp. in *attrib.* use), occas. early **Armed Police** (or **Constabulary**) **Force** (see quots. 1851, 1991).
a. The name from c1846, freq. from 1867 to 1886, for a national force formed from various militia as the first national police force, orig. to combat Maori 'hostiles' and to keep civil order.

ARMED OFFENDERS SQUAD

1846 *10 Victoria No.2* 201 (9 Oct.) For the purpose of providing for the establishment maintenance and discipline of an armed Constabulary Force. **1851** *NZGG* (New Munster) IV. 5.25 Colonial Secretary's Office, Wellington, 14th February, 1851. His Excellency..has been pleased to appoint Mr. Robert Smith, Sergeant in the Armed Police Force, to discharge the duties of Inspector of Sheep and Slaughter Houses. **1867** *31 Victoria No.37* 449 (10 Oct.) An Act to provide for the establishment and maintenance of an Armed Constabulary... The designation thereof shall be 'the New Zealand Armed Constabulary' hereinafter called the 'Armed Constabulary'. **1868** *Richmond-Atkinson Papers* (1960) II. 278 Whitmore has only gone as a Volunteer to the front. I need hardly say that he is Commandant of the Armed Constabulary. **c1875** MEREDITH *Adventuring in Maoriland* (1935) 83 Things looked a trifle ugly for a short time; the armed constabulary were mustered and dispatched to the vicinity to be in readiness for any emergency. **1904** *NZ Observer* 27 Aug. 5 Some particulars were given of Mr Kirk's meritorious career..as a member of that splendid force, the Armed Constabulary. **1922** COWAN *NZ Wars* (1955) I. 177 He became captain in 1863, and served in the Military Settlers, and later in the Armed Constabulary as Sub-Inspector. **1935** MAXWELL *Recollections* 73 During earlier Maori disturbances [t]here was also a force called the 'Forest Rangers' which saw much service in the wars of the eighteen-sixties. That force and the Colonial Defence Force merged into one that was known as the 'Armed Constabulary'. It was quite a misnomer, for the term Constabulary gives the impression that it was more or less a kind of police force. It was distinctly a field force. **1964** NORRIS *Settlers in Depression* 27 With the transfer of the Armed Constabulary headquarters from Hamilton, this building..was removed to Cambridge. **l972** *Dominion* (Wellington) 26 Oct. 13 The redoubt [at Taupo] was constructed by the Armed Constabulary in about 1870. **1986** BELICH *NZ Wars* 214 In 1867, this miscellany of units was greatly reduced in numbers and formed into a colonial regular army, euphemistically named 'the Armed Constabulary'. **1991** LA ROCHE *Hist. of Howick & Pakuranga* 232 Howick was served in 1849 by one corporal..and two privates of the Armed Police Force [NZ Gazette, 18 Aug. 1849].

Hence **armed constable**. See also TROOPER.
1984 BARBER *Red Coat to Jungle Green* 48 During operations in the bush the armed constables wore 'bush outfits'.

b. As **A.C.**, occas. also in the sense armed constable (see quots. 1885, 1895).

1873 *Weekly Herald* (Wanganui) 7 June in Swan *Hist. NZ Rugby Football* (1948) I. 16 A little loose play on the part of the A.C. half-backs allowed the ball to break through. **1885** VINCENT *Forty-Thousand Miles* 106 There are about fifteen of these A.C. stationed [in Auckland]. **1895** *Diary Jonathan Roberts* 14 If you darted straight among a number of private citizens the A.C.'s couldn't use their arms. **1904** *NZ Observer* 24 Sept. 4 At that time he was a member of the A.C. Force. **1922** COWAN *NZ Wars* (1955) II. 261 Tu-Patea pointed out..the place where the body of the A.C. man was eaten. **1935** COWAN *Hero Stories NZ* 138 And then the lads in blue, sixty of them (No.5 Division, A.C.) came up at the double, with fixed bayonets. **1972** *Dominion* (Wellington) 26 Oct. 13 The hotel was originally the A.C. wet canteen. It was first built there about 1870... The A.C. Baths, off Spa Road, mark the spot where tired members would bathe in the hot thermal stream from huts erected..in 1889.

Armed Offenders Squad. A special police group trained and equipped to deal with situations involving firearms.

1980 LELAND *Kiwi-Yankee Dict.* 9 *Armed Offenders Squad:* A S.W.A.T. team. As the police are normally unarmed (as are criminals) this is a very special group of armed police called out to deal with armed criminals who have shown a willingness to use their weapons. **1987** *Dominion* (Wellington) 10 Oct. 3 The police armed offenders squad surrounded a Lower Hutt house early this morning after a man had barricaded himself in with a machete knife, numchakas and a rifle. **1989** THOMSON & NEILSON *Sharing the Challenge* 255 The concept of New Zealand Police Armed Offenders' Squads emerged after the tragic shooting..on 6 January 1963. **1992** *Dominion* (Wellington) 12 Dec. 10 Most of them fall as short of their target as a barrage of shots from an armed offenders' squad.

armoured cow: see COW 5.

aroha /ˈʌrʌu(w)ə/. [Ma. /ˈaroha/: Williams 16 *Aroha. 1.* n. *Love, yearning* for an absent relative or friend... *2. Pity, compassion... 3. Affectionate regard.*]
1. Sympathy, understanding, love, fellow-feeling; also used (occas. as **arohanui** 'much love') to end a personal letter.
   [**1815** KENDALL *New Zealanders' First Book* 40 Aróha Affection love] **1863** MAUNSELL *Let.* 28 May in Wily & Maunsell *Robert Maunsell* (1938) 150 Now, dearest George, adieu. All send much *aroha*. **1905** BAUCKE *White Man Treads* 90 Sing songs of sentiment, with deft allusion to that tender yearning of the heart, that mystery, which answers to the call of 'Aroha' (love). **1933** BAUME *Half–caste* 52 Dear Paul,..your very, very loving Ngaire, so aroha nui, Paul. **1969** BAXTER *Collected Poems* (1980) 442 And the rainbow of aroha shine on each one's face Because love is in the look. **1971** DRUMMOND in *Auckland Jrnls. Vicesimus Lush* 265 Mary Anne Parker..emerges from this journal—and from her own unselfconscious account of life in early Auckland—as a remarkable woman in many ways, with an *aroha* for the Maori people that is remembered still. **1983** KING *Whina* 219 The chairman [of the Auckland Harbour Bridge Authority] relented and even signed his telegram 'Arohanui'. **1986** O'SULLIVAN *Pilate Tapes* 45 Who was it I began to write to? Arohanui. P. **1992** *Listener* 13 Jan. 10 There was aroha between the health professionals and the people.
2. Special Comb. **aroha job**, work done free for love not money; or at *mates' rates* (MATE 5) q.v.
   1985 MITCALFE *Hey Hey Hey* 84 All right. Give you half and hour [to produce the stolen article]... That set's too expensive to be just another 'aroha job', 'fa'a Samoa', all that stuff.

arohanui: see AROHA 1.

aro(h)i, varr. ARUHE.

arrow squid: see SQUID 2 (1).

arse. *Usu. impolite*. There are a few verbal uses of *arse* not yet recorded elsewhere which are poss. New Zealand variants. See also A INTO G.
1. In phrases reflecting a person's ignorance, innocence, confusion: **not to know one's arse from one's elbow**, **not to know if one's arse was on fire**.
   1947 DAVIN *For Rest of Our Lives* 258 Oh, a lot of profanity about..colonels who were too dumb to know if their arses were on fire. *Ibid.* 329 They're all to hell out there, sir. Don't know whether they're on their arse or their elbow. Tanks all over the place. **1959** MIDDLETON *The Stone* 43 That fleeco won't know whether he's on his arse or his elbow in the morning. **1980** SMITHYMAN in *Te Reo* 22–23 109 Nothing is said [in the *Heinemann NZ Dict.*] of..*arse over kite*..or *'got his arse* where his elbow ought to be', or 'can't *tell his arse* from his elbow' or '*get his arse into gear*'.
2. In the phr. **arse over kite** [f. northern Brit. dial. *kite* stomach], var. of general Eng. uses *arse over tip* or *tilt*, head over heels; **on the bones of one's arse**, see BONE 1.
   1965 GEE *Special Flower* 144 'And tell her not to come near me again. I'll kick her arse over kite if she does.' **1972** *James K. Baxter 1926-72* 20 Arse over kite I [*sc.* Brian Bell] went into the gutter, and a bottle of Red Band ale shattered in my gaberdine pocket. **1979** WILLIAMS *Skin Deep* 65 But try as he might to pick his way through the swirling ranks of choppers to get to them, he's downed, arse over kite. **1983** HENDERSON *Down from Marble Mountain* 141 And Ted obeying. And instantly going arse over kite into the six-foot ditch.

arsehole. *Usu. impolite*. In the phrases **from arsehole to breakfast (table)**, indicating entirety; **not to be** (a tradesman's, etc.) **arsehole**, said of an inexpert or inefficient tradesman, practitioner, etc.; **to give** (someone or something) **arseholes**, to attack or compete wholeheartedly, also to revile, to ill-use; **arsehole of the world** (occas., **of New Zealand**), an unlovely place, esp. if windy, and often applied to Wellington or to the Bluff.
   1948 *Landfall* 7 178 It's absolute comfort from **arsehole to breakfast-table**. **1984** BEATON *Outside In* 22 Sandy: A fucken soap up! Foam from arse'ole to breakfast. **c1962** BAXTER *Horse* (1985) 15 'He's not a blacksmith's **arsehole**,' said a voice from the door... 'He's an old brown-hatter. Watch out, Tim. He'll be up you like a rat up a drainpipe.' **1968** SLATTER *Pagan Game* 174 And the only pep talk [the coach] ever gave them, all he ever said every Saturday, was go out there and **give them arseholes**. **1971** SHADBOLT *Bullshit & Jellybeans* 47 It was strange wandering through the snow utterly stoned, in the middle of the Southern Alps down in the **arsehole of the world**. **1982** PEAT *Detours* 229 'People are coming back [to Nightcaps, Southland] for the cheap rates and country lifestyle. You're not in the arrrsehole of New Zealand yet, boy.'

arsepaper: *to tear someone up for arsepaper*, see TEAR v.

Arse-ups. *WW1*. [f. the shoulder patch, an inverted triangle.] See quot. 1937. See also DINK *n.* 1 b.
   1937 PARTRIDGE *Dict. Slang* 18 *Arse-ups, the*. The 4th Battalion of the N.Z. Rifle Brigade: New Zealand military in G.W. Ex the shape of the battalion shoulder-patch. [**1953** *2ZB Wellington* (Lux Money-go-round programme) 12 Feb. In the Great War there were the Square Dinks, the Triangle Dinks, and I won't tell you what we called the other ones but their triangle was upside down—you know what soldiers mean.]

artesian bore: see BORE 1.

Arthur or Martha. In phr. **not to know whether one is Arthur or Martha** [Wilkes 1957], in a state of confusion, not to know whether one is coming or going.
[*Note*] Noel Hilliard (Titahi Bay), p.c. November 1994, notes that a variant 'I didn't know if I was Arthur or Martha or General MacArthur' was current in the 1950s after MacArthur's removal from his Korean war command by President Truman in April 1951.
   1968 SLATTER *Pagan Game* 167 The new man didn't know whether he was Arthur or Martha even though he'd got his way at the Parent Teacher meeting. **1971** TAYLOR *Plekhov Place* 22 We've been here a fair stretch and up till now they've not cared to find out whether we're Arthur or Martha... It's all Arthur and Martha round here. Not like home. **1988** CRUMP *Barry Crump's Bedtime Yarns* 116 [Of a mixed-up booking.] The bloke who jacked it up wouldn't know whether he was Arthur or Martha. **1993** *Dominion* (Wellington) 15 Jan. 6 I didn't know whether I was Arthur or Martha. Neither, I suspect, did my minister, who was at the scene [of the Aramoana massacre].

articulated. Also **articulator**. [Ellipt. or altered form f. *articulated truck*: see OED *articulated* 2 b.] An articulated truck.
   1959 SLATTER *Gun in My Hand* 22 The lorries crowding in..to be loaded..sometimes over ten tons on the articulateds. **1984** WILSON *S. Pacific Street* 10 He'd hitched a ride into Auckland with the Maori driver of a big food transport truck articulator.

artist. [AND 1889.] An expert or expert performer in a field usu. indicated by a defining suffix often with derogatory connotations of illegality, impropriety, excess; or in ironic or pejorative use, suggesting a hard-case or inveterate performer in a field disapproved of. Cf. earlier -KING (KING *n.*² 1).
1. *Military*, esp. *WW1*. Indicating (often pretentious) expertise or rank, esp. WW1 **one-pip artist**, **one-star artist**, second lieutenant.
   1919 *Chron. NZEF* 24 Jan. 312 A one-pip artist, just newly born, was scandalised..at Tony's appearance. **1936** TREADWELL *Recolls. Amateur Soldier* 3 Many [volunteers] were soon after given the opportunity of joining some other company..as second lieutenants, or, as these most important gentlemen became known during the war, 'one-pip artists'. **1938** *Press* (Christchurch) (McNab Slang) 2 Apr. 18 [Slang of the N.Z.E.F.] There is a touch of irreverence in 'the trump of the dump', for O.C., and in 'one-star artist'. **1945** HENDERSON *Gunner Inglorious* 19 Shortie, the one-pip artist, comes up to us around the gun.
2. a. Indicating a seasoned or inveterate performer, often in something reprehensible; a devotee to excess.
   1912 *Truth* 14 Sept. 6 Since Percy took up the T.P. jewellery business—he had come to be regarded as something of a 'hot air artist' and customarily made the statement that he carried five hundred quids' worth of jewellery in his bag. **1941** in Reid *Book NZ* (1964) 287 Then we heard the wireless news, Old bluff-artist Winston giving his views. **1942** *NZEF Times* 25 May 4 [A WW1 publication is quoted.] Scene: Any dugout... 'As a matter of fact I used to be a bit of a blackboard artist'. **1944** FULLARTON *Troop Target* 25 Hood, you bloody clifty artist, where are my matches? **1955** *BJ Cameron Collection* (TS July) artist (n). An adept or specialist in some activity. Used in compound words and in a derogatory sense e.g. booze-artist.
b. With a defining word: **booze artist**, a confirmed drinker, a drunkard; **bull (bulldust, bullshit** [Wilkes 1941]) **artist**, one who deals in lies or boastful nonsense, an empty boaster; **con artist**, a confidence trickster, a shrewdie; **grog-artist**, see *booze artist* above; **soapbox artist**, a street speaker, a soapbox orator. See also *tank-artist* (TANK *n.*² 2).
   [**1949** DAVIN *Roads from Home* 49 A real artist for

the booze, isn't he?] **1959** SLATTER *Gun in My Hand* 167 Drunken sot. I'd do it with pleasure. No-one would miss this **booze artist. 1971** TAYLOR *Plekhov Place* 104 They reckon he was sozzled. A right booze artist they're saying he was. Bottle a night and all that. **1992** ANDERSON *Portrait Artist's Wife* 81 They seldom spoke about their experiences except for an occasional story of..a heavy session with a booze artist named Arnold in Noumea. **1959** SLATTER *Gun in My Hand* 203 I can see him out on his rounds. The real **bull artist**..walking into the shops with his blah-blah salesmanship. **1960** HILLIARD *Maori Girl* 233 She told him about an artist who came in each day and asked her to pose for him, 'Booze artist, or bull?' Arthur wanted to know. **1987** NORGROVE *Shoestring Sailors* 125 Now I know you're a bull artist. **1961** *Truth* 4 Apr. 1 'Professor' William Boyd, as he once styled himself, has thus reached the high point of his career in the ranks of the..professional **bulldust artists**. **1983** HULME *Bone People* 170 Whoever coined that was an unmitigated fuckwit, a bullshit artist supreme. **1976** *Evening Post* (Wellington) 29 June 14 **Con artist**: good talker. **1992** SINCLAIR *Frontman* 148 Hey..it's the fucken **grog-artist**! Have one on us, Johnny! **1938** HYDE *Nor Yrs. Condemn* 267 'From what you can read about Hyde Park, the lungs do a bit of squawking...' 'That's only the Reds gabbing. **Soapbox artists**, we call them.'

art union. *Hist.* Often init. cap. [See OED *art* 18 a union of persons for the purpose of promoting art by purchasing the works of artists, and distributing them among their members, which is usu. done by lottery, 1839; AND 'lottery', 1849.] Also *attrib.* and *fig.*

1. a. A local raffle or lottery, often for a charitable cause. Also *transf.*
     1864 *Marlborough Express* (Blenheim) 4 Jan. 6 The origin of the affair [*sc.* a practical joke] was, we understand, in connection with the Art Union of last week. **1874** *NZ Herald* (Auckland) 4 Sept. 1 [Advt] Art union of sewing machines. Second distribution. Fourteen first-class sewing machines as prizes... Tickets—10s. each. **1886** *Napier Telegraph* quoted in Wood *Victorian New Zealanders* (1974) 18 'By permission of the Colonial Secretary Miss Bacon [of the School of Art Needlework, Auckland] will hold a grand art union of works of art, comprising handpainted brackets, diapers, cushions, wax work, art needlework. Tickets 2s 6d.' **1890** *Otago Witness* (Dunedin) 25 Sept. 23 For cool impudence..it is the art union lottery man with 20,000 tickets to sell at a shilling a piece... Accompanying this letter..is a printed circular setting forth the merits of the engravings. **1913** *NZ Observer* 9 Aug. 17 The secretary of a hospital bazaar committee was fined for submitting a prize cow as a fit prize for an 'art union'. **1921** *Quick March* 10 Mar. 39 An art union with attractive prizes has been arranged. **1931** *Dominion* (Wellington) 26 Dec. 13 Here we have art unions freely sanctioned..for every conceivable object from sports of every kind to first aid. **1941** *Sports Post* (Wellington) 11 Jan. 4 [Advt] Art Union for the thoroughbred yearling colt 'War Effort'..in aid of Patriotic funds. **1984** *Listener* 28 Apr. 30 The Auckland Aero Club, the first in the field, netted £12,905 from their art union.

b. *transf. Hist.* As **Jimmy Allen's Art Union** (also **Allen's sweep**) [from the name of Sir James Allen (1855–1942), Minister of Defence during WW1], a facetious name for the ballot for (overseas) service in the armed forces during WW1.
     1917 *Chron. NZEF* 18 Apr. 89 When a fellow in business or on a farm draws a prize in 'Jimmy Allen's Art Union' he has to go whatever happens to his affairs. [1917 *Note*] Colonel Sir James Allen is Minister for Defence, and in that capacity controls the ballots which are made use of to fill the drafts after voluntary recruiting fails. **1918** *Ibid.* 5 July 243 I want a P.T. sergeant's job at Trentham from the day That father draws a prize in Allen's sweep.

2. The name of the former State lottery (see esp. quot. 1961). Cf. *Golden Kiwi* (GOLDEN *a.* 2).
     1924 *Star* (Christchurch) 24 Dec. 14 Mr. Smith..is not charging anything for his open sesame to the winning of prizes in art unions. **1926** *NZ Dairy Produce Exporter* 27 Nov. 60 [Advt] Positively the last Art Union with a £5,000 Prize List. **1937** FINLAYSON *Brown Man's Burden* (1973) 29 The..little settlement..hadn't seen..such lavishness since Timi Kaituna won the Art Union. **1948** BALLANTYNE *Cunninghams* (1963) 124 But it would be a long, long time before she got a new dress—unless her ship came home and she won an art union. **1959** STONE *Verdict on NZ* 14 They have..set their seal of approval on what is euphemistically known as an 'art union.' **1961** *Evening Post* (Wellington) 1 Dec. 17 Under the law operating when the art unions began in 1929, raffles or lotteries could only have works of art for prizes. Alluvial gold had apparently qualified as a work of art and for some years the prizes were £4000 in alluvial gold, which had to be deposited in the Bank of New Zealand and paid for before any tickets could be sold. Cash finally replaced the alluvial gold prizes, but the name 'art union' stuck. **1988** SMITH *Southlanders at Heart* 125 Just an old Art Union ticket.

aruhe. Also early **anoohe** (poss. erron. for *aroohe*), **aro(h)i, arue**. [Ma. /ˈaruhe/: Williams 17 *Aruhe... Edible fern root.*] FERN-ROOT a.
     [**1770** PARKINSON *Journal* (1773) 127 Hèanoohe, [=he aruhe] *Fern root*.] **1843** DIEFFENBACH *Travels in NZ* II. 357 Aruhe, *also* aroi, arohi, *and* arue—fernroot. **1906** CHEESEMAN *Manual NZ Flora* 971 Common fern; Bracken; Rau-aruhe; Rahurahu; of the root, *Aruhe, Roi.* **c1920** BEATTIE *Trad. Lifeways Southern Maori* (1994) 298 Aruhe, or fernroot to eat, was sought after... Bishop Selwyn said that he thought the South Island product better than the North Island aruhe. **1930** NGATA *Let.* 22 May in *Na To Hoa Aroha* (1987) II. 22 The 'tangata whenua' stuck to the hinter-land and forests, faring on 'mamaku', 'aruhe', eels and huahua. **1946** *JPS* LV. 151 *aruhe*, a plant (Pteridium esculentum), edible fernroot; bracken-fern. **1978** FULLER *Maori Food & Cook.* 7 The perei had a mass of tubers which were cooked in the same way as aruhe. **1990** CROWE *Native Edible Plants of NZ* 114 The roots of bracken may be eaten after proper preparation, i.e. soaking, roasting and pounding... Good bracken fern (aruhe), is found only in rich loose soil.

arvo. Also **avo**; **sarvo**. [AND 1927.] (This) afternoon. Cf. AFTO.
     1953 17 M A35 Thames DHS 15 Sarvo (the sarvo) **a1974** SYDER & HODGETTS *Austral. & NZ Eng.* (TS) 1031 This afternoon. 'See you this arvo. About three o'clock, O.K.?' **1976** *Evening Post* (Wellington) 29 June 14 *S'arvo*... words and sayings sent in by 'Tuesdate' readers—things their parents said when they were at school. **1980** *Islands* 29 131 'Going to this arvo's session?' he asked. **1988** *Listener* 19 Nov. 97 It's the arvo in Wellington, where men and women of affairs ask nothing more than to make peace with their stomachs. **1992** *Dominion* (Wellington) 14 Jan. 21 [Heading] *Lost. Swatch* watch. Sat. Avo. Tinakori Road.

ash. As **New Zealand** (or **native**) **ash**, TITOKI 1.
     1871 *TrNZI* III. 186 *Alectryon excelsum*, DC. The Titoki, or New Zealand Ash, is far from uncommon in many districts. **1889** KIRK *Forest Flora* 183 It is sometimes termed 'the New Zealand ash', doubtless on account of its resembling that tree in the shape of its foliage and the toughness of its wood, but it is most generally known as 'the titoki'. **1900** *Canterbury Old & New* 184 Broadleaf, five-fingered Jack, New Zealand coffee, titoki or native ash..jostle..in the dense dry bush. **1907** LAING & BLACKWELL *Plants NZ* 225 This tree is sometimes called *The New Zealand Ash*, and its timber is largely used. Maori name, *Titoki*. **1960** *Campbell Paterson's Catalogue NZ Stamps* (1978) permanent page 02 2¹/₂d Titoki. A handsome tree, sometimes called the New Zealand Ash, which grows up to 60 feet high. **1982** HARRIS *Field Guide Common NZ Trees & Shrubs* 24 Titoki (New Zealand Ash) *Alectryon excelsus*.

ashet. *Otago-Southland.* [f. n. English and Sc. dial. *ashet* (ad. French *assiette*) a dish or large flat plate: see OED.] A large serving dish or platter, esp. for serving joints, etc. of meat.
     1913 BATHGATE *Sodger Sandy's Bairn* 12 'Surely the laddie'll ha'e his supper first, Mr. Tamson,' said Mirren, as she put on the table an ashet containing savoury-smelling mutton pies. **1943** HISLOP *Pure Gold* 16 [Stanley's Hotel at Macraes Flat, Central Otago] was one of the best tucker houses on the road, and..the hungry C.T. who was usually found stopping there would have a full ashet to help himself from, placed before him. **1950** *Listener* 10 Nov. 19 The process of yielding to the environment is illustrated in the case of the word 'ashet', meaning a large meat plate. A Dunedin Scottish lady explained : 'Mother would have said 'ashet' always. I might say 'ashet', or I might say 'the big meat dish'. The family would say 'the big meat dish'. (There are signs, however, that this word is returning to use.) **1960** SUMMERS *Moon Over the Alps* (1974) 48 He looked at the ashet. It was heaped with rice... In the middle..were deliciously tender lamb shanks. **1992** *NZ English Newsletter* 6 10 (Bartlett *Regional Variation: Southland*) *Ashet* has been reported as *ash* (which is clearly a shortening), *hashet* (predictably, by a speaker of Irish descent), and *hatchet* [erron.]... Some interviewees have said that an *ashet* can be used for serving food other than meat.

asphalt /ˈæʃfɒlt/. *West Coast. Obs.* As **asphalt hut**, see quot. Also **asphalter**, a tourist from the town, a 'townie'. Cf. LOOPIE.
     1890 *Otago Witness* (Dunedin) 23 Oct. 27 After disembarking we came to another Government hut erected for the convenience of tourists, known as asphalt hut—so termed on account of its being for the use of those who usually walk on hard city pavements and are called 'asphalters' by the West Coasters, who hold them in somewhat low esteem.

Assembly: see GENERAL ASSEMBLY.

Assessor. *Hist.* Also **Maori** (or **Native**) **Assessor**. A Maori appointed by the Crown to assist with expert advice the settlement of (esp. land) claims between Maori and Pakeha. Also **Native Assessorship**.
     1858 *NZPD* (1856–58) 18 May 444 The characteristic feature [of the Resident Magistrates Ordinance] is the institution of Native Assessors. *Ibid.* 445 The Native Assessorship is a most valuable and essential institution in this country. **1859** *Richmond-Atkinson Papers* (1960) I. 486 Mr Turton is also of opinion that it will be adviseable [*sic*] to appoint Taati te Waru as a Maori assessor. **1864** *AJHR* E-7 26 Return of Officers Employed in Native Districts. Names of Native Officers... Nature of Appointment. Te Warena Mahuri... Warden. Te Huhuna... Karere. Te Hira Wanui ... Assessor. **1866** GRACE *Jrnl.* 28 Nov. in Grace *Pioneer Missionary* (1928) 150 On reaching the village of Parawai, the Native Assessor, who lives here, stopped me to say that he could not get on with the trial of Mr. —'s case to-morrow unless my son Tom stayed to

interpret for him. **1877** [see QUARTER *n*.]. **1993** *Dominion* (Wellington) 9 Oct. 13 For most of the nineteenth century, following British annexation in 1840, justice was administered by a system of resident magistrates, assisted by salaried Maori assessors (local chiefs) and Maori police.

assisted, *ppl. a.* Of or pertaining to (later usu. State) subsidized passages to New Zealand, esp. in collocations with **emigrant** [AND 1848], **immigrant, emigration, immigration, passage.**
1856 FITTON *NZ* 211 In the Chapter on 'Assisted Emigration' will be found the regulations..respecting assisted passages for labouring persons and domestic servants to Canterbury. *Ibid.* 299 [Canterbury regulations] 1. Assisted passages [of half passage-money] will be granted by the Provincial Government to *bonâ fide* labouring men, country mechanics, their wives and families, and female domestic servants only. *Ibid.* 312 Assisted immigration. **1857** *Lyttelton Times* 4 July 6 Notice is hereby given, that if any Immigrants who have given Promissory Notes in part payment of assisted passages to this Province, and of which payment will be required a year after their landing, are willing to pay the whole or any part of their engagements before that time, they will be allowed a Discount. **1876** ADAM *Twenty-five Yrs. Emigrant Life* 56 Assisted emigration will likely take the place of free emigration. **1881** INGLESON *Battle of Life* 69 Wanted assisted emigrants to proceed to the Canterbury Province. **1892** *NZ Official Handbook* 60 The following table shows the immigration—distinguishing between the unassisted and the assisted... Unassisted Immigrants... Free and Assisted Immigrants... Total Immigrants. **1913** CARR *Country Work* 7 Assisted passages are also granted to farm labourers by the High Commissioner's Office in London. **1948** *Dominion* (Wellington) 9 Feb. 6 With more than 500 assisted immigrants..the Government-chartered ship Atlantis berthed at Wellington..yesterday. **1958** MILLER *Early Victorian NZ* 36 Besides the forecastle where the sailors slept, the sleeping accommodation usually consisted of six cabins..a house on the deck for the second-class passengers, and several long dormitories..for the assisted emigrants in a ship of 250 to 500 tons. **1964** ANDERSON *Doctor in Mountains* 27 Assisted immigrants of course had to travel steerage, and the food was not the best. **1987** HARTLEY *Swagger on Doorstep* 31 The hard-working colonist who arrived on an assisted passage of a very different sort..had scant respect for remittance men.

associate. [Spec. use of *associate* a partner.]
1. A female partner or companion of a gang member.
1991 *Sunday Star* (Auckland) 4 Aug. A3 Two Mongrel Mob associates were interviewed in Wellington.
2. As **associate teacher**, an experienced teacher to whose class teacher-trainees are assigned for supervised training in the classroom.
1987 *Metro* (Auckland) May 58 We [teacher trainees] went on section and I fell silently in love with 23-year-old associate teachers.

association, *n.*[1] *Hist.* Used of various early 19th c. bodies arranging or sponsoring organized emigration to New Zealand. **a. The New Zealand Association**, the fore-runner and supporter of the New Zealand Company (cf. COMPANY *n.*[1]).
1840 HOBSON 20 Feb. in *GBPP House of Commons 1841 (No.311)* 13 I have not yet had any communication with the emigrants who were sent from England by the association..but I have heard that several ships have reached Port Nicholson. **1901** FAWCETT *Sir William Molesworth* 178 The Association then [c1838, after failing to secure Government support] dissolved and re-formed itself as a limited liability company under the title of the New Zealand Land Company. **1966** *Encycl. NZ* II. 658 The genesis of the New Zealand Company is to be found in the New Zealand Association, which took shape in the spring of 1837 as a practical expression of Wakefield's challenging theories concerning emigration and colonisation.
b. The Canterbury Association, the body sponsoring emigration to the Canterbury Settlement.
1849 TORLESSE *Papers* (1958) 61 Settled accounts with Bruce. Expended £3/9/- for Association and gave Bruce an order for £13 on D. W[akefield]. **1864** CHUDLEIGH *Diary* 25 Sept. (1950) 145 We talked about the days of the Province before the Association came here.

association, *n.*[2] *Prison.* A cell designed to accommodate several people.
1980 MACKENZIE *While We Have Prisons* 95 *association* more than one occupant of a cell (*see* bridal suite). **1982** NEWBOLD *Big Huey* 244 Association (n) A cell designed to accommodate more than two people.

astelia. [The name *Astelia*, a latinised adaptation of the Greek ἀ without, στελεά stem, was given to the plant genus in 1810 by the British botanist Robert Brown, referring to the apparently stemless nature of some species.]
1. A perennial tufted herb of the predominantly southern hemisphere genus *Astelia* (fam. Liliaceae), occas. epiphytic ('perching lily' so-called, esp. *A. solandri*) but in most species a ground plant (e.g. *A. nervosa*), having heads of sword-like leaves and frequently long sprays of berries of intermingled colours. See also *bush* or *treeflax* (FLAX III), *bush lily* (LILY 2 (2)), KAHAKAHA, KAKAHA, KOWHARAWHARA, *tree-tussock* (TUSSOCK 3 (12)), WHARAWHARA.
[**1835** YATE *NZ* (1970) 16 At the tops, and on some of the higher branches of some of the forest-trees, grows a sedgy, succulent plant (*Astilia angustifolia*), much valued for the sweetness of the stem.] **1870** *TrNZI* II. 90 The slopes of the hills are usually covered with a dense forest..the forms being..Toro..and immense tussocks of an undescribed Astelia. **1922** COWAN *NZ Wars* (1955) I. 281 Some of the Maoris climbed the tree, and from the cover of the thick flax-like growth of *wharawhara*, or astelia, in the forks of the main branches, fired over the log wall. **1926** CROOKES *Plant Life Maoriland* 3 Most striking among them are the perching lilies (the Astelias) with their great fans of stiff bright green pointed leaves. **1935** *Tararua Tramper* July 2 Many fruits can be eaten raw. Amongst these are the wine-berry, the konini, the tawa, the matai, the totara, astelia berries. **1938** *Ibid.* June 6 The leading features of this side of the range are the danthonia (snowgrass) meadows and the astelia beds. **1968** SLATTER *Pagan Game* 120 He loved to scramble through the maze of angled rock in a mountain gorge..that unrestrained world of rock and snow grass and astelia and mountain flax. **1981** DENNIS *Paparoas Guide* 159 On damper parts of the forest floor astelias..are plentiful among the more open, stunted trees. **1995** coastal astelia (*A. banksii*) [see KOWHARAWHARA].
2. astelia moth, see MOTH 1.

aster. [Transf. use of *aster* for various similar plants.]
1. *Obs.* Also **native** (or **New Zealand**) **aster**, any of several aster-like plants, esp. of the genus *Celmisia* (see also CELMISIA).
1773 FORSTER *Resolution Jrnl.* 11 Apr. (1982) II. 253 Here and there this slope [in Cascade Cove] was variegated by large branches of a white fine new Aster. **1855** TAYLOR *Te Ika A Maui* 443 Peke, (Celmisia holocericeus,) a large broad-ribbed leafed aster. **1868** LINDSAY *Contribs. NZ Bot.* 53 They [*sc.* native celmisias] are also known partly as the 'Native Aster,'—a term applied, however, equally to species of *Olearia* and *Mesembryanthemum*. **1879** HAAST *Geol. Canterbury & Westland* 73 *Celmisia coriacea*, and *spectabilis*, the gigantic New Zealand asters, were also very frequent. **1883** GREEN *High Alps* 173 Large white asters (*Celmisia*) [*sic*], with flowers four inches in diameter, peeped forth from the boulders [in the Southern Alps].
2. With a modifier: **Chatham Island** (or **cliff**) **aster**, *Olearia semidentata* (fam. Asteraceae), a small Chatham Islands shrub of peaty or boggy ground.
1910 COCKAYNE *NZ Plants & Their Story* 122 These [bogs] are frequently occupied by a close growth of the Chatham Island aster.., a truly lovely shrub in every respect. **1952** RICHARDS *Chatham Is.* 68 [*Olearia semidentata*] Found only on the Chathams... Chatham Island Aster. Hanga-tare. **1956** *Bull. Wellington Bot. Soc. No.28* 6 This tree-daisy, or cliff aster as it is locally known [on Chatham Is.] is still abundant on the cliff tops. **1984** HOLMES *Chatham Is.* 93 Areas of heaths, Rautini, Chatham Island Aster, Corokia Macrocarpa.

ataata. [Ma. /aˈtaːtaː/: Williams 18 *Ata* (i)..*ataata*..2. [formerly] *Lunella smaragda*.] CAT'S EYE 1.
1947 POWELL *Native Animals NZ* 26 Cat's Eye... The circular greenish operculum, the cat's eye, is its most conspicuous feature. The Maori name is Ataata. **1966** *Encycl. NZ* I. 319 Cat's Eye... This is the best known of all our shellfish of the inter-tidal rocks... The Maori name is ataata. **1981** O'BRIEN *AA Book NZ Wildlife Turbo smaragdus* Cat's eye snail. Ataata.

atua /ˈʌtuə/. Formerly **Ea-tooa, Eātua** (=he atua), often init. cap. [Ma. /ˈatua/: Williams 20 *Atua. 1.* n. *God, demon, supernatural being...* 2. *Object of superstitious regard.*: cf. OED 1769 (Tahitian).] A spirit, god, or demon; occas. a figure representing such a concept; in Christian contexts 'God'. Occas. in transf. use, and also *attrib*.
1769 MONKHOUSE *Jrnl.* 9 Oct. in Cook *Jrnls.* (1955) I. 569 Gave us the names of three of their *Eātuas* or *demigods* and spoke of the custom of eating human flesh... The names of the Eātuas were Torònomŷ [Te Rongomai]—Tahòugoona [Te Kahukura]—Ohŷere. **1804** COLLINS *Eng. Colony in NSW* 345 While the soul is received by the good Ea-tooa, an evil spirit is also in readiness to carry the impure part of the corpse..to Terry-inga. **1823** CRUISE *Journal* (1957) 184 They believe in a Supreme Being, designated the Atua, or something incomprehensible. **1834** MARKHAM *NZ* (1963) 66 The old people believe that the (Atua) God of the Parkiars Strangers is killing or eating the Mouries. **1842** SELWYN *Lett.* 11 Dec. in Taylor *Early Travellers* (1959) 79 Various causes had led to the relapse of the chiefs, among which was the death of some of their children, which they attributed to the displeasure of their own *Atua* (spirit) at the introduction of Christianity. **1851** *Richmond-Atkinson Papers* (1960) I. 103 You are pretty sure that though he may have some faith in the atonement as a charm to exorcise 'atuas' that his Xtianity does not go a great deal further. **1871** MEADE *Ride through Disturbed Dist.* in Taylor *Early Travellers* (1959) 491 There must first be a great *karakia*, or ceremony of worship, to induce the great *Atua* (spirit) to inspire them rightly as to what was to be done with the pakeha. **1884** MARTIN *Our Maoris* 35 He..told us that an Atua Maori,—that is to say a man who professes

to be possessed by a spirit,—had been disturbing the neighbourhood. **1904** Chudleigh *Diary* 30 May (1950) 422 Packed a Moriori Atua for Dr. Benjamin Moorhouse. It is a human figure after a fashion, scraped not cut on the bark of a kopi. **1916** Cowan *Bush Explorers* (VUWTS) 15 Puhi says he [*sc.* a morepork] is an Atua, a god, and has a hundred eyes. **1946** *JPS* LV. 151 *atua*, god, demon, supernatural being, ghost; anything malign, disagreeable. **1976** Wilson *Pacific Star* 92 If I hadn't hauled back on the stick. I must have done it instinctively. Unless it was some atua, powerful joker in the sky. **1988** Mikaere *Te Maiharoa* 47 [Mitai Tuture records] Te Maiharoa went ahead to Awakino to kill the 'taipo' of that place and I think he killed two there. Taipo is the name used now but we called those evil spirits atua then [c1860s].

atwai, var. HUTIWAI.

aua /ˈæuə/. Also **awa**. [Ma. /ˈaua/ or /ˈawa/: Williams 21 *Aua* (i)..*Agonostomus forsteri*.] MULLET 2 (3). See also HERRING 1.

 1843 Williams *NZ Jrnl.* (1956) 41 Of this variety of 78 species [of fish on the NZ coast] I will name a part, viz... Anwa [poss. miscopied from *Auwa] species of whiting. **1848** Wakefield *Handbook NZ* 161 Both they [*sc.* smelts] and the fish called herring, (*aua* of the natives,) readily take a fly in the estuaries of rivers, which they enter with the tide. **1855** [see HERRING 1]. **1872** Hutton & Hector *Fishes NZ* 114 The Makawhiti or Aua of the Maoris (*Agonostoma Forsteri*)..is a common fish. **1888** Buller *Birds NZ* II. 151 When the pouch is emptied, the mother [shag]..goes off for a fresh supply of *auas*. **1892** *NZ Official Handbook* 167 Of the sea-fishes that are used as food in New Zealand, we have..the hapuku..moki, aua, rock-cod [etc.]. **1903** *TrNZI* XXXV. 319 Large numbers of aua or kataha. **1921** [see MULLET 2 (3)]. **1947** Powell *Native Animals NZ* 67 Yellow-eyed Mullet..Awa of the Maoris, is usually called the Herring. **1970** Thomas *Way Up North* 24 The Maoris knew to a nicety when to expect the Aua, or herring, or to be correct, the yellow eyed mullet. **1982** Burton *Two Hundred Yrs. NZ Food* 78 New Zealand has two species: the grey mullet or *kanae*, and the yellow-eyed mullet or *awa*.

auata, var. AWHATO.

Auckland, *n.* [f. the name of the city or provincial district.]

1. *WW1.* Usu as **The Aucklands**, occas. **the Aucklanders**, until the formation of the New Zealand Division in 1916, the Auckland Battalion of the Infantry Brigade; thence, either the 1st or 2nd Auckland Battalions of variously organized Infantry Brigades. Occas. early in WW1, the Auckland Regiment of the Mounted Rifles.

 1919 Waite *New Zealanders at Gallipoli* 125 The Wellingtons were on the left, the Aucklands in the centre, and the Canterburys on the right. **1919** [see DAISY PATCH]. **1984** Pugsley *Gallipoli* 197 The Aucklands and Otagos grimly held on to the fringes of the woods.

2. Used *attrib.* as a modifier in the names of animals, see: MULLET, *rock oyster* (OYSTER 2 (4)).

Aucklander. One born or resident in greater Auckland. See also AUCKLAND 1.

 1846 Marjoribanks *Travels in NZ* (1973) 43 Now, in the *Gazette* of 1st December, 1841, opposite to the word '*Tea*' there is still marked '*none*', so that..the Aucklanders had it not in their power to become *tea*-totallers. **1859** Thomson *Story NZ* II. 223 [Provincialists] were anxious to be Wellingtonists or Aucklanders, not New Zealanders. **1882** Hay *Brighter Britain* I. 21 Passing up Queen Street..[we notice] a rather singular feature in the Aucklanders we meet..the fact that all have strangely aquiline noses. **1912** Herz *NZ* 189 I fear the new town Hall..will not bring much balm or consolation to the Aucklander's soreness over the ugliness of his buildings. **1920** Bolitho *With the Prince in NZ* 143 It is said that Aucklanders are superficial and fond of outdoor life. **1948** Lipson *Politics of Equality* 45 Up to 1876 political sentiment was regionalized... Provincial loyalties were paramount; people considered themselves Aucklanders or Wellingtonians rather than New Zealanders. **1963** *Dominion* (Wellington) 23 Sept. 1 It was found that the big Aucklander B.T. Thomas was unable to pass. **1972** Mitchell *Pavlova Paradise* 33 Dunedinites think of Auckland as another country. Aucklanders advise South-bound trippers to take enough overcoats..for the South Pole. **1987** *Metro* (Auckland) May 61 I had started to become a Wellingtonian, one of the most horrible things that can happen to a New Zealander; and I remember thinking from that sad perspective how different Aucklanders were from the denizens of the capital.

Auckland Island. In the names of animals, see: CRAB 2 (3), SHAG 2 (1), SNIPE *n.* 2, TEAL 2 (1).

auction block. *Hist.* Applied to a former system of hiring wharf labour. Also as **on the block**, applied to an allocation of wharf-labouring work.

 c1926 The Mixer *Transport Workers' Song Book* 20 Ah, what a picture to behold If you lined up to the [wharf-labour] stand With a string of ducks around your neck And a rooster in each hand [to bribe the overseer]... What a symbolic design To hang above the 'auction block' For the fringe of the bread-line. **1948** *Our Own Country* 91 The Lyttelton waterfront has been working under the bureau system of engaging labour for nine years now... 'And,' the bureau manager said, 'the men wouldn't like to go back to the old way again.' Under the old system, foremen of the various shipping companies stood on a small platform or block with the men awaiting employment before them and nominated those they required to work their own ships. The trouble with this 'auction block' system, as it was called, was that each company tended to give preference to a certain group of men. It engaged the same men first all the time and employed others only when the preferred group were all at work. **1988** Jackson *Rainshadow* 134 There was seldom a day when I didn't get work on the block. With bonuses of dirt money and danger money, I calculated I'd easily save enough for a year's studies.

aue, *exclam.* [Ma. /ˈau'e:/: Williams 21 *Auē. 1.* int. expressing astonishment or distress. *Alas*.] Mainly in Maori use, 'Alas!', 'Goodness me!'

 1863 Maning *Old NZ* x 159 'Is it you?—is it you?—truly is it you?—*aue! aue!* they hold me, they restrain me. **1927** Donne *Maori Past & Present* 258 Today that land is worth about £200 an acre. Heigh Ho! and *Aue!* **1939** Grieve *Sketches from Maoriland* (1961) 46 And here was the *rangatira Pakeha* a whole day before his time. *Aue Aue*. [**1939** *Note*] *Aue—a wailing expression of grief*. **1955** Campbell *By Reef & Range* 14 Aue! I shall be the crown upon your brow, my warriors, the cloak about your shoulders. **1964** Middleton *Walk on Beach* 171 'Aue!' growled Dad, smiting his thigh. **1986** Hulme *Te Kaihau* 115 Aue, I know you recall. You lost your good temper and yelled at me all kinds of rude names and swearing, taureka and sloven, 'pokokohua and bitch.

aukati. *Hist.* Also occas. init. cap. [Ma. /ˈaukati/: Williams 22 *Aukati 1.* Prohibition... 3. n. *Line which one may not pass*.]

1. Mainly in *attrib.* use in Comb. with **boundary, line, pole**: a line or boundary which may not be passed or crossed; also, a prohibition, *spec.* a prohibiting of Pakeha travel, land-purchase, etc.

 1869 *Richmond-Atkinson Papers* (1960) II. 281 On their side the chiefs [were] to withdraw their *aukati* and openly and public[ly] disavow..the murderous tribes of Hauhau, to allow needful roads and royal rights over the territory etc. **1915** *Canterbury Times* 3 Mar. (VUW Fildes Clippings 421:59) [He] did not worry himself over the chances of retribution [in the King Country] for evading the 'Aukati', the Hauhaus' 'Thou-shalt-come-no-further.' **1916** Cowan *Bush Explorers* (VUWTS) 1 Not a pakeha farm..southward of the Puniu, the old Aukati pole. **1922** Cowan *NZ Wars* (1955) II. 468 The Kingites strictly enforced their *aukati*—that is, they forbade *pakeha* intrusion on the Maori side of the frontier line. **1935** Cowan *Hero Stories NZ* 158 Sometimes the farthest-out farmers went across the Aukati line to trade with Maoris..and they were on friendly terms with many of the Kingites. **1940** Cowan *Sir Donald Maclean* 113 But they enforced the 'Aukati' order of the Kingite chiefs against the *pakeha*. **1955** *NZ Geogr. Soc. Rec.* July–Sept. 6 But the Maori Wars and the aukati closed the area until the latter was lifted and the railway was again pushed southwards. **1964** Norris *Settlers in Depression* 49 The Waikato adherents of the Maori King..kept all Europeans from crossing the Puniu River... The firmness of this decision was emphasised by the deaths of Europeans who had..crossed the Aukati Line, the boundary over which the white people were forbidden to pass. **1990** *Landfall* 173 87 Kingites frequently crossed the boundary, the *aukati*, to buy kegs of rum. **1993** Geering in *Of Pavlovas, Poetry and Paradigms* 252 Of the 436 words [from Maori] found [in the *Auckland Weekly News*] in this period [*sc.* the 1860s], apart from *Maori*, which occurred 171 times, the two of next greatest frequency were *Hauhau* (79) and *aukati* (29). *Hauhau* was found only 3 times thereafter [to the 1890s], and *aukati* not at all.

2. *transf.* A boundary line.

 1887 *Auckland Weekly News* 11 June 21 I had dinner with them [*sc.* MPs], for the 'aukati' was as distinctly marked in this two-pounds-a-night hovel as in the Parliamentary Chambers.

aunt: *not to call the Queen one's aunt*, see CALL *v.* 3.

auntie. Also **aunty**.

1. *Derog.* An older effeminate male homosexual, or suspect-homosexual.

 1946 Sargeson *That Summer* 84 The cook got my goat when he started trying to do the same thing [*sc.* pinch my backside]. He was a tonk all right, just a real old auntie.

2. [AND Aborig. Eng. 1963; OED US for an elderly woman esp. negress; also Brit. dial.] Used mainly by Maori speakers of English as a form of address to an older woman one does not know; or in reference when Mrs., etc., would be too formal and the use of a forename alone precluded by the addressee's advanced age.

 1988 *Short Stories NZ* 133 'No Aunty,' said Tom. 'I don't know Wellington. I thought you fellas would know all that!' 'Aue!'... 'Hey, does anyone know how to get to Government House?' 'You mean the Beehive, Aunty?' **1991** *Evening Post* (Wellington) 18 July 3 Coastlands manager..worked all night to have everything ready for the formal opening..by Ngahina trustee 'Auntie' Ngapera Taupiri Teira. **1995** *Ibid.* 30 Nov. 7 Ria Moheko Taiaroa Wi Neera (Aunty Leah) was one of the venerable Ngati Toa kuia.

Aussie [/'ɒzi/, occas. /'ɒsi/, *n.* and *attrib.* Also **Ossie**.

A. *n.*

1. [AND 1918.] An Australian, esp. an Australian soldier of WW1.

1917 *NZ at the Front* xiii Aussie, or Ossie.—The 'Tommy' of Australia. *Ibid.* 90 If you want a good electric torch I'll get one from the Ossies; they're white, they are. **1918** *NZ at the Front* 35 [Caption] 'And now we hear from Palestine that our dear old comrades the Aussies have entered Bethlehem on Christmas Eve, and we may be sure the shepherds watched their flocks by night.' **1939** McKinley *Ways & By-ways* 28 I did not hear the term ['digger'] applied to the Australians until much later in 1917, they being known to everyone in France as the 'Aussies'. **1944** Fullarton *Troop Target* 104 On his own the Aussie's a regular guy. **1964** Middleton *Walk on Beach* 91 Although he laid down three Jacks to the Aussie's thirty days, Johnson still looked white. **1987** *Sunday News* 4 Jan. 3 It's really gone down well with the Aussies.

2. [AND 1915.] Australia.

1928 Smyth *Jean of Tussock Country* 215 You meet a few bums from Aussie. **1944** *NZ New Writing* III. 28 'Billy Norfolk?' I said, 'You were never a banker here, and you were never a banker in Aussie.' **1965** Watson *Stand in Rain* 111 And Paul and June were off to Aussie on Friday.

B. *attrib.* passing into *adj.* Australian.

a1910 Goldstone 'Man From Kaiveroo' in Woodhouse *Farm & Station Verse* (1950) 49 We'd a bunch of Aussie shearers, and they come from New South Wales. **1917** Nuttall, G.W. *MS Papers 2192* (ATLTS) 10 Nov. Spent the evening at the 'Aldwich Theatre' which is the Aussy Y.M. and well run. **1936** Hyde *Passport to Hell* 143 At Mudros we met up with the Aussies, and started to buy cake..from them, for it looked as if the Aussie women remembered the troops better than the New Zealanders. **1943** Hislop *Pure Gold* 86 Now feel the weight of this..for your Aussie article is as hollow as the bung-hole in a barrel. **1956** Wilson *Sweet White Wine* 138 The Aussie Major's shirt was wet from collar to waistband. **1965** Watson *Stand in Rain* 101 The new wife was a tall dark Aussie girl called June.

austral, *a.* [Spec. use of *austral* southern: see OED; AND 'Australian', 1823.] Of or pertaining to New Zealand, Australia and offshore islands.

1875 Hogg *Lays & Rhymes* 175 I love New Zealand—for 'tis destined yet To be the first, the greatest, and the best Of lands on which an Austral sun can set. **1875** *TrNZI* VII. 182 The attention of the Austral Colonies has not been directed to the conservation and creation of forests one moment too soon. **1890** *NZ Observer* 1 Feb. 7 Auckland! Queen City of the Austral Seas. **1898** Morris *Austral-English A Dictionary of Australasian Words Phrases & Usages* [Title] **1928** Davis *Dainty Dishes* 20 *Austral Trifle*..sandwich cake..whipped cream..passionfruit.. jelly..walnuts..put one round of the sandwich cake in a glass dish..whipped cream on it,.. other half of cake on top..spread the passionfruit..when jelly is nearly set pour it over the whole..whipped cream on top. **1961** *Merriam-Webster Third Internat. Dict.* 145 *austral english n, cap A & E*: the language of most inhabitants of Australia and New Zealand—used esp. with the implication that it is a variety of English distinct from that used in Great Britain yet not so divergent as to be a separate language; compare American English, Australian English, British English.

Australasia. [AND *Hist.* 'Australia' (1794–1890), f. French *Australasie*, the Australian continent and neighbouring islands.] New Zealand with Australia and their outlying islands. (Often felt as a patronising term and replaced by locutions as *Australia and New Zealand*, *New Zealand-Australia(n)*, *Anzac*, etc.)

1838 Polack *NZ* II. 376 The most southerly group in Australasia was discovered in 1811, by a Sealing Master. **1859** Thomson *Story NZ* II. 195 Around the iron-bound coasts were rising up..a numerous race of daring sailors, a class almost unknown in Australasia. **1877** *TrNZI* IX. 86 Australasia can supply these vessels better and cheaper than any other country. **1885** *TrNZI* XVII. xxiii The security against attack of certain ports in Australasia is an essential part of the maritime defence of this portion of the empire. **1892** *NZ Official Handbook* 7 Total [square miles] Continent of Australia 3,030,771. Tasmania..26,375. New Zealand..104,471. Total Australasia..3,161,617. **1902** Lancaster in *Happy Endings* (1987) 101 She's a young country, I grant you, but she's got the biggest future of all Australasia. **1915** Algie, Colvin *MS Papers 1374* (ATLTS) 25 Apr. It has been a trying test for new soldiers but they are magnificent. Australasia can be justly proud. **1935** Guthrie *Little Country* (1937) 102 The second..was the conviction that the Little Country was part and parcel of the continent of Australasia..largely due to the current use of that canopian word Australasia. **1946** Soljak *NZ* 3 The tendency to confuse New Zealand with Australia has been encouraged by the use of the term 'Australasia', which Australians naturally favour but New Zealanders dislike intensely. **1960** Curnow ed. *Penguin Book NZ Verse* 27 If New Zealand's littleness cramped that 'elasticity of pride', there was always the capacious term 'Australasia'. Little as it means on either side of the Tasman Sea today, it meant a great deal to the New Zealand poet or journalist of the nineteenth or early twentieth century... The term 'Australasia' has been banned for many years—informally, as far as I know, but by common consent—in the New Zealand press. **1985** Sherwood *Botanist at Bay* 18 He also uses expressions like 'down under', which implies that there's something wrong with the Southern Hemisphere, and 'Australasia', which implies a close connection between New Zealand and her bullying barbaric neighbour.

Australasian, *a.* and *n.*

A. *adj.* [AND *Hist. adj.* Of, pertaining to, or characteristic of Australia, 1802; see also OED.]

1. Of or pertaining to New Zealand and Australia; of or relating to New Zealand, Australia, and their offshore islands.

1838 *Dublin Rev.* July 276 New Zealand is included in the vast diocese of our Australasian Bishop. **1849** Arnold *Letters* (1966) 164 Yesterday we saw the great Taranaki, the king of the Australasian mountains. **1853** Swainson *Auckland* v It [*sc.* Auckland is]..about to become the nearest of our [*sc.* British] Australasian possessions. **1868** *Marlborough Express* (Blenheim) 25 Jan. 5 Two courses seem to be open to the Australasian colonies. **1875** Hogg *Lays & Rhymes* 196 That the Australasian Colonies may never know the sufferings to which the factory children of Great Britain have been subjected, is the prayer of the writer of this note. **1894** *NZ Official Year-book* 70 There is not in New Zealand, as in each of the other Australasian Colonies, one metropolitan centre of population overshadowing, by comparison, the other towns of the colony. **1914** Algie, Colvin *MS Papers 1374* (ATLMS) 23 Dec. General Birdwood, who commands the Australasian corps (N.Z. and Australia). **1918** *NZ at the Front* 16 But the overwhelming majority, the flower of Australasian youth and manhood—these were..men indeed. **1937** Cowie *NZ from Within* 253 [New Zealand] refuses to allow the term 'Australasian' to be used in her hearing. **1978** Moore & Irwin *Oxford Book NZ Plants* 138 *Cassinia* is a genus of Australasian and South African shrubs. **1987** *Listener* 12 Dec. 11 When New Zealanders use the term Australasian they invariably mean the geographical and cultural combination of Australia and New Zealand. Some authoritative Australian definitions still hold that it means Australia, New Zealand and the Pacific Islands south of Asia.

2. In the names of animals, see: BITTERN 2 (1), GANNET 1, HARRIER.

B. *n.* [AND a non-Aboriginal Australian, 1819; an Aboriginal, 1845.] A person from Australia or New Zealand; an antipodean.

1905 *Truth* 26 Aug. 5 Alibil on Australasians. **1915** *Otago Witness* (Dunedin) 12 May 17 The Australasians did not wait for orders or for boats to reach the beach [at Gallipoli]. **1950** Joseph *Imaginary Islands* 24 The Australasians hate him Loathe and abominate him Because he is swift and gay.

Australian, *a.* Spec. uses mainly as a (usu. vernacular) modifier in the names of plants, animals, and foods originating (or thought to originate) in, or passing into New Zealand English from, Australia.

1. In the names of plants and animals, see: BURR $n.^1$ 2 a, COOT 2, FIREWEED, FLAX 7, GANNET 1, HEATH 5, PIRIPIRI $n.^1$ 1 c, TAUHINU 3 (1).

2. In recipes for various foods and food dishes, esp. those containing tropical fruits, or brown ingredients.

1908 *Souvenir All Nations Fair, Gisbourne* 3 *Australian Soup*..clarified brown stock..tapioca..add tomatoes; rub through a sieve. **1913** *Australasian Cook. Book* 34 *Australian Apples*..good dessert apples..scoop out..cores..fill the hollows with cream or custard [after stewing in water and sugar until transparent]. *Ibid.* 38 *Australian Cakes* 5 eggs..sifted sugar..flour..pineapple flavouring..bake..cut into fingers..sprinkle with sugar... *Australian Trifle* 1 dozen bananas..1 dozen oranges..layer with sugar..and grated cocoanut..boiled custard..whites of eggs. **1915** McCredie *Patriotic Fete ... Bungalow Recipe Book* 21 *Australian Soup*..brown stock..salt..tomatoes..tapioca. Crush tapioca..boil. **1936** *Home of Compassion Recipes* 111 *Australian Shortbread*..butter..brown sugar..syrup..vanilla..rolled oats..cocoanut..bake slowly.

3. In special collocations: **Australian fashion**, in rough outdoors style; **Australian invasion**, referring to the influx of esp. Victorian miners in the 1860s; **Australian language**, a euphemism for any colourful oathing; **Australian summer**, a dry, droughty summer.

1860 Begg *Diary* (1960) 26 Came upon a surveyor's tent and had dinner there, regular **Australian fashion**—damper tea and mutton cooked in the open air. **1914** Pfaff *Diggers' Story* 2 The commencement of the **Australian Invasion** to the [West] coast must be dated from March, 1865. Our neighbours in Victoria tried to check it, and said it was only a 'steamboat rush'. **1922** Burton *Auckland Regt.* 77 These donkeys are noteworthy, because their driver was reputed to have the most forcible and fluent command of the **Australian Language** in the Brigade. **1868** Barker *Station Life* (1870) 209 Every one was anxiously looking for rain..and people were beginning to talk of an **Australian summer** and to prophesy dismal things of a drought.

Austrian. *Hist.* DALMATIAN. Also *adj.*

1894 *NZ Official Year-book* 340 A Commission appointed last year..gives the number of persons on the gumfields in May, 1893, as under: British, 4,303;

settlers, 416; Maoris, 1244; Austrians, 519; other foreigners, 415. **1913** CARR *Country Work* 42 It is estimated that there are 8,000 Croatians, Austrians they are commonly called, on the fields. **1914** MASSEY in Thorpy *Wine In NZ* (1983) 39 Austrian wine had caused loss of life and it should be put down with very drastic measures. I do not know whether the name is a misnomer or not; but it is a liquor that is sold in the district north of Auckland. **1917** *Free Lance* (Wellington) 11 May 22 It is Town Talk..that the Austrian gum-digger is still steadily purchasing Maori land in the far North. **1924** LYSNAR *NZ* 14 Thousands of pounds worth of gum have been obtained from it, first by the surface digger, and latterly by the industrious Austrian. **1956** SUTHERLAND *Green Kiwi* (1960) 135 When the first Dalmatian and Croatian settlers arrived their provinces were under the rule of the Austro-Hungarian Empire and the inhabitants suffered political and cultural oppression, but because their passports were written in the Italian and German languages they became known as 'Austrians' on their arrival in this country. **1965, 1970, 1987** [see DALMATIAN A]. **1991** *North & South* (Auckland) May 74 'Oh, where the Austrians live,' said the truckie. 'No, we're not Austrians, we're Yugoslavs,' Belich replied. 'Oh, same thing,' was the driver's reply.

aute. *Hist.* Also early **Aouta, Eaowte** (=he aute). [Ma. /'aute/: Williams 23 *Aute..1. Broussonetia papyrifera, paper mulberry... 2. Cloth* made from the bark of this tree.] *Broussonetia papyrifera* (fam. Moraceae) brought to New Zealand by the early Polynesian immigrants, and formerly cultivated by the Maori for its bark as useful for cloth-making until replaced by FLAX I. See also *paper mulberry* (MULBERRY 1).
    1769 PARKINSON *Journal* (1773) 110 We saw many plantations of the Koomarra, and some of the Eaowte, or cloth trees. **1769** BANKS *Endeavour Jrnl.* I. 444 After this they shewd us a great rarity 6 plants of what they called *Aouta* from whence they made cloth like the Otahite cloth; the plant proved exactly the same, as the name is the same, as is usd in the Islands... They seemd to value it very much and that it was very scarce among them I am inclind to beleive. **1869** [see MULBERRY 1]. **1905** *TrNZI* XXXVII. 95 And before being hung up the *iho* is wrapped up in *aute* or *raukawa* (the paper-mulberry and *Panax edgerleyi*, a scented shrub), and bound with *aka* (a climbing plant). **1924** *Otago Witness* (Dunedin) 17 June 4 An aute kite can be made to fly fast. **1930** NGATA *Let.* 22 May in *Na To Hoa Aroha* (1987) II. 19 Your general conclusions in 'The Evolution of Maori Clothing' of local development based on phormium as opposed to 'aute' and the necessities of a colder climate, may have to be reviewed.

autumn muster: see MUSTER *n.* 2.

avalanche grass: see GRASS 2 (1).

avo, var. ARVO.

avocet /'ævəset/. [Spec. use of *avocet* a wading bird, esp. one with a flexible upturned beak: see OED.] *Recurvirostra novaehollandiae* (fam. Recurvirostrinae), the Australian Red-necked avocet, at one time common in New Zealand, now a very rare straggler.
    1870 *TrNZI* II. 48 Those less common birds, the great White Crane, the Avocet, and Spoonbill Duck were seen at rarer intervals. **1875** *TrNZI* VII. 206 Recurvirostra novae-hollandiae... Red-necked Avocet. **1883** DOMETT *Ranolf & Amohia* II. 63 Bluff *oyster-catcher, avocet,* And tripping beach-birds, seldom met Elsewhere. **1904** HUTTON & DRUMMOND *Animals NZ*

212 *The Avocet. Recurvirostra novae-hollandiae...* At one time, our Avocet was seen fairly frequently in some localities... Now, however, it is very rare. **1990** *Checklist Birds NZ* 131 *Recurvirostra novae-hollandiae..Australian Red-necked Avocet...* In the latter half of the 19th century, New Zealand received a minor irruption, during which (1859–92) Avocets were reported widely.

Avondale spider. Often *ellipt.* **Avondale** /'ævən‚deɪl/. [From *Avondale*, an Auckland suburb with which it is associated.] **a.** An Australian huntsman spider *Delena cancerides* (fam. Sparassidae) introduced to New Zealand, and found orig. and mainly in the Avondale area of Auckland city.
    1978 *Western Leader* (Auckland) 3 Oct. 4 It appears that the Avondale spider is not as recent an immigrant as we thought and one elderly Avondale woman says her acquaintance with him goes back 50 years. **1988** *Central Leader* (Auckland) 3 Feb. 5 Grace Hall is launching the first major research project on Avondale spiders. **1990** *DSIR Plant Protection Leaflet* 90/1 Avondale spider; *Delena cancerides* Walckenar (Araneae: Sparassidae). The large harmless spider found around the Avondale area is an Australian huntsman spider. This spider found its way to New Zealand in the early 1920s, with the first specimen found in 1924... It has not spread very far from Avondale, so it has received the popular name of *Avondale Spider*. **1991** *Auckland City Harbour News* 17 Jan. 5 The Avondales are harmless, despite their appearance and reputation.

b. *Fig.* and *transf.* in trade-names.
    1988 Dix *Stranded in Paradise* 211 Working-class teenagers hailing from the western suburbs, they [*sc.* a pop group] were originally called the Avondale Spiders. **1990** *Western Leader* (Auckland) 2 Apr. 33 [Advt] Buying or selling. Still the best deal for Your Furniture & Appliances only at Avondale Spiders Ltd.

aw /o/, *int.* [Cf. OED *int.* quots. (1852–1932) seem mainly drawn from non-British (or provincial or dial.) English; see also EDD: also used by lower class British TV characters.] A speech prefix, particularly frequent in New Zealand, usu. indicating entreaty, doubt or patient disapprobation; often followed by **heck, hell, come off it,** etc.
    1928 SMYTH *Jean of Tussock Country* 46 'Aw—yes, you want a job!' the manager muttered. 'Can you ride?'.. 'Aw—you can.' **1935** GUTHRIE *Little Country* 66 ''Allo.' 'Fine day.' 'Yair.' Pause, 'Going far?' 'Aw no. Up along.' Long pause, 'Aw well, Hooray!' 'Hooray!' **1943** MARSH *Colour Scheme* 119 'How could he stand?' 'Aw heck!' **1945** HENDERSON *Gunner Inglorious* 182 Aw..break it down, fella. **1950** *Landfall* 13 20 Aw, hell! **1959** MIDDLETON *The Stone* 35 Aw he goes out after sheilas in the park with those jokers from Central. **1963** WALLIS *Point of Origin* 10 'Aw, they're all right,' said Bert. 'Want to give a man a fair go, Charlie.' **1970** MASON *Solo* (1981) 15 Aw, break it down, Robbie. **1984** *NZ Short Stories* 7 'You're not to touch those afghans.' 'Aw, Mum.' **1985** JONES *Gilmore's Dairy* 206 'Aw, I hoped so. Terry'll be rapt.' **1987** Norgrove *Shoestring Sailors* 43 'Aw, c'mon now, I told you it was dinkum!'

awa, var. AUA.

awailago, var. WAYLEGGO.

awake up (to): see WAKE UP.

award, *n.* and *attrib. Hist.*

A. *n.* [AND 1886.] A determination of the Arbitration Court on wages or conditions of work, or the legal agreement which ratifies this. Cf. ARBITRATION.
    1898 in 1900 *Awards, etc.* 6 [Auckland Seamen's Award] That this award shall come into force on the 1st of February next..until the 28th of February, 1899. **1904** *Awards, etc.* 3 [North Auckland Timber-Workers' Award] The Court doth..order, award, and declare that during the currency of the said award band-mill men shall be paid at the rate prescribed in the said award for No. 1 circular-saw men. **1926** DEVANNY *Butcher Shop* (1981) 67 Now the men are organised into a union and work under a Dominion award. **1946** [see ARBITRATION]. **1948** *Public Holidays Amendment Act* s2 'Award or industrial agreement' includes any instrument or contract relating to the terms of employment of any worker. **1955** BOWEN *Wool Away* 16 In New Zealand the shearers' award sets out a nine-hour day. **1964** HINDE *Mozley & Whiteley's Law Dict.* (NZ edn.) 36 *The award of the Court of Arbitration,...* or any reference to it under the provisions of the Industrial Conciliation and Arbitration Act 1954. 'An industrial award is in form a judicial decree, but in substance it is an act of legislative authority. It is the establishment of a set of authoritative rules regulating an industry, and determining not the present rights and obligations of litigants, but the future relations and mutual rights and obligations of all persons who thereafter during the currency of the award choose to enter into contractual relations with each other as employers and employed in that industry.' **1980** LELAND *Kiwi-Yankee Dict.* 10 *award:* an award, or more properly an Industrial Award, is the contract between union and employers. Awards specify pay, fringe benefits, types of work etc. [**1991** *Dominion* (Wellington) 3 Sept. 11 The wider shears were faster and New Zealanders were accused [in Australia] of undercutting the award.]

B. As an *attrib.* in special Comb. **award rate** [AND 1919], **award wage** [AND 1941], the minimum legal rate of pay for a particular type of work.
    1972 MITCHELL *Pavlova Paradise* 182 **award rate:** Pay no one actually gets. Discussions on wages and salaries concentrate on this so that no one is embarrassed by having his income revealed, and no one feels involved. **1955** *BJ Cameron Collection* (TS July) **award wage** (n) The minimum wage permitted in an industry under its award. Equivalent to the basic or minimum wage. **1964** *Evening Post* (Wellington) 16 Jan. 12 Employers are prepared to pay above award wages to attract staff.

awaruite. [f. *Awarua* a locality associated with Big Bay on the sw. coast of the SI + *-ite*.] A nickel-iron alloy occurring naturally.
    1891 *NZJSc.* (NS) I. 60 In October 1885, Mr. W. Skey..read a paper before the New Zealand Philosophical Society..announcing the discovery of a Nickel-Iron Alloy, which he recognised as a new mineral species and named 'Awaruite.' The discovery was made in a collection of minerals sent..by the Warden of Jackson's Bay District, which includes Big Bay (Maori name, 'Awarua'). **1911** *TrNZI* XLIII. 451 [Milford Sound] is remarkable owing to the presence with the platinum of that peculiar nickel-iron mineral awaruite. In appearance it is not unlike platinum, and was mistaken by the miners for that mineral... Both the metal and the awaruite occur in a district composed..of serpentine and dunite. **1993** [see TARANAKITE].

awato, var. AWHATO.

away back, var. WAYBACK.

away laughing: see LAUGH.

away with the fairies: see FAIRY 2.

aweto, var. AWHATO.

awhato /əˈwetʌu/, /əˈwatʌu/. Also **auata** and commonly (poss. from Ma. dial.) **awato, aweto; awheto, hawhato.** [Ma. /ˈaːfato/, /ˈaːfeto/: Williams 24 *Āwhato* = *āwheto* 1... *Cordiceps* species. 2. A large caterpillar, larva of *Sphinx convolvuli.*]

[*Note*] In Maori use *āwhato* (and a dial. var. *hōtete*) denote a class of caterpillars some of which (*Wiseana* formerly *Porina* spp.) are invaded by the *Cordyceps* fungus, some (*Agrius* formerly *Sphinx* spp.) are not. In English use *awhato* and *hotete* (often in confusing spellings) became mainly synonyms for *vegetable caterpillar*, the fungally transformed entity, but were still occas. used for the various moth caterpillars themselves.

1. VEGETABLE CATERPILLAR.
    1845 MEURANT *Diary* 24 [We] walked into a forrest [*sic*] to look for the Awato, or Otete (the large caterpillar). **1848** TAYLOR *Leaf from Nat. Hist.* xii The most singular thing is the *aweto* or vegetating caterpillar. **1867** HOCHSTETTER *NZ* 171 The Aweto or Hotete the large (ni[g]ht-butterfly) caterpillar, from the head of which a parasitical fungus, *Sphaeria Robertsii*, grows out; hence the name 'Vegetating Caterpillar' amongst the colonists. **1869** *TrNZI* I. (rev. edn.) 267 The black pigment [for tattooing] was obtained..also from the ashes of the curious vegeto-caterpillar fungus, the Hawhato. **1889** WAKEFIELD *NZ after Fifty Yrs.* 81 The *aweto*, or vegetable-caterpillar... It is a perfect caterpillar in every respect, and a remarkably fine one too, growing to a length, in the largest specimens of three and a half inches and the thickness of a finger, but more commonly to about a half or two thirds of that size... When fullgrown, it undergoes a miraculous change. For some inexplicable reason, the spore of the vegetable fungus *Sphaeria Robertsii*, fixes itself on its neck, or between the head and the first ring of the caterpillar, takes root and grows vigorously..exactly like a diminutive bulrush from 6 to 10 inches high without leaves, and consisting solely of a single stem with a dark-brown felt-like head, so familiar in the bulrushes. **1904** TREGEAR *Maori Race* 259 Soot for use as colouring matter for tattooing the body was sometimes made from the burnt *awheto* or 'vegetable caterpillar' (Cordiceps robertsii). **1924** *School Jrnl. Part III* Nov. 318 He probably referred to the insect called the 'vegetable caterpillar', called by the Maoris *awheto*. **1930** REISCHEK *Yesterdays in Maoriland* (1933) 70 Under the rata roots I also found the Aweta, or plant-caterpillar, which to change into a chrysalis creeps underground, and in many cases instead of becoming a moth becomes—a mushroom! **1955** MILLER *Nature NZ* 21 Other Ghost Moths are the several species of porinas... These larvae are attacked by..a Cordyceps fungus. The fungus spores invade and germinate in the larvae, producing thread-like masses..then the fungus sends out, from the head of the larval remains, one or more long stalks which grow..until their swollen, spore producing ends project above ground. These objects are 'vegetable caterpillars', the *awhato* of the Maori. **1964** BACON *Along the Road* 129 The Maoris knew them [*sc.* vegetable caterpillars]; they called them awhato and ground them up for tattooing pigment. **1982** SHARELL *NZ Insects* 59 The awheto has not been used for tattooing the face, as it proved to be an insufficiently deep black.

2. A caterpillar esp. that of the convolvulus hawk moth (*Agrius convolvuli*), which feeds on kumara leaves but is not invaded by *Cordyceps* spp. See also HOTETE b. (Quot. 1848 refers prob. to the greasy cut-worm caterpillar.)
    1848 WAKEFIELD *Handbook NZ* 170 There is, especially, a black caterpillar, (*auata* of the natives,) which attacks potatoes, eating the young holm off level with the ground. **1856** SHORTLAND *Traditions & Superstitions* 293 Its [*sc.* sphinx moth's] caterpillar, called by the natives *awheto* or *hotete*, makes its appearance in the eighth month, viz. the end of January. **1896** *TrNZI* XXVIII. 624 The *aweto* (larva of the sphinx-moth) may often be observed on the convolvulus... Some people fancy that the *aweto* is the vegetating caterpillar; but this is a mistake. **1904** TREGEAR *Maori Race* 86 Careful watch was also kept upon the growing plants to guard them from the ravages of a certain caterpillar; the larva of a large moth (*anuhe*, *awhato*, *hotete*...) which preyed on the *kumara* leaves. **1931** *JPS* XL. 1 The most destructive of pests among the sweet potato plants is the *awheto*, *awhato*, *hotete*, or *anuhe*, a large caterpillar that often appeared in great numbers.

awheto, var. AWHATO.

axe.

1. [Transf. use of *axe*.] In Maori reference, ADZE; early MERE 1 or TEWHATEWHA. Cf. TOKI 1.
    1826 SHEPHERD *Jrnl.* in Howard *Rakiura* (1940) 364 [New Zealanders] generally kill the person with a Maree or axe or spear before he has time to make a second thrust. **c1835** BOULTBEE *Journal* (1986) 82 Most of these men had their stone marees (axes) slung to their wrists. **1864** CAMPBELL *Martin Tobin* I. 125 The other [hand] frequently grasps a long-handled spear, or native axe made of the magical green stone. **1889** *TrNZI* XXI. 338 I can see no difference in the stone axes or adzes found at the exposed pa. **1903** *TrNZI* XXXV. 241 The axes, adzes,.. are also made from a hard kind of stone not found on the mainland. **1935** GUTHRIE *Little Country* (1937) 18 A greenstone mere or Maori axe..with a written guarantee that it had passed through many a skull. **1943** MARSH *Colour Scheme* 110 I can't see anything amusing in your..suggestion that a Maori axe should be discovered in Mr. Gaunt's room.

Hence **axe-stone,** GREENSTONE 1.
    1869 *TrNZI* I. (rev. edn.) 352 Their stone Axes of various sizes..were made of..the green jade, or axe stone.

2. See AMERICAN AXE, KELLY, PLUMB, *racing axe* (RACING *ppl. a.*). (Another favoured brand was the *Sharp's* or *Sharps* axe.)

3. Special Comb. **axe-handle** [AND 1958], as a rough measure of breadth, often, of a man's shoulders or, patriarchally, of a woman's buttocks (see also PICK HANDLE); **axework,** the exercise or result of an axeman's skill.
    1961 CRUMP *Hang On a Minute Mate* 189 About four **axe-handles** across the shoulders, face on him like a pine-cone. **1978** in *Listener Short Stories 3* (1984) 75 She smokes a pipe and can still push the lawn-mower. My father reckons she's nearly two axe-handles across the arse. But I never meshua her. **1993** *Sunday Times* (Wellington) 27 June 35 Scores of league players, shoulders six axe handles wide, snuggled up with Bob on the couch. **1986** OWEN & PERKINS *Speaking for Ourselves* 62 His **axe-work** was a mighty necessary part of his makeup.

axeman. [Spec. use of *axeman* woodman: see OED 1.] An experienced tree-feller or bushman; one who takes part in log-chopping competitions.
    1878 BULLER *Forty Yrs. NZ* 28 They worked as axemen, sawyers, etc., for the few traders. **1905** *Weekly Press* (Christchurch) 8 Feb. 50 [Caption] Axemen's carnival. **1920** *Quick March* 10 Dec. 11 Can any old-timer axeman give any information concerning this liquor [*sc.* matai beer]? **1933** *Tararua Tramper* Feb. 1 While the axe-men cut huge quantities of wood the wireless expert supervised the erection of a very satisfactory aerial. **1947** *Weekly News* (Auckland) 9 Apr. [Caption] Axemen Compete in Carnival at Taumarunui for Championship Titles. **1950** *Weekly News* (Auckland) 19 Apr. [Caption] Great Easter carnival in Central North Island: Axemen, Cyclists and Athletes. **1979** WILLIAMS *Skin Deep* 63 True, there is only one axeman's carnival per year scheduled for Carlton, the choppers being booked up well ahead, weekend after weekend. **1991** *Dominion* (Wellington) 5 Jan. 10 Seventeen-year-old Jason Winyard has been included in the New Zealand Axemen's team to compete against Australia for the Tasman Cup at the Easter Show in Auckland.

B

babbler. [AND 1904.] BABBLING BROOK.
　1944 BRUNO *Desert Daze* 33 Arch, the cook—oh, how how that bold 'babbler' could curse. **1963** *Weekly News* (Auckland) 5 June 37 We worked it out that old babbler made 112,000 rock cakes during those four months. **1973** NEWTON *Big Country SI* (1977) 60 Another..character was an old 'babbler', George Frizzel.

babbling brook. [AND 1913.] Rhyming slang for 'cook', esp. a camp (or army) cook.
　1918 *Kia Ora Coo-ee* 15 Oct. 14 He reviled the officers' cook for being a..thieving, dirty, greasy, 'babbling brook'. **1921** LORD *Ballads of Bung* (1976) 14 Ryan, T.P., ex-soldier, a 'babbling brook' at the war. **1939-45** *Expressions and Sayings 2NZEF* (*Nat. Archiv. TS WAII DA 420/1*) Babbler, Babbling brook or greasy babbler—Cook. **1947** NEWTON *Wayleggo* 83 Another character was the cook (in mustering parlance—the babbling brook). **1955** *Upper Hutt Leader* 4 June 5 Said the Grim Dig. 'We never saw food in its natural state, but..there was plenty wrong after the Army babbling brooks got hold of it.' **1963** *Weekly News* (Auckland) 5 June 37 That got us started on the 'babbling brooks'. I've got a few memories of station cooks. **1989** RICHARDS *Pioneer's Life* 30 I'm Barb Lindsay da babbling brook (cook).

baby-farm. *Hist.* [A spec. use of *baby-farm* a derogatory term for a place where the lodging and care of babies is undertaken for profit (see OED *baby-farm*, 1868), poss. popularized in NZ by the notoriety of Minnie (Williamina) Dean (1847-95), a Winton (South Island) baby-farmer executed 1895.] **a.** A term for a place where under a pretence of accepting illegitimate or unwanted babies or small children for fostering or fostering out, a profit is made by killing them through neglect or other means.
　1890 *NZ Mail* 14 Nov. 25 [Heading] A Baby Farm. Shocking Disclosures. **1933** SHEEHAN *Famous Murders in NZ* 22 As a foster-mother to many unwanted children Mrs Dean's baby-farm had been the object of the constable's suspicions. **1991** *Short Hist. of Newlands* 2 In 1922/23 the Baby farm scandal broke, and as a result of this people did not want to live in Newlands.

b. Also frequently in quasi-verbal derived forms **baby-farmer**; **baby-farming**.
　1895 *Otago Witness* (Dunedin) 27 June 13 The trial..was concluded here at 1 o'clock today, Minnie Dean, the now notorious **baby-farmer**, being found guilty and sentenced to death for the murder of Dorothy Edith Carter. **1933** SHEEHAN *Famous Murders in NZ* 27 Eager eyes were turned upon the infamous baby-farmer [Dean] as she was escorted to the dock. **1966** *Encycl. NZ* III. 449 [Minnie Dean] has been known, with approximate accuracy, as the Winton Baby Farmer. Under the guise of benevolent motive she received unwanted children and apparently destroyed them... For a premium..[she] adopted unwanted infants, but the payment of the fee invariably marked the disappearance of the child into the care of a 'lady' whose name or abode was never disclosed. **1890** *NZ Mail* 14 Nov. 25 A **baby-farming** case was before the police court today, when..an elderly lady, was separately charged with having wilfully ill-treated and neglected two children in a manner likely to cause unnecessary suffering and injury to health... There was a burial four months ago, and last year, and the year before two deaths had occurred. **1893** *AJHR H-26* 3 Attention is called to what appears to be a growing evil in this colony—viz., 'baby-farming'... It appears that children, either by advertisement or otherwise, are placed in most unsuitable homes, where it is perfectly well understood that the sooner the child dies the better pleased all concerned will be. **1923** *NZ Times* 18 May 9 It was held..that the Crown Prosecutor..could bring evidence to prove systematic baby-farming on the part of both accused. *Ibid.* 24 May 4 The crime of which Daniel Cooper has been convicted is, like the crime of the baby-farming murderess Dean.., a horror and a revelation. **1953** *NZ Observer* 3 June 7 There has been more than one case in New Zealand of what became known as 'baby-farming'—the maintenance of illegitimate children for a period followed by their murder without the knowledge of their parents. **1983** [see BULLY *n.*²].

bach /bætʃ/, *v. intr.* or *absol.* Also **batch**. [Prob. in NZ a shortened form of BACHELORIZE; poss. f. US *bach v.* 1862 (HDAS) (itself, so OED, directly f. US *bach n.* a bachelor): AND 1882.] To live alone as a bachelor, to 'do' for oneself (often in the temporary absence of a spouse); to share living quarters, domestic chores and expenses, usu. with a person (occas., persons) of the same sex. Also *quasi-trans.* **bach with** (another). Cf. BACHELORIZE.
　1890 *NZ Observer* 26 July 6 A rather good story is told of two young embryo lawyers who are at present 'baching' not too far from Newton. **1905** CLYDE *Pagan's Love* 26 You would live in a cheap lodging-house or batch with another girl. **1913** *NZ Observer* 28 June 17 Those boys who 'batch' and grow fretful when their turn at the frying pan comes around can comfort themselves by remembering that they are qualifying themselves for a happy married life. **c1924** ANTHONY *Me & Gus* (1977 Gus Tomlins) 41 When he was a young man he bached in a tin shanty for years. **1934** LEE *Children of Poor* (1949) 234 'Mrs. Axeldeen is away,' he informed me. 'I'm batching.' **1959** DAVIN *No Remittance* 56 He'd bought a patch of bush..and cleared it himself, while he batched in a tent. **1970** MCNAUGHTON *Tat* 69 Baldy [the station fencer] bached in a hut down the road a bit. **1986** RICHARDS *Off the Sheep's Back* 60 Despite the fact that we lived on boiled rice for a week, it has remained my favourite dish when baching.

Hence **baching** *vbl. n.* [AND 1936], esp. of a male, living usu. apart from a family and without domestic help; 'doing for oneself' in various circumstances.
　1916 in Malthus *ANZAC* (1965) 4 Mar. 156 Sometimes I think of Opihi and trout fishing and 'batching', sometimes of Peel Forest and the rata blossom. **1937** *NZ Railways Mag.* Jan. 47 To get the full flavour of baching you hire a bach as big as a piano case and fill it with three times as many people as it will hold. **1947** SMITH *From N to Z* 129 'Baching' is a universal sport for men of all ages. **1964** DICK *High Country Family* 29 Three years of baching, and coping with the idiosyncrasies of a male cook-housekeeper and young shepherd, followed his purchase of Lilybank.

bach /bætʃ/, *n.* Also **batch**. [f. BACH *v.*: AND *batch n.* a holiday house, 1929, 'prob. infl. by N.Z. *bach*'.]

1. a. A detached or semi-detached simple habitation, often merely a single room, with no or primitive conveniences, rented as a cheap lodging; occas. applied to a bachelor establishment (see quot. 1913).
　[**1864** CAMPBELL *Martin Tobin* II. 290 I..supplied him with..a *carte blanche* to take up his quarters in my bachelor's hut.] **1911** *Truth* 28 Jan. 6 Henry..was made acting secretary to the Brigade, and was given the key of a room in the 'batch' formerly occupied by Munn. **1912** *Truth* 24 Feb. 6 The 'bach,' said the doctor was absolutely unfit for human habitation... The owner of the place, who used to draw three shillings a week in rent for the rotten crib, was feverishly engaged in pulling it down on the following day. **1912** [see CRIB 1 a]. **1913** *NZ Observer* 5 Apr. 16 Some suburban bloods lately gave a more or less 'fancy dress' ball at a 'bach,' where six young men and a housekeeper manage to keep the wolf from the door. **1939** CRESSWELL *Present Without Leave* 211 And seeing a small hut in a back garden by the road, of the sort called a bach in this country (after bachelor and the habit of young men to keep house for themselves in surroundings where women are scarce) I inquired at the house if I might inhabit it. **1946** MILLER *There Was Gold* 93 The three of them lived together in a small hut known as the 'bach' and worked by day in their orchards. **1974** AGNEW *Loner* 26 They found me a small bach behind a large, two-storied building [in Wellington]... A small room simply furnished with a bed, and a dressing table. **1985** *Evening Post* (Wellington) 24 Dec. 1 The armed offenders squad surrounded a Wainuiomata house last night after a 69-year-old locked himself into a bach with a high-powered rifle. After repeated calls the man came out of the shed. **1988** *Sunday Star* (Auckland) 5 June A6 I remember quite clearly as a primary-school child walking to Mosston School past a little bach-type house wherein lived an old bachelor gentleman called Charlie Roots.

b. A cottage, hut or whare occupied by a farm worker.
　c1924 ANTHONY *Me & Gus* (1977) 52 The second year Gus Tomlins and I were farming, Gus came over to my bach. **1932** *Tararua Tramper* Dec. 3 Mr. Baine..directed the festivities at Mr. Jones' [*sc.* a farmer's] bach. **1950** CHERRILL *NZ Sheep Farm* 63 An untidy two roomed cottage. Could that be the batch of which Julius had so often spoken. **1965** WATSON *Stand in Rain* 118 There's an empty bach up in the scrub a bit, we can have it for free. **1980** MANTELL *Murder & Chips* 153 Mr Robinson was a share-milker on a local farm. He lived by himself in a bach on a back paddock.

2. (The main modern sense.) A weekend or holiday cottage or second residence, esp. at the beach. See also CRIB *n.*¹ 2.
　1924 *Otago Witness* (Dunedin) 30 Dec. 71 My girl friend and I had a batch at Takapuna for a fortnight.

1934 Cresswell *Letters* (1971) 90 Soon after you left I took a bach by the outer channel at Castor Bay [Auckland]... I was never so close to the sea, in my feelings. **1957** Frame *Owls Do Cry* (1967) 21 Francie Withers is poor. The Withers haven't a week-end bach..nor have they got a vacuum cleaner. **1964** [see CRIB n.¹ 2]. **1977** O'Sullivan *Butcher & Co.* 60 Likes to think..of queen of pig island of pylon-tall Circe a batch at Taupo swinging one starry boob. **1986** *NZ Census Form: Population & Dwellings* Quest.2 Is this dwelling 01 separate house..05 Bach, crib or hut (*not in a work camp*) 06 Caravan, cabin or tent in a motor camp. **1993** *Evening Post* (Wellington) 10 Feb. 24 A Christchurch businessman who applied for unemployment benefit arranged a scheme so that he could keep a $300,000 bach.

3. A period of baching.
  1935 *NZ Free Lance* (Wellington) 2 Nov. 19 Be practical and do a weekend 'bach'.

Hence **bacher** *n.* [AND 1895], one who baches, or lives in, uses, or owns a bach; **bachy** *a.*, suitable to, or of the manner of, a bach.
  1928 Devanny *Dawn Beloved* 153 Dawn..asked a young **bacher** living near her to mend the step. **1947** Smith *From N to Z* 129 The normal bacher makes his bed once. **1933** Cresswell *Letters* (1971) 83 I am writing snugly in bed in my new apartment, what they call a bach in this barbarous land, though it is simply a self-contained room like many I've had in London, but rather nicer..because of its..nice new **bachy** furniture and things.

4. Comb. **bach-owner**, **bach-user**.
  1993 *Press* (Christchurch) 22 Jan. A Lincoln University student lives with the..knowledge that her workplace was formerly a long-drop toilet... The [park toll-]booth..had been acquired by a bach-owner and installed atop a deeply-dug hole for the convenience of bach-users.

bachelorize, *v. Obs.* Often **bachelorize with**. [Cf. OED *v.* 2, 'N.Z.', with an 1854 Brit. nonce use.] BACH *v.*
  1879 *Auckland Weekly News* 20 Dec. 19 At one time, he and two other young men..'bachelorised,' together in Wellington. **1887** Hopeful *Taken In* 133 They [*sc.* Chinese] of course live very cheaply, because these communities are composed of men bachelorizing together, they have no wives or children to support. **1895** Roberts *Diary of Jonathan Roberts* 9 Whom should I see but Mr — from Timaru, with whom, in days gone by, I had bachelorized. **1906** *Truth* 10 Mar. 5 Single men [at Cross Creek] had either to bachelorize in their whares or board with one or another of the married men. **1912** Baughan *Brown Bread* 129 So he's bachelorisin', and I'm keeping house for him.

Hence **bachelorizing** *vbl. n.* and *ppl. a.*
  1883 A Lady *Facts* 8 Bachelorising, to use a Colonial term, is not a disagreeable life. **1912** Baughan *Brown Bread* 191 He was reduced to a most forlorn 'Bachelorising' existence in a one-roomed hut. **1924** Gibson *Gibbie Galoot* 16 He promised..to show me a few more points in Bachelorising.

bachelor's button. Also **bachelors' button**, and freq. in *pl.*

1. [Spec. use of *bachelor's buttons* any of various plants with round or button-like flowers.] The perennial herb *Cotula coronopifolia* (fam. Asteraceae), having bright yellow flowerheads and widespread in damp sites in New Zealand; occas. other similar flowers. See also *soldier's button* (SOLDIER n.¹ 3), *yellow-button* (YELLOW 2).
  1920 *Otago Witness* (Dunedin) 23 Nov. 52 One could find thousands of little yellow 'bachelor's buttons', a daisy-like plant (Cotula) which is only found where the marsh or damp soil is distinctly salt. **1943** Mannering *Eighty Years NZ* 27 I recollect one grand fight we had [at Christ's College]..with bachelor's buttons—yellow flowers collected from a tree growing just through the gate. **1961** Martin *Flora NZ* 243 Where a fresh-water stream meanders through the saltmarsh one may expect to see..Bachelors's Button (*Cotula coronopifolia*), a robust succulent with conspicuous bright yellow rayless flowers. **1980** Lockley *House Above Sea* 201 A whole range of salt-marsh plants delights the eye:.. the golden discs of *Cotula coronopifolia*, sometimes called 'bachelor's button' (a name given to a very different wayside land plant in Britain). **1995** Crowe *Which Coastal Plant?* 60 Because bachelor's button is so widely distributed across the world, it was long thought that it might not be native to this country. Yet native it most likely is since..Banks and..Solander collected it here on Cook's first voyage.

2. A button put into a Christmas pudding with the small coins indicating that a man finding it will remain a bachelor (that is, will have to provide and sew on his own buttons).
  1938 Hyde *Nor Yrs. Condemn* 62 'Like old times..Mother always used to make us boys stand on a stool and stir in threepences [to the Christmas puddings]... But you'll see; if there's anything, I'll get the bachelor button. I'll never get a woman to love and care for me.'

3. [Poss. f. a resemblance to the plant *bachelor's button* 1.] A small cake.
  1924 *Otago Witness* (Dunedin) 7 Oct. 59 Batchelor's Buttons. Required: 10 ounces of flour, six ounces of castor sugar. **1961** *'Sure to Rise' Cook. Book* 12 *Bachelor's Buttons*. Sift flour and baking powder together, rub in butter, add sugar, then beaten eggs, roll into small balls, dip in sugar, and bake on shelf in quick oven.

bachsceach, var. BUCKSHEE.

back, *n.*¹, *a.*, and *adv.*

A. *n.*

1. [AND 1878.] Often in the phr. (**at** or **in the**) **back** (**of**), indicating a place remote or distant from the speaker's point of reference, esp. the part of a farm or station remote from the homestead. Cf. BACK COUNTRY.
  1853 Rochfort *Adventures of Surveyor* 13 At the back of these hills is a level plain, forty miles in width. **1867** Barker *Station Life* (1870) 197 We used to have a quiet old station-horse saddled..and start off miles away to the back of the run. **c1875** Meredith *Adventuring in Maoriland* (1935) 65 The wild dogs had been among the sheep, and were evidently camped in the ranges at the back of the outstation. **1897** Wright *Station Ballads* 57 I went poisoning out at the back. **1917** *Triad* 10 Apr. 66 The musterers are away 'in the back'... The [mustering] team came in yesterday, after a month 'at the back'. **1932** Mason in *Phoenix I* No.2 9 [He] came out on the 'back', as they called the main body of the sheep-run. **1946** Sargeson *That Summer* 173 I'm going to bring some sheep down from the back, he said. **1986** *Evening Post* (Wellington) 21 June 27 He went bush in the back of Golden Bay. **1988** Shadbolt *Voices of Gallipoli* 60 I was on a bush-felling contract, back of Gisborne, in the winter of 1914 when the war began.

2. [AND 1897.] BACKBLOCK A 2 a.
  a1922 Turner *Happy Wanderer* 146 These trips from 'the Back' to the town in August are stern affairs. **1987** Ogonowska-Coates *Boards, Blades & Barebellies* 94 Remote stations are often referred to as being *up the back*.

B. *adj.*

1. [AND 1800.] Remote from the coast or a main access route; away from urban areas; of a station or run, remote from the homestead.
  1873 Barker *Station Amusements* 92 Miles of bush, and hundreds of acres of steep hill-side, formed the *back-est* of the 'back country'. **1874** Kennaway *Crusts* 83 As the value of back runs began to be proved, explorers pushed back in greater numbers into the interior to look for them. **1878** *TrNZI* X. 323 The furthest back settler at the time was Mr. Charles Hopkinson. **1883** *Brett's Colonists' Guide* 214 Shearing usually commences on the farms near the coast somewhat earlier than in the back districts. **1896** O'Regan *Poems* 35 So he left his back-gully, secluded and still. **1934** Scanlan *Winds of Heaven* 181 He would take them riding over the back hills to look at a boundary fence. **1951** Levy *Grasslands NZ* (1970) 249 [Caption] Hill country in back Taranaki successfully converted from forest. **1960** Masters *Back-Country Tales* 15 Back huts were few and far between then, and a Swede..was employed building them.

2. In special collocations: **back bush**, the remote forested areas; **back land** [AND 1824], the immediate hinterland (of a port, etc.); **back paddock** [AND 1898], a paddock remote from the farm homestead, or the main access route; **back range**, a mountain range distant from the coast; **back section**, a remote block of surveyed land; **back station** [AND c1887], a remote stock station. See also BACKBLOCK, BACK COUNTRY.
  1854 *Richmond-Atkinson Papers* (1960) I. 145 Thus our neighbour Gilmour in the **back bush** wants £1 per acre for his uncleared land not so well situated as ours. *Ibid.* I. 154 We have 36 head of cattle running this winter on the back bush land. **1905** Thomson *Bush Boys* 171 The men are in from the back-bush then [*sc.* on Sunday] and use it for hammering and carpentering in their shanties. **1840** Mathew to Hobson 23 Mar. in GBPP 1842 (No.569) 145 I have most carefully examined every part of it, and although the **back-land** is rugged and precipitous there is a much larger portion of it level than I have yet seen in the Bay, and fully sufficient to afford space for a very pretty and convenient town. **1876** Peache *Journal* in Gray *Quiet with Hills* (1970) 49 Front paddock 80 acres Upper paddock 50 [ditto] **Back paddock** 10 [ditto] Middle paddock 20 [ditto]. **1899** Bell *In Shadow of Bush* 43 Of course, by this route he could have a look round the sheep in Ashwin's back paddock on the way in or out. **1907** Koebel *Return of Joe* 131 A couple of shepherds..were riding through one of the back-paddocks. **1948** Finlayson *Tidal Creek* (1979) 37 So Uncle Ted..goes off to catch the little brown pony..in the corner of the back paddock. **1965** Watson *Stand in Rain* 58 It was quite a walk from the hut to where they were working in the back paddock. **1982** Sutton-Smith *Hist. Children's Play* 154 Somewhat later, farmers were urged to arrange the mating of bulls and cows in back paddocks, because although it was a necessary activity it was immodest. **1862** Chudleigh *Diary* 13 Dec. (1950) 70 You see the river flowing down between mountains 3 and 4000 ft., the lofty **back ranges** looking blue and the tops covered with snow. **1882** Potts *Out in Open* 76 Look about the slopes of our alpine back-ranges. **1895** *TrNZI* XXVII. 278 After a number of years, when sheep were mustered in from the back ranges, it was noticed that several would die in the yards. **1912** Rutherford *Impressions NZ Pastoralist on Tour* 147 [Every] gully and every mountain side of our back ranges will be cultivated. **1902** *NZ Illustr. Mag.* V. 381 Your poor, rough, **back section**. It has been forfeited twice, and you'll never make a do of it. **1874** Kennaway *Crusts* 204 The cattle..were half-wild, restless brutes, imported from Australian

back-stations, or bred on the equally wild ranges to the north of our own island. **1874** KENNAWAY *Crusts* 208 One evening, I remember a neighbouring back-station holder, after a long day's journey, rode up late along the fence-side of our home-paddocks.

C. *adv.* [AND 1878.] At or to the back (of); away from a settled area or from the coast. See also WAYBACK A.

1853 *Richmond-Atkinson Papers* (1960) I. 132 I am v. sorry that this new land is so far back, as we can only see Js. once a week. **1874** KENNAWAY *Crusts* 181 Having proved..that the Burke's pass country..could be safely held during the winter..we started from it to explore still further back. **c1875** MEREDITH *Adventuring in Maoriland* (1935) 129 I went to a very jolly country dance at a station about fifteen miles back. **1882** HAY *Brighter Britain* II. 326 The..groups of men and dogs are divided into three bodies, two of which will proceed right and left..and the third will go directly 'back' from the farm. **1897** *NZ Mines Rec.* Aug. 14 If tracks were cut along the main spurs..and underscrubbed for 6 ft. or 8 ft. wide, prospectors could get back [i.e. get to the 'back-blocks']. **1948** *Our Own Country* 43 She was one of the district nurses from 'further back'; her work was among the Maoris. **1966** SCOTT *Days That Have Been* 103 It was summed up for me in the words of a settler who lived further back than we did. **1984** WILSON *S. Pacific Street* 9 There was a lot of rough country back in from our place. **1986** OWEN & PERKINS *Speaking for Ourselves* 150 I've known of cases where men were working out in the bush a long way back.

back, *n.*² [Spec. uses of *back* (at) the rear (of a building or section).]

1. *Obs.* As **the back**, a detached earth closet; a 'little house' (usu. placed at the *back* of a house or section).

c1920 p.c. W.H.B. Orsman, Marlborough. Usage esp. *to go out* (or *to*) *the back*, to go to the lavatory. **1948** *Landfall* 7 196 He would..get into bed after a visit to the back. **1957** FRAME *Owls Do Cry* (1967) 65 But your father's up the back, he's been there for half an hour... He just keeps taking those pills. **1985** LANGDALE-HUNT *Last Entail Male* 150 The Archdeacon set off with me and no sooner had we got out the door when he suddenly said, 'May I see your back?' I obligingly showed him my back—but that is not what he meant. It was the lavatory or toilet and I am afraid I had been much used to coarser language.

2. *Prison.* [AND 1896, 2 quots. only.] In the phr. **down the back**, (in) solitary confinement.

1980 MACKENZIE *While We Have Prisons* 95 *back down the back*, solitary confinement or punishment.

back, *n.*³ [Used elsewhere but recorded earliest in NZ: see OED *back n.*¹ 24 f.] In the phr. **to get one's back up**, to become angry or annoyed.

1840 *NZ Jrnl.* I. 206 Captain Nias had 'got his back up'.

back, *v.*

1. *trans.* [Orig. US and Brit. dial.: see OED *v.* 23; EDD 2.] To carry on the back or shoulders.

1851 TORLESSE *Papers* (1958) 190 Backed the loads across the Courtenay, and built a warré.

2. *trans.* and *absol.* [AND 1942.] Of a sheep-dog, to run across the backs of sheep in a pen or yard (in the manner of a BACKING DOG).

1934 LILICO *Sheep Dog Memoirs* 26 Any keen dog constantly forcing in yards can be trained to back when there are other dogs doing so, but stockmen in Addington have evolved a race which take naturally to backing. **1949** HARTLEY *Shepherd's Dogs* 38 Teaching a dog to back sheep is something for which provision must be made in the puppy's early tuition. **1956** DARE *Rouseabout Jane* 165 I even managed to make him 'back' the sheep, a job a great many dogs will refuse. When sheep are being driven into the woolshed, there is a great tendency for them all to get jammed up and no amount of barking will make them move, and it is at this moment that a 'backing dog' is needed. **1971** LETHBRIDGE *Sunrise on Hills* 120 He had been taught to 'back' the sheep.

Hence **backer**, BACKING DOG; **backing** *vbl. n.*, the action of a backing dog.

1934 backer [see BACKING DOG]. **1934** backing [see 2 above].

backblock, *n.* and *attrib.* [AND *back block* 1870, *back-blocks* 1872.] (Now usu. as **the backblocks**, taking both *sing.* and *pl.* verbs.)

A. *n.*

1. Usu. uncompounded **back block**, a (surveyed) block of grazing land remote from a main station or homestead, or from the coast.

1852 *McLean Papers* (ATLTS) X. 156 The back Block here. **1895** CHAMIER *South Sea Siren* 161 [The house] was used as head-station for a sheep run, comprising several 'back blocks'..that extended for many miles over bleak and rugged country. **1904** *NZ Illustr. Mag.* Apr. 48 This whare was..the furthest back habitation [on the station]... It was erected for the accommodation of shepherds when mustering the back-blocks. **1915** MACDONALD *NZ Sheepfarming* 37 The Merino provides good wool returns in its natural quarters—the mountainous back blocks. **1939** BEATTIE *First White Boy Born Otago* 117 In the fifties he early became aware of the efforts of the Runholding class to open up the backblocks. **1969** NEWTON *Big Country NI* 245 From the road it seems only a stone's throw across [the Mata River] to that station's back block.

2. In present use mainly a compounded form **back-blocks** or **backblocks** often functioning as a grammatical singular. **a.** The remote hinterland; the sparsely settled hinterland of more closely-settled districts, having few urban facilities. See also BACK A 2, BACK COUNTRY A, BOOHAI 1, BUSH A 2 a, NEVER-NEVER, WAYBACK C 1.

1901 *NZ Illustr. Mag.* VII. 266 Far away in the bush backblocks. **1907** MANSFIELD *Letters* 20 Nov. (1984) I. 32 We sleep tonight at the Rangataiki & then the plains & the back blocks. **c1910** MACDONALD *Reminiscences* (VUWTS) 18 When I come to write of the outsettlements from Wellington, or as they are now called, the 'back blocks'. *Ibid.* 29 Neither had we a 'township'.. racecourse, newspaper, lawyers and due proportion of loafers in every back block as you appear to have now. **a1927** ANTHONY *Gus Tomlins* (1977) 90 Living out in the back-blocks, miles away from any town, a motor-bike is not to be despised. **1930** PINFOLD *Fifty Yrs. Maoriland* 14 In the 'back blocks' and new places, tracks, through the bush or just formed over clay hills, were mostly what one might expect to find. **1945** *JPS* LIV. 97 Tokotoko says she is not going to Kawa. She can't be bothered going to the 'backblocks' she says. **1959** SINCLAIR *Hist. NZ* 149 The pioneering father-figure of contemporary New Zealand imagination was a man who went out to the 'back-blocks' (a term which originally referred to blocks of land purchased from the Maoris, but came to mean remote farming districts). **1964** DAVIS *Watersiders* 70 I headed for my father's broker's place up the Taihape road. Real backblocks, I can tell you. Plenty of scrub, gorse, and pigs. **1981** HUNT *Speaking a Silence* 25 They wanted my brother to go back and manage the show but he said he'd had enough, way out in the backblocks like that.

b. *transf.* In jocular use, the suburbs reputedly farthest from a city or town centre.

1987 *Karori News* 16 June 16 [Heading] Bus visits backblocks of Karori.

B. *attrib.* or *adj.* **backblock** or **backblocks**. [AND *back-block* 1868.] Characteristic of areas remote from a town; self-reliant, or (pejoratively) rough in form or manner, makeshift. Cf. BUSH B 2, WAYBACK B.

c1875 MEREDITH *Adventuring in Maoriland* (1935) 55 The first thing I had to do [on arriving at Wellington] was to get a new rig-out, as my backblock clothes were not in keeping with my important duties [as a civil servant]. **1900** WRIGHT *Wisps of Tussock* 24 His back-block talk he can never forget. **1901** *NZ Illustr. Mag.* III. 254 The clean-limbed hard backblocks-men mustering in the river arm. **1910** *Kai Tiaki* Jan. 28 Slowly perhaps, but surely, we hope the Back-blocks District Nursing Scheme is progressing... No back-block settler..will be too far away to get help in their time of trouble. **c1920** BEATTIE *Trad. Lifeways Southern Maori* (1994) 355 Kirimuka meant the skin and leaves of a tree and was applied to manuka when it was steeped in boiling water to make 'backblocks tea' (in the absence of proper tea). **1926** DEVANNY *Butcher Shop* (1981) 86 The apt cunning of Taihape's hotel-keeper, long inured to back-blocks men's customs.., saw to that. **1933** SCANLAN *Tides of Youth* 55 Each little group was dependent upon itself for amusement and entertainment, and visitors were a peg on which to hang some simple backblock festivities. **1947** BEATTIE *Early Runholding* 41 All the early runs and backblocks settlements could have much easier done without horses than without draught bullocks. **1959** SHADBOLT *New Zealanders* (1986) 10 I grew to awareness rejecting as alien our scrubby backblocks farm. **1967** ELLIOTT & ADSHEAD *Cowshed to Dog Collar* 14 A little house still standing today in the backblock settlement of Apiti. **a1973** FINLAYSON *Brown Man's Burden* (1973) 128 Well, it looked a mighty big town to my backblock eyes but *you'd* think it pretty quaint... 'You can't go about the city looking like a little backblock Maori,' she said.

backblocker. [AND 1870.] A person from the backblocks; a rustic. Cf. WAYBACK C 2.

1910 *Truth* 8 Jan. 6 Your back-blocker, who hasn't seen a woman for months, often keeps painful control of his tongue until he gets a beer or two in. **1914** *Poverty Bay Herald* 5 Nov. (Leading Article) Our New Zealand backblockers are eager to show their love and loyalty to the Empire. **1927** *NZ Dairy Produce Exporter* 3 Sept. 43 In the backblocks, we backblockers have to lead a pretty quiet life. No picture shows, or even shops. **1930** DEVANNY *Bushman Burke* 32 It is one of the back-blocker's pleasures, taking tea in restaurants in town. **1966** SCOTT *Days That Have Been* 103 If the backblockers didn't stick together, they couldn't exist. **1989** VIRTUE *Upon Evil Season* 19 Sometimes in the city they were treated like real backblockers

backblocks, var. BACKBLOCK.

backblocksy, *a.* Also **backblocky**. In semi-humorous use, having rough or makeshift characteristics usu. associated with the backblocks.

1913 *NZ Observer Christmas Annual* 7 St Petersburg, said Nicholas..was too 'backblocky' to do the thing in style. **1916** CHURCH *Tonks* 271 I have been told of your sporting adventure... It sounds rather backblocksy.

backbone.

1. Usu. in the phr. **the backbone of the country** (or occas., **island**), the main mountain range(s) or divide, esp. the Southern Alps. Also *attrib.* See also ALPS.

c1837–40 *Descr. View Bay of Islands* A chain of mountains running through the whole [of the islands]—not inaptly termed their back-bone. **1838** SYMONDS *Cloudy Bay* (Royal Geog. Soc., London: Jrnl. & Proc. 418) The Waipa is believed to rise in the high snowy mountains behind Tui..being a spur from the great range or back-bone of this island. **1866** BARKER *Station Life* (1870) 48 As a background we have the most magnificent chain of mountains—the back-bone of the island—running from north to south. **1894** ARTHUR *Kangaroo & Kauri* 120 [The Southern Alps] is called 'the backbone of the island'. **1951** LEVY *Grasslands NZ* (1970) 137 Strangely enough, it is a really important clover in the higher backbone country of the Southern Alps. **1959** SINCLAIR *Hist. NZ* 32 The southern island has a mountainous backbone, rising to over 12,000 feet, which was Tasman's first glimpse of the country.

2. Usu. in the phr. **the backbone (of the country, or land, or New Zealand)**, farmers or the farming community (occas. their sheep), regarded as the main producers of natural wealth. (Often ironically or jocularly applied, suggesting that farmers and ranges are both solid, dense, and tend to divide the community.)

1905 BLOMFIELD in Grant *Unauthorised Version* (1980) 48 [Cartoon caption] Spineless N.Z. Farmer: Remember I am the backbone of the country. **1906** *Truth* 9 June 5 The noble farmer is the backbone of this great, young land. *Ibid.* 14 July 1 'One of the backbone', as they love to call themselves—especially when they are bulldozing Governments for a helping hand..was charged at the Rangiora Court with sooling dogs on to an insurance agent, using indecent language, and assault... Insurance agents among the wild and whiskerous 'backbone' down south have lively experiences, sure pop. **1913** CARR *Country Work* 17 Sheep are the backbone of New Zealand. **1927** DEVANNY *Old Savage* 200 Just one of those ordinary, common farmer women that Bill Massey called the backbone of New Zealand. **1934** HYDE *Journalese* 76 Backbone of the country he is, of course, and sees no need for a headpiece to complete the job. **1947** SMITH *N to Z* 95 A famous statesman once said that farming was the backbone of New Zealand. Unfortunately, the Press Association sent out a distorted message, substituting 'farmers' for 'farming', and this has given rise to endless misunderstanding ever since. **1988** *Dominion* (Wellington) 16 Apr. 9 Motto: Agricolae pro patria laborant—Farmers are the backbone of the nation. **1990** *Dominion* (Wellington) 21 Aug. 2 Manufacturers have accused farmers of becoming the jawbone rather than the backbone of the economy.

back-burn, *v.* [Used elsewhere but recorded first in NZ: cf. OED *back-* B.] *trans.* To burn (grass, scrub, bush, etc.) against the wind; to set a (grass, etc.) fire against the wind. Also as a *vbl. n.* **back-burning**.

1878 ELWELL *Boy Colonists* 90 The 'back-burning' of the fire, which though very slow, is always the most steady and most effective. **1978** JARDINE *Shadows on Hill* 40 As it was not possible to fight the fire directly in the six-foot-high bracken, it would have to be back-burned from specially cleared breaks well out on each side.

Hence as a *n.*, the process or result of burning grass, scrub, bush, etc. against the wind.

1957 *NZ Farmer* 8 Aug. 3 Fire is hard to control and it takes a fierce intense back burn to kill the scrub.

back carting, *vbl. n.* The carrying of loads on a return journey. Cf. BACK-LOAD *v.*

c1885 ACTON-ADAMS *Letters* in McCaskill *Molesworth* (1969) 57 You would earn at least £3 a week..as I pay 50/- a ton for wool with a lot of back carting at half price.

back country, *n.* and *attrib.* [Orig. US: AND 1798.] Cf. BACK *n.*[1]

A. *n.* /ˈbæk ˌkʌntri/. The land remote from coastal settlements or from settled districts; the hinterland of a settlement or of a port; the parts of a sheep-station remote from the homestead. Cf. *front country* (FRONT A 2).

1840 *NZ Jrnl.* I. 208 Hobson is founding a town at the Bay of Islands, but we have an assurance that there is no back-country there. **1841** *Mathew to Hobson* 20 Oct. in *GBPP 1842 (No.569)* 184 The land [at Wellington] rises suddenly into bold and rugged hills..as to render the back country exceedingly difficult of access. **1860** BUTLER *First Year* 24 Mar. (1863) iv 48 At last I have been really in the extreme back country, and positively, right up to a glacier. **1871** MONEY *Knocking About NZ* 21 His station..was situated in what [in Canterbury] was called the back country, *i.e.*, close to the ranges. **1882** POTTS *Out in Open* 41 It is only in the 'back country' as it used to be called, that we can hope to find its breeding place. **1902** *Settler's Handbook NZ* 32 There has been a marked abatement of the pest, even on high back-country. **1930** GUTHRIE *NZ Memories* 111 A good story is told by a friend who was going into the back country on a visit. **1949** REED *Story Canterbury* 128 Another wily plan was to run a fence up a valley..and thus deprive any intending purchaser of water or the use of the back-country. **1966** TURNER *Eng. Lang. Austral. & NZ* 143 *Back country*, suggesting big Canterbury sheepruns, is a term of approval. **1987** OGONOWSKA-COATES *Boards, Blades & Barebellies* 94 *Back-country*. Land extending beyond and including the foothills; land beyond the river gorges. Remote stations are often referred to as being *up the back*.

B. *attrib.* Often **back-country**.

a. /ˈbæk ˌkʌntri/ [AND 1888.]

1860 BUTLER *Forest Creek Manuscript* June (1960) 37 I may as well say a word on the nature of back country travelling in the Canterbury settlement. **1867** BARKER *Station Life* (1870) 173 The distant 'back-country' ranges must have felt the storm more severely even than we have. **1882** POTTS *Out in Open* 187 Within the last few years [the kea] has discovered the out-stations of some of the back-country settlers. **1909** OWEN *Philip Loveluck* 82 He considered it a luxury for a man who was often reduced to *rou-rou* on a back country block. **1934** MULGAN *Spur of Morning* 262 And he saw..that these big sheep people—whether they owned their land or leased it, as many back-country squatters did..were a distinct class. **1953** SUTHERLAND *Golden Bush* (1963) 41 Many memory-pictures of back-country loveliness..we keep stored in the mind. **1968** GRUNDY *Who'd Marry a Doctor?* 49 Twice each day the operators at the [Chatham Island] radio station called all the back-country people. **1990** EDWARDS *AWOL* 4 I drove the old Morris eight along the back country road to the hostel.

b. In special collocations: **back-countryman** (also **back country man**) [orig. US: see OED], **back-country woman**, one who lives or works in the back-country.

1942 MARSH & BURDON *NZ* 9 The shepherds, musterers, shearers and drovers, the **back-countrymen** of New Zealand. **1952** BLAKISTON *My Yesteryears* 16 In those days [1883] there were no luxuries like butter, condensed milk or jam for back country men. **1966** NEWTON *Boss's Story* 59 I'd say that any woman who has spent a winter in at Mount White could truly qualify as a **back-country woman**.

back-cut. [AND *back n.*[2] 1901; DARE 1958.] A cut with a saw or axe on the side of the trunk opposite to the direction the tree is meant to fall. Cf. BACK-SCARF *v*, BACK UP *v.*[1]

1961 CRUMP *Hang On a Minute Mate* 47 Always make your back-cut a bit higher than the scarf and leave plenty of wood so if she leans back you can wedge her over. **1964** FRANCES *Johnny Rapana* 28 He knew that, here in this confined space, Dinny would put in the back cut himself, one mistake crashing a tree on to house or barn.

back delivery. *Hist.* A reaping machine delivering its sheaves at the rear rather than at the side. See also TILTER.

1937 AYSON *Thomas* 41 Instead of the crops being cut by the hook with women and children sharing the work, back deliveries came into use. **1948** SCOTTER *Run Estate & Farm* 41 Then at the beginning of 1869 this firm demonstrated their reaping machine... Meek used as many as ten of these back deliveries in a paddock, seven men were required to each machine and perhaps thirty more were stooking... The side delivery, the binder, took its place. **1954** MILLER *Beyond the Blue Mountains* 64 In the Heriot district..McKay had a Nicholson back-delivery [c1870s]... Then Reid and Gray started making back-deliveries. **1980** NEAVE *Land of Munros* 90 [He] got a job binding sheaves behind a back delivery, an early [c1868] machine for cutting crops, and he got a job on a farm. **1990** MARTIN *Forgotten Worker* 123 The 'tilter'—also known as the 'back-delivery' because it dropped the sheaves from the back of a tilting hinged platform—was drawn by two horses and was first used in the early 1860s.

backing dog. [f. BACK *v.* 2: AND 1941.] A dog trained to run across the backs of yarded sheep. See also *yard dog* (YARD *n.* 2).

1934 LILICO *Sheep Dog Memoirs* 26 A bitch pup I sold..went direct to freezing works to pen up and developed into a first class forcer and backer... The finest backing dogs I have ever seen are in the saleyards at Addington. **1949** HARTLEY *Shepherd's Dogs* 38 *Training the backing dog* Teaching a dog to back sheep is something for which provision must be made in the puppy's early tuition. **1956** [see BACK *v.* 2]. **1966** *NZ Short Stories* (1976) 126 You wouldn't notice Dan, the yellow backing dog until the mob got boxed at a gate way... He'd be up over their backs barking. **1966** [see *yard dog* (YARD *n.* 2)]. **1971** LETHBRIDGE *Sunrise on Hills* 120 Instead of climbing out of the the yard and along the rails, a backing dog would jump up on top of the sheep and run along their backs pushing the front one right up into the head of the pen. **1982** *Agric. Gloss.* (MAF) 24 *Backing dog*: Dog that will jump on to the backs of sheep to help move them.

backing gate. A gate which opens to allow a beast to move forward but prevents it moving backward.

1974 *NZ Agric.* 83 The backing gate is used to bring cows from the yard into the dairy. Its main purpose is to keep stock near the milking area. As each cow is taken in to be milked, another fills up the space she has left and there are no delays in milking. The gate is controlled by the milker, who can bring in the next cows without having to leave those already being milked.

back-load, *n.* Freight carried on a return journey from carrying a main load.

1874 BAINES *Edward Crewe* 205 Reserving some 30lbs..for my back-load home. **1878** ELWELL *Boy Colonists* 112 He would get two or three back-loads of manuka. **1981** PINNEY *Early N. Otago Runs* 34 They contracted [in 1881] to cart to Kurow for 34s 4d a ton, and to backload at 23s. Many of these backloads were of coal.

back-load, *v. intr.* To carry on a return or 'back' trip; *trans.* to load (a ship, vehicle, etc.) with a back-load. Cf. BACK-CARTING.
1943 HISLOP *Pure Gold* 117 But the usual thing for the Styx settlers so far inland was to back-load with a year's supply of good quality coal. **1953** SUTHERLAND *Golden Bush* (1963) 76 Sometimes our trips to the Bend were profitable for there were wool and hides to be taken out and fertilizers and general cargo to backload. **1961** HENDERSON *Friends in Chains* 122 Bush rats at night sometimes made their way into our schooners when they were..back-loaded with small quantities of farm produce. **1981** [see BACK-LOAD *n*.].

Hence **backloading** *vbl. n.* [AND 1925], freight carried on a return journey.
1933 JONES *Autobiogr. Early Settler* 52 We had to order a year's supply of provisions, etc., which came up as backloading when the wool was sent down. **1946** ACLAND *Early Canterbury Runs* 166 In those days [c1877] the wool was carted to Albury by bullock wagon at 5/6 a bale—back loading 25/- a ton. **1960** SUMMERS *Moon Over Alps* (1974) 34 'When Nanna..first came up here [to the isolated sheep station] they only had backloading [to bring in stores]..' 'Backloading?'... 'Yes—once a year. The wagons that came in to take the wool out brought in the stores.'

back-log. [Orig. N. American (OED 1684).] Orig. a large log placed at the back of an open fire; thence, any sizeable log for an open fire.
1873 PYKE *Wild Will Enderby* (1889, 1974) III. vi 93 Having thus spoken, he..discharged a liquid shot [*sc.* a tobacco spit] at an aggravating knot in the back-log. **1895** TWISLETON *Poems* 28 The back-log's yellow light. **1901** *NZ Illustr. Mag.* IV. 596 He cut up a lot of maire backlogs. **1910** COCKAYNE *NZ Plants & Their Story* 152 The rather tall story goes how a trunk, which had been used for a back log to a fire for a whole year, upon being finally cast into the open air as worthless, put forth green shoots, and grew again into a tree! **a1927** ANTHONY *Gus Tomlins* (1977) 174 I was forced to go out into the wet again and cut off a couple of big back-logs. **1937** AYSON *Thomas* 83 The log being drawn by bullocks on the other side right into the chimney for a back log. **1945** HARPER *Camping & Bushcraft in NZ* 18 A good rata back-log [to hold the fire in]. **1981** HENDERSON *Exiles Asbestos Cottage* 60 Rata for heat and backlog.

back of beyond. [Spec. use of *back-of-beyond* 'a humorous phrase for..some very out of the way place': see OED *beyond, quasi-noun* b.; AND 1888.] A remote, outlying place or district; BACKBLOCK A 2 a, BOOHAI 1.
1911 *Triad* 11 Sept. 46 'Very good,' I said, 'then you shan't go home. I'll wheel you to the back of beyond. I'll take you miles.' **1912** WILLIAMS *Letter* 19 Aug. in Jones *Samuel Butler* (1919) I. 85 I shall never forget the small dark man who took up a run at the back of beyond, carted a piano up there on a bullock dray, and passed his solitary evenings playing Bach's fugues. **1924** *NZJST* VI. 441 Some, like the house-sparrow, cling tenaciously to the settled areas, while others, like the chaffinch,... sometimes occur in the very 'back of beyond.' **1943** HISLOP *Pure Gold* 57 Late that afternoon saw me over the ten miles of up-hill road which seemed..to be leading to the back of beyond. **1967** MAY *West Coast Gold Rushes* 281 Duffer rushes collapsed so quickly that storekeepers could find themselves in the back-of-beyond with a fully-stocked shanty and no sales. **1985** MCGILL *G'day Country* 78 Eketahuna itself enjoyed the dubious notoriety in the seventies as *the* back of beyond. *Ibid*. 97 This was so back of beyond they [*sc.* NZ Railways] still had a water tank at Whanga.

back round, *v.* [Extended use of *back v.* of the wind, to change direction: see OED *v.* 17.] Of a fire in bush or open country, to change direction relative to the direction of the wind; to burn against the wind. See also BACK-BURN.
1933 SCANLAN *Tides of Youth* 66 As a last resort, get under a culvert. But it [*sc.* a bush-fire] is backing round this way, and the whare will probably go later.

back-scarf, *v.* [f. *back*, the side of a standing tree behind or away from the direction of fall.] *trans.* To scarf (a tree) on the side opposite the direction of intended fall.
1892 KIPLING *One Lady at Wairakei* (1983) 36 He went out into the bush and backscarfed a big tree so that it would fall in one particular direction. **1928** KENWAY *Pioneering Poverty Bay* 38 He will 'belly-scarf' and 'back-scarf' the lot, that is to say he will cut about one third through on the lower and upper sides [of the tree].

Hence as a *n.*, a scarf or cut so made. See also BACK-CUT.
1955 WILSON *Land of My Children* 24 If you go too deep [with the belly-scarf], the tree might split and fall before you put in the back-scarf.

back-slack, *v. trans.* To answer back, to cheek, to 'back-chat'.
1929 SMYTH *Bonzer Jones* 237 Think I'm going to sit here and let this — this farm labourer back-slack us.

back to back. *Mining.* See quots.
1907 *NZGeol.SB* (NS) No.4 106 The ore-shoots of all the approximately parallel Hauraki veins occurred in corresponding positions in the veins, and pitched in the same direction as the main shoot. This is the structure termed in the older mining phraseology 'ore to ore', or shoots 'back to back'. **1912** *NZGeol.SB* (NS) No.15 107 [At Waihi] the shoots being disposed 'back to back' in these parallel veins.

back to the mat: see MAT 3 a.

back track. Esp. in the phr. **to take the back track (back trail)**, to retrace one's steps.
1870 WHITWORTH *Martin's Bay Settlement* 34 There was nothing for it but to turn back..so I determined to take the back track as soon as possible. **1916** ANZAC *On Anzac Trail* 105 Our little party now came to the conclusion that it was time to take the back trail.

back up, *v.[1]* *Logging.* Of a tree being felled, to put in a back-cut with a saw; or, to open up a back-cut with a **backing-up wedge** (see quot. 1995) or several wedges placed (i.e. 'backed up', see quot. 1904) one on the other. Cf. BACK-CUT *v.*
1864 *Weekly News* (Auckland) in Reed *Story Kauri* (1953) 159 It is agreed to bring him down with an axe instead of backing him up with a cross-cut. **1904** *NZ Illustr. Mag.* Dec. 178 'Don't you hear her talkin'?' as a gentle ticking would indicate the act of partition had commenced. Then the wedges were 'backed up,' and a few solid blows from the heavy mauls would complete the operation [of felling]. **1961** HENDERSON *Friends in Chains* 11 I soon learned [c1890] how to chop a scarf in a standing pine, how to pull on..a crosscut saw, to back up with hammer and wedges. **1981** MARRIOTT *Life in Gorge* 95 When we were well in with the saw-cut, Cyrus started backing the tree up—driving two wedges into the saw-cut and actually lifting the back of the tree, from the lean it had, to the perpendicular. **1995** *NZ Geographic* Jan.–Mar. 16 The front scarf was cut in the next tree and the bushmen were backing it up with the six-foot crosscut saw... The other took the broad-bladed backing-up wedge and drove it into the saw-cut with the maul.

Hence **backing** *vbl. n.*, putting a back-cut in (a tree to be felled).
1961 CRUMP *Hang On a Minute Mate* 42 During the next few weeks Jack learned about scarfing, backing, limbing, deeing, sniping [etc.].

back up, *v.[2]* In the phr. **to back up on** (someone), to gang up on (for retaliation).
1982 NEWBOLD *Big Huey* 168 In our gang we all used to back up on Barclay because we'd all talked it over and decided to stick together.

Hence **back-up** *n.*, retaliation, revenge.
1982 NEWBOLD *Big Huey* 79 It was rare for a dispute to take place without at least talk of a back-up (retaliation) afterwards.

badeek, var. PATIKI.

bag.
1. *Horseracing.* [Fig. use of (bookmaker's) *bag*: AND 1903.] In the phr. **to be in the bag**, of a horse, to be certain to lose.
1900 SCOTT *Colonial Turf* 33 The neddy was in the bag in the Cup; he was no trier.

2. *WW1.* [f. *sand-bag*: AND *over the bags* 1918.] A military sandbag, esp. in the phr. **to go over the bags, to hop the bags**, to leave one's trenches on attack; to go 'over the top'. Also *fig.*
1917 in Boyack *Behind the Lines* (1989) 76 The boys went over the bags at 3.15 a.m. **1918** *NZ at the Front* 69 Toasted their health while he vowed to fight, in the good old 'Digger' way, And then 'hopped the bags' with the photo fair of the girl in the estaminet. *Ibid*. 78 'We're just out training for another little stunt.' 'Stunt! What's that?' 'Hopping the bags.' 'Hopping the bags? Is that "going over the top"—an attack?' 'Yes.' **1936** TREADWELL *Recolls. Amateur Soldier* 201 It was a rule of our battalion that any man awaiting trial..should go 'over the bags' at zero hour. **1976** LEE *Soldier* 1 Three times I had been over the bags. Three times the blood of mates had spattered my khaki, seeped into my being.

3. *transf.* See *rough as bags* (ROUGH *a.* 2 a (a)).

4. [f. the plastic bag into which suspected drinking drivers are required to blow.] The breathalyser, esp. in the phr. **to put the bag on**, to have (someone) blow into the breathalyser.
1986 *Listener* 22 Nov. 46 Lenny [a traffic cop]: Should we put the bag on him. Hound: Why? Lenny: Well, he reckons he's drunk.

5. Special Comb. **bag hole** *farming obs.*, a hole dug under the grain-outlet of a threshing-machine to facilitate the filling, ramming, and sewing up of the grainsacks; **bagman (bag-rammer, bag-sewer)**, BAGGIE.
1954 MILLER *Beyond the Blue Mountains* 65 When baggers came in it made a big difference, and before that [chaff]cutters with a portable engine and a **bag hole** to fill and tramp the bags were in vogue. **1892** COX *Diaries 1888–1925* (ATLMS) 15 July We threshed the oats... I was **bagman** and the oats were very dirty, I was nearly smothered. **1908** *Awards, etc.* 618 [Enforcements of Awards] Same... v. James Keane, for employing two bagmen instead of three. **1913** CARR *Country Work* 13 The mills carry their own forkers, band-cutter, weigher and bagman (one man), and sewer and stacker. **1954** MILLER *Beyond the Blue Mountains* 112 I have seen

him [sc. Ferguson, the poet], when I was a girl taking lunch out to the threshing mill hands..standing gazing into space..and the **bag-rammer** would look up and say, 'Dugald's got it now'. **1984** *Knapdale Run* 148 Sheets were placed under the [threshing] mill [c1900] to catch any seed that leaked out and the bag hole men would dig out the bag hole so that the bags could be rammed full... The usual gang for stack threshing was 12 men. The boss kept steam up and attended to the mill adjustments and lubrication, three men worked in the bag hole, the bag-rammer, the bag-sewer, and the bag-carrier; two men were on top of the mill, a band cutter and a man to turn the sheaves to the band cutter.

baggie. [f.*bag*(man + -IE.] A member of a thrashing-mill or header-harvester gang who attends to the filling and often sewing-up of the grain-sacks. See also *bagman* (BAG 5).

1963 WALLIS *Point of Origin* 80 Not much room [on the header] for the baggie, is there? How many bags does the chute hold? **1971** HENDERSON *Our Open Country* 63 At the grain chutes perspiring 'baggies' toiled with needle and twine, carrying the sewn bags to a growing pile. **1985** STUDHOLME *Coldstream* 128 The grain emerged from one corner of the mill into sacks. These were stitched up by the 'baggies', using, as with the wool packs, large curved needles threaded with twine.

Bagush Box: see BOX *n.*² 5.

bail, *n.* [f. Brit. dial. *bail* a barrier, a bar: see OED *n.*³; EDD *n.*² 1; AND 1843.]

1. Orig. a wooden device for securing the head of a cow during milking, or occas. of a beast in a race (a **head bail**, see quot. 1982); thence, an open wooden framework or stall of poles, stakes, or pieces of timber (the orig. 'bails'), etc. in which a cow is restrained during milking, with often a head bail (or headrope) and poss. a bar or rope at the hinder end of the 'bail', and in recent times, a 'legrope' (also occas. as **milking-bail**, see quots. 1859, 1982); thence, *pl.* or collective, the group of stalls or pens for milking many cows at once; a COWSHED. See also COWBAIL. **a.** *pl.* As **the bails.** (In quot. 1859 poss. the pieces forming the 'head bail'.)

1849 [see COWBAIL]. **1859** FULLER *Five Years Residence* 170 A heifer being taught to go into the milking-bail usually has a rope passed over her horns by means of a long stick, so..she can be drawn into the position required, where she is secured by fastening the bails, and then, her leg being tied, she can be milked safely. This being repeated a few times with each cow, is generally sufficient to teach them to walk in of themselves afterwards when driven up to the bail. **1882** HAY *Brighter Britain* I. 200 They [sc. cows] are brought up to the bails morning and evening, fastened up and given a feed of koraka. **1908** BAUGHAN *Shingle-Short* 84 For the curv'd Three (that yonder So glitter and sparkle There, over the bails), This morning, at dawn, At the start of the milking. **1924** *Otago Witness* (Dunedin) 5 Feb. 15 He..spends an incredible number of hours in a draughty shed that he refers to as the 'bails'. **1944** *Te Awamutu Courier* 30 June 4 When the last of the cows are in the bails I gather up the jug of milk and set sail for home. **1960** MUIR *Word for Word* 122 Like the froth on the creamy buckets of milk..when the handyman brought them in from the bails in the back paddock. **1988** WARR *Bush-burn to Butter* 33 Almost without exception [in the 19th century] cows were milked in the open stockyard or field. They were usually put into bails formed by two upright poles driven into the ground and drawn together over the beast's head to secure the animal during milking.

b. *sing.* (Usu.) a stall in a milking-stand, and occas. a similar holding space for other animals (see quot. 1991); occas. as **head bail**, movable bars or a similar device to secure the head of a cow in the milking stall (see quots. 1903, 1982, 1989).

1855 CAVERHILL in Deans *Pioneers Port Cooper Plains* (1964) 95 The general state of the herd is very satisfactory..and the heifers that have calved have all been broken in to bail. **1859** milking-bail [see a above]. **1862** BUTLER 4 Oct. in Maling *Samuel Butler* (1960) 58 She [sc. a cow] was so quiet that we milked her there and then with no leg rope, and without putting her into the bail. **1874** BAINES *Edward Crewe* 225 It would have been impossible to milk [the cow] without a 'bail.'.. It is in very general use in the Australian colonies; and my advice to any one troubled with a naughty cow, who kicks like fury during the process of milking, is to have a bail constructed in their cow-house. **1888** BARLOW *Kaipara* 92 To milk her it was not only necessary to put her in the bail—an arrangement which secures the head of the cow in somewhat the same manner as some of the old-fashioned instruments..used to secure the head of a man—but it was also necessary to rope both her hind legs to prevent her from kicking. **1903** *Otago Witness* (Dunedin) 25 Nov. 74 All the animals looked so intelligent as they went into the stalls..and put their heads between the bails. **1906** ROBERTS in *Hist. N. Otago from 1853* (1978) 16 She soon broke in some heifers to be milked, by putting a rope over their horns and dragging them up into the bail. **1920** POWDRELL *Dairy Farming* 24 A 20-bail shed of this type six years ago cost £105. **1925** [see BYRE]. **1936** BELSHAW et al. *Agric. Organiz. NZ* 457 Cows become so trained that they enter the bail themselves as soon as one becomes vacant. **1956** DARE *Rouseabout Jane* 147 The cows were driven into a small yard and then into the bail, which held two at a time. They walked into position and were not tied up, but a chain hooked around their hindquarters kept them from backing out. **1970** McNAUGHTON *Tat* 103 He noticed a red-headed girl releasing a cow from a bail in a small cowshed. **1982** *Agric. Gloss.* (MAF) 4 *bail.* A frame for holding an animal, e.g. milking bail, head bail. **1989** RICHARDS *Pioneer's Life* 50 A strong bail was made at the end of the race to secure his head. **1991** LA ROCHE *Hist. of Howick & Pakuranga* 198 The ostriches would go into sheds, being driven by the dogs..and held in a little bail [for plucking].

2. Special Comb. **bail-peg**, a wooden peg used to hold in place the moveable arm of a device ('head bail') holding the head of a cow while in the bail.

1967 McLATCHIE *Tang of Bush* 106 A two bailed cowshed by the road gave us shelter... I took the bail peg, split it with the shears and used it to splint the broken [bicycle] bar, binding it round with twine.

bail, *v.* Also occas. **bale**, and freq. with **up**. [f. Brit. dial.: see EDD *bail v., bail up* tie up, fasten; and used as an imperative in calling cows.]

I. As **bail up. 1. a.** *trans.* [AND 1874.] To put (a cow) into a bail (or 'head bail') preparatory to milking.

1841 BEST *Journal* 6 Apr. (1966) 285 Imagine my delight when I saw a small herd of Cows driven into a little stockyard bailed up and milked all by a *mauri* lad. **1849** *Notes on NZ* II. 22 Bailed the cows up and milked them. **1853** ROCHFORT *Adventures of Surveyor* 24 We were just in time to see his men bailing up some cattle; *i.e.* the cow is made to put her head between two posts, when a bar slides across the space and catches her by the neck, rendering it impossible to get her head back. A slip knot is then fastened to one of her hind legs, which is drawn up tight in a horizontal position to a strong post. She is then milked with safety. **1856** FITTON *NZ* 218 A young cow when first milked is generally 'baled up'. **1895** *Ann. Rep. Dept. Agric.* III. 88 When the milker has bailed-up and leg-roped the cow..he should..wash the cow's udder and teats and his hands. **c1924** ANTHONY *Follow the Call* 101 I had just got one tin full when I went out to bail up my quietest cow. **1948** FINLAYSON *Tidal Creek* (1979) 68 After the cows are bailed up and Uncle Ted busy milking them, Jake pauses happily leaning on the yard gate. **1966** BARRY *In Lee of Hokonuis* 37 We bailed her up at night and morning to the dray wheel and as she gave a lot of milk we had a plenteous supply. **1984** WILSON *S. Pacific Street* 5 She used to help me bail up the cows for Dad.

b. *intr.* Of a cow, to go into a bail; of a person, to put a cow into a bail.

1880 CRAWFORD *Recoll. of Travel* 127 The cow would not 'bail up' as the young [Maori] lady correctly expressed it in English. **1936** BELSHAW et al. *Agric. Organiz. NZ* 457 It is seldom essential for the attendant to go into the yard to bail up. Cows become so trained that they enter the bail themselves as soon as one becomes vacant.

2. *transf.* **a.** [AND 1838.] *trans.* To halt (a person or group) forcibly, to hold up. Often as *imp.* **Bail up!** Also *absol.* and *fig.* Cf. STICK UP *v.*¹ 2. Also as *vbl. n.* **bailing-up,** the holding up for purposes of robbery (see quots. 1881, 1888).

1863 MOSER *Mahoe Leaves* 67 You are losing caste fast among your European flock, and I fear among your Maori one. They are shutting their toll gates against ministers, and 'bailing up' Bishops. They are a bad lot my dear friend. **1866** BURGESS *Confessions* (1983) 123 They came within 15 yards of me when I stepped out and called on them to 'stand, bail up'—such being the phraseology in vogue, which means 'get together'. **1881** CAMPBELL *Poenamo* 42 [The bush rangers'] mode of proceeding was something after this fashion: on arriving they collected all the inmates of the house..and placed a sentry with a loaded gun over them, with the instructions to shoot, without compunction, any recreant individual who dared to stir 'a — inch', in the delicate language employed. This was termed 'baling up'. **1883** *Auckland Weekly News* 4 Aug. 6 The [Parihaka] Maoris were somewhere about ready to 'bail us up'. **1890** *Otago Witness* (Dunedin) 18 Dec. 16 Our Outram correspondent..supplied the following information with reference to the 'bailing-up' of a station in the Strath-Taieri district. **1908** *Truth* 13 June 5 The nocturnal persons asked Mather for a match, and as he was producing a lucifer, the redoubtable Johnstone presented a revolver at his head, remarking fiercely, 'Bail up!' **1910** *Truth* 16 Apr. 5 However, a man alleged to be Powelka is said to have bailed up a house at Terrace End. *Ibid.* 7 May 5 She went out and the man holding the six-shooters addressed her: 'Bail up!' She put her hands up. **1925** BATHGATE *Random Recolls.* 27 I thought..the men I had seen might come by that route, and bail me up. **1965** *Dominion* (Wellington) 13 Mar. 3 Te Au, masked and armed with a rifle, bailed up Mr D.R. Hensleigh, a former policeman, and demanded money.

b. Usu. *passive.* To be held up or constrained by the elements or occurrences of nature.

a1862 THATCHER in Duncan *Wakatipians* (1888) 105 We are bailed up by the snow, And look like frozen Esquimaux.

c. To accost and halt (often for a favour, loan, etc.); to 'buttonhole'.

1879 BARRY *Up & Down* 112 She bailed me up and asked if I was going to keep my promise and marry her. **1895** CHAMIER *South Sea Siren* 205 He was immediately 'bailed up' [by the surveyors], and made to dismount against his will to partake of some refreshment. **1900** WRIGHT *Wisps of Tussock* 50 He bailed me up straight for a shilling. **1910** *NZ Free Lance* (Wellington) 2 July 12 A well-known barrister..was immediately 'bailed up' by a couple of student policemen..who charged him with being Powelka. **1930** GUTHRIE *NZ Memories* 16 Toby, who was too courteous to break away from his lady admirer when once 'bailed up', as he called it, tried all the same politely to evade her. **1951** COMPTON *Through the Open Door* 42 One day in Morrinsville an evangelist had baled up Uncle in the street. **1968** SLATTER *Pagan Game* 106 There was no hope of getting away from him once he bailed anybody up in the staffroom or in the corridor or in the men's lavatory. **1963** MORRIESON *Scarecrow* 74 Pop seemed to lack the sense..just to say 'Good day' to Doc, instead of trying every time to bail him up and talk importantly. **1982** BREAM *Island of Fear* 67 He pays a lot of attention to us... He bailed me up outside Tarn's yesterday.

3. a. *trans.* To halt and restrain (quarry, esp. wild pigs) usu. with dogs; to bring to bay. Also *transf.* to force (a person or animal) into a difficult or inescapable position, to 'corner'.

1863 CHUDLEIGH *Diary* 9 Sept. (1950) 101 The dogs bailed it [*sc.* a wild pig] up in a stream of water & I..killed it. **1872** BARKER *Christmas Cake* i He and his dogs had bailed [the boar] up unsuccessfully 'many a time and oft'. **1880** SENIOR *Travel & Trout* 36 His troutship having neglected to secure a line of retreat, was, in colonial parlance, 'bailed up'. **1888** BARLOW *Kaipara* 123 We could see the man in the tree,..and wondered..until he shouted out that he was bailed up by the bull. **1916** COWAN *Bush Explorers* (VUWTS) 19 One morning..we found that they had bailed up an old boar..by the side of a little stream. **1939** *Te Aroha Times* 20 July 4 Intent on following the sounds of the dogs which frequently bailed up the pig, the party lost its bearings. **1960** MASTERS *Back-Country Tales* 12 From the sound of things Brave was on to an old boar that wasn't for bailing up. **1975** ANDERSON *Men of Milford Road* 162 We could have believed that there were a number of pigs baled up. **1986** RICHARDS *Off the Sheep's Back* 30 He was a very good pig dog, but when he was with us he only hunted for kiwis. Joe would bail up a kiwi while we grabbed it.

b. *intr.* Of quarry, to halt at bay.

1894 ARTHUR *Kangaroo & Kauri* 98 The pigs will often 'bale up', or stop, with their back to a rock, tree or other obstacle, keep two or more dogs at bay for a long time.

Hence **bailed(-up)** *ppl. a.*, of quarry, brought to bay; **bailing-up**, the action or process of fastening cows in a bail; **bail-up** *n.*, a halting and holding of (wild) cattle.

c**1875** MEREDITH *Adventuring in Maoriland* (1935) 64 It sometimes takes up to half an hour to scramble through the rough gullies to where the dogs have the pig stuck up... A **bailed-up** pig makes periodical rushes at the baiting dogs. **1937** BUICK *Moa-Hunters NZ* 185 The kick of the Moa is said to have been a forward one, and it is narrated that the ruse was to place a hunter in front of a bailed-up bird. **1960** CRUMP *Good Keen Man* 84 I couldn't see eye-to-eye with Jim on the matter of going in on bailed boars with a slasher. **1984** HOLDEN *Razorback* 71 Obviously there wasn't much fight in this particular boar. Walking briskly towards the bailed animal, Bob shook his head in outright disgust. **1912** BAUGHAN *Brown Bread* 142 There was no leg-roping, and hardly any **bailing-up**. **1990** EDWARDS *AWOL* 55 I had enough know-how..to do the baling up and leg roping. **1966** SHARPE *Fiordland Muster* 57 It looked to me as if the **bail-up** [of cattle] was about ten chains in from the forest fringe.

II. As **bail. 4.** *trans.* To put (a cow) into a bail. (**bail up** is the preferred transitive use.)

1860 DONALDSON *Bush Lays & Rhymes* 14 A young cow must be bailed.

Hence **bailed** *ppl. a.*, of a cowshed, comprising a stated number of bails (e.g. four-bailed); **bailing** *vbl. n.*, a gathering of cows into the bails.

1924 ANTHONY *Follow the Call* (1975) 3 Two-roomed house and **four-bailed** cowshed on property. Will milk twenty cows. **1967** two bailed [see BAIL *n.* 2]. **1912** *Otago Witness* (Dunedin) 23 Oct. 78 The byre itself is a new-fangled invention... It holds 16 cows at one **bailing**, and has double bails on each side.

5. a. *trans.* Of a hunting dog, to corner and hold quarry.

1952 BLAKISTON *My Yesteryears* 17 In the hunting of..pigs..we used..two terriers which would bail any pig. One would swing on an ear while the other grabbed the tail. **1960** CRUMP *Good Keen Man* 170 He'd cast out..in all directions until he found a pig..then he'd bail it till the other dogs got there. **1982** HOLDEN *Wild Pig* 62 On the few occasions that the dogs had actually managed to bail a deer, they had killed it.

b. *intr.* or *absol.* Usu. of pig-dogs, to corner and hold a pig.

1962 *Listener* 19 Apr. 5 The other three [dogs] were finding and bailing. **1986** CARR *Diary Pig Hunter* 19 There's Tip and Roy bailing good-oh.

c. *intr.* Of an animal (esp. a wild pig), to be cornered and held.

1922 *Auckland Weekly News* 5 Oct. 47 The dogs got on the scent of a large boar, that did not 'bail' until it reached the thick undergrowth. **1960** CRUMP *Good Keen Man* 127 The pig broke and charged back down the hill, to bail again in a steep creek. **1963** CAMPBELL *Golden North* 20 The pig usually bailed against a fallen log. **1982** HOLDEN *Wild Pig* 111 Obviously the pig had bailed at once.

Hence **bailing** *vbl. n.*, in pig-hunting, the cornering and holding of quarry; occas. applied to the sound or barking ('speaking') of a dog bailing a pig.

1960 CRUMP *Good Keen Man* 127 There was a furious bailing half-way up to the top of the ridge. The confounded dog had got on to something he couldn't handle, probably a rank old boar. **1962** *Listener* 19 Apr. 5 What about giving the lowdown on terms like bailing and finding... A good bailing dog will hold right in close on the nose, bark at him, snarl at him, kick up all the commotion he can and keep the pig occupied until you get down there.

bailer. Also **bailing dog**. A pigdog trained to bail wild pigs. Cf. HOLDER.

1951 *Here & Now* Dec. 15 Pig-dog types are many... The writer's considered classification is straight finders, straight bailers, straight holders and straight killers... Inside it we have finder-bailers; bailer-holders; finder-bailer-holders; bailer-holder-killers and holder-killers. **1960** MASTERS *Back-Country Tales* 201 All our sheep dogs had a go at Kooti at some time, but they were only bailers and far too cunning to go within range of Kooti's tusks. **1982** HOLDEN *Wild Pig* 156 Pigdogs are classified into three groups: finders, bailers, and holders. The name of each type indicates perfectly what they are expected to do. **1986** CARR *Diary Pig Hunter* 19 Now this is where I made a big mistake. Mine were holding dogs and, when asking Tony whether his dogs would help I was thinking along the lines of holding something like an ear, a leg, or a snout. Tony, however, had only bailing dogs with him.

bailing dog: see BAILER.

bait. Also **'bait.** Abbrev. of WHITEBAIT.

1972 *Sunday Times* (Wellington) 8 Oct. 3 [Heading] Coast 'bait are running. For the first time in years West Coast whitebaiters are getting their share. **1982** *Listener* 6 Nov. 131 On a good day, when the bait was really running, a halt would be called when more than one kerosene tin was full. **1986** HULME *Windeater* 37 One thing everybody does know about the Coast is bait. Whitebait.

Also **bait** *v.*, to take whitebait; **baiter**, a whitebaiter.

1989 HULME & MORRISON *Homeplaces* 108 Whitebaiting is in earnest now. I've seen people 'baiting—I've been 'baiting—when there's a lightning storm raging. **1992** *NZ Tablet* (Dunedin) 6 Jan. 9 Watch the resident 'baiter dragging in one or two pint hauls with each scoop when the 'bait were running truly good.

bake, *v.*[1] *Obs.* [f. Brit. dial.: see EDD *v.*[1] 4 *obs.*] Usu. **as be baked**, to become exhausted.

1861 *Puketoi Station Diary* in Beattie *Early Runholding* (1947) 82 In 1860 one [bullock] would not drive; in 1861 one 'baked' (i.e., knocked up) at the Gimmerburn. **1863** CHUDLEIGH *Diary* 2 Nov. (1950) 108 We had not 5 minutes spell all day... We were quite baked at the end of the day. **1900** SCOTT *Colonial Turf* 83 My horse is already baked and could not carry two.

bake, *v.*[2] *Drug-users.* To manufacture HOMEBAKE q.v.

1986 *Evening Post* (Wellington) 5 Apr. 19 Then he met someone who knew how to bake.

Hence **bake** *n.*, the process of making a batch of homebake; **baker** *n.*, one who manufactures homebake.

1986 *Evening Post* (Wellington) 5 Apr. 19 Homebake's popularity has also declined with the influx of bakers and subsequent plummet in quality. *Ibid.* 5 Apr. 19 You might go out on a Friday night to a house where someone is doing a bake... It takes about two hours to complete a bake excluding 'shelling time'. (Taking pills out of packets.)

bakshee(sh), varr. BUCKSHEE.

bald, *a.* In special collocations: **bald coot, bald pate** *West Coast obs.* [orig. US. *bald coot* a duck: AND 1829], PUKEKO. See also COOT.

c**1875** MEREDITH *Adventuring in Maoriland* (1935) 134 The only birds [at Tolaga Bay] are wild ducks of many varieties, pheasants, and *pokeko* (bald-coots). c**1899** DOUGLAS in *Mr Explorer Douglas* (1957) 234 I have heard..[the pukeko] also called bald pate and New Zealand turkey.

Baldwin. *Obs.* [f. the name of Thomas Scott *Baldwin* (1860–1923), b. Illinois, touring showman, balloonist, parachutist, parachuting from a hot-air balloon: first appearance in England at Alexandra Palace 1888, first New Zealand appearance at Dunedin 21 Jan. 1889, thence elsewhere.] In the phr. **to go up as high as Baldwin**, to meet the full rigour of one's lack of success or wrong-doing, etc; to go up 'sky-high'.

1900 SCOTT *Colonial Turf* 34 You wait till you come before the stewards; we don't stand no shenannikin. It's for crooked behaviour..and you'll go up as high as Baldwin. **1946** ALISON *A New Zealander Looks Back* 63 All countries have their slang expressions, and New Zealand is no exception to the rule. 'To go up for a skate' is one colonial idiom, and 'To go up as high as Baldwin' is another... 'To go up as high as Baldwin' had its origin in the [18]90's, after a visit to this country of the balloonist, Professor Baldwin. *Ibid.* 68 Poor Captain Lorraine [a balloonist killed in an accident]. He met with disaster. To use a colloquial expression 'He went up as high as Baldwin'.

baldy. [Origin uncertain: see quot. 1966.] A cry of pax used in children's games.
 1941 Baker *NZ Slang* 56 Other twentieth century New Zealand expressions of varied use include *baldy!* a schoolboy term synonymous with the English *fain I!* implying refusal. **1966** Turner *Eng. Lang. Austral. & NZ* 158 The way to ask for a truce in a game is to call *Pax*... Apparently some New Zealand schools use or have used *baldy*, which sounds like a variant of English *barley*.

bale, var. BAIL.

bale. [Spec. use of *bale* a large package closely pressed, wrapped in material and corded: see OED *n*.³ 1325.] **a.** In New Zealand from 1838 usu. a bale of wool (occas. a hay-bale); used distinctively mainly in combination.
 1838 *Cargo Statements* 16 Aug. in McNab *Old Whaling Days* (1913) 224 [The *Minerva* brought up] 4 bales wool, shorn from the back of sheep at Mayna [*sc.* Mana Island] N.Z. and the first imported into this Colony [N.S.W.]. **1982** *Agric. Gloss.* (MAF) 52 *Bale*: Package of wool in a regulation wool pack, weighing at least 100 kg. Maximum packed weights allowed under regulations are 181 kg for fleece and lambs wool and 204 kg for oddments.

b. Special Comb. **bale-box**, the box holding the wool-pack in a press; **bale-board, bale-sheet**, the board or paper on which details of each bale are recorded as it is pressed; **balehook**, a hook attached to a handle used for moving bales of wool, sacks, etc.
 1875 Rives *Jottings on the Spot* 15 Feb. (Cant. Pub. Lib. TS) 3 Rained all day to-day and I was engaged in making the frame for a **bale box** in the shed, while the *other* station hands were in the shed making posts. *Ibid.* 22 Feb. 5 We finished the bale-box today and pressed ¾ of a bale of wool. **1922** Perry *Sheep Farming* 125 As each bale is pressed its number, weight, and description should be recorded on the '**bale board**' for future reference. **1940** Meek in Woodhouse *Farm & Station Verse* (1950) 152 There are stackers swinging **balehooks** and barrows shifting wool. **1955** Bowen *Wool Away* 95 When the bale is branded enter up on the **bale sheets** its number, grade and contents.

 Hence **bale** *v.*, to press (usu. wool) into standard packs; **baler** *n.*, a woolshed hand who operates the wool-press.
 1881 Campbell *Poenamo* 41 He was busy 'baling his clip' to send down to Sydney for shipment home. **1981** Charles *Black Billy Tea* 27 In the shearing shed there is a strict social order... Below [the gun shearers] are the 'learners'... Then the shed-hands..the 'fleecies'..and the 'balers' who man the presses.

ball. In various phrases.
1. to be at long balls with *hist.* [f. cannon-(*ball*), to be in long-range conflict with.
 1839 Chapman *Lett. & Jrnls.* I. 145 The fight..had made their appearance at nine that morning and had been at long balls with the Pa all day and were just then retired.
2. ball of fire *WW2* (N. Africa), the nickname of the Second New Zealand Division in North Africa.
 1942 *NZEF Times* 21 Aug. 1 In England, not long before I left, I heard someone say that the New Zealanders were a 'ball of fire'. It was said by someone quite impartial. **1944** *Ibid.* 4 Dec. 5 How does that help us who roll the old ball of fire? **1942** Churchill 11 Nov. in *War Speeches* (1952) II. 357 [To the House of Commons.] For the purpose of turning the breach to fullest account, an entirely new corps, the 10th, was formed, consisting of two British armoured divisions and the New Zealand Division—that 'ball of fire' as it was described to me by those who had seen it at work. **1946** Soljak *NZ* 129 In the great Eighth Army attack of November 1, the New Zealand Division, with two British armo[u]red divisions, comprised the Tenth Corps. This 'ball of fire', as Montgomery described it, broke through on a front of four miles. **1949** Partridge *Dict. Slang Addenda* 983 As the *Ball of Fire*: the 2nd New Zealand Division: Army in North Africa: 1941-3.

3. (a) ball of muscle [AND 1914], used of a physically fit, vigorous person.
 1964 Sargeson *Collected Stories 1935-63* 297 ball: *a ball of muscle*, fit and energetic. **1980** Leland *Kiwi-Yankee Dict.* 11 *ball of muscle*: usually referring to children: (A) a ball of fire (complimentary) (B) a hyperactive child (derogatory) Which of the two meanings is employed, depends more on the circumstances than the child.

4. up with the ball [poss. a var. of *on the ball*, and *up with the play*], in touch with the latest methods, improvements, etc.
 1984 *Marlborough Express* (Blenheim) 20 Jan. 22 Dairy farmers in the Blenheim district are 'up with the ball' as far as herd leptospirosis vaccinations are concerned.

5. to have balls on one like a scoutmaster, see quot.
 1984 Partridge *Dict. Slang* (8edn.) 45 *balls on him like a scoutmaster* (, *he has*). A low NZ c[atch]p[hrase], dating from ca. 1930 and based upon the scurrilous idea, popular among the ignorant, that scoutmasters are active homosexuals. Can. also.

6. to pick up (the ball) and run with it, see PICK UP *v.* 2.

Ballarat. *Obs.* [f. *Ballarat*, a town in Victoria, Australia, the site of a famous early goldfield.] In full **Ballarat lantern**. See quot. 1875. See also LANTERN.
 1875 Wood & Lapham *Waiting for Mail* 21 He lit a candle, and dropped it into the Ballarat lantern, and away they went... [1875 *Note*] A 'Ballarat lantern' is formed by knocking off the bottom of a bottle, and putting a candle in its neck. **1911** Boreham *Selwyn* 103 More than once he [*sc.* Selwyn] rushed, half-clothed, into some little bush settlement at dead of night. In his hand was a *ballarat*—an impromptu lantern, consisting of an inverted bottle with the bottom broken off, and a candle fixed in the neck.

ballhead. Also **bald'ead.** [f. *bald* having relatively less hair, or a shaven head: reinforced by *ball* a head like a ball, shaven smooth.] A Mongrel Mob gang term for an outsider.
 1989 *Press* (Christchurch) 14 Feb. 19 Ballhead: derogatory term, used by one Maori to another, meaning 'Pakeha'. **1991** Payne *Staunch* 19 A bald'ead—an outsider whom the Mob go to great lengths to be different from.

ballie. Also **boldie.** A familiar term for a ball-bearing used as a marble.
 1983 Stewart *Springtime in Taranaki* (1991) 100 Boldies, or bole-bearings, were big silvery ball-bearings, and when you hurled them into the centre of the ring the dakes would fly out in all directions. **1984** *NZ Yesterdays* 288 The march of technology added ball bearings—ballies or steelies—which were unbeatable when it came to smashing an opponent's miserable glassie.

bamboo.
1. As **native** (or **New Zealand**) **bamboo**, *Microlaena polynoda* (fam. Poaceae).
 1927 *TrNZI* LVII. 938 native bamboo [The author, Andersen, quotes Duncan and Davies Descriptive Catalogue of 1917.] **1966** *Encycl. NZ* I. 872 Coastal cliffs are the habitat of the straggling New Zealand Bamboo, *Microlaena polynoda*.
2. bamboo orchid, see ORCHID 1.

banana boat. A Pacific Island trading ship engaged in the fruit (esp. banana) trade and formerly a vehicle for Island immigration to New Zealand.
 1987 *Metro* (Auckland) May 62 In the centre of the city..Polynesian families who had arrived on the *Tofua* and the *Matua*, the banana boats, in the fifties and sixties, felt the pressure of rising rents. **1991** Payne *Staunch* 100 I arrived here as a young boy on one of the banana boats—which brought most of the Islanders to New Zealand in those days.

banana passion-flower, passionfruit: see PASSION-FLOWER 2.

banded. In the names of birds and fish in the senses having bands of different coloured feathers or scales; or having characteristic band(s) rather than blocks of colours, see: BELLOWSFISH 2, DOTTEREL 2 (1), KOKOPU 2 (1), PARROTFISH 2 (1), RAIL 2 (2).

bandfish. Either of two unrelated ribbonlike fish, as **crested bandfish** *Lophotes capellei* (fam. Lophotidae), a widespread, silvery fish; and (more usu.) as **red bandfish** *Cepola aotea* (fam. Cepolidae), a reddish-pink fish.
 1881 *TrNZI* XIII. 196 In shape, [the family Trachypteridae] are usually long, deep, and very much compressed and flattened on the sides, so much so that their local appellations always embody some idea of these peculiarities—such as ribband-fish, lath or deal fish, band fish or blade fish. **1927** Phillipps *Bibliogr. NZ Fishes* (1971) 27 *Cepola aotea* Band-fish. **1956** Graham *Treasury NZ Fishes* 404 Bandfish *Cepola aotea*. **1982** Ayling *Collins Guide* (1984) 188 The crested band fish is an elongate ribbon-like fish... On top of the forehead the front portion of the dorsal fin is abruptly elevated to form a high curving crest. *Ibid.* 249 The red band fish [*sc. Cepola aotea*] has a tapering eel-like body... Although it is found throughout New Zealand this fish is rarely seen because of its secretive habits. **1986** Paul *NZ Fishes* 68 Crested bandfish... Body smooth, silvery, with red fins. *Ibid.* 116 New Zealand has one species, the red bandfish *Cepola aotea*.

bandicoot, *n.* [See AND 2: 'as an emblem of deprivation and desolation': *miserable as*, 1845.] In the phr. **as barmey as a bandicoot**, very eccentric; **as miserable as a bandicoot**, in a very miserable or pitiful physical state; **as useless as a bandicoot**, very useless.
 1891 Chamier *Philosopher Dick* 246 Hullo, Raleigh, is it yourself that's there? Looking as miserable as a bandicoot, and doing *nothing* as usual. **1891** Cottle *Frank Melton's Luck* 111 You go about looking as miserable as a bandicoot, and expect a girl to smile at you. **1950** Gaskell in *Some Other Country* 91 What have you been doing to Norman? He's as miserable as a bandicoot. I'll have to go in and sweeten him up as soon as I finish this. **1955** BJ *Cameron Collection* (TS July) barmey as a bandicoot Very mad. **1992** Anderson

bandicoot, v. Obs. Also **bandycoot**. [f. some alleged habits of the Australian *bandicoot*: AND 1896.] *trans.* and *intr.* To steal (usu. potatoes) by removing the tubers without disarranging the haulms. See also RABBIT v.³

c1940 *To bandicoot* used of potatoes in Marlborough (Ed.). **1974** SIMPSON *Sugarbag Years* 108 There was a paddock of potatoes around the road from us... And the people had been going at night and bandycooting. **1976** ANDERSON *Water Joey* 11 They raided the farmer's orchard, pinched his eggs, and bandycooted his potatoes and vegetables.

bang. As **bang slap** [cf. OED *slap-bang*], an intensifying elaboration of *bang* a hit; also used adverbially.

1922 MANSFIELD *Stories* (1984) 488 'You see, with a thing like a marquee..you want to put it somewhere where it'll give you a bang slap in the eye, if you follow me.' Laura's upbringing made her wonder whether it was quite respectful of a workman to talk to her of bang slaps in the eye. **1989** example (Ed.): 'I ran bang-slap into him in the street.'

banger. [Spec. use of *banger* that which bangs: see OED n.¹ 1.] A (large) firecracker. See also DOUBLE-BANGER 1 a.

1937 *King Country Chronicle* 3 Nov. 6 Some years ago big 'bangers' were prohibited because the Government liked the future citizens to be as complete as possible. **1972** *Evening Post* (Wellington) 31 Oct. 11 The 80 stores would not be selling the small units of crackers or bangers, said Mr Liddle. **1987** *Listener* 8 Aug. 67 For Guy Fawkes we used to have a few pennyworth of small 'bangers' and, if we were lucky, some bigger 'silver powder' crackers. **1988** SOMERSET *Sunshine & Shadow* 57 Their Jimmy yelled every time there was a burst of a cracker or a banger [c1897–1907]. **1989** *Dominion* (Wellington) 31 Dec. 6 Only people with a permit to provide a public display of fireworks will be able to purchase 'bangers'. 'Bangers' relate to any fireworks which rely principally on percussion for their main effect and basically include all crackers. **1990** *Dominion* (Wellington) 5 Apr. 3 Bangers were still terrifying pets despite last year's law banning them.

banjo. [f. a resemblance to a 'banjo' shape.]
1. [AND 1915.] A (usu. long-handled) shovel having a rounded ('spoon-like') rather than an oblong-shaped blade; occas. applied to any long-handled shovel. Also in Comb. **banjo shovel**, (esp.) a coalminer's large-bladed shovel.

1912 *Maoriland Worker* 22 Mar. 9 He performed the herculean..task of turning the first sod of the Waihi-Tauranga railway, with a specially sand-papered and varnished 'banjo' of rather less than the orthodox No. 5 size. **1913** CARR *Country Work* 20 The use of the pick and 'banjo' (as the long-handled shovel is termed) is very useful accomplishment. **1919** HOLLAND *Armageddon or Calvary* 65 He [sc. an NCO of a Field Punishment Centre] immediately ordered me to 'grab a banjo' and go over and help fill sandbags. **c1926** THE MIXER *Transport Workers' Song Book* 105 It's a long time since you handled a 'banjo'. **1960** *Listener* 21 Oct. 7 'It's interesting work—anything's better than the banjo.' 'The banjo?' 'A shovel. Some people call it a Mexican side-loader.' **1973** NEWTON *Big Country SI* (1977) 205 He took on a job with the local county council—on the pick and shovel... Jimmy claimed that [his] old dog was so humiliated at seeing his boss using a 'banjo' that he lay down and died. **1981** HUNT *Portrait Artist's Wife* 53 The girls were as useless as bandicoots.

Speaking a Silence 133 And they'd go down the mine,.. scrape the coal down and load it into the skips by hand with great big 'banjo' shovels. **1984** BEARDSLEY *Blackball 08* 128 You filled the tub [with coal], shoving the big banjo into the soft heap at your feet.

2. WW1. An entrenching tool.
1918 *Chron. NZEF* 30 Aug. 57 We [sc. Maori Pioneer Battalion] were still wielding the old 'Banjo' in good style. **1982** SHADBOLT *Once on Chunuk Bair* (1990) 53 On the end of a shovel, boss. Swinging the old banjo.

bank, n.¹ [f. *bank* a raised ridge or shelf of ground.]
1. *Goldmining*. Special Comb. **bank claim** [AND 1931], **bank diggings** [AND 1851], indicating a claim, etc., in or on a bank rather than in the bed of a river or creek.

1873 PYKE *Wild Will Enderby* (1889, 1974) I. iv 17 The Dunstan gold workings were of two kinds—technically known as 'beach claims' and '**bank claims**'. The latter were on the gravelly river banks which the miners sluiced away bodily for..the golden grains therein deposited. **1900** KITTO *Pract. Dredgeman's Manual* 18 If you are working a bank claim it is important that you keep the hole or paddock wide.

2. Obs. **a.** As **the bank**, an earth embankment (occas. so called) used as a grandstand in many New Zealand sports (esp. rugby union) fields, and often associated with the rowdier spectators; by metonymy the 'regulars' of the bank as a group.

1921 *Quick March* 10 Mar. 15 [Title] On the 'Bank'. On the Bank! 'Struth, don't it 'urt,... The team is filin' thro' the gate—just 'ear the shout. **1944** *NZEF Times* 24 Jan. 11 The mists coming down on the Western Bank [of Athletic Park], just before the final whistle blows. **1959** SLATTER *Gun in My Hand* 78 A vast concave mass of humanity tightly packed on the curving embankment... The bank, a corporate mass willing their [rugby] team to win, quick to applaud, and quicker to censure. **1968** SLATTER *Pagan Game* 115 Rugby Football was a game to be observed from the bank. **1981** *St Patrick's College, Silverstream 1931–80* 27 My contemporaries will recall..hitching their way into Wellington to get into one of those seemingly never-ending queues for the 'Western Bank' [of Athletic Park]. **1986** HOLCROFT *Sea of Words* 38 The only protesters [at Lancaster Park, 1938] were on the Bank, old-timers who never missed a match and who felt entitled to chide players.

Hence **banker**, formerly, a spectator on the bank of a rugby union field.
1911 *Truth* 13 May 3 Roberts (Oriental) got a bone in his cheek injured, and it is..odds on that he joins the 'bankers' for a bit. **1928** NICHOLLS *With the All Blacks in Springbokland* 34 If I ever become a Saturday afternoon 'banker'..I should insist loudly..that there be as little as possible of the..heaving and struggling in the game.

b. In the phr. **to send** (one) **to the bank**, **to give an order for the bank**, to send (a rugby player) off the field of play as a penalty. Cf. *early shower* (EARLY 3).
1906 *Truth* 19 Aug. 2 The referee was guilty of a grave dereliction of duty in not giving the suburbanite an order for the bank.

3. See DITCH AND BANK.

bank, n.² [f. *bank* a custodian of money.]
1. In the phr. **to be right as a bank**, to be completely right, fit, safe, etc.
1947 DAVIN *For Rest of Our Lives* 301 'How's the leg, Rusty?' asked Frank... 'Right as a bank. No trouble at all.' **1959** SLATTER *Gun in My Hand* 165 I'm all right I tell ya. Right as a bank... I'm not drunk I tell ya.

2. Special Comb. **bank cheque**, a cheque (in Australia and the US termed a *cashier's cheque*) issued and guaranteed by a trading bank, having in law the nature of a promissory note, and treated popularly as equivalent of cash esp. in respect of property transactions.

1993 *Capital Letter* (Wellington) 7 Sept. 1 (No.737) [Heading] 'Bank Cheques' – as good as cash?.. The supposed sanctity of bank cheques featured this year in a High Court judgment (16 TCL 8/5)... The Court of Appeal has now overturned..[the] decision..(CA 24/93; 1/9/93)... The High Court pointed out that bank cheques are neither bills of exchange nor cheques but bank promissory notes... The essential point was conveniently summed up in Justice Mckay's [Appeal] conclusion: 'The use of bank cheques payable to order is commonplace for the settlement of commercial and conveyancing transactions, and they are generally treated as equivalent to cash to the extent that the only risk is that of the solvency of the bank.'

bank and bank, *a.* or *adv.* Also **bank high**. [AND 1847.] Of a river, in flood. See also BANKER.

1860 in Butler *First Year* (1863) vi 79 Sometimes..the river is what is called bank and bank; that is to say, one mass of water from one side to the other. **1862** CHUDLEIGH *Diary* 26 Sept. (1950) 60 There is every chance of the river being bank high and not passable for a week, the first fresh is always the highest. **1864** *Ibid*. 30 Jan. (1950) 120 I heard the Rakaia was bank and bank so I went to Harman's to see O'Brien. **1933** *Press* (Christchurch) (Acland Gloss.) 9 Sept. 15 *Bank and Bank.*—A river runs b[ank] and b[ank] when all the streams join into one; i.e., when in high flood.

banker. [AND 1848.] A river in high flood, with the bed fully covered from bank to bank, esp. in the phr. **to run a banker**, to be in high flood. See also BANK AND BANK.

1914 PFAFF *Diggers' Story* 122 When the party woke..they found the 'Terry Mick Ow' [Teremakau river, West Coast] running a banker. **1933** *NZ Alpine Jrnl.* V. 20 235 The rains made the Whitcombe [River] rise to a 'banker', and the performances closed with nine inches of snow. **1948** HAAST *Julius Von Haast* 128 When the snow melts, the streams swell and swirl and the river may be running a 'banker', spreading from bank to bank and covering the whole of the shingle beds. **1950** *Canterbury Mountaineer* 25 The rain came down in sheets..and the river was a banker, with boulders rolling a yard or two from the tent. **1977** BRUCE *Life in Hinterland* 40 However, owing to heavy rain in the mountains, when they arrived at the Ashley River it was running a banker.

bank high: see BANK AND BANK.

bantie. Also **banty**. [f. *bant*(am + -IE: poss. orig. US: see DARE, *banty* in widespread US use from 1890.] A bantam, esp. as a pet; also a call to bantams.

1936 HYDE *Passport to Hell* 13 Within, a mellow voice says reproachfully, 'Hey, Banty! Banty!' The four little bantam hens..quarrel bitterly for a place on Starkie's shoulders. **1938** HYDE *Nor Yrs. Condemn* 318 You don't want to sleep with the old banties, Flo. You'll get things in your head. **1983** HENDERSON *Down from Marble Mountain* 120 The special brown part-bantie pecking with deft little darts the wheat in my cupped hand. **1986** *Landfall 158* June 142 Things look up when..Curnow..explains exactly what happened

banty, var. BANTIE.

bar, *n.*[1] *Goldmining.* [Transf. use of *bar* bank of sand at a river mouth: AND 1843.]

1. a. A bank of material, often auriferous, formed in a river or creek by the action of currents, or by a ridge of rock on the stream bed.

1852 *NZGG* 9 Nov. V. 26:165 (Rep. Gold Discovery in Coromandel) A favourable indication was noticed at a bar in the creek [in the Coromandel] *Ibid.* 10 Dec. V. 30:187 Down to bar at junction of path and stream... The earth passed through the 'Tom' was top stuff, incidental to opening a new bar. 1864 THATCHER *Songs of War* 5 They work on the bars of the river, And in many a crevice, I'm told, With knives they can pick out the nuggets. 1874 PYKE *George Washington Pratt* 47 They had found a 'bar', such as satisfied George's critical discernment. They then went to work to turn the creek above the bar, and by nightfall the water was running in their new channel. 1896 MOFFATT *Adventures* (1979) 58 As the bar commenced to dry in patches [as the river dropped], our hopes were high... The wash was about six inches thick. 1902 *Brett's Colonists' Guide* 1030 The contained gold..has been concentrated in *leads* and *bars*. 1918 *NZJST* I. 12 The best [gold] was found on the beaches and shallow bars of the stream.

b. A ridge of rock on a stream bed which traps gravel, sand, etc.

1879 HECTOR *Handbook NZ* 171 The wash everywhere resting on water-worn bars and ledges of greenstone. 1887 PYKE *Hist. Early Gold Discoveries Otago* (1962) 75 Further up the river they observed on the eastern bank a series of long rocky bars projecting into the stream. 1908 *NZGeol.SB (NS)* No.5 40 On a favourable bottom gold will lodge on the down side of a bar of rock running across the bed of a stream. 1983 NOLAN *Gold Fossicker's Handbook* 111 *Bar*: a ridge of rock crossing or nearly crossing a stream. Also, in North America, a gravel bank or a protruding beach.

2. As **blue bar,** see quot. (cf. *blue bottom, blue reef* (BLUE *a.* 3)); **hard bar,** in quartz-mining, a band of hard non-auriferous rock separating veins of auriferous material.

1896 *AJHR* C-3 50 The andesites occur in bars, varying from 20ft. to 300ft. in width, and are termed by the [Thames] miners 'hard country', or '**blue bars**'. 1900 *NZ Mines Record* 16 Mar. 305 The miner took the naming of rocks into his own hands, and pronounced the softer country 'sandstone,' where this had not to be called 'puddingstone,' 'mullock-bands,' or '**hard-bars**'. 1906 *TrNZI* XXXVIII. 22 In almost every instance the [parallel] veins are separated from each other by a narrow belt of hard unaltered andesite. These hard bands, or 'bars' as the miners term them, possess the same general strike and dip as the veins. 1907 *NZGeol.SB (NS)* No.4 101 These ribs or dyke-like masses [of country rock separating two veins] are the 'hard bars' of the miners. In some cases, however, these 'hard bars' are probably due to dykes. 1948 *Ibid.* No.42 39 Further, the 'hard' bars most probably interrupted the shoot, more or less horizontally.

3. A mineralised stratum associated with an auriferous ore-shoot or vein; see quot.

1907 *NZGeol.SB (NS)* No.4 122 In the upper levels of the mines the ore-shoots are said to have been intimately associated with what are termed 'mineral heads' or 'bars'. These are apparently layers of sedimentary rock, which originally proved more permeable to the circulating ground-waters than the general mass of rock, and supplied aqueous precipitants of gold and silver to the vein channels.

bar, *n.*[2] [f. *bar* a rod or oblong block of a substance.]

1. *Ellipt.* for a crowbar.

1902 LANCASTER 'Our Lady of the Plains' in *Happy Endings* (1987) 105 She came out to watch him sinking a post-hole, and to explain the uses of a 'bar' in clayey soil.

2. In the phr. **not to know** (someone, something) **from a bar of soap,** not to recognize, to know nothing of; also humorously re-formed, see quot. 1968.

1903 *NZ Bulletin* 24 Oct. 15 Didn't know the game [of golf] from a bar of soap, and now that I know something about it, would certainly give the cake to the soap. 1938 *The Standard* 16 June in Gustafson *Cradle to Grave* (1986) 72 The workers made a presentation to their cook..whom Savage as he later recollected, didn't know 'from a bar of soap'. 1959 SLATTER *Gun in My Hand* 146 And even if they don't know me from a bar of soap they do know I was in the Battalion. 1968 SLATTER *Pagan Game* 163 Didn't know him from a bottle of detergent. 1995 COCHRANE *Tin Nimbus* 137 And where's your ID, you?.. I don't know you from a bar of soap.

bar, *n.*[3] [Origin uncertain, poss. the reference was originally to a bar of music: AND 1933.] In the phr. **not to have a bar of,** not to tolerate; to reject; to dislike thoroughly.

1986 *Marist Messenger* Dec. 33 'We're set to do a record shear.' 'Not a hope,' he said, 'not with these new handpieces... The shearers over at Fairview won't have a bar of them.' 1987 *Dominion Sunday Times* (Wellington) 27 Sept. 11 And he [*sc.* Prime Minister Kirk] was shouting back, 'I won't have a bar of that, get out of here Patrick Millen', and all that sort of thing. 1990 *Dominion* (Wellington) 31 Mar. 1 Opposition education spokesman Lockwood Smith said National would not have a bar of the legislation. 1992 ANDERSON *Portrait Artist's Wife* 180 'They [*sc.* undertakers] hold you to ransom,' she used to say. 'Take advantage of your grief. Don't have a bar of it.'

bar, *v.*[1] [f. *bar the dice* to declare a throw void: AND 1897.] Usu. *imp.*, in the game of two-up, cancel the spin! (of the coins): esp. in the calls **bar 'em** or **barred!**

1912 *Truth* 20 Jan. 7 Even the metallic ring of the coins could be heard, followed by the suppressed sighs of 'heads' bettors as 'tails' were cried while 'two ones,' 'barred,' 'heads a dollar,' 'tails' ditto, 'pass the bat,' and other equally quaint and even classic chants, were wafted on the midnight breezes. 1912 *Magpie* (Mar.) 'Bar!' shouted somebody. 1928 DEVANNY *Dawn Beloved* 162 As the pennies flew into the air a man in the circle called sharply 'Bar 'em'... The man who barred 'em didn't like the way they were spun. Any man has the right to bar 'em so long as he speaks while they are in the air.

bar, *v.*[2] To carry a passenger on the bar of a bicycle, DOUBLE-BANK *v.* 2.

c1954 p.c. R. Mason. Heard in Christchurch. 'He used to bar me home to Burwood before we were married.' 1959 *Star* (Christchurch) 5 Aug. 19 Mr McCormick..used to bar Fergus to his school boy matches.

baracoota, baracouta, barakuta, varr. BARRACOUTA.

barbed wire. WW1 (Egypt). A name for the places where those infected with venereal disease were isolated. Also as **barbed wire soldier**, one with a venereal disease.

1936 TREADWELL *Recolls. Amateur Soldier* 48 The women [*sc.* Cairo prostitutes] of the old area were examined, and those infected were immediately placed in a concentration camp, known as the 'barbed wire', behind which she remained until she received a clean bill of health. 1984 PUGSLEY *Gallipoli* 76 A large venereal disease hospital was established near the Australian lines and run by the Australians for both Australians and New Zealanders. It was surrounded by barbed wire and guards to prevent men breaking out. Men unfortunate enough to be so caught earned the sobriquet 'barbed wire' soldiers.

barber.

1. [f. being keen enough to shave one: orig. e. Canada, Nova Scotia, Newfoundland (and also Shetland Islands) *barber* a mist or keen wind containing ice-crystals (1830); frost-smoke arising from water; a bitterly cold wind (1830): see OED 1 c, DARE, DCan, DNFE.] Usu. as **the barber,** a keen, cutting wind, often with mist or fog, orig. and usu. associated with Greymouth on the West Coast.

[1867 PHILLIPS *Point Journal* 31 July (ATLTS) 110 A *fearful* day—wind like an extra sharpened double bladed super fine razor. Snow drifted 6 feet in places.] 1908 BARR *Brit. Rugby Team in Maoriland* 75 They have a prevailing wind at Greymouth called 'The Barber', which..smites the inhabitants hip and thigh..a keen, biting wind which cuts like a sabre-thrust, nips like an ant, and stings like a whip-lash. 'What do you think of 'The Barber'?' in Greymouth is synonymous with 'What do you think of our harbour?' in Sydney. 1933 *Press* (Christchurch) (Acland Gloss.) 16 Sept. 15 *Barber, the.*—A very bitter cold wind which blows down the gorge of the Mawhera and afflicts the river front, railway station, and adjacent streets of Greymouth. The miners and drovers used the word in the 'sixties, and it is still in use. 1937 ELLIOT *Firth of Wellington* 22 There [*sc.* West Coast, Grey Gorge] in winter raged an icy blast known as 'the barber', for it was as keen as any razor. 1942 *Blue & White* 31 As often as not, there would be a real barber of a wind sweeping down the wadi, enveloping everything in dust. 1963 PEARSON *Coal Flat* 393 This day was clear. There was a frost on the grass in the morning, and a 'barber'—the keen wind and night mist blowing down from the Grey Valley—was pushing across Blaketown..and disappearing over the sea. 1979 CRUMPTON *Spencer: Gold Seeker* A low ceiling of cloud engulfed the summits, and fog could be seen swirling down the ranges. 'The barber is coming down and he'll shave you.' 1981 DENNIS *Paparoas Guide* 197 On fine, still nights, the air cooled in the inland valleys drains down the Grey and Buller Rivers producing a keen and cutting morning wind near the coastal towns known locally as 'The Barber'. 1991 *Evening Post* (Wellington) 1 May 24 He was out of the reach of the 'barber'—the wind that slices down the river from the hills—so he was, by current standards there, pretty warm anyway.

2. [f. *barber* an obsolete nickname for a shearer: AND 1898.] In special collocations: **barber's annual clip,** the annual shearing; **barber's breakfast,** see quot.

1952 MEEK *Station Days* 110 **Barber's Annual Clip**: The annual shearing. c1962 BAXTER *Horse* (1985) 101 After a **barber's breakfast**—the dry retches, a bottle of beer and a cigarette—Horse went to a phone box and dialled Zoe's number.

3. [The reference is obscure: poss. to a 'cut cat' as one (sexually) useless. Cf. J.C. Hutten *Slang Dictionary* (1865 edn) 'Barber's cat, said of a half-starved, sickly-looking person, in connexion with an expression too coarse to print.'] In the

phr. **all piss and wind like the barber's cat**, all pretence, useless.
  1983 Cooper *Wag's Tales* 62 Therefore [the horse] was tall and slab-sided, with huge feet. Paddy described him as like the 'Barber's cat'. (Politeness forbids me to explain that simile.) **1987** Norgrove *Shoestring Sailors* 65 He'll be all piss and wind for a while..just like the barber's cat. Crap, too.

barbie. Also **barby**. [f. *barb*(ecue + -IE: AND 1976.] A barbecue; (the occasion of) a meal cooked on (or at) a barbecue.
  1986 *Evening Post* (Wellington) 12 Dec. 1 [Heading] Watch the barbie! Paper and kindling wood is still the best way to light a barbecue, says a Wellington safety officer. **1989** *Pacific Way* Jan. 11 One feature of New Zealand speech that is often commented on by visitors is our inordinate fondness for abbreviations which end in 'ie' or 'y'... It's good to have a barbie on the back lawn. **1991** *Dominion Sunday Times* (Wellington) 27 Oct. 21 While meat is traditionally the basis of a barbecue, peppers..and corn cobs are just a few of the vegetables which can be delicious..cooked on the barby. **1994** *City Voice* (Wellington) 15 Dec. 25 [Heading] Barbie kai for vegetarians... Whack another sausie on the Barbie, mate!

bar-bound, *a*. Of a boat, grounded on, held up or confined to port by a river-mouth bar. (Occas. used jocularly of one seemingly held up in a hotel bar.)
  1876 Chudleigh *Diary* 1 Aug. (1950) 250 Still in Ch.Ch. looking for a ship... The Cleopatra is the one expected to go down but she is bar bound in the Grey and may stay so for a month. **1914** Pfaff *Diggers' Story* 146 Hearing at the latter port that the first boat had arrived at Hokitika [1864], but was bar-bound, we decided to travel overland. **1971** Watt *Centenary Invercargill* 82 Ships which used it, were not infrequently bar-bound or weather-bound for lengthy periods.

barby, var. BARBIE.

barcoo. [See AND: of the w. Queensland Barcoo River and hinterland connoting a remote district with barely civilized inhabitants.] Special Comb. **barcoo challenge** *shearing*, see quot.; **barcoo rot**, see quot.
  1934 *Press* (Christchurch) (Acland Gloss.) 13 Jan. 13 *Barcoo challenge*.—(1) to scrape the points of the shears on the floor or wall; or (2) to throw the belly over another shearer's head, indicating a challenge for the day's tally. **1990** Martin *Forgotten Worker* 137 This diet with its lack of fresh vegetables left station hand, shearer and farm alike susceptible to vitamin C deficiency and scurvy (so-called '**Barcoo rot**').

bare, *a*.
a. In special collocations in the sense 'lacking wool': **bare-back** [f. Brit. dial.: see EDD *adj*. 1 (2) (b)], a newly-shorn sheep; **bare-belly** [AND 1897], a sheep with (much of) its belly-wool scraped off or shed; **bare-bellied** *ppl. a*. [AND 1912], of a sheep, having no wool on the underside of the belly (and the inside of the legs); **bare-point**, a sheep with no wool on the points, hence **bare-pointed** *ppl. a*.
  1846 Pharazyn *Journal* (ATLMS) 62 Dressed one lamb and also six **bare-backs** (new lot). **c1875** Meredith *Adventuring in Maoriland* (1935) 143 Naturally, the easiest-shorn sheep — '**bare-bellies**' and 'bare points' — are selected first [by shearers]. **1921** Guthrie-Smith *Tutira* (1926) 157 A considerable proportion of our flock appeared on the shearing-board with bellies, sometimes with sides too, bare of wool,— 'Pare perries'—bare bellies—joyfully the shearers hailed them in the catching-pens. **1934** *Press* (Christchurch) (Acland Gloss.) 13 Jan. 13 *Barebelly*.—Sheep (generally a ewe) with no wool on the belly. **1955** Bowen *Wool Away* 9 In the old days, there were a lot of bush burns, with the result that bare bellies and bare points were much more frequent than today. **1982** *Agric. Gloss.* (MAF) 52 *Bare-belly*: Sheep with all the wool scraped or shed from its belly. **1878** Elwell *Boy Colonists* 109 The [merino] ewes have many of them at shearing time no wool on the legs or under the belly, and hence are called 'bare-bellies'. Of course these '**bare-bellied**' ewes..are very quickly shorn. **c1875, 1955 bare points** [see *bare-belly* above]. **1960** Mills *Sheep-O* 104 The Bowens are no 'Sunday' shearers. Rams..**bare-pointed** sheep..these hold no terrors for these class shearers.

b. In special collocations: **bare-bottom haka**, a haka which includes the presentation of bare buttocks (Maori *whakapohane*) to the recipient, as a mark of contempt (cf. BROWN-EYE); **bare tucker**, see TUCKER *n*. 2.
  [**1953** Cody *Man of Two Worlds* 122 When the old-time Maoris wished to demonstrate their most extreme measure of contempt for any person they danced a haka standing naked and waist high in a river and at appropriate times in the dance turned their posteriors towards the unwelcome visitor.] **1967** *Pol. Science* Dec. 76 The ceremonial contumely of the '**bare bottom haka**' has been often enough described. [A description of a woman performing it for Maui Pomare follows.]

baricouta, var. BARRACOUTA.

bark, *v.*[1] *trans*. and *intr*. Also **bark up**. To make sheep-dogs bark.
  1933 *Press* (Christchurch) (Acland Gloss.) 16 Sept. 15 *Bark*.—Make dogs bark; e.g., 'Bark your dogs well when you get on to the top'. **1951** McLeod *NZ High Country* 23 They..stand and bark their dogs and give a long 'Yahoooo' or a high yodelling hoot. **1960** *Proc. of 10th Lincoln College Farmers' Conference* 71 I can well remember high-country sheep being so thin in the spring that when one barked a dog, many would fall over. **1970** McLeod *Glorious Morning* 53 *Bark up*: The musterer often stands on a point of vantage and makes his dogs bark to start sheep moving or to show his position. **1978** Jardine *Shadows on Hill* 9 He knew the rule that if you sang out and barked up, the man on the next beat was supposed to answer. *Ibid*. 76 I could hear the boss barking-up occasionally and I answered him.
  Hence **barking-up** *vbl. n*., see quot. 1966; **bark up**, *n*.
  1966 Newton *Boss's Story* 185 *Barking-up*: During the course of his mustering work the musterer frequently gets his team to bark while at heel (i.e. alongside him) the object being to frighten sheep along without actually running a dog. This is known as 'barking-up'. **1959** McLeod *Tall Tussock* 118 A good 'bark up' soon had them [*sc*. sheep] travelling out again.

bark, *v.*[2] *Obs. trans*. To line (a hut or roof) with bark.
  1837 *Piraki Log* (1911) 63 [Dec. 21] the Men employed Putting Bark on the Capt's House and other necessary things. [Dec. 22] The men employed in barking the Capt's House and carrying clay.

barker. [Prob. f. the barking or yapping sound of its call; poss. an alteration [b(w)akə] of Ma. POAKA stilt.] *pied stilt* (STILT 2 (2)).
  1966 Falla et al. *Birds NZ* 147 *Pied stilt Himantopus leucocephalus. Other names*: Stilt, Barker, Poaka, White-headed Stilt, Daddy Long-legs, Torea (Rotorua), Pip (Kaipara)... *Voice*: A puppy-like yapping *yep yep*. The call of the young is a shriller *kip kip*.

bark hut, bark whare. [AND 1810.] In early New Zealand, a bush hut, often made from totara bark. Cf. BARK *v*.[2]
  1851 Weld *Hints to Intending Sheep-farmers* 12 Such accomplishments as painting and music, far from being out of place in a bark or wooden hut, are invaluable there. **1885** W.J. Swainson let. in *William Swainson* (1992) 108 The first and only hut we had there [on the station] was just a common Maori bark whare.

barley grass: see GRASS 2 (2).

barney. [Prob. f. Brit. dial.: see OED 1 c; AND 1858.] A rowdy argument or dispute; a quarrel, a fight; esp. in the phr. **to have (a bit of) a barney**.
  1873 Pyke *Wild Will Enderby* (1889, 1974) I. v 19 [Chapter title] A Barney [*sc*. about a fight and row with claim-jumping 'rowdies']. **1879** *Auckland Weekly News* 20 Sept. 7 He often told me about the 'barney' he had with his brother. **1897** Wright *Station Ballads* 53 The yarns of strikes and barneys will be told till all is blue. **1946** Sargeson *That Summer* 153 I'd hook off while they [*sc*. a husband and his estranged wife] had their barney. **1978** Mantell *Murder in Fancydress* 131 Heard Keith Hounsell and Mrs White having a bit of a barney so I looked out. **1980** Lawry *Good Luck & Lavender* 52 'There was a bit of a barney down in Werry's this afternoon'... 'And I got into a fight'.
  Hence **barney** *v. intr*. [AND 1861], to argue, dispute.
  1880 *Evening Post* (Wellington) 13 Jan. 2 He saw the prisoner and prosecutor 'barneying' in the middle of some strangers. **1913** Bathgate *Sodger Sandy's Bairn* 76 I can't barney with you all day.

barra: see BARRACOUTA.

barrack, *v*. [Prob. f. N. Irel. dial. (see EDD) *barrack* to brag: AND considers any connection with *borak* unlikely.]
1. (The action of the verb is directed against the object.) **a.** [AND 1878.] *trans*. To jeer at, to tease (a person, esp. a performer or an opponent).
  1897 [see *vbl. n*. below]. **1905** *Truth* 16 Sept. 6 The fellow, who must have been thoroughly ashamed of himself,.. had been barracked by his toffy friends who had seen his name in the Christchurch papers. **1917** let. 14 Dec. in *Boots, Belts* (1992) 52 Although we had a great reception..we put in the time barracking Uncle Sam's soldiers. **1928** Smyth *Jean of Tussock Country* 88 'You cut along first, Ben,' he barracked. **1937** Ayson *Thomas* 31 The diggers caught sight of his bell-topper and began greeting him with cries of 'Joe, Joe.'.. The minister was puzzled to understand why he was being barracked so freely. **1945** *Arts in NZ* June-July 19 It is tiresome and ungrateful to continue barracking the Academy. **1956** Dare *Rouseabout Jane* 185 They would enjoy a few minutes rest while barracking us slower ones. **1984** Marshall *Day Hemingway Died* 40 The others began barracking his impotence.
  Hence **barracking** *vbl. n*. [see EDD, 'boastfulness'; AND 1878: cf. also BARRAGIN], chaff, teasing; *ppl. a*., teasing; noisy or persistent adverse criticism.
  1897 Wright *Station Ballads* 41 While we coves all laughed and shouted, and the barracking began. **1905** *Truth* 19 Aug. 5 The butt of a good deal of barracking from the disappointed ones. **1937** Ayson *Thomas* 28 All the fight was taken out of the bully, and

it was not many days before the barracking he had to undergo caused him to take himself to fresh fields. **1947** NEWTON *Wayleggo* 106 To sit there like Jacky in front of a mob of grinning, barracking station hands..made me feel a perfect fool. **1993** *Dominion* (Wellington) 12 Feb. 3 Mobil had treated a service station proprietor fairly despite his constant bellyaching and barracking about his rent.

b. *Obs. intr.* To argue, to row.

1914 GRACE *Tale Timber Town* Come in, come in..and stop barracking like two old washerwomen.

2. (The action of the verb is directed to the support of the object.) **a.** *intr.* Of sports spectators, to support noisily.

1904 MCMURRAN *New York to NZ* 136 Thousands of people are..shouting themselves hoarse or 'barracking', as it is called, in support of good play. **1919** *Quick March* 10 June 82 Some girls barrack quite seriously [at football matches]. **1948** BALLANTYNE *Cunninghams* (1976) 171 'Struth it would be great all right to..stand on the sideline barracking his head off. **1968** *NZ Contemp. Dict. Suppl.* (Collins) 3 *barrack..v.* in Australia , loudly jeer, banter or criticize in chorus the players of a game; support, cheer; in..N.Z. to encourage, not jeer at.

b. As **barrack for**, to voice public, often noisy, partisan support for (often a contestant or team).

1905 *Truth* 16 Sept. 5 The Wellington 'E[vening] P[ost]' is busy barracking for J.J. Michell. **1908** FINDLAY *Humbugs & Homilies* 254 The maids began to openly barrack for the cook. **1928** REES *Wild Wild Heart* 26 Biddy always barracks for me as a rider. **1944** GASKELL in *Listener Short Stories* (1977) 9 I'll not say which side I'll be barracking for. **1959** SLATTER *Gun in My Hand* 75 I don't care which side wins. There was a time when I would barrack for a team, but that was before I went on my trips overseas. **1980** *National Radio* 'Morning Report' 10 Dec. For many years, hospital boards here have been barracking for a new system of funding.

Hence **barracking** *vbl. n.*, noisy verbal support. Also *ppl. a.*

1890 *NZ Observer* 26 July 15 The jockey boys have taken to 'barracking'. **1910** FANNING *Players & Slayers* 70 The difference..is that in America 'rooting' is a well-established art, and in New Zealand barracking is merely a haphazard business. **1919** *Quick March* 10 June 81 Few people go to a match deliberately to yell... For this lack..in the barracking department one is rather grateful than regretful. c**1930** *Whitcombe's Etym. Dict. Aust.-NZ Suppl.* 1 *barracking n.* shouting and cheering in chorus with a view to encouraging or discouraging one of the participants in a game, such as cricket.

barrack, *n.* Noisy (usu. good-humoured) chaff or argument in support of or opposing the actions of others.

1895 *Otago Witness* (Dunedin) 7 Nov. 37 And spite of the fact that our papers tried to rouse public disgust thereupon, there was really very little barrack against it. **1897** *Ibid.* 29 Apr. 39 Oh, there's music in the barrack of the gay sparks in the pit. **1914** in *Hist. N. Otago from 1853* (1978) 68 By this time my bandmates entered into the spirit of the thing and backed him up with good natured 'barrack' such as 'Give it a go, Bill', 'Have a shot', 'Be a sport'. **1949** NEWTON *High Country Days* 46 The other four, full of noisy barrack, were playing pitch and toss with a set of old horse shoes.

barracker. [AND 1889; cf. EDD, 'a braggart'.] An enthusiastic supporter, or vociferous spectator (esp. at sports gatherings); occas. a vociferous critic.

1887 *NZ Mail* (Wellington) 15 July 9 (NZ Slang) People who go to football matches and howl encouragement to either side are 'barrackers', 'chiakers'. **1890** *NZ Observer* 12 July 11 Any good play..was loudly applauded by the respective barrackers of each club. **1890** *Otago Witness* (Dunedin) 10 July 28 Fitchett..muffed the ball a good deal, thus bringing himself under the lash of the merciless 'barracker'. **1910** FANNING *Players & Slayers* 69 The barracker is the peculiar produce of the football field. **1921** *Ensign* (Mataura) 28 Sept. in Barry *In Lee of Hokonuis* (1966) 320 After the battle players and barrackers adjourned to J. Johnston's lawn for afternoon tea. **1934** MULGAN *Spur of Morning* 23 When the attack was pressed, the barrackers of each side roared encouragement together.

barracks, *n. pl.*

1. *Hist.* In full *emigration* (*emigrant, immigrant, immigration*) *barracks* (see EMIGRATION 2, EMIGRANT B 2, IMMIGRANT 2, IMMIGRATION 2). Temporary accommodation for immigrants newly arrived in New Zealand.

1849 in *Lett. from Otago* 3 Dec. (1978) 43 On our landing here, we resided at the emigrant's depot or 'barracks', until we had our house ready. Of these there are two; they are large wooden houses, with four windows and two doors, and a fireplace, and fitted up like a ship, with berths on one side. **1878** BULLER *Forty Yrs. NZ* 159 I felt particularly interested in the immigrants [to Christchurch] and used to visit them in the 'Barracks' on their arrival. **1886** HART *Stray Leaves* 8 As the last comers [to Canterbury settlement], we had..to take our chance of accommodation on arrival in the barracks—the range of buildings a little lower down than Mr. Godley's house. **1898** HOCKEN *Contributions* 97 The shelters or barracks, as they were called, were situated along the beach. **1930** GUTHRIE *NZ Memories* 37 Here most of the emigrants from the first three ships had squatted, but there were no barracks or shelter of any kind.

2. *Secondary schools.* Also **barracks week**. [Transf. use of *barracks* military accommodation.] A period of military cadet training when usual schooling is replaced by military exercise and discipline.

1935 *St Patrick's College 1883–1935* 117 Barracks were held in the week following Easter, and culminated in a miniature battle on Mt Victoria for the infantry. **1958** MCDONALD *Hist. Waitaki Boys' High School* 201 The second camp, which lasted four days and was held in April was more correctly a 'barracks', the boys sleeping in the school buildings. **1959** SLATTER *Gun in My Hand* 149 The names of boys who used to swank in the school cadets and faint with the heat of form fours in barracks week in February. **1961** *Dominion* (Wellington) 7 Feb. 7 A new venture in military cadet training was ushered in today when 'Barracks Week' began for about 600 Southland Technical College Students. **1968** in *NZ Short Stories III* (1975) 71 On the first day of barracks an instructor had made a fool of him over a bren. **1985** SANGSTER *Pathway to Establishment* 164 The 'barracks' week—the School under military administration and usually immediately after Easter—stuttered along from about 1917 with occasional gaps of three or four years until from 1930 (when cadets were 'astonished' to fall under a military regime in the first week) it became a regular feature. **1990** MCKAY *Baxter* 54 Barracks, as cadet training was called, took place early in his first term... Mercifully, war conditions..meant the school was without military uniforms. Over the next three years it was different, with khaki replacing the school uniform during barracks. **1991** *St Patrick's College Silverstream 1931–91 A Diamond Jubilee Magazine* 12 Military training was serious business..with Barracks Week in the first term.

barraconda. [Origin unknown.] HAKE (*Jordanidia solandri*).

1936 *Handbook for NZ* (ANZAAS) 72 *Jordanidia solandri*: Hake (Wellington), kingfish (Otago), barraconda (Auckland and Napier). **1966** DOOGUE & MORELAND *Sea Anglers' Guide* 280 Southern Kingfish... kingfish, hake, barraconda; king barracouta, Tasmanian kingfish (Australia); tikati (Maori). **1981** WILSON *Fisherman's Bible* 201 [The Southern Kingfish is] called Hake in southern fish shops... Tasmanian kingfish, barraconda and 'tikati' (Maori) are other names.

barracouta. Also with much variety of form as **bar(r)acoota, baracouta, barakuta, baricouta, barrac(o)uda, barracouter, barrakuda;** (early) **benecootoo** (?-*n-* erron. for -*rr*-), **boracoota; paracuta.** [Transf. use of W. Indian *barracuda*, *barracouta* a predatory tropical fish: AND 1835.]

1. *Occas. ellipt.* **barra** (see quot. 1970). *Thyrsites atun* (fam. Gempylidae), a slender, commercially important snake-mackerel reaching 120 cm in length, abundant in southern hemisphere coastal waters. See also COUTA, MANGA 1. Contrast KING BARRACOUTA.

1770 PARKINSON *Journal* (1773) 15 Jan. 114 All the coves of this bay teem with fish of various kinds, such as..large breams, small and large barracootas. **1817** NICHOLAS *Voyage NZ* II. 14 The canoes came alongside, bringing us..snappers, bream, parrot-fish, benecootoos. c**1826–27** boracoota [see MANGA 1]. **1837** *Piraki Log* 18 Nov. (1911) 60 Instead of a load of Whale Bone they brought a Cargo of Barakuta. **1840** BEST *Journal* July (1966) 230 Port Nicholson abounds with fish the principal are the Kawa Kawa, Snapper, Harbouker, Barracouta. **1863** WALKER *Jrnl. & Lett.* (ATLTS) 30 June There was a grand procession [in Dunedin] to which the fishermen persisted in being admitted.. represented by five men slightly inebriated in a pony truck decorated with boughs and 'Baracouta' fish. **1872** HUTTON & HECTOR *Fishes NZ* 109 A very common fish..is well known throughout the colonies as the Barracoota (*Thyrsites atun*), which name is no doubt borrowed from the Barracouda Pike of the tropical parts of the Atlantic. **1886** SHERRIN *Handbook Fishes NZ* 12 Dried barracouda—or snook as it is called [at the Cape of Good Hope]. **1890** *Otago Witness* (Dunedin) 30 Jan. 17 The barracouta is in nowise particular about the colour of the wood [of the lure] if in a feeding mood. **1949** BUCK *Coming of Maori* 220 A specialized but rather crude hook..was used for catching barracouda (*Mangā*). **1956** GRAHAM *Treasury NZ Fishes* 310 Barracouta (Manga)... Incredible as it may seem these fish, with their well-armed jaws of sharp fang-like teeth, were usually caught on a slightly curved stick about four feet in length. **1966** SHERRARD *Kaikoura* 31 He had heard Chief Rerewaka of Kaikoura scornfully boast, 'Let this Te Rauparaha come to Kaikoura, and I will rip him open with a barracouta tooth!' **1970** SORENSEN *Nomenclature NZ Fish* 11 *Barracouta..* (b) Suggested commercial name[s]: Sea Pike; Couta; Snoek; Barra Fillets. (c) Other common names: B/couta; Bait. **1993** *Evening Post* (Wellington) 8 July 30 The barracouta is one of the few fish New Zealand anglers will encounter with teeth sharp enough to cut through most monofilament lines with ease.

2. Special Comb. **barracouta bird**, *white-fronted tern* (TERN 2 (10)), **barracoota hook**, a lure for catching barracouta (see quots.); **barracouta season**, see quot. c1835.

1878 HEBERLEY *Autobiogr.* (ATLTS) 35 [Caption c1835] green stone maree Long Club or Mire. **Baracoota hook**. **1845** WAKEFIELD *Adventure NZ* I. 183 This is a piece of red wood with a nail driven through it and bent round in the shape of a hook commonly called a Barracoota hook. **1928** BAUCKE *Manuscript* in Skinner & Baucke *Moriors* (Bishop Museum Memoirs Vol.IX No.5 82) The 'barracouter' hook is a canoe-shaped bit of wood inlaid on the one side with a strip of bright shell of *Haliotis*. **1942** ANDERSEN *Maori Place Names* 284 The Maori used [paua] as the lure of the kahawai or barracouta hooks. **1966** PHILLIPPS *Maori Life & Custom* 25 Barracouta hooks, known as Okooko, were in common use in pre-European times. **c1835** BOULTBEE *Journal* (1986) 75 The **Baracoota** season had now commenced and we had abundance of these fish [1986 *Note*] The barracouta..season ran from November until April.

3. *transf.* In full **barracouta loaf.** Formerly a nominal one-and-a-half pound (510 g) loaf, baked long and narrow in an open-topped tin to give a raised crust which fancifully resembled the (back of a) barracouta fish, and often indented in the middle to enable breaking into two 'quarter' loaves. (But see also quot. 1990.)
1916 MANSFIELD *Aloe* (1982) 121 She had a..plate of butter..on the table before her and a big loaf called a 'barracouta'. **1920** MANSFIELD *Stories* (1984) 250 Alice was making water-cress sandwiches. She had a lump of butter on the table, a barracouta loaf, and the cresses tumbled in a white cloth. **1934** BYCROFT LTD *Bread Baking NZ* (page unknown) Single or straight Barracuda. **1963** FRAME *Snowman Snowman* 15 All the cars huddled in the streets, look like barracuda loaves of bread without any crust, only crisp snow for tasting by the saw-toothed wind. **1972** *Marlborough Express* (Blenheim) 29 Sept. 6 Barracouta loaves of bread will no longer be available in Nelson as from Monday... The withdrawal of barracoutas will mean that no longer will unsliced quarter loaves be available. **1985** MCGILL *G'day Country* 9 I grew up haunting the Matata bakery, offering to help spoon out the tins of barracuda loaves just to enjoy the smell. **1990** BROWNE et al. *Cook's Bread Book* 4 These free standing loaves were sold under such names as French or Turnover, Barracouta (oval with a split centre) and scone (round).

barracuda. [Transf. use of W. Indian *barracuda* a predatory tropical fish.] The sea-pike *Sphyraena novaehollandiae* (fam. Sphyraenidae), a smallish relative of the aggressive tropical barracuda. See also PIKE.
1989 PAULIN et al. *NZ Fish* 206 Barracudas are carnivorous pike-like fishes found in tropical and temperate seas... *Sphyraena novaehollandiae*, barracuda.

barracudina. Any of several slender, predatory, mid-water fishes of the fam. Paralepididae, cosmopolitan in range, esp. *Magnisudis* (formerly *Paralepis*) *prionosa* caught off New Zealand in depths of 600–1000 m.
1956 GRAHAM *Treasury NZ Fishes* 401 Barracudina *Paralepis brevis* Zugmayer. **1982** AYLING *Collins Guide* (1984) 125 The barracudina is a midwater pelagic fish that averages 40 to 50cm in length... These fishes have an elongate body with a pointed snout and moderately large eyes. **1989** PAULIN et al. *NZ Fish* 109 Barracudinas are mid-water fishes common in all oceans.

barragin. *Circus argot.* [Cf. OED *baragouin* jargon, double Dutch 1613–1860: in the form *barrakin* 1851 Mayhew (sole quot.).] Teasing, chaff.
c1872 WHITWORTH *Spangles & Sawdust* 4 Johnny..said to the boss, 'Twig his nibs,' and was immediately shut up by being told to 'cheese his barragin'... [=] Cease his chaff.

barrakuda, var. BARRACOUTA.

barred trout: see TROUT 2 (1).

barrel. [Transf. use of *barrel* a cylindrical container with bulging sides for other objects of similar or tapering shape.] The stem or trunk of a tree.
1878 *NZ Country Jrnl.* II. 394 The barrels of trees average 30ft quite clean. **1888** BARLOW *Kaipara* 153 To secure this it is necessary to climb the [Kauri] tree; but the barrel being of such huge dimensions..it cannot be climbed in the ordinary manner. **1950** p.c. R. Gilberd (Okaihau). 'Stringers' or 'drawers' are drawn out of the barrel of a falling tree.

barrel: see *orange barrel* (ORANGE 3).

barrier pine: see PINE 2 (1).

barrow, *n.*[1] [f. Brit. dial.: see OED *n.*[2]] A castrated boar.
1850 TORLESSE *Papers* (1958) 128 Being out of meat we sallied forth to the chase and caught 2 boars and 1 barrow near the 'Eaikuku'. **1852** in *Canterbury Rhymes* (1866) 16 While both barrows and boars, and sows by the scores Cut their sticks with the wind at their tail. **1949** NEWTON *High Country Days* 193 Barrow: A male pig which has been desexed. Musterers often catch young pigs and perform this operation.

barrow, *n.*[2] In the phr. **to be in the same barrow as,** to be in the same situation (or 'boat') as.
1960 MASTERS *Back-Country Tales* 152 As far as capital for breaking in the land was concerned, Jack was in the same barrow as the rest of the bush settlers; he just didn't have any.

barrow, *v. Shearing.* [Orig unknown: see OED '?cf. Gaelic *bearradh*, shearing, clipping'; AND 1891.] See quots.
1933 *Press* (Christchurch) (Acland Gloss.) 16 Sept. 15 *Barrow*.—To shear or partly shear a sheep for a shearer. 'No barrowing allowed on the board' was at one time a rule which the Shearers' Union got into the award. Boys often finish or begin a sheep for a shearer. **1989** RICHARDS *Pioneer's Life* 44 Each of the other shearers had rousies 'barrowing' for them. The rousies were allowed to shear as learners five minutes before the whistle for their favourite shearer.
Hence **barrowing** *vbl. n.* [AND 1887], the shearing of sheep by learners or shed hands outside official shearing periods, the sheep so shorn being credited to a professional shearer.
1933 [see *v.* above]. **1949** NEWTON *High Country Days* 54 Some of the more energetic [shed hands] tried their hand at shearing, a practice known as 'barrowing'. **1989** *NZ Eng. Newsletter* III. 21 *barrowing*: A term to describe the action of a shed hand who finishes off a sheep for a shearer after the bell has gone for the end of a run.

barrowman. [See BARROW *v.*] One who barrows sheep for a shearer. Also as **barrow-boy,** a lad or learner who helps a shearer by barrowing.
1940 STUDHOLME *Te Waimate* (1954) 129 There were always a certain number of 'barrowmen' and 'learners' on the board... Friends of the shearers, who came on to the board for a chat and, while yarning, frequently shore a few sheep for their pals. **1986** RICHARDS *Off the Sheep's Back* 94 The following day, Jim (later Sir Eruera [Tirikatene]) became my 'barrow-boy' and washed and dried my used gear each run for the privilege of shearing the first sheep.

bar-the-door. Also **bar-the-gate.** [See OED *bar n.*[1] 17 d *bars* in northern dial.] A name for a common 'tag' variety of children's game.
1932 p.c. G. W. Turner Among the [children's] games that I remember [from school near Dannevirke in the 1930s] are two varieties of hide-and-seek, called *All Home*..and *Hawk and Pigeon*, a game sometimes known as *Bar the Gate*. **1971** SHADBOLT *Bullshit & Jellybeans* 25 It was [at Blockhouse Bay school c1950s] Kingaseeny (or Bulldog, King Dick or Bar-the-Door for those outside Auckland) at lunchtime, rugby on Wednesday, the gang after school.

base. WW1, WW2. [f. *base* the place from which a commander conducts military operations.] In special Comb. **base-bludger, base-walloper** (often *ellipt.* **walloper**), **base-wallower** (alterations of milit. *base-wallah*), contemptuous names for an officer serving at base, occas. transferred to other (alleged) 'layabouts'.
1959 SLATTER *Gun in My Hand* 92 Nobody put up stripes in our outfit. That was for **base bludgers**. **1935** STRONG in Partridge *Slang Today* 287 He is a shrewd head, but I think he would give a man a fair go although he is a **base-walloper**. **1937** PARTRIDGE *Dict. Slang* 36 *base wallah*. A soldier employed behind the lines..1915-18... The New Zealanders preferred *base walloper*. **1944** *NZEF Times* 14 Aug. 4 The rest of you wallopers can sit around in tanks and tents and ACV's all day. **1947** DAVIN *For Rest of Our Lives* 147 'The working class can kiss my arse, I've got a bludger's job at last,' sang Smithy to the tune of the Red Flag. 'All the boys sing it whenever they pass Bludger's Hill... Makes the base-wallahs mad'... 'Almost makes a man want to be a base walloper... A nice quiet life. Nothing to do except get up in the morning and have the shaving water [etc.]. **1959** SLATTER *Gun in My Hand* 154 I soon wangled my way to platoon headquarters as platoon runner. Bloody base walloper the others said. **1947** DAVIN *Gorse Blooms Pale* 193 'Good old Plugger,' said Alec. 'Too old to be anything but a **base-wallower** himself but never lets the fighting-man down.'
Hence **base-walloping** *ppl. a.*
c1945 *Sixes & Sevens* (Troopship magazine) 16 'Why! You two-timin', back-stroppin', base-wallopin'...'

bash, *n.*[1]

1. In the phr. **on the bash** [Ayto & Simpson 1 a 'Scottish and NZ'; see also OED *n.* 2.], on the spree, on the booze.
1945 HENDERSON *Gunner Inglorious* 182 When you get back, we'll..go on a dirty great bash together, won't we, Eddie? **1951** in *Listener Short Stories* (1978) 20 'I know,' I said, 'but if you go on the bash and start abusing these people, they'll lock you in the cooler'. **1959** SHADBOLT *New Zealanders* (1986) 156 Jack and I went on the bash every Saturday... Drink all day. **1964** MORRIESON *Came a Hot Friday* (1981) 122 'Where you been?' said Bishop angrily. 'On the bash?' **1988** MCGILL *Dict. Kiwi Slang* 79 *on the bash* an alcoholic drinking bout, particularly in New Zealand and Scotland; eg 'I feel ghastly. I was on the bash most of the night.'

2. A booze-session or drinking bout; a party.
1948 *Landfall* 6 June 111 What he spent on beer week-nights would total no more than what most jokers spent on their Saturday bashes. **1950** in *Some Other Country* (1984) 98 'Hell, he has had a bash,' said Cliff. 'Spent the whole night on the tiles, eh?' **1966** TURNER *Eng. Lang. Austral. & NZ* 132 In New Zealand, the term *bash* for a party where drink is the chief attraction is heard (or was, some years ago among Wellington students). **1984** MANTELL *Murder in Vain* 164 They tell me Breck held his liquor pretty well. Had to be really tanked up to show any signs. That sounds

like a bash. **1994** *Dominion* (Wellington) 24 Nov. 35 TV3 celebrates its fifth birthday..but plans for a big bash have had to be put on hold.

bash, *n.*²

1. *Shearing.* [Spec. use of *bash* a wild blow.] A wild uncontrolled shearing stroke (cf. BLOW *n.*³). Also **basher** *n.*, one whose shearing style admits 'bashing'.
 1955 BOWEN *Wool Away* 155 Bash. A wild uncontrolled blow by a shearer. Basher. A shearer who uses the above type of blows. **1982** *Agric. Gloss.* (MAF) 52 *Bash*: Wild uncontrolled blow by a shearer.

2. Usu. *pl.*, cane strokes as a means of secondary school discipline.
 1984 17 F E54 Pakuranga Coll. 23 Bashes [school discipline]

bash, *v.* [Transf. use of *bash* to strike.]

1. Common in boys' speech, and in a weakened sense applied esp. to corporal punishment in schools by strapping or caning.
 1951 16+ M 26 Marlborough C. 30A Bash [M7], bash up **1951** 14–15 M 33 Wellington H.S. 30A Bash [M7] **1953** 13–16 M A1 Thames DHS 30 Bash [M18] Bash up [M3] **1975** in *NZ Short Stories* (1984) 96 I used to bash you up. Give you the old Chinese burn. **1984** 16 F E4 Pakuranga Coll. 30A Bash [F3] **1984** 14 F E130 Wgton Girls C. 30A Bash; bash up

2. Applied to rough travel (1906 quot. poss. formed f. *knock about*), esp. in tramping to rough and difficult travel through scrub, up river-beds, etc., demanding vigour in making progress. Cf. *boulder bash* (BOULDER 2), *bush-bash* (BUSH-BASHING).
 1906 *Truth* 6 Jan. 5 I've bashed about the land some. **1958** MASON *Tararua* Sept. 30 'Push', 'bash', 'crash' occur pretty frequently in describing progress in accounts of tramping trips, and tell a tale of scrub and tangled bush. **1971** *Listener* 19 Apr. 56 He sidled up the spur but he got off the discs and had to bash through the lawyers and windfalls. **1978** *Manawatu Tramping Club Jubilee* 71 We would stream bash or plod our way up the ridges. *Ibid.* 90 We dropped into the Arahura River valley and bashed over some of the biggest boulders I ever want to see.

3. bash up, a var. of *knock up*, to build, make (quickly or inexpertly).
 1945 HENDERSON *Gunner Inglorious* 163 Take p.-o.-w. duff for example. Everyone had bashed up a duff for himself at one stage or another.

basic wage. [AND 1911.] A national minimum wage set according to age and gender.
 1936 *Tomorrow* 17 Mar. 310 The fixing of the basic wage by the Court of Arbitration at £3/16/- for men at 21 years old and £1/16/- for women has provoked much adverse comment. **1937** *King Country Chronicle* 29 Apr. 5 No good purpose would be served by attacking the basic wage. **1945** *NZPD* CCLXXII. 463 The Court of Arbitration..also found that an adult female worker should have a basic wage of £1 16s. **1951** *PSA Jrnl.* Mar. 9 The wage level will remain below what it ought to be, and this is particularly true of those on or near the basic wage.

basin, *n.*¹ [Used elsewhere but freq. in rural NZ use esp. among high-country people: see OED *n.* 13.] A depression or small, open, usu. rounded, valley in a hillside.
 1864 BARRINGTON *Diary* 27 Mar. in Taylor *Early Travellers* (1959) 404 This place forms a basin with low ranges and made hills. **1882** HAY *Brighter Britain* I. 179 An abrupt succession of ranges, gullies, and basins. **1907** *TrNZI* XXXIX. 73 I went out to the tops: in a small basin under the top..facing a rocky country that we called 'skay', there was a mob of sheep snowed in. **1933** *Press* (Christchurch) (Acland Gloss.) 9 Sept. 15 *Basin*.—Open valley near the top of a hill; all the very highest tops of a run are sometimes called 'the basins'. **1947** NEWTON *Wayleggo* 153 *Basin*: a depression or basin in a hillside. Most creeks originate in a basin. **1958** *Tararua* Sept. 41 From the top basin we sidled up tiresome scree. **1978** JARDINE *Shadows on Hill* 5 We'll hunt the basin back out to you, so keep quiet. **1981** PINNEY *Early N. Otago Runs* 53 Even though there was a thaw in early May, the snow returned and lay deep on the tops and halfway down the basins.

basin, *n.*² Usu. cap., in full **the Basin (Reserve).** A Wellington municipal sports ground formed from a reclaimed tidal basin.
 [**1841** *Mathew to Hobson* 20 Oct. in *GBPP 1842 (No.569)* 185 The second [Wellington reserve] was intended for a basin, an idea suggested probably by the swampy character of the ground around it; but besides that, such a project is of very questionable advantage.] **1910** *Truth* 2 Apr. 6 If the Wellington Cricket Association has any sort of a surplus, it should at once indulge in the luxury of a more up-to-date scoring board at the Basin. **1982** *Dominion* (Wellington) 20 Feb. 9 Will New Zealand sink at the Basin? Full coverage of the final day of the Rothman's International One Day Cricket Series.

basket.

1. Special Comb. **basket social** [see OED basket *n.* B 2; DARE chiefly Midwest, Northwest, 1895 (=box social)], see quot. 1955.
 1918 *Hawkes Bay Herald* 18 July 8 18 July 5 A basket social and dance..for Maori soldiers..turned out an unqualified success. **1921** *Ensign* (Mataura) in Barry *In Lee of Hokonuis* (1966) 363 A well attended basket social was held..on Friday evening. **1955** BOSWELL *Dim Horizons* 153 A basket social took the form of a dance [in Northland before WW1], with an auction of supper baskets. Each girl would make a pretty basket and fill it with good things for supper. When supper-time came, the baskets were auctioned from the stage and keen was the rivalry and competition for some of the baskets, young blades emptying their pockets and often dipping into their bank accounts in trying to out-bid their rivals. **1986** OWEN & PERKINS *Speaking for Ourselves* 150 A common method of raising money [for a country family in need] was called a 'basket social'. A hall would be used for the function, and the people of the district would be invited to bring along baskets... In the basket its maker put a supper... They would then be auctioned, and the purchaser of the basket would have the pleasure and the honour of having supper with the provider of the basket. **1987** BATISTICH *Sing Vila* 146 Basket socials were always a stir [in Northland c1920s]... The baskets were put up for auction just before the supper waltz; highest bidder got basket and girl.

2. In the phr. **Ladies bring a basket,** see LADY 1 a.

3. basket fungus, see FUNGUS 2 (1).

basking shark: see SHARK 2 (1).

bass. Also **bass groper,** and with a modifier **black bass, sea bass.** *Polyprion moeone* (fam. Percichthyidae), a large food fish often confused with and marketed as HAPUKU. See also MOEONE.
 1913 *TrNZI* XLV. 215 The fishermen who go out to the 100–150-fathom water off [Otago] frequently catch..a huge groper, which they call 'bass groper', and which seems to be specifically distinct from the ordinary hapuka. They say it is common off Wellington, and is there known as 'black bass'. **1928** *TrNZI* LVIII. 126 After examination of numerous hapuku and bass in our local markets my conclusion is that we have in the indigenous bass a new species..to be known as *moeone*, the present name in common use among the Maori. **1947** POWELL *Native Animals NZ* 69 Most of the very large [hapuku or groper] are from 100 fathoms or more and are a different species, the Bass, *P[olyprion] moeone*, distinguished by having a much larger head and a deeper body. **1957** PARROTT *Sea Angler's Fishes* 169 Bass... Black Bass; Bass Groper. **1972** DOAK *Fishes* 35 Bass... This fish used to be considered the deepwater form of the hapuku, but it is quite a separate species. **1985** BINNEY *Long Lives the King* 52 'Sea-bass; caught the bugger out at Awatuna Mouth on Sunday,' said Les. **1986** PAUL *NZ Fishes* 83 Bass... Sometimes (and correctly) called bass groper.

bass groper: see BASS.

bastard, *attrib.*

1. In the names of plants and animals which resemble (but often cannot match the qualities of) their namesakes; or, occas., have displeasing or nasty ('bastardly') qualities (e.g. *bastard-grass*), see: BIRCH 3 (1), COD 2 (1), GRASS 2 (3), SANDALWOOD 2, TRUMPETER 2 (1).

2. *Goldmining.* **bastard quartz,** see quot.
 1875 *AJHR H-3* 31 A small, shallow excavation in trachyte..which is here full of silicious segregations of irregular outline..of a quartz-like character and bluish-white colour ('bastard quartz', in miners' phrase).

bat, *n.*¹ Any of three species (see quot. 1990) of native flying mammals of the order Chiroptera: *Chalinolobus tuberculatus* (fam. Vespertilionidae), *Mystacina tuberculata* and *Mystacina robusta* (fam. Mystacinidae), often distinguished by various defining words. See also PEKAPEKA.
 1773 FORSTER *Resolution Journal* 18 May (1982) II. 283 George drew the Shag and a new *Bat*, which we got. **1838** [see PEKAPEKA]. **1842** GRAY *Fauna* in Dieffenbach *Travels in NZ* (1843) II. 181 As yet, no terrestrial beast, except bats, has been found wild in these Islands. **1867** [see PEKAPEKA]. **1872** *TrNZI* IV. 184 Only two species of bats are at present known to inhabit New Zealand, and both of these are found anywhere else. **1894** *TrNZI* XXVI. 220 We have two species, which are familiarly known by the names of the short-eared bat (*Chalinolobus tuberculatus*), and the long-eared bat (*Mystacina tuberculata*). **1899** DOUGLAS in *Mr Explorer Douglas* (1957) 224 Rabbits, ferrets and stoats had their passage paid by a far seeing paternal government, but there is no evidence that the bat was imported, so he ought to be proud of himself. **1921** *NZJST* IV. 140 Examples of the short-tailed bat so far recorded have been taken in widely separated localities. **1947** POWELL *Native Animals of New Zealand* 92 Our only native land mammals are..small species of bats... They are known respectively as the Long-tailed Bat and the Short-tailed Bat. Alternatively, they could be referred to as the 'Short-eared' and the 'Long-eared'. **1959** *Forest & Bird* 131 8 We could see it crawl up the outside of his coat sleeve, rather in the manner of a spider. This is..one of the distinguishing features of the New Zealand short-tailed bat..for it may feed off non-flying insects on trees, as well as catching moths, etc., on the wing. **1966** *Encycl. NZ* I. 169 Long-tailed Bat... [This bat] is easily recognised, when caught, by the 1½ in. tail which is almost as long as the rest of the animal, and is included in a large tail-membrane which

stretches between the legs. *Ibid.* 170 *Short-tailed bat...* It is recognised..by its long and rather pointed ears, by its prominent nostrils, and by its short stumpy tail which projects for about ½ in. from the upper surface of the small, leathery tail membrane. **1984** *NZJ Ecol* VII. 10 The three bats are small... *Mystacina* has a broad diet of ground and flying arthropods, nectar, fruits and pollen; but *Chalinolobus* is exclusively insectivorous. **1990** *Handbook NZ Mammals* 117 *New Zealand long-tailed bat...* Also called New Zealand short-eared bat..pekapeka. *Ibid.* 122 The small endemic family of New Zealand short-tailed bats contains only one genus with two species; until recently only one species was described. *Ibid.* 123 *Lesser short-tailed bat Mystacina tuberculata...* Also called northern short-tailed bat, New Zealand long-eared bat..pekapeka. *Ibid.* 131 *Greater short-tailed bat Mystacina robusta...* Also called southern short-tailed bat, Stewart Island short-tailed bat..pekapeka.

bat, *n.*² *Two-up.* [Transf. use of *bat* a flattish implement for striking a ball.] KIP 1.
 1912 *Truth* 20 Jan. 7 Some of them [*sc.* labourers] have engaged in the simple yet sinful process of tossing two bright copper pennies, with a bit of wood, popularly known as 'the bat' or 'the kip'. **1917** *Chron. NZEF* 16 May 137 The spinner's eyes began to gleam.. The big brown paw that held the 'bat' Was trembling like a leaf.

bat, *n.*³ *pl.* [A shortened form of *pl.* DINGBATS, poss. infl. by *bats* eccentric.] In the phr. **in the bats**, drunk; in the DTs.
 1921 LORD *Ballads Bung 'Stunology'* (1976) We say a man is..'on a bender,' 'in the bats' if he don't pull His heroic self together.

batch, var. BACH.

batfish. [Named from a fancied resemblance to the mammalian bat.] Applied in New Zealand to at least two unrelated fishes which in some way resemble a bat, *Pteraclis velifera* (fam. Bramidae) (with very large membranous fins), the WINGFISH q.v. and *Halieutaea maoria* (fam. Ogcocephalidae) (which is superficially like a crawling bat). **a.** *Pteraclis velifera.*
 1927 PHILLIPPS *Bibliogr. NZ Fishes* (1971) 35 *Pteraclis velifera...* Batfish. **1942** *TrRSNZ* LXXI. 242 *Pteraclis velifera...* Batfish. **1967** NATUSCH *Animals NZ* 221 Family Pteraclidae is represented by the extraordinary batfish.
 b. *Halieutaea maoria.*
 1956 GRAHAM *Treasury NZ Fishes* 413 Batfish *Halieutaea maoria.* **1984** AYLING *Collins Guide* (1984) 137 Batfishes are so grotesquely shaped that they do not appear to be fishes at all... The limb-like jointed pectoral fins are set at the hind corners of the head and are used to 'walk' slowly across the bottom. **1989** PAULIN et al. *NZ Fish* 135 Batfishes are rare, bottom-dwelling..fishes that walk on the sea-floor with their pectoral and pelvic fins.

bathers' itch. Also occas. **swimmers' itch.** A skin irritation first recorded from Lake Wanaka in 1944 by W.V. Macfarlane who attributed it to the larvae of the schistosome *Cercaria longicauda* n. sp. See also *duck itch* (DUCK 3 a).
 [**1944** *NZ Med. J.* XLIII. 136 Some twenty years ago it became increasingly recognised that swimmers in Lake Wanaka suffered an itch and urticarial wheal [*sic*] some time after leaving the water.] **1967** NATUSCH *Animals NZ* 50 People bathing in some of our larger lakes sometimes get 'bathers' itch', caused by a free-swimming stage of a blood fluke or schistosome. The intermediate host is in this case the native freshwater snail... The adult blood fluke cannot live in man, so the itch is the only harm done. **1982** PEAT *Detours* 209 But..what about..the dreadful 'Swimmers' Itch' which affects summer holidaymakers [at Lake Wanaka].

bathing togs: see TOGS.

Bathurst burr. [AND 1853: 'f. the name of a town in central New South Wales.'] Usu. first init. cap. A tall S. American weed introduced from Australia, *Xanthium spinosum* (fam. Asteraceae), having fruiting burrs covered in hooked prickles, a troublesome weed in sheep country. Cf. BIDDY-BID 1 b, BURR.
 1879 *Auckland Weekly News* 3 May 8 Recently reference was made to the existence of the Bathurst burr in Auckland. **1896** *Otago Witness* (Dunedin) 23 Jan. 36 'Biddybids detract very materially from the value of the wool... They are not quite so bad as the Bathurst burr, but are certainly in the same category. **1902** *Brett's Colonists' Guide* 242 Bathurst burr.—A shrubby annual from 9in. to 3ft. high... The seed is..thickly studded with hooked prickles. Believed to be a native of Chili. **1928** REES *Wild Wild Heart* 58 'What are those things in the wool of the sheep?' 'Bathurst burr'... 'What the children call biddy-biddy?' 'Yes.' **1982** *Dominion* (Wellington) 16 Feb. 4 The noxious weed bathurst bur, considered extremely dangerous to pasture could have been growing on a Richmond farm for two years before its discovery last week.

batt. [Extended use of Brit. *bat(t)* a felted mass of fur, etc. used in hat-making: see OED *n.*¹ 12.] Also often as **pink batt** (a proprietary name, f. the usual colour), a thick rectangular piece of matted fibre or fibreglass, usu. intended for insulation of buildings.
 1969 *Evening Post* (Wellington) 3 Apr. 16 [Advt] Our fuel bills were monsters until we got the Batts. Batts in the attic cut fuel bills 40%. **1974** *NZ Patent Office Jrnl No.1143* 11 Nov. Batts 105507 [filed] 27 August 1973..insulating materials. New Zealand Fibre Glass Limited. **1985** *NZ Patent Office Jrnl* [pending] 28 Jan. Pink batts 156731 [filed] 28 January 1985 in the name of A.H.I. Operations Ltd for 'insulating materials'. **1985** *Listener* 13 July 22 So we built a big oven. Built it cheaply out of 4 x 2 and fibreglass batts. **1988** MACRAE *Awful Childhoods* 154 'They had bales of batts lying around at one stage,' Chris said. **1992** *Listener* 24 Feb. 37 [Advt] Just as new Pink Batts control heat, new Sound Barrier reduces sound.

batten. [Spec. uses of *batten* a strip of wood: see OED *n.*¹ 1, 2, the general sense being recorded from 1844 in NZ.] Orig. and usu. a light piece of wood, but also more recently a strip of steel, wire, chain or plastic, used to strengthen wire fences, or to keep the wires at equal distances apart; DROPPER *n.*¹ Also in the phr. **batten and wire (fence).**
 c**1875** [see DROPPER *n.*¹]. **1883** *Brett's Colonists' Guide* 77 This will place [posts] 16½ feet apart, and then they require an equal number of battens or stakes placed alternately. **1895** *Fencing Act in Settler's Handbook NZ* (1902) 161 Batten and wire fence..with one or more wires..battens either driven securely into the ground and securely stapled, or intertwined in wires in an upright position. **1913** CARR *Country Work* 19 In the North Island the bulk [of fences] is constructed with wooden posts and battens. c**1924** ANTHONY *Me & Gus* (1977 Gus Tomlins) 14 Then he ran to a seven-wire fence and tore a batten off it with a single jerk. **1955** WILSON *Land of My Children* 177 They were scientific, too, these fences... Six posts to the chain, six battens between each. **1961** [see STRAINER-POST]. **1988** *Dominion* (Wellington) 23 July 8 The typical new..farm fence is a glittering grid of gleaming and galvanised No 8 wire, with battens and strainers ranked like troops at a passing-out parade. **1991** *Dominion* (Wellington) 9 Feb. 9 Liefting picked up a bundle of battens in one hand and a chainsaw in the other.

 Hence **batten** *v. trans.* and *absol.*, to fix (battens) horizontally to a stake-and-batten fence, or vertically to a wire fence.
 1882 HAY *Brighter Britain* I. 191 After the stakes were set up we had to batten them together. We bought..battens—rough outside boards split up, and the like—for next to nothing, at the Wairoa sawmills. **1959** MIDDLETON *The Stone* 51 When all the posts were in and we had strained-up the wires, we started battening. I would hold my axe against the backs of the battens and Dan would drive staples into the tough honeysuckle.

 Hence **battening up** *vbl. n.*, the stapling of battens to a wire fence.
 1981 *Listener* 21 Mar. 67 The 'battening up' was done next day. At 6.30am I heard the sound of a hammer.

battery. *Goldmining.*
 1. [Used elsewhere but freq. and significant in NZ goldmining use: AND 1858.] A crushing-mill consisting of a group of stampers or stamps for crushing (auriferous) quartz.
 1868 *Thames Miner's Guide* 93 Kurunui Battery..of six stampers, and one stamper specimen battery with Berdans at the end of tables to grind the tailings. **1882** HAY *Brighter Britain* II. 279 The next objects of interest are the quartz-crushing batteries... The smallest has four stampers, and the largest sixty-two. **1894** *NZ Official Year-book* 369 The ore..when brought to the surface, is committed to 'batteries' or crushing-mills, where the stone is stamped or ground into powder. **1907** *NZGeol.SB (NS)* No.4 112 The mill on the Hauraki claim consists of a fifteen-stamper battery, Wilfley, vanner, berdans, and accessories. **1935** BLYTH ed. *Gold Mining Year Book* 11 *Battery*: Any number, more than one, of stamp mills would constitute a battery. **1963** AUDLEY *No Boots for Mr. Moehau* 28 A great dream..that golden enterprise, with forty head of stampers thudding at the battery day and night. **1985** HUNT *I'm Ninety-five* 29 Then sometimes of an evening we'd all meet up at the boarding house, right near the gold battery.

 2. *Special Comb.* **battery-box,** a box-like receptacle in which ore is crushed by the 'battery' and the metal amalgamated with mercury; **battery hand,** one who works at a crushing-mill.
 1868 *Thames Miner's Guide* 93 The battery has three stampers in each box, double cams, quicksilver placed in **battery boxes,** grating perpendicular, with round holes. **1911** *Maoriland Worker* 7 July 13 I want to say, though, that none but the **battery hands** [out of the Waihi miners] signed it.

battik, var. PATIKI.

battle-axe. An early name for a Maori weapon, usu. MERE; occas., TEWHATEWHA.
 1774 FORSTER *Resolution Jrnl.* 15 Mar. (1982) III. 470 They are short but almost shaped like the N.Z. battle Axes. **1777** FORSTER *Voyage Round World* I. 137 Standing on the shore we perceived one of the natives... He stood with a club or battle-axe in his hand. **1807** SAVAGE *Some Acc. of NZ* 27 (Griffiths Collect.) He is attended by..dauntless warriors, armed with spears and battle-axes, and decorated with war-mats. **1873** *TrNZI* V. 26 On presenting the conquerors with a greenstone

battle axe (the *mere pounamu*), they were again allowed to be called a tribe. **1913** [see SPEAR *n.*¹]. **1936** LAMBERT *Pioneering Reminisc. Old Wairoa* 45 With a famous greenstone battle-axe he killed Kiwi.

battle of the Wazza: see WAZZA.

battler.

1. *Obs.* [AND 1898.] A street-walker.
1908 *Truth* 18 Jan. 6 The grim constable stated..that whether Lady Malkin was married or not, she was one of the most persistent battlers in Upper Willis and Ghuznee-streets, and both women were known to the police as Magdalenes of an unrepentant sort. **1909** *Ibid.* 13 Mar. 1 Mary Collins is a hard-faced, Christchurch battler, who serves as a sort of human football for the local Harvey Duffs, who shoot her between the gaol ports of the booby hatch on the slightest provocation.

2. [AND 1896: in NZ use much earlier than the quots. suggest.] One who doggedly or courageously struggles or battles on against odds. Cf. TOILER.
1943 BENNETT *English in NZ* in *Amer. Speech* XVIII. 88 A *toiler* or *battler* is a hard, conscientious worker—both are used with a shade of condescension. **1966** TURNER *Eng. Lang. Austral. & NZ* 144 In New Zealand..*battler* is used for a person who puts up a hard fight against adverse conditions without giving in, and is thus a general term of praise. **1972** *Truth* 19 Sept. 7 A battler all his life..but now he's going broke... It would be a tragedy if, after a lifetime of effort, he is thrown on the scrapheap. **1986** *Evening Post* (Wellington) 4 Sept. 9 'Now the old battlers of Kainga will be able to own their own flush loo like every other New Zealander,' he said.

batwing. Also **batwing tent.** See quot. 1896.
1896 HARPER *Pioneer Work* 50 Our camp has not yet been described, and..it is the simplest and best form of shelter for a party of two... It is an invention of Douglas's, and we call it a 'batwing'... We..could not afford to take..a weighty camp. We therefore pitch an ordinary 6 ft. by 8 ft. canvas tent, on a ridge pole, with an 8 ft. by 10 ft. fly six inches above it; and cut the tent in half along the ridge, and taking away one half, leave the other half standing. This is just large enough to allow two men to lie 'heads and tails'. [The side is left open.] **1935** MURRAY in *Mr Explorer Douglas* (1957) 39 [Douglas's] camping equipment then [c1880s], as ever, was a batwing tent, one blanket sewn into a bag... [1957 *note*] The batwing tent was a shelter devised by Douglas. It allowed a fire to be lit under the lee of a fly.

bay.

1. [Cf. AND 1841 (for Botany Bay).] As **the Bay**, used locally to refer to various popularly known 'bays'. **a.** The Bay of Islands.
1831 WILLIAMS *Early Jrnls.* 20 Aug. (1961) 189 Capn. Dean..mentioned that the Brig at Kororarika was in a state of mutiny... Told him that he was in the Bay we should not interfere. **1843** CHAPMAN *NZ Portfolio* 126 The Bay was for many years the resort of escaped convicts and runaway sailors. **1855** *Richmond-Atkinson Papers* (1960) I. 176 [Dr Montgomery and C.W. Richmond] had a long korero about New Zealand and the Bay, where the Doctor has been quartered for 5 years. **1876** *TrNZI* VIII. 428 Mr. Stewart said the opinions commonly entertained as to the relative advantages of Newcastle and Bay of Islands coal were clearly erroneous. In many respects the Bay coal was the best of the two.

Hence **Bay-of-Islander** (also **Bay of Islander**) *hist.*, a resident, Maori or Pakeha, of the Bay of Islands.

1828 WILLIAMS *Early Jrnls.* 15 Mar. (1961) 111 At 6 p.m. letters arrived..with most distressing news that considerable fighting had taken place with the natives there and the Bay of Islanders. **1835** YATE *NZ* (1970) 151 The Bay-of-Islanders have latterly introduced iron.

b. Orig. Hawke Bay, then (usu.) the Hawke's Bay province or district. (Now esp. used in giving a concise and easily vocalized identity to Hawke's Bay representative sports teams.)
1885 *NZJSc.* II. 485 The first specimen was..killed by whalers at Port Mahia, at the north head of the Bay. **1927** *Wairarapa Times-Age* in Bromby *Eyewitness Hist.* (1985) 150 The Bay owed its win principally to the superiority of their forwards. **1952** *The Standard* (Wellington) 8 Oct. 4 The Bay teams. **1959** SLATTER *Gun in My Hand* 170 Picking fruit up the Bay and forking peas into the cannery. **1973** FERNANDEZ *Tussock Fever* 14 A mountain of potatoes, kumara brought from the Bay, peas from the station garden. **1989** *Dominion* (Wellington) 23 Sept. 10 [Caption] Man dies in Bay car crash. A man was killed..just north of Waipukurau. **1992** ANDERSON *Portrait Artist's Wife* 127 Nelson had played hooker for the Bay in the twenties, the golden days of Hawke's Bay rugby.

c. Often *pl.* as **the Bays**, the Golden Bay-Motueka district in the nw. South Island, used esp. of sports teams.
1970 SLATTER *On the Ball* 132 In the 1967 season Marlborough went to Motueka to play the Bays [for the Seddon Shield] and to Greymouth to play the West Coast.

d. The Bay of Plenty.
1987 *National Radio* 'Morning Report' 23 Mar. Housing is still a problem in parts of the Bay [after the recent earthquake].

2. *Whaling.* Special Comb. **bay fishery**, **bay fishing** *hist.*, see *bay whaling*; **bay whale** *obs.* [by back-formation from **bay-whaling**: AND 1820], the southern right whale (see WHALE 2 (14)); **bay whaler**, a person [AND 1867], or a ship [AND 1913 McNab], engaged in bay whaling (but see also quot. 1882); **bay whaling** *hist.* [AND 1837], whaling carried out in coastal waters from a base on shore or often on an anchored whaling-ship; also *attrib.* (see also *shore whaling* (SHORE 1)).
1838 BALLENY *Journal 'Eliza Scott'* 10 Dec. in McNab *Old Whaling Days* (1913) 464 We have seen some marks of visitors [in Chalky Inlet] but whether natives or whites for the **bay fishery**..I do not know. **1842** *Lett. from Settlers* (1843) 32 [Wellington, 5 Sept.] Up to this time, the **bay fishing** has been almost a failure, and unless the off-shore fishing has been more fortunate, you need not look for much oil. **1947** CLARK in Belshaw *NZ* 32 Fur seals and **bay whales** (i.e., the right whales) which once frequented the island are now virtually extinct. **1882** ANDERSON *Chatham Islands* 25 The curse..of the island then was what Mr. Hunt calls 'the **Bay whalers**', a set of men from the Bay of Islands. **1905** BAUCKE *White Man Treads* 36 This [immorality] was not true of olden days—not until the Maori had noticed how the skin-bleached newcomer, the lawless pakeha bay-whaler, conducted his festivities with limitless rum. **1913** MCNAB *Old Whaling Days* 110 The *Lucy Ann*, as a bay whaler instead of a trader, began to seek for fresh places for the pursuit of whales and sailed on 1st June [1835] for Port Cooper. **1971** *New Zealand's Heritage* I. 427 Mostly the bay whalers operated from shore stations, which saved the cost of a ship. **1982** MORTON *Whale's Wake* 141 They seldom sought right whales, the usual prey of bay whalers. **1837** RHODES *Jrnl. Barque 'Australian'* 6 May (1954) 102 The season also would be far advanced for **Bay**

Whaling. 1853 EARP *NZ* 95 The Wellington settlers..were ardent followers of the whale fishery, carried on chiefly on the coasts of the northern and middle island by means of boats—a method technically called 'bay-whaling'. **1866** HUNT *Chatham Is.* 60 The old bay whaling parties have long since ceased to trouble the Islands. **1882** HAY *Brighter Britain* II. 230 There are eight kinds of whales, so bay-whaling is carried on round the coast. **1905** BAUCKE *White Man Treads* 75 An old-time bay whaling station consisted..of at least two boats, with their crew of six men each. The headsman, or mate, four ordinary oarsmen, and the harpooner, or 'boat-steerer,' who pulled the bow-oar, and drove in the harpoon, and who, when the whale had been struck and 'fastened on,' went aft and steered the boat, while the mate took his place, and by repeated lance-thrusts killed it. **1917** HOWES *Marlborough Sounds* 8 Many of these whalers settled on the coast and confined themselves to bay whaling, selling the oil and bone to visiting ships. **1933** OMMANEY *Whaling in NZ* in *Discovery Rep.* VII. 243 Much of the Right whale industry was carried on by the method known as 'bay whaling'. This branch of the fishery derived its name from the Right whales' habit of entering shallow bays and inlets of the coast for the purpose of..calving. **1949** MCLINTOCK *Hist. Otago* 66 The female or cow whales, accompanied by their young calves, appeared in such numbers in the sheltered bays that the whaling vessels were accustomed to anchor at these favoured spots and carry on the fishing under less arduous conditions than on the open sea. Under such circumstances 'bay whaling' originated. **1954** in Rhodes *Jrnl. Barque 'Australian'* (1954) xvi The pursuit in coastal waters of black whales was known as 'bay whaling', and the procedure followed was for the ships to lie at anchor in a convenient harbour or bay, sending out their boats to cruise in nearby waters for 'fish'. **1959** MCLINTOCK *Descr. Atlas* 5 A more positive step to permanent settlement came with the establishment of 'bay whaling' stations at points along the coastline of both islands. **1982** MORTON *Whale's Wake* 17 From 1831 to 1837 Cloudy Bay..attracted..ships, which anchored and whaled within the bay in competition with local shore stations. By 1837 this 'bay whaling' had spread south to Banks Peninsula, and to Otago and Bluff harbours. *Ibid.* 230 The writer has adopted as logical a terminological distinction between 'bay whaling', which is whaling from anchored ships in bays, and 'shore whaling', which is whaling from a base on shore. It is a distinction not always made and indeed there was a major overlap in technique.

bayonet grass. Also **bayonette-grass**. [Fig. from its sharp-pointed bayonet- or spear-like leaves: see OED *bayonet* 5 *Spanish bayonet*: a species of *Yucca*, 1865.] A now rare name for SPEARGRASS 1.
1860 in Butler *First Year* (1863) v 72 The Spaniard (spear-grass or bayonet-grass) 'piked us intil the bane'. **1868** bayonette-grass [see SPANIARD 2 (1)]. **1879** HAAST *Geol. Canterbury & Westland* 25 They formed with the gigantic *Aciphylla Colensoi*, the Spaniard or Bayonet grass..which..most severely punished man and horse. **1899** KIRK *Students' Flora* 207 Spaniard, Bayonet-grass. **1946** *JPS* LV. 158 *Taramea*, a plant..spear-grass, bayonet-grass, spaniard: a hill and mountain plant from whose spiny blades the Maori by heat and torsion extracted a valued scent.

bay villa: see VILLA 1 b.

beach.

I. [In various spec. uses of *beach* sea-beach.] **1. a.** In New Zealand the usual word for the *seaside*, as a place of enjoyment or recreation. (In early whaling use, often also a place of work.)

[**1769** Cook *Journals* 16 Nov. (1955) I. 204 We found it first in small lumps upon the Sea beach.] **1831** Bell *Let.* Nov. in McNab *Old Whaling Days* (1913) 9 If the fishing is to be carried on by a shore party, the try pots and huts are erected on the beach. **1843** *Lett. from New Plymouth* (1968) 7 My brother Peter was on the beach waiting for me. **1910** *Truth* 16 Apr. 4 It is horrid to contemplate a young lady, who regards the beach as sacred to the uses of a Lovers' Paradise, coming home from church and seeing a surf-bather's bare feet as he toddled home to kai. **1934** Scanlan *Winds of Heaven* 181 Another day he would rush them all off..down to the beach for a picnic and a swim. **1951** Frame in *Some Other Country* (1984) 102 The Beach. Why wasn't everyone going to the Beach? **1965** Sargeson *Memoirs of Peon* 16 I would..be handed over to some family friend for a visit to the zoo.., the pantomime, or in summertime the beach. **1988** *New Women's Fiction* 33 It's a beauty day; I thought we might go to the beach.

b. *Hist.* As **The Beach**, an early name for any of several various localities. (a) The sea-front of early Wellington, later to become Lambton Quay. Also *attrib.*

1841 *NZ Gaz. & Spectator* (Wellington) 6 Mar. quoted in Richards *Whaling & Sealing Chatham Is.* (1982) 22 A person calling himself Captain Richards..has beguiled and smuggled from the beach, four to five young females to carry with him to the Chatham Islands. **1850** Godley *Letters* 27 Aug. (1951) 94 What is called 'the Beach'; that is the long [Wellington] street (about a mile and a half)..that has houses only on one side and runs along by the sea. **1885** *Wanganui Chronicle* 8 Sept. in Arnold *New Zealand's Burning* 193 The average Wellingtonian recommend[s] to the visitor..a stroll 'down the beach', in other words a walk along Wellington's longest, most important street, Lambton Quay. **1917** *Free Lance* (Wellington) 2 Nov. 4 In the early eighties, he was the..senior partner in the butchery business..whose shop was on Lambton-quay, then colloquially known as 'The Beach'. **1931** Coad *Such Is Life* 42 [Making his fortune] he evidently thought could be done by strolling about the beach [at Wellington] with his hands in his pockets, grumbling. **1940** *Tales Pioneer Women* (1988) 104 The anniversary of the landing of the first settlers was celebrated..usually with aquatic sports off the Queen's wharf, which was much nearer to 'The Beach,' as Lambton Quay was then called, than it is today.

(b) The sea-front at Kororareka.

1840 in Wilkes *US Exploring Exped.* (1852) I. 296 [Kororarika] is chiefly inhabited by the lowest order of vagabonds, mostly runaway sailors and convicts, and is appropriately named 'Blackguard Beach'. **1842** *Bay of Islands Observer* in Cowan *NZ Wars* (1955) I. 12 [Thomas Spicer,] 'Kororareka Beach'[, announced that he had for sale such articles as] duck frocks and trousers..tomahawks..and crockery. [**1906** Bullen *Cruise 'Cachalot'* 30 Terrible scenes were enacted upon its [*sc.* Russell's] 'blackguard beach', orgies of wild debauchery and bloodshed.] **1938** Lancaster *Promenade* 22 Since Hobson had landed on the Beach this morning, reading England's Proclamation of Annexation in the little wooden church..the Beach's principal business had been to get drunk. **1959** Sinclair *Hist. NZ* 45 'The Beach', as Kororareka was called, was not that fabled 'Beach' which the explorers had sought: the dissolute men known as 'the beachcombers' found no gold nuggets; they made a living by preying on seamen in one way or another.

2. Special Comb. **beach ranger** *obs.* [poss. beach 1 b (b) 'Kororareka' + bush-)ranger *n.*²], a beach-side robber (cf. the Maori transliteration *pihareina)*; **beach-trader** *obs.*, one who engaged in occasional trade from the beach side.

1832 Earle *NZ* (1966) 82 There is another class of Europeans here [in the Bay of Islands], who are both useless and dangerous... These men are called '**Beach Rangers**'; most of whom have deserted from, or have been turned out of whalers for crimes, for which, had they been taken home and tried, they would have been hanged. [**1852** *He Korero Tipuna Pakeha no mua, ko Ropitini Kuruho, tona ingoa* (trans. of *Robinson Crusoe* by H.T. Kemp. Wellington, Government Printer) 40 Ko te tino pouritanga i pouri iho ai toku ngakau, ka whakaaro iho hoki ahau, ma te Pihareina, ma te kararehe ranei, ma te hemo kai ranei au e patu. 'My heart was filled with sorrow as I contemplated being killed by beach rangers or wild beasts, or overcome by starvation.' (trans. T. Duval). Defoe's text follows, with poss. relevant passages italicised (Everyman's Library 1945 (1960) ed. Guy N. Pocock p.53, 'The Journal' September 30, 1659): All the rest of that day *I spent in afflicting my self at the dismal circumstances I was brought to,* viz. I had neither food, house..*and in despair* of any relief, saw nothing but death before me, either *that I should be devour'd by wild beasts, murther'd by savages, or starved to death for want of food.* **1941** Sutherland *Numismatic Hist. NZ* 37 Although at the outset the Maori got rid of his coins..by purchasing 'anything and everything' from **beach-traders**, he later found that his visible riches were an embarrassment.

3. In the phr. **on the beach** [f. nautical usage], unemployed; broke. See also beached.

1946 Sargeson *That Summer* 77 I'm on the beach myself, I said, but I can make it a deener. **1971** Shirley *Just a Bloody Piano Player* 61 When the 'Niagara' left Sydney on her next trip I found myself 'left on the beach'.

II. [In various uses mainly in a sense of *beach* river-beach, in goldmining contexts.] **4. a.** Applied to a river beach usu. as a source of auriferous material or a site of gold-claims, and often surviving in place-names.

1861 Haast *Rep. Topogr. Explor. Nelson* 12 We camped on the sandy beach of the river. **1864** Barrington *Diary* 19 Apr. in Taylor *Early Travellers* (1959) 407 I believe there is plenty of gold on this river, but I also believe that there must be pumps to work the ground, as they are all heavy beaches. **1873** Pyke *Wild Will Enderby* (1889, 1974) I. xiv 47 The Co. were enabled to work claim after claim of a really rich beach. **1923** *NZJST* VI. 137 His statement that it was found on the beach after a heavy flood suggested to his London friends that it was obtained on the sea-beach near the river-mouth. But in New Zealand miners apply that term to sandy deposits along the sides of rivers and in all probability it was a river-beach that Mr Marmaduke Sellan referred to. **1930** Dobson *Reminiscences* 141 A number of gold-diggers were working in the neighbourhood, some on the beaches and some on the adjoining terraces. **1983** Nolan *Gold Fossicker's Handbook* 111 Beach: flattish gravel deposit at a riverside.

b. *attrib.* With reference to river beaches, but occas. to ocean beaches, esp. in respect of ('black sand') claims and workings (see quot. 1967).

1930 Dobson *Reminiscences* 154 In the terraces on the adjoining hills, old beach leads were worked up to 500 feet above sea level. **1953** Sutherland *Golden Bush* (1963) 38 'Beach gold!' I once heard an old-timer remark with heavy scorn, it's like feathers. **1967** May *West Coast Gold Rushes* 219 The sinking was shallow, the ground dry, and the gold coarser than usual for beach-gold.

5. Special Comb. **beach claim**, see quot. 1873, occas. also applied to a claim on a West Coast ocean beach; **beach diggings (diggins)**, a claim working black sand on a West Coast ocean beach; **beach-workings**, claims worked on both river and ocean beaches.

1864 *AJHR* C-4 14 **Beach claims** shall mean claims situated between ordinary high flood mark and the edge of the water on the beaches of rivers. **1873** Pyke *Wild Will Enderby* (1889, 1974) I. iv 17 The Dunstan gold workings were of two kinds—technically known as 'beach claims' and 'bank claims'... The former were on the sandy margins of the river, and were often extended by means of 'wing-dams' and other ingenious devices far into the rushing waters. In these claims the gold was found lodged in 'pockets' or fissures formed by the slate bars. **1892** Pyke *Gold-Miners' Guide* 7 Claims are classified as follows:—Alluvial deposits, and river- or creek-beds; Quartz lodes, reefs, and leaders; Sea-beach claims; Prospecting claims. **1967** May *West Coast Gold Rushes* 170 Collet's quicksilver plates rapidly became common on the beach-claims. **1866** Mueller *My Dear Bannie* 2 Jan. (1958) 100 The greatest drawback with **beach diggins** is, they are so quickly washed out. **1926** Cowan *Travel in NZ* II. 90 From the..beach diggings in the neighbourhood [of Okarito] tons of gold were won; and a little is still obtained by industrious beach-miners. **1873** Pyke *Wild Will Enderby* (1889, 1974) I. viii 30 When the river is 'up' the **beach workings** are covered and the occupants cease from their labours. **1967** May *West Coast Gold Rushes* 186 The beach-workings of south Westland, stretched along sixty miles of coastline.

beachcomb, *v.* [Prob. by back formation f. beachcomber, beachcombing.] *v. intr.*

1. 'To live off the land' without taking up regular work.

1959 Shadbolt *New Zealanders* (1986) 110 He was..a rolling stone who moved about the country..beachcombing with Maoris in Northland. **1961** Crump *Hang On a Minute Mate* 61 I remember when I was beachcombing up in the Bay of Islands... What, just living off the beach, Son?... Yeah. Bit of fishing and mussel-picking, sheep-stealing and garden-raiding when a man felt energetic or hungry.

2. To work at beachcombing for gold.

1914 Pfaff *Diggers' Story* 45 For a considerable time [in 1860s] I was coasting and beach combing until Wakamarina rush took place.

beachcomber.

1. *Hist.* [f. comb *v.* search thoroughly: recorded early in NZ: see OED beach 4, 1840, HDAS 1836.] A dissolute vagabond preying on seafarers. [*Note*] Quot. 1840 may allude to beach 1 b (a), *The Beach* of early Wellington.

1840 Revans *Lett.* 15 May (ATLMS) 42 While putting up printing office [in Port Nicholson] I picked up two wanderers, who I engaged to saw... I adopted them because they were shaved and clean... They appeared to me to contrast to great advantage [?with (paper torn away)] the regular 'beach comber'. I write the phrase large because I think it is [?new (paper torn away)] to you. It is appropriate to the class. Its meaning I assume is evident. The 'beach combing' class is large. The fellows are daring, dirty, requiring much excitement, accustomed to work on shore and on board, generally about the beach, and take what they find without any very strong sense of doing that which is improper. **1845** Wakefield *Adventure NZ* I. 339 Idle, drunken vagabond..he wanders about without any fixed object, cannot get employed by the whaler or anyone else, as it is out of his power to do a day's work; and he is universally known as the 'beach-comber'. *Ibid.* II. 4 Even the corrupt beachcombers and whalers of Kapiti would go out of their way to say a good word..for Mr. Hadfield. **1850** Torlesse *Papers* (1958) 131 Lyttelton..by all accounts is the receptacle of loose

BEACHCOMBING

beachcombers and escaped lags and convicts, who have been employed in preference to honest and able men from the settlements. **1859** THOMSON *Story NZ* I. 285 It was impossible that a community [*sc.* Kororareka in 1838] composed of sailors..convicts, traders, beachcombers, sawyers, and New Zealanders could live together. **1936** BUICK *Treaty of Waitangi* 149 During the remainder of the day [in February 1840] a strong effort was made by the beachcombers and whisky sellers of Kororareka to spread dissension among the chiefs. **1959** [see BEACH 1 b (b)].

2. *Modern.* A person who searches beaches for interesting or valuable objects.
 1972 *Marlborough Express* (Blenheim) 30 Sept. 3 A strong smell seems to be considered a necessary attribute of ambergris by the average beach-comber.

3. A prospector or miner who works claims on black-sand beaches for gold (see also BEACHER 2, *blacksander* (BLACK-SAND *v.*), SURFACER 1).
 1881 BATEMAN *Colonist* 36 The small quantity of gold under the boulders, which lie on the sandy beach [on the West Coast, South Island] is generally supposed by gold prospectors, otherwise termed 'beach-combers', to be due to the lifting action of the surf. **1887** *Handbook NZ Mines* 217 The beaches..have now been worked for many years, but the yields are not so good... still, the 'beach-combers' make fair wages. **1959** MILLAR *Westland's Golden Sixties* 161 Blotting paper sales mounted as beachcombers [on West coast black sand] got to work.

beachcombing, *ppl. a.* and *vbl. n.* [See BEACHCOMBER.]

1. *ppl. a.*, also *transf.*, pertaining to or characteristic of beachcombers as a socially reprehensible class.
 1840 [see BEACHCOMBER 1]. **1853** *NZ & Its Six Colonies* 58 Except among the old whalers, and the 'beachcombing population', marriages with native women seldom take place. **1912** *Hutt Valley Independent* 21 Dec. 3 Such political beachcombing vituperation as has been indulged in [by the *Petone Chronicle*].

2. *West Coast goldmining.* [Poss. a new formation from *beach* + *combing* searching, influenced by the older forms.] The washing of gold from sea-beach black sand. Cf. *blacksanding* (BLACK-SAND *v.*).
 1868 HAAST in May *West Coast Gold Rushes* (1967) 222 This method of working the [West Coast blacksand] beaches was also called 'haymaking' or 'beachcombing'. These terms were not applied to beach-workings above high-water mark. **1896** HARPER *Pioneer Work* 83 A few diggers live here [Gillespies Beach, West Coast], working for gold on the beach... This 'beach combing' is sometimes profitable, as a great deal of 'surfacing', or black gold-bearing sand, is now and then deposited after a storm. **1910** *NZ Geol. SB (NS)* No.11 37 Along the beach north of the river 'beach-combing' is sometimes resorted to after heavy weather, to extract the precious metal from the leads of 'black sand'.

beached, *ppl. a.* Hard up. Cf. *on the beach* (BEACH 3).
 c**1872** WHITWORTH *Spangles & Sawdust* 5 I was down there with Old Ashmore's lot, doing the trampoline... I was reg'lar beached, and I tell you when a cove 'as to spout his smish it's about time to look out... [1872 *Note*] 7. [beached] Hard up.

beacher. *Hist.*

1. *Otago whaling.* A settler living on the beach; a retired shore-whaler or sailor.

 1844 TUCKETT *Diary* 22 May in Hocken *Contributions* (1898) 223 Thus at Kurreroo or Molineux, where there are now half-a-dozen natives, they say that formerly..there were above a thousand; and in many other places within the last sixteen years, which is about the extent of the experience of the older beachers, there has been..a corresponding diminution of numbers.

2. *West Coast goldmining.* BEACHCOMBER 3.
 1879 HAAST *Geol. Canterbury & Westland* 159 As soon as a storm has subsided, the 'beachers' or 'surfacers' as they are called, examine the coastline near their houses. When they come upon one of the rich spots, the fine particles of gold being often visible to the naked eye, they at once remove the black layer of sand out of the reach of the tide, and wash it when convenient. **1930** ELDER *Goldseekers & Bush Rangers* 155 On this..beach he found..a number of miners who worked..amid the black-iron sands to be found on the beaches. In the early days of the gold-rush many of these 'beachers' or 'surfacers' had prospected the whole southern part of the coast from Riverton to Okarito. **1967** MAY *West Coast Gold Rushes* 526 Beacher: a miner working a sea-beach claim.

beachmaster. *Whaling. Hist.* [Poss. a transf. use of *beachmaster* one who supervises the disembarkation of troops.] The man in charge of a shore-whaling party and operations.
 1982 GROVER *Cork of War* 53 The chief-headsman, or beachmaster, as he was often known, did not keep order [among a shore party in the 1830s]..by knocking down any man who argued with him.

bean. In the phr. **to think no small beans of**, to think a great deal of, to have a high regard for.
 1906 *Truth* 4 Aug. 3 All loyal Wanganuites think no small beans of the local fire brigade, and they have the same opinion of themselves.

beat, *n.* [Spec. use of *beat* a round or course habitually traversed: see OED 10 e.]

1. *Obs.* A drover's round while patrolling a resting mob of cattle.
 1862 CHUDLEIGH *Diary* 28 Apr. (1950) 35 All hands walked centry [*sic*] [over the cattle] all night... Here ended my beat. Draper's began, and went to another fire and to the sea.

2. a. The stretch of country over which a musterer (earlier, a shepherd) operates.
 1873 TINNE *Wonderland of Antipodes* 38 As they complete [the muster of] each flock, it is turned over to a shepherd, who would drive it off with the aid of his dogs to a beat, possibly ten or twenty miles distant. **1874** CAIRD *Sheepfarming NZ* 20 When a considerable stretch of country had to be mustered each man got his separate beat. **1906** CHUDLEIGH *Diary* 25 Oct. (1950) 436 That awful Wilson did not muster his beat at all, fiend of a fellow. **1940** STUDHOLME *Te Waimate* (1954) 122 The men were out on their beat by daylight, sometimes well before. The beats were about half a mile apart, or more if the country was open. **1978** JARDINE *Shadows on Hill* 28 On the beat, Ben [a sheep-dog] was always happier if you put him out above or below to take a beat through on his own.

b. Often prec. by a modifier: **bottom** (also **middle, top**) **beat,** see quot. 1934; **lambing beat,** a patrolling of ewes about to lamb; **outside beat,** see quots. 1949, 1953.
 1934 *Press* (Christchurch) (Acland Gloss.) 13 Jan. 13 *Beat.*— A musterer's *b[eat]* is the ground off which he has to clear the sheep each day; often **top** *b[eat]*, **bottom** *b[eat]*, **middle** *b[eat]*, etc., also hard and easy *b[eat]s*. The word is also applied to the ground on

BEAUT

which a rabbit poisoner has to lay his poison. **1975** DAVIES *Outback* 75 The Boss was adamant that the two boys couldn't miss their **lambing beat. 1949** NEWTON *High Country Days* 196 **Outside Beat**: The farthest beat on a block is known as the outside beat. Quite often the course of the outside beats may be a complete half circle, the outside man travelling almost right round the whole block. **1953** STRONACH *Musterer on Molesworth* 24 The beat on the top of the hill is known as 'the **top beat**' and the one along the bottom as 'the bottom beat'. This is rather obvious—but the longest and most strenuous, whether top or bottom, is known as the 'outside beat'. **1969** MOORE *Forest to Farm* 18 On one occasion I had the top beat and had to wait for the men below me. **1981** CHARLES *Black Billy Tea* 35 There's no place I'd rather be, Than the top beat With a snow-line boundary.

3. The stretch of country over which a rabbiter lays poison.
 1934 [see 2 b above].

4. A usual haunt (of wild cattle).
 1937 AYSON *Thomas* 86 They got a good muster of cattle..kept those that were to be tamed in the paddock, and let the rest out in a mob, each to find its way to its own beat. **1940** STUDHOLME *Te Waimate* (1954) 135 I don't think she was ever yarded, though many attempts were made to get her in; finally she had to be shot on her beat in the bush at the Upper Hook.

5. A swagger's usual or set round.
 1899 BELL *In Shadow of Bush* 11 He has crossed the Straits, then. Times must be bad among the stations when Davie [Dunlop, the Sundowner] has come so far out of his beat. **1986** OWEN & PERKINS *Speaking for Ourselves* 68 I..swagged with a character that was well known on the track at that time. They were fellows that were on the track permanently, and they all had their beats.

beat, *v.*

1. In the phr. **to beat the feet,** to move, to run; occas. to abscond.
 1973 *Salient* (Wellington) 19 Sept. 10 Everyone who is anyone in the underworld..when needing to sell a radio, hide out some place if 'beating the feet' [orig. erron. *fleet*] or just wanting a few jugs. **1982** NEWBOLD *Big Huey* 244 Beat the feet (v) Run away, escape.

2. *Logging.* **to beat off,** to cut or strip off outer bark and wood.
 1953 REED *Story of Kauri* 165 The axe was used to beat off the depths of the scores [*sc.* the guide marks cut in the log].

beaut /bjut/, *n., a.,* and *adv.* Also **bute.** [Shortened form of *beauty* or *beautiful:* recorded earliest in US 1866: AND 1898.]

A. *n.*

1. a. Anything that is excellent, superior or enjoyable of its kind; a term expressing approbation and delight. Also used as an exclamation.
 1906 *Truth* 7 Apr. 1 Lord! a smash From someone's boot Caught him a 'bute' Now he's a mash. **1919** *Quick March* 10 July 17 A curse of a Fritz... Guv me a prick... A beaut of a Blighty, be Gosh! **1929** SMYTH *Girl from Mason Creek* 161 We didn't quite get the hang of things first go off, but now I reckon it will be a 'beaut'. **1937** *Auckland Univ. Carnival Book* 24 Solo: She was cute. *All:* You betcha! Gee! Solo: What a beaut! **1944** *NZEF Times* 24 Jan. 11 'You're a beaut,' I said. 'Wouldn't it rotate you!' **1950** *Landfall* 13 20 I'm reading a beaut. It's a corker. **1984** 14 F E120 Wgton Girls C. 4 Beaut [F2] [something or someone good or liked]

b. In ironical use from the prec. sense, often suggesting that the object is a 'character'. Cf. DAG n.² 1 a, *hard case* (HARD *a.* 1 a).

1944 FULLARTON *Troop Target* 26 Pommie officers are beauts... Hasn't anyone told them that we are fighting for democracy. **1961** CRUMP *Hang On a Minute Mate* 159 Missus Wagner's a bit of a beaut, isn't she. She's a hard case all right.

c. With a defining word: **real beaut, wee beaut; you beaut** (in address).

1947 DAVIN *For Rest of Our Lives* 51 She was a real beaut. Only cost me fifty ackers. **1964** HARVEY *Any Old Dollars Mister?* 6 I let out a real beaut [*sc.* a bad word] at the table one night and Dad grabbed me by the collar and took me into the bathroom. **1969** MASON *Awatea* (1978) 34 Gilhooly, *rapturous*: You beaut! You bloody beaut! I could kiss the face off yer! **1987** VIRTUE *Redemption of Elsdon Bird* (1988) 54 My grandad was one of them [*sc.* Poms] and he was a real beaut... He was a boozer and loved the trots.

2. *Ellipt.* for, e.g., *beaut trick*, in the phr. **to put across a beaut**, to successfully trick a person.

1938 *Press* (Christchurch) (McNab Slang) 2 Apr. 18 'To be a dag at,' 'to put across a beaut,' 'to jerry to'..need no explanation. **1944** *NZEF Times* 23 Dec. 14 A certain Kiwi..put what may justly be called 'a real beaut' over 'George'. **1950** *Landfall* 13 39 Did I rub it into him... I put a beaut across him.

B. *adj.* [AND 1918.] BEAUTY B 1. Also used as an exclamation of pleasure.

1948 BALLANTYNE *Cunninghams* 8 A beaut pair of gossips. **1964** HARVEY *Any Old Dollars Mister?* 1 Under our house was a beaut basement where Dad put all his tools and things. **1973** FERNANDEZ *Tussock Fever* 29 Aw, that's a kid's dress... There's a beaut style in your Woman's magazine. **1988** FRAME *Carpathians* 66 Wouldn't it be beaut if they abolished distance?

Hence (*rare*) in the comparative, **beauter**.

1960 KEINZLY *Tangahano* 25 Gee, it must be a beaut! But he bet the one his father was going down to finish would be beauter.

C. *adv.* Beautifully, corker.

1986 MILLER *Gemina* 23 She's bloody beaut looking too!

beauty /ˈbjuti/, /ˈbjudi/, /bjuˈtiː/, *n.* and *a.* Also **beaudy, beaut-ee-e, bewdy, bjudee**, etc. following various *joc.* or emphatic pronunciations. [A shortened form of *beautiful*: AND *n.* 1852; see OED 5.]

A. *n.*

1. a. Anything superior, excellent, admirable, or to one's liking. Often with a defining word: **little (wee) beauty, you beauty**, expressing approval in varying degrees and often represented in writing by elongated spelling forms (cf. quot. 1964).

1897 SCOTT *How I Stole 10,000 Sheep* 11 Our own dogs..turned out to be 'beauties'. **1907** *Truth* 28 Sept. 3 His try was a real 'beauty'. He took a pass cleverly, and dashed over in an instant. **1924** *Otago Witness* (Dunedin) 28 Oct. 72 My brother..said I was a beauty to go eeling with. **1935** GUTHRIE *Little Country* (1937) 62 A tall fellow caught the ball..and dived over the line to score. The people clapped and roared, 'You beauty, you little beauty!' **1936** HYDE *Passport to Hell* 174 [Of a wound.] Jakeloo, Starkie; she's a little beauty, clean through my arm! **1947** DAVIN *For Rest of Our Lives* 247 'You little beauty,' said Bluey. The last [shell] had gone nicely over the rim. **1950** GASKELL in *Some Other Country* (1984) 92 But auntie was yelling 'You beauty. You beauty,' and hammering my shoulder. **1964** MORRIESON *Came a Hot Friday* (1981) 45 He pronounced to be a hero and a little 'bee-yu-tay'. **1970** MASON in *Solo* (1981) 50 Come on Firpo! Oh, you beauteeee! **1979** *Islands* 27 462 If I get one of them big hooers [*sc.* frozen carcasses] up my arse, you'll get one of my size nine kadoodies up yours! Oh, I'll root you a bewdy with me size nine kadoody. **1986** *Listener* 27 Sept. 32 [Cartoon: after-match function] He's a little beaudy in the ruck—I'll say that for him.

b. Mainly by or to children, as a quasi-adverbial intensifier, **beauty of a**.

1899 BELL *In Shadow of Bush* 46 'Look here, Billy!' said Maurice,.. 'I saw a beauty of a two-bladed knife in at Buncombe's store, the other day.' **1923** MANDER *Strange Attraction* 71 I had a beauty of a little boat. **1963** in *Listener Short Stories* (1978) 65 A long time ago I made a beauty of a kite.

2. In the phr. **to put across a beauty**, to successfully perpetrate a smart trick, joke, or sly manoeuvre. Cf. BEAUT A 2.

1935 STRONG in Partridge *Slang Today* 287 I put across a beauty when I found the double-headed penny in the ring, and that's how I won 200 francs. **1988** McGILL *Dict. Kiwi Slang* 89 *put across a beauty* make a smart or tricky move; eg 'Sims put across a beauty with that double dummy.'

B. *adj.*

1. [AND 1971.] Superior, excellent; admirable; enjoyable.

1963 CASEY *As Short a Spring* 276 The beauty times are when you get in with the mob and do the rounds of the brothels and grog-shops. **1965** ANDERSON & AITKEN *Speech & Idiom Maori Children* 94 The noun + y..method of forming adjectives may help to explain the use of such a word as 'beauty' for 'beautiful': Beauty smell, eh? Yeah, they're beauty, eh? **1974** MORRIESON *Predicament* (1981) 93 'Nah,' she said. 'It's good: beaut-ee-e.' **1992** *Marlborough Express* (Blenheim) 31 Jan. 5 'It [*sc.* a high-country farm] was a beauty possie up the Puhi..' Sam says wistfully. **1992** *Sunday Times* (Wellington) 29 Nov. 23 I asked him what it was like when the tree fell. His face lit up: 'It was bewdy, bloody bewdy.'

2. *exclam.* [AND 1968.] Expressing delight, approval, etc.

1951 14 M 10 Wellington H.S. 18 Beauty [exclam. of delight] **1977** HALL *Glide Time* 36 The Boss has got promotion. Going to Ag. and Fish. *Jim.* Fair go? *Hugh.* True. *Jim.* Beauty. About time. **1984** 16 M E77 Pakuranga Coll. 35A Beauty [exclam. of approval] [M2]

beaver. For a so-called 'beaver', a rumoured native animal, see WAITOREKE.

beazer, *a.* Obs. [f. Sc. dial.: see SND *beez n.* Children's expression for something supremely good; similarly *beezer*.] Of a person or thing, excellent or superior in its class; 'corker', 'grouse'.

1933 PRUDENCE CADEY *Broken Pattern* 136 It will be a bonzer day and you will make a pinger hostess..and you a beazer host.

B Ech: see ECH.

bed.

1. [Extended use of *bed* the bottom of the channel of a river or stream: see OED *n.* 9.] The areas of boulders, shingle, etc. forming a path, usu. marked by banks, where a river runs, has run, or may again run. See also *river-bed* (RIVER 2 a).

1862 CHUDLEIGH *Diary* 16 Mar. (1950) 28 The bed [of the Rakaia] is two miles across, the water a mile but split up into many branches. **1878** ELWELL *Boy Colonists* 42 The Waitaki like many other New Zealand rivers is bordered on each side throughout its course by steep banks, and the whole space of ground thus hemmed in by its banks is generally termed loosely 'the bed', though seldom, if ever, covered by the river. **1917** *TrNZI* XLIX. 4 Strictly speaking, the term 'bed' is applicable only to that part of the valley actually covered by the flowing water... In this paper the term 'river-bed', following the colloquial usage, is used to include that part of the valley liable to be covered with water in times of severe floods.

2. a. [Spec. use of *bed*: see OED *n.* 13 b (Geol).] The bedrock.

1862 CHUDLEIGH *Diary* 2 June (1950) 41 The digers [*sic*]..told us we should have to sink deep to get to the bottom. We got some 7 feet below the bed.

b. [Spec. use of *bed* the level surface on which anything rests: see OED *n.* 12.] The surface over which gold-bearing material is washed to extract the gold.

1882 HAY *Brighter Britain* II. 279 We see this liquid [*sc.* puddled ore] sent over 'beds', and 'floors', and 'ladders', and 'blanketings', and washed again and again.

bedroll. [f. *bed* + *roll*: orig. US, see Mathews.] Bedding rolled into a bundle for carrying, or for neat storage.

1947 NEWTON *Wayleggo* 153 Bluey: bedroll, or swag. **1951** WILSON *Brave Company* 20 I can distinguish the long vermouth stain above Hope's bedroll. **1959** SLATTER *Gun in My Hand* 228 Can't line up life with a long string like bed-rolls in an army hut.

bee.

1. a. As **bush-bee**, a wild honey bee *Apis mellifera* (fam. Apidae).

1871 BRACKEN *Behind the Tomb* 63 [Bush children] hunting for the hidden sweets where the bush-bees are humming. **1902** SATCHELL *Land of Lost* (1971) 156 And the earth is bare and barren where the bush-bee used to hum.

b. As **native bee**, any of some 40 endemic species of families Colletidae and Halictidae, solitary bees which make burrows in clay and sand, holding stores of pollen as food for larvae.

[**1843** DIEFFENBACH *Travels in NZ* I. 143 I am not aware that there is any native bee in New Zealand.] **1892** HUDSON *Elementary Manual of NZ Entomology* 34 This [*Leioproctus fulvescens*] is the true native bee of New Zealand, and may be taken abundantly during the whole summer. **1902** DRUMMOND & HUTTON *Nature in NZ* 60 Though the colony has several *native bees* none of them makes honey. **1929** MARTIN *NZ Nature Book* I 131 Of the shiny flower-frequenting native bees the black *Hylaeus capitosus* is the commonest species. **1947** POWELL *Native Animals* 52 A native bee (*Paracolletes fulvescens*) is typical of several species of native bees, all of which are smaller than the introduced honey-bee and are noted for their extremely hairy pollen-carrying hind legs. They are mostly dark grey with golden-brown hairs. These bees burrow in the ground, especially in clay and are solitary in the sense that each builds its own nest and gathers its own supply of honey. **1974** *NZ Bee Keeper* May 47 The first native bees from New Zealand were described by F. Smith in 1853, and to date about 26 species have been described. **1986** JOHNSON *Wildflowers Central Otago* 51 When in flower..they are smothered with native bees, active little creatures that I always avoided until recently, when I learned that they have no sting. **1992** PARK *Fence around the Cuckoo* 8 We searched for..an obscure burrow in a sandy bank where a native bee, small and dowdy, dwelled with her eggs or larvae.

BEEBYISM

2. In the phr. **as the bee flies**, in a straight line, 'as the crow flies'.
 1863 Lush *Auckland Jrnls.* 28 Sept. (1971) 251 Wairoa, 6 miles as the bee flies from the redoubt.

Beebyism. [f. the name of Clarence E. *Beeby* (b.1902), Director of Education 1940–60.] The educational reforms, esp. in primary education, encouraged and implemented during Beeby's term as Director of Education. Contrast PLAYWAY.
 1983 Sinclair *Hist. Univ. of Auckland* 182 Some of the professors quite literally hated the local dominant education trends called 'Beebyism'. **1985** *National Bus. Rev.* 16 Dec. 9 For impressive contributions one had to look to the junior ranks [of M.P.s], to Ruth Richardson, who has challenged many of the fundamentals in education after 40 years of Beebyism. **1992** *Dominion* (Wellington) 7 Feb. 6 Director of Education from 1940 to 1960, Beeby's introduction of civilising disciplines like arts and crafts to the school curriculum has yet to be overturned. On the contrary, 'Beebyism', as his reforms came to be known, has been reinforced and amplified.

beech. [Transf. use of *beech*, a northern hemisphere forest tree of the genus *Fagus*.]
1. Also **native** or **New Zealand beech**. Any tree of the ancient southern hemisphere genus *Nothofagus* (until 1873 *Fagus*) (fam. Fagaceae), four species of which are endemic and form extensive forests esp. in southern and mountainous regions; also the timber of beech species. See also BIRCH (freq. in popular but technically incorrect use), TAW(H)AI (the Maori generic name, esp. in NI use), KAMAHI (erroneously, in SI use).
 [**1773** Bayly *Journal* 12 Apr. in McNab *Hist. Records* (1914) II. 206 The next biggest is a tree whose wood resembles beach tree in England.] **1845** Taylor *Journal* 10 Nov. (ATLTS) III. 166 [Near Hikurangi] we passed through a noble forest of beech trees (Tawai) some were 8 feet in diameter and of great height. **1869** *TRNZI* I. (rev. edn) 171 The city of Nelson is now almost entirely dependent for its supply of firewood upon the beech forests. **1871** *TrNZI* III. 200 Four species [of *Fagus*] are recognized by botanists; these are known to settlers [of Otago and Canterbury] by the names of Black, White or Red *Birch*, not *Beech*, which would be their more correct designation. **1891** *NZJSc.* (NS) I. 202 Our first excursion was through..beech forest in which we noted..the gorgeous crimson mistletoe. **1940** [see BIRCH 1]. **1953** *Evening Post* (Wellington) 9 Mar. 8 Fire eats further into [State] beech forest. **1966** *Encycl. NZ* II. 680 The native beech, *Nothofagus*, has been called *birch* since the early days and is still often so called by bushmen. **1984** Wardle *NZ Beeches* 15 The New Zealand beeches belong to the genus *Nothofagus* or 'false beeches'.

2. With modifiers denoting appearance of tree (**black, silver**), quality of timber (**hard, red**), appearance of leaves (**tooth-leaved**), habitat (**mountain**), locality (**Southland**): **black, Blair's, clinker, entire-leaved, hard, mountain, red, round-leaved, silver, southern, Southland, tooth-leaved**.
 [*Note*] Species and varieties hybridize, often compounding a confusion of vernacular names. See esp. J.C. Andersen *Popular Names of New Zealand Plants* (1926 *TrNZI* LVI. 663f.), and T. Kirk *On New Zealand Beeches* (1885 *TrNZI* XVII. 298 ff.).

(1) **black beech.** A beech, usu. *N. solandri* var. *solandri*, having dark bark, or bark blackened by sooty mould. See also *tawhai-rauriki* (TAWAI 2).

 1848 Taylor *Leaf from Nat. Hist.* 444 Black birch or beech tree—Tawai. **1879** Haast *Geol. Canterbury & Westland* 81 Along the rather wet track appeared..here and there black beeches (*Fagus fusca*). **1936** Belshaw et al. *Agric. Organiz. NZ* 578 The chief indigenous trees of commercial value are..red and hard beech (*Nothofagus f[u]sca* and *Nothofagus truncata*), silver beech... (*Nothofagus Menziesii*), black beech (*Nothofagus Solandri*). **1940** Laing & Blackwell *Plants NZ* 140 *Solander's Beech*... Bark white in young trees, black in old. North Island: mountain forests... The Black Beech. **1978** Moore & Irwin *Oxford Book NZ Plants* 80 *Nothofagus solandri* variety *solandri*, black beech. A tall tree of lowland sites whose precise distribution is uncertain because of crossing with mountain beech. **1988** Dawson *Forest Vines to Snow Tussocks* 121 *Nothofagus solandri* var. *solandri*: black beech (the bark is very dark partly due to the growth of a sooty mould).

(2) **Blair's beech.** *Obs. Nothofagus blairii*, a hybrid of *N. solandri* var. *cliffortioides* and *N. fusca*.
 1890 *PWD Gen. Catalogue* (NZ & South Seas Exhib.) 23 Lithograph of 'Blair's beech' foliage. **1898** Morris *Austral-English* 24 In New Zealand, there are six species of true beeches, which according to Kirk are as follows. Blair's B[eech] *Fagus blairi* [etc.].

(3) **clinker beech.** *Obs.* [Poss. from the furrowed appearance of mature bark giving an appearance of 'clinkered' or overlapping boards.] See *hard beech* (5) below.
 1937 *Tararua Tramper* Mar. 3 Here black beech (N. Solanderi) [*sic*] and clinker beech (N. truncata) are abundant. **1940** Laing & Blackwell *Plants NZ* 139 A somewhat similar species is *N. truncata*, the Clinker Beech, often called the Hard Beech.

(4) **entire-leaved beech.** *Nothofagus solandri*.
 1875 Kirk *Durability NZ Timbers* 17 With the view of obviating the confusion caused by the misuse of the common names hitherto applied to the New Zealand beeches, I would suggest the adoption of new names based on the obvious characteristics of their foliage:- For *Fagus fusca*, tooth-leaved beech; for *Fagus solandri*, entire-leaved beech; and for *Fagus menziesii*, round-leaved beech. **1885** [see BIRCH 3 (2) a]. **1890** *PWD Catalogue Timbers* (NZ & South Seas Exhib.) 9 Beech, entire leaved..Fagus Solandri..Heavy, tough, strong timber; used for sleepers, fencing, bridges, &c. **1902** [see (9) below].

(5) **hard-beech.** [f. hardness or brittleness of the timber.] *Nothofagus truncata*. See also TAWHAI-RAUNUI.
 1933 *NZJST* XIV. 233 *Nothofagus truncata* (Hard Beech). **1936** [see (1) above]. **1940** [see (3) above]. **1978** Moore & Irwin *Oxford Book NZ Plants* 80 Hard beech, the only *Nothofagus* native to north Auckland, is absent from the east and south of the South Island. **1988** Dawson *Forest Vines to Snow Tussocks* 121 *Nothofagus truncata*: hard beech (the wood has a high silica content making it hard).

(6) **mountain beech.** *Nothofagus solandri* var. *cliffortioides*, a beech common in dryer subalpine forest.
 1886 Kirk in *Settler's Handbook NZ* (1902) 121 [Settlers' name] Mountain beech. **1891** *NZJSc.* (NS) I. 202 Mr. Enys' house..is 2,500 feet above the sea, and is beautifully situated in a clump of Mountain Beech. **1900** Dendy in *Canterbury Old & New* 186 As we ascend the character of the vegetation changes, the mountain beech replaces that of lower altitudes. **1918** *NZJST* I. 308 *Fagus cliffortioides*.—This tree much resembles *F. Solandri*, but it is found generally only at high altitudes... The most suitable name for it is 'mountain-beech.' **1937** *Tararua Tramper* Mar. 3 The mountain beech cannot compete..with the silver beech in such high rainfall areas [in the Tararuas]. **1960** Masters *Back-Country Tales* 77 The track..leads along the crest of a main ridge, and passes..through an area of native mountain beech forest. **1970** [see BIRCH 3 (11) a]. **1978** *Manawatu Tramping Club Jubilee* 99 [We] take the track into splendid..mountain beech bush. **1981** Dennis *Paparoas Guide* 159 Mountain beech (*N. solandri* var. *cliffortioides*) descends to river terraces.

(7) **red beech.** *Nothofagus fusca*. See also *tawhai-raunui* (TAWAI 2).
 1910 Cockayne *NZ Plants & Their Story* 49 *N. fusca* and *N. Menziesii*, called respectively the red and silver beeches. **1918** *NZJST* I. 308 *Fagus fusca*.—In Auckland this tree is called 'black-birch'; in Wellington 'red-birch'; in Nelson, Marlborough and Westland it is called 'brown-birch'; and in Otago it is called both 'red-birch' and 'bull-birch.' The most suitable name is 'red-beech.' **1936** [see (1) above]. **1940** Laing & Blackwell *Plants NZ* 139 *N. fusca* (The Red Beech)... North Island: mountainous districts; South Island: abundant. The Red Birch. **1971** *VUWTC* 71 20 Built of red beech slabs, the hut had a tin roof, a clay floor..and accommodated eleven (in five sacking bunks). **1981** Henderson *Exiles Asbestos Cottage* 60 Red or brown beech/birch, 'steaming wood', good fill-in wood. **1995** [see *tawhai-raunui* (TAWAI 2)].

(8) **round-leaved beech.** *Nothofagus menziesii*. See quot. 1875, (4) above.

(9) **silver beech.** [f. colour of its bark.] *Nothofagus menziesii*, a variety of native beech found mainly in rainy areas, often popularly and locally called 'silver birch'.
 1885 *TrNZI* XVII. 298 [*Notho*]*fagus menziesii*... Silver Beech. Brown Birch, White Birch, Red Birch. Silver Birch. **1889** [see BIRCH 3 (10)]. **1902** *Settler's Handbook NZ* 120 Silver-beech and entire-leaved beech are found as far south as Preservation Inlet and the Tautuku Forest, while the mountain-beech prefers higher levels. **1918** *NZJST* I. 308 *Fagus Menziesii*.—The commonest name of this tree is 'silver-birch,' but it is often called 'brown-birch,' 'red-birch,' and 'white-birch' in different localities. It would be best to call it 'silver-beech,' though it is gaining an Australasian reputation as 'Southland beech.' **1937** [see (6) above]. **1950** *Bull. Wellington Bot. Soc. No.23* 16 The principal forest trees [at Manaroa, Pelorus Sound]..are silver beech, (*Nothofagus menziesii*) in this locality known as cherry birch. **1978** Moore & Irwin *Oxford Book NZ Plants* 80 *Nothofagus menziesii*, silver beech. A hardy tree, growing from sea level to timber line and often forming pure forests, especially in Nelson and Southland. **1983** *Land of Mist* 60 Above about 1200 m, red beech disappears and pure silver beech continues to the timberline which reaches nearly 1400 m on Mt Manuoha.

(10) **southern beech.** A general name for native *Nothofagus* spp.
 1912 *TrNZI* XLIV. 63 I am using, at Dr. Cockayne's suggestion, the term 'southern beech' (*Nothofagus*) to distinguish our forests from the beech (*Fagus*) forests of the Northern Hemisphere. **1951** Levy *Grasslands NZ* (1970) 265 The southern beech country around Wellington and the Hutt Valley. **1980** Mantell *Murder & Chips* 5 Sawmills..chewed up southern beech..into small flat chips around an inch square.

(11) **Southland beech.** The wood of *Nothofagus menziesii* used in cabinet making and furniture.
 1918 *NZJST* I. 308 [*Notho*]*fagus Menziesii*.—The commonest name of this tree is 'silver-birch'... It would be best to call it 'silver-beech,' though it is gaining an Australasian reputation as 'Southland beech.' **1955** *BJ Cameron Collection* (TS July) southland beech (n) A species of beech the wood of which is valued for furniture making. **1959** Slatter *Gun in My*

Hand 129 I pick up the wedding photo from the Swedish-style china cabinet in Southland beech. **1966** McLintock *Encycl. NZ* III. 710 Beech... Silver or Southland..tawhai..*N. menziesii*.

(12) **tooth-leaved beech**. *Nothofagus fusca*.
1875 [see (4) above]. **1885** *TrNZI* XVII. 302 All the men engaged at the sawmills [of West Oxford] had heard of 'tooth-leaved beech', but only one or two of them had seen it growing, and no one had seen it converted.

3. Special Comb. **beech burr**, a form of external growth found on beech trees, in appearance something like a pumpkin covered with round knobs of bark (cf. BURR *n.*²); **beech bush**, see BUSH A 1 d; **beech fever**, prob. an allergic sickness associated with beech trees (cf. *birch itch* (BIRCH 4)); **beech forest butterfly**, see quot. 1980; **beech potato**, see quot. 1961; **beech strawberry**, the spherical honeycombed sporing bodies of the fungus *Cyttaria gunnii* (Order Pezizales) an obligate parasite of silver beech (*Nothofagus menziesii*) (see also FUNGUS 2 (2), (9)).
1975 Anderson *Men of Milford Road* 62 The head sawyer called me over and said, 'I've got a **beech burr** for you. It'll make a lovely clock for your bedroom.' **1958** *Tararua* Sept. 31 **Beech fever**. An Otago term which refers to a sickness which affects some people in beech country. It may be the same as *birch itch*, suffered by people allergic to beech pollen. **1980** Gibbs *NZ Butterflies* 184 Although sometimes referred to as the **beech forest butterfly** (Salmon, 1964) [the forest ringlet, *Dodonidia helmsii*] is by no means limited to this type. **1961** Martin *Flora NZ* 37 The most conspicuous of these [pouch fungi which develop underground] is the violet-tinted **Beech Potato** (*Hysterangium scerodermum*), a tuberous-looking fungus resembling a small Derwent potato. **1961** Martin *Flora NZ* 43 Finally, there are those curious, yellow, spherical 'fruit' of the so-called **beech strawberry** (*Cyttaria gunnii*), a fungus which attacks the silver beech. These strawberry-like fruits form clusters on the twigs at the end of the branches, their honey-combed surface making recognition easy and certain. **1978** Fuller *Maori Food & Cook*. 85 Beech strawberry—*Cyttaria gunnii*.

Beehive. [f. a resemblance to an old-fashioned *beehive*, a dome-shaped structure built of straw and housing bees.]

1. *Hist.* The name given, from its appearance, to the Williams family's first raupo house at Paihia, completed September 1823.
1823 Williams *Early Jrnls*. 13 Dec. (1961) 90 My brother and myself engaged..this day..plastering and repairing some of the cells of the Beehive.

2. a. The dome-roofed building in Wellington, designed by Sir Basil Spence, and housing Cabinet, ministerial and some parliamentary offices.
1976 Harrison *Broken October* 44 Some of them went for a..walk along Willis Street and Lambton Quay and round the great circular Beehive Building of Parliament. **1981** Kennedy *Straight from Shoulder* 94 I had an hour with [the Prime Minister] in his office in the Beehive. **1984** Ovenden *Ratatui* 13 In the middle of them all..the Beehive Building, with its multitudinous combs, the centre of the hum of government activity. **1995** *Sunday Star-Times* (Auckland) 19 Feb. sect. C3 Legend has it the Beehive started life as a playful sketch on a Bellamy's napkin, as an eminent visitor sought to amuse then Prime Minister Sir Keith Holyoake.

b. *fig.* The Government or Cabinet. Also *attrib.*

1986 *National Bus. Rev.* 28 Mar. 10 That figure is denied by a Beehive aide. But the Beehive source admits 'there is a possibility it [*sc.* the tax take] is down'. **1987** *Sunday Star* (Auckland) 26 July A9 The Beehive's well-oiled publicity machine appears to have run away with itself. **1993** *Dominion* (Wellington) 15 Jan. 6 I leave Wellington and my Beehive job with regret.

beer.

1. In the phr. **to have a beer in**, to be tipsy or drunk.
1907 *Truth* 7 Dec. 6 The well-dressed blackguard had a beer in and commenced patting the shoulder of the pretty girl beside him in the car on Courtenay Place section.

2. [Transf. use of *beer* a refreshing drink.] BROSE (see 1933 quot.).

3. Special Comb. **beer-barn**, *booze barn* (BOOZE); **beer-biter**, **beer-bummer** *obs.*, a person who habitually begs a drink from another (that is, 'puts the bite' on); **beer-chewer**, [AND 1895], **beer-eater** [AND 1891] *obs.*, a (practised) beer drinker; **beer goitre**, a protruding stomach, a 'pot', from continual beer-drinking; **beer shell**, an empty beer bottle; **beer strike**, a strike by brewery and/or hotel workers; **beer tanker**, a vehicle for the transport of bulk beer.
1976 Johnston *New Zealanders* 147 But the suburban tavern is frequently a '**beer-barn**', continuing the old mass-consumption methods. **1987** *Listener* 23 May 34 The beer-barn image has been replaced in most areas by well-appointed clubrooms run in a professional manner. **1919** *Quick March* Feb. 5 Can't the civilian police do something with that fiend who accosts the lately returned soldier..then he tries the beer-bite with 'How is it for a couple of bob?' Inquiry shows that some of these '**Beer-biters**' are ordinary 'civvy' loafers... The R.S.A. has denounced the 'beer-biter'. **1906** *Truth* 21 July 1 Barry [charged with using obscene language] was a **beer-bummer** and his lawyer pleaded that the language was used only in an hotel bar. **1905** *Truth* 12 Aug. 5 The wicked **beer-chewer**. **1906** *Truth* 10 Mar. 1 'Sing a song of sixpence.' That is the immelodious chant of the beer-chewer when he's biting your lug for a sprat. **1906** *Truth* 21 July 6 [Heading] The Beer-chewers Call. It is, however, the '**beer-eater**', the chewer of swipes whom we have in our mind's eye just now. **1917** *Chron. NZEF* 18 Apr. 84 I know an old beer eater that will answer your calls for twenty-four hours for half a crown. **1988** McGill *Dict. Kiwi Slang* 14 **beer goitre** a large stomach or pot induced by too much of the amber fluid, aka beer; high incidence of goitre into this century here, until iodine deficiency was rectified. **1905** *Truth* 30 Sept. 7 The 'Bottle O' belted the back gate and called for the 'dead marines'..hunter of **beer shells**. **1970** *Dominion* (Wellington) 30 Jan. 2 Mr Neylon..was delighted to hear that a Whangarei group was considering joining in on the **beer strike**.

beetle. [In locally significant use only with a defining word.]

1. black beetle. a. *Platyzosteria novaeseelandiae* (fam. Blattidae), a native stinkroach. See also *kauri-bug* (KAURI 5), KEKERENGU, *Maori-bug* a, STINKING BUG, *whare bug* (WHARE 7 b), *wood bug* (WOOD *n.*¹ 2 b). Also *fig.* and *attrib.* a dark-suited person, esp. a clergyman (see quots. 1874, 1906).
1844 Williams *NZ Journal* (1956) 111 One kind of Black Beetle is worthy of particular notice on account of its troublesome nature, and known by the appellation of Kekerere, by the natives. If molested throws off the most disgusting smell imaginable, but not a venomous insect. **1863** Walker *Journal and Letters* 4 May (ATLTS) You have no idea what a hubbub there is here [at the Molyneux] some times, it is infinitely worse than 'Blackbeetles, Bluebottles and Flies.' **1874** Kennaway *Crusts* 209 A ball being imminent, our late guest..had to reduce himself to the black-beetle appearance of the evening exquisite of the nineteenth century. **1882** Hay *Brighter Britain* I. 151 [The kauri bug] is flat, black, hard and shiny, and resembles a cross between a black-beetle and the woodlouse or slater. It stinks. **1906** *Truth* 14 July 1 Of course the 'black beetle' denied that he had done so [i.e. 'aspersed the moral character of the young people of Motueka']. **1916** Mansfield *The Aloe* (1982) 121 To dream of four black beetles dragging a hearse is bad. **1952** *JPS* LXI. 21 Though the term, as 'fusty', could apply to some species of ground beetle (*Carabidae*), it is more likely applicable to the stink-roach (*Platyzosteria novae-seelandiae*), often called 'black-beetle.' **1984** Miller *Common Insects* 148 The best known native species is the Black Cockroach..which produces an objectionable stink when alarmed; it is about 40mm long, and commonly called the 'Maori bug,' or 'black beetle,' but it is neither a bug nor a beetle. **1993** [see MAORI-BUG a].

b. The introduced *Heteronychus arator* (fam. Scarabaeidae), a pasture pest.
1971 Miller *Common Insects in NZ* 143 The Black Beetle..has become an important pest of pastures... The beetle varies from chestnut-brown to shining black and is about ½″ long. **1974** Helson *Insect Pests* 93 Black beetle is the common name given to a 13-mm long, glossy black beetle (*Heteronychus arator*). A native from South Africa, it was first recorded in New Zealand in March 1937 from Waiheke Island. **1982** *NZ Entomologist* VII. 227 Black beetle, *Heteronychus arator*..is a major pest of pastures and crops in northern areas of the North Island.

2. brown beetle. GRASS GRUB 1 b. See also TURNIP FLY. (The Maori name *tutae-ruru* 'owl-shit' recalls the beetle's colour, size and shape.)
1934 [see TURNIP FLY]. **1943** *NZJST* XXIII. 322A One of the most destructive pests in New Zealand is the grass grub or brown beetle... (*Odontria* [now *Costelytra*] *zealandica*). This insect..has been responsible for the destruction of..crops. **1960** Matthews *Matthews on Gardening* 23 The brown beetle is a dun-coloured insect some three-eighths of an inch long, which swarms through one's garden at dusk with a droning noise. **1971** Miller *Common Insects in NZ* 143 The common Brown Beetle and similar species were known [to the Maori] as *papapapa* and *tutaeruru*, and the larvae as *moeone* (to sleep in the ground). **1981** O'Brien *AA Book of NZ Wildlife* 43 The most common of the grass grub adults is the brown beetle which lays its white globular eggs in the top 15cm of soil.

3. butcher beetle, see BUTCHER 1 a.

4. giraffe beetle, see GIRAFFE BEETLE a.

5. grass grub beetle, see GRASS GRUB 1 b.

6. green beetle. See *manuka beetle* 8 below.
1964 Hintz *Trout at Taupo* 123 How many times on smaller streams have I spent glorious days with puffs of wind shaking the green beetle from the manuka bushes and with the trout rising madly after them!

7. huhu beetle, see HUHU.

8. manuka beetle. *Pyronota* spp. (fam. Scarabaeidae), a small green beetle which feeds on manuka. See also KEREWAI; also *green beetle* 6 above.
1918 *TrNZI* L. 141 Among the beetles the green manuka-beetle (*Pyronota festiva*) is sometimes common. **1926** Tillyard *Insects of Austral. and N.Z.* 229 The Manuka Beetle, *Pyronota festiva* is a beautiful

green cockchafer about 10mm. long, found clustering in large swarms on Manuka..during November and December. **1934** MILLER *Garden Pests in NZ* 58 Another common cockchafer which is on the wing most of the summer and autumn is the green manuka beetle (*Pyronota festiva*). **1954** BEATTIE *Our Southernmost Maoris* 68 The Maori seems to have taken little notice of insects..naming only the more noticeable kinds such as..kekerewai the manuka beetle, also called Te Manu-a-Rehua. **1967** NATUSCH *Animals NZ* 150 Other common chafers include the metallic green manuka beetles, a colourful species being *Pyronota festiva* with its crimson edges and orange legs. **1986** *Campus News III* June 21 Persistent walking brings these rewards: one high garland of clematis one green manuka beetle. **1991** *Dominion* (Wellington) 24 July 8 Fine art quality reproductions, including..the manuka beetle..are intended to highlight the urgent need to preserve native..animals.

9. matai beetle. *West Coast*. HUHU.
1943 MANNERING *Eighty Years* 218 It [Lake Brunner] is a good place for night trolling with minnow or a big lure, or the local 'Huhu', the larva of the matai beetle.

10. Napier beetle. *Obs*. [From Napier, Hawke's Bay, where it was observed by Mr. A. Hamilton in the 1880s.] *Rodolia cardinalis* (fam. Coccinellidae), the cardinal ladybird as a predator of the cottony cushion scale (*Icerya purchasi*).
1890 *NZ Country Jrnl*. XIV. 148 *Icerya* will not be absolutely exterminated by *Vedalia* (the *Napier beetle*). *Ibid*. 149 [Mr. A. Hamilton of Napier writes:] I learn that both the Icerya and the Napier beetle have totally disappeared from the neighbourhood, and that there are still a few to be found at Hastings; which is now probably the only place in New Zealand where the beetle can be procured.

before! *Exclam*. *Obs*. A bushman's warning of the imminent falling of a tree to any who may be in its path.
1986 OWEN & PERKINS *Speaking for Ourselves* 156 Presently they would see the trunk lifting and starting to move, and then there would be the call 'Before!' and it would ring right through the bush, and everbody would be ready and get out of the way.

beggar.
1. *pl*. In the phr. **beggars on the coals** [AND 1848], DAMPER 1. Cf. *buggers afloat* (BUGGER 2).
1871 MONEY *Knocking About NZ* 31 These and other employments, such as baking my dampers, or 'beggars on the coals', exploring the creeks..kept my time fully occupied.
2. beggars' or **beggar's ticks** [f. US or Brit. dial.], *Bidens frondosa*, a weed resembling a dahlia having seeds which stick to wool.
1969 *Standard Common Names Weeds* 4 *beggars' ticks Bidens frondosa* L. **1981** TAYLOR *Weeds of Roadsides* 15 *Beggar's Ticks*... Annual with general likeness to the garden dahlia..introduced from Europe..a weed whose seeds fasten so readily to wool and clothing.

begonia fern. Also **native begonia**. [Transf. use of *Begonia* (fam. Begoniaceae).] PARATANIWHA (*Elatostema rugosum*).
1961 MARTIN *Flora NZ* 246 Another herb with attractive foliage is the Parataniwha or so-called Native Begonia (*Elatostema rugosum*), though it is in no way related to the begonia. **1978** MOORE & IRWIN *Oxford Book of NZ Plants* 82 Parataniwha. The botanically improbable name 'begonia fern' is heard in the Far North. Like a begonia, the plant has thick rhizomes and juicy stems... Like a fern, it grows in great drooping cascades on damp banks.

beg pardon. [AND 1906.] Usu. in the phr. **no beg-pardons** (occas. **no asking pardons**), without apology; with no quarter given. Also occas. *attrib*.
1905 SATCHELL *Toll of Bush* 399 There's no askin' pardons about the bush; it's just life and death. **1910** *Truth* 27 Aug. 6 There are no beg pardons about Susan, who gave a gasp of scornful incredulity when Marshall accused her. **1927** DONNE *Maori Past & Present* 248 In those days men..fought to a finish, there were no 'beg pardons'. **1948** *Our Own Country* 145 As soon as the last load is brought in, without word or a beg-pardon to any one, she [a horse] trundles herself, her cart, and her daughter round to the stable. **1968** SLATTER *Pagan Game* 209 Use yourselves. No beg pardons... Start playing like a First Fifteen for a change. **1975** HOWITT *NZ Rugby Greats* 61 We used to hit each other really hard. There were no beg pardons. **1983** *National Bus. Rev*. 4 July 32 It's got to be uncompromising, no-beg-your-pardons stuff. 'Hit 'em right from the opening whistle.'

behind, *adv*. In the phr. **in behind a**. Esp. **get in behind**, a command to a working-dog to come to heel, or to the rear of a mob of sheep; also used joc. as a catchphrase to people, 'behave yourself'; or expressing mild disbelief, 'I don't believe that'.
1951 [see WAYLEGGO]. **1953** STRONACH *Musterer on Molesworth* 11 Each man took care to keep his dogs in behind, and each dog tried his or her darnedest to get in front. **1964** DICK *High Country Family* 64 Life had been tame for the dogs for many days, so, heedless of their master's cries to 'Wayleggo there, Tip', 'Get in behind, Jock', 'Siddown, Ben'.., they rushed madly hither and thither. **1980** LELAND *Kiwi-Yankee Dict*. 44 Get In Behind: An instruction to working dogs that has become a national in-group joke. In general usage it says, in a humorous way, 'Keep your (subordinate) place'.
b. *transf*. Behind the scenes, 'in camera'.
1991 *Evening Post* (Wellington) 30 Nov. 1 [Wylie, the All Black coach] said it hadn't been an easy decision to make, but 'knowing very well the sort of things going on in behind', he had little option [but to resign].

be in: see IN.

Belgian, *n*. and *a*.
A. *n*. WW1. *Obs*. In the phr. **to give it to the Belgians** [f. a wartime stereotype of an oppressed or starved people], see quot.
1937 PARTRIDGE *Dict. Slang* 45 *Belgians!, give it to the*. C[atch]p[hrase] advice to a man complaining about his food or clothing or inquiring what to do with some superfluity: New Zealand soldiers': 1916-18.
B. *adj*. Also occas. **Belgium**. Used during and after WW1 in special collocations as a patriotic prefix to various items of prepared food, often replacing a traditional epithet *German* (cf. GERMAN *a*.): **Belgian biscuit (cake)**, see quots.; **Belgian** (occas. **Belgium**) **sausage** (or **roll**), and occas. *ellipt*. **Belgium**, LUNCHEON SAUSAGE.
1926 FUTTER *Home Cook. NZ* 209 *Belgian biscuits*..Flour..Brown Sugar..Butter [etc.]... Put together with jam while hot. Ice. **c1939** BASHAM *Aunt Daisy's Book of Recipes* 143 *Belgian cake*..Beat butter and sugar, add eggs..flour..baking powder. To a small half of the mixture, add..cornflour. Spread in tin, then..jam, then remainder of mixture... Bake. **1968** GRUNDY *Who'd Marry a Doctor?* 138 A set of scales appeared from somewhere and a brisk trade was started in sausages, saveloys, **belgian roll**, ham and chicken, and black pudding. [**1914** *Hawke's Bay Tribune* 17 Sept. in Boyd *City of the Plains* (1984) 210 E.H. Green's butchery advertised **Belgian** (not German) **sausage**.] **1916** *Hawkes Bay Herald* 12 Aug. 4 [Advt] Whether it's pork sausages, Belgians, saveloys..or bacon, and you mention 'Morepork', you've said it. **1927** *NZ Dairy Produce Exporter* 28 Apr. 39 Half a pound of Belgian sausage for a pale little office girl who 'rooms' by herself. **1938** [see *German sausage* (GERMAN)]. **1940** STUDHOLME *Te Waimate* (1954) 142 In those days most of the bulls ended their days as pig food, whereas nowadays a large number of them become involved in the luscious Belgian sausage. **1957** FRAME *Owls Do Cry* (1967) 140 If it were mealtime she would..help distribute the Belgian sausage, Sunday. **1984** MARSHALL *Day Hemingway Died* 44 He ate damaged cheese... furrowed snouts of Belgium sausage rolls that were left lying by the slicer. **1992** *NZ English Newsletter* 6 11 (Bartlett *Regional Variation: Southland*) [Other items which may be diagnostic of Southland English are:] *Belgium/Belgium roll/Belgium sausage* (a specific type of luncheon sausage, also used as the generic term)—the adjectival form *Belgian* is occasionally heard. *Belgium* was known as *German sausage* until c. World War I. **1996** *Tablet* (Dunedin) 21 Jan. 8 Shifting from the South Island to the North— from Invercargill all the way up to Morrinsville... Things that stick out most is we roll our R's, we call 'luncheon' 'belgium' and we call 'vacuum cleaning' luxing.

bell. *Obs*. [f. the manufacturer's name *Bell* and Co.] The round top of a cylindrical 'Bell' matchbox; in *pl*., a children's game. See quots.
1903 in Lawlor *Old Wellington Days* (1959) 62 1903 October 15... Commenced collecting bells. **1959** LAWLOR *Old Wellington Days* 62 The bells I collected were the tops of those round two-piece cardboard matchboxes of the period [made by Bell and Co.]. **1972** SUTTON-SMITH *Folkgames Children* 170 Next in order of importance [to Egg Cap] in the pitching games was *Bells* (K-23). This was based on the game of Pitch and Toss..., but had a more innocuous character. The coins for this game, that is the 'bells', were the round, flat tops of the cylindrical Bell [Company] Wax Vesta matchboxes. The head was the blue end with the red flowers in the middle. The 'sugaries' at the other end of the box (the spot on which the match was struck) were not often used, although there is one report in which they were said to represent half the value of the bell.

bellahonie. *Obs*. [Poss. an alteration of Engl. dial. *ballow* or *balla my hand* + *home*: cf. EDD *ballow v*. Yks, Lanc., Chesh.; also written *balla*. 1. To lay claim to an object, partner in a game (=Bags I) 2. *balla my hand* Lancashire signal for truce or a temporary stoppage of the game for rest, etc. by boys at play.] A tagging game.
1972 SUTTON-SMITH *Folkgames Children* 80 In a few tagging games the players joined hands with the He when they were caught and helped him catch the other players. These games were known as *The Bellahonie* (E-21) (Wellington, 1910), Kick Post One (Hampden, Otago, 1880), and Ballyhooley (Wellington, 1920). **1982** SUTTON-SMITH *Hist. Children's Play* 231 There are games recorded in this period for which there is no record before 1900 though they may well have existed under other names... *Wellington*: Who Goes Round My Stone Wall, Beg o' My Neighbor, Bellahonie.

Bellamy's.
1. The British House of Commons term transferred to the dining and drinking establishment of the New Zealand House of Representatives.

1875 HOGG *Lays & Rhymes* 228 Those who talk to Dillon Bell, Or do not talk, but only vote, Or act in Bellamy's the sot. **1880** CHUDLEIGH *Diary* 10 July (1950) 289 Wellington. Interviewed the premier Sir John Hall... Dined at Bellamys. **1919** FANNING *Politics and the Public* 71 Then when work is done he [*sc.* an M.P.] discovers it's too late to go home, and again he has a meal in his room or at Bellamy's. **1934** HYDE *Journalese* 30 There too is Bellamy's, which was forbidden territory to every petticoat whatsoever. **1963** BAXTER *Collected Poems* (1980) 266 The dead who drink at Bellamys Are glad when school kids clap. **1986** GUSTAFSON *Cradle to Grave* 230 Although friendly with many journalists, with whom he would often have 'a great "schooner" of beer' in the press bar in Bellamy's, Savage disliked many of the papers for which they worked.

2. *Hist.* Similarly used in respect of the Canterbury Provincial Council Chambers.

1874 TROLLOPE *NZ* 59 The Provincial Assembly will be a real Parliament with a 'Bellamy'—as the parliament refreshment rooms are called, in remembrance of the old days in the House of Commons at Home. **1882** *TrNZI* XIV. 509 I succeeded, also, in having the fine room above Bellamy's—the so-called coffee room, afterwards the Superintendent's Office—set apart for Museum purposes.

bellbird. [AND 1799.]

1. a. *Anthornis melanura* (fam. Meliphagidae), a bush song-bird renowned for its bell-like notes. See also BLACKSMITH BIRD, KORIMAKO, MAKOMAKO *n.*¹ 1, MOCKER *n.*¹, MOCKIE *n.*¹, MOCKING-BIRD.

[**1770** BANKS *Journal* 17 Jan. (1962) I. 455 This morn [at Queen Charlotte Sound] I was awakd [*sic*] by the singing of the birds ashore. *Ibid.* 456 Their voices were certainly the most melodious wild musick I have ever heard, almost imitating small bells but with most tuneable silver sound imaginable to which maybe the distance was no small addition.] **1845** WAKEFIELD *Adventure NZ* 23 The melodious chimes of the bell-bird were especially distinct. **1866** BARKER *Station Life* (1870) 93 Every now and then we stood..to listen to the Bell-bird, a dingy little fellow nearly as large as a thrush with the plumage of a chaffinch, but with such a note! **1873** [see KORIMAKO]. **1883** DOMETT *Ranolf & Amohia* II. 96 And *honey*-bird and *mocking*-bird And he of clearest melody, The blossom-loving *bell*-bird. **1914** GUTHRIE-SMITH *Mutton Birds & Other Birds* 143 The Bell-bird's eggs are pinkish-white marked with blotches of richest brown; the nest, too, is a beautiful structure firmly set in position and lined with many feathers. **1933** *Press* (Christchurch) (Acland Gloss.) 9 Sept. 15 *Bell bird*.—Mako-mako, or Moki-mok... The name is still sometimes used [in Canterbury]; but the bird is now generally called a 'Mokky'. **1959** WILSON *Bird Is. of NZ* 98 On the Poor Knights the bellbird were in hundreds of thousands, and in the morning their chorus was deafening and so continuous that one got quite bored with it. **1990** *Listener* 16 July 14 Although it's a relatively familiar creature in forests further south, the bellbird has been regionally extinct in Northland for at least a century.

b. *Obs.* Occas. formerly applied to the KOKAKO and TUI (poss. with reinforcement from the synonym KOKO for the latter suggesting the form *kokako*).

c1835 BOULTBEE *Journal* (1986) 104 The Bell-birds are very fond of these flowers, and early in the morning they are to be heard chirping amongst the flax in great quantities... The Bell-Bird is of a purple colour, with a white spot on the breast, shaped like a bell. **1905** THOMSON *Bush Boys* 174 Hark! It [*sc.* the sabbath bell] is ringing now, not the clang of harsh metal hanging in church steeple, but the mellow note of the *Tui*, the bell-bird of our Northern Isle. **1924** *Otago Witness* (Dunedin) 16 Dec. 6 The North Island crow, which is sometimes given the title of bell-bird on account of its notes, is larger than a tui, dark bluish-grey, and has blue wattles. **1932** STEAD *Life Histories NZ Birds* 145 In different parts of New Zealand, the name Bell-bird is applied to different birds. In Canterbury, and, indeed, to a large extent, throughout the South Island, it referred to *Anthornis melanura*; but it was frequently applied to the Tui. In the North Island, it was applied to both these birds; but, particularly among the bushmen, of the central portion of the island, it was used almost exclusively for the Crow. **1946** [see KOKAKO 1]. **1949** BUCK *Coming of Maori* 7 When [Kupe was] asked if it was inhabited, he said that all he saw was a *weka* (wood hen) whistling in the gullies, a *kokako* (bell bird) tolling on the ridges, and a *tiwaiwaka* (fantail) flitting about before his face.

2. With a regional modifier: **Chatham Island**, **Poor Knights**, **Three Kings**.

(1) Chatham Island bellbird. *A. m. melanocephala.*

1873 BULLER *Birds NZ* 96 Anthornis melanocephala. (Chatham-Island Bell-Bird.) **1884** *NZJSc.* II. 279 *Anthornis melanocephala*... Chatham Island Bell-bird. **1904** HUTTON & DRUMMOND *Animals NZ* 109 *The Chatham Island Bell-bird. Anthornis melanocephala*... The Chatham Islands have a Bell-bird of their own. Its note is said to be much richer and fuller than that of the New Zealand species. **1955** BAILEY *Birds NZ* 107 Two other races of the bellbird are recognised, one restricted to Three Kings Island (*obscura*), and the Chatham Island form (*melanocephala*) which has been extinct since about 1906. **1985** *Reader's Digest Book NZ Birds* 290 *Chatham Island Bellbird A. m. melanocephala*... Probably extinct. **1990** *Checklist Birds NZ* 215 *Chatham Island Bellbird*;..finally on Mangere Island; extinct since about 1906.

(2) Poor Knights bellbird. *A. m. oneho.*

1990 *Checklist Birds NZ* 214 *A. m. oneho*..Poor Knights Bellbird... Poor Knights Islands: throughout the group.

(3) Three Kings bellbird. *A. m. obscura.*

1955 OLIVER *NZ Birds* 505 *Three Kings Bellbird*... When Cheeseman visited the Three Kings in 1887 he saw a bird which he described as common, about the size of a Bellbird but the underparts were greyish white. **1985** *Reader's Digest Book NZ Birds* 290 *Three Kings Bellbird*... Most common bird on the Three Kings Islands.

bellies: see BELLY 1 a.

bellman. *Hist.* [Used elsewhere, but of historical interest in its association with early (esp. West Coast) goldfields settlements.] Also **bellringer**. A town crier or public announcer drawing attention to the announcements by ringing a bell.

1857 HURSTHOUSE *NZ* I. 401 But New Zealand..is..a land of which some future bellman may some day sing. **1868** *Shortland Town by Night* in Cooper *Digger's Diary* 12 Mar. (1978) 30 Bell-men pervade the thoroughfares and announce various entertainments. **1878** BULLER *Forty Yrs. NZ* 121 The services were published by the bellman [in Hokitika, 1865]. **1914** in *Hist. N. Otago from 1853* (1978) 99 About this time [c1880s] the town's bellman was Jimmy Reid, who..was in great demand by the auctioneering firms on sale days. **1925** BATHGATE *Random Recolls.* 16 Amongst [the capsized ferry's] passengers was one of the bellmen who plied their trade, and often made a hideous noise in the city streets. This man had been engaged to announce the different events on the day's programme [at Vauxhall Gardens, Dunedin, c1860s], and as he landed dripping on the Vauxhall jetty he exclaimed: 'Oh! What'll I do? I've lost my bell.' 'Wring your clothes,' said a bystander. **1961** HENDERSON *Friends in Chains* 45 One of the last of the bellringers to parade the streets of Maoriland could often be heard [at Reefton c1900], ringing out his sad or glad, or indifferent tidings.

bellowsfish.

1. Also occas. **bellowfish**. Any of several species of small marine mid-water snipefish (fam. Macrorhamphosidae), of a shape recalling a fire-bellows.

1911 WAITE *Rec. Canterbury Museum* I. 169 *Centriscops Humerosus*..Bellows Fish. **1927** SPEIGHT et al. *Nat. Hist. Canterbury* 198 Snipe fishes (or bellows fish)..which have the front of the head produced into a snout with small jaws at the tip, are a group regarded as an offshoot from the Garfish. **1956** GRAHAM *Treasury NZ Fishes* 402 Bellows Fish *Centriscops humerosus*... Bellows Fish *Notopogon xenosoma*. **1967** NATUSCH *Animals NZ* 211 The bellows fish..has scales too small to see clearly, though their roughness can be felt. **1981** WILSON *Fisherman's Bible* 25 Bellowfish. Deep-bodied fish of the family *Macrorhamphosidae* which resemble related pipefish and seahorses, with their mouths at the end of a tube-like snout... Whitley suggests that they get their name from the closeness with which they resemble the old-fashioned bellows for blowing fires.

2. With a modifier: **banded (blue banded) bellowsfish**, *Centriscops obliquus*; **banded (red banded) bellowsfish**, *Centriscops humerosus*; **crested bellowsfish**, *Notopogon lilliei*; **orange bellowsfish**, *Notopogon fernandezianus*.

1982 AYLING *Collins Guide* (1984) 192 *Banded Bellowsfish Centriscops obliquus*... The banded bellowsfish is a deep-bodied species that attains a maximum size of about 25cm. *Ibid.* 193 *Crested Bellowsfish Notopogon lilliei*... The crested bellowsfish is a deep bodied species similar in shape to the banded bellowsfish but lacking the hump behind the head... They are found south of Cook Strait in water between 100 and 600m deep. **1989** PAULIN et al. *NZ Fish* 164 *Centriscops obliquus* bluebanded bellowsfish... *Centriscops humerosus* redbanded bellowsfish. *Ibid.* 165 *Notopogon lilliei* crested bellowsfish... *Notopogon fernandezianus* orange bellowsfish.

bellringer: see BELLMAN.

Bell's brick: see BRICK 1.

bell sheep. *Shearing.* [f. the *bell* rung to mark the end of a shearing run: AND 1897.] See quot.

1989 *NZ Eng. Newsletter* III. 21 *bell sheep:* The last sheep shorn by any shearer in any run of the day and it has to be clear of the catching pen before the bell goes.

belltopper. *Obs.* Also **bell-topper**; rarely **belles-topper**. [Poss. f. a type having a bell-shaped crown: but cf. EDD (N. Ireland and Manx) *belles-topper*, a woman's high hat, and the 1874 quot. below.] One of various kinds of (often black, silk) top hat.

1853 in *Canterbury Rhymes* (1866) 30 The life-nominees shall wear long-faced bell-toppers. **1862** THATCHER *Auckland Vocalist* 5 His volunteer cap's on whenever I meet him, He wears it to save a belltopper no doubt. **1873** TINNE *Wonderland of Antipodes* 57 No tall black hats ('bell-toppers', à la coloniale). [**1876** ADAM *Twenty-five Yrs. Emigrant Life* 79 In the last generation some of the Manx women wore men's hats; my grandmother was married in one of these Belles-Toppers.] **1884** *Daily News* 30 Aug. in Clayden *Handbook NZ* (1886) 209 The outlandish gear [*sc.* wide-awake hat] is put aside [by the new chum], a 'bell-topper' is bought, gloves are resumed, and a first illusion over. **1905** FERGUSON *Poems & Sketches* 149 And when his 'bell topper' he puts on, his looks there's no withstanding. **1916** MANSFIELD *Aloe* (1982) 71 He liked to dance and attend pic-nics—to put on his 'bell topper'. **1934** SCANLAN *Winds of Heaven* 143 Did you go to school in a belltopper hat? Mike says the boys do at Eton. **1959** MASTERS *Tales of Mails* 148 When on his rounds [a1910] he rode an old horse and always wore a bell-topper hat. **1961** HENDERSON *Friends In Chains* 185 Bell-topper: High hard hat with wide flat crown. **1979** *Evening Post* (Wellington) 12 May 12 He was observed walking briskly to his 8am appointment with his work, dressed in the invariable belltopper, frock coat, check trousers. **1984** BOYD *City of the Plains* 23 'A very fine man in appearance, stature and spirit' he disembarked wearing a bell-topper and swallow-tails in 1859.

belly. [Spec. or transf. uses of *belly* the stomach, the underside, or the bulging part or something or someone: see OED.]

1. a. [AND 1928.] Usu. *pl.* as **bellies**. *Ellipt.* for BELLY-WOOL.
1920 MACDONALD *Austral. & NZ Sheepfarming* 144 The big stations..may even divide up the skirtings..besides keeping the bellies, locks, and stained wool separate. **1936** SARGESON *Conversation with My Uncle* 24 After we'd pulled the bellies off the fleeces we had to roll them up and put them in the press. **1944** MARSH *Died in the Wool* 16 It's not bellies in that pack, either. Bellies smell a bit but nothing to touch this. **1950** *NZJAg.* Oct. LXXXI. 311 Frames hinged to a wall can be very useful to support a wool pack for bellies, necks, etc. **1964** ANDERSON *Doctor in Mountains* (1974) 32 They also swept up the bellies and pieces, and so kept the shearing board clean and tidy. **1973** FERNANDEZ *Tussock Fever* 166 'What's 2nd Pcs H?' 'Grade 2, pieces'... 'And Bls E?' 'That's belly wool. E grade bellies.' **1989** *NZ Eng. Newsletter* III. 21 *belly, belly wool:* The wool shorn from the sheep's belly.

b. By back formation, **bellied** *ppl. a.*, of a sheep, shorn of belly-wool before the main shearing.
1989 *NZ Eng. Newsletter* III. 21 *bellied sheep:* A sheep that has had the belly wool shorn off it prior to the main shearing.

2. *transf.* The thick or bulging part of a stockwhip.
1933 *Press* (Christchurch) (Acland Gloss.) 9 Sept. 15 *Belly...* The thick part of the lash of a stock whip, towards the middle. **1940** STUDHOLME *Te Waimate* (1954) 150 The standard measurements [of a stockwhip]: Handle 10 to 12 inches; thong: say 11 ft. six inches; the fall: eighteen inches; and the cracker, twelve inches or more. Total length, about 15 feet... The strands were made gradually thicker up to the belly then trimmed off to the 'tail' of the whip. The belly, or thickest part of the thong, was filled out with pieces of leather laid lengthwise and the strands plaited round them.

3. Special Comb. **belly-buster** [AND 1941], **belly-flop (-flopper)** [as a dive into water, recorded earliest in NZ: see OED *belly n.* 17; cf. EDD *belly-flop*], an awkward or failed dive in which the diver lands on the stomach, also *transf.* to a business or other failure; **belly-rope** *farming*, see quot. 1878; **belly-scarf** *v. logging* [AND *n.* 1909], to cut a scarf in a standing tree on the side of the intended direction of fall (contrast BACK-SCARF).
1953 14 M A4 Thames DHS 16 **Belly buster** [M2] **1960** KEINZLY *Tangahano* 161 Lunch hour was what Gus expected it to be. Jeering kids called him Glider, Ole Dusty, and Belly Buster. **1980** LELAND *Kiwi-Yankee Dict.* 13 *belly-buster:* is not an excess of candy and ice cream. It is the inexperienced swimmer's least favourite dive—a belly flop. (see *honey pot/bomb, duck dive*). **1937** HYDE *Wednesday's Children* 49 'It hurt,' she added... 'So I didn't do any more worshipful **belly-flops.**' **1964** HARVEY *Any Old Dollars Mister?* 67 He trotted down into the surf and did a beaut belly flop into the water. **1988** MCGILL *Dict. Kiwi Slang* 14 *belly-buster* disastrous dive where stomach hits water; aka 'bellyflop'. **1995** *Dominion* (Wellington) 3 June 22 Really, it's [*sc.* a film] better described as a disaster area... Huge expectations, lots of pretension in the air, and a painful bellyflop. **1959** SLATTER *Gun in My Hand* 10 Climbing over the tin fence into the town baths and heaving the stand planks into the water when we tired of bombs from the side and **bellyfloppers** from the board. **1965** HILLIARD *Power of Joy* 63 How white his father looked..poised for a bellyflopper. **1878** ELWELL *Boy Colonists* 190 The animal was at length brought with its head close up to the corner post; the end of a small rope fastened to one of the rails was now passed..rapidly round its body, and handed to the men outside to put round another rail and hold... Almost at the same time that this '***belly-rope***', as it was called, was being fastened to keep the body of the animal upright, Harold would be putting a rope round one of the hind legs. **1928** KENWAY *Pioneering Poverty Bay* 38 He will '**belly-scarf**' and 'back-scarf' the lot, that is to say, he will cut about a third through on both the lower and higher sides.

belly-pieces: see BELLY-WOOL.

belly-wool. [AND 1871.] Inferior wool on or from a sheep's belly; also **belly-pieces**, oddments of belly-wool. See also BELLY 1 a.
1851 WELD *Hints to Intending Sheep-farmers* 10 Their mothers do not lose the belly wool, as they would do by lambing in the spring, when their wool is long, and the heat of the body renders it liable to peel off. **1875** *Otago Witness* (Dunedin) 18 Sept. 18 First, clean all the points, the crutch and the belly wool, and let this be swept aside. **1901** *TrNZI* XXXIII. 196 The black fleece was rolled up just as taken from the sheep's back, the belly-pieces being also left in... For example, white wool divides, when skirted by the roller at the wool-table, thus: Belly pieces, say, 6d. per pound; first pieces, 8d. per pound. **1920** MACDONALD *Austral. & NZ Sheepfarming* 148 The belly wool and the pieces or locks are kept separate from the fleece when rolling it. **1959** MIDDLETON *The Stone* 42 The shearers wandered over to the yards and caught a few sheep and felt their belly wool. **1973** FERNANDEZ *Tussock Fever* 166 'And [what's] Bls E?' 'That's belly wool. E grade bellies.' **1986** RICHARDS *Off the Sheep's Back* 55 I was allowed to miss school to help in the shed by picking up the bellywool.

belt, *n.*¹ [Spec. use of *belt* a zone or district: see OED 5 a; EDD *n.*¹ a narrow strip of wood or plantation.]

1. Orig. as **the Belt** (usu. cap. and occas. *pl.*, see quot. 1948, with *spec.* Christchurch reference), now usu. (and felt as a short form of) TOWN BELT q.v., an urban recreational and environmental reserve kept mainly in parkland or trees.
1848 WAKEFIELD *Handbook NZ* 96 It is to be hoped, that as they [*sc.* the wooded Tinakore heights] are included in the Belt of land reserved all round the Town for public purposes, strict precautions may be taken to preserve the timber from depredation. **1890** *TrNZI* XXII. 486 *P. heterophylla* was more abundant on the Belt than it is now. **1904** ADAMS *Tussock Land* 61 Their way lay along 'the Belt' that broad band of Native bush which encircles Dunedin. **1922** *NZJST* IV. 278 The wax-eye..used to build in the bush on the Belt. **1948** HAAST *Julius Von Haast* 462 If the citizen [of Christchurch c1866] went out to the Belts, the boulevards of the City, he found..the trees that had been planted in the East [Belt] had been neglected. *Ibid.* 490 On May 13 [1867], the [Christchurch] City Council received a report from a committee on planting, recommending planting the Belts in the following manner. A footpath, 10 ft. wide on each side of the Belt, two roadways running parallel to the footpaths, each half a chain in width, leaving 46 ft. clear in the middle of the Belt, to be planted with trees, so as to allow a 10 ft. grass-walk down the centre of each block between the intersecting streets. Each block was to be planted with one variety of tree. **1976** SARGESON *Sunset Village* 31 On the suburban side of the Belt all to the eye was uniform and conforming. **1980** BRASCH *Indirections* 26 We shot..arrows of..the whitey wood that grew in the Belt just outside the back gate.

2. [Poss. ellipt. for *shelter-belt*.] A strip of trees or bush.
1853 SWAINSON *Auckland* 38 These belts and clumps consist of a rich variety of wood; the graceful tree-fern..clustering..around the tall stems of the statelier forest trees. **1899** *The Lash* in Woodhouse *Farm & Station Verse* (1950) 47 You rattle thro' the belt and scrub and up the little hill.

belt, *n.*² [Transf. use *belt* a prize in boxing, and later, in shooting: see OED *n.*¹ 1 b.] In the phr. **to give (one) the belt**, to give the prize to; **to hold the belt**, to win the prize.
1910 *Truth* 24 Dec. 1 It is reported from across the Tasman that when a sheep was being shorn at a station near Penhurst, a starling's nest with one egg in it was found in the wool. To hold the belt, Zealandia will require to produce a duck that has hatched a sitting of eggs in a collection plate. **a1974** SYDER & HODGETTS *Austral. & NZ Eng.* (TS) 53 *The belt.* The ensign of a champion bestowed in name only. 'Harry can talk longer, and on more different topics than any of us, and after he had gone on non-stop most of the evening, we told him we'd give him the belt for the greatest talker known among us all.'

bench, *n.*

1. [Extended use *bench* a shelf or ledge left in steep earth: see OED 7.] A ledge or sheep-track along a hillside. See also BENCH *v.*
1946 *NZJST* XXVII. 159 On inland northerly and westerly situations..these breaks [in the surface] develop successively in definite steps or benches... Near the crests of hills sheep aggravate the position by camping on these terracettes. **1984** HOLDEN *Razorback* 14 He thumbed back..the hammer of his rifle, before warily continuing along the ever-narrowing bench. Soon it was no more than ten paces across.

Hence **benchy** *a.*
1944 *NZ New Writing* III. 56 Upon the benchy hillside Where hoggets love to lie. **1970** MCNAUGHTON *Tat* 99 It was a slow process, getting those sheep down. The hillside was benchy and rough.

2. Special Comb. **bench loader** *flaxmilling*, see quot.; **bench seat**, a, usu. front, seat of a motor vehicle in the form of a single upholstered bench extending from one side to the other.
1913 CARR *Country Work* 43 When the flax arrives at the mill it is weighed and credited to the cutter. The '**bench loader**' then takes two or three bundles and puts them in a barrel (heavy end down). He then takes the longest leaves and places them on a bench convenient to the 'feeder'. **1986** *Listener* 20 Dec. 13 Tell-tale signs: car obviously belonging to mum..two in the front (no **bench seat**), four in the back with crates on their knees, zinc on their noses.

bench, *v.* Usu. as *ppl. a.*, **benched (out)**, of a track, road, etc., cut out or formed as a ledge (on a hillside or sloping ground).

1932 *Canterbury Mountaineer* 34 Our directions were difficult to follow for a benched track, over 30 years old 'was supposed to be somewhere'. **1937** *Tararua Tramper* June 12 In order to be sure of picking up a benched track we kept in the river. **1960** *Over Whitcombe Pass* 14 Where the boulder beaches merge into gorges well-benched foot-tracks make delightful walking. **1961** Crump *Good Keen Man* 21 In some places the track had to be benched into the side of the hill with axe and spade, and paved with pongas. **1984** *Listener* 28 Apr. 62 One of my correspondents, tramping with her husband, referred to the 'benched-out' track they were following up the hillside... She, on the other hand, knew of no other name for the kind of farm track that at one time was dug and is now more commonly bulldozed along and up a hillside. 'Benched-out' roads, she assures me, climbed all over Banks Peninsula where she was brought up and it had not occurred to her that the phrase was in any way unusual.

benchie: see BENCHMAN (1971 quot.).

benchman. *Sawmilling.* Also **benchie**. [AND 1895.] The mill-hand on the sawbench who feeds the log or flitch into the saw; occas., one who works on or operates a sawbench.

1894 *NZ Official Year-book* 334 In Southland, at this date (May, 1894) benchmen are paid at the rate of 9s. per day. **1908** *Awards, etc.* 337 [Wellington Sawmills Award] [Rates of wages] Head benchman is a man who sharpens and sets his own saws per week [£]3 6[s.] 0[d.] But hammering a saw being the work of a specialist shall not be included in the duties of a sawyer. **1923** *Awards, etc.* 111 [Westland Timber Yards and Sawmill Employees] [Rates of wages] Dray-drivers [£]4 0[s.] 0[d.] Benchman and band-sawyer 0 15 6 Sawyer keeping up to three saws 0 18 4. **1936** Rust *Whangarei & Dist.* 163 Hundreds of bushmen, loggers..and rafters were employed besides stackers, saw doctors, benchmen and mill-hands in the different sawmills [at Maungakaramea in the 1860s]. **1952-53** *NZ Forest Service Gloss.* (TS) Benchman. Head-sawyer of a breast-bench. **1971** in Cleveland *Great NZ Songbook* (1991) 54 From the bushmen to the breaker-out, From the breaker-out to the bench; From the benchie to the tailer-out, From the tailer-out to the yard. **1988** Gibbons *Recollections* 39 He was one of the best benchmen on native timber.

Hence **benching** *vbl. n.*, in sawmilling, the occupation of benchman.

1965 Hilliard *Power of Joy* 45 He would go among the men from the mills..asking if there were any jobs going. 'Benching?—any benching?

bend. *Goldmining.* [Orig. US: see DAE *n.* 1 b; AND 1860.] The land partly enclosed by a bend or curve of a river.

1862 *Otago Goldfields & Resources* 21 Should they prove auriferous, these flats, or bends, will afford room for thousands [of diggers].

bender.

1. [f. the bending of the knees in ritual genuflection.] A derogatory term for a Catholic.

1974 Hilliard *Maori Woman* 91 'If they found out I'd joined the Catholic Church'... Maisie Hobson must have heard. She called out... 'Are you still with the benders? I bet the knees of your stockings don't last long with that crowd.'

2. Usu. *pl.* [f. bending over to receive punishment on the buttocks.] (A stroke of) corporal punishment at secondary school.

1953 14-17 M A10 Thames DHS 23 Benders [M16]

benecootoo, var. BARRACOUTA.

beneficial, *a.* [Spec. use of *beneficial* enjoying as a usufruct: see OED 3 (*Law*) b.] In special collocations: **beneficial** (also **beneficiary**) **island,** one of various statutorily named islands in the south of New Zealand, the breeding places of the MUTTONBIRD, to which certain Maori people (**beneficial owners**) have an inherited sole right (**beneficial right**) to a TAKE q.v. Cf. BENEFICIARY 2.

1949 *Land Act Regs.* in Wilson *Titi Heritage* (1979) 174 '**Beneficial island**' means any one of the following Titi Islands. **1979** Wilson *Titi Heritage* 21 There is a schedule to the agreement which sets out the areas reserved and ninth in the schedule is a list of the Titi Islands which have become known as the Beneficial Islands. **1995** *Sunday Star-Times* (Auckland) 22 Jan. sect. C 15 [Heading] Titi (Muttonbird) Islands. Annual Permit Meeting 1995... A meeting will be held..in connection with the issue of permits to take muttonbirds from Crown Islands, for the appointment of supervisors for both Crown and Beneficial Islands. **1982** Sansom *In Grip of Island* 69 Herekopare and Woman's Island are the only two **beneficiary** muttonbird **islands**. All the rest are Crown lands. **1949** *Land Act Regs.* in Wilson *Titi Heritage* (1979) 174 '**Beneficial owner**' means a Rakiura Maori who holds a succession order from the Maori Land Court entitling him to any beneficial interest in any beneficial island. **1979** Wilson *Titi Heritage* 27 **Beneficial rights** to each island were very jealously guarded, and any natives landing on an island to which they had no hereditary right, and taking birds, were very severely punished.

beneficiary. [Spec. use of *beneficiary* a debtor to another's bounty: see OED B 3.]

1. One who receives regular payment or assistance (a 'benefit') from the State or an institution.

1950 *Growth & Development of Social Security* 71 The 25-per-cent subsidy on personal earnings of blind beneficiaries was retained in the Social Security Act. **1988** *Dominion* (Wellington) 11 Nov. 2 Social Welfare minister Michael Cullen spoke out yesterday against those who criticised beneficiaries as 'undeserving' or 'idle bludgers'. **1988** *Dominion* (Wellington) 25 Nov. 10 [Heading] Beneficiary admits breaking windows. —, 38, invalid beneficiary, admitted intentionally damaging six windows at the property. **1989** *Dominion* (Wellington) 22 Apr. 6 The defendants are..—23, writer,—31, scallop opener,—47, welfare beneficiary.

2. A registered member of an iwi entitled to receive benefits due to the tribe. Cf. BENEFICIAL.

1995 *NZ Herald* (Auckland) 20 Jan. sect. 1 11 The Tainui Maori Trust Board will travel the country telling its beneficiaries what the Crown's offer was for the settlement of the tribe's raupatu (confiscation) land claim.

Benghazi burner. WW2 (N. Africa). Also **Benghasi, Benghazi boiler.** [f. the name *Benghazi* a coastal town in Libya.] A portable makeshift device for heating containers of water within an open-ended jacket fired usu. by petrol. See also THERMETTE.

1945 Uren *Diamond Trails of Italy* 90 This type of water heater we called a 'Benghazi Burner'—it is sometimes advertised commercially as a 'Thermet'. The fire burns in the funnel, the water being on the outside of the funnel. The water boils in two minutes. **1949** The Sarge *Excuse My Feet* 28 From out of his bundle of gear, Herbert produced a small Benghazi, a present from a Taranaki Old Dig, who had returned after service in the desert. **1956** Davin *Sullen Bell* 114 'Time to brew up,' Alec said. He set a light to the Benghazi boiler he had made out of odds and ends of tin. **1967** Elliott & Adshead *Cowshed to Dog Collar* 90 The Kiwis had to have their boilup. The Benghazi burner would quickly oblige with a brew. Its principle was simple in the extreme:.. one 4-gallon tin with holes pierced in the top. First sand was dropped in, next a little petrol, and finally a lighted match. **1982** Burton *Two Hundred Yrs. NZ Food* 32 An ingenious contraption was developed for brewing water for tea. Known as the Benghazi burner, it consisted of an upright cylindrical sleeve inside which a diesel or petrol fire was made. The jacket was filled with water which boiled with the rising heat. **1991** Benghazi boiler [see THERMETTE].

benny, *n.* and *attrib.*

1. [f. an alteration of BENE(FICIARY.] A familiar form of BENEFICIARY.

1994 *Evening Post* (Wellington) 25 Oct. 8 [Heading] Bennys who neglect their kids.

2. [Prob. from an alteration of *bene*(fit a State allowance paid to the variously needy.] As **benny day,** a day on which a State benefit is paid out.

1994 *Evening Post* (Wellington) 25 Oct. 8 [The Special Education people] 'd know to be around on a Tuesday, what they call 'Benny Day', there being two of these weekly, the other on Thursday.

benzine.

1. [Cf. OED b, 1865.] Until approx. WW2, the preferred name for petrol in New Zealand, and still in occasional use.

1904 *NZ Herald* (Auckland) 3 June in La Roche *Hist. of Howick & Pakuranga* (1991) 161 The motor 'bus is named 'Pioneer'... The fuel is benzine. **1910** *Truth* 8 Jan. 5 The furniture, including a saddle-backed couch and sofa, had been piled against the wall. Benzine was poured on them, and..ignited. **1923** *NZJST* VI. 52 Benzine is supplied by the company at pre-war rates— £1 5s. per case. **1931** Ngata *Let.* 15 May in *Na To Hoa Aroha* (1987) II. 143 I have taken revenge on him and appointed him welfare officer pro tem at £3 a week and a small benzine allowance. **1943** Bennett *English in NZ* in *Amer. Speech* XVIII. 87 And petrol is generally known as *benzine*, though it is now coming to be advertised as *gas* at the more modern 'service stations'. **1960** Masters *Back-Country Tales* 163 As they jolted out of the last of the holes, Mrs. Caunce noticed a strong smell of benzine. **1985** Langdale-Hunt *Last Entail Male* 103 A very necessary job was greasing the tins that held petrol, or as it was known on the Chathams, benzine.

2. a. *attrib.*

1911 *Maoriland Worker* 30 June 12 The speakers were looking towards a benzine 'bus, and didn't see the kids. **1928** *Free Lance* (Wellington) 8 Feb. 17 On Anniversary week-end..the Benzine Brigade—gently melted away into the surrounding country by car and motor-bike. **1946** Sargeson *That Summer* 34 We talked and he pumped some air into a benzine lamp and it fizzed and lit up bright enough to blind you. **1990** *Listener* 27 Aug. 114 This city is an abuse. Concrete medians..four-way off-ramps, triple channel replays of benzine sunsets.

b. Special Comb. **benzine bowser,** a petrol pump (cf. BOWSER); **benzine box,** a wooden case capable of holding two four-gallon tins of benzine and used as a makeshift article of furniture, or as a building material; **benzine engine,** a petrol-powered engine; **benzine tin,** a four-gallon container orig. for benzine, but put to various domestic, farm, etc. uses.

1966 Turner *Eng. Lang. Austral. & NZ* 172 The word **benzine** for petrol and **benzine bowser** for petrol pump seem to be fading from use. 1926 *NZ Dairy Produce Exporter* 30 Oct. 39 Writing about the use of **benzine boxes** I said 'Six would make a fowlhouse'. a1927 Anthony *Gus Tomlins* (1977) 89 I was little better off. Both of us used benzine boxes for chairs. 1949 Hartley *Shepherd's Dogs* 39 A benzine box lying on its side is sufficiently high for a three-months' puppy to climb upon. 1963 Morrieson *Scarecrow* 64 Victor Lynch got off the benzine box he was sitting on. 1988 Gibbons *Recollections* 17 A benzine box was a box which held two four-gallon tins. 1923 *NZJST* VI. 52 A small **benzine-engine** of, say, 1 horse-power to drive the dynamo would be very useful. a1927 Anthony *Me & Gus* (1977 Gus Tomlins) 86 He spoke of the dangers of benzine engines. 1910 *Truth* 26 Mar. 1 He took with him a **benzine tin**, upon which he sat down every now and again. 1953 *NZ Observer* 25 Mar. 12 They arrived in oblong cases, two to a case..those benzine-tin buckets so familiar to the old-time cocky.

berdan. *Quartz-gold mining.* [Origin unknown: AND 1901.] A revolving circular iron pan in which an iron ball grinds ore concentrates with mercury and water, the whole tilted so that the excess water can escape. Also *attrib*.
1867 *Trip to Thames Goldfields* 27 Oct. in Cooper *Digger's Diary* (1978) 28 There are but two or three small Berdan machines on the spot [for crushing stone]. 1868 *Thames Miner's Guide* 93 Kurunui Battery..of six stampers, and one stamper specimen battery with Berdans at the end of tables to grind the tailings. 1876 [see drag *n.* 1]. 1908 *NZGeol.SB (NS)* No.6 26 The crushing machinery in all these batteries consisted of four to ten heads of light stamps, and the gold-saving plant of amalgamated copper plates, with or without the addition of a small berdan. 1978 McAra *Gold Mining Waihi* 312 Berdan pan: An annular-shaped cast-iron bowl or basin about four feet in diameter containing heavy weights which were revolved slowly to grind the ore, particularly concentrates, finely. Sometimes mercury was added to the berdans to form an amalgam with the finely-ground gold.

bergoo, var. burgoo.

Berka. *WW1* and *WW2* (Egypt). Also **berker**; occas. (**Wagh el**) **birka, Birkett, burka.** [Poss. orig. *Wagh-el-Burka* f. *Wagh* street, *burka* Hindi ad. Arabic *burga* (see OED *burka*[1]) a long enveloping garment worn in public places by Muslim women to screen them from the view of men and strangers.] As **the Berka**, the red-light district of Cairo; **Berka 8**, a joc. name for the Africa Star medal or ribbon (see quot. 1939–45). Cf. Wazza.
1915 Comyns in Boyack *Behind the Lines* (1989) 27 At about 4 pm a serious riot occurred in Eharia, Wagh-el-Birkett in a street which bears an unenviable reputation. 1917 Thornton *With Anzacs in Cairo* 65 I picked up the man, carried him into the Wagh el Birka..and sent him in a cab back to Zeitoun. 1939–45 *Expressions & Sayings 2NZEF (TS N.A. WAII DA 420/1)* Lady Astor–Africa Star. Also called Berka 8 and Zib-bib Star. 1943 'Berker' [see Wazza]. 1947 Davin *For Rest of Our Lives* 147 And a man would get very meskeen too, losing his kale on two-up at the Naafi and bints in the Berka. 1978 Tucker *Thoroughbreds Are My Life* 23 I may say that during my stay in Cairo I did all the things that young soldiers do, visiting such places at the Burka, which is the red-light district of Cairo. 1982 Sandys *Love & War* 216 But he knew how his cobber felt about Anna, and suspected he disapproved of his own infrequent sorties into the Berka. 1990 Birk[a] [see Wazza].

berko /'bɜkʌʊ/, *a*. [Alteration of *ber*(ser)*k* + -o.] Usu. as **go berko**, to go 'berserk', to become uncontrollably violent or emotional.
1961 Crump *Hang On a Minute Mate* 163 He's okay when he's sober but when he's got a few in he goes berko. 1963 *Salient* (Wellington) 18 June 2 Sales affect me in an odd way. I seem to go a trifle berko and rush round buying tomes on pot plants. 1972 *Otago Daily Times* (Dunedin) 4 Apr. (Griffiths Coll.) A 23-year-old housewife..was convicted of breaking property valued at $120, assaulting a police constable and using obscene language... 'You went what is commonly called berko,' Mr Ross said when remanding the defendant for sentence. 1989 *Listener* 25 Mar. 12 Grey Panthers go berko in this very odd geriatric vigilante movie.
Hence **berky** *n*., a 'berserk' fit.
1985 Mitcalfe *Hey Hey Hey* 102 'Suppose you boys tell me just exactly what happened yesterday'. 'Joe did a "berky". Reckoned we wrecked his machines!'

berl, var. burl *n*.[1]

berley. [Of unknown origin: AND *n*. 1874, *v*. 1852.] Ground bait for fish. Also *vbl. n.*
1968 *NZ Contemp. Dict. Suppl.* (Collins) 3 *berley..n.* ground bait for fish. 1981 Wilson *Fisherman's Bible* 31 Berleying: *see Ground-baiting*. 1991 *North Shore Times Advertiser* (Auckland) 13 Use lots of berley which slimies respond extremely well to... The baitfish jigs should be jigged in the berley.

berm. [Extended use of *berm* narrow ledge, esp. in fortifications: see OED *n*. 1; DARE 4 esp. Great Lakes, 1965.] Locally in New Zealand a grass strip, often mown, between the hard surface of a, usu. suburban, road and the footpath; occas. (Lower Hutt, 1951, p.c. Professor W. Cameron) the square plots of lawn on the street frontage of state houses.
1939–45 *Expressions & Sayings 2NZEF (TS N.A. WAII DA 420/1)* Verges, shoulders, **berms**... Edges of road off the bitumen or metalled surface. 1954 *berm* first heard by Ed. in Upper Hutt for the grassed strip between the roadway and footpath. 1961 p.c. Jack Columbus, Blenheim. Used in Blenheim for the strip between the road and the gutter. 1979 *SANZ Gloss. Bldg. Terminol.* 14 Berm 1. Continuous horizontal bench (or benches) cut into a batter to ensure slope stability. 2. Narrow strip of land separating footpath from carriageway or between footpath and boundary of road reserve used for underground services, and often widened to include planting.

Bermuda buttercup. *Oxalis pes-caprae* (fam. Oxalidaceae), a South African herb with showy golden flowers, a common weed in New Zealand lowlands.
1980 Adams *Wild Flowers* 20 Bermuda buttercup is neither a buttercup nor from Bermuda... Botanical name: *Oxalis pes-caprae*, South Africa. Family: Oxalidaceae. 1980 Taylor *Weeds of Crops* 72 Bermuda Buttercup (*Oxalis pes-caprae*)... A South African weed of flower and vegetable gardens, very common in Auckland.

beta-beta, var. biddy-bid.

beyond: see back of beyond; *beyond the blue mountains* (blue *a*. 1).

Bible.
1. As the first element (usu. init. cap.) of derog. special Comb. **Bible-banger** [AND 1904], **Bible-basher** [AND 1958], **Bible-puncher, Bible-thumper** [both used elsewhere but recorded earliest in NZ: see OED *bible* III], an outspoken religious zealot or vigorous preacher of usu. fundamentalist Christian belief; often in a weakened sense, any minister of religion.
1905 *Truth* 19 Aug. 3 Baptist **Bible-banger**. 1935 Strong in Partridge *Slang Today* 287 I might even go to the Sallies; they have the shortest service. You can take my word I am no Bible-banger. 1948 Ballantyne *Cunninghams* (1976) 110 Gil reckoned that Kent was better than most of the Bible-bangers who visited the hospital... He didn't force the Bible down your throat. 1963 Adsett *Magpie Sings* 45 He was probably going somewhere quiet to read the Bible. Everyone said he was a Bible-banger and he would be worse today because it was Sunday. 1953 16 M A32 Thames DHS 24 **Bible basher** [name for clergy] 1972 *Sunday Times* (Wellington) 8 Oct. II. 7 In those days he could be seen at Albert Park 'jumping Sundays' berating the Bible-bashers and ridiculing religion. 1980 Leland *Kiwi-Yankee Dict.* 14 Bible-basher. A very religious, often aggressively religious person. This term is often applied to the door-to-door advocates of religion, usually Fundamentalists..; however, anyone more religious than the speaker can earn this appellation. 1984 16-17 F E16 Pakuranga Coll. 24D Bible basher [F14M23] 1917 *Tiki Talk* 10 Synonyms: clergyman, parson, minister, pastor, sky-pilot, preacher, **bible-puncher**, padre, chaplain. 1938 Hyde *Nor Yrs. Condemn* 93 Tommy was the only one in a dog-collar that I'd have called a man at all. When the war finished up, he could have gone back and been a **Bible-thumper**, same as the rest.
Hence **bible-banging, bible-bashing** *vbl. n.* and *attrib.*, outspoken or vigorous sermonizing.
1964 Middleton *Walk on Beach* 40 That **bible-banging**, psalm-singing old crawler! 1989 Virtue *Upon Evil Season* 21 His **Bible bashing** wasn't liked much in some areas.
2. In the phr. **to bang the Bible**, to moralize in a loud-mouthed fashion.
c1962 Baxter *Horse* (1985) 21 'I don't believe in gambling'... 'Leave the boy alone,' said a grey-headed rollsman. 'It's not his fault. His old man's always banging the Bible.' 'Banging the bishop more likely,' Gandhi muttered.

biccies, var. bickies.

bickies, *n. pl.* Also **biccies, bikkies**. [Extended use of hypocoristic *bicky* biscuit.]
1. As **big bickies**, abundant or 'big' money or salary; in *attrib.* use, of grandiose design or great worth; also, ironically, **small bickies**.
1980 Leland *Kiwi-Yankee Dict.* 14 *big bickies*. Lots of money. 'Sam just got promoted, he's in the big bickies now'. 'Sam just got promoted, he's in the high income bracket now'. 1992 *Evening Post* (Wellington) 27 June 13 With a sale quota of $60 a kilogram, and export markets in Hong Kong, Asia and Canada, it is not small bikkies. *Ibid*. 25 July 14 Answering critics who say even more thermal generation should have been committed late last year, Dr Deane says that costs 'big bikkies'.
2. Preceded by **tough, stiff**, a variant or euphemism of 'tough titty', tough or hard luck.
1977 Eldred-Grigg *Of Ivory Accents* 42 Tough biccies on me, I suppose, she said. 1992 *NZ Tablet* (Dunedin) 1 July 22 That is stiff bikkies.

bidabid, bid-a-bid, varr. biddy-bid.

biddy. Also (children's occas.) **bizzy.** BIDDY-BID *n.* 1 a.

1905 *Otago Witness* (Dunedin) 22 Feb. 74 After tea we went further up the creek..throwing bid-a-bids at each other. Those throwing 'biddies' must have been enjoying themselves. 1911 MORELAND *Through South Westland* 109 He was completely stuck over with 'biddies'—the hateful little hooked seeds of a species of acaena, that cling so persistently nothing but scraping with a knife will dislodge them. 1938 LAWLOR *House of Templemore* 131 There would be 'bizzies' on his stockings.

biddy-bid, *n.* Also with much variety of form as **beta-beta** (rare), **bidabid, bid-a-bid, biddy-biddy, bidi-bid, bidibidi, bidy-bidy.** [ad. Ma. *piripiri* with change of Maori /p/ to English /b/, medial /r/ to /d/.] See also PIRIPIRI *n.* 1.

1. a. Occas. also **biddy-burr** (see quot. 1933). Native species of *Acaena* (fam. Rosaceae), esp. *A. anserinifolia* (formerly *A. sanguisorbae*) and occas. *A. novae-zelandiae* and other spp., a creeping plant and its burr, a many-seeded fruit with hooked spines which catch in clothing, the wool of sheep, etc. See also BIDDY, BURR *n.*¹ 1, HUTIWAI, PIRI-KAHU.

1866 'bidy-bidy' [see 3 below]. 1868 LINDSAY *Contribs. NZ Bot.* 59 To the Otago settler the plant is also known as the 'Bidi-bidi', or 'Beta-beta'; to the North Island Maori as 'Hutiwai', 'Piri-piri', (Colenso), or 'Piri-kahu', (Colenso). 1870 WHITWORTH *Martin's Bay Settlement* 12 That troublesome, burr-bearing plant called by the natives bidi-bidi. 1880 POTTS *Out in Open* in *NZ Country Jrnl.* XII. 195 Piri-piri (*Acaena sanguisorbae*) by the settlers has been converted or corrupted into *biddy-biddy*; a verb has been formed on it, which is in very constant use for a great part of the year at least. To biddy is to rid one of burrs, as 'I'll just biddy my clothes before I come in'. 1896 *Otago Witness* (Dunedin) 23 Jan. 36 Biddybids detract very materially from the value of the wool. 1904 LANCASTER *Sons o' Men* 245 Them's his breathin' words, but I aint producin' his tongue. That's c'lonial Scotch wi' a sprinklin' o' biddy–bid. 1913 bidabid [see HUTIWAI]. 1926 CROOKES *Plant Life in Maoriland* 57 To this class [of plant] belong the different species of 'bidi-bidi'. 1933 BAUME *Half-Caste* 221 I've got biddy-burrs on my stockings and crawlies over my feet. 1949 SARGESON *I Saw in My Dream* (1974) 120 Jack's dog was..pulling with his teeth at the biddy-bid that had got entangled in his hair. 1951 FRAME *Lagoon* (1961) 19 Father shook the bidi-bids off the big red and grey rug. 1966 *Encycl. NZ* II. 680 Many native plants have Maori names more or less mutilated such as..*biddy bid* (piri piri). 1973 FERNANDEZ *Tussock Fever* 37 The clumps of tussock..sheltered a scattered growth of English grasses..and..the bidibid which hooked itself on to the sheep's wool. 1986 [see HUTIWAI]. 1992 *Dominion Sunday Times* (Wellington) 26 July 21 You will gather the heads of bidibidi..in your socks.

b. Loosely and occas. for *sheep's burr* (BURR *n.*¹ 2 a) *Acaena agnipila* (formerly *A. ovina*), BATHURST BURR, or other wool burrs.

1926 bidi bid [see BURR *n.*¹ 2 a]. 1967 HILGENDORF & CALDER *Weeds* 161 Horehound (*Marrubium vulgare*), is actually called piri piri and bidi bid in some localities. It is common in waste places and sheep camps in both islands. The dried flower head acts as a burr and sticks to wool. 1928 biddy-biddy [see BATHURST BUR(R)].

2. *transf.* or *fig.* In the phr. **to stick like biddy-bids,** to stick or cling firmly.

1889 LANGTON *Mark Anderson* 115 They stick like mud, or bid-a-bids. 1981 HENDERSON *Exiles Asbestos Cottage* 92 But for all their air of imminent irredeemable disaster, stick like bidi-bids they did to their slips and shingle slides. 1993 *Evening Post* (Wellington) 21 Aug. 10 I was a good teacher, but Shaw said something like 'He who can does, and he who can't teaches', and that has stuck like a biddy-bid in my mind all my life.

3. *Obs.* Special Comb. **biddy-biddy season,** the period during which the seed burrs ripen and are likely to infest fleeces; **biddy-bid tea,** an infusion of biddy-bids formerly occas. used as a substitute for tea; **biddy-biddy wool,** wool infested with seed burrs.

1942 *NZEF Times* 9 Feb. 6 The **bidi-bidi season** is approaching and if shearing is delayed until the wool becomes seedy, its value is expected to drop. 1866 MUELLER *My Dear Bannie* 9 Jan. (1958) 110 The last of our tea and sugar we shall have tomorrow..and after that **'bidy-bidy' tea**, or 'Manukau' tea, without sugar. [1889 [see HUTIWAI]. 1893 JACOBSON *Tales of Banks Peninsula* 226 The pioneers were reduced..to using..seeds of biddy-biddy for tea. 1940 *Tales Pioneer Women* (1988) 30 For tea, a concoction of bidi-bidi was used, and I have heard it described by one of these early pioneer women as horrible stuff too!] 1986 *NZ Herald* (Auckland) 1 Mar. 1 Despite these difficulties their shanty has been recorded in Puhoi history as..a hospitable place to stop for a cup of bidibidi tea. 1918 *Dannevirke Evening News* 20 Apr. 3 [Heading] Biddy Wool... At the present time **biddy biddy wool** was only worth about 5d... The French were the only people in the world who had the machinery for cleaning seedy wool.

biddy-bid, *v.* Also **biddy.** *trans.* To extract biddy-bids from (wool, clothing, etc.).

1880 biddy [see BIDDY-BID *n.* 1 a]. 1942 ANDERSEN *Maori Place Names* 380 In the early days a verb 'to biddy-bid' was in use, a man having to biddy-bid or biddy his clothes before entering the house.

biddy-biddy, biddy-burr, bidi-bid(i), bidibidi, bidy-bidy, varr. BIDDY-BID.

biff, *v.* [Transf. use of *biff* to hit: see OED *biff v.* 1 c.] *trans.* and *intr.* To throw (usu. a stone). Also as **biff out,** to throw out. Cf. BISH *v.*

1910 *Truth* 3 Sept. 1 Hon. Tam Mackenzie surely cannot be..sure of his Taieri seat..and constituencies have a habit of biffing out turn-coats. 1964 *Listener* 1 May 4 'All I can do is biff'. 'Then just biff—as hard as you can.' 1964 HARVEY *Any Old Dollars Mister?* 115 'Gee,' said Nuts in disgust. 'We're not too hot at biffin' rocks, are we?' 1984 *Motor World* Oct.-Nov. 34 And how better to accommodate our vacation paraphernalia than to biff it in the back of our all-purpose family wagon? 1991 *Dominion Sunday Times* (Wellington) 29 Dec. 17 Smith picked up a smooth stone and biffed it underarm.

Hence **biffed** *ppl. a.*, struck or taken (pleasantly) by (something).

1989 VIRTUE *Upon Evil Season* 8 But Lubin was pretty biffed by it. As soon as he got back to Effie, he told her, 'It's a real dag.'

big, *a.* As a modifier denoting severity as well as size. In special collocations: **Big Ben** *obs.* (a) [f. a proprietary name derived from London's 'Big Ben', the clock (chime) of the Houses of Parliament], an alarm clock; (b) *pl. whaling obs.*, see quot; **big bickies,** see BICKIES 1; **big boy,** *school shark* (SHARK 2 (15)); **big country** [AND 1970], open country; **big diver,** see DIVER; **bigeye,** a small deep-bodied reef- and cave-dwelling fish of the family Pempheridae having relatively large eyes (see also BULLSEYE 1); **big house** [AND 1881], HOMESTEAD *n.*¹ 2; **big islander** *obs.* [f. relative size of Australia and NZ, with a play on *pig* islander], an Australian; **big jingles,** a name for a play in the game of knucklebones; **big-note** *v.* [AND 1953], to act the big person; to try to impress, or make a great impression (as with continually flashing big bank notes); **big-noter** [AND 1967], one who pretentiously seeks to impress; **big one (the Big One),** a prospective disastrous earthquake; **big picture** [see OED *big* B 2, 1927 (sole quot.)], the main or feature film of a programme as distinct from the newsreels, etc.; **Big Red** *Wellington City obs.*, a bus of the former Wellington municipal fleet, having red as the standard colour; **big ring** [AND 1947; also US: see DARE 1, 1934], a marble game played from the edge of a ring; **big spit** [AND 1959], the act of vomiting or its result, esp. in the phr. **to go for the big spit,** to vomit.

c1924 ANTHONY *Me & Gus* (1977 Gus Tomlins) 47 Next morning my **Big Ben** went off as usual, and I sat up and reached for my pipe. c1940 Marlborough, *Big Ben* a popular brand of cheap alarm clock sold in the general store at Havelock (Ed.). 1983 COOPER *Wag's Tales* 7 At the far end was a huge fireplace, with a mantelshelf on which stood a Big Ben clock [c1913]. 1986 RICHARDS *Off the Sheep's Back* 60 A large 'Big Ben' clock, placed in a kerosene tin, saw to it that we did not sleep in [in the 1920s]. 1982 GRADY *Perano Whalers* 226 ***Big bens***—Adult bull killer whales. 1970 SORENSEN *Nomenclature NZ Fish* 42 Shark, School..: *Galeorhinus australis* (principally)... Other common names: B.B., **Big Boys**; Soupfin; Grey Boys; Tope or Topi. 1953 SUTHERLAND *Golden Bush* (1963) 171 The trained observation of a man who has travelled '**big**' **country** from childhood gleans detail unconsciously. 1972 DOAK *Fishes* 33 **Bigeye** *Pempheris adspersa* (Aust: bullseye). 1982 AYLING *Collins Guide* (1984) 227 The big eye is a small deep bodied fish... Most of the head is taken up by the huge eyes. 1986 PAUL *NZ Fishes* 98 **Bigeye** *Pempheris adspersa* Family Pempheridae (bullseyes). Coppery brown, deep bodied... Sometimes entering shallow estuaries. 1926 DEVANNY *Butcher Shop* (1981) 33 These [men's] quarters..opened into a passage leading to the '**big house**' as the homestead is generally called. 1933 *Press* (Christchurch) (Acland Gloss.) 16 Sept. 15 *Big House*.—The owner's residence on a station. The men called it b[ig] h[ouse], even though their own hut[s] were larger. 1939 BEATTIE *First White Boy Born Otago* 29 When he came across to live here his first residence was a cottage... He left there to reside in the 'big house'. 1946 [see HOMESTEAD *n.*¹ 2]. 1954 [see FORTY-ACRE]. 1987 OGONOWSKA-COATES *Boards, Blades & Barebellies* 94 *Big house*. The runholder's residence. 1990 MARTIN *Forgotten Worker* 52 The runholder or manager lived in the 'Big House' and ate separately from the hands who had their own quarters some distance away. 1916 *Chron. NZEF* 30 Aug. 10 All colonials, '**big islanders**' included..agree with the speaker that in the past there has been too much Anzac; it's about time we heard of the brave and glorious [deeds] accomplished by the British Tommies in France. 1982 MARSHALL *Master Big Jingles* 55 'What do you think is the hardest of all?' said Creamy. Ken considered. He pushed the knuckle bones about the ground with his finger as he thought. 'I reckon **big jingles**,' he said. 'Ten big jingles on the go,' said Creamy. 'I challenge you to ten big jingles without a fault.' 1987 *National Bus. Rev.* 11 Sept. 10 Our only overseas presence was a handful of non-achievers..supplemented by Muldoon's regular forays **big-noting** around the international financiers. 1993 *Evening Post* (Wellington) 24 Apr. 2 It [sc. National government's 'good news' debate] was to be a big-noting debate. And then along came Mr Trouble..

Richard Prebble. **1986** *Metro* (Auckland) Dec. 142 You need guts to go up to some **big-noter** businessmen and ask for $20,000 or even $60,000 for the theatre. **1980** HENDERSON *New Zealanders* in McLauchlan ed. *Acid Test* (1981) 192 'This is an earthquake'... In Napier, the gravedigger..leaning out [of a newly dug grave] to avoid burial in **The Big One**. **1946** SARGESON *That Summer* 58 She was a bit like the girl in the **big picture**. **1982** FRAME *To the Is-land* (1984) 108 We went to every film, watching through the news, the cartoon, the Pete Smith Novelties, the James Fitzpatrick travel talks, the serial, and, after halftime or interval, the 'big picture'. **1973** *Evening Post* (Wellington) 29 June 1 [Heading] Citizens find their feet to beat the **Big Red** bus stoppage. **1984** *Islands* 33 10 Men..sat peacefully waiting for their bus while the big reds came and went in clouds of blue exhaust. **1993** *North & South* (Auckland) July 67 Wall's also the man who got Wellingtonians referring to their buses as 'the big reds'. At the time of full employment, the council couldn't then attract bus drivers, and Wall's advertising slogan, 'Are You Man Enough To Drive The Big Reds?' was the key to a successful recruiting campaign. **1972** SUTTON-SMITH *Folkgames Children* 175 In the nineteenth century the ring game [as distinct from a game played with holes] seems to have been the most popular marble game... There was **Big Ring**, in which a circle a yard or more in diameter was drawn on the ground; there was the mullibar variation, in which an outsize taw was catapulted amongst the marbles in this circle. **c1963** p.c. V. O'Sullivan. Heard at Auckland. A Maori says: 'I'm going outside for the **big spit**'. **1988** McGILL *Dict. Kiwi Slang* 14 *big spit, the* vomit, often in phr. 'to go for the big spit'.

big smoke. Often with init. caps. **a.** Orig. London [see OED *smoke* n. 1 d, 1864], adopted mainly by servicemen.
 1905 *Truth* 24 June 1 Tory papers in the 'Big Smoke'. **1917** 24 Apr. in Miller *Camps, Tramps & Trenches* (1939) 61 My first day in 'the Big Smoke'. **1922** TURNER *Happy Wanderer* 18 My knowledge of the Big Smoke ceased at Algate Pump. **1941** HAYDON *NZ Soldiers in England* 10 Most of us made tracks for London or the 'Big Smoke', as we affectionately termed it.

b. Also occas. **big smoker**. [See OED 1848 'chiefly Austral.'; AND 1848.] Extended, from a rural perspective, to any New Zealand town or city.
 1904 *NZ Observer* 13 Feb. 7 Wellington is to share with Auckland the distinction of being the 'big smoke' of the colony. **1947** *NZ Observer* 17 Sept. 27 Among those living out of town who visited the 'big smoke'..were All Black Mick Lomas, 'Circus' and Morgan Haywards. **1964** MIDDLETON *Walk on Beach* 190 Well Sonny! What do you think of the big smoke? **1979** WILLIAMS *Skin Deep* 14 The car head[ed] back towards the big smokers, leaving Carlton's [a small country town] little puff behind. **1985** McGILL *G'day Country* 66 When we were kids, Whakatane was the nearest Big Smoke. **1991** *Listener* 7 Jan. 42 I left a radio/tape recorder running..to find out what this signal from the big smoke was all about.

bike. [Fig. use of *bike* a bicycle.]

1. In various phr. **a.** [AND 1938.] In the negative phr. **don't get off your bike!**, don't get excited or angry. Cf. HORSE *n.*[1] 2.
 1943 BENNETT *English in NZ* in *Amer. Speech* XVIII. 90 'Don't get off your bike' (from 'don't get off your horse', via a music-hall song?) means 'don't get rattled, excited'. **1944** FULLARTON *Troop Target* 75 Don't get off your bike, Jock. **1955** *BJ Cameron Collection* (TS July) bike get off one's bike (v) To get mad.

b. (to be) on one's bike, to be annoyed.
 1945 GASKELL *All Part of the Game* (1978) 45 She wouldn't let Jack sing... He reckoned she was on her bike. So they went on Mac's bike. [**1978** *Note*] 'be on one's bike', to be uppity and cross.

c. to get on one's bike, to make a move (to another job or place).
 1959 SLATTER *Gun in My Hand* 21 So I got on my bike and went down the road. Cursing the easterly and cursing life. **1990** SMITH *Will the Real Mr NZ Please Stand Up* 38 One day I was sitting in the pub and I thought, 'This isn't for me.'..I was young and confused but knew I had to get on my bike.

2. See TOWN BIKE.

3. Special Comb. **bike-spanner**, a special spanner designed for adjusting the various push-bicycle nuts and attachments.
 1903 *The Huia* Dec. 11 I don't kill things with a bike-spanner.

bikie. *Often derog.* [AND 1967.] Usu. a member of a motorcycle gang. Also *attrib.*, esp. as **bikie gang**.
 1971 SHADBOLT *Bullshit & Jellybeans* 36 We..got his bike off him. That was the last time that snake [i.e. traffic cop] gave a Queen Street bikie a ticket. **1972** *Otago Daily Times* (Dunedin) 26 Jan. 7 (Griffiths Collect.) He called me a 'dirty bikie bastard'. **1980** MANTELL *Murder & Chips* 69 Kind of totem thing. Bikie gangs in Auckland—all the rage. Sort of paramilitary thing. **1991** *Evening Post* (Wellington) 4 Jan. 4 Yes, we are bikers, but bikies we are not... The hoon of yesterday is reborn as a true motorcyclist; the bikie image is dead.

bikkies, var. BICKIES.

billet.

1. [Transf. use of military **billet** an order requiring the giving of board and lodging to a soldier: see OED 4 c; AND 1843; a common term in early rural NZ.] A position or appointment; a permanent job. Occas. as **board and billet**, board and lodging.
 1860 in Butler *First Year* (1863) vi 75 When a man takes a cadet's billet, it is a tolerably sure symptom that he means half-and-half work. **1871** MONEY *Knocking About NZ* 17 The owner of the machine..gave me the billet of outside porter to a wholesale store. **1887** HOPEFUL *Taken In* (1974) 135 If you are out of place, out of work, or out of a situation as we say, here it is called 'out of billet.' **1903** KING *Bill's Philosophy* 23 He couldn't get a billet, tho' he tramped it up and down. **1933** *Press* (Christchurch) (Acland Gloss.) 16 Sept. 15 *Billet.*—In the 'nineties, station hands spoke of 'a permanent b[illet]', where they now [1933] speak of a 'job'. In those days a man's job was his allotted task, and his billet was his appointment.

2. *Obs.* [AND 1909.] A job given as a political favour; an appointment to a government or public service post. Occas. as a verb.
 1866 SMALL *NZ & Austral. Songster* (1970) 33 For I've promised each [friend] a billet should I get elected. **1894** *The Argus & Newtown Chron.* 10 Aug. 3 [The Premier, Seddon] does all the billetting... Dick never gives a billet to any but his friends... Why I heard of him giving a billet of £4 a week to a fellow. **1905** BAUCKE *White Man Treads* 295 After a lot of waiting and jawing we [*sc.* a farmer] get what the chap with a billet to keep [*sc.* a departmental valuer] shies at you.

billey, var. BILLY *n.*[1]

Bill Massey. [f. *William* (familiarly *Bill*) Ferguson Massey (1856–1925), Prime Minister 1912–25.]

1. *pl. WW1.* Occas. felt as a possessive. (A pair of) army boots. See also MASSEY 1.
 [**1916** in Boyack *Behind the Lines* (1989) 89 We have boots which weight [*sic*] about one stone, regular Bill Massey's farm yard brand with nails in the soles very handy for in fighting. **1918** let. 26 Jan. in *Boots, Belts* (1992) 68 I'm afraid my 13 stone..is much too big to fly along, particularly in Bill Massey's boots.] **1928** *Free Lance Christmas Annual* (Wellington) 1 Dec. 11 Many of our party had already..provided themselves with more or less comfortable boots of the type known amongst the Diggers as 'Bill Masseys'. **1938** *Press* (Christchurch) (McNab Slang) 2 Apr. 18 [Slang of the NZEF] Issue boots were 'Bill Masseys.' **1941** BAKER *NZ Slang* 50 Among numerous terms originated in the first Great War we may note *Bill Masseys* for army boots issued in this country. **1989** *Those Were the Days* 17 The black boots which soldiers of the First New Zealand Expeditionary Force christened, not entirely with humorous intent, their 'Bill Massey's'.

2. *WW1.* As **Bill Massey's tourists, Bill Masseying**, see TOURIST 1 a.

billy, *n.*[1] Also occas. **billey**. [Prob. f. Scots dial. *billy* a pot (see SND *n.*[1] 7 (6) *billy-pot* cooking utensil: Aberdeen 1828), poss. reinforced by the early immigrant BOUILLI(-TIN) in various pronunciations for a utensil often orig. improvised from *bouilli* (tinned meat or stew) containers (cf. BOUILLI, and BULLY POT (1846): see also Morris *Austral-English*); AND 1849.]
 [*Note*] Billy was not the only or preferred word in pre-1850 use for a utensil of a 'billy' kind. Cf. **1839** TAYLOR *Journal* 30 Apr. (ATLTS) II. 122 W. is kneading a damper in a tin pot. **1846** JOHNSON *Notes from Jrnl.* in Taylor *Early Travellers* (1959) 119 A tin pot serves as tea-kettle and tea-pot, and each man carries a 'pannikin' for a cup. **1850** GODLEY *Letters* Nov. (1951) 143 We hung [on three flax-sticks] just such a tin can and cover as one of your Welsh women..would bring for broth. **1861** *Otago Witness Suppl.* 19 Jan. 2 Each [soldier] will carry a hatchet..and a tin pot to boil his tea in a bivou[a]c.]

1. a. A cylindrical tin-plate (later enamelled, or aluminium) vessel with a swinging arched wire handle, and often a lid, used orig. for boiling water, or for cooking in the open, and later for holding milk and other liquids. Also called **billy-can** (6 below), **tin billy**, or for specific uses, **milk billy**, **tea billy** etc., and occas. *joc.* as **william** (see quot. 1898).
 1853 ROCHFORT *Adventures of Surveyor* 63 We must needs purchase a 'billy' (a tin pot for boiling tea, coffee, meat or anything you may have the luck to get), to make our tea in. **1858** THOMSON *Reconn. Survey S. Dist. Otago* in Taylor *Early Travellers* (1959) 333 We are now existing in the manner of savages, boiling our flesh or fowl in our tea-can (called a *billy*). **1863** WALKER *Jrnl. & Lett.* (ATLTS) 8 Jan. Monday, got in stores at the following rates and pitched tent. Flour 9d. tea 4/6 a good handful... Tin dish 6/- Billy 3/6 small swing pot for boiling. **1866** billey [see PANNIKIN 1 a]. **1882** POTTS *Out in Open* 189 A prospector returning to the pale of civilization..brought with him..his camp kettle or billy. **1898** *Otago Daily Times* (Dunedin) 17 Feb. 6 In a few minutes the 'william' was boiling merrily. **1901** BUTLER *Erewhon Revisited* ch. ii (Everyman edn. 1932 (1960) 207) I should, perhaps, explain to English readers that a billy is a tin can, the name for which (doubtless of French-Canadian origin)

is derived from the words '*faire bouillir*.' **1912** MANSFIELD *Stories* (1984) 112 I'll send the kid down with..a billy of milk. **1925** BATHGATE *Random Recolls.* 12 There were large tins of boeuf bouilli containing not very palatable boiled beef, with a good deal of liquid, which were obtainable and used for ships stores. The contents were commonly called soup and bully, and the cannisters bully cans, from which the popular name of 'billy' for a tin pitcher is undoubtedly derived. [Bathgate is possibly following E.E. Morris's etymological surmise (1898 *Austral-English* 30).] **1933** WASHBOURN *Reminisc. Early Days* 5 The term billy for tin can also originated on the digging [*sc.* Collingwood 1856-57] and is still in general use. **1943** BENNETT *English in NZ* in *Amer. Speech* XVIII. 86 *Billy*..is now also applied to any can which will contain household milk. **1967** MCLATCHIE *Tang of Bush* 108 E[th]el made a very good brew; four tablespoons of oatmeal and a little water into a seven pound treacle[-tin] billy. **1989** RICHARDS *Pioneer's Life* 9 His cry was 'Milko!' but some of the wags added, 'Milko, if you haven't got a billy bring the po.' **1991** *NZ Geographic* Apr.–June 24 [Caption] A fully kitted-out gumdigger with spear, spade and axe on his shoulder, a bucket for sluicing, a billy for the midday brew.

Hence **billied** *ppl. a.*, equipped with a billy.
1910 FANNING *Players & Slayers* 81 I was tramping with a mate..to Westland, and it was our whim to be slouch-hatted, and 'blueyed', 'billied', unshaven, and otherwise orthodox swaggers.

b. *attrib.*
1941 MYERS *Valiant Love* 35 She was on her way across the paddocks, carrying the 'Billy'-tin and the basket of good things for tea. **1949** *Tararua Tramper* Feb. 7 Plenty of time..to see if you can still master the art of billy cooking.

2. a. In the phr. **to boil the billy** [AND 1867], **to swing the billy** [AND 1928], to make, or pause for, tea or a tea-break, occas. with a snack; to make (often picnic) tea in a billy. See also BOIL-UP.
1863 WALKER *Jrnl. & Lett.* (ATLTS) 19 Jan. It was as much as Bill could do to bake some bread..and **boil the billy** while I dug a trench around the tent. **1878** HEBERLEY *Autobiogr. 1803-43* (ATLMS) 87 [We] boiled the Billy and made some Tea out of tawa bark [c1839]. **1887** PYKE *Hist. Early Gold Discoveries Otago* (1962) 80 Pegs [for marking claims] were not to be had..and when introduced stood a great chance of helping to boil the neighbour's 'billy'. **1897** WRIGHT *Station Ballads* 80 We..boiled the billy and feasted on damper and tea. **1907** MANSFIELD *Urewera Notebook* (1978) 48 We stop—boil the billy and have tea and her[r]ings. **1911** KOEBEL *In Maoriland Bush* 150 When you boil the 'billy', you make tea, *voilà tout*. **1925** MANDER *Allen Adair* (1971) 91 He moved on till he found a safe place to make a fire to boil the billy for tea. **1943** HISLOP *Pure Gold* 20 A visitor..may wash his colours of gold from almost anywhere while his wee wife boils the billy. **1957** FRAME *Owls Do Cry* (1967) 13 [They] spent every day..going for picnics and boiling the billy and drinking tea. **1960** ROGERS *Long White Cloud* 12 'Looks like the billy's boiling,' Broker said, nodding toward the kitchen. **1986** RICHARDS *Off the Sheep's Back* 59 I was the 'new chum' so it was my job to boil the billy [for the bush gang]. **1934** *Press* (Christchurch) (Acland Gloss.) 27 Jan. 15 **Swing the billy**.—Put the b[illy] on to boil. **1951** MCLEOD *NZ High Country* 26 Then the horses and dogs are tied up, somebody swings the billy and lunch precedes the serious business of the day. **1965** SHADBOLT *Among Cinders* 138 'Let's swing the billy again'... I filled the billy with water and fixed it over the flames. When the water bubbled, Hubert threw a fistful of tea into the billy.

b. Hence in combination with suffixed participles or in noun phrases: **billy-boiled** (also **billy-made**) [AND 1898], of tea, made in a billy; **billy-boiler**, one who boils the billy; **billy-boiling** *quasi vbl. n.* [AND 1961]; **boiled billy**, applied to a campfire or makeshift meal taken outdoors.
1898 HOCKEN *Contributions* 54 The sole comforts of this miserable night were boiled ducks and **billy-boiled** tea, unless one might add that the soaking clothes..were..dried..by frost. **1900** SCOTT *Tales of the Colonial Turf* 230 Sat down to Christmas dinner of pork, doughboys and **billy-made** tea. **1978** JARDINE *Shadows on Hill* 36 Packers, **billy-boilers** and bastards—and you're third class. **1916** COWAN *Bush Explorers* (VUWTS) 10 Grateful were the spells for rest and smoke and the midday **billy-boiling** half-hour; more grateful still the sundown halt for rest. **1947** *NZ Forest Service Official Advice Note* (MS) 23 Sept. In the matter of billy-boiling along roadsides, drovers are a class apart and there is little prospect of suppressing what has been a universal custom, since the earliest days of settlement... Permission to light billy-fires should be granted. **1951** HAY *Swagger Jack* 19 And so remembers all a lively store Of billy-boilings to the evening star; outdoor tea-making. **1953** *Onslow News* (Wellington) 4 The Guides' break–up was to have been..a boiled billy supper, but the rain came down.

c. In the noun phr. **boiling (of) the billy**.
1922 *Weekly News* 5 Jan. [Caption] Boiling the billy at the camp. **1930** GUTHRIE *NZ Memories* 70 The lapping of the sea mingled with the bell notes of the moko moko and tui and..that of the burning bush wood in the boiling of the 'billy'. **1964** HOSKEN *Life on Five Pound Note* 34 One day, a resident of the Mackenzie Country, when travelling in a dray on the Braemar Road, overtook a young swagger. 'Throw your swag up, and get in,' he remarked, 'and we'll boil the billy soon.' But this young Englishman..not knowing what 'boiling the billy' meant..refused the kind offer and decided to push on. **1981** HENDERSON *Exiles Asbestos Cottage* 24 So that 'Mother' would know he was nearing home, Chaffey habitually hung a piece of white calico on a tree stump, a boiling-the-billy distance away from the whare.

d. In quasi-proverbial comparison. (See also the occas. (orally attested) use **to keep the billy boiling** to keep things going, as in 'Keep the billy boiling; I'll be back in a few minutes'.)
1899 BELL *In Shadow of Bush* 199 'Not as much firewood left as would boil the billy,' Maurice said afterwards, with much exaggeration.

3. In the phr. **to sling the billy**, to stop (outdoor work, etc.) for refreshment.
1883 FERGUSON *Castle Gay* 178 The billy he would sling afresh. That they might have... 'A snack before they went to bed'. **1894** *TrNZI* XXVI. 620 Its buttressed roots offer a too-convenient place for the road-contractor to 'sling his billy'. **1973** WALLACE *Generation Gap* 71 You gentlemen would like a cup of tea?.. They insisted on helping us sling the billy.

4. With a modifier indicating the appearance or the predominant use. [See AND 4 (in collocations), 1862.] **black billy**, often in modern literary use in the collocation **black-billy tea**, tea made outdoors in a fire-blackened billy; **milk billy** *obs.* [AND 1935], a billy as a container for milk; **tea-billy** [AND 1889], one used for (outdoor) tea-making; **tin billy** [AND 1881], the common billy made from tinplate.
1864 *Otago Witness* (Dunedin) 16 Apr. 16 Heavily swagged diggers and heavily swagged horses, whose heavy swags consist of all the household gods [*sic*] of a mining party, from the black billy which boils the tea, to the tom cat which kills the rats and mice. **1915** *Canterbury Times* 3 Mar. (VUW Fildes Clippings 421/59) A tin wash-dish for testing the creek gravels, and his old black billy, made [the prospector's] 'pikau'. **1962** SEVERINSEN *Hunter Climb High* 23 Our evening meal was a sparse affair consisting of copious supplies of strong black billy tea and little else. **1979** CRUMPTON *Spencer: Gold Seeker* 43 He awoke about midday and..demanded a quart of black billy tea. **1981** CHARLES *Black Billy Tea* 6 Black billy tea, boy, Black as it can be. **1988** SOMERSET *Sunshine & Shadow* 5 [The swagger, c1900] threw a few leaves of tea into the old black billy that had begun to boil on the fire. **1912** MANSFIELD *Stories* (1984) 113 She trailed over to us with a basket in her hand, the **milk billy** in the other. **1963** CASEY *As Short a Spring* 232 He was clutching the handle of a battered milk billy, which he was waving wildly about to help explain to Rex. **1899** BELL *In Shadow of Bush* 7 His swag generally contained some [eatables] that, with the help of the ever-present **tea-billy** which he carried, could supply a meal if necessary. **1922** COWAN *NZ Wars* (1955) II. 515 They observed [c1873] that the tea-billy was upturned on the fire, things were in general disorder, and Sullivan and Jones were missing. **1874** BAINES *Edward Crewe* 142 The **tin 'billy'** had been slung over a roaring fire, and the tea made. **1930** DOBSON *Reminiscences* 156 Boiling was done in light tin billies. **1960** HILLIARD *Maori Girl* 221 Netta bought a shiny tin billy without any clear idea of what she would do with it.

5. Comb. indicating various foods baked orig. in a billy: **billy bread**, **billy cake**, **billy loaf**, **billy sponge**, see quots.
1929 MCKAY *Pract. Home Cook.* 176 Brown **Billy Bread** wheatmeal..baking powder..salt..treacle..cream and milk... Let the mixture rise in billy ten minutes (on the rack) before baking. **1934** *Marigold Book Recipes* 35 *Billy Bread*..flour..wheatmeal..salt..B.P...golden syrup..milk. Mix..into a wet dough, grease and flour the billy, bake for 2 hours with lid on. **1924** *Help the Babies Cook. Book* 113 *Billy cake*..flour..sugar.. butter..sultanas or currants [etc.] place in billy, and bake..until cooked. **1948** SCANLAN *Rusty Road* (1949) 56 Pooh! I'd rather have billy cake with raspberry jam. Scones aren't very special; we often have them. c**1916** *Edmonds 'Sure to Rise' Cook. Book* (4edn.) 8 *Billy Currant Loaf*..flour..sugar..Edmonds' Baking Powder..1 egg..butter..milk..salt..Bake 1 hour not removing the lid till cooked. **1961** *Ibid*. 9 Billy Currant Loaf. **1924** *Help the Babies Cook. Book* 90 *Billy Loaf*..flour..wheatmeal..golden syrup..salt..baking powder..Bake in No. 3 billy with lid on. **1915** MCCREDIE *Patriotic Fete..Bungalow Recipe Book* 67 *Billy sponge Cake*... Have ready a 3-quart billy with buttered paper; cook with lid on 1½ hours. Do not have fire too fierce and do not take lid off till the cake comes out. c**1929** *Nelson Cookery Book* 66 Billy Sponge... Bake for one hour in moderate oven with lid on billy. **1950** CHERRILL *NZ Sheep Farm* 106 And in true New Zealand style, I suppose I had better send her the recipe of a billy-sponge. c**1964** *Atlas Cook. Book* 44 Billy Sponge... Pour into a greased and floured billy or loaf tin.

6. Special Comb. **billy boy** [AND 1944], a boy, or cadet, who carries the billy, makes tea, and does the rouseabout work for field parties, shearing gangs, etc.; **billy-can** [f. *billy* + *can*: AND c1870], *billy* 1 a above; **billy-can farm**, a small dairy-farm; **billy fire**, an outdoor fire made to boil a billy; **billy-full** (**billy-ful**) [AND 1861], the amount contained by a full billy; **billy-hook**, a (usu.) S-shaped hook on which a billy is suspended over an open fire; **billy-lid**, the lid of a billy; **billy milk**, milk collected or carried in a billy; **billy tea** [AND 1890], tea made outdoors by throwing tea-leaves into a billy of boiling water (see also *black-billy tea* 4 above).

1960 *Rep. Ninth Science Congress May 12-17: Proc. RSNZ* 144 My experience of mountains is lengthy although it may not be deep—**billy boy** to the botanists of the 'twenties', mountaineering and field collecting for geologists in the 'thirties'. **1982** *Dominion* (Wellington) 27 Aug. 8 Starting as a billy-boy, he worked at just about every [sawmill] job in the next 3 and a half years. **1986** RICHARDS *Off the Sheep's Back* 60 As the 'billy boy', it was my job to get back to camp before dark, get the water, light the fire and start the dinner. **1907** KOEBEL *Return of Joe* 13 He presented himself at the door of the homestead, with a request for water to fill his **billy-can**. **1911** *Truth* 7 Jan. 4 Having rolled my swag up..and having provided myself with billy-can and nosebag, I made a start from Woodville. **1914** PFAFF *Diggers' Story* 113 Mr. McParland sent to Dunedin for 100 billy cans, but..abbreviated by writing 100 billies, first boat. The boat duly arrived with the 100 billies, but..they turned out to be goats. **1946** SIMPSON *If You'd Care to Know* 99 This billy is an article much like an outsize in preserved-peach cans; indeed, its real name is billy-can. **1951** *Here & Now* 27 May 1 In many suburbs billy cans are still used for deliveries, the milk being ladled out of a container that is open to germs and dust. **1963** CAMPBELL *Golden North* 5 The tea and sugar came in bulk [in the 1880s] and the tea in ten-pound billy cans. These cans had many uses, and often hung over the fire cooking vegetables and meat. **1976** MASON in *Solo* (1981) 121 One afternoon..four of us..took our billycans to the mudflats and began to fill them [with blackberries]. **1992** SMITHYMAN *Auto/Biographies* 15 Now let us our billycans clink clink clink. **1982** MALCOLM *Where It all Began* iv The 1939-40 era of the numerous small dairy farms, some being little more than '**Billy-can**' farms, is also gone. **1953** SUTHERLAND *Golden Bush* (1963) 240 A cluster of stones plus a bushland river still charred by a **billyfire** of long ago. **1861** HAAST *Rep. Topogr. Explor. Nelson* 14 Mr. Burnett went down for a **billy-full** of water. **1866** MUELLER *My Dear Bannie* 22 May (1958) 174 I also turned out Bob and ordered him to boil a billy-full of tea. **1871** MONEY *Knocking About NZ* 62 Billy-ful after billy-ful did we consume of the raw fish. **1881** *TrNZI* XIII. 188 I myself put away nearly a whole 'billy' full of new potatoes. **1892** HOCKEN & FENWICK *Holiday Trip Catlins* 14 We had a hurried lunch and a billyful of tea. **1981** MARSH *Black Beech & Honeydew* 86 'Here you are, old fellow,' said my father coming through the stunted manuka scrub with a billy-ful of spring water. **1988** PICKERING *Hills* 80 Strong Y-supports were set in the ground either side of the fire and from the cross bar would hang **billy-hooks**, which everyone carried. **1865** MUELLER *My Dear Bannie* (1958) 55 We have no plates—only pannikins, so I ate my stew out of one, while Price had a **billy lid** for a plate. **1875** WOOD & LAPHAM *Waiting for Mail* 23 Some other facetious person had crowned him with a billy lid. **c1890–1900** in *Penguin Book NZ Verse* (1985) 93 Oh, the days of Hughey's tribute and the doings that they did! You had to drink your grog those times from out a billy lid. **1960** CRUMP *Good Keen Man* 46 Often I was driven to frying myself a steak in the billy-lid. **1950** *NZJAg.* Oct. LXXXI. 306 In New Zealand about 85 per cent. of all town milk sold in urban areas is pasteurised... Too much '**billy**' milk is still sold. **1897** WRIGHT *Station Ballads* 27 The spuds and meat were nicely done, The **billy tea** was made. **1906** *Tetaka Kai Book Well Tried Recipes* 138 Billy Tea A clean billy, good water that has percolated through pumice... Have ready a white linen rag in which is placed ¼oz of tea, loosely tied... Let the water simmer..take out the bag. Drink without milk. **1926** *NZ Dairy Produce Exporter* 18 Dec. 39 With..a generous plate of good things on our knees and a cup of steaming hot 'billy tea', we feel it is indeed a happy..Christmas Day. **1936** HYDE *Passport to Hell* 70 Rannock fed his prison labour on honest bush food: fresh meat, billy tea, enormous flat damper scones. **1950** CHERRILL *NZ Sheep Farm* 54 Is that what you call 'billy tea'? She had watched him throwing in tea by the fistful. **1965** SHADBOLT *Among Cinders* 139 Just smell it, will you? Nothing to beat it. Billy tea boiled over manuka. **1970** THOMAS *Way Up North* 106 His technique for making billy tea was correct. He waited for the water to boil, then dropped into it a little less tea than would be used in a teapot and allowed it to boil just briefly before taking the billy off the fire. **1988** PICKERING *Hills* 8 Of billy tea. Waiting until the billy boils, throwing in half a handful of tea..and tapping the side with a spoon to settle the leaves.

billy, *n.*² [Used elsewhere but recorded earliest (as is *billy goat* in 1840) in NZ: see OED *n.*² 1 c.] Abbrev. of *billy goat*.
  1849 PHARAZYN *Journal* (ATLMS) 281 All hands on right hill hunting goats Robin shot a Billy [*sic*]. **1914** [see BILLY *n.*¹ 6]. **1981** HENDERSON *Exiles Asbestos Cottage* 81 Chaffey came over one day..saying: 'I've brought you over a bit of young billy.'

billy-be-damned. [DARE chiefly northern US, 1914.] Used as an intensifier in comparative phrases, 'to a great extent'.
  1940 STUDHOLME *Te Waimate* (1954) 75 A cook once said to the manager, 'I wish you would speak to that there bullocky. He walks about with as much sangfroid as billy-be-damned.'

billycart. *Obs.* [Perh. f. *billy*(goat + *cart* orig. a strong hand-cart (occas. formerly drawn by a goat): AND 1923.] A boys' two-wheeled go-cart or shafted push-cart; later also applied to a four-wheeled 'trolley'.
  c1905 The name 'billy-cart' known to W.H.B. Orsman (p.c. 1972), from childhood, as a two-wheeled pushcart with shafts. **1982** SUTTON-SMITH *Hist. Children's Play* 269 Billy carts were absolutely essential for a boy. Originally this was a box—butterbox or slightly larger—set on an axle and with, preferably, a pair of high wheels off a discarded pram, about an 18- to-20-inch diameter, and having long shafts. **1986** OWEN & PERKINS *Speaking for Ourselves* 101 And then we had [c1913] a little 'billy-cart'—a box with a couple of wheels on it and a shaft. **1988** GIBBONS *Recollections* 24 Then we had to catch the billy cart. [The children had a shafted cart and harnessed a billygoat to it.]

billycock. *Obs.* or *Hist.* [Orig. Brit. f. *bully-cocked*, prob. a hat cocked in the style of a *bully* a hectoring blade of the 18th c.: so OED 1862, a round, low-crowned felt hat; EDD *billy n.*⁵ 1 a, wideawake hat. Also called *billycock* (1889); AND 1867.] Often as **billycock hat**, any of various low, round-crowned hats worn by men, orig. soft-crowned, later occas. applied to hard-crowned hats such as the 'bowler'.
  1865 FARJEON *Shadows on Snow* 61 All are alike attired in rough jackets, moleskin trousers, and billycock hats. **1873** PYKE *Wild Will Enderby* (1889, 1974) I. iii 14 Only cherubs don't wear 'billy-cock' hats, nor carry 'swags', as a general rule. **1889** SKEY *Pirate Chief* 48 Now this your stiff belltoppers won't do, One kick and their day is done; So the billycock soft my looks shall renew, And let off my innocent fun. **1891** COTTLE *Frank Melton's Luck* 32 He [*sc.* a rough-looking old fellow] was attired in a blue serge shirt stuffed into a pair of moleskin pants... A billy-cock hat..completed his outfit. **1970** JENKIN *NZ Mysteries* 77 She saw a man standing at the foot of the bed, dressed in a check coat and a billycock (or bowler) hat. **1977** EBBETT *In True Colonial Fashion* 37 The billycock hat which was worn a great deal was a low-crowned round felt hat which suggests that billycock was just another name for the bowler.

bin, *n.*

1. a. [AND 1867.] One of several receptacles or compartments in a woolshed or woolstore for holding the variously classed fleeces. See also *wool-bin* (WOOL 3).
  1865 BARKER *Station Life* (1870) 33 [Fleeces] were laid on the tables before the wool-sorters, who opened them out, and pronounced in a moment to which *bin* they belonged. **1881** BATHGATE *Waitaruna* 173 The best of the fleece was quickly classified, rolled together, and deposited in a kind of bin, according to its quality. **1894** WILSON *Land of Tui* 242 At the main entrance of the shearing-shed..stands a wool-press, and behind this are the bins into which the fleeces, after having been classed, are placed preparatory to being pressed. **1913** CARR *Country Work* 15 The wool rollers take off the dirty portion of the fleece and throw it into a bin, the dag cutter..cuts off all the wool he can, which he throws into another bin. **1982** *Agric. Gloss.* (MAF) 52 *Bin*: Receptacle for holding loose wool prior to pressing in either a shearing shed or woolstore.

b. Special Comb. **bin-boy**, a woolstore employee engaged to carry wool to bins; **bin-room**, a section of a woolstore containing the bins in which various classes of wool are stored.
  1987 *More* (Auckland) Apr. 43 A series of unskilled, low-paid jobs followed [for her]..as **bin boy** in a woolstore. **1936** BELSHAW et al. *Agric. Organiz. NZ* 711 When a clip is received by the store for classing, all the fleece wool goes to the fleece classing-room which in most stores is on a different floor from the '**bin room**' where all the pieces and oddments are sent.

2. *Goldmining*. A hopper or container for holding ore.
  1978 MCARA *Gold Mining Waihi* 312 *Bins*: Ore hoppers.

3. Also **dump bin**, and formerly in Wellington, **Burke(s bin)**, also *fig.* [from the name of a Wellington transport firm] (see quots. 1982, 1995). A very large open container for rubbish and spoil, designed to be picked up by a special truck. See also SKIP.
  1982 *Listener* 4 Dec. 21 'Get yourself a Burke,' he says. 'I've already got a boss,' I say. 'But does he help you shift rubbish?' he asks... And then I realise we are at cross purposes... The Burke's bin. **1985** *Listener* 30 Nov. 11 As the skinny joker from the centre curses the thing into gear and collects a dump bin on his way to temporary safety. **1992** ANDERSON *Portrait Artist's Wife* 169 Jack lifted an outraged face from his skip and roared at Tony. 'Is this your bloody ngaio in my bin?' **1995** *Evening Post* (Wellington) 26 Aug. 13 Although similar bins were in use in Europe, Burke was the first operator in the world to recognise the possibilities of their widespread popular use. Launched in 1956, Burkes Bins became almost a generic term for the big, heavy iron containers. Many people still refer to them by that name, although Burkes stopped handling bins a few years ago. **1995** *Sunday Star-Times* (Auckland) 28 Jan. A1 [A] Department spokesman..said Internal Affairs, as the oldest government department, had a few 'culture problems'. 'It's been seen as the Burke's Bin of the state sector, for things that don't fit anywhere else.'

4. CHILLYBIN.
  1983 *Truth* 23 Mar. 2 The security man at the gate inspected the bin and took away their grog.

bin, *v. trans.* To sort (fleeces or wool) into bins according to type; *spec.* in woolstores, to class or sort (small parcels of wool) into bins for eventual rebaling and sale.

1936 BELSHAW et al. *Agric. Organiz.* NZ 710 They are either mixed with the pieces or sent to store to be binned. 1974 *NZ Agric.* 67 Wool may be opened and reclassed in the broker's store, repacked in the owner's bales, and sold under his 'brand'; or it may be opened, classed, and then 'binned'. Binning is a system of pooling similar wools from a number of properties, allowing the smaller quantities to be grouped for sale. The farmer is credited according to the weight of his wool that has been assigned to each bin. This wool is sold under the broker's brand.

Hence **binning** *vbl. n.* and *ppl. a.,* see quots.
1936 BELSHAW et al. *Agric. Organiz.* NZ 710 'Crutchings' are seldom if ever classed except by the wool brokers when the wool is sent to them for binning. *Ibid.* 711 In 'Binning', the bales are broken up and classed into lines. This method of building up saleable lines is generally used in the case of small parcels of fleece wool and bales of oddments which cannot be included in the main lines without destroying their evenness. As each vendor's wool is classed in the binning-room, the wool in each class is weighed and credited to the owner before being placed in its appropriate bin. 1938 WINTER *King Country* 15 I found..that I had contributed no less than 8/11 to the revenue of our railways..that receiving, storing, lotting, weighing..ran away with 1/11, while somebody called Binning had secured 3/9 out of the scramble. Now who is Binning? 1950 *NZJAg.* Oct. LXXXI. 313 The broker has a good binning system and can handle most of the oddments. If a line of four bales cannot be made, send the wool in for binning. 1982 *Agric. Gloss.* (MAF) 52 *Binning*: Broker service for the disposal of small or mixed lots of wool. Each grower's wool is classed and weighed to bins with similar types from other [growers].

binder, *n.*[1] [f. Brit. dial. *binder* a large quantity, esp. of food: see OED 9; also EDD.] A solid meal, esp. one eaten when very hungry.
1915-17 MOLONEY in Boyack *Behind the Lines* (1989) 17 The idea is to go in [sic] have a real good binder and on a given signal all hands make for the tall timbers. 1917 *Chron. NZEF* 19 Sept. 55 I was hungry, so I turned my eyes away from the promising binder. 1925 *Auckland Capping Book* 13 If you hunger there is the 'binder for a bob'. 1937 *Canterbury Mountaineer* 13 We had also counted on a really good 'binder' at the Ball [Hut]. 1946 SARGESON *That Summer* 58 I shouted him a bob dinner and I could tell by the way he ate he was in need of a binder. 1953 SUTHERLAND *Golden Bush* (1963) 32 No, he didn't want a feed, he said; he's just got up from an 'almighty binder,' thanks just the same. 1964 HELMER *Stag Party* 80 This little hori's damned hungry..I could scoff a real binder, just quietly! 1981 SUTHERLAND & TAYLOR *Sunrise* 109 Better give our pony a binder and let her go in the horse paddock.

binder, *n.*[2] [Spec. use of *binder* piece of cloth used to bind parts of the body: see OED 3 a.] A strip of flannel worn (usu. by outdoor workers) across the lower back to prevent chills.
[*Note*] The term was used much earlier. Flannel 'binders', so called, were sewn in Marlborough at least as late as c1938 for bushmen and miners with 'bad backs'; and also, earlier, as cloth or gauze pieces specially prepared for 'binding' a newborn baby's umbilicus and navel (cf. M. Shepherd *Some of My Yesterdays* (1989) 94). (Ed.))
1986 RICHARDS *Off the Sheep's Back* 55 They suffered agony with backache and cramp [in learning to shear]. Each wore a wide red flannel 'binder' to keep their back warm.

bindweed. [Local or spec. use of *bindweed* for members of the fam. Convolvulaceae.] In New Zealand applied to native and naturalized (esp. *Convolvulus arvensis*) species of the family Convolvulaceae (esp. *Calystegia* spp.), climbing plants of waste places, forest margins, or sandy country, CONVOLVULUS.

1. *Calystegia* spp. See also ICE-PLANT. **a.** *C. sepium.* POHUE a.
1777 ANDERSON *Journal* Feb. in Cook *Journals* (1967) III. 805 Amongst the known kinds of plants are common and rough Bindweed, Nightshade and Nettles. 1838 POLACK *NZ* I. 105 The..bell flower, whose hues, white, red, and yellow, with the convolvulus, or bindweed, and innumerable indigenous liands, hung around in pleasing disorder. 1853 HOOKER *II Flora Novae-Zelandiae I Flowering Plants* 183 *Calystegia sepium...* 'Panake and Pohue'... This beautiful plant, the English 'Bind-weed', is as common in the Southern Hemisphere as it is in the Northern, being found in Chili, Australia, Tasmania, and Java. 1906 CHEESEMAN *Manual NZ Flora* 476 *Pohue; Panahe;* Bindweed... Widely dispersed in most temperate countries and everywhere highly variable. 1917 WILLIAMS *Dict. Maori Lang.* 7 *Akapohue..*A creeping plant. = *pohue* (*Calystegia sepium, bindweed*). 1969 *Standard Common Names Weeds* 5 *bindweed, greater Calystegia sepium* agg. 1981 BROOKER et al. *NZ Medicinal Plants* 44 *Calystegia sepium...* Bindweed... Pohue, pohuhe... A common weed of many forms, found in most temperate countries.

b. As **shore** (also **sea**) **bindweed** (or *sand convolvulus* (CONVOLVULUS)), *C. soldanella,* a species widespread in sandy habitats behind beaches.
1940 LAING & BLACKWELL *Plants NZ* 364 *Calystegia soldanella* (*The Sea-bindweed*). Stems prostrate, often buried beneath the sand;... *Nihi-nihi...* Sea-bindweed. 1969 *Standard Common Names Weeds* 68 *sea bindweed* [=] *shore bindweed.* 1982 WILSON *Stewart Is. Plants* 148 Shore Bindweed... Creeping in sand, rarely ascending through other vegetation... Flowers pink with white stripes, occasionally all white. 1993 GABITES *Wellington's Living Cloak* 31 Other native plants, like Strathmore weed, New Zealand ice plant and shore bindweed have creeping, prostrate forms and bind the shingle.

c. *Stewart Island.* As **native bindweed,** *C. tuguriorum.*
1982 WILSON *Stewart Is. Plants* 42 *Calystegia tuguriorum* Native Bindweed... Convolvulus... High climbing, twining stems with thin leaves. Flowers white, conspicuous.

2. As **black** (or **field**) **bindweed** (*Convolvulus arvensis*).
1926 HILGENDORF *Weeds* 135 Convolvulus (*Convolvulus arvensis*), is also called bindweed and black bindweed, cornbind, and morning glory. 1969 *Standard Common Names Weeds* 5 *bindweed, black* [=] *cornbind... bindweed, field.*

bingy /ˈbɪndʒi/. *Obs.* Also **bingey, bingie, bingjey, binjie.** [AND *bingy* (in non-Aboriginal use, 1892) ad. Aboriginal Dharuk *bindhi* (1791) 'belly'.] Stomach, belly.
1910 *Truth* 23 July 1 If the wowsers got their way boxing championships of the future will be decided by the candidates being required to answer certain questions, as, for instance..what to do upon receipt of a prod in the bingie. 1913 *NZ Bulletin* 8 Feb. 16 Not Understood! Yer cop one in the bingie, jis' when yer think you got 'im dead to rights; yer claim a foul, but referees are stingy. 1941 BAKER *NZ Slang* 51 The following [slang terms], which I have noted in constant use by our youngsters, [include]..binjey, skite. c1945 *Sixes & Sevens* (Troopship pub.) 7 'My oath,' I said. 'Many a Jap binjie is going to get a hoodickey stuck in it before sparrow-hiccough.' 1984 BEARDSLEY *Blackball 08* 33 I tell you there's times my tucker burns in my bingy all afternoon.

binjey, binjie, varr. BINGY.

biobio, var. PIOPIO.

birch. *Obs.* [Colloq. transf. use of northern hemisphere *birch* (*Betula* spp., fam. Betulaceae) for southern beech (*Nothofagus* spp., fam. Fagaceae), earlier erron. placed in the *Fagus* genus).]

1. Occas. as **New Zealand birch,** BEECH esp. 1. Often *attrib.*
[*Note*] Birch was the preferred familiar common name (esp. in the South Island) until c1960.
1796 MURRY *Journal* Jan. in McNab *Hist. Records* (1914) II. 534 The Birch would only fit for fuel—Its uncommon whiteness would cause it to be preferred for decks, &c. but it splits with the smallest blow, and, of all the woods at Duskey Bay it is the least durable. 1842 *NZ Jrnl.* (1843) IV. 185 There are also some hilly points upon which the birch grows. 1853 HECTOR *Handbook NZ* 125 White-birch of Nelson and Otago (from colour of bark), Black-heart Birch of Wellington, *Fagus solandri*..a lofty, beautiful ever-green tree, 100 feet high. Black-birch (Tawhai) of Auckland and Otago (from colour of bark), Red-birch of Wellington and Nelson (from colour of timber), *Fagus fusca*..a noble tree 60 to 90 feet high. 1866 BARKER *Station Life* (1870) 94 [Ferns] contrasting..with the black stems of the birch-trees around them. 1889 KIRK *Forest Flora* v At least a dozen kinds of small-leaved trees are termed 'birch', with the prefix 'black', 'white', 'red', 'brown', 'grey', or even 'yellow', applied as the imagination of the bushman may suggest, scarcely any two bushmen being agreed as to the correct application of the qualifying term, while architects and contractors for the most part are but little better informed. The brown-birch of Otago is the white-birch of Nelson; the white-birch of Westland..is a totally different tree; the black-birch of Auckland is termed red-birch in Wellington, brown-birch in some parts of Nelson, while in Otago it appears to be termed indifferently black-birch or red-birch. 1891 *NZJSc.* (NS) I. 50 The perversity with which the true 'beeches' have become popularly known as 'birches'..is enough to fill with despair any botanist who desires to foster a system of popular names that will be free from misleading and inaccurate suggestions. c1899 DOUGLAS in *Mr Explorer Douglas* (1957) 259 At one time the Kakapo screamed in that birch country from the sea beach to near the snow line. 1917 WILLIAMS *Dict. Maori Lang.* 475 *Tawai*..the birch of the colonists. 1940 LAING & BLACKWELL *Plants NZ* 136 The species of the genus *Nothofagus* in New Zealand..are known to bushmen as 'birch', but should more correctly be termed beech. It is perhaps futile to hope that the more exact name will become popular... At present the various species are designated almost indifferently, white, red, black, silver birch, etc. 1966 [see BEECH 1]. 1972 *Otago Daily Times* (Dunedin) 11 Mar. 1 Mr Lyn Thompson yesterday inquired about the difference between red, black and brown birch. It was 'clearly' explained for him by a prominent axeman, Mr Bill Evans. The bark of the red birch is silver, but the timber is pink when it's green. Brown birch often has black bark, but the green timber is red. Sometimes the bark of the black birch is white, but the timber is yellow and sometimes it's brown when it's green.

2. Misapplied locally in the South Island to (usu. small-leaved) genera other than *Nothofagus,* esp. KAMAHI 1, *Weinmannia racemosa* (cf. 3 (1) below), from a vague similarity between kamahi adult foliage and the leaves of *N. fusca* (red beech) and *N. truncata* (hard beech), poss. reinforced by a

similarity of the Maori word-forms TOWAI (for *Weinmannia*) and TAWAI/TAWHAI (for beech).
1877 *TrNZI* IX. 148 Kamai is called black birch in the Catlin River District and Southland... I cannot understand how such an idea could have originated, for except in the case of the bark of one there is not the slightest resemblance between the birches and kamai. 1889 KIRK *Forest Flora* 133 [*Weinmannia racemosa*] is..generally known as 'kamahi' in the South Island and in Stewart Island. In common with other trees characterized by small leaves, it is termed 'birch' by the bushman, or 'red birch' or 'brown birch', the names being applied with strict impartiality and without any definite meaning. 1892 DOUGLAS in *Mr Explorer Douglas* (1957) 175 Young Totara, however large they may be, are no better than mountain birch or Kaimai. 1940 LAING & BLACKWELL *Plants NZ* 197 *Kamahi W. racemosa*. Kamahi..is particularly common in the forests of Westland where it is usually termed red birch. 1963 PEARSON *Coal Flat* 420 Birch: Common West Coast bushman's name for two kinds of tree, the *kaamahi* and the New Zealand beech. 1965 HENDERSON *Open Country* 72 Dick..had found..a big old hollow-butted kamahi (a sort of red birch) with a fair-sized hole among its twisting roots.

3. With a modifier: **bastard**, **black**, **black-heart**, **brown**, **bull**, **cherry**, **entire-leaved**, **mountain**, **red**, **silver**, **white**, **yellow**.
[*Note*] Prefixed vernacular modifiers, similar to but more various than those of BEECH (see esp. quots. 1853, 1889 and 1972 in 1 above), attempt to distinguish species and varieties by colour of bark or wood, texture of timber, appearance of leaf, etc. (see note at BEECH 2).

(1) **bastard birch**. KAMAHI. Cf. 2 above.
1966 NEWTON *Boss's Story* 107 This birch timber—commonly known [in Canterbury] as 'bastard' birch—rots in no time. 1969 *Standard Common Names Weeds* 4 *bastard birch* [=] *kamahi*. 1973 NEWTON *Big Country SI* (1977) 10 The Nelson hill country was predominantly 'bastard' birch and of comparatively low fertility.

(2) **black birch**. **a.** Various *Nothofagus* spp. often locally so-called.
1841 *NZ Jrnl.* II. 51 The forest is again formed of one sort of trees, the tawai, or black birch as it is called. 1844 BARNICOAT *Journal* (ATLTS) 19 Jan. 150 The timber of the [Nelson] hills is chiefly..of a kind called black birch which is..almost invariably hollow. 1846 HEAPHY *Exped. S.W. Nelson* 10 Feb. in Taylor *Early Travellers* (1959) 193 The forest was of black birch, almost the only timber in these high elevations. 1853 HOOKER *II Flora Novae-Zelandiae I Flowering Plants* 229 *Fagus fusca*... Mountains of the Northern Island... Common in the Middle Island... Nat. name, 'Tawai', Bidwill. 'Black Birch' of the colonists. 1860 BUTLER *Forest Creek MS* (1960) June 52 After tea..cut up black birch boughs or tussock grass or snow grass..and make yourself a deep warm bed. 1869, 1875 [see (9) below]. 1882 HAY *Brighter Britain* II. 190 The Tawairaunui (*Fagus fusca*) is..known as 'black birch'. 1885 *TrNZI* XVII. 301 [*Notho*]*fagus solandri*... Entire-leaved Beech. Black Birch of Wellington, Canterbury, and in part of Otago and Southland. 1889 KIRK *Forest Flora* 201 *Fagus cliffortioides*, in common with the other New Zealand species of *Fagus*, is perversely termed 'birch' by the bushman, who prefixes the adjective 'black' if he looks at the dark bark of an old tree, or 'white' if he has before him the pale bark of a young tree. 1896 HARPER *Pioneer Work* 35 There is also the rata tree, the prince of firewoods,... so-called red-birch, white and black birches (which are really beeches). 1906 CHEESEMAN *Manual NZ Flora* 641 *F. fusca*... A noble forest-tree 60-100 ft. high, bark dark-brown or black in old plants, deeply furrowed, smooth and greyish-white on young trees;.. rare in Canterbury and eastern Otago... *Black-birch*; *Red-birch*. Ibid. 643 *F. Solandri*... A lofty forest-tree 40–60 ft. high, bark black..in old trees..pale and smooth on young ones... *Tawhai*; *Tawhai-rauriki*; *Black-birch*; *White-birch*. 1918 *NZJST* I. 307 *Fagus Solandri*.—The most common name of this tree is 'black-birch,' but it has several other names... In Canterbury it is called 'black-birch,' 'white-birch,' 'red-birch,' and 'brown-birch'; in Otago it is known as 'white-birch,' 'black-birch,' or 'black-heart birch.' Young specimens of this tree that have no dark heart-wood are often called 'white-birch.' 1972 MCLEOD *Mountain World* 310 *Black birch*: Common misnomer of mountain beech [in SI high country].

b. Other than *Nothofagus* spp. *Weinmannia racemosa* (fam. Cunoniaceae). KAMAHI 1, TAWHERO 1.
1848 WAKEFIELD *Handbook NZ* 142 Tawai, (*Leiospermum racemosum*.)..is commonly called 'black birch' by the sailors and other Europeans acquainted with it. 1875 KIRK *Durability NZ Timbers* 19 Tawhero.- (*Weinmannia racemosa*)... Often called black birch, and substituted for that timber, to which it is greatly inferior in strength and durability. 1877 *TrNZI* IX. 148 The kamai is called black birch in the Catlin River District and Southland, which name is given on account of a supposed resemblance to the 'birches', or more correctly, 'beeches'. 1889 FEATON *Art Album NZ Flora* 136 Weinmannia Racemosa... The 'Tawhero' or 'Kamai'... In Otago the tree is popularly known as the 'Black Birch'.

c. In *attrib*. or collocative use, esp. **black birch bush**, **black birch country**.
1847 BRUNNER *Exped. S.W. Nelson* 25 Jan. in Taylor *Early Travellers* (1959) 266 We found none [*sc.* eels]..or anything else fit to eat in the black birch forest. Ibid. 26 Feb. 268 Passing over about a mile of very good pine forest, but again came to our black birch country—precipices and granite rocks. 1863 HARPER *Lett. from NZ* 1 Oct. (1914) 72 Noticing a clump of black birch trees which might shelter my horse for the night. 1878 JOLLIE *Reminiscences* (ATLTS) 35 Clearing the road through black birch bush. 1890 *PWD Gen. Catalogue* (NZ & South Seas Exhib.) 21 Black birch burr (entire leaved beech).

(3) **black-heart birch**. *N. solandri*, having dark-streaked heartwood.
1877 *TrNZI* IX. 164 The utmost confusion prevails among the common names of the birches... I would suggest the retention of the common Otago names Fagus fusca—Red birch; F. solandri—Black-heart birch; F Menziesii—Silver birch. 1883 HECTOR *Handbook NZ* 125 *Nothofagus solandri*... White-birch of Nelson and Otago (from colour of bark), Black-heart Birch of Wellington. 1885 *TrNZI* XVII. 301 [*Notho*]*fagus solandri*... Black-heart Birch of Otago. 1890 *PWD Gen. Catalogue* (NZ & South Seas Exhib.) 16 Hand specimen, entire leaved beech (black heart birch). 1918 [see (2) a above].

(4) **brown birch**. *N. menziesii* and *N. solandri*.
1885 *TrNZI* XVII. 298 [*Notho*]*fagus menziesii*... Silver Beech. Brown Birch, White Birch, Red Birch. Silver Birch. Ibid. 301 [*Notho*]*fagus solandri*... White, Black, Red, and Brown Birch of Oxford and Alford Forests. 1889 [see (10) below; also 1 above]. 1918 [see (2) a above; (9) below]. 1981 HENDERSON *Exiles Asbestos Cottage* 60 Red or brown beech/birch, 'steaming wood', good fill-in wood.

(5) **bull birch**. *N. fusca*.
1885 *TrNZI* XVII. 300 [*Notho*]*fagus fusca*... Black or Bull Birch of Lake Wakatipu. 1902 *Settler's Handbook NZ* 125 Bull-birch, of southern lakes district. 1918 *NZJST* I. 308 *Fagus fusca*... In Otago it is called both 'red-birch' and 'bull-birch'. 1961 *Merriam-Webster Third Internat. Dict.* 293 *bull birch n, NewZeal*: Beech 4

(6) **cherry birch**. Marlborough Sounds. *N. menziesii*. See *silver birch* (10) below.
1950 *Bull. Wellington Bot. Soc. No.23* 16 The principal forest trees [at Manaroa, Pelorus Sound]..are silver beech, (*Nothofagus menziesii*) in this locality known as cherry birch.

(7) **entire-leaved birch**. *N. solandri*. See also *black-heart birch* (3) above.
1886 KIRK in *Settler's Handbook NZ* (1902) 121 [Native name] Tawhai..[Settlers' name] Entire-leaved birch. 1890 [see (3) above].

(8) **mountain birch**. *N. solandri* var. *cliffortioides*. See also *white birch* (11) a below.
1861 HARPER *Lett. from NZ* 20 July (1914) 57 The house nestles under a forest of Mountain Birch, so-called, but really a beech, with very small leaves. 1906 CHEESEMAN *Manual NZ Flora* 643 *F. Cliffortioides*... A small tree, usually from 20 ft. to 40 ft. high..Mountain districts... *Tawhai-rauriki*; *Mountain Beech* or *Birch*. 1918 *NZJST* I. 144 *Fagus cliffortioides*... Mountain beech or birch.

(9) **red birch**. **a.** Various *Nothofagus* spp., their wood or timber, so-called from the colour of the wood or bark.
1853 HOOKER *II Flora Novae-Zelandiae I Flowering Plants* 229 *Fagus Menziesii*..Nat. name, 'Tawai', Col. 'Red Birch' of the colonists. 1869 *TrNZI* I. (rev. edn.) 193 Red Birch of Otago, Black Birch of Nelson, Beech, etc. (*Fagus Menziesi*). Ibid. 44 The Tawhai, and Tawhai-rau-nui, or Black and Red Birches, (*Fagus Solandri* and *F. Fusca*,) often form large..trees. 1875 KIRK *Durability NZ Timbers* 15 Black Birch of Auckland and Otago, Red Birch of Wellington and Nelson: Hutu-Tawhai.—(*Fagus fusca*). Ibid. 17 Red Birch.—(*Fagus menziesii*). 1882 HAY *Brighter Britain* II. 190 The Tawai (*Fagus Menziesii*), called 'red birch' by settlers, is a favourite for fencing when young. 1885 [see (4) above]. 1890 *PWD Gen. Catalogue* (NZ & South Seas Exhib.) 19 Test piece, red birch (tooth leaved beech). 1906 [see (2) a above]. 1918 *NZJST* I. 307 *Fagus Menziesii*.—The commonest name of this tree is 'silver-birch,' but it often called 'brown birch,' 'red-birch,' and 'white-birch' in different localities... *Fagus fusca*.— In Auckland this tree is called 'black-birch'; in Wellington 'red-birch'. 1970 MCLEOD *Glorious Morning* 83 In the forests on the north side of the Waimakariri there are substantial stands of *Nothofagus fusca*, the red beech, which we called 'red birch' in those days [*sc.* late 1920s]. 1981 HENDERSON *Exiles Asbestos Cottage* 60 Red or brown beech/birch, 'steaming wood', good fill-in wood.

b. Genera other than *Nothofagus*, KAMAHI; *red matipo* (MATIPO 2 (2)).
1889 [see KAMAHI 2]. 1892 *NZ Official Handbook* 150 Mapau, red-mapau, or red-birch (*Myrsine urvillei*). 1896 HARPER *Pioneer Work* 35 There is also the rata tree, the prince of firewoods,... miki-miki, kamahi, or so-called red-birch, white and black birches (which are really beeches). 1910 COCKAYNE *NZ Plants & Their Story* 160 *Weinmannia racemosa*, called red-birch in Westland, is very common, and belongs to the Cunoniaceae, a most closely related family. 1922 *Auckland Weekly News* 23 Nov. 17 Racemes of small white flowers of the red birch—kamahi in part of the South Island, tawhera in the North Island, Weinmannia racemosa to botanists..are reflected in magic mirrors while they drink the waters of the lake. 1926 CROOKES *Plant Life in Maoriland* 42 It has been found growing on the hange hange, one of the coprosmas, the 'red birch' (myrsine), one of the beeches, and some five other trees. 1940 LAING & BLACKWELL *Plants NZ* 197 [The Kamahi]..is particularly common in the forests of Westland.. where it is usually termed red birch (!). 1969 *Standard Common Names Weeds* 63 *red birch* [=] *kamahi*.

BIRD

(10) **silver birch**. *N. menziesii*. See also *cherry birch* (6) above, *white birch* (11) below.

1877 [see (3) above]. 1885 [see (4) above]. 1889 KIRK *Forest Flora* 175 The silver-beech [*Fagus menziesii*], in common with all the New Zealand species of Fagus, is known as 'tawhai' or 'tawai' by the Natives. To settlers and bushmen it is known under various names, as 'brown-birch', 'red-birch', 'white-birch', and 'silver-birch'. 'Brown-birch' is the name most generally used. I have proposed the name of 'silver-beech' for general use, on account of the pale-grey silvery bark. 1890 *PWD Gen. Catalogue* (NZ & South Seas Exhib.) 19 Test piece, silver birch (silver beech). 1906 CHEESEMAN *Manual NZ Flora* 641 *F. Menziesii*... bark white or silvery, especially in young trees;.. *Tawhai; Tawai; Silver-birch; Red-birch*. 1918 *NZJST* I. 144 [*Fagus*] *Menziesii*... Silver or red birch. 1926 COWAN *Travel in NZ* II. 140 Beeches (*tawai*), *rata*, silver-birch and other fine trees tower around us. 1939 BEATTIE *First White Boy Born Otago* 111 On the face to the south the bush was either silver pine or silver birch and so open you could drive cattle through it. 1968 HALL-JONES *Early Fiordland* 44 His collection of specimens [from Dusky Sound] included two fine New Zealand trees, the silver birch (*Nothofagus menziesii*) and the pineapple scrub.

(11) **white birch**. **a.** *Nothofagus* spp. (mainly from the colour of the bark or wood), esp. *N. solandri* var. *cliffortioides, N. solandri* and also *N. menziesii*. See also *mountain birch* (8), *silver birch* (10) above.

1844 TUCKETT *Diary* 24 May in Hocken *Contributions* (1898) 223 The bush-like woods on the east side [of Colac's, Otago] are of white birch, likewise no recommendation of the soil. 1853 HOOKER *II Flora Novae-Zelandiae I Flowering Plants* 230 *Fagus Solandri*... English name, 'White Birch'... *Fagus Cliffortioides*... Very similar indeed to *F. Solandri*, and also called 'White Birch', but a more alpine plant. 1869 *TrNZI* I. (rev. edn.) 193 White Birch of Otago, Beech, etc. (*Fagus Solandri*). This has the greatest distribution of the three [Red, Black, White]. Wood white, soft, decays easily. 1879 HAAST *Geol. Canterbury & Westland* 35 Almost up to the terminal moraine of the Tasman glacier, small groves of the obtuse leafed *Fagus Cliffortioides*, the White Birch of the settlers, is [*sic*] found in many localities. 1882 HAY *Brighter Britain* II. 197 The Tawai-rauriki (*Fagus Solandri*) is the 'White Birch' of the settlers. 1885 [see (4) above]. 1885 *TrNZI* XVII. 304 [*Notho*]*fagus Cliffortioides*... Mountain beech...White Birch of Nelson, and in part of Otago and Southland. 1889 [see (2) a above]. 1890 *PWD Gen. Catalogue* (NZ & South Seas Exhib.) 16 Silver beech (white birch) slab. 1906, 1918 [see (2) a above]. 1970 MCLEOD *Glorious Morning* 254 *Birch trees/Beech trees*: Bush or forest in the high country consists almost entirely of *Nothofagus cliffortioides*, the mountain beech. These were always known as birch by the early settlers, and high country men usually call them 'white birch' (from colour of wood).

b. Genera other than *Nothofagus*, poss. in districts where the relevant *Nothofagus* spp. are not common, spec. *Carpodetus serratus* (PUTAPUTA-WETA) and *Quintinia* spp. (LILAC 1).

1883 HECTOR *Handbook NZ* 132 *Carpodetus serratus*... Tawiri, White Mapau, White-birch (of Auckland). 1889 KIRK *Forest Flora* 77 [Putaputaweta] is frequently applied by settlers, who also term it 'mapau', 'white mapau', 'white maple', and 'white birch', so that it affords a good instance of the misuse of both Native and common names. *Ibid*. 255 On the west coast of the South Island it [*sc. Quintinia serrata*] is known as 'white-birch'—perhaps the most unmeaning application of the comprehensive word 'birch' that has yet been recorded.

(12) **yellow birch**. *N. solandri*, from the colour of the wood.

1885 *TrNZI* XVII. 303 [In Oxford Forest] I learned that the tree [*N. solandri*, entire-leaved beech] was termed 'red birch', 'brown birch', 'white birch', 'black birch' and 'yellow birch' at different stages of its growth, but the application of these terms differed greatly.

4. *Special Comb.* **birch itch** (occas. in s. New Zealand, **birch fever, birch sickness**), an allergic reaction to New Zealand beech trees. Cf. *beech fever* (BEECH 3), *bush itch* (BUSH *n*. C 3 a).

1951 p.c. R. Mason. In Otago and Southland an allergic reaction to beech trees is known as birch (or beech) fever, or birch sickness. 1952 THOMSON *Deer Hunter* 119 Cliff developed a kind of skin rash, sometimes called 'birch itch'. This rash usually occurs with people who are allergic to bush localities, especially when the pollen is released from the trees in the spring. 1974 PRESTON *Lady Doctor* 28 A child from the Catlins district was admitted suffering from 'bush (or birch) itch'. This was a common affliction in the more southerly parts of Otago and Southland, cases seldom coming into hospital unless very severe; it was thought to be a form of scabies. Today it would be recognised as an allergy..; it is still common among trampers and mountaineers. 1975 ANDERSON *Men of Milford Road* 93 (Griffiths Collect.) Some people are allergic to beech trees and the local name for this allergic condition was birch itch. On one occasion a compensatory claim was sent to Wellington advising that the condition suffered was birch itch. Back came a reprimand about this use of the term birch—it should be *beech*.

bird, *n*.

1. *Ellipt.* for MUTTONBIRD 1.

c1835 BOULTBEE *Journal* (1986) 77 We went a few yards and made a fire and ate our dinner of birds and potatoes. *Ibid*. 81 [At Ruaboka (Ruapuke Island)] were crowds of natives collected together..who were on their way to the islands in the Straits in search of birds. 1952 SANSOM *Diary* 20 Apr. *In Grip of Island* (1982) 153 Birds in kelp bags with totara bark wrapping, looking fine in their new flax baskets.

2. *Prison* and *WW1*. [Transf. or fig. use of *bird* as one confined in a cage (cf. *gaol-bird*): see OED *bird n.*[4] 4 c.] One imprisoned in prison or detention camp. Cf. BIRD-CAGE 4.

1908 *Truth* 2 May 1 The 'Harmy' [*sc.* Salvation Army] always hangs around 'Prison Gates' to get hold of discharged 'birds' to give them a helping hand. 1937 PARTRIDGE *Dict. Slang* 54 *bird*... 2. A prisoner: New Zealand military: 1915-18. Ex *cage*, a detention-camp. Prob. ex earlier *cage*, a prison. 1938 *Press* (Christchurch) (McNab Slang) 2 Apr. 18 [Slang of the N.Z.E.F.] A 'blue duck' was a rumour; but a 'bird' was a prisoner in a cage.

3. In various *transf.* or *fig.* uses. **a.** A success, in the phr. **to make a bird of** (a job, an opportunity), to complete successfully.

1963 PEARSON *Coal Flat* 12 Well, you'll get a clear run this time, son, and you make a bird of it and get ahead in your job.

b. box of birds, see BOX *n.*[2] 6 a.

4. In various special Comb. and collocations: **bird islands**, the far southern islands on which muttonbirds breed (see 1 above); **birdseed**, (a) *broadleaved plantain* (PLANTAIN); (b) see *live on birdseed* (LIVE *v*. 1 a); **bird's eye**, used attributively of wood the grain of which when polished resembles a bird's eye, esp. **bird's eye totara**, totara timber showing a mottled pattern reminiscent of a bird's eye; **bird sheep** *obs.*

BIRD-CAGE

?*Norfolk Island*, MUTTONBIRD 1; **birdsmouth** or **birdsmouth joint**, see quots.; **birdsnest fungus**, see FUNGUS 2 (4); **bird-stone** usu. *pl.*, a gizzard-stone of a moa, MOA STONE.

1965 bird islands [see BIRD *v*.]. 1926 birdseed [see PLANTAIN]. 1925 bird's-eye totara [see MOTTLED *ppl. a.* 2]. 1987 MASSEY *Woodturning NZ* 93 *Bird's eye figure* Small rounded grain figure resembling a bird's eye. 1952 RICHARDS *Chatham Is*. 84 Muttonbirds were so called from their fancied flavour of mutton. The first known mention of the name is in a letter from an officer stationed on the newly-founded convict station on Norfolk Island. He writes in 1793 that the island swarms with muttonbirds so called by the convicts or sometimes **bird sheep**. 1968 SLATTER *Pagan Game* 17 The rafters that broke without warning, the **birdmouths** that would not fit on the top plate, the undulating soffits. 1979 *SANZ Gloss. Bldg. Terminol*. 15 *Birdsmouth joint (metal)*... *Birdsmouth joint (timber)*— An angle checked near or at the lower end of a rafter for connection to the wall plate. 1991 LA ROCHE *Hist. of Howick & Pakuranga* 90 The eaves protected the windows and walls, and a 'birds mouth'—a right angled cut in the rafter gave a snug joint with the top plate. 1890 *TrNZI* XXII. 410 Many small stones, well-worn—unquestionably '**bird-stones**'—can be picked out of the clay immediately beneath the ashes of the burned peat-bed. *Ibid*. 411 Bird-stones are to found in the present soil and subsoil, but they are so rare that the search for them is disheartening work.

bird, *v. intr*. To take muttonbirds.

1965 GILLHAM *Naturalist in NZ* 29 I knew that birding rights are closely guarded; that even among the Maoris only those whose ancestors have birded from times long past are allowed ashore on the bird islands in the harvest season. 1979 WILSON *Titi Heritage* 64 The old birders said there was always a queer unfriendly feeling about these places, as though unseen eyes were watching them and they were reluctant to 'bird' there.

bird-cage. [Transf. or fig. use of *bird-cage* a confining or protective wire structure.]

1. *Obs*. (Of a) type of railway carriage having a viewing corridor the outside wall of which was enclosed only by wire mesh.

1900 LLOYD *Newest England* 60. There is not on our [U.S.] 'Sunset' or 'Cannon-ball' limited trains any car equal to the 'Bird-cage' car on the New Zealand express trains, composed of compartments with an outside corridor up and down which the passengers can walk under shelter, but with a full view of the scenery. This corridor is inclosed with a wire grating breast high, and hence the name 'bird-cage'. 1904 *NZ Observer* 2 Jan. 5 He [*sc*. the Minister of Lands] received a deputation in one compartment of a 'bird-cage' carriage. 1912 *Otago Witness* (Dunedin) 17 July 89 Well, there's three bird-cage compartments, that's sleeping quarters at night. 1965 SARGESON *Memoirs of Peon* 105 We all returned from Rotorua by train [*circa* WW1].., a first-class compartment being reserved for us in that kind of carriage which used to have a birdcage walk all along one side. 1972 LEITCH *Railways of NZ* 198 In the 1890s the unusual 'birdcage' cars were built... They featured an open saloon in one half of the car, and two small compartments in the other half opening on to an open corridor or passage protected by heavy grillwork. 1982 FRAME *To the Is-land* (1984) 147 We went for our first family holiday, on the train to Rakaia, travelling in a first-class 'bird cage' on our annual free ticket.

2. *Horseracing*. [Transf. use of *birdcage* the paddock at Newmarket race-course in which horses are generally saddled: see OED 2, 1884; AND 1893.] **a.** The area on a racecourse, often enclosed with high wire-mesh fence, where horses are paraded before a race, and to which they return after racing. Used also in show-jumping of the area in which ponies and riders wait their turn to compete.

[**1897** *NZ Times* (Wellington) 30 Oct. Suppl. [6] A Melbourne writer says that those who looked at [Aurum] in the birdcage at Caulfield would recognise that his portraiture..was tolerably faithful.] **1914** *PSA Jrnl.* 21 Dec. 17 'Oh! 'ere they come,' as the horses filed out of the bird-cage to do their preliminary. **1928** *NZ Free Lance* (Wellington) 4 Jan. 32 Our photograph shows the horses parading in the birdcage prior to the start of one of the races. **1934** *Weekly News* 3 Jan. [Caption] 10. The candidates for the Auckland Cup parading in the birdcage prior to the start. **1940** SARGESON *Man & His Wife* (1944) 64 And didn't Fred and me get a kick out of taking the horses into the birdcages and leading them around. **1954** JOURNET *Take My Tip* 45 [Heading] The Birdcage This is one of racing's most inappropriate terms. The birdcage is a large open space in which all the horses parade before the start of the race. **1985** STEWART *Gumboots & Goalposts* 46 The jockey brought her into No. 4 stall in the birdcage.

b. Used *attrib.* in Comb. **birdcage artist**, one aware of the illicit practices connected with a race course birdcage; **birdcage steward**, the course steward who oversees the birdcage.

1924 *Otago Witness* (Dunedin) 20 May 24 Witness was the **birdcage steward** at the meeting. Jury had the evidence of Wilson, 'the **birdcage artist**'. **1968** *Evening Post* (Wellington) 2 Jan. 15 —, trainer..was fined $50 for failing to obey an instruction by the birdcage steward.

3. *Obs.* Mainly *attrib.* [Cars, new or used, were a scarce and valuable commodity in the 1950s and early 1960s.] A strongly-fenced enclosure, often protected with barbed-wire, where used-car dealers displayed their wares. Also in Comb. **birdcage boys**, used car dealers or salesmen.

1954 *PSA Jrnl.* May 20 That dealing in the sale of second-hand cars is a lucrative profession can be gauged by the very numerous 'bird-cage' businesses that now abound... *Ibid.* 21 These used car dealers, perhaps more colloquially known as the 'bird-cage boys'. **1976** *Evening Post* (Wellington) 13 Nov. 6 Clearly the days of 'bird-cage' dealers (so called because their lots are usually surrounded by wire netting) are on the way out. **1988** MCGILL *Dict. Kiwi Slang* 15 *birdcage* used car dealer's lot post-war; died out as dealers got rid of the chicken wire; may revive along with new security fences.

4. *Prison.* A security exercise yard. Cf. BIRD *n.* 2, BUDGIE-CAGE.

1982 NEWBOLD *Big Huey* 245 Birdcage (n) Security exercise yard.

5. bird-cage fungus, see FUNGUS 2 (3).

birdcatching tree. Also **bird-catcher**, **birdcatching plant**. *Pisonia brunoniana* (formerly *Heimerliodendron brunonianum*) (fam. Nyctaginaceae), a small tree confined to coastal regions of the northern North Island, having extremely viscid fruits capable of trapping small birds. See also BIRD-KILLING TREE, PARAPARA.

1889 KIRK *Forest Flora* 293 Mr. Colenso informs me that this plant [*Pisonia brunoniana*] is the parapara of the northern natives... It is sometimes termed the 'bird-catching plant' by settlers and bushmen... It will always be a plant of special interest, as small birds are often found captured by its viscid fruits, to which their feathers become attached as effectively as if they were glued. **1898** MORRIS *Austral-English* 31 Bird-catching plant..a New Zealand shrub or tree..*Parapara*. **1907** LAING & BLACKWELL *Plants NZ* 159 Maori name *parapara*, sometimes called by the settlers the *Bird-catching plant*. North Island: Auckland province chiefly. **1924** *NZJST* VII. 186 The third..is..the parapara, or 'bird-catcher' of the settlers... As is well known, the seed-pods of the *Pisonia* exude a sticky substance, which it is stated will ensnare the smaller birds that come into contact with the gluey mass—hence the name 'bird-catcher plant'. **1943** *NZEF Times* 26 July 11 Some mysterious person every year..breaks off the branches of the bird-catching tree in Pukekura Park..so that it cannot trap birds or insects. **1957** WILLIAMS *Dict. Maori Lang.* 262 *Parapara,...* n. *1...the bird-catching tree.* **1965** GILLHAM *Naturalist in NZ* 229 Trees on Little Barrier include the nikau palm, the Maori cork tree, ngaio, and the birdcatching tree. **1988** DAWSON *Forest Vines to Snow Tussocks* 110 On the mainland as well as on islands, and extending to East Cape and beyond, are the small trees parapara or the 'bird catching tree'..and tawapou.

birder. [f. MUTTON–)BIRDER rather than a specific use of obsolete Brit. *birder*: AND 1896.] A shortened form of MUTTONBIRDER; but also locally, esp. in the Chatham Islands, one who catches (the young of) other birds (mainly seabirds) for food.

1918 *TrNZI* L. 145 Mr. Smith informed me that partially white mutton-birds are..yet sufficiently rare as to make a specimen of special interest even to the birders. **1928** BAUCKE *Manuscript* (Bishop Museum Memoirs Vol.IX No.5 343-382) in Skinner & Baucke *Moriorīs* (1928) 372 When we were younger [Chatham Island] birders grumbled at delays. **1940** HOWARD *Rakiura* 211 European wives or husbands of legitimate 'birders' may..accompany their partners to the islets. **1952** RICHARDS *Chatham Is.* 84 In March, while in the burrows, the chicks are pulled out and killed by the birders, split, salted, roasted over a fire. **1966** *Dominion* (Wellington) 5 Mar. 8 The bird is caught by hand and dragged out to receive a sharp rap over the head from a club, or a crushing bite from the birder's strong teeth. **1979** [see BIRD *v.*]. **1985** *Reader's Digest Book NZ Birds* 97 Muttonbirding begins on 1 April. Formerly the birders travelled by sea, but now many hire a helicopter.

birding, *vbl. n.*

1. [AND 1896, Tasmania.] A shortened form of MUTTONBIRDING, but also occas. (esp. in the Chatham Islands) used of the taking for food of the young of other seabirds such as the albatross.

1878 CHUDLEIGH *Diary* 25 Sept. (1950) 272 Got letters from the Chathams... Hood has been delayed birding with the natives. **1900** *NZ Illustr. Mag.* II. 920 Some of the families or tribes [of Maoris] hold the right of 'birding' on certain islands. **1918** *TrNZI* L. 145 On the 14th June, 1916, I had an interview with Mrs. Sidney Ladbrook..who had just then returned from a birding expedition to Evening Island. **1928** BAUCKE *Manuscript* (Bishop Museum Memoirs Vol.IX No.5 343–382) in Skinner & Baucke *Moriorīs* (1928) 362 These sea birdings [on the Chathams] were preluded and attended by special rituals; for instance, no birder must coite with a female the night before the expedition. *Ibid.* 372 Hence those repeatedly successful birding expeditions, almost incredible to such as know..the fierce currents between the main island and the Motuhara—birding rock. **1952** BLAKISTON *My Yesteryears* 39 During one long vacation, he [Maui Pomare] returned to the Chathams, and one day went out with a birding party. **1965** [see BIRD *v.*].

2. Special Comb. **birding island**, an offshore breeding-place for muttonbirds over which certain families usu. have the rights to take muttonbird young; **birding season** (also **muttonbird(ing) season**), the season for taking muttonbirds (see quot. 1949).

1925 GUTHRIE-SMITH *Bird Life on Island & Shore* 113 As on all 'birding' islands paths—of a sort—were numerous and well-defined. **1918** *TrNZI* L. 145 During the birding season of 1917 [they] went to the same island again. **c1920** BEATTIE *Trad. Lifeways Southern Maori* (1994) 176 In the muttonbird season [the Titi islands] are visited by the Maori and halfcaste families whom the law recognises as owners. **1930** *Wanderlust Magazine* II No.1 58 The mutton-birding season opens on April 1st. **1949** *Land Act Regs.* in Wilson *Titi Heritage* (1979) 174 'Birding season' means a period commencing on the 1st day of April in any year and ending with the 31st day of May in the same year. **1964** DEMPSEY *Little World Stewart Is.* 49 The weeks of the birding season went by. **1979** WILSON *Titi Heritage* 38 Over the years since 1864 they had controlled their islands during the birding seasons with stern and strict discipline.

bird-killing tree. BIRDCATCHING TREE.

1884 *TrNZI* XVI. 364 A Bird-killing Tree... In a shrub growing in my father's garden at New Plymouth, two Silver-eyes..had been found with their wings so glued by the sticky seed-vessels that they were unable to move. **1926** CROOKES *Plant Life Maoriland* 57 [The parapara's] seeds exude a glutinous substance, which enables them to adhere very readily to the wings of birds... If the bird happens to be a small one, it may become firmly glued on to the fruit, and unable to escape. For this reason the parapara has been called by the settlers 'the bird-killing tree.'

birl, var. BURL *n.*[1]

biscuit.

1. New Zealand follows British rather than N. Amer. usage in traditionally preferring *biscuit* to *cracker* (except in Comb. *water-, cream-, sao-cracker*, etc.) or *cookie*. In early use (see quot. 1860) *biscuit* often denotes the hard, dry 'ship's biscuit', still extant in the name of the commercially available CABIN BISCUIT q.v.

1860 *Richmond-Atkinson Papers* (1960) I. 671 A remark of Manuka's was rather good—Maori chiefs (leaders) were toas & went out at the head of their men, Pakeha chiefs stayed in Town and ate biscuit. [1860 Note] Their notion of luxury. **1980** LELAND *Kiwi-Yankee Dict.* 14 Any sort of cookie or cracker is a biscuit. What you [*sc.* an American] think is a biscuit is a scone.

2. *Railways. Obs.* See quot. 1950.

1950 28 Dec. p.c. F.M. O'Brien, Invercargill. *The Biscuit*: The tablet used in N.Z. railways signalling. **1957** FRAME *Owls Do Cry* (1967) 61 Oh my papa, retired, cut off from all that mattered to him, the railway..meeting his cobbers and talking their private language of the biscuit, She's got too much of a grade. **1985** MCGILL *G' day Country* 32 Inside the station they had the big red metal boxes that work the old-fashioned tablet signalling system. If you ever wonder what drivers are picking up or unloading on the end of a curved piece of wood, it is the tablet or biscuit. A train cannot get through a section of rail without the biscuit matching the one in the red metal box, which is connected to the manually operated signals. Automatic signals are phasing this system in to rural museums.

3. Special Comb. **biscuit class** [a play on *business class*, but with a biscuit rather than a more elaborate meal being served in flight], air travel on provincial routes.

1987 *National Bus. Rev.* 20 July 4 Spokesman Bob

bish, v. [An alteration of BIFF: see OED v.²] trans. To throw, to biff.
   1941 MARSH *Surfeit of Lampreys* (1951) 142 They'd just sort of bished them [*sc.* the things used for charades] into the cupboard and they were bulging out. **1981** GEE *Meg* 94 Someone must have bished a beer bottle in.

Bishopscourt. Also **Bishop's Court.** The general name of the residences of Anglican bishops. (Contrast the use in English church law as a term for an ecclesiastical court held in the cathedral of a diocese: see OED *bishop* 10 a.)
   1863 CHUDLEIGH *Diary* 22 Aug. (1950) 99 Fine. Dined at Bishopscorte at one. **1875** LUSH *Thames Jrnls.* 22 Feb. (1975) 159 At 1.30 I dined at Bishop's Court [Auckland]. The Bishop seemed pleased to see me. **1911** BOREHAM *Selwyn* 57 The house of a Mr Clarke had been secured as a 'Bishopscourt' for the present. **1948** *Our Own Country* 7 Bishop Selwyn lived at Waimate, where his house, the first Bishopscourt, still stands as the second oldest wooden building in New Zealand. **1967** HARPER *Kettle on Fuchsia* 40 Plans for the future were discussed at Bishop's Court [at Christchurch] when Ellen went there.

bite, v.

1. *Obs.* [Abbrev. of Brit. slang *bite the ear*: see OED v. 16; AND 1912.] *trans.* CHEW v. a.
   [**1906** *Truth* 10 Mar. 1 'Sing a song of sixpence.' That is the unmelodious chant of the beer-chewer when he's biting your lug for a sprat.] **1946** BRUNO *Maleesh George* 38 They had to bite a Red-cap for the fare home. **1951** PARK *Witch's Thorn* 53 I'd feel the same way if I had a mug biting me for money all the time. **1960** CRUMP *Good Keen Man* 146 I'd been bitten for money often enough before, but this was the best I'd come across yet.

2. [Survival of active use of Brit. dial. and slang *bite* to cheat, deceive: see OED v. 15 a 'Now only in passive.' 'The biter bit.'.] *trans.* To defraud; to trick (out of money, property, etc.).
   1877 CHUDLEIGH *Diary* 23 June (1950) 258 The fellow could hardly conceal his chargrin [*sic*] at my having done him and his knavery [in trying to get Chudleigh's land away from him] saying that though he would not have bitten me he should have been able to do so had his lawyers been half smart with his deed and not let mine get in first. **1943** HISLOP *Pure Gold* 28 The other chap who had been taking it all in had a good laugh at the expense of this shrewd head who I bit for a sixpenny bit [*sc.* in context 'tricked the trickster out of sixpence'].

3. In a negative construction, **not to bite**, not to oblige.
   1964 SARGESON *Collected Stories 1935–63* 298 bite: *he wouldn't bite*, he wouldn't oblige.

4. bite your bum (or **back**), an *imp.* phr. expressing contemptuous dismissal.
   1955 *BJ Cameron Collection* (TS July) bite your back Go and jump in the lake. **1988** MCGILL *Dict. Kiwi Slang* 15 *bite your bum* get lost! eg 'I'm sick of you, go bite your bum!'

bite, n.¹ [f. *bite* v. to speak sharply: see OED v. 4.] An irritable, sharp-tongued person.
   1917 *Chron. NZEF* 5 Sept. 28 Two..[sergeants] were universally known as 'C.B. Kings', and were the worst 'bites' in their respective battalions.

bite, n.² [AND 1919.] An instance of cadging; esp in the phr. **to put the bite on** (someone), to pressure (someone) for (money, a favour, etc.). See also COLD BITE, NIP n. 1.
   1918 *Chron. NZEF* 7 June 199 A fellow can't look at him now without risking a 'bite'. **1951** *Landfall* 17 21 Lola comes up and tries to put the bite on me because I am a stranger. **c1962** BAXTER *Horse* (1985) 43 Tony would have the kale. But he did not like putting the bite on Tony. **1974** AGNEW *Loner* 68 From him I learned..that it was smart to drop your swag in small towns and put the bite on the butcher, baker and grocer. **1990** EDWARDS *AWOL* 4 I would have to put the bite on Daisy's father for the minister's fee.

bitsa, bitser, varr. BITZER.

bitter-cress. [Transf. use of European *bitter cress Cardamine hirsuta* for native *Cardamine* spp. (fam. Brassicaceae).] Also **native, New Zealand cress.** Small herbs, esp. *Cardamine debilis*, with pinnate leaves and a taste similar to that of hot cress. See also PANAPANA.
   1926 HILGENDORF *Weeds* 95 Bitter Cress..also called lady's smock, is found in native pastures and cultivated gardens throughout the islands. **1964** TUWHARE *No Ordinary Sun* (1977) 21 No one comes..through straggly tea tree bush and gorse, past the hidden spring and bitter cress. **1969** *Standard Common Names Weeds* 52 native bitter cress [= *New Zealand bitter cress*.. *Cardamine debilis*. **1989** JOHNSON *Wetland Plants NZ* 180 Cardamine debilis DC. bittercress, panapana.

bittern.

1. Either *Botaurus poiciloptilus* (2 (1) below) or the now extinct *Ixobrychus novaezelandiae* (2 (2) below).
   1841 BEST *Journal* 15 May (1966) 311 This end of the lake abounds with wild duck I also saw a fine Bittern. **1845** DEANS in *Pioneers* (1964) 43 And a large bittern, which only cries in the spring, like the roar of a bull. **1853** MACKIE *Traveller under Concern* 31 Mar. (1973) 95 I saw a small bittern. **1869** *TrNZI* I. (rev. edn.) 105 Botaurus poicilopt[il]us. Matuku-hurepo. Bittern... Rare. **1875** *Richmond-Atkinson Papers* (1960) II. 399 I have got a great many birds since you have been away... One of them is the New Zealand bittern. **1882** [see MATUKU 1 a]. **1909** CHUDLEIGH *Diary* 26 Nov. (1950) 449 Heard the bitterns boom like great bulls a long way off, a rather terrible sound when you think they are bulls. **1939** BEATTIE *First White Boy Born Otago* 121 I never actually saw the bittern but I heard its whoop. **1946** [see MATUKU 1 b]. **1955** OLIVER *NZ Birds* 395 The Brown Bittern, or as it is usually called, the Bittern, was first collected in New South Wales... It was recorded from the Bay of Islands by Yate in 1835 and by Colenso in 1842. **1990** *NZ Geographic* VII. 5 Bitterns stalk eels, frogs and fish and are not averse to taking the odd duckling.

2. With a modifier: (**Australasian** or **Australian**) **brown**; (**New Zealand**) **little**.

(1) **brown** (**Australasian** or **Australian brown**, occas. early **black–backed, common**) **bittern**. *Botaurus poiciloptilus* (fam. Ardeidae), a secretive, tawny, long-legged marsh bird with a characteristic loud booming call, and a range which includes New Caledonia, Australia, and New Zealand. See also MATUKU-HUREPO.
   1888 BULLER *Birds NZ* II. 141 (Black-backed Bittern)... Matuku-hurepo. Ibid. 142 The Common Bittern is very generally distributed..in places suited to its habits of life, such as raupo swamps, sedgy lagoons. **1947** POWELL *Native Animals NZ* 79 Brown Bittern.., Matuku-hurepo of the Maoris, is a bird of the swamps and lagoons throughout the country, but now less common than formerly owing to the advance of settlement. **1966** FALLA et al. *Birds NZ* 79 Australian Brown Bittern..Brown Bittern, Black-backed Bittern, Matuku, Matuku-hurepo... Rises with dangling legs. Flies with neck tucked in. **1985** *Reader's Digest Book NZ Birds* 135 Australasian Bittern... Australian brown bittern, brown bittern, matuku-hurepo... Australasian Bitterns are heard more often than they are seen. **1990** *NZ Geographic* VII. 50 Well camouflaged in a bed of rushes a brown bittern assumes its characteristic pose used to disguise its presence when disturbed, and also when hunting.

(2) **little** (**New Zealand little**) **bittern.** *Ixobrychus novaezelandiae* (fam. Ardeidae), an extinct species.
   1871 HUTTON *Catalogue Birds NZ* 27 Ardea pusilla... Little Bittern. **1885** *NZJSc.* II. 557 Little Bittern.—Its breeding habits to the present have not been observed or recorded. **1904** HUTTON & DRUMMOND *Animals NZ* 194 *The Little Bittern.—Kioriki...* 'They breed on the ground, in very obscure places, and are, on the whole, a rare bird.' **1917** WILLIAMS *Dict. Maori Lang.* 139 *Kioriki, n...little bittern.* **1955** OLIVER *NZ Birds* 398 In captivity the Little Bittern has eaten mudfish..and worms when given to it in water. **1990** *Checklist Birds NZ* 93 *Ixobrychus novaezelandiae*... New Zealand Little Bittern... New Zealand. Allegedly first obtained at Tauranga, the sole North Island record; but no longer traceable. Fewer than ten specimens from the South Island..Tasmania; straggling to New Zealand. Recorded about twenty times in South Island..but has not been seen for many years.

bitumen.

1. [AND 1948.] Esp. as **the bitumen**, a tar-sealed road (surface). Cf. TAR-SEAL n. 1.
   [**1930** PINFOLD *Fifty Yrs. Maoriland* 15 There are now good new roads: the main ones being finished with bitumen and the side ones macadamized.] **1938** HYDE *Nor Yrs. Condemn* 101 The lighter bread-carts slapped the bitumen young fellows in white aprons shouted 'Giddap, giddap'. **1949** SARGESON *I Saw in My Dream* (1974) 247 The dust of the sidestreet was a relief after the bitumen. **1960** MUIR *Word for Word* 87 'Those autumn trees,' Arthur said, as they turned back [from the metal] towards the bitumen. **1971** WATT *Centenary Invercargill* 70 They [*sc.* boys aged 9 to 13] played the game of side skidding on the bitumen. **1984** WILSON *South Pacific Street* 59 Then the big black taxi accelerated fast and drove away with a squeal of its tyres on the bitumen.

2. Special Comb. **bitumen man**, see quot.
   1966 NEWTON *Boss's Story* 185 *Bitumen Man*: A town-dweller—one who has spent his time in the bitumen-sealed streets.

bitza, var. BITZER.

bitzer. Also **bitsa, bitser, bitza.** [Alteration of *bits o'* (this), *bits o'* (that); cf. Charles Dickens's (*Hard Times*) character *Bitser*, whose knowledge was made up of bits of facts.]

1. [AND 1924.] Anything made up or appearing to be made up of odd bits and pieces; used esp. of cars and (by schoolchildren) of bicycles.
   1946 *Farmers Weekly* 30 May 8 It is a perfectly ordinary machine—a 'bitza' in fact, being made up of parts from four different machines. **1968** SLATTER *Pagan Game* 230 He acquired a succession of grids... One he called the Herk Bitsa, being mostly Hercules with bits of stolen B.S.A. **1988** MCGILL *Dict. Kiwi Slang* 15 *bitser* made from bits and pieces, such as mongrel [*sic*]

or home-made trolley. **1996** *Independent* (Auckland) 15 Mar. 19 Some of them [*sc.* Otago cribs], bitsers and oddities certainly, are ingenious constructions.

2. [AND 1936.] A mongrel dog.
1969 Hascombe *Down & Almost Under* 32 Although his official description is humiliatingly described as 'bitsa' he is passed off by us..as a 'Surrey setter'. **1985** *Dominion* (Wellington) 5 Mar. 4 [The fireman] received a standing ovation when he was pulled by a rope from the bottom of a 16-metre cliff yesterday with an ageing grateful bitser [*sc.* dog] in his arms.

bivouac. [In non-military use, the noun *bivouac* is found elsewhere but recorded earliest in NZ (see OED 2): also *bivvy* OED Army slang 1916.] A camping out; a temporary camp or camping-place; a hut, or tent, etc. built or used as a temporary shelter; and esp. as **bivvy** (or **biv**) freq. among outdoors people for a purpose-built rough shelter or sheltered camping place. Also recorded as a verb, to shelter (see quot. 1938).
1844 Monro *Notes of a Journey* in Hocken *Contributions* (1898) 257 We found a nice grove of wood on the banks of the Waihola lake, and had a most comfortable bivouac. **1853** Adams *Canterbury Settlement* 40 The first bivouac must always be united with something strange and even impressive to the feelings. **1936** *Hills & Valleys* II. 3 [A picture of a frame-tent with the legend] 'Building the Hutt Valley Tramping Club's Bivouac in the Otaki Valley.' **1938** *Canterbury Mountaineer* 28 A yodel ahead announced Conway and Co..who had been forced to bivvy. **1940** Gilkison *Peaks, Packs & Mountain Tracks* 54 We were back at the bivouac. **1958** *Tararua* Sept. 34 We found a good bivvy in a rock about as large as a church, riddled with cracks and caves complete with upholstered sleeping bench. **1965** Shadbolt *Among Cinders* 144 Hubert and I was just slept in a bivvy made of manuka and fern; there was just enough room for us both to crawl inside. **1988** *Dominion* (Wellington) 30 Dec. 11 For the first three months they gravitated between..a pup tent camp up the valley, where they built brush bivvys [*sic*]- their first homes. **1988** Pickering *Hills* 82 [Caption] Bivouacs are shrunken versions of huts and affectionately called dog kennels. Winchcombe Biv, Tararuas. **1995** Crump *Bushwoman* 96 I finally reached the bivvy in the upper Landsborough... The bivvy was situated above the river..and could sleep many in a normal position.

bivvy: see BIVOUAC.

bizzy: see BIDDY.

black, *n.*¹ and *a.*¹ [Spec. use of *black* dark-skinned (person).]

A. *n.*

1. a. *Derog.* An Australian Aborigine.
1827 Williams *Early Jrnls.* 5 May (1961) 54 The [New Zealand] natives have had much conversation, relative to the projected settlement in New Holland... They wish to be distinct from the whites or blacks, to retain their own teachers.

b. *Offensive.* Also occas. **Blacky.** A Maori or Pacific Islander.
1843 *NZ Jrnl.* IV. 34 The way in which the Maories make the responses is singular. I must say the Blackies are very civil. **1845** Whisker *Memo. Book* in Barthorp *To Face the Daring Maori* (1979) 71 The Blacks or Mowreys acted very well... The Natives ware [*sic*] no clothes at all but some old shirt tied around there weastes. **1863** Carberry *Journal* (ATLMS) 18 Nov. [The Waikato] will eventually fall into the Hands of the Whites when the Blacks go to the wall. **1971** *Otago Daily Times* (Dunedin) 31 Aug. 7 (Griffiths Collect.) A further charge..was of robbing Ariki Akamoeua of a transistor radio... Murray is reported to have said, 'I'm going to get a black tonight.'

c. A Melanesian.
1855 Patteson in Yonge *Life John Coleridge Patteson* (1874) I. 234 [Picton tangata whenua to Rev. J.C. Patteson] 'We want *you*!..we can understand you!' 'No, I am going to the islands [*sc.* to Melanesia as Missionary] to the blacks there.' (N.B. The Maoris speak of the *Blacks* with a little touch of contempt.) 'You are wanted here! Never mind the blacks.'

2. *Ellipt.* for a Black Power gang member.
1983 *Dominion* (Wellington) 10 May 1 We thought it was the blacks. **1991** Payne *Staunch* 37 White Power don't like the blacks; blacks are the scum of the earth.

B. *adj.*

1. *Offensive.* **black** introducing an intense or derog. comparison referring to a dark complexion or skin colour. **black as Maoris, black as the ace of spades, black as B-flat.**
1864 Nicholl *Journal* 27 Apr. (ATLMS) 200 By the time we got back we were as **black as Maoris** from the dust. **1915** *Great Adventure* (1988) 48 Just then he came out and to my astonishment he was an Indian, as **black as the ace of spades**. **1973** Wallace *Generation Gap* 215 After this fire they arrived back tired, hungry, black as the ace-of-spades, eyebrows singed. **1964** Morrieson *Came a Hot Friday* (1981) 84 Two-ton Tilly, **black as B flat**... I wouldn't have widdled on a bag like that if she'd been on fire.

2. In various special collocations of offensive reference to dark-skinned people usu. Maori or Polynesian. **black man** *obs.*, a Maori; **black velvet** (cf. *brown velvet* (BROWN *a.* 3)), a Maori female as a sexual object.
1815 Kendall *New Zealanders' First Book* 22 [Sentences] Na! Iesu Christ ta Atua Nue, ta Atua Pi, ta wanhoungha Nue, ta wanhoungha Pi, ke ta notungata na, Pakkahah, ke ta na tangata maoude, ke ta tungata katoa katoa. *Ibid.* 23 [translation] Behold! Jesus Christ is the great and good Atua, the great and good friend to white and **black men**; to all men. **1948** Ballantyne *Cunninghams* (1976) 214 'I'd like a nice piece of **black velvet**,' Clive said. 'One of those quarter-castes, boy.' **1964** Frances *Johnny Rapana* 121 All they want is to get you in the dark and then go off and boast they've had a bit of black velvet. That's what they call us [Maori girls], Johnny. Black velvet!

black, *n.*² and *a.*² [Spec. use of *black* characterized by the colour.]

A. *n.*

1. Usu. *pl.* as **the Blacks,** see ALL BLACK 1.
1905 *Evening Post* (Wellington) 2 Nov. 7 This the wily Blacks invariably smothered in an early stage... The passing of the Blacks was often very pretty and fine to see. **1910** *Evening Post* (Wellington) 4 July 3 Australia pressed from the start, and..nearly crossed the line, but the blacks, with a great rush, carried the ball down the field. **1922** *Quick March* 11 Sept. 20 A penalty try..was awarded [in the first test] for obstruction to Stanley who was racing..for the ball, which had been kicked over the Blacks' line. **1991** *Evening Post* (Wellington) 4 Oct. 5 The Blacks are back. The World Cup has begun in the best possible way for New Zealand—victory over the home favourites.

2. Usu. *pl.* Of animals, a black sheep; *black flounder* (FLOUNDER 2 (1)).
1921 Guthrie-Smith *Tutira* (1926) 362 I remember..watching the well-known dealer..picking 'fats.' When asked by me for his..discrimination in regard to several apparently prime blacks, his answer was that they 'killed' badly. **1970** Sorensen *Nomenclature NZ Fish* 24 *Flounder* (four species) (a) Scientific name..*Rhombosolea retiaria*... Other common names..Blacks, Black Flounder.

B. *adj.*

1. In the names of plants and animals, see: ANGELFISH, BASS, BEECH 2 (1), BINDWEED 2, BIRCH 3 (2), *black beetle* (BEETLE 1), *black-bug, black cap,* see 2 below, BREAM 2 (1), COD 2 (2), DIVER, EEL 2 (5), FLOUNDER *n.* 2 (1), MAIRE 1 a and 2 (1), MAPAU 2 (1), MATIPO 2 (1), MUSSEL 2 (1), OREO 2 (1), OYSTERCATCHER 2 (1), PERCH 2 (1), PETREL 2 (1), PINE 2 (2), ROBIN 2 (a), SCRUB *n.* 2 (1), SHAG 2 (2), SHARK 2 (1), SNAPPER *n.*¹ 2 (1), STILT 2 (1), TEAL *n.*¹ 2 (2), TIT *n.*¹ b, *tree-fern* (FERN 2 (20) b (a)), WHALE 2 (2). See also BLACKFISH.

2. In special collocations: **black-bug,** BEETLE 1; **black cap,** *white-fronted tern* (TERN 2 (10)); **black damp** *coalmining,* see quots; **black gold,** a dark-coloured gold, the residue from electrolytic de-silvering; **black ground,** see quot.; **black iron** [poss. as a contrary of *white iron* tinned iron: see OED 2 a, note], ungalvanized iron (wire) (cf. *black wire* below); **black joe** *gumdigging* [an alteration of BLACK-JACK 1 b infl. by a play on the black minstrel refrain 'Old Black Joe'], BLACK-JACK 1 b; **blackman** [f. the colour, with a play on the *Blackman,* an Irish children's bogeyman], treacle; **black Maori,** see MAORI A 6 b; **black molly** [prob. f. MOLLY(MAWK)], PETREL 2 (10); **black scrub,** see SCRUB *n.* 2 (1); **black singlet,** see SINGLET 2 a; **black sugar** *gumdigging,* an inferior grade or type of kauri gum referring to the colour and size of the granules (cf. BLACK-JACK 1 b); **black tea,** strong tea without milk, often brewed outdoors or for outdoors folk (contrast *black billy tea* (BILLY *n.*¹ 4)); **black-tracker** *obs. tramways* [transf. joc. use of *black-tracker* an Aboriginal tracker], one who cleans tram-tracks; **black vine** *obs.* [f. the colour of the bark], SUPPLEJACK; **black whale, black whaler, black whaling,** see WHALE 2 (2); **black wire** *obs.,* non-galvanized fence-wire (see also *black iron* above).

1924 *Otago Witness* (Dunedin) 26 Feb. 6 [The wasp] searches amongst the wi-wi..for the **black bug** or Maori bug, kikereru, twice its size. **1948** Finlayson *Tidal Creek* (1979) 67 And he's sick of black-bugs. Just leave your coat hanging on the wall and there'll be a black-bug in it. **1955** B.J. Cameron Collection (TS July) maori bug (n) A repulsive cockroach-like insect, which makes an unpleasant smell when squashed. Also known as *black bug.* **1966** Falla et al. *Birds NZ* 164 White-fronted Tern *Sterna striata. Other names*: Sea-swallow, Kahawai Bird, Tara, **Blackcap. 1985** *Reader's Digest Book NZ Birds* 237 *White-fronted Tern*... *black cap, grenadier, swallowtail, noddy.* **1980** Bennett *Canterbury Tale* 128 There was much **black damp** (carbon dioxide), a gas so heavy that a candle burning brightly at one level might be extinguished two inches lower. **1984** Beardsley *Blackball 08* 242 Black damp air that is low in oxygen content and high in carbon dioxide as a result of an explosion in a mine. **1978** McAra *Gold Mining Waihi* 225 By electrolytic action, [the anodes] deposited the silver in the form of silver crystals, while the gold—then called '**black gold**'—was caught on the canvas trays. *Ibid.* 312 Black gold: The residue after the bullion anodes had been treated in the electrolytic de-silvering cells. **1933** *Press* (Christchurch) 16 Sept. 15 **Black ground.**—As ground clears after a fall of snow it is spoken of as 'black' ([1890-1910]). **1895** *Fencing Act* in *Settler's Handbook NZ* (1902) 161 Batten and wire fence..with one or more wires, not lighter than No. 8 in steel, or **black** or galvanised **iron**. **1937** BEALE *Seventy Yrs. Auckland* 11 An inferior residue of gum known as '**Black Joe**' is still eagerly sought for and even salvaged from muddy creeks. **1980** MCGILL *Ghost Towns NZ* 93 'Would you like some bread and **blackman**?' Paddy would ask the kids, meaning bread and treacle. **1966 Black Molly** [see PETREL 2 (10)]. **1956** SUTHERLAND *Green Kiwi* (1960) 70 Some of the classifications under which gum was exported give an indication of the appearance of some of the grades:..black flour dust..bright seeds and **black sugar** are some of the names. **1909** THOMPSON *Ballads About Business* 44 Then with this eternal mutton, sodden brownie he will spread, An' **black tea** with a little sugar. **1938** HYDE *Godwits Fly* (1970) 129 When the Boss called, 'Smoke-oh,' the men scrambled down like baboons, sprawling themselves out on the..grass..their throats scalded by the black tea stewed up every few hours. **1963** BACON *In the Sticks* 89 The foreman nodded..squinting up at us from where he sat nursing a mug of black tea. 'Goodday, mates. Like a mug of brew?' **1971** NEWTON *Ten Thousand Dogs* 22 I was shown how to make an 'oil drum' stew and, apart from a few slabs of toast and black tea, that was about the musterers' sole diet. **1908** *Truth* 4 Jan. 5 The latest boorish boss that deserves pillorying is one Francis, who is held [to be] of what are called the '**black-trackers**' who clean [tram] lines or something of that sort. **1869** *TrNZI* I. (rev. edn.) 185 And..the *Rhipogonum scandens*, or **Black vine**, with its numerous smooth black stalks..is also a very striking plant. **1962** EVANS *Waikaka Saga* 131 Then [after the early non-galvanized triangular wire] the first round wire or '**black wire**' as it was more often referred to.

3. Introducing figurative comparisons denoting an intensity of darkness: of the weather, **as black as a bull's backside**; of the night, **as black as a musterer's billy**, **as black as the inside of a cow**.

1983 *Press* (Christchurch) 10 May 1 It was '**as black as a bull's backside**' and the Westport dredge they were in was rolling heavily in the swell. **1948** *Our Own Country* 132 All through a night **as black as a musterer's billy** we had seen nothing but..the black form of black hills. **1991** *Dominion* (Wellington) 28 Oct. 1 The men were all in good spirits and he was keeping contact by shouting to them. 'It's **as black as the inside of a cow** out here.'

black, *a.*³ [Spec. use of *black* disastrous, malignant.] In the special collocations: **black budget** *hist*. (also with init. caps.), a name given to a severely deflationary, and hence unpopular, budget, esp. one which increases taxation on popular consumer items; *spec*. the name given to a 1930 budget, and esp. to Labour Finance Minister Nordmeyer's deflationary budget of 1958 (see quot. 1976); **black hole** [a short form, figuratively used, of *The Black Hole of Calcutta*], the grain exit hole of an old-fashioned threshing-mill.

1930 *NZPD* CCXXIV. 843 We had a contribution to this debate to-day from one of the Ministers of the Crown..about the so-called '**black**' Budget. **1931** *NZPD* CCXXIX. 88 When the last Budget was introduced, the leader of the Opposition described it as the 'Black Budget.' I think we could describe the present document as the 'Black and Blue' Budget. **1963** *Comment* 17 Oct. 5 Mr Lake and the government are lucky that the country's condition permitted them to avoid a Black Budget. **1971** *Speeches & Documents* 434 [Heading] The 'Black Budget' 1958. In his Budget speech, 26 June 1958, the Labour Minister of Finance, Arnold Nordmeyer, increased taxes in order to reduce demand for imports, encourage local manufacturing and conserve foreign exchange. **1976** SINCLAIR *Nash* 309 In 1930 J.G. Coates had called Ward's budget 'the Black Budget' [see quots. 1930, 1931 above]—but that was long forgotten. This time the label stuck. Nordmeyer's budget [of June 1958] was remembered as 'the black budget' for many years. **1991** *Dominion* (Wellington) 8 July 1 Just what impact will the Budget have on the over sixties, and will the pressure being applied..by Grey Power stop what will be a Black Budget for older people? **1992** ANDERSON *Portrait Artist's Wife* 136 Her lack of concern at the Labour Government's suicidal 1958 Black Budget depressed him. **1937** AYSON *Thomas* 42 A boy had to stand with fork in hand and a veil over his face forking ceaselessly to keep the hole through which the grain fell clear. It was no wonder that this was known as 'The **Black Hole**,' for out of it fell straw, dust and smut as well as grain.

blackback, black-backed gull: see GULL 2 (1).

blackball. [f. Brit. dial. *blackball*: see OED *n.*³ 1851.] A hard, round, black 'boiled' sweet with white stripes, similar to a 'brandyball'.

c1910 p.c. W.H.B. Orsman (1972). *Blackballs* were common lollies before WW1. **1925** MANDER *Allen Adair* (1971) 50 That night he added ju-jubes, liquorice, blackballs..and sugar-candy sticks to his next [store] order. **1939** GRIEVE *Sketches from Maoriland* (1961) 65 Our latest 'stunt' is to reward the tidiest with blackballs (in the case of infants). **1957** FRAME *Owls Do Cry* (1967) 47 It is not an aniseed ball or acid drop or blackball, but a little black pipe or whistle. **1964** HOWE *Stamper Battery* 34 But Mum had foresight. She stood at the finishing line with a blackball, a popular lolly [c1880] which was Johnny's favourite. **1978** in *Listener Short Stories 3* (1984) 75 You can buy some meat..some nails..and blackball lollies all in the one shop there. **1987** BATISTICH *Sing Vila* 63 She called us 'kids' collectively and never came without a brown paper poke of blackballs.

blackberry. The common term (rather than *bramble*) for the introduced *Rubus fruticosus* aggregate, and related species (fam. Rosaceae), both for the vine and the fruit. Also occas. (as was *bramble*) applied to the native *Rubus cissoides* and *R. australis*, the BUSH LAWYER *n.*¹ Compare BRAMBLE.

1842 WADE *Journey in Nthn Is.* 196 Tataramoa: the Bramble or Blackberry of New Zealand. **1926** HILGENDORF *Weeds* 97 Blackberry (*Rubus fruticosus* and [*R. laciniatus*]), occasionally called bramble, is commonest in the middle and south of the North Island, and on the West Coast of Nelson.

black billed gull: see GULL 2 (2).

blackbird.

1. A coloured person. **a.** *Obs. Derog.* A Maori. Cf. BLACK *n.*¹ A 1 b.

1849 TORLESSE *Papers* (1958) 49 Captain Thomas, Wills and party arrived..having bushed it last night at the edge of the big swamp, and leaving their blackbirds [*sc.* Maori porters] behind, who would not move on Sunday.

b. *attrib*. An extended use of Austral. *blackbird* for indented (often kidnapped) labour from the Pacific Islands: here used of a scheme to import Polynesian servants.

1911 *Truth* 9 Sept. 4 Up Auckland way the crusade in favour of cheap domestic labor [*sic*] has resulted in a scheme for the importation of a number of black 'boys' from the islands, said 'boys' being men who are sent to the Dominion under contract by their relatives or owners with whom a regular slave or 'blackbird' traffic will be initiated.

2. In rare early use, as **New Zealand blackbird**, TUI 1.

1832 EARLE *Residence NZ* 174 Tooee or New Zealand Blackbird.

black-browed mollymawk: see MOLLYMAWK 2 (1).

black-capped petrel: see PETREL 2 (2).

blackfellow. *Obs. Offensive*. [AND 1798.] BLACK *n.*¹ A 1 b.

1859 THOMSON *Story NZ* II. 49 The Anglo-Saxon feeling, that one Englishman was a match for several 'black fellows,' the term frequently applied to the natives, was now universal. **1868** TAYLOR *Past and Present of NZ* 111 The Maori is constantly being called a nigger and a black fellow to his face, and viewed as an inferior being.

blackfish, *n.*¹ [Spec. uses of *blackfish*: see OED 2 a small species of whale.]

1. *Whaling*. Any of several small black whales or dolphins, esp. the pilot whale *Globicephala melaena* (fam. Delphinidae). See also *pilot whale* (WHALE) 2 (10)).

1793 CHAPMAN *Letter from Norfolk Island* 19 Nov. in McNab *Hist. Records* (1908) I. 186 We fell in with a school of black fish, which is a sort of whale. **1837** RHODES *Jrnl. Barque 'Australian'* Feb. (1954) 42 Saw nothing worthy of notice, excepting blackfish and porpoises. **1846** HEAPHY *Exped. to Kawatiri* 26 Mar. in Taylor *Early Travellers* (1959) 205 The flats off Taupata Point..are strewn with the bones of the grampus, or black-fish of the whalers. **1851** STEPHENS *Journal* (ATLTS) 488 Grampuses, or black fish as they are called by the whalers. **1875** *TrNZI* VII. 261 Globicephalus macrorhynchus... Blackfish. **1911** SHAND *Moriori People* 6 The Rongomoana, or black-fish, and other kinds of whale. **1924** *Otago Witness* (Dunedin) 3 June 4 The blackfish (Globicephalus melas) is a gregarious and timid species of whale which feeds on cuttle fish. **1935** *Free Lance* (Wellington) 25 Nov. 28 [Caption] Eighty-eight blackfish were recently stranded at Tokerau Beach. **1951** RICHARDS *Chatham Islands* 93 There is a long-beaked blackfish that also comes ashore in shoals. It is quite inedible; even dogs die after a feed of it. **1972** GASKIN *Whales Dolphins & Seals* 116 Pilot whales, or 'blackfish' as they are known locally, are regarded as common animals by most New Zealand coastal authorities. **1990** BAKER *Whales & Dolphins* 97 Long-finned Pilot Whale *Globicephala melaena*. The name 'Blackfish' is also applied to this species and it is sometimes confused with the False Killer Whale.

2. Special Comb. **blackfish-oil**, the oil tried out from blackfish blubber.

1895 CHUDLEIGH *Diary* 10 July (1950) 391 Bob McLurg tryed out blackfish oil, a nice job for a cold day. **1985** LANGDALE-HUNT *Last Entail Male* 25 Some of the oil (black fish or bottle-nosed grampus) was still in the workshop in my time, until my brother, Reg tried it out on his mustering boots one day and was begged..to leave them outside.

blackfish, *n.*² PARORE.

1922 *NZJST* V. 92 *Mangrove-fish*, or *Blackfish*. Common in Auckland throughout the year. Sold as 'blackfish'. **1957** PARROTT *Sea Angler's Fishes* 103 The Blackfish... Maori name: Parore. The body of the blackfish is robust, covered with moderately large scales. **1966** DOOGUE & MORELAND *Sea Anglers' Guide*

242 Blackfish, black perch; black bream (Tasmania)... Frequents mangrove swamps and muddy river mouths. **1986** PAUL *NZ Fishes* 101 *Parore*... Known variously as blackfish, black snapper, black bream, and mangrove fish.

black-fronted dotterel, tern: see DOTTEREL 2 (2), TERN 2 (2).

black-heart birch: see BIRCH 3 (3).

black-jack.

1. a. *Mining.* [See OED *black-jack* (1747-1812).] A miner's name for zinc sulphide or blende.

1868 *Thames Miner's Guide* 53 Black-jack, or Blende.- Sulphide of zinc.

b. *Kauri gumdigging.* [Prob. taken over from mining usage.] A type of dark inferior kauri gum, or gum residue. Cf. *black joe* (BLACK *a.*² B 2).

1951 LEVY *Grasslands NZ* (1970) 100 There is also ample evidence in the gum residues, black-jack..that intensely hot fires have destroyed the forests. **1953** REED *Story of Kauri* 103 Inferior sorts [of kauri gum]— brown, sugary, and what was known as 'black jack', were generally found in swampy ground. **1960** BOSWELL *Ernie* 154 He made delicate posies and circlets of flowers from the white 'candle-gum', and clusters of 'grapes' from the smoky 'black-jack'.

2. [Prob. a new formation describing a black or dark blue old-fashioned liquor bottle; poss. a continuation of an extended use of *obs. blackjack* a large leather jug for beer, coated externally with tar: cf. OED *black-jack* 1.]

1970 SANSOM *Stewart Islanders* 45 He stepped off, but with no confidence, in another direction; we scrabbled around and there it was, an old 'black-jack' or 'square-face' which had held gin in the early days.

black oil. *Whaling. Hist.*

1. The dark oil tried out from rancid blubber, compared with whitish fresh right-whale oil and golden-tinted fresh sperm oil.

1836 *Addison Log* 26 Aug. in Morton *Whale's Wake* (1982) 57 Found the blubber so bad that it made black oil. **1853** WELLER *Lett. of Weller Bros. 1833-40* Dec. in McLintock *Hist. Otago* (1949) 69 There is a great deal of black oil in the cargo.

2. The oil from a black whale, see esp. quot. 1954.

1831 *Let.* 27 July in McNab *Old Whaling Days* (1913) 14 The following fishers are in Cloudy Bay:- The *Dragon*, full; *Courier*, 300 barrels; *William Stoveld*, 300 barrels of black oil, and 400 of sperm. **1846** MARJORIBANKS *NZ* 78 It is evident that a great part of the black oil..which was procured at New Zealand..will..be conveyed in the boats..which they have begun to use on the spot. **1856** FITTON *NZ* 83 [Prices of]..sperm oil, none; black oil, none; 3-bushel bags, 24s..per dozen. **1949** McLINTOCK *Hist. of Otago* 75 The season proved most successful and yielded the partners ninety-five tuns of black oil. **1954** in Rhodes *Jrnl. Barque 'Australian'* xvi [1954 *Note.*] The oil of black whales was usually called 'black oil', not because the oil was black, but because of the colour of the whales producing it.

black sand, *n. West Coast.* Also **black-sand** in *attrib.* use. A dark-coloured sand of New Zealand west coast ocean beaches, usu. auriferous in the South Island, and 'iron sand' in the North Island. See also IRONSAND.

1862 *Otago Witness* (Dunedin) 23 Aug. 7 The gold is very fine, and accompanied by a great quantity of black sand, from which it is difficult to separate it. **1879** HAAST *Geol. Canterbury & Westland* 364 I have already alluded to the black-sand beachers, who watch the coast principally..where small indentations favour the preservation of magnetic..iron-sands. **1888** PAYTON *Round About NZ* 292 The town [*sc.* New Plymouth] is built close down to the sea, and almost on those wonderful black sands which contain..as much as 75% of iron. **1902** *Brett's Colonists' Guide* 1030 The common associate of alluvial gold is the *black sand* of the miner, principally composed of magnetite..which from its great weight is left behind with the gold. **1935** BLYTH ed. *Gold Mining Year Book* 11 *Black Sand*: These deposits occur all along the West Coast of the South Island and are composed of black iron and other metals sometimes carrying gold in alluvials also. **1958** *NZJGeol.* I. 615 At Gillespie's Beach drill records show blacksand at depths of over 50ft from the surface. **1981** HENDERSON *Exiles Asbestos Cottage* 113 Luring, encouraging, enticing, odd nuggets up to the size of a small fingernail bare their beauty in black sand in pan or sluicebox.

black-sand, *v. intr.* To work black sand for gold.

1896 *AJHR* D-4 67 There were about forty men black-sanding, and they make a bare livelihood. **1977** *Sunday Times* (Wellington) 27 Nov. 17 Ken Nolan started his blacksanding more than 25 years ago.

Hence *West Coast hist.* **blacksander,** one who works sea-beach black sand for gold (cf. BEACHCOMBER 3); **blacksanding** *vbl. n.*, the working of black sand for gold (cf. BEACHCOMBING 2).

1906 *NZ Mining Rec.* 124 The '**blacksanders**' reaped their harvest. **1967** MAY *West Coast Gold Rushes* (1962) 198 Eighteen weeks had been time enough for the black-sanders to extract the accumulated wealth of centuries. **1977** *Sunday Times* (Wellington) 27 Nov. 17 Ken..is a '**blacksander**', one of the few left on the Coast. His mine is the beach where the high tides wash away the top layers of white sand to reveal the gold-bearing black stuff. **1906** GALVIN *NZ Mining Handbook* 122 At present there are small parties who earn a good average living by what is known as '**blacksanding**'..between Jackson's Bay and Karamea. **1906** *NZGeol. SB (NS)* No. 1 4 The operation of working the beach sands on a small scale is known as 'blacksanding', because the gold is associated with ironsand (magnetite).

blacksmith bird. [f. the sound, poss. reinforced by allusion to the 'Anvil Chorus' or Handel's *Harmonious Blacksmith.*] BELLBIRD 1 a.

c1861 STACK in Reed *Annals Early Dunedin* 15 We were delighted to hear [near Paieri] the bellbirds or, as they called them, 'blacksmith birds', ringing out their sweet notes.

black-winged petrel: see PETREL 2 (3).

blacky: see BLACK *n.*¹ 1 b.

blade, *n.*¹ [AND 1897.]

1. a. Usu. *pl.* as **the blades,** a set of sheep-shears manually operated by the shearer's hand. See also DAGGER 2, *hand shears* (HAND *n.*² 3), SWORD, TONGS 1.

1917 *NZJAg.* Sept. XV. 134 The majority of the larger sheepowners..have come to recognize the advantages of 'machines' over 'blades'. **1926** DEVANNY *Butcher Shop* (1981) 44 She shut her eyes and pictured the pens of excited animals waiting for the blades. **1933** *Press* (Christchurch) (Acland Gloss.) 16 Sept. 15 *Blades.*—Hand shears as opposed to shearing machines. Hence also *blade shearer.* **1946** MULGAN *Pastoral NZ* 32 'Blades'—that is hand-shears—are still used for fine-woolled sheep in the high-country. **1951** McLEOD *NZ High Country* 26 So most of us stick to 'the blades', the big shining steel shears eight and a half inches long, with a double spring 'bow' on the end to keep them apart. **1960** MILLS *Sheep-O* 19 This establishes the date [17 Nov. 1900] of the change-over from blades to machines. **1990** MARTIN *Forgotten Worker* 83 The hand shears or combination 'blades' comprised two steel shears, eight or nine inches long, joined at their ends by a spring bow to spring the shears apart again after being closed.

b. *attrib.* (Always *sing.*)

1960 MILLS *Sheep-O* 40 Well, the calm, peaceful atmosphere of a blade shed is much more to my liking than the constant din of handpieces and machinery. **1973** NEWTON *Big Country SI* (1977) 61 He first went to the Muller [station] in the old blade days. **1978** JARDINE *Shadows on Hill* 129 The machines were closed down..and operations reverted to an eight-man blade gang until 1956.

2. In the phr. **off the blades,** of sheep, newly shorn, *off the shears* (SHEAR *n.* 1 b); **gone out with the blades** [AND 1958], see quot. 1989.

1947 NEWTON *Wayleggo* 39 It was the practice then to dip the wethers **off the blades** (straight after shearing). **1966** NEWTON *Boss's Story* 188 *off the blades*: Newly shorn, i.e. sheep dipped straight after shearing are dipped 'off the blades'. **1989** *NZ Eng. Newsletter* III. 24 **gone out with the blades**: An expression used *outside* of blade shearing that means old fashioned and no longer wanted.

3. Special Comb. **blademan** or **bladesman** [AND 1918], **blade shearer** [AND 1924], one who shears sheep with hand-shears; **blade-shearing** *vbl. n.* [AND 1945] and *attrib.* [AND 1949], hence, occas. and prob. by back-formation, **blade shear** *v. intr.* to use blade shears in shearing; **blade-shorn,** shorn by hand-shears, leaving a residual wool-cover greater than with machine-shearing.

1951 McLEOD *NZ High Country* 16 Lean Australian **blademen** from 'the other side' across the Tasman [and] tough old Merino shearers. **1973** NEWTON *Big Country SI* (1977) 20 A top blade-man in his day he claims that his 164 ewes, at Molesworth, is the blade record for that shed. **1989** *NZ Eng. Newsletter* III. 21 *bladesman:* Handshearer. **1933 blade shearer** [see 1 a above]. **1950** *NZJAg.* Oct. LXXXI. 351 Owing to the acute shortage of blade shearers..the owners [of Glenaray station] were forced to change to machine shearing. **1962** SHARPE *Country Occasions* 40 When one blade shearer starts on five thousand sheep the end is a long way ahead. **1988** *Press* (Christchurch) 24 Aug. 18 Ivory Poi [—], aged 35, a blade shearer..was remanded to September 6. **1922** PERRY *Sheep Farming* 83 Nowadays shearing is mostly done with machines, although in some parts there is a reaction in favour of **blade shearing. 1955** BOWEN *Wool Away* 1 Right back in early **blade-shearing** history, it [*sc.* shearing] was always a race. *Ibid.* 8 Most of our good blade shearers today are veterans, and one foresees that this age-old art of blade shearing may die out. **1962** SHARPE *Country Occasions* 35 As blade shearing is slow, and the merino sheep..are very difficult to shear, the back-country station is usually last on any shearer's itinerary. **1975** HARPER *Eight Daughters* 41 Ernie Radford..gave the girls lessons in blade-shearing, and on one day Kathleen shore thirteen. **1981** CHARLES *Black Billy Tea* 39 Sure I'll sing you a song Of the blade-shearing days. **1990** MARTIN *Forgotten Worker* 85 Blade shearing placed a tremendous load on the wrist ligaments in particular because of the special pivoting action and the force necessary to close the blades against the bowsprings.

1993 *Straight Furrow* 22 The annual round of the blade shearing gangs..still features on the calendars of high country stations. **1995** National Radio 20 Sept. 10.05 a.m. (Kim Hill programme): New Zealander, Ian Rutherford, has taught a number of South Africans to **blade shear**. **1966** Newton *Boss's Story* 30 Although late March was late enough, **blade-shorn** lambs could come to little harm.

blade, *n.*[2] By synecdoche, a knife as a weapon.
1982 Newbold *Big Huey* 245 Blade: (n) Knife. Recorded as British criminal slang in 1929, but probably in use long before that. **1986** *Evening Post* (Wellington) 7 May 1 When he joined gang members used blades but today's weapon was the gun and 14-year-olds were not mature enough for this.

blade, *v. trans.* To remove (material) usu. with a bulldozer blade.
1958 *NZJAg.* Nov. XCVII. 402 Two drivers were killed when they were root-raking or blading scrub into gullies. **1961** Crump *Hang On a Minute Mate* 32 Had to take the scarfs out in sections and blade them out of the way with a dozer.

blanket. [Spec. and fig. uses of *blanket* a covering, esp. with reference to its former use by the Maori as an external garment.]

1. *Hist.* In various phr. referring to Maori people or Maori ways. **a. to return (go back) to the blanket,** to return to Maori ways. See *back to the mat* (MAT 3 a).
1912 *Truth* 17 Aug. 5 Then came the agony between a young European wearing the tartan name of Stuart McIvor and his erring half-caste Maori missus called by the festive name of Pehipa, who has, to use a current term, returned 'to the blanket' in preference to Stuart's manly buzzim.

b. to take the blanket, of a Pakeha, to live as a Maori.
1922 Cowan *NZ Wars* (1955) II. 14 Sometimes renegade white men joined with the Maoris in the ceremonies around the *niu*. One of these runaways from civilization who had 'taken to the blanket' was Kimble Bent. **1931** *Taranaki Herald* 22 May (VUW Fildes Clippings 621/38) [Heading] The Pakeha-Maori... Whites who took the blanket. Bent and Cockburn and their like, the renegade soldiers who 'took the blanket' represented the lowest stratum in Pakeha-Maoridom.

c. See *flour and blanket policy* (FLOUR AND SUGAR).

2. *Mining.* [AND 1862.] A piece of blanket-material (later often baize) placed over a board or 'table' to catch particles of precious metal washed over it. Usu. *attrib.* or in special Comb.: **blanket-board,** boards surfaced with blanket material as part of a gold collection process (see also *gold–saving cloth* (GOLD 3)); **blanket-table** [AND 1862], a flat table-like construction lined with blanket material to catch precious metal; **blanket tailings,** BLANKETINGS.
1876 *TrNZI* VIII. 179 The blanket strakes below the silver tables are about 20 feet long; they are so arranged that any part of them may be washed from time to time... Instead of blanket, baize & coarse plush have been used with advantage. **1868** *Thames Miner's Guide* 93 The copper-plate tables [of the mine battery] are about 12ft. long by 5ft. wide, and raised about 14in. above the **blanket boards**... [The blankets] appear to be ordinary grey blankets of a very inferior description. **1876** *TrNZI* VIII. 177 The constant outflow of crushed quartz and water from the stamp boxes is received on a table, having on it grooves or ripples, containing quicksilver and a large extent of amalgamated copper plates smoothly nailed on. This may be called the silver table;... The flow then passes over **blanket tables**, which arrest mechanically all the heavier particles. **1876 blanket tailings** [see BLANKETINGS].

3. Special Comb. **blanket-bag,** a rolled blanket used as a carrying-bag slung over the shoulder; a blanket pack; also an early version of a sleeping-bag; **blanket piece** *whaling*, a piece of blubber stripped from a whale.
1854 Malone *Three Yrs. Cruise* 17 About four miles from Pokatutu's pah, we stopped, opened our ***blanket-bags***, and took a hearty lunch. **1896** Harper *Pioneer Work* 90 On turning in we lie 'heads and tails' in our blanket bags. **1838** Polack *NZ* II. 420 [The whale] is then raised as high as the main mast head, and another tackle is applied to a fresh piece of blubber, technically called **blanket pieces**, during which the preceding piece is lowered into an inclosed place below the deck, called the blubber room. **1892** Osborn in Richards *Foveaux Whaling Yarns* (1995) 20 From eighteen to twenty men, with handspikes heave away at the windlass, and the blanket piece begins to rise, peeling off from the carcass as fast as the men cut the body of the animal rolling in the water.

blanketings. *Mining.* Usu. *pl.* The auriferous and other material caught by a blanket board or table.
1876 *TrNZI* VIII. 179 The blanket tailings or blanketings, as they are otherwise called, consist mostly of iron pyrites and other sulphides, combined with quartz, and contain a fair proportion of gold..that had escaped over the silver tables. **1882** Hay *Brighter Britain* II. 279 We see this liquid [*sc.* puddled ore] sent over 'beds', and 'floors', and 'ladders', and 'blanketings', and washed again and again. **1992** Latham *Golden Reefs* 427 Blanketings: The heavy sand, consisting largely of sulphides, caught by the blankets of the amalgamating-table.

blast, *v. Whaling.* [f. Brit. dial. *blast* swell up: see OED *v.* 4; EDD 5.] *intr.* Of a dead whale, to swell up during decomposition. Also *ppl. a.*
1982 Grady *Perano Whalers* 188 When the *Orca* finally refound their 'lost whale' it had blasted (blown up like a balloon) to twice its normal size owing to decomposition gases. *Ibid.* 226 Blasted—Swollen whale advanced in decomposition after death.

blatherskite, *n.* Also occas. **blatherskyte.** [An altered form of Brit. and US dial. *blatherskate.*] A boaster, blowhard. See also SKITE *n.* 2.
1865 *McLean Papers* (ATLTS) XXIV. 279 His lordship blatherskate makes writing impossible. **1986** Richards *Off the Sheep's Back* 35 He was never known by his Christian name. It was always Mr Clemett. Out of earshot he was known as Old Clem, or the South Island blatherskite.

Hence also **blatherskite** *v. intr.,* SKITE *v.* 1 a.
1865 *McLean Papers* (ATLTS) XXIV. 114 That talking fellow Russell has spread the news right and left. When he arrived he was blatherskyting about how secure everything was at Hawkes Bay.

blaze, *n.* [f. *blaze n.* and *v.* mark (made) by chipping off bark.] A blazed track; a rough track marked by blazes.
1939 *NZ Alpine Jrnl.* VII. 26 98 David Gunn had run a blaze from the top of the Kaipo slip..south along a ridge for 'three hours'. **1958** *Tararua* Sept. 69 An indifferent blaze was picked up which led through bush and scrub to the tussock line.

bleaching paddock. *Flax-milling.* A paddock in which flax fibre was hung to dry and bleach in sunlight. Cf. PADDOCK *n.*[1] 2.
1966 Barry *In Lee of Hokonuis* 280 The flax fibre produced from the mill was hung in the bleaching paddock. **1980** McGill *Ghost Towns NZ* 221 [Caption] Fibre is being carted from the mill to the bleaching paddocks.

bleed, *v. Obs.* [Spec. use of *bleed* to draw blood from.] *trans.* and *intr.* To release blood (from a sheep) to remedy poisoning by tutu or, occas., ergot.
1863 Chudleigh *Diary* 19 Nov. (1950) 110 One ram was tooted and we had to bleed him freely. **1960** Scrymgeour *Memories Maoriland* 145 The seed ripened on the ryegrass, and with it came the legacy of 'ergot'... Too much blood obtained..and the remedy was..'to bleed' and take from the patient the overflow of red corpuscles. **1968** Tomlinson *Remembered Trails* 19 Odd sheep started to get 'tooted' and instead of pushing on the men started bleeding the sheep. This was done by cutting a vein under the eye.

bleeder. One who obtains kauri gum from the living tree.
1991 *NZ Geographic* Apr.–June 32 Gum climbers and bleeders scaled kauri using a weighted line and rope.

Hence **bleeding** *vbl. n.,* the process of obtaining such gum. Cf. *bush-bled* (BUSH C 1 a).
1991 *NZ Geographic* Apr.–June 29 It was found that if slashes were made in the trunk of the tree, it would bleed, and the resin could be harvested later. Initially, it was thought that bleeding did not harm the tree.

blenny.

1. [Spec. use of *blenny* (ad. Lat. *blennius*) a name used elsewhere, but recorded earliest from NZ waters, for a widespread genus of small fishes, fam. Blenniidae: see OED.] Applied to small spiny-finned fish found in rock pools, weeds and shallow coastal waters belonging to the families Blenniidae (true blennies), Tryperygiidae (triplefins) and Clinidae (weedfishes): often (esp. by children) popularly called 'cockabully'.
1773 Forster *Resolution Jrnl.* 8 Apr. (1982) II. 250 We got some other new fish, viz. a small Lumpfish, a small Blenny, both caught under the rocks at low water mark. **1885** *TrNZI* XVII. 168 *Trypterygium compressum.* The Blenny... This specimen of a blenny was caught off Otago Heads. **1927** Speight et al. *Nat. Hist. Canterbury* 200 More numerous still in both species and individual members are the Blennies, small spiny-rayed fishes in which the pelvic fins are placed far forward under the throat. **1967** Natusch *Animals NZ* 228 [Caption] Blennies or Cockabullies. 1. Threepenny, *Gilloblennis* 2. Blenny, *Ericentrus*. 3. Cockabully, *Forsterygion*. **1982** Ayling *Collins Guide* (1984) 278 They are normally referred to as blennies in New Zealand but they are not true blennies..and are best referred to as triplefins in reference to their three dorsal fins.

2. With a modifier: **crested, mimic.**

(1) crested blenny. *Parablennius laticlavius.*
1982 Ayling *Collins Guide* (1984) 277 The crested blenny is a small fish..that like most blennies has a smooth scaleless skin and a blunt head. It has..[a] distinctive crest, made up of a large forked cirrus above each eye, that suggested the name crested blenny. **1989** Paulin et al. *NZ Fish* 222 Head square, blunt; body with prominent horizontal stripe..crested blenny.

(2) **mimic blenny**. *Plagiotremus tapeinosoma*.
1982 AYLING *Collins Guide* (1984) 277 The name mimic blenny comes from this fish's habit of hiding amongst schools of somewhat similar but harmless oblique swimming triplefin in an attempt to get closer to potential prey without being detected. **1986** PAUL *NZ Fishes* 135 The mimic blenny..is more aggressive, hiding amid schools of similar but harmless species and darting out to bite pieces from larger fish.

blight-bird. Also **blightie, blighty.** SILVEREYE.
1870 *TrNZI* II. 61 We first noticed this bird..in the Rockwood Valley, Malvern Hills, July 28th, 1856... It very soon obtained the name of Blight-bird..from its habit of feeding on the American blight [aphis], with which apple trees in this colony are so generally infested. **1888** BULLER *Birds NZ* I. 79 I was in Auckland..on the 20th of May [of 1868], when the so-called Blight-birds appeared here. **1897** *TrNZI* XXIX. 285 It is well known that the bittern varies its feeding..adding still another enemy to our useful little migrant blight-bird. **1917** WILLIAMS *Dict. Maori Lang.* 325 Pihipihi, n. *1. Zosterops caerulescens*, wax-eye, blight-bird. **1926** GREY *Angler's Eldorado* 170 The trees were full of the little yellow blighties, named from their very good habit of eating the insect blight. **1946** *JPS* XV. 159 *Tauhou*, a wandering bird.., blight-bird; twinkie; button-eye; wax-eye; ring-eye. **1967** NATUSCH *Animals NZ* 282 *Zosterops lateralis*..called ring-eye in the south, wax-eye, white-eye, silvereye, blightie, etc., elsewhere. **1988** McGILL *Dict. Kiwi Slang* 15 *Blighty* blight bird, now better known as waxeye, white-eye or silver-eye.

blightie, blighty: see BLIGHT-BIRD.

blind, *a.*, *attrib.*, and *n.*

A. *adj.* and *attrib.*

1. [Spec. use of *blind* (of a geographical feature) terminating abruptly: see OED 11 c.] Of a (geographical) surface or under-surface feature, leading nowhere, terminating abruptly or, occas., with a suggestion of being partially hidden by growth. **a.** Used *attrib.* in collocations: **blind creek** [AND 1834], **blind gully** [AND 1852], **blind pakihi**, **blind spur** (for further definitions see noun element).
1888 BULLER *Birds NZ* II. 142 The Common Bittern is very generally distributed..in places..such as..those '**blind creeks**', covered over with a growth of reeds and tangle. **1933** *Press* (Christchurch) (Acland Gloss.) 16 Sept. 15 *Blind*.—(1) Unseen, hard to see (creek, gully, etc.). (2) leading nowhere (spur, creek, gully, etc.). I think (1) is the commoner usage. **1848** PHARAZYN *Journal* 15 Jan. (ATLMS) 97 Teddy and W. to lambs to drive them to pen, smothered 10 in a **blind gully**. **1862** *Otago Goldfields & Resources* 23 The principal workings here are blind gullies and streams. **1988** *In Their Own Words* 36 After lying up all day in a blind gully..the battalion moved up along a deep sap up the beach for about two miles. **1951** McLEOD *NZ High Country* 43 A clearing completely surrounded by bush will be called a '**blind Parkee**'. **1970** McLEOD *Glorious Morning* 255 *Pakihi*: A clearing in the bush, perhaps only a bay. If totally enclosed, a 'blind' pakihi. **1861** HAAST *Rep. Topogr. Explor. Nelson* 8 We descended..but soon discovered that we had selected a so-called **blind spur**, which fell abruptly into a deep gully.

b. *Mining.* [See DARE *blind lead* one not visible from the surface, 1874.] Of mineral veins, lodes, reefs, etc., petering out, or not developing into a rich seam; also (esp. **blind leader**) not visible by surface inspection.
1861 *NZ Goldfields 1861* (1976) 12 At present the diggings are believed to be confined to Tuapeka..where Gabriel's Gully..and a few blind leaders have been opened. **1882** HAY *Brighter Britain* II. 299 Eventually it was proved that the find was but a 'blind reef', a 'pocket', a mere isolated dribble from the main continuous vein we had at first supposed we had struck. **1912** *NZGeol.SB* (NS) No.15 126 These particular veins are 'blind', or feather out in the enclosing dacites.

2. In special collocations in various senses of *blind*: **blind dipping** *vbl. n.* goldmining, dipping a gold-pan indiscriminately or blindly into a stream-bed on the chance of washing out gold; **blind-drag** *v.* West Coast, to dip the net into a whitebait run blindly, without directed aim or because of water discolouration; **blind-dragging** *vbl. n.*; **blind eel**, see EEL 2 (1); **blind roller** West Coast, a large wave which does not break; **blind stabbing** *vbl. n.* [f. *blind* without sight of an object + *stab* an attempt], see *blind dipping* above; **blind tiger** *obs.* [orig. US: see DARE a place that sells liquor illegally; poss. f. its disguise as an exhibition hall to conceal illegal selling of liquor; or perh. from the one-eyed peephole through which the proprietor of such an establishment monitored customers (1857–1965): person who sells illegal liquor (1966)], a sly-grogger; a seller or provider of illegal liquor.
1887 PYKE *Hist. Early Gold Discoveries Otago* (1962) 104 When matters had settled down a bit the miners spread themselves along the river, getting gold almost everywhere on the beaches, and following it in until they stood up to their thighs in the stream '**blind dipping**'. **1974** in *Listener Short Stories* (1977) 119 And every beginning spring, Coasters in their hundreds flock to the rivers and streams to swoop and scoop and **blind-drag** as many [whitebait] as possible out of sanctuary. *Ibid.* 120 I was newly arrived from Christchurch, and unaware of Coast ways... **Blind-dragging** was peculiar terminology. **1888** PRESHAW *Banking Under Difficulties* 155 A few of us landed in one of the ship's boats; not a safe thing to do as a rule on the Coast, what are known as '**blind rollers**' often rising and swamping a boat. **1950** p.c. L. Cleveland (Wellington). **blind-stabbing**: Used by Jack Sweeney, prospector, to describe a traditional method of getting gold-bearing wash out of glacial rivers. The prospector is anchored by a rope which is controlled by a mate on the bank. He wheels a wheelbarrow as far into the torrent as is possible, shovels the alluvial wash into it blindly, because the water contains glacial silts and is milky white, and returns to the bank with as much as he can shift. This is processed at leisure for gold. **1912** *Truth* 26 Oct. 6 The man who enters a boarding or 'temperance' house is..suspected of designs of all descriptions. He is dubbed 'a dropper', or 'a **blind tiger**.'

B. *n.* In the phr. **on the blind a.** [AND 1929.] Of sheep-dogs, working out of sight of the shepherd; or working with no direct sight of the object sheep.
1934 LILICO *Sheep Dog Memoirs* 6 Though he was very perfect on sheep within sight of him [sc. his master], he was no use at running on the blind in rough ground. **1949** HARTLEY *Shepherd's Dogs* 25 *Casting 'On the Blind'*... A good opportunity is often presented when driving a mob through a paddock. A few will go off on a side track over a ridge. The trainer is certain of their whereabouts but it is a run 'on the blind' to the young dog. **1951** McLEOD *NZ High Country* 22 Gradually the [dog's command] distance is lengthened until you hunt him as far as you can see. Then he must be taught to run 'on the blind'—that is, to go up or down hill as directed, looking for sheep he hasn't seen. **1966** NEWTON *Boss's Story* 189 *Running on the Blind*: When a dog is being sent after sheep which are out of his sight he is running on the blind.

b. [AND 1917.] Of an action, done without prior information or proper sight or foresight.
1952 LYON *Faring South* 168 It used to be rather shrewdly suspected that tributors were not 'working on the blind' but had as former employees of the company marked a lead and covered the same by a piece of mine timber or rubble till a later date give them the chance to profit by their knowledge. **1953** SUTHERLAND *Golden Bush* (1963) 175 Alan then recounted his movements. He had stalked a roaring stag on the blind for the greater part of the morning. **1955** BOWEN *Wool Away* 131 The short staple of wool on the Merino allows a shearer to see and handle his work more easily. With the long wools, quite a lot of hand-work is done 'on the blind'. **1978** TUCKER *Thoroughbreds Are My Life* 26 It was a question of backing on the blind because nobody was supposed to know in advance which mule carried which saddlecloth [indicating the number carried in the race].

blister. [Transf. use of *blister* a summons to court.] A strong, usu. official, written reprimand.
c1926 THE MIXER *Transport Workers' Song Book* 44 Note how the Labour Department always like to get your 'goat.' When you refuse the overtime..how they chase you round with 'blisters'. **1939** GRIEVE *Sketches from Maoriland* (1961) 68 I was sanguine enough to believe that a parental application of *hot* water and soap, administered with the added impetus of an official 'blister' delivered in an envelope bearing the awe-inspiring legend 'On His Majesty's Service', might have the desired effect.

blister: see *cheese blister* (BUSTER *n.*[4]).

block: see also AUCTION BLOCK.

block, *n.*[1] [f. *block* a large quantity, a mass.]

1. a. *Hist.* In land purchase or subdivision, a large area of land intended for European settlement, in the SI esp. the *Canterbury Block* and the *Otago Block* forming the regional nuclei of their respective settlements, later provinces (see further b below).
[Note] Orig. reference is mainly to Crown and New Zealand Company purchase of Maori land, but usage also reflects the sense of *block* as a surveyor's name for a division of a Land District.
1841 DEANS *Letters* 25 Mar. (1937) 31 The boundaries of the block are now pretty well defined. **1843** DEANS *Pioneers Port Cooper Plains* (1964) 18 We are to take a lease of a block of land from the natives for 99 years, paying them a small yearly rent; this the Government can't forbid. **1848** EARP *Emigrant's Guide* 47 Several settlers are ready to cultivate land in the new 'block' south of the Sugar Loaves [New Plymouth]. **1848** WAKEFIELD *Handbook for NZ* 308 North of the Otago block, the country is said to resemble that described as within it. **1851** *Lyttelton Times* 26 July 5 They [sc. the colonists] found that the Canterbury block was part of the plain lying in the vast segment of the wide circle between the sea and a range of mountains, entirely cut off from all other settlements by natural boundaries, and formed, as it were by nature, to consist of one district in itself. **1855** *Austral. & NZ Gaz.* 27 Jan. 88 The land between the Inch Clutha and these ranges, much of which is swampy, is laid off in sections extending sixteen miles from the coast, and containing nearly one half of the Otago block. **1862** AYLMER *Distant Homes* 44 He had travelled through most of the settlement looking at the different 'blocks' or divisions of land the Government buys from the natives to sell to

the settlers. **1898** HOCKEN *Contributions* 58 This Otago block contains 400,000 acres, and extends from Taiaroa Head down the coast to Tokata Point or the Nuggets. **1949** REED *Story Canterbury* 112 In 1853 the Canterbury block was enlarged and became known as the Canterbury Province. **1957** [see MAORI WAR 1 b]. **1959** SINCLAIR *Hist. NZ* 81 Large areas of land were purchased in the North Island. Almost the entire South Island was bought in a few huge 'blocks'. **1966** *Encycl. NZ* I. 298 In 1850 the Canterbury Association was granted powers to dispose of land within 2,500,000 acres, generally known as the 'Canterbury Block', between the Waipara and Ashburton Rivers and occupying about half the Canterbury Plain.

b. Esp. in the NI, a named area of alienated Maori land.

1854 *Taranaki Herald* in Fitton *NZ* (1856) 153 To enforce this *tapu* they have constructed a pa on Rawiri's section on the Bell Block. **1863** CAREY *The Late War in NZ* 27 The word *block* is used in New Zealand to designate a portion of land purchased at a particular time, and opened to settlement; thus the Omata block, the Bell block, the Grey block etc. **1936** LAMBERT *Pioneering Reminisc. Old Wairoa* 20 When Dr. F.F. Ormond purchased the Orangitirohia block on the north side of the river, not all the Natives had been satisfactorily dealt with. **1952–53** *NZ Forest Service Gloss.* (TS) In land-subdivision, a term relating to a defined area of Maori land and bearing the original Maori tribal name.

c. Special Comb. **block committee**, see quot.

1983 KING *Whina* 36 Native Land Court sittings were held there in the late 1890s and early 1900s... These sittings were not of the court proper, but of 'block committees' of chiefs responsible for parcelling out shares in land allocated to particular hapu in earlier court sittings presided over by a judge. The block committees' decisions were subsequently ratified by court.

2. a. *Surveying.* In land survey a major subdivision of a Survey District. See quot. 1952–53.

1851 *Lyttelton Times* 27 Sept. 4 That desirable Block of Land, Number 114 on the Surveyors' Map. **1898** HOCKEN *Contributions* facing 130 [Caption] Dr. Stewart's cowhouse on Sec. 20, Blk VI. **1952–53** *NZ Forest Service Gloss.* (TS) *Block.* In land-subdivision, a major subdivision of a Survey District... A Block is usually 1/16 of a Survey District and is square, with sides 250 chains long. Block numbers are indicated by roman numerals **1954** MILLER *Beyond the Blue Mountains* 122 The Merino Downs district..comprised parts of Blocks 1 and 5, Glenkenich Survey District,.. Block 5 [being] part of Merino Downs station... John McNoe also purchased another section (No. 27, Block 1) of 200 acres at the station sale in 1894.

b. A surveyed holding of land within a survey district.

1888 D'AVIGDOR *Antipodean Notes* 65 Roads at right angles to each other cut up the cultivated land into 'blocks', and..there are many landowners in Canterbury who farm several of these huge divisions. **1894** *NZ Official Year-book* 206 On the line of railway..blocks of Government land were laid off into sections, varying in area from one quarter to five acres. **1955** WILSON *Land of My Children* 25 I've a section m'self in this Block, and I'm tellin' you plain that I'll knock any man down who as much as offers to put match to twig before the right time [for burning felled bush]. **1960** *Dominion* (Wellington) 29 June 14 A stopbank protecting twenty farms in a block west of Kerepehi broke this afternoon and a number of settlers were forced to leave. **1976** BROWN *Difficult Country* 47 Those [sections surveyed in the township of Hampden] sold were bought by residents of Nelson as a spec., and several country blocks had absentee owners.

3. a. An area of bush to be worked for timber or cleared for farmland.

1852 in Beattie *Pioneers Explore Otago* (1947) 27 Our day's travelling was over some high undulating land with..several blocks of bush land with very good timber. **1899** BELL *In Shadow of Bush* 42 On Robinson's section the last remaining block of standing bush had already been felled earlier in the season. **1902** *Settler's Handbook NZ* 17 In the neighbourhood of Kaikoura..there is another small block of forest land, in which three small sawmills have been erected. **1986** RICHARDS *Off the Sheep's Back* 45 Each year after a new block of fallen bush had been burned off, we would have a wonderful harvest of cape gooseberries.

b. In forest management. See quot.

1952–53 *NZ Forest Service Gloss.* (TS) *Block.* In forest management, a major subdivision of a forest, generally bounded by natural features and bearing a local name. In some of the first established exotic forests, block was used in place of *Compartment* [sc. a subdivision of a forest]. **1961** CRUMP *Hang On a Minute Mate* 97 Tony..and I were working a block of pine bush up at Tokoroa.

4. An area of land taken up for farming; a management subdivision or other identifiable area of a large farm or station.

1875 CHUDLEIGH *Diary* 2 Aug. (1950) 237 About £1 3/- per acre for fencing if done in blocks of not less than 640 acres. **1907** *TrNZI* XXXIX. 292 On going over a block about a mile long and a quarter wide we found close on three hundred dead sheep. **1922** PERRY *Sheep Farming* 90 These sheep will thrive far better on one block with plenty of room to move about than they will if constantly moved from one block to another. **1946** ACLAND *Early Canterbury Runs* 18 As wire became more plentiful the runholders divided their runs into blocks. At first a block each for ewes, wethers and hoggets was as much as the runholder cared to pay for. **1951** McLEOD *NZ High Country* 11 Besides the buildings there have to be many miles of fencing dividing the country into 'blocks' for the various classes of sheep and seasons of the year. **1969** HAMILTON *Wild Irishman* 107 Leaving the homestead at daybreak we mustered half the block, hunting the sheep across a small creek by dark. **1978** JARDINE *Shadows on Hill* 34 This block faced north, only five miles long. **1981** ANDERSON *Both Sides of River* 8 A greater number of stations were using snowline fences on their winter blocks. **1992** *Marlborough Express* (Blenheim) 31 Jan. 5 His first farm was a 400 acre block in Southland.

Hence a verbal form **blocking** *vbl. n.*, inspecting stock on a farm block.

1981 SUTHERLAND & TAYLOR *Sunrise* 83 But early in July Mr Knox set Bill the job of blocking—daily riding round the ewes.

5. An area of land being developed by the State from bush or scrub to farmland (often called **development block**), or being made available by the Crown ('settled') for farms (often called **settlement block**). Also **block manager**, the manager of a development or settlement block.

1904 LANCASTER *Sons o' Men* 193 He..went away to ride..to the home [*sc.* a sod whare] that he had built her. It stood on a new-leased Government block. **1963** BACON *In the Sticks* 87 'But surely it'd take some time before this block was ready for settlement?' I asked. 'Yeah, mate... They [*sc.* Lands and Survey Department] usually send in a block manager with half a dozen other jokers..to clear it up and get the place a bit straight for the permanent settlers.' **1982** *Agric. Gloss.* (MAF) 5 *Block*: An area of land, e.g.: Development block—an area being developed from bush or scrub to farmland. Settlement block—an area made (settled) into farms. **1988** *More* (Auckland) Mar. 30 On arrival at the Maori Affairs block shed the two women who'd been in the car took me aside.

6. a. The area (or 'beat') usu. of Crown Land, State Forest or other public land allocated by an authority, over which an opossum-trapper is licensed to operate, or an official culler or a private sportsman is permitted to shoot, or which is assigned to a rabbiter to clear of rabbits. Also occas. an area authorized for prospecting for minerals.

1946 MILLER *There Was Gold* 82 They once saw a couple of poachers working their rabbiting block across the gorge. **1948** *Our Own Country* 23 The blocks of land [at Thames] in which prospecting was allowed by the Maoris were limited. **1950** *Tararua Tramper* Nov. 6 Knowing a shooter's favourite block..will give a clue as to where to look for him. **1959** McLEOD *Tall Tussock* 27 At the end of the [mustering] season they took a rabbit block together, and had quite a good winter. *Ibid.* 124 *Rabbit block*: A contract to catch rabbits on a certain piece of country, either for wages or for the skins. **1960** CRUMP *Good Keen Man* 31 Jim..sent me down to a possum block in the Ruahines for the winter. **1964** HELMER *Stag Party* 6 It reproduces the atmosphere of a deer block in the Urerewa very nicely. **1965** MACNICOL *Skippers Road* 47 The men had long heavy days on the rabbiting blocks. **1978** MANTELL *Murder in Fancydress* 87 A cast antler caught in a bush and he had to barge right into it. Halfway through shooting out a block so his mate patched him up and he carried on. **1980** HOLDEN *Stag* 20 He'd spent the last five years as a professional hunter... So he now knew the block reasonably well. **1992** *Evening Post* (Wellington) 30 Apr. 3 Mr H— and three companions..were hunting in a private block in the middle of Kaimanana Forest Park. **1995** CRUMP *Bushwoman* 34 When I went tramping I kept my eyes open for a possum block.

b. In the phr. **to take (up) a block**, of a rabbiter, to hunt rabbits on an assigned area.

1933 *Press* (Christchurch) (Acland Gloss.) 18 Nov. 15 *Rabbit...* To kill r[abbit]s, to be employed as a *rabbiter.* He may be a permanent or a temporary hand, or may *take a block* for the skins. He may use dog, gun, and spade, poison, or traps.

block, *n.*² Obs. [f. *block* a city block: AND 1868 (Melbourne).] In the phr. **to do the block**, to promenade or parade the streets.

1891 WILLIAMS & REEVES *In Double Harness* 54 You do the block in swagger style, in *such* a clever gown. **1894** [see FOSSICKER]. **1909** *Truth* 18 Dec. 5 The writer of this was almost gathered to his fathers the other night when he met a fat Chow 'doing the block' in the dour city. **c1952** in SUTTON-SMITH *Hist. Children's Play* (1982) 67 Once or twice we [*sc.* a boys' impromptu band c1880–90] 'did the block', but I am afraid our collection was even more inadequate to our supposed needs than the Army's was to theirs.

block, *n.*³ [f. *block* head.] In various phrases:

1. to lose one's block [AND 1907], to lose one's head, to become angry or excited.

1911 *Maoriland Worker* 7 July 9 Mr. — of the Trades Hall, Wellington, seems to have lost his block... The general displeasure hardly seems sufficient grounds for..taking leave of his senses. **1918** *Chron. NZEF* 21 June 221 If you can keep your block while those about you Are losing theirs.

2. to do one's block, to go mad; to become angry, excited; to lose self-control. Cf. *do one's bun* (*scone*) (BUN *n.*¹, SCONE *n.*).

1910 *Truth* 16 Apr. 7 A Christchurch bookmaker..'did his block' with the aid of hops on March 31, when he went temporarily insane in the Star and Garter Hotel. **1921** *Quick March* 11 July 15 Dicken! I done me block right enough! I come home and the old finger hit the roof. Tike it from me, he's gotter rat. **1935** Young to Roberts 11 Feb. in Gustafson *Cradle to Grave* (1986) 161 Savage started off and completely did his block; made a vicious attack upon those who supported the resolution. **1945** HENDERSON *Gunner Inglorious* 48 In the dark, my [disturbed] mind cries out... 'Break it down,' reproves Pilling. 'Don't do your block.' **1959** SLATTER *Gun in My Hand* 114 A leader of men. He was tough and reliable and never did his block. **1961** CRUMP *Hang On a Minute Mate* 163 He got kicked out of the ring for doing his block... He goes berko. **1987** VIRTUE *Redemption of Elsdon Bird* (1988) 39 He really felt like doing his block and telling them just what he was thinking. **1990** EDWARDS *AWOL* 7 'My bloody oath I do!' I was beginning to do my block.

3. to be off one's block, to act crazily or unintelligently; **to use one's block**, to act intelligently.

1936 SARGESON *Conversation with my Uncle* 20 You'd almost believe they think I'm off my block which is just plum ridiculous. **1940** SARGESON *Man & His Wife* (1944) 303 [also 1939 *Tomorrow* 18 Jan. 18] Use your block and in no time you'll be unlucky if you don't have them [*sc.* women] eating out of your hand. **1984** PARTRIDGE *Dict. Slang* 96 *block*..2. The head:.. In Aus. and NZ, to *use* (one's) *block* = to use one's common sense; to act sensibly, hence to act intelligently: C20.

block, *n.*[4] A self-contained module of off-job training or study, esp. as **block course**, a continuous period of institutional instruction for apprentices or other trainees normally receiving training on the job. Also as **on block**, taking part in the study section of a trainee's programme.

1952 p.c. R. Mason 7 June *On block*. In earlier days nurses trained and nursed at the same time, a system replaced c1939 by a 'block' of study. *On block* signifies that the whole time for a specified period is being devoted to study. *Block courses* are used in many trade training schemes. **1956** *AJHR E-1* 9 There has been a growing preference in some trades for 'block' courses, involving continuous attendance at a school for forty hours a week during one or more weeks a year. **1965** *Report of Commission of Inquiry into Vocational Training* 33 [We] expect boys to spend seven and a half to eight hours each day at school or day classes or block courses. **1978** *Review of Apprenticeship, Vocational Training Council* 9 Engineering apprentices have an 18-week block course, in three six-week blocks, in the first year.

block, *n.*[5] [f. *block* a solid piece of wood.]

1. As **house-block**, see HOUSE 5.

2. *Axemen.* A block of wood trimmed to a standard diameter, often fastened to another, and drawn by ballot among the competitors, to be chopped through in an axemen's competition.

1963 BACON *In the Sticks* 135 At intervals, Mac would call for competitors to draw their blocks; the selected blocks, trimmed to a uniform diameter, and securely nailed into position ready for the next event.

block, *n.*[6] [f. BLOCK *v.*[1], poss. influenced by *butcher's block, chopping block.*]

1. a. A session of serial group intercourse, rape, or sodomy. Cf. BLOCK *v.*[1]

1973 *Truth* 9 Oct. 5 Dick was alleged to have said he was at the party and was aware 'a block was going on' but he repeatedly denied having intercourse with either of the females... Spence told the court he heard a discussion about one or two girls 'going on the block'. **1980** MANTELL *Murder & Chips* 103 'Possible. What did that stupid goon say in that Auckland trial? Blocking was ceremonial. There was no way the pigs were going to stop it'... The block. Multiple rape. Gang rape. **1991** PAYNE *Staunch* 43 Then there was this cultural change within the group where the block, the rape of women, was no longer an acceptable thing.

b. In the phr. **to put (a female) on the block**, to subject (a female) to serial intercourse, rape, or sodomy.

1973 *Truth* 4 Dec. 5 Later she heard the boys talking about 'putting a girl on the block'. Mr Rowan: What does that expression mean to you? Witness: It's when a whole heap of jokers have intercourse with one girl. **1974** *Truth* 18 June 11 A girl was told: 'you have got your head on the chopping block.' Then she was raped by several youths. **1982** NEWBOLD *Big Huey* 131 One time a bunch of gang members from the other side of the compound decided they were going to put her on the block.

c. In the phr. **to go on the block**, of a female, to be subjected to serial rape.

1973 *Truth* 4 Dec. 5 Home had told the girl: 'You've got between now and the time I finish this cigarette until you go into the bedroom and go on the block.'

2. A girl so treated, or considered for such treatment.

1974 *Truth* 2 Apr. 18 He said he knew her as 'the block', and he had sex with her. 'She looked 17 or 18. I thought she was "easy",' he added.

block, *v.*[1] [Cf. Partridge 8: to coit with a woman.] To rape or sodomize in serial fashion. Cf. DIG *v.*[2]

1978 *Truth* 14 Feb. 3 'The Black Power boys will block you if you struggle'... That was a threat allegedly made..to a 16-year-old girl. **1986** *Sunday News* (Auckland) 10 Aug. 9 Bloat..Peanut..L.T..and Gab all pleaded not guilty to sexual violation of a 17-year-old who confessed to smoking several joints before being 'blocked'. **1991** PAYNE *Staunch* 109 When a sheila came she knew what was going to happen, she was going to be blocked, gang raped.

Hence **blocking** *vbl. n.*

1980 [see BLOCK *n.*[6] 1 a]. **1988** MCGILL *Dict. Kiwi Slang* 16 *blocking* group rape; aka 'gang rape' or 'gangbang'.

block, *v.*[2] *Goldmining. Obs.* [Spec. use of *block* to cut out: AND *Obs.*, 1862.] As **to block out**, to excavate auriferous washdirt, or a gold-vein, in sections.

1952 HEINZ *Prospecting for Gold* 11 Under many of the mining camps there were tunnels from which the miners were 'blocking out' the rich wash dirt clear to bedrock.

Hence **blocking out** *vbl. n.*, see quot.

1935 BLYTH ed. *Gold Mining Year Book* 11 *Blocking out*: Describes the process of exposing, on at least three sides, any ore vein, also describes the working of auriferous alluvial deposits in square blocks.

bloke.

1. See ORDINARY BLOKE.

2. In composition, often in jocular nonce use: **blokeish** *a.*, stereotypically male; **blokery**, see quot.; **blokess**, a female bloke (see also ORDINARY BLOKE); **blokeism**, male chauvinism.

1994 *North & South* (Auckland) July 16 For a man called Swami Hansa, he's very New Zild *blokeish*; speaks English with a perfect New Zild accent. **1941** BAKER *NZ Slang* 56 Other twentieth century New Zealand expressions..include..*blokery*, the male sex in general and bachelors in particular. **1993** *Of Pavlovas, Poetry and Paradigms* (1993) 42 Forms such as *hackettes, chapesses* and even **blokesses** which I [*sc.* Prof. Janet Holmes] have noted in the current usage of male journalists can probably be regarded as nonce forms. **1993** *Salient* 12 July 21 *Seventeenth Doll* is offensive in its attitudes towards women and its rampant '**blokeism**'.

blood.

1. As **blood and money**, also **blood and treasure**, applied as an epithet to Governor George Grey's despatch accusing missionaries (and the Williams family in particular) of obtaining excessive Maori land.

1846 GREY in Carleton *Life of Henry Williams* (1877) II. Appendix D li His Majesty's Government may also rest assured that these individuals cannot be put in possession of these tracts of land without a large expenditure of British blood and money. **1848** WILLIAMS 5 Apr. in *Turanga Jrnls.* (1974) 487 As the editor [of the *New Zealander*] says if he [*sc.* Governor Grey] has compounded many such documents as the Blood & Treasure despatch, he is a ruined man. [**1866** *Richmond-Atkinson Papers* (1960) II. 213 [Jane Maria Atkinson referring to the Austro-Prussian War, and manoeuvrings of France under Louis Napoleon] I have such a dread of that horrid long-headed Louis Napoleon that I rather expect after all the the misery is gone thro', all the 'blood & treasure' spent, it will turn out that France alone is the gainer.] **1877** CARLETON *Life of Henry Williams* II. Appendix D l The confidential despatch to Mr. Gladstone, known in the colony by the name of 'Blood and Treasure', is of historical interest. **1974** PORTER in *Turanga Jrnls.* 441 There were several despatches attacking these [northern landholding] missionaries, but the 'celebrated one' [mentioned by W. Williams, Journal 1847 August 19] was that of Grey to Gladstone, 25 June 1846, which came to be known as the 'Blood and Money' or 'Blood and Treasure' despatch.

2. In the phr. **(to have) blood worth bottling**, see BOTTLE *v.*[2] 3.

3. Special Comb. **blood alley** [f. Brit. dial.: see OED, EDD], a white marble streaked with red, but cf. quot. 1972 (see also *bloodshot* below); **blood and bone**, dried blood mixed with bonemeal for use as a garden fertilizer; **blood blister** [f. Brit. dial.: see EDD 1 (1) Cheshire], a blister-like small bruise caused by a pinching or striking injury; **blood house** [f. *blood*(shed + *public) house*: AND 1952], a rough-house hotel; **blood nose**, a bleeding or bloody nose; **blood room** *obs.*, described as a place in or near a hotel where drunken shearers, etc., were put to sleep off a spree; a DEAD HOUSE q.v.; **bloodshot** (also **bloodie**), see *blood alley* above.

1972 SUTTON-SMITH *Folkgames Children* 176 [Waitara, Taranaki, 1899] A 'taw' was usually an 'alley' or '**blood alley**' made of agate. We used to take them home and burn them in a fire to convert them into 'blood alleys'. **1984** PARTRIDGE *Dict. Slang* 97 *blood alley*. A white, or whitish, marble streaked with red: Aus. and NZ children's: late C.19-20. Adopted ex. common English dialect. **1975** *Yates Garden Guide* 12 Bonedust and **Blood and Bone** are organic (animal) manures. **1982** PEAT *Detours* 236 As industry and port affairs encroach. There's salt air mixed with phosphate fine, A stench of blood and bone. **c1920** p.c. R. Mason (1953). A **blood blister** was the small blue-red 'blister' which came up when the flesh was severely pinched. We used it in my childhood, about 1920. **1938** *Blood blister* commonly used in Marlborough for the small blister-like bruise caused by, e.g., striking a fold of flesh with a hammer. (Ed.) **1951** *Evening Post*

(Wellington) 13 Jan. 12 For many years [the Royal Tiger's] customers [sailors] earned it [c1900] the reputation of a '**blood house**' and the licensee's job of keeping the peace was a hard one. **1942** GILBERT *Free to Laugh* 14 He threatened his mother with a **blood nose** and a black eye and demanded to become a cowboy. **1973** FERNANDEZ *Tussock Fever* 14 Henare with an angry glare flashed back, 'You clever bastard. You want the blood nose, eh?' **1992** SINCLAIR *Frontman* 97 The fight became real..one of them retired with a blood nose. **1984** *National Radio* 'Morning Report' 27 Nov. **Blood room** used and described [as in the definition above] in an interview with two Australians doing a history of New Zealand hotels. **1995** *Independent* 8 Dec. 20 **Bloodshots** or **bloodies** – white marbles with red stripes running through them – were special taws and greatly prized [by Dunedin boys].

bloodie: see *blood alley* (BLOOD 3).

bloody, *a.* and *adv.*

A. *adj.* [OED 1785; AND 1814.] A colloquial intensifier, used, so EDD, by the 'lower classes' 'indifferently as a term of depreciation or appreciation'; early and frequent in a NZ connection, but by no means a New Zealandism.
   [**1837** in RHODES *Jrnl. Barque 'Australian'* 11 July (1954) Walter [3rd Mate]..said it was a dam'd lie and that all who said so were bloody liars.] **1840** J. Watkin *MS Jrnl* 14 June in Evison TE WAI POUNAMU (1993) 151 The horrible use of the word 'bloody' is universal. **1859** SWAINSON *NZ & Colonisation* 37 When the heathen Maories see their men made drunk, their women debauched, and their chiefs called 'bloody Maories', no wonder our religion shall appear to them but little better than the empty profession of a barren creed.

B. *adv.* [OED 1676; AND 1823.] Also as **bloody well**. A colloquial intensifier, 'very'.
   1867 BUTLER *Letter* in Jones *Samuel Butler* (1919) I. 128 I was telling them at the [art] school I go to..about your man and his [mate] [*sic*] saying 'bloody' 72 times in 10 minutes. **1900** ASHCROFT *Public Morals* 13 [Against the over-use of bugger, bloody and hell]... One of [these], the word b—y, is simply coarse and nasty, but it may have had a perfectly harmless, even pious, origin... Its absurd uses now... 'That's a high building, Tom'... 'Not so bloody high.' **1933** BAUME *Half Caste* 14 The kind [of woman] that shouldn't bloody well exist. **1944** WILSON *Moonshine* 88 The sanguinary adjective too that sounds so daring but really has no significance whatever, he used [c1880s] between every second word, even between syllables as 'I bloody well told the bloody mongrel that he was too ego-bloody-tistical.' After the first few sentences this gave no gain in force and much loss in time.

bloody Spaniard: see SPANIARD 2 (1).

blow, *v.*[1] [Mainly Brit. dial. *blow* to deposit eggs: see OED *v.*[1] 28 c; EDD *v.*[1] 10; AND 1827.] *trans.* and *intr.* Of a fly, to deposit eggs on (food, blankets, clothing, etc.).
   1860 in Butler *First Year* (1863) iv 52 The bluebottle flies blow among blankets that are left lying untidily about... Fly-blown blankets are all very well, provided they have been quite dry ever since they were blown. **1878** *TrNZI* X. 308 [The blankets] would then not be 'blown' [by flies]. **1967** MAY *West Coast Gold Rushes* (1962) 277 Bush flies, mosquitoes and sandflies were numbered among the lesser scourges. Food, blankets and clothes were quickly 'blown'.

   Hence, of sheep, **blowing** *vbl. n.*, the inflicting of fly-strike; **blown** *ppl. a.* [AND 1910], suffering from fly-strike.

1922 PERRY *Sheep Farming* 145 The blowing of sheep is most common during the spring. *Ibid.* 146 A blown sheep is generally noticed to stamp its feet. **1951** DUFF *Shepherd's Calendar* (1961) 17 When I was able to make an examination I found a nest of maggots from an earlier strike at work under the skin... To reach the blown ewe the other one had to stretch across an intervening back.

blow, *v.*[2] [AND 1858.] *intr.* Occas. as **blow off**. To boast; to brag. Also *vbl. n.*
   1864 BARRINGTON *Diary* 19 Jan. in Taylor *Early Travellers* (1959) 398 Found my mate..had been on the spree ever since I left, and had also been blowing about the country we had been to. **1873** BARKER *Station Amusements* 237 I only mention this, not out of any desire to 'blow' about our sheep, but because I want to account for my tender-heartedness. **1887** *Auckland Weekly News* 23 July 7 They compare Auckland with Naples, Nice, Genoa, and Constantinople, and Auckland surpasses all. This is what they call in the colonies 'blowing'. **1888** D'AVIGDOR *Antipodean Notes* 171 To '*blow*' is, in the colonies, to brag or boast; this is graphic if not elegant. **1917** *Chron. NZEF* 5 Sept. 35 I [didn't] care about blowin' about it. **1946** SOLJAK *NZ* 116 The following New Zealand expressions derive from British dialects. *blow*: to boast **1988** MCGILL *Dict. Kiwi Slang* 16 *blowing/blowing off* boasting or talking too much; eg 'Bill's blowing off again about his prowess with the cue.'

blow, *v.*[3] [AND *dry blow*, 1894: see OED *v.*[1] 16.] *trans.* To clean (a mineral, esp. gold) by blowing air over it to remove the particles of the material in which it was found. Cf. DRY-BLOWING.
   1874 BATHGATE *Col. Experiences* 217 'By the time I [*sc.* a bank clerk] had cleaned, or 'blown' the gold, it was too late to think of returning. *Ibid.* 220 The gold is placed on a flat pear-shaped metal dish, with a perpendicular rim or edge except at the point of the pear, where there is no rim. This is moved in such a manner that the gold is tossed up, and all the finer particles and dirt are worked forward towards the opening, out by which the operator blows the sand.

blow, *v.*[4] Forming various phrasal verbs.

1. As **blow in** [see OED *v.*[1] 9 d 'Chiefly *U.S.*', 1886], to spend recklessly, to squander. Also *absol.* See also BLUE *v.*[1]
   1906 *Truth* 31 Mar. 6 If you 'blew in' at the races, Then you 'whip the flaming cat'. **1910** *Truth* 5 Mar. 7 John Richard Bourke got his wages last Saturday..and at once started to blow in for a lot of it on booze. **1939** BEATTIE *First White Boy Born Otago* 170 It appeared that from October to Christmas he had made £2000 and he was now engaged in 'blowing it in'. He was reeling down the street. **1946** SARGESON *That Summer* 34 He'd go to town and blow his money in.

2. With senses 'clear out', leave (hurriedly): as **blow off (blow out, blow through)**. Cf. SHOOT THROUGH.
   1917 *NZ at the Front* 9 And Sol 'blew' off, happy in the thought that the 'bull-ring' was dodged for that day, anyhow. **1938** HYDE *Nor Yrs. Condemn* 213 But that night..Starkie packed his bags and blew out. **1941** Used in the Royal NZ Air Force p.c. M. Singe May 1951 (Wellington). I'll just blow through now. **a1974** SYDER & HODGETTS *Austral. & NZ Eng.* (TS) 76 *To blow through*. To depart quickly, in order to avoid trouble of his own making. a. 'There was a lot of money unaccounted for in the ledgers and he was the bookkeeper. So he blew through. He hasn't been heard of from that day to this.' b. To depart quickly with very little announcement. 'Oh, he blew through—he went off up North somewhere, I think.'

blow, *v.*[5] In the phr. **to blow out** (someone's) **light(s)**, to give someone a beating.
   1982 NEWBOLD *Big Huey* 245 Blow (someone's) lights (v) Knock somebody out, kill somebody. **1984** BEATON *Outside In* 23 Sandy:.. An' Ginny yelled... an' up an' rushes this chick, like she was gunna blow her [*sc.* the chick's] lights out. *Ibid.* 109 *blow out (someone's) light*: to give someone a good hiding.

blow, *v.*[6] In the phr. **blow that for a joke**, an elaboration of *blow*! or *blow that*!, an expression of exasperation, or dismissal of an unwanted suggestion.
   a1974 SYDER & HODGETTS *Austral. & NZ Eng.* (TS) 75 *Blow that for a joke*. An acid dismissal of a proposition, in which the speaker has been asked to participate; in the daily round of work, or in social life. 'What! Mac and I've done all the organizing and you others won't do a little job like this. Blow that for a joke!' 'I've done the late shift for three weeks, because none of you other jokers was willing. I won't do it continuously. Blow that for a joke!' **1988** MCGILL *Dict. Kiwi Slang* 16 *blow that for a joke!* emphatic rejection; 'blow' euphemistic curse; eg 'Me referee that lot? Blow that for a joke!'

blow, *n.*[1] Mining. [f. *blow* to erupt: see OED *n.*[1] 1 d, and *v.*[1] 26 c *blow out*; AND 1871.] An isolated outcrop of mineral (esp. quartz).
   1879 BARRY *Up & Down* 224 I came to the conclusion that the lode was not a permanent one, but only what is called a 'blow' of quartz. **1897** *AJHR* C-9 9 This great 'blow' of quartz, as the miners term it, strikes to the north-west. **1908** *NZGeol.SB (NS)* No.5 65 So far as one could judge from a surface examination, the outcrops appear to be isolated blocks of quartz or 'blows' that follow the foliation planes of the schist. **1939** *Ibid.* No.39 104 In places [scheelite] occurs as blows in the quartz in sufficient quantity to be sorted by hand-picking. **1948** *Ibid.* No.42 54 An immense 'blow' of quartz 150ft by 100ft on the surface, and standing 30ft above the surrounding ground was located in 1872 on the Rainy Creek property. **1983** NOLAN *Gold Fossicker's Handbook* 111 Blow: a large outcropping reef, usually of barren quartz.

blow, *n.*[2] [AND 1867.] Boasting; skite.
   1885 *Lyttelton Times* in Bailey & Roth *Shanties* (1967) 74 They'll give that cruising Russian lot, Some real Colonial 'blow'. **1890** FIRTH *Nation Making* 307 His merry laughter at our 'blow.' **1908** *Truth* 14 Mar. 3 Blow, pure blow; much more of it and you'd bust. **1953** 15 M A28 Thames DHS 17 Blow [boasting]

blow, *n.*[3] Shearing. [Prob. f. Brit. dial.: see EDD Suppl. *blow* 5. a sheep shearing term; the mark or ridge left by the shears. (Somerset); OED *n.*[1] 1 c; AND 1870.] **a.** A stroke of the shears or handpiece.
   1875 *Otago Witness* (Dunedin) 18 Sept. 18 Every sheep to be shorn closely and cleanly, and the fleece taken off whole. 'Tomahawking' will in no case be allowed, neither will clipping or chopping be tolerated; the wool must be taken off at first blow. **1938** BURDON *High Country* 84 The sheep they shore were not so well woolled on the belly..so that fewer short blows were required to take off the trimmings. **1949** NEWTON *High Country Days* 49 With a few deft 'blows' the ringer had cleaned out the crutch. **1955** BOWEN *Wool Away* 6 A minimum of blows applied on the sheep should be aimed at... On good average-shearing crossbred sheep anything from fifty to sixty blows is satisfactory. **1973** FERNANDEZ *Tussock Fever* 3 Ten bodies bent over the sheep, bring off the fleeces with deft, sweeping blows.

b. As **long blow** [AND 1904], a shearing stroke which extends from the tail to the neck. See esp. quots. 1968, 1990.

c1927 SMITH *Sheep & Wool Industry* 77 The shearer now gets in a long blow with the machine, running from the britch end to the top of the neck. **1949** NEWTON *High Country Days* 49 Laying his sheep full length he swung into the 'long blow'—from rump to neck. **1955** BOWEN *Wool Away* 30 The shearer still has a long awkward long blow, almost from the tail to the head, and tends to make more second cuts than with the new style. **1968** *Straight Furrow* 21 Feb. 20 Long blow: The shearing strokes, usually five in number, along the sheep's back as it lies on the board. 'The finest blow in shearing'. **1986** RICHARDS *Off the Sheep's Back* 97 It made a fast neck and long blow. **1990** MARTIN *Forgotten Worker* 90 Two changes of technique in the early twentieth century revolutionised shearing—the 'long blow' and the 'Maori belly wool'. The long blow was developed by Jim Power, who held the machine-shearing record at that time, and involved laying the sheep flat on the board. Godfrey Bowen describes this as 'one of the hardest positions to master', but the key to quick shearing. The long blow entailed about half a dozen long unbroken movements along the back of the sheep from tail to neck.

Hence **long blow** v.

1989 RICHARDS *Pioneer's Life* 51 Six shearers 'long blowing' together would cause [the engine] to grunt and groan.

blow, n.[4] *Mining*. [Cf. OED n.[2] 1 d *Obs.* by 1720, a blast of gunpowder.] A rock-blasting explosion.

1973 MCCARTHY *Listen..!* 52 They were all good miners..Jimmy and Jack were putting up the set, that is, were timbering the walls and roof, which was necessary to prevent the walls and roof collapsing when the next 'blow' took place.

blow, n.[5] [Apparently rare in Brit. English: see OED n.[2] 1611, 1875 only.] A deposit of blowfly eggs. Cf. BLOW v.[1]

1952 THOMSON *Deer Hunter* 71 In the summer months, with the countless number of 'blue-bottles' (blowflies) the 'blows' would hatch out in a few hours, and by the end of the day a carcass would be a seething mass of maggots.

blow-fly.

1. As **Maori** (or **native**) **blow-fly**, either of two large indigenous blowflies *Calliphora stygia* or *C. quadrimaculata* (fam. Calliphoridae).

1882 HAY *Brighter Britain* I. 155 There is another of our insect enemies which must have special mention and that is the Maori blow-fly. **1922** *NZJST* IV. 275 Native blow-flies (*Calliphora quadrimaculata*) were very much more abundant in the country districts than they are now.

2. In the phr. **as busy as a blowfly**, very busy.

1951 PARK *Witch's Thorn* 140 The two bartenders..were all as busy as blowflies.

3. Special Comb. **blowfly cake**, see quot.

1992 PARK *Fence around the Cuckoo* 87 With the tea I bore a large wedge of what was known as blowfly cake, light fruit cake composed of fossilised lemon peel and raisins loosely connected by vivid yellow material.

blowhole.

1. [Prob. f. a resemblance to the water-jet effects associated with *blow-hole*, the breathing hole of a whale: AND 1849.] A small surface vent of a sea-cave through which water spurts in response to the pressure of waves.

[**1838** POLACK *NZ* II. 138 One of the caves on Poriwoa, is excavated close to the water's edge, and, refilling at half flood tide, the approaching waves cause a peculiar hollow noise on entering this submarine cavern, and are again spouted forth to some height, with a noise and appearance similar to the spouting from the spiracle of the right whale; it is named in consequence, by the natives, *Mungi no te tohora*, (Whale's Mouth.)] **1892** CARRICK *NZ's Lone Lands* 59 One or two blow-holes..through which the water rushed with incessant roar, did attract attention; but they failed to inspire either wonder or admiration. **1916** *TrNZI* XLVIII. 249 [They] inform me that during southerly weather the waves strike these cliffs and splash right over the top. They were under the impression that there was a 'blowhole' in the island. **1939** BEATTIE *First White Boy Born Otago* 19 The blowhole was at the Point [near Waikouaiti], and there was another one at Bobby's Head farther north. **1966** *Encycl. NZ* II. 889 When it is rough, thunderous booming and rumbling noises accompany geyser-like jets of water and compressed air from the blowholes as the sea rushes in and out of the caves and chambers. **1970** JOHNSON *Life's Vagaries* 59 The ocean swell slid up the faces of those high jagged rocks to..enter some narrow cave to be driven out by the compressed air with the report of a gun and a column of spray: a true blowhole. **1987** *Dominion* (Wellington) 7 Dec. 6 The Punakaiki blowholes turned on a spectacular display for a crowd..at the opening of the Paparoa National Park.

2. A volcanic steam or gas vent.

1957 GOLDBLATT *Democracy at Ease* 19 Not many miles away, the ceaseless deafening roar of Wairakei's blow holes. **1962** *Listener* 11 Jan. 57 The whole thermal area of the North Island [of New Zealand], with its hot pools and geysers and blowholes.

blowie. [AND 1916.] A blow-fly.

1985 MCGILL *G'day Country* 98 We stopped. You could hear two sounds, a blowie and a bellbird. **1987** SLIGO *Final Things* 40 Benedict didn't roast blowies any more over a candle. **1989** *Pacific Way* Jan. 11 In summer we buy aerosols to ward off the mossies and blowies.

blubber, *attrib. Whaling*. [Various *attrib.* uses of *blubber* the fat of cetaceans.] Special Comb. **blubber boat**, a small boat used for transporting blubber from a whale carcass to the try-works; **blubber-flencher**, one who strips blubber from whales; **blubber knife**, a knife or knife-like instrument used to slice (blocks of) blubber usu. for the try-pot (cf. also *bounding knife* (BOUND v.); **blubber room**, a place below deck where blubber is tried out; **blubber spade**, see quot. 1892 (see also *boat spade* (BOAT); **blubber way**, the skids or sloping platform up which blubber is hauled.

1836 *Piraki Log* 18 June (1911) 37 Carpenter repairing old **blubber boat**. **1922** COWAN *NZ Wars* (1955) I. 10 Lean, hard-worked hunters of the world's biggest game; harpooners, and oarsmen, and **blubber-flenchers** from all the sea-faring countries of the world. **1836 blubber knife** [see *blubber room* below]. **1837** *Piraki Log* (1911) 49 1 Cutting Spade 8/-... 2 Boat Spades ... 4 Boat axes -..4/- ea... 5 Boat Knives -..2/- ea... 2 Blubber Knives. **1924** *Otago Witness* (Dunedin) 18 Mar. 44 Mata, and blubber knives, are another important link. **1836** RHODES *Jrnl. Barque 'Australian'* 5 Sept. (1954) 15 The 3rd Mate having a slight quarrel with one of the men in the **blubber room** about a steel to sharpen the blubber or bounding knife, and the work being retarded by his not bounding, the Captain took the knife and bounded. **1837** *Piraki Log* (1911) 51 The Peple Employed in Macking the Blubber Rum. **1838** blubber room [see *blanket piece* (BLANKET n. 3)]. **1892** Osborn in RICHARDS *Foveaux Whaling Yarns* (1995) 20 This operation continues until the blubber is all peeled off and deposited in the blubber room, where it is cut up into 'horse chunks' about eight inches square. **1892** *op. cit.* 20 Two men now [after the whale is fastened alongside] get on the outside of the ship on a platform, each armed with a sharp **blubber spade**, which is about six by eight inches, welded to a shank of iron half an inch thick and four feet long, the whole being fastened to a wood handle twelve feet long, with which they begin to cut out a strip of blubber about three feet in width. **1838** *Piraki Log* 19 Mar. (1911) 68 men employed making the **Blubber way**.

blucher. *Hist.* [Not exclusively NZ, but of special significance as part of the early colonial outdoors costume: see OED 1831; AND 1839.] Usu. *pl.* In full **blucher boot**. A strong leather half-boot.

1856 FITTON *NZ* 83. Boots and shoes... Napoleons, 35s... per pair; Wellingtons, English, 30s..; colonial, 35s..per pair; Bluchers and Oxford..12s. **1863** STICHBURY *Diary of Capt. James Stichbury* 24 July in Cowan *NZ Wars* (1955) I. 461 Served out with regimental clothes. They were forage cap with topknot, blue-serge shirt, trousers.., blucher boots, short leggings. **c1875** *Otago Guardian* in Tonkin *Dunedin Gaol* (1980) 17 Bluchers of good hard leather, flat and thick in the soles. **1906** PICARD *Ups & Downs* 7 The waster that has a bad word for him isn't fit for you to wipe your hob-nailed bloody bluchers on. **1912** MANSFIELD *Stories* (1984) 111 Her front teeth were knocked out, she had red pulpy hands, and she wore on her feet a pair of dirty 'Bluchers'. **1922** MANSFIELD *Stories* (1984) 475 A pair of old bluchers was on one side of the door, and a large red watering-can on the other. **1963** CAMPBELL *Golden North* 111 I wore long dungarees and blucher boots and stood by a planing machine at the mill. **1972** REED *Gumdiggers* 51 [The gumdigger's] essentials were dungaree trousers, with leather belt, short-sleeved flannel shirt, blucher boots (socks were rarely worn), a cap or wide-brimmed felt hat. **1982** AYTON *Diary* x Working in the wet was hard on footwear, and boots were a heavy item in clothing expenditure. Some wore 'bluchers', a short boot; gumboots do not seem to have been in general use until the twentieth century.

bludge, v. [A back-formation f. BLUDGER: AND (in various senses) 1899.]

1. [AND v. 4, 1954.] *trans.* and *intr.* Often with **on**, to cadge, scrounge; sponge (on). Often with a weakened sense in mod. use (see quot. 1986).

1945 WEBBER *Johnny Enzed in Middle East* 43 Those oysters you bludged from me. **1950** *Canterbury Mountaineer* 93 We bludged our way into a bus and went down to the Franz Joseph. **1959** SLATTER *Gun in My Hand* 44 What in hell are ya doin in Christchurch anyway? Bludgin on social security, I spose. *Ibid.* 47 I was nearly bowled over by some officer being thrown out. Trying to bludge in on their party he was. **1964** HELMER *Stag Party* 103 We strolled up to see Russ Tullock. 'Maybe bludge a drink,' Crump said. 'Haven't a drop in the house, lads,' said Russ. **1986** ROBINSON *Heroes & Sparrows* 70 I sometimes joke about what I call 'the worldwide freemasonry of runners' which makes it possible..to bludge a spare bed in any city in the world. **1991** *Dominion Sunday Times* (Wellington) 8 Dec. 9 Streetlife remembers Joseph starting Wednesday morning downtown, 'bludging, looking for a feed'.

2. *intr.* or *absol.* Orig. WW2. *Army*. To enjoy a job at base; to live at ease or in apparent safety at the front-line soldier's expense: hence to cadge, to live by cadging.

1939–45 *Expressions and Sayings 2NZEF* (Nat. Archiv. TS WAII DA 420/1) Bludge—Procure by any means, dishonest or otherwise. Dodge work and risks. **1944** FULLARTON *Troop Target* 186 He'll immediately assume that you were one of the 95% who bludged at base in Enzed or England or Yankee Land.

Hence **bludging** *vbl. n.* and *ppl. a.* [AND 1903], cadging, loafing; in WW2 (North Africa), being, or playing the part of, a 'base bludger' or one with a job at base; *spec.* **dole-bludging** [AND 1978], an offensive term for living on State benefit payments.

1942 *NZEF Times* 21 Dec. 17 Back at base, they set the pace, when bludgin' was an art. **1947** DAVIN *For Rest of Our Lives* 304 Well, how do you like the idea of a bit of bludging at Div HQ, Curly? **1960** BAXTER *Collected Poems* (1980) 219 He's got no time for any man bludging. I owe him [*sc.* the publican] for a grunter and a bottle And he'll think I'm dodging. **1963** CASEY *As Short a Spring* 194 We came on a bludging trip. Can you let John have Padre to ride for a day or two? **1988** *Listener* 24 Dec. 6 Although there is less talk of dole-bludging these days there is still an unrelenting criticism from pockets in the community.

bludge, *n.* [A back-formation from BLUDGER.] An act (or the process) of cadging or sponging. In the phr. **on the bludge**, on the cadge, intent on borrowing.

1948 in Pearson *Six Stories* (1991) 31 The Egyptian kids..were more than usually on the bludge. **1974** MORRIESON *Predicament* (1981) 202 I suppose you're on the bludge as usual? Why don't you earn it this time? **1985** *Listener* 9 Feb. 28 Don't you know that. It's a bludge. I'm just a bludger.

bludger. [A shortened form of *bludgeoner* a prostitutes' pimp.]

1. *Obs. Rare.* [OED 1842.] A criminal who uses a bludgeon.

1906 *Truth* 10 Feb. 7 Was Griffiths Brutally Butchered by Bludgers?

2. *Obs.* [AND 1882.] A man who lives with or on the earnings of a prostitute; a prostitute's pimp.

1906 *Truth* 11 Aug. 5 Bludger and Bawd and Their Brats:.. He allowed his wife to go out battling..of nights while he stayed home. *Ibid.* 25 Aug. 5 What, in slang phrase, we call a 'bludger', or a species of un-human being that lives on the proceeds of an 'unfortunate's' prostitution. **1936** HYDE *Passport to Hell* 103 In the noon heat everything in Cairo slept except..the male defenders of the prostitutes' quarters, known to the dictionary as *souteneurs*, and to the troops as bludgers.

3. a. [AND 1900.] A useless person; one who avoids responsibility or (*fig.*) 'lives on the back' of deserving people; a loafer, an idler. Often merely a term of abuse.

1906 *Truth* 8 Sept. 4 What type of skunk Costello is can be gathered from the fact that he is an individual of the bludger class, who will never attempt anything in the form of honest hard work. **1953** HAMILTON *Till Human Voices Wake Us* 89 But connected with him it didn't mean what it was supposed to mean. A bludger is a pimp, a man who lives on women, but I doubt if anyone thought specifically that of him. Bludger is also what it sounds, a fairly indiscriminate term of abuse. When the boobheads called him that they meant a lot of things. A bully, something sly, a chap who'd put a dirty one on to you, not necessarily for any purpose other than it gave him pleasure to do so. **1960** CRUMP *Good Keen Man* 60 As far as he was concerned, he said, bludgers [*sc.* members of a search-and-rescue party] could stay lost if they didn't have the sense to follow a creek. **1963** MORRIESON *Scarecrow* 3 Uncle Athol is a bludger, a prize bludger... If [he] ever whipped up a bead of honest sweat in his whole life I would appreciate finding out just where. **1988** *Dominion* (Wellington) 11 Nov. 2 Social Welfare minister Michael Cullen spoke out yesterday against those who criticised beneficiaries as 'undeserving' or 'idle bludgers'.

b. *spec.* as **dole bludger** [AND 1976], an offensive term for an unemployed person living on a State benefit and regarded as a scrounging loafer.

1983 *Listener* 20 Aug. 136 The term 'dole bludger' was not, for instance, uttered even once from the [National Party] conference floor during the recent party get-together in Dunedin. **1984** *Landfall* 150 148 She never used the term 'dole bludger' except in the most ironic tones. **1991** *Metro* (Auckland) Apr. 142 200,000 dole bludgers queuing up in the Hawkes Bay to pick squash.

4. a. WW2. A serviceman who has a safe job at base or who shirks, or appears to shirk, active service.

1943 WAGENER *Kiwi's Soliloquy* 7 'The Bludger' typifies the Div. man's contempt for a certain type who were numerous enough at one time in a certain part of Maadi Camp to earn for it the title 'Bludgers' Hill'. **1959** SLATTER *Gun in My Hand* 92 Nobody put up stripes in our outfit. That was for base bludgers. **1975** DAVIN *Breathing Spaces* 124 You should be jake sitting out the rest of the war in some bludger's job in Trentham [Military Camp]. **1986** DAVIN *Salamander & the Fire* 79 As if a man could sign off like that and let his cobbers go out on their own while he sat on his arse in Maadi, being a bloody bludger.

b. In the collocation **Bludgers' hill** (also **Daffodil Hill**). WW2. A piece of rising ground in Maadi Camp near Cairo, on which the NZ Divisional Headquarters was established.

1942 *NZEF Times* 21 Dec. 18 They sent ole Bill to Bludgers' Hill, and jacked him up a stripe. **1944** HELM *Fights & Furloughs* 8 The hill that has since become famous in the 2NZEF, Bludgers' Hill, or Daffodil Hill (beautiful but yellow) as it is now known. **1949** KIPPENBERGER *Infantry Brigadier* 10 The Fourth Brigade Headquarters was established on the Hill..to be derisively and unfairly known as 'Bludgers' Hill'. **1968** SLATTER *Pagan Game* 66 This chap finally admitted he had never come down from Bludgers' Hill. **1982** *Evening Post* (Wellington) 4 Oct. 41 Maadi, once known to thousands of New Zealanders as 'Bludger's Hill'—the site of Freyberg's headquarters, the training camp and the main camp for those on leave from the front—is unrecognisable.

5 a. [AND 1955.] A persistent scrounger; an inveterate cadger; a sponger.

1942 *NZEF Times* 21 Dec. 17 Some bludger's got my tin hat. **1968** BAXTER *Collected Plays* (1982) 39 We'll go up North and start a boarding house. No bludgers allowed. **1970** Baxter in Moeller *In their Own Words* 60 They'd say you must have a lot of bludgers and parasites. I've said sometimes, yes, the bludger or the parasite is a jewel hidden in a ball of mud. **1980** LELAND *Kiwi-Yankee Dict.* 15 To bludge is to borrow. It's socially acceptable to say 'may I bludge a cigarette (or a cup of sugar)' but calling someone a bludger can be a fighting insult.

b. In the collocation **bludger's fish.** WITCH, which has little flesh on its bones. Cf. CADGER'S FISH.

1981 WILSON *Fisherman's Bible* 74 Megrim... Known to Christchurch fishermen in early years as the Bludger's Fish. It was the fish they handed out to well-known bludgers who came down to the docks to cadge fish.

blue, *a.*

1. In special collocations of *blue* in literal or fig. uses: **blue blind** *a. obs.* [f. *blue* drunk + *blind* drunk: see OED; AND *Obs.*, 1911–18], very drunk; **blue blister** *Otago obs.*, a familiar term (prob. f. the colour), for an early form of local currency; a promissory note on a prominent businessman; **blue boy** a *WW1* (also **blue coat**) [f. the colour of the special hospital clothing], a convalescent wounded serviceman; **b** [f. the colour], the twopenny value of the 1931 Health Stamps; **blue fit** [transf., orig. a fit of apoplexy] in the phr. **to have a blue fit**, to become very angry or shocked (esp. at untoward or unexpected behaviour); **blue flu** *police* [a play on colour of the police uniform], the taking of unjustified sick leave by police, esp. mass sick leave in lieu of striking; **blue lady** [f. the bluish colouring of the emetic additive], among street alcoholics, methylated spirits as a drink; **blue lips** [f. the colour of the lower lip moko], a Maori woman (see also *blueskin* below); **blue meanie**, a variety of 'magic mushroom'; **Blue Mountains** in the phr. **beyond the Blue Mountains**, used of an early children's game (the name *Blue Mountains* is well-known as a place-name in Australia, and locally in New Zealand); **blue orchid** WW2 [f. the colour of uniform, and an allusion to supposed hothouse cosseting: AND 1940 for RAAF], a derisive Army name for RNZAF and other airforce men; **blue peter**, see PETER $n.^2$, cf. BLUEY $n.^1$ 7; **blue pugaree** WW1, usu. *pl.*, a military policeman; **blue shirt**, *obs.*, see quot.; **blue skin** *hist.* [f. the colour of moko], an early whalers' nickname for a tattooed Maori (cf. *blue-lips* above); **blue-tongue** (a) [AND 1900: f. the reputed sleepiness of blue-tongued lizards], a ROUSEABOUT; (b) applied offensively to a Maori; **blue vein** [mainly provincial in Brit. use in the form *blue-veined* or *blue-veiny* (Dorset 1892): see OED *blue-veined*], also **blue-veined cheese**, see quot. 1982.

1921 LORD *Ballads of Bung 'Stunology'* (1976) I nearly forgot to mention '**blue blind**', 'bunkered', and 'brimful', As well as on 'a bender'. **1912** WILSON ed. *Reminisc. Early Settlement Dunedin* 68 We got no ready money as pay [for shearing c1860s] but a '**blue blister**', i.e., a cheque on Johnny Jones. **1916** *Chron. NZEF* 30 Aug. 12 [The patients you meet at every corner, landmarks of blue—those well-fitting faultlessly tailored blues!] *Ibid.* 29 Sept. 59 It was infinitely touching to see some of the Blue Boys making the beds..for their wounded comrades. **1917** INGRAM *Anzac Diary* 28 Oct. (1987) 73 Our host was one of the many kindly Londoners who call at Hospitals on Sundays and take out 'Blue-boys' for an airing. **1947** *NZ Observer* 29 Jan. 8 Roughly 75,000 of the 'red boy' and 112,000 of the '**blue boy**' were sold. **1977** *Captain Cook* V. 105 This..was the first that most New Zealanders read about the two stamps now known as the 'Red and Blue Boys'. **1988** GWYNN *Collecting NZ Stamps* 93 The 1d 'red boy' was sold in considerably smaller quantities than the 2d 'blue boy', and is the scarcer of the two stamps in used condition. **1936** HYDE *Passport to Hell* 131 'Yes,' nodded a fellow **blue coat**, 'I could do with a popgun like that myself. How does he work, Starkie?' **1938** HYDE *Nor Yrs. Condemn* 35 Sister Collins went out into the thankful darkness of the hall, and sat behind the Bluecoats. **1946** SARGESON *That Summer* 139 He was a regular hard case to talk to, his aunt would have a **blue-fit** [*sic*] if she found out. **1990** *Dominion* (Wellington) 16 Feb. 3 Christchurch police say they are threatening to take '**blue flu**' sick leave to get around illegal strike action out of bitterness toward planned cuts to their superannuation scheme. **1988** *Dominion Sunday Times* (Wellington) 14 Feb. 19 Meths is **blue** or white **lady**, and steam is a mixture of meths and sherry. **1871** MEADE *Ride through Disturbed Dist.* in Taylor *Early Travellers* (1959) 441 The custom of tattooing is now falling out of fashion amongst the rising generation of both sexes, and it is to be hoped that before many years have passed, the nickname of '**Blue-lips**' will no longer be applicable to the native girls of New Zealand. **1924** LYSNAR *NZ* 72 For the young women this ornamentation [*sc.* moko] was limited to the lips, and the name 'blue-lips' was given to them by the English. Red lips were looked upon as a reproach or disfigurement. **1991** *Dominion* (Wellington) 13 May 1 Invercargill police said..there had been an upsurge in the number of people out looking for the mushrooms, colloquially known as **blue-meanies** and gold tops. [**1863** PYKE *Report* in *Handbook NZ Mines* (1887) 9 There was indeed, a small rush to what were termed [in Otago] the Blue Mountains. **1932** *Tararua Tramper* Nov. 4 Tramp from Silverstream to Blue Mountains and camp on Mr. Jones' place [in the Hutt Valley].] **1899** MANSFIELD *Stories* (1984) 7 I played a game which had no ending or beginning, but was called 'Beyond the **Blue Mountains**'. The scene was generally placed near the rhubarb beds, and Pat officiated as the villain, the hero, and even the villainess, with unfailing charm. **1941** p.c. Professor R. Clarke, Wellington (1972). **Blue Orchid** used in 1941 by New Zealand soldiers in the Pacific for Air Force personnel. **1944** *Korero* (AEWS Background Bulletin) 17 July 24 Whereas the B.E.F. has its name for the R.A.F. 'Brylcreem boys', the New-Zealander prefers 'blue orchids', thus perpetuating the name of a happily long-forgotten blues dance-number. **1945** HENDERSON *Gunner Inglorious* 160 'Oh Christ.... oh whackoh! Oh boy, see that one! That'll show the greasy bastards.' 'Oh you beautiful blue orchids, oh you beauties, you'll do us.' Cruuuuump! **1959** SLATTER *Gun in My Hand* 59 We hated those damned blue orchids laughing at us from the cockpit and flying home to sheets on the bed. **1970** SLATTER *On the Ball* 139 All of us jammed together on the terrace, New Zealanders to a man, soldiers, sailors and blue orchids, too. **1914** in *Hist. N. Otago from 1853* (1978) 117 Shouting colourful epithets at them, and waving a Maori kit which contained her supper in a '**Blue Peter**', she [*sc.* the tipsy woman] chased them down the platform. *Ibid.* 125 It is doubtful if ever again [as in the 1890s] we will see..men and women drinking beer from 'square-riggers' and 'blue peters' in doorways or on the sidewalks. **c1930s** [see PETER *n.*²]. **1949** DAVIN *Roads From Home* 50 I've got a couple of Blue Peters at my place. **1955** [see PETER *n.*²]. **1937** PARTRIDGE *Dict. Slang* 70 *blue pugaree.* (Gen. pl.) A military policeman: New Zealand soldiers': 1915–18. Ex the distinctive colour of their hat-bands. **1874** BAINES *Edward Crewe* 39 [Heading] *Bush fashion.* He [a Northland sawmiller] wore what is called a '**blue shirt**', that is, a sailor's shirt of serge, fitting very closely, and a pair of moleskin trousers..and a wideawake hat. **1939** BEATTIE *First White Boy Born Otago* 22 I do not know Tommy Roundhead's Maori name, but there was a heavily tattooed Maori known to the whalers as **Blueskin**, and Blueskin Bay at Waitati was named after him, although Blueskin Beach at Goodwood was named because of a plant with berries with a blue skin... The old chief at Blueskin Bay was very blue in his tattoo. **1988** *More* (Auckland) Mar. 31 A rouseabout—also variously known as a rousie, woolhandler, shedhand, fleeco..or a **blue tongue**. **1960-70s** p.c. 1980 H. Wilford (Hastings). Blue tongue heard in Whakatu Freezing Works, Hastings, as an offensive reference for a Maori. **1959** MCLINTOCK *Descr. Atlas* 58 The main kind of cheese produced is 'cheddar', with one factory at Eltham producing '**blue vein**' cheese. **1977** HUNT *Drunkards' Garden* 11 Don't ever trust that guy, The one with freckled knees A stutter and a sly Old dog called Blue Vein Cheese. **1982** BURTON *Two Hundred Yrs. NZ Food* 51 Blue vein belongs to that family of cheeses which in England is called stilton, in France roquefort,

in Italy gorgonzola, and in Denmark Danish blue. New Zealand blue vein is recognised as a blue cheese in its own right and can be distinguished from its Continental counterparts by the deeper yellow colour of its curd. This arises from a difference in milk colour.

2. In the names of plants and animals. a. As a modifier, see: BORAGE, COD 2 (3), CRANE a, DUCK 2 (2) a, GRASS 2 (5), GRENADIER *n.*², HAKE 2 (1), MACKEREL 2 (1), MAOMAO 2 (1), MUSSEL 2 (1), PENGUIN 2 (1), SHAG 2 (3), SHARK 2 (3), TUSSOCK 3 (1), WAREHOU 2 (1), WHALE 2 (3).

b. In special collocations: **blue-billy** *Chatham Islands,* broad-billed prion (PRION 2 *Pachyptila vittata vittata*, see also quot. 1952); **blue-bone,** BUTTERFISH 1; **blue-bonnet** (also familiarly **bluey**), a small bottom-living marine fish *Hemerocoetes artus* of the opalfish family Percophidae, having bright blue head markings; **blue-cap** [f. Brit. dial.: cf. OED 3 'a salmon in its first year;.. so called because it has a blue spot on its head'], see *blue-bonnet* above; **bluefin (bluefin tuna)**, see TUNA *n.*²; **bluefish** [AND 1790, 2 quots. only], an uncommon bright blue edible marine fish, *Girella cyanea* (fam. Kyphosidae) often found near reefs and headlands (see also KOROKORO-POUNAMU); **bluegill** (also **blue-gills**) (a) KOKAKO 2 (1), (b) *blue-gilled bully* (BULLY *n.*¹ 2 (1)); **blue-heeler** [AND 1908], any of a breed of medium-sized dogs with a dappled or bluish red-flecked coat, bred in Australia and New Zealand as cattle-dogs; **blue-hen** *West Coast obs.*, grey kiwi (KIWI 2 (3)); **blue-jaw,** BLUENOSE; **blue moon** [see quot. 1924], an Australian butterfly *Hypolimnas bolina nerina* (fam. Nymphalidae), the male having a large rounded white central spot on each wing broadly margined with iridescent purplish blue; **blue pointer**, see SHARK 2 (4); **blue top** [f. its flowers], naturalized *Verbena* spp. (fam. Verbenaceae) perennial weeds from tropical and subtropical America (see also GRIFFIN WEED, *missionary weed* (MISSIONARY *n.* 2 b)); **blue weed**, *blue borage* (BORAGE), and occas. applied to a vervain; **blue whistling duck**, see DUCK 2 (8).

1872 *TrNZI* IV. 65 Amongst birds he has obtained [at the Chathams] are..a sea-bird, called by the whalers the '**Blue Billy**', the beak of which is singularly shaped, and of a blue colour, hence its trivial name. [**1952** RICHARDS *Chatham Is.* 86 *Prion..vittatus...* These tiny birds are light grey above. The blue bill is very wide and edges of the upper mandible turn upwards.] **1966** FALLA et al. *Birds NZ* 38 Broad-billed Prion *Pachyptila vittata...* Parara, Blue Billy (Chathams). **1985** [see PRION 2]. **c1920** BEATTIE *Trad. Lifeways Southern Maori* (1994) 501 The kelp fish of Canterbury is the **Blue–bone** of Nelson and may be the Green–bone of Southland. **1956** GRAHAM *Treasury NZ Fishes* 316 *Hemerocoetes Waitei...* The..anglers and fishermen [of Port Chalmers] had various names to distinguish this fish from Opal-fish—which are as follows: Bluey, Blue-cap, **Blue-Bonnet**, which I have used. **1967** NATUSCH *Animals NZ* 226 The opal fish and blue bonnet are two handsome and colourful species of *Hemerocoetes*. **1956 blue-cap** [see *blue-bonnet* above]. **1892** *TrNZI* XXXIV. 210 From Cape Maria van Diemen a number of fish termed '**blue-fish**' are recorded... I am quite unable to suggest what fish is meant by 'blue-fish,' unless, indeed, the observer has used the names indiscriminately. These fish were very numerous, were taken during every month of the year... They weighed from 1lb to 2lb each. **1921** *NZJST* IV. 116 *Blue-fish; Korokoropounamu.* A rare and highly esteemed fish,

secured up to 6lb. in deep water off Cape Brett and headlands round Hauraki Gulf... Unknown south of Hauraki Gulf. **1957** PARROTT *Sea Angler's Fishes* 106 The Bluefish... Maori name Korokoropounamu... This beautiful fish has been recorded from the Hauraki Gulf, but is seldom seen south of Whangarei. **1967** NATUSCH *Animals NZ* 221 The handsome bluefish, is bright blue above, paler below, with a sprinkling of golden specks. **1982** AYLING *Collins Guide* (1984) 229 *Bluefish* (Blue drummer, korokoropounamu)... As the name suggests their body colour is a uniform bright blue and all the fins are a similar colour. (a) **1874** *TrNZI* VI. 147 The writer found that in the Wairarapa the *Glaucopis wilsoni* is sometimes familiarly known as '**the blue-gills**.' **1885** *NZJSc.* II. 377 Wattle-bird, Blue Gills, Kokako. **1966** FALLA et al. *Birds NZ* 236 Kokako... Wattled Crow, Organ-bird, Gill-bird, Bluegill (N.I.). **1985** *Reader's Digest Book NZ Birds* 303 North Island Kokako... Other names: *Blue wattled crow, blue gill.* **1989** PARKINSON *Travelling Naturalist* 76 Piopio, whekau..were all present then, together with the kokako, which early Pakeha settlers called 'blue-gills'. (b) **1981** DENNIS *Paparoas Guide* 189 Bluegills are seldom seen owing to the turbulent nature of their habitat. **1960** CRUMP *Good Keen Man* 163 We..went out to the dog-breeder's place. The Waiau blokes bought four bully-looking mongrels..and Vince got himself another **blue-heeler**. **1976** *Spleen* Dec. No.6 19 He starts boiling about three hundred yards away... Jed, the blue-heeler and Puke race after him. **1981** CHARLES *Black Billy Tea* 34 I've lost my dog—my best blue heeler! **1872** *TrNZI* V. 188 Straight-billed kiwi, Grey Kiwi, **Blue-hen** of the [West Coast] diggers. **1885** *NZJSc.* II. 505 *Apteryx oweni*, Gould. Kiwi, Straight-billed Kiwi, Grey Kiwi, Blue hen of the diggers. **1966** DOOGUE & MORELAND *Sea Anglers' Guide* 223 Griffin's Silverfish... *Other names: Seriolella amplus;* **blue-jaw**, bonito; matiri (Maori). **1924** *School Journal* Sept. 249 I [*sc.* Johannes Andersen] have called it the '**blue-moon** butterfly' because it is so rare; it is found only 'once in a blue moon'. Besides, it carries the blue moon on its wings, and it is like other blue moons—it is there all the time, but it is only when you are in certain positions that you can see it. **1936** *Weekly News* 6 May [R. A. Falla Column] Fortunately, Mr. Johannes Anderson [*sic*] has suggested an appropriate trivial name and we may refer to it as the Blue Moon butterfly. **1947** POWELL *Native Animals* 54 Blue Moon (*Hypolimnas bolina*). A great rarity in New Zealand, where it occurs from time to time as a chance migrant, probably from Australia, where it is common. **1954** *NZ Entomologist* I(4). 13 A tattered female specimen of the 'Blue Moon' butterfly was captured by F.C. Caughley on 16.2.54 in a garden in Tinakori Rd Wellington. **1971** *NZ Entomologist* V(1). 75 It is appropriate here to mention the origin of the name Blue Moon Butterfly for *Hypolimnas* in New Zealand. In Australia it is called the Common Eggfly. **1989** PARKINSON *Travelling Naturalist* 170 Butterflies, too, arrive in Westland, some annually. The blue moon, one of the most striking species, turns up each year. **1990** *West Coast Times* 16 May 1 Mr Palma says blue moon butterflies have been reported here as far back as the 1850's. **1926** HILGENDORF *Weeds* 146 Vervain (*Verbena officinalis*), also called **blue top**, griffin weed, and missionary weed, is a slender tough-stemmed perennial 1 to 2 ft high, with a few opposite rough, cleft leaves, and small lilac flowers. **1969** *Standard Common Names Weeds* 6 *blue top* [=] *vervain.* **1926 blue weed** [see BORAGE]. **1969** *Standard Common Names Weeds* 6 *blue weed* [=] *vervain: viper's bugloss.*

3. In mining applications referring to the bluish colour of a particular ground or formation: **blue bottom (reef)** *goldmining* and *geol.*, a blue clay or sandstone formation, auriferous, or underlying auriferous ground (see also BOTTOM *n.* 1); **blue country (ground)** *goldmining*, CEMENT. See also BAR *n.*¹ 2, BLUESTONE.

1892 Pyke *Gold-Miners' Guide* 110 Tunnelling and Driving—Through drift or **blue reef**: 1s.6d. per foot for the first 500ft, 3s.6d. per foot for next 500ft, 4s.6d. per foot for next 500ft. or any portion of 500ft. **1906** *NZ Geol. SB (NS)* No.1 20 The clays and sandstones are called the '**Blue Bottom**'. *Ibid.* 86 The Blue Bottom is so called because it forms the basement formation of the extensive unconsolidated later Tertiary and more recent deposits of the coastal plain, and consists chiefly of blue clay. **1938** *NZ Geol. Memoir* No.4 25 A thin zone of soft decomposed rock which has been buried and preserved beneath overlying beds. This decomposed surface is the 'blue reef' or 'bottom' of the miners, and has been vigorously worked for gold throughout Central Otago. *Ibid.* 55 And it is here assumed to be the marine sandstone of the Blue Bottom. **1898** 'H' *The Grain of Gold* 13 He told of the hard long weeks of 'driving' through 'tight **blue country**' to pick up a reef. **1932** '**blue ground**' [see CEMENT].

blue, *n.*[1] [f. *blue* applied to things (orig.) coloured blue or perceived as blue, often in figurative or transferred use.]

1. [Spec. use of Brit. dial. *blues, blue devils* depression; delirium tremens: see OED *n.* 12; EDD 7 *blue devils*.] As **the blues**, an alcoholic depression; D.T.s.

1867 Thomson *Rambles with Philosopher* 50 There is no keeping him from [drink] as long as there is a *shot in the locker*... I have seen him, when he is in the blues run up the gully as if he had a thousand devils after him. *Ibid.* 51 He said he had been [on the spree] for three weeks, and did not expect *the blues* for a fortnight yet.

2. [f. the colour of the paper orig. used: AND 1939.] **a.** Also as **a bit of blue**, *ellipt.* for BLUE PAPER, a notice of summons to a court. See also BLUEY *n.*[1] 4 a.

1909 *Truth* 13 Mar. 5 He is still a conductor in the tram service, and was shown the blister when Bailey was served with a bit-o'-blue.

b. A hotelkeeper's notice banning an offending customer from admission to or service on the premises.

1988 *Dominion* (Wellington) 4 June 3 The group was issued with 'blues', banning them from the hotel for two years after they began fighting among themselves about 9pm.

3. Mainly WW1 and WW2 (N. Africa) and *mountaineering*. [Prob. f. *blue* the blue sky indicating great distance, infl. by the phr. 'the wild blue yonder': see OED *blue n.* 5, 16 b.] Often as **the blue**, and preceded by prepositions **into, out, up. a.** WW1. Far away from base or a main body of troops.

1918 *Chron. NZEF* 24 May 175 After they were far beyond their guns they led their men on 'into the blue'. **1921** Stewart *NZ Div.* 114 [In the advance by Eaucourt, September 1916] the companies..reported their location..by runner to Battalion Headquarters... It was with some consternation that General Braithwaite.. found his troops in a position so much 'in the blue' as to invite disaster.

b. WW1. and WW2. (Far into) the desert.

1938 Robertson *Cameliers in Palestine* 27 As each man always had to have in stock five days' supply of food and water for himself, and a similar supply of grain for his mount.., the whole [Camel] Brigade could, at an hour's notice, go off into the 'blue' for five days without any communication with or assistance from its base. **1943** *NZEF Times* 12 Apr. 3 We were striking out into the blue... In the desert the unknown is always 'the blue', whether it be Egypt, Cyrenaica..or Tunisia. **1943** Jackson *Passage to Tobruk* 104 Early in the month of September, 1941, the whole battalion moved 'up the blue' (a term used to indicate any portion of the sterile Western Desert) to a place called Baguish. **1947** Davin *For Rest of Our Lives* 209 Those bastards [*sc.* MPs] are too bloody fond of poking the borax at a bloke just back from the blue.

c. *Mountaineering.* In the phr. **into the blue**, into the back country.

1948 *Canterbury Mountaineer* 300 An exceedingly soggy packing-up followed next morning and then it was once more 'into the blue'.

4. *Ellipt.* in the names of animals considered to be of blue appearance: MUSSEL 2 (1), WHALE 2 (3).

1982 Morton *Whale's Wake* 28 The sperm and right whalemen shied away from attacking..rorquals, which is the generic name for finbacks and blues. **1989** *Marlborough Express* (Blenheim) 10 May 20 Blues [*sc.* mussels] are farmed prolifically along the coast of Galicia, Spain's Atlantic seaboard.

5. [AND 1932.] BLUEY *n.*[1] 6 a, a (nickname for a) redhead.

1961 Crump *Hang On a Minute Mate* 80 There was Brian, the young chap;.. Nick, with the ginger beard; and Blue, with red hair. **1987** *Sunday Star* (Auckland) 11 Jan. A7 Andrew James (Blue) Kennedy... Never one to dodge a 'blue' with employers..he was in fact nicknamed for his wiry crop of ginger hair. **1991** Eldred-Grigg *Shining City* 79 Blue was our coach. 'Me name's Blue cause me head's red,' he added.

6. [By metonomy, a wearer of a blue uniform.] *Mount Eden Prison.* A 'trusted' prisoner having special prison duties and privileges.

1989 Newbold *Punish. & Politics* 76 Most inmates [of Mt Eden] still wore brown or white moleskins but trusties, known as 'Blues', wore blue denim trousers.

blue, *n.*[2]

1. [Orig. uncertain, poss. f. *bloomer* a mistake: AND *n.*[2] 3, 1941.] A bad or embarrassing error or blunder, a bloomer, esp. in the phr. **to make** (occas. **put up**) **a blue**.

1954 *Evening Post* (Wellington) 14 July 12 He rang Mr McGavin, Cromwell's solicitor, asking if there could be any 'blues' or defects in title. **1961** Crump *Hang On a Minute Mate* 17 Trouble with your blokes is you won't admit when you've made a blue. **1981** put up a blue [see DONK *n.*[2]]. **1985** Sherwood *Botanist at Bay* 42 Oh Rosie, forgive us, what have we done? Have we made a blue? **1990** Edwards *AWOL* 132 The sailor walked out of the door..and, as far as he was concerned, I'd made a blue.

2. a. [AND *n.*[2] 1, 1943.] An argument, a tiff; a fight.

1956 *Evening Post* (Wellington) 11 Aug. 15 Some brawlers left before the police arrived. 'The bloke who really started the blue isn't here—he shot through,' said Purda. **1965** Watson *Stand in Rain* 110 Abungus came home one night and said he'd had a blue with six Irish seamen, he'd beaten up one of them. **1980** *Evening Post* (Wellington) 25 July 1 Mr Coleman said: 'About six months ago I had a blue with the council about this but I've since straightened it out.' **1988** *Evening Post* (Wellington) 22 Sept. 11 [Heading] Pub notice stops blues. **1995** *Sunday Star-Times* (Auckland) 16 Apr. A5 We ended up in a blue over it. I thought we were going outside for a smoke... I just lost my rag.

b. In the phr. **to send off the blue**, to start a brawl.

1971 *Truth* 20 July 21 Injuries suffered by other trainees included a fracture of the skull, head, face, shoulder and arm lacerations... When arrested..Brown told the police that he 'sent off the blue' because the trainees had been 'razzing' his 'Hell's Angels' associates.

3. A misdemeanour in the eyes of the police or other authority; 'a spot of bother'.

1932 in 1949 Partridge *Dict. Underworld* (1961) 54 *in the blue.* In trouble, esp. with the police: New Zealand: 1932, Nelson Baylis (private letter); extant. Perhaps there is a reference to the blue paper on which summonses are written. **1950** *Here & Now* Nov. 15 For a man on the Collar, every blue he gets in means maybe another two years. **1953** Hamilton *Till Human Voices Wake Us* 127 Bluey had lost his seaman's ticket over his jail blues, and I don't suppose he'll ever get it back. **1982** Newbold *Big Huey* 245 Blue (n) Criminal charge

blue, *v.*[1] [Used elsewhere (OED *v.*[2] 1 1846) but, as in Austral. (so AND 1881), has a distinctive local resonance.] *trans.* In the phr. **to blue a cheque**, to spend recklessly, to blow.

1904 Lancaster *Sons o' Men* 289 If I blue twenty cheques they'll never come back. **1916** Anzac *On Anzac Trail* 72 The boys had had fixed to give us a boncer welcome, but..in the words of our informant, 'they blued their cheques, got shikkared and the show was bust up'. **1952** Meek *Station Days* 110 Blued their cheques: Spent their money mostly on liquor.

blue, *v.*[2] [f. *blue n.*[2] 2: AND 1969.] *intr.* To become noisily angry; to 'go off pop'; to fight, brawl (as *vbl. n.* **blueing**). Also occas. *trans.*, to scold or abuse (someone).

1963 *Truth* 21 May 19 Apparently, I had made a meet at the Johnny Horner for that afternoon and when I didn't front she blued. to blue..to abuse someone. **1991** Payne *Staunch* 103 We all went back to jail because we had this big blue with a group called the Peacemakers; they were a bunch of big Maori guys who wanted to stop all the blueing.

bluebell. [Transf. use of northern hemisphere *bluebell Campanula* spp. (fam. Campanulaceae) for New Zealand *Wahlenbergia* spp.] Also **native** (or **New Zealand**) **bluebell**. Any of several small slender-stemmed herbs of *Wahlenbergia* spp. (fam. Campanulaceae) having blue or white bell-shaped flowers, esp. *W. gracilis*.

1867 Hooker *Handbook* 764 Bluebell, native. *Wahlenbergia*, several sp. **1868** Lindsay *Contribs. NZ Bot.* 66 *W[ahlenbergia] gracilis*... Known to the settlers, in common with the following [*W. saxicola*], which better deserves the name, as 'the Blue Bell'. *Ibid.* 67 *W. saxicola*... The 'Native Blue Bell' of the settler. **1878** Buller *Forty Yrs. NZ* 502 The *Rimuroa* is the bluebell. **1922** *Auckland Weekly News* 4 May 15 A native bluebell..is accompanied by interesting notes. **1940** Laing & Blackwell *Plants NZ* 430 *Wahlenbergia gracilis* (The Graceful Blue-bell). *Ibid.* 431 *W. gracilis* is one of the commonest of flowers in dry situations on open plains, and grassy hill-sides. It might be described as the New Zealand blue-bell, except that the application of the term to a flower, which is more often white than blue, is scarcely appropriate. **1973** Fernandez *Tussock Fever* 37 The clumps of tussock..sheltered a scattered growth..of dainty wild flowers..a delicate little bluebell..and..the bidibid.

blueberry. *Dianella nigra* (formerly *intermedia*) (fam. Phormiaceae), a native herb having sedge-like leaves and characterized by its small flowers and large glossy violet-blue berries containing inky juice. See also INKBERRY, TURUTU 1, WHISTLES.

1890 Harris *NZ Berries* (*Blue berry*). A grass-like plant. Leaves 1-5 feet long; very slender, much branched stems, flowers small greenish white, berries a lovely blue. **1908** *AJHR* C-14 37 Turutu Blue berry..Iris-like herb with creeping rhizome. **1940** Laing & Blackwell *Plants NZ* 99 *Dianella intermedia* (The Blueberry).

This plant is found in woods or open fern lands... Maori name, *Rena*. **1961** Martin *Flora NZ* 245 Lilies are represented by..the Blueberry (*Dianella*). **1978** [see whistles]. **1981** Dennis *Paparoas Guide* 161 Among the lilies are the blueberry *Dianella nigra*.

blue duck.

1. [Poss. an alteration of (orig. US) *dead duck* a failure: AND 1895.] Something unprofitable; a failure, a lost cause, esp. in the phr. **she's** (or **it's**) **a blue duck**. Also as **blue-ducked** *Auckland cabmen's slang*, done out of a fare, swindled.

1890 *Otago Witness* (Dunedin) 27 Feb. 29 It's a case of 'blue duck' with my Deception money. **1918** *Kia-ora Coo-ee* (1981) 15 May III. 15 [Answers to correspondents] 'Blue Duck': your mss. [*sic*] is synonymous [*sic*] with your nom de plume. **1944** *NZEF Times* 25 Sept. 4 She's away for a blue duck. **1948** Mundy *There's Gold* 112 I said to Mack 'she looks like a blue duck' [*sc.* an unprofitable gold-mining venture or claim]. **1951** McLeod *NZ High Country* 43 Another expression for a hopeless day when rain or fog prevents any chance of mustering is a 'blue duck', and I don't know the origin of this either. **1960** Scrymgeour *Memories Maoriland* 173 With 30 love and Mabel serving [her too often repeated 'double fault'], the result looked like a 'blue duck'. **1974** Henderson *Open Country Muster* 62 We could talk learnedly of wash, blue ducks, seepage races, benching, californian riffles, and all the terms that go with prospecting. **1983** *Metro* (Auckland) July 81 *Blue duck*. Origin unknown. ??South Auckland cabese for slinter. However, drivers more inclined to make quacking sounds into their RT's than report 'I've just been blue ducked'. **1988** *Karori News* (Wellington) 11 Oct. 1 A petition to force a by-election for two new trustees for the Terawhiti Licensing Trust never got off the ground. Organiser Norm Thomas says the petition is a 'blue duck'.

2. [Perh. from 1 above.] A baseless rumour.

1935 Mitchell & Strong in Partridge *Slang Today* 286 [The] following [was] employed by those who served in the [Great] War..*blue duck*, a rumour, esp. a baseless one. **1938** *Press* (Christchurch) (McNab Slang) 2 Apr. 18 [Slang of the NZEF] A 'blue duck' was a rumour; but a 'bird' was a prisoner in a cage. **1941** Baker *NZ Slang* 50 Among numerous terms originated in the first Great War we may note..*blue duck*, a rumour.

bluenose. Also **bluenose warehou**. *Hyperoglyphe antarctica* (fam. Centrolophidae), a bluish-grey food fish of moderately deep water, related and somewhat similar to blue warehou. See also *blue-jaw* (blue *a.* 2 b), bonita, bream 1 d, griffin's silverfish (*obs.*), stone-eye.

1978 *Catch* Oct. 18 Bluenose..Griffins Silverfish, bonita, stoney-eye... Distinguished from the hapuku and bass by a laterally compressed body, a larger eye set lower on the head, and a blunt snout. **1982** Ayling *Collins Guide* (1984) 301 *Blue-nose Warehou*..(Blue-nose grouper, griffins silverfish, bonita, deepsea trevalla)... The blue-nose warehou is a large heavy bodied fish... It is remarkably similar to the hapuku and bass, although completely unrelated, and as a result is often known as the blue-nose grouper. Blue-nose warehous are locally common all around New Zealand, mainly over rocky ground in 100 to 500m of water. **1986** Paul *NZ Fishes* 138 *Bluenose Hyperoglyphe antarctica*... Alternative New Zealand names include stoneye [*sic*], bonita, bream, Griffin's silverfish. **1991** *Evening Post* (Wellington) 20 Feb. 46 Offshore fishing for longnose and bluenose are still good at such places as Nicholson Trench and along the south coast. **1993** *Evening Post* (Wellington) 14 Jan. 21 We settled our mains of beef fillet..and poached Bluenose with smoked salmon cream.

blue paper. *Obs.* [f. the blue laid paper on which a summons was orig. printed: AND see *bluey* 4, 1895 C. Crowe *Austral. Slang Dict.* 58 *Piece of blue paper*, a summons.] A notice of summons to a court. Also *attrib.* Cf. blue *n.*¹ 2 a, bluey *n.*¹ 4 a.

1906 *Truth* 5 May 5 Mr Taylor might be served with a piece of blue paper calling on him to show some good and valid reason. **1910** *Truth* 2 July 4 Whenever a defendant's appearance before a court can be ensured by serving him with a blue-paper 'stiff,' it is right and proper that that course should be adopted, rather than that he should be submitted to the indignity of arrest.

Hence *v. trans.*, to summons.

1909 *Truth* 24 July 6 Sergt. Burrows had a little quiet conversation with Grant as a result..that individual was blue-papered to appear in the S.M. court on a charge.

bluestone. [AND 1850.] Basalt and similar blue-black volcanic rocks used as road aggregate, building blocks and building rubble, esp. in the se. South Island.

1875 *Official Handbook NZ* 133 dolorites (bluestones) **1876** *TrNZI* VIII. 134 *Bluestone*, which is so largely used for road metal..is to be found in almost all districts that have been disturbed by volcanic agencies... The basements of nine-tenths of the buildings in Dunedin are built of bluestone rubble. **1886** Hector *Handbook NZ* (4edn.) 58 Basalts, locally called 'blue-stones', occur of a quality useful for road-metal, house-blocks, and ordinary rubble masonry. **1900** *Canterbury Old & New* 129 There is abundance of good building stone [in South Canterbury], chiefly bluestone..and white stone something like the famous Oamaru stone. **c1930** *Whitcombe's Etym. Dict. Aust.-NZ Suppl.* 2 *blue*..bluestone n. a durable basaltic rock used for buildings, road-making, etc. **1944** Hislop *Pure Gold* 16 [At Macraes Flat, Central Otago] the old cock [carved in stone] is still there, stretching its neck to breaking point against the bluestone wall of Stanley's Hotel. **1951** *NZ Draft Standards Inst. Draft for Code of Bldg. Terminology D 3701* (TS) 27 Apr. 8 Blue Stone: A term correctly applied to basaltic rock and loosely applied to any similar volcanic rock. **1980** MacKenzie *While We Have Prisons* 14 The installation of plumbing in the bluestone fortress [Mt Eden prison] would cost a fortune.

blue-wattled crow: see crow *n.*¹ 2 (1).

bluey, *n.*¹ Also occas. **bluie**. [f. *blue* applied to things (orig.) coloured blue, or perceived as blue + -y.]

1. a. *Obs.* [f. the traditional *blue* of the blanket roll: AND 1878.] swag *n.*¹ 1 a. Esp. in various phr. **(with) bluey up**, on the swag; **to hump** (one's) **bluey**, see hump *v.* 2 b; **to pick up one's bluey**, or **up bluey (and away)**, to leave (home, work) for a travelling life. Contrast *blanket-bag* (blanket 3).

1896 O'Regan *Poems* 29 You can fancy, old mate, now I'm longing..To flee with 'billy' and 'bluey' To the spot where our spring-time we spent. **1904** *NZ Observer* 20 Aug. 5 As he had a wife and child to support, he 'up bluey' and away. **1911** *Poo-Bah of the Pacific* 2 [The new Resident of Rarotonga declared] that: 'He did not care for...[*sic*] anyone; he was there to govern, and govern he would, and that for two pins he would pick up his "bluie" and clear out.' **1913** *NZ Observer* 13 Sept. 5 When he heard that Hartly and Williams had taken thirteen pounds..of first-class gold at one wash in the Dunstan River, he 'up bluey' and away. **1927** Duggan *NZ Artist's Annual* 18 We'd sell and pack our things My oven and his axe—If they had seen us then With blueys [**1940** *NZ Poems* 38 read 'swags'] on our backs. **1933** *Press* (Christchurch) (Acland Gloss.) 16 Sept. 15 *Bluey*.— Swag. A nickname for a swag common in the 'nineties. In those days most station blankets were blue (earlier still, I believe, they were red). Hence *bluey up*—carrying a swag. **1951** in Pearson *Six Stories* (1991) 54 I've never been in one [city] more than a week but I've packed my bluey and got out into the open air. **1970** Johnson *Life's Vagaries* 73 If folks were reduced to walking and humping the bluey the least one could do was to give a lift, was his unvoiced attitude. **1986** Owen & Perkins *Speaking for Ourselves* 70 He [*sc.* the swagger] said to me, 'Well, I'm going through to the coast, and if you like you can roll up your bluey and come along with me.'

Hence **bluey-humper**, swagger 1 a; **blueyed**, with swag up, swagged.

1903 King *Bill's Philosophy* 28 That is, if we wear slouchers, And boots a bit square-toed—It ain't for bluey-humpers To travel on his road. **1910** Fanning *Players & Slayers* 81 I was tramping with a mate..to Westland, and it was our whim to be slouch-hatted, and 'blueyed', 'billied', unshaven, and otherwise orthodox swaggers.

b. [AND 1888.] *Obs.* A (usu. swagger's) blue blanket.

1906 *Truth* 26 May 7 We are told..that each [West Coast prospector in 1860] carried his swag of provisions, with the necessary 'bluey' and 'matilda'. **1917** Glen *Six Little New Zealanders* (1983) 84 'The hose!' shouted Uncle John. 'Wet the blueys!' cried Uncle Stephen [to put out a grass fire on a Canterbury station]. **c1930** *Whitcombe's Etym. Dict. Aust.-NZ Suppl.* 2 bluey n. a blue blanket in which the bushman wraps his belongings.

c. *Obs.* Occas. by metonymy, swagger 1 a.

1897 A Tramp, Esq. *Casual Ramblings* 87 In other countries tramps have a language of their own. Our 'blueys', however, are only in the rudimentary sign stage.

2. [Transf. use of 1 prec.: AND 1959.] Luggage, esp. a suitcase; things packed for a journey.

1909 Thompson *Ballads About Business* 91 'Come along with me to Southland,' said my old mate then to me... I agreed. We packed our blueys, and together then we went By train to Invercargill. **1961** Crump *Hang On a Minute Mate* 122 Her old man packed his bluey in the finish... He tried to get a divorce.

3. [AND 1917.] Usu. pl. Blue denim working overalls or trousers.

1901 *College Rhymes* (1923) 15 Rank oil is not in sympathy with Gallienic tears, Though lovely on the blueys of our College Engineers. **1957** Frame *Owls Do Cry* (1967) 43 And when Bob Withers came home, with his workbag of coal in one hand, and his dirty blueys in the other..he kissed his wife..and his overalls dropped on the floor and unrolled. **1967** McLatchie *Tang of Bush* 117 The girls were shown into Jim's [*sc.* the hotel's hired hand's] room, complete with razor strop..and his old blueys hanging on the red rail. **1981** Hunt *Speaking a Silence* 29 We'd have a pair of dungarees—that's like the blue jeans they wear today—denims they call them but we used to call them blueys. **1982** Frame *To the Is-land* (1984) 146 In his work he didn't get covered with oil and coal on his blueys.

4. a. [f. the blue laid paper on which it was orig. printed: AND 1909 (Thompson, as below).] A notice of summons to a court. Cf. blue *n.*¹ 2 a, blue paper.

1909 Thompson *Ballads about Business* 13 I'll show you valls papered mit blueys, and cracks in dem closed up mit scrip. *Ibid.* 48 [Title] How they served the 'blueys' [sc. 24 summonses on a defaulting mine owner]. **1938** Hutcheson *H.B. & J's Handbook* Pt II. 5 Blue laid: Paper that is 'legal' blue in colour and shows *Laid* watermarks. Gives its name to the ever-unwelcome 'Bluey.' **1949** Partridge *Dict. Underworld* (1961) 55 A summons by the police: New Zealand and Australian: since ca1910: 1932, Nelson Baylis (private letter). **1984** Beardsley *Blackball 08* 131 'Ickey. Oi 'ave 'ere a bluey for you to appear in the Warden's Court at Greymouth on the fourteenth inst.

b. *Obs.* A traffic offence notice or ticket. (No longer printed on blue paper.) See also sticker *n.*[1]
   1942 *NZEF Times* 16 Mar. 6 The speed cop who gave me my last bluey.

c. *transf.* Any sort of official summons or information.
   1947 *Sports Post* (Wellington) 13 Dec. 9 The hundreds of 'blueys' which summoned guests to the Law Ball, resulted in..a nice variety of finely-worded replies. **1951** Frame *Lagoon* (1961) 116 But all that was before the headmaster sent Mum a bluey saying action would be taken unless.

5. *transf.* A publican's written notice banning a person from a hotel bar.
   1987 *Press* (Christchurch) 11 Sept. 1 Hotel patrons who misbehave in Christchurch hotels will soon be served with a 'bluey'—a legal notice warning them to stay off the premises. **1988** *Evening Post* (Wellington) 22 Sept. 11 The 'Bluey,'—a legal notice aimed at keeping troublemakers out of pubs—has been an outstanding success... The 'Bluey' combines provisions of the Trespass and Sale of Liquor Acts.

6. A name or nickname, for an animal or human, based on perceptions of shades of blue. **a.** [AND 1906.] A nickname for a ginger- or red-headed male. See also blue *n.*[1] 5.
   1936 Hyde *Passport to Hell* 59 'Bluey' Jameson next morning told him to fall in line with Dave Lester's squad. **1946** Soljak *NZ* 115 Following are examples of colloquialisms common to New Zealand and Australian English, with their English or American equivalent..*bluey*: redhead; also, a court summons **1953** Hamilton *Till Human Voices Wake Us* 123 He..had red hair and of course, he was called Bluey. **1978** Tucker *Thoroughbreds Are My Life* 16 In our ranks at the time [c1940, Army Camp] was a very tough citizen by the name of Bluey Drysdale... In addition he had a shock of curly red hair. **1986** Richards *Off the Sheep's Back* 35 Fyffe was a typical redhead... The Maoris called him Puni-whero (redhead)... He was later nick-named Bluey.

b. A name for a draught bullock with a bluish (poss. a reddish) coat.
   1939 Beattie *First White Boy Born Otago* 154 [The bullocks'] names were Nimble and Nobby, both poleys, and Bluey and Yellowburn.

c. A shortened familiar form of *blue-bonnet* (blue *a.* 2 b).
   1956 [see *blue-bonnet* (blue *a.* 2 b).].

7. *Obs.* blue peter (blue *a.*[1] 1). Cf. peter *n.*[2]
   1994 McLauchlan *Story of Beer* 155 The half-gallon jar was preceded by the 'flagon' which, in turn, was preceded by the 'square rigger' and the 'bluey'.

bluey, *n.*[2] blue *n.*[2] 1.
   1964 Summers *Smoke and the Fire* 88 'Oh, Dinah, did you see that frightful bluey in our ad?'... 'They got the captions under the blocks mixed. Look.' **1995** *Sunday Star-Times* 13 Aug. B3 Yesterday, Southland, in a challenge which aimed to end its..36-year Ranfurly Shield drought, committed a double bluey.

bluff, *n.*

1. [Used elsewhere but in frequent use as a significant feature of NZ landscape and an accompaniment of much back-country outdoor activity: cf. OED *n.*[1] 1 a.] **a.** A broad and steep or precipitous headland face.
   1844 Tuckett *Diary* 19 Apr. in Hocken *Contributions* (1898) 208 Walked to the north headland of the bay, called the north bluff, about seven miles; and to the north bluff river. **1851** Shortland *S. Dist. NZ* 9 A shoal..extends from this towards the eastern Head [of Otakou inlet]—a steep round bluff—leaving a channel..running close to the bluff. **1879** Haast *Geol. Canterbury & Westland* 162 A high bluff on the northern side..which cannot be passed by travellers except by climbing over its summit, was next examined. **1907** *TrNZI* XXXIX. 74 It would either go over a bluff or drop down from exhaustion. **1943** Marsh *Colour Scheme* 100 It's a bit of a bluff that sticks out on the other side of the inlet. **1951** McLeod *NZ High Country* 23 Someone asked me the other day what I meant by a bluff. To us a bluff is any precipitous outcrop of rock or any steep broken face where the rock is bare and the fragments fall away below in scree and shingle slide. **1978** Jardine *Shadows on Hill* 7 She [sc. a heading dog] pulled too hard and nearly put them [sc. sheep] over a bluff.

b. *Special Comb.* **bluff road**, one cut out of the side of a bluff, gorge, etc.
   1883 Partington *Random Rot* 325 The road is what is called a bluff road, that is, it is cut out of the side of the precipice.

2. With Init. cap. in the phr. **from Bluff to Cape Maria (to the Cape)** [f. *Bluff*, a town in the far south of the SI; *Cape Maria van Diemen* or the *North Cape* on the northern tip of New Zealand], from one end of New Zealand to the other. See also North Cape (or Cape Reinga) to the Bluff.
   1902 Nalder *Battle-smoke Ballads* 11 From Bluff to Cape Maria New Zealand is agreed. **1919** *Quick March* Oct. 33 There ain't a dug-out..nor an armed Hun from here to the Bluff, or from the Bluff to the Cape.

bluff, *v. trans.* To drive (sheep) over a bluff.
   1934 *Press* (Christchurch) (Acland Gloss.) 13 Jan. 13 *Bluff.*—Used in some parts as meaning, to drive sheep over a b[luff]. **1953** Stronach *Musterer on Molesworth* 40 But we got through, though one man had bad luck bluffing twenty sheep. They all ran out on to a rocky ledge.

bluffed, *ppl. a.* [Prob. f. bluff *n.* 1.] Usu. in the phr. **to be (get) bluffed**, to be stopped or hindered by a bluff or cliff; to be forced to retrace one's steps; to get lost.
   1933 *NZ Alpine Jrnl.* V. 20(177) We traversed beyond the correct spur, were 'bluffed', and retreated. **1953** Stronach *Musterer on Molesworth* 24 Sheep often get stuck in the cliffs—'bluffed'—and so do the dogs; and so, sometimes, do the men. **1965** Macnicol *Skippers Road* 37 Sheep drifted down..seeking young green food about the terraces and often got 'bluffed' on the almost sheer rock faces. *Ibid.* 38 It wasn't until his sons grew old enough to be interested in 'bluffed' sheep that he decided a bullet was the best..answer to this problem. **1975** Newton *Sixty Thousand on the Hoof* 15 Several sheep had become bluffed and..Charlie Gilman went back..to try and retrieve the sheep... He was found dead at the foot of a fearsome bluff.

Hence **bluffing** *vbl. n.*, see quot.
   1950 Wilson *My First Eighty Yrs.* 139 The first three days of the journey were spent walking up the river-bed, crossing the stream from side to side to avoid rough going (bluffing, the mountaineers call it).

Bluff oyster: see oyster *n.* 2 (1).

bluie, var. bluey.

blunty. A Strikemaster aircraft.
   1991 TV3 6.30 p.m. 15 Oct. Strikemasters, called 'blunties' by their pilots. **1991** *Dominion* (Wellington) 2 Nov. 9 The Strikemasters were so cuddly nobody really took them seriously and they were given the nickname of Blunty... The Blunty was simple enough for a fledgling pilot and stern enough to be adequate schooling for hard operational flying.

board, *n.*[1]

1. a. [AND 1870.] Usu. as **the board** (occas. **the boards**), the area in a woolshed on which shearers work; *shearing-board* or *shearing floor* (shearing B 3). Cf. all aboard, *clear the board* (clear *v.* 2).
   [**1857** Paul *Lett. from Canterbury* 90 One of these huts must serve you for your first year's wool-shed, with the help of a few hurdles in front, and a tarpaulin or a few boards to shear on. **c1875** Meredith *Adventuring in Maoriland* (1935) 130 The dance was held in the woolshed. The boards of the shearing floor were not particularly even; so a tarpaulin was spread over the floor.] **1900** Acton-Adams *Letters* 22 May in McCaskill *Molesworth* (1969) 83 I have arranged with the Smoko Shearing Company of Wellington, to erect 10 machine shears on the western board of the shed. **1904** Lancaster *Sons o' Men* 78 Twenty-four held place on the boards alone. **1912** [see expert]. **1925** Rees *Lake of Enchantment* 113 The shed hands with brooms [swept] the 'board' clean. **1949** Sargeson *I Saw in My Dream* (1974) 113 Wally took the broom to sweep up stray bits of wool from the board. **1986** Richards *Off the Sheep's Back* 73 I, being a learner, was on the traditional 'drummer's' stand, at the far end of the board. **1995** *Listener* 1 Apr. 42 Out in the shearing shed, he looks a good foot taller up on the board, wielding a handpiece.

b. [AND 1904.] Often as **full board**. The complement of shearers on a shearing floor or in a woolshed.
   1894 Wilson *Land of Tui* 242 At one side [of the shearing shed], down the whole length of the building, the shearers work, thirteen of whom are called a 'full board.' **1913** Carr *Country Work* 14 Half the board (i.e., half the total shearers) are Maori, and the other half Pakeha (white). **1941** [see boss 3]. **1952** Meek *Station Days* 110 Board... When there is the full number of shearers required, a shed is said to have a 'full-board'. **1964** Deans *Pioneers Port Cooper Plains* 113 The week after Christchurch Show, shearing commenced at Homebush, with a board of ten Maoris and ten white men. **1981** Pinney *Early N. Otago Runs* 36 Middleton got a full board [in 1885], though fewer Australians had come than usual.

c. [AND 1879.] In various uses of the phr. **on the board**. (a) **to be on the board**, to be at work on the board shearing, to be shearing.
   1940 Studholme *Te Waimate* (1954) 210 When this station was at its zenith over 120,000 sheep were shorn each year, 34 shearers being on the board. **1960** Scrymgeour *Memories Maoriland* 48 Perhaps a week had passed, 26 men on the board, mostly Australians. **1986** *National Radio* 'Landline' (Farming Programme) 11 Oct. You have to help your local shearers; some wives are on the table, and we're often on the board too.

(b) **all on the board**, a call given near the end of shearing when the last sheep to be shorn are in the catching pens. Contrast all aboard.
   1955 Bowen *Wool Away* 155 'All on the board'. The call given when the last sheep of the mob are all in the catching pens. **1982** *Agric. Gloss.* (MAF) 52 *All on*

BOARD   72   **BOB**

the board: Call given to shearers when the last sheep of a mob has been caught for shearing.

d. In the phr. **to put** (someone) **off the board**, to dismiss or stand down from shearing.

   1955 BOWEN *Wool Away* 46 No learner has ever been put off the board because he has shorn sheep well, but many have lost their run through..rough shearing.

e. In the phr. **to walk the board**, to be in charge of the shearing (see also *board-walker* 3 below). Cf. *boss of the board* (BOSS 3).

   1960 SCRYMGEOUR *Memories Maoriland* 49 William Steuart, with the solemnity of one who views things going wrong, walked the board, with a quiet mien, but with an ever rising hostility in his Celtic nature. *Ibid.* 110 The only European [in the shearing gang] was the classer..and Joe Gillies walked the board as boss.

2. The killing floor of a freezing works.

   1910 *Awards, etc.* 388 Gut hands may be allowed to learn on the boards, provided they leg for slaughtermen equally and in rotation. **1951** *Awards, etc.* 323 [NZ Freezing-Workers Award] In the event of a cut-out on any board and slaughtermen are required to wait ten minutes or more, they shall be paid at the rate of 5s. 4^{1}/2d. per hour from the time the last sheep leaves legging-table to go on the chain until the next sheep following is ready to go on the chain. *Ibid* 335 [NZ Freezing-Workers Award] In engaging learners for the mutton-board preference..shall be given to men who have been members of the union for the previous twelve months. **1981** *Evening Post* (Wellington) 24 Jan. 7 The best men on the killing board [c1914], called the Ringers were Ellis and Pettit.

3. Special Comb. **board-walker** (a) *shearing,* the person in charge of shearing or the shearing board; the *boss of the board* (BOSS 3); (b) *freezing works,* one who is in charge of the chain or a particular part of it.

   1949 NEWTON *High Country Days* 193 **Board walker**:.. His main job is to patrol the board to see that the shearers are making a satisfactory job. **1989** RICHARDS *Pioneer's Life* 57 [The shearers] nearly drove the board-walker crazy with ridiculous requests for the unobtainable. **1951** May 17 Feilding Freezing Works terms p.c. Colin Gordon The *department-boss* is in charge of the **board-walkers**.., who are in charge of the chain etc.; they vary the speed of the drive on the chain. **1959** SLATTER *Gun in My Hand* 13 I slipped on the bloodied floor and the carcase should have fallen on me... The board-walker had to climb up on the wall and saw through the hind leg.

board, *n.*² [Spec. use of *board,* a tablet or frame on which some games are played: see OED 2 c.] A crown-and-anchor board, usu. a square piece of cloth with the game's symbols painted on.

   1916 GRAY, Norman *MS Papers 4134* (ATLMS) 9 Feb. They carry a table, acetylene plant and Crown and Anchor Board over to this place, and carry on a great business. **1936** TREADWELL *Recolls. Amateur Soldier* 31 One of the Crown and Anchor 'kings' was reported to have said, 'That damned sergeant has..taken the boards as security for the moneys..owing to him!' **1956** WILSON *Sweet White Wine* 138 I squatted beside the piece of baize. The Maori did not twitch a muscle of his face... I said, 'This is a raid. Fold up your board, Kiwi, for half an hour.' **c1962** BAXTER *Horse* (1985) 26 He turned to the Maori. 'You remember me, Joe? I've lost a few quid up at your place. On the board. On Saturday.' **1964** MORRIESON *Came a Hot Friday* 113 Replacing the usual poky little square of canvas or oilcloth, Sel Bishop owned a really impressive board some four feet square.

boarfish. [Spec. use of a cosmopolitan fish-name for any of various fishes with protruding or upturned snouts.] A name applied (often with genera distinguished by a modifier: **giant, long-finned, southern, yellow,** etc.) to species of the fam. Pentacerotidae, but also occas. to the *silver dory* (DORY 2 (2)) *Cyttus novae zelandiae* (fam. Zeidae).

   1872 HUTTON & HECTOR *Fishes NZ* 112 The term Boar Fish (*Cyttus australis*) has been applied to a fish of which several specimens were cast up on the shore of Cook Strait during the south-east gale of November last. **1911** *Rec. Canterbury Mus.* I. 216 *Zanclistius Elevatus*... Long-finned Boar Fish. **1927** PHILLIPPS *Bibliogr. NZ Fishes* (1971) 37 *Paristiopterus labiosus.* Giant Boarfish. **1956** GRAHAM *Treasury NZ Fishes* 181 Boarfish *Cyttus australis. Ibid.* 247 Boarfish *Griffinetta nelsonensis. Ibid.* 407 Boarfish *Paristiopterus labiosus*... Boarfish *Zanclistius elevatus*. **1967** NATUSCH *Animals NZ* 222 In the common boarfish, *Paristiopterus* (not really common, but perhaps less rare than other kinds), the sexes are markedly different. The long-finned boarfish (*Zanclistius*) rather resembles the tropical angel fish of aquariums; very rare indeed is the Nelson boarfish, *Griffinetta nelsonensis,* collected once from its nameplace, and once from the Chathams. **1970** SORENSEN *Nomenclature NZ Fish* 74 Sowfish— *Paristiopterus labiosus,* also known as Boarfish. Taken occasionally in the north and as far south as Cook Strait. **1982** AYLING *Collins Guide* (1984) 233 The long-finned boarfish has a body as high as it is long... There is a projecting bump on the forehead above the eye and the tubular snout ends in a small mouth... The long snout enables this fish to probe the cracks and crevices. *Ibid.* 236 *Richardsons Boarfish*..(pelagic armourhead, southern boarfish)... [It] is often seen on the surface at night gulping down the longer planktonic animals and small fishes attracted to a light hung from a boat. **1986** PAUL *NZ Fishes* 99 Boarfishes. A small family (Pentacerotidae) of fishes which have very hard, finely patterned exposed head bones; their alternative name is 'armour heads'... Giant boarfish... Adults..are good eating, with a sweet flavour. **1989** PAULIN et al. *NZ Fish* 97 *Pentaceros decacanthus* yellow boarfish.

boat. *Whaling. Hist.* As an *attrib.* or in Comb., *ellipt.* for *whaleboat* (WHALE 3). **a.** A prefix identifying various sharpened tools used in the capture or flensing of whales, such as **boat-axe, boat knife, boat spade** (see also *blubber spade* (BLUBBER)).

   1837 *Piraki Log* (1911) 49 1 Cutting Spade—..8/-.. 2 Boat Spades—... 4 Boat axes—..4/- ea... 5 Boat Knives—..2/- ea... 2 Blubber Knives... [Boat] Traveller.

b. Special Comb. **boat-steerer,** see quots. 1845, 1905; also in modern use, the crew member in charge of the steering oar of a surf-boat.

   c1835 BOULTBEE *Journal* (1986) 36 Our Captain [on 5 April 1826] advised the Boatsteerer to take 6 muskets, but he refused. **1845** WAKEFIELD *Adventure NZ* I. 317 The *boat-steerer* pulls the oar nearest the bow of the boat, fastens the whale with the harpoon, and takes his name from having to steer the boat under the headsman's directions while the latter kills the whale. **1905** BAUCKE *White Man Treads* 75 An old-time bay whaling station consisted..of at least two boats, with their crew of six men each. The headsman, or mate, four ordinary oarsmen, and the harpooner, or 'boat-steerer', who pulled the bow-oar, and drove in the harpoon, and who, when the whale had been struck and 'fastened on', went aft and steered the boat, while the mate took his place, and by repeated lance-thrusts killed it. **1985** LANGDALE-HUNT *Last Entail Male* 128 The 'Port Waikato' wanted a boat steerer for the surfboat to land stores there.

boatgirl. SHIPGIRL.

   1978 HILLIARD *Glory & Dream* 210 And a boatgirl with tired eyes said to him, You got a moneys eh I saw you give that kid a moneys.

boatie. Someone who runs a small boat, especially one which is power-driven.

   1972 *Marlborough Express* (Blenheim) 29 Sept. 6 'Skippers and boaties have to be very careful when using the channel... Some boaties take little notice of the markers and navigation aids,' he added. **1988** *North & South* (Auckland) Sept. 41 Where else are they so big on hypocorisms?.. Boatie (person who sails boats), yachtie (person who sails yachts). **1990** *Evening Post* (Wellington) 1 Oct. 4 A Cook Strait lighthouse demanned earlier this year, is the new headquarters for a boaties' association.

bob, *n.*¹ *Obs.* [Mainly transf. or fig. uses of *bob* a shilling(-piece), recorded in NZ use from 1841 to 1967 (the introduction of decimal currency when the *shilling* was replaced by the 10–cent piece).] Also *half-a-bob* sixpence, *two-bob bit* a two-shilling piece. Cf. COLONIAL ROBERT.

1. In special Comb. **bob-day** *a.,* describing one who would work for a shilling a day; **bob in** [AND 1919], a bar-game in which participants contribute a shilling each, the winner buying a round of drinks; **(to have a) bob in,** a former bar-room drinking system whereby a participant pays a shilling (more or less) into a round of drinks, and can withdraw from the school when the money is spent (also *attrib.*).

   1841 REVANS *Lett. to Chapman* (ATLTS) 96 I told him to work as a **bob-day** labourer, rather than be idle and starving. **1889** DAVIDSON *Stories NZ Life* 5 From tricks at cards, the fun changed to '**a bob in**' the winner shouting. **1925** HICKEY *'Red' Fed. Memoirs* 31 [A] goodly number were non-drinkers, and those who did take a 'spot' confined their imbibing to 'bobs in'. **1948** *NZ Geogr.* 166 Drinking on the West Coast has an etiquette of its own. It condones none of the 'bob-in' touch of a city bar when the man will have the two drinks he wants and then leave.

2. In the formulaic phr. **to be** (or **pay**) (**only**) [x] **bob in the pound,** see SHILLING 1 a; **to be two bob short,** see SHILLING 1 b.

bob, *n.*² [The entry for OED *n.*¹ 7 suggests that the use is mainly Brit. dial., US, and NZ.] Meat bait, worms, etc. threaded on string or held in a tangle of twine or shredded flax-blade and attached to a line, used for catching eels by entangling their teeth; see *eel-bob* (EEL 3). Also *vbl. n.* **bobbing** (see quot. 1874).

   1874 BATHGATE *Colonial Experiences* 243 The manner most frequently adopted for catching eels, called 'bobbing', is primitive enough, and is by means of a line formed of narrow strips of flax leaves, to the end of which is tied a bundle of earth worms. The eels bolt the 'bob' and are readily pulled out of the water. **1899** DOUGLAS in McDowall *JRSNZ* (1980) X. 316 But fishing for eels with hook or *bob* is foolishness; there is not much fun sitting all night devoured with mosquitoes. **c1920** BEATTIE *Trad. Lifeways Southern Maori* (1994) 143 The Maori had various ways of securing eels. One of these was by 'bobbing'. A bob was made of worms threaded with flax strings and this was dropped into the water. The eel sank its teeth into the bob and was hauled out before it could let go. **1967** McLATCHIE *Tang of Bush* 104 With a darning needle and thread..they soon had a five foot string of worms which they coiled into a bob and tied in several places.

This was fastened with flax to a strong stick about six feet long. We went down to the river about dusk, each of us with a rod..our bobs suspended in a deep pool. **1976** LORETZ *Moments of Life* 6 A 'bob' is simply a bunch of worms strung on flax fibre and tied to a light pole.

bob, *n.*³ [Poss. f. *bob up and down* with anger, annoyance.] In the phr. **(to be in a) state of bob**, (to be in a) state of excitement or confusion; (to be) extremely nervous.
    1862 CHUDLEIGH *Diary* 26 July (1950) 50 We struck the river opposite the A.C. house and came out 5 miles up the stream. Cooper and I had a swim and we were always in a state of bob... It took us over three hours to cross.

bob, *v.* See quot.
    1952–53 *NZ Forest Service Gloss.* (TS) Fiddle. To crosscut logs using a singlehanded saw; syn. Bob.

bobby: see BOBBY CALF.

bobby. *Northland kauri logging.* [Prob. an extended or spec. use of Brit. and N. Amer. dial. *bob* a short sleigh runner; hence, a timber carriage of the catamaran type: see OED *n.*¹ 2 d; EDD *n.*⁴ 1: it is unlikely to be a fig. or transf. use of *bobby policeman* in a sense 'guard-timber'.] An upright placed against the bank on a bend in a skidded log-road to prevent timber catamarans from striking the bank.
    [**a1914**] MCCARROLL *The Days of the Kauri Bushmen* (Radio Talk 4 (1951): TS) On the bank side, that is, the uphill side of the road, there would be short pieces let into the ground and standing up against the bank and placed just in front of the skid. These were called bobbies, and were to prevent the cat from jamming against the bank of the road [c1914]. **1953** REED *Story of Kauri* 181 Curves were laid with a camber..to prevent the cat from 'pulling off', and these bends were laid with much longer skids, to widen that part of the road. At such points too, a 'bobby'—a short skid extending from the bank to the road—was placed to prevent the cat from running into the bank [c1900].

bobby calf. Also *ellipt.* **bobby.** [f. Brit. dial. *bob* a very young calf: see EDD *bob n.*⁶ Cornwall, Austral.; OED *bobby* 4.]

1. An unweaned, usu. male, calf for slaughter as veal. See quot. 1982. Also *attrib.*
    1928 *Weekly News* (Auckland) 26 July 58 30,000 bobby calves, mostly from the Waikato, were exported..last season as boneless veal. **1936** BELSHAW et al. *Agric. Organiz. NZ* 470 Prior to the season 1927–28, it was customary to kill all surplus calves on the farm, and dispose of their skins only. The trade, which is known locally as 'The Bobby Calf' trade, developed during that season, and has extended rapidly each year since. Under this system of disposal, calves are collected by motor lorry and delivered at freezing-works, where they are slaughtered and packed as boneless veal. **1938** *NZ Statutory Regs.* 334 'Bobby calf' means a calf which is intended for slaughter for human consumption as boneless veal. **1939** BROWN *Farmer's Wife* 261 The Bobby Calf lorry, with its sadly vocal load, struck..a dissonant chord. **1955** WILSON *Land of My Children* 201 Mati was somewhat out of her depth in explaining the workings of the bobby-calf trade. **1959** SLATTER *Gun in My Hand* 13 And the bobby calves, poor little beggars. Hanging from the [freezing works] chain in horrible bunches of ten or a dozen at a time. **1968** *Crime in NZ* 180 E.V. was seen by some children behaving unnaturally with a dog. He admitted to indecency with a sheep and a bobby calf as well. **1971** *NZ Dairy Exporter* Sept. 130 Most of the calves go off as 'bobbies'. **1982** *Agric. Gloss.* (MAF) 19 *Bobby-calf*: Calf to be slaughtered when over 4 days old that has been fed solely on whole milk... They are calves defined as under 45.5 kg live weight with carcasses of not less than 9.98 kg. **1992** ANDERSON *Portrait Artist's Wife* 65 She was still staring, her eyes wide, vulnerable as a bobby calf's. **1992** *North & South* (Auckland) Nov. 84 Small male calves, 'bobbies', cute and appealing..are left at the farm gate to be collected and killed as vealers.

2. *Special Comb.* **bobby-veal** [cf. OED *bob-veal* 'U.S.', 1855], veal obtained by slaughtering bobby calves.
    1974 *NZ Agric.* 185 Veal is produced from young animals of 3 to 10 months, and from calves of up to 3 months old ('bobby' veal).

Bob Munro. [Origin unknown; poss. merely a rhyming catchphrase.] In the phr. **in** (occas. **out**) **you go says Bob Munro**, indicating encouragement for entry into (or exit from) an enterprise, competition, etc.
    1959 SLATTER *Gun in My Hand* 45 'Well, in ya go says Bob Munro,' he toasts and we drink some slowly. **1988** MCGILL *Dict. Kiwi Slang* 61 *in you go, says Bob Munro* an encouraging c[atch]p[hrase].

bob's-a-dying: see BOBSY-DIE.

Bob Semple, *n.* and *attrib.* [f. the name of *Robert Semple* (1873–1955), Minister of Works in the first Labour Government.]

1. Bob Semple tank, a makeshift tank for home defence during WW2, comprising a protective iron shell on a bulldozer body, an enterprise attributed to Semple, then Minister of Works.
    1970 PORTER *Nor'west Arch* 23 I had to wear [the armband of c1940)] that way the next day in a big parade of the different services, following a huge Bob Semple tank, carrying a banner emblazoned with 'Law & Order'.

2. *Railways.* See quot.
    1990 CHURCHMAN & HURST *Railways of NZ* 196 The mixed train which arrived at Rewanui about 11.30 pm Sunday to Thursday was known as the 'Paddy Webb' or 'Bob Semple' after the miners who became Cabinet Ministers in the first Labour Government, and who first arranged this train to make it easier for the miners changing shift at midnight.

bobsidie, var. BOBSY-DIE.

bobsy-die /ˌbɒbziˈdaɪ/. Also **bob's** (or **Bob's**)-**a-dying**; **bobsidie.** [f. Brit. dial. *Bob-a-dying*, *bobs-a-dial*, *bobs-a-dilo*: see OED *Bobs-a-dying*; EDD.] A great fuss, esp. in the phr. **to kick up bobsy-die**; also **to play bobs-a-dying with**, to affect badly.
    1935 *Canterbury Mountaineer* 36 The brown torrent kicked up 'Bobsie Die' in deafening manner. **1941** MARSH *Surfeit of Lampreys* (1951) xvi 251 'If she's right,' said Fox 'it plays Bobs-a-dying with the whole blooming case.' **1949** PARTRIDGE *Dict. Slang Addenda* 1092 *kick up Bob's-a-dying*. To make an unnecessary fuss or noise or commotion: New Zealand: since ca. 1890. (Prof. Arnold Wall, letter of Aug. 1939.) **1952** *Here & Now* Jan. 25 Or Dido kicked up quite such bobsy-die If she had a squint in her left eye. **1960** MUIR *Word for Word* 181 'Been running round kicking up bobsy-die all morning. Must have a hangover, I reckon.' **1974** SIMPSON *Sugarbag Years* 72 They had paper down—but me mother kicked up bobsydie about that place. **1986** *NZ Times* 12 Jan. 1 Local publican Bruce Ford said the two youngsters had 'kicked up bobsie die' on the boat during the journey from Bluff to Stewart Island. **1988** *Listener* 13 Feb. 25 For eight months [he]..kept watch for villains, 'not only burglars but the ratbags coming in and kicking up bobsydi'. **1992** ANDERSON *Portrait Artist's Wife* 205 Why doesn't she cry?.. She'll kick up bobsy-die later, poor little pet.

bocacker /ˈbʌuˌkækə/, /ˌbʌuˈkækə/, var. PUKEKO.

bodgey, var. BODGY.

bodgie. *Hist.* [Prob. f. Austral. *bodg(er* a fake, worthless thing or person + -IE: AND 1950.] A male member of a street group of the 1950s distinguished by peculiarities of dress and behaviour. Often *attrib.* Contrast WIDGIE.
    1955 *NZ Herald* (Auckland) 31 Oct. 8 Young New Zealand servicemen decided last night to clean Queen Street of the 'teddy boy' and 'bodgie' element. **1955** *BJ Cameron Collection* (TS July) bodgie cut (n) A hairstyle affected by bodgies. **1956** *Street Society Christchurch* 1 During the early months of this year [1956] much publicity was given..to the fact that large numbers of young people were to be seen, especially at the weekends, in the central areas of the city. These young people congregated in the streets and milk-bars. Many of them had motor-cycles... At various times these young people were referred to as 'Teddy Boys', 'Milk Bar Cowboys' and 'Bodgies and Widgies'. *Ibid.* 2 Many boys and girls imitate its [*sc.* the Australian bodgie cult's] fashions and share with its adherents an interest in jive. The dress of these youngsters resembles that of the Teddy Boy and Girl, but is not so immaculate; hair is worn long and brushed back, without the characteristic Teddy Boy tuft; behaviour tends to be more boisterous and 'attention provoking'. In this report such phrases as 'Teddy Boy style' or 'Bodgie type' are used purely as descriptive terms, to indicate certain fashions of dress which show these overseas influences. **1964** DAVIS *Watersiders* 141 The ultra-short haircut and tight, tailored jeans he affected [in the 1950s] were the trademark of both respected athletic types and harum-scarum bodgies. **1965** WATSON *Stand in Rain* 80 I gave our name as Haversham, might as well have an interesting bodgie name I thought. **1974** HILLIARD *Maori Woman* 293 Up in Newtown and you were talking with two bodgie-looking types on bikes. **1986** *Manukau Courier* in *Listener* (1986) 9 Aug. 4 Attention Sth Auckland Rock'n'Roll club presents Budgie & Wedgie Nite. **1987** HUTCHINS *Tall Half-backs* 81 In his dirty denim jeans, with his slickered, swept back hair, with his battered..motor bike and jar of malt, Schmidt was the closest I'd been to a bodgie—or the external image of what I perceived a bodgie to be. **1988** LAY *Fools on Hill* 10 'Listen to it, it's all the same, that bodgie music!' 'That's Neil Sedaka. He's not a bodgie.'

Hence **bodgiedom**, bodgies and their subculture; **bodgieism**, the state or condition of being a bodgie.
    1993 *Landfall* 185 65 I remember once [c1956] writing an anonymous article..on the phenomenon of bodgiedom. **1958** *NZ Herald* (Auckland) 5 Nov. 14 Some of New Zealand's suggested cures for 'bodgieism' were not only 'wide of the mark' but surprisingly 'vindictive', says Dr. D. P. Ausubel.

bodgy, *a.* Also **bodgey.** [f. Austral. *bodger* (1945), *bodgy* (1952) fake: see AND.] False; 'unofficial'; unsatisfactory; amateurish, makeshift.
    1989 *Sunday Star* (Auckland) 16 July A1 The freelance writer insists that the booklet..is a souvenir to

mark Rotorua's first league international. Angry officials claim it is a bodgy programme. **1992** *Evening Post* (Wellington) 18 June 14 It did stage too many bodgey and bogan gigs. **1992** *Dominion* (Wellington) 27 Nov. 10 Anyone who zizzles a neighbour or friend through a bodgey toaster repair will be prosecuted.

body. *Obs.* [Spec. use of *body* the main part of a collection: AND *body bullock*, 1872.] The centre pair of a bullock team; also **body-bullock**, one of the centre pair.
1860 in Butler *First Year* (1863) vii 105 The leaders..slewed sharply round, and tied themselves into an inextricable knot with the polars [*sic*], while the body bullocks..slipped the yoke under their necks, and the bows over. **1940** Studholme *Te Waimate* (1954) 153 In breaking in a young bullock to the team [c1900] the first step was to couple the young beast to a steady near-side bullock used to working in the body (centre) of the team.

bog, *v. West Coast mining.* [Prob. f. Brit. dial. *bog*, *budge* to shovel, to remove by shovelling; cf. AND *West Austral. bogger* one who works underground shovelling ore, 1935.] To shovel.
1973 McCarthy *Listen..!* 51 The same thing applied after the face had been 'shot': before shovelling (or bogging, as it was called) the stone down the pass it had to be thoroughly drenched with water. **1992** Latham *Golden Reefs* 427 *Bog-out/up* (Waiuta): To bog meant to shovel; to bog-out was to shovel quartz out of the stope through a pass to a lower level; to bog-up was to clear all the quartz in the drive into trucks after firing a round of shots.
Hence **bogging** *vbl. n.*, shovelling.
1978 McAra *Gold Mining Waihi* 182 The routine of shovelling, or bogging as it was called, followed by drilling and blasting, was continued until..the shaft had been sunk about fifty feet below the timbers.

bog, *attrib.* In the names of plants, see: CELMISIA, CLUB-MOSS, GENTIAN, HEATH, LILY, PINE 2 (3), POA, RUSH.

bogan. Of uncertain origin: a recent Australian borrowing (Wilkes 1988, in a quotation associated with Melbourne's western suburbs). An uncouth or stupidly conventional person, a 'nerd'. Also *attrib.*
1992 *Evening Post* (Wellington) 18 June 14 It did stage too many bodgey and bogan gigs. **1996** *Dominion* (Wellington) 29 April 21 No one will ever know just how many bogans—'Wellington westies'—lie on the ocean floor stretching out beyond Paraparaumu beach (having failed in their intoxicated attempts to swim out to Kapiti Island wearing upward of two pairs of black jeans).

bogey, var. BOGIE.

boghee-boghee, var. PAKE 1 (*pakapaka*).

bogie, *n.* Also **bogey.** [Spec. use of n. Brit. dial. *bogie* a small, low, four-wheeled truck: see OED *n.*[1]] A wheeled frame for carrying coal-bins or logs.
1948 *Our Own Country* 103 At the bins, the tubs having been emptied into enormous containers, the coal is screened (sifted)..and loaded into hoppers..[which] are fitted into a four-wheeled frame called a bogie. **1952-53** *NZ Forest Service Gloss.* (TS) Bogey: A framework consisting of a carriage and 4 wheels used for carrying logs on bush tramways.

bog in, *v. intr.* Also *trans.* **bog into.** [AND 1907.] To start or take on (a task, etc.) enthusiastically or vigorously, esp. to begin eating.
1952 MEEK *Station Days* 74 With his 'Burgon's' then to the shed [he] tore, Where into the sheep he bogged. **1980** LELAND *Kiwi-Yankee Dict.* 16 *bog in*: begin to engage enthusiastically in an activity usually eating. *Ibid.* 58 *Kiwi grace*: (before meals): '2, 4, 6, 8; bog in, don't wait'. **1993** RENÉE *Daisy & Lily* 38 Ignoring the fact that the bread was supposed to last for Monday's lunches, they all bogged in.

boil, *n.* [Spec. use of *boil* an act of boiling.] Also in the noun phr. **boil the billy.** BOIL-UP 1.
1940 GILKISON *Peaks, Packs & Mountain Tracks* 82 But the best part of the tramp on the home hills is the mid-day 'boil'. **1953** STRONACH *Musterer on Molesworth* 8 We halted at the Saxon for a 'boil'. Each filled his small mustering billy and held it over the fire on the end of the mustering stick. *Ibid* 26 We had a boil and then started the ascent. **1974** SIMPSON *Sugarbag Years* 90 No break for a smoke, no boil the billy, only your cold tea to drink at mid-day.

boil, *v.*[1] *Hist.* [Spec. uses of *boil down* to reduce by boiling; *boil out* to render animal fat.]
1. As **boil** (or **boil out**) whaling, TRY OUT *v.* a.
1836 *Log 'Mary Mitchell'* 31 May in McNab *Old Whaling Days* (1913) 444 Began to boil at 7 our boats returned. *Ibid.* 445 June 5 cut in our whale and began to boil this is a Monstrous whale. **1836** RHODES *Jrnl. Barque 'Australian'* (1954) 17 Began to boil out. *Ibid.* 20 Two strange sail in sight boiling out. *Ibid.* 22 Oct. 23 Employed clearing the decks and boiling out.
Hence **boiling out** *vbl. n.*
1982 [see BOOK *n.*[3]].
2. As **boil down** *farming* [AND 1843], to reduce (sheep carcasses) by boiling to produce tallow. See also BOILING DOWN *vbl. n.*
1850 in *Speeches & Documents* (1971) 27 As yet the sheep-owners have not been driven to 'boil down' but expect to do so as their stock increases. **1875** *TrNZI* VII. 184 If a squatter..should proceed to boil down the whole flock..he would be denounced as a lunatic. **1936** LAMBERT *Pioneering Reminisc. Old Wairoa* 159 Then came the outbreak of scab, and thousands of sheep had to be slaughtered to boil down for tallow. **1969** McCaskill *Molesworth* 53 Five thousand sheep were boiled down soon after [the autumn of 1881].

boil, *v.*[2] In the phr. **to boil the** (or **one's**) **billy**, see BILLY *n.*[1] 2 a.

boiled dog. Side, affectation.
1937 PARTRIDGE *Dict. Slang* 75 *boiled dog*. 'Side': New Zealanders': from ca. 1910. Perhaps on *boiled shirt*. **1941** BAKER *NZ Slang* 56 Other twentieth century New Zealand expressions..include..*boiled dog*, 'side' or affectation.

boiled lolly. A sweet made of sugar hardened by boiling (Brit. 'boiled sweet'.) Cf. LOLLY 1.
1959 LAWLOR *Old Wellington Days* 21 Also, there would be boiled lollies and cherries [c1905]. **1984** HOLCROFT *Way of Writer* 6 Early evening..I was given one boiled lolly—a blackball—from an old, curiously ornamented tin. **1990** CONEY *Out of the Frying Pan* 16 There were always shortbread and a huge jar of boiled lollies in the pantry. **1992** *Landfall 183* 277 There was always a tin of brightly coloured boiled lollies on the mantelpiece.

boiler.
1. *Obs.* [AND 1884.] An animal fit only for boiling down.
1951 DUFF *Shepherd's Calendar* (1961) 11 A neighbour whose bull I had arranged to hire told me a few days ago that 'the old fool had knocked himself out' and was now 'finished—a boiler'.
2. In the phr. **to bust** (or **burst**) **one's boiler**, see BUST *v.* 2.

boiling down. *vbl. n. Hist.* [f. BOIL *v.*[1]]
1. Also **B.D.** The process of, or tanks and establishment for, boiling down sheep or cattle carcasses to extract tallow.
1847 in Deans *Pioneers of Canterbury* (1937) 114 Wethers are worth from 5/-..and bullocks from £2 to £3 for boiling down. **1861** HURSTHOUSE *NZ* 374 'Boiling-down establishments' were formed in the pastoral districts, and the process became a regular business. The sheep or cattle were killed and skinned, the carcass thrown into the boiling vat, the fat skimmed off for export tallow, and the meat thrown away. **1870** *Benmore Diary* 25 May in Pinney *Early N. Otago Runs* (1981) 24 On 25 may, B.D. started on Benmore. **1938** BURDON *High Country* 112 Boiling down did not begin in New Zealand until later [than in Australia], as there was no need for it. **1944** WILSON *Moonshine* 7 [In the 1880s] some run-holders set up boiling-downs.
2. a. *attrib.* passing into Comb.
1855 SEWELL *Journal* 27 May (1980) II. 147 Assuming..surplus stock worth something above boiling down rate, they will give a large return for the capital laid out. **1864** MARSHMAN *Canterbury 1862* 41 The ultimate value when the boiling-down point has been reached, will be..the worth of the wool and tallow. **1867** *NZ Herald* (Auckland) in Burdon *High Country* (1938) 112 It is said there are thousands of fat wethers..ready..and as no market can be found for them a 'boiling down' company has been established. **1890** *Otago Witness* (Dunedin) 7 Aug. 36 We..dream'd of great flocks to be drafted off every year to boiling-down yards. **1935** JACKSON *Annals NZ Family* 132 I believe [the kea] acquired his liking for fat in the old 'boiling down' days. **1969** McCASKILL *Molesworth* 53 There [at Tarndale station] he..ordered a boiling-down plant from Andersons in Christchurch.
b. Special Comb. **boiling-down house**, a place or building on a sheep-station where boiling-down is carried out; **boiling-down price**, the lowest or bedrock price at which it is more profitable to 'boil down' than to sell sheep for other purposes; **boiling-down works**, a regional plant, or one on a sheep station, where boiling down is carried out.
1875 RIVES *Jottings on the Spot* (Cant. Pub. Lib. TS) 16 After lunch I walked down with W. to look at the [sheep station's] **boiling down house**... The boiling down house is about two miles from the homestead to avoid the stench. **1888** D'AVIGDOR *Antipodean Notes* 79 The latter [*sc.* offal] are taken to the boiling-down house, on the opposite side of the road, where tallow is made. **1851** WELD *Hints to Intending Sheep-farmers* 5 In prudence a man should not calculate on a higher than the minimum, or **boiling-down price** of about 5 *s.* a-head for male (wedder) [*sic*] stock. **1859** FULLER *Five Years Residence* 166 A boiling-down price for wethers would be reached in a few years. **c1875** MEREDITH *Adventuring in Maoriland* (1935) 96 There is a **boiling-down works** at Featherston..where thousands of..large fat sheep..are boiled down. **1885** CHUDLEIGH *Diary* 31 Aug. (1950) 335 Drove with W. Beetham to his boiling down works and meat preserving factory [at Masterton]. **1921** *Quick March* 10 Feb. 36 In the succeeding two years the ex-coke-shoveller..boiling-down works labourer, shearer..examined a mining boom. **1937**

AYSON *Thomas* 153 Boiling down works had also been started at Green Island. Merinos were boiled down for their fat and pelts. **1950** WILSON *My First Eighty Yrs.* 20 I do not want to leave station life without mentioning one feature that was beginning to appear on most stations in the 'seventies. These were the boiling-down works. **1992** PARK *Fence Around the Cuckoo* 27 Day by day [in the Depression] we saw mobs of dusty sheep... They were *en route* to the boiling-down works.

boilly, var. BOUILLI.

boilover. [AND 1871.] An unexpected result.
   1979 *Star* (Christchurch) 5 Apr. 19 The first of his victories was achieved at his debut, and it was a real boilover.

boil-up. [Spec. use of *boil-up* an act of boiling.]
1. Esp. in outdoors work or life, the act of making (or boiling) a brew of tea in a billy, or a brew or tea so made, esp. in the phr. **to have a boil-up**.
   1918 *Kia-ora Coo-ee* (1981) 15 Aug. II. 16 On patrols, [the NZ Mounted Rifleman] is characterised by..a passion for innumerable 'boil-ups' for the ever welcome mug of tea. **1933** *Tararua Tramper* Feb. 1 Then a long climb..then another boil up when we reached the Green lake. **1946** JOHNSTON ed. *Twenty-one Yrs. with Boots & Pack* 4 First 'boil up', Rangitoto, 18th October, 1925. **1952** ORBELL *Comfort & Commonsense in Bush* 66 At the midday stop, some people always insist on a boilup. **1964** HELMER *Stag Party* (1990) 42 We stopped near..Sonny White's clearing for a 'boil-up' of tea. **1988** McGILL *Dict. Kiwi Slang* 17 *boil-up* tea-break, mostly among thirsty trampers boiling the billy.
   Hence **boil-up** *v. intr.*, BOIL *v.*²
   1947 NEWTON *Wayleggo* 35 In some back-country districts in Canterbury, it is the practice for musterers to carry billies..and to 'boil-up'..when circumstances permitted during their beat. **1971** *Listener* 19 Apr. 56 They cooeed out, and while he skinned the spiker they found a possie in a bit of a trog and boiled-up. **1978** JARDINE *Shadows on the Hill* 2 The pauses to boil up for the ever-welcome billy tea.
2. Esp. in the phr. **to have a boil up** [cf. OED *v.* 3 c '*U.S. and N.Z.*'], to boil clothes (in a copper).
   1949 *Here & Now* Oct. 17 So long as there are babies.., there is washing to be done daily,... Once a week or once a fortnight there's a copper boil-up.

bokak(k)a, bokak(k)er, boke, bokie, varr. PUKEKO.

bolar. [Origin unknown: cf. *Macquarie Dictionary* (1981) *bolar blade* cut of beef from the blade.] Also **beef bolar**, and often *attrib*. as **bolar roast, bolar steak**. A cut of beef from the hindquarters adjacent to (or from) the blade.
   1982 *Agric. Gloss.* (MAF) 37 Beef cuts [illustrated]... Roll of blade and bolar. **1995** *Evening Post* (Wellington) 1 Nov. 24 [Advt] Fresh Tenderbeef Bolar Roasts.

boldie, var. BALLIE.

bolter. [Wilkes 1941] A (usually successful) outsider.
   1995 *Sunday Star-Times* 9 Apr. B1 Other features are... Several bolters making their way into the New Zealand XV from outside the two summer World Cup squads... I repeat, we cannot close off to the bolters.

bolter's chance. Also **bolter's show**. [f. *bolter* an absconder: AND 1941.] Constr. with indef. article. An outsider's chance, or no chance at all. Compare BUCKLEY'S CHANCE.
   1928 *Free Lance* (Wellington) 4 Jan. 45 Edwards was not given a 'bolter's chance' to fight for what is really his title. **1990** *Evening Post* (Wellington) May 6 Today, tobacco wouldn't have a bolter's show of being approved by anybody, other than perhaps as a restricted chemical to kill off garden pests.

bomb, *n.*¹ [Transf. or fig. use of *bomb* an explosive, dangerous, or noisy object or projectile.]
1. [With poss. ironic play on the phr. *to go like a bomb*: AND 1950.] An aging or dilapidated car, occas. motorcycle; occas. also applied to any dilapidated moveable mechanical object, e.g. 'My old bomb of a lawnmower'.
   1959 SLATTER *Gun in My Hand* 14 And then it was racing back to town in the Beat-Up Bomb, everybody jammed in. **1960** MUIR *Word for Word* 231 It's bad enough down on the flat with every street full of louts in jalopies and Dad taking the kids for a spin in the family bomb. **1979** *Dominion* (Wellington) 10 Oct. 5 Old bombs—ageing cars peculiar to New Zealand roads—should be scrapped, motor vehicle dealers say. **1980** LELAND *Kiwi-Yankee Dict.* 47 *bomb*: Usually refers to a car, but any mechanical device can 'go like a bomb'. Strangely enough this means that it is going well.
2. *Children*. A (running) jump into water, from a height, and usually with hands clasped around drawn-up legs, the object being to make the biggest splash and noise possible, hence the name.
   1959 [see BELLY 3]. **1993** *Evening Post* (Wellington) 4 Mar. 32 [Caption] Rangi's city cousin is having her first swim in a country swimmin' hole... No pushin'! No shovin'! No bombs!
3. *Whaling*. A grenade or explosive charge in the head of a whale-lance; also in Comb. (see quots.).
   1968 JOHNSON *Turn of Tide* 34 One bomb was darted and the whale rose and floated on its back. **1982** MORTON *Whale's Wake* 39 In 1859 the captain of the American whaler *Florida*, which visited New Zealand in January of that year, tried out a new 'whaling gun' or 'Bomb lance gun'—it was referred to by both names—and later his first mate 'fired three bomb lances' into a whale. **1982** GRADY *Perano Whalers* 226 *Bomb-poles*—The steel pole that was used by the Peranos to thrust the bomb-lance into the whale... *Bomb-wire*—The electric flex that connects the bomb-charge with a control on the whale-chaser. When the electrical circuit is closed, the bomb explodes.
4. *Prison*. An illegal water-heater or water-boiling device.
   1982 NEWBOLD *Big Huey* 85 Every smoko time..[they] would pull their bombs out of snooker and brew up a cup of tea or cocoa. *Ibid*. 245 Bomb (n) Illegal water-boiling device.
5. *Rugby football*. A high up-and-under punt near an opponent's try-line.
   1983 *National Bus. Rev.* 4 July 32 And rugby types jeer at players who leave the high balls ('bombs' in league) to others.

bomb, *n.*² Also and orig. **bom**. [f. *bom*, a proprietary name, prob. suggested by the shape (see quot. 1989).] A chocolate-covered ice-cream of cylindrical shape eaten from a cone.
   1942 *Blue & White* 45 While we feel grateful to the turfing squad we note that they were daily furnished with an ice-cream 'bomb' and a bottle of fizz. **1989** BARNETT & WOLFE *New Zealand! New Zealand!* 45 The competitive nature of the [ice cream] novelty business was expressed by W.J. Carbines of Mt Eden in 1939. His chocolate-coated Boms had a truly military flavour. **1991** MELVILLE *My Home Town* 28 In later days choc bombs and Eskimo pies joined the frozen menu.

bomb, *v.*
1. *trans*. Also **bomb out**. To end a relationship, esp. in the phr. **to get (be) bombed**, to be blacklisted by one's union.
   1973 *Salient* (Wellington) 19 Sept. 11 To bomb someone out is to tell them you've finished with them. **1986** *Sunday News* (Auckland) 2 Nov. 8 John Doran had a go at me for not asking his permission to go overseas. I got bombed and I couldn't get a job as a rigger in the Labourers' Union after that... He just told me I'd be getting no f—..work, he told me I'd be bombed—and I'd be yard bombed.
2. *Tramping*. **bombed** *ppl. a.*, bombarded with loose debris or scree.
   1971 *Listener* 19 Apr. 56 They [Pete and Sam] got up the low scree, sidled across the first face..but they were getting bombed so they cramponed up to just below a gendarme.
3. *Whaling. trans*. To kill or disable a whale with a bomb–lance.
   1982 GRADY *Perano Whalers* 226 Bombed [*sic*]— To thrust a bomb-lance into a whale and then to electrically detonate the grenade-head.
4. *Deer-culling*. As **bomb up**, to bombard animals with shots; to release wild shots at a herd.
   1984 DINGLE *Two Against Alps* in *Thousand Mountains Shining* (1984) 172 Private shooters they come here And bomb up all the easy deer. **1970** bombing up [see *bush-happy* (BUSH C 1 b)].

Bombay. [f. the name of the early immigrant ship 'Bombay'.]
1. *Hist. pl*. A name applied to a body of immigrants brought out in 1863 in the 'Bombay' to settle in Williamson's Clearing on the military road south of Drury, later the township of Bombay.
   1865 LUSH *Waikato Jrnls.* 19 July (1982) 52 These people came in a vessel called the *Bombay*—so they go by the name of 'Bombays'.
2. [From the place-name 'Bombay Hills', occas. familiarly 'the Bombays', a group of hills about 30 miles south of Auckland and forming a natural barrier between greater Auckland and the Waikato.] As **Bombay hills** or **hills**, esp. in the phr. **north (south) of the Bombay Hills**, alluding to that part of New Zealand within (or outside) greater Auckland's influence or purview. Hence *joc*. **Bombayan**, one who lives north of the Bombay Hills.
   1986 *Listener* 11 Jan. 22 I am moving to Auckland and I am taking my off-pat Wellington phrases: New Zealand stops at the Bombay Hills. **1991** *Dominion Sunday Times* (Wellington) 8 Dec. 10 One decision for the cardinals of rugby is whether to stick with someone of the proven ability of Hart, however much he irritates people south of the Bombay hills. **1992** *Evening Post* (Wellington) 16 Apr. 6 Find me a local tragedy, preferably north of the Bombay Hills. *Ibid*. 1 May 4 As a lifelong resident north of the Bombays, my moving to Windy Wellington was to be a traumatic affair. **1995** *Dominion* (Wellington) 16 Aug. 10 We Bombayans will forgive everything in the rich except a failure to show off.

Bombay bloomers, *n*. WW2 (N. Africa). [Origin uncertain: prob. nicknamed f. the city of Bombay.]

Also *ellipt.* **Bombays**. Loose and baggy summer-issue military shorts able to be fastened below the knee (see quot. 1953).

1941 *Tararua Tramper* July 1 We are being re-equipped with 'Glamour Pants' or 'Bombay Bloomers'. These are long khaki shorts (or short longs), the legs of which can be turned down below the knee and drawn in, to keep off the wicked mosquito. **1942** *NZEF Times* 29 June 11 [Caption] If they think I'm going to be seen on leave..with my Bombays rolled up... **1945** WEBBER *Johnny Enzed in Middle East* 7 'Have you thought about the wider issues?' 'Not Bombays again.' **1953** CODY *21 Battalion* 29 These ['Khaki drill other ranks shorts long'] were weird garments..and had the legs lengthened to about eight inches below the knee, buttons and button holes permitting the extensions to be fastened above the knee [and below the knee]... The troops disliked intensely these 'Bombay bloomers'. **1994** *North & South* (Auckland) July 36 He wore Bombay bloomers – huge, wide, grey drill shorts that made his legs look like peasticks – and white singlets. Legs 11! Mum would call him.

bombflet. WW2. Also **bombphlet**. [f. *bomb* + lea)*flet*, or pam)*phlet*.] A leaflet dropped from an aeroplane.

1940 *NZ Stamp Collector* XXI. 26 Souvenirs of interest to air mail collectors were provided during two flights over Christchurch and one over Nelson. With the purpose of assisting the drive for the Red Cross funds and to stimulate recruiting, leaflets were dropped from the 'planes and as the wording contained a warning that 'this might have been a bomb', the leaflets have been called 'bombphlets'. **1940** *Evening Post* (Wellington) 3 Aug. 11 [Heading] Nazi 'Bomphlets'. Hitler's Peace Speech Dropped in England. **1978** *The Philatelist* Dec. 86 Yet another word has been added by New Zealanders, to the philatelic language. The word 'Bombphlet' applies to the leaflets dropped from the air in 1940 over Christchurch and Nelson. **1986** *Captain Coqk* XIV. 94 Another bomphlet! Illustrated on the front page of 'Captain Coqk'..of September 1978..was a leaflet, dropped from a plane over Christchurch in 1940.

bombie: see BOMB-SQUASHER.

bomb-squasher. *Marble players*. Also **bombie**; and occas. heard as **bum-squasher**. [Compare DARE *bombsies* a dropping shot in marbles.] A large marble often used in a dropping shot in the game of eye-drops.

1972 SUTTON-SMITH *Folkgames Children* 174 There were the terms referring to particular kinds of marbles: for example..blood alleys, bomb-squashers, bonies, bonsers. **1989** MCGILL *Dinkum Kiwi Dict.* 15 *bomb-squasher* big marble, a menace to small marbles. **1995** *Independent* 8 Dec. 20 Eye drops were of no interest. But if you were going to play the rule was no bombies; no giant marbles called bomb squashers.

bommy-knocker: see DONGER-KNOCKER.

bonamia /bəˈnæɪmɪə/. [f. the generic name which was coined in 1979 from the name of J-R. *Bonami*, a French biologist.] *Bonamia ostreae*, a protozoan parasite of esp. Bluff oysters.

1986 *Catch* May-June 2 The Foveaux Strait oyster fishery was closed from 27 July 1986... This was in response to the serious threat from the parasite *Bonamia* which has infected the oyster beds. **1992** *Dominion* (Wellington) 15 Feb. 3 Scientists from Maffish begin a two-week survey of the bonamia-afflicted Foveaux Strait oyster beds on Monday. **1995** *Dominion* (Wellington) 9 Dec. 17 The problem was diagnosed..as the parasite named bonamia—pronounced for some reason as bonemia in the deep south.

boncer, var. BONZER.

bone.

1. [See also OED *bone* 3 b, *near the bone* destitute.] In the phr. **on the bone(s) (of one's arse)**, hard up.

1935 GUTHRIE *Little Country* x 178 Mr. Winks, who had no other living but politics, had 'been on the bone'..scratching an existence from commission work. **1988** SCOTT *Glory Days* 8 Lived on the bones of their arse for years before they got a break.

2. In the phr. **to give it a bone** [f. quieting a (hungry) dog's barking], be quiet!

1982 SHADBOLT *Once on Chunuk Bair* (1990) 30 Holy: Shut up. Smiler: Give it a bone, Porky. Mac: Put a sock in it or I will.

3. Special Comb. with reference to things Maori: **bone carver**, one who carves latter-day Maori artifacts from bone, usu. for sale to tourists; **bone people**, also **bone–wearer**, usu. a middle-class white, or often a Maori, who flaunts carved bone ornaments to advertise solidarity with Maori aims; **bone-scraper** *hist.*, one who 'scraped' or cleansed the bones of Maori dead in preparation for ritual disposal in a private or secret place; also **bone-scraping** *vbl. n.*, HAHUNGA.

1993 *Dominion* (Wellington) 15 Sept. 3 [X], a 29-year-old **bone-carver** of Kohimarama, earlier admitted one charge of rape. **1990** *Dominion Sunday Times* (Wellington) 2 Dec. 12 [Heading] Schoolchildren saved from crusading feminists and **bone people**. **1990** *Dominion Sunday Times* (Wellington) 30 Dec. 8 Liberals of the type generally known as 'bone people', have endeavoured to elevate the Treaty of Waitangi to almost mystical status. **1873** TINNE *Wonderland of Antipodes* 69 Separated from the rest of the inhabitants..were the **bone-scrapers**, who had performed the last offices to the dead. *Ibid.* 66 The most..interesting ceremonial..was a 'huhunga,' or **bone-scraping**. [**c1920** BEATTIE *Trad. Lifeways Southern Maori* (1994) 269 In regard to the scraping of the bones of the dead he fancied it was called ahu. It was done up at the Bay of Islands but he did not think it was done in Canterbury or Otago.] **1994** *Dominion* (Wellington) 7 Sept. 10 The central messages of the film [*Once Were Warriors*] offer..support for what might be called the **bone–wearers** of all races and a silly and damaging prescription for..the plight of the urban Maori... Maori activists and white liberals will like the idea that the answer is in 'culture', from which not a few already make a living.

bone *v. Freezing works*. To remove (bones) from carcases, used distinctively mainly in derived special combinations **boner, boning**.

1. As **boner. a.** A cattle beast graded as providing manufacturing beef rather than prime cuts.

1963 CASEY *As Short a Spring* 159 I ran into a packet of mastitis that first season—a lot of them had to go to the freezing works as boners. **1974** *NZ Agric.* 188 Culled dairy cows and culled beef animals are sent directly to the works as 'boners'—that is, the bones are removed from the carcasses and the meat is used for manufactured products (as distinct from meat that is used for prime cuts). **1982** *Agric. Gloss.* (MAF) 19 *Boners*: Old cows or bulls for slaughter to produce manufacturing (grinding) beef. Also young stock in very lean condition. *Ibid.* 33 *Boner*: Carcasses of animals intended for use as manufacturing meat (mince, hamburger, sausages, etc.) and usually graded as manufacturing.

b. Also **meat-boner**. A meat-worker who removes bones from carcasses.

1908 *Awards, etc.* 211 [Meat-workers award] [Rates of wages] Cooling-floor and gut-house hands, per day, 7s. 6d.; boners, per day, 8s. 6d. **1951** *Awards, etc.* 324 [NZ Freezing-Workers Award] [Rates of wages] Cattle, per head—Boners [£]0 3[s.] 0[d.] Freezers 0 3 2¼ Chillers 0 3 8. **1968** *Evening Post* (Wellington) 9 Aug. 10 [Heading] Striking boners have support of their union. **1974** *Dominion* (Wellington) 8 Mar. 1 At Longburn the boning room is idle because 12 boners have been dismissed. *Ibid.* 9 Mar 1 Meat boners and chiller hands were among those immediately affected. **1986** *Metro* (Auckland) July 76 Across in the boning room, the sides of beef are put through a band saw, and the pieces travel down a conveyer belt to the boners, working at tables in pairs. Theirs is heavy work as they cut the meat from the shoulder blade, ribs and thigh bone and slice it into the different cuts.

2. As **boning**, denoting the removal of bones from a carcase in a meatworks, in special Comb. **boning foreman**, the person in charge of a boning section or gang; **boning room**, the space in a meatworks where the bones are removed from (usu.) beef carcases.

1993 *Dominion* (Wellington) 16 Apr. 11 The pioneer of **hot-boning** in the New Zealand beef industry..says rivals' criticism of his end product is unjustified. **1992** *Evening Post (Wellington)* 7 Dec. 3 Company Directors were..a former Railcorp executive;.. and Jamie McGregor, previously a **boning foreman** at Whakatu. **1974** *NZ Agric.* 189 Meat is processed in a **boning** or cutting **room**, after it comes (whole or in quarters) from the cooling floor or from the chiller. 1974, 1986 [see 1 b prec.]. **1989** STIRLING *On Four Legs or Two* 12 Me mate here works in the boning room in the freezer.

bones-eye, var. BONES I.

bones I. Also **bones-eye**. [f. dial. *bunce* or *bonus*: cf. DARE *boners*, also *boney*, 1895, 1966.] A children's assertion of a prior claim or possession; occas. used for the usual 'bags I; I bags'.

1915 PEACOCKE *My Friend Phil* 37 Bones-eye first hide..unless you want it very much.

boney. A marble made out of, or having the appearance of, bone.

1972 SUTTON-SMITH *Folkgames Children* 174 There were the terms referring to particular kinds of marbles: for example, agates..bonies, bonsers.

bong. *Otago students*. [Perhaps from drug-users' *bong* a water-pipe for smoking marijuana; reinforced by *bong, bung* unconscious.] See quot. Also *v.* and *vbl. n.*

1985 *Sites* (Hodges 'Drinking Vernacular') XI. 13 An alcohol bong is constructed of a plastic funnel joined by a plastic tube. There are both large and small bongs. The smaller model holds one large bottle of beer, while the bigger bong can hold up to four. Once a bong has been filled with the desired amount of beer, one person holds the contraption high in the air while the intended recipient opens his mouth over the outside of the end of the plastic tube and allows the beer to rush in a torrent into his stomach... Bonging In the philosophy of practitioners of alcohol bonging, the whole exercise is undoubtedly fun.

bong(a), var. BOONG(A).

boning: see BONE *v.* 2.

bonita /bəˈnitə/. [Var. of *bonito*: also US, see Webster 1961 *bonito*.] Either of two marine species: (more usu.) *Brama brama* (fam.

BONITO

Bramidae) *Ray's bream* (BREAM 2 (2)); or *Hyperoglyphe antarctica* (fam. Centrolophidae) BLUENOSE. Contrast BONITO.

1970 SORENSEN *Nomenclature NZ Fish* 12 *Bonita*—Two fish species are taken in small quantities, Ray's Bream (*Brama raii*) and, chiefly in Cook Strait, *Hyperoglyphe porosa*. Both are commonly called Bonita or Bream and usually marketed as Groper. The common name Bonita is not to be confused with Bonito which is Skipjack Tuna, (*Katsuwonus pelamis*). **1982** [see BLUENOSE]. **1986** *Dominion* (Wellington) 28 Nov. 1 The fish were warehou and bluenose, also known as bonita. **1986** [see BLUENOSE].

bonito. [Spec. use of northern hemisphere *bonito* (ad. Spanish *bonito*, of doubtful origin) striped tunny.] In New Zealand waters *Katsuwonus* (formerly *Gymnosarda*) *pelamis*, *skipjack tuna* (TUNA *n.*²), often as **striped bonito**. Contrast BONITA. (*Bonito* is obsolescent in New Zealand use.)

1921 *NZJST* IV. 118 *Gymnosarda pelamis. Bonito...* Distribution: North Island coasts. Examples have been caught as far south as the Kaikoura Peninsula. **1927** PHILLIPPS *Bibliogr. NZ Fishes* (1971) 45 *Katsuwonus pelamis*. Bonito. **1936** *Handbook for NZ* (ANZAAS) 72 *Euthynnus pelamis*: Bonito. **1967** MORELAND *Marine Fishes* 52 Striped Bonito [*Katsuwonus pelamis*]... Striped tunny or tuna, skipjack, bonito, and sometimes skipper, are alternative names in use. **1970** SORENSEN *Nomenclature NZ Fish* 12 The common name Bonita is not to be confused with Bonito which is Skipjack Tuna.

bonsa, bonser, bonsor, varr. BONZER.

bonus bond. Often with init. caps. A New Zealand state security carrying a chance of a cash prize if its number is drawn.

1976 *Dominion* (Wellington) 22 Mar. 3 Bonus Bonzer: The prize of $6,000 in the Post Office Bonus Bonds weekly prize draw for March 20 went to bond unit No.490 962691. **1988** FRAME *Carpathians* 67 He'd spent the day like many other Pumaharians..searching through the Golden Kiwi results; or on Tuesdays waiting for the Bonus Bond results.

bonza, var. BONZER.

bonzer /ˈbɒnzə/, /ˈbɒnsə/, *n.* and *a*. Also **boncer, bonsa, bonser, bonsor, bonza**. [Poss. f. Brit. dial. *bouncer* anything very large of its kind; itself poss. ultimately f. Brit. dial. *bonce, boncer* var. *bounce, bouncer* a very large marble (orig. used for 'bouncing' or playing checkstones, a kind of knucklebones) (see EDD, DARE); and poss. influenced by *bonanza* (see quot. B 1, 1900): see also BOSKER and its variant *boshter* which may have related derivations.]

A. *n.*

1. [AND 1904.] Something or someone outstanding, fine, splendid, superior of a kind.

1906 PICARD *Ups & Downs* 26 America said she was a real boncer. **1930** *NZ Short Stories* 126 The fireman drank half of it, and said it was a 'bonzer'. **1970** *Truth* 29 Dec. 19 The [Manawatu judicial] committee committed a bonzer when it fined Otaki trainer Clem Bowry $100.

2. *Marble-players*. Also **bonzie**. A taw, or big marble.

1972 SUTTON-SMITH *Folkgames Children* 174 There were the terms referring to particular kinds of marbles: for example, agates..bomb-squashers, bonies, bonsers.

1978 p.c. Professor Graeme Kennedy *Bonzer* or *bonzie* used by an Auckland man of 66 years for a big marble: remembered from his boyhood c1918. **1989** MCGILL *Kiwi Baby Boomers* 45 Your shooting marble was usually a bonzer... One day I dug up an old purple bonzer... It was like finding a nugget of gold.

B. *adj*. Mainly in *attrib*. use.

1. [AND 1906.] Splendid, fine; beautiful.

[**1900** SCOTT *Colonial Turf* 11 [She] would inherit..bonanza dividends paid out by Reefers pork sausage mysteries. [An allusion to quartz-mine shareprofits.]] **1906** *Truth* 25 Aug. 3 Wallace made one 'bonsor' shot at goal from a difficult angle. **1910** FANNING *Players & Slayers* 13 Their joy [at seeing old-fashioned wing-forwards] was like the thrill of the alleged Spaniard, who watched a game in the heyday of 'wingerism': 'Caramba! eet ees splendida! Eet ees to me your bonsa or bosca.' **1916** ANZAC *On Anzac Trail* 27 The boys had fixed to give us a boncer welcome, but..in the words of our informant, 'they blued their cheques, got shikkared and the show was bust up'. **1917** *Tiki Talk* 35 Bonser little nurse goes past; comes to light with lollies an' tips a cove a smile. **1920** MANSFIELD *Stories* (1984) 246 Now that they lived in this fine house and boncer [1916 version *Aloe* 109 has bonzer] garden they were inclined to be very friendly. **1937** *Tararua Tramper* Dec. 8 [Advt] Denhard Bonza loaf. An ideal picnic loaf. **1947** *NZ Woman's Weekly* 2 oct. 17 She's got bonzer muscles, mum, and can race every boy and girl in the school. **1949** SARGESON *I Saw in My Dream* (1974) 52 No need to worry, he said. Be a bonzer afternoon. **1951** PARK *Witch's Thorn* 87 He knew a secret, scrub-hidden place under the bridge where a fellow could..have a bonzer view of Mrs Hush's place. **1973** *Sunday Times* (Wellington) 14 Oct. 44 The film quarterlies discovered Buster was bonzer. **1982** PRAIN *Seized* 26 Maggie:.. thanks Mo for a bonza night. **1991** VIRTUE *Always the Islands of Memory* 58 Sister had thought it a bonzer painting.

2. A male nickname.

1938 WINTER *Northern King Country—Random Sketches* 36 [In the 1890s] 'Bonser' Watts was the principal 'bookie'.

boo. In the phr. **before one can say boo**, very quickly.

1952 *Here and Now* Oct. 18 But before we could say boo, the constables had marched us down to the cell-block.

boo-ai, boo-ay, booay, varr. BOOHAI.

boob. [f. *boob* a prison cell: cf. also older *booby-hatch*, used in NZ (as in the US: DARE 1859) for a gaol or lock-up (elsewhere, often a lunatic asylum), see quot. 1909 BATTLER 1.]

1. In various attrib. uses as special Comb. in senses 'prison': **boob-blue**, an illicit prison-made alcohol; **boob dot**, a small tattoo under or at the side of the eye indicating a stay in borstal or prison; **boob-happy**, deranged by prison confinement; **boobhouse**, a prison; **boob tat**, a tattoo applied in prison; **boobweed (boob weed)**, prison-issue tobacco.

1984 BEATON *Outside In* 64 Kate: What is it, Boss? Di: A drop of the ol' **Boob Blue**! *Ibid*. 109 *boob blue*: alcohol obtained by straining brasso polish. **1991** DUFF *One Night Out Stealing* 10 [Crims] with their obvious histories tattooed all over em, and the rare ones who had..hardly any, like Sonny here who had only a very old boob dot under his right eye from his first borstal lag at age sixteen. **1953** *Here & Now* Nov.-Dec. 44 He'd done nearly nine years in three three-year sessions and he was **boob-happy**. **1953** HAMILTON *Till Human*

BOOHAI

Voices Wake Us 186 A blushing young maiden from the backblocks has nothing on the **boobhouse** leaders when it comes to avoiding the public eye. **1981** HARRISON *Quiet Earth* 153 'You know what a **boob tat** is?'... 'A tattoo done in jail. Or borstal. Or D.C... Detention Centre. Or remand home' **1989** *Metro* (Auckland) Mar. 51 His left arm (and hand) have been heavily (and badly) tattooed, first by the kids at the Owairaka boys' home and later by the men of Mount Eden jail. Edmonds calls them 'boob tats'. **1982** NEWBOLD *Big Huey* 245 **Boobweed** (n) Prison tobacco. **1991** STEWART *Broken Arse* 42 *Henry pulls out his boob weed. Piggyscrew. Not this. Have a roundy. He offers him a tailor-made.*

2. Special Comb. **boobhead** [f. *boob* + (*piss*, etc.) *head*] **a.** a prison inmate, one conditioned to prison life.

1950 *Here & Now* Nov. 14 Glossary of technical terms: A boobhead is a prisoner. **1953** HAMILTON *Till Human Voices Wake Us* 72 Of course, when it comes to smuggling things in, the boobhead always has one advantage over the screw. **1971** BAXTER *Collected Poems* (1980) 526 For the fate of a boobhead is That men do him bind And plant him in the digger Till he goes out of his mind. **1980** MACKENZIE *While We Have Prisons* 79 He lived in Mt Eden jail for many years, to become an accepted 'boob-head' character. *Ibid*. 95 *boob* prison; mental hospital. Boob-head—a person conditioned to life in a prison or mental hospital. **1991** DUFF *One Night Out Stealing* 45 Oh fuckem all, the boobheads of the world.

b. A fool; one who has 'blown' the wits with alcohol or other drugs.

1982 NEWBOLD *Big Huey* 245 Boobhead (n) Moron, imbecile. **1986** WEDDE *Symmes Hole* 70 How did they know he wasn't a Courtenay Place bus-shelter sherry boob-head?

boo-eye, var. BOOHAI.

boof. [A short form of *boofhead* a person or animal having a large head: cf. EDD *boof n.*²; cf. AND.] STARGAZER.

1986 PAUL *NZ Fishes* 118 *Monkfish Kathetostoma giganteum...* Known by a number of local names: giant stargazer, flathead, bulldog, boof, etc.

boohai /ˈbuːˌwaɪ/. Also with much variety of form as **boo-ai, boo-ay, booay, boo-eye, booeye, boo-hai, boohoy, bouai, Buhoi, buwai, Puhoi**. [Prob. an alteration of the place-name *Puhoi*, a township and district north of Auckland, once remote and difficult of access, orig. settled by German-speaking Bohemian immigrants.]

1. Often *joc*. A remote place or district. See also BACKBLOCK A 2 a, BACK OF BEYOND, BUSH A 2 a, CACTUS 2 a, WOOP-WOOPS, WOP-WOPS 1. **a.** Esp. in the phr. **in (up) the boohai**.

1922 p.c. R. Mason (1955). *boohai* heard and used in Pukekohe, Auckland, c1922 **1946** SIMPSON *If You'd Care to Know* 101 Another New Zealand expression is 'Up the Bouai' (pronounced boo-eye). There was a place near Auckland city which many years ago was somewhat isolated, and it was called the Bouai... To go 'up the Bouai' has become fairly general in use. Today, if a person comes to town from any lonely place in the forests or mountains, and a friend asks him where he has been, most likely the answer will be, 'Oh, I've been up the Bouai.' It is a general word for an isolated region. **1959** SINCLAIR *Hist. NZ* 97 The Bohemians.. founded Puhoi (the name of which, corrupted, is apparently the origin of the slang term 'the Boo-ay', a synonym for 'the out-backs'). **1963** BACON *In the Sticks* 184 *sticks*- 'out in the sticks', 'out in the backblocks', 'out in the bush', 'out in the booay', 'out in the cactus', all have the same basic meaning of 'fifty miles from nowhere'. **1963** CASEY *As Short a Spring* 244 You fancy them up here in the boo-eye, mortgaged up to their necks for the rest of their lives. **1966** *Encycl. NZ* II. 678 An example [of local slang terms] is the Auckland term *up the Puhoi* or *Boohoy* (its form varies a good deal) meaning 'gone somewhere or other' and this is a genuine local product referring to an old German settlement on the coast north of Auckland and little, if at all, in use elsewhere in New Zealand. *Ibid.* II. 680 Examples of slang and colloquial expressions of local origin are..*up the boohai* (and other forms) for 'off in some unknown locality', an Aucklander's idiom. **1969** *A.U.T.C. Song Book 3edn.* Song No.36 It's a long drive up from the buwai By Woodcocks and Kairpara [*sic*] flats. **1971** *Listener* 19 Apr. 56 Well, out of the boo-ai comes three trampers. One was a nuggety bloke in a sou'-wester. **1986** *NZ Herald* (Auckland) 1 Mar. 1 The oldest son, John, left Puhoi [c1900] when he was 16 to settle in Auckland... 'The expression "up the Buhoi" was said to have originated with him because when he was asked where he came from, that was what he replied in his strong accent—the same pronunciation of the name of our village can still be heard in Puhoi today,' said Mrs Williams. **1988** LAY *Fools on Hill* 220 Living in a shack in the middle of the boo-ai with a load of strangers, doing the washing by hand under a tilly lamp?

b. In the phr. **way to boohai**, intensifying remoteness or distance; 'way to blazes'.
1981 HUNT *Speaking a Silence* 88 When we got there, way to boo-eye up Lake Rotoiti way, we had to shovel the snow away before we put the tent up.

2. In the phr. **up the boohai**, completely awry, astray. Cf. *in the cactus* (CACTUS 1).
1955 BJ Cameron Collection (TS July) bouai up the bouai (adv.) Up the spout. **1959** SLATTER *Gun in My Hand* 91 Got the pricker with me. Slingin off at me he was. You're up the boo-ay he told me. **1960** MUIR *Word for Word* 171 'She'll be right? She'll be right up the boo-ay if we're not lucky,' Arthur said.

3. In elaborations, often associated with PUKEKO 3 a, forming evasive or dismissive replies to children or importunate questioners.
1930 p.c. W.J. Morrell (Wanganui) letter (30 Apr. 1984) to *Heinemann Dict. of NZ Quotations* 'Up the booeye for the rhubarb season'. Saying of the 1930s. Source unknown. **1988** *Through the Looking Glass* 126 Of the boys' funny sayings [in the 1930s] two live on in my memory... If he was asked where he was going, he would answer: 'Up the boo-ai in a matchbox hunting pukakers [pukekos] with a long-handled shovel.' **1988** McGILL *Dict. Kiwi Slang* 18 *up the boohai—shooting pukakas* (pukekos) an amusing extension of notion of being lost, possibly in the head, Sue Budd recalls. Grant Tilly recalls its completion: *up the boohai shooting pukakas with a popgun.* 'Boohai' c.1920. **1989** p.c. Mrs Lois Bieder 9 Nov. *Up the boohai*: My father, who would be 101 if he were alive, and my whole family, were frequent users of such happy expressions. This one can mean nothing else but 'Up the Blue Sky', and to couple, 'in a match box', a throw away evasive reply to such a question as 'Where have you been?'

boohoy, var. BOOHAI.

book, *n.*[1] [AND 1891.] A bookmaker; bookie.
1883 *Auckland Weekly News* 24 Mar. 10 A number of 'books' from Auckland were present, but business was not brisk. **1900** SCOTT *Colonial Turf* 134 If the 'books' did not see the horse doing good work, they would not bide. **1917** *Free Lance* (Wellington) 9 Mar. 21 One of the city's best-dressed 'books' has gone to Sydney for a change of clothes. **1934** *Truth* 18 Apr. 6 A bunch of [pukekos] were passed and the bookmaker ejaculated: 'Look at them, protected like the "books".

book, *n.*[2] *Farming.* [Cf. AND *book muster*, an inventory based on a stockbook.] In the phr. **off the books**, of stock, present and correct in number and type on the authority of the farm tally-book.
1921 GUTHRIE-SMITH *Tutira* (1926) 153 Instead, therefore, of collecting the sheep from every part of the run and counting them in the yards, we took delivery 'off the books'—that is, we accepted the flock on the previous shearing and lambing tally.

book, *n.*[3] *Whaling.* [See OED *book* 1 d (1840 Dana only): poss. f. the appearance of the blocks, resembling books.] See quots.
[*Note*] Such a 'book' when further sliced, and the slices themselves, were called a 'bible' or 'bibles': cf. OED *bible* a holystone block.
1982 RICHARDS *Whaling & Sealing Chatham Is.* 72f [Caption] Cutting Blackfish blubber for boiling down.— The blubber is cut into blocks then chopped into 'Books' to speed up the oil extractions. [The 'books' pictured appear to be about 150 x 75 mm, and about 25 mm thick.] **1982** MORTON *Whale's Wake* 55 Seamen sliced the blubber chunks thinly to make the boiling-out quicker and easier. Usually they left the slices together at one edge to facilitate handling; the chunk sliced in this fashion was called a 'book' for obvious reasons.

book, *v.*[1] *Sealing.* intr. To fold sealskins into layers like the leaves of books. Cf. BOOK *n.*[3]
1940 HOWARD *Rakiura* 40 If the cargo is intended for the European or American market, the skins are removed from the animal [*sc.* seal] with an inch of blubber adhering, and in the final simple treatment are washed, heavily slated, and then folded or 'booked' into rectangular shape for packing.

book, *v.*[2] [f. *book* account or invoice book.] As **to book up**, to charge on an account.
c1940 Used in the Havelock (Marlborough) store. Will you pay cash or book it up? **1960** MASTERS *Back-Country Tales* 173 As previously instructed Bill arranged for a wreath from the station people, including himself. This he booked up against the station.

booka-booka: see PUKAPUKA.

bookau /ˈbuˌkæu/, var. PUKAHU.

boom. [f. N. Amer. *boom*: see OED *n.*[2] 4 a.] Often *pl.* A chain of logs across a creek mouth or a river to retain floating logs; occas. the logs retained by a boom (see quot. 1911).
1874 BAINES *Edward Crewe* 177 It is nine miles from the dam to the 'boom' at the mouth of the creek. **1889** KIRK *Forest Flora* 151 Taking advantage of the first 'fresh'..the sluices of the dams are opened, and the [kauri] logs..are 'driven' to the booms by the volume of water suddenly liberated. The booms are formed by large logs secured to each other and to the bank by strong chains; they often enclose an area of several acres, which, after a successful 'drive', is crowded with thousands of logs. **1894** *NZ Official Year-book* 365 At the mouths of streams a line of floating [kauri] logs have been previously fastened together with iron 'dogs' and short chains; this is called a 'boom', and prevents the timber getting away to sea. **1907** LAING & BLACKWELL *Plants NZ* 63 Here [the felled kauri trees] lie until a 'fresh' drives them down to the creek or harbour where the 'boom' lies waiting. This boom is formed of a circle of logs fastened together with chains. **1911** *Weekly News* 2 Feb. [Caption] A boom of kauri logs waiting shipment at Whangarei. **1920** MANDER *Story NZ River* (1974) 198 They watched the progress of the log from the booms up the skids to the side of the breakdown platform. **1930** PINFOLD *Fifty Yrs. Maoriland* 60 On his return [from Upper Thames] he took us to what were called 'The Booms'. These were great logs of wood driven into the ground across the mouth of a river that opened out toward the sea. The bushmen..felled the trees. Afterwards, when a good rain came and flooded the river, the 'logs' would come down, and the 'booms' were expected to stop them from going out to sea. **1953** REED *Story of Kauri* 228 A boom consisted of heavy piles driven into the bottom of the river or harbour, strengthened by heavy stays, and giving support to a chain of stout barricading logs. The structure had to be strong enough to withstand the pressure of thousands of logs. **1964** HOWE *Stamper Battery* 15 We had certainly expected life in Thames to be more lively than it was at the 'booms' [of a timber camp].

boomer. [f. Brit. dial.: see EDD *n.*[1] 'anything very large of its kind'; AND 1843.]

1. Also as **little boomer**. A 'whopper'; anything very large of its kind.
1889 SKEY *Pirate Chief* 168 Here lies a man who lied so long... When, lo! one day, ourselves in luck, A boomer in his throttle stuck. **1905** THOMSON *Bush Boys* 65 It must have been a boomer of a slip, for it held together in one piece in a wonderful way, and so it was a boomer as you can see by the pile of stuff there now. **1910** *Truth* 26 Mar. 8 My word, he's a boomer. Must be over a hundred pounds, by the way he tugs. **1974** *Listener Short Stories* (1977) 120 Take half a pound of bait per person... Or take a very large one, for the season's started out a boomer. **1987** *Sunday Star* (Auckland) 14 June A13 The budget next Thursday, the Prime Minister says, will be a 'little boomer.' That threw various political soothsayers into a panic. Was he, they wondered, emphasising the word 'boomer'— or the adjective? **1991** *Sunday Star* (Auckland) 6 Oct. D1 It's the 'get to the point' attitude which is the hallmark of the Communicado product and the Communicado story..is a boomer because of it.

2. In *attrib.* or adjectival use. Very good, hugely successful.
1974 GIFFORD *Loosehead Len's Big Brown Book* 60 *Boomer*: Good (to describe play, or player, in Rugby). **1988** *Dominion* (Wellington) 23 Apr. 8 On behalf of all those who watched this year's boomer Christmas parade, may I thank all..who helped to make this fantastic occasion.

booming, *vbl. n. Otago goldmining.* [Orig. US mining: see OED.] Ground sluicing by accumulating and suddenly discharging a volume of water. Also *attrib.*
1939 BEATTIE *First White Boy Born Otago* 168 The Arrow is also a booming river when in flood. **1952** HEINZ *Prospecting for Gold* 48 Booming is ground sluicing by means of an intermittent supply of water.

boonga /ˈbʊŋ(g)ə/. *Offensive.* Also **bong** /bɒŋ/, **boong** /bʊŋ/, /bʊŋ/, **boonger, bung, bunga**. [Altered transf. use of Austral. *boong* an offensive name for an Aborigine or other coloured person, AND 1924: orig. uncertain, but prob. not from an Australian language.] A coloured person, esp. a Polynesian Pacific Islander.
1957 *Star* (Auckland) 29 Nov. 4 Aucklanders called Maoris niggers, blacks and 'boshees' a long-forgotten mid-century fore-runner of such terms as wog, gook, boong and hun. **1964** BOOTH *Footsteps in Sea* 174 The labels they pin on people and things, the queers, the coms., the bungs, the Poms, the Nips, and the rest of them. **1977** *Dominion* (Wellington) 17 Aug. 8 The

Labour Department sent a boy to a job which fellow workers told him was only done by 'boongers' (Islanders) because it was dirty and dangerous and the pay was poor. **1980** LELAND *Kiwi-Yankee Dict.* 16 *bong*: A term borrowed from Australia where it is used to refer to aborigines; in New Zealand, it is a derogatory reference to Maoris and occasionally Pacific Islanders. **1982** O'SULLIVAN *Rose Ballroom* 28 [Skull had] sunk piss with a bishop and mouthed more damns when the world didn't shape up than a bunga eats yams. **1985** MITCALFE *Hey Hey Hey* 148 Maoris is 'Boongers', right? And Polynesians is 'Coconuts', right? And Winston's half Boonger and half Coconut. **1987** *Evening Post* (Wellington) 22 July 12 Paul started the fight with three Samoan men after calling them 'boongas'. **1988** *Dominion Sunday Times* (Wellington) 3 Apr. 8 Other [White Club] members feel perfectly free to talk to me about 'bongas', 'a touch of the tar brush', 'the jungle coming out in him' and 'bloody Maoris'. **1990** KIDMAN *True Stars* 199 There was a bunch of Islanders playing their bloody boong music on the beach. Not that I'm racist or anything. **1991** *Evening Post* (Wellington) 26 Oct. 25 She called the Samoans 'bongas' and 'coconuts' and told them they should go home to Samoa.

booreedy, var. PURIRI.

booster. [Poss. a play on *boost* to give a lift up, and *lift* steal.] A shoplifter.
    1953 *NZ Observer* 23 Sept. 7 An expert 'booster' (shoplifter), he goes into shops..and starts a conversation with the assistant.

boot, *n.*

1. As **the boot**, a kicking attack.
    1907 *Truth* 23 Mar. 4 The tough's 'cobbers'..are not particular whether it is 'the boot'..or even a bottle that is brought into action. **1959** SLATTER *Gun in My Hand* 205 Some pakehas got him outside and into him with the boot.

2. In the phr. **to put (sink) the boot in** (occas. heard as **plant the boot**). **a.** [AND 1915.] To kick a prostrate foe, to kick a vulnerable or disabled person.
    1906 *Truth* 24 Nov. 5 They have no notion of what is called British fair play..the moment a man is down they put the boot into him. **1911** *Truth* 26 Aug. 5 According to McCowan..he remarked, with vehemence, 'Put in the boot low down; don't go any further.' **1953** *Truth* 3 Mar. 9 Raymond attacked him 'putting the boot in'. **1971** CRUMP *Bastards I Have Met* 19 He dropped two of the blokes who butted in to stop him putting the boot into Ted while he was on the ground.
    b. *fig.* [AND 1916.] To treat unfairly; to attack a disadvantaged opponent; to play rough.
    c1926 THE MIXER *Transport Workers' Song Book* 107 All of them keeping the worker down, by putting in the boot. **1929** DEVANNY *Riven* 293 She had done him dirty. She had 'put in the boot'. **1935** MITCHELL & STRONG in Partridge *Slang Today* 286 [The] following [was] employed by those who served in the [Great] War..*put the boot in*, to take an unfair advantage. **1959** [see PANNIKIN BOSS]. **1972** *Sunday Times* (Wellington) 8 Oct. 2 In full evangelistic cry Marcus is likely to shout 'hallelujah', and urge his audience to sink the boot into Satan. **1986** CRANE *I Can Do No Other* 100 The police had found him sleeping out in one of the city gardens and had 'put the boot in'.

3. [AND 1950.] In the phr. **boots and all**, with no holds barred, wholeheartedly, esp. in the phr. **to go in boots and all**, often alluding more specifically to the over-enthusiastic use of questionable, often violent, tactics.
    1924 *Free Lance* (Wellington) 28 May 38 They were [betting] on him [*sc.* a racehorse] 'boots and all' at Wanganui. **1947** NEWTON *Wayleggo* 78 We encountered a clutch of young Paradise ducks, just in the flapper stage..so we went in boots and all. **1968** SLATTER *Pagan Game* 123 Got held up last Monday night..but this time I'm in, boots and all. She's not sixteen remember, said Dick Howell. **1988** MCGILL *Dict. Kiwi Slang* 18 *boots and all* no holds barred, complete or enthusiastic commitment; eg 'What better title for big lock Andy Haden's story than *Boots 'n' All*?'

4. *Shearing.* In the phr. **boots (boots on the board, boss's boots)**, shearers' warning calls on the approach of the owner or farmer.
    1955 BOWEN *Wool Away* 4 Yet I believe that if a shearer does continually cut sheep in these places he shears less in a day, as he is mentally conscious of his shearing, looking for the 'boss's boots.' **1987** OGONOWSKA-COATES *Boards, Blades & Barebellies* 95 *Boss's boots*. Whenever the boss is sighted the shearers pass on the phrase 'boss's boots' or 'boots on the board' as a warning. Not only was the boss the only person in the shed to wear boots, but from the doubled-up position of the blade shearer working over a sheep, the boss's boots were the first thing he saw. **1989** *NZ Eng. Newsletter* III. 21 *boots on the board:* The boss is in the vicinity.

5. In the phr. **there's an old boot for every sock**, said to longtime bachelors and spinsters as an expression of hope.
    1980 LELAND *Kiwi-Yankee Dict.* 103 *there's an old boot for every sock*: a phrase bearing reassurance for all those seeking spouse or paramour.

bootlace. *Shearing.* Mainly *pl.* [f. a resemblance to the formerly common bootlaces cut from strips of leather.] A narrow strip of skin cut off by rough shearers. See quots. 1934, 1955.
    1934 *Press* (Christchurch) (Acland Gloss.) 13 Jan. 13 *Boot laces*.— Narrow strips of skin cut off by rough shearers, generally when opening up the neck. Hence the verb, to *b[oot]l[ace]*. **1955** BOWEN *Wool Away* 155 Bootlace. A long thin strip of skin cut off a sheep, seen mostly on last side. It usually comes from wrinkled skin. **1986** RICHARDS *Off the Sheep's Back* 97 Several sheep went out the port hole minus a few 'boot laces' from their neck.
    Hence *v. trans.*, to take a strip of skin off (a sheep) while shearing.
    1934 [see above]. **1955** BOWEN *Wool Away* 41 Also, having the skin wrinkled does not make for quite such a good job, and you are more likely to bootlace the sheep—i.e. cut the wrinkles off in long thin strips of skin.

bootleg. *v. Mining. intr.* Of an explosive charge, to explode incompletely.
    1953 *Evening Post* (Wellington) 12 Apr. 6 An accident which took place in the course of tunnel operations..A charge had 'bootlegged' on March 28 at 9 p.m.—that was, some holes had not blown completely.

boozaroo, var. BOOZEROO.

booze. In special Comb. **booze artist**, see ARTIST; **booze balloon**, a protruding stomach reputedly caused by excessive drinking of alcoholic liquor; **booze barn**, a tavern or a hotel with extensive bars given over to the rapid serving of liquor (see also *beer barn* (BEER 3)); **booze-rooster**, an over-indulgent drinker (a play on BOOZEROO 1).
    1979 WILLIAMS *Skin Deep* 17 That's a **booze balloon** around his middle region, and his shoulders slope a bit. **1979** GEBBIE & MCGREGOR *Incredible 8-Ounce Dream* 94 While there appears to be some general consensus that a small cosy neighbourhood tavern..is a preferable alternative to a **boozebarn** sited in the middle of a concrete wasteland, no one wants them in the street. **1984** *Evening Post* (Wellington) 20 Aug. 14 The new bottle stores and parlour bars..are part of moves by the Wellington South Licensing Trust to get away from the 1970s image of taverns as large booze barns. **1989** HALEY *Transfer Station* 41 They were going flat out in the booze barn pulling in as much coin as they could while things were sweet. **1992** ANDERSON *Portrait Artist's Wife* 260 No booze barns here. Not in 1972, my word. Those days are gone. **1962** JOSEPH *Pound of Saffron* 253 'The way she talks..you'd think I was a regular **booze-rooster**.'

boozelum: see BOOZEROO.

boozeroo. Also **boozaroo.**

1. [An elaboration of *booze* + -EROO 'a factitious slang suffix' (OED): occas. + *-elum*.] In early use, occas. **boozelum** (see quot. 1911). (A bout of) heavy drinking, a drinking party; a spree.
    1908 *Truth* 4 Jan. 6 Walker's explanation was that he was on the boozeroo, and didn't know what he was doing. **1910** *Truth* 5 Mar. 5 The face of Elizabeth Sheehan, next charged, reminded one of a lost soul plunging violently in a sea of boiling beer. She pleaded guilty to boozeroo, but denied with vehemence that she was a rogue and vagabond. **1911** *Truth* 30 Sept. 5 His good lady had got him sundry jobs which he had promptly lost through the 'boozelum.' He was all right when he was sober, only he was never sober. **1943** BENNETT *English in NZ* in *Amer. Speech* XVIII. 89 A 'good spree' would be described as a 'a proper old boozeroo', this word being of the same pattern as various American words in *-eroo*. **1947** DAVIN *For Rest of Our Lives* 75 All the boys still drinking to celebrate the Second Ech coming from England... And the whole lot of them thinking: well here's for a last good boozeroo. **1952** *Landfall 23* 224 His [beer] party is not so different from the Saturday night boozeroo in the Sydenham side-street with the keg on the kitchen-sink. **1960** BOSWELL *Ernie* 106 'Meeting!' retorted Mother, witheringly. 'Boozeroo you mean!... I'm glad the old Soak had to walk home.' **1970** *Listener* 12 Oct. XII. It's going to be a real boozeroo. **1992** *Evening Post* (Wellington) 17 Jan. 3 I must here confess I've never been to a Legion boozaroo.

2. [An elaboration of *booz*(er + -*eroo*.] A (low) pub.
    1963 BAXTER *Collected Poems* (1980) 290 Till any Scotsman with the shakes Can pile on your head his mistakes And petrify a boozaroo Reciting *Tam o' Shanter* through. **1988** MCGILL *Dict. Kiwi Slang* 19 *boozeroo* drinking bout.—pub.

bo-peep, *n.* [A play on *peep* and *Bo-peep* the nursery-rhyme character: AND 1941.] A look, a peep.
    1946 SARGESON *That Summer* 61 I'd seen a smart-looking piece of goods drying her face and having a bo-peep out of the bathroom window. **1961** CRUMP *Hang On a Minute Mate* 91 Have a bo-peep at this little lot, Jack. **1964** HORI *Fill It Up Again* 94 The men promised not to have a bo-peep at [Godiva]. **1976** WILSON *Pacific Star* 84 So we went over to have a bo-peep.

borage. Mainly *Sl.* Usu. as **blue borage.** Transf. mistaken use of the name *borage* (*Borago officinalis* fam. Boraginaceae), a blue-flowered European herb, for the similarly blue-flowered hairy weed *viper's bugloss* (*Echium vulgare* fam. Boraginaceae), common in dry inland parts of esp. Marlborough and North Canterbury. See also *blue weed* (BLUE *a.* 2 b).

1926 Hilgendorf *Weeds* 143 Viper's Bugloss..also called blue weed and by mistake, blue borage, occurs on roadsides, river-beds, and fields in both islands, though it is commoner in the south, and especially in Marlborough. **1954** *Bull. Wellington Bot. Soc. No.27* 11 [Clarence Valley, Marlborough] Tussock is continuous..except for occasional patches of scree, colonized by blue borage. **1959** McCaskill *Molesworth* 248 Small local hives of wild bees produced honey with a special flavour due to the mixture of nectar from white clover, viper's bugloss (known locally [on Molesworth] as blue borage) and various wildflowers. **1969** *Standard Common Names Weeds* 7 borage, blue [=] *viper's bugloss*. **1980** Adams *Wild Flowers* 32 Viper's bugloss, or blue devil, often incorrectly called 'borage', makes a sea of blue on open ground, particularly..in the South Island. **1993** *Listener* 15 May 54 The beautiful blue flowers of vipers bugloss, also known as blue borage, which clothes high-country hills.

borak /'boræk/. Now more commonly **(the) borax**. [AND *borak* ad. Aboriginal Wathawurung language *burag* 'no, not', orig. used in Austral. pidgin to express negation, 1839; as a *n.* nonsense, 1845; *poke borak* 1873, *borax* 1902.]

1. a. In the phr. **to poke borak (the borax) (at)**, to chaff, tease; to ridicule.

1887 *Auckland Weekly News* 17 Sept. 21 My first thought was that the gentle shepherd was 'taking a rise out of me,' 'poking borax,' 'playing a little game,' and so forth. **1904** *NZ Observer* 27 Aug. 2 Notwithstanding all the 'borak' that has been poked at the Premier, Richard is plainly in earnest on the subject of stimulating the birth rate. **1914** [see chiack *v.*]. **1935** Marks *Memories* 60 As soon as the boss left the room (always an opportunity for us to 'poke borak' at one another). **1945** *NZPD* CCLXXII. 254 It is all very well for Opposition members to 'poke borax' at this sort of thing. **1959** Slatter *Gun in My Hand* 224 Taffy was always poking the borax at the queers. **1974** Sargeson in *Islands* 7 91 It was Brixton's habit—talking to himself, a long monologue which reproduced the slang of forty years ago..tell about some bloke he had a snicker on, some joker who would work a slinter if you didn't watch out—or he might start poking borax. **1984** Ovenden *Ratatui* 189 I was only poking the borax. **1990** *Sunday Mag.* 20 May 21 You can poke the borax at one another.

b. Nonsense, 'bulldust'.

1904 *NZ Observer* 23 Apr. 4 If one could only think that Attic salt was a commodity that you could buy at the grocers..it would be easier to determine how much of the eloquence poured out at..meetings of the Natives' Association is genuine and how much 'borak'.

2. As **the borax**, the blame; occas. concretely, a scolding.

1946 Cooze *My Little State Home* 54 All the borax cannot, in fairness, be heaped upon her permed head. **1986** *Metro* (Auckland) July 80 Frank Barnard comments: 'We got borax from the members, and congratulations from the Prime Minister.' **1992** *Dominion Sunday Times* (Wellington) 26 July 27 We've had the borax thrown at us, and I can't say it didn't have a detrimental effect on some of the players.

bore.

1. Esp. as **artesian bore** [spec. use of **artesian**, orig. of the type of well found in Artois, France: AND *artesian bore* 1897], an artesian well. Also *attrib.*

1867 Hochstetter *NZ* 509 The depth of these bore-holes in the street of Christchurch averages about 83 ft. **c1875** Meredith *Adventuring in Maoriland* (1935) 157 At Makaraka..an artesian bore was put down which struck water at about a hundred feet. **1882** *TrNZI* XIV. 121 A recent bore put down at Clinton to a depth of 102 feet, presented..the same features, so far as the constant inrush of water was concerned. **1943** *NZJST* XXIII. 98B A few households and business concerns obtain excellent water from bores sunk in the old sedimentary rocks. **1971** Taylor *Plekhov Place* 91 'Water, bloody water. Where is it?' another bellowed. A fruitless search ensued. No tanks. 'Must have sunk a bloody bore.' **1981** Gee *Meg* 48 He had rainwater tanks and an artesian bore and compost bins. **1988** *Dominion* (Wellington) 6 May 3 Kut and Kolour salon owner..said many of her customers had had problems with their hair since the town switched to bore water supply.

Hence **artesian boring** [OED *n.* 1830].

1864 Williamson *Rep. Timaru Rd. Bd.* in Gillespie *S. Canterbury* (1958) 473 I would urge upon the Board that they..make a survey of the neighbourhood with a view to artesian boring.

2. A (geo)thermal bore, for the supply of hot mineral water for bathing, heating, or the generation of electric power.

1962 Farrell *Power in NZ* 67 Bores in the first stage of blowing-in have been heard from as far as eighteen miles away. **1988** Stafford *New Century in Rotorua* 250 Hot water had been extracted from the ground by hand-sunk bores since the 1920's. **1991** *Dominion* (Wellington) 24 Sept. 12 [Heading] Rotorua bore users seek 'fairer' charge... Taupo geothermal users have escaped charges on domestic bores.

borer: see *oyster borer* (oyster 4 b).

borer, *n.*[1] [Spec. use of *borer* a wood-boring insect: cf. OED *borer* 1 c.]

1. Usu. as **the borer**. Any of various wood-boring insects, chiefly *Anobium* spp., infesting houses.

1883 *Brett's Colonists' Guide* 227 The Borer.— Figure 11 is the likeness of a longicorn beetle (*Navomorpha*), which is often called the 'borer'. **1911** *Maoriland Worker* 6 Oct. 7 If their hearts are not broken before then or the borers have not eaten the house, in 20 years they will own their own homes. **1927** *Wairarapa Times-Age* in Bromby *Eyewitness Hist.* (1985) 150 If possession of the Ranfurly Shield is to encourage this class of warfare, the sooner the borer consumes this trophy the better. **1939** Beattie *First White Boy Born Otago* 56 The talk of borers in these wooden houses has only been during the last 30 or 35 years [*sc.* from c1900]. **1959** Slatter *Gun in My Hand* 228 I lived in an old house with borer. **1969** [see duchesse]. **1982** Hulme *Silences Between* 10 My flat is old dust from borer tunnels.

2. As **borer dust** [if not idiolectal, a euphemism for bull-dust], nonsense.

1988 McGill *Dict. Kiwi Slang* 112 *that's borer dust* that's a lot of nonsense or rubbish.

3. Special Comb. **borer bomb**, a proprietary device emitting fumes poisonous to the borer.

1979 *Salient* (Wellington) 1 Oct. 17 A borer bomb was thrown into a Committee meeting..in the Lounge. **1990** *Sunday Magazine* (Auckland) 6 May 45 A school hall was evacuated after they let off borer bombs to add atmosphere to the performance.

borer, *n.*[2] A machine which drills artesian bores.

1863 *Report* 19 June in Haast *Geol. Canterbury & Westland* (1879) 58 In summing up I may..state, that the strata through which the borer has to go will not..offer any serious obstacle.

boride, var. puriri.

born in a tent: see tent 2.

borough. *Hist.* [Spec. use of *borough* a town having a municipal corporation: see OED *n.* 3.]

1. An urban unit of local government controlled by an elected borough council, replaced by **District (Council)** since 1974 through the Local Government Act.

1867 Acts NZ 31 Vic No.24 [Para.] 29 There shall be in and for each single borough a council consisting of nine councillors. **1955** *BJ Cameron Collection* (TS July) borough (n) The ordinary unit of town government. An area with a certain minimum density of population and having a mayor and council elected by the residents. **1974** *NZ Statutes* II. No.66 1538 Every reference in this [Local Government] Act... To a borough or borough council shall..be read as including a reference to a district or district council, as the case may be: To a county or county council shall be read as a reference to a district or district council.

2. Comb. **borough-council** (occas. **Boro' Council**). **a.** A council elected to administer a borough.

1885 *Wairarapa Daily* 8 Oct. 2 If the Brigade breaks up, the duty of providing efficient means for protection from fire will devolve on the Borough Council. **1904** *NZ Observer* 6 Feb. 4 In the local governing body, which began as a road board and developed into a borough council, Knox was always prominent. **1913** *NZ Bulletin* 8 Feb. 16 [Heading] Hastings Boro' Council. **1921** *NZPD* CLXXXVIII. 177 The late Henry Serjeant..had left a considerable amount of landed property in Wanganui to the Borough Council. **1930** *NZPD* CCXXVI. 866 The Borough Council was desirous of making certain of the sections available as sites for workers' dwellings. **1945** *Korero* (AEWS Background Bulletin) 29 Jan. 19 Strictly speaking, a Borough Council is the highest unit of local government in New Zealand. **1951** *AJHR H-28* 15 The West Harbour Borough Council had..done practically nothing to improve the area.

b. *fig.* [A play on (*city*-)*corporation*.] A (small) 'corporation'; a pot-belly.

1934 Tararua Tramper Mar. 4 Mr. Scully won the gentleman's prize; he was a fat and dissipated person with a point lace cravat, heavy nose, ginger whiskers, and a borough council.

borra borra, var. poroporo.

boscar, var. bosker.

boshter: see bosker.

bosker /'bɒskə/, *a. Obs.* in modern speech. Also occas. **boscar**, also **boshter** (see quots. A 1906, B 1916); and occas. as a noun (see quots. A 1906, 1910). [Origin unknown; poss., with some alteration, from the same source as bonzer q.v.]

A. In attributive use. [AND *bosker* 1905, *boshter* 1908.] bonzer B 1.

1902 in Lawlor *More Wellington Days* (1962) 28 1902 January 4 Went for a picnic in a drag to York Bay and had a bosker time. **1906** *Truth* 8 Sept. 12 'Do you like going to church?' asked a visitor of a Methodist minister's son. 'My oath!' said the lad. 'It's a real boshter to hear Dad talking for a solid hour and a half, and Ma never allowed to say a word!' **1910** *NZ Free Lance* (Wellington) 8 Jan. 12 You're a bosker, Ma! **1911** Kiwi *On the Swag* 14 We gave him a boscar funeral. **1922** Mulgan *Three Plays NZ* 36 [Young flapper speaks] That's a boscar song. **1934** Scanlan *Winds of Heaven* 143 He says it would be a bosker game kicking them [*sc.* top hats] round the yard. **1942** *NZEF Times* 21 Dec. 18 Makes a boska big blaze, doesn't it? **1947** *Landfall 3* 219 [Sargeson's] ear is fine [in *That Summer*] so that the exact out-of-dateness of schoolboy argot, regional relics, as for example 'bosker'..are registered as neatly as the rise and fall of his lines. **1953** 14 M A19 Thames DHS 4 Bosker (boscer) **1963** KINROSS *Please to Remember* 85 'By crikey!' we said. 'What a bosker cop!'

B. In predicative use. [AND 1923.] BEAUTY B 1.
1910 *Truth* 23 Apr. 1 He said: 'It smells bosker.' I said: 'It smells rotten.' **1916** *Weekly News* (Auckland) 23 Mar. 14 The thrill of a bayonet charge is, as I am informed, boshter. **1937** SARGESON 'Cow Pats' in *Tomorrow* 6 Jan. He said it made his feet feel bosker and warm. So we all stuck our feet into cow-pats, and after walking over the frost it was bosker and warm sure enough. **1978** *Islands 21* 240 I tell people to read [Sargeson's 'Cow Pats'], especially the young, for it shows so precisely how it is against dignity to do certain things simply because it feels 'bosker'. I quote that last word because to the young..the use of once current slang is a little impediment.

boss.
1. [Spec. use of *boss* master.] **a.** A (term of address to a) station-owner.
1874 CAIRD *Sheepfarming NZ* 12 The owner of the station commonly called the 'Boss.' **1888** D'AVIGDOR *Antipodean Notes* 160 Occasionally, during those early days, the 'boss' (proprietor) would come round and scold men for not working hard enough. **1891** CHAMIER *Philosopher Dick* 5 The 'residence' stood close by..[where] 'the Boss' and 'the Missus' lived. *Ibid.* 33 'Is the boss at home?' I shouted to him trying to appear colonial. **1933** *Press* (Christchurch) (Acland Gloss.) 16 Sept. 15 If the owner manages his place himself, he is called, and addressed as, 'boss'. If not, the boss is whoever gives the men their orders. Presumably it comes (via Australia or America?) from the South African 'Baas'. **1947** BEATTIE *Early Runholding* 35 On Christmas or Boxing Day..the hands would run a picnic, the biggest donation being from the 'boss' or owner [of the station]. **1955** BOWEN *Wool Away* 2 Good weather, good shed, good sheep, good boss, and a good gang create an atmosphere of work and action. **1987** OGONOWSKA-COATES *Boards, Blades & Barebellies* 95 Boss. The runholder or his/her manager. The term is loosely used by the shearers to refer to whoever gives the men their orders.

b. In special collocations: **boss's boots!**, see BOOT *n*. 4; **boss's royal**, see ROYAL 1.

2. Special Comb. **boss-cocky** [AND 2, a leader, 1902], often ironical, a leader who is given, or who assumes, authority.
1910 *Truth* 5 Mar. 4 All these men are responsible to Mr. Robinson, who, in turn, is responsible, during the session only, to the Speaker. Out of the session he would appear to be absolute 'boss cocky'. **1951** PARK *Witch's Thorn* 71 I have been baptized by the boss cocky, old Bishop Lenihan, long time ago now. **1968** *NZ Contemp. Dict. Suppl.* (Collins) 4 *boss cocky n.* any farmer who employs men, hence, any one who is undisputed leader.

3. In the phr. **boss of the board(s)** (**boss over the board** [AND 1893]), the overseer of a shearing board or shed. Cf. *board walker* (BOARD *n*.[1] 3 a).
1912 *Maoriland Worker* 29 Mar. 12 When the boss of the board was in a bad humor [*sic*]..he used the raddle on the sheep shorn by the shearer and the raddle sheep were counted out and the shearer not paid for them. **1941** BAKER *NZ Slang* 39 The use of *board* for the floor of a shearing shed is also slang. Whence comes *a full board* and *boss-over-the-board*. **1947** Ross in Beattie *Early Runholding* (1949) 59 He acted as shepherd, wool-classer, 'boss of the board' in the shearing shed, and wool scourer. **1967** HARPER *Kettle on Fuchsia* 92 Among all those men in dungarees..was one man with a high starched collar and tie. Systematically he walked the woolshed floor, saw that every sheep was thoroughly shorn, not a tuft left, and kept an account of the tallies. He was known as 'the boss of the boards.' **1975** HARPER *Eight Daughters* 25 Each shearing season, for many years he came..to be 'boss of the shearing board'. **1981** SUTHERLAND & TAYLOR *Sunrise* 43 And he acted as boss-of-the-board when Mr Knox wasn't in the shed.

bot, *n*.[1] [Transf. use of *bot(t)* a parasite or parasitical worm afflicting farm animals; or as *the bot*, the affliction so caused.]

1. a. Usu. as **the bot**, a passing illness such as a cold, esp. **to have (catch) the bot**, to have or catch a cold, to feel unwell; formerly applied specifically to lung or bronchial infection (so Partridge and McNab, but not elsewhere well-attested, and poss. recalling lungworm in sheep).
1937 PARTRIDGE *Dict. Slang* 83 *bot*... A germ: New Zealand medical: from ca.1928. Perhaps ex the *bot(-fly)*, which, in horses, lays eggs that are said to penetrate into the animal when they hatch. 3. Hence, a tubercular patient: id. from ca. 1929. **1938** *Press* (Christchurch) (McNab Slang) 2 Apr. 18 'Bot' is a rare example of medical slang, meaning a germ or a tubercular patient. **1941** BAKER *NZ Slang* 51 Emerging originally from children's slang to bulk quite considerably in a grown-up world is the serviceable term *bot*. Its origin seems to be medical, since in early uses *bot* is rendered as a germ, doubtless from *bot-fly*. From this comes the phrase of greeting, *How are the bots biting?*.. Of fairly recent development in New Zealand is the phrase *to have the bot*, to be sick or out of sorts, moody or disagreeable. **1953** 14–15 M A2 Thames DHS 31 The Bot [sickness] [M7] **1968** SLATTER *Pagan Game* 144 And if you have a good rub down and wrap up warm after, nobody will catch the bot. **1987** GEE *Prowlers* 45 'How are you mate? Off colour, eh? Got the bot?' **1992** *Evening Post* (Wellington) 4 Nov. 2 He had been feeling 'a bit nauseous, hot and crabby' after taking antibiotics for 'a bit of the bot'.

Hence **botty** *a*., (suggestive of) chesty (illness).
1995 *Dominion* (Wellington) 10 Apr. 8 Q. What are the latest excuses when ringing in sick?.. A. Try: a severe biliousness, crook guts, gout, migraine..nasal squeaks, botty coughs.

b. *Obs.* **how are the bots biting?**, 'how's things?, how are you getting on?', a humorous greeting.
1937 PARTRIDGE *Dict. Slang* 83 *bots biting?, how are the*. How are you?: New Zealand medical: from ca. 1929. **1941** [see 1 a above]. *c*1941 Used freq. as a greeting or friendly phrase by Miss Johannah O'Connor (Wellington), a retired nurse (Ed.).

2. *Obs.* [AND cadger, 1916.] A smalltime financial parasite, a cadger, a bludger. Hence *v*. [AND *v. trans.* 1921, *intr.* 1934] *trans.*, to cadge from, to borrow from (someone); also hence **on the bot**, on the cadge. Cf. **cold bite**.
1941 BAKER *NZ Slang* 52 By the 1920s a *bot* is being used extensively for a troublesome person, for a persistent borrower, a financial parasite. By 1925 the noun *bot* was translated to a verb, and as a result we have *to bot*, to borrow money, to impose on others, and *botting*, the practice.

bot, *n*.[2] Short for *bottle* (of liquor).
*c*1945 *Sixes & Sevens* (Troopship pub.) 7 'It's a grim show,' I said. 'You can't have a victory on one bot of Canadian.' **1984** *Cosmo* July-Aug. 56 You'd con the girls into hiding a couple of 'bots' in their enormous stoals [*sic*] and stash the grog up the chimneys [of the Majestic Cabaret].

Botany Bay. *Obs.* [f. *Botany Bay* as an Australian home of convicts.] In the special Comb. **Botany Bay language**, abusive or foul language. Cf. *Australian language* (AUSTRALIAN 3).
1866 HENDERSON *Otago & Middle Is. NZ* 20 I am credibly informed that the person this letter is for, is a cattle stealer, a swindler and a bastard..choice Botany Bay language.

bottle, *n*.

1. *pl.* A drinking game.
1988 *Dominion Sunday Times* (Wellington) 13 Mar. 16 Other well-known [drinking] games are Hokonui Swindle, Bottles, Fluffy Ducks, Bunnies are Hovering, Cardinal Huff.

2. Used *attrib.* in special Comb. **bottle boy**, a young collector of refundable bottles from the litter left after sports gatherings; **bottle-drive**, the organized collection of refundable bottles, esp. empty beer or soft-drink bottles, to raise money for charitable or public causes; **bottle lantern**, see quot. (see also LANTERN for synonyms); **bottle licence** *hist.*, a licence to sell bottled liquor; **bottle top** *obs.* [a transf. use from the shape, and poss. a play on *bluebottle* policeman], a policeman's helmet.
1959 SLATTER *Gun in My Hand* 78 The **bottle boys** will have a good collection after this game. **1976** JOHNSTON *New Zealanders* 149 Most take their bottles home, and the '**bottle-drive**'—collecting empties to gain the deposit on them—is a frequent method of raising money for several organisations. **1977** HALL *Glide Time* 17 Plus a bottle drive for the Girl Guides. **1988** McGILL *Dict. Kiwi Slang* 19 *bottle drive* fund raising by collecting empty bottles from residences for the miniscule deposit; now declining. **1940** McBRIDE in Heinz *Bright Fine Gold* (1974) 17 **Bottle lanterns** were made by knocking off the bottom of a bottle and dropping a candle in, which was held firmly in place by the narrow neck. **1868** GRACE *Journal* June in *Pioneer Missionary* (1928) 192 Europeans on all sides are trying to get what they call '**bottle licenses**'—which, if they succeed, will mean that the Natives may be paid their rents in grog! **1894** *NZ Official Year-book* 258 Bottle licenses can be granted only in the Provincial Districts of Hawke's Bay, Otago, Westland, Marlborough, and Nelson; and in those districts there are not more than sixty. **1952** *Here & Now* Oct. 19 Bluey got smart and..knocked a constable's **bottletop** off his head.

bottle, *v*.[1] *Obs. intr.* To dash, to bolt.
1907 *Truth* 18 May 6 One day when he went round to the back of the house from the street two men bottled out of the front door.

bottle, *v*.[2]

1. [AND 1917.] *trans.* To strike or attack (someone) with a (broken) bottle. Cf. JUG 1.
1971 SHADBOLT *Bullshit & Jellybeans* 82 A real tough guy smacked another guy in the face with a bottle. It was the first time most of the students had seen a guy get bottled. **1974** *Evening Post* (Wellington) 2 Oct. 19 He said that James—had been 'bottled' by McCormick and would be scarred for life. **1980** *Truth* 25 Nov. 5 On both occasions he had denied 'bottling' Tuohy. **1991** *North & South* (Auckland) June 85 Minty had been to the hospital to have his head stitched up because he'd been bottled, and they'd followed him back.

2. [Also Brit. dial.: see EDD 6.] *trans.* To feed (young animals) from a bottle.
1981 *Listener* 14 Nov. 7 The pupils were allowed to bottle the young lambs.

3. [f. *bottle* to preserve in a glass container: the phr. ***blood's worth bottling*** expressive of admiration is recorded in Austral. in 1919 (*Digger Dial.* (1990) 23).] Usu. in the phr. **(to have blood) worth** (or **worthy of**) **bottling**, to be a valuable or staunch person (or thing), to be well worth preserving.

1959 SLATTER *Gun in My Hand* 147 His blood's worth bottling. He won't be beat that bloke. **1976** MCCLENAGHAN *Travelling Man* 18 'Your blood's worth bottling, boy,' said Sam appreciatively. **1989** *Dominion* (Wellington) 8 Aug. 1 [Caption: referring to Prime Minister Lange's resignation.] A smile worth bottling. **1991** *Evening Post* (Wellington) 14 Dec. 52 His remarks..were eloquent; his language worthy of bottling and preserving. **1993** *Evening Post* (Wellington) 14 June 10 Hawkesby's blood's worth bottling: 22 hours of non-stop live TV must be tough enough.

bottlee, var. BOTTLIE.

bottle-oh /ˈbɒtəlˌʌu/, *n.*[1]

1. Also **bottle-o**, and occas. **bottle-o-er**. [AND 1898.] A professional dealer in refundable bottles.

1905 *Truth* 30 Sept. 7 The 'Bottle-O' belted the back gate and called for the 'dead marines'..hunter of beer shells. **1910** FANNING *Players & Slayers* 50 The cavalry charger yoked to a 'bottle-oh's' decrepit vehicle, can be galvanised by the old sounds. **1915** *Countess of Liverpool's Gift Book* 92 The King of Bottle-o-ers. **1918** *Kia-ora Coo-ee* (1981) 15 Nov. V. 14 We find our old friend the bottle-o doing a great business. Does he buy the bottles? No,... he gets them baksheesh. **1938** HYDE *Nor Yrs. Condemn* 337 'Our Daddy *does* drink.... he's got lots and lots of bottles, and we sell them to the bottle-oh.' **1944** BRUNO *Desert Daze* 10 He was bottle-oh [that is, he collected the empties at a picture theatre]. **1953** *NZ Observer* 30 Sept. 12 If you don't know Sydney Claridge—Sid the bottle-o, to you—then you don't know your Wellington. **1987** *Those Were the Days (1930s)* 23 At regular intervals a bottle collector led his huge draught horse down the street shouting out his trade—'bottle-o, bottle-o.'

2. *Obs.* **bottle-oh!** formerly used as a street cry by some itinerant bottle dealers.

1938 HYDE *Godwits Fly* (1970) 36 The only other queer person in Calver Street [Newtown] was old Nigger Jack, who drove about with a dusty sack round his shoulders, chanting, 'Bottle-oh, bottle-oh,' in his strong, sad voice.

bottle-oh, *n.*[2] Also **bottle-o**. [AND 1956.] BOTTLIE.

1951 PARK *Witch's Thorn* 176 He took a green bottle-o from the unresisting hand of an open-mouthed, dismayed child... 'Gimme back me marble... Whatcher let him take the glassy for?. **1988** MCGILL *Dict. Kiwi Slang* 19 *bottle-oh*..a green marble.

bottler. [AND 1855.] Someone or something that is considered outstanding, excellent, superior. Occas. used ironically, e.g. for a blatant lie, a 'whopper' (see quot. 1945). Also *attrib.* Cf. CORKER A.

1941 BAKER *NZ Slang* 51 Of children's terms..we may note..*bottler*..descriptive of something superlative or excellent. **1945** *NZEF Times* 26 Feb. 3 [heading] 'A Bottler'... On cleaning the fish he discovered it had swallowed a beer bottle shortly before being hooked. **1959** SLATTER *Gun in My Hand* 181 Ya know old Donovan? He was a bloody bottler. A real beaut. **1960** *Dominion* (Wellington) 17 Jan. 8 Concerning the book 'Lolita', your columns on Thursday contained a 'bottler.' **1979** MARSHALL *Supper Waltz Wilson* 46 'Arthbutt's [sledge] is a bottler.' 'Yeah, but he didn't build it. I reckon ours is faster.' **1982** SHADBOLT *Once on Chunuk Bair* (1990) 35 Here, Mac, you can use my special pocket knife. Mac: You bottler, Scruff.

bottle store. [Cf. OED *bottle n.*[2] 5 *South Africa* a bottle-shop, 1862.] (Usu.) the retail outlet of a hotel or tavern licensed to sell liquor by bottle lots for consumption off the premises.

1944 *NZ Short Stories* (1953) 104 There are rats in the bottle store, dozens of them! **1964** BOOTH *Footsteps in Sea* 64 The boys had abandoned their kicking..to head for the show via the bottle store. **1976** WILSON *Pacific Star* 42 I..went into the bottle store and bought three bottles of beer in a paper bag. **1980** LELAND *Kiwi-Yankee Dict.* 17 *bottle store*: Attached to every licensed hotel is not only a boozer, but a separate shop which sells your home supplies of booze. In other words, a liquor store or package store. **1991** *Contact* (Wellington) 5 Dec. 4 [Advt] Dominion Tavern Bottlestore F.Y.O. 2 Ltr Flagons Lion Brown $4.70

bottlie /ˈbɒtli/. Also **bottlee, bottley**. [AND 1956.] The spherical, clear glass stopper of an old-fashioned patent soft-drink bottle used as a marble. See also BOTTLE-OH *n.*[2], GLASSIE.

c1910 p.c. W.H.B. Orsman (1972), *bottlie* used by boys before WW1. **1959** bottlee [see GLASSIE]. **1972** SUTTON-SMITH *Folkgames Children* 174 When I first went to school, bottlies were good currency, being classed as two-ers, but usually sodawaters and black-bottlies counted as the equivalent of six-ers [for exchange purposes] (Petone, Wellington, 1913). **1987** *Alfredton* 75 Colin Houlbrooke's glossary of marbles [of the period 1927–46] lists... Bottlies—the glass marble stoppers from the top of bottles. These worked perfectly well but were not considered to be high class.

bottom, *n.* Goldmining.

1. [AND 1853.] Also **bottom rock**. The gold-bearing stratum, or the bedrock on which it lies. See also *blue bottom* (BLUE *a.* 3), *Maori bottom* (MAORI B 5 a), *old man bottom* (OLD MAN B 3).

1862 CHUDLEIGH *Diary* 2 June (1950) 41 The digers [*sic*]..told us we should have to sink deep to get to the bottom. We got some 7 feet below the bed. **1862** LINDSAY *Nat. Hist. in Coloniz.* 12 You may see the same series of clays..the same 'chopped slate' or slatey debris..the so-called gravel of the digger—the same 'wash dirt'—the same 'bottom rock'. **1864** BARRINGTON *Diary* 29 Mar. in Taylor *Early Travellers* (1959) 404 The creeks look very well for gold; splendid quartz boulders, and a fine wash, but could not get bottom anywhere, as it is too deep. **1871** MONEY *Knocking About NZ* 16 Our cradle was set,... and we began to take up the ground in the bed of the creek to get down to the bottom, where the heaviest gold always lies. **1887** CHUDLEIGH *Diary* 29 July (1950) 356 Fraser thinks there must be gold in quantity deeper. Noone has seen any bottom yet at 30 ft. **1967** MAY *West Coast Gold Rushes* (1962) 526 Bottom: the bed-rock where the richest deposits are expected. **1983** NOLAN *Gold Fossicker's Handbook* 111 *Bottom*: the hard floor of rock or clay forming the base of an alluvial deposit. On and just above it generally lies the heaviest concentration of gold.

2. In the phr. **to knock the bottom out** (of a claim), to extract all the auriferous material from the 'bottom'.

1887 PYKE *Hist. Early Gold Discoveries in Otago* (1962) 61 [It] happened that in some of the richest claims on the Sailor's Gully Reef..the surface claim-holders knocked the bottoms out of their shafts at a depth of about 20 feet.

bottom, *v.* Goldmining. Also **bottom on**.

1. *trans.* [AND 1852.] To work (a claim) to its bottom, or to bedrock or pay dirt, esp. in the phr. **to bottom a hole**. Cf. BOTTOM *n* 1.

1855 *Nelson Examiner* 28 Jan. 2 The first hole was imperfectly bottomed, owing to the quantity of dead wood. **1862** WEKEY *Otago As It Is* 64 'To bottom a hole', is a peculiar expression used on the mines in Australia; it means to convey the sinking of a shaft down to the bed-rock on which the auriferous drift generally rests. **1866** SMALL *NZ & Austral. Songster* (1970) 27 I marked out a claim... To bottom it took me a week. **1897** WRIGHT *Station Ballads* 20 Someone..bottomed the old shaft.

2. *intr.* or *absol.* [AND 1862.] To reach a BOTTOM q.v.

1862 *Otago Witness* (Dunedin) 23 Aug. 7 Having the misfortune to break our shovel..we were not able to bottom. **1863** WALKER *Jrnl. & Lett.* (ATLTS) 22 Jan. Managed to bottom but did not even find colour. **1914** PFAFF *Diggers' Story* 56 There were over a thousand diggers..waiting to see the result of the prospect when we bottomed. We..struck very good gold. **1967** MAY *West Coast Gold Rushes* (1962) 526 When a shaft reaches bed-rock it has 'bottomed' and the prospect taken is said to be 'off the bottom'.

3. In the phr. **to bottom on** [AND 1855.], to reach (bedrock), or to strike (gold or paydirt).

1887 *Handbook NZ Mines* 130 The party bottomed on a bluish-grey wash. **1892** WARDON *MacPherson's Gully* 14 They bottomed on gold.

bouai, var. BOOHAI.

bouilli /ˈbwɪli/, /ˈbuˌɪli/. Also **Boilly** /ˈboili/. [*bouilli* (OED 1664–1821), recorded elsewhere for boiled or stewed meat, is of significance in early immigration and settlement as a usual fare, and for the container as a useful object.]

1. Tinned meat, stew, or soup; a camp soup made from ingredients at hand.

1843 STEPHENS *Lett. & Jrnls.* (TS) 171 Dinner off preserved soup & bouilli. **1849** TORLESSE *Papers* (1958) 57 Sent him my Shakespeare, some brandy and bouilli soup. **1855** *Nelson Examiner* 23 Dec. 2 Schooner Auckland..49 tins bouilli. **c1890** BODELL *Soldier's View Empire* (1982) 176 At last we managed to get a hot pannikin each of what I called Boilly Soup a Mixture of Tea Sugar Biscuit and Pork fat, anything better than hunger.

2. As **bouilli tin**, a tin which has contained bouilli, serving, when empty, as a utensil or source of useful material. Cf. BILLY *n.*[1] 1 a, BULLY POT.

1852 *Austral. & NZ Gaz.* 21 Feb. 57 My parcel consisted of a blanket, my Mackintosh, a bouilli tin (that is a tin in which 6lbs. of preserved meat is packed for the voyage) to put my small things in. **1866** NORMAN & MUSGRAVE *Voyage & Proc. HMCS 'Victoria'* 29 We found a soup-and-bouillie tin. **1877** PRATT *Col. Experiences* 15 There was another of these low chimneys the architect of which..had inserted a boulli soup tin (minus the bottom) in the clay..as an aperture.

boulder.

1. In the special Comb. **boulder bank**, a large natural bank of deposited alluvial boulders, *spec.* (and often with init. caps) the **Boulder Bank** of Nelson harbour.

1844 TUCKETT *Diary* 6 Apr. in Hocken *Contributions* (1898) 204 The Waiola appeared to be at points scarcely separated from the ocean by a narrow sand, or bolder [*sic*] bank. **1853** EARP *NZ* 134 At the point where the high [Nelson] bluffs cease, a very irregular bank of boulder-stones detaches itself from the main land, and, at the distance of about half a mile, runs parallel with it for eight or nine miles, nearly to the bottom of the bay. The space between this boulder-bank and the main land..is filled by a flax swamp. **1868** *Marlborough Express* (Blenheim) 8 Feb. 4 A considerable portion..of the Boulder Bank at the Wairau River mouth has been washed away. **1892** CARRICK *Romance Wakatipu* 8 The walls of huge boulder-banks. **1935** GUTHRIE *Little Country* (1937) 194 The moonlight silvered the quiet harbour, and showed the outline of a long, natural boulder bank.

2. With suffixed verbs **bash** (cf. BASH *v.* 2), **hop, jump, scramble**, forming combinations alluding to the difficulty of traversing boulder-strewn areas. Often as *vbl. n.*

1932 *Diary* 26 Dec. in *NZ Alpine Jrnl.* (1933) XX. 233 All 'beaches' obliterated and boulder-hopping a necessity. **1937** *NZ Alpine Jrnl.* VII. No.24 57 It was a mixture of boulder-scrambling and 'bush-hiking' interspersed with a few shingle flats. **1939** *Tararua Tramper* Feb. 5 After a little more boulder hopping we arrived at the Waiohina Park Forks. **1948** *Canterbury Mountaineer* 299 After tea we boulder-hopped up to the wee Macgregor moraine. **1950** *Tararua Tramper* Apr. 5 The fact that the others boulder-hopped across, indicates that the water was not deep. **1958** *Tararua* Sept. 48 We were able to stay on the east bank all the way, travelling along flats or the hillside, or boulder-hopping. **1962** GLOVER *Hot Water Sailor* (1981) 77 There were..a host of others who were boulder-hopping and climbing in country that was little known. **1970** SEVERINSEN *Hunt Far Mountain* 116 I tried to reach base by boulder-jumping and cliff-climbing along under the bluffs on the seashore. **1971** *Listener* 19 Apr. 56 Pete..forded the creek beside the shingle slip just below the confluence. Then he boulder-hopped along through the burn. **1978** *Manawatu Tramping Club Jubilee* 90 We boulder bashed out to Klondyke Corner. **1988** PICKERING *Hills* 31 Boulder-hopping alongside a river also requires that essential rhythm and..a certain minimum speed so that you have enough momentum to recover from a stumble.

bound, *v. Whaling. Hist.* To slice up (blocks of blubber) for the try-pot. Also **bounding-knife**, *blubber knife* (BLUBBER).

1836 RHODES *Jrnl. Barque 'Australian'* 5 Sept. (1954) 15 The 3rd Mate having a slight quarrel with one of the men in the blubber room about a steel to sharpen the blubber or bounding knife, and the work being retarded by his not bounding, the Captain took the knife and bounded.

boundary.

1. [AND 1808.] The perimeter or limits of a rural property; a boundary line or fence. Often *attrib.* passing into Comb. as **boundary peg (post)**.

1851 *Lyttelton Times* 14 June 6 I..was occupied two hours in searching amongst the tutu and fern for the boundary posts of the section required. *Ibid.* 16 Aug. 1 [Request for such information] as will lead to the conviction of parties removing, obliterating, or destroying Trigonometrical Stations, Boundary Pegs of Sections. **1853** ROCHFORT *Adventures of Surveyor* 25 The run is bounded on one side by the Turakina river, on the other three by a good post-and-rail fence. The sheep require but little looking after, as they cannot get over the boundary. **1864** *The Sheep Ordinance* Session xxii No.13 in *Canterbury Ordinances 1857-67* 71 s.27 If any sheep infected with scab or catarrh shall be found..within half-a-mile of the boundary of the run or land..such boundary not being a natural barrier or guarded by a sheep-proof fence the owner of such sheep shall be subject to a penalty. **1872** in Meredith *Adventuring in Maoriland* (1935) 27 My duties are to look after the boundaries, as the fences are often knocked about by wild pigs. *Ibid.* 33 As my time is not fully occupied with 'boundary' work, I have taken a contract to split posts for fencing. **1873** ALEXANDER *Bush Fighting* 23 A boundary stake; that is, a staff driven into the ground to mark a boundary. **1938** [see *sheep-proof* (SHEEP 1)]. **1970** MCNEISH *Mackenzie* 68 Sometimes at a boundary post a lone dog would rush forward barking excitedly.

2. a. *Hist.* In the phr. **to keep a** (or **the**) **boundary**, to patrol a stock station boundary to control and monitor stock, and (if fenced) to keep fences in repair (but see also 1864 quot.).

1864 CHUDLEIGH *Diary* 29 Jan. (1950) 120 Left Ch.Ch. I had next door to an offer of £300 [*sic*] p.a. from Government to keep the boundary of Canterbury and Otago but I could not accept. *Ibid.* 6 Oct. 147 Had dinner and started after a mob of sheep that had broken away from the man that was keeping a boundary. **1874** BATHGATE *Col. Experiences* 203 Wire fences..save the cost of a shepherd to 'keep the boundary'. **1881** BATHGATE *Waitaruna* 170 I did not think you would have got into such a scrape when I sent you to keep the boundary. **1940** STUDHOLME *Te Waimate* (1954) 103 The open places [on the run] were guarded by shepherds, 'keeping boundary', who as well as they were able, prevented the sheep from straying. **1953** STRONACH *Musterer on Molesworth* 15 It was one man's duty to 'keep boundary'; that is, to sit at the mouth of the creek and keep all the sheep from going back—a lazy man's job, and one not sought. **1975** ACLAND *Early Canterbury Runs* 267 The chief station work in those days [c1847] consisted of milking, keeping boundary on the sheep and hunting for lost cattle.

b. *Hist.* [AND *boundary-ride v. trans.*, 1889.] As **boundary-ride**, **ride boundary**, to keep boundary. Also *fig.*

1881 NESFIELD *Chequered Career* 36 In Australia, sheep are either in large paddocks which are boundary-ridden, or else they are shepherded and yarded every night. **1912** BOOTH *Five Years NZ* 26 A shepherd resides at some convenient place on the boundary, whence it is his duty to walk or ride this boundary at least once a day, and see that no sheep have crossed it. **1939** CURNOW *Not in Narrow Seas* 6 The bishop boundary-rides his diocese. **1969** MCCASKILL *Molesworth* 181 From then on they rode boundary, hundreds of miles of it, to ensure that the Molesworth cattle stayed on Molesworth.

3. Special Comb. **boundary dog** *hist.*, a dog chained permanently somewhere on the boundary of a (usu. SI) sheep-run (for example, at a break or gateway in a fence) to prevent stock straying; also *transf.* a guard dog (cf. *fence dog* (FENCE *n.*[1] 3)); **boundary fence** [AND 1843], a fence on the perimeter of a rural property (also *fig.*); **boundary hut** *hist.*, the living-quarters of a boundary-keeper (see also OUT-STATION 2); **boundary keeper** *hist.*, a shepherd who patrolled (mainly SI) sheep-run boundaries doing the work of a boundary-dog and mending fences (see quot. 1933); **boundary-keeping** *vbl. n.*; **boundary-rider** *hist.* [the term preferred in Austral.: AND 1864], a stockman who patrols boundaries or fences; **boundary-shepherd** (see also quot. 1890), **boundary watcher** *hist.*, see *boundary-keeper* above.

1876 KENNEDY *Colonial Travel* 196 The first [dog] seen [past the Rangitata] was a **boundary-dog**, chained to a break in a fence, to prevent sheep straying from one run to another. **1902** LANCASTER in *Happy Endings* (1987) 105 For fences were not..and kennelled boundary-dogs strung off the invisible line that severed the runs throughout the plains. **1904** *NZ Illustr. Mag.* July 278 The cruel fate which had condemned him to the living death of a boundary dog, had not yet wholly..embittered him. **1933** *Press* (Christchurch) (Acland Gloss.) 16 Sept. 15 *Boundary Dog.*—A dog chained to his kennel at a gateway on a road to keep the sheep from passing through. Now that most roads are fenced, boundary dogs are only used temporarily. **1975** NEWTON *Sixty Thousand on the Hoof* 41 From the Dog Kennel Corner—its name dating back to the days when a 'boundary' dog was left there to stop straying sheep—the road skirts the foot of the Dalgety Range. **1992** LASENBY *The Conjuror* 30 We've got expectations for you. You're going to beat the boundary dogs! **1857** PAUL *Lett. from Canterbury* 27 The **boundary fence** which separated the poor man from the rich. **1866** BARKER *Station Life* (1870) 76 After we passed our own boundary fence we came upon a very bad *track*. **1873** WILSON *Diary* in Wierzbicka *Wilson Family* (1973) 149 Immediately to our left is the home station of another settler..who has taken the trouble of planting a Hawthorn Hedge all away along the Boundary Fence. **1882** POTTS *Out in Open* 72 Thin lines, drawn straight across the landscape as far as the eye can follow, show the boundary fences or their subdivisions of tightly strained wire. **1895** *Fencing Act* in *Settler's Handbook NZ* (1902) 159 The [Fencing] Act deals with the nature of boundary fences, the cost thereof and its apportionment, and the obligations, rights, and duties of settlers in connection therewith. **1926** DEVANNY *Butcher Shop* (1981) 32 They shortly came to the boundary fence of the station, and slipped through..on to the public road. **1934** SCANLAN *Winds of Heaven* 181 He would take him riding over the back hills to look at a boundary fence. **1940** STUDHOLME *Te Waimate* (1954) 105 'Bad fences make bad neighbours', is one of the truest sayings..for many quarrels have arisen from boundary fences not being stock-proof. **1953** SUTHERLAND *Golden Bush* (1963) 178 The wild pigs..ignored his boundary fences and slashed his lambing percentages every spring. **1968** JOHNSON *Turn of Tide* 62 'Found two sheep worried inside the boundary fence,' he muttered. **1970** MCNAUGHTON *Tat* 61 The dogs had about one hundred and fifty ewes mobbed against a boundary fence, and were worrying for all they were worth. **1987** SLIGO *Final Things* 12 He could look over his land, well enough kept what with a manager... He climbed the boundary fence. **1981** PINNEY *Early N. Otago Runs* 68 The old mustering and **boundary huts** were of stone and the fences were rabbit-netted. **1933** *Press* (Christchurch) (Acland Gloss.) 16 Sept. 15 *Boundary Keeper.*—A shepherd who keeps sheep from passing an unfenced boundary. He goes along the boundary once or twice a day or, if he has a convenient lookout, watches the sheep all day. In the old days any boundary keepers lived on their boundaries all the year and never saw anyone, except at mustering or by chance. **1947** BRERETON *No Roll of Drums* 21 His next effort to raise money entailed a three-days' walk to the Wairau where he had four months' work as 'Boundary Keeper' to a runholder. **1952** NEWTON *High Country Journey* 60 A base camp is set up at Butlers hut and the boundary-keeper spends night about at the homestead and the hut. **1978** JARDINE *Shadows on Hill* 48 With the release of the sheep to their winter range the work of the boundary-keeper begins. **1873** WILSON *Diary* 2 Feb. in Wierzbicka *Wilson Family* (1973) 165 There are 13 shepherds but the run is very well fenced in and there are only three men **boundary keeping**. **1938** BURDON *High Country* 85 Quite apart from the long, expensive business of dipping scab-infected sheep, the lack of wire fences entailed constant vigilance in tailing and boundary keeping. **1965** MACNICOL *Skippers Road* 19 He spent the next three years shearing, mustering, and boundary-keeping on Coronet Peak [station]. **1975** NEWTON *Sixty Thousand on the Hoof* 179 As with most high-country stations of this sort boundary-keeping after the autumn muster is a regular practice. **1875** Cockburn-Hood *Chowbokiana* 89 It is not to be wondered at, that so many of the shepherds become insane..when the wretched **boundary rider**, who may once perhaps have sat at some merry mess-table surrounded by his brother officers, or amongst pleasant companions at Oxford or Cambridge..sits with his dog cowering over a small stove. **1881** Nesfield *Chequered Career* 32 [We were] sent to learn the art of sheep-farming at different out-stations. At these out-stations are shepherds and boundary-riders stationed. **1921** *Quick March* 10 Feb. 36 In the succeeding two years the ex-coke-shoveller, boundary-rider, stockman..examined a mining boom. **1947** Beattie *Early Runholding* 12 Before fences were erected, the man who patrolled the edges of the run was a boundary-keeper if on foot or a boundary-rider if mounted. **1970** Severinsen *Hunt Far Mountain* 86 Burwood Station is probably the only station in New Zealand to warrant a boundary rider: all summer a Burwood shepherd rides herd on thousands of ewes on unfenced open ranges. **1984** Boyd *City of the Plains* 43 Edward Kirk..worked as a boundary rider and ploughman at Roy's Hill. **1875** Rives *Jottings on the Spot* (Cant. Pub. Lib. TS) 9 One of Caverhills's **boundary shepherds** who was on the look-out for me set me right and walked about four miles with me. **1878** Elwell *Boy Colonists* 78 He..knew nothing whatever about sheep or dogs, but..soon learnt enough to be of service as a boundary-shepherd. **1890** *Otago Witness* (Dunedin) 4 Sept. 35 These dogs, called 'boundary shepherds', are placed wherever two roads meet to act as deterrents towards sheep which would otherwise cross the boundary line. **1947** Beattie *Early Runholding* 45 Before fences were constructed, **boundary watchers** were employed to patrol the run boundaries.

boundary-line. [AND 1808.] A surveyor's line cut to mark the boundary between land still in Maori ownership and alienated land (or land to be alienated); or to mark the boundary of a rural property.
    1858 Grace *Journal* 24 Mar. in *Pioneer Missionary* (1928) 77 The war at Taranaki commenced by a land agent inducing a Chief to cut a boundary line (for the purpose of sale) through land of which he was, at most, a part owner only! **1884** Chudleigh *Diary* 20 Aug. (1950) 329 Robertson cutting my boundary line. **1986** Mitcalfe *Look to Land* 29 Te Whiti sent the fencers of Parihaka to restore every boundary line, regardless of road and roadmaker.

bounty. *Obs.* [An extended use of *bounty* a payment for the killing of dangerous animals: see OED 5 e 'chiefly N. Amer.'.] A payment for evidence of the destruction of a noxious animal.
    1938 Hyde *Nor Yrs. Condemn* 155 Some of them are back in the bush trapping 'possums. There's a bounty on 'possums. **1952** *Tramper* Dec. 7 The Government last year introduced a bounty of 2s. 6d. for every token representing an opossum killed. **1952** Wilson *Julien Ware* 17 He was provided with a home, with food and with a small wage, but received also a bounty for each [rabbit] tail.

bow /bʌu/. [Spec. uses of *bow* an object of curved shape.]
1. *Obs. Bullock-driving.* [f. Brit. dial.: see OED *bow* n.¹ 5 'obs. or dial.'.] An iron contrivance in the shape of a double bow which fitted to the underside of the necks of a pair of draught bullocks and was fastened to the *yoke* across the upper side of the pair's necks.
    1848 Wakefield *Handbook NZ* 261 You would have only to buy another [bullock] plough and two yokes and bows. **1856** [see *bullock-yoke* (bullock n. 3 a)]. **1860** Butler *First Year* (1863) vii 105 The body bullocks, by a manoeuvre not unfrequent, shifted..the yoke under their necks, and the bows over. **1933** *Press* (Christchurch) (Acland Gloss.) 23 Sept. 13 The iron which passed under the bullocks' necks to keep the yoke in place was called the *bow*. The *bow* was held to the yoke by a *yoke key* which passed through a hole in it. **1940** *Tales Pioneer Women* (1988) 151 They were returning [in a bullock dray]..when a carelessly tied 'key' that held the 'bow' into the 'yoke' dropped out and let one bullock free. **1947** Beattie *Early Runholding* 42 Very seldom was harness used [to attach bullocks to the vehicle], and then without winkers, and it was called branks. The pulling strain came on the bows, and a yoke joined two bows and went over each neck of a pair of bullocks. If there were five pairs, say, a chain ran from the yoke of the first pair to the yoke of the second pair, and another chain from the second to the third, and another chain from the third to the fourth. These chains were lighter between the first pairs and heavier as you got further back. The two rear bullocks were yoked to the pole of the dray or waggon. As there were no reins, the driving was all by commands and cracking the whip. **1953** Reed *Story of Kauri* 182 A suitable piece of kauri ricker..shaped at each end to receive the ends of the bows or loops by which the yokes were fastened to the bullocks' necks.

2. [OED records this sense at *bow* n.¹ 11 b, no quot.; EDD n.¹ 10.] One of the several bow-like half-hoops over a wagon or dray to hold the canvas cover or tilt. (Quot. 1961 may be a transf. use of *bow* the front end of a boat; or may rest on a misconception.)
    c**1871** Masters *Autobiography* (ATLMS) 45 I took my primitive dray, now made like a large basket, with bows and a tilt over it. [**1961** Henderson *Friends in Chains* 185 Bow: Term used [c1900–20] for front of horse-drawn vehicle.]

3. *Shearing.* Usu. *pl.* [Spec. use of *bow* a ring or hoop of metal forming a handle: see OED n.¹ 11 a.] See 1933 quot.
    1933 *Press* (Christchurch) (Acland Gloss.) 16 Sept. 15 *Bow*.— (1) The bows are the curved parts at the top of the handle of a pair of sheep shears. They give the shears their spring open after the shearer has made his blow. All shears are now made with double bows; but until about the 'seventies single bows were the only kind. **1938** Burdon *High Country* 84 The shears they used were one inch and a half shorter in the blade and, being joined by a single instead of a double bow, required a wrist of iron to drive them continuously throughout a summer's day. **1951** [see blade n.¹ 1 a]. **1989** *NZ Eng. Newsletter* III. 22 bow: The curved handle top of hand shears. The grip is against the bows which causes the blades to spring open after each cut.

bowcaker /bʌuˈkækə/, var. pukeko.

bowing-bird /ˈbæuwɪŋ/-. *Chatham Islands.* The *shore plover* (plover 2 (6)).
    1873 *TrNZI* V. 217 *Thinornis novae-zealandiae.* I only found this bird on Mangare and parts of the coast of Pitt Island. It has been called the 'bowing-bird' by the settlers, from its habit of bowing its body when approached.

bowl of fruit: see box n.² 8.

bowser /ˈbæuzə/. [f. a proprietary name (see quot. 1920): AND 1918.]
1. Also occas **bowzer**. A pump (in first uses also a proprietary system) for dispensing filtered petrol from a holding tank; also by synecdoche, a petrol station (see quot. 1959). Often *attrib.* Occas. early **bowserized** *ppl. a.*, of petrol, dispensed by the bowser method.
    1918 *Hawkes Bay Herald* 27 Aug. 6 [Advt] Bowserized... All Benzine and Oils are now retailed from the Famous Bowser Steel Tanks. **1920** *NZ Patent Office Jrnl* [no number given] 2 Dec. Bowser 15293 [filed] 19th March, 1919 [Trademark Logo includes 'Established 1885']. Application No. 16973 has been proceeded with by order of the court for goods of a similar nature, and the present mark has been in use in New Zealand for a considerable time. S.F. Bowser and Co., Inc., a corporation organized and existing under the laws of the State of Indiana, of corner of Bowser and Creighton Avenues, in the City of Fort Wayne, County of Allen, State of Indiana, in the United States of America, Manufacturers and Merchants. Class 6. Storage, distribution, dispensing, measuring, clarifying, and filtering systems and equipments for oils and other liquids. **1929** *NZJST* X. 214 A similar danger frequently occurs during the time a tank is being filled, especially in the case of underground tanks of the kind popularly referred to as 'bowser' tanks (although not necessarily made by the firm of Bowser) which are connected to kerbside pumps. **1933** Graeme-Holder *Restless Earth* 103 'O.K.!' said the bowser-hand as they paid him. **1935** Guthrie *Little Country* (1937) 410 On the first corner was a building of flats with a bowser station on the ground floor. **1943** Bennett *English in NZ* in *Amer. Speech* XVIII. 87 A pump at a filling station is a *bowser*. **1959** Slatter *Gun in My Hand* 151 Tobacconists selling magazines, pubs selling cigarettes, petrol bowsers selling sweets. **1961** Crump *Hang On a Minute Mate* 101 Food, cried Jack, and a petrol pump! They pushed the Ford the last thirty yards to the bowser. **1965** Hilliard *Power of Joy* 34 They knew the names of the drivers, too..overheard them at the bowzer when the trucks stopped. **1970** Duggan *O'Leary's Orchard* 95 How's it going, then, Adam? I hear you're doing a stint on the bowsers, Saturday. **1982** Tuwhare *Year of Dog* 10 The car never played up at all. And after we'd given it a second gargle at the all-night bowser it just zoomed on. **1990** *Dominion* (Wellington) 4 July 1 [Caption] No benefit at bowser from fall in oil price... The downward trend..has yet to yield any change at petrol pumps.

2. [AND 1976.] A dispenser attached to an inverted spirit-bottle in a hotel bar which automatically measures and dispenses a standard 'nip'.
    1957 Wilson *Strip Jack Naked* 23 The barman..picked up a glass which he held under the bowser of a hanging bottle. **1958** *Star-Sun* (Christchurch) 24 Apr. 3 One licensee said there was a growing embarrassment at the necessity to place inferior brands of spirits on sale in bars... He predicted that wartime rationing with bowser sales restricted to a one-hour period may have to be re-introduced. **1979** Gebbie & McGregor *Incredible 8-Ounce Dream* 10 He's [sc. a sophisticated cocktail barman] probably..filled up an empty bottle of black-label Johnnie Walker with local whisky and popped the bottle back up on the bowser.

3. *fig.* As a male nickname.
    1938 *NZ Observer* 1 Sept. 17 'Bowser' Toogood..was best man.

bow tie. A married woman's boy-friend or fancy man.
    1948 Ballantyne *Cunninghams* (1976) 125 Come off it. You wouldn't like your sister-in-law to park her ears to all I know about you. You and your bow-tie.

bowyang /ˈbʌu.jæŋ/. Also **bo-yang**. Usu. *pl.* [f. Brit. dial. *bow-yanks:* see EDD *bow yankees* leather leggings; cf. also SND *booyangs, bonanks;*

AND 1893.] **a.** String or lace ties below the knees of a workman's trousers intended to keep knee movement free of constriction and trouser cuffs above ground level.

1910 *Truth* 14 May 5 The afore-mentioned mere males, one old with grey whiskers and wearing bowyangs..procured liquor for Jane. **1919** *Quick March* 10 July 21 A seedy-looking man in bow-yangs..approached Bill. **c1927** SMITH *Sheep & Wool Industry* 75 The shearers..[were] arrayed in their working clothes, with bowyangs (a strap over their trousers, below the knees, which allows them to bend with more comfort). **1944** *NZEF Times* 8 May 4 Boyangs are not an issue. **1955** BOWEN *Wool Away* 15 'Bowyangs' are essential to shearing, more so than plus-fours are to golf. Straps are better than twine and will not cut off blood circulation. **1962** WILSON *Linkwater* 124 He rode through the capital city..dressed as usual in bo-yangs and hard knocker. **1978** JARDINE *Shadows on Hill* 131 They [*sc.* shearers] were all dressed in the recognised style..white moleskin trousers supported by bowyangs below the knees. **1986** RICHARDS *Off the Sheep's Back* 61 If bowyangs were not worn, the weight of the wet trousers suspended entirely by the hips would become very tiring by the end of the day.

b. *transf.* [Apparently from their 'navvying' duties.] A nickname of the Maori Pioneer Battalion in WW1.

1917 *Chron. NZEF* 18 Apr. 78 The Infantry called us [Pioneers] 'bow-yangs'.

bowzer /ˈbæuzə/, var. BOWSER.

box, *n.*[1]

1. *Farming.* Also **box-up.** [A back-formation from BOX *v.*[1], to mix mobs of sheep.] The mixing of two drafts or mobs of sheep.

1883 FERGUSON *Castle Gay* 174 That swiftly darting 'twixt the flocks, Just barely saved a three-fold box. **1933** *Press* (Christchurch) (Acland Gloss.) 16 Sept. 15 When two mobs of sheep get mixed accidentally it is called a box. **1972** GOULTER in Mcleod *High Country Anthol.* (1972) 226 You see we're driving through the middle of a ewe block and 'boxes' are frowned on. **1989** RICHARDS *Pioneer's Life* 27 I usually stayed in the lead to guard against overtaking another mob and having a 'box up'.

2. *fig.* As **box-up**, or in the phr. **to be in a box,** (to be in) a confused state.

1941 BAKER *NZ Slang* 39 When flocks are mixed they are said to be *boxed*, and from this peculiar use of the verb we have derived the term a *box-up*, a state of confusion, and *to be in a box*, to be in a confused state of mind. **1988** MCGILL *Dict. Kiwi Slang* 20 *box up* state of confusion; eg 'It's a total box up, nobody seems to know what his position is, or what he's s'posed to do.'

box, *n.*[2] [Spec. or fig. or transf. uses of *box* container.]

1. *Mining.* A high-sided truck for carrying coal or ore from a mine.

1900 *NZ Illustr. Mag.* II. 507 Let the boxes go, let the jig chains rattle away. **1904** *Awards, etc.* 91 [Otago Coal-Miners Agreement] In headings where a sprag has to be used for any trucking..the miners shall be paid 1d. per box for the next 10 yards or part thereof. **1906** *TrNZI* XXXVIII. 480 The rock [is] immediately loaded into trucks or 'boxes' and drawn to the burning-ground. **1963** PEARSON *Coal Flat* 27 He swung the last box of coal round on to the rails and pushed it up the incline, trundling it along the unevenly fixed rails. *Ibid.* 420 box: A metal truck used in coal-mines. **1980** THOMPSON *All My Lives* 40 Two shifts a day she [*sc.* the mine-horse] would drag upwards of 200 half-tonne boxes, six at a time, into the lay-by. **1981** *Listener* 2 May 43 The wheeled vehicles that transport the coal (trucks, tubs, or skips elsewhere) are in the Strongman [Mine] called *boxes*, and linked together in a string they become a *race of boxes*. **1992** LATHAM *Golden Reefs* 427 *Boxes*: Timber trucks with steel bands were used in the Blackwater mine from about 1930; they held half a ton of ore and were hauled up the shaft.

2. *Goldmining.* **a.** *sluice-box* (SLUICE 2).

1870 in Evans *Waikaka Saga* 30 Nov. (1962) 18 Can the miners erect a small dam, thereby to save the night water, to work a box with during the day. **1983** NOLAN *Gold Fossicker's Handbook* 111 *Box*: abbreviation for sluice box.

b. See *battery-box* (BATTERY 2).

3. [f. US *out of the band box* brand new: AND *n.*[6], 1926.] In the phr. **to be one out of the box,** (of a thing or person) to be outstandingly fine, esp. of a day's weather. Occas. formerly in adjectival use.

1907 *Truth* 14 Dec. 3 He..received one of 'Cobby's' 'out of the box' balls and was bowled after. **1933** PRUDENCE CADEY *Broken Pattern* 109 One straight out of the box, he is. **1946** SARGESON *That Summer* 173 It was a fine hot day, one right out of the box. **1947** DAVIN *For Rest of Our Lives* 301 But you've no idea what a good joker Alister was. He was one out of the box, was Alister. **1950** WHITWORTH *Otago Interval* 108 What a morning... It's one out of the box. **1968** SLATTER *Pagan Game* 129 All right then, said the Coach... I know Geoffrey will play one out of the box on Saturday. **1976** WILSON *Pacific Star* 152 'She's a beauty, all right,' I said. 'One out of the box. The best looking piece I've seen since I got back.' **1987** HARTLEY *Swagger on Doorstep* 62 I believe he was his favourite niece. He told my parents, 'She's one out of the box.' **1991** ELDRED-GRIGG *Shining City* 17 Modern progress... It's something out of the box. No more piss buckets or coal ranges.

4. A *wool-box* (see WOOL 3), the lower part of a patent wool-press.

1913 CARR *Country Work* 16 Pressing.—When there is sufficient wool in one bin, the pressers (generally two) get to work. One gets into the 'box' as the lower portion of the patent presses is called, while his mate..hands him..the fleeces. These are placed in tiers, and tramped down until the lower box is full. An upper box is then swung..or lowered on to the lower one, and the process repeated.

5. *WW2* (N. Africa). A flat coastal plain bordered by escarpments, the whole resembling the floor of a box; *spec.* **the Bagush** (also **Baagush, Baggush, Baguish**) **Box**.

1943 JACKSON *Passage to Tobruk* 104 Baguish Box..is a flat coastal plain bordered by an escarpment, and resembles the ground floor of an outsize packing-case. **1944** FULLARTON *Troop Target* 56 The Box..that outpost of Egyptian empire fully a hundred and fifty miles from Alex. The first batch of Kiwis went there in the summer of '40 to do a spot of digging. I believe they were bombed once. Anyway, they strung a few strands of barbed wire around their diggings and called it the Bagush Box. **1947** DAVIN *For Rest of Our Lives* 133 4 and 6 Brigades back in Baagush box. **1953** CODY *21 Battalion* 110 The brigade had its first lessons in desert mobile operations at the Kaponga Box... The brigade joined the Division in the Baggush Box on the coast... The Baggush Box was a defensive position named after one of the two small oases in the area (Baggush and Burbeita); there was a railway station at Sidi Haneish, inside the Box.

6. a. In the phr. **(to be) a box of birds,** (to be or feel) fine, fit, in health, 'chirpy'; often used as a reply to a greeting.

1943 JACKSON *Passage to Tobruk* 126 Friday, and I was 'a box of birds'. **1947** DAVIN *For Rest of Our Lives* 194 'Glad to see you're alive. You're looking fit.' 'A box of birds, a box of birds.' **1950** *Here & Now* Dec. 19 Hans was the clever one, who already knew all the expressions of New Zealand slang. 'I'm a box of boids,' he would say. **1959** SLATTER *Gun in My Hand* 144 'How's yaself?' 'Boxa birds,' he tells me with a wink. **1962** CURNOW *Four Plays* (1972) 140 George: How are you, Bill? Bill: Box o' birds. And you? George: I'm fine, thanks. **1978** BALLANTYNE *Talkback Man* 164 'Good morning, Phil. How are you, today?' 'Box of birds, Miss. How would you be yourself?' **1986** HULME *Windeater* 133 'How yer gettin' on mate?' Boxa birds, eh?' 'Boxa birds all right, mate. All shit and feathers, eh.' **1991** *Dominion* (Wellington) 28 Oct. 1 We're keeping the rafts in sight, everyone's a box of birds.

b. In an elaborated phr. **a box of fluffy ducks**.

1980 LELAND *Kiwi-Yankee Dict.* 17 I'm a box of fluffy ducks? I'm just as well/happy/successful as can be. **1993** *Evening Post* (Wellington) 4 Mar. 3 [He] said the break would not deter her from standing at the next election. 'She's a box of fluffy ducks. She will be standing.'

7. In the phr. **the whole box and dice** [f. Brit. dial. *box and dice* the sum total: see EDD *n.*[1]; SND; AND 1888], everything, the 'whole works'.

1962 CRUMP *One of Us* 169 He must have used about ten plugs [of gelignite]. Blew the whole box and dice to bits. **1962** HORI *Half-gallon Jar* 52 Put the whitebait into the pan... Heave the whole box and dice onto the brown paper, add pepper and salt..and serve. **a1974** SYDER & HODGETTS *Austral. & NZ Eng.* (TS) 1098 *Whole box and dice*. Everything in that connection, every person in that group. Often derogatory. 'They are all scroungers, the whole box and dice of them.'

8. As **box (bowl) of fruit,** rhyming slang for a 'suit'.

1963 *Truth* 21 May 19 I decked myself out in a box of fruit, with knife creased terrace of houses, polished up the mary lous, locked up the shovel and headed for the racetrack. box of fruit..suit. **1982** NEWBOLD *Big Huey* 245 Bowl of Fruit (n) Suit

9. GLORY BOX a.

1957 FRAME *Owls Do Cry* (1967) 75 I got the blankets for my box almost as soon as I started at the mill. **1967** MACNICOL *Skippers Canyon* 19 Even her sisters..had started sewing and saving for their 'boxes'. **1983** KIDMAN *Paddy's Puzzle* 64 She wanted to leave [school] and start getting her box together..they were going to get married.

10. *Rugby union.* [Prob. transf. from the soccer use for the penalty area.] The unmanned area, a kind of no man's land, behind an opponent's scrum but in front of the defending winger and fullback.

1968 SLATTER *Pagan Game* 141 They practised five yard scrums on attack and on defence, the up and under, the kick into the box, the reverse kick to the blindside wing. **1975** HOWITT *NZ Rugby Greats* 42 In 1953 Pat Vincent kicked 'into the box' and upset our fullback.

box, *n.*[3] [Transf. use of *box Buxus* spp.] As **New Zealand** (occas. **mountain**) **box,** *Hebe odora* var. (formerly *Veronica buxifolia*). See also BOXWOOD, KOROMIKO.

1908 *AJHR* C-11 39 [*Veronica*] *buxifolia* New Zealand box [Endemic].. Wet ground of shrub steppe. **1926** CROOKES *Plant Life in Maoriland* 144 But as we mount upwards, this veronica disappears and its place is taken by one such as the New Zealand box (Veronica buxifolia). The New Zealand box has its leaves arranged in fours like its lowland brother, but there the resemblance ends. **1961** *Merriam-Webster Third*

Internat. Dict. 1477 *Mountain box* n : a common New Zealand shrub (*Veronica buxifolia*) with white flowers and leaves resembling heath.

box, *v.*[1] *Farming*. [Origin uncertain: AND 1870.]
1. *Farming*. **a.** *intr*. Of separate drafts of sheep, to be allowed to join or mix either accidentally or for some purpose, esp. in passive uses **to be (get) boxed**.
   1864 *Puketoi Station Diary* (Hocken TS) 19 Apr. Grant unwell; lambs boxed [Apr. 20] Fine. Drafted lambs out of John Murray's ewes. **1872** BARKER *Christmas Cake* iii He [*sc.* a shepherd] couldn't cross [his mob] over a river..and never a week passes without his getting boxed. That's mixed-up ma'am. **1883** FERGUSON *Castle Gay* 172 When he beheld in act to fuse With his, an adverse flock of ewes. One startled glance told plain enough That he had boxed with Harry Ruff. **1910** *Truth* 31 Dec. 6 To hear the drover at his best—or his worst—it is desirable to be near him when..the mob gets 'boxed' with another mob round the corner. **1933** *Press* (Christchurch) (Acland Gloss.) 16 Sept. 15 (1) When you put two mobs of sheep together on purpose, you *box* them. (2) When they join by accident they are said to *get boxed*. In fact, the active voice of the verb signifies intention; the passive, accident. **1947** BEATTIE *Early Runholding* 12 When two mobs ran into each other and intermingled, they were said to be 'boxed'. **1960** MASTERS *Back-Country Tales* 118 It was Andrew's job to patrol the rugged boundary each day, hunt the sheep back to keep them from getting boxed. **1970** MCNAUGHTON *Tat* 95 Be careful not to hunt them [*sc.* escaped wethers] further back... They'd get boxed with the ewes if they got out that way.

b. *intr*. To combine drafts or mobs of sheep for driving (to a sale, etc).
   1986 RICHARDS *Off the Sheep's Back* 84 I was no longer asked to help with the droving of stock to the sale. If one of my sisters could not help he would 'box' with a neighbour.

Hence **boxing** *vbl. n.* [AND 1868], the inadvertent or purposeful mixing of drafts of sheep.
   1872 BARKER *Christmas Cake* ch. iii We calls it boxing when your sheep go and join another mob feeding close by, and you can't tell one from another except by the brand or the earmark. **1939** BEATTIE *First White Boy Born Otago* 152 Fear of boxing was the origin of this custom of giving notice [of driving sheep through another's property]. **1947** BEATTIE *Early Runholding* 84 Boxing.—Sometimes different lots of sheep would fail to keep separate, and entanglement followed.

2. *trans*. To mix (drafts of sheep) either accidentally or for a purpose.
   1904 LANCASTER *Sons o' Men* 95 That's pretty well boxed 'em [*sc.* two mobs of sheep]. **1913** BATHGATE *Sodger Sandy's Bairn* 51 He 'boxed' more than half his mob with your sheep. **1930** *NZ Short Stories* 171 Once I left the gate open and boxed some sheep. **1970** MCLEOD *Glorious Morning* 52 He then emerged into an open plain, where he must try and hold his mob to box them with those emerging from some other valley. **1981** PINNEY *Early N. Otago Runs* 26 In 1886 there was a bad drought... Middleton boxed the 9,000 cull ewes with the wethers, and in February pushed them well into the back country.

3. *transf*. for other mixtures. **a.** To mix paint.
   1953 Wellington paint dealer used the expression: You've got to box the paint well by pouring half of it off first.

b. *Dog-racing*. As a *vbl. n.*, a combination bet involving taking dogs selected to finish in any order.
   1993 *Dominion* (Wellington) 16 Jan. 3 All picked the result with a single combination rather than taking the dogs selected to finish in any order—known as boxing—which would have cost $60 for a $10 bet.

4. *transf*. and *fig*. [Poss. influenced by *boxed in*: AND *transf*., 1911.] Of trampers and others, **to get (be) boxed** (or **boxed up**), to get lost, to become bluffed.
   1936 *NZ Alpine Jrnl.* VI. (23) 228 All the mercies we had to be thankful for..how we were safe on this side of the Godley and not boxed up in Scone Creek. **1939** *Ibid.* VIII. (26) 45 If you do get lost don't get rattled... You are not the first to get boxed.

box, *v.*[2] [Spec. use of *box* store away.]
1. *trans*. To settle; to render innocuous.
   1919 MANSFIELD in *Let. to Murry* 24 Nov. (1951) 409 It's a regular German stove with a flat top... I should think it would box it—the cold I mean. [Murry's *Note*] To 'box' something, in K.M.'s private language, was to settle it satisfactorily.

2. As **box off** [poss. also influenced by *box off* of cargo, to stow it away, with a play on *box* a cargo container]. See quot.
   1972 *Dominion* (Wellington) 2 Oct. 1 [Heading] Containers could box off 1000 watersiders. About 1000 watersiders could become redundant within the next 18 months.

box, *v.*[3] *Hist. trans*. To confine (someone) in a box-like punishment cell. Hence **boxed up** *ppl. a.*, gaoled.
   1837 BEST *Journal* 12 July (1966) 81 July 12 Reported convict for insolence [on journey to antipodes] to a sentry..[he] was boxed..July 13 convict's..meat was stopped and he was put in the box [during voyage to Australia and New Zealand]. **1961** PARTRIDGE *Dict. Slang* 1012 *boxed-up*, adj. In prison; gaoled: New Zealand:C. 20

box, *v.*[4] [f. *box* to take part in a boxing match.]
1. [AND 1919.] In the phr. **to box on** (often **box on regardless**), to keep going, to persevere (in a job, task), to get on with one's life.
   1959 SLATTER *Gun in My Hand* 239 I'd better slope off. I'll box on somewhere. **1968** SLATTER *Pagan Game* 107 Kevin boxed on in his own way, the honest teacher, the man with a conscience..and no hope of becoming a headmaster. **1981** GEE *Meg* 99 It's best not to tell her anything, Meg. Just let her keep boxing on. **1988** MCGILL *Dict. Kiwi Slang* 20 *box on box on regardless* keep going, endure; eg 'I know we've no chance of winning, but just box on regardless.'

2. In the phr. **to box out of the ring**, of a married person, to have an illicit sexual encounter.
   1978 TUCKER *Thoroughbreds Are My Life* 61 Four of us have a mousy brown hair colouring, but I have one sister who had beautiful titian red hair. Once I became interested in genetics I began to wonder how 'Ginger' had turned up. My mother was a very dignified English schoolmistress and I certainly could not suspect that she had 'boxed out of the ring'. **1991** *Examiner* (Auckland) 22 Aug. 6 Sydney businessman is caught out by the missus doing—shall we say—a bit of boxing outside the ring... The missus knew the sweet young lady involved.

3. Of deer, to spar to establish an order of precedence. Also **boxing** *vbl. n.*
   1991 LENTLE & SAXTON *Red Deer* 182 *boxing* technique of fighting used by deer of the same sex who are in dispute in a pecking order. Hinds often box one another. Stags do also, particularly when in velvet. Contestants rear up on their hind legs and approach each other with downward-kicking forelegs.

boxer, *n.*[1] Also **boxer hat**. [Prob. f. Brit dial. *box* or *box hat* a tall hat: see OED *n.*[4]; EDD Suppl. *Box n.*[1] *Box-hat*, a tall hat. Cornwall.] A bowler hat. Cf. HARD-HITTER.
   1863 CHUDLEIGH *Diary* 27 Jan. (1950) 74 Started Mr and Mrs Acland and their belongings in their carriage. Mrs Harper and son in boxers. [*Ed. Note.*] bowlers, i.e., hats. **1898** *Merriam-Webster Internat. Dict.* (Australasian Supp.) 2018 *Boxer..*, *n.* A kind of stiff round hat;—called in England *bowler* or *deerstalker*. **1906** *Truth* 5 May 8 Another man who wore a 'boxer' hat..he saw the accused and the 'bloke' in the 'boxer'.

boxer, *n.*[2] *Two-up*.
1. [Poss. also influenced by a play on *boxer*, one who boxes in a ring: AND 1911.] The ring-keeper, the person in charge of (the bets in) a two-up game. Cf. RINGIE.
   1920 *NZ Free Lance* (Wellington) 9 June 24 The 'boxer'—the man in charge of the school—without hesitation or ceremony laid out the owner of the double-header. **1951** LAWSON *Gold in Their Hearts* 90 Percy Gray was the spinner, and Alf Burke, the boxer—you know the man who takes the bets [c1880s].

2. [Poss. f. *one for the box*, i.e. for kitty: AND 1949.] A gratuity or percentage of winnings paid to the person in charge of a two-up ring.
   1935 STRONG in Partridge *Slang Today* 287 When the ring-keeper said 'Up and do 'em,' I collected 200 francs. Of course I had to give the ring-keeper a boxer. **1937** PARTRIDGE *Dict. Slang* 87 *Boxer*. A gratuity; esp. to the 'ringie' (in two-up) from the winning betters: New Zealand and Australia (-G[reat] W[ar]+). ex *Christmas box*. **1938** *Press* (Christchurch) (McNab Slang) 2 Apr. 18 A 'boxer' is a gratuity to the 'ringie' at two-up.

box-fish. [Spec. use of *boxfish Ostracion* spp.: see OED *n.*[2] 24.] Any of various marine fishes of the fam. Ostraciidae having the body enclosed in a box-like armour of bony plates.
   1932 *NZJST* XIII. 233 Box-fishes. *Ostracion eco* n. sp. **1956** GRAHAM *Treasury NZ Fishes* 413 Box Fish *Ostracion eco*. **1967** NATUSCH *Animals NZ* 233 Family Ostraciidae. The box fish (*Ostracion..*) and trunk fish (*Paracanthostracion*) have the head and body completely encased in an armoured box of welded hexagonal plates. **1981** WILSON *Fisherman's Bible* 31 Two species of Boxfish inhabit New Zealand waters and both make their appearances from time to time, usually as curiosities taken from fishermen's nets and displayed in fish shop windows. **1982** AYLING *Collins Guide* (1984) 315 *Box Fish*... This distinctive little fish is enclosed in a rigid box-like armour of bony plates that protects all but the eyes, mouth, fins and tail. **1989** PAULIN ET AL. *NZ Fish* 244 Boxfishes are slow swimming bottom-living..fishes of tropical and subtropical seas... Rare in New Zealand waters. Flesh of all species is extremely toxic.

boxhead. [f. (empty) *box* + *head*.] A fool.
   1951 PARK *Witch's Thorn* 67 She says not to be big boxhead. **1981** JOHNSTON *Fish Factory* 75 'What a cruel thing to say box-head,' Jackpot returned sadly.

box seat. [A figurative use of *box-seat*, (the favoured position on) the coach-driver's high seat on the box (in which luggage, etc. was stored).] In the phr. **to be on the box-seat**, to be on top of the situation, in a favourable position; to have the upper hand; to be 'sitting pretty'.
   1950 CHERRILL *NZ Sheep Farm* 95 They're [*sc.* shearers] on the box-seat now..and they don't forget to

let you know it, either. **1959** SLATTER *Gun in My Hand* 147 Livin in a good paddock. Never had it better. On the box seat. **1988** MCGILL *Dict. Kiwi Slang* 20 *box seat* favoured position; originally the driver's box or seat... Modern eg: 'After bowling Australia out for 125 on the first day, New Zealand look to be in the box seat in the third test at the Basin.'

boxwood. [Transf. use of *box Buxus* spp. (fam. Buxaceae) and the hard-grained wood.] Applied to any of various native plants resembling the European box (*Buxus sempervirens*) either in wood-quality (esp. MAIRE), or in other ways (esp. KOROMIKO (*Hebe odora*) and *golden tauhinu* (TAUHINU 3 (2)) *Cassinia fulvida*). Cf. HEATHER, BOX *n*.³
 1898 MORRIS *Austral-English* 51 *Box-wood*..a New Zealand wood, *Olea lanceolata*.. *N.O. Jasmineae* (Maori name, *Maire*.) Used by the 'Wellington Independent' (April 19, 1845) for woodcuts, and recommended as superior to box-wood for the purpose. See also *box*. **1953** [see HEATHER]. **1961** ALLAN *Flora NZ* I. 887 In the high country the name 'boxwood' us[ually] refers to some small-l[ea]v[e]d *Hebe*. **1969** *Standard Common Names Weeds* 7 *boxwood* [=] *golden tauhinu*. **1970** MCNAUGHTON *Tat* 59 For several days they travelled over miles of silver tussock country with, here and there, clumps of..boxwood growing in patches of peaty swamp.

boy. *Derog.*
 1. *Hist.* Often *pl.* [Spec. use of *boy* a coloured servant, slave: see OED *n*.¹ 3 c; AND 1864.] A Maori (occas. Pacific Island) male (as a servant, porter, Christian convert, attendant, rugby footballer).
 1826 WILLIAMS *Early Jrnls.* 22 Dec. (1961) 31 Some of our boys [*sc.* ?converts] returned from Taramai where they had been to visit their sick friends. **1827** WILLIAMS *Early Jrnls.* 6 Nov. (1961) 82 After breakfast our boys urged us to move on. **1834** MARKHAM *NZ* (1963) 40 I was certainly ashamed that Europeans could degrade themselves so before their New Zealand Boys, but so they did. *Ibid*. 72 They picked out two of the strongest of the Boys (as they call the Men) about the place. **1840** *NZ Jrnl.* I. 287 My boys, as native attendants are always styled by both natives and white men, started away early to a native settlement. **1841** JAMESON *NZ, S. Austral. & NSW* 293 Gangs of *boys* (as the New Zealanders of all ages call themselves when in the service of Europeans). **1851** GRACE *Journal* Mar. in *Pioneer Missionary* (1928) 10 We had not been long here before my boys had dressed the pig in the Maori fashion. **1911** *Truth* 9 Sept. 4 Up Auckland way the crusade in favour of cheap domestic labor [*sic*] has resulted in a scheme for the importation of a number of black 'boys' from the islands, said 'boys' being men who are sent to the Dominion under contract by their relatives or owners with whom a regular slave or 'blackbird' traffic will be initiated. **1946** SOLJAK *NZ* 117 New Zealanders have coined or adapted many expressions to meet local requirements, as illustrated by the following:.. *boy:* native servant; recorded in 1840.
 2. With prefixed **Maori**, a belittling term for a Maori man of any age.
 1952 *Here & Now* Jan. 21 'D'ere d'hino,' said the Maori boy at the pool table. **1956** WILSON *Sweet White Wine* 140 'Escort this man to the brig'... The Maori boy [*sc.* the prisoner] said, 'I do what I like.' *Ibid*. 141 Fourteen stone of burly Maori was sitting on a mess table... His eyes met mine... He was close to hysteria, this Maori boy. **1959** SLATTER *Gun in My Hand* 99 I've seen some very good Maori boys on the paddock. Real good boys. Winnin or losin. They got a flair for the game. **1966** *NZ Short Stories* (1976) 86 She was..working the pump and filling handles four at a time for a bunch of Maori boys.
 3. Often formerly, esp. among Maori youths, a term of address.
 1960 CRUMP *Good Keen Man* 45 I'd ask Mori for his tally and he'd reply, 'Found a beauty huhu log, boy.' **1964** MORRIESON *Came a Hot Friday* (1981) 208 My wrist's broken, you can put a ring around it... You'll have to get me to a quack, boy. **1976** WILSON *Pacific Star* 70 'Hit the sack, eh, boy? We're going to be flying in the morning.'

bo-yang: see BOWYANG.

brace. *Goldmining.* [f. *brace* the mouth of a mineshaft: see OED *n*.¹ 18; EDD.] The deck or platform at the mouth of a mineshaft on which men and materials are loaded and unloaded.
 1961 HENDERSON *Friends In Chains* 185 Brace: Type of platform around the top of a mine shaft. **1978** MCARA *Gold Mining Waihi* 313 Brace: The covered deck surrounding the poppet-head on the surface and used for loading and unloading men and materials from the cages.
 Hence **braceman**, one who works on or is in charge of the brace of a mine (see quot. 1978).
 1875 *Official Handbook NZ* 259 [Wages on goldfields] bracemen..8/4, feeders..6/-, amalgamator..9/-. **1892** PYKE *Gold-Miners' Guide* 82 No *youth* shall be employed as lander, or brace-man over any shaft. **1911** *Maoriland Worker* 29 Sept. 6 Brace and chambermen not to be employed in any other occupation. **1908** *Awards, etc.* 235 [Inangahua gold-miners award] [Rates of wages] Blacksmiths' assistants, strikers 8[s.] 0[d.] Bracemen 9 0 Chambermen 10 0. **1978** MCARA *Gold Mining Waihi* 313 *Braceman*: A man employed on the brace where the cages were loaded and unloaded. He had to remove and tip the full trucks and replace them with empties as they arrived in the cage, and had to load men and materials going down the shaft.

bracken. Also early **brackens**, **brackins**. [Transf. use of *bracken* a fern, usu. *Pteridium esculentum*: AND 1844.] Also **bracken fern**, and occas. with a modifier **common bracken**. The fern *Pteridium esculentum* (fam. Dennstaedtiaceae), occurring elsewhere, but widespread and of special significance in New Zealand. See also FERN 1 a.
 1834 MARKHAM *NZ* 29 The Southern side is..dark from being covered with Fern or Brackens. **1849** DEANS in *Pioneers* (1964) 56 [On land] which was, when we came here, entirely covered with fern or brackins, we have sown grass..after burning off the fern. **1873** PYKE *Wild Will Enderby* (1889, 1974) I. iii 16 Trailing 'bush-lawyers', intermingled with coarse 'bracken', cling lovingly to the rude stones. **1882** [see FERN 1 a]. **1891** WALLACE *Rural Econ. Austral. & NZ* 230 The common fern resembles very closely, if it is not identical with, the brake or Bracken..of this country. **1905** WHITE *My NZ Garden* 51 The common 'Bracken' grows and spreads everywhere where the soil is good. **1910** COCKAYNE *NZ Plants & Their Story* 51 The bracken fern..is a common constituent of heaths, and is frequently the most important plant. **1933** [see FERN 1 a]. **1946** *NZJST* XXVII. 432 Bracken fern..was originally widespread..on the hill country of Hawke's Bay. **1966** *Encycl. NZ* I. 647 The ubiquitous bracken..the farmer's misery, grows to 6 ft in height and spreads rapidly by means of rhizomes. **1988** DAWSON *Forest Vines to Snow Tussocks* 107 Where the previous forest cover is completely removed..the first coloniser is bracken fern.

bracket, *n. Horseracing.* [An extended or transf. use of *bracket* one of the marks used to enclose figures or words, in this case the names of horses placed within brackets.] Each horse (or the pair of horses) paired ('bracketed') in a race or race-meeting. See note to verb 1 below.
 1938 *Auckland Weekly News* 19 Oct. 76 With Crocus and Nervie's Last, F.J. Smith has a powerful bracket. **1945** SUTHERLAND *The NZ Turf* 33 Regarding brackets, whereas in the galloping branch horses which are raced by the same owner are bracketted [*sic*], in the trotting branch all horses trained by the same mentor starting in the same race are also bracketted. **1986** *NZ Rules of Racing* 117 In the event of there being a greater number of starters in a race than there are numbers available on the totalisator the Stewards or Committee may create a sufficient number of brackets to meet the position by including two horses for each bracket so required beginning with the two lowest weighted horses and working up from them.

bracket, *v*.
 1. *Horseracing.* [See BRACKET n.: to have names paired by or placed within a bracket.] Usu. as a *pa. ppl.* or *ppl. a.* As a totalisator or betting convenience, to pair horses in certain circumstances so that if either is placed a dividend is paid on both.
 [*Note*] The circumstances are these: (a) horses beyond 18 in any race are paired ('bracketed') with a number, and hence a horse, already given (e.g. in a race of 20 entries, the last numbers would be 17, 17a, 18, 18a); (b) similarly, when entries are more than can be safely run at one time and the race must be run in two divisions, each horse in the first division is paired ('bracketed') with each horse in the second; (c) (formerly) horses of the same ownership (galloping) or of the same ownership and trainership (trotting and pacing), running in the same race were bracketed.
 1938 *Auckland Weekly News* 11 May 76 Charlie Chan..is a useful improver..and bracketed with the consistent Sandusky, the combination will find strong support. **1944** *Wanganui Chronicle* 30 Dec. 7 In the Marton Cup, Betterman and Skydonna will be bracketed. **1970** *Horse Racing, Trotting & Dog Racing in NZ* 233 The Rules of Trotting... say that all horses shall be bracketed: (a) Which are owned wholly or partly by the same owner... (f) Which the stipendiary stewards order to be bracketed.
 Hence **bracketing**. Also *attrib*.
 1970 *Horse Racing, Trotting & Dog Racing in NZ* 233 In horse racing, bracketing is the coupling of two or more horses under one number on a race card and on the totalisator. The bet is recorded against the number, not the individual horse... Bracketing policies differ between racing and trotting.
 2. [f. *bracket* to parenthesize.] *trans.* To relegate or stand down (esp. a member of a sports team).
 1988 *Dominion* (Wellington) 15 July 28 [Heading] Injured Jones bracketed for test... It will..be touch and go whether he is fit in time to regain his test spot.

brackins, var. BRACKEN.

braeburn. [Named from *Braeburn* Valley, Nelson, the locality of the orchard in which it was discovered in 1950.] A variety of dessert apple having an excellent response to cool-storage.
 1974 *Orchardist NZ* Nov. 337 Braeburn. This is a marvellous apple out of the cool store, and would be one of the few that improves with cool storage. **1986** *Illustr. Encycl. NZ* 46 Braeburn—A new variety with crisp, juicy flesh and a distinctive flavour. **1991** *New Zealand's Best Apple Recipes* 13 Braeburn. This popular

apple originated from a chance seedling on Mr William's Nelson orchard.

brain.

1. In the phr. **to need** (or **want**) **one's brains brushed**, to need one's thoughts clarifying.
  1908 *Truth* 25 Apr. 1 Whoever conceived the idea of taking a vehicle over that country wants his brains brushed.

2. Brains Trust (also early **brains pool**). [Transf. f. *Brain Trust* the popular name of a politico-economic advisory group set up in 1933 by US President F.D. Roosevelt: see OED.] The nickname of an advisory group of economists set up in the early 1930s to advise the Minister of Finance, the Hon. Gordon Coates.
  1933 BUCK in *Na To Hoa Aroha* 12 May (1988) III. 80 [Roosevelt] is credited with being advised on the side by a group of professors who are known as the 'brains pool'. **1936** *Ibid*. 6 Jan. III. 205 The post-election inquests have attributed the defeat of the nationalists to various causes. Coates' unpopularity and the Brains Trust. [**1988** *Note*] Economists, including the civil servants, R.M. Campbell, W.B. Sutch, and Professor Horace Belshaw (of Auckland University College), who advised Coates. The name was derived from Roosevelt's 'Brain Trust'. **1992** *North & South* (Auckland) Dec. 75 It was..[Paul Verschaffelt] who worked alongside Dr W.B. (Bill) Sutch in then Prime Minister Gordon Coates's 'brains trust'—developing economic and fiscal policy in the period 1933 to 1935.

bramble. [AND 1827.] Also **native bramble, New Zealand bramble**, in occasional early use for BUSH LAWYER *n*.¹, native species of *Rubus*. Compare BLACKBERRY.
  [*Note*] *Bramble* as a general term for 'blackberry' is an occasional and early use only: cf. **1978** WATSON *World Is an Orange* 58 I wonder why I used the word 'Brambles'. I'm disturbed by it, because really only the Poms call them 'brambles'! We say 'blackberries'! It is really discouraging to catch a note of pretension or plagiarism, as if while composing my poems, I had some one else's poems in my head.
  1777 ANDERSON *Journal* Feb. in Cook *Journals* (1967) III. 805 Amongst the known kinds of plants are..Brambles. **1838** POLACK *NZ* I. 295 *Knot-grass, brambles, eye-bright, groundsell*..supposed to be solely indigenous to New Zealand, abound throughout the country. **1853** [see BUSH LAWYER *n*.¹]. **1866** ANGAS *Polynesia* 47 Dr. Bennett says, '..After passing through a dense forest, annoyed by the 'tataramoa', or New Zealand bramble..we descended a hill covered with exuberant vegetation.' **1889** FEATON *Art Album NZ Flora* 120 The Maori name of the plant is 'Tataramoa', whilst the settlers designate it as the 'Native bramble', or 'Bush lawyer'. **1908** BAUGHAN *Shingle-Short* 190 *Bramble*: Better known to New Zealanders as 'Bush Lawyer'. **1940** LAING & BLACKWELL *Plants NZ* 205 The New Zealand Bramble is of the same tribe as the raspberry and the blackberry, though its fruits are not so fine. **1978** FULLER *Maori Food & Cook*. 10 A drink was also made from the bark of the houhere and rata, and from the New Zealand bramble. **1982** [see BUSH LAWYER *n*.¹].

branch. Mainly *SI*. [Spec. use of *branch* a lateral extension from a main trunk: see OED *n*. 2.] Applied to any of the various subsidiary streams (or beds) into which a plains river is divided.
  1844 DEANS *Pioneers* (1964) 38 The river divides into several different branches near to our houses, and it is between them that our cattle feed; they serve as fences. **1862** CHUDLEIGH *Diary* 16 Mar. (1950) 28 The bed [of the Rakaia] is two miles across, the water a mile but split up into many branches. **1874** KENNAWAY *Crusts* 170 At one of the most dangerous crossings of the river,—increased now by swollen branches which had joined it on all sides,—a man was camped. **1896** BIGGAR *Diary* in Begg *Port Preservation* (1973) 344 It was plainly to be seen that it [*sc*. Wilson's River] had three branches instead of two as marked on the map. **1983** FRANCIS *Wildlife Ranger* 56 Do you remember old Shirty and the time his dogs got away up the top branch?

branchman. *Goldmining*. [f. *branch* the metal piece on the end of a hose, to which the nozzle is screwed (see OED *n*. 11) + *man*.] One who operates the nozzle of a sluice-head.
  1904 *NZ Illustr. Mag.* X. 182 We saw some sluicers at work further on. The branchman had a big nozzle on a stand, and was directing a powerful jet of water..against the face of gravel.

brand, *v. Obs*. [Spec. use in children's games of *brand* to mark as one's own.] *trans*. See quots. Also **branding** *vbl. n*.
  1966 TURNER *Eng. Lang. Austral. & NZ* 159 In small schools without proper playing fields, games were spontaneous and enjoyable, and holes could be dug freely in the school grounds for *Rotten Eggs*, in which a tennis ball is rolled into the nest of one of the players and all run while the boy with the ball has to *brand* another player (i.e. hit him with the ball). **1982** SUTTON-SMITH *Hist. Children's Play* 231 There are games recorded in this period for which there is no record before 1900 though they may well have existed under other names... *Golden Bay*:.. Creeping, Branding, O'Leary.

branding, *vbl. n. Farming*. Used *attrib*. in various special Comb., of or pertaining to the branding of stock: **branding-muster** [AND 1954], a muster (of stock) for branding; **branding race**, a narrow race in which sheep or cattle are branded.
  1907 LANCASTER *Tracks We Tread* 64 The **branding-muster** was heavy work on the Mains, with three sets of irons going at once. **1933** *Press* (Christchurch) (Acland Gloss.) 16 Sept. 15 *Brand*.—(1) The letter or other mark which each owner has to identify his own stock... Hence *branding race*, a narrow race for branding sheep. **1950** *NZJAg*. July LXXXI. 7 In addition..there may be units such as a branding race. **1978** JARDINE *Shadows on Hill* 129 Branding paint had to be mixed..and yard books made ready at the branding-race shed.

brass razoo: see RAZOO a.

brattice. *Mining*. Also **brattis**. [f. Sc. or northern Brit. dial. *brattice*: see EDD 2.; SND 2.] A canvas or coarse cloth, or wooden partition, used to control ventilation in a mine.
  1928 DEVANNY *Dawn Beloved* 172 All that the doctor could do was..to cover the whole with a piece of brattis ripped down from the stenton. **1978** MCARA *Gold Mining Waihi* 313 *Brattice*: A curtain erected across an airway to control ventilation. **1980** BATTYE & EAKIN *Shadow of Valley* 72 *Brattice*. Coarse canvas screen hung at intervals through the mine to contain foul air and distribute fresh air from the ventilation system. **1984** BEARDSLEY *Blackball 08* 242 brattice: partition of wood used to control ventilation in a mine.

bravo duck. *Stewart Isd*. [Orig. unknown.] *blue shag* (SHAG 2 (3)).
  1989 PARKINSON *Travelling Naturalist* 178 The blue shag..goes under the rather unusual local [Stewart Island] name of the bravo duck.

break, *v*.¹ [Spec. use of *break, v*. to escape from restraint.]

1. [Orig. US: see OED 38 b; AND 1888.] **a**. Of a mob (or part of a mob) of sheep or (esp.) lambs, and occas. cattle (see quot. 1904) to bolt or stampede.
  1865 CHUDLEIGH *Diary* 25 Oct. (1950) 202 The sheep broke repeatedly before we could get them in. I..rode home after the yarding and had a plunge bath. **1889** REISCHEK *Wonderful Dog* 34 If the sheep broke he ordered a second dog to assist. **1904** LANCASTER *Sons o' Men* 21 With a crash the mob broke. **1934** *Press* (Christchurch) (Acland Gloss.) 13 Jan. 13 *Break*.— Break away, usually of lambs. Both as noun and as verb. **1947** NEWTON *Wayleggo* 153 *Break: Lamb Break*:.. Great care must be exercised, as a false move by man or dog will have the lambs, ever on their toes, stampeding or breaking. **1952** BLAKISTON *My Yesteryears* 22 Now and then, one [lamb] will try to bolt back over the ground along which it has come, and, if one gets past the shepherds, several hundreds will follow. When lambs 'break' as this bolting is termed, they may run for miles before they stop, for no dog can turn them.

b. As **break away** (occas. **break** *intr*.), of stock, to break free or bolt from a herd or mob.
  1864 CHUDLEIGH *Diary* 6 Oct. (1950) 147 Started after a mob of sheep that had broken away from the man that was keeping a boundary. **1874** KENNAWAY *Crusts* 135 The wild brutes tried to break away in every direction. **1994** LASENBY *Dead Man's Head* 101 A drover came running a bull fast so it wouldn't break off the road.

c. As **break back**, of sheep, to run or dash in the reverse direction of the drive.
  1864 CHUDLEIGH *Diary* 13 Oct. (1950) 148 A mob broke back when we where [*sic*] crossing a small stream and [we] ran over two miles before we could turn them. **1933** JONES *Autobiogr. Early Settler* 59 If a mob..broke back..the rest of us would have to wait while the shepherd on whose beat the sheep had broken back, went for them.

2. As **break for** (a destination), to escape to a new locality, from the constraints of an old.
  1909 *Truth* 21 Aug. 11 In September, 1901, George broke for 'Roo land', his avowed intention being to 'place his children in life'.

break, *v*.² In various phr.

1. to break the back of (some heavy task) [see OED *v*. 7 b *break the neck of*], to get the worst or heaviest or largest part done.
  1950 CHERRILL *NZ Sheep Farm* 85 I've had a time grubbing old Tom's gorse. However, I've broken the back of it now.

2. to break the drought, to take up drinking liquor after abstinence.
  1909 *Truth* 29 May 7 But as some of the exiles [to 'dry' districts] escape from the desert of despair, they promptly embark on their glad programme of breaking the drought.

3. *Two up*. **to break the ring** [an alteration of the gambling term *break the bank*: see OED *v*. 11], to 'break the bank' (as in other gambling), to win all the ringkeeper's cash.
  1937 LEE *Civilian into Soldier* 99 Sometimes a man would succeed daringly, doubling up and breaking the ring with a long run of heads, 'throwing a trot'.

break, *n*. [f. BREAK *v*.¹ 1.]

1. A stampede or panic rush (usu. of sheep), often away from the main mob. See also BREAKAWAY 1.
  1934 *Press* (Christchurch) (Acland Gloss.) 13 Jan. 13 *Break*.— Break away, usually of lambs. Both as

noun and as verb. **1947** NEWTON *Wayleggo* 48 [The dog] made his name..by his masterly handling of a 'break' of lambs. **1951** MCLEOD *NZ High Country* 25 A 'break' and a bad break of lambs is a thing you won't forget in a hurry. Twenty or thirty of the little brutes will dash off, their heads turned towards the friendly hill, racing and jumping. **1962** SHARPE *Country Occasions* 173 To the drover..a 'break', as we call a stampede, is just an unmitigated nuisance.

2. Special Comb. **break-fence**, a fence fixed across a hillside, gully, etc. to prevent a 'break' or any quick movement or stampede of stock downhill or in a confined space. Also *ellipt.* as **break**.

1952 NEWTON *High Country Journey* 185 All that was needed to hold cattle in the valley above was the erection of a short 'break' across the neck of the gorge. **1959** MCLEOD *Tall Tussock* 37 This was the repair of a 'break fence' crossing a leading spur above the bush. **1973** WALLACE *Generation Gap* 230 The men were..putting up breaks for stock. **1975** NEWTON *Sixty Thousand on the Hoof* 199 Most of the paddock fences were renewed and attention was then directed to the hill; numerous 'break' fences (short lengths of two or three barbs spanning gullies or running from existing fences up steep faces and into bluffs) were put in at strategic spots.

break: see *break-fence* (BREAK *n.* 2).

breakaway, *n.*

1. [AND 1881.] BREAK *n.* 1.

1934 [see BREAK *n.* 1]. **1968** *NZ Contemp. Dict. Suppl.* (Collins) 4 *breakaway n.* panic rush of stock. **1970** MCNAUGHTON *Tat* 99 But once they [*sc.* sheep] were started on the downward journey, the danger of a breakaway was past, and all that remained was hard punching to keep them together.

2. [Cf. AND 1926: a rush of floodwater bursting from its usual course; the channel thus eroded.] A piece of land washed out by rain or flood.

1897 *TrNZI* XXIX. 515 Larger landholders [on the Hawke's Bay plain] supplied estimates of 'breakaways' in their land as a result of the excessive rainfall that then took place.

break camp: see CAMP *n.* 2 b.

break down, *v.*[1] [f. *break v.* destroy cohesion: see OED 51 f.]

1. *Sawmilling.* To take (usu. the first) cuts off a log; occas. also, to saw logs or flitches into timber.

1875 *TrNZI* VII. 186 If 'broken down' or cut into suitable boards for wainscoting and furniture, [the timbers] would be highly appreciated for their striking beauty. **1892** [see FLITCH].

Hence **breaker-down**, a sawmill worker who operates a break-down saw.

1923 *Awards, etc.* 112 [Westland Timber Yards and Sawmill Employees] [Rates of wages] Sawyer keeping up to three saws [£]5 7[s.] 6[d.]... Slipman 0 13 0 Leading breakerdown 0 14 0. **1951** *Awards, etc.* 453 [Westland Timber-Workers Award] [Rates of wages] Sawyer who does no saw keeping 4[s.] 4[d.] Leading breaker-down, circular saw 4 3 Second breaker-down, circular saw 3 11¾. **1951** p.c. R. Gilberd, Okaihau. A log comes off 'the skids'..and on to a travelling platform which carries it on to the 'breaking-down' saw. The man who works this saw is the 'breaker-down' and his offsider is 'the slabby'. **1952–53** *NZ Forest Service Gloss.* (TS) Breaker-down. The head-sawyer of a breaking-down bench.

2. To make (a task, a problem) easier or lighter.

1937 PARTRIDGE *Dict. Slang* 91 *break down.* v To make lighter: C. 20 New Zealand c[ant]. **a1974** SYDER & HODGETTS *Austral. & NZ Eng.* (TS) 111 You expect too much. 'Break it down—that job's too much for a new chum—he can't handle that until he's had a bit of practice.'

break down, *v.*[2] [f. *break down* to demolish: AND 1941.] To desist from (something annoying); usu. in *imp.* phr. **break it down!**, stop it! cut it out! be quiet!, usu. as a reprimand or indicating disbelief.

1940–41 *H.M. Transports* 23 & 23A (Troopship pub.) 16 Break it down, gunner, how often have I told you to answer your name properly. **1943** *NZEF Times* 16 Mar. 6 Break down the swearing... The padre doesn't like it. **1949** COLE *It Was So Late* 13 'Break it down!' Wood shouted from the telephone. 'I can't hear a thing.' **1959** SLATTER *Gun in My Hand* 202 Drink and be merry for tomorrow we die he yelled and the boys said break it down, cut out that sort of talk. **1976** WILSON *Pacific Star* 52 Steady on, Ted. Break it down, boy. Watch she doesn't stall. **1988** MCGILL *Dict. Kiwi Slang* 21 *break it down* demand to stop unacceptable behaviour; eg 'Break it down, will ya! Some of us are trying to sleep!'

breakdown, *n. Sawmilling.* [f. BREAK DOWN *v.*[1] 1.] Used mainly in special Comb.

1. In full **breakdown saw**, a large circular saw, or set of two such (one upper, one lower), taking the first cuts from rough logs to convert them to flitches.

1920 MANDER *Story NZ River* (1974) 159 By day the whole bay vibrated with the whistle and screech of the circular saws, the tear of the break downs, the rasp of the drags. **1923** MALFROY *Small Sawmills* 17 The laying of the foundations of the breakdown should first be proceeded with. **1981** CHARLES *Black Billy Tea* 70 And sawdust in a shower The 'break-downs' thump, And the logs go bump.

2. In various technical uses in special Comb. **breakdown bench**, the sawbench on which logs are converted to flitches; **breakdown benchman**, **breakdown man**, the sawmill worker who operates the breakdown bench; **breakdown platform**, breakdown bench.

1921 *Ensign* (Mataura) 24 May in Barry *In Lee of Hokonuis* (1966) 144 There are **break down benches** and two large saws of five and a half feet and four and a half feet. **1923** MALFROY *Small Sawmills* 19 A good..breakdown bench can be built locally on the principle of the 'Bullock' bench which has been used in some parts of New Zealand for the last fifty years. *Ibid.* 28 The **breakdown benchman** should be able to keep his own saws, and break the logs down to suit the cutting at the sawyer's bench. **1943** BENNETT *English in NZ* in *Amer. Speech* XVIII. 85 [The timber trade] has supplied a wide variety of occupational terms... A *bush skiddy* is a man who works on the cleared tracks which carry logs to the mill, where it is [*sic*] handled by a **break-down man** ('to break down' in New Zealand means 'to make lighter'). **1920** MANDER *Story NZ River* (1974) 198 They watched the progress of the log from the booms up the skids to the side of the **breakdown platform**... Halved and quartered, it was then levered..on to greased rollers and rushed towards the big circulars, which turned it into flitches.

break in, *v.* [Orig. f. Brit. dial.: see EDD *break v.* II 1.] To clear and prepare virgin land for cultivation, or occas. for planting. Cf. *bring in* (BRING *v.* 2).

1836 [see *vbl. n.* below]. **1856** FITTON *NZ* 99 Considering the facility of breaking in land here..the clearing and burning off for the entry of the plough varying from ten to twenty shillings per acre. **1891** WALLACE *Rural Econ. Austral. & NZ* I. 24 The single-furrow plough is employed to break in the land. **1899** BELL *In Shadow of Bush* 222 I am supposed to be here for the purpose of gaining 'colonial experience'..here, where men are hourly engaged in breaking-in the wilderness, and all that sort of thing. **1927** REES *Life's What You Make It* 118 Breaking in country means clearing it, doesn't it? **1946** SARGESON *That Summer* 173 It was years now since he had finished breaking in his farm from heavy bush country. **1963** BACON *In the Sticks* 87 It isn't far to where they'll be breaking in this land you've heard so much about. **1984** *Listener* 11 Aug. 29 Jim and Rose Henare set out to break in a farm at Motatau that people said would never pay its way. **1991** *More Earlier Days on the Coast* 35 Gradually, as the land was broken in, Grandpa began milking his Jersey cows.

Hence **breaking in** *vbl. n.* and *attrib.*, of virgin land, the bringing into cultivation; **broken in** *ppl. a.*, brought into cultivation; also as **unbroken**, of virgin land, with its original vegetation, etc. intact.

1836 *Letter* 5 Jan. in Matthews *Matthews of Kaitaia* (1940) 80 The latter part I was engaged in attending to the **breaking in** of land, and planting corn and potatoes for native food. **1930** *NZJST* XI. 279 From 1902 onwards the breaking-in of the swamp was undertaken on a large scale. **1951** LEVY *Grasslands NZ* (1970) 250 Following the initial primary forest burn, secondary scrub fires and logging-up burns continue the breaking-in process. **1964** SARGESON *Collected Stories 1935-1963* 298 breaking in (land or a farm): clearing of its original vegetation and preparing for sowing or ploughing. **1924** *Otago Witness* (Dunedin) 4 Nov. 54 Wakawai consisted mostly of what is known as '**unbroken** country'... The bush would have to be felled and burnt off before the station could be put down in grass, and used for sheep and cattle. **1940** COWAN *Sir Donald Maclean* 3 The experience he gained in work on the newly **broken-in** settlements was useful..when he came to take up a pastoral block in Hawke's Bay. **1952** FINLAYSON *Brown Man's Burden* (1973) 112 Beyond the weatherbeaten old Tairua village, on the river flats amid newly broken-in land, were neat new houses.

breaking-down, *vbl. n. Sawmilling.* [f. BREAK DOWN *v.*[1] 1.]

1. The conversion in a sawmill of logs to flitches.

1894 *NZ Official Year-book* 332 Breaking-down is commonly effected by the circular-saw, and in the case of very large logs by two circular-saws, an upper and a lower working in the same vertical plane. **1928** *Free Lance* (Wellington) 25 July 7 When the loco arrives at the..skids, the logs are hauled off by two winches, cut to the required length by the fiddling saw, then kicked to the Pacific bench which does the 'breaking down'. **1965** HILLIARD *Power of Joy* 45 He would go among the men from the mills..asking if there were any jobs going. 'Benching?—any benching? How about breaking-down?'

2. *attrib.* passing into special Comb. **breaking-down bench**, the moving platform in a sawmill where logs receive their first cut; **breaking-down saw**, see BREAKDOWN *n.* 1 and 2; **breaking-down shed**, a sawmill building housing the breaking-down saw.

1889 KIRK *Forest Flora* 32 In Southland small mills are furnished with a **breaking-down bench** and twin circular saws, working one above the other, to cut deep logs. *Ibid.* 151 A vertical frame-saw for breaking-down work is invariably in use. **1949** DE MAUNY *Huntsman in His Career* 162 Leaving the mill, the scream of the bandsaws on the breaking-down bench..he was struck once more by the extraordinary silence of the bush. **1951** *Awards, etc.* 452 [Westland Timber-Workers Award] 'Breaking-down bench' means any type of bench used for the purpose of reducing logs to flitches, irrespective of the type of saws used. **1952–53** *NZ Forest Service Gloss.* (TS) Breaking-down bench. A sawbench used for the purpose of reducing logs to flitches. **1981** MARSH *Black Beech & Honeydew* 103 The next morning we saw them thunder down skids to a breaking-down bench in the mill. **1889** KIRK *Forest Flora* 32 The **breaking-down** frame-saw common in other districts is almost unknown in Southland. **1894, 1913** [see FLITCH]. **1951** p.c. R. Gilberd, Okaihau. A log comes off 'the skids'..and on to a travelling platform which carries it on to the 'breaking-down' saw. **1967** GROVER *Another Man's Role* 34 Breaking-down saws—most efficient amputators of arms and legs. **1988** JACKSON *Rainshadow* 90 He was answered by the..drone of the breaking-down saw as it bit into a pine log. **1964** BACON *Along the Road* 31 The **breaking-down shed** [was] more decrepit than when we first saw it.

break out, *v.*¹ [Used elsewhere but recorded earliest from NZ: see OED *break v.* 55 g, 1840 (Dana).] To open up a receptacle or place of storage and remove articles from it.
  1835 *Piraki Log* 29 Dec. (1911) 21 Commenced breaking out the After hold to recooper the provisions &c. **1838** POLACK *NZ* II. 418 After the ship has had a quantity of oil within her hold some length of time, the casks are taken again upon deck, termed broke out.
  Hence **break-out** *n.*, the unloading of a receptacle.
  1964 DAVIS *Watersiders* 36 They've opened the VB [wagon] and she's crammed to the door... Only room for one joker to work. He hops up does the break-out.

break out, *v.*² [AND 1855.] Of a new goldfield, to come into full operation, to become the centre of a rush; of a goldrush, to start; of a locality or district, to suffer a goldrush; of gold, to be first discovered.
  1861 *NZ Goldfields 1861* (1976) 20 Since the goldfields have broken out, the face of things has greatly changed. **1873** BARKER *Station Amusements* 88 The West Coast Diggings had just 'broken out' (as the curious phrase goes there). **1874** TROLLOPE *NZ* 90 When gold 'broke out', as the phrase goes, on the western side of the Middle Island. **1881** BATHGATE *Waitaruna* 139 There was a rush broke out over at Blackman's and some of the diggers began leaving here for there. **1894** O'REGAN *Voices of Wave & Tree* 14 An' after, when the Coast broke out, we roughed it through the bush An' beat the boats..in gettin' to the rush. **1914** PFAFF *Diggers' Story* 121 Okarito had broken out, and some very dangerous..characters had collected there. **1939** BEATTIE *First White Boy Born Otago* 121 [The white crane] was always rare and was never seen after the diggings broke out. **1947** BEATTIE *Early Runholding* 12 These 'gentlemen of the swag' were not in evidence until after the gold diggings broke out.

break out. *v.*³ [AND 1965.] To go on a drinking bout; to go on a spree (occas. of vandalism).
  1899 BELL *In Shadow of Bush* 101 Davie..had thought it best on the one occasion in which Dan had 'broken out' [*sc.* 'on the burst'], to give him a wide berth. **1904** *NZ Illustr. Mag.* IX. 429 Bill did 'break out'.
  Hence **breaking out** *vbl. n.*, an outburst of violence.

c**1875** *Otago Guardian* in Tonkin *Dunedin Gaol* (1980) 9 The governor informs us that the penal servitude men often have what is termed a 'breaking out',—that is to say, after having behaved..remarkably well for several months, they must give way to their feelings by smashing everything they can lay their hands upon... Only a short time ago one of the long-sentence men had a 'breaking out', and smashed everything in his cell.
  Hence by back-formation **break-out** *n.* [AND 1847], a drinking bout, a spree.
  1908 KOEBEL *Anchorage* 49 A break-out don't seem to oil your tongue.

break out, *v.*⁴ *Shearing.* To open up (a part of a sheep's fleece) with the first shearing cuts.
  1955 BOWEN *Wool Away* 24 The next blow is from the off side of the brisket down to the opposite flank, and if possible the belly wool is broken out. If this is found too difficult to break out, then leave it for the third blow. **1986** RICHARDS *Off the Sheep's Back* 97 My style of breaking out the neck by turning the head and coming out behind the ears could not be applied on these loose, wrinkle-necked half-breds.

break out, *v.*⁵ *Logging.* To haul (logs) from the bush to a collection point, or to the mill skids.
  1969 MOORE *Forest to Farm* 42 [Logs were] then 'broken out' or dragged through a roughly cleared bush track to a central point or 'landing' where the skidded road started.
  Hence **breaker-out**, the workman who supervises the hauling of the logs from the bush; **breaking-out** *vbl. n.* and *ppl. a.*, (pertaining to) the hauling of logs from the bush.
  1943 BENNETT *English in NZ* in *Amer. Speech* XVIII. 85 Other [timber-trade] terms..are **breaker-out**..(pl *breakers-out*). **1951** *Awards, etc.* 520 [Marlborough Timber-Workers Award] [Rates of wages] Other crosscutter and scarfer 4[s.] 2¹/₂[d.] Breaker-out, snigger, ropeman (hauling rope), to apply to only one man in each hauling team 4 4¹/₂. **1952–53** *NZ Forest Service Gloss.* (TS) Breaker-out. The bushman who attaches the cable to trees or logs being hauled from stump to landing. **1971** in Cleveland *Great NZ Songbook* (1991) 54 From the bushmen to the breaker-out, From the breaker-out to the bench. **1992** *Dominion* (Wellington) 9 Jan. 15 Following after him was the breaker-out, hooking the fallen trees up to the hauler with heavy wire strops. **1953** REED *Story of Kauri* 151 The cost of filling and cross-cutting might be set down, say, at fourpence per hundred feet; **breaking out** (separating the logs), sniping and chuting into creeks, one-and-two per hundred. **1961** CRUMP *Hang On a Minute Mate* 37 And what's breaking out? Oh, you just get the log ready and hook her on to the winch-rope when the tractor swings to swing her out to the skids. [a1914] McCARROLL *The Days of the Kauri Bushmen* (Radio Talk 2 (1951): TS) The roads bringing the logs out of the bush from the stump are called [c1914] **Breaking-Out** Roads, and are really only bush tracks along which the bullocks haul the logs out to the main road.

breaksea devil. *Obs.* [f. the name of *Breaksea Island*, in Breaksea Sound, on the sw. coast of the South Island.] A sound of rushing air, attributed to a phantom bird; or the bird species (HAKUWAI q.v.) that causes the noise. See also HOKIOI.
  1844 TUCKETT *Diary* 24 May in Hocken *Contributions* (1898) 224 All the people frequenting this coast [*sc.* west coast of Otago] believe in the existence of an extraordinary bird, or phantom, which they can never see, but only hear rushing past them through the air with the rapidity of a rocket, and making a terrible rushing sound. The Maories declare that it is a bird possessing many joints in its wings. The whalers call them *break-sea-devils*, after the name of an island where this phenomenon is of most frequent occurrence. **1970** JENKIN *NZ Mysteries* 157 A similar strange bird [*sc.* to the hakuwai], called by the whalers the Breaksea Devil, was said to be heard on Breaksea Island. **1988** *Notornis* XXXV. 216 Either of the group [of islands] off Shelter Point..or the small islet south of Great Island..could have held Hakawai, Break-sea Devils—or Stewart Island Snipe. **1990** FORD *NZ Descriptive Animal Dictionary* 188 Hakawai:.. Other names: Hakawai, Breaksea Devil.

break water, *v.* *Whaling.* [A specific use.] Of a whale, to rise to the surface (after sounding).
  1838 POLACK *NZ* II. 421 After the whale is pierced, they frequently remain from twenty to sixty minutes previous to rising again on the surface of the ocean, termed breaking water.

breakwind. [AND 1840.] A wind-break.
  1838 *Piraki Log* 27 Feb. (1911) 67 The Men employed cutting wood in the Bush for building a Breakwind round the Try work. **1879** FEATON *Waikato War* 87 (Griffiths Collect.) Breakwinds of titree and flax were erected. **1904** LANCASTER *Sons o' Men* 9 The breakwind was close-packed manuka-scrub and birch logs. Behind it cowered the ten-by-twelve wharè. **1917** let. 13 Aug. in *Boots, Belts* (1992) 24 In one place they have breakwinds to protect the train... The wind sweeps over the railway and down a big gully. **1955** BJ Cameron Collection (TS July) breakwind (n) A line of trees or other obstacle serving to break the force of the wind.

bream. [Transf. use of northern hemisphere *bream*, a sea-fish: AND 1699.]
1. a. In New Zealand applied, occas. as **sea-bream**, to often quite dissimilar sea-fish of several families, esp. to (small or young) SNAPPER *n.*¹ 1, 2 (5), to WAREHOU 1, and to BLUENOSE.
  1769 PARKINSON *Journal* (1773) 24 Nov. 107 We..caught a great number of large fishes of the scienna or bream kind; we therefore named this Bream Bay. **1777** ANDERSON *Journal* Feb. in Cook *Journals* (1967) III. 807 Those [fish] which the Indians mostly supply'd us with are a sort of sea Bream of a silver colour with a black spot on the neck. **1807** [see SNAPPER *n.*¹ 1]. **1835** YATE *NZ* (1970) 71 Those saltwater fish most plentiful, and of greatest note, are..snapper, mullet, bream. **1842** HEAPHY *NZ* 49 The bream, ling, gurnard..and a species of mackarel, are all in abundance. **1910** *TrNZI* XLII. 430 The crew caught with lines an astonishing quantity of fine fish belonging to the species *Dorade unicolor*... It is the same fish that Cook calls 'bream'. **1970** [see b following].

b. Also **brim.** SNAPPER *n.*¹ 1, esp. young snapper.
  1820 LEE & KENDALL *NZ Gram. & Vocab.* 206 Támure *s.* Bream fish. **1967** MORELAND *Marine Fishes* 42 Snapper... The name bream is applied to small examples, and the Maori name tamure is still in use about northern coasts. **1970** SORENSEN *Nomenclature NZ Fish* 12 *Bream or Brim*—A loose term for Black Bream (Auckland); small snapper at Nelson; and small Groper at Dunedin. **1981** WILSON *Fisherman's Bible* 31 Bream Small snapper, at a certain stage of their development, are known as 'bream' around Nelson. **1986** PAUL *NZ Fishes* 96 Small snapper are quite often called bream or brim.

c. Also **sea-bream**, applied to WAREHOU.
  1872 [see WAREHOU 1]. **1922** *TrNZI* LII. 22 Common Name of Fish... Sea-bream (warehou). **1957** PARROTT *Sea Angler's Fishes* 170 Warehou *Seriolella brama* Trevally; Sea Bream. **1970** SORENSEN *Nomenclature NZ Fish* 50–51 *Warehou*... Suggested commercial name[s]: Sea Bream; Bream.

d. BLUENOSE (*Hyperoglyphe antarctica* (formerly *porosa*)).
1927 PHILLIPPS *Bibliogr. NZ Fishes* (1971) 32 *Hyperoglyphe porosa*..Bream. **1956** GRAHAM *Treasury NZ Fishes* 222 Bream *Hyperoglyphe porosa*... Before deep sea fishing came into practice the Bream was not common but once line fishermen began fishing from the reefs off Otago Heads this excellent fish became common. **1981** WILSON *Fisherman's Bible* 60 Deep-sea Trevally A name once used for Bream (*Hyperoglyphe porosa*) when they were common around Otago.

2. With a modifier: **black**, **Ray's**.

(1) **black bream**. *Girella tricuspidata* (fam. Kyphosidae). PARORE.
1970 [see 1 b above]. **1986** PAUL *NZ Fishes* 101 *Parore*... Known variously as blackfish, black snapper, black bream, and mangrove fish.

(2) **Ray's bream** *Brama brama* (formerly *raii*) (fam. Bramidae), see esp. quot. 1981. See also BONITA.
1925 *Evening Post* (Wellington) 1 Aug. 13 'I am sending the enclosed photograph of a rare fish which I caught in Karehana Bay, Plimmerton last week...' This fish is a specimen of Ray's Seabream (Brama raii). **1938** *TrRSNZ* LXVIII. 410 *Brama raii*... Ray's bream. **1966** DOOGUE & MORELAND *Sea Anglers' Guide* 237 Rays Bream... *Brama raii;* sea bream. **1976** *Catch* Sept. 9 Ray's bream (*Brama brama*) were extremely abundant off the Westland and Cape Farewell regions. **1981** WILSON *Fisherman's Bible* 182 Ray's Bream. A beautiful, blue-black fish with a most unusual iridescent marking which has been described as 'though a paint brush had been drawn from the head to the tail on each side'.

breast, *v.* [Fig. use of *breast* to face: AND 1909.] *trans.* To stand up close to (a barrier, counter, etc., esp. in the phr. **to breast (up to) the bar**, to approach a (hotel) bar with an air of confidence.
c**1926** THE MIXER *Transport Workers' Song Book* 19 What odds, what chance have you each day As you 'breast' the labour stand [for wharf-labouring work]. **1981** CHARLES *Black Billy Tea* 67 The driver comes in & breasts up to the bar. He says, 'Give me a jar & a couple of crates.'

breast-bench. *Sawmilling.* [Origin doubtful; perh. f. a bench which one 'breasts' or faces; or f. a 'breast-high' bench.] A saw-bench with reversible rollers which takes flitches of timber direct from the breaking-down saw and converts them into planks, etc. (see also quot. 1952-53).
1913 CARR *Country Work* 40 Old fashioned 'Breast' benches (where flitches from the breaking-down saw are cut into commercial sizes) are still used in many mills. **1944** *Korero* (AEWS Background Bulletin) 8 May 27 The system of delivery line..is duplicated in another carrying sawn lengths down from the breast benches to what is called the 'docking' table. **1952–53** *NZ Forest Service Gloss.* (TS) Breast-bench. A table-high sawbench with a single circular saw and with reversible rollers for feeding flitches in and out. The flitches are set against a fence and the whole rig is designed to give the maximum flexibility in sawing to grade. **1981** CHARLES *Black Billy Tea* 69 I went back to work on the 'breast bench' and as the fragrant slabs of pine timber came screaming off the saw and I threw them up on to the truck I sang a little song.

brew. [f. *brew* a boiling of tea.]
1. *Prison.* An illegal alchoholic beverage made in prison.
1982 NEWBOLD *Big Huey* 245 Brew (n) Illegal, locally made alcoholic beverage.

2. *Drug-users*. In the phr. **to make a brew**, to 'cook up' homebake drugs.
1985 *Press* (Christchurch) 24 May 9 He had heard about 'this stuff you can make to get a buzz'. When the police came in he was just thinking about 'making a brew'.

brewer.
1. *Obs.* [Cf. EDD *boorey*, 1869.] A children's game, origin and reference uncertain, but poss. a colonial form of the Northumberland *boorey*, var. *brewery*, a ring for marbles or a marble ring-game of 'keeps' for the marbles players in turn can knock out of the ring.
1905 THOMSON *Bush Boys* 84 Others wanted [to play] 'Prisoners' Base' or 'Chivvy', 'Brewer', 'Egg-in-the-hat', 'Duck-stone', 'Red Rover', or 'Kingy-seeny'.

2. In special collocations: **brewer's asthma** [AND 1953], a hangover; also a fit of coughing or wheezing associated with a hangover; **brewer's goitre** [AND], a fat belly or 'pot' associated with too much beer-drinking. (Known to Ed. from 1945–46.)
1968 SLATTER *Pagan Game* 164 He's a moral to get potted—Shock treatment for the old **brewers' asthma**. **1963** MORRIESON *Scarecrow* 61 I wondered..how a person could answer to the description 'spindle shanked and herring gutted' yet still run to a **brewer's goitre**.

briar. *Obs.* Occas. in early writing for native *Rubus* spp. (fam. Rosaceae), BUSH LAWYER *n.*[1]
1777 FORSTER *Voyage Round World* I. 127 The prodigious intricacy of various climbers, briars, shrubs, and ferns which were interwoven throughout the forests, rendered the task of clearing the ground extremely fatiguing. **1844** TUCKETT *Diary* 24–25 Apr. in Hocken *Contributions* (1898) 212 For the first two hours I almost despaired.., so impenetrable was the forest... Frequently I could only get through the briars by cutting a way with my knife. Nature be thanked, there is only one species of briar to punish invading man in the woods of New Zealand, but that one scratches cruelly.

brick.
1. Also **brickie**. [See OED *n.*[1] 3. (1735), prob. f. French *brique* a loaf.] A loaf shaped like a brick, esp. as **Bell's brick** *Canterbury trampers obs.*, a brick-shaped wholemeal loaf formerly baked by Bell's Bakery in Christchurch and favoured by trampers for its keeping qualities.
1869 THATCHER *Wit & Humour* 24 There's a baker as well, who no longer needs bread, He doesn't sell French bricks, but gold bricks instead. **1934** *Bread Baking NZ* [Caption] facing 128 Brickie or small flat. **1949** *Canterbury Mountaineer* 290 Except for a loaf of Bell's Brick sliding into Bill's back..travelled happily to Glenthorne. **1958** *Tararua* Sept. 26 *Bell's bricks*, the brick-shaped, wholemeal loaves of bread produced by Bell's bakery in Christchurch, were not unknown further afield, but no doubt are being forgotten since the firm closed down a few years ago.

2. a. [Transf. use of *brick* to an object with brick-like qualities.] A rock or stone (to be thrown); also occas. as a *v. trans.*, **to brick** (a person), to throw stones at).
1950 SUTTON-SMITH *Our Street* 25 He used to..throw bricks if the others teased him.

b. *Fishermen.* A rock likely to be struck by a boat.
1982 p.c. Tim Brosnahan, Wellington fisherman.

A rock which can be hit by a boat (Fiordland, West Coast, Wellington, Napier).

3. [f. the shape.] 12-bottle pack of beer in its carton. Cf. Slab *n.*[1] 3.
1986 *Dominion* (Wellington) 15 May 7 [Advertisement : Robbie Burns Liquor Store] DB Draught bricks $7.99 per dozen **1993** *Evening Post* (Wellington) 29 Apr. 2 [Advt] DB Bitter bricks $11.45 1 Doz.

4. [f. the shape.] A Morris 'mini' motorcar.
1981 *Star* (Christchurch) 5 Feb. 4 'Brick' is the half affectionate, half derogatory slang term for a Mini.

5. In the phr. **to be a few bricks short of a load**, to be intellectually wanting, to have an intellectual handicap.
1985 BINNEY *Long Lives the King* 72 'I think that little Haywards kid's a few bricks short of a load. What normal boy of that age spends all day swinging on the gates. **1989** CRANNA *Visitors* 105 Sounds like this dame's a few bricks short of a load, mate.

6. brick veneer [AND *adj.* 1935; *n.* 1968], a brick exterior over wooden framing.
1952 *Evening Post* (Wellington) 2 Apr. 6 In the single brick, or brick veneer, there is still a large quantity of timber that has to be placed in a house so constructed.

brickie: see BRICK 1.

bridal-tree. [f. the flower bunches resembling a bride's bouquet.] *Pennantia corymbosa* (fam. Icacinaceae), a small native tree having bunches of white flowers carried on fine white stalks; KAIKOMAKO.
1927 *TrNZI* LVII. 912 bridal tree *Pennantia corymbosa* [Vernacular names supplied by B.C. Aston, Dept. of Agriculture, collected in various parts of New Zealand.] **1946** *JPS* LV. 151 *Kaikomako*, a small tree (Pennantia corymbosa), bridal-tree, Maori fire. Sometimes kahikomako. The softer of the two woods used by the Maori for producing fire by friction. **1961** MARTIN *Flora NZ* 178 The kaikomako, also known as Cheesewood and Bridal tree, commences life as a bushy shrub.

bridal suite. *Prison.* See quot.
1980 MACKENZIE *While We Have Prisons* 70 The whole problem of homosexuality came into prominence when prison populations rose beyond the single-occupant cell capacity. With great reluctance two-man cells were officially approved. In Mt Eden they became known as 'bridal suites'. *Ibid.* 95 *bridal suite* cell containing two prisoners

bride-cut. *Whaling. Obs.* First or 'virgin' cut (in a whale's carcass).
1854 MALONE *Three Yrs. Cruise* 70 One of the whale captains with a long-handled kind of sharp-edged spade, made the first, or as they called it, the bride-cut [in the whale's carcass].

bridle. [f. *bridle* 'fit or designed for horse rather than wheeled traffic'.] The special Comb. **bridle-path**, **bridle-road**, **bridle-track** are used elsewhere but very frequently (esp. **bridle-track**) in early colonial New Zealand.

1. a. bridle-path [OED 1811].
1842 HEAPHY *NZ* 78 The other road, or rather 'bridle path', commences at the Scotch village of Kaiwarawara. **1852** *Austral. & NZ Gaz.* 1 May 156 I pay my shilling and commence a steep ascent on the 'bridle-path' along the face of a hill with great care. **1867** BARKER *Station Life* (1870) 176 At last we mounted

and rode by a bridle-path among the hills. **1879** HAAST *Geol. Canterbury & Westland* 119 Mr. Greenlaw was in charge of the road party, which..had been sent up to form a bridle-path over the Pass. **1958** [see *bridle-track* 3 below].

b. *Canterbury Hist.* Usu. init. cap., **the Bridle Path**, the track over the hill from Lyttelton to Christchurch.
1851 WARD *Journal* 23 Jan. (1951) 115 I went to the ferry instead, along the Bridle Path which finished so far. **1853** ADAMS *Canterbury Settlement* 27 Two or three hundred yards in advance, is the foot of the 'bridlepath', a steep and narrow road leading directly over the range of hills..to the ferry across the Heathcote on the way to Christchurch. **1867** THOMSON *Twelve Yrs. Canterbury* 7 'Dear me!' petulantly exclaimed a lady who had lately landed, and was being conducted over the bridle-path by a friend. **1951** CRESSWELL *Canterbury Tales* 26 Although the Pilgrims could cross the hills to the Plain over the Bridle Path..all heavy luggage had to go to Christchurch by sea.

2. bridle road *Obs.* [OED 1833].
1841 *NZ Jrnl.* II. 224 Colonel Wakefield is also about to direct a line or bridle road (the basis of the future road) to be cut.

3. bridle-track [EDD 1879]. (Also occas. used (see quot. 1862) for *bridle-path* 1 b above.) See also *saddle-track* (SADDLE 2).
1851 *Lyttelton Times* 12 Apr. 3 Moved by Mr. Shand..That the bridle track be made practicable from the bridle-path to Christchurch. **1862** CHUDLEIGH *Diary* 14 May (1950) 38 We at last got to the Bridle track which we followed to the top of the hill. **1868** *Marlborough Express* (Blenheim) 6 June 6 The road would be longer..than the present bridle-track over the Maungatapu, but then it would be a dray-road. **1871** MONEY *Knocking About NZ* 85 I was soon trudging away along the winding bridle track which wound up the gorge. **1902** *Settler's Handbook NZ* 33 The history of road-making is as follows: First comes the bridle-track, that gradually grows into the dray-road; and then comes the metal. **1920** [see TUMATAKURU]. **1958** *Tararua* Sept. 24 [*Path*] is the word that is most often used by Englishmen for we call a track, but its use in this sense survives here only in *bridle path*, and that has a rival in *bridle track*. **1986** RICHARDS *Off the Sheep's Back* 6 During the early days.., the only access to Waihi was by bridle track over the range.

bright, *a.*

1. In the name of a grade of gold or kauri gum, pure, clean.
1862 *Otago Goldfields & Resources* 20 The gold [from Waipori] is very fine, but very bright and pure. **1862** in *Canterbury Rhymes* (1883) 129 Gold, gold, fine bright gold, Tuapeka, Wangapeka, bright red gold. **1956** SUTHERLAND *Green Kiwi* (1960) 70 Some of the classifications under which gum was exported give an indication of the appearance of some of the grades: bright..bright chips..bright seeds and black sugar are some of the names.

2. bright and shiny swords, see SWORD.

brill. [Transf. use of *brill* a European flatfish.] Usu. the large edible New Zealand flounder *Colistium guntheri* (fam. Pleuronectidae), superficially resembling the European brill. See also BRILL (occas.), TURBOT.
1872 HUTTON & HECTOR *Fishes NZ* 51 Pseudorhombus scaphus... Brill. **1886** SHERRIN *Handbook Fishes NZ* 26 It has been termed brill on account of its being the only one of our flat-fish with the eyes on the left side of the head; but it is small in size, and so full of bones, that it cannot be eaten with comfort. **1898** MORRIS *Austral-English* 56 *Brill*..a small and very bony rhomboidal fish of New Zealand, *Pseudorhombus scaphus*, family *Pleronectidae*. **1906** *TrNZI* XXXVIII. 543 *The Brill*... The fish known by this name is occasionally taken by the trawlers outside Otago Heads. **1925–26** *NZJST* VIII. 100 The principal fishes caught in the trawl [off Otago] are soles..flounders, and brill among the flat-fishes. **1938** *TrRSNZ* LXVIII. 407 *Colistium guntheri*... Brill. **1956** [see SOLE 2 (2)]. **1960** PARROTT *Queer & Rare Fishes NZ* 120 The Brill is generally distributed throughout New Zealand, but usually the supply is never sufficient to meet the demand. **1982** *Evening Post* (Wellington) 8 Dec. 37 Brill is a handsome, well-proportioned flatfish with long black lines down its brownish-grey body.

brim, var. BREAM.

bring, *v.*

1. As **bring down** [in NZ, Austral. and Canadian but not Brit. use: poss. a variant of general (incl. NZ from 1854) English *bring in* (= introduce legislation), see OED *bring* 18 e (1602)] (occas. as **bring forward**), to introduce into Parliament a Bill or other proposed legislation.
1876 *NZPD* XXI. 417 The question was whether the Bill, as now brought forward, would act beneficially or not. *Ibid.* 459 I cannot expect that the Government themselves will be in a hurry to bring down here a Bill, the passing of which must rob them of support of that kind. **1935** *NZPD* CCXLII. 237 I would like to compliment the honourable Member for Napier on again bringing down the measure. **1953** *Ibid.* CCXCIX. 728 I would like to congratulate the member..for bringing this bill down. **1953** *Ibid.* CCXCIX. 279 The Minister has not given us a very satisfactory reason for bringing this bill forward.

2. As **bring in** [used elsewhere but recorded earliest in NZ: see OED *bring* 18 k], to bring land into cultivation or production. Cf. BREAK IN *v.*
1860 CARGILL *Otago* 29 Open land is covered with either fern or grass..and is easily brought in. **1929** *TrNZI* LIX. 406 The operation of 'bringing in' the bush-country, or in other words of quickly converting forest-land to a sheep and cattle-grazing pasture. **1933** REES *NZ Holiday* 111 Approved method of 'bringing in' bushed country. **1950** *NZJAg.* Oct. LXXXI. 371 Swedes and turnips..their usefulness as feed for dairy cows and in the bringing in of new land. **1988** MCGILL *Dict. Kiwi Slang* 21 *bring in* in the process of introducing land to cultivation.

3. In the phr. **to bring the stone to grass**, see STONE *n.* 1 b.

4. [AND 1967.] **bring your own (liquor)**, see BYO.
1971 TAYLOR *Plekhov Place* 151 On the fifth I rested and threw a bring-your-own-booze party.

brisket.

1. [A Sc. dialectal transf. use of *brisket* the human breast: see OED 1 b.] The (human) chest; occas. the diaphragm.
1938 HYDE *Godwits Fly* (1970) 129 The men formed a ring... Larry Kirst said, 'Sock 'im in the brisket, Kid, 'e's all wind downstairs,' and Timothy nodded.

2. *Freezing works.* Comb. **brisket-puncher, -punching**, see quot. 1951.
1951 17 May Feilding Freezing Works terms p.c. Colin Gordon *Brisket-puncher*, *-punching*: One who 'punches' or pulls, or the action of so removing, a pelt from the brisket of a carcass. **1959** SLATTER *Gun in My Hand* 85 Their fullback, a brisket-puncher on number one chain, kicks it into the stand. **1975** *NZ Short Stories III* 4 His one..companion was a freezing-works chain slaughter-man (with appropriate gestures he explained his job as a brisket-puncher). *Ibid.* 7 The slaughter-man withdrew..but this was no occasion for brisket-punching.

bristle tussock: see TUSSOCK 3 (2).

brit. [Transf. use of Brit. dial. *brit* fry (of fish, etc.): see OED.] WHALE-FEED 1.
1838 POLACK *NZ* II. 402 [Right Whales' food] is principally spawn of a pabulous nature, of a red and yellow hue, called by the fishermen brit; which is sometimes seen supernatant on the surface of the ocean, many miles around.

Britain of the South. *Hist.* Also (**Great** or **Greater**) **Britain of the Southern Hemisphere** or **South Sea(s)**, an early nickname for New Zealand. Also *attrib.*
1839 *Glasgow Constitutional* (New Zealand Colonization Dinner) 26 Oct. [Sir Archibald Alison Sheriff of Lanarkshire, at a New Zealand Colonization Dinner.] No one can doubt from its physical situation, natural advantages and close proximity to the Great Continent of Australia, that it is destined to become at no distant period the Great Britain of the Southern Hemisphere. (Loud cheers.) **1848** WAKEFIELD *Handbook NZ* 29 New Zealand, the Queen of her own Hemisphere, the Britain of the South, has been added to the domain of the Crown without a violence. **1859** THOMSON *Story NZ* I. 5 Sentimental settlers designate New Zealand the Britain of the Southern hemisphere, on the same principle that the Dutchman Tasman, who discovered the country, called it New Zealand. **1867** HOCHSTETTER *NZ* iii Albions [*sic*] enterprising sons..are wont to call [New Zealand] 'the Great-Britain of the South Sea'. **1886** HART *Stray Leaves* 52 The foundations of a nation which is yet to rise up in this Greater Britain of the South. **1892** *NZ Official Handbook* 116 Much more might be said in praise of the colony, which is rapidly gaining for itself the right to be called the 'Britain of the South'. **1905** *Truth* 24 June 2 The hospitality of this Britain of the South. **1930** PINFOLD *Fifty Yrs. Maoriland* 13 Some of the names given to it [*sc.* New Zealand] are very suggestive and often throw light upon its position, character and destiny. It has been called the Britain of the South; the Wonderland of the Pacific; and God's Own Country. **1946** SOLJAK *NZ* 49 Pioneer leaders had planned to make of New Zealand a veritable 'Britain of the South', preserving much of the old economic order. **1958** GOLDMAN *Hist. Jews in NZ* 29 [Joseph Barrow Montefiore] was the first to call New Zealand the 'Britain of the South' [c1838]. **1970** MCNEISH *Mackenzie* 22 In jail he conceived of a plan of the perfect Anglican settlement, a little Britain of the South.

Briton. In the phr. **a (regular little) Briton**, used to encourage a child to put a brave face on a hurt or setback.
1938 HYDE *Godwits Fly* (1970) 105 'A little Briton,' he said, patting Simone's shoulder, 'game as a regular little Briton.' **1949** SARGESON *I Saw in My Dream* (1974) 5 Mother dried his eyes..And she told Arnold to take his hand, and father..told him to be a Briton.

bro. [Spec. use of *bro* abbrev. of brother.] Used by Maori young people or to or of Maori, esp. among gang members, or among members of the extended family. In *pl.* as **the Bros**, one's Maori gang associates; Maori collectively. (Often used humorously or ironically.) Cf. CUZ.
1984 16 F E37 Pakuranga Coll. 24E Bro (brother) [F2] **1989** TE AWEKOTUKU *Tahuri* 58 Hey Milt! C'mere!

Hurry up bro. [Spoken to a Maori adolescent who is raping his own sister.] **1991** PAYNE *Staunch* 74 Everyone's sitting around [at gang H.Q.], the bro's, the prospects and even the gash... 'You scared, bro?' sneers a prospect. 'Got no balls, cuz?' says another.

broadleaf. Also occas. **broadleafed**.

1. Either of two small trees of genus *Griselinia* (fam. Griseliniaceae), having distinctive broad glossy leaves, esp. *G. littoralis* common in lowland and upland forests; also the wood of such trees. See also KAPUKA, PAPAUMA 1, PUKA 2.

    1844 *Monro Notes of a Journey* in Hocken *Contributions* (1898) 242 Its leaf is of a smooth, glossy, green colour, about the size of the leaf of a Portugal laurel, but more heart-shaped. The native name of the tree is kapuka. It is commonly called broad-leaf by the white men there [at Waikouaiti]. **1869** *TrNZI* I. (rev. edn.) 199 Broad leaf (*Griselinia littoralis*). A large tree, with large ovate, shining leaves. **1879** BLAIR *Bldg. Materials Otago* 155 There are few trees in the [Otago] bush so conspicuous or so well known as the broad-leaf... It grows to a height of fifty or sixty feet, and a diameter of from three to six; the bark is coarse and fibrous, and the leaves a beautiful deep green of great brilliancy. **1890** *PWD Catalogue Timbers* (NZ & South Seas Exhib.) 13 Papauma (broadleaf)..Griselinia littoralis..Timber heavy, dense, and of great strength, grain prettily marked, but timber liable to warp. **1906** [see PAPAUMA 1]. **1940** STUDHOLME *Te Waimate* (1954) 104 Later, broadleaf was the timber chiefly used for fencing, because it was much less inflammable than totara. **1975** DAVIN *Breathing Spaces* 34 You remember how old Andy Keogh brought that big broadleafed down right on top of his own kitchen. Only the real bushmen can do it properly. **1988** DAWSON *Forest Vines to Snow Tussocks* 81 Broadleaf..is the only other species of its genus in New Zealand.

2. Less commonly applied to other native shrubs or small trees with broad glossy leaves, esp. *Meryta* (PUKA 1) and (also as **shining broadleaf**) *Griselinia* spp. (PUKA 2); and *Coprosma* spp. (fam. Rubiaceae).

    1867 HOOKER *Handbook* 764 Broadleaf, *Hector. Griselinia lucida*. **1868** LINDSAY *Contribs. NZ Bot.* 71 The 'Broad-leaf' or 'Orange-leaf' tree of the settler [*C. lucida*]; terms, however, which are probably not only applied to other species of the genus *Coprosma*, (*e.g. C. robusta*, Raoul,) but to species of genera belonging to very different families—and especially to *Griselinia lucida*..whose foliage closely resembles that of *Coprosma lucida*. **1922** [see PUKA 1]. **1930** REISCHEK *Yesterdays in Maoriland* (1933) 97 On December 8 I found..a tree which..was only to be found here. It is some 12 feet high, has leaves some 12 inches long, and is of a dark green colour. It is called the 'broadleaf' tree by the colonists [*Meryta sinclairii*]. **1940** LAING & BLACKWELL *Plants NZ* 316 *Griselinia lucida* (*The Shining Broadleaf*)... From 3 ft.-30 ft in height, often epiphytic. Leaves 4 in.-8 in. long, very thick, shining... Native name *Puka*. A name given to any broad-leaved tree. **1966** *Encycl. NZ* III. 710 Broadleaf, shining . . puka . . G[*riselinia*] *lucida*.

Brogdenite. *Hist.* Occas. **Brogdenman**. One of the labourers imported by the railway contractors, J. Brogden and Sons, to work on the railway development instigated by Vogel's public works policy in the 1870s.

    1914 *Hist. N. Otago from 1853* (1978) 48 The first immigrants [c1870s] consisted of a number of workers with others, known as Brogdenites, who had been selected by Messrs Brogden and Co., the contractors for the Oamaru-Moeraki section of the railway. *Ibid.* 107 [At the Oamaru sports meeting c1880s] there were Chinese, Cingalese, Germans,.. shearers, gold miners, Brogdenites, sailors and swaggers. *Ibid.* 108 Commencement of railway line. The Brogdenites. The [railway building] contractors, Messrs Brogden and Sons, had a bullock prepared [for the ceremony of turning the first sod]. The Brogdenmen were all there, and a very fine type of navvy they were. **1945** BEATTIE *Maori Place-names Canterbury* 11 In their absence a party of Brogdenites (railway construction gangs) broke in to the Maoris' huts [at Waimate] and used them as their own.

broken-arse. *Prison*. A prisoner who has submitted to the authorities and become of lowest status in the inmate hierarchy.

    1987 *National Radio* 'Spectrum Documentary' 12 Apr. [A psychiatrist discussing the difficulties of drug therapy for disturbed prisoners says:] Drug therapy can give the inmate the status of a 'broken arse'—if you'll forgive the expression—at the bottom of the [status] heap. **1991** STEWART *Broken Arse* 44 *Whimple:* Hey, you're a scab, man! You've sold out!.. *Tu*... Broken arse, Broken arse. Broken arse.

broken down swell.

1. An 'upper-class' emigrant reduced through circumstances (usu. alcoholic) to manual or menial labour. Contrast *paper-collared swell* (PAPER-COLLAR).

    1862 THATCHER *Auckland Vocalist* 1 First we notice the broken down swells, Once wealthy, but now very needy. **1891** CHAMIER *Philosopher Dick* 6 There was another shepherd of a very different type; he came under the category known as 'broken-down swells'— a numerous class in the country at that time [ca1850–1860s].

2. *Prison*. See quot.

    1982 NEWBOLD *Big Huey* 245 Broken down swell (n) Emotionally distressed person.

bronze. In the names of birds and fish, see: CUCKOO 2 (1), SHAG 2 (5), *bronze whaler* (SHARK 2 (6)).

bronze-winged cuckoo: see CUCKOO 2 (1).

bronzie: see SHARK 2 (6).

broom. [Transf. use of *broom* for plants of fam. Fabaceae.] Any of various brooms or broom-like native plants of fam. Fabaceae, mostly leafless as adults with stems carrying out photosynthesis, esp. the genera *Carmichaelia*, *Corallospartium*, *Notospartium*; and (as **tea-broom**) *Leptospermum*.

1. *Carmichaelia* spp. Also **alpine** or **mountain broom** (*C. odorata*), **native broom**, **New Zealand broom**. See also MAKAKA.

    1867 HOOKER *Handbook* 764 Broom, native. *Carmichaelia*, various sp. **1869** *TrNZI* I. (rev. edn.) 196 *Carmichaelia grandiflora*. This may be called the New Zealand Broom, being generally found with leaves. **1889** FEATON *Art Album NZ Flora* 110 Carmichaelia flagelliformis... The 'native broom'.—This species, which is well known by its long whip-like branches, is found along the East Coast of the Northern, and in many parts of the Middle, Island, from Nelson down to Otago. It is the most common species in Southland. **1896** HARPER *Pioneer Work* 35 There is also the rata tree,.. the mountain broom. **1897** *TrNZI* XXIX. 501 Carmichaelia is perhaps the most characteristic of the many endemic genera..represented from the North Cape to Foveaux Strait by numerous species..but in all localities recognised by the settler as native broom and by the Maori as *makaka*. **1900** *Canterbury Old & New* 203 The air [of the sub-alpine areas] at a certain season of the year is full of the fragrance of the Alpine Broom... *Carmichaelia grandiflora*, var. *alba*. **1910** COCKAYNE *NZ Plants & Their Story* 60 Similar experiments with certain of the New Zealand brooms (Carmichaelia)..will lead to a similar result. **1926** COWAN *Travel in NZ* II. 95 We have climbed above the pines [on the West Coast];... and up here on the mountain side the vegetation is..the native alpine broom..and whole forests of fern trees. **1938** *Tararua Tramper* Feb. 15 Celmesias and ranunculus gave way to gaultheria and native broom, alpine scrub to ribbonwood. **1962** EVANS *Waikaka Saga* 239 The whole [Waikaka] valley and the..ridges were covered [in 1876] with..shrubs comprising Mauko[r]o, or native broom (Carmichaelia australis). **1988** *New Women's Fiction* 52 At the brow the naturalists stopped to beat the native broom.

2. *Corallospartium crassicaule*. **coral broom**. [f. its stems resembling coral growth.]

    1900 *Canterbury Old & New* 190 As we ascend the grassy slopes we may note the curious leafless coral-broom, with its stiffribbed stems. **1924** *Otago Witness* (Dunedin) 18 Mar. 10 I came across a fine clump of the coral broom. **1961** ALLAN *Flora NZ* I. 371 Montane and subalpine grassland..east of divide..*Coral broom, sticks*. **1973** MARK & ADAMS *Alpine Plants* (1979) 76 Genus Corallospartium 'Coral Broom'—referring to the stems. Consists of a single species, confined to the South Island. **1986** JOHNSON *Wildflowers Central Otago* 15 Coral broom..is another native.

3. *Notospartium* spp., usu. as **Canterbury broom** (*N. torulosum*), and **pink broom** (*N. carmichaeliae* and *N. torulosum*).

    1867 HOOKER *Handbook* 764 Broom, pink. *Notospartium Carmichaeliae*. **1889** FEATON *Art Album NZ Flora* 113 The 'Notospart[i]um' or 'Pink Broom'. This beautiful tree is indigenous to the Middle Island..It blossoms in December,... having its long weeping branches adorned with the beautiful pink pea-flowers, plentifully displayed. **1961** ALLAN *Flora* I. 372 *N. torulosum*... foothills east of divide. *Pink Broom*. **1982** *Press* (Christchurch) 9 Oct. 15 Notospartium torulosum' the Canterbury broom: Notospartium from Greek, notos, the south wind, and spartium, broom—literally, the southern broom, torulosum from Latin, torula, diminutive of torus, a protuberance or bulge, describing the characteristic 'waisted' seed-pods.

4. *Leptospermum scoparium*. **tea-broom**. MANUKA 1 a.

    1883 DOMETT *Ranolf & Amohia* I. 303 In the poem it is called indiscriminately manuka, broom, broom-like myrtle, or leptosperm. The settlers often call it 'tea-broom.'

broomie. *Shearing*. [f. *broom*(hand + -IE: AND 1895.] A worker who sweeps the shearing board clean during shearing. See also SWEEPER 1.

    1933 *Press* (Christchurch) (Acland Gloss.) 16 Sept. 15 *Broomie*.—A boy who keeps the board swept of locks, etc., at shearing. **1940** STUDHOLME *Te Waimate* (1954) 208 At shearing time [at Benmore, 1892] about 55 men were employed in the shed: 28 to 30 shearers, 2 penners-up, 4 pickers-up, 2 broomies, 6 rollers. **1955** BOWEN *Wool Away* 65 Very often shearers are blamed for not making clean blows when it is the fault of the 'Broomie'. **1968** *Straight Furrow* 21 Feb. 20 *Broomie:* The sweeper on the shearing board. **1982** *Agric. Gloss.* (MAF) 53 *Broomie*: Person who sweeps the shearing board clean during shearing (also called sweepo).

brose /brʌuz/. *SI farming. Obs.* [f. Sc. dial. ad. *browis* usu. an oatmeal gruel: see SND 1.] OATMEAL WATER q.v. as a sustaining thirst-quencher for shearers or field workers. See also BEER 2, BURGOO 2.

1883 Brett's Colonists' Guide 649 'Brose', a common article of diet in Scotland, is not boiled at all, but is made by pouring boiling water on the oatmeal, and stirring briskly till it becomes thick and smooth. 1933 *Press* (Christchurch) (Acland Gloss.) 23 Sept. 13 *Burgoo*.— Sailors' word for porridge. Here the word is applied to the oatmeal and water taken to the woolshed or harvest field to be drunk between smoke-ohs. I have also heard it called *beer* and *brose*.

brown, *n.*[1] *Obs.* [AND 1812 (Vaux), 1845.] A penny, a copper. Cf. BROWNIE 3.

1864 THATCHER *Songs of War* 18 There are lots of little swindles In all New Zealand towns, Got up by folks for easing you Of your superfluous browns. 1896 *Bracken's Annual* 41 You can't turn an honest brown anyhow. 1909 THOMPSON *Ballads About Business* 64 But 'twere even half a crown You'd get it if I had it, but I haven't got a 'brown'. 1943 BENNETT *English in NZ in Amer. Speech* XVIII. 91 In New Zealand Slang a penny is a *brown*. 1977 *NZ Numismatic Jrnl.* Oct. 16 For the penny nicknames used were *copper* and *brown* (sometimes *Brownie*), while the halfpenny was called a *half-copper*, a *mag*, or a *rap*.

brown, *n.*[2] A situation or mood unpleasing or unpleasant.

1984 17 M E103 Pakuranga Coll. 5 What a brown [indicating annoyance] 1988 McGILL *Dict. Kiwi Slang* 21 *brown* in phr. *do a brown* act shy or sulky or ashamed; eg 'What's wrong with Jill?' 'Nothin', Miss. She does a brown for no reason, eh.'

brown, *a.*

I. [Spec. use of *brown* the colour.] **1.** In the names of plants and animals, see: BEETLE 2, BIRCH 3 (4), BITTERN 2 (1), CREEPER *n.*[1], DUCK 2 (3), KIWI 2 (1), MUDFISH 2 (2), PARROT 2 (1), SHARK 2 (2), TEAL 2 (3), TUSSOCK 3 (3) a.

2. In special collocations: **a.** [Alluding to the brown colour of the anus or excrement.] **brown ankles** *prison* [f. the metaphor of being so far up a boss's arse that even the ankles are brown], esp. in the phr. **to have brown ankles**, to have 'crawled' to authority; **brown eye**, (a display of) the anus (as an expression of contempt, esp. formally by Maori from pre-European times: see 1769 quot.); **brown nose** *prison*, a sycophant (cf. *brown ankles* above).

1976 *Salient* (Wellington) 12 July 6 The Prisoner's code: I can't crawl to screws (cops, prison officers, etc), anyone who does is a 'Nark',... or has '**Brown Ankles**'. [1769 MONKHOUSE 12 Oct. in Cook *Journals* I. 576 Finding we took no notice of his signal to wait for him his people [*sc.* Maori] set up a loud shout and brandished their paddles in the air—one of them very civilly turned up his breach [*sic*] and made the usual sign of contempt among the Billingsgate ladies.] 1981 *Avondale College Slang Words* (Auckland) (Goldie Brown Collect.) *brown eye*: bare bum display 1984 MIHAKA *Whakapohane* 51 But not only that, you [Sergeant Rattenbury] said that I clasped, or this Maori gentleman clasped, the cheeks to his..you know, that area of his body and pulled them apart? [Sergeant] Yes, what I would call a 'brown eye'. [Mihaka] Is that what you call it? And you are positive of that are you? 1989 *Dominion* (Wellington) 10 June 10 [British] Good for you [NZ] good on yu [*sic*]... [Bri.] Royal greeting [NZ] brown eye. 1991 PAYNE *Staunch* 90 I turned around, dropped my trousers and..bent over and gave her the 'brown-eye'. 1980 **brown noses** [see CANARY *n.*[1] 3].

b. brown backs *pl.*, an endemic subalpine shrub daisy *Brachyglottis rotundifolia* (formerly *Senecio elaeagnifolius*) (fam. Asteraceae), having soft brown hairs on the undersides of leaves, LEATHERWOOD; **brown bomber** *obs.*, DB bottled brown ale, an Auckland Dominion Breweries beer.

1888 HETLEY *Native Flowers NZ* 3 The short scrub [at New Plymouth]..was greatly composed of *Senecio eleagnifolius* or '**brown backs**.' 1927 *TrNZI* LVII. 913 Brown backs... Because of the brown hairs on the backs of the leaves. 1952 *Here & Now* Jan. 15 But he [barman] missed one clink, and counted wrong, and felt wild because someone had pinched a bottle of the **brown bomber**, and it wasn't him this time. 1968 *NZ Contemp. Dict. Suppl.* (Collins) 4 *brown bomber n.* (*Coll.*) name given..in N.Z., beer.

II. [Spec. use of *brown* brown-skinned (person).] **3.** In special collocations (cf. BROWNIE 1): **brown flight** [a variant of *white flight* the removing of white children from predominantly black schools], a term for Pacific Islanders removing children from predominantly Maori schools; **brown man's burden** [an alteration of *white man's burden*], the social, etc. burden imposed by European society on the Polynesian; **brown velvet** *offensive*, a Maori woman as a sexual object (cf. *black velvet* (BLACK *a.*[1] B 2)).

1986 *Sunday Star* (Auckland) 10 Aug. A1 The poor standard of some schools denied them a fair chance and led to '**brown flight**' as parents directed their children to high achievement schools, many of them Catholic. Senior lecturer in Maori studies at Auckland University Pat Hohepa rejects Mr Ioane's comments and suggests Islanders involved in 'brown flight' should go home. 1986 *Dominion* (Wellington) 12 Aug. 3 Porirua secondary school principals say 'brown flight' is not a significant problem in their schools, and has been largely contained by strict enforcement of zoning schemes. 1938 FINLAYSON ***Brown Man's Burden*** [Title] 1986 SORRENSON *Na To Hoa Aroha* (NZPD, v. 154 (1911) 728) I. 25 Once he [Ngata] intervened in a debate on the Cook Islands to remind Opposition speakers who had been lamenting the 'white man's burden' that they should be concerning themselves instead with the 'brown man's burden'. 1933 BAUME *Half Caste* 64 There's a new bank-clerk..[who's] certain to fall for you Ngaire, though it's **brown velvet** he likes. [Ngaire is a 'white' half-caste Maori.]

brownie. Also **browny.** [Spec. or transf. uses of *brownie* something of brown colour.]

1. *Obs.* A (hypocoristic or patronizing term for a) Maori.

1850 LUSH *Auckland Journals* 1 Nov. (1971) 34 Charlie and the 3 girls played with Hakopa's little daughter. This is the first day we have managed to get the little browny in the slightest degree sociable.

2. a. Mainly *SI rural*. Also **browny**. [AND 1883.] A currant or raisin loaf sweetened with (brown) sugar, esp. as sheep-station fare. See also SPOTTED TOMMY.

1883 PARTINGTON *Random Rot* 312 It was an amusing sight to see the three of us, each with a huge hunch of 'brownie' (bread sweetened with brown sugar and currants) in one hand, and a lump of ice in the other. 1900 *Auckland Weekly News* (Suppl.) 26 Jan. 2 May there never be less than cold meat and 'browny' (currant bread) in their tucker boxes. 1913 [see DUFF *n.*]. 1926 DEVANNY *Butcher Shop* (1981) 33 [Shepherds speak] Here, jerk the brownie along, Potts. Think you've got the only guts at the table. 1940 *Tales of Pioneer Women* (1988) 256 The sweet station 'brownie', rich in brown sugar and heavy with Merino dripping and a few rare raisins, is being cut up for supper. 1952 LYON *Faring South* 166 The digger's fare..included..a curr[a]nt or raisin cake risen with soda and acid, which was usually the full width of the camp oven and termed a brownie. 1973 WHEELER *Hist. Sheep Stations NI* 97 The [station] boss said 'brownie' was cake. We knew it only as bread dyed with bullocky's joy (treacle), and sparingly dotted with currants. 1981 MARRIOTT *Life in Gorge* 59 Brownies were the bushman's staple diet. Made in a camp oven, they were like a big brown scone with a nice crisp crust.

b. Special Comb. **brownie-gorger**, a shearing shed hand.

1988 McGILL *Dict. Kiwi Slang* 21 brownie gorger shearing shed hand. 1989 *NZ Eng. Newsletter* III. 22 *brownie gorger:* Old expression for a shedhand.

3. [AND 1899.] A penny (piece); a copper. Cf. BROWN *n.*[1]

1899 *Bulletin* (Sydney) 14 Jan. (Red Page) [Letter from *Loafer*, Tauranga.] Following are other local money-names..1d.—*Maori half-crown*, *brownie* or *copper*. 1977 [see BROWN *n.*[1]].

4. *Otago rural.* (A dried-up) dwarf-dock.

1908 DON *Chinese Mission Work* 22 On these Rough Ridge foothills the light olive-brown dwarf-dock is in great abundance; so there will be many 'brownies' next Autumn.

5. A local name for a young SADDLEBACK q.v.

1925-26 *NZJST* VIII. 337 The plumage of the yearling [saddleback] was the hue of blended chocolate and black..these first-season birds, or 'brownies' as we called them.

6. An empty brown-glass beer-bottle, a 'dead marine'.

1979 *Star* (Christchurch) 3 Jan. 2 There's something depressing about beer bottles... You return your empties... You know they've sunk as many as you have and it's a fair bet their own garden sheds are bursting with brownies.

Brown's cow. [A var. of *all behind like Barney's bull*, perh. also a play on the elocutionary 'How now, brown cow'.] In the phr. **to be all behind** (or **all over the road**) **like Brown's cow(s)**, to be disorganised; behind with a job, etc. (Occas. said of a fat or big-rumped woman.)

1920 p.c. W.H.B. Orsman (1972). Used in Marlborough in the sense of being behind with work, etc. 1988 McGILL *Dict. Kiwi Slang* 21 *Brown's cows* in phr. *all over the road like Brown's cows* disorderly, disorganised or making a dreadful mess; Joy Shepard's two country aunts were crossing Christchurch's Cathedral Square with the red light flashing, and Cousin Jack said 'Oh gosh, Joy, look at them..ooh..all over the road like Brown's cows!'; curious recycling of the elocution improving phrase 'how now Brown cow'.

browny, var. BROWNIE.

brumby. [Orig. unknown: AND 1880.] A wild horse, mainly of the central North Island plateau; occas. an inferior or rough-looking horse. Also *transf.* Cf. KAIMANAWA WILD HORSES.

1916 THORNTON *Wowser* 111 I've got that there brumby in; he's a beauty. *Ibid.* 256 These [Taupo] plains were the habitation of hundreds of wild horses, or 'brumbies', as they were generally termed. 1953 *Sports Post* (Wellington) 21 Feb. 1 Brumby to Represent NZ [*sic*]... One of the five New Zealand riders to compete at the Sydney Royal Show..on her mount Rum. A brumby is a common description of a wild horse, and Rum was formerly among the many running round the Galatea district [of the central North Island plateau]. **1969** HAMILTON *Wild Irishman* 84 Duff..took us chasing brumbies through the manuka scrub [at Tokaanu]. **1989** RICHARDS *Pioneer's Life* 48 Wild horses and cattle roamed and bred on the Maori block... There were some quite good horses among them but some were so inbred that they were just brumbies. **1991** *Contact* (Wellington) 28 Nov. 8 In the past, many 'brumbies' were captured and tamed... This practice ceased when they were given protected status under the Wildlife Act. **1993** MILNER *Intersecting Lines* 119 I was very fond of Winty, as we called her, though she looked on me as a raw young brumby.

brummy. [Transf. use of *Brum* (f. *Brum*(magen (Birmingham) counterfeit) + -Y: AND 1900.] Ill-made and cheap. Occas. as a noun, a cheap or ill-made object.
    1912 *Dominion* (Wellington) 4 Apr. 3 'I bought a brummy'—meaning a brummy ring—'with my last two bob.' **1914–1918** NICHOLLS in Boyack *Behind the Lines* (1989) 12 The Arab jabbers and annoys, And pesters you with Brummy toys.

brush, *n.*[1]

1. [AND 'vegetation', 1789.] In occas. early New Zealand use as a shortened form of BRUSHWOOD, in the sense 'scrub'.
    1839 WHITE *Important Information Relative NZ* 9 Burning away the brush and underwood. **1840** MATHEW *Journal* (ATLTS) II. After scrambling for ten minutes through the brush, we came upon a full view of the fall.

2. Special Comb. **brush harrow** *v.*, to harrow with a rough or makeshift harrow made of brushwood; **brush hook** [AND 1904-1979], long-handled arcuate tool for cutting light scrub; **brush yard** [AND 1835], a makeshift sheepyard built of brushwood.
    1860 DUPPA in Crawford *Sheep & Sheepmen Canterbury* (1949) 45 Seed should be **brush harrowed** in, that is wild Irishman should be interlaced in the crossbars of the harrows. **1821** KENDALL 27 Sept. in Elder *Marsden's Lieutenants* (1934) 174 Will not these islanders convert anything and everything they can into war instruments? Even axes, hatchets, reaping hooks, **brush hooks**, or anything else that has a sharp edge. **1881** NESFIELD *Chequered Career* 74 We built a yard for the sheep—that is, we chopped down a lot of scrub, and made what is termed a '**brush**' **yard**—and then my 'boss' left me. **1898** MEREDITH *Reminisc. & Experiences* 20 Having made a small brush yard, Dent and 'old Lass' were put in charge of the main mob of sheep. **1902** *Settler's Handbook NZ* 281 A brush yard will do well enough for a small flock which does not require to be very often in it.

brush, *n.*[2] Pl. *brush* or *brushes*. [f. *brush* in various senses suggesting (ironically) women's long hair, poss. reinforced by use of *brusher* young person, or a rhyme with *thrush*: AND 1941.] A girl or woman, esp. as a sexual object. Cf. CROW *n.*[1] 5.
    1941 SARGESON *When Wind Blows* 55 I don't go looking for trouble with brushes that are under age. **1947** DAVIN *Gorse Blooms Pale* 200 What comes along but an Iti bint, a real grouse brush she was, with bonzer black eyes and nice charlies. **1951** *Landfall 17* 21 There were about a dozen brush in the place and about three times as many jokers. **1960** HILLIARD *Maori Girl* ix 239 It's the good-looking brush that give a man all the trouble. **1963** MORRIESON *Scarecrow* 144 Who would have thought it in a burg like this? What a piece of lush brush! This sheila oughta be a film actress. **1980** MACKENZIE *While We Have Prisons* 95 *brush* girl, woman

brushwood. [*Brushwood* (OED 2, 1732) is recorded from 1817 in early New Zealand use, to be quickly replaced by SCRUB.] Occas. used attributively in the sense 'cut scrub used as a building material'.
    1937 AYSON *Thomas* 121 Thomas got his assistants to erect a brushwood yard on the bank of the river, well above the ford, so that the lambs could be forced to jump over the bank into the deep water. **1938** HYDE *Nor Yrs. Condemn* 167 Alex Mounter..helped Starkie to build a big board and brushwood shack at Waikaremoana.

bubu /ˈbubu/, var. PUPU.

buccatea, var. PUKATEA.

buck, *n.*[1] [Spec. use of *buck* a male (animal): see OED 1, 2.]

1. a. A (young) male, esp. a Maori.
    1892 Osborn in RICHARDS *Foveaux Whaling Yarns* (1995) 34 When it comes a very warm day [in the 1840s], there will be seen several old bucks together, each standing back of his neighbour, picking out the greybacks from his blanket and conveying them to his mouth as sweet morsels. **1933** BAUME *Half Caste* 23 Four bucks from Raglan came in drunk and there was a fight. **1960** SCRYMGEOUR *Memories Maoriland* 110 The Maori buck did the shearing, with machines, boys penned, and did pick-up work. Wahines..did the sorting, and Maori girls did the sweeping on the shearing board.

b. A male crayfish.
    1977 FISHER *Angels Wear Black* 40 When there is a group of crayfish in a cave it is usually the biggest that stands vigil... We have witnessed how a big buck would face up to a fully grown conger eel.

2. Special Comb. **a. buck dance** [AND 1898], **buck hop**, an exclusively male dance, a 'stag' dance; **buck-dancing**; **buck Maori** *obs.*, occas. formerly used for a (young) male Maori.
    1961 HENDERSON *Friends In Chains* 185 **Buck-dance**: All men dancing together. **1922** TURNER *Happy Wanderer* 143 On Saturday nights..[the shearers] had '**buck**' **dancing** in the sheds. **1914** in *Hist. N. Otago from 1853* (1978) 127 It may not be out of place to mention Jack Burns' '**buck hop**' on the top floor of the old bacon factory... There were no lady partners. **1941** BAKER *NZ Slang* 55 Other terms which probably hailed originally from the country are..a **buck Maori**, a large well-built native (a somewhat unwarranted construction on *buck nigger*). **1945** *JPS* LIV. 231 *Buck Maori* (slang) a male Maori, especially a well-built man. Recorded post-1920, but possibly used before. **1960** SCRYMGEOUR *Memories Maoriland* 67 Finally the College Fifteen wound up a close second in the season's fixtures,.. for a team with several big 'Buck Maories' from Leeston settled all other teams in that year.

b. In mining applications [poss. from *buck* male: hence, of itself, non-fruitful]: **buck-quartz**, **buck reef**, barren, yielding no gold or ore; **buckreefy** *a.*, applied to non-auriferous country.
    1971 BALE *Maratoto Gold* 23 Quartz that contained no impurities was termed by the goldminers '**buck**' **quartz**. **1897** *AJHR* C-9 31 There is evidence to show that occasionally..[small branching veins] lead into large veins of nearly barren quartz called '**buck reefs**'. **1909** *TrNZI* XLI. 81 *Barren Reefs, or Buck Reefs*... In Otago they consist of very wide, massive, bold outcrops of 'hungry' glassy quartz. **1978** MCARA *Gold Mining Waihi* 28 [Prospectors in the 1870s] seem to have ignored the Martha outcrop entirely—describing it as a 'buck', or barren, reef. **1992** LATHAM *Golden Reefs* 133 Morning showed the find to be nothing more than a barren or 'buck' reef. **1897** A TRAMP, ESQ. *Casual Ramblings* 116 It presents itself to me as a '**buckreefy**' 'mullocky leadery' sort of country.

buck, *n.*[2] [f. *buck* an act of bucking.]

1. In the phr. **to have a buck at**, **to give it a buck**, to have a try at, to give (something) a go.
    1899 BELL *In Shadow of Bush* 84 By Jove! I mean to have a buck at some of those sections in the Whakatangi Block that'll be thrown open shortly. **1913** BATHGATE *Sodger Sandy's Bairn* 71 I've a mind to have a buck at this new rush myself. **1941** ALLEY & HALL *Farmer in NZ* 104 One of the most striking features of modern New Zealand farming is its..readiness to 'try anything once' or to 'give it a buck' when some innovation swims into its ken.

2. fair buck. [Poss. a development of 1 above, 'a try, a go'; perh. related to *buck*, an abbrev. of *buck-horn knife* formerly used as a token in the game of poker (see DARE *n.*[3]), esp. as *pass the buck*.] Usu. as an exclamation expressing disbelief, incredulity, or an appeal for fair play or a fair hearing.
    1941 *Convoyager II* (H.M. Transport 22 Troopship pub.) He was clearly uncertain whether or not to believe him. 'Fair buck!' another digger chimed in. **1985** O'SULLIVAN *Shuriken* 22 He'd go up behind her and grab her arse like half a ton of blancmange... He did, fair buck. **1988** MCGILL *Dict. Kiwi Slang* 44 *fair buck* appeal for fairness or reasonable treatment; eg 'Fair buck, you guys, I've only been batting a few minutes.'

buck, *n.*[3]

1. *Obs.* A sixpence, esp. in the phr. *two-and-a-buck*, for 'two-and-six', a half-crown piece. Cf. KICK *n.*
    1899 *Bulletin* (Sydney) 14 Jan. (Red Page) [Letter from *Loafer*, Tauranga.] Following are other local money-names... 2.6d *half-bull, half-caser* or *two-and-a-buck*. **1977** *NZ Numismatic Jrnl.* Oct. 15 The half crown was called a *half-dollar..two-and-a-kick*, and *two-and-a-buck*. In the latter instance *buck* stands for sixpence, though apparently this term was rarely used by itself for that coin denomination, but almost always in association with a number of shillings.

2. [Orig. US, in freq. NZ informal use since 1967, the year of the introduction of decimal coinage and the change from *pound* to *dollar* as the name of the main unit of currency.] The New Zealand dollar.
    1977 *NZ Numismatic Jrnl.* Oct. 17 A permanent slang term introduced into New Zealand during the late 1960's early 1970's is the American *buck* for dollar. Kelly (1970:463) noted its appearance in Auckland in mid 1969. In Dunedin, the term apparently became popular in 1972, for when I left the city at the end of 1971 for a year's residence in Australia the term was not widely used, but on my return in late January 1973 I was immediately struck with the common use of the term.

buck, *v. Obs.*

1. In the phr. **to buck a town down**, of horses, to buck violently.
    c1875 MEREDITH *Adventuring in Maoriland* (1935) 70 These horses would 'buck a town down', as the saying is. I saw one sailor get a cropper.

2. In various phrasal constructions: **buck at**, to object; **buck in**, to pitch in; **buck on**, to renege on; ?to object to performing (a task).
    1937 PARTRIDGE *Dict. Slang* 99 *buck*... Also, v.i., to object, be reluctant (vt. with *at*): coll[oquial], from ca. 1890; mainly Australia and New Zealand. **1980** LELAND

Kiwi-Yankee Dict. 19 The Mayor of Greymouth was on TV recently, praising the townsfolk for the way they **bucked in** (pitched in) to help the city and each other during a flood. **1910** *Truth* 17 Sept. 5 A porter at Palmerston had the duty of clearing the car, but he apparently **bucked on** the job and on the morning of August 29 the car was returned to Dunedin without being cleaned.

buckaroo, buckeroo, varr. PAKARU, PUCKEROO.

buckateer, bucketeer, varr. PUKATEA.

bucket-of-water-wood. *Obs.* Also **bucket-of-water-tree.** Any tree or wood rich in sap and useless for firewood. **a.** FUCHSIA 1.
 1889 KIRK *Forest Flora* 54 The [fuchsia] wood is extremely difficult of combustion, and like the rewarewa is often termed 'bucket-of-water wood' by the bushman; even when thoroughly dry it can scarcely be burned in an open grate. **1910** COCKAYNE *NZ Plants & Their Story* 152 As a firewood [fuchsia's] badness is almost incredible, and truly none but the newest of chums would dream of using it when camped in the forest. 'Bucket-of-water wood', it has been termed; and the rather tall story goes how a trunk, which had been used for a back log to a fire for a whole year, upon being finally cast into the open air as worthless, put forth green shoots, and grew again into a tree!
 b. Occas. REWAREWA.
 1889 [see above]. **1907** LAING & BLACKWELL *Plants NZ* 146 *Knightia excelsa* (The [Maori] Honeysuckle)... Maori name, *Rewa-rewa*. It is sometimes called the *Bucket-of-water-tree*, because it is so slow of combustion.
 c. KOHUHU.
 1889 FEATON *Art Album NZ Flora* 32 Pittosporum tenuifolium... Even as firewood it is despised, and bears the all too suggestive name of 'Bucket of Water Wood', so little is it calculated by its combustive qualities to enliven the domestic hearth.

buckjump, *v.* [f. *buck* a male deer + *jump v.*: AND *v. intr.*, 1838.]
 1. *intr.* Of a horse, to leap from the ground in the manner of a startled deer, with head down, feet drawn together and back arched.
 1853 in MacKenzie *Overland Auckland to Wellington* (1893) 45 Saddled my mare and gave her to Mr Shepherd to hold. She got away and buck-jumped fearfully. **1873** *TrNZI* V. 99 I had scarcely remounted my horse before the animal began to buck-jump most violently. **1912** BOOTH *Five Years NZ* 50 Eight out of every ten horses could and did buckjump.
 2. buck-jumping *vbl. n.* and *attrib.* **a.** Of a horse [AND 1848], see quot. 1856.
 1856 ROBERTS *Diary* 23 Aug. in Beattie *Early Runholding* (1947) 35 Buckjumping is a horrid vice... The horse tries to roll itself up into a ball, with all four feet close together, head down as near the ground as possible between the forelegs, tail well down, back stuck up like the hump of a camel when in good condition. Attitude is everything. Then commences the performance. With an active spring and rather a forward motion up you go in the air, and down again with a jerk, then up and down like an india-rubber ball, occasionally varying the action by jumping forward and kicking out behind with both legs at once, returning to the oval position as rapidly as possible, then turning round like a teetotum at lightning speed. **1857** PAUL *Lett. from Canterbury* 43 A few tumbles from a buck-jumping brute. **1874** CAIRD *Sheepfarming NZ* 29 Buck-jumping is, I believe, an art only known by the colonial horses at the Antipodes. I imagine it is generally caused by the horse being broken in too quickly, and backed too soon. **c1891** COTTLE *Frank Melton's Luck* I had never experienced the sensation of buck-jumping, which in its true significance is peculiar to colonial horses. **1912** BOOTH *Five Years NZ* 50 The faculty of buckjumping is..almost confined to Australian horses... It was a fact that eight out of every ten horses could and did buckjump, and with many of them the vice was incurable. **1981** CHARLES *Black Billy Tea* 10 The term 'buck-jumping show' has given way to the American 'rodeo', although in fact the only real similarity is in the riding of bucking horses. **1992** PARK *Fence around the Cuckoo* 251 As a curate he had scandalised his prim world by winning a buckjumping contest.
 b. *transf.* The name of a boys' game of riding a springy tree branch.
 c1938 Buckjumping was a popular game among Havelock (Marlborough) boys, played by riding up and down on a low springy tree branch. (Ed.) **1953** SUTTON-SMITH *Unorganized Games NZ Primary School Children* (VUWTS) II. 744 The athletic games of strength include Bull in the Ring, Buck Jumping, Cock-Fighting. **1982** SUTTON-SMITH *Hist. Children's Play* 112 There was.. Rough-riding, in which one player sat on a fir tree branch while the others took the end of it and pulled it up and down and then let it go flying up in the air. The player who could stay on the longest was the rough-riding champion. Of a similar nature was Buck-jumping, in which individual players rode a macrocarpa or gum branch to see who could rise the highest.

buck-jump, *n.* [f. prec.: AND 1882.] Of a horse (or bullock), an act of buck-jumping. Also *attrib.*
 1873 BARKER *Station Amusements* 233 The process called 'gentling' was a complete misnomer for the series of buck-jumps, of bites and kicks, with which [the mare] received the slightest attempt to touch her. **1981** CHARLES *Black Billy Tea* 9 I used to go to every show Where they ran a buck-jump ring. The wildest moke I thought a joke, I really had a fling. *Ibid.* 18 A bullock-busting sideshowman Who knew the buck-jump stunts.

buck-jumper. [AND 1838.] A horse which buck-jumps.
 1866 *Canterbury Rhymes* 18 Clarke's horses are notorious buck-jumpers. **1879** INNES *Canterbury Sketches* 94 My dear fellow, can you sit a buck-jumper. **1889** MITCHELL *Rhymes & Rambles* 28 It was in 1875 I..proposed to a girl, and was rejected... I felt as if I had been thrown from a buck-jumper. **1911** BOREHAM *Selwyn* 92 The chief..had deliberately placed at his disposal an animal of..vicious propensities, and the natives were applauding the skill with which he was managing the worst buck-jumper in the country! **1937** AYSON *Thomas* 66 Thomas soon realized that riding a buckjumper meant more than just sticking to the saddle and allowing oneself to be jerked up, down, here, there and everywhere. **1948** FINLAYSON *Tidal Creek* (1979) 100 When all is fixed and the big tent up, there's a hoop-la stall..a line of piebald ponies and wicked buckjumpers. **1969** MOORE *Forest to Farm* 54 The pack-saddles..were not of a class to stand up to a buckjumper determined to dump his load. **1981** CHARLES *Black Billy Tea* 11 There were just rough buck-jumpers, in an A. & P. sideshow.

Buckleys, *n. pl. Obs.* [Poss. reinforced by BUCKLEY'S CHANCE in a sense of no chance of working, or (later) by the dramatically advertised *Buckley's Canadiol* cough-mixture involving the noise of howling storms.] A holiday from logging owing to wet weather.
 1953 REED *Story Kauri* 135 These wet-day holidays were known as 'buckleys'... The term 'buckleys' is said to have originated from a place called Buckley's Gully, which was always heavily shrouded in mist when a storm was approaching.

Buckley's chance. Usu. *ellipt.* as **Buckley's, Buckleys;** occas. **Buckley's show.** [AND 1895: poss. f. the name of William *Buckley* (1780–1856), an escaped convict who lived for 32 years with Aborigines in s. Victoria.] Little or no chance at all; a forlorn hope. Compare BOLTER'S CHANCE.
 1906 *Truth* 28 July 3 The [Boxing] Association is making a 'dead set' against the professional talent which has come into such prominence in Wellington of late, and the stoushers' chance of fixing up 'shleinter goes' is 'Buckley's'. **1911** *Maoriland Worker* 11 Aug. 8 To oust Hereditary Ward's Government, Massey will have to hold all the seats that he has got and capture fifteen more. He has got two chances of doing this—his own and Buckley's. **1934** *Press* (Christchurch) (Acland Gloss.) 13 Jan. 13 *Buckley's chance, Buckley's.*—No chance whatever. Does anyone know who Buckley was? *Ibid.* 27 Jan. 15 *Buckley's chance.*— A correspondent from Kirwee, the same as explained *Jimmy Woodser* for me, writes that Buckley was one of the earliest convicts (perhaps the first) to escape from Botany Bay and take to the bush. It was then thought impossible to do this and live... Any other convict who talked of escaping was invariably told that he would have 'Buckley's chance'—hence the saying. **1944** FULLARTON *Troop Target* 38 We've Buckley's Chance of getting there first. **1955** BJ *Cameron Collection* (TS July) buckleys: have buckleys (v) have buckleys chance (v) To have no chance at all. **1960** BOSWELL *Ernie* 140 'You haven't got Buckley's chance.' (Buckley's chance was a colloquialism for an impossible hazard.) **1985** O'SULLIVAN *Shuriken* 47 Personally I wouldn't give you Buckley's show against a third-form team with a couple of girls on the wing. **1993** O'SULLIVAN *Let the River Stand* 231 There wouldn't be Buckley's of them going on if he was crook.

buck rat. [Prob. an alteration of Brit. dial. *fierce as a buck rat*: see EDD.] In the phr. **as fit as a buck rat,** or occas. **buck rabbit** [by mishearing or from s. US, DARE *buck*[1] 1 c], very fit and vigorous; **as wild as a buck rat,** very wild, completely untamed.
 1953 SUTHERLAND *Golden Bush* (1963) 154 A dozen dogs got after them but the sheep were as wild as buck-rats and wouldn't be headed. **1958** MCCARTHY *Rugby in My Time* 48 Everybody thought, 'I'm as fit as a buck rat, good as gold.' **1968** SLATTER *Pagan Game* 172 Tank Tarrant the greatest thing since sliced bread. Fit as a buck rat. **1983** *National Bus. Rev.* 21 Nov. 57 It used to be accepted that people who were 'as fit as buck rats'..were likely to be very eager for sex. **1993** *Evening Post* (Wellington) 8 Apr. 36 I was always as fit as a buck rabbit.

buck saw. [f. *buck* a saw-horse + *saw*: see OED *n.*[7]: prob. orig. a saw used with a saw-horse.] A hand frame-saw.
 1879 FEATON *Waikato War* (frontispiece advt) Try the Cheap Hardware House for..colonial ovens, &c... Hand, Rip, Tennon, Cross-cut, Pit, and Buck Saws.

buckshee /ˌbʌkˈʃi/, *n.* and *a.*

A. *n.* Also **bachsceach, bakshee(sh).** [Spec. use of orig. Army *buckshee* and varr. (f. *baksheesh* a present, an adaptation of a common Middle Eastern Arabic form) something free or extra.] A superficial wound meriting a return home; 'a blighty'; 'a homer'.

1917 in Miller *Camps, Tramps & Trenches* (1939) 164 Nearly got a buckshee. **1917** Gray, Norman *MS Papers 4134* (ATLMS) 7 Dec. Many men would have given 5 years of their life to have got my 'buckshee'. **1918** *Chron. NZEF* 2 Aug. 8 He may have even been lucky enough to get an N.Z. buckshee. **1918** *Shell-Shocks* 24 'Joe Robinson..got a decent baksheesh' (all slight wounds are classed as baksheesh). **1927** Burton *Auckland Regt.* 155 A 'buckshee' was all very well, a neat little hole through the arm or leg, with a trip to 'Blighty' at the end of it; but some frightful smash..was another thing. **1937** Partridge *Dict. Slang* 28 *bakshee...* A light wound: military, esp. New Zealanders': in G[reat] W[ar].
B. *adj.* Orig. WW1, **buckshee leave**, unofficial or unapproved leave.
1960 Scrymgeour *Memories Maoriland* 123 The ride down [on business] was uneventful, and though the 'Electricity Station' [where a pair of good-looking girls lived] was only a few miles off the bridle track, Jim like a good Anzac, faithfully refrained from taking 'Bachsceach Leave' and held to the paths of duty, that led in this case 'not to glory, but nearly to the grave'.

buckyteer, var. PUKATEA.

budgie-cage. *Army.* WW2. A military prison or field punishment centre. Cf. BIRDCAGE 4.
1943 *NZEF Times* 25 Oct. 11 And he says to me that a little more lip like that and he'd shove me in the budgie cage for longer than a month or two. **1944** *Coral Dust* Dec. Don't walk down Queen St in your underpants or you'll probably spend a night in the 'Budgie Cage.' **1945** Webber *Johnny Enzed in Middle East* (Glossary) R.P.C., Budgie Cage, Rock College, Field Punishment Centre.

buffalo chips. [Transf. from an orig. US use.] The dried dung of animals as fuel.
1976 Veitch *Clyde on Dunstan* 17 Waggoners used wood substitutes for fuel for cooking during the journey from Central to Dunedin. 'Buffalo chips' (dried dung), 'yellow pine' (straw), or 'kaladdies' (the flower and stem of flax) were burned in a can which was hung behind the waggon.

buffalo grass: see GRASS 2 (7).

buff weka: see WEKA 2 (2).

bugabuga: see PAKE.

bugger. As widely and variously used as a verb and noun in NZ as elsewhere. The earliest recorded NZ use (the noun) is from the trial of the Maungatapu murderers (**1866** *Lyttelton Times* 26 Sept. Yes, you old bu— if you pay out—that is scream.). Distinctive or frequent local uses may include the following.
1. Elaborations of general English *bugger (me)!* expressing surprise, disbelief, or disapproval: **bugger me Charlie**, **bugger me days**, **bugger that for a joke!**
1948 Ballantyne *Cunninghams* 237 'Bugger me Charlie,' he shouted, jumping up. **1984** 16 M E89 Pakuranga Coll. 35B Bugger me days **1949** Davin *Roads from Home* 223 I'd say: Bugger that for a joke!
2. As a noun, usu. *pl.* in the word-groups **buggers afloat (buggers-to-float)**, dumplings boiled or fried, also known as 'doughboys'; occas. applied to fried scones, or kinds of doughnuts. Cf. FRIED SCONE.
c1940 Buggers-to-float for fried scones used by Mrs N. Ngatai of Taranaki: p.c. Helen Small (1983) **1969** Henderson *Open Country Calling* 122 I make what my family calls 'B——s Afloat', but we'd better call them: Sinkers. **1978** Jardine *Shadows on Hill* 32 The artistry and ingenuity he could display in the use of a camp oven,.. in producing such delicacies as..scones, 'buggers-to-float' (doughnuts)..were a wonder to behold. **1985** Hunt *I'm Ninety-five* 29 We'd make dumplings, too, fried up in the camp oven. Buggers afloat we called them [c1916].

bugger-lugs. Also **bugalugs.** [Prob. northern Brit. dial.: see EDD *begger-lug, -leg*, a term of mock anger applied to children; see also in somewhat different sense, Partridge 8 : *buggerlugs* 'A not necessarily offensive term of address: orig. mainly nautical: late C. 19–20'.] A term of slightly irritable endearment often formerly to children and not felt as offensive or impolite. Also pronounced as *buggy-lugs*.
c1914–18 In spoken use in Marlborough from at least WW1 (p.c. W.H.B. Orsman). **1986** TV1 Advertisement for Smith & Brown 5 Apr. A woman says (excitedly): 'These old buggerlugs at Smith and Brown are offering [etc.]' **1992** Park *Fence Around the Cuckoo* 142 The Brigadier was Brigadier, sir. Alas..in the smoky privacy of the bunkhouse, these two grand people became [c1932] Bugalugs and Ma Bugalugs.

buggy.
1. [See OED (1773), 'but in recent [1860–70] use esp. *U.S.* and the Colonies'.] A (usu.) four-wheeled vehicle; thence any light passenger vehicle, as distinct from the main, light freight vehicle, the express wagon.
1862 *Puketoi Station Diary* (Hocken TS) 1 June Thomson came in buggy. **1874** Merewether *By Sea & By Land* 172 There was Mr. Allen with a very nice pair-horse buggy built on the American principle. **1888** D'Avigdor *Antipodean Notes* 170 *Buggy*, originally an American expression for a specially-constructed four-wheeled vehicle, is in the colonies often applied to every sort of light open trap. **1894** Wilson *Land of Tui* 76 The buggy, a peculiarly Colonial contrivance, most convenient for going through rivers. **1907** Chudleigh *Diary* 6 Oct. (1950) 443 The old American buggy that used to be in N.Z. was the best carriage for rough ground I ever knew. **1920** Mansfield *Stories* (1984) 223 There was not an inch of room for Lottie and Kezia in the buggy. **1939** Vaile *Pioneering Pumice* 299 *Buggy*. An antiquated vehicle for light transport—usually to carry four persons and drawn by two light horses. **1940** Studholme *Te Waimate* (1954) 164 My father always drove an Abbott buggy, and would go right across country in this conveyance,... [1954 *Note*] American four-wheeled buggy built of hickory wood by a man named Abbott. **1978** Preston *Family of Woolgatherers* 104 Mother and father, we three children..travelled [c1901] in convoy in two buggies, a light one with small, fast horses and a large 'express' pulled by half-draughts. **1984** Boyd *City of the Plains* 10 A buggy became the status symbol of a rangatira.
2. *attrib.*, often tending towards Comb. See quots.
1869 *Puketoi Station Diary* (Hocken TS) 8 Apr. Burns got in Buggy horses. **1879** Barry *Up & Down* 283 The horse managed to break the buggy-pole. **1883** Brett's *Colonists' Guide* 11 One of the side-buildings to be..formed into a four-stall stable, buggy-house, harness-room, and cart-shed. **1938** *TrRSNZ* LXVIII. 7 As a source of electricity he used a battery of Grove cells, the box for which he constructed in his father's buggy-shed at Pongarehu while on holiday. **1968** Seddon *The Seddons* 14 At one side of the yard [c1880s] was the stable, the buggy-house, the fowl-house, the cowshed and a sty for our pig. *Ibid.* 17 As a buggy mare Daisy was ideal. *Ibid.* 30 When the shadow of night had fallen and the buggy lamps shed a faint yellow glow on the white road. **1986** Richards *Off the Sheep's Back* 41 One winter three buggyloads of our relatives.. arrived from Horotiu to stay with us during the shooting season.

buhai, var. BOOHAI.

build, *v.* [Prob. f. US: see DARE B2 To prepare something to eat or drink, 1907.] To prepare or put together a recipe, a dish or a meal; to cook. (Also, to roll a cigarette.)
1897 Wright *Station Ballads* 16 'Look here, old mate,' says he, 'I'll cook the spuds... And you can build a duff!' **1947** Newton *Wayleggo* 118 The packie had built us a stew. **1965** Macnicol *Skippers Road* 101 Archie declared he was pretty good at the cooking, and was always threatening to 'build' a pot of soup. **1974** Agnew *Loner* 80 I stretched out my hand for the rest of the tobacco and began building a smoke. **1989** McGill *Dinkum Kiwi Dict.* 17 *build a feed* preparing food in the bush, used among forestry workers and musterers in the South Island.

builders' mix. A mixture of shingle and sand used for making concrete; aggregate.
1979 *Heinemann NZ Dict.* 136 *builders mix*, see aggregate. **1987** Willson *Home Building* 46 You will need to purchase a quantity of 'builders' mix'—a mixture of the fine and coarse aggregates (stone and sand) which make up the bulk of the concrete—and cement. **1991** *Wellington 1991/92 Yellow Pages* 124 Sand—Gravel—Roading—Builders Mix..All Delivered or Ex Yard.

Building. Usu. collective *pl*. **Government Building(s)**, often **the Buildings** or **the wooden buildings**, the large wooden building near Parliament Buildings in Wellington, reputedly 'the biggest wooden building in the Southern Hemisphere', built originally to house the offices of Ministers of the Crown and public servants.
c1870s Meredith *Adventuring in Maoriland* (1935) 23 There is quite a lot [of land] reclaimed already [in Wellington], and enormous government buildings are in process of erection on part of it. **1882** Skey *Pirate Chief* (1889) 172 So poor that a desk in the 'Big Buildings' new, Bad though it seemed, was the best of the two. **1883** *Bishop's Guide to Wellington* 22 'The Buildings', as they are locally designated, have the appearance of being thoroughly substantial and permanent in character, and it is not a little surprising to a stranger..to find that the ponderous edifice is constructed of wood. **1889** Knox *Boy Travellers* 248 The Government Building is an immense structure in Italian style; it covers an area of two acres, and is said to be the largest wooden edifice in the world. **1890** *Richmond-Atkinson Papers* (1960) II. 559 A deputation of representatives of the Trades and Labor [*sic*] Unions waited on the Hon the Premier at the Government Buildings. **1911** *Triad* 11 Sept. 45 I..found the Premier wanted a private secretary. When I got to the Buildings, I was told Sir Cornelius was busy. **1954** Winks *These New Zealanders* 162 Proud residents of Wellington are quick to point out one of the government buildings as 'the largest wooden building in the world'. **1963** Morrieson *Scarecrow* 132 The house looked as big as the government buildings. **1990** *Telephone Directory* (Wellington) 48 Education Ministry of..National Office Government Bldgs 55 Lambton Quay

bukaka, var. PUKEKO.

bukatea, bukitea, varr. PUKATEA.

bulbul, var. BULL-A-BULL.

bulk funding. Alluding to a system of funding teachers' salaries from a block amount given to each school to manage.
   1991 *Evening Post* (Wellington) 7 Nov. 2 Trustees of St Patrick's College, Kilbirnie, have rejected the Government's teacher salaries bulk funding trial. **1992** *PPTA News* Nov. 5 The report stated that bulk funding was implemented in New Zealand primary schools from 1878 until 1901, and in secondary schools from 1903 to 1920, but both systems were rejected because of the inequities they created between schools and their staffs and between teachers in particular schools.

bulkie /ˈbʊlki/. A labourer employed to load railway wagons and trucks.
   1991 *Dominion* (Wellington) 9 Nov. 14 Much of the work performed by railway staff is now carried out by the 'bulkies' who load wagons, etc., and former railway staff who are now 'owner drivers'.

bull, *n.*
   1. *Obs.* In early New Zealand use (1869), as elsewhere (see OED *bull n.*[1] 7, 1812), a crown or 5-shilling piece, esp. as **half-a-bull, half-bull,** half-a-crown.
   1977 [see DOLLAR *n.* 2].
   2. In the phr. **not to come within a bull's roar of,** to come nowhere near, not to come within coo-ee of.
   1967 (8 May) Lynch in memo to *NZBC Wellington Programme Advisory Committee* (p.c. L. Cleveland) They create an atmosphere that the happiness boys cannot come within a bull's roar of equating. **1987** TV1 Cricket Test Commentary NZ & West Indies 3 Mar. Chatfield was not within a bull's roar of that [ball]. **1989** MCGILL *Dinkum Kiwi Dict.* 17 *bull's roar, you wouldn't come within a* you are not even close; eg 'I'd flag away the sprints if I was you, Norty. You're not within a bull's roar of qualifying, let alone winning.' **1993** O'SULLIVAN *Let the River Stand* 216 Poor dead ungainly Emily! Did she ever come within a bull's roar of it, he wondered?
   3. In comparisons, see *full as a bull* (FULL *a.* 1) or *black as a bull's backside* (BLACK *a.*[2] B 3).

bull, *v.*[1] *Obs.* [Poss. f. *bull* water put in an empty spirit cask to draw the spirit out of the wood; hence watered-down spirit (see OED *n.*[6], 1830), as a noun recorded in NZ c1871.] *trans.* To falsify or adulterate; to (surreptitiously) alter the characteristics of.
   1913 CARR *Country Work* 21 Some parties were in the habit of 'bulling' the time-sheet, i.e., putting down days worked when they were absent. **1934** *Press* (Christchurch) (Acland Gloss.) 13 Jan. 13 *Bull the tea.* —Put soda in it to make it stronger.

bull, *v.*[2] *Mining.* [f. northern Brit. dial. *bull* an iron rod used to enlarge a hole in the process of blasting: AND 1889.] *trans.* To enlarge (the bottom of holes) with a light charge to enable the holes to hold a larger charge of explosive.
   1907 *Truth* 22 June 5 In the first place they do not use enough dynamite to 'bull' the holes which are from 18ft to 20ft... At Sydney Street one permanent hand..'bulls' the hole then puts on his coat and inspects the scenery. **1956** SUTHERLAND *Green Kiwi* (1960) 191 The contractors..knew their gelignite inside out,... to what extent it was wise to 'bull' the end of a deep borehole with one or more comparatively light untamped charges so as to form a chamber deep in the rock into which could be loaded the heavy, concentrated charge that would break out the living rock in jagged blocks. **1978** MCARA *Gold Mining Waihi* 191 Hand-drilling continued to be used in the stopes to avoid wetting the fill and it was customary to bull these holes, that is to enlarge the bottom of the hole by firing a small charge in it to make room for a larger charge.

bull-a-bull /ˈbʊləˌbʊl/. Also with much variety of form as **bulbul, buli-buli, bullabulla, bullibull, bullibulli, bullybul,** an adaptation of Ma. POROPORO. For varr. **borra borra, burra burra, pura-pura,** see POROPORO, the preferred form in recent speech and writing, and the form underlying the common transliterations which illustrate the usual substitutions by English speakers of [p>b], [o>u], [r>l] and the freq. perception of a Ma. final vowel as silent or barely audible. Usu. applied to either of two native soft-wooded shrubs of coastal and lowland forest margins and clearings, *Solanum aviculare* and *S. laciniatum* (fam. Solanaceae), having fleshy berries edible when ripe; occas. to the small black nightshades, the native *S. americanum* and the naturalized *S. nigrum*; also the berries of these plants. See also POROPORO.
   1840 TAINE in Patrick *From Bush to Jubilee* (1990) 12 Alongside it ran a clear stream, on the banks of which wild fuchsia and bulbuls grew luxuriously. **1844** 15 July in Hursthouse *Emigration* (1853) 111 [Song in honour of New Plymouth] And as for fruit, the place is full Of that delicious bull-a-bull. **1856** TANCRED *Nat. Hist. Canterbury* 21 [Near the sea coast] also grows a shrub, called by the natives bulbul (Solanum aviculare) with handsome, deeply-cut leaves, and bearing a yellow fruit which is eaten. **1868** TAYLOR *The Past and Present of NZ* 209 Bull-a-bull. The common way of pronouncing Poro-poro, a solanum producing an edible berry. **1897** *Otago Witness* (Dunedin) 16 Dec. 7 The inconspicuous scented tufts of the green clematis mingled with the purple blooms and big yellow berries of the bulibul. **1898** MORRIS *Austral-English* 62 *Bull-a-bull,* or *Bullybul, n.* a child's corruption of the Maori word *Poroporo.* **1906** THOMSON *Introductory Classbook of Botany* 69 Poroporo, or, as it is commonly pronounced, Bullibulli..&c.,... are more or less common. **1927** *NZ Tablet* (Dunedin) 14 Sept. 37 We came across many bushes of buli-buli, which is a plant something like the cape gooseberry, but its fruit is twice its size. **1946** *JPS* LV. 145 *poroporo,* a plant..with beautiful large blue flowers and large orange-coloured berry eaten by boys and birds: often corrupted to bullybul. **1969** *Standard Common Names Weeds* 9 bullibul, bullibulli [=] poroporo. **1975** KNIGHT *Poyntzfield* 18 We could often get a good feed of ripe pura pura (mostly called bulla bull) berries [in Wellington c1850s]. **1981** BROOKER et al. *NZ Medicinal Plants* 93 *Solanum aviculare... Bullibulli... Poroporo, kohoho...* Some authors have identified 'poroporo' as *S. nigrum* [Black Nightshade], a smaller, weedy plant, and it is possible that the Maori did not distinguish the species. **1982** WILSON *Stewart Is. Plants* 77 *Solanum laciniatum* Poroporo... Bullabulla.

bullabulla, var. BULL-A-BULL.

bulla bulla: see BULLY *n.*[1]

bull-artist: see ARTIST 2 b.

bull-bar. [AND 1967] A sturdy frame of metal bars fitted to the front (occasionally also to the rear) of vehicles to reduce damage from a collision, esp. with straying stock. Compare *cow-bar* (COW 6).
   1994 *AA Directions* May 48 Some love them, others detest them. Known as roobars in Australia, and nudge bars in the UK, bullbars adorn the front and rear of thousands of vehicles in New Zealand.

bull birch: see BIRCH 3 (5).

bulldog. [A name given by fishermen from a fancied resemblance of the head to that of a bulldog.] *giant stargazer* (STARGAZER 2 (3)) or MONKFISH.
   1970 SORENSEN *Nomenclature NZ Fish* 37 *Monkfish..Geniagnus monopterygius..* [and] *Kathetostoma giganteum...* Other common names (both): Monkfish, Monks, Stargazer, Flathead (also applied at times to export gurnard); Churchills, Toebiters, Bulldogs, Spotted Stargazer, Maori Chief (Dunedin); Muddies. **1986** [see MONKFISH].

bulldust. [A euphemism for *bullshit*: AND 1951.] (Boastful) nonsense, rubbish. Also an exclamation of disbelief. See also *bulldust artist* (ARTIST 2 b), BULLSWOOL.
   [**1923** *Aussie* (NZ Section) 15 Aug. I The Duchess of Dillwater and the Dishonourable Percy Prig will..see nothing but mutton and eggs, and bonedust [?a euphemism for *bulldust*] from Maoriland.] **1961** [see ARTIST 2 b]. **1982** *Listener* 24 July 21 The farmer just said, 'Bulldust, Southlanders always do well in the north'. **1992** *Sunday Star* (Auckland) 25 Oct. A10 There's something deliciously satisfying about witnessing the sanctimonious being revealed..as just as full of bulldust and methane gas as the rest of us.

bullet, *n. Drug-users.* [Transf. use of *bullet,* so called f. the shape.] A portion of cannabis leaf wrapped for sale usu. in plastic or aluminium foil. Also **bullet house,** see quot. 1995. Cf. TINNY *n.*[2]
   1979 *Press* (Christchurch) 21 Aug. 19 When a search warrant was executed at the defendant's flat they found 19 cannabis 'bullets', 20 cannabis roaches. **1984** *Press* (Christchurch) 7 Dec. 4 Entering the toilet he saw Mr Maddox handing over money for marijuana. He snatched the bullet out of his hand. **1993** *Metro* (Auckland) Sept. 122 Dean smoked dope every day... Scoring a bullet (about three joints)..on a Thursday was almost a ritual. **1995** National Radio 'Morning Report' 4 Apr. [Auckland detective explains:] Drug distributors organize young people to run drug houses, with the locations continually changing, and deal drugs to customers from them. The drug is usually cannabis in the form of 'bullets', that is enough cannabis for about 3 cigarettes wrapped in aluminium foil. Hence they get their names 'bullet houses' or 'tinny houses' [the latter from the aluminium foil wrappers].

bulley, var. BULLY *n.*[1]

bulleye, var. BULLSEYE 1.

bullhead. [Cf. OED: any of various N. Amer. freshwater fish.] *giant bully* (BULLY *n.*[1] 2 (4) *Gobiomorphus gobioides*).
   1870 *TrNZI* II. 85 The Bull-head..is an Acanthopterygious fish. **1886** SHERRIN *Handbook Fishes NZ* 129 Bullhead (*Eleotris gobioides*). **1892, 1902** [see BULLY *n.*[1] 1]. **c1920** BEATTIE *Trad. Lifeways Southern Maori* (1994) 501 The patete is a form of 'bullhead' (kokopu) but is flat. **1942** ANDERSON *Maori Place Names* 301 The bull-head, or bully..is a sluggish fish, resting mostly on the bottom, or lurking beside or

under stones, or among the weeds if present. **1955** [see BULLY *n.*¹ 2 (6)]. **1981** WILSON *Fisherman's Bible* 24 Probably our most common freshwater fish the Bulley is also known as the Bullehead [*sic*] and is a basic staple diet of our trout.

bullibull(i), varr. BULL-A-BULL; BULLY *n.*¹

bullie, var. BULLY *n.*²

bull kelp. [Transf. use of *bull kelp*, N. American *Nereocystis* spp., for New Zealand *Durvillaea* spp.: cf. OED *n.*¹ 11.]

1. *Durvillaea antarctica* (fam. Durvillaeaceae), a robust brown seaweed of Pacific waters, several metres long, and having a massive holdfast against violent seas on exposed rocky coasts. Also *attrib.* See also KELP, RIMU *n.*² 1 a, RIMURAPA.
  1904 LANCASTER *Sons o' Men* 113 He took part in the landing through the bull-kelp of Auckland Island. **1911** SHAND *Moriori People* 11 The kelp used to make [the Moriori canoe] buoyant was of the *Rimurapa*, or broad, flat, bull kelp. **1922** *Auckland Weekly News* 14 Sept. 18 The meat was packed in bags made of seakelp, known..to the pakeha sea-farer as 'bull kelp'. **1928** [see RIMURAPA]. **1940** HOWARD *Rakiura* 208 The [muttonbird] containers are made of bull kelp.., which grows in profusion on the rocky fringes of the islets. **1961** MARTIN *Flora NZ* 4 [Caption] Seaweeds of the intertidal belt, Stewart Island, here consisting mainly of Bull-Kelp (*Durvillea*), Strap-weed (*Xiphophora*). **1982** BURTON *Two Hundred Yrs. NZ Food* 6 Alternatively, it [tutu juice] was boiled with the pith of the pitau fern or pieces of bull kelp seaweed (*rimurapu* [*sic*]). **1990** *Sport* 5 15 A cynical piece about a worldweary young idealist..who throws himself over Highcliff, down into the heaving bull-kelp.

2. Special Comb. **bull-kelp bag**, a bag made of split kelp in which fresh muttonbirds are preserved or kept for transportation. See also POHA.
  1952 *Diary* 20 Apr. in Sansom *In Grip of Island* (1982) 153 Out on line by door bull-kelp bags blown up and drying. Under the table finished pohas stacked. Birds in kelp bags with totara bark wrapping, looking fine in their new flax baskets.

bullock, *n*. *Obs*. or *Hist*. [Spec. or transf. uses of *bullock* a draught animal: cf. Acland's note in 1933 *Press* (Christchurch) (Acland Gloss.) 23 Sept. 13 *Bullocks*. Never called oxen in New Zealand, whether working bullocks or otherwise.]

1. Abbrev. of *bullock language*, esp. as **talk bullock**, the rough language used by a bullockdriver to his team. See also BULLOCKY *n.* 2.
  1889 *TrNZI* XXI. 450 We hear of men on upcountry stations who can do nothing but 'talk bullock'; and so all men did to a great extent in days when both word and idiom had origin in cattle-speech. **1941** BAKER *NZ Slang* 47 As long ago as 1864..Thatcher..used the expression *to talk bullock*.

2. a. Used *attrib*. in special Comb, mainly *obs*. and not always exclusive to New Zealand: **bullock-cart** [AND 1805], a two-wheeled cart drawn by bullocks attached to it by neck-yokes and chains; **bullock-chain**, a chain used to attach bullocks to carts, drays, sledges, etc.; **bullock-drawn** *a.*, of a vehicle, drawn by bullocks; **bullock-dray** *hist*. [AND 1847], a two- or four-wheeled vehicle, with a pole rather than shafts, drawn by a team of bullocks (also *attrib.*, see quot. c1875); **bullockdriver** *hist*. [AND 1836], one who drives a bullock-team, a BULLOCKY; **bullock-driving** *vbl. n.* [AND 1847]; **bullock-fence**, one strong enough to contain bullocks; **bullock-horse**, a bullockdriver's hack; **bullock janker** (or **jinker**), a wagon or catamaran consisting of a pole with a pair of wheels at one end and drawn by bullocks; **bullock language**, (a) strong language reputedly or proverbially associated with bullock-drivers' urging on their animals (see also 1 above), also *transf.*, any coarse language; (b) the practical language of command used by bullock-drivers to bullocks; **bullock-plough**, a heavy plough drawn by bullocks; **bullock-puncher** *obs*. [f. *bullock* + *puncher* one who 'punches' or drives animals along: AND 1859], see *bullock-driver* above (see also PUNCHER); **bullock-punching** *vbl. n. obs.* [AND 1886]; **bullock-sledge**, a heavy sledge designed to be drawn by bullocks; **bullock team** [AND 1829], a team of two to twenty or more paired bullocks, used as a draught instrument; **bullock teams**, a children's game; **bullock tie** *logging*, a wishbone shaped device attached to a bullock yoke to facilitate the hauling of logs; **bullock-wagon** [AND 1909], a two- or fourwheeled vehicle drawn by bullocks; **bullock whip**, see quots.; **bullock-yoke**, see quot. (see also BOW 1).
  1851 *Richmond-Atkinson Papers* (1960) I. 89 We..heard..that he had mounted a **bullock cart** & was doing very well. **1853** MACKIE *Traveller under Concern* (1973) 102 C. D[illon] at one time farmed his own land in the Waimea and was in the habit of driving his own bullock cart into Nelson. The bullock cart is the general and almost only vehicle in this district. It is a two wheeled cart with a pair of bullocks; occasionally we see 4–6 or 8 bullocks yolked [*sic*] according to circumstances. **1860** *Richmond-Atkinson Papers* (1960) I. 590 Went to Merton with young Sartin & his bullock cart & brought back a load of board for shutters to keep Maories out. **1922** COWAN *NZ Wars* (1955) I. 166 Soon a hundred bullock-cart loads of timber were on the spot selected for the post. **1874** KENNAWAY *Crusts* 155 There was a rattle of the yokes and **bullock-chain** as the sledge tried to follow. **1947** BEATTIE *Early Runholding* 41 Now a generation has arisen to whom a **bullock-drawn** vehicle would be as strange as a Roman chariot. **1848** WAKEFIELD *Handbook NZ* 447 The **bullock-dray**, used instead of a waggon, has a pole, to the end of which the yoke is fastened. **1854** *Richmond-Atkinson Papers* (1960) I. 146 There are other carriages very interesting to me—the bullockdrays with their teams of ten oxen and loads of groceries. **1863** BUTLER *First Year* viii 128 I hardly know why I introduced this into an account of a trip with a bullock dray. **1874** WILSON *Diary* May in Wierzbicka *Wilson Family* (1973) 188 Linton..ordered a Bullock Dray seven feet by five feet, for Body, three inch axles and four feet eight wheels, four inch tires with an Iron Bark pole running right through the Dray. c**1875** MEREDITH *Adventuring in Maoriland* (1935) 38 Up to now, there have only been bullock-dray tracks. **1912** SIR JOSHUA STRANGE *Letter* 19 Aug. in Jones *Samuel Butler* (1919) I. 85 I shall never forget the small dark man who took up a run at the back of beyond, carted a piano up here on a bullock dray, and passed his solitary evenings playing Bach's fugues. **1930** PINFOLD *Fifty Yrs. Maoriland* 15 By means of a bullock-dray families could sometimes be brought to church. **1933** *Press* (Christchurch) (Acland Gloss.) 23 Sept. 13 *Bullockdray* was a rough cart with two wheels and a pole, to which the bullocks were attached by yokes over their necks, and a chain. It was usually drawn by a team of six or eight. **1947** [see *bullock sledge* below]. **1968** TOMLINSON *Remembered Trails* 52 Many sheep, and later..bullock drays, were taken through this track to the Wairau. **1981** HUNT *Speaking a Silence* 34 We'd all have to go to school on the bullock dray. It was a great big square, open thing; they'd put seats across it and away we'd go. **1846** *McLean Papers* (ATLTS) III. 226 **Bullock-drivers**, stockmen and carpenters. **1857** PAUL *Lett. from Canterbury* 27 As soon as maybe after his arrival, [the new settler] engages himself as a shepherd, or bullock-driver. **1860** BUTLER *First Year* (1863) iv 50 I am informed that he..has so far mollified his morals that he is an exceedingly humane and judicious bullockdriver. c**1875** THATCHER in *NZ Songster* V. 64 If nice expressions you would learn, Colonial and new, Some bullock driver who is bogged, Is just the man for you. **1881** NESFIELD *Chequered Career* 118 The station bullock-driver was, like all bullock-drivers, addicted to swearing. **1891** COTTLE *Frank Melton's Luck* 2 As long as a man earns what he wants on the square..we don't care a rap whether he is a Member of Parliament or So-and-so's bullock-driver. **1905** *Truth* 12 Aug. 4 She heard Bloomfield say that Price was a dirty bullockdriver. **1913** CARR *Country Work* 40 Bullock drivers who handle from 12 to 24 animals are also employed [in the sawmills]... The saying..to 'swear like a bullock driver', is common. **1933** *Press* (Christchurch) (Acland Gloss.) 23 Sept. 13 *Bullock Driver*.—Man employed to drive bullocks... They were famous for swearing, and the old story of the parson who said, 'Even a bullock driver has a soul to be saved' is still told up country. **1959** [see BULLOCKING 2 a]. **1860** BUTLER *First Year* (1863) iv 50 [H]e then returns to his shepherding, cooking, **bullock-driving**, &c. &c., as the case may be. **1871** MONEY *Knocking About NZ* 146 I took the job of hedge-trimming at first, and, after having finished this..I began to pick up bullock-driving. **1881** BATHGATE *Waitaruna* 67 Talking of bullock-driving reminds me of an incident that occurred the other day. **1947** BEATTIE *Early Runholding* 42 Bullock-driving is now a lost art. **1851** SHORTLAND *S. Dist. NZ* 28 I was once called upon to endeavour to obtain compensation from a native who had destroyed..several hundred yards of stout **bullock-fence**. **1940** STUDHOLME *Te Waimate* (1954) 156 The bullockies invariably took their hack, known as the '**bullock horse**' with them... These horses were tied on behind the drays by a neck-rope, and dragged along if they were not inclined to go willingly. Sometimes, when the dray was being driven through low scrub, the bullock horses would get some nasty knocks from the stems flying up and hitting them. **1981** HUNT *Speaking a Silence* 34 If it was fine but muddy he'd send a man to take us in the old **bullock janker**; it was just too [*sic*] big wheels with a long pole and two bullocks, one each side, hooked on with great big yokes around their necks. (a) c**1860** *Wiener Zeitung* (Vienna) Nos 57-65 transl. in Haast *Julius Von Haast* (1948) 36 If the English sailors have acquired a not undeserved reputation for their curses, surely the New Zealand bullock-drivers must be reckoned superior to them in this accomplishment, for such an assortment of fantastic oaths from all kingdoms of Nature, Heaven and Hell I have never heard before from mortal lips. Astounded I listened to this blue-eyed son of Albion and was at last impelled to ask him why he cursed so horribly; it could serve no purpose and only made the beast more stubborn. 'You don't understand, Sir,' the young man answered. 'I'm only speaking the **bullock language**. The animal certainly wouldn't understand or obey me if I spoke to him as I would to my horse. The bullock has been brought up to carry in this way, and if I want to get on fast, I've got to talk to him like this.' **1886** HART *Stray Leaves* 27 Bullock drivers are seldom choice in their language under the most favourable circumstances, but to drive a team with a load of firewood..from Papanui to Christchurch [in 1852], was a work of so much difficulty, that the flow of bullock language was more than ordinarily profuse. **1992** *Evening Post TV Week* (Wellington) 21 Sept. 9 I probably have a much

BULLOCK

fuller range of 'bullock driver's' language than these two [commentators]; the difference is that I use due respect..to those within earshot. (b) [**1947** BEATTIE *Early Runholding* 42 As there were no reins, the driving was all by commands and cracking the whip. The calls were 'Get up' or 'Gee up' to start, 'Whoa' to stop, 'Come here' to turn to left, and 'Gee off' to turn right. If you came to a sharp corner, you would often say persuasively, 'Way! Way! Come here.' There is a general impression that bullocks could not be successfully driven without roaring oaths and curses at them, but this idea is a relic of early-day humour.] **1953** REED *Story of Kauri* 180 Nearly all the drivers used the same **bullock language**, giving the command always in the same words..*wo* 'halt'; *back*; come here. **1848** WAKEFIELD *Handbook NZ* 247 The first day was devoted to a ploughing match, for **bullock-ploughs**. **1939** BEATTIE *First White Boy Born Otago* 95 A season or two later bullock ploughs were used. **1856** ROBERTS *Diary* 19 Sept. in Beattie *Early Runholding* (1947) 43 [The bullock whip] was a powerful flagellator in the hands of an experienced '**bullock puncher**'. **1888** D'AVIGDOR *Antipodean Notes* 170 A *bullock-puncher* is a man engaged to drive bullocks to market or port. The expression is painfully true, as these men, who receive but very poor wages, and are recruited from the worst class, ill treat the poor animals by *punching* their sides with a pointed stick. **1892** BROOKES *Frontier Life* 27 One of the bullock-punchers did his duty for him. **1905** *Truth* 1 July 2 A stream of adjectives one would hardly expect from a bullock-puncher. **1912** BOOTH *Five Years NZ* 39 [In the accommodation house was] the bullock puncher, whose every alternate word was a profane oath. **1921** GUTHRIE-SMITH *Tutira* 382 Owners and employees had worked shoulder to shoulder..as bullock-punchers. **1939** BEATTIE *First White Boy Born Otago* 136 The next day the snow had almost ceased so the 'bullock-puncher' pushed his mob on as fast as conditions allowed. **1868** PHILLIPS *Point Jrnl.* 9 Nov. (ATLTS) T.A.P. & J.P. **bullock punching**—carting stones into creek &c... Tuesday 10th very fine & hot N.E Heavy bullock punching—stone carting &c. **c1875** MEREDITH *Adventuring in Maoriland* (1935) 61 After a spell of 'quill-driving' it takes one a week or so to get into one's stride of splitting, fencing, bullock-punching again. **1891** CHAMIER *Philosopher Dick* 411 He soon got charge of a team and was loud in expatiating upon the art of bullock-punching. **1844** in *NZ Co. Reports* (1854) XVII. 62 It would be easy to bring a **bullock-sledge** thus far. **1898** HOCKEN *Contributions* 176 The day before [the wedding] she drove there in her bullock sledge in charge of the bridecake, which..was wrapped in her macintosh. **1947** BEATTIE *Early Runholding* 33 He has made a rough track to this rough home by smoothing one or two extra rough bits and sloping off a few creek banks to allow bullock drays or sledges to get through. Sledges were the common vehicle of the earliest times, followed by bullock drays, and then, after the diggings broke out, by the long-bodied, four-wheeled bullock wagon and also by horse-drawn drays and wagons with greatly increased accommodation. **1848** WAKEFIELD *Handbook NZ* 247 Only eleven ploughs were on the ground, seven of which were **bullock-teams**. **c1872** in Meredith *Adventuring in Maoriland* (1935) 34 They [sc. grasshoppers] actually stopped a bullock-team this week [by flying in the faces of the leaders]. **1884** CHUDLEIGH *Diary* 14 Feb. (1950) 326 Willie Dix and bulock [sic] team arrived in the morning and Martin with horse team in the afternoon. **1892** *NZ Official Handbook* 158 In the south, rough tramways are laid down in the bush, and the logs hauled on low carriages to the mills by horse- or bullock-teams. **1992** PARK *Fence around the Cuckoo* 12 The old people of Te Kuiti competed against each other with mud stories. 'Remember the time a bullock team and jinker sank in the main street?' **1982** SUTTON-SMITH *Hist. Children's Play* 64 Another play unknown at a later date was the widespread **Bullock Teams**: It was easy to make a team of working bullocks from pieces of supplejack, with their opposite branches doing duty as horns. The manufacture of yokes, substitutes for chains and model sledges gave a boy the pleasant feeling that accompanies successful achievement. Leading the team by a piece of string was the next step. (1870; Waipu) **1973** WHEELER *Hist. Sheep Stations NI* 34 [Caption] Logging pan for dragging logs, **bullock tie** (or wishbone) used on the yoke, and in front a logging dog [i.e. an iron spike or hook] that grips the log to prevent it from falling off the logging pan. **1873** BARKER *Station Amusements* 18 A turn of the track showed us a heavy timber-laden **bullock-waggon** labouring slowly along. **1933** *Press* (Christchurch) (Acland Gloss.) 23 Sept. 13 A *Bullock-waggon* was much the same as a bullock-dray, but had four wheels and was drawn by 10 or 12 bullocks. **1938** HYDE *Godwits Fly* (1970) 144 Our mother came here by bullock-wagon, when she was eighteen. **1947** [see *bullock sledge* above]. **1951** DUFF *Shepherd's Calendar* (1961) 13 Bullock-wagons were still in use when I was a boy, but the noises I heard the drivers make were certainly not music. **1962** EVANS *Waikaka Saga* 112 [Caption] The true bullock wagon had two wheels only. Note the wide wheels, the chain shoulder high... Such a team of up to six bullocks was common. **1973** WHEELER *Hist. Sheep Stations NI* 10 The dumped wool was taken by bullock wagon into the surf [and] transferred to surfboats. [**1856** ROBERTS *Diary* 19 Sept. in Beattie *Early Runholding* (1947) 42 The [**bullock**] **whip** was rawhide plaited sinnet, about six feet long, thick at the upper end, where it was fastened to a handle as long as itself, but tapering nearly to a point, to which was attached a narrow strip of rawhide, called 'the fall', finishing off with a twisted 'cracker' made of 'weetau' or dressed flax in place of whipcord, and was a powerful flagellator in the hands of an experienced 'bullock puncher.'] **1933** *Press* (Christchurch) (Acland Gloss.) 23 Sept. 13 *Bullock Whip.*—Whip used by bullock driver. It was made with a very long handle (perhaps eight feet) and a long lash. **1939** BEATTIE *First White Boy Born Otago* 154 In driving bullocks the best bullock-whips were made from the skins of plump wild sows—these skins pleated [sic 'plaited'] well and lasted well. **1960** BOSWELL *Ernie* 142 'Bullocky' whips were not so long in the leather as stockwhips, but had very long, flexible handles. **1856** ROBERTS *Diary* 19 Sept. in Beattie *Early Runholding* (1947) 42 I yoked up the bullocks. The **bullock yoke** was a square piece of white pine smoothed and hollowed out to fit the necks of the two bullocks, with holes for the iron bows which went round the neck and through the yoke, being fastened above with a key tied with a bit of greenhide; in the centre a bolt with a ring called 'the start' passed through the yoke, to which the chain was fastened from the sledge.

b. In the collocation **bullock's kai**, RAUREKAU (*Coprosma australis*).

1892 KELLY *Journey through Waitara* 3 [The eels] are then covered with the broad leaves of the raurikau (or bullock's kai as it was known by the early settlers).

bullock, *v. Hist. trans.* See also BULLOCKING *vbl. n.* and *ppl. a.*

1. To shift, haul, etc. (a load) with bullocks.

1890 *Otago Witness* (Dunedin) 6 Mar. 9 The seed has to be packed on horses..to tracks, where a sledge will take it to the main road, to be bullocked to the different bays for transport by steamer. **1953** REED *Story of Kauri* 255 Here [c1900] Caldow and Malone worked 6 million feet, which was bullocked, and then trammed, to the mouth of the Kaimarama River near the old booms. **1973** WHEELER *Hist. Sheep Stations NI* 78 I ask Bert about transporting [kauri] logs. 'The [Kauri Timber] Company bullocked the kauri logs to the streams, and the logs were floated out from trip dams on the Pungapunga.'

2. To drive (horses) hard; to 'bucket'.

1876 KENNEDY *Colonial Travel* 307 Here comes Yankee George, a-bullocking his horses along,—he's a card, an' no mistake.

3. [AND 1875.] Also *intr.* To work hard and vigorously; to tackle (a job, etc.) with rough-and-ready strength.

1887 *Auckland Weekly News* 20 Aug. 8 It seemed as though the horses would be unable to 'bullock' the heavy vehicle through the mud. **1905** *Truth* 9 Sept. 8 We should make it a condition that [assisted immigrants] be strong and willing to go up-country and bullock hard. **1922** *Quick March* 11 Sept. 20 The first Rubgy test [was] one in which the heavier New Zealand forwards..'bullocked' their way to victory. **1949** BAXTER *Collected Poems* (1980) 80 In mine and threshing-mill he had his day Bullocking, a strong back and a weak head. **1956** BAXTER *Collected Plays* (1982) 15 Webfoot Charlie bullocks the dead Cornishman's body to the side of the sleeping Dane. **1968** SLATTER *Pagan Game* 217 The Ruamahanga forwards bullock into the ruck and Keith Maxwell, given the ball, takes a snap pot at goal. **1973** *Islands* 5 272 He..saw, bullocking in through the gate, 1650s, red, and orange. **1988** McGILL *Dict. Kiwi Slang* 22 *to bullock* is still regarded as acting belligerently, and rugby forwards, in commentator's parlance, *bullock over* for tries.

bullocker: see BULLOCKY *n.* 1.

bullockeys' joy, var. BULLOCKY'S JOY.

bullocking.

1. *vbl. n.* [AND 1888.] Hard manual work; an activity demanding more physical vigour than intelligence or grace.

1890 *NZ Observer* 30 Aug. 11 Mansfield did some good work for Ponsonby, though still inclined to do a little 'bullocking'. **1893** FROBISHER *Sketches of Gossiptown* 15 To use his won emphatic expression, he set his face against all such senseless 'bullocking' [*sc.* in dancing]. **1905** SATCHELL *Toll of Bush* (1985) 37 There's no bullocking attached to the job; all that'll be done for you.

2. *ppl. a.* **a.** Pertaining to hauling, drawing, carting by bullock team.

1935 COWAN *Hero Stories NZ* 223 In his crippled old age he was cheered..by a visit from some old friend of his bush-scouting, bush-clearing, bullocking days. **1953** REED *Story of Kauri* 186 During bullocking operations in a portion of Puhipuhi, a nineteen foot log was being taken out on a catamaran. **1959** MASTERS *Tales of Mails* 115 Sam hadn't long been here before..becoming a professional bullock driver. Early in his bullocking career Sam and three other bullockies..were engaged in carting stores from Napier to Te Aute.

b. Aggressively and sturdily vigorous, used esp. in reference to rugby forward play to describe one who actively takes play to the opponents.

1947 GASKELL *Big Game* 8 Big bullocking bastards always mauling each other about. **1959** SLATTER *Gun in My Hand* 80 Now the bullocking forward is king of the field.

bullocky, *n. Hist.*

1. Occas. as **bullocker** (AND 1889). [AND 1869.] *bullock-driver* (BULLOCK *n.* 2 a).

1854 COX *Recollection* (1884) 67 Clear the road, make room for the bullocky from Australy. **c1875**

BULLOCKY

MEREDITH *Adventuring in Maoriland* (1935) 72 To my astonishment, the bullocky headed his team straight for the river where it was quite unfordable. **1894** ARTHUR *Kangaroo & Kauri* 91 I once saw..a bullocker who was working with his team. **1897** WRIGHT *Station Ballads* 64 When the bullockies came with their load, boys, The days of the first of the gold! **1913** CARR *Country Work* 40 A good 'Bullocky' is like a good shepherd, his voice is seldom heard. **1925** ANDREW in Neave *Land of Munros* (1980) 58 About this time [1860] it was necessary to go the Christchurch for stores and the Dad and bulloc[k]y went. **1933** *Press* (Christchurch) (Acland Gloss.) 23 Sept. 13 The old nickname for [bullock-driver] was *bullocky*. **1947** BEATTIE *Early Runholding* 43 The 'bullocky' and his whip (and language) have a fairly conspicuous place in the early colonial literature. **1959** [see BULLOCKING 2 a]. **1970** MCNEISH *Mackenzie* 17 He smiled as the bullocky screamed again, firing the whip with one horny hand while the other attacked a boil on his neck with a pruning knife. **1981** *Dominion* (Wellington) 6 Feb. 7 [Caption] Working team is pride and joy of bullocky... Mr Falconer owns one of the country's last [bullock] teams.

2. [AND 1879.] *bullock language* (BULLOCK *n.* 2 a).
1941 BAKER *NZ Slang* 47 The noun *bullocky* has even been evolved to describe the language used by such men. **1966** *Encycl. NZ* II. 680 *Bullocky* has been used to describe the language supposed to be characteristic of bullock-drivers.

bullocky, *a.*

a. [AND 1876.] Like a bullock, vigorous or physically strong.
1910 FANNING *Players & Slayers* 61 Those were the times [20 years ago] of packs of [rugby] Goliaths, brawny but 'bullocky'. **1940** STUDHOLME *Te Waimate* (1954) 179 Then the swine made a bullocky rush for home, though too late, the gate withstanding the impact.

b. Characteristic of or pertaining to bullocks or bullock-driving.
1922 *Quick March* 11 Sept. 13 Those days..were the good old 'bullocky' years; at one time the Ketemarae miller..had seventy bullocks in the teams carting sawn timber about the district.

bullocky's joy. [AND 1901.] Treacle or golden syrup. Cf. COCKY'S JOY.
1933 *Press* (Christchurch) (Acland Gloss.) 23 Sept. 13 *Bullocky's Joy*.—Golden syrup or treacle. **1946** MACFARLANE *Amuri* 109 Out in camp he lived on hard bread, meat and bullockeys' [*sic*] joy. **1954** MACFARLANE *Te Raka* 11 He might be given [by the station cook] a fresh bun with treacle, 'Bullocky's joy'. **1960** MASTERS *Back-Country Tales* 166 The bread was no good because it had to be made in bullocky's joy tins. **1973** [see BROWNIE 2 a]. **1981** CHARLES *Black Billy Tea* 27 For when dad was a boy, Bullocky's joy, The only jam they knew, Was treacle—black As an old coal sack And as thick as rubber glue.

bull ring. *WW1, WW2.*

1. [Used elsewhere but recorded first as a NZ use: see OED *bull n.*¹ 11, 1928.] A training-ground at a military base; in WW1, esp. that of Etaples.
1916 HEALEY, C.A. *MS Papers 2244* (ATLTS) 27 Aug. In the bullring from 7.30 am till 12.30. **1917** GRAY, Norman *MS Papers 4134* (ATLMS) 27 Apr. The 'Bull ring'. Here are rows of bags filled with shavings, rags etc. and smeared over the 'heart', 'lungs', 'abdomen', etc. with blobs of red paint. **1944** *Korero* (AEWS Background Bulletin) 17 July 24 Amongst the older expressions still used [in NZ Army slang]..'burgoo' for porridge..'bull-ring' for the training-ground, still retain their popularity. **1949** DE MAUNY *Huntsman In Career* 13 Drawing equipment at the Q.M., drilling on the bull-ring.

2. *WW1. transf.* WAZZA.
c1914-18, 1919 [see WAZZA].

bullrush, var. BULRUSH.

bull rush, *n.* Also **bullrush.** A children's game. Cf. KINGY-SEENY.
1978 SUTHERLAND *Elver* 61 'Do you play Bull Rush at your school?' John asked. 'Bull Rush?' said Ewan... 'You get out on the field and draw a line at the ends. You pick someone to be He to stand in the middle. He calls out someone's name, and he has to get across to the other end. The guard has to try to tackle the runner and hit him three times. But if the runner gets across he calls out Bull Rush and everyone runs ...[*sic*]' 'That's King-a-Sene!' said Ewan. 'But we're only allowed to tag the player, we're not allowed to tackle him.' **1986** WATSON *Address to a King* 58 Some other children have come over from the neighbouring farm and they're all playing *bullrush. Bullrush!* they shout, and Ida runs across the lawn with flying hair and Selby, the youngest, trails the others as they dive after her. **1984** 16–17 M E77 Pakuranga Coll. 21 Bullrush [games out of school] M2 **1989** MCGILL *Baby Boomers* 41 Bullrush involved as much of the school as possible, all at one end of the paddock, one person in the middle. At the cry of 'bullrush' we all ran and he had to catch one of us. **1992** *North & South* (Auckland) Feb. 37 The street..was still as good for a game of cricket or bullrush as it had been a generation before.

bullseye, *n.* [f. a resemblance in form to a 'bullseye' target.]

1. Also **bulleye.** *big-eye* (BIG *a.*).
1928-29 *TrNZI* LVIX. 380 *Pempheris compressa*, Bullseye. **1956** GRAHAM *Treasury NZ Fishes* 407 Bullseye *Pempheris adspersa*. **1982** AYLING *Collins Guide* (1984) 227 *Big eyes, Bullseyes: Pempheridida*e. **1989** PAULIN et al. *NZ Fish: A Complete Guide* 192 Family Pempheridae: *bulleyes*... Bulleyes are coastal fishes of tropical, subtropical and temperate seas.

2. A kind of marble.
1972 SUTTON-SMITH *Folkgames Children* 174 Then there were the terms referring to particular kinds of marbles: for example, agates..bull's eyes..cat's eyes.

3. A small cake or biscuit.
1934 *Marigold Book Recipes* 27 *Bulls' Eyes*..butter..icing sugar..flour..cornflower[*sic*]..B.P.. 2 eggs, roll into balls, press out flat, make hole in middle, fill with jam..bake.

bullseye, *v. Farming.* [f. the resemblance of the rear of a ring-crutched sheep to a 'bullseye' target.] *trans.* RING CRUTCH *v.*
1950 COOP *Shearing Ewes before Lambing* 28 With August shearing it is customary and generally advisable to 'ring-crutch' or 'bullseye' the ewes before putting the rams out at tupping.

bullswool /ˈbʊlzˌwʊl/. Also **bull's wool.** [AND 1933.] A euphemism for *bullshit*; nonsense. Also as an exclamation. (Quots. 1921, 1934 prob. involve a play on *bull's wool* 19th c. army slang for a coarse woollen cloth (so Partridge), and listed in Isabel B. Wingate (ed.) *Fairchild's Dictionary of Textiles* (6edn.) 1979 as 'Bull's Wool. Formerly a woolen [*sic*] trade term for very coarse, low grade woolens'.)
1909 *Truth* 6 Nov. 7 [letter ending]—I am etc., 'Boolz Wool.' [**1921** *Quick March* 11 Apr. 46 Suppose we had to discuss the much-advertised 'Bulls wool', and I wanted to say in Italian: 'Do not hesitate to use "Bulls wool" on any washable fabric.' **1934** *Otago Univ. Capping Book* 44 [Cartoon] In an interview after bathing at Mt. Maunganui in his red bullswool costume G.B.S[haw] said 'The Beach was the finest in the world.'] **1935** *Star Sun* (Christchurch) 16 Dec. 8 We live in a land of beautiful bullswool. **1946** SARGESON *That Summer* 149 I know she's dead. Bull's wool, I said, she's not dead. **1953** SUTTON-SMITH *Unorganized Games NZ Primary School Children* (VUWTS) II. 677 Some of the [slang] expressions listed by children in two schools are: 'Up the shoot..bullswool, go jump in the lake. **1963** MORRIESON *Scarecrow* 3 'Bull's wool rules the world' is his motto. **1984** BEARDSLEY *Blackball 08* 98 I've unlearned a lot of bullswool, that's all, and it allows me to think straight now. *Ibid.* 242 *bullswool* nonsense.

bull trout. *Obs.* Also occas. **bulla bulla, New Zealand bull trout.** [Transf. use of Brit. *bull-trout*, a freshwater fish of large size found in some British rivers: see OED.] Poss. KOKOPU 2 (2).
[**1842** HEAPHY *NZ* 49 In fresh-water rivers and streams, a fish resembling the bull-trout is to be met with at times, and which rises readily at a bait.] **1856** TANCRED *Nat. Hist. Canterbury* 16 There is also a bull-trout [in fresh water] and shoals of smelts. **1868** *Province of Otago* 32 A spotted fish—called 'bull-trout'—seldom weighing more than half-a-pound, and averaging much less, is found in clear streams. **1879** HAAST *Geol. Canterbury & Westland* 162 We also obtained [in Lake Hall] a number of the large New Zealand bull-trout (*Galaxias alepidotus*), which provided us with a good meal. **1889** [see BULLY *n.*¹ 1].

bully, *n.*¹ Also **buli bul, bulla bulla, bulley.** [f. Brit. dial. *bully* the name of a fish; poss. perceived as a familiar shortened form of *bullhead* or *cockabully*: see OED *n.*⁷]

1. Any of various small, stocky, scaled spiny-rayed freshwater fishes of the genus *Gobiomorphus* (fam. Eleotridae); occas. applied to *Galaxias* spp. (see quot. 1889). See also TOITOI *n.*² Cf. BULLHEAD, COCKABULLY.
1889 *TrNZI* XXI. 215 [Kingfishers] descend..to the..sunny flats on the Grey River, subsisting on insects and small bull-trout or 'bullys' until the arrival of the whitebait. **1892** SPACKMAN *Trout in NZ* 35 In all the [Wellington] rivers is the bullhead or 'bully' (*Eleotris gobioides*), on which the trout largely feed. **1898** MEREDITH *Reminisc. & Experiences* 17 I threw my line into a little water-hole..and..pulled out a fish about 1 lb in weight, which proved to be the New Zealand trout, or bulla bulla. **1902** DRUMMOND & HUTTON *Nature in NZ* 74 The bully, or bull-head, and the kokopu, or native trout, live entirely in fresh water. **1912** BAUGHAN *Brown Bread* 2 The beloved creek where bullies wait the hook. **1925-26** *NZJST* VIII. 296 The bulley, or toitoi, is known from the Bay of Islands to the Bluff, and abounds in almost every stream in New Zealand. **1933** *Press* (Christchurch) (Acland gloss.) 13 Jan. 13 *Cockabully*.—Often shortened to *bully*, especially by fishermen. **1946** *JPS* LV. 152 Kokopu..name corrupted by children to cock-a-bully and abbreviated bully. **1956** GRAHAM *Treasury NZ Fishes* 318 The bulley is one of the most abundant of our native freshwater fish... The Bulley, or Bullhead as it is known in some parts, forms an important food for the introduced Trout throughout New Zealand. **1967** NATUSCH *Animals NZ* 226 Bullies are not the same as cockabullies. The family these rather severe-faced fishes belong to is widely distributed over moderately warm and even tropical countries, and reaches its southernmost

distribution in New Zealand... Bullies are spiny-rayed fishes with the paired ventral fins placed well forward. **1981** DENNIS *Paparoas Guide* 189 Tiny, largely transparent bullies are also amongst the migrants..common bully..redfinned bully..and bluegilled bully... These are sometimes caught in large quantities by whitebaiters. **1988** SOMERSET *Sunshine & Shadow* 8 A quiet little brook..a home for bullies, tadpoles and sometimes even freshwater crayfish. **1990** MCDOWALL *NZ Freshwater Fishes* 295 The bullies, and their relatives, are found in coastal seas and freshwaters throughout the tropical Pacific and South-East Asia... Not many inhabit New Zealand where they reach their worldwide southern limits in Stewart Island. **1995** WINTER *All Ways Up the Hill* 135 Once outside [the school], he threw a couple of pieces of wood on the roof... Then he trotted off to the creek to catch buli buls [c1880s].

2. With a modifier: **blue-gilled, common, Cran's, giant (large), red-finned, upland**.

(1) **blue-gilled bully**. *Gobiomorphus hubbsi*. See esp. quot. 1963.
1955 STOKELL *Freshwater Fishes NZ* 59 Blue-gilled Bully... This is the smallest bully known in New Zealand. **1963** WOODS *Freshwater Fishes* 44 Blue-gilled Bully... Its name refers to the vivid iridescent blue-green curtain underneath the gill covers... The Blue-Gilled Bully lives under stones in the fastest parts of rivers. **1978** MCDOWALL *NZ Freshwater Fishes* 157 The Bluegilled Bully is a stocky, tubular little fish. **1984** MCDOWALL *NZ Whitebait Book* 21 The bluegilled bully is distinguished by a steely-blue stripe on the gill membranes and its distinctly dark-spotted, almost leopard-like pattern on the head.

(2) **common bully**. *Gobiomorphus cotidianus*.
1955 STOKELL *Freshwater Fishes NZ* 51 Common Bully... This fish is usually distinguishable from other bullies by the occurrence of seven rays in the first dorsal fin. **1967** NATUSCH *Animals NZ* 226 The common bully..is plentiful at river mouths, and occurs also in some upland lakes like Te Anau and Alexandria. **1978** MCDOWALL *NZ Freshwater Fishes* 158 The Common Bully is the species familiar to most people near lake shores and gently flowing streams. It is well-known because it is less secretive than other bullies. **1983** *Freshwater Catch* XVIII. 18 The use of submerged platforms in studies of plant growth..has been temporarily thwarted by the common bully... A succession of night dives revealed that the bullies were sucking up mouthfuls of sediments from the pots, swimming to the edge of the platforms, and spitting them over the edge.

(3) **Cran's bully**. [f. the name of H.J. ('Cran') Cranfield (b. 1936) fisheries biologist.] *Gobiomorphus basalis*.
1978 MCDOWALL *NZ Freshwater Fishes* 167 This species was 'rediscovered' in 1962 by H. J. Cranfield; as it has no common name, I suggest the name 'Cran's Bully'. **1983** *Land of Mist* 73 Both the common bully..and Cran's bully..may occur within the park. **1993** *Evening Post* 20 Jan. 22 Koru Aquaculture went to the High Court..seeking an injunction to stop the drainage, on the grounds that it was killing a native fish, the cran's bully.

(4) **giant** (occas. *obs.* **large**) **bully**. *Gobiomorphus gobioides*. See also BULLHEAD.
1955 STOKELL *Freshwater Fishes NZ* 55 Large Bully... Favourite habitats are lowland swamps and spring-fed creeks, within fifty feet of sea level. (Is same as giant bully but name never ever used today). **1963** WOODS *Freshwater Fishes* 46 Giant Bully... A giant indeed compared to its relatives and having a stout body, it appears very large for a bully. **1981** *Freshwater Catch* X. 4 The giant bully..closely resembles the common bully and for many years the two were regarded as one species. **1990** MCDOWALL *NZ Freshwater Fishes* 301 The giant bully is a chunky fish with a stout, tapering trunk.

(5) **redfinned bully**. *Gobiomorphus huttoni*. See esp. quot. 1963.
1955 STOKELL *Freshwater Fishes NZ* 55 Red finned Bully... This is the smallest of the scaled-headed bullies, its maximum length being about three inches. **1963** WOODS *Freshwater Fishes* 45 The red-finned bully does not always have red fins, but it need not be confused with other bullies because it has distinctive stripes on the head. **1990** MCDOWALL *NZ Freshwater Fishes* 296 The Redfinned Bully is one of the commonest and most widespread New Zealand freshwater fishes, and yet the handsome males of this species are virtually unknown to the general public, who usually express great surprise when they first see them.

(6) **upland bully**. *Gobiomorphus breviceps*.
1955 STOKELL *Freshwater Fishes NZ* 57 Upland Bully... This is probably the broadest-headed of the New Zealand bullies and probably inspired the original name 'bull-head', but the failure to distinguish between the various species occurring in this country led to the general application of the name and its familiarized version (debatable!). **1963** WOODS *Freshwater Fishes* 42 The Upland Bully..has a characteristic speckled pattern of orange and dark spots over its head and body. **1978** MCDOWALL *NZ Freshwater Fishes* 16 The Upland Bully is probably the commonest and most widespread bully in the South Island. Its common name is somewhat misleading, as the fish may occur commonly at quite low altitudes.

bully, *n.*² Also **bullie**. A pig-dog with some bulldog in its genetic makeup.
1983 *Listener* 23 July 51 The talk ranges from the value of the 'bullie' (collie-bulldog cross) in pig-hunting, the Hokonui coalmine and Minnie Dean's baby farming.

bully, *n.*³ [f. *bull*(dozer + -Y.] A shortened form of bulldozer.
1981 JOHNSTON *Fish Factory* 156 Anchor the bully over there and winch her across.

bullybul, var. BULL-A-BULL.

bully pot. *Obs.* [ad. *bouilli* boiled beef + *pot*.] A stock-pot. Cf. BILLY *n.*¹ 1 a, BOUILLI.
1846 WHITE *Journal* (ATLMS) 21 The young one looks as if he had be [*sic*] fed on cabbage and water, and imprisoned in a scrap and bully pot all the days of his life.

bulrush. Also **bullrush**. [Transf. use of British *bulrush* for local species: AND 1793.] Usu. RAUPO *n*. 1 a; less commonly applied to other tall robust marsh plants.
1777 ANDERSON *Journal* Feb. in Cook *Journals* (1967) III. 805 Amongst the known kinds of plants are..Nettles..rushes..Bullrushes, Flax. **1820** MARSDEN *Lett. & Jrnls.* Aug. (1932) 289 He had got the stump of a tree placed where he intended I should sit, and had made a cushion of bulrushes which was placed upon it. **1835** YATE *NZ* (1970) 153 [New Zealanders' houses] are built of bulrushes and lined with the leaves of the palm-tree, neatly platted [*sic*] together. **1840** POLACK *Manners & Customs* II. 82 Among the circumstances that entitle a native to become a claimant of land, unpurchased by a European, the following may be mentioned:.. For having been in the habit of cutting bulrushes (*raupo*) in the marshes (if any) for covering houses. **1869, 1881** [see PUNGAPUNGA]. **1892** WILLIAMS *Dict. NZ Lang.* 70 *Raupo... Typha angustifolia*; bulrush. **1906** CHEESEMAN *Manual NZ Flora* 743 T[ypha] angustifolia, Linn... Bulrush; Raupo. **1939** [see RAUPO 1 a]. **1966** *Encycl. NZ* III. 712 Raupo, bulrush . . koreire, raupo . . *Typha muelleri*.

bulrush caterpillar. *Obs.* [f. the resemblance of the spore-bearing stalk to the flower-head of the bulrush (RAUPO).] VEGETABLE CATERPILLAR.
1855 TAYLOR *Te Ika A Maui* 422 Description of the Bulrush Caterpillar (*Sphaeria Robertsia..Aweto-Hotete*). This singular plant, which is a native of New Zealand, may be classed amongst the most remarkable productions of the vegetable kingdom. **1888** BARLOW *Kaipara* 184 [I] will proceed to describe the most curious of the New Zealand native insects I have seen, called the *bulrush caterpillar..Aweto*. **1986** ANDREWS *Southern Ark* 108 His account of the Bulrush Caterpillar reflected a fascination with the 'vegetable caterpillar' which was later revealed as a caterpillar of *Wiseana* spp. infected with a fungus (*Cordyceps robertsi*) which transformed it internally.

bum.

1. In the phr. **to be up one's bum to the neck**, to be very snobbish or 'stuck-up'.
1984 BEATON *Outside In* 39 Ginny: Stuck up! She thinks she's God all-fucken-mighty,.. She's fucken up her bum to her neck!

2. Special Comb., often suggesting sycophancy or homosexuality: **bumboy**, a sycophant, or (*prison*) an assistant superintendent; **bum buzzard** WW2, one who sits out the war, usu. at (or on) Base; **bumchum** [AND 1972], an intimate; **bum-slide** *v.* mountaineering, to slide down a snow-slope in a sitting position; **bum-sliding** *vbl. n.*; **bumsquat** WW2, to sit out the war at Base (see also *bum buzzard* above).
1959 SHADBOLT *New Zealanders* (1986) 50 The job you people promised me. Now your **bum boy** out in the office tells me I can't have it. **1986** IHIMAERA *Matriarch* 374 'Erina darling,' she smiled, oozing charm and sweetness, 'be a dear and see whether your mother and father are tucked up safely away from our gossip.' 'When did your last bumboy die,' Erina grumbled as she got up. **1982** NEWBOLD *Big Huey* 246 **Bumboy** (n) Assistant superintendent. **1947** DAVIN *For Rest of Our Lives* 148 As Tony displayed his identity card to the Cypriots at the gate he savoured..the palpable back-from-the-desert air with which he passed these base wallahs and **bum buzzards**, deflating the pale pigs' bladders of their importance as they flitted from office to office. **1984** 17 M E98 Pakuranga Coll. 29 My **bumchum**. **1991** *Dominion* (Wellington) 28 Dec. 1 He said the avalanche was probably started by them as they **'bum-slid'** down the slope... They sat down and started sliding down... **Bum-sliding** is good fun but you should only do it if you have a run-out at the end. **1947** DAVIN *For Rest of Our Lives* 288 By God, if it isn't old Frank. What the devil are you doing here. Thought you were **bumsquatting** at GHQ or something.

bump. *Rugby Union*. *Obs*. To fend an opponent by use of the shoulder or hip-thrust. Also *vbl. n.*
1900 *NZ Illustr. Mag.* III. 237 A favourite mode of attack in New Zealand is the bump, that is the player with the leather crouches himself while going at full speed, and butts with all his force (using hip or shoulder) at the opponent who is essaying to tackle. **1902** ELLISON *The Art of Rugby Football* 26 Bumping is done by the timely transmission of the weight and momentum of a runner to a would-be tackler. *Ibid.* 71 I never saw a Britisher who knew anything about the 'bump'.

bumper. *Obs.* [Poss. f. *bu*(tt + st)*ump* + -ER: AND 1899.] A cigarette butt.

1916 *Anzac Book* 47 ['Enessy] lights up a bumper... Along comes the bloomin' officer... The officer..asks 'Ennessy: 'Are you smoking?'.. So 'Enessy sticks 'is lighted bumper down south in 'is overcoat pocket. **1956** SUTHERLAND *Green Kiwi* (1960) 203 Coins, cigarette 'bumpers' and odds and ends fell from George's pockets on to the ground. **1968** *NZ Contemp. Dict. Suppl.* (Collins) 5 *bumper n.* cigarette butt.

bump noses: see NOSE *n*.¹ a.

bumpout, *n.* An extension to the external wall of a room used as an alcoved breakfast nook, etc.

1990 JEWET-PATTERSON *Real Estate Advertising Flier* The rimu kitchen with breakfast bar in sunny glass bumpout, leads to large family/dining room with French doors to private deck.

bun, *n.*¹ [Orig. unknown: poss. a variant of or play on *scone* head.] In the phr. **to do one's bun,** to lose one's head; to lose one's temper or self-control. Cf. *do one's block (scone)* (BLOCK *n*.³ 2, SCONE *n*.).

1939-45 *Expressions and Sayings 2NZEF (Nat. Archiv. TS WAII DA 420/1)* Do the Scone (or bun)—Lose the temper—panic. **1944** *Korero* (AEWS Background Bulletin) 17 July 24 The most important of Army slang expressions..has been 'doing the scone' with its variant 'doing the bun', used for losing one's grip or one's temper. **1950** THE SARGE *Excuse My Feet* 128 'O.K.! O.K.! don't do your bun,' he answered. **1955** *BJ Cameron Collection* (TS July) do one's block do one's bun do one's lolly (v) To get excited, lose one's head. **1960** CRUMP *Good Keen Man* 76 Jock did his bun properly. 'So my money's not good enough, eh mate?' he snarled at the driver. **1980** LELAND *Kiwi-Yankee Dict.* 32 *Do your bun or do your scone:* is to blow your fuse. This is a temper tantrum but is less general and more directional than to throw a wobbly. One does one's bun at someone. **1993** *Evening Post* (Wellington) 9 July 13 A Wellington fisherman..has said he 'did his bun' when he found out the fish receivers had rejected some of his catch.

bun, *n.*² *Obs.* [f. the shape.] In full **bun hat.** A bowler hat.

1914 *History of North Otago* (1978) 131 In the 90's the younger generation discarded their beards... The flat-topped hat gave place to the 'bun' or 'hard-hitter'. **1917** INGRAM *Anzac Diary* (1987) 9 What a motley looking mob we were!..Some wearing 'bun' hats, some straws and others felts. **1924** *Otago Witness* (Dunedin) 15 July 74 Our victim removed an antiquated bowler hat (referred to by the vulgar as a 'bun'). **1941** BAKER *NZ Slang* 52 A bowler hat has become *bun* in colloquial speech, taking its place beside the Australian *boxer* or *peadodger* and the American *derby*. **1947** *NZ Woman's Weekly* 17 Apr. 17 His hat, an old 'bun', went bowling up the street. **1955** DUFF *Shepherd's Calendar* (1961) 247 'What do you think of the bun hats?' Ng. asked, as the saddle horses were passing. **1967** MILLER *Ink on My Fingers* 27 With his bun hat, steel-rimmed glasses..he was a well-known figure [in Dunedin]. **1992** LATHAM *Golden Reefs* 418 'Jock' Robertson is remembered by many Greymouth people as a small man always completely dressed with a 'bun' or bowler hat.

bundle. In the phr. **to drop (do) one's bundle.**

1. [AND 1897.] To lose self-control; to become uncontrollably excited by fear or anger; to 'lose one's head'. Cf. *do one's bun* (BUN *n.*¹)

1935 STRONG in Partridge *Slang Today* 287 He absolutely dropped his bundle, and, to make matters worse, I had started off with a duck's breakfast. **1947** NEWTON *Wayleggo* 115 My confidence immediately disappeared. However, I could not drop my bundle, so into the jungle I went [after the wounded beast]. **1960** SCRYMGEOUR *Memories Maoriland* 173 From thence on Mabel [after losing the tennis set] began to drop her bundle... Jim fought valiantly..but still Mabel wilted. **1976** HILLIARD *Send Somebody Nice* 97 She was not the sort that anyone was likely to do his bundle over. **1984** BEARDSLEY *Blackball 08* 124 Well, he wouldn't drop his bundle. There might be something doing at the mine today.

2. Of a woman, to give birth. See also DROP *v.* 1 a.

1948 BALLANTYNE *Cunninghams* (1976) 25 If he doesn't hurry she'll be dropping her bundle at our place. **1972** p.c. G.J. Griffiths (Dunedin) *drop one's bundle* has changed slightly to mean also 'to give way to an element of panic', or 'to lose control'; about the 1940s, & probably other times it also meant for a woman to give birth. **1989** *Pacific Way* Jan. 10 Suppose a friend says to me..'[It] seems that he's shacked up with some pluty Remmers sheila and she's about to drop her bundle.'.. A non-New Zealander will probably require a translation... [He] is now cohabiting with a wealthy woman from the affluent Auckland suburb of Remuera. This woman is soon to give birth.

bung, *a.* [AND orig. Austral. pidgin: prob. ad. Aborig. Yagara (Brisbane region) *baŋ* 'dead'.]

1. In predicative use as **go bung.** [AND 1885.] **a.** Of a business or businessman, to go bankrupt, to fail.

1887 *Auckland Weekly News* 22 Oct. 21 You Auckland men, look to mining as [the] only salvation from going 'bung'. **1888** A TRAMP, ESQ. *Ramblings* 21 The local Press is being run at a loss now..and when the big dailies pour in..something must go 'bung.' **1894** *NZPD* 2 Aug. 292 Upon the Bank of New Zealand there'd have been a run And, a thousand chances to one, It would have jolly well gone bung. **1902** SATCHELL *Land of Lost* 47 The merchant princes who have gone bung, and the geniuses who have gone bunger. **1951** LAWSON *Gold in Their Hearts* 169 The Bank of New Zealand which someone had discovered was insolvent and would go bung unless the Government saved it. **1978** SUTHERLAND *Elver* 27 Dad had bought it cheap when Mr Brooks went bung.

b. Of a working mechanism, object, scheme, etc., to become broken or ruined; to fail, to stop; to come to an end. Also occas. **gone-bung** *n.*, a (personal) failure (see quot. 1907).

1894 *Waikato Times* in Norris *Settlers in Depression* (1964) 227 [Advt] The state now guarantees the Bank, We guarantee the leather. For honest boots that won't go bung, And stand all tear and weather, Go straight to D. Salmon. **1905** *Truth* 12 Aug. 1 The man who has gone bankrupt for a large amount of splash..all his schemes going bunger. **1907** *Truth* 28 Sept. 4 It is not often that measures of usefulness emanate from the Legislative Council, but still that body of political gone-bungs, or dead-beats, must occasionally do something to show that they are still in the political game. **1920** *Hawkes Bay Herald* 9 Mar. 3 I was hoping the springs would go bung. **1951** LAWSON *Gold in Their Hearts* 48 Charleston might go bung some day, and then where would we be. **1962** HOGAN *Billy-Can Ballads* 31 In '69 the field went 'bung', And the diggers moved on, broke. **1978** HILLIARD *Glory & Dream* 8 'Crook valve. More expense.' 'You mean it's gone bung?'

2. Broke, having no money left.

1948 MACFARLANE *This NZ* 137 We were bung, completely down and out.

3. Esp. of parts of the body, injured, broken, failed in use.

1952 WILSON *Julien Ware* 68 'Why aren't you playing?'... 'Got a bung ankle. Don't want to hurt it again when there's a big match next week.' **1963** ADSETT *Magpie Sings* 96 Pet's two front teats were what his father called 'bung' but the back ones made up for them. **1968** SLATTER *Pagan Game* 189 I played one game too many and got a bung knee for life out of it. **1965** ANDERSON & AITKEN *Speech and Idiom Maori Children* 37 [Maori child speaks] He's got a bung eye. **1970** PORTER *Nor'west Arch* 61 I developed a very sore ankle which I must have twisted... I didn't fancy living in a tent with a bung leg. **1979** TOOGOOD *Out of the Bag* 38 I was worried that my bung eye would get me rejected as unfit.

Hence **bung out** *v.*, to die.

1908 *Truth* 9 May 1 It's good policy to keep the premiums paid up. Rather-r-r-r, especially if it's the wife's, and she bungs out first.

4. In the collocation **bung juice**, strong alcoholic liquor.

1906 PICARD *Ups & Downs* 7 Got too full of bung juice, dropped dead.

bunga, var. BONGA, BOONGA; PONGA.

bungalow. [Spec. use of *bungalow*: see OED.] As **California(n) bungalow**, see quots. 1987, 1991.

1978 SINCLAIR & HARREX *Looking Back* 118 After about 1910 probably the commonest type of new house was the bungalow, which was influenced by the earlier Californian bungalow. **1987** *Listener* 8 Aug. 61 The house..was a Californian bungalow, New Zealand version, built in the late 1920s... Our house had a corner-bow window, with a window-seat, a small side porch and a back verandah. There was a coloured-glass window picturing a sailing ship and—the other mark of the Californian bungalow—a feature area of wood shingles beneath the bow window. **1989** DUDER *Alex in Winter* 83 Along the [Auckland] street..stood rows of fifty-year-old kauri villas and thirty-year-old California bungalows; comfortably bourgeois. **1991** SHAW *NZ Architecture* 47 By 1910 the impact of the Californian bungalow was being felt and many architects, while continuing to design houses according to the traditional villa plan, began to incorporate bungalow features into house facades. Roof angles were flattened, fretted and turned verandah decorations were simplified, and double-hung sash windows were replaced with casement-and-fanlights. The transition between villa and bungalow lasted some ten years; Jeremy Salmond has noted that 'after 1918 no speculative builder with any commercial sense would have bothered to advertise a new house in the villa style'.

bunger, bungi(e), bungy, varr. PONGA.

bun hat: see BUN *n*.²

bunk, *n.* [Transf. and extended use of *bunk* a box or recess in a ship's cabin serving as a bed: see OED *n.*¹ 1 a.]

1. Used elsewhere, but in widespread and freq. use in New Zealand for the 'shelf-beds' in men's quarters on rural properties, in work-camps, or in tramping huts and other communal sleeping quarters. See also *double-bunking* (DOUBLE B), MAORI BUNK.

1845 WAKEFIELD *Adventure NZ* I. 205 A 'bunk', or wooden shelf, supported Colonel Wakefield's bed. *Ibid.* I. 330 For the information of those who do not know what a *bunk* is, I must explain that it is a bed place built against the wall of a house or ship. **1847** CHAPMAN *Lett. to His Father* 24 Nov. (ATLTS) in Miller *Early*

Victorian NZ (1958) 140 The squatters' huts..are native built whare's... The sleeping place is a 'bunk' or standing bed place as on board ship. **1855** PHILLIPS *Rockwood Jrnl.* 30 Oct. (TS) 18 John jobbing—Harry putting up Bunk in back room. **1867** BARKER *Station Life* (1874) 190 [The bushman] began to make plans for F- and me to stop [at a back-country station hut] all night, offering to give up his 'bunk' (some slabs of wood made into a shelf, with a tussock mattress and a blanket). **1873** PYKE *Wild Will Enderby* (1889, 1974) III. iv 85 The bunks—rude structures of bush poles, with flour bag sacking—had been torn down. **1921** FOSTON *At the Front* 54 [New chum asks] 'What is a bunk, sir?' 'Oh, a rough bedstead.' **1933** *Press* (Christchurch) (Acland Gloss.) 23 Sept. 13 *Bunk.*— A bed, whether made of wood in a hut, like a berth in a ship, or of fern and tussock in a tent. **1947** BEATTIE *Early Runholding* 12 The ship term 'bunk' was applied to the beds built against the walls in the men's huts. **1989** *NZ Eng. Newsletter* III. 22 *bunk:* The name for a shearer's bed. Years ago shearer's bunks were often in three tiers and made up with straw filled palliasses for mattresses and borrowed woolpacks for warmth.

2. In widened modern colloquial use, any bed, esp if makeshift. Also **to go to bunk**.

1903 *Huia* 12 Think I'll go to bunk. **1961** BAXTER *Collected Poems* (1980) 237 Hunting pignuts on all fours In the great funfair none do well. Tom likes boys and Bob likes whores And both will share a bunk in Hell.

bunk, *v.* [A var. of (DOUBLE-)BANK.] *trans.* To carry (someone) on a bicycle (bar); DOUBLE-BANK *v.* 2.

1963 ADSETT *Magpie Sings* 175 I'm not fussy so long as she keeps her skirts out of the bloody spokes. Last [girl] I bunked home took me hours to unwind her.

bunking, *vbl. n.* [f. *bunk* to decamp.] Playing truant from school.

1981 WILKINSON *NZ Way* 24 'Truancy' is by no means an objective word... 'Why are you bunking?' I said to a Maori pupil I met in the Square an hour before school officially finished... 'Sir, I'm on my way home. Bunking is when you hang around the square instead of going to school or home.' **1988** MCGILL *Dict. Kiwi Slang* 23 *bunking* wagging school.

bunny-hop, *v. intr.* Of a motor vehicle, to move by stops and starts.

1990 *Dominion* (Wellington) 19 Oct. 9 Paiti returned alone. Police stopped him on April 19 driving Ms Junge's car because it was 'bunny-hopping'. **1991** *Metro* (Auckland) Jan. 91 Two young cops..saw the blue Suzuki bunnyhopping down Ryan Place.

bur, var. BURR.

burg. [Orig. US: see OED *burg* 2, town, city.] A place, a town; occas. **my burg**, my place, home (quot. 1976).

1925 CLYDE *NZ, Country & People* 47 In smaller towns there is sometimes indifference to anything outside 'the murmur of their burg'. **1927** DEVANNY *Old Savage* 167 You know, there's not much to choose between the men and women in this little burg. **1976** MORRIESON *Pallet on Floor* 29 What say we go down to my burg and scoff some home-brew. **1978** MANTELL *Murder in Fancydress* 131 Coupla years. Must be. When I first came to this burg. **1985** O'SULLIVAN *Shuriken* 21 Tiny:.. Not as if this [*sc.* prison camp] is a submarine or something. Jacko: Might as well bloody be. Locked up in this burg.

Burgon. *Shearing. Obs.* [Ellipt. f. the trading name *Burgon and Ball*, as the makers of former single-bow hand-shears.] The name of an old-fashioned single-bow hand-shears.

1952 MEEK *Station Days* 74 With his 'Burgon's' then to the shed [he] tore, Where into the sheep he bogged. *Ibid.* 110 Burgon and ball: Hand shears with a single bow. Present-day shears have a double bow. **1989** *NZ Eng. Newsletter* III. 22 *Burgon and Ball:* Brand of sheep-shears with a single bow.

burgoo /bɜˈguː/. Also **bergoo**, **bergou**. [f. nautical and Brit. dial., ultimately ad. Arabic *burghul* (cf. OED): used elsewhere, but freq. in NZ.]

1. Coarse, esp. institutional, porridge; in later use joc. for any porridge. Also *fig.*

1862 HODDER *Memories NZ Life* 7 Breakfast..generally consisted of a pot of bergou each—a farinaceous dish, known by the Scotch as 'porridge'. **1864** *Saturday Rev.* IV. 15 The [prisoners] partake of..a pewter plateful of porridge, or bergoo. **1871** MONEY *Knocking About NZ* 111 Though rationed off for a short time to a pannikin of burgoo morning and evening..we ran short. **1907** *Truth* 19 Oct. 6 Probably the collections were too small or the burgoo preaching did not suit the high-class natives of Pareora. **1918** *Chron. NZEF* 7 June 204 I want 'em for the 'bergou' in the morning. *Ibid.* 16 Aug. 37 See-saw, Johnny McGraw Ate Burgoo till he strained his jaw. **1941** *Troopship Tattoo* (H.M. Transport 32, Troopship pub.) 9 Burgoo: porridge (used by seamen). **1959** SLATTER *Gun in My Hand* 43 Ya couldn't get work shovellin burgoo to a Scotchman. **1971** *Listener* 19 Apr. 56 It was hard yakka, nothing but a plate of burgoo and a handful of scroggin since sparrow-chirp. **1980** MACKENZIE *While We Have Prisons* 95 burgoo porridge

2. BROSE.

1933 [see BROSE]. **1952** LYON *Faring South* 122 Some of the old country farmers supplied beer with the food [for mowers], but as a general rule, excesses led to tea or water from soaked oatmeal, called burgoo, as being more suitable.

buridi, var. PURIRI.

burl, *n.*¹ Also **berl**, **birl**. [App. a var. of Brit. dial. *birl* a whirring sound, a rapid turn; hence, a 'spin'.]

1. *Two-up.* **Fair burl!** Of pennies, 'fair spin!'

1917 *Chron. NZEF* 16 May 137 So up they [*sc.* coins] went and spinning well, And betters cried 'Fair burl!'

2. [AND 1924.] In the phr. **to give it a burl**, to give it a go, a 'spin', a try.

1945 *NZEF Times* 22 Jan. 4 Something's got to be done to encourage the right class of hommes to give it a burl. **1947** DAVIN *For Rest of Our Lives* 227 And so while [my wounded leg] was still ugly and they weren't worrying I'd give it a burl. And I made it, got clean away. **1955** *BJ Cameron Collection* (TS July) *burl* give it a burl (v) To give it a go. **1959** SLATTER *Gun in My Hand* 181 Come round, she said, it'll be open slather. Might as well give it a birl. **1963** MASON *Pohutukawa Tree* 44 Mrs Johnson..: I don't know how I'll sing without a piano. Johnson: Give it a burl, old girl. **1976** MCCLENAGHAN *Travelling Man* 21 He's all right. We'll give it a burl for a while. **1981** GEE *Meg* 192 Come on. Give it a birl. **1992** *North & South* (Auckland) June 8 He'd thought: 'Yeah, OK, give it a berl,' and found he liked it.

Hence **burl** *v. intr.*, to roll or spin.

1986 O'SULLIVAN *Pilate Tapes* 38 Yet Rat gets toey As the veil rends, Mr P. edgy as a knife drawer When the sky burls up.

burl, *n.*² [f. Old French *bourle* tuft of wool: see OED *n.*¹ 1 and 2.]

1. A matted tuft in wool.

1857 TIFFIN in Hursthouse *NZ* (1857) II. 393 The fleeces should not be tied up with strings; the lint mixes with the wool, and makes what are called 'burls;' no tying is requisite.

2. A knot in wood; BURR *n.*²

1952-53 *NZ Forest Service Gloss.* (TS) Burl. A tumour-like woody swelling on the trunk or branch of a tree. **1980** Goldie Brown Collection (Auckland) *burl:* Common in NZ pine timber.

burn, *v.* See also BURN OFF.

1. Mainly *NI. intr.* To clear or improve land by burning standing or felled cover. **a.** *intr.*

1846 PHARAZYN *Journal* (ATLMS) 27 Commenced burning on the flat on this side the creek up the Valley. **1856** *Richmond-Atkinson Papers* (1960) I. 201 As there was a nice breeze we lighted our clearings. Bill and the Ronalds also burnt—in all about 46 acres. **1899** BELL *In Shadow of Bush* 198 A few, fearful of a change in the weather, had already burned with fairly satisfactory results; and the general topic of conversation..was of bush-burning.

b. *trans.*

1854 *Richmond-Atkinson Papers* (1960) I. 143 They wanted to burn the large clearing that day. **1863** BUTLER *First Year* x 151 You will have burnt a large patch of feed at the outset. Burn it in early spring, on a day when rain appears to be at hand.

2. Mainly or orig. *SI.* To fire (tussock grassland, scrub or fern country) to bring on new growth; to create stock feed by burning; to periodically fire pasture. See also BURN OFF 2, BURN OVER. (The effect of the verb seems applied to the land or country rather than to the vegetation to be burnt.)

a. *trans.* Often as **to burn country**, **to burn a run**.

1857 HARPER *Lett. from NZ* 1 Sept. (1914) 21 One day we went on an expedition [on Mt. Peel station] into the mountain valleys to 'burn country', a process adopted here for the improvement of pasture. **1864** CHUDLEIGH *Diary* 22 Sept. (1950) 145 We are going to burn the country to prepare it for sheep. **1867** BARKER *Station Life* (1870) 194 I am quite sorry that the season for setting fire to the long grass, or, as it is technically called, 'burning the run', is fairly over at last. **1891** *NZJSc* (NS) I. 199 They disappear as the country is burnt by the runholder. **1947-48** BEATTIE *Pioneer Recolls.* (1956) 49 When they got on to the Waimea Plains a dense smoke assailed them from fires set alight by newly-arrived runholders 'burning the country' around the Five Rivers vicinity.

b. *intr.*

1865 CHUDLEIGH *Diary* 3 Oct. (1950) 201 Went on the hills burning and Greenly lit a fire on a spur that had grass and flax six feet high on it. **1940** STUDHOLME *Te Waimate* (1954) 96 There are many things to be taken into consideration when burning... If your country is warm and early, with a small rainfall, it is a good rule to burn early in the season.

Hence **burning** *vbl. n.*, the process or action of clearing land by fire.

1989 RICHARDS *Pioneer's Life* 49 Farm work, scrub cutting, logging up and burning went on as usual.

burn, *n.*¹ [Orig. N. American: see OED *n.*³ 1 b and c; AND 1849.]

1. a. (An instance of) clearing bush, scrub, unpalatable grass, etc. from land by means of fire, to bring it into cultivation or to improve pasture. Cf. BUSH-BURN 2.

[*Note*] In 19th century NI use, mainly applied to burning bush previously felled to clear land for agriculture; in SI and later general use, applied to burning rank growth to improve pasture.

1850 *Otago Jrnl.* VI. 108 Everything depends on a successful burn. **1854** *Richmond-Atkinson Papers* (1960) I. 172 Arthur is going to make a clearing on our land this year, and..after the burn would put up a slab house of two rooms. **1867** BARKER *Station Life* (1870) 194 [The wind] must not be *too* violent, or the flames will fly over the grass, just scorching it instead of making 'a clean burn'. **1877** [see BURNING SEASON]. **1887** *Auckland Weekly News* 26 Feb. 8 We had just had what is called a 'good burn'. **1899** [see BUSH-BURNING *vbl. n.*]. **1921** GUTHRIE-SMITH *Tutira* (1926) 170 The 'burn' of 1902..was not what is technically known as a 'clean' fire... This fire left unburnt ridge-caps, the tops, sometimes even the upper slopes. **1936** BELSHAW et al. *Agric. Organiz. NZ* 359 These [sown pastures] may be divided into two groups—(a) sown on cultivated land, and (b) surface sown after forest, scrub or fern burn. **1955** WILSON *Land of My Children* 25 A bad burn [of cleared bush] may spell ruin to a man with limited capital. **1973** WALLACE *Generation Gap* 228 Although we'd had a good burn the giant logs and candlewick stumps hemmed the stock in. **1981** MCLAUCHLAN *Farming of NZ* 177 If the summer rains came and spoilt the burn, it meant a great loss for the farmer.

b. As **white burn**, **black burn**. See quot.

1951 LEVY *Grasslands NZ* (1970) 87 It was not so difficult to replace the forest with grass where the climate made intense white-ash burns possible after the felling of the forest... But in higher rain-fall belts, when poor burns (black burns) only occur, much forest litter remained unconsumed. *Ibid.* 241 A steady, hot fire was desired in order to burn all fallen timber and leaf mould, seeds, and fern spores lying dormant on the forest floor. A white ash, called a *white burn*, was the objective; a black burn resulted from a less intense fire where the heat was not sufficient to burn the timber, leaf mould, seeds, and spores on the forest floor.

2. The area of land so 'burnt' or cleared by fire.

1879 KIERNAN *Diary* 5 Feb. in Guthrie-Smith *Tutira* (1921) 125 Saw large mob of sheep on the new burn outside Hughie's fence. **1893** *TrNZI* XXV. 504 Perhaps to their position on the edge of a previous burn..[the moa-bones] may in a measure owe their preservation. **1905** BAUCKE *White Man Treads* 147 Suddenly, like a slap in the face from an unseen hand, where one had looked for fresh wonders of forest beauty, spread a settler's recent burn! Gaunt and charred, prone on their mother's bosom, lay the mighty monarchs of the woods. **1915** *TrNZI* XLVII. 79 This fern springs up in countless thousands on neglected burns. **1935** MCKENZIE *Gael Fares Forth* 80 Settlers of a later generation discontinued the practice of clearing a new 'burn' of all logs. **1951** LEVY *Grasslands NZ* (1970) 243 [Heading] Sowing the Burn. **1981** CHARLES *Black Billy Tea* 74 There is a good cheque you can earn, seeding a burn, Or cutting some cow-cocky's scrub.

burn, *n.*² *Otago Scots*. [f. Sc. dial.] A creek or stream.

1871 *TrNZI* III. 271 This river is fed by the Swine and other burns. **1873** WILSON *Diary* 26 Jan. in Wierzbicka *Wilson Family* (1973) 152 Below us to the East the creek, a small tiny burn, rushes and tears away over crags and stones making a great noise. **1939** BEATTIE *First White Boy Born Otago* 132 We have crossed several burns of respectable size and many minor creeks during our journey, but we have now to cross a river. **1944** BEATTIE *Maori Place-names Otago* 36 On the other side of the [Taieri] river the flow of 'animal' burns [Ewe, Gimmer, Sow, etc.] is interrupted by the intrusion of a mere 'creek', even if it is named Eden after the place where Adam named all the animals.

burning season. *Hist.* For felled bush, the late summer. Occas. in modern use, **firing season**.

1877 *NZ Country Jrnl.* Oct. quoted in *NZJAg.* (1958) Apr. XCVI. 375 The time for felling the bush in order to ensure a good burn in at the proper burning season—which is generally most favourable about the beginning of February—is from August to October. **1904** *NZ Illustr. Mag.* Nov. 112 Before the burning season had arrived they [*sc.* pigeons] had successfully hatched..three young ones. **1981** MCLAUCHLAN *Farming of NZ* 176 As the homes were set in clearings in the middle of the bush, the firing season was an anxious one for all.

burn off, *v.*

[Cf. AND *burn* (*off*) *v.* 1 *trans.*, 1793.]

1. *quasi-trans.*, *quasi-intr.* or *absol.* To clear land for agricultural or pastoral use by burning. **a.** By burning felled bush or logs.

1817 NICHOLAS *Voyage NZ* I. 342 On our way we had to pass through another wood, part of which the natives had cut down, and were burning off, for the purposes of cultivation. **1842** *NZ Jrnl.* III. 5 Nature, in a few years after the trees have been cut down and burnt off, will..have completed the task necessary to have a farm in fine working condition. **1857** HURSTHOUSE *NZ* II. 331 The fallen-stuff lies withering and drying through the summer, and is burnt-off in early autumn. **1902** [see SELECT *v.*]. **1986** RICHARDS *Off the Sheep's Back* 45 Each year after a new block of fallen bush had been burned off, we would have a wonderful harvest of cape gooseberries.

b. By burning fern, scrub, or light vegetation.

1819 MARSDEN *Lett. & Jrnls.* (1932) 176 The land is generally clear from timber, excepting small brushwood and fern, which can with little trouble be cut down and burnt off. **1840** *Rep. Protector of Aborigines* Dec. in *GBPP 1842 (No.569)* 96 No further labour to commence ploughing than burning off the fern. **1849** ALLOM *Letter* in Earp *Handbook* (1852) 126 Grass everywhere makes its appearance wherever fern and brushwood are burnt off.

2. *quasi-trans.* To burn (country) to improve or renew pasture. See also BURN *v.* 2.

1860 DUPPA in Crawford *Sheep & Sheepmen Canterbury* (1949) 45 Burn off portions of a run for winter feed.

Hence **burning-off** *vbl. n.* [AND 1804], the burning of bush, logs or scrub in land-clearing, or of rank growth to improve pasture; **burnt off** *ppl. a.*, of land, cleared by fire.

1844 CHAPMAN in Drummond *Married & Gone to NZ* (1960) 69 Xmas is the time for **burning off**, and the clearing must go on. **1856** FITTON *NZ* 99 The clearing and burning off for the entry of the plough [vary] from ten to twenty shillings per acre. **1862** *Otago Witness* (Dunedin) 23 Aug. 6 The soil being mostly alluvial, the 'burnings-off' and grass-fostering influence of stock will rapidly improve it. **c1875** MEREDITH *Adventuring in Maoriland* (1935) 134 Burning-off is the easiest part of the business [of clearing flax land]. **1891** WALLACE *Rural Econ. Austral. & NZ* 232 Falling is done in winter, and burning off in the middle or end of summer. **1907** *TrNZI* XXXIX. 82 The burning-off of the alpine scrub and the bush in the gullies..would deprive the bird of its normal food. **1963** BACON *In the Sticks* 154 When they've done the burning off, the aeroplanes are going to come in and plant the grass. **1973** in *NZ Short Stories III* (1975) 212 Those concrete posts must be good for burning-off. **1938** HYDE *Godwits Fly* (1970) 128 This was **burnt-off** country, black-and-green on top, blue papa underneath, too poor for the grass to be more than a bristling crop. **1984** BOYD *City of the Plains*

27 Ploughing burnt-off land proved 'a sorry business for horses', until he put a heavy piece of leather next to the hoof before he nailed on the shoe.

burn-off, *n.* An instance of *burning-off* (BURN OFF *v.* 2.); also the land cleared by burning off. See also BUSH BURN.

1850 *Otago Jrnl.* VI. 103 The completion of the burn off. **1861** MORGAN *Journal* 27 Feb. (1963) 28 Not an over excellent burn off—there having been of late a good deal of wet. **1869** MAY *Guide to Farming* 18 In due time we fired [the bush] and had a clean burn off. **1928** MORTON *Along the Road* 64 Smoke of fresh burn-offs. **1975** in *NZ Short Stories III* (1975) 141 So I ask my Dad about a burn-off, and we take the kerosine and matches and set the whole hillside alight. **1976** HILLIARD *Send Somebody Nice* 18 We passed..three Maori women..stooping to cut puha from a manuka burn-off. **1987** HARTLEY *Swagger on Doorstep* 75 The farmers..roundly cursed the settler who had started them [*sc.* fires] with an imprudent burn-off. **1993** *Sunday Star* (Auckland) 18 July A9 The Department of Conservation has invoked an unused power to save 2000ha of red tussock in Central Otago from a burnoff.

burn over. To set fire over (an area of vegetation). Also as *ppl. a.* **burnt over.**

1882 *TrNZI* XIV. 77 The surface vegetation..had been systematically burnt over, year after year, in order to encourage fresh growth for the use of stock. **1968** SLATTER *Pagan Game* 20 There were the scrublands of blackened second growth..the reproachful columns of burnt-over bush.

burnt, *ppl. a.* In various phrases and collocations.

1. *Mustering*. In the phr. **to take the burnt chops** or **to take to the burnt spur**, see 1934 quot.

1934 *Press* (Christchurch) (Acland Gloss.) 13 Jan. 13 *Burnt chops.*—An expression somewhat akin to the expression *Burnt Spur* which denoted the business of high country mustering: 'So and so has taken to the b[urnt]s[pur]' meaning he has taken on mustering. **1941** BAKER *NZ Slang* 54 Here are a few more [rural terms] that appear to have originated this century; *to take the burnt chops* (said of a person), to take on work as a musterer.

2. As **burnt feed** [AND 1837], juicy, tender grass that springs up from the ashes of a pastoral 'burn'.

1863 BUTLER *First Year* x 152 Burnt feed means contented and well-conditioned sheep... Your sheep will not ramble, for if they have plenty of burnt pasture they are contented where they are.

3. As **burnt gully** *fig.*, in the phr. **to look as if one has lived** (or **been up**) **a** (**the**) **burnt gully for the winter**, **to look as if one has spent the winter up a burnt gully**, to look, or be, very thin, emaciated, underfed (like a sheep which has spent a winter up a gully where the feed has been burnt off in the autumn).

1962 HORI *Half-gallon Jar* 63 The pakeha lady she is nearly always skinny and looks as if she has been up the burnt gully for the winter. *Ibid.* 72 This coot is about five feet high and very pale. He looks as if he had been living on bird seed or had spent the winter up a burnt gully.

4. In the phr. **to stand** (**like**) **a burnt stump**, to stand immobile. Usu. in neg. constr., in a sense 'Move!'.

1976 MCCLENAGHAN *Travelling Man* 87 Don't stand there a burnt stump. Come back up here. **1986** Remarks on NZ idiom made by Ms. Ostmann, a US food writer: *p.c. Tui Flower of NZ Woman's Weekly* (14 Jan. 1987) When someone says, 'Don't just stand around like a burnt stump,' it means, do something!

burr, *n.*[1] Also **bur**. [Restricted use of *bur(r)* a burr-bearing plant for mainly local *Acaena* spp.]

1. Also **common** (or **native**) **burr**. Any of various native *Acaena* spp.; BIDDY-BID *n.* 1 a.

   1848 WAKEFIELD *Handbook NZ* 123 Another advantage is to be found in the absence of *burrs* in the New Zealand runs... In some parts of New Zealand there does exist a small *burr*, called *otiwai*. **1849** PHARAZYN *Journal* (ATLMS) 234 Burn[ed] off a lot of burr on top of ridge. **1854** TAYLOR *Journal* (ATLTS) VIII. 165 Our camping place was on a bed of burrs which covered [our] blankets all over. **1868** LINDSAY *Contribs. NZ Bot.* 59 Hence the plant [*Acaena sanguisorbae*] is only too familiar, as the 'Native Burr' to the sheep farmers alike of New Zealand, Australia, and Tasmania. **1889** FEATON *Art Album NZ Flora* 125 The Native Burr... The 'Hutiwai', or 'Piripiri'. **1907** *AJHR* C-8 19 *Acaena sanguisorbae*..Piripiri common burr. **1911** [see PIRIPIRI *n.*[1] 1 a]. **1952** RICHARDS *Chatham Is.* 31 *Acaena..sanguisorbae*... Burr, Biddi-biddi.

2. Applied to introduced burr species. **a.** **Australian (Australian sheep's) bur(r)**. *Acaena agnipila* (formerly *A. ovina*) (fam. Rosaceae), a naturalized Australian weed. See also BIDDY-BID *n.* 1 b.

   1921 GUTHRIE-SMITH *Tutira* 245 That period [1870s] was marked by the establishment of plants carried..in the wool of sheep, as Australian bur (*Acaena ovina*). **1926** HILGENDORF *Weeds* 99 Sheep's Burr (*Acaena ovina*), called also Australian burr, false bidi bid, and very loosely piri piri or bidi bid, is not uncommon in fields and waste places in certain localities of both islands, but is commoner in the north. **1969** *Standard Common Names Weeds* 3 Australian sheep's bur *Acaena ovina*. **1981** TAYLOR *Weeds of Lawns* 9 Australian Sheep's Bur (*Acaena ovina*)..is widespread in New Zealand, frequently seen in poor pasture and on roadsides.

b. See BATHURST BURR.

   Hence **burry** *a.*, of wool, contaminated with burrs.
   1982 *Agric. Gloss.* (MAF) 53 *Burry Wool*: Wool containing burrs such as clover burr and Bathurst burr.

burr, *n.*[2] See quot. See also BEECH 3, BURL *n.*[2] 2, TOTARA *n.*[1] 3.

   1987 MASSEY *Woodturning NZ* 93 *Burr* Contorted growth on the tree trunk closest to the stump.

burrow. [Extended use of *burrow* underground rabbit nest.] The underground nesting place of the muttonbird.

   1844 MONRO *Notes of Journey* in Hocken *Contributions* (1898) 254 As the mutton-bird seldom makes a new burrow, but returns to the old ones year after year, and as these burrows are nearly horizontal, the natives have made vertical openings into them, through which they extract the young one. **1914** GUTHRIE-SMITH *Mutton Birds & Other Birds* 28 Many of the Kuaka [*sc.* diving petrel] burrows were really alive with revelry... Often a Kuaka would sit for long periods just outside a burrow mouth, gazing, and I believe at intervals, singing into its cavernous depths. **1925** GUTHRIE-SMITH *Bird Life on Island & Shore* 128 From twos and threes, from dozens, from hundreds, from thousands, from tens of thousands of burrows, rose an intensifying babel of sound. **1932** STEAD *Life Histories NZ Birds* 78 When a stick is thrust into the burrow the sitting bird gives a loud double hiss, and then often 'Ti-ti-ti'. **1993** *News Vuw* (Wellington) 20 Apr. 9 During the full moon the birds often stayed at sea..returning..just long enough to feed their anxious young cheeping in the burrows.

burst, *n.*[1] *Obs.* [f. Brit. dial. *burst* an outburst of drinking: see EDD *burst* 4; SND 4; AND 1852.]

a. A spree (esp. a drinking or drunken spree), usu. in the phr. **on the burst**, occas. early, **to have a burst**. (Replaced in modern use by BUST *n.* q.v.)

   1861 HARPER *Lett. from NZ* 20 July (1914) 65 You may argue with them [*sc.* station hands], and they gravely plead that to 'have a burst' is necessary for health after the long monotony of station life and fare. **1873** BARKER *Station Amusements* 221 'Hisabella' had gone on the 'burst', having bought..a bottle of rum from a passing swagger. **1874** KENNAWAY *Crusts* 167 Once or twice a year, he went..to Christchurch..and, like hundreds of his class, he went down with the set resolution '*to have a burst*'. **1889** SKEY *Pirate Chief* 200 Like a fish on land I thirst,... Oh, give me the drunken burst, The song, and the thick voice loud. **1896** HODGSON *Poems* 3 'Tis worth a pint..To..coach a bagman 'on the burst', With candlestick, to bed. **1904** *NZ Illustr. Mag.* Dec. 179 He would purchase half a dozen bottles of rum..and go on a regular burst. **1925** BATHGATE *Random Recolls.* 36 Every now and again he gets a remittance from Home, and has a tremendous burst for a week or two. **1933** *Press* (Christchurch) (Acland Gloss.) 23 Sept. 13 *Burst, Bust*.—Drinking bout. E.g., 'He has been on the burst for a week', 'He has had an awful bust'.

   Hence (poss. a modern back-formation from the noun) **burst** *v. trans.*, to spend (a pay-cheque) on a drinking spree.
   1990 MARTIN *Forgotten Worker* 3 Many workers succumbed to the temptations of infrequent but expensive drinking sessions in which they would 'burst' or 'dissolve' their pay cheques and rapidly dissipate their earnings in the local public house.

b. A spending spree.
   1934 SCANLAN *Winds of Heaven* 129 'It's appalling..the price they charge.' 'Oh, well, this is London... And it's the first burst we have had.'

burst, *n.*[2] *Canterbury.* [AND 1894 only.] BURSTER.

   1851 TORLESSE *Canterbury Settlement* 9 The north-west wind..somewhat resembling the 'hot winds' of Australia..is almost invariably succeeded by one from the south-west, which in the summer time is a cool and pleasant guest, but in the winter season what is aptly denominated 'a burst', and sometimes lasts for two or three days, being generally accompanied by rain, if not by snow and sleet.

burst, *n.*[3]

1. Of stock, a sudden break or movement away from a controlled path. Cf. BREAK *n.*[1] 1.

   c**1860** MURDOCH in Beattie *Early Runholding* (1947) 116 The cattle broke away..and this burst put any chance of my seeing..Moa Cottage..at an end. **1863** BUTLER *First Year* x 156 [Sheep] will race off helter-skelter to feed... Therefore have some one stationed a good way off to check their first burst, and stay them from going too far and leaving their lambs.

2. In the phr. **on the burst**, of esp. rugby players, making a vigorous movement into and through opponents' defences. Also *transf.*

   1987 *National Bus. Rev.* (Budget Special) 9 June 6 [Heading] Douglas [Finance Minister] and pack are on the burst. **1989** *Evening Post* (Wellington) 13 Oct. [Caption] Joe Ropati on the burst—top performances on return to Warrington.

burst, *v.* [f. a fig. sense of (the body) bursting (like a boiler), or being broken up, by too vigorous effort.] See also BUST, the preferred modern usage.

1. *Canterbury. Hist.* Usu. as **burst up**, of landed estates, to break up or to be broken up into smaller holdings by deliberate policy. Also as a *vbl. n.* and *ppl. a.*

   1890 *Otago Witness* (Dunedin) 27 Nov. 15 Setting aside the absurdity of buying land for settlement while there are millions of acres of Crown lands to burst up, I'll tell you what that means. **1891** A TRAMP ESQ. *Casual Ramblings* 47 There are no natural grasslands in the North, consequently no squatter, and no big estates to burst up. **1898** HOCKEN *Contributions* 145 One of the results of this policy..was the creation of those vast estates which some recent legislation has been busied in 'bursting up'. **1904** *NZ Observer* 30 July 3 The policy of 'bursting up' large estates by rating on unimproved value..is scarcely consistent with the non-taxation of native lands. **1913** *NZ Observer* 4 Oct. 3 We have heard a great deal about the desire to 'burst up' the large estates. **1959** SINCLAIR *Hist. NZ* 175 The Government hoped that 'the graduation screw', as the landowners called the tax, would 'burst up' the estates by making it costly to retain large, undeveloped properties. **1980** ELDRED-GRIGG *Southern Gentry* 132 Estates began to 'burst' everywhere [from 1893 to 1896]. [Cheviot's] 84,000 acres..were cut up into 150 farms and farmlets. *Ibid.* 133 In South Otago the Pomahaka Downs estate was 'burst' in 1893.

2. Often reflexive, or in the phr. **to burst one's boiler**, to overexert (oneself), often at heavy work, see BUST *v.* 2.

burster. *Obs.* [AND 1854.] A sudden change of wind direction or force, esp. as *southerly burster* or *southerly buster* (SOUTHERLY 2, 3). See also BURST *n.*[2]

   1857 *Lyttelton Times* 29 July 5 The weather..was exceedingly cold, but has now changed to fine again, proving that the sum of a few 'bursters' which blow from time to time, at long intervals, is our real winter; that, as a season, we have scarcely one to be called. **1858** SHAW *Gallop to Antipodes* 128 When within a few miles of Wellington Harbour, a wind came on in the opposite direction, or, as they term it, a 'burster but-end first'. *Ibid.* 183 We had a favourable wind in the straits when all of a sudden..an opposite burster came on in a manner so furious that the captain..declared it was blowing a hurricane.

bush, *n.* and *a.* [See OED *n.*[1] 9. 'Recent, and probably a direct adoption of the Du. *bosch* [woodland] in colonies originally Dutch'. 1779 US (DARE), 1780 S. Africa (OED); AND 1790.]

The BUSH entry is laid out as follows: **A.** *n.* **1.** 'forest' **a.** *the bush, patch of bush* **b.** *a bush, bushes* **c.** with modifiers defining nature of the bush *heavy, light,* etc. **d.** defining composition *beech bush,* etc. **e.** defining locality *back bush.* **2. a.** 'the backblocks' **b.** in Maori reference *Nga Bush,* etc. **3.** In verbal phrases **a.** *take to the bush* **b.** *go back to the bush* **c.** *go bush.* **B.** as an *adj.* or *attrib.* **1 a.** 'of the bush' **b.** 'covered with bush' **c.** 'made of bush materials'. **2.** 'of the backblocks'. **C.** In combination and composition. **1. a.** with a participle (e.g. *bush-clad*) **b.** with an adjective (e.g. *bush-dark*). **2. a. b. c. d.** in combinations and **3. a. b. c. d.** in special combinations in senses (respectively) of *bush adj.* B 1 a, b, c, 2, above. **4.** In the names of plants and animals.

A. *n.* Freq. with *the*.

[*Note*] (1) Eighteenth century and early 19th century writers apparently preferred *woods* and its derivatives, to *forest*, etc. Twentieth century usage seems to prefer *forest* and derivatives for 'exotic forest, plantation' (following technical forestry usage), and *bush*, etc., for 'native forest'. See also WOOD *n.* (2) Some early 19th century evidence suggests that *bush* could be used collectively for 'brush(wood), 'shrubbery': e.g. 1773 Forster *Resolution Jrnl.* 20 Apr. (1982) II. 262 The Capt went up to them & nosed them..and several of our people came up to them: there were girls behind the Indians in the bush. 1838 Polack *NZ* I. 110 On emerging from Pámáki we ascended another plain..covered with fern and bush, above which the tupákihi..occasionally shewed its bending stem. *Ibid.* I. 111 We pursued our route over a succession of hill and valley, bush and plain, swamp and forest.

1. [AND 1790.] (Land covered with) native rainforest. **a.** (a) Usu. as **the bush**, and (b) often with a *quasi-pl.* of the type **patches of bush**. See also *native bush* (NATIVE B 2 a).

1810 [see A 3 a (a) below]. **1815** KENDALL 19 May in Elder *Marsden's Lieutenants* (1934) 83 Warrakkee expressed..his fears lest the English should..increase their numbers, drive the natives into the bush, and take away their land from them. **1820** LEE & KENDALL *NZ Gram. & Vocab.* 181 Móe kóroha: Asleep in the bush. **1823** KENT *Journal* in Begg *Port Preservation* (1973) 321 Caddell..put us on our guard in case the natives..had secreted themselves in the bush, to make an easy prey of us. **1834** MARKHAM *NZ* (1963) 65 Now in Ho-kiangar there were few or no walks. [Markham's *note*] Except in the bush or Forrest, when Pidgeon shooting. **1841** *NZ Jrnl.* II. 35 The bush or jungle can only be penetrated by natives. **1851** *Richmond-Atkinson Papers* (1960) I. 83 We encamped at nightfall on the margin of a small forest, or technically a small piece of bush. **1860** in Butler *First Year* (1863) iv 47 Here [at Oxford], for the first time, I saw the bush; it was very beautiful; numerous creepers, and a luxuriant undergrowth among the trees, gave the forest a wholly un-European aspect, and realized, in some degree, one's idea of tropical vegetation. **1889** WAKEFIELD *NZ After Fifty Yrs.* 139 'Bush' means, in general parlance, the native forest in its virgin state, lofty trees, with dense undergrowth covering the whole ground. **1896** HARPER *Pioneer Work* 32 In New Zealand the forest is always spoken of as 'bush' as opposed to lower growth of vegetation, which is called 'scrub'. **1909** THOMPSON *Ballads About Business* 103 Past fern-girt gully and gurgling creek, with a wealth of bush beside. **1920** BOLITHO *With the Prince in NZ* 159 There were stretches of bush which fed the sawmills nearby. **1935** MITCHELL & STRONG in Partridge *Slang Today* 286 During the Maori War, the natives had an exasperating habit of retreating to 'the bush', wooded country. **1964** JEFFEREY *Mairangi* 23 [New chum.] 'They're p-pongas.' [New Zealander.].. 'They belong to the bush.' 'W-what bush?' '*The* bush, silly. Native bush.' 'You mean f-forest?' 'Help! You're funny, aren't you? Forests are only in stories.' **1983** *Land of Mist* 69 [Caption] The North Island robin prefers the shade of the forest to the edge of the bush.

(b) As **patch of bush** forming a distributive or quasi-plural (cf. 1 b below).

1856 FITTON *NZ* 12 The singing birds..are only found on the outskirts of woods and small patches of bush. **1866** BARKER *Station Life* (1870) 64 It is a constant object for my walks up the gullies, exploring little patches of bush to search for the ferns. **1886** *TrNZI* XVIII. 79 Mr. Henry states that the skeleton..was found at the edge of a patch of bush, about 200 acres in extent. **1907** MANSFIELD *Urewera Notebook* (1978) 51 Past the shearing shed—past the homestead to a beautiful place with a little patch of bush—tuis—magpies—cattle. **1958** *Tararua* Sept. 23 Even those later scientists who use *forest* as a general rule usually write of..*patches of bush*, and the *bushline*. **1966** TURNER *Eng. Lang. Austral. & NZ* 52 The loss of singular and plural *wood* and *woods* leaves a gap, because *bush* is not normally used with an indefinite article... My way out would be to say 'patch of bush', and I think this is fairly usual in New Zealand. **1970** THOMAS *Way Up North* 77 It was fully fenced..with the exception of patches of bush he had been wise enough to leave standing.

b. (a) Esp. *Canterbury and Otago*. As *sing.* **a bush**, *pl.* **bushes**, often with a prefixed defining word. [See OED 9 c.] A patch of bush; a clump of native trees.

1844 MONRO *Notes of a Journey* in Hocken *Contributions* (1898) 235 Leaving this pa, we passed through a very pretty bush, which runs up nearly to the top of the range. **1848** TORLESSE *Papers* (1958) 43 After leaving the bushes the soil was inferior... Dec. 21 Over the low table spurs..till we came to a bush at 6½pm. **1858** MOON *Wreck of Osprey* 119 They are called long and short bush, from the shortness or length of time it takes to travel through them. **1867** THOMSON *Rambles with Philosopher* 133 A clump of trees, colonially termed a bush. **1898** HOCKEN *Contributions* 50 The first night was passed in the shelter of a small bush, whose last few trees yet remain. **1902** *Settler's Handbook NZ* 30 The timbers of commercial value are totara, rimu, [etc.] in mixed bushes. **1920** MANDER *Story NZ River* (1974) 179 In the remote districts of the northern bushes it was not regarded as important. **1939** BEATTIE *First White Boy Born Otago* 86 [Drayroad Bush] was a long narrow bush..and a dray-road had been cut through its narrowest part, hence its name. **1982** NEWBOLD *Big Huey* 209 In the summer we worked in the smaller bush, cutting posts.

(b) With a defining word or modifier forming a place-name or local name, often for a once-bushed area subsequently clearfelled, or for the remnant of bush reserved when this was done. (For example, the 'Bush' district of Wairarapa; or Wilton's Bush of Wellington: poss. *ellipt.* for *bush reserve*).

1877 *TrNZI* IX. 142 The Otatara, Waikiwi, and Makarewa bushes in the vicinity of Invercargill are also of considerable extent..the next large forest is the Tautuku bush, extending from Waipapa point to the Clutha river, a distance of forty-five miles. **1958** *Tararua* Sept. 23 The settlers gave their settlements or localities names such as Wright's Bush, Ryal Bush, Pigeon Bush, or Kowhai Bush; they cleared the Seventy Mile Bush so thoroughly that it is now but a memory; they left remnants that are now reserves, such as Barton's Bush and Wilton's Bush. **1968** TOMLINSON *Remembered Trails* 28 The bush in the locality [of Tophouse], known as Big Bush Settlement, was cut into sections in 1906. **1991** DALLAS *Curved Horizon* 110 That coastal Southland was heavily forested originally may be discerned today from the place-names on a map: Longbush..Myross Bush, Grove Bush, Pine Bush, Roslyn Bush, Ryal Bush, Mabel Bush..and so on.

c. With modifiers defining the nature of the bush: **heavy** (also **heavily-bushed**) or **light bush** (also *attrib.*), comprising respectively larger trees and undergrowth, or smaller trees, including shrubs and second growth; **open bush**, not dense and having little undergrowth, often spaced with natural clearings; **standing bush**, comprising timber trees on the stump; **timber** or **milling bush**, standing bush being or able to be worked for timber; **virgin bush**, forest in its original state untouched by human hand or axe (in Southland occas. called **maiden bush**); **working bush**, a timbered block being milled or assigned to a sawmiller for clearfelling.

1865 HAYNES *Ramble in NZ Bush* 5 It is only in the '**heavy bush**' and the ti-tree bush (that is the larger variety) that the undergrowth..is seen to any extent. **1882** HAY *Brighter Britain* II. 184 The woodlands of Northern New Zealand may be divided into two general classes, the heavy bush and the light bush. The light bush..is not dissimilar to a very wild and luxuriant English wood. **1913** CARR *Country Work* 31 The bulk of this is cut with a slasher in the same manner as underscrubbing heavy bush. **1935** MAXWELL *Recollections* 99 There was between the tall bush and the sea a coastal belt of flax, cabbage tree and scrub-covered land. It is described as open land to distinguish it from that covered with big heavy bush. **1946** SARGESON *That Summer* 173 It was years now since he had finished breaking in his farm from heavy bush country. **1952** THOMSON *Deer Hunter* 146 Usually in this heavily-bushed country..it is so damp that one has difficulty in getting enough dry kindling wood to light a fire. **1978** MCARA *Gold Mining Waihi* 46 The country was mostly covered with heavy bush. **1849** HURSTHOUSE *New Plymouth* 17 Of smaller trees, and shrubs forming the '**light bush**', there is great variety. **1857** HURSTHOUSE *NZ* I. 135 The smaller trees and tree-shrubs, ('light bush',) growing about the edges of the great forests, or clothing the dells and valleys of the open country. **1882** [see *heavy bush* above]. **1892** BROOKES *Frontier Life* 174 I wish to notice the ornamental trees on the outskirts of our forest scenery—what we call the light bush. **1902** *Settler's Handbook of NZ* 111 The more timber is used in what is called a '**milling bush**', the more economical to the State is the use of that portion of its forests. **1904** CRADOCK *Sport in NZ* 21 [Heading] Camp in the **Open Bush**. **1911** *TrNZI* XLIII. 204 This is a small plant..probably not uncommon in open bush and scrub throughout. **1882** HAY *Brighter Britain* II. 238 [The sown grass] ran in and out of the **standing bush**..spreading altogether over a good stretch of country. **1883** *Brett's Colonists' Guide* 18 No good permanent fence should ever be erected within half-a-chain of standing bush. **1893** *TrNZI* XXV. 439 As regards the **timber bushes** and the forests of the North Island generally, the case..is hopeless. **1925** BEST *Tuhoe* 9 The bush which still covers the greater part of Tuhoeland is what an European bushman would term 'light bush'. A sawmiller would not describe it as a 'timber bush'. **1887 Virgin Bush** [see BUSH-FARM]. **1891** *NZJSc.* (NS) I. 69 I hope some naturalist living near a piece of virgin bush will undertake its investigation. **1914** PFAFF *Diggers' Story* 42 At this period the place where Hokitika stands was all virgin bush. **1936** BELSHAW et al. *Agric. Organiz. NZ* 30 Of the 43 million acres of occupied land, about 24 million acres are 'unimproved', and are under native grasses, phormium, fern, scrub and virgin bush. **1966** TURNER *Eng. Lang. Austral. & NZ* 167 *Virgin bush*, too, carried all the nineteenth-century overtones of the word *virgin* (and little protection they offered). **1986** RICHARDS *Off the Sheep's Back* 10 The land was virgin bush. **1906** *Red Funnel* II. 13 It was as if all the hands from all the **working bushes** in the district had congregated.

d. With modifiers defining the major element in the botanical composition of the bush: **beech bush**, **black birch bush**, **kauri bush**, etc.

1850 MCLEAN in Cowan *Sir Donald Maclean* (1940) 59 We passed through a *totara* bush, across the Manawatu and Tamaki rivers, through a second *bush*. **1863** MOSER *Mahoe Leaves* 4 It is a picturesque spot by the edge of a river flanked by a noble pine bush, the most noble of all the New Zealand forests. **1869** *TrNZI* I. (rev. edn.) 190 The undergrowth of this Beech bush is composed chiefly of *Coprosma lucida*. **1878** JOLLIE *Reminiscences* (ATLTS) 35 Clearing the road through black birch bush. **1888** BARLOW *Kaipara* 112 There is a Kauri bush at the present time on fire in this riding. **1952** THOMSON *Deer Hunter* 32 Jack escorted us to the main base camp of the shooters, pitched in beech bush. **1971** LETHBRIDGE *Sunrise on Hills* 44 I'd never been into beech bush before. It reminded me of England with its open forest floors.

e. With modifiers defining locality in respect of access: **back bush**, see BACK *n.*[1] B 2.

2. Usu. as **the bush**. **a.** In early settlement, the mainly forested, often Maori-populated, hinterland (esp. in the North Island) awaiting European occupation or 'civilization', the 'backwoods' (see also A 3 a (a) below); thence, esp. in the South Island, any district (forested or unforested) remote from urban company, conveniences and way of life, a use prob. influenced by prior Austral. usage (see AND *bush* 3, 1825), eventually often being replaced in informal use, esp. in the North Island, by numerous congeners such as BACKBLOCK A, BOOHAI 1, CACTUS, WOPWOPS. Cf. B 2 below.
[*Note*] Compare a similar use of *forest* in 1865 LUSH *Waikato Jrnls.* 21 Sept. (1982) 57 [The] house is—or rather was—in the depth of a dense forest: now the clearing around is considerable..the excuse for the higgledy-piggledy style of serving up the meal is too often—'Oh, I know you'll excuse it—we are in the Forest—not in the Town'.
1841 BRIGHT *Handbook Emigrants* 99 [The Maories] retire into the bush (or wilds). **1842** HEAPHY *NZ* 46 These two plants [manuka and kawakawa], together with the fern root..are of much dietary service in the 'bush'. **1844** ASHWORTH *Jrnl. of Edward Ashworth* 28 Jan. (1992, VUWTS) 65 Whalers crews are formed of raw heads 'green as cabbages' from the bush. 'They hav'nt [*sic*] yet got the hayseeds out of their hair.' **1849** TORLESSE *Papers* (1958) 117 I am buried in the bush, and know but little even of our Canterbury politics. **1851** [see B 2 below]. **1853** SWAINSON *Auckland* 71 To those who live in the bush, or at a distance from the town, the cost of living in the northern part of New Zealand is very cheap. **1862** HODDER *Memories NZ Life* 56 Life in the bush, or backwoods, in districts far remote from town or village..has circumstances peculiar to itself. **1875** COCKBURN-HOOD *Chowbokiana* 74 The Bush in colonial parlance means everywhere out of the towns, the bleak plains of Canterbury and the dreary uplands of Otago destitute of all vegetation save coarse tussock grass..are called the bush, as well as the impenetrable forests of lofty trees..which cover the western portions of both islands. **1876** KENNEDY *Colonial Travel* 284 By nightfall we arrived at an inn..and though there was not another house within miles, yet when we commended the tidiness of her rooms, [the hostess] exclaimed in injured tones 'You didn't think you was in the bush, did you?' **1882** HAY *Brighter Britain* I. 81 'Bush' has a double signification, a general and a particular one. In its first and widest sense it is applied to all country beyond the immediate vicinity of the cities or towns. Thus Riverhead may be described as a settlement in the 'bush', and our road lies through the 'bush', though here it is all open moorland. **1892** SWANTON *Notes on NZ* 93 [A sheep run] is an immense tract of open country either in the bush, among the mountains, or upon the plains. **1910** *Kai Tiaki* July 100 Nurses seem to have passed through many countries, especially countries with large, sparsely settled country parts, 'bush', 'back-blocks', or 'out West' as it may be. **1959** SLATTER *Gun in My Hand* 82 Fancy you not knowin old Wilkie... Don't you follow the game [*sc.* rugby]? Or you been up in the bush or what? **1963** BACON *In the Sticks* 184 'Out in the sticks', 'out in the backblocks', 'out in the bush', 'out in the booay', 'out in the cactus', all have the same basic meaning of 'fifty miles from nowhere'. **1971** NEWTON *Ten Thousand Dogs* 26 Those three [musterers] were 'Bush Rats'. They came from the Alford Forest district, commonly known as 'The Bush'.

b. As **Nga Bush**, applied to a Maori (or collectively to a particular group) from areas remote from towns; *spec.* a nickname for (members of) the Northland Ngapuhi tribe, incorporating a bilingual pun (Nga a shortened form of NGATI; *puhi* a Maori transliteration of 'bush'); used in phrases as **straight from the bush**, to allude in a similar way as a stereotype of 'uncivilized' Maori. Also as **the bush**, applied to early settlers on back bush sections (see quot. 1856). Cf. BUSH NATIVE.
1856 *Richmond-Atkinson Papers* (1960) I. 195 Lieut. Crosse..and his party of 50 men of the 58th, challenged the settlers [to cricket] and 'the bush' took up the glove. **1960** HILLIARD *Maori Girl* 34 Dad's view was that since they [*sc.* members of a Maori family] would have to make their way in a *pakeha* world they must know English well or for ever bear the brand of 'straight from the bush'. **1971** WILLIAMS *Dict. Maori Lang.* 157 Kahore he kupu a te mohoao (*The man from the bush* [previous editions use *wood*: see p. ix] *has not anything to say*). **1983** HULME *Bone People* 63 See? Bloody superstitions Nga Bush? Get the Maori a bad name eh? *Ibid.* 465 Nga 'bush' = bush people, primitives. **1989** MCGILL *Dinkum Kiwi Dict.* 71 *Nga bush* nickname, not necessarily a very nice one, indeed offensive, for the Ngapuhi tribe.

3. In verbal phrases (often in *transf.* use) implying some movement in space or time, esp. a reversion to earlier or less civilized ways. **a. to take to the bush**, occas. **to go (in) to the bush** [AND 1826].
(a) In early use, usu. of the Maori, to seek refuge in the bush; in later use, often *transf.* or *fig.*, to hide, to 'go to ground'.
[*Note*] The phr. is a variant of Brit. or US *take to the woods* (or *hills*, etc.), the former recorded in a New Zealand context in Nov. 1792 in Murry's *Journal* in McNab *Hist. Records* (1908) II. 512 At [Breaksea, Dusky Cove at] this moment one of our people made a noise which roused the inhabitants who issued from their abode and took to the woods.]
1810 Berry to Gov. Macquarie 6 Jan. in McNab *Hist. Records* (1908) I. 296 [On the rescue of the Boyd massacre survivors, and the apprehension of a perpetrator, the chief Te Pahi.] Tippahee has betaken to the bush and eluded my researches. As there is no opportunity of sending the chiefs to Port Jackson it will be necessary to liberate them. [Berry is using formal 'dispatch' style.] **1836** MARSHALL *Narr. Two Visits* 152 They [*sc.* the interpreters] took to the bush for shelter, by day and night. **1837** *Piraki Log* 14 Apr. (1911) 52 Captain Harled the Canous up to Hous [on the beach] Nativs went to the bush again. **1839** WHITELEY in *NZ Jrnl.* (1840) I. 200 [William White] took to the bush until we returned. **1840** BEST *Journal* 21 Oct. (1966) 252 [Kikora]..ended by saying had I killed the white men I could not have concealed it. I must have taken the bush & the other tribes would have given me up when they caught me. **1863** *Richmond-Atkinson Papers* (1960) II. 52 They fired 40 rounds..but it is very doubtful if they killed any one, because of course the Maoris took to the bush. **1881** BATHGATE *Waitaruna* 44 There was nothing for it but to shut the door and take to the bush again. **1938** [see FRIENDLY ROAD 1]. **1947–48** BEATTIE *Pioneer Recolls.* (1956) 46 The erstwhile captive lost no time in 'taking to the bush' which then surrounded Invercargill and made good his escape. *a*1974 SYDER & HODGETTS *Austral. & NZ Eng.* (TS) 1008 *To take to the bush*. To hide, as in the bush. Used commonly in a figurative sense. 'Now all you blokes are to keep quiet about this. If the wife gets to know I'm playing poker again I might as well take to the bush straight away.'

(b) Of domestic and farm animals and birds, to escape to or return to the wild.
1847 BRUNNER *Exped. Middle Is.* 5 Jan. in Taylor *Early Travellers* (1959) 263 These birds..[have] been destroyed by wild dogs belonging to the natives, but which have taken to the bush. **1849** POWER *Sketches in NZ* 189 From the number of swarms that take to the bush, there is promise of an abundance of wild honey and wax. **1851** *Richmond-Atkinson Papers* (1960) I. 99 [The hens] cunningly take to the bush so that chickens are plenty though eggs are scarce.

(c) To live in, take up life in, or make a living in, (remote) areas not yet cleared of bush, or still barely settled.
1849 POWER *Sketches in NZ* 189 Great numbers of labourers have taken to the bush, squatting down on an acre or two of partially cleared land which furnishes them with potatoes. **1850** WARD *Journal* 16 Dec. (1951) 86 [The Governor's Private Secretary] gave us some good advice—among other things to cut the town and take to the bush. **1886** CLAYDEN *Handbook NZ* 225 [Hints to intending emigrants include:] If you do 'go into the bush', meaning really going in for country life, be on your guard against the common danger of relapsing into barbarism. **1943** BENNETT *English in NZ* in *Amer. Speech* XVIII. 85 *To go into the bush* is to go into the wild, uncultivated parts of the country.

(d) Of explorers, trampers, hunters, etc., to be forced to leave a passable track or easier going (e.g. along a river bed) and proceed through (usu.) untracked bush.
1861 HAAST *Rep. Topogr. Explor. Nelson* 11 The river, too, deepened a good deal, and we had again to take to the bush, and camped, after a walk of another mile, on its banks. **1896** HARPER *Pioneer Work* 127 Rocky bluffs against which the river ran very deep, compell[ed] us to 'take to the bush'. I have already described what 'taking to the bush' involves in the way of track cutting, so need only add that when compelled to leave the open river-bed, the loads had to be put down, a track 'blazed' round or over the obstacle.

b. In the phr. **to go bush (back to the bush)**. Of a Europeanized Maori, to revert to traditional tribal ways. See also *go back to the mat* (MAT 3 a).
1888 BALLOU *Under Southern Cross* 334 We are told amusing anecdotes of their going back to the 'bush' from time to time, solely to indulge in the old savage habit of nudity, and to enjoy a sense of entire freedom from the conventionalities of the whites.

c. *transf.* **go bush** [see OED *bush n.*[1] 9 e]. (a) To leave urban life for that of the rural outdoors; to practise or revert to a rough or outdoor way of life.
1941 BAKER *NZ Slang* 15 There are several dozen derivatives from the term [bush] commonly used both in New Zealand and Australia, [including]..go bush. **1965** SHADBOLT *Among Cinders* 201 You not keen about going bush? That it? You not so keen about the bush any more? **1986** *Listener* 5 July 23 Fleur Grenfell describes the benefits of some of her officers and inmates going bush together on an Outward Bound-style weekend. **1986** *Evening Post* (Wellington) 21 June 27 But it appeared it [*sc.* the priesthood] was not his calling, so he went bush in the back of Golden Bay..to save money to study law.

(b) *fig.* To leave suddenly (often under duress), or to escape from, one's usual haunts; to seclude oneself.
1934 *Truth* 20 June 11 [Heading] Went Bush after Theft. **1955** *Truth* 23 Nov. 16 One of this year's new All Blacks has 'gone bush'—but not to dodge creditors or military service. **1973** HAYWARD *Diary Kirk Years* (1981) 157 The media have been busy criticising Hugh Watt for 'going bush'. **1985** *Dominion* (Wellington) 23 July 4 Police were disturbed at the indications that the boys intended to 'go bush'. **1986** *Evening Post* (Wellington) 12 Mar. 1 Hadlee left Christchurch immediately after the second test and went 'bush' for four days to 'think things out'. **1986** *Dominion*

(Wellington) 29 Jan. 2 Overseas Trade and Marketing Minister Mike Moore will 'go bush' today for a two-day discussion of the work of the new Market Development Board. He will join 18 other..people at the Waitomo Hotel till Friday night. **1991** *Landfall 178* 172 I caught a glimpse of the escaper's face... 'I thought he had gone bush forever and a day,' a voice said behind me.

(c) In modern quasi-literal use (prob. re-formed from senses (a) and (b) above), to go into the native bush (to hunt, hide, etc.).

1982 *NZ Times* 5 Sept. 3 An alleged hit-and-run driver punched a traffic officer then went bush in Wellington's Island Bay yesterday. He was punched by the man who then leapt into nearby bush and disappeared. **1985** *National Bus. Rev.* 4 Nov. 26 [Heading about a hunting trip.] Six go bush and bag a whitetail on Rakiura. **1987** *Sunday News* (Auckland) 24 May 2 'Well son,' said the helicopter shooter [to a new-chum hunter], 'if you want some advice from an old hand then the next time you go bush you'd be well-advised to take your cheque book with you.'

B. *adj.* and *attrib.* (*bush* is rarely used predicatively.)

1 a. Pertaining to, or found, growing, living, ranging, situated, etc. in, the New Zealand forest.

1852 GRACE *Journal* 31 Dec. in *Pioneer Missionary* (1928) 19 Now they are making every effort to reclaim their bush cows, and great numbers are milked regularly. **1853** SWAINSON *Auckland* 68 Riding, boating, cricket, and bush excursions, are the favourite out-door amusements. **1857** HARPER *Lett. from NZ* 4 Nov. (1914) 36 We found ourselves barred by a line of 'bush' trees growing thick together. **1858** YOUNG *Southern World* 14 Mr Whiteley, who occupies a 'bush' station. **1897** *TrNZI* XXIX. 496 So long as the gum-digger and bush-larrikin are allowed to put a match into anything that will burn, there is not much hope for..restoration. **1906** *TrNZI* XXXVIII. 339 A beautiful bush-musician..is the bell-bird. **1914** GRACE *Tale of Timber Town* 67 There's no water like bush water. **1921** *Quick March* 10 Mar. 11 While on the subject of bush medicine, I may as well mention a few others. **1922** COWAN *NZ Wars* (1955) I. 52 The outer wall..was formed of stout timbers..all bound firmly together with..bush-vines. *Ibid.* II. 281 An Armed Constabulary scout..shared in the bush chase. **1959** MASTERS *Tales of Mails* 13 Mr McPherson was one of the real old time bush pioneers. He had felled trees..and built his own house with the timber. **1984** HOLMES *Chatham Is.* 25 Initially..they [*sc.* the Maori invaders] set about felling and clearing areas of bush in readiness for cultivation... This forming of 'bush gardens' was the traditional means of claiming invaded territory. **1986** RICHARDS *Off the Sheep's Back* 59 A bush gang must always work as a team and work a block accordingly.

b. Covered with or surrounded by bush. See also BUSHED *ppl. a.*

1901 *NZ Illustr. Mag.* VII. 266 Far away in the bush backblocks. **1939** *Tararua Tramper* Feb. 6 We struggled over a bump..then on to the next low bush saddle there to pitch tent on a mud flat. **1940** STUDHOLME *Te Waimate* (1954) 247 Many of the bush and scrub gullies extended from the Waihao River to the top of the range. **1942** ANDERSEN *Maori Place names* 124 [The birds] of the plains, swamps and bush-lagoons. **1980** HOLDEN *Stag* 13 Over the years, this saddle had become a..natural gateway linking two huge bush valleys.

c. Composed or made of materials from the bush.

1849 PHARAZYN *Journal* (ATLMS) 275 One wether lamb staked in bush pen and after drowned. **1873** PYKE *Wild Will Enderby* (1889, 1974) III. iv 85 The bunks—rude structures of bush poles, with flour bag sacking—had been torn down. **1904** *NZ Illustr. Mag.* Dec. 165 It was only needful to sling our tent and fly over the poles..and give it a good sweep out with a bush broom. a**1927** ANTHONY *Gus Tomlins* (1977) 89 Both of us..slept in bunks made of bush poles nailed together and covered with sacks of hay. **1936** HYDE *Passport to Hell* 111 A world which.., behind the bush-veils and the mist-veils of the New Zealand hills, had silenced their childhood with a memory.

2. Of or pertaining to remote rural, as distinct from urban, areas and life, often depreciatory in connotation ('rough', 'makeshift', 'uncivilized'), occas. appreciatory ('inventive', 'practical', 'hospitable', 'communally helpful').

1851 WAKEFIELD *Let. to Sir George Grey* 31 The stockowner, though brought up as a gentleman, if he lives long in the 'bush', learns first to be proud of the 'bush' manners, and then becomes unfit for any but 'bush' society. **1859** *Richmond-Atkinson Papers* (1960) I. 486 A knowledge of Maori ought to be essential to a bush appointment [as a Maori assessor]. **1870** WHITWORTH *Martin's Bay Settlement* 48 I found..tied to a stick, (a bush candlestick), about two inches of candle. **1881** NESFIELD *Chequered Career* 37 In a few months' time I had learnt all the most important items of a bush education: how to cook, make bread or damper..work a dog. **1898** HOCKEN *Contributions* 201 The verses refer to the little bush congregation by the clay cottage at Green Island. **1906** *Truth* 25 Aug. 5 [Shotover Bill's] brains were like those of a chimpanzee A Maori hen, or a bush J.P. **1910** *NZ Free Lance* (Wellington) 3 Sept. 13 The 'deadhouse' is a familiar adjunct to a bush pub. **1922** COWAN *NZ Wars* (1955) II. 508 The Maori had used [for percussion caps] match-heads, cut off and inserted in eyelets..and this bush contrivance failed to detonate. **1947** BEATTIE *Early Runholding* 40 Some of the bush runs in Western Southland had no choice in the matter, as the country was unsuitable for sheep. **1960** MASTERS *Back-Country Tales* 150 Nevertheless with the customary bush hospitality, he invited the man in for a drink of tea. **1960** CRUMP *Good Keen Man* 114 I..put nine stitches in his [*sc.* the dog's] side with a sack-needle and string... He recovered all right from both the wound and the bush surgery. **1965** SHADBOLT *Among Cinders* 91 She claimed to have built all her children up on smoky, burnt bush porridge. **1986** OWEN & PERKINS *Speaking for Ourselves* 150 The way in which the bush people—the bushmen and their wives—stuck to one another is shown by the way they rallied round in the case of a family that was in need. **1990** *Dominion Sunday Times* (Wellington) 4 Mar. 19 Bush bands started in New Zealand last century. The music is essentially a mix of Irish, Scottish and English influences. *Ibid.* 4 Mar. 19 The bush dance developed as a means for people to get together.

C. In combination or composition.

1. a. With a *pa. ppl.* forming compound adjectives: **bush-bled**, of kauri-gum, taken from a living tree (see also *gum-bleeding* (GUM 3 b)); **bush-bordered**; **bush-bound**, bounded or enclosed by bush; **bush-bowered**; **bush-bred** [AND 1833], born or reared in a forested or in a rural district; **bush-browned**, of a creek or river, coloured with detritus from the bush; **bush-canopied**; **bush-clad** [AND 1838], the most freq. of these compounds, very often collocated with 'hills'; **bush-clothed**; **bush-covered** [AND 1948]; **bush-crowned**; **bush-draped**; **bush-fringed** [OED 10 a, 1891]; **bush-raised**, of stock, raised in the forest on bush feed rather than in a paddock on pasture; **bush-scented**; **bush-shadowed**; **bush-shrouded**; **bush-sited**; **bush-surrounded**; **bush-trained**, of settlers, trained in bush-fighting during the New Zealand Wars.

1948 REED *Gumdigger* 78 This harvest of the living [kauri] tree is called '**bush-bled** gum'. **1956** SUTHERLAND *Green Kiwi* (1960) 70 Gum was also won by tapping, the exuded or 'bush-bled' gum being chipped off at regular intervals. **1959** SLATTER *Gun in My Hand* 227 [The tourists] never see the wood-chopping at the **bush-bordered** showgrounds at Tuatapere. **1946** ACLAND *Early Canterbury Runs* 210 There was a wedge-shaped block of ninety thousand acres of high tops, mostly **bush-bound**, in the middle. **1952** THOMSON *Deer Hunter* 100 I had previously shot two or three on every clearing while travelling up the bush-bound valleys. **1966** NEWTON *Boss's Story* 120 The Poulter and Riversdale country is practically all bushbound. **1973** NEWTON *Big Country SI* (1977) 28 These [ewes] could not be let go..with safety [because of lack of fences] so he put them out on some bush-bound tops away in behind the Mataki country. **1930** *NZ Short Stories* 30 The canoe came from the mouth of a **bush-bowered** river. **1896** *Bracken's Annual* 39 His mare was one of those wiry **bush-bred** ones. **1920** *Quick March* 10 May 39 I'm hanged if it would deceive any New Zealander country-born or bush-bred. **1935** COWAN *Hero Stories NZ* 225 There were three stalwart brothers..men of bush-bred strength and hardihood. **1947** BEATTIE *Early Runholding* 43 The musterers..were mounted on tough, bush-bred ponies. **1961** HENDERSON *Friends in Chains* 63 Farther back was McMurray's Creek, the **bush-browned** waters of which idled along..parallel with the more rapid and clear river flow. **1987** *Dominion Sunday Times* (Wellington) 30 July 24 [Heading] Trek in beech forest leaves lasting memory of **bush-canopied** trails. **1873** BARKER *Station Amusements* (1973) 2 Behind the Malvern Hills..lies many and many a mile of **bush-clad** mountain. **1885** *TrNZI* XVII. 351 The hardy miner..has penetrated the dark bush-clad and rugged ranges. **1905** SATCHELL *Toll of Bush* 5 Low scrub-covered hills walled it in; beyond rose great bush-clad ranges. **1921** *Quick March* 10 Sept. 23 In those low ridges and bush-clad hills roamed herds of red deer. **1940** MCINTOSH *Marlborough* 289 About two-thirds of this consists of bush-clad hills and narrow valleys in the Sounds. **1979** MORRIESON *Pallet on Floor* 139 Sam regarded the high opposite bank of the river. It was bush clad. **1986** BELICH *NZ Wars* 29 The basic pattern of military operations..was a series of British forays into the hilly and bush-clad interior. **1882** HAY *Brighter Britain* II. 280 So we see as much of the place as we can..the **bush-clothed** heights upon the further shore. **1849** POWER *Sketches in NZ* 19 On two sides it was nearly perpendicular **bush-covered** mountain; and in front was..the hill, densely covered with forest. **1873** ST JOHN *Pakeha Rambles* in Taylor *Early Travellers* (1959) 517 The dark bush-covered hills of the Hunua. **1894** *TrNZI* XXVI. 361 [They] form the high bush-covered ranges on the east side of the river-valley. **1907** MANSFIELD *Letters* 20 Nov. (1984) I. 31 You draw rein at the top of the mountains & round you everywhere are other mountains—bush covered. **1930** GUTHRIE *NZ Memories* 87 So on their way back they again sailed into the beautiful, bush-covered bay. **1945** JONES *Diversions of Professor* in *Centennial Treasury Otago Verse* (1949) 71 The little beaches..bush-covered all the way. **1965** *NZ Geogr.* Oct. 154 The counties which constitute the lowest group [of fenced land] were to be found primarily in the bush-covered or formerly bush-covered areas..of both islands. **1983** *Land of Mist* 72 Its habitat is a pool in a small bush-covered stream. **1946** REED *Farthest North* 15 Over to the north-east,.. can be seen a **bush-crowned** hill, the site of a famous pa, Ruapekapeka. **1978** *Islands* 21 239 Over in the low bush-crowned hills some bird or other seemed to pluck its breast two or three times. **1986 bush-draped** [see BUSHED *ppl. a.*² 2 a]. **1968** SEDDON *The Seddons* 30 Whether it were through the **bush-fringed** Christchurch road or along the straight stretches..those drives were a joy. **1985** *Dominion* (Wellington) 10 Dec. 11 Two communities at the end of five kilometres of bush-fringed gravel road in Golden Bay are fed up with raids on their quiet valley by police squads searching for cannabis. **1882** HAY *Brighter Britain* I. 200 The pasture-fed cattle of the South are not in prime condition..during the dry season. Our **bush-raised** beasts are, and this gives us a pull. **1980** BENNETT *Canterbury Tale* 152 The air is clean again, the **bush-scented** air of the Coast. **1949** COLE *It Was So Late* (1978) 63 The rattle of their implements, and the deepening engine note of a passing vehicle as it changes into low gear on the..slippery **bush-shadowed** bends, seem only to nibble at the vast silence. **1954** McDONALD *Stinson's Bush* 216 Perhaps even now he was in some secluded hut drinking the potent whisky which was the secret of the **bush-shrouded** hills. **1985** *National Bus. Rev.* 13 May 6 A newspaper advertisement offers for auction a **bush-sited** home with an 'irreplaceable Northcote beach frontage'. **1951** HUNT *Confessions* 24 Potatoes, kumeras, taros, and water melons were the chief crops grown in the..humid **bush-surrounded** plots. **1922** COWAN *NZ Wars* (1955) I. 268 The **bush-trained** settlers of Papakura, Hunua, and the Wairoa were the dependable nucleus of the corps.

b. With an adjective, adverb, or other suffix, forming compound adjectives: **bush-dark**, of the dark green colour of New Zealand bush; **bush-happy**, slightly mad or eccentric from living in the remote bush; **bushless**, of country, lacking in forest cover, 'open'; **bush-like** [AND 1848], resembling the New Zealand bush; **bush looking**, suggesting from appearances an origin in the remote wilds; **bush-shy**, shy or retiring from being too long isolated in a remote area, hence **bush-shyness**.

1949 COLE *It Was So Late* (1978) 32 He stood for an instant surveying the bungalows..and in the background the purple **bush-dark** hills. **1970** SEVERINSEN *Hunt Far Mountain* 42 No wonder [the Wild Life Division's] cullers got **bush-happy** and once every month or so had to be carried off down to Poronui for a long weekend bombing up the sika [deer]. **1959** MILLAR *Westland's Golden Sixties* 45 In **bushless** Central Otago they had been able to move freely from point to point. **1844** TUCKETT *Diary* 16 Aug. in Hocken *Contributions* (1898) 223 The **bush-like** woods on the east side are of white birch. **1838** POLACK *NZ* II. 209 A new company arrived on the land,.. they were a wild **bush looking** race. **1984** BEARDSLEY *Blackball 08* 74 What a life for them..Could anything be lonelier, harder, less rewarding? You'd soon get **bush-shy** like that. *Ibid.* 242 *bush-shy* shy of people from being too long isolated. **1910** GROSSMAN *Heart of Bush* 3 Across this charmed circle [the boy] gazed..in a mingling of **bush shyness** and curiosity.

2. Comb. **a.** In sense *bush* B 1 a above: **bush-bird, boar, chalet, chopping, district, -drive, -dweller, -edge, fairy, flower, fly** [AND 1838], **-journey, -living, -lore** [AND 1862], **lover, -missionary** *obs.*, **outfit, party, path, picnic** [AND 1901], **pork, -roughing, township** [AND 1880], **travel** (also *v.*), **-traveller** [AND 1834], **-travelling** [AND 1844], **-wandering**. **b.** In sense B 1 b: **bush-creek, -face, -gully, -range. c.** In sense B 1 c: **bush fireplace. d.** In sense B 2: **bush architecture, -ball, bun, dress, -fare, language**.

a. In sense *bush* B 1 a 'pertaining to the bush'.

1866 BARKER *Station Life* (1870) 100 The first awakening of the myriads of **Bush-birds**. **1894** *TrNZI* XXVI. 602 The little bush-birds flew in or out amongst them with unerring accuracy. **1910** GROSSMAN *Heart of Bush* 26 The first morning..she was wakened by a chorus of bush birds. **1929** *NZJST* XI. 127 Many of our bush-birds play an important part in the fertilization of our native trees and shrubs. **1937** BUICK *Moa-Hunters NZ* 132 The Moa was not a bush bird: it was too large and clumsy for that. **1946** *JPS* LV. 156 *piopio*, a bush-bird.., the North Island thrush. **1959** SHADBOLT *New Zealanders* (1986) 15 In sudden queer silence among the sounds of cicadas and bush birds, we glided up to a fern-fringed jetty. **1962** HOGAN *Billy-Can Ballads* 6 Where the bush birds all sing in the springtime As the Kowhai pours gold in his lap. **1989** PARKINSON *Travelling Naturalist* 25 What trees there are also support tui, kereru and the smaller bush birds. **1859** THOMSON *Story NZ* (1974) II. 62 Spearing **bush boars** on horseback occasionally equalled the same gallant sport in the Deccan. **1926** COWAN *Travel in NZ* II. 134 There are Government shelter huts, iron-roofed little **bush chalets**..10 and 19 miles from Glade House [Te Anau]. **1881** HURNDALL in Warr *Bush-burn to Butter* 24 Feb. (1988) 52 1881 February 24: many burnings off and **bush choppings**. **1899** BELL *In Shadow of Bush* 1 In one of the lately settled **bush districts** of the Wellington Province, where the clearings were as yet comparatively few..this story opens. **1935** MAXWELL *Recollections* 65 There were..many labourers..employed by the Government on road construction in bush districts, even as far afield as Taranaki. **1985** *NZ Times* 3 Feb. 12 Those great crashing **bush-drives**, when one tree was aimed to hit another partly-cut tree, which in turn smashed into another half-severed tree, and so on smashing and roaring downhill to the gully's bottom. **1920** *Quick March* 10 Jan. 42 Anyway, whoever heard of a **bush-dweller** going home with an unblown cheque in his pocket. **1935** COWAN *Hero Stories NZ* 84 Now..there was some hard fighting..in the clearing at the **bush-edge**. **1958** *Tararua* Sept. 48 Behind the bush-edge fringe of mountain beech, silver-beech extended some hundreds of feet up the mountainside. **1961** CRUMP *Hang On a Minute Mate* 53 They rode along the bush-edge to where long tussock clearings fingered up the gullies. **1990** *Dominion* (Wellington) 5 June 3 Ngawaka Bedggood was helped out of the bush by **bush fairies**, local Maori elders believe. **1870** *TrNZI* II. 44 The [captive] Tui..has to exchange for the dewy nectar of **bush flowers**, a monotonous diet of soaked bread. **1888** BULLER *Birds NZ* I. 90 [The Bell-bird's] food consists of..the honey of various kinds of bush-flowers. **1967** MAY *West Coast Gold Rushes* 277 **Bush flies**, mosquitoes and sandflies were numbered among the lesser scourges. **1853** SWAINSON *Auckland* 128 For such [who declare all travel barren], a **bush-journey** in New Zealand will have neither pleasure nor profit. **1940** COWAN *Sir Donald Maclean* 54 As they arrived there, after their rough bush journey of ten days they were received with loud cries..from the women. **1881** NESFIELD *Chequered Career* 40 It is all very fine to read about **bush-living**, or listen to men talking of the 'dampers' that they have made. **1921** *Quick March* 10 Mar. 11 A great deal of the **bush-lore** of the Maoris has vanished with the wise old men and women. **1955** BOSWELL *Dim Horizons* 110 My father, who knew Maori bush-lore as well as the natives themselves, heard of the trouble and decided on treatment. **1920** *Quick March* 10 Feb. 38 As a **bushlover** I regret the practice. **1858** YOUNG *Southern World* 69 The labours and sufferings of a New Zealand **bush-missionary**. **1849** TORLESSE *Papers* (1958) 100 Packed up my boxes and prepared [my surveyor's] **bush outfit**. **1984** BARBER *Red Coat to Jungle Green* 48 During operations in the bush the armed constables wore 'bush outfits'. **1853** *Richmond-Atkinson Papers* (1960) I. 133 The **bush party** have now been away a fortnight. **1850** McLEAN *Journal* (ATLTS) III. 33 The road had been a tolerable **bush-path**. **1867** LUSH *Waikato Jrnls.* 15 Mar. (1982) 109 It is a very long time since I had such a thorough bush path to traverse. **1907** MANSFIELD *Letters* 20 Nov. (1984) I. 31 We got great sprays of clematis..and drove first through a bush path. **1938** HYDE *Nor Yrs. Condemn* 245 She started to walk to the [Auckland] Domain by a little bush path which lanced the side of the reserve. **1905** FERGUSON *Poems & Sketches* 125 [Heading] A **Bush Picnic** **1924** ANTHONY *Follow the Call* (1975) 74 My mind kept returning to the events of that bush picnic. **1967** HOLDEN *Empty Hills* 49 It was obvious that Felicity was not at all an outdoor girl, nor was she dressed for a bush picnic. **c1871** MASTERS *Autobiography* (ATLMS) 41 I may here mention that **bush pork**, is superior to home fed, as the pigs live upon roots, berries. **1936** LAMBERT *Pioneering Reminisc. Old Wairoa* 147 How thankful I was for a pannikin of tea and a slice of bush pork and damper. **1871** MONEY *Knocking About NZ* 81 They had neither of them seen much of real **bush-roughing** before. **1899** BELL *In Shadow of Bush* 20 The promoters of these **bush townships**—whether it were the Government, private companies or individuals..made the boundaries of them wide enough. **1873** TINNE *Wonderland of Antipodes* 7 A 'new chum'..was consulting my friend as to what amount of luggage he would advise for **bush travel**. **1916** COWAN *Bush Explorers* (VUWTS) 9 I have done some alpine climbing and rough bush travel since those days. **1922** COWAN *NZ Wars* (1955) II. 458 As the summer drew on the conditions of bush travel improved. **1847** *NZ Jrnl.* VII. 240 Sunrise, after which no **bush-traveller** ought to be in bed. **1853** SWAINSON *Auckland* 123 Nor should a stranger, or novice in bush travelling..be advised to start alone. On the contrary he should..secure as a companion some experienced bush traveller. **1881** CAMPBELL *Poenamo* 155 [Supple-jack] sometimes catches you by the neck, the most temper-provoking..thing that ever tried the temper of a bush traveller. **1851** *Richmond-Atkinson Papers* (1960) I. 83 We have with us tea & sugar which are considered almost indispensable in **bush travelling**. **1857** HURSTHOUSE *NZ* I. 251 Visitors and colonists 'bush travelling' in New Zealand, generally provide themselves with a native attendant, as guide... New Zealand 'bush travelling'..beats a Highland tour by a hundred per cent. **1879** HAAST *Geol. Canterbury & Westland* 58 I parted with this gentleman, who had..been accustomed for years to New Zealand bush travelling. **1896** *TrNZI* XXVIII. 88 Three of them (strong and determined, and used to heavy bush-travelling) arranged to visit that out-of-the-way spot. **1921** *Quick March* 10 Dec. 9 The old-timer was talking of bush-travelling and the difficulty in rough forest country of maintaining one's direction. **1935** ODELL *Handbook Arthur Pass National Park* 39 The old pipe-line..eliminates the worst of the bush travelling. **1871** MARCUS CLARKE in Money *Knocking About NZ* vi He asked me to write a preface to this record of rough and ready **bush-wandering**.

b. In sense *bush* B 1 b 'forested', or 'surrounded by bush'.

1873 BULLER *Birds NZ* 246 It frequents rivers, **bush-creeks**, lagoons and swamps. **1912** *TrNZI* XLIV. 64 Here the edge of a bush-creek is fringed with *Muehlenbeckia*. **1947** NEWTON *Wayleggo* 110 It was mainly heavy flats bounded by..high **bush faces**, topped by ragged peaks. **1960** CRUMP *Good Keen Man* 32 All the bush faces were spotted with the dead branches of trees. **1938** LANCASTER *Promenade* 133 'I'm going to be a Mohammedan,' announced Tiffany..sneaking down to the **bush-gully** to conduct her orisons among the birds. **1992** SMITHYMAN *Auto/Biographies* 9 Now the fish steers towards the bush gully..and disappears. **1879** GUDGEON *Reminisc. War in NZ* 70 The men did little but scout and forage..allowing the Hauhaus to erect a strong pah in the **bush-ranges**. **1953** SUTHERLAND *Golden Bush* (1963) 41 The cleared country narrowed and ran out in the higher ground of the bush range at the head. **1982** KEENE *Myrtle & Sophia* 26 'My farm extends right to the top of those bush ranges,' he said proudly.

c. In sense *bush* B 1 c 'composed of bush materials'.

1960 Masters *Back-Country Tales* 266 The party had to leave without having a chance to try the **bush fireplace**, always a touchy thing to build.

d. In sense *bush* B 2 'non-urban, rough in manner or style'.

1862 Wekey *Otago As It Is* 45 Most of these [indigenous timbers]..serve to supply the limited demand created by what is called '**bush architecture**'. **1882** Hay *Brighter Britain* I. 268 Bright and cheerful, neat and comely, pleasant partners at a **bush-ball** are these half-Anglicized daughters of the Ngatewhatua. **1953** Reed *Story of Kauri* 138 Some **bush buns**. These were made [c1900] from pieces of left-over dough, kneaded and made into handy sizes, and containing a sprinkling of currants and raisins. **1986** *Sunday News* (Auckland) 16 Nov. 5 Self-consciously clad in their **bush dress**, 'essential attire', they were hanging-on in there for what had been billed as the most incredible book launch of the year. **1856** Abraham *Walk with Bishop NZ* in Taylor *Early Travellers* (1959) 111 Instead of the old proverb, 'Good wine needs no *bush*', the Bishop..always reads it, 'Good bush needs no wine'... I feel as if I have a lee-way of a fortnight's **bush-fare** to make up. **1986** Richards *Off the Sheep's Back* 38 [To our British teacher] a paddock was now a field, our tucker or crib bags (made out of sugar bags) became satchels or lunch bags and our oilskin coats became macs. We preferred to retain our **bush language**. **1988** Pickering *Hills* Mar. With the bush language there comes a certain attitude to the hills, a conviction that the bush is a great place to be.

3. Special Comb. **a.** In sense *bush* B 1 above 'pertaining to the bush': **bush boss** (or **bush manager**), the person in charge of the logging operations in the bush as distinct from the operations at the sawmill; **bush-boy**, (a) [AND 1856], also **bush girl, bush children** *pl.*, a boy or girl, or children, born and raised in a (recently cleared) bushed area, (b) one employed at bush work, felling, logging, etc.; **bush cane**, supplejack; **bush-clerk** *obs.*, a clerk dealing with the bush operations of a sawmill; **bush-clerking**, (following) the occupation of bush-clerk; **bush contractor**, one who contracts to clear-fell or log bush (see esp. quot. 1969); **bush-cutting** *vbl. n.*, see bushfalling; **bush disease** *obs.*, bush sickness; **bush-fed** *a.*, cattle raised on *bush feed*; **bush feed** [AND 1841], the leaves of forest plants as green-feed for stock; **bush fever**, a fever of cattle caused by the ingestion of certain bush plants; **bush food**, food gained from the bush, food usual or suitable for bushmen; **bush-fright**, a sense of panic brought on by being lost in the bush or feeling totally immersed in its solitude; **bush girl**, see *bush-boy* above; **bush gum**, solidified kauri-gum found on living trees (see gum 2); **bush-hand** [AND 1850], (a) one experienced in bushcraft, or in rural or backblocks life and work, (b) a man employed in the bush work of a sawmill, clearing-gang, etc.; **bush-hat**, a hat suited for wear in the bush; **bush honey** [AND 1907], wild honey, or, occas., honey made from nectar collected from native forest; **bush horse** [AND 1842], one trained for bush conditions; **bush inspector**, see quot.; **bush itch**, see *birch itch* (birch 4); **bush legs** [an extension of *sea-legs*], in the phr. **to get one's bush legs**, to learn how to walk through the bush; **bush level**, **bush limit**, bushline; **bush manager**, see *bush-boss* above; **bush railway**, see *bush tram(line)* below; **bush scout** *hist.*, one employed as a military scout in the bush warfare associated with the New Zealand wars; **bush-scouting**; **bush section**, a parcel of forested land, or an urban or suburban section with some trees on it (see also section 3); **bush selection**, see *bush section* prec.; **bush settlement**, a small settlement in a remote area recently cleared of bush, having few amenities (see also *bush settler* 1889 quot.); **bush settler** *obs.*, one who brings bush land into cultivation, or a settler in (originally) bushed back-country (see quot. 1889); **bush shooting** *vbl. n.*, shooting deer (often at close range) in the bush as distinct from in open country, also *v. intr.*; **bush skiddy** *forestry*, see quot.; **bush skids** *n. pl.*, see skids; **bush stalking** *vbl. n.*, stalking deer in the bush as distinct from shooting them in the open (cf. *bush shooting*); **bush swag**, a type of swag (or pack) best suited to use in the bush; **bush track** [AND 1837], a track through or in the bush (cf. *Maori track* (maori B 5 a)); **bush tram** *obs.* (a) the locomotive of a bush tramway system (see loci, tram 1 a) (b) see next entry; **bush tramline**, **bush tramway**, a light railway system, usu. with wooden rails, used to haul logs from the bush to sawmill (see esp. *tramway* (tram 2); **bush uniform**, see bush costume; **bushwoman**, a white woman living in the bush or backblocks; **bush-work** [AND 1846], work done in the bush, or as part of any bush operation such as felling, logging, etc.; **bushworker** [AND 1891], one who does bush-work; **bush-working** *vbl. n.*, usu. *pl.*, an area where bush is being, or has been, 'worked' or logged for timber; as *attrib.*, utilized in logging or other bush work.

1924 Gibson *Gibbie Galoot* 72 The **bush bosses** gave the Saturday as a whole holiday. **1950** p.c. R. Gilberd (Okaihau) Next in importance to the bush-boss is the 'breaker-out', where steam haulers are still in use. **1952-53** *NZ Forest Service Gloss.* (TS) Bush Boss A logging foreman. **1905** Thomson *Bush Boys* 11 Hugh was truly a 'boy' and a '**bush-boy**'. **1910** Cockayne *NZ Plants & Their Story* 33 Very frequently, as bush boys and girls well know, their [*sc.* Muehlenbeckia] rope-like stems hang swaying from the forest roof. **1910** in *Dominion* (Wellington) 31 Aug. (1963) 7 [Taihape in those early days] carried a big floating population of bushmen... Those bush boys were game... Upwards of 30 of them came forward to try their luck [at bareback riding]. **1992** Park *Fence around the Cuckoo* 8 Like so many bush boys he was a brilliant observer and often intelligent theorist about his own environment. **1871** Money *Knocking About NZ* 115 A piece of gauze fastened to a circle of supple-jack or **bush cane**..was all that was required for their [*sc.* whitebait] capture. **1955** Boswell *Dim Horizons* 78 The Katui school!... How I adored the succession of teachers who came to impart at least the rudiments of knowledge to us 'bush children'. **1994** Arnold *New Zealand's Burning* 155 We turn now to bush children. They too were part of the family team, contributing to the farm economy from an early age. **1924** Gibson *Gibbie Galoot* 65 [A bush-boss c1890 speaks:] You're now a **bush-clerk**, and that's the Kauri analogy to a midshipman's job in the Navy. **1924** Gibson *Gibbie Galoot* 71 **Bush-clerking** [c1890] requires but little brains. **1875** *TrNZI* VII. 183 It is the utter recklessness displayed by..**bush contractors**.. which is destroying our forests at a rate constantly increasing. **1916** Stallworthy *Early N. Wairoa* 39 An enterprising bush contractor..purchased and improved land at Arapohue. **1927** *NZJST* IX. 166 The writer is indebted to Mr R H Gibbons, bush contractor for the logs. **1969** Moore *Forest to Farm* 39 The bush contractor was the man who..usually contracted with a sawmill owner to fell the trees, crosscut them into logs, and deliver [them to the mill skids]. **1865** Mueller *My Dear Bannie* (1958) 56 The work consists chiefly of **bush-cutting**, which certainly is as bad as can be, owing to the many creeping plants, supplejacks, &c., growing in these old forests. **1941** Baker *NZ Slang* 15 New Zealand originals include *bush-cutter* and *bush-cutting* (both used before 1863). **1899** *Ann. Rep. Dept. Agric.* V. 68 '**Bush' Disease.** This affliction appears to be due rather to innutrition [*sic*] than to any disease, and is apparently confined to the Rotorua district. The animals seem to pine away, but if removed to other and older pastures they usually recover. **1899** *Ann. Rep. Dept. Agric.* VII. 11 Mr Gilruth visited the Rotorua bush lands re 'bush disease'. **1911** *NZJAg.* Sept. 394 The evidence adduced..goes to show that the condition in stock known locally as 'bush disease' or 'bush sickness' which occurs in the Rotorua, Matamata and Tauranga Counties..is not a disease in the proper sense of the term, but a physiological condition. **1882** Hay *Brighter Britain* I. 207 As **bush-fed** beasts are in good condition at the end of the dry season, when pasture-raised cattle are poor, we do as well by them as could be desired. **1854** *Richmond-Atkinson Papers* (1960) I. 154 The **bush feed** keeps the cattle in fine order in winter time. **1882** Hay *Brighter Britain* I. 207 He [*sc.* the open-land farmer] has no bush-feed for cattle as we have. **1967** McLatchie *Tang of Bush* 61 Those [cattle] accustomed to hina-hina could eat it with impunity, but to strangers it was poison... We had no further trouble with **bush fever** unless strange cattle were brought in. **1922** Cowan *NZ Wars* (1955) II. 428 A rather good bush vegetable is the *pikopiko*, the curled shoots of the *mauku* fern. The natives have long given up the use of these **bush foods**. **1948** Finlayson *Tidal Creek* (1979) 80 There's a loneliness about the bush and something that pulls taut the nerves... Jake remembers old settlers speaking about such experiences. **Bush fright**, they reckoned. **1955** *BJ Cameron Collection* (TS July) bush-fright (n) The panic which follows the knowledge of being lost. **1910** Grossman *Heart of Bush* 139 As there were only the family and two little **bush girls** who had played at being bridesmaids, formality was dispensed with. **1863** Butler *First Year* x 147 How many hands shall you want? We will say a couple of good **bush hands**, who will put up your hut and yards and wool-shed. **1871** *TrNZI* V. 182 A bush-hand, living the life of a hermit in his little whare of tree-fern stems, up in the Waio river-bed. **1894** *NZ Official Yearbook* 333 In the kauri district, bush-hands are commonly paid 20s., or rarely 18s. per week, with board and lodgings. **1925** Mander *Allen Adair* (1971) 90 He had the gumfield trade in full, and most of that now done by the bush hands. **1964** Howe *Stamper Battery* 7 When he heard that bush-hands were wanted, he and Mum moved into the Kanaeranga bush. **1891** Marriott-Watson *Web of Spider* 14 Throwing himself again on the bracken, he pushed his **bush-hat** from his head. **1988** *Through the Looking Glass* 63 This usually consisted of my brother's..boots..my cherished bush hat (a cross between an Australian outback hat and a Daniel Boone cap) and my..parka. **1952** Lyon *Faring South* 105 I never knew the pakeha to suffer any after-effects from the use of **bush honey**, and I have felled many bee trees. **1967** McLatchie *Tang of Bush* 61 We usually had a good supply of bush honey [c1900]. The most likely place to find it was in a hollow tree. **1982** Burton *Two Hundred Yrs. NZ Food* 102 A strongly flavoured New Zealand bush honey is best for this dish [*sc.* Canterbury lamb with honey]. **1995** *Contact* (Wellington) 27 Apr. 12 Manuka, Kamahi, Rewarewa.. and pasture honey..all have different tastes. As well there is bush honey which can incorporate a variety of tastes. **1867** Lush *Waikato Jrnls.* (1982) 109 The Bishop has often told me she is a first-rate **bush horse** and so she proved herself to be—she went on and on—in and out—struggling through this and plunging through that and at last..emerged [from the bush]. **1912** Booth *Five Years NZ* 42 The trained bush horse will stand quietly where his rider leaves him. **1982** *Dominion* (Wellington) 27 Aug. 8 Merv is one of 13 **bush inspectors** employed..by the Department of Labour... Their principal concern is the safety and welfare of all persons in 'bush undertakings and sawmills'. **c1882–83** WILMOT *Diary* in Hall-Jones *Early Fiordland* (1968) 159 Homer unable to work today because of the '**bush itch**' and the men got their blankets flyblown. **1974** [see *birch itch* (BIRCH 4)]. **1922** COWAN *NZ Wars* (1955) II. 210 The recruits from Wellington knew nothing of the bush... They were falling over logs and vines; a man needs to get his **bush-legs** just as a sea passenger needs to get his sea-legs; he must learn where to place his feet and how to get through the bush with the greatest speed and the least trouble. **1897** *AJHR C-1* 121 There is a pass below **bush-level**, at the head of the Hauroto Burn. **1923** *NZJST* VI. 87 Thus Philpott (1919) describes it as 'plentiful in all forests and extending to the bush-level on the mountains'. **1952** THOMSON *Deer Hunter* 123 The bush-covered mountains reached from the water's edge up to the natural bush level. **1896** HARPER *Pioneer Work* 39 The robin..is a constant companion in some localities, as far as the **bush limit**. **1902** *Settler's Handbook NZ* 18 The greater part [of the Nelson Land District is]..high and mountainous, and on the western and inland ranges covered with dense forest to the bush-limit, at from 4,000 ft. to 4,500 ft. **1953** REED *Story of Kauri* 263 Ted Thompson, who was **bush manager** for the K[auri] T[imber] C[ompany] at No Gum Camp..attended to the cleaning up of all the old logs in the various driving creeks. **1979** *Islands* 25 267 We sat around a German coal range the couple had hauled by means of wood-track **bush railway** to the top of the hill on which they had built their house. **1986** OWEN & PERKINS *Speaking for Ourselves* 161 In some cases steam engines were employed [to get logs out of bush], or locomotives running on a bush railway, or 'tram'. **1935** COWAN *Hero Stories NZ* xi Soldiers and Maori warriors, missionaries, settlers, **bush scouts**, sailors, heroic women are the leading figures in these tales of true romance. *Ibid.* xi Memories of old Ben Biddle and Donald Sutherland..telling the tales of their **bush scouting**. *Ibid.* 223 In his crippled old age he was cheered now and again by a visit from some old friend of his bush-scouting, bush-clearing..days. **1851** *Richmond-Atkinson Papers* (1960) I. 95 One great blessing in a **bush section** is the abundance of firewood. **1905** THOMSON *Bush Boys* 137 He was an expert bushman, and Mr. MacLean considered himself fortunate in securing his services from the time of taking up his bush-section. **1959** MASTERS *Tales of Mails* 141 The early settlers.., for a number of years after taking up their bush sections, had to rely on packhorse transport from Dannevirke. **1973** MCELDOWNEY *Arguing with My Grandmother* 10 He first had a sawmill at Ngaere, later a bush section many miles inland from Stratford. **1989** *Sunday Mag.* 29 Oct. 8 It is a cosy..home [in Titirangi] on a large bush section. **1907** GIPPS *Outward Bound* 27 On this spacious **bush-selection**. **1892** *NZ Official Handbook* 151 The New Zealand fungus known to commerce is found upon various kinds of decayed timber in the North Island, in what are called new **bush settlements**. **1905** THOMSON *Bush Boys* 11 There were only two 'Misters' there, the schoolmaster..and the young Minister, who paid periodical visits to this bush-settlement. **1911** BOREHAM *Selwyn* 63 Whenever he came upon some rustic township, bush settlement or native *pa*, he at once..threw all his energy into his ministration to the deepest needs of the people. **1853** in Macmorran *Octavius Hadfield* (1969) 81 We started about 5.30, and at 11 reached the place of a **bush settler** named Cowell. **1860** *Voices from Auckland* 67 The bush-settler must lop and log, the nine acres already fallen. **1889** WAKEFIELD *NZ after Fifty Yrs.* 140 When..bush settlers are spoken of, they are to be understood to be those who buy or lease forest land, covered with heavy timber, and clear it for the purpose of sowing the land with grass..or..growing..crops. **1905** [see BUSH LIFE]. **1911** *TrNZI* XLIII. 440 During late years the dairy industry has been one of the most popular..industries of the bush settler. **1930** GUTHRIE *NZ Memories* 107 In the outlying districts the life of bush settlers was very strenuous and terribly lonely. **1940** COWAN *Sir Donald Maclean* 51 No one imagined fifty..years ago..that the South Auckland ranges would be ruined..by the joint efforts of bush-settler and sawmiller. **1965** *NZ Geogr.* Oct. 147 The bush settler rarely attempted to keep the tops of the palings [of fences] at the same height. **1952** THOMSON *Deer Hunter* 42 Some say the open sight is better for snap or **bush shooting** and the aperture more suitable for long range shooting. *Ibid.* 44 In bush shooting our range would vary from a few yards up to seventy or eighty depending on the thickness of the undergrowth. **1943** BENNETT *English in NZ* in *Amer. Speech* XVIII. 85 A **bush skiddy** is a man who works on the cleared tracks which carry logs to the mill. **1952-53** *NZ Forest Service Gloss.* (TS) **Bush Skids** A platform made of logs and used to assist in loading logs or trees on to vehicles. **1952** ORBELL *Comfort & Commonsense in Bush* 50 Stalking generally takes two different forms:- (1) High tops open country stalking: (2) **Bush stalking**. **1892** MCHUTCHESON *Camp Life Fiordland* 46 The horse-shoe [swag] won't do in the bush... I'll show you the '**bush**' **swag**... When the compact knapsack had been slung between our shoulders, leaving the arms quite free, and no projecting ends to catch, we recognised how convenient the bush swag was. **1865** CHUDLEIGH *Diary* 13 May (1950) 184 Another forde [*sic*], another **bush track**. **1874** BAINES *Edward Crewe* 231 On most bush tracks men follow each other—Indian file. *Ibid.* 281 After dinner we rode along a bush track through the forest to call on Mr. Page. **1888** BULLER *Birds NZ* I. 162 At the time..this place could be only reached by a canoe journey..from Foxton, or by a rude bush-track—one of the Maori war-paths of former times. **1907** MANSFIELD *Letters* (1984) I. 31 He guided us through the bush track by the river. **1916** GASCOYNE *Soldiering NZ* 26 There in an open spot in *manuka* I left my horse and saddle (for the bush track was impassable for a horse in the dark). **1922** COWAN *NZ Wars* (1955) I. 117 The hostile Maoris maintained their communication with Rauparaha..either by canoe at night or by the bush tracks. **1940** *Tales Pioneer Women* (1988) 33 She..struggled through the bush tracks..taking three days to reach the school. **1965** GILLHAM *Naturalist in NZ* 23 The trunks may be..laid side by side across the bush tracks to offer a footing above the peaty mud. **1982** SANSOM *In Grip of Island* 31 Trampers who walk the four-mile bush track from Halfmoon Bay..come out on the open green patch. **1952–53** *NZ Forest Service Gloss.* (TS) **Bush tram** a, usually steam driven, locomotive hauling bogeys of logs from the bush to mill, usually on wooden rails. **1970** DAVIN *Not Here Not Now* 125 The cart track petered out and became the track of the old bush trams. They could see the wooden rails along which the logs had been brought. **1952-53** *NZ Forest Service Gloss.* (TS) **Bush tramline** A light logging railway, usually on wooden rails. **1965** MCLAGLAN *Stethoscope & Saddlebags* 174 It was an extraordinary journey, mostly on one of those amazing bush tramlines built for timber trucks by amateur engineers who worked in the mills. **1958** *Tararua* Sept. 32 We crossed the Routeburn on a good swing bridge and picked up an old **bush tramway** which led us well up the river. **1969** MOORE *Forest to Farm* 38 Ofte[n] it [*sc.* a log] was 'fleeted up' on the skids ready for loading on to a bush tramway, the motive power for which was supplied either by draught animals or small steam locomotives. **1984** BEARDSLEY *Blackball 08* 161 The little mill unions..were always in the most inaccessible parts of the Coast and..you had to ride by rickety bush tramway. **1922** COWAN *NZ Wars* (1955) II. 342 [The Maori scouts] marched barefoot.

Steve's **bush uniform** consisted of a blue jumper and a pair of trousers cut short at the knees. **1874** BAINES *Edward Crewe* 192 Truly this poor Maori girl was superior to her degraded and brutish mate, who was only fit to be yoked to one of those demons in human form—I allude to the white **bushwoman**—creatures of a mature age, hideous to look upon..always drunken when opportunity was found, excelling the rough, reckless bushman as the female can and will excel the male in the vices. **1940** DUGGAN *NZ Poems* 38 [Title] The Bushwoman. They're bidding me to town. They say they are ashamed That I should live alone... It's strange that sons of mine Should love the town the best. **1864** MARSHMAN *Canterbury 1862* 48 There are other kinds of unskilled labour going on as road-making, fencing, **bush-work** etc. **1878** ELWELL *Boy Colonists* 238 Sledges were necessary for bush work, for the bush roads were too narrow..for a dray to be worked in them. **1878** BULLER *Forty Yrs. NZ* 316 It was his first acquaintance with our [*sc.* missionary] bush-work. **1898** HOCKEN *Contributions* 59 Colonel Wakefield..had despatched..surveying cadets, and seven men selected for their knowledge of bush work. **1922** COWAN *NZ Wars* (1955) II. 210 I had done pioneering bush-work before the Waikato war began. **1939** BEATTIE *First White Boy Born Otago* 45 As bush work proved too heavy the father returned to Waikouaiti. **1986** OWEN & PERKINS *Speaking for Ourselves* 68 At the end of seven months' bushwork we didn't have a brass razoo. **1910** *Triad* 10 Jan. 43 Did you ever hear a New Zealand **bushworker** talk like that? **1936** BELSHAW et al. *Agric. Organiz. NZ* 590 The higher wages paid to bush workers are accounted for partly by the more exacting nature of the work, longer hours, remoteness and consequent lack of social intercourse. **1897** *TrNZI* XXIX. 412 A fire ran through the old **bush-workings**. **1948** *Our Own Country* 26 One shop [at Thames] specialized in the manufacture of sawmilling and bush-working machinery, log-haulers in particular.

b. In sense *bush* B 1 b 'forested', 'surrounded by bush': **bush flat** [see OED 10 c], a flat area having some tall cover, or enclosed by bush; **bush paddock** [AND 1847], a paddock made by clearing standing bush.

1847 *NZ Jrnl.* VII. 90 Another very considerable stream running through fine **bush flats**. **1889** *TrNZI* XXI. 220 Secluded lagoons on the bush-flats in the vicinity of Lake Brunner. **1960** CRUMP *Good Keen Man* 136 Four deer and three hours later we came to a long bush-flat where the trees were enormous. **1872** *TrNZI* IV. 297 In the North it is usually relied upon for the staple, especially on **bush paddocks**.

c. In sense *bush* B 1 c 'composed of bush material': **bush bunk** [AND 1910], a makeshift bunk constructed from materials taken from the bush; **bush chimney**, a chimney constructed of green slabs or other bush materials, often daubed with mud, and having a large base area serving as a hearth; **bush fence** [AND 1828], a crude fence made of logs and branches; **bush fencing**; **bush harrow** *obs.* [spec. use of *bush harrow*: see OED], a makeshift harrow made from materials taken from the bush; **bush hearse**, see quot.; **bush house** *obs.* (a) [AND 1837], see *bush-hut* (b) [AND 1890], a garden summer-house; **bush-hut** [AND 1830], a hut erected in the bush from materials at hand; **bush mattress** *tramping*, dry moss, etc. for makeshift bedding; **bush stain**, see quot. (see also *log stain* (LOG *n.*[1])); **bush stretcher**, a rough or makeshift bedstead consisting of a rectangular frame covered with planks, laths, branches or wire-netting, the whole supported by four (often folding) legs (cf. STRETCHER a);

bushwood [AND 1945], (fire)wood cut from the bush.
    1920 *Quick March* 10 Jan. 41 The construction..was that of most **bush bunks**; the main supports consisting of a section of 'bungi' laid on the ground at each end. These supported wine-berry poles. **1924** ANTHONY *Follow the Call* (1975) 46 He knocked up an extra bush bunk in the bach, and came to live on the job. **1960** MASTERS *Back-Country Tales* 158 Among his other accomplishments, he was an adept at erecting **bush chimneys**. **1986** *Islands* 37 Aug. 41 Blue Knee went to the bush chimney and stirred embers below the water tin suspended from the cooking rail. **1849** PHARAZYN *Journal* (ATLMS) 293 Making a **bush fence**. **1958** PERHAM *Kimberley Flying Column* 32 A kind of yard fenced with logs piled one on top of the other. In New Zealand it would be called a 'bush fence'. **1985** LANGDALE-HUNT *Last Entail Male* 8 In my time we would make an early potato garden by felling the trees in a sheltered hollow where there was no growth underneath, making a bush fence of the trunks and branches round the plot which made it both sheltered and stock proof. **1888** CHUDLEIGH *Diary* 25 June (1950) 362 All hands at **bush fencing** and all very tired. Karawas [supplejacks] as thick as a cloud, every tree hung together like wax. **1858** BEETHAM *Diary* 9 Oct. in Rickard *Strangers in Wilderness* (1967) 98 Made a **bush harrow** and sowed all the land I had grubbed. **1869** WAITE *West Coast Goldfields* 21 The seed was merely thrown down, and a large bush harrow drawn by four or five Maoris, with two women riding on the brush to keep it down, was all the cultivation thought of. **1952** NEWTON *High Country Journey* 144 The accident took place..twenty miles in from Mt. White and the wounded man was sledged out on a '**bush hearse**'. A bush hearse, I should explain, is a forked branch dragged V end first with a litter rigged up on the fork of the branches. **1848** BRUNNER *Exped. Middle Is.* 21 Mar. in Taylor *Early Travellers* (1959) 310 Having constructed our framework, the thatch..was the difficulty... We would..brave the storm for another handful of grass, toitoi..so that about midnight, we could call our covering water-tight for a **bush house**. **1902** SATCHELL *Land of Lost* 164 'Come around to the bush-house'... They seated themselves together on a rustic seat among the ferns. **1905** WHITE *My NZ Garden* 23 Glass structures can be too hot here in summer, so my plants are migratory, and go out..into a skeleton shed with bushes round the sides and forming the roof, commonly called a 'bush-house,' and for summer these places afford much pleasure and occupation. **1915** TrNZI XLVII. 20 Common in damp bush; also cultivated in bush houses on the island. **1920** *Yates Garden Guide* (14edn.) 93 The main objects of a bush-house is [*sic*] to subdue the intense sunlight, keep a cool moist atmosphere around the plants, and to protect them from hot or dry winds. **1850** MCLEAN *Journal* (ATLTS) III. 72 We slept at the Heu Heu posts, where Pohe erected a good **bush-hut**. c**1860** MURDOCK in Beattie *Early Runholding* (1947) 116 The floor of [Moa Hut] is of clay, and the roof without any ceiling. Still, it is warm and comfortable enough, and is a very good example of a bush hut. **1867** BARKER *Station Life* (1870) 181 The mistress of this charming 'bush-hut' [previously described as a picturesque gable-ended little cottage surrounded by a rustic fence] insisted on our having some hot coffee and scones and wild honey. **1981** HUNT *Speaking a Silence* 87 The little hut was quite comfy for a bush hut: just two rooms and no luxuries. **1986** RICHARDS *Off the Sheep's Back* 14 It was not long before the Rongo family instructed the brothers in building a ponga and nikau whare (bush hut) alongside their tent. **1938** *Tararua Tramper* Dec. 4 We helped ourselves liberally to '**bush mattresses**' by stripping thick, heavy fleeces of dry moss from the trunks of old fallen trees. **1958** *Tararua* Sept. 24 Bush mattresses, i.e. dry moss for bedding, I have not heard used, but it occurs in *The Tramper* for 1938. **1982** *Agric. Gloss.* (MAF) 53 **Bush Stain**: Discoloration of wool with charcoal from bush burns. More commonly referred to as log stain. **1924** ANTHONY *Follow the Call* (1975) 5 I didn't have a bed, so I knocked up a **bush stretcher**, with some rails, and nailed sacks across. **1860** SCOTT *Rough Notes on Travels* 55 The **bush-wood** after it is cut down is generally disposed of by burning. **1869** PHILLIPS *Rockwood Jrnl.* 30 July (ATLTS) 191 J.P. for a dray load of bushwood [for firewood] **1930** GUTHRIE *NZ Memories* 70 The lapping of the sea mingled with [the sound]..of the burning bush wood in the boiling of the 'billy'. **1937** MARSH *Vintage Murder* 243 I longed for the smell of burning bush-wood.

d. In sense *bush* B 2 'non-urban, rough in manner or style': **bush baptist** [see OED 11, 1902], a person given to expressing strong religious (usu. fundamentalist) views; one who is not a member of an organized church or group; **bush bread** [AND 1840], DAMPER 1; **bush cattle**, see CATTLE 1; **bush cook** [AND 1887], a camp cook, or one who provides rough–and–ready meals in a camp or outdoor setting ; **bush doctor** [AND 1928], a doctor who practises in the backblocks; **bush-edition** *obs.*, the 'rural' or country edition of a newspaper; **bush hotel** [AND 1865], a hotel in the backblocks; **bush-inn** *obs.* [AND 1847], a remote country inn or accommodation house; **bush jacket**, a bush-shirt or swanndri; **bush justice** [AND 1959], rough justice; **bush-lamp**, SLUSH LAMP or *bush lantern*; **bush lantern**, a bottle lantern (see quot., also LANTERN); **bush nightie** *joc.*, a bush-shirt or swanndri; **bush-philosopher**, a backblocks or rural moralizer given to expressing opinions; **bush poet** [AND 1846], a rural versifier celebrating legends and other matters dear to the heart of the colonial-born; hence **bush poetry**; **bush post-office** [AND 1908], a rural mail-box; **bush-pub**, a backblocks hotel or public house; **bush school** [AND 1852], a country or backblocks school; **bush scone**, a scone baked over embers, a damper; **bush shirt**, a thick, woollen shirt, dark green, or of a vari-coloured check pattern, worn outside the trousers (cf. SWANNDRI); **bush singlet**, see SINGLET 2; **bush-store**, a rural general store; **bush style** [AND 1838], in the style of the bush or of bush life or dress; roughly but often hospitably, with few comforts; makeshift;; **bush-talk**, vernacular backblocks speech; **bush tea** [AND 1848], *billy tea* (BILLY *n.*¹ 6); **bush wagon**, see quot.; **bush whisk(e)y**, illicitly distilled whisky (cf. HOKONUI 1).
    1908 *Truth* 15 Feb. 6 [A correspondent writes] I am a solicitor and likewise a **bush baptist**. **1935** STRONG in Partridge *Slang Today* 287 Good job I'm a bush baptist; I can please myself as to what rank I parade with. **1941** BAKER *NZ Slang* 15 Derivatives..commonly used both in New Zealand and Australia [include]..bush baptist. **1988** MCGILL *Dict. Kiwi Slang* 24 *bush baptist* religious fundamentalist or religious poseur. **1849** *Otago Jrnl.* 5 Nov. 71 Dampers, that is flour & water mixed together..& thrown on the ashes..; this is **bush bread** & I had rather have it than any bread I ever tasted. **1873** ST JOHN *Pakeha Rambles* in Taylor *Early Travellers* (1959) 554 Good, nay delicious, as the *kora* is when boiled..or even when knocked up in a curry by the untutored paws of a **bush cook**. **1906** *Truth* 20 Jan. 1 When the bush cook is not using heavy damper as a slow poison. **1925** MANDER *Allen Adair* (1971) 43 He had known that Allen was not a bush cook, but he had said it because a cook was the most urgent need. **1953** REED *Story of Kauri* 124 Someone with a craving for more dainty fare than that provided by the bush cook [in a logging contractor's camp]. **1969** MOORE *Forest to Farm* 40 The bush gang..would include first of all a good bush cook, used to cooking over an open fire..and able to bake and roast in the 'camp ovens' generally used. **1986** OWEN & PERKINS *Speaking for Ourselves* 153 Bush cooks that I knew were tremendous fellows at preparing sweets of various kinds. **1873** BARKER *Station Amusements* 150 A **bush doctor**, name of Tomkins, who was likely to be round by Simmons' 'cos o' his missus. **1903** *NZ Illustr. Mag.* VIII. 128 The **bush-edition** howls out innumerable orders. **1947–48** BEATTIE *Pioneer Recolls.* (1956) 38 The 'old hands' used to tell some queer stories about this '**bush hotel**' [at Pyramid] and did so with an amusing mixture of condemnation for its worst features and pride in its eccentricities. **1853** ROCHFORT *Adventures of Surveyor* 23 The 'house of call' was..situated on the opposite side of the river... The landlord, came over and ferried us across to his house, which is the best **bush inn** in New Zealand—containing six or seven good-sized rooms with glass windows. **1907** GAMBIER *Links in My Life* 116 We..marched [c1860] on foot through the wonderful forest to a small bush inn kept by a man called Selby. **1985** *NZ Herald* (Auckland) 4 June 2 Mr Johnstone [a Kaikohe fisherman] was wearing knee-length gumboots and a **bush-jacket**. 'I..had to get down under the water to pull my swanny over my head,' he said last night. **1979** *Evening Post* (Wellington) 13 Nov. 32 The penalty he had already suffered was substantial, a penalty by way of '**bush justice**'. **1990** *Dominion Sunday Times* (Wellington) 5 Aug. 3 He..had gone to the..house to deliver some bush justice. He said he would 'deal to' the person involved. **1891** CHAMIER *Philosopher Dick* 36 The **bush-lamp** had burned low. **1963** CAMPBELL *Golden North* 96 Those who remained made bush lamps by knocking the bottoms off bottles and putting lighted candles inside them. **1873** PYKE *Wild Will Enderby* (1889, 1974) I. xii 42 A **bush lantern** is constructed by placing a candle within the neck of a clear glass bottle, the bottom of which has..been knocked off. **1991** *National Radio* (Jack Perkins interview) 12.45 p.m. Everyone wore the old bush shirt or Swanndri—the **bush nightie** as it was called. **1882** HAY *Brighter Britain* I. 127 The Old Colonial is a **bush-philosopher**, and delivers himself of moral orations in the shanty of nights. **1903** KING *Bill's Philosophy* Intro. The moralisings of his bush philosopher Bill. **1890** *Otago Witness* (Dunedin) 18 Dec. 21 The New Zealand **bush poet**—I speak of him in the singular, but his name is legion—is not dead, nor even seriously discouraged. **1952** NEWTON *High Country Journey* 105 Another story is commemorated by a piece of rough **bush poetry** which still adorns the wall of the Glenthorne musterers' hut. **1876** KENNEDY *Colonial Travel* 196 In the middle of the [Canterbury] plains we drew up alongside a post, on which was nailed what looked like a small writing-desk. The driver leant out, lifted the lid, took out a small leather bag, and drove off. It was a **bush post-office**—a very private letter-box, belonging to some sheep-station. **1890** *NZ Observer* 22 Mar. 9 At 4 o'clock he had started with two two-gallon billies to fetch beer from the nearest **bush-pub**. **1852** MUNDY *Our Antipodes* 61 There was a humble hedge-school—or rather **bush-school**..and a crowd of flaxen..children rushing from its porch. **1906** *Truth* 27 Jan. 4 Bush Schools: Low wages, hard graft, and unnecessary worry is the lot of the out-back schoolteacher. **1950** WILSON *My First Eighty Yrs.* 141 That evening [c1897] we baked **bush scones** on sticks to the delight of our friends. **1949** THE SARGE *Excuse my Feet* 110 He went away in search of his *Groppi mokka*, which consisted of a freshly pressed..pair of slacks and a **bush shirt**. **1970** PORTER *Nor'west Arch* 66 The rest of the audience turned up in bush shirts and woolly jumpers. **1985** *Evening Post* (Wellington) 16 Feb. 1 His bush shirt was described as

a knee-length Swandri, worn with blue jeans and the boots. **1990** CHAVASSE *Integrity* 25 There were several four-wheel-drive vehicles there..and maybe thirty or forty solid-looking young men in swandrys and colourful bush shirts getting ready to go. **1882** HAY *Brighter Britain* II. 27 When enough [gum] has been collected and scraped it is carried down to the nearest **bush-store** or settlement, where it is at once sold. **1914** HALL *Woman in Antipodes* 86 I had time to..see some of the typical bush-stores, with their disordered medley of merchandise. **1890** *Otago Witness* (Dunedin) 23 Dec. 18 They..proceeded to 'knock down' their cheque in approved **bush style** at the first grog shanty. **1891** CHAMIER *Philosopher Dick* 141 The table was laid in regular bush style, with tin plates and pannikins, iron forks and spoons. **1959** MASTERS *Tales of Mails* 18 Tents had been erected to accommodate the numerous [wedding] guests from distant parts, in true bush style. **1907** LANCASTER *Tracks We Tread* 87 Then Steve's heart leapt in him at the sound of the **bush-talk**, which is a language all of its own. **1891** WALLACE *Rural Econ. Austral. & NZ* 43 **Bush tea** is..boiled in a can. **1925** WEBB *Miss Peters' Special* 19 Peter used to take the milk to the factory, driving Dolly in a **bush wagon**— the low, four-wheeled springless cart so popular in the bush districts of New Zealand. **1899** *Hawera & Normanby Star* 17 May 2 Quite a lot of people do not..like hare. They seem to think it is like **bush whisky**: 'the flavour is pretty strong'. **1906** *Truth* 7 Apr. 1 Bush whisky makes the boozer think the world is upside down. **1918** CLARK *My Erratic Pal* 45 Vile bush whiskey.

4. In the names of plants and animals (often in the sense of 'wild' as distinct from 'domestic'), see entries for: BEE 1 a, CLEMATIS b, CREEPER *n*.[1], CROW 1, DOG 2 a, FALCON, FLAX 8 (ASTELIA), FUNGUS 1 a, GRASS 2 (32), HAWK 2 (1), LILY 2 (2), MANUKA 2 (1), MOA 1 b, NETTLE 2 b, PAINKILLER 2, PARROT 2 (2), PIG *n*.[1] 1 a, PIGEON 2 (1), RAT *n*.[1] 2, ROBIN 1, SARSAPARILLA, WARBLER 2 (1), WREN 2 (1). Also **bush devil**, the *tree weta* (WETA 2 (5), see also TAIPO 5); **bush hen** *obs.*, WEKA 1; **bush snail**, any of various land snails of the genus *Paryphanta* or *Powelliphanta* (fam. Paryphantidae), KAURI SNAIL, PUPURANGI; **bush thistle** *South Island*, the sowthistle (THISTLE 2 (5) a).
1957 *Star Sun* (Christchurch) 9 Nov. 2 On the West Coast of the South Island, 'taipo', or what is supposed to be the English translation of that word, '**bush devil**', is the name generally given to the common tree weta. **1882** HAY *Brighter Britain* II. 219 The Weka..is found plentifully in the woods. Settlers call it the '**bush-hen**'. *Ibid.* II. 337 We wish it had been a weka, or bush-hen, as that is more succulent eating. **1959** MCLINTOCK *Descr. Atlas* 27 Students of the large **bush snails** (*Paryphanta*) have found this an interesting area. **1983** HENDERSON *Down from Marble Mountain* 127 Where..woodhens once stalked..and bush snails made slow and thoughtful circles in time. **1985** *NZ Times 3* Feb. 12 The bush snails [were] dying, the woodhens confounded. **c1920** bush thistle [see PUHA 1 a].

bush, *v. intr.* Usu. as **bush it** (the simplex verb is recorded only as a *vbl. n.*). **a.** [AND 1825.] To camp in the bush (for a night); to camp out.
1848 TORLESSE *Papers* (1958) 42 We could not cross the Coldstream and bushed it on the banks. **1862** GOLDIE 5 May in Beattie *Pioneers Explore Otago* (1947) 98 I resolved to scramble along the side of the lake..even though we had to 'bush it' for a night or two.

b. *Obs.* [AND 1839.] To live in the bush; to live a bush life.
1853 *McLean Papers* (ATLTS) XI. 110 But for them, he might still be 'bushing' it in the Omata.

Hence **bushing it** (also **bushing** [AND 1839]) *vbl. n.*, living (or camping) in the bush.
1848 BRUNNER *Exped. Middle Is.* 12 Apr. in Taylor *Early Travellers* (1959) 313 There being no material for erecting a shelter, we had to hoist our blankets for a shed, but found a year's bushing had made a sad alteration in their waterproof qualities. **1850** SYMONDS *Journal* 26 Jan. in Pascoe *Explorers & Travellers* (1983) 31 These Mokau natives seem more apt to bushing than most I have seen owing to the rough country they inhabit. **1851** WARD *Journal* 7 Apr. (1951) 164 Robert..proved his inexperience in 'bushing' by insisting on taking a cup and saucer and teaspoon..and other most unnecessary articles for tent life. **1846** *NZ Jrnl.* VI. 166 I passed the night under a pine-tree..and awoke, after my first experience of 'bushing it', exceedingly refreshed. **1853** ADAMS *Canterbury Settlement* 40 A little more experience in 'bushing it' would have taught us to have left the bush at once to its fate [*sc.* by fire]. **1854** RICHARDSON *Summer's Excursion* 159 We decided on encamping for the night, or colonially speaking, 'bushing it'.

bush-bashing, *vbl. n.* Moving or tramping through undergrowth off a formed track. Also *transf.* driving a four-wheeled vehicle off a formed road. Also *ppl. a.* Cf. BASH *v.* 2.
1958 *Tararua* Sept. 39 We had the alternatives of facing a wet crossing..or staying on our own side [of the river] and perhaps getting involved in a bush-bashing session. *Ibid.* 43 The following day our bush-bashing commenced... A good deer track came to an abrupt end at a cliff face. **1985** *NZ Times* 28 Apr. 29 [Heading] Bush-bashing comes easily in Suzuki's dinky little wagon... It has always been a source of amazement..just how many people use the little Suzuki off roader as a round-town hack.

Hence, by back-formation, **bush-bash** (also occas. **bush-crash**) *v. intr.* [AND 1967], to tramp with difficulty through undergrowth off a formed track; **bush-basher** *transf.*, a four-wheel–drive off-road vehicle.
1967 *Evening Post* (Wellington) 6 Dec. 16 But half the track had been washed away so we decided to '**bush bash**' to get to Cone Ridge. **1981** *Dominion* (Wellington) 2 Feb. 3 They were lifted out..after losing their way..bush-bashing till 3am on Saturday morning. **1988** PICKERING *Hills* 8 So to cope with the rituals of tramping..a slang language has developed to suit... 'Crud' (cloud), 'bush-bash'..and many, many more. **1991** *Dominion Sunday Times* (Wellington) 17 Nov. 23 We chose the wrong spur to climb and..had to bush-bash our way to where the ridges converged before we met the track. **1985** *NZ Times* 28 Apr. 29 Ostensibly designed as a mini **bush-basher**, the Suzuki has nevertheless proved to be a winner among the rich and trendy people. **1965** SHADBOLT *Among Cinders* 33 We followed a faint track as far as it went, then we just **bush-crashed**.

bush burn.

1. a. Land cleared by felling and burning off the bush. See also BURN *n*.[1] 1.
1861 MORGAN *Journal* 27 Apr. (1963) 29 Last week sowed some grass seed on bush burn. **1936** *Introduction to the Grasses of New Zealand* 64 It [*sc.* cocksfoot] is especially valuable on certain classes of 'bush-burns'. **1958** *Tararua* Sept. 24 We also have *bush burns*, areas where the bush has been recently burnt off. **1960** MASTERS *Back-Country Tales* 34 About half a mile in from the Inland road, the track passes through an old bush burn. **1981** BROOKER et al. *NZ Medicinal Plants* 50 *Aristotelia serrata*... This handsome shrub is common on bush burns and the outskirts of forests.

b. Used *attrib.* in Comb. as **bush-burn country, farmer, mixture, sowing**.
1945 *Korero* (AEWS Background Bulletin) 26 Mar. 10 The 'bush burn' farmer at least replaced the forest with grass. **1951** LEVY *Grasslands NZ* (1970) 244 Much undressed seed and even seed cleanings were used in the so-called cheap mixtures for rough bush-burn country. *Ibid.* 251 The weak, weedy swards..are often found, particularly where poor seed mixtures were used in the original bush-burn sowings. **1959** MCLINTOCK *Descr. Atlas* 39 In Taranaki and the Manawatu..good pastures were established on the 'bush burn' country. **1985** *NZ Times* 3 Feb. 12 Harry Barrow..nipping in and around the logs, flicking to and fro handfuls of grass seed, the grand old bushburn mixture.

2. The act or process, or an instance, of clearing bush by felling and burning.
1893 *TrNZI* XXV. 436 As may easily be seen after a bush-burn. **1930** *NZJST* XII. 4 Now that the effect of the early bush-burns is disappearing sheep are showing signs of malnutrition over considerable areas. **1932** *Ibid.* XIII. 57 After the bush-burns, the sheep did well for a time. **1936** BELSHAW et al. *Agric. Organiz. NZ* 81 A soil on which 'dopiness' develops [in sheep] is..found on deteriorated lands, i.e., lands which originally were highly fertile due to the ashes from the 'bush burn'. **1959** MCLINTOCK *Descr. Atlas* 39 The settlers..soon learned the art of the 'bush burn'. **1964** *Weekly News* (Auckland) 22 Jan. 39 To burn everything cleanly but the heavy trunks is so important to the success of the bush burn.

bush-burning, *vbl. n. Hist.* [See OED 11, 1898.] The process of bringing forested land into cultivation by clearfelling and burning. See also BURN OFF *n.*, BUSH-FIRING.
1899 BELL *In Shadow of Bush* 198 The season promised to be a good one for bush-burning; and those who had bush-felled were congratulating themselves on the prospect of getting excellent 'burns'. **1980** *National Radio* (Rural Programme) 22 Dec. 12.50 p.m. I hadn't heard the term 'bush-burning' for ages and I thought it a thing of the past.

Hence **bush-burnt** *ppl. a.*
1912 *NZJAg.* Dec. V. 585 Much of the damage caused to grass in recently bush-burnt country..will be found to be due to the little green cockchafer.

bush camp. [AND 1846.]

a. A bushman's habitation or camp in the bush.
1916 COWAN *Bush Explorers* (VUWTS) 11 But all the little troubles of the day's tramp were forgotten when the night came down upon us in our snug little bush camp. **1922** COWAN *NZ Wars* (1955) II. 294 Early in March of 1869 Titokowaru had established himself in a bush camp at Otautu. **1935** MAXWELL *Recollections* 196 The log-cabin kind of structure was not often resorted to in New Zealand, except in cases of bush camps, or bushmen's habitations. **1986** OWEN & PERKINS *Speaking for Ourselves* 151 The the camp had to be near running water... It was usually made of the trunks of sapling trees..and the walls were made from leaves of the nikau palm... I have slept many times in those bush camps, and I was always conscious of being very comfortable indeed.

b. A camp or collection of (temporary) dwellings of, or for, bush workers.
1905 THOMSON *Bush Boys* 160 I warn't done with the parson yet. He axed me if there were any other bush-camps about as 'e wanted to visit 'em all. **1914** PFAFF *Diggers' Story* 166 [Advt] For 33 years 'K' Jam has been known and appreciated in all parts of the coast—in bush camps and mining townships. **1934** MULGAN *Spur of Morning* 162 The best thing that could

happen to him would be six months in a bush camp getting down to things. **1956** Sutherland *Green Kiwi* (1960) 150 His father had been called out to a remote bush camp to perform a marriage ceremony. **1964** Howe *Stamper Battery* 11 But I can remember that I was glad to get back to the bush camp. **1986** Richards *Off the Sheep's Back* 62 For the first time I realised the importance of teamwork... The bond that grew and existed in that bush camp was never broken.

bush carpenter.

1. *Obs.* An itinerant carpenter seeking odd jobs.
1873 Barker *Station Amusements* 101 He was what is called a bush-carpenter: *i.e.* a wandering carpenter, who travels from station to station, doing any little odd rough jobs wanted.

2. [AND 1841.] A self-trained rough handyman; a rough-and-ready carpenter with no formal training.
1902 *Brett's Colonists' Guide* 1131 A large proportion of the country settlers of New Zealand are compelled..to become their own architects, or to appeal to some bush carpenter, who has no skill in the art of designing, though, perhaps, a good enough mechanic. **1925** Bathgate *Random Recolls.* 27 I found that Fletcher..had secured an iron building, which was being converted by a bush carpenter into suitable premises for a bank. **1933** Jones *Autobiogr. Early Settler* 52 As it was too far to get a tradesman up for any repairs, we were all, what was called, 'Bush Carpenters'. **1953** *Evening Post* (Wellington) 26 Aug. 10 Registration of builders now being carried out by the New Zealand Master Builders' Federation would eventually provide a safeguard..against the activities of 'bush carpenters'. **1955** Wilson *Land of My Children* 65 That bush-carpenter's economy in doing without piles had been a disastrous mistake. **1968** Slatter *Pagan Game* 171 [They were] vowing eternal friendship in the face of all drongos, no-hopers, wowsers and bush carpenters. **1987** Batistich *Sing Vila* 33 Taddi was a good bush carpenter; he soon knocked up a rough cottage for the men to live in.

Hence **bush-carpentered** *ppl. a.*, built (as) by a bush-carpenter; **bush carpentry** (also *transf.*).
1905 Baucke *White Man Treads* 296 By eye-metry the house measures 10 ft. by 20 ft.; the walls and roof are of split palings, **bush-carpentered**, but storm excluding. **1938** *Tararua Tramper* July 2 Let me assure you who would try your hand in this intricate mosaic of **bush carpentry** that there is still much to do. **1939** Alexander in Partridge *Dict. Slang Addenda* (1949) 1005 In New Zealand [*bush*] also [='rough and ready']; *esp.*, *bush carpenter* (or *carpentry*): since ca. 1910. (Niall Alexander, letter of Oct. 22, 1939.) **1993** *Sport 11* 39 He rhymed Lenin with some word I can't remember, then crossed it all out and did a bit of quick bush carpentry with *brain* and *Ukraine*.

3. *transf. WW1.* A rough or unskilled doctor; a 'sawbones'.
1937 Lee *Civilian into Soldier* 147 Too many bush-carpenters & vets. in the Medical Corps.

bush-clearing.

1. *n.* An area (often still surrounded by bush) cleared of its original bush cover. See also clearing *vbl. n.* 1.
1851 *Canterbury Papers* XI. 308 Self-sown wheat that I have seen stood taller than my head..but that is in a bush-clearing. **1867** Turner in Neal *London to Lonely Rai* (1969) 47 Last year I used to look at [the peach trees] from our bush clearing. **1888** Buller *Birds NZ* II. 259 In the settlers' bush-clearings at Eketahuna, in the Forty-mile Bush, I found them [*sc.* ducks] long after dark. **1899** Bell *In Shadow of Bush* 2 To the artistic eye, the bush clearings..may appear as a sore blemish on the face of the landscape. Thickly strewn with blackened logs and branches,... these clearings stand out in ugly contrast with the virgin native bush. **1907** Hawdon *New Zealanders & Boer War* 100 I'll be back in time for shearing, And to burn the new bush clearing. **1930** Reischek *Yesterdays in Maoriland* (1933) 169 The bridle-track led past little bush-clearings with fenced-in Maori plantations. **1960** *Penguin Book NZ Verse* 257 No more fearful than was the pa Te Huripapa In the bush clearing, where the river Opened its mouth. **1981** Marsh *Black Beech & Honeydew* 108 She lived in a deserted lumberman's shack in a bush-clearing. **1995** Anderson *House Guest* 99 The searches were all televised, or rather the bush clearing where the Search and Rescue team was based was shown.

2. *vbl. n. Hist.* The act or process of clearing native bush by felling (and, usu., subsequent burning). Also *attrib.*
1852 Southey *Col. Sheep & Wool* 63 As workmen they are sought after for bush-clearing. **1895** *TrNZI* XXVII. 423 Bush-clearing has destroyed many of the habitats of this moss. **1935** Cowan *Hero Stories NZ* 223 In his crippled old age he was cheered..by a visit from some old friend of his bush-scouting, bush-clearing, bullocking days.

bush costume. *Hist.* [AND 1847.] A costume or outfit suitable or usual for early New Zealand rural outdoor wear (cf. bushman 1 (quot. 1846) and cabbage-tree hat (quot. 1853)); often *spec.* that for military manoeuvres in the forest during the New Zealand Wars (cf. *bush uniform*, (bush C 3 a); and ranger *n.*¹ (quot. 1935)).

1847 Angas *Savage Life* II. 3 Clad in our 'bush' costume, but without weapons, and each with a *toko toko* or long walking-staff in our hands, my fellow traveller and myself set off in excellent spirits. **1849** Power *Sketches in NZ* 38 The bush costume of the [Artillery] officers in New Zealand [c1846] consists of a blue serge shirt, coarse trowsers, hobnail boots, and a cabbage-leaf hat or cap. **1854** Young *Southern World* 24 He was accompanied by some of the Missionaries in their 'bush' costume, consisting of a white 'wide-awake' and other articles to correspond with it.

bush country. [AND 1870.] bush-land 1.

1859 Rochfort *Jrnl. Two Expeds.* 297 In looking across this lake you perceive a flat bush-country. **1902** *Settler's Handbook NZ* 259 The back bush country is being rapidly cleared for pastoral purposes, chiefly sheep-grazing. **1905** Thomson *Bush Boys* 171 Have we not heard of that rough God-forsaken and God-forgotten place the bush-country, with its profane Sabbaths that have horrified us? **1915** *TrNZI* XLVII. 71 The best fern-root grew on freshly burnt bush country. **1935** Cowan *Hero Stories NZ* 223 His capacity for hard marching in rough bush country with a heavy swag of..provisions. **1955** Wilson *Land of My Children* 17 Theirs was to be a bush farm, for the Government was opening up some bush country said to be the finest land in all New Zealand. **1980** Holden *Stag* 76 The dawn chorus of the birdlife in bush country during the late spring..is an awe-inspiring sound.

bushcraft. [AND 1851.]

1. Skill in, or knowledge of, matters pertaining to life or survival in the bush.
1871 Money *Knocking About NZ* 29 He gave me my first lessons in bushcraft, such as a knowledge of edible herbs and roots, modes of crossing rivers, snaring birds, and many other invaluable 'wrinkles'. **1888** Buller *Birds NZ* I. 144 Except to the lovers of nature and bush-craft its [*sc.* the parakeet's] very existence is almost unknown to the colonists. **1892** McHutcheson *Camp Life Fiordland* 42 Mac proved himself an adept..at all other wrinkles of bush-craft. **1906** *TrNZI* XXXVIII. 337 My chief informants were..elderly men..who are more reliable on matters..of bushcraft than other southern Natives. **1916** Cowan *Bush Explorers* (VUWTS) 8 The white and Maori explorers experimented with such onga-onga poison antidotes as their bushcraft suggested. **1958** *Tararua* Sept. 23 *Bushcraft* refers to those skills necessary for anyone to find his way around and to exist comfortably in bush country. **1970** *Evening Post* (Wellington) 5 Feb. 16 He regarded the skill and ability in bushcraft of Johnston and Crump as extremely high.

2. Skill in, or knowledge of, matters pertaining to the occupation of bushman or bush-faller.
1953 Reed *Story of Kauri* 120 He had to find dependable answers to problems peculiar to kauri bushcraft. *Ibid.* 122 they took a pride in their work, and knew all there was to know about the bush-craft of their day—cross-cutting [etc.].

bush devil. *Fencing.* [Poss. f. a proprietary name.] See quot.

1966 Sharpe *Fiordland Muster* 32 In the middle of that cable there was a hell of a sag, and we could see no way to evade the tightening job. As equipment we had a 'bush devil', a sort of wire-straining outfit on which two men are expected to apply a pressure up to twenty tons, and a massive wrench. Hooking the strainer on to the base of a handy tree we got its claws, or whatever you call them, gripped on the long cable, above the turn buckle, and worked the lever until the joined sections were slack.

bushed, *ppl. a.*¹ [Used elsewhere (see OED *ppl. a.* 2, 1741) but early and freq. in New Zealand.] Covered with bush. See also bushy *a.*

1865 Chudleigh *Diary* 15 Apr. (1950) 174 We moved along the shores of Lakes Katherine and Sumner, the latter a very fine lake..and bushed down to the waters [*sic*] edge. **1917** Howes *Marlborough Sounds* 19 One may voyage..by a picturesque road to Havelock, from whence one may explore Pelorus Sound, more bushed and therefore even more beautiful than Queen Charlotte Sound. **1930** Guthrie *NZ Memories* 89 High, heavily bushed hills appeared to rise straight out of the water. **1941** *Tararua Tramper* Oct. 2 No depth [of snow] was encountered until we arrived at that bushed stretch facing south. **1952** Thomson *Deer Hunter* 164 We found ourselves on a partly-bushed plateau. **1971** Bale *Maratoto Gold* 106 The following morning he found himself in a thickly bushed gully with a small stream at the bottom. **1981** Hooper *Goat Paddock* 193 The dark, bushed hills seemed to be pushing the town into the river and the sea.

bushed, *ppl. a.*²

1. [AND 1844.] Caught by nightfall in, or lost in, the bush. **a.** In predicative use.
1882 Potts *Out in Open* 108 On one occasion when 'bushed' (that is lost in the forest)... **1896** Harper *Pioneer Work* 32 Even the oldest bushman may find himself temporarily 'bushed', but a good man can..generally find his way out somewhere. **1904** *NZ Illustr. Mag.* Mar. 429 Late at night, having been temporarily 'bushed', he wandered, footsore..into camp. **1914** Pfaff *Diggers' Story* 43 You had to follow down a track or run the risk of being bushed. **1923** Skinner *Morioris Chatham Is.* 11 In the southern part of the island the bush was so dense that two members of Mr. Percy Smith's party..were 'bushed' and very nearly lost their lives. **1938** Wily & Maunsell *Robert Maunsell* 24 One night the Bishop and the Doctor were 'bushed' and forced to bivouac where they were till morning.

1971 *Listener* 19 Apr. 56 Before long he [*sc.* a tramper] was fair-dinkum bushed. 1981 CHARLES *Black Billy Tea* 92 If you ever get bushed, boy, follow a creek.

b. In occas. *attrib.* use.
1930 GUTHRIE *NZ Memories* 101 The secret of safely finding their way through densest forest..was theirs... They could track a 'bushed' calf and return it to its proper mother.

2. a. [AND 1885.] Lost in the general outback or outdoors (as distinct from the forest); also *transf.* bewildered or overcome by circumstances, baffled.
1889 WILLIAMS & REEVES *Colonial Couplets* 45 I live in a country where drought is unknown, Where the poor stockman, bushed, need be never athirst. 1900 SCOTT *Colonial Turf* 197 'You wouldn't suppose a fellow could get lost on those Plains, would you? I was bushed here once!' 'After that you'd get bushed in an empty packing case.' 1924 *Otago Witness* (Dunedin) 17 June 68 We were..anxious about getting 'bushed' among the wire fences in the dark. 1933 *Press* (Christchurch) (Acland Gloss.) 23 Sept. 13 *Bushed.*—Lost (of people) whether in the bush or anywhere else. (A taxi-driver got 'bushed', he said, in finding a street. [Professor Arnold Wall's example.]) 1944 FULLARTON *Troop Target* 45 'Have you any idea where we are?' 'We're bushed behind the enemy lines about a hundred miles from nowhere.' 1958 *Whitcombe's Modern Jun. Dict.* (8edn.) 55 *Bushed* Lost or astray anywhere. One who loses his way among city streets will say he is bushed. 1963 BACON *In the Sticks* 64 'You've got me bluffed properly,' I said. 'I'm properly bushed.' Each tree, each fallen log, was the same as the last to me. 1964 *Listener* 2 Oct. 5 [A prisoner speaks.] Something seemed to move behind him; he jumped. Nothing... 'Now, don't go getting bushed,' he said. 1986 *Sunday News* (Auckland) 16 Nov. 5 [Heading] Barry's big day had 'em bushed! Being flipped about in a four-wheel drive..high above bush-draped ravine [*sic*] made things just authentic enough for 'townies' to think they'd gone native.

b. Beaten (at sports, games, etc.).
1973 *Dominion* (Wellington) 11 Sept. 18 Second-half burst leaves Bay [*sc.* the Hawke's Bay rugby team] bushed.

bushfaller. One who fells bush or timber-trees for a living. See also BUSHMAN 1, BUSHFELLER.
1864 TEMPSKY *Memoranda* (ATLTS) 13 The bushfallers fled, were fired upon ineffectually at the same time that the sentry was shot. 1888 PAYTON *Round about NZ* 48 I watched the noble game of 'Euchre' being played by some bush-fallers and Scandinavians. 1892 BROOKES *Frontier Life* 11 Immigrants..were not long in becoming..good axemen and bush-fallers. 1899 BELL *In Shadow of Bush* 48 Those bushfallers..were asking where they could get a regular supply of good butter. 1912 FERGUSON *Castle Gay* 63 Once the bushfaller's camp, now the deer-slayer's haunt.

bushfalling, *vbl. n.* The clearfelling of bush or timber-trees. Also *attrib.* See also BUSHFELLING, FALLING.
1866 MURRAY *Descr. Prov. Southland* 37 Bush Falling is never done in quantity. 1879 VOGEL *Land & Farming NZ* 68 There is still a great demand for labour. Bush falling, road making and harvest. 1882 HAY *Brighter Britain* I. 187 When bush-falling is performed by hired labour, it usually goes by contract. 1899 BELL *In Shadow of Bush* 9 This was Maurice McKeown, employed..to assist..in doing a little bushfalling, though the latter work was usually let by contract. *Ibid.* 86 I know who you are—you're one of the bushfalling chaps that get butter here. 1913 CARR *Country Work* 29 I class the men who follow up bushfalling as physically the finest..in the colonies. 1920 *Quick March* 10 Jan. 41 Bill was cook of a bushfalling camp. 1933 *Press* (Christchurch) (Acland Gloss.) 23 Sept. 13 *Bush Falling.*—Never 'felling'.

bush farm. *Hist.* [Recorded elsewhere but of historical significance in NZ: see OED *bush n.*[1] 10 c, 1851.] A farm cleared from the bush in a remote country district.
1883 *Brett's Colonists' Guide* 80 On bush farms..it is usual to sift the seed. 1887 *Auckland Weekly News* 4 June 2 [Advt] 146 Acres—Workingman's Bush-farm, about 16 miles from Auckland... The property consists of about 90 acres of Virgin Bush. 1918 *Quick March* 1 Nov. 15 Diggers, Go for the bush farm If you like, but take a 'orrible example of me, and beware of widders all yer life! 1922 COWAN *NZ Wars* (1955) I. 253 A settler..and his young son had been found tomahawked on their bush farm..about four miles from Drury. 1930 REISCHEK *Yesterdays in Maoriland* (1933) 63 I found a haven with Mr. Wilson at his bush farm, which was only connected with the outside world by water. 1956 SUTHERLAND *Green Kiwi* (1960) 38 Several miles beyond this block, out across the rolling gumland hills..lay a back-block section, a bush farm in the early stages of development. 1965 SHADBOLT *Among Cinders* 115 He married her and took her off to his first bush-farm.

bush farmer. *Hist.* [AND 1852.] One, usu. a pioneer, farming on (recently cleared) bush land.
1858 *Richmond-Atkinson Papers* (1960) I. 338 I also found that I was a bush farmer with 60 acres of clearing. 1874 ADAM *Twenty-five Yrs. Emigrant Life* 128 I have often seen on a stormy night a bush farmer take an American axe and cut [hine hine] for food for his cows. 1882 HAY *Brighter Britain* I. 207 It is eight or twelve years before the bush-farmer gets a chance of ploughing. 1891 *TrNZI* XXIII. 526 The logs..cumber the clearings of the bush-farmer. 1905 THOMSON *Bush Boys* 13 His father..was a simple bush-farmer, and funds are none too plentiful with such. *Ibid.* 31 A clean sweep [of fire during a burn] is a delight to the heart of the bush-farmer. 1952 LYON *Faring South* 180 Posts and battens..transported to the fencing site on the shoulders of the bush farmers themselves. 1988 WARR *Bush-burn to Butter* 42 A bush farmer, with about 200 acres, would be felling the last 20-30 acres of his holding after about ten years.

bush farming, *vbl. n.* [Used elsewhere but recorded earliest in New Zealand: see OED 10 c.] Farming on, or bringing into cultivation, land cleared of bush.
1857 *McLean Papers* (ATLTS) XIV. 35 Bush Farming has been such a failure with me in Taranaki. 1874 BAINES *Edward Crewe* 279 [Friends] had sent out the young gentleman to the Antipodes, giving him an outfit of things supposed necessary for the proper management of bush-farming in New Zealand. 1889 WAKEFIELD *NZ after Fifty Yrs.* 143 This is..the whole process of bush farming. 1899 BELL *In Shadow of Bush* 26 He hasn't had much experience of bush farming, I fancy. 1952 LYON *Faring South* 177 As the trend of bush farming became more general, the skill of the bushman became more in evidence. 1960 *Richmond-Atkinson Papers* (1960) I. 138 The energies of the community in Taranaki were hopefully absorbed [in the 1860s] in bush farming on their holdings. 1988 WARR *Bush-burn to Butter* 57 Walter Riddell was an early bush-farming pioneer on the Otago Peninsula.

bush-fell, *v.* To fell forest, or timber-trees.
1894 *TrNZI* XXVI. 221 He and another man were engaged in bushfelling near Reweti. 1902 *Settler's Handbook NZ* 11 This industry gives employment.. indirectly to those who labour at bushfalling..fencing, and otherwise opening up new country. 1930 DOBSON *Reminiscences* 168 But on reaching Lake Sumner, the bush began, and we commenced bush felling. 1967 ELLIOTT & ADSHEAD *Cowshed to Dog Collar* 16 When the men were out bushfelling it was standard practice to give the pungas a hearty whack and then leap back to dodge at least a couple of rats.

bushfeller. [Not recorded elsewhere.] BUSHFALLER.
1863 MORGAN *Journal* 31 Oct. (1963) 107 The bush-fellers..have proceeded to Wairoa. 1864 TEMPSKY *Memoranda* (ATLTS) 25 This post was also the headquarters of the bush fellers, who..were cutting down the forest on each side of the road. 1905 BAUCKE *White Man Treads* 229 Two were paid-off bushfellers. 1905 SATCHELL *Toll of Bush* 353 At McGregor's store a party of native bush-fellers were at work extending and burning the clearing. 1920 BOLITHO *With the Prince in NZ* 152 The party started out for the famous Buller Gorge, a mountain pass which defies civilisation and the ruthless hand of the bush feller. 1937 DUGGAN *Poems* 43 [Heading] The Bushfeller. 1938 HYDE *Nor Yrs. Condemn* 145 The town, to which many bushfellers and men from the outback came when they drew their pay cheques, was accustomed to small troubles. 1952-53 *NZ Forest Service Gloss.* (TS) Bushfeller [=] bush whacker 1986 OWEN & PERKINS *Speaking for Ourselves* 149 When the bushfellers came to take timber from a pure kauri stand, they worked the bush on a face.

bushfelling, *vbl. n.* [Recorded elsewhere only in Webster (1961), labelled *Australian.*] BUSHFALLING. Also *attrib.*
1910 *NZGeol.SB* (NS) No.9 4 In the process of clearing the land the necessary burning which follows the bush-felling often destroys such reserves as may have been left. 1930 GUTHRIE *NZ Memories* 107 He could make no headway..without first clearing the land of forest, so they were obliged to continue the..work of bush felling. 1962 in *Listener Short Stories* (1978) 63 In mining and bushfelling country bad news travels quickly. 1988 SHADBOLT *Voices of Gallipoli* 60 I was on a bush-felling contract, back of Gisborne, in the winter of 1914, when the war began.

bush fighting, *vbl. n. Hist.* [Spec. use of orig. US *bush-fighting* guerilla warfare in the bush: see OED.] The name during the New Zealand Wars for irregular or guerilla fighting in the bush. Also *transf.* (see quot. 1856). Cf. BUSH WARFARE.
1847 MATHEW *Reports* (ATLTS) IV. 15 [The natives] beat us in skirmishing & bush fighting. 1853 ROCHFORT *Adventures of Surveyor* 26 They [*sc.* officers] can fancy them [*sc.* invasive bush-rats] to be Maories, by a little stretch of imagination, and practise bush-fighting from behind the bedposts. 1856 SEWELL *Journal* 11 May (1980) II. 236 There was a good deal of what I call bush-fighting in the Debate, and the Opposition tried to prevent me from replying by refusing to speak. 1873 ALEXANDER *Bush Fighting* 1 Bush fighting is a comprehensive term for warfare conducted in forests, in broken ground, and on the hill-side. Wherever cover can be got, in attack and defence, under the canopy of heaven, there bush fighting can be practised. 1922 COWAN *NZ Wars* (1955) I. 211 But it was not until 1863 that the value of..bush-fighting companies was recognized. 1946 SOLJAK *NZ* 42 Finally the British Government withdrew the bulk of the Imperial forces and Frederick Weld..proceeded to employ the New Zealand militia in unconventional bush fighting better suited to cope with the elusive Maori. 1974 BARTLETT *Emigrants* 78 'Von' [Tempsky] was dead, famed through New Zealand for his reckless bravery and his skill in bush fighting.

Hence by back-formation **bush fight**, an instance of bush-fighting; **bush-fighter**, an irregular skilled at fighting in the bush during the New Zealand Wars (see also BUSH RANGER *n.*[1] 2).

1922 COWAN *NZ Wars* (1955) II. 281 Those who escaped from Ngatapa..includ[ed] a number of women who survived the terrors and hardships of the bush fight. **1873** ALEXANDER *Bush Fighting* 1 Active and wiry men, of sound constitutions, are best adapted for bush-fighters.

bush-fire.

1. *Obs.* [AND 1832.] A campfire in the bush.

1851 WELD *Hints to Intending Sheep-farmers* 11 If provisions run short [the sheepfarmer] should not think it a degradation, gentleman born though he might be, to heap fresh logs on the bush fire, to put on the soup pot, or to bake a damper in the ashes. **1862** HODDER *Memories NZ Life* 72 That night I enjoyed—what had often pleased me to read of in books—a bush-fire. Six or seven large old dry trees had been chopped down and cast onto the already large fire, which..lit up the whole of the bush surrounding us. **1871** MONEY *Knocking About NZ* 31 I smoked my evening pipe. This I did by the light of a good bush-fire, that danced and flickered on the trees and scrub around me.

2. [AND 1832.] A fire in uncleared bush land; a forest fire.

1853 ADAMS *Canterbury Settlement* 14 As the night darkened we saw far in the distance the red glow of a huge bush-fire. **1862** WALKER *Jrnl. & Lett.* (ATLTS) 17 Oct. Last night we saw a light..which turned out to be a bush fire. **1870** *TrNZI* II. 49 The constantly recurring bush fires have cleared off the stately Ti palms (so fragrant in early spring). **1882** POTTS *Out in Open* 49 After a wide-spread bush-fire..almost the entire surface of a wide extent of country lies temporarily a blackened waste. **1899** BELL *In Shadow of Bush* 199 Bush fires were now more frequent. **1905** WHITE *My NZ Garden* 69 Bush-fires have burnt it [*sc.* the native quail], and dogs, cats, and rats have eaten it. **1939** BEATTIE *First White Boy Born Otago* 142 This was in the big bush fire that destroyed so much property at Waimate in November, 1878. **1948** *Our Own Country* 15 And from the engine-room there was enough smoke to make you think there were not two kerosene engines below, but a bush fire. **1952** *Landfall* 23 Sept. 213 It was like reading those school essays we used to write, before Professor Gordon, in which every noun had to have at least one 'expressive adjective', in which a bush fire was a fierce holocaust raging down stately corridors of ancient rimus. **1993** *The Hutt News* (Lower Hutt) 17 Aug. 25 The bushfire force currently stands at 38 members... The number of bushfires vary [*sic*] from year to year.

3. *transf. or fig.* In various phr. **a. to run (spread) like a bush-fire**, of news, etc., to spread quickly.

1875 HOGG *Lays & Rhymes* 176 'Twas when the Rocky River rush began... The news like bush fire thro' the diggings ran. **1905** *Truth* 28 Oct. 6 The news spread round..Gore like a bushfire. **1974** PRESTON *Lady Doctor* 92 As suddenly as a bush fire, the new pestilence spread through the land. **1993** MILNER *Intersecting Lines* 107 The news spread like a bush-fire round the campus.

b. to rage (roar) like a bush-fire, to rage fiercely, noisily, out of control.

1959 DAVIN *No Remittance* 146 The flu came raging south like a bushfire. **1975** DAVIES *Outback* 136 You'd have gone roaring round the place like a bush fire.

c. to get on like a bush-fire, of people, to 'get on like a house on fire', to be very friendly with, to suit.

1964 MIDDLETON *Walk on Beach* 162 But what about Sally Smith? She likes dancing with me. We get on like a bush fire.

bush-firing, *vbl. n.* The act or work of burning fallen bush as part of land-clearing operations. Cf. BUSH-BURNING.

1854 *Richmond-Atkinson Papers* (1960) I. 141 The houses in this neighbourhood have been in some danger from the bush firings. **1889** *Collinson's Col. Mag.* 26 Bush-firing and logging up is a job which is often given to a new chum.

bushie. Also **bushy.** [f. BUSH(MAN + -IE: AND 1887.] BUSHMAN in various senses: *occas. spec.* a bush-hand of a sawmill; a person lacking 'civilized' or town manners.

1890 *NZ Observer* 15 Feb. 4 Two bushies, passing, helped the first to carry To his lost home this legal luminary. **1905** *Truth* 11 Nov. 7 A bushman [speaks]... 'Look here,' said the bushie..said the man from the outback. **1924** GIBSON *Gibbie Galoot* 66 The unlucky 'bushie' whose mannerisms and objectionable traits attract overmuch attention from his mates. **1936** MASON *Collected Poems* (1962) 85 The lone hand digging gum and the starving bushie outback. **1944** *Korero* (AEWS Background Bulletin) 9 Oct. 28 These are the 'bushies' and 'sailors' on horseback who have no idea of riding, but simply mean to stick there by brute force. **1968** *NZ Contemp. Dict. Suppl.* (Collins) 5 *bushie n.* rough yokel.

bush-land. [AND 1827.]

1. a. Usu. as **bush land**, land covered (or once covered) with bush as distinct from originally open land. See also BUSH COUNTRY.

1842 HEAPHY *NZ* 103 The bush land will be cleared with less attendant expense than at Wellington. **1848** EARP *Handbook* 13 [Quoting Land Regulations] All reserves for townships or agricultural establishments shall have reserves marked off of one-twentieth of all bush-land within the limit of such block, or if there be no bush within such block. **1851** *Richmond-Atkinson Papers* (1960) I. 81 The land is cleared bush land full of stumps, only fit for grazing. **1860** WILLOX *NZ Handbook* 80 The 'Bush' or forest land, although most difficult to reclaim, becomes most speedily productive. **1881** BATEMAN *Colonist* 183 The forest, or what is colonially termed 'bush-land' takes some time to clear. **1899** *TrNZI* XXXI. 7 Large areas of bush land are being annually cleared. **1920** BOLITHO *With the Prince in NZ* 113 In another stretch of country there would be unbroken bush-land, wild and wonderful, and illustrating the regrettable necessity of the feller who must clear the land to cope with the demand for pasture and timber. **1955** WILSON *Land of My Children* 19 Soon came bushland with here and there a small clearing where a few houses and perhaps a store, huddled beside the railway. **1968** JOHNSON *Turn of Tide* 69 Their way still led through bush-land, and..tiny birds began to appear. **1985** LANGDALE-HUNT *Last Entail Male* f42 Frederick Hunt gave quite a nice piece of bushland to Isabella.

b. As **bush-lands**, areas of land covered, or once covered, with bush regarded collectively or extensively.

1860 *Voices from Auckland* 67 [New comers] are puzzled by what is said about *fern-lands* and *bush-lands*. **1889** *TrNZI* XXI. 209 I have seen most of the great bush-lands of New Zealand. **1896** *TrNZI* XXVIII. 155 Bush-lands are put up for sale. **1915** MACDONALD *NZ Sheepfarming* 106 The fallen bush lands and some of the scrub lands have been surface sown in English grasses. **1953** SUTHERLAND *Golden Bush* (1963) 69 The pastures being encircled by unhunted bushlands, signs of pigs moving in..had to be watched for constantly. **1984** HOLDEN *Razorback* 11 [Pigs] infested the wild bushlands that lay beyond [the station boundary].

2. Farmland from which the original bush cover has been cleared.

1842 in *Lett. from Settlers* (1843) 153 The bush-land is the best land. **1844** TUCKETT *Diary* 23 May in Hocken *Contributions* (1898) 223 It [*sc.* wheat] was in very good condition and heavy, grown on cleared bushland, a nice sandy loam. **1856** FITTON *NZ* 101 I know that when I left New Plymouth district..the bush land crops of wheat were deemed inferior..to those of open fern lands. **1870** *TrNZI* II. 117 Cleared bush-land is suitable for the cultivation of the flax plant. **1886** CHUDLEIGH *Diary* 6 Oct. (1950) 348 My meadow fescue sown on the 15 acre of bushland felled by Manuel is a perfect failure. **1902** *Settler's Handbook NZ* 13 It takes from ten to fifteen years before the plough can be used in bush land. **1919** *TrNZI* LI. 366 Bush land has not been sown with cocksfoot.

3. A rural district still (or once) covered by bush.

1873 PYKE *Wild Will Enderby* (1889, 1974) III. v. 88 They lighted a fire, and 'slung the billy', (..a tin vessel used for preparing tea)..the chief luxury of dwellers in bush land. **1960** BOSWELL *Ernie* 102 I recall his chuckle when we showed him..the huge white caterpillar known throughout bushland [in North Auckland] as the 'rata grub'.

bush lawyer, *n.*[1] [f. Brit. dial. *lawyer* the long thorny stem of a bramble or briar: poss. *lawyer* is a variant of *layerer*, a plant which lays down trailing stems; prob. the name is, as usu. perceived, a fig. use of *lawyer* a member of a profession from whose entanglements it is difficult for lay-folk to imagine an escape: OED 3; cf. EDD Kentish dial. *bramble* a lawyer (see EDD *bramble* 5) alluding to 'the tangle of the law'; AND (*lawyer vine*) 1878.] Any of several native thorny plants of the blackberry family Rosaceae, esp. *Rubus cissoides* (formerly *R. australis*). See also BLACKBERRY, BRAMBLE, *Captain Cook's ropes* (CAPTAIN COOK), LAWYER, STOP-A-BIT CREEPER, SUPPLEJACK 2, TATARAMOA, WAIT-A-BIT 1.

1853 ADAMS *Canterbury Settlement* 44 Hour after hour we toiled on, sometimes making our way through..the long and clinging bramble, called by colonists the 'bush-lawyer'. **1867** HOCHSTETTER *NZ* 135 *Rubus Australis*, the thorny strings of which scratch the hands and face, which the colonists, therefore, very wittily call the 'bush lawyer'. **1873** PYKE *Wild Will Enderby* (1889,1974) I. iii 17 *Bush-lawyer*—Native name, Tataramoa—A disagreeable bramble, very tenacious of grasp. **1882** POTTS *Out in Open* 71 Torn by the recurved prickles of the bush-lawyer (*rubus*). **1894** WILSON *Land of Tui* 234 Everywhere the self-asserting 'Bush Lawyer', which has gained its name from the tenacity of its prickly spikes that cling and hold everything as surely in their toils as could the most persistent member of the legal profession. **1908** *AJHR* C-14 16 The thin-leaved juvenile form of the rose-leaved bush-lawyer (*Rubus schmidelioides*) creeps over the wet ground. **1938** HYDE *Godwits Fly* (1970) 79 The girls laughed and screamed as the tiny thorns of bushlawyer tugged their filament hair. **1940** MATTHEWS *Matthews of Kaitaia* 17 There was no path..and the thorny vines of the 'bush lawyer' or, as Pene called it, Taihoa (Wait-a-bit) made travelling difficult. **1960** HILLIARD *Maori girl* 103 Sloshing about in the bush..with stinging cuts in your flesh from chips and bush-lawyer and cutty-grass. **1982** WILSON *Stewart Is. Plants* 40 *Rubus cissoides* Bush Lawyer... Tātarāmoa. The commonest and most savagely prickly of the native brambles. **1990** *Listener* 23 July 2 Andrew comes in, sticking-plaster over one ear. Ripped it on a bit of bush lawyer, Andrew explains.

bush lawyer, *n.*² [f. BUSH B 2 + *lawyer*: AND 1835.]

1. *Hist.* A mining agent. Cf. *goldfields agent* (GOLDFIELD 2).

1874 BATHGATE *Col. Experiences* 225 One species of the genus lawyer is rapidly becoming extinct in Otago. They are called 'bush lawyers' and flourished chiefly on the goldfields and in up-country towns, whence they are being supplanted by younger branches of the profession. The bush lawyers, or mining agents, which is a name they accept, are often men who have acquired some knowledge of the law as lawyers' clerks and are of great use to the diggers. **1925** BATHGATE *Random Recolls.* 30 Very often some of the litigants were represented by an ex-policeman.., who combined the practice of mining agent (as such bush lawyers were called) with keeping a public house. **1967** MAY *West Coast Gold Rushes* 244 The amount of litigation in a gold-mining community was extraordinary; the West Coast diggings must have produced as many 'bush-lawyers' as the West Coast bush.

2. A layman who likes to display, often argumentatively, some knowledge of law or regulations.

1890 *NZ Observer* 15 Feb. 4 [Headline] A Bush Lawyer **1910** FANNING *Players & Slayers* 76 [The players] knew that he [*sc.* the referee] was a bush-lawyer, but they also knew that he would act fairly and squarely, and promptly. **1912** CHUDLEIGH *Diary* 2 Sept. (1950) 460 Scott the policeman..served summons on Himeona and Co. This makes no sort of difference to the enemy... The bush lawyer Te Hau Materau was with them. **1933** *Press* (Christchurch) (Acland Gloss.) 23 Sept. 13 *Bush Lawyer.*—Argumentative, agitating workman. **1933** SCANLAN *Tides of Youth* 91 You're a regular bush lawyer. **1946** SIMPSON *If You'd care to Know* 99 And when you come up against some fellow with a smattering of legal knowledge that he likes to display, you call him a bush-lawyer. **1955** *Waikato Times* (Hamilton) 24 May Unfortunately in institutions like borstal there were a number of bush-lawyers who were past graduates in the school of criminal law. **1965** SHADBOLT *Among Cinders* 69 He learned his law sitting in smoky little huts in the bush, and I suppose that's why he was called a bush-lawyer. **1976** *Progressive Youth Movement* [Title] The bush lawyer's handbook... A guide to the individual's legal rights and the power of the police. **1981** JOHNSTON *Fish Factory* 93 Jamie's defence counsel..judging by the fee the man charged..was definitely no bush lawyer. **1990** *Dominion Sunday Times* (Wellington) 30 Sept. 3 Successful Auckland bush lawyer Bob Coombridge plans to appeal against the conviction of a second woman serving life imprisonment.

Hence, by back-formation, **bush-law**, a body of non-professional or pseudo-legal opinion.

1967 MAY *West Coast Gold Rushes* 252 [May quoting a correspondent]..sham, humbug, bush-law, vanity, and vexation of the spirit..a gathering of quacks.

bush licence, *n.*¹ *Obs.* [f. BUSH B 2 + *licence.*] A special licence, granted in respect of a remote accommodation-house or public house, entitling the holder to sell liquor esp. as a convenience to the travelling public.

1848 WAKEFIELD *Handbook NZ* 195 Under the Amended Licensing Ordinance Session III., No.21, 1844, 'Bush Licences' are granted for the convenience of Travellers, at rates fixed by the Governor and Executive Council, according to the traffic of the place. **1849** *McLean Papers* (ATLTS) VI. 285 Mr. Secombe, the brewer, applied for a fresh Bush Licence, for a country Inn and Beer Shop at Omata. **1857** *Richmond-Atkinson Papers* (1960) I. 278 Bush licenses in remote country districts do not answer the purpose for which a license is granted. They are the resort of all the idle dissipated characters in the district. **1862** *Otago Prov. Government Gaz.* 23 July V. 197(23) Publicans' Licenses. The following list of Licenses..is published... Bush Licenses.—E.N.T. Smith to Donald McLean, Tokomairiro, 18 June. **1873** *Licensing Act* in *Acts of Wellington Provincial Legislature* (1873) 277 [Heading] Publicans' Licenses. 13. Every person who shall desire to obtain a publican's or bush license..under this Act shall [etc.]. **1911** MACTIER *Miranda Stanhope* 60 You could get a bush-licence. **1947-48** BEATTIE *Pioneer Recolls.* (1956) 37 The original Pyramid accommodation house..was owned by White and had a bush license. **1959** BOLLINGER *Grog's Own Country* 17 Especially after the widespread granting of 'bush licences' in the 1860s, liquor was deliberately used by unscrupulous Pakehas as a means of debauching individual Maoris..and swindling them of their tribal lands. **1980** MCGILL *Ghost Towns NZ* 63 Many bush licences disappeared when [the] county clerk..raised the licence fee from £15 to £20.

bush licence, *n.*² *Obs.* [f. BUSH B 1 a + *licence.*] A licence to fell Crown-owned bush for timber.

1869 *AJHR* D-22 6 The system of granting bush licenses leads to an extravagant waste of forest. *Ibid.* 9 I am of opinion that bush licenses are not advisable... They give men the right to go anywhere through the forests in their district, and to cut and destroy any quantity of timber. **1880** *TrNZI* XII. 7 The interest that the bush licence or leasing system affords to the State is 'nil'. **1893** JACOBSON *Tales of Banks Peninsula* 158 He took out a bush licence for splitting shingles and posts and rails.

bush life. [AND 1831.] Life in remote forested places or in the backblocks.

1844 in SWAINSON *William Swainson* 3 Apr. (1992) 106 We shall be obliged to live in a tent. [For] a person who has been any time in this country it is no inconvenience, indeed in my opinion a bush life as it is called, is anything from disagreeable. **1859** *Richmond-Atkinson Papers* (1960) I. 473 My youthful spirits are required..to keep Bessie [Domett] from drooping under the depressing influence of bush life. **1862** in Haast *Julius Von Haast* (1948) 283 He did not understand the poetry of bush life. **1871** MONEY *Knocking About NZ* 36 [He acquired] such a passion for a wandering bush life, that he afterwards threw up his billet at Mr Taylor's. **1905** THOMSON *Bush Boys* 48 Such is the typical log-whare in which the pioneer bush-settler and family..have to spend years of a rough, bush life. **1912** BOOTH *Five Years NZ* 15 According to bush custom it was usual to dub all fresh arrivals 'new chums' until they had satisfactorily passed certain ordeals in bush life. **1914** PFAFF *Diggers' Story* 110 I saw plenty of bush life and was twelve months at one time up the Totara River..without once going to Ross. **1922** COWAN *NZ Wars* (1955) II. 15 He was a deserter from the colonial forces..and had already lived a bush life with the Piri-Rakau and Ngati-Raukawa..Tribes.

bushline. The altitude or limit beyond which trees do not grow; occas. (as in quot. 1960) the silhouette of unfelled bush along the crest of ridges or spurs. See also *bush-level*, *bush-limit* (BUSH C 3 a), *forest-line* (FOREST), *timber-line* (TIMBER *n.*¹).

1889 PAULIN *Wild West Coast* 119 Fresh snow..came down to within 2000 feet of sea level—*i.e.*, considerably below the bush-line. **1896** HARPER *Pioneer Work* 151 If we are above the bush line, snow or creeks wet us daily. **1905** *TrNZI* XXXVII. 336 From the bush-line to the top of the mountain the..ascent is very easy. **1929** *Tararua Tramper* Apr. 2 An excellent track..leads down from the bushline. **1947** NEWTON *Waylego* 134 Above the bushline it [*sc.* the mustering block] reared in innumerable ledges and little basins. **1958** *Tararua* Sept. 24 *Bushline*, the upper limit of the bush, would be the *timberline* in North America. **1960** CRUMP *Good Keen Man* 82 His place was spread against one side of a leading ridge, along the top of which was the bushline. **1971** BERTRAM *Occasional Verses* 11 Sheep on the hills, and a grazing horse by the ragged Edge of the bushline. **1988** PICKERING *Hills* 43 Traditionally all the landforms above the bushline have been regarded as tops country.

bushman. [f. BUSH B 1a (occas. B 2) + *man.*]

1. [AND 1847.] **a.** One who fells bush professionally for land-clearing or timber-getting purposes.

1846 *NZ Jrnl.* VI. 166 In a belted blue bush man's frock, hatchet in hand..he looked in truth the scholar disguised as a wood-chopper. **1855** *Richmond-Atkinson Papers* (1960) I. 160 Some of the bushmen are such enthusiastic dancers, that after a hard day's felling they will come a six miles rough walk. **1861** HARPER *Lett. from NZ* 20 July (1914) 61 It was growing dark, and in amongst the trees I caught a glimpse of a fire, round which a group of bushmen were discussing their supper. They were employed in cutting timber for neighbouring settlers. **1873** BARKER *Station Amusements* 3 The next step was to engage 'bushmen', or woodcutters by profession, who felled and cut the timber into the proper lengths. **1888** BARLOW *Kaipara* 116 The bushman who fells the timber and rolls out the logs receives an average wage..as well as his food. **1902** *Brett's Colonists' Guide* 20 A good bushman will underscrub and fell an acre of average bush in a week. **1905** THOMSON *Bush Boys* 174 No Sabbath bell rings for bushmen. **1922** COWAN *NZ Wars* (1955) I. 261 On the 25th August [1863] twenty-five men of the 40th..besides some bushmen, were engaged in felling timber. **1975** DAVIN *Breathing Spaces* 34 You remember how old Andy Keogh brought that big broadleafed down right on top of his own kitchen. Only the real bushmen can do it properly.

b. A sawmill employee or logger who works at the bush (as distinct from the milling) operations of a sawmill.

c1870 *The Bushman's practical measure* [title: *NZNB* I. 148, item 835] [A set of tables.] **1882** HAY *Brighter Britain* II. 13 Still, some of us [farmers] have..acted the part of lumberers, or bushmen proper. **1894** *NZ Official Year-book* 331 The logs are forced along this road by timber-jacks, which the bushmen use with remarkable skill. **1916** THORNTON *Wowser* 189 These bushmen, of whom I am speaking [*sc.* land-clearing farmers], lead a very different life from that of the woodcutters and sawyers (although they too are called bushmen) employed at the saw-mill. **1923** MALFROY *Small Sawmills* 27 The *head bushman* should be..capable of acting as bush foreman on a small operation. **1936** RUST *Whangarei & Dist.* 163 Hundreds of bushmen, loggers, jackers..were employed in..different sawmills. **1951** *Awards, etc.* 452 [Westland Timber-Workers Award] A 'leading bushman' shall be engaged at each particular logging operation, such as a winch or tractor, and shall be the man whom the employer selects to 'lead' or direct each such particular logging operation. **1958** *Star-Sun* (Christchurch) 23 Apr. 18 [Advt] Bushman wtd. Apply Wairakei Road Sawmills. **1961** HENDERSON *Friends in Chains* 69 When we reached the bushmen, we found them busy on their knees, cross-cutting the sloven..off a fallen silver pine. **1971** [see BREAKER-OUT]. **1986** *Listener* 28 June 39 A bushman who leaves a good stump, that's his signature, and you can tell what bushman fells a tree by the stump he leaves.

2. [AND 1825.] One proficient in bushcraft or bush-lore; one skilled in bush travel.

1842 Heaphy *NZ* 56 They [*sc*. Taupo Maori] have the reputation of being the best bush-men in the country; and in their instinctive sagacity they approach near to the character of the Red Indian of America. **1847** Brunner *Exped. Middle Is.* 21 Oct. in Taylor *Early Travellers* (1959) 288 I believe I have now acquired the two greatest requisites for bushmen in New Zealand, *viz*., the capability of walking barefoot, and the proper method of cooking and eating fern-root. **1859** *Richmond-Atkinson Papers* (1960) I. 453 The cutting of the supple-jacks marks the line, & a good bushman will be able to find some traces for years after. **1867** Hochstetter *NZ* 285 The woollen blanket..I had sewed up..into a kind of sack..an excellent invention of experienced 'bush-men'. **1873** Pyke *Wild Will Enderby* (1889, 1974) III. v. 88 Amongst the party were old bushmen, to whose experienced eyes it was evident that the Prospectors had not crossed the creek. **1881** Douglas in *Mr Explorer Douglas* (1957) 32 Every Bushman carries a piece of candle. **1896** [see BUSHED *ppl. a*.² 1 a]. **1903** *TrNZI* XXXV. 46 Each month as it came round..had its task for the [Maori] bushmen, birds or rats to be caught or certain berries to be gathered. **1922** Cowan *NZ Wars* (1955) II. 210 The practised bushmen among us, like myself..had grown to look on a tree as a friend. **1937** Buick *Moa-Huniers NZ* 177 The numerous smaller birds which the skilled Maori bushman knew so well how to lure and snare. **1958** *Tararua* Sept. 24 A *bushman* is one who lives and works in the bush, or sometimes one skilled in bushcraft. **1964** Helmer *Stag Party* 6 Helmer had picked up in a couple of months more than a lot of bushmen have understood in a lifetime.

3. [AND 1832.] **a.** One who lives, farms or otherwise works in the bush or in a rural district; one who displays skills appropriate to such places.

1848 Godley *Letters* 8 May (1951) 206 Sometimes (on rainy days) he is the 'bushman', in a blue shirt etc; sometimes the sportsman. **1855** Anderson *Diary* in Manson *I Take up My Pen* (1971) 63 During the whole time I was employed at this farm, I heartily enjoyed myself... I like the life of a bushman and its healthy recreations. **1867** Barker *Station Life* (1870) 180 The 'bushmen'—as the men who have bought twenty-acre sections and settled in the bush are called—had scattered English grass-seed all over the rich leafy mould. **1871** Money *Knocking About NZ* 115 The surveyor in charge of the work was a thorough specimen of a gentleman, combined with the character of a rough colonial bushman. **1889** Williams & Reeves *Colonial Couplets* 3 You will never, I'm afraid, hear a self-respecting bushman call a bush a leafy glade. **1910** Grossman *Heart of Bush* 13 Out of its [*sc*. the bush's] recesses there came a rough-coated primitive bushman..riding a bay horse. **1930** *NZ Short Stories* 13 A country impossible for settlement, impenetrable to anybody save a trained bushman, armed with axe and billhook. **1959** Masters *Tales of Mails* 25 At one part in the early motoring days on the road, a bushman character..landed what he considered to be one of the softest jobs of his varied career.

b. *Joc*. Usu. *pl*. Country people regarded as uncouth or lacking the amenities of 'civilization'.

1858 Smith *Notes of Journey* in Taylor *Early Travellers* (1959) 379 The inhabitants of Okataina are called bushmen by their more civilised brethren of Wairoa, on account of the few white people who visit them. **1984** Edmond *High Country Weather* 21 Left to ourselves we're hicks, bushmen—uncouth louts—without your [*sc*. townsfolk's] new roads and drains... We'll go on living like animals.

4. Special Comb. **bushman-settler**, a settler proficient in bushcraft.

1922 Cowan *NZ Wars* (1955) I. 225 Day after day Atkinson led out his war-party of practised bushmen-settlers and scoured the forest and the native tracks, and soon had the country free from hostiles.

5. In special collocations: **bushman's bunk**, MANGEMANGE, the tangle of whose wire-like stems can make a springy mattress foundation; **bushman's friend**, the leaves of any large-leaved bush plant (such as RANGIORA or FLANNEL-LEAF) which can be used as emergency toilet paper, and, in the case of rangiora with its white underside, as writing paper; also (?*obs*.) applied to a bush wren (see quot. 1922); **bushman's mile**, a rough underestimate of a distance (cf. *Irishman's mile*); **bushman's shirt**, *bush shirt* (BUSH C 3 d); **bushman's singlet**, SINGLET 2; **bushman's sprig**, a square-headed hobnail designed to give a better grip in slippery places; **bushman's steak**, see quot.; **bushman's toilet paper**, see *bushman's friend* above; **bushman's trousers** (mainly *tramping*), see quot.

1943 *Botany of Auckland* 22 They are climbing ferns such as mangemange or '**Bushman's Bunk**'..whose wire-like stems were once much used in binding thatches and in making hinaki or eel-traps. **1922** *Auckland Weekly News* 26 Jan. 47 He had seen..the little wren known as 'the **bushman's friend**'. **1980** Lockley *House Above Sea* 200 [Flannelweed] is a handsome plant with big, pointed, pale-green leaves ('the bushman's friend', as a tramper once called it, although this vulgar name has been applied to other large-leaved New Zealand plants—for practical reasons readers will guess). **1985** *Evening Post* (Wellington) 4 Jan. 9 Bushman's friend, or rangiora, was not only used for letter writing and toilet paper. Tom Paul shows how the Maori used the leaves for a bandage tied with flax. **1890** Firth *Nation Making* 253 If you are ever in this Colony, let me advise you, if you are pressed for time, to beware of the '**bushman's mile**' or an 'Irishman's quarter of an hour'. **1984** Edmond *High Country Weather* 33 Mr McLachlan, his red-checked **bushman's shirt** with the sleeves rolled up. **1986** Richards *Off the Sheep's Back* 61 A bushman always wore a special type of boot known as 'ferntights'... Round-headed hobnails were replaced with with square-headed '**bushman's sprigs**'.. It was essential..to have a good firm footing and 'bushman's sprigs' helped to prevent us losing our foothold on a slippery bank. **1905** Brandon '*Ukneadit*' 102 ***Bushman's Steak***... For two men..steak on a long stick..roasted to a nice brown..pour little water into pan; add..flour..vinegar..pepper..salt..pour over steak. **1965** Gillham *Naturalist in NZ* 21 The fuchsia is a useful tree, for its papery bark which is easy to peel off has been dubbed in some parts '**bushman's toilet paper**'. **1990** Crowe *Native Edible Plants* 68 *Rangiora*..bushman's toilet paper; *pukapuka*... [69] The more practical and better known use of rangiora is described by the plant's European name. **1933** *Tararua Tramper* Oct. 2 '**Bushman's trousers**' are very good. These are extra heavy underpants, dark colour, hip pocket, and cost 10/-. **1954** p.c. R. Mason (Wellington). Concerning *bushman's trousers*: according to two old bushmen, Joe Gibbs and Sandy Donaldson, bushmen wore (and may still wear) long, red, woollen underpants at work. They do not get wet as quickly as trousers, do not flap uncomfortably around the legs when wet, and keep the legs warm. Trampers often do likewise in snow and in cold wet windy weather when it is too cold for shorts. **1958** *Tararua* Sept. 24 Judging by a remark in the *Tramper* of 1933 there were articles known as *bushmen's trousers* on sale. These were a type of garment pretty much the same as long woollen underpants, but made for outer wear and provided with pockets.

6. In combination: **bushmanlike** *a*. [AND 1862], having the appearance or air of one skilled in bushcraft; **bushmanship** [AND 1848], a capability for or knowledge of bushcraft.

1916 Cowan *Bush Explorers* (VUWTS) 9 Led by Julian with his slash-hook..**bushmanlike** figure enough was 'Wirihana'. **1902** Walker *Zealandia's Guerdon* 44 Arthur had been much struck with his.. **bushmanship**. **1934** Harper *Windy Island* 147 A friendship based on bushmanship. **1968** *NZ Contemp. Dict*. (Aust.-NZ Suppl.) 612 *bushman n*. one skilled in bush lore, and able to find his way in the bush; whence *bushmanship*, skill in bushcraft.

bush native. *Obs*. Also occas. in later use **bush Maori**. A former name for a Maori whose life was spent only or mainly in non-European surroundings or in the remote bush. See also BUSH A 2 b.

1835 Yate *NZ* (1970) 194 Whatever might be the value of what was to be sent, I had no hesitation in giving it in charge to a bush-native, accustomed to Europeans, but has all his life resided among his own people. **c1835** Boultbee *Journal* (1986) 75 It was rather a hazardous undertaking..as it sometimes happens in these parts, that straggling bush-natives attack and kill such persons as they fall in with, helpless. **1840** *NZ Jrnl*. I. 221 The Naticahouns are a very warlike tribe; they are bush natives and all heathens. **1843** Dieffenbach *Travels in NZ* I. 86 From all I have seen in New Zealand, I am convinced that the formidable pictures of bush-natives which have been drawn are purely the result of imagination. The natives in general..know their own interests too well, to live in a gloomy and inhospitable forest. **1846** Heaphy *Exped. to Kawatiri* 26 Apr. in Taylor *Early Travellers* (1959) 223 Ekehu discovered signs of the place having been recently occupied by natives... We were yet 75 miles from..the Ngaitahu tribe... Were they bush natives? Jacky and Etau appeared to think the vicinity of such individuals rather objectionable. **1955** *BJ Cameron Collection* (TS July) bush-Maori (n) A Maori little influenced by European ways.

bushranger, *n*.¹

1. a. [AND 1805.] One who travels in or explores ('ranges') the New Zealand bush.

1843 Stephens *Letters* (ATLTS) 168 But rough as this style of living may be thought it is luxurious to the bushranger's life which I myself have been accustomed to for the greater part of the time I have been in New Zealand. **1848** Brunner *Exped. Middle Is*. 14 Mar. in Taylor *Early Travellers* (1959) 308 The weka, or wood-hen, is the most useful..bird to a bush-ranger.

b. *transf*. A sheep which has escaped from the flock, thus missing being shorn.

1921 Guthrie-Smith *Tutira* (1926) 139 Of Newton's 4000 sheep, 1200 or so would have died..; about 200 of them would have became what we used to call 'bushrangers'; from 500 to 700 would have straggled off the run. **1947** Brereton *No Roll of Drums* 120 Roger Salisbury had killed a big bushranger wether and dogs and men had a good meal.

c. *fig*. A perapatetic reporter.

1934 Hyde *Journalese* 189 All Sun reporters were 'bush-rangers'—wandering hither and thither to pick up local incident, tint with local colour, and present in 'snappy' style.

2. As **Bush Ranger**. Usu. *pl*. A member of a settlers' volunteer unit or militia engaged in bush fighting during the New Zealand Wars. See also *bush-fighter* (see BUSH FIGHTING), FOREST RANGER *n*.¹, RANGER *n*.¹

1863 Richmond *Papers* (ATLTS) I. 593 [They] both belong to the Guerillas or Bush Rangers. *Ibid*. II. 59 Our company of *Bushrangers* (which is *the* company being the pick of No. 2 Rifles). **1865** *Punch in Canterbury* 19 Aug. 89 Send up the friendly natives, and the bushrangers too. **1879** GUDGEON *Reminisc. War in NZ* 6 A company of Bush Rangers under Major Von Tempsky..arrived. **1922** [see FOREST RANGER *n.*¹].

bushranger, *n.*² [f. Austral. *bushranger* a bush bandit often in transf. use.]
1. [AND 1801.] An armed robber operating on country roads.
[**1842** HEAPHY *NZ* 9 The sight of 'mounted police',—men whose business it was, in the penal colonies to apprehend escaped convicts and hunt down 'bush-rangers'—patrolling the beach [at Wellington] with fetters in their hands, for the intimidation of the inhabitants, served but to prepare them [*sc.* the Company settlers] for the still harsher usage they were to meet from local government.] **1863** CHUDLEIGH *Diary* 6 May (1950) 86 A notorious Australian bushranger has been caught here [at Timaru]. **1866** FARJEON *Grif* 233 We're not good gentlemen—we're bushrangers. **1874** KENNAWAY *Crusts* 136 The great break or rift..was named '*McKenzie's Pass*', after a bush-ranger who..tried to push through with a thousand sheep which he had succeeded in carrying off. **1914** in *Hist. N. Otago from 1853* (1978) 169 Some excitement was caused on the road, when in 1865, two bushrangers, Davis and Everest, stuck up Fricher's Hotel. **1925** BATHGATE *Random Recolls.* 27 I saw that the supposed bushranger was a compact bush of matakoura or wild Irishman. **1949** SHAW & FARRANT *Taieri Plain* 36 In the spring of 1861 drama stalked on to the scene—bushrangers were reported in the district under the leadership of Garrett. **1968** SEDDON *The Seddons* 34 Bushranger tragedies held us spellbound [in the 1880s]. Towards the end of one blood-curdling melodrama the heroine was in dire distress.
2. *transf.* **a.** A Maori 'bandit' operating from the bush. **b.** A black cricket.
1850 TAYLOR *Journal* 5 Feb. (ATLTS) VII. 62 The natives say that until lately these remote forests [near Mokau] were infested with 'Parau' native bushrangers or slaves who had run away from their masters and were guilty of every enormity, and woe to the unfortunate traveller who went alone through these forests. **1921** GUTHRIE-SMITH *Tutira* (1926) 319 The black cricket, *puharanga*—'bush-ranger'—of the natives..is reputed to have reached New Zealand either in matting from the islands, or in the bedding of troops from India.
3. *transf. Joc.* **a.** An elusive child sneak-thief.
1888 BARLOW *Kaipara* 162 This lollipop-sucking bushranger for several weeks completely baffled all efforts..leaving behind him..jam tins, lolly bottles, pie dishes..and rural policemen.
b. An overcharging or dishonest storekeeper. Also as **bushrangering** *vbl. n.*, dishonest or sharp practices.
1938 HYDE *Godwits Fly* (1970) 77 Nearly everyone in the new district was sedate, except..the harness-maker, who was a Bolshie, and had in his shop window a large, unsteadily-lettered notice, 'No Bushrangering Done Here.' **1951** PARK *Witch's Thorn* 190 Consequently her thoughts went: 'Two shillings for that smoked snapper! That Solivich is a bushranger.'
4. *Hist.* A boys' game.
1984 KEITH & MAIN *NZ Yesterdays* 288 In the last years of the 19th century a battle game of 'bushrangers' was popular.

bushranging, *vbl. n. Hist.*
1. *Rare.* [AND travelling cross-country, 1821.] Wandering in the bush.
1852 GOLDER *NZ Minstrelsy* 10 Let's go a bushranging, thou fairest of lassies; Let's go a bushranging, and visit each scene. **1996** *Dominion* (Wellington) 12 Feb. 3 But the days of solo bush ranging are over for Mr Evans. 'I'm getting a bit old for all this,' he said... Mr Evans will return to the ranges next week to retrieve Binney [his dog].
2. Guerilla-patrolling in the bush as carried out by Bush Rangers (see *n.*¹ 2).
1863 *Richmond-Atkinson Papers* (1960) II. 53 Paraded at 9 when the men were picked out for the bush ranging. **1863** MORGAN *Journal* Dec. (1963) 135 The importance of bushranging corps..has been urged repeatedly. **1879** FEATON *Waikato War* 38 Let me tell you young men so eager for the eight shillings per day for bushranging, that..you had better think twice before you venture on such work. **1935** bush-ranging costume [see RANGER *n.*¹].
Hence by back-formation **bushrange** *v. intr.*, to be active as a Bush Ranger.
1864 *Richmond-Atkinson Papers* (1960) II. 117 I had a skirmish with Arthur, who tho' off duty..wished to go as he scented fighting... I have let him bush range for months uncomplainingly.
3. a. [AND 1813.] Armed highway robbery.
1868 LINDSAY *Contribs. NZ Bot.* 6 The risks of travel were considerable: 'Sticking-up', and other features of 'Bush-ranging'..were rife in Otago. **1924** *Otago Witness* (Dunedin) 22 Jan. 7 The first instance of bushranging was when Garrett stuck up persons travelling over Maungatua range. **1968** *NZ Contemp. Dict. Suppl.* (Collins) 5 *bushranging*, the practice of the bushranger.
b. In modern *transf. attrib.* use, of a wild boar raiding lamb paddocks, etc.
1955 CAMPBELL *By Reef & Range* 9 Meanwhile men spoke of this [*sc.* a wild boar's] bushranging nuisance..of some footprints,... or a recent raid on sheep.

bush road. [AND 1827.]
a. A road formed, often crudely, through, or in, the bush; occas. *spec.* a logging road or track to a mill or to a log collection point.
1850 MCLEAN in Cowan *Sir Donald Maclean* (1940) 59 A bush road, tolerably level for a mile. **1864** TEMPSKY *Memoranda* (ATLTS) 23 After having waded through the bottomless bush road to Pukekohe, I stood before the Church of the settlement. **1878** ELWELL *Boy Colonists* 238 Sledges were necessary for bush work, for the bush roads were too narrow and too full of stumps for a dray to be worked in them. **1882** HAY *Brighter Britain* II. 224 It [*sc.* the pihoihoi] is a ground pipit, and may often be seen fluttering and chirping about a bush road. **1891** *TrNZI* XXIII. 190 The bird in question was captured..by a man who stated that he saw it walking on an unfrequented bush-road. **1916** *TrNZI* XLVIII. 254 In one instance I found a a single 'seedling' plant growing on a bush-road clay-cutting.
b. [AND 1827.] A back-country road.
1871 MONEY *Knocking About NZ* 115 To describe..so strange an assortment..as the labourers on the bush-roads in the colonies would require the pen of Dickens. **1874** TROLLOPE *NZ* 47 The road [to Wakatip was] fairly good—for a 'bush' road. The name must be taken in a colonial sense. There was hardly a tree to be seen throughout the journey... A country road which is merely formed and not metalled is a bush road, though it pass across an open plain, or up a treeless valley. **1895** *Pictorial NZ* 2 Is the road difficult? And the answer was, Not as bush-roads, so called, go. **1938** HYDE *Godwits Fly* (1970) 156 They were on the bush road, curved like a bow. **1959** MASTERS *Tales of Mails* 33 At first he conducted business from his farm house, about a mile and a quarter up the little bush road at Puketitiri. **1968** SEDDON *The Seddons* 23 The two men and the two boys in that dog cart went their way along the long bush road past Marsden township.

bush shanty.
1. [AND 1885.] An unlicensed back-country grog-shop. See also SHANTY 2.
1881 DOUGLAS in *Mr Explorer Douglas* (1957) 30 Scene a bush Shanty among the [West Coast] ranges. A number of Diggers sitting Drinking and talking. **1986** DEVANNY *Point of Departure* 48 Next morning found him in the grip of a terrific hangover... He rose..and left the house. I watched him take the road that led up to a bush shanty [c1905].
2. A bushman's hut.
1924 GIBSON *Gibbie Galoot* 66 Most bush shanties possess such a butt. **1961** MACKAY *Puborama* 94 When he arrived at the little bush shanty, Mr Jones was away in the tall timber.

bush-sick, *a.*
a. Of stock, suffering from bush sickness.
1912 *TrNZI* XLIV. 288 A steer..was killed..as being a typical bush-sick animal. **1928** *TrNZI* LVIII. 538 The trial of iron medicines was indicated as a logically correct remedy for bush sick stock. **1938** *NZJST* XX. 193A [Caption] Bush-sick sheep, Sherry River.
b. Of land or soil, capable of inducing bush-sickness in stock.
1912 *NZJAg.* Aug. V. 123 Lime..has an injurious action on the feeding quality of pasture on 'bush-sick' lands. **1928** *TrNZI* LVIII. 539 Those in the 'bush sick' area were inspected and a dozen found to have died. **1938** *NZJST* XX. 14A Pastures from typically bush-sick country contained..less than 0.04 p.p.m. cobalt. **1950** *NZJAg.* Jan. LXXX. 31 The amount of cobalted fertiliser used..in 1949..would be sufficient to correct cobalt deficiency in 940,000 acres of bush-sick pasture. **1978** PRESTON *Woolgatherers* 51 Like a large part of Southland..that place, as well as having an extremely high rainfall, was 'bush-sick', a condition not understood at that time. **1987** CHRISTIE *Candles & Canvas* 104 At that time it was not known that the land was 'bush sick', that it lacked the all-important element cobalt.

bush sickness. A term denoting a disease of herbiferous ruminants, or its cause, a deficiency of certain minerals (specifically cobalt) in the soil. See also *bush-disease* (BUSH C 3 a), *cattle sickness* (CATTLE 2), SKINNIES, *Tauranga disease* (TAURANGA 2). **a.** Of stock.
1897 *Ann. Rep. Dept. Agric.* V. 4 Over a small extent of wooded country between Waikato and Tauranga, a percentage of cattle kept on clearings become affected with what is locally called 'bush sickness', recovering when removed. **1911** [see *bush-disease* (BUSH C 3 a)]. **1912** *TrNZI* XLIV. 288 The mysterious wasting condition locally known as 'bush sickness', which always eventually appears in ruminating herbivora pastured on certain areas of pumice-country in the North Island. **1928** *NZ Free Lance* (Wellington) 22 June 7 For long the 'coasty sickness', 'pluing', 'vinguish' and 'daising' of stock on King Island off the coast of Tasmania, in the Kedong Valley of Nairobi, and among the Cheviot Hills of the North of England were not associated with New Zealand 'bush sickness' or 'the skinnies' as it is graphically labelled by the farmers of this country. **1936** BELSHAW et al. *Agric. Organiz. NZ* 71 Bush-sickness has long been recognised as a serious stock ailment affecting ruminant animals on several localities in the vicinity of Rotorua. **1951** LEVY *Grasslands NZ* (1970) 334 Cobalt deficiency..caused a condition known

as bush sickness in stock. **1966** *Encycl. NZ* I. 44 *Cobalt deficiency* or 'bush sickness' occurs widely. **1973** WHEELER *Hist. Sheep Stations NI* 58 Years of inevitable hardship caused by..bush sickness in stock caused by an unsuspected cobalt deficiency in the soil. **1987** [see LICK *n*.²].

b. Of land.
1927 MULGAN in Woodhouse *Farm & Station Verse* (1950) 84 Farming was handicapped by 'bush-sickness' and ragwort. **1928** *Sixteen Yrs. Progress 1912-28* 90 *Bush-sickness and neglect*: The country has its deteriorated lands it is true—lands suffering from bush-sickness and the neglect of their occupiers. **1939** *NZJST* XX. 14A The analysis of New Zealand soils has revealed that bush sickness is in general associated with soils of very low cobalt content. **1950** *NZJ Ag.* July LXXXI. 67 Development of former bush-sick areas in Tauranga county... The discovery [in 1935] that cobalt was a cure for bush sickness came at a most opportune moment.

bushwack(er), var. BUSHWHACK(ER).

bush walk.
1. [Contrast the Australian sense of 'a hike, a tramp': AND 1892.] A walk in the bush.
1851 *Richmond-Atkinson Papers* (1960) I. 79 [We] had our first bush walk over matted roots and stumps amidst tree fern, cabbage palm, supple jack, not to name a long list of timber trees. **1936** HYDE *Passport to Hell* 43 May wasn't exactly the same as the Sunday-walking brigade... On May's unorthodox bush-walks, of a sudden he would find himself sitting beside her.

2. A path in or through bush.
1987 *Evening Post* (Wellington) 21 Sept. 36 The woman, who was only two days into a scheduled New Zealand holiday, was approached by a man wielding a pistol on a bush-walk adjacent to the Stone Store in Kerikeri River basin. **1988** *Haeremai Hicks Bay* (Information Sheet Hicks Bay Motel Lodge) 25 Apr. Recreation—Pool table. Golf course. Bush walks. Glow-worm grotto. **1989** *Dominion* (Wellington) 10 June 8 'Heaps of good bush walks round here,' says the motelier up the coast next day... 'My bush walks aren't like that. I concreted the path all the way.'

bush-walking. *Obs.* Walking in, or through, the bush.
1840 *NZ Jrnl.* I. 232 We came soon by a little bush-walking..to Okewi. **1853** *Richmond-Atkinson Papers* (1960) I. 133 There is what we call a *good* bush road to Rata Nui but beyond it there are two miles of bush walking along what is called 'a line'. **1867** BARKER *Station Life* (1870) 179 No paths but real rough bush-walking.

bush warfare. *Hist.* BUSH FIGHTING.
1843 *NZ Jrnl.* IV. 327 It would be found with their [*sc.* the natives'] present mode of *bush* or guerilla warfare..that not much success would attend the most numerous and well disciplined British troops, opposed to them. **1870** *Evening Post* (Wellington) 15 Dec. 2 I..venture to..affirm 'that the native policy of the present government has been eminently successful'—that the late government had not 'formed a strong and reliable force accustomed to bush warfare'—and that 'bribing the Maoris to peace' is sound in practice..and kind as it is useful and wise. You cannot shoot Maoris down one by one like snipe—the process is too costly. **1922** COWAN *NZ Wars* (1955) II. 157 It was typical bush warfare for a few minutes.

bushwhack, *v.* Also **bushwack**. [Back-formation f. BUSHWHACKER.]

1. [AND 1946.] *intr.* To fell standing timber. See also WHACK *v.* 1.
1900 SCOTT *Tales of the Colonial Turf* 40 He..went bushwhacking in the Rangitikei district, but the contract did not pay a dividend. **1907** KOEBEL *Return of Joe* 287 You new chums cuttin' good terbaccer as if you was bushwackin'. **1924** ANTHONY *Follow the Call* (1975) 89 I'm out at Whanga now, bush-whacking.

2. *trans.* and *intr.* To hack one's way (through bush).
1936 *Tararua Tramper* Mar. 3 We girded our empty stomachs into the prospect of bushwhacking the bluffs back to the flat opposite Arapito Creek. **1952** *National Geographic* Mar. 397 Since 1948 six expeditions have bushwhacked into the 685-square mile zone [in Fiordland].

bushwhacker. Also occas. **bushwacker**.
1. BUSHFALLER.
1899 BELL *In Shadow of Bush* 18 Accidents [*sc.* a broken axe-handle] will happen, you know. Davie isn't qualified as a bush whacker yet. **1905** THOMSON *Bush Boys* 138 They could swing an axe and fell a tree in real bushwhackers' style. *Ibid.* 145 The sawmill hands were there almost to a man, and many also of the 'bush-whackers' from away back. **1916** *Chron. NZEF* 30 Oct. 104 And so, with the philosophy of the average bush-whacker and stockman, they contentedly went to sleep. **1920** *Quick March* 10 Feb. 37 He said it was the practice of many bush-whackers to set the big hollow ratas ablaze when they cut out a bush. **1933** SCANLAN *Tides of Youth* 59 The bushwhacker with his axe had become the spearhead of civilization. **1946** SIMPSON *If You'd Care to Know* 99 A man who fells trees is not a lumberjack or a woodsman but a bushwhacker. **1952–53** *NZ Forest Service Gloss.* (TS) Bushwhacker. A workman engaged in clearing forest for settlement. **1961** CRUMP *Hang On a Minute Mate* 164 Some gate-crashing bush-whackers had picked on one of their blokes. **1977** MACMORRAN *In View of Kapiti* 156 Her future husband..was working there as a 'bushwacker' for a mill when Helen..first arrived. **1983** HENDERSON *Down from Marble Mountain* 129 Old Naish Cook, a great old bushwhacker and scrubcutter..in his day but now a bit ringbarked himself.

2. Often *joc.* [AND 1896.] A (rough) country person; a person from the bush.
1960 ROGERS *Long White Cloud* 13 Hislops are holding a *tangi* tonight... I'm taking Concertina Charlie over with me. Special invitation to bushwhackers. **1985** SHERWOOD *Botanist at Bay* 45 'But princess,' he drawled, 'us sex-starved bushwhackers buried out here in the sticks have to make do with what we can get.' 'Queen Street bushwhackers from a commune in Auckland, more likely.'

3. *attrib.* passing into adjective. Rough, homely; makeshift; rough-and-ready.
1948 FINLAYSON *Tidal Creek* (1979) 57 After the meal the whole Crummer tribe squat around the big bushwhacker chimney-place and roll cigarettes. *Ibid.* 109 Jake thinks how nice it is after Uncle Ted's bush-whacker style to see a table with a crisp white cloth and crystal and all the fittings.

bushwhacking.
1. *vbl. n.* [AND 1929.] BUSHFALLING.
1904 *NZ Observer* 8 Oct. 16 Clerks don't, as a rule, tear their collars out by the roots when the slump comes, and take to bushwhacking. **1906** ELKINGTON *Adrift in NZ* XVI 262 Bushfelling, or as it is termed, bush-whacking was a favourite pastime of mine. **1924** *Aussie (NZ Section)* 15 July XV They were Bush-Whackers, and they lived by Bush-Whacking. **1930** SMYTH *Wooden Rails* 39 Don't you like saw-mills and bush whacking and all that. **1955** WILSON *Land of My Children* 7 In fact, bush-whacking was the refuge of one type of destitute who could hardly..have been induced to take work in shop, gravel-pit, railway or any of the recognized avenues of trade or labour. **1959** DAVIN *No Remittance* 56 He'd..had a go at everything—mining, bullock-driving, bush-whacking, shearing. **1967** MCLATCHIE *Tang of Bush* 100 'What is your job, McLatchie?' 'Bushwhacking, Sir.' 'What, exactly, is a bushwhacker?' 'A man who fells bush.' **1983** PASCOE *Explorers & Travellers* 150 Grave's daughter published a record of his bush-whacking and mountaineering that added up to genuine exploration.

2. *ppl. a.* [AND 1927.] Pertaining to bushfalling, occas. (as in quot. 1960) in a weakened transf. use.
1920 *Quick March* 10 Nov. 13 It's the only way I feel safe in this blasted bushwhacking job. **1960** *Over Whitcombe Pass* (Pascoe ed.) 14 The new tracks were not maintained and..in the thirties..the Whitcombe Pass was considered to be one of the really tough bushwhacking feats. **1986** RICHARDS *Off the Sheep's Back* 148 Outside bushwhacking contracts and shearing had given them cash.

bushy, *a.* [AND 1843.] Wooded; covered with bush. See also *bush-clad* (BUSH C 1 a), BUSHED *ppl. a.*¹.
1844 BARNICOAT *Journal* (ATLTS) 24 Apr. 168 The harbour of Otago forms a magnificent sheet of land-locked water, surrounded by wooded or bushy hills. **1855** *Sidebottom's Let.* 6 Mar. in Gillespie S. *Canterbury* (1971) 459 That day..we followed the track..to the bushy gorge of the Pureora. **1864** BARRINGTON *Diary* 30 Apr. in Taylor *Early Travellers* (1959) 409 Continued on our course up the river..a very bushy sideling of a steep mountain gorge. **1870** *TrNZI* II. 57 As soon as one ascends the bushy gullies of the hills, the Canary is sure to pay a reconnoitering visit. **1889** WILLIAMS & REEVES *Colonial Couplets* 3 *Bushy gully* suits me better, serves my purpose just as well. **1920** MANSFIELD *Stories* (1984) 227 Now the big dray rattled into unknown country..up steep, steep hills, down into bushy valleys. **1932** *Tararua Tramper* Jan. 2 Near the old trypot sites, facing the bushy slope, are old rubbish heaps. **1948** FINLAYSON *Tidal Creek* (1979) 28 Beyond, on the coastal hills, little cotton wool clouds hide the bushy valleys. **1958** *Tararua* Sept. 68 Some..hours later we had negotiated the last bushy knob and were descending the final slope towards the hut. **1980** HOLDEN *Stag* 76 Only when the warming face of the sun cleared a bushy ridge..did he turn away. **1986** *Evening Post* (Wellington) 7 Jan. 2 [Heading] Bushy sites soon on sale.

bushy *n.*: see BUSHIE.

bust, *n.* [Brit. dial. *bust* var. BURST *n.*¹: see OED *n.*³ a; AND 1865.] Occas. as **bust up**, and esp. in the phr. **on the bust**. BURST *n.*¹ a.
1907 *Truth* 30 Mar. 6 He works for a few days, and then goes on the bally bust for a month. **1914** PFAFF *Diggers' Story* 14 It is true that many of them had periodical 'busts', but these were more in the way of social re-unions than debauches. **1920** *Quick March* 10 Jan. 41 He swore after every 'bust' that it was his last. **1946** SARGESON *That Summer* 34 If you once went on the bust in a place like this it was good-bye McGinnis, he said. **1960** MASTERS *Back-Country Tales* 169 He had been to town on the bust. **1966** BALLANTYNE *Friend of Family* 10 Our days in the coaster..., the old port-to-port beat with a bust-up in every port and Ted Cullers matching me on every boozy run.

bust, v.

1. As **bust up** intr., often as **busted** ppl. a., (to go) bankrupt or broke; to (reach a state of) collapse.

1865 THATCHER *Otago Songster* 12 Publicans bust up I am told every day, For the rents in this town are excessive. **1892** JENKYNS *Hard Life* 221 All the mines..are 'bust up', and hundreds of men are out of work. **1916** ANZAC *On Anzac Trail* 27 The boys had fixed to give us a boncer welcome, but..in the words of our informant, 'they blued their cheques, got shikkared and the show was bust up'. **1946** MORRIESON *Came a Hot Friday* (1981) 84 He drank his whisky. 'Fill her up, shag,' he said. That left him busted.

2. *reflexive*. In collocations or phrases suggesting rupture (as of a steam-boiler bursting) from excessive pent-up effort or over-exertion: **to bust** (occas. **burst**) **oneself**, to overwork or overexert oneself to a point of breakdown; also figuratively expressed as **to bust** (occas. **burst**) **one's boiler (foofer, guts)** [see OED boiler 2 c, US].

1891 CHAMIER *Philosopher Dick* 247 We must have a spell, anyhow. Nobody has ever bust himself as I have done for the old man. **1938** SCANLAN *Guest of Life* 326 You don't want to burst yourself one week and be useless for two. **1946** SARGESON *That Summer* 41 And there's no need to bust your boiler. **1948** HENDERSON *Taina* 4 'I guess and calculate, stranger,' drawled Ben, 'that you'll burst your boiler if you let the angry passions burn.' **1959** SLATTER *Gun in My Hand* 23 He got on to me about smoking in the shed. No sense bustin ya guts out. **1966** TURNER *Eng. Lang. Austral. & NZ* 120 The expression *busting one's guts out* is a common New Zealandism. **1963** MORRIESON *Scarecrow* 128 I nearly burst my boiler getting home to rip the remaining wallpaper down, and generally make Prudence's bedroom presentable for a working-bee. **1978** SUTHERLAND *Elver* 58 Uncle Angus never let himself become excited... The old girl will bust her boiler if she's not careful, he thought. **1985** MITCALFE *Hey Hey Hey* 26 Gee man, you don't want to work so hard... You might bust a boiler or something. **1988** MCGILL *Dict. Kiwi Slang* 61 *I've nearly bust my foofer* I have overexerted and almost ruptured something; foofer probably 'foofoo' or 'poopoo valve', the mythical gadget the Royal Navy blames for anything that goes wrong. **1990** VIRTUE *In the Country of Salvation* 82 'We've all got to pull together,' Mr Young told her. 'Bust our boilers until the rain comes.' **1994** *Dominion* (Wellington) 20 July 3 Oncology unit head John Carter said yesterday that staff were 'busting their guts' working to treat as many patients as possible.

3. bust (it)!, expressing annoyance.

1937 PARTRIDGE *Dict. Slang* 113 *bust*! Dash it!: New Zealanders': C. 20. Also *bust it!* **1953** 14–17 M A5 Thames DHS 5 Bust [expressing annoyance] [M5] **1988** MCGILL *Dict. Kiwi Slang* 24 *bust it!* dash it!; eg 'I almost had it that time. Oh bust it!'

4. [AND 1878.] Of money (esp. a cheque), to squander, esp. on drink. See also BLOW, BURST n.[1] b.

1924 ANTHONY *Follow the Call* (1975) 90 Came in [to town] to bust the cheque. Out again tomorrow. **1930** DEVANNY *Bushman Burke* 24 He has a very good cheque to draw, and then 'busts' it in riotous living. **1944** LEE *Shining with the Shiner* 47 Don't I bust my harvest cheque every year in this town. **1953** SCOTT *Breakfast at Six* 181 Have a good time with it. Bust it any way you like. **1981** CHARLES *Black Billy Tea* 58 To bust one cheque a year On racehorses and beer.

buster, n.[1]

a. [AND 1873.] A short form of *southerly buster* (SOUTHERLY 3), occas. for any strong, cold wind. See also BURSTER.

1868 LINDSAY *Contribs. NZ Bot.* 28 [Otago's] winds..include all forms between the cold gales locally known as 'Busters', and the hot dust winds that sweep across Australia. **1887** *Auckland Weekly News* 14 May 22 On Sunday we were favoured with a stiff easterly buster. **1891** CHAMIER *Philosopher Dick* 268 The young man had gained the reputation of being 'weatherwise'... On the present occasion he predicted 'a buster'. **1915** HAY *Reminiscences Early Canterbury* 83 The quarter from which we got the most rain was the southwest. It came in what we called 'busters'. **1921** GUTHRIE-SMITH *Tutira* (1926) 394 In March a 'buster' blew up from the South, a foot and a half of rain falling in three days. **1962** LAWLOR *More Wellington Days* 191 Oh wilful wild wind of Wellington city, Hats off to you, Buster, you make us alive. **1988** SMITH *Southlanders at Heart* 24 Did I speak about the weather—blowing hard and wet, From a buster out of Foveaux.

b. Of a season, or weather, **to come a buster**, to blow up cold and windy.

1897 WRIGHT *Station Ballads* 19 Then winter came a buster, with its wind and driving snow.

buster, n.[2] *Obs.* [Poss. Brit. dial.: see OED *buster* 3 b, and *burster* 1 c; AND 1878.] A heavy fall, esp. in the phr. **to come a buster**, to come a cropper, to take a fall. Also *transf.*

c1875 MEREDITH *Adventuring in Maoriland* (1935) 156 The ferns were sufficiently thick to break his fall [from his horse]. He appeared to be more mortified at missing the dogs than by the buster he got. **1902** *NZ Illustr. Mag.* V. 488 What a buster I came on that stone. **1905** *Truth* 26 Aug. 7 You will meet him when you're busted When you're broken by the 'books' And he knows you've come a buster. **1953** 15 M A23 Thames DHS 16 Buster (a fall) [M2] **1960** SCRYMGEOUR *Memories Maoriland* 183 Hearing of the buster [sc. a fall from a horse] at Fern Flats, Jack put together a par. concerning young Steuart.

buster, n.[3] *Obs.* [Origin uncertain.] As **the buster**, a local newspaper, esp. a country newsheet or newspaper.

1893 FROBISHER *Sketches of Gossiptown* 73 How vain the thought to get such grace Within the roll of Fame's bright muster, Whose rhymes are scarce permitted space Of print within our local 'Buster'. **1914** GRACE *Tale Timber Town* 39 I bought the gold myself. I gave the information to the 'buster'. **1924** GIBSON *Gibbie Galoot* My visitor showed me a copy of the Chronicle, his own paper, a typical country 'buster', consisting mainly of advertisements and stale telegrams. **1984** p.c. Martine Cuff, *buster* for newspaper used in c1950 at Milton, Otago.

buster, n.[4] [Poss. f. *Obs.* Brit. *buster*, *burster* a small loaf, a bun: cf. OED n. 1 (not defined); Partridge 8 c1850.] As **cheese buster** (also occas. **cheese blister**), a plain or savoury thin biscuit or pastry traditionally flavoured with cheese; often a 'cheese straw'.

1916 *Celebrated Amuri Cook. Book* (1927) 112 Busters. Two cups flour, dessertspoon butter, pinch salt, small cup milk and water... roll out [dough] half at time very thin, cut into strips or large blocks. **1928** *Everybody's Cook. Book of Tested Recipes* 45 Cheese Busters..flour..salt..butter..grated cheese... Roll out very thin, cut into squares and place on cold oven shelf. Bake. **1934** *Marigold Book of Recipes* 26 *Cheese Busters..butter..flour..grated cheese..cayenne pepper..salt..B.P... stiff paste with..water.* **1936** *Merry Meal Maker Cook. Book* 31 *Cheese Busters..*Roll out, cut into strips about three inches long and brush over with egg. Bake. **c1939** BASHAM *Aunt Daisy's Book of Recipes* 109 *Cheese Blisters..*Roll out thinly, and cut into oblong pieces... Bake. **1955** *Cook. Book NZ Women's Inst.* 109 Busters. Two cups wholemeal, 2 teaspoons baking powder, 1 cup milk, rub in 2ozs butter, salt. Stiff dough. Roll very thin and cut into long strips. *Ibid.* 156 Blisters. One cup flour, 1 tablespoon butter, ½ cup milk or water, ½ teaspoon salt. Mix to a stiff dough and roll out very thinly... *Cheese Busters.* Eight ozs flour, 2ozs butter, 4ozs grated cheese..½ teaspoon baking powder...Roll very thin, cut and bake on cold slide.

buster-cut. *Hist.* [Poss. f. *buster* boy; fellow.] A young woman's hair style fashionable in the late 1920s, consisting of a boyish close crop.

1924 *Star* (Christchurch) 12 Dec. (Xmas Number) 5 I thought you hated buster cuts. **1926** GLEN *Uncles Three* 134 Though it was not a buster-cut the effect was really pretty. **1950** *Landfall* 13 15 She had her hair short in a buster-cut. **1988** HOOD *Sylvia* 49 I cut off my hair [c1926] in a buster cut.

Hence **bustered** a., of hair, cut in a buster-cut.
1926 DEVANNY *Butcher Shop* (1981) 73 Her bustered yellow hair stood out from her head in a beautiful crisp frizz. **1992** PARK *Fence around the Cuckoo* 45 After I'd had my hair 'bustered' and slicked down with bay rum, he said that I looked like a wet ferret.

but. [AND 1853, then 1938.] As sentence or clause final, 'though, however'.

1966 TURNER *Eng. Lang. Austral. & NZ* 113 There is no local grammar. The local usage which comes to mind, and it is not widespread, is the use of *but* as an adverb at the end of a sentence, an equivalent of *however*... I first heard this usage in 1945 in Auckland among students at a Teacher's College, where it was a bit of an affectation or craze rather than established unconscious usage, but. **1983** p.c. Professor C. Corne (Auckland). but—'though', sentence or clause finally. 'Jeez, this is strong piss! Nice, but'. 'X's are good cars, I wouldn't buy one, but': Whangarei, widely used in 50s and 60s. Also current in Hawaiian Creole English. **1986** *New Outlook* XXI. 49 It's true but... Caleb still caught untold kutus that year but.

butcher, n.

1. a. In special Comb. **butcher-bee** (prob. erron. confused with MASON-WASP or BEE: see quot. 1983), **butcher-boy**, the larva, and as **butcher-beetle**, the mature form, of the tiger beetle *Neocicindela* spp. (fam. Cicindelidae), referring to the predatory habits of both in searching out prey. See also PENNY DOCTOR.

1891 TREGEAR *Maori-Polynesian Comparative Dict.* 247 Moeone, a kind of grub, the larva of the Butcher Beetle (Ent. *Cicindella*, sp.). **1935** DIXON *Nature Study Notes* 34 The grass grub is sometimes confused with the larva of the Tiger Beetle, called by children 'Butcher Boy' or 'Penny Doctor'. **1948** MARTIN *NZ Nature Study* 190 Tiger Beetles (about 16 species). The larvae are the butcher-boys or penny doctors to be seen on sunny summer days at the entrance of their circular burrows in clay banks facing the sun. **1952** *JPS* LXI. 9 Larva of *Cicindela tuberculata* (WD. 2), the tiger, or butcher, beetle. The term could apply to any of the several species of *Cicindela*. **1965** BEGGS *Nature Study* 270 f. [Caption] Parents of the 'butcher boy.' Tiger beetles may be observed running and flying near the circular mouths of 'butcher boy' tunnels. **1971** SHARELL *NZ Insects* 85 The tiger beetle larva is popularly known as butcher boy or penny doctor. While the first name clearly derives from a first-hand observation of slaughter, penny doctor is less obvious. **1983** STEWART *Springtime in Taranaki* (1991) 72 A butcher-bee is a small, black, busy insect, perhaps really a kind of wasp rather than a bee, which lives in a hole in a clay bank.

You fished for them by poking a straw down the hole, whereupon..the butcher-bee would seize it and you could pull him out, still clinging to it.

b. *transf. pl.* **butcher-boys** (also **butcher bats**) *butcher-beetles*, esp. as used in a children's game (see quots.), known from at least 1902 (cf. Drummond & Hutton *Nature in NZ* (1902) 62); also the name of the game itself.

1951 *JPS* LX. 104 *Penny Doctor* beetles, also known as 'Butcher bats' is a game widely reported by Wellington Training College students as being played in many parts of the North Island. In this game straws moistened by spittle are pushed down the hole of the appropriate beetle. The beetle seizes the end of the straw. When the player feels the straw moving he or she flicks out the beetle. The player who can catch the most beetles wins the game. **1953** SUTTON-SMITH *Unorganised Games NZ Primary School Children* (VUWTS) I. 404 The most widely known game with insects is a game named variously by T.C. students as Butcher Boys (Gisborne, New Plymouth, Kaponga, Te Pohu, Newall, Sth. Wellington), Butcher Bats (Ohau, Takaka), Penny Doctor Beetles (Tauranga, Pipiriki, Rotorua), or Fishing (Morunui)... Most of the reports of this practice come from the North Island, though it was known in the South as early as 1900 (Waikouaiti). **1984** WALKER *Common Insects 2* 27 In the past children nicknamed the larva 'butcher boy' or 'penny doctor' and made a game of fishing out the larva with a piece of straw poked down the burrow. *Ibid.* 100 Children often play a game called 'drawing the butcher', or 'penny doctor', by inserting a grass stem into the larval tunnel, when it is tenaciously seized by the inmate.

2. As **butcher-bird** *Taranaki* [origin unknown], TOMTIT.

1966 FALLA et al. *Birds NZ* 200 Tomtit *Petroica macrocephala* Other names: Miromiro (North Island), Ngirungiru (South Island), Wheedler, Butcher-bird (Taranaki).

butcher's.

1. In full **butcher's hook(s)** [AND *n.*² 1 b, 1918], rhyming slang for 'CROOK' B 2, angry, in the phr. **to go (off) butchers' hook(s)** (at a person), to become angry (with), to go off (at), to scold or reprimand severely. Occas. *fig.* **a. go (off) butcher's hook.**

1918 *Kia-ora Coo-ee* (1981) 15 Aug. II. 5 A certain New Zealand Regiment, camped on the Jordan flats, recently came under the eagle eye of brother 'Jacko', who immediately went 'butcher's hook' or 'ram's horn' and launched forth much frightfulness by lugging a 5.9 up on to one of the spare hills and chucking ironmongery promiscuously about the place. **1943** BENNETT *English in NZ* in *Amer. Speech* XVIII. 90 *To go crook* is to show anger or annoyance, to 'sling off at'; and *to go butcher's hook* is presumably a development of this rhyming slang. **1950** CHERRILL *NZ Sheep Farm* 206 You should have heard him go off butcher's hook. **1951** FRAME *Lagoon* (1961) 20 I'll come back with a salmon or I'll go butcher's hook. **1960** BOSWELL *Ernie* 119 'Mum'll go butchers' hooks at us if she finds out,' said Ted. **1963** CASEY *As Short a Spring* 275 The old man had come home full as a bull one night..all his money gone. The old woman had gone butcher's hook and they'd got stuck into one another.

b. As **go butcher's.**

1955 *BJ Cameron Collection* (TS July) *go butchers* (v) *go butchers hook* (v) To get furious. Rhyming variation of '*go crook*'. **1963** CASEY *As Short a Spring* 212 And that was either a nasty burst of static or old Ma Bower going butcher's. **1973** WILSON *NZ Jack* 124 Gil went really butcher's at her to me for a minute. 'Don't be a flaming galah, Ken,' he said. **1995** ANDERSON *House Guest* 229 She went butchers... Gave the woman both barrels, told her what she thought of her.

2. In the phr. **to be in like a butcher's cat**, to attack or be 'stuck in' vigorously, without restraint.

1959 *The Standard* (Wellington) 19 Aug. 9 Once in the bar..make sure you do not get 'full of bull' unless the 'shout' is 'on' someone else, when of course you will be 'in like a butcher's cat'.

3. In the phr. **as greasy (slippery) as a as a butcher's apron (pup)**, see GREASY *a*.

4. As **butcher's board**, a marble game.

1972 SUTTON-SMITH *Folkgames Children* 175 (In more recent years marble games with holes have had the greater role [than ring games].).. There were Little Ring, Liney, Follows..and then, on a less important scale, Butcher's Board, in which the marbles were bowled through the holes in a board, Eye-Drop, Knock-Backs.

5. [Poss. a var. of *tinker's damn* or *curse*.] In the phr. **not to give a butcher's**, not to care a whit, not to give a 'tinker's curse'.

1982 SANDYS *Love & War* 19 So long as the meals are on time I don't give a butcher's what the place looks like.

butt-ender. *Obs.* [Poss. Brit. dial., see EDD *butt* Westmoreland, in the phr. *the butt of the wind* 'the wind's eye, the point from which it comes'; poss. a nautical use: cf. James Cowan's foreword to Eaddy '*Neath Swaying Spars* (1939), about sailing scows 'Pushed along by the butt-end of a sou'wester'; also 1858 Shaw *Gallop to Antipodes* 128 When within a few miles of Wellington Harbour, a wind came on in the opposite direction, or, as they term it, a 'burster but-end first.'] A northerly gale. Cf. *southerly buster* (SOUTHERLY 3).

1858 SHAW *Gallop to Antipodes* 184 Some of these winds [in Cook Strait] come on gradually until they reach their greatest force..others burst upon the crew with all their fury and then gradually decline. This latter has received the name 'butt-ender' from its resemblance to that part of a gun which is the heaviest, strongest and broadest.

butter.

1. In various special Comb. alluding to the New Zealand dairy industry: **butter-box** *obs*., formerly a box, usu. of white-pine timber, designed to hold approx. 56lb. [25.4 kg] of butter, used also for many other domestic and general purposes; also **butter-box timber**, *white pine* (PINE 2 (19)); **butter cheque** (usu. **cream cheque**), money paid to a supplier by a dairy company; **butter country**, Taranaki, from its predominant dairy industry; **butter factory** [not exclusively NZ, but of great local social and economic significance], a factory, usu. cooperatively owned by the contributing farmers, receiving cream and manufacturing butter and related products (also called *dairy factory*, see DAIRY 4); **butterfatter**, a former colloquial name for a dairy farmer as a supplier of butterfat (now 'milk fat') to a dairy factory.

1907 COX *Diaries 1888–1925* (ATLMS) 2 Jan. I worked all day, had some **butter-box timber** to stack and since was carrying timber into the Mill. **1917** *Free Lance* (Wellington) 20 July 16 Anybody with a sense of humour would have laughed..if he had been a witness of the butter-kings' very solemn deputation to Premier Massey... They asked..for State aid to preserve supplies of butter-box timber. **1938** *Auckland Weekly News* 12 Jan. 15 [Heading] Butter-box Timber. Survey for White Pine Resources. **1980** YORKE *Animals Came First* 46 We found that the invaluable butterbox could be made to fulfil our most pressing needs. A set of them..on top of one another provided storage places for clothes, more butterboxes became chairs. **1991** *Listener* 16 Dec. 21 When he married his wife Margaret they had 'a butterbox and a couple of shearer's beds'. **1919** CHUDLEIGH *Diary* 31 Mar. (1950) 466 I also start them with 20 cows apiece at a fixed price to be paid for out of the **butter cheque**. **1905** *Truth* 24 June 7 Billy Murphy now knocking out a crust in the **butter country**. **1892** *NZ Official Handbook* 128 It is true that cheese factories are becoming numerous in Otago and Southland, with a few **butter-factories**. **1902** *Settler's Handbook NZ* 14 Eighty-seven butter- and cheese-factories were returned to 1st November, 1900, as at work in the Wellington Provincial District. **1925** WEBB *Miss Peters' Special* 123 We have no wealthy capitalists,... no manufactories save the butter factory, which takes our milk. **1934** SCANLAN *Winds of Heaven* 174 Lack of cleanliness in the milking shed had caused his test to fall to second grade at the butter factory. **1957** FRAME *Owls Do Cry* (1967) 18 Also a photograph of the Freezing Works..; of the Woollen Mills,... the butter factory..all meaning prosperity..and a fat filled land. **1986** DEVANNY *Point of Departure* 19 The coming of the butter factory [c1900] I felt to be of the nature of a curse. **1917** *Stratford Evening Post* 3 July 4 'Butter fat' is a word that will be heard frequently in the House this session... [Farmers' representatives] are out for a refund of the butter-fat tax, which the Government says is not a tax... The struggle between the **butterfatters** and the Government will be worth watching.

2. With a modifier defining the place or type of manufacture, broadly distinguishing that made in a dairy factory (**factory (creamery, shop) butter**), from that made in a farm dairy from skimmed or hand-separated cream (**farm, farmers', separated butter**, also freq. formerly heard as *dairy*, or *separator butter*).

1894 *Ann. Rep. Dept. Agric.* II. 202 They [sc. English merchants] comment very favourably concerning the quality of our 'factory' or 'creamery' butter. **1946** BEAGLEHOLE *Some Modern Maoris* 95 Home-made butter is used (the family will eat only shop butter on bread, so the home-made butter is all used for cooking). **1985** HUNT *I'm Ninety-five* 70 Factory butter was one and two a pound, separated farmers' butter one shilling a pound [c1910].

buttercup.

1. Transf. use of *buttercup* for any of various native spp. of *Ranunculus*. See also BERMUDA BUTTERCUP, WAORIKI.

2. With a modifier: **Castle Hill, Kaikoura, mountain (great mountain, great white), Mount Egmont**.

(1) **Castle Hill buttercup**. [f. the name of *Castle Hill* sheep station: see quot. 1984.] *Ranunculus crithmifolius* (formerly *pauciflorus*).

1984 *Dominion* (Wellington) 4 Dec. 4 He first began his fight to preserve the Castle Hill buttercup in the early 1940s. The low yellow-flowered buttercup grows only..on a harsh limestone environment on the historic Castle Hill station 85 kilometres northwest of Christchurch. **1985** SHERWOOD *Botanist at Bay* (1986) 14 [*Ranunculus paucifolius*] was listed as an endangered plant, but a widely publicized rescue operation had made it well known in international conservation circles. It was known as the Castle Hill Buttercup, and its range was limited to Castle Hill, wherever that might be.

BUTTERFISH 124 **BUTTERFLY**

1989 Parkinson *Travelling Naturalist* 134 Castle Hill is also known for its flowers... Best known among them is the Castle Hill buttercup—a spectacular plant with large golden flowers growing on shortened stems among brown-green leaves.

(2) **Kaikoura buttercup**. [From the name of the type locality *Kaikoura* on the east coast of Marlborough province.] *Ranunculus insignis* (formerly *lobulatus*).

1919 Cockayne *NZ Plants & Their Story* 139 Under certain circumstances..the Kaikoura buttercup (*R. lobulatus*) produces leaves of this kind. **1961** Martin *Flora NZ* 254 Very choice rock-frequenting, floriferous herbs native to Marlborough include the Kaikoura Buttercup. **1966** *Encycl. NZ* I. 713 The yellow-flowered *Ranunculus lobulatus* is known as the 'Kaikoura buttercup'.

(3) **mountain buttercup**. *Ranunculus insignis*. Also as **great mountain buttercup**, **great white buttercup**. *R. lyallii*, LILY 2 (9) and (10). See also KORIKORI.

1909 *AJHR* C-11 6 *Ranunculus insignis* Mountain-buttercup. **1969** McCaskill *Molesworth* 14 On the higher levels, up to 5,000 feet and over, a scattered alpine vegetation, including pen-wiper and mountain buttercups. **1978** [see KORIKORI]. **1979** Mark & Adams *Alpine Plants* 34 *Ranunculus lyallii*... Great Mountain Buttercup... A magnificent, glabrous, summer-green buttercup, reaching 1m. high, often wrongly referred to as a lily. **1982** Wilson *Stewart Is. Plants* 126 Mountain Lily... Mount Cook lily... Great white buttercup.

(4) **Mount Egmont buttercup**. [f. the type locality, *Mount Egmont*, now Mt Taranaki.] *Ranunculus nivicolus*, a golden-flowered buttercup of high mountain country.

1910 Cockayne *NZ Plants & Their Story* 94 The Mount Egmont buttercup..is one of the features of that mountain.

3. *transf.* [Prob. an abbrev. of US *buttercup squash*, so called from its green skin over yellow flesh: cf. DARE *buttercup squash* (1949), 'chiefly Nth. A cultivated variety of fall squash (*Cucurbita maxima*)'.] A small, usu. green, squash pumpkin with yellow flesh; see also quot. 1962.

1962 *NZJAg.* CV. 237 Buttercup, another small-fruited variety [of squash], was developed at the North Dakota Agricultural College. It is turban-shaped, 5 to 7 in. in diameter, and very slightly ribbed. The colour is deep, dull green, faintly striped, and flecked with dull grey, and there is a prominent button at the blossom end. The flesh is golden yellow, fine grained and dry, and of pleasing flavour. **1971** Flower *NZ Woman's Weekly Cookbook* 89 Stuffed Buttercup... With the buttercup stalk side uppermost, place a cup on end cut out a circle ½ inch through the skin. **1976** Scarrow *NZ Vegetable Gardening Guide* 56 'Buttercup': A true winter squash. The small fruit average about 15cm in diameter, and mature early. **1987** *Yates Garden Guide* 84 Buttercup: finest quality summer and autumn squash... The flesh is firm, deep orange, sweet and dry... Rind is dark green with pale green flecks and stripes.

butterfish. [f. the slippery ('buttery') coating of mucus on the skin: AND 1849.] Any of various fishes having a coating of mucus on the skin.

1. Any of several fishes of the family Odacidae esp. *Odax* (formerly *Coridodax*) *pullus*. See also *blue-bone* (BLUE *a*. 2 b), GREENBONE, KELPFISH 1, KELPIE *n*.[1], KELP-SALMON, MARARI, RARI *n*.[1]

1872 Hutton & Hector *Fishes NZ* 114 Butter Fish... The Marare of the natives, known as the Kelp Fish among the fishermen and the Butter Fish in the market (*Coridodax pullus*), is the fish most commonly sold in Wellington during the winter months. It has a rather forbidding appearance, having a dark coloured slimy skin and inelegant form; it is nevertheless very good food. **1886** Sherrin *Handbook Fishes NZ* 14 Known by many as the kelpfish, and by the fishermen in some places as the butter-fish. **1902** Drummond & Hutton *Nature in NZ* 73 The butterfish lives amongst kelp, or sea-weed, and is generally found where kelp is plentiful. **1913** *TrNZI* XLV. 231 The butter-fish, kelpfish or kelp-salmon, as it is variously called, is very common in Otago Harbour. **1921** *NZJST* IV. 117 Butterfish; Marari. Sold as 'greenbone' or 'kelp-salmon' in Dunedin. **1936** *Handbook for NZ* (ANZAAS) 72 *Coridodax pullus*: Butter-fish (Wellington and Marlborough), green-bone or kelp-fish (Otago). **1945** Beattie *Maori Place-names Canterbury* 61 Marari (or marare in other provinces)—the butter-fish, or kelp fish. **1957** Parrott *Sea Angler's Fishes* 130 It is unfortunate that the Butterfish has been given a variety of local names which have originated either from their habit of associating with kelp, their body form, or from the colour of their bones, as for example, Kelpfish, Kelp-salmon, Greenbone, and several other names not so easy to explain. **1966** Doogue & Moreland *Sea Anglers' Guide* 258 Butterfish... greenbone; marari, rari (Maori)... Variable fat content, flaky delicate fish with high iodine content. Can be baked, steamed, fried and grilled. **1970** Sorensen *Nomenclature NZ Fish* 14 Butterfish... Suggested commercial name[s]: Butterfish; Greenbone. Other common names: Southern Kelpfish. **1982** Ayling *Collins Guide* (1984) 265 Butterfish (Greenbone, marari)... Small individuals have a markedly different colour pattern from that of the adults and until recently were thought to belong to a separate species named the kelpfish, *Odax vittatus*. **1986** Paul *NZ Fishes* 110 Internationally the name butterfish is used for the family to which our warehou belong, but in New Zealand the name is so firmly associated with the species described below [*sc. Odax pullus*] that a change is unlikely. **1993** Bertram *Capes of China* 282 Sandy Bay..recalled..notable childhood feasts of butterfish and crays.

2. SPOTTY 1 (*Notolabrus celidotus*).

[*Note*] Butterfish was the usual early Otago name for the *spotty* (*N. celidotus*, a wrasse) of other localities, poss. deriving from the yellow or 'buttery' colouring of the undersurface. Perh. as a consequence of this, the name *butterfish*, which was more generally used in other localities for *Odax pullus*, gave way in Otago (and other parts of the SI) to *greenbone*.

1878 *TrNZI* X. 329 The true butterfish was caught several times during the year. It must, however be considered a rare fish in our [Otago] waters... The spotty, or butterfish of our local fishermen, has been very plentiful this year. **1886** Sherrin *Handbook Fishes NZ* 92 The spotty [fam. Labridae] is also known in Dunedin as the butterfish. **1906** *TrNZI* XXXVIII. 551 *Pseudolabrus bothryocomus*. Locally known as 'butterfish' or 'spotty'; very common. **1921** [see SPOTTY 1]. **1966** Doogue & Moreland *Sea Anglers' Guide* 257 Spotty... *Pseudolabrus celidotus*; butterfish, kelpie, guffy. None is widely used. Paketi, pakirikiri (Maori). **1986** Paul *NZ Fishes* 107 Spotty *Pseudolabrus celidotus*. Alternative names include paketi, kelpie, and butterfish (the last two being misleading).

3. As **deepsea butterfish**, a (retail) trade name for *girdled parrotfish* (see PARROTFISH 2 (2)).

butterfly, *n.* and *attrib.*

A. *n.*

1. Suffixed (but often omitted) in names of New Zealand butterflies: **little blue**, **mountain ringlet**. See also *beech forest butterfly* (BEECH 3), *blue moon* (BLUE *a*. 2 b), COMMON COPPER, RED ADMIRAL, *southern* (occas. *New Zealand*) *blue* (SOUTHERN 3), *tussock butterfly* (TUSSOCK 5 b), *yellow admiral* (YELLOW 2).

1984 *Hanmer Forest Park* 65 Mountain ringlet butterfly—*Percnodaimon pluto*: This black butterfly may be seen skipping around the higher screes on hot summer days. *Ibid.* 66 Little blue butterfly—*Zizina oxleyi*: This is the most common butterfly in the [Hanmer] district.

2. [In transf. use for sea animals which in some features resemble a butterfly.] See quots.

1947 Powell *Native Animals NZ* 29 Sea Butterfly (*Cavolina telemus*). A small fragile inhabitant of the open seas, which washes ashore at rare intervals on our ocean beaches. The Sea Butterfly is a Pteropod (wing-footed), which name refers to the expansion of the foot of the animal into two spreading lobes used for swimming. **1966** *Encycl. NZ* I. 340 One species [of chiton], *Cryptoconchus porosus*, has beautiful greenish-blue internal valves. These are the 'butterflies' so keenly sought by amateur collectors.

3. *Obs.* In the phr. **to fly a butterfly**, to raise money on worthless cheques or bills.

1868 *Auckland Punch* 67 With regard to their currency some of them live by flying butterflies, pieces of paper of peculiar form and stamp.

B. *attrib.*

1. a. In the names of fish, see: PERCH 2 (2).

b. As **butterfly fish (tuna)** [f. the resemblance of its pelvic wings to those of a butterfly], *Gasterochisma melampus* (fam. Scombridae), a large (180–200 cm), deepwater tuna, the 'scaled tunny', having distinctive fan-like pelvic wings, taken occas. on longline or in trawling in New Zealand waters.

1872 Hutton & Hector *Fishes NZ* 20 *Gasterochisma melampus*... Butterfly Fish. **1886** Sherrin *Handbook Fishes NZ* 301 *Gasterochisma melampus*... Butterfly-fish. **1898** Morris *Austral-English* 74 Butterfly-fish... New Zealand sea-fish, *Gasterochisma melampus*... The ventral fins are exceedingly broad and long, and can be completely concealed in a fold of the abdomen. The New Zealand fish is so named from these fins. **1913** *TrNZI* XLV. 230 The 'butterfly-fish', as it is called when young, has been taken in Otago Harbour, and is now known to be the young of the scaled tunny. **1927** Phillipps *Bibliogr. NZ Fishes* (1971) 45 *Gasterochisma melampus*... Butterfly-fish. **1957** Parrott *Sea Angler's Fishes* 156 The Butterfly Fish is also known as the Scaled Tunny, and is closely related to the Bonito and Albacore. **1982** Ayling *Collins Guide* (1984) 295 Butterfly Tuna (Scaly tuna)... The butterfly tuna..changes considerably in appearance as it increases in size. **1986** Paul *NZ Fishes* 128 The butterfly tuna..is an unusual, silvery grey, laterally compressed fish with large scales and ventral fins (large in small fish) which fold into a groove.

2. In the names of plants: **butterfly bush**, a naturalized Chinese shrub *Buddleja davidii* (fam. Buddlejaceae) with dense panicles of fragrant flowers which attract butterflies.

1943 Matthews *NZ Gardening Dict.* (3edn.) 27 Buddleia (Butterfly Bush);... which proves such an attraction for butterflies, the Red Admiral in particular. **1969** *Standard Common Names Weeds* 10 butterfly bush [=] buddleia. **1988** Webb, Sykes, Garnock-Jones *Flora NZ* IV. 449 Buddleia or butterfly bush is abundantly naturalised to the point of being a nuisance in some areas.

3. *fig.* or *transf.* In special collocations denoting things or operations, (parts of) which resemble butterfly wings: **butterfly hammer-drill**, see quot.; **butterfly marble**, a playing marble having interior whorls and colours resembling those of butterfly wings; **butterfly-stoper** *mining*, see quot.; **butterfly scarf** *logging*, a scarf, or cut in the trunk of a standing tree, which resembles butterfly wings.

1978 McAra *Gold Mining Waihi* 313 **Butterfly hammer-drill**: The original swing-stoper was known as a butterfly stoper. It used an anvil block in addition to the piston and was equipped with a new type of valve known as a butterfly valve. 1989 Virtue *Upon Evil Season* 48 I'se getting some **butterfly marbles** for Christmas. 1978 McAra *Gold Mining Waihi* 319 *Drill, popper or butterfly stoper*: A fairly light drill mounted vertically on a pneumatically-operated telescopic leg; used for boring uppers, and rotated by a swinging by hand. 1944 *NZ New Writing* III. 54 Only the brain can decide when a *butterfly scarf* is work wasted.

butternut. [An abbrev. of US *butternut squash*, so called from its light orange-brown (US 'butternut') colour; cf. Webster (1961): also *Austral.*, p.c. Dr. W.S. Ramson.] *Cucurbita moschata* (fam. Cucurbitaceae), a small bottle-shaped type of pumpkin with a smooth buff to pale orange skin and orange-yellow flesh, cultivated in warm areas of the North Island.

1962 *NZJAg*. CV. 237 *Butternut* is the most widely grown of the small types [of squash of North American origin]. It is 6 to 12 in. long, 3 to 5 in. in diameter... The shape ranges from short and squat to elongated, the flower end being bowl shaped and containing a small seed cavity... The skin is smooth, hard, and thin, creamy yellow to orange brown. The flesh is a rich golden orange, free of fibre. 1976 Scarrow *NZ Vegetable Gardening Guide* 56 '*Butternut*': Has a small pear-shaped fruit, is quite dry and has an excellent flavour. 1987 *Yates Garden Guide* 84 *Butternut*: a favourite, small fruited squash. Delicate nutty flavour. Distinctive, buff-coloured, pear-shaped fruits. Rind is thin, hard and very smooth.

buttoner. *Obs.* [AND suggests a survival of Brit. *buttoner* accomplice, decoy, 1882, citing OED *button n.* 9 and *buttoner* 3.] The accomplice of a confidence man.

1910 *Truth* 26 Nov. 4 The [Auctioneers Amendment] Bill could also have been improved by a clause or two dealing with 'buttoners' the individuals employed, mostly at furniture sales, to run up prices.

Hence **button** *v.*, to act as a tout or swindler; **button** *n.*, in the phr. **to do a button**, to tout or cadge for money.

1908 *Truth* 11 Jan. 2 The [racing] club had one of its employees 'buttoning' for the machine. He stood beside the machine's notice board informing all and sundry that 'Now's yer time, only half a minute more.' 1906 *Truth* 31 Mar. 6 If you've got to cadge for boodle, Then you're said to 'do a button'.

button-eye. [f. the button-like appearance of its ringed eye.] silvereye.

1946 *JPS* LV. 159 Button-eye, a wandering bird (Zosterops halmaturina), blight-bird; twinkie; button-eye; wax-eye; ring-eye.

buwai, var. boohai.

buzzy bee. [f. a proprietary name given c1947–49: (p.c. George D. Steel, Auckland, May 1994.] A wooden toy originated in New Zealand in the form of a brightly coloured bee on wheels which emits a sharp clackety-clacking noise when drawn along a surface.

1978 *NZ Patent Office Jrnl No.1183* 2 June Buzzy Bee 114123 [filed] 8 December 1975..games and playthings in the nature of bees or suggestive of bees. H.E. Ramsey & Company Limited. 1989 *Truth* 1 Dec. 2 They reveal..that our old mate Buzzy Bee, that venerated toy of thousands of New Zealand children and developed by Aucklanders Hec and John Ramsey, of Onehunga, is now being manufactured in China. 1990 *Listener* 3 Aug. 11 Mention culture, they say, and it's beginning to sound too important, the role of Buzzy Bee or Wattie's peas in our national psyche notwithstanding. 1992 *Dominion Sunday Times* (Wellington) 30 Aug. 9 [He] had intended to make most of his returns on franchising the *Buzzy Bee* label. 1994 *Herald* (Auckland) 2 May (correspondence page) [George D. Steel, Milford, writes] The Buzzy Bee was first introduced to Ramsey's [H. and E. Ramsey and Co., repetition wood turners] by myself. The idea came from a toy gift from my sister's mother-in-law who had returned from the United States with a flat wooden version with printed paper glued over it.

by Christchurch!; corry, gorry, korry: see Christchurch; korry a.

BYO, BYOB, BYOG. [AND 1968.] Abbrev. of **bring your own** (usu. liquor), **bring your own beer** (**booze**, **bottle**, **grog**), applied to and used by restaurants which, though not fully licensed to sell liquor, may serve liquor brought by a customer; also used on or with party invitations to indicate the nature of the event; occas. transferred to other activities.

A. *n.* A BYO restaurant so licensed; occas. applied to the liquor brought.

1985 Marshall *Secret Diary Telephonist* 157 The breakaway group hadn't been able to decide whether to go to a licensed restaurant or a B.Y.O. 1988 McGill *Dict. Kiwi Slang* 24 *BYO* acronym for bring your own, usually meaning the wine you take to an unlicensed restaurant. 1989 *Contact* (Wellington) 8 Dec. 4 It has always surprised me that more restaurants don't open them—particularly the smaller BYOs which are mainly owner-operated. 1990 *Contact* (Wellington) 19 Jan. 2 After a massive campaign to try to persuade the city's BYOs to stay open during the Christmas period.

B. In *attrib.* use passing into Comb.

1976 *NZPD* CDVII. 3574 The creation of a permit to allow the consumption of a customer's liquor in an unlicensed restaurant—known overseas as a BYO licence—will..receive almost universal support. 1985 McGill *G'day Country* 151 There was a BYO restaurant, but I had not brought my own booze. 1986 *Evening Post* (Wellington) 11 July 11 BYO ad functions illegal, police say... Senior Sergeant Max Moore said this when commenting on recent advertisements on radio and newspapers in Oamaru advertising functions as 'bring your own liquor'. 1988 Hill *More from Moaville* 45 A ute boot sale, BYO gumboot throwing, raffles [at School Gala day].

C. In *verbal* use.

1976 *NZPD* CDVII. 3561 The need for a provision of this nature—sometimes known as BYOG, 'bring your own grog'—has been widely recognised. 1976 Johnston *New Zealanders* 150 The invitation probably said 'BYOG' (bring your own grog) and 'Ladies a plate'. 1980 Leland *Kiwi-Yankee Dict.* 20 B.Y.O.B. on a party invitation, means bring your own bottle. 1986 *Metro* (Auckland) July 20 Fed Up. 244 Ponsonby Rd. BYO. No bookings. Small, crowded with drabbies. Menu long overdue for a change, but still good value. 1986 *Victoria Univ. Weekly Staff Circular* 21 Mar. No.782 *Progressive Dinner*... BYO and $2.00 to cover costs.

byre. *Otago-Southland.* [f. Sc. dial. *byre* cowshed.] cowshed. See also *cow-byre* (cow 6).

1883 Ferguson *Castle Gay* 251 And the farmstead... With stables, outhouse, barn and byre,... Were all a farmer could desire. 1899 *Ann. Rep. Dept. Agric.* IV. 33 There was only one byre out of a number visited that I consider milk should have been allowed to be sold from. 1912 *Otago Witness* (Dunedin) 23 Oct. 78 The byre itself is a new-fangled invention... It holds 16 cows at one **bailing**, and has double bails on each side. 1925 *NZ Dairy Produce Exporter* 30 Sept. 40 One day when Dad had a dancing turn, there was a big bony cow looking round the corner of the byre, chewing her cud and waiting for a bail. 1943 Bennett *English in NZ* in *Amer. Speech* XVIII. 86 The Scottish *byre* is used for a cattlepen in the south of the South Island—a reminder of the origin of the first settlers there. 1959 Slatter *Gun in My Hand* 41 Sitting around in the cattle byre. 1960 Summers *Moon Over Alps* (1974) 37 They had hunted systematically..in shearing sheds, in the men's quarters, the outbuildings, byres, even in the cool store. 1977 Sargeson *Never Enough!* 76 And in case of readers who might say that last word ['husbandry'] is archaic I would remind that I was now in a [Southland] countryside... Also I saw nothing so ordinary as a cowshed, no indeed, instead there was Romance: byres. 1982 Frame *To the Is-land* (1984) 185 The cow..was already named Scrapers after her habit of scraping her hooves on the concrete floor of the byre. 1991 La Roche *Hist. of Howick & Pakuranga* 263 The cowshed [built at Howick c1863] had 8 byres or cowbails, each with a leather hinge.

C

cabbage.

1. Any of several naturalized forms of *Brassica* (fam. Brassicaceae), usu. European cabbage *B. oleracea*, less commonly wild turnip *B. rapa*; usu. with a modifier: **Maori (colonial, native, wild)**. Cf. MACQUARIE CABBAGE.

[**1807** SAVAGE *Some Acc. of NZ* 57 The diffusion of cabbage seed has been so general..that you would suppose it an indigenous plant of the country.] **1847** ANGAS *Savage Life* I. 278 The whole island was thickly overrun with wild cabbage. **1849** TORLESSE *Papers* (1958) 94 By the time I returned to the pah I..was out of provisions, indeed had already experienced the nutritious qualities of Maori cabbage and fernroot. **1852** *Austral. & NZ Gaz.* 10 Jan. 11 After dinner went about two miles down the river to a spot where a plant grows called the 'Maori Cabbage'... I believe this plant is a turnip which has degenerated for want of proper cultivation, so that the roots are too small to be of much use, but the tops are excellent boiled as greens. It is supposed to have been introduced by Captain Cook. **1852** TAYLOR *Journal* 3 Nov. (ATLTS) VIII. 50 My party made an oven in which they placed a large quantity of native cabbage. **1863** BUTLER *First Year* ix 131 The only plant good to eat is Maori cabbage, and that is Swede Turnip gone wild, from seed left by Captain Cook. **1873** BULLER *Birds NZ* 154 It is said to feed also on the leaves of the thistle and wild cabbage. **1880** MUELLER *My Dear Bannie* 1 Dec. (1958) 78 The use of these [native greens] in modern times..was commonly superseded by that of the extremely useful and favourite plant—the Maori cabbage, Brassica oleracea—introduced by Cook. **1884** MARTIN *Our Maoris* 42 Sometimes the Maoris would bring a basket of wild cabbage. **1898** HOCKEN *Contributions* 54 These [odds and ends] well mixed with a few potatoes, some wild native cabbage, and above all the optimum condimentum [=salt] added, made a most sumptuous feast. **1903** *TrNZI* XXXV. 87 What is known as 'Maori cabbage' is here [among the Tuhoe] termed *paea*. **1914** PFAFF *Diggers' Story* 76 They used up everything, and had to live on shellfish and Maori cabbage. **1926** HILGENDORF *Weeds* 93 Wild Cabbage..often called Maori cabbage, is a rape-like annual found on sea cliffs in both islands. **1940** *Tales Pioneer Women* (1988) 104 [In early Wellington] the children were sent out to gather sow-thistle, and what they called Colonial Cabbage... 'Colonial' or 'Maori Cabbage' resembled rape and was plentiful in the early days. **1957** WILLIAMS *Dict. Maori Lang.* 222 *Niko..Wild cabbage, Brassica* sp. **1963** MCRAE *By the Braes of Balquether* 40 The meal that night would be a typical colonial one—boiled mutton and potatoes, Maori cabbage and sago pudding, washed down with strong tea and brown sugar. **1969** *Standard Common Names Weeds* 86 *wild cabbage Brassica oleracea*. **1978** FULLER *Maori Food & Cook.* 8 Paea, says Elsdon Best, was the name for a Maori cabbage. **1979** STARK *Maori Herbal Remedies* 28 Kapeti (Wild Cabbage) *Brassica oleracea*. This is doubtless a garden escape plant.

2. Occas. as **Maori cabbage**, PUHA 1 a.

1871 MONEY *Knocking About NZ* 68 A fine piece of bacon was quietly simmering..with plenty of sow thistles or Maori cabbage to give it a flavour. **1952** REED *Coromandel Holiday* 48 Another suggestion [about the name 'Cabbage Bay'] is that the native cabbage (puha) was cultivated here. Mrs. Bridge says that a kind of wild cabbage, like turnip tops, still grows around the shore. **1962** HORI *Half-gallon Jar* 98 *Puha*: Maori cabbage.

3. By synecdoche, applied to systems transporting vegetables: **cabbage boat**, one used to transport vegetables to market; **cabbage train** (also **the Cabbage**), the overnight Picton-Christchurch express goods train carrying vegetables for the Christchurch market.

1987 *Evening Post* (Wellington) 26 Sept. 2 'I think it is important,' he said, 'that people get a perspective of me as not someone that comes from a background of pink gins, quiche and Parnell but someone who had to come up the river in a **cabbage boat**'. **1972** *Dominion* (Wellington) 31 Oct. 7 Frank Andrew..telephoned to tell me how the Picton-Christchurch express got lumped with the name 'The Cabbage'... The express goods train was so nicknamed because it regularly delivered vegetables from Marlborough to the hungry people in Christchurch. **1976** JOHNSTON *New Zealanders* 114 Other links are..in passenger wagons attached to freight services (such as the overnight 'cabbage train' from Picton to Christchurch. **1989** CHURCHMAN *Route of the Coastal Pacific Express* 15 [Caption] The Dashwood Pass crash of the 'Cabbage Train' on 19 May 1966.

4. *transf.* Low-grade cannabis leaf.

1986 *Listener* 26 Apr. 15 They [*sc.* male plants] were ripped out and the low-value leaf ('cabbage' in dope jargon) rushed onto the market before Christmas when supplies were low and prices high.

5. *fig.* [Cf. HDAS *n.* 5. *Mil.*, citing only Hamman *Air Words*: *Cabbage*. Medals and decorations.] Braid, or other decoration, on uniform peaked caps.

1991 STEWART *Broken Arse* Weazel [a prison officer] wears his uniform as though he is a general. There is extra cabbage on his hat.

cabbage-garden hat. *Hist.* [f. *Cabbage Garden* an old New South Wales nickname for the Austral. state of Victoria: AND 1882.] CABBAGE-TREE HAT.

1905 *Truth* 19 Aug. 1 A lady went to the Wanganui theatre last week wearing a big cabbage-garden hat.

cabbage hat, cabbage-leaf hat: see CABBAGE-TREE HAT.

cabbage-palm. Also occas. **cabbage-palm-tree, cabbage-tree palm.** [AND 1770.]

1. a. CABBAGE-TREE 1 (*Cordyline australis*).

1769 PARKINSON *Journal* (1773) 20 Nov. 107 They also saw several young cabbage palm-trees, and a new species of Pandanus, or palm-nut. **1773** FORSTER *Resolution Jrnl.* 13 May (1982) II. 277 An infinite variety of high trees..[in Dusky Bay], among which the New-Zeeland Dragon-tree (*Dracaena antarctica*) is very remarkable; (*NB* Our Sailors called them the *Cabbage-palm*, but it is different; though the middle most leaves may be eaten & taste almost like sweet fresh Almonds). **1838** POLACK *NZ* I. 67 The guardian..pointed to a small bunch of human hair made fast to a *ti*, or cabbage palm-tree. **1870** WHITWORTH *Martin's Bay Settlement* 5 The hills rise very rapidly from the coast, being thickly wooded with..flax, grass-tree, cabbage-palm. **1874** cabbage-tree palm [see WHANAKE]. **1882** HAY *Brighter Britain* II. 187 There is the cabbage-tree palm, with bare shank and top-knot. **1904** TREGEAR *Maori Race* 224 The other fibres..used in making garments were those of the Cabbage Palm. **1938** HYDE *Godwits Fly* (1970) 32 And the cabbage-palms and tree-ferns people grew in their backyards—like beasts in a zoo—looked cowed and sick.

b. Special Comb. **cabbage-palm moth**, see MOTH 2.

2. *Obs.* NIKAU 1.

1777 FORSTER *Voyage Round World* II. 451 In our rambles through the woods at this place we found a true cabbage-palm (*areca oleracea*). **1843** DIEFFENBACH *Travels in NZ* I. 223 The cabbage-palm (Areca sapida) grows in the deepest recesses. **1847** ANGAS *Savage Life* I. 263 The houses or huts were many of them thatched with the leaves of the *nikau*, or cabbage-palm (*areca sapida*).

cabbage-tree. [Spec. use of *cabbage-tree*: AND 1778.]

1. *Cordyline australis* (fam. Asphodelaceae), a striking, palm-like tree having a tall bare trunk topped with clusters of sword-shaped leaves, the young growing shoot of which is edible. See also CABBAGE-PALM 1, DRAGON-TREE, GRASS-TREE 1, *mountain palm* (PALM 2), PALM-LILY, PALM-TREE 1, TI *n.*[1], TI-PALM, occas. TI-TREE, WHANAKE. Often *attrib.*

1769 COOK *Journals* 29 Oct. (1955) I. 186 We..found one Cabbage tree which we cut down for the sake of the Cabbage. **1836** [see MUTTONBIRD 1]. **1847** BRUNNER *Exped. Middle Is.* in Taylor *Early Travellers* (1959) 265 *19th* [January]. Collected a quantity of the roots of the ti, or cabbage-tree. **1856** HARPER *Lett. from NZ* 25 Dec. (1914) 2 On the steep shelving sides of the sheltered valleys there are..tall palm trees, locally termed Cabbage trees. [**1856** *Note*] Ti-Ti palm. **1865** BARKER *Station Life* (1870) 25 Nothing seems so wonderful to me as the utter treelessness of the vast Canterbury plains; occasionally you pass a few Ti-ti palms (ordinarily called cabbage-trees). **1889** KIRK *Forest Flora* 295 This grand palm-lily is commonly termed 'ti', or..properly ti-kouka... Settlers and bushmen generally apply the unmeaning name 'cabbage-tree'. **1905** WHITE *My NZ Garden* 50 Parallel with the happy family on the trellis I planted a row of twenty Cordylines, or Palm Lilies, commonly called New Zealand Cabbage Trees, for the uninteresting reason that someone once boiled some and ate them as a vegetable. **1924** *Otago Witness* (Dunedin) 3 June 71 Have you ever tried sliding down a hill on a cabbage tree? **1939** BEATTIE *First White Boy Born Otago* 98 I once listened to an account of an early resident of Waikouaiti who made whisky out of cabbage-tree juice and sold it to the Maoris. **1959** SHADBOLT *New Zealanders* (1986) 15 A grove of cabbage trees..screened off the milking-shed and the hay-barn. **1967** *Listener* 29 Sept. 10 A New Zealand play without sentimentality, brashness or cabbage trees. **1978** FULLER *Maori Food & Cook.* 34

The bushy crowns (kouka) of *Cordyline australis*..were relished..also by early European settlers, who found the kouka tasted like cabbage and named the tree accordingly. **1987** WILSON *Past Today* 152 The cabbage tree which stood in front of one of the houses was protected by the local council.

2. mountain (or **Waimarino**) **cabbage tree**. [*Waimarino* is a district in the s. central North Island.] *Cordyline indivisa*, a plant of wet mountain regions; see TOI *n*.[1]

1904 TREGEAR *Maori Race* 238 The Tuhoe tribe found a substitute for flax in the leaves of the mountain cabbage-tree (*toi*: C. indivisa). **1946** *Bull. Wellington Bot. Soc. No.14* 8 Here are some [vernacular names]... *Cordyline indivisa*, Waimarino cabbage tree. **1966** *Encycl. NZ* III. 710 Cabbage tree, mountain broadleafed . . toi . . C[*ordyline*] *indivisa*. **1988** DAWSON *Forest Vines to Snow Tussocks* 103 A few other small trees prefer higher altitudes in northern New Zealand and they include..the mountain cabbage tree (*Cordyline indivisa*).

3. Occas. the NIKAU 1.

1774 FORSTER *Resolution Jrnl.* 20 Dec. (1982) IV. 673 I found there [in Queen Charlotte Sound] a young Stock of a true *Cabbage-Tree (Arecca oleracea)*, which is the more remarkable as this place is so much to the South.

4. Special Comb. **cabbage-tree hut**, a hut made of cabbage-tree stems; **cabbage-tree kit**, a basket made out of plaited cabbage-tree leaves; **cabbage-tree moth**, see MOTH 2; **cabbage-tree rum**, a spirit distilled from the fermented juice of the cabbage-tree; **cabbage-tree sheep** *obs.*, HERMIT, esp. one having a cabbage-tree for a companion.

1887 PYKE *Hist. Early Gold Discoveries in Otago* (1962) 98 We immediately turned to and built a **cabbage-tree hut**. **1989** TE AWEKOTUKU *Tahuri* 33 A tukohu—**cabbage tree kit**—was hanging in its place..close to the steaming pool. **1945** HALL-JONES *Hist. Southland* 45 The manufacture of **cabbage-tree rum** by McShane the Cooper and the occurrence of two wrecks earned the place [*sc.* Sandy Point] an unsavoury reputation. **1891** *TrNZI* XXIII. 215 On the Canterbury Plains in the early days, when all the runs were unfenced for many years, we used to find **cabbage-tree** or hermit **sheep**. These were merino sheep living alone, and having a cabbage-tree or a flax-bush for a mate or companion; and they could not be made to leave, always keeping within a certain radius of that special tree, which they considered their especial friend.

cabbage-tree hat. *Hist.* Also **cabbage hat**, **cabbage-leaf hat**. [AND 1841.] An imported wide-brimmed hat made out of the leaves of the Australian cabbage tree.

1849 cabbage-leaf hat [see BUSH COSTUME]. **1853** ADAMS *Spring Canterbury Settlement* 57 My costume consisted pair of white duck trousers, checked shirt, stout boots, large cabbage-tree hat and a sort of blue flannel frock confined at the waist by a leather belt. **1869** *TrNZI* I. (rev. edn.) 278 The fibrous leaves of the Kiekie (*Freycinetia Banksii*), is an excellent article for men's hats,—far better than the largely imported common 'Cabbage-tree' hat, but little inferior to a coarse Leghorn or Manilla one. **c1875** MEREDITH *Adventuring in Maoriland* (1935) 135 The Maoris make excellent hats resembling the celebrated 'cabbage-tree' hats, from the fibre of the [kiekie] leaves. **1885** W.J. Swainson let. in *William Swainson* (1992) 107 The universal dress in those days [c1843] for country settlers and travellers was moleskin trousers, blue serge shirt, and travellers was moleskin trousers, blue serge shirt, and that much prized head covering, when it could be obtained, a New South Wales cabbage tree hat with a long black ribbon (a broad brimmed hat plaited from the leaves of the Australian Cabbage Tree), the older the hat the more it was valued. Indeed I have known a new one willingly exchanged for a much older article—perhaps because it did not look so 'new chummy'. They were difficult to procure, having to be ordered from Sydney, and the price was high, from twentyfive shillings to two pounds. **1900** *Canterbury Old and New* 109 I therefore dressed myself in the garb of an up-country 'Shagroon' [c1855–56]... I took off my cabbage-tree hat, loosened my neckerchief and shirt-band. **1912** FERGUSON *Castle Gay* 48 The cabbage hat and the blouse were then Insignias of the flow'r of men. **1933** *Press* (Christchurch) (Acland Gloss.) 23 Sept. 13 *Cabbage Tree hat.*—These were made in Australia, whence both the name and the article were imported. Both had dropped out of use in New Zealand long before the 'nineties, but I heard old hands speak of them.

cabbage-tree palm: see CABBAGE-PALM.

cabin biscuit. Also **cabin bread**. A large, thick, hard plain cracker biscuit, a domestic form of ship's biscuit. (Quot. 1853 may indicate a mishearing by Lush of *cabin('s) biscuit*.)

[**1853** LUSH *Auckland Jrnls.* 25 Dec. (1971) 146 Returned to breakfast at 8: fried captain's biscuit and very good it is—the biscuit is soaked in water overnight and then fried in a little butter the next morning.] **1886** *Brett's NZ and South Pacific Pilot* xix John Lamb,.. Biscuit Manufactory..has for sale—Wheat meal, Sharps, Cabin Biscuits. **1902** SATCHELL *Land of the Lost* (1971) 25 Having nibbled some cabin-bread and made himself a panikin of tea. *Ibid.* 188 The establishment [*sc.* gum-digger's tent] contained nothing save cabin-bread. **1982** *Listener* 31 July 70 The grey man gnawed at the biscuits and cheese. 'It's all right, tasting the old cabin bread again.' **1983** COOPER *Wag's Tales* 21 I remember one winter just to make sure we would never go hungry, he bought a whole crate of cabin bread biscuits. **1983** BUCKLEY *Of Toffs and Toilers* 150 In 1866 the [Victoria Flour Mills and Steam Biscuit Factory] advertised—Best Cabin Biscuits £18 per ton. **1991** *Dominion* (Wellington) 26 Dec. 8 [On Pukapuka] there [is] no time in the morning to prepare an adequate meal in the absence of 'fast foods' like cabin bread and other flour-based products.

caca, var. KAKA.

cactus.

1. [Poss. an extension or euphemistic variation of *in the cack* in difficulties.] In the phr. **in the cactus** [AND 1943], in trouble, in difficulties; **out of the cactus**, free from a difficult situation, 'in the clear'.

1944 FULLARTON *Troop Target* 57 Now we're in the cactus [*sc.* way off course]. *Ibid.* 114 Now we're going flat out to pull them [*sc.* our column in difficulties] out of the cactus. **c1945** *Sixes and Sevens* 18 Just read this and climb out of the cactus. **1953** *Evening Post* (Wellington) 9 Mar. 12 Rather funny you being in the cactus at home—I'm in the dog box with my wife too. **1958** *Tararua* Sept. 44 Here we camped... We were all tired, and relieved to be out of the cactus. **1969** MASON *Awatea* (1978) 75 *Matt.* What did they say? *Brett.* That I was taking a risk; that if it fizzled, I'd be in the cactus. **1977** HALL *Glide Time* 54 Why should I get in the cactus just because you make a muck-up? **1984** WILSON *South Pacific Street* 52 'I'm in the cactus. Done a flip. Just lost three thousand smackaroos on the big race on Wednesday.'

2. a. *fig.* [AND 1945.] A remote place; the backblocks; BOOHAI 1. (Poss. orig. WW2 (North Africa) for 'the desert'.)

1944 FULLARTON *Troop Target* 202 Where do we go from here? Into the cactus every time. **1960** MUIR *Word for Word* 79 A fat lot of use a map would have been. He knew where he was. In the cactus. **1963** [see BOOHAI 1 a].

b. Special Comb. **cactus stove** WW2 (Pacific Islands), a rough and ready 'bush' stove. (Poss. influenced by *cactus*, a military code-name for Guadalcanal.)

1944 *Coral Dust* Dec. ['Cactus Stoves'] have nothing to do with cactus, and they are as much like a stove as a mountain range is a heating appliance... Just how they came to be called 'cactus stoves' is more than I can say and I don't propose to hazard a guess.

3. In the imperative phr. **cut the cactus** [poss. an alteration of *cut the cackle*], keep quiet, 'cut the cackle'.

1952 *Here & Now* June 13 'Mmm,' I murmur (but I think, 'Cut the cactus, Colonel, the ole dragon wouldn't have me before!').

caddie, var. CADY.

cadet, *n.* [Spec. uses of *cadet* a junior or inexperienced person, esp. one under instruction: AND 1879.]

1. a. *Hist.* Also occas. early **colonial cadet** (poss. here an immigrant 'minor', see quot. 1841), a young man learning sheep farming.

1841 JAMESON *NZ, South Austral. and NSW* 337 We [are] in want of a college for colonial cadets. *Ibid.* 339 The [New Zealand] Company should take charge, during his minority, of the landed property intended for a cadet. **1857** PHILLIPS *Rockwood Jrnl.* (Canterbury Pub. Lib. TS) 30 Oct. 71 Herbert Matthias came over to take Mrs. Leech home—Jem his cadet. **1863** BUTLER *First Year* vi 74 I..must explain that a cadet means a young fellow who has lately come out, and who wants to see a little of up-country life. He is neither paid nor pays. He receives his food and lodging *gratis*, but works (or is supposed to work) in order to learn. **1871** MONEY *Knocking About NZ* 6 This military designation of cadet was applied to any young fellow who was attached to a sheep or cattle station in the same capacity as myself... In consideration of his 'education', he was permitted to reside and take his meals with the master, but was sent to work with the men. **1898** VOGEL *Maori Maid* 147 A cadet is a young man, generally from England, who is paying a run-holder so much a year for the honour and privilege of working for him. **1910** *Truth* 23 Apr. 1 From a Dunedin paper:—'Wanted, a cadet for a sheep farm'. **1928** STAPLEDON *Tour in Austral. & NZ* 29 The lucky young man may get placed as 'Jackaroo' on an Australian station, or as 'Cadet' on a New Zealand station. **1934** MULGAN *Spur of Morning* 310 They climbed into a four-wheeled buggy..which a bright-faced cadet (who had failed his army examinations and had been shipped oversea) had driven down the day before. **1946** ACLAND *Early Canterbury Runs* 222 Heath had been a cadet with Savill at..Craigieburn. **1964** ANDERSON *Doctor in the Mountains* (1974) 27 We were met [at Wellington in 1907]..by..the stock manager through whose agency I had secured the cadet job. **1975** HARPER *Eight Daughters* 78 Two more cadets came in 1921.

Hence **cadetship** (occas. **colonial cadetship**), the position or status of a cadet.

1841 JAMESON *NZ, S. Aust. and NSW* 337 Colonial cadetships. **1853** ROCHFORT *Adventures of a Surveyor* 20 The other two..had just finished their 'cadetship', that is, they had been learning sheep-farming under a settler. **1921** GUTHRIE-SMITH *Tutira* (1926) 156 Our three months' cadetship on Captain..Russell's Tunanui station had taught us that indiscriminate burning of fern was unwise.

b. In modern use, usu. **farm cadet**, an apprentice farmer.
 1981 *Press* (Christchurch) 16 Jan. 6 There will be some changes in the format of the North Canterbury farm cadet scheme this year... Mr Simpson said it was expected that there would be about 120 cadets training.

2. In full **surveying cadet**. A young person learning surveying.
 1843 *Lett. from Settlers* (1843) 73 From Mr. Thomas Bremner, one of the Cadets on the Nelson Surveying Staff. **1845** WAKEFIELD *Adventure NZ* II. 162 He was accompanied by a large suite of young gentlemen engaged by the company for three years as 'Surveying Cadets'. **1878** JOLLIE *Reminiscences* (ATLTS) 2 Two of the Cadets were requested [c1842] by one of the Asst. Surveyors to take a chain... The cadets were gentlemen and they were quite right to refuse to do labourers' work. **1898** HOCKEN *Contributions* 59 Colonel Wakefield..had despatched the *Carbon*..having on board Messrs. Richard Nicholson and Albert Allom, who were surveying cadets.

3. *Obs.* A young person learning the work of a State department.
 1951 HUNT *Confessions* 55 The work of a cadet included clerical work, portering, shunting trucks, etc.

4. Usu. as **school cadet**. Often *attrib.* A member of a school CADET CORPS; usu. as **the (school) cadets**, the cadet training programme. Cf. BARRACKS 2.
 1907 *Free Lance* (Wellington) 20 Apr. 12 Down South lately a school cadet route march was about to take place. **1923** *Invercargill Middle School Jubilee* 53 These charges no doubt inspired the formation of school cadets. **1932** *Short Hist. of Boys' District High School..at Wanganui* 27 In August, 1894, Mr. Aitken commenced the school cadets... At various times cadet camps were held at Tayforth and on the Racecourse. **1959** SLATTER *Gun in My Hand* 149 The names of boys who used to march in the school cadets. **1962** GLOVER *Hot Water Sailor* (1981) 34 It was at New Plymouth Boys' High School that I first entered into the hazards of compulsory school cadet training..I was unable in the school cadets to deal..with any problem. **1989** *Illustr. Encycl. NZ* 1094 School cadets began in New Zealand when corps were established in an ad hoc manner during the 1860s and early 1870s, at such schools as Auckland Grammar, King's College, Wellington College and Christ's College.

cadet, *v. intr.* To be, or to work as, a cadet.
 1890 *Zealandia* I. 487 Frank was cadeting. **1933** *Press* (Christchurch) (Acland Gloss.) 23 Sept. 13 *Cadet.*—(1) A young man working on a station to learn sheep farming... (2) To be, or to work as, a cadet.

Hence **cadetting** *vbl. n.*, the practice of working as a cadet.
 1891 COTTLE *Frank Melton's Luck* 91 [Heading] Cadetting—Baronet's Son Again to the Fore. **1898** VOGEL *Maori Maid* 147 Otherwise cadetting..is a swindle. **1902** LANCASTER *Our Lady of the Plains* in *Happy Endings* (1987) 103 [He] doubted that the wisdom gained in a year's cadetting on Jamison's station would over-pay for the raw newness of life lived on the level of strenuous fact.

cadet corps. [Used elsewhere but recorded earliest in NZ: see OED *cadet* 3 b, 1873.] Also now usu. called **School Cadet Corps**, a uniformed company of secondary schoolboys receiving basic military training as part of a special programme of school activities. See also *school cadet* (CADET 4).
 1864 *AJHR G-1* [24th November 1864] Petition of the Scholars of the High School, Dunedin. Your memorialists learn that the establishment of a Cadet Corps, duly instructed, armed, and in uniform, is likely to inlist [*sic*] a spirit into the rising generation which would materially nourish the most patriotic feelings. **1875** *Richmond-Atkinson Papers* 16 Aug. (1960) II. 400 I get quite enough of lessons in school [*i.e.* Nelson College] so I will go on to our gallant cadet corps. **1902** *AJHR E-1D* 1 All the public-school cadet corps which were under the Defence Department were armed with [Snider Carbines]. **1933** SCANLAN *Tides of Youth* 241 He was proud of his uniform in the school cadet corps..but the majority regarded drill night as a nuisance. **1956** *Nelson College Old Boys Register 1856–1956* 603 The year 1875 saw the formation of the Nelson College Cadet Corps... The corps was the first of its kind to be established in New Zealand. **1968** SLATTER *Pagan Game* 86 I sometimes wonder if the Cadet Corps is worthwhile in this day and age. **1971** *Defence Act* s57 There may from time to time be raised and maintained under the direction of the Defence Council cadet forces, comprising the Sea Cadet Corps, the School Cadet Corps and the Air Training Corps. **1981** *St Patrick's College, Silverstream 1931–80* 67 The Cadet Corps did not really die, but like a good Old Soldier just faded away at the end of 1969. **1990** MCLEAN *Otago Boys' High School* 13 As officer commanding the school cadet corps, 'Blobs'..was a force not to be reckoned with.

cadger's fish. WITCH. See also *bludger's fish* (BLUDGER 5 b).
 1956 GRAHAM *Treasury NZ Fishes* (2edn.) 187 Another name given to this useless fish [*sc.* witch] by local fishermen, in Port Chalmers at least, was that of Cadger's-fish. **1967** NATUSCH *Animals NZ* 217 The megrim, once dubbed 'cadgers'-fish' because of its suitability for palming off on those who hover round landing fishing-craft in the hope of perks, especially flatfish! **1981** WILSON *Fisherman's Bible* 44 Cadger's fish... Name give by early South Island fishermen to the Megrim, or Witch, flatfish. This 'fake' flounder was frequently caught and kept to hand out to cadgers who frequented the docks in search of a few fish from the commercial fishermen just returned from sea.

cady /'kæidi/, /'kædi/. *Hist.* Also **caddie, kadi.** [f. northern Brit. dial. *cady, cadey, caddy* a (straw) hat: see EDD *cadey.*] **a.** A felt hat with a wide brim.
 [**1898** MORRIS *Austral English* 76 *Cady, n.* a bush name for the slouch-hat or wide-awake. In the Australian bush the brim is generally turned down at the back and sometimes all round.] **1906** *Truth* 31 Mar. 6 A 'kadi' is a hat. **1909** *Truth* 13 Mar. 2 Fred Leslie kinked his knees so as to come down to camera height, and dear boy Bradshaw artistically polished the nap of his cady. c**1930** *Whitcombe's Etym. Dict. Aust.-NZ Supplement* 3 *caddie n.* sl. a slouch hat, or wide-awake.
 b. A straw hat; a 'boater'.
 1938 HYDE *Godwits Fly* (1970) 92 School regulation costume [c1919-23]: navy serge gym. costume..black band with college colours about your hat, which is in winter a straw cady, making a thick red furrow on your forehead. **1941** BAKER *NZ Slang* 55 Other terms which probably hailed from the country are..*cady* or *kadi*, a straw hat. **1977** *Dominion* (Wellington) 20 Aug. 11 The correct headgear for the boy of the period was either a tight-fitting college cap..or, at holiday time, a 'cady' (straw hat) or a cast-off panama of your dad's. **1981** GEE *Meg* 103 [The Grammar boys] named me Plumb Jam because of my straw cady.

cage. [Prob. a transf. or spec. use of a mining *cage*: see OED 5 a.] A crude but effective means of transport over a back-country river, consisting usu. of a platform with a safety enclosure of wire or wood, suspended on wires and capable of being drawn back and forth. See also *miner's cage* (MINER). Cf. FLYING FOX.
 1903 COX *Diaries 1888–1925* (ATLMS) 24 Dec. I had a good walk..to the bridge over the..river at Ngatairi, I crossed the river in 1892 with my swag, on a wire rope in a cage, things are greatly changed since then. **1908** *NZGeol.SB (NS)* No.6 21 Half a mile above the junction the Hokitika River is crossed by means of a wire rope and cage. **1930** GUTHRIE *NZ Memories* 170 Later they were swinging across the great Teramakau river in a cage which was simply a box with sides not quite waist-high, and suspended from wire ropes above; it would require some nerve to be shot across the..torrent in this fashion. **1962** SHARPE *Country Occasions* 80 One of the most unlucky country children..fell out of a 'cage' slung on a cable across a river, landing face down on shingle. **1983** NOLAN *Gold Fossicker's Handbook* 111 *Cage*: the elevator ('lift') used for the transport of men and material up and down a mine shaft. Also, a suspended cable and pulley device for crossing rivers.

calabash, *n. Hist.* [Transf. use of *calabash* a vessel made from the shell of a gourd.] *Lagenaria siceraria* (fam. Cucurbitaceae), a trailing vine (see also HUE) introduced to New Zealand in pre-European times but not naturalized, and its fruit which, having a hard smooth rind, was mainly used as a container (see also TAHA).
 [*Note*] Botanical (e.g. Webb et al. *Flora of NZ* (1988) IV. 593) and other authorities (e.g. Webster 1961) describe the fruit of the *Lagenaria siceraria* as 'inedible'. Marie C. Neal *In Gardens of Hawaii* (1965) 812 states: 'In some forms, the rind of the ripe fruits is hard, woody, long-lasting. Fruits of a form grown for food are picked when green.' The Yate and Dieffenbach (quots. 1835, 1843 below) prob. refer to an immature *Lagenaria* gourd, or perh., esp. the 1843, to a gourd-like fruit (see HUE esp. quot. 1820) other than that of *Lagenaria siceraria*.
 1777 FORSTER *Voyage Round World* I. 220 They have nothing in which to keep liquids except a minute kind of calabash or gourd. **1835** YATE *NZ* (1970) 107 [Among New Zealand vegetables] the green calabash. *Ibid.* 108 A calabash-full of water. **1843** DIEFFENBACH *Travels in NZ* I. 314 Long rows of baskets filled with articles of food, such as green calabashes, kumeras, pumpkins, water-melons, and dried fish. **1863** MOSER *Mahoe Leaves* 34 Things..were got ready at last, and served up in baskets made of flax, known as kits, calabashes, pots and kettles. **1882** POTTS *Out in Open* 16 Women are bringing water in calabashes (taha). **1904** TREGEAR *Maori Race* 113 At one [hakari] feast there has been seen 2,000 one-bushel baskets of *kumara*,.. calabashes of oil, etc. etc. **1924** LYSNAR *NZ* 20 The calabash, the kumara, the taro, and the yam, were carried in the fleet. **1948** HENDERSON *Taina* 112 [The chiefs] had their share brought to them in calabashes called *taha*.

Hence **calabashed** *ppl. a.*, served up in calabashes.
 1894 *TrNZI* XXVI. 579 When the bodies placed in the *hangis* were cooked they were calabashed, and formally handed over to the Ngatitoa as payment for the children of Te Rauparaha who had been treacherously killed by the Muaupoko.

calawar, var. KAREAO.

Calcutta sweep(stake). Also *ellipt.* **Calcutta, calcutta.** [Also US: see Webster (1961) *Calcutta* 2 pool (esp. in golf or bridge).] A method of gambling on horse-races, golf matches and other forms of competitive sport (see quot. 1939).

1937 *Truth* 24 Nov. 22 Throughout New Zealand..thousands of pounds are invested on the eve of important races in Calcutta sweepstakes. *Ibid.* The auctioneer told the crowd that the last Calcutta sweep at this club..was worth £100 to start. **1939** BELTON *Outside the Law in NZ* 169 A sweep had been drawn [at Te Aroha] on the Champion Hack Handicap, and in accordance with the 'Calcutta' sweep practice, the horses drawn were in the process of being sold... The method of conducting a 'Calcutta' differs entirely from the more common form of sweep whereby a subscriber who draws a horse retains his interest in it. In a 'Calcutta' subscriptions are usually £1 each, and they are not governed by the number of horses in the race upon which the sweep is based. Assuming that there are 16 horses in the race, it may be that there will be 60 subscribers at £1 each. Slips of paper on which the name of the horse is written are then placed in a hat, and also some blank slips, and in another hat are placed the names of the subscribers. The promoter..takes the role of auctioneer and explains that each horse drawn will be offered at auction and sold to the highest bidder. The full amount bid has only to be paid if the buyer is not the drawer of that particular horse. If the drawer should buy the horse in, then he pays only half the amount bid, and the money goes into the pool. If the..buyer does not draw the horse, the amount bid is divided, half to the drawer and half to the pool. *Ibid.* 170 It is generally considered that in a 'Calcutta' the pool, when all the horses have been sold, will be about double the amount at which subscriptions closed. **1952** *Truth* 28 May 18 A number of people..pleaded guilty to being found in a common gaming house, the South Featherston Hall, while a Calcutta Sweep was in progress. **1971** NEWTON *Ten Thousand Dogs* 45 Another memory of that meeting [*sc.* dog trials at Springfield, c1928] is the 'Calcutta Sweep'... The evening before the event concerned the crowd would get together and every dog on the programme would be put up for 'auction'. The proceeds of the 'sale' would be pooled, divided into first, second and third money, and after the actual event was finished this went to the men who had 'purchased' the placed dogs. **1974** *Sunday Times* (Wellington) 23 June 20 [The] system, known casually as the Calcutta sweep, is practised in most clubs round the country and makes amateur golfers wealthy men through golf as an amateur sport. Basically, the idea works on the system of paired golfers who compete for prize-money put up by their fellow club-members... The pairs are deemed horses and are bought at local club auctions by other club members. I know of one team that went for $3 all up and won a calcutta. **1991** MCCARTEN *Modest Apocalypse* 81 He..could hardly remember his days as a parish priest..when Joe Mullins had managed his illegal Calcutta evenings to raise badly needed funds for the church. **1993** *Evening Post* (Wellington) 26 Feb. 13 A calcutta sweepstake on the Terrace regency Weight-For-Age [race] will kick off proceedings tomorrow night [at Otaki Racing Club's meeting].

cale, var. CALLY.

calf day. A competition in rural schools to allow pupils to show off their calves and to determine the best calf among them.
   1985 HILL *Moaville Magic* 22 The principal [of the school] also has to organise Calf Day—the uniquely rural occasion when the children's pet is exercised, shampooed, brushed, perfumed, has its hoofs vaselined and polished and its muzzle wiped, and is then carried tenderly to school in the back seat of the car in case it gets dirty before judging.

calfeteria /ˌkafəˈtiriə/. *Farming.* [f. *calf* + caf)*eteria*.] See quot. 1987.
   1986 *National Radio* 'Landline' (Farming Programme) 30 Aug. I'll feed the calves from a mobile calfeteria [in Taranaki]..I won't feed them so much meal this year—milk is cheaper. **1987** *Te Reo 30* 132 One coinage which turned up years ago and which I thought was a nonce word. It turned up again recently: *calfeteria*, a bowl with several teats from which a number of calves may feed at the same time.

Cali /ˈkæli/. An informal short form of *Californian thistle* (THISTLE *n.* 2 (1)).
   1926 HILGENDORF *Weeds* 187 Of the fourteen districts into which the country was divided, 'Cali' was considered one of the three worst weeds in no fewer than twelve. **1966** *NZ Farmer* 28 Apr. 37 Digging 'Cali' thistles, a legacy of hay–carting, out of one's fingers. **1981** SUTHERLAND & TAYLOR *Sunrise* 61 Calies aren't killed by cutting..the seed blows across.

califont /ˈkæləˌfɒnt/. [?a proprietary name: ?f. Latin *cali*dus hot (also 'quick, ready') + English *font* a source of water.] A gas-fuelled water heater over a bath, sink, etc. Cf. British *geyser.*
   1921 *NZJST* III. 259 Tests were made on a bathroom califont of the ordinary type shown in fig. 2. [Caption] Gas-califont of the ordinary type. **1964** MORRIESON *Came a Hot Friday* (1981) 33 A gas califont that could have been an enormous money box for all the hot water it reciprocated. **1973** DRYLAND *A Multiple Texture* 31 He would have nothing to do with the gas califont in the bathroom, preferring cold baths to being blown up. **1980** LELAND *Kiwi-Yankee Dict.* 20 Califont. You may rent a flat that has a small gas waterheater over the tub or shower. You switch this on and it roars into life, startling the hell out of you and providing the frightening sight and sound of a violent conflagration that quickly heats the water. **1988** *Through the Looking Glass* 94 In the bathroom..resided my enemy—the califont, a silver contraption that you lit and from which hot water flowed into the bath. **1993** O'SULLIVAN *Let the River Stand* 180 Overnight [he] left them..above the califont.

Californian, *a.*

1. As a modifier (often replacing the *California* used in technical and other varieties of English) in the names of plants and animals, see: QUAIL 2, **Californian stinkweed** see *digger's weed* (DIGGER *n.*[1] 3 c), THISTLE *n.* 2 (1).

2. As **Californian (California) bungalow**, see BUNGALOW.

3. As **Californian (California) pump** *goldfields hist.* [AND 1853], an endless belt with buckets attached moving over rollers and designed so that when the lower end is placed in water the moving buckets are filled, carry the water to the top, and, as they turn over, discharge it into a flume or race for disposal (see also quot. 1967).
   1861 27 Sept. in *NZ Goldfields 1861* (1976) 28 Almost every claim [at Tuapeka] was a wet one, and Californian pumps had to be kept constantly going to prevent the water rising to too high a level. **1861** Letter 14 Aug. from Tuapeka in Hochstetter *NZ* (1867) 110 I would also advise parties of six to..provide themselves with a California pump, sluice, picks, shovels. **1874** BATHGATE *Colonial Experiences* 129 We could hear..the creaking of their Californian pumps. **1891** COX *Diaries 1888–1925* (ATLMS) 28 May The Californian pump broke twice this morning and we lost more than an hour [of work flax–stripping]. **1967** MAY *West Coast Gold Rushes* (1962) 190 Pumping gear became more elaborate with the introduction, in the deeper paddocks, of the ingenious Californian pump. This comprised a long narrow box, open at each end but otherwise completely enclosed. Through it ran an endless canvas belt with wooden cleats fitting neatly into the inside of the box. The belt passed over rollers at the upper and lower ends of the box; the lower end was immersed in the flooded paddock and as the belt turned clockwise over its rollers the water was drawn up through the box and delivered to a tail-race. The motive power was commonly an overshot water-wheel.

call, *v.*

1. [Spec. use of *call* to announce: AND 1906.] To give a running commentary on (a sporting event, esp. a horse-race) to spectators, radio listeners, etc.
   1951 *call* used on 2ZB Wellington in the sense 'to give a running (radio or amplified) commentary on a horse-race' (Ed.). **1986** *Listener* 23 Aug. 35 He became the NZBC's first 'sole charge' television rugby commentator, calling his first test match at home in 1973 and away in 1974. **1989** DUDER *Alex in Winter* 1 And then, as the announcer called the placings, two steps up on to the top level of the dais. **1991** *Listener* 5 Aug. 40 We [*sc.* TVNZ] would be much the poorer if he wasn't calling games for us... He's the consummate commentator.
   Hence **caller** *n.*, a sports commentator (see also RACE-CALLER); **calling** *vbl. n.*
   1984 *Listener* 16 June 21 Now, as the **caller** of most races in the north, and part-owner of the highly successful McGinty, he is perhaps the best-known commentator in the country. **1992** *Dominion* (Wellington) 4 Sept. 19 [Heading] Legendary caller's efforts recognised. **1991** *Sunday Star* (Auckland) 15 Sept. B1 The ministerial committee into racing **calling** has been demanding professional judicial committees.

2. In the phr. **to call the game in**, to call off; to cease doing (something); to admit defeat.
   1937 PARTRIDGE *Dict. Slang* 121 *call the game in*. To cease doing something; to admit one has had enough: New Zealand coll[oquial]: from ca. 1912. **1941** BAKER *NZ Slang* 53 To call the game in, to cease any activity, has been current since early in the twentieth century. **1955** BJ Cameron Collection (TS July) call the game in (v) To cry quits, admit defeat.

3. In the negative phr. **not to call the king (one's) uncle**, **not to call the Queen (one's) aunt**, expressions of positive independence. (Partridge *Dict. Catch Phrases* 149 (2edn 1986) notes the 'queen' variant as a Brit. expression from 1977.)
   1899 BELL *In Shadow of Bush* 84 If I had a couple of hundred acres of good bush land, and a wife like that girl down there would make, I wouldn't call the Queen my aunt. **1992** PARK *Fence around the Cuckoo* 200 Topped with this [hat]..Grandma declared she wouldn't call the King her uncle.

call, *n.* Also **race-call.** [f. *v.*] A running commentary on (a sporting event, esp a horse-race) for spectators, radio listeners, etc.
   1986 *Sunday News* (Auckland) 24 Aug. 23 Seifert's one-eyed call of the national men's basketball final last weekend left many Canterbury fans seething. **1988** COSTELLO & FINNEGAN *Tapestry of Turf* 208 Kell..was to do the race-calls at Trentham and most other lower North Island courses until his retirement. *Ibid* 501 Clarkson called both trots and gallops in Canterbury and also did the calls at Trentham.

Calley /ˈkæli/, var. CALLY.

callie /ˈkæli/, an informal short form of *Californian quail* (QUAIL 2) q.v.

Cally /ˈkæli/. *Dunedin.* Also **Cale** /ˈkæli/, **Calley**. [f. *Cale*(donian.] As **The Cally**, an abbrev. of the Caledonian Sportsground, Dunedin.

1934 LEE *Children of the Poor* (1949) 14 'Where are you going on New Year's Day? Oot to the Cale. (Caledonian Grounds), To hear John Hogg and hear his pipers play, Oot at the Cale.' **1936** ALLEN *Poor Scholar* 18 The Cally. **a1950** WHITWORTH *Otago Interval* 51 [Father] took me..to the Caledonian Grounds on New Year's Day. 'Where are ye going to on New Year's day? Oot to the Calley, oot to the Calley.'

caltha /'kælθə/. [Transf. use of European genus name *Caltha*, the marsh marigold.] Usu. with a modifier: **native** (or **New Zealand**) **caltha**, **white** (or **yellow**) **caltha**, *Caltha* spp. esp. *Caltha novae-zelandiae* (fam. Ranunculaceae).

1889 FEATON *Art Album NZ Flora* 10 *Caltha novae zelandiae*... The New Zealand Caltha... The 'Native Caltha'. **1909** *AJHR* C-12 54 New Zealand caltha or marsh-marigold..Bog, sub-alpine meadow. **1940** LAING & BLACKWELL *Plants NZ* 179 (*The New Zealand Caltha*). A stout, fleshy plant, with heart-shaped auriculed leaves... Petals none... This is a little alpine marsh-marigold. **1973** MARK & ADAMS *Alpine Plants* (1979) 44 *Caltha obtusa*..White Caltha. A low-growing herb... *Caltha novae-zelandiae*... Yellow Caltha. **1982** WILSON *Stewart Is. Plants* 274 Yellow Caltha... New Zealand marsh marigold... Small, hairless rosettes... Flowers pale yellow.

camp, *n*. [Spec. use of *camp* temporary quarters.]
1. a. *Obs*. A Maori settlement.
1840 MATHEW *Jrnl*. 27 Feb. in *Founding of NZ* (1940) 65 After a walk of about four hours we..were glad to rest for a while at the native camp.

b. *Archaeol*. A Moa-hunters' camp or camp-site.
1937 BUICK *Moa-Hunters NZ* 132 This camp site also is involved in another interesting problem.

2. a. [AND 1845.] A sheltered place where sheep or cattle regularly choose to congregate; a resting or assembly place for farm stock. See also *sheep-camp* (SHEEP 2), *stock camp* (STOCK 2 a).
1863 CHUDLEIGH *Diary* 17 May (1950) 87 Reached Ontopope in good time but we could not get a good camp and the consequence was the cattle broke camp at the back. **1883** FERGUSON *Castle Gay* 193 The ewes in camp all safe and fast And all the lambs composed at last. **1907** *TrNZI* XXXIX. 291 The sheep have favourite places for sleeping... These spots are called 'camps'. **1951** LEVY *Grasslands NZ* (1970) 300 Bareground camps may be the inevitable outcome of a high carrying capacity. **1978** JARDINE *Shadows on the Hill* 134 The sheep had not yet risen from their camps. **1990** MARTIN *Forgotten Worker* 68 Many 'camps' of dead sheep were discovered as the snow retreated.

b. As **break camp**, of stock, to move from a (night) camping-ground.
1863 [see a above]. **1874** KENNAWAY *Crusts* 211 Got up from the ground by daybreak and let the sheep break camp at once. **1933** *Press* (Christchurch) (Acland Gloss.) 16 Sept. 15 *Break Camp*.—Move away from camp, shift camp. Sheep which camp together are also said to 'break camp' when they move off to feed at dawn. **1952** BLAKISTON *My Yesteryears* 18 Next morning we had to be up early to reach the tops before the merinos broke camp and started back for the country off which they had been mustered.

3. In special Comb. **camp keeper**, one of a group of people camping appointed to look after a camp; **camp pie** [AND 1909], a shepherd's pie; **camp stretcher**, see STRETCHER a.
1878 LINDSAY-BUCKNALL *Search for Fortune* 30 One of our party was to be appointed cook and '**campkeeper**' week about. **1902** *Brett's Colonists' Guide* 833 **Camp Pie** Chop cold beef..add pepper and salt; make gravy from the bones; put..in a piedish, and add mashed potato. Beat up an egg with flour, pour it on the top, and bake.

camp, *v*.
1. a. *intr*. [AND 1843.] Of farm stock, to rest, assemble, usu. at a preferred place.
1846 PHARAZYN *Journal* (ATLMS) 40 Inspected Ewes and Hogs, the former all camped on the left hand hill. **1863** CHUDLEIGH *Diary* (1950) 14 Mar. 80 I was with the sheep till 8 p.m. when they camped and I turned into the tent. **1909** MOWATT *Diary* 24 Dec. in McCaskill *Molesworth* (1969) 104 On 24 December 1909 a mob of 5,600 shorn hoggets were taken from Molesworth to the sheep yards..where they camped for the night. **1936** BELSHAW et al. *Agric. Organiz. NZ* 358 Where sheep 'camp' there is invariably abundance of *Marrubium vulgare*. **1946** *NZJST* XXVII. 159 Near the crests of hills sheep aggravate the position by camping on these terracettes. **1952** BLAKISTON *My Yesteryears* 31 Merino ewes always camp just below the highest top on what they regard as their own piece of country.

b. *trans*. [AND 1847.] To assemble (stock) for the night, or for an extended rest.
1862 CHUDLEIGH *Diary* 21 Apr. (1950) 33 We followed [the cattle]..and camped them on a triangle formerly the junction of the Timooka and Opihi. **1915** MACDONALD *NZ Sheepfarming* 120 Footrot appears through the dry-foot loving sheep being camped..too long on damp ground. **1937** AYSON *Pioneering Otago* 40 I had to follow the lambs about all day, bringing them home at night to camp them near the homestead.

Hence **camping** *vbl. n*., of stock, assembling or resting in a preferred place.
1874 KENNAWAY *Crusts* 153 But for the sheep there were only a few quiet campings at sunset, and a few dewy mornings to come. **1951** LEVY *Grasslands NZ* (1970) 32 The East Coast country in question is not alone in being denuded of vegetation on the knolls and ridges by the camping of stock.

2. [AND 1861.] Of wild dogs, to establish a permanent resting-place.
c1875 MEREDITH *Adventuring in Maoriland* (1935) 65 The wild dogs had been among the sheep, and were evidently camped in the ranges at the back of the outstation.

3. *Shearing*. [Cf. AND *camp* 2, 1848 to take a short rest.] To slow up one's shearing pace in order to force a pen-mate to choose a difficult sheep. Also as a *vbl. n*.
1934 *Press* (Christchurch) (Acland Gloss.) 13 Jan. 13 *Camp*.—As transitive verb, *e.g.*, to *c[amp]* the sheep. A shearer's expression meaning to go slow (so as to let a pen mate in for a bad cobbler). **1989** *NZ English Newsletter* III. 22 (Wallace Shearing Gloss.) *camping*: This often occurs when two shearers are catching from one pen. One slows down to force his pen mate to catch the cobbler.

Campbell Island. In names of birds, see: SHAG 2 (6), TEAL *n*.¹ 2 (4).

camping ground.
1. [AND 1845.] A usual or preferred resting place (of farm stock); CAMP *n*. 2 a.
1860 *Notebook* 4 Apr. in Kennaway *Crusts* (1874) 111 Reached sheep about two o'clock..and began driving at once. Reached our proposed camping-ground about sundown. **1867** BARKER *Station Life* (1870) 135 We saw strings of sheep going down from their high camping-grounds to feed on the sunny slopes. **1878** ELWELL *Boy Colonists* 182 They came on some very old camping-grounds where numbers [of sheep] had clearly at one time encamped. **1918** *NZ at the Front* 77 They've turned the sheep on the long fern hill..Stringing far out to their camping ground in the ti-tree on the ridge. **1921** GUTHRIE-SMITH *Tutira* (1926) 181 [Sheep-paths] are, in fact, roads from a city, for to sheep their camping-ground is as his town to man, at once a refuge and a resting-place. **1951** DUFF *Shepherd's Cal*. 21 Feb. (1961) 22 But always she [*sc*. an old ewe] is..the first on to the camping ground when the sun sets, and the first off it when day returns.

2. [See OED *vbl. n*.² 2, 1867.] A place to camp at; now usu. an area set aside for camping or camping sites.
1861 *NZ Goldfields 1861* 1 Oct. (1976) 31 A few small meetings have been held on the wharf, in the immigrants' camping ground, to consider their position. **1878** LINDSAY-BUCKNALL *Search for Fortune* 30 Having landed our stores and worldly goods, we proceeded next to select a 'camping ground'. **1883** DOMETT *Ranolf & Amohia* II. 55 In search of some good camping-ground They paddled up Mahánas Lake. **1897** *TrNZI* XXIX. 341 No change took place until we reached the Parerau camping-ground, where there is a patch of bush, and a pretty little stream. **1900** CANTERBURY *Old & New* 195 [The wekas] visit every camping ground, investigating the empty tins. **1939** *Te Aroha Times* 28 Sept. 5 The object of the ground is to provide accommodation for the moving public and it should be left as a camping ground. **1986** *National Bus. Rev*. 5 Sept. 3 The resort is on land valued at $280,000 which was formerly occupied by a camping ground and baches paying peppercorn rentals. **1991** COWLEY *Bow Down Shadrach* 83 They found the camping ground quite easily.

camp oven. [Used elsewhere but of special significance in pioneer New Zealand: AND 1832.] **a**. A three-legged iron cooking pot designed to stand in a fire or bed of hot coals, having a heavy (occas. concave) lid on which hot coals may be heaped, and often a swinging handle. Also *attrib*.
1842 WEEKES *Journal* (ATLTS) IV. 3 Camp oven and gypsy kettles. **1850** LUSH *Auckland Jrnls*. 25 Oct. (1971) 30 Learned how to make bread with flour, buttermilk and carbonate of soda, baked in a camp oven. **1860** BUTLER *First Year* (1863) vii 111 We carried down a kettle, a camp oven, some flour, tea, sugar, and salt beef..also two cats. **1870** PRENTICE *A Tale of NZ* (GALMS) 32 The cooking gear comprised..a frying pan and a circular iron pot called a camp-oven. **1908** STEWART *My Simple Life* 105 Tinker Simmonds..showed me how to use a 'camp-oven'—a 15-inch round iron pot on legs, and with a handle, so that it could either stand or hang. **1920** MANDER *Story NZ River* (1974) 52 Just then his eye rested on a heavy iron camp oven set on the hearth. **1949** NEWTON *High Country Days* 193 Camp oven: A broad, rather shallow iron 'pot'. It has three short legs and a handle like that of a bucket. Very good for cooking mutton. **1951** CRESSWELL *Canterbury Tales* 21 Mrs Godley and young Arthur..had an open-air dinner of camp-oven mutton, potatoes and cabbage. **1962** HOGAN *Billy-Can Ballads* 6 We buried Old Frank by the Kowhai, Our champion camp oven cook. **1991** *NZ Geographic* Apr.-June 22 There'd be an open fireplace and a camp oven. They were round, cast iron, with a lid, on three legs. You made a bed of charcoal, and put the oven on it, then put hot coals on the lid, too.

b. Used *attrib*. in Comb. **camp-oven bread**.
1890 *Otago Witness* (Dunedin) 7 Aug. 36 We ate our campoven bread and our fat chops, and dream'd of great flocks to be drafted off every year to boiling-down yards. **1912** *Otago Witness* (Dunedin) 31 July 17 He sat down and had a refreshing drink of tea and a slice of camp-oven bread. **1981** CHARLES *Black Billy Tea* 25

[Title] *Camp Oven bread* Bread in those early days was baked in a camp oven. **1985** HUNT *I'm Ninety-five* 28 We made camp oven bread, too—beautiful. **1987** *Listener* 21 Feb. 56 Years ago I used to make a camp-oven bread with cooked potatoes and eggs, flour, salt, yeast and milk.

Canadian. Also occas. **Canada**, in the names of plants and animals, see: GOOSE *n.*¹ 2, THISTLE *n.* 2 (1).

canary, *n.*¹

1. [Transf. use of *canary* a small yellow bird.] Also with a modifier: esp. **bush canary** (occas. **native**, **New Zealand canary**). YELLOWHEAD, occas. also WHITEHEAD (see quot. 1924).
   1870 *TrNZI* II. 57 Mohoua ochrocephala, Mohoua. Canary. As soon as one ascends the bushy gullies of the hills, the Canary is sure to pay a..visit. **1886** *TrNZI* XVIII. 102 New Zealand Canary, two species (*Popokatea*). **1896** HARPER *Pioneer Work* 39 The canaries..are useful as foretellers of the weather. **1904** HUTTON & DRUMMOND *Animals NZ* 91 The Bush Canary.—Mohua... The New Zealand Canary has a sharp, strident call, and its movements are quick and active. **1904** *TrNZI* XXXVI. 119 I have paid special attention to the nests of three birds, the Native Canary..the Robin..and the Tomtit. **1924** *Otago Witness* (Dunedin) 16 Dec. 6 [The whitehead] is best known to bushmen, probably, as the bush canary, although it is not a canary. **1936** GUTHRIE-SMITH *NZ Naturalist* 65 Mohua ochrocephala has been well named the Bush Canary. Its commonest call is a trill or rapid shivering rattle not unlike the pea whistle note of the popular cage bird. **1966** FALLA et al. *Birds NZ* 210 Yellowhead... Mohua, Bush Canary. **1983** *Land of Mist* 70 There are many song bird species in the park, including the whitehead or bush canary.

2. *fig. Hist.* [AND 1898.] An illegal Chinese immigrant.
   1907 *Truth* 9 Mar. 1 It would be interesting to know how many 'canaries' (Chow stowaways) are landed in the diminutive wayside ports of this colony.

3. *fig. Prison.* [f. *sing (like a canary)* to inform.] An informer.
   1980 MACKENZIE *While We Have Prisons* 16 Prisoners who did converse [with officers] were accused of 'sucking up' to officers, and were held in contempt by their fellows. They were known as 'brown noses', 'toppers' or 'canaries'. *Ibid.* 95 *canary* squealer; a songbird

canary, *n.*² *Obs.* A used bus-ticket. Also in the phr. **to sell a canary**, to give a free ride on public transport.
   1958 *Truth* 24 June *Made Bird Of Old Tickets.* Sales of 'canaries'—used tickets—by drivers and conductors of buses have been giving the Auckland Transport Board a headache. **1978** *Dominion* (Wellington) 24 May 1 If drivers were 'selling canaries'—giving free or cheap rides—they faced dismissal and the union would not support them.

cannibal. *Derog. Obs. Hist.* In early pre-colonial and colonial times applied to the Maori. Also *attrib.*
   1815 KENDALL in Elder *Marsden's Lieutenants* (1934) 89 I cannot conclude..without returning thanks to the Almighty God for delivering us from the hands of a set of desperate cannibals. **1826** BUSBY *Letter* 13 Feb. in McNab *Hist. Records* (1908) I. 652 I was not deterred by the consideration of the dangers and hardships of a sojourn on a stormy coast and among a race of cannibals. **c1835** BOULTBEE *Journal* (1986) 76 Now to be a lost man in the midst of strange people, and cannibals tho' in justice to the New Zealanders, I have seen more friendship amongst them than I have subsequently amongst the white people who formed the crew of the boat I was in. **1847** ANGAS *Savage Life* I. 280 'Black Charley' the Australian [aborigine], who had heard much of the cannibal propensities of the New Zealanders, was afraid to go ashore for fear of being devoured. **1856** HODGKINSON *Emigration to NZ* 13 Besides great numbers slain in battle many of the prisoners were killed and eaten by this sanguinary chieftain [Rauparaha] and his cannibal followers. **1958** MILLER *Early Victorian NZ* 20 At the age of nineteen, Jerningham Wakefield, son of the theorist, heard that his Uncle William was going to lead an expedition to the Cannibal Isles.

Hence **cannibalism**.
   1840 *NZ Jrnl.* I. 62 Let it be further duly noted, that the colonization which must so go on, is daily introducing vices among the Aborigines, to which even their own cannibalism must yield in atrocity.

canoe, *n.*¹ *Hist.* A Maori dugout canoe; WAKA 1. See also WAR CANOE. (Also used in reference to the Maori 'founding' canoes: cf. FLEET.) Also *attrib.*
   1769 COOK *Journals* 8 Oct. (1955) I. 168 We saw in the Bay several Canoes, People upon the shore and some houses in the Country. **1777** FORSTER *Voyage Round World* I. 132 Here [at Dusky Bay] we found a double canoe hauled upon the shore... The canoe..consisted of two troughs or boats joined together with sticks, tied across the gunwales with strings of the New Zeeland flax-plant. **1807** SAVAGE *Some Acc. of NZ* 3 Immediately upon coming to an anchor we were surrounded by a great number of canoes. **1837** *Piraki Log* 14 Apr. (1911) 52 Captain Harled the Canous up to Hous [on the beach]. **1849** TORLESSE *Papers* (1958) 79 Returned up the Avon in canoe having shot a bittern and grey teal which J. Deans stuffed. **1858** SMITH *Notes of Journey* 4 Jan. in Taylor *Early Travellers* (1959) 352 Putting our packs in the canoe, we walked down the bank till opposite the pa, where they put us across. **1873** TINNE *Wonderland of the Antipodes* 70 [He] would receive two canoe-loads of provisions, if he came to a bone-scraping in his official capacity. **1881** BATHGATE *Waitaruna* 74 It was really a canoe of native manufacture, and was simply a log of Totara, which had been hollowed out by some patient Maori. **1924** LYSNAR *New Zealand* 65 Few savage races were greater adepts in the art of canoe-building than the Maoris. **1936** HYDE *Passport to Hell* 141 The Maori girls sing them, weaving lithe arms and bodies in the canoe *pois*, the graceful dance of the womenfolk.

Hence *v. intr.* (also as **canoe it**), to travel by, or in a, canoe.
   1874 BAINES *Edward Crewe* 95 When night came we camped, building a very rough hut..and this..made us as comfortable..as travellers canoeing it could desire. **1930** DOBSON *Reminiscences* 156 When working with the Maoris, we were so much in and out of the water, canoeing and travelling along the beaches.

canoe, *n.*² A solemn procession of believers in the teachings of Te Whiti, a Maori spiritual leader. Also *v.* See also TE WHITI.
   1952 RICHARDS *Chatham Is.* 125 The rest of the natives held a 'canoe' or solemn, silent procession consisting of over forty people on forty horses and accompanied by more than that number of dogs. Te Whiti told them that they must canoe seven times before the Europeans would leave the Chathams.

Cantabrian /kənˈtæbrijən/, *n.* and *a.* Also **Canterburian**. [A pseudo-learned formation confusing Brit. *Cantabrian* of Cambridge (University) with *Cant*(er) + *b(u)rian*.]

A. *n.* One born or resident in the provincial district of Canterbury.
   1969 HASCOMBE *Down & Almost Under* 57 Riccarton Bush..called 'Deans Bush' by any Cantabrian worthy of the name. **1987** ELDRED-GRIGG *Oracles and Miracles* 226 'He's a fine little Cantabrian,' she said. **1992** *Dominion* (Wellington) 20 July 8 To my mind, 'Cantabrians', the name for the inhabitants of Canterbury, is not a happy choice. It seems to be a result of a misconception about the meaning of the British abbreviation 'Cantab'... 'Canterburians' is not too difficult to pronounce.

B. *adj.* Of or pertaining to the provincial district of Canterbury.
   1983 *Evening Post* (Wellington) 21 May 6 Your news item of May 11, 'Unashamedly Cantabrian' quotes the chairman of a Christchurch City Council committee saying some development project was 'unashamedly parochial and unashamedly Cantabrian'... [1983 *Note*] The 'Post's' chief reader Ian Spicer says 'Cantabrian' to describe a resident of, or phenomenon related to Canterbury—and more particularly Christchurch—has been around for a long time. Usage appears to be peculiar to Christchurch newspapers... Arguments about the word have waxed at least as long with Canterburians being preferred by some as being etymologically more valid. However, Canterburians looks awkward and is a mouthful to pronounce: for those reasons Cantabrian appears to have scored the victory.

Canterburian, var. CANTABRIAN.

Canterbury, *n.* and *attrib.*

A. *n. WW1.* Usu. as **the Canterburys**, until the formation of the New Zealand Division in 1916, the Canterbury Battalion of the Infantry Brigade; thence, either the 1st or 2nd Canterbury Battalions of variously organized Infantry Brigades. Occas. early in WW1, the Canterbury Regiment of the Mounted Rifles.
   1916 *Chron. NZEF* 16 Oct. 81 The Canterburys have continued fighting with dash and gallantry. **1919** [see AUCKLAND 1]. **1966** [see OTAGO A]. **1984** PUGSLEY *Gallipoli* 178 His party was joined by more Canterburys.

B. *attrib.*

1. In the names of plants and animals, see: BROOM 3, MUDFISH 2 (3), SMELT.

2. In special collocations: **Canterbury Block**, see BLOCK *n.*¹ 1 a; **Canterbury lamb** [see OED 4], a term used in Great Britain for lamb or mutton imported from New Zealand; in New Zealand for certain grades of such meat (also *ellipt.* **Canterbury**).
   1898 *NZ Farmer, Bee & Poultry Jrnl.* July 232 Does he mean to say that intrinsically as food..English mutton is worth about three times as much as prime Canterbury frozen? **1903** *Cyclopedia NZ* III. 80 We are basking in prosperity, now that we can turn off a large quantity of 'Prime Canterbury' from the plains. **1917** *Chron. NZEF* 14 Mar. 37 The last I remembered I was a prime Canterbury in the freezer at Islington. **1928** STAPLEDON *Tour Australia and NZ* 58 A brief reference to the New Zealand 'Canterbury lamb'..may not be out of place. **1936** BELSHAW et al. *Agric. Organiz NZ* 636 'Canterbury' lamb and mutton is now a trade term and because of consistent high quality usually has had a premium over other New Zealand supplies. **1959** PASCOE *NZ Sheep Station* 3 Every time we buy Canterbury lamb from the butcher we are reminded that the meat we are going to eat has come from a New Zealand

sheep-farm. **1960** SCRYMGEOUR *Memories Maoriland* 146 Even with this and other complaints, sheep throve, and put 'Canterbury lamb' on the map... 'Prime Canterbury' was mostly the result of Southdown or Border mated to half-bred merinos. **1966** TURNER *Eng. Lang. Austral. and NZ* 146 The term *Canterbury lamb* must not be overlooked, though it has now become a victim of standardization, being replaced by the term *down grade*.

Canterbury Pilgrim. *Hist.* [A play on *Pilgrim* (*Father*) an original (religious) settler, a newcomer (see OED, *pilgrim* 5) overshadowed by the inevitable pun on Chaucer's *Canterbury Pilgrims* first expressed by Tupper.] Usu. *pl.* One of the Canterbury Association's founding immigrants, or as plural, the group as a whole (see quot. 1850) who travelled in 1850 by 'the first four ships' to the Church of England settlement of Canterbury. See also PILGRIM 1 a.
1850 TUPPER *'Canterbury Pilgrims'* in *The Canterbury Papers* (1850) IV. 116 Heaven speed you, noble band! Linked together heart and hand, Sworn to seek that far-off land Canterbury Pilgrims. **1851** *NZ Spectator & Cook's Strait Guardian* (Wellington) 7 May 'Dream of the Shagroon' in Reed *Story of Canterbury* (1947) 111 Lo! the land which was to have been sacred to the orthodox foot only of a 'body of English gentlemen', was in possession of the 'stragglers, the whalers, and the stock-drivers from other settlements'. Alas! for the goodly land,—the land of the Canterbury Pilgrims. **1855** SEWELL *Journal* 27 May (1980) II. 147 I have been gathering all the information I can on the subject from old settlers, old Australians and Canterbury Pilgrims, who are *novis homines* in the pastoral world. **1859** THOMSON *Story NZ* II. 188 It is worthy of notice, that the colonists, soon after the formation of all the settlements, acquired distinguishing epithets; thus there was an Auckland cove..and a Canterbury pilgrim. **1866** [see PROPHET *n*.¹]. **1874** TROLLOPE *NZ* 78 We found ourselves..among the people..who are still called the Canterbury Pilgrims. **1886** HART *Stray Leaves* 7 In the month of September [1850] the band of Canterbury Pilgrims..set sail for Canterbury from Gravesend. **1898** HOCKEN *Contribs*. 94 Probably the last of the 'send-offs' [i.e. functions for departing emigrants] was in 1850, when the 'Canterbury Pilgrims' sailed. **1927** *Press* (Christchurch) 15 July 6 Some interesting records..are gradually being collected by the Canterbury Pilgrims Association. **1933** SCANLAN *Tides of Youth* 120 Walton Kite's father had arrived from England on the heels of the Canterbury Pilgrims, who had laid out that lovely city of Christchurch. **1951** CRESSWELL *Canterbury Tales* 19 At the same time frequent letters kept him appraised of what was happening to the Canterbury Pilgrims of the *Southern* seas. **1969** HASCOMBE *Down & Almost Under* 56 We learnt that those who can claim to belong to a family who came out to New Zealand in one of the first four ships..in 1850 belong to an *élite* society known as the Canterbury Pilgrims.

canvas.

1. [AND 1855.] Used *attrib*. of buildings made of canvas.
1879 HAAST *Geol. Canterbury & Westland* 85 We found everywhere [near Teramakau] tents and canvas stores, often comfortably fitted up, and the people hard at work... At the mouth of..the Waimea river..we found a settlement..consisting of about thirty shanties and canvas houses, mostly stores and public-houses.

2. Special Comb. **canvas town**, **Canvastown** [AND 1853], orig. a goldfields tent settlement; thence (with caps.) a place-name.
1861 in *NZ Goldfields 1861* 23 Sept. (1976) 18 Mr. Cairns..pointed out the nature of the case [about shortage of accommodation], and urged that a space of ground should be allotted to the new comers, somewhat after the fashion of the 'Canvas Town' of 1852 and 1853. **1864** *Nelson Examiner* 11 June 3 A wet day at Canvas Town is only surpassed in misery by a wet night at the same place, as most of the tents leak. **1865** BARKER *Station Life* (1870) 16 The gold-fields on this coast were only discovered eight months ago, and already several canvas towns have sprung up. **1866** FARJEON *Grif* 78 Nothing further was known of him, than that he had sprung up suddenly in Canvas Town. **1868** CHUDLEIGH *Diary* 18 Apr. (1950) 220 I went up to Dunedin and how it has grown since I was here last. Then it was a canvas town. **1892** REEVES *Homeward Bound* 3 Round Dunedin [in 1860s] rose a 'canvas town' for miles. **1904** *NZ Observer* 6 Aug. 4 Te Aroha was a canvas town. **1914** GRACE *Tale of Timber Town* 152 Across the scarred, disfigured valley, over the mullock heaps,.. bearded men..collect in Canvas Town's one ramshackle street. **1924** *Otago Witness* (Dunedin) 21 Oct. 54 Hokitika was known then as Canvas Town. **1948** *Our Own Country* 23 Within three years there was a population [at Thames] estimated at 20,000... Canvastown, the hundreds of bell-tents, had been replaced by wooden buildings. **1951** HUNT *Confessions* 13 Most of the inhabitants of 'Canvastown' might well have been described as the scum of the earth. **1963** PEARSON *Coal Flat* 46 She knew it rained hard [on the West Coast]..that there had been a violent history of gold-rushes and canvas-towns. **1981** HENDERSON *Exiles of Asbestos Cottage* 131 He sent notes..picturing.. lacebark or ribbonwood in flower bringing thoughts of white glimpses of miners' sudden canvastowns.

cap, *n.* [Spec. use of *cap* a cap-like cover or similar part on the end of anything: see OED *n*.¹ 12.] The loose 'top' of a wool-pack, sewn or fastened on to the packed bale.
1949 NEWTON *High Country Days* 52 The lid of the press, to which was attached the 'cap' of the pack, would be winched down. **1986** RICHARDS *Off Sheep's Back* 113 While one press was being filled and pressed, the already pressed bale would have the cap clipped (not sewn), and then it would be branded and wheeled away.

cap, *v.* [f. Scottish University use, orig. to place a cap on a person's head esp. as a sign of conferring a University degree: see OED *v*.² 1.] *trans.*, usu. constr. in the passive. To confer a University degree (usu. at a graduation ceremony). See also CAPPING *vbl. n.* 1, the most freq. use.
1912 *Auckland Univ. College Students' Capping Carnival Programme* 10 [Advt] 'Economy' George Court..Is still teaching Economy to a Discerning Public The Students Admit that Our Value 'Caps All'. **1937** HYDE *A Home in This World* (1984) 82 Grave lines of girls going up to be capped, each bearing a little posy.

capai, var. KAPAI.

cape, *attrib*. and *n.*

A. *attrib.* As a modifier in the names of plants and animals deriving orig. from the Cape of Good Hope. **a.** See DAISY 2 (1), IVY 2 a, PETREL 2 (5), PIGEON 3 a; see also CAPE WEED a.

b. Cape barley. [AND 1825.] A hardy variety of barley.
1890 CHUDLEIGH *Diary* 19 Mar. (1950) 371 I was cutting cape barley with machine and then drafting sheep. **1892** *NZ Official Handbook* 120 *Cape Barley*... Its extreme hardiness renders it peculiarly adapted for autumn sowing. **1902** *Settler's Handbook NZ* 98 A breadth of oats or Cape barley is usually sown to come in at early spring. **1921** GUTHRIE-SMITH *Tutira* (1926) 306 Record of early connection with South Africa, with the Cape of Good Hope, is preserved by such plant-names as 'Capeweed'..'Cape gooseberry'..and 'Cape barley'.

c. Cape tulip. [*Cape* (of Good Hope) + transf. use of *tulip*, *Tulipa* spp. (fam. Liliaceae), for various unrelated plants with funnel-shaped flowers.] Either of two plants introduced from South Africa: formerly, species of *Protea* (fam. Proteaceae); or (usu.) *Homeria collina* (fam. Iridaceae) a poisonous plant with a long solitary leaf and attractive orange-pink flowers.
1905 WHITE *My NZ Garden* 97 Among exotic things worth having are the Proteas, or Cape Tulips— handsome shrubs, with large tulip-shaped flowers. **1926** HILGENDORF *Weeds* 60 One-leaved Cape Tulip (*Homeria collina*). A single leaf arising from a corm. **1969** *Standard Common Names Weeds* 11 Cape tulip *Homeria breyniana*. **1981** TAYLOR *Weeds of Roadsides* 33 Cape Tulip (*Homeria collina*) South Africa perennial..with grass-like leaves,... and pretty flowers with six reddish orange petals..extremely poisonous to stock.

B. *n.* A short form of *Cape gooseberry* (recorded in NZ from 1841), *Physalis peruviana* (fam. Solanaceae), a South American plant naturalized and growing wild in the warmer areas of New Zealand.
1975 DAVIES *Outback* 123 I hope Max doesn't find that patch of Capes up there.

Cape Reinga: see REINGA 2.

Cape weed. Applied to either of two introduced weeds of the daisy family. **a.** [AND 1878.] *Arctotheca calendula* (formerly *Cryptostemma calendulacea*) (fam. Asteraceae), a South African annual herb, a poisonous weed of coastal sand and wasteland in the North Island and parts of the South. See also *Cape daisy* (DAISY 2 (1)).
1878 *TrNZI* X. 367 *Cryptostemma calendulacea*... The Cape weed, which is plentiful in Auckland, is with us confined to the vicinity of Wanganui, where it is spreading rapidly. **1926** [see DAISY 2 (1)]. **1969** *Standard Common Names Weeds* 11 Cape weed *Cryptostemma calendula*. **1981** TAYLOR *Weeds of Roadsides* 35 Cape weed (*Arctotheca calendula*)... This South African plant is well-established [on] the west coast of the North Island.

b. (*Obs.*). In the South Island, the European catsear *Hypochoeris radicata* (fam. Asteraceae), a widespread perennial weed of open ground and pasture.
1898 MORRIS *Austral English* 78 *Cape Weed*... In New Zealand, name given to the European cats-ear. **1905** *TrNZI* XXXVII. 336 The only introduced plant I noticed [on Mt Holdsworth] was the 'cape-weed' (*Hypochaeris*), which was in profusion at about 4,000 ft. **1921** GUTHRIE-SMITH *Tutira* (1926) 285 Throughout this block..'capeweed' or cat's-ear..germinated in millions of millions. **1933** *Press* (Christchurch) (Acland Gloss.) 23 Sept. 13 *Cape Weed.*—Hypochaeris radicator [*sic*]. The English catsear so called in Canterbury. **1952** BLAKISTON *My Yesteryears* 45 When the sour clay beneath was turned up, it would grow nothing but Cape weed and Yorkshire fog. **1984** *Standard Common Names Weeds* 18 Cape weed [=] *catsear: hawksbeard*.

capi, var. KAPAI.

CAPPING

capping, *vbl. n.* [See CAP *v.*]

1. A university graduation ceremony (held usu. in May), and its attendant student activities. Often *attrib.*

1890 *Otago Witness* (Dunedin) 28 Aug. 25 The annual 'capping' of graduates who have kept their classes at the University of Otago took place in the Garrison Hall last evening. **1905** *Westminster Gazette* 28 Aug. II. 3 Sir Robert Stout..announced at the last capping at Wellington that..if the students persisted in their senseless conduct there would be no more capping ceremonies in public. **1907** HULL *College Songs* (Preface) 7 Capping Songs are a matter of yearly duty, but these lyrical pieces are spontaneous... The greater part of these poems are Capping Songs—irresponsible expressions of College opinion, and humorous criticisms of ephemeral events in College life. **1912** *Otago Witness* (Dunedin) 10 July 34 The 'douce', sober..air supposed to be so characteristic of Dunedin, was rudely disturbed at midday..by the University students' annual capping procession. **1914** *Auckland Univ. College Students' Carnival Programme* 5 List what the Senate has said—'Capping for ever is dead' Gone is our function of solemn state. **1934** MULGAN *Spur of Morning* 60 'Capping' was the one day in the year when the college came before the public. **1936** *Auckland University College Programme* [cover] Auckland University College Students' Association present the Capping Revue 1936. **1962** JOSEPH *Pound of Saffron* 171 It's the students' capping procession. **1980** LELAND *Kiwi-Yankee Dict.* 21 Capping. In May of each year, the seven University level institutions hold their graduations after a week of traditional hi-jinks.

2. Special Comb. **capping ball**, a formal ball often held as part of university capping festivities; **capping book (capping mag)**, a magazine of student humour published at capping; **capping ceremony**, the public ceremony at which graduates formally receive their degrees; **capping concert** (see also EXTRAV(AGANZA)), a humorous, satirical and often lewd revue (formerly) performed during capping festivities; **capping day** (usu. init. caps., also *attrib.*), the day on which the University confers degrees at a public ceremony; **capping week**, usu. with reference to the continual student activities during the week in which a capping day occurs.

1968 SLATTER *Pagan Game* 81 The riding of bicycles around the dance floor at the **Capping Ball**. **1934** *Otago University Capping Book* [inside cover] Capping Committee, 1934... Capping Concert, May 16th... **Capping Book**, May 15th. **1936** *Otago University Capping Book* 1936 1 [Title] **1890** *Otago Witness* (Dunedin) 4 Sept. 24 At the **'Capping' ceremony** last week, everything went as merry as a marriage. **1899** *NZ Times* (Wellington) 14 June 7 At the 'capping' ceremony in connection with Auckland University College, the Governor is reported to have said:—'Knowledge produced by cramming..was not what was wanted'. **1913** *Auckland University College Student Carnival Programme* 6 June 20 They have given us a bad name and hanged us: and taken our Capping Ceremony from us. **1925** *Auckland University College Students Association Souvenir Programme* [cover] Official Capping Ceremony Friday, June 12th. Presentation of Diplomas. **1934 Capping concert** [see *capping book* above]. **1980** LELAND *Kiwi-Yankee Dictionary* 21 Capping concert. At graduation time each year, the students of a number of New Zealand's Universities put on a musical stage show. **1912** *Auckland Univ. Capping Carnival* 6 June 9 We're students gathered here for fun on this our **Capping Day**. **1919** *Quick March* 10 July 49 On Capping Day students of Victoria College had a procession. **1928** *Free Lance* (Wellington) 2 May 5 The Hon. W. Downie Stewart suggests that politicians should be caught young. How about introducing the Capping Day spirit and a few Varsity students? **1934** MULGAN *Spur of Morning* 57 Two or three had made names for themselves..and their records were cited with pride on 'Capping day'. **1959** LAWLOR *Old Wellington Days* 64 It may even inspire our Capping Day Processions to better things. **1962** JOSEPH *A Pound of Saffron* 171 Brendan Keogh jumped down from the Art School truck..and watched the capping-day procession. **1968** SEDDON *The Seddons* 136 The brave band of early students on Capping Day processed and emulated the carryings on of their brethren in larger colleges elsewhere. **1938** *Auckland Univ. College Carnival Book* 1938 [Cover] Auckland University College **Capping Week**. **1959** SLATTER *Gun My Hand* 36 Before the war the wind-whipped gowns of hurrying students..the laughter and explosions and grease paint of Capping Week. **1976** HARRISON *Broken October* 48 A woman on Oriental Parade..said to her husband: 'Aw look, Jeff. Is it Capping Week again?' **1985** STEWART *Gumboots & Goalposts* 41 I'm sure she thinks they are marks painted on the road by..university students during capping week.

cap rail. [AND *cap* 1849, *cap rail* 1897.] The top rail of a post-and-rail (esp. stockyard) fence.

1856 ROBERTS *Diary* 18 Dec. in Beattie *Early Runholding* (1947) 44 When released the poor beast is not in an amiable temper... The idea that it may catch you before your legs are safely over the cap rail certainly accelerates one's movements. **1867** BARKER *Station Life* (1870) 163 The gentlemen sallied forth once more to the stock-yard, and with great difficulty got off two of the cap or top rails. **1934** *Press* (Christchurch) (Acland Gloss.) 13 Jan. 13 *Cap rail.*— Top rail of a yard fence. **1951** MCLEOD *NZ High Country* 24 The yard consists of a netting enclosure and a smaller pen beyond, built of posts or stakes, with a cap rail to hold the lambs upon. **1982** *Agric. Gloss.* (MAF) 27 *Cap rail*: Top rail on cattle yards used for walking on. Top rail on wooden fence.

Captain Cook. Also *ellipt.* **Cook's**. [f. the proper title and surname of *Captain* James *Cook* (1728–1779), navigator and explorer, used allusively in collocations.]

1. a. In special collocations: **Captain Cook's cress**, **scurvy grass**, see CRESS, SCURVY GRASS b; **Captain Cook's ropes**, BUSH-LAWYER *n.*[1]

1868 PYKE *Province Otago* 35 Two species of wild vines. One of these is known to the settlers as 'supplejack' and the other has received the fantastic name of 'Captain Cook's ropes'.

b. In allusive reference to wild pigs reputedly descended from domestic pigs released by Captain Cook, according to a longstanding tradition or legend, viz. 1840 Apr. 25 *Sarah Mathew Jrnl.* in 1940 *Founding of NZ* 128 We passed numerous traces of wild pigs [in Northland], which are said to be very numerous, the descendants of those left by Captain Cook. **1881** BATHGATE *Waitaruna* 282 He stayed only..to examine its long tusks..which told that the boar was a patriarch of its kind. 'He is evidently what the doctor calls "one of Captain Cook's original lot"', muttered Gilbert. **1889** DAVIDSON *Stories NZ Life* 25 As the dogs do most of the [pig-hunting] work, the knives..are used principally to inspire Captain Cook's protegés with a due sense of respect. **1960** SCRYMGEOUR *Memories Maoriland* 147 There, with much natural cover, were a number of wild pigs, descendants of the once liberated 'Captain Cook' progeny.

2. *Obs.* CAPTAIN COOKER. Often *attrib.*

1879 *NZ Country Jrnl.* III. 55 The immense tusks at Brooksdale attest the size of the wild boars or Captain Cooks, as the patriarchs are generally named. **1880** BATHGATE *NZ* 7 Wild boars are usually known by their name 'Captain Cooks.' **1892** BROOKES *Frontier Life* 122 Before many years have passed over pig-hunting (of what is termed the Captain Cook breed) will be one of the past sports of New Zealand. **1898** MORRIS *Austral-English* 79 *Captain Cook*, or *Cooker*, *n*. New Zealand colonists' slang. First applied to the wild pigs of New Zealand, supposed to be descended from those first introduced by Captain Cook; afterwards used as term of reproach for any pig which, like the wild variety, obstinately refused to fatten. **1907** *TrNZI* XXXIX. 228 In later years the 'Captain-Cooks', as they were called, afforded splendid diet for the Maoris and early European visitors. **1916** COWAN *Bush Explorers* (VUWTS) 19 Most of us, being ill-equipped for an argument with a Captain Cook tusker, shinned up a tree. **1935** MAXWELL *Recolls.* 99 About Opunake this belt [of open land] was about two miles wide, and into it came numbers of cattle and wild pigs of the 'Captain Cook' type. **1945** *JPS* LIV. 225 The pig was introduced by Captain Cook... [1945 *Note*] Hence modern Newzealand slang a *Captain Cook* or *Captain Cooker*, for a wild pig. **1951** *Here & Now* Dec. 14 Only Captain Cook in an ungetatable 'bail' warrants the full-stop bullet. **1977** BRUCE *Life in Hinterland South Island* 75 Here too is fresh evidence of the Captain Cook habitat (pig rootings). **1983** HENDERSON *Down from Marble Mountain* 134 A shorthaired collie..superb at bailing up wild cattle or Captain Cook pigs, plump from hinau berries.

3. Any sorry-looking domestic pig (see also 2 above, quot. 1898).

1879 *Auckland Weekly News* 24 May 8 Many of them [*sc.* pigs] were of a fair breed and in good condition, while others were of that nondescript or mongrel character that is generally known as 'Captain Cook's'. **1889** WAKEFIELD *NZ after 50 Years* 85 The lean-ness and roughness of the wild pig gives it quite a different appearance from the domesticated variety; and hence a gaunt, ill-shaped, or sorry-looking pig is everywhere called in derision a 'Captain Cook'.

Captain Cooker. Also **cooker**. [f. CAPTAIN COOK + -*er*.] A New Zealand wild pig, *Sus scrofa* (fam. Suidae) (esp. a boar) of the lean, blue-gray, razor-backed variety descended from domestic pigs reputedly released by Captain Cook. See also CAPTAIN COOK 2, PIG *n.*[1] 1.

1893 CRAIG *Hist. Rec. Jubilee Reunion Old Colonists* 7 A real 'Captain Cooker' came along. **1906** *Truth* 5 May 1 A Marlborough sport..advanced into a gully where his two dogs had bailed up a Captain Cooker. **1917** *Chron. NZEF* 25 July 244 I just dived like a flash uv greased lightnin'..an' stuck 'im like I uster a Captain Cooker. **1921** *Quick March* 10 Sept. 23 In those low ridges and bush-clad hills roamed herds of red deer and thousands of 'Captain Cookers'. **1938** HYDE *Nor Yrs. Condemn* 128 They..heard wild pig crashing in the undergrowth. 'Old Captain Cooker, eh?' said Starkie softly. **1940** STUDHOLME *Te Waimate* (1954) 258 After being ripped by a pig..most dogs soon dropped to the fact that some of these old 'Cookers' should be approached with caution. **1951** HUNT *Confessions* 34 'Captain Cookers', with sharp snouts and formidable tusks, waged constant war with a group of dogs. **1966** SCRYMGEOUR *Memories Maoriland* 148 Running lightly to the fatter 'Captain Cooker' Jim slipped out his sheath knife. **1974** BARTLETT *Emigrants* 57 In this great forest there were..wild pigs, the long-legged descendants of Captain Cookers. **1981** HENDERSON *Exiles Asbestos Cottage* 61 Some of these free Captain Cooker hams and bacon were delicious. **1990** *Dominion Sunday Times* (Wellington) 30 Sept. 11 Mr Garnett recalls a long chase after a large Captain Cooker that had escaped from the city saleyards.

caraceer, var. KARAKA.

Caravan. WW2. Also **Caravan A**. [A play on *Craven A* a popular brand of cigarettes, with reference also to the droppings of passing camel caravans.] A nickname for a brand of issue cigarettes.
1942 NZEF Times 9 Feb. 6 Unless I bought some Caravan A instead of just Caravan he would view it with even more concern. **1946** WEBBER *Johnny Enzed Italy* A brand of alleged cigarettes issued free to the troops. In the same classification as V's. Correct name 'Caravans'—others deleted by censor. **1970** SLATTER *On the Ball* 136 'Clueless, that's what he is. Gonna cost me dough. *Cinque mille* and a carton of Caravan A thrown in.'

carbie. Also **carby**. [f. *carb*(urettor + -IE: AND 1957.] A carburettor.
1956 SUTHERLAND *Green Kiwi* (1960) 126 If you was to stir your old wreck along a bit faster she wouldn't get flyblown—you never hear of Harrington getting maggots in the carbie, do you now? **1979** *Otago Daily Times* (Dunedin) (Dunedin) 28 Mar. 21 The new [Heinemann's] dictionary..does not contain diff and carby (which have now moved from slang into general use among at least half the population).

Carbine. [Transf. use of the name of *Carbine* (1885–1912), a New Zealand racehorse very well known internationally.] Used, often ironically, of a horse either surprisingly fast or slow.
1943 HISLOP *Pure Gold* 124 He asked me if I would mind putting a bullet in [the sheep-worrier's] head..[and burying it] near the road boundary—'about opposite the old horse will do,' he said, as he pointed to his old Carbine taking it easy in his old age. **1960** SCRYMGEOUR *Memories Maoriland* 180 Charlie Eager shouted with approval [at the win in the cross country horse race], 'Hell, Stewie old horse, had I known you were such a carbine, would have had a placard on your back "Dalgety's for Woolpacks".'

carbonette /ˌkabə'net/. [Poss. f. a proprietary name: ? *carbon* + briqu)*ette*.] A briquette of compressed coal dust, used as a domestic fuel.
1964 HORI *Fill It Up Again* 18 It's a carbonette, isn't it. **1972** in Baxter *Collected Poems* (1980) 593 Tonight the carbonettes Are glowing in the fire at Kathy's house. **1979** FRAME *Living in the Maniototo* 51 That evening we sat in our armchairs..by the carbonette fire. **1980** LELAND *Kiwi-Yankee Dictionary* 22 Carbonettes (North Island): hard packed briquets of coke. Long and hot burning. The biggest bit of culture shock I've experienced in New Zealand was moving from the North Island, where these are sold in every neighbourhood store (dairy) and gas (petrol) station, to the South Island and trying to buy some. No one knew what I was talking about. **1989** *Pacific Way* Jan. 11 In the north we refer to little lumps of coal dust as carbonettes.

carby, var. CARBIE.

cardie. Also **cardy**. [f. *cardi*(gan + -IE, used elsewhere but of high frequency in NZ: Ayto & Simpson 1966.] A cardigan.
1964 MORRIESON *Came a Hot Friday* (1981) 79 There's..a cardy Mum knitted for me you can have. **1983** HULME *Bone People* 31 This godzone baby talk. Hottie, lolly, cardie, nappy, crappy, the lot of it, she snarls to herself. **1991** *Dominion* (Wellington) 12 Oct. 13 It's [*sc.* the body's] just like an old cardy—when you finish with it, you throw it away.

card rug. A piece of material, having the icons of a gambling game (esp. *Crown and Anchor*) painted on it, on which gamblers place their bets.
1956 WILSON *Sweet White Wine* 138 But all round the perimeter [of the two-up ring] sat solemn cross-legged men with their crown and anchor boards and their card rugs set out before them.

cardy, var. CARDIE.

CARE /'keə/. Also occas. **Care**. The acronym of Citizens Association for Racial Equality, an organization set up in 1964 to combat apartheid and racial disharmony.
[**1965** *NZ Herald* (Auckland) 30 June 2 The meeting, organised by the Citizens' Association for racial equality, heard four speakers..declare that the Springboks should not be welcomed in New Zealand because of the apartheid policies of their country.] **1971** *Otago Daily Times* (Dunedin) (Dunedin) 23 Sept. 3 Anti-apartheid groups split last night over the controversial visit of the South African golf team. The Citizens Association of Racial Equality (Care) entered a pact not to disrupt the tourney featuring the South Africans in Auckland. **1975** THOMPSON *Retreat from Apartheid* 54 C.A.R.E.'s objections to the tour were summarised in one of its leaflets. **1981** CHAPPLE *The Tour* 6 Then in 1964 one organization, CARE, the Citizens' Association for Racial Equality..had as its twin aims the promotion of racial equality and opposition to apartheid. **1989** NEWNHAM *25 Years of Care* 3 The meeting chose the titles Citizens' Association for Racial Equality, whose initials spelled the felicitous acronym CARE..which..became a household word throughout New Zealand in the years which followed.

cark, *v. intr.* Often as **cark it**. [Of uncertain ultimate origin. The NZ use is a late borrowing from the Australian, AND deriving *kark* 'to die' (1977) from an earlier *cark* 'to caw', from the association of crows with carrion; it is poss. simply a play on a shortened form of *carc* (ass 'a dead body'; or perh. an intensification of Sc. and northern English dialect *cark* 'to fret; to worry; to complain' or (Scots) 'to cause trouble or anxiety' (SND *cark* v. 2).] To die.
1995 *Dominion* (Wellington) 18 Feb. 23 Rhett came up trumps after his namby-pamby wife Ann..obligingly carked it with yellow fever. **1995** *Ibid.* 17 June [Hayden column] Doubt exists about the origin of *cark*, though not about its meaning; 'to collapse', or in extreme cases 'to die'. There is a sloppy variant, *cark it*.

carless day. *Hist.* A fuel conservation measure introduced for a time in 1979. See quot. 1980.
1979 in JONES *Letters* 30 July (1982) 106 All this car-less day nonsense is ludicrous. If the government is really serious about saving 10 per cent of petrol consumption they should simply shoot every tenth motorist. **1980** LELAND *Kiwi-Yankee Dict.* 22 *carless days*: On the 30th July 1979, New Zealand introduced a drastic fuel conservation measure... This was the banning of the operation of all privately [*sic*] petrol powered motor vehicles weighing 4,400 lbs or less (except for motor-cycles) for one day per week. That day to be chosen by the owner of the vehicle in question... You will see a green sticker with a white X upon it next to the red carless day sticker on the windscreens of exempt vehicles. **1986** *NZ Times* 13 Apr. 8 My carless day was Thursday. With oil prices dropping through the sump I can probably scrape the sticker off my windscreen now. **1991** *Dominion* (Wellington) 4 Nov. 4 Car pooling, the sending to bed of the country an hour earlier by turning off the Government television transmission switch, carless days—remember them?

carnie. Also **carny**. [f. unlawful) *carn*(al knowledge 'unlawful sexual connection with an under-age girl' + -IE.]
1. A nubile girl under the age of 16 years as an underage (and therefore unlawful) sexual object.
1962 *Truth* 27 Nov. 13 He used to call her 'Carny', a popular term for anyone who had carnal knowledge and was underage. **1971** SHADBOLT *Bullshit & Jellybeans* 34 All these little teenybopper girls used to hang around trying to look tough, but none of the guys would touch them because they were all carnies. **1988** MCGILL *Dict. Kiwi Slang* 25 *carnie* sexually desirable and probably available female under the lawful age of 16 for sexual intercourse, short for 'carnal knowledge'; aka 'jailbait', because of jail sentence for male convicted of carnal knowledge.
2. A young street-kid.
1991 *Dominion Sunday Times* (Wellington) 8 Dec. 9 In street lingo the younger streetlifes are called 'younglings' or 'carnies' and the older ones 'originals' or 'old boys'.

carny, var. CARNIE.

carpet. *Obs.* A one-pound note.
1899 *Bulletin* (Sydney) 14 Jan. (Red Page) [Letter from *Loafer*, Tauranga.] Following are other local money-names:—1 pound note—*flimsy*, *rag* or *carpet*. **1977** *NZ Numismatic Jrnl.* Oct. 16 The pound note of pre-decimal days was var[i]ously known as a *quid*, *nicker*, *smacker*, *flimsy*, *rag*, and *carpet*. The latter term was apparently peculiar to New Zealand and Australia.

carpet grass, carpet shark: see GRASS 2 (10), SHARK 2 (7).

carrier shell. [See OED *carrier* 7.] The deepwater shellfish *Xenophora neozelanica* (fam. Xenophoridae) so called because it cements empty shells to itself as camouflage from predators.
1909 CHUDLEIGH *Diary* 26 Nov. 449 It is called the Carrier Shell... It protects its own shell by sticking small flat shells on its back like slates. **1947** POWELL *Native Animals NZ* 26 Carrier shell (*Xenophora neozelanica*). A rare deep water species of the northern part of the North Island... In order to evade detection the carrier cements to the back of its shell bits and pieces of rock or shell from the surrounding debris of the sea-bottom. **1970** PENNIKET *NZ Sea Shells in Colour* 26 Carrier Shell (*Xenophora neozelanica*)... Empty shells are always cemented with the concave side uppermost.

carrot.
1. Any of various members of the carrot family (Apiaceae). **a.** As **wild carrot**, *Daucus carota*, an introduced carrot, a common wild plant of lowland open spaces, characterized by its slender white taproot.
1848 WAKEFIELD *Handbook NZ* 150 There are..*wild carrots, turnips,* and *cabbages*, whose origin, from their similarity to ours, may be attributed to the visits of some European shipping. **1926** HILGENDORF *Weeds* 132 Wild carrot (*Daucus carota*) is common in fields and waste places in scattered localities. It is annual or biennial, with a distinct white tap root only faintly suggestive of its cultivated descendant. It grows 1 to 2 feet high, and the leaves and flowers are like those of

an ordinary carrot. **1969** *Standard Common Names Weeds* 86 *wild carrot Daucus carota.* **1981** TAYLOR *Weeds of Roadsides* 169 Wild carrot..has a smaller root and more hair than the garden carrot... introduced from Eurasia, is very common on roadsides.

b. As **native** (or **New Zealand**) **carrot**, *Daucus glochidiatus,* a small native carrot, an uncommon plant of lowland open sites.
1853 TAYLOR *Diary* 30 Jan. in Mead *Richard Taylor* (1966) 192 An epacris and several other pretty flowers, a wild carrot also abounded. **1961** MARTIN *Flora NZ* 288 Eight genera have but a single species, the Native Carrot..and the Mountain Myrrh..being two with no very attractive features. **1984** *Standard Common Names Weeds* 70 *native carrot* [=] *New Zealand carrot* [*Daucus glochidiatus*].

c. *Anisotome* spp., native herbs. Cf. *wild parsnip* (PARSNIP).
1870 *TrNZI* II. 177 The M'Quarrie cabbage, cotton plant..and wild carrot grow abundantly [on Campbell Island]. **1946** ACLAND *Early Canterbury Runs* 15 There were some very valuable plants growing between the tussocks, such as wild parsnip, wild carrot and aniseed. **1986** JOHNSON *Wildflowers Central Otago* 71 [Caption] Native carrot *Anisotome cauticola.* **1988** *Pacific Way* June 48 Above on the rocky bluffs [at Nugget Point, South Otago] the hardy native carrot *anisotomi* [sic] *lyalli*..and the tiny blue grass..cling resolutely to small cracks.

2. Special Comb. **carrot country**, the Ohakune district of the North Island, well known for its commercial carrot crops.
1984 *Evening Post* (Wellington) 4 Feb. 2 A Tuwharetoa elder from 'carrot country' (Ohakune, his words), offered me bites of his melting lemonade iceblock.

carry, *v.* [Used elsewhere but recorded earliest in NZ: see OED *v.* 40.] *trans.* Of land, to support or maintain (stock).
1849 DEANS *Pioneers* (1964) 56 The pasture will now carry as much stock per acre as the bank in front of your house. **1897** SCOTT *How I Stole 10,000 Sheep* 24 We had not grass to carry them for many days. **1933** *Press* (Christchurch) (Acland Gloss.) 23 Sept. 13 *Carry.*—Country is said to c[arry] so much stock, meaning that it will grow enough feed to support them.

carrying-capacity. [Used elsewhere but recorded earliest in NZ in this sense: see OED *carrying* 4.] The number of stock a given area of land will support. See also *stock carrying capacity* (STOCK 2 a).
1902 *Settler's Handbook NZ* 8 The carrying-capacity of the land is, on an average, three sheep to the acre. **1916** *TrNZI* XLVIII. 156 This gives a carrying-capacity of one-thirtieth of a sheep per acre. **1930** ACLAND *Early Canterbury Runs* 151 Hoare.., by ploughing, had raised the carrying capacity to over 30,000 sheep in 1890. **1959** MCLINTOCK *Descr. Atlas* xxi Throughout this hill country aerial topdressing has made spectacular progress in improving the carrying capacity of the land. **1974** *NZ Agriculture* 40 The fertility and the carrying capacity of much of this 'hill country' have been increased through aerial topdressing.

carshed /'ka:ˌʃed/. *Rural.* [Cf. DARE 1861, then 1930–65 a shelter for a motor vehicle.] A free-standing garage housing the family vehicle(s) on a rural property or farm.
[*Note*] *carshed* was the usual term in rural Marlborough in the 1930s and early 1940s replaced by modern 'garage', a word then used for the mechanic's workshop where a vehicle was serviced and benzine bought (Ed.).

1992 *Taranaki Property Guide No. 315* (New Plymouth) 1 [Farm Sales] 12.21 ha rolling contour, 15 paddocks, implement shed, hayshed, 3 brm w/b renovated home, lock-up carshed, schoolbus at gate.

carved house. A Maori MEETING HOUSE q.v. (The concept is post-European, the earlier carved house being apparently a chiefly dwelling or used for a special purpose.)
1895 *TrNZI* XXVII. 674 The carved house, which..has just been purchased for the Auckland Museum, was the property of Te Pokiha Taranui. **1930** NGATA *Let.* 20 Sept. in *Na To Hoa Aroha* (1987) II. 56 Here is a list of projected carved houses... There is some talk of a carved house at Nelson, one at Dunedin. **1938** FINLAYSON *Brown Man's Burden* 44 But back at the fine new carved house the old lady, wrapped in her shawl, did not think of burying. **1950** *NZJAg.* Aug. LXXXI. 187 [Caption to scene from Waitangi museum] The whare-runanga, carved house, with war canoe house in the background. **1976** FINLAYSON *Other Lovers* 100 'You're our visitor and you sleep tonight in the whare runanga—you know, the meeting-house...' Johnny took Jim over the paddock to the carved house. **1983** KING *Whina* 125 Ngata wanted all Maori tribes to revive the building and use of carved houses. **1992** PARK *Fence around the Cuckoo* 37 Sometimes I crept into the carved house... I had an uneasy feeling that the people didn't like it.

case. *Whaling.* [Recorded earliest on the NZ coast: see OED *n.*⁴] The (back part of the) skull or head of a sperm whale which contains the spermaceti.
1837 RHODES *Jrnl. Barque 'Australian'* (1954) 59 At 6pm got one case baled and the junk cut up. Hung the other head astern. **1838** POLACK *NZ* II. 420 The case or occipital part [of the sperm whale is] opened and the spermaceti, which is entirely pure is then baled out. This head matter bears the highest price in the market. **1982** GRADY *Perano Whalers* 226 *Case*—Upper portion of the head of a sperm whale which contains oil and spermaceti.

case: see *hard case* (HARD *a.* 1 a).

cashgora. [f. *cash*(mere + an)*gora*.] A fine goat-hair with properties of cashmere and angora; also occas. the breed of goat producing it.
1985 *More* (Auckland) Oct. 71 But the buzz word in goat farming is 'cashgora'. This stuff, hailed as the first new natural fibre to hit the world for 35 years, is an intermediate grade of fibre culled from crossbred goats. **1986** *Nat. Bus. Rev.* 1 Aug. 41 The high profile of the industry has forced investors to become familiar with the three types of goat breeds—cashmere (feral), angora and the hybrid cashgora. **1986** MCCALLUM *Meeting of Gentlemen on Matters Agricultural* 199 Suddenly goats were in great demand... So valuable are they for their fibre 'cashgora', that is in world-wide demand. **1989** *Marlborough Express* (Blenheim) 10 May 17 As a generic term, cashgora received international recognition at Avignon (France) in June last year when the International Wool Textile Organisation approved the name. It now appears in the organisation's 'Blue Book' which lists all internationally-recognised generic fibre names.

cashie, *n* and *attrib. Car salesmen.* See quots.
1995 *Sunday Star-Times* (Auckland) 17 Dec. A4 The [used–car] empire was propped up by tax-free car trading—known in the trade as 'cashies'... The accountant advised the Parsons in 1993 to stop trading in 'cashie' cars... The purpose of 'cashie' cars was to turn a quick profit of 100% with no paperwork and no tax cut.

cash up, *v.* [AND 1930.]

1. cashed up *pa. ppl.*, well supplied with money.
1961 CRUMP *Hang On a Minute Mate* 191 I couldn't even go on the bash when we were cashed-up because me mate wasn't the sort of bloke a man likes to lead astray. **1990** *Sunday Star* (Auckland) 23 Sep. 1 Honniwell told her [*sc.* a prostitute] he was cashed up. He asked her if she would like to go back to his place.

2. To put up cash, to 'front up'.
1982 *Dominion* (Wellington) 16 Feb. 10 He said he had told Williams that: '..I just want to see you about getting them off you at a decent price.'.. Williams had replied: 'That would be no problem. I could let you have them if you cashed up.'

casing. *Goldmining.* [Recorded early in NZ: see OED *casing* 3 c, 1881 *Raymond*..(Pacific slope) Casings are zones of material altered by vein-action, and lying between the unaltered country rock and the vein.] See 1881 quot. preceding.
1869 *TrNZI* I. (rev. edn.) 480 A great deal of the soil that was thrown away..contained..gold. Captain Hutton asked whether the earth was meant, or the casing of the veins. Dr. Purchas said it was the casing he was referring to. **1914** in *Hist. N. Otago from 1853* (1978) 178 [Reference Maerewhenua goldfield 1869] Several quartz-leaders are being followed up, and look very 'likely'. Gold has..been washed out of the 'casing' but no gold has been yet found in the quartz itself. **1992** LATHAM *Golden Reefs* 427 *Casing*: The clayey matter on the walls of a reef between it and the country rock.

cask. [AND 1974.] A cardboard box containing a plastic bladder with a tap attached and holding table wine or fruit juice. Also *attrib.* esp. in the Comb. **cask wine**. Cf. CHATEAU CARDBOARD, CHATEAU DE CASK.
1986 *Metro* (Auckland) June 110 Cask wine made up 65 to 70 percent of their total product. **1987** *NZ Times* 18 Jan. 9 What has caused this mushroom-like growth of Chateau Cardboard? As a simple matter of economics it is cheaper to put wine into a cask than a bottle. **1993** *Listener* 8 May 10 Imagine yourself stuffed..with..smorgasbord delicacies and compli-mentary cask white. **1995** *North & South* Sept. 135 The consumption of cask wine (also known as bag-in-box or 'chateau cardboard') is gradually declining here.

caspian tern: see TERN 2 (3).

cast, *n.* [f. *cast* the spreading out of hounds in search of a lost scent: see OED *n.* 41; AND 1929.]

1. The sweep a working dog makes when mustering sheep.
1933 *Press* (Christchurch) (Acland Gloss.) 30 Sept. 15 *Cast...* A *heading dog*..goes wide round sheep so as not to disturb them and make them go faster. This curve or sweep is called a c[ast]. **1947** NEWTON *Wayleggo* 28 [The dog] had a tremendous cast and I used to marvel at the unerring way he would land out at the head of sheep in country where his cast took him..out of sight of them. **1970** MCNAUGHTON *Tat* 97 It was a blind cast for both man and dog, for neither had been over the country before. **1982** *Agric. Gloss.* (MAF) 24 *Cast*: Action of a dog when it leaves its handler to encircle or gather sheep. It can be a right- or left-hand cast.

2. In the phr. **to cross the cast**, of a dog on the long pull at a sheep-dog trial, to move from one side to the other of the specified field of action.
1970 MCNAUGHTON *Tat* 119 You get your signal from the judge, and you send your dog out from the side he's standing on. You have to be careful about this: if your dog crosses over to the other side it's called 'crossing his cast' and you lose twenty points.

cast, v.[1] [See prec. and OED v. 60.] Also **cast out**.
a. trans. [AND 1920.] In mustering, to direct (a working dog) to make a wide sweep around stock.
 1911 KOEBEL *In Maoriland Bush* 77 He must acquire the art of 'casting' a sheep-dog. **1949** HARTLEY *Shepherd's Dogs* 25 If a trainer casts the young dog out to head when sheep cannot escape..it will quickly become a habit with him. **1953** SUTHERLAND *Golden Bush* (1963) 154 Tazzy got annoyed and told them to call their mongrels in and he'd cast the old dog. **1966** NEWTON *Boss's Story* 185 *Catching sheep:* A heading dog when cast out to head running sheep is catching them. (Quite a different thing from his actually catching *hold* of a sheep.)

b. intr. Of a working dog, to make a wide sweep when mustering stock or hunting quarry.
 1947 NEWTON *Wayleggo* 153 It is instinctive for a heading-dog to cast when running out, i.e., to make a wide detour so as to get round his sheep without disturbing them. **1949** HARTLEY *Shepherds' Dogs* 24 When the young dog is ready to work, the trainer's foremost aim should be to ensure that his dog will learn to cast out fast and free. **1960** CRUMP *Good Keen Man* 170 [Rip would] cast out through the scrub..until he found a pig.

cast, v.[2] [f. Brit. dial. *cast* to shed hair, horns, etc.: see OED v. 20 a 'somewhat *arch.* or *dial.*'] *trans.* and *intr.* **a.** Of sheep, to shed (wool).
 1933 *Press* (Christchurch) (Acland Gloss.) 30 Sept. 15 *Cast...* A sheep whose wool has fallen off before shearing is said to have *cast* it, and the wool is classed as *cast*. **1953** SCOTT *Breakfast at Six* 145 As their fleeces grew heavy..they began to cast with monotonous regularity.

b. Of deer or wapiti, to shed (antlers).
 1965 BANWELL *Wapiti Hunters* (TS) The old antlers are generally shed from early October to November, the larger bulls casting first.

cast, a. [f. *cast* v. throw (a beast) on its back or side: used elsewhere esp. in Brit. dial. (see EDD v. III), but in this sense apparently recorded earliest in NZ: see OED v. 12 *ppl. a.*, b and c.]
1. a. Of a sheep, unable to rise from a lying position.
 1877 *TrNZI* IX. 310 Sheep that were 'cast' were soon attacked by the blow-fly. **1922** PERRY *Sheep Farming* 55 Owing to their wide level back they [*sc.* Southdown sheep] are frequently unable to right themselves when cast. **1936** BELSHAW et al. *Agric. Organiz. NZ* 425 A small percentage of deaths is incurred through woolly sheep getting entangled in second growth or cast in hollows. **1949** NEWTON *High Country Days* 193 Cast: When a sheep gets down and, through weakness or heavy condition, cannot get up again it is known as being cast. **1951** DUFF *Shepherd's Calendar* 22 Aug. (1961) 45 I caught a hawk in the very act of tearing out the eye of a cast sheep. **1963** BACON *In the Sticks* 180 *cast sheep*—Sheep, particularly when carrying a heavy fleece, have a habit of becoming cast, that is, lying flat on their backs with their four legs pointing skyward. In this position, they are quite unable to regain their feet, and must be hoisted right side up. **1982** *Agric. Gloss.* (MAF) 49 *Cast sheep*: A sheep found lying on its back that cannot get onto its feet unaided, usually because of advanced pregnancy, heavy fleece, or lying in a hollow.

b. *transf.* (a) [Cf. Partridge 8: Anglo-Irish: -1935.] Very drunk, 'paralytic'.
 1949 NEWTON *High Country Days* 116 It was not long before he was discovered 'cast', and dead to the world, out on the grass in front of the hotel.

(b) Of a person, unable to rise after a fall.
 1958 *Tararua* Sept. 56 We put skis on and it was then a hilarious progress... Crashes were frequent, as we had fairly heavy packs, and we often had to stop to help 'cast' companions.

2. In the collocation **cast-for-age** [AND 1930] (also **c.f.a.**), esp. of old breeding sheep, culled for age.
 1933 *Press* (Christchurch) (Acland Gloss.) 30 Sept. 15 *C[ast] for age,* etc., means 'culled' for [age], etc. This term is used for stud rather than flock sheep. **1949** NEWTON *High Country Days* 193 Cast sheep—sheep which have been culled out of the flock, mainly refers to age, i.e. cast for age. **1966** *Encycl. NZ* III. 235 The ewes, which are bred on the farm, pass into the breeding flock, where they remain for four or five years. They then leave the farm in the autumn and appear in the ewe fairs to be bought by fat-lamb breeders as 'cast for age' (or 'C.F.A.') ewes. **1974** *NZ Agric.* 59 The products from this type of farm are..some culled hoggets, store cattle, varying numbers of store or fat wethers, and a draft of 'cast-for-age' (c.f.a.) ewes. **1982** WHEELER *Hist. Sheep Stations NZ* 25 Most surplus lambs go to the works at weaning, and cast-for-age sheep sell well at the end of their useful life here.

castaway hut. A shelter, often holding a survival cache, erected on an uninhabited island for the use of survivors of shipwreck or other misadventure.
 1991 HIGHAM *NZ's Subantarctic Islands* 18 After the earlier wrecks, castaway huts were erected on all the New Zealand subantarctic islands.

caster, a. [AND 1945: ?'f. *castor sugar* (something) sweet'.] Fine, 'OK', 'sweet'.
 1963 *NZ Truth* 21 May 19 I was caster for Gene Tunney [=money], so I took a slapsie maxie [=taxi] to the course. **1982** NEWBOLD *Big Huey* (Glossary) 246 Caster (adj) Good, OK, fine. caster..well off

Castle Hill buttercup: see BUTTERCUP 2 (1).

cat. [Ellipt. for *catamaran.*] **a.** A twin-hulled pleasure craft.
 1966 DYSON *Yachting the NZ Way* 98 Because a 'cat' or a 'tri' has such shallow draft, it can sail right up to the beach. **1987** *Chosen Place* 5 Yahooing for joy as the 'cat' gave a slight shudder, he pulled the tiller towards him, sending the craft skimming across the sheltered lagoon waters.

b. See CATAMARAN 1.

cat: see *whip the cat* (WHIP v.).

catamaran /ˈkætəməˌræn/.
1. Also **cat**. *Northland logging*. [f. a resemblance, when dragging logs, to the catamaran raft of the East and West Indies (see OED 1): used earliest in Newfoundland and Western Canada (see DNE 1, 1810); prob. taken to northern NZ by Nova Scotian immigrants in the last century.] A logging sledge on to which the front end of the log was raised and secured for towing ('snigging') out of the bush.
 1902 *NZ Illustr. Mag.* V. 375 In the winter-time [the log] is jacked on to a large catamaran. **1951** MCCARROLL *The Days of the Kauri Bushmen* (TS) Radio Talk 4 The catamaran, more commonly known [c1914] as the cat, would be anything up to 30 feet long and made with two runners (usually Rata) and a bolster about five feet long bolted across the runners at each end. **1953** REED *Story of Kauri* 180 A kind of sledge, known as a catamaran, or, in bushmen's language, the 'cat'. It consisted of two hard wood runners, about thirty feet in length, with two mortised and cross-bolsters about ten feet apart, on which the logs were placed, and well chocked. **1969** MOORE *From Forest to Farm* 40 To transport the timber on these [skidded, *i.e.* corduroy] roads a 'catamaran' would be constructed. This consisted of two heavy hard-wearing pieces of timber, rata for preference, with up-turned ends and 20-30 feet in length. They formed runners, spaced apart by two heavy crosspieces bolted to them... This 'cat', loaded with one or more logs, with grease sloshed on the skids, enabled a team of bullocks to move surprisingly heavy loads. **1986** OWEN & PERKINS *Speaking for Ourselves* 160 In many places the logs were brought out on what was called a 'cat', which was short for catamaran. A catamaran was a big heavy sledge made of bush timber.

2. Any of various kinds of farm sledges, often with a set of wheels to raise either the front or the back (of esp. a long load) clear of the ground. See also JANKER, KONAKI 1.
 1970 THOMAS *Way Up North* 93 Harry built a catamaran; a vehicle which is perhaps best described as a cross between a sledge and a trolley. It has one central runner in front and two wheels towards the rear.

catch, n. *Shearing.*
a. The sheep a shearer takes from the catching-pen; the catching of such a sheep.
 1952 MEEK *Station Days* 110 Catch: When a shearer takes a sheep from the catching pen, that's his catch. **1955** BOWEN *Wool Away* 19 The Catch. The first part of shearing is to catch your sheep and get it onto the board in the correct starting position.

b. In the phr. **to get** (or **go for**) **a** (or **the**) **catch** [AND 1965], to take, or attempt to take, a sheep from the catching-pen just before the signal for the end of a run sounds (see esp. quot. 1987).
 1933 *Press* (Christchurch) (Acland Gloss.) 23 Sept. 13 *Catch.*—Just before stopping time in a wool shed, a shearer tries to finish the sheep he is on and catch another which he can finish at ease after knock-off. This is called *getting a c[atch]*. E.g., 'How many more can you do this run?' 'Two and a catch.' **1949** NEWTON *High Country Days* 53 For the last 10 minutes..of each run, the men would endeavour to select sheep which would enable them to just beat the gong and get an extra sheep. This was known as 'getting the catch'. **1986** RICHARDS *Off the Sheep's Back* 94 He thought he would be able to put one around me and get the catch, thus putting his tally two up on the rest of us. **1987** OGONOWSKA-COATES *Boards, Blades & Barebellies* 95 In the few minutes before knock-off, each shearer tries to finish the sheep actually being shorn and catch another one, which, if started before the bell, can be finished at leisure and is an easy addition to one's tally. Aiming to get a sheep before the bell is termed 'going for the catch'.

catch, v. *Shearing*. trans. and (occas.) intr. To take (a sheep) from the catching-pen.
 1880s *Teviot Station shearing rules* in Martin *Forgotten Worker* (1990) 95 No Shearer shall go into a pen to catch a Sheep after 'Smoke-oh' or any interval, or 'Clear the Board' has been called. **1912** *NZ Shearers... Report Third Annual Conf.* 16 Oamarama Remit No. 1... 'That any shearer catching a sheep or bringing one on the board after the signal to cease work shall be fined £1.' **1913** *NZ Observer Christmas Annual* 4 He had put up a rather willing fight with the man who had been..'catching' from the same pen that day. **1955** BOWEN *Wool Away* 155 Very often this sheep produces one extra for the tally of the shearer who shears well enough to catch it first. **1965** *Listener* 26 Feb. 15

CATCHING DOG 137 **CATTLE**

Catching pen: The pen in which sheep are held ready for shearing. In competition the shearer is not permitted assistance in catching his sheep.

Hence **catcher**, one who catches sheep for another to work on.

1940 STUDHOLME *Te Waimate* (1954) 114 One man tailing could keep three catchers going at top speed.

catching dog. A dog which catches animals for its owner; *spec.* a pig-dog trained to catch wild pigs.

1940 STUDHOLME *Te Waimate* (1954) 133 [Grass-thieving] quickly came to an end, one old Scot [shepherd] looking his country with a catching dog and a sharp knife [to kill foreign trespassing sheep]. **1986** CARR *Diary Pig Hunter* 19 Tony..had only bailing dogs with him; his catching dog, Rock, was tied up at the cowshed.

catching-pen. *Shearing.*

1. Also **catch pen.** [AND 1867.] A small pen adjacent to the shearing board from which the shearer selects sheep. Also *attrib.*

1857 PAUL *Lett. from Canterbury* 88 I should say make it [*sc.* the sheep-yard] of short, stiff hurdles with a post and rail catching pen. **c1875** MEREDITH *Adventuring in Maoriland* (1935) 143 When the word is given to start, the shearers go into the 'catching-pen' and feel over the sheep, select one, carry it out on to the shearing-floor, and commence shearing. **1897** *Otago Witness* (Dunedin) 2 Dec. 58 The men rushed into the catching pens. **1904** CRADOCK *Sport in NZ* 172 The 'wool-shed' where all shearing is done has a row of pens ('catching-pens', they are called) in it reaching from one end to the other, each pen holding some 25 to 30 sheep. **1912** *Sheepowners' Handbook* 26 No shearer shall enter the catching pen after the bell rings. **1926** [see *bare-belly* (BARE *a.* 1)]. **1933** *Press* (Christchurch) (Acland Gloss.) 30 Sept. 15 *Catching pens.*—Pens built small, and next the board in a woolshed, from each of which one or two shearers catch their sheep. **1934** HARPER *Windy Island* 240 Behind each pair of shearers was a small catch pen with a swing door. **1940, 1953** [see PENNER-UP]. **1960** SCRYMGEOUR *Memories Maoriland* 50 The bell rang, the whole procedure stopped..half shorn sheep were pushed back into the catching pens. **1988** *More* (Auckland) Mar. 30 The shearers were leaning on their catching pen doors.

2. A pen for catching sheep for purposes other than shearing: at a sheep-dip, in a paddock, or in a freezing works.

1903 CHUDLEIGH *Diary* 18 June (1950) 418 I worked at the dip yards making a catching pen so that men can catch and slide each sheep in head first. **1922** PERRY *Sheep Farming* 79 The material required in making a small catching pen are two coils of netting, stakes, and about six or seven hurdles. **1982** *Dominion* (Wellington) 12 Mar. 9 [The solo butcher relied very] much on the support of the other butchers, in particular the mate with whom he was sharing the catching pen.

catch pen: see CATCHING-PEN 1.

caterpillar: SEE VEGETABLE CATERPILLAR.

catfish. [Transf. use of *catfish* a N. Amer. freshwater fish.] A marine fish *Genyagnus monopterygius* (fam. Uranoscopidae), *spotted stargazer* (STARGAZER 2 (5)).

1838 POLACK *NZ* I. 323 Many other fish are equally numerous..various kinds of *skate* and *cat-fish*, *sting-ray* and *dog-fish*. **1872** HUTTON & HECTOR *Fishes NZ* 23 Kathetostoma monopterygium..Cat Fish. **1886** SHERRIN *Handbook Fishes NZ* 301 Cat-fish, Hard-head, or Ngu.

1906 *TrNZI* XXXVIII. 549 The cat-fish or hard-head. **1938** *TrRSNZ* LXVIII. 413 *Genyagnus monopterygius*..Catfish. **1967** NATUSCH *Animals NZ* 224 The catfish [is]..mainly found in southern waters, it is recorded also from Canterbury rivers. **1986** PAUL *NZ Fishes* 119 *Spotted stargazer*... Listed alternative common names include catfish and dogfish, both inappropriate.

Cathedral City. [f. the Anglican cathedral in its central square.] A name for Christchurch. See also GARDEN CITY.

1902 WALKER *Zealandia's Guerdon* 16 Christchurch, the Cathedral City of New Zealand. **1920** BOLITHO *With the Prince in NZ* 167 The north had a different way from the south; the coast expressed itself more noisily than the Cathedral city. **1928** *Free Lance* (Wellington) 1 Aug. 6 Some call her the Cathedral City, the most English City, the City of the Plains. **1943** HISLOP *Pure Gold* 90 That was by no means the best of the many sales I made in the Cathedral City. **1985** MCGILL *G'day Country* 159 Coasters never miss a chance to poke the borax at the Cathedral City.

cats' bar. *Obs.* Also **cat('s) bar**. [f. *cat* a prostitute.] Formerly, orig. a bar other than a public bar, where a woman and her 'escort' could be served liquor; a 'Ladies and Escorts' bar.

1953 *NZ Observer* 1 July 6 They could not help being brought into close personal contact with what some of them coarsely termed 'the cats' bar' or 'the mares' nest'. **1959** SLATTER *Gun in My Hand* 23 He's a randy old coot always hangin around the cats' bar. **1966** TURNER *English Lang. Aust. & NZ* 120 There are..expressions with which I am not personally directly familiar, *cat's bar*, presumably 'ladies bar'. **1976** MCCLENAGHAN *Travelling Man* 118 'What bar's that?' 'The cat bar,' said Eton Junior. 'I'd rather walk into a lion's den than a cat's bar.'.. It was explained that this bar..was used by women. *Ibid.* 119 Hogan leaned forward again and looked into the cat bar.

cat's eye.

1. Also **catseye**. *Turbo smaragdus* (fam. Turbinidae), a univalve shellfish having a heavy greenish-black shell and found on mainly rocky shores; or its round, spirally-marked operculum or lid fancifully resembling a cat's eye and used to close the shell aperture. See also ATAATA, PUPU.

c1920 BEATTIE *Trad. Lifeways Southern Maori* (1994) 159 The bubu (pupu) is a black, round shellfish good to eat. The door of its house forms the 'kanohi pupu', or 'cat's eye' as the pakeha calls it. **1937** POWELL *Shellfish NZ* 30 In the Turbinidae it [*sc.* the operculum] is shelly, a familiar example being the well-known *cat's eye*. **1951** FRAME in *Some Other Country* (1984) 102 Look at all of the coloured shells, look a little pink one like a fan, and a cat's eye. **1967** NATUSCH *Animals NZ* 72 Familiar examples [of door-like opercula] are the 'cat's eye' of *Lunella smaragda*. **1970** SANSOM *Stewart Islanders* 184 [Horse Shoe Bay] is a good beach on which to find the big strong shells, the ostrich-foot, a big whelk, and the southern volute, or dog shell, the lunella or catseye shell, and the rare modelia, also with a catseye to close its door. **1978** FULLER *Maori Food & Cook.* 49 Catseyes, preserved (pupu) The catseye..is a small helical shellfish common on rocky beaches. **1983** GUNSON *Collins Guide to Seashore* 90 The common cat's eye *Turbo smaragdus* (30mm) is one of the best-known univalves of the north, and is sometimes mistakenly referred to as a periwinkle. The operculum is thought to resemble a cat's eye, hence the shell's name.

2. [Also in US regional use, see DARE 1, 1955.] A marble coloured like a cat's eye.

1930 *NZ Short Stories* 237 Granny's needs [for Christmas presents] were simple and few..a dozen assorted marbles of the genus 'Cat's eye' for five-year-old John. **1962** LAWLOR *More Wellington Days* 128 Cat's-eyes were a variety [of marble]..and I think they came in early in my marble-playing time [c1905]. **1972** SUTTON-SMITH *Folkgames Children* 174 Then there were the terms referring to particular kinds of marbles: for example, agates..bum-squashers, cat's eyes. **1983** [see GLASSIE].

cat's meat. Something easy or light to do or suffer; a 'pushover'.

1962 HORI *Half-gallon Jar* 84 I sure got an ear bashing for being late, but I knew it was only cat's meat to what I would get when I got home.

cattle.

1. As **wild cattle** (also occas. **bush cattle** [AND 1842]), unearmarked or unbranded stock orig. from domesticated beasts escaped from farm or cattle-run.

1848 TORLESSE *Papers* (1958) 30 Dec. 45 Saw 3 wild cattle—2 cows, 1 bullock- on high bank of R. Coldstream. **1848** WAKEFIELD *Handbook for NZ* 170 It has already been observed, that there are some *wild cattle* on the island of Kapiti. **1861** HAAST *Topographical Exploration of Nelson* 136 In the open country near Mount Murchison..we met with numerous tracks of wild cattle. **1867** BARKER *Station Life* (1870) 175 [Heading] *Wild cattle hunting in the Kowai Bush*. **1874** BAINES *Edward Crewe* 152 We saw many wild cattle, of which, at the time I write..there were upwards of a thousand head on the [Barrier] island. **1882** HAY *Brighter Britain* I. 212 Wild cattle abound there [Hokianga], possibly in hundreds; and the Maoris make a good thing by hunting them for their hides. **1922** THOMSON *Naturalisation Animals Plants NZ* 51 Wild cattle have been very abundant in the back country for the last seventy years. **1945** HALL-JONES *Historical Southland* 107 [The early runholders] had good sport together among the native game and the wild cattle and the hunting of the kuri. **1950** WODZICKI *Introduced Mammals NZ* 152 With the recent considerable reduction in the wild cattle and sheep populations, the problem of their control is mainly only of historical interest. **1967** GROVER *Another Man's Role* 5 Who would they ask when they needed a drover for a herd of bush cattle that had to be driven a hundred miles? **1971** NEWTON *Ten Thousand Dogs* 74 I had a go at the wild cattle at Lake Coleridge. These cattle, all cleanskins, were mainly in the bush-bound Harper country. **1990** *Handbook NZ Mammals* 373 *Feral cattle*... The alternative common name, 'wild cattle', is best avoided, to save confusion with the true wild cattle of Asia. *Ibid.* 375 On the main islands of New Zealand, feral cattle [*sc.* domesticated cattle escaped to the wild] were most widespread and in greatest numbers (sometimes in mobs of 100 or more) from the 1860s to the 1880s.

2. Special Comb. **cattle banger**, COW-BANGER; **cattle catcher**, CATTLE-STOP, see quot. *cattle-pit* below; **cattle country**, farmland potentially suited to the maintenance of cattle rather than sheep; **cattle-driver** [AND 1843], DROVER; **cattle-driving** [AND 1843] *ppl. a.*, pertaining to the work of driving cattle usu. over long distances; **cattle-hunting** *vbl. n.*, searching for stock in the bush; **cattlelick** [orig. US], a (usu.) salt block used as a dietary supplement to be licked by cattle; **cattle-man**, a man who farms or works with cattle; **cattle-pit**, CATTLE-STOP; **cattle-puncher**, one who works with or drives cattle; **cattle-punching** *vbl. n.*; **cattle run** [AND 1823], a tract of land or large farm on which beef cattle are grazed, RUN *n.*¹ 2; **cattle-sick** *a.*, suffering from BUSH SICKNESS; **cattle sickness**, BUSH SICKNESS; **cattle station** [AND 1832], a station or large farm on which beef-cattle are raised; STATION 3 a; **cattle-yard**, YARD *n.* 1.

1941 BAKER *NZ Slang* 41 *Cowspank*, to be a dairy farmer or a farmhand, whence *cowspanker* (we also use *cattle-banger* and *cow-banger*). **1892** *NZ Official Handbook* 115 The west coast of the island is essentially a **cattle-country**. **1862** *Puketoi Diary* (Hocken MS) Apr. A mob of cattle-beasts..and '**cattle-drivers**' from Cambers. **1879** HAAST *Geol. Canterbury & Westland* 82 Numbers of tents were put up..for the accommodation of gold-diggers, cattle-drivers, and storekeepers. **1882** HAY *Brighter Britain* I. 209 I have had some experience of this **cattle-driving** work; and of all the aggravating jobs I know, it certainly is the very worst. *Ibid.* I. 203 He [*sc.* the stockman] has to go out with the dogs almost every day to hunt up some mob or other... **Cattle-hunting**, as we term this employment, has a certain charm. **1948** FINLAYSON *Tidal Creek* (1979) 134 Oh, that was a **cattlelick** salesman... He said it was full of minerals and things. Well, I always reckon a bit of rock-salt's all right but with these patent mixtures you don't know what you're getting. **1907** ROBIN *Trip to Maoriland* 26 [A herd]..surrounded by a number of '**cattlemen**'... The term cowboy is not known here. **1883** PASH *Report on NZ* 5 Cattle, sheep, horses etc., are prevented from straying on the [railway] line by what is termed a '**cattle-pit**' or '**catcher**'. This is a pit sunk between the rails and fences about 2 feet 6 inches deep and 10 feet wide, covered by bars of wood and placed parallel with the lines and about 5 inches apart. **1902** in *Happy Endings* (1987) 103 A dashed **cattle-puncher**, I tell you. He nailed forty of my calves, and banged 'em along with his own mob 'fore I could get on his trail. **1952** RICHARDS *Chatham Is.* 137 There was no skilled labour as generally understood on the Chathams. We were our own sheep shearers, cattle punchers, horse breakers... Working with or herding cattle. **1907** KOEBEL *Return of Joe* 282 During no time of..that first eventful day of '**cattle punching**'..did the Gunner put in an appearance. **1834** McDONNELL *Extr. from Jrnl.* (1979) 35 You may travel for miles..over..very gently undulating Country—the very model, in fact, of a sheep or **cattle run**. **1840** *Bunbury's Report* 28 June in *GBPP House of Commons 1841* (No.311) 106 A Captain Lethart, of Sydney, also here [at Akaroa] since the 10th of November last, has established a cattle run, with about thirty head of horned cattle. **1849** POWER *Sketches in NZ* 113 The only plan will be to lease sheep and cattle runs, at a cheap rate for a long term of years. **1860** BUDDLE *Maori King Movement* 21 [The Maori] desire [is] to have large tracts of land for pig and cattle runs, over which the herds may range without danger of trespass on the white man's cultivation. c**1875** MEREDITH *Adventuring in Maoriland* (1935) 93 I told them that it is quite an easy thing for a horseman to throw a beast, and described how I had done so several times on the cattle-run at home. **1892** *NZ Official Handbook* 157 On a cattle-run the tasks of mustering and drafting the stock and branding the youngsters are very heavy work. **1926** DEVANNY *Butcher Shop* 181) 28 Sawmills, flaxmills, sheep-stations and cattle-runs encircled it in all directions. **1939** BEATTIE *First White Boy Born Otago* 160 Wilkin and Thomson owned The Forks, which was a cattle run. **1927** *NZ Dairy Produce Exporter* 23 July 43 We were in a '**cattle-sick**' area, and Arabella was developing signs of the disease. **1929** *TrNZI* LX. 47 The first three local names of the disease 'Tauranga disease', 'Bush sickness' and '**Cattle sickness**', are misleading... Sheep are more susceptible than cattle to the ailment. **1950** *NZJAg.* July LXXXI. 67 This theory [of its being due to iron deficiency] was exploded when it was found that certain brands of limonite were ineffective in remedying 'cattle sickness' or 'bush sickness' as it was called. **1843** DEANS *Pioneers* (1964) 80 William Rankin has gone up to the **cattle station** for a month to see how he likes it. **1848** *NZ Jrnl.* VIII. 71 There are thirteen sheep and cattle stations established in the district, the runs being leased from the natives. **1851** *Lyttelton Times* 8 Mar. 2 A Canterbury Colonist..wishes to meet with a Gentleman whom he would assist in working his farm, or he would undertake the entire management of a cattle Station or Farm. **1871** MONEY *Knocking About NZ* 85 He was one of the owners of Tarndale, the largest cattle-station in the country. **1928** *Weekly News* 12 Jan. [Caption] White Rock is one of the largest sheep and cattle stations in the Dominion. **1945** HALL-JONES *Hist. Southland* 86 He acquired the stock at McKoy's cattle station, Sandy Point. **1902** *Settler's Handbook of NZ* 281 With **cattle-yards**, yards for dairy purposes, the dearest are from start to finish the cheapest.

cattle dog.

1. [AND 1868.] A dog trained to work cattle.

1843 DEANS *Pioneers* (1964) 18 Good cattle and sheep dogs are indispensable and difficult to be got. **1865** CHUDLEIGH *Diary* 26 Oct. (1950) 202 He is very sharpe [*sic*], his fighting qualities will make him a good cattle dog and I have named him Thug. **1878** ELWELL *Boy Colonists* 48 Fricker..[was] delighted to shew the 'new chum' how to work a cattle dog. **1882** HAY *Brighter Britain* I. 204 But clever, well-trained cattle-dogs are a treasure beyond price in the bush. **1966** *Encycl. NZ* I. 493 *Cattle Dogs:* Most of the cattle in New Zealand are worked by sheep dogs. **1986** CARR *Diary Pig Hunter* 30 And there was Tiger, a big black dog—part cattle dog, part boxer and part kelpie—but wholly pig dog.

2. *transf.* [An alteration of a play on *Cathol*(ic ['kætəlɪk] + *dog*.] (Usu.) a State schoolchild's abusive term for a Catholic schoolchild. (Often found in children's rhymes. e.g. Cattledogs, cattledogs, Live in trees and under logs... And don't eat meat on Fridays.)

1962 LAWLOR *More Wellington Days* 132 Protestants used to call the Catholic schoolchildren 'Cattle Dogs'. **1973** McCARTHY *Listen..!* 21 It was only natural that we 'Cattledogs' [from Marist Brothers School, Tasman Street, c1916] were frequently ambushed by those 'Proddyhoppers' [from Mount Cook State School]. **1988** McGILL *Dict. Kiwi Slang* 26 *cattle dog* Protestant term of abuse for a Catholic. **1992** PARK *Fence around the Cuckoo* 94 We children had a kind of good humoured rivalry, admittedly, often shouting, 'Yah yah, Cattledog!' or 'Proddyhopper!' as the case might be, but that was all.

cattle-stop. A device in a roadway or track, esp. at a farm road-entrance (or earlier, at a railway crossing), usu. made of spaced (often loose) wooden bars or steel pipes over a pit. See also *cattle-catcher*, *cattle-pit* (CATTLE 2).

[*Note*] In Austral. and Brit., use and also occas. in NZ, (*cattle-*)*grid* is preferred.

1934 SCANLAN *Winds of Heaven* 176 Mike knew there was a cattle-stop between the road and the [railway station] platform. **1949** DAVIN *Roads from Home* 250 John worked his way round the cattlestops by the..glare of the engine's firebox. **1952** RHODES *Fly Away Peter* 108 He passed the Mount Solomon [station] mail-box, rattled over a cattle-stop and drew up in a small paddock. **1973** WHEELER *Hist. Sheep Stations of NI* 67 'Today, Colin,' he goes on, as we rattle over the cattlestop, 'farmers tend to bend with every breeze.' **1988** FRAME *The Carpathians* 194 A man stood in front of the gate of the village, by the cattle-stop. **1991** *Dominion* (Wellington) 2 Nov. 10 First-time cattle-stop crossers often clutch nervously at their steering wheel, as their entrance is greeted by what sounds like a burst of heavy machine-gun fire beneath their bows.

caucus /'kɔkəs/. [Transf. use of US *caucus* a private meeting of the leaders or representatives of a political party: see OED 1; AND 1887.] A meeting in committee of the parliamentary members of a political group, faction, or party; such members as a group (see also 1886 quot.). Also *attrib.* or Comb. **caucus meeting**; and, rarely, **caucus** *v. intr.*, to meet in caucus (see quot. 1995).

1876 *NZPD* XX. 73 [Robert Stout] I am not aware that Ministers of the Crown have been in the habit of bringing before Parliament what took place at a meeting of their supporters. It is supposed that these things are done secretly; and if it is parliamentary to refer to such things as a caucus meeting, I can only assume we are getting sort of Americanized in some of our proceedings, and this serves as the first step in making us acquainted with caucuses and rings. **1876** *Saturday Advertiser* (Dunedin) 22 July 11 Wellington, July 21st. The Mimbers are wastin' the counthry's time houldin Kaukass meetins. *Ibid.* 5 Aug. 9 ['Paddy Murphy' reporting House of Representatives from Wellington] At a Kawkass meetin' held a few nights since, wid miself in the chair, it was unanimously resolved that the country be cut up into three powerful inchular kingdoms, to consist of the North, the Middle, and the South Islands. **1886** *NZ Herald* (Auckland) 1 June 4 The Auckland members are to have a caucus this morning, to consider what action should be taken in connection with the appropriation. **1896** SAUNDERS *History of NZ* I. 446 The debate was adjourned from the 26th to the 28th of June [1861], when the Government avoided defeat by adopting an amendment..which had been.. unanimously adopted at an Opposition caucus. **1907** in *Fowlds Papers—Politics* (1980) 6 1907, 8 July—Last week..one of the most successful caucus meetings of the Party I have ever seen and Sir Joseph handled it with consummate skill. **1936** LEE *Diaries* (1981) 18 29 March Caucus on superannuation. Caucus committee brought down a magnificent report. **1948** LIPSON *Politics of Equality* 123 Sporadically for two decades parliamentary party meetings were held as occasion required, though not until 1876 was the term 'caucus' introduced to describe them. *Ibid.* 127 The very word 'caucus', which was first used by Stout in 1876 as opprobriously as Disraeli applied it in England in 1878, soon lost its early unsavory connotation. **1962** SCOTT *NZ Constitution* 110 In recent years the organization of caucus in both parties has become more formal. **1979** PALMER *Unbridled Power?* 25 The role of caucus is one of the minor mysteries of New Zealand government. **1995** *Sunday Star-Times* (Auckland) 10 Sept. C2 Labour has been caucusing in Whangarei, honing its strategy —and wisely so.

Cavalier. [A play on *Cavalier* both as a noun self-righteously suggesting (but also subverting) an association with the 17th century Royalist favourite of popular romance; and as an adjective applied to one who 'behaves arrogantly without considering the feelings of other people or the seriousness of a situation' (*Collins Cobuild Eng. Language Dict.* (1987).] In *pl.*, a name taken by a group of rugby union players who in 1986 chose to play representative games in South Africa against the wishes of the New Zealand rugby authorities; a member of that team. Also *attrib.*

1986 *Listener* 7 June 31 Ces Blazey promised that the business of the rebel Cavaliers tour would *not* be swept under the carpet. **1986** *Dominion* (Wellington) 21 Aug. 22 With the All Blacks assembling to prepare for the second test, captain David Kirk says he hopes the word 'Cavalier' will slip from New Zealanders' vocabulary. **1986** *Illustr. Encycl. NZ* 517 [Caption] Andy Haden, All Black and Cavalier rugby player, during his 11th game and 39th test for New Zealand... He was a member of the Cavaliers team whose surreptitiously arranged tour of South Africa took place in 1986. **1988** HADEN *Lock, Stock 'n Barrel* 88 The birth and bringing together of the Cavaliers was a fragmented business bubbling with intrigue. **1991** *Dominion* (Wellington) 30 Mar. 10 He returned to South Africa, was arrested and interrogated at the same time as our odious 'Cavaliers' were sneaking out the back door of New Zealand in order to play rugby with South Africa. **1995** *Metro* (Auckland) Dec. 113 Luyt paid teams like the infamous Cavaliers to ignore the ban [on playing sport in South Africa].

cave: see SNOW CAVE *n.*

cavel /'kævəl/. *Coalmining.* Also **cavil.** [f. northern or Northumberland dial. *cavel* a lot (that is cast), applied to lots drawn to determine in which 'bord' each miner should work: see OED *n.*[1] 1.] A drawing of lots among miners to determine their places (and mates) at the coalface, esp. for the easiest or most profitable place. Also as *v.* **cavil for** (places), and *vbl. n.* **cavilling.**

1897 in 1900 *Awards, etc.* 186 All coal to be cavilled for every three months... All men who are competent to be included in the cavil. **1904** *Awards, etc.* 8 [Hikurangi Coal-Miners Agreement] If there be more than one man to shift from any district at one time, they cavil for the fresh places; the truckers to cavil for places the same as general cavil... Should the manager have any special work inside the mine he must call for volunteers, to be approved by the manager, three clear days before a cavil. *Ibid.* 101 Men wishing to change mates can do so at cavilling. **1963** PEARSON *Coal Flat* 420 cavel: The casting of lots by which miners are assigned their places on the coal-face and the mates they will work with. *Ibid.* 206 In the last cavel Jock had been paired with Ben Nicholson. **1981** *Listener* 2 May 43 The extinct *cavel*—the drawing of lots for places in the mine is anything but extinct. The *cavel* takes place every three months on the West Coast and, apart from the chance of a change, 'the cavel day' is looked forward to by all at the mine as it involves a short, two-hour shift.

cave weta: see WETA 2 (1).

caw, *v.* Also **core.** [Prob. f. Sc. *caw*: cf. SND *ca, caw*[1]. 4. 'to set or keep in motion'.] *intr.* To turn a skipping rope.

ca1920-28 p.c. Les Souness. Southland and Dunedin. The usual children's term for turning a skipping rope, e.g. 'your turn to caw', also wind (*sc.* a handle on top of a well). **1982** FRAME *Is-land* 72 Nora Bone..whose need [to join in] was so strong that she always offered to 'core for ever', that is, turn and turn the skipping rope and never herself join in the skipping.

cawcaw, var. KAKA.

cawdi(e), var. KAURI.

cawpie, var. KAPAI.

cedar. [*Spec.* use of *cedar* for any of various trees more or less resembling those of the genus *Cedrus.*]

1. Any of three trees of genera thought to resemble the European cedar: *Dysoxylum* (KOHEKOHE) and *Libocedrus* (KAWAKA, PAHAUTEA).

1830 CRAIK *New Zealanders* 175 Crozet..asserts in his account of Marion's voyage that they found what he calls the cedar of New Zealand to weigh no heavier than the best Riga fir. **1848** New Zealand cedar [see KOHEKOHE]. **1869** *TrNZI* I. (rev. edn.) 192 Cedar (*Libocedrus Doniana*), a handsome conical tree, with reddish wood, fit only for inside work. **1875** KIRK *Durability NZ Timbers* 13 Cedar—Pahautea.- (*Libocedrus bidwillii*). *Ibid.* 14 In the North Island the native kohe-kohe (*Dysoxylum spectabile*), which yields a tough reddish-coloured wood..is also called cedar by the settlers. **1883** HECTOR *Handbook NZ* 122 *Libocedrus doniana*... Kawaka, Cypress, Cedar. This handsome tree attains a height of 60–100 feet, and a diameter of 3–5 feet. Wood reddish, fine-grained and heavy. *Ibid.* 123 *Libocedrus bidwillii*... Pahautea, Cedar. A handsome conical tree 60–80 feet high, 2–3 feet in diameter. **1890** *PWD Catalogue Timbers* (NZ & South Seas Exhib.) 10 Kawaka (cedar)..Timber dark red colour, straight and even in grain. *Ibid.* 11 Kohekohe (cedar)..Dysoxylum spectabile..Wood light, soft, and easily worked, heart blood-red in colour. **1896** HARPER *Pioneer Work* 35 It is always possible to build a good..'mai-mai' with bark stripped from the rata.., totara..or cedar (*Libocedrus Bidwillii*) trees. **1902** *Settler's Handbook NZ* 119 Cedar, or pahautea, pokaka, and hinau are not unfrequent. **1936** [see KOHEKOHE]. **1958** *Tararua* Sept. 13 Still foreign to my Tararua-trained eyes were the handsome, symmetrical cedars..of the [Ruahine] forest. **1966** *Encycl. NZ* III. 711 Cedar, New Zealand . . kawaka, kaikawaka . . *Libocedrus plumosa* . . pahautea . . *L. bidwillii.*

2. With a modifier: **mountain**, **native** (or **New Zealand**).

(1) **mountain cedar.** (*Libocedrus bidwillii*), PAHAUTEA (syn. KAIKAWAKA).

1865 CHUDLEIGH *Diary* 9 Jan. (1950) 158 The mountain cedar is found here [past Mesopotamia]. **1909** *AJHR* C-11 2 Here, the mountain-cedar or pahautea, locally kaikawaka (*Libocedrus Bidwillii*)..appear..among the conifers. **1936** BELSHAW et al. *Agric. Organiz. NZ* 578 The chief indigenous trees of commercial value are:.. Miro.., Kaikawaka or mountain cedar. **1961** MARTIN *Flora NZ* 171 [Kawaka] is the commoner species in the North Island as the Pahautea or Mountain cedar is in the South Island. **1978** *Manawatu Tramping Club Jubilee* 117 [Ruapehu] At times the bush turned from beech to silver pine and the long lanky boles of the mountain cedar with its sparse foliage and naked trunk stood out above the canopy. **1988** DAWSON *Forest Vines to Snow Tussocks* 82 I have observed it [*sc.* mountain five-finger] growing as an epiphyte on kaikawaka or mountain cedar..on Mt. Taranaki.

(2) **native** (or **New Zealand**) **cedar.** *Libocedrus plumosa,* KAWAKA, KOHEKOHE.

1867 HOCHSTETTER *NZ* 159 Kohekohe N.Z. cedar. **1889** FEATON *Art Album NZ Flora* 83 The Kohekohe..is indigenous to the Northern Island, but is often local... The tree is generally called by the settlers 'The native Cedar'. **1889** *Canterbury Resources and Progress* 35 Venetian Blind, manufactured from New Zealand Cedar. **1907** [see KOHEKOHE]. **1908** *AJHR* C-14 35 *Libocedrus Doniana* Kawaka New Zealand cedar, New Zealand arbor vitae..Tall tree, with deciduous bark. **1922** COWAN *NZ Wars* (1955) I. 452 This Pukekohe East stockade..consisted of New Zealand cedar (*kohekohe*) logs. **1957** WILLIAMS *Dict. Maori Lang.* 110 *Kawaka..Libocedrus plumosa,* New Zealand cedar. **1981** [see KAIKAWAKA].

celery.

1. Applied to two *Apium* species (fam. Apiaceae), esp. to the native coastal herb of variable form *Apium prostratum* (formerly *A. australe* and *A. filiforme*) and, less commonly, to the introduced Eurasian erect biennial *A. graveolens.*

1769 COOK *Journals* 27 Oct. (1955) I. 184 The other place I landed at was at the north point of the Bay where I got as much Sellery and Scurvy grass as loaded the Boat. **1777** FORSTER *Voyage Round World* I. 187 Another inconvenience of Dusky Bay is the want of celery, scurvy-grass, and other antiscorbutics. **1869** *TrNZI* I. (rev. edn.) 203 Celery. *Apium australe.*

2. With a modifier: **Maori** (or **native**), **wild**.

(1) **Maori** (or **native**) **celery.** *Apium prostratum.* See also PARSLEY 1.

1867 HOOKER *Handbook* 764 Celery, native. *Apium australe.* **1882** HAY *Brighter Britain* II. 211 Then there is the native celery..which might be eaten. **1907** Maori celery [see PARSLEY 1]. **1952** RICHARDS *Chatham Is.* 37 *Apium..prostratum...* Native celery has a root as thick as a thumb and thick prostrate stems 10–24 in. long. **1969** *Standard Common Names Weeds* 12 celery, Maori *Apium australe.* **1981** BROOKER et al. *NZ Medicinal Plants* 96 *Apium australe.* Common names: *Maori celery, green celery, prostrate parsley.* Maori name: *Tutae koau.* **1982** WILSON *Stewart Is. Plants* 148 *Apium prostratum* Native celery... Shore parsley..Variable, sprawling almost hairless herb with glossy green leaves tasting of celery... Common, coastal rocks, banks, turf, saltmarsh.

(2) **wild celery.** *A. prostratum.* [AND 1788].

1769 COOK *Journals* 22 Oct. (1955) I. 183 There is plenty of wild sellery and we purchased of the natives about 10 or 15 pounds of sweet Potatous.' [*sic*] **1773** FORSTER *Resolution Jrnl.* 8 June (1982) II. 297 The wild *Sellery* was not in flower & we could not determine to which genus of Umbellated plants it belongs. **1817** [see PARSLEY 1]. **1838** POLACK *NZ* I. 291 The *turnip* is found in a wild state over the entire country, as also wild *radishes, garlick, celery..&c.* **1841** WEEKES *Journal* Aug. in Rutherford & Skinner *Establish. New Plymouth* (1940) 53 There is some clayish soil..with some..wild celery and various native plants. **1911** *TrNZI* XLIII. 200 Among the herbs may be mentioned the wild celery (*Apium prostratum*). **1925-26** *NZJST* VIII. 200 Among the shore-plants..are the wild celery. **1968** JOHNSON *Turn of Tide* 74 On making New Zealand, Cook was pleased to find wild celery growing in profusion. **1971** *New Zealand's Heritage* I. 113 Wild celery was used, too. Its botanical name is *Apium prostratum*, and it is still plentiful along our shores. **1995** [see ICE-PLANT].

celery(-leaved), celery-top(ped) pine: see PINE 2 (4).

celmesia, var. CELMISIA.

celmisia. Formerly also **celmesia.** [The plant genus *Celmisia* was named by Count Cassini in 1825 from Celmis, a corybantic priestess of the goddess Cybele.] A plant of the predominantly New Zealand genus *Celmisia* (fam. Asteraceae); COTTON PLANT, *mountain daisy* (DAISY 2 (7)). See also ASTER 1, TIKUMU.

1856 ROBERTS *Diary* in Beattie *Early Runholding* (1947) 18 A large celmesia, or cotton plant, [was] growing very abundantly, the leaves long and narrow with a soft down on the under part of the leaf and a white flower like a large moon daisy. **1869** *TrNZI* I. (rev. edn.) 85 Near the summit..a Celmisia..was collected. **1889** *Zealandia* I. 27 [We left] a wooden cross, wreathed with beautiful celmesias and alpine lilies, to mark the spot where he was last seen. **1911** MORELAND *Through South Westland* 6 All this alpine meadow was beautiful with flowers: giant celmisias with satiny-white petals like enormous daisies. **1926** COWAN *Travel in NZ* II. 70 Most abundant are the..celmisia or mountain daisy, called by the Maoris *ti-kumu*. **1938** *Tararua Tramper* Feb. 15 Celmesias and ranunculus gave way to gaultheria and native broom. **1945** BEATTIE *Maori Place-names Canterbury* 65 Tikumu, the mountain celmisia, is also mentioned. The white fibrous down was scraped from its under side and manufactured in[to] taupa (leggings). **1968** SEDDON *The Seddons* 57 Daisy-like celmisias grew in drifts and between rocks near the series of little lakes at the top of the pass. **1988** DAWSON *Forest Vines to Snow Tussocks* 179 Mountain daisies or celmisias are probably the most frequently encountered of our alpine herbs.

cement. *Goldmining.* [AND 1858.] The layer at the base of, or within, an auriferous deposit consolidated by the chemical deposition of a natural cement, usu. iron oxide or silica. See also *blue country* (BLUE *a*. 3).

1862 WEKEY *Otago As It Is* 21 The mere prevalence of blocks of 'cement', as it is technically termed..forms no sure indication of the presence of a lead. **1865** *AJHR* C-4A 1 The discovery..of an immense belt of auriferous tertiaries—the 'cement' of the miners—in the District of Gabriel's. **1871** *TrNZI* III. 276 I will also direct your attention to the specimens of light-coloured cements, which I chipped from blocks of various sizes weighing from several tons to a few pounds... The brown-coloured cement I have seen in the Shag Valley, at Mount Watkin, and along the lower spurs of ranges of the West Taieri. **1887** PYKE *Hist. Early Gold Discoveries in Otago* (1962) 141 Beneath the [underlying soil of the old tertiary] is a bed of 'cement', which has not yet been determined. Gold was found in each and all of these. The deposit spoken of as 'cement' had been traced in a direct and continuous line from the Blue Spur. **1896** MOFFATT *Adventures* (1979) 58 The wash was about six inches thick, lying on a false bottom, consisting of a thin layer of rusty cement, and under that thin white gravel [at Gabriel's Gully]. **1907** *NZGeol.SB (NS)* No.3 93 On the vein stuff pinching out, attention was turned to the highly brecciated, recemented surface débris from the gossan of the reef, locally known as 'cement'. **1918** *NZGeol.SB (NS)* No.19 13 This conglomerate, which will be shown subsequently to be of Early Tertiary age, received the local name of 'cement', and this has been retained to the present day. *Ibid.* 52 The boulders and pebbles of the conglomerate are firmly united together by fine-grained detritus. Slight chemical changes within this fine-grained matter have caused it to set relatively hard, and thus justify the application of the miners' term 'cement' to the whole deposit. **1932** *NZJST* XIII. 263 The cementing medium of the deposit is finely comminuted fresh mica-schist, resembling coarsely ground cement, hence the term 'cement' applied by the miners to this and similar deposits. In the zone of weathering the 'cement' is a rusty-brown colour. Below the zone of weathering lies the unaltered 'cement' which forms the 'blue ground' of the miners. **1967** MAY *West Coast Gold Rushes* (1962) 226 Diggers on these earliest-discovered cement-leads had pioneered techniques generally adopted in the lower Waimea. **1983** *NZ Geol Memoir No.4* 30 The so-called gold-bearing cements.

centennial /sənˈtenjəl/ or /-ˈtinjəl/. [As a noun used occas. in US (see OED *centennial* B, 1876): used in NZ from c1940, first as a shortened form of *Centennial Exhibition*.] A hundredth anniversary or its celebrations, *spec*. the hundredth anniversary in 1940 of the signing of the Treaty of Waitangi; a centenary. Cf. SESQUI. [*Note*] R. Mason states (1953, *fide* her father, the Hon. H.G.R. Mason, a Labour Cabinet Minister at the time): 'New Zealand had a *centennial* in 1940, not a *centenary*. Australia had a *centenary*. No one could decide whether to pronounce the second *e* in *centenary*, [e] or [i], and *centennial* was deliberately chosen by the NZ Government to attempt to avoid the difficulty.' Mason Collect. (1953).

1940 MCCORMICK *Lett. & Art in NZ* viii Some readers will have seen..the Centennial Exhibition of New Zealand Art. *Ibid*. 194 Government patronage of artists has more recently marked the celebration of New Zealand's Centennial. **1946** SOLJAK *NZ* 102 Celebration of the Dominion Centennial in 1940 impressed on New Zealanders the fact that their country had attained its place in history. **1968** SLATTER *Pagan Game* 172 Here he collapsed..his head whirling and glowing like a fireworks display at the Centennial. **1989** *Dominion* (Wellington) 14 Mar. 8 The Netherton School and District celebrates its centennial on March 2–3, 1990.

Central.

a. Usu. in the collocation **Central Otago** (or **Otago Central**) but also *ellipt*. **Central, the Central**, an area of Otago generally taking in the broad catchment of the Upper Clutha River, and characterized by a dry climate, seasonal extremes of temperature, generally arid vegetation, schist outcrops, a history of goldmining, orcharding and tourism, and a largely self-contained structure of local government. See also b below, quot. 1948.

1899 *TrNZI* XXXI. 400 Such scrub occurs more or less on all the high mountains; but on the drier ones— such as those of Central Otago, East Nelson, Marlborough, or the eastern portions of the Southern Alps. **1909** THOMPSON *Ballads About Business* 89 From the wild Otago Central to Otago's biggest town. **1929** SMYTH *Bonzer Jones* 94 Know th' Central. **1930** *NZ Short Stories* 13 Our station was in Central Otago, high up on the slopes of the great ranges. **1939** BEATTIE *First White Boy Born Otago* 116 The Central was an area of far horizons then. *Ibid*. 118 Some of the Central runs had been applied for at the Dunedin Land Office late in 1857 and others during 1858. **1943** HISLOP *Pure Gold* 28 Fresh fish is a luxury in the Central in the summer. **1947** BEATTIE *Early Runholding* 25 Two travellers through Otago Central in 1859 saw only one woman. **1948** *Our Own Country* 132 If we were thinking of taking up farming in Central his advice was, 'Clear out the rabbits and get a good wife.' **1959** DAVIN *No Remittance* 42 He'd arrived too late for..the big strikes round Central Otago but he'd..gone back to Central later with the dredgers. **1992** ANDERSON *Portrait Artist's Wife* 263 Max had disappeared, he was reputed to have gone down to Central but no one was sure.

b. In the phr. **up Central**.

1948 COWAN *Down the Yrs. in the Maniototo* 2 At one time then the Maniototo County..was practically Central Otago itself. Indeed, there are many people even to-day who visualise only this area when they talk about 'up Central'. **1963** DUCKWORTH *Barbarous Tongue* 181 'Is Timothy in with Mrs Flint?' 'No, she's gone to her brother's crib for the weekend—up Central.' **1971** ARMFELT *Catching Up* 151 People from Waitapa often went 'up Central' to Alexandra. **1995** ANDERSON *House Guest* 176 He laughed with..the pleasure of being up Central where the air is.

Centralism. *Hist*. The name for the point of view, or the movement, current until the abolition of provinces in 1876, supporting the absolute authority of the central General Assembly over that of the several Provincial Councils, or over provincial government *per se*. Contrast PROVINCIALISM.

1856 *Richmond-Atkinson Papers* (1960) I. 214 [Sewell] is inclined to Centralism in every thing but finance but is not strong enough to face the [Provincial] Superintendents. **1856** FITZGERALD *Lett. to Electors Lyttelton* 5 Half the recent session was occupied in a struggle between Centralism and Provincialism. **1862** *NZ Advertiser* 26 Sept. 'Centralism' and 'provincialism' were the watchwords used by the contending parties to represent the same thing. **1953** [see PROVINCIALISM]. **1966** *Encycl. NZ* I. 144 In 1873 Ballance entered politics... The main issue was provincialism versus centralism.

Hence (often init. cap.) **centralist**, *n*., one advocating or supporting Centralism. Also *attrib*.

1858, 1859 [see *Provincialist* (PROVINCIALISM)]. **1865** HURSTHOUSE *England's NZ War* 49 In civil matters we are not Whigs and Tories in New Zealand, but 'Centralists' and 'Provincialists', that is those who would govern New Zealand by *one* Parliament, and those who should govern her by many. **1868** *Punch in Wellington* 34 Mr. John Cargill begs to call the attention of recently elected Members of Parliament to his Stock of *Centralist Opinions*. **1875** MACANDREW *Address to People of Otago* 14 If there should be more than one anti-Centralist candidate for the same seat, the chances are that the centralist candidate..may be a minority of the constituency. **1948** LIPSON *Politics of Equality* Centralists [in the 1870s], when they sought to cripple the provinces, naturally aimed first at their lands. **1959** SINCLAIR *Hist. NZ* 106 There were in the House of Representatives in the fifties, less clearly thereafter, two loose groups which were called the 'Centralist' and the 'Provincialist' parties. **1966** *Encycl. NZ* I. 144 As a supporter of Stafford's..'Centralist' policy, Ballance retired in favour of Sir Harry Atkinson. **1987** *NZJH* Apr. 48 With..two new members, Harry Atkinson and Charles Bowen, representing Stafford's centralist faction in the government, the opposition was made up of an angry rump of provincialists, mainly from Auckland and led by Grey.

centurion. A member of a Wellington rugby union club or team formed from senior or experienced players (orig. from past provincial representatives) to foster and encourage the game at all levels; a rugby player invited to play for a centurion club or team. Also in Canterbury and Otago (see 1971, 1979 quots.) a player who has played 100 games as a provincial representative. Usu. init. cap. in the name of a team.

1971 *Evening Star 7 O'clock* (Dunedin) 18 Sept. 6 (Griffiths Collect.) Salute Mike Hanham, who became Mid-Canterbury's second only rugby centurion when he led his team against North Otago at Oamaru this week. **1979** *Otago Daily Times* (Dunedin) 28 Mar. 21 (Griffiths Collect.) The 'centurion' still wears a sword and armour, though the New Zealand centurion is more usually a much-capped rugby hero. **1982** *Dominion* (Wellington) 7 July 20 The Wellington Centurions rugby team to play Marlborough at Blenheim's Lansdowne Park on Sunday, July 18, is a mixture of old and new. **1984** *Dominion* (Wellington) 23 Mar. 19 [Advt] Festival Rugby..Auckland Barbarians XV v Wellington Centurions. **1985** JONES *Gilmore's Dairy* 44 Terry left school at the end of the fifth form, although he would have been a dead certainty for the Centurions next season. There were All Blacks who had been Centurions.

cervena /sɜːˈvenə/. A commercially generated trade-name for farm-produced venison.

1993 *North & South* (Auckland) June 60 We started with 4500 names before coming down to Cervena [pronounced sir-venn-ah, derived from the Latin family name for deer, Cervidae, plus ven for venison and 'a' for premium, in total meaning nothing, like Kodak or Lego].

c.f.a.: see *cast-for-age* (CAST *a.* 2).

chaffie, *Obs.* Also **chaffy**. [f. *chaff* chopped straw (or perh. *chaff*(hand))+ -IE.] A threshing-mill hand dealing with the straw.
1917 *Otago Witness* (Dunedin) 11 Apr. 23 The mills here are now equipped with pipes and fans to blow a strong current of air through them to carry away the chaff, thus dispensing with the services of a 'chaffy'. **1951** DUFF *Shepherd's Calendar* 17 May (1961) 30 Today I was No. 4 of the crew of a header harvester... Fifty years ago I would have been No. 12, 'Chaffy', the dirtiest and most despised member of the gang. **1954** MILLER *Beyond the Blue Mountains* 112 Dugald was chaffy and had time to stand and muse while the chaff sheet filled. **1971** OGILVIE *Moonshine Country* 151 About a dozen men were needed [c1880] to operate such a [threshing] mill. The engine driver who was the boss, the 'feeder' who fed in the sheaves, three men at the bags, three who forked the sheaves to the 'feeder', a cook, a 'water joey', and a 'chaffie'. **1984** *Knapdale Run* 148 [When the threshing mill was working] the 'chaffy'..brought round threshed straw to the bag hole end to make a bed and cover for the heap of [full wheat] bags. **1990** MARTIN *Forgotten Worker* 130 There had to be enough of this [*sc.* straw], pulled round by the 'chaffy' at the beginning of the day to also cover the bags with a thick layer at the finish.

chaffy, var. CHAFFIE.

chain: see *drag the chain* (DRAG *v.* 1), *Queen's chain* (QUEEN 4 b).

chain, *n. Freezing works.* [Transf. use of *chain* a linked series.]
1. a. Also **killing chain**. The overhead moving chain on which carcasses are carried for processing in a freezing works, specifically often **beef chain**, **mutton chain** dealing respectively with beef or mutton carcasses; (any of) the group of various workers who work at different points on the chain.
1951 *Awards, etc.* 333 [NZ Freezing-Workers Award] *Chain Slaughtering.-* (*a*) Wherever used in this Section or any other part of this award, the term 'chain' shall mean and include every system whereby the killing and dressing of sheep and lambs is carried out in a series of successive operations executed by a number of slaughtermen, each of whom is engaged in one of the operations of the series, whatever may be the form of the system or whatever variation may be introduced into it... Not more than thirty-five men shall be employed on any mutton and lamb chain. **1959** SLATTER *Gun in My Hand* 67 Lambs hooked on to the chain and progressing slowly along while the row of men standing alongside slash and tear and nick with knives while others punch briskets or pull the skins from the swinging carcases. **1972** *Press* (Christchurch) 17 Oct. 1 Mutton chains throughout the country were idle yesterday over a dispute concerning the rate to be paid for a new job on the chain. **1974** beef chain [see CHILLER 2]. **1980** LELAND *Kiwi-Yankee Dict.* 23 The chain. In the freezing works where meat animals are butchered for New Zealand's most lucrative export trade, there is a kind of dis-assembly line where each person chops out the same portion of each carcass as it reaches him on an endless belt. **1986** *Metro* (Auckland) July 76 Across the road at Hellaby's they have a beef chain killing up to 850 a day, two mutton chains killing 3,200 each. **1991** *Metro* (Auckland) Nov. 76 He was working on the killing chain at the now defunct Feilding freezing works.

b. learners' chain, the chain on which beginners or 'apprentices' work.
1951 17 May Feilding Freezing Works terms p.c. Colin Gordon The *learners' chain* is called the *monkey chain*, and the new chaps are called *skulls*, from the chaffing at the beginning: e.g., 'Look at the skulls on them!', 'They've got the right-shaped head for it'. Learners retaliate by calling the old hands 'lavatory chains' or more frequently 'shithouse chains'. **1951** *Here & Now* Oct. 14 He shifted Alasdair out of the learners' chain into the professional gang. **1973** *Truth* 18 Dec. 56 Went Waingawa [freezing works] and got a job on the learners' chain. He worked his way on to the 'gun' chain in a couple of seasons. **1995** SLATTER *One More River* 53 [It was] not as well paid as a seagull on the wharf or a freezing worker on the learners' chain but a holiday job none-the-less. Then back to varsity.

2. Special Comb. chainman, an employee who works on the chain; **chain slaughtering**, **chain system**, the system of mass handling of the killing and processing of animals for meat, replacing the 'solo butcher' system in the 1930s.
1982 *Dominion* (Wellington) 10 Feb. 4 [The accused] **chainman**, was giving evidence in his trial. **1951** *Awards, etc.* 324 [NZ Freezing-Workers Award] [Rates of wages] Hourly rates of pay for **chain slaughtering**—All sheep and lambs, per hour [£]0 5[s.] 4½[d.]. **1956** DARE *Rouseabout Jane* 188 All the work was done on the **chain system**, each man doing the same job all the time, the carcass going slowly down the line until it was finished. **1974** *NZ Agric.* 189 The 'chain' system is used for slaughtering lambs, sheep, bobby calves, and pigs. **1982** *Dominion* (Wellington) 12 Mar. 9 At least eight of the present employees..were solo butchers at the time the chain system was introduced in 1956. **1989** PERRIAM *Where it all Began* 87 Under the chain system a recruit soon learned the knack of carrying out the specialised but limited job required of him.

chain lightning. Also **chained lightning**. [f. US *chain-lightning* inferior whisky.] Crude, often illicit, liquor. Cf. LIGHTNING-ROD.
1908 *Truth* 7 Nov. 8 Where as if they did likewise with good, wholesome beer—not chain-lightning brands—not half the harm would result. **1916** ANZAC *On the Anzac Trail* 77 Shebangs [in Cairo]..sell you whisky that takes the lining of your throat down with it..; a soothing liquid that licks 'forty-rod', 'chained lightning', or 'Cape smoke' to the back of creation. **1933** EADDY *Hull Down* 95 Most of the masters being well 'under the influence', and nearly all supplied with a parting gift of 'chain-lightning' whiskey. **1976** LEE *Soldier* 60 There's about two or three barrels of chain lightning. You can't have the chain lightning.

chalkie, *n.*¹ A cheap marble.
1938 HYDE *Godwits Fly* (1970) 26 Once Curly Adams' bag of marbles, glimmers and chalkies, came up [from the street-sewer] on the shovel. **1943** [see DUMP *n.* 2].

chalkie, *n.*² *Obs.* Also **chalky**. [Perh. reinforced by the general English term *chalkie* for a school-teacher.] A person who records on the chalk board of the Stock Exchange the quotation for each share traded. (Replaced by computerization, 21 June 1991.)
1986 *Consumer* June 144 As the sale [of shares on the Stock Exchange floor] proceeds, a 'chalky' records the quote for each share traded. **1988** *Listener* 12 Nov. 36 Chalkies were on television a lot last October..flitting from blackboard to blackboard, armed with chalk and duster, squiggling the hieroglyphs that rule the world via the stock exchange. **1991** *Dominion* (Wellington) 21 June 12 When the [Exchange trading] floor closes today, four staff including one chalkie will lose their jobs.

chalky, var. CHALKIE *n.*²

chalky, *a.* See GUM 2.

Chalon head. [f. the name of Alfred Edward Chalon (1780–1860), a fashionable portraitist (the first to paint Queen Victoria after her accession, who provided the design of the FULL FACE QUEEN) + *head* the image of a monarch on a stamp or coin.] FULL FACE QUEEN.
1967 *NZ Stamp Collector* XLVII. 96 Many early stamps—including our own Chalon heads—have been issued..in a multiplicity of shades. **1977** FRANKS *All the Stamps of NZ* 18 The design is from a painting of the young queen in her coronation robes, by Chalon, and this design..is sometimes referred to as the Chalon head. **1988** GWYNN *Collecting New Zealand Stamps* 4 This Chalon Head or Fullface Queen design..was magnificent; a British collector..called it 'the Rembrandt of philately—the most beautiful stamp in the world'.

chamber. *Freezing works.* [Spec. use of *chamber* a space or room for a purpose: see OED 9.]
1. Usu. short form of **freezing-chamber**, a room in a freezing works where carcasses can be frozen rapidly.
1900 *Auckland Weekly News* (Suppl.) 2 Feb. 6 [The carcasses] were sent gliding smoothly to the cooling chamber. **1901** *Awards, etc.* 438 [Canterbury Freezers Award] No freezers shall be asked to work outside at a lower rate of pay while work is going on in the chambers. **1986** *NZPOD* 118 *chamber..NZ & Austral.* room in freezing works where carcasses are frozen.

2. Special Comb. **chamberhand**, one who works in the freezing-chamber of a freezing works;.
1950 *Landfall* 14 125 The gang of chamber-hands..are already crossing the loci tracks up in front. **1985** LIND *Cut Above* 327 In the past, chamberhands had serviced the old cutting department. **1989** PERRIAM *Where it all Began* 130 The chamber hands were next to make an award.

change-house. *Mining.* [A var. of *changing-house*: see OED *changing vbl. n.* 4, 1884.] A place where miners can clean themselves and change clothes after an underground shift.
1911 *Maoriland Worker* 25 Aug. 10 It was pointed out by witnesses that without change-houses near the mine mouth, men were compelled to walk home..in their wet clothes. **1978** MCARA *Gold Mining* 315 *Changehouse*: The building in which the miners changed from their street clothes into their underground clothes and vice-versa. It had hot showers and equipment for washing and drying work-clothes.

changer. A marble so called because it could be changed or exchanged as the game demanded.
1951 FRAME *Lagoon* (1961) 116 I had pee-wees and bully taws and changers that weren't made of glass mind you. **1972** SUTTON-SMITH *Folkgames Children* 174 There were terms for marbles such as..'dubs', 'dates', 'stakes', 'dukes', or 'changers', referring to the marbles put down to be fired at.

changing shed. A building at a beach or swimming-baths in which one can change into or out of a bathing costume; a dressing-shed.
1985 MARSHALL *Secret Diary Telephonist* 10-11 Suzie..settled down for the day behind the changing sheds with ten men and a dozen half G's. **1987** HUTCHINS *Tall Half-Backs* 48 Mind you, he..spent..time..peeping..through the knot holes in the wall of the main girls' changing sheds. **1989** MARSHALL *Divided World* 188 Dusty suggested we spend time drilling a hole in the girls' changing sheds.

chaser: see *whale chaser* (WHALE 3).

chat, *n. Obs.* [See *v.*] In the phr. **to give** (occas. **get**) **the chat,** to give (or get) firm advice or remonstrance.
   1909 *Truth* 10 Apr. 3 Skipper Roberts had better give the 'chat' to play the game as it should be played. **1910** *Truth* 3 Sept. 3 The unspeakable dens..naturally attracted the attention of the police. The Mt. Cook officers were always on the alert, and, though powerless of take any action, the women were given the 'chat', and their business was conducted as privately as possible.

chat, *v.*
   1. [Spec. use of *chat* to advise, to 'chat up'.] *trans.* To give firm advice to (a person, often with an implication of reproof); to point out another's fault.
   c1926 THE MIXER *Transport Workers' Song Book* 69 He don't like to see others toiling, And he proves he's a 'tiger-skin', When he drinks with a bloke and chats him 'Why don't you join up and dig in.' **1971** SHIRLEY *Just a Bloody Piano Player* 112 I found out that other members of the band were being paid..more than I was. I talked to Bert and we both chatted the Manager. To my surprise..the discrepancy was removed.
   2. In the phr. **let me chat you,** let me tell you; take my advice!
   1937 PARTRIDGE *Dict. Slang* 478 *let me chat yer* (or *you*)*!* Let me tell you!: a New Zealand soldiers' c[atch] p[hrase] in the G.W.

chateau cardboard, chateau de cask. A joc. term for cask wine (see CASK).
   1986 *Metro* (Auckland) June 110 When it came to bulk wine the cheapest Chateau Cardboard is the best in the eyes of the average consumer. **1987** *Salient* (Wellington) 9 Mar. 2 Apparently..Jenny got a bit under the weather—but who wouldn't surrounded by such a bunch of socially diverse [student] politicos all hitting the chateau de cask on a Sunday avo? **1989** *Dominion* (Wellington) 1 Nov. 6 [Heading] Chateau cardboard expected to decline. A top Australian winemaker believes that the day of bag-in-the-box wines will soon be on the decline in New Zealand. **1994** *Cuisine* July 4 The everyday wine of a typical French family is of equal or less quality than some of our domestic 'Chateau Cardboard'.

Chatham Island.
   1. In the names of plants and animals, see: ASTER 2, BELLBIRD 2 (1), CRANESBILL, FANTAIL 2 (2), FERNBIRD 2, FLAX II 6, FORGET-ME-NOT, GERANIUM, LILY 2 (3), MOLLYMAWK 2 (4), OYSTERCATCHER 2 (2), PARAKEET 2 (2) and (3), PETREL 2 (4), PIGEON 2 (2), PIPIT, RAIL 2 (3), ROBIN 2 b, SHAG 2 (7) and (14), SMELT, SNIPE *n.*, TAIKO 2, THISTLE 2 (2), TIT *n.*¹ b, WARBLER 2 (2).
   2. Special Comb. **Chatham Island truck,** see quot. See also KONAKI 2.
   1984 HOLMES *Chatham Islands* 59 Before the coming of motorised transport, the mode of transportation was the 'Chatham Island Truck' (Konake), a wooden flat-decked horse or bullock-drawn vehicle, with iron or wooden wheels at the back and sledge runners on the front.

Chatham Islander.
   1. *Hist.* MORIORI 1 a.
   1841 DIEFFENBACH in Skinner *Moriorisof Chatham Is.* (1923) 35 The greater hue of the Chatham Islanders may be in great measure attributed to their greater exposure and still greater uncleanliness. **1881** *Auckland Star Saturday Suppl.* in Richards *Chatham Is.* (1982) 22 We had a Chatham Islander on board [in 1807], Hororeka. **1904** TREGEAR *Maori Race* 577 The Chatham Islanders were clever in making their sea-craft from the most unpromising materials.
   2. One born or resident in the Chatham Islands.
   1879 CHUDLEIGH *Diary* 23 June (1950) 281 Hood, Shand, Naera and three Maories and a white girl servant for some Chatham Islander. **1906** *Ibid.* 12 Mar. 432 Went to the Chief Postmaster..and stated that the Chatham Islanders..had gone too far to withdraw from the Canterbury Steamship Coy. **1989** *Listener* 13 Nov. 110 He has spoken with many of the present-day Chatham Islanders and to Moriori descendants in New Zealand. **1995** *Sunday Star-Times* (Auckland) 28 May sect. B 6 A breed apart from the English, [Manx people are] distinctive as the fiercely independent Chatham Islanders.

chaw, var. CHEW.

CHE /tʃi/. *pl.* **CHEs** /tʃiz/. [f. the acronym of *Crown Health Enterprise.*] A name chosen to replace *(Public) Hospital* in a modern context of managerial accountability and competition for health product.
   1992 *Evening Post* (Wellington) 7 Dec. 17 [Heading] 'Politics' behind creation of competing CHEs... We think it can be made line-ball, but that depends on each CHE Board.

check-pen. A stockyard pen in which sheep are held for checking.
   1922 *NZJAg.* Sept. XXV. 152 A further lot of sheep [can be] placed in the check-pen. **1947** HUTCHINSON *At Omatua's Fireside* 29 The manager [was] at race and check-pen. **1950** *NZJAg.* July LXXXI. 7 In larger sets of yards one or more of these drafting pens communicate, via a gate, with *the check pen(s)*... Since their purpose is to hold sheep while they are being checked over for mistakes in drafting and for treatment, these pens must be small. **1955** [see *drafting pen* (DRAFTING 2)].

check-shirt bird. *Obs.* [f. the banded appearance of its breast.] *shining cuckoo* (CUCKOO 2 (3)). Cf. ZEBRA BIRD.
   1896 HARPER *Pioneer Work* 147 On the way down [the Cook river from Tony's Rock] we saw a cuckoo, and his usual companion the 'check-shirt' bird... The former is the Maori koe-koea... The 'check-shirt' follows him in his migrations, and is often seen with him in the lower hills. **c1899** DOUGLAS in *Mr Explorer Douglas* (1957) 273 The Check Shirt or Spirit Bird. *Ibid.* The name check shirt is local and was given on account of its breast being marked with black and white like scotch [*sic*] tweed shirts.

cheerio. [Prob. formed from the drinking salutation *Cheerio:* AND 1965.] A small party sausage of the saveloy or frankfurter kind.
   1953 *NZ Observer* 11 Feb. 14 I'll get tomatoes and ham and cheerios... The cheerios went on, and the making of sandwiches, coffee and cocktails began. **1963** DUCKWORTH *Barbarous Tongue* 170 'It must be a party.'.. Peanuts and chippies and cheerios and cheese. **1986** RICHARDSON *Choices* 58 Sixth birthday... Cheerios on sticks and sauce to dip them in. **1991** *More* (Auckland) Mar. 66 I felt there should have been cheerios and tomato sauce, meat pies..pavlovas, lamingtons, sausage rolls..and thick cups of steaming tea.

cheese buster: see BUSTER *n.*⁴

cheese factory. A, usu. cooperative, dairy factory manufacturing cheese.
   1887 INGLIS *Our NZ Cousins* 91 A cheese factory has been started here [Gisborne] lately [c1885], and the cheese I tasted was exquisite in flavour. **1892** *NZ Official Handbook* 128 It is true that cheese factories are becoming numerous in Otago and Southland, with a few butter-factories. **1902** *Settler's Handbook NZ* 14 Eighty-seven butter- and cheese-factories were returned to 1st November, 1900, as at work in the Wellington Provincial District. **1957** *Mangamaire School 1897–1957* 5 Mangamaire was a dairying district and there was a busy cheese factory where farmers brought their milk daily.

cheese roll. Mainly *southern SI.* A thin slice of bread spread with a savoury cheese mixture, rolled up so that it keeps its roll form, then toasted.
   1979 *Favourite Recipes—Milton Home & School Cookery Book* 70 Cheese Roll Mixture 1 cup milk 1 chopped onion 1 cup tasty cheese grated 1 tbsp cornflour 55g butter... Spread the cooled mixture on fresh bread and roll up. These keep well in the freezer. To serve, toast or grill without thawing. Spread with margarine before grilling if frozen.

cheque. [AND 1857.] See also *bank cheque* (BANK *n.*²).
   1. The wages of esp. a seasonal worker paid usu. as a lump sum at the end of a job; the payment esp. to a farmer for produce sold, *spec. butter cheque, milk cheque, wool cheque* (see BUTTER 1, MILK, WOOL 3).
   1861 [see KNOCK DOWN *v.* 1]. **1890** *Otago Witness* (Dunedin) 30 Oct. 32 Whence [to our port of shipment] came all the bullock drivers' and shearers' cheques, to be 'knocked down' on their periodical 'bursts'. **1899** BELL *In Shadow of Bush* 22 When men were paid off from a contract, and came in with their cheques, a hearty welcome awaited them at the Cosmopolitan. **1903** *NZ Illustr. Mag.* VIII. 349 All parts of New Zealand send their quota of cocksfooters to 'make a cheque'. **1911** *TrNZI* XLIII. 440 Every acre..of grass represents a cow, whose yield of milk helps to swell the monthly cheque from the factory. **1924** ANTHONY *Follow the Call* (1975) 46 All through the winter Clive and I hoed into the firewood and knocked up a fair-sized cheque. **1938** HYDE *Nor Yrs. Condemn* 222 He comes back from New Zealand woolsheds each year with a big cheque. **1947** NEWTON *Waylego* 153 A musterer is usually paid by cheque at the end of the season, and refers to his pay as his cheque. **1960** SCRYMGEOUR *Memories Maoriland* 48 26 men on the board..making a good cheque on the soft cutting New Zealand flocks. **1981** [see BURN *n.*¹ 2].
   2. In the phr. **to knock down a cheque,** see KNOCK DOWN *v.* 1.
   3. Special Comb. **cheque proud. a.** [f. analogy with *collar-proud,* fretting at having to wear a collar, thus anxious to get rid of it.] Anxious to dispose of or 'knock down' a cheque.
   1934 *Press* (Christchurch) (Acland Gloss.) 13 Jan. 13 *Cheque proud.*—A station hand becomes c[heque] p[roud] when he wants a bust. He will be no good to himself or anyone else until he has spent his wages.
   b. Mean or 'tight' with money; not anxious to pay out.
   1978 PRESTON *Woolgatherers* 108 Next morning Jack [the overseer] solemnly paraded from one end of the shed to the other, ey[e]ing every shorn sheep critically and saying not a word... 'Look out fellers, the young bugger's cheque proud!'

cherry. *Obs.* Either MIRO or LACEBARK, two unrelated trees whose fruit was thought to resemble cherries.
1843 *Lett. from New Plymouth* (1968) 2 Mar. 22 There was one tree, which they call the cherry-tree, nineteen feet round. **1889** FEATON *Art Album NZ Flora* 54 Owing to the flowering habit of the tree [*sc.* lacebark], and its fruit being a depressed sphere, hanging on a long..stalk, it is commonly known by the settlers as the 'Wild Cherry'.

cherry birch: see BIRCH 3 (6).

Cherub. A fanciful name given to a 12 foot (3.66 m) sailing dinghy (designed by John Spencer in 1950 and built by R.G. Earley in 1951) which became the prototype of a popular national class, also later becoming established in Britain (1957) and Australia (1962).
1953 *Sea Spray* Apr. Nearly a full season has passed since the first Cherubs appeared. This 12 footer to the design of John Spencer was featured in the June 1952 issue of *Sea Spray*, and building plans and instructions offered to readers. **1974** *DB Yachting Annual* 125 The 1974 World Cherub Championships in Britain will go down as the series which New Zealand should have won but didn't.

chew, *n.* Also **chaw.** *Usu. pl.* A youngsters' name for a sweet or lolly.
1948 BALLANTYNE *Cunninghams* (1976) 97 He could buy things like chaws and pies out of his own earnings. **1950** SUTTON SMITH *Our Street* 48 He would spend it on biscuits and chews. **1964** HARVEY *Any Old Dollars Mister?* 122 People running up and down with luggage..and buying books and chews. **1982** SUTTON-SMITH *Hist. Children's Play* 115 It appears that the children then were more often urgently hungry than is the case today, when there is an ever-ready supply of school milk and 'chews' available. **1991** ELDRED-GRIGG *Shining City* 120 And then he said to me, ya want a chaw? And I said, nah, I've got my chuddy.

chew, *v.*
a. In the phr. **to chew** (one's) **ear** or **lug** (a var. of **bite**), to apply to and borrow (esp. money) from, to 'put the bite on' (someone). See also BITE *v.* 1.
1906 *Truth* 31 Mar. 6 If you ask a pal for money When you cannot 'strap a beer', Then you 'chew his lug', how funny, And what's more you 'bite his ear'. **1909** *Truth* 15 May 7 He 'made his marble good', he alleged, by paying up a score he owed, having for that purpose chewed the ear of an acquaintance he had providentially met in the street.
b. Esp. in quasi-passive constr. **to get (have) one's ear chewed,** to be wordily reprimanded, instructed, etc.
1918 *NZ at the Front* 109 And the Sergeant-Major's genial, And he doesn't 'chew your lug'.

Chewing's (fescue): see GRASS 2 (17) b.

chiack /ˈʃaiæk/, /ˈtʃaiæk/, /ˌʃaiˈæk/, *v.* Also **chiak, chyack, chyik, shi-ack, shyack.** [f. Brit. slang *chi-hike,* orig. a London cry of praise: see OED; AND 1853.] *trans.* To taunt, tease (a person); *intr.,* to indulge in (often friendly) teasing.
1889 in Bailey & Roth *Shanties* (1967) 120 Every man who dared 'chyack' her Found how well her arms were hung. **1904** LANCASTER *Sons o' Men* 42 [Station hand speaks] You're always chiackin' a fellow. **1908** *Truth* 7 Nov. 4 Did not 'chiack' Curran about his hat, and Curran did not tell him that he was always interfering with things that had nothing to do with his business. **1914** GRACE *Tale of Timber Town* 88 Go on chiacking—poke borak—it don't hurt me. *Ibid.* 116 You won't chiack or poke borak at his grey and honoured head. **1944** FULLARTON *Troop Target* 36 He was 'chyiked' unmercifully. **1951** PARK *Witch's Thorn* 67 She sat down at the table, looking..shyly at the boys who elbowed and kicked and chiacked their way to the table. **1988** MCGILL *Dict. Kiwi Slang* 26-27 *chiack* mock, tease, disparage, usually by sporting spectators, used by commentator in 1987 World Rugby Cup. **1993** *Evening Post* (Wellington) 23 Apr. 5 Just outside you can hear the Harawene whanau shyacking on Christmas Day as it lines up its families for commemorative photos.

Hence **chiacker,** one who chiacks; **chiacking** *vbl. n.* [AND 1853], cheeking, teasing.
1887 [see BARRACKER]. **1904** LANCASTER *Sons o' Men* 30 [Station hand speaks] Stop off yer **chiackin',** you fellers, can't yer? **1927** DEVANNY *Old Savage* 171 Something was wrong with him apart from the ass he had made of himself and Phillips' 'shi-acking'. **1975** *Press* (Christchurch) 1 Nov. 17 I will not say that this [neighbours' quarrel] has been an entirely one-sided affair as there has been chyacking from both camps over many months. **1978** JARDINE *Shadows on Hill* 44 After tea, during which he had to endure the usual chiacking from the other members of the team he caught and saddled his horse. **1993** O'SULLIVAN *Let the River Stand* 15 And because it was then so clear that no amount of shiyacking was going to touch him, the class laid off.

chiack, *n.* [f. verb.] Teasing, banter.
1955 BOWEN *Wool Away* 2 Shearers (all you good 'cobbers' that have shorn sheep) know the romance, glory, 'shi-ack' and fascination of this grand job. *Ibid.* 157 Shi-ack. The usual shed banter, from which none are excused. All in the shed from the boss to the 'rousie' can be the target of good-natured teasing. **1963** AUDLEY *No Boots for Mr. Moehau* 16 But everyody put theirs [*sc.* food offerings] into a pile..to make a beaut feast, girls too; everyone hoeing in with plenty of laughing and chiack.

chickweed. Also **native** (or **New Zealand**) **chickweed.** Any of several weedy herbs of *Stellaria* spp. (fam. Caryophyllaceae), esp. the native *S. parviflora* and the European weed *S. media.*
1843 DIEFFENBACH *Travels in NZ* I. 393 [Mokoia Island, Rotorua] was always well cultivated, and..European plantain, chickweed, and others, which in such cases generally spring up, vary agreeably the usually brown tint of the lower native vegetation. **1892** WILLIAMS *Dict. NZ Lang.* 64 *kohukohu,* n. *1 chickweed*; *Stellaria* sp. **1952** RICHARDS *Chatham Is.* 28 *Stellaria..parviflora...* New Zealand chickweed. **1982** WILSON *Stewart Is. Plants* 270 *Stellaria parviflora* Native chickweed.

chief. *Hist.* [Spec. use of *chief* a tribal leader.] Often with init. cap. MAORI CHIEF *n.*[1]
1769 COOK *Journals* 27 Nov. (1955) I. 213 In each of the Canoes were two or three Cheifs [*sic*] and the habits of these were superior to any we had yet seen, the Cloth they were made on was of the best sort and cover'd on the out side with Dog skins put on in such a manner as to look agreeable to the Eye. **1777** in Ledyard *Journal* Feb. (1963) 13 The New-Zealanders are generally well-made, strong and robust, particularly their chiefs, who among all the savage sons of war I ever saw, are the most formidable. **1814** MARSDEN *Lett. & Jrnls.* (1932) 86 The chiefs were all seated on the ground, according to their custom. **1839** JONES in Eccles & Reed *John Jones of Otago* 6 July (1949) 25 The stations generally occupied are purchased from the Native Chiefs. **1853** ROCHFORT *Adventures of Surveyor* 35 The old chief led me into his whare, where I was received by his wife, and the petty chiefs and women of the tribe. **1860** [see BISCUIT 1]. **c1875** MEREDITH *Adventuring in Maoriland* (1935) 151 As a rule Maoris are not allowed at the table d'hôte [in the Poverty Bay hotel]; but at one of the hotels the chiefs are permitted to have their meals with the pakehas. **1901** KEMP *Early Coloniz. Hist. NZ* 7 The chiefs demanded payment in gold within 48 hours. **1927** DONNE *Maori Past & Present* 97 The word 'Chief' is in general use in New Zealand to indicate the head man of a tribe or section of a tribe. **1949** BUCK *Coming of the Maori* 36 All the tribes trace their aristocratic lineages back to the chiefs of the voyaging canoes. **1960** SCRYMGEOUR *Memories Maoriland* 14 An aged chief remembered his ancestors playing each other and the forfeit was a Moriorie slave, who would be knocked on the head and roasted for a tribal feast. **1973** WALLACE *Generation Gap* 142 [The minister and his wife] lived on his mission station, a 100-acre block of land which was presented to him by..the local paramount chief.

Hence **chieflet,** a petty chief.
1952 RICHARDS *Chatham Islands* 128 Her marriage twenty years previously with Wi Te Tahuhu, a chieflet of the East Coast Maoris..who held no land in the Chathams.

chiefess: see CHIEFTAINESS.

chieftain. *Hist.* [Spec. use of *chieftain* a tribal or clan leader.] CHIEF.
1807 SAVAGE *Some Acc. of NZ* 12 The island is appropriated to the residence of a chieftain and his court. **1935** MAXWELL *Recollections* 120 Many writers have..failed to..recognise the great difference between the chieftain, or rangatira, class, and the ordinary, let alone the slave class. **1990** *Dominion* (Wellington) 22 Jan. 6 They took very great pains to ensure that the chieftains really understood the treaty.

Hence **chieftainship.**
1848 *McLean Diary* 26 May in Cowan *Sir Donald Maclean* (1940) 36 The elder men were dressed in their best dogskin..not neglecting their *méré pounamu* (greenstone clubs), and every other ancient emblem of chieftainship.

chieftainess. *Hist.* Also **chiefess, chieftess.** A Maori woman of chiefly rank.
1840 POLACK *Manners and Customs* II. [1] [Caption] A Haupatu, Chieftess of Waipoa. **1873** TINNE *Wonderland of the Antipodes* 66 The first visit we had was from Maria, a 'chiefess', who owns most of the estate on which we live. **1881** CAMPBELL *Poenamo* 161 Young chieftainesses were a cheap bait with which to lure and secure the Pakeha. **1905** *Weekly Press* (Christchurch) 25 Jan. 47 [Caption] Airini Karauria (Mrs G.P. Donnelly) a chieftainess of the Maoris. **1951** KOHERE *Autobiog. of a Maori* 54 The [war-]party would have succeeded if the chieftainess had not put out to sea in a canoe. **1972** *Marlborough Express* (Blenheim) 25 Sept. 6 The great-nephew of the chieftainess..and relatives followed Mrs Rongo into the tomb to tangi over the remains.

chieftess: see CHIEFTAINESS.

child. Used *attrib.* as special Comb. **child allowance,** a payment formerly made to the care-giving parent (usu. the mother) of children under 16 years (in some cases 18 years) of age; often called *family benefit* (as in Britain: see OED *family* 22); **Child Welfare,** a familiar shortening of the title of the former Child Welfare Division of the Department of Education, having statutory

responsibilities for children and young people now exercised by the Department of Social Welfare; also often used of the child welfare system in general.
1959 SLATTER *Gun in My Hand* 225 People in the pubs spending the **child allowance** on booze. **1964** ASHTON-WARNER *Bell Call* 57 I like the Child Allowance. And there'd be none of that without a government. *Ibid.* 56 And all this brandishing of paper we get from the Education Board these days. And from the **Child Welfare** and the court. **1980** THOMPSON *All My Lives* 12 Later when my mother's periods of disturbance become worse..the children are farmed out under Child Welfare.

children of the mist.

1. An early term for an isolated Maori tribal group.
1866 ANGAS *Polynesia* 120 Here and there [in the wild mountain region of south-west Nelson], in some secluded nook, a few miserable natives, the remnants of early fugitives from the massacres on the eastern side, true 'children of the mist' and 'wild men of the woods', have raised their little huts.

2. Also with init. caps. A name for the Tuhoe people.
1925 BEST *Tuhoe; the children of the mist* [Title]. **1938** HYDE *Nor Yrs. Condemn* (1986) 146 Tuhoe... Children of the Mist: a man named Elsdon Best had written a book about them, but books weren't much in Starkie's line. **1983** *Land of Mist* 19 The first people of the Urewera, the Tuhoe, are known as 'the Children of the Mist', because they are believed to be descendants from the marriage of Hine-pukohu-rangi, the celestial Mist Maiden, with the mountain. **1986** IHIMAERA *Matriarch* 5 And the Tuhoe, Children of the Mist, are to our west.

Chile(an). Also **Chilian**, in the names of plants, see: GRASS 2 (11) and (26) b.

chiller.

1. A farm animal (usu. a bullock) the carcass of which is to be chilled after slaughter.
1951 *Awards, etc.* 324 [NZ Freezing-Workers Award] [Rates of wages] Cattle, per head—Boners [£]0 3[s.] 0[d.] Freezers 0 3 2¼ Chillers 0 3 8. **1959** *NZJAg.* Aug. XCIX. 101 The field day demonstration at this unit showed how to attain the objective of putting off 12 chillers every three months from 150 acres carrying 600 ewes!

2. A cool-room for esp. beef carcasses, having a low temperature but above freezing-point. Also *attrib.*
1974 *Dominion* (Wellington) 8 Mar. 1 It is thought the beef chain will stop..when the chillers are full. *Ibid.* 9 Mar. 1 Beef boners and chiller hands were laid off. **1982** *Agric. Gloss.* (MAF) 33 *Chiller*: Cool room with temperature above freezing point.

chillybin. [f. a proprietary name.] A portable insulated (polystyrene) container for food and drink. Also *transf.* (see quot. 1995).
1974 *NZ Patent Office Records* CHILLYBIN Trade Mark application 110542 by Skellerup Industries Ltd: Cooling containers: abandoned 19 November 1979. **1976** MCDERMOTT *How to Get Lost and Found in NZ* 18 A chilly-bin is a polystyrene picnic hamper which will keep ice, cold drinks..cold up to ten hours, dependably. **1986** *Truth* 23 Mar. 2 The booze ban at Eden Park was carried too far. Two middle-aged ladies took their chilly-bin with lunch etc. and two cans of beer to wash the food down. Hard luck. **1990** DUFF *Once Were Warriors* 110 At the table with the borrowed from next-door's chilly bin on the table. **1995** *House &* *Home* (Wellington) July 11 [Heading] 'Chillibin' houses are good for warmth. A system of exterior cladding that is finding increasing acceptance..is the use of plastered polystyrene (known technically as EIFS—Exterior Insulation Finishing Systems).

chimney. *Whaling. Fig.* In the phr. **the chimney is on fire**, used of a dying sperm whale spouting blood and water.
1982 GRADY *Perano Whalers* 181 A soft groan comes from his [*sc.* the sperm whale's] open jaws. The sea is crimson with his blood, As he spouts, a crimson mist blows upwards, In old whaling vernacular 'the chimney is on fire'.

Chinaman, *n.*¹ *Otago goldmining.* [Prob. from the yellowish-brown colour of the stone.] Usu. cap. Also as **Chinaman stone**, a large stone composed of quartzite or ortho-quartzite found in auriferous gravels in Central Otago. Cf. *white Maori* (MAORI A 6 a).
1897 MCKAY *Older Auriferous Drifts Central Otago* 51 Making here careful inquiries as to the occurrence of the white cement stones derived from the older grits... It was also stated that a great number of 'Chinamen' or 'white Maoris', as these boulders are called by the miners, were met in sinking the shaft. *Ibid.* 56 In the face of this can be seen a stratum of the cement-stone, 'Chinaman' or 'White Maori', as boulders of it are called indifferently by the miners in different parts. **1908** *NZGeol.SB (NS) No.5* 33 The cement stones or 'Chinamen' of the miners, occur in the basin, but are never abundant. **1918** *NZGeol.SB (NS)* No.19 54 These sands have, owing to the deposition of secondary silica, become consolidated into hard flinty concretionary boulders, often of large size. These boulders locally called 'chinamen', are quite analogous to the sarsen stones of English geology. **1933** *NZJST* XIV. 263 Quartz pebbles and cemented silts or quartzite boulders derived from the quartz conglomerate formation, and locally called 'chinamen', also occur in the gravel bands. **1943** HISLOP *Pure Gold* 104 In sluicing big stones are pitch-forked out of the gutter before they block the intake, but should a 'Chinaman'—(as the miners call the extra large sand stones)—come within the force of the nozzle it is blown aside unless it is of exceptional size. Some of these 'Chinamen' are very queer in shape and colour, and are taken away as ornamental stones for the garden. **1974** WILLIAMS *Economic Geology of NZ* 80 A notable feature of the basal sediments over much of Otago is the presence of 'chinaman' stones—the Sarsen stones of English geology... As this silica-cemented material is very hard, the chinaman stones have been recycled through later Tertiary rocks and pervade the Quaternary gravels as rounded boulders often coated with iron stain. **1989** *Sunday News* letter of Aug. cited in *NZ Skeptic* (1989) 26 May 6 The land slide [near Tapanui] contains 'China-man stones' (not China-stones as reported).

Chinaman, *n.*² [Origin unknown.]
a. Usu. as **the chinaman**, a chute (usu. with a gate at the bottom to control flow of material), or a hopper device, for loading trucks, etc. with spoil; also the process of loading with a chinaman.
1921 FOSTON *At the Front* 65 [In working down a big cutting] a small drive [was] put into the hill. Into this rails were laid for trucks to run on. A hole was then made overhead, into which soil and debris was allowed to slide. The trucks when full were drawn by horses, which, after starting, were quickly unhooked. Once going, the truck gathers momentum and automatically tips itself. It is then returned again and again by the horses and again and again tipped in a like manner, until the work is completed. This device is called 'the Chinaman', because it was a Chinaman who is credited with being first to introduce it into New Zealand. **1956** July p.c. C. Peters. *Chinaman* was the name for a loading chute in Second Field Squadron during WW2. **1973** TROUP *Steel Roads of NZ* 146 [Caption] The navvies have built a wooden 'Chinaman', or earth-hopper, holding the spoil loosened above, until the trucks are backed in to be filled.

b. As **chinaman chute**, see quot.
1978 MCARA *Gold Mining* (Glossary of Waihi Mining Terms) 315 *Chinaman chutes*: These were used for feeding the surface filling into two-and-a-half-ton trucks. They generally consisted of a few planks laid across the drift timbers under which the trucks were placed while the material was 'rilled down' from the sloping face above and checked by dropping a plank into position.

chinaman, *n.*³ *Quarrying.* [Origin unknown.] See quot.
1950 p.c. R. Gilberd (Northland). Sometimes a drill-hole develops a 'chinaman', a ridge running down one side of the hole which prevents the drill from turning freely, and if not cut out, will eventually cause the drill to jam.

chinaman, *n.*⁴ *Shearing.* An unshorn lock on a sheep's rump, reminiscent of an oriental pigtail.
1955 BOWEN *Wool Away* 155 Chinaman. A lock of wool missed by the shearer and left unshorn on the sheep's rump. **1965** *Listener* 26 Feb. 15 *Chinaman*: An unshorn lock on a sheep's rump reminiscent of the pigtail worn by Orientals in earlier years. **1989** *NZ English Newsletter* III. 24 *flag*: Lock of wool left unshorn on a sheep's rump, and sometimes called a 'chinaman'.

Chinaman, *n.*⁵ [Origin uncertain: see quot. 1956.] Either of two unrelated fish, the FLATHEAD 1 or (on Stewart Island) the *banded parrotfish* (PARROTFISH 2 (1)).
1922 [see PARROTFISH 2 (1)]. **1938** *TrRSNZ* LXVIII. 413 *Katheostoma giganteum* Haast. Flathead (Chinaman). **1956** GRAHAM *Treasury NZ Fishes* 286 Other names for the Flathead are Chinaman and Frenchman, but where these names originated and for what reason I do not know with certainty. One theory is that when Chinamen hawked fish about Dunedin they kept Flatheads for their own consumption, as they preferred them to all other fish. **1967** [see FLATHEAD 1]. **1981** WILSON *Fisherman's Bible* 100 Frenchman Another name for Flathead. Also known as Chinaman. The latter name apparently derives from the fact that Chinese fish merchants in Dunedin in the early days always kept these fish for their own consumption.

Chinaman, *n.*⁶

1. In collocations: **Chinaman's digging(s)**, a great deal of work for a small return of gold; **Chinaman's luck**, very good luck.
1933 REES *NZ Holiday* 109 'But this is just **chinaman's digging**,' he said. **1908** BARR *British Rugby Team in Maoriland* 111 **Chinaman's luck**, thought our hero, as 'John' entered. **1940** LORD *Old Westland* 246 Success was entirely due to what was known as 'Chinaman's Luck', which diggers held to be infallible.

2. In the phr. **(to have) the luck of a Chinaman**, (to be) very lucky.
1902 SATCHELL *Land of Lost* 243 Hanged if he hasn't the luck of a Chinaman. **1955** *BJ Cameron Collection* (TS July) luck of a Chinaman (n) Extraordinary luck.

Chinese.

1. In the names of plants, see CHINESE GOOSEBERRY.

2. In collocations: **Chinese ballast**, rice; **Chinese burn**, a children's torture executed by taking the arm or lower part of the leg in both hands and twisting the skin; **Chinese rocks**, uncut heroin; **Chinese smoking**, (occas. orally recorded as **Chinese drawback**), see quot.

1987 *Chosen Place* 60 Ah, good old **Chinese Ballast**! You know, our old dad always called rice that! Hated the stuff. 1951 PARK *Witch's Thorn* 89 He..slowly twisted the flesh on her wrist... 'That's called the **Chinese burn**. Does it hurt?' 1963 FRAME *Reservoir* 49 And she twisted my arm once more, and caught at my wrist, giving me a vicious Chinese and Maori burn combined. 1975 in *NZ Short Stories* (1984) 96 You remember. I used to bash you up. Give you the old Chinese burn. You used to enjoy it too. 1983 HENDERSON *Down from Marble Mountain* 83 I was initiated [at Riwaka School, 1920s]..into the misery of 'Chinese Burns', inflicted by anyone larger, swiftly screwing the skin of a wrist clockwise and anti-clockwise almost simultaneously. 1993 SINCLAIR *Halfway Round the Harbour* 43 There was [at school] the painful Chinese burn, when the bully..would grasp a boy's forearm and twist the skin in opposite directions. 1986 *Evening Post* (Wellington) 5 Apr. 19 Will he stay off it? He wants to, but if someone offered him some **Chinese rocks** (uncut heroin), 'I would be sorely tempted.' 1964 HARVEY *Any Old Dollars Mister?* 72 [The boy] sat back..and let smoke trickle from his mouth and up through his nostrils. '**Chinese smoking**,' he said proudly and started to cough.

Chinese gooseberry. *Hist.* [Cf. OED *Chinese* 2 'the N.Z. name for the plant and fruit'.] Also familiarly **china** (see quot. 1982). KIWIFRUIT.

1925 *Auckland Weekly News* 1 Oct. 62 The Chinese gooseberry..has been introduced into Auckland. 1937 *King Country Chronicle* 3 Apr. 8 A fruit with great possibilities as a market crop for the small orchardist, the Chinese gooseberry, has come into prominence of late years. 1944 *NZJAg.* Feb. LXVIII. 111 The Chinese gooseberry, the fruit of a vine imported from China, is gaining increasing popularity in New Zealand. 1963 DUCKWORTH *Barbarous Tongue* 148 Oh, look, I forgot—your Chinese gooseberries. 1970 *NZ Listener* 2 Nov. 57 Chinese Gooseberry Ring. I refuse to call these exotic fruits 'Kiwi Fruit' as there is, for me, a slight suggestion of cruelty to animals about their new name. 1982 PEAT *Detours* 165 The [tobacco] industry was being asked to cut back production and go into..crops like kiwifruit, which the [Riwaka] growers referred to as 'chinas' because of the vine's origin.

Chink. *Offensive.* Also **Chinkie**, **Chinko**. [An altered form of *Chinese*: used elsewhere (see OED *n.*⁵) and recorded earliest in Austral. (AND 1887), much used (with earlier varr. *Chinkie*, *Chinko*) in New Zealand in a context of early racism.] A Chinese. See also CHOW.

1. As **Chink**. Often *attrib.*

1905 *Truth* 2 Sept. 5 Chinks and Japs. 1913 MANSFIELD *Stories* (1984) 132 He thought he heard one of the Chinks after him and he slipped into a timber-yard. 1936 HYDE *Passport to Hell* 229 The little Chinks [*sc.* of the Chinese Labour Corps] hated the Boche like hell. 1947–48 BEATTIE *Pioneer Recolls.* (1956) 39 Later they put on Peter, a modern 'Chink,' to help him but Ah See chased him off saying 'Him no Chinese—him no pigtail.' 1988 SMITH *Southlanders at Heart* 119 The Chinese were highly respected as industrious and law-abiding citizens but that didn't prevent us referring to them as 'Chows', 'Chinks' or even 'Chinkies'— terms that would never do today! 1991 *Metro* (Auckland) Nov. 117 The latest trend is T-shirts emblazoned with 'No Chinks in Chowick'. [A play on the name *Howick*, a middle-class Auckland suburb with a noticeable contemporary Asian immigrant inflow.]

2. As **Chinkie. a.** [AND 1876.] A Chinese.

1879 BARRY *Up & Down* 284 One of the Chinkies threw a stone at me. 1883 FERGUSON *Castle Gay* 201 And Chinkies, Malay, Fiji cannibal All had a dab at thee, yet didst thou 'scape them all. 1897 WRIGHT *Station Ballads* 60 For the country as far as I've seen it's as chock full of holes as a sieve. With the Chinkies a-mullocking through it and yet those coves manage to live. 1905 *Truth* 24 June 5 One Christchurch daily includes Chinkies in its passenger list if they travel first class. 1988 [see 1 above].

b. *transf.* A name for a (yellow) marble.

1972 SUTTON-SMITH *Folkgames of Children* 174 There were the terms referring to particular kinds of marbles: for example..blood alleys..bottlies, bull's eyes, bum-squashers, cat's eyes, chinkies..Greeks, milkies.

3. As **Chinko**.

1866 SMALL *NZ and Australian Songster* (1970) 22 ('Paddy's Fight with the Chinamen') Now the 'bamboos' they were flashing, And poor Pat at them was dashing; But he very soon discovered that the 'Chinkos' had the best.

chip, *n.*¹ [Spec. use of *chip* a small piece of a substance.]

1. A kind of confectionery.

1902 *Brett's Colonists' Guide* 807 Chips.—Centennial, Opera, Florence, Boston, and other 'chips' are merely refined sugar, boiled to the crack, and flavoured to taste.

2. A small piece of kauri gum; in *pl.*, a grade of kauri gum comprising small pieces. See also *digger's chips* (DIGGER *n.*¹ II 5).

1916 *Chambers Jrnl.* Aug. 542 The chief factor influencing sales and prices of kauri-gum in recent years has been the request for the poorer qualities, called 'chips' and 'dust'. 1936 *NZJST* XVII. 371 It is no doubt also responsible for the dark coloured varnishes produced from the chip grades... The terms dust, seeds, chips..&c., are the names given to certain of the lower kauri gum grades according to the relative sizes of the pieces. 1956 [see GUM *n.* 2]. 1966 *Encycl. NZ* II. 207 An increasing demand for poorer grades of gum [after 1900], used in making linoleum, made it profitable to search for smaller gum: 'nuts', 'chips', 'seeds', and 'dust'. 1991 *NZ Geographic* Apr.–June 41 In order of decreasing size, the pieces of gum were known as nuggets, nubs, peas, chips, and dust.

3. [Ellipt. for *wood-chip*.] Usu. *pl.* Small pieces of wood sliced from logs for sale to paper or chipboard manufacturers, etc. Also as **chip-pile**, a large pile of such chips awaiting loading for export.

1980 MANTELL *Murder & Chips* 5 The chip pile!.. Anyone living in Nelson was intensely aware of the chip pile. Sawmills to the west chewed up southern beech, radiata pine, into small flat chips around an inch square.

4. *Farming.* See quot.

1982 *Agric. Gloss.* (MAF) 53 *Chip*: Small pieces of dried faeces in crutchings.

5. *transf.* **do one's chips**, see DO *v.*¹

chip, *n.*² [Prob. f. Brit. dial. *chip n.* disagreement, or CHIP (AT) *v.*¹ find fault with: see OED *n.*², *v.*¹ a; EDD *n.*³ 6.] A reprimand or warning about faulty workmanship, esp. to a shearer.

1910 *Maoriland Worker* 15 Oct. 4 During shearing at one station in the early days, the boss came along and gave him a chip for shearing roughly, and asked him how it was that he shore all right in the morning but got rough after dinner. 1986 RICHARDS *Off the Sheep's Back* 122 Les always held to the opinion that if you did not get 'chipped' at least once a day, you were shearing entirely for the boss. A 'chip' meant you were on the borderline and shearing a few for yourself as well. *Ibid.* 123 The shearing is below my standard of workmanship... You can take this as a general chip—or else. 1989 *NZ Eng. Newsletter* III. 22 *chip:* This is a reprimand handed out to a shearer by a station owner/manager.

chip, *v.*¹ Also **chip at**. [See CHIP *n.*²] *trans.* To find fault with (someone); to reprimand; to carp at or nag; to tease; esp. or *spec.* to caution or reprimand a shearer about poor workmanship.

1906 *Truth* 11 Aug. 5 Why the policeman had been called to the pub was the fact that Milligan was 'chipping' at the proprietor and wouldn't desist. 1933 *Press* (Christchurch) (Acland Gloss.) 30 Sept. 15 Chip.—Shearer's slang. To c[hip] a shearer is to find fault with work, or to caution him ([c1890-1910]). 1936 HYDE *Passport to Hell* 252 And there's the way they all chip me about what I said when I was delirious. 1959 SLATTER *Gun in My Hand* 218 I don't want to keep chipping at you, Ron, but I'm still a bit worried about that gun. 1963 PEARSON *Coal Flat* 95 When he got home Myra chipped him about staying out spending money. 1973 NEWTON *Big Country SI* (1977) 196 On one occasion he chipped Jack Murchison because the chaff wasn't too good. 1986 [see CHIP *n.*²]. 1989 RICHARDS *Pioneer's Life* 64 My words muttered between clenched teeth were, 'Now, chip me on them [*sc.* shorn sheep], you bastard.' 1993 O'SULLIVAN *Let the River Stand* 36 [His father said] 'Stops you believing bullshit...' 'In front of Dick, if you don't mind,' his mother chipped.

chip, *v.*²

1. As **chip in** [AND 1797], to hoe seed in, or to turn seed in with a harrow.

1846 PHARAZYN *Journal* (ATLTS) 61 Sowed 4 rods more barley chipped it in after dusk. 1849 HURSTHOUSE *New Plymouth* 98 For its first grain crop the seed can be 'chipped-in' for 10*s.* per acre more. 1869 MAY *Guide to Farming NZ* 21 It is advisable to chip in [wheat] seed. c1910 MACDONALD *Reminiscences* (VUWTS) 36 The first settlers [c1840s]..'chipped' in their little patches of wheat among the stumps.

2. *trans.* To remove (weeds, tussock, etc.) with a sharp spade or grubber.

1905 in Barry *In Lee of Hokonuis* 9 Sept. (1966) 162 First the tussocks are burned off, the roots are chipped with a sharp spade, thrown into heaps and burnt again, leaving an untrammelled course for the plough. 1966 BARRY *In Lee of Hokonuis* 100 At this stage communication with English speaking people was almost impossible and Mr. Kubala senior worked at ditching, chipping tussock etc.

chip heater. Also occas. **chippee** (see quot. 1989). [AND 1946.] A domestic heater (often with a wet-back) fuelled by small pieces of wood.

[1916 *Rangitikei Advocate & Manawatu Argus* 23 Sept. 1 [Advt] The Chip Bath Heater. Your warm baths from waste fuel.] 1938 HYDE *Nor Yrs. Condemn* 218 Starkie did their cooking, lit the chip-heater, tidied up, minded the flat. 1973 FERNANDEZ *Tussock Fever* 99 There were fowls to feed..kindling to chop for the chip heater and sitting room fire. 1987 *Dominion* (Wellington) 28 June 8 The school has the best bark garden in the district. The schoolteacher's house has one of the best-fed chip heaters in the country. **1989** McGill *Dinkum Kiwi Dict.* 20 *chippee* wood-burning wetback stove, short for a chip heater. **1991** *Listener* 10 June 34 I asked, how did the army come to have a chip heater? I was told that John Hart sold one of his Thermettes to an army sergeant who in turn, extolled its virtues to his superiors.

chippee: see CHIP HEATER.

chippie, *n.*[1] [f. *chip* + -IE.] Usu. *pl.*, a thin slice of potato fried until crisp and eaten cold; a potato crisp.
  1963 [see CHEERIO]. **1980** Leland *Kiwi-Yankee Dict.* 25 Chippies: Those crunchy thin slices of fried potato (potato chips). One of my first language laughs in New Zealand was a sign in the Palmerston North Opera House which said: No Chippies Allowed: I hadn't realized that soliciting was such a serious problem. **1986** McCauley *Then Again* 30 They can't be too far from civilisation; cigarette packets and ice-cream wrappers and chippie packets mark out a trail. **1988** *Short Stories from NZ* 82 This story spans quite a few years, so you may need a large packet of lollies, chippies, or whatever, to help you through.

chippie, *n.*[2] A kind of cheap marble which chipped easily.
  1972 Sutton-Smith *Folkgames Children* 174 There were the terms referring to particular kinds of marbles: for example..aggies..and in more recent years ball-bearings, chippies, plastics, and woodies. **1982** Sutton-Smith *Hist. Children's Play* 261 Elsewhere the [marble] tradition has continued unbroken (with 'chippies' throughout the war), and strong seasons still flourish.

chisel-mouth(ed), *n.* and *a. Farming.* [f. having teeth sharply bevelled at the ends, thus resembling a chisel.] See quot. 1949.
  1933 *Press* (Christchurch) (Acland Gloss.) 9 Sept. 15 Dealers and stock-agents use various terms, such as chisel-mouthed, to make failing mouthed sheep sound younger; but these terms are not in common use by sheepfarmers or shepherds. **1949** Newton *High Country Days* 193 Chisel Mouths: A fresh full-mouthed sheep whose teeth have not yet been worn down level; sheep grow two teeth each year; they grow only eight, and at four years are chisel mouths. With age the teeth wear down until each tooth is level.

chivoo, var. SHIVOO.

chocka, var. CHOCKER.

chocker, *a.* Also **chocka, chokka, chockers.** [f. *chock*(-a-block + *-er(s)*; OED records only the slang sense 'fed up', from 1942.] Completely full, packed.
  1980 Leland *Kiwi-Yankee Dict.* 25 *chocka:*... Chocka means full to bursting. **1985** Stewart *Gumboots & Goalposts* 39 They can't lean across the front seat. It's usually chockers anyhow. **1991** Virtue *Always the Islands of Memory* 142 It was chocka with other things Parnell had shifted out there. **1992** *Evening Post* (Wellington) 11 Aug. Traffic was chokka. Cars were queued up stationary along the motorway.

chocolate.
1. Special Comb. **chocolate alley** *obs.*, ?a fun parlour or amusement arcade with prizes of bars of chocolate; **chocolate fish,** a chocolate covered marshmallow bar shaped like a fish; occas. **chocolate frog,** a frog-shaped confection of solid or peppermint-filled chocolate.
  1926 *NZ Observer* 22 May 7 Wellington business men have complained that the '**chocolate alleys**', which have come north from the Dunedin Exhibition, are affecting trade and they are calling upon the City Council to exercise more care in the issue of licenses for these 'amusement' parlours. **1926** *NZ Dairy Produce Exporter* 30 Apr. 31 Chocolate Alley was an outstanding feature. **1935** Guthrie *Little Country* (1937) 113 God bless my soul..if that grocer fellow hasn't sent me **chocolate fish** instead of tobacco. **1947** Davin *Gorse Blooms Pale* 11 'How much are the pencils, please?' 'A penny each.' So was the chocolate fish. **1955** *Truth* 22 June 4 When I get a bit pettish with them they merely give me a gentle slap and hand me a chocolate fish..to keep me quiet. **1978** Gee *Plumb* (1979) 198 Bluey lumbered round the table and put a chocolate fish on the children's side plates. **1990** *Evening Post* (Wellington) 22 Aug. 20 Mayell Foods makes chocolate fish, but the popularity of these marshmallow-based sweets seem to be peculiar to New Zealand. **1992** *Evening Post* (Wellington 8 July 5 The leak of the chocolate fish scandal from Cabinet should be enough to rouse the country's corporate diners from their state of post-Budget shock. **1960** Keinzly *Tangahano* 147 He bought Cinta a bag of jelly beans, a chocolate fish and a **chocolate frog** and he played a record for his mother.

2. In the phr. **(not) to have the brains of a chocolate fish,** to be very stupid.
  1981 *Avondale College Slang Words in Use* (Auckland) (Goldie Brown Collect.) *brains of a chocolate fish:* no brains. **1984** *Pakuranga College* (questionnaire) 10 Brains of chocolate fish [for a useless person]

chokee, chokey, varr. CHOKY.

chokka, var. CHOCKER.

choko /'tʃʌukʌu/. [ad. Brazilian Indian *chuchu:* OED (1902) *Austral.* and *N.Z.* variation of *chocho* (1756); AND 1909.] The introduced tropical American vine *Sechium edule* (fam. Cucurbitaceae) and its green-coloured fruit eaten as a vegetable.
  [**1989** Brucher *Useful Plants of Neotropical Origin & Their Wild Relatives* 268 Sechium edule (Jacq.) Swartz Chayote, christophin, chocho, cayotle, xuxu. The common designation 'chayote' for this vegetable has been derived from the Nahuatel language. Most probably the region of domestication has to be sought in Central America, where the highest grade of genetical variation exists.] **1917** *Otago Daily Times* (Dunedin) 2 May 6 Tree tomatoes, amalfi citron, choko (something like a vegetable marrow), guavas..and grapes are included in the [Auckland] display. **1922** *Auckland Weekly News* 1 June 46 Chokos, 6d to 1s per dozen. **1934** Tannock *Practical Gardening in NZ* 195 Choko.- This is a perennial climber, a member of the gourd family with a green squash-like fruit. **c1943** McPherson *Whitcombe's Complete New Zealand Gardener* 226 Choko (Mexican marrow): This member of the melon family grows like a climbing cucumber. **1956** *NZ Gardener* Sept. 57 The Choko, or Mexican Marrow (*Sechium edule*) is a curious sub-tropical edible fruiting vine which may be planted this month, placing the whole fruit in the ground. **1965** *NZJAg.* Apr. CX. 357 The bland flavoured choko, though uninteresting alone, blends very well with other flavours, especially cheese. **1988** *NZ Herald* (Auckland) 28 June 5 Choko is our name for a squash-type vegetable known in other countries as chayote, pepinello, custard marrow or vegetable pear. **1991** McDonnell *Grow Your Own Fruit* 77 Choko... The fruit looks like a cucumber and tastes rather like a marrow.

choky. Also **chokee.** [f. Anglo-Indian *choky* a police station, lock up: used also in Brit. slang from 1873, and in Austral. 1840–1962: see OED 2; AND.] A lock-up; gaol.
  1844 *NZ Jrnl.* IV. 343 If the Whaler does not keep within bounds, he is soon an inmate of the 'chokee', id est 'lock up'. **1852** *McLean Papers* (ATLTS) X. 146 A few hours rest in 'choky' to teach him better manners for the future. **1869** Thatcher *Wit & Humour* 4 'Come along now,' says Plummer, 'and let us away, No longer in Chokee will we be confined, And long ere the warders turn out for their breakfast We'll have left the Stockade and Mount Eden behind.' **1888** Duncan *Wakatipians* 39 We [*sc.* sailors] found ourselves in 'chokey' before we had fairly begun to enjoy our spree. **c1890** Bodell *A Soldier's View of Empire* (1982) 137 I considered this very bad Conduct on the Part of the Sergt..to put me in Chokey to save himself. **1909** Owen *Phillip Loveluck* 84 Oh, te case, werry goot. Three month's choky. **1982** Newbold *Big Huey* 246 Chokey (n). Prison, detention block.

chook /'tʃʊk/. Also **chookie;** occas. **chuck, chucky** /'tʃʊki/. [f. (esp. n.) Brit. dial. varr. of *chick*, a chicken or fowl, or a call to fowls: AND 1900 (*chuckey* 1855).]

1. A domestic fowl (usu. a hen); a call to fowls; also *fig.*, a very silly person (see quot. 1993). **a.** As **chook.**
  1905 *Truth* 2 Sept. 7 The rooster had cornered 17 chooks. **1919** *Quick March* 11 Aug. 26 She warned the family..to feed the pigs. 'And the chooks'. **1948** Scanlan *Rusty Road* (1949) 58 'Chook! chook! chook!' the children called, and the hungry hens, the rooster and the two ducks came crowding around for their evening meal. **1951** Frame *Lagoon* (1961) 66 My big mother with a big blue pinny to shake at me as if it were wheat for a little chook. **1973** Fernandez *Tussock Fever* 99 He had mixed the pollard into the aromatic chook pot of peelings Bessie had cooked for him. **1982** Sutton-Smith *Hist. Children's Play* 89 We would imitate a rooster in the evening and set all the chucks [hens] in the valley going. (1895; Takaka) **1988** Jackson *Rainshadow* 59 'After tea you children can take Nicholas out to feed the chooks,' she rattled on. **1993** *Dominion* (Wellington) 3 Apr. 10 We have never argued that our treaty rights should be calculated by 'coastal length'—that's a northern fiction which the journalistic chooks have been feeding on.

b. As **chookie.**
  1895 Chamier *South Sea Siren* 195 You will let me carve the chucky? **1905** Lancaster *Sons o' Men* 266 Whaur did ye pit thae chuckies, Sandy? **1928** *Free Lance* (Wellington) 11 July 9 [Heading] Chilled 'Chookies': Prospect of new export industry. **1934** Scanlan *Winds of Heaven* 79 Here's your grannie, darling; she'll take you down the garden to see the chookies. **1959** Lawlor *Old Wellington Days* 22 Christmas dinner of 'chookie', pork, or roast beef. **1989** Te Awekotuku *Tahuri*, 103 chooks: chickens; also chookies; domestic fowl.

2. Special Comb. **chook-house (chook-run)**, a fowl-house, fowl run; **chook raffle**, a (usu.) quickfire raffle with a frozen chicken as prize.
  1986 Richards *Off the Sheep's Back* 95 Some of the boys decided they wanted some fresh eggs and raided the farmer's **chookhouse**. **1989** Te Awekotuku *Tahuri* 23 She splashed round the back to the chook house. **1992** *Dominion* (Wellington) 29 June 6 If fund-raising were limited to the cake-stall and the **chook raffle**, politicians who represented the poorest and least-privileged could foot it with those who represent the richest and most powerful. **1989** Richards *Pioneer's Life* 44 I was like a new rooster in a **chook run**.

3. In various phrases: **a. like a headless chook**, mindlessly in panic; in a 'flap'.

1991 *Dominion* (Wellington) 20 Dec. 9 The nats are running like a bunch of headless chooks. **1992** *Listener* 24 Feb. 38 I'll enjoy watching them run round like headless chooks.

Hence **headless chookery**.

1987 *Dominion* (Wellington) 11 Mar. 2 Mr Lange said the Cabinet had not discussed assistance for insurable damage this week, because it had not known the extent of the damage before it met. 'We rely on facts, not some sort of headless chookery,' Mr Lange said.

b. pissed (or **silly**) **as a chook**, very drunk. (*silly as a chook* can also mean 'very silly': p.c. Simon Cauchi (Hamilton), 1996.)

1964 Morrieson *Came a Hot Friday* (1981) 136 And in the end..when you're as silly as a chook and you've done your akkers you wend your way to a smelly [hotel] lavatory and piddle it all out. **1985** Binney *Long Lives the King* 53 Your mate's as pissed as a chook and you don't look too steady on your pins.

choom /tʃʊm/. [Imitative of Brit. dial. pron. of *chum*: AND 1916.] **a.** WW1. As a name for, or reference to, an English soldier. (Also occas. in WW2.)

1918 *Kia Ora Coo-ee* Oct. 14 'Jock', 'Choom', 'Dinkum' and 'Cobber' are standardised monikers that do yeoman service. **1937** Partridge *Dict. Slang* 150 *choom*; properly, but less gen., *chum*. A term of address much used by the Australian and New Zealand soldiers to an unknown English (not Welsh, Scottish or Irish) soldier: 1915-18. **1995** Slatter *One More River* 90 British troops, pongos or chooms we called them, thronged the town.

b. An English immigrant.

1941 Baker *NZ Slang* 43 *Choom*, also a New Zealand use for an Englishman, is merely the lengthening (as in English Midland dialects) of the vowel in *chum*. **1959** Slatter *Gun in My Hand* 220 'They're all right really. The Pommies, I mean. The Homeys, the Chooms, the Pongos...' 'They did a good job during the war, remember.' **1966** *Encycl. NZ* II. 680 An English immigrant is *choom*.

chop, *n.*[1] [An application of *chop* quality, class, ad. Hindi *chhāp* a brand, mark of quality: AND 1847; see also OED *n.*[5] 4 b.] In the negative phr. **no chop(s)**, **to be not much chop(s)**, to be not up to much, to be of little or no good. Cf. COP.

1909 *Truth* 20 Nov. 3 Harry is no 'chops' as regards elegance, but he gets runs, and that is the whole kernel of the run-making game. **1909** Vogel *Tragedy of Flirtation* 219 He ain't much chops, that doctor, I reckon. **1945** *NZ Dairy Exporter* 1 Nov. 67 It wasn't much chop being let down by someone who had crept into your heart and thoughts. **1947** Davin *Gorse Blooms Pale* 207 It's not been much chop so far.

chop, *n.*[2] [AND 1899.] Often *pl*. as **the chops**. A log-chopping contest involving skill and speed; or a series of such events. Also *spec.* as *jigger chop* (JIGGER *n.*[2] 2); **standing (or upright) chop** (or occas. **cut**), where the axeman stands to a vertical log fastened to an upright block; **underhand chop**, where the axeman stands on a horizontal log fastened to a cradle or secured on the ground; **chop off**, the final or deciding round of a chopping contest (see quot. 1934).

1905 *Weekly Press* (Christchurch) 8 Feb. 50 [Captions] Winner of the Boys' Chop. After the champion chop. On the grand stand [Kumara]: watching the champion chop. **1910** in McGill *Ghost Towns NZ* (1980) 188 [1910 photograph of competitors with a block on which is written] Mokai Bush Chop 1910 **1926** Devanny *Butcher Shop* (1981) 31 The quickest time through a two-foot upright or an underhand cut carried weighty honours. **1930** Smyth *Wooden Rails* 108 There were standing chops, underhand chops, single and two-handed sawing contests. **1934** *Feilding Star* 27 Jan. 4 Patrons are advised to..obtain a good view of the competition, which will be run in two heats and a final chop off. **1942** *NZEF Times* 5 Oct 4 This year New Zealand won only..the 12-inch standing chop, and..the 14-inch cross-cut sawing... Sapper T. Jackson, West Coast, was second in the 14-inch underhand chop. **1947** *Weekly News* (Auckland) 9 Apr. [Caption] J. Witika..winner of the 14-inch handicap standing chop. **1963** Bacon *In the Sticks* 131 Mac Harris was saying they want a Chops Steward. You could do that, couldn't you?..The Chops are the most important part of the Sports. **1984** *Dominion* (Wellington) 31 Aug. 13 Eddie is a competitive axeman and attends around 20 chops each season... Sometimes he'll return from a chop with as many as 40 [axes] in the boot of his car for re-grinding. **1989** Richards *Pioneer's Life* 34 I won the 10-inch and 12-inch chops. **1992** Boyd *Pumice & Pines* 127 [caption] The Kaingaroa Forest Axeman's Chop in 1963, 'the biggest chop yet organised by the N.Z. Forest Service'..was a most successful carnival. **1993** *Sport 11* 38 Then I won the underhand chop..working to a handicap of dummy one.

Hence **chopper** [AND 1901], an axeman who takes part in chopping contests.

1955 Bowen *Wool Away* 66 You never see a good chopper without a good axe or a good shearer without good gear. **1979** Williams *Skin Deep* 63 There is only one axeman's carnival per year scheduled for Carlton, the choppers being booked up well ahead.

chop, *n.*[3] [f. *chop* something cut out, a share: see OED *n.*[1] 1 e; AND 1919.] A share, esp. in the phr. **to be in for** (or **get**) **one's chop**. See also *be in* (IN 1).

1960 Crump *Good Keen Man* 101 Don't worry mate... Be in for your chop! Make the most of it while you've got the chance. **1961** Cross *After Anzac day* 11 First it was free milk at schools. 'Fill up on it, girl,' he would tell her. 'Get your chop, because we workers are getting our money back now.' **1968** Slatter *Pagan Game* 102 That Cheryl Thomas... Now there's a piece if I ever saw one. They tell me Colin Harrington is in for his chop there. **1988** McGill *Dict. Kiwi Slang* 27 *chop* share or cut; phr. *in for one's chop* selfishly interested in getting one's share and perhaps more..eg 'Any hint of extra profits and Nat's in for his chop, no worries.'

chop, *v*. [Extended use of *obs*. Brit. *chop v.* (cf. OED *v.*[3]) to snap, bite: f. *chop pl*. jaws.] To made continual snapping movements with the jaws; of a boar, to gnash the tusks.

1947 Newton *Wayleggo* 112 The [mad] boar..was content to stand and chop in the creek. **1953** Stronach *Musterer on Molesworth* 42 The dogs began to get distemper..; their jaws began to 'chop', or open and shut convulsively.

chopper, *n.*[1] [f. *chop* to mince.] See quots.

1951 *Awards, etc.* 325 [NZ Freezing-Workers Award] [Rates of wages] Skinning chopper pigs, mechanically skinned, all weights, per head [£]0 3[s.] 7³⁄₄[d.]. Skinning chopper pigs, hand skinned, all weights, per head 0 4 8³⁄₄. **1961** *Merriam-Webster Third Internat. Dict.* 398 *chopper n -s 3* : a meat animal not esp. suitable for sale in fresh butcher's cuts—used of an overweight or aged hog in Australia and New Zealand. **1974** *NZ Agric.* 188 Other types of pig are sold at weekly sales; they include..aged sows and boars (classified as 'choppers'). These choppers are used for sausages, brawn, and other pork smallgoods.

chopper, *n.*[2] [Transf. use of *chopper* that which chops.] Usu. *pl*. The teeth. See quot.

1980 Leland *Kiwi-Yankee Dict.* 25 (A) 'Sink your choppers into that chook and you'll think you died and went to heaven.' Teeth... (B) Slang term for Malaysians, used on some University campuses.

chou /tʃæu/. Also **chow**. *Ellipt*. for CHOU MOELLIER.

1952 *Tasmanian Jrnl. Agric.* (1) 1 Feb. 23 Another excellent crop inspected was one of chou moellier, commonly called 'Chow' in New Zealand. **1973** Newton *Big Country SI* (1977) 207 Winter feeding is now a big item and the normal practice is to grow about 100 acres of turnips and chou. **1992** Anderson *Portrait Artist's Wife* 37 He nodded at the choumollier in the next paddock. In the winter it would be nibbled to the ground by the sheep... 'Chou,' said Dougal.

chou moellier /ˌtʃæu ˈmɒlijə/. [Ad. French *chou mollier* marrow-filled cabbage.] *Brassica oleracea* (fam. Brassicaceae), a kind of kale grown as a root-crop for stock feed.

1910 *NZJAg.* Oct. I. 354 *Chou moellier* (*Marrow Cabbage*): Ruakura. This comparatively new plant is proving valuable as a fodder crop. **1912** *NZJAg.* Jan. IV. 25 The photograph below illustrates a very promising crop of chou moellier at Ruakura Farm of Instruction. **1951** Levy *Grasslands NZ* (1970) 70 A like area of chou moellier..is often used for winter feed. **1992** [see CHOU].

chow, var. CHOU.

Chow. *Offensive*. Also occas. **chow-chow**. [f. an earlier pidgin-English *chow-chow* 'mixture, medley', esp. of yellow pickles: see OED 1, 1872; AND 1876.] A Chinese. Also *attrib*. Cf. CHINK 1.

1872 in Meredith *Adventuring in Maoriland* Oct. (1935) 22 History does not report what induced the solitary Chinaman to take up his abode amongst the hardy Scots of Dunedin. Possibly this 'Chow' wanted to study economy in its higher branches. **1905** in Lawlor *Old Wellington Days* (1959) 102 September 25... A man shot a Chow in Haining Street. **1910** *Truth* 1 Jan. 1 All over New Zealand the unfortunate white woman has been pushed out of the laundry business by the smellful, evil, industrial law-breaking Chow. **1913** *NZ Bulletin* 7 June 13 Would it not be more dignified to have Municipal buildings without any Chow fruit shops? **1921** *Auckland Capping Book* 21 [Humorous play on the name of the musical 'Chu Chin Chow'.] Ousted from the Theatre by the 'Chows'—will the President of the White Australasia League please note. **1931** Coad *Such Is Life* 51 The old Chow who sold it took us in nicely. **1943** Bennett *English in NZ* in *Amer. Speech* XVIII. 89 A Chinese (generally known as 'John') is a *Chow* (a derivative of 'chow-chow' [the yellow pickle]). **1959** Lawlor *Old Wellington Days* 84 They were fierce competitors of 'The Chows' or 'The Johns' as the Chinese fruiterers were called. **1988** [see CHINK].

chow-chow: see CHOW.

Christchurch, *int*. [f. *Christchurch*, the name of a SI city, with a past reputation for anglophile gentility.] As (**by** or **oh**) **Christchurch!**, euphemistic for '(by or oh) Christ!'.

1941 Baker *NZ Slang* 50 Need to find some outlet for pent up feelings resulted in..*by Christchurch!* **1947** Smith *N to Z* 25 [Christchurch] derived its name from a remark passed by the first settler who..was so overcome by the magnificent sight that all he could exclaim was 'Oh, Christchurch!' **1963** Casey *As Short a Spring* 129 Christchurch, look at your *bed*. You can't see a doctor like *that*. **1987** Eldred-Grigg *Oracles & Miracles* 6 'Oh Christchurch!' is what some people used to say when they wanted to swear.

Christmas tree.

1. pohutukawa, most species of which flower prolifically in late December.
 1864 Lush *Waikato Jrnls.* 24 Dec. (1982) 43 Charlie and Martin accompanied to the beach for Pohutakawas (our Xmas tree—our substitute for holly). **1867** Hochstetter *NZ* 240 About Christmas these [pohutukawa] trees are full of charming..blossoms; the settler decorates his church and dwelling with its lovely branches, and calls the tree 'Christmas-tree'! **1882** Hay *Brighter Britain* II. 191 The Pohutukawa..is called 'the Settlers' Christmas Tree', as its scarlet flowers appear about that time. **1905** White *My NZ Garden* 87 They are called the Christmas-tree because they flower about that time. **1934** Mulgan *Spur of Morning* 197 He..looked up past the still leaves of the Christmas tree to the darkening blue of the sky. **1977** Sargeson *Never Enough* 11 And a great Christmas tree in flower reached out far enough to colour the tide. **1992** Park *Fence around the Cuckoo* 149 His farmhouse was..sheltered by unkempt pohutukawas, the pakeha's Christmas tree.

2. *Mussel-farming.* As **Christmas-tree rope**, a hairy rope of intertwined black and silver threads used by mussel-farmers as a settling place for spat or small mussels. See also *mussel-rope* (mussel 3).
 1981 *Marlborough Sounds Marine Farming Association Newsletter* 7 Oct. 5 Rope for Sale—5 coils of 12mm black and 2 coils of xmas tree.

chub. [f. Brit. dial. *chub* a chunky piece of wood: see OED 3.] Any of various cold cooked sausages, stubby in shape, and enclosed in plastic.
 1982 *Evening Post* (Wellington) 22 Feb. (Wardells advertising insert.) Total Pet Food—2.25 kg Chub.

chuck, *v.* [An informal substitution for *throw*.] Cf. chuck-in.

1. In the phr. **to chuck off (at)** [AND 1901], to chaff, to sneer (at).
 1909 *Truth* 23 Jan. 7 The man then started to chuck off at him. *Ibid.* 18 Sept. 6 At the [dance] he didn't hear gentle Ellen chuck off... He heard Arthur say he had enough of her slinging off. **1917** Pilling *Anzac Memory* 21 Jan. (1933) 119 Everyone is eating my lollies. They chuck off when a parcel of lollies arrives, but none are lacking on the eating stakes. **1982** *Collins Concise Eng. Dict.* 198 *chuck off vb.* (intr.) Austral. & N.Z. inf. to sneer (often foll. by *at*).

2. chuck (up) [AND 1957], to vomit, to throw up. Also occas. as a noun.
 1981 Auckland Secondary Teachers College (Goldie Brown Collection) *chuck*: vomit. **1984** 16-17 F E53 Pakuranga Coll. 31 Chuck, chucks up [F1 M4] **1984** 17 M E117 Pakuranga Coll. 31 Chucks up **1988** McGill *Dict. Kiwi Slang* 28 *chuck* to vomit: often 'have a chuck'.

chuck, chuckie, /tʃʊk/, varr. chook, chookie.

chuckie-chuck ?/ˈtʃʌkɪtʃʌk/. [Orig. unknown: Morris presents *Chucky-chucky* as an Aboriginal name for a berry, quoting 1885 Mrs. Praed; in Austral. and NZ, the fruit of species of *Gaultheria* (fam. Ericaceae): OED suggests Austral. 'a native name'.] The calyx of *Gaultheria* spp. (prob. *G. antipoda*) eaten as a fruit.
 1871 *TrNZI* III. 194 Two other *Gaultheriae* are very distinct; one, of prostrate habit, bears a round white flower, which is eaten, under the name of 'chuckiechuck.' **1891** Potts *Out in Open* in *NZ Country Jrnl.* XV. 198 When out of breath, hot and thirsty, how one longed for a handful of chuckie-chucks. In their season how good we used to think these fruits of the *gaultheria*, or rather its thickened calyx. A few handfuls were excellent in quenching one's thirst, and so plentifully did the plant abound that quantities could soon be gathered... [The] notable [pioneer housekeepers] sometimes encouraged children to collect sufficient chuckie-chucks to make preserve. The result was a jam of a sweet mawkish flavour that gave some idea of a whiff caught in passing a hair-dresser's shop.

chuck-in. [AND 1916.] Something thrown in to make up weight, advantage, etc.; a bonus, an advantageous happening.
 1888 McHutcheson *New Zealander Abroad* 84 The watch was a 'chuck in' at $40. **1912** *Truth* 11 May 4 Fancy landing thousands of the starving humans from Bull's country... What a chuck-in for the local squatters!

chuckstones, chuckystones: see chucky.

chucky, var. chookie.

chucky /ˈtʃʌkɪ-/. Also **chuckstones**, **chuckystones, chukky.** [f. Sc. dial. *chucky* a quartz pebble (used in *chucky-stones*): see OED *chuck n.*³ 5, *chuckie*.] A piece of stone found in coal; also as **chucky-stones**, the game of knuckle-bones.
 c**1920** Beattie *Trad. Lifeways Southern Maori* (1994) 73 Ruke..was a favorite [Maori] game of old and was of a similar nature to the game of 'chuckystones' played by white children. **1972** Sutton-Smith *Folkgames Children* 177 Knucklebones (K-34) was played in both Europe and Polynesia, independently at first... Occasionally it was known as Chucks, Chuckstones, Chuckystones, Fingerstones, Hucklebones, Jacks, Jackstones, Knuckles, or Knucklestones. Children still played it here and there throughout the country in 1949, but they knew little about it until plastic knuckles were imported in 1954 in large quantities and revived the game. **1981** *Listener* 2 May 43 West Coast miners call these [bits of stone in coal] *chukkies*, another north-country term. A chukky in the north was (and is) a pebble, and the children's game of knuckle-bones was there called chukkies or chukky-stones, played with sheep's bones but with pebbles. It was—like skipping-ropes—a purely female sport and no six-year-old male chauvinist would touch a *chukky*—unless he wanted to use it as a projectile.

chuddy. Also **chuddygum, chutty.** [Orig. uncertain: prob. an alteration of *chew(ed)*.] A children's word for chewing gum.
 1904 in Lawlor *More Wellington Days* (1962) 53 January 15 Wally gave me some chuddy. Its corker for playing games with. **1941** Baker *NZ Slang* 51 In constant use by our youngsters [is]..chutty. **1950** Sutton-Smith *Our Street* 35 A boy put a big lump of 'chutty' on the top of the seat in front. **1962** Lawlor *More Wellington Days* 53 In my boyhood days it [sc. chuddy] was the equivalent of today's chewing gum, but different in shape or for mastication. The generation of 'chuddy' per medium of teeth, tongue and saliva was a minor work of art. **1963** Hilliard *Piece of Land* 32 They were all chewing chuddy, smoking, tramping butts into the litter on the floor. **1982** Sutton-Smith *Hist. Children's Play* 228 Chuddy—now called 'chewing gum'—was then [c1910] in the zenith of its popularity. **1982** Frame *To the Is-land* (1984) 90 'O.K., chief' was best said while you were chewing *chutty* or chewing gum, drawing the chutty out of your mouth..and stretching it as you watched the adult alarm at this apparent irresponsibility. **1991** Mitchell in *My Home Town* 73 Capstan..or Craven A [cigarettes] were snapped up with a packet of Wrigley's chuddy gum to..cover up the breath.

chug-a-lug. [Cf. Partridge 8: an Austral. drinking toast.] Also **chug** *n.* and *v.* See quots.
 1987 Sligo *Final Things* 100 All dancing around, passing the whisky bottle after a good swig..and trying a few passes and a few more chug-a-lugs. **1988** McGill *Dict. Kiwi Slang* 28 *chug* to drink alcohol; *chugalug* act of drinking, usually a beer, in one gulp, or a drinking bout; eg 'Fancy a few chugs after work, Nobby?'

chukky, var. chucky.

chum. [A shortening of *new chum*: AND 1846.] new chum A 1. See also choom b.
 1926 Cook *Far Flung* 14 Who is the big, smiling chum gettin' out the luggage?..came out to learn sheep farming, eh? **1945** Macdonald *Away from Home* 124 A 'chum' whom we picked up on the way in. **1959** Masters *Tales of Mails* 69 The chum thought the story sounded feasible, so he wrote home [a1900] and told his people about it.

chunder, *v.* [AND 1950 'Prob. rhyming slang *Chunder Loo* for "spew", after a cartoon figure *Chunder Loo of Akim Foo* orig. drawn by Norman Lindsay (1879-1969), and appearing in advertisements for Cobra boot polish in the Sydney *Bulletin* between 1909 and 1920'; cf. WW1. *chunder* a nickname for an Egyptian, (?ad *Chand(r)a*) (see quot. 1918 below) and the transitional quots. given in AND.] To vomit, to spew, esp. after excessive drinking. Also *transf.* or *fig.* **chunder out**, to pour out in a great flow. [*Note*] First heard by Ed. among University students c1963, and given impetus (as was *technicolour yawn*) by the Barry Humphries 'Bazza McKenzie' comic strips.
 [**1918** *Kia-ora Coo-ee* (1981) 15 June 15 So questioned 'Chunder' (a walid, who, for a few piastres per week, acted as 'batman' to myself and a couple of mates.] **1971** in *NZ Short Stories III* (1975) 194 'For Christ's sake!' says the medal..'not there, eh? Don't chunder there, boy.' **1976** McLeod in McLauchlan *Acid Test* (1981) 171 Then this friend of Nigel's..chundered all over the supper table. **1984** Cox *Einstein* 63 Some fuckwit chundered in our bed—lucky I didn't have to sleep in it! **1992** *Sunday Star* (Auckland) 19 Jan. A8 N[ational] B[usiness] R[eview] had been chundering out not much more than regurgitated PR handouts..since it had been taken over by Aussies in 1989. **1995** *Sunday Star-Times* (Auckland) 25 June A1 There are 1200 advisers..all chundering out paper to just 20 ministers.

Hence **chundering** *vbl. n.*
 1976 Johnston *New Zealanders* 148 Even to vomit publicly (chundering is the local term) is frequently applauded [as part of the male ethos]. **1982** Kidman *Mrs Dixon & Friend* 143 The plane rocked

CHUNDER

dangerously... There was much talk of chundering. Most of them were hungover.

chunder, *n.* [f. prec.: AND 1960.]
1. Vomit; an act of vomiting.
1979 *Islands* 25 237 I hear a cleaning woman at the station say, 'Imagine what it does to me, coming in every morning and seeing all this chunder lying round.' **1979** GEBBIE & MCGREGOR *Incredible 8-Ounce Dream* 15 Not too many years ago the New Zealand diner's wine-tastes stopped at a bottle of Waihirere Sauterne followed by a chunder on the carpet. **1988** *Dominion Sunday Times* (Wellington) 13 Mar. 16 Four bottles [of beer] is said to test the digestive system to the limit and is almost impossible to keep down and so usually leads to what is called a 'power chunder' or projectile vomiting.

2. In special Comb. **chunder bunny**, a person not able to hold large amounts of liquor without vomiting.
1985 *Sites* XI. 14 On one side were Men, resolutely with a capital M, while the other were 'chunder bunnies' or 'coma kids'. **1988** *Dominion Sunday Times* (Wellington) 13 Mar. 16 A game called Anchorman.. requires participants to consume six jugs of ale in four hours without being sick... [It is] regarded as a way of sorting out 'Men' from the 'chunder bunnies' or 'coma kids'.

chute /ʃut/. Also **shoot**.
1. *Shearing.* **a.** [AND *shoot* 1900.] The passage or ramp from which shorn sheep leave the shearing board.
1960 SCRYMGEOUR *Memories Maoriland* 50 Rousies..followed out from the side door to where the shoots from the stands gave the nearest exit. **1982** *Agric. Gloss.* (MAF) 53 *Chute*: Ramp from the porthole in a shearing shed taking sheep to a lower level. **1989** *NZ English Newsletter* III. 23 *chute:* Also called the 'porthole', this is a low opening and ramp through which the shorn sheep are passed down to the counting out pen.
b. Special Comb. (a) **chute-shed**, a shearing shed designed on a plan different from that of the conventional board type; (b) **chute cowshed**, SHED *n.*¹ 4 b.
1955 BOWEN *Wool Away* 109 Competition was held in true shed conditions, the five-stand chute-shed being conducted in the same way as for its usual shearing activities. *Ibid.* 110 These two plans illustrate the two main types of shed—the board shed and the chute shed. **1956** *NZ Farmer* 23 Feb. 10 A South Island farmer once said this to me: 'I don't like a chute shed'.

2. In the phr. **up the chute (shoot).** [A formulaic phr. (cf. *up the spout, wop,* etc.) the reference being prob. to going in the wrong direction or against gravity, the right direction in reality being usu. 'down the chute': Partridge 8 labels the phr. 'Aus.: since ca. 1920'.] Awry, wrong; in grave difficulties; pregnant (see quot. 1994).
1953 SUTTON-SMITH *Unorganized Games NZ Primary School Children* (VUWTS) II. 677 Some of the [slang] expressions listed by children..are 'Up the shoot..shivery dick, shiver me timbers'. **1955** *BJ Cameron Collection* (TS July) *chute up the chute.* Up the spout. **1966** TURNER *Eng. Lang. Austral. & NZ* 122 It must be pointed out that my meaning for *up the booay* [='altogether wrong'] is already supplied by *up the chute*, however. **1981** *Evening Post* (Wellington) 20 Nov. 14 Miss Firth said pupils would be 'up the chute' with one section, containing a difficult word list which had to be incorporated into a paragraph. **1990** *Listener* 1 Oct. 109 I stopped laughing when two pair of eyes

looked at me crosseyed and very grim. I thought everything was goin' up the shoot. **1994** CLEVELAND *Dark Laughter* 82 [WW2 (Egypt) soldiers' song] Old King Farouk Put [Queen] Farida up the chute.

chutty, var. CHUDDY.

chya(c)k, chyik, varr. CHIACK.

circular saw (shell). Also occas. called **spur (star, sun) shell**. *Astraea heliotropium* (fam. Turbinidae), a large (10 cm) purplish-grey or pinkish-grey univalve, having a spirally toothed shell.
1924 BUCKNILL *Sea Shells NZ* 34 The Circular Saw shell... Fifty years ago, when trawling and dredging were not carried out to any extent, a good pair of these shells would fetch £60 in the London salerooms. **1947** POWELL *Native Animals* 25 Circular saw (*Astraea heliotropium*)... Dead shells wash ashore on ocean beaches, but living ones are obtainable only by dredging. **1955** DELL *Native Shells* 16 The Circular Saw Shell (sometimes known as a Spur Shell) was once considered very rare... The oyster boats in Foveaux Strait sometimes bring up hundreds of these shells. **1970** PENNIKET *NZ Seashells in Colour* 20 Star Shell (*Astraea heliotropium*) 3in. Often known as the Circular saw shell, this species is one of the finest and most interesting of a worldwide family and is deservedly popular with collectors. **1971** CHILDS *NZ Shells* 60 Sun Shell or Circular Saw Shell... This is perhaps the most distinctive shell in New Zealand waters, with its strange spiral of projecting teeth. **1983** GUNSON *Collins Guide to Seashore* 90 The star shell, *Astraea heliotropium* (80mm)..has a remarkable spiral of sharp horns or teeth giving rise to the alternative name of the circular saw shell.

City of the Plains. The South Island city of Christchurch situated on the Canterbury Plains. See also GARDEN CITY.
1851 *Lyttelton Times* 23 Aug. 7 Public meeting at Christchurch... this 'City of the Plains' has become the scene of the first political demonstration in the Canterbury settlement. **1870** *TrNZI* II. 69 [The bittern] was once very common about Christchurch, 'the City of the Plains'. **1887** HOPEFUL *Taken In* 75 It is generally called the 'City of the *Plains*', and is named after Christ Church, Oxford—and well indeed it deserves its former title. **1909** THOMPSON *Ballads About Business* 92 From the Bluff I shipped to Christchurch or the City of the Plains, As the cultured people call it. **1928** *Free Lance* (Wellington) 1 Aug. 6 Some call her the Cathedral City, the most English City, the City of the Plains. **1959** SLATTER *Gun in My Hand* 76 Christchurch, The City of The Plains, a city of long straight streets and the gently curving Avon, a fine city.

civilization. *Hist.* The imposing of a European way of life (on the Maori).
1825 MARSDEN *Lett. & Jrnls.* 17 Mar. (1932) 415 He was so far lost to all religious feelings when I was in New Zealand that he would contend that the civilization of the young women was promoted by their living as prostitutes on board the whalers. **1845** MATHEW in *Founding of NZ* (1940) 220 Truth to tell however, the New Zealanders are acute, intelligent Savages, susceptible no doubt of a considerable degree of civilization. **1858** *Memo. by Native Secretary* 13 Oct. in Rutherford *Sel. Documents* (1949) 105 In these and many other ways the efforts of the Government have been successfully directed to the improvement and civilization of the Maori race. **1862** *Otago Witness* (Dunedin) 23 Aug. 2 The Natives were, however, in a state of retreat from civilization before the wa[r]s, from various causes. **1900** CANTERBURY *Old & New* 177

CLAIM

[Maori art] is a vigorous, earnest expression of the minds of the people before their 'civilization' commenced.

civilize, *v. Hist.* [Spec. use of *civilize* to reclaim from barbarism; to educate into a superior culture.] *trans.* To impose a European way of life on (Maori). Also *ppl. a.* **civilized, civilizing**.
1826 SHEPHERD *Journal* 25 Mar. in Howard *Rakiura* (1940) 364 He said Arms is the only sure method of sivilizing [*sic*] them that Missionaries were of little or no use. **1834** MARKHAM *NZ* (1963) 65 It is a curious Thing that the Chiefs have married of late years often the Girls who have been living on Board of Whalers, and I do believe that the Sailors have done as much towards Civilizing the Natives as the Missionaries have, or more. **1841** in *Establishment of New Plymouth* (1940) 71 The Missionaries have done much to civilize the New Zealanders both by themselves, and indirectly by educating and sending among them native teachers. **1851** SHORTLAND *S. Dist. NZ* 81 We were much amused at the pride the whalers evidently took in him [*sc.* Tuhawaiki]... [He] was appealed to as evidence of what they had done towards civilizing the New Zealanders. **1859** THOMSON The story of New Zealand: Past and present—savage and civilized [title: *NZNB* I ii 1023, iten 5537] **1971** *New Zealand's Heritage* I. 253 Marsden had thought that the best approach to mission work would be to 'civilise' the Maoris first and then to introduce them to Christianity. **1989** [see WAKEFIELD 1].

Hence **civilizer** *n. joc.* or *ironic*. A European as a pretender to a civilization supposedly superior to that of the Maori.
1852 MUNDY *Our Antipodes* II. 393 Many a reeling and reeking wretch among the white civilizers of the savage I saw [at the race-course]..but I saw only one native who had fallen a victim to the rum-booths,—and alack! it was a woman.

civil servant: see PUBLIC SERVANT.

clad(d)ie, clad(d)y, varr. KORARI.

clagger. [f. northern Brit. dial. *clag* a heavy viscid mass (*e.g.* of mud) + *-er:* see OED, EDD *clag.*] A heavy steamed pudding. Cf. SINKER 2.
1976 ANDERSON *Water Joey* 10 The [threshing-] mill-hands usually feasted on mutton and clagger (a heavy plum pudding).

claim. [Spec. use of *claim:* orig. US: AND 1851.]
1. a. A piece of land marked off or taken for (esp. gold) mining purposes. Also with a defining word, see: ALLUVIAL C 1, AMALGAMATED CLAIM, BEACH 5, CREEK 3 b, DREDGING CLAIM, EXTENDED CLAIM, FRONTAGE CLAIM, ORDINARY CLAIM, *prospecting claim* (PROSPECT *v.* 2), *river claim* (RIVER 2 b), *sluice claim* (SLUICE *n.* 2), *special claim* (SPECIAL *a.*), *wet claim* (WET *a.* 3).
1852 *Coromandel Gold Field. Provisional Regs.* in Swainson *Auckland* (1853) 161 Every person desirous of establishing a claim to a particular portion of unoccupied ground, by working in the ordinary method, for alluvial Gold, may have his claim marked out on the following scale, viz.,.. 15 feet frontage to either side of a River. **1862** HODDER *Memories NZ Life* 74 We marked out our 'claim' through the bed of the stream, according to the published regulations which allowed twenty square feet of land to each man for surface digging or 30 square feet for deep sinking. **1881** NESFIELD *Chequered Career* 75 We spent many jolly evenings in the claims, and met men in rough flannels and dirty soil-stained moles. **1892** PYKE *Gold-Miners' Guide* 7

Claims are classified as follows:—Alluvial deposits, and river-or creek-beds; Quartz lodes, reefs, and leaders; Sea-beach claims; Prospecting claims. **1940** *Nelson Evening Mail* 1 Aug. 10 Twelve subsidised men employed on claims situated on the Baton and Wangapeka Rivers produced 26 oz. of gold. **1953** MUNDY *Days That are No More* 124 They came across Sam's little claim and just cleaned up the box as if it was theirs. **1964** *Dominion* (Wellington) 6 Mar. 7 The Westland District Progress League may soon own its own gold-panning claim to be worked as a tourist attraction. **1978** MCARA *Gold Mining* 316 *Claim*: A title to mine issued by the Warden's Court under the Mining Act. A claim might be granted for any period up to 42 years. An annual rental was payable.

b. *transf.* A find of moa-bones treated as a mining claim.

1937 BUICK *Moa-Hunters NZ* 137 A few of the bones were taken into Waimate, and an account of the find..attracted the attention of Professor Hutton, who at once entered into negotiations for the purchase of the 'claim'; and..the said 'claim' passed into his hands.

2. Special Comb. **claim holder** [AND 1853], the holder of a mining claim; **claim jumping** *vbl. n.* [AND 1863], the illegal occupation, often by force, of another's claim (see also JUMP *v.*[1] 1).

1867 COOPER *Digger's Diary* 22 Nov. (1978) 15 If the charges..are persisted in, then very few, except the first-class **claim-holders**, can by any possibility avail themselves of [the crushing machine]. **1887** PYKE *Hist. Early Gold Discoveries Otago* (1962) 61 In some of the richest claims on the Sailor's Gully Reef at Forest Creek the surface claim-holders knocked the bottoms out of their shafts at a depth of about 20 feet. **1943** HISLOP *Pure Gold* 100 His claim produced a real good patch of gold..but although..he had to do no **claim-jumping** to get it, I cannot say it was quite above board. **1959** MILLAR *Westland's Golden 'Sixties* 146 At the field, there was a spectacle of claim-jumping that almost baffled description.

clap, *v.* [Transf. use of Brit. dial. *clap* of an animal, to sit down suddenly: see EDD *v.* 8.] **a.** *trans.* To make (a dog) sit or lie.

1934 *Press* (Christchurch) (Acland Gloss.) 13 Jan. 13 *Clap*.—To *c[lap]* a dog is to make him sit down. I am told the expression is in frequent use at dog-trials. I have never heard it on a station except from one very Scotch shepherd who used '*c[lap] down*' as a word of command.

b. *intr.* Of a dog, to sit or lie.

1971 NEWTON *Ten Thousand Dogs* 27 He was plain-eyed and barked when pulling, but was an outstanding hill dog... He used to 'clap' and would lie there barking.

Hence **clapping** *vbl. n.*

1984 RENNIE *Working Dogs* 37 Clapping is considered a fault in heading dogs by most trainers in New Zealand. The term describes the habit of some heading dogs particularly those with a strong eye, of lying down every time they stop moving. *Ibid.* 38 If you decide clapping is a fault you wish to correct, the time to do it is when the dog..'claps' for the first time.

clapmatch. *Sealing.* Also **clap match.** [Recorded earliest from NZ waters: cf. OED, ad. Dutch *klapmuts* 'a sailor's cap', apparently from a hood-shaped cartilage over the eyes of some northern seals to which the term was first applied.] A Pacific whalers' name for a female (usu. fur) seal. Cf. WIG *n.*

1815 *Sydney Gaz.* in McNab *Murihiku* (1907) 172 The Clap Match, or female seal, furnish great proportion [of kills]. **c1824** LETTER in McNab *Murihiku* (1909) 271 I do assert of late the southern and western coasts of New Zealand have been infested with Europeans and New Zealanders, who, without consideration, have killed the pups before they are prime, and the clap matches before pupping, for the sake of eating their carcasses. **c1920** [see KEKENO]. **1940** HOWARD *Rakiura* 40 Incoming skins are sorted to arbitrary standards—wigs (old males), clap-matches (females), bulls, yearlings, grey or silver pups (under one year), black pups. **1950** BEATTIE *Far-Famed Fiordland* 2 [Beattie comments] 'the explanation of *our own usage* of wigs and clapmatches is not meant for refined ears.'

class /klæs/, *n. Prison.* The classification block at Paremoremo prison.

1982 NEWBOLD *Big Huey* (Gloss.) 246 Class (n) Classification block. **1985** *NZ Times* 12 May 4 Classification Block slowly evolved into a de-classification block. True, all new 'Parry' residents were initially sent there for observation and assessment. But 'Class' was also the home of prisoners who did not quite fit elsewhere—inmates who needed protection from others.

class, *v. Shearing.* [AND 1889.] *trans.* To grade fleeces in a shearing-shed, or wool for sale according to type, quality, etc.

c1875 MEREDITH *Adventuring in Maoriland* (1935) 41 Fortunately, pater showed me how to class wool. **1879** *Auckland Weekly News* 25 Oct. 13 Why is the wool classed or sorted in the colonies? **1889** WILLIAMS & REEVES *Colonial Couplets* 10 Is there any advantage in classing each fleece? Does it pay to wash wool, or send them to market in the grease? **1894** [see BIN *n.* 1 a]. **1900** *Letter* in McCaskill *Molesworth* (1969) 83 I do not think my classer, who has classed for me for 4 or 5 years, understands scouring. **1933** *Press* (Christchurch) (Acland Gloss.) 30 Sept. 15 *Class*.—The woolclasser decides under what description each fleece shall be sold, or *classes* the clip. **1952** BLAKISTON *My Yesteryears* 30 The parents of Harry Smith, who classed the Gorge wool for forty years, came..by bullock dray in 1856. **1986** RICHARDS *Off the Sheep's Back* 113 Close by stood the classer's table, where he sat and classed each fleece before it was carried by a shed hand to its respective bin.

Hence **classing** *vbl. n.* [AND 1845.] Also *attrib.* In full *wool-classing* (WOOL 3).

1920 MACDONALD *Austral. & NZ Sheepfarming* 144 The big stations may make classing a very simple business. **1922** PERRY *Sheep Farming* 17 There should be good large windows in the roof over the classing or wool tables. **1951** MCLEOD *NZ High Country* 27 [The classer] is expected to be highly skilled in the classing and preparation of wool for sale. **1981** PINNEY *Early N. Otago Runs* 23 The Benmore classing was a big job, as some 3,000 fleeces came over four tables each day.

classer. [AND 1874.] In full *wool-classer* (see WOOL 3).

1878 *Country Jrnl.* (1877) II. 400 When shearing commences, a sorter or classer's table, be it ever so simple should be erected. **1894** WILSON *Land of Tui* 244 The shorn fleeces are..spread out by four wool-pickers, who tear away the bad parts and fold the fleeces square, passing them to the classer. **1913** CARR *Country Work* 15 The Classer, by feel, sight, and general knowledge, decides what class it [*sc.* the fleece] belongs to. **1926** DEVANNY *Butcher Shop* (1981) 68 Here the broad benches were piled high with golden fleeces which the classers..were sorting into various grades. **1940** STUDHOLME *Te Waimate* (1954) 208 At shearing time [at Benmore, 1892] about 55 men were employed in the shed: 28 to 30 shearers..1 classer. **1951** MCLEOD *NZ High Country* 28 The classer stands beside the gong..and when the clang of the old disc blade rings through the shed, the catching pen doors are flung open. **1973** FERNANDEZ *Tussock Fever* 3 Erina had gathered up Mutu's last fleece and thrown it expertly on the table before the classer. **1985** BREMNER *Woolscours of NZ* (Gloss. of Old Wool Terms) 9 *Classer* hand who groups together fleeces of similar style—length, fineness, quality—usually in shearing shed.

Classic Maori. Also **Classical Maori.** Usu. *attrib.* Applied by students to the period in Maori culture after the 'moa-hunter' but before the main European settlement.

1978 FULLER *Maori Food & Cook.* 10 Some time after the Moa-hunters came the Classical Maori. **1984** *Te Maori* 35 David Simmons follows with an essay that describes the tribal styles, beginning with those known in literature as Classic Maori, which belong to the Puawaitanga period (1500–1800), and extending to the varied styles of more recent times.

clayey. Also **clayie.** A clay marble.

1984 KEITH & MAIN *NZ Yesterdays* 288 World War II brought 'clayeys', often imperfectly spherical they were pathetic terracotta substitutes for real marbles. **1988** MCGILL *Dict. Kiwi Slang* 28 *clayie* clay marble.

Claytons. Also **Clayton's, claytons.** [The proprietary name of a substitute for hard liquor: see AND (1984) for details of the 1980 TV advertisement with its punch-line 'It's the drink I have when I'm not having a drink.'] Usu. as a quasi-adjective indicating a pretence to or a largely unsuccessful imitation of the 'real thing'.

1983 *National Bus. Rev.* 15 Aug. 7 To those criticising Muldoon for producing a Claytons Budget I say: 'Be thankful you're still living. He could have done worse.' **1984** *Evening Post* (Wellington) 6 July 8 Counsel..asked the jury of five men and seven women to see the trial for what it was—a 'Clayton's' conspiracy, the conspiracy that really isn't a conspiracy. **1992** *Dominion* (Wellington) 31 Mar. 10 Just when we thought we had heard the last of Clayton's, the Government introduces the referendum you have when you're not having a referendum. **1993** *Dominion* (Wellington) 29 Mar. 8 Then they [*sc.* banks] imposed a clayton-style receivership on the board.

clean, *a.*[1] *Farming hist.*

1. Free of disease, esp. of scab or pleuro-pneumonia. Hence also **unclean** (see b quot. 1912). **a.** [AND 1839.] Of farm animals.

1848 [see SCAB 1]. **1850** FOX in *Dillon Lett.* 8 Feb. (1954) 106 I hear awful accounts of scab in the Wairau. Only three flocks are said to be clean. **1872** in Cresswell *Canterbury Tales* 18 May (1951) 137 Mr Pasley inspected 16,000 sheep and finding all clean he left this afternoon on his way to Nelson. **1913** CARR *Country Work* 28 A means of keeping [ragwort] under by grazing clean sheep (i.e., sheep off clean pasture) has been found.

b. [AND 1840.] Of grazing country.

1885 ACTON-ADAMS in McCaskill *Molesworth* July (1969) 56 The only point I would mention is the *scab* question... At last after enormous effort the Amuri is clean. **1912** BOOTH *Five Years NZ* 28 At the time [c1860].., most of the runs in Nelson Province were 'unclean'—that is, infected with scab. **1938** BURDON *High Country* 79 It is notorious that, whereas the whole of the province of Nelson is scabbed, Canterbury is clean. **1968** TOMLINSON *Remembered Trails* 56 It was mostly clean country, and McCallum had built up a well known Merino flock.

Hence **clean** *v.* [AND 1845.] *trans.* To free (country) from scab.

CLEAN

1885 ACTON-ADAMS in McCaskill *Molesworth* July (1969) 56 The only point I would mention is the *scab* question... I have kept mustering [the Severn Block] to get in the wild sheep and my station diary will show that I have spent about £300 cleaning it... And after the country has been cleaned at my expense..you propose..to place the whole of the Amuri in danger.

2. In collocations: **clean certificate**, a certificate of freedom from scab; **clean hundreds**, the areas free from scab.

1863 CHUDLEIGH *Diary* 3 Nov. (1950) 108 Arthur had to go to Lyttelton to get a **clean certificate** from the scab inspector. **c1875** MEREDITH *Adventuring in Maoriland* (1935) 146 The Government is going to have a lot of bother with this [East Coast Maori] flock, in getting rid of the scab... Otherwise the sheep will constitute a bar to the issue of a 'clean certificate' for the colony. **1937** AYSON *Thomas* 99 The beasts were being inspected by the stock inspector for cases of pleuro-pneumonia to allow them to pass over the Wyndham River which was the boundary at that time for what was called the **clean hundreds**.

clean, *a.*[2]

1. Of a muster, complete, without stragglers.

1865 CHUDLEIGH *Diary* 24 Oct. (1950) 202 There were eight fellows spread about the face of the range below us but we did not make a very clean muster notwithstanding. **c1875** MEREDITH *Adventuring in Maoriland* (1935) 87 On these fern-clad [Wairarapa] runs, it is almost impossible to get an absolutely clean muster of the sheep.

2. a. Of the act of shearing, without difficulties or hold-ups.

1905 LANCASTER *Sons o' Men* 81 A big Maori was making the [shearing] pace; opening up in a scientific fashion with a clean-run cut over the ear-root. **1955** BOWEN *Wool Away* 78 One comb should do a run if properly ground on average clean shearing.

b. Of wool, scoured.

1982 *Agric. Gloss.* (MAF) 53 *Clean wool*: Scoured wool.

3. Of country, freed from scrub, fern, etc.

1951 LEVY *Grasslands NZ* (1970) 265 There are great areas of relatively clean country in the Wellington district.

clean, *a.*[3] *Prison.* [Transf. use of *clean* of a report bearing no adverse point or remark, listing no offence: see OED 3 c.] Of a person, innocent; of a prison inmate, free from a wish to inform on a fellow. See also CLEANSKIN 2.

1982 NEWBOLD *Big Huey* 246 Clean (adj) Innocent, free from incriminating evidence. **1984** BEATON *Outside In* 42 Di: Someone told her [the new inmate] I could score, so I helped her out... Ma: Bit risky, weren't it? Di: Nah, she's clean. You know how I feel about dogshit.

clean potato. [Prob. f. Brit. dial.: see OED *potato* 5 c; AND 1853.] In the negative phr. **not the clean potato**, of not unblemished reputation.

1907 *Truth* 20 July 6 A rag like yours can only circulate among a certain set, who like yourself are by no means very clean potatoes. If you were put upon the market I don't think 160 sacks of your kidney would even fetch 10/-. **1984** BEARDSLEY *Blackball 08* 743 clean potato (wasn't the c– p–) wasn't the honest person.

Clean-Shirt Ministry. *Hist.* [f. a remark by Thomas Spencer Forsaith (1814–98) an Auckland draper, politician, and Congregationalist pastor, b. London, emigrated to New Zealand 1858.] See quots.

c1898 *Gentleman's Mag.* vol. 284 No.2010 [Article by J.F. Hogan 'The Clean-Shirt Ministry'] 1st September 1854. T. Forsaith was asked..(when at work at his business) to form a Ministry. [He said] 'I put on a clean shirt and waited on His Excellency.' **1930** *Evening Post* (Wellington) (VUW Fildes Clippings 621:33) 16 Oct. The name 'Clean Shirt' Ministry arose from the fact that Mr. Forsaith announced in the House, in his Ministerial explanation, that he changed his shirt when summoned from his shop to the Governor's presence. **1934** HYDE *Journalese* 222 The Governor called on an Auckland baker to form a new Ministry. The said gentleman popped upstairs to don a clean shirt before calling on His Excellency, thereby providing his cabinet with the splendid title, 'The Clean-Shirt Ministry.' **1977** SINCLAIR *'Experiences of Auckland'* in *Auckland at Full Stretch* 31 When Thomas Forsaith, a draper, was asked to call on the administrator about forming a ministry in 1854 he first went home from his store to change his clothes. His government was called the 'clean shirt ministry'. It only lasted two days.

cleanskin.

1. *Farming.* [AND 1881.] See CLEAR-SKIN (the preferred New Zealand use).

1947 NEWTON *Wayleggo* 98 [The cattle] were of course real wild stuff—cleanskins born and bred in the bush. **1966** [see CLEARSKIN]. **1975** NEWTON *Sixty Thousand on the Hoof* 220 There were always the odd little bunches of 'cleanskins' that had either been missed or had beaten the dogs in previous musters.

Hence **clean-skinned** *a.*, of cattle, without brand or earmark.

1960 MASTERS *Back-Country Tales* 221 All were clean skinned wild cattle bar one, a 15-year-old steer with the old Willow Flat ear mark.

2. *Police.* [AND 1945.] A person without a police record. See also CLEAN *a.*[3]

1966 TURNER *Eng. Lang. Austral. & NZ* 148 In the underworld, *cleanskin* has been used for a man who has not crossed with the police before. **1981** *Dominion* (Wellington) 11 Mar. 7 Williams ran checks on [the man], tossing his name round experienced drug squad detectives and checking police files. Nothing came back. He was what police call a 'cleanskin'—a person with no police record.

clean up, *v. Goldmining.* To extract gold (from a tailrace, crushed ore, etc.); or from mercury amalgam by squeezing through chamois leather.

1874 BAINES *Edward Crewe* 259 After one day's wash with the machine, or when all the quicksilver..had become thickened by amalgamation, he would 'clean up,'—a process much the same with our little toy..as it is with the great quartz-crushing mills. **1881** BATHGATE *Waitaruna* 183 The trial crushing had commenced.... When they were to 'clean up' he did not know. **1907** COWAN *NZ* 34 The tail races..are periodically 'cleaned up' for gold.

Hence **cleaning-up** *vbl. n.*, the action or process of thus extracting gold. Also **clean-up**.

1903 *TrNZI* XXXV. 403 Mr. William Beetham..in Nelson, mentioned the trouble..occasioned at the periodical 'clean-up' by the presence of..lead which collected in the ripples with the gold. **1967** MAY *West Coast Gold Rushes* (1962) 528 Washing-up: the whole operation of saving gold from the wash-dirt. 'Cleaning up' had the same meaning. **1992** LATHAM *Golden Reefs* 1332 It would start stamping the six hundred tons of quartz about 'to grass' before cleaning up.

CLEARING

clear, *n. Chatham Is.* Usu. collective *pl.* **the clears**. [f. *clear adj.* of land, free from trees or forest.] The mainly fern-covered peaty land on Chatham Island, orig. unforested open or barren peat country.

1875 MCLEAN *Papers* (ATLTS) Vol. 42 [Sheep] feed on the open ground ('clears' as they are called here) in fine weather. **1897** *TrNZI* XXIX. 166 Having by observation found its [*sc.* a bird's] sleeping-place on the 'clears', the Moriories made long tracks leading up to it. **1902** *TrNZI* XXXIV. 253 When the sea-birds came to lay their eggs in the 'clears' in the south of the island the Moriories would live in that part. **1911** SHAND *Moriori People* 6 They [*sc.* Chathams duck] were driven from the lagoons into the..coarse growth of the 'clears', or open land. **1934** *Press* (Christchurch) (Acland Gloss.) 13 Jan. 13 *Clears, the.*—Great areas of barren, peaty land growing nothing but stunted fern and a few weakly plants of fog. A term confined to the Chatham Islands. **1956** *Bull. Wellington Bot. Soc. No.28* 3 The visitor to Chatham island is at first puzzled when he hears local residents referring to the 'clears'... The term was originally used to refer to those extensive areas on Chatham Island which, on account of wind exposure.., have always been 'clear' of forest. **1968** GRUNDY *Who'd Marry a Doctor?* 66 'Well,' she explained, 'the men get up early morning and ride into the clears'... Peaty areas covered with tussock, flax and bracken. **1985** LANGDALE-HUNT *Last Entail Male* 142 There were three paddocks named after Moriories that had lived there: Meinui Field..Kapata on the Paynter block, and Coachies Clear at Rauceby.

clear, *v.*

1. [See CLEARING 1.] *trans.* and *intr.* To free (land) from forest and other cover; to bring land into cultivation by clearfelling and burning bush.

1837 *Piraki Log* 27 Oct. (1911) 58 Sawyers clearing the Bush for their Work. **1846** CHAPMAN *Let.* 16 Dec. in Drummond *Married & Gone to NZ* (1960) 72 We have some Maories clearing for us [in Karori, Wellington]. They are burning off all logs.

2. In the phr. **clear the board!**, a woolshed cry or order to stop shearing.

1878 *Otago Witness* (Dunedin) 28 Sept. 3 Some men are good pen-men. Those who have watches are working hard to get the sheep they have on the board off, and catch another, before the manager calls out: 'Clear the board.' **1880s** *Teviot Station Shearing Rules* in Martin *Forgotten Worker* (1990) 95 No Shearer shall go into a pen to catch a Sheep after 'Smoke-oh' or any interval, or 'Clear the Board' has been called. **1897** WRIGHT *Station Ballads* 101 Clear the board! Clear the board! is the shout... Big Mick is smiling grimly as he takes the cobbler out. **1904** CRADOCK *Sport in NZ* 172 The wool-classer, or shed manager, as the case may be, roars out for the final time 'Clear the Board!' **1933** *Press* (Christchurch) (Acland Gloss.) 30 Sept. 15 *Clear the board.*—Order given (now usually by a gong or bell) to the shearers to stop shearing.

clearing, *vbl. n.*

1. [Spec. use of *clearing vbl. n.* f. *clear* to free (land, etc.) from trees, etc.: see OED *clear v.* 10 b (b) 1697: of special significance in NZ in respect of the clearing of native bush for settlement.] **a.** An area cleared of its original bush cover; a cleared part of a bush farm. See also BUSH-CLEARING 1.

1848 ARNOLD *NZ Lett.* 24 July (1966) 60 She is one of a lot of cattle that have just been landed..but she is now out on the clearing..and feeding away heartily. **1855** *Richmond-Atkinson Papers* (1960) I. 797 My old clearing is pretty clear but in parts of the new one they [*sc.* thistles] absolutely cover the ground. **1882** Hay *Brighter Britain* II. 226 It is much seen about gardens and clearings, and settlers know it as the 'blight-bird'. **1899** Bell *In the Shadow of the Bush* 8 A large clearing opened out on the right, and a little way back from the road-line stood a slab hut. **1905** Thomson *Bush Boys* 83 A tall 'Kahikatea' (white pine)..stood gaunt, bare, and solitary in the 'clearing'.

b. In place-names. With init. cap. and a prefixed defining word, a place-name denoting a specific clearing.

1879 Featon *Waikato War* 43 [S]ome bushmen..were busy at work felling and clearing away the bush alongside the road, a short distance past Williamson's Clearing. **1959** *TrRSNZ* LXXXVII. 27 A much larger natural clearing in a beech forest (Littles Clearing) on the flat summit of the Black Birch Range.

2. a. [Used elsewhere but recorded earliest in NZ: see OED *clearing* 3, 1860.] The (process of) clearing from land of bush, scrub, and other hindrances to cultivation.

1842 Heaphy *NZ* 74 Evidently the best way of clearing..is thus always employed either in the cultivation of the ground, or on fresh clearings. **1899** Bell *In Shadow of Bush* 9 This was Maurice McKeown, employed..to assist..in the work of the farm..in logging up and clearing..and also..in doing a little bushfalling.

b. Occas. as **clearing off**, the felled debris, slash, etc. cleared and left for burning. See also clear off *v.*

1854 *Richmond-Atkinson Papers* (1960) I. 141 The houses in this neighbourhood have been in some danger from bush firings..then just as several people had lighted their clearings a strong gale..sprang up. In a few hours all the dead trees and stumps in the neighbourhood were on fire. **1883** *Brett's Colonists' Guide* 18 Start the fire at noon all round the clearing..and let them burn towards the centre. **1892** *TrNZI* XXIV. 704 When burning the rest of the clearing-off in March, however, the trees caught fire, and several of them were burnt through and fell.

clearing sale. A sale to dispose of superfluous stock at greatly reduced or unreserved prices; a clearance sale.

1915 *Rangitikei Advocate & Manawatu Argus* 15 May 8 [Heading] Unreserved Clearing Sale. **1924** Anthony *Follow the Call* (1975) 23 On Sunday morning I ran my gig out of the shed... I had bought it at a clearing sale for £4, and it wasn't exactly a model turnout. **1992** *TV1* 22 Mar. 5.20 p.m. [Advt] Motown's end of season crazy clearing sale.

clear off, *v. trans.* To rid land of felled debris, logs, etc. usu. by burning.

1899 Bell *In the Shadow of the Bush* 198 Many, who..had been unfortunate in getting bad 'burns', were now hopeful of clearing off much of the timber by means of a second fire.

Hence **clearing-off** *ppl. a.*

1936 Belshaw et al. *Agric. Organiz. NZ* 581 Fires, originating generally from settlers' clearing-off operations..have in the past done considerable destruction.

clear-skin. [AND 1884.] An unbranded, unearmarked wild cattle-beast. Cf. cleanskin 1.

1898 *Merriam-Webster Internat. Dict.* (Australasian Supp.) 2020 *Cleanskins..Clearskins..n. pl.* Unbranded cattle. **1904** Cradock *Sport in NZ* 173 The station..caused a reward to be offered of £2 per head for all cattle..bearing the station brand, and a further reward of £1 per head for all 'clear skins'. **1947** Newton *Wayleggo* 153 *Clearskins*: Cattle which have not been ear-marked. Really wild cattle are referred to as clearskins. **1952** Lyon *Faring South* 85 In this large area [of Rangitikei flax swamp]..cattle bred unmolested, and it was the custom of early settlers to shoot a clearskin, or unbranded young animal for meat. **1966** Turner *Eng. Lang. Austral. & NZ* 148 *Clearskin* or *cleanskin* are names for unbranded animals.

clematis. [Spec. use of *clematis* a flowering climber.] **a.** Also **New Zealand clematis**, **white clematis**. Any of eight native species of *Clematis* (fam. Ranunculaceae), climbing plants or suckering subshrubs common in forest and scrub. See also *Our Lady of October* (lady 3), pikiarero, puawananga.

1833 Williams *Early Jrnls.* 27 Nov. (1961) 351 We landed on Motu tapu in a lovely retired sheltered spot, where the clematis and convolvulus and other creeping plants hung beautifully around. **1844** Colenso *Excurs. Northern Is.* in Taylor *Early Travellers* (1959) 12 I detected a rambling *Clematis* with ternate, coriaceous, and glabrous leaves. **1850** Angus *Savage Life* I. 289 The large and star-like flowers of the *clematis*, or pikiarero of the New Zealanders. **1867** Barker *Station Life* (1870) 180 Their stumps were already hidden by clematis and wild creepers of other kinds. **1883** Domett *Ranolf & Amohia* I. 132 No clematis, so lovely in decline, Whose star-flowers when they cease to shine Fade into feathery wreaths silk-bright. **1907** Mansfield *Letters* 20 Nov. (1984) I. 31 We got great sprays of clematis—and konini, and drove first through a bush path. **1910** Cockayne *NZ Plants* 38 The large-flowered clematis (*Clematis indivisa*, puawhananga) is esteemed by all, and its snowy blossoms are frequently torn from their forest home only to wither. **1922** *NZJST* IV. 281 The sweet-scented clematis (*C. foetida*) flourished on the Cattlemarket Reserve. **1933** Scanlan *Tides of Youth* 59 Supplejack vines, clematis, bush lawyer..twined and wreathed both trunk and branch. **1969** Harvey & Godley *Botanical Paintings* 22 *Clematis paniculata* White clematis Puawananga Ranunculaceae Puawananga is the most beautiful of our nine native species of *Clematis*. **1985** *NZ Times* 3 Feb. 12 Up to 10 years after such a bushfire,... some stumps were soothed with a brief cool bandage of white native clematis, which is called, charmingly, Our Lady of October over The Hill in Takaka.

b. As **bush-clematis**, the wild native species as distinct from introduced ornamentals.

1965 Shadbolt *Among Cinders* 33 Around one twist in the creek we came to a fantastic display of bush-clematis. The white flowers, all shimmering with sunlight, dripped from every tree in sight. **1971** *New Zealand's Heritage* I. 267 Bush Clematis, *Clematis paniculata*. Large strong woody vine which climbs trees. Produces lovely white flowers. **1981** Dennis *Paparoas Guide* 158 From early in spring the..kowhai and occasional treetop white of the climbing bush clematis (*C. paniculata*) are common sights.

Cleopatra (apple). [Transf. use of *Cleopatra* the name of a queen of Egypt famous for her beauty: AND (chiefly Tasmania) 1936.] A variety of eating apple, no longer grown commercially.

1887 *Auckland Weekly News* 30 July 34 Five included lists of apples for export, the following varieties have been recommended:—Blenheim Orange.. Wellington Pippin..Northern Spy..Cleopatra. **1890** *Otago Witness* (Dunedin) 24 July 5 Mr. J.G. Sharpe..has given..some particulars regarding a box of sample apples..sent to England... Cleopatra—Both sound. **1913** *NZJAg.* Jan. VI. 388 The New York Pippins (Cleopatras) were a nice line. **1939** Bensemann *Apple Culture* 68 A photo is taken of the six varieties as follows..Cox Orange Pippin..Cleopatra..Delicious.. Sturmer..Jonathan..Dunn's Favourite. *Ibid.* 89 [Caption] Fig. 40 showing Sturmer and Cleopatra apples. **1950** *Royal NZ Inst. Hort. Official Judging Rules* 21 In the case of yellow and green apples, the appearance of such apples is enhanced if a blush is present, such as may be found in Cleopatra.

clever. [f. Brit. dial. *clever* in health: see OED 4 b; EDD 1.] Esp. in the negative phr. **not too clever**, not very well in health or mood.

1937 Partridge *Dict. Slang* 158 *clever*... Esp. *not too clever*, indisposed in health; the health sense is common in Australia and New Zealand. **1938** *Press* (Christchurch) (McNab Slang) 2 Apr. 18 [The traveller to New Zealand] might be..told..that his acquaintance, somewhat indisposed, did not 'feel too clever'.

clianthus. [f. *Clianthus* (fam. Fabaceae) a genus of two Australasian shrubs named by English botanist J. Lindley in 1835.] In New Zealand *Clianthus puniceus*, a native shrub rare in the wild, kaka-beak 1.

1841 Mrs Loudon *Ladies' Compan. Flower Garden* 56 [OED] Clianthus..the crimson Glory Pea, is a magnificent half-hardy shrub..with bright crimson flowers, a native of New Zealand. **1853** Mackie *Traveller under Concern* 23 June (1973) 119 The only native plant grown in the gardens for the beauty of its flowers is the Clianthus. **1907** [see kaka-beak 1]. **1921** Tannock *Manual of Gardening* 140 The clianthus is a most showy plant.

climbing fern: see fern 2 (1).

climb into. [Cf. Wentworth & Flexner *climb v.t.* To reprimand, scold, or criticize (someone) severely. *W.W.II Army use.*] To criticize (someone) severely; to attack with words (occas. also, physically).

1993 *Dominion* (Wellington) 6 July 1 You can go to certain suburbs in this country of middle-class New Zealanders where you will have people climbing into Polynesians for under-achieving and in the next breath criticising Asians for over-achieving.

clina, var. clinah.

clinah /ˈklaɪnə/. *Obs.* Also **clina**. [AND *cliner* ad. Germ. *kleine* feminine of *klein* little, 1895.] A girl or girl-friend.

1906 *Truth* 31 Mar. 6 [Bloke's Patter] For he tells you, not being prudy, That your love's a 'Tom' or 'Tart', Or a 'Clinah' or a 'Judy', Likewise 'Bit of Skirt' or 'Tart'. **1906** Picard *Ups & Downs* 26 No thanks to this party who had been smoodging to a clina up the line instead of slinging the roaring lion his hash.

cliner, var. clinah.

cling fish.

1. In New Zealand applied to various small fishes of the fam. Gobiesocidae using modified ventral fins to form a strong suction disc for clinging to rocks. See also *suckerfish* (sucker *n.*[1]).

1927 Phillipps *Bibliogr. NZ Fishes* (1971) 55 *Trachelochismus littoreus*... Clingfish. **1938** *TrRSNZ* LXVIII. 418 *Trachelochismus littoreus*... Cling-fish. **1947** Powell *Native Animals NZ* 65 Cling fish (*Diplocrepis puniceus*). This is found by turning over stones at low tide, for it frequently makes no attempt to escape, but clings tightly to the stone by means of a specially designed suction disc on the under side of the body..common in Auckland waters. **1956** Graham *Treasury NZ Fishes* 413 Clingfish *Trachelochismus* *melobesia*... Clingfish *Dellicthys morelandi*. **1967** Natusch *Animals NZ* 233 Family Gobiesocidae. Small clingfish are found inshore, under stones in intertidal pools. **1982** Ayling *Collins Guide* (1984) 133 Clingfishes are small fishes of shallow water with a distinctive large-headed flattened shape.

2. With a modifier: **orange**, **urchin**.

(1) **orange clingfish**. See quot.
  1982 Ayling *Collins Guide* (1984) 134 *Orange clingfish Diplocrepis puniceus*... Orange clingfish are common on rocky coasts throughout New Zealand but are restricted to a narrow band reaching from immediately above low water level down to about 5m depth.

(2) **urchin clingfish**. *Dellicthys morelandi*, named from its association with the sea-urchin.
  1982 Ayling *Collins Guide* (1984) 133 Another common species is the urchin clingfish, *Dellichthys morelandi*... A peculiarity of this species is that it is only found..living between the sheltering spines of the common sea urchin or kina. **1983** Gunson *Collins Guide to Seashore* 174 The urchin clingfish *Dellichthys morelandi* (30mm) can be found hiding under the spines of the common sea urchin *Erechinus choroticus*, and is distinguished from its larger relations by the bright blue spots on its upper surfaces.

clinker beech: see BEECH 2 (3).

clip. [Recorded elsewhere but of special significance in the NZ farming economy: see OED *n.*² 2 b, 1825 (dial.).] All the wool shorn from sheep from one farm, area, or the whole country; the wool shorn in a season.
  1848 Cargill in Eccles & Reed *John Jones Otago* (1949) 49 Mr. Jones's clip (and he began with but a handful) amounted last year to £4,500. **1851** Weld *Hints to Intending Sheep-farmers* 5 I think that this sum, the proceeds of two clips of wool, should carry your station over the first two years. **1879** Chudleigh *Diary* 5 Dec. (1950) 282 My shearing has been a long one and my clip a light one. **1892** *NZ Official Handbook* 122 The average clips for the various breeds of sheep are approximately as follow: Merino, from 4lb. to 7lb. [etc.]. **1909** Owen *Philip Loveluck* 172 They're not half a bad flock... It ought to be a good clip. **1929** *NZJST* X. 326 Regarding the respective values of the clips..fleeces from March-shorn sheep were not able to be rolled. **1936** Belshaw et al. *Agric. Organiz. NZ* 710 In large clips of 100 bales or more each of these lines would usually be subdivided into two lots. **1951** Hunt *Confessions* 71 The phenomenal growth of my company aroused certain of our competitors from whom we were taking scores of clips of wool that they had handled for many years. **1964** Dick *High Country Family* 25 In the 1915-16 shearing season the whole clip was sold privately for 10d per pound. **1982** *Agric. Gloss.* (MAF) 53 *Clip*: Quantity of shorn wool from a defined area (farm or locality) or group of sheep.

clippie. *Obs.* A tram or train conductor; one who 'clips' passengers' tickets.
  1944 *NZEF Times* 13 Mar. 7 Things are bad in New Zealand now for such women. What with clippies on the trams, land girls and meat factory girls. **1952** *Here & Now* Sept. 29 Your tram ticket is punched by the same Maori clippie you meet every day. **1980** *Dominion* (Wellington) 25 July 1 'Where's the guard, where's the guard?,' she said. We had this clippie with us and she said 'What's the matter?' **1988** Smith *Southlanders at Heart* 25 Tramway rules would not permit him help a 'clippie' with his grab.

clobbering machine. Also **the (great) Kiwi clobbering machine**. [f. *clobber* to strike down, to defeat.] A metaphor for the local or bureaucratic conservatism allegedly responsible for quashing individual creativity or enterprise.
  1972 Mitchell *Pavlova Paradise* 45 The New Zealand Clobbering Machine is the national equivalent of small town community pressures. **1987** *Listener* 3 Oct. 12 The musical clobbering-machine in New Zealand is not short on frenzied moral outrage. **1988** *Evening Post* (Wellington) 14 July 37 'The great Kiwi clobbering machine does not exist in the bookworld, as people do take a pride in their country and their heritage,' Mr King said. **1989** Bioletti *The Yanks Are Coming* 39 It is part of the Kiwi clobbering machine that our own are put down and the visitor exalted. **1989** *Press* (Christchurch) 14 Feb. 19 The 'great brown clobbering machine' is a major obstacle to Maori achievement at school, say two researchers... Achievers are labelled 'mallowpuff Maoris'. **1992** *Evening Post* (Wellington) 27 Mar. 4 The Great New Zealand Clobbering Machine which keeps our heroes down to a manageable number goaded him on to triumph.

clock, *v.*¹ [Extended use of *clock* to hit on the face: see OED *v.*¹ 3.] To hit, to punch.
  1947 Davin *For Rest of Our Lives* 51 So then I clocked him and we beat it. **1951** 15–16 F 23 Marlborough C. 30A Clock [F1M1] **1970** Davin *Not Here Not Now* 308 You're a hypocritical bastard yourself, shaking his hand instead of clocking him one. **1974** Mason *Hand on the Rail* (TS 1987) 37 June:.. Jimmy was the on'y friend he ever had. On'y one! Then he had to go and clock him. **1984** Wilson *South Pacific Street* 51 Going off with Martha like that. I ought to sock you one. I'll clock you, you bloody mongrel!

clock. *v.*² [f. *clock* an odometer.] *trans.* To wind back the odometer of a used vehicle to increase its value. Also as *vbl. n.*
  1995 *Sunday Star-Times* (Auckland) 23 July C13 [Heading] Customs official warns of 'clocking'... About 90% of the used cars coming into New Zealand had done more miles than their odometers [sic] indicated. They had been 'clocked'.

Cloudy Bay cod: see COD 2 (4).

clout, *v.* Also **clout on**. [f. obs. Brit. slang *clout* to steal (perh. orig. to steal 'clouts' or handkerchiefs): see Partridge *Dict. Underworld*.] To steal; to 'get down on'.
  1937 Partridge *Dict. Slang* 161 *clout*... To seize; to steal: New Zealanders': C. 20. **1938** *Press* (Christchurch) (McNab Slang) 2 Apr. 18 [In local criminal slang] 'to clout', 'to pole', 'to fend off' are to steal. **1962** Hori *Half-gallon Jar* 16 [The mussels] have all gone. The wife's brother has clouted on them while we are [sic] away. **1964** Hori *Fill It Up Again* 4 That brother-in-law of mine had clouted the lot. **1991** Duff *One Night Out Stealing* 102 Sonny thinks he's gonna keep that stuff he clouted on the stereo and tv.

club. [Spec. use of *club* a heavy stick for use as a weapon.] A Maori or Moriori short hand-weapon (see MERE, PATU); also a pestle or pounder.
  1777 Forster *Voyage Round World* I. 137 Standing on the shore we perceived one of the natives... He stood with a club or battle-axe in his hand. **1791** *Jrnl. 'Chatham'* 29 Nov. in McNab *Hist. Records* (1914) II. 506 Both their [sc. Moriorisʼ] Spears and Clubs were subject to great variety... Their Clubs were rough pieces of Wood,.. and a very few had two stones lashed on at one end, which gave them the appearance of a double-headed maul. **1904** *TrNZI* XXXVI. 460 As affording some guide..two clubs of black-maire (*Olea cunninghamii*)—the kind used by the natives in crushing fern-root—were found.

clubbie. [f. life-saving *club* (member) + –IE.] A surf patrol member.
  1995 *Sunday Star–Times* (Auckland) 22 Jan. C6 We went and told the surf patrol, not 10 metres away... The clubbies said they had contemplated throwing a bucket of water over [the drunk youth].

clucky, *a.* [f. the noise made by a broody or 'clucking' hen.] Of a woman, showing a desire for children.
  [**1883** Ferguson *Castle Gay* 213 And those who cannot shake theirs, fegs! Are deemed no more than 'Chinkies', Or left like clocking hens, on eggs.] **1988** McGill *Dict. Kiwi Slang* 29 *clucky* showing signs of wanting children, being pregnant, or being fussy about children, akin to the clucking of a brooding hen; eg 'Win's been quite clucky of late. You haven't duffed her, have you, Brian?' **1990** *NZ Herald* (Auckland) 13 Jan. sect. ii (leader page) We all get clucky. And, by the sound of all the oohing and aahing, the sight of Romanian orphans on television has set off a small epidemic of cluckiness.

c'mon. A common familiar representation of 'Come on!', a cry of encouragement.
  1986 *Listener* 19 Apr. 28 The Telethons and the Live Aid concerts indicate that we are generous but they are no more culturally us than jogging or 'C'mon, Kiwi, c'mon'. **1992** Sinclair *Frontman* 50 Ten bucks if ya skull a bottle of DB, c'mon, ya fucken wanker.

CMT, *Hist.* An acronym of *Compulsory Military Training*, the name commonly given to a scheme for peacetime conscription and military training, introduced 1949–50 and abolished in 1959.
  1993 Yska *All Shook Up* 32 By 1952, compulsory military training, popularly known as CMT or 'the call-up', attracted controversy when it was revealed that teenage conscripts were indoctrinated at camp.

coal-fish. *Obs.* Also **cole-fish**. [Extended use of *coal-fish* applied to various species having a dusky skin: see OED.] blue cod (COD 2 (3) *Parapercis colias*).
  1770 Banks *Journal* Mar. (1962) II. 7 Besides these there were many species which tho they did not at all resemble any fish that I at least have before seen, our seamen contriv'd to give names to, so that hakes, breams, Cole fish &c. were appellations familiar with us. **1777** Forster *Voyage Round World* I. 126 The best and most savoury fish was a species of cod, which, from its external colour, our sailors called a coal-fish. **1793** Raven in McNab *Hist. Records* 19 Nov. (1908) I. 178 Coal-fish are innumerable [at Dusky Sound] and may be caught with hooks and lines in almost any quantity. **1838** Polack *NZ* I. 323 Many other fish are equally numerous, answering to our *hakes, tench..cole-fish..*and *dog-fish*. **1842** Gray *Fauna* in Dieffenbach *Travels in NZ* (1843) II. 222 The 'polach' he [sc. Polack] speaks of are, perhaps, the young of the *Percis colias*, the adult of which are known to the settlers as the 'cole-fish'. **1872** [see COD 2 (3)]. **1957** Parrott *Sea Angler's Fishes* 141 This [Blue Cod], is the fish known to Captain Cook as the 'Coal-fish'. **1967** Moreland *Marine Fishes* 28 Blue cod... A very old name from Cook's time, coalfish, is still in use. A variety of Maori names are now little used. **1986** [see COD 2 (3)].

coarimika, var. KOROMIKO.

coarse, *a.* Of gold, granulated in comparatively large particles. Contrast FINE.
  1914 Pfaff *Diggers' Story* 64 We made a good haul of very coarse gold. **1918** *NZJST* I. 12 The gold occurring in the quartz was very fine, and it was

considered that the coarse alluvial gold found in the creek-beds could not have been shed from the lodes discovered. **1976** BROWN *Difficult Country* 38 He was shown fine gold from from the Matakitaki and coarse gold from the Mangles. **1981** DENNIS *Paparoas Guide* 68 The gold soon gained a reputation for being coarse and nuggety.

Coast. Usu. as **the Coast.** Often *attrib.*

1. EAST COAST.

1853 GRACE *Let.* 29 Apr. in *Pioneer Missionary* (1928) 24 A week ago I received a letter from the Revd. R. Barker telling me that he is leaving the Coast. **1934** NGATA *Let.* 17 Mar. in *Na To Hoa Aroha* (1988) III. 132 Already the Coast and Bay of Plenty tribes were moving to Waitangi. **1948** BALLANTYNE *Cunninghams* (1976) 25 I got nothing against Maoris, Fred... Especially these coast Maoris. **1973** WHEELER *Hist. Sheep Stations NI* 71 The ram type press..is not uncommon on the Coast. **1986** IHIMAERA *Matriarch* 25 There's something about Maori women from Gisborne or up the Coast.

2. WEST COAST.

[*Note*] 'The Coast' seems preferred to 'The West Coast' by those born or longtime resident in the area.

1866 MUELLER *My Dear Bannie* 2 Jan. (1958) 100 Unless they find gold..there is very little prospect of the diggers now at the Coast remaining long. **1878** *TrNZI* X. 481 The Coast was..too powerful a magnet to be counteracted by the simple chances of finding gold in a district where possibility was the only inducement held out. **1888** PRESHAW *Banking Under Difficulties* 155 A few of us landed in one of the ship's boats; not a safe thing to do as a rule on the Coast. **1896** O'REGAN *Poems* 37 An' after, when the Coast broke out, we roughed it thro' the bush. **1908** FINDLAY *Humbugs and Homilies* 258 Who talks as fast as a Coast cockatoo? **1912** MANSFIELD *Stories* (1984 Alpers) 113 She'd be a barmaid down the Coast—as pretty as a wax doll. **1926** COWAN *Travel in NZ* II. 90 Only one Chinaman, says Coast gossip, ever ran the gauntlet. **1959** SLATTER *Gun in My Hand* 76 To him the Coast was home and there was no place like it. **1966** *Encycl. NZ* II. 680 The west coast of the South Island is *The Coast* and residents there are *Coasters*. **1974** in *Listener Short Stories* (1977) 120 I was newly arrived from Christchurch, and unaware of Coast ways. **1986** HULME *Windeater* 37 One thing everybody does know about the Coast is bait. Whitebait.

3. Other local applications. **a.** The north-east coast of the SI.

1934 ACLAND *Press* (Christchurch) (Acland Gloss.) 13 Jan. 13 *Coast, the.*— Short for West Coast, but since the [1914-18] war I have heard people who live between Kaikoura and Blenheim speak of the country as the C[oast].

b. The west coast of Wellington province from roughly Paremata to Paekakariki (or further north); also occas. called the GOLD COAST.

1963 *Comment* 17 Oct. 11 Golden Coasters are not, by and large, keen gardeners. Perhaps the heavy clay deters them. More likely the Coast attracts a different type: the open air fraternity which prefers boating and fishing.

coast(al), *a.* In names of plants, see: MILK-TREE, *sowthistle* (THISTLE *n.* 2 (5) b).

Coaster.

1. A shortened form of WEST COASTER.

1907 DRUMMOND *Life & Work R.J. Seddon* 349 [Seddon] was assisted by his good wife (who shared the love of all Coasters, with her husband) and their daughter. **1914** PFAFF *The Diggers' Story* 36 Among the old Coasters..the question is always asked: 'Did you ever hear about the fight at the Big Dam?' **1924** *Otago Witness* (Dunedin) 4 Mar. 69 To the Coasters the Coast is God's best creation. **1935** ODELL *Handbook Arthur Pass National Park* 13 When the problem of travelling stock was solved by the Coasters raising their own meat, the efforts to construct a track over Browning Pass were discontinued. **1959** SLATTER *Gun in My Hand* 76 To him the Coast was the rattling bridge at Hokitika..and the friendly ways of the real Coasters. **1965** GILLHAM *Naturalist in NZ* 94 Coasters can also claim that their region is the only home of the true Maori greenstone or jade. **1974** in *Listener Short Stories* (1977) 118 Coasters in their hundreds flock to the rivers and streams to swoop and scoop..as many [whitebait] as possible. **1986** HULME *Windeater* 37 Well, I mean, Coasters have their channels for spreading news, mainly ex-Coasters. **1992** *NZ Encycl.* 551 The 'Coaster' has always been a legendary character of independence who ignored the six o'clock closing of hotels and other petty bourgeois laws, and has always retained an image that is macho, but self-reliant and friendly.

2. Occas. also **Coastie.** A shortened form of *East Coaster* (EAST COAST).

1987 *Dominion* (Wellington) 2 Jan. 3 Mr Haenga, a coaster born and bred in the area, has no doubts Ruatoria will soon return to the lifestyle of the good old days. **1993** *North & South* (Auckland) Feb. 90 So I went for the audition... 'Are you Ngati Porou?' They're the coasties—staunch. Syd Jackson, Hone Kaa, those kind of people. **1995** *National Geographic* Oct.–Dec. 19 Poor as can be, but living the lives of kings—a Coastie's description of the laid-back lifestyle on New Zealand's easternmost seaboard.

coast grass: see GRASS 2 (12).

Coastie: see COASTER 2.

coat. In various phrases.

1. to put (one) **on the coat** [AND 1940], to ostracize, to excommunicate.

1982 NEWBOLD *Big Huey* 66 This is one of the reasons that informal social control mechanisms at Paremoremo are so strong. Anybody who deviates from the required standard of thought or behaviour— the criminal standard—is quickly observed and 'put on the coat' by the rest of the community. *Ibid.* 130 A lot of my old mates..disapproved totally of what was happening and put me on the coat. We remained on speaking terms, but it wasn't the same as it had been before.

2. Shearing. **to pull the coat,** see quot.

1989 *NZ English Newsletter* III. 26 *pulling the coat:* Walking out of a shed before the shearing has finished.

cob, *n.*¹ *Hist.* [f. *cob* a building material used esp. in the south-west of England (see OED *n.*²), of significance in early colonial New Zealand.]

1. A mixture of clay or mud and straw or grass formerly used in building.

1842 in *Lett. from New Plymouth* 16 Sept. (1968) 52 The Devonshire and Cornish emigrants build excellent houses of mud and straw mixed, which they call *cob.* **1866** BARKER *Station Life* (1870) 49 Some of the houses are built of 'cob,' especially those erected in the very early days, when sawn timber was rare and valuable: this material is simply wet clay with chopped tussocks stamped in. **1894** *Richmond-Atkinson Papers* (1960) II. 595 Reached this house [the Hermitage] [*sic*]..a long low building—the old part cob, the new part galvanised iron. **1913** BATHGATE *Sodger Sandy's Bairn* 51 It was a primitive structure, being built of 'cob', or, as Mr Beauchamp preferred to call it, 'adobe'. **c1937** in Hyde *Selected Poems* (1984) 44 Swarming down from their lone-set mountain cabins, Tramping from cob and raupo, wattle and daub. **1948** SCOTTER *Run Estate & Farm* 18 The building of a hut made of cob—clay mixed with grass—for shepherds has been mentioned. **1986** SALMOND *Old NZ Houses* 231 Cob. a mixture of clay, water, chopped straw or grass (in New Zealand tussock or wiwi), and often animal manure, all thoroughly mixed and trodden in layers to form walls.

2. Used *attrib.* in Comb. in the sense 'built of cob' as **cob chimney, house, hut.**

1851 *Richmond-Atkinson Papers* (1960) I. 82 The kitchen has a wide **cob chimney**, & is roughly floored with wide planks just laid on the ground. **1842** in *Lett. from New Plymouth* 28 Sept. (1968) 56 At the Hua-Toki, we have several excellent wooden and **cob houses**, building or built. **1851** *Lyttelton Times* 5 July 1 Contract for Ditch and Bank Fencing, the erection of Cob-Houses, Excavations, &c. **1944** *Fielding Express* 29 June 4 The difference between a sod house and a cob house is that the former is made of sods cut square and laid like bricks to form a wall, while a cob house is built of clay cemented with tussock. **1952** THOMSON *Deer Hunter* VII [Caption] **Cob huts** are common in Marlborough; made from clay and chopped tussock, they are warm in winter, cool in summer and have stood the test of time. **1964** ANDERSON *Doctor in Mountains* (1974) 53 The tiny building where I saw my patients was little more than a cob hut.

cob, *n.*² Abbrev. of COBBER.

1956 *Street Society Christchurch* 20 [At a Christchurch youth club] Oh, a great party. You had somewhere to have it? Yeah, at a cob's place. **1959** SLATTER *Gun in My Hand* 45 Too proud to drink with ya old cobs? A man oughta dong ya. **1960** MUIR *Word for Word* 254 You weren't actually married, of course. Not me, cob. She was keen enough, though. **1970** SLATTER *On the Ball* 140 'Righto, Spandau, me old cob,' I say.

Cobb. *Hist.* A term for specific type of coach, thorough-braced rather than sprung, popular in New Zealand and Australia in the 19th and early 20th centuries; hence used (poss. illicitly) in quasi-proprietary names for particular coach-lines having no connection with the genuine Cobb and Co.

[*Note*] Cobb and Co. never operated in New Zealand, but it was usual for coach-line proprietors to use the name *Cobb and Co.* for promotional purposes. See J. Halket Millar, *High Noon for Coaches* (1965) pp.40–41 on the coach and the company name.

1. The name of a type of coach; occas. (?quot. 1863) of a coach line. **a.** As **Cobb('s) coach.**

1863 WALKER *Jrnl. & Lett.* (ATLTS) 4 Jan. Sent our swags by Cobb's coach. They took them for £1 each. **1870** SEWELL *Lecture on NZ* 16 Cobb's Coaches were first established in Australia from thence they have been transplanted to New Zealand, and have taken root; strange vehicles they are with springs of leather. **1888** D'AVIGDOR *Antipodean Notes* 190 The 'Cobb' coaches—as these vehicles are termed from their original proprietor—are very strongly built; the body is borne by a combination of leather and iron, called a 'thorough brace'. **1898** HOCKEN *Contributions* 108 At length the gold days and Cobb's coaches ended this uncertain travel, and now that..journey is accomplished in an hour-and-a-half. **1931** LOVELL-SMITH *Old Coaching Days* 117 The last two or three years of coaching saw a well-equipped 'Cobb' coach, painted red, and drawn by four good horses, meet the train at Riversdale. **1980** NEAVE *Land of Munros* 48 The coaches [c1900] were very like the Cobb Coach, and were set on springs above the axles of the four wheels.

b. As Cobb.
    1874 MEREWETHER *By Sea & By Land* 170 Into ruts plunged the vacillating & fluctuating 'Cobb.' **1914** PFAFF *Diggers' Story* 73 Cobb and Co. (Mr.Beamish) had to remain until we were ready to start. Cobb, in trying to pass me to get the road, smashed several splinters off my hind wheels.

2. As Cobb and Co. (occas. Cobb and Company, Cobb's Mail), in the names of coach-lines.
    1865 *Southland News* in Lovell-Smith *Old Coaching Days* (1931) 99 The tender of Cobb and Co. has been accepted for the conveyance of mails inland. **1865** CHUDLEIGH *Diary* 9 June (1950) 189 We ride as far as the Rakaia and then on by Cobs Mail. **1875** *Ibid.* 26 Aug. 237 From Mercer to Hamilton is some 50 miles..I took Cobb & Co. coach for 16 miles. **1968** SEDDON *The Seddons* 12 Cobb and Company's coaches stopped at our place and the horses were stabled right alongside our home.

cobber, *n.* [Prob. f. Brit. dial. *cob* to take a liking to: see EDD *v.*² Suffolk; AND 1893.]

1. a. A close friend, a mate, occas. work-mate. Also in the phr. **to be cobbers with**, to be (close) friends with.
    1897 WRIGHT *Station Ballads* 59 The man who is 'cobbers' with Christ comes off best if he's ever so poor. **1905** *Truth* 23 Dec. 5 Young Graham and some cobbers were out for the usual spree. **1917** *NZ At the Front* 180 Digger and cobber, mate and chum—Who says there is nothing in a name? **1926** DEVANNY *Butcher Shop* (1981) 90 He had deprived himself of his mate, his 'cobber' for twenty and odd years. **1936** ALLEN *Poor Scholar* 67 Had Andy and Ponto belonged to a later decade, they would have been described in the jargon of the 'Cally' as 'cobbers.' The word so exactly hits off their relationship, that I must use it. The bond between cobber and cobber has about it no taint of sentiment. **1943** MARSH *Colour Scheme* 100 He's cobbers with some of the wharfies, him and Eru Saul. **1953** *NZ Observer* 25 Mar. 4 There is a world of difference between 'friend' and 'cobber'. **1957** [see BISCUIT 2]. **1968** SLATTER *Pagan Game* 150 I've just about had this cobber thingo, said Erik Johansen. Cobbers are cobbers when it suits them. **1978** MANTELL *Murder in Fancydress* 85 You're cobbers with Wilkins, aren't you? Blaney? **1986** DAVIN *Salamander & the Fire* 71 Herbie was cobbers with everyone. Everyone was Herbie's best cobber.

b. In use by or of a woman, a friend.
    1924 *Otago Witness* (Dunedin) 22 Apr. 64 My 'cobber', A Little French Maid, cuts my letters out of their paper. **1928** *NZ Free Lance* (Wellington) 17 Mar. 15 Come with me after work tonight, Ethel. Bring a cobber along with you if you like. **1964** HARVEY *Any Old Dollars Mister?* 89 Anyhow, she didn't seem to mind and after that we were real cobbers for a while. **1984** MIHAKA *Whakapohane* 105 But Hinekatorangi was in fact a Queen of the Hawkes Bay Maoris. She came over to mourn for her lifetime cobber, Te Aputa O Ngati Raukawa [a kind of Queen of the Ngati Raukawa].

2. As term of address among males. MATE *n.*² 4, SPORT.
    1917 *NZ at the Front* 78 Never come at that game, cobber. **1921** *Quick March* 10 Aug. 27 [The game is crown-and-anchor.] 'Murder on the old sergeant-major [=crown].' 'Ten frog [=pound (note)] half-way, cobber. Right, she's set.' **1933** GRAEME-HOLDER *Restless Earth* 75 Sorry, cobber,.. I betcha they was on the beach... Awright, cobber. **1981** *Staff Officer NZ Police National Headquarters* (Goldie Brown Collection) cobber: pal or friend; e.g., 'Hello there cobber.'

Hence **cobbery** *a.*, friendly.
    1959 SLATTER *Gun in My Hand* 51 He's pretty cobbery with some of the owners and trainers and he wouldn't miss a meeting for quids. **1968** SLATTER *Pagan Game* 161 He had been cobbery with them for years.

cobber, *v.* [See *n.*: AND 1918.] Usu. as **to cobber up (with)**, to become mates (with), to make friends (with).
    1916 *Chron. NZEF* 29 Sept. 66 We took train..about six, and cobbering up with an 'Ossie' at Salisbury I was safely escorted to Waterloo. **1955** *BJ Cameron Collection* (TS July) cobber up with (v) To become matey with. **1963** PEARSON *Coal Flat* 104 You wait and see, they'll cobber up in no time. It's natural for a young chap to cobber up with chaps his own age. **1971** ARMFELT *Catching Up* 125 Yes, Graham, I knew from your first game that we'd cobber up beaut. **1988** MCGILL *Dict. Kiwi Slang* 29 *cobber up with* make friends with; eg 'I cobbered up with Barry over the duck-shooting season, but I haven't seen him since.'

cobbler, *n.*¹ [f. a pun on (*cobbler's*) *last* a shoemaker's model: AND 1871.]

1. *Shearing*. The last sheep in the shearing pen, and usu. the hardest to shear. See also SANDY-BACK, SNOB *n.*²
    c**1875** MEREDITH *Adventuring in Maoriland* (1935) 143 It is amusing to watch the tactics of some of the shearers to dodge the Kapara (Cobbler) the last sheep in the pen, which, presumably, is the worst shearing sheep of the lot. **1894** WILSON *Land of Tui* 243 The last sheep to be shorn is often the most difficult to catch, and is called the 'cobbler'. **1904** CRADOCK *Sport in NZ* 172 Each man tries to pick a sheep that looks easy to shear, so the last one is generally a great ugly brute with matted wool and his fleece full of sand. This fellow is invariably nicknamed the 'cobbler'. **1913** CARR *Country Work* 17 The shearer who takes the last sheep (called the 'cobbler') calls out 'Sheep O!' when the boy..immediately fills up the back pen. c**1927** SMITH *Sheep & Wool Industry* 76 They always leave the 'cobblers', or hard sheep, until the last. **1940** STUDHOLME *Te Waimate* (1954) 130 When an old hand and a young one were sharing a catching pen, the former would let the learner in for the 'cobbler', or hard shearing sheep, at the end of every pen. **1986** RICHARDS *Off the Sheep's Back* 95 I found I could hold him on the good ones, but he had the edge on me when it came to the 'cobblers'.

2. [Poss. a transf. use of prec., but see EDD *cobble n.*² 5 a large cock of hay made previous to carrying or moving it (Northhamptonshire).] The last load of hay in the harvest field.
    1934 *Press* (Christchurch) (Acland Gloss.) 13 Jan. 13 *Cobbler*... A correspondent points out that this word is also applied to the last load of hay, etc., in the harvest field. **1968** *NZ Contemp. Dict. Suppl.* (Collins) 6 *cobbler n.*...last load of hay in harvest.

cobbler, *n.*² [f. Brit. dial. *cobbler* (ad. French *cabot, chabot*) bullhead) a fish with a large head: see EDD *n.*¹ 2; also called a *shoemaker*: *cobbo* in Kent, Sussex for 'miller's thumb'.] Applied in New Zealand to either of two *Scorpaena* spp. (fam. Scorpaenidae), *S. papillosus* SCORPIONFISH or *S. cardinalis* red rock cod (COD 2 (7)).
    1932 *NZJST* XIII. 233 This fish [sc. scorpion-fish *Scorpaena cruenta*] is the common scarpee of Cook Strait and the cobbler of Napier... The cobbler differs from the sea-perch in having more pronounced ridges on the head. **1957** PARROTT *Sea Angler's Fishes* 164 [The Red Rock Cod] is also known as the 'Common Scarpee' and in Napier it is known as the 'Cobbler.' Perhaps 'Cobbler' would be the best to use for this fish, but it is unfortunately not known under this name outside Napier. **1960** DOOGUE & MORELAND *Sea Anglers' Guide* 271 [Red scorpionfish] *Scorpaena cardinalis;* red rock cod, scarpee, grandfather hapuku, cobbler.

cobbler, *n.*³ Also **cobler**. [Poss. a reflex of SHOEMAKER q.v. a name for any of various petrels from their chattering cries reminiscent of the sound of an old-time cobbler cobbling.] A (Chatham Island) seabird.
    c**1843** HEAPHY 'A Chapter on Sealing' in *Southern Monthly Magazine* (1863 June) I. iv 172 As we got closer to the reef [of Jackson's Keys] we could hear the wailing cry of the penguins—like babies crying; then the 'coblers' from the rocks would come wheeling round us.

cobler, var. COBBLER.

cockabulla, cock-a-bulli(e), varr. COCKABULLY.

cockabully. Also **cockabulla, cock-a-bulli(e), cocker bully, kokobula**. [Usu. taken to be an alteration of Ma. *kōkopu*, but phonologically more probably from dialectal or other cognate Maori forms or variants such as *kokopuru*; or *kōkopuruao* (Williams 130) 'a large variety of *Galaxias*'; or (Williams 130) *kokopara*, a 'small fresh-water fish' (Whanganui), a 'variety of *Galaxias*' (Ngaitahu) (see also quot. 1942 below, and also KOKOPARA (KOKOPURU)); poss. reinforced by Brit. dial. names for small fish, *bull-head, bully.*
[*Note*] It is unlikely that *kokopu* is derived from *cockabully*, as the former is attested from 1820, the latter only from c1880, and then only in NZ English and not (as would be expected) in a Brit. dialect.

1. Any of various small freshwater fishes. Cf. BULLY *n.*¹, COCKY *n.*², KOKOPARA, KOKUPU 1.
    1882 STUART *Sir George Grey* 6 Shall Green and Fish, and even smaller fry, (mere cockabullies) claim the public eye. **1889** DAVIDSON *Stories NZ Life* 74 They had got a broken trycicle [sic]... and in the box a little dead cock-a-bullie. **1896** *The Australasian* 28 Aug. 407 During my stay in New Zealand my little girl caught a fish rather larger than an English minnow. Her young companions called it a 'cock-a-bully.' It was pretty obvious to scent a corruption of a Maori word, for, mark you, cock-a-bully has no meaning. It looks as if it were English and full of meaning. Reflect an instant and it has none. The Maori name for the fish is 'kokopu'. c**1899** DOUGLAS in *Mr Explorer Douglas* (1957) 261 Some people are so eager to get their name in print as the discoverer of something new, that if those beings found a cock-a-bulla with its tail bit off, they would put it down as a new fish and murder the Latin language and their own name in fixing that fish's position in the world of waters. **1900** *Canterbury Old & New* 129 There were no fish in the rivers and creeks except the cockabully, and in season whitebait. **1920** *TrNZI* LII. 60 Another of the old men said 'The correct name of the cockabullies is *kokopara*...' In the early days of the Otago settlement the name of this fish was spelt 'kokobula', or sometimes 'cockabulla'. c**1920** BEATTIE *Trad. Lifeways Southern Maori* (1994) 137 Kokopara or Kokopura—These names in the rude speech of the old Maoris sounded like kokobala and kokobula and hence we get the familiar name 'Cockabully' known to all New Zealand boys... The flesh of the kokopara is sweet but it is unusually full of bones. **1939** COMBS *Harrowed Toad* 31 He cast an eagle glance over the swimming-hole, whence emerged..a small boy who had fallen in..while angling for cocker bullies. **1942** ANDERSEN *Maori Place Names*

300 The Waimate creek, flowing through the town of Waimate in South Canterbury, was formerly, and still is locally, known as the Waikokopuru, not Waikokopu, and some of the Pakehas thought that when the Maori used the name kokopuru he was trying to say 'cock-a-bully'. **1964** HINTZ *Trout at Taupo* 66 The cockabully is almost exclusively a marginal fish, although he frequents weed beds in water of moderate depth. **1990** *Listener* 20 Aug. 97 No you can't take it home, she said. It'd miss the other cockabullies. Momma bully, Poppa bully, all the little bullies.

2. Any of various small, salt-water rock-pool fishes of the family Tripterygiidae (triplefins). See also TWISTER 1.

c**1900** West Coast children's rhyme, as reported to the Editor (1960s). Cockabully, cockabully, Care for a swim? Yes by golly When the tide comes in. **1906** *TrNZI* XXXVIII. 550 *Tripterygion tripinne*... Popularly known as the 'cock-a-bulli' (perhaps a corruption of 'kokopu'); abundant near the beach. **1921** THOMSON & ANDERTON *Hist. Portobello* 95 Kokopuru. *Tripterygion tripenne*... This fish (locally known as 'cock-a-bully,' which is a corruption of its Maori name) is abundant in [Otago] harbour. **1952** BAXTER *Collected Poems* (1980) 122 Cockabully finned with the fire of summer. **1967** NATUSCH *Animals NZ* 229 Is 'cockabully' a transliteration and transference of 'kokopu', the Maori word for a different fish, the galaxiid; or does 'kokopu' come from 'cockabully'? In any case, cockabully, kokopu and bully are used for quite different fishes. All cockabullies look much alike, dashing about, jewel-eyed and lightning-swift. All have a three-piece dorsal fin; all are blotched with squares or diamonds, or marked with fine-drawn, coloured lines. **1990** *Landfall* 173 58 A flicker of transparent tail as a cockabully betrayed itself above the matching bottom of sand. **1996** *Dominion* (Wellington) 19 Mar. 10 The triple fin (ika) is one of about 20 varieties of rock pool fish called cockabullies. They can be beautifully coloured.

cockatoo, *n*. [AND derives *cockatoo* (*n*.²) f. the name *Cockatoo Island* in Sydney harbour, formerly a prison for intractable convicts, hence *cockatoo*, a Cockatoo Island convict; thence, transferred to a small farmer orig. with reference to tenant farmers brought from Sydney and settled in the Port Fairy district: *Cockatoo settler* 1845, *cockatoo farmer* 1849, *cockatoo* 1853.]

1. Also **cockatoo farmer**, **cockatoo settler**. A small farmer. See also *forty-acre farmer* (FORTY-ACRE).

1859 *Let.* 25 Sept. in *Voices from Auckland* (1860) 51 [Signed] 'A Cockatoo Settler' **1867** BARKER *Station Life* (1870) 109 We suddenly dropped down on what would be called in England a hamlet, but here it is designated by the extraordinary name of a 'nest of cockatoos'. *Ibid.* 110 Small farmers [who have started from next to nothing] are called Cockatoos in Australia by the squatters or sheepfarmers who dislike them for buying up the best bits of land on their runs; and say that, like a cockatoo, the small freeholder alights on good ground, extracts all he can get from it, and then flies away to 'fresh fields and pastures new'. **1874** TROLLOPE *NZ* 61 The squatters, the miners, the cockatoo farmers..all say the same thing. They regret that they ever left England. **1877** BROOMHALL *Fragments from the Jrnl.* 41 A man who farms less than 100 acres is a *ground parrot*; more than 100 acres but less than 1000 acres, he is a *cockatoo*; over 1000 acres, he is a *gentleman*. **1888** BULLER *Birds NZ* II. 255 When riding between Woodville and the Manawatu Gorge, I saw, at a 'Cockatoo homestead', a flock of domestic ducks. **1897** SCOTT *How I Stole 10,000 Sheep* 7 We'll get a job on a 'Cockatoo' farm somewhere. **1901** *Letter* in Hawdon *New Zealanders & Boer War* (1907) 188 The stock is miserable, especially sheep, beside which the scrubbiest 'cockatoo' sheep would look prizewinners. **1913** CARR *Country Work* 35 The bulk of this class of agriculture is carried on by comparatively small holders, commonly called 'Cockatoos', or for endearment 'Cocky'. **1933** *Press* (Christchurch) (Acland Gloss.) 30 Sept. 15 *Cockatoo*.—Now usually abbreviated to *cocky*. An agricultural farmer, a small farmer, as opposed to a squatter or sheep farmer. *C[ockatoo]* is also used as a verb. **1947** NEWTON *Wayleggo* 153 Cocky: Cockatoo. A flat country man with a small farm. **1973** WILSON *NZ Jack* 84 Among the crowd of fast young marrieds and all the rest of the country club cockatoos..he apparently became a gallant hero. **1980** ELDRED-GRIGG *Southern Gentry* 80 Shepherds and cockatoo farmers came from miles away.

2. As **cockatoo's weather**, see quot.

1934 *Press* (Christchurch) (Acland Gloss.) 13 Jan. 13 *Cockatoo's weather.*—Fine by day and rain at night; or, sometimes, fine all the week and wet on Sunday.

3. In jocular composition.

1887 *Auckland Weekly News* 12 Mar. 14 There are some half-score of these sets, ranging from the milky way of the *creme de la creme* of the cockatoocracy to the long-beer constellations that gyrate round the 'luminous' Hebe. **1887** *Auckland Weekly News* 13 Aug. 8 Bidding adieu for a while to my friends, the village, and special settler and other, the cockatoo-ralloos of the bush settlements, I entrain at Woodville.

cockatoo, *v. Obs.*, [AND *Obs.* freq. as *vbl. n.* 1875, 1880.] *intr.* To work or live as a small farmer. Also as *ppl. a.*

1877 *Tapanui Courier* 11 Apr. in Marks *Hammer & Tap* (1977) 11 No doubt land and sheep lords have good grounds of complaint against being mixed up with the higgledy-piggledy cockatooing and digging settlers, forming the bulk of the ridings contiguous to [the town of] Lawrence. **1889** MITCHELL *Rhymes & Rambles* 21 It was early in the year 1870..that I composed..*The Levanting Cockatoos*. In summer time, when work was slack..says C. to Jack, 'Let's go a cockatooing'. **1896** O'REGAN *Poems* 30 They tell me you're now 'cockatooing', And worried to death, I suppose, With striving and riving and sueing. **1927** DONNE *Maori Past & Present* 11 Some [Maoris] are dairying, others 'cockatooing' with a few acres of land, three or four cows, half a dozen pigs. **1933** [see COCKATOO *n*. 1].

cockatoo, var. KAKAHU.

cocker bully, var. COCKABULLY.

cockey, var. COCKY.

cockfighting, *vbl. n.* [See OED, EDD, SND for the various Brit. (esp. Sc.) dial. uses of *cock* (*cock's-headlin*, *to ride cockie-breekie*, *cock-a-legs*) in the names of a boys' game in which one mounts on another's shoulders.] A boys' game in which a boy mounted on another boy's shoulders tries to topple or unseat an opponent similarly placed. Occas. as **cockfight** *n*., an instance of cockfighting (see quots. 1981, 1992).

1953 SUTTON-SMITH *Unorganized Games NZ Primary School Children* (VUWTS) II. 619 Wrestling..Cock-fighting and boys' behaviour in Forts and Dens are characteristic activities which reflect.. aggressive and physical solidarity. **1965** HILLIARD *Power of Joy* 133 They played cock-fighting..and stuffed grass down the necks of girls who gave cheek. **1974** HEINZ *Bright Fine Gold* 38 Some of the simple games played by the [West Coast] children were rounders, shinty, duckstone..cockfighting..and leapfrog. **1980** BENNETT *Canterbury Tale* 34 There was cockfighting in which each of two players, mounted pick-a-back, tried to resist dislodgement. **1982** SUTTON-SMITH *Hist. Children's Play* 27 A variety of games were [*sic*] played with stilts... They had races with them..and had 'cockfights' in which great groups of boys jostled each other in a struggle on sticks. **1987** *Alfredton* 75 A somewhat more violent playtime activity [c1927–46 at Alfredton school] was 'cock fighting'. In these piggy-back fights one tried to pull an opponent off his 'horse'. **1992** CONDON *Hurleyville* 25 Other games played by the whole school from time to time included rounders, bedlam, tick-tack, tiggy tiggy touchwood..and cock fights—a form of piggy back.

cockie, var. COCKY.

cockle. [Transf. use of *cockle*, the name in Britain for a bivalve shellfish of *Cardium* spp.]

1. In New Zealand usu. either of two bivalve shellfish of *Austrovenus* (fam. Veneridae) or *Paphies* species (fam. Mesodesmatidae); and also, usu. with a modifier, any of several other bivalves. (Now often termed commercially *clam*.)

a. In early use, a general name of uncertain attribution.

1769 COOK *Journals* 6 Nov. (1955) I. 194 The Natives brought to the Ship and sold to our people, small Cockles, Clams and Mussels enough for all hands. **1773** WALES *Journal* in Cook *Journal* (1961) II. 787 Amongst the crustaceous Tribe we found Craw-Fish, Muscles [*sic*], Cockles, Scollops Whelks Periwinkles. **1807** SAVAGE *Some Acc. of NZ* 11 To such as are fond of cockles, muscles, and all the varieties of small shell-fish, the bay of islands [*sic*] must prove a most desirable place to visit. **1816** KENDALL in Elder *Marsden's Lieutenants* 16 Oct. (1934) 129 They then generally leave the school, and repair to the rivers or bush in pursuit of fish, fern-root, cockles, etc. **1834** MARKHAM *NZ* (1963) 45 The Dog [*sc*. a sawyer] was a bit of an Epicure in his way and gave me a sauce of Cockles done in hot Lard as there is nothing else in the Country.

b. Also **New Zealand** (or **common**) **cockle**. *Austrovenus* (formerly *Chione*) *stutchburyi* (fam. Veneridae), a small whitish edible bivalve with a strongly sculptured shell, its beds being common throughout New Zealand in sheltered beaches and estuaries. See also PIPI 1 b, TUANGI.

c**1826–27** BOULTBEE *Journal* (1986) 110 Cockles, tòàkki **1879** HAAST *Geology Canterbury and Westland* 416 Then follows a series of shell beds, consisting of the remains of the following species, now still inhabiting the estuary..*Chione stutchburyi* (Cockle); *Huai* or *Pipi*. **1924** BUCKNILL *Sea Shells NZ* 106 *Chione stutchburyi*... This fairly large, bluish or greyish-white or reddish-brown cockle, with curved beaks directed forwards, is called the Pipi by the Maoris, and is highly esteemed by them as one of their standing dishes. **1955** DELL *Native Shells* (1957) 46 New Zealand cockle... Maori *Tuangi*... This shell is often wrongly called 'pipi' which was the Maori name for a completely different shell. **1966** *Encycl. NZ* III. 456 *Tuangi* (*Chione stutchburyi*). Well known as the New Zealand 'cockle', it is not a true cockle; venus shell, or the Maori name, tuangi, is preferable. **1968** MORTON & MILLER *NZ Sea Shore* 443 Their most typical bivalves are the pipi, *Amphidesma australe*, higher up the shore, giving place lower down to the cockle or tuangi, *Chione stutchburyi*, in places designated 'pipi' as well. **1986** *Shellfisheries Newsletter* 29 6 The 'New Zealand cockle' (*Chione* (*Austrovenus*) *stutchburyi*) is in fact not a cockle but a clam... The US Food and Drug Administration approved the use of the name 'New Zealand littleneck clam' for *Chione*.

COCKROACH

c. PIPI 1 c (*Paphies australis*).
   1834 MARKHAM *NZ* (1963) 45 Now Why heckie was the name of a bed of Pippies or Cockles, in the River [*sc*. saltwater estuary]. **1841** BIDWILL *Rambles in NZ* (1952) 115 Other shell-fish are also abundant, particularly Cockles—of these I have seen more than a man could carry collected by one woman during the space of a tide. **1878** BULLER *Forty Yrs. NZ* 27 On those shoals the women gather cockles (pipi). **1966** *Encycl. NZ* III. 709 Cockles, *see* Pipi.

2. With a modifier: **dog, lace, nestling** (or **dog's foot**), **purple, strawberry.**

(1) **dog cockle**. Either of two species of fam. Glycymeridae, *Glycymeris laticostata*, a large bivalve having a reddish-brown almost circular shell, or *Glycymeris modesta*, a small white or brown bivalve having striking and variable shell patterns in shades of brown.
   1924 BUCKNILL *Sea Shells NZ* 87 *Glycymeris laticostata*... The Large Dog cockle or Comb shell. A thick solid bivalve, brown or brown and white... *Glycymeris modesta*... This is the lesser Dog cockle or Comb shell. A small, thick, circular bivalve..of a yellow, light or dark brown colour, either splashed with white or simply plain. **1967** *Encycl. NZ* I. 372 *Cockle, dog*... The dog cockle grows up to 3 in. across, is thick and radially ridged, with a speckled pattern in reddish brown. **1970** PENNIKET *NZ Sea Shells in Colour* 70 Large Dog Cockle (*Glycymeris laticostata*)... Thick heavy shells... Small Dog Cockle (*Glycymeris modesta*)... A cream shell with an infinitely variable pattern of brown splashes and dashes. **1984** *Marlborough Express* (Blenheim) 22 June 23 The cockle tribe also includes the glycymeridae family to which the local large and small dog cockles belong. The small one is known as glycymeris modesta and is plentiful. The large dog cockle..is also common, and can grow to 10cm.

(2) **lace cockle**. *Divaricella huttoniana* (fam. Lucinidae).
   1955 DELL *Native Shells NZ* (1957) 41 The Lace Cockle has a snowy white shell marked with a pattern of raised divaricating lines. **1971** POWNALL *NZ Shells & Shell Fish* 53 Lace Shell... *Divaricella..huttoniana*.

(3) **nestling** (or **dog's foot**) **cockle**. *Cardita aoteana* (fam. Carditidae).
   1955 DELL *Native Shells* 40 The Nestling Cockle lives attached to the undersides of rocks and in the holdfasts of seaweeds. **1971** POWNALL *NZ Shells & Shell Fish* 53 Nestling Cockle... *Cardita..aoteana*... Clustering under rocks at extreme low tide and in deeper water. **1990** FOORD *NZ Descr. Animal Dict.* 271 Nestling Cockle. *Cardita aoteana*. A distinctive bivalve 2 cm long with a very inequilateral wedge shape, brownish, with large, rounded, radial ribs... Other names: Dog's Foot Cockle.

(4) **purple cockle**. [f. its interior colour.] *Venericardia purpurata* (fam. Carditidae).
   1947 POWELL *Native Animals NZ* 20 Purple Cockle (*Venericardia purpurata*)... It is pinkish to light brown on the outside, which has heavy banded radial ribs, and pinkish to reddish purple within. **1955** DELL *Native Shells* (1957) 40 The Purple Cockle is one of our very common shells, usually found washed ashore on sandy, open beaches. **1970** PENNIKET *NZ Seashells in Colour* 88 Purple Cockle... This attractive shell lives just below low tide on many of our sandy open beaches throughout New Zealand.

(5) **strawberry cockle**. [f. its pinkish exterior colour.] *Nemocardium pulchellum* (fam. Carditidae).
   1955 DELL *Native Shells* (1957) 48 Strawberry Cockle... *Nemocardium pulchellum*... A good specimen of this delicate little shell with its fine structure and pink flushed surface ensures for it a place of honour in the collection. **1970** PENNIKET *NZ Seashells in Colour* 88 Strawberry Cockle... Found throughout New Zealand but more often in the south. **1984** *Marlborough Express* (Blenheim) 22 June 23 Locally the only true cockle is the strawberry cockle. It belongs, like all true cockles, to the [Carditidae] family, not the Veneridae.

cockroach. As **Gisborne cockroach**, *Drymaplaneta semivitta* (fam. Blattidae), a large dark brown cockroach introduced from Western Australia and associated with Gisborne, a city on the east coast of the North Island.
   1975 *NZ Entomologist* VI. 71 Specimens of the Gisborne cockroach received at the Auckland Plant Diagnostic Station, during the past year, were... identified as *Drymaplaneta semivitta* (Walker). **1988** *Dominion* (Wellington) 6 Feb. 3 The roach, originally from Western Australia, was thought to live only around the Gisborne and Auckland areas but some appear to have found their way south... National Museum entomologist Ricardo Palma identified them as genus drymaplaneta, commonly known as the Gisborne cockroach. They are thought to have lived in Gisborne since the late 1960s.

cocksfooter. *Obs*. One who gathers for sale the seed of wild cocksfoot grass. See also GRASS-SEEDER.
   1903 *NZ Illustr. Mag.* VIII. 349 All parts of New Zealand send their quota of cocksfooters to 'make a cheque'.

cocksfooting. *Obs*. The gathering of wild cocksfoot seed for sale. See also *grass-seeding* (GRASS-SEEDER).
   1903 *NZ Illustr. Mag.* VIII. 349 [Title] Cocksfooting on Banks Peninsula. In many ways cocksfooting resembles shearing. **1913** CARR *Country Work* 8 Cocksfoot cutting on Banks' Peninsula..follows. Before 'cocksfooting' (as it is termed) is finished, i.e., about the middle of January, Canterbury..will be crying out for men. *Ibid*. 12 To get back to cocksfooting. The grass is cut with a sickle. **c1940** *cocksfooting* in use in Marlborough for collecting wild cocksfoot seed from roadsides, etc. (Ed.).

cockspur. *Shearing*. Also *ellipt*. **spur**. A device to stop the blades of hand-shears opening so wide as to overlap wrong sides together when closed again for the cutting stroke.
   1951 MCLEOD *NZ High Country* 26 The shearers buy their shears from the station and then proceed to cut them and bend them, and embellish them with 'drivers,' 'knockers,' 'jockeys' and 'cockspurs' until their makers would hardly recognise them. **1978** JARDINE *Shadows on Hill* 130 They had received their two free pairs of blades..and had spent many hours at the two big grindstones 'taking them down', attaching drivers, jockeys, spurs and knockers. **1989** *NZ English Newsletter* III. 23 *cockspur*: A metal guard fitted to shears to stop the blades from overlapping when opened wide.

cocky, *n*.¹ Also **cockey, cockie**. [f. COCK(ATOO *n*. + -Y.]

1. [AND *n*.², 1871.] COCKATOO *n*. 1; thence (occas. as **cocky-farmer**) any farmer. See also COW-COCKY, *sheep-cocky* (SHEEP 2).
   1890 *Otago Witness* (Dunedin) 16 Oct. 17 Even if oats don't pay, it is to be hoped that the 'poor cockie' will have some other means of paying his way. **1891** WILLIAMS & REEVES *Double Harness* 34 I made a little poem on the cockey and the squatter. **1906** *Truth* 9 June 5 ['Jim the Milker', Taranaki] But I must tell you that the cocky I graft for ain't a bad sort of chap. **1913** [see COCKATOO *n*. 1]. **1934** MILTON *Waimana* 215 They were 'cocky-farmers' in well-pressed navy blue suits. **1949** SARGESON *I Saw in My Dream* (1974) 185 After all, lots of cockies had to turn their stock out on the road when they were short of feed. **1953** HAMILTON *Till Human Voices Wake Us* 8 And that's the house of the New Zealand small farmer. They call him the squealing cocky and no wonder. **1956** DARE *Rouseabout Jane* 190 They were just smallholders, or 'cocky farmers'. **1966** TURNER *Eng. Lang. Austral. & NZ* 149 Any disparagement remaining in the term *cocky*..is not enough to shake a belief held by all dairy farmers that they form the 'backbone of the country'. **1972** MITCHELL *Pavlova Paradise* 182 *cockie:* Farmer who turns mud into milk. **1991** *Sunday Star* (Auckland) 1 Dec. A8 As a contractor who gets 90% of his living from the cockies..I know he's wrong.

   Hence **cockydom** *n*., the universe of small farmers.
   1913 *NZ Observer* 1 Mar. 9 This highly intellectual sample of cockeydom admits that the fires are destructive.

2. a. As **cocky's dog**, an indifferently bred or trained working dog of doubtful intelligence.
   1971 NEWTON *Ten Thousand Dogs* 18 Although he was just an ordinary cocky's dog, to me he was about the best ever.

b. In the phr. **as dry as a cocky's selection (after a long drought)**, very dry.
   1905 *Truth* 26 Aug. 7 She was an old tart with a high-bridged smelling apparatus and a dial that looked as dry as a cocky's selection after a long drought.

cocky, *n*.² [f. COCK(ABULLY + -Y.] A familiar shortened form of COCKABULLY 1.
   1924 *Otago Witness* (Dunedin) 12 Feb. 71 I forgot we did catch a great number of 'cockies'. **1947-48** BEATTIE *Pioneer Recolls.* (1956) 30 In these streams eels and cockabullies abounded. These 'cockies' grew to an eatable size and were preferred to eels.

cocky's joy. [f. COCKY *n*.¹, alluding to the freq. impoverished circumstances of the small farmer: AND 1902.] Golden syrup or treacle. Cf. BULLOCKY'S JOY.
   1947 DAVIN *Gorse Blooms Pale* 194 Go easy on that Cocky's Joy. **1969** HILLIARD *Green River* 45 Martha Nelson put out a freshly cooked plate of hot hinu-bread and a tin of golden syrup... 'Homai te cocky's joy!' [*homai* 'give me'.] **1974** SIMPSON *Sugarbag Years* 64 Sometimes [during the Depression c1931] we'd have 'cocky's joy'—fried scones with golden syrup. **1986** OWEN & PERKINS *Speaking for Ourselves* 71 The [swagger's] billy was ninety-nine times out of a hundred an old 'cocky's joy' tin—the old golden syrup or treacle tin, because the seven-pound treacle tin was the ideal brewing billy. **1992** PARK *Fence around the Cuckoo* 29 Most ate their breakfast, bread and cocky's joy—golden syrup—on the horse's back.

cocoi, var. KOKOWAI.

coconut. *Offensive*. Also in shortened form **coco** (see quot. 1992). [Fig. use of *coconut* a common fruit of the Pacific Islands.] A Pacific Islander.
   1964 FRANCES *Johnny Rapana* 121 This is the elite part of town. Islanders, Chinamen and Maoris. Coconuts, horis and chinks. **1984** *Dominion* (Wellington) 28 Mar. 7 She heard Britt making comments about 'blacks and coconuts should not be allowed in the country', referring to Polynesians generally. **1985** MITCALFE *Hey Hey Hey* 16 Samoa, eh?

Another coconut, eh? We got to crack these coconuts, eh Gary, else there be no room for us kumaras, what you reckon? **1991** *Evening Post* (Wellington) 26 Oct. 25 She called the Samoans 'bongas' and 'coconuts' and told them they should go home to Samoa... 'It was the first someone had called me a coconut.' **1992** *Dominion* (Wellington) 28 Jan. 6 Bad enough calling an Islander a coco. Though they are.

coconut bomber. WW2. [f. the dismissive implication that the NZ Division in the Pacific theatre saw no real action.] Used in the Middle East theatre as a nickname for members of Third New Zealand Division who had earlier served in the Pacific.

1941 *NZEF Times* 22 Dec. 22 Dave rose to great heights—heights that would make the tales of 'glamour boys' or 'cocoanut [*sic*] bombers' pale into comparative insignificance. **1952** *Landfall* 23 223 The intellectual is as snobbish in his attitude to..writers as other New Zealanders are to many things, notably to returned soldiers—whether they had been 'cocoanut bombers' in the Pacific or had been 'really overseas' to Africa. **1983** HENDERSON *Down from Marble Mountain* 252 We Coconut Bombers, the defenders (sic!) of the Pacific, closest to home if the Japanese come south with their firecrackers, and our glamour is nil, we rate nothing. **1990** *Evening Post* (Wellington) 27 Oct. 29 [Heading] After months of frustration, 'The Coconut Bombers' finally saw action in the Solomons. *Ibid.* 29 They were members of the Third NZ Division, 'The Coconut Bombers'. This ironic description, which the troops applied to themselves, reflected frustration with their lot in serving in the Pacific on mainly garrison and other routine duties.

cod. [The name of the Atlantic *Gadus* genus, transferred to various cod-like and often unrelated fishes of NZ waters, the simplex often preceded by a modifier usu. indicating a skin colour or shade: AND 1821.]

1. As **cod** (unmodified), or, in early use, **codfish**. **a.** Esp. in modern use, mainly the *blue cod* 2 (3) below, but also applied to other species.

1777 FORSTER *Voyage Round World* I. 126 The best and most savoury fish was a species of cod, which, from its external colour, our sailors called a coal-fish. **1886** SHERRIN *Handbook Fishes NZ* 15 Under the popular name of cod, at least four kinds of fish are recognised. **1930** *Wanderlust Magazine* II 29 The eating capacity of mollymawks is amazing—one bird will make no bones about stowing away several fair-sized cod. **1967** NATUSCH *Animals NZ* 224 The 'cod' mentioned in books about the subantarctic islands is *Notothenia*. **1986** PAUL *NZ Fishes* 56 The name 'cod' is applied to many fishes, often quite unrelated. True cods (family Gadidae), typified by the common Northern Hemisphere cod, are represented in New Zealand by only two species. The so-called 'cods' of our waters belong to other families.

b. *Obs.* Often HAPUKU 1.

1820 LEE & KENDALL *NZ Gram. & Vocab.* 225 Wapúku, *s.* The cod-fish. **1838** cod-fish [see HAPUKU 1]. **1844** SELWYN in *NZ Part III (Church in the Colonies VIII)* 7 Feb. (1851) 29 In a moment the little population [of Stewart Island] was alive—children dragging up cod-fish (*hapuka*) nearly as large as themselves. **1855** TAYLOR *Te Ika A Maui* 411 Hapuku or whapuhu commonly called the cod, but a much richer fish in flavo[u]r. **1872** HUTTON & HECTOR *Fishes NZ* 102 [The hapuku] is also occasionally called the Cod fish, which is altogether erroneous. **1904** TREGEAR *Maori Race* 106 The cod (*hapuku*) is a fine sea fish, sometimes attaining a weight of 50 pounds.

2. With a modifier: **bastard red**, **black**, **blue**, **Cloudy Bay**, **New Zealand**, **red**, **red rock**, **rock (kelp, southern rock)**.

(1) **bastard red cod.** Either of two species of *Pseudophycis* (fam. Moridae) which are often confused: *Pseudophycis breviuscula* **northern bastard red cod** and *P. barbata* **southern bastard red cod.** See also WHITING d.

1938 *TrRSNZ* LXVIII. 405 *Pseudophycis breviusculus...* Bastard red cod. **1956** GRAHAM *Treasury NZ Fishes* 173 Bastard Red Cod *Physiculus* (*Pseudophycis*) *breviusculus...* The vernacular name of this fish was first given to it by commercial fishermen who, when one was hooked and brought to the surface, would exclaim: 'another bastard Red Cod!' meaning to say it was not a true Red Cod; the name stuck to this fish and was used by line fishermen of Otago. **1966** *Encycl. NZ* I. 372 The bastard red cod (*Pseudophycis breviusculus*) is stouter, a deeper red in colour, and has a rounded tail fin. **1986** PAUL *NZ Fishes* 58 *Bastard red cods* There are two species related and rather similar to the red cod..they are not easily separated from each other. *Pseudophycis barbata* occurs round the South Island..and *P. breviuscula* around the northern North Island.

(2) **black cod.** Various species of *Paranotothenia* (formerly *Notothenia*) (fam. Nototheniidae, the ice-cods). See also MAORI CHIEF $n.^2$ 1.

1877 *TrNZI* IX. 486 Two different fishes are included in this term [*sc.* blue cod], and one of them is sometimes called black cod. **1886** SHERRIN *Handbook Fishes NZ* 302 *Notothenia microlepidota*..Black Cod. **1906** *TrNZI* XXXVIII. 550 *Notothenia microlepidota...* Not uncommon outside the [Otago] Heads, and sold as 'black cod'. **1938** *TrRSNZ* LXVIII. 414 *Notothenia microlepidota...* Black cod. **1956** GRAHAM *Treasury NZ Fishes* 297 The Black Cod [*Notothenia*] is closely related to the Maori Chief, being of the same genus... It is an inhabitant of the wider southern waters and only stray specimens begin to make their appearance (1931) off the Otago coast. **1966** DOOGUE & MORELAND *Sea Anglers' Guide* 265 Black Cod... Other names: *Notothenia microlepidota*; southern rock cod, nototheniid, Maori chief. **1972** DOAK *Fishes* 101 [The red and rock cod] as well as the blenny-like black cod, *Notothenia microlepidota*, are southern and antarctic fishes. **1982**, **1986** [see MAORI CHIEF[2] 1].

(3) **blue cod.** *Parapercis colias* (fam. Pinguipedidae, formerly Mugiloididae), a fine food fish, popular for recreational fishing. See also COAL-FISH, PAKIRIKIRI, POLLOCK, RAWARU and *rock cod* ((8) a below).

1872 HUTTON & HECTOR *Fishes NZ* 113 Rock cod... This..is the Coal Fish of Captain Cook and Blue Cod of the settlers in the South, and the Pakirikiri of the Maoris and is the most commonly caught fish among rocks on the coast. **1892** [see (8) a below]. **1918** *NZJST* I. 270 A large proportion of the blue cod which arrives in this city comes from the Chatham Islands; but the supply is seldom equal to the demand. **1938** *TrRSNZ* LXVIII. 413 *Parapercis colias...* Blue cod. *Rawaru*. **1946** *AJHR* H-15 40 Chatham Island blue cod are at least equal and probably superior to the best landed in New Zealand and Stewart Island. **1953** KEITH SINCLAIR in *Landfall* 27 174 Friday and he were the terror of the blue cod. Where they sailed the groper fled. **1967** [see COAL-FISH]. **1970** JOHNSON *Life's Vagaries* 46 I hauled in a blue cod..large enough for the whole family. **1986** PAUL *NZ Fishes* 114 *Blue cod Parapercis colias*... Found only in New Zealand. Known almost exclusively by this common name, the occasionally listed coal-fish being a name used only by Captain Cook and some early writers, and derived from an unrelated European fish.

(4) **Cloudy Bay cod.** [f. *Cloudy Bay* in se. Cook Strait.] **a.** A mainly central New Zealand name for LING (*Genypterus blacodes*).

1872 HUTTON & HECTOR *Fishes NZ* 116 Ling... This fish, also known as the Cloudy Bay Cod, is exceedingly common in Cook Strait. It is, however, seldom brought to market, not being as much appreciated as food as it deserves. **1957** PARROTT *Sea Angler's Fishes* 159 The Ling was known to the Maoris as Hokarari. Some years ago large catches were made in Cloudy Bay, and were placed on the Wellington market as 'Cloudy Bay Cod'. **1981** WILSON *Fisherman's Bible* 143 [Ling is] known around Wellington as Cloudy Bay Cod.

b. See *rock cod* (8) c below.

1957 PARROTT *Sea Angler's Fishes* 43 [The rock cod] occurs not uncommonly in Cloudy Bay, and Mr. W. J. Phillipps records that, in 1924, small numbers were sold in Wellington as 'Cloudy Bay Cod.' **1966** *Encycl. NZ* I. 373 The Cloudy Bay cod (*Lotella rhacinus*), also known as rock cod and southern hake, is rather more brown and lacks the dark blotch by the pectoral fin [of the red cod]. **1981** WILSON *Fisherman's Bible* 38 [Rock cod] Known also as Cloudy Bay Cod in some areas.

(5) **New Zealand cod.** *Obs.* HAPUKU 1.

1856 CHAPMAN *Lett. & Jrnl.* (ATLTS) III. 621 A hundred hapuku (New Zealand Cod). **1880** SENIOR *Travel & Trout* 294 Another native fish, the hapuku, is commonly called the New Zealand cod, although properly it is a sea-perch.

(6) **red cod.** *Pseudophycis bachus* also listed as *Physiculus bac(c)hus* (fam. Moridae), an often abundant food fish of mainly SI waters. (In early writings occas. and confusingly referred to as *rock cod* or *yellowtail*.) See also FINDON HADDOCK, HADDOCK, HOKA, *nightwalker* (NIGHT 1). Contrast *bastard red cod* (1) above.

1773 FORSTER *Resolution Jrnl.* 2 May (1982) II. 269 The day before, the *greater Dog fish*..was caught, & likewise a new kind of Codfish..it has 2 dorsal-fins, & one beard under the Chin, a dark back, but is all over reddish, & even under the belly & on the fins. I had got such another *red Codfish* some days before. **1872** HUTTON & HECTOR *Fishes NZ* 115 Red cod..is a well known fish on some parts of the coast, being the species that is cured and sold as the Findon Haddock at Port Chalmers. **1880** SENIOR *Travel & Trout* 298 There is another fish somewhat resembling [the haddock] cured and sold in Dunedin as the Findon haddock. This is in reality a red cod, and is beautifully coloured. **1902** DRUMMOND & HUTTON *Nature in NZ* 71 The snapper..and the trevally are essentially northern; while..the red cod, and the ling are just as essentially southern. **1921** THOMSON & ANDERTON *Hist. of Portobello* 74 The red cod in an immature condition is taken all the year round, often in enormous numbers. **1937** [see HOKA]. **1957** PARROTT *Sea Angler's Fishes* 47 The Red cod *Physicubus bachus...* When removed from the water the grey colour rapidly gives place to a uniform red: hence the common name 'Red Cod'. **c1961** BAXTER *Collected Poems* (1980) 230 For the fat red cod and small-mouthed greenbone. **1982** BURTON *Two Hundred Yrs. NZ Food* 70 [Heading] Cod, red. This stout, reddish-grey fish, known to the Maori as *hoka*, more closely resembles its English counterpart than other New Zealand 'cod'. **1990** *Dominion Sunday Times* (Wellington) 19 Aug. 11 He was getting 45 cents a kilo for red cod that sold in the shops for ten or so dollars.

(7) **red rock cod.** Any of several small scorpionfishes (fam. Scorpaenidae) of coastal reefs, esp. *Scorpaena cardinalis*. See also COBBLER $n.^2$, MATUAWHAPUKU.

1921 *NZJST* IV. 121 *Red Rock-cod; Matuawhapuku.* Very common throughout the year in rocky localities around North Auckland Peninsula, but not greatly utilized as a food fish. **1938** *TrRSNZ* LXVIII. 417 *Scorpaena cruenta*... Red rock cod. (Australia). **1957** PARROTT *Sea Angler's Fishes* 163 The Red rock cod *Ruboralga cardinalis*... The Red Rock Cod is a fairly common fish in the North Island but becomes less plentiful in southern waters. **1965, 1982** [see SCORPIONFISH].

(8) **rock cod**. Any of various marine fishes, esp. *blue cod*. **a**. See *blue cod* (3) above.
1841 WEEKES *Journal* 24 Mar. in Rutherford & Skinner *Establish. New Plymouth* (1940) 39 The emigrants have been engaged in fishing over the vessels side [in Cloudy Bay] with a hook and line, catching a number of ling and rockcod. **1855** [see PAKIRIKIRI 2]. **1868** PYKE *Province of Otago* 32 Many..varieties of sea-fish are caught round the coast, such as barracouta, groper, rock-cod, ling, flounders. **1872** [see (3) above]. **1892** *TrNZI* XXIV. 209 Rock-cod or Blue-cod—*Percis colias*... Localities—Reported from all the stations. **1903** [see RAWARU]. **1927** SPEIGHT et al. *Nat. Hist. Canterbury* 200 For instance the Rock-cod (*Parapercis colias*) a comparatively rare line fish in Canterbury waters, has spiny-rayed fins. **1957** PARROTT *Sea Angler's Fishes* 141 This [Blue Cod] is the fish known to Captain Cook as the 'Coal-fish', and it has frequently been referred to by older authors as the 'Rock Cod'. It was known to the Maoris as 'Rawaru' or 'Pakirikiri'. **1983** [see c below].

b. *Obs*. HAPUKU 1.
1849 *NZ Jrnl*. IX. 125 English Name: Rock Cod Native Name: Whapuku. **1851** SHORTLAND *S. Dist. NZ* 131 The 'hapuku' or rock cod, as it is called by the whalers—the finest fish of these seas. **1882** [see HAPUKU 1].

c. Also occas. **kelp cod**. *Lotella rhacinus* (fam. Moridae), a dark purplish-brown morid cod of coastal reefs. See also *Cloudy Bay cod* (4) b above, and (the inappropriately named) *southern hake* (HAKE 1 d, 2 (4)).
1925 *NZJST* VII. 369 A specimen of this rather rare fish [*Physiculus (Lotella) rhacinus*] was captured off Cape Saunders early in 1924, and kept in captivity for several months. Before its death my curiosity was aroused by one of the staff calling it a 'rock-cod' and stating that that was the name used in the north even where the 'blue-cod'..was also caught. **1938** *TrRSNZ* LXVIII. 405 *Lotella rhacinus*... Rock cod. **1956** [see HAKE 2 (4)]. **1966** DOOGUE & MORELAND *Sea Anglers' Guide* 210 Rock cod... Other names: *Lotella rhacinus*; Cloudy Bay cod, southern hake. **1970** SORENSEN *Nomenclature NZ Fish* 18 Cod, rock..*Lotella rhacinus*... Suggested commercial name[s]: Rock Cod; Kelp Cod. **1983** HULME *Bone People* 251 Simon made the acquaintance of..red cod, kelp cod, and rock cod.

d. southern rock cod, see *black cod* (2) above, quot. 1966.

3. As **deep sea cod**, a retail trade name for any of several fishes, see esp. MONKFISH (quot. 1993), RIBALDO; as **googly-eyed cod**, see RIBALDO (fam. Moridae).

codfish: see COD 1.

co-e, var. COO-EE.

coffee. *Obs*. [Transf. use of *coffee Coffea* spp. (fam. Rubiaceae).] As **New Zealand coffee** or in Comb. **coffee-bush**, **coffee-plant**, **coffee-shrub**, the shrub KARAMU, *Coprosma lucida* (fam. Rubiaceae), having coffee-like berries and seeds.
1867 HOCHSTETTER *NZ* 337 The slope..was overgrown with bushes of the New Zealand coffee-shrub—karamu of the natives (*Coprosma lucida*..)—full of red berries. [**1877** *TrNZI* IX. 545 I have seen it stated that coffee of fine flavour had been produced from the karamu, *Coprosma lucida*.] **1883** DOMETT *Ranolf & Amohia* I. 154 Let but a grass-green *parrakeet* alight To pluck from some wild *coffee*-bush in sight, And nibble... The scarlet berries. **1898** MORRIS *Austral-English* 94 *Coffee-bush*..a settlers' name for the New Zealand tree the *Karamu*... Sometimes called also *coffee-plant*. **1900** *Canterbury Old & New* 184 Broadleaf..New Zealand coffee..jostle one another in the dense dry bush. [**1900** *Note*] Species of *Coprosma*.

cohi, var. COO-EE.

cohou-cohou, var. KOHUKOHU.

coinleaf. [f. the rounded shape of the leaf.] *Epilobium* spp., a willowherb. Cf. THREEPENNY BIT.
1952 RICHARDS *Chatham Islands* 35 *The coinleaf* or *threepenny bit* [*Epilobium* sp., a willowherb] has dull green fleshy round leaves and forms a valuable food for sheep on account of the creeping root system and its rapid growth.

cokiddi, var. KOKIRI.

cold bite. *Obs*. [f. *cold* clever, impudent, 'cool'.] A person who is an easy touch for money. Cf. BITE *n*. 2, BOT *n*.¹ 2.
1944 BRUNO *Desert Daze* 19 Leo was renowned as the best 'cold bite' in the entire Brigade. All creeds..made a bee-line for his tent with hard-luck tales when the feloose ran out.
Hence **cold biting** *vbl. n*.. Also **cold-botting**. A beggar's or cadger's frank request for money, food, etc.
1941 BAKER *NZ Slang* 52 Here we find that *cold biting* is rendered as a straight-out request by a tramp or dead-beat for money. On the other hand *cold botting* is a straight-out request for food at house-doors.

cold-botting: see COLD BITE.

cold country.
1. High (or shady) country. Cf. *winter country* (WINTER).
1873 BARKER *Station Amusements* 69 New Zealand sheep-farmers are not sentimental. Beyond a rapid thought of self-congratulation that such 'cold country' was not on *their* run, they did not feel affected by its eternal silence and gloom.
2. [A play on *Old Country*: AND 1906.] A nickname for Britain.
1909 *Truth* 9 Jan. 6 Mr Hoban remarked that the wife viewed with alarm a promise made by Holbrook's father of £50 to enable Walter to visit friends in the Cold Country.

cold lake. Usu. *pl*. A non-thermal lake of the southern South Island. Contrast *hot lake* (HOT *a*. 2).
1905 *Weekly News* 14 Sept. [Caption] A morning scene at Queenstown, the well known tourist centre of the cold lake regions of Otago. **1924** LYSNAR *NZ* 15 [South Island] lakes are sometimes called the Cold Lakes, in order to distinguish them from the Hot Lakes in the North Island. **1934** LEE *Children of Poor* (1949) 28 In New Zealand we designate lakes hot or cold. Our thermal regions give us the hot lakes in the north as a set-off to the cold lakes of Alpine temperatures. **1955** *BJ Cameron Collection* (TS July) cold lakes (n) The large lakes of Otago and Southland, in contrast with the *warm lakes* of the Rotorua area.

cold tea. *Hist*. Alluding derog. to Prohibitionism, its ideology, or its political platform.
1904 *NZ Observer* 16 Apr. 3 Mr. Seddon's opponents will most certainly have the cold tea party against him. *Ibid*. 27 Aug. 3 The wash of Cold Tea is undermining the basis of Seddon's fortress at last. **1911** *Maoriland Worker* 30 Oct. 17 Before the worker decides to support a candidate he should consider the candidate's platform and record. As to Mack's platform, it is a nauseous mixture of Lib.-Labism and Cold Tea. **1913** *NZ Observer* 20 Sept. 3 The Maoriland Cold Tea people are aghast at the idea of a dissolution just now for..if this Parliament is killed..no Prohibition referendum can be taken at the general elections.
Hence **cold teaite**, a prohibitionist.
1906 *Truth* 28 July 1 He is a bigot of the worst type, a rabid cold tea-ite, and was secretary of the N.S.W. Alliance, which, like its Maoriland prototype, is down on all the good liquid things of the world.

cole-fish, var. COAL-FISH.

colladdy, var. KORARI.

collar.
1. *Obs*. As **the collar**, and in full **dog collar**, a name for the Habitual Criminals and Offenders Act, 6 Edw. VII s2(1)(a) 1906 (absorbed into the 1908 Crimes Act) providing for an indeterminate sentence for any person declared a 'Habitual Criminal' by the Court (now replaced in practice by preventive detention); a declaration or indeterminate sentence given under this act. Cf. ACT, KATH, KATHLEEN MAVOURNEEN 1.
1945 BURTON *In Prison* 133 This is an indeterminate sentence, and can only be given to a man who has been declared an Habitual Criminal... Unless the 'Act' is lifted from him by a judge of the Supreme Court it will continue in force for the rest of his life. Among convicts this particular sentence is known as the 'dog collar' for obvious reasons. **1950** *Here & Now* Nov. 14 The Act or the Collar—The Habitual Criminals Act, under which persons declared habitual criminals can have their sentences increased by the Prisons Board for offences against prison discipline during their incarceration. *Ibid*. 15 That's Joe, they said, doing six years and the Act for shooting a copper... Joe was doing six years and the Collar, which meant he didn't know when he'd get out. **1980** [see KATHLEEN MAVOURNEEN 1].

2. As **collar**, a deep topping of white froth, or 'head', on a glass of beer, reminiscent of a clerical collar. Occas. heard as **Roman collar**.
1955 *Truth* 26 Jan. 4 A bloke's a mug to pay a sprat at the rubbitydub for nine ounces with a collar on. **1963** PEARSON *Coal Flat* 18 'One without a collar, Paul?' old Dan said with just a little more pep in his voice than usual: he had evidently had one or two with Jimmy too.

3. *Obs*. In the phr. **out of collar** [poss. an allusion to a draught-horse being in or out of harness], out of work; **up to the collar**, hard at work, 'up to the mark'.
1881 NESFIELD *Chequered Career* 51 If a man is willing to work..he need never be long 'out of collar'. **1897** WRIGHT *Station Ballads* 30 But for coves that's out of collar, mate, there's hunger in the air. **1983** WILSON *Rutherford, Simple Genius* 28 And there is no doubt that his mother kept him and his brothers and sisters 'up to the collar' (the local phrase [?c1880s]) with their school work.

College. In New Zealand a usual name for a secondary school; at tertiary level, formerly applied to each of the six original 'University Colleges' affiliated to the University of New Zealand, now independent universities (see OED 4 d), and to any of the Teachers Training Colleges, now termed Colleges of Education. **a.** A common name (or title) of a secondary (post-primary) school.

1860 [see UP-COUNTRY A]. **1892** *NZ Official Handbook* 107 Number of public (primary) schools, colleges, grammar and high schools, private schools, industrial schools, orphanages, and native schools, in the colony of New Zealand, on 31st December, 1890. **1905** THOMSON *Bush Boys* 14 We'll get to College together, eh? **1914** MCCANDLISH *Let.* 6 Oct. in Pugsley *Gallipoli* (1984) 54 A greater part of the chaps here have been to College and every other one comes from the Wanganui School. **1952** BLAKISTON *My Yesteryears* 15 On a later date, while I was on my way back to college, we found that the flooded Ashburton river had washed away the ford. **1974** in *Listener Short Stories* (1977) 124 I say, wait for me, he would call in that strange sort of English English we all somehow picked up when we went to college. **1987** CHISHOLME *From the Heart* 10 Streamed into the B class in his first year at college... Brian finished second for the year.

b. A University college.

1901 *NZJE* III. 134 This appears to us to be superfluous in centres provided with university colleges. **1926** [see UNIVERSITY ENTRANCE]. **1934** MULGAN *Spur of Morning* 56 To take a degree you had to pass matriculation and keep terms, but the college also welcomed anybody who cared to come to lectures.

c. As **College of Education**, or formerly **(Teachers) Training College** (also **Teachers College** and, familiarly, **Training Coll.**), the name of a tertiary training institution for school-teachers.

1880 *AJHR H-1A* 16 When the four training colleges at Auckland, Wellington, Christchurch, and Dunedin are in full operation [etc.] **1984** WILSON *S. Pacific Street* 91 So she had no one to turn to for comfort except her training coll friend. **1987** *Dominion* (Wellington) 6 Aug. 11 Wellington Teachers College will get a new..name next year. From January it will become the Wellington College of Education. **1990** *Dominion Sunday Times* (Wellington) 1 July 16 The teachers colleges, now officially colleges of education.

Colonel Peerless's Light Infantry. *WW1.* [f. the name of the medical officer in charge of Etaples base.] A nickname for New Zealand medical personnel working at the Etaples base.

1935 STRONG *WW1 scene* in Partridge *Slang Today* 287 If any of you fellows put the boot into me in any way, I'll parade sick and join Colonel Peerless's Light Infantry at the base. **1938** *Press* (Christchurch) (McNab Slang) 2 Apr. 18 [Slang of NZEF] 'Colonel Peerless's Light Infantry' served at the base at Etaples under a medical officer, Colonel Peerless. There were many titles of that kind.

colonial, *a.* and *n.* Mainly *Hist.*

A. *adj.*

1. a. [AND 1793.] Of, belonging to, manufactured in, or characteristic of the colony (or the colonies) of New Zealand or of the Australasian colonies; in pre-1840 use, often synonymous with AUSTRALASIAN *a.*

1822 KENDALL in Elder *Marsden's Lieutenants* 1 Aug. (1934) 191 Perhaps some captains of colonial vessels may be induced to put into this river occasionally. **1836** GREENE *Report* in McNab *Old Whaling Days* (1913) 155 After having recourse to the same manners as our Colonial and other English whalers thereat..we [*sc.* Americans] departed. **1855** *Richmond-Atkinson Papers* (1960) I. 159 I have often been at parties [in Britain]..which might be called clumsy and vulgar in comparison with this colonial and servantless entertainment. **1863** BUTLER *First Year* viii 128 I hardly know why I introduced this into an account of a trip with a bullock dray; it is, however, a colonial incident, such as might happen any day. **1874** CAIRD *Sheepfarming NZ* 12 He very soon discovers that..he cannot crack a stock whip..in these and many other things he will find himself far from being up to the colonial standard of efficiency, so he must bear the name of new chum with equanimity, till..he is capable of performing his various duties in true colonial fashion. **1890** COLENSO *Treaty of Waitangi* 6 He [*sc.* the author] applied to the Government of the colony to publish his MSS., deeming them, though brief, to be not merely interesting, but also of a colonial, if not of a national, importance, especially in days to come. **1904** *NZ Illustr. Mag.* Dec. 177 We were all bursting with new-chum energy as we took our first steps in colonial life. **1907** KOEBEL *Return of Joe* 137 You shouldn't squeal for the sake of a drop of water like that. It isn't colonial. **1934** MULGAN *Spur of Morning* 27 He had superimposed on a Rugby education a dozen years of colonial shepherding and sawmilling. **1948** LIPSON *Politics of Equality* 493 The colonial outlook is a still-surviving heritage of the days when pioneers hacked their homes from the 'bush' and wrestled with the physical problems of mountains and Maoris, of sheep and shipping. **1959** SHADBOLT *New Zealanders* (1986) 18 The homestead..was often visited by those who wished to find an authentic colonial atmosphere.

b. With reference to a sports team, nationally representative; NEW ZEALAND B 2.

1904 *NZ Free Lance* (Wellington) 25 June 14 It was possible that the various interprovincial teams will make a better stand against the visitors than the colonial team.

2. [AND 1808.] In usu. pejorative, often jocular, use, inferior in some respect, provincial, rough, makeshift.

1846 FITZROY *Remarks on NZ* 28 The very few persons who are not (to use the current expression) 'colonial' in their ideas and conduct, are neither understood nor estimated as they deserve to be, or as they would be in old countries. **1849** MCKILLOP *Reminiscences* 132 We had become quite colonial—an expression very common both in New South Wales and New Zealand, and means that we had learned how to sleep in the bush with a blanket round us..build a waré or hut. **1850** *Emigrants Lett. from Brit. Colonies* 94 The cut of the people here [in Wellington] is very peculiar, and is only explained by the term colonial. **1853** SWAINSON *Auckland* 67 The colonial practice of standing idly smoking at the shop doors in broad daylight, and of wearing bush costume is more honoured in the breach than the observance. **1910** GROSSMAN *Heart of Bush* 48 There was a dash of colonial wildness about her that would have to be subdued before she took her place in English society. **1943** MARSH *Colour Scheme* 14 Simon [an English boy]..had attended the Harpoon State schools and, influenced..by his schoolfellows' suspicion of 'pommy' settlers, had become truculently colonial..and defiantly uncouth.

3. Of architectural style. See quot. Cf. *colonial house* (4 below), *colonial villa* (VILLA 1 a).

1905 BAUCKE *White Man Treads* 296 Its [the outback house] style is the undecorated early colonial: two front rooms and a lean-to.

4. In collocations: **colonial ale** [AND 1853], **beer** [AND 1831], **blanket**, **born** *a.* and *n.*, **brew**, **Church**, **debt**, **furniture**, **government**, **-grown** *a.*, **house**, **-made** *a.*, **museum**, **papers**, **twang** [AND 1859], **varnish**.

1865 *Punch in Canterbury* 15 Apr. 3 Kaiapoi Hotel..English and **Colonial ale** and porter, on draught or in bottle, always at hand. **1867** JKM *Mary Ira* 9 A glass of thick, saltish, mess called Colonial ale. **1859** in *Canterbury Rhymes* June (1866) 64 Fetch in some fresh **colonial beer**! **1870** *Evening Post* (Wellington) 29 Dec. 2 There was some stale Colonial beer in the sale room. **1892** *NZ Official Handbook* 166 Beer, colonial..per h[ogs]hd... £4 to £4 10 Beer, english, bottled..per doz. qrts. **1922** *Evening Post* (Wellington) 3 July 6 All-wool **Colonial Blankets**... Special Prices in Manchester Goods. **1877** *TrNZI* IX. 43 In New South Wales and Victoria the **colonial born** grow tall and thin. **1882** HAY *Brighter Britain* 9 In the colonies Great Britain is always spoken of as 'home', even by colonial-born people. **1973** MCELDOWNEY *Arguing with My Grandmother* 38 They were both English gentlemen, who..found a refuge from colonial crudity in one another's company. Their wives were both colonial-born. **1887** 'HOPEFUL' *Taken In* 147 Beer is 6*d.* a pint,... and this alludes only to **Colonial brew**, much of which is inferior. English beer is 6*d.* a small glass. **1884** MARTIN *Our Maoris* 1 Some years later, a great man, preaching in London on the wants of the **Colonial Church**, talked of the coral reefs in New Zealand! **1968** DALZIEL *Vogel* 32 **Colonial debt**: The money a colony owes to its mother country. **1873** *Nelson Colonist* 28 Jan. [Advt] Also on hand a large assortment of **colonial furniture** comprising chiffoniers, chests of drawers, washstands..couches and other goods. **1971** NORTHCOTE-BADE *Colonial Furniture in NZ* 15 Colonial houses are the setting for colonial furniture. **1861** FOX *Memo. of Ministers* 8 Oct. in Rutherford *Sel. Documents* (1949) 111a Now this has..been practically reserved in the hands of the Governor as the representative of the Imperial Government, and the **Colonial Government** in fact has had little or nothing to do with it. **1939** *NZJST* XX. 100A In the past there has been in the minds of the New Zealand farmer and merchant a prejudice against **colonial-grown** Brassica seed. **1935** MAXWELL *Recollections* 192 Particular types of buildings were evolved; these types might well be termed '**colonial houses**', just as the particular style of oven of the early days went by the name 'colonial oven'. **1865** *Punch in Canterbury* 15 Apr. 3 Diggers, Station-holders, and Farmers supplied with the best **colonial made** boots and shoes cheap for cash. **1985** MCGILL *G'day Country* 55-56 And then on to the partridge hatchery, another **colonial museum** and a Devonshire tea without the double Devonshire clotted cream. **1887** 'HOPEFUL' *Taken In* 73 A free public reading-room; where a number of London, as well as **Colonial papers** are to be seen. [**1892** KIPLING *One Lady at Wairakei* (1983) 34 [Colonial twang.] He loved a woman at a sheep station..a red-faced raddled woman who talks about 'ke-ows', and 'bye-bies'.] **1917** *NZ at the Front* 105 Above the babel of **colonial twang**, the noise and din in the estaminet near, rose the raucous shout of the proprietor of the royal and ancient game of chance. **1881** SOUTHAN *Two Lawyers* 23 These shelves [in the hut] are also papered with a light-brown wrapping paper, which has been varnished with what is termed '**colonial varnish**'—made from a little of any kind of spirit, and mixed with some of the gum which is very plentiful in Victoria and Tasmania.

5. In special collocations: **colonial adjective**, 'bloody'; **colonial allowance** *obs.*, an allowance paid to troops serving outside Britain; **colonial boy**, a joc. or ironic transf. use of 'wild colonial boy', a larrikin (cf. the occas. use heard for a town-bred convention-breaker *eau-de-colonial boy*); **colonial cabbage**, see CABBAGE 1; **colonial cadet (cadetship)** *obs.*, see CADET *n.* 1 a; **colonial**

couch, a kind of 'daybed' usu. with a raised support (or arm-rest or back-rest) at one end and along part of its back; **colonial cringe** [prob. f. Austral. *cultural cringe*: AND 1950], an attitude of deference in cultural matters esp. to Europe, particularly to Britain; **Colonial Defence Force** *hist.*, a regular force of mounted men formed under provisions of the Colonial Defence Act, 1862 (see esp. quot. 1966); **colonial fever** *obs.* [AND 1857], typhoid fever; **colonial half-bred** *obs.*, see quot.; **colonial language** *obs.*, coarse language (see also *colonial adjective* above); **colonial lantern** *obs.*, a bottle lantern (see quots., see also LANTERN); **colonial meal** (or **menu**), usu. mutton, damper and tea; **colonial oath** [AND 1859], OATH 1; **colonial pudding**, any of several kinds of 'steamed' pudding often using ingredients easily to hand; **colonial saddle**, see quot. 1933; **Colonial Secretary** *hist.* [AND 1810], a chief adviser to the Governor in early colonial New Zealand, whose office was primarily responsible for domestic affairs (see quot. 1958); **colonial stove** *obs.*, COLONIAL OVEN; **Colonial Treasurer** *hist.* [AND 1826], see quot. 1968; **colonial villa**, VILLA 1 a; **Colonial Volunteers** *hist.*, a local militia raised to control Maori 'hostiles', FOREST RANGER *n.*[1];

1907 *Truth* 24 Aug. 5 The word ['bastard'] is usually preceded by the great **colonial adjective**, which flourishes in the vocabulary of assorted sizes and degrees of luridity. **1872** 'J.H.K.' *Henry Ancrum* 55 He exchanged to [a regiment] in New Zealand, where what are called **colonial allowances**, though paid by the home government, would enable him to support himself. **1981** CHARLES *Black Billy Tea* 55 Our bold **colonial boy** was completely overcome. He dropped his gun And turned to run And hide behind his mum. **1874** *NZ Herald* (Auckland) 4 Sept. 4 [Advt] Furniture, Groceries, &c... W. Dowden will sell by auction ... Bedsteads, Cots, **Colonial Couches**. **1874** *Otago Daily Times* (Dunedin) 16 July 4 [Advt] 100 Colonial Sofas and Couches. **1925** WEBB *Miss Peters' Special* 37 She invited me to be seated, and settling herself upon the end of the colonial couch, prepared for a comfortable chat. **1971** NORTHCOTE-BADE *Colonial Furniture in NZ* 144 The term 'colonial couch' is a survival..: the style differs from place to place. From the advertisement quoted it obviously meant 'colonial made'. **1984** DAVIES *Bread & Roses* 21 The house had a huge kitchen with..a colonial couch where the Dad read the *Auckland Weekly* and farming magazines. **1991** *Metro* (Auckland) Nov. 156 Her clipped British accent would be hard to replace as most of us speak like New Zealanders now that the **colonial cringe** has left us. **1881** NESFIELD *Chequered Career* 117 The Colonel was at that time chief officer of the **Colonial Defence Force**. **1892** *Roll of the Colonial Defence Force (Cavalry) Auckland Division: New Zealand* 1892 [title: NZNB III. ii. 291, item N539]. **1966** *Encycl. NZ* I. 462 Colonial Defence Force... The Colonial Defence Act of 1862 authorised the formation of the first Regular Force, a mounted body, not to exceed 500 men, enrolment being voluntary and for a three-year period of service. Maoris as well as Europeans were eligible, and officers and non-commissioned officers were appointed by the Governor. Of divisions formed in Auckland, Napier, and Wellington, the Auckland Division..played a significant role during the Waikato Wars. **1935** MAXWELL *Recollections* 73 That force [*sc.* Forest Rangers] and the Colonial Defence Force merged into one that was known as the 'Armed Constabulary'. **1883** *TrNZI* XV. 498 *Typhoid*, sometimes recognised and very often not, goes by many names, *e.g.* **colonial fever**, low fever, gastric or bilious fever, blood poisoning, swamp fever etc. **1964** NORRIS *Settlers in Depression* 12 An epidemic of typhoid and 'colonial fever' in Hamilton in 1876 was blamed on the immigrants. **1974** *NZ Agriculture* 57 The Merino was crossed with two of these breeds, the Lincoln and the English Leicester, to produce the '**Colonial Halfbred**'. **1862** HAAST in Haast *Julius Von Haast* (1948) 282 With the rain, the sandflies, and the mosquitoes we passed our existence, now and then indulging in a little **Colonial language** in our impatience. **1925** BATHGATE *Random Recolls.* 18 Every guest [at a private dance in Dunedin c1860] carried a parcel containing dancing footwear..and **colonial lanterns**, which consisted of a clear bottle with the bottom removed, and a candle dropped into the neck. **1982** DRUMMOND in Lush *Waikato Jrnls.* (1982) 191 A weekly dance [c1860]..followed by a walk home of two or three miles through the bush by the light of a 'colonial lantern', a bottle with the bottom knocked out and carried upside-down with a candle in its neck. **1925** BATHGATE *Random Recolls.* 19 We were invited to lunch [at the Greenfield run c1860s], which we had in a hut, and there I partook of my first old-style **colonial meal**, consisting of mutton chops, colonial oven bread, and tea without milk. **1939** BEATTIE *First White Boy Born Otago* 122 The traditional fare of the backblocks stations was the traditional **colonial menu** of tea, damper and mutton for breakfast. **1915** McCREDIE *The Bungalow Recipe Book* 57 **Colonial Pudding**.. eggs..butter..sugar..flour..jam..baking powder... Steam. **c1920** Stevens' *'Cathedral Brand' Essences Cookery Book* 34 *Colonial Pudding*..Minced Suet [etc.] Breadcrumbs..Milk..Sugar..Flour..Baking Powder.. Raisins..Grated Carrots..steam for 2½ hours. **1866** BARKER *Station Life* (1870) 82 All our luggage consisted of my..'swag'..fastened with two straps to the 'D's', which are the steel loops let in in four places to all **colonial saddles**. **1929** [see MONKEY 1 b (a)]. **1933** *Press* (Christchurch) (Acland Gloss.) 30 Sept. 15 A c[olonial] saddle has large knee pads, a very dipped seat, and numerous dees. **1839** *Instructions from Secretary of State* C.O. 209(4) pp. 2–81, 14 Aug. in *Speeches & Documents* (1971) 16 Amongst the Officers thus to be created, the most evidently indispensable are those of a Judge, a Public Prosecutor, a Protector of Aborigines, a **Colonial Secretary**, a Treasurer, a Surveyor General of Lands, and a Superintendent of Police. **1843** CHAPMAN *NZ Portfolio* 122 At the present moment New Zealand is governed by the governor and council, the latter comprising the attorney-general, the colonial secretary and treasurer. **1854** *Richmond-Atkinson Papers* (1960) I. 151 With this you will probably receive an official letter from me with a copy of my communication on the subject of the native Hiriwanu to the Col. Secretary. **1898** HOCKEN *Contributions* 115 A month later the money was returned with a polite letter from the Colonial Secretary, who explained that it had been removed to Wellington solely for 'greater security'. **1948** LIPSON *Politics of Equality* 98 The head of the ministry [from 1856] and leader in Parliament was at first known as the colonial secretary. In the early sixties..the highest position was designated by the title and office of premier; and the colonial secretaryship..was allotted to a different member of the cabinet. **1958** POLASCHEK *Government Administration in NZ* 4 Hobson modelled his administration on the typical Crown Colony pattern. He brought with him a Colonial Secretary, and a Colonial Treasurer and Collector of Customs. *Ibid.* 6 The Colonial Secretary's Office was the focal point of the newly-formed administrative structure. It was through this Office that a settled form of government was introduced into the country. Until 1848 all correspondence between the Governor and government employees passed through the Colonial Secretary's hands, as also did letters between the administration and the public. The Colonial Secretary was the Governor's chief aide, the head of the Public Service, ranking in precedence next after the Chief Justice. **1979** HILTON *Wellington Racing Club* 10 In March of 1896 the Chairman..was concerned by a letter that the Colonial Secretary was not prepared to approve the use of totalisator at Wellington district meetings. **1851** *Lyttelton Times* 15 Mar. 1 To sell by auction..a new **Colonial Stove**. **1883** 'A LADY' *Facts* 18 A Colonial stove is simply an iron box with a door, and in it everything is baked—on it the fire is set. *Ibid.* 21 With a little patience a Colonial stove can be made to answer all purposes, and it bakes well. **1841** *Gov. Hobson's Proclamation* 3 May in Rutherford *Sel. Documents* (1949) 11(a) And I do hereby further proclaim..that Her Majesty has been further pleased to appoint a Legislative Council for the said colony of New Zealand..and to..direct that such Legislative Council shall..consist of..His Excellency the Governor for the time being, the Colonial Secretary..the Attorney-General..the **Colonial Treasurer**. **1843** [see *Colonial Secretary* above]. **1863** MANING *Old NZ* ii. 26 The whole upshot of this treatise on political economy..(which I humbly lay at the feet of the Colonial Treasurer), is this:- I would not give one of your locks, my dear, for all the gold, silver, pearls, diamonds, *mere pounamus*—stop, let me think,—a good *mere pounamu* would be a temptation. **1958** [see *Colonial Secretary* above]. **1968** DALZIEL *Sir Julius Vogel* 32 Colonial Treasurer: The cabinet member responsible for finance, similar to the Minister of Finance of today. **1988** *Through the Looking Glass* 154 They shifted..to a large old **colonial villa**..overlooking Glenfield. **1863** MOSER *Mahoe Leaves* 48 **Colonial volunteers** are not as a body the most indisposed for a joke.

B. *n. Hist.* [AND 1827.]

1. An early name for usu. a non-Maori immigrant settler (also (rarely) a Maori settler: see quot. 1873) or native-born New Zealander. (In non-New Zealand use *colonial* often connotes inferiority.)

1873 TINNE *Wonderland of Antipodes* 31 The korero might have been indefinitely prolonged, for, like all colonials, they [*sc.* the Maori] are much given to 'yarning'. **1885** *Wairarapa Daily* 26 May 2 When he was first returned by an Auckland constituency, he made it a boast that he was a 'colonial' born and bred, and while all colonials were duly proud of him, colonists generally were on the tip-toe of expectation. **1889** PAULIN *Wild West Coast* 2 M. was almost a colonial, having come out to New Zealand when very young, and being now about 27. **1905** BAUCKE *White Man Treads* 148 I am a colonial, and sweet to me are the scents of the land of my birth. **1917** *NZ Free Lance* (Wellington) 26 Jan. 5 The principal speakers [to the Catholic Federation Council] [included]..Father D. Hurley, of Wellington..a young colonial whose pleasant voice gives an additional charm to his interesting speech. **1939** BEATTIE *First White Boy Born Otago* 138 The two of us, new-chum and colonial, got on well together. **1959** DAVIN *No Remittance* 23 But the first-class passengers were all a much more refined set, even the New Zealanders among them—colonials, as we [English] used to say. **1969** HASCOMBE *Down & Almost Under* 50 We know there are still people who will never be convinced that we do not refer to them or think of them as 'colonials'..that the only occasions when we have heard the word 'colonials' used to describe the people of New Zealand have been when New Zealanders themselves have used the expression. **1988** SOMERSET *Sunshine & Shadow* 13 Once she told us [c1897–1907] that Aunt Amy had very little taste, being a Colonial.

2. In specific uses: *pl.* as (**the**) **Colonials**, one of the names applied in the British press to the 1905 'All Blacks'.

1905 *South Wales Echo* 16 Dec. in *The Wales Test 1905* (1983) 20 The Colonials stood in the centre of the field and sang this weird war cry: Ka mate ka mate [etc.].

COLONIAL EXPERIENCE

3. In *ellipt.* use: *colonial ale* or *beer* (see A 4 above); the English used in the Colony of New Zealand as distinct from British English.
1912 *NZ Free Lance Christmas Annual* (Wellington) 25 Foaming jugs of 'colonial' decked the board. **1888** D'AVIGDOR *Antipodean Notes* 48 The chap would hang about till some digger would *shout* to all comers. [1888 *Note*] Shout: Colonial for offering drinks. **1924** *Otago Witness* (Dunedin) 17 June 74 It is 'not so bad'—Colonial for very good.

colonial experience. *Hist.* [AND 1838.] The practical experience of life in (esp. rural) colonial New Zealand to be gained by new immigrants; the conventional wisdom and self-reliance of an OLD HAND 2. Contrast *Overseas Experience* (OVERSEAS B).
[**1840** REVANS to CHAPMAN (ATLTS) 15 May 40 Partridge will do well—Our Colonial experience is useful, and we know how to buy and sell quickly.] **1853** in *Canterbury Rhymes* (1866) 18 Sowing at once, with a double stitch, Colonial experience and groans. **1874** BATHGATE *Col. Experiences* 1 'New Chums'..hear a great deal said on all sides about 'Colonial Experience', and are apt to imagine..that this phrase means a great deal, and that a man possessed of this quality has acquired a degree of infallibility to be gained nowhere out of the colonies. **1892** REEVES *Homeward Bound after Thirty Years* 25 As far as I can see Colonial Experience means the rapid power of adaptability to circumstances and the faculty of unlearning. **1930** *NZ Short Stories* 12 [Clarence] had come straight out from England with a letter of introduction to the boss, 'to learn colonial experience'. **1951** CRESSWELL *Canterbury Tales* 115 He had arrived in Victoria as early as 1838, and when he judged in Market Square had had 14 years colonial experience. **1991** *Dominion* (Wellington) 9 Feb. 7 [Samuel Butler] repaid the debt by creating, in Erewhon and Erewhon Revisited, two of the finest of all renderings of colonial experience.

colonial goose. [f. the shape resembling a stuffed goose: AND 1882.] **a.** Also occas. *ellipt.* **goose.** Orig. a leg (occas. shoulder) of mutton boned and stuffed with a savoury stuffing and roasted; now often applied to mutton flap, etc., rolled and similarly stuffed. See also *Dominion goose* (DOMINION 2).
1891 A TRAMP, ESQ. *Casual Ramblings* 61 The goose was mutton. **1892** KIPLING *One Lady at Wairakei* (1983) 34 He loved a woman at a sheep station—one of the women who serve up the 'colonial goose' to the tourist when he stops at the wooden shanties. **1905** CLYDE *Pagan's Love* 38 Colonial goose, a savoury variant on the usual mutton. **1939** *Bread—Basic Food: Facts & Recipes* 37 Colonial Goose..shoulder of mutton..pepper..breadcrumbs..egg..suet..minced onion..sage..flour..salt..dripping... Fill the cavity with stuffing... Serve with good gravy..and apple sauce. **1952** *Listener* 4 Apr. 7 Colonial Goose, which is strong mutton sliced wafer thin and served with onion stuffing and an almost black gravy. **1982** BURTON *Two Hundred Yrs. NZ Food* 99 [Title] Colonial goose. This is a true national dish. 1 leg mutton..115g fresh breadcrumbs.. 60g suet..1 large onion, finely diced..1 Tbs chopped parsley..½ tsp sage..½ tsp thyme..salt and pepper.. 1 egg..beaten milk.
b. *fig.* and *joc.* for a New Zealander.
1984 HORTON *Memoirs of a Colonial Goose* [Title]

colonialism. NEW ZEALANDISM 2.
1916 THORNTON *The Wowser* 45 He was—to use a colonialism—'a white man'.

colonially, *adv. Obs.* With the sense 'in New Zealand', in collocations forming adjectives: **colonially-manufactured, -reared.**
1892 *NZ Official Handbook* 132 A considerable trade is also done in **colonially-manufactured** jams. **1857** *Richmond-Atkinson Papers* (1960) I. 318 His wife is a pretty little person with the limited experience and ideas..of a **colonially-reared** girl.

colonial oven. *Hist.* [AND 1867.] A long narrow iron box in the form of an oven set into a hearth, with fire under the bottom and also on the top to heat the oven, and superimposed over the top an iron grill or bars on which to place pots (for boiling and stewing). See also *colonial stove* (COLONIAL A 5).
1879 *Auckland Weekly News* 11 Jan. 14 Some years ago Mr. H.H. Smith began the manufacture of what was called 'colonial ovens'. **1904** *NZ Illustr. Mag.* Apr. 48 Batch after batch he..gloated over as they came out of the long-suffering Colonial oven, nicely risen and browned. **1908** STEWART *My Simple Life* 13 We..had friends to early dinner of roast sirloin, admirably cooked..in a 'Colonial oven', a sort of iron box with a wood-fire under and over it. **1925** BATHGATE *Random Recolls.* 19 I partook of my first old-style colonial meal, consisting of mutton chops, colonial oven bread, and tea without milk. **1933** *Press* (Christchurch) (Acland Gloss.) 30 Sept. 15 Colonial oven.—A plain oven without divisions, trays, or dampers, like a box with the door at one side. It is set a little above the floor of the fireplace so that a fire can be put under it for baking, but most of the cooking is done on an open fire lighted on top of it. **1962** EVANS *Waikaka Saga* 221 The colonial oven was an elongated iron box affair, bricked into place, with provision for a fire underneath it. On top was the main cooking fire, and kettles and pots rested on iron bars above the flames or were suspended on chains. **1970** JOHNSON *Life's Vagaries* 47 At Redheugh we graduated in bread baking from the camp oven to the Colonial. **1985** LANGDALE-HUNT *Last Entail Male* 130 It was only a punga house with a corrugated iron roof, but beautifully kept inside and the cooking was done with a colonial oven.

colonial Robert. *Obs.* Also *joc.* **Robert, roberto** (see quot. 1917). [An extended play upon BOB *n.*[1] a shilling: AND 1869.] Often with init. caps. A shilling or shilling-piece.
1869 WHITWORTH *Grimshaw Comic Guide to Dunedin* 39 Shall we strike the happy mean by investing our two Colonial Roberts in a seat each in the stalls? **1899** *Bulletin* (Sydney) 14 Jan. (Red Page) [Letter from *Loafer*, Tauranga.] Following are other local money-names..1s.—*deener, bob, colonial robert* or *penny*. **1905** *Truth* 19 Aug. 5 Caused to spend two lovely Colonial Roberts under false pretences. **1913** *NZ Observer* 15 Feb. 7 The new helmets worn by the police cost 9s 3d each. Nine 'Roberts' and three coppers. **1917** *Truth* 13 Oct. 5 [The doorkeeper] gave evidence of having been told off to collect the 'robertos' at the main door. **1977** *NZ Numismatic Jrnl.* Oct. 16 A *colonial robert* is obviously a play on the English slang *bob* for a shilling. (*Colonial robert* was in use in New Zealand before the turn of the century, and was also recorded about the time of the first World War.)

colonist. *Hist.*
a. [AND 1790.] A European early or founding settler in New Zealand; thence, one who has gained 'colonial experience' (see quot. 1864). Compare COLONIAL B 1, EMIGRANT A 1, IMMIGRANT 1a, SETTLER 2 a.
[*Note*] In the 1840s, esp. in the propaganda of

COLONIZATION

colonization schemes, *colonist* connoted a higher class of settler (a land-purchaser or 'cabin passenger', or 'gentleman colonist' of quot. 1853) as distinct from an (assisted) 'immigrant' (or 'emigrant') or other 'steerage' passengers. By about WW1, *colonist* had been overtaken by *settler* as the common term for mainly rural, landholding Europeans.
1834 MCDONNELL *Extracts from Journal* (1979) 14 [New Zealanders] would..prove good subjects, and become a valuable acquisition to the colonist. **1843** SWAINSON in Manson *I Take Up My Pen* (1971) 25 Papa has taken a great deal of pains with [our section], indeed I think he has too much taste for a Colonist, for he cannot bear to see the beautiful trees and tree-ferns cut down. **1853** ADAMS *Canterbury Settlement* 19 It could not be expected that a vast and uncultivated plain should present an inviting prospect to the unpractised eye of a 'gentleman colonist'. **1853** EARP *NZ* 9 No greater fallacy can occupy the mind of an emigrant, than that by becoming a colonist he is about to acquire a *sudden* fortune. *Ibid.* 226 The better class of colonist is always distinguished by plainness, but excellence, of costume. **1864** CHUDLEIGH *Diary* 12 July (1950) 138 Here he is known and appreciated as a good Colonist and has had numerous offers as manager but he has settled that N.Z. is rotten and he means to leave it. **1874** KENNAWAY *Crusts* 9 We left the ship, slept upon the new and almost unpaced ground of the antipodes—and our experiences as colonists began. **1888** PAYTON *Round About NZ* viii A colonist would no more dream of calling a Maori *whare* 'a house,'.. than he would of saluting Tawhias [*sic*] as King of New Zealand. **1907** LAING & BLACKWELL *Plants NZ* 272 *Leptospermum scoparium* (*The Manuka*)... Maori names *Manuka, Kahikatoa*. Colonists' [1940 edn., English] name, Tea-Tree. **1910** CHUDLEIGH *Diary* 16 Aug. (1950) 451 Poor Alex. He lived a hard life and a long one as regards home... He was a good Colonist and a most useful Islander, also a good brother. **1959, 1980** [see EMIGRANT 1].
b. *transf. joc.* A bumblebee.
1889 in Wilson *Land of Tui* 27 Oct. (1894) 41 The innumerable big, brown, humblebees are called here the 'latest colonists', and were imported to propagate clover.

colonization. The European settling of New Zealand; the Europeanization of the Maori. Cf. CIVILIZATION.
1842 in Wily & Maunsell *Robert Maunsell* 31 Mar. (1938) 75 At the three principal posts of colonization, the Bay of Islands, Auckland (the metropolis near us), and at Wellington, the Company's town at the western part of Cook's Straits. **1845** INGESTRE *Let.* 5 May in Rutherford *Sel. Documents* (1949) 12 The avowed object of the missionaries has been to prevent colonization, to preserve the nationality of the New Zealanders. **1853** SWAINSON *Auckland* 1 It was seen..that an irregular species of colonization was already going on..'fatal to the natives'; that the New Zealanders were improvidently divesting themselves of their territorial possessions. **1868** LINDSAY *Contribs. to NZ Botany* 59 Like the *Leptosperma*, in the early days of colonisation, the plant [*Acaena*] was much used, in bush journeys. **1871** *Evening Post* (Wellington) 11 Feb. 2 This means that an old, obstinate, sulky savage has the power to arrest the progress and colonization of this island. **1877** GRACE *Let.* 18 Nov. in Grace *Pioneer Missionary* (1928) 286 In early years they [Natives] received Christianity—and I may say Colonization—at our hands without doubting, and, to a great extent, on credit. **1882** POTTS *Out in Open* 34 Native birds have to contend against the effects of the changes which colonisation has wrought. **1899** BELL *In the Shadow of the Bush* 25 [The old gentleman] seems to be rather too far gone in the sere and yellow leaf to give promise of much success in the glorious work of colonisation, as

you would call it. **1943** Marsh *Colour Scheme* 64 He showed little of his Maori blood, but..he might have served as an illustration of the least admirable aspect of colonisation in a native country. **1983** Marshall *Memoirs* 24 It is strange that this part of New Zealand [*sc.* Northland], where colonisation began..should have slipped back into an isolated backwater.

colonize *v. Hist.*

1. *trans.*, occas. *intr.* **a.** To settle (New Zealand) with non-Maori immigrants.

1841 in *Estab. New Plymouth* 13 Feb. (1940) xv With sixty persons Taranaki may be considered as colonised. **1845** Ingestre *Let.* 5 May in Rutherford *Sel. Documents* (1949) 12 The Crown devolved on [the NZ Company] the function of colonizing New Zealand; that is, of filling it with inhabitants. **1851** *Lyttelton Times* 19 Apr. 5 The *Spectator* is dreadfully scandalized that New Zealand should be colonized by Companies in whose management the settlers have no voice. **1897** Courage *Lights and Shadows* 354 In the early days, settlers felt they were 'colonizing', now the new arrivals immigrate in the same way.

Hence **colonizer** *n.*
1853 in *Canterbury Rhymes* (1866) 22 Among her colonizers brave Shall many a soul be found To make the Southern wild and wave Henceforth poetic ground.

b. *Rare.* To settle (New Zealand) with Maori immigrants.

1906 Cheeseman *Manual NZ Flora* 99 The Maoris assert that it [*sc.* tainui] sprang from the rollers or skids that were brought in the canoe 'Tainui' when they first colonised New Zealand.

2. As a *ppl. a.* predicatively used. **to be (come, get) colonized** (occas. **colonialized**), to become adjusted to New Zealand ways and life; to become a colonial.

1874 Bathgate *Col. Experiences* 9 If an unfortunate new chum ventures mildly to protest against some trifling hardships he is at once silenced by being told that it is evident he is not 'colonised' yet, and that he must get used to such things. If any particular philologist should read this, he will probably object to the word colonised in place of the more correct but uglier colonialised, but he would find it a vain task to attempt to argue the colonists into the use of any other. **1882** Hay *Brighter Britain* I. 21 After inhaling this magnificent air of ours for a year or two, your nose will grow bigger to receive it; and about the same time you will have spent the money you brought with you, gone in for hard work, learnt common sense, and become 'colonised.' **1891** Chamier *Philosopher* 149 'You ain't colonised yet,' remarked Jack [to the new chum].

3. To turn (or force) Maoris into a European way of life. Cf. civilize.

1978 Hilliard *Glory & Dream* 126 'It looks different to me. You've always got to be the boss. Is that just pakeha, or is it being a man? Let me just be myself. Don't try to make me be like you. Then we'll get along fine. But don't try to colonize me. You do it all the time.' Colonize. A strange word for her; must have learnt it in school. Why the English came out here: to colonize New Zealand. That would be pretty hard for them to take: Maori kids, being told how they were colonized.

colony. *Hist.*

1. Used in *sing.* and *pl.*, with and without init. cap. (occas. as **the Colony**), to denote any one or several of the original local settlements made in New Zealand, later called 'province(s)', *viz.* Auckland, Wellington, Taranaki, Nelson, then Canterbury and Otago. See also settlement 2 a.

1840 Weekes *Letter* in *Establishment New Plymouth* (1940) 4 On landing in the Colony the Storekeeper..is authorised to allow you these amounts. **1842** Deans *Pioneers* (1964) 13 I have now made up my mind to leave this Colony and to settle in another part of New Zealand. **1848** Wakefield *Handbook NZ* 2 These [details] will comprise..a separate description of each of the existing Settlements, and of the several districts of country..which appear to offer eligible sites for the Canterbury Colony. **1851** Gov. Grey in Rutherford *Sel. Documents* 30 Aug. (1949) 44.25 These five colonies were settled at different times, each upon a totally distinct plan of colonization, and by persons who proceeded direct to their respective colony, either from Great Britain or from the neighbouring Australian colonies, and who rarely passed through any other New Zealand settlement previously to reaching the colony which they now inhabit. **1861** *NZ Goldfields 1861* (1976) 31 Public Notice. The largely increasing immigration to this province from adjacent colonies..makes it imperative on the part of the Government..to come forward with an authoritative declaration. **1959** Sinclair *Hist. NZ* 105 Until late in the nineteenth century, however, most of the settlers thought of themselves as belonging to the colony of Otago or Wellington, not the colony of New Zealand.

2. Usu. as **the Colony**, New Zealand regarded as a country existing as a political or administrative whole.

1840 *Lord Russell to Hobson* in *GBPP House of Commons 1841* (No.311) 27 The colony of New Zealand will..be indebted to the colony of New South Wales for any advances made from the one treasury to the other. *Ibid.* 106 [Bunbury's report] I obtained..the signature of a very intelligent well-dressed native, who spoke English better than any that I have yet met with in this colony. **1857** *Lyttelton Times* 1 July 2 The Imperial Parliament having conferred upon the Colony of New Zealand a constitution of unparalleled liberty..I am wishful to see that constitution properly..carried out. **1864** *Richmond-Atkinson Papers* (1960) II. 117 But anything more treacherous than the conduct of the Home Govt. [*sic*] in luring on the Colony to such..expenditure for the final settlement of this Maori question..I never heard of. **1888** D'Avigdor *Antipodean Notes* 160 This was one of the few places in the Colony where the eight hours rule was ignored. **1907** *TrNZI* XXXIX. 227 I have lately collected a great deal of information dealing with the position that has arisen in New Zealand since acclimatisation was commenced in this colony. **1938** Burdon *High Country* 150 The first two stages of the Colony's growth..had clashed. **1968** Seddon *The Seddons* 199 In 1908 he [*sc.* Sir Joseph Ward] attended an Imperial Conference. When he returned home he announced that we were no longer a Colony but a Dominion.

3. As **the Colony**, in early (pre-1840) New Zealand use, New South Wales.

1815 Burnett in Elder *Marsden's Lieutenants* 31 Aug. (1934) 90 Mr. John O'Neal, mate of the vessel and a native of the Colony, for some time defended Mr. Burnett against the attacks of several adversaries. **1823** Marsden *Lett. & Jrnls.* Nov. (1932) 401 The whole of his misconduct would soon spread through the Colony after our arrival. **1833** Williams *Early Jrnls.* 4 June (1961) 317 Ship arr'd from the Colony for Liverpool to sail in the morning. **1878** Buller *Forty Yrs. NZ* 28 Rafts of long spars..were floated down to the ships -..to be taken..to New South Wales, or to 'the colony,' as it was then [1836] called.

colour, *n.*[1] *Goldfields.*

1. [AND 1859] **a.** As a collective singular, **the colour**. A speck or particle of gold, usu. one of many, indicating a prospect.

1861 *NZ Goldfields 1861* 1 Oct. (1976) 30 Mr. Read's researches..have resulted in his finding only the 'colour' of gold. **1879** Haast *Geol. Canterbury & Westland* 84 I instructed my men to dig for gold; we found, to use a technical expression, 'the colour everywhere'. **1974** Heinz *Bright Fine Gold* 200 *The colour*: Specks of gold visible in a prospector's pan or in a sample of quartz.

b. As a distributive plural.

1863 Young *West Coast Notes* (ATLMS) 30 The gold will be remarkable -..a few colours to the pan. **1888** Payton *Round About NZ* 271 Beard's party found gold 'colours' in 1884. **1893** *TrNZI* XXV. 354 Aided by..an old alluvial miner—the locality was diligently prospected, and one or two 'colours' are said to have been found in the wash. **1906** in Evans *Waikaka Saga* 7 Dec. (1962) 39 Dredging through false bottom of green sandy pug..about 8 colours to the dish. **1943** Hislop *Pure Gold* 20 A visitor..may wash his colours of gold from almost anywhere while his wee wife boils the billy.

2. In the phr. **to find (get, raise) colour (the colour)**, to discover signs of gold.

1862 Chudleigh *Diary* 3 June (1950) 41 This man and his mates afterwards worked it [*sc.* a claim] in this way... They got colour. **1863** Walker *Jrnl. & Lett.* (ATLTS) 9 Jan. Tuesday 9th bottomed the hole, found colour, but not enough quantities to pay for working. **1867** Barker *Station Life* (1870) 186 They talk of having 'found *the* colour' (of gold) in some places. **1906** *Red Funnel* XXIII. 202 Got a colour or two in the dish. **c1930** *Whitcombe's Etym. Dict. Aust.-NZ Suppl.* 3 *to raise the colour*, to obtain signs of gold in the pan. **1967** May *West Coast Gold Rushes* (1962) May 526 When small specks of gold are found in a 'prospect' the miner has got a 'colour'.

colour, *n.*[2] Usu. *pl. colours.* A gang identification patch, esp. in the phr. **to run for (one's) colours**, of a probationary gang member, to serve a probationary period before being admitted to the status of a full, 'patched' member.

1975 *Dominion* (Wellington) 17 June 3 In December, 1974, there were about 20 patch members and there were also a few 'running for their colours'— serving a probationary period. **1975** [see patch *n.*[2]].

coloured. Of sheep, 'non-white', having black or brown fleeces.

1901 *TrNZI* XXXIII. 197 My own coloured flock was commenced about ten years ago from a mixed lot of merino and Lincoln-merino ewes. **1986** *NZ Pocket Oxford Dict.* 142 *coloured sheep NZ* one of some small flocks mostly black or grey, yielding wool suitable for home-spinning and weaving.

colt. A New Zealand representative in team sports under a certain age, usu. 21 years; in *pl.*, a junior representative team. **a.** In cricket.

1955 *Weekly News* (Auckland) 28 Dec. 39 The New Zealand Colts team to tour New South Wales country districts has been chosen. **1992** *Western News* (Wellington) 27 Nov. 16 Karori cricket's colt grade had an easy win over Onslow...The team of mostly form one boys is on track to win its grade before Christmas.

b. In rugby football.

1982 Mourie & Palenski *Graham Mourie Captain* 54 The following year marked my first class debut— for Wellington Colts against Horowhenua. **1986** Knight *Shield Fever* 278 In 1980 Warwick [Taylor] had also been in Bryce Rope's New Zealand colts side. **1992** *Dominion* (Wellington) 9 July 30 New Zealand Colts rugby manager..is confident his side won't be beset by the same problems which affected the last national under-21 tourists in Queensland.

comb, *n.* Shearing. [AND 1887.] The lower, stationary unit of a shearing handpiece having teeth which enter and hold the wool as it is cut. Also with a defining word: **wide (widecut) comb**, occas. **narrow comb**, in New Zealand mainly termed GEAR (*n.*¹ 3).

1890 *Otago Witness* (Dunedin) 11 Dec. 7 A man is also required to sharpen knives and keep combs in order. **1891** WALLACE *Rural Econ. Austral. & NZ* 379 The cutter..moves from side to side 4,000 times per minute over the comb, which rests upon the skin of the sheep, and threads its way among the wool close to the surface. **1906** *Awards, etc.* 626 In sheds where machines are used..the shearers to pay for combs and cutters at cost price. **1911** *Maoriland Worker* 11 Aug. 11 That Rule 99 in regard to widecut combs and cutters be strictly adhered to. **c1927** SMITH *Sheep & Wool Industry* 70 Each shed employs an expert, who sharpens the shearers' combs and cutters and looks after the machinery. **1950** *NZJAg.* Oct. LXXXI. 310 Dust can lower the value of a clip..besides being hard on combs and cutters. **1955** BOWEN *Wool Away* 84 There are many types of gear, ranging from round comb..to a straight comb and on to a hollow comb in which the outside teeth are longest. There is also narrow gear, as used in Australia, and wide gear as used in New Zealand. *Ibid.* 86 Finally there is the argument about which is best—wide gear or narrow... The present narrow comb is wider than the early narrow comb. On wrinkly Merino sheep a narrow comb is probably better than a wide one... The wide comb [is] better on all smooth-skinned sheep. **1973** FERNANDEZ *Tussock Fever* 3 The pumice in the wool played up with the gear, blunted the cutter and combs, ruined a man's tally. **1988** *More* (Auckland) Mar. 32 We worked for a contractor..who had just weathered a storm of controversy over the wide combs he and his shearers wanted to use to help them shear more sheep each day. **1991** *Dominion* (Wellington) 3 Sept. 11 New Zealanders were resented when they started migrating to Western Australia with their wide-comb shears in the 1960s.

comb, *v.* Goldmining. [Transf. use of *comb* to search minutely (see OED *v.* 4 b), or a back-formation from BEACHCOMBER.] **a.** *West Coast.* As **comb up**, to sift (black sand) for gold.

1914 HALL *Woman in Antipodes* 99 They work on the [West Coast] beach 'combing' up the black sand..with which the flour-like gold dust is associated.

Hence **comber** *n.*, BEACHCOMBER 3.

1946 SMITH *Poetical Works* 200 Biddy had the 'comber's' art of panning off a dish.

b. In the phr. to **comb for gold**, to comb country in search of gold. *gold-combing* (GOLD 3).

1938 HYDE *Nor Yrs. Condemn* 129 He thought of Macnamara, combing for gold up in the mountains of Otago central, and wondered if he had found any.

Hence **comber** *n.*, a prospector who searches ('combs') a place (esp. old workings) for gold.

1938 HYDE *Nor Yrs. Condemn* 54 The hills was stiff with combers..but none of them had any luck [finding a lost reef]. *Ibid.* 56 'There's not much [gold] to be picked up in the hills now.' 'Oh, the combers make a living, if they can stand the cold.'

comb fern: see FERN 2 (2).

come, *v.*

1. In various phrasal verbs. **a. come at** [AND 1911], in New Zealand use mainly in negative constructions, not to accept, to refuse to consider (a suggestion, way of acting, etc.); esp. in the phr. **don't come at** (that, etc.), don't try (that) on.

1944 FULLARTON *Troop Target* 95 Don't come at that [*sc.* cheating], you *wog* bastard. **1949** DAVIN *Roads from Home* 44 Barry won't come at it. Says he's not going to start the Mission with a skinful of piss. **1960** CRUMP *Good Keen Man* 26 'Who'd get up to that sort of thing?' Jim looked sideways at me. 'Don't come at it too often,' he said. **1960** MASTERS *Back-Country Tales* 85 He reckoned a man needed experience before coming at that sort of thing.

b. As **come down** [see OED *come v.* 60 j 'Austral., N.Z. and S. Africa'], of a river, to develop a sudden fresh, to flood; of a flood, to flow suddenly.

1863 BUTLER *First Year* vii 83 The river had come down the evening on which we had crossed it, and so he had been unable to get the beef and himself home again. **1903** *NZ Illustr. Mag.* VIII. 367 The flood came down with a rush..but it backed up terrific. **1933** *Press* (Christchurch) (Acland Gloss.) 30 Sept. 15 *Come down.*—To flood (of a river). **1975** ACLAND *Early Canterbury Runs* (4edn.) xi 325 His brother was grazing a mob of sheep there when the Bowyer Stream came down in flood and drowned most of them. **1988** SOMERSET *Sunshine & Shadow* 150 I learned that when the snow on the hills melted the river flooded or 'came down' and filled the dry riverbed.

c. As **come out** *obs.*, to emigrate to New Zealand.

1863 BUTLER *First Year* vi 74 I..must explain that a cadet means a young fellow who has lately come out, and who wants to see a little of up-country life. He is neither paid nor pays. **1955** *BJ Cameron Collection* (TS July) come out (n) To immigrate to NZ.

2. In various phr. **a. to come a thud**, see THUD.

b. to come good [spec. use of *come v.* with a complement: see OED 25 a 'Often expressing passage from one condition into another.'; see also EDD *come v.* (10) Of anything injured or hurt, to recover.] (a) To recover after a setback (physical, physiological, financial); (b) to produce money due; to settle a debt; (c) to establish a good character, reputation after unsatisfactory conduct, work, etc.

a1974 SYDER & HODGETTS *Austral. & NZ English* (TS) 202 *To come good.* To recover from an illness. 'I'm a lot better than I was. Oh, I'll come good, it's just a matter of time.' *Ibid.* 204 To produce the amount of money due, rather against expectations. 'Oh, yes. He paid me what he owed. He came good.' *Ibid.* 205 To establish good character for oneself after a poor standard of conduct previously. 'When he was a young fellow, Alfred was a regular no-hoper... Now he's settled down, got a nice wife and a good job—he's come good.'

c. to come to light [see OED *come v.* 48 i 'Austral. and N.Z.'] (a) As **to come to light with**, to produce (in response to a request); to come up with (money, etc.).

1908 *Truth* 15 Aug. 4 Quite a number of ardent Chow-haters have 'come to light' with their 'half-dollars'. **1917** [see BONZER B 1]. **1944** MARSH *Died in Wool* 156 You come to light with them two books. **1960** MASTERS *Back-Country Tales* 42 I came to light with a Spanish kid skin wine bag which I had filled with sherry..and secretly planted in my swag.

(b) *absol.* To produce (money, racing-form, etc.).

1911 *Truth* 11 Mar. 2 We in New Zealand always hoped against hope, that he [*sc.* a horse] would come to light if only for a decent race, and show them what he could do. **1917** *Chron. NZEF* 5 Sept. 28 We hit him up for a loan for weeks afterwards and he always came to light too.

comeback: see QUARTER-BACK.

commercial, *a.* Applied in various collocations to that section of the New Zealand radio network which was permitted to broadcast paid advertisements and had a call-sign ZB: **commercial broadcasting (broadcasting service), commercial network, commercial radio (radio station)** or **commercial station**.

1937 *NZ Railways Mag.* Apr. 33 [Advt] Another achievement by the **Commercial Broadcasting Service. 1939** *Taranaki Herald* (New Plymouth) 25 Aug. 8 The commercial radio service shows [a] profit for the first time. **1940** in Edwards *Scrim* (1971) 125 After listening to another sermon..by the controller of commercial broadcasting, I desire..to lodge a protest. **1966** *Weekly News* (Auckland) 26 Jan. 62 I suppose commercial broadcasting cannot..be curtailed. **1971** EDWARDS *Scrim* 92 Three months later, 1ZB was operating as first station of the state **commercial network. 1976** DOWNES & HARCOURT *Voices in the Air* 146 On the commercial network radio was unashamedly designed to attract the masses. **1947** *NZ Observer* 14 May 13 No one considered seriously what an effect **commercial radio** has had on our thinking in the past 10 years. **1976** DOWNES & HARCOURT *Voices in the Air* 129 In 1940 commercial radio stations had great success with a nation-wide campaign to sell within the country over a million cases of apples. **1937** *NZ Railways Mag.* May 20 [Advt] Wellington's new **commercial station**, 2ZB, offers entertainment never before equalled in New Zealand's radio history. **1947** SMITH *From N to Z* 144 The object of the Commercial Stations is to provide entertainment. **1953** *NZPD* CCC. 1647 One step..would be to extend the broadcasting hours of commercial stations to eleven o'clock. **1966** *Encycl. NZ* I. 250 Within 18 months of the 1936 Act, 12 non-commercial stations and four commercial stations were being operated by the Government. **1976** DOWNES & HARCOURT *Voices in the Air* 107 Commercial stations opened after 1ZB in sequence—2ZB in Wellington in April 1937.

Hence **non-commercial**, esp. **non-commercial station**, one funded from an official licence fee or by the State.

1962 *NZPD* CCCXXXI. 1930 The television licence fee did not..cover the cost of running the non-commercial side. **1976** DOWNES & HARCOURT *Voices in the Air* 150 It happened also with 'Dad and Dave' on 2YD and other non-commercial stations. **1986** *Illustr. Encycl. NZ* 1003 Several non-commercial stations also gained licences.

commercial, *n.* Also **commercial traveller**.

1. *Obs.* [f. either a transf. use of Brit. slang *commercial* a vagrant; or an interplay of two senses of *drummer*, a swagger (who carries a *drum* or swag) and commercial traveller (who drums up business): see OED 6 b.] SWAGGER 1 a.

1933 *Press* (Christchurch) (Acland Gloss.) 30 Sept. 15 *Commercial*, or *c[ommercial] traveller.*—Slang for *swagger*. Probably so called because they travelled. Cf. *drummer*, another nickname they were given. **1946** ACLAND *Early Canterbury Runs* 122 On one occasion [a1880] Mr Reed..was taking a mob of sheep out to one of the paddocks when he met two 'commercials' (swaggers). One of them said to him 'Good day, mate, is old Scabby at home?'

2. [Alluding to folk stories of commercial travellers' sexual appetites or proclivities.] See quot.

1989 *NZ Eng. Newsletter* III. 23 *commercial traveller:* Rams are sometimes called this in humorous allusion to the notion that they satisfy a large number of females.

commissioner. *Hist.*

1. The title (also with init. cap.) given to a goldfields magistrate, the official responsible (among other matters) for the issue and administration of miner's rights and licences on a goldfield. See also *gold commissioner*, *Goldfields Commissioner*, (GOLD 3, GOLDFIELD 2), WARDEN 1 a.

1864 *Gold Digger's Notes* (1950) 51 My mate..then heard of a job at the camp at the Arrow..., putting up quarters for the commissioner, troopers, etc. **1873** PYKE *Wild Will Enderby* (1889, 1974) I. v 20 Commissioner was the title then given to the Goldfield's magistrates. **1887** PYKE *Hist. Early Gold Discoveries Otago* (1962) 62 I must premise that for some unexplained reason the title of 'commissioner' was at first assigned to these gentlemen in place of that of 'warden' as directed by the Goldfields Act. **1967** MAY *West Coast Gold Rushes* (1962) 527 'Joe! Joe!' was the old Australian warning-cry signalling the approach of 'the traps' (the police) or of commissioners checking for gold-digging licences. **1976** VEITCH *Clyde on the Dunstan* 13 It was thought best to appoint Jackson Keddell, who was already in charge of the Gold Escort, as Commissioner.

2. (Native) Land Purchase Commissioner, see LAND 1.

commo. [f. *comm*(unist + -o: see OED 'Chiefly *Austral.* and *N.Z.*'; Austral. 1941.] Often init. cap. A member, or alleged member, of the Communist Party, or one thought to support Communist principles. Cf. REDFED.

1960 HILLIARD *Maori Girl* 245 I know all about it now. Going behind my back, you and that Commo you live with. **1963** PEARSON *Coal Flat* 355 If they would just look at the ringleaders of this boycott they would soon find out that they were commos. **1988** McGILL *Dict. of Kiwi Slang* 30 *Commo* a Communist.

common. When prefixed to the name of a plant or animal, *common* is usu. disregarded as an independent modifier in *Dictionary* entries.

common copper. A book-name for *Lycaena salustius* (fam. Lycanidae), a small, ubiquitous orange and black butterfly.

1929 MARTIN *NZ Nature Book I* 146 The Common Copper... The complete life history of this common butterfly is still imperfectly known. **1947** POWELL *Native Animals NZ* 54 Common copper... This has a span of up to 1½ inches and the wings are bright coppery orange, bordered and veined in black. **1965** MANSON *Nature in NZ* 28 The Common Copper... In the latter part of the summer this butterfly is quite common, frequently flying close to the ground in waste places and open areas throughout the country. **1971** SHARELL *NZ Insects* 50 The most variable species is perhaps the Common Copper butterfly... The wings of this are a rich orange with a brilliant coppery sheen, patterned with dark transverse bands. **1986** ANDREWS *Southern Ark* 41 For some time it has been assumed that *Lycaena salustius* (the Common Copper) was based on specimens of *Lycaena* that are part of the Banks collection currently in the British Museum.

Company, *n.¹ Hist.* In early New Zealand, usu. the New Zealand (Land) Company (NEW ZEALAND B 4 b). (The 1826 quot. prob. refers to an earlier New Zealand Land Company.)

1826 SHEPHERD *Journal* 22 Mar. in Howard *Rakiura* (1940) 362 The advantages to be derived from this Island to the Company is of so very little importance. **1840** BEST *Journal* 27 July (1966) 231 The 27th had been the day appointed for the holders of land [in Wellington] under the Company to choose their Town Acres. **1848** WAKEFIELD *Handbook NZ* 278 A bridle-road has been marked out by the Company..round the eastern spurs of Mount Egmont. **1856** FITTON *NZ* 17 The Company was finally broken up in 1851.

company, *n.² Whaling. Obs.* Usu. in the phr. **to keep** (**keep in** or **join**) **company**, of whaling ships, to sail together in each other's sight. (Called by American whalers 'mating'.)

1831 BISCOE *Journal* in McNab *Old Whaling Days* (1913) 419 At 8 the Cutter joined Company. **1836** RHODES *Jrnl. Barque 'Australian'* (1954) 19 Spoke to the Tamar [whaler]... We decided to keep in company. **1878** HEBERLEY *Autobiography* (ATLTS) 18 We asked him [*sc.* a whaler c1828] where he was going to cruise... We kept company together till we arrived at Japan.

competitions, *n. pl.* [Spec. use of *competition* a contest for some prize: cf. OED 2.] Any of various local events, often fairly regularly held, comprising a series of competitive graded exercises displayed publicly before judges for children of various age-groups in the areas of singing, dancing, dramatic and elocutionary arts, with higher placings hotly competed for.

1903 *Otago Witness* (Dunedin) 4 Nov. 16 [Heading] Dunedin Competitions Society. The Competitions brought to a close. **1910** *Triad* 10 Feb. 41 If you have never attended Competitions, you can have no fair beginning or suspicion of an idea of what you are in for. **1929** *Evening Post* (Wellington) 9 Sept. 11 While in England and America competitions were growing in popularity, in New Zealand they appeared to have reached the beginning of their decay. **1932** *Oamaru Mail* 29 June 4 At a meeting of the Oamaru Competitions Society it was decided to hold a two-days competition on August 19 and 20. **1932** *Oamaru Mail Extra* 8 May 6 Competition week in Oamaru was at one time a very important event, bringing large numbers of visitors to the town. **1988** *Metro* (Auckland) Aug. 221 The [North Shore] competitions cover the whole range of performing arts from instrumental to choral and solo singing, ballet, jazz and tap dancing.

compo. [Abbrev. of (workers') *comp*(ensation + -o: AND 1949.]

1. A compensation payment or allowance under the Worker's Compensation Act (now Accident Compensation Commission) for an injury received in the course of employment (now, any injury); the compensation system in general; a particular compensation payment. Also *attrib.*

1949 *Here & Now* Oct. 34 The wharfies..must also of necessity carry their own insurance against damage and loss—as well as workers' compo. **1956** *Street Society Christchurch* 17 'Yeah. That's how I lost ma finger—va top of one finger.'... 'Did you get any compo?' 'No.' 'Why not?' 'Not the first joint.' 'Oh, a pity.' **1969** MASON *Awatea* (1978) Appendix II 111 A week ago, a carcase fell on Tane; he was give three week's [*sic*] compo. **1975** ANDERSON *Milford Road* 92 Compo is the universal term for payments made to workers injured on the job, and denotes a payment under the Worker's Compensation Act. **1981** *Evening Post* (Wellington) 11 Dec. 4 Compo rises to keep pace with wages. Substantial increases are to be made in accident compensation payments. **1991** *Dominion* (Wellington) 31 July 1 [Heading] Compo changes lift taxes... Changes to the accident compensation scheme will see workers paying an effective tax increase.

Hence **compo-itis**, a *joc.* formation indicating a propensity to feign or extend disability to gain compensation payments.

1986 OWEN & PERKINS *Speaking for Ourselves* 197 I think compo-itis was the most striking disease. I imagine that's disappeared with the advent of Accident Compensation.

2. a. In the phr. **on compo** [AND 1941], (absent from work) receiving compensation payments.

1959 SLATTER *Gun in My Hand* 225 Men off work on compo with a strained back. **1962** CRUMP *One of Us* 49 He'd made friends with..a wharfie who was 'on compo' with a sprained thumb. **1988** McGILL *Dict. Kiwi Slang* 30 *compo* compensation for lost wages from work-related injury, formalised as Accident Compensation.—*on compo* in receipt of such.

b. *transf.* Of a dog, refusing to work after an injury.

1986 CARR *Diary of a Pig Hunter* 171 [Caption to photograph of a dog] Tiger throwing a 'sickie'—on compo after that dunking in the dark.

3. Special Comb. **compo artist**, **compo king**, one who suffers continual compensatable (often cleverly feigned or exaggerated) injuries to take advantage of workers' compensation payments. Cf. ARTIST, -KING.

1938 *NZ Observer* 24 Nov. 7 Non-unionists have been recipients of much unwelcome publicity, due..also to the operations of 'compo' artists. **1941** BAKER *NZ Slang* 52 **Compo king**, a social parasite who makes a practice of injuring himself or malingering in order to secure workers' compensation. **1975** ANDERSON *Milford Road* 95 In the PWD there was a sprinkling of what were known as 'compo kings'. These were men who always seemed to be on compo and they fell into well-defined categories. **1986** *NZ Times* 20 July 5 An Auckland dentist who led a campaign against the accident compensation scheme six years ago has surfaced again to take on who he describes as the criminal 'Compo Kings'.

conciliation. *Hist.* [See OED 7, 1902 NZ.] Used *attrib.*, in special Comb. **conciliation board**, **conciliation court**, institutions for the settling of industrial disputes by a meeting of the parties for discussion.

1894 *Industrial Conciliation and Arbitration Act* 58 Vict. [preamble] An Act to encourage the formation of Industrial Unions and Associations, and to facilitate the settlement of Industrial Disputes by Conciliation and Arbitration. *Ibid.* s43 *Boards of Conciliation*..Every [Conciliation] Board shall..carefully and expeditiously inquire into and investigate any industrial dispute of which it shall have cognisance..and, for the purposes of any such inquiry, shall have all the powers..which are..conferred on the Court of Arbitration. **1900** Conciliation Board [see LARRIKIN 3]. **1908** *Industrial Conciliation and Arbitration Act* s36 In and for every industrial district there shall be established a Board of Conciliation, which shall have jurisdiction for the settlement of any industrial dispute which arises in such district and is referred to the Board under the provisions in that behalf hereinafter contained. **1910** *Truth* 11 June 4 Canterbury wool kings..motored to the Conciliation Court, Christchurch, last week..for the purposes of demanding a reduction of the shearing rates. **1959** SINCLAIR *Hist. NZ* 180 The country was divided into districts in which Conciliation Boards, elected by masters and workers, were set up.

confiscated lands: see CONFISCATION.

confiscation. *Spec.* the confiscation of Maori land, esp. in the Waikato, Bay of Plenty, and Taranaki regions and esp. as a result of the wars of the 1860s, of those tribes opposing land sales. Also as **confiscation line**, the line dividing land under Maori control from confiscated land under control of the Crown (see quot. 1964). See also RAUPATU.

1882 POTTS *Out in Open* 20 He [Ta Kerei Te Rau] was amongst the number of those chiefs who lost the whole of their possessions by the Waikato confiscation. **1964** NORRIS *Settlers in Depression* 151 Although the chiefs disapproved of the murder, they would neither allow Winiata to be arrested in the King Country, nor return him over the Confiscation Line to be taken in charge by the Europeans. **1991** *Dominion* (Wellington) 16 Jan. 7 Arguments over the findings of a 1927 Royal Commission look likely to delay the current Waitangi Tribunal hearing into widespread land confiscations in Taranaki... The claimants asked that the Crown accept their interpretation of the findings:.. that there should have been no confiscations in Taranaki.

Hence **confiscated lands**, the term for land taken from tribes opposing land sales, often by force of arms.

1882 POTTS *Out in Open* 28 We were soon clear of the forest and descending the fertile spurs of beautiful Pirongia, from whence we got extensive prospects of 'the confiscated lands'. **1887** *Auckland Weekly News* 18 June 8 There is another class of land..known as 'Confiscated Lands'. These lands are situated in the provincial districts of Auckland and Taranaki, and were principally the property of natives who rebelled against the Queen's Authority, and took part in the Waikato and Taranaki Wars.

conger (eel): see EEL 2 (2).

consultation. *Obs.* [Euphemistic use of *consultation* the seeking of advice; AND 1880.] A sweepstake; an illegal (esp. Australian) lottery. See also HOBART, TATTS 1.

1885 *Wairarapa Daily* 15 Mar. 2 A young man was much surprised because I did not know the price of horse-racing 'consultation' tickets. *Ibid.* 6 Nov. 2 It is to be hoped that everyone feels better, purer, and generally higher toned, through the coming in[to] force today of the Act prohibiting consultations. **1897** *NZ Times* (Wellington) 25 Oct. 2 The success of certain New Zealand investors in the 'sweeps' or 'consultations' promoted in Tasmania, will have the effect of increasing the sum sent from this colony by people who are desirous of putting their luck to the test. **1934** *Feilding Star* 16 Mar. 6 The syndicate of five which last week won a £12,000 first prize in Tattersalls consultation is a case in point. **1953** *Truth* 21 Jan. 5 The only way I can see for a [Tattersalls] customer to be hoodwinked is for an agent to..purchase another ticket in the same name in a later consultation. **1976** [see HOBART].

contestability. [Spec. use of *contestability* having the ability to be competed for.] The principle of being in competition for scarce or inadequate resources (financial, human, etc.) rather than taking an allocation by right or by tradition. As **union contestability**, allowing other unions' rights to enter into contest for any union's membership coverage.

1986 *Dominion* (Wellington) 30 Sept. 1 Mr Cullen said Mr Rodger was trying to disguise the fact that union contestability would be introduced, and to mount an attack on the national award system. **1986** *National Bus. Rev. 3 Oct.* 14 Putting aside the two most difficult points for the unions, contestability under the guise of a provision for union coverage and demarcation..the FOL has fared relatively well.

contingent. [Spec. use of *contingent* a force contributed to form part of an army, etc.] A name for the various large groups of New Zealand troops sent overseas during the Boer War and WW1. Contrast WW2 ECHELON.

1899 in Hull *College Songs* (1907) 31 We'd best muster up the lot, And send a sixth contingent to the war. **1900** *Eighth Rep. Dept. Agric.* 200 Had it not been for the pressure of other work, notably examination of horses for South African contingents, certain doubtful points might have been elucidated. **1916** ROSS *Light & Shade* 177 The men from the Antipodes have brought with them a..slang of their own... The first contingent became known as 'The Tourists'.

Hence **contingenter** (*WW1*), one who having enlisted was assigned to a contingent for overseas service.

1914 *Wanganui Herald* 12 Aug. 6 The hall is constantly full of waiting contingenters and volunteers saying 'Goodbye'.

continuance. *Hist.* Usu. as **National Continuance**, the name for a voting option (withdrawn after the 1987 election) which if carried would allow the public sale of liquor to continue, latterly one of three options given usually at the time of a general election, the others being *no licence* or *national prohibition*, and *State purchase and control*.

1910 *NZPD* CLIII. 603 In the first [voting paper], the voter is asked whether he votes for continuance or no-license. **1910** *NZ Statutes* No.46 208 [Licensing Amendment Act] I vote for Continuance I vote for No-License. **1946** *AJHR H-38* 46 In 1910 the Licensing Amendment Act of that year..made provision as follows... For a poll in all districts on the question of national continuance or national prohibition. **1959** BOLLINGER *Grog's Own Country* 62 For a Continuance vote implies not merely continuance of the sale of liquor, but continuance of the licensing system and the whole fabric of law under which it is sold. **1966** TURNER *Eng. Lang. Austral. & NZ* 156 In New Zealand a triennial poll is held to decide whether drink should be prohibited... The voting is for one of three alternatives, 'National Continuance', 'State Purchase and Control' or 'National Prohibition'.

Continuous Ministry.

1. Also occas. **Continuous Government**. A name applied to any of various Ministries formed from Ministerial reshuffles in the 1870s and 1880s.

1877 *NZPD* XXVI. 31 An attempt has been made by the Attorney-General to show that the present Ministry are not responsible at least for some part of the matter of which they are accused, inasmuch as they were not in office at the time when the libel was printed. But that is a prevarication, for this is a continuous Ministry. *Ibid.* 106 Did any honourable member ever imagine or infer that the Government of which Sir Julius Vogel became Premier was a different Government from that over which the Hon. Fox had been Premier? It was to all intents a continuous Government. **1884** *NZPD* XLVIII. 74 The 'Continuous Ministry' is one of those political catch-words which have become very common, and it has become as familiar as a household word. **1890** *NZ Observer* 13 Dec. 4 The Continuous Ministry is as dead as Queen Anne. **1898** REEVES *Long White Cloud* 335 When we come to look at the men as distinct from the measures of the parliament of New Zealand between 1870 and 1890, perhaps the most interesting and curious feature was the Continuous Ministry... The Continuous Ministry was a name given to a shifting combination, or rather series of combinations, amongst public men, by which the cabinet was from time to time modified without being completely changed at any one moment. **1913** *NZ Observer* 15 Feb. 17 The continuous Ministry, which for years held office, robbed the people of the country of their lands. **1940** WEBB *Govt. in NZ* 16 The Continuous Ministry, it is clear, was a phenomenon made possible by the absence of organised political groups in the General Assembly. **1959** SINCLAIR *Hist. NZ* 160 Despite the frequent reshuffling of the cabinet, it was so obvious that the changes of personnel involved no change that the Government came to be called 'the continuous ministry'. **1987** Dalziel in *NZJH* Apr. 49 The 'Continuous Ministry' label was established by frequent reiteration. Samuel Hodgkinson..flatly asserted: 'this is a continuous Ministry. There may have been a new material put into it, but it is much the same Ministry as an old garment is the same garment though it has been patched from time to time.'

2. *transf.* Any series of ministries formed by the same party under successive leaders.

1992 *Dominion Sunday Times* (Wellington) 2 Aug. 11 With a weak Labour Party and a divided opposition, National might under present voting conditions establish a near continuous ministry as it did from 1949-84.

contract. Used *attrib.* in special Comb.

1. a. contract shearing. A system in which gangs contract to complete shearing and related activities for a price of so much per hundred sheep. Also *ellipt.* and *attrib.*

[**1856** FITTON *NZ* 220 The shearing of the sheep is generally done by contract;.. at so much per 100 sheep shorn—their [*sc.* hands'] rations, in addition to their pay, being provided for the shearers.] **1911** *Maoriland Worker* 6 Oct. 17 I do not think that many of the boys across the water [in Australia] approve of contract shearing, but the system has taken root and will be hard to abolish. **1974** *NZ Agric.* 66 Contract shearing gangs (consisting of shearers; shed hands; and, usually, a cook) travel from farm to farm. **1986** RICHARDS *Off the Sheep's Back* 95 I was very fortunate in having had a couple of days to settle in and get the 'feel' of contract shearing. **1995** *Mana 9* (Winter issue) 73 Our contract business at Milton was shearing well over a million sheep.

b. contract shed, a farm or station subscribing to contract shearing.

1911 [see GUN *n.*[1] 1]. **1986** RICHARDS *Off the Sheep's Back* 94 Otoro was George's first contract shed... But all his shed hands, shearers and his wool classer had been with him before.

2. contract boarder *obs.*, a usu. male boarder who gives his pay cheque to his landlord and helps himself to what he wants in the way of food, drink, and facilities.

1902 SATCHELL *Land of Lost* 30 Clifford looked about for the contract boarder [at the inn], but he was nowhere to be seen... 'His time is nearly up,' said the innkeeper. 'Most men would have turned him out before this, but I like to give full value.'

contributing school. A state primary school providing for the first six years of a child's education which, with others, 'contributes' its senior pupils to intermediate, form II to VII, or area schools.

1932-33 *Education Amendment Act, Interpretation* 'Contributing school' means a public school or a Maori school from which the pupils of the senior division have been removed to an intermediate school or to the intermediate department of a school. **1944** *Education Gaz. Vol. 23* (No.6) 1 As the intermediate system extends, the number of contributing schools will keep increasing. **1964** *Education Act, Interpretation* 'Contributing school' means a State primary school that is for the time being established under this Act without provision for classes for pupils of forms 1 and 2 or either of those forms. **1989** *Education Amendment Act* s14 The Minister shall from time to time determine which primary schools are to be contributing schools.

conversation. *Obs.* Also **conversation** (occas. **conversational) lolly**. [Perh. an alteration of Sc. dial. *conversation (lozenge)*: see EDD Suppl. 1896; AND 1901.] A flat sweet cut into various shapes, with a usu. sentimental message or motto stamped on it.

1862 HOBHOUSE *Selected Let.* 9 Sept. (1992) 95 'Mrs 'obhouse are you fond of conversation lollies?' was a question with wh [*sic*] she [*sc.* a badly-spoken Nelson servant] mystified me one day. **1880** *Evening Post* (Wellington) 11 May 2 The party were amusing themselves with 'conversation lollies'. **1885** *Wairarapa Daily* 13 June 2 He sat Tommy on the counter and bought him two brandysnaps and a packet of conversational lollies. **1934** SCANLAN *Winds of Heaven* 42 Kitty remembered she always asked for 'Conversation Lollies' with those touching little phrases to aid a laggard in love: 'Meet me to-night', or 'Are you my true love?' **1951** PARK *Witch's Thorn* 78 And Mrs Bedding, the lolly-shop lady, poured out all the wonders she had stored... Green, white, yellow conversation lollies with inscriptions of 'Oh, you kid!' and 'Is that so?' and sometimes, blushingly, 'You're the cat's pyjamas.' **1955** BOSWELL *Dim Horizons* 74 Most wondrous of all [lollies] the variously-coloured 'conversations' with their entrancing mottoes—'I love you', 'Meet me by moonlight', 'Love me alone', and a dozen others. **1983** STEWART *Springtime in Taranaki* (1991) 91 Another of our entertainments..was to pass 'conversation lollies' to the girls. Conversation lollies came in flat pink or yellow squares and circles and heart-shapes of some sugary substance, on one side of which were imprinted such tender messages of passion as 'Hug me tight'.

convert /kən'vɜt/, *v.*[1] *Forestry.* [Spec. use of *convert v.* to transform something material.] *trans.* To turn (logs) into sawn timber.

1885 *TrNZI* XVII. 302 All the men engaged at the sawmills [of West Oxford] had heard of 'tooth-leaved beech', but..no one had seen it converted. **1889** KIRK *Forest Flora* 19 The timber has been utilised only to a limited extent..although..it is occasionally converted at the Southland sawmills.

Hence **conversion** *n.*, the sawing of logs into timber.

1889 KIRK *Forest Flora* 32 The most important centres of conversion are Southland and Wellington. In Southland the timber-supply is obtained almost entirely from State forests.

convert /kən'vɜt/, *v.*[2] [Spec. use of *convert* to change.] *trans.* Esp. in legal use, to take unlawfully (another's property, *spec.* a motor vehicle) for one's own use.

1919 *Police Offences Amendment Act 10 Geo.V* s3 Every person commits an offence and is liable on summary conviction to a fine..or imprisonment..who unlawfully and without colour of right, but not so as to be guilty of theft within the Crimes Act 1908, takes or converts..any horse, motor-car or other vehicle or carriage of any description. **1938** *Auckland Weekly News* 30 Nov. 17 [Heading] Motor Cars 'Converted'. **1966** SCOTT *Days That Have Been* 83 Obviously the Minx had been stolen—for I don't think you can 'convert' a horse. **1980** LELAND *Kiwi-Yankee Dict.* 28 In this genteel society, 'down under' one does not do anything so crass as to steal a car, one merely converts it to one's own use.

Hence **conversion** *n.*, the unlawful taking of another's property (*spec.* and usu. a motor vehicle) for one's own use.

[*Note*] Conversion, an often temporary deprivation of another of the use of property, is distinguished from *theft*, a permanent deprivation.

1924 *Police Offences Amendment Act 15 Geo.V* s10(2) The Magistrate or Justices..may order the person so convicted to pay to the owner a sum..by way of compensation for any damage arising out of the unlawful taking or conversion. **1938** *Auckland Weekly News* 30 Nov. 17 The theft and unlawful conversion of 10 motor cars..were referred to in 28 charges preferred against seven youths. **1956** *Police Offences Amendment Act* s4 Conversion or attempted conversion of motor cars, etc.—The principal act is..amended by.. s32(1) Every person commits an offence who without colour of right but not so as to be guilty of theft..takes or converts to his use... (a) Any motor car or other vehicle. **1961** CRUMP *Hang On a Minute Mate* 67 Two minutes later a police car pulled across in front of the one Tonker was in and they ran him in for conversion. **1983** *Listener* 20 Aug. 101 Some [NZ] words and senses get left out [of the Collins *Concise Dictionary*]... *pikelet, car conversion* and *Taranaki gate*. **1991** *Metro* (Auckland) Jan. 88 His criminal record by then included theft..burglary, car conversion and dishonesty.

convictism. *Hist.* [AND 1834.] The use of a colony as a place of penal servitude.

1856 FITTON *NZ* 342 In New Zealand, too, convictism has not spread its moral blight as in Van Diemen's Land or New South Wales, for convicts have never been sent to New Zealand. **1859** THOMSON *Story NZ* II. 309 The antipodeal colonies, separated by half the globe from England, are tainted with convictism and cannibalism. **1881** CAMPBELL *Poenamo* 141 The arrival at Waiomu was not the arrival of Pakehas tainted with convictism or ship-run-awayism.

convolvulus. [Transf. use of *Convolvulus* (fam. Convolvulaceae) a genus of twining and trailing plants named by Swedish botanist C. von Linné in 1753.] Also **New Zealand** (or **wild) convolvulus.** Applied to both native and introduced species of *Calystegia*, but usu. to the introduced *C. sepium*, and to the indigenous *C. tuguriorum*, and (as **sand**, earlier **shore, convolvulus**) *C. soldanella*. See also BINDWEED, PARAHA, POHUE a, POWHIWHI.

1833 WILLIAMS *Early Jrnls.* 27 Nov. (1961) 351 We landed on Motu tapu in a lovely retired sheltered spot, where the clematis and convolvulus and other creeping plants hung beautifully around. **1840** MATHEW *Journal* 27 Feb. in *Founding of NZ* (1940) 64 It [*sc.* fern] is entangled..with the vines of the wild Convolvulus, which grows everywhere in the greatest luxuriance. **1873** BULLER *Birds NZ* 95 The nest is a rather loose structure..sometimes interlaced with the wiry stems of the bush convolvulus. **1908** BAUGHAN *Shingle-Short* 54 Manuka dark-ey'd, Convolvulus star-ey'd—The glittering of you that morning! **1910** COCKAYNE *New Zealand Plants* (1edn.) 66 Where the shore is sheltered, the shore convolvulus (*Calystegia* [s]*oldanella*)..is often present. **1915** *AJHR* C-6 14 *Calystegia tuguriorum* New Zealand convolvulus. Forest. **1946** [see PARAHA]. **1966** *Encycl. NZ* III. 711 Convolvulus, New Zealand..pohue, pouwhiwhi, powhiwhi..*Calystegia tuguriorum*. **1967** COCKAYNE *New Zealand Plants* (4edn.) 50 Where the shore is sheltered, the sand convolvulus (*Calystegia soldanella*)..with its large whitish flowers striped with lilac, and kidney-shaped or heart-shaped fleshy green leaves, is often present. **1971** WILLIAMS *Dict. Maori Lang.* 256 *Panake*, n. *Calystegia sepium*; wild convolvulus. =*poohue*. **1986** HULME *Windeater* 43 There, suitable low sandhills are covered with marramgrass [*sic*] and pingao and sand convolvulus. **1995** sand convolvulus [see ICE-PLANT].

coo couper, var. KUKUPA.

cooe(e), varr. COO-EE.

coo-ee /ku'wi/ (as a call), /'ku,wi/, *n.* Also with much variety of form as **co-e, cohi, cooe(e), coo'ee** (prob. indicating stress on the second syllable), **cooey, coo-ey, coohee, cooi, ko-hi, kuhi,** etc. [AND ad. Aboriginal Dharuk language *guwi*: orig. in Aboriginal use, 1790: in settlers' use, 1831.]

1. a. An outdoor call formerly often used as a signal to attract attention.

1838 POLACK *NZ* I. 104 Támároa..requested to carry me over. He would admit of no refusal, but..we heard a native *kuhi*, or halloo, which came from two of our comrades who had halted here, to relieve Támároa carrying me. **1845** TAYLOR *Journal* 29 Nov. (ATLTS) III. 185 [He] did not succeed in finding his way through the wood that when the natives heard his co-e they came straight to the spot where he was. **1853** in Cutten *Cutten Lett.* (1979) 47 He is just beginning to speak but his vocabulary is confined to Poppa Ann (the servant) and Coo-ee, a native cry corresponding to ahoy there; it is used to guide people lost in the woods as it can be heard at a far greater distance. **1860** BUTLER *Forest Creek MS* June (1960) 45 Coo-ey can be heard for a very very long way—the 'Coo-' is dwelt on for some time and the 'ey' is brought out sharp and quick in high relief as it were from the Coo—and at an unnaturally high pitch. **1872** DOMETT *Ranolf & Amohia* 474 No sight—no sound of anything that lives—A 'cooey!' low and cautious, then he gives. **1882** POTTS *Out in Open* 227 It is analogous to the bushman's 'coo-ey' attracting instant attention. **1906** ELKINGTON *Adrift in NZ* 259 Suddenly we were startled by hearing a faint coo-ee. **1918** *Kia-ora Coo-ee* (Cairo) (1981) 15 Mar. I. 1 Coo-ee—strange, strong, resonant sounding syllables... The hillsides of Gallipoli have resounded with it. **a1927** ANTHONY *Me and Gus* in *Gus Tomlins* (1977) 80 His last 'Cooee' brought him within a chain of me, and when he heard me answer he started to go crook. **1936** HYDE *Passport to Hell* 50 George gave a long cooee of warning from the higher hills. **1950** CHERRILL *NZ Sheep Farm* 108 She was standing at the gate and gave me a coo-ee. **1960** MASTERS *Back-Country Tales* 94 I cupped my hands and cooeed. A few minutes later Margaret's responding cooee, was borne back to me on the still night air.

b. In transf. use for the call of the weka.

1907 LAING & BLACKWELL *Plants NZ* 132 With sunset the north-wester always lulls for a short time, and then its roar gives place to the coo-ee of the weka and the melancholy cry of the owl.

2. In the phr. **within coo-ee (of)** [AND 1836]. **a.** Within earshot; hence, within reach, near.

1865 CHUDLEIGH *Diary* 15 June (1950) 190 We fussed about all day and by night got all necessary things within cohi as we say here, that is, able to put your hand on them at a moments notice. **1880** BRACKEN *Paddy Murphy's Budget* 60 Within a long 'cooey' Av ould Wanganui Ye couldn't raitch, darlint, yer out in the could. **1905** THOMSON *Bush Boys* 16 Sandy knew he had only to keep within 'Cooee' of Dennis, and he would have him 'clean-beat' in the end. **1913** *NZ Observer* 2 Dec. 21 It is really most interesting to watch the women when they get within coo-ee of a mirror. **1930** *NZ Short Stories* 219 No auriferous reef could possibly be found within 'cooee' of the spot where

Michael's pegs were placed. **1944** *Korero* (AEWS Background Bulletin) 11 Sept. 7 Out of over a score of bombs not one landed within 'cooee' of the mark. **1964** SARGESON *Wrestling with the Angel* 81 The town shows no sign of a hill anywhere within coo-ee. **1980** LELAND *Kiwi-Yankee Dict.* 113 *within coo-ee*:.. Originally it meant within calling distance, but now it usually just means handy or around. 'Is your mate Bazzer within cooe?' Is your friend Barry around?

b. Mainly in neg. constructions **not to come (be) within coo-ee (of)**, not to come near or approach (in quality, accuracy, etc.).

1896 *AJHR I-4A* 2 Melbourne, in all its dishonesty and mad-brained speculation, was not within 'cooey' of the present idiotic boom in Auckland. **1916** ANZAC *On the Anzac Trail* 39 Even the niggers..wouldn't come within cooee of our mob. **1938** *NZ Observer* 20 Jan. 7 Since the Seddon administration, no other government can come within 'cooee' of the first Labour Government's record for endeavour performance. **1978** MANTELL *Murder in Fancydress* 153 Kept telling him how good you were, how well-liked. Sniping at him because he wasn't within cooey [of you]. It got on his nerves. **1988** *Contact* (Wellington) 13 May 2 No other oyster in the world comes within cooey of the Bluff oyster.

coo-ee /ˌkuˈwi/, *v.*

a. [f. prec.: AND 1824.] *intr.* To cry out 'coo-ee' to attract attention.

1843 *Journal of Excursion to find a Route to..Wairoo Valley in NZ* in *Jrnl. Royal Geog. Soc.* 186 We sat down and cooi-ed..but without effect... Still cooi-ing at intervals. **1855** *Lyttelton Times* 18 Apr. 6 After talking with him..the dogs began to ko-hi. Upon being questioned what he was kohi-'ng for, he stated that 'they were his mates,' but witness was not to be afraid, they would not hurt him. **1860** BUTLER *Forest Creek MS* June (1960) 46 The butcher boy is coming up with the meat. He Coo-eys a long way off and by the time he has got up to the house the door is opened to receive the meat. **1862** CHUDLEIGH *Diary* 7 Aug. (1950) 52 People were cooheeing all over the plains last night, they lost their ways. **1871** MONEY *Knocking About NZ* 29 We 'coo'ed' instantly, and after a few minutes were joined by one of Howitt's party. **1919** MANSFIELD *Letters* 2 Oct. (1993) III. 5 After you had gone I coo-eed when I saw you on a part of the road which was visible. **a1927** ANTHONY *Me & Gus* in *Gus Tomlins* (1977) 80 I sat up there for an hour before I thought of cooeeing for Gus. I heard Gus cooee back. **1946** SARGESON *That Summer* 178 He cooeyed, and Rex answered. **1971** *Listener* 19 Apr. 56 Well, out of the boo-ai comes three trampers... They cooeed out. **1981** HUNT *Speaking a Silence* 66 I cooeed for the puntman but got no response.

b. In transf. use for a cry of the laughing owl.

1985 *Reader's Digest Book NZ Birds* 308 Apparently it [*sc.* the now-extinct laughing owl] was easily kept in captivity, and reports say that it cooeyed in the evening, yelped like a young dog and mewed and chuckled.

Hence **coo-eeing** *vbl. n.* [AND 1845].

1857 PAUL *Lett. from Canterbury* 18 Cooeings—a sort of shriek, distinctly audible at great distance. It is uttered by bush-travellers in Australia and New Zealand to indicate their whereabouts. **1871** MONEY *Knocking About NZ* 71 While we were waiting we heard a 'cooing' to our left..and presently a number of men appeared coming towards us. **1924** *Otago Witness* (Dunedin) 22 Jan. 7 I..heard..loud and prolonged cooeeing proceeding from the river. **1982** *Evening Post* (Wellington) 11 Aug. 18 The art of cooeeing is probably not familiar to many New Zealanders.

cooey, coohee, cooi, varr. COO-EE.

cookee. *Hist.* Also **cookie, kuki**. [A Maori alteration of Eng. *cook(y)* to *kuki* which was then re-formed to *cookee*: see Williams Appendix *kuki* [from English] cook.]

a. A slave in early Maori society.

1817 NICHOLAS *NZ* 115 He held no rank among his countrymen, but was one of the common men, or what they themselves call *cookee*. **1829** ATKINS in McNab *Hist. Records* 2 Mar. (1908) I. 696 They are divided into two classes, viz., *ranghateeroos* (or chiefs)..and *cookees* (slaves), who are nearly black, and much shorter, and appear a different race of people. **c1835** BOULTBEE *Journal* (1986) 71 Tarboka had taken a woman as his cookie or slave. **1840** POLACK *Manners & Customs* I. 25 The term of Cookee is incorrect for that of a slave; this word is derived from the word cook, an office on board British ships, accounted as only fit for a slave by the New Zealanders—hence the term. **1853** EARP *NZ* 50 According to New Zealand notions of rank he being the highest in the scale, and his tormentor being regarded as a *cookee*, or slave, the lowest. **1948** HENDERSON *Taina* 26 The *tohunga* made it..*tapu*, so that the *kukis*, *taurekarekas*, *tutuas*, and other varieties of slaves..would be afraid to meddle.

b. *transf.* A European 'slavey' or servant.

1899 GRACE *Sketch of NZ War* 67 A great chief like you ought to be afraid of a mere Queen's servant (*cookie*) like Donald McLean.

Cooker: see CAPTAIN COOKER.

Cookham boots. *Canterbury. Obs.* [f. a proprietary name.] Also *ellipt.* **Cookhams**. *pl.* Strong outdoor or working boots.

[**1860** in *Canterbury Rhymes* (1866) 76 Softgoods, and hard, and holloware, With Stringers buns and toffees; And Cookham's famous boots are there, So is the Union Office.] **1872** BARKER *Christmas Cake* iii I took off my Cookhams and worsted socks at each ford. **1873** LADY BARKER *Station Amusements* 15 [The bushmen's] working dress of red flannel shirt, and moleskin trousers, 'Cookham' boots, and diggers' plush hats. **1879** HINGSTON *Australian Abroad* 320 Here and there, over [Christchurch] shops, one sees this mysterious inscription, 'Cookham Boots'—only that, and nothing more. **1970** McNEISH *Mackenzie* 58 It was necessary for Mackenzie to remain in Christchurch until the celebrations ended, for he needed a new pair of Cookham boots, size ten.

cookhouse. [Spec. use of *cookhouse* a building or room where cooking is done.] The cooking-shed of a pa or kainga; the kitchen building on a marae; KAUTA.

1847 ANGAS *Savage Life* I. 332 The cook-house [of a kainga] is merely a shed, built of posts or slabs of wood placed several inches apart, so as to admit the air and wind. **1866** ANGAS *Polynesia* 153 In each court [yard of a pa] stands the house and cook-house. **1924** *TrNZI* LV. 367 In many places, the tribal meeting-house stands alone or flanked by a solitary cook-house.

cookie, var. COOKEE.

Cook Islander: see ISLANDER 1.

Cook Medal. Also **Cook's Medal**. [f. the surname of Captain James *Cook* (1728-1779), navigator and explorer.] See quot. 1941.

[**1773** FORSTER *Resolution Jrnl.* 7 Apr. (1982) II. 249 Capt Cook gave the old man a Medal & I gave one glass bead, the only thing we had about us.] **c1835** BOULTBEE *Journal* (1986) 54 We found one of Cook's Medals amongst a heap of rubbish on Iron Island [Dusky Bay]. it was a composition piece, of the size of a penny; on one side, was the head of George the Third, and the other was the representation of 2 ships, and 'Resolution and Adventure, sailed from England March 1772'. **1941** SUTHERLAND *Numismatic Hist. NZ* 209 *Cook Medals. Ibid.* 210 The first medallic link between Great Britain and New Zealand was..forged by Captain James Cook who arranged (in 1772), with the approval of the Lords of the Admiralty, to strike silver, copper and brass medals bearing, on the obverse, a portrait of King George III, and on the reverse a representation of two sailing ships—*Resolution* and the *Adventure*—with which Cook was to undertake his second voyage of discovery.

cookshop. A stock station, camp or army cookhouse.

1857 *Diary St. Leonard's Station* 1 Jan. in Macfarlane *Amuri* (1946) 123 Rum and plum duff at the cook shop. **1909** THOMPSON *Ballads About Business* 44 Go trampin' through the snow, To the [station] cook-shop for yer breakfast. **1917** let. 30 Sept. in *Boots, Belts* (1992) 27 We got down here [to Trentham army camp]..and were put in huts for the night, then the next morning 20 of us were put in the cook shop. **1933** *Press* (Christchurch) (Acland Gloss.) 30 Sept. 15 *Cookshop*.—Kitchen and dining room where station hands' food is cooked and eaten. It is sometimes a separate building, sometimes part of the men's hut. **1940** STUDHOLME *Te Waimate* (1954) 216 They [*sc.* swaggers] generally arrived at the homestead in the evening, and were given some food at the cook shop. **1965** McLAGLAN *Stethoscope & Saddlebags* 147 The schoolmaster's house had been co-opted as a cookshop and hostel for the volunteer nurses. **1978** JARDINE *Shadows on Hill* 173 Halfway..was sited the working centre of the station—men's quarters, cookshop, stables. **1981** HUNT *Speaking a Silence* 85 At the Cobb [hydro] they went and put in a flash new cookshop.

Cook's Medal, var. COOK MEDAL.

cook's offsider: see OFFSIDER 2 b.

Cook's scurvy grass: see SCURVY GRASS.

Cook's Tourists. *WW2.* [f. a play on the name of Thomas *Cook* and Sons, travel agents.] Also as **the tourists**, a jocular or ironic name for the Second Echelon 2NZEF (who were sent first to Britain and then to Egypt). Cf. DEBT-DODGER, TOURIST.

1941 HAWDON *NZ Soldiers in England* 4 These are the experiences of a soldier of the Second Echelon, 2NZEF, the 'Cook's Tourists'. **1978** SINCLAIR & HARREX *Looking Back* 215 The troops left home in three 'Echelons'... The second was diverted to the United Kingdom and its members were known as 'the tourists'. **1983** HENDERSON *Down from Marble Mountain* 261 The Second Echelon are 'Cook's Tourists'. **1995** [see DEBT-DODGER].

Cook's turban shell. Also **turban shell**. [f. the name of (Captain) James *Cook.*] *Cookia sulcata* (fam. Turbinidae), a large univalve (up to 12 cm) found among seaweed on rocks below low-tide level.

1947 POWELL *Native Animals of New Zealand* 25 Cook's Turban Shell... Maori names for this shell are Karaka, Toitoi and Ngaruru. **1955** DELL *Native Shells* (1957) 16 Cook's Turban Shell... *Cookia sulcata..Karaka, Toitoi* or *Ngaruru*... When alive the shell is usually covered with marine growth which, when cleared off, reveals a beautiful pearly shell. **1966** *Encycl. NZ* I. 398 Cook's Turban Shell... This fish is quite common, and lives under rocky ledges at low tide, in clean water along the coasts. **1970** PENNIKET *NZ Seashells in Colour* 22 *Cooks Turban Shell...* Perfect specimens are almost impossible to obtain as adult shells are rarely seen without a snowy summit of white limey deposit. **1984** *Listener* 22 Sept. 30 Tiger shells, turban shells, the southern volute, a mass of empty oyster shell.

cooma-cooma, var. KAMOKAMO.

coom(e)ra, varr. KUMARA.

coon. [Transf. use of *coon* a negro.] An offensive name for usu. a Pacific Islander, occas. any Polynesian.
  1981 *Avondale College (Auckland) Slang Words in Use* (Goldie Brown Collect.) Feb. *coon*: Maori or Islander **1987** *Evening Post* (Wellington) 15 June 3 The head doorman explained the rules to me as no jeans, no people who were drunk and no coons, which I knew meant no Pacific Islanders.

co-op. A farmers' co-operative dairy factory. As **co-op store**, the general store attached to a dairy factory.
  1911 *Maoriland Worker* 20 Mar. 8 Have sent your letter to R. Ross, storekeeper, Glen Oroua, who has been manager of a large co-op. store and is in full sympathy with the movement. **1959** SINCLAIR *Hist. NZ* 201 The farmers were not as individualistic as they imagined. For instance they combined to form their own butter and cheese factories, over half of which, by 1903, were 'co-ops'. **1988** HILL *More from Moaville* 57 The calendars on the walls of all sets are always from the Moaville Co-Op Dairy Factory.

co-operative. [Spec. use of *co-operative* of a business, etc., owned and run by its members on a profit-sharing basis: see OED *cooperative a.* and *n.* 2.] Usu. applied to a dairy company or factory complex which is co-operatively owned by its farmer-suppliers.
  1899 *Hawera & Normanby Star* 13 Aug. 2 Suppliers to co-operative dairy factories are looking forward..to September when the balance sheets..will be presented. **1912** *Otago Witness* (Dunedin) 25 Sept. 16 The above incident was brought under the attention of a calm, cool and canny Scot, who is the chairman of a co-operative dairy factory in Southern Taranaki. **1959** *NZ Dairy Exporter* 10 Sept. 20 The recently-celebrated golden jubilee of the Tamaki-Kiritaki Co-op Dairy Co...calls to mind some of the earlier proprietary co-operative struggles in the district before the co-operative system had become universal in our dairy industry. **1971** *NZ Dairy Exporter* Sept. 43 One hundred years ago this month, New Zealand's co-operative dairy industry was brought into being by the enterprise and courage of seven forward-looking settlers on the Otago Peninsula.

cooper's flag. *Obs.* RAUPO *n.* 1 a, the stems of which were used by early ships' coopers for sealing whale-oil and water casks. See also FLAG 1, quots. 1773 and 1939.
  1834 *Log 'Lucy Ann'* 26 Apr. in McNab *Old Whaling Days* (1913) 102 [Cargo from NZ.] 10 logs of timber, 890 rickers..13 casks of black whale oil..3 tons flax, 86 bundles coopers' flags. **1878** JOLLIE *Reminiscences* (ATLTS) 57 Raupo, a sort of Cooper's flags. **1898** MORRIS *Austral-English* 97 *Cooper's-flag..* another name in New Zealand for *Raupo*.

Coopworth. [f. the name of I. E. *Coop* (1914–), Professor of Animal Science and later Vice-principal of Lincoln University College + *worth*.] A New Zealand sheep breed yielding both wool and meat.
  1978 BLAIR *Seed They Sowed* 158 I.E. Coop..reported on his interbreeding of Border Leicester and Romney with the objective of producing a high-fertility Border-Romney breed by interbreeding the crossbreds. This notable first in Lincoln history culminated in the establishment of a new breed registered [in 1968]..as the Coopworth. **1989** *Illustr. Encycl. NZ* 249 *Coopworth* is a breed of sheep developed in the 1960s from Border Leicester and Romney, and named after Professor Coop of Lincoln College in Canterbury. Coop initiated the research on which the Coopworth Society bases its strict breeding requirements. **1990** CROSS *NZ Agriculture* 104 The Coopworth, developed in the 1960s from Border Leicester and Romney breeds, is a dual-purpose sheep with equal emphasis on meat and wool.

coot.

1. Also **coote**. Any of various rail-like birds including the PUKEKO *Porphyrio porphyrio* (*obs.*), and possibly the New Zealand DABCHICK *Podiceps rufopectus*, thought to resemble the northern hemisphere (*bald*) *coot*. See also *bald coot* (BALD *a.*).
  1769 PARKINSON *Journal* (1773) 11 Oct. 89 We found here [at Poverty Bay]..a Fulica, or bald Coot, of a dark blue colour; and a Black-bird, the flesh of which was of an orange colour, and tasted like stewed shellfish. **c1899** DOUGLAS in *Mr Explorer Douglas* (1957) 234 Some people call..[the pukeko] the coote, from some fancied resemblance to the water hen of the Old country [*sic*]. **1955** OLIVER *NZ Birds* 91 Another specimen [of *Podiceps rufopectus*]..is that which was given to Colenso..on the Waikato River below Ngaruawahia and was by him mistaken for a coot and described as a new species (*Fulica nova-zealandiae* [*sic*]).

2. Usu. as **Australian coot**, *Fulica atra australis* (fam. Rallidae), a small black waterbird with a prominent white frontal shield, self-introduced from Australia.
  1955 OLIVER *NZ Birds* 381 *Coot Fulica atra australis* Seven instances are on record of this widely ranging species having been taken in New Zealand. The first specimen to be taken was shot at Lovells Flat, about 1875. **1966** FALLA et al. *Birds NZ* 107 Australian Coot... Rare but increasing in New Zealand, especially in the last decade. **1970** *Annot. Checklist Birds NZ* (1980) 43 *Australian Coot* Australia and Tasmania; straggling to New Zealand; eight records, all in South Island, between 1875 and 1953... There appears to have been an invasion of coots..in, or before 1957. **1984** SOPER *Birds NZ* 85 The Australian Coot has black plumage, a conspicuous white bill and shield and olive-green legs.

coota, cooter: see BARRACOUTA; COUTA.

cooter, cootie, varr. KUTU.

cop. [f. *cop n.* a catch, a capture: see OED *n.*[7] b, 'Chiefly *Austral*. and *N.Z.*'] A valuable catch, a 'good thing'. Cf. CHOP *n.*[1]
  1916 GRAY, Norman *MS Papers 4134* (ATLMS) 26 Aug. I still have my sanitary work, but there is practically nothing to do and it's a pye-on kop (excuse)! *Ibid.* 14 Oct. The hours are 9–12 and 2–4 and all the men are free until 9 p.m...we are constantly saying that it is the best 'kop' since we left new Zealand. **1944** BRUNO *Desert Daze* 11 Any other bottles [other than the three that paid for his seat at the pictures] that fell into his maw were distinct 'cop'. **1951** p.c. Pugh-Williams. I have often heard seamen and watersiders use *on a cop* when they are paid overtime till, for example, 9am and complete the job at 6.30.

copa-, coppa (maori), varr. COPPER MAORI.

copper maori. *Hist.* Also with considerable early variety of the form *copper*: **copa, coppa, coppre, copu, kaipa, kapa-, kápá, kapura, kopa, koppa**; occas. with init. cap. [f. Rawara Maori dialect *kopa* (*maori*) a Maori (i.e. 'the usual New Zealand') oven, reinforced by *kāpura* 'fire' (recorded as *Ka poola* from 1815 in Kendall *New Zealanders' First Book* 17; see also 1 c below) with a suggestion of English *copper* 'boiler'.]
  [*Note*] *Copper Maori* seems to have been used by Europeans in the North Island (esp. Northland) for the more usual HANGI, UMU. Though eventually felt as English (a more complete anglicization is represented by the occasional **Maori copper**), and susceptible to early use of an -*s* plural, the orig. *copper maori* is essentially a construct which follows Maori grammar in placing the defining word after the noun. *Maori* (variously spelt in early texts) can thus be interpreted as the traditional 'usual, ordinary' rather than as an early Maori use of the modern sense 'Maori'. Therefore *kopa maori* (or *Maori*) may be the 'ordinary' or 'traditional' earth oven as distinct from a **kopa pakeha*, an iron (try)pot or GOASHORE, more akin to an English *copper*, and used as a boiler rather than a steam cooker. (The English word *boiler* was transliterated to Maori as *paera*, possibly from a 19th c. English dial. pron. [baila(r)].) Thus *copper maori* would seem from earliest times to be open to the influence of the English word *copper* 'boiler' for which **kopara* or **kapara* are possible early 19th c. transliterations. English *copper* and (or) its transliterated forms could easily be linked or confused (in spite of a difference in vowel length) with Maori *kāpura* fire (see 1 c below). Cf. the following early use of *copper oven*: 1773 WALES *Journal* 5 Nov. in Cook *Journals* (1961) II. 816 It having been discovered on board that most of [the bread] which we had in Butts was damp and Mouldy; to day a Copper Oven was brought on Shore and fixed up by the Tent to rebake it.

1. The following entry is arranged under the predominant spelling forms: **a. copper maori; b. kopa** or **kapa (maori); c. kapura maori.** *Pl.* often -*s*. Also with init. cap. *Maori.* HANGI 1. See also *Maori copper* (MAORI B 5 a). **a.** As **copper maori.**
  1834 MARKHAM *NZ* (1963) 44 Coppre Mourie, or the Native Ovens are described I rather think in Captain Cookes Voyages. They are done this way. They scratch a hole 8 or 10 inches deep and two Feet in Diameter and then light the Fire in the hole; when the fire is at its best. They cover it all over with Stones The size of Potatoes or what you would put on the roads in England. They are well heated and [when] the fire dies down a wet cloth of Mat is put round the edge. **1841** BIDWILL *Rambles in NZ* (1952) 30 I saw all the native ovens (copper mowries, according to English pronunciation) in which the cooking had been performed. **1843** *NZ Journal* IV. 216 We cooked some meat in a copper mauri, or *hangi* being the native term. **1858** MOON *Wreck of HMS Osprey* 83 This peculiar mode of cooking is called by the natives a Hangi, but more commonly by Europeans, a Copper Maori. **1864?** VON TEMPSKY *Memoranda* (ATLTS) 78 They could not fail to see now that this smoke was such as issues, of a sudden, from a Copa-Maori. **1873** TINNE *Wonderland of the Antipodes* 16 We watched..the preparation of our food in a genuine copu-maori, or native oven. **1878** HEBERLEY *Autobiography* (ATLTS) 13 They sucked [the slave girl's] blood till [she] was dead, then they cut

her up and cooked her in a copper Maori [c1826]. [Heberley also uses *Maori copper*.] **1891** PRICE *Through the Uriwera [sic] Country* 17 The native women busied themselves with their 'copper-maoris'. **1905** BAUCKE *White Man Treads* 101 'Coppa Maori', 'Maori oven', etc.—these are the slang names given by those who know no better. By the natives it is called an 'Umu' and universally a 'Haangi'. **1908** *Souvenir of All Nations Fair, Gisbourne* [sic] 11 The hangi, or koppa maori... An hour is long enough for a moderate sized hangi. **1923** [see KOPA]. **1933** WASHBOURN *Reminiscences of Early Days* 47 For a long time after the arrival of the pakeha the Maoris did their cooking in a 'koppa Maori'. **1968** *NZ Contemp. Dict. Supp.* (Collins) 6 *copper Maori n.* Maori earth oven which cooks food on heated stones, more often called a *hangi*.

b. As **kopa** or **kapa (maori)**; also ?erron. **kaipa maori**.

1838 POLACK *NZ* I. 399 The only method of cooking formerly in use [by the New Zealanders] was by the *kápá* or *angi maori*, the native oven, already described. **c1875** MEREDITH *Adventuring in Maoriland* (1935) 37 These natural utensils are called *kaipa maoris*, generally pronounced 'copper maori'. *Ibid.* 89 They had cooked some pork, maize, and *kumaras* in a *kapa-maori*. **1882** HAY *Brighter Britain* II. 153 The earth-oven, the kopa or hangi. **1889** *TrNZI* XXI. 417 So they set to work and dug holes on the flat..and shaped something like a *Kopa Maori*. **1894** *JPS* IV. 224 The kapas continued in use [in the Pelorus district, Marlborough] until superseded by the kohua, or iron pot. **1904** W.A.Q. *The Story of Hawera* 7 The stray embers from a 'kopa maori' or 'hangi'. **1913** *NZ Observer* 22 Feb. 22 They made a huge 'Kapa Maori' (native oven) and spread 60 magnificent flounder. **1923** *Northlander* (Hare Hongi) (VUW Fildes Clippings 461a:130) 11 Jan. We youngsters haunted the hakis (miscalled kapa Maori). **1938** *Auckland Weekly News* 2 Mar. 42 Immediately above the beach the trampers saw the burnt stones of many old-time hangis or kapas Maori. **1940** MATTHEWS *Matthews of Kaitaia* 20 And so the first sermon was preached in Kaitaia, with the kapa Maoris heating to cook the preacher! **1982** BURTON *Two Hundred Years of NZ Food* 22 [Quoting a poem *The Candidate*] And can you cook wild pork, man, Well—a la kopa Maori?

Hence *v. joc. trans.*, to hangi.

1900 *Auckland Weekly News Xmas Number* 17 Her mother was dead—Koppa-Maoried, I was told, by a neighbouring tribe.

c. As **kapura maori**. [Ma. /ˈkaːpura/: Williams 97 *Kāpura*, n. Fire: Markham's spelling *corpora* suggests that some English perceptions of Ma. *kāpura* tended towards an [ɒ] or [o] realization which could suggest English dial. pronunciations of *copper* with various vowel lengths and qualities differing from the modern standard: 1834 MARKHAM *NZ* (1963) 38 The Natives told him to his Teeth, that if he got it, they would put (Corpora) Fire to it.]

c1849-50 RICH in *Aust and NZ Gazette* (1853) 62/14 This [with hot stones, etc.] is an excellent way of cooking and is called Kapura Maori. **1865** LEVY in Williams *East Coast Hist. Records* (1932) 25 Mar. 91 The females were all now getting the kapura maoris ready for a grand feed when..there arrived..some hundreds of kits of potatoes. **1866** CARTER *Life & Recoll.* 427 These cooking pits were hongis [sic] or kapura maories. **1890** *TrNZI* XXII. 104 In two distinct places..there were a number of *kapura Maori*, or native ovens.

2. The contents of a **copper maori**; HANGI 2.

1879 GREY *His Island Home* 21 It was intimated to us that the copper-maori was ready for consumption... [It] consisted of kumeras..Indian corn, mullet etc.

coppre (maori), var. COPPER MAORI.

coprosma.

1. A genus of sub-shrubs, shrubs and small trees of the family Rubiaceae named by the botanists J.R. and J.G. Forster in 1776 (see quot. 1898), and represented in New Zealand by 50 or so species occupying habitats from coastal to subalpine zones. Often with a prefixed modifier. See also COFFEE, COPROSMA, KARAMU 1, KARANGU, TAUPATA, *yellow-wood* (YELLOW 2).

1871 WILLIAMS *Dict. NZ Lang.* 45 *Karamuu*, n. *coprosma*, a shrub, of various species. **1882** POTTS *Out in Open* 114 The berries of the konini, of various species of coprosma, ripening early, furnish some part of its food supply. **1898** MORRIS *Austral-English* 98 *Coprosma*..scientific and vernacular name for a large genus of trees and shrubs of the order *Rubiaceae*. From the Greek [κοπροσ] dung, on account of the bad smell of some of the species... The Maori name is *Karamu*. **1911** *AJHR* C-13 40 *Coprosma acerosa*... Dune-coprosma. Shrub dune. **1915** *AJHR* C-16 15 [*Coprosma*] *propinqua*... Common coprosma... Bank of streams. **1929** *Tararua Tramper* Oct. 2 Along the creeks or in shady gullies fuchsias, coprosmas and the N.Z. privet..are plentiful. **1951** LEVY *Grasslands NZ* (1970) 87 Toetoe, phormium, cabbage tree, with swamp coprosma and hupiro may figure as a developmental phase on wet soils. **1968** SLATTER *Pagan Game* 120 To the townies matai and kahikatea..were just street names, to him they were familiar foes of the formidable bush, as familiar as the..coprosmas..and fern. **1972** McLEOD *Mountain World* 310 Coprosma: A large genus of dense shrubs described as dung-smelling. **1980** MANTELL *Murder & Chips* 35 The garden had been allowed to revert to wild-garden..green on green, splashed by an occasional yellow-leafed coprosma. **1988** DAWSON *Forest Vines to Snow Tussocks* 104 The coprosma is sometimes known as 'stinkwood' because the crushed leaves smell like rotten cabbage. **1992** *Dominion Sunday Times* (Wellington) 26 July 21 There may be..other coprosmas fruiting pale red berries.

2. Comb. **coprosma hedge**.

1936 HYDE *Passport to Hell* 42 Over a coprosma hedge he fell in love..with Fanny's little sister, May. **1938** HYDE *Godwits Fly* (1970) 12 He flung his bicycle against the coprosma hedge, and Carly and Eliza came running out to meet him.

co-provincials: see PROVINCIAL *n.*

cop the damper: see DAMPER 3.

copu (maori), var. COPPER MAORI.

coraddee, coraddie, varr. KORARI.

coral broom: see BROOM 2.

corduroy, *n.* Also **corderoy**. [Orig. US: f. the ribbed appearance resembling *corduroy cloth*: see OED *n.* A 3, B 3; AND 1875, *-road* 1861.]

1. A road(-base) formed of logs, poles, etc. placed usu. side by side (at a right-angle to the direction of traffic) across a swampy track or ground; the logs, etc. so used.

1866 [see 2 below]. **1923** MALFROY *Small Sawmills* 38 Corduroy..Small saplings placed side by side across a soft wet track to avoid the sinking of the load. **1938** *Tararua Tramper* Jan. 7 A great deal of willing work is often wasted by not making a good job of the corduroy. **1940** *Tales Pioneer Women* (1988) 157 There were no roads; we followed narrow, boggy tracks, where there was..corduroy where the bottom was undiscoverable. **1959** MASTERS *Tales of Mails* 148 The corduroys of the track had broken or slipped away. **1981** HENDERSON *Exiles Asbestos Cottage* 123 The worst parts of mud and ooze were covered with 'corduroy', short small logs from saplings pegged tight one against the other. **1992** PARK *Fence Around the Cuckoo* 132 At the worst places..[the road] was corduroy—rows of small tree trunks hammered down into the mud.

2. In special Comb. **corduroy pathway, road, track**, a pathway, etc. formed with a corduroy base.

1961 REED *North Cape to Bluff* 46 The **corduroy pathway** to these mighty trees has been constructed of the trunks of tree-fern. **1866** CARTER *Life & Recoll.* II. 107 The roads over the swampy flats were..made possible by means of bush poles, which were laid close together across the middle of the roads. These were—as in America—called '**corduroy roads**'. **1931** LOVELL-SMITH *Old Coaching Days* 19 The formation of the road surface..consisted of tree trunks fastened together and laid across the road going over the swamp. It was known as a 'plank' or 'corduroy' road. **1951** CRESSWELL *Canterbury Tales* 122 Here was a muddy creek where drays often stuck fast and when this happened bundles of sticks were laid down to form a corduroy road. **1986** [see SKIDDED ROAD]. **1934** *Press* (Christchurch) (Acland Gloss.) 13 Jan. 13 **Corduroy track**.—Roadway made by laying poles across it to stop wheels sinking in the mud. (More used in the North Island than the South.) **1948** FINLAYSON *Tidal Creek* (1979) 119 Might be caught after dark on..one of them long narrow corduroy tracks across a swamp. **1951** ACLAND *Early Canterbury Runs* 363 Corduroy track: Roadway made by laying poles across it to stop wheels sinking in the mud. **1978** *Manawatu Tramping Club Jubilee* 86 The corduroy track was still sound in many places and a big help in the swampy areas.

corduroy, *v.* [AND 1879.] *trans.* To surface (a swamp track, etc.) with logs, etc.

1868 DILKE *Greater Brit.* I. 340 The highway is 'corduroyed' with trunks of the tree-fern. **1922** COWAN *NZ Wars* (1955) I. 104 A rough and narrow bush road, 'corduroyed' with fern-tree trunks in the marshy portions, wound through the forest. **1967** MAY *West Coast Gold Rushes* (1962) 359 Corduroying bush tracks was not the only lesson the American backwoods could teach. **1968** TOMLINSON *Remembered Trails* 52 A great deal of it [*sc.* a bush track] was corduroyed, that is saplings or split timber, perhaps up to ten feet wide, laid close together and covered with dirt or gravel.

core: see CAW.

corero, var. KORERO.

Corinth. *Obs.* [f. the name of the Greek city, famous for its beautiful situation on an isthmus.] In the phrases **the Corinth of the North** (or **Southern Hemisphere, South Pacific**), Auckland city, from its having a situation similar to that of Corinth.

1860 *A Handbook for Emigrants* 13 Auckland..has been termed by the Bishop of New Zealand, and men of classic recollections, 'the Corinth of the Southern Hemisphere'. **1889** KNOX *Boy Travellers* 186 'It reminds me of Corinth, in Greece,' said Fred,.. 'No doubt it does,' said the officer.. 'Auckland is called the Corinth of the South Pacific.' **1899** BULLOCK *Wonderland* 2 Beautiful for situation, [Auckland] has therefore been styled the 'Corinth of the North'.

corker, *n., a.,* and *adv.*

A. *n.* [Used elsewhere but recorded earliest in NZ: see OED *corker* 2 b, 1882.] Something or someone of surpassing size or excellence; also used ironically. Cf. BOTTLER.

c1862–63 THATCHER in Mosley *Illustrated Guide to Christchurch* (1885) 11 I'm down at last; I own [the walk] has been a *corker*, To go back now would be a bitter pill. **1919** MANSFIELD *Letters* 9 Dec. (1993) III. 15 Next year well [*sic*] do a korker... The copy all in advance—a dummy ready to be taken round for the ads. **1948** BALLANTYNE *Cunninghams* 20 Isn't Marjorie a corker, Fred? Think she'd write and let her mother know. You'd better watch it too. The road down to the woolshed's a corker.

B. *adj.* [f. *corker n.*] Fine, excellent; enjoyable; very well. Also in a joc. play **fun of cork**, corker fun (see quot. 1918).

1904 in Lawlor *More Wellington Days* (1962) 53 Wally gave me some chuddy. It's corker for playing games with. **1918** let. 22 June in *Boots, Belts* (1992) 107 The best of the lot was a hurdle race for mules. It is the fun of cork to watch a mule hurdling. **1937** MARSH *Vintage Murder* 72 He talks with a corker sort of voice. Not queeny, but just corker. *Ibid.* 174 The idiom is a bit puzzling but 'corker' seems to be the general adjective of approbation. *Ibid.* 49 We tried her out till we was sick and tired of her and she worked corker every time. She worked good-oh, didn't she? **1944** GASKELL in *All Part of the Game* (1978) 24 It's such a corker name for a small country pub. **1945** TEXIDOR *In Fifteen Minutes* (1987) 179 They must have been interested in the Islands, or why did..Miss Massey say so many times, How corker. **1951** FRAME *Lagoon* (1961) 64 Minnie agreed. Yes it's a corker kite. **1964** HARVEY *Any Old Dollars Mister?* 15 He had beaut savs, that butcher—they were smoked and went corker with lots of tomato sauce. **1987** GEE *Prowlers* 179 She dredged up language no one had heard in years. Dinky-di. Corker. Biff him on the nose. **1992** PARK *Fence Around the Cuckoo* 255 A little stove, a *corker* little stove with bandy legs.

cork tree. [f. the light weight of the wood.] Also **Maori** (or **New Zealand**) **cork tree.** WHAU.

1817, **1830** [see WHAU]. **1869** *TrNZI* I. (rev. edn.) 389 The paper mulberry tree and the New Zealand cork tree. **1889** FEATON *Art Album NZ Flora* 61 The 'Whau', or 'Hauama'.- This very beautiful small tree is peculiar to the Northern Island of New Zealand, but is not common... Owing to the extreme lightness and buoyancy of the wood, the tree is known to the Colonists as the 'Cork Tree'. **1965** GILLHAM *Naturalist in NZ* 229 Trees on Little Barrier include the nikau palm, the Maori cork tree, ngaio, and the birdcatching tree.

corkwood. WHAU; also its wood. See also CORK TREE.

1885 *TrNZI* XVII. 426 At the head also of these glens are some very fine 'corkwood' trees about one foot through, the largest I have seen; this wood is called 'corkwood' by bushmen from its being, like cork, very buoyant in water. **1890** [see WHAU]. **1907** LAING & BLACKWELL *Plants NZ* 243 [The wood] is about half the weight of cork, and the whau is sometimes, therefore, termed 'the cork-wood tree'. Mr T. Kirk suggested that it might be utilized for life-belts. **1946** [see WHAU]. **1978** MOORE & IRWIN *Oxford Book NZ Plants* 70 *Entelea arborescens, whau, corkwood*. A round-headed tree up to 10m tall, remarkable for its light wood.

cormorant. [Specific use of *cormorant* for local shag species.] SHAG. (New Zealand usage prefers *shag* to *cormorant*.)

1773 FORSTER *Resolution Jrnl.* 9 May (1982) II. 273 He brought in all 41 Ducks..and Shags on board, one of them was the common Cormorant (*Pelecanus Carbo*). **1861** HAAST *Rep. Topogr. Explor. Nelson* 137 In speaking of cormorants, I may add that there are several species which exist all along the rivers and sea coast. **1898** HOCKEN *Contributions* 79 As the boat speeds round the various points, flocks of seagulls and cormorants rise. **1984** [see SHAG 1].

corn. Modern New Zealand usage follows N. American in applying *corn* to (usu.) the 'sweet corn' varieties of *maize*, *Zea mays* (fam. Poaceae) (see quot.), rather than to *grain*, as in most British usage. (The sense 'grain' is also occas. recorded from NZ in the first half of the 19th century.)

1833 WILLIAMS *Early Jrnls.* 7 Nov. (1961) 341 They brought however a basket of stinking corn which had been soaking in water for some weeks. [1961 *Note*] *Kanga pirau*. This is still a Maori method of preparing corn.

corner dairy: see DAIRY 3 a.

cornstalk. *Obs.* [AND 1851.] The Austral. nickname for, orig., a man from New South Wales, recorded in New Zealand from 1859, applied to NSW sports teams, and during WW1 (and occas. in WW2) as a general term for an Australian.

1859 THOMSON *Story NZ* II. 230 'Sydney cornstalks', as the youth of that city are denominated, are no match in intellect against men brought up in colder countries. **1890** *NZ's Jubilee 1840-90* 87 [In an intercolonial cricket match] Yates showed fine form, and appeared to master the Cornstalks' bowling. **1905** *Truth* 1 July 2 Footballers in almost every part of the Colony will be given the opportunity of seeing the Cornstalks and the Bananalanders [*sc.* the NSW and Queensland football teams] rushing the leather. **1915** MCCANDLISH *Let.* 5 Jan. in Pugsley *Gallipoli* (1984) 81 For instance in the route march through Cairo the Australians were there. The papers..did not mention the Cornstalks at all. **1933** SCANLAN *Tides of Youth* 52 Geoffrey..was an Australian, a typical Cornstalk in appearance. **1944** FULLARTON *Troop Target* 104 On his own the Aussie's a regular guy... Three cornstalks for every Kiwi in the Middle East.

coromica, coromico, varr. KOROMIKO.

corpse-reviver. *Obs.* [Orig. US: see OED.] An alcoholic pick-me-up drink; a first drink to dispel a hangover, the 'hair of the dog'.

1888 MCHUTCHESON *New Zealander Abroad* 128 (Griffiths Collect.) The holiday throng..are evidently having a 'high old time' of it without the aid of brandy cocktails and gin-slings, sudden-deaths and corpse-revivers, elsewhere considered so absolutely indispensable. **1889** DAVIDSON *Stories NZ Life* 38 Another [man] seized the whisky bottle, and like a good Samaritan, went round to each recumbent form, and applied that wonderful elixir, which is termed in the language of the poets, a 'corpse reviver'. **1910** *Truth* 12 Mar. 7 When he awoke, thirsty and thick-headed, he grabbed his coat, looked for his quondam friend, and made a beeline for the bar and a corpse reviver.

corraddi, var. KORARI.

correspondence school. Usu. with init. caps.; often *ellipt.* **correspondence**. A State institution using various media (orig. correspondence through the post) to provide 'distance' education for those unable to attend ordinary primary and secondary schools.

1924 *Otago Witness* (Dunedin) 18 Mar. 59 The Minister of Education..spoke particularly of the excellent work accomplished by the correspondence school which had been started four years ago [*sic*] with only 40 pupils. **1939** *Taranaki Herald* (New Plymouth) 6 May 6 Every one of the pupils of the correspondence school is isolated from the railroad and other recognised means of transport. **1945** *AJHR E-2* 4 The Correspondence School, established in 1922, is organized to provide educational facilities for persons, whether children or adults, who are unable to attend school owing to personal disability, distance or employment. **1965** MACNICOL *Skippers Road* 118 The children were educated by correspondence school. **1974** *Educ. Devel. Conf. Report of Working Party on Organiz. & Admin.* 26 In addition, the Correspondence School provided tuition for over 1,200 primary, over 700 full-time secondary, and over 1,500 part-time secondary pupils. **1988** *Rep. of Working Party to Review School Library Service* 25 The National Library would supply books to the secondary students of the Correspondence School for five years.

correspond with Hobart: see HOBART.

Corriedale. [f. the name of the estate in North Otago where the breed was evolved.] A breed of New Zealand sheep evolved from Romney, Lincoln, Merino and Leicester to yield both wool and meat.

1902 *Rep. Conference Del. Agric. Soc.* (Dunedin) 64 The amendment in favour of naming the breed 'Corriedale' was..put and carried. **1902** *Settler's Handbook NZ* 93 Some breeders claim that the new breed, Corriedale, is a class of sheep which embraces these desired qualities and possesses a fixity of type. The generally accepted meaning of the Corriedale is a sheep resulting from the fourth cross of half-bred Lincoln-merino, and the rams Lincoln. The progeny of these is half-bred. These in turn are bred, half-breds to half-breds, for four generations, and a Corriedale is the result. It was Mr. James Little, of Allandale, Waikari, Canterbury, who gave sheep bred on these lines the distinctive name of 'Corriedale.' **1915** MACDONALD *NZ Sheepfarming* 27 The Corriedale is a well woolled sheep. **1920** MACDONALD *Austral. & NZ Sheepfarming* 43 The Corriedale has been negatively yet appropriately described as a 'purebred-crossbred'. **1936** BELSHAW et al. *Agric. Organiz. NZ* 296 The wool industry, however, has been markedly affected by the scientific breeding work carried out by James Little, the founder of the Corriedale. **1948** MARTIN *NZ Nature Study* 156 Corriedale. A New Zealand sheep resulting from inbreeding a cross between Merino ewes and long-wool rams. **1951** CRESSWELL *Canterbury Tales* 57 Before long he had begun experiments on fixing a breed of sheep we call to-day 'Corriedale'... Little gave it the name of the estate he managed—Corriedale.

corrirow, var. KORERO.

corroboree. Also **corrobery, corroborry**. [AAW ad. Aborig. Dharuk (Sydney region) prob. *garabari* 'a style of dancing': AND a dance ceremony (1791), hence a meeting (1833).] In New Zealand, occas. applied to a Maori KORERO; also to a discussion among Europeans.

1853 ROCHFORT *Adventures Surveyor in NZ* 35 After a smoke a corrobery ensued. [1853 *Note*] Conversation. **1887** PYKE *Hist. Early Gold Discoveries Otago* (1962) 39 We had a 'corroboree' over our digging experiences. **1906** GAMBIER *Links in My Life* (1907) 161 After a day or two of Corrobries (called in Maori Koren [*sic*], more war-dancing and races..between the huge war canoes.

corrugated iron. Also *ellipt.* **corrugated**. Used elsewhere (see OED *corrugated* 2 b, 1887) but in freq. and significant New Zealand use as a common roofing and building material. See also IRON *n*.

1848 WAKEFIELD *Handbook NZ* 446 [What to Buy for Exportation]..some *corrugated iron* or *zinc* will be found very handy for roofing houses or verandahs quickly. 1864 *Nelson Examiner* 7 May 8 A corrugated iron house will speedily, I am told, be erected here. 1888 PRESHAW *Banking Under Difficulties* 142 The first building erected by the Bank of New South Wales at Hokitika was a corrugated iron one. 1925 MANDER *Allen Adair* (1971) 54 There was a sizeable shanty down there, built of wood and roofed with corrugated iron. 1965 SHADBOLT *Among the Cinders* 9 Bricks had tumbled from the chimney on to the rusty corrugated roof. 1988 HILL *More from Moaville* 34 'Play your part in the restoration of this public facility [sc. Town Hall]', urged the Moaville Messenger. 'Sponsor a sheet of corrugated iron.'

corry: see KORRY.

CORSO /'kɔsʌu/. Occas. also **Corso**. The acronym of Council of Organisations for Relief Services Overseas. See quot. 1966.

1953 BRASCH in *Landfall Country* (1962) 446 This quality [sc. humanity] implies a religious attitude to life, which indeed underlies so much of our co-operative social activity as well as our social legislation, and the application of these abroad, as in Corso's work. 1966 *Encycl. NZ* I. 403 The New Zealand Council of Organisations for Relief Service [sic] Overseas, familiarly called CORSO, coordinates the work of many religious, national, youth, labour, medical, relief, and charitable organisations which are interested in relief of distressed areas throughout the world. It was formed on 16 August 1944. 1974 *Dominion* (Wellington) 7 Feb. 4 CORSO—the initials stand for Council of Relief Services Overseas [sic]—was set up in August 1944 when the National Council of Churches, the New Zealand Red Cross Society and the Society of Friends met to form an organisation for post-war relief work. 1979 *Dominion* (Wellington) 29 Aug. 6 The correct full name of Corso since 1972 has been simply CORSO (Incorporated). Before then its name was the New Zealand Council of Organisations for Relief Services Overseas (Incorporated), from which the acronym Corso was formed. 1984 BOYD *City of the Plains* 388 [The] wife of a local doctor, who had come from England 6 years earlier, was a member of the CORSO committee.

Cossack: see *Massey's cossacks* (MASSEY 2).

cot. [Transf. use of *cot* matted wool: see OED *n*.² 1.] A sheep with matted wool.

1955 BOWEN *Wool Away* 155 Cot. A sheep with matted wool. 1966 TURNER *Eng. Lang. Austral. & NZ* 147 There are [shearers'] names for types of sheep, the *cot* with matted wool; the *cobbler*, a difficult sheep.

Hence **cotty** *a*.[f. Brit. dial.: see OED, 1789 sole quot.], of wool, matted; of a sheep, having a matted fleece. As an occas. *n.*, a lump of matted wool.

1955 BOWEN *Wool Away* 32 [One blow is made]..with the comb on the side to cut the morty neck wool (the first few inches up the neck) that is always a bit cotty and is the hardest to break. 1986 RICHARDS *Off the Sheep's Back* 130 In the afternoon we got ahead of the musterers, so the manager had to run in a mob of undagged cotty sheep that were being held until the cut out. 1995 *Mana* 9 (Winter issue) 73 There may be wool that's stained from mud and dung or raddle – or matted into 'cotties'.

cot-case. [f. *cot* a hospital bed + (medical) *case*: Wilkes 1932.]

1. A person very sick or injured, thus often confined to bed.

1916 *Chron. NZEF* 15 Nov. 124 There were many cot cases... The Medical Service chose to call them cot cases, and cot cases they were to be. 1918 *Quick March* 2 Dec. 18 [Title] A Cot Case... sketch..of his first day in a military hospital. 1929 WILSON *Let.* 23 Mar. in Wierzbicka *Wilson Family* (1973) 218 He said those who were not cot cases were not allowed to smoke in the Ward but cot cases could. 1939 ALISON *New Zealander Looks On* 56 The doctor considered him a 'cot-case', giving him only two years to live. 1946 SARGESON *That Summer* 133 No rough house, he said. No, I said, because we don't want any more cot cases. 1950 CHERRILL *Story NZ Sheep Farm* 173 He almost looks like a cot-case. 1961 CRUMP *Hang On a Minute Mate* 42 You take it easy for a few days, lad. We don't want to make a cot-case out of you. 1986 KNIGHT *Geriatrics* 104 The unfortunate result..was that his nervous system and glands were undermined and soon he was a cot case.

2. A person incapacitated esp. by drink; one hopelessly drunk.

1968 SLATTER *Pagan Game* 162 There we were arse up with care over the bank... A real cot-case. 1988 McGILL *Dict. Kiwi Slang* 30 *cot case* lunatic or very drunk.

3. *transf.* As an *attrib.* hopeless; producing very bad results.

1995 *Dominion* (Wellington) 28 July 7 Professor Matthews says he picked up the phrase 'cot case schools' over the teacups with an education review office inspector. The term refers to those schools where, in contrast to the undoubtedly good schools available, 'kids can't read, can't add up'.

cotton daisy: see COTTON PLANT.

cotton fireweed. *Senecio quadridentatus* (formerly *Erechtites quadridentata*) (fam. Asteraceae), an erect daisy, a common weed of open sites, having narrow silvery leaves covered with fine hairs (or 'cotton').

1969 *Standard Common Names Weeds* 16 *cotton fireweed Erechtites quadridentata.* 1981 TAYLOR *Weeds of Roadsides* 53 Cotton Fireweed (*Erechtites quadridentata*)... Many fine hairs give the whole plant a silvery appearance. Cotton fireweed is native to New Zealand and also to Australia.

cotton-grass: see COTTON PLANT.

cotton plant. Mainly *SI*. Also **cotton daisy**, and (formerly) **cotton-grass**. Any of several plants of the genus *Celmisia*, esp. *C. coriacea* and *C. spectabilis*, whose leaves have dense white hairs (or 'cotton') on the lower surface. See also CELMISIA. Cf. LEATHER-PLANT, TIKUMU.

1856 [see CELMISIA]. 1867 HOCHSTETTER *NZ* 491 Snowgrass and the leaves of the *Celmesia coriacea*, called 'cotton plant' by the settlers, are often the only feed procurable. 1874 *TrNZI* VI. 56 The various species of *Celmisia*, chiefly known by the settlers as cotton-grass or leather-plant, appear well adapted for our purposes. 1879 HAAST *Geol. Canterbury & Westland* 11 We returned..to give our horses..food, they..having..principally fed on the leaves of the *Celmisia coriacea*, the cotton plant of the settlers. 1900 *Canterbury Old & New* 190 The great white buttercup of the Southern Alps..[is] only rivalled in beauty by the marguerite-like flowers of the numerous different kinds of 'cotton plant' or mountain daisy. 1933 *Canterbury Mountaineer* 43 What should have been grassy flats..were covered..for acres at a time with dense cushions of the common cotton-plant, Celmisia spectabilis, the leaves dark glossy green above and very woolly beneath. 1941 MYERS *Valiant Love* 160 Here, also are mountain daisies called cotton plants. 1952 NEWTON *High Country Journey* 73 The bulk of the country lies into the south and is cold, unattractive, cotton-plant country. 1961 [see LEATHER-PLANT]. 1973 MARK & ADAMS *Alpine Plants* (1979) 22 The common cotton daisy (*C.[elmisia] spectabilis*) has become important over much of its range, more especially in parts of Marlborough and Canterbury.

cottonwood. [Local uses of *cottonwood* for any of various plants having cottony hairs on the leaves or surrounding the seeds.]

1. TAUHINU 1.

1874 *TrNZI* VI. 50 *Cassinia leptophylla*, cottonwood. Common on sand-hills all round the coast; seeds abundantly. 1910 COCKAYNE *NZ Plants & Their Story* 72 Taranaki, Hawke's Bay, and the shores of Cook Strait have the tauhinu or cottonwood. 1940 LAING & BLACKWELL *Plants NZ* 467 (*The Narrow-leaved Cassinia*)... Local name Cottonwood, Maori name *Tauhinu*. In Marlborough particularly a troublesome weed. 1951 LEVY *Grasslands NZ* (1970) 293 Gorse..cottonwood, tauhinu, and other scrub growths are neglected on the hills. 1962 EVANS *Waikaka Saga* 239 The whole [Waikaka] valley and the..ridges were covered [in 1876] with..trees and shrubs comprising..cottonwood (Cassinia fulvida),..and mingimingi. 1978 MOORE & IRWIN *Oxford Book NZ Plants* 138 Cassinia is a genus of Australasian and South African shrubs. The five New Zealand species, known as 'cottonwoods' or 'tauhinu'.

2. With a modifier as **golden**, **mountain**, **New Zealand cottonwood**, different forms of *Cassinia leptophylla* (formerly treated as separate species).

1951 LEVY *Grasslands NZ* (1970) 35 The harsh patotara, golden cottonwood, cushion-like pimeleas, and the..scabweeds are characteristic of the low tussock country. 1969 *Standard Common Names Weeds* 52 *New Zealand cotton-wood* [=] *golden tauhinu*: *mountain Tauhinu*: *niniao*: *tauhinu*. 1973 MARK & ADAMS *Alpine Plants* (1979) 166 *Cassinia vauvilliersii*... Mountain Cottonwood. 1981 DENNIS *Paparoas Guide* 164 Mountain cottonwood..and *Senecio bennettii* are also common plants in the region immediately above the bushline. 1991 *Victoria University Weekly Staff Circular* 20 Dec. 2 The mountain cottonwood (an alpine daisy..) is flowering for the first time... It has grown from seed collected on Mt Taranaki four years ago.

cotty: see COT.

cou couper, var. KUKUPA.

coudie, var. KAURI.

cough one's cud. [With reference to the sound of a ruminant animal's regurgitation.] To vomit.

1989 RICHARDS *Pioneer's Life* 91 The poor townie turned green..and as we say in the country, coughed his cud.

coumalla, var. KUMARA.

Council: see *County Council* (COUNTY 2), EXECUTIVE COUNCIL, LEGISLATIVE COUNCIL, *Provincial Council* (PROVINCIAL 2).

counter-lunch. *Hist.* Also occas. **counter snack.** [AND 1880.] A savoury snack formerly provided free to drinkers in hotel bars.

1913 *NZ Observer* 8 Nov. 20 Counter lunch was on at a neighbouring hostelry. **1918** *Chron. NZEF* 24 Apr. 130 The N.Z.Y.M.C.A. provides backshee cocoa..for the wounded, and a 'counter lunch' for the staff. **1924** *Grey River Argus* 13 June 4 A counter lunch was put on consisting of baked potatoes, rissoles, sausage rolls or lamb's fry. **1936** Hyde *Passport to Hell* 202 There were always huge door-step sandwiches..with slices of ham and sweet pickles in them, just like the old counter-lunches you could once get in any New Zealand pub by putting down sixpence for a handle of beer. **1946** Sargeson *That Summer* 71 I had to go into the pub because I wanted to pick up a bit of counter-lunch. **1952** *Here & Now* Dec. 5 Cheese is bung... Something to fill up on..or to toss on the bar as counter-lunch. **1966** Baxter *Collected Poems* (1980) 359 Nobody gets a look in When Caelius cleans up the counter-lunch... Cheese, chicken, savelovs, black pudding, It all goes down the hatch. **1974** Simpson *Sugarbag Years* 29 They told us about one hotel that put on a counter-lunch at midday. It was apparently a pretty good one with cheese on toast, roast rabbit, rissoles and the like. **1982** Burton *Two Hundred Years of NZ Food* 33 The old custom of counter snacks was well dead by the 1960s. At one time the hotels in New Zealand would regale their customers with all sorts of savouries..and, what is more, it was all on the house. **1983** Henderson *Down from Marble Mountain* 218 And the pig's trotters and savelovs and cheese and onions, chips and sausage rolls, and sometimes even oysters, of the free 'counterlunches' the pubs served up then.

count out. *v. Shearing.* [Spec. use of *count out* to count while taking from a stock.]

1. To count or tally the number of sheep shorn. Usu. as a *vbl. n.*

c1875 Meredith *Adventuring in Maoriland* (1935) 144 As I was finishing the counting-out, the boss came towards the shed. **1986** Richards *Off the Sheep's Back* 122 After 'count-out' he flew at Les..and condemned the quality of his work. **1989** Richards *Pioneer's Life* 29 Breakfast wasn't..until our first knock-off time at 7 a.m. when he had to count out the sheep. *Ibid.* 64 When I slammed the porthole shut at the end of the run I called to the manager not to 'count out' until I arrived.

2. Special Comb. **counting-out pen** [AND c1914] (also **count-out pen** [AND 1874]), a pen where shorn sheep are held for accounting to a shearer's tally.

1874 Caird *Sheepfarming* 23 A small door for each shearer to put his shorn sheep out of the shed, and into the counting out pens. **1913** [see PORTHOLE]. **1922** Perry *Sheep Farming* 18 Counting-out pens [pictured on a diagram of woolshed, behind the shearing board, and entered by] port 'Holes'. **1933** *Press* (Christchurch) (Acland Gloss.) 30 Sept. 15 *Counting out pens.*—Narrow pens outside the woolshed. **1982** *Agric. Gloss.* (MAF) 54 *Count-out pen*: Pen adjacent to a shearing stand into which sheep are released after shearing to be counted. **1987** Ogonowska-Coates *Boards, Blades & Barebellies* 95 Each shearer passes the shorn sheep through a porthole and into an individual counting-out pen that adjoins the woolshed on the outside. **1989** Richards *Pioneer's Life* 29 Each shearer has a porthole leading to his own count-out pen, as shearers are paid by the number they shear.

country. *Country* in New Zealand common usage is frequently defined by reference to land use. See also BACK COUNTRY, BUSH COUNTRY, COLD COUNTRY, *cow-country* (COW 6), *dead country* (DEAD *a.*¹ 2), *fern-country* (FERN 3 b), HARD COUNTRY

2, *sheep country* (SHEEP 1); SHADY *a.*, SUNNY *a.*

1. a. [AND 1855.] Land suitable for (esp. pastoral) farming (occas. for the extraction of commercial timber); a rural landholding.

1860 in Butler *First Year* Apr. (1863) v 71 A mountain here is only beautiful if it has good grass on it. Scenery is not scenery—it is 'country', *subauditâ voce* 'sheep'. **1898** Reeves *Long White Cloud* 403 'Country' is used as a synonym for grazing; 'good country' means simply good grazing land. **1922** Perry *Sheep Farming* 91 This tendency to fret is well seen in the case of half-bred sheep that have..been moved from one man's country to that of another some miles away. **1933** Scanlan *Tides of Youth* 17 I'll get on some up-country place, and later I may be able to pick up a bit of new country cheap, and clear it. **1934** *Press* (Christchurch) (Acland Gloss.) 13 Jan. 13 *Country*, adjectives applied to.—Country is sometimes hard but never soft, cold but never hot. Other words used to describe it are warm, sunny, shady, sweet, easy, steep, sour, and rideable. **1940** Studholme *Te Waimate* (1954) 96 There are many things to be taken into consideration when burning. Climate—is your country early or late?.. In what state is your neighbour's country? **1966** Newton *Boss's Story* 21 The sheep will be shorn and out on their country again with the least possible delay. **1977** Bruce *Life in Hinterland South Island* 99 Another experience was when helping another neighbour to muster his country. **1981** Pinney *Early N. Otago Runs* 77 The old Hawkdun [station] country can now be seen..from the curve of the Ranfurly–Omakau road.

b. Mainly *Canterbury*. In the phr. **to find (look for, look at) country**, to search for (or find) unoccupied Crown land suitable for leasing or purchasing for pastoral purposes. Cf. TAKE UP 1.

1860 in Butler *First Year* 24 Mar. (1863) iv 48 I left Christchurch..in the hopes of finding some considerable piece of country which had not yet been applied for. **1863** Chudleigh *Diary* 10 Sept. (1950) 101 He has just been looking at some new country Butler brought [*sic* =bought] in the McKinsey Country. **1891** Chamier *Philosopher Dick* 90 [He was] bound for the north, where he was looking out for 'country'. **1906** Roberts in *Hist. N. Otago from 1853* (1937) 7 If a traveller was asked where he was going to, the answer would be, 'I'm looking for country'. A newcomer, if asked what he was going to do, would answer 'Take up country'.

2. *Mining, Quarrying.* Also **country rock**. **a.** [f. Brit. dial. (chiefly Cornish) *country* or *country rock* the rock in which a lode of ore occurs: see OED 11; EDD; AND 1848.] The material surrounding a lode of ore.

1868 *Thames Miner's Guide* 53 Country or Ground.- Same as bed-rock. [*sc.*: 'The mass of rock in which the veins or lodes occur.'] **1911** *TrNZI* XLIII. 261 His work on the silicified rocks plainly pointed the way to a theory of metasomatic replacement of country by vein-material.

b. As **country rock**. See also quot. 1983.

1909 *TrNZI* XLI. 79 The country rock is little altered, except for about 2 ft. from the vein-walls, where the alteration is considerable, the rock being soft and 'mullocky'. **1911** *TrNZI* XLIII. 261 The term 'country rock', now so commonly employed by writers on economic geology, is, strictly speaking, tautological. The miners of the Hauraki Goldfield, as a rule, employ the more correct expression, 'country'. **1965** Williams *Econ. Geol. NZ* 58 The country-rock strikes north-westerly. **1971** Bale *Maratoto Gold* 23 In the Thames and Coromandel areas..the rocks are volcanic in origin, composed mostly of andesites. This was called 'country rock' by the miners, the term simply meaning the rock through which the quartz reefs ran. **1983** Nolan *Gold Fossicker's Handbook* 111 *Country rock*: the chief foundation rock or rocks of a region; the rock into

which a vein or reef has been intruded. **1992** Latham *Golden Reefs* 428 *Country Rock*: Strata on each side of an ore deposit.

c. The ground including its various compositional elements; earth. See also HARD 1, KINDLY.

1897 *AJHR* C-9 21 Above this is a belt of so-called 'kindly sandstone', and then a band of what is known as 'jointy' or 'shingly' country occurs, and consists of a fine-grained light-brown rock, which is much shattered and traversed by joints in every direction. **1921** Foston *At the Front* 69 The thickness of the concrete on the one side [of the tunnel] was 18 inches, but at the other end, where the country consists of papa, it was reduced to 14 inches. **1938** Hyde *Nor Yrs. Condemn* 172 He had a job..cutting wild country at 1s. 3d. per cubic yard, wheeling and trucking, shifting the side of a mountain. **1978** McAra *Gold Mining at Waihi* 183 Chamber sets had to be well anchored in the country.

d. With a defining word: **favourable** (or **unfavourable**) **country, kindly country**, country whose appearance indicates, or does not indicate, a prospect of gold.

1922 *NZJST* V. 115 The miner, quickly recognising these characters, uses them in his search for ore-bodies, and calls any rock exhibiting them 'favourable' or 'kindly' country... The cause of the ore is the cause of the 'favourable' country, and it is not correct to say that 'favourable' country (in the sense used by the Hauraki miners) is the cause of ore-deposition. *Ibid.* 119 This, from its appearance, and from the fact that the Martha and Edward lodes become poor where, in the deeper levels, it impinges on them, has been regarded as 'unfavourable' country.

country-acre. In early settlement, an allotment, usu. by a land company, of 'rural' land outside a planned town boundary. See also *country section* (SECTION *n.*¹ 2). Compare *town-acre* (TOWN 2).

1839 *Terms of Sale of NZ Land Company; GBPP 1852, xxxv. 570, p.18*, 1 June in *Speeches & Documents* (1971) 19 These doubly-selected lands will be divided into 1100 sections, each section comprising one town-acre, and 100 country-acres. **1840** Deans in *Pioneers* (1964) 6 I expect soon to go far into the bush to survey the country acres.

Country Library Service. *Obs.* An organization formerly providing public library services to rural areas.

1938 *NZ Libraries* I. No.8 78 The Country Library Service..will lend books free to a Borough or Town District Library. **1949** Cole *It Was So Late* (1978) 75 I had seen him with books from the Country Library Service. **1964** *AJHR* H-32A 7 Country Library Service help was given in preparing book orders, in planning the layout of the building, and at the time of opening. **1973** *AJHR* G-13 23 The general function of the Country Library Service is to help public libraries..to give a service..comparable in quality to that given by the largest libraries. **1980** *AJHR* G-13 12 It was then considered appropriate that the term Country Library Service should be replaced by that of Extension Service. **1988** Jackson *Rainshadow* 102 To this end we borrowed books from the Country Library Service van which stopped at Hikuwai every Saturday morning.

country quota. *Hist.* The artificial weighting of voting power in favour of rural electorates, in operation from 1881 to 1945.

[**1881** *NZPD* XXXIX. 472 [Hall] We therefore propose in this Bill [*sc.* the Representation Bill] that the quota for country districts shall be less than the quota for town districts by..25 percent.] **1938** *Tomorrow* 29 Dec. 102 Country quota has often been described as votes for cows. **1948** Lipson *Politics of Equality* 29

[The Representation Act of 1881] modified the population basis by conceding to all rural electorates a far smaller number of inhabitants than was required of the urban. This 'country quota' as it came to be called, was not incorporated in the main texts of the law; it appeared only in the accompanying schedule. **1950** *NZPD* CCLXXXIX. 600 Here was a Bill..which removed the country quota entirely. **1966** *Encycl. NZ* I. 861 The electoral device known as the 'country quota' was first used in New Zealand in 1881 when, for the purposes of maintaining the existing balance between urban and rural parliamentary constituencies, a 'quota' equivalent to 33$^1/_3$ per cent of the population was added to rural constituencies. **1986** *Illustr. Encycl. NZ* 255 Country quota was a percentage once added to the population of rural electorates to give them what was seen as a finer balance.

country service. *Hist.* The period during which a teacher in the State service was required to teach in rural schools.
   1938 *NZ Educ. Gaz.* Oct. CLXXXIV. 1 Unless specifically exempted no teacher shall be eligible to apply for a [Grade A] position..unless he has completed..three years' country service. **1968** SLATTER *Pagan Game* 92 His three years at Ruamahanga College had not had such an impact on him..for it was mainly a matter of getting his country service over. **1971** *Dept. Education Circular E* 38:2:19 18 June These positions are not deemed to be country service for the purpose of removal expenses. **1988** SOMERSET *Sunshine & Shadow* 127 Connection was made..with the little Oxford train... I was to begin my 'country service' as a teacher. **1990** *Dominion* (Wellington) 27 June 14 The country service requirement once provided a pool of teachers who could be placed to fill the needs of rural New Zealand.

county. [Transf. use of Brit. *county* a territorial unit for various administrative, judicial, etc. purposes: AND 1892.]
1. A former rural territorial or administrative unit of local government controlled by an elected council. Often *attrib*.
[*Note*] Counties have now been replaced by district councils.
   1856 *Counties Act* 19 & 20 Vict. s1 It shall be lawful for the Governor..to divide such Provinces into counties, and to subdivide such counties into hundred and parishes. **1876** *Counties Act 40 Vict.* s6 Until as otherwise provided, there shall be within New Zealand the several counties having the names and boundaries set forth in the first schedule. Boroughs shall not be included in counties. *Ibid.* s9 There shall be in every County a governing body, consisting of a Chairman and Council, elected as hereinafter provided. **1888** BARLOW *Kaipara* 95 The main road through the county is supposed to be constructed by the County Council. *Ibid.* 96 The main county road here is not yet formed in places. **1902** *Settler's Handbook NZ* 142 When the nine provinces were abolished in 1876 the colony was divided for local government purposes into counties, regard being had to boundaries of existing road districts, and the counties were subdivided into ridings, each riding being empowered to elect a certain number of members of the Council of the county. **1996** BOSTON et al. *Public Management: the NZ Model* 184 Essentially, local government now consists of regional councils and city and district councils (replacing boroughs and counties).
2. Comb. **County Council** (also *ellipt.*); **county councillor**, **county councilman**.
   1882 *Public Works Act 46 Vict.* s81 The **County Council** may make country roads throughout the county, except within the limits of a borough. **1886** *Counties Act 50 Vict.* [preamble] An Act to consolidate and amend the Law relating to the Constitution of County Councils, and the Powers and Duties of such Councils. **1897** A TRAMP, ESQ. *Casual Ramblings* 11 Another remedy that might be tried with advantage is the abolition of the County Councils and Road Boards. **1904** *NZ Observer* 5 Mar. 3 Who is there to prevent the local bodies—County Councils, Borough Councils, Road Boards—from being empowered to elect members of Land Boards, just as School Committees now have power to elect members of the Provincial Education Boards? **1935** GUTHRIE *Little Country* 15 The Government, county councils, harbour boards..had gone in for a race of borrowing from overseas. **1943** *NZ Farmers' Weekly* 26 Aug. 7 Reports from County Councils have shown a marked improvement in rate payments from Maori land. **1967** MACNICOL *Skippers Canyon* 75 I'll come back with the county truck in the morning. **1971** TAYLOR *Plekhov Place* 12 Gray says he'll go to the County about it after Christmas. **1969** HENDERSON *Open Country Calling* 273 Night time is a pretty good time to get hold of a **county councillor**. **1887** *Auckland Weekly News* 21 May 21 From the Prime Minister to the meanest West Coast member, from the Speaker of the House to the buffoon and 'chawbacon' of the Lower, Waste Lands Board, **County Councilmen**, prigs and policemen, all are travelling on us.

courad, var. KORARI.

courie, var. KAURI.

Court of Arbitration: see ARBITRATION.

cous, var. CUZ.

Cousin Jack. *Obs.* [AND 1863.] A Cornishman. Also occas. **Cousin Jinny**, a Cornishwoman.
   1861 *NZ Goldfields 1861* (1976) 6 Scotchmen, Welshmen, 'Geordies', and 'Cousin Jacks' were they. **1916** ANZAC *On Anzac Trail* 52 [The Egyptians] were as saving as a Cousin Jack, investing their earnings in donkeys and wives. **1938** HYDE *Nor Yrs. Condemn* 196 There were a couple of Cousin Jacks in there [*sc.* gaol]—English fellows—and were they disgusted? **1940** STUDHOLME *Te Waimate* (1954) 175 We might have English, Irish, Scotch, Cornish (Cousin Jacks) or German gangs working. **1965** Howitt in *Looking at the West Coast* in LATHAM *Golden Reefs* (1992) 312 Came many from the Old Country—especially came Cousin Jacks and Cousin Jinnies.

couta /'kutə/. Also **'coota**, **'couta**. [AND *coota*, 1933.]
1. A shortened form of BARRACOUTA 1.
   1872 in Meredith *Adventuring in Maoriland* (1935) 1 Oct. 9 I amused myself catching barracouta... Directly the line is slackened on deck the 'coota lets go the bait. **1911** *Truth* 1 Apr. 6 Hampton said that the 'couta [hawked in Sumner] were rotten and stinking. **1968** BALLANTYNE *Sydney Bridge* 148 Dad's got plenty of lines. He doesn't care when we use them. Specially if we catch a 'couta or kingie. **1981** WILSON *Fisherman's Bible* 26 Although they are basically surface pelagics, the coutas are met in shoals at all depths down to forty fathoms.
2. Special Comb. **couta lure**, a lure for attracting barracouta; **couta stick**, a stick or pole used to attract barracouta (see also PA $n.^2$).
   1981 WILSON *Fisherman's Bible* 26 '**Couta' lures** In selecting lures it should be borne in mind that this fish's teeth are particularly sharp and strong. **1956** GRAHAM *Treasury NZ Fishes* 310 Barracouta... These fish..were usually caught on a slightly curved stick about four feet in length. Fastened to this stick was a piece of stout fishing line about three to four feet in length, carrying a piece of red-coloured wood—usually cedar—about five to six inches in length. A bent nail was secured to this piece of wood in the form of a hook but no bait was used. When a school of Barracouta was found the **Couta stick**, or paw, was brought out ready for fishing. From the cockpit of the launch the piece of wood with the nail was violently swirled with a circular motion in and out of the water, causing a disturbance of the water in a good imitation of a number of Sprats, Pilchards or other small fish jumping in and out of the sea. The Barracouta would swim for such a place. Seeing the piece of red wood moving rapidly through the water they would take it for a fish, snap at it or even jump out of the water for the lure and were caught by the crude iron hook.

cove. [f. Brit. (orig. thieves') slang: OED $n.^2$ notes 'Frequent in the 20th century in Austral. sources.'; AND 1828: freq. in early NZ use, though after WW1 progressively replaced by BLOKE, JOKER.]
1. A fellow, bloke, chap.
   1859 THOMSON *Story NZ* II. 188 It is worthy of notice, that the colonists, soon after the formation of all the settlements, acquired distinguishing epithets; thus there was an Auckland cove, a Wellington swell. **1865** THATCHER *Otago Songster* 6 A cove there with a camera The sports was photographing. **1887** INGLIS *Our NZ Cousins* 40 If I wasn't workin', some blasted cove, wot wants my billet 'ud be making remarks. **1900** WRIGHT *Wisps of Tussock* 24 He'll talk of a 'bloke', and a 'cove', and a 'joker', And the luckless days when he was a 'broker'. **1917** *Chron. NZEF* 5 Sept. 28 Tom Smith, some of you coves know him. **1929** SMYTH *Girl from Mason Creek* 149 Got to have some cove massage me. **1934** MASON *Collected Poems* (1962) 56 Let the fruit be plucked and the cake be iced;... and the wine be spiced in the old cove's night-cap. **1962** WEBBER *Look No Hands!* 93 'You coves from Scott Base beat me,' said the Bloke. **1973** FERNANDEZ *Tussock Fever* 40 The visitor was a Government rabbiter, Pat, a cheerful cove, talkative and delighted to have company. **1980** LELAND *Kiwi-Yankee Dict.* 29 'He's a right rum cove, that bartender', translates as he's a very peculiar person, that bartender.
2. *Obs.* [f. Brit. dial. *cove* overseer: see EDD $n.^2$; AND 1837.] Usu. as **the cove**, the owner of a sheep-station or the boss overseer.
   1874 KENNAWAY *Crusts* 175 [The squatter] fancies the sheep upon his run are only being half-shepherded while 'the cove' (as *he* is called) isn't on the ground. **1883** FERGUSON *Castle Gay* 175 Then in the fence we'll mak[e] a breach, And to the cove a yarn we'll pitch. [1883 *Note*] Bush term for boss.

covey, var. KAWE.

cow. [In senses 1 to 3 below an extended use of Brit. slang *cow* a derog. term for a woman: see OED $n.^1$ a, b; AND 1864.]
1. A term of abuse for a person, thing or situation; occas. used good-humouredly. Often preceded by an intensifying or defining word esp. **fair**, **dirty** (or **rotten**), **silly**. **a.** In earliest use applied to a quiet or unspirited ('cow-like') horse.
   1862 CHUDLEIGH *Diary* 26 July (1950) 50 We had breakfast and I changed the yellow cow, a fine horse in the water, for the old mare Sprightly. **1891** COTTLE *Melton's Luck* 78 The less spirited [horses] become regular cows (as we called them) and only go because they are obliged to. **1907** KOEBEL *Return of Joe* 285 That old cow [*sc.* an old stallion] is the Gunner's particular property. **1965** McLAGLAN *Stethoscope & Saddlebags* 172 Finally he called them the most insulting

name he could think of. 'You two *rotten* old cows,' he shouted, then plunged into the icy water above his knees and tugged them out by the reins.

b. Applied to people.

1908 *Truth* 18 July 1 'What did you do to him?' inquired a sport. 'I called him a blanky cow,' replied the indignant cove. **1913** *NZ Bulletin* 8 Feb. 16 Suspicious cow! 'e wants a flamin' biff. **1918** *NZEF Chron.* 7 June 204 I'll get even with the cows for that. **1936** LAWLOR *Murphy's Moa* 87 Is everyone in this carriage prepared to shell out threepence to make this cow turn off his music? **1944** *Short Guide to NZ* 39 Cow—may just mean cow, but may also mean an unpleasant man, woman, or situation. **1951** DUFF *Shepherd's Calendar* 20 May (1961) 31 'What, is someone else using your possie?' 'Two or three of the cows.' **1964** HARVEY *Any Old Dollars Mister?* 24 'You stupid little cows,' he said right in our ears. **1988** McGILL *Dict. Kiwi Slang* 31 *cow* unpleasant, mean, ill-tempered person or uncooperative thing, such as 'a cow of a lawnmower'.

c. Applied to things and situations.

1962 HOGAN *Billy-Can Ballads* 21 We were making for the irrigation drain Both our billy cans were empty So we hardly spoke a word Except to say, 'The cow will never rain.' **1964** MORRIESON *Came a Hot Friday* (1981) 110 'This is the crookest road I've ever struck,' said Cyril negotiating a fern-draped hairpin bend... 'It's a cow all right,' said Penelope. **1988** [see b above].

2. a. As **fair cow**, see FAIR *a.* 5.

b. As **silly cow**.

1929 SMYTH *Girl from Mason Creek* 164 'What th' hell you silly cows want to ring th' church bell for,' the publican demanded. **1944** GASKELL *All Part of the Game* (1978) 26 Well to hell with him, I thought. Silly useless old cow. **1956** *Numbers* May I. 7 What's the silly old cow done now? he shouts. **1964** HARVEY *Any Old Dollars Mister?* 23 Then the silly cow threw out both arms and his fingers went *squ-eek* on the glass. **1984** 15–17 F E2 Pakuranga Coll. 1 Silly cow [F2M1]

c. In compassionate use, as **poor cow**, an unfortunate or pitiable person or creature.

1945 HENDERSON *Gunner Inglorious* 120 'The poor cow,' say his cobbers. 'What rotten luck.' **1959** SLATTER *Gun in My Hand* 201 I saved a joker from drowning once... Pulled the poor cow out. **1964** HARVEY *Any Old Dollars Mister?* 49 Some flies were sleeping on the wall over the stove, so I gave them a heck of a scare with the gas gun. I kept pulling the trigger and all the sparks shot out and scared the daylights out of the poor cows.

3. In various phr.: **a.** As **a cow of a, cows of**, indicating an extremely unpleasant variety or occurrence of that which is denoted by a following noun.

1918 *NZEF Chron.* 5 July 251 Well, of all the undiluted cows of places, that there Terrynikow took the cake. **1929** SMYTH *The Girl from Mason Creek* 15 These tricky cows of horses. *Ibid.* 163 'A cow of a job' he muttered 'a bit crook for yer.' **1938** HYDE *Nor Yrs. Condemn* 12 It's been blooming wet lately. A cow of a climate, and no error. **1944** *Short Guide to NZ* 38 If something is godawful, they'll say it's a 'fair cow', or they'll call a bad day a 'cow of a day'. **1959** *Truth* 2 June 16 'That was a cowardly thing to do,' said Mr W.A. Harlow, S.M., sternly rebuking a man... In an evening newspaper, Mr Harlow was reported as saying: 'That was a cow of a thing to do.' **1964** DAVIS *Watersiders* 133 Blue and me and the dogs..snuggling up to that cow of a dead pig all freezing night. **1979** ROCHE *Foreigner* 187 When they [New Zealanders c1939] meant 'think' they said 'reckon'. When the weather depressed them they grunted, 'Cow of a day!'

b. As **to be a cow**, esp. **it's a cow**, alluding to an unpleasant or difficult situation.

1937 in **1976** SINCLAIR *Nash* 147 [Jordan *NZ High Commissioner*] asked why the menu was in French..and went on, 'When I asked them this in a West End restaurant a few weeks ago, they said, 'The chef's a Frenchman'. I said, 'It would be a cow, wouldn't it, if he were a Maori?' **1943** *NZEF Times* 25 Oct. 11 Bit of a cow nickin' all of your tobacco. **a1974** SYDER & HODGETTS *Austral. & NZ English* (TS) 570 *It's a cow*. An expression describing a situation which may be unhappy, annoying, distressing, exasperating, unfortunate, perplexing, disappointing, a cause for pity or commiseration, anger or consternation. Common. 'It's still raining, the paddock's 're all under water—it's a cow.' 'It's a cow—I've left my hammer at home.' 'This is a cow of a teapot. My wife likes the shape, but I can never see the shape matters if it won't pour properly.'

4. In the phr. **black as the inside of a cow**, see BLACK *a.*[2] B 3.

5. [Partridge 8: Canada, Aust.] *fig.* Milk, 'cow-juice'; often with a defining word (esp. in WW1 and WW2 contexts), **armoured cow**, **tinned (tin) cow**, condensed milk in a tin.

1916 THORNTON *Wowser* 90 'Have some tinned cow?' He..explained that 'tinned cow' was a 'bushism' for condensed milk. **1949** THE SARGE *Excuse My Feet* Gloss. Armoured Cow: (Kiwi-ism) 'tinned milk'. **1953** 16 M A34 Thames DHS 22B Tin cow. **1971** *Listener* 19 Apr. 56 She boils! Mugs up, here's the cow; who's got some grit.

6. Special Comb. often reflecting the central importance of dairy-farming in the New Zealand economy and society: **cow-bar**, a frame of steel bars or pipes fitted to the front of farm vehicles to protect them from stock; **cow-byre** *southern South Island*, COWSHED (see also BYRE); **cow-catcher** [orig. a railways term for the frame in front of a locomotive], see *cow-bar*; **cow-country**, land (or a district) suitable for or given over to dairy-farming; **cow-dog**, a dog trained to bring home milking-cows; **cow-dollop**, see *cow-pat*; **cow-gravy**, see *cow-pat*; **cow-grid**, an occas. form of CATTLE-STOP; **cow-house** *obs.* (or occas. modern jocular), COWSHED; **cow-jerker** [f. 'jerking' a cow's tits, with reference to milking], a dismissive term for a milker or dairy-farm-hand; **cow-jockey**, *jocular* for COWBOY; **cow-kick** [AND *n.* 1936, *v.* 1911], of a horse to kick out violently to one side; **cow-paddock** [AND 1908], a paddock near a house, or farm homestead holding the house cow(s) conveniently for milking; **cow-pat** (also **pat**), a polite term for (a round of) cow-dung; **cow-pie**, see *cow-pat*; **cow-punching** [?transf. (via 'western' stories) f. US beef- to NZ dairy-cattle application infl. by *cow-banging*, etc.], dairy-farming, occas. specifically, milking; **cow-stop**, see *cow-grid*; **cow-testing** *obs.*, HERD-TESTING; **cow-time** [AND 1906], milking-time; **cow-track**, a rough track made (or as though made) by cows making their way to milking; **cow-tucker**, feed for cows.

1982 *Evening Post* (Wellington) 2 Jan. 3 **Cowbars** originally designed to protect farm vehicles from stock are being increasingly used on the roads... Commonly called **cow-catchers**, these cowbars are not catching cows but are catching motorcyclists. **1912** RUTHERFORD *Impressions NZ Pastoralist on Tour* 148 **Cow-byre** manure is packed in on mules. **1936** HYDE *Passport to Hell* 156 Nevertheless, you could never forget [the]..red-cheeked women who came into the estaminets, still smelling of soil and cow-byre. **1946** MILLER *There Was Gold* 88 There was an old galvanised iron bath in his cowbyre. **1960** SCRYMGEOUR *Memories Maoriland* 17 Many stables, cow byres, men's quarters and other buildings graced 'Teviot' [Station]. **1985** FRAME *Envoy from Mirror City* 129 The ground was like a Southland cowbyre in winter, churned with mud and hoofmarks. **1982 cow-catcher** [see *cow-bar* above]. **1938** LAWLOR *House of Templemore* 144 The first trip had been to the **cow country** of Taranaki. **1955** BJ *Cameron Collection* (TS July) cow country (n) Land used or suitable for dairying. **1960** HILLIARD *Maori Girl* 9 This valley was once all Maori land... The best of the cow-country is owned by the *pakehas*. **1987** VIRTUE *Redemption of Elsdon Bird* (1988) 46 Morrinsville was almost right in the middle of the Waikato cow country. **1986** *Islands* 37 Aug. 40 'He's a good enough **cow-dog**,' he said, soon calm again. **1959** SLATTER *Gun in My Hand* 14 Basil in the willows scraping the **cow dollop** from his shoe. **1906** PICARD *Ups & Downs* 3 I got over to Taranaki, the place where the **cow gravy** and buttermilk hails from. **1987** VIRTUE *Redemption Elsdon Bird* (1988) 84 By the time they'd reached the farm, rattled over the **cow-grid** at the gate..Elsdon had forgotten feeling bothered. **1851** *Key to 'View of Dunedin...'* in Hocken *Contributions* (1898) [facing 130] 25. Dr. Stewart's **cowhouse** on Sec. 20, Blk. VI. **1874** BAINES *Edward Crewe* 225 My advice to any one troubled with a naughty cow..is to have a bail constructed in their cow-house. **1883** *Brett's Colonists' Guide* 11 The cow-house open to the stockyard, round which arrange..pig-styes, fowl-houses, and open sheds for cattle. **1906** PICARD *Ups & Downs* 12 Aggie [from the dairy] is a champion **cow jerker**, can do seven an hour... She has a goo-goo eye and a blameless past. **1973** NEWTON *Big Country SI* (1977) 205 Among the many who came to Algidus [Station in 1920]..was a new '**cow jockey**'... From cowboy he graduated to 'the dogs', he was later promoted to head shepherd. **c1875** MEREDITH *Adventuring in Maoriland* (1935) 70 I saw one sailor get a cropper; he regained his feet quickly,... and caught hold of the stirrup; whereupon the neddy '**cow-kicked**,' and caught him in the stomach. **1912** in *Studholme Coldstream* 26 Dec. (1985) 129 He levelled an area near our cottage in the **cow paddock**. **1925** MANDER *Allen Adair* (1971) 118 He went through the house, the gardens, the cow paddock, the horse paddock, searching carefully. **1936** HYDE *Passport to Hell* 201 When a German 'plane broke its back in a cow-paddock overnight, the pilot and his mechanic..looked like toy figures. **1956** DARE *Rouseabout Jane* 155 The manager..put those more heifers and two bulls into my cow paddock. **1966** *Encycl. NZ* II. 679 Terms like *cow paddock* and *horse paddock*..took on their special use in Australia **1985** JONES *Gilmore's Dairy* 110 Raymond left town for..a rock festival held on a cow paddock somewhere outside Hamilton. **1937** *Tomorrow* 6 Jan. 153 [Title of a Sargeson story] Cow Pats. [**1940** SARGESON *A Man and His Wife* (1944) 22 On cold mornings we'd watch out, and whenever a cow dropped a nice big pat we'd race for it, and the one who got there first wouldn't let the others put their feet in.] **1954** *Landfall 31* 273 These green paddocks dotted with thistles and cow-pats. **1963** KINROSS *Please to Remember* 36 The ball struck a tuft of cocksfoot at the edge of a dry cowpat. **1978** SUTHERLAND *The Elver* 64 He picked up an old dry cowpat from the paddock. **1992** *Dominion* (Wellington) 27 Jan. 1 [Heading] Bliss found in cowpat **1986** ROBINSON *Heroes & Sparrows* 125 For the trouble of..getting **cow-pie** on your Nikes you can run almost anywhere without trespassing. **1905** *Truth* 9 Sept. 1 Taranaki can't get a sufficient supply of schoolteachers... **Cow-punching** affords more possibilities. **1982** MARSHALL *Master Big Jingles* 127 They pull over when the car has rattled past the **cow stop**. **1912** *NZJ Ag.* Jan. IV. 98 I started testing my herd when the Dairy Division of the Agricultural Department opened the **Cow-testing** Association at Kaupokonui at the beginning of the season a year ago. *Ibid.* 258 Some cows tested in connection with the cow-testing associations gave as much as 300 lb. fat in the season. **1913** *NZJAg.* Mar. VI. 308 The extension of the cow-testing movement this season has been gratifying. **1966** TURNER *Eng. Lang. in Austral. & NZ* 45 But the point to note is that another set of references could be got from the same journal [*sc.* of Agriculture] for a word *cow-testing* with the same meaning [as *herd-testing*]; this word is never used now. **1966** TURNER *Eng. Lang. Austral. & NZ* 150 [In winter] a farmer does not have to be mindful of **cow-time** or milking time on *town day* (or *sale day*, equivalent to English 'market day'). **1902** *NZ Illustr. Mag.* V. 379 Your section is behind that. You have two razor-backs and a gully and no way in except a **cow-track**. **1963** CASEY *As Short a Spring* 108 Terrible pity to see good **cow-tucker** going to waste like that. *Ibid.* 156 Nobody's got cow-tucker to burn. I started feeding out before the end of April.

cowbail. Also **cowbale.** [AND 1936.] Often (collective) *pl. cowbails.* BAIL *n.* 1; occas. in later use synonymous with COWSHED (see quot. 1982 below).
 1849 ALLOM *Letter* in Earp *Handbook* (1852) 123 The [stock] yard is generally divided into..a large yard for the whole herd, a drafting yard, and a milking yard, at one end of which is placed the milking shed, cow bails, and calf house. **1861** *Puketoi Station Diary* (Hocken TS) 18 July Cleaned out stockyard and flagged cowbale. **1882** CHUDLEIGH *Diary* 4 Nov. (1950) 314 Made a cow bale in the morning, worked at the punga fence in the afternoon. **1908** BAUGHAN *Shingle-Short* 81 Yet, see! past the cow-bails, Down, deep in the gully, What glimmers? **1924** *Otago Witness* (Dunedin) 5 Feb. 15 Several hours a day must be spent in the cow bails and in mustering the sheep. **1940** *Tales Pioneer Women* (1988) 213 In the cold grey light of dawn she would rise and share with her husband the work of the cowbails. **1956** DARE *Rouseabout Jane* 7 This consisted of a very small cowyard and a corrugated iron cow-bail holding two cows at a time. **1967** MCLATCHIE *Tang of Bush* 58 Two cowbails were made against a huge rata log over six feet through. **1982** MALCOLM *Where It All Began* 171 During the depression he built a cowbail and bought a herd of 70 cows. **1987** HARTLEY *Swagger on Doorstep* 182 As I opened the cowbail door I saw Tony with his wife in his arms.

cow-bang *v.*: see COW-BANGER.

cow-banger. [f. Brit. dial. *cow-banger* one who attends on cows: see OED *cow n.* 8 (Yorkshire 1892).] A dairy-farmer; occas. a milker. See also COWSPANKER.
 1915 *Hutt Valley Independent* 3 July 3 A certain money-grubbing Mangaroa cow-banger. **1917** *Truth* 20 Oct. 1 If the 'rumoured' surprises..really happens [*sic*] in Taranaki, the cow-bangers must have taught them an exceedingly bad habit. **1941** BAKER *NZ Slang* 42 *Cow spank*, to be a dairy farmer or a farmhand, whence *cowspanker* (we also use *cattle-banger* and *cow-banger*). **1988** MCGILL *Dict. Kiwi Slang* 31 *cowbanger* dairy farmer.
 Hence, by back-formation, **cow-bang** (also occas. **bang**) *v. intr.* and *trans.*, to dairy farm; to milk (cows); **cow-banging** *vbl. n.*
 1905 *Truth* 9 Sept. 8 These new chums should not get into the employ of a Taranaki farmer, whose aim in life is to..make them **cow-bang**. **1926** *NZ Dairy Produce Exporter* 28 Aug. 29 I think any boy that works hard on a farm should get a couple of holidays a year if he is 'banging cows'. **1988** MCGILL *Dict. Kiwi Slang* 31 *cowbang* to run a dairy farm... Also *cowspank.* **1912** BAUGHAN *Brown Bread* 118 It's a poor job, *cowbangin'* all alone.

cowboy. *Obs.* [Spec. use of Brit. provincial English *cowboy* a boy who attends cows.] A (junior) station-hand responsible for milking and other domestic chores; now often COWMAN or *cowman-gardener* (see COWMAN).
 1854 in Cutten *Cutten Lett.* (1979) 56 The cow boy is leaving..so I expect I shall have to scamper after the cows myself. **1875** WOOD & LAPHAM *Waiting for Mail* 83 It did not take Frank long..to..drive the cow down. In the township he met Edwards, who..said..'Hallo! have you turned cow-boy?' **1891** WILLIAMS & REEVES *Double Harness* 8 Michael Miggs the station cowboy was invariably there. **1903** *NZ Illustr. Mag.* VIII. 365 The cow-boy was waitin' with a dog-cart to take her up to the station. **1913** CARR *Country Work* 34 I nearly forgot the cow-boy. Where the gardener does not milk, a boy of 14 or 16 years old is generally employed. His duties are to milk..chop wood, carry in and out washing, etc. **1933** *Press* (Christchurch) (Acland Gloss.) 7 Oct. 15 *Cowboy.*— The boy who milks, etc. Not the romantic American horseman. **1947–48** BEATTIE *Pioneer Recollections* (1956) 16 When I was a cowboy I made up my mind I was going to be a farmer. **1956** DARE *Rouseabout Jane* 63 I used to try..and get the cowboy to teach me the rudiments of milking. **1964** DICK *High Country Family* 28 1932 saw Allan as a lad of seventeen, and out to his first job: cow boy to a farmer near Oamaru. **1985** LANGDALE-HUNT *Last Entail Male* 136 On the way back to the [Chatham Island] hotel the cowboy, quite a young lad, said in a quavering voice, 'Do you think she will die, Mr Hunt?'

cow-cocky. Also **cow-cockie.** [AND 1902.] A dairy-farmer. Also *attrib.* Cf. COCKY *n.*[1] 1.
 1924 *Otago Witness* (Dunedin) 5 Feb. 15 He is referred to by public speakers..as a dairy farmer, by his neighbours (and in particular sheep farmers) as a 'cow-cockie'. **1933** SCANLAN *Tides of Youth* 17 He sat in the bar and drank beer with a couple of the cow-cockies. **1948** SCANLAN *Rusty Road* (1949) 68 'You cow-cockies are never satisfied,' Whitton said. **1959** DAVIN *No Remittance* 136 I began to dream what I'd have done if I'd had a couple of thousand acres of sheep country instead of a miserable little cow cocky's place in land that would go back to bush. **1966** TURNER *Eng. Lang. in Austral. & NZ* 148 The real cow-cocky country is in the North island of New Zealand, especially in Taranaki and the Waikato. **1987** VIRTUE *Redemption of Elsdon Bird* (1988) 44 Going to the Waikato seemed like going to the other side of the world. 'They'll be a bit cow-cocky up there, I reckon,' he told himself. **1989** HOGG *Angel Gear* 16 The economic downturn? Well... the rich cow cockies get by.

cow-cockying, *ppl.a.* [AND 1936.] Dairy-farming.
 1942 *National Education* May 146 Southill, the cow-cockying district.

cowdee, cowdie, cowdy, varr. KAURI.

cowfish. [Applied to various sea animals from a fanciful resemblance to the appearance, habits, or milk-producing faculty of a cow.]
 1. The adult INANGA *n.*[1] (see esp. quot. 1956).
 1903 *TrNZI* XXXV. 311 They are what we call 'cowfish' or 'inanga'. **1956** GRAHAM *Treasury NZ Fishes* 119 Previously men who had seen Minnows congregating at high tide gave the fish [*Galaxias maculatus*] the name Cowfish because of the milkiness of the water, due to the amount of milt from the males and ova from the females which they extruded as they were lifted in a net from the river. **1978** MCDOWALL *NZ Freshwater Fishes* 69 *Galaxias maculatus*..(Inanga)... Various common names are used for the adult, including Minnow and Cowfish. **1990** [see INANGA[1]].

2. The *bottlenosed dolphin* (DOLPHIN 2 (1)).
 1917 WILLIAMS *Dict. Maori Language* 483 *Terehu n. Tursiops tursio*, cow-fish. **1920** *Quick March* 10 Apr. 37 The Marlborough Sounds..are the haunts of the cowfish—a mammal whose scientific name is Tursiops..the popular name of 'porpoise' applied to it by steamer passengers is..wrong. **1922** *NZJST* V. 139 The cowfish..is a large dolphin occasionally seen off the coast of the South Island... It has a distinct but short beak, a high falcate dorsal fin, and 22 or 23 pairs of teeth. **1930** REISCHEK *Yesterdays in Maoriland* (1933) 70 Next morning I found a stranded cow-fish, whose carcass it took me four days to get clean. **1966** DOOGUE & MORELAND *Sea Anglers' Guide* 302 Bottlenosed Dolphin... *Tursiops truncatus;* cowfish. **1966** *NZ Short Stories* (1976) 33 Once, too, we passed a school of cowfish—smaller cetaceans allied to the porpoises, but fifteen feet long, salty in colour and having a falcate dorsal fin in place of the more usual rounded one. **1982** SANSOM *In the Grip of an Island* 78 Wonderful days those were, when we might be amongst the dolphins (cow-fish we called them). **1990** BAKER *Whales & Dolphins* (2edn.) 107 Bottlenose dolphins or 'cowfish' are amongst the largest dolphins, reaching nearly 4 m in length.

cowleaf. *Banks Peninsula. Obs.* MAHOE, the leaves of which are useful cattle fodder. Cf. COWTREE 1.
 1871 *TrNZI* III. 184 In many parts of Banks Peninsula... [*Melicytus ramiflorus*] is known as 'Cowleaf', from the avidity with which its leaves are devoured by cattle. **1907** LAING & BLACKWELL *Plants of NZ* 266 On Banks Peninsula [mahoe] is sometimes called the *cow-leaf*, as cows are are very fond of its foliage. **1911** *AJHR* C-13 38 *Melicytus ramiflorus...* Mahoe. Whitewood; cowleaf.

cowman. Also **cowman-gardener.** A general station-hand or farm hand responsible for milking and for other domestic chores, esp. attending to the homestead vegetable garden. See also MILKMAN. **a.** As **cowman**.
 1892 COX *Diaries 1888–1925* (ATLMS) 2 Nov. Wyatt the cowman here is a Wiltshire man. **1914** *Normanvale, Canterbury, Wages Book* in Hayes *Toss Of Coin* (1978) 156 F. Denham (cowman). **1941** CURNOW *Island and Time* 20 Wasn't this the site, asked the historian, Of the original homestead? Couldn't tell you, said the cowman; I just live here, he said. **1951** MCLEOD *NZ High Country* 16 In winter time the number of men [on a station] is small, perhaps only a single shepherd and a cowman. **1973** FERNANDEZ *Tussock Fever* 26 Any old station hand—even the cowman—gets more than me.
 b. As **cowman-gardener**.
 1956 DARE *Rouseabout Jane* 28 The vegetable garden..was looked after by a cowman-gardener. **1965** WATSON *Stand in Rain* 139 The only suitable job was a cowman-gardener on a station. **1980** WATSON *Flowers from Happyever* 11 [On the Queensland sheep station there were] the head shepherd and the shepherds, the cowboy (which is the Australian term for cowman-gardener).

cowree, cowri(e), cowry, varr. KAURI.

cowshed. [Used elsewhere but recorded earliest, and of freq. use, in NZ: see OED *cow* 7 a.] A farm building in which cows are milked rather than sheltered. See also BAIL *n.* 1, BYRE, COWBAIL, *cow-byre, cow-house* (COW 6), MILKING SHED, SHED *n.*[1] 4 b (esp. for the various types of cowshed, *angle-park, tandem, walk-through*, etc.).
 1830 MARSDEN *Lett. & Jrnls.* (1932) 490 What they have at present are as bad as cowsheds. **1849** POWER

Sketches in NZ 89 On entering the cowshed I was horror-struck by the most dreadful sight my eyes ever beheld. **1855** *Richmond-Atkinson Papers* (1960) I. 172 Arthur..would put up a slab house of two rooms which might serve afterwards for cowshed or kitchen and workshop. **1860** *Richmond-Atkinson Papers* (1960) I. 617 Harry has lent his large cowshed to the military authorities for a guardhouse. **1899** BELL *In Shadow of Bush* 36 A neat dairy was to be seen..and..a comfortable cowshed and yards, where milking operations were in progress. **1902** *Settler's Handbook NZ* 281 The dearest cowsheds are in the Taranaki country. **1912** RUTHERFORD *Impressions NZ Pastoralist on Tour* 148 This cowshed manure is a priceless treasure on the Continent. **1924** ANTHONY *Follow the Call* (1975) 3 Two-roomed house and four-bailed cowshed on property. **1930** GUTHRIE *NZ Memories* 164 On it came, this avalanche of mud, tearing up..the cow-sheds 80 feet in length. **1959** DAVIN *No Remittance* 69 He went back towards the cowshed and I took the path to the house. **1970** McNAUGHTON *Tat* 103 He noticed a red-headed girl releasing a cow from a bail in a small cowshed. **1986** *Islands 37* Aug. 40 I never saw his cowshed, nor the cows.

cowspanker.

1. [AND 1919.] A dairy farmer; occas. a milker. See also COW-BANGER.
  1887 *Auckland Weekly News* 8 Oct. 8 He entered on the profession of a 'cow spanker', as they call it here. **1890** *NZ Observer* 1 Nov. 4 This [*sc.* a circus] just makes Mr Cowspanker real hilarious. **1906** *Truth* 11 Aug. 3 The king of Okoia cow-spankers rules his small boggy kingdom with a rod of iron. **1917** in Miller *Camps Tramps & Trenches* 13 Mar. (1939) 50 I am sure he [*sc.* an English staff officer] tries to look aristocratic in contrast to these scummy Colonial cow-spankers and bush-whackers. **1926** *NZ Dairy Produce Exporter* 18 Dec. 35 From the worried gentlemen in Tooley Street to the humblest cow-spanker, we all look to the cow. **1934** *Press* (Christchurch) (Acland Gloss.) 13 Jan. 13 *Cowspanker.*—Station slang for cowboy; but a correspondent points out that to people in the town it connotes a dairy farmer. **1946** SOLJAK *NZ* 117 New Zealanders have coined or adapted many expressions to meet local requirements, as illustrated by the following:.. *cowspank:* to milk cows; *cowspanker:* dairy farmer **1950** THE SARGE *Excuse my Feet* 7 'Cow spanker,' said Herbert proudly. **1966** *Encycl. NZ* II. 680 Dairy farmers are (or were) *cowspankers.*

2. *Obs.* COWBOY, one who milks the house-cow (on a stock station).
  1932 SCANLAN *Pencarrow* 87 Kitty decided that she was not meant for a life of dullness and drudgery among ploughmen, and drovers and cowspankers. **1934** [see 1 above].

cow-spanking, *vbl.n.* and *ppl. a.*

a. The work or process of (hand-)milking cows; dairying.
  1899 *Taranaki Herald* (New Plymouth) 9 Jan. 3 Cow-spanking evidently agrees with many people. **1900** *NZ Illustr. Mag.* II. 592 There would in time be an end to the eternal round of cow-spanking, school, and getting up. **1966** NEWTON *Boss's Story* 98 When I come to look back on my own cow-spanking days I can't say I broke any records myself as a gardener. **1980** WOOLLASTON *Sage Tea* 187 With milking machines..the ghastliness of cow-spanking was a thing of the past.

b. [AND 1896.] Dairyfarming.
  1904 *NZ Observer* 11 June 5 All..are residents of the town, and know too much to embark in cow-spanking. **1909** THOMPSON *Ballads About Business* 94 So I tried my hand at dairyin', but soon began to see Cow spankin' wasn't quite the game they cracked it up to be. **1960** McMEEKAN *Grass to Milk* 2 'Cow-spanking', or a job in town!

Hence **cow-spank** (occas. **cow-spang**) (?*spank* + *bang*) v. intr. [by back-formation f. *cow-spanker, -spanking*], to run a dairy farm; to milk cows.
  1921 FOSTON *At the Front* 154 He had got a job cow-spanging on a good farm. **1920** *Otago Witness* (Dunedin) 30 Nov. 56 Before that I was 'cow-spanking' in the Waikato. **1934** *Press* (Christchurch) (Acland Gloss.) 13 Jan. 13 A correspondent points out..that to *cowspank* is to run a dairy farm. **1934** SCANLAN *Winds of Heaven* 189 If it hadn't been for Michael, Kelly would still be cow-spanking somewhere up-country.

cowtree.

1. Any of several native trees with leaves palatable to cattle, esp. KARAKA and MAHOE. Cf. COWLEAF.
  1860 BENNETT *Gatherings of Naturalist* 346 The Karaka-tree of New Zealand..also called Kopi by the Natives, and Cow-tree by Europeans (from that animal being partial to its leaves.) **1898** MORRIS *Austral-English* 103 *Cow-tree, n.* a native tree of New Zealand. Maori name *Karaka.* [cites Bennett.] **1912** *TrNZI* (Proceedings) XLIV. 22 The partiality which stock exhibit for..mahoe or hinahina, the so-called 'cow-tree' of the settler (*Melicytus ramiflorus*)..led to the practice among stockmen of cutting the shrubs down for fodder. **1930** DEVANNY *Bushman Burke* 9 And watch the lesser forest folk; the cowtree and five-finger;.. the hen and chickens; all their brood, and the lawyer sneaking under.

2. [f. its producing a milky sap.] MILK-TREE.
  1956 DAVIES *NZ Plant Studies* 154 The sweet milky sap of *P. microphylla* was frequently used by the settlers as a substitute for milk in their tea. Hence the popular name and its variation 'cow tree'.

coz, var. CUZ.

crab.

1. [An extended use of *crab* for any of various species found in New Zealand waters.] In significant New Zealand use for three families of true crabs (Majidae, Portunidae and Raninidae), and one family (Lithodidae) not a true crab, each with a variety of common names.

2. With a modifier: **king** (**southern king,** or **stone, southern stone**), **paddle** (**sand, surf, swimming**), **spider** (**giant spider, southern spider,** or **giant, New Zealand giant,** or **Auckland Islands**), **tojo**.

(1) **king** (**southern king,** or **stone, southern stone**) **crab.** *Lithodes murrayi* (fam. Lithodidae), a large deepwater 'Anomuran crab' (a crab-like crustacean, not a true crab) with only three pairs of fully developed walking legs with a spread of up to 1 metre.
  1963 DELL *Native Crabs* 62 Southern stone crab... Crayfish pots set in very deep water (about 1,800 feet) off Solander Island in Foveaux Strait were found to contain numbers of these huge crabs with their long powerful legs. **1970** *Fisheries Tech. Report* 97 1 There is only one previous recording of the southern stone crab (*Lithodes murrayi*) in New Zealand waters, that by Yaldwyn and Dawson (1970) found..in 1960..at western approaches to Cook Strait in 209 metres. **1986** FRASER *Beyond the Roaring Forties* 36 A lively scientific interest makes no direct impression on the coastal waters or shore life of the subantarctic islands, but the commercial exploitation of the southern king crab, *Lithodes murrayi*, found in deeper waters on the Campbell Plateau, is always a possibility. **1986** PAUL *NZ Fishes* 154 There are two true king or stone crabs, *Lithodes murrayi* and *Neolithodes brodiei*, present in our deep waters and increasingly encountered on orange roughy grounds in 700m or more.

(2) **paddle** (**sand, surf, swimming**) **crab.** *Ovalipes catharus* (fam. Portunidae), a commercially exploited native swimming crab.
  1947 POWELL *Native Animals* 38 Swimming crab... This is common on most exposed sandy beaches throughout New Zealand. It is at once distinguished by the broad paddle shaped back legs which are admirably adapted for both swimming and digging in loose sand. **1963** DELL *Native Crabs* 43 The common swimming crab is found throughout the North and South Islands and at the Chathams. **1979** *Catch* Sept. 3 There may be enough swimming crabs around New Zealand to support a commercial fishery... The common swimming crab (*Ovalipes catharus*) is also known as the 'paddle crab' or 'sand crab'. **1983** *Evening Post* (Wellington) 29 June 23 The paddle crab (Ovalipes catharus) is also known as the swimming, surf or sand crab... It is particularly aggressive, emerging from the sand to nip the soles and toes of bathers and the fingers of pipi diggers. **1992** *Dominion Sunday Times* (Wellington) 25 Oct. 24 Late in the summer there was an invasion of paddle crabs in the bay.

(3) **spider** (**giant spider, southern spider,** or **giant, New Zealand giant,** or **Auckland Islands**) **crab.** *Jacquinotia edwardsii* (fam. Majidae).
  1963 DELL *Native Crabs* 35 *Jacquinotia edwardsii* New Zealand Giant Crab... This is New Zealand's largest known true crab. It is unfortunate that although it occurs in countless thousands around Campbell and the Auckland Islands it is very seldom seen by the average New Zealander. **1970** *Fisheries Tech. Report* 52 2 It is proposed that the full common name of *Jacquinotia edwardsii* be: 'Jacquinot's southern spider crab' normally abbreviated to southern spider crab. **1986** PAUL *NZ Fishes* 154 *Giant spider crab Jacquinotia edwardsii*... A spider crab (family Majidae) restricted to southern New Zealand. Also known as the southern spider crab and Auckland Islands crab... The giant spider crab is not related to the large North Pacific king crab (family Lithodidae).

(4) **tojo crab.** [Orig. uncertain: poss. from its appearance being fancifully considered to resemble that of Hideki Tojo (1884–1948), the much-caricatured Japanese wartime prime minister.] *Lyreidus tridentatus* (fam. Raninidae), a relatively large, smooth, narrow-fronted frog crab.
  [c**1957** The name *tojo crab* known to Dr Desmond Hurley from its use by central NI fishermen.] **1994** *Occasional Papers of the Hutton Foundation* (Wellington) No.6 2 This [*L. tridentatus*] is a northern continental shelf and upper slope species not found south of Cook Strait, commonly referred to as 'tojo crab' on Bay of Plenty trawlers, and harp crab or smooth frog crab in Australia.

crab-hole. *Obs.* [Fig. use of *crab-hole*: AND 1847.] A hole or deep depression filled with water, usu. in a swamp or in swampy ground.
  c**1850** in Hall-Jones *Mr Surveyor Thomson* (1971) 45 The bearers stumbled in the crab-holes on either side, or over the tussocks. **1856** ROBERTS *Diary* in Beattie *Early Runholding* (1947) 32 We went down a spur for two miles that was very soft from the late rain, and full of waterholes, called crab-holes. **1867** THOMSON *Rambles With Philosopher* 22 We had to hold by the lower spurs of the ranges..now floundering in a swamp, then stumbling into crab-holes. **1873** PYKE *Wild Will Enderby* (1889, 1974) I. iii 16 Ages ago..was..drained the great network of lakes, whereof the existing representatives..are mere 'crab-holes' by comparison. **1890** *Otago Witness* (Dunedin) 2 Jan. 4 Once Bob disappeared altogether in a treacherous crab-hole. **1910**

CHUDLEIGH *Diary* 13 Apr. (1950) 450 We both fell into crab-holes a name given to swampy country when full of holes and full of water in wet weather but dry now. **1937** AYSON *Thomas* 84 Thomas found that he had to ride..over very rough country consisting of rocks, scrub, flax, crab holes. **1964** DEANS *Pioneers* 114 Most of this area consisted of low-lying swamp and crab holes covered with flax and toetoe.

crack, *v.*

1. In various phr. with sexual implications: **to crack it**, of a woman, to have, offer, or provide sexual intercourse. See also *crack a fat* FAT *n.*[3]
  1972 *Truth* 17 Oct. 26 He further said: 'You know Shirley's been cracking it.'..'I understand 'cracking it' means a person selling their body for money.' **1984** *Metro* (Auckland) Apr. 42 I've been on the game 11 years and first cracked it for a chemist in return for dope.

2. a. As **to crack it** [AND *v.*[2], 1936], to succeed in an enterprise; to bring something off.
  1982 NEWBOLD *Big Huey* 120 And you always got the feeling..that by not smiling and waving, and by not cracking it for a chat with the screws..you were blowing your chances of work-release. **1984** BEATON *Outside In* 21 Kate:.. Ginny might pull one. Sandy: No way, she's fucken in for it, boy..Ginny's cracked it before now. *Ibid.* 109 Crack it—to succeed in an enterprise; bring something off.

b. In the phr. **to crack one's whip**, to stand one's shout; to take one's turn.
  1953 SUTHERLAND *Golden Bush* (1963) 166 'That being so we'll have one [*sc.* bottle of beer],' I told him. 'You've carried it all the way up here and now you can crack your whip.' **1966** TURNER *Eng. Lang. Austral. & NZ* 148 I have heard 'Can he crack his whip?' used..to mean 'Does he join us for a drink in the pub?' or 'Is he a good drinking man?' **1971** NEWTON *Ten Thousand Dogs* 85 When one did get a win he had to crack the whip. *Ibid.* 168 *Crack your whip*: To shout or stand drinks.

c. In the phr. **to crack hardy (hearty)** [AND *crack hardy*, 1904], to put on a tough or bold front (in the face of difficulties, pain); to endure patiently.
  1944 FULLARTON *Troop Target* 67 Hark at the four-figure man cracking hardy. **1949** SARGESON *I Saw in My Dream* 177 Daley's got a big family to keep... So he cracks hearty. **1975** DAVIES *Outback* 104 You were always a battler, Dad... But don't crack too hardy. **1980** MANTELL *A Murder Or Three* 34 Gave me the willies just looking at it. So I thought maybe Angela was cracking hardy—y'know. **1992** PARK *Fence Around the Cuckoo* 118 What a lot we were..perished with cold most of the time, and yet ostentatiously cheerful. This was called *cracking hardy*.

crackee crackee, var. KARAKIA *n.*

cracker, *n.*[1]

1. [f. Brit. dial and US (1855) *cracker* a small cord on the end of a whip which makes it crack: see EDD; AND 1852.] A short piece of plaited (usu. shredded) flax-leaf, etc. at the end of a stockwhip to make it sting and crack.
  1856 ROBERTS *Diary* 19 Sept. in Beattie *Early Runholding* (1947) 42 The [bullock] whip was rawhide plaited sinnet, about six feet long, thick at the upper end..but tapering nearly to a point, to which was attached a narrow strip of rawhide, called 'the fall,' finishing off with a twisted 'cracker' made of 'weetau' or dressed flax in place of whipcord. **1862** CHUDLEIGH *Diary* 9 Dec. (1950) 69 Did a little to a great many things. One was to milk some cows, make some crackers, cross-cut and chop some fire-wood. **1907** KOEBEL *Return of Joe* 164 Fresh and efficient crackers swing continually at the ends of the stockwhips. **1925** BATHGATE *Random Recolls.* 24 Flax proved useful..providing a temporary boot lace or a cracker for a whip. **1940** STUDHOLME *Te Waimate* (1954) 151 The thong was fastened to the wooden handle [of the whip] by a leather loop or keeper. The fall was made from a tapered piece of greenhide. The crackers were made from native flax. **1975** HARPER *Eight Daughters* 108 The older children made her ask the musterers for flax 'crackers' for the stockwhips.

2. [Transf. use of fire)*cracker* firework.] A cartridge.
  1937 PARTRIDGE *Dict. Slang* 188 *cracker*... (Gen. pl.) A cartridge: New Zealanders': from ca. 1910. **1938** *Press* (Christchurch) (McNab Slang) 2 Apr. 18 [Slang of the NZEF]..a 'cracker' was a cartridge. **1941** BAKER *NZ Slang* 55 Probably..originally from the country are..*crackers*, cartridges.

cracker, *n.*[2] [Fig. use of *cracker* a thin dry biscuit: cf. a similar use of *bean*.] Usu. in negative constr. **a.** [AND 1934.] The smallest amount of money, esp. as **not to have** (etc.) **a cracker**, to have no money at all, not to have a cent.
  1955 *BJ Cameron Collection* (TS July) not to have a cracker (v) Not to have a bean. **1960** HILLIARD *Maori Girl* 240 I've got nothing, Harry: not a cracker. **1986** OWEN & PERKINS *Speaking for Ourselves* 76 Months of bushwork, with hardly a cracker coming from it, made me carry a swag. **1990** EDWARDS *AWOL* 3 I haven't got a cracker to my name... I'm just a bum salesman.

b. In the phr. **not to be worth** (etc.) **a cracker** [AND 1953], not to be worth even the smallest amount, to be worthless.
  1963 CASEY *As Short a Spring* 89 She's a dead-end show round about four o'clock of a week-day, isn't she?..Nothing doing worth a cracker, eh.

cracker, *a.* [An adjectival use of the Brit. and US slang noun *cracker* something outstanding of its kind (see OED *n.* a 1, HDAS *n.* 3: also recorded in NZ use from 1908); poss. infl. by *crackerjack a.* fine, outstanding.] Fine, excellent, outstanding (of a kind).
  1964 HARVEY *Any Old Dollars Mister?* 41 The huge Maori put the Yank down... 'By Kori,' he said with a kind smile. 'That was a cracker yarn, mate.' **1978** BALLANTYNE *Talkback Man* 112 'On a cracker day like this?' she asked. 'I'm hot enough as it is.' **1982** HOLDEN *Wild Pig* 45 'They're cracker tusks all right, too,' Stan said. **1986** *Listener* 27 Sept. 32 [Cartoon of an after-match function] No doubt about it—she's a cracker game, Bruce.

cracker, var. KARAKA.

craddie, var. KORARI.

cradle, *n.* Goldmining.

1. *Hist.* [f. US *cradle* a goldmining apparatus: AND 1851.] A box on rockers used for washing away sand or gravel to extract any alluvial gold.
  1852 *NZGG* 10 Dec. V. 30:183 (Heaphy's Rep.) The implement most effectual in economising labour is the 'Long Tom', or trough strainer, cradles are but of little comparative service. **1862** HODDER *Memories NZ Life* 74 We worked a 'cradle'..a machine into which the earth is thrown and rocked about until merely a small residue remains under a sheet of perforated iron amongst which the gold is found. **1873** PYKE *Wild Will Enderby* (1889, 1974) III. vii 95 Alone and unaided he scooped the wash-dirt into his cradle, which he vigorously rocked with his left hand, whilst with the right he ladled water from the river into the 'hopper' or s[ie]ve. **1911** BREMNER in *Mt Ida Goldfields* (1988) 10 The days of the tub and cradle were past, and unless water could be obtained for sluicing, the field was played out. **1937** [see LONG TOM 1]. **1946** MILLER *There Was Gold* 41 It took two men to work the cradle satisfactorily—one to shovel and one to rock it violently..and at the same time to dash water on to it by means of a dipper fastened to a stick. **1962** EVANS *Waikaka Saga* 11 If a claim was very rich and localised the cradle could be used. **1970** WOOD *Gold Trails Otago* 7 In the cradle the gravel was separated from the sand and gold through a perforated metal hopper and the gold remained in the short segments of riffle box and matting below.

2. The mounting of a drifter-drill.
  1978 MCARA *Gold Mining* 317 *Cradle*: The mounting of a drifter-drill equipped with manual screw-feed. In setting up the machine the cradle was usually placed on an arm attached to a vertical column wedged between the roof and the floor of the working.

3. See *miner's cradle* (MINER), a form of flying fox.

cradle, *v.* Goldmining. [f. prec.: AND 1851.] *trans.* and *absol.* To wash (goldbearing washdirt) in a miners' cradle. Also *vbl. n.*
  1858 HODGKINSON *Descr. Canterbury* 19 A claim for the purposes of sinking, surface digging, tomming or cradling. **1862** CHUDLEIGH *Diary* 23 May (1950) 39 [The gold] is not of a very good quality, too fine, not nuggety enough to use a sluice well so they adopt the slower and surer way of cradling. **1871** MONEY *Knocking About NZ* 18 I started them [the diggers] to cradle some 'headings', or dirt thrown out of deserted holes. **1887** PYKE *Hist. Early Gold Discoveries Otago* (1962) 79 The miners..strained every effort to obtain the auriferous 'dirt'..leaving the washing up and 'cradling' to be done when the getting more dirt was impossible. **1889** BLAIR *Lays of the Old Identities* 47 He puddled and cradled, and digged all he knew When the claim proved a regular duffer. **1914** PFAFF *Diggers' Story* 42 We passed some men cradling on the river bank near Kanieri. **1946** MILLER *There Was Gold* 31 When we were not cradling for gold we made furniture for our camp. *Ibid.* 69 I decided, as long as I had the water for cradling to work the gold in this way. **1959** MILLAR *Westland's Golden Sixties* 161 Wash-dirt..is quickly removed..into the bucket, wound [up the mine-shaft] to the daylight and cradled. **1962** EVANS *Waikaka Saga* 228 In order to have a daily supply of water for cradling and panning many miners combined to build this dam.

  Hence **cradler** *n.*
  1977 MURRAY *Costly Gold* 21 Many of the cradlers found it expedient to live close to their claims.

crake. [Spec. use of *crake* a ralline bird as a general name (usu. with a modifier) for any of various small, secretive New Zealand water-birds, species of *Porzana* (formerly *Ortygomera*) of fam. Rallidae.] **a.** *Porzana pusilla affinis.* **marsh crake,** a small, shy, rarely seen swamp bird. See also KOITAREKE, *marsh rail* (RAIL 2 (8)).
  1873 BULLER *Birds NZ* 183 *Ortygometra affinis.* (Water-crake.)... Koitareke... This handsome little Crake is found in both Islands; but it is everywhere extremely rare and difficult to obtain. **1886** *TrNZI* XVIII. 113 *Ortygometra affinis.*—Koitareke, Water Crake. Both Islands, Extremely rare everywhere. **1955** OLIVER *NZ Birds* 359 *Marsh Crake. Koitareke Porzana pusilla affinis. Ibid.* 360 The Marsh Crake..inhabits both fresh and saltwater swamps and also the marshy banks of rivers. **1966** FALLA et al. *Birds NZ* 106 Marsh Crake. The smallest of our rails... Call notes a harsh *krek-krek*

or *creak-creak*. **1985** *Reader's Digest Book NZ Birds* 166 *Marsh Crake Porzana pusilla affinis... Koitareke...* The marsh crake, a secretive swampland bird, is heard rather than seen. **1990** *Checklist Birds NZ* 122 *Porzana pusilla affinis... Marsh Crake (Koitareke)...* New Zealand and Chatham Islands. Widespread.

b. *Porzana tabuensis plumbea.* Formerly **swamp crake** or *swamp rail*, now usu. **spotless crake**, a small slate-coloured rail. See also PUTOTO, PUWETO, RAIL 2 (10).

1873 BULLER *Birds NZ* 181 Ortygometra tabuensis. (Swamp-crake)... Pueto and Pututo. **1886** *TrNZI* XVIII. 117 *Ortygometra tabuensis.*—Pututo, Swamp Crake. **1900** CANTERBURY *Old & New* 196 In the rail family we have..the striped rail, the water crake, the swamp crake, and the swamp hen. **1908** *TrNZI* XL. 498 Our striped rail, water-crake, and swamp-crake, with the bittern and pukeko, remain only..so far as swamp exists. **1955** OLIVER *NZ Birds* 357 *Spotless Crake. Puweto Porzana tabuensis plumbea...* On Raoul Island, the Spotless Crake is found in the forest, but resorts to a raupo swamp to breed. **1966** [see RAIL 2 (10)]. **1976** SOPER *NZ Birds* 210 In New Zealand Spotless Crakes are birds of dense cover and swampy ground. **1983** *Whakarewarewa Forest Park* 64 Should you hear strange sounds from the reeds and sedges it is almost certainly a spotless crake. **1990** *Checklist Birds NZ* 122 *Porzana tabuensis plumbea... Spotless Crake (Puweto)...* Australia, Tasmania and New Zealand. In New Zealand, widespread.

crane. [Transf. use of *crane* for species of *heron* (fam. Ardeidae).]

[*Note*] Modern New Zealand usage prefers *heron* to *crane*.

1. blue crane. *reef heron* (HERON 2 (1) *Egretta sacra sacra*).

1844 WILLIAMS *NZ Jrnl.* (1956) 114 The Matukutuku, or Crane, of this there are several kinds in New Zealand; the blue crane or that which inhabits the seashore is common to every one. **1883** DOMETT *Ranolf & Amohia* II. 153 'Twas that *blue crane* with bristly crown—You recollect? **1899** [see HERON 2 (1)]. **1936** GUTHRIE-SMITH *NZ Naturalist* 77 In the neighbourhood of Takaka..we watched the nesting customs of the Blue Crane. **1966** FALLA et al. *Birds NZ* 78 Blue Reef Heron *Egretta sacra sacra Other names*: Blue Crane, Matuku-moana. **1985** [see HERON 2 (1)].

2. *Obs.* **white crane.** *white heron* (HERON 2 (3)). See also KOTUKU.

1849 TORLESSE *Papers* (1958) 68 After some manoeuvring, I shot a white crane in one of the lagoons about Timaru. **1856** SHORTLAND *Traditions & Superstitions* 143 If the feathers are those of the bird called *huia*, it is a sign the child will be a girl; if those of the *kotuku* (a white crane), the dream prognosticates a male child. **1863** BUTLER *First Year* ix 136 I must not omit to mention the white crane, a very beautiful bird, with immense wings, of purest white. **1870** *Evening Post* (Wellington) 16 Dec. 2 A gentleman who can propose to pay off Britain's national debt..is as rare a stranger as the 'white crane of the Maoris'. **1883** DOMETT *Ranolf & Amohia* I. 279 There, as the shy *white crane*, so rarely seen, Stands. **1894** WILSON *Land of Tui* 92 B. wished to show us..the country round Lake Brunner ('Kotuku waka oka'—home of the white crane). **1904** [see HERON 2 (3)]. **1917** STRACHAN in Neave *Land of Munros* (1980) 65 Just as we were passing..lake [Ohau in 1858], we saw what I never saw again..- it was a beautiful white crane. **1939** BEATTIE *First White Boy Born Otago* 121 I saw a white crane at Taieri Lake. **1948** HAAST *Julius Von Haast* 106 Haast recorded..an unsuccessful attack by three sparrow-hawks upon a white crane fishing. **1958** GILLESPIE *S. Canterbury* (1971) 7 White herons have been reported from various parts of South Canterbury for many years and were often referred to as 'white cranes'.

Hence **cranery** [a nonce-formation on *rookery*], the breeding place of the white heron at Okarito.

1872 HON. W. FOX *Let.* 17 Apr. in Buller *Birds of NZ* (1873) 227 Do you know of the existence of a 'Cranery' of the White Crane at Okarita, on the West Coast?..The Okarita 'Cranery' is, I suspect, nearly the last.

cranesbill. Also **crane's-bill.** [Transf. use of *cranesbill Geranium* spp. of Europe and Asia.] Any of various native species of *Geranium* (fam. Geraniaceae), perennial herbs of grasslands and shrublands with fruits shaped like the beak of a crane. Also with a modifier: **Chatham Island (mountain, soft) cranesbill.** See also DOVE'S FOOT, GERANIUM.

1777 ANDERSON *Journal* Feb. in Cook *Journals* (1967) III. 804 Amongst the known kinds of plants are..Nettles..and Cranes bill. **1838** POLACK *NZ* I. 295 *Vanilloe*, or *willow*, *euphorbia*, *cudweed*, *crane's-bill*. **1867** HOOKER *Handbook* 764 Cranesbill. *Geranium*. **1910** COCKAYNE *NZ Plants & Their Story* 124 The Chatham Island cranesbill (*Geranium Traversii*), of which there are white and pink varieties. **c1919** COCKAYNE in McCaskill *Molesworth* (1969) 154 [On Molesworth there are] the small rosettes of mountain cranesbill dotted here and there, a remnant of the primitive plant-covering not eaten even by rabbits. **1926** [see DOVE'S FOOT].

crape fern: see FERN 2 (3).

craptogram: see LATRINOGRAM.

crate. A beer-crate holding two dozen quart bottles or six half-gallon flagons; its contents. (Often used *joc*. **Ladies a plate, gentlemen a crate**, as an invitation to a party.)

1981 CHARLES *Black Billy Tea* 67 He says, 'Give me a jar and a couple of crates, For I am running the cutter tonight for me mates!'. **1991** *Evening Post* (Wellington) 26 Oct. 25 The three decided to go to the pub, have a few drinks and fill a crate.

crawfish. *Obs.* [A var. of CRAYFISH common in the early and mid 19th c.]

1. CRAYFISH 1 a.

1777 FORSTER *Voyage Round World* I. 150 Here [at Anchor Island] they sat down by the side of a pleasant brook, and made a slight repast on some boiled craw-fish. **1821** MAY in McNab *Hist. Records* May (1908) I. 550 There is..abundance of lobsters, or a fish between a lobster and a craw-fish. **1838** POLACK *NZ* II. 136 [The cavern] is mostly in request by parties fishing for the kohuda, (craw fish), and other fish. **1848** WAKEFIELD *Handbook NZ* 161 A large *Craw-fish*, obtained by diving among the rocks, supplies the place of the lobster. **1858** *Puketoi Station Diary* 27 Dec. in Beattie *Early Runholding* (1947) 76 27th Dec.—Visitors went down to Taieri; came back with pig, ducks and crawfish. **c1920** BEATTIE *Trad. Lifeways Southern Maori* (1994) 326 The koura-waitai or sea crawfish boiled red as is commonly known. **1978** NATUSCH *Acheron* 155 A fishing party came back with Kahawai and 'crawfish'.

2. CRAYFISH 1 b, CRAWLER 2 (the freshwater crayfish, *Paranephrops* spp.).

1843 DIEFFENBACH *Travels in NZ* II. 45 Fresh-water crawfish, which are common in the inland lakes and rivulets, are taken with bait. **1851** *Richmond-Atkinson Papers* (1960) I. 79 After tiring of [singing] they set off with burning brand & tomahawk to catch crawfish..in a little brook near our encampment.

Hence **crawfish** v. WW1. *fig.*, see quot.

1937 PARTRIDGE *Dictionary Slang* 189 *Crawfish*. To withdraw unreservedly from an untenable position: New Zealand soldiers' in G.W. The crayfish swims backwards.

crawler. [f. *crawl* to move slowly across a surface + *-er*.]

1. *Farming*. [AND 1838.] A slow-moving sheep, or one in bad condition.

[**1858-69**] *Puketoi Station Diary* in Beattie *Early Runholding* (1947) 85 In connection with stock the following terms were used:—'Let the sheep draw down to the Taieri'; 'stags', 'crawlers', 'stragglers'. **1877** RITCHIE in Crawford *Station Yrs.* (1981) 113 His sheep are crawlers..of merinos which have shorn only 4lb of greasy wool. **1889** WILLIAMS & REEVES *Colonial Couplets* 21 Be they freezers or crawlers or wethers or ewes. **1891** CHUDLEIGH *Diary* 24 Nov. (1950) 378 Had splendid muster. Sheep very large and fat with heavy fleeces. No crawlers. **1981** CRAWFORD *Station Yrs.* 33 In the springtime of 1869 there were held on these paddocks 1,000 sheep which were described as 'crawlers', a term used to describe sheep that were too weak or lame to keep up with the mob.

2. [Poss. reinforced by an anglicized pronunciation /korə/ of Maori *koura*.] A mainly children's name for the *freshwater crayfish* (CRAYFISH 2 (1)), KOURA b. See also CRAWFISH 2, CRAWLIE.

1948 FINLAYSON *Tidal Creek* 40 'They was only crawlers, mighty small fry,' he says cheerlessly. **1949** SARGESON *I Saw in My Dream* (1974) 82 And in the creek they saw the crayfish and Mr Jones said he called them crawlers, but the Maoris called them koura. **1959** SLATTER *Gun in My Hand* 10 Hunka Harris..went in the creek after crawlers in his bare feet. **1989** GIBBONS *Recollections* 40 The three of us..went off with a bucket to catch the crawlers.

crawlie. Also **crawly.** CRAWLER 2.

1893 SEDDON *Let.* 3 Feb. in Seddon *The Seddons* (1968) 42 Dear old Stuart. That crawly catching should be stopped. **1942** ANDERSEN *Maori Place Names* 351 A stream with fresh-water crayfish (crawlies). **1955** WILSON *Land of My Children* 195 Catching crawlies in the little spring..one of the children found a *mere* (a Maori axe). **1967** NATUSCH *Animals NZ* 109 A disturbed crawlie, as the children call it, rears upon its four pairs of legs, brandishing its pincers. **1980** THOMPSON *All My Lives* 31 Other boys pulled freshwater crawlies from the creek above the town with bare hands, holding them amidships so as to avoid their nippers.

crawly, var. CRAWLIE.

cray. Pl. often *cray*. [AND 1909.]

1. A shortened form of CRAYFISH 1, (usu.) a marine crayfish, but also occas. a freshwater crayfish.

1773 BAYLY *Journal* 9 Nov. in McNab *Hist. Records* (1914) II. 212 There is plenty of Cray & other fish in this Bay. **1840** POLACK *Manners & Customs* I. 202 [There is] a great variety of testaceous and crustaceous fishes..such as clams, muscles, oysters, crays. **1935** LAWLOR *Confessions of Journalist* 216 To him a crayfish became a cray only when it poked its nippers through the clumsy parcel under a drunk's arm. **1944** ANDREWS *Something to Tell* 21 It hadn't been a fresh cray for ever so long. **1953** SUTHERLAND *Golden Bush* (1963) 44 The cray allowed itself to be sniffed [by the dog] all along the back without protest. **1960** BAXTER *Collected Poems* (1980) 219 There's twenty other good men..Have sold their crays and terakihi. **1979** *Commercial Fishing* Oct.

CRAYFISH

7 [Heading] Export market seen for fresh water crays. **1993** BERTRAM *Capes of China* 282 Sandy Bay..recalled..notable childhood feasts of butterfish and crays.

2. *fig.* See quot. See also CRAYFISH 4.

1988 MCGILL *Dict. Kiwi Slang* 31 *cray* 100 dollar bill; from its colour red, same as a crayfish; eg Bold poker player to the table: 'His cray and up two.'

3. Special Comb. **cray boat**, a crayfishing boat; **cray diver**, a crayfisher who dives for the catch; **cray-diving** *vbl. n.*; **cray-pot**, a crayfish pot.

1963 *Commercial Fishing* July 32 [Heading] Coroner says **cray-boat** was torn apart by mountainous seas. **1979** *Commercial Fishing* 18/2 74 Quite a large commercial cray boat. **1987** *National Radio Rural Programme* 11 Sept. We'll be back aboard the cray-boat in a few minutes. **1991** *National Business Review* 13 Sept. 9 What is happening to the **cray divers** [*sc.* outlawing of commercial crayfish diving] can happen to any business sector when bureaucrats are delegated power to make regulations without reference to parliament... **Cray diving** is not a big industry. **c1937** HYDE *Selected Poems* (1984) 59 An absent face..as far As fisher's boats that bob across the bay Setting their **cray-pots** in the island's shadow. **1964** DEMPSEY *Little World Stewart Is.* 121 It was the first time I had seen the cray-pots hauled aboard. **1979** MARSHALL *Supper Waltz Wilson* 31 As George turned back to the fence he noticed a fishing-boat setting cray-pots off the point. **1981** JOHNSTON *Fish Factory* 86 Instead of going down to the wharf to throw himself off the end of it with a few cray-pot weights tied around his neck he could now see a faint ray of light. **1991** *National Business Review* 13 Sept. 9 A cray fisherm[a]n with $100,000 or so tied up in a boat, cray pots, and other gear doesn't like competing with a younger and fitter man catching the same amount of crays with a couple of thousand dollars' worth of gear.

Hence **cray** *v. intr.*, to fish for crayfish.

1963 *Evening Post* (Wellington) 31 Aug. 31 It was ideal weather for craying.

crayfish. [Transf. use of *crayfish* for any of various edible aquatic decapod crustaceans: AND 1770.] See also CRAWFISH, KOURA, LOBSTER. [*Note*] The preferred trade name for the marine species is now 'rock lobster'.

1. a. Also **New Zealand crayfish**. Any of several marine crustaceans of the family Palinuridae, esp. the common rock lobster *Jasus edwardsii* (formerly *lalandii*).

1769 PARKINSON *Journal* 22 Oct. (1773) 99 This bay abounds in a variety of fish, particularly shell and cray-fish. **1773** FORSTER *Resolution Jrnl.* 10 Apr. (1982) II. 251 Since two or three days some crayfish (*Cancer Homarus*) but better than the Lobster, were caught in great Numbers. **1807** SAVAGE *Some Acc. of NZ* 11 The cray fish and crabs are excellent. **1831** BISCOE *Journal* 30 Oct. in McNab *Old Whaling Days* (1913) 415 At 11 A.M. some New Zealanders came alongside in a Canoe, but had nothing with them except a few Cray Fish. **1842** GRAY *Fauna* in Dieffenbach *Travels in NZ* (1843) II. 266 *Palinurus* sp. 'Lobster, or Sea Cray-fish'. *Cook*... 'Kohuda or cray-fish', Kohura. **1850** LUSH *Auckland Jrnls.* 19 Nov. (1971) 38 At Hall tasted for the first time some New Zealand crayfish; like immense lobsters but *without* claws. **1889** SKEY *Pirate Chief* 17 On pipis he lives—on cockles and eels, And lobsters so fine and so red;.. And kakapos stewed for dessert. [p.ix errata] Page 17—6 for *lobsters* read *crayfish*. **1937** HYDE *Wednesday's Children* (1989) 62 The crayfish was a terrible..monster, rusty-brown with its years. **1950** *Zool. Publ. VUC* 7 25 Most of the crayfish caught in Wellington waters were taken in supplejack pots baited with fish-heads. **1986** PAUL *NZ Fishes* 150 'Crayfish' has been regularly used as a common name, although it is more properly applied to freshwater species. Some combination of 'red', 'spiny', and 'rock lobster' is more appropriate. **1990** *Dominion* (Wellington) 28 Aug. 3 The rock lobster (crayfish) fishery is worth about $112 million a year.

b. Any of several species of *freshwater crayfish* (see 2 (1) below).

1847 [see KOURA b]. **1858** SMITH *Notes of Journey* 27 Jan. in Taylor *Early Travellers* (1959) 378 A Maori who was with us caught some crey [*sic*] fish, and taking them to a boiling spring just above our bath, cooked and presented them to us. **1883** DOMETT *Ranolf & Amohia* I. 184 The small *cray-fish* in myriads bred, With sunk fern-bundles lifted from the Lake. **1905** *Jrnl. Polynesian Soc.* XIV. 135 Like many rivers Whanganui has its poetical..names:.. Te koura-puta-roa, the crayfish's deep chasm.

2. With a modifier: **freshwater**, **packhorse** (or **green**, **smoothtail**), **run**, **spiny** (or **red**).

(1) **freshwater crayfish**. Any of several spp. of *Paranephrops*, a small lobster (fam. Parastacidae). See also CRAWFISH 2, CRAWLER 2, CRAWLIE, KOURA b.

1873 TINNE *Wonderland of Antipodes* 17 I had heard..of the fresh-water cray-fish (goura) that are found in these lakes. **1899** *TrNZI* XXXI. 32 In the North Island there is only one genus of fresh-water crayfish..while in the South Island there are three species. **1915** *TrNZI* XLVII. 47 The fresh-water crayfish become sexually mature a considerable time before they attain their full size. **1929** BEST *Fishing Methods* 71 Fresh water crayfish (koura) were taken in considerable numbers in some districts. **1947–48** BEATTIE *Pioneer Recolls.* (1956) 6 They noticed an occasional koura or freshwater crayfish. **1964** HINTZ *Trout at Taupo* 67 The trout will take the smaller freshwater crayfish whole, but even the smaller koura can be bigger than a man's thumb. **1981** HENDERSON *Exiles Asbestos Cottage* 114 Those little freshwater crayfish up the Cobb tasted sweet. I could go one now.

(2) **packhorse** (or **green**, **smoothtail**) **crayfish**. *Jasus verreauxi* (fam. Palinuridae), a large dark-green marine lobster. Also *ellipt.* **packhorse**.

1960 DOOGUE & MORELAND *Sea Anglers' Guide* 281 Smooth tail Crayfish... *Jasus verreauxi*, green crayfish, pack-horse. **1966** *Encycl. NZ* III. 706 Crayfish, 'packhorse' or 'green' . . koura papatia . . *Jasus verreauxi*. **1970** *NZJMFR* IV. 46 *Jasus verreauxi*.. known locally as the packhorse crayfish—is the less common of the two New Zealand species of spiny lobster (marine crayfish). **1981** WILSON *Fisherman's Bible* 39 The biggest saltwater variety is the Packhorse Crayfish, so named because he grows to a prodigious size compared with his offsider, the spiny, or red crayfish. **1991** *NZ Geographic* Jan.-Mar. 106 The introduction of air travel by flying boat in the 1950s made the commercial exploitation of packhorses possible.

(3) **run crayfish**. See quot.

1981 WILSON *Fisherman's Bible* 41 Fishermen often use the term 'run crayfish' for light-coloured crayfish, with yellow being a more prominent colour than usual. These runcrays are either males or juvenile females.

(4) **spiny** (or **red**) **crayfish**. *Jasus edwardsii*, the common New Zealand crayfish.

1960 DOOGUE & MORELAND *Sea Anglers' Guide* 280 Common Crayfish... *Jasus lalandei*; spiny crayfish; koura, koura-papatea (Maori). **1971** *New Zealand's Heritage* I. 71 *Spiny crayfish*..found anywhere along coastline below tide level. **1981** spiny, or red crayfish [see (2) above].

CREAM

3. a. Used *attrib.* in Comb. **crayfish pot**, **supper**.

1966 *Commercial Fishing* IV. 9 May 11 Use of **crayfish pots** with escape gaps to permit the escape of crayfish has been studied in Western Australia. **1984** HOLMES *Chatham Islands* 65 So began the 'Crayfish Bonanza Years' in the Chathams—'an ocean-going stampede to make a fortune from the "gold" which came slithering and splashing out of the sea when the crayfish pots were hoisted in'. **1990** *Dominion Sunday Times* (Wellington) 19 Aug. 11 She can see right over the patch of sea where he's set his crayfish pots. **1922** *Auckland Weekly News* 15 June 49 The night after the match..a big **crayfish supper** was held.

b. Special Comb. **crayfish spider**, the body and legs remaining after the crayfish has been tailed; **crayfish tailing**, the removal of the commercially valuable tails of crayfish.

1991 *Dominion Sunday Times* (Wellington) 31 Mar. 21 The Hokitika Dramatic Society sold off 180 **crayfish spiders** (crayfish minus the tails) fresh from Jacksons Bay in South Westland. **1966** *Commercial Fishing* IV. 11 July 20 The Fishing Industry Board has recommended to the Minister of Marine that **crayfish tailing** at sea be permitted to continue in the Southland and South Westland areas.

4. *fig. Obs.* A fifty-pound note, from its crimson colour. CRAY 2.

1963 *NZ Truth* 21 May 19 I plonk 10 rogue and villains on it I suppose, home it rolls and I'm winning a crayfish. crayfish..£50.00

crayfisherman. Also **crayfisher**, **crayman**. **a.** One who catches crayfish for business or pleasure.

1967 NATUSCH *Animals NZ* 107 A crayfish which has been in hiding while its shell hardened comes out in a very hungry state to forage for food, and itself falls easy victim to the crayfisherman's pots. **1981** HENDERSON *Exiles Asbestos Cottage* 219 And the craymen, the scollopmen, the fishermen who look at you through cracked eyes. **1982** WHEELER *Hist. Sheep Stations NZ* 69 The men in my drawing are crayfishers awaiting the tide before they cruise round their pots. **1986** *Listener* 16 Aug. 82 This is big cray country; squadrons of jet-boating crayfishers make their way..to the fast refrigerator trucks. **1991** cray fishermen [see *cray-pot* (CRAY 3)].

b. A crayfishing boat.

1986 BROWN *Weaver's Apprentice* 13 The inlet was a harbour within a harbour, with some forty vessels, trawlers and crayfishers, passing the sabbath afternoon over slumped mooring lines and lazy reflections.

crayfishing, *vbl. n.* The catching of crayfish for business or pleasure.

1949 *Auckland Weekly News* 5 Jan. 37 [Caption] Cray-fishing at the Bay of Islands. **1953** *AJHR H-15* 21 The principal increases occurred at those ports or places where crayfishing has only recently developed. **1968** SLATTER *Pagan Game* 165 He had been up and down the island picking up jobs... Crayfishing and scrubcutting. Contract fencing.

crayman: see CRAYFISHERMAN.

cream. *Obs.* Used *attrib.* in special Comb. with reference to the production and processing of cream for dairy products: **cream-can**, a can in which farm cream was stored ready for transport to a butter factory; **cream cheque** [OED 7 'Austral.', 1921], the money received by a dairy-farmer for cream sold to the local dairy factory; **cream factory**, a dairy factory making butter; **cream launch**, in lake or marine districts, a launch collecting farmer's cream-cans for delivery to a dairy factory; **cream-lorry**, see *cream-truck*; **cream stand**, a stand, usually at a farm gate, holding cream-cans for collection; **cream-truck**, a vehicle collecting farmers' cream-cans for delivery to a dairy factory.

1948 *Our Own Country* 25 Dairy and cheese factories are dotted over the plains, **cream-cans** stand at farm gates. **1959** SHADBOLT *New Zealanders* (1986) 16 Father mounted me..on the konaki beside the cream-cans. **1963** AUDLEY *No Boots for Mr. Moehau* 25 The cream cans jumped and crashed with greater hilarity [on the back of the lorry]. **1987** HARTLEY *Swagger on Our Doorstep* 188 After breakfast Dad left the house with mugs and a cream can of oatmeal water—a refreshing drink of rain water, lemon juice and a large handful of oatmeal. **1931** *NZJST* XIII. 59 The best that could be done was to keep the food bill paid out of the **cream cheque**. **1933** *Na To Hoa Aroha* (1988) III. 88 The first collections from cream cheques came to a little under £140. **1948** FINLAYSON *Tidal Creek* (1979) 30 What's money to me? The cream cheque goes to the store and pays the month's bills and everything. **1953** *Here & Now* Apr. 31 When secondary school assistants wed A cocksfoot man from the cream-cheque land There's no time for books and less for bed, But tits and cups in your early hand. **1959** SHADBOLT *New Zealanders* (1986) 12 Results were slow: the cream-cheques were never large; money was always short. **1973** FINLAYSON *Brown Man's Burden* 140 cream cheque: the monthly payment to a farmer from the local dairy factory for milk and cream supplied. **1987** HARTLEY *Swagger on Our Doorstep* 148 I am mystified as to know how my parents achieved such stylish comfort in the early 1930s on their share of the cream cheque. **1925** MANDER *Allen Adair* (1971) 48 Already he saw the **cream factories** which men down south were dreaming as part of every township. **1959** SHADBOLT *New Zealanders* (1986) 16 Father..took me, with the cans, down to our jetty, there to await the **cream-launch**. **1965** GILLHAM *Naturalist in NZ* 104 The homesteads dotted along the steep [Sounds] coastline have each their..wooden jetty where the 'cream launch' delivers mail and stores, collects the farmer's cream. **1991** *Dominion* (Wellington) 13 Apr. 9 It only takes a few words for us to recognise the shots of scenic New Zealand:.. the cream launch, the happy campers. **1929** *Northern Advocate* (Whangarei) 5 Jan. 8 As driver of the **cream lorry** which serves part of the district, [he] has won the esteem and regard of all. **1936** SCOTT *Barbara and the Backblocks* 14 Send us bread by the cream-lorry. **1946** SARGESON *That Summer* 13 A man who ran the cream lorry would give her a lift into town. **1959** SLATTER *Gun in My Hand* 77 The bulldozers nudging a slippery track for the cream lorries waiting in the rain. **1978** SUTHERLAND *The Elver* 20 A Goosman cream lorry, Wills' Reo Speedwagon Big Tree petrol tanker, the T model Ford fire engine. **1986** O'REGAN *A Changing Order* 45 We arrived back that night in triumph, on the back of the cream lorry driven by an exuberant Snowy Walker. **1939** GRIEVE *Sketches from Maoriland* (1961) 104 On another occasion a..bump-bump-bump in the vicinity of the **cream-stand** drew me as a glittering object draws the curious *weka*. **1960** *Weekly News* (Auckland) 8 June [Caption] A stop to pick up a party of school children by a cream stand on the Takatu road. **1977** HOLCROFT *Line of the Road* 108 Cream stands then appeared on the roadsides, causing uneasiness to the Council. **1987** HARTLEY *Swagger on Doorstep* 97 Mr Davis put a large box of groceries in our cream stand once a week. **1960** HILLIARD *Maori Girl* 9 The county council built a wooden bridge which somehow still stands..its stringers creaking beneath every **cream-truck** and tractor. **1986** *NZ Sunday Times* 21 Dec. 2 The cream truck in the 50s, with few private cars around, was one of the favoured..means of transport into town. **1992** *Listener* 13 Jan. 10 We went there [*sc.* north Hokianga] by launch and the only access to other parts was by cream truck.

creamery. *Hist.* [Used elsewhere but of historical significance in NZ.] An establishment where farmers or dairy-cow owners formerly took their milk to be separated; often, also, a butter manufactory, later giving place to *dairy factory* (DAIRY 4) or *butter factory* (BUTTER 1).

1887 *Auckland Weekly News* 26 Nov. 29 These creameries represent an important epoch in the dairying industry in Waikato for they purpose to do for butter what the freezing meat company should do for beef and mutton—produce an export market for the produce. **1890** *NZ Observer* 22 Nov. 17 It's buttermilk that makes the creamery boys spooney. **1892** *NZ Statutes* No.30 178 [Dairy Industry Act] 'Factory' or 'creamery' shall mean a place established for receiving the milk or cream of cows from the public for the purpose of manufacturing the same or any portion of the same into butter or cheese, or both, as the case may be. **1899** *Taranaki Herald* (New Plymouth) 25 May 2 Hitherto, that policy has been to discourage creameries, or as they are more correctly called—skimming stations, and deal with all the milk at the large central factory. **1904** LANCASTER *Sons o' Men* 206 The district [*sc.* Taranaki] reeks with creameries. **1913** CARR *Country Work* 39 Creameries are run where there are not sufficient cows to warrant a factory. **1938** *Auckland Weekly News* 16 Feb. 60 All that remains..is..a neglected ruin of what was an important creamery. **1957** *Mangamaire School 1897–1957* 29 It is said that at a later date there were as many creameries as there were sawmills. **1978** SINCLAIR & HARREX *Looking Back* 97 Creameries or skimming stations were established in dairying districts so that farmers didn't have to maintain their own dairies, and so that they could produce a more uniform butter by pooling their milk. **1983** COOPER *Wag's Tales* 67 Until about 1917 Patutahi boasted a 'Creamery', where all the dairy farmers took the milk in huge cans, to be separated. **1992** CONDON *Hurleyville* 72 Under Dairy Industry Act, 1898, the term 'creamery' was defined as a butter manufacuring plant. Petch Road and Gentle Annie [creameries] were registered as skimming stations—where milk was separated only.

creamfish. A trade name for LEATHERJACKET 1 (*Parika scaber*).

1921 *NZJST* IV. 123 *Leather-jacket; Kōkiri.* Large numbers are skinned and sold in Auckland as 'cream-fish'. **1947** POWELL *Native Animals NZ* 73 [Leatherjacket] is a good food fish and is sold in the Auckland markets in the form of skinned fillets under the name of 'cream-fish'. **1970**, **1982** [see LEATHERJACKET 1].

creek. [f. Brit. *creek* a narrow inlet in the sea-coast, an estuary; thence applied in US (1622), Austral. (1795), NZ (1815) to a freshwater tributary of a river.] Early, esp. northern, New Zealand examples retain the Brit. meaning.

1. Now mainly *Northland* or *Obs.* **a.** A 'saltwater creek' or narrow coastal inlet; a narrow arm of the sea; a harbour. Cf. RIVER 1.

1773 COOK *Journals* 13 Apr. (1961) II. 120 After securing the Boat in a little creek, I proceeded to the place. **1820** MARSDEN *Lett. & Jrnls.* 18 July (1932) 260 A creek of salt water, about one hundred yards wide, runs from the main river round to the rear of the hippah till it meets a fresh-water stream. **1826** SHEPHERD *Journal* 10 Mar. in Howard *Rakiura* (1940) 359 The name of this part of the harbour is called Seal Cove we saw a great number of Creeks and little bays on each side as we went along in the boat. **1843** *First Rep. Committee Auckland Agric. Soc.* in Swainson *Auckland* (1853) 38 This [Papakura] district is bounded on the west by the waters of the Manukau, which deeply indent it in various directions, with its numerous creeks. **1874** BAINES *Edward Crewe* 38 It was a place [16 miles by boat from Auckland] we never could have found without a guide, there were so many creeks, as big as the main one apparently, branching off on both sides. **1883** DOMETT *Ranolf & Amohia* I. 138 As, when you turn upon a sea-creek's shore, Some limpet-crusted boulder o'er. **1892** *NZ Official Handbook* 242 This great inlet [*sc.* Pelorus Sound]..extends in a southerly direction about 25 miles, branching of to the eastward and westward into numerous arms and creeks. **1970** THOMAS *Way Up North* 39 He carted sacked..gum from the fields to the wharf or to the landing places on the harbour front and creeks.

b. As **tidal creek**, a freshwater creek or narrow inlet susceptible to tidal flows.

1882 POTTS *Out in Open* 3 From the shallows at the heads of harbours, where wide mudflats receive the waters of tidal creeks, nearly every stream..must have..often reflected the quaint attitudes of this watchful fisher [*sc.* kotuku.] **1926** COWAN *Travel in NZ* II. 169 Three of us once cruised about [Stewart Island's] secret coves and in and out of its tidal creeks in a whaleboat carrying mainsail and jib. **1934** MULGAN *Spur of Morning* 44 Little steamers sailed every week from Eden to mainland harbours, tidal creeks, and islands. **1959** SHADBOLT *New Zealanders* (1986) 32 The barbecue was held on a sandy spit about a mile, by water, from the place where the town met the tidal creeks; there the creeks became sea, and the sea swelled out to the harbour heads. **1974** PRESTON *Lady Doctor* 79 We had a call to a farm well up the [Hokianga] river, at the head of one of the tidal creeks.

2. A running freshwater stream; a brook.

[*Note*] In early use often collocated with *freshwater* and distinguished from the *saltwater* or *tidal* (see quot. 1959) *creek* of 1 above.

[**1773** FORSTER *Resolution Jrnl.* 6 Apr. (1982) II. 247 We entered a spacious long Cove with fine fish & plenty of fresh water-brooks..& midst of the woods a fine stream, forming another cascade.] **1815** *Deeds ceding land to Missionaries* 24 Feb. in Nicholas *NZ* (1817) II. 194 All that piece and parcel of land situate in the district of Hoshee, in the Island of New Zealand, bounded on the south side by the bay of Tippoona and the town of Ranghee Hoo, on the north side by a creek of fresh water, and on the west by a public road into the interior. **1820** MARSDEN *Lett. & Jrnls.* 8 May (1932) 249 There are two warm springs opposite each other, one on each bank of the creek, about ten feet above the level of the fresh water, which runs between them. **1838** POLACK *NZ* I. 129 The young females are generally very cleanly in their habits; in summer, often bathing during the day, in the sea or fresh-water creeks. **1841** SINCLAIR in *GBPP 1842 (No.569)* 19 July 134 Two of the best of these [Auckland waterside allotments], bordering on a fresh-water creek, which runs down through the valley, have been selected by Government officers. **1857** PAUL *Lett. from Canterbury* 65 In the Australian Colonies, as in America, brooks are called creeks. **1860** in BUTLER *First Year* 13 Feb. (1863) iv 46 A little river, brook, or stream, is always called a creek; nothing but the great rivers are called rivers. **1889** WILLIAMS & REEVES *Colonial Couplets* 2 What they call a brook or brooklet or a streamlet or a rill, I do only, I confess it, call a *creek* and always will. **1896** HODGSON *Poems* 8 Vale, brook, and grove, to poet dear, Here changing name and dress, As *gully*, *creek*, and *scrub* appear, In conscious ugliness. **1912** MANSFIELD *Stories* (1984) 109 At noon we lunched off fly biscuits and apricots by the side of a swampy creek. **1929** *Tararua Tramper* Oct. 2 Along the creeks or in shady gullies fuchsias..are plentiful. **1959** SHADBOLT *New Zealanders* (1986) 30 We walked to the back of the farm, to a place where a fresh-water creek [*sc.* non-tidal] spilt down terraces of rock. **1960** SCRYMGEOUR *Memories of Maoriland* 30 She fished, waded in the creeks. **1971** OGILVIE *Moonshine Country* 135 Eels have always been common along this stretch of the Opihi, its side-creeks and back-waters. **1984** WILSON *S. Pacific Street* 7 In my spare time I went continually down to our muddy creek.

3. a. *Comb.* **creek-bank** [AND 1849], **-bed** [AND 1847], **-head, -side**.
1911 *TrNZI* XLIII. 198 In damp places on **creek-banks**.. *Elatostemma rugosum*..is a characteristic covering. **1871** MONEY *Knocking About NZ* 78 On my return to the lower world we used to bathe and basks in the **creek-bed**, I found the party broken up. **1892** *NZ Official Handbook* 172 In July, 1867, gold was discovered in a creek-bed at the Thames. **1918** *NZJST* I. 12 It was considered that the coarse alluvial gold found in the creek-beds could not have been shed from the lodes discovered. **1958** MULGAN *Making of New Zealander* 34 The once open creek-bed, where we used to bathe and bask in the sun. **1973** HENDERSON in *Islands 4* 117 The man's hobnails struck fire in the dried-up creekbeds. **1985** HILL *Moaville Magic* 63 There *had* been blue herons in the creekbeds up Murphy Road—until the executives moved in and the creekbeds and blue herons moved out. **1960** CRUMP *Good Keen Man* 13 I..told and retold a bored Stan..how I shot that old hind in the **creek-head**. **1957** FRAME *Owls Do Cry* (1967) 59 There on the **creekside** the bird refugees were free to waddle and preen. **1967** MAY *West Coast Gold Rushes* (1962) 148 For many miles along the creek-sides lay likely looking terraces, all of them auriferous. **1979** ADCOCK *Butter in Lordly Dish* 49 We went along the creekside, pushing our way through the wild mint. **1982** SANSOM *In Grip of Island* 32 Mint, watercress and pennyroyal by the creek-side scent the air.

b. *Special comb.* **creek-claim**, see quot.; **creek fern**, an occas. name for KIWAKIWA q.v.
1862 WEKEY *Otago As It Is* 61 Claims shall be classified thus..Creek or river claims, *i.e.*, alluvial claims in the bed of creeks or rivers.

creeper, *n*.[1] [Spec. use of *creeper* or *tree-creeper*, a name given to any of various small birds which run or creep up and down trunks and branches: see OED 3.] Also **tree-creeper**, and usu. with a modifier **brown**, occas. **bush**, or **New Zealand creeper**. *Finschia novaeseelandiae* (fam. Pachycephalidae), a small attractive, grey and reddish-brown insect-eating bush bird. See also LINNET, PIPIPI, TOITOI *n*.[1]
1777 FORSTER *Voyage Round World* I. 148 The birds seemed to retire from it to a little distance, where the shrill notes of thrushes..and the enchanting melody of various creepers resounded on all sides. c**1835** [see LINNET]. **1870** *TrNZI* II. 59 Brown creeper; Brown Canary. Although this Creeper may be seen in almost every bush, from the coast to the distant Alpine Ranges, we have only once found its nest. **1871** HUTTON *Catalogue Birds NZ* 11 Brown Creeper. Brown Linnet. Toitoi. **1888** BULLER *Birds NZ* I. 51 Certhiparus novae zealandiae. (New-Zealand Creeper)... *native names.-* Pipipi and Toitoi. **1908** *TrNZI* XL. 491 [Brown creepers] are seen at Wyndham in little flocks, and are often called the 'grey creeper' and 'the other canary'. **1917** WILLIAMS *Dict. Maori Lang.* 328 Pipipi... *Finschia novae-zealandiae*, tree-creeper; a bird. *Ibid.* 506 Toitoi..brown creeper; a bird. **1936** GUTHRIE-SMITH *NZ Naturalist* 55 A few Brown Creepers..were also seen. *Ibid.* 62 From one or other of a Bush Creeper pair came the note that told us..of their two babies. **1940** STUDHOLME *Te Waimate* (1954) 230 The discordant notes of the Brown Creepers, as they flitted from tree to tree, also warned the other forest inhabitants of the stranger's coming. **1946** *JPS* LV. 156 *Tree-creeper*, a gregarious bird..the flock sings a long song in time and in unison. **1955** OLIVER *NZ Birds* 472 *Pipipi*... The Brown Creeper was discovered in 1773 by the Forsters at Dusky Sound during Cook's second voyage. **1967** NATUSCH *Animals NZ* 277 The brown creeper..is an inconspicuous bush-warbler of the South Island and Stewart Island back country. It is not easy to get a clear view of the bird behind the outpourings of 'szzzzt! (Ka ke kau!) whp! whp! whp! -p-p-p! (Ka ke kau!)' **1976** SOPER *NZ Birds* 53 Brown Creepers have a remarkable ability to exist unsuspected near inhabited areas. **1984** SOPER *Birds NZ* 140 Brown Creepers occur only in the South Island, Stewart Island and some of the Stewart Island off-liers such as Codfish Island.

creeper, *n*.[2] [Cf. OED 2 b, 1867, the larva of the stone-fly.] As **black creeper**, the Dobson fly larva, *Archichauliodes* spp. See also TOEBITER 1.
1921 *NZJST* III. 273 Order 4 (alder-flies) is represented in New Zealand by only a single species *Archicauliodes dubitatus*, an insect of large size, whose fat, succulent larva is found under rocks in streams, and forms excellent food for trout. This larva is called the 'black creeper', or sometimes the 'toe-biter'. **1967** NATUSCH *Animals NZ* 151 The Dobson fly..is a speckled orange-winged insect which flits weakly over streams at dusk. The larva (known as the black creeper or toe-biter)..hides under stones in the creek bed by day, coming out for a night's career with its powerful jaws ready to seize and devour whatever comes its way.

cress. [Transf. use of *cress Lepidium sativum* (fam. Brassicaceae).] Applied in New Zealand to species of the native and introduced genera of fam. Brassicaceae, esp. *Cardamine, Lepidium*, and *Rorippa*, usu. with a modifier: **Captain Cook's cress** (*Lepidium oleraceum*), **Kawarau cress** (*Lepidium sisymbrioides* subsp. *kawarau*), **New Zealand marsh cress** (*Rorippa palustris*), **New Zealand bitter cress** (*Cardamine debilis*), **wild cress**, and others. See also PANAPANA, SCURVY-GRASS.
1838 POLACK *NZ* I. 291 The *turnip* is found in a wild state over the entire country, as also wild *radishes, garlick, celery, cress*, &c. **1867** HOCHSTETTER *NZ* 157 Panapana, Hanea, Nau, *(Cardamine)* New Zeal. cress. **1882** [see PANAPANA]. **1889** FEATON *Art Album NZ Flora* 17 Nasturtium palustre *(D.C.)*... The New Zealand marsh cress is edible, and was formerly eaten by the natives. **1926** HILGENDORF *Weeds* 95 Narrow-leaved cress (*Lepidium ruderale*) is also called swine cress, wart cress, way-side cress, wild cress, pepper cress, pepper weed, and scurvy grass. It is common on waste lands, especially near the sea. **1951** 31 Oct. 2ZB Wellington (Nature session) Dr Cohen [speaks of]..Captain Cook's cress or as some people call it Captain Cook's Scurvy Grass. It is edible. **1952** land cress [see PANAPANA]. **1969** *Standard Common Names Weeds* 18 *cress*, native bitter [=] *New Zealand bitter cress... cress, New Zealand bitter Cardamine debilis*. *Ibid.* 47 *marsh cress Rorippa islandica*. *Ibid.* 119 *cuckoo cress Cardamine pratensis*. **1986** JOHNSON *Wildflowers Central Otago* 36 From Kawarau Gorge Petrie collected [in the 19th century] a native cress which he named *Lepidium kawarau*... It has turned up again..in the Kawarau Gorge, on dry rocky bluffs..where it grows with the cryptic purple-grey coloration typical of many scree plants. *Ibid.* 37 [Caption] Kawarau cress *Lepidium sisymbrioides* subspecies *kawarau*.

cresset. [See OED *cresset* 'Frequent as a historical word; in actual use applied to a fire-basket for giving light on a wharf, etc.': last use 1853.] An iron vessel often suspended as a container (e.g. hung from a ceiling).
1940 *Tales of Pioneer Women* (1988) 212 We wonder if..Grandmother said something under her breath when the 'cresset', made by amateurish hands and often slightly larger at the bottom than at the top, defied all her efforts to get the cheese out.

crested. In the names of animals, see: GREBE 2 (1), PENGUIN 2 (2), (3) and (7), SHAG 2 (14) and (16), WEEDFISH.

crevicing, *vbl. n.* Goldmining. [f. US: see OED 1851.] Fossicking in crevices of rocks, esp. those in stream beds, for alluvial gold.
1952 2YA Wellington: W.S. Hynds programme *Gold Prospecting* 22 Aug. Some days when the creeks are too low for sluicing, we go crevicing. **1970** WOOD *Gold Trails Otago* 81 Crevicing can be a fascinating occupation, for one never knows when one might find a virgin crevice with its quota of shotty gold and even a small nugget. **1976** NOLAN *Hist. Gold Trails Nelson & Marlborough* 88 Crevicing: This simple method consisted of scraping out cracks in rock bars or in rock masses once covered by the river.

crib, *n.*[1] [Spec. use of *crib* a small habitation; cabin; hovel: see OED 3 a.]

1. a. *Obs.* Also **crib log hut**. A hut, shanty; in some 20th century uses poss. BACH *n.* 1 (see quot. 1912).
1856 PHILLIPS *Rockwood Jrnl.* 30 Dec. (Canterbury Pub. Lib. TS) 62 It now began to rain and the party were not at all sorry to find themselves comfortably housed in Mr. O's snug little crib. **1862** THATCHER *Auckland Vocalist* 16 The [Post-]office is an ancient crib, Built several years ago, When Auckland was a tiny place. **1874** *Southern Mercury* 24 Jan. 5 In [your] last issue you expressed surprise that the signal-master should be housed in a crib not more than 6 x 8. **1891** CHAMIER *Philosopher Dick* 177 I was welcomed like the prodigal son, hugged all round, installed in my old crib, and made drunk every night. **1906** *Truth* 25 Aug. 1 It appears [the constable] got wind of a crib in Utiku [Taihape] where the illicit whiskey bottle was wont to go the rounds. **1912** *Otago Witness* (Dunedin) 9 Oct. 79 When the mater returned to Dunedin after her holidays..I determined to try 'baching', and after having been six months in my crib at the top of the hill, I am more than ever resolved not to descend again to town level... My 'bach' is perched..about 7000ft above sea-level. **1929** SMYTH *Bonzer Jones* 213 'Here's my crib,' he announced. **1947** BEATTIE *Early Runholding* 33 [The pioneer pastoralist] may call it various names according to its materials, but three names would not enter his head—i.e., crib, bach, or shack. He may call it a cabin, a shanty, a cottage, a warrie [whare] [*sic*], but probably he would use the commonest term of all—hut. [**1952** LYON *Faring South* 173 It was after the foregoing incident that [the two diggers] occupied a crib log hut on the hillside leading to the mine they worked [120 miles from Nelson]. **1980** NEAVE *Land of Munros* 75 [Caption] 'Westmere'..was built by Christian Hille in the 1860's. The original crib was burnt.

b. [f. Brit. dial. or slang *crib* a lock-up: see OED 3 c.] A lock-up; a confined sleeping-place or cell (usu. in the gaol).
1864 *Saturday Review* (Dunedin) IV. 15 [The prisoners] are then at liberty to arrange their cribs and go to sleep. **1869** THATCHER *Wit & Humour* 35 For the weather and time had so peppered This tumble-down crib, I declare That it didn't require a Jack Sheppard To find his way quick out of there.

c. *Spec.* a sleeping space (or a hut or detached building) in which a pregnant woman was housed to have her baby with a view to giving it up illicitly. (The reference is poss. merely to a BACH *n.* 1.)
1964 *Truth* 29 Sept. 27 He [*sc.* Cooper, a Newlands, Wellington, baby-farmer c1922] told her she could

occupy a 'crib' on his place at Newlands, at a rent of 15/- a week. **1984** *Dominion* (Wellington) 13 Oct. 10 The murder charge, however, had been narrowed down..to a baby born to [name omitted], who for a fee, had arranged to rent a crib in the Coopers' house during her pregnancy... It had also been established that a [name omitted] who shared the crib with [name omitted], had also given birth to a baby on the Cooper property... The woman confined in the crib with [name omitted] had testified under cross-examination.

2. *Orig. and mainly southern South Island.* A weekend or beach cottage; BACH *n.* 2.
[*Note*] This use pre-dates the similar general use of BACH *n.* 2.

1909 *Otago Daily Times* (Dunedin) 30 Dec. 10 [Advt] A Crib at Puketerahi. Beautifully-built weekend Crib... Everything that four fellows could possibly require. **1912** *Kai Tiaki* July 59 A mental expert..ordered her removal to a quiet seaside resort, under the care of a mental nurse. As the crib which was taken for our habitation was built facing a river with the ocean to one side, and the bush behind, one can realise the opportunities afforded to one who was admittedly 'tired of life'. **1920** *Otago Witness* (Dunedin) 23 Nov. 1 As a result of complaints from the owners of the cribs at Tomahawk..the police have been watching the locality. **1927** *Otago Daily Times* (Dunedin) 8 Jan. 14 [Advt] Wanted, crib at seaside for two months or longer; rent must be reasonable. **1943** HISLOP *Pure Gold* 80 As for the old horse trams..several of them made their last run to many of our bonnie [Otago] coastal camping grounds converted into real good cribs. **1947** SMITH *From N to Z* 132 Cribs vary greatly in size and cost... You might have a modest crib built out of a couple of motor car cases... The idea of a weekend crib is to give you some place to go at the weekends. **1950** *Truth* 15 Nov. 11 He had two young girls..staying..under his care at a crib beside Waituna Lagoon, Southland. **1964** DEMPSEY *Little World Stewart Is.* 6 Where the North Islander talks of his beach cottage, or bach, we call these little places *cribs*, a much more euphonious name. **1973** DOWLING *Unreturning Native* 25 Far off..the majesty of Aspiring; At hand, campers and cribs, bathers, and boats for hiring. **1980** GLEN *Bush in Our Yard* 63 Jock closed the gears and began to edge slowly out of our Te Anau crib driveway. **1986** [see BACH *n.* 2]. **1991** *Listener* 18 Mar. 15 Its [*sc.* Aramoana's] cribs, as these cottages are known south of the Waitaki, circulate amongst insiders.

Hence **cribbie** *n.*, a person who owns or uses a crib.
1985 *Karitane postcard* Karitane, Otago, New Zealand... During the summer months 'cribbies', as the holiday vacationers who spend time in their little cottages are termed, swell the small population of permanent residents.

crib, *n.*² [f. Brit. dial *crib* a light meal at work; a break from work: see OED *crib* 66 (OED quots. are mainly of Cornish and mining provenance); AND 1890.]

1. In local use, esp. by coal-miners and tunnellers, lunch, usu. a cut lunch eaten at work; meal-time at the workplace.
[*Note*] The word is usu. associated with the West Coast, but has spread widely among miners, tunnellers, and other occupations.

1904 LANCASTER *Sons o' Men* 159 Sereld..growled because someone had spilt tobacco-ash into his crib— which is bushman for dinner. In the Southland timber country the hands..cook for themselves. **1911** *Maoriland Worker* 20 Apr. 2 The other day we received the sad intelligence that William Young was killed in one of the Westport mines while sitting at crib! **1917** *Thames Goldfield Jubilee Booklet* in Williams *Racing for Gold* (1987) 49 After the men had fired their holes we went to crib at about three o'clock in the morning. **1925** HICKEY *Red Fed. Memoirs* 11 One of the standing grievances [at Blackball, 1908] was the time allowed for 'crib' (meal-time) underground. **1930** DEVANNY *Bushman Burke* 290 My crib is along with Crighton's. **1967** *Manapouri Power Project Employees' Industrial Agreement* (TS) (Schedule) 12 Apr. 3(c) A worker shall not be required to work more than five hours continuously without being granted a break for a meal or supper or crib. **1979** *Otago Daily Times* (Dunedin) 28 Mar. 21 (Griffiths Collect.) It was a running argument over the time taken for the miners' crib which led to trouble in the Blackball mine. **1985** HUNT *I'm Ninety-five* 28 We'd take our crib into the [gold]mine with us [c1916]: a cut lunch wrapped up in newspaper, cold meat, stew or bacon sandwiches and tea. **1988** *NZ Herald* (Auckland) 13 Feb. sect. ii 2 When her husband was on the surface working on the [Martha Hill mine] crusher [c1900], she would take him his crib (lunch), and hurry back.

2. *Special Comb.* **crib bag** [AND 1898], TUCKER BAG; **crib-box** [AND 1947], a lunch-box; **crib cuddy**, see quots. (see also CUDDY); **crib hut** [AND 1986], **crib-shed**, a building set aside for workers to eat their cribs in; **crib table**, a table provided in a crib-hut; **crib-time** [AND 1890], a meal-time or meal break (see also SMOKO), a snack taken at work; **crib-tin** [AND 1919], a tin holding a cut-lunch or snack.

1986 RICHARDS *Off the Sheep's Back* 38 [To our British teacher] a paddock was now a field, our tucker or **crib bags** (made out of sugar bags) became satchels or lunch bags and our oilskin coats became macs. **1971** HUTCHINSON *Forbidden Marriage* 49 Men, coming off and going on shift [at Thames mines], carrying their **crib-boxes**, met them. **1940** *Otago Daily Times* (Dunedin) 10 Feb. 12 Two of the tunnellers were interested enough to chalk up on the walls of the 'crib-cuddy', where the mid-shift lunches were eaten, account of progress made. **1978** MCARA *Gold Mining* 317 Crib cuddy: A warm dry disused underground working used as a place where miners could have their meals. **1986** RICHARDS *Off the Sheep's Back* 5 The miners looked for a dry spot in a worked-out section of tunnel in which to leave their gear. This was known as the 'crib cuddy'. **1992** LATHAM *Golden Reefs* 428 Crib Cuddy: A drive of thirty feet or so off the main drive, where out of the smoke from blasting the miners would have their crib (lunch) on seats along each side. **1960** KEINZLY *Tangahano* 124 'Didn't I tell you blokes a man needs drink to live?' The **crib hut** laughed and Janiss went back out to the truck. **1968** *Report of Industrial Relations Manager on a Work Stoppage at Manapouri Power Project* (p2) (MOW 92:12:70:5) 9 Mar. (TS) The Union terms were set out as follows:- 3) The crib huts walled-in or crib huts provided in place of tables. *Ibid.* Unless the Company provided properly closed-in **crib sheds**, washing facilities, and additional toilets..the men..would refuse to work there. *Ibid.* The Union was advised that the Company did not propose to provide an alternative to the **crib tables** currently being used as these had been approved by the Mines Inspector... The clean up and disinfecting of the crib tables..would be put in hand as soon as work resumed. **1901** in 1900-01 *Awards, etc.* 74 [Auckland (Waihi) Gold-Miners Award] That the week's work consist of forty-six hours for men working day-shifts..including **crib-time**. **1908** *Western Gaz.* 13 May 6 Half an hour's 'crib' time [at Blackball] is also granted. **1911** *Maoriland Worker* 3 Nov. 5 The shot firer charges the hole. He does it during crib time. **1925** HICKEY *'Red' Fed. Memoirs* 15 I was approached by the local constable, who informed me that he had a warrant for my arrest for refusing to pay the fine..arising out of the 'crib'-time incident. **1951** *Awards, etc.* 323 [NZ Freezing-Workers Award] A shift shall consist of eight consecutive hours, including twenty minutes' crib-time and two 'smoke-ohs'. *Ibid.* 529 [Marlborough Timber-Workers Award] Where temporary shelters are required for the convenience of workers during crib-time, the employer shall provide the necessary material for same. **1961** HENDERSON *Friends In Chains* (1961) 185 Crib Time: Meal time at quartz and coal mines [c1900–20]. **1962** HOGAN *Billy-Can Ballads* 2 Miners [at Waihi] are a knowledgeable clan and down below as crib time discussions took place that would have done credit to the back-room boys. **1987** WILSON *Past Today* 107 Miner militancy made its first successful appearance at Blackball with the crib time strike in 1908. **1928** DEVANNY *Dawn Beloved* 273 Val stopped in the porch to hang up his towel and **crib tin**. **1963** PEARSON *Coal Flat* 17 There were a dozen familiar faces of miners on their way home, in rough clothes, their sugar-bags and crib-tins laid on a bench. **1986** RICHARDS *Off the Sheep's Back* 5 The miners always carried their food (crib) to work in a specially designed tin box called a crib tin.

crib, *n.*³ [f. US *crib* a bin or place with slatted sides for storing Indian corn: see OED *n.* 15.] Usu. as **hay crib**, or **maize crib**, a platform with raised slatted sides in which hay or maize is stored.

1928 *Weekly News* 21 Aug. [Caption] The largest maize crib of the district..near Gisborne. It is 100 yards in length, 10ft. high, and 6ft. wide, holding the crop from 85 acres. **1931** *Na To Hoa Aroha* (1987) II. 146 They were kids who crawled into the maize cribs to sleep. **1945** *NZ Dairy Exporter* 1 Dec. 7 [Caption] With sleds fitted to its base, the hay-crib..can be moved around the paddock at will. **1966** FINLAYSON *Brown Man's Burden* (1973) 120 Here and there you see the nikau thatch roofs of our maize cribs.

cricket: see TREE-CRICKET.

crim. [Ellipt. for *criminal*, prob. orig. US slang: see OED 1909; AND 1953.] A (convicted) criminal. See also CRIMMO.

1980 LELAND *Kiwi-Yankee Dict.* 30 A crim is a criminal, this term is used by police, social workers, prison officers, criminals, etc. **1988** *Listener* 18 June 17 There were 70 people [in Oakley psychiatric hospital]; the majority of those were crims, most were stir-crazy. **1991** DUFF *One Night Out Stealing* 10 He looked around at the human scenery of crims.

Crimean shirt. *Hist.* Also **crimea.** [f. the name of the s. Russian peninsula, chief seat of the Russo-Turkish war 1854–56, prob. with reference to the warmth of the material: AND 1864.] A long, usu. grey or blue, flannel shirt resembling a bush-shirt, a common article of the early colonial bush costume, often worn outside the trousers.

1862 HODDER *Memories NZ Life* 137 Our..swags.. each contained a pair of blankets, Crimean shirt, biscuits..and a tolerably good supply of powder and shot. **1864** CHUDLEIGH *Diary* 11 Nov. (1950) 152 I had nothing on all day but moleskin trousers and a crimean shirt minus arms. **1870** *Letter* in King *Moriori* (1989) 112 This to let you know the things I asked for:.. 1 Hat 1 Monkey Jacket 1 Necktie 1 Crimea. **1887** *Auckland Weekly News* 1 Jan. 23 He came down for breakfast that morning dressed in..a soft wideawake hat, a Crimean shirt. **1896** O'REGAN *Poems* 39 The moleskin an' Crimean shirt are growing scarce apace Like the sturdy men that wear them. **1902** SATCHELL *Land of Lost* 14 He wore a blue Crimea shirt, open at the throat. **1914** in *Hist. N. Otago from 1853* (1978) 130 The men's dress of the 70's and 80's was usually composed of rough working clothes... A heavy grey twill Crimean shirt with a red bandana handkerchief..tied around the neck. **1937** *NZ Railways Mag.* Nov. 17 The young officer's costume was as primitive as his river-boat—a cabbage-tree hat, a Crimean shirt, and a kilt mat of woven flax belted round his waist. **1977** EBBETT *In True Colonial Fashion* 30 Crimean shirts were also part of working dress for men, particularly in winter. They were of grey wool, made without a collar, just a simple neckband, and were pulled over the head. Diggers on the goldfields wore them outside their trousers.

crimmo. [f. CRIM(M) + -O.] CRIM.
  1950 *Here & Now* Nov. 14 Most crimmos don't take much notice of that five times daily insult, the search. **1953** HAMILTON *Till Human Voices Wake Us* 99 When you're in jail your sympathy is with the crimmos, unless you're just a natural topper. **1972** *Jerusalem Daybook* 42 Everybody knows that the Jerusalem community is a crowd of wierdos [*sic*], no-hopers, drop-outs, mad people, crimmos, thieves and junkies. **1984** *Listener* 13 Oct. 47 He supports his arguments with vivid word pictures of [prison] incidents and inmates, both crimmo and conchie.

crimp. *Obs.* [Transf. use of *crimp* one who procures seamen, etc. by entrapment.] **a.** One who dishonestly procures seamen to desert in New Zealand ports, usu. to work up-country; one who takes money for helping seamen jump ship. See CRIMPING *vbl. n.*
  1862 *AJHR* D-5 4 They must first escape the control of their own Officers before they can fall under that of the crimps. **1910** *Truth* 29 Jan. 7 He admitted taking Krause and another German to Zimmer's German hashhouse at 2 a.m. and letting them in by the back door and providing accommodation for them... Counsel alleged that Buhler was a crimp, but the 'Square-head' was discreetly unintelligent and nothing could be got from him.

b. *transf.* ?A dishonest power-broker.
  1907 *Truth* 20 July 4 As was to have been expected, that crimp of corrupt capitalism, Clemenceau the French Premier, has, after the manner of his kind, climbed down in the most cowardly fashion.

crimping, *vbl. n. Obs.* [Transf. (or reverse) use of *crimping* the seducing of men into the navy or army: see OED *vbl. n.* 1.] The enticing of seamen off ships to become farm labourers.
  1861 Commodore Seymour in *AJHR* D-9 19 Feb. 3 (Griffiths Collect.) I cannot..consent to allow another of Her Majesty's ships to be stationed at Wellington, so long as the crimping which prevails there both for the Sheep Farms and the Coasting Trade is allowed to remain on its present footing. **1862** Commodore Seymour in *AJHR* D-5 18 Apr. 4 (Griffiths Collect.) A total of 112 men and boys..have been lost to Her Majesty's service through the disgraceful system of crimping. **1862** Commissioner Naughton (Police) in *AJHR* D-5 23 May 7 (Griffiths Collect.) I believe 'crimping', in its proper light, is not known in the Province. Many of the bush settlers have..been deluded by these runaways, who describe themselves as newly-arrived immigrants.

cronk, *a. Obs.* Also **kronk**. [Prob. f. Brit. dial. *crank* infirm, crooked, distorted, rather than an adaptation of (Yiddish) German *krank* ill.] CROOK in senses 'ill', 'bad'.
1. a. [AND 1891.] Ill, unwell, infirm (of men and animals, esp. horses); CROOK A 4.
  a1899 p.c. Prof. P.S. Ardern (Auckland, 1953) I don't remember hearing *cronk* after my schooldays (which ended in 1899), nor any other sense than 'ill'. I suggest a derivation from a Yiddish pronunciation of German *krank*, as does Morris. **1906** *Truth* 17 Mar. 3 [Christchurch corresp.] Eventually he took ill and died..and before his death he was in a very cronk state, being practically [comatose]. **1933** *Press* (Christchurch) (Acland Gloss.) 7 Oct. 15 *Cronk.*—Ill, not at all well.

b. [AND 1890.] Crooked, counterfeit, spurious. Cf. CROOK A 1.
  1905 *Truth* 23 Sept. 5 The swindling wool-kings of the Canterbury Plains who make up cronk bales of wool and palm them off..as the best. **1906** *Ibid.* 4 Aug. 8 Yet this stuff [*sc.* a patent medicine] is sold..as the genuine article, and every week you will see it advertised in big type, and backed up with a lot of cronk testimonials. *Ibid.* 8 Sept. 3 Getting a good fiver for a cronk tenner.

c. In various senses in context: bad; inferior; not genuine; ill-considered; worthless.
  1905 *Truth* 24 June 1 And the financing of the Bank of New Zealand has been the cronkest thing in financial history. *Ibid.* 9 Sept. 8 So many sly grog shops about ladling out kronk stuff warranted to kill at a thousand yards. *Ibid.* 7 Oct. 5 The Public Works Committee ought to drive this cronk notion out of their brain-boxes for good. *Ibid.* 4 Nov. 4 Some cronk-craniumed cove. **c1930** *Whitcombe's Etym. Dict. Aust.-NZ Suppl.* 3 *cronk a.* cranky; unsteady; of racehorses, unfit to run;-sl. dishonestly obtained. [Ger. krank, sick, ill] **1941** BAKER *NZ Slang* 62 *Cronk*, sick, worthless, or illegal.

2. As a predicative adjective in the phr. **to go cronk**, to go bad, to go 'astray' (morally); to 'go off the rails'.
  1905 *Truth* 19 Aug. 6 Help save the country from going completely cronk. **1906** *Ibid.* 3 Nov. 5 There are plenty of girls named Selina about, which is not wonderful, but what is so is that so many of them go cronk.

crook, *a.* [Prob. an abbrev. of *crooked* bent, not straight, hence dishonestly come by, [etc.] (see OED *crooked* 3 b): poss. influenced by several words similar in form or range of meaning: *cronk* (associated with the first recorded use of *crook* in AND), or Brit. dial. *crock* a broken-down ewe or horse, a sick or injured human; or orig. US *crook* a swindler. See also CROOKED *a.* 1 below.]
A. In attributive use, and in predicative use after the verb 'to be'.
1. a. [AND 1898.] Dishonest, crooked; wrong or wrongful (of a trick, business, etc.); occas., immoral.
  1905 *Truth* 29 Aug. 4 One or two of the head officials..seem to be also agents for private companies. If this is so we wouldn't be surprised if things are crook. *Ibid.* 4 Nov. 5 He has interviewed Dwyer..in connection with this crook conviction but has been ordered out of the office every time. **1910** *Ibid.* 15 Jan. 5 The poor plucked pigeon of a punter..imagines he is capable of holding his own against the 'smarties' who take up 'crook' pony racing as a livelihood. **1916** ANZAC *On Anzac Trail* 44 They were ignominiously herded in, protesting..in lurid language against what they styled 'a crook trick'. **1928** SMYTH *Jean of Tussock Country* 78 'I reckon, though he don't let on, that he knows all about station work. If that don't make him queer and crook I'd like to know what does!' **1936** SARGESON *Conversation with Uncle* 18 He'd pulled a horse and got disqualified. They said it was a crook business right through like they say all racing is. **1951** PARK *Witch's Thorn* 52 'That Georgie Wi must be a crook cow,' whispered his fellow penitents. 'Look at the time he's in there [*sc.* a confessional box]!' *Ibid.* 93 'I done something crook, Dad, I hit her.' **1962** WEBBER *Look No Hands* 25 Point is, how *does* a joker register a protest about buying crook articles at a crook price?

b. Dishonestly obtained or produced.
  1907 *Truth* 21 Sept. 5 A Chow on a deserted goldfield can always show colo[u]r, and if it is not on a deserted field, the Chow, too, can always be found on the 'cross' (viz.) buying crook stuff. **1910** *Ibid.* 12 Mar. 7 I told them I couldn't have crook stuff on my place, and he carted them [*sc.* potatoes] over to Maurice O'Connor's. **1919** *Hawkes Bay Herald* 9 Oct. 5 Some 'crook' totalisator tickets got into circulation at the Hastings races yesterday.

2. [AND 1900.] Of events, situations, work or objects, bad or badly made, ill-fitting; unfortunate, unpleasant, unsatisfactory; of persons, inferior, unpleasant. See also *crook spin* (SPIN *n.* 2 a).
  1906 PICARD *Ups & Downs* 33 That's dead crook. Look here, I'll write to the War cry about it. **1915** PILLING *Anzac Memory* (1933) 62 Had a very crook night, sickness, cramp, dysentery. **1929** SMYTH *Girl From Mason Creek* 163 'Cow of a job,' he muttered... 'It's a bit crook for yer.' *Ibid.* 76 His temper's that crook. **1930** LAWLOR in *NZ Short Stories* 176 'Crook health and crook times,' he explained in a small asthmatic voice. **1941** *NZEF Times* 22 Dec. 24 'Soldier, didn't you notice my uniform?' Recruit: 'Yes, it's crook all right, but look at what they gave me.' **1945** GASKELL *All Part of the Game* (1978) 43 Isn't it crook about Keith and Gordon [being killed]? **1964** MORRIESON *Came a Hot Friday* (1981) 110 'This is the crookest road I've ever struck,' said Cyril negotiating a fern-draped hairpin bend. **1968** SLATTER *Pagan Game* 161 This is crook beer. I'll be glad when I've had enough. **a1974** SYDER & HODGETTS *Austral. & NZ Eng.* (TS) 233 *Crook*. An unsatisfactory situation which irritates the speaker. 'Well, this is a crook sort of a turnout—the doctor was supposed to be here this morning.'

3. Of a thing (including a part of a human body), 'dud', disabled, damaged, out of order, broken.
  1915 Duncan in Boyack *Behind the Lines* 2 May (1989) 39 My knees very crook too and I am sore all over. **1917** in **1939** MILLER *Camps, Tracks & Trenches* 52 The rifle issued to me was a crook one that fired high and left. **1938** HYDE *Nor Yrs. Condemn* 106 'You at the war?' 'That's where I got my crook arm... That's where I buggered up this arm.' **1945** MACDONALD *Away from Home* 151 That awful word 'crook'—how they loved it. It was 'Sister, me arm's crook'; or 'Gee, I've come over all crook.' **1960** CRUMP *Good Keen Man* 45 It saves you from getting the crook guts, boy. **1993** *Sunday Star* (Auckland) 16 May B 3 I thought the phone line was a bit crook.

4. [AND 1908.] Ill, out of sorts; injured.
  [*Note*] Of the approx. 30 responses in the secondary schools' questionnaire (1951–84) all but 3 recorded *crook* as a synonym for *ill*. See also *feel crook* B 1 below.
  1917 in Miller *Camps, Tracks & Trenches* (1939) 42 Crook with dysentery all day. **1929** SMYTH *Girl from Mason Creek* 52 You're a bit crook about the eyes. **1948** BALLANTYNE *Cunninghams* (1976) 60 [He] wasn't feeble-minded because he was crook... Maybe he'd feel better by Christmas. **1959** SLATTER *Gun in My Hand* 34 I wasn't there. I was out crook at the time. **1960** HILLIARD *Maori Girl* 124 Boy, you were sure out to it. I thought at the time, 'By crikey, I bet she's crook tomorrow.' **1972** MITCHELL *Pavlova Paradise* 182 *crook:* State of health after eating local food. **1987** VIRTUE *Redemption of Elsdon Bird* (1988) 28 'Mrs Nation must be real crook the way she carried on,' Elsdon said... 'She's a bit crook in the head.'

B. In predicative use with verbs other than the verb 'to be'.

1. [AND 1908.] Indicating illness, bad health, esp. as **to feel (get, look) crook**, to feel, become

or look ill, sick or unhealthy. Occas. as **to go crook** (see quot. 1980).
   1903 Bill Reardon's roadman's diary 17 Feb. in *Alfredton* (1987) 162 Came from hospital to Alfredton to day, feeling very crook. **1916** *Oil Sheet* (Troopship pub.) Dec. 7 I've just been vaccinated, and am feeling pretty crook. **1937** Marsh *Vintage Murder* 116 'He was looking horribly crook'. 'Ill?' asked Alleyn cautiously. 'Too right, sir.' **1947** Davin *For Rest of Our Lives* 199 'Poor old Frank. He's not what he was.' 'Yes, he looks bloody crook.' **1963** Bacon *In the Sticks* 180 To feel crook is to feel unwell; to be pretty crook is to be extremely ill. **1976** Wilson *Pacific Star* 136 It made me feel pretty crook when she told me. **1980** Marsh *Photo-Finish* 31 'Take the dog... The boss give it to her. Well, it goes crook and they get a vet and he reckons it's hopeless and it ought to be put out of its misery. So *she* goes crook. Screechin' and moanin'.' **1992** *Listener* 4 May 38 Can you assure me..that in order to safeguard my profit margin, enough Kiwis will continue to get, as you say, crook?

2. [AND 1910.] Indicating anger, vexation, frustration, esp. as **to go (off) crook (at**, occas. **on**, see quot. 1933), to become angry (at, with), to 'go off (at)'; to complain vehemently.
   1917 Fraser *in* Boyack *Behind the Lines* (1989) 184 Well of course the chap went crook at them for pushing him around. **1917** *Chron. NZEF* 3 Oct. 86 Many of his friends went crook whilst acquaintances remained neutral. **a1927** Anthony *Me and Gus* in *Gus Tomlins* (1977) 80 He had been rambling about since dusk looking for me... When he heard me answer he started to go crook. **1933** Prudence Cadey *Broken Pattern* 197 If Phoebe's gone crook at you..she's had some good reason for it. *Ibid.* 199 It's a queer thing the way the law goes crook on a chap for a natural instinct like assault. **1947** Davin *For Rest of Our Lives* 116 They'd all been going crook something awful about the cold. **1950** Sutton-Smith *Our Street* 77 They would go off crook at him. **1959** Slatter *Gun in My Hand* 14 Annie was always going crook about it and finally she drove us out with shrill vehemence. **1962** Hori *Half-gallon Jar* 53 The boss who owns the big flash Jaguar looks plurry crook because the production manager has just bought the Cadillac. **1987** Sinclair *Rail* 128 The guards were very tolerant and only occasionally 'went crook' when the van was cluttered with sleeping bags.

3. In the phr. **to go crook (on)**, to go bad (on a person), to deteriorate, to cease functioning adequately, to break down.
   1929 Smyth *Girl from Mason Creek* 149 Got to have some cove massage me arms so's they won't go crook on me. **1937** Marsh *Vintage Murder* 165 'Pardon, It's gone crook on my digestion.' Berry doubled up. **1943** *NZEF Times* 19 July 5 On sick parade with a toe that looked as if it was going to go crook. **a1964** Texidor in *In Fifteen Minutes* (1987) 152 They have to send for the doctor when they're ill, and you'll see, if the fridge goes crook they'll send for me. **1993** O'Sullivan *Let the River Stand* 42 He said he was collecting them for a sow that had gone crook on him.

4. Indicating an unpleasant or dishonest result, or deteriorating function.
   1934 Scanlan *Winds of Heaven* 78 Surely they don't expect to win all that on her in one race, unless Pencarrow is running crook. **1945** Henderson *Gunner Inglorious* 24 A cigarette first thing in the morning, before a cup of tea, tastes crook.

5. Indicating deterioration in personal relationships as **to be in crook with** (a person), to be lowered in the estimation of, or on bad terms with, another, to be in another's 'bad books'; **to put** (one) **crook (or in crook) with**, to lower a person's standing, reputation, etc. in the estimation of another.
   1951 Young in *Listener Short Stories* (1978) 20 Stone the crows. I've got no monkey suit. I dont want to put you in crook, boy, but... **1959** Slatter *Gun in My Hand* 91 Got a snitch on me and put me in crook with the boss. **1965** Shadbolt *Among Cinders* 202 Right now he's in crook with his bosses in Wellington on account of him being too lenient on the after-hours liquor trade round here. **a1974** Syder & Hodgetts *Austral. & NZ Eng.* (TS) 895 *To put (one) in crook with (someone)*. To refer to a person, to his disadvantage, with the third person. 'You'd made it look as if I'd been having a good time with Val while she was away. You silly bastard, now you've put me in crook with her.'

6. Indicating wrong (occas. deceitful) advice, **to put** (one) **crook**, to put (one) on the wrong track, to lead (one) astray.
   1960 Radio 2ZB Wellington: quizmaster Selwyn Toogood to a contestant who had given a wrong answer: 'The audience put you crook, boy.' **1961** Crump *Hang On a Minute Mate* 86 We'll follow the pack-horse from here on and hope he doesn't put us crook. **1965** Shadbolt *Among the Cinders* 187 He's put us crook. That's not Gum Bay. **1995** Crump *Bushwoman* 154 That was Barry's advice and he has never put me crook.

crook, *n.* [A survival of obs. Brit. dial. or shipbuilding technical usage: see OED 5 c (quots. 1802, 1806).] A naturally in-curved piece of timber.
   1982 Sansom *In Grip of Island* 36 It was an established custom to go out looking for crooks in the bush. 'Crook' is a word that needs some defining. It can be a rogue, or in this case, a natural bend from either a suitable broadleaf or totara tree... A planned new dinghy or fishing boat would begin with the procuring of a natural bend or crook from the bush. **1987** Massey *Woodturning in NZ* 93 *Crook* A tree trunk with a natural curve. (Noun) To warp longitudinally in board form. (Verb)

crooked, *a.* ?/krŏkt/ Wrong, astray; angry. Cf. crook B 2.
   c1872 Whitworth *Spangles & Sawdust* 5 I was down there with Old Ashmore's lot, doing the trampoline, and so on; but things was very quizby. Everything went crooked somehow, and the gorger had a hawful cramp in his kick. **1961** Crump *Hang On a Minute Mate* 62 When I saw the [small] size of it I went a bit crooked on him.

crookie. [f. crook *a.* + -ie.] Someone or something 'crook' in various senses of crook A.
   1953 *Here & Now* Mar. 14 A gammey leg and one glass eye... The good eye always looked at the cash, But the crookie looked you full in the gob. **1962** Crump *One of Us* 104 These West Coast publicans are usually a pretty good team but there's a crookie in every bunch of blokes.

cropper. *Obs.* [OED, locally in US and elsewhere; DARE 1 =sharecropper.] See quots. 1883, 1885.
   1883 Pash *Report on NZ* 5 Croppers..pay a price per acre for the privilege of taking off a crop of corn after the land has been fed a couple of years in clover or grass. **1885** Vincent *40,000 miles* 217 We passed a few huts and tumble-down shanties [in Canterbury] belonging to 'croppers', or men who break up and 'crop' the land for a couple of years, at a rent of 10 shillings per acre, after which it is sown in grass for the owner, the cropper moving elsewhere. **1891** Wallace *Rural Econ.* 285 The land [near Oamaru] is let for one crop of wheat..to a class of contractors called 'croppers'.

Cross. [AND 1872.] As **the Cross,** abbrev. of Southern Cross 1.
   1847 [see Southern Cross 1]. **1897** *TrNZI* XXIX. 147 Midnight is past, the Cross begins to bend. **1905** Thomson *Bush Boys* 135 The brilliant Cross looked down in resplendent state from our Southern sky. **1920** *Quick March* 10 July 41 It was Ack Ack Emma, A Moon or two swayed in the welkin, And the Cross resembled many 'milky' ways. **1952** [see Southern Cross 1].

crossbred, *n.* and *a.*

A. *n.* [Used elsewhere but of great commercial significance (and recorded earliest) in NZ.]

1. Also **x-bred**. A sheep of the result of crossing two or more breeds, lines or strains, a 'two-way cross' being made up from crossing two basic breeds, a 'three-way cross', from three; the wool from such a sheep.
   [**1851** Weld *Hints to Intending Sheep-farmers* 8 The Merino has the more valuable wool, being finer, and particularly superior in the 'skirts', which are remarkably deficient in the crossed sheep.] **c1875** Meredith *Adventuring in Maoriland* (1935) 41 Most of the crossbreds would have about an inch thick of fat on the ribs. **1879** Kiernan *Diary* 1 Feb. in Guthrie-Smith *Tutira* (1921) 125 Put X-breds in Newton block, and T.S. took the Mer[ino] wethers over Papa creek. **1883** Pash *Report on NZ* 8 11,700 crossbreds, bred from Merino ewes by Lincoln rams. **1892** *NZ Official Handbook* 121 The dapper little Southdowns flourish wherever crossbreds thrive. **1915** [see half-bred B]. **1922** Perry *Sheep Farming* 65 The class of cross-bred chiefly in evidence varies considerably in different parts of the Dominion. **1934** *Feilding Star* 6 Feb. 7 The same could not be said of crossbreds..the majority of which met with disappointing bidding [at the woolsale]. **1936** Belshaw et al. *Agric. Organiz. in NZ* 415 The term 'cross-bred' is used to define any long-woolled sheep which has been produced by..mating cross-breds with each other. **1982** *Agric. Gloss.* (MAF) 15 *Crossbred*: The result of crossing two breeds, lines or strains...*Criss-cross*: Crossbred produced after a period of using each of the two parent breeds alternately. **1985** Bremner *Woolscours of NZ* 9 *Crossbred* cross of coarse-woolled breeds.

2. *fig.* Alluding to other forms of hybridization.
   1889 *Zealandia* I. 15 I hate your milk-and-water crossbreds between a Sunday School pic-nic and a Methody prayer meeting.

B. *adj.* Of or pertaining to cross-bred sheep or their wool; see also quot. 1982.
   1879 Kiernan *Diary* 23 Mar. in Guthrie-Smith *Tutira* (1921) 129 600 ewes, 100 wethers, and 800 cross-bred wethers. **1892** *NZ Official Handbook* 121 *Crossbred Sheep*: Those bred from Merino ewes and long-wool rams are the most suitable for the frozen-meat trade. **1900** *Egmont Star* (Hawera) 25 Aug. 17 There's a tweed spun from crossbred wool... It's out of fashion now, and we cannot sell any of it. **1922** Perry *Sheep Farming* 65 The half-bred ewe [*sc.* obtained by crossing a long-woolled ram..on the Merino ewe] is then crossed with a ram of a mutton breed to obtain the cross-bred ewe, which is the chief type of sheep found on the majority of farms in Canterbury. **1955** Bowen *Wool Away* 3 Fine-wool sheep, expecially Merinos, are much slower than crossbred sheep. **1982** *Agric. Gloss.* (MAF) 54 Crossbred wool: Type of wool grown by Romney, Perendale, Coopworth, Leicester, and Lincoln sheep and their crosses with other than Merino or part-Merino breeds.

crosscut, *v.* Also **cross-cut**. [Spec. use of *crosscut* to cut across or transversely: see OED *v.* 1;

CROSS-CUT

EDD.] *trans.* and *intr.* To cut transversely through (a log or tree-stem) with a cross-cut saw. Also as *vbl. n.*

1844 PARNELL *Notebook & Farm Diary* (ATLMS) Cross-cutting Mairi. **1859** *Richmond-Atkinson Papers* (1960) I. 476 The rest goes for cross cutting and heaping [logs]. **1862** CHUDLEIGH *Diary* 9 Dec. (1950) 69 Did a little to a great many things. One was to milk some cows, make some crackers, cross-cut and chop some fire-wood. **1874** BAINES *Edward Crewe* 170 A bushman..entered into a contract with me to fall, cross-cut, and roll handy to the creek's side 200,000 feet of timber. *Ibid.* 174 [He was] falling and cross-cutting logs, from ten to twenty-five feet in length. **1881** INGLESON *Battle of Life* 74 Often I have cross-cutted with a handsaw fallen logs a foot or more through. **1894** *NZ Official Year-book* 331 The trees are felled and cross-cut into suitable lengths for conversion, the logs being conveyed to the mill. **1948** HENDERSON *Taina* 26 It was cross-cut into three lengths and then sawn up into boards and scantlings. **1953** REED *Story of Kauri* 162 Two good men might crosscut a four-feet log in less than a couple of hours. **1961** CRUMP *Hang On a Minute Mate* 32 Jack and I were cross-cutting in the last stand of kauri.

cross-cut, *n.*

1. [Used elsewhere but recorded earliest in NZ: see OED *cross-cut* 5.] A short form of CROSSCUT SAW.

1848 *Otago Journal* III. 46 Pit saws; whit saws; and cross-cuts, and files for ditto. **1860** BUTLER in Jones *Samuel Butler* (1919) I. 82 Woolbales Sewing twine Grave stone..Files, for crosscut and handsaw. **1919** WAITE *New Zealanders at Gallipoli* 2 The bushman put away his crosscut and axe. **1946** *Tararua Tramper* May 7 Material carried in from the road included..grubber pick, shovels, mawl, steel wedges, four cross-cuts. **1960** ROGERS *Long White Cloud* 91 Those blokes walking out to the gig with a fence-puller in one hand and a cross-cut in the other.

2. In the phr. **to be on the cross-cut** *obs.*, to be angry or at odds, or crossgrained (with a person).

1902 SATCHELL *Land of Lost* 69 Me an' your mate..had a bit of a barney some days ago. I thought I'd just step round and bury the hatchet... Yes, 'tain't the square thing to be on the cross cut at Xmas time.

crosscut saw. [f. US and Brit. provincial use; see Mathews 1645; EDD; OED *crosscut a.* 1.] A long two-man saw for cutting across the grain of a log.

1774 FORSTER *Resolution Jrnl.* 19 Oct. (1982) III. 672 One tree was cut down with a crosscut-Saw, which we had left standing. **1815** MARSDEN *Lett. & Jrnls.* (1932) 138 [Heading] A List of Articles Wanted for the Use of the *Active* and the Settlement in New Zealand, 1815. Twenty dozen tommy hawkes..eight pit and four crosscut saws. **1826** SHEPHERD *Journal* 8 Mar. in Howard *Rakiura* (1940) 359 All hands..proceeded immediately to cut down the timber and with the use of cross cut saws and axes cut down 15 trees before dinner. **1840** POLACK *Manners & Customs* I. 168 A stage is generally erected about three feet from the ground, when, with a cross-cut saw, the party (chiefs included,) work in turn until the tree is levelled. **1857** HURSTHOUSE *NZ* II. 331 The trees are thrown with the x [*sic*] cut saw and American axe. **1877** PRATT *Col. Experiences* 16 The cross-cut saw..had a great deal of what is technically called 'set' upon [its teeth], being especially adapted for cross-cutting green..white-pine logs. **1900** *Egmont Star* (Hawera) 2 June 17 A trial of the thin black racer cross-cut saw..was a success.

cross-cutter. [Used elsewhere but recorded earliest in NZ.] One (of usu. two persons) operating a crosscut saw.

1902 *NZ Illustr. Mag.* V 374 Having severed the head from the trunk, the crosscutter's work is considered accomplished, and they pass on to another tree. **1936** 'A' in Rust *Whangarei & Dist. Early Reminisc.* 163 Hundreds of bushmen, loggers, jackers, bullock-drivers, cross-cutters and rafters were employed..in the different sawmills. **1953** REED *Story of Kauri* 156 Good crosscutters can tell to an inch where the tree will land.

crow, *n.*[1]

I. Transf. use of *crow* a northern hemisphere bird of the genus *Corvus.* **1.** Also **bush, native** (or **New Zealand**) **crow.** KOKAKO.

1835 YATE *NZ* (1970) 64 *Kokako*; called, by some, the New-Zealand crow. **1849** TAYLOR *Journal* (ATLTS) VI. 37 The natives have a saying that the huia stole the plumage of the kokako, the native crow, and gave its own tail instead. **1855** [see KOKAKO 1]. **1868** HARPER *Lett. from NZ* 20 July (1914) 130 [The Otira Pass area] is also the haunt of the New Zealand crow, a shapely bird, purple, shot with black, and reddish yellow rings under the eyes, very tame. **1871** MONEY *Knocking About NZ* 33 The crow being very similar to our black bird, and seldom flying further than a few yards at a time, is generally found in low bushes, hopping from bough to bough. *Ibid.* 43 I always had..a couple of wood-hens and ducks, or bush-crows, suspended from the ridge-pole of my tent. **1888** BULLER *Birds NZ* I. xvi I have accordingly commenced my history of our Avifauna with an account of the New-Zealand Crow. **1896** HARPER *Pioneer Work* 41 If one is hard pushed for food, the smaller birds, such as the crow, tui, paraquet, and saddle-backs, are all acceptable. **1904** HUTTON & DRUMMOND *Animals NZ* 58 The note of the New Zealand Crow is in pleasing contrast with the harsh and dissonant croak of the Old Country Crow. **1922** *Auckland Weekly News* 3 Aug. 17 Native crows—the Maori's kokako— which were very plentiful a few years ago, are being driven further back. **1936** GUTHRIE-SMITH *NZ Naturalist* 57 The New Zealand Crow..were still to find [in Nelson province]. **1945** BEATTIE *Maori Place-names Canterbury* 64 The matuku, or bittern..is not mentioned, nor is the kokako or crow. **1966** *Encycl. NZ* II. 235 Commonly called the native crow, the kokako does not belong to the crow family, but is, instead, a member of a family of birds peculiar to New Zealand, the Callaeidae, or wattle-birds. **1973** SARGESON *Once Is Enough* 14 Higher up still there was the ding dong of the New Zealand crow.

2. With a modifier: **blue (blue-wattled,** or **North Island), orange-wattled** (or **South Island**).

(1) **blue (blue-wattled,** or **North Island) crow.** *Callaeas cinerea wilsoni* (fam. Callaeidae), KOKAKO 2 (1).

1871 HUTTON *Catalogue Birds NZ* 16 Glaucopis wilsoni... Blue-wattled Crow. Kokako. **1890** *Otago Witness* (Dunedin) 17 Apr. 18 The blue-wattled crow is of a dark bluish-grey colour, with the lower part of the back and abdomen tinged with rufous-brown. **1904** *TrNZI* XXXVI. 119 Sir Walter Buller says..that the Blue Crow..lays a single egg, and..leaves the care of the chick to the Popokatea. **1904** HUTTON & DRUMMOND *Animals NZ* 57 The North Island Crow.—Kokako. **1921** GUTHRIE-SMITH *Tutira* (1926) 113 Thus I learnt that the Blue Wattled Crow..was at one time common also on Tutira. **1946** [see KOKAKO 1]. **1957** MONCRIEFF *NZ Birds* (5edn.) 51 Blue-wattled Crow or North Island Crow... Haunts, wooded hills of North Island. Flight a succession of hops. **1988** MORRIS & SMITH *Wild South* 28 His song, combined with images of shafts of sunlight and early morning mist in the forest, and the 'blue-wattled crow' singing his own song, gave a deeper feeling to the scenes we'd filmed. **1990** [see KOKAKO 2 (1)].

(2) **orange-wattled** (or **South Island**) **crow.** *Callaeas cinerea cinerea* (fam. Callaeidae), KOKAKO 2 (2).

1871 HUTTON *Catalogue Birds NZ* 16 Glaucopis cinerea... Orange-wattled Crow. **1882** POTTS *Out in Open* 194 The Orange-wattled Crow or wattle-bird..still seems to be an almost unknown bird. **1893** *TrNZI* XXV. 56 *Glaucopis cinerea*... (The South Island Crow.) **1904** HUTTON & DRUMMOND *Animals NZ* 60 The South Island Crow, besides frequenting the bush, haunts open places and light scrub. **1914** GUTHRIE-SMITH *Mutton Birds & Other Birds* [iii] He, too, was an enthusiast, and even waist deep in water chilled with melted hail..was still able to note the discovery of a pair of Orange-Wattled Crows in the flooded scrub. **1923** *NZJST* VI. 97 Orange-wattled Crow. With the spread of settlement the diminution of the numbers of this tame species was almost inevitable. **1936** GUTHRIE-SMITH *NZ Naturalist* 175 The species we hoped to make friends with [off Stewart Island] were the Snipe..the South Island Crow..., and the South Island Thrush. **1944** *NZEF Times* 4 Sept. 10 The orange-wattled crow is sometimes mistaken for [the huia] by trampers. **1957** MONCRIEFF *NZ Birds* (5edn.) 50 Orange-wattled or South Island Crow... Travels Indian file through bush by hops, carrying wattles compressed under jaw. **1985** *Reader's Digest Book NZ Birds* 303 South Island Kokako... orange wattled crow.

3. *Obs.* In the phr. **not to know** (someone) **from a Maori crow,** not to recognize.

c**1900** Nelson district p.c. Miss McKenzie (1952). I didn't know him from a Maori crow.

II. In transf. uses of *crow* a black bird. **4.** In exclamations of surprise, disbelief, exasperation or disgust, **(God) spare, stiffen** [AND 1932: poss. from *stiffen* 'kill'], **stone (stun) the crows** [AND 1927].

1917 *Chron. NZEF* 17 Oct. 114 Oh, God stiffen the — crows. Strike me dead, and pink and blue and blind and pretty. **1938** *Auckland Weekly News* 23 Nov. 96 Spare the crows! Come to buy that fight have yer! **1944** FULLARTON *Troop Target* 65 God stun the crows! Look who's here! **1951** PARK *Witch's Thorn* 111 His heart was jumping delightedly. Spare the crows, what a thing to tell the gang! **1951** YOUNG in *Listener Short Stories* (1978) 20 Stone the crows. I've got no monkey suit. **1953** *Here & Now* Nov.–Dec. 40 God stiffen the crows, I thought, even the lowest swagger..would spit in your eye if you offered him clothes like that. **1960** KEINZLY *Tangahano* 110 God stiffen the crows! Here, eat this and get in to your brother. **1960** HILLIARD *Maori Girl* 150 [Man thinks] Stone the crows, would you believe it? Coming out on a night like this in white shoes! God! **1962** HORI *Half-gallon Jar* 3 'Stiffen the crows,' I say, 'that is good stuff.' **1963** MORRIESON *Scarecrow* 19 Stone the crows, if she isn't the aunt as well of this poor girl that's gone and got her throat cut. **1981** ANDERSON *Both Sides of River* 76 'What the bloody hell are you talking about?' he guffawed in sarcasm. 'Stone the blasted crows, I'd walk that trickle.' **1981** STEWART *Hot & Copper Sky* 188 'Gawd stiffen the crows.'

5. *Obs.* [f. the resemblance to a crow's appearance of the former standard girls' school uniform of black or navy gym frock and black cotton stockings.] A male (usu. adolescents' or schoolboys') contemptuous name for a girl (-friend), a young woman; or collectively, girls or women in general. Compare BRUSH *n.*[2]

c**1941** *Crow* known to Ed. for, in particular, St Mary's College (Wellington) girls in their uniform of black gym frock and stockings. **1951** 14 M 141 St

Bede's, Chch 28 [M4] 'crow' **1953** Baxter in *Here & Now* Sept. 27 In the sad New Zealand summer when the rainclouds clog the sky and in the quiet boozer roost my loving crow and I. **1974** Morrieson *Predicament* (1981) 203 You might get yourself a crow out there, Merv. Some of the crows out there might want to come back with you.

crow, *n.*² *Farming*. Also **crower**. [Fig. use of *crow*, or a playful allusion to a *crow's-nest*.] The worker on a haystack (or grainstack) who pitches sheaves to the stacker or stack-builder.

1885 *Tokarahi Estate Diary* in Martin *Forgotten Worker* (1990) 104 [In March they began harvesting.] Six drays leading in..3 crowers, 3 forkers, & six draymen... For each stack (1 builder, 1 crower, 2 draymen, 1 forker). **1888** Bradshaw *NZ of Today* 171 When harvest came..he ought to have taken his place as 'crow' upon the stack. [1888 *Note*] A 'crow' is the man who pitches the sheaves to the stacker. **1913** Carr *Country Work* 11 Haymaking... A 'crow' is also employed, whose work consists of passing the forkfulls thrown up by the carter to the stacker. **a1927** Anthony *Me & Gus* in *Gus Tomlins* (1977) 72 Gus says he wouldn't mind being crow, if he got any credit for it. **1946** Miller *There Was Gold* 134 I found keen enjoyment in forking [the new-mown hay] to the stack and keeping the crow busy spreading the hay along the top. Generally the boss was the crow. **1956** Dare *Rouseabout Jane* 185 When it came to stacking the corn, my job was to be 'crow'. **1964** *Weekly News* (Auckland) 22 Jan. 37 While the stack [of oats] was building the sheaves were passed to the builder by the 'crow'. **1973** Fernandez *Tussock Fever* 145 Back at the stack these [sheaves] were then forked off [the truck] to the crow who fed them to the stacker. **1984** Kerse *Knapdale Run* 146 At the stack the [dray] load was forked to the 'crow' who in turn moved the sheaves to the builder.

crow, *n.*³ *Obs.* [Poss. a pun on *crow-bar*, or a fig. use of *crows-nest*.] As **the crow**, the bar-counter of a hotel.

1887 *NZ Mail* (Wellington) 15 July 9 (NZ Slang) A few miscellaneous expressions are..'a cocktail', a coward; 'behind the crow', behind the bar, that is to be a barmaid or barman. **1909** *Truth* 25 Sept. 6 He used to keep the Eastern Hotel, but has been three years without a hostelry, and when sixpences cease to come across the 'crow' for three years, a financial gap is created. **1952** Meek *Station Days* 75 This shearer's roll and six quid as well..Went over the 'crow' at the bush hotel For a riotous non-stop jag. *Ibid.* 110 Crow: The counter in the bar of an hotel. **1957** *Press* (Christchurch) 17 Oct. 3 The Government of 1911 said that 'the crow' is no place for barmaids.

crow, *v.* [f. crow *n.*²] *intr.* In building a (hay)stack, to fork the sheaves (or hay) across to the stacker.

1913 Carr *Country Work* 13 Stacking.—The stacker is boss of the paddock... The only way to learn is to take on jobs at 'crowing'. **a1927** Anthony *Me and Gus* in *Gus Tomlins* (1977) 72 He usually ends up by putting Gus crowing for him on the stack—says he can keep an eye on him there. **1944** *Korero* (AEWS Background Bulletin) 10 Apr. 8 Instead [of stacking] you may 'crow'. **1966** Barry *In the Lee of the Hokonuis* 370 My first job was crowing, for a neighbour.

crower: see crow *n.*²

Crown. [*Attrib.* use of *crown* for the authority so symbolized.] In special Comb. in a sense 'pertaining to land tenure', esp. **Crown grant**, **Crown land. a.** As **Crown grant** [AND 1840], a grant of land to which the Crown has title, made to an individual or incorporation; the instrument validating such a grant.

1844 Shortland *Letter* 10 June in *Traditions & Superstitions* (1856) 309 And as the Commissioners may recommend the issue of Crown grants to lands..cases will probably occur where the lands may be resold. **1848** Wakefield *Handbook NZ* 297 The New Zealand Company has received a Crown grant, under the seal of the territory, dated 13th of April, 1846, of the portion of this District [of Otago]. **1851** *Richmond-Atkinson Papers* (1960) I. 82 The aforesaid two individuals have refused to cash up [their payment for the NZ Company section] until they receive a crown grant. **1868** Taylor *Past & Present of NZ* 116 He indignantly threw down the Crown grant and left, to become a leader of the king party. **1874** Bathgate *Col. Experiences* 202 The lessee is entitled to a 'Crown grant' or transfer of the freehold without further payment. **1892** *NZ Official Handbook* 284 On the fulfilment of conditions, which are five years' residence, the erection of a house, and the cultivation of one-third of the selection if open land, and one-fifth if bush-land, the Crown grant is issued.

Hence **crown-grant** *v.* [by back-formation f. the noun] *trans.*, to make a crown grant of (an area of land).

1899 Williams *Page from History* 9 [The land] is wretched stuff, not worth crown-granting.

b. As **Crown land** (also in *pl.*) [AND 1814], unalienated land to which the Crown has title.

1841 in Deans *Pioneers of Canterbury* (1937) 33 The Commissioners for the sale of Crown Lands in the colonies have since determined that a uniform price of £1 per acre is all that is to be asked for land in the new colonies. **1863** *Hearing before Waste Land Board* Feb. in Griffiths *King Wakatip* (1971) 99 Where the pre-emptive rights of a runholder interfere with the sale of Crown Lands, the Government has the power to disallow those rights. **1879** *Auckland Weekly News* 13 Sept. 8 [The judgement] embraces several important collateral points, such as..the 'extinction of native title', the distinction between 'Crown lands and the demesne lands of the Crown'. **1889** Kirk *Forest Flora* 155 The [gum-]digger pays no fee..for digging on open Crown lands. **1902** *Settler's Handbook NZ* 1 Of Crown lands there are available, roughly speaking, some 11,000,000 acres. **1937** *King Country Chronicle* 26 Jan. 4 The question of unpaid rates on Crown lands was brought to the notice of the Minister. **1970** Thomas *Way Up North* 29 With the exception of a few individuals engaged in raising cattle on unfenced Crown land..the whole population of the far north of New Zealand at the turn of the century depended on..kauri gum. **1989** *Dominion Sunday Times* (Wellington) 15 Oct. 13 Huts are frequently built on crown land or road reserve.

crown fern: see fern 2 (4).

crow's nest. *Obs. Canterbury local.* See quot. 1933.

1933 *Press* (Christchurch) (Acland Gloss.) 7 Oct. 15 *Crow's nest.*—Platform built on poles or in a cabbage tree from which a shepherd could see his sheep. C[row's] n[est]s were used on the old plains stations until the runs were fenced about 1860. **1946** Acland *Early Canterbury Runs* 17 On some of the plains stations 'crow's nests' were built—platforms on poles or up cabbage trees from which the shepherd could watch the sheep without disturbing them. **1949** Crawford *Sheep & Sheepmen Canterbury* 39 In order to disturb the sheep as little as possible..'crows nests', platforms on poles or in cabbage trees, were frequently built on the plains as look-out stations [for boundary keepers].

crud. *Tramping.* [Spec. use of slang *crud* (a var. of *curd*) something or someone dirty or unpleasant.] Cloud or mist.

1988 Pickering *Hills* 8 To cope with the rituals of tramping, its pains and camaraderie, a slang language has developed to suit... 'Crud' (cloud), 'bush-bash'.

cruise. *Forestry.* [f. US forestry use.] See quot.; also used as a verb.

1948 Jewell *Accounting in Timber Industry* 128 *Cruise.* Survey of forest land to locate timber and estimate quantities.

Hence **cruiser** *n.*, one who assesses the quantities of standing timber.

1961 Mackay *Puborama* 95 [Matai beer] went out of favour when 'cruisers' for the various timber mills complained that much good yellow pine was being ruined through the number of deep axe cuts and even auger holes in the standing trees.

crush. *Farming.* [AND 1872.] In full **crush-pen**. In a stockyard, a narrowing race, or pen narrowing in one end, for confining or controlling an animal or animals before drenching, branding, tailing, etc. See also crush-yard, *drafting pen* (drafting *vbl. n.* 2), forcing-pen.

1856 Roberts *Diary* 18 Dec. in Beattie *Early Runholding* (1947) 43 As there was no crush pen, or drafting race, we had to head rope those [cattle] requiring branding. **1892** Swanton *Notes on NZ* 124 The [unbroken] horses are put in a stockyard and there roped and driven into a crush, the head stalls and breaking rollers are put on. **1912** *NZJAg.* Jan. IV. 534 Can you please let me know the dimensions, structure, &c., of a crush-pen for cattle. **1931** Harper *Windy Island* (1934) 225 The lean-to in its turn was divided into crush-pens and a large receiving pen. **1949** Newton *High Country Days* 93 The 'crush'—a race perhaps ten yards in length and just wide enough for a grown beast to pass through... Beyond the [drafting] gate the race terminated in the crush itself, the end being blocked by a rudely constructed bail. **1950** *NZJAg.* July LXXXI. 7 *The crush or forcing pen(s)*: These are usually one or two long, small pens, frequently tapering at one end, and holding about 50 sheep. **1966** Sharpe *Fiordland Muster* 76 Dave's [stock-]yards consisted of two main pens and one small one, known as the 'Crush', into which calves could be driven for earmarking and castration. **1973** Wheeler *Hist. Sheep Stations NI* 14 [Caption] Rebuilding the cattleyards, showing the..cattle crush. **1989** Richards *Pioneer's Life* 26 All the ewes..would be mustered and sorted in the 'crush pen'.

Hence **crush** *v. trans.*, to confine (a beast) in a crush(-pen).

1962 Sharpe *Country Occasions* 63 He [*sc.* the farmer] has no yard into which he can crush a beast so that it has to stand still.

crusher: see *dag-crusher* (dag *n.*¹ 2), *shingle crusher* (shingle *n.*² 3 b).

crushing: see *fern-crushing* (fern 3 d).

crushings, *vbl. n. pl. Goldmining.* [Used elsewhere but recorded earliest in NZ: see OED *vbl. n.* 3.] Crushed metalliferous ore.

1868 *Shortland Town by Night* in Cooper *Digger's Diary* (1978) 31 Proprietors..are contributing to the working of some claims..or are drawing dividends from good 'crushings'. **1874** Baines *Edward Crewe* 266 [We] were now tired..with the poor return our crushings at this time yielded, and determined to abandon the mine.

Hence **crushing room**, the place on a mine site where ore is crushed to render it more susceptible to the extraction of metal.
  1898 'H.' *Grain of Gold* 5 They saunter into the roaring 'crushing room', and watch the hard quartz rock slowly passing under the relentless stampers.

crush-pen: see CRUSH.

crush-yard. [See OED *crush* n. 6 a, 1888 'Austral.'] A funnel-shaped stockyard designed to direct stock towards a narrow race for easier handling. Cf. CRUSH.
  1879 KIERNAN *Diary* in Guthrie-Smith *Tutira* (1921) 132 Got 482 sheep shorn, and would have done more but for the number of previously shorn sheep being mixed up with the woolly, making it necessary to fill the crush-yard more often. **1950** *NZJAg.* Apr. LXXX. 377 For handling large herds a crush yard is recommended.

crust, n.[1] [AND 1888.] Often as **a crust**, a living, a livelihood.
  1905 *Truth* 24 June 1 Billy Murphy [a boxer] now knocking out a crust in the butter country. **1906** PICARD *Ups & Downs* 7 He's a man for pushing ahead for a crust and not hanging round chewing hops. **1947** NEWTON *Wayleggo* 36 I was deer shooting for my crust. **1967** HENDERSON *Return to Open Country* 91 What have they got you doing for a crust these days? **1979** WILLIAMS *Skin Deep* 71 Vic's in his office..prior to accommodating any of the local work force determined to squander their credits of lethargy carefully accumulated during the average man's 'just making a crust' day. **1981** JOHNSTON *Fish Factory* 148 As long as..the sun rose..and gave them light to do something about earning a crust, they were happy.

crust, n.[2] *Obs.* [AND 1910.] A charge of vagrancy.
  1912 *Truth* 13 Jan. 7 As a consequence Albert, the mendicant, was charged with 'vag', otherwise known as 'the crust'.

crutch, n. [AND 1879, 1965 only.] A crutch-shaped wooden implement designed to submerge sheep during dipping.
  [**1881**] [see CRUTCH v.[2]]. **1916** *NZJAg.* Sept. XIII. 228 It is necessary to hold each lot of sheep in the bath for the time necessary to secure thorough immersion. This may be done..by the use of the crutch. **1933** [see CRUTCH v.[2]]. **1949** NEWTON *High Country Days* 102 Armed with a 'crutch' it was his job to duck each sheep. **1953** STRONACH *Musterer on Molesworth* 55 We had two men on the 'crutch' pushing the sheep's heads under, and seven men at the race. **1968** TOMLINSON *Remembered Trails* 11 We children [c1890s] used to plunge empty dip packets attached to a sheep crutch into a long swim sheep dip made of wood. **1986** RICHARDS *Off the Sheep's Back* 48 Dad was 'crutch' man and also responsible for timing each dip full of sheep. **1986** BROWN *Weaver's Apprentice* 87 Matthew walked with them [*sc.* the ewes], shoving their heads twice under the yellow liquid with a dipping crutch.

crutch, v.[1] [f. *crutch*, the usual term in NZ for the bifurcation of the hind legs of a sheep and the adjacent area; AND 1913.] *trans.* and *intr.* To remove wool from the hindquarters of a sheep. See also RING CRUTCH v.
  1913 [see CRUTCHING *vbl. n.*]. **1920** *NZJAg.* July XXI. 8 The keeping-lambs are crutched, branded, dipped. **1933** *Press* (Christchurch) (Acland Gloss.) 7 Oct. 15 *Crutch.*—(1) to cut away the wool round a sheep's tail and hind legs so that he will not foul himself. **1944** MARSH *Died in the Wool* 28 We're crutching now. **1955** BOWEN *Wool Away* 53 Sheep that are crutched heavily are usually fat-lamb ewes. **1975** HARPER *Eight Daughters* 43 The sheep were drafted, then crutched and dipped. **1989** *NZ Engl. Newsletter* III. 23 *crutch:* To cut away the wool from the tail and hind legs so that the sheep will not foul itself.

Hence **crutcher**, occas. **crutcher-and-dagger** [AND 1943], one who crutches sheep.
  1958 FAIRBURN & GLOVER *Poetry Harbinger* 21 A drunken swagger, a crutcher-and-dagger. **1964** DICK *High Country Family* 70 A room full of crutchers, rough diamonds all of them. **1978** FISHER *Dolphins & Killer Whales* 45 Ralph's attitude towards the..gangs of scrubcutters, shearers, crutchers..and dockers was quite different. **1989** RICHARDS *Pioneer's Life* 52 He spent the entire day..at the end of the shearing board watching the crutchers at work.

crutch, v.[2] *Obs.* [f. CRUTCH *n.:* see OED v.[1] 4 'Chiefly *Austral.* and *N.Z.*', 1886.] *trans.* To submerge (sheep) in a swim-dip with a crutch-like implement.
  1933 *Press* (Christchurch) (Acland Gloss.) 7 Oct. 15 *Crutch...* (2) When sheep are dipped they are shoved under with a thing like an inverted c[*rutch*]. This is called *crutching.* (3) The implement used for (2). **1940** STUDHOLME *Te Waimate* (1954) 117 One day whilst trying to 'crutch' (push under) some slippery-backed old ewe, my brother Geoffrey fell in amongst the sheep.

Hence **crutcher** n., one who with a crutch submerges (occas. early, scrubs the backs of) sheep in a dip or wash.
  [**1881**] BREMNER *Woolscours of NZ* (1985) 15 A description of an unidentified sheepstation in 1881 recorded that a twenty-two man gang..put through [the sheep-wash] 1250 sheep in a..day... The trough was divided into four partitions with a 'crutcher' at each... Four times each sheep was soaped, its back scrubbed with a crutch.

crutching, *vbl. n.*

1. a. The removal of wool and excrement from a sheep's hindquarters. Also occas. in a more limited sense, **crutch** (see quots. 1982, 1989). Also *attrib.*
  1913 *NZJAg.* Jan. VI. 577 Proper dipping, crutching, dagging, &c., are necessary; and if scouring be present care should especially be taken to keep the posterior parts clear of dung-clogged wool. **1920** MACDONALD *Australian & NZ Sheepfarming* 156 Cleanliness by way of proper dipping, crutching, etc., assists towards suppression of the fly. **1936** BELSHAW et al. *Agric. Organiz. in NZ* 710 The wool removed by crutching is of low value and the amount per clip is usually small. **1955** BOWEN *Wool Away* 53 Heavy crutching can spoil the fleece when it comes to shearing time. **1966** MIDDLETON in *NZ Short Stories* (1976) 128 But aside from shearing and crutching times, life was good at the station. **1982** *Agric. Gloss.* (MAF) 49 *Crutching*: Removal of wool from the tail end of sheep. *Ring crutch*—removal of minimal area of wool from around the vulva and anus. **1989** RICHARDS *Pioneer's Life* 52 Crutching consisted in catching the ewes in the catching pen..clipping the wool from any that were getting wool-blind, two blows on the belly above the udder, a complete crutch and a full blow above the tail.

b. Usu. collective *pl.* The wool removed by crutching. Occas. (in *attrib.* use) *sing.*
  1929 *NZJST* X. 326 A star bale sold at a crutching sale made 101/4d. **1936** BELSHAW et al. *Agric. Organiz. in NZ* 710 'Crutchings' are seldom if ever classed except by the wool brokers when the wool is sent to them for binning. **1966** BARRY *In Lee of Hokonuis* 373 He recalls a bale of crutchings from Friedlander, weighing 950 lbs. **1987** HUTCHINS *Tall half-backs* 79 We used to roam the district..picking up wool bales, crutchings and dags. **1990** MCKAY *Baxter* 86 Baxter's duties..were with the sheep, drafting, and picking over crutchings.

2. *Shoplifters.* See quot.
  1994 *Dominion* (Wellington) 8 Aug. 9 Clothes, especially jeans, are always vulnerable... It's under the coat, under the skirt – 'crutching' – and they're off.

Cuba Street Yank. *Wellington. Obs.* [From *Cuba Street* one of Wellington's main streets.] One who parades a main street with the (reputedly) dressy confidence of an American serviceman. See also *Queen Street Yank* (QUEEN STREET 2).
  c**1947–52** *Cuba Street Yank* was a Wellington name for a 'wide-boy', often in distinctive dress, who spent the evening promenading various streets, or holding court in milk-bars. (Ed.) **1952** *Evening Post* (Wellington) 6 Feb. 14 [Columnist 'Candid Comment' on narrow-legged trousers] 'Cuba Street Yank': I don't mind them narrow, but I sure wouldn't want them that narrow.

cuckoo. [Transf. use of northern hemisphere *cuckoo*, *Cuculus* genus.]

1. Also **New Zealand cuckoo**. Applied to two migratory birds of the fam. Cuculidae which lay their eggs in the nests of other birds, the *long-tailed cuckoo* (2 (2) below), and the *shining cuckoo* (2 (3) below).
  1773 FORSTER *Resolution Jrnl.* 5 Nov. (1982) III. 419 The native of *Bolabola*..shot a fine green new Cuckow with a white belly, barred transversally with green. **1777** ANDERSON *Journal* Feb. in Cook *Journals* (1967) III. 806 Two sorts of Cuckoos, one as large as our common sort, of a brown colour variegated with black..the other not larger than a sparrow..of a splendid green cast above & elegantly varied with waves of a gold, green, brown, & white colour below. **1838** POLACK *NZ* I. 297 *Cuckoos..*are also found, with various plumage. **1843** [see KOEKOEA]. **1873** [see KOHOPEROA]. **1914** PFAFF *Diggers' Story* 11 All night the More-pokes..and, in summer, the Cuckoos, kept up their cries. **1939** BEATTIE *First White Boy Born Otago* 121 I never saw the native quail, the cuckoo nor the morepork in the Central [Otago, c1860s].

2. With a modifier: **bronze (bronze-wing(ed)), long-tailed, shining** (or **Australian**) **cuckoo**.

(1) **bronze (bronze-wing, bronze-winged) cuckoo.** See *shining cuckoo* (3) below.
  1870 *TrNZI* II. 45 How true is the Bronze-winged Cuckoo to his appointment. **1885** *NZJSc.* II. 477 *Chrysococcyx lucidus...* Whistler, Bronze-winged Cuckoo, Pipiwarauroa. **1930** REISCHEK *Yesterdays in Maoriland* (1933) 72 Once, hearing the chirp of a chick in a tree, I climbed up and saw a young bronze cuckoo in the nest of one of these warblers. **1946** *JPS* LV. 156 *pipiwharauroa,* often shortened to wharauroa, a migratory bird (Chalcococcyx lucidus), shining- or bronze-wing cuckoo: winters in New Caledonia and adjacent islands: the long-tailed cuckoo is koekoea[a]. **1985** [see (3) below].

(2) **long-tailed cuckoo.** *Eudynamys taitensis*, a migratory bird larger than a thrush, with upper parts dark brown with rufous bars and spots, and having a tail longer than the body, and a harsh, strident call. See also KAWEKAWEA, KOEKOEA, KOHOPEROA, *kumara bird* (KUMARA 2), SCREAMER.
  1869 *TrNZI* I. (rev. edn.) 224 During the quiet

summer nights the deep rich notes of the Koheperoa, or Long-tailed Cuckoo, may be heard at intervals till break of day. **1873** BULLER *Birds NZ* 73 Eudynamis taitensis. (Long-tailed Cuckoo.).. Koekoea, Kawekawea, and Koheperoa. **1882** POTTS *Out in Open* 197 We are inclined to believe that eggs of this bird are often destroyed by the long-tailed cuckoo. **1914** GUTHRIE-SMITH *Mutton Birds & Other Birds* 15 The Long Tailed Cuckoo was very plentiful and very noisy. Its screech..almost as it were, spat forth, so vehement was the utterance, and sometimes it was answered from a distance by a note not unlike a rapid, low tapping or hammering. **1926** COWAN *Travel in NZ* II. 170 The shining cuckoo, or *pipi-wharauroa*, and the long-tailed cuckoo, called koekoea and also kohoperoa, are regular summer migrants from the tropics. **1954** STUDHOLME *Te Waimate* (1954) 238 The Long-tailed Cuckoo is now extremely rare, if not extinct, in South Canterbury, though the Shining Cuckoo is still seen occasionally. **1967** NATUSCH *Animals NZ* 288 The long-tailed cuckoo..is known by its strident rising screech, which, if uttered non-stop, is said to 'forecast' rain. **1976** SOPER *NZ Birds* 50 Yellowheads are exploited by the Long-tailed Cuckoo, which not only lay eggs in their nests for them to rear but also eat the eggs and nestlings. **1985** *Reader's Digest Book NZ Birds* 255 *Long-tailed Cuckoo...Koekoea, kohoperoa, screecher, screamer...* Because of its predatory habits the long-tailed cuckoo is heartily disliked by other birds.

(3) **shining cuckoo**. *Chrysococcyx* (formerly *Chalcites*) *lucidus lucidus*, a small migratory bird, with upper parts deep glossy green and underparts white finely barred with green, and having a musical whistling call. See also *bronze cuckoo* (1) above, CHECK-SHIRT BIRD, PIPIWHARAUROA, RAINBIRD, WHISTLER *n.*² 1, ZEBRA BIRD.
1869 *TrNZI* I. (rev. edn.) 225 The Pipiwarauroa, or Shining Cuckoo, is of milder disposition. **1873** BULLER *Birds NZ* 77 Chrysococcyx lucidus. (Shining Cuckoo.)... Warauroa, Pipiauroa, and Pipiwarauroa. **1904** HUTTON & DRUMMOND *Animals NZ* 120 *The Shining Cuckoo.— Pipiwarauroa. Chalcococcyx lucidus...* Our Cuckoos do not possess the 'cuckoo' note which has given the bird its name. *Ibid.* 123 The cry of the Shining Cuckoo is described as being an exceedingly pleasant one. **1926** [see (2) above]. **1946** [see (1) above]. **1955** OLIVER *NZ Birds* 533 Latham, who described Forster's specimen, called it the Shining Cuckoo, a title adopted by Gmelin when founding the specific name [*sc. lucidus*]. **1967** NATUSCH *Animals NZ* 287 The shining cuckoo..really does shine; I saw one on wet grass in a dazzling burst of sunshine after a downpour, its metallic green back alight with coppery gleams, set off by the cream and rust striped 'football jersey' beneath. **1985** *Reader's Digest Book NZ Birds* 254 *Shining Cuckoo... Pipiwarauroa, bronze cuckoo, whistler...* The shining cuckoo breeds wherever the grey warbler or Chatham Island warbler are found. It lives in native forest, pine forest, wooded farmland and suburban gardens, and is particularly fond of willow trees along water courses.

3. *fig*. Applied to those who impose on others' goodwill. **a**. Of unfaithful lovers or husbands.
1934 LEE *Children of Poor* (1949) 18 Evidently he was a ne'er-do-well rather than a domesticated parent— one of those human shining cuckoos who play at love and leave hedge sparrows to mourn the consequences.

b. *Watersiders. Obs*. One who does not pay union fees but receives union benefits.
c1926 *Transport Workers' Song Book* 28 Get rid of the Union 'cuckoo' And the 'stool pigeon' as well. The 'arrear fiends' and the 'ring-necks'.

cucumber. *Ellipt*. for CUCUMBER FISH 1.
1978 McDOWALL *NZ Freshwater Fishes* 40 *Retropinna retropinna..*common names..include..cucumber-fish or just cucumber. **1986** PAUL *NZ Fishes* 49 *Common smelt...* Also called silvery, estuarine smelt, or cucumber (from the smell of freshly caught fish). Silvery, particularly along the sides. **1990** [see CUCUMBER FISH 1].

cucumber fish. [AND 1843.]
1. The estuarine SMELT *Retropinna retropinna* (fam. Retropinnidae).
c1899 DOUGLAS in McDowall *JRSNZ* (1980) X. 320 The cucumber fish, trout, and blenny are too few in number to represent all that are left of the whitebait swarms. **1940** [see SMELT]. **1956** GRAHAM *Treasury NZ Fishes* 113 Smelt (Paraki)..They are often referred to as Silvery, while in other parts they are called Cucumber Fish. **1960** DOOGUE & MORELAND *Sea Anglers' Guide* 186 Smelt... *Retropinna sp.*; silvery, cucumber-fish; inanga-papa (Maori). **1981** WILSON *Fisherman's Bible* 208 Smelt..He is the bitter, silver fellow the sharp-eyed whitebaiter discards from his nets. Smells like cucumber, hence one of his other names Cucumber-fish. **1990** McDOWALL *NZ Freshwater Fishes* 65 *Common Smelt...* Common names for the species include silvery, cucumberfish (or just cucumber) and estuarine smelt. The purplish iridescent band along the sides once prompted the name violets (Archey, 1927 [*The native Fishes of Canterbury*]), although this is rarely if ever used today.

2. *Chlorophthalmus nigripinnis* (fam. Chlorophthalmidae), a pale green and silver marine fish.
1911 *Rec. Canterbury Mus.* I. 164 *Chlorophthalmus Nigripinnis..*Cucumber Fish. **1960** PARROTT *Queer & Rare Fishes NZ* 39 Cucumber fish *Chlorophthalmus nigripinnis...* The Cucumber Fishes are related to the Lizard and Lantern Fishes. *Ibid*. 40 This fish must not be confused with the Smelt, a fresh-water fish which is often called the Cucumber Fish, because of the faint smell of cucumber in freshly caught specimens. **1967** NATUSCH *Animals NZ* 209 Cucumber fishes... Similar to the lantern fishes..green above and silvery below, averages seven inches in length. **1982** AYLING *Collins Guide* 124 The cucumber fish is an elongate cigar-shaped species that reaches a maximum length of about 20 cm... This fish derives its name from the strange cucumber-like smell it emits.

cuddy. [Local, often *transf*., use of nautical *cuddy* the saloon or cabin of a large ship where officers and cabin passengers have meals, etc., well-known to early 'colonist' immigrants: see *OED n.*² 1.]

1. *Hist*. The saloon or cabin of an immigrant ship.
1851 KENNAWAY *Biscuit & Butter* (1973) 78 Our delicate..stomachs received the most racy and highly esteemed dainties peculiar to the *cuddy* table. **1853** ADAMS *Spring in Canterbury Settlement* 21 Every few minutes a shower of hail..would compel us to make a precipitate retreat into the cuddy. **1871** MONEY *Knocking About NZ* 2 Half of the entire cuddy berths were occupied by a wealthy Canterbury squatter, who..had taken such good care of the pence that the pounds tumbled into his pocket.

2. *transf*. **a**. *Obs*. The parlour or saloon of an accommodation-house.
c1850s in Hall-Jones *Mr Surveyor Thomson* (1971) 48 (Griffiths Collect.) Our host asked us into the 'cuddy', as he called the parlour [of his accommodation-house].

b. *Hist*. The first rough station house at Te Waimate. (Here, and in 3, poss. also a joc. *transf*. use of *cuddy* small room, closet (cf. *cubby*): see *OED n.* 2.)
1940 *Reminiscences of 1860 by Effie Studholme in Studholme Te Waimate* (1954) 59 M.'s [*sc.* Studholme's] pillows..were brought from the hut, or 'cuddy', as it was called to distinguish it from the men's hut. I should have liked to have lived in the 'cuddy', but M. would not hear of it. **1984** STRONGMAN *Gardens of Canterbury* 59 Michael Studholme's first home, The Cuddy, was constructed in 1854 from a single totara tree and the roof was thatched with snowgrass. In the winter of 1860 the small vegetable garden belonging to the cuddy was empty.

3. A stall for animals.
1965 MACNICOL *Skippers Road* 84 Warm 'cuddies' were built along a shed wall to house his pets [goats].

4. See *crib-cuddy* (CRIB *n.*² 2).

cudweed. [Transf. use of Brit. *cudweed* a plant (*Gnaphalium* spp.) administered to cattle that had lost their cud.] In New Zealand, applied to native and naturalized daisies of *Gnaphalium* and the related genera *Anaphalis* and *Pseudognaphalium* (fam. Asteraceae), in particular *Pseudognaphalium luteoalbum*. See also SILVERWEED 2.
1777 ANDERSON *Journal* Feb. in Cook *Journals* (1967) III. 804 Amongst the known kinds of plants are common and rough Bindweed..also Cudweed. [1967 *Note*.] 3. Possibly *Gnaphalium* sp. or *Helichrysum* sp. **1838** POLACK *NZ* I. 295 *Speedwell, sow,* and *melon thistles* (coetus)..*euphorbia, cudweed, crane's-bill*. **1909** *AJHR C-12* 63 *[Gnaphalium] luteo-album..*white cudweed..Dunes, heath. **1926** HILGENDORF *Weeds* 171 Cudweed (*Gnaphalium luteo-album*). This or an allied species is sometimes called silver weed. It is found all over the world including New Zealand, in all soils and climates. It is an annual or rarely biennial with a weak stem reaching a height of 15 or 18 inches. Clothed in all its parts..with soft white woolly down. **1975** *Tane 21* 8 Compositae *Gnaphalium luteo-album..*cudweed.

cuff. [Poss. rhyming slang for *a bit rough* or *tough*.] In the phr. **a bit on the cuff**, beyond what is normal; excessive; too severe.
1942 *NZEF Times* 16 Nov. 8 A bit on the cuff, that sort of thing. **1944** FULLARTON *Troop Target* 85 That's a bit on the cuff, Dig. **1988** McGILL *Dict. Kiwi Slang* 32 *cuff* phr. *on the cuff* excessive or unfair or inappropriate... 'Steady on, old boy, that language is a bit on the cuff.'

culch /kʌltʃ/. *Bluff oystering*. [f. Brit. dial. *culch, colch* the mass of stones, old shells, and other hard material to which the oyster spat adheres: see EDD *n.*² Norfolk, Essex, Kent, Cornwall; OED *culch*.] As a *n.*, the rubble of old shells, sand, weed, etc. which is part of the oyster-bed dredged up with the oysters; also as a *v. trans.*, to remove (saleable oysters) from the mass of *culch*; or to remove (culch) from saleable oysters. Also as *vbl. n.* See also MULLOCK *n*. 1 c.
1899 *NZ Illustr. Mag.* Dec. 183 They culch each dredge, (that is, take all the saleable oysters and throw the rubbish overboard). **1921** *Quick March* 10 Aug. 31 The mess [from the oyster dredge] is dumped on the deck and picked over—'culched'—while the next 'drift' goes on. **1973** *NZ Heritage* XCIX. 2771 Large clumps of animal life which come up in the culch in the dredge are known as 'mullock'. **1983** *Catch '83* Sept. 17 The catch is then [*sc*. after washing by dipping in the sea] ready to be culched, ie, the takeable oysters are sorted from the unwanted material and undersized oysters... The traditional method of hand culching is used by most of the fleet. The contents of each dredge are dumped onto waist-high sorting benches... The second method is mechanical culching... Four men stand alongside the conveyor culching-off unwanted material (rather than takeable ousters).

cull, *v.*

1. *trans.* [See OED *v.*¹ 4 a, 'The earliest examples are from *Austral.* and *N.Z.* but the word is now widely used in Britain and elsewhere'.] To select (livestock) according to quality.

1889 WILLIAMS & REEVES *Col. Couplets* 9 I'd far sooner choose To be writing to you, than be culling the ewes. **1914** *Stratford Evening Post* 24 Oct. 2 The sheep in question was not a culled ewe.

2. [An extended use of *cull* to select and kill (wild animals or birds), usu. in order to improve the stock or reduce the population: see OED *v.*¹ 4 b.] *trans.* and *intr.* To kill (noxious wild animals, esp. deer) or to reduce or attempt to exterminate professionally the populations of such animals. Also as a *vbl. n.* and *ppl. a.*

1934 *Evening Post* (Wellington) 12 Apr. 10 With the object of determining the best method of culling deer in the Tararuas..the sum of £10 was granted by the Acclimatisation Society last night. **1951** DUGGAN *More Poems* 22 If you must cull, oh make of death an art, Shoot at short range and only through the heart. **1952** culling [see CULLER]. **1953** SUTHERLAND *Golden Bush* (1963) 69 Some of the high tallies taken in the early days of the so-called 'culling' operations..show that the shooters learned the wisdom of concentrating their fire on the leader hinds. **1982** MARSHALL *Master Big Jingles* 78 Raf thought we should cull the rabbits before we had too much beer. **1994** *Evening Post* (Wellington) 5 Dec. 3 [Heading] 74 goats culled in reserve... Seventy-four goats were shot last month in Speedy's Reserve... The cullers were called in by the Hutt City Council because of damage to native trees.

culler. [f. CULL *v.* 2 + -ER.] **a.** A professional hunter employed, usu. by the State, to kill wild animals selectively, later to exterminate noxious animals, esp. deer. See also *deer-culler* (DEER).

1934 *Canterbury Mountaineer* 72 With the cullers broke camp at 8.30 a.m. **1948** *Dominion* (Wellington) 4 June 8 One experienced culler said yesterday that the culling season had been very successful. **1952** THOMSON *Deer Hunter* 18 Though we are still graced with the name of cullers, culling out is no longer our job. Now we are killers, with orders to clean out every deer. **1964** REID *Book NZ* 225 Some 100,000 deer are shot every year in New Zealand, about half by amateurs, the rest by professional deer-cullers... Here four cullers display wapiti and red deer antlers. **1982** YEREX *Farming Deer* 73 Although the work of reducing deer numbers was assigned to government-employed shooters (termed 'cullers', but quite wrongly) there had always been private individuals who shot deer for sport or in order to sell skins. **1994** [see CULL *v.* 2].

b. One hired to kill wild geese.

1981 ANDERSON *Both Sides of River* 110 The Government had cullers smashing eggs and shooting the old geese.

cuma, *var.* KUMUKUMU.

cumalla, *var.* KUMARA.

cunning, *a.* Used in various (often *derog.*) phr. having the meaning 'very cunning or sly'. **a. cunning as a Maori dog** (or **kuri**); also occas. **to have Maori dog** (in one), to be cunning.

1947 DAVIN *For Rest of Our Lives* 239 Innocent as a child and cunning as a Maori dog, Bert had once called him. **1949** NEWTON *High Country Days* 59 Cunning as Maori dogs, the musterers omitted to mention that the Craiglea gang that year included a man whose spin bowling found him knocking at the door for provincial honours. **1953** SCOTT *Breakfast at Six* 30 'Cunning as a Maori dog', supplemented Sam vulgarly. **1962** *Australasian Universal Dict.* 1 'As cunning as Maori dog' is a common simile in New Zealand, although there is not the same local flavour in the slang there. **1972** HAYWARD *Diary Kirk Years* 18 Apr. (1981) 30 He's told us about being at a Maori gathering when a pakeha said unthinkingly, 'He's as cunning as a Maori dog'. It appeared to have gone unnoticed until a Maori remarked, 'He's as cunning as a pakeha dog'. Mr K enjoyed that. **1982** KEENE *Myrtle & Sophia* 49 Now, Platypus was, as Bert would say, as cunning as a *kuri*, and while she was in sight of the house, she ambled along innocently. **1995** *Dominion* (Wellington) 7 June 44 He denied a magazine article which..questioned Tatarangi's will to win. 'I'd say that [another Maori golfer] [*sic*] Michael Campbell will turn out the better of the two. He's got more "Maori dog" in him,' the latest issue of *New Zealand Golf* quotes the official as saying.

b. cunning as a Maori hen.

1926 COWAN *Travel in NZ* II. 63 'As cunning as a Maori hen' [*sc.* weka] is a familiar New Zealand bush simile.

c. cunning as a (in speech usu. **shithouse** but also euphemised to **backhouse, bush, mad, outhouse**) **rat.**

c1915 in Bailey & Roth *Shanties* (1967) 115 Old Abdul under cover was as cunning as a rat; As yet we'd done no shootin'—saw nothin' to shoot at. **1947** *NZ Woman's Weekly* 21 Aug. 3 She can be as cunning as a bush rat sometimes. **1964** HELMER *Stag Party* (1990) 52 And cunning, eh? Like a backhouse rat. **1990** KIDMAN *True Stars* 43 *Cunning as a bunch of shithouse rats you lot* O'Meara said, last time he came round; *shithouse rats*. **1993** *Listener* 29 May 42 He is variously described as stealthy as a wolf, cunning as a mad rat, hungry as a shearing-gang at teatime. **1993** TV3 Ralston Group discussion 15 Dec. He's as cunning as an outhouse rat. **1996** *Sunday Star-Times* (Auckland) 7 July A5 Fulton is described as being as cunning as the proverbial outhouse rat.

cup. [Transf. use for objects resembling a cup in shape.]

1. Usu. *pl.* A metal sheath lined with rubber designed to fit over a cow's teat and transmit a pulse imitating the action of hand milking, and so encourage her to let down milk. Also as a *v. trans.* **to cup** (a cow), to attach cups to a cow's teats.

1926 *NZ Dairy Produce Exporter* 31 July 21 [Advt] Free Trial of these Real Money-making Teat Cups. Your Milking Machine is no better than the Teat Cups you use on it. **1953** *Here & Now* Apr. 31 When secondary school assistants wed A cocksfoot man from the cream-cheque land There's no time for books and less for bed, But tits and cups in your early hand. **1959** *NZ Dairy Exporter* July 37 Most farmers wait after washing and stimulating, before putting their cups on. **1963** DUGGAN *Collected Stories* (1981) 199 I was bent double stripping old Daisy..after the cups came off. **1984** KEITH *NZ Yesterdays* 102 By 1902 the double-chambered teat cup with a flexible rubber liner was patented.

2. [f. the shape of early insulators resembling inverted tea-cups, occas. having a curved stem, reminiscent of a handle, with which they were fixed to the pole-arms.] A china or pottery insulator on telephone or electric-power poles.

c1940 Among Havelock (Marlborough) boys, 'cup' was the usual name given to esp. telephone 'cups', and breaking them with stones a common pastime. (Ed.) **1959** SLATTER *Gun in My Hand* 9 Juvenile delinquency. What about us? Breaking cups on the power posts along the country roads. **1986** O'REGAN *A Changing Order* 44 Such public offences might include raiding an orchard..or throwing stones at the cups on telegraph poles. **1994** LASENBY *Dead Man's Head* 71 [Constable Heath] said the gang had smashed all the cups on three telegraph posts.

curl: see CURLER.

curler. Also occas. **curl.** A curling wave; the 'curl' of a wave.

1872 in *Otago Daily Times* (Dunedin) (1972) 17 May (100 Years Ago) (Griffiths Collect.) The steamer struck on the bar and was swept by three 'curlers'. **1933** SCANLAN *Tides of Youth* 145 The tide-rip off Terewhiti came in great..curlers. **1968** WARWICK *Surfriding in NZ* [Gloss.] Cutback—A stall method of bringing the board back into the curl. **1979** *Otago Daily Times* (Dunedin) 28 Mar. 21 Ironically 'curler' is equated with 'roller' only in the beauty salon, though it had exactly the same meaning at the seaside, too.

curlew. [Spec. use of *curlew*: AND 1834.]

1. *Obs.* OYSTERCATCHER 1.

1773 FORSTER *Resolution Jrnl.* 27 Mar. (1982) II. 240 Saw on the beach [at Dusky Bay] some black birds, with red bills & feet; the people who had been here before, called them Curlews, but they had rather the appearance of Sea Pies. **1838** POLACK *NZ* I. 72 Large detached masses of black rocks lined the shore, on which the gannet, curlew, pelican, and gulls..sat perched.

2. *Numenius madagascariensis* (fam. Scolopacidae), a large, long-legged migratory wading bird, having a very long down-curved bill. In ornithological use usu. with a modifier, esp. **eastern** (or **far-eastern, long-billed**) **curlew**. Also (formerly) the GODWIT a *Limosa lapponica* and various other long-legged shore-birds.

1791 BELL *Jrnl. Voyage H.M.S. 'Chatham'* (Vancouver exped.) (ATLMS) 50 The Best kinds were Ducks, Curlews, a bird very much resembling a Wood Cock & Sea Pies. **1849** POWER *Sketches in NZ* 72 A few curlews, whale-birds, sand-pipers, and wild ducks frequent the coast and river swamps. **1871** [see GODWIT a]. **1882** HAY *Brighter Britain* II. 222 The Kuaka (*Limosa Baueri*) is the bird spoken of as 'curlew' and 'grey snipe' by the colonists. Large flocks are to be seen on our rivers, feeding on the mud-banks. **1901** [see GODWIT a]. **1966** FALLA et al. *Birds NZ* 131 Long-billed (Eastern) Curlew *Numenius madagascariensis*... Godwits tend to resent stray curlews and have been seen to mob and chase them. **1976** SOPER *NZ Birds* 245 Giant among the waders, standing head and shoulders above all others, is the Long-billed Curlew. **1985** *Reader's Digest Book NZ Birds* 190 *Far-eastern Curlew Numenius madagascariensis*... Eastern curlew, long-billed curlew, Australian curlew... Sightings of far-eastern curlews have increased steadily over the past 30 years, but the summer total in New Zealand probably still does not reach 100.

3. Special Comb. **curlew-shooting**, the former seasonal shooting of the godwit.

1888 BULLER *Birds NZ* II. 43 'Curlew-shooting' (as it [*sc.* godwit-shooting] is termed in the colony) sometimes, however, becomes more legitimate sport... [Quoting a New Zealand correspondent of *The Field*:] 'Curlew-shooting has just begun; I had a day last week (early in March). The best locality for this kind of shooting is the upper part of Auckland harbour.'

curly *n.*: see WENTLETRAP and quots. there.

curly, *a.* In NZ use in two apparently contradictory senses: in the phr. **a curly one**, difficult, esp. of a question; and as **curly** *a.* [poss.

ellipt. for *curly-mo* (AND *curl-the-mo*): cf. 1982 NEWBOLD *Big Huey* 248 Curly Mo: (adj or adv) All right, fine, go ahead], impressive; fine, pleasant.
1981 *Avondale College* (Auckland) Feb. Slang Words in Use (Goldie Brown Collection) *very curly*: difficult; or pleasant **1984** PARTRIDGE *Dict. Slang* 280 *curly* adj... 2. But in NZ, e.g. as 'That was extra curly' (Slatter), it seems to mean 'excellent' or 'attractive' and to date since ca. 1935. **1988** McGILL *Dict. Kiwi Slang* 33 *curly* a difficult situation, derived possibly from googly ball in cricket; eg 'That second question on the exam paper's a curly one.'

curly grass: see GRASS 2 (13).

Curnow's curse. [Origin uncertain: prob. from the name of the family from whose farm the weed was reputed to have spread.] Either of two N. American weeds naturalized locally in New Zealand, *Calandrinia compressa* or *C. menziesii* (fam. Portulaceae). See also HORGAN'S WEED. Contrast PATERSON'S CURSE.
1967 HILGENDORF & CALDER *Weeds* 78 Curnow's Curse (*Calandrinia ciliata* var. *caulescens*) is also called portulaca, horgan's weed, and purple calandrinia. It has spreading fleshy stems and somewhat fleshy leaves. **1969** *Standard Common Names Weeds* 19 *Curnow's curse* [=] calandrinia.

currant. *Obs.* Also **currant-tree.** [Transf. use of *currant*, *Ribes* spp. (fam. Glossulariaceae), shrubs with clusters of small berries.] Usu. as **mountain** (or **native, New Zealand**) **currant**, WINEBERRY 1, which has clusters of dark-red to black berries resembling red or black currants.
1842 SWAINSON in *William Swainson* Oct. (1992) 91 There is another tree which is in flower now: we call it the Currant, although it grows to the size of a tree—its flowers are shaped like the Lily-of-the-valley, but instead of being white they are pink. **1864** BARRINGTON *Diary* 16 Mar. in Taylor *Early Travellers* (1959) 402 The native currant also makes first-rate wine, and grows very profusely. **1890** *PWD Catalogue Timbers* (NZ & South Seas Exhib.) 11 Makomako (currant-tree)..Aristotelia racemosa..Timber light and straight grained. *Ibid.* 19 Makomako (wine berry or currant tree) slab. **1892** HUDSON *Elem. Manual NZ Entomology* 32 This curious species is found abundantly in the stems of dead currant trees (*Aristotelia racemosa*). *Ibid.* 70 The plant most usually selected by the caterpillar is *Aristotelia racemosa*, called by the settlers 'New Zealand currant', from its large clusters of rich-looking black berries, which appear in autumn. **1909** *AJHR C-12* 56 [*Aristotelia*] *fruticosa*... Mountain-currant, or wineberry. Scrub in river-valley. **1909** *AJHR C-12* 56 *Aristotelia racemosa*... Makomako. Wineberry, native currant. **1910** COCKAYNE *NZ Plants & Their Story* 60 The mountain-currant (*Aristotelia fruticosa*). **1940** LAING & BLACKWELL *Plants NZ* 258 In Otago, it [*sc.* *Aristotelia* sp.] is the New Zealand Currant, or 'Mokomok'. **1961** MARTIN *Flora NZ* 235 Aristotelia fruticosa. Mountain Currant.

curry.
1. *Offensive.* [f. *curry* as an item of Indian diet.] An Indian.
1979 *Evening Post* (Wellington) 26 Sept. 48 'The curries are just like the Jews,' a youth said about the fire-bombing of the shop of a Petone Indian... 'This reference I [*sc.* Mr Johnson] took to mean the Indians.'

Hence **curry-muncher**, *offensive*, an Indian.
1981 *Avondale College* (Auckland) Feb. Slang Words in Use (Goldie Brown Collection) *curry muncher*: Indian **1988** McGILL *Dict. Kiwi Slang* 33 *curry muncher* Indian; offensive. **1991** *Dominion* (Wellington) 6 May 9 One Fiji Indian representative at the meeting said Indian children were generally referred to as curry-munchers and niggers.

2. [AND 1936.] Physical or verbal violence or abuse, esp. in the phr. **to give someone curry**.
1983 HUTCHINS *Rugby Rabbits* 37 If a forward whispered compliments in his [*sc.* the rugby union selector's] ear at after match functions and indulged in the occasional curry on the paddock he would invariably get the nod. **1988** McGILL *Dict. Kiwi Slang* 49 *give someone curry* to abuse or razz vigorously, often in sport; from the heat associated with curry; eg 'That useless Aussie bowler, did we give him some curry!' **1989** *Listener* 7 Jan. 13 And it's anybody's guess what Japanese tourists make of such Kiwisms [*sic*] as 'She's apples' 'put the nips in' 'feeling crook' or 'give him some curry'.

cut, *v.*[1]
1. a. *trans.* Of a sheep, to produce (wool) from a shearing.
1892 *NZ Official Handbook* 123 Until the commencement of the frozen-meat industry, in 1882, sheep-farmers in New Zealand confined their attention exclusively to producing the class of sheep that would cut the heaviest fleece. **1933** *Press* (Christchurch) (Acland Gloss.) 7 Oct. 15 A sheep is said to *c[ut]* so many pounds of wool; i.e., produce.

b. *trans.* Of a farmer, to produce (wool) by shearing.
1968 TOMLINSON *Remembered Trails* 58 These [Merino wethers] did very well..and he cut about sixty-five bales of wool.

2. [Cf. OED *v.* 21 c outdo, 1884.] *trans.* Of a shearer, to outshear another shearer.
1986 RICHARDS *Off the Sheep's Back* 137 On the next run I cut Mack by three, so I knew he was working at top speed... On the last run I cut him by five.

3. *trans.* (also *absol.*). To cut (a sheep's skin) by rough shearing.
c1875 MEREDITH *Adventuring in Maoriland* (1935) 143 Two of them [*sc.* shearers]..were cutting the sheep rather badly, necessitating the constant application of the Stockholm-tar brush to the cuts. **1904** LANCASTER *Sons o' Men* 79 I don't deny 'e [*sc.* a rough shearer] is cuttin' 'is jumbucks into fancy pattrons all right. **1960** SCRYMGEOUR *Memories of Maoriland* 49 Passing down the board towards the end, he saw Jack Gwydir cutting badly..and said, 'Try not to cut too much, I don't like it.'

cut, *v.*[2]
1. *trans.* Usu. of liquor, to finish (off); to empty.
1945 HENDERSON *Gunner Inglorious* (1974) 117 Let's cut the lot. **1952** WILSON *Julien Ware* 241 Here, drink it down. We must cut this bottle tonight. **1981** HENDERSON *Exiles Asbestos Cottage* 14 Plenty of garrulous half-shot but willing hands..had all the wool stacked safely in the store by 1 am, when they turned to even more willingly and cut the keg.

Hence **cut** *ppl. a.* Used predicatively, often of consumables esp. liquor, finished, cut out.
1946 WEBBER *Johnny Enzed in Italy* 5 She's [*sc.* the keg's] cut, is she? **1956** DAVIN *Sullen Bell* 214 No need to worry about [giving me a rise]. The gratuity's not cut. **1963** CASEY *As Short a Spring* 168 Anyway the plonk's cut. **1976** McCLENAGHAN *Travelling Man* 45 Dropsy tapped the keg... 'Our form is good today. We'll soon have this cut.' **1988** McGILL *Dict. Kiwi Slang* 33 *cut* to finish or finished; eg 'Let's cut all the beer.' 'Too late. It's all cut.'

2. In the imperative phr. **cut the rough**, **cut out the rough stuff** [perh. an extension of *cut it out!* stop it!], usu. as an exclam. or command to cease doing or saying something considered rough or offensive by the speaker: also in neg. constr. **don't go the rough stuff**, don't attempt violence.
1933 *Auckland Univ. Capping Book* 27 'That's why I kicked it.' 'Well, cut out the rough stuff. This isn't a test match.' **1937** PARTRIDGE *Dict. Slang* 202 *cut the rough (stuff)*. To cease doing or saying something obnoxious to another: Australian and New Zealand (lower classes), then military) coll.: C. 20. i.e. *cut out*, desist from. **a1974** SYDER & HODGETTS *Aust and NZ English* (TS) 241 *Cut out the rough stuff!* A rebuke. Your language or your topic, or both, offend. 'Hey cut out the rough stuff! That old bag you're talking about happens to be my mother-in-law.' No more of this! or, cease this disorderly conduct! 'Cut out the rough stuff! These boxes are marked "Fragile", they're full of glassware. You can't throw them on any old how.'

cut, *n.*[1] *Farming.*
1. [AND 1895.] A job as a shearer.
1912 *Maoriland Worker* 16 Feb. 12 Organiser John Mee..went to Christchurch with the intention of perhaps getting a cut in at a late shed or taking part in the straw rush.

2. A style of shearing.
1934 *Press* (Christchurch) (Acland Gloss.) 20 Jan. 15 *Cut*... Style of shearing; e.g., 'They have a very rough *c[ut]* at So-and-so's' means that 'So-and-so' does not care whether his sheep are neatly shorn or not. **1960** SCRYMGEOUR *Memories of Maoriland* 49 The advancement [in numbers shorn] went on but with a different and a rougher cut than was usual... The cut was becoming rougher and numbers spoilt good work.

cut, *n.*[2] [AND 1915.] Usu. *pl.* A stroke of the strap or cane given (usu. on the hand) as a school punishment, esp. in the phr. **to get the cuts**, to get the strap, to receive corporal punishment.
1913 *Truth* 12 Apr. 1 A country journal records..that one poor little boy who made 'a [April] fool' of his master received no fewer than 'ten cuts', as the boy put it. **c1920** p.c. R. Mason (p.c. 1953) quotes a Pukekohe, Auckland, skipping rhyme of c1920: 'Andy pandy sugary candy, French almond nuts, If you don't behave yourself You're sure to get the cuts'; or, alternatively, 'If you stay away from school You will not get the cuts.' **1938** LAWLOR *House of Templemore* 123 'Urry or yer'l git the cuts. **1945** SARGESON *When Wind Blows* 14 [You] would get the cuts for sure. **1951** 15–18 M 3 Marlborough College 23 Cuts [F10 M3] **1962** LAWLOR *More Wellington Days* 100 I think it was brother Augustine who initiated the lay-by system of 'cuts'. **1986** DAVIN *Salamander & the Fire* 158 The other [teacher] we called Deathknell or Clapper because whenever he asked you a question you always ended by getting six cuts of the cane on each hand. **1992** *North & South* (Auckland) Apr. 39 I once got the cuts for leaving out an apostrophe. **1995** WINTER *All Ways Up Hill* 212 [The teacher] dealt out a cut with the strap for every question that was not answered correctly and at once.

cut, *n.*[3] [AND 1874.] Esp. in the phr. **to take a cut of**, a part of a mob of sheep or cattle detached for a purpose. See also CUT OUT *v.*[1]
1933 *Press* (Christchurch) (Acland Gloss.) 7 Oct. 15 If a mob of sheep is too large for any purpose, you *c[ut]* them or take *c[ut]s* of the required size. Taking a *c[ut]* of ewes and lambs from a paddock for shearing is one of the most delicate and responsible jobs a shepherd has to do. **a1947** MACGIBBON in Beattie *Early Runholding* (1947) 50 The snowgrass was so long that

it was necessary to take a small cut of the main flock of sheep and drive them ahead a half-mile or so. **1953** STRONACH *Musterer on Molesworth* 68 At last we got a small cut of our mob over and the rest was easy. **1960** MASTERS *Back-Country Tales* 239 Jackaroo and Bluey held the main mob while I took a small cut..and tried to ease them down to water. The cut I had, on scenting the water, started bleating and tearing forward. **1978** JARDINE *Shadows on Hill* 88 The previous owner..had mustered in a good cut [of cattle] for inspection by a buyer. **1981** SUTHERLAND & TAYLOR *Sunrise* 49 After tea Bill had to help pack the [shearing] shed with another cut of dry-fleeced sheep for the morning run.

cut, *n.*[4] *Mining*. See quot.
1978 MCARA *Gold Mining Waihi* 179 Holes [for blasting-charges] were drilled about two feet apart and four or five feet deep in the bottom of the shaft, in accordance with the pattern or 'cut' being used. *Ibid.* 318 *Cut*: The pattern of drill-holes used to make the initial penetration of a face, for the purpose of creating a second 'free face', to facilitate the breaking of the rock.

cut and tail. *Farming.* [Cf. OED *cut v.* 26, castrate.] *trans*. To castrate and dock lambs usu. perceived as one process or operation. See also MARK a *v*.
1857 TRIPP *Diary* 29 Oct. in Harper *Kettle on Fuchsia* (1967) 32 We all helped at cutting, tailing etc. the lambs. 470 were cut. **1867** PHILLIPS *Point Jrnl.* 5 Dec. (Canterbury Pub. Lib. TS) 134 Cut and tailed 2740 lambs and brought ewes up to hills in evening. **1876** PEACHE *Journal* in Gray *Quiet with Hills* (1970) 52 We cut and tailed the lambs. **1889** WILLIAMS & REEVES *Col. Couplets* 9 Cutting and tailing the poor little lambs.

Hence **cutting and tailing** *vbl. n.*, the farming process of castrating and docking lambs, usu. done at the one time.
1858 ACLAND *Notes on Sheepfarming NZ* 10 About a fortnight after lambing is over the operation of 'cutting and tailing' is performed. **1862** *Puketoi Station Diary* 6 Nov. (Hocken TS) Cleared out pens and prepared yard for cutting & tailing. **1878** ELWELL *Boy Colonists* 172 The sheep had to be mustered..in the latter part of the spring for cutting and tailing. **1933** *Press* (Christchurch) (Acland Gloss.) 7 Oct. 15 *Cut.*— (1) Castrate. *Cutting and tailing* was the old name for earmarking, castrating, and taking the tails off lambs, all of which operations are performed together. *C[utting] and t[ailing]* is still the general name mostly used by shepherds, but..is being replaced by *tailing* or *marking*.

cut cat. A (newly) castrated cat, usu. in the phr. **to go (run) like a cut cat**, indicating speedy (often noisy) withdrawal (occas., noisy argument) as a variation of 'go like a scalded cat'.
1965 SHADBOLT *Among Cinders* 263 They might have gone on for hours like a pair of cut cats, but then Jim walked into the argument carrying his crate. **1968** SLATTER *Pagan Game* 162 Off down the road like a cut cat. Pandebloodymonium— **1988** MCGILL *Dict. Kiwi Slang* 51 *go like a cut cat* go or depart fast; eg 'Whatever you think of motor scooters, these new Vitas go like a cut cat. True!'

cut in, *v.* *Whaling*. [Recorded earliest on the NZ coast: see OED *v*. 55 b, 1839.] *trans.* and *intr*. To incise and then strip blubber from a whale. Also as *vbl. n.* and *ppl. a.*
1835 *Piraki Log* 5 Dec. (1911) 17 People employed fitting Boats, Cutting in gear, &c. &c. **1836** RHODES *Jrnl. Barque 'Australian'* (1954) 6 Got the whale along side and commenced cutting in. **1836** *Piraki Log* 22 May (1911) 36 Brought the whale alongside, and in the afternoon cut her in. **1844** TUCKETT *Diary* 3 May in Hocken *Contributions* (1898) 215 They were busy cutting in a captured whale of large size. **1905** BAUCKE *White Man Treads* 76 Then the 'cutting in' is begun; the huge slabs of fat are sliced and allowed to 'ripen' in casks. **1954** STRAUBEL in Rhodes *Jrnl. Barque 'Australian'* (1954) xvi The whales when caught were towed back to the ships to be 'cut in' (i.e. to be stripped of their blubber). **1968** JOHNSON *Turn of Tide* 29 A Mr Wilkins from Wellington had arrived at Te Awaiti to take.. films of a chase and of the cutting-in and drying-out process. **1982** GRADY *Perano Whalers* 226 *Cutting-in*—Making the guideline cuts or directions on a dead whale for taking the blubber off.

Hence **cutter-in** *n.*, the person responsible for incising and removing the blubber of a whale.
1843 DIEFFENBACH *Travels in NZ* (1974) I. 51 [The tongue of the whale] is the monopoly of the 'tonguer', or 'cutter-in'.

cut lunch. [f. *cut* sliced: AND 1937.] Sandwiches and other snacks to be eaten elsewhere than at home or at a formal eating-place.
1983 FRANCIS *Wildlife Ranger* 2 The [station] midday meal was more often a cut lunch eaten on the job. **1985** HUNT *I'm Ninety-five* 28 We'd take our crib into the [gold]mine with us [c1916]: a cut lunch wrapped up in newspaper, cold meat, stew or bacon sandwiches and tea. **1990** KIDMAN *True Stars* 39 He had only finished his cut lunch ten minutes before, eating on the run.

cut out, *v.*[1] [AND 1844.] Also **cut** (see quot. 1933). *trans*. To separate or detach (part of a mob of stock) usu. for a particular purpose. Also as *vbl. n.* [AND 1848]. Cf. CUT *n.*[3]
1859 *Puketoi Station Diary* 26 Dec. (Hocken TS) Cut out about 25 wethers from Hume's flock and joined them with Duncan's ewes. **1862** CHUDLEIGH *Diary* 13 Mar. (1950) 28 Draper..and myself were on the run all day cutting out bullocks we succeeded in yarding about 60. It is very hard to cut out so many. **1867** THOMSON *Rambles with Philosopher* 149 The Squire was now on his metal, his nostrils dilated with eagerness to commence the..operation of cutting-out the fattest bullock. **1874** KENNAWAY *Crusts* 206 The horses were often..wonderfully eager and clever at it [*sc.* handling cattle], cutting out and dodging single beasts with extraordinary sagacity and spirit. **1904** LANCASTER *Sons o' Men* 152 Suppose a man can cut a steer, or wheel a mob... Your colonial reverences that man. **1933** *Press* (Christchurch) (Acland Gloss.) 7 Oct. 15 If a mob of sheep is too large..you *c[ut]* them or take *c[uts]* of the required size. *Cut out...* To draft cattle in the open. **1940** STUDHOLME *Te Waimate* (1954) 135 Most of the drafting was done in the open by a process known as cutting out. **1973** FERNANDEZ *Tussock Fever* 44 When you are well on the way I'll cut out the next third and go on up the valley.

Hence **cutter-out** *n.* [AND 1873], a farm worker who cuts stock out from a mob.
1940 STUDHOLME *Te Waimate* (1954) 136 Several men would hold the cattle together..while the 'cutter-out' rode through them, and after spotting the beast that he wanted, would follow it out to the edge of the mob, when the holders would open out and allow both beast and cutter-out to pass through.

cut out, *v.*[2] [In various uses of *cut out* to bring, or come to an end.]

1. a. *Shearing*. [AND 1882.] To complete shearing (a run of sheep or a whole mob).
c**1875** MEREDITH *Adventuring in Maoriland* (1935) 96 Shearing is early here this year. The Brancepeth flock was cut out last week. **1910** *Maoriland Worker* 15 Dec. 3 (Suppl.) Fairfield was cut out by the beginning of December. **1933** *Press* (Christchurch) (Acland Gloss.) 7 Oct. 15 *Cut out.*- (1) To finish the whole shearing... (2) To finish shearing a particular mob and then stop the shearers before starting on different sheep. **1940** STUDHOLME *Te Waimate* (1954) 128 After 'cutting out' the Waimate shed, they would go on to the back country stations. **1986** RICHARDS *Off the Sheep's Back* 68 When we had 'cut out' John's flock and packed our shearing gear, we returned..to pack our swags and get 'squared up'. *Ibid.* 74 I was sorry when the last sheep was cut out and it was time to pack. *Ibid.* 93 When he had cut-out his pen and called 'sheepo', he changed his cutter and comb.

b. [AND 1899.] *absol.* Of a shearer, to complete a shearing contract, to finish shearing; of a farm or mob, to have shearing completed. Also as *ppl. a.*
1877 PEACHE *Journal* in Gray *Quiet with Hills* (1970) 54 Three of the men had to move on and the others cut out the next day. **1892** COX *Diaries 1888–1925* (ATLMS) 23 Nov. They were shearing today but got cut out soon after dinner, no more sheep in. **1911** *Maoriland Worker* 20 Feb. 1 (Suppl.) Glenthorne cut out today after a run of seven days fine weather... This shed follows Lake Coleridge, which cut out on February 3. *Ibid.* 6 Oct. 17 The 'boss' knows when the 'gun' is cutting out. **1925** REES *Lake of Enchantment* 94 If they 'cut out' (or in other words get all their shearing over) by the end of the week the shearers would start in at the River View shed on Monday. **1955** BOWEN *Wool Away* 156 Cut out. Finished; the end of the mob. This call is made to the tally clerk before the new mob is started. **1960** MILLS *Sheep-O* 24 We're cutting out here in the morning and will be with you tomorrow night. **1968** *Straight Furrow* 21 Feb. 20 *Cut-out*: Finished—the end of [shearing] a flock or line of sheep. **1986** RICHARDS *Off the Sheep's Back* 74 A few days before we cut out, Harold Wilson informed us that one of his horses was to race at Auckland. **1992** ANDERSON *Portrait Artist's Wife* 46 They'd cut out in the sheds the day before.

2. a. *absol*. Of work other than shearing, to finish.
a**1974** SYDER & HODGETTS *Austral. & NZ Eng.* (TS) 240 To finish the job. 'When do you reckon we'll cut out—about four o'clock?'

b. To finish off (a job). Also as *ppl. a.*
1988 RENNIE *Super Man* 159 Thirty tons [topdressed] today, there's about nine left. Should cut it out easily by lunch time tomorrow.

3. Of resources or consumables. **a.** [AND 1907.] Of bush, to complete clearfelling (standing timber over an area); often in a passive construction: to be stripped of millable timber.
1889 KIRK *Forest Flora* 229 The amount of totara converted in the South Island is but small; in many districts it is completely cut out. **1900** *Regulations* in *Settler's Handbook NZ* (1902) 135 The areas and fees to be paid vary: In forests 'cut out' or not heavily timbered, the areas and corresponding fees are—200ft. by 200ft., £2 10s per annum per man [etc.]. **1904** *TrNZI* XXXVI. 204 After twenty-five years of great activity in the sawmilling industry these richly timbered forests are now almost 'cut out'. **1926** *Prospectus Waitane Saw-milling & Afforestation Ltd* in Barry *In Lee of Hokonuis* (1966) 145 In 1920 Messrs. Hallidays having cut out their bush at Kamahi began to look around for suitable timber areas. **1940** LAING & BLACKWELL *Plants NZ* 10 A forest that has been 'cut out' will, in time replace itself.

b. *absol*. Of a resource of standing millable timber, flax, gold, etc., to be completely used up, to come to an end; of a mill, to come to an end of its usable resource.

1905 *AJHR C-1* 74 I have had the opportunity of making minute inspections of several 'cut-out' kauri bushes, as well as two or three areas of kauri forest. **1944** GASKELL in *All Part of the Game* (1978) 19 The sawmills had just about cut out, and farming was the thing then. **1948** *Landfall 2* 123 After the flax cut out..it [*sc.* a house] had been used for camping in. **1948** *NZGeol.SB (NS)* No.42 49 [T]he shaft was progressively deepened, but at No 11 level several shoots cut out. **1986** RICHARDS *Off the Sheep's Back* 45 Shortly after we arrived..the timber mill..operating on Albert Tapp's bush 'cut out'.

c. As a predicative *ppl. a.*, of any consumable, (to be) used up. Cf. CUT *v.*² 1.

1960 MASTERS *Back-Country Tales* 158 By the time the wine was cut out, he'd worn the fiddle strings out, and the days were beginning to lengthen anyhow. **1963** CASEY *As Short a Spring* 156 'I started feeding out before the end of April.' 'How are you off for hay, then?' 'Just about cut out, what the hell do you think?'

4. to spend (money) (usu.) on liquor, esp. in the phr. **to cut a cheque out** [AND 1913], to spend its entire amount.

1906 *Truth* 8 Dec. 1 A young man is reported to have 'cut out' a cheque for £93..within the space of a fortnight, and was begging a drink when last heard of. **1924** ANTHONY *Follow the Call* (1975) 89 'Not a stiver,' he returned... 'I've never been able to save since I cut out the roll I collected there.' **1959** MASTERS *Tales of Mails* 52 When he had cut his cheque out, he would..ride right into the bar of the Hotel for what was supposed to be a final drink. **1961** MACKAY *Puborama* 12 Over the [shanty hotel] counter went his hard-earned cheque and, when that cheque was 'cut out'..the celebrant was kicked out. **1963** MORRIESON *Scarecrow* 5 After the flicks, Les and I cut out what was left of the cone money on a milk-shake. **1986** RICHARDS *Off the Sheep's Back* 96 Many a bushman..came into town with his cheque, handed it to the publican and..told the publican to tell him when it was 'cut out'.

cut-out, *n.*¹ *Farming.*

a. [AND 1896.] The completion of shearing (a line of sheep, or the whole shearing).

1910 *Awards, etc.* 111 [Otago Shearers Award] When shearing wet ewes, the shed-manager may..extend the hours..in order to complete the cut-out. **1922** TURNER *Happy Wanderer* 143 The songs they sang when an issue of rum followed a 'cut out'—the finishing of a line of sheep or of the shed itself. **1926** DEVANNY *Butcher Shop* (1981) 70 Another two days would have seen the cut out. **1959** MIDDLETON *The Stone* 49 On the day of the cut-out Mr Silva made a special trip..to pick up a ten-gallon. **1986** RICHARDS *Off the Sheep's Back* 138 Stan engaged a full-time accountant to keep in touch with the gangs and pay the men at 'cut-outs'.

Hence spec. Comb. **cut-out party**, a celebration to mark the end of shearing on a farm or station.

1995 Radio Pacific talkback 26 Nov. A former itinerant wool-classer reminiscing about shearing in the 1940s–50s: 'I had adventures with the shearing gangs that I couldn't talk about on air—cut-out parties that went on for days.'

b. The end of a job other than shearing; esp. in a freezing-works, the completion of processing of a batch of stock for slaughter.

1951 *Awards, etc.* 323 [NZ Freezing-Workers Award] In the event of a cut-out on any board and slaughtermen are required to wait ten minutes or more, they shall be paid at the rate of 5s. 4½d. per hour from the time the last sheep leaves legging-table to go on the chain until the next sheep following is ready to go on the chain. **1960** MASTERS *Back-Country Tales* 249 I wasn't sorry to see the cut out of that job [*sc.* mustering], and to be on my way again.

cut-out, *n.*² *Freezing works.* See quot.

1982 *Agric. Gloss.* (MAF) 33 *Cut-out:* The term often applied to the proportion of saleable product obtained from a carcass excluding fat and other trim, and bone where this is normally removed as for beef.

cuts: see CUT *n.*²

cutter, *n.*¹ In the phr. **to run the cutter**. [Prob. f. Brit. dial. *cutter* a bottle holding half a mutchkin of whisky (see SND), with a poss. a play on smuggling applications of the phrase in the sense of evading the revenue cutter; see EDD *run v.* 2 (17); AND 1904.] To fetch liquor for another. Also *transf.*

1906 *Truth* 22 Dec. 5 'He runs the cutter between a brothel in Frederick-Street and a nearby hotel,' remarked Tec. Cassells of a crook in the S.M.'s court during the week. **1910** *Ibid.* 4 June 7 It is not quite certain..what one should call the bottles which are usually requisitioned for the gentle duty of 'running the cutter'. **1933** AUGUST *Oreti Anthol.* 12 I used to 'run the cutter' with a dish from Side Street where we set the Daily Sun. **1943** BENNETT *English in NZ* in *Amer. Speech* XVIII. 89 *Running the cutter* (i.e. obtaining liquor for people who cannot get it themselves) is used without any appreciation of its original meaning of smuggling. **1953** *Evening Post* (Wellington) 4 Feb. 8 The party [of railway track layers] is provided with..a jigger to maintain communications with the tunnel-mouth—and to 'run the cutter' for the morning lunch and afternoon tea which is brewed outside. **c1962** BAXTER *Horse* (1985) 20 And Horse had run the cutter down to the pub to bring back three gallon jars of beer. **1981** CHARLES *Black Billy Tea* 67 The expression 'running the cutter' has its origins in the whaling days... When a ship lay at anchor, most of the crew would go ashore and an 'anchor watch' would be left aboard. Very often, some thirsty soul..would 'borrow' the cutter and slip ashore for rum... This was 'running the cutter'. Later, in days when some areas were under prohibition, the term was used for the job of going to the nearest licensed hotel for liquor. *Ibid.* 67 And the driver comes in and breasts up to the bar. He says, 'Give me a jar and a couple of crates, For I am running the cutter tonight for me mates!'... 'We are fresh out of beer, So that's why I'm here, Running the cutter tonight.'

cutter, *n.*² *Shearing.* [AND 1891.] The reciprocating unit or blade of a shearing handpiece which cuts the wool against the stationary comb.

1890 *Peache Jrnl.* in Gray *Quiet with Hills* (1970) 82 I saw a new shearing machine for shearing the wool off sheep... I think the stroke of the cutter might be lengthened. **1906** *Awards, etc.* 626 [Otago Shearers Award] In sheds where machines are used..the shearers to pay for combs and cutters at cost price. **1912** *Rep. Third Annual Conf. NZ Shearers* 23 Assets Shearers' Combs, Cutters, etc. **1915** [see HANDPIECE]. **c1927, 1950, 1973** [see COMB *n.*]. **1989** RICHARDS *Pioneer's Life* 30 Back at the shed our first job was to collect our gear of comb and cutters out of our water pots and clean, dry and grind them ready for the next 'run'.

cutter, *n.*³ *flax-cutter* (FLAX I 5 c).

1913 CARR *Country Work* 43 The cutter, armed with a sickle, stoops down and cuts the plant as near the base as he can get without taking in too much of the white growth, commonly called 'rhubarb'.

cutter, *n.*⁴ *Gumfields.* A gumdigger.

1916 *Truth* 11 Mar. 6 A gun cutter, swamp lingo for a good man.

cuttigrass, var. CUTTY-GRASS.

cutting, *ppl. a.*

1. *Whaling.* In special collocations: **cutting-block**, the block of the block-and-tackle used to haul the strips of cut blubber from the whale carcass (it is unlikely to be a wooden block on which whale blubber is sliced); **cutting-spade**, an implement for cutting into and removing a whale's blubber.

1840 *Piraki Log* 23 Apr. (1911) 107 People employ'd stropping **cutting-blocks** and laying Blubberways. **1837** *Piraki Log* (1911) 49 List of gear lost. 38 Irons—..8/- ea... 14 Lances—..8/- ea... 1 **Cutting Spade**—..8/-..2 Boat Spades... 4 Boat axes—..4/- ea... 5 Boat Knives—..2/- ea... 3 Pughs... 2 Blubber Knives... 1 [Boat] Traveller.

2. Of sheep or fleece-wool, usu. with a modifying adverb, indicating the ease or otherwise of shearing.

1960 SCRYMGEOUR *Memories of Maoriland* 48 26 men on the board, mostly Australians, who came over in the off-season making a good cheque on the soft cutting New Zealand flocks. **1981** CHARLES *Black Billy Tea* 53 Good cutting sheep they were—shore a thousand head. **1986** RICHARDS *Off the Sheep's Back* 68 My two mates selected a easy cutting ewe hogget each and got 'stuck into it'. *Ibid.* 82 The farm itself was very poor and covered with hutiwai (biddy bids), so the sheep were fairly slow cutting.

cutting-grass. [AND 1831.] Any of several grasses, sedges or grass-like plants having sharp-edged leaves or stems. See also CUTTY-GRASS.

1. *Gahnia* spp. (fam. Cyperaceae).

1864 VON TEMPSKY *Memoranda* (ATLTS) The bush was open on account of the absence of supplejack and cutting grass. **1867** HOOKER *Handbook* 764 Cutting grass. *Gahnia*, various sp. **1874** *TrNZI* VI. 56 Cutting grasses, *Gahnia setifolia* and *Gahnia ebenocarpa*, appear well adapted for the manufacture of coarse papers. **1887** *Auckland Weekly News* 17 Dec. 8 I..was in great difficulties among tall cutting grass (gahnia). **1897** *TrNZI* XXIX. 493 The tufts of the toe-kiwi—the 'cutting-grass' of the bushmen—which are a feature of the kauri bush, are set in a blaze. **1909** *AJHR C-11* 12 [*Gahnia*] *xanthocarpa* Cutting-grass.

2. *Cyperus* (formerly *Mariscus*) *ustulatus* (fam. Cyperaceae).

1888 *TrNZI* XX. 155 Our 'cutting-grass' or toe-toe (*Cyperus ustulatus*) is everywhere present at low elevations, readily taking possession of the abandoned cultivations. **1925-26** *NZJST* VIII. 203 Various grass-like sedges occupy the moist ground..and these include the..cutting-grass (*Mariscus ustulatus*).

3. *Cortaderia* spp. (fam. Poaceae).

1904 TREGEAR *Maori Race* 18 Sometimes a plaster of the leaves of cutting-grass (*toetoe*) was applied and sometimes the wounds were held in the smoke of a fire.

Cutts, see THEY'RE OFF MR CUTTS.

cutty-grass. Also *occas.* **cuttigrass**. A frequent familiar (esp. children's) alteration of CUTTING-GRASS q.v., often *spec.* TOETOE.

1889 PRINCE *Diary of Trip* 11 The Falls were soon arrived at, and standing..upon a little terrace of cutty grass, a full..view was obtained. **1900** *NZ Illustr. Mag.* III. 203 Spidery tafia [*sic*] and cutty grass. **1910**

COCKAYNE *NZ Plants & Their Story* 109 Here is also the home of the sedge family to which the so-called 'cutty-grasses' belong. **1920** MANDER *Story NZ River* (1974) 20 She saw an astonishing figure making its way among the rushes and cuttigrass bushes. **1939** BEATTIE *First White Boy Born Otago* 127 This greenness is not caused by grass or verdant pasture but by a 'water cutty grass'. **1948** FINLAYSON *Tidal Creek* (1979) 80 Cutty grass scars his arms and cheeks, bush-lawyer vines hook into clothes and flesh. **1953** MAGEE in Heinz *Bright Fine Gold* (1974) 37 Some huts [on the early diggings] were built with logs, criblogged, and the roof thatched with rushes or cutty grass. **1960** ROGERS *Long White Cloud* 12 A voice said: 'About time. I could eat cutty grass.' **1987** SLIGO *Final Things* 44 Natalia..looked at her son's legs, scratched by the cutty-grass down at the river paddock. **1992** LASENBY *The Conjuror* 215 Tendons severed, legs trailing, he was pulling himself through the cutty grass with both hands.

cut up. In various senses not *spec.* recorded in OED.

1. To cut (an animal) with a stockwhip.
  1862 CHUDLEIGH *Diary* 2 Apr. (1950) 30 I am..much improved with the stockwhip. I can crack it well enough but the thing is to be able to cut up your beast. An old Australian will cut a rat in two at full gallop and take the sight from a bullock.

2. Depleted, 'cut out'.
  1866 HUNT *Chatham Is.* 59 The busy [whaling] seasons lasted about five years; the ground then became pretty well cut up.

3. *Prison.* To mutilate oneself.
  1982 NEWBOLD *Big Huey* 248 Cut up (v) Mutilate oneself.

cuz /kʌz/. Also **cous'**, **coz**; **cuzzy**, **cuzzy-bro** (the last prob. the invention of Billy T. James (d. 1992), Maori entertainer and comedian). [A specific use of shortened (or elaborated) forms of *cous*(in, elsewhere usu. archaic.] **a.** Among Polynesians often in address, a cousin, a member of the family at large; also, in mainly non-Polynesian use, a Polynesian. Cf. BRO.
  1985 MITCALFE *Hey Hey Hey* 20 'Howdy, cous',' said he extending a hand. 'What you mean, cous'?' said Sefulu... 'I mean cousin, what else? Vaine, she my Auntie, small world, eh, man.' **1986** *Metro* (Auckland) Sept. 33 This you understand, is an intensely Maori group. It would seem that Billy's [*sc.* T. James, a Maori entertainer] not entirely joking when he talks about his countless cuzzies. **1988** MCGILL *Dict. Kiwi Slang* 31 *coz* greeting of friend, short for cousin; a Kiwi revival of archaic greeting used by likes of Romeo and Benvolio in Shakespeare's *Romeo and Juliet.* **1990** *Listener* 11 June 14 [Heading] Cuzzybro Comedy. **1991** PAYNE *Staunch* 74 Everyone's sitting around, the bro's, the prospects and even the gash... 'You scared, bro?' sneers a prospect. 'Got no balls, cuz?' says another. **1991** *Dominion* (Wellington) 14 Aug. 1 I want to give these chaps responsibility..they're the 'cuzzie-bros' from in these gangs. **1991** *Examiner* (Auckland) 29 Aug. 6 Either the Tongans didn't want curly locks..or some of the wrinkly Kiwi cuzzies put a sour note in a Tonga-bound wine bottle to spoil the benefit-cutting MP's hols. **1991** *Dominion* (Wellington) 23 Nov. 9 Nga Tama Toa members would come..and just say to everyone, 'Don't say a thing, cuz, till you get out of there.'

b. *transf.* in jocular or slightly derogatory reference to Australians as sharing the stereotype of the technologically disadvantaged Polynesian.
  1992 *Dominion IT Weekly* (Wellington) 21 Sept. 4 Under closer economic relations IBM PCs made by our Digger cuzzy-bros are apparently as good as home-made. **1995** *Dominion* (Wellington) 26 Jan. 2 C'mon. Deenkie-die folks. I love my Aussie cuzzies—and not just because they make rip-snorter wines.

cypress. *Obs.* [Transf. use of northern hemisphere *cypress*, an evergreen coniferous tree of the genus *Cupressus* (fam. Cupressaceae): AND 1820.] Formerly occas. applied in New Zealand to the tall native evergreen trees KAHIKATEA (rarely), and KAWAKA.
  1820 MARSDEN *Lett. & Jrnls.* 21 June (1932) 256 The quality of the timber is not considered good enough for masts, especially a species of the Cyprus (cypress) which composes the principal forests here and is called by the natives kikatea. **1867** HOOKER *Handbook* 764 Cypress. *Libocedrus Doniana.* **1883** HECTOR *Handbook NZ* 122 *Libocedrus doniana*, Endl. Kawaka, Cypress, Cedar. **1916** COWAN *Bush Explorers 'More Reminisc.'* (VUWTS) Here the trees are totara, manuka, and a kind of cypress, or arbor vitae, no kareao.

D

D /di/: see DEE *n.*[1]

dab, *n.*[1] Also occas. **dab flounder**. [Transf. use of *dab* a small flatfish.] *Rhombosolea plebeia* (fam. Pleuronectidae), the common sand flounder (FLOUNDER 2 (9)); also formerly used as a general term for any flounder. See also DIAMOND.
1770 PARKINSON *Journal* 15 Jan. (1773) 114 All the coves of this bay teem with fish of various kinds, such as..dogfish, soles, dabs. **1910** *Truth* 30 July 7 'The position is scandalous,' said Mr.Coltman, J.P...when a fish inspector candidly confessed that he did not know the difference between a dab and a flounder. **1936** [see FLOUNDER *n.* 2 (9)]. **1956** [see PATIKI 1]. **1967** [see FLOUNDER *n.* 2 (9)]. **1970** [see PLAICE]. **1982** [see FLOUNDER *n.* 2 (9)]. **1985** McGILL *G'day Country* 56 A fishshop [at Thames] was selling dabs (baby flounder) and crab sticks.

dab, *n.*[2] *Rugby football*. [Fig. use of *dab* a sharp, quick blow: see OED *n.*[1]] A short darting run.
1970 SLATTER *On the Ball* 110 An audacious dab by Mill surprised Southland and Stringfellow cut past..to score halfway out. **1979** *Otago Daily Times* (Dunedin) 28 Mar. 21 The three meanings given for 'dab' do not include the short darting run made by a rugby player.

dab: see WATTLE-AND-DAUB a.

dabchick. Also **New Zealand dabchick**. *Poliocephalus* (formerly *Podiceps*) *rufopectus* (formerly *rufipectus*) (fam. Podicipedidae), a small, dark, water bird having a reddish-brown fore-neck and upper chest and lobed feet. See also DIVER, *little grebe* (GREBE 2 (2)), TOTOKIPIO, WEWEIA.
1869 *TrNZI* I. (rev. edn.) 23 A small dab-chick (*Podiceps rufipectus*) is common in our freshwater lagoons. **1873** BULLER *Birds NZ* 350 (New-Zealand Dabchick)... *Native names.*—Weweia, and Totokipio. **1900** *Canterbury Old & New* 197 The divers are represented by the almost cosmopolitan crested grebe and the dabchick. **1922** *NZJST* IV. 279 The little grebe (or dabchick) was not uncommon in the quiet reaches of the river or deeper lagoons. **1949** *NZ Bird Notes* III. 170 Dabchick (*Poliocephalus rufopectus*).—This species seems quite common on lakes in the central plateau. **1955** OLIVER *NZ Birds* 91 *New Zealand Dabchick. Weweia*... The first specimen of the New Zealand Dabchick that came into the hands of ornithologists was collected by Dr. A. Sinclair and..described..as a new species. **1973** POWER *NZ Water Birds* (unpaged) The Dabchick, widely distributed through the larger lakes of the North Island, can also be seen on the small sand dune lakes of the Wellington Province. **1989** PARKINSON *Travelling Naturalist* 42 One of the main populations of the rare New Zealand dabchick (weweia) is to be found here. **1990** *Checklist Birds NZ* 10 *Poliocephalus rufopectus..New Zealand dabchick (Weweia)*... New Zealand only... Total population, perhaps 600–700 breeding pairs.

dack up. [f. *dacca*, *dack(a)* marijuana ad. S. African *dagga* /ˈdʌxə/ wild hemp or marijuana ad. Khoi *daxah*; DSADT *dagga* marijuana; cf. Wilkes *dacca*, *dakker* drugs, esp. marijuana.] To light up or smoke (up) a marijuana joint.
1991 DUFF *One Night Out Stealing* 102 You all moved up the street..and drank more piss, went outside to dack up with a few of the boys, back inside for more laughs.

dactylanthus. [ad. Greek (prob. through modern Latin) δακτυλος finger + ανθος flower.] *wood rose* (WOOD *n.*[1] 2 b).
1963 BACON *In the Sticks* 57 It was a small twig, of reddish wood, with three delicately shaped wooden flowers clustered towards the end. They were hard, beautifully fashioned, securely fastened to the stem. 'No, they won't come off,' said Les. 'That's dactylanthus; *Dactylanthus Taylori*. It's a parasite that gets into the roots of various native trees, usually five finger or lancewood.' **1992** *North & South* (Auckland) June 18 Ecroyd recently succeeded in germinating dactylanthus seeds.

Daffodil Hill: see *Bludgers' Hill* (BLUDGER 4 b).

dag, *n.*[1] [f. Brit. dial. *dag*: see OED *n.*[1] 3; AND 1891.]

1. Often pl., a clot of matted wool and excrement found on (or cut from) the hindquarters of a sheep; such daggy wool removed from a sheep. Also green dags, those still soft or moist. See also *sheep-dag* (SHEEP 1).
1912 *NZ Shearers... Rep. Third Annual Conf.* 16 Sheep did not do well with daggs [*sic*] on. **1933** *Press* (Christchurch) (Acland Gloss.) 7 Oct. 15 *Dag, dags*.—Hard or soft dung hanging from the breech of a sheep. Cutting this off the sheep with an old pair of shears is called *dagging*. The *d[ag]s* are afterwards gone through by a *d[ag]-picker* or *d[ag]-boy*, who cuts out any wool worth saving. **1959** SHADBOLT *New Zealanders* (1986) 113 [They met] in the dust and dag-stink of a woolstore. **1983** HENDERSON *Down from Marble Mountain* 267 Talks sheepdogs day and night at the drop of a dag. **1991** TV3 *Nightline* 26 Sept. Interest rates are dropping like dags on shearing day. **1991** *NZ Gardener* Dec. 5 The lanolin [i.e., wool-fat] is bad for possums, good for the hands..and is dag-free. **1995** *Dominion* (Wellington) 24 Nov. 19 Bulk Green Dags are now no problem. We can dry them at no extra cost to clients.

2. Special Comb. **dag-boy**, a young *dag-picker*; **dag-crusher** (a) a machine to crush dags to enable the removal of wool; (b) a person who operates a dag-crusher or dag-crushing plant; **dag-crushing**, the crushing of dags preparatory to removing the wool (also *attrib.*); **dag-cutter**, a dag-picker who cuts wool from dags; **dag cutting**, the cutting of wool from dags; **dag-heap**, the pile or heap of daggy wool awaiting picking; **dag-picker** [AND 1907], a shedhand who removes wool from dags; **dag-picking** *vbl. n.*, the cutting of wool from dags; **dagwool**, wool cut or otherwise produced from dags; **dag-rattling** *ppl. a.*, see RATTLE *v.*

1933 dag-boy [see 1 above]. **1985** BREMNER *Woolscours NZ* 9 **Dag-crusher** machine to remove wool from dags. **1987** HUTCHINS *Tall Half-Backs* 80 And then the dag bags had to be manhandled to the dag crusher down by the pond. Bill Schmidt was in charge of the dag crusher. *Ibid.* 86 Bill Schmidt, the dag crusher..remained faithful to his fibrolite bach, and..one suspects, true to Elvis Presley. **1985** BREMNER *Woolscours NZ* 33 One of the woolscouring industry's most historic landmarks is now a **dag-crushing** plant, known far and wide as the 'Old Fellmongery' on the Waikaka River at Gore. **1913** CARR *Country Work* 15 **Dag Cutting**.—The wool rollers take off the dirty portion of the fleece and throw it into a bin, the **dag cutter**..with a pair of shears cuts off all the wool he can, which he throws into another bin. It is then called 'second pieces'. **1991** *Dominion Sunday Times* (Wellington) 20 Oct. 25 I saw my outline in the **dag heap**. **1933 dag-picker** [see 1 above]. **1951** DUFF *Shepherd's Calendar* (1961) 40 They were inferior to everybody but dag-pickers and swaggers, and this was her hour of brief authority. **1975** NEWTON *Sixty Thousand on the Hoof* 87 I was very thankfull [*sic*] for your reply to my application for the job **Dag picking** but I am sorry to say that I carn't [*sic*] feel confident in fieting [*sic*] with any contractor at my age 72 on the first [T]hursday. **1995** *Dominion* (Wellington) 24 Nov. 19 We have the ability to manufacture your dags into the best possible product. Because of this our company has a strong demand from the wool exporters for scoured dagwool.

3. In the phr. **rattle one's dags**, see RATTLE *v.*; **dags do not wag the sheep** (a var. of 'the tail does not wag the dog') indicating that a (contemptible) minority does not control the majority.
1983 *National Bus. Rev.* 26 Sept. 9 Lange came back from Australia after the debacle of two MPs who had supported him in his drive last year for the leadership fulminating that in Australia 'the dags did not wag the sheep' in the Labour Party. The inescapable inference from that is that here the sheep is being wagged by the dags (a choice of phrase hardly likely to enthuse those accused of doing the wagging).

dag, *n.*[2] [Transf. use of Brit. dial. (esp. among boys) *dag* a daring feat, a challenge: see EDD *n.*[2] 11: 'There's a dag for you..do it if you can.'; AND 1875, 1916. There is no direct evidence to suggest that early NZ uses may have referred primarily to a memorable event rather than to a person; there is some slight indirect evidence that usage may have been influenced by a rhyme with *wag*. (Cf. Fraser & Gibbons *Soldier and Sailor Words* (1925) 70 *Dag, A*: A funny fellow. A wag.)]

1. a. Esp. as **a real dag**, someone or something extraordinary or entertaining; an amusingly eccentric or impudent person; a character, a 'hard case.'
1916 *Anzac Book* 47 'Anzac Types 2—The Dag'... Yes, 'Ennessy was a dag if ever there was one! **1919** *Quick March* 10 Sept. 17 I do remember though..three Diggers, real 'dags', the three of them. **1945** *NZ Geogr.*

Apr. I. 19 'Dag'..is a word used first to describe a tuft of wool fouled by excrement... Used personally, 'dag' was earlier a term of some approbation. Its meaning has widened, however, and now signifies no more than 'hard case', or 'tough guy', or 'card.' *Ibid.* 21 'Real dags' they were; there was one fellow, like, who cut off the leg of his engine-driver's overalls to wrap a billy in. *Ibid.* 35 He was a tough old dag, and no mistake. **1959** SLATTER *Gun in My Hand* 45 For once in ya life ya right. But you're a dag, you are. **1973** WILSON *NZ Jack* 162 'Perfidious males,' she said, smiling. 'Oh, you're a real dag.' **1985** McGILL *G'day Country* 160 Two handsome middle-aged women boarded... They looked a couple of dags. The driver asked if their husbands had let them out on the town. They laughed. **1993** *Capital Times* (Wellington) 22–28 Sept. 7 Dominique is a smart girl's dag: ribald and honest, but with the ability to assume total control.

b. In the phr. **a bit of a dag**, **a dag of a**, used of an amusing, extraordinary, etc., person, thing, or situation.

1948 *Canta* July in McKay *James K. Baxter* (1990) 58 In *Canta*, July 1948, he wrote of King's: 'By the time I'd been there a year or two I was counted all right and a bit of a dag.' **1965** HILLIARD *Power of Joy* 252 Had a dag of a French period this week—teacher was reading..and when she translated 'quite naked' she blushed all over. **1971** *Listener* 19 Apr. 56 Old Pete's a real scrounger, a bit of a dag. **1978** HALL *Middle-Age Spread* 44 I said 'What did you do that for?' and he said 'Just wanted to see what it was like to score a goal. Bit of a dag, eh Sir?' **1981** HENDERSON *Exiles Asbestos Cottage* 38 'Saying "tock-tick" too,' Bertie loved to say. 'A dag of a watch.' **1987** VIRTUE *Redemption of Elsdon Bird* (1988) 95 I heard a lady up the road..saying that they all thought Dad was a pommy holy roller and it [*sc.* a fire] was all a bit of a dag, a way of getting rid of him.'

2. An extraordinary or amusing situation or event, esp. in the exclam. **what a dag!**, How amusing!

1960 18 C M B 11 Nelson Boys C. 8 Dag, what a dag (=how funny) **1979** ROCHE *Foreigner* 187 [New Zealanders c1939] larded their conversation with strange, uncouth expressions. 'What a dag!' they said. (She was horrified when she found out what a dag was.) **1980** LELAND *Kiwi-Yankee Dict.* 31 [Dag] has..become part of the language as in 'What a dag!'—an admiring statement directed at someone who has done something slightly risque. **1991** *Listener* 16 Dec. 16 She was peeved but amused. What a dag!

dag, *n.*³ [Poss. an alteration *be a dab at*.] In the phr. **to be a dag at**, to be extremely good at.

1937 PARTRIDGE *Dict. Slang* 204 *dag at, be a*. To be extremely good at: from the middle 1890's: Australians'; hence, by 1920, New Zealanders'. Ex [dag 'hard case']. **1938** *Press* (Christchurch) (McNab Slang) 2 Apr. 18 'To be a dag at,'.. 'to jerry to,'..need no explanation.

dag, *v.*

1. *Farming*. [f. Brit. dial.: AND 1867.] *trans.* To remove dags or daggy wool from (a sheep's hindquarters).

1878 *Country Jrnl.* (1877) II. 400 With reference to cleaning or dagging crossbred sheep. **1889** WILLIAMS & REEVES *Colonial Couplets* 9 Dagging the hoggets, or drafting the rams. **1912** *NZ Shearers... Rep. Third Annual Conf.* 15 It was decided: 'That all members refuse to dagg [*sic*] sheep during shearing except the dagging rate be added to the shearing rate, as we are of the opinion that dagging is not shearing.' **1922** PERRY *Sheep Farming* 83 It is advisable to dag all dirty sheep before shearing. **1948** *NZJAg.* Feb. LXXVI. 157 Good flockmasters dag breaking ewes when they put them out to the ram. **1974** *NZ Agric.* 66 Any dirty animals are 'dagged' (any stained wool and pieces of dung hanging around the tail are clipped off). **1991** *Dominion Sunday Times* (Wellington) 10 Nov. 24 We'd been dagging hoggets in the woolshed.

Hence **dagging** *vbl. n.* [AND 1867] and *ppl. a.* (pertaining to) the removal of dags or daggy wool from the hindquarters of sheep; also special collocation **dagging shears**, see quot. 1989; but also (see quot. 1938) a name for short-bladed specialist shears more able than full shears to deal with the awkward angles of a sheep's crutch during dagging or crutching (p.c. Dr S.R. Pennycook).

1871 MONEY *Knocking About NZ* 146 Dagging and paring sheep, tailing lambs, etc, felling timber,.. were the other employments..at Mr. McBeth's farm. **1898** VOGEL *Maori Maid* 147 When the docking, and dagging, and cutting comes he is worked as hard as any man. **1902** *Brett's Colonists' Guide* 319 Lamb dagging. **1912** dagging rate [see preceding section]. **1913** *NZJAg.* Jan. VI. 577 Proper dipping, crutching, dagging, &c., are necessary. **1926** DEVANNY *Butcher Shop* (1981) 29 The dust of the yards in the dagging season... One could not free one's throat from it. **1938** *Auckland Weekly News* 26 Oct. 84 Many accidents occur on farms and stations through men being careless when carrying dagging shears. **1953** STRONACH *Musterer on Molesworth* 31 So, after three days of mustering about the paddocks, with a dagging thrown in, we were glad to get away up Yoe Creek again, to straggle the ewe country. **1985** LANGDALE-HUNT *Last Entail Male* 79 I found on this heavy grass country carrying a flock of Romney sheep that there was continual dagging and crutching to keep the wool clean. **1986** RICHARDS *Off the Sheep's Back* 130 The drafting yards and dagging pens were concreted and all under cover. **1989** *NZ Eng. Newsletter* III. 23 *dagging shears*: Handshears that are too worn for shearing but still suitable for cutting dags or for gardening.

2. *transf.* To shorten trousers (etc.) roughly by cutting off excess length.

1940 *National Educ.* 16 Feb. 16 The [Maori boy] is wearing the [cast off] 'pant' well up under the armpits... They had been dagged at a convenient length round the ankles also.

dag! *exclam. Obs.* [f. Brit. dial.: see EDD *dag v.*³ Sc. Yks 1: Used in imperative as an imprecation 'confound!' 2 *dag on't* (*dagont*): cf. *doggone*.]

1917 MUSGRAVE *Myola* 65 He laughed contemptuously at the curious expletive 'Dag!'

dagger.

1. One who dags sheep.

1889 WILLIAMS & REEVES *Colonial Couplets* 28 He would take what came, nor shirk or fret, Be 'brander', 'rouse-about' or 'dagger', Yet work he never seemed to get. **1892** COX *Diaries 1888–1925* (ATLMS) 1 Oct. The daggers worked today so we had a few to dinner but a good crowd this evening, six swaggers here tonight. **1966** *NZ Short Stories* (1976) 127 What with the dogs..and daggers brought to give them a hand in the shed and yards.

2. *pl.* [AND 1876.] Dagging handshears.

1989 *NZ Eng. Newsletter* III. 23 *daggers*: See dagging shears. [*sc.* Handshears that are too worn for shearing but still suitable for cutting dags.]

daggings, *n. pl.* [Formed on analogy with CRUTCHINGS.] Dags with wool attached.

1883 *Brett's Colonists' Guide* 172 Fleeces should be carefully skirted, and all daggings and faulty parts removed. **1917** *Fielding Star* 29 Jan. 3 [Advt] Daggings, Daggings, Daggings. We have a buyer for good dried woollied Daggings.

daggy, *a.*¹ [AND 1895.] Of a sheep or a fleece, with dags attached; discoloured by dags.

1912 *NZ Shearers Rep. Third Annual Conf.* 15 Mount Watkins Remit No. 3: 'That an allowance in the case of daggy sheep be arranged for', was dealt with. **1922** PERRY *Sheep Farming* 75 It is not advisable to carry out this work [*sc.* crutching] too early or else the ewes will be very daggy by the lambing season. **1940** MEEK in Woodhouse *Farm & Station Verse* (1950) 153 May they dump them [*sc.* Nazis] with Joe Goebbels in a truck of daggy wool. **1950** *NZJAg.* Oct. LXXXI. 310 One daggy sheep can stain quite a few clean sheep when penning up is in progress. **1960** *Dominion* (Wellington) 12 Feb. 11 [Freezing Companys' Advt] *Notice to Fat Stock Producers Daggy and Dirty Stock...* All stock for slaughter must be free of dags and dirt. **1981** CHARLES *Black Billy Tea* 72 Then it's grab a daggy ewe and drag her to the board, Pick up your hand-piece and pull on the cord.

Hence **dagginess** *n.*, the state of being daggy.

1941 *NZJAg.* Feb. LXII. 107 The control of dagginess on the farm is an important factor in lessening the incidence of strike. **1958** *Ibid.* Dec. XCVII. 507 The degree of dagginess is affected by the type of country being grazed.

daggy, *a.*² Of the nature of a DAG *n.*²; amusing in an out-of-the-way fashion. Occas. heard as **daggish**.

1966 *Dominion* (Wellington) 15 Oct. 3 Daggy..Fantabulous. **1985** *Listener* 3 Aug. 54 Cropdusting, as seen by Stephen Woodman and Andrew Niccol in their daggy *Paying Through the Nose...* Wry cartoons give ingenious literal interpretations of English expressions. **1995** *Sunday Star-Times* (Auckland) 21 May sect. D 21 *Jools* and *Lynda Topp*..were magnificent in gorgeous long frocks – which they later switched for their usual daggy cowgirl look.

dago. *Obs. Offensive.* [Spec. use of *dago* a dark-skinned person, esp. one of Mediterranean origin.]

1. a. A Maori.

1905 *Truth* 24 June 3 At a recent Otaki meeting an intoxicated Dago assured me that..he was the 'pest plurry chockey in New Zealand.' **1911** [see NIGGER]. **1912** *Truth* 20 Jan. 7 Among the many things for which New Zealand is noted is the manner in which the native population, i.e. the Maoris, commonly and contemptuously called by the pakeha, 'the dago', has been cared for by a paternal-like Government. **1946** [see NIGGER]. **1946** SARGESON *That Summer* 34 Oh boy, but it's a quiet dump he [*sc.* the barman] says. All Dagoes. Do I have some long serves. **1951** PARK *Witch's Thorn* 83 So, you're mucking around with dagoes now. Mum's going to be interested.

b. DALMATIAN A.

1904 *NZ Observer* 23 July 7 'Dago' oyster saloons are springing up everywhere in Auckland's principal streets.

2. *Boarding school.* [f. *day*(boy with a play on *dago*.] A day-boy.

1951 16-18 M 32 St Bede's, Chch 25 Dagos, day-goes [M16]

3. [Poss. a play on *borsalino*, a famous Italian brand of hat.] A round black hat.

1965 SARGESON *Memoirs of Peon* 186 It was not merely that Tony..dashingly wore a round black hat of the variety known as dago, and was further very elegant in an expensive winter overcoat.

DAIRY

dairy. [Senses 1 and 2 below are found elsewhere but are of historical significance for NZ.]

1. *Hist.* **a.** A dairy-farm, one which produces milk or milk products.

1844 DILLON *Letters* 10 Apr. (1954) 40 He has very large herds and a large dairy where he makes a great deal of butter and cheese. His dairy is of about 40 cows. **1853** MACKIE *Traveller under Concern* (1973) 86 We reached the hospitable roof of Geo. McRae who has an extensive sheep run and a large dairy. **1898** *Dairy Industry Act* in *Settler's Handbook NZ* (1902) 148 A 'dairy' is: (*a*) a milk-house, milk-shop, dairy factory, and any other place where dairy produce is collected, deposited, treated, separated, prepared, or manufactured, or is sold or offered or exposed for sale; and includes (*b*) a farm, stockyard, milking-yard, paddock, stable, stall, and any other place where cows from which the milk-supply of a dairy is obtained are depastured or kept. **1986** HENDERSON *Jim Henderson's People* 33 I've had my days of dairies.

b. *Rare.* [Poss. orig. *dairy shed.*] A milking shed.

c1910 MACDONALD *Reminiscences* (VUWTS) 15 There were 7 or 8 of us lads and our chief business [c1840s] was a dairy—but not such a dairy as we have now. **1974** *NZ Agric.* 81 'Herringbone' dairies, developed in New Zealand, are increasing rapidly in number. *Ibid.* 83 The backing gate is used to bring cows from the yard into the dairy.

2. *Hist.* The building or place on a farm where milk, cream, etc., were formerly kept and butter made.

1844, 1898 [see 1 a above]. **1928** SEDDON *The Seddons* (1968) 14 The dairy, a cool building shaded by a pine-tree, stood near the house. On a bench which extended along the interior stood large shallow metal dishes in which the milk was placed [c1880]. **1967** MCLATCHIE *Tang of Bush* 58 A dairy made from packing cases was attached to the back of the house; and shelves to hold the milk pans were made from split rails. **1984** HENDERSON *Tales of the Coast* 126 The stumps and the trees burned for months but we were out of danger... The dairy and the cowshed were gone.

3. a. A small, mixed-grocery store (orig. selling, then licensed to sell, milk, eggs, and dairy products, and other perishables after normal trading hours). Occas. (poss. orig.) **dairy shop**; in recent use, on the model of Brit. 'corner shop', **corner dairy**.

[*Note*] The sense 'small mixed-grocery shop' is not recorded unambiguously before the early 1940s: *cash grocer* seems to have been a usual term then. The 1938–39 entries suggest a transition from a 'lolly-shop' to one selling dairy products, ice-cream, confectionery, and possibly other convenience items; perhaps further suggesting that the expansion of the sale by 'dairies' of a wider range of items than the 'dairy products' they were legally entitled to sell may have been a function of the development of the NZ 'long weekend'—i.e. the moving of the (traditional) Wednesday half-holiday to Saturday morning.

[**1908** *Truth* 25 Jan. 5 T.J. O'Hagan's Aberdeen Dairy... Fresh Milk, Butter and Eggs Delivered Daily] **1938** *Wise's NZ Post Office Directory* 1071 Upland rd [Wellington]... 92 Skelton Mrs H. cnfr [confectioner] **1939** *Ibid.* 1093 Upland rd 92 Loblan Andrew. dry [dairy] **1939** *Wellington Telephone Directory* (Trade Directory) Dairies... Upland Rd Dairy, 92 Upland Rd Kelburn [sole entry in this category]. **1945** *NZPD* CCLXXII. [263 If a milk-bar or dairy establishment sells, say tea or sugar, it must observe the award conditions applicable to grocers.] *Ibid.* 268 In Auckland a large number of shops close on Saturday... The result is that all these little dairies have arisen. In a city in which milk is delivered every morning irrespective of the dairies, there are twenty-nine dairies in one road. It is not milk they are selling, but groceries. **1948** BALLANTYNE *Cunninghams* (1976) 30 He entered the dairy... Mrs Morpeth sold milk, cream, ice cream, bread, scones, all sorts of sweets..and blocks of cake and tins of biscuits. **1950** *NZJAg.* Oct. LXXXI. 306 There is still a danger where dairy shops buy raw milk for use in milk shakes. **1963** DUCKWORTH *Barbarous Tongue* 181 We didn't put any [milk] bottles out. I'll have to go to the dairy. **1985** FRAME *Envoy from Mirror City* 165 I bought supplies from the dairy and I stared curiously at the dairy owner..who had been named next-of-kin when my father collapsed outside the shop. **1987** WILSON *Past Today* 122 The town is devoid of embellishments that signify life styles of the 1980s. There is no theatre, no hotel, no corner dairy. **1991** *North & South* (Auckland) June 75 Corner dairies and other strip-retailers, [etc.]—all form New Zealand's mass of small businesspeople.

b. Special Comb. **dairy porn**, sexually explicit magazines sold at local dairies.

1993 *National Radio* 'Sunday Supplement' 31 Jan. The exotica [in the local grocery shop]..includes a large and varied selection of magazines, a disproportionate number of which are what has come to be known as dairy porn.

4. Used *attrib.* in special Comb. **(New Zealand) Dairy Board** (orig. **Dairy-produce Control Board**, a statutory body, operating from 1924, having authority over various aspects of dairy production and marketing; **dairy co-op**, a dairy factory, or factory company owned cooperatively by its suppliers; **dairy factory** [OED 'Chiefly N.Z.'], a factory where usu. cream is made into butter, or milk into cheese, and other dairy products are manufactured (cf. FACTORY 1); **dairy run** *obs.*, **dairy station** [AND 1838] *obs.*, a large dairy-farm (cf. STATION 3 a).

1924 *AJHR* H-29 4 The Dairy-produce Control Board subsequently elected got to work quietly and effectively. **1938** *Auckland Weekly News* 4 May 82 The New Zealand **Dairy Board** to be empowered to organise a national co-operative system of local pools for the collection and disposal of bobby calves and all bobby calf products. **1959** SINCLAIR *Hist. NZ* 245 At the farmers' instigation, in 1922 the Government set up a Meat Board, and a year later..a Dairy Board. **1986** *Listener* 12 July 15 It was the sharemilker and **dairy co-op** director and its accountant revealed that next season their industry was facing an almost 50 per cent drop in payments to farmers on their production's butter fat content. **1888** MCCALLUM *Rep. Dairy Factories NZ* 5 I have inspected a number of the **dairy factories** in the colony. **1895** *Ann. Rep. Dept. Agric.* III. 90 I will explain what a dairy-factory manager must be: he must be a man with a perfect practical and theoretical knowledge of his business. **1898** [see 1 a above]. **1948** *Our Own Country* 25 Dairy and cheese factories are dotted over the plains. **1959** SLATTER *Gun in My Hand* 150 Frank..used to fly model aeroplanes of balsa and tissue in the big paddock behind the dairy factory. **1966** *NZ Short Stories* (1976) 200 Milking cows and sending cream down river to the dairy factory. **1989** *Sunday Star* (Auckland) 4 June A6 Last year, the gang tried to buy a dairy factory at Piriaka. **1861** *Otago Witness* (Dunedin) 2 Feb. 10 Wanted, a partner, sleeping or active, to take a share in a good **Dairy Run**, near a thriving town. **1848** WAKEFIELD *Handbook NZ* 124 Butter and cheese, the product of **dairy stations** at Wairarapa, are sent to Wellington. **1851** *Lyttelton Times* 5 July 7 There are..also six dairy stations, which supplied about 12 tons per year of the celebrated Port Cooper cheese.

DAISY

daisy.

1. Applied to any of various daisy-like species (esp. *Celmisia*), usu. with a modifier. See also DAISY-TREE, TREE DAISY.

1982 SALE *Four Seasons* 33 The shrub called Kirk's daisy wears flowers so dazzling white that from a distance they look like a cascade of clematis. **1988** *Pacific Way* June 48 Above on the rocky bluffs [at Nugget Point, South Otago]..the local daisy *celmisia lindsayii* and the tiny blue grass..cling resolutely to small cracks.

2. With a modifier: **Cape, cotton, dog, everlasting, horse, Marlborough, mountain, native (New Zealand)**.

(1) **Cape daisy**. CAPE WEED a (*Arctotheca calendula*).

1926 HILGENDORF *Weeds* 184 Cape Weed..or Cape daisy is abundant in pastures and waste places in the North Island and is also recorded from Greymouth. **1969** *Standard Common Names Weeds* 11 Cape daisy [=] Cape weed.

(2) As **cotton daisy**, see COTTON PLANT.

(3) **dog daisy**. [f. Brit. dial.: cf. EDD *dog-flower*.] (Usu.) *Leucanthemum vulgare* (formerly *Chrysanthemum leucanthemum*) (fam. Asteraceae), an introduced daisy-like plant with a strong odour.

1905 COX *Diaries 1888–1925* (ATLMS) 4 Feb. I have now got a job on the Borough Council to grub the Dog-daisies in the Domain. **1910** COCKAYNE *NZ Plants & Their Story* 135 But..the dog-daisy..and the foxglove, to mention only a few British plants, are now wild in various places. **1911** *Truth* 2 Sept. 4 It was then thought that the..scandal had been deeply and irrevocably buried, and that dog da[i]sies six feet in height were growing on its grave. **1926** HILGENDORF *Weeds* 176 Oxeye Daisy... also called dog daisy, moon daisy and poached eggs, is common in pastures on somewhat heavy and damp land throughout the islands. **1934** LEE *Children of Poor* (1949) 44 Sometimes I would gather a handful of buttercups or white dog daisies and gallop the tribute home to Big Mother. **1965** FRAME *Adaptable Man* 113 The smell of dog-daisies was unpleasant.

(4) **everlasting daisy**. (Usu.) *Helichrysum bellidioides*, also known familiarly (from a jocular alteration of its scientific name) as **hells bells** (see quot. 1990).

1952 RICHARDS *Chatham Is.* 47 *Helichrysum.. bellioides...* False Edelweiss. Everlasting Daisy. **1969** *Standard Common Names Weeds* 20 daisy, everlasting *Helichrysum bellidioides*. **1970** JOHNSON *Life's Vagaries* 54 In November we would have the added pleasure of seeing the everlasting daisies *Helichrysum*, in bloom, scrambling over the great boulders. **1980** BRASCH *Indirections* 18 We drove round..the rocky upper [Otago] Peninsula road..to pick everlasting daisies. Grandmother probably first told me their name... Their dry silver-white petals enclosed an eye of clear honey or pale lime green,.. the dark green leaves, silver beneath... I pressed everlastings in books. **1990** WEBB et al. *Flowering Plants NZ* 28 [Caption] *Helichrysum bellidioides* (or hells-bells for short) is a widespread native everlasting daisy. In this daisy tribe it is the persistent white bracts which give each flower cluster the appearance of being a single flower.

(5) **horse daisy**. Any of various plants of the genus *Celmisia*.

1981 BROOKER et al. *NZ Medicinal Plants* 41 *Celmisia coriacea*..and allied spp. Common names: *Cotton plant, horse daisy* Maori name: *Tikunu*.

(6) **Marlborough rock daisy**. *Pachystegia* spp., usu. *P. insignis* (fam. Compositae). See quot. 1988.

1988 *Evening Post* (Wellington) 9 Dec. 32 [Advt] Marlborough Rock Daisy Pachystegia insignis. Gorgeous, low growing..shrub has the most exquisitely formed brilliant white, yellow centred daisy flowers! An incredibly beautiful native plant from the cliffs of Marlborough. **1990** *NZ Gardener* Feb. 55 The pick of the native flowering plants seen in November were the Pachystegias or Marlborough Rock Daisies. **1990** WEBB et al. *Flowering Plants NZ* 29 [Caption] The Marlborough rock daisies, *Pachystegia*, are a genus of woody daisies.

(7) **mountain daisy**. Any of various plants of the genus *Celmisia*. See also CELMISIA.

1848 *NZ Jrnl.* VIII. 198 The last plant the party observed, as they wended their way upwards, was..the mountain daisy. **1858** THOMSON *Reconn. Survey S. Dist. Otago* in Taylor *Early Travellers* (1959) 335 Half-way up the mountains some pretty flowers were gathered, amongst which the mountain daisy deserves notice. **1889** PRINCE *Diary of Trip* 9 The Saddle itself is..studded with..several forms of Celmesia (*mountain daisy*), and with Edelweiss plants. **1900** *Canterbury Old & New* 210 The great Mountain Daisies and other plants which fleck the upland meadows with purest whites and softest yellows... Celmisias of various species. **1926** COWAN *Travel in NZ* II. 70 Most abundant are the giant alpine buttercup..and the celmisia or mountain daisy, called by the Maoris *ti-kumu*. **1940** LAING & BLACKWELL *Plants NZ* 449 Most of the [Celmisia] species are found in sub-alpine regions, and are termed by the inhabitants Mountain Daisies or Cotton Plants. **1971** LETHBRIDGE *Sunrise on Hills* 91 Tussock grass and beech forest had given way to monowai bushes and mountain daisies. **1991** *NZ Gardener* Aug. 62 Clumps of mountain daisies (*Celmisia* species) displayed silver leaves and white daisy flowers too.

(8) **native** (or **New Zealand**) **daisy**. **a.** *Lagenifera* (formerly *Lagenophera*) spp. (fam. Compositae). See also PAPA-TANIWHANIWHA.

1867 HOOKER *Handbook* 764 Daisy, native. *Lagenophera*, various sp. **1899** KIRK *Student's Flora NZ* 257 Papataniwhaniwha. Native daisy. The leaves are usually pale-green and rather fleshy; the bracts are frequently erose or almost ciliate. **1926** [see PAPA-TANIWHANIWHA]. **1940** LAING & BLACKWELL *Plants NZ* 439 *Lagenophora pumila*... Leaves roundish, obtuse, lobed or crenate... Native Daisy: Maori name *Papataniwhaniwha*. **1952** RICHARDS *Chatham Is.* 45 *L...pumila*... A small perennial daisy... Native Daisy. Papa-taniwha-niwha. **1979** New Zealand Daisy [see PARANI]. **1981** BROOKER et al. *NZ Medicinal Plants* 42 *Lagenifera petiolata*... Common name: *Native daisy*. Maori name: *Parani*.

b. Any of various plants of the genus *Brachycome* (fam. Compositae).

1899 KIRK *Student's Flora NZ* 260 *B. Sinclairii*... A rather coarse glandular pubescent herb, 4 in.–12 in. high or more... *Native daisy*. **1907** LAING & BLACKWELL *Plants NZ* 410 *Brachycome Sinclairii* (*Sinclair's Brachycome*). A shining herb with radical leaves..*Native Daisy*. **1947–48** BEATTIE *Pioneer Recolls.* (1956) 5 The children rambled and scrambled through the tussock and among this rather dreary but prevailing vegetation they were delighted to find wild flowers such as the dainty native daisies.

c. *Celmisia spectabilis*, probably the commonest sub-alpine *Celmisia*.

1958 *Tararua* Sept. 12 We were..surprised, also, to find that the patches of green all through the tussock [in the Ruahine range] were mats of the native daisy, *Celmisia spectabilis*.

Daisy Patch. *WW1*. A level daisy- and poppy-filled field on Gallipoli, the scene on 8 May 1915 of the wholesale killing by Turkish machine-gunners of advancing New Zealand troops; hence, similar high-casualty places or situations.

1915 *Auckland Weekly News* 23 July 17 'I was hit in the famous daisy patch,' said Lieutenant Fletcher. **1916** *Alexandra Herald* 23 Feb. 5 Our orders were to double across a fire-swept ridge ('Daisy patches' we call them) and take up our positions upon a small hill opposite the ridge. **1918** *NZ at the Front* 9 The brusquely-interrupted tea and the race over the paddock next to the 'Daisy Patch' with one or two of us dropping in the machine-gun fire. **1919** WAITE *New Zealanders at Gallipoli* 125 When some Munsters and Essex [soldiers] saw the preparations, they shouted, 'You're not going to charge across the daisy patch, are you?' 'Of course we are,' the Aucklanders answered. 'God help you,' they said, and watched with admiration as the New Zealanders flung themselves over the top. **1921** BYRNE *Official History Otago Regiment* 37 It was across this open space, to be remembered as the 'Daisy Patch' that four successive waves of Auckland Infantry advanced, each to be swept away by the concentrated fire of Turkish machine guns concealed in the dead scrub to the left... 10th and 14th Companies [of Otago battalion] moved up..each exposed to enemy fire as it hurriedly crossed the short stretches of level fields to be remembered as 'Daisy Patches', but not such bloody patches as that crossed by the Auckland Battalion. **1960** *Review* Jan. 15 Now we are in billets at Rue des Fiefs and in a brigade that never heard of Quinn's Post, the Apex or the Daisy Patch. **1973** *NZ Heritage* LXXIV. 2060 On the 8th [of May] they [*sc.* NZ infantry] charged across the notorious Daisy Patch into machine-gun fire so fierce as to put the capture of the village..out of the question. **1984** PUGSLEY *Gallipoli* 197 We retired over the open area—the Daisy Patch—where the dead and survivors lay among the poppies and daisies, the cries and moans followed us in our retreat.

daisy tree. Any of various woody members of the family Asteraceae, less commonly, any of various related plants of the genera *Brachyglottis* (formerly *Senecio*) and *Olearia* (fam. Asteraceae or Compositae), bearing clusters of flowers. See also TREE DAISY. Cf. OLEARIA, TETEAWAKA, TUPARE.

1867 HOOKER *Handbook* 764 Daisy-trees. *Olearia*, various sp. **1900** *Canterbury Old & New* 188 The [sub-alpine] vegetation..consists largely of shrubby veronicas, white and yellow-flowered daisy trees... *Olearia* and *Senecio*. **1910** COCKAYNE *NZ Plants & Their Story* 116 These are composed of the truly magnificent daisy-tree (*Olearia Lyalli*), found only in these islands. **1940** HOWARD *Rakiura* xvii Along the coastal fringes [of Stewart Island] it consists of..'Mutton-bird scrub', the principal constituents..being Puheretaiko..Tete-a-weka..and Daisy Tree (*Olearia Colensoi*). **1965** GILLHAM *Naturalist in NZ* 21 Trees belonging to the daisy family often don a protective coat of woolly hairs, colourful Stewart Island examples being the mauve-flowered daisy trees (*Olearia* spp.). **1988** DAWSON *Forest Vines to Snow Tussocks* 156 Also in Fiordland and Stewart Island are distinctive coastal shrubberies of 'daisy trees'.

dake. Also occas. **daker**. [Prob. f. Sc. dial. *daich* soft, flabby (a variant of *dough*): cf. EDD 1877 They daichy peasmeat trash (of marbles).] A cheap fired-clay marble.

c1930–35 West Coast children p.c. R.B. McLuskie. A cheap ceramic-clay marble—often when playing marbles children cry—'No dakes'. **1951** PARK *Witch's Thorn* 176 A mob of little boys had their tails up over a marble game... They fired their taws..at the squares richly laid with the weatherbeaten old clay soldiers which sold at twelve a penny and were known as dakes. **1972** SUTTON-SMITH *Folkgames Children* 174 There were terms for marbles such as..'dubs', 'da[k]es', 'stakes', 'dukes', or 'changers', referring to the marbles put down to be fired at. **1983** [see GLASSIE]. **1993** SINCLAIR *Halfway Round the Harbour* 24 The bigger and more skilful boys won most of my marbles off me [at Auckland c1931], their glassies or steelies (ball-bearings) blasting my clay dakers ruthlessly out of the ring.

Dally, *n.* and *a.* Occas. *derog.*

A. *n.* Also **Dallie**. [f. DAL(MATIAN + -Y.] DALMATIAN A.

1940 SARGESON *Man & His Wife* 10 Two young dallies who ran an orchard... These two had come out from Dalmatia. **1955** *Numbers* 3 June 13 The father's a Dally, but the mother is Irish, as far as I know. **1965** SHADBOLT *Among Cinders* 190 You fullows guess I am bloody Dally from Dalmatia, eh? **1975** SARGESON *More Than Enough* 43 He was young, tall, strong, handsome, with cut of features besides dark eyes and colouring which suggested Croat descent what an earlier generation of New Zealanders would have called Austrian before the latter-day settling for Dally or Dalmatian. **1985** ROSIER-JONES *Cast Two Shadows* 129 'Emma has got Dally in her y'know, Fred,' the manager says. **1991** *NZ Geographic* Apr.–June 42 Northlanders were gumdiggers, Maori and 'Dallies', and none of these epithets was a compliment.

B. *adj.*

1. DALMATIAN B.

1950 *Landfall 14* 127 You can buy an awful lot of Dally plonk for four pounds. **1961** CRUMP *Hang On a Minute Mate* 77 Broke off his engagement..and got this dog off an old Dally scrub-cutter. **1965** GEE *Special Flower* 38 'She knows I like my vino,' he explained. 'Where did you get it, Corrie? Is it dally stuff?' 'Henderson special'..'Not dally though.' **1986** *Sunday News* (Auckland) 12 Oct. 1 Tim's [Shadbolt's] Team sank the Dally mafia without trace in yesterday's local body election. *Ibid.* 2 Nov. 19 Our society, which represents a very large percentage of Yugoslav Dalmatians, is concerned that any paper can slander our community by calling them Dally mafia. **1991** *NZ Geographic* Apr.–June 40 There was social card playing and Dally bowls with a round bowl—not off-centre—and grape wines, and dances like the kolo, done in a circle.

2. In the collocation **Dally plonk**, cheap wine made and sold by Dalmatian settlers.

1950 [see 1 above]. **1965** WATSON *Stand in Rain* 111 On Sunday we..had a barbeque on the beach with the fowls and a bottle of cheap Dally plonk. **1979** BAXTER *Collected Poems* 429 I do recall one evening, drunk In Devonport on Dally plonk. **1984** *NZ Yesterdays* 38 This industrious production of wine was a constant irritant to the prohibition lobby. 'Dally plonk', as it was widely known in the 1950's, had a long and bitter fight before it transformed drinking habits.

Dalmatian, *n.* and *a.* Also often erron. **Dalmation**.

A. *n.* An immigrant settler from Dalmatia; a New Zealand resident of Dalmatian extraction. See also AUSTRIAN.

1916 COATES speech in Scott *Seven Lives on Salt River* (1987) 148 *Coates*: We have difficulty in the north in connection with the Dalmatians. **1919** CHUDLEIGH *Diary* 22 Mar. (1950) 465 Twelve people at work [in Waikato]. English French Swiss Dalmatian. **1940** SARGESON *A Man and His Wife* (1944) 13 Nick was saying he was a New Zealander, but he knew he wasn't a New Zealander. And he knew he wasn't a

DALMATION

Dalmatian any more. **1955** BOSWELL *Dim Horizons* 59 The [gum-]diggers, more especially the Austrians—or Dalmatians as they later insisted on being called—paid well for the service. **1965** SHADBOLT *Among Cinders* 156 Crawling with Dalmatians. Only they were called Austrians then. **1970** THOMAS *Way Up North* 35 The Austrians soon established themselves as fine, hard-working and law-abiding people... When the map of Europe was changed after the First World War they changed with it and became known as Dalmatians. **1975** [see DALLY A]. **1987** BATISTICH *Sing Vila* 24 Austrian was our first name here and it stuck. But it wasn't the name of a country the New Zealanders invoked when they said it; it was the name of a fear... With every shipload of Dalmatians coming to work on the gumfields that fear grew... But to my child's mind it was all a confusion—all those names. Austrian. Dalmatian. Some said Croatian. And now Yugoslavs. **1991** *NZ Geographic* Apr.–June 24 Known then as Austrians, later as Dalmatians, they were a collection of distinct and separate peoples from the states of Dalmatia, Macedonia, Bosnia-Hercegovina, Croatia, Slovenia, Serbia, and Montenegro.

B. *adj.* Originating in Dalmatia; pertaining to Dalmatian settlers in New Zealand.

1931 *NZJAg.* Nov. XLIII. 356 A method of herbaceous grafting of grape-vines introduced by Dalmatian settlers..is giving very good results. **1940** SARGESON *A Man And His Wife* (1944) 12 Why? I said, there are plenty of Dalmatian girls out here. I bet you could get New Zealand girls too. **1959** SHADBOLT *New Zealanders* (1986) 32 When we declined their beer they triumphantly produced some sherry from a Dalmatian vine-yard. **1967** BAXTER *Collected Poems* (1980) 392 I'd bought a peter of wine From the owner of a Dalmatian vineyard. **1984** *NZ Yesterdays* 38 At the beginning of the 20th century there were three major Dalmatian settlements—Herekino, near Kaitaia; Te Kopuru, near Dargaville; and Henderson, north of Auckland. The first Dalmatian settler arrived in Henderson in 1895. **1991** *North & South* (Auckland) May 74 He remembers growing up amid fierce political discussions between the large numbers of Dalmatian gum-diggers who regularly gathered at the Belich house.

Dalmation, erron. var. DALMATIAN.

dam. [f. Brit. dial.: AND 1843; cf. EDD *n.*[1] 1; NewSOD 'Now local.'] Also **farm dam.** An artificial pond or reservoir; a body of water stored behind a dam or embankment.

c1930 *Whitcombe's Etym. Dict. Aust.-NZ Suppl.* 3 *dam n.* an embankment for restraining the flow of water; the water so collected. **1948** *NZJAg.* Jan. LXXVI. 64 The dam, generally located at the head of a gully, and so situated as to supply more than one field, has been adopted as the least expensive and best method of providing water for stock. **1959** *NZ Farmer* 7 July 38 If there is any likelihood of delay in planting..it is a good plan to put the butt ends of the wands or poles in a dam. **1965** *NZJAg.* May CX. 405 A basic requirement for a reliable farm dam is a well chosen site that offers maximum water storage for each cubic yard of soil shifted.

damper. [Poss. f. Brit. dial. *damper* food which damps down the appetite: see EDD *damp n.*[1], hence *damper*..2. a luncheon, a snack between meals (Lancashire); AND 1825.]

1. An unleavened camp bread or flour-and-water dough baked on hot coals or in a frying pan, camp oven, etc.; a loaf or portion of damper. Cf. *beggars on the coals* (BEGGAR 1), *bush bread* (BUSH C 3 d), *camp-oven bread* (CAMP OVEN b).

[*Note*] Tea, mutton and damper were typical fare in early colonial times.

1839 TAYLOR *Journal* 20 Apr. (ATLTS) II. 111 We have been busy frying pancakes and making a damper for our Sabbath's provision. **1842** *NZ.Jrnl.* III. 223 Salt beef and damper (that is to say, flour and water baked in hot ashes), with tea and sugar, constitute in almost every place in the interior the daily fare. **1848** in *Lett. from Otago* 20 July (1978) 16 We call our loaves dampers. I will give you a short sketch how we make the damper; first, we make the dough any size we wish, then let it stand two hours at the fire to rise, then take a spade and scrape out the bottom of the fire, then lay in the damper and cover it over with the ashes, and again with the red embers, let it lie for about two hours, take it out and beat it well with a towel to clean it of ashes, when we have an excellent loaf. **1856** SEWELL *Journal* 2 Mar. (1980) II. 214 That [*sc.* a damper recipe] is what is called fat damper, otherwise Scones, a Bushman's delicacy. **1863** TRIPP *Lecture* in Harper *Kettle on Fuchsia* (1967) 47 A damper is made of flour and water, mixed as you would bread, and when you retire for the night you scrape away most of the ashes from the fire and put the dough there. **1875** WHITWORTH *Cobb's Box* 6 Half a damper and a piece of mutton lay on the table. **1883** DOMETT *Ranolf & Amohia* II. 109 And bread in its primeval form of 'damper'— Unleavened cakes of palatable maize Well pounded. **1914** GRACE *Tale Timber Town* 83 They sat and ate their simple fare—'damper' baked on the red-hot embers of their fire. **1933** *Press* (Christchurch) (Acland Gloss.) 7 Oct. 15 *Damper.*—Flour and water kneaded into dough..and baked in the ashes of a wood fire. Tea, mutton and d[amper] formed the whole diet of the earliest squatters and station hands. **1951** in Pearson *Six Stories* (1991) 53 Red Flaherty was hanging a damper over the open fire when they walked in. **1980** *Woman's Weekly* 7 Jan. 83 *Menu* Tramper's Milford Stew Damper Scroggin Apricot Chew

2. Used *attrib.* in special Comb. **Damper Hall,** a jocular name for an early colonial house; **damper scone,** a ('fried') scone made in a frying pan or camp oven.

1859 *Richmond-Atkinson Papers* (1960) I. 452 Harry's house is distinguished as 'Kai kai Lodge' (in reference to the uniform abundance of meat & drink) whilst Henry's mansion is named '**Damper Hall**'. **1936** HYDE *Passport to Hell* 70 Rannock fed his prison labour on honest bush food: fresh meat, billy tea, enormous flat **damper scones** cooked on the three-legged camp oven. **1970** SEVERINSEN *Hunt Far Mountain* 104 Towards dusk Russell turned out a reasonable line of damper scones, cooked in the frypan.

3. *transf.* In the phr. **to cop the damper,** an obsolete jocular variant of 'take the cake' (or 'bun').

1917 BROWN *Lay of Bantry Bay* 29 Those woolly bounders fairly cop the damper.

dancing dolly. The white-faced storm petrel (PETREL 2 (19) b (e)), from its apparent ability to walk or dance on water. Compare the names JESUS CHRIST BIRD, SKIPJACK 2.

1979 FALLA et al. *New Guide Birds NZ* 55 White-faced Storm Petrel *Pelagodroma marina*... Takahikare-moana, Skipjack, Jesus Christ Bird (shortened to 'J.C. Bird'), Dancing Dolly. **1985** *Reader's Digest Book NZ Birds* 104 White-faced Storm Petrel *Pelagodroma marina*... Tahaki-kare-moana, frigate petrel, J.C. bird, skipjack, dancing dolly.

dandelion. [Spec. use of *dandelion Taraxacum* spp.] Usu. as **native dandelion** *Taraxacum magellanicum* (fam. Asteraceae), a perennial rosette herb of montane grasslands and herbfields.

DAPHNE

1907 *AJHR* C-8 21 *Taraxacum glabratum*... New Zealand dandelion... Rocky ground near coast. **1915** *AJHR* C-6 15 *Taraxacum magellanicum*... New Zealand dandelion..Tussock pasture. **1917** WILLIAMS *Dict. Maori Lang.* 504 *Tohetaka..Taraxicum officinale,* native dandelion. **1973** MARK & ADAMS *Alpine Plants* (1979) 164 *Taraxacum magellanicum*... Native Dandelion. **1982** WILSON *Stewart Is. Plants* 214 Native Dandelion... Hairless rosettes like [the dandelion] but usually much smaller.

Dan Doolin. *West Coast.* [Origin unknown.] As **Dan Doolin bait** (or **spawn**), a local name for migrating young of freshwater galaxiads esp. *Gobiomorphus hubbsi.* See also BULLY *n.*[1]

1978 MCDOWALL *NZ Freshwater Fishes* 157 *Gobiomorphus hubbsi*..Blue-gilled Bully..The migrating young are known to whitebaiters on the West Coast as 'Whalefeed' or 'Dan Doolin Spawn'. **1981** [see WHALE-FEED 2]. **1989** HULME & MORRISON 104 There are local names for them [*sc.* fry of Galaxiads], too—elephant-ears and Dan Doolin 'bait (which isn't true whitebait at all).

danthonia. [f. a Latinization of the name Étienne Danthoine, a 19th c. French botanist.] Any of various native perennial, tufted pasture grasses of the genera *Rytidosperma* and *Chionochloa,* formerly *Danthonia.* See also *bristle tussock* (TUSSOCK 3 (2)).

1910 COCKAYNE *NZ Plants & Their Story* 87 This must not lead the farmer to suppose that 'danthonia', as all these different forms are called in the papers and by seed-merchants, will ever replace ryegrass, cocksfoot, or red-clover in the better land. **1922** PERRY *Sheep Farming* 103 During the past few years the use of danthonia, the best of the native grasses, has considerably increased. **1936** BELSHAW et al. *Agric. Organiz. NZ* 81 The land becoming gradually less productive owing to the replacement of good by poor pasture plants such as..Danthonia. **1952** FAIRBURN *Three Poems* 59 In time of drought The danthonia shines like a flame. **1961** MARTIN *Flora NZ* 133 Soils of poor quality both upland and lowland are commonly known as *Danthonia* country, by which is inferred their poor quality. **1978** JARDINE *Shadows on Hill* 37 Above the bracken line lay the sweeping face of the hill—silver tussock and danthonia. **1983** HENDERSON *Down from Marble Mountain* 116 I started a fire.., the danthonia dry as a county chairman's speech.

daphne. [Transf. use of *daphne* a genus of flowering shrubs bearing fragrant flowers.] Usu. with a modifier **Maori (native, New Zealand, sand) daphne,** a shrub of the chiefly Australasian genus *Pimelea* (fam. Thymelaeaceae) found mainly on coastal sands. See also STRATHMORE WEED, TARANGA.

1952 RICHARDS *Chatham Is.* 55 *Pimelea..arenaria*... Sand daphne. Aute taranga. **1961** MARTIN *Flora NZ* 204 [Another very floriferous shrub to be seen on the] drier hillsides of Nelson and Marlborough and of North Island hills is that known as the Native Daphne or Taranga (*Pimelea longifolia*). **1966** *Encycl. NZ* III. 711 Daphne, New Zealand . . taranga . . *Pimelea longifolia*. **1982** WILSON *Stewart Is. Plants* 114 *Pimelea lyallii* Sand Daphne... Low, sprawling sub-shrub... Flowers white, strongly scented, attractively clustered at branchlet tips. **1986** HOLCROFT *Sea of Words* 190 We returned from North Canterbury with a spread of native daphne donated from a garden..a few miles from Rangiora. **1995** CROWE *Which Coastal Plant?* 38 Native daphne [*Pimelea prostrata*] is a useful mat-like plant to use in rock gardens... Sometimes known by the less complimentary sounding name of Strathmore weed. A

DARG

close relative, autetaranga or sand daphne (*Pimelea arenaria*) is technically more of a coastal plant..but is becoming much harder to find.

darg. [f. Sc. and n. Brit. dial. *darg* a day's work: see EDD.] An amount of work done (in a day).
 1924 *Otago Witness* (Dunedin) 29 July 1 The perusal of Hansard is not part of my daily darg, thanks be! **1967** MILLER *Ink on My Fingers* 165 For a good many years I have run a daily column in the *Southland Daily News* called 'The Day's Darg'... 'Darg' is a coalmining term meaning a norm of work. Theoretically, when you have finished your darg you go home.

dark chocolate. In New Zealand the usual name, synonymous with Brit. *plain*, distinguishing the darker-coloured (often termed 'energy') chocolate from 'milk' chocolate.
 c1940 *Dark* and *milk* chocolate were the usual terms known to Ed. **1957** FRAME *Owls Do Cry* (1967) 18 And glass cases packed with chocolate, dark or milk, fruity or plain. **1961** MESSENGER *Dine with Elizabeth* 51 Boffins... 2 oz. dark, sweet, chocolate. **1978** *Edmonds Cookery Book* 47 Santé Biscuits... Butter..Flour..Sugar..Sweetened Condensed Milk..Baking Powder..*Dark* Chocolate. **1989** *Cuisine* Dec.–Jan. 50 While velvety milk chocolate has received most attention in dairy-festooned New Zealand..dark chocolate is the silkier sweet.

darkie. Also **darky**, occas. **dark skin** (see quot. 1866). An offensive (see quot. 1991) transf. use of *darkie* a (North American) negro (recorded in NZ from 1872 for a black sea-cook) for a Polynesian, occas. as a term of address, or as a nickname. Compare NIGGER.
 1863 MOSER *Mahoe Leaves* 31 'Halloa', cried Harry, as we pulled up our horses about a mile from the pah, 'there go a string of darkies a-head.' **1866** HUNT *Chatham Is.* 11 This concluded my first commercial transaction with a dark skin, and each party was well satisfied. **1984** CAMPBELL *Island to Island* 93 In those days [c1939] racism was more blatant than it is now... I had become accustomed to being addressed as 'snow', 'darky', and even 'Hori', often by adults who would have been surprised had they known they were giving offence. **1991** DUFF *One Night Out Stealing* 129 The black arseholes did it to him, and Sonny..if you could call his a beating..they let him off cos he was a darkie like they were.

dark rock shell. *Haustrum haustorium* (fam. Muricidae), a common carnivorous intertidal univalve.
 1947 POWELL *Native Animals NZ* 28 Dark Rock Shell (*Lepsia haustrum*)... Easily recognised by the large open mouth with a conspicuous brown patch. **1955** DELL *Native Shells NZ* 28 Dark Rock Shell..*Kaeo* or *Ngaeo*... Like all the Rock Shells this species is carnivorous and preys upon other shell fish. **1983** GUNSON *Collins Guide to Seashore* 94 In similar situations [amongst rocks] lives the slightly smaller dark rock shell... This creature has no respect for relatives.

darky, var. DARKIE.

darl. [Short form of *darling*: AND 1930, chiefly a mode of address.] A term of affectionate address, esp. in women's prisons usu. with lesbian overtones; a woman's girlfriend. Compare MRS, DOLLY *n.*[2]
 1968 TAYLOR in *Genetic Psychology Monographs* (1970) No.81 92 Female offenders of all ages were tattooed almost exclusively with tattoos that marked homosexual relationships they had with their young 'Mrs.', teenage 'Darls', or adult 'Dollies'. **1976** HILLIARD *Send Somebody Nice* 58 [Two Maori girls in prison writing notes to each other.] I don't need you really because I got all the darls I need just now... I will tell you who my darls are and that will make you jelous [*sic*]. **1984** BEATON *Outside In* 53 Sandy: Nah. She don't mean a sugar daddy, darl. *Ibid.* 96 Helen: Don't let her get to you, Darl. Di: 'Darl'. No wonder your boyfriend did a bunk. *Ibid.* 109 Darl: a term of affectionate address in women's prisons.

Dart: see *Old Dart* (OLD *a.* 1 b).

Darth Vader's pencil box. [f. the shape, and the black, non-reflective colouring, suggesting the sinister villain of the 'Star Wars' movies.] The Bank of New Zealand Head Office building in Wellington.
 1984 *Listener* 5 May 43 I am truly appalled by the effrontery of that foreigner from Southland..with his reference to the BNZ Building as being 'Darth Vader's pencil box'. **1985** *NZ Times* 19 May 18 It's Friday, 7.15am. The sun streams across Wellington harbour directly into the 21st floor dealing room of the BNZ. The building forex dealers term Darth Vadar's [*sic*] pencil box. **1989** KERNOHAN *Wellington's New Buildings* 83 Known as 'Darth Vader's pencil box' or 'the great safe deposit box in the sky' it is variously liked and disliked.

dash. [Spec. use of *dash* a small amount of a liquid.] A small portion of lemonade added to a glass of beer.
 1905 *Truth* 11 Nov. 1 Beer and a dash. **1966** *NZ Short Stories* (1976) 88 'Three straights and a dash?' she [*sc.* the barmaid] said to the Maoris, and gathered the empty handles in her fingers. **1972** MITCHELL *Pavlova Paradise* 182 *dash:* Mild expletive uttered when lemonade is found in beer.

date. [AND 1961.] Anus, arse.
 c1940 (esp. schoolboys) 'Up your date for two-and-eight (2/8)', a catchcry. (Ed.) **1988** McGILL *Dict. Kiwi Slang* 35 *date* anus; 'get off your date' was common army advice WW2.

date mussel, date shell: see MUSSEL 2 (2

dawn.
 1. Often with cap. Used *attrib.* in special Comb. associated with the commemoration of Anzac Day, 25 April: **dawn address**, **dawn ceremony**, **dawn parade** (also occas. **dawn parader**), **dawn service**, an address, ceremony, military parade, or religious service taking place at dawn on Anzac Day.
 1982 MARSHALL *Master Big Jingles* 68 Each year on Anzac Day he emerged to lead the R.S.A. parade and make a **dawn address** at the lawn cemetery in town. **1939** *Evening Post* (Wellington) 24 Apr. 11 The following is the order in which services will take place tomorrow. 5 a.m.—War Veterans will assemble at Railway Station for the **dawn ceremony** of remembrance. **1938** *NZRSA Review* June 45 Wanganui Anzac Day (1938)... We will also have our **Dawn Parade**, which is considered by the men to be their special ceremony of homage in token of memories of the past, which are dear to all of us. **1939** *Evening Post* (Wellington) 12 May 15 The introduction of 'dawn parades' similar to those held in Australia was advanced at a meeting of the [R.S.A., at Dunedin]... They were peculiarly Australian in origin, their particular association with that country being derived from the fact that the Australians went over the top at Anzac at dawn. **1950** *RSA Review* June 10 We old blokes of 1914 vintage..find that after attending Dawn Parade..we are just too tired to go to town for the afternoon service. **1968** SLATTER *Pagan Game* 176 The vicar would drone on about this Anzac Day, this day of remembrancer. Years ago and now the rum and milk after Dawn Parade. **1972** *Consultation on Observance of Anzac Day, Church and Society Commission* 11 In fact, there was only one major innovation in the Observance of Anzac Day between the two wars—the institution of the Dawn Parade. 1939 was the first year when the Dawn Parades were held throughout the country, although in some of the smaller centres they had begun about 1937. The Dawn Parade was a ceremony essentially for the returned servicemen. **1982** MARSHALL *Master Big Jingles* 72 When I was really young I thought Dawn Parade was a girl, but as I grew up I came to realise the solemn implications of the Anzac Day ceremonial. **1991** *Dominion Sunday Times* (Wellington) 21 Apr. 11 Most of the medals worn at the dawn parades and other ceremonies are campaign medals and stars. **1987** HUTCHINS *Tall Half-Backs* 34 It was the **Dawn Paraders**. The R.S.A. men marching. Marching in honour of their fallen comrades. [**1937** *NZRSA Review* Aug. 41 New Plymouth Anzac Day 1937. At dawn the local members of TOCH held a brief and simple service at the Cenotaph, including the 'Light' ceremony.] **1938** *NZRSA Review* June 6 Soon afterwards the troops were lined up on the wharf, ready to move off for the **Dawn Service**. **1972** *Consultation on Observance of Anzac Day, Church and Society Commission* 24 The dawn service was essentially an ex-servicemen's service for ex-service personnel, though others were also present. **1990** MACLEAN & PHILLIPS *Sorrow & the Pride* 124 The Dawn Service was introduced to New Zealand in 1939 by Australian veterans who had attended a similar service in Sydney the previous year.

2. Special Comb. **dawn raid**, a term (prob. suggested by Nazi raids on Jews' houses) for the early-morning raids on houses suspected of harbouring esp. Polynesian 'overstayers' or others suspected of overstaying their temporary residence permits. Also *fig.* a sudden or unexpected 'raid' on company shares with a view to a takeover (see quot. 1983); also *transf.* in an historical use (see quot. 1990).
 1981 KENNEDY *Straight from Shoulder* 9 There was the advantage that these [Pacific island] people were not admitted permanently, and if things got tough, we could..round up, with dawn raids in the best totalitarian tradition, those who had overstayed and forcibly depart them. **1983** *Dominion* (Wellington) 6 Oct. 9 Lightning and unexpected company takeovers—dawn raids—could become outlawed under proposed changes to existing takeover law. Securities Commission chairman..described dawn raids as 'entirely unacceptable'. **1986** *Evening Post* (Wellington) 12 Aug. 6 A stereotype of Pacific Islanders as overstayers, established during the 'dawn raids' of a decade ago, remains an influence in the Labour Department's immigration division. **1990** *Te Karanga* Nov. 3 The tension level was raised even higher when Grey had Te Rauparaha, then aged 77, 'arrested'. During a dawn raid on 23 July [1846], the chief was dragged from his whare and made a prisoner on board the warship *Calliope* for 10 months.

day.
 1. In the phr. **that'll be the day!**, see THAT *pronoun* 1.

2. In the phr. **(to have) a day for a king, a day for (on) the king (queen), it's a day for (on) the**

king (queen), (to take) a day off, esp. when conditions do not allow outdoor work.

1947 NEWTON *Wayleggo* 119 He and his dogs have a day off [on a foggy day]—in musterers' parlance—'a day for a king'. **1951** MCLEOD *NZ High Country* 43 When you wake up in the morning in a mustering hut and hear the rain beating on the roof someone is sure to poke his head out of the door and look around and say: 'Its a day for the King boys!' I don't know how this saying originated but it means a day of enforced idleness. **1954** LILEY et al. *The Health of Fieldworkers in the NZ Forest Service* (TS) 16 Although no objection is made to 'having a day on the king or queen', nearly every day is worked in the bush regardless of the weather. **1978** PRESTON *Woolgatherers* 96 The next day being wet, all [mustering] hands stayed in camp—a 'Day for the King'. **1982** GRADY *Perano Whalers* 140 As well as superstitions, the whalers of Tory Channel had a few time-honoured habits. One of these was known as 'a-day-for-the-Queen'. Its main application seems to have been when a whaler had had a heavy day on the grog and had butterflies in his stomach and head the next day in the form of a hangover.

daylighting, *vbl. n. Tunnelling.* Opening up the roof of the tunnel.

1982 *Evening Post* (Wellington) 12 Mar. 1 The Railways will have to knock the top off five tunnels... The tunnel jobs—termed 'daylighting' in rail jargon—are required because the tunnels are not wide enough to take the new electric locos plus overhead wires... 'We have to daylight five tunnels.' **1987** *Karori News* 24 Mar. 1 'Daylighting' of the Karori [motor vehicle] tunnel so that it could be widened was another possibility discussed.

Hence **daylight** *v. trans.*

1985 MCGILL *G'day Country* 38 'They can't daylight it [*sc.* the tunnel],' said Bill discouragingly. 'There's a lake above. I never feel safe going through it.'

dead, *a.*[1]

1. In the phr. **dead as a moa**, long dead, outmoded; **dead as Ned Kelly**, see NED KELLY.

1955 *BJ Cameron Collection* (TS July) dead as the moa Dead as the dodo.

2. *Mining.* [f. *dead* unproductive: see OED *a.* 10.] **dead country**, ground in which there is little or no auriferous material. Cf. KINDLY *a.*

1913 *NZGeol.SB (NS)* No.16 98 In the Aroha Subdivision..of the Hauraki Peninsula, a distinction between 'kindly' and 'dead' country is made by miners... 'Kindly' country for each locality is country in which lodes of that locality may carry valuable ore, while 'dead' country is country in which the lodes become barren and small, or pinch out altogether.

3. *Mining.* [Cf. OED *dead work* 2.] **dead work**, preparatory work unproductive of ore or gold.

1910 *NZGeol.SB (NS)* No.11 36 Its close proximity to the vein would obviate the necessity of much 'dead work' before the vein was reached. **1967** MAY *West Coast Gold Rushes* 526 Dead work: all preparatory work on a claim—sinking shafts, driving tunnels, constructing a race—before gold-saving commences.

4. As **dead ground**, unperceived but distance-distorting country between a viewer and a distant landmark.

1961 CRUMP *Hang On a Minute Mate* 76 Dead ground? Yeah, dead ground is the country in hollows and between ridges that you can't see when you're looking at something a long way off, like those mountains there. Distances are very deceptive in this sort of country. You can travel all day towards a landmark and never seem to get any closer. Then bang, you're suddenly there. Something to do with dead ground I suppose.

dead, *a.*[2] [f. *dead* exact.] In phrases meaning 'the exact likeness': **the dead ring (of)** [f. orig. US *dead ringer*: AND 1899], **the dead spit (of)** [f. *dead* + the very *spit* of: see OED *n.*[2] 3], the exact likeness (of).

1948 BALLANTYNE *Cunninghams* (1976) 72 Bob said they were **the dead ring of** Gil, especially Gilbert. **1952** *Evening Post* (Wellington) 15 Nov. 9 You are the dead ring of that chap [Jiggs] in the skit in the back of the 'Evening Post.' **1988** MCGILL *Dict. Kiwi Slang* 35 *dead ring* exact likeness. **1891** A TRAMP, ESQ. *Casual Ramblings* 91 That horse..is the '**dead spit**' of the steeplechaser Orangeman. **1912** MANSFIELD *Stories* (1984) 112 'She's not like you—takes after her father?'... 'No, she don't; she's the dead spit of me. Any fool could see that.' **1959** SLATTER *Gun in My Hand* 231 He belted my bare bottom and shouted you're like your parents no damn good you're the dead spit of your old man. **1980** LELAND *Kiwi-Yankee Dict.* 61 *look the dead spit*: 'Beaut baby! Looks the dead spit of his dad!' Just alike.

deadbeat. [AND 1892.] A person down on his luck, but not (as in the orig. US sense) a loafer; a person completely broke.

c1875 MEREDITH *Adventuring in Maoriland* (1935) 156 A deadbeat appealed to the owner for a job, and wouldn't take no for an answer. **1902** SATCHELL *Land of Lost* 18 This [gumfield] is the stamping-ground of the dead-beats of the World. **c1930** *Whitcombe's Etym. Dict. Aust.-NZ Suppl.* 3 deadbeat n. a person down on his luck. **1955** *BJ Cameron Collection* (TS July) deadbeat (n) A person down on his luck. (In U.S. it means a sponger). **1963** MASON *Collected Poems* 56 The cold wet dead-beat plods up the track.

dead horse. [f. Brit. dial. and nautical usage: see OED *horse* 19 b; EDD *dead adj.* 2 (10).] In the phr. **to work (off) a dead horse** (occas. **to bury a dead horse**). **a.** To work off a debt, esp. an advance on wages.

1842 THOMPSON *Journal* 16 Feb. in *Nelson Evening Mail* (1978) It was customary for crews to receive two months' wages before going on board, and this they spent promptly, so that for the first part of the voyage they were 'working off a dead horse'. **1862** BRETT *Diary* June in Brett & Hook *Albertlanders* (1927) 45 One uncommon thing noted [was] the old sailoring custom, now a thing of the past, of 'working off a dead horse'... In those days a sailor had a month's wages advanced to him before leaving Port. As he invariably spent it, he called the first four weeks at sea 'working off a dead horse', and the end of the term was signalised by the heaving overboard, with much ceremony, of an effigy of the defunct equine. **1863** BUTLER *First Year* x 146 They [*sc.* station hands] will come back [from a spree] possibly with a *dead horse to work off*—that is, a debt at the accommodation house—and will work hard for another year to have another drinking bout at the end of it. **1933** *Press* (Christchurch) (Acland Gloss.) 7 Oct. 15 *Dead Horse, Working a.*—Working off an old debt, usually for overdrawn wages. **1941** BAKER *NZ Slang* 54 *Work a dead horse*, a New Zealand variation of the Australian *ride the dead horse* and *work off a dead horse*, meaning to perform work that has already been paid for or to redeem a debt. **1983** BUCKLEY *Of Toffs & Toilers* 58 The passing of the first month [at sea in the *Westminster* in 1842] brought the sailors' ceremony of 'burying the dead horse'. When engaged, the men received one month's pay in advance to enable them to outfit themselves. Few would have much left, so for the first month they felt themselves to be working for nothing, or 'working a dead horse' which must now be buried. An equine effigy was placed on a wooden frame with four wheels, and amid loud singing was drawn around the deck three times by sailors dressed as policemen bearing staves of sailcloth filled with straw, hats of the same material and whiskers and long wigs of white yarn. The 'horse' was put up for auction (the money being for liquor afterwards) and was then hoisted to the main yard-arm mounted by a sailor, during another chorus. Duly hoisted with this ceremony the 'horse' was set alight by a long squib, the rope was cut, and the 'poor old man' (as the song went) fell into the sea. Thus was the dead horse buried. [Possibly from William Harris's MS Journal of a voyage; or John Newland's diary 1841.] **1986** RICHARDS *Off the Sheep's Back* 107 With the promise of a weekly wage I would no longer be compelled to shear for three months each year which would mostly go in paying off a 'dead horse' (store account).

b. *transf.* A mortgage.

1900 *NZ Illustr. Mag.* May 591 We are only working a dead horse here, what with the mortgage and one thing and another.

dead-house. *Obs.* [AND 1855.] A hotel shed used to accommodate drunken customers until they had slept off their over-indulgence. (The 1867 quot. may refer to a makeshift morgue.) See also *blood room* (BLOOD 3).

1867 COOPER *Digger's Diary* 17 Dec. (1978) 23 The body was then taken back to the dead-house. **1876** *Weekly Herald* 10 June in Scott *Seven Lives on Salt River* (1987) 52 When 'the heroes of a hundred drunks' are helplessly prone on the floor [of a Kaipara bar]..a couple of stretcher men speedily whip away the 'dead drunk' off to an outbuilding in the rear..known as 'the dead house', there to sleep off the effects of the debauch. On one Sunday, 18 bushmen and gumdiggers were lying 'heads and tails' in the deadhouse. **1892** KIPLING *One Lady at Wairakei* (1983) 42 Dreams of lost loves and lost hopes in the dead-houses of country pubs. **1902** SATCHELL *Land of Lost* 15 [To publican] 'Where is the guest?' 'In the dead-house... We have to put him in there at times; he won't keep out of the bar.' **1910** *NZ Free Lance* (Wellington) 3 Sept. 13 The 'deadhouse' is a familiar adjunct to a bush pub. **1933** *Press* (Christchurch) (Acland Gloss.) 7 Oct. 15 *Dead House.*—A rough room with bunks round it, which was kept by country publicans to put the dead drunks in. **1953** REED *Story of Kauri* 121 And the 'deadhouse', at that time [c1900] a necessary adjunct to every country hotel, wherein the paralytic drunks were thrown, is now known only in history. **1970** THOMAS *Way Up North* 34 If he became drunk enough [in the gumfields hotel] to be a danger to himself or to anyone else accommodation would be provided in the dead house. This institution..was a small, strongly built shed with no windows. Auger holes provided light and ventilation. The door was locked outside by a strong hasp and padlock.

dead man. In fanciful descriptive names of food items.

1. dead man's bread. Prob. TUTU 1 a.

[*Note*] The Mansfield reference suggests a well-trained child's perception that 'all berries are poisonous'.

1916 MANSFIELD in *Poems* (1923) 47 To L.H.B. (1894–1915)... We were at home again beside the stream Fringed with tall berry bushes, white and red. 'Don't touch them: they are poisonous,' I said... And as you stooped I saw the berries gleam. 'Don't you remember? We called them Dead Man's Bread!' **1938** HYDE *Godwits Fly* (1970) xx But ours [*sc.* leaves of history], darker, might cry, 'Where is Selwyn? Where is Rutherford? Where is Katherine, with weeds on her grave at Fontainebleau, when what she really wanted was the dark berry along our creeks? (Don't you remember? We call them Dead Man's Bread.)'

2. deadman's arm, a steamed (currant) roll pudding; **dead man's ears**, stewed dried apricots; **dead man's head**, a round steamed plum pudding eaten cold or hot.

1985 *NZ Times* 3 Feb. 5 You [bush-felling] contractors in black singlets and bowyangs, fuelled on spuds and mutton and pumpkin and rice and spotted dog or **deadman's arm** and black billy tea..come into our art galleries, on to our stamps. **1986** HENDERSON *Jim Henderson's People* 154 Karamea..where bread, scones, pastries, pikelets, cakes, pavlovas, spotted dick and deadman's arm come singing out of oven and camp oven. **1992** GRACE *Cousins* 139 Have you heard of having frog's eggs and **dead man's ears** for pudding? **1994** LASENBY *Dead Man's Head* 151 He took down and undid a flourbag, and rolled out something round and pale like a cooked human head... '**Dead Man's Head!**' said Uncle Ted. 'See his eyes?'.. They..ate their slice of plum pudding. Denny picked out his raisin eyes and swallowed them whole.

dead meat ticket. WW1. [f. *dead meat* a corpse: AND 1920.] An identity disc.

1917 in Miller *Camps, Tramps & Trenches* (1939) 15 Our Dead Meat Tickets (identity discs) were issued.

dead wool. [f. Brit. dial.: cf EDD *dead* 1 (23); AND 1899.] Wool plucked from the skin of a dead sheep.

1936 BELSHAW et al. *Agric. Organiz. NZ* 710 'Dead Wool', removed from dead sheep, has little commercial value and is never an important item. **1944** MARSH *Died in the Wool* 15 When did we start buying dead wool?.. The smell of dead wool goes off when it is plucked. **1982** *Agric. Gloss.* (MAF) 54 **1990** McKAY *Baxter* 86 Baxter's duties, as recorded in the station journal kept by the manager..were..drafting, and picking over crutchings and dead wool in the paddocks.

deal, *v.* [Extended use of *deal* to hand out.]

1. As **deal to** (someone). **a.** To give a hiding or bashing to. Also as *vbl. n.*

1980 BERRY *First Offender* 147 Jim talking of bread, grass, acid, boob, screws and dealing to people, while Ben spoke of money, marijuana, LSD, prison officers, and good hidings. **1984** *Dominion* (Wellington) 28 Mar. 7 Britt had learned that a group of Rastafarians at the party had 'dealt to' Miss Edwards and her friend Kim McFarlane. **1985** *Metro* (Auckland) Oct. 24 [The bouncer] descended, seized one of the chaps and hauled him away..for a dealing to. **1990** *Dominion Sunday Times* (Wellington) 5 Aug. 3 He..had gone to the..house to deliver some bush justice. He said he would 'deal to' the person involved.

b. *transf.* To treat roughly.

1987 30 May *TV1 Rugby Commentator*. Most of the team that dealt to Tonga are still with [the Canadian rugby team]. **1989** *Broadsheet* Nov. 5 I feel I have been dealt to by the male media and subjected to men's rules. **1990** *Dominion* (Wellington) 17 June 7 The bikies then dealt to the car by smashing windows.

2. In the phr. **to deal** (someone) **one** [cf. AND *deal it out to* (someone), 1901], to attack, to assault; to give (somebody) a blow or a hiding.

1984 BEATON *Outside In* 17 Ma: Y'want me to deal ya one! *She holds up her arm in a backhand, threateningly. Ibid.* 30 Ginny: Told her that new chick was gettin' on me nerves. Bad mouthin' me work. She had it comin'. I dealt her one. *Ibid.* 109 Deal Somebody One: to assault; pay somebody back.

debt-dodger. WW2. Usu. *pl.* Also as **debt-evader, one-stepper, wife-beater, wife-dodger,** jocular nicknames for an early volunteer of the First Echelon, 2NZEF. Cf. **Cook's Tourists.**

1944 BRUNO *Desert Daze* (Foreword) Certain near-sober First Echelon wife-beaters and debt-dodgers. **1946** FULLARTON *We Walked Alone* 62 'Truth' said last week..that this First Echelon was made up of debt-evaders and wife-deserters and out-of-works. **1979** *Evening Post* (Wellington) 26 Sept. 2 [Arthur Helm, writing on a First Echelon reunion.] Their lot was made no easier by the knowledge that, in some unthinking quarters back in New Zealand they had been dubbed 'wife-beaters and debt-dodgers'. **1995** SLATTER *One More River* 62 Every reinforcement [of the 2NZEF] was given a satirical name by those that had preceded it, such as The Wife-Dodgers or One-Steppers who kept one step ahead of the law or conscription or whatever, or The Cook's Tourists or some such. We were called The Rainbow Boys because we appeared after the storm, the war was over.

deck. [Cf. OED *deck n.* 2 c, *on deck* at hand, alive.] In the phr. **to keep on deck**, to remain alert, awake, sober.

1947 NEWTON *Wayleggo* 31 The [hotel] proprietor managed to keep on deck for the first two nights, but was forced to take to his bed on the third night. **c1955** Heard at Kaingaroa Forest Headquarters (Ed.) I'll keep on deck for the first two hours then you can relieve me [*sc.* for a fire patrol].

Declaration of Independence. A declaration signed at Waitangi 28 October 1835 by thirty-five Northland chiefs at a meeting convened by the British Resident, James Busby, asserting the independence of the New Zealand Maori under the United Tribes of New Zealand (as against Baron de Thierry's proposal to declare a personal sovereignty over the north), and a preference for British protection.

1835 BUSBY Let. 2 Nov. to Under Secretary of State in *Facsimiles of the Declaration of Independence and the Treaty of Waitangi* (1877) [unpaged 2] I have the honour to enclose herewith a copy of the Declaration, by the chiefs of the Northern parts of New Zealand, of the Independence of their country, and of their having united their tribes into one State, under the designation of 'The United Tribes of New Zealand'. In this Declaration the chiefs entreat that His Majesty will continue to be the parent of their infant State. **1840** Hobson to Bunbury 25 Apr. in *GBPP House of Commons 1841 (No.311)* 17 The treaty which forms the base of all my proceedings was signed at Waitangi on the 6th February 1840, by 52 chiefs, 26 of whom were of the confederation, and formed a majority of those who signed the Declaration of Independence. **1877** *Facsimiles of the Declaration of Independence and the Treaty of Waitangi* (1877) [unpaged 1] The Declaration of Independence was adopted and signed at a meeting of Northern chiefs convened at Waitangi on the 28th of October, 1835. **1993** *Dominion* (Wellington) 16 June 17 A High Court judge at Auckland says the court has no jurisdiction to rule on the the significance of the 1835 Declaration of Independence signed by Northern Maori chiefs. Mr Justice Temm..said that the 1835 document was a declaration of an assertion of right and did not fall into the category of a pact, a treaty, an agreement or a contract.

decoy pen. Also *ellipt.* **decoy.** A pen holding decoy sheep to attract others for dipping, etc.

1865 CHUDLEIGH *Diary* 11 Apr. (1950) 173 They run up the rise frightened by the dogs in the yard and seeing the sheep in the decoy immediately slip into the dip off a smooth sheet of iron. **1949** NEWTON *High Country Days* 102 The tip, a small pen capable of holding a dozen sheep, was situated a foot or so above and partly overhanging the dip... With the aid of a lever it could be tipped and the sheep sent slithering into the dip below. The decoy pen was so situated that two or three sheep placed in it decoyed others on to the tip.

dee, *n.*¹ Also **D, D-man.** [Abbrev. of *detective*, or poss. *demon*: used elsewhere but recorded earliest in NZ: see OED *D* III. *Dee.*] *Pl.* often as **the Dees**. A policeman, now esp. a detective. See also DEMON.

1869 WHITWORTH *Comic Guide to Dunedin* 27 These..are gentlemen who give their talents and time to the paternal government for a certain modicium [*sic*] of payment, and are known as D.s. **1895** ROBERTS *Diary of Jonathan Roberts* 18 I was informed that the D's were hanging around that vicinity. **1911** *Truth* 22 July 1 Wellington Detective Department showed a mean sort of spirit over Detective Sergeant Cassell's farewell. As is well known the popular 'demon' has been transferred to Napier... The uniformed branch of the police..wished him all sorts of good wishes, but the other branch, the 'Dees', was not represented. **1930** *National Educ.* May 197 I asked a young man what was the matter, and got the reply, 'Oh, it's nothing! Only the d's pinchin a little piece'... I found that d's were detectives. **1946** SARGESON *That Summer* 74 Not letting that bloody dee bulldoze me. **1960** MUIR *Word for Word* 252 The bloody Ds told me she was..bloody lucky she didn't get clink. **1986** *Listener* 26 Apr. 15 To stay away from the forces of law and order means avoiding..the D-man, the under-cover detective. **1992** PARK *Fence Around the Cuckoo* 119 Occasionally he was raided, noisy stormings by bulky gentlemen referred to as The D's.

dee, *n.*² *Logging.* Also **D.** [Spec. uses of *D(ee)* for anything shaped like the letter D.] See quots.

1950 p.c. R. Gilberd (Okaihau). A 'ropey' will learn to snipe—which is a highly-skilled operation. The butt end of a clean-trimmed log is trimmed of angles. V's are cut at points opposite each other at the butt end (usually) and are connected by a Dee which runs round in a D from one to the other. In the Dee is laid a 'strop', a short length of cable with an eye in each end. **1952–53** *NZ Forest Service Gloss.* (TS) Dee: A groove in the front end of a log into which a strop is fitted for hauling. **1953** REED *Story of Kauri* 197 R. Ross describes 'D-ing' thus: These 'Ds' are grooves cut with the axe a foot or two back from the sniped end of the log. On a large log the groove might start as far back as three feet, coming to a halt in the centre of the sniped end, and of a depth and width just sufficient for the insertion of a wire-rope strap... The groove—semi-circular, combined with the square of the log, resembled a capital 'D', hence the name. **1969** MOORE *Forest to Farm* 42 [The log] was hauled by wire rope or chain bridle. This was attached sometimes by cutting a 'D' in the top half of the nose of the log, or more often by two heavy spiked 'dogs' which were driven in each side of the log.

dee, *v. Logging.* Usu. as **deeing** *vbl. n.*, the cutting of dees in logs to be hauled from the bush.

1953 [see DEE *n.*²]. **1961** CRUMP *Hang On a Minute Mate* 42 During the next few weeks Jack learned about scarfing, backing, limbing, deeing, sniping, [etc.].

deener. *Obs.* [f. Brit. slang *deaner* a shilling: once esp. freq. in NZ and Austral.: AND 1882.] Also **denah.** A shilling (piece). Cf. ZWEIDEENER.

1887 denah [see HERRING *n.*²]. **1899** *Bulletin* (Sydney) 14 Jan. (Red Page) [Letter from *Loafer*, Tauranga.] Following are other local money-names..1s.—*deener, bob, colonial robert* or *penny*. **1912** *Truth* 20 July 7 Grasping that piece of current coin known to wicked bookies and others as a 'deener', he banged gaily on the counter. **1946** Sargeson *That Summer* 77 I'm on the beach myself, I said, but I can make it a deener. **1952** *Here & Now* Jan. 21 I couldn't even drink beer as I was down to my last deener. **1970** Duggan *O'Leary's Orchard* 130 Obol and diobol, the two in the one like a symbol of something... Two zacs to the deener, too.

deep, *a*. *Mining*. [Spec. uses of *deep* well underground.] In special collocations: **deep ground**, ground in which the gold-bearing material lies well beneath the surface; **deep lead** [AND 1858], a lead which can be tapped only by deep-mining operations; **deep sinking** [AND 1853], the mining of deep ground or deep leads.
 1967 May *West Coast Gold Rushes* 526 Deep sinking: putting down a shaft to tap a deep lead. No absolute figure can be given but '**deep ground**' usually required shafts of over sixty feet. **1914** Pfaff *Diggers' Story* 146 We had a claim..over the terrace on a **deep lead**. **1933** *NZJST* XIV. 272 The alluvial miners thought they were dealing with superficial alluvial deposits... Deeper workings showed that the beds dipped steeply, and the gold continued downwards, the conglomerates were then called 'deep leads', probably in the belief that they resembled the deep leads of Victoria. **1962** Evans *Waikaka Saga* 39 This dredge received its name from the fact that the McGeorge Brothers prospected for and found a new 'deep lead' or layer of gold-bearing wash deeper down. **1970** Wood *Gold Trails Otago* 81 The downfolded remnants in the valleys now form the 'deep leads', the white 'quartz wash' of many areas. **1862** *Otago Goldfields & Resources* 18 The **deep sinking** has not, so far, realised the sanguine expectations once entertained regarding it. **1862** Lindsay *Nat. Hist. in Coloniz.* 13 Diggers need make neither 'shallow' nor 'deep sinkings' there. **1866** Mueller *My Dear Bannie* (1958) 100 Unless they find gold in the Ranges, and have deep sinking, there is very little prospect of the diggers now at the Coast remaining long.

Deepfreeze. Also **Deep Freeze**. The operational name ('Operation Deepfreeze') for the original 1955–56 summer US Navy Expedition to the Ross Sea and Antarctica in preparation for the International Geophysical Year, subsequently applied to later expeditions, and, with the establishment of a Deepfreeze Base in Christchurch, applied in New Zealand to any US Navy or US Science Foundation operations or personnel associated with the Antarctic. Freq. *attrib.*
 1955 *Dominion* (Wellington) 19 Sept. 8 The [American] Ambassador said the surface unit component of Task Force 43, which would carry on 'Expedition Deepfreeze' would include two Navy icebreakers. **1955** *Truth* 14 Dec. 15 [Heading] Police Not Told, How to Deal with 'Deepfreeze' Offenders... There were rumours in Christchurch before the arrival of 'Deepfreeze' that an understanding had been reached between the New Zealand and American authorities about maintaining shore discipline. **1971** Young *Penguin Summer* 29 We promptly put them to work unloading all the packs and sledge boxes from the car and carting them in to the Deep Freeze desk. *Ibid.* 15 The New Zealand Post Office or Deep Freeze took it into their hands to collect the mail. **1980** Hickson *Flight 901 to Erebus* 89 He heard reports from Deep Freeze of conditions in the area during the day when the flight was lost.

deep sea.
1. In the names of fish, see Groper 2 (2); **deep sea cod**, see Cod 6.

2. *Obs*. As **deep sea diver**, rhyming slang for 'fiver', a five-pound note.
 1963 *NZ Truth* 21 May 19 I had promised to give her a deep sea diver for the Duke of Kent. deep sea diver..fiver.

3. *Whaling*. **deep sea fishing**, whaling carried on from ocean-going ships as distinct from shore-whaling.
 1842 Terry *NZ* 241 [Whaling] is carried on in two ways—either by vessels that remain absent from their port for a certain period, which is termed 'deep sea fishing', or by establishments in the large bays..denominated 'shore-fishing'.

deep south. In New Zealand, usu. s. Otago, Southland, and Stewart Island. Contrast Far North.
 1980 Mantell *Murder & Chips* 150 Mightn' mean anything but he comes from the deep south. Dunedin. **1985** Stewart *Gumboots & Goalposts* 67 He was a South Islander from the deep South and he rolled his r's. **1995** *Dominion* (Wellington) 9 Dec. 17 The problem [with Foveaux Strait oysters] was diagnosed..as the parasite named bonamia—pronounced for some reason as bonemia in the deep south.

deep thinker. *WW2*. A nickname for a member of later reinforcements of 2NZEF. Contrast Debt-Dodger.
 1983 Henderson *Down from Marble Mountain* 260 Puzzled, we hear of 'Deep Thinkers'. A member of the 5th Reinforcements, nearing the last of the volunteer New Zealand soldiers because 'the rush to the colours' in this war was much more subdued, was heard to observe: 'Yes, I must admit I did some deep thinking before joining up.' From then to the end of World War Two, the 5th Reinforcements were known as the 'Deep Thinkers'.

deer, *attrib*. In special Comb. referring to the hunting or farming of deer: **deer bed**, see quot. 1991; **deer-culler**, a professional deer shooter employed (formerly, usu. by the State) to kill wild deer (see also Culler a); **deer-culling** *vbl. n*. and *attrib*., the professional killing of wild deer; **deer farm**, a farm whose livestock comprise deer; **deer farmer**, one who owns or runs a deer farm; **deer farming** *vbl. n*., the domestication and breeding of orig. (and usu.) ferile or occas. imported deer for venison, velvet, and other by-products; **deer puller**, a hunting-dog which 'pulls' or moves the deer nearer to its master, the hunter.
 1991 Lentle & Saxton *Red Deer* 183 **deer bed** position repeatedly used by deer for sitting and cudding. These places often become slightly hollowed out. **1939** *Tararua Tramper* July 2 We..made for home accompanied by the **deer-cullers**. **1947** Newton *Wayleggo* 153 Deer Cullers: Men who shoot deer professionally for the Government or an acclimatization society. **1959** Slatter *Gun in My Hand* 169 I could get right back into the bush and live in deer cullers' huts. **1964** Hintz *Trout at Taupo* 88 In spite of the efforts of the deer cullers, whose mission it is to exterminate a forest pest, the deer stalking outside the State forest areas can still be exciting. **1973** Dryland *A Multiple Texture* 157 I was a deer-culler for a couple of years before I took up teaching. **1989** *Dominion Sunday Times* (Wellington) 12 Feb. 17 If a Swanndri survives two months on a deerculler, it's a winner. **1935** *Tararua Tramper* Feb. 3 The Internal Affairs Dept. would like the Club to co-operate with its Tararua **deer culling** scheme. **1952** Newton *High Country Journey* 73 Deer culling is one of the roughest and hardest of jobs, but it is a life with an appeal of its own. **1978** Mantell *Murder in Fancydress* 87 Tried different jobs, finally settled for deer culling. **1981** Hooper *Goat Paddock* 28 There had been a boy Parkin, who had wanted to spend a year deer-culling in the South Island. **1995** Crump *Bushwoman* 86 I often felt the bush was forgotten when I came across old camps and huts from the deer-culling days. **1977** *NZJAg.* June CXXXIV. 3 There are, today, perhaps 100 **deer farms** in this country. The New Zealand Deer Farmers' Association has about 80 members with deer. **1985** *NZJAg.* Aug. CLI. 22 During a recent visit to the Waikato/Bay of Plenty I saw many deer farms grossly under-stocked. **1985** *NZJAg.* Aug. CLI. 4 TB in deer poses a threat to much of farming but finding an eradication programme acceptable to **deer farmers** is no easy task... The 10th Annual Conference of the Deer Farmers' Association, held recently in Queenstown, decided that a compulsory test should have a back-up system. **1986** Bateman *Illust. Encycl. NZ* (1989) 294 Deer farmers had established a Deer Farmers' Association shortly after deer farming was legalised. **1967** *NZPD* CCCLXIV. 4422 Members should know..the recommendations of the Noxious Animals Committee for the basis of the future administration of **deer farming**. **1970** *NZJAg.* Mar. CXX. 51 Applications for deer farming licences have already been received from places as far apart as Northland and North Canterbury. **1985** McGill *G'day Country* 98 Olly said this town had sawmilling, deer farming, a hospital. **1991** Eldred-Grigg *Shining City* 275 I see the Hawdons have gone ahead with deer farming. **1951** *Here & Now* Dec. 15 These crosses, sometimes euphemistically called lurchers, are excellent **deer-pullers**... Only with great luck and fitness..can the hunter be in on the pull with the knife. On the whole it is better not to have dogs so fast as to be able to pull deer unless you are going in for that line exclusively.

de facto /dəˈfæktʌu/, *n*. [Spec. use of the Latin phr. *de facto* in fact, in reality (often as distinct from *de jure* by law); in Brit. use, an *adj*. or *adv*.: see New SOD; AND 1952.] Also *transf*. (see quot. 1986). A common-law spouse, as distinct from a *de jure*, or legally married one; one who has a permanent, live-in extra-marital relationship with a partner.
 1972 *Salient* (Wellington) 7 June 16 Radicals are not race-conscious. To prove this, radical girls like to have a tame Polynesian boyfriend/de facto to show off to their friends. **1980** Glen *Bush in Our Yard* 116 Each one of the girls was quietly living with her own fears for husband, boyfriend, de-facto..and parents. **1986** Knight *Geriatrics* 9 Dalton had previously captained the All Blacks against the Springboks in 1981 when..Mourie had been unavailable. Dalton believed this question implied his role in 1981 had been that of a de facto and he judged this to be demeaning of both himself and his team.

delayed telegram. *Obs*. A telegram not sent or delivered out of office hours. Cf. Tannergram.
 1885 Vincent *Forty-Thousand Miles* 158 A system of 'delayed telegrams'. **1890** Moore *NZ for the Emigrant* 173 'Delayed telegrams' [sixpence for 20 words] **1894** in Wilson *Land of Tui* 52 B. also sent me several messages, which they call here 'delayed telegrams', because delivered by the postman with the letters instead of by special messenger, which would be costly.

demo, var. Rimu

demolition party. A party held on the last night of a tenancy for the purpose of deliberately destroying furniture and fittings. Cf. *house-trashing* (House 5).

demon. [Prob. a pun on *dee-man* + *demon* devil; or a playful extension of *dee* detective: AND 1889.] Often in *pl.* as **the demons**. A policeman, esp. a detective. See also DEE *n.*[1]
1906 *Truth* 31 Mar. 6 [Bloke's patter] And a 'Demon' is a 'Nark.' **1908** *Truth* 1 Aug. 1 According to a well-known Christchurch demon, the slang of three months in thieves' argot is 'a drag'. **1911** [see DEE *n.*[1]]. **1932** Nelson Baylis let. in Partridge *Dict. Underworld* (1961) 183 A detective: New Zealand: 1932, Nelson Baylis (private letter). **1946** SARGESON *That Summer* 64 The barman winked at me and said he was a demon. **1950** *Here & Now* Nov. 16 When they got to the station a big demon walked into Joe's cell with his coat off. **1963** *Truth* 30 July 5 Talk of 'demons' and 'jokers' being 'hooked'..proved too much for Mr L.G.M. Sinclair, S.M., in Auckland Court. Te Atatu mussel curer, Benjamin Patrick —, 28, explained. 'Demons,' he said, were detectives. **1974** MORRIESON *Predicament* (1981) 36 'What sort of questions did the demons ask you?' 'The demons?' 'The police,' said Mervyn. 'The bulls'. **1987** NORGROVE *Shoestring Sailors* 14 'The police!' 'Yeah, he wanted to get the demons in on the act.'

dental clinic. A shortened form of *school dental clinic* (see SCHOOL 2).
1947 *NZ Woman's Weekly* 15 May 3 For the rest of the day there was a constant stream of children to and fro from the Dental Clinic. **1961** *Carterton District School Centennial Celebration* 13 The first dental clinic was established in Greytown on March 1st, 1928, the intention being to establish rooms in the schools at Featherston, Martinborough and Carterton, the nurse travelling to these schools in turn. **1988** JACKSON *Rainshadow* 61 Crouched under the lawsonianas by the Dental Clinic, a sense of loss..seized me. **1991** [see MURDER HOUSE].

dental nurse. A shortened form of *school dental nurse* (see SCHOOL 2).
1921-22 *AJHR* H-31 32 A school for dental nurses has been housed in the old war-records building in Whitmore Street, and is now at work. **1947** *NZ Woman's Weekly* 15 May 3 In the afternoon..there was the dental nurse's lesson. **1966** *Encycl. NZ* II. 522 The first Dental Nurses School was established in Wellington in 1921, with 35 students. **1974** *Islands* IX. 271 She was four-and-a-half years old when she got the first filling in her teeth. A big smiling dental nurse drilled out the tiny little bad bit. **1986** *Illustrated Encycl. NZ* (1989) 299 Such has been the improvement in the dental health of young people in recent years that two of the three training schools for dental nurses have been closed and there was no intake at the remaining school in 1989. **1993** *Dominion* (Wellington) 6 Nov. 11 New treatments and equipment..had lifted the image of dental therapists (formerly dental nurses).

depasturage licence. *Hist.* Also **depasturing licence.** [AND 1841–51.] **a.** The right, by payment of a fee, to graze stock on specified Crown land. Cf. *pastoral lease* (or *licence*) (PASTORAL *a.* 3 a), PASTURAGE LEASE, *run licence* (RUN *n.*[1] 4 b).
1856 FITTON *NZ* 338 The land department (sales and depasturage licences) to be administered by a Board of not less than three commissioners. **1856** in Evans *Waikaka Saga* (1962) 88 Depasturing Licence No. 111 'Whereas Alexander McNab of Knapdale has made application for a Licence to Depasture Stock upon the Waste Lands of the Crown... Dated at Dunedin this 4th day of November, one thousand eight hundred and fifty six.' **1879** *Auckland Weekly News* 16 Aug. 15 It was assumed the Board had power to grant a depasturing licence to the Union Sash and Door Company. **1898** HOCKEN *Contributions* 59 When the selection [of the N.Z. Company share of the Otago Block] had been made the Crown grant was to be issued, and there was an understanding that if Colonel Wakefield desired still more land he was to have it. This was the origin of what was afterwards known as the depasturage licences, under which settlers were authorised to run cattle and sheep in the adjoining districts. **1948** SCOTTER *Run Estate & Farm* 15 There was also [in Otago] the unsold land open for grazing. Each year, therefore, those who wished to graze stock on this open country applied for a depasturing licence. **1982** WHEELER *Hist. Sheep Stations NZ* 1 A race for the Lands Office would follow, there to fill in a 'Depasturing License'. **1991** LA ROCHE *Hist. of Howick & Pakuranga* 232 [Wardens] were responsible for allocating.. 'depasturing' licences for g[r]azing on Crown owned 'Waste Land'.

b. As **depasturage licensing system**, the system within which such licences were formerly granted.
1898 HOCKEN *Contributions* 149 Much of the country [in Otago] had been taken up as runs under the depasturage licensing system.

depasture. *Obs.* [*depasture* for *graze v.* was in common use esp. in the South Island during the years 1840–70, poss. felt as a back-formation from *depasturing licence*: AND 1841.] *trans.* and *intr.* To put sheep or stock to pasture, often under a depasturing licence. Also as *vbl. n.*
1844 MONRO *Notes of Journey* July in Hocken *Contributions* (1898) 235 Both the herbage and the nature of the ground are admirably adapted for the depasturing of sheep. **1851** *Lyttelton Times* 19 July 1 Wanted to purchase, 500 scabby sheep, to depasture at Rhodes Bay. **1879** *Auckland Weekly News* 26 Apr. 16 Four horses were depasturing in the immediate vicinity. **1882** POTTS *Out in Open* 47 Years ago, on the Rakaia, the writer depastured a large herd of breeding cattle. **1922** *Auckland Weekly News* 27 Apr. 15 Mr. J.D. Enys..while depasturing his flocks, gathered wild flowers on the mountains. **1932** *Oamaru Mail* 7 May 6 Farmers depasturing sheep near the confines of the borough are suffering severe losses by the ravages of dogs.

depatch: see PATCH *v.*

de-rail /ˈdiːreɪl/. *Obs.* [Poss. f. the notion that its strength 'puts one off the rails'.] Illicit raw spirits.
1938 HYDE *Godwits Fly* (1970) 129 It was Maori country, which meant no licensed hotels, but plenty of sly grog—the good stuff down to de-rail, denatured alcohol and meths.

derb /dɜb/. Mainly *students*. Also **durb.** [Orig. unknown: poss. f. an obsolete brand-name, or a var. of DURRY.] A roll-your-own, handmade cigarette.
[*Note*] A fairly freq. use, but not yet found in written sources.
1941 Derb used frequently at St Patrick's College, Silverstream. (Ed.) **1960** 14 Oct. C. Corne Letter **1983** (Auckland) Derb—handrolled cigarette; cigarette butt (student slang, 1960) **1981** *Avondale College Slang Words* (Auckland) (Goldie Brown Collect.) *der/derb; durb:* smoke.

dere /ˈdɛrə/. *WW1. Gallipoli.* [f. Turkish *dere* a valley.] A small valley or gully.
1918 WESTON *Three Years with the New Zealanders* 48 Our last thin line of sentries would file out of the deserted trenches and slip down the Dere to the waiting lighters. **1919** WAITE *New Zealanders at Gallipoli* 286 Up the deres, great wire gates had been erected so that if the force was attacked the gates would be shut down. *Ibid.* 318 Dere—Valley with stream. **1928** CUNNINGHAM et al. *Wellington Regiment* 64 The Dere itself, as it ascended towards the hill, grew gradually narrower. **1935** BURTON *The Silent Division* 104 The second [stage] was through the long and winding Dere. **1984** PUGSLEY *Gallipoli* 276 His men then piqueted either side of the dere and the two remaining squadrons passed through.

derision. *Wellington tramping.* [A euphemistic shortening of *shit and derision* applied to bad weather (cf. Partridge 8: used by air-crews, WW2).] Cold wet weather.
1939 *Tararua Tramper* Jan. 5 We jiggy-jagged on to Maungahuka, where we erected the dead marine as a propitiation to the Gods of derision. **1946** *Tararua Tramper* June 4 Of course it rained; nice, steady Tararua 'derision'. **1947** *Ibid.* May 2 The stars still blazed, but a quarter of an hour later they were concealed by derision. **1952** PASCOE *Land Uplifted High* (1961) 11 Of the crossing in blizzard conditions over Mounts Alpha... I can only remember..the surprise when Kime Hut flung itself out of the derision at us. **1958** MASON *Tararua* (Track & Trail) Sept. 27 Derision has been an accepted term among trampers and climbers for at least twenty years for bad weather—cold, stormy, and wet.

dero /ˈdɛrʌu/. Also **derro.** [f. *der*(elict + -o: AND 1971.] A human 'derelict'.
1987 MOORE *Hard Labour* 18 I took it [*sc.* a job] and rented a room in a shabby Ponsonby boarding house, which I shared with 'deros' and down-and-outers. **1988** JACKSON *Rainshadow* 170 Outside the Hotel Hollywood, the deros sat in the gutter amidst broken glass. **1988** SCOTT *Glory Days* 98 It was the room of a person no longer bound to life, an old derro, impersonal and final. **1992** *Metro* (Auckland) Oct. 126 I know most of the deros by sight and I say hello to them.

derry. [Prob. f. the refrain *derry, down, derry* used humorously for *down* a dislike: AND 1882.] In the phr. **to have** (occas. **get**) **a derry on**, to have a down on, a strong dislike for or aversion to.
1887 *NZ Mail* (Wellington) 15 July 9 (NZ Slang) Colonial Colloquialism provides many opprobrious epithets.. to a person you have 'a derry on' (a grudge against). **1897** WRIGHT *Station Ballads* 30 They hadn't such a derry on the bloke upon the track. *Ibid.* 58 I ain't down on them if they ain't got a derry on me. **1912** *Truth* 1 June 7 You seem to have a derry on the Home people. **c1930** *Whitcombe's Etym. Dict. Aust.-NZ Suppl.* 4 *derry n.* sl. prejudice.—*to have a derry on* to be prejudiced against, have a 'down' on (playful allusion to 'hey derry down derry', as refrain of old songs). **1943** BENNETT *English in NZ* in *Amer. Speech* XVIII. 90 Another familiar variant is 'to have a derry on', *derry* being a substitute for *down*, apparently from the association of the two words in the refrain 'derry down', 'to have a derry on blowflies' is to have a strong dislike of them.

deviation. A rail (or road) detour, now commonly used of any (esp. new) formation which deviates from an old route.
1885 in Wright *Clifton* (1989) 15 [County Council minutes] G. Pott was authorised to..lay off a cutting and procure estimates for a deviation north of the Mimi Bridge. **1894** DOUGLAS in *Mr Explorer Douglas* (1957)

209 But the new [road] deviation will be beyond the funds of the county council. **1911** *Truth* 7 Oct. 7 Dryden was acting under the instructions of..the engineer in charge of a gang of men engaged on 'The Deviation' on the Waiouru section of the North Island Main Trunk line. **1952** *Evening Post* (Wellington) 3 July 10 Connection of the Wilson deviation to the main railway line. **1980** *Evening Post* (Wellington) 29 Dec. 28 Construction of the South Rangitikei railway bridge..is getting close to completion. The 300-metre bridge is the longest of three on the nine kilometre Mangaweka deviation... The deviation is being constructed to eliminate a steep winding section of the North Island Main Trunk. **1994** *Evening Post* (Wellington) 14 Nov. 5 A $13 million plan to realign State Highway 2..has been given resource assent... The Kaitoke deviation is a key element in a proposed major upgrading of the Rimutaka Hill Road.

devil.

1. *Hist.* [Spec. use of *devil* Satan, poss. influenced by *devil's missionary* 2 below.] Contrast MISSIONARY *n.* 1. **a.** Often *pl.* A European or settler not considered favourable to early missionary interests.

1839 8 Apr. in Matthews *Matthews of Kaitaia* (1940) 121 Of great numbers of our countrymen I truly say that they are the vilest of the vile; and such Europeans are distinguished by the name of 'devils' by those natives who know them. **1840** *NZ Jrnl.* I. 202 The rangatira missionary will come out along with the *devils*, as the missionaries have kindly christened every European not of their own cloth. **1841** BEST *Journal* 30 May 319 In fact Hospitality is the universal attribute of all white men 'Devils' (a term used to distinguish them from the members of the Mission) residing in New Zealand?

b. A Christian convert's name for a Maori unconverted to Christianity.

1841 BIDWILL *Rambles in NZ* (1952) 44 It sounds rather curious to hear a native, in answer to a question as to whether he is a missionary or not, reply quite coolly, 'No, I'm a devil!' **1842** HEAPHY *NZ* 53 [The old native replied] 'the converts need be under no apprehension of danger from them [*sc.* sharks], but that the 'dewaras' (devils) or unbelievers would certainly be devoured'. **1847** ANGAS *Savage Life* II. 152 Those natives who are still heathen are generally styled 'devils' by the Christianized people; and they themselves adhere to the appellation.

2. In special collocations: **devil's darning needle** [Brit. and US dial.: see EDD II 1 (13), Sc. & Lancashire; DARE 1809], see quot. 1982; **devil's half acre**, see quot. 1991; **devil's highway** *obs.*, a fanciful name for terraces formed by glaciation; **devil's missionary** *hist.*, a name given to pre-1840 Europeans, who were not associates of the Christian mission (cf. 1 above); **devil's purse**, **devil's stink egg**, *basket fungus* (FUNGUS 2 (1));

1982 SALE *Four Seasons* 91 I surmise from their size and general colour on the wing that they are probably what some simply call large dragonflies, or others name more colourfully **Devil's Darning Needles**, or Horse Stingers (or, in Scotland, Flying Adders). *Ibid.* 92 My book on native insects says the 'darning needle' nickname derives from a tradition that the dragonflies sew up the ears of delinquents. **1991** *Dominion Sunday Times* (Wellington) 17 Feb. 15 During the Otago gold rushes..the early cottages of the lower side [of Walker Street]..gained an unsavoury reputation, with a red light district and much criminal activity reported there. The nickname '**The Devil's Half Acre**' was born and it was a label that stuck for years. **1879** HAAST *Geol. Canterbury & Westland* 121 With every step, the effects of the enormous glaciation become more manifest, all mountains and hills have not only the *roche moutonnée* form, but glacier shelves at different altitudes and lying one above the other, are cut deeply into the hillsides. Some of these are so regular that the settlers have called them carriage roads, **devil's highways**, or by some similar epithets. **1837** WAKEFIELD *Brit. Coloniz. NZ* 31 [The lawless whites] really deserve a name which has been given them—that of '**Devil's missionaries**.' **1840** WARD *Information Relative NZ* 108 There are upwards of two thousand British subjects now settled in different parts of the islands, of whom several hundreds consist of a most worthless class of persons... They really deserve a name which has been given them, 'Devil's Missionaries'. **1922** *NZJST* V. 247 *Clathrus cibarius*, the 'Bird-cage Fungus'... This fungus, known variously as 'basket fungus', 'lattice fungus', '**Devil's purse**', '*tutae whetu*', '*tutae kehua*', belongs to the Phallaceae, a family included in the Basidiomycetes. **1938** HYDE *Godwits Fly* (1970) 107 It's a toadstool. It's a **Devil's Stink Egg**. You'll turn black in the face and die.

diamond. *Ellipt.* for *diamond-back flounder* (FLOUNDER 2 (9)). See also DAB *n.*¹

1960 DOOGUE & MORELAND *Sea Anglers' Guide* 203 Sand Flounder... Other names: *Rhombosolea plebeia*; diamond, tinplate, dab, square; patiki. **1967** [see FLOUNDER 2 (9)]. **1970** [see PLAICE].

Diamond Dinks: see DINK *n.* 1 b.

dicken. Also **dickin**, **dikkon**. [AND 1894; var. of *Dickens*!] As **(aw) dicken!** or **dicken on that!**, an exclamation or interjection of disbelief, disgust, etc., now in infrequent use. **a.** As **dicken!**

1911 *Truth* 1 Apr. 4 'It has not been restrained by any fear of the penalties that are provided for the offence known as "contempt", but by a desire to assist in preserving the dignity of the court and in upholding its authority.' Dicken! **1918** *Chron. NZEF* 10 Apr. 101 [Caption] 'Say Kiwi, some coot told me you were a wingless bird.' 'Dicken Yank, yer gotter have arms when there's a war on.' **1937** MARSH *Vintage Murder* 238 'Aw dikkon, Mr Alleyn!' said Wade. 'What did you say?' 'Haven't you heard that one, sir? I suppose it's N.Z. digger slang. "Dikkon". It's the same as if you'd say "Come off it". Used to hear it on the Peninsula. "Aw dikkon, dig".' **1941** BAKER *NZ Slang* 51 In constant use by our youngsters..dickin! **1950** GASKELL *All Part of the Game* (1978) 140 'Ow, Cliff,' I said. 'Cut it out. You're hurting. Oo. Dicken.' **1970** *Listener* 12 Oct. 13 'You don't lie and cheat the way my mother does.' 'Ah, dicken.' **1984** WILSON *S. Pacific Street* 58 Ah, dicken! I know what makes things tick between you and Bert. He's a decent joker.

b. In the phr. **dicken on that**, an elaboration of **dicken**.

1949 DAVIN *Roads from Home* 237 Dicken on that for a joke. **1950** *Evening Post* (Wellington) 6 Nov. 8 The accused said: 'Murder..dicken on that, me murder anyone.' **1959** SLATTER *Gun in My Hand* 44 'What in hell are ya doin in Christchurch anyway? Bludgin on the social security, I spose.' 'No. Dicken on that.' **1988** MCGILL *Dict. Kiwi Slang* 36 Dicken on that! go easy, will you!; eg 'You want me to help you lift that dirty big post? Dicken on that, mate.'

dickey, var. DICKY.

dickin, dickon, varr. DICKEN.

Dick Seddon: see SINCE.

dicky, *a.* Also **dickey**. [f. modern *dick*(-head fool + -Y.] Stupid.

1982 MCCAULEY *Other Halves* 20 'I thought your husband looked a bit dicky if you ask me.' 'Why would I ask you?' **1988** MCGILL *Dict. Kiwi Slang* 36 dickey stupid; eg 'Well, I don't think Billy T's dickey at all, I think he's neat.'

dictionary: see MAORI DICTIONARY.

die, *v. intr.* Usu. as **die well**, **die badly**, etc., of stock killed for meat, to provide a high or low quality carcass. Cf. KILL *v.*

1922 PERRY *Sheep Farming* 56 They [*sc.* Southdown sheep] die well, *i.e.*, have a small percentage of offal, and the bones being small there is little waste. *Ibid.* The Ryeland kills well, and produces meat of a fairly good quality.

Dieffenbach's rail: see RAIL 2 (4).

diehard. *Hist.*

1. In *pl.* as **Diehards**, the name of a former Christchurch (street) gang.

1912 *Truth* 3 Feb. 7 There used to be much more of the push element around Christchurch than there is now, and it frequently occurred that pushes [*i.e.* youths belonging to these groups] like the 'Tigers', the 'Diehards', the 'Scalpers', and the 'Skull-Draggers', faced the music before the beak.

2. *WW1*. Any one of those choosing to be evacuated last from Gallipoli, to help conceal the evacuation from the Turks. See also LAST DITCHER.

1916 GRAY, Norman *MS Papers 4134* (ATLMS) 5 Jan. The new camp was pitched before nightfall, and seeing that there were four Diehards in our tent, we managed to collar a few mats. **1919** WAITE *New Zealanders at Gallipoli* 285 By 4.30 a.m. on December 19 [1915], the last beetle cleared from the shore leaving the 'Diehards' of the Division, only 3,000 strong, to hold the line against a mighty army. *Ibid.* 286 The 'last ditchers' were to be sacrificed for the army. There was no lack of volunteers..men of Anzac and Suvla alike—vied with each other in an endeavour to become included in the 'Diehards'. **1935** BURTON *The Silent Division* 132 After the evacuation, the troops assembled in a tented camp outside Mudros. The 'diehards' of the last party were welcomed with great joy.

diffy. [f. *diff*(erential + -Y.] A differential (of a motor vehicle).

1955 p.c. R. Mason *Diffy* occurs in a set of instructions for running the ski-tow (Christchurch Ski Club) at Temple basin. **1956** SUTHERLAND *Green Kiwi* (1960) 199 In affectionate terms we discussed the innards..of their 'carbies' and their 'diffies' and their 'con-rods'.

dig, *n. WW1* and *WW2*.

[Note] Orig. (WW1) and usually a term of address among New Zealand soldiers, a shortened (and by New Zealanders, the preferred) form of DIGGER, increasingly the form preferred by Australians (see AND *digger* 2). In WW2 the substantival use was popularized, often with a defining word, as **grim dig**, **old dig**, later to be used (esp. in the late 1940s and 1950s) in non-military contexts.

1. See also COB, COBBER, MATE *n.*², SPORT. **a.** [AND 1916.] As a term of address, orig. and mainly used by and among New Zealand soldiers.

1917 FRASER in Boyack *Behind the Lines* (1989) 137 [Women] just came up with all the soft stuff imaginable [*sic*] shout for me dig, and so on. **1918** *Chron. NZEF* 21 June 221 Be shrewd, sweet Dig, and let those who will die working. *Ibid.* 22 Nov. 198 'How far's the war, Dig?' was the first question we asked. **1921** *Quick March* 10 Aug. 27 Come on me lucky lads, you pick 'em. Hop in, digs, and have a fly with the old man.

b. *WW2 and after.* Often also as a term of address to a stranger.

1944 *Listener* 28 Jan. 20 Talking to each other, the Kiwis [of the 2NZEF] use the terms 'Soldier' or 'Dig' mostly. **1945** MACDONALD *Away from Home* 12 [To a nurse] Roll a bloke a cigarette, Dig. **1959** SLATTER *Gun in My Hand* 178 'Howya doin, Dig?' 'Good,' I tell him. **1973** WILSON *NZ Jack* 14 But his hair was white now. 'Ah, hullo, Dig,' he said.

2. a. A New Zealand soldier in WW2.

1944 *Dept. Short Guide NZ* 39 *Dig, digger*—Australian or New Zealand soldier. **c1945** *Sixes & Sevens* (Troopship pub.) 7 'And the digs back in Italia,' I said. 'Bet they're a bit umbriago oggi.' **1959** SLATTER *Gun in My Hand* 92 Sleep it off, Dig. He called me Dig. I was one of the Digs. The nicest thing anybody ever said to me. **1975** DAVIN *Breathing Spaces* 95 'Talks just like a dinkum dig,' Ted said.

b. grim dig, see GRIM *a.* b.

c. Often with init. caps. **old dig** [f. *old* experienced], an experienced soldier; also occas. [f. *old* former] (also **ex-dig**), a returned serviceman.

1944 *Listener* 28 Jan. 20 1st, 2nd and 3rd Echelon men are naturally known as the 'Old Digs'—men who were there almost before the Pyramids. **1945** WEBBER *Johnny Enzed in Middle East* 4 The war has finished. A large number of Old Digs have bustled their way down various gangways. **1947** *NZ Observer* 6 Aug. 11 It has been particularly noticed in the South Island where 'ex-digs' are reported to be feeling great dissatisfaction. **1959** SLATTER *Gun in My Hand* 144 The grey jersey and the grey flannel shirt as worn by the Kiwi. Walking back from the tailor in Maadi camp with my old dig shirt. *Ibid.* 220 'We're just old digs now, Ron,' he is saying. 'Returned men.' **1962** WEBBER *Look No Hands* 124 You remember telling me you didn't want any of your grogged-up Old Dig friends giving her the lowdown on you?' **1977** HOLMES *Best of Homespun* 64 Thus old digs could carouse snugly in their clubrooms. **1982** OLIVER *Poor Richard* 22 For he can't stop himself spending Saturdays up and down the sideline Sundays in bed with whatever's left of the dozen other old digs. **1991** *Evening Post* (Wellington) 13 May 6 There are..vital issues that I think all Old Digs will agree on. You cannot do precision ceremonial drill with present day weapons.

dig, *v.* [Spec. uses of *dig.*]

1. [f. *dig* to seek by digging.] *intr.* To work a claim as an alluvial goldminer or DIGGER *n.*¹ 1.

1852 *Agreement between Government & Native Tribes for Gold Fields on the Thames* 30 Nov. in Swainson *Auckland* (1853) 158 A Fund shall be created by a Tax of *two* shillings on every License, for the purpose of..rewarding the native owners..as well as recompensing them for any damage, annoyance, or inconvenience they may experience from Europeans while digging on their lands. **1863** CHUDLEIGH *Diary* 20 Aug. (1950) 99 He has been diging [*sic*] for 7 months more for amusement than aught else. **1871** MONEY *Knocking About NZ* 147 A neighbouring settler, who remembered me years before when I was digging..in Otago. **1881** BATHGATE *Waitaruna* 142 I am going to try digging at Muttontown, as I spoke of doing before.

2. [f. *dig* to poke, to thrust.] *trans.* To (gang) rape. See also BLOCK *v.*¹

1974 *Truth* 2 Apr. 13 Eight members of a gang took a girl to the stockyards in Cemetery Road, where they 'dug' her.

3. As **dig in** [f. Brit. (also US) dial.: OED 11 e] *intr.*, to set to (work) energetically, to 'hoe in'.

a1927 ANTHONY *Me & Gus* (1938) 21 We'll dig in like niggers, Mark, and show those old jokers over the fence how to smack up wood.

digger, *n.*¹ [Spec. or transf. uses of *digger* a miner, esp. one who works shallow deposits.]

I. *Goldmining.* **1.** [AND 1849.] A miner on the New Zealand goldfields, esp. one working alluvial or surface gold (see quot. 1869).

1852 *Gold Circular* 13 Dec. in Swainson *Auckland* (1853) 107 Considering the small number of diggers yet upon the ground..and the large proportion of the time of each digger employed in exploring, we hail this commencement of the Auckland gold diggings as affording the most brilliant promise of ultimate productiveness. **1869** *AJHR D-6* 3 The alluvial diggings..in Otago and on the West Coast can hardly with any propriety be termed mines, or those who work them, miners... For the sake of convenience, I shall, in the following essay observe a distinction between the alluvial digger, by whom I understand one who gathers gold from the surface and from later deposits only, and the alluvial miner, that is, one who works the deeper deposits, or deep placer mines as they are called. **1871** MONEY *Knocking About NZ* 74 The true digger, whether Irish, Scotch, or English, is a brave, high-spirited working-man, ready with his purse as a friend, or with his fist as a foe. **1881** [see DIGGING 1]. **1899** GRACE *Sketch NZ War* 120 Dressed in a blue jumper, with a pair of brown tweed trousers on tucked into digger's knee-boots, I wore a forage cap with the Army Medical Staff badge. **1920** *Otago Witness* (Dunedin) 28 Dec. 53 These Irish diggers (they hated to be called miners) made the place as bad or worse than Donnybrook. **1950** *Review* June 13 The Central Otago association with Australians went back to the early days when the term 'digger' was first used on Otago goldfields. **1967** MAY *West Coast Gold Rushes* 526 Digger: commonly applied to all men who searched for gold but apparently not always synonymous with 'gold-miner'. **1991** *NZ Geographic* Apr.–June 110 Diggers (or 'hatters' as they were often termed) persisted, a few into the last decade.

2. a. As a supposed term of address or salutation on the New Zealand goldfields. (This use is unsupported by contemporary NZ or Austral. evidence.)

1938 *Press* (Christchurch) (McNab Slang) 2 Apr. 18 'Digger' was a familiar greeting of the 50s. **1948** SUMPTER in *Search of Central Otago* 73 We [miners] reckon we'll pack our swag and head back to California. What do you think, digger?

b. In a weakened sense, 'fellow', 'joker'.

1940 MEEK in Woodhouse *Farm & Station Verse* (1950) 152 The Stock and Station diggers have got it on the brain.

3. In *attrib.* use. **a.** [AND 1854.] Of or pertaining to an alluvial miner.

1875 HOGG *Lays & Rhymes* 183 Drenched till my digger boots were running o'er. **1881** NESFIELD *Chequered Career* 75 Their manner of accosting me was simply their 'digger' style of humour. **1894** O'REGAN *Voices Wave & Tree* 10 But that was digger nature. Was the digger ever seen Who..dreamt of dearth?

b. Special Comb. **Digger Dick** *hist.*, a nickname for Premier *Richard* John Seddon (cf. KING DICK); **digger-mania, digger-phobia** [cf. AND *digging-mania* (*digging* 2), 1857], *gold fever* (GOLD 3).

1904 *NZ Observer* 6 Feb. 3 Who is better equipped..than 'Digger Dick', practical miner, Empire builder, and the very active personality behind 'Seddon, New Zealand'? **1919** FANNING *Politics and the Public* 23 It was one of those paternal days, dear to the heart of 'Digger Dick'. After this..Mr. Seddon returned to Wellington at top speed. **1867** COOPER *Digger's Diary* 19 Dec. (1978) 23–24 It is called by some **digger-mania**, by others **digger-phobia**. This dire disease is usually developed about a month after the victim has commenced digging; its symptoms are very varied and curious, and are anything but agreeable to those who are unfortunately connected with the poor afflicted one.

c. In special collocations: **digger's costume**, the usual clothing of a gold-digger (see also quot. 1867 below); **digger's delight, digger's hat**, a wide-brimmed felt hat [AND military only]; **digger's lantern**, a bottle lantern (see quots., see also LANTERN); **digger's shirt**, a blue (?Crimean) woollen shirt, part of a miner's or bush costume; **digger's weed** [?f. the epithet *Californian* in its common name *Californian stinkweed*], see quot. 1967.

1857 *Richmond-Atkinson Papers* (1960) I. 308 A man in a blue serge shirt and **digger's costume** accosted me [in Nelson]. **1941** BAKER *NZ Slang* 46 New Zealand terms, recorded during the closing twenty years of last century, [include]..**digger's delight**, a large felt hat worn by gold-diggers in New Zealand. **1867** BARKER *Station Life* (1870) 182 I must say, [the bushmen] were the most picturesque of the party, being..dressed in red flannel shirts and leathern knickerbockers and gaiters; they..wore '**diggers' hats**,' a head-dress of American origin—a sort of wide-awake made of plush, capable of being crushed into any shape, and very becoming. **1869** LUSH *Thames Jrnls.* 8 Sept. (1975) 67 I had taken up as I left home, a '**digger's lantern**'; this is usually made out of a brandy bottle with the bottom broken off and a candle stuck in the neck and which, held by the neck, makes a capital..lantern. **1952** HEINZ *Prospecting for Gold* 11 The other went off in the dark to search the creek bed, using a digger's lantern which was a glass bottle with the bottom removed and a candle stuck in the neck. **1894** O'REGAN *Voices Wave & Tree* 11 Men now..dress fine, and do the grand, For the age of **digger's shirts** has passed away. [*Ibid.* 15 The moleskin an' the Crimean shirt are growing scarce apace Like the sturdy men that wear them.] **1895** *Leaflets for Farmers* (NZ Dept. Agric.) No.22 1 Californian Stinkweed, **Digger's Weed** (*Navarettia* (*Gilia*) *squarrosa*). *Ibid.* 2 It is sometimes erroneously called 'Bathurst burr'. **1922** THOMSON *Naturalisation Animals & Plants* 443 *Gilia squarrosa*... Californian Stink-weed; Digger's Weed. **1967** HILGENDORF & CALDER *Weeds* 150 Stinkweed (*Navarettia squarrosa*), formerly named *Gilia squarrosa* and called Californian stink weed, digger's weed, and yeast plant, occurs chiefly in river beds on dry cultivated pastures and fields in Marlborough and Otago, where it sometimes becomes dominant over all other herbage. **1969** *Standard Common Names Weeds* 22 *digger's weed* [=] *Californian stinkweed.*

II. *Gumdigging.* [Prob. partly an extension of sense 1 to gum-digging; partly a shortened form of GUMDIGGER *n.*¹] **4.** GUMDIGGER *n.*¹ 1.

1867 LUSH *Waikato Jrnls.* 4 Feb. (1982) 105 There are..plenty of immense trunks lying all about..and near to these trunks especially the diggers found the gum. **1873** LUSH *Thames Jrnls.* 2 Dec. (1975) 143 It must have taken years and years to have brought the gum to the hardness in which the 'diggers' find it. **1882** HAY *Brighter Britain* II. 26 Sometimes a digger will not get a shillings worth of gum in a whole week's work. **1904** *NZ Illustr. Mag.* Mar. 429 One might have scraped gum..among less interesting surroundings than those of the diggers' camp. **1920** MANDER *Story NZ River* (1974) 228 In keeping with the usual custom, the diggers bought their gum to the boss's store for sale at the current rates. **1946** REED *Farthest North* 45 Half a century ago hundreds of diggers were camped hereabouts, and..took out of the ground some four hundred tons of gum annually. **1963** CAMPBELL *Golden North* 61 The children went into the gumfields and collected sugar bags full of the smaller nuts that the diggers considered too small to scrape and clean. **1970** THOMAS *Way Up North* 30 When the spear met with obstruction an experienced digger knew at once..whether he had located gum. **1992** SMITHYMAN *Auto/Biographies* 29 A few regulated water soaks..a whare..and traces of diggers.

5. As **digger's chips**, kauri-gum 'chips' with a high impurity content (see CHIP *n.*¹ 2).
1935 *NZJST* XVII. 374 The so-called **diggers' chips** varying from about 15 per cent to 30 per cent gum-content can be purified still further by primitive flotation processes.

III. *WW1, WW2.* **6.** [Transf. use of 1 and 2 above; *digger* 'gumdigger' was still in active use in NZ at the time of WW1: AND 1916. Cf. also 1918 *Kia-ora Coo-ee* (1981) 15 Dec. VI. 5 [Butler Gye, as an Australian, writes from France confirming a goldfields theory of origin expressed in a previous issue.] 'The term "Digger" is as old as the most ancient goldfield in Australia or Maoriland, and it has nothing whatever to do with digging-in [in trench warfare]... The Maorilanders applied the term to members of the A.I.F. soon after arrival in France implying that the Aussies were real dinkum mates.' The frequently invoked folk derivation from the supposed superior capacities of New Zealanders in trench-digging is difficult to validate (see quots. 1918¹, 1924, 1994).] Usu. init. cap. In WW1 and less frequently in WW2, a New Zealand soldier, usu. a private. See also *Anzac(ian)* (ANZAC A 3 a), DIG *n.* 2. **a.** In *WW1*.
1917 *Chron. NZEF* 5 Sept. 28 He ain't no digger; that's the colonel or the sergeant-major. **1917** *Digger* (41st Reinforcement at Sea, Troopship pub.) 2 The term 'digger' has lately come to be a term of common use among our New Zealand soldiers and those who meet with them in the training camps and at the Front. The New Zealander is the 'Digger' as the Australian is the 'Ossie'. **1918** let. 26 July in *Boots, Belts* (1992) 113 It is a well known fact that the N.Z. Division does more work behind the lines than any other crowd in France. The place is nothing but wire and trenches... We have done most of the work here... Why are we called diggers but for this. **1918** *Chron. NZEF* 30 Jan. 186 Tommies and overseas Kangaroos and Diggers enter into conversation with the peasants. **1918** *NZ at the Front* 32 Throughout these pages the term 'Digger' stands for a New Zealand soldier... More than a year ago it became general throughout the Division. **1919** *Quick March* Oct. 61 Some of the Mounted Rifles who have recently returned to Christchurch, are objecting to being called Diggers. **1921** *Ibid.* 10 June 27 'Digger' was first applied on active service to the members of a company of the Auckland Infantry Battalion of New Zealand. The company consisted largely of gum diggers from the Hauraki Gulf. They had a battle cry which went something like this : 'Who are, who are, who are we? We are diggers from Hauraki, Oamaru, Timaru, Waipukurau. Yah!' To distinguish this particular company from the others it was known as 'the Diggers'. **1924** AUSTIN *Official Hist. NZ Rifle Brigade* Appx vii 586 A temporary unit formed of drafts from the 3 Brigades, occasionally addressed one another as 'Digger' when cable-burying in March, 1917, in preparation for the Messines battle. In our Brigade it became fairly common when we were engaged on similar work for the French Army on the northern part of the line in the following July. **1935** [see FERNLEAF 2 a]. **1948** BALLANTYNE *Cunninghams* (1976) 143 He wondered if many other diggers would get [George VI] Coronation souvenirs. **1971** MCKEON *Fruitful Yrs.* 129 We had learned that 'Digger' was the general nickname applied to the Australians and the New Zealanders, and with some pride we assumed the title, conferred only on those who had served or were serving in the battle areas. **1984** BOYD *City of the Plains* 312 The way in which the executive committee of 'diggers' immediately opened its ranks to 'kiwis' and gradually made way for them ensured the RSA strong, continuing support. **1994** *NZ Defence Quarterly* Autumn 36 [Chris Pugsley, 'Putting the NZ back in Anzac'] 'Digger' first became a common term after the Battle of the Somme in September–October 1916. During this battle, the British forces praised the work of the New Zealand engineers and the..Pioneer battalion as the 'digging battalions' in pushing two communication trenches forward..after the attack on 15 September 1916.

b. In *WW2*, more usually applied to an Australian than to a New Zealand (private) soldier.
1941 *Sports Post* (Wellington) 25 Jan. 5 A present-war Digger..was one of the many patrons at Trentham on the opening day. **1972** *Islands I* 19 'There's ways of telling a soldier naked as sky' B. argues one day with a digger.

7. A term of address, a salutation. See also DIG *n.* 1. Cf. COBBER *n.* 2.
[*Note*] In WW1, orig. among soldiers; thence popular among civilians (esp. returned soldiers) as expressing comradeship; revived (often as *dig*) in WW2, thence for a short time again in 'rehab' civilian life, as a term of address or salutation.
1917 INGRAM *Anzac Diary* 7 Oct. (1987) 54 I ask him how he feels. 'Not so bad Digger,' he replies. **1920** BOLITHO *With the Prince in NZ* 61 Somebody shouted 'Hullo, Digger,' and the Prince caught the greeting and smiled back. **1936** TREADWELL *Recolls. Amateur Soldier* 198 A Canadian officer rushed towards me yelling... 'Digger,' he cried, 'come over here with me.' **1938** HYDE *Godwits Fly* (1970) 123 He was disappointed when the tramp called him 'Sir', instead of 'Digger' or 'Mate'. **1948** FINLAYSON *Tidal Creek* (1979) 22 The travelling men laugh too, but one of them says [to the boy], 'Put your bag under the seat, digger. This is our cabin.'

8. *WW1*. As **The Diggers**, a name given to a professional concert party performing immediately after WW1, and formed from an NZEF entertainment troupe 'the Pierrots'.
1944 HURST *Music and the Stage in New Zealand* 60 Another aspect of the influence of the Great War was evident in 1919, with the appearance of the Diggers. **1979** DOWNES *Top of the Bill* 58 The New Zealand Pierrots were at a loose end by this time [*sc.* 1919] and, more or less as a body, they became the principal members of the new group—the Diggers... For the next twelve years the name of Pat Hanna's Diggers became a byword throughout both countries [*sc.* Australia and New Zealand]. **1991** WOLFE *Kiwi* 34 Formed in 1917, this group eventually evolved into the Diggers and were led by Pat Hanna.

9. In *attrib.* use. *WW1.* **a.** [AND 1922.] Of or pertaining to the New Zealand military.
1917 in Miller *Camps, Tramps & Trenches* (1939) 192 A digger officer would have worded the message quite differently. **1918** *NZ at the Front* 69 There's many a good New Zealand lad... Who has learnt love's lesson while things looked bad, from girls with faces fair, Toasted their health while he vowed to fight, in the good old digger way. **1918** let. 29 Sept. in *Boots, Belts* (1992) 127 She [*sc.* a Scottish nurse] got a shock when Mac dropped his digger language and spoke in broad Scotch. **1933** FIELD *Money Spider* 29 A nickname of my 'digger' days.

b. Special Comb. **Diggerland** [by analogy with MAORILAND], New Zealand; **Digger Prince**, a returned soldiers' nickname for the Prince of Wales during his 1920 visit.
1918 *NZ at the Front* 77 [Title] **Diggerland**... Can you see the waving tussock grass that yellows in the sun [etc.]. **1920** BOLITHO *With the Prince in NZ* 34 Amid repeated cheering somebody shouted 'Three cheers for the **Digger Prince**', and this popular expression aroused the mass to still further shouting.

c. As **diggers' goodbye**, a rousing patriotic farewell.
1920 BOLITHO *With the Prince in NZ* 137 The only lady to drive the Prince during his New Zealand tour..drove the Royal car to the station after Trentham had farewelled the Prince with what they called a '**Diggers' Goodbye**'.

digger, *n.*² Prison. [Poss. an alteration of or influenced by *jigger* a prison cell (OED *n.*¹ 6 b); prob. an alteration of *dig-out*, orig. an excavation into which prisoners were put for punishment, hence punishment cell.] A punishment or solitary confinement cell in prison; the punishment block of a prison; the punishment cell or room in a Boys Welfare Home. See also DIG-OUT, DUMMY *n.*² Cf. POUND *n.*²
1941–45 p.c. members of the Riverside Community (Nelson). *Digger*, a prison punishment cell. **1971** SHADBOLT *Bullshit & Jellybeans* 10 Another feature of prison life..is 'the digger'. Solitary confinement. One visit a fortnight, one letter a week, very few blankets. **1982** *Dominion* (Wellington) 2 Sept. 5 A boy described Cell 7, in the secure block at Owairaka [Boys Welfare Home] in these terms. 'Number 7, that's the digger. There's no light or anything in there. There's two beds, they're single, one is on one side of the wall and there's another bed on the other side of the wall, the toilet's in the middle of the two beds. There's a sink joined to the toilet. **1984** BEATON *Outside In* 23 Ma: Ginny's been actin' crazy, lately. Ever since she got back from digger. *Ibid.* 109 Digger—punishment cell for solitary confinement. **1991** DUFF *One Night Out Stealing* 43 Insolence to an officer... Seven days in the Digger on number two diet.

digging, *vbl n. Hist.* Usu. in *pl.* [Spec. use of *digging(s)* a place where digging is done; as applied to goldfields, orig. US, thence Austral., thence NZ.]

1. *Pl.* [AND 1851.] **a.** Also **diggins, digins**. A place where gold is found, a goldfield. See also GOLD-DIGGING 1.
1851 M.F. Marshall let. in *William Swainson* 20 Dec. (1992) 162 Mrs. Petre had a cousin in the 'Clara', he..has finally gone to the diggings. **1853** ADAMS *Canterbury Settlement* 57 At length for the sum of 37l. I obtained an excellent little mare, 'the ppty of a gentleman going to the diggins'. **1862** CHUDLEIGH *Diary* 9 May (1950) 37 Met some mourays who told us of the new digins. **1869** [see DIGGER *n.*¹ 1]. **1881** NESFIELD *Chequered Career* 76 We travelled to..the Grey, and back to the Buller..all familiar diggings to any west-coast digger, and very rowdy diggings too. **1896** O'REGAN *Poems* 39 An' I trust on fairer diggins you have made a grander find. **1995** ANDERSON *House Guest* 197 They explored the diggings first... The

broken-down crushers, the remains of a sluice, an old race.

b. In the phr. **on the diggings**, within the precincts of a goldfield.
1871 Money *Knocking About NZ* 10 I slept for the first time 'on the diggings'; and..I confess I would have preferred a warm bed. **c1875?** Thatcher in *NZ Songster* No.5 49 He'd a mart on the diggings here, and in addition, He did a great deal selling things on commission.

c. A deposit of gold; a claim.
1857 *McLean Papers* (ATLTS) XIV. 272 Someone found a 'diggins' at the Hutt. 1878 Elwell *Boy Colonists* 184 The men were only diggers who had caught sight of the tent, and thought that Ernest and Harold had a good 'diggings' there in a quiet way.

2. *sing.* **a.** A hole, a claim.
1852 *NZGG* 9 Nov. V. 26(165) (Rep. Gold Discovery in Coromandel) Mr. C. Ring found it necessary to abandon the first digging, owing to the obstruction offered to his reaching bed rock by the presence of large Quartz Boulders.

b. *digging* 1 a above.
1874 Bathgate *Col. Experiences* 138 There are always a few of these unsocial miners [hatters] about every digging. 1930 Dobson *Reminiscences* 137 He had to hold a service at Antonio's Flat (a digging on the Grey Valley) next morning. 1933 Washbourn *Reminisc. Early Days* 5 The term billy..originated on the [Collingwood] digging and is still in general use.

c. The occupation of gold-digging.
1896 Biggar *Diary* in Begg *Port Preservation* (1973) 346 Our friends informed us they were Orepuki natives and had been following digging since boyhood.

3. In *attrib.* use **a.** Pertaining to digging, diggings, or diggers.
1856 Fitton *NZ* 344 The digging population is not now what it used to be. Diggers are now hard-fisted in more senses of the word than one. 1864 Harper *Lett. from NZ* 20 Dec. (1914) 79 I went amongst them every day, and we talked of their digging experiences. 1871 Money *Knocking About NZ* 121 [Prospective diggers] had only arrived to find the whole thing what is called in digging parlance a 'duffer'. 1896 Harper *Pioneer Work* 30 [The West Coast] has become, from a digging point of view, a field of far less importance. 1933 Washbourn *Reminisc. Early Days* 4 These [large specks floating in a dish] in digging terms are 'floaters.'

b. Special Comb. **digging town(ship)**, the dwellings and other buildings on a goldfield. Cf. *canvas town* (canvas 2).
1868 Dilke *Greater Britain* I. 335 A gang of diggers and sailors, dressed in the clothes which every one must wear in a digging town unless he wishes to be stared at by every passer-by. 1873 Wilson *Diary* 23 Jan. in Wierzbicka *Wilson Family* (1973) 146 At dinner we had the pleasure of the company..of a publican from Nokomai, a digging township on the road we were going. 1904 *NZ Illustr. Mag.* Dec. 163 Lyell is a picturesque little digging township.

diggins, digins: see digging *vbl. n.* 1 a.

dig-out. *Obs. Prison.* An excavation into which a prisoner was put for special punishment; a place for solitary confinement. Cf. digger *n.*²
1905 *Truth* 19 Aug. 3 Prisoners [in the Terrace Gaol, Wellington] frequently complain that if the chief gaoler gets a snout on them they go into the dig-out on the slightest provocation.

dike, *n.*¹ *Goldmining.* Also **dyke.** [f. Brit. mining use *dike* a fissure or fault in a stratum: see OED 9; EDD 13.] A vein or outcrop of quartz.
1853 Swainson *Auckland* 91 Quartz occurs in detached blocks of various sizes, mixed with fragments of slate, granite and trap; but regular dykes of quartz are not generally met with, although they are reported to exist. 1908 *NZGeol.SB (NS)* No.5 29 Near Carricktown..several dyke-like outcrops were found, locally known to the miners as 'dykes'. They are not dykes, but outcrops of hard, bluish-grey, flinty or horny quartz, often much slickensided on one wall.

dike, *n.*² Also **dyke.** [f. *dike* a ditch or watercourse, a water closet or urinal: OED 2 c, 1923.] Any privy (not necessarily a water-closet).
1944 *Short Guide to NZ* 38 A 'john' means a cop, not a toilet, and the latter is sometimes called (between men only) a 'dyke' or 'house of parliament'. 1960 Hilliard *Maori Girl* 74 But the dyke's in the bathroom. 1962 Baxter *Collected Poems* (1980) 250 The new guitar of sex I kept on twanging Inside the iron virgin Of the little smelly dyke. 1972 *Islands* I. 27 A corrupt man can sit on a dike and watch a tree beginning to blossom in the yard.

dikkon, var. dicken.

dill. Also **dilberry, dillbrain.** [A back-formation, often with elaboration, from dilly silly: AND 1941.]

1. As **dill**, a stupid, foolish, or naive person; a fool.
1941 *Dill* used at St Patrick's College, Silverstream for a 'fool' (Ed.). 1953 Sutton-Smith *Unorganized Games NZ Primary School Children* (VUWTS) II. 677 Some of the [slang] expressions listed by children..are:..you're bats, dronk, drongo, dill, dip, dippy..(South Wellington). 1960 Muir *Word for Word* 261 Yeah. The others are proper dills. Except Arthur's side-kick. 1978 Mantell *Murder in Fancydress* 85 I'd have looked a bit of a dill reporting something like that to the police. 1991 Eldred-Grigg *Shining City* 86 You're a dill... You're just a stupid dill.

2. As **dilberry, dillbrain** [elaborations of *dill*], a witless or stupid person; a 'lame-brain'.
1952 *Landfall* 23 221 Any man who thinks and reads beyond the immediate requirements of getting a good job is a fool—'wet', 'gormless', 'dilberry', etc. 1981 *Avondale College Slang Words* (Auckland) (Goldie Brown Collect.) dillbrain: idiot. 1987 *Sunday News* (Auckland) 19 July 37 The minute they [*sc.* Nats) get the Government on the ropes, the dill-brains start slogging themselves on the chops instead.

dilly, *a.* [f. Brit. dial.: *daft* + *silly*: EDD Somerset 1873; AND 1905.] Silly; cranky; cracked; foolish. See also dill.
1910 *Truth* 16 Apr. 1 His Worship: 'Was the accused sober?' Witness: 'Well, he looked muzzy.'.. His Worship: 'I don't understand you.' Witness: 'He seemed to have a rat in his garret.' His Worship: 'Oh, speak English!' Witness: 'Off his dot—balmy [*sic*]—dilly.' Sergeant: 'He says the man was mad, your Worship.' 1989 Heinemann *NZ Dict.* 313 dill (2) *noun (informal)* a stupid person. *Word Family:* dilly, *adjective,* stupid, silly.

dimu(dimu), varr. rimu.

ding. [f. *ding* a small dent in a surfboard: (cf. OED *ding* *n.*² 2 *Surfing,* 1962): thence extended to a dent in car bodywork (DARE 1988), and poss. more generally used in NZ than elsewhere; the 1879 verb use is prob. nonce.] A small dent, orig. in a surfboard, now usu. in a car bodywork.
1968 Warwick *Surfriding NZ* 72 When repairing a ding or damaged area on your board, don't rush. 1988 McGill *Dict. Kiwi Slang* 36 *ding* a dent, usually in a car, of a minor nature; also the minor accident itself. 1990 *Motoring Today* Apr. 11 Always call the MoT. I lay down the same rule for all my staff—even where it is only a small ding.

Also **ding** *v.*, to dent.
1879 *Auckland Weekly News* 13 Sept. 8 You may judge the reckless way the [tins of confectionery] have been handled when I tell you that some of the tins are actually dinged in the corner from the sudden jerking of the cases. 1994 *Listener* 11 June 7 God help me if, in a moment's inattention, I ding a Rolls.

dingbat. [Poss. f. *ding* + *bat*, perh. a play on *ding-dong* with *bats in the belfry*.]

1. Usu. *pl.* [AND 1920.] Fits of madness, delirium, esp. delirium tremens. **a.** In the phr. **to give** (one) **the dingbats**, to drive (one) crazy; also in a weakened sense.
1911 *Truth* 4 Nov. 6 Lord! how the writer remembers that dreadful disaster..which gives me dingbats every time I remember it! 1946 Sargeson *That Summer* 56 The youngster got spanked and the way she yelled gave me the dingbats. *Ibid.* 72 Being all on my pat up there..somehow gave me the dingbats properly.

b. In the phr. **to get** (or **have**) **the dingbats, to be in the dingbats**, to be silly or mad, esp. with delirium tremens.
1918 *Chron. NZEF* 27 Sept. 109 'Ave you got the dingbats. 1926 Devanny *Butcher Shop* (1981) 84 George, 'e 'ad the dingbats. 'Ad 'em bad. 1933 *Press* (Christchurch) (Acland Gloss.) 14 Oct. 15 *Dingbats.*—Slang, of Australian origin, for delirium tremens. The *d[ingbat]s*, I believe, are really the snakes, weasels, etc., which a sufferer sees. 1959 Slatter *Gun in My Hand* 42 Boozin' again! You'll end up with the dingbats, you will. **c1962** Baxter *Horse* (1985) 25 When I had the dingbats there was a bloody great Negro's face an inch away from me all the time. It must have been the bad grog. 1964 Morrieson *Came a Hot Friday* (1981) 210 You've gone crackers. You're in the dingbats, Jackson. 1963 Morrieson *Scarecrow* 73 He had been called out..to attend Uncle Athol whose mysterious ailment turned out to be ye olde fashioned dingbats.

c. In a transf. or concrete use **to rain dingbats**, suggestive of a mood of near madness.
1993 *NZ Skeptic* Mar. 17 By sundown I was on the brink of madness. It was as though the sky had opened up and rained dingbats.

Hence **dingbatitis**, drunkenness or excessive drinking.
1921 Lord *Ballads of Bung 'Stunology'* (1976) 10 'Dingbatitis', 'drinking', 'doped', 'dizzy', or on 'the drunk'.

2. *sing.* [Orig. US slang: AND a halfwit, 1918.] **a.** An eccentric or crazy person.
1976 Hilliard *Send Somebody Nice* 32 'Drongos,' Max hisses. 'Wart-heads. Dingbats. Halfwits.' 1988 McGill *Dict. Kiwi Slang* 36 *dingbat* odd or silly person. 1992 Park *Fence around the Cuckoo* 115 These Socialists... They say they'll take over the world. Dingbats.

b. *transf.* A difficult sheep.
1970 McLeod *Glorious Morning* 147 'I don't know what the hell I'm doing up here shearing these f——dingbats,' he would say. '... Look at these dingbats—wool all over their eyes;.. A man must be bloody mad to shear them?'

3. As a predicative *adj.*
1949 *Landfall II* 146 [Children yell] Your mother's dingbats.

dingle stick. [Poss. f. Brit. dial.: cf. EDD *dingle* v.² to dangle, hang loosely.] A stick fastened over an open fire from which a billy hangs.

1964 HELMER *Stag Party* 80 'This little hori's damned hungry,' Crump said, lifting the tea billy from the dingle stick. 'I could scoff a real binder, just quietly.'

dining room. In an older New Zealand house, often a name for the 'best' sitting room. Cf. FRONT ROOM.

1948 BALLANTYNE *Cunninghams* (1976) 159 He said he wouldn't mind [a cup of tea], so she went out to the kitchen... When she returned to the dining-room he was sitting on the chesterfield. **1974** BARTLETT *Emigrants* 102 On the mantelpiece in the dining room, among the ornaments and family photographs, stood an especially fine piece of kauri gum.

Dink, *n. WW1.* [Transf. use of an abbrev. of *dinkum*.]

1. a. A member of the 'Dinkums', the New Zealand Rifle Brigade; usu. as a collective *pl.*, the Rifle Brigade itself (see DINKUM B 3). See also TRENTS.

1916 *Let. from Egypt* 11 Mar. in Malthus *ANZAC* (1965) 156 I have seen a number of university men of the Rifle Brigade, generally known to us as the Dinks—a name they have cheerfully accepted and try to live up to... The newspapers urging enlistment in 1915 declared that the later men, joining the forces with motives of reasoned patriotism, would be more praiseworthy than the 'impetuous spirits' of the Main Body. Hence the sardonic nickname of 'the Dinks'—dinkum soldiers—attached to the new brigade. **1917** *Chron. NZEF* 14 Mar. 41 We were talking to the 'Dinks' that evening. **1918** let. 28 Oct. in *Boots, Belts* (1992) 137 A big Dink came strolling along and this joint [*sc.* a Tommy officer] hauled him up and asked him why he did not salute. **1921** STEWART *NZ Div.* vi Colloquially the Rifle Brigade Battalions were known as 'Dinks', a term applied to them on their arrival in Egypt, 1916, and alluding to the special patronage which they enjoyed of the Governor-General of the Dominion, and to their peculiarities of drill and dress. **1927** REES *Life's What You Make It* 177 The Dinks were the men of the Rifle Brigade. I believe Lord Liverpool told the original draft, before they left NZ, that they were fair dinkum soldiers—or words to that effect. Anyhow we were always known as the Dinks. **1936** HYDE *Passport to Hell* 204 The Dinks—the New Zealand Rifle Brigade—had been getting it in the neck. **1950** *Review* July 4 The big smoke concert will be held..on the Saturday night, and it is anticipated that more than one thousand Dinks will be there. **1968** SLATTER *Pagan Game* 153 He spent most of his time..with..his old cobbers who were in the Dinks in the first war. **1978** HENDERSON *Soldier Country* 123 A few days after Messines, D Company 4 Battalion, NZRB walked out of Plocgsteert Wood... A complete mystery. Can any old Dink throw any light on it? **1987** KNOX *After Z-Hour* 171 The Dinks were laying cable in the forward areas.

b. With modifiers indicating the shape or orientation of shoulder patches, hence forming names for various battalions of the Brigade: **Arse-up Dinks**, Fourth Battalion (an inverted triangle: also called the **Inverteds** see quot. 1917); **Diamond Dinks**, First Battalion; **Square Dinks**, Second Battalion; **Triangle Dinks**, Third Battalion. See also ARSE-UPS.

1917 *Chron. NZEF* 5 Sept. 28 Said Martin of the Dinks, Why, he was the greatest 'swi-up' king in the 'Inverteds'. **1939** MCKINLEY *Ways & By-Ways* 24 The sobriquet for the Third Brigade had many variants from the original 'Dinks', one of the battalions being known as the 'Square Dinks' and another as the 'Fair Dinks'. **1953** 2ZB Wellington (Lux Money-Go-Round radio programme) 12 Feb. In the Great War there were Square Dinks, the Triangle Dinks and I won't tell you what we called the other ones but their triangle was upside down—you know what soldiers mean. **1963** AITKEN *Gallipoli to the Somme* 46 Next came the New Zealand Rifle Brigade from Mersa Matruh, first the 2nd Battalion, nicknamed the 'Square Dinks' (a 'square dinkum bloke' being idiomatic Australian for a genuine fellow) from the distinctive black patch on the upper sleeve; later the 'Diamond Dinks', who wore a diamond patch. **1988** MCGILL *Dict. Kiwi Slang* 114 *Triangle Dinks* Third Battalion, NZ Rifle Brigade, WW1, from shoulder flash.

2. *attrib. WW1.* Pertaining to the Rifle Brigade, or a member of it.

1917 in Miller *Camps, Tramps & Trenches* (1939) 159 A Dink officer got one in the arm. **1918** INGRAM *Anzac Diary* 13 Sept. (1987) 112 At about 9.30 last night we started off in the pouring rain to relieve the Fourth Dink Battalion.

dink, *complement.* Usu. **dinks**. [Abbrev. of DINKUM *a.* and *adv.*: AND 1906.] Mainly with a defining word: **fair dink(s), true dink(s)**, to express or imply (with a querying tone) doubt, or to assert the truth of a statement.

1939 COMBS *Harrowed Toad* 47 He asked me would we get the threepence and buy some comics and I said, 'No don't, Burton.' 'True dink, I did,' Mr. Bojis. **1943** BENNETT *English in NZ* in *Amer. Speech* XVIII. 91 The Australian asseverations 'Dinkum', 'fair dinkum' (honest, 'straight') have produced in New Zealand the meaningless variant 'feather dinks'. **1989** EVANS *Making It* 51 'You're making it up.' 'Fair dinks,' he said.

dinkie, var. DINKY.

dinkum /ˈdɪŋkəm/, *a., n.* and *adverbial*. [f. Brit. dial. *fair dinkum* fair play!: see EDD *fair* 1 (6), *fair dinkum* (Lincolnshire, 1881), =(7) *fair dos* 'fair dealing'; also *dinkum* (a due share of) work (n. Lincolnshire, Derbyshire, 1891).]

A. *adj.*

1. 'Honest-to-god'; genuine; true; first-rate. **a.** With a prefixed intensifier: **square** (prob. *obs.*), occas. (see quot. 1915) **real**, and (usu.) **fair** [perh. associated with the rhyming phr. *fair and square*: AND 1890].

1895 GRACE *Maoriland Stories* 105 Well it ain't goin' to be *honest injun*, that's plain; not what I call *square dinkum*. **1915** *Rangitikei Advocate & Manawatu Argus* 17 June 4 I will give you a brief description of the little I saw of the real dinkum part of soldiering. **1917** THORNTON *With Anzacs in Cairo* 43 Another restaurant [in Cairo] had for its sign these cryptic words: 'Square dinkum feed'. **1924** AUSTIN *Official Hist. NZ Rifle Brigade* 586 It must have been a 'fair dinkum' fight! **1935** STRONG in Partridge *Slang Today* 287 Anyhow, to give you the fair dinkum guts I put across a beauty when I found the double-headed penny in the ring, and that's how I won 200 francs. **1945** SARGESON in *Listener Short Stories* (1977) 20 But everybody always said the butcher was exaggerating... The butcher would say no, it was the fair dinkum truth. **1959** SLATTER *Gun in My Hand* 45 I didn't know you read poetry, Willie. Well I'll go he. Is that fair dinkum? **1962** HORI *Half-gallon Jar* 59 Well, this wahine Tui was a fair dinkum pulse-quickener. **1976** MORRIESON *Pallet on the Floor* (1983) 87 'Is this fair dinkum?' said Breen, completely amazed. 'Fair dinkum.' **1985** O'SULLIVAN *Shuriken* 78 You can always tell when they're fair dinkum. They don't line up..for nothing.

b. Without an intensifier (but cf. quot. 1909). See also OIL *a*.

1905 *Truth* 10 Oct. 3 Why, our Sergeant said he would walk from [Palmerston North] to Ashhurst..to see a 'dinkum go' [*sc.* boxing match] through a crack. **1909** *Truth* 21 Aug. 4 Mahony invited witness out on to the 'Kings Highway' to settle the disputed point... Witness accepted cheerfully, and he and Mahony had a good, fair 'dinkum go'. **1910** [see STRAIGHT *a.²* a]. **1917** INGRAM *Anzac Diary* 10 July (1987) 35 However I shall not feel like a dinkum soldier until I get my regimental badge and battalion patch. **1927** REES *Life's What You Make It* 177 'What does dinkum mean?' 'You've been in New Zealand for months and months and you don't know what dinkum means?' 'It's good, excellent, superlatively fine, genuine, not faked. That's what dinkum is.' **1938** HYDE *Nor Yrs. Condemn* 177 Some of them hadn't seen it before, and they cried, dinkum tears. **1944** GASKELL *All Part of the Game* (1978) 26 'No, fair go Bomb. This is dinkum.' **1963** CASEY *As Short a Spring* 211 Even if he is dinkum about this, I don't want him to go mucking up the show in his usual style. **1986** *Woman's Weekly* 30 June 18 When Stand In The Rain appeared in 1965 the dust jacket hailed it as the women's side to the New Zealand legend of the hard case dinkum-type Kiwi. **1991** *North & South* (Auckland) May 96 Sprinkled among the beautiful backpackers are some dinkum Mark I Zephyr youths and the odd fresh-air superannuitant.

2. In collocations: **dinkum Anzac**, **dinkum kiwi** [poss. a local var. of *dinkum Aussie* (AND 1920)], **dinkum New Zealander**, a name applied (occas. ironically) to people and things perceived to be quintessentially of New Zealand, 'honest', 'egalitarian' and 'open-hearted' to the point of stupidity.

1961 *Review* Aug. 2 [Heading] Gold Badge for 'Dinkum' Anzac. **1966** *NZ Short Stories* (1976) 100 'She's a **dinkum Kiwi**, our Joan,' smiled Bernard, waving his pipe. *Ibid.* 102 'Not a dinkum Kiwi attitude,' Don joked. **1971** SHADBOLT *Bullshit & Jellybeans* 115 For Normal Norm [Kirk] and Kiwi Keith [Holyoake] the battle was to determine who was the most average, fair-dinkum Kiwi. **1988** MCGILL *Dict. Kiwi Slang* 36 *dinkum* genuine or fair, often expressed as *fair dinkum*, *dinky-di* and *dinkum oil* (the truth), and as *dinkum Kiwi*. **1916** Dinkum New Zealander [see DINKUM B 3]. **1964** *Review* Dec. 2 Contact is being sought with those 'fair dinkum New Zealanders' who befriended Mr. Sid Jones of Kent, England, on their return to New Zealand in the RMS Rimutaka after World War I.

B. *n.* [AND work, exertion, 1888.]

1. *Obs.* Occas. as **Dinkums** (or **Dinks**) occas. used as a boy's nickname and as an adaptation of *Denis*.

1905 THOMSON *Bush Boys* 10 Whoever heard of one boy calling another by his proper name? So to each other it was Dinkums [for Denis] and Mac. Sometimes even Dinkums proved too long and was shortened to 'Dinks'. **1905** [see 2 following].

2. Ready money; hard cash.

[*Note*] Alistair Campbell p.c. 1951 notes that *dink* 'cash money' was current in Dunedin in 1932.

1905 *NZ Times* 21 Oct. [From a review of Thomson's *Bush Boys*.] 'Dinkum' is familiar to every Colonial boy. It is harmless slang for 'money', loose cash, silver, and has in it something not inappropriate. It has also a secondary meaning, denoting true value. 'Dinkums', as a nickname, might originate with a fond mother and apply to an infant in its early years, but to an ablebodied bush-boy, never... 'Dinkums' and 'Mac' are not representative New Zealand boys.

DINKUM OIL

3. *WW1 Hist.* As **The Dinkums**, perh. earlier, **the Square Dinkums** (see quots., Pilling 1916, 1924). Also occas. (perh. facetiously) **Dinkumites** (see quot. 1917). [Prob. from such collocations as *dinkum New Zealanders*, *dinkum soldiers* applied ironically (by Main Body men) to battalions of the distinctive Rifle Brigade, the name becoming obsolescent when the New Zealand Division was formed: AND 1916, applied to the Austral. Second Division.] (Battalions of) the New Zealand Rifle Brigade. See also DINK *n.* 1 a.

1916 in Pilling *Anzac Memory* (1933) 76 The Square Dinkums, or in other words, the Second Battalion of the Rifle Brigade, had just returned from the lines of communication on the Western Front... Out on the Peninsula we heard from the later reinforcements various accounts of two new battalions that were being formed in New Zealand under the name of 'Lord Liverpool's Own'. Among the older hands at Anzac it was felt that New Zealand people felt the Main Body was chiefly composed of men who had rushed away to the war, merely under the strain of excitement, not impelled by any true spirit of patriotism; but these new battalions had realised what they were doing, had counted the cost and should, therefore, prove the better soldiers. Amongst us, therefore, they sarcastically became known as the 'Dinkum New Zealanders'. However, we find them not unlike ourselves and our old friends are none the worse for their new name. **1916** TWIDLE *Diary* (MS) 5 June I. 48 Went up in the trenches again tonight, but this time not on our own, but up with the Dinkums and Second Brigade. **1916** [see TOURIST 1 b]. **1917** *Chron. NZEF* 14 Mar. 41 Up to muddy Trentham came the Dinkumites one day. **1918** *Chron. NZEF* 13 Sept. 82 Ehoa! 'member the days when the Dinks were christened 'Dinkums' as a term of derision? And today the name 'Dinks' stands for a record as proud as any in the good old Division. **1918** *Shell-Shocks* 56 [Caption] A 'Square Dinkum'. **1924** AUSTIN *Official Hist. NZ Rifle Brigade* 586 The application of the term [(*fair*) *dinkum*] to the NZ Rifle Brigade as a nickname dates from the early days of 1916. On its return from Dabaa, the Second Battalion joined the veterans from the Dardanelles... The Riflemen..relaxed nothing of their old smartness on parade, more particularly at guard-mounting, and were more punctilious than usual in their soldierly conduct when off duty. The old ill-feeling, almost akin to animosity, was still in the air, and the general bearing of the Riflemen evoked considerable comment, mainly of a derisive nature. No distinguishing colour patch had yet been adopted outside the Rifle Brigade, except by the Samoan Relief Force, and the square 'blaze' on the puggance of the men of the Second Battalion was thus all the more conspicuous. With the idea of conveying the impression that the Riflemen were inordinately proud of themselves, the term '*The Square Dinkums*' was, in derision, applied to the Second Battalion, and afterwards, when the other units arrived, to the whole Brigade. This is the generally accepted opinion as to the origin of the nickname... Shortened to '*The Dinkums*', and again to '*the Dinks*', it was an appellation fully recognized within and without the Brigade, becoming eventually almost official. **1936** LAMBERT *Pioneering Reminisc. Old Wairoa* 28 It is worthy of note here..a 'Digger', one of the 'dinkums', who saw service in the Great War.

4. *Obs.* [Cf. DAE *dinky* sweetheart, 1908.] As **little dinkum**, a 'true' sweetheart; a 'steady' girlfriend; a loving wife.

1917 *Tiki Talk* (Troopship pub.) 35 Ter dream an' think yer back at 'ome with yer little dinkum. *Ibid.* 36 When we're comin' home..with all the little dinkums waitin'.

5. [Ellipt. for *dinkum oil* (OIL *n.* a): AND 1916.] The truth.

1973 WILSON *NZ Jack* 75 He liked to fray the edges between truth and fantasy, or between dinkum and lies.

C. *adv.* or *quasi-adv.* [AND 1915.]

1. [AND 1890.] With a defining word (most freq. **fair**) forming emphatic adverbials or asseverations, 'most certainly'. **a. sure dinkum**, most certainly, 'sure thing'.

1917 *Chron. NZEF* 22 Aug. 16 'You'll see me again soon, "sure dinkum!"' 'Yes! You *are* a New Zealander.'

b. straight dinkum [AND 1905], truly.

1919 MANSFIELD *Letters* 5 Dec. (1993) III. 143 I shall send (cross my heart straight Dinkum) Kuprin..on Sunday. **1922** MANSFIELD *Stories* (1984) 449 Promise not to tell... Say, cross my heart straight dinkum.

c. fair dinkum [AND 1890] (occas. **fair-dinkumly**) (a) really.

1917 *Chron. NZEF* 5 Sept. 35 Fair Dinkum now. **1924** AUSTIN *Official Hist. NZ Rifle Brigade* 586 [Among soldiers] Like many other slang expressions, the term 'fair dinkum' is not easy of definition... It would seem to convey the idea that any statement with which it may be used is to be looked upon as absolutely reliable and true. **1929** MILTON *Love & Chiffon* 137 Fair dinkum, I'll tell the world he's some steed. **1938** HYDE *Nor Yrs. Condemn* 31 Worth dyin' for. Fair dinkum, it is. **1946** SIMPSON *If You'd Care to Know* 97 This 'fair dinkum' really has a widespread application. Should you go to the horse races and win a big dividend, you are fair dinkum lucky, and when you wake up and find you have been dreaming, you are fair dinkum annoyed. **1949** SARGESON *I Saw in My Dream* (1974) 67 All right mate, I'll tell you the trouble fair dinkum, only it's just between you and me. **1959** MIDDLETON *The Stone* 33 'But fair dinkum!' he used to say, 'if anyone liked to look at it..there's not another traveller..who provides the service I do.' **1963** MORRIESON *Scarecrow* 67 'Sounds like a lotta bull to me.' 'No, fair dinkum. They all said yuh were.' **1985** 2YA Wellington 7 Aug. 8.55 p.m. Noel Scott MP (for Tongariro) speaking in Parliament on the Adoption Bill. 'Let us treat the matter completely fair-dinkumly.'

(b) Often with a rising intonation, an interrogative expressing surprise, and often implying (slight) disbelief: 'You don't mean to tell me?'; 'I wouldn't have believed it'. See also *fair go*, *fair do* (FAIR 1, 2).

1976 WILSON *Pacific Star* 17 'The Americans are coming. A whole division of troops, so they tell me.' 'Fair dinkum?' **1981** *Avondale College Slang Words* (Auckland) (Goldie Brown Collect.) *fair dinkum*: real, true; go on! you reckon!

d. *Now rare.* **square dinkum**. [AND 1894.]

1929 *Spike* 52 Square dinkum, I thought the Association had got me.

2. In adverbial use, for emphasis, or to assert truth in the face of doubt; absolutely, 'without a word of a lie'. **a.** [AND 1919.] Really; 'honour bright'; 'fair go'.

1908 *Truth* 18 Apr. 2 I kin understand 'ow pubs feel when they loose [*sic*] their license, dinkum I can. **1924** *Otago Witness* (Dunedin) 19 Aug. 73 I haven't been doing anything—dinkum I haven't. **1937** MARSH *Vintage Murder* 73 She'd write to her old man and complain..give you a pain in the neck, dinkum, she would. **1945** HENDERSON *Gunner Inglorious* 157 But dinkum, I mean it. And when you get back, we'll..go on a dirty great bash together, won't we, Eddie?

b. [AND 1915.] Occas. as an adverbial intensifier: 'really', 'truly'; 'bloody well'.

1934 HYDE *Journalese* 19 I never thought of asking him whether he gave away Free Lances, really dinkum free..when a patriotic object was in view. **1943** *NZEF Times* 5 July 6 I've dinkum swallowed it this time.

dinkum oil: see OIL a.

dinky, *a.* [f. Brit. and N. Amer. dial.: see OED.] Something commendably small and neat or trim.

1918 *Shell-Shocks* 57 An' this dinky bit o' skirt Smiles jes' at me an' no one else. **1938** HYDE *Nor Yrs. Condemn* 281 Look at that dinky red hat. **1941** BAKER *NZ Slang* 51 In constant use by our youngsters..dinky. **1946** COOZE *My Little State Home* 25 The icecream man had a dinky little cart.

dinky di /ˈdɪŋki ˈdaɪ/, *n.* [f. *di*(amond, with a play on DINKY-DI *adv.*] The diamond in Crown and Anchor.

c1945 *Sixes & Sevens* (Troopship pub.) 16 Six hearts—no bid. Who'll back the Dinky Di, come on, all you lucky players... Well, up they come, and it's Charlie pays Jim and the old man gets Miss Adams [*sc.* sweet Fanny Adams or nothing]. **1964** MORRIESON *Came a Hot Friday* (1981) 115 'Any more for the dinky-di?' called Kohi.

dinky-di /ˈdɪŋki ˈdaɪ/, *adv.* Also **dinky-die** and elaborated to **dinky die do** (/ˈdaɪdʌu/). [AND *adj.*, 1918; *adv.*, 1915.] Truly, certainly. (Also occas. as an *adj.* 'excellent of its class'.)

1938 LAWLOR *House of Templemore* 194 'Dinky die?' asked Percy Andrews. **1941** BAKER *NZ Slang* 51 In constant use by our youngsters..dinkydie. **1976** WILSON *Pacific Star* 96 'Pretty dicey trip,' he said when I'd finished. 'Dinky die do,' Ted said, and laughed. **1987** NORGROVE *Shoestring Sailors* 48 'This is straight up, Blue?' 'Absolutely dinky-die!' **1987** GEE *Prowlers* 179 She dredged up language no one had heard in years. Dinky-di. Corker. Biff him on the nose. **1995** *Dominion* (Wellington) 26 Jan. 2 C'mon. Deenkie-die folks. I love my Aussie cuzzies—and not just because they make rip-snorter wines.

dinner.

a. [AND 1911.] The midday meal whether the main meal of the day (as often in rural New Zealand) or not (as is usual in towns).

1883 *Brett's Colonists' Guide* 589 *Dinner.*—Dinner at one p.m. Wholesome fresh meat and vegetables..plainly cooked, served hot, and properly masticated... *Tea.*—Tea may be taken at six or half-past, and include one or two small cups of black tea... If it be the last meal of the day..the meal may include some light meat, chicken, or white fish. **1890** *Otago Witness* (Dunedin) 4 Sept. 36 After dinner, another lounge and gossip, afternoon tea, another drive to the baths, bathing, home again, tea time. After tea, walking or riding. **a1927** ANTHONY *Gus Tomlins* (1977) 143 Before milking, they made a hearty meal of cups of tea and bread and butter and cake. After milking, they made a hearty meal of breakfast, porridge with cream, then ham and eggs. About half past ten in the forenoon, a jug of hot tea and a basket of scones was always taken out into the paddock..as a refresher, and at mid-day they had a three-course dinner. Then at four in the afternoon, afternoon tea was served before the evening milking, and at six the family sat down to tea. Then supper at nine o'clock, and they were ready for bed. **1964** HARVEY *Any Old Dollars Mister?* 120 Nuts came down soon after [half-past nine]... When Nuts got his breath back he said, 'I'm allowed out until dinner-time.'

b. As elsewhere and esp. in urban use, a main meal taken at evening. Cf. TEA.

DINNYHAYSER

1962 Curnow *Four Plays* (1972) 97 I must go and get the tea—? The *dinner* ready. **1979** Simons *Harper's Mother* 97 'Tea won't be long.' She always calls it tea. My mother said that a meal of meat and vegetables was called dinner but that on no account was I to correct Mrs Turbett. I never know whether to thank her for the 'tea' or for the 'dinner'. **1987** *Chosen Place* 22 My girlfriend almost *did* get presented with 'a plate' (empty), when she asked me to meet some folks at her place for dinner—whoops, sorry tea.

dinnyhayser /ˌdɪniˈhæɪzə/. Also **dinny hazer**. [Origin unknown: Partridge derives the word from the name of a famous boxer, *Dinny Hays*.]
1. [AND 1907.] A king hit.
  1910 *Truth* 21 May 2 He turned round, and seeing who it was, shot out an iron-clad mauler that caught the obliging young fellow a 'dinny hazer' on the point.
2. [AND 1949.] Anything superior, excellent (of its kind).
  1941 Baker *NZ Slang* 51 In constant use by our youngsters..dinnyhazer. **1988** McGill *Dict. Kiwi Slang* 37 *dinnyhayser* anything first-rate; eg 'So that's your new yacht. She's a dinnyhayser, boy.'

Dio /ˈdaɪʌʊ/. *Auckland local. Ellipt.* for the Diocesan Girls' High School, an 'exclusive' Auckland girls' secondary school.
  [**1919** *Great Adventure* 22 Jan. (1988) 250 A 'Queenie' who is talking to a Y.M.C.A. girl and making me sick so I must close. A queenie wears its hair brushed straight and kept in position with Anzora Cream. It talks with a vile affected accent like the Diocesan girls and crawls round the women for buckshee trips.] **1987** *Metro Fiction* 28 Kids who would do anything for a buzz, bored malcontents straight from the hot-house of Dio and Kings with skin like cream and hard eyes.

dip, *n.* [Used elsewhere but of significance for NZ farming: see OED, the bath 1871, the liquid 1877.] A sheep-dipping bath.
  [*Note*] *dip* the disinfectant liquid is recorded in NZ from much later; *dip v.* and *dipping vbl. n.* from 1864 and 1856: OED 1840.]
  1865 Barker *Station Life* (1870) 35 Our last visit was to the Dip... These poor [scabby sheep] are dragged down a plank into a great pit filled with hot water, tobacco, and sulphur, and soused over head and ears two or three times. **c1875** Meredith *Adventuring in Maoriland* (1935) 88 The dip consists of a wooden launder, about twenty feet long by about six deep, and three wide at the top, tapering to almost one foot wide at the bottom. **1900** Blacke *Flights from Land* 16 The 'dip' beyond, where the sheep were washed. **1933** *Press* (Christchurch) (Acland Gloss.) 2 Dec. 15 Y[ards] for dipping [sheep]..are generally called *dip y[ard]s*. **1940** *NZJAg.* Feb. LX. 101 The early pasturalists were faced with the necessity of treating their ever-increasing flocks in an expeditious manner—and so were evolved the swim dips and draining pass. **1972** *Ibid.* Oct. CXXV. 25 [It] should give protection against maggot fly for two to three months when used in plunge or shower dips. **1983** Henderson *Down from Marble Mountain* 36 The wonder of the dip itself, a filthy skinny concrete corridor of woe where terrified sheep were heaved into foul waters.

dip, *v.*
1. *Forestry. Obs.* scarf *v.* 2.
  1877 *NZ Country Jrnl.* I. 244 On the side the tree will most easily fall [the experienced bushman] dips it—that is, he cuts in a deep notch from the circumference towards the centre.

2. In the phr. **to dip south,** see south *n.* 2.
3. In the phr. **to dip the billy,** to fill the billy.
  1934 *Press* (Christchurch) (Acland Gloss.) 20 Jan. 15 *Dip the billy.*—Fill the billy—dip it in the creek.

dipchick: see petrel 2 (7).

dip out. [AND 1965.] Also as **to dip out (on),** to miss out (on); to be unsuccessful; to fail.
  1968 Slatter *Pagan Game* 163 Never dipped out, that boy. In for his chop, Old Tank. **1985** Gordon & Deverson *NZ Eng.* 48 *dip out* (to be unsuccessful, miss out) **1988** McGill *Dict. Kiwi Slang* 37 *dip out* fail; eg 'You'll need a good line with her, Clem. Better men than you have dipped out there.'

dipper. *Obs.* [prob. f. Brit. provincial use (see EDD Supp. *dipper* a mug); poss. from, or influenced by, Brit. and US regional *dipper* a long-handled ladle.] A large vessel of up to a gallon capacity, usu. tin-plated and shaped like a large mug with a handle fixed vertically to the side, used mainly for ladling liquid.
  1873 Pyke *Wild Will Enderby* (1889, 1974) III. vii 95 He vigorously rocked [his cradle] with the left hand, whilst with the right he ladled water from the river... He cast aside the 'dipper', and hastened towards the reefs. **c1930** *Whitcombe's Etym. Dict. Aust.-NZ Suppl.* 4 *dipper* n. a can of tin or iron, about one gallon capacity with a fixed handle on one side, used for scooping water out of a water-butt, barrel, etc. **c1940** *dipper* as defined in quot. c1930 was the only Marlborough use known to the Editor in the 1930s and 1940s.

dippy *a. Shearers.* Of sheep, having wool impregnated with organophosphatic sheep-dip sufficient to affect shearers.
  1995 *Sunday Star-Times* (Auckland) 4 June. A10 The dip made from organophosphates..can damage the nervous systems of people and animals. Occupational Safety and health spokesman Mel Tyson said he had been contacted by..shearers who have suffered blurred vision, dizziness and nausea after handling sheep that had been recently dipped. The risky animals were known in the trade as 'dippy sheep'.

directly /dəˈrek(t)li/, *adv.* In modern New Zealand use the sense 'shortly, soon, by-and-by' (see OED 6 c *dial.* and *U.S.*) is preferred to the sense 'immediately' (OED 6 a). (*Presently adv.* is used in a similar way.)
  1842 Wade *Journey in Nthn Is.* 66 'Taihoa'. This word has been translated, By and by; but in truth, it has all the latitude of directly,—presently,—by and by,— a long time hence,—and nobody knows when. **1883** Domett *Ranolf & Amohia* II. 259 ''Twas nothing—he was not to mind her—she Was foolish—was '*porangi*'—and would be Better directly.

dirt. *Goldmining.* [AND *Obs.* 1852.] The alluvial deposit in which gold is found; occas. (in quartz-mining) ore. Also *attrib.* See also *washdirt* (wash *n.*² 2).
  1861 Haast *Rep. Topogr. Explor. Nelson* 18 I gave orders again to wash for gold, and every dishful of dirt yielded some specks. **1887** Pyke *Hist. Early Gold Discoveries Otago* (1962) 79 The miners..strained every effort to obtain the auriferous 'dirt', and stacking it on their claims, leaving the washing up and 'cradling' to be done when the getting more dirt was impossible. **1909** Thompson *Ballads About Business* in *Centennial Treasury Otago Verse* (1949) 59 In the seeming open sewer that extends beyond the claim... And the stones are ever coming, While the dirt-pipes keep a-drumming.

DISC

1935 Blyth *Gold Mining Year Book* 11 *Dirt*: Paydirt or gravel wash containing metal. **1967** [see *washdirt* (wash *n.*² 2)]. **1970** Wood *Gold Trails Otago* 7 On the claim the gold-bearing dirt, usually stream gravel, was shovelled into a dirt-bucket, which was then levered to the surface by a manuka pole and weight arrangement. **1978** McAra *Gold Mining Waihi* 318 *Dirt*: The common mining term for ore.

dirty point: see show *v.* 1.

disaster. *WW1.* Also familiarly **dizzy.** [A rhyming alteration of *piastre.*] A piastre.
  1918 *Kia-ora Coo-ee* (1981) 15 Nov. V. 14 The buns are sold at the rate of three for two dizzies, and they are really worth the money. **1937** Partridge *Dict. Slang* 223 *disaster.* A piastre: Australian and New Zealand soldiers' (Eastern front): 1915–18. By rhyme and pun—the coin being of low value. **1938** *Press* (Christchurch) (McNab Slang) 2 Apr. 18 [Slang of the N.Z.E.F.] From Egyptian [came] 'buckshee' and 'disaster' for piastre. **1945** *NZEF Times* 16 Apr. 5 When soldiers found they would have to refer to their money as piastres, it did not take them long to substitute 'disaster'... It may have been a concert party gag at first..to talk of owing a friend five 'accidents,' and the abbreviation to 'aker' or 'akker'..followed as a matter of course.

disc, *n.* [Spec. use of *disc* a round flat metal or plastic plate.]
1. *Farming.* Also **disk.** [Ellipt. for *disc cultivator, disc harrow.*] Usu. *pl.*, esp. as **a set of discs,** disc-harrow.
  1938 *NZJAg.* July LVII. 52 The soil should be stirred occasionally during the summer with disks and harrows until late February or early March. **1940** *Ibid.* Dec. LXI. 415 Where rolling has been left rather late, a cut with the disks will be helpful in preparing the land for subsequent rolling. **1961** Crump *Hang on a Minute Mate* (1970) 'Never heard of anyone ever using six horses in the discs,' he cried. **1988** Hill *More from Moaville* 63 A set of discs is a real bonus when it comes to dealing with the paspalum.

2. A metal or plastic marking or identification disc. **a.** *Watersiders.* The personal marker in the form of a disk uplifted to show that one is on the job.
  1964 Davis *Watersiders* 55 And then the eight o'clock siren sounded. 'Sorry, I've got to go. Haven't lifted my disc yet.'

b. A bright-coloured metal disc, often makeshift, used to mark back-country tramping tracks.
  1971 *Listener* 19 Apr. 56 At the first bluff he sidled up the spur but he got off the discs and had to bash through the lawyers and windfalls.

  Hence **disced** *ppl. a.,* of a track, marked with discs.
  1946 *Tararua Tramper* Nov. 10 From here down through the bush was straightforward going, especially when the disced portion of the track was reached some half an hour down from the top. **1988** Pickering *Hills* 24 Old tin can tops, often painted, became a cheap way of marking a track, and some of the older maps and guidebooks still refer to a track as being 'disced'.

disc, *v. Farming.* Also **disk.** [Cf. OED *v.* 'Chiefly *U.S.*' (1884) 'and *N.Z.*'] *trans.* and *intr.* To cultivate with a disc harrow.
  1928 *NZ Free Lance* (Wellington) 28 May 45 I have ploughed 1,250 acres, hustled 1,000 and disced, drilled, harrowed, etc., a fair amount. **1938** *NZJAg.* Sept. LVII. 234 Should the land have been ploughed and worked down or disked and harrowed..all

cultivation possible should be given while the fern is growing. **1950** *Ibid.* Mar. LXXX. 314 Stalks should be ploughed or disced in..after the tobacco harvest. **1961** CRUMP *Hang On a Minute Mate* 38 I'd been discing a few hundred acres of fern for a bloke in Taranaki with a six-horse team. **1984** HENDERSON *Tales of the Coast* 129 I was out one day on the tractor disking a paddock and I was singing away to myself and disking and along came this big flash car.

Hence **discable** /'dɪskəbəl/ *a.*, of land, flat enough to enable the use of disc cultivation; **discing** or **disking** *vbl. n.*, disc cultivation or harrowing.

1951 LEVY *Grasslands NZ* (1970) 7 [Caption] Northland. Broad, open valleys, for the most part ploughable or **discable** are characteristic. **1958** *NZ Farmer* 11 Dec. 4 One who had taken a block of 560 acres of hill land..with only 60 acres discable. **1952** HOLCROFT *Dance of Seasons* 75 After the ploughing came the discing, a confused and bumpy distribution of clods which marred the beauty of the furrows.

disc-harrow. Also **disk.** [See OED *disc* 8, 1884.] A farm harrow or cultivator comprising rows of sharp-edged concave discs set obliquely on axles.

1883 *Brett's Colonists' Guide* 20 A *stolen* crop of white turnips can be sown on light land by the free use of the scarifier or the disc harrow on the stubbles. **1891** WALLACE *Rural Economy* 270 The Disc-Harrow..with its saucer-shaped discs strung on two axle-shafts. **1938** *NZJAg.* July LVII. 52 In the early spring disk harrows should be used..and further disking to break up the soil before summer dryness makes the work difficult.

Hence **disc-harrow** *v. trans.*, to cultivate (land) with a disc-harrow.

1883 *Brett's Colonists' Guide* 78 It should be ploughed, disc-harrowed, and worked as fine as possible. **1917** *Truth* 20 Oct. 6 He was disc-harrowing in a paddock on the Saturday. **1922** *Auckland Weekly News* 26 Jan. 39 [Caption] Disc-harrowing with a bullock team.

dish, *n.*[1] Goldmining. [AND 1852.] A special pan or like receptacle in which alluvial material is washed to separate out the gold; the total amount of alluvial material contained in a dish. See also PAN *n.*[1], *prospecting dish* (PROSPECT *v.* 2), *tin dish* (TIN *n.*[1] 1).

1861 *NZ Goldfields 1861* (1976) 16 This morning a man..showed me a prospect which he had obtained from several dishes of washing-stuff. **1906** in Evans *Waikaka Saga* (1962) 39 Dredging through false bottom of green sandy pug..about 8 colours to the dish. **1931** *NZJST* XII. 159 The first miners used only the pick, the shovel, the dish, and the cradle. **1968** SEDDON *The Seddons* 44 Could I peg out a claim of my own and in a dish swill dirt to find if there were any specks of gold in the pan?

Hence **dishful** *n.* [AND 1852], the amount of alluvial material held by a dish; **dishing** *vbl. n.*, separating out gold by washing (dirt) in a dish.

1861 [see DIRT]. **1864** *Press* (Christchurch) 6 May in Turner *Eng. Lang. Austral. & NZ* (1966) 17 He scooped out a dishful, washed it, and in five minutes took close on half an ounce of gold. **1959** MILLAR *Westland's Golden 'Sixties* 51 The shingle and sand..[were] moved to the bank for **dishing** and cradling.

dish, *n.*[2] *Forestry.* SHOE. See also *snigging-shoe* (SNIGGING 2).

1952–3 *NZ Forest Service Gloss.* (TS) Dish. 1. A snigging-pan or shoe.

disk, var. DISC.

district.

1. An officially demarcated region or a unit of local administration, esp. one marked off for administrative or other purposes, such as an *electoral district*, *postal district*, or that served by a district high school; any one of the 58 territorial units of local government outside major urban areas, such as *Marlborough District*.

1858 *Native Districts Regulation Act 21 & 22 Vict.* s1 It shall be lawful for the Governor in Council from time to time to appoint districts for the purposes of this Act, being districts over which the Native title shall not for the time being have been extinguished, and any such appointment to vary or revoke. **1862** LINDSAY *Nat. Hist. in Coloniz.* 11 I do not refer to any of the 'districts' of your excellent Survey Office, but to the natural district formed by the range of the Green Island hills.

2. As. **district high school** *hist.*, orig. a rural primary school incorporating one or more senior classes studying 'secondary' subjects; thence often a name for a local secondary school.

[*Note*] In New Zealand *high school* 'secondary school' (recorded from 1856) is interchangeable with *college* and occas. with *grammar* (*school*).

[**1856** *Educ. Ordinance* 59 There shall be established a Public School to be called the 'High School of Dunedin'.] **1876** ADAM *Twenty-five Years Emigrant Life* 107 Wherever fifty children are found located three miles distant from another school, the Government erect a school-building and endow it with £50 annually from public funds until the district increases in size. When this occurs, the 'side-school' has its designation changed to a district school. **1877** *Educ. Act* s55 Any Board..may..convert any public school in the district into and establish the same as a district high school. **1900** *NZ Illustr. Mag.* Jan. 280 There are also established..what are termed District High Schools. These schools correspond to the *Superior Public Schools* in New South Wales; they are merely primary schools with additional courses for secondary work. **1949** McDONALD in *Education* II. No.5 13 Today, June 1949, it is a District High School with sixteen primary teachers, four full-time and three part-time secondary assistants. **1959** TUNNICLIFFE in *Education* VIII.No.7 216 The secondary departments of New Zealand's district high schools serve the educational needs of almost 10,000 pupils. **1969** HENDERSON *Open Country Calling* 298 The school was to be closed and we were to attend the District High School in our county town. **1977** BROOKING *Massey—Its Early Years* 19 Tate suggested that the solution to New Zealand's agricultural education problem lay with the District High Schools.

ditch. As **the ditch**, the Tasman Sea, usu. in phrases with reference to Australia.

1906 PICARD *Ups & Downs* 7 I've crossed you away..that big drought sun-blazed continent the other side of the ditch. **1994** *Dominion* (Wellington) 20 Aug. 23 Before kick-off [in the Australia–NZ rugby test], you could smell the liniment waft..from the screen. The chaps from each side of the ditch were put to the test.

ditch and bank. *Hist.* Also **ditch and bank fence**, **ditch and embankment**. See quot. 1856.

1848 DEANS *Pioneers* (1964) 51 We have now all but finished one paddock of about 400 acres, with a ditch and bank. **1849** *Ibid.* 150 The system of fencing which would be generally in use here would be by ditch and embankment, similar to what you have seen at our station, of which a good labourer would do at least two rods a day. **1856** FITTON *NZ* 257 The most usual mode of enclosing a new section is by a 'ditch and bank fence', the ditch being made six feet wide at the top, and three feet deep; a compact bank being built of the soil excavated from the ditch, and the turf sods removed from the surface of the ground forming a coping. **1874** WILSON *Diary* 23 Apr. in Wierzbicka *Wilson Family* (1973) 180 He talks of 11/- and 12/- for ditch and bank, but I really think that 16/- is little enough for a four foot sod 2ft. 6in. ditch and good wattle on top. *Ibid.* 187 D. and B. is the best fence. **1883** *Brett's Colonists' Guide* 78 A ditch and bank, on heavy wet land, makes a good fence. **1902** *Settler's Handbook NZ* 162 Ditch and bank dividing-fences may be half on adjoining land. **1965** *NZ Geogr.* Oct. 149 Where timber was scarce and therefore expensive, as in most of Canterbury and Otago, fencing by ditch-and-bank, associated with a live hedge.., was the most common method employed in the earlier years before wire was available cheaply.

Hence **ditch and banking** *vbl n.*, the work of forming a ditch and bank fence.

1862 CHUDLEIGH *Diary* 29 Mar. (1950) 30 Did some ditch and banking in the morning and gardening in the afternoon.

div., *n.*[1] [Ellipt. for DIVIDEND or DIVVY: AND 1891.] DIVIDEND. Cf. DIVVY *n.*[1].

1887 *Auckland Weekly News* 26 Feb. 35 None of the Bullstown 'pubs' are paying heavy 'divs'. **1916** *Triad* 10 Jan. 43 'What you've got to do is to keep up agin the tote and when I signal, bung in and get the div. quick,' a youth was explaining to his 'cobber'.

Div., *n.*[2] *WW2.* Also **divvy**. Usu. as **the Div.**, the familiar name among New Zealand soldiers for the Second New Zealand Division in the Middle East. Cf. DIVVY *n.*[2]

1943 CLEWS in *Review* Jan. (1960) 5 The Hun was advancing on old Alex town When our Kiwi div. went to the fore. **1959** SLATTER *Gun in My Hand* 152 'Cheeri,' he calls. I don't like these new slangs. Hooray is the word. Everybody in the Div said hooray. **1986** DAVIN *Salamander & the Fire* 53 Anyhow by the time I got back the Div. was getting ready for the left hook round Agheila.

diver. [Spec. use of *diver* for any of several water birds notable for a diving habit.] Usu. with a modifier as **big diver**, **black diver**, **little diver**, various diving birds, mainly grebes. See also DABCHICK, GREBE 2 (1), WEWEIA.

1838 POLACK *NZ* I. 306 *Black divers*, rails of various kinds and variegated colours. **1842** HEAPHY *NZ* 47 The Paradise and common duck, teal, widgeon, water-hen, and diver are all found in great numbers on the rivers. **1892** WILLIAMS *Dict. NZ Lang.* 226 *weiweia*, n. *diver*; a bird. **1900** [see DABCHICK]. **c1920** BEATTIE *Trad. Lifeways Southern Maori* (1994) 164 An early settler told the collector that he remembered the birds called 'divers' by the colonists. If fired at these birds could dive so fast that the shot did not hit them. **1945** BEATTIE *Maori Place-names Canterbury* 64 Totokepio is the 'little diver' of the settler to distinguish it from the 'big diver' (the crested grebe). **1966** FALLA et al. *Birds NZ* 28 Dabchick... *Local names*: Diver, Weweia.

divide. Occas. with init. cap. [Local use of *divide* high ground dividing two watersheds.]

a. Also **Great Divide**. The Southern Alps. Cf. RANGE *n.* 1 b.

1932 *Tararua Tramper* Nov. 2 The peaks of the Arrowsmith Range, running in an easterly direction from the Divide, are often clear when the main range is shrouded in mist. **1951** CRESSWELL *Canterbury Tales* 75 To-day you may do this trip across the Divide in comfort with your post-war sedan, but it is the same road. **1981** CHARLES *Black Billy Tea* 23 There is no gold... On this side of the mountain. But on the other side of the great divide, Are riches beyond countin'.

1984 BEARDSLEY *Blackball 08* 243 Great Divide: common name for the Southern Alps which run down the middle of the South Island of New Zealand

b. As **Main Divide**. (Often heard in national weather forecasts with reference to the Southern Alps.) See also RANGE *n.* 1.

1935 *Tararua Tramper* Mar. 2 We sidled round above some schrunds and then up some good scree slopes..to the main divide. 1951 CRESSWELL *Canterbury Tales* 149 And every season now, hundreds of young people visit the snowfields and glaciers of the Main Divide and have the time of their lives. 1978 MOORE & IRWIN *Oxford Book NZ Plants* 50 *M. ephedroides* is..more common in the South Island, east of the Main Divide. 1981 MARSH *Black Beech & Honeydew* 94 We began to climb in earnest: up into the outer ramparts of the Main Divide.

dividend. *Horseracing.* Often *pl.* The amount paid out (esp. by the totalisator or T.A.B.) to betters on a winning or placed racehorse. Also *attrib.* See also DIV(VY).

1891 COX *Diaries 1888–1925* (ATLMS) 30 Mar. I went to the C.J.C. Autumn Races... Some good dividends were paid. 1941 *Sports Post* (Wellington) 11 Jan. 5 Vermette brought off a big surprise at New Plymouth to return backers a dividend around the century. 1951 *Sports Post* (Wellington) 17 Feb. 4 The amount of the place pool available for dividend computing purposes shall be divided into as many equal parts as there are horses placed in the dividend-bearing places and allocated accordingly. 1964 MORRIESON *Came a Hot Friday* (1981) 72 A sports flash from the radio had given the results and dividends of the first race. 1970 *Weekly News* (Auckland) 20 Jan. [Caption] The possibility of winning a dividend without making any investments whatsoever was not overlooked by this small collector of discarded tote tickets. 1991 *Dominion Sunday Times* (Wellington) 7 Apr. 44 The concession dividend, any five winners, paid $7064.75.

dividing mate: see MATE *n.*[2] 1 c.

dividing range: see RANGE *n.* 1 b.

diving petrel: see PETREL 2 (7).

divvy. Also **divvie**, **divy**. [A spec. use of *divvy* share, percentage paid out; an abbrev. of DIVIDEND.] Also in transf. use. DIVIDEND. **a.** A horseracing dividend; the money gained from betting.

1887 *Auckland Weekly News* 16 Apr. 21 A few 'mugs,' who didn't know anything, scooped in a £24 divy. 1890 *NZ Observer* 12 July 9 He found himself in the happy position of being able to draw three good 'divvies'. 1926 *NZ Observer* 24 Apr. 6 No. 13, Letter of Credit, won that race and paid a rattling good divvy. 1959 SLATTER *Gun in My Hand* 164 A man shoulda been in on the big divvy on the last race. 1966 TURNER *Eng. Lang. Austral. & NZ* 174 The respectability of racing is enhanced by the use, even in official publications such as the *Yearbook*, of the term *investments* for bets and *dividends* (popularly *divvies*) for money won. 1977 HALL *Glide Time* 55 Gets his *radio out and starts listening*. Wonder what the divvy was.

b. *Transf.* to other payments.

1912 *NZ Free Lance* (Wellington) 9 Mar. 22 The light-fingered pick-pocket profession struck..a 'divvy' of over £250. 1962 WEBBER *Look No Hands* 147 You get..the Arbitration Court saying they'll only pay a divvy of sixpence in the quid..and Nordy saying that's just a spiel.

Divvy, *n.*[2] *WW1*, *WW2*. The First or Second New Zealand Divisions. Cf. DIV *n.*[2]

1918 let. 6 Oct. in *Boots, Belts* (1992) 129 The old Divvy is having a rough time over there as you can see by the casualty lists. ?1941 *NZEF Times* 22 Dec. 17 Who will race to Divvy Base and fetch a Christmas duff?

divy, var. DIVVY.

dizzy: see DISASTER.

do, *v.*[1] Also **do in**, occas. **do up**. *trans.* To consume, to use up (food, drink, money); esp. in the phr. *to do one's dough*, *to do one's chips*, to spend all one's money. As **do** (something) **in**, to get rid of (see quot. 1910).

1889 DAVIDSON *Stories NZ Life* 3 His friend Kelly could always do a stiff nip when off duty. 1906 *Truth* 20 Nov. 6 Does his dough on [nags]. 1909 THOMPSON *Ballads About Business* 27 I'd never make for home again until I'd 'done it [*sc.* money] in'. 1910 *Truth* 29 Jan. 7 John Thomas said he had sacked him for intemperance, which time John [Sullivan] had got another job and 'done it in' for the same reason. Ibid. 17 Dec. 6 The watchhouse-keeper asked where the ring was, and accused said he had 'done it in', meaning that he had got rid of it. 1935 STRONG in Partridge *Slang Today* 287 When I done all my sugar and never even had the makings, he went very hostile because I never told him I was swept. 1944 do up [see ONKUS]. 1947 BEATTIE *Early Runholding* 54 The Maori shearer of the early 'sixties..unfortunately..proved a ready convert to the custom of..'doing-in' his cheque at the nearest grog shanty. 1959 SLATTER *Gun in My Hand* 23 An it ran like a hairy goat an I did me chips. 1964 MORRIESON *Came a Hot Friday* (1981) 159 Six hundred quid!.. But I did it in! I did it in! 1964 HORI *Fill It Up Again* 7 No. 2 dead-heats for ninth, so I do my dough. 1976 MORRIESON *Pallet on Floor* 48 Jack does up all our dough on booze and I need it. 1981 CHARLES *Black Billy Tea* 34 I've done my dough and my wallet is missing.

do, *v.*[2] *intr.* To weigh, to not exceed a certain weight.

1910 *Truth* 14 May 6 Therefore his rides this season will be fewer, as he may not often 'do' under 9 stone... His horsemanship is superb, whilst this weight—for he can 'do' 7st 4lb.—is a very big advantage.

do, *v.*[3] *Farming.* [f. Brit. dial.: see EDD *do* 6. *n.*; OED 11.] *trans.* To provide fodder for (stock); in the phr. **to do** (stock) **hard**, to keep (stock) short of feed; **to do** (stock) **well**, to keep (stock) plentifully fed.

1916 *NZJAg.* Sept. XIII. 174 Ewes have been..'well done by' during the winter. 1923 PERRY *Sheep Farming* 116 Besides the usual pasture, roots and green feed given to the flock it is often found profitable to 'do' the show sheep especially well. 1924 ANTHONY *Follow the Call* (1975) 87 The two farms together were capable of 'doing' forty cows. 1950 *NZJAg.* Oct. LXXXI. 347 The successful management of a sheep run calls for..an appreciation of the carrying capacity of tussock land to 'do' sheep well without either overstocking or understocking. 1955 BOWEN *Wool Away* 138 When the [Romney] sheep have been 'done hard', they can be among the toughest a man can put a handpiece into.

Hence **doing** *ppl. a.*, see quot.

1982 *Agric. Gloss.* (MAF) 4 *Doing*: To describe how stock are growing or their state of health, e.g. doing well or badly. 'Not doing' = performing badly.

do, *v.*[4] In various phr.: *to do a get*, see GET *n.*; *do one's block* (*bun, melon, scone*), see BLOCK *n.*[3] 2, BUN *n.*[1], MELON 3, SCONE *n.*

do, *n.*

1. A success, a 'go'; esp. in the phr. **to make a do of**.

1902 *NZ Illustr. Mag.* V. 381 Your poor, rough, back section. It has been forfeited twice, and you'll never make a do of it. 1911 *Truth* 16 Sept. 5 The rent is raised on..the butcher and baker.., and the butcher and baker, to 'make a do of it', pass the liability on the consumer. 1945 *NZ Geogr.* I. 36 High-country men..take to the back-country because they can make a better 'do' of it than on a mixed farm. 1947 DAVIN *Gorse Blooms Pale* 91 Another go at making a do of things with his wife.

2. fair do (fair doos), see FAIR *a.* 11.

dob, *v.* [Cf. Brit. dial. *dob* to put down: see EDD *v.*[1] 1; AND 1955.] *trans.* and *intr.* Usu. as **dob in** to inform on, to betray (someone) to authorities, to make an accusation against (a person).

a1974 SYDER & HODGETTS *Aust & NZ English* (TS) 273 *To dob (someone) in.* To deliberately betray, or, in a less serious situation, to deliberately reveal detrimental information concerning another—naturally to his disadvantage. 'They reckoned nobody had the slightest clue, but it looks as if someone was watching them. The police walked up to their tent while they were still asleep. Somebody dobbed them in alright.' 1986 *Sunday News* (Auckland) 19 Oct. 7 The pre-teen courier was dobbed in by a nine-year-old classmate and taken away for a chat with some friendly policemen. 1991 *Evening Post* (Wellington) 9 Feb. 3 The fact one of the daughters lied about sexual misconduct and then 'dobbed' her mother in did not mean the mother had lied about being raped by Farmer.

Hence **dobber** *n.*, an informer; **dobbing in** *vbl.n.* and *ppl.a.*, (pertaining to) the act or process of informing on a person.

1995 *Evening Post* (Wellington) 6 Feb. 4 Dobbers are not accountable—it stinks. [Heading] This community road watch, as they're calling the dobbing-in campaign on motorists by their ratfink fellow and fellowesses, is monstrous. The old Soviet Union made a culture out of dobbing in and ended up with five million citizens...who'd dob to order. Or just dob regardless.

dobbin. [f. Brit. dial.: see EDD *dobbin n.*[2] a small three-wheeled cart; OED Irish *dobbin-cart* a four-wheeled cart.] A small, wheeled truck as used in mining (for moving ore), and later in woolstores (for moving wool). See also SKIP.

1953 DEWAR *Chaslands* 113 The most advanced innovation on this line was the dobbin, a wheeled truck that would hold about a yard of material. It was run on wooden rails extending from the cutting face to the adjacent gully or filling and added to as the work advanced. Ibid. 114 On reaching the end of its run the dobbin was either spragged or tipped by means of a cradle. 1982 [see SKIP]. 1993 MARSHALL *Ace of Diamonds Gang* 129 The sacks [of pine cones] had to be dragged out on sledges, or dobbins, to the road.

dock.

1. [Spec. use of *dock Rumex* spp.] In New Zealand use, *Rumex flexuosus* (fam. Polygonaceae), usu. as **Maori (native, New Zealand) dock**. Also as **rolling dock**, a dock the dry branched fruiting stalk of which can be blown about by wind. See also RUNA.

1915 *AJHR* C-6 12 *Rumex flexuosus*... New Zealand dock. Tussock pasture. 1926 HILGENDORF *Weeds* 65 Maori Dock..is called also native dock, New Zealand dock, and rolling dock. It occurs throughout both islands on native and artificial pastures, showing no preference for moist country... When it ripens the whole stalk often breaks off, and is blown about by the wind (whence the name rolling dock). 1946 *Bull. Wellington Bot. Soc.* No.14 5 The native dock..was flowering in the swamp [in the Rakaia]. 1969 *Standard Common Names Weeds* 46 Maori dock *Rumex flexuosus*. Ibid. 52 New Zealand dock [=] Maori dock 1980 GIBBS *NZ Butterflies* 159 *L. boldenarum* eggs and larvae have also been found on the native 'Maori dock'. 1982 WILSON *Stewart Is. Plants* 164 *Rumex flexuosus* Native Dock... Runa... Leaves brown-green.

2. As **dockdigging** *obs. fig.* [f. the apparent aimless wandering of those working at digging up docks from a paddock], doing nothing in particular; walking around looking for work.
1892 JENKYNS *Hard Life* 228 It was the Dane's turn to stay in the house, so Gilbert and I set out 'dockdigging' as it was called.

docket. A retailers' invoice or cash-register receipt for goods or services supplied.
1974 SIMPSON *Sugarbag Years* 152 While I'd no objection to seeing on a return docket sometimes a packet of cigarettes..if I found there was not food for the family as well, I would then make out the order to the wife only. 1979 *Otago Daily Times* (Dunedin) 28 Mar. 21 It is a great pity that sharp differences of meaning explained in the publisher's publicity for such Anglo-New Zealand words as mall, docket, jack-up, social studies, etc. were not included in the dictionary proper. 1993 *Hutt News* (Lower Hutt) 44 Tens of thousands of dollars worth of yellow supermarket dockets, collected by students to exchange for new computer equipment, were saved from the [school] blaze.

docking, *vbl. n. Farming.* [f. *dock* to remove most of an animal's (esp. lamb's) tail leaving a short stump: see OED v.¹ b, 1491.] Of significance as *attrib.* 'pertaining to, used in the process of docking' esp. in Comb. **docking area, iron, knife, muster, pen, yard**. See also TAILING *vbl. n* 1.
1960 MASTERS *Back-Country Tales* 124 As a young and silly lamb, without any proper knowledge of what is liable to happen in this hard old world, Hermit followed his mother into a **docking area**. 1950 *NZJAg.* Oct. LXXXI. 199 The searing or **docking iron** must be at 'black heat', not red hot. 1963 WALLIS *Point of Origin* 18 In Awatere there had been sacks of grain and seeds,.. boxes of nails, **docking knives**. 1953 STRONACH *Musterer on Molesworth* 6 Most were bearded, as they had arrived that day after the **docking muster** on the Ewe Country—twelve days' hard going. 1966 *NZJAg.* July CXIII. 55 The **docking pen** must be strong enough to hold the ewes and lambs. 1969 MCCASKILL *Molesworth* 99 The **docking yard** was made of hurdles in the conventional way.

doctor, *n.*¹ [f. *doctor* ship's cook (OED *n.* 11, 1821), thence a station or camp cook: AND 1868.]

1. a. In the sense 'ship's cook' recorded early on the New Zealand coast and prob. well-known to early immigrants.
1839 *Piraki Log* 16 June (1911) 89 At 11 a.m. the Doctor and Jim Robinson from Wongooloa, with a Crew. 1842 *Piraki Log* 29 Apr. (1911) 126 The Doctor and Mate spent the day on shore. 1850 *Richmond-Atkinson Papers* (1960) I. 75 [On the way to New Zealand] a fat black fish was seen swimming along following a sheep which had been hung out by 'the doctor' to wash. c1900 BAILEY & ROTH *Shanties* (1967) 132 The old man's full of she-oak—..The 'doctor's' boilin' stinkin' beef and drinkin' hell-fire rum. 1933 EADDY *Hull Down* 101 The Doctor, as all sailing-ships' cooks are dubbed.

b. *Transf. Obs.* In early whalers' or traders' parlance, a Maori slave who prepares meals; a COOKEE.
1845 WAKEFIELD *Adventure NZ* I. 319 A chief was called a '*nob*'; a slave, a '*doctor*'; a woman, a '*heifer*'; a girl, a '*titter*'; and a child, a '*squeaker*'.

2. The men's cook on (orig. South Island) sheep stations, thence to camps and gangs of outdoor workmen. (Cf. the occas. use of *galley* for the usual 'cookhouse' on some stations.)
1898 ANDERSON *Bushfalling Reminisc.* in Mulinder *Pioneer Family* (1947) 42 I was known in the [bush fellers'] camp as the 'doctor', and the men came to me for things they needed from a little store I made a point of carrying. 1902 WALKER *Zealandia's Guerdon* 55 Cook-shop for all hands..the 'doctor's—cook's—residence. 1933 *Press* (Christchurch) (Acland Gloss.) 7 Oct. 15 *Doctor*.—Slang name for station cook. Given as S[outh] Australia in [1898 Morris *Austral-English*] but very commonly used here. 1947 BEATTIE *Early Runholding* 12 On many stations the cook was almost always known as 'the doctor'. 1968 *NZ Contemp. Dict. Suppl.* (Collins) 7 *doctor n.* bush term for cook.

doctor, *n.²* *Obs.* [Cf. Partridge *Doctor* 4, 1770-1880.] Rum and milk as a 'pick-me-up'.
1864 LUSH *Waikato Jrnls.* 26 Nov. (1982) 37 After breakfast the Doctor gave me a 'Doctor'—*i.e.* a tumbler of new milk well mixed with a glass of [—] shall I tell?—a glass of rum. 1895 CHAMIER *South Sea Siren* 206 Let's have a *doctor* Joe! Fetch that rum and milk... Raleigh expostulated that at so early an hour 'doctors' did not agree with him.

doctor, *n.*³ [A transf. use of the literal phr.: AND 1949.] In the phr. **to go for the doctor**, to make an often final supreme effort; to risk all on a main chance.
1952 *Standard* (Wellington) 24 Sept. 4 Once again Mullet 'went for the doctor' in the ninth round and this time a right-cross put Hall down for another count of eight. 1971 NEWTON *Ten Thousand Dogs* 112 Anyway Jim knew what he had to beat and 'he went for the doctor' and turned in a winning run. 1980 MCGILL *Ghost Towns NZ* 127 Gambling was poker or 45s, a diggers' card game from California involving legs, queer suits and Maggie, cries of 'Get Jinx!' and 'Go for the Doctor!' 1987 *National Radio* 'Morning Report' 19 June [Dick Griffin, Political Commentator, on Finance Minister Roger Douglas's budget] He's going for the doctor and apparently doing it quite well.

doer /ˈduə/. [Transf. use of *doer* a horse or other animal that 'does' or thrives well: see OED 3; see also DO v.¹]

1. Of a racehorse, one which runs or races well.
1891 A TRAMP, ESQ. *Casual Ramblings* 114 The Priest [a racehorse] is a good 'doer'.

2. [AND 1902.] Of a person, a *hard doer* (HARD *a.* 1 b).
1916 TWIDLE *Diary* (MS) 18 May I. 33 Thursday 18th I was a hard looking doer covered with mud, thigh [gum]boots and steel helmet. 1943 BENNETT *English in NZ* in *Amer. Speech* XVIII. 88 A *doer* is a jester, or an eccentric. 1968 *NZ Contemp. Dict. Suppl.* (Collins) 7 *doer, hard doer..n.* tough character, hard case.

dog, *n.*
[*Note*] It is often difficult to determine whether a particular quotation refers to the Polynesian or the European breed.

1. Usu. as **Maori (native, New Zealand) dog**, *Canis familiaris* (fam. Canidae) the Polynesian breed of the domestic dog introduced to New Zealand by the Maori. See also KURI.
1770 COOK *Journals* 31 Mar. (1955) I. 277 The country is certainly destitute of all sorts of beasts either wild or tame except Dogs and Ratts, the former are tame and live with with people who breed and bring them up for no other purpose than to eat. 1777 FORSTER *Voyage Round the World* I. 219 A good many dogs were observed in their canoes, which.. they kept tied with a string, round their middle; they were of a rough long-haired sort, with pricked ears, and much resembled the common shepherd's cur... They were of different colours, some spotted, some quite black, and others perfectly white. 1807 SAVAGE *Some Acc. NZ* 10 They have no larger animal than the dog, which is a native here, usually black and white, with sharp, pricked up ears, the hair rather long, and in figure a good deal resembling the animal we call a fox-dog—the native name of which is Coraddee [= Ma. *kararehe*]. 1821 *Evidence of Ensign McCrae before Commissioner Bigge* in McNab *Hist. Records* (1908) I. 536 Q. Are there any quadrupeds in New Zealand, wild or tame? A. None but the native dog that resembles that of New Holland, tho' in New Zealand it is capable of being domesticated and they are trained to catch pigs. 1840 BEST *Journal* (1966) 9 Dec. 263 As we approached one of the Mauri dogs jumped over board and swam towards some rocks. 1859 TE HEU HEU in *NZ Yesterdays* (1984) 40 As clover killed the fern, and European dog the Maori dog;.. so our people will gradually be supplemented by the pakeha. 1861 HAAST *Topographical Exploration of Nelson* 135 The old native dog (kuri) seems to be extinct. 1890 COLENSO *Treaty of Waitangi* 11 Whilst here and there a *hani*..was seen erected, adorned with the long flowing white hair of the tails of the New Zealand dog. 1904 TREGEAR *Maori Race* 166 The Maori dog (*Kuri ruarangi*) has now entirely disappeared. 1925 BEST *Tuhoe* 11 The native dog, now extinct, is said to have been introduced by old-time Polynesian voyagers from the isles of Polynesia. 1939 BEATTIE *First White Boy Born in Otago* 148 These wild dogs [of early Otago] were the real Maori dogs, and were sometimes yellow and sometimes black-and-white. 1946 *JPS* LV. 153 kuri, Maori dog, brought with him from the Pacific; now applied to any mongrel: long extinct, and only surviving in the strips of skin with hair attached used as ornaments on the Maori valued cloaks (kaku-waero). 1981 *NZJ Archaeology* III. 16 The descriptions of 'Maori dog' by early settlers in the southern back-country fit perfectly with those of the pure indigenous breed observed in the eighteenth century. 1990 *Handbook NZ Mammals* 281 *Kuri Canis familiaris*... Also called guri (southern Maori)..; Maori dog, native dog, Polynesian dog, wild dog (English). This account..includes the wild kuri-European cross-breeds of last century.

2. As **bush, Maori (native)** or **wild dog**, *Canis familiaris*, the dog introduced by European settlers, often escaped into a wild state. **a. bush dog**. A wild dog (living in the bush); occas. a working-dog trained to work or hunt in the bush (see quot. c1899).
1847 ANGAS *Savage Life* II. 130 The dogs belonging to the native who was our fellow-traveller..put up a wild bush-dog... It was covered with long bushy hair, and in appearance greatly resembled a jackall. c1899 DOUGLAS in *Mr Explorer Douglas* (1957) 231 I have seen..[wekas] by sheer cheek and audacity route [*sic*] an experienced bush dog. 1984 BOYD *City of the Plains* 11 'I was tired of you and Hamlin,' he [*sc.* Manaena]

told Tanner at the Commission hearing: 'you were like bush-dogs chasing me'.

b. *Hist.* **Maori (native) dog**, occas. **pa dog**. (a) A mongrel dog associated with Maori settlements. See also KURI 2.

1841 *Establishment of New Plymouth Colony* in *Establishment of New Plymouth* (1940) 76 And yet, strange to say, the numerous half-starved native dogs never think of destroying them. **1857** *Lyttelton Times* 8 Aug. 3 If the measure [*sc.* dog-registration] can be made to affect the intolerable Maori-dog nuisance, it will be of great service. **1859** THOMSON *Story New Zealand* I. 22 What are called native dogs by the Middle Island shepherds are English animals, free, not wild. **1868** CHUDLEIGH *Diary* 20 Feb. (1950) 216 Two of old Jims dogs are slain on suspicion [of sheep-worrying] and two other Maori dogs are tied up to die as soon as their owner returns. **1881** NESFIELD *Chequered Career* 36 There is nothing to..worry the sheep in New Zealand unless it is a Maori dog or two; and a few carefully laid baits in the neighbourhood of a Maori Pah soon make the owners of the dogs more careful. **1892** *TrNZI* XXIV. 16 I have seen the Australian dingo, and this Maori dog is very much like him, only not nearly so large. **1900** *Canterbury Old and New* 29 The Maori dogs and pigs were so numerous as to be a constant source of trouble, allowed as they were to wander about. **1917** *NZ Free Lance Christmas Annual* (Wellington) 51 The pah dogs with their eager barking heralded the day. **1939** BEATTIE *First White Boy Born in Otago* 118 [Central Otago] was a silent land, voiceless save for..the long-drawn, eerie howl of a wild native dog. **1951** HUNT *Confessions* 22 Maori dogs were a continual source of trouble to the struggling settlers. **1973** WHEELER *Historic Sheep Stations of the North Island* 101 The early sheepmen did not appreciate the Maori dog. At Ernscliffe we were told that, roaming in packs of forty or fifty, from Rotorua, they were the 'worst curse of the times'.

(b) In phr. of odious comparison: **cunning as a Maori dog**, see CUNNING *a*. a; **lazy as a Maori dog**, very lazy.

1955 BJ *Cameron Collection* (TS July) maori dog (n) A stock peg on which to hang all manner of vices, e.g. *cunning as a maori dog*. *Ibid.* lazy as a maori dog Very lazy.

c. wild dog. A dog having no owner and living in a wild state.

1853 MACKIE *Traveller under Concern* (1973) 11 Mar. 86 We found the shepherd..unwell, having met with a serious accident whilst hunting wild dogs. These dogs are of English origin, they are often met with and are destructive to the sheep. **1856** FITTON *NZ* 5 The renegade curs, which now haunt the unfrequented parts of the mountains..and are dignified by the name of 'Wild Dogs' by the English settlers, are evidently the neglected produce of some European mongrels. **1892** *TrNZI* XXIV. 16 Goodall explicitly pointed out that this breed [*sc.* the Maori kuri] was not to be confused with either the 'wild dogs' of the Southland coast or the 'cur dogs' of many breeds which he had seen in the Wairarapa during the 1850's. **1938** BURDON *High Country* 53 In the unlikely event of their surmounting all these dangers, they would find the country useless for pasture and inhabited by nothing but wild pigs and wild dogs. **1946** ACLAND *Early Canterbury Runs* 79 Like all runholders in the 'fifties the Halls were much bothered by wild dogs. I don't know whether these dogs were descended from Maori dogs or from pre-Adamite settlers' dogs gone wild.

4. With a modifier distinguishing various kinds of working dog, see: BACKING DOG, *eye-dog* (EYE 3 b), HEADING DOG, HUNTAWAY 1, LEADING DOG, STOPPING DOG, *Sunday dog* (SUNDAY).

5. Special Comb. **dog bludger**, a nickname for a musterer; **dog-boots** *mustering* [DCan. of a sled-dog, 1871], protective coverings for a working-dog's feet; **dog driver**, see quot.; **doghair**, see quot.; **dog-hole** *obs*. [f. obs. Brit. slang: see OED], a place unfit for human habitation; **dog-hunting**, the hunting of wild dogs; **dogman** (a) [AND 1948], one who gives directions to a crane-driver, and attaches loads to the crane's *doghook*; (b) a musterer or dog-trialist; **dog-money** *deerculling*, an official (Public Service) allowance for the upkeep of working dogs; **dog-poor** [Austral., orig. applied to a horse: see OED *dog* 19 d], of sheep, very unthrifty; **dog pound**, a solitary confinement cell at Tongariro Corrective Training Centre (cf. POUND *n.*²); **dog's cake**, see quot.; **dog-slow** *adv*., very slowly; **dog tax** *obs*., a tax on dog-owners; **dogtown**, an early derog. name among coastal seamen for Port Chalmers.

1989 *NZ Eng. Newsletter* III. 23 *dog bludger*: A musterer. **1978** JARDINE *Shadows on Hill* 30 I used to keep a pair of **dog-boots** for his front feet. **1933** *Press* (Christchurch) (Acland Gloss.) 7 Oct. 15 *Dog Driver*— Slang word for shepherd or musterer. **1928** *NZJST* IX. 182 There is in some South African sheep an occurrence of 'kempy' fibres with even thicker medulla than in ordinary kemp, and these are known as '**doghair**' and 'gare'. **1869** MAY *Guide to Farming* 42 The country was a **dog-hole**..the forty-acre system a most villainous take-in. **1859** *Puketoi Station Diary* (Hocken TS) 29 May Rode **dog hunting** on Rowleys run. **1987** TVNZ1 news 28 Jan. of crane mishap in Auckland. [Crane-driving] is helped by men on the ground called **dog-men**. **1990** *Dominion* (Wellington) 22 Feb. 10 [Heading] Crane ballast fall hurts dogman... Part of the block fell on to the rear of the truck, missing the injured dogman by about two metres. **1975** NEWTON *Sixty Thousand on the Hoof* 247 Ron Donald is a familiar name among **dog-men**. **1960** CRUMP *Good Keen Man* 14 You'll get five shillings a week **dog-money** if your pup turns out any good. **1978** PRESTON *Woolgatherers* 108 In the Spring we had only 30% of lambs and the sheep were **dog-poor**. **1982** *NZ Times* 19 Sept. 16 Then there's 'the **dog pound**'. That's solitary confinement. It's the only part of the institute that looks like a real prison. A concrete cell, bars on the window. Cold in the winter, hot in the summer. **1940** *Tales Pioneer Women* (1988) 153 After the bread came out, trays of apples..would go in to bake,... or a special '**dog's cake**' made of pollard, bran, suet, and butter-milk. **1988** TV1 News 15 Sept. [A NZ yachtsman speaks about racing at the Seoul Olympics preliminaries.] Think you're getting up in the water, but find you're going **dog-slow**. **1861** *Puketoi Station Diary* (Hocken TS) 23 Mar. A constable from Dunedin called to collect **dog tax**. **1883** *Brett's Colonists' Guide* 173 The dog tax of New Zealand has had the very beneficial effect of reducing the number of useless curs that were formerly the terror of sheepowners. **1939** BEATTIE *First White Boy Born Otago* 99 I remember in the [eighteen] fifties that men used to come to collect the dog tax, and..the amount was 10/- for any kind of dog. **1988** MIKAERE *Te Maiharoa* 82 Parliament introduced legislation to limit the number of Maori-owned dogs, by imposing steep registration fees, or dog taxes. **1911** *Truth* 8 July 7 The quickest way to cause a riot and to raise an insurrection is to call an inhabitant of Port Chalmers a dweller in **Dogtown**. **1920** p.c. Pugh-Williams May 1951 Port Chalmers was nicknamed *dog town* perhaps because it comprised the proverbial 'only one man and a dog' only.

6. Spec. use of *dog* a contemptible person. **a.** In the phr. **to turn dog on** [AND 1863, f. *dog* informer (1848).] (a) To inform on.

1908 *Truth* 4 Apr. 5 It was a very contemptible thing, added the beak for Machray to 'turn dog' on his mates. *Ibid.* 11 Mar. 7 Constable Maher magnanimously offered to see what he could do to secure the husband work as compensation for loss of employment through turning 'dog' on Shears.

(b) Also as **to go dog on**, to go bad on, to turn sour on.

1910 *Truth* 5 Mar. 1 Latest political small talk is that Masterton's member..is turning dog on it. Next election will..see him wooing an Auckland electorate. **1953** MUNDY *Days That Are No More* 25 Fred struggled along not doing so well, complaining that he had no help, and that the rest of the family had turned dog on him. **1974** MORRIESON *Predicament* (1981) 207 The bottle of 'the red' he had tossed off in such high spirits had turned dog on him. He was on the verge of nausea. **1995** ANDERSON *House Guest* 183 Should've warned you. The hot [water] goes dog on you if I turn her on in here.

b. Esp. among prisoners and adolescents, a low contemptible person, MONGREL 1; also applied to undesirable or ill-performing things.

1982 NEWBOLD *Big Huey* 32 'You're a dog!' [the prison warder] shouted into my face. 'You're a filthy bastard and a pig!' **1984** BEATON *Outside In* 70 Sandy: Arselicker! Dog! Cunt! *Ibid.* 109 Dog. An abusive term for a person. **1990** *Dominion Sunday Times* (Wellington) 22 Apr. 4 If you're called [by adolescents] a..dog..you've been insulted. **1991** DUFF *One Night Out Stealing* 103 Might be you woke up with a sheila beside ya... But afraid to check her out too closely in case she was a dog, cos she was sure to be at least half a dog. **1992** *Dominion* (Wellington) 28 Feb. 9 The Rolls Royce..was not a 'dog' despite 21 faults, the court was told. Auckland Rolls Royce franchise dealer..said the car was neither a 'lemon' [i.e. a car hard to sell] nor, to use a New Zealand expression, 'a dog'. **1993** p.c. Dr Chris Harfoot (Waikato University) The term 'dog' is used among the New Zealand sailing fraternity to describe a yacht, sailing dinghy, etc. which is a sluggish sailer.

c. With init. cap. As a play on *Mongrel (Mob)*, an intra-gang name for a patched member.

1991 PAYNE *Staunch* 19 If a bald'ead..is angered or upset by their lifestyle then, to a true 'Dog', this is simply a reaffirmation of the life he has chosen to lead. **1994** *Dominion* (Wellington) 11 Oct. 6 The 'dogs', as Mongrel Mob members called themselves, punched, kicked and hit him with a dumbbell.

7. In various phrases: **to have a dog tied up** [AND 1905], see quot. 1988; **to try (something) on the dog** [fig. use of *dog* in a sense 'the public', 'others'], to try something out on the public; **done like a dog's dinner** [cf. AND *do like a dinner*, 1847], usu. *pass*. **to be done like a dog's dinner**, to be soundly defeated, to be completely worsted; **to keep a dog and bark oneself**, see quot.

1988 *Dominion Sunday Times* (Wellington) 14 Feb. 19 If they [*sc.* vagrant alcoholics] **have a dog tied up** somewhere, that means they owe someone in the place money. **1903** *Evening Post* (Wellington) 17 Feb. The opera ['Tapu'] was shelved until lately, when it was handed over to Mr Tom Pollard to '**try on the dog**', as the saying goes, in the very town in which the authors lived and worked for many years. **1931** *Tararua Tramper* Jan. 2 You're the winner—the coves in front are all **done like dogs' dinners**. **1989** MCGILL *Dinkum Kiwi Dict*. 26 *done like a dog's dinner* comprehensively defeated; eg 'Last year just about every other province was done by Auckland like a dog's dinner.' **1991** *Evening Post* (Wellington) 1 Aug. 12 [Heading] Done like a dog's dinner. Done over by Ruth Richardson one night and the Okkers the next. What a week! [Reference to a 'Black Budget' and a crushing defeat in a rugby league test.] **1993** *Dominion* (Wellington) 2 Mar. 7 In [striking] Telecom workplaces the faxes ran hot with amateur cartoons of Spot [a dog featuring in Telecom advertising] being done like a dog's dinner. **1955** *BJ Cameron Collection* (TS July) **keep a dog and bark oneself** To duplicate one's effort needlessly.

dog, *v*. In the phr. **to dog it over** (someone), to lord it over; to play the boss in a pretentious fashion.
  1936 TREADWELL *Recolls. Amateur Soldier* 233 There were a good many non-combatant units at headquarters, and many of the non-commissioned officers used to think it smart to dog it over the man who was across on leave.

dogbox.
1. *Railways*. [Cf. AND a carriage with compartments but no internal corridor, 1905.] **a.** *Obs*. A type of railway goods wagon.
  1917 in Miller *Camps, Tramps & Trenches* (1939) 2 Our crowd moved off from Headquarters in the railways goods waggons known as 'dog-boxes'.
b. A special box or cage, or space for carrying dogs in the guard's van; also the guard's storage compartment at the rear end of an electric unit.
  1969 HASCOMBE *Down & Almost Under* 31 'The dog in the carriage with you?... He'll have to go in the dogbox'... Because there was not enough room for us all in the dogbox..we were allowed to stand in the guard's van. **1981** *Dominion* (Wellington) 23 Apr. 1 Lower Hutt police said last night it appeared the [injured] boy had tried to get into the dogbox part of a carriage while the train was moving.
2. a. A poor or cramped quarters, or office; a small sub-standard house.
  1952 2YA Wellington: Parliamentary Broadcast 4 July Mr Connolly, MP, Dunedin, said: 'Houses for 700 pounds?—substandard housing, that's what it is.' *Interjector*: 'Dog-boxes, I'd say.' **1982** NEWBOLD *Big Huey* 248 Dog box (n) Prison official's office. **1988** McGILL *Dict. Kiwi Slang* 37 *dogbox* cramped quarters, originally the guard's van cage; *in the dog box* out of favour, in disgrace; eg 'I see Jim's staying at the pub again. In the dogbox with the missus, eh?'
b. *Obs*. See quot.
  1980 NEAVE *Land of Munros* 90 Later, traction engines [for threshing]..had their own galley and cook, and it was a great sight to see engine, mill, water-cart and dog joey—a two wheeled hut [where the boss and water joey slept].
3. A wooden box-like cover over the engine of an open boat.
  1925–26 *NZJST* VIII. 100 Nearly all the [Otago fishing-] boats are fitted with good cabins and weather-dodgers, the open boat with only a dog-box over the engine having fallen into disuse.
4. In the phr. **to be in the dog box** (with a person) [var. of US *in the doghouse*], to be in disgrace (with), be out of favour (with).
  1953 *Evening Post* (Wellington) 9 Mar. 12 Rather funny you being in the cactus at home—I'm in the dog box with my wife too. **1972** *Marlborough Express* (Blenheim) 21 Oct. 6 What's this to do with errant husbands?.. 'Well, they're either in the dog box or leading a dog's life,' he explained. **1988** [see 2 *a* above].

dog cockle: see COCKLE 2 (1).

dog collar *Obs*.

1. In the phr. **to take the dog collar**, to take the prize.
  1906 *Truth* 19 May 6 We find in proportion to population..New Zealand takes the dog collar [for incidence of lunacy].
2. An habitual criminal's indeterminate sentence. See COLLAR 1.

dog daisy: see DAISY 2 (3).

dog dosing.
1. See quot. 1982.
  [**1959** *NZPD* CCCXXI. 2171 First, there will be the compulsory dosing of dogs.] **1963** AUDLEY *No Boots for Mr. Moehau* 134 As for the..President of the Farmers' Federation, he arrived at ten to nine, having been on the telephone to the Matamata branch over the matter of dog-dosing. **1966** TURNER *Eng. Lang. Austral. & NZ* 142 *Dog dosing* needs no further explanation in New Zealand. **1982** *Agric. Gloss.* (MAF) 24 *Dog Dosing*: Act of drenching and purging a dog to obtain a sample of faeces to be examined for parasitic worms.
2. Special Comb. *Obs*. **(dog) dosing-strip**, formerly an area or enclosure set aside for the treatment of dogs for hydatids.
  1960 *NZPD* CCCXXII. 710 It is not necessary for a dog owner to present his dog at a dosing strip..if he produces a certificate by a veterinary surgeon that the dog has been treated for hydatids. **1968** SLATTER *Pagan Game* 162 On the dog-dosing strip at Kuripuni I fell in love with you. **1971** TAYLOR *Plekhov Place* 20 We're pretty solitary except when we throw a party. Me more so than Gray who at least sees the other chaps at the dog-dosing strip. **1974** AVERY *The Ken Avery Songbook* [Title 'By the Dog Dosin' Strip'] By the dog dosin' strip at Dunsandel I fell in love with you... The hydatids hinderers, by the way, don't like the term 'dog dosing strip'; they prefer to call it 'hydatids testing area'. **1982** *Agric. Gloss.* (MAF) 24 *Dosing strip*: an area of ground where official dosing by hydatids control officers is carried out. **1991** *Dominion Sunday Times* (Wellington) 31 Mar. 21 Over in the big marquee a country and western singer crooned away about a romance that blossomed on the dog dosing strip at Dunsandel.

dogfish. [Transf. or extended use of the northern hemisphere name *dogfish*.]
1. Any of various small sharks, a valuable food source of the early Maori, and of the modern New Zealander as very often the fish of 'fish and chips', having many and various common names applied, often only occasionally, to members of the two dogfish families: (a) fam. Triakidae, the smoothhound or smooth dogfish family, esp. *Mustelus lenticulatus*, having the names **spotted** (or **smooth** or **smooth-hound**) **dogfish** (occas. called 'spotted shark'), GUMMY *n*.³ or *gummy shark* (SHARK 2 (9)), PIOKE, RIG *n*.¹; and *Galeorhinus galeus*, having the names *school shark* (SHARK 2 (15)), TOPE: or (b) fam. Squalidae, the spiny dogfish family, esp. *Squalus acanthias*, having the names **southern** (or **spotted spiny**) **dogfish**, KOINGA, and also the occasional familiar names of *spineback*, *spiky*, *spiky dog*, *spiny*, *spurdog* (see quot. 1986 below); and *Squalus mitsukuri* (formerly *blainvillei*), having the names **grey spiny** (or **northern** (**spiny**)) **dogfish**; and *Scymnodon plunketi Plunket's shark* (SHARK 2 (13)). See also MANGA 2; and occas. MANGO, OKEOKE.
  1770 [see DAB *n*.¹]. **1777** FORSTER *Voyage Round World* I. 181 [We] indeed caught some fish [near Long Island] which are common to Europe, viz. the horse-mackarel, the greater dog-fish, and the smooth hound. **1817** NICHOLAS *Voyage NZ* I. 269 On these stages were placed a quantity of the dog-fish and sting-ray, which were drying there as a supply against the winter. **1838** POLACK *NZ* I. 323 Many other fish are equally numerous, answering to our *hakes*,... various kinds of..*dog-fish*. **1848** WAKEFIELD *Handbook NZ* 160 The *Shark* is rarely seen near the coast, though small *Dog-fish*, from *one to three feet* in length, are very common. **1884** MARTIN *Our Maoris* 26 After this we came to a long row of poles, on which was hung an immense supply of dried shark (the dogfish split in two). **1898** [see MANGO 1]. **1922** *Auckland Weekly News* 9 Mar. 15 [A female] contained 26 young, spiny dogfish. **1956** GRAHAM *Treasury NZ Fishes* 80 There are several species of small sharks that are known as dogfish. **1986** PAUL *NZ Fishes* 31 Spiny dogfish *Squalus acanthias*... Other names include southern dogfish, spurdog, spineback, or spiky. Occurs almost world wide in cool temperate seas. **1991** BRADSTOCK *Fishing* 22 Southern spiny dogfish, spiky dog or koinga (*Squalus acanthias*) is brownish grey with a few white spots...As it makes poor eating and often is abundant, it is regarded as a nuisance... The dogfish with many white spots and no spines is..good eating—it's often what you get in fish and chips. Known variously as rig, lemon fish, gummy shark, smooth-hound dogfish, pioke, manga or *Mustelus lenticulatus*, it grows to more than 1 m.
2. With a modifier: **spotted dogfish**. *Mustelus lenticulatus*, GUMMY *n*.³ See also RIG *n*.¹
  1966 *Encycl. NZ* III. 708 Dogfish, spotted, or shark, gummy . . manga, mango . . *Mustelus lenticulatus*. **1981** WILSON *Fisherman's Bible* 224 Gummy Shark... Also known as Sweet William Shark, Spotted dogfish, gummy, and by the Maori name 'mango'. **1983** *Dominion* (Wellington) 2 Apr. 5 It seems mystery surrounds the fish commonly served..in our fish and chip shops—the rig, or spotted dog fish.

dogged, *a*. Farming. Equipped with, possessed of working dogs.
  1947 NEWTON *Wayleggo* 57 The gang that year [1932–35] was the most capable and strongly dogged I have ever worked with. *Ibid*. 89 Early November found me riding up country again newly dogged and horsed. **1971** NEWTON *Ten Thousand Dogs* 90 He wasn't very strongly dogged and, of course, that didn't help matters. His mainstay was a dog called Wad.

dogger-on. *Logging*. A workman who attaches the log strop to the log-hauling line. Cf. DOGHOOK 1, *dogman* a (DOG 5).
  1923 *Awards, etc*. 112 [Westland Timber Yards and Sawmill Employees] [Rates of wages] Horse log-trollyman [£]0 15[s.] 0[d.] Dogger-on and tracker 0 15 0 Winchman 0 14 0. **1951** *Awards, etc*. 454 [Westland Timber-Workers Award] [Rates of wages] Second bushman 4[s.] 1³⁄₄[d.] Skiddy 4 0¹⁄₄ Dogger-on and tracker 4 1³⁄₄ Snigger 4 3¹⁄₂.

doggin. [Poss. an alteration of *dog-end* a cigarette butt.] A cigarette-butt.
  1945 HENDERSON *Gunner Inglorious* 170 By crikey..wouldn't it be great to collect all the cigarette butts chucked away at the old cinemas back home? Remember all the 'doggins' round the lounges and entrances?

doghook. *Obs*. [Spec. or extended use of *doghook* a bale-hook, a small hook with handle attached.]
1. *Logging*. An iron bar with a bent prong or 'dog' for securing or hoisting logs, etc.
  1863 WELLS *Diary* (TS) (1970) 4 May 51 Tools hid in the bush under the first pine log west of my stream: Auger, truck irons, axe, mattock, doghook, hoe.

2. *fig.* In the phr. **to hang on with both hands and a doghook**, to hang on very firmly or tightly.
 1905 *Truth* 30 Sept. 7 I don't take much stock of texts, mum, but I reckon that one over your head is the real straight griffin, and a fellow ought to hang on to it with both hands and a doghook.

dog-leg. Also **dog-legged fence**. [f. the shape of the fence or fence-line: AND *dog-leg*, 1836; *-legged*, 1901.] A rough fence composed of crossed uprights at intervals, with poles resting one end in the crook and the other (often) on the ground, and often with a horizontal rail on top, the construction enabling the fence to follow the contours or lie of the land.
 1883 *Brett's Colonists' Guide* 18 The log fence and the dog-leg are the cheapest, and most common on new clearings. **1935** McKenzie *Gael Fares Forth* 88 The 'dog-legged' type of fence..was apparently a purely Canadian type..made of stakes of varying length and the trunks of small trees. **1943** *Memoirs of Pioneers* 6 We had to make [in Auckland c1865] what is called a 'dog-leg fence'. This was composed of stakes driven crossways in the ground and the long sticks laid with one end on the ground and the other end on the crossed stakes. **1955** Boswell *Dim Horizons* 45 Small paddocks were fenced, first the crude 'dog-leg' of roughly-split light posts..and later barbed wire. **1965** *NZ Geogr.* Oct. 147 The dog-leg fence, found in North America only in the Maritime Provinces of Canada, reappeared in the Nova Scotian settlement at Waipu, and from there spread to some other bush settlements in the north. It was constructed by driving two crossing stakes into the ground, and in the notch of these placing a third rail which followed the direction of the fence. **1988** McGill *Dict. Kiwi Slang* 38 *doglegged* shape of a crooked fence; from the proverbially crooked nature of a dog's hind leg.

dogskin.
a. The skin of the kuri or Maori dog (DOG *n.* 1), used to make or decorate early Maori clothing.
 1769 Cook *Journals* 27 Nov. (1955) I. 213 The habits of these [chiefs] were superior to any we had yet seen, the Cloth they were made on was of the best sort and cover'd on the out side with Dog skins put on in such a manner as to look agreeable to the Eye. **1777** Forster *Voyage Round World* I. 214 They had bits of dog-skin at the four corners of their cloaks. **1840** Mar. in Wilkes *US Exploring Exped.* (1852) I. 303 In his hand [Pomare] usually carries a short cloak of dog-skin, called *topuni*, *shupuni*, or *patutu*. **1869** *TrNZI* I. (rev. edn.) 344 [The Maori men to the making] of their prized dog-skin, or Kiwi-feather, clothing mats. **1882** Potts *Out in Open* 23 Robes of piu piu, korowai, or of dogskin, contributed a great variety of costume.
b. Used *attrib.* in Comb. **dogskin cloak**, **mat**, **robe**.
 1941 Sutherland *Numismatic Hist. NZ* 15 The most valuable gifts that can be bestowed include the **dogskin cloak**. **1832** Williams *Early Jrnls.* 6 Mar. (1961) 231 He stood in silence leaning on the end of his musket, a bill-hook bright as silver in his belt in front, and a handsome **dogskin mat** thrown carelessly over his shoulders. **1848** McLean in Cowan *Sir Donald Maclean* (1940) 36 The elder men were dressed in their best dogskin and *kaitaka* mats. **1894** *TrNZI* XXVI. 219 It [sc. the Maori dog] was a purely domesticated species..valued..for supplying the material for their much prized dogskin mats. **c1920** Beattie *Trad. Lifeways Southern Maori* (1994) 46 Kakahu ihupuni..is a dogskin mat. It has a whitau foundation to which are attached narrow strips of dogskin. **1940** Cowan *Sir Donald Maclean* 42 Te Rangihaeata rose, a tall gaunt savage in appearance, clothed in a dogskin mat. **1840** Mar. in Wilkes *US Exploring Exped.* (1852) I. 307 He was very feeble,... and clad in an old **dog-skin robe**.

dog trial. Usu. *pl.* Also (early) **sheep-dog trial(s)**. A trial or contest of sheep-dog and sheep-dog-handling skills.
 1890 *Otago Witness* (Dunedin) 20 Mar. 10 [Heading] The Sheep Dog Trial. The Waitaki Collie Dog Club's annual meeting commenced on Thursday morning. **1918** *Fielding Star* 20 Apr. 4 [Advt] National Dairy Show... Leaping Competitions and Sheep Dog Trials. **1947** Newton *Wayleggo* 31 The event of the year was my trip to the Springfield dog trials. **1948** *NZJAg.* Jan. LXXVI. 46 Sheep dog trials are tests of efficiency. The trial grounds are not training tracks, but testing grounds. **1959** Masters *Tales of Mails* 63 Kuripapanga was the scene of the first dog trial ever to be held in the North Island, and a hill there is still called Dog Trial Hill. **1960** Masters *Back-Country Tales* 163 Owing to dog trials being held that day at Patoka, Mr. Fitzpatrick, the hotel keeper was the only one left in the village with a car. **1975** Newton *Sixty Thousand on the Hoof* 111 It is in the dog-trial game that the Anderson family will be best known.
 Hence **dog-trialling** *vbl. n.*, the sport of running sheep-dogs in dog-trials; **dog-trialler**, one who competes in the sport of dog-trialling.
 1991 *Dominion* (Wellington) 24 Oct. 1 The show also features down-on-the-farm Kiwi entertainments, in keeping with the Bay's rural history, such as **dog trialling**. **1995** Anderson *House Guest* 176 He's a **dog trialler** then?

dog tucker.
1. Meat (esp. mutton) as food for working dogs. (Occas. applied to any inferior meat or food.)
 1933 *Press* (Christchurch) (Acland Gloss.) 7 Oct. 15 *Dog-tucker.*—Food for dogs. Old sheep kept for the purpose are called *d[og]-t[ucker]s*. **1947** Newton *Wayleggo* 42 He..was only luring the stag to the hut for dog-tucker. **1953** Stronach *Musterer on Molesworth* 13 From these we selected three for dog tucker and one for mutton, and four of us were told off to kill them. **1973** Fernandez *Tussock Fever* 42 As his first deer had been shot only half a mile from the hut, he staggered back a little later with a load of dog tucker.
2. a. An old or unsaleable sheep intended to be killed for (mainly farm) dog-tucker.
 1933 [see 1 above]. **1934** *Press* (Christchurch) (Acland Gloss.) 20 Jan. 15 *Dog tucker*... In the old days when Merino sheep were worth even less than they are now, it was the custom to throw in a few to the drover on delivery to make up for the losses on the road. They were called *d[og]t[ucker]*. E.g. 'I'll throw ten in for your dogs.' **1951** [see *red collar* (RED *a.* 2)]. **1965** Macnicol *Skippers Road* 90 'I'll kill a mutton and a dog-tucker after tea,' Archie remarked one night. **1971** Taylor *Plekhov Place* 59 'What are you doing tomorrow?' she asked. 'As little as possible. I have to kill a dog tucker.' **1981** Sutherland & Taylor *Sunrise* 72 'I suppose I'll have to kill a sheep now,' said Bill... 'Yeah. There's that dog tucker tomorrow.' **1995** *Dominion* (Wellington) 14 Jan. 14 She can do anything on a farm except kill dog-tuckers.
 Hence **dog tucker** *v. trans.*, to kill or prepare (an animal) for dog-tucker.
 1986 *Sunday Star* (Auckland) 20 July B16 He [a horse] had the most unusual formline in yesterday's Te Rapa racebook—BLORF—short for brought down, lost rider not in the first nine, ran off and fell. Laugh as much as you like, says Wilson, Blorf isn't ready to be dog-tuckered. **1994** Lasenby *Dead Man's Head* 109 He'll skin it [sc. a dead horse] and boil it down... Or dog-tucker it. There's a lot of meat on a horse.

b. *attrib.* Also **dog-tucker**. Of, or pertaining to, an inferior animal 'fit only for dog tucker'.
 1947 Newton *Wayleggo* 14 With the killing of mutton and dog tucker sheep, the musterers are finished for the day. **1961** Crump *Hang On a Minute Mate* 165 It only takes one swipe and you've got no more life expectancy than a dog-tucker ram. **1978** Sutherland *Elver* 74 Take a bit of meat for bait from the dog-tucker calf hanging in the pine tree by Pup's kennel. **1993** *Dominion* (Wellington) 23 Apr. 5 The round-up was a kneejerk reaction that would see 220 horses disposed of at 'dog-tucker' value.

3. *fig.* or *transf.* **a.** A poorly performing person, system, etc., or animal, a loser; *spec.* a racehorse given to losing or poor performance.
 1995 *Dominion* (Wellington) 7 Nov. 8 [Cartoon bubbles from a punter watching the race on TV.] Ah! The Melbourne Cup! The excitement, the colour. The glamour, the thrill. The anticipation. [The horse is not placed.] The bloody dogtucker! **1995** *Ibid.* 27 Nov. 1 [According to the Hon. Simon Upton, the industry] 'was seen five years ago as dog tucker but instead we've seen a far more efficient industry emerge'. **1996** *Western News* (Wellington) 3 May 1 Mr Prebble believes he has a great chance of beating Mrs Gardiner saying she is now 'dog tucker' since leaving National.
b. In the phr. **he wouldn't go out to a dog-tucker's picnic**, said of a reclusive person; **to be dog-tucker**, to be in a losing or 'no-win' position or situation.
 1984 Aug. p.c. Rosemary A Barnes, Spotswood, Cheviot. Local oral traditional use in Cheviot when speaking of recluses: he wouldn't go out to a dog-tucker's picnic. **1990** *Sunday Star* (Auckland) 28 Oct. 1 David Lange said it all in the 1987 campaign: 'If Labour fails to turn around the economy and reduce unemployment by 1990, then surely we will be dog tucker.' **1993** *Dominion* (Wellington) 25 Oct. 9 At that stage we knew we were dog tucker, but I couldn't have gone around saying we'd lose, because negativity breeds negativity.
c. Special Comb. **dog-tucker country**, lean and hungry unproductive country; **dog-tucker years**, the last, unproductive, and painful years of life; the declining years.
 1984 Marshall *Day Hemingway Died* 18 I'm not much interested in stretching out the dog-tucker years... I'd rather keep on going here a bit. **1992** Anderson *Portrait Artist's Wife* 49 He was too tall and skinny. 'Raised on dog tucker country,' sighed Nelson.

dog watch. [Transf. from nautical usage.] **a.** In various trades, the midnight to morning (occas. the whole-night) shift.
 1939 Belton *Outside the Law* 88 I had not forgotten the morning 'dog-watch' as we [police] called it [c1928]. This duty occurred about once in ten days. **1950** *NZ Post Office Eng. Course* (TS) 14 The Post Office likewise has its own phrases: 'clear down', 'six to clear', 'dog watch'. **1962** Evans *Waikaka Saga* 273 After this he went to the West Coast and worked in the Blackball [coal] mine on what was called 'the dog watch' because it was an all-night shift. **1983** *Metro* (Auckland) July 81 *Dog watch*. The late, late shift (usually 11 p.m.–7 a.m.) for [taxi] despatchers. A naval term—thought to have been coined by those who thought that particular watch to be 'a dog of a job'. **1992** Latham *Golden Reefs* 433 The 'day-shift' at Waiuta [goldmine] was 8 a.m. to 4 p.m., the afternoon or 'back-shift' was 4 p.m. to 12 midnight, and the 'night-shift' or 'dog-watch' from midnight to 8 a.m.

b. *Obs. fig.* A collective name for those who kept debate alive during the late-night parliamentary sessions of the 1890s.

dole bludger: see BLUDGER 3 b; **dole-bludging:** see BLUDGE *v.* 2.

dollar.

1. *Hist.* [AND 1 *Hist.* Spanish dollar circulating in NSW 1803–44.] As in early 19th century New South Wales, a Spanish dollar.
1826 BUSBY *Letter* 13 Feb. in McNab *Hist. Records* (1908) I. 653 Mr. Kent..in addition to his pay..had 940 dollars paid him, being one fourth of the value of the flax, for his merit in collecting it. **1833** WILLIAMS *Early Jrnls.* 21 Apr. (1961) 308 It appears that Satan through the means of these his agents has been very industriously circulating the idea of our intention to seize the Chiefs in a short time..and that for those who receive our instruction we are to receive dollars according to the rank of the individual. **1840** MATHEW *Journal* 16 Feb. in *Founding of NZ* (1940) 53 [The Governor's] distribution of presents [to the natives] gave..much dissatisfaction; and one vagabond who actually begged a Dollar of him had the impudence..to bring it back, and at Captain Hobson refusing to accept it, threw it in the River. **1840** POLACK *Manners & Customs* I. 183 The Spanish dollar is the favorite [*sic*] coin, as in all barbarous countries, where the distinction in coinage is known.

2. [AND 1902.] Before the introduction of decimal currency, the sum of five shillings, esp. as *half-dollar* (HALF- 2) a half-crown.
1908 *Truth* 22 Apr. 2 The average racecourse frequenter growls when he has lost a dollar. **1925** SCANLON *Much in Little* 31 Could you lend me a dollar till tomorrow? **1936** HYDE *Passport to Hell* 73 You can have a job at a ha'penny a day blocking the swamps, or a job at a dollar a day fighting for your King. **1941** [see 3 below]. **1964** DAVIS *Watersiders* 51 'What you boys want, Curly?' 'Dollar'... 'Yes. Dollar it is'... 'A whole five bob?' **1977** *NZ Numismatic Jrnl.* Oct. 15 The crown was called a *bull*, a *cartwheel*, a *caser*, *five bob*, and most familiar of all a *dollar*, the latter dating from the time when the rate of exchange was four US dollars to the pound... The half crown was called a *half-dollar*, a *half-bull*, *half-caser*.

3. *fig. pl.* Money in general.
1892 *Star* (Auckland) in Bailey & Roth *Shanties* (1967) 82 Down to Wellington we travel, M.H.R. and M.L.C., Where we blow the hard-earned dollars of our bleeding counteree. **1905** *Truth* 30 Sept. 1 She ought to be worth some dollars. **1914** GRACE *Tale Timbertown* 117 Where's the gold, the dollars. **1941** SUTHERLAND *Numismatic Hist. NZ* 63 Dealing with the tendency of the Maori to refer to all money as 'dollars'—a practise persisting to some extent with the Pakeha today—.. [1941 *Note*] Some New Zealanders use the term 'half-dollar' for 'half-a-crown'. **1987** *Chosen Place* 23 I'd better..buy some morning tea (which we'll eat, not drink) and pay for it in dollars and cents.

4. Since July 1967, the name of the standard unit of New Zealand currency.
1959 *NZPD* CCCXXXVIII. 351 The names for the major and minor units will be 'dollar' and 'cent'. **1964** *NZ Statutes* I. No.27 122 [Decimal Currency Act] The monetary unit of currency of New Zealand shall be the 'dollar'. **1974** MULDOON *Rise & Fall of a Young Turk* 76 We had had trouble with the name of the major unit. We [on the Decimal Currency Board] favoured dollar but did not want to say so too loudly... A weekly newspaper took a poll which showed that nearly half the people preferred to wear dollar as in Australia, so we went ahead with that.

dolly, *n.*[1] *Obs.* [Transf. use of Brit. dial. *dolly* a clothes-washing stick; an injured finger bound up in rags (cf. sense 2 below).]

1. *Fellmongering.* **a.** A tub with revolving blades or paddles (the 'dollies' proper) in which pelts are washed (or, occas., cured) (see also quot. 1908 b below).
1918 *NZJST* I. 165 Sheep and lamb skins are conveyed into another building, called the fellmongery, and after being washed in a 'dolly' they are painted on the flesh side. **1921** *Ibid.* IV. 158 The pelts are first washed in pits or 'dollies', with paddles revolving, in order to thoroughly remove as much as possible of adhering detritus. **1957** MACDONALD *Canterbury Frozen Meat Co.* 69 Generally there has been little change in fellmongering practice since 1892. Skins are still cold-water washed in 'dollies' or paddles.

b. Special Comb. **dollyman,** one who cleans skins in a fellmongery.
1908 *Awards, etc.* 211 [Meat-workers award] [Rates of wages] Fellmongery hands, pullers, painters, fleshers, pelt-classers, curing-dolly, steam-drier, dollymen, scudders, skin-washers, wool scourers and trimmers, 8s. per day. **1951** *Awards, etc.* 328 [NZ Freezing-Workers Award] [Rates of wages] *Pelt Department*—Lime dollymen and limers, per hour [£]0 4[s.] 7[d.].

2. A device to help sit a fractious horse.
1943 MANNERING *Eighty Years NZ* 42 The only way I could sit him was to have a 'dolly' in front and crupper behind... (A 'dolly' was a stout stick wrapped in a sack and held with straps on the dees of the saddle.)

Dolly, *n.*[2] *Prison.* A lesbian's fancy woman. Cf. MRS, DARL.
1968 TAYLOR in *Genetic Psychology Monographs* (1970) No.81 92 Female offenders of all ages were tattooed almost exclusively with tattoos that marked homosexual relationships they had with their young 'Mrs.,' teenage 'Darls,' or adult 'Dollies'.

dolly, *v. Obs.*

1. [Transf. from Brit. dial. and technical *dolly* to wash clothes in a dolly-tub.] *trans.* **1.** To wash by moving and rubbing in water.
1886 BUTLER *Glimpses Maoriland* 128 As there is barely room in this passage for [the sheep] to swim up and down, they 'dolly' one another, and rub all the dirt out of their fleeces.

2. [AND 1893.] *trans.* To crush (auriferous quartz) with a dolly, an apparatus for crushing and extracting gold. Also *intr.*
1978 MCARA *Gold Mining Waihi* 29 It may have been that the white 'hungry' appearance of much of the quartz on the surface discouraged earlier prospectors and they did not bother to test it by 'dollying' and washing a few samples. **1981** HUNT *Speaking a Silence* 47 I dolly in it [*sc.* a *dolly pot*] too if I come across quartz reef. **1992** LATHAM *Golden Reefs* 428 *Dolly*: To break up quartz with a piece of wood shod with iron in order to wash out the gold.

Hence **dolly pot,** see quot. 1938.
1938 *Auckland Weekly News* 28 Dec. 33 The dolly-pot..is the goldminer's morter [*sic*] and pestle, with which gold-bearing rock is powdered for the pay-dust. **1981** HUNT *Speaking a Silence* 47 He dug up a complete dolly pot, lid and all. That's what the real old-time miners used when they found a quartz reef; they were very heavy pots with extra thick bottoms. **1986** DEVANNY *Point of Departure* 11 Dad, the only man owning a dolly pot, had used to dolly the stolen gold for the men on tribute, amassing by this means a large collection of nuggets.

dolly's wax. [Poss. f. a rhyme for (*up to*) *tin tacks*, and/or a play on the fact that only the head and bust of a 'wax' doll were made of wax.] In the phr. **up to dolly's wax,** to the utmost; to the top. [*Note*] The phr. can have a sense 'up to scratch', up to a reasonable standard: e.g., The concreting is not up to dolly's wax. It must be done again.
1944 *Coral Dust* This box [*sc.* cactus stove] has to be filled up to dolly's wax with really hot flames.

dolphin.

1. Usu. with a modifier, any of the various marine mammals of the family Delphinidae, having a long beak and many pointed teeth.
[*Note*] In popular New Zealand use 'porpoise' is often erroneously used for 'dolphin', though the true 'porpoise' (currently defined in scientific use as a delphinid with no beak and spade-shaped teeth) is absent from New Zealand waters.
1885 *TrNZI* XVII. 198 There are also two species of dolphin very plentiful, which could be easily secured and used for oil and their skin for leather. **1918** *NZJST* I. 137 *Porpoises* and *dolphins* are most valuable for their skins and oil.

2. With a modifier: **bottlenose(d), common, dusky, Hector's, Risso's.**

(1) **bottlenose(d) dolphin.** *Tursiops truncatus*, a large (3–3.6 m) heavily-built beaked dolphin. Occas. *ellipt.* **bottlenose.** See also COWFISH 2.
1966 DOOGUE & MORELAND *Sea Anglers' Guide* 302 Bottlenosed Dolphin... *Tursiops truncatus*; cowfish. **1971** GASKIN *Whales Dolphins & Seals* 128 The Bottlenosed Dolphin or Cowfish *Tursiops truncatus*. **1985** DAWSON *NZ Whale & Dolphin Digest* 67 Bottlenose dolphins are by far the most studied and familiar cetacean, as they are the species most often kept in marinelands. **1990** BAKER *Whales & Dolphins* 108 In New Zealand, the sudden appearance of a group of bottlenose in such enclosed harbours as the Bay of Islands and Marlborough Sounds has been regarded as a forerunner to stormy weather.

(2) **common dolphin.** *Delphinus delphis*, a strongly-beaked dolphin of up to 2 m in length with a distinctive colour pattern of a purplish-black, saddle-shaped dorsal surface and a white ventral surface, frequently with a light blaze on the dorsal fin.
1922 *NZJST* V. 141 The common dolphin (*Delphinus delphis*) has a well-marked beak and a high falcate dorsal fin. **1966** DOOGUE & MORELAND *Sea Anglers' Guide* 303 Common Dolphin... *Delphinus delphis*. **1971** GASKIN *Whales Dolphins and Seals* 137 The common dolphin was the first species to be held in captivity in New Zealand. **1985** DAWSON *NZ Whale & Dolphin Digest* 64 Usually found in schools of about a dozen, Common Dolphins occasionally form schools of several thousand. **1990** BAKER *Whales & Dolphins* 112 The common dolphin can be recognised by its colour, distinct beak, and low, smoothly-sloping head. Each jaw bears 45–51 pairs of small teeth less than 3mm in diameter.

(3) **dusky dolphin.** Occas. *ellipt.* **dusky.** *Lagenorhynchus obscurus*, an almost beakless, streamlined dolphin, completely patterned in grey and white, up to 2 m in length and easily identified by its noisy, acrobatic behaviour.
1922 *NZJST* V. 140 The dusky dolphin..is perhaps as plentiful round the coast of New Zealand as the common porpoise. It can be distinguished from it by the falcate dorsal fin and the more pointed snout. It is black above and white below, with an oblique white band on the flanks. **1971** GASKIN *Whales Dolphins & Seals* 124 [Caption] The dusky dolphin: 1. ploughshare-

shaped head. 2. large dorsal fin, and black streaks invading the white flanks of the caudal range. **1985** Dawson *NZ Whale & Dolphin Digest* 71 There are several accounts of Dusky Dolphins attempting to rescue school-mates from nets. They are among the most altruistic of the dolphins... they will readily assist other dolphin species in distress, and there are reports of duskies coming to the aid of humans. **1994** *Evening Post* (Wellington) 17 Jan. 11 [I] am suddenly the focus of attention for three of the little duskys who are swimming around..me... At one stage we see a group of four duskys mating.

(4) **Hector's dolphin**. [f. the name of Sir James *Hector* (1834–1907), an eminent NZ scientist.] *Cephalorhynchus hectori*, a small species confined to New Zealand coastal waters. Also called *puffing pig* (see quot. 1993).
1966 Doogue & Moreland *Sea Anglers' Guide* 305 Hector's Dolphin... Confined to New Zealand..; native dolphin, New Zealand porpoise. **1971** Gaskin *Whales Dolphins & Seals* 61 Small dolphins, black and grey above, white colour. Dorsal fin very bluntly triangular... Hector's Dolphin. **1988** *Dominion Sunday Times* (Wellington) 22 May 1 New Zealand's only native dolphin is under threat of extinction... The total population of the rare hector's dolphin is 3000 to 4000, with about 660 living in the Banks Peninsula area. **1990** Baker *Whales & Dolphins* 118 On very calm days Hector's dolphins surface very quietly, just drifting to the surface with little or no splash. **1993** *Listener* 2 Jan. 29 Fishermen have nicknamed Hector's dolphins 'puffing pigs'.

(5) **Risso's dolphin**. [f. the name of Giovanni Antonio *Risso* (1777–1845), Italian naturalist.] *Grampus griseus*, a uniformly grey, but in older specimens extensively scarred dolphin, up to 3–4 m in length with underslung mouth and bulbous shallowly-grooved forehead. Of special significance in New Zealand as the dolphin Pelorus Jack.
1904 *NZ Gazette* 26 Sept. 2302 It shall not be lawful for any person to take the fish or mammal of the species commonly known as Risso's dolphin (*Grampus griseus*) in the waters of Cook Strait or of the bays, sounds, and estuaries adjacent thereto. **1922** *NZJST* V. 137 Risso's dolphin..is the first of the dolphin family to be mentioned. **1947** Powell *Native Animals* 90 *Risso's Dolphin*... This is best known to New Zealanders by one example, the famous 'Pelorus Jack,' which for many years attracted wide interest from its regular habit of playing about the bows of steamers in the vicinity of Pelorus Sound. **1960** Alpers *Book of Dolphins* 197 It was as Risso's Dolphin that Pelorus Jack was protected in 1904, not by an 'Act of Parliament' as the postcards said, but by an Order in Council, signed by the Governor of the Colony, Lord Plunket. **1971** Gaskin *Whales Dolphins & Seals* 132 Stranded Risso's dolphins can be positively distinguished from pilot whales by an examination of the teeth... Risso's dolphin almost invariably lacks teeth in the upper jaw, and those in the lower are confined to the anterior margin only. **1990** Baker *Whales & Dolphins* (2edn.) 103 The head of Risso's dolphin has a distinct 'melon'— it bulges forward and slopes very steeply down to the mouth, and has a vertical median crease on the forehead. There is no trace of a beak.

domain /dəˈmeɪn/. [Spec. use of a shortened form of *public domain* land reserved to the Crown; cf. 1860 *NZ Statutes* No.32 486 [Public Domains Act] An Act to provide for the Management of the Public Domains: see OED 3 b; AND Sydney Domain only.] A public park or reserve; often in local use as **the Domain**.

1. As **Government Domain** *obs.*, orig. the grounds surrounding Government House, Auckland; also those surrounding Government or Parliament House, Wellington.
1841 *Mathew to Hobson* Oct. in *GBPP 1842* (No.569) 185 As it is only five acres in extent, and is situated in the very centre of the town, overlooked from every part, it is utterly unfit for a Government Domain. **1857** Askew *Voyage Austral. & NZ* 350 [In Auckland] on the right, is the Government domain, a large tract of land reserved for botanical gardens. **1872** *TrNZI* IV. 301 A large coarse grass, common in woods and warm gullies, not hardy in the Government Domain; eaten by cattle.

2. As **the Domain**, land reserved by the Crown to be used as a park or other public purpose. **a.** In Auckland.
1860 *Richmond-Atkinson Papers* (1960) I. 645 Read the papers & did Maori, went for about half an hour in the Domain & found a fantail nest. **1874** Baines *Edward Crewe* 20 I was sitting on a hill side in the [Auckland] Domain when up came my two Antipodean aboriginals. **1890** Weston *Ko Meri* 111 They all passed..through Parnell into the shady Domain. **1919** Wilson *NZ Cities* (Auckland) 44 Then there is the Auckland Domain with its two hundred acres of native bush and..a tree-circled cricket ground. **1938** Hyde *Nor Yrs. Condemn* 236 There was a church service..and laying of wreaths at the foot of the Cenotaph, which would follow in the Domain grounds. **1983** *Evening Post* (Wellington) 2 July 14 Auckland possesses a vast, open stretch of tree-fringed village common called The Domain. **1990** *Listener* 30 July 8 As debates go, it's the most bizarre I've heard since they passed a law permitting the Pope to play cricket in the Auckland Domain.

b. In Christchurch.
1875 Rives *Jottings on the Spot* (Cant. Pub. Lib. TS) 7 Mar. 10 I took a constitutional in the domain before lunch but owing to the flatness of the country there is little to be admired. **1902** *Settler's Handbook NZ* 55 The whole is admirably set off by Hagley Park (400 acres in extent), the Domain and Botanical Gardens (79 acres).

c. In other local and general use, a public park, recreation ground, etc.
1920 Bolitho *With the Prince in NZ* 20 The Domain is a far spreading park land, with undisturbed native bush, botanical gardens, and recreation grounds. **1935** *Patea & Waverley Press* 14 Jan. 2 Not content with damaging property, they [*sc.* larrikins] annoyed some tourists who were camping in the Domain. **1952** *Here & Now* Sept. 30 And two pimply boys Whisper tales Of intercourse with schoolgirls In playgrounds and domains. **1964** Howe *Stamper Battery* 99 When the train arrived, most people made straight for the [Te Aroha] Domain to secure a shady spot for their picnic lunch. **1976** McDermott *Lost & Found NZ* 32 When you read 'domain' think 'park'. **1984** Edmond *High Country Weather* 5 It was a hundred small towns. You used to drive through them.., anywhere in the North Island. Fair Square grocery... A stringy little park labelled Town Domain. **1992** *Dominion* (Wellington) 16 Apr. 3 Mourners turned up for a public memorial service..at the Brighton domain.

3. Special Comb. **Domain Board**, a local, often elected, body set up to control a local domain.
1887 *Auckland Weekly News* 15 Jan. 17 The Domain board is defunct. **1890** *Otago Witness* (Dunedin) 25 Sept. 19 Our Domain Board (if there is such a body) have [*sic*] surely gone to sleep. **1908** *Consolidated Statutes* Appendix D. IV. 798 The Governor may..appoint such persons..as he thinks fit to be a Domain Board. **1925** *Patea & Waverley Press* 16 Mar. 2 Patea Domain Board: The matter of an extra cow for the Domain paddock was left in the hands of the Secretary. **1964** Norris *Settlers in Depression* 201 He will be best remembered for his work on the local Domain Board.

dome. Applied to dome-shaped objects.

1. [Ellipt. for *dome fastener*: used elsewhere but the common term in NZ for a *snap-*, *spring-* or *stud-fastener*: see OED.] A stud-fastener.
c1914 W.H.B. Orsman p.c. 1972: sold in the Havelock (Marlborough) store as 'domes' or 'dome fasteners' from at least the Great War. **1963** Frame *Reservoir* 39 The pair of little blue glass slippers..which now housed buttons, domes, needles, hooks and eyes. **1980** Leland *Kiwi-Yankee Dict.* 33 Dome. The snaps that you commonly find on garments in North America.

2. As **the Dome**, an area within Mount Eden Prison under a dome-shaped roof.
1980 MacKenzie *While We Have Prisons* 96 *dome* central area of Mt Eden from which the cell wings radiate

domestic purposes benefit. Usu. as **DPB**, **dpb**, often in the phr. **on the dpb**. A State benefit payable to a family care-giver who has little or no other income.
1972 *Social Security in NZ* 243 To overcome certain inconsistencies it was decided in 1968 to group emergency benefits payable to women who have lost the regular support of their husbands and who qualify for an emergency benefit, under one generic term of 'domestic purposes benefit'. *Ibid.* 260 We recommend that: (17) A statutory domestic purposes benefit..be provided for solo parents, for women required to care for an infirm or sick person and for women whose previous domestic commitments have affected (or are deemed to have affected) their ability to obtain employment. **1973** *Social Security Amendment Act* s27(b)(2) Subject to the provisions of this Part of this Act, an applicant shall be entitled to receive a domestic purposes benefit if the Commission is satisfied that— (a) The applicant has attained the age of 16 years and; (b) The applicant is caring for a dependent child or children. **1982** Oliver *Poor Richard* 18 She's a good little mother is kanga scraping along on the d p b no mr about the place just roo. **1988** Macrae *Awful Childhoods* 24 It was a cheap loan but while she was on the DPB, more than enough to cope with. **1991** *Listener* 11 Mar. 35 The bottom line is we wouldn't have cut the dpb. I'm telling you the case, we wouldn't have done it.

dominican: see GULL 2 (1).

Dominion.

1. a. Also *joc.* **Dominyong** (parodying the pronunciation of esp. Peter Fraser, Labour Prime Minister 1940–49), New Zealand as a self-governing country of the British Empire (now Commonwealth), esp. as **the Dominion**, a designation or title accepted in 1907, formally defined in 1926 in the Balfour Report, integrated into the Imperial Statute of Westminster in 1931, and, being considered inappropriate as a descriptive title of an independent member of the Commonwealth, replaced by 'Realm' in the Royal Style and Title adopted in 1953. Contrast COLONY.
1907 *NZ Gaz.* (Suppl.) in *Speeches & Documents* (1971) 269 By resolutions passed by the House of Representatives on the 12th July, 1907, and by the Legislative Council on the 16th July, 1907, addresses were forwarded to His Majesty the King respectfully requesting that the necessary steps might be taken to change the designation of New Zealand from the

Colony of New Zealand to the Dominion of New Zealand; and it is hereby notified that His Majesty the King, by Order in Council dated 9th September, 1907, and by Proclamation issued 10th September, 1907, has been graciously pleased to change the style and designation of the Colony of New Zealand to 'The Dominion of New Zealand'; such change to take effect on and from Thursday, the 26th day of September, 1907. **1913** CARR *Country Work* 9 The Dominion consists of three main islands, the North, the South, and Stewart Island. **1921** *NZJST* III. 259 The Shacklock range is used practically universally in the Dominion. **1943** *NZEF Times* 30 Aug. 6 It's grim in the old Dominyong, all right. **1968** SEDDON *The Seddons* 199 In 1908 he [Sir Joseph Ward] attended an Imperial Conference. When he returned home he announced that we were no longer a Colony but a Dominion... A few Government members were luke-warm about saying good-bye to the term 'Colony'.

b. *attrib.* or *adj.*
1910 *Truth* 1 Oct. 4 The proposal of the Government to brand all Dominion productions, 'Made in New Zealand', is viewed by manufacturers with the feelings of a patent medicine fiend who is compelled to swallow his own concoctions. **1918** *Kia-ora Coo-ee* (1981) 15 Nov. I. 6 The Dominion Government is giving £ for £ toward the total sum required. **1925** WEBB *Miss Peters' Special* 99 If a few of our Dominion boys got on to the Germans they'd have it all settled up quick and lively. **1946** [see SILENT DIVISION]. **1959** SINCLAIR *Hist. NZ* 238 Just as Massey had in 1907 opposed the adoption of the title 'Dominion'.., now, in office, he declined to participate in the formulation of the concept of 'dominion status'.

2. Special Comb. **Dominion Day**, September 26 observed in New Zealand as a bank holiday only celebrating the anniversary of the coming into Dominion status; **dominion goose**, a joc. var. of COLONIAL GOOSE; **dominion pudding**, a steamed pudding often containing dried fruit; **dominion sausage**, an orig. patriotic name replacing *German sausage* (GERMAN) during WW1 and after, now usu. LUNCHEON SAUSAGE; **Dominion-wide**, *a.* and *adv.*, national, throughout New Zealand;
1907 *NZ Mail* in Bromby *Eye Witness Hist.* (1985) 90 Yesterday, September 26, will stand in the records as the first **Dominion Day**. **1910** *Public Holidays Act* 1 Geo.V s2(b) Where in any Act or in any award or industrial agreement reference is made—.. (b) To Dominion Day, such reference shall hereafter be deemed to be the fourth Monday in September. **1987** *Evening Post* (Wellington) 26 Sept. 5 The Dominion Day birthday shared. Eighty years ago tomorrow New Zealand became a dominion and Frances Flett Dominion Daker was born at Arrowtown. **1943** CAMPBELL *Postscripts of Crowbar* 78 **Dominion Goose.** [1943 *Note*] Formerly Colonial. **1987** ELDRED-GRIGG *Oracles & Miracles* 114 She'd just opened the pudding bag to show off a big puffy white **dominion pudding**. **1989** McGILL *Dinkum Kiwi Dict.* 26 *The Dominion pudding* raisins and batter, first appearing to celebrate our Dominion status in 1907. **c1938 Dominion sausage** known to Ed. as a common alternative Marlborough name for *German sausage*. **1953** *Evening Post* (Wellington) 24 Mar. 3 [Advt] A **Dominion-wide** organisation has a vacancy for a male clerk aged 17-20 for duties of a general clerical nature.

dommyknocker: see DONGER-KNOCKER.

don. *Obs.* RINGER *n.*[1] 1.
1876 *Otago Witness* (Dunedin) 11 Nov. 130 The crack shearer in a shed can often shear 100, 120, and even 180 sheep daily... And such a man..will very frequently make the greatest possible exertion to keep up his high daily score, and have the high honour..of being termed 'the don' or 'the ringer of the shed'.

donah /ˈdʌunə/. *Obs.* [f. Brit. slang ad. Spanish *doña* a woman: AND 1874.] A girlfriend; a sweetheart.
1896 *Tom Bracken's Annual* I. 38 [Lad of the smart set speaks.] Girls were never punctual—even 'Donahs'. **1905** *Truth* 12 Aug. 8 He was trailing a spoony couple and became..excited when viewing the manner in which the young fellow kissed his 'donah'. **1906** *Ibid.* 20 Oct. 6 [Heading] Dancing Donahs.

Donald Duck. Rhyming slang for 'fuck', an act of sexual intercourse.
1982 NEWBOLD *Big Huey* 248 Donald Duck (n) Act of sexual intercourse. Rhyming slang. **1985** *Metro* (Auckland) June 65 'Women sleep under here [*sc.* Grafton Bridge, Auckland] too,' says Brian. 'All over 18. They like a 'donald duck'..I don't say no.'

dong, *v.* [AND 1916.] *trans.* To hit, to strike (esp. to punch). Also *fig.*, to 'hit' with a fine.
c1900 p.c. C.R. Carr, Mowai Red Cross Home, 1951: used by Dunedin schoolchildren c1890–1900 for 'hit, punch'. **1938** *Press* (Christchurch) (McNab Slang) 2 Apr. 18 [Slang of the N.Z.E.F.] 'To dong' and 'to knock cold' are plain. **1943** MARSH *Colour Scheme* 220 They [*sc.* Maori warriors] used to dong one another with those things [*sc.* adzes]. **1959** MCLEOD *Tall Tussock* 72 Joe was trying to dong him [*sc.* a wild pig] with his mustering stick and swearing and shouting. **1968** BALLANTYNE *Sydney Bridge* 6 'I'll dong you, boy!' he shouted. **1986** *Listener* 25 Oct. 48 I read in the paper the other day of a man who was fined $100 with court costs $35, and was then donged $3.50 GST on the court costs.

donga /ˈdɒŋə/. [f. South African *donga* a Zulu native name for a steep-sided gully: AND 1902.]
1. *Boer War, WW1, WW2.* A (small) gully, or dry water course.
1907 HAWDON *New Zealanders & Boer War* 64 [Trooper Barry quoted] 'some of our scouts were down a donga and could not get out in daylight.' **1915** *NZ Herald* (Auckland) in Bromby *Eye Witness Hist.* (1985) 126 The land [at Anzac] rises gradually in a series of hills and ridges... It is broken by deep nullahs and dongas. **1924** AUSTIN *Official Hist. NZ Rifle Brigade* 41 Our battalion was held up for some time by hot rifle and machine-gun fire from a donga. **1959** SLATTER *Gun in My Hand* 225 The O.C. said when the Japs land we'll chase them into the donga, we'll chase them into the matagouri and he really believed it because he was in the first war.

2. *Golfing local.* A dip or hollow in the course.
1948 p.c. K.J. Cullinane. *donga* used by Featherston golfers. **1960** *Hutt Municipal Golf Links: Card of Local Rules.* No 7: Tee shot finishing in 'Donga' may be brought back on to fairway without penalty.

3. *transf.* In the phr. **in the donga**, in trouble.
1955 *BJ Cameron Collection* (TS July) donga in the donga In the cart.

donger /ˈdɒŋə/. [f. DONG *v.* + -ER.]
1. Mainly *fishermen.* A heavy wooden club (for stunning fish).
1960 HILLIARD *Maori Girl* 84 Netta saw..the donger on a loop of leather. **1963** *Evening Post* (Wellington) 4 Apr. 29 Within seconds a beautiful blue [Mao Mao] was threshing in the bottom of the boat and Johnny was reaching for the cray and his donger... Doubling the crayfish over he pounded the claws into a pulp.

2. One who stuns (animals) with a club.
1984 TRAIL *Child of the Arrow* 87 I did not fully understand what this dawn ritual was all about and was horrified to discover that some of the trapped rabbits were still alive and had to be donged on the head. I was to be the donger while he was busy skinning the dead ones.

3. *fig.* [Poss. an extension or elaboration of *dong* penis.] The penis.
1985 BENTLEY & FRASER *Grand Limerick Tour* No.40 During choir practice at Otorohanga The bell-ringer displayed his new donger; Some thought it much thicker Than the curate's or vicar's, And everyone said it was longer. **1988** LAY *Fools on Hill* 51 'How's the donger?' 'Bit of suturing, but still in one piece.'

donger-knocker /ˈdɒŋə-/, /ˈdɒŋgə-/, *n. Children.* [Poss. orig. a familiar alteration of DONG a hit, a blow (or DONGER) + *knocker*, or *bomb(y)* + *knocker*; or an interaction of both as in *dommy-knocker*.] Also as **bommy-knocker** (popularized by Cowley and Melser in the book quoted below), **dommy-knocker, dongyknocker.** In mainly children's fanciful use, a striking weapon or club to use on enemies.
c1938 *donger-knocker* was a Marlborough nursery word for a stick or other 'bludgeon' usu. the implement of a humorous threat. **1980** COWLEY & MELSER *The Hungry Giant* 2 'I want some bread!' roared the giant. 'Get me some bread, or I'll hit you with my bommy-knocker'. **1988** McGILL *Dict. Kiwi Slang* 38 *dommyknocker* a stick to beat other kids with, aka *bommyknocker*; origins unknown. **1989** McGILL *Dinkum Kiwi Dict.* 26 *dongyknocker* a club, cousin of dommyknocker, invoking the concept of a dong or knock, familiar among possum poppers, or trappers.

donk, *n.*[1] [A shortened form of *donkey.*]
1. [AND 1907.] A donkey or mule.
1915 BENNETT in Manson *Doctor Agnes Bennett* (1960) 75 All the villages alive with blue-gowned fellaheen marketing; dear little donks and groaning old camels. **1919** WAITE *New Zealanders at Gallipoli* 33 [Caption] 'Donks.' These big mules of the N.Z. Divisional Train were bred in North America.

2. A horse, esp. a racehorse.
1952 NEWTON *High Country Journey* 76 However the station still has a few old donks at the homestead. **1959** SLATTER *Gun in My Hand* 71 She was always doing her money cold on the donks. **1960** MUIR *Word for Word* 224 'There's no such horse as Kiwi Song.' 'Too right, there is. Just a young donk but not a bad pacer at that.'

donk *n.*[2], **donkey** *n.*[1] [Abbrev. and transf. use of *donk*(ey-engine.]
1. *Forestry.* HAULER.
1952–53 *NZ Forest Service Gloss.* (TS) Hauler. A portable engine equipped with drum and cable, and powered by steam or internal combustion. syn Donkey (a)

2. An engine, prob. orig. an aircraft engine.
1981 JOHNSTON *Fish Factory* 121 Better pull the motor and gear-box out and get them both done up, Jamie. I've heard your donk in the mornings and it's running rough. **1981** CHARLES *Black Billy Tea* 89 Young Bradshaw's the boy who is flying this plane, She is as full as a tick and it's pouring with rain. Things are not going good—his donk's on the blink—Then he puts up a blue and she dives in the drink. [1981 *Note*] his donk's on the blink: his engine is giving trouble (airman's slang).

donkey *n.*[2] Special Comb. **donkey-deep**, in the phr. **to be donkey-deep in** [the original reference is obscure], to be immersed in, 'up to one's neck' in; **donkey lick** [AND 1890], to defeat decisively (esp. in sport); **donkey vote** [AND 1962], the vote of those whose choice is made from the candidates' names occurring first in alphabetical order on the ballot paper.
  1918 *Chron. NZEF* 2 Aug. 12 The T.M.'s are **donkey-deep** in cricket. **c1926** THE MIXER *Transport Workers' Song Book* 67 I'm 'donkey-deep' in fractions Since I got the ha'p'ny rise I'm on the 'skin' in decimals, And my brain is all afire To try and make the increase spread. **1960** *Dominion* (Wellington) 8 Aug. 13 In the expressive idiom of New Zealand rugby the All Blacks '**donkey licked**' Transvaal... Their victory, decisive. **1987** *Sunday News* (Auckland) 2 Aug. 27 Road safety campaigner Herb Bickley is hoping to win more than the '**donkey vote**' at the general election on August 15.

donkey room. *Watersiders.* [Orig. uncertain: p.c. Ron Smith (Wellington, 1994), poss. derives from the name orig. given to an enclosed area on the Wellington wharves containing a donkey engine in which room watersiders would find shelter and warmth during inclement weather in the days before permanent shelter was built.] A room or space at the work-place where (wharf) workers congregate for various purposes. See also DONKO.
  1926 DEVANNY *Lenore Divine* 257 On the first payday they each had about five pounds to draw. At eleven o'clock..Lafe and Holly ranged themselves in the queue in the [wharf] 'donkey room'. **1975** *Evening Post* (Wellington) 17 May 2 The mission was still hoping to move into the upstairs section... This was formerly the watersiders' dining and meeting area and was known in the old days as the 'donkey room'.

donko /ˈdɒŋkʌu/. [Poss. an abbrev. and alteration of DONKEY ROOM q.v.] A room in a workplace set aside for workers' smoko, meals, etc.
  1976 MORRIESON *Pallet on Floor* 53 Hastening..up the stairs to the 'donko' to wrap the sacking known as 'sneakers' around his boots; going down these same old slippery stairs from one of the freezing chambers. **1981** p.c. Stone in a letter to Editor *Heinemann NZ Dict.* 28 Apr. May I suggest the inclusion of the word 'Donko' in any subsequent edition of your New Zealand Dictionary. The word, which appears to mean 'the lunch room or similar facilities for workers in a factory'. The word appears to have fairly wide usage in New Zealand and I have spoken to several Australians and found them unaware of it. **1982** *Listener* 21 Aug. 49 Can you tell me the origin of the word 'donko'? My correspondent assures me it is a New Zealand term for 'the tea room of a factory or work-place'. The report comes from Wanganui. **1984** *Listener* 14 Apr. 13 In the woolstores..smoko was held in the donko, where we'd adjourn after working like billyo.

donnie. Also **donny.** [Ellipt. for *donnybrook* a brawl or noisy argument: f. *Donnybrook fair* held in Donnybrook a suburb of Dublin.] A brawl or violent argument.
  1960 HILLIARD *Maori Girl* 257 'There was a donny down at the Foresters tonight,' he said 'Couple of them..was belting him with a bottle.' **1961** CRUMP *Hang On a Minute Mate* 164 Some gate-crashing bushwhackers had picked on one of their blokes and it looked like a real donnie coming up.

donny, var. DONNIE.

doodackie /ˈduˌdæki/.
1. A thingumebob; HOODICKY. (In use c1940 much earlier than the quot. (Ed.))
  1988 McGILL *Dict. Kiwi Slang* 38 *doodackie* thingummybob, or humorous word for something you have no name for; a local variation of doodad, doodah, dooflickey, etc.
2. As **doodackied up** [poss. f. an elaboration of joc. *doed up*], spruced up; dolled up.
  1947 WALSH *Fourth Point of Star* 12 Anyway..Matron must have seen John waiting here, all doodackied up [to meet his girlfriend].

doodee, var. DUDEE(N).

doodle-em (doodlum) buck, varr. TOODLE-EM-BUCK.

doolan.
a. Occas. **doolin.** Also init. cap. [f. the common Irish surname.] Also in familiar form **doolie.** A, usu. Irish, Catholic; occas. an Irish person. See also MICKY DOOLAN.
  c1935 'doolies' [see MICKY DOOLAN]. **1940** SARGESON *Man & Wife* (1944) 19 It sounded pretty awful to me, that sort of praying. Because I'm a Doolan myself, and Mrs. Bowman was always down on the churches. **1959** SLATTER *Gun in My Hand* 60 And in peace the civilians must have something to hate too. The Dutchies or the Pommies or the Doolins or somebody. **1963** PEARSON *Coal Flat* 63 They had called him 'the Doolan bugger'—*Doolan* on their tongues meant an Irish Catholic. **1980** LAWRY *Good Luck & Lavender* 77 This fellow measured far short of what they wanted for their daughter, and anyway, he was a 'doolan'. **1984** CAMPBELL *Island to Island* 87 We'd gang up on kids who chucked off at us—like the boys from the Catholic home... We'd call them 'doolans', 'doolies', 'Mickey Doolans'—or worse. **1993** *Contact* (Wellington) 5 Aug. 3 The classics are ignored by St Patrick's College band, Downstream Doolies.
b. *attrib.* passing into *adj.* (Roman) Catholic.
  c1962 BAXTER *Horse* (1985) 42 Horse had not been in a Doolan church before. **1987** SLIGO *Final Things* 8 The Doolan priest who was always hanging around the convent, as everybody knew.

doolie: see DOOLAN.

doos, dos: see FAIR *a.* 1.

do over, *v.* [AND 1944.] To treat (usu. a person) harshly, roughly or dishonestly; to thrash; to scold severely.
  1866 BURGESS *Confessions* (1983) 118 And since we are going to do these people over (his very words) I think we had better prevent him from doing us any harm hereafter. **1959** SLATTER *Gun in My Hand* 44 The terror of Featherston camp he was. I tried to trim him down but he did me over proper. **1960** MUIR *Word for Word* 255 You're bloody lucky I don't do you over just for being such a nark. **1984** *Evening Post* (Wellington) 6 Apr. 20 [Comic strip] The Murphy's pigs are gonna do me [*sc.* the Dog] over because they think I'm responsible for the pig carcass in the river mud. **1991** [see DOG *n.* 7].

dopiness. *Farming.* [f. *dopey* stupid, half-asleep + *-ness.*] A name given to deficiency disease(s) in sheep marked by debility or sluggishness.
  1929 *TrNZI* LIX. 412 The worst soils for 'dopiness' as the local farmers call the disease [*sc.* bush-sickness]. **1932** *Discovery* Nov. 357 Recent investigations in New Zealand testify to..the value of top dressing of pastures with lime and superphosphate where sheep are affected with dopiness diseases. **1936** BELSHAW et al. *Agric. Organiz. NZ* 81 'Dopiness' [or calcium deficiency is found] on soils derived from fine volcanic dust or mud showers. A soil on which 'dopiness' develops is a leached loam and is found on deteriorated lands. **1943** *NZJST* XXIII. 323A The result [for sheep] is a high mortality in young lambs, an increased susceptibility of the ewe to 'dopiness'. **1950** *NZJAg.* July LXXXI. 3 Some green, succulent feed just before and at lambing assists in the prevention of diseases associated with lambing—dopiness (twin lamb disease or ante-partum paralysis) and milk fever.
  Hence **dopie** *a.* or *adv.*, applied to a sheep suffering from a deficiency disease. Cf. DOZY *a.*
  1933 *Press* (Christchurch) (Acland Gloss.) 7 Oct. 15 *Dozie.*—Country where sheep lose condition and do not thrive—go *dopie*, in fact—is called d[ozie]. I have heard shepherds speak of d[ozie] sheep also. It is very likely the Scots for *dopie*.

do-ray-me /dʌuræiˈmi/. [A play on and elaboration of the homophones *dough*, and *do(h)* from the Tonic Solfa.]
  1985 MITCALFE *Hey Hey Hey* 64 'What you doin' out so late, small fry? You got no do-ray-me?' 'Do-ray-me?' 'You know, gold. What it takes. Green stuff, money, boy, money!'

dory. [Spec. or transf. use of northern hemisphere *dory.*]
1. Any of various thin, deep-bodied sea-fish of the fam. Zeidae having capacious, tubelike mouths. See also *oreo dory* (OREO).
  1842 GRAY *Fauna* in Dieffenbach *Travels in NZ* (1843) II. 211 *Capros australis*... This is probably the Dory mentioned by Polack. **1855** TAYLOR *Te Ika A Maui* 625 The *Dory* also belongs to New Zealand, but is very rarely captured. **1880** SENIOR *Travel & Trout* 288 Amongst the sea-fishes fit for food there are..a number of periodical fishes..and these include frost-fish..dory..and garfish. **1892** *NZ Official Handbook* 167 Of the edible [pelagic] fishes [are]..the frostfish.. kingfish, dory, warehou, mackerel, and garfish. **1986** PAUL *NZ Fishes* 73 Dories are thin, deep-bodied fishes and apart from the common John Dory are generally found in deep water.
2. With a modifier: **mirror, silver.**
  (1) **mirror dory.** *Zenopsis nebulosus.* See quot. 1982.
  1922 *NZJST* V. 95 *Mirror Dory.* During April the trawler 'Nora Niven' secured small numbers of mirror dory in about 40 fathoms in Cook Strait... They were sold in Wellington as 'silver dory'. **1957** PARROTT *Sea Angler's Fishes* 52 The Mirror Dory is found, as far as is known in northern waters, and, as far as I know, has not been recorded off the coast of the South Island. **1982** AYLING *Collins Guide* (1984) 181 Mirror dories are a uniform silver in colour, so bright as to be almost mirror-like... They are commoner around northern New Zealand where they have been caught commercially.
  (2) **silver dory.** *Cyttus novae-zealandiae.* (See also quot. 1922 (1) above.) See also BOARFISH.
  1911 *Rec. Canterbury Mus.* I. 190 *Cyttus Novae-Zealandie... Silver Dory.* **1921** *NZJST* IV. 121 *Silver-dory.* A deep-water species secured by line fishermen. **1956** GRAHAM *Treasury NZ Fishes* 182 When taken from the net the Silver Dory has a habit of distending its mouth and ejecting regurgitated quantities of Shrimps and other food in a partly digested state. **1967** NATUSCH *Animals NZ* 216 *Cyttus*, the silver dory, is similar [to the John Dory], but without the dark marking, and its

DOSING-STRIP

'silver' is a bit tarnished. **1984** *Marlborough Express* (Blenheim) 22 Aug. 6 There are also ling and school shark..squid and silver dory..electric skates and others with saw toothed snouts.

dosing-strip: see DOG DOSING 2.

doss, *v.*

1. As **doss down** [a var. of Brit. *doss*: recorded earliest in NZ], to get a shakedown or temporary sleeping-place for the night; to sleep in rough circumstances.
   1896 *NZ Alpine Jrnl.* II. 9. 169 Hodgkins and I 'dossed down' by the side of the rock. **1904** CRADOCK *Sport in NZ* 17 Allow [the swagger] to 'doss down' in a barn.

2. As **doss out**, to sleep outdoors.
   1909 *Truth* 3 July 4 His offence, if it can so be called, consisted in 'dossing-out', or in begging food to keep body and soul together.

Hence **doss-down, doss-out** *n.* [*doss* used elsewhere but recorded with a suffix earliest in NZ: see OED *n.*² 1], a shakedown; a rough, makeshift bed; an outdoor sleep or sleeping place.
   1892 CARRICK *Romance Wakatipu* 16 [The bed] was accounted a luxury..compared with the doss-down the digger in pursuit of his calling was accustomed to. **1943** HISLOP *Pure Gold* 117 I thought it..a great place for a doss-out.

dotterel. Also **dotteril, dottrel**. [Transf. use of the northern hemisphere name *dotterel*.]

1. Any of several wading birds of the family Charadriidae (plovers) resembling the European dotterel (*Eudromias morinellus*). See also PLOVER, POHOWERA, TUTURIWHATU, TUTURUATU.
   1871 HUTTON *Catalogue Birds NZ* 24 Charadrius bicinctus... Dotterel. **1882** POTTS *Out in Open* 131 Of the wilder ground birds, swift of wing, of wandering or migratory habits; the dotterel (*Charadrius bicinctus*), the oyster-catcher or sea-pie.. both..do 'yeoman's service' as insect feeders. **1904** HUTTON & DRUMMOND *Animals NZ* 202 *The Dotterel.—Tuturiwatu. Ochthodromus obscurus.* Ibid. 203 The Dotterel is another bird that has had to beat a retreat before civilisation. At one time it was found on the Canterbury Plains, but it has now gone up into the mountains of the back country. **1919** *TrNZI* LI. 224 Dotterel *Pluviorhynchus obscurus...* In Stewart Island it occurs in fair numbers..visiting the bare tops of the high country. **1928** BAUCKE *Manuscript* (Bishop Museum Memoirs Vol.IX No.5 343–382) in Skinner & Baucke *Moriorls* 358 The most important [Chatham Island] edible sea-birds: turiwati tchūriwat' dottrel [sic].

2. With a modifier: **banded, black-fronted, New Zealand**.

(1) banded dotterel. *Charadrius bicinctus,* a small brown and white shore bird, with two bands of colour across throat and breast, and having two subspecies, the **banded dotterel** (*C. b. bicinctus*) and the **Auckland Island banded dotterel** (*C. b. exilis*). See also TUTURIWHATU.
   1870 *TrNZI* II. 48 The banded Dotteril [sic] flies around with warning note, whilst its grey-clad young hide cunningly behind some stick or stone. **1904** HUTTON & DRUMMOND *Animals NZ* 204 *The Banded Dotterel.— Pohowera. Ochthodromus bicinctus.* **1914** GUTHRIE-SMITH *Mutton Birds & Other Birds* 108 The spots most closely searched had been where Banded Dotterel or Stilt would have chosen to lay, that is, on slightly raised terraces of broken stone. **1921** GUTHRIE SMITH *Tutira*

222

208 The Banded Dotterel..following the plough and harrow may become a common sight perhaps where before it was unknown. **1932** STEAD *Life Histories NZ Birds* 87 At his best the cock Banded Dotterel in his breeding dress is an exceedingly handsome bird. **1947** POWELL *Native Animals NZ* 81 Banded Dotterel..or Tuturuwhatu is a characteristic little bird of the sand dunes, river beds and tussock clad plains. **1955** OLIVER *NZ Birds* 262 *Auckland Islands Banded Dotterel Charadrius bicinctus subsp...* A male, nearly mature, bird from Adams Island is similar in coloration to the New Zealand mainland form. **1966** FALLA et al. *Birds NZ* 123 Banded Dotterel *Charadrius bicinctus..*Double-banded Dotterel, Mountain Plover, Tuturiwhatu, Pohowera... A handsome small plover easily recognised in breeding dress..when both male and female have *two bands*—one black and narrow on the lower neck, the other chestnut and wider on the breast. **1967** NATUSCH *Animals NZ* 261 The banded dotterel..runs very fast, as if on wheels. **1985** *Reader's Digest Book NZ Birds* 180 *Banded Dotterel Charadrius bicinctus... Pohowera, tuturiwhatu, double-banded plover.* **1995** ANDERSON *House Guest* 72 The maternal behaviour of a banded dotterel mother..left Lisa speechless with joy.

(2) black-fronted dotterel. *Charadrius melanops*, a small distinctively marked bird self-introduced from Australia.
   1955 OLIVER *NZ Birds* 265 A black-fronted Dotterel was observed..at Ahuriri Lagoon, near Napier, on August 29th, 1954. **1966** FALLA et al. *Birds NZ* 125 First recorded in New Zealand in 1954, near Napier, the Black-fronted Dotterel is now strongly established in Hawke's Bay. **1984** SOPER *Birds NZ* 93 Black-fronted Dotterels are birds of stony riverbeds, over which they run at great speed.

(3) New Zealand dotterel. *Charadrius obscurus*, a large native species nesting mainly in the n. North Island and in the s. South Island, the males in their breeding dress (June to December) having red breasts and bellies. See also *dusky plover, red-breasted plover* (PLOVER 2 (2), 2 (4)), TUTURIWHATU, TUTURUATU.
   1888 BULLER *Birds NZ* II. 1 (New-Zealand Dottrel)... Tuturiwhati and Tuturuwhatu... It subsists chiefly on small crustaceans, mollusca, and sand-hoppers, and pursues its prey on foot. **1897** *TrNZI* XXIX. 191 *Charadrius obscurus* (New Zealand Dottrel) [sic]. Mr Marklund has sent me two skins of this well-known species, in summer plumage, which he obtained..on Stewart Island. **1914** GUTHRIE-SMITH *Mutton Birds & Other Birds* 104 On these several hundred acres of sand drift, dune, and stone strewn plain, each year a few of the New Zealand Dotterel breed. **1949** *NZ Bird Notes* III. 128 In the small bays in and near the Hokianga Harbour..New Zealand dotterels were quite numerous and many had young birds on the wing. **1955** OLIVER *NZ Birds* 257 *New Zealand Dotterel. Tuturiwhatu...* The New Zealand Dotterel breeds in sandy places along the coast or it moves to higher ground perhaps far inland. **1966** FALLA et al. *Birds NZ* 125 Red-breasted (New Zealand) Dotterel... A squat, broad-winged dotterel with a robust bill. **1970** SANSOM *Stewart Islanders* 204 North of Duck Creek..is the place to see the red-breasted New Zealand dotterel, the size of a slim bantam hen but not as fussy. **1980** LOCKLEY *House Above Sea* 181 New Zealand boasts four endemic waders not found elsewhere in the world. These..[include] the New Zealand dotterel, red-breasted in summer, rather curiously nesting in two discrete groups, one in the Hauraki Gulf, the other far away at and around Stewart Island.

dotteril, dottrel, varr. DOTTEREL.

doub: see DUB *n.*¹ 2.

DOUBLE

double, *n., a.* and *adv.* [Various uses of *double* two(fold), twice as much, two of a sort together, twice the size, to twice the extent, etc.]

A. *n.*

1. *Farming.* See *double-fleecer* (DOUBLE B).
   1972 MCLEOD *Mountain World* 310 *Double:* Sheep which has missed shearing once or more. **1973** NEWTON *Big Country SI* (1977) 86 When he took over [the station], the only domestic sheep were 'roughies'—long tailers and doubles.

2. *Prison.* A two-ounce packet of prison tobacco.
   1982 NEWBOLD *Big Huey* 248 Double (n) Two-ounce packet of prison tobacco. **1989** NEWBOLD *Punish. & Politics* 83 A 'fig' is a one- or two-ounce ration of tobacco. A two-ounce ration is also called a 'double'.

B. *a.* and *adv.* In collocations in various senses: **double All Black**, a player who has represented New Zealand at both rugby and cricket; **double-bottoming** *vbl. n. goldmining*, striking two layers of paydirt in a claim, one below the other; **double-bunk** *v. tramping*, to sleep two to a bunk in a tramping hut; **double-bunking** *vbl. n.*; **double-cut** *n.*, **double-cutting** *vbl. n.*, SECOND CUT 1; **double-dipping** *vbl. n.* [transf. use of *dip*, the action of making a 'lucky dip' for a hidden prize: Wilkes 1983 (of welfare beneficiaries)], of those on State or institutionally funded pensions, bursaries, welfare benefits, etc., obtaining money (often illicitly) additional to one's original entitlement, e.g. of tertiary students, claiming both student allowance and the unemployment benefit; **double-dump** *n.* [AND 1955], DUMP *n.* 1 a; **double-dump** *v.*, **double-dumped** *ppl. a.*, **double-dumping** *vbl. n.* [AND 1936], see DUMP *v. a*; **double-fleece** *n. farming*, a fleece of more than 12 months' wool growth; also *attrib.* applied to a sheep carrying such a fleece; **double-fleeced** *ppl. a.*, of a sheep, carrying a double-fleece; **double-fleecer** *n.*, a sheep which has missed a shearing and thus has more than 12 months' wool growth; **double G** *hist.*, a nickname given by political opponents to Sir George Grey, prob. from joining his initials with an allusion to his reputed double-dealing (cf. GREY *n.*²); **double gate** *farming*, see quot. (see also DRAFTING GATE, SWING GATE); **double-ground (claim)** *goldmining*, a claim of double the usually permitted area; **double-headed Jack** *obs.*, a double-headed coin used in two-up or pitch-and-toss, often called a *double-header*; **double-header** [AND 1898], a 'double'. or twice the standard nip of spirits served in a single glass (see also DOUBLER 1); **double unit house**, a semi-detached house; two house-units having one common fireproof wall; **double-yolker** *prison*, a stupid person, a buffoon.
   1966 *Encycl. NZ* I. 33 *Double All Blacks.* One of the highest honours that a New Zealand sportsman can receive is to represent his country both at rugby and at cricket. The following is the list of double All Blacks who have represented New Zealand in these games. **1986** BATEMAN *Illustrated Encycl. NZ* 305 Dickinson, George Ritchie (1903–78) was the first so-called 'double All Black' representing New Zealand at rugby and cricket. **1993** *Evening Post* (Wellington) 22 Nov. 1 The 20-year-old double All Black [sc. Jeff Wilson, also a NZ cricket representative] is taking the rugby world by storm. **1861** *NZ Goldfields 1861* 16 Oct. (1976) 45 Unless new discoveries—for **double-bottoming** still appears to be a myth—..are made..the approach of winter will find Gabriel's Gully deserted. **1984** *Story Nelson Lakes National Park* 154 Huts... **Double bunk**

if necessary to permit all to have a bed. a1940 GRETTON in Bailey & Roth *Shanties by the Way* (1967) 144 I heard this sad song O In the Orongorongo, 'No more double-bunking, **double-bunking** for me.' 1946 *Tararua Tramper* Apr. 7 Eleven bunks between eighteen meant a little double bunking—there were no complaints. 1883 *Brett's Colonists' Guide* 215 Care must be taken to guard against..making **double cuts** in the fleece. **Double cutting** is a serious fault in a shearer, and is generally owing to carelessness or undue haste. 1890 *Otago Witness* (Dunedin) 27 Nov. 11 The fleece, being free from double cuts, is worth considerably more. 1991 *Dominion* (Wellington) 9 Jan. 1 University Students Association president..said she did not believe **double-dipping** was a big problem. Those committing fraud were undermining the system for others. 1964 DAVIS *Watersiders* 24 And when a stevedore asks you to lift and slide **double dumps** through something the size of rat-hole—don't have it on. *Ibid.* 42 She had nearly been bowled by an incoming heave of double dumps for the second time in ten minutes. 1949 *NZJST* XXX. 170 One part was baled, **double-dumped** and shipped the return journey from New Zealand to England. 1968 *NZ Contemp. Dict. Suppl.* (Collins) 8 *dump, to double dump v.t.* compress wool bales, as by hydraulic pressure. 1949 *NZJST* XXX. 170 The **double-dumped** scoured wool was given an extra passage. 1974 *NZ Agric.* 67 A powerful hydraulic press forces two bales into the space formerly occupied by one, and they are bound with steel bands, or wires. (This process is called '**double dumping**' or 'dumping'.) 1933 *Press* (Christchurch) (Acland Gloss.) 7 Oct. 15 **Double-fleece**.—A sheep that is missed at one shearing and comes in the next has a *d[ouble]-f[leece]*. He is called a *double-fleecer*. 1968 TOMLINSON *Remembered Trails* 58 Most of the sheep went on, except about fifty wild and double-fleece sheep that were put in a scrubyard. 1982 *Agric. Gloss.* (MAF) 54 *Double fleece:* Fleece wool which is more than 12 months wool growth (also called overgrown). 1895 *TrNZI* XXVII. 278 When sheep were mustered in from the back ranges, it was noticed that several would die in the yards... These dead sheep would be mostly sheep which had missed a shearing, and were **double-fleeced**, having very long wool. 1904 *NZ Illustr. Mag.* Apr. 48 A few hundred sheep annually evaded the shearing muster, and became among the scrub and flax bushes to develop into '**double-fleecers**'. 1921 GUTHRIE-SMITH *Tutira* (1926) 224 We lived on wild pig..and the fat wild sheep and double-fleecers that could be raked in from river cliffs. 1877 *Richmond-Atkinson Papers* (1960) II. 440 The great landed estates have originated in Sir G. Grey's 5/- an acre regulations... The result ought to be a caution to working settlers against such friends as **double G**. 1933 *Press* (Christchurch) (Acland Gloss.) 7 Oct. 15 **Double Gate**.—Two gates from the race in a sheep yard, which allow the sheep to be let into any of three pens, so that a mob can be drafted into three lots at once. *D[ouble] g[ate]s* were introduced into Canterbury about 1868. 1892 PYKE *Gold-Miners' Guide* 7 Claims are classified as follows..and comprise ordinary claims, **double ground**, extended claims, frontage claims, special claims and dredging claims... *Ordinary claim* in alluvial.—An area *n[ot] e[xceeding]* 100ft. by 100ft. for each miner, and not more than 100,000 square feet in one claim. But the Warden may grant *double ground* on being satisfied that such extension is necessary for working the ground. 1938 HYDE *Nor Yrs. Condemn* 59 Wallie Black..was said to spin a penny or a **double-headed Jack** better than any other man in the N.Z.E.F. *Ibid.* 60 While he had his double-headed Jack the cupboard never went bare. 1957 WILSON *Strip Jack Naked* 111 Then he goes on drinking these **double 'eaders**, but he don't get noisy, just..glaring round the bar. 1964 HARVEY *Any Old Dollars Mister?* 37 Fancy watching grown-ups standing around drinking those things like double-headers and spots..Dad was always talking about. 1986 RICHARDS *Off the Sheep's Back* 124 The boat had a liquor licence... Singles soon turned to 'double-headers' as we headed into the..semi-darkness of the canyons. 1957 Dec. p.c. Professor J.H. Robb: N.Z. usage includes '**double unit house**', a semi-detached house. 1966 TURNER *Eng. Lang. Austral. & NZ* 172 *State houses* (owned and let by the government) are occasionally *double-unit* houses. 1982 NEWBOLD *Big Huey* 197 I was very annoyed and went around referring to Kapua as a weak mug and a **double-yolker**. *Ibid.* 248 Double-yolker. (n) Stupid person, buffoon. See also Egg.

double, *v. trans. Ellipt.* for DOUBLE-BANK 2. *v.* Also occas. as a noun [also US, see DARE]. See also DUB *v.*
  1959 SLATTER *Gun in My Hand* 187 San Severino and coming down the track on the company bike with Mick doubling me on the bar. 1963 HILLIARD *Piece of Land* 57 A bike came past: a big boy doubling a girl on the crossbar. 1963 MORRIESON *Scarecrow* 63 'Hop on the bar of my grid,' said D'Arcy. 'I'll double you round to meet some pals of ours.' 1988 *Through the Looking Glass* 67 Once I did let my legs dangle too close to the wheel as I was doubled somewhere on the back of a bike. 1994 LASENBY *Dead Man's Head* 127 'We've got to go,' Bob said. 'We've only got two grids.'.. Denny trotted beside Joe who was doubling Polly.

double-banger.
1. a. A large cracker allegedly making twice the bang of the ordinary 'double-happy'; applied in recent times to a double-happy as distinct from the small 'tom thumb' cracker. See also BANGER.
  1928 *Evening Post* (Wellington) 6 Nov. 10 One a 'double-banger' was thrown through an open window, and its explosion caused a commotion in the crowd. c1940 Used by Marlborough children of a very large cracker (approx 50 mm length, 10 mm diameter) (Ed.). 1981 PETERSON *Glasshouses* 7 One of my earliest recollections is of watching..one 5th November [in the 1890s], while the boys let off their crackers..One double banger seemed a dud. 1983 STEWART *Springtime in Taranaki* (1991) 78 There would be the bonfire..and double-bangers dancing as they double-banged.
b. *fig.* A woman of reputedly intense sexual response.
  1987 GRAY *Stepping Out* 59 Giving you your bit is she, then? She'd be a double banger I bet. The quiet ones always are.
2. Something in two conjoined parts. (In the quot., specifically a lottery with two separate prizes to be won with the same ticket.)
  1986 *Evening Post* (Wellington) 10 Apr. 4 [Heading] Double-banger winner elusive. Golden Kiwi lottery organisers may spend several thousands dollars searching for the winner of a $150,000 unclaimed prize in November's double banger Melbourne Cup sweepstake.

double-bank, *v.* [Transf. use of *double-bank* to double (up), orig. (so AND) of rowers either in pairs or two to an oar.]
1. Of horses. **a.** [AND 1863.] *intr.* Of horse-traction, to augment a team in difficult or steep places by hitching on a second team. Also as *vbl. n.*
  1897 WRIGHT *Station Ballads* 65 There the teams double-banked when they tackled the hill. 1961 HENDERSON *Friends In Chains* 130 My three leaders were hooked in front of Tommy's team. Having given him a pull to the crest, they were brought back. This practice was known as double-banking [West Coast, c1900]. *Ibid.* 186 Double Banking: One horse team added to assist another.
b. *intr.* and *trans.* [AND 1876.] To ride two on a horse; to carry two people on one horse. Also as *vbl. n.*
  1883 *Auckland Weekly News* 2 June 6 Some [children] were on foot, some what is called 'double-banking' on their pony. 1934 SCANLAN *Winds of Heaven* 42 As children they had walked along it to school, before they had a pony, on which they 'double-banked'. 1952 NEWTON *High Country Journey* 105 And as the horse was too touchy to 'double bank', the shepherd had to leave the cook..and head..for another horse. 1960 SCRYMGEOUR *Memories Maoriland* 178 Ruefully he noticed a pal..sitting on his well-groomed chestnut galloway. 'Reg,' called Jim, 'double bank me to the start.' 1983 COOPER *Wag's Tales* 19 We were cantering along, Jess and I double banked, bare-back on one horse. 1992 PARK *Fence Around the Cuckoo* 29 Times were harder still for many of their pupils, especially farmers' children from the backblocks, double-banking on a barebacked horse.

2. [AND 1960.] *intr.* To carry someone on the bar (less often the handlebars or rear-carrier) of a bicycle, occas. of a motorcycle. Also *trans.* and as *vbl.n.* See also BUNK *v.*, DOUBLE *v.*, DUB *v.*
  1916 *Evening Post* (Wellington) 1 Apr. 9 [Heading] Double-banking on motor cycles. 1917 *Otago Witness* (Dunedin) 11 Apr. 23 May Taylor and another girl were 'double-banking' down a hill on their way to school. 1917 *Stratford Evening Post* 3 May 3 Two boys..who were riding home from school 'double-banked', collided with a telegraph pole. 1945 *NZ Dairy Exporter* 1 Sept. 90 Of course you soon learned to double-bank and take your girl-friend for a spin on a Saturday afternoon. 1955 *BJ Cameron Collection* (TS July) double-bank (v) To carry a passenger on the bar of a bicycle.

3. *Railwaymen. intr.* To split a train in half to enable one engine (otherwise insufficiently powered) to draw each section up a hill.
  1985 McGILL *G'day Country* 120 We might make Wharanui in a couple or so hours. Unless..we stopped on the hill... When it did, you had to split the train in half, double-banking. Took one half at a time.

4. In various transf. uses of two people, things, situations conjoined or doubled up together. Also *fig.*
  c1926 THE MIXER *Transport Workers' Song Book* 86 And the growlers double-bank him In the way they alway[s] fight. 1938 LANCASTER *Promenade* 134 'I have to inform you..that I engaged myself to two gentlemen last night...' 'Two gentlemen. Double-banked.' 1946 *Tararua Tramper* Dec. 7 Bodies double-banked in the five bunks.

double-decker.
1. *Hist.* Prob. a shortened altered form of *double-deck car* (see 1904 quot.²) or *double-deck tram*, a tramcar with seating at upper and lower levels.
  1890 *Otago Witness* (Dunedin) 24 Apr. 35 These trams are all what we call double-deckers, and it is the fashion in Christchurch for the ladies to ride on the top instead of inside, so that on a summer's day these vehicles present a..flower-like appearance. 1904 *NZ Observer* 16 Jan. 2 Whatever the Company may think of the recommendations to abolish the double-decker cars, the proposal is one that finds considerable sympathy with the travelling public. 1904 *Weekly News* 10 Mar. [Caption] Wellington's electric trams: a double-deck car packed up ready to be mounted on the truck. 1912 *NZ Free Lance* (Wellington) 3 Mar. 15 Some of the double-deckers [*sc.* trams] run on the long routes... All the provision that is made for smokers on double-decker cars is needed. 1959 LAWLOR *Old Wellington Days* 84 Evidently my parents wished to

see how the trams behaved before allowing me to try them out some three weeks later [c1904], and then recklessly..on the top of a double-decker. **1991** *North & South* (Auckland) May 33 Our favourite was the 8-25 double-decker, a tram like an unroofed London bus.

2. *Farming.* [Transf. from tramways use.] See *double fleecer* (DOUBLE B).

1960 MASTERS *Back-Country Tales* 25 The mob were started over, but the double deckers, those with two years' wool. **1967** HENDERSON *Return to Open Country* 163 In the wool boom in 1951 an orchardist in Hamilton had five 'double-decker' sheep in his orchard (they'd missed one shearing and had a double crop of wool)... Being double deckers each sheep clipped close to twenty pounds. **1971** LETHBRIDGE *Sunrise on Hills* 95 A hermit [sheep] must be distinguished from a 'double-decker', which is simply a sheep that had missed the muster once and consequently had a double layer of wool. **1981** HENDERSON *Exiles Asbestos Cottage* 80 Young Roy Mytton so proudly succeeded in rounding up twenty-odd old hermits, defiant woolly sheep also known as 'double deckers', which had been wily enough to dodge last season's muster.

double-happy.

a. [f. the proprietary name on packet, poss. a translation of the Chinese.] A children's name for a Chinese firecracker.

1984 *Dominion* (Wellington) 1 Nov. 5 Burglars who took $2000 worth of fireworks from a Kilbirnie fruit shop left only one packet of double happys on the shelves. **1985** MCGILL *G'day Country* 62 It was round the store we would have our first late October battle with lighted Tom Thumbs and Double Happys. **1988** *Press* (Christchurch) 17 Feb. 9 I had a fair idea it was lightning. There was a roar like a double happy (fire cracker) going off inside a rubbish bin.

b. *transf.* A (nuclear) explosion.

1972 *Truth* 25 July 2 Does it mean that the protestors approve Communist Chinese doctrines, the thoughts of Mao—and the Nanking nuclear double-happy.

doubler. *Obs.*

1. A 'double', or twice the standard nip of spirits, served in a single glass.

1871 MONEY *Knocking About NZ* 141 Taking turn about at the duty of shouldering the stretchers, we reached the Wanganaro Redoubt early in the afternoon, and we were served out with a 'doubler', or two lots of grog in one.

2. An extra condenser for refining illicitly-distilled spirit.

1971 OGILVIE *Moonshine Country* 110 For good measure the distillate would be put through a 'doubler' for further refinement and strengthening. At this stage a copper 'worm' was used to lead the vapour to its condensation point.

doughboy. [f. Brit. dial. and nautical use: freq. in (esp. outdoor) NZ use: AND 1827.]

1. a. A plain flour and water mixture, occas. with suet or sugar added, boiled, steamed or fried.

1860 BURNETT *Diary* Mar. in Haast *Julius Von Haast* (1948) 87 A glorious feast last night of potatoes, bacon, doughboys, and sweetened coffee, as I sat up in my sleeping-bag. **1871** MONEY *Knocking About NZ* 29 We had a billy of 'skilligolee' to warm us up while the..dough-boys..were being got under weigh. **1896** HARPER *Pioneer Work* 139 We could only afford two small 'dough-boys'—or suet dumplings—for each meal. **1905** BRANDON *Ukneadit* 105 Dough boys, 'sinkers,' or 'water boys' are prepared in exactly the same manner as damper, except that the dough need not be so stiff. **1928** KENWAY *Pioneering Poverty Bay* 7 Flapjack and a doughboy (dumpling). **1933** *Press* (Christchurch) (Acland Gloss.) 14 Oct. 15 *Doughboy.*— A dumpling made of flour, sugar, and suet, boiled. It was a favourite dish out mustering. **1962** EVANS *Waikaka Saga* 30 They bought rice and a little flour to make doughboys. **1988** PICKERING *Hills* 73 Doughboys are dumpling-like globules of flour and baking powder, milk and water, dropped into stews and cooked. Neither damper nor doughboys feature greatly on modern menus. **1996** *Capital Times* (Wellington) 24 Jan. 6 The title *Doughboy* comes from the traditional Maori boiler, a pot of puha, pork bones, potatoes and a lump of wet dough, broken into little round balls, thrown in. These little dumplings are called doughboys (Mutumutu), and by some cruel or happy fate, depending on how you look at it, this has become one Maori slang name for gays.

b. In local use, LILIPI.

1951 KOHERE *Autobiog. of a Maori* 17 The principal food eaten and enjoyed [at a hui on the East Coast c1870s] was what is called doughboy, that is, flour boiled and stirred in water and sweetened with sugar or wild honey. Potfuls of the preparation were poured into canoes around which sat the guests, each armed with mussel and paua shells.

2. *Mining. Obs.* In transf. use, a dumpling-like stone.

1897 MCKAY *Older Auriferous Drifts Central Otago* 72 Everywhere they are formed exclusively of quartzose materials, with the exception of a few feet at the base of the deposit, which is sometimes made up of local rocks occurring as highly-decomposed breccia conglomerate, occasional boulders of which are sometimes met with in the quartz sands, called 'dough-boys' by the miners.

dover. *Obs. Farming.* [Transf. f. *Dover* a proprietary name of a once-popular clasp-knife.] In the phr. **the run of the dover(s)**, 'all found', provided with all necessary food (see quot. 1933).

a**1890** in Kerse *Knapdale Run* (1984) 18 This 'big house' [built of slabs in 1860]..was very draughty and McNab at a time when he was suffering from a bronchial ailment, was heard to remark... 'I tell you what, Johnson, these big houses are a curse. I wish I were back in the maimai with a plate of bark and a run of the dover'. **1933** *Press* (Christchurch) (Acland Gloss.) 14 Oct. 15 *Dover*... George McMillan, who came out in 1858, told me that when he arrived it was the custom for hands to find their own knife, fork, spoon, plate, and pannikin, which were all called dovers. A man would offer work for 'a pound a week and the run of my dovers'. The expression died out in Canterbury before 1860. **1947** BEATTIE *Early Runholding* 11 The saying then [c1870] in engaging a hand was 'so much a week and the run of the dover'. The dover was a Dover knife, and the 'run of the dover' was as as much food as one could eat.

Dover stove. Occas. *ellipt.* **Dover.** [f. a proprietary name.] A free-standing small iron wood-burning stove.

c**1940** An instruction to the editor as a boy: 'Go and get another armful of wood for the Dover' [*sc.* the general store's Dover stove]. **1951** HUNT *Confessions* 56 My pay as a cadet was so small..[that] I induced the management to provide me with a 'bach' fitted up with a Dover stove for cooking and warmth. **1952** PASCOE *Land Uplifted High* 150 We snuggled into the hut..and built up the scrub fire in a Dover stove. a**1973** FINLAYSON *Brown Man's Burden* (1973) 127 The stove was going good, that old cast-iron Dover there that was secondhand when I got it..ages ago. **1982** GRADY *Perano Whalers* 3 The Lookout Hill shelter gained a wooden floor, a Champion Dover wood stove,.. 'gib' board lining, bookshelves. **1995** *Dominion* (Wellington) 5 Jan. 10 While his Dover wetback wood stove is heating up the kettle, Mr Webber is..plucking 20 fresh leaves for the tea-pot.

dove's foot. Also **dovesfoot.** [f. the shape of the leaf.] An introduced weed-geranium. See also CRANESBILL, GERANIUM.

1926 HILGENDORF *Weeds* 122 Dovesfoot (*Geranium molle*), or soft geranium or wild geranium or soft cranes bill, is common in all soils and situations, and has been considered a native. It is a diffuse much-branched annual or perennial, softly hairy in all its parts. **1969** *Standard Common Names Weeds* 22 dove's foot *Geranium molle*. **1980** TAYLOR *Weeds of Crops* 40 Dove's Foot (*Geranium molle*)... This weed introduced from Eurasia, is common throughout New Zealand.

dovie /'dʌvi/. *dove petrel* (PETREL 2 (8)).

1938 *Auckland Weekly News* 23 Mar. 42 At times, some defect in the tunnelling leads to the reappearance of a 'dovie'. **1980** *Star* (Christchurch) 25 Feb. 26 Tuataras often share their burrows with fairy prions or dove petrels, little seabirds about the size of a dove. These are known to Stephens Island lighthouse keepers as 'dovies'.

down, *adv.* [Local uses of various senses of *down adv.*] Indicating direction of travel, or locality reached, in relation to a starting point (within New Zealand of indicating a point south of the user). Contrast UP *adv.* See also DOWN-COUNTRY, DOWN SOUTH, DOWN UNDER. **a.** *Obs.* From Sydney to New Zealand.

1827 WILLIAMS *Early Jrnls.* 16 Mar. (1961) 45 It was determined the *Herald* should return to the Colony for stores, as none had come down exceptg. flour. **1847** 22 Oct. in Wakefield *Handbook NZ* (1848) 249 I brought down from Sydney [to Nelson] thorough bred Merino rams.

b. The Chatham Islands in relation to New Zealand (esp. to Lyttelton), esp. as **to get down**, **to go down**, to travel from New Zealand to the Chatham Islands.

1876 CHUDLEIGH *Diary* 1 Aug. (1950) 250 Still in Ch.Ch. looking for a ship. Mrs Briscoe of the Islands is here and very anxious to get down. The Cleopatra is the one expected to go down but she is bar bound in the Grey. **1985** LANGDALE-HUNT *Last Entail Male* 148 One thing that was rather bad in my early years down there [in the Chathams] was the fact that there was no branch of the Post Office Savings Bank.

c. *Canterbury.* From the hinterland to the coast.

1856 FITTON *NZ* 220 There are the drays..for carrying down the wool after the shearing season, to the ports for shipment.

down, *prep.* [Local uses of various senses of *down prep.*]

1. [OEDAS II. 12 marks the usage '*colloq.* and (chiefly *south.*) *dial.*' from 1899; AND 1911.] With ellipsis of a following modified **at**, **in**, **to**, etc., esp. as **down the** (coast, paddock, etc.).

1857 PHILLIPS *Rockwood Jrnl.* 24 Jan. (Canterbury Pub. Lib. TS) 66 John & Seal out shooting down the River and to old Whare swamp. **1947** DAVIN *For Rest of Our Lives* 209 Had a bit of a run-in with a pongo MP down the Berka last night. **1959** SLATTER *Gun in My Hand* 45 I used to read whole books of it [*sc.* poetry] while you was sleepin between the rows down the back paddock. **1985** MCGILL *G'day Country* 35 I was down Whangarei port loading fertiliser. *Ibid.* 159 Young women down the back of the bus were talking about guys putting the hard word on them.

2. *Southland.* **down below**, in Invercargill.
  1936 HYDE *Passport to Hell* 49 Breaking the boss's jaw won't half get you a sweet time down below.

3. In the phr. **down the road (track)**, esp. as **to go (get, be sent) down the road (track)**, to get, be given the sack; also *transf.*, to be in an unfortunate state.
  1952 THOMSON *Deer Hunter* 21 If we find any [workers] that don't pull their weight on the open range, there is no enthusiasm about being mates with them. Usually they are not long in going down the track. **1973** WHEELER *Hist. Sheep Stations NI* 99 Remote stations usually have labour problems, and I couldn't imagine the man in question going down the road because of his language. **1973** WALLACE *Generation Gap* 194 For Gawd's sake, boss, get him [*sc.* a violent camp cook] down the track fast. It can't be too fast for us. **1981** ANDERSON *Both Sides of River* 109 The cook's in bed, and when he recovers he'll be going down the track. Can you cope? **1986** 23 Mar. *Radio New Zealand* discussion. In five years' time..if these conditions continue I put it to you farming will be down the track. **1994** LASENBY *Dead Man's Head* 13 'I'm not having any red-fed Bolshy working for me,' Old Man Wilson said. 'You're down the road.' **1995** WINTER *All Ways Up Hill* 116 Experience had taught..[the boss] that when a man was sacked the others worked a little harder. He picked on a man wearing braces one night. 'You git down the track after breakfast,' he snarled.

4. In the phr. **down the gurgler**, see GURGLER; **down to a fine art**, see FINE *a.* 2.

down, *n.* [AND 1828.] In the phr. **to have (get) a down on**, to have a set on, a grudge against; to be prejudiced against. See also DERRY.
  1862 THATCHER in *Canterbury Songster* 10 I've got no 'down' on Travers, For he's a clever chap; 'Twas but in self-defence I Gave him a gentle rap. **1883** BRADSHAW *NZ As It Is* 3 Sun and wear have had too much of a 'down' on that suit for much colour to survive. **1890** *Evening Post* (Wellington) 10 Nov. 2 He has a decided 'down' on Trade Unionism. **1906** *Truth* 22 Sept. 6 The lad stated that Taubman had ordered him to stand there till the night-watchman came, because Taubman 'had a down on him'. **1940** STUDHOLME *Te Waimate* (1954) 135 My father had a great down on light-coloured beasts. **1988** MCGILL *Dict. Kiwi Slang* 39 *down*, in phr. *have a down on* a grudge, hostile or at least poor opinion of someone.

down country, *n.* Mainly *SI.* [Cf. DOWN *adv.* 1 c.]

a. The (esp. coastal) plain or lowland as distinct from the hinterland high country. Often *attrib.*
  1904 LANCASTER *Sons o' Men* [Chapter heading, chapter xvi] In the down-country. [The reference is to Christchurch.] **1933** *Press* (Christchurch) (Acland Gloss.) 30 Sept. 15 *Down c[ountry]*, used (chiefly by people in the hills) to describe the localities near town or on the plains. They also speak of *d[own] c[ountry]* people or sheep. 'Wakatip Mail', April 4, 1872. **1940** STUDHOLME *Te Waimate* (1954) 113 At Waimate we ran Cross-bred sheep on the down-country and Merinos or Half-breds on the hills. **1952** THOMSON *Deer Hunter* 20 There's a subtle difference between back-country men and those enslaved to industry and commerce... 'Down country they only think with their heads.'

b. *attrib.* Pertaining to or situated in lowland as distinct from high-country districts.
  1932 *Rep. Pyne, Gould & Guiness & Co.* Down country, used (chiefly by people in the hills) to describe localities near town or on the plains. They also speak of down country people or sheep. **1943** HISLOP *Pure Gold* 126 'Shiner'..had called with his usual thirst at one of the down-country hotels. **1953** SUTHERLAND *Golden Bush* (1963) 188 It was a down-country drover returning from an assignment to the west coast. **1969** MCCASKILL *Molesworth* 192 How many down-country paddock farmers would be happy with an equal result? **1978** PRESTON *Woolgatherers* 112 While the tussle was going on I managed to get in touch with a down-country drover whose dogs could manage these sheep.

down-country, *adv.* Mainly *Canterbury and Otago*. [AND *adv.* 1875.] Towards or situated on lowlands near the coast, or in the towns found there.
  1874 BATHGATE *Col. Experiences* 135 A dozen or more [packmen] with their pack-saddles empty..were returning down country. **1939** BEATTIE *First White Boy Born Otago* 133 Once or twice he had gone down-country with an empty dray. **1946** ACLAND *Early Canterbury Runs* 168 After this [disastrously cold] year they always bought turnips and wintered their hoggets down country. **1948** *Our Own Country* 122 When an inhabitant of the Mackenzie goes beyond Burke's Pass, he talks of going 'down country'. The phrase implies a moral as well as a physical descent. **1953** STRONACH *Musterer on Molesworth* 20 And Christmas at Tarndale was better held drunk than sober, because down country all our people were hanging up stockings. **1960** MASTERS *Back-Country Tales* 59 It was high time I headed down country and started associating with people before I went crackers. **1970** MCNAUGHTON *Tat* 91 When Bluey finished at the station, he headed down country for his sister-in-law's place. **1986** *Southland Times* 29 July 19 He was puzzled why any kea would be found so far down-country.

down south, *adv.* and *n.* Also often **down South**. [Local uses of *down south* esp. freq. in NZ, a country whose main axis is north-south.] Applied to any place considerably to the south of the speaker's geographical reference, esp. to the (southern) South Island. Cf. UP NORTH.

A. *adv.*

a. In adverbial use.
  1867 BARKER *Station Life* (1870) 137 [Heading] A Journey 'Down South' [*sc.* Canterbury to Otago.] **1874** TROLLOPE *NZ* 117 'A railway for you gentlemen down South!' [*sc.* South Island] says a northern member. 'Certainly,—but on condition that we have one here, up North.' **1881** LUSH *Waikato Jrnls.* 22 May (1982) 175 'Very cold this morning, Mahon.' 'Very Sir: there's been a heavy fall of snow somewhere down-south.' **1896** HARPER *Pioneer Work* 147 On one occasion he was 'down South', below Gillespies [Beach, West Coast]. **1902** SATCHELL *Land of Lost* 18 [A Northland man speaks] 'What part of the country do you come from?' 'Down South.' 'Taranaki or Hawkes Bay way?' **1910** *Truth* 3 Sept. 1 Hon. Tam. Mackenzie surely cannot be to a sure of his Taieri seat down south. **1925** MANDER *Allen Adair* (1971) 48 Already he saw the cream factories which men down south were dreaming as part of every township. **1948** BALLANTYNE *Cunninghams* (1976) 21 'Reminds me of the time down south when I was watchman at a brewery,' Simmons said. **1951** FRAME *Lagoon* (1961) 12 Once she went for a holiday down South [from Canterbury to Otago]. **1961** CRUMP *Hang On a Minute Mate* 74 Sam got the cowman-gardener's beardie to train for him 'like we handle 'em down South.' **1988** SOMERSET *Sunshine & Shadow* 13 Aunt Amy would spend her Christmas holidays either 'up North' or 'down South'. **1992** SMITHYMAN *Auto/Biographies* 32 Down South they are going to call this..the Auckland Attorneys' War.

b. *fig.* [AND 4 b, 1916.] In a bottom (or trouser) pocket.
  1916 *Anzac Book* 47 'Enessy sticks 'is lighted bumper down south into 'is overcoat pocket. **1917** *Chron. NZEF* 16 May 137 He dreamt he'd got his fourteen 'peg' And buttoned it 'Down South'.

c. In the phr. **It's snowing down south**, see SNOW *v.* 1.

B. *n.* and *attrib.* The South Island.
  1906 *Truth* 7 Apr. 1 Bush whisky makes the boozer think the world is upside down. After three glasses of a brand retailed by a down South publican. **1949** NEWTON *High Country Days* 69 Lofty in happy mood, and unfailing in his praise of his native province [Southland], delighted young Wallace with tall stories of 'down South.'

down under, *adv.*, *n.*, and *attrib.*

A. *adv.* To or in Australasia.
  1886 FROUDE *Oceana* 92 We were to bid adieu to the 'Australasian'... She had carried us safely *down under.*

B. *n.*

1. New Zealand, esp. as part of Australasia.
  1905 *Daily Mail* (London) (?)24 Oct. in *Why the 'All Blacks' Triumphed* (1906) 21 Smith..is the champion hurdler 'down under'. **1916** ANZAC *On Anzac Trail* 72 Anyway, the men from Down Under were real glad to see them. **1916** *Chron. NZEF* 27 Dec. 199 Let them pause, and hear when nights are still The other girl who coo-ees from 'down under'. **1934** LEE *Children of Poor* (1949) 10 In those days Antipodes meant more than 'down under'. The term imaginatively suggested the edge of the world. **1946** SIMPSON *If You'd Care to Know* 7 The little Dominion of New Zealand is the more or less happy land popularly known as 'Down Under'... It is doubtful whether the origin of the term 'Down Under' will ever be known. It first came into general use during the World War of 1914–18, when the New Zealanders who fought in the ill-starred Gallipoli campaign were referred to as 'the men from Down Under'. **1985** SHERWOOD *Botanist at Bay* 18 He also uses expressions like 'down under', which implies that there's something wrong with the Southern Hemisphere, and 'Australasia', which implies a close connection between New Zealand and her bullying barbaric neighbour. **1991** *Dominion Sunday Times* (Wellington) 10 Nov. 3 The invasion of New Zealand by 500,000 American soldiers..began in Auckland on June 12, 1942, and a group called Operation US Down-Under hopes to bring some of them back next year.

2. *Whaling.* Chatham Island waters.
  1984 HOLMES *Chatham Is.* 20 The time of migration of sperm whales around 'Chatham waters' ('Down Under' as it was called by the whalers) was November to April each year.

C. *attrib.* New Zealand; occas. Australasian.
  1916 ANZAC *On Anzac Trail* 2 Trained for service with the 'Down Under' contingents. **1916** *Chron. NZEF* 27 Dec. 199 'Down Under' boys on furlough are in town, Discharged from hospital, repaired and braced. **1946** SIMPSON *If You'd Care to Know* 6 A Down Under book for overseas friends and relations. **1987** *Sunday News* (Auckland) 8 Nov. 21 As well, her Downunder Mr Wonderful had to be warm, caring, considerate..a man of strict Christian principles.

dozy, *a.* Also **dozie**. Of land, deficient in minerals and causing sheep to lose condition; of sheep, affected by such a deficiency disease. Cf. *dopie* (DOPINESS).
  1933 *Press* (Christchurch) (Acland Gloss.) 7 Oct. 15 *Dozie.*—Country where sheep lose condition and do not thrive—go *dopie*, in fact—is called *d[ozie]*. I have heard shepherds speak of *d[ozie]* sheep also. It is very likely the Scots for *dopie*.

dpb: see DOMESTIC PURPOSES BENEFIT.

dracophyllum /drækʌuˈfɪləm/. Also *ellipt.* **draco**. [f. the generic name *Dracophyllum* 'dragon leaf' (i.e. with leaves as in *Dracaena* spp.) given in 1798 by the French naturalist J.J.H. de Labillardière.] A predominantly New Zealand genus of trees and shrubs, having linear leaves (fam. Epacridaceae); INANGA *n*.², NEINEI. Also **dracophyllum scrub**, an area covered predominantly with various *Dracophyllum* spp.

1841 BIDWILL *Rambles in NZ* (1952) 100 I here first saw the great Dracophyllum; it formed a small tree about six inches in diameter, and twenty feet high; it is one of the most curious plants in the world. **1946** *Tararua Tramper* July 15 When night fell..we had been able to pitch the tent..and, with plenty of dracophyllum, had a good fire. **1977** *The Islander* Sept. 112 Much of the water's edge on the east side has..draco down to the high tide level. **1989** *NZ Geographic* I. 26 [Caption] Dracophyllum scrub forms a dense manuka-like cover around parts of the coast [of Campbell Island]. **1992** *Dominion Sunday Times* (Wellington) 26 July 21 Straggly dracophyllums, grasses trying to be trees..continue above the line of beeches.

draft, *n.* [Spec. use of *draft* a detachment from a main body: AND 1813.] A group of animals separated from a main mob for a special purpose; a line of stock so separated for sale.

1933 *Press* (Christchurch) (Acland Gloss.) 14 Oct. 15 *Draft...* A number of stock sent for sale. E.g., 'The annual Stonyhurst *d[raft]* of four-year-old ewes will be offered.' When the *d[raft]* is actually offered it is usually spoken of as a *line*. **1937** *King Country Chronicle* 22 Nov. 5 He obtained a good average of 49 guineas for his draft. **1960** SCRYMGEOUR *Memories Maoriland* 162 That evening a Mr. Wright..asked casually if an offer could be procured of 800 to 1000 lambs for immediate fattening. 'Yes,' said Jim, 'I know of a draft,' roughly describing same. **1966** NEWTON *Boss's Story* 88 We had a small draft of sale ewes that year.

draft, *v.* [Spec. use of *draft* to draw off, to detach: AND 1837.]

1. a. *trans.* To sort (farm animals) into particular groups; to separate a large mob into smaller groups for a special purpose.

1859 *Puketoi Station Diary* (Hocken TS) 11 Nov. finished drafting wethers which were put acrorss [*sic*] Wedderburn. **1867** *Richmond-Atkinson Papers* (1960) II. 237 The armies of sheep were only being drafted (that is sorted) for sale. **1889** WILLIAMS & REEVES *Colonial Couplets* 9 Dagging the hoggets, or drafting the rams. **1894** WILSON *Land of Tui* 242 The sheep..are..placed in smaller..enclosures adjoining the wool-sheds, from which are drafted..a number sufficient to keep the pens..full. **1924** *Otago Witness* (Dunedin) 23 Sept. 54 Sheep drafted in through a race from the yards into pens..were taken from these pens by the shearers. **1950** CHERRILL *NZ Sheep Farm* 113 Sometimes she would draft a mob to the stock yards, but..prices ran low. **1970** MCLEOD *Glorious Morning* 253 *Drafting sheep*: The process of dividing a mixed mob into sexes or ages or any other required types.

b. *intr.* To undertake the sorting of farm animals into particular groups.

1867 PHILLIPS *Point Jrnl.* 3 Jan. (Canterbury Pub. Lib. TS) 91 All hands drafting at woolshed. **1879** KIERNAN *Diary* 27 Feb. in Guthrie-Smith *Tutira* (1921) 127 C.H.S. and T.S. drafting and putting shorn sheep out to the paddocks.

Hence **drafted** *ppl. a.*, of stock (or a group of farm animals), separated from a main mob for a special purpose.

1865 CHUDLEIGH *Diary* 5 May (1950) 181 It being too late to get down the river tonight I only crossed the drafted cattle over one stream and took them on one mile.

2. draft off, draft out, to separate out, and remove, certain animals from a group or mob.

1860 *Puketoi Station Diary* (Hocken TS) 18 Feb. Templars sheep came in the morning—Drafted out most of Newton's. **1863** BUTLER *First Year* x 154 Should you be drafting out sheep or taking your rams out, let the sheep..be let into yards D and E. **1879** KIERNAN *Diary* 27 Feb. in Guthrie-Smith *Tutira* (1921) 127 Drafted out all woolly sheep and took them to the shed. **1888** DUNCAN *Wakatipians* 64 First we had to draft [the sheep] off and boat them across the arm of the lake. **1890** *Otago Witness* (Dunedin) 7 Aug. 36 We ate our campoven bread and our fat chops, and dream'd of great flocks to be drafted off every year to boiling-down yards. **1953** STRONACH *Musterer on Molesworth* 37 Arriving at Tarndale, we drafted off the woollies and sent them to Molesworth to be shorn. **1982** *Agric. Gloss.* (MAF) 5 *Draft off or drafting*: Removing certain animals from a group. This can be done by driving the animals out of a group (cut off or drift off) or driving them up a race and removing them through a special gate (drafting gate).

drafting, *vbl. n. Farming.*

1. [AND 1845.] The process of separating a group of farm animals from a main mob.

1864 CHUDLEIGH *Diary* 9 Jan. (1950) 117 Finished drafting and when we came to take the rams out..we found 40 of them had nocked [*sic*] down a rail. **1883** PEACHE *Journal* in Gray *Quiet with Hills* (1970) 63 Think some got out as made out there were 14,000 in hand after drafting. **1899** BELL *In Shadow of Bush* 79 The yards were small and inconvenient, and of a temporary character, and the work of drafting was difficult. **1913** CARR *Country Work* 33 All station hands are liable to be called upon to assist in drafting, etc. **1928** *Weekly News* 12 Jan. [Caption] A mob of nearly three thousand cattle was mustered and yarded for branding and drafting. **1947** BEATTIE *Early Runholding* 44 One who was present has told me of a cattle drafting on the Beaumont Run..rounding-up the remainder..exciting work done that day. **1953** GUTHRIE-SMITH *Tutira* (3edn.) 160 It was no rare sight, during a spell of hot, wet autumn weather, to see sheep come into the draftings distinctly green on the back with sprouting grass. **1989** RICHARDS *Pioneer's Life* 26 All the ewes..would be mustered and..then 'raddled' (chalk marked) ready for drafting.

2. Special Comb. **drafting gate** (also erron. **draughting**) [AND 1882], a two-way gate in a drafting-race for separating farm animals into special groups (see also *double gate* (DOUBLE *a.*), SWING GATE); **drafting pen** [AND 1854], a pen into or out of which animals are drafted; **drafting race**, a fenced passage in a stockyard with room only for a single file of animals, and leading to a drafting gate allowing the animals passing through to be separated into various groups (see quot. 1949); **drafting yard** [AND 1832], an enclosed yard into or out of which animals are drafted; also *pl.*, the complex of pens, yards, and races used esp. for handling stock.

1875 RIVES *Jottings on the Spot* (Cant. Pub. Lib. TS) 26 Feb. 7 A devilish hard job I had standing at one of the **draughting gates** counting out the woolly ones. **1916** *NZJAg.* Sept. XIII. 220 Drafting gates 3ft. wide. **1940** STUDHOLME *Te Waimate* (1954) 136 These yards were specially built for handling wild cattle, and had narrow gaps between the hinge of the drafting gate and post, through which a man could escape from a charging beast. **1961** CRUMP *Hang On a Minute Mate* 169 Jack was working on a drafting-gate that wasn't swinging properly. **1973** FERNANDEZ *Tussock Fever* 1 The boss was there working the drafting gate—two-tooths to the left-hand gate, six-tooths to the right. **1982** drafting gate [see DRAFT *v.* 2]. **1934** MULGAN *Spur of Morning* 314 There were stables and..a huge wool-shed and **drafting pens**. **1955** BOWEN *Wool Away* 120 This drafting race divides sheep into the separate lots required, and these are then handled by the *drafting pens*, *check pens*, and *holding yards*, which should correspond in size to the receiving yards. **1963** WALLIS *Point of Origin* 18 Somewhere outside..there were salesmen talking to farmers,.. sitting astride the drafting pens discussing dips and shearing machines. **1856** ROBERTS *Diary* 18 Dec. in Beattie *Early Runholding* (1947) 43 As there was no crush pen, or **drafting race**, we had to head rope those [cattle] requiring branding. **1883** *Brett's Colonists' Guide* 173 [Sliding gates] make the sheep run more freely into the small yards which lead into the drafting races. **1922** PERRY *Sheep Farming* 16 [The sheep yards] should consist of receiving yards at each end, forcing pen, and drafting race. **1933** *Press* (Christchurch) (Acland Gloss.) 14 Oct. 15 About 1864 it was found possible to run sheep one at a time through a *drafting race* and move a *single gate* as they came, so drafting into two lots. See *double gate*. **1949** NEWTON *High Country Days* 194 Drafting: The main feature of sheepyards is the drafting race. This race, perhaps eight yards in length, is only wide enough for sheep to pass through in single file; at the end of the race are two swinging gates which can be manipulated to turn the sheep into different yards, and so separate them into different 'lines' or mobs. **1955** [see *drafting pen* above]. **1960** SCRYMGEOUR *Memories Maoriland* 17 'Teviot' had a magnificent stone and steel woolshed [built 1880]..with two complete drafting races. **1975** NEWTON *Sixty Thousand on the Hoof* 107 Sandy told me he once saw 40,000 wethers come into the Benmore yards in one mob and that the whole lot went through the drafting race in the one day. **1849** ALLOM *Letter* in Earp *Handbook* (1852) 123 The [stock] yard is generally divided into..a large yard for the whole herd, a **drafting yard**, and a milking yard. **1864** CAVERHILL in Deans *Pioneers* (1964) 103 Improvements on sheep station, consisting of dwelling house... Woolshed and yards, drafting yards and shearers' hut. **1874** WILSON *Diary* 29 Apr. in Wierzbicka *Wilson Family* (1973) 186 Donald and Mick went over to the Bush at Sandy's to cut posts for the Drafting yard. **1922** PERRY *Sheep Farming* 16 The erection of drafting yards is one of the first improvements to be attended to by the young sheep farmer. **1956** DARE *Rouseabout Jane* 167 We had to move the whole lot to the drafting yards. **1973** FERNANDEZ *Tussock Fever* 1 Barbara..dawdled across the horse paddock by the homestead heading for the dusty, noisy, drafting yards.

drag, *v.*

1. In the phr. **to drag the chain** [prob. fig. from draught animals in harness allowing the draw-chain to slacken and drag instead of pulling on it: AND 1912 (shearing), 1954 (drinking)], to be slow or behindhand and thus to slow the progress of the group; to lag behind one's fellows; *spec.* applied to the slowest shearer in a shed, or the slowest drinker in a school.

1934 *Press* (Christchurch) (Acland Gloss.) 20 Jan. 15 *Drag the chain, to.*—To be the slowest shearer in a shed. **1939** in Partridge *Dict. Slang Addenda* (1949) 1035 *drag the chain*. To be at the rear in a race or in a game (of, e.g., cribbage): New Zealand: C. 20. Niall Alexander, letter of Oct. 22, 1939, 'The ploughman's term to designate his slow horse that does not keep its chains tight'. **1941** BAKER *NZ Slang* 39 From the New Zealand shearing sheds came those effective expressions *to drag the chain* and *swing the gate*,

DRAG

phrases applied to the slowest and the fastest shearer in the shed respectively. **1959** SLATTER *Gun in My Hand* 45 But stop draggin the chain. Drink up and have one on me. **1966** TURNER *Eng. Lang. Austral. & NZ* 122 *Stop dragging the chain* supplies a need where the etiquette of drinking requires rapid consumption of liquor: it means 'hurry up with your drink so that the next round can begin'...*To drag the chain* is a shearer's term meaning 'to be a slow worker'. **1989** *NZ Eng. Newsletter* III. 24 *dragging the chain:* A shearer is said to do this when he lags behind the rest because he is slow, lazy or inexperienced. The origin is from bullock driving where it is said that the rear bullock attached by a chain to the wagon, 'drags the chain' if it slows down. **1994** *Dominion* (Wellington) 23 June 6 [Heading] *Stop dragging the dog chain.* If the Government can shake off its seemingly terminal bout of canine torpor, New Zealand may one day have a dog law that fits the times.

2. In the phr. **to drag one's hook** [prob. an alteration of *take one's hook*; or f. a fig. use of *hook* anchor, to raise anchor], to leave (a place).
1962 CRUMP *One of Us* 105 I think it's time we dragged our hook, Sam. It's about time a man had a little holiday. I can feel the itchy feet coming on.

drag, *n.*

1. Mining. a. As **drag ball**, a loose iron ball attached to a chain for crushing ore in a berdan (see quot.).
1876 *TrNZI* VIII. 179 These tailings are treated in berdans with extra quicksilver and ground up. The berdans now in use at the Thames..are generally five feet in diameter... At one time a couple of rotating balls were considered sufficient for the amount of crushing required; now, the general practice is to have a loose ball as well as a stationary one attached to a chain, and it is called a drag ball; this drag does more work than a loose ball..for the drag grinds the bowl as much as the tailings.

b. As **dragstone**. [Cf. OED *drag n.* 9 *drag-fold, drag-line*; Webster (1961) *drag* 5 b (6) a bending of rock strata adjacent to a fault. Cf. **1907** *NZGeol.SB (NS)* No.4 114 This faulting has effected a considerable 'drag' of the vein to the eastward.] Deposits of loose rock produced by a geological fault.
1938 *NZ Geol. Memoir No.4* 74 Buhman further casts doubt on the so-called 'dragstone', the position of which influenced prospecting for the lost portion..; he mentions that drag quartz diminished when followed up the fault-plane and along the strike of the fault, whereas the amount of dragstone should have increased as the lost portion of the ore-body was approached. **1948** *NZGeol.SB (NS)* No.42 53 The continuation of the lode was relatively upthrown south-west of the fault, as appeared to be suggested by the up-turning of the lode against the fault and drag-stone... The channel may be offset, but dragstone should indicate in which direction to seek.

2. Sawmilling. a. *Ellipt.* for 'drag-saw', a *drag-tooth* saw (that is, one equipped with *drag-teeth*, b below), smaller than a breaking-down saw and used for converting flitches into timber.
1920 MANDER *Story NZ River* (1974) 159 By day the whole bay vibrated with the whistle and screech of the circular saws, the tear of the break downs, the rasp of the drags. *Ibid.* 198 [The log] was then levered..on to greased rollers & rushed towards the big circulars, which turned it into flitches. Then the small circulars, the drag, & the goose completed its metamorphosis into the regulation strips.

b. drag-tooth, a tooth in a (crosscut) saw shaped to clear the saw-cut of sawdust.
1874 BAINES *Edward Crewe* 173 Cross-cut saws

have what is called a peg-tooth and cut both ways. It is a great improvement to sharpen every fifth tooth, counting from the centre to the ends, as a drag tooth, that is, a tooth filed square across and with a considerable hook, this arrangement tends to keep the cut clear of sawdust.

dragon-tree. *Obs.* [Spec. use of *dragon-tree* plants of the *Dracaena* genus.] CABBAGE-TREE 1.
1773 FORSTER *Resolution Jrnl.* 13 May (1982) II. 277 An infinite variety of high trees & shrubbery [in Dusky Bay], among which the New-Zeeland Dragon-tree (*Dracaena antarctica*) is very remarkable. **1817** NICHOLAS *Voyage NZ* II. 247 [Cook's people] found here also..a new species of dragon-tree, the central shoot of which partook at once both of the flavour of cabbage and of an almond kernel. **1847** ANGAS *Savage Life* I. 240 The tropical-looking dragon-trees (dracaena), called *ti* by the natives..grow up the steep sides of the hills. **1853** EARP *NZ* 92 The sides of the [Wellington] hills.. are almost tropical in their character, from the abundance of the *ti*, or dragon trees, with which they are covered.

draining-pen. [AND 1886.] A pen in which animals emerging from a dip can shed the surplus liquid, which then drains back into the dip.
c1875 MEREDITH *Adventuring in Maoriland* (1935) 88 At the end of the dip are two draining-pens, used alternately. **1986** RICHARDS *Off the Sheep's Back* 48 Dad was..responsible for timing each dip full of sheep before opening the gate and letting them out into the draining pens.

draught, draughting, varr. DRAFT, DRAFTING.

draw, *v. Whaling. intr.* Of a harpoon, to disengage from a whale, or fail to remain fixed in its target.
1836 *Piraki Log* 16 July (1911) 39 1 P.M. saw a whale... Mate got fast but his Iron drew.

draw, *n. Logging.* Also **drawer**. A long sliver of wood drawn out of the barrel of a tree being felled and usu. remaining attached to the stump when the tree falls. See also STRINGER *n.*[2]
1950 p.c. Roy Gilberd (Northland). [The fibres of wood in a tree just about to fall] do not part all in one plane and 'stringers' or 'drawers' are drawn out of the barrel, sometimes several feet long. Sometimes men on contract, trying to save timber, place their saw-cut too low and some of the wood-fibres break off up in the barrel. These are 'stringers' while they are breaking, and 'slivers' or 'drawers' when they are left upright in the sloven. **1953** REED *Story of Kauri* 151 A 'draw' was a serious defect, but was not due to any fault in the living tree. When a tree fell before it was quite severed, it sometimes, in the act of falling, wrenched or 'drew' out a portion of the butt, leaving great jagged, fang-like splinters adhering to the stump. The damage was, of course, always to the heart wood... *Ibid.* 156 Very often, before the saw got within a foot or so of the front scarf, the tree would start to fall gradually, and the uncut timber between the saw and the front scarf would have to break, and seldom cleanly; the heart, being more brittle than the sap, would break here and there, several feet above where the sawcut would have been standing straight. As the tree fell, these pieces, still attached to the stump, would draw out of the tree, and being almost heart-wood became the chief defect we call 'draws'.

dray, *n.*

1. In early New Zealand, usu. a two-wheeled cart, orig. drawn by bullocks (see also *bullock-dray* (BULLOCK *n.* 2 a), *pack-dray* (PACK *n.*[1] 3)),

DRAY

and later usu. a high-platformed single-horse-drawn shafted cart with sides (if sprung, called a 'spring-dray'; if with a tipping mechanism, a 'tip dray'); often in early settlement also (as in Britain) a four-wheeled wagon or *draycart* (OED 1719) as in the 1848 quot. See also *horse-dray* (HORSE *n.*[1] 5).
1846 WHISKER *Memo. Book* (ATLMS) 21 One of the Drays broke down about one mile from the camp with shot and rum on it. [**1848** WAKEFIELD *Handbook NZ* 97 Except for the conveyance of heavy goods, for which dray-carts drawn by bullocks are chiefly used, locomotion [in Wellington] is much easier on foot.] **1857** *Lyttelton Times* 1 July 5 A ford has been opened for drays opposite the seventh mile post on the North road. **1868** LYTTELTON *Two Lectures* 31 But drays are much used, open in front and behind, and like an improved costermonger's barrow. **1882** POTTS *Out in Open* 72 That object that seems all but motionless is the store-laden dray, slowly, painfully dragged onward towards the station by the patient efforts of the straining bullock team. **1900** WRIGHT *Wisps of Tussock* in *Centennial Treasury Otago Verse* (1949) 58 And the fork tines flash as the sheaves are turned on the frame of the one-horse dray. **1904** LANCASTER *Sons o' Men* 72 None of them had a hope [of beating me] if they'd come singly. But they spilt on me like shingle from a tip-dray. **1951** MCLEOD *NZ High Country* A fine new dray..left Windwhistle..with a shiny new body and red painted wheels, only to arrive next day at the station with every speck of paint blown off. **1994** NOTT *Sound Living* 12 I would harness up the old horse into the dray and swing the cans of cream into the dray to go off down to the wharf to put them on the mail launch which came in twice a week to deliver the mail and stores and collect cream.

2. *attrib.* and *Comb.* **a.** *attrib.*
1866 BARKER *Station Life* (1870) 49 It was preceded by two dray-loads of small rough-hewn stone piles. **1874** KENNAWAY *Crusts* 155 After picking up our fourteen pigs,—and with the assistance of a couple of dray-ropes piling them on the sledge as securely as dead pigs may be piled,—we started for home. *Ibid.* 169 The driver had succeeded in freeing an axe which was..lashed to the guard-irons, with the intention of cutting the dray-pole, and so letting the team escape. **1939** BEATTIE *First White Boy Born Otago* 120 [Matagouri] had been killed by fires..leaving blackened sticks which could be gathered by drayloads and carted away for firewood.

b. Special Comb. **dray-cloth**, a tarpaulin or other cover to protect a dray load; **drayman** [AND 1831], one who earns a living driving a dray; **dray-road** [AND 1843], **dray-track** *obs.* [AND 1843], a road or track negotiable by drays (including bullock-drays) but difficult or impossible for other kinds of wheeled vehicle.
1874 KENNAWAY *Crusts* 72 We stretched the **dray-cloth**, or tarpaulin, full-spread over the loaded dray, pinning it to the ground all round. **1866** BARKER *Station Life* (1870) 62 [We have to] hire a **drayman** who possesses a team of bullocks and a dray of his own, to fetch it to us. **1939** BEATTIE *First White Boy Born Otago* 129 In Shag Valley draymen and others can get charred timber on the hills. **1959** MASTERS *Tales of Mails* 68 On the way up the Blowhard the drayman ran into a bad storm. **1845** WAKEFIELD *Adventure NZ* II. 159 The proprietors constructed a **dray-road** down the steep side. **1849** ALLOM *Letter* in Earp *Handbook* (1852) 116 A dray road has been formed from the most northern station to Tekopi. **1868** *Marlborough Express* (Blenheim) 6 June 6 The road would be longer..than the present bridle-track over the Maungatapu, but then it would be a dray-road. **1902** *Settler's Handbook NZ* 33 At the fringes of settlement..the history of road-

making is as follows: First comes the bridle-track, that gradually grows into the dray-road; and then comes the metal. **1930** Dobson *Reminiscences* 171 One brilliant genius proposed to build a railway on a dray road, which was to be made on dray road gradients and curves. **1949** Shaw & Farrant *Taieri Plain* 22 To begin with a 'dray' road was completed as far as the Saddle Hill coal mines—that is to say a track wide enough for a wagon, for as yet there was no metal. **1967** May *West Coast Gold Rushes* 158 The dray road terminated at the Howard River and coaches ran part of the distance. **1859** Fuller *Five Years Residence* 149 Improvements to a Run..[consist of] partial cuttings for a **dray-track** when required to be made. **1862** *AJHR E-9* 25 There would be no difficulty..in making a practicable dray-track... Above that point, the great height..would make it difficult to get even a good bridle-track. **1898** Hocken *Contributions* 198 Some old Australian diggers, engaged in cutting a dray track..discovered the precious metal. **1931** Lovell-Smith *Old Coaching Days* 19 It was not until 1860 that money was forthcoming to make a dray track from West Taieri to Black's station.

dray, *v. Obs.* [Used elsewhere but recorded earliest in NZ: OED 1857.] *trans.* To carry in or transport by dray.
1857 *Richmond-Atkinson Papers* (1960) I. 318 We found him away 'draying' Mr Moore's wool. **1866** Barker *Station Life* (1870) 39 My house..is being *cut out* in Christchurch, and will be drayed to our station next month.

Hence **draying** *vbl. n.* and *ppl. a.*, (pertaining to) the action or process of transporting by dray.
1857 *Lyttelton Times* 13 May 8 Stock owners have been enabled to complete their draying operations with ease. **1863** Butler *First Year* x 159 Then follows the draying of the wool to port, and the bullocks come in for their full share of work. **1866** Barker *Station Life* (1870) 62 Most stations have a bush near to the homestead, or greater facilities for draying than we possess.

dredge, *n.*
1. Special Comb. **dredge paddock**, the area being worked by a gold-dredge inclusive of its pond; **dredge pond**, the pool of water on which a dredge floats, being constantly formed as the dredge moves forward, and filled with tailings behind; **dredge oyster**, see oyster 2 (1).
1919 *Alexandra Herald* 20 Aug. 5 Five to six heads of water came continuously from the dam to the dredge paddock. **1962** Evans *Waikaka Saga* 38 'Lines' here refers to ropes, and the punt for carrying the coal across the dredge pond to the dredge. *Ibid.* 80 A Mr. Lusk was drowned in one of the United dredge ponds.

2. As **dredgie**, a worker on a gold-dredge, a dredge-man.
1963 Pearson *Coal Flat* 275 But, bugger me, these bloody miners and dredgies come along and spoil it.

dredge, *v.*
1. As **dredge out** [f. *dredge* to dig out as with a dredge], to extract with difficulty or in a messy or slovenly fashion.
1960 Crump *Good Keen Man* 14 I'd sat on the wood block, dredged out the letter Jim Reed had given me, and worked the flap open with a knife.

2. dredgeable *a.*, able to be worked with a gold-dredge; country on which a gold-dredge can work.
1906 Galvin *NZ Mining Handbook* 276 This is a valley about nineteen miles in length and containing over 5,000 acres of dredgable land.

dredging claim. A claim worked by a dredge or by dredging.
1892 Pyke *Gold-Miners' Guide* 7 Claims..comprise ordinary claims..frontage claims, special claims and dredging claims. **1902** *Settler's Handbook NZ* 59 Crossing the Beaumont Bridge the road follows the west bank of the Clutha, passing numerous dredging-claims. **1914** Pfaff *Diggers' Story* 120 Meeting a miner on the road, he asked him if he knew the site of such-and-such a dredging claim.

dried hash: see dry hash.

drift, *n.*[1] [Spec. use of Brit. dial *drift* something driven: see OED *drift* 7.] draft *n.* Also as *v.* **drift off**, to draft out certain animals by driving them from a main mob.
1856 *Richmond-Atkinson Papers* (1960) I. 201 After dinner Henry, Brind & I took up a 'drift' of cattle & then as there was a nice breeze we lighted our clearings. **1982** *Agric. Gloss.* (MAF) 5 *Draft off or drafting*: Removing certain animals from a group. This can be done by driving the animals out of a group (cut off or drift off) or driving them up a race and removing them through a special gate (drafting gate).

drift, *n.*[2] *Goldmining.* [AND 1852.] A deposit of sand, gravel, etc. left by (flood) water. Also *attrib.* passing into special Comb. **drift gold**, gold found in drift.
1862 Wekey *Otago As It Is* 64 'To bottom a hole'..means to convey the sinking of a shaft down to the bed-rock on which the auriferous drift generally rests. **1870** *TrNZI* II. 371 The source of these..is from the disintegration of a parent rock, and together with the other elements of the rock, they constitute what is known as 'drift'. Gold drift consists of sand and gravel containing gold. **1890** *TrNZI* XXII. 403 There is a nuggety..appearance about drift-gold which reef-gold does not present. **1892** Pyke *Gold-Miners' Guide* 110 *Tunnelling and Driving*—Through drift or blue reef: 1s.6d. per foot for the first 500ft. **1906** Galvin *NZ Mining Handbook* 129 The gold that has been got has been technically called 'drift'—that is, simply thrown up on sheltered beaches where there has been a sharp bend. **1914** Morgan *Rep. Geol. Survey* in Evans *Waikaka Saga* (1962) 4 A rich layer in the fault-involved older quartz drifts..was worked from the surface. **1970** Wood *Gold Trails of Otago* 81 The gold from the..sediments became re-concentrated in the younger terrace gravels and alluvium, or 'younger drifts' of the miners.

drink *v.*: *drink with the flies*, see fly *n.*[2] 1.

drinking funnel. *Hist.* A special funnel (Maori *ngutu*) for feeding a Maori tohunga, who cannot through tapu touch food or drink.
1927 Donne *Maori Past & Present* 76 [Caption] Drinking-funnel for tohunga when tapu. **1955** Phillipps *Maori Carving* 9 Four beautifully-carved drinking funnels are on exhibition.

drinking horn. Also **Drinking Horn contest**. A drinking contest among New Zealand university students involving the timed emptying of glasses of beer.
[**1935** Smad 1 May 2 Shortly before Easter, Ian Campbell presented a priceless drinking horn, mounted on priceless wood, to be the trophy for an inter-Varsity drinking contest.] **1939** *Salient* (Wellington) 19 Apr. 2 'Salient'..interviewed the Professor, and endeavoured to ascertain if he was training for future Drinking Horn Contests. **1945** *Ibid.* 9 Apr. 2 Take twenty four husky Varsity men, surround 'em with two hundred shouting, singing, hakaing supporters, place 'em under the eagle eye of mine host of the Occidental..put thirty-six handles of the best..and the answer's The Drinking Horn. **1956** *Ibid.* 3 May 1 First move to ban the Drinking Horn contest held in conjunction with New Zealand University tournaments was checked temporarily by a procedural motion. **1963** Casey *As Short a Spring* 8 Like a drinking-horn, all you had to do was to get it down soon enough and keep it down long enough. **1979** *Salient* (Wellington) 23 Apr. 9 [Heading] Drinking Horn Mon 23rd. Starts 12.15. **1986** *Campus News* 8 Sept. 17 He must be [politically unsound]: he organised this year's drinking horn. **1992** *Metro* (Auckland) Mar. 105 The Drinking Horn is the big event of the year.

drive, *v.*
1. *Northland logging.* [Cf. OED 7 b '*U.S., Canada and N.Z.*', US 1848.] *trans.* Also **drive out**. To move (a mass of floating logs) downstream by opening a flood-dam, or by a natural flood.
1874 Baines *Edward Crewe* 170 The 'stand of kauri' I had acquired..was estimated to contain upwards of a million feet of timber, capable of being 'driven out' by placing a flood-dam in a suitable position..too great a body of water filling the creek at one time for a 'drive'. **1889** [see boom]. **1894** *NZ Official Year-book* 332 Often it is necessary to construct costly dams to impound the water in the upper parts of the creek, in order that it may be suddenly liberated..so that the entire assemblage of [kauri] logs may be 'driven' to the booms. In dry seasons the logs may remain in the bed of the creek for months, and, occasionally, after a successful 'drive', the harvest of logs is carried out to sea and lost. **1906** Laing & Blackwell *Plants NZ* 63 Here [the kauri logs] lie until a 'fresh' drives them down the creek or harbour where the 'boom' lies waiting. **1913** *NZGeol.SB (NS)* No.16 19 The logs were transported to the mill in the case of the Waitanui by a wooden-railed tramway; in the case of the Tamaki they were 'driven'. **1951** McCarroll *Days of Kauri Bushmen* [Radio Talk 4: (TS)] It was a great dam and [c1914] drove 10,000,000 feet of timber out.

Hence **driving** *vbl. n.*, the action or process of moving a mass of timber downstream; also used *attrib.* in special Comb.: **driving creek**, a creek, either naturally suitable or prepared by damming, down which a mass of logs can be driven; **driving dam**, a dam which includes a tripping device to release the water and the logs trapped behind it, or placed in the channel before it.
1889 Kirk *Forest Flora* 151 In back-country where the mills depend upon **driving** for the supply of [kauri] logs..dry weather..may prevent conversion. **1912** *NZGeol.SB (NS)* No.15 34 The 'driving' of the large kauri-logs in the creeks by 'tripping' dams during flood-time has had a marked effect on many of the watercourses. **1896** *AJHR I-4A* 20 You have been in that district, about the creeks where the driving of logs takes place? **1875** *TrNZI* VII. 186 Stripped of their branches they could be floated down the **driving creeks** with the ordinary logs. **1889** *TrNZI* XXI. 38 My son..took a leading spur on the right bank of what had been a driving-creek for kauri logs. **1953** Reed *Story of Kauri* 215 In a steep driving creek..the sub-contractor had built a dam in very much of a hurry. **1904** *TrNZI* XXXVI. 464 When the natural supply of water is not sufficient to float these [logs] they are forced along by **driving-dams**. **1991** *Historic Places* Sept. 27 Inventive methods of transportation were devised to get logs to the mills. One of the most ingenious involved the use of timber dams, known as driving dams... When enough water had built up, the dam would be tripped and the logs carried down stream to the sawmill on the resulting flood.

2. [Perh. transf. f. *drive* 1.] *intr.* and *trans.* To scarf a group of trees in such a way as to cause all to fall in serial fashion when a key tree falls; of a key tree, to topple (a group of scarfed trees) in its line of fall; of a group of scarfed trees, to fall serially. Often as a *vbl. n.* [AND 1909].

1899 BELL *In Shadow of Bush* 83 Harry had just given the last cut of the axe to a big rimu, which, after a few premonitory cracks as it began to move, fell, driving before it in its line of fall a dozen or so of the smaller trees, which had been 'scarfed' or cut partly through in readiness, and skilfully, so that each, when struck, might again in its turn strike and bring down another. The noise of a fall or drive of this kind is like thunder. **1904** LANCASTER *Sons o' Men* 286 That kahikitea [sic] 'll drive like skittles wi' a good man atop. **1951** LEVY *Grasslands NZ* (1970) 241 Next, the forest trees up to approximately 30 in. in diameter were felled by a system of driving, the trees being notched on the upper and lower side of the drive, which commenced at the top of the slope and proceeded downwards. **1952** LYON *Faring South* 179 The bushmen developed an expert knowledge of driving, or directing one tree against another, or a body of trees, which swept a great weight in one irresistible drive of crashing and thunderous timber. **1986** RICHARDS *Off the Sheep's Back* 15 The three brothers spent the first few weeks clearing, learning the art of chopping, scarfing, driving and working a face.

Hence **driver** *n.*, a 'key' tree chosen and prepared to start the driving process.

1952 LYON *Faring South* 178 Again, a tough old rata or hinau often had a tall pine felled and lodged in its branches, with the result that the weight of the driver and the lower tree were too much for the supporting one, and a few cautious axe strokes completed the job.

drive, *n.*[1] *Mining.* [f. DRIVE *v.* (*Mining*) to excavate horizontally (OED *v.* 10): AND 1857.] A horizontal tunnel.

1867 COOPER *Digger's Diary* 27 Oct. (1978) 27 Taking the claims as they came, the first..consisted of a drive of about a hundred feet into a prominent looking 'spur'. **1874** BAINES *Edward Crewe* 262 Our reef, or leader, measuring only four inches in thickness, a drive for a considerable distance following the course of the gold-bearing quartz had to be carried out. **1880** LAPHAM *We Four* 18 There was a deserted 'drive' up on the spur. **1912** PURNELL *Modern Arthur* 17 Then rushed the [coal] miners from their hollow 'drives'. **1928** DEVANNY *Dawn Beloved* 169 Drives were broken off at right angles to [the dip heading] at distances of two chains apart thus forming pillars on either side of the dip, two chains square. These drives were called main levels. **1973** McCARTHY *Listen..!* 54 Paddy made bigger money than most of the miners, taking on contracting work in driving the levels, or drives. These drives were the roadways where we trucked the stone from the stopes.

drive, *n.*[2] *Northland logging.* [Cf. DRIVE *v.*]

1. [OED *drive n.* 1 a 1860 (N. Amer.) the impelling of a mass of logs; 3 b 1878 (N. Amer.) the mass of timber driven.] The moving, or movement, of a mass of logs by a rush of water; the mass so moved.

1874 BAINES *Edward Crewe* 176 When all was completed I had one hundred logs rolled into the stream below, and thirty above the dam. I then fixed upon a day and an hour to have a 'drive,' and mustered all the men I could. **1889** [see BOOM]. **1894** [see DRIVE *v.* 1]. **1913** *NZGeol.SB* (NS) No.16 27 During a 'drive' the logs, driven by the rush of the waters, scour out the bottoms of the creeks, and create artificial floods, by which logs, dragged to the creeks, may be transported. **1922** *Auckland Weekly News* 9 Mar. 33 [Caption] When there are sufficient logs for a 'drive', the dam is 'tripped' during a 'fresh' or flood. **1953** REED *Story of Kauri* 221 Other men, if available, would at the same time be preparing the creek bed for the 'drive'. **1991** *Historic Places* Sept. 28 The release of water and logs by tripping the dam was known as a drive.

2. [Cf. OED 3 b, 1899 (NZ), then 1940: AND 1904.] The serial felling of a group of trees by causing each to fall so as to topple the others.

1899 [see DRIVE *v.* 2]. **1913** CARR *Country Work* 31 Even the most experienced men sometimes get caught by a falling tree or branch, or clearing a 'drive' that has missed. **1947** KENWAY *Quondam Quaker* 53 Selecting a certain group of trees he will 'belly scarf' and 'back scarf' the lot... If this 'drive' as it is termed, has been well-managed the whole lot will came down together. **1951** [see DRIVE *v.* 2]. **1961** CRUMP *Hang On a Minute Mate* 42 Jack learned about scarfing, backing, limbing,...toms, strops, drives, triggers. **1972** NEWTON *Wake of Axe* 117 He had seen as many as twenty-four men in a single [professional bushfalling] gang and they worked 'drives' of up to five acres and more [in the King Country]. **1986** RICHARDS *Off the Sheep's Back* 22 It was quite a common practice for experienced bushmen, to have a 'drive'. If you are chopping up a 'face' and there is a large tree behind you further up the face, you select that as the 'key'. To save time..you do not waste time by chopping down each tree individually, but just 'scarf' and partly chop each tree. When all is ready and you have worked back to the key, you scarf it very carefully... If everything goes according to plan it will 'drive' the one below, which will in turn drive the next, and so on.

3. In competition chopping, the stroke which leads up to that which severs the block. Compare PUNCH *v.*

1983 TV1 Programme showing axemen chopping competitively: the commentator uses 'drive' freq. for the stroke which leads up to the *punch*, the blow which severs the block.

driver. *Shearing.* [AND 1905.] A strap of leather or other suitable material on hand shears (see quot. 1989).

1933 *Press* (Christchurch) (Acland Gloss.) 14 Oct. 15 *Driver.*—A leather strap on the handle of a pair of shears, which fits over the back of the shearer's hand. **1951** McLEOD *NZ High Country* 26 The shearers buy their shears from the station and then proceed to cut them and bend them, and embellish them with 'drivers', 'knockers', 'jockeys' and 'cockspurs' until their makers would hardly recognise them. **1978** JARDINE *Shadows on Hill* 130 They had received their two free pairs of blades..and had spent many hours at the two big grindstones 'taking them down', attaching drivers, jockeys, spurs and knockers. **1989** *NZ Eng. Newsletter* III. 24 *driver*: A leather strap on hand shears. This fits firmly round the handle and over the back of the shearer's hand, thus allowing more drive to be given to a blow while preventing the hands from slipping over the blades. Sometimes this is also called the 'monkey'.

drongo /ˈdrɒŋɡəʊ/. Occas. abbrev. **dronk**. [AND 1941: transf. use of *drongo* the name of a bird, perh. influenced by the name of an Austral. racehorse running between 1923 and 1925.] A stupid or clumsy fool. Also *transf.* (see quot. 1990).

1951 *Moa on Lambton Quay* 21 Some drongo's beer spills on your tweeds As you're drinking. **1953** SUTTON-SMITH *Unorganized Games NZ Primary School Children* (VUWTS) II. 677 Some of the [slang] expressions listed by children..rag bag..dronk, drongo, dill, dip, dippy..(South Wellington). **1963** CASEY *As Short a Spring* 251 If you gave that drongo fifty bucks he'd still think you were holding out on him. **1976** HILLIARD *Send Somebody Nice* 32 'Drongos,' Max hisses. 'Wart-heads. Dingbats. Halfwits.' **1984** WILSON *S. Pacific Street* 43 You're sure we wouldn't be just two lousy drongoes and get in everyone's way? **1990** *Dominion Sunday Times* (Wellington) 4 Mar. 19 The extra men get to stand in the middle of a circle of eight and feel silly. This dance is known as the drongo. She'll be coming round the drongo when she comes.

dronk: see DRONGO.

drop, *v.*

1. a. [Transf. f. an orig. reference to farm animals, esp. sheep, giving birth: cf. OED 14.] In male informal use, to give birth to a baby (see also *to drop one's bundle* (BUNDLE 2)).

1964 HARVEY *Any Old Dollars Mister?* 71 Well, we started talking about this and that and ended up on Nuts's sister Violet, the one who was having this baby. 'When's she goin' to drop it?' Jim Dickson asked Nuts. 'Drop what?' 'The kid.' Snigger, snigger. 'She's not goin' to drop it,' said Nuts angrily. 'It's goin' to be born.' 'Same thing.'

b. In the phr. **to drop** (someone) **in it**, to land (someone) in a difficult situation.

1988 McGILL *Dict. Kiwi Slang* 40 *drop in it* put someone in trouble; eg 'You really dropped me in it with the wife telling her I was the one wanting another round.'

c. In the phr. **to drop** (a person or thing) **like a hot scone**, to get rid of, to eliminate from a team or activity.

1968 SLATTER *Pagan Game* 155 Dropped him [from the first fifteen] like a hot scone.

d. In the phr. **to drop one's bundle**, see BUNDLE.

2. *trans.* To cut down (trees, scrub, etc.), to fell.

1904 LANCASTER *Sons o' Men* 165 Their cross-cut bit through a trunk and dropped it for the [timber] shoe. **1964** FRANCES *Johnny Rapana* 27 'We're dropping the trees on Marsden's place—which we should have started this morning.' **1981** *Evening Post* (Wellington) 5 Mar. 28 [Cartoon] Push off young Pew! It'll take a lot more than one scrawny little magpie to stop me dropping this tree mate. **1983** *Evening Post* (Wellington) 7 Nov. 36 These scrubcutters are supposed to be cuttin' the barbery [sic] but they're droppin' the kanuka as well.

drop, *n.* [f. *drop* something dropped.]

1. *Farming.* **a.** [AND 1838, 1903.] The number of farm animals (esp. lambs) born on a farm in a season.

1977 *Dominion* (Wellington) 20 Sept. I. 9 Lamb losses were staggering. One farmer had lost 1850 lambs out of 2100—90 percent of his drop. **1986** *National Radio* 'Landline' (Farming Programme) 20 Sept. Lambing has gone well with Nelson farmers reporting the highest drop ever.

b. In the phr. **on-the-drop**, of a farm animal, about to give birth.

1982 *Agric. Gloss.* (MAF) 13 *On-the-drop*: Animal about to give birth.

2. [Back formation f. DROPPER *n.*[2]] A delivery of sly-grog liquor.

1976 McCLENAGHAN *Travelling Man* 21 I'll take care of the bill until you're able to yourselves, which should be when you've made your first two drops.

Hence **dropping** *vbl. n. obs.*, the delivery of an order of sly-grog.

1973 SARGESON *Once Is Enough* 81 When I first visited the farm he had told me stories about King Country drinking, that was to say, 'sly-grogging' and 'dropping'. **1976** McCLENAGHAN *Travelling Man* 19 'You think we could do a little dropping?' he said...

The sale of liquor was prohibited in the King Country..that didn't mean people couldn't drink.

3. [Extended use of *drop* a small quantity of liquid: cf. OED *n.* 6.] A brew or selection of liquor.

1974 Agnew *Loner* 180 They've got a good drop at the Park Hotel. I can recommend it.'

drop on. To happen on (esp. gold).

1862 Chudleigh *Diary* 28 Oct. (1950) 64 I went in the other direction and droped [*sic*] on the [strayed] horses about 3 miles from home. **1862** *Otago Goldfields & Resources* 25 The most inexperienced man.. has..every prospect of 'dropping' upon one of those rich patches which are the object of every miner's ambition. **1864** Thatcher *Songs of War* 6 And each steamer will bring up a cargo Of Victorian diggers... They're the boys that can drop on the metal.

dropper, *n.*[1] *Fencing*. [Orig. perhaps laths 'dropped' through slots in the rails of a post and rail fence to keep them rigid as distinct from posts fixed in ground (see quot. 1904, Lancaster): AND 1897.] A vertical lath (or, later, a steel strip) stapled (or wired) into a wire fence in the spaces between posts to increase the rigidity and to fix wire-spacing. See also BATTEN. Cf. STANDARD a.

c1875 Meredith *Adventuring in Maoriland* (1935) 68 Between the posts the wires are stapled to 'droppers', consisting of about three by one battens. **1904** Lancaster *Sons o' Men* 93 It was a viciously strained ten-wire, with close standards; and every other wire was a barb. Condy, who had prayed for slotted droppers, collapsed in the saddle. **1912** *Otago Witness* (Dunedin) 29 May 33 In the erection of a wire fence it is usual to put the posts in the ground at a comfortable distance apart, droppers being used as intermediate attachments to the wires to keep them from opening or contracting so that animals are prevented from forcing their way between the wire. **1927** *NZ Dairy Produce Exporter* 26 Feb. 39 She grabbed something between a dropper and a post. **1965** Henderson *Open Country* 55 When all the wires are strained tightly the battens or droppers, which are split to about two inches square, are stapled at spaces varying from two to three feet. **1982** *Agric. Gloss.* (MAF) 27 *Dropper*: Same as batten... Used in parts of South Island and Australia.

dropper, *n.*[2] *Obs*. [f. *drop* (sly-grog) *off* a train, truck, etc.]

1. *Orig. King Country*. One who delivers (i.e. drops off) sly-grog supplies in a dry district, either by lorry or from a train; a sly-grog retailer or wholesaler.

1911 *Truth* 28 Oct. 4 It is possible to get as much liquor as one wants in Masterton, and while much of it..is of good quality, much more (surreptitiously dispensed at sly-groggeries and by what are locally termed 'droppers' at enhanced prices) is atrocious and harmful liquor. **1912** Ibid. 26 Oct. 6 The man who enters a boarding or 'temperance' house is immediately accused of having rolled a beer barrel through the maze of the Licensing Act. He is suspected of designs of all descriptions. He is dubbed 'a dropper', or 'blind tiger.' **1949** Sargeson *I Saw in My Dream* (1974) 247 When the police raided her [*sc.* a sly-groggery]..they reckoned they'd got her this time, because they'd found out a dropper had been through the town just a few nights before on his lorry. So they reckoned she'd be well stocked up. **1952** p.c. from a King Country informant. A gang of the boys often beat up the local 'dropper' in Raurimu, who can't say anything or else he'll get had up for 'dropping'. The police usually allow only one 'dropper' in the town and clamp down on the others. **1976** McClenaghan *Travelling Man* 20 They could bring in their own liquor..and there was no reason why they should when they could rely on the droppers. **1985** Hermans *Capital Coppers* 12 [The introduction of No-licence to the Waiararapa] brought a new problem in the form of the sly grog seller (or '*dropper*')... One well known '*dropper*'..used to plant his bottles under street culverts for his clients.

2. In the hotel trade during the period of six o'clock closing, a hotel worker who acted as a look-out for police, and handed out illegal after-hours take-away liquor.

1951 *Dominion* (Wellington) 5 Apr. 8 We [*sc.* hotelworkers] want £2 a week extra for the 'looker-out' and the 'dropper'. **1974** Morrieson *Predicament* (1981) 61 Have a swig for Christmas... A man isn't a big time dropper for nothing.

dropper, *n.*[3] *Farming*. [f. *drop v.* to hang down.]

1. Carrying-sacks or receptacles hooked on to pack saddles. Cf. POCKET *n.*[2]

1949 Newton *High Country Days* 38 Potatoes and vegetables were in sacks known as 'droppers' which would hang from the hooks on each side of the pack saddles.

2. Usu. *pl.*, see quots.

1951 p.c. G.W. Turner: Droppers are the two small pipes to which the tubes with suction cups are attached. They hang or 'drop' into the bail from the main pipeline of the milking machine. **1982** *Agric. Gloss.* (MAF) 40 *Droppers*: Tubes which hang down and carry the milk[,] or pulsation tubes

3. In a shearing-shed, a flexible tube which hangs down from above the shearer and carries a revolving drive-shaft which powers the mechanism of machine shears.

1955 Bowen *Wool Away* 4 When the comb digs in it makes the sheep kick and the dropper moves around and loses its true swing. **1989** Richards *Pioneer's Life* 41 I now have a collection of antiques..old handpieces, combs, cutters, droppers.

droppie. *Rugby football*. Also **droppy**. [f. *drop*(kick + -IE.] A dropkick; a dropped goal.

1970 Slatter *On the Ball* 138 Down slams the scrum, Wales hook, and Cleaver has a droppy that spins just wide of the post. **1975** Howitt *NZ Rugby Greats* 17 I scored a try, kicked a droppie and played a blinder. **1981** *Dominion* (Wellington) 6 Apr. 20 [Heading] Droppie undoes Hutt. A 40 metre dropped goal by Porirua City centre Don Baker enabled his side to score a grand 11–10 last minute rugby league victory.

droppy, var. DROPPIE.

drover. [AND 1841.] One whose occupation is driving stock usu. over long distances. Cf. *cattle-driver* (CATTLE 2); *stock driver*, (STOCK 2 a).

1842 *Smith's Rep.* Nov. in Wakefield *Handbook NZ* (1848) 343 Cattle have been driven from Oihoa (or Go-ashore),.. to Akaroa in about eight hours;.. my informant was one of the drovers. **1856** Fitton *NZ* 278 The vulgar delusion that, in order to be a colonist in earnest, it is expedient to dress like a drover..is now quite out of fashion. **1904** Chudleigh *Diary* 2 Mar. (1950) 420 Took the sheep over the hill [to Lyttelton] myself with 2 drovers. **1910** *Awards, etc.* 584 [Drovers and Shepherds Award] A 'drover' shall mean a person who is hired from time to time for the purpose of driving stock, and trucking stock if required. **1933** *Press* (Christchurch) (Acland Gloss.) 14 Oct. 15 *Drover*.—One who drives stock for a living. In Canterbury they were usually spoken of as sheep- or cattle-drivers until about 1900. There is a newly formed verb, *to drove*, trans and intrans, coming into use. **1947** Beattie *Early Runholding* 12 In my boyhood [1880s] we called a man driving sheep a drover, and a man driving cattle a stock-driver or stock-rider or stockman. **1952** Meek *Station Days* 110 Drovers: Men who drive sheep or cattle on the road. **1970** Thomas *Way Up North* 55 Starting in the extreme north these drover buyers would buy any cattle they found for sale, mostly store steers.

Hence **drove** *v*. [f. *drover* by back-formation: AND 1847], to drive animals in an organized mob on the hoof, usu. over long distances; **droving** *vbl. n.*, the occupation of a drover, or the method or result of carrying it out.

1910 *Truth* 23 Apr. 1 Counsel: 'You drive for a living?' Witness: 'No, I'm a drover.' Counsel: 'Well, you drive sheep for a living?' Witness: 'No; I drove.' Counsel: 'Do you mean you used to drive?' Witness: 'No, I drove now.'

drum, *n.*

1. *Obs.* [Poss. from the cylindrical drum-like shape of a rolled *swag*: AND 1866.] A rolled swag (see SWAG *n.*[1] 1 a). See also *hump one's drum* (HUMP *v.* 2 c).

1889 Ross *Complete Guide Lakes Central Otago* 44 'Time's up!' is called, the 'drum' (the local [*sc.* Mt. Earnslaw] for swag) hoisted on, and the final ascent begins. **1906** Picard *Ups & Downs* 7 You may look down on a man who gives his swag, drum, knot, or parcel of bags a shove round the land. **1911** [see SWAG *n.*[1] 3 c]. **1933** *Press* (Christchurch) (Acland Gloss.) 14 Oct. 15 *Drum*.—Swag, obviously from the shape. Hence **drummer**. **1947–48** Beattie *Pioneer Recolls.* (1956) 55 When passing Jimmy Holland's, I felt a wee bit queer; I thought I'd throw the old drum down And have a pint of beer.

2. [See OED *n.*[1] 9 e; AND 1879.] A house or lodgings; *spec*. a brothel.

1906 *Truth* 8 Sept. 4 Rossini had been fined for keeping a 'drum' in Auckland. **1980** MacKenzie *While We Have Prisons* 96 *drum* house, lodgings.

Hence **drum** *v.*, to steal from a house or dwelling.

1980 MacKenzie *While We Have Prisons* 96 *drum* (*v.*) steal from a dwelling

3. [f. a transf. use of *drum* as a signalling instrument: AND 1915.] Usu. **the drum**, correct (esp. horseracing) information. Cf. OIL.

1962 Hori *Half-gallon Jar* 23 [The race-course tout] says, '... wait till I get the drum.' I say, 'What's this drum business?' He says: 'It's the same as the oil, the griffin, and the low down.' **1980** MacKenzie *While We Have Prisons* 96 *drum*... Information. **1982** Newbold *Big Huey* 61 Taylor gave me the usual drum on the rules of the block.

Hence **drum** *v. obs.* [AND 1919] *trans.*, to give (misleading) information to.

1908 *Truth* 18 Apr. 2 The unsuspecting lad [=jockey] fell in and drummed everybody that the horse was oomey [=?certain to lose]. **1911** Ibid. 6 May 4 As to sheep, some of the mob have drummed me they'll bite if they're disturbed during nesting season.

drum, *v.* [f. a resemblance of the booming sound to drumbeats.] *intr.* Of kakapos, to make their peculiar call. Also *vbl. n.* and *attrib*.

1903 Henry *Flightless Birds of NZ* 20 Months before the appointed breeding season the male is developing an air sac in his throat, which he can puff up like a drum, and which may act as a sounding board to assist in making the curious drumming notes in spring.

Ibid. 25 I thought the drumming was just at my feet... On this ridge we got quite close to one when drumming, and it was a powerful note. **1968** HALL-JONES *Early Fiordland* 126 On one occasion the noise of the kakapos drumming on the northern side of the Sound was so loud that he had to put in at Cooper Island for the night.

drummer.

1. [Poss. a play on *drummer* as one fit only to look after *drums* (i.e. swags): AND 1897 *Obs.*] **a.** Also **drummer boy**. The slowest (often the learner) shearer in a gang.
    1911 *Maoriland Worker* 7 July 14 A 'drummer' is the man with the lowest tally—perhaps because he is likeliest to take and keep the track with his 'load'. **1934** *Press* (Christchurch) (Acland Gloss.) 20 Jan. 15 *Drummer.*—The slowest shearer in a shed. **1949** NEWTON *High Country Days* 55 Hewett, the learner, and 'drummer', of the gang, with seventeen to his credit had also shown an improvement. **1960** MASTERS *Back-Country Tales* 255 I was [c1925] only the drummer (slowest shearer) of that particular gang. **1989** RICHARDS *Pioneer's Life* 35 Already I was referred to as the Drummer Boy, a title always given to the slowest man or learner who shore on the far end of the board.

b. The youngest, least experienced or useful member of a bushfelling gang.
    1995 WINTER *All Ways Up Hill* 114 There was one exception [to the rule of matching the boss's rate of axe-work], the 'drummer'. He was a mere lad. At half past eleven his hopeful eye caught a nod from the boss, and he was off to boil up.

2. *Obs.* [Cf. DRUM *n.* 1 a swag, poss. also infl. by US *drummer* commercial traveller: AND 1898.] SWAGGER 1 a.
    1933 *Press* (Christchurch) (Acland Gloss.) 14 Oct. 15 *Drum.*—Swag, obviously from the shape. Hence *drummer*. **1988** MCGILL *Dict. Kiwi Slang* 40 *drummer* swagman or tramp.

drummer boy: see DRUMMER 1.

drunk, *a.* In comparisons **(as) drunk as a skunk (wheelbarrow** [f. *obs.* Brit. usage: see G.L. Apperson *English Proverbs* (1929)]), in the sense 'very drunk'. Cf. FULL *a.* 1.
    1953 *Here & Now* Mar. 14 Drunk as a skunk, with his whiskers skewed. **1961** CRUMP *Hang On a Minute Mate* 182 Drunk as a skunk he was. **1982** SANSOM *In Grip of Island* 41 Adam's ale is the only tipple on tap there today. No one will get as drunk as a wheelbarrow on that. **1992** ANDERSON *Portrait Artist's Wife* 8 Kindly, avuncular and drunk as a skunk.

dry, *a.*

1. *Goldmining.* **a.** Of a claim or workings, removed from water; occas., not liable to flooding or seepage.
    1861 *NZ Goldfields 1861* (1976) 13 His opinion is that a party can make an ounce a man, as the sinking is very shallow, and the working dry.

b. Usu. as **dry diggings** [AND *dry digging*, usu. in *pl.* 1851: orig. US], a claim or diggings above water-level. Contrast *river diggings* (RIVER 2 b), *wet-diggings* (WET *a.* 3).
    1853 *NZGG* 12 Jan. VI. 1:2 The slip has filled with a mass of decayed vegetation, gravel..the former hollow of a small rivulet, and in this, at a depth of about 3½ feet, in what is denominated a 'dry diggings', the Gold is found. *Ibid.* 3 Latterly the removal of the miners from the creeks to the dry diggings. **1857** HURSTHOUSE *NZ* 101 [There are] two kinds of diggings—the 'river diggings' in the beds of streams, or 'dry diggings' in the conglomerate or gravel on the sides of mountains. **1862** HODDER *Memories NZ Life* 224 The nature of gold in dry-diggings is nuggety. [**c1860** *Wiener Zeitung* (Vienna) Nos 57–65 in German] in Von Haast *Sir Julius Von Haast* (1948) 35 The dry diggings, which generally require more capital and strength, are to be found mostly on the heights or in the higher diluvium. The water must often be brought long distances in sluices.

2. In phr. formed from **(as) dry as a** prefixed to various nouns or noun phrases, of a person, very thirsty; in need of liquid or alcoholic liquor: **as dry as a cocky's selection (after a long drought)**, see COCKY *n.*[1] 2 b; **as dry as the rim of a lime-burner's hat** [cf. Brit. dial. *dry as a lime-burner's clog* (EDD, Cumberland)]; **as dry as a sack of gum dust**; **as dry as a wooden god** (occas. heard **dry as a wooden cow**, with a poss. play on *dry* not in milk).
    1895 SATCHELL *Toll of Bush* 154 He approached the storekeeper and whispered something in his ear. 'Not a taste,' said the latter aloud. 'Dry as a sack of gum dust, I give you my word.' **1918** *Chron. NZEF* 7 June 205 I'm as dry as the rim of a lime-burner's hat. **1950** *Listener* 3 Mar. 9 I went to sleep with the light on and woke up at one-thirty in the morning dry as a wooden god. **1959** SLATTER *Gun in My Hand* 181 Let's get crackin on our own tank-up. Over to the bar at the high port. I'm dry as a wooden god. **1988** MCGILL *Dict. Kiwi Slang* 40 *dry as a wooden god* very dry or thirsty; popular NZ Navy WW2.

3. As **dry horrors** [AND 1913], the D.T.'s, delirium tremens; often in the lesser sense of 'suffering alcoholic dehydration'. See also HORRORS.
    1934 *Press* (Christchurch) (Acland Gloss.) 20 Jan. 15 *Dry horrors.*—State of a shepherd when back from a bust in town.

dry blowing, *vbl. n.* [AND 1881.] A process where a draught of air is used to separate esp. gold particles from attendant rubbish.
    1941 BAKER *NZ Slang* 28 The finding of gold brought..nuggeting, dryblowing... and *fossicking*. **1968** *NZ Contemp. Dict. Suppl.* (Collins) 8 *dry-blowing n.* gold-mining term, separating gold by placing pounded material in one dish, pouring it slowly from a height into another, and allowing the wind or a bellows to blow the dross away.

dry hash. Also **dried hash**. [Spec. use of *hash* a dish of seasoned chopped ingredients, esp. leftovers.] A baked (highly seasoned) dish made out of leftovers or oddments of meat, vegetable, breadcrumbs, without the addition of water; a dry kind of 'shepherd's pie'.
    1902 WALKER *Zealandia's Guerdon* 57 Moist and 'dry' hashes. **1905** *Truth* 7 Oct. 4 There was a pretty hubbub in a toney Wellington hash-house last week..the bachelors in these dry-hash establishments. **1936** HYDE *Passport to Hell* 223 ''Ere, take this. Not much, it ain't. Dry 'ash'... Dry hash, sailor. **1983** *NZ Times* 4 Dec. 8 [Miss Wilson] accomplished the impossible by abolishing Tuesday's abomination called Dry Hash [at Nelson Boy's College, c1930s].

drying green. An outdoor paddock so arranged that fibrous material can be spread or hung out to dry or bleach: of a wool scour, for the drying of scoured wool; of a flaxmill, for the drying and bleaching of dressed flax fibre. See also GREEN *n.* 1, PADDOCK *n.*[1] 2.
    1913 CARR *Country Work* 18 A number of stations..run a scour... From five to seven men are generally employed..at the wash, and the balance on the drying green... The work on the green [at the port scour] is practically the same as on a sheep station. *Ibid.* 44 [The flax fibre] is carted..to the drying green, generally called the 'paddock', where it is spread out to dry and bleach.

Drysdale /ˈdraizˌdæil/. [Named after Dr Francis Williams *Dry*, 1891–1979, agricultural geneticist]. A New Zealand breed of sheep which yields a coarse wool used in carpet manufacture.
    1970 *NZJAg.* Dec. CXXI. 69 The Drysdale.. produces the best carpet wool in the world... The Drysdale is taking the place of the Scottish Black face wool and is better suited to the extent that it has no coloured fibres... The needs of local manufacturers for Drysdale wool have not yet been met. **1977** BROOKING *Massey—its early years* 87 Much of the credit for producing the Drysdale breed must go to its original ancestor the Neilson ram lamb named 'Pa Neilson', which..had..a hairy coat. **1979** *Dominion* (Wellington) 17 July V. 1 The man who developed the Drysdale sheep breed, Dr Francis William Dry has died in Palmerston North... Dr Dry discovered a ram lamb in a flock near Palmerston North which had an extremely hairy fleece due to an abundance of halo-hairs. Dr Dry's successful efforts to isolate the gene in Romney led to the development of the Drysdale. **1988** *NZ Patent Office Jrnl* New Zealand Drysdale 181073 [patent filed] 2 May 1988 in the name of Drysdale Wool Cooperative Company Limited for wool material treatment services. **1991** *NZ Post Brochure NZ Sheep Stamp Issue* Drysdale. Of Romney extraction, bred in New Zealand.

dry-skin. *Whaling.* A whale having little blubber.
    1837 'Bowditch' *Log* 14 Nov. in Morton *Whale's Wake* (1982) 54 Found him to be a dry skin [so] threw it overboard again. **1982** MORTON *Whale's Wake* 54 Occasionally there was not even enough blubber on the whale to make it worth cutting, a condition called 'dry skin'.

dub, *n.*[1] [A shortened and altered form of *double*.]

1. A 'doubles' bet on horse-racing.
    1934 *Truth* 23 May 3 Those who try to get a King's Birthday present for themselves from the books over the Canterbury Park 'dub' will need to remember that mud mokes are a necessity at this meeting.

2. Also **doub**. *Ellipt.* for DOUBLE-BANK *n.* (unrecorded in written form), a ride on the bar, rear-carrier or handlebars of a bicycle.
    1940 p.c. R. Mason: *doub* heard in Wellington; also freq. as *n.* and *v. trans.* among Marlborough boys (Ed.). **1966** *Sunday Times* (Wellington) 30 Oct. 44 [Heading] 'Dub Ends In Death'... Philip was being doubled on the bicycle. **1991** ELDRED-GRIGG *Shining City* 19 I sung out if [*sic*] she wanted a dub.

3. DOUBLE-DECKER 1, a tram-car.
    1954 *Parson's Packet* Mar.–Apr. 3 So that our next-to-eldest can get away at 7.45 to catch the '8 o'clock dub.' This double-decker tram must have been on the tracks for close on fifty years.

4. *Ellipt.* for WC /ˌdʌb(ə)ljuːˈsiː/, DUNNY 1.
    1983 COOPER *Wag's Tales* 8 The only time I remember Dad scolding us was when Jess was scared to go on her own in the dark to the 'Dub' which seemed to us to be quite a long way along a spooky path.

dub, *n.*[2] [f. Brit. and US dial.: cf. EDD 1: a term used in the game of marbles in various senses, but not, as in NZ, of the marble itself: poss. in NZ infl. by DUB IN.]

1. Often *pl*. A cheap clay marble, esp. one put down (often as a substitute for a better marble) to be fired at; a marble game or action where marbles are laid down, usu. in a ring, to be fired at.

1953 Sutton-Smith *Unorganized Games NZ Primary School Children* (VUWTS) II. 770 It is important to distinguish..'Action-Terms'..from the innumerable merely descriptive marble terms which have no effect on the course of the action—terms such as..Dubs, Kills, Funs, Keeps. **1982** Sutton-Smith *Hist. Children's Play* 269 Here are some [marble] terms from Taranaki around 1880–90..dubs, finking..and from Dunedin School in 1949: knee high, manyies..dig, dubs, cheats. **1991** O'Regan *Aunts and Windmills* 14 We would each have a bag with a draw-string tie for..our carefully guarded supply of dubs. We would race out each playtime to 'dub in' and the game would begin within seconds. On a good day you would go home with your bag weighed down with dubs won from other players. **1995** *Independent* 8 Dec. 20 Like most kids [in Dunedin] I wouldn't play for stinkies, wouldn't let others put up stinkies as dubs—substitutes or changes.

Hence **dub** *v*. [spec. use of *dub in* to make a contribution], to put a 'dub' marble in the ring in a game of keeps.

1972 Sutton-Smith *Folkgames Children* 175 An oval ring was described in the earth by means of a stick, and each player would 'dub in' one marble. **1991** [see above].

2. The throwing-stone in the game of duckstones.

1972 [see DUCKSTONE].

dub, *v*. Also **doub**. *Ellipt*. for DOUBLE-BANK *v*. 2 (on a bicycle).

1955 *BJ Cameron Collection* (TS July) dub (v) Abbreviation of *double-bank*. **1963** Adsett *Magpie Sings* 177 No luck tonight, I'll have to dub you home to keep me hands in practice. Never touched the handle-bars once last time. **1987** *Evening Post* (Wellington) 20 July 18 I was dubbing my little brother down the footpath and this van comes out from behind these bushes. **1989** McGill *Kiwi Baby Boomers* 58 The crossbar allowed you to 'doub' kids. The first time I doubted a girl on it I was on fire with the new feeling of being close to her. **1994** *Dominion* (Wellington) 30 Aug. 13 As we cycled back from Hoi An's beach a woman asked us to dub her child to school.

duchesse /'dʌtʃes/. Also **duchess**. [In Brit. use apparently usu. *attrib*.: cf. OED *duchesse-dressing chest* 1863, *ellipt*. 1881.] Also as **duchesse chest**, a name applied to a dressing-table or chest of drawers usu. with a mirror on top.

[**1884** *Nelson Mortgage Deed*, 18 Apr., Mary Hunt listing her chattels: Cedar bedstand Duchess dressing table in Cedar..Cedar chest of Drawers. **1900** *Taranaki Herald* (New Plymouth) 3 Jan. 4 [Advt] Dingle bros Reliable Furnishing Emporium... Duchess Suites, Combination Chests, Couches in endless variety.] **1905** *NZ Herald* (Auckland) 14 Jan. 6 [Advt] Duchesse Pair, Latest Design, Bevel Mirror, Brackets, Tile Back Washstand. **1907** *Dominion* (Wellington) 20 Dec. 11 Duchesse Chests..from 42s. to £10. **1924** *Grey River Argus* 1 Apr. 1 [Advt] Harley and Co., Ltd., will submit to Public Auction..Oak Bedroom Suite comprising Duchesse, Wardrobe, Bedstead and Pedestal. **1938** *Ibid*. 19 Jan. 1 [Advt] Modern Reflex Mirror Duchess, with Cabriolet Legs... Now only £4/10/- **1943** Hislop *Pure Gold* 17 In my hurry into tea [at the hotel] I planted them [*sc*. the watches] all in a small drawer at the side of the old-fashioned duchesse. **1957** Frame *Owls Do Cry* (1967) 50 She had a case with a paua shell cover, on the duchesses in front of her, and a powder puff in her hand. **1969** Hascombe *Down & Almost Under* 35 Suddenly a woman hisses, 'There's borer in the back of this duchess'... What is a duchess? What is borer? **1980** Leland *Kiwi-Yankee Dict*. 35 Duchesse: The hereditary New Zealand title for a Low Chest of Drawers With A Mirror on it so it can double as a dressing table. **1987** Eldred-Grigg *Oracles & Miracles* 3 After we was born we was put in a drawer in a duchesse.

duck.

1. Applied to any of numerous native web-footed swimming birds of the fam. Anatidae, esp. of the genus *Anas*, or to introduced species breeding in the wild. See also PARERA, PUTANGITANGI, WHIO. Cf. SCAUP, SHOVELLER, SPOONBILL, TEAL *n*.¹, WIDGEON.

1770 Cook *Journals* 31 Mar. (1955) I. 276 Those known in Europe are Ducks, Shags, Gannets & gulls all of which were eat by us and found exceeding good. **1791** Bell *Jrnl. Voyage H.M.S. 'Chatham'* Nov. (ATLMS) 50 The Best kinds were Ducks, Curlews. **1853** Swainson *Auckland* 120 Pigeons, ducks, teal, and other water-fowl abound. **1889** Parker *Catalogue NZ Exhib*. 117 in Morris *Austral-English* (1898) 128 There are eleven species of Native Ducks belonging to nine genera, all found elsewhere, except two—the little Flightless Duck of the Auckland Islands (genus *Nesonetta*) and the Blue Mountain Duck (*Hymenolaemus*). Among the most interesting of the non-endemic forms, are the Paradise Duck or Sheldrake (*Casarca variegata*), the Brown Duck (*Anas chlorotis*), the Shoveller or Spoonbill duck (*Rhynchaspis variegata*), and the Scaup or Black Teal (*Fuligula Novae-Zealandiae*).

2. With a modifier: **Auckland Islands** (or **flightless**), **blue** (**mountain, blue mountain**), **brown**, **grey**, **painted**, **paradise**, **spoonbill**, **whistling** (**blue whistling**), **white-eyed** (**Australian white-eyed, white-winged**), **wild**.

(1) **Auckland Islands** (or **flightless**) **duck**. *Anas aucklandica aucklandica*. TEAL *n*.¹ 2 (1).

1889 Flightless Duck [see 1 above]. **1890** *Otago Witness* (Dunedin) 13 Feb. 14 At another landing [on Adam's Island] I saw more specimens of the rare flightless Auckland Island duck. **1923** *NZJST* VI. 83 Auckland Islands Duck. Captain Bollons sees no reason to suppose that the numbers of this bird have diminished since its discovery. **1955** Oliver *NZ Birds* 412 Auckland Island Flightless Duck... The Auckland Island Duck was discovered by the naturalists of the *Erebus* and *Terror* under the command of Sir James Ross, who called at Port Ross in 1840. **1986**, **1990** flightless duck [see TEAL *n*.¹ 2 (1)].

(2) **a. blue** (**blue mountain, mountain**) **duck**, *occas*. **blue grey duck**. *Hymenolaimus malacorhynchos*, a native duck of turbulent mountain rivers noted for its hoarse whistling cry, having a pale pink bill and an upper plumage dove-grey with a bluish sheen. See also *whistling duck* (8) below, WHIO 1. For transferred and figurative senses see the separate entry BLUE DUCK.

1773 blue grey duck [see (8) below]. **1846** Heaphy *Exped. S.W. Nelson* in Taylor *Early Travellers* (1959) 198 Great quantities of blue ducks, apparently a species of shoveller, are to be met with on this stream. **1849** McLean *Diary* 16 July in Cowan *Sir Donald Maclean* (1940) 48 Pigeon, *weka*, duck, and *whio* (blue mountain duck) are included in the *papa*. **1855** Taylor *Te Ika a Maui* 407 Whio (*Hymenolaemus malacorhynchus*), the blue duck, is found abundantly in the mountain-streams, and in the Middle Island. It takes its name from its cry. **1860** Butler *Forest Creek MS* (1960) June 44 I have seen the rarest kind of mountain duck swimming within five yards of me..as though I had no soul for roast duck seasoning. **1870** *TrNZI* II. 48 From the swift stream below..arose the plaintive whistle of the Blue Duck, as with soft-fringed bill it explored each little foaming eddy. **1896** Harper *Pioneer Work* 42 Blue or mountain ducks..are not now found in any numbers except in the upper parts of hitherto unvisited rivers. **1906** *TrNZI* XXXVIII. 341 The *whio*, or 'whistler'..generally called the blue mountain duck, is much more abundant in the South Island than the North. **1916** Cowan *Bush Explorers* (VUWTS) 24 We saw little squadrons of 'whio' the blue mountain duck..; they called to each other in the whistling cry that has given them their Maori name. **1927** Guthrie-Smith *Birds* 41 The geographical formation of Tutira..is well suited to the 'Blue', or 'Mountain Duck'. **1967** Natusch *Animals NZ* 271 It is certainly a 'break from the troubles of the world' to see a pair of blue ducks and their flotilla of chicks navigating mountain creeks..with the aplomb of rubber 'dinghies'. **1976** Soper *NZ Birds* 25 The New Zealand Blue Duck, or Mountain Duck, is something of an oddity among ducks, for it shows no obvious relationship to any other duck species. **1990** *Listener* 8 Oct. 116 There was a pair of blue ducks and a kea.

b. In the phr. **a blue duck's trip** [alluding to the blue mountain duck's liking for mountain torrents], a wet or rough tramping trip.

1934 *Canterbury Mountaineer* Aug. 4 Easter, 1933, was disastrous with evil storms. Len Boot..made a blue duck's trip down the Whitcombe.

(3) **brown duck**. *Anas aucklandica chlorotis*, a now rare duck, warm brown in general colour. See also *brown teal* (TEAL *n*.¹ 2 (3)), PATEKE.

1843 Dieffenbach *Travels in NZ* I. 276 Flights of the common brown duck..people these swamps. **1873** Buller *Birds NZ* 248 Anas chlorotis. (Brown Duck)... Tarawhatu, Pateke, and Tete-whero. **1886** *TrNZI* XVIII. 113 Pateke, Brown Duck. Both Islands and Chatham Islands. A very indifferent flier. **1904** Hutton & Drummond *Animals NZ* 313 The Brown Duck inhabits the Chatham Islands as well as New Zealand. **1927** Guthrie-Smith *Birds* 55 When quietly floating in shaded waters, and many of the birds together, the Brown Duck has a curious habit of sometimes striking the water violently. This, apparently, is done with its foot. **1955** Oliver *NZ Birds* 414 During the daytime, the Brown Duck hides in the thick growth of raupo or sedges found along the edges of creeks. **1966** Falla et al. *Birds NZ* 88 Brown Duck (Brown Teal)... Pateke. *Ibid*. 89 Once very widely distributed... Widely taken for food in the period of European settlement. **1970** Sansom *Stewart Islanders* 143 The now rare native brown duck is still to be seen. **1985** [see TEAL *n*.¹ 2 (3)].

(4) **grey duck**. *Anas superciliosa*, having a striped face, and brown feathers with grey edges; formerly common but now scarce. See also PARERA.

1845 Deans in *Pioneers* (1964) 43 A species of grey duck very like the wild duck at home. **1856** Phillips *Rockwood Jrnl*. (Canterbury Pub. Lib. TS) 28 Dec. 60 Seal killed a Grey Duck. **1867** Barker *Station Life* (1870) 181 I don't think a minute passed without a brace of wild ducks flying past,—grey, blue, and Paradise. **1870** *TrNZI* II. 72 Parera. Grey Duck... One of the commonest game-birds left to us by the eager sportsman. **1894** *Richmond-Atkinson Papers* (1960) II. 597 Once coming up the Waikato in 1851 your Uncle James got a pot-shot at a lot of parera (grey duck). **1904** Hutton & Drummond *Animals NZ* 311 The Grey Duck, fortunately, still maintains its ground, in spite of heavy losses each year in the shooting season. **1927** Guthrie-Smith *Birds* 13 They have become more cautious of their enemies; certainly the

Grey Duck is a wilder bird than he was forty years ago. **1946** [see PARERA]. **1950** *NZ Bird Notes* III. 235 My attention was attracted by a grey duck..flying low along the main thoroughfare [of Whakatane]. **1962** *Landfall Country* 326 At night a boss grey duck will quack authoritatively to a few companions. **1985** *Reader's Digest Book NZ Birds* 144 Until about 1960, grey ducks made up 95 per cent of New Zealand's dabbling duck population. Now..they comprise less than 20 per cent.

(5) **painted duck**. *Obs*. See *paradise duck* (6) below.

1773 WALES *Journal* in Cook *Journals* (1961) II. 786 One [duck] which on account of its varigated [*sic*] plumage we called The Painted Duck was the most beautiful bird I ever saw. **1793** MURRY *Journal* 12 Oct. in McNab *Hist. Records* (1914) II. 516 We shot about 6 [ducks]—the last of which was a Painted one. **1907** MCNAB *Murihiku* 21 Cook saw the paradise duck for the first time here [at Dusky Sound], called by him the painted duck.

(6) **paradise duck** (occas. also **paradise drake**). *Tadorna variegata* (fam. Anatidae), a shelduck, the male being predominantly black, the female having a conspicuous white head, rusty brown body with a darker back. See also *painted duck* (5) above, PARRIE, PUTANGITANGI, RANGITATA GOOSE, SHELDUCK.

1813 WILLIAMS *Report* Sept. in McNab *Murihiku* (1909) 196 We found the large bay..covered with paradise ducks which induced me naming it Duck Bay. **1826** SHEPHERD *Journal* 9 Mar. in Howard *Rakiura* (1940) 359 This day returned to Albion cove saw..a large black and white Duck called a Paradise Duck. **1848** WAKEFIELD *Handbook NZ* 164 The *paradise duck*, or *Pu-tangi-tangi*..is remarkable for its size, for the beauty of its plumage, and the delicacy of its flesh. **1851** SHORTLAND *S. Dist. NZ* 312 Putakitaki.., a duck with beautiful plumage, rather larger than the common grey variety. It is very common in the south of New Zealand, and is generally known as the paradise duck. **1867** *Richmond-Atkinson Papers* (1960) II. 237 As I write I hear the quacking, or rather cawing, of a paradise drake... The drake caws exactly like a 6d. woolly dog. **1873** BULLER *Birds NZ* 241 New Zealand Sheldrake... Putangitangi; Putakitaki in the South Island; 'Paradise Duck' of the colonists. **1894** WILSON *Land of Tui* 176 Her precious Paradise ducks had discovered that their wings..were now strong enough for flight. **1926** COWAN *Travel in NZ* II. 64 The handsome paradise-duck (*putangitangi*) and blue mountain duck (*whio*) are numerous in the streams and lakes [of Western Southern Alps]. **1947** POWELL *Native Animals NZ* 80 Paradise Duck.., Putangitangi of the Maoris, is a handsome bird variously mottled, freckled and lined with brown and white on a brownish to black ground. **1968** BAXTER *Collected Poems* (1980) 431 There is more than one Schoolhouse looking at itself in a lagoon Where paradise ducks come down. **1985** MCGILL *G'day Country* 149 A pair of paris (paradise ducks).

(7) **spoonbill duck**. SHOVELLER. See SPOONBILL 1 for quotations.

(8) **whistling (blue whistling) duck**. See *blue duck* (2) above. Cf. WHIO.

1773 COOK *Journals* 11 May (1961) II. 136 The third sort is the blue grey Duck..or the whistling Duck as some called them from the whistling noise they made. **1851** WELD *Letter* Jan. in *NZGG* 21 Feb. (1851) 33 Woodhens and blue whistling and paradise ducks formed our chief food in the latter part of an expedition. **1871** MONEY *Knocking About NZ* 32 There was a species of grey duck [near the Grey river] with white bills, often described as the whistling duck. **1917** WILLIAMS *Dict. Maori Lang.* 583 *Whio..blue duck*; sometimes called *whistling duck*. **1946** [see WHIO 1].

(9) **white-eyed (Australian white-eyed, white-winged) duck**. *Aythya australis australis*, an Australian diving duck occas. straggling to New Zealand but never permanently established. See also KARAKAHIA.

1886 *TrNZI* XVIII. 117 Karakahia, White-winged (white-eyed?) Duck. Both Islands; Australia. **1893** *TrNZI* XXV. 63 *Nyroca* [*sic*] *australis*... (The White-eyed Duck.) **1900** *Canterbury Old & New* 196 As regards the duck family we are also well off, with our paradise ducks, brown ducks, grey ducks, white-winged ducks and blue mountain ducks. **1955** OLIVER *NZ Birds* 419 *Karakahia*... The White-eyed Duck was first noticed by Hutton in 1867 on Whangape Lake, in the Lower Waikato. **1966** FALLA et al. *Birds NZ* 93 Australian White-eyed Duck..Karakahia. *Ibid*. 94 This duck has apparently disappeared after an early period (1867–95) of some abundance in some districts. **1984** SOPER *Birds NZ* 73 The white-eyed Duck is an Australian species with the habit of dispersing widely in times of drought.

(10) **wild duck**. Orig. any of various native species; later also applied to introduced species living in the wild, esp. the now dominant mallard *Anas platyrhynchos*.

1777 FORSTER *Voyage Round World* I. 137 In this fine place, we found a number of wild fowl, and particularly wild ducks..from whence we gave it the name of Duck Cove. **1815** MARSDEN *Lett. & Jrnls.* (1932) 99 We dined off a wild duck and potatoes. **1841** *Rep. Protector of Aborigines* in *GBPP 1842 (No.569)* 98 Here the banks of the river [Waipa] were covered with wild-ducks. **1867** [see (4) above]. **1883** DOMETT *Ranolf & Amohia* II. 95 The wild-ducks' black and tiny fleet Shot in-and-out their shy retreat. **1899** *TrNZI* XXXI. 9 On any quiet evening now at the lake you may hear..the pleasant chattering of numberless Wild-duck and Teal. **1930** *Taranaki Herald* 5 May 6 It was a great place for wild duck and other water-fowl..that Ngaere Swamp. **1956** BAXTER *Collected Poems* (1980) 163 Who knows what fear the raupo hides Or where the wild duck flies? **1961** *Edmonds 'Sure to Rise' Cookery Book* 72 Sauce for wild duck, teal, etc. Take a quantity of good stock, pepper and salt to taste; squeeze in the juice of 2 good oranges, add a little wine.

3. a. Special Comb. **duck itch**, BATHERS' ITCH; **duck-scarer** *Marlborough Sounds obs*., the little pied shag (formerly called the 'frilled shag'), see SHAG 2 (8) and (11).

1980 LELAND *Kiwi-Yankee Dict.* 35 **Duck itch**: a rash that develops as a result of contact with a waterborne parasite that infests some of New Zealand's southern lakes. It has just left its snail host and is looking for a duck to grow up in. Look for warning signs. **1896** '**duck-scarer**' [see SHAG 2 (8)].

b. In special collocations: **ducks and geese** *prison* [AND 1950], rhyming slang for 'police'; **duck's breakfast** *joc*., occas. **duck's dinner**, a drink of water and nothing to eat; **duck's egg** [transf. from cricketing use of *duck*: see OED 1868], a complete or severe loss; ?a bankruptcy; **ducks on the pond**, a shearers' call of warning to all in the shed that a woman is approaching (cf. SIXTY-NINE).

1963 *Truth* 21 May 19 Her pot and pan had smacked it for a blue with the **ducks and geese**, but was out on ginger ale. ducks and geese..police. **1935** STRONG in Partridge *Slang Today* 287 He absolutely dropped his bundle, and, to make matters worse, I had started off with a **duck's breakfast**, but I saw a cookhouse and decided to give it a pop for a binder. **1938** *Press* (Christchurch) (McNab Slang) 4 Apr. 18 'ducks' breakfast', 'to float up to', 'to blow up to', 'to sleep in the Star Hotel' need no explanation. **1988** MCGILL *Dict. Kiwi Slang* 40 *duck's breakfast* or *dinner* a drink of water to WW1 soldiers. **1858** *Richmond-Atkinson Papers* (1960) I. 396 I sounded Hirst & found him..impracticable... Cutfield's aid would scarcely have saved him from a **duck's egg**. The whole affair put the Ministry in a very ungraceful position. **1988** MCGILL *Dict. Kiwi Slang* 40 **ducks on the pond** warning of a woman in a male environment; shearing term.

4. See BRAVO DUCK (*blue shag*).

duckfart. [f. the imagined sound and appearance of a duck's underwater farting.] A schoolboys' term for the noise of a small stone plopping into water; occas. the stone itself.

c1940 p.c. Rodney Simonsen (1951): *duckfart* was used in a game of skimming stones by Palmerston North boys. **1968** SLATTER *Pagan Game* 51 The hurling of stones straight up in the air so they would fall into the back-water with that satisfying plup known as a duck fart.

duck-shove, *v*. Also **duck shuffle** (see quot. 1938). *trans*. and *absol*. Esp. in public life, to evade responsibility for a decision by claiming that it belongs with another person or office; to 'pass the buck'.

1938 *Auckland Weekly News* 23 Nov. 96 No duck shufflin', yer cow. **1960** *Spectator* (London) 4 Nov. 677 As the leader of the [New Zealand] Opposition complained, the Government has 'dodged and duckshoved' the issue. **1988** MCGILL *Dict. Kiwi Slang* 40 *duckshove* to cheat or pass responsibility on to someone else, perceived as a typical bureaucratic trick; eg 'The public is always complaining of duckshoving in that department.'

duck-shoving, *vbl. n*. [f. DUCK-SHOVE *v*.]

1. *Obs*. [AND 1870 Melbourne.] Of cab-drivers, touting for passengers in the street instead of waiting one's turn on the rank.

1896 *Otago Daily Times* (Dunedin) 25 Jan. 3 The case was one of a series of cases of what was technically known as 'duck shoving', a process of getting passengers which operated unfairly against the cabmen who stayed on the licensed stand and obeyed the by-law.

2. [AND b, 1942.] Indecisiveness; 'passing the buck'.

1972 *Press* (Christchurch) 20 Oct. 1 We have been the perfect vehicle for duck-shoving from one department to another. We have been shunted from the Health Department to the Social Welfare Department to the Education Department. Each in turn has declined responsibility for us. **1985** SHERWOOD *Botanist at Bay* 26 The words flew, and enriched Celia's [an English visitor's] vocabulary. 'Duck shoving' was the local name for buck-passing between government departments. **1985** STEWART *Gumboots and Goalposts* 115 I want a straight answer now and no duckshoving.

duck shuffle: see DUCK-SHOVE *v*.

duckstone. Also **duckstones**. [A term and game widely known in 19th c. Brit. provincial and boys' use: see EDD *duck n.²*] A children's stone-throwing game; a target stone in the game.

1905 THOMSON *Bush Boys* 84 Others wanted [to play] 'Prisoners' Base' or 'Chivvy', 'Brewer', 'Egg-in-the hat', 'Duck-stone', 'Red Rover', or 'Kingy-seeny'. **1953** PATRICK MAGEE 'Growing Up at the Diggings' in Heinz *Bright Fine Gold* (1974) 38 Some of the simple games played by the [West Coast] children [c1870] were rounders, shinty, duckstone..and leapfrog. **1972** SUTTON-SMITH *Folkgames Children* 166 A game that was based directly upon children's interest in throwing stones was *Duckstones* (K-16)... In the simplest form, the players put one stone on top of a larger stone and then attempted to knock the top one off by throwing other stones at it. The player who knocked off the most stones won... (South Clutha, 1875; Stillwater, Nelson, 1885; Wakefield, Nelson, 1875). *Ibid.* 167 In this [West Coast version of Duckstones] the duckstone belonged to the He. As soon as he put his duckstone on the big stone the game commenced and the others began to fire their own 'dubs' at the duckstone. **1982** SUTTON-SMITH *Hist. Children's Play* 217 At school, however, there was little place for Duck Stones, with its dangerous stone-throwing.

duds, *n. pl.* [Poss. an alteration of *bubs* breasts.] A woman's breasts.
1968 SLATTER *Pagan Game* 165 Telling her he hadn't seen such lovely duds outside a garage calendar.

dudee /duˈdiː/. *Obs.* Also **doodee, dudeen, dudheen.** [Used elsewhere, but freq. in early NZ use: cf. OED *dudeen*: 'Irish name for a short clay tobacco-pipe; in the late 19th c. generally known in Great Britain, and esp. in the British Colonies and *U.S.*', 1841.] A short clay tobacco-pipe.
1853 ROCHFORT *Adventures of Surveyor* 12 We no sooner brought up [at Lyttelton] than..our little craft was crowded with persons, eager for news, smoking their short dudees. **1871** MONEY *Knocking About NZ* 95 We were roused by a roaring in our ears, and had only time, the one to snatch his pocket-book..the other his black dudheen..before the hut was a raging furnace. **1880** SENIOR *Travel & Trout* 100 [He] knocks the ashes out of his dudheen. **1891** A TRAMP, ESQ. *Casual Ramblings* 141 The boss of [the Cathedral] is Bishop Julius..who smokes a 'dudeen' and reads shilling shockers. **c1940** *doodee* known to Ed. as an occas. joc. term used by Marlborough elderly for a pipe: 'Here comes your father with his old doodee.'

dudheen, var. DUDEE.

duff, *n.* [f. a northern Brit. dial. pron. of *dough* (cf. *rough*), used elsewhere but very freq. in NZ use from colonial times, and of special significance as the name of a regular item of camp and cookhouse fare.] Boiled or steamed suet pudding, often with dried fruit in it; esp. **plum duff,** a plum pudding or 'Christmas' pudding.
1851 KENNAWAY *Biscuit & Butter* (1973) 78 Our delicate..stomachs received the most racy and highly esteemed dainties peculiar to the *cuddy* table, and which when you all come out you will soon discover, such as 'Duff & Treacle', Boiled Pudding, Plum Duff..and bread in particular. **1862** HODDER *Memories NZ Life* 10 I chopped suet and plums to make a 'duff' for dinner. **1872** BARKER *Christmas Cake* ch.iii 'Duff'—that's colonial for pudding, ma'am. **1888** DUNCAN *Wakatipians* 28 If we drew their attentions to..the inevitable currant pudding on Sunday, their only answer was 'Take the whole blooming "duff".' **1890** *Otago Witness* (Dunedin) 16 Oct. 30 And this, too, to colonials who had known most of them what..it had been to partake of 'Sunday duff' boiled in a kerosene tin. **1913** CARR *Country Work* 17 Anyone who can bake, make a decent 'brownie' (as the plain cake is called) and a plum duff is fit for a shearers' cook. **1933** *Press* (Christchurch) (Acland Gloss.) 14 Oct. 15 Duff.—A very plain plum pudding, which was the invariable second course at Sunday dinner on stations. **1945** *NZ Dairy Exporter* 2 Apr. 71 'Got a duff?'.. 'Oh, yes, I made two, filled ours with thrums.' **1983** FRANCIS *Wildlife Ranger* 2 The main [station] meal, 'tea', was basically mutton, potatoes, onions..and, for afters, stewed dried fruit, plum duff or rice and prunes.

duff, *v.* [f. general English slang *up the duff* pregnant.] *trans.* To make (a woman) pregnant.
1974 MORRIESON *Predicament* (1981) 72 He duffed one of the maids up at his old man's house and she died having an abortion. **1974** MAUGHAN *Good & Faithful Servants* 7 Still he had changed all that, moving into practice and duffing Elizabeth. **1981** JOHNSTON *Fish Factory* 65 When Ma-Mac finds out I've duffed her daughter there'll be a bloody massacre in the village!

duffer. *Goldfields.* [f. *duffer* something counterfeit.]
1. [AND mine, claim 1855, goldfield 1873.] An unproductive claim, mine, or goldfield.
1863 *AJHR D-6* 3 The place was 'rushed' by about 500 men, who speedily deserted it, and declared the Waitahuna to be a 'duffer'. **1871** MONEY *Knocking About NZ* 121 They had only arrived to find the whole thing what is called in digging parlance a 'duffer'—i.e., that there was comparatively 'nothing' to repay them for even the trouble of digging a single hole. **1887** HOPEFUL *Taken In* 135 Supposing a man is digging, but without success, and he therefore abandons his hole, it is called a 'shicer'—that is, the *ground* was called a 'shicer' or duffer, thus the origin. **1897** WRIGHT *Station Ballads* 19 He was working like a nigger, sinking duffers here and there. **1914** PFAFF *Digger's Story* 56 I sunk a shaft on the Larrikins' Terrace there, but it proved a duffer. **1948** HAAST *Julius Von Haast* 26 This visit was commemorated by miners who took up 'Hochstetter' and 'Haast' claims, which..proved 'duffers'. **1974** HEINZ *Bright Fine Gold* 200 *Claims* Worthless claims or ground were called schicers or duffers.

2. As **duffer (duffers') rush** [AND 1876], a rush to an unproductive goldfield.
1869 WAITE *West Coast Goldfields* 15 Those first disappointed arrivals chose to call the expedition a duffer rush. **1870** *AJHR D-40* 4 More than ordinarily rich the last six months seems to have been in 'duffer rushes'. **1914** PFAFF *Diggers' Story* 151 He was among the earliest at Hokitika, Grey..Jackson's Bay (a duffer's rush), etc. **1924** *Otago Witness* (Dunedin) 11 Nov. 66 It was soon found to be a 'duffer' rush. **1967** MAY *West Coast Gold Rushes* 281 Duffer rushes collapsed so quickly that storekeepers could find themselves in the back-of-beyond with a fully-stocked shanty and no sales. **1992** LATHAM *Golden Reefs* 133 On occasion it seems that 'duffer rushes' were deliberately engineered by unscrupulous promoters.

3. *transf.* **a.** A fake; a washout.
1865 *Evening Post* (Wellington) 3 Aug. 2 The township..is full of life and excitement caused by the crowds of diggers, packers and storekeepers, all anxiously waiting to be off to..the Golden Grey. Affairs will not take their usual course if we do not have numbers coming back to the Hokitika, loudly declaring the whole thing a 'duffer' and a 'sell'.

b. A dry cow, or one not producing milk in commercial quantities.
1902 *Brett's Colonists' Guide* 28 If the cows are themselves duffers, and are mated to a mongrel bull, the heifer calves cannot turn out very good. **1912** *NZJAg.* Jan. IV. 382 The following tables very well illustrate the value of culling out those cows that the system of testing reveals to be 'duffers'. **1920** POWDRELL *Dairy Farming* 42 Practical farmers sometimes put two calves on to one duffer cow, or to a run cow for five or six weeks. **1920** POWDRELL *Dairy Farming* 45 First he must weed out the 'duffers'.

duffer out, *v. Goldfields.* [AND 1880.] *intr.* Of a mine or claim, to prove a failure; to become unproductive.
1897 WRIGHT *Station Ballads* 59 A good bit of ground duffers out. **1907** *TrNZI* XXXIX. 395 Since the house had been abandoned many years ago when the Owen reefs duffered out. **1967** MAY *West Coast Gold Rushes* 198 The Auckland Lead on the beach was all but duffered out.

Hence **duffered (out)** *ppl. a.* [AND v. 2 *duffered out*], exhausted; ended. Also *fig.*
1894 O'REGAN *Voices Wave & Tree* 10 Life's claim is almost duffered, the washing-up is near. **1967** MAY *West Coast Gold Rushes* 526 A claim which was exhausted was said to be 'duffered out'. **1974** HEINZ *Bright Fine Gold* 200 *Duffered out*: All the gold has been mined.

dug-out.
1. *Hist.* [Orig. US: see OED 1.] A name applied in the 19th century to a Maori canoe formed by hollowing and shaping a log.
[**1842** HEAPHY *NZ* 94 Canoes resembling the Canadian 'dug-out' loaded to the water's brim with pigs, potatoes, fern, kumeras, corn.] **1867** HOCHSTETTER *NZ* 293 I counted not less than twenty-four of us..the 'dug-out' had to carry. [**1867** *Note*] 'Dug-out' is the name of these canoes among the backwoodsmen of North America. **1896** HARPER *Pioneer Work* 45 On the 22nd [October, 1893] we started in a small 'dug-out', or canoe hollowed out of a tree, down the outlet... Our craft was only 6 ft. by 2 ft., and very clumsily made. **1927** DONNE *Maori Past & Present* 54 It was a Maori dug-out canoe.

2. *transf.* Somebody rough or primitive in appearance or manner, as if roughly fashioned, or (poss.) dug out of the ground.
1943 MARSH *Colour Scheme* 102 I think he's [sc. a cantankerous older man] a nark and a dug-out. **1953** SCOTT *Breakfast at Six* 116 An old car with its exhaust off and its horn on... Couldn't catch sight of the driver, but I'll bet he was a real old dug-out too.

3. A hole in the ground (often lined with polythene or other impervious sheeting) used for storing water for fire-fighting.
1958 *Rep. Soil Conservation & Rivers Control Council* 24 The preparations, however, convincingly demonstrated the usefulness of low-cost sheet-polythene as a means of lining dugouts in porous country such as pumice so that water can be stored cheaply for fire fighting.

duke /duk/. [Origin unknown.] An inferior marble.
1972 SUTTON-SMITH *Folkgames Children* 174 There were terms for marbles such as..'dubs', 'dates', 'stakes', 'dukes', or 'changers', referring to the marbles put down to be fired at.

Duke of Yorks. *Hist.* [A variation on PRINCE ALBERTS q.v.] *pl.* A makeshift foot-wrapping.
1955 WILSON *Land of My Children* 6 They [sc. contract bushmen] did not wear socks: they cut an old tent into squares and pushed their feet, with the squares round them, into boots—they called these 'Duke of Yorks', and said that changing them daily they protected the feet better than socks.

dummy, *n.*[1]
1. *Hist.* [Spec. use of *dummy* one who is a mere tool of another: AND 1865.] In New Zealand from the time land laws were applied, one paid to acquire the title to a parcel of Crown land on behalf of another who was not legally entitled to do so.
1873 *Weekly News* (Auckland) 26 Apr. 4 Mr. Browning held the shares in question..and transferred

them to Mr. Martin Sholl, sharebroker, who transferred them to William Lestrange, a well-known 'dummy'. **1884** TREGEAR *Southern Parables* 17 He can go and be a Dummy on the Otago runs. **1897** WRIGHT *Station Ballads* 44 And yet the talk is evermore, 'The people want the land!'... A dummy grabbing what he can is not the people's friend. **1933** *Press* (Christchurch) (Acland Gloss.) 14 Oct. 15 *Dummy.*—A man who takes a run in his name for the benefit of another; hence to d*[ummy]* and *dummyism*. **1948** LIPSON *Politics of Equality* 58 A man who wished to conceal the extent of his acquisitions could take out a title in another person's name, using him as a 'dummy' owner. **1969** MCCASKILL *Molesworth* 114 It would appear that a syndicate of directors and senior officials of the Farmers' Coop Association were the prime movers in the purchase [in 1917] and that the Lockheads were really 'dummies' whose initial contributions towards the purchase [of the station] were soon lost. **1977** MARKS *Hammer & Tap* 510 For a time [after the passing of the land Act in 1872] the squatters seem to have found a means of counter attack by employing 'dummies' to apply to purchase land on the runs for repossession by the runholder.

Hence **dummyism** [AND 1865], the action or process of *dummying*.

1883 *Illustrated NZ News* 3 Sept. 10 The Committee on Alleged Dummyism have brought up their report. **1890** *NZPD* LXVIII. 413 He said that he had not meant 'dummyism', and that he had made a mistake, for he intended 'gridironing', and wished that word in its place. **1898** [see DUMMY v.]. **1933** [see 1 above]. **1948** SCOTTER *Run Estate & Farm* 14 The Kakanui area was not entirely a stranger to a third practice of the large landholder, dummyism, that is land acquisition under cover of different names. **1959** SINCLAIR *Hist. NZ* 156 Where leaseholders were not permitted to 'select' land, or where conditions of residence were enforced, 'dummyism' was rife—that is, a leaseholder would pay some 'swaggie' to act as the ostensible selector and fulfil the requirements for him. **1966** *Encycl. NZ* I. 235 As a member of the Otago Wastelands Board from 1878, he opposed 'Dummyism' and similar abuses. **1977** MARKS *Hammer & Tap* 510 By 1890 large scale dummyism had disappeared.

2. [f. *dummy* something that imitates or counterfeits the action of the real thing.] **a.** A lure or imitation fishing bait.

1926 GREY *Angler's Eldorado* 33 The boatmen began trolling with hand-lines for bait. They used a small gig, dark in color, shaped like a canoe, which they called a dummy.

b. In a double bail in a milking shed, a structure which does the work of an internal bail by separating the foreparts of the two cows and keeping them in position for milking, and also serving as a stand for parts of the milking machine.

1950 *NZJAg*. Apr. LXXX. 378 The use of galvanised iron piping or iron piping for erection of internal dummies and partitions. *Ibid.* May 479 [Caption] A small dairy with suspended dummy and bucket milking machine for one cow.

dummy, *n.*[2] *Prison*. [Poss. a play on *dummy* an abusive term for a fool or halfwit, hence a cell where the 'dummies' are put; poss. *dummy* false, that is orig. not a standard (or 'real') cell but merely a place of confined punishment.] **a.** Also **dummy cell**. A punishment cell or block. Cf. DIGGER *n.*[2]

1909 *Truth* 5 June 5 The young prisoner [in the Terrace Gaol]..was unable to work, and was placed in 'The Dummy', a building which the prisoner described to 'Truth' as an old chicken house. Whilst in 'The Dummy' he received no attention whatever, except that his meals were brought to him. **1936** HYDE *Passport to Hell* 62 He was taken in front of the Governor and sentenced to three days in the Dummy. It is always dusk in the Dummy, which lies underground... At six in the morning the door is unlocked, and the prisoner gets his clothes, all except boots. **1945** BURTON *In Prison* 107 The aggressor in this case was promptly led off and incarcerated in the 'dummy' [for attacking a warder]. *Ibid.* 109 Someone else had seen a bloodstained towel coming from the 'dummy'. **1950** *Here & Now* Nov 15 They took him down to the dummy yard where the flogging framework was set up. **1953** HAMILTON *Till Human Voices Wake Us* 112 When a three-striper came down they [sc. warders] locked Barney up in a dummy cell and carted Alec up to the hospital. **1965** LEE *Rhetoric at Red Dawn* 127 When one of the prisoners was put in the dummy for misbehaviour, Jim O'Brien..wanted to bring the jail out on strike. **1980** MACKENZIE *While We Have Prisons* 14 The punishment block, known as the 'pound' or the 'dummy', was a prison within the [Mt Eden] prison. In the basement, through a steel grille and a wooden door, it was a dimly lit and silent annexe leading at its far end to the tiny execution yard.

b. Solitary confinement, a spell in the dummy.

1953 HAMILTON *Till Human Voices Wake Us* 57 He'd think nothing of snooping into the cell of a man doing his dummy. *Ibid.* 159 Sometimes, during the strain of that long dummy I'd burst out in a stream of curses at a screw.

dummy, *v. Hist.* [f. DUMMY *n.*[1] 1: AND 1878.] In Crown land purchase, to purchase (land) as an agent for another who is not legally entitled to purchase the land in question.

1898 REEVES *Long White Cloud* 356 The attempts often ingeniously made to evade these [land] restrictions by getting the land in the name of relatives, servants, or agents are called 'dummyism', and may be punished by imprisonment—never inflicted—by fines, and by forfeiture of the land 'dummied'. **1933** [see DUMMY *n.*[1]].

Hence **dummying** *vbl. n. hist.* [AND 1873], the practice of hiring an agent to acquire Crown land on behalf of one not entitled to do so.

1948 LIPSON *Politics of Equality* 58 Liberal politicians had inveighed against 'dummying', 'spotting', and other favorite devices of land monopolists. **1981** PINNEY *Early N. Otago Runs* 65 The upper Ahuriri and the hills..were now legally tenanted. Any suggestion of dummying is no more.

dump, *n.*

1. [Spec. use of *dump* something squat, perh. f. *dumpy adj.*] **a.** Two bales of wool reduced under high pressure to approx. the size of one; also in modern use (as **double dump**, see quot. 1993) a machine for dumping bales. Also called a **double dump**.

1883 CHUDLEIGH *Diary* 27 Jan. (1950) 317 Wi Te Tahuhu shore 300 sheep and had 5 bales and a dump of wool. **1964** DAVIS *Watersiders* 105 On wool, when three men work elbow to elbow on seven-hundred-pound dumps and one slip means a hook through your mate's hand. **1968** TOMLINSON *Remembered Trails* 33 Twenty-five dumps, or 50 bales, was a wagon-load for eight horses. **1993** *Taranaki Farmers Co-op. Annual Report* 8 Wanganui Wool Dumpers again made a significant contribution to the annual result. An additional double dump was..commissioned during the year. This investment increased dumping capacity.

b. Special Comb. **dump-shed (dumping shed)**, a place where wool-bales are dumped, or dumped bales stored, preparatory to shipment.

1899 *NZ Times* (Wellington) 28 Dec. 2 Wool wagons are daily to be seen on almost every road bringing down wool from the various farms..to the dumping sheds..and from thence to the wool ships which roll at anchor in the Bay. **1973** WHEELER *Hist. Sheep Stations NI* 14 [Caption] The woolshed. From left, dump shed (formerly sited on the shore..) woolroom, toolshed, carpenter's shop, saw bench.

2. [Poss. because it is a dispensable marble 'dumped' in the ring.] An inferior marble; or, often *pl.*, a marble-game.

1943 HISLOP *Pure Gold* 22 I suppose at that time [c1860s goldrush] I would be more interested in grabbing my 'dumps' out of the ring at school, when some quick eye had noticed that a young pointer had tried to get away with placing a stinkie or a chalkie into play with the rest of his marbles. The 'Grab your dumps' was the roar, as we all rushed in for our own, and anybody else's one could get. **1953** SUTTON-SMITH *Unorganized Games NZ Primary School Children* (VUWTS) II. 719 There is only one record of a New Zealand game in which a formal penalty element entered. This was a game of marbles called Dumps and was played at Wakefield in 1875. In this game the loser, in a marble game of Holey, was required to hold his marble partially exposed between the fingers of his closed fist [for others to shoot at].

dump, *v.*

a. [AND 1849.] *trans.* To compress (two bales of wool) into approx. the size of one to save transport space. See also *double-dump* (DOUBLE *a.*).

1881 CAMPBELL *Poenamo* 41 Under his hospitable roof I took my first lesson in 'dumping wool', for he was busy 'baling his clip' to send down to Sydney for shipment home. **1885** *Wairarapa Daily* 28 Nov. 2 [Heading] The Wool-Dumping Charges... That the present charge for dumping wool be reduced..from 2s to 1s 9d per bale. **c1930** *Whitcombe's Etym. Dict. Aust.-NZ Suppl.* 4 *dump v.t.* to press closely, esp. as in compressing bales of wool for economy in freight during shipment overseas. **1968** TOMLINSON *Remembered Trails* 33 [Wool] was dumped in a hydraulic press that compressed two bales into one space for carting on wagons. **1969** MCCASKILL *Molesworth* 103 The cleanest and best wool was dumped in the grease on the station and taken to Blenheim for shipment to London.

b. *trans.* To compress (bales of material other than wool).

1902 WALKER *Zealandia's Guerdon* They [press in a wool-press] rabbit skins properly dressed..and dumped in bundles of two dozen. **1944** *NZJST* XV. 204B The dry [sea]weed..is packed most commonly into woolbales, either by tramping or with a wool-press... [In Auckland] the weed is checked over..before being 'dumped' for final despatch to the factory.

Hence **dumped** *ppl. a.*, of wool(-bales), so compressed.

1973 WHEELER *Hist. Sheep Stations NI* 10 It was customary, as at Waipiro Bay..to have a wool store and a dump press near the beach. The dumped wool was taken by bullock wagon into the surf, transferred to surfboats, and rowed out to the..steamer lying offshore.

dumper.

1. [f. DUMP v.] A hand in a woolshed or wool-store who (or a commercial enterprise which) dumps wool.

1868 *Marlborough Express* (Blenheim) 18 Jan. 3 A number of shearers and dumpers having secured a fiddler and fifer, paraded the town with green ribbon round their hats.

2. [Origin unknown.] A criminals' name for a race-course detective.

dumping, *vbl. n..*

1. [See DUMP v.: AND 1980.] The operation or process of compressing two bales of wool into the size of one. Also *attrib*.

1894 *NZ Official Year-book* 494 A dumping-plant has been erected by the Harbour Board; and last year (1893) 5,703 bales of wool..were shipped. **a1914** MOWAT *Diary* in McCaskill *Molesworth* (1969) 103 The dry wool was pressed at the scour and the bales taken to the woolshed for dumping ready for shipment. **1922** PERRY *Sheep Farming* 138 It is a mistake to think that seed..in wool is crushed to dust in the dumping. **1958** *NZ Farmer* 30 Oct. 20 The Shaw Savill & Albion Company last year 'dumped' 100,548 bales of wool... 'Dumping' is the pressing of two bales of wool into the space of one, thus conserving shipboard storage space. **1974** *NZ Agric.* 67 A powerful hydraulic press forces two bales into the space formerly occupied by one, and they are bound with steel bands, or wires. (This process is called 'double dumping' or 'dumping'.) **1993** dumping [see DUMP *n.* 1 a].

2. [f. a transf. use of DUMP v. to compress or make squat.] The forcing of a sheep into a compressed posture to enable easier shearing.

1952 LYON *Faring South* 194 When shearers are striving for a tally, or a big output of shorn sheep, dumping is the act of pushing the lamb's head downward when seated on the boards, in such a way that the lamb's lungs are pushed down on his diaphragm causing great agony and often fatal injury... The idea is that by dumping the sides of the lamb are flattened and permit a larger flat surface of fleece to be exposed to the shears. **1955** BOWEN *Wool Away* 5 There are several known styles of shearing. They range from the old blade method of stretching the sheep and shearing more round and round, to the modern method of dumping or crimping the sheep and following the blows right through more along the body of the sheep.

dumpy. Also **dumpty**. [A var. or alteration of *dunny* + *dump*: AND 1965.] An outdoor privy.

1957 FRAME *Owls Do Cry* (1967) 84 Her husband was up in the dumpy. **1981** ANDERSON *Both Sides of River* 101 'Thank heaven for that [*sc.* a flush toilet],' I said. 'I had visions of tramping some lonely path to an old dumpty, perched over a big hole full of spiders and wiggly things.' **1982** FRAME *To the Is-land* (1984) 29 The lavatory, or 'dumpy' as we called it, was the usual enclosure about a deep hole, with a railway-red seat.

Dunedinite /dəˈnidənˌait/. One born or resident in Dunedin.

1864 *Smith Diary* (Hocken MS) 9 Feb The 11 of All-England and the 22 of Otago, and as a matter of course the Dunedinites were beat. **1874** BATHGATE *Col. Experiences* 13 There is nothing..in the natural situation..of the town itself which recalls the 'Modern Athens', although a Dunedinite might well exclaim with Scott 'mine own romantic town'. **1887** INGLIS *Our NZ Cousins* 224 The Dunedinites..have rather arrogated to themselves the reputation of being preternaturally knowing. **1926** *NZ Observer* 20 Mar. 2 There is a modicum of truth in the Dunedinite's facetiousness. **1952** LYON *Faring South* 131 No wonder the old Dunedinite of a former generation referred to them [*sc.* barracouta]..as 'Old Identities'. **1961** REED *N. Cape to Bluff* They found the evening a little chilly, and even the Dunedinite found the warm glow acceptable. **1972** MITCHELL *Pavlova Paradise* 33 Dunedinites think of Auckland as another country. **1987** SLIGO *Final Things* 172 Each brick..was dense with the thickness of the Dunedinites' lives. **1990** *NZ Gardener* Oct. 14 Tony Wyber, a Dunedinite,.. provided the..photographs.

Dunedin sound. A characteristic musical sound emphasising jangly guitar, said to distinguish Dunedin pop groups from other New Zealand bands.

1981 *In Touch* (Wellington) 15 Dec. 6 'Do you consider that there is such a thing as a distinctive "New Zealand" sound?'... 'No, but I think there's a "Dunedin Sound"'. **1986** *Listener* 17 May 68 I'm worried that the 'Dunedin sound' will begin to parody itself very soon. **1991** *North & South* (Auckland) Nov. 74 Empty white-sand beaches, the very good university and the famous 'Dunedin Sound' pub music attract people too. **1992** *Salient* (Wellington) 13 Apr. 12 Cited by many as the headlining band of a 'new Dunedin Sound', *Hellzapoppin*' has entered the national chart at no. 24.

dunger /ˈdʌŋə/. [Imitative of the sound of an old or mechanically deficient engine, 'dung-a dung-a'.] Often as **old dunger**, something (sounding) mechanically worn out or not in first-class order, esp. an old car.

1980 *In Touch* (Wellington) May 7 We had to take out a commercial motor vehicle policy on our old dunger of a station wagon. **1982** *Evening Post* (Wellington) 24 Mar 8 Judge P.J. Bate said Rawhiti might have made an initial mistake in purchasing a car which in common parlance might be called a 'dunger'. **1983** *Truth* 30 Nov 23 And Crump has written another book, using his 'old dunger' of a typewriter which he describes as 'a real antique'. **1983** *Dominion* (Wellington) 7 Apr. 7 Those cars, doesn't matter whether its a brand new Mercedes, or an old dunger, are all somebody's pride and joy. **1992** *Contact* (Wellington) 18 Nov. 1 Newtown, Berhampore and Island Bay are the worst spots for old 'dungers'.

dunite /ˈdʌnait/. *Geol.* [Named by Hochstetter (see quot. 1867) from *Dun* Mountain, Nelson.] An olivine rock composed mainly of the iron-magnesium silicate mineral.

1867 HOCHSTETTER *NZ* 474 [Dun Mountain, Nelson] consists of a very peculiar kind of rock, of a yellowish-green colour when recently broken, but turning rusty-brown on the surface when decomposing. The mass of the rock is olivine..; it is distinguished from serpentine for which it was formerly taken, especially by its greater hardness, and its crystalline structure. I have called it Dunite. **1883** HECTOR *Handbook NZ* 56 Chrome ore.., which is a mixture of chromic iron and alumina, is chiefly associated with magnesian rock, resembling olivine in composition, named Dunite by Dr. Hochstetter. **1898** MORRIS *Austral-English* 132 *Dunite*..an ore in New Zealand, so called from Dun mountain, near Nelson. **1911** *TrNZI* XLIII. 451 Both the metal [platinum] and the awaruite occur in a district composed..of serpentine and dunite. **1939** *Taranaki Herald* (New Plymouth) 19 May 4 A large Sydney firm is at present interesting itself in the deposits of dunite, a mineral containing copper, on Dun Mountain. **1966** *Encycl. NZ* II. 92 His [*sc.* Hochstetter's] name 'dunite' for the olivine rock of Dun Mountain is firmly established. **1974** KINGMA *Geological Structure NZ* 73 The rocks of Red Mountain lens..commonly consist of unaltered..dunites, harzburgites, wehrlites.

dunnekin /ˈdʌnəkən/. Also **dunneken, dunnican**. [f. Brit. dial., of unknown orig., poss. *dung* + *ken* a cant term for 'house': cf. OED at *dunny*, a1790; EDD *dunnekin;* AND 1843.] A (usu. outside) privy; DUNNY.

1837 BEST *Journal* 23 Oct. (1966) 142 They soon came out saying that the water was pouring in forward through the Dunnekin and that everything was afloat. **1968** TURNER *Rev. Pitcairnese Lang.* in *Anglia* LXXXVI. 359 Thus, to go beyond the several examples already given in the book, *cack* and *dunnekin* survive in New Zealand as well as Pitcairnese (though in New Zealand, as in Australia, the shorter *dunny* is much commoner than *dunnekin* now), but presumably these are independent survivals. **1982** LYNN *Lynnwood Tree* 75 We built a little dunnican out in the paddock with a three by two rail, so there was not much we could wish for.

dunney, var. DUNNY.

dunnican, var. DUNNEKIN.

dunny. Also **dunney**.

1. [A familiar shortened form of Brit. dial. *dunneken* a privy: see EDD *dunnekin*; AND 1933.] A privy. See also DUNNEKIN.

1941 CURNOW 'Country School' in *A Small Room with Large Windows* (1962) 4 How small Are the terrible doors; how sad the dunny And the things you drew on the wall. **1952** BAXTER *Collected Poems* (1980) 122 Dark as a dunny the under-runner The green flax plaited for whiplashes. **1960** HILLIARD *Maori Girl* I iii 19 She delighted in giving cheek to the boys and taking refuge in the girls' dunny. **1978** SUTHERLAND *Elver* 33 The dunny was a small house over a hole in the ground. **1982** LYNN *Lynnwood Tree* 125 One local builder..gave instructions to one of his old carpenters to build the dunney for a job... The old Privy..WC..Lavatory.. Dunney..Netty. **1987** HARTLEY *Swagger on Doorstep* 43 For a different visual encounter we had only to visit the lavatory (our family called it the 'lav', others preferred the terms dunny or outhouse) outside. **1992** *Salient* (Wellington) 28 Sept. 32 New Zealand is still the land of the milk-can dunny.

2. a. Comb. **dunny door, hole**.

1991 *Dominion* (Wellington) 9 Feb. 9 No 8 was called on to form makeshift kitchen implements, latch a million **dunny doors** and hang out the nation's laundry. **1986** TAYLOR *Shooting Through* 42 'What're **dunny holes**?'... 'Dunny holes are loos. They used to have them in the olden days.'

b. Special Comb. **dunny box**, the wooden commode which fits over the hole in the ground or over the dunny bucket; **dunny brush**, a long-handled brush for cleaning water-closets, also in *transf.* or *fig.* use; **dunny-paper**, toilet paper; **dunny rat**, as an emblem of cunning or luckiness, prob. a euphemism for *shithouse rat*; **dunny rose**, a trailing rose grown to hide or beautify an outdoor dunny.

1981 JOHNSTON *Fish Factory* 175 '**Dunny box** for a new long drop,' Hec grunted and continued with his work. **1982** MARSHALL *Master Big Jingles* 62 Arty couldn't meet our eyes as the car pulled away. 'What a **dunney brush** he turned out to be,' said Mathew, and we laughed. **1987** *Listener* 25 July 49 Chatterton passed a hand over his own stiff, grey hair. A dunny brush, he'd heard it called. **1987** SLIGO *Final Things* 88 Their cavalcade passed by, streaming with pink **dunny paper**. **1983** HULME *Bone People* 220 Joe tells her, adding with a laugh that Simon has the luck of a proverbial **dunny rat**. **1951** FRAME *Lagoon* (1961) 35 They had a nice trellis-work too, with **dunny roses** growing up it. **1985** FRAME *Envoy from Mirror City* 167 I..looked out along the path to the cypress tree and the old dunny with its dunny roses spilling in a mass of white buds over the corrugated tin-hat roof. [**1990** LANGFORD *Newlands* 31 The other place Dad got away from Mum was the dunny out the back, hidden from the house by a hedge of wild roses.]

3. In the phr. **to go down the dunny**, of an enterprise, scheme, idea, etc., to come to an end; to be put out of action; to be ruined.
  1993 *Metro* (Auckland) Feb. 12 Malcolm Walker was *The Examiner* cartoonist before it went down the dunny.

durb, var. DERB.

durry. [Orig. unknown: AND 1941.] A (roll-your-own) cigarette.
  1984 16 F E30 Pakuranga Coll. 33 Durree, durrey, durry [F1M6] **1985** McGILL *G'day Country* 120 He had worked out of Christchurch..he said as he carefully rolled a durry. **1988** McGILL *Dict. Kiwi Slang* 41 *durry* cigarette, usually roll-your-own, the makings often called *durries*, perhaps associated with Bull Durham brand tobacco.
  Hence **durry** *v. intr.*, in adolescents' use, for to smoke (illicitly).
  1960 18C M B11 Nelson Boys C. 21 Durry [to smoke a cigarette] **1984** 17 M E115 Pakuranga Coll. 33 Durrying [F2 M1]

dusky plover: see PLOVER 2 (2).

dust.
1. *Obs.* In early whalers' or traders' parlance, gunpowder.
  1845 WAKEFIELD *Adventure NZ* I. 319 Every article of trade with the natives has its slang term,—in order that they may converse with each other respecting a purchase without initiating the natives into their calculations. Thus pigs and potatoes were respectively represented by '*grunters*' and '*spuds*', guns, powder, blankets, pipes, and tobacco, by '*shooting-sticks*', '*dust*', '*spreaders*', '*steamers*', and '*weed*'.

2. *Goldmining.* [Orig. US: AND 1851.] Ellipt. for 'gold dust'.
  1852 *Gold Circular* in Swainson *Auckland* (1853) 106 The dust consisted of flaky gold, of a pale lemon colour, largely intermixed with auriferous quartz. *Ibid.* 109 These parties also brought up..various other specimens; one parcel of which, consisting of large rich dust and flakes, and exceedingly auriferous quartz. **1938** HYDE *Nor Yrs. Condemn* 54 Hadn't so much as a pick, he hadn't, and when he came down again he was carrying his dust in a sugar-sack on his back.

3. An inferior grade of kauri gum. See also *gum-dust* (GUM 3 a).
  1916 STALLWORTHY *Early N. Wairoa* 54 At one time the dust, and scrapings, of the gum were not saleable... Since then there has always been a price of some sort for all dust and scrapings. **1936** [see CHIP *n.*¹ 2]. **1948** REED *Gumdigger* 56 Black sugar, Chalk, Bright Seeds..Black Flour Dust, Bright Dust, Rescraped Bush, Bright Chips. **1956** black flour dust [see GUM *n.* 2]. **1966** [see CHIP *n.*¹ 2]. **1972** REED *Gumdiggers* 82 The [1920 Kauri Gum Industry] report stated that during the preceding few years the proportion of low-grade gum, chips and dust (scrapings) had increased in volume..to about two-thirds of the total gum exports.

4. As **the dust** [AND 1937], a term for miners' phthisis or silicosis.
  1978 McARA *Gold Mining Waihi* 320 *Dust*: Quartz dust was a major menace to the health of miners. It blocked up the microscopic air-sacs in the lungs, producing hardening of the tissues and impairing the function of the lungs. Eventually, sometimes after many years, death resulted. The disease miners' phthisis was commonly called 'the dust.' It gradually came to an end after the introduction of axial-water-feed drills.
  Hence **dusted** *ppl. a.* [AND 1942], suffering from silicosis.
  1986 RICHARDS *Off the Sheep's Back* 5 The greatest occupational hazard of mining was the dust... Drilling was all done dry in those days. The air was laden with particles of flint and quartz, ground to the consistency of flour... Once a man was 'dusted', there was no cure. **1992** LATHAM *Golden Reefs* 356 The author recalls, in childhood years, hearing adults on Broadway [Reefton] speaking with an air of hopeless resignation if some miner was said to have been 'dusted'.

dustie. [f. *dust*(man + –IE.] A rubbish collector.
  1985 *Listener* 8 June 11 No one told me that the dusties collected the rubbish around the back. Early. And no one told the dusties that a white robed flailer was not a kehua, a ghost. **1993** *Dominion* (Wellington) 8 July 10 If too many extra [rubbish] bags went out the council might have to negotiate new contracts with the dusties.

Dutchie. [f. *Dutch*(man + –IE.] A Dutch person.
  1959 SLATTER *Gun in My Hand* 60 And in peace the civilians must have something to hate too. The Dutchies or the Pommies or the Doolins or somebody. **1960** MASTERS *Back-Country Tales* 116 Mr. Jock Anderson..arranged to met [*sic*] a new-Dutchman... As he came on to a small bluff he called out. The Dutchie responded.

Dutchman. In early New Zealand applied, as elsewhere, to any North European, esp. to a sailor; also giving rise to an appellation or nickname (Dutch Charlie, Dutch Harry, etc.). Compare SCANDY A.
  1909 *Truth* 29 May 5 Many expressed regret when the 'blasted Dutchman' succeeded in clearing his name. The tendency to call every foreigner 'a Dutchman' is well known and amazing. **1939** BEATTIE *First White Boy Born Otago* 47 Take 'Dutch Harry' for instance. His name was Henry Wickson (or Wixon), and it was said he was an Austrian and came from Memel... To the whalers any foreigner was Dutch so that is how he got his nickname. **1939** EADDY *Neath Swaying Spars* 26 Quite a number of the trading scows were manned wholly with Scandinavians. They were very clannish, these people, and should a 'Dutchman' as they were always dubbed, be appointed master of any scow, generally speaking, that vessel would eventually be manned entirely by 'Dutchmen'.

dwang. [f. Sc. dial.: OEDAS II. 22 '*Sc.* and *N.Z.*', 1497 (*Sc.*); SND *dwang* 3, 1849: cf. also J. Jakobsen *An Etymological Dict. of the Norn Language in Shetland* (1928) I. 136, *dwang* 'a piece of wood..(doubtless orig. for fastening something); in a special sense of a wedge' ad. Old Norse *þvengr* a strap, latchet.] A short piece of timber fixed horizontally between vertical framing timbers. See also NOG(GING).
  1914? *N.Z. Building Trades Guide & System of Measurement* 27 Solid dwangs and those formed by cross pieces shall be measured by the lineal foot. **1951** *NZ Standards Institute: Draft code Bldg. Terminol. D 3896* (TS) 16 Nov. 17 Dwang: A short member, also known as 'nogging', fixed between the framing timbers to form a support for the attachment of linings or coverings. **1966** TURNER *Eng. Lang. Austral. & NZ* 178 The Scottish word *dwang* for a strut between studs seems to be used generally as a builder's term in New Zealand, but, oddly enough, a builder told me it is not used in Otago, where dwanging is called *nogging*. **1979** *SANZ in Reverse* 12 To specify the drilling pillars And regulate amalgam fillers While perforated plates and dwangs Defy the rat and mouse's fangs—Put up to us a plaque. **1986** SALMOND *Gloss. Bldg. Terminol.* 232 *Nog (or dwang)*..a short piece of framing timber fixed tightly between *studs*, to which lining materials are fixed. **1988** *Dominion* (Wellington) 23 July 8 Fitted over the exposed wooden dwangs inside corrugated iron walls, it becomes hooks upon which one may hang hats. **1992** [see NOG].

dyer's weed. [Orig. unknown.] A wild mignonette. See quots.
  1926 HILGENDORF *Weeds* 96 Mignonette (*Reseda luteola*) is called wild mignonette, scentless mignonette, giant mignonette and dyer's weed. It is not uncommon in fields and waste places in both islands. **1969** *Standard Common Names Weeds* 23 dyer's weed, [=] *wild mignonette*.

dyke, var. DIKE.

E

e. Usu. an altered form of the Ma. indef. art. HE, often prefixed to early transliterations of Ma. nouns: e.g. **e-taboo** =he tapu.

eagle.

1. Often also **Haast's eagle** (see quot. 1893), also **giant eagle**, **native eagle**, **New Zealand eagle**. *Harpagornis moorei* (fam. Accipitridae), an extinct, carnivorous, giant (13 kg) forest eagle, with a wing span of up to 2.8 m and believed capable of killing small moa.

[**1872** *TrNZI* IV. 194 As the small Harrier now flies leisurely during the day time over the plains and downs in search of food..so the *Harpagornis* doubtless followed the flocks of Moas feeding either upon the carcases of the dead birds, or killing the young and disabled ones.] **1888** BULLER *Birds NZ* II. 183 Sir George Grey is of the opinion that the extinct New-Zealand Eagle (*Harpagornis moorei*) was the bird to which the tradition [of the 'Hokioi'] relates and he may be right in this conjecture. **1893** *TrNZI* XXV. 92 Pride of place will certainly be yielded to the great extinct eagle, first made known by the excavations of Sir Julius von Haast at Glenmark. **1948** HAAST *Life & Times von Haast* 756 People still hunting the moa feasted long enough above the site to form a midden-layer above it, with boulders, oven stones, and charcoal, shellfish, bones of moa, extinct swan..and extinct eagle. **1955** OLIVER *NZ Birds* 604 Greater Extinct Eagle... The first discovered bones of this species were found in 1871 when the moa deposits of Glenmark were being investigated by Haast. **1969** KNOX *Nat. Hist. Canterbury* 565 Glenmark swamp..also produced the first recorded bones of the giant eagle, *Harpagornis moorei*, which Haast named, after finding the bones, in honour of Mr G. H. Moore, manager of Glenmark Station. **1988** STEVENS et al. *Prehistoric New Zealand* 101 [Caption] Haast's eagle..the largest, most powerful eagle in the world. **1990** HAYWARD *Trilobites, Dinosaurs & Moa Bones* 86 In addition to moas, other spectacular birds have disappeared including the world's largest and most powerful eagle, Haast's eagle with a wing span close to 3m. **1994** *Evening Post* (Wellington) 1 July 3 [Caption] Dave Maguire with his model plane in the shape of the extinct native eagle harpagornis.

2. [f. US services' slang *the eagle shits* for 'payday'.] The freezing works, esp. in the phr. **the eagle shits**, 'it's payday'.

1976 MORRIESON *Pallet on Floor* 29 'If that's on the cards, let's get few flagons,' said Entwhistle quickly. 'After all the eagle shits tomorrow'. This was freezing workers' slang for pay-day. *Ibid.* 119 Here was the siding to the sprawling empire of the Freezing Works, the 'Eagle' as the men called it.

eagle ray: see RAY 2 (1).

eaglewist: see EDELWEISS.

ear.

1. Special Comb. **ear-piece** *freezing works*, the detached scalp of a sheep including the ears; **eartag** *n.*, a distinguishing marker attached to the ear of a cattle-beast; **eartag** *v. trans.*, to distinguish beasts by attaching tags to their ears; also *transf.* to 'earmark' or set aside for a particular purpose. See also EAR-SHELL, *sea-ear* (SEA 1 b).

1951 17 May Feilding Freezing Works terms p.c. Colin Gordon The *chopper* also *scalps* them which gets taken off as the ***ear-piece***, and goes down to the *pie-house*, on to the *pie-heap* where it rots and is plucked by the *pie-pickers*. **1930** *NZ Dairy Produce Exporter* 23 Jan. 33 [Advt] Everything for stock breeders. We can supply Earmarks, **Eartags**, Brands, (Burning or Fleece), Ram Clamps. **1960** *The NZ Dairy Exporter* 11 Jan. 9 [Advt] The Farm-acy (N.Z.) Ltd. Makers of: Sheep and Cattle earmarkers; Eartags (brass and plastic). **1988** HILL *More from Moaville* 62 Each year, the $1 donation..has been **eartagged** for some worthy community cause.

2. See *chew one's ear* (CHEW v. a).

earbash, *v.* [AND 1944.] To talk long and hard at (a person); to bore (one) with words; to nag. Occas. as a *n.* (see quot. 1995).

1955 BJ Cameron Collection (TS July) earbash (v) To talk on and on. earbasher (n) One who so talks. earbashing (n) The infliction of a long wearisome discourse. **1957** CROSS *God Boy* 81 We went on earbashing each other like that for the next hour or so. **1964** FRANCES *Johnny Rapana* 183 Now, after ear bashing you like that, the least I can do is take you out to lunch. **1991** *Examiner* (Auckland) 2 May 6 Wellingtonians ear-bashed by anti-government community groups..might not realise it but they've been paying for this propaganda. **1995** *Sunday Star-Times* (Auckland) 26 Feb. sect. C1 Staff say that [Lange] made great use of the Beehive's circular prime ministerial offices..to evade anyone he suspected was going to nobble him for a gratuitous earbash.

Hence **earbasher** *n.* [AND 1941], one who talks incessantly, a loudmouthed bore (see quot. 1955 above); **earbashing** *vbl. n.* [AND 1945], a lengthy talking to; a talking at length.

1951 16+ M 26 Wellington H.S. 23 Ear-bashing. **1973** *Islands* 6 385 The phys ed teacher complains that a whole period of ear-bashing..cannot make 14 yr old boys dance with girls. **1980** LELAND *Kiwi-Yankee Dict.* 36 Ear Bashing. Talking to excess. **1995** *Dominion* (Wellington) 18 Sept. 2 The luckless Mr Godfrain had been dispatched to Papua New Guinea to endure a succession of ear bashings from South Pacific forum countries over nuclear testing.

early.

1. Used of the pioneering period of colonial settlement in New Zealand, esp. in the collocations **early colonist**, **early settler**.

1859 HOBHOUSE *Selected Let.* 24 Nov. (1992) 41 The early Colonists tell me of the days when there was no way of crossing the rivers but by driving in a bullock & holding on by his tail. **1917** HOWES *Marlborough Sounds* 13 The early settlers burnt the bush that clothed the hills and held their soil in place. **1930** *NZ Fishing and Shooting Gaz.* 1 Feb. 10 Early settlers often netted quantities [of inanga] and preserved them in bottles with weak vinegar and cloves. **1938** *With Rod and Gun in NZ* NZ Govt. Tourist and Health Resorts Dept. 2 To the early settlers whose memories were stirred by thoughts of the happy days spent with rod and line in the 'Old Country' such a state of affairs was a challenge to inherited sporting instincts. **1952** BLAKISTON *My Yesteryears* 9 I had known the Orari Gorge Station since 1869 and so many of the old hands and early day doings.

2. Special Comb. **early cup**, **early morning (cup of) tea**, a cup of tea given to a guest on waking. (A former New Zealand rural and hotel tradition.)

1875 LUSH *Thames Jrnls.* 22 Feb. (1975) 159 Felt inclined to have an extra hour's rest in bed, but the recollection that the servant might soon be bringing the early cup of tea made me hurry up... The 'early cup' came as I had expected at half past six. **1935** GUTHRIE *Little Country* (1937) 108 She was always cross when wakened early, even if it was for her early morning cup of tea. **1961** BOOTH *Long Night* 104 He was under the shower [at the hotel] when the early-morning tea came in..It was the old stuff, tepid with soggy biscuits. **1979** BELSHAW *Man of Integrity* 64 I remember my father being highly amused when the owner brought in early morning tea. **1986** HULME *Windeater* 38 Setnets were strangers, and the joys of very early morning tea in a tin shack on a river-side also unknown.

3. Special Comb. **early shower**, often in the phr. **to take (be sent for) an early shower**, in team sports (esp. rugby), to be sent off the field of play as a penalty; also in transf. use, to be dismissed from a job or position (see quot. 1985).

1978 *Dominion* (Wellington) 14 July 16 Petone beat Porirua 2–0..but lost Pickering to an early shower after she apparently kicked an opponent. **1981** *Dominion* (Wellington) 2 Oct. 8 Koteka's indiscriminate booting of his opposite..deserved the early shower but the punishment did not fit the crime. **1985** *NZ Times* 18 Aug. 1 [Heading] Varnham takes early shower A second press officer has made an abrupt departure from Parliament. Mary Varnham, press secretary to Women's Affairs Minister Ann Hercus, left Tuesday in a surprise move. **1992** *Dominion* (Wellington) 23 Apr. 1 [He] had not known that Roumat had been ordered off. He was receiving attention to his head when the Frenchman headed for an early shower.

4. As **early opener**, an hotel which opens its bars earlier than, say, 9.00 a.m.

1988 *Dominion Sunday Times* (Wellington) 14 Feb. 19 When they [*sc.* vagrant alcoholics] go to bed fully dressed that's 'marching orders' and their 'dawn parade' will be held at an early opener.

ear-shell. *Obs.* [Spec. use of *ear-shell* for species of fam. Halitodae: f. the shape of the univalve shell.] PAUA. Cf. *sea-ear* (SEA 1 b).

1769 MONKHOUSE in Cook *Journals* 11 Oct. (1955) I. 574 Its whole length does not exceed two feet, ending in the representation of a face..two large Saucer-eyes formed of broad rings of Ear-Shell. **1777** FORSTER *Voyage Round World* I. 132 [The canoe] had a carved head..with eyes made of round pieces of ear-shell, which somewhat resembled mother of pearl. **1791** *Jrnl.*

HMS *Chatham* 29 Nov. in McNab *Hist. Records* (1914) II. 505 In the centre of this circle [on Chatham Island] was the mark of a fire place, and a great number of Fish Shells lay about, particularly the Earshell. **1807** SAVAGE *Some Acc. of NZ* 58 The hooks are formed of the outer rim of the ear-shell, well polished, and barbed at the extremity. **1856** TANCRED *Natural Hist. Canterbury* 16 Shell, called from its shape the ear-shell. **1872** *TrNZI* V. 367 The ear-shell was used by the Maoris in the manufacture of fish-hooks.

earth oven. HANGI 1. Cf. MAORI OVEN 1, *native oven* (NATIVE B 3 a), OVEN 1.
1879 *TrNZI* XI. 103 From another very old chief I had heard of two having been once cooked in a Maori earth-oven. **1904** TREGEAR *Maori Race* 109 Food was generally cooked in an earth-oven. **1920** [see HANGI 1]. **1938** HYDE *Nor Yrs. Condemn* 147 After dinner, he walked back to the back of the shack, where two little brown men were still fiddling with an earth-oven. **1946** ZIMMERMAN *Where People Sing* 65 She showed me, too, how to make the little baskets called *konae* that are used to hold the food that is put into the earth ovens to be cooked by the heat of hot rocks. **a1973** FINLAYSON *Brown Man's Burden* 134 Such hui were always accompanied by mass cooking, for the visitors, in the earth ovens or haangi.

earthquake.
1. As an *attrib.* or in combinatory uses recalling New Zealand's propensity for earthquakes.
c1875 MEREDITH *Adventuring in Maoriland* (1935) 57 It [the earthquake] did us no damage, as all the shelves are made specially earthquake-proof. **1889** *TrNZI* XXI. 337 One strange feature of the country [in northern Wairoa] is the presence of a layer of blue clay or mud in a liquid state at varying depths... This mud or clay is just like what the early Wellington settlers used to call earthquake mud or clay, because it always ran out of cracks and holes in the ground at the time of an earthquake. **1983** *Nelson Evening Mail* 13 Jan. 4 Over the years different parts of the Karamea River have become blocked through earthquake slips. Locally known as earthquake lakes many are scattered throughout the area. They are quite distinctive with large numbers of dead trees littering the lakes.
2. Special Comb. **earthquake weather**, still, warm, humid oppressive weather, thought to forebode an earthquake; also in composition **earthquaky**, foreboding an earthquake (see quot. 1919).
[**1841** WEEKES *Journal* Sept. in *Establishment of New Plymouth* (1940) 55 The atmosphere was peculiar the evening before the earthquake, and an old Mauri 'Huniko' told Lakeman at tea that we should have one, their name being *Mumu* for it.] **1919** MANSFIELD *Letters* 30 Nov. (1993) III. 128 Weather report: Dead calm, warm—some sun, earthquakey. **c1942** St Patrick's College, Silverstream (Hutt Valley) (Ed.) *Earthquake weather* was often used in 1942–43 in connection with the severe earthquakes in the Hutt Valley and the Wairarapa. **1956** SUTHERLAND *Green Kiwi* (1960) 169 The phrase 'earthquake weather' did not then [17 June 1929] have currency in the district [*sc.* Murchison]. **1968** SLATTER *Pagan Game* 230 The summers were hot then, earthquake weather my mother always said. **1977** DRYLAND *Curious Conscience* 112 'Earthquake weather,' Aunty Mag said. **1986** *Evening Post* (Wellington) 3 Sept. 60 It's very still..and it's gone quiet... It's what they used to call 'earthquake weather'. **1993** *Marist Messenger* Nov. 39 [Heading] Earthquake weather. We're told, living here in Wellington, to be prepared..to know what to do in the event of 'the big one'.

easer. *Mining.* A charge which breaks up rock or other material.
1965 *Evening Post* (Wellington) 17 Feb. 18 Mr Taurima said the face measured about 30ft square. Seven shots were were laid—four lifters and three easers—and 150lb of gelignite was used. **1978** MCARA *Gold Mining Waihi* 189 The usual method of drilling was to start with the right-hand lifter, then the centre lifter, next the bottom right-hand cut hole, the knee hole, the stab (to break the outer part of the face and assist the cut) the bottom cut easer, then the hip hole, the right-hand cut easer, the two shoulder holes, the top right-hand cut hole, the top easer, the centre and right-hand back holes.

easies, *n. pl.* A woman's elasticized foundation garment.
1980 LELAND *Kiwi-Yankee Dict.* 36 *easies*: Girdle; foundation garments. **1988** MCGILL *Dict. Kiwi Slang* 42 *easies* women's elasticised foundation garment, called 'step-ins' in Australia. **1991** *NZ Women's Weekly* 24 June 40 Later came rubberised latex girdles, sometimes called easies or roll-ons.

East Coast.
a. Usu. as **the East Coast** (or **the Coast**), the eastern North Island from Tikirau (Cape Runaway) to Te Toka-a-Taiau (the northern bank of the Turanganui River) at Gisborne. See also COAST 1.
1840 *Williams to Queen* 1 Feb. in *GBPP House of Commons 1841 (No.311)* 140 That while your petitioner makes mention of the progress of the natives on the east coast, he begs to observe he is only describing the condition of the inhabitants generally throughout the northern island. **1868** *Richmond-Atkinson Papers* (1960) II. 269 You ask what I think about the East Coast. I say do not yield. **1873** ST JOHN *Pakeha Rambles* in Taylor *Early Travellers* (1959) 576 The reader who has good-naturedly followed me in my rambles about the East Coast must be by this time as tired of mountain scenery as I. **1922** *Auckland Weekly News* 12 Jan. 17 Aucklanders commonly call [the area between Poverty Bay and the Bay of Plenty] 'The East Coast', but there is an East Coast all the way from Parengarenga to the Bluff. **1936** LAMBERT *Pioneering Reminisc. Old Wairoa* 160 The new firm..will..do its utmost to further develop this fertile portion of the East Coast. **1948** HENDERSON *Taina* 96 Then Hineato stood up and sang a song, still very popular all over the Bay of Plenty and East Coast. **1959** SLATTER *Gun in My Hand* 43 And she would get me hoeing again and tell me about the East Coast up there under Hikurangi. **1963** HILLIARD *Piece of Land* 12 Other Maoris, you ask them where they come from, they'll tell you straight away. Up North, or East Coast, or Down South, wherever it is. **1980** LELAND *Kiwi-Yankee Dict.* 36 The area known as the East Coast..consists of the peninsula that forms the northeastern bulge of the North Island plus the area immediately inland from that bulge.
b. In *attrib.* use.
1866 *East Coast Land Titles Investigation Act 1866* **1869** HAWTHORNE *Dark Chapter NZ Hist.* 10 By 1867, manifold conflicting interests had grown up in Poverty Bay and East Coast districts, in the shape of land purchases. **1897** *TrNZI* XXIX. 161 On the completion of their school career they should be permitted to attend public schools like Napier and Gisborne along the east Coast district. **1916** GASCOYNE *Soldiering NZ* 88 We East Coast fellows [from Gisborne] had nearly forgotten what tents were like. **1925-26** *NZJST* VIII. 40 These carved designs are simple in comparison with some east-coast forms. **1951** *Here & Now* July 35 His [*sc.* Ballantyne's, in *The Cunninghams*] slang rings true and his people move, live, act and talk just like the people in his East Coast town. **1960** HILLIARD *Maori Girl* 218 When Shirley put a cigarette-butt down the sink..Netta would say, 'That's a real Maori trick, that one! Real East Coast!'

Hence **East Coaster** (also occas. familiarly **East Coastie**), a person (usu. a Maori, of (usu.) Ngati Porou affiliation) born or resident on the East Coast. See also COASTER 2.
1877 PRATT *Col. Experiences* 156 There is a story current in Wellington of a confiding East-Coaster. **1939–45** [see GEAR *n.*[1] 2]. **1969** HILLIARD *Green River* 22 He had teamed up with a young East Coaster named Bill Ehau. **1984** WILSON *S. Pacific Street* 91 He was an East Coaster who'd come over from Gisborne to work in Auckland. **1994** *Dominion* (Wellington) 29 July 3 [The gang] has run into stiff opposition from East Coasters. Gang members camped near Ruatoria were shot at and chased from the area. **1995** *Mana* 9 (Winter issue) 41 For most East Coasties, forestry is a curse.

Easter orchid: see ORCHID 4.

eat, *v.* In various phrases: **a. to eat cigarettes**, to chain-smoke.
1930 DEVANNY *Bushman Burke* 164 Lighting up the pipe he had been smoking. 'Eating too many cigarettes, so took to the old gun, Bert,' he explained.
b. *Women's informal.* **to eat sausage** [cf. OED *eat* 1 b, *U.S.*], to engage in fellatio with a male.
1984 BEATON *Outside In* 94 Ginny: Yeah. Had a film on VD. Fascinatin'! Put you off eating sausage, Kate!
c. *Obs.* **to eat the leek**, to be brought to face unpleasant consequences.
1889 CHUDLEIGH *Diary* 13 June (1950) 367 Both refused to be arrested so force will have to come from N.Z. Summonses will have to be served on every person..who has not registered their dogs. Wi and co must be made to eat the leek to the last root.
d. *Obs.* **to eat** (one's) **toot** (*tutu*), see TUTU 4 a.
e. to eat (someone) **without salt (and pepper)**, to be able to overcome (someone) easily; to 'gobble up'; to 'have for breakfast'.
1864? TEMPSKY *Memoranda* (ATLTS) 19 Snap!—and very flat—goes a cap of a carelessly handled piece of one of our men! Talk about cannibals, I could have eaten that man without salt and pepper—a sudden silence amongst the Maoris announced their having heard the suspicious sound.

Ech. /eʃ/ *WW2.* Abbrev. of ECHELON, esp. as a suffix in compounds such as **B-Ech, First Ech**.
1941 *NZEF Times* 22 Dec. 22 'First Ech'. Jim already had a Vat 69 at his elbow. *Ibid.* 30 Nov. 6 Second Ech., after their Queen St parade, will be nothing to it. **1946** WEBBER *Johnny Enzed in Italy* B-*Ech*: contraction for B-Echelon — reserve section of a unit — Lotus Eaters **1947** DAVIN *For Rest of Our Lives* 75 All the boys [were] still drinking to celebrate the Second Ech coming from England. *Ibid.* 104 'Where are they [*sc.* German prisoners] now?' 'I sent them over to "B" Ech'. **1970** SLATTER *On the Ball* 136 He is really getting on my nerves as he natters on and on, a lot of nonsense about getting out of B Ech and back into the sharp end with the boys.

Echelon. [Spec. use of *echelon* a formation of troops, ad. French *échelon* rung of a ladder.] In the New Zealand Army, a contingent or specific part of an expeditionary force; used in WW2 for a contingent of the Second New Zealand Expeditionary Force. See also ECH. Compare WW1 CONTINGENT.

1919 WAITE *New Zealanders at Gallipoli* 71 The troops were organised into three groups, labelled Echelon A, B, and C. Echelon A was composed of the portion first to land. **1939** *Chief General Staff to War Office* 6 Dec. (London) in *Documents Relating to Second World War* (1951) II. 22 The following provision is being made here for reinforcements for the 2nd NZEF: Every echelon will include normal first reinforcements. The Second Echelon will include second reinforcements for the First Echelon on a similar scale. The Third Echelon will include third reinforcements for the First Echelon and second reinforcements for the Second Echelon, also on a similar scale. **1940** *Tararua Tramper* Apr. 1 Some left in the First Echelon, others are in camp with the Second Echelon, and others are expecting to be called up for the Third Echelon. **1966** *Encycl. NZ* I. 464 Recruits for this [volunteer 'Special Force' for service overseas]— the First Echelon—entered camp in November [1939]. This First Echelon (approximately one-third of a division) became the nucleus of the Second New Zealand Expeditionary Force which left New Zealand on 6 January 1940, being followed by the Second Echelon on 2 May, and by the Third on 27 August. **1979** *Evening Post* (Wellington) 26 Sept. 2 The use of the word 'echelon' in the sense of First, Second or Third Echelon has puzzled many people, for though it is a military term it does not normally denote a 'contingent'. Echelon refers to the position of an army in the form of steps or parallel lines... A new name was sought for Second World War soldiers, and 'echelon' was the word chosen. It was first used in this context on August 29, 1939. While in the Middle East—in September 1940—an attempt was made to alter it to 'contingent', but this was not successful, and 'echelon' it remained. **1987** *Metro Fiction* 89 They'd both been in the first Echelon of the 2nd NZEF.

economic unit: see UNIT *n.*² 2 a.

edelweiss. Also *joc.* **eaglewist**, and erron. **eidelweiss** /ˈaɪdəlˌvaɪs/. [Spec. use of European *edelweiss Leontopodium alpinum* (fam. Asteraceae).] Also as **New Zealand edelweiss**, a native alpine daisy of the fam. Asteraceae, *Leucogenes* (formerly *Helichrysum*) *grandiceps* (often **South Island edelweiss**) and *L. leontopodium* (often **North Island edelweiss**) with silvery leaves and flowering heads surrounded by a ring of radiating bracts covered in white woolly hairs.

1883 GREEN *High Alps* 196 Here..we found the New Zealand edelweiss..and my men seemed to take fresh heart..when we had our hatbands adorned with the familiar little felt-like flowers. **1894** *TrNZI* XXVI. 343 Because we have here in New Zealand on our mountains two closely-allied plants resembling the Swiss one, which are usually known as the New Zealand edelweiss—viz. *Gnaphalium (Helichrysum) colensoi,* and *Gnaphalium (Helichrysum) grandiceps*. **1900** *Canterbury Old & New* 190 Ours is my assemblage of [mountain] plants belong the New Zealand 'Edelweiss' (no mean representative of the Swiss plant from which it derives its name). **1919** COCKAYNE *NZ Plants* 97 On Mount Hikurangi, the next high-mountain community appears..some of them the most beautiful of the alpine flora: *e.g.,* the North Island edelweiss (*Leucogenes leontopodium*)—a fine-sounding name for a noble plant. **1923** COCKAYNE *Cultivation NZ Plants* 86 *Leucogenes grandiceps* (South Island edelweiss..) is a most beautiful, glistening, silvery everlasting growing on subalpine and alpine rocks and stones, with large white bracts to the flower-heads... *L. leontopodium* (North Island edelweiss..) is even more beautiful, with larger bracts. **1946** *Tararua Story* 7 And above the bush lies the alpine meadow, tiny white blooms of euphrasia..clumps of North Island edelweiss—the club badge. **1951** MCLEOD *NZ High Country* 44 In spite of their life they [*sc.* musterers] are usually ignorant of natural history; the alpine plants all round them they seldom know by name; even the snowy eidelweiss [*sic*] they know, if at all, as 'eaglewist'. **1971** *New Zealand's Heritage* I. 266 *North Island Edelweiss, Leucogenes leontopodium.* Small prostrate plant with upward-curving stems the tips of which pass into thick woolly flower-stalks bearing beautiful flower heads. **1982** WILSON *Stewart Is. Plants* 202 *Leucogenes grandiceps* South Island Edelweiss.

Eden of the Southern Sea. *Obs.* A (satirical) name for New Zealand.

1867 THOMSON *Twelve Yrs. Canterbury* 7 This 'Eden of the Southern Sea', as it is was termed..had its defects. **1883** ROUSE in *Canterbury Rhymes* 68 Land where all is dear and bad, Comfort scarcely to be had;.. Oh! I'm sadly sold on thee, Eden of the Southern Sea.

Edinburgh of the South. Also early **New Edinburgh**. Former descriptive by-names for Dunedin, orig. named after Edinburgh and settled by Scottish emigrants.

1862 LINDSAY *Nat. Hist. in Coloniz.* 26 Let us hope that ere many years elapse, 'New Edinburgh' may possess in the Southern Hemisphere, a University rivalling that of 'Old Edinburgh'. **1902** IRVINE & ALPERS *Progress of NZ* 167 Colonel Wakefield..had in 1844 commissioned Frederick Tuckett..to examine the eastern coast of the Middle Island with a view to selecting a site for the 'New Edinburgh' settlement. **1926** DEVANNY *Butcher Shop* (1981) 92 To Wellington, the capital city, to Auckland, the Queen city of the North, even down to Dunedin, the Edinburgh of the South. **1927** *Glasgow Herald* 18 Mar. 13 The Mayor [of Dunedin] hoped [the address of welcome] would always remind [the Duke of York] of 'the Edinburgh of the South'. **1989** *Those Were the Days* 19 Golf had been introduced, naturally enough to the Edinburgh of the South, in 1870.

eel. [Spec. use of *eel* a snake-like fish for native freshwater and marine spp.]

1. Any of various eels esp. freshwater spp. of fam. Anguillidae, but also marine spp., the blind eel or hagfish (fam. Myxinidae), the conger eels (fam. Congridae), and the moray eels (fam. Muraenidae). See also HAGFISH, LAMPREY, NGOIRO, PUHARAKEKE, SILVERBELLY, TUNA *n.*¹

1821 *McCrae's Evidence before Commissioner Bigge* May in McNab *Hist. Records* (1908) I. 550 Q. What sort of fish did you obtain at New Zealand? A... There are snappers (schnapper), mullet, bream, soles, eels. **1846** HEAPHY *Exped. to Kawatiri* 7 May in Taylor *Early Travellers* (1959) 230 How else can an eel be cooked to equal its flavour when roasted on a supplejack? **1855** TAYLOR *Te Ika A Maui* 383 The small eels are often dried by being hung up in the sun, when it becomes like a bag of rancid oil. **1880** *TrNZI* XII. 316 In December and January millions of small eels from 2–5 inches in length and the thickness of a steel knitting needle may be seen crawling up the face of the overhanging rock. **c1899** DOUGLAS in McDowall *TRSNZ* (1980) X. 316 When an eel is landed you don't take it up stroking it gently and point out its beauties to your pupils and remarking that mine hostess will cook it for supper stuffed with parsley and merrigold. No when an eel is landed you are dancing and howling around the wriggling monster trying to stun it with a club sufficiently to get it into the sack without its taking a finger along with it. **1918** *TrNZI* L. 296 The New Zealand eel is a mysterious creature as to which one would like more in information. He reaches an immense weight, and has been credited with being dangerous even to human beings when they are bathing. **1925** *Evening Post* (Wellington) 1 Aug. 13 According to Maori myth..it was an eel, not a serpent, which tempted the first woman, who in her turn tempted man to a knowledge of good and evil. **1946** *AJHR H-15* 41 Experiments were continued on canning eels... Packs were prepared in several different ways, including eels in agar, vinegar, and oil and smoked eel. **1966** *Encycl. NZ* I. 565 Many people are loath to believe that our eels proceed to the open sea to breed, but the fact remains that the leaf-shaped larvae of our eels have never been taken in local waters. **1990** MCDOWALL *NZ Freshwater Fishes* 425 During the Second World War there was extensive exploitation of eels.

2. With a modifier: **blind, conger, glass, long-fin(ned), mud (black), sand, short-fin(ned), silver, spring**.

(1) **blind eel.** *Eptatretus cirrhatus* (fam. Myxinidae), HAGFISH.

1917 WILLIAMS *Dict. Maori Lang.* 324 *Pia..*2. *Blind eel.* = *napia.* **1922** *Auckland Weekly News* 9 Mar. 15 The repulsive blind eel is very much in evidence. **1945** BEATTIE *Maori Place-names Canterbury* 62 The..list of fish to be caught along the Canterbury coast has some notable omissions... Omitted are the..koiro (conger eel), tuere (blind eel). **1956** GRAHAM *Treasury NZ Fishes* 51 The Hagfish, or Blind-eel as the fishermen call it, is one of the most unpleasant-looking creatures of the sea. **1967** MORELAND *Marine Fishes* 30 Hagfish and blind eel are widely used alternative names, while the Maori tuere and napia are still in use. **1986** PAUL *NZ Fishes* 23 Hagfish..also known as blind eel; it is eel-like, but not a true eel. **1990** *Evening Post* (Wellington) 21 Nov. 59 Horrible blind eels are abundant too.

(2) **conger eel.** Also *ellipt.* **conger.** Either of two marine eels of fam. Congridae, the larger **southern conger** *Conger verreauxi,* and the **northern conger** *C. wilsoni.* See also NGOIRO.

1774 FORSTER *Resolution Jrnl.* 30 Oct. (1982) IV. 677 The Natives have been fishing..& brought Congers, & large Breams to sell. **1848** WAKEFIELD *Handbook NZ* 160 Fish of all sorts and sizes abound on every part of the sea-coast. The only sorts similar to ours are the *Conger-eel, Sole, Plaice,* and *Flounder.* **1855** [see KOIRO]. **1886** SHERRIN *Handbook Fishes NZ* 18 Congers are captured by hooks and lines. **1905** [see KOIRO]. **1918** *NZJST* I. 136 Conger-eel is occasionally smoked, and I have often met with it at Wellington hotel-tables under the name of 'smoked hake'. **1932** *NZJST* XIII. 229 *Conger-eel...* This is the koir[o] of the Maoris, common around Wellington... In the common New Zealand conger the male is readily recognized by its greatly flattened head and small anus. **1945** [see (1) above]. **1956** GRAHAM *NZ Fishes* 138 The Conger Eel is known to the Maori as Koiro, and is considered a fine eating fish, either fresh or smoked. **1986** PAUL *NZ Fishes* 44 The..northern conger, *C[onger] wilsoni,* is smaller (70–80cm) [than the southern] and its dorsal fin originates well behind the pectoral fin.

(3) **glass eel.** A transparent larval eel of *Anguilla* spp. (fam. Anguillidae).

1876 *TrNZI* VIII. 125 *Leptocephalus altus. Glass eel.* **1977** *NZJMFR* XI. 193 In pre-European times, the Maoris were well acquainted with the upstream migration of glass-eels..and took advantage of natural obstacles in the waterways to collect large quantities for food. **1982** JELLYMAN & TODD *MAF Fish. Res. Div. Info. Leaflet* XI. 1 The larvae drift north with the ocean currents back towards land. Once they arrive over the continental shelf they metamorphose into small, transparent glass eels and then enter fresh water. **1990** MCDOWALL *NZ Freshwater Fishes* 52 As they come into contact with fresh water flowing out to sea from rivers along the coast, the glass eels stream up the rivers in countless thousands.

(4) **long-fin (long-finned) eel**. *Anguilla dieffenbachii* (fam. Anguillidae), a native freshwater eel, distinguished by having its dorsal fin considerably longer than its ventral fin. See also SILVERBELLY, TUNA *n.*[1]

1927 SPEIGHT et al. *Nat. Hist. Canterbury* 197 They are the long-finned (*Anguilla aucklandii*) and the short-finned (*A. australis*) the first of which frequents quick-running rivers, while the latter is found more often in lakes or sluggish streams. **1946** *AJHR H-15* 41 Apart from smoked eel, the straight pack of large long-finned eels with the addition of salt only gave the most satisfactory product for New Zealand. **1950** *Tuatara* III. 43 [Griffin established] the names *Anguilla dieffenbachii* for the commonly called 'long-finned' eel and *A. australis schmidtii* for the 'short-finned' eel. **1978** McDOWALL *NZ Freshwater Fishes* 34 The young of the Longfinned Eel penetrate the farthest reaches of river systems throughout New Zealand to become the most widespread species of fish in our rivers and streams. **1982** JELLYMAN & TODD *MAF Fish. Res. Div. Info. Leaflet* XI. 1 The term 'yellow-belly' applies almost always to longfins, whereas 'silver-belly' describes either species from a stony habitat or migrating shortfins.

(5) **mud (occas. black) eel**. A name applied to any of various (usu. freshwater) eels living or burrowing in mud.

1892 WILLIAMS *Dict. NZ Lang.* 21 *hao,.. 2* mud-eel. **1900** [see (8) a below]. **1967** MORELAND *Marine Fishes* 30 Longfinned Eel [*Anguilla dieffenbachi*]... Mud-eel and black eel are alternative names, while a variety of Maori names are in use. Tuna is widely used. **1978** [see MUDFISH 2 (2)].

(6) **sand eel**. An alternative (but inappropriate) name for the SANDFISH *Gorynchus gonorynchus* (fam. Gonorynchidae) and other small eel-like marine fishes.

1872 HUTTON & HECTOR *Fishes NZ* 119 Sand Eel... This curiously formed fish is remarkable for its eel-like shape and projecting snout, from beneath which its mouth protrudes like a sucker. It is caught..near the entrance to the Hutt River. **1886** SHERRIN *Handbook Fishes NZ* 84 The flesh of the sand-eel is firm, of a white colour, and delicate in flavour. **1898** MORRIS *Austral-English* 135 The *Sand Eel* does not belong to the Eel family, and is only called an Eel from its habits. **1938** *TrRSNZ* LXVIII. 402 *Gonorhynchus gonorhynchus* [*sic*]..Sandfish (sand eel). **1940** [see SANDFISH]. **1982** AYLING *Collins Guide* (1984) 133 *Sand Fish Gorynchus gonorynchus* (*Gorynchus greyi*) (Beaked salmon, sand eel).

(7) **short-fin (short-finned) eel** (occas. *ellipt.* **shortfin**). *Anguilla australis* (fam. Anguillidae), a native freshwater eel distinguished by having its dorsal fin only slightly longer than its ventral fin. See also SILVERBELLY, TUNA *n.*[1]

1927 [see (4) above]. **1936** *Handbook NZ* 73 *Anguilla australis*: [European Name] Short-finned eel [Maori Name] Tuna. **1947** POWELL *Native Animals NZ* 64 Short-finned Eel (*Anguilla australis schmidtii*). These are the common freshwater eels called Tuna by the Maoris. **1967** NATUSCH *Animals NZ* 209 There are two species of freshwater eels in New Zealand, one, the short-finned *anguilla australis schmidtii*..having the dorsal fin about the same length as the ventral fin. **1979** *Catch* Mar. 16 The Lake Ellesmere eel fishery..is based on the shortfinned eel (*Anguilla australis*). **1986** PAUL *NZ Fishes* 43 Male shortfins migrate when between six and twenty-four years (average fourteen), females at an average twenty-two years (range ten to thirty-five). **1990** McDOWALL *NZ Freshwater Fishes* 61 *Anguilla australis..shortfinned eel..*The shortfinned eel is the eel of the lowland lakes and creeks and is usually the most common species where eel populations are very dense.

(8) **silver eel**. In New Zealand applied to **a.** *Anguilla* spp. of freshwater eels (see also SILVERBELLY); and **b.** the silver conger, *Gnathophis habenatus*. **a.** *Anguilla* spp. (fam. Anguillidae).

1856 TANCRED *Nat. Hist. Canterbury* 30 These [fresh-water eels] are..species of silver eel. **1857** HURSTHOUSE *NZ* I. 122 Silver eels attaining a goodly size are found in every stream. **1900** *Canterbury Old & New* 129 Mud eels and silver eels were very plentiful. **1918** *TrNZI* L. 306 *Kopakopako*. Silver-eel. The Ngai-Tahu people call this *pakeha*, a name they used long before the advent of the Europeans. **1956** GRAHAM *Treasury NZ Fishes* 123 The Short-finned Eel varies from dark brown to very light brown on the back, with silvery sides and belly, and is known as the Silvery-eel or Silver-belly. **1970** SORENSEN *Nomenclature NZ Fish* 21 *Anguilla dieffenbachi* and *Anguilla australis* respectively... Suggested commercial name[s]: (i) Longfin Eel—Eel (ii) Shortfin Eel—Silverbelly; Silver eel.

b. *Gnathophis habenatus* (fam. Congridae).

1872 HUTTON & HECTOR *Fishes NZ* 66 *Congromuraena habenata*... Silver Eel. **1886** SHERRIN *Handbook Fishes NZ* 89 Silver Eel (*Congromuraena habenata*). **1898** MORRIS *Austral-English* 135 The New Zealand Eels are..Silver Eel—*Congromuraena habenata*. **1921** *NZJST* IV. 119 *Silver-eel*. Called 'hao' by the Arahura Maoris. Rare in Auckland and Wellington markets, and not greatly utilized as a food fish. Distribution: New Zealand coasts. **1957** WILLIAMS *Dict. Maori Lang.* 317 *Putu..Gnathophis habenata, silver eel,* =hao. **1967** MORELAND *Marine Fishes* 30 Silver Eel [*Gnathophis habenata*]... It is also known as little conger.

(9) **spring eel**. *Neochanna apoda* (fam. Galaxiidae), MUDFISH.

1926 *NZJST* VIII. 297 Mudfish... With the help of..[the] curator of the Masterton trout hatchery, an example was taken among stones in a spring close to the hatchery building. These fish are there termed 'spring eels'. **1940** PHILLIPPS *Fishes NZ* 41 [The Mudfish] is not uncommon in the spring time in running water in the horse-shoe bends of the springs and rivulets which surround Masterton, and is there called 'spring eel'. **1978** [see MUDFISH 2 (2)].

3. Special Comb., often with reference to Maori practice: **eel-basket**, a woven basket-like construct designed to trap eels; **eel-bob** [see OED *eel* 6 b, 1883], a device made from flax fibre with bait mounted in it used for catching eels by entangling their teeth in the threads, hence **eel-bobbing** (see also BOB *n.*); **eel-house, eel-lodge, eel-pa, eel (or eeling) station, eel-trap, eel-trap, eel-weir** [OED 5, 1868], any of various kinds of devices or structures designed to trap eels; usu. translations of Maori *pā-tuna* a construction built in a stream to facilitate the trapping of eels; **eel pass**, a channel on or beside the face of a dam to allow passage of eels; **eel-pot**, see *eel-basket* above; **eel-station, eel-trap, eel-weir**, see *eel-pa* above.

1844 TAYLOR *Journal* 2 Oct. (ATLTS) III. 26 [Otaki] my boys are feasting on a large tuna they caught as they came along... They have found a native **eel basket** which they have set..they went to the hinaki and found it almost full they took about 2 doz. **1860** BURNETT *Diary* 22 Mar. in Haast *Julius von Haast* (1948) Went in canoe with old Chief and Mackay to shoot ducks and set eel-baskets. **1904** TREGEAR *Maori Race* 188 The eel-basket (*hinaki*) was nearly the same as that used in England for the same purpose. **1939** BEATTIE *First White Boy Born Otago* 16 The white man always tries to catch eels with a bob or hook, but when I was a boy I saw the Maoris get them in eel baskets.

1946 BEAGLEHOLE *Some Modern Maoris* 98 Trout are occasionally tickled in nearby streams and eels are more frequently caught with an eel basket. **1962** SHARPE *Country Occasions* 186 The only way to get eels out of deep water is with an eel basket, or hinaki. **1980** [see HINAKI 1]. **c1875** MEREDITH *Adventuring in Maoriland* (1935) 43 [We] undertook to risk the reptile [*sc.* taniwha] if the Maoris would make us two '**eel-bobs**'. These are made by stringing worms on flax-fibre, which is attached in a loose lump by a cord to the end of a stick. *Ibid.* 44 The Maoris had our 'bobs' ready... Presently an old chap named Paitai got very excited because a large eel was 'stripping his bob'. The fibre was not strong enough to lift the large eel out of the water. **1943** HISLOP *Pure Gold* 74 **Eel-bobbing** and rabbit-potting usually filled the summer evenings in slack periods for me at Taieri-side. **1921** GUTHRIE-SMITH *Tutira* (1926) 86 At the crossing itself stood also a *whare-tuna*, an **eel-house** or **eel-lodge**... After a heavy haul from the many *patunas* along the creek Tutira, the surplus fish were often placed in a large reserve eel-pot—*hinaki-ruru*. **1847** ANGAS *Savage Life* II. 97 At one bend of the stream, where it breaks into foam over masses of rock, we observed an **eel-pah**, whither the natives occasionally resort for the purpose of taking these fish in their *kupengas* or nets. **1990** McDOWALL *NZ Freshwater Fishes* 55 Such an **eel pass** was successfully constructed up the face of the dam on the Patea River, to a height of 75m. **1845** WAKEFIELD *Adventures NZ* (1908) 185 They placed **eel-pots** called hinaki, which are very artistically made, as the lower extremity of funnels formed by series of upright poles driven into the bed of the river, the interstices being filled up with fern. **1858** THOMSON *Reconn. Survey S. Dist. Otago* in Taylor *Early Travellers* (1959) 329 There is an improved mode..by the eel-pot. This consists of a tube made of wicker work, or bark, having a funnel-shaped mouth. **1882** POTTS *Out in Open* 171 They adopted a variety of methods for their capture, as by eel-pots or baskets in connection with the weir or warri-tuna; by means of the spears of different forms, or by the patu or club. **1918** [see HINAKI 1]. **1929** BEST *Fishing Methods* 128 A weir was constructed in a stream; eel-pots were set at it in the evening, and in the morning they were lifted, full of eels, brought to land, and the eels in them killed. **1847** BRUNNER *Exped. Middle Is.* 25 Feb. in Taylor *Early Travellers* (1959) 268 [We] encamped at an apparently good **eel-station**. **1861** HAAST *Rep. Topogr. Explor. Nelson* 26 On the 16th of March we reached a fine **eeling station**, and..we all started to different places in the deep water to fish. **1844** TUCKETT *Diary* 6 Apr. in Hocken *Contributions* (1898) 205 The track conducting into the Raupo became wetter and wetter, until it terminated at an **eel-trap** in deep-standing water. **1938** HYDE *Nor Yrs. Condemn* 126 It was a good life on the hydro. Men dragged home quarters of deer from the ranges..or learned from the Maoris to make eel-traps, wickerwork structures which caught the big black-sided fellows down in the stream. **1943** *NZJST* XXII. 69B The eels are easily caught in giant hinakis (eel traps)) at the seaward margin of the lakes [Ellesmere, Onoke, Eversyth] during the evening hours. **1972** BAXTER *Collected Poems* 585 Or lift the eel-trap from the river As fog shifts from the highest hill. **1843** SELWYN in *NZ Part II* (Church in the Colonies VII) 25 Oct. (1845) 25 On a small stream, a few feet in width, we found a native **eel-weir**, with a net full of eels. **1879** *Auckland Weekly News* 12 July 13 I..saw several eel-weirs which being made in the water-courses, they had of course become blocked up. **1918** *TrNZI* L. 307 The *pa-tuna* or eel weir is of two or three types, one for small streams and others for rivers. **1921** GUTHRIE-SMITH *Tutira* (1926) 87 Rights to these eel-weirs descended from father to son, but this natural transmission of property could be disturbed by force. **1930** *Wanderlust Magazine* I. (4) 22 On the river..was a large eel-weir, a rough palisade running down the centre of the stream. **1987** WILSON *Past Today* 59 Eel weirs were still a common sight on the Wanganui River at the time of the 1921 Dominion Museum expedition.

4. In the names of plants: **eel-grass (eelgrass)** [OED 'Chiefly *U.S.*', 1790], *Zostera* spp. (fam. Potamogetonaceae), a grass-like plant of tidal areas.

1909 *AJHR C-12* 49 *Zostera nana* Grass-wrack, eel-grass. Sandy shores between high and low water-mark. Plentiful [on Stewart Is.] where sheltered and water shallow. **1968** MORTON & MILLER *NZ Sea Shore* 541 Zostera Flats. Green swards of eel grass often spread acres wide over the harbour flats below half tide and may extend out to shallow depths offshore. **1972** *Press* (Christchurch) 21 Oct. 12 They live along the shoreline, generally among seaweeds or eel-grass down to depths of about 20 fathoms. **1982** WILSON *Stewart Is. Plants* 320 *Zostera novazelandica* Seagrass..Eelgrass. Green grass growth on intertidal flats, often forming extensive 'sea meadows'... Stewart Island: Common, intertidal sandy mudflats. **1995** CROWE *Which Coastal Plant?* 53 *Nana*[,] *Eelgrass Zostera* species... With the tide in, the leaves stand upright like an underwater lawn. At low tide they lie flat... This is our only native flowering plant that is capable of living below mid-tide. Also known as seagrass, karepō, rehia or rimurehia.

eel-trout. Prob. *mountain trout* (TROUT 2 (4)). [Cf. 1851 *Lyttelton Times* 5 July 7 (Torlesse) There are eel pouts (a species of trout) in some of the streams.]

1851 *Austral. & NZ Gaz.* 13 Dec. 499 Found some fine eel-trouts at the end of my lines this morning, which I intend to have pickled. **1855** TAYLOR *Te Ika a Maui* 383 The 'Tikihemi' [Williams glosses 'a fish'] corresponds with our trout; in shape and appearance it is much like an eel. The settlers have named it the eel-trout. *Ibid.* 414 *Takaruwha*, a fresh-water fish a foot long, and thick in proportion, found in the Waingongoro; this is called the eel trout, and rises at the fly.

egg.

1. In the phr. **full as an egg**, see FULL *a.* 1.

2. egg-bird. *Hist.* [Transf. use of *egg-bird*, a West Indian tern whose eggs are collected for food: cf. OED *egg* 7.] A species of tern.

1772 FORSTER *Resolution Jrnl.* 6 Dec. (1982) II. 190 An *Eggbird* & the *Quackerbird*, both which I wish to examine. [1982 *Note*] *Pachyptila* spp. **1777** FORSTER *Voyage Round World* I. 113 We saw..[in s. Indian Ocean] a single tern (*sterna*) or as the seamen call it an egg-bird, which had a forked tail. **1985** *Reader's Digest Book NZ Birds* 233 *Sooty Tern Sterna fuscata*... Wideawake tern, *whale bird, egg bird*... The sooty tern is the most oceanic of all terns; it ranges over most tropical and sub-tropical seas and comes to land only to breed.

3. In the names of early children's games: **egg cap** (see also *rotten eggs* (ROTTEN *a.*)), **egg-in-the-hat**.

1905 THOMSON *Bush Boys* 84 Others wanted [to play] 'Prisoners' Base' or 'Chivvy', 'Brewer', '**Egg-in-the hat**'..or 'Kingy-seeny'. **1953** SUTTON-SMITH *Unorganized Games NZ Primary School Children* (VUWTS) II. 74 1 Pitching games were Pitch and Toss, Quoits, Ninepins, **Egg Cap** and Toodle-em-buck... There is still occasional mention of Egg Cap (Horoeka, Alexandra). **1972** SUTTON-SMITH *Folkgames Children* 168 Nevertheless, [pitching games] had their place [in the play of New Zealand children], and most important of all was undoubtedly *Egg Cap* (K-21), known also as Egg in Cap, Egg in the Nest, Egg Cup, Rotten Egg, and Mingle the Bonnets. It was a pitching, chasing, and ball-tagging game in which a ball was pitched into school caps or holes in the ground. Fortunately the game is still played at Alexandra, Central Otago, and has been recorded in some detail. [Holes or 'nests' are 6 inches apart.]..(Naseby, Otago, 1900; Nelson, 1875; Dunedin, 1885).

4. *Prison*. Also **eggroll**. A stupid or dull person.

1982 NEWBOLD *Big Huey* 248 Egg, eggroll (n). Stupid, incompetent person. **1991** DUFF *One Night Out Stealing* 13 Plus the fact that these kinda people [*sc.* crims] are eggs, as they call it in the vernacular here.

5. Special Comb. **egg-fart**, a particularly noisome kind of fart redolent of rotten eggs; **egg** (or **egg marketing**) **floor**, formerly the building or 'floor' where eggs were graded and packed under Egg Marketing Regulations; also the licensed marketing agent appointed by the Poultry Board in all egg marketing areas, to receive, grade and distribute eggs to retailing outlets.

1986 MACRAE in *New Outlook* XXI. 46 A big kid of 12 we call Eggy because he does **egg farts** was first in our class to get into trouble this term. **1943** *Timaru Herald* 7 July 4 The reason for the visit is to have a final discussion..for the purpose of establishing an **egg marketing floor** in Timaru. **1945** *Korero* (AEWS Background Bulletin) 12 Feb. 30 The wholesale handling of eggs has been centralized in what are known as 'egg floors'. **1953** *NZ Observer* 27 May 10 One grocer I know is sure that the answer to the bad egg mystery can be found on the poultry farm instead of in the egg floor buildings. **1982** *Agric. Gloss.* (MAF) 47 *Egg Floor*: Licensed marketing agent appointed by the Poultry Board in all egg marketing areas, to receive, grade and distribute eggs to retailing outlets.

egg-shell blonde. [Austral., Baker *Australia Speaks*, 1953.] A bald man.

1949 In Marlborough use, *egg-shell blonde* applied to a bald man (Ed.). **1974** MORRIESON *Predicament* (1981) 64 No wonder he's gone bald. He never did have much hair but..he's an egg-shell blonde now.

egret. Usu. with a modifier, a name for any of several herons of the genus *Egretta* (fam. Ardeidae), non-breeding in New Zealand except for the KOTUKU. See also *white heron* (HERON 2 (3)); also applied to the Cattle Egret (*Bubulcus ibis*), an annual migrant from Australia.

1946 *JPS* LV. 153 *kōtuku*, a bird (Egretta alba), white heron or egret, always rare even in Maori regard. **1955** OLIVER *NZ Birds* 384 *Eastern Great White Egret. Kotuku. Egretta alba modesta* The White Egret was first observed in New Zealand by Captain Cook during his second voyage. **1966** FALLA et al. *Birds NZ* 77 Little Egret *Egretta garzetta*... Pure white... Flying away looks not unlike a very white Caspian Tern. **1985** *Reader's Digest Book NZ Birds* 130 The first little egret recorded in New Zealand stayed on the Hawke's Bay coast for more than a year in 1951–52. *Ibid.* 131 *White Heron Egretta alba modesta*... *great white heron, white egret, large egret, kotuku*. **1990** *Checklist Birds NZ* 91 *Bubulcus ibis coromandus*... Cattle Egret... Since..[1956] there has been a spectacular increase in the number of winterers, sizable flocks reappearing annually in many favoured localities from Northland to Southland.

eh /æ/. Also **ay, aye**; in Maori contexts often **ne**, erron. **nei**. A frequent speech particle reinforcing or emphasising a question or request, often in the form: positive statement + *eh*. In some New Zealand uses, a development of the Ma. particle *nē* /ne:/ (Williams 220 '*Nē* ad[v]. interrogative, giving emphasis to a question, request, or proposal.').

1. ne (erron. **nei**) forms, used in representations of Maori speakers' use of English giving emphasis to an interrogative statement, esp. one expecting the answer 'yes', rather like French '*n'est-ce pas*'.

1881 CAMPBELL *Poenamo* 269 In vain my protestations. '*Taihoa, taihoa*, all in good time—what's the hurry, O Pakeha!' time was made for slaves—hurry no man's cattle, as we in the classics say. 'What's the odds, a day or two sooner or later? There's Motu-Korea; it won't run away—*taihoa nei*?' with a chuck back of the head as they ended with the interrogative. **1898** VOGEL *Maori Maid* 32 'I will be back...' [A Maori girl answers] 'And be with me all the summer, *ne*?' **1909** VOGEL *Tragedy of Flirtation* 45 'You big chief, *ne*?' the [Maori] woman said in a tone that suggested an assertion rather than a question—though the 'ne' is a verbal note of interrogation. **1969** MASON *Awatea* (1978) 17 Kani. Dug it, Pera... Five feet, almost roast an ox in it [*sc.* hangi], whole, Time for a beer, ne? **1974** MASON *Hand on Rail* (TS 1987) 20 Hingawaru..When Rangi chooses his wahine, someone else pays, ne? **1983** HULME *Bone People* 5 Then, he had only chuckled again and said, 'Well, we got him on the way, nei?' **1986** IHIMAERA *Matriarch* 132 'You hate me now, ne?' the matriarch called. 'Yes!' he shouted. 'I hurt you, ne?' she asked.

2. eh forms. (Also occas. **heh**.) **a.** In representations of Maori speakers' use of English, in the sense of *ne*, 1 above.

1905 BAUCKE *White Man Treads* 161 The next day, Taupoki came to me and said: 'Yesterday's degradation; you saw it, hey?' **1938** HYDE *Nor Yrs. Condemn* 113 The Maori mother laughed, showing broken teeth. 'She got a rash, eh?' **1948** FINLAYSON *Tidal Creek* (1979) 40 The fat brown man leers broadly. 'How you like, eh?' asks Fatty-face, swinging the full kit forward for Uncle Ted to see. **1955** WILSON *Land of My Children* 203 'I t'ink he pay,' exclaimed Mati, with her usual little interrogative 'Eh', meant to soften the positiveness of her assertions. **1959** SLATTER *Gun in My Hand* 154 Just one of those Maori girls eh. Descended from the plurry cannibals eh. *Ibid.* 206 He could speak beautiful English but often he put on the plurry Maori eh just to have a crack at us. **1963** PEARSON *Coal Flat* 43 I'm a full Maori and proud, too... Old Mum she meant I'm still a savage, that's what she meant. Just quietly, eh? **1978** HILLIARD *Glory & Dream* 210 And a boatgirl with tired eyes said to him, You got a moneys eh I saw you give that kid a moneys. **1985** ROSIER-JONES *Cast Two Shadows* 63 So it's you. Not a bad looker. Take after your mother, e? **1989** TE AWEKOTUKU *Tahuri* 101 e: pronounced as in 'ten'. Interrogative, or a way of finishing a comment. **1995** *Victoria Quarterly* (VUW quarterly magazine) Summer issue 15 *New Zealand English, eh.* 'Eh', as in 'It's really good, eh', is extensively used among Maori people and by many Pakeha [as shown by the two-million word corpus of New Zealand English]. It is a distinctively New Zealand tag meaning, are you following, do you agree, or are you with me?

b. By non-Maori, usu. 'working-class' speakers, not always as an interrogative, or with an interrogative intonation; often expressing a slight uncertainty, or merely implying an expectation of agreement from a listener. At times tends to be replaced in modern New Zealand English by the high-rising terminal intonation. See also quot. 1995 in a above.

1905 THOMSON *Bush Boys* 14 We'll get to College together, eh? **1918** *NZ at the Front* 110 [If you] asked 'How are you Tom?' he'd invariably answer, 'I'm thirsty, Nugget; you ain't got a pint about yer, eh?' **1920** MANSFIELD *Stories* (1984) 230 'How long do you think it will take to get straight—couple of weeks—eh?' he chaffed. **1926** Devanny *Lenore Divine* 141 We'll have some supper, eh? **1936** Hyde *Passport to Hell* 120 Money belt? I think the Turks got it, eh? **1944** Fullarton *Troop Target* 29 'Which way did you come?' 'Through Larissa, eh?' The final 'eh?' spoken on a rising inflection, is a meaningless Kiwi-ism common to many North Islanders. It defies either explanation or translation. **1950** *Here & Now* Nov. 9 By and large..there is remarkably little difference in English here and in Britain. That is..after making due allowance for such atrocities as..the ubiquitous 'Eh' at the end of every other sentence, and the normal vowel flattening. **1963** Casey *As Short a Spring* 283 Chased him for three days up that valley, *ey*. **1973** Wilson *NZ Jack* 11 'Can I speak to your husband?'... 'He's down at the back catching the bull, eh?' She spoke sullenly and her diction was slovenly. **1986** *Evening Post* (Wellington) 22 Sept. 36 Sorry Wal. I was a burk tryin' to be a big man for the sheilas, eh? **1987** Gray *Stepping Out* 61 Mum said I can go away at Labour Weekend. Neat eh? **1987** Gee *Prowlers* 60 'What a beach,' Phil said. 'I'd like to own this place, eh.'

ehoa /ˈeho/, /ˈæɪˌho/, /ˈæɪˌhoə/. Also **e hoa**.

1. [Ma. /e'hoa/ formed from two words *e*, vocative particle; *hoa*: Williams 54 friend, mate.] Used in address as 'friend, mate' orig. and mainly among Maori speakers, but also formerly by Eng. speakers as a term of familiar address chiefly among or between men, often to a person whose name is not known; occas. formerly *joc.* or contemptuously **hee-haw**.

[**1778** Forster *Observations* 284 A Comparative Table of the Various Languages in the Isles of the South-Sea. [English] *A Friend*..[New-Zeeland] *Hòa*.] **1881** Campbell *Poenamo* 71 E hoa ma, Cookie, why do you frown? [**1881** *Note*] E hoa ma, my friend. [=O friends. *ma* is a pluralizer.] **1917** *Chron. NZEF* 18 Apr. 79 EHOA is the Vocative or form of address and means O Friend. It is sufficient. To say 'Dear O Friend' sounds queer. To cut the O out before friend, you must drop the E before Hoa, and then you have 'Dear Hoa', which sounds rotten. **1938** Hyde *Nor Yrs. Condemn* 170 'I'll be getting back. *Haere ra, e hoa*.' She drew the shawl over her black feathers and slipped away. **1943** Bennett *English in NZ* in *Amer. Speech* XVIII. 93 *e hoa*, an exclamation with the value of 'look here', 'I say', has become corrupted to the tag Heehaw (as in 'give us that fork, heehaw'). **1959** Shadbolt *New Zealanders* (1986) 33 'One an one are three!' cried another [Maori child]. 'You don' know your sums, ehoa,' **1960** Hilliard *Maori Girl* 219 Worst of all [Pakehas] were the amorous ones who knew only one or two words: *haeremai* or *e hoa*, or obscenities; they seemed to think that the only way to ingratiate themselves with a Maori girl was to demonstrate their familiarity with Maori filth. **1983** Hulme *Bone People* 241 I know you're close to them, e hoa, but I've never quite worked out who they are.

2. *WW1. Obs.* A Maori (soldier).

1918 *Chron. NZEF* 30 Aug. 56 It is not at all unusual to see an Ehoa [*sc.* a member of the Maori Pioneer Battalion] and a Yank, arm-in-arm. *Ibid.* 13 Sept. 81 The Pioneers—I mean our Pioneers, the Ehoas, were throwing the earth about and fast getting a road through.

ehogoa: see Hoka.

eight, Used in various combinations and collocations where the number (of) *eight* is of significance: **eight** *hist.*, *ellipt.* for *eight-ounce* below; **eight-hour** *attrib.* (also **eight hours**) [with reference to the slogan 'eight hours work, eight hours play, eight hours rest' in the context of the movement for a fair working-day associated with Samuel Duncan Parnell, and introduced into NZ c1840: AND 1856; OED 1845], connoting the duration of a fair working day; **eight ounce**, an eight-ounce beer, or its glass container (227 ml); **eight penn'orth**, **eight pen'worth**, an eight week or eight month prison sentence; **eight-tooth** *farming*, FULL-MOUTHED.

1962 Crump *One of Us* 11 'I'll try an **eight**,' he said to the only-just-sober barman. *Ibid.* 100 If you can't handle an eight you want to drink five-ounce beers. **1988** Lay *Fools on Hill* 29 He found a gap and reached the bar. 'Three eights!' he yelled, and a short, portly barman grabbed the glasses from a rack. **1886** Froude *Oceana* 209 **Eight hours** work, eight hours play, Eight hours rest, eight bob a day. **1888** D'Avigdor *Antipodean Notes* 160 This was one of the few places in the Colony where the eight hours rule was ignored, where men worked ten hours daily. **1890** Cox *Diaries 1888–1925* (ATLMS) 28 Oct. Today was Demonstration Day of the Eight hours work and was kept up in Wellington but not by all, some of the shops were open. A procession of the trade societies walked in the morning.., they also held sports in Newtown Park and a concert in The Opera House this evening. **1898** Hocken *Contributions* 103 The Eight Hours movement has always been one of interest, and to Mr. Burns must be accorded the credit of its introduction to New Zealand. **1913** Beattie *Trade Hunting* 10 I was one of a little colony of men who had no respect for the eight-hour day, and to whom any semblance of government stroke was anathema. **1963** *Evening Post* (Wellington) 19 Oct. 21 *Eight-Hour Day Pioneer Is Remembered* A special ceremony to mark the Labour Day anniversary on Monday, October 28, is to be held by the Socialist Forum. **1988** *Heinemann Dict. NZ Quotations* 11 Labour Day was instituted in 1899 to celebrate the introduction of the eight-hour day. **1993** *Dominion* (Wellington) 27 Apr. 7 Plaque to commemorate the eight-hour day man [S.D. Parnell]. **1964** Davis *Watersiders* 43 Standing in the pub I was... And then suddenly, up he [*sc.* a leprechaun] pops and sits on the edge of my **eight-ounce**. **1964** Booth *Footsteps in Sea* 9 He was a beer boy, and he found his stomach gurgling..at the thought of an eight-ounce glass. **c1875** *NZ Songster No.5* 50 Of him an example the magistrates made now, And he's doing **eight pen'north** in Pentridge stockade now.

elder. [Spec. use of *elder* an older person as a respected authority.] A person of recognized authority in a Maori community; KAUMATUA.

1860 *Richmond-Atkinson Papers* (1960) I. 562 We found him [Wiremu Kingi] & some of the elders together, but.. [*sic*] they all declined the discussion. **1879** *TrNZI* XI. 72 Many a deliberation of the *Kaumatuas* or elders took place over the prepared model. **1882** Potts *Out in Open* 27 Amongst the old men, the elders of the land..they have gained..such ripe experience as makes their voices to be valued in council. **1959** Shadbolt *New Zealanders* (1986) 17 She began to play an active part in tribal affairs, and her voice was heard with respect by the elders. **1980** Marsh *Photo-Finish* 97 Rangi Te Pokiha?... He's one of our most prominent elders. **1990** *Dominion* (Wellington) 5 June 3 Waimaman Ngawaka Bedggood was helped out of the bush by bush fairies, local Maori elders believe. **1995** *Dominion* (Wellington) 26 Aug. 16 The trouble with *elder* is that we are now using it all over the place when we talk about Maori *elders*, our translation of *kaumatua*, so your listeners are likely to prick up their ears in surprise if you use it for anything else.

elderberry. *Obs.* [Transf. use of *elderberry*, the berry of the European elder *Sambucus nigra* (fam. Caprifoliaceae), esp. as used for making wine and jelly.] Also *ellipt.* **elder**, the TUTU, and its berry, resembling the European elderberry, and used by the Maori to make a beverage, *tutu wine* (TUTU 3 c).

[**1817** Nicholas *Voyage NZ* 111 We met with..one [shrub] which, from the pithiness of its wood, and the conformation of its leaves, resembled very much the elder-tree. This bore a fruit hanging down in thick clusters of small berries, the juice of which afforded a delicious treat to the natives, who appeared to relish it exceedingly. They express it through their fingers, and I should suppose that the elder-berry yields in our own country. **c1835** [see TUTU 1 a (a)].] **1838** Polack *NZ* I. 110 On emerging from Pámaki, we ascended another plain..above which the tupákihi, or native elder-berry, occasionally shewed its bending stem, yielding to the weight of the fruit, which hung in purple clusters.

electorate. [Transf. use of *electorate* the body of people entitled to vote; OEDAS II 34 3. *Austral. and N.Z.*, Austral. 1866.] The area represented by a Member of Parliament, a constituency.

1906 *Cyclopaedia of NZ* V. 45 Mr Atmore..travelled over a great portion of the electorate, delivering as many as five speeches in a day. **1946** *AJHR* H-38 46 These six electorates, with the others which had retained no-licence, made a total of twelve electorates under no-licence. **1959** Sinclair *History of NZ* 61 Its programme..was not sufficiently plausible to win a majority of voters in a single electorate. **1977** *Dominion* (Wellington) 22 Sept. 6 It is reported that the Labour Party ticket formed by Island Bay electorate chairman Mr. Joe McTaggart consists of all but one of Labour Party members. **1980** *Electoral Amendment Act* s2(1) (1) Section 2(1) of the principal Act is hereby amended by inserting in the definition of the term 'district', after the words 'electoral district', the words 'or "electorate"'.

electric puha, ray, skate: see PUHA 2, RAY 2 (2), SKATE 2 (1).

elephant ear.

1. [from the size and shape of the leaf.] *Alocasia macrorrhiza* (fam. Araceae), an introduced arum.

1980 Adams *Wild Flowers* 10 Elephant ear is widely naturalised in northern districts. Its inconspicuous flower has a delicious fragrance... The fruit head is crimson ... Botanical name: *Alocasia macrorrhiza*, tropical Asia.

2. As **elephant ears** *pl. West Coast* [see quot. 1981], a kind of whitebait.

1981 Wilson *Fisherman's Bible* 61 Elephant Ears A species of whitebait. The young of the native Koaro, so named by West Coast whitebaiters because of their large and projecting pectoral fins. **1983** *Dominion* (Wellington) 3 Apr. 6 Here on the Coast, there is a kind of whitebait called 'elephant ears'. It is fat and clear and larger than other varieties, but no one can give a definitive answer as to why it got stuck with the label 'elephant ears'.

elephant fish. Also *ellipt.* **elephant**. [from its trunk-like snout.] *Callorhinchus milii* (fam. Callorhinchidae), a large (up to 120 cm) commercially important cartilaginous fish having a prominent trunk-like snout. See also REPEREPE, *silver trumpeter* (TRUMPETER 2 (2)).

1770 Banks *Journal* Mar. (1962) II. 7 We also [took] that fish describ'd by Frezier in his voyage to Spanish South America by the name of Elefant, Pejegallo, or Poisson Coq, which tho coarse we made shift to Eat. **1777** ANDERSON *Journal* 12 Feb. in *Cook Journals* (1967) III. 797 Caught as many Elephant Fish and Mullet [in Queen Charlotte Sound] as serv'd both Ships crews. **1838** POLACK *NZ* I. 323 Many other fish are equally numerous, answering to our *hakes, tench..elephant-fish*. **1842** GRAY *Fauna* in Dieffenbach *Travels in NZ* (1843) II. 226 It is the 'erhe-perhepe' of the natives, and the 'elephant-fish' of the English settlers. **1855** TAYLOR *Te Ika A Maui* 626 Of the Fam. Chimaeridae, is that singular fish the..(Repe repe,) or elephant fish, which attains a size of fully two feet. **1877** *TrNZI* IX. 489 I have seen over a dozen sorts of fish in one haul, ranging from Barracoota and Elephant Fish down to Garfish and Herrings. **1906** *TrNZI* XXXVIII. 552 The elephant-fish; a migratory species, occasionally occurring in large numbers. **1927** SPEIGHT et al. *Nat. Hist. Canterbury* 193 The strikingly-patterned elephant fish..with large flopping fins is well known (as 'Silver Trumpeter') to all fishermen along the coast. **1938** *TrSNZ* LXVIII. 401 *Callorhynchus milii*... Elephant-fish. *Reperepe*. **1947** POWELL *Native Animals NZ* 60 The elephant-fish is confined to the Antarctic Basin and the South Pacific seas. The New Zealand species..is common along the whole of the East Coast of the South Island. **1956** GRAHAM *Treasury NZ Fishes* 86 Having a most unusually-shaped mouth may be the reason Elephant-fish do not take a baited hook readily. **1967** NATUSCH *Animals NZ* 201 The common elephant fish..grows up to forty inches long. The long trunk-like proboscis is thought to be an organ of touch. **1986** BROWN *Weaver's Apprentice* 91 A good proportion of cod and elephants with a few rig sharks..thrown in for good measure.

elephant seal. Also in early *ellipt.* use **elephant**. [From the elephantine size, and the enlarged inflatable proboscis of the adult male thought to resemble an elephant's trunk: DANTE *elephant* 1811 (Tristan da Cunha).] *Mirounga leonina* (fam. Phocidae), a large (6 m, 3700 kg) southern marine mammal.

1832 let. from Capt. Harvey of *Venus* whaler in Kerr *Campbell Isd* (1976) 27 McQuaries is entirely cut up. I landed on both ends of the Island, but could see no sign of an Elephant whatever. **1852** COOK *Jrnl. MacQuarie Is.* (ATLTS) 1 We have killed all the Elephants that have come up here as yet. **1913** McNAB *Old Whaling Days* 88 She first made Macquarie Island and the captain [of the *Venus*, c1831]..could see no signs of elephants. **1951** SORENSEN *Wild Life in the Subantarctic* 7 Elephant seals, although not entirely devoid of intelligence, are rather stupid. **1966** *Encycl. NZ* III. 203 Elephant seals or sea elephants..are found throughout the sub-Antarctic islands of the Atlantic, Indian, and Pacific Oceans. **1983** KING *Seals of the World* 124 Elephant Seal oil has very much the same properties and uses as whale oil, but was not mixed with it. **1986** GRADY *Sealers and Whalers* 53 The name 'sea elephant' comes from the inflatable, trunk-like proboscis which is very conspicuous in bulls. Early sealers simply called them 'elephants'. **1986** FRASER *Beyond the Roaring Forties* 30 Elephant bulls are often heavily scarred from territorial battles, and can be up to six metres in length. **1990** *Handbook NZ Mammals* 267 The southern elephant seal was harvested in great numbers on Campbell and Macquarie Is. and elsewhere throughout its range in the 19th century, primarily for its blubber oil but occasionally for hides.

Hence **elephant sealing** *hist.*, the taking of elephant seals commercially.

1983 KING *Seals of the World* 124 The story of Elephant sealing on South Georgia is well known by now.

emigrant, *n.* and *attrib.*

A. *n.* [AND 1820.] One who leaves another country to settle in New Zealand. Also *hist.*

labouring emigrant, one assisted by a subsidized passage, often in the 19th century distinguished as a class from a *cabin* passenger or 'colonist'; in modern use often *assisted emigrant* (see ASSISTED). Cf. COLONIST a, IMMIGRANT, SETTLER 2 a.

1840 *Let. Instruction* 9 Nov. in Rutherford & Skinner *Establish. New Plymouth* (1940) 3 I..am to draw your serious attention there to as also the regulations to be observed on board the Ship by the labouring Emigrants. **1840** WEEKES *Journal* 4 Dec. in Rutherford & Skinner *Establish. New Plymouth* (1940) 18 A school commenced among the emigrants' children—the cabin passengers kindly assisting the schoolmaster. **1841** Diary in *William Swainson* 28 May (1992) 84 The Captain used to read prayers on the Quarter deck and the Doctor to the Emigrants..all the Emigrants were obliged to be on deck by half past seven clean and tidy. **1844** ASHWORTH *Jrnl. of Edward Ashworth* 28 Jan. (1992, VUWTS) 65 The schooner was close under the bows of a large scotch ship that had..lately brought 'emigrants' to the colony. [1844 *Note*] Emigrants as applied in the colonies means only those whose passage is paid for them. **1850** WARD *Journal* (1951) 19 The condition of the poor emigrants whom I had induced to follow me. [1951 *Ed. Note*] The term 'emigrant' was applied only to steerage passengers. The cabin passengers, mainly land-purchasers, were styled colonists. **1853** [see COLONIST a]. **1854** CHOLMONDELEY *Ultima Thule* 41 'Emigrant' and 'Colonist' are used by some as simply convertible terms; though the life of every settler compared with itself, the condition of every colony, refute the mistake. Others, who are aware of the great difference that exists between the two, are yet very far from knowing wherein it consists. They sometimes speak of emigrants..and colonists as two distinct classes, or rather, castes of men. One who flies from his native land driven by want..who sets his life on a venture because it is worth so little..these are Emigrants; while farmers, tradesmen, gentlefolks, those who have something, all, in short, who can make up a purse full enough to depart respectably, all who have prospects however distant; these are Colonists. I remember well on board the Charlotte Jane on the voyage out to New Zealand, certain friends of mine always called the common passengers—'the emigrants'. Evidently they considered themselves in all respects above the condition of 'emigrants'. **1863** MORGAN *Journal* (1963) Aug. 68 Emigrants are arriving every week... What disappointment awaits them! **c1871** MASTERS *Autobiography* (ATLMS) 49 In 1857, the Government employed a batch of emigrants to clear a cart track, through the three mile bush. **1894** *TrNZI* XXVI. 564 About twelve months afterwards [*sc.* late 1850s] four English emigrants arrived, wearing the smock-frock then worn by farm-labourers. **1911** *TrNZI* XLIII. 439 'We never used to have these heavy frosts before the emigrants came in,' said the old Taranaki settlers some twenty-five years ago. **1959** SINCLAIR *Hist. NZ* 94 On board the Company ships the cabin passengers, who paid their own fares, and who called themselves 'colonists', while referring to the assisted passengers down below as 'emigrants', amounted to twelve or fourteen per cent of the total passengers. **1980** GRANT *Unauthorised Version* 12 Events quickly caught up with most of the New Zealand Company's methodical planning, but the colonists (cabin) and the emigrants (steerage) were shipped to the new colony with model and thoughtful efficiency.

B. *attrib.*

1. In early *attrib.* use with reference to the (usu. British) colonization of New Zealand.

1856 FITTON *NZ* 88 Auckland is more likely to have attracted the attention of persons, who form their ideas of a whole country from the most salient points of interest..than the less populous, but, perhaps, more strictly *emigrant* settlements in other parts of New Zealand. **1861** *Otago Witness* (Dunedin) 30 Mar. 4 Arrived per 'Melbourne':..12 Emigrant Stoves, with Ovens and Galvanized Boilers complete **1898** HOCKEN *Contributions* 94 In the early days of New Zealand emigration, it was a not unusual custom to speed a departing emigrant vessel by means of some function... Probably the last of the 'send-offs' was in 1850, when the 'Canterbury Pilgrims' sailed.

2. Special Comb. **emigrant barracks** [AND 1840], *emigration barracks* (EMIGRATION 2), see also BARRACKS 1; **emigrant ship** [AND 1837], a vessel chartered (or converted) to carry emigrants to New Zealand.

1853 ROCHFORT *Adventures of Surveyor* 13 [There are] several good hotels [in Lyttelton]..also a custom-house and **emigrant barracks**. **1930** GUTHRIE *NZ Memories* 120 Some of them remained in the emigrant barracks at Port Cooper for a few days. **1840** WAKEFIELD 8 Jan. in Miller *Early Victorian NZ* (1958) 12 Then in September 1839..the first fleet of **emigrant ships** was despatched 'to the Cannibal Lands when all seemed uncertainty and risk'. **1841** Diary in *William Swainson* 1 July (1992) 85 A boat load of wood and the old fittings came up off an Emigrant Ship. **1853** ADAMS *Canterbury Settlement* 18 They had been greeted on their arrival (as indeed, singularly enough, had almost every emigrant ship) with a '*sow-wester*'. **1864** CAMPBELL *Martin Tobin* III. 219 He had come out as chaplain on board an emigrant ship. **1961** *Distance Looks Our Way* 28 Emigrant ships generally took four..months to reach New Zealand in the forties and fifties. **1992** SCHOUTEN *Tasman's Legacy* 83 [The Johan van Oldenbarnevelt] in 1951 was converted into an emigrant ship with accommodation for more than 1400 passengers. Her first voyage as an emigrant ship began badly.

emigrate. To choose to leave a home country to settle in New Zealand. Cf. IMMIGRATE.

1821 *Sugden to Earl of Bathurst* 18 Jan. in McNab *Hist. Records* (1908) I. 516 A party about emigrating [*sic*] to New Zealand begs most respectfully to solicit the assistance of Government in their undertaking. I am (with several who have resided on the island) convinced an English colony would soon become flourishing and happy. **1843** CHAPMAN *NZ Portfolio* 90 No *data* derived from a penal settlement can apply to one to which the persons who emigrate have to produce testimonials of character and respectability—of which description the mass of the present settlers in New Zealand are composed.

emigration.

1. [AND 1820.] The leaving by choice of a home country to settle in New Zealand.

1840 *NZ Jrnl.* I. 3 His instructions, as the agent for the West of Scotland to the New Zealand Land Company, charged him not to over-state the benefits of emigration to New Zealand, but rather to under-rate them, in order to avoid exciting undue expectations. **1853** EARP *NZ* 98 Emigration to New Zealand has given way to the *mania* for the Australian gold diggings. **1857** *Lyttelton Times* 1 July 1 Arthur Willis, Gann, & Co. will readily afford every facility to intending emigrants for Canterbury, until definite arrangements by the Provincial Government can be transmitted to England to promote a continuous stream of emigration to this Province.

2. Special Comb. **emigration agent** [AND 1833], a company or Government employee responsible for arranging emigration and, at times, the matters to do with the arrival of emigrants; **emigration barracks**, *immigrant barracks* (IMMIGRANT 2), see also BARRACKS 1, EMIGRANT 2; **emigration commissioner**, one responsible for supervising emigration to New Zealand; **emigration fever**, an over-powering urge to emigrate to New Zealand.

1898 HOCKEN *Contributions* 160 The *auri sacra fames* was..the all-powerful **emigration agent**, for in the three years of the goldrush, 1861 to 1863, no less than 78,000 souls quickened the old life into wonderful progress and activity. *Ibid.* 173 The efforts of the [Otago] Provincial Council to induce a fresh stream of emigration from the home country now began to bear good fruit... Mr. Adam, who at the beginning of 1857 had been despatched as Emigration Agent, discharged his duties with remarkable energy and success. **1842** SELWYN in *NZ Part I* (Church in the Colonies) Aug. (1844) 40 I arrived here [in Nelson] on Sunday, August the 21st and preached at the afternoon Service in the **Emigration Barrack**. **1850** GODLEY *Letters* 23 Apr. (1951) 24 There are several long-looking cottages together which are 'Emigration Barracks'; that is, houses ready for the emigrants to get into on first landing, while they make their selection of land and raise a house. **1898** HOCKEN *Contributions* 173 Emigration barracks, very different from those poor constructions raised for the shelter of the first pioneers, were erected at the south corner of Princes and Police Streets [for the fresh emigrants arriving in 1857]. **1863** BUTLER *First Year* i 2 The **emigration commissioner** was taking a final survey of the ship and shaking hands with this, that, and the other passengers. **1840** WEEKES *Voyage* in Rutherford & Skinner *Establish. New Plymouth* (1940) 9 In the autumn of the year 1840 I was attacked by the ***emigration fever***, to which there had been evidently a predisposition in my system for some time.

Empire.

1. Special Comb. **Empire ring**, a kind of cake; **Empire disease**, a patronizing attitude to non-European members of a colonial community.

1934 *Marigold Book Recipes* 13 **Empire Ring**..butter..sugar..flour..egg..peel..currants..almond essence [etc.] B.P... Form into a long roll and twist into a ring. Brush with beaten egg and decorate with blanched almonds. **1979** ASHTON-WARNER *I Passed This Way* (1980) 19 Strange that Mumma should mention Queenie, as her attitude to Maoris was strongly affected by **Empire disease**.

2. In the collocation **the Empire's (dairy) farm**, a catchphrase once applied to New Zealand.

1959 SINCLAIR *Hist. NZ* 234 The premise of Massey's political philosophy, a cliché of the nineteen-twenties, was that New Zealand was 'the Empire's outlying farm'. **1973** SARGESON *Once Is Enough* 41 It was all very well for the Empire's dairy farm to be momentarily annihilated.

Empire City. *Hist.* [OED, also applied to New York.] Applied to two New Zealand cities. **a.** Auckland.

1858 in *Speeches & Documents* (1971) 106 Mr Secretary Stafford..is it right that Her Majesty's lieges should be in fear lest the magnates of the 'Empire City' should declare war against the rest of New Zealand. **1883** *Auckland Weekly News* 10 Nov. 14 He arrived in the Empire City at six o'clock on Thursday night. **1908** *Truth* 18 Apr. 2 When they [sc. the bookies] returned to the Empire City, they found an S.P. [sc. Starting Price] commissioner had been at work and depleted their coffers of several hundred pounds.

b. Wellington.

1868 *Marlborough Express* (Blenheim) 18 Jan. 3 Our Wellington contemporary [sc. *Evening Post*] seems to have lost the pointent... As the gentleman last named has gone to the Empire City on a visit..he may call and make this correction himself. **1879** HINGSTON *Australian Abroad* 363 [Wellington] has taken now to call itself 'the Empire City', since its acquisition of Government business. **1880** *Evening Post* (Wellington) 7 June 2 The wharf is the only Sunday promenade in the Empire City, and its approaches might well be kept clean and sweet. **1889** SKEY *Pirate Chief* 3 To night [*sic*] from lofty shapes in trappings gay, The Empire City's bathed in mellow day; To night a thousand suns resplendent shine, From Lambton's curve to Newtown's far confine. **1894** WILSON *Land of Tui* Feb. 72 After the Bush, breezy Wellington looked somewhat tame, notwithstanding its smart name of 'Empire City', bestowed on it by the newspapers, a designation which appears characteristic of London alone. **1905** *Truth* 12 Aug. 2 The boys from Wellington..would have decided to walk back to the Empire City. **1914** ALGIE *MS Papers 1374* (ATLMS) 14 Oct. The contrast between Auckland and Wellington was most marked. The Empire city also kept up its 'windy' reputation as during the whole day a biting cold wind has been blowing. **1930** PINFOLD *Fifty Yrs. Maoriland* 86 For many months preceding the Prince of Wales's visit to the 'Empire City', much interest had been taken in matters masonic. **1952** *Evening Post* (Wellington) 14 Oct. 8 About 60 years ago four or five of us young men came down [from Taranaki] to see the sights of what we then called the Empire City.

empty house. In the phr. **an empty house is better (better an empty house) than a bad tenant**, said when farting in public.

c1938 used by Jane Morison, Havelock (Marlborough): 'An empty house is better than a bad tenant.' (Ed.) **1984** BEATON *Outside In* 27 *Lou farts,... Ma*: Better an empty house than a bad tenant.

emu.

1. *Obs.* An early sealers' and whalers' name for a (South Island) KIWI. Occas. applied to the MOA (see 1849, 1892 quots.).

1820 CRUISE *Journal* 21 Aug. (1957) 142 Wheety, who was now a very important personage, laid aside his European clothes, and putting on his emu-feathered mat.., seated himself upon the deck to receive his countrymen. *Ibid.* 216 The emu is found in New Zealand, though we were never fortunate enough to meet with one... Their feathers are black, smaller and more delicate than the emu of New Holland, and a mat ornamented with them is the most costly dress a chief can wear. **c1835** BOULTBEE *Journal* (1986) 104 There are green parroquets..besides Emus, greenbirds and woodhens. **1844** MONRO *Notes of Journey* in Hocken *Contributions* (1898) 261 The kivi [*sic*], called by the sealers the emu, is met with in great abundance on the west side. **1849** ASHWELL *Lett. & Jrnls.* (ATLTS) I. 147 The moor [*sic*], the New Zealand Emu was found. **1858** THOMSON *Survey S. Dists. Otago* in *Jrnl Royal Geogr. Soc.* (London) XXVIII. 318 Mr. Bates also informs me, that a bird, called by the 'old hands' the 'Emu' (Apteryx), exists in the woods [on the sw. coast]. **1863** CAPLES *Diary* in Hall-Jones *Early Fiordland* (1968) 103 Near the mouth of the Middle Fiord [of Te Anau], they..shot a 'native emu'. The bird is described as being 'curious among the feathered tribe, having neither wings nor tail'... I [sc. Hall-Jones] favour the conclusion that their 'native emu' was the large type of kiwi (roa). **1892** OSBORN in Richards *Foveaux Whaling Yarns* (1995) 33 Then there is the emeu [*sic*]—the big emeu is nearly or quite extinct... A couple of weeks or so after digging the pit, we returned and found the emeu in our trap. He was a monster bird and weighed about five hundred pounds...The little emeu is about the size of a large turkey, but heavier.

2. As **emu parade** (occas. *ellipt.* **emu**) *orig.* *army* [AND an assembly esp. of soldiers to pick up litter, 1941], also **emu-scratching** (see quot. c1951), a parade, or often a school detention, directed towards picking up paper and rubbish from, or otherwise cleaning up, an area or playground.

1939–45 *Expressions and Sayings 2NZEF (Nat. Archiv. TS WAII DA 420/1)* Emu—A parade for cleaning up an area, picking up paper, etc. **1944** *Korero* (AEWS Background Bulletin) 17 July 24 The best of these [newer Army slang terms] is 'emu parade' for an organized sanitary scavenge (obviously Australian in origin). **c1951** p.c. Les Souness. Emu-scratching is the term applied at Petone West School to detentions involving picking up paper etc. in the school grounds. **1954** *Upper Hutt Leader* 2 June [The Heretaunga College grounds were] littered with small stones, and at the end of last term an 'emu parade' was organised in which the pupils worked methodically across the fields clearing the stones as they went. **1990** EDWARDS *AWOL* 18 I was delegated [in the army] to cleaning toilets and picking up rubbish and cigarette butts (Emu Parade) more than anyone else. **1992** *North & South* (Auckland Sept. 97 The company..organises, in conjunction with ski-club members (it's called the 'emu parade'..because everyone's bending over) a massive cleanup at the end of each season, during which several tonnes of rubbish are removed from the slopes.

e-muka, var. MUKA.

enaki, var. INANGA (INAKA).

English, *a.*

1. a. Associated with Britain as a 'home' country; originating in Britain.

1853 ROCHFORT *Adventures of Surveyor* 13 The town [of Christchurch] lay in a hollow..; the snug little weather-boarded houses..each standing in the midst of a neat little English garden, formed a delightful contrast to the wild hills around. **1862** CHUDLEIGH *Diary* 4 Dec. (1950) 69 I must begin my English letter on the first opportunity, I have not any time to do anything. *Ibid.* 71 Dec. 21 Enys brought my English letters. **1898** REEVES *Long White Cloud* 19 With trees and plants which the Colonists call specifically 'English'—for the word 'British' is almost unknown in the colony—the native flora is beginning to be cultivated in gardens and grounds.

b. Also as noun, European, PAKEHA 1 a.

1852 *Agreement between Government & Native Tribes for..Gold Fields on the Thames* in Swainson *Auckland* (1853) 157 All owners to be free to dig Gold on their own land, without payment to Government, but not to permit other persons, whether Natives or English, to dig without a License. **1931** *Na To Hoa Aroha* (1987) II. 227 *St. Stephens*. This institution is now out at Bombay. I attended the opening ceremony, and hearing that the Trustees have decided to introduce a large number of English [*Ed. Note* Pakeha boys, not English migrants] boys and to raise the fee to £60 a year had a go at the Trustees over the new policy.

2. In special collocations: **English axe**, a usu. single-bitted axe as distinguished from a usu. two-bitted AMERICAN AXE; **English biscuit** (formerly *German*, but with name-change due to anti-German prejudice during WW1), see quot.; **English sunbathing**, ironically applied to sitting fully clothed in the sun.

1848 WAKEFIELD *Handbook NZ* 447 The Colonist's attention should be directed to the following articles, with which he must provide himself according to his means and his intentions. For clearing and cultivating *timbered land*:—American axes, of various sizes,... Common **English axes**. (The natives can use these best). **1892** OSBORN in Richards *Foveaux Whaling Yarns* (1995) 38 Captain Howell set me to chopping down an ironwood tree three and a half feet in diameter, with an English axe that weighed two pounds with the edge beveled on both sides the same as a hatchet is on one side. After chopping with it for some time I..went up to the captain... I told him I could not chop with that axe... He said I could have an American axe... I found one that weighed four and a half pounds. **1915** *Our Boys Cook. Book* 123 **English Biscuits** Beat butter and sugar... Add spices and salt. Beat eggs... Add eggs, cornflour and..flour..to butter and sugar... Add baking powder... Roll out... Cut in rounds... Bake... Place in pairs with jam between and icing on top..sprinkle with coloured sugar. **1980** LELAND *Kiwi-Yankee Dict.* 36 **English Sunbathing**. The risky and risque exposure of one's ankles (possibly even the whole leg below the knee) to the rays of the sun while ensuring the rest of one's body is swathed in thick layers of woollen clothing.

3. As an antonym of NATIVE *a*. B 2, distinguishing those plants and animals associated with an English (or British) provenance or name, see HAKE 2 (2), MACKEREL 2 (1), SOLE 2 (1). See also ENGLISH GRASS.

English grass. Often *pl.* Occas. **England grass**. Any of various introduced high-yielding pasture grasses, esp. rye-grass *Lolium perenne* and cocksfoot *Dactylis glomerata*. Contrast *native grass* (NATIVE B 2 a).
1834 *NZ in the 1830s* (1979) 9 Aug. 33 [Hokianga] would be splendid sheep country; if English grasses could be got to grow upon it. **1848** DEANS *Pioneers* (1964) 51 We have..four acres around the house fenced and sown down with English grasses which do remarkably well. **1853** MACKIE *Traveller under Concern* (1973) 104 In his paddocks he has several of the english grasses, they are found to be very advantageous here, being hardier than the native grasses, they produce more herbage through the winter. **1866** BARKER *Station Life* (1870) 63 The ground immediately outside the house..is awaiting the spring to be sown with English grass. **1889** SKEY *Pirate Chief* 144 Ay, much he likes to see the grass, The English grass once more; To see a waving toothsome mass, Where stood the waste before. **1910** GROSSMAN *Heart of Bush* 2 He climbed through the bush towards 'The House', with steps that..were finally arrested just outside the cleared ground where English grasses and gowan daisies and daffodils grew wild. **1936** BELSHAW et al. *Agric. Organiz. NZ* 281 The grasses used were largely the best of the English grasses and clovers such as perennial rye grass, cocksfoot, dogstail and white clover which, incidentally, are not found to any marked extent in hill pastures in Great Britain. **1951** LEVY *Grasslands NZ* (1970) 166 The early settlers of a century ago introduced to New Zealand various 'English' grasses and clovers to supplement and later to replace the native grasses on the average-to-superior soil types. **1975** ACLAND *Early Canterbury Runs* ix 278 Glenmark was probably the only place in Canterbury where pastoralists tried to get English grass paddocks back into native pasture before sowing tussock seed. **1989** RICHARDS *Pioneer's Life* 48 They were more interested in returning to their natural feeding grounds and English grasses.

entire-leaved beech: see BEECH 2 (4).

enunga, var. INANGA.

Enzed /en'zed/, *n*. and *a*. Also **En-Zed, En Zed, N.Z.** [f. a pronunciation of the individual letters of the standard abbrev. N.Z.]

A. *n*. (See also NEW ZEALAND D.)
1. New Zealand.
1917 *NZ at the Front* 56 Call I 'lucky' one who's surely dead?... He has gone—just back to old N.Z. **1918** *Chron. NZEF* 30 Aug. 57 Baseball—a game something similar to what is known in En Zed as 'rounders'. **1924** *Aussie* (NZ Section) 15 July VIII This is a pity when we consider the infinite possibilities the scenic grandeurs of Enzed offer. **1931** *Aussie* (NZ Section) 15 Aug. 51 London *Times* recently paid a graceful, if very sincere compliment to Enzed's financial stability. **1944** *NZEF Times* 27 Mar. 7 They talk Enzed, they act Enzed, they think Enzed, and They eat butter. **1946** HAUGHEY *Railway Reminisc.* 6 He was back in En-Zed for a holiday. **1959** SLATTER *Gun in My Hand* 184 You could kid those Pongos up a gum tree. Told them I had a big cattle ranch back in Enzed. **1964** MORRIESON *Came a Hot Friday* (1981) 140 Guy who said Enzed was the backside of the world sure must have been around. **1976** SARGESON *Sunset Village* 35 Poor old Enzed!—sometimes he thought it might be just as well if it was called Small Beer.

2. A New Zealander; *spec.* in WW1, a New Zealand soldier. [AND *Enzed* a New Zealander, 1915.]
1917 *Press* (Christchurch) 29 Dec. 9 The 'Fernleaves' are known as equally courageous in battle and methodical in trench making... The forces call each other respectively 'Aussies' and 'Enzeds'. **1918** *Chron. NZEF* 30 Jan. 283 [Caption] 'Say, N.Z., I suppose you feel a bit lonely here all on your own!' *Ibid.* 24 May 179 Another interesting struggle was the tug-of-war between the 'En-zeds' and 'Ossies'. **1922** *Free Lance* (Wellington) 27 Sept. 1 The Anzacs' Response. [Caption to cartoon] The Two Anzacs (Aussie and En Zed): 'Here we are, Dad. If the Turk wants another scrap we're ready to do our bit.' **1991** *Dominion Sunday Times* (Wellington) 17 Nov. 9 [George Bernard Shaw] attacked the illusions of imperial-patriotic 'En-Zeds' who called England 'Home'.

Hence **Enzedder** (also **N.Zedder, N-Zer, N.Zder**) [AND 1933], a New Zealander.
1917 *NZ at the Front* 79 And there arose a certain Bull which had his Ring not far from the En Zedders. **1918** *Chron. NZEF* 19 July 272 I heard a Tommy telling some Enzedders that they did not speak proper English. **1923** *Aussie (NZ Section)* 14 July I [Heading] The Silent Enzedder. **1934** HYDE *Journalese* 44 A young Enzedder, free-lance journalist..went to a show one night with three fair young maidens. **1943** *NZEF Times* 28 June 5 Where there are Enzedders, there is beer and where there is beer there are Enzedders. **1943** *Fourth Generalities* (Troopship magazine) 14 Big gang of N-Zers [*sic*]. **1947** FAIRBURN *Letters* 30 May (1981) 162 I have something to say about the inferiority feelings of NZders when they're dealing with Englishmen. **1950** *Here & Now* Nov. 9 I am left with a feeling that Mr Average N.Zedder is of necessity patron, president, secretary..of something or other. **1972** SARGESON *Man of England Now* 26 Anyway they'd soon be meeting the missis..she was an Enzeder like himself. **1982** *Pacific Index Abbrev.* 223 *NZedder(s)* (En-zed-der(s))—New Zealander(s)..*NZer, NZ'er* New Zealander. **1990** *Dominion Sunday Times* (Wellington) 22 Apr. 8 I am not an Enzedder, or a Kiwi, or an Antipodean, or an Anzac..I am a New Zealander, of northern European descent, as it happens.

B. *adj.* Of, from, or pertaining to New Zealand.
1918 *NZ at the Front* 65 Would that our ain folk knew what an En Zed mail means to us. **1926** LAWLOR *Maori Tales* 20 Official Enzed time. **1929** MILTON *Love & Chiffon* 167 Good old N.Z. mutton. **1941** *Convoyager* (H.M. Transport 22, Troopship pub.) The back-country Enzed lad. **1943** *NZEF Times* 1 Mar. 5 During the advance from Alamein an Enzed driver came upon a deserted German truck full of most desirable articles. **1960** MUIR *Word for Word* 202 She has penned a sprightly novel with a contemporary Enzed backdrop.

eppa(h), var. PA.

escort. *Hist.* Often with init. cap. *gold escort* (GOLD 3); occas. *transf.*, the gold carried (see quot. 1861).
1851 *Lyttelton Times* 13 Sept. 3 His Excellency..had made arrangements for an armed escort to convey gold from the diggings to Sydney once in each week. **1861** *NZ Goldfields 1861* (1976) 40 Of the first two escorts there is no official record at hand, but they may be roughly estimated at a total of 3,500oz. **1862** *Otago Witness* (Dunedin) 23 Aug. 4 The Escort arrived in town Thursday evening bringing down the following quantities of gold [from Tuapeka, Waipori, etc.] **1866** FARJEON *Grif* 7 'We can stick up the escort in the Black Forest,' he ses.

eskimo pie. [See OED *eskimo* 4 'Chiefly U.S.', 1928: orig. a proprietary name.] A bar of vanilla icecream coated with chocolate.
1922 *NZ Patent Office Jrnl.* [no number given] 30 Dec. Eskimo Pie 19290 [filed] 2nd August, 1922..Russell Stover Co.. Chicago.. Confectionery, including ice-cream covered or coated with chocolate. **1947** *NZ Observer* 3 Dec. 10 I may be able to do a little better with Eskimo pies to-morrow. **1963** GLOVER *Bedside Book* 143 And if I die and if I die then bye and bye and bye and bye you'll be eskimo pie up in the sky up in the sky. **1970** DAVIN *Not Here Not Now* 219 'Let's bring her back some eskimo pies,' Martin said. 'I haven't had one since I was at school.' **1974** *Sunday Times* (Wellington) 3 Feb. 63 Men, women and children and even some of the news media watching at night, were as frozen as eskimo pies in the stand. **1991** MELVILLE *My Home Town* 28 In later days choc bombs and Eskimo pies joined the frozen menu.

etaboo, e-taboo, varr. TAPU.

etohora, var. TOHORA.

e-to-ki, var. TOKI.

e-tootoo, var. TUTU.

European, *n*. and *a*.

A. *n*. [Spec. use of *European* (cf. OED B 2) one of European extraction who lives away from Europe: AND 1832.] A non-Maori white immigrant to, later resident of, New Zealand. See also PAKEHA 1 a.
[**1778** BOWMAN *Travels of Hildebrand Bowman* 29 As I had no further business in that part of the country, and knew from charts, that New Zealand (as it is called by the Europeans) is a great extent of country.] **1817** KENDALL 25 July in Elder *Marsden's Lieutenants* (1934) 141 The natives approve of Europeans settling amongst them, through motives of self-interest. **1823** CRUISE *Journal* 24 Sept. (1957) 163 During the week the Europeans employed in the woods received little or no assistance from the natives. **1832** HAY *Notices of NZ* (1979) 10 F. Mascetu—a flax settlement; four Europeans here; likely to—be permanent. **1841** *Gov. Hobson's Proclamation* 3 May in Rutherford *Sel. Documents* (1949) 11(a) The Governor avails himself of this occasion to appeal to the good feelings of the colonists generally in favour of their fellow-subjects of the native race, who require only instruction and good example to become equal to Europeans in moral, as they already are in physical attainments. **1851** WELD

EVAI 247 EXPRESS

Letter Jan. in *NZGG* 21 Feb. (1851) 31 [We descended] upon the site of the old fishery of Amuri; there are no Europeans living there now. **1869** HAWTHORNE *Dark Chapter NZ Hist.* 5 Several settlers of thirty, and even forty years' standing yet reside in Turanga, or Poverty Bay, as it is named by Europeans. **1909**, **1967** [see PAKEHA A 1].

B. *adj.* Pertaining to a non-Maori white immigrant or resident.

1849 WELD in Bidwill & Woodhouse *Bidwill of Pihautea* (1927) 9 One of the newest features of the valley is the appearance of cottages belonging to the wives and children of European settlers. **1891** *NZJSc.* (NS) I. 204 I made inquiries of old residents (European and Maori). **1983** LAMBERT *Illustr. Hist. of Taranaki* 34 Under the guidance and leadership of Wiremu Kingi, they adopted European farming technology.

evai, var. WAI.

even terms. *Obs.* [A euphemism prob. developed from the phraseology of running sheep 'on terms'.] Working for keep only. See TERMS *n.*[1]

1933 *Press* (Christchurch) (Acland Gloss.) 14 Oct. 15 *Even Terms.*—'Working for his tucker'; a polite expression only applied to cadets. **1955** *BJ Cameron Collection* (TS July) even terms (n) Working for food and keep merely. The expression has little application in these prosperous days.

ewe. Special Comb. **ewe block**, a set of yards etc. set aside for ewes; **ewe country**, easy country suitable for lambing etc.

1952 BLAKISTON *My Yesteryears* 21 As every **ewe block** had a set of yards and a mothering paddock, ewes and lambs were mustered in sections, with very early starts to avoid the summer heat. **1953** STRONACH *Musterer on Molesworth* 25 The next job was mustering the **ewe country**, and we began to prepare. *Ibid.* 25 The Molesworth ewe country has a reputation.

Executive Council.

1. *Hist.* An appointive body responsible to the Governor of New Zealand.

1848 WAKEFIELD *Handbook NZ* 195 Under the Amended Licensing Ordinance Session III., No.21, 1844, 'Bush Licences' are granted for the convenience of Travellers, at rates fixed by the Governor and Executive Council, according to the traffic of the place. **1940** WEBB *Government in NZ* 4 New Zealand received a governor of its own [*sc.* in 1840], an executive council, and a legislative council. **1957** SINCLAIR *Origins of Maori Wars* 129 On 12 February 1858, Stafford laid before the Executive Council a memorandum by the Ministers on the state of affairs in Taranaki. **1986** *Illustr. Encycl. NZ* 847 Edward Eyre was appointed Lieutenant-Governor of New Munster and a Legislature and Executive Council was set up under the control of Governor-in-Chief Grey.

2. Also as **Council**. The Ministers of the Crown sitting as a Council presided over by the Governor-General, and offering advice on matters of statutory law and regulation, and specifically on Orders-in-Council.

1893 *AJHR* A.-7A 38 The Executive Council are the men who have for years headed the popular party unanimous in its demands for the Land Bills. **1934** MULGAN *Spur of Morning* 212 If they can't block us in the House, they'll do it in the Council. **1962** SCOTT *NZ Constitution* 78 Cabinet and the Executive Council are two bodies with the same membership and different functions. **1989** *Illustr. Encycl. NZ* 379 Executive Council is the legal entity which formally transforms decisions of Cabinet into law.

Exodus. *Hist.* As **the (Great) Exodus**, the emigration of New Zealanders to Australia during the depression of the 1880s.

1946 SOLJAK *NZ* 52 The seventeen years' depression between 1876 and 1893 was marked by a movement known to New Zealanders as 'the exodus', when over 150,000 people, or approximately 25 per cent of the total population, migrated from New Zealand to Australia. **1951** LAWSON *Mary Smith's Hotel* (1957) l 73 The country was slowly recovering from the dreadful days of unemployment that led to the Great Exodus—a name given to the migration of thousands of people from New Zealand to Australia in the late 80s. **1959** SINCLAIR *Hist. NZ* 160 During the late eighties the departures exceeded the arrivals by many thousands. During 'the Exodus', as it was called, most of the emigrants went to Victoria.

exotic, *a.* and *n.* [Spec. use of *exotic* introduced from a foreign country.]

A. *adj.* A term applied (esp. in forestry use) to an introduced tree (occas. plant) species as distinct from endemic; or to a forest composed of exotic species.

1894 *TrNZI* XXVI. 622 Every description of fern, whether native or exotic. **1946** SOLJAK *NZ* 11 These exotic forest resources [insignis pine, Douglas fir, etc.] are being expanded to..facilitate preservation of the native forests, which the early settlers wastefully reduced. **1960** MASTERS *Back-Country Tales* 193 What eventually happened to that great wild stallion, will probably always remain just another of the secrets of the huge exotic forests of the wild and lonely Rangitaiki Plains. **1971** ARMFELT *Catching Up* 20 But here on the Flat almost all the trees were exotic: the windbelts of radiata pine or macrocarpa..(it sounded peculiar to hear them called 'exotic'). **1987** CHRISTIE *Candles & Canvas* 79 It [Tarawera Hotel] nestled on a flat piece of ground between hills devoid of any growth except for a thin line of exotic pines.

B. *n.* An introduced tree species.

1936 LEE *Hunted* 50 Across the plains ran belts of exotics. **1938** HYDE *Nor Yrs. Condemn* 191 In the country back towards Auckland and civilization, north of Arapuni, there had been a conquest by exotics; close-growing old puriri trees disputed the soil with little plantations of pine. **1951** LEVY *Grasslands NZ* (1970) 16 The region is noted for its indigenous trees and also for exotics planted for shelter or for farm firewood and timber.

Expeditionary Force. *WW1.* As **New Zealand Expeditionary Force** (often as **NZEF**), the general name for the troops sent overseas to fight during WW1; as **Second New Zealand Expeditionary Force** (or **2NZEF**), for those sent during WW2.

1916 *NZ Statutes* No.8 97 [Military Service Act, Clause 37] The Expeditionary Force may be divided..into such units and other divisions as the Commandant..thinks fit. **1918** WESTON *Three Yrs. with New Zealanders* 7 In October the main body of the New Zealand Expeditionary Force, with its first reinforcement, also sailed for Egypt. **1933** SCANLAN *Tides of Youth* 243 New Zealand was equipping an Expeditionary Force which was to sail in a few weeks. **1940** *Weekly News* 7 Feb. [Caption] Soldiers of the Second Echelon in training at Burnham Camp, Christchurch, for service with the Second Expeditionary Force. **1990** *Listener & TV Times* 4 June 50 The actual position was that, as with all other units in the Expeditionary Force, the battalion's officers..had to be drawn from the small..pool of experienced personnel.

expert /ˈekspɜt/, *n. Shearing.* [Spec. use of *expert* a person who has special skills or knowledge: AND 1910.] A term for the person who sets up and grinds handshears, and keeps handpieces and other shearing gear and plant in order.

1913 CARR *Country Work* 14 The owner or manager generally gets his own pressers and expert (where machines are run). **1955** BOWEN *Wool Away* 156 Expert. The man who grinds the gear, and keeps the handpieces and plant in order. This man is often a retired shearer. **1989** RICHARDS *Pioneer's Life* 43 George Stuart, being the contractor and the expert, was on Number One stand. **1990** MARTIN *Forgotten Worker* 86 The changeover from hand shearing required an 'expert' to be hired specifically for setting up and maintaining the machines, and for grinding 'combs' and 'cutters'.

expert, *v. trans.* and *intr.*, to keep (shears and plant) in order. Also as a *vbl. n.*

1912 *NZ Shearers Rep. Third Annual Conf.* 11 To Shear and Expert 'That Remit No. 7 be struck out, i.e. ... 'That no shearer be allowed to shear and expert on the same board.'... 'That no shearer expert and shear on a board of more than five shearers.' **1955** BOWEN *Wool Away* 74 The next phase of experting a new comb is to scrape or rub the tips on wood. *Ibid.* 75 I trust that the experting as set out in this text will be a practical guide and help to all, as good gear is the foundation of all good shearing. **1986** RICHARDS *Off the Sheep's Back* 121 He was always 'ringer' of the gang besides doing the experting.

export. In the phr. **export of brains**, used to describe the emigration from New Zealand of educated or highly-trained people in search of higher pay.

1948 LIPSON *Politics of Equality* 493 Yet persistently New Zealand refuses opportunities to its most talented sons and daughters, denies them the chance of creative expression, and often drives them from its own shores in the annual 'export of brains' which is its greatest tragedy. **1966** TURNER *Eng. Lang. Austral. & NZ* 85 It may seem that science is something that very intelligent people go abroad to pursue, a process which in England has recently been called the 'brain drain' and has in New Zealand..been called the 'export of brains' for at least twenty years.

express. *Obs.*

1. *Ellipt.* for EXPRESS WAGON.

1889 DAVIDSON *Stories NZ Life* 5 The station [*sc.* sheep station] express was got out..and away drove Duncan. **1914** GRACE *Tale Timber Town* 69 The man..ran round to the back of his 'express'—a vehicle not unlike a square tray on four wheels. **1921** *Quick March* 10 Feb. 35 He had hitherto not heard the term 'express' applied to these tempestuous vehicles. **1959** LAWLOR *Old Wellington Days* 64f [Caption] In the days of 'the Express'. **1968** TOMLINSON *Remembered Trails* 29 My father was able to get Harry Stone..to do the driving of the express. **1978** [see BUGGY 1]. **1980** NEAVE *Land of Munros* 42 [Caption to picture showing an 'express'—a 4-wheeled open spring wagon with raised sides, and moveable front wheels.] T.A. Munro's Stables... The dark horse in the express is a young horse being broken in.

2. Special Comb. **expressman**, one who operates or drives an express (wagon).

1939 BEATTIE *First White Boy Born Otago* 180 One of my brothers was an expressman in early Dunedin. **1959** LAWLOR *Old Wellington Days* 49 No wharfie, even of the old days, ever caught the eye of his pannikin boss as smartly as these express men when you signalled them for a job.

express wagon. *Obs.* [Spec. use of *express* a wagon in which packages etc. were taken to and from an express office: cf. OED *express a.* C 3.] In New Zealand, commonly a light four-wheeled horse-drawn sprung vehicle usu. for goods delivery. See also EXPRESS 1.
   1862 THATCHER *Dunedin Songster 1* 8 There was a little express wagon waiting to convey these Melbourne notables to Dunedin. **1883** BRADSHAW *NZ As It Is* 81 Our 'buggies', a generic name in the colony for every description of vehicle on springs short of the 'express' waggon, were carefully overhauled.

extended claim. [AND 1869.] A (usu. frontage) claim which has been increased in area by the incorporation in the original claim of additional ground or length of lead, or, by amalgamation, of one or more other claims.
   1892 PYKE *Gold-Miners' Guide* 7 Claims are classified as follows:—Alluvial deposits, and river- or creek-beds; Quartz lodes, reefs, and leaders; Sea-beach claims; Prospecting claims; and comprise ordinary claims, double ground, extended claims, frontage claims, special claims and dredging claims.

extra, *n.* Usu. *pl.* Occasional dance music played by others than the band, group, or person hired to provide the main music for the dance, often to give the main musicians a rest or break.
   1915 *Rangitikei Advocate & Manawatu Argus* 15 May 4 Music was supplied by Mr. C. Edwards (piano) and extras were played by Mrs. J Cameron and Mr. J. Deehan. **1919** *Stratford Evening Post* 17 May 5 Dancing was kept going during the evening to music by Mrs. Bennett (piano), extras being supplied by Mrs. Middlemass and Miss Keegan. **1945** *Taranaki Daily News* (New Plymouth) 8 June 7 Music was played by Messrs. W. Aorere, W. Aaiaroa, and B. Mata, extras being played by Miss M. Pringle.

extra, *adv.* [Prob. a shortening of *extraordinar(il)y.*] Used frequently in speech to intensify a following adjective, and having a sense 'very; really'; also in the collocations: **extra curly, extra early** (*obs.*), **extra good,** fine, excellent.
   1961 PARTRIDGE *Dict. Slang* 1081 *extra early.* First rate; very good, excellent: New Zealand: since ca. 1945. **1966** TURNER *Eng. Lang. Austral. & NZ* 30 We do not know whether an affable New Zealander about to agree to something is going to say *extra good* or *good as gold* or simply *all right* or even *O.K.* **1988** McGILL *Dict. Kiwi Slang* 43 *extra* enhancing intensive which can reverse the meaning of the parent word, as in the first of the two common uses of it following:—*extra curly* first rate; eg 'That last four Martin Crowe belted was extra curly';...*extra grouse* exceptionally attractive; eg 'The spread put on by Ken's Mum after the game was extra grouse.' Often applied to a desired woman.

extrav: see EXTRAVAGANZA.

extravaganza. Also in shortened form **extrav**. [Spec. and joc. use of *extravaganza* a literary or musical composition of an extravagant or fantastic character.] The traditional name of the Victoria University (College) student revue.
   1924 *Otago Witness* (Dunedin) 24 June 30 Victoria College is now recovering from its extravaganza, which was quite the best thing ever produced by the students. **1926** FAIRBURN *Letters* 21 July (1981) 5 Cheeking the examiner in an Economics Paper..throwing a roll of toilet paper..on to the stage from the Gods on the last night of the extravaganza. **1935** *Free Lance* (Wellington) 5 June 5 The students of Victoria College put on a successful extravaganza in the Town Hall. **1949** BEAGLEHOLE *Victoria Univ. College* 128 More uniformly satisfactory [than capping ceremonies] was what came to be called the 'Carnival',... Starting, therefore, with concerts of miscellaneous songs, hakas [etc]..the revellers went on to develop the 'extravaganza'—or rather a number of different sorts of extravaganza; for no attempt to stabilize permanently the pattern of that combination of buffoonery and satire has ever been successful. **1956** WILSON *Sweet White Wine* 72 She had performed with distinction in the dramatic club and in the annual [Victoria University College] extravaganza. **1965** HILLIARD *Power of Joy* 295 The barman slapped a fellow on the shoulder. 'When are you going to give that suit back to the Varsity Extravaganza?' **1966** *Cappicade* (Wellington) 9 Agitators generally provoke demonstrations under the guise of 'Proceshes' and 'Extravs'. **1978** HARCOURT *A Dramatic Appearance* 41 The typical university extravaganza is a show apart, conforming to no finely drawn lines of difference, but usually savours more of musical comedy than anything else. **1992** *NewsVUW* 6 Oct. 10 Students would never again be able to take time out for activities such as Victoria's legendary 'extravaganzas', the traditional highlight of the May graduation festivities, which have since died.

eye.

1. In the adverbial phrase **eyes out**, esp. **to go eyes out,** (to proceed) at top speed, at full stretch.
   1863 CHUDLEIGH *Diary* 8 Jan. (1950) 73 My horse turning to[o] quickly while I was going eyes out, fell and rowled oaver [*sic*]. **1895** ROBERTS *Diary of Jonathan Roberts* 28 You weren't travelling 'eyes out' were you? **1906** *Truth* 18 Aug. 2 Jack Spencer, King, Bill Adams and Sullivan went 'eyes' out after a win which didn't come their way, however. **1945** *NZ Geogr.* Apr. 24 Musterers go 'eyes out' to keep the sheds fed with sheep. **1966** TURNER *Eng. Lang. Austral. & NZ* 177 In a light poem, Butler uses the expression *eyes out* to mean as fast or as energetically as possible. One still hears 'We'll have to go eyes out to get finished in time'.

2. *Obs.* or *hist.* **to pick** (occas. **take**) **the eyes out (of land).** [Transf. use of Cornish dial. *eye* a mass of ore left in a mine to be worked when others are scarce; hence, a 'plum', a titbit left to last: cf. OED *n.*¹ 16 b; AND 1865.] **a.** To buy or alienate the choicest pieces in a block of land. Cf. GRIDIRON *v.*, SPOT *v.*¹ 1. (More freq. in Austral. than NZ use, which latter preferred *spot*.)
   1891 WALLACE *Rural Econ. Austral. & NZ* 24 The original settlers..have in colonial phraseology 'picked the eyes out of the country' in making their selection. **1895** CHAMIER *South Sea Siren* 165 I took 'the eyes out of it', as we say—spotted all the best patches, secured all the waterholes. **1907** ALLOM note to Jollie *Reminiscences* (ATLTS) (1878) 39 [When Allom borrowed the MS from Jollie's wife he added this note to Jollie's account of buying the best parts out of a run in 1856.] This was probably about the beginning of the grid-iron process of picking the eyes out of the country, so much practised afterwards. **1930** DAVIDSON *Sketch of His Life* 18 With free selection of land at £2 per acre everyone had the same opportunity to buy, and a leaseholder ran the risk of waking any morning to find the eyes picked out of His [*sic*] run by some outsider.

b. Transferred to timber blocks and county boundary-setting.
   1936 BELSHAW et al. *Agric. Organiz. NZ* 567 The system [of granting timber rights] allowed for 'picking the eyes out' of areas of standing timber and leaving the less advantageous parts to future operators. **1958** *Star-Sun* (Christchurch) 31 May 9 They pick the eyes out of the country. The populous areas are taken [*i.e.* transferred to the city] and we are left with the rural districts.

3. *Farming.* **a.** Of a sheep-dog, esp. as **show eye**, the quality of being able to command or work sheep by gaze; a deep concentration on the movements of the sheep. Also *attrib*. Cf. STRONG-EYED. Contrast *plain-eyed* (PLAIN *a.* 1 a).
   1934 LILICO *Sheep Dog Memoirs* 1 These dogs had any amount of eye and style and yet they were powerful forcers with plenty of noise. **1949** HARTLEY *Shepherd's Dogs* 2 The dog shown on page 13 is a huntaway..that showed a considerable amount of eye. **1956** SUTHERLAND *Green Kiwi* (1960) 115 For straight-out 'eye' work he's a pretty nice dog. **1966** [see PLAIN 1 a]. **1971** NEWTON *Ten Thousand Dogs* 168 *Eye*: Common to our heading dogs. This is the action of 'setting' sheep—as some of our sporting dogs set game—and exercising extreme concentration on the sheep they happen to be working... A very strong-eyed dog ('stinking' with eye) works sheep in a manner similar to a cat stalking a bird. **1982** *Agric. Gloss.* (MAF) 24 *Eye*: Trait of a dog to stare at a sheep; deep concentration on the movements of the sheep. 'Strong-eye' or 'plain-eye' dogs. **1985** RENNIE *Working Dogs* 37 When a heading dog first begins to eye sheep it is important to break the eye by calling it so that it looks at you.

b. *Special Comb.* **eye-dog,** a dog which controls sheep by concentrated gaze. Also *transf.*, a censorious person (see quot. 1995).
   1934 *Press* (Christchurch) (Acland Gloss.) 20 Jan. 15 *Eye dog*.—Dog that commands sheep by his eye. I daresay he acts by the same instinct that makes a pointer or setter 'stand' to game. **1959** McLEOD *Tall Tussock* 124 Eye Dog: Heading dog which controls sheep by a concentrated stare. **1966** *NZ Short Stories* (1976) 128 Someone would always trot out the old theory about eye dogs being biters. **1982** *Agric. Gloss.* (MAF) 24 *Eye-dog*: Same as a heading dog. One that shows 'eye'. **1995** *Dominion* (Wellington) 24 Aug. 10 I visualise them [*sc.* the National Council of Women]..as the eye dogs..of our sinful society..glowering, tense..with a sinner like myself..as a sort of recalcitrant ewe.

Hence **eye** *v. trans.*, of a sheep-dog, to control or work (sheep) through eye-contact.
   1953 STRONACH *Musterer on Molesworth* 43 At Molesworth in those days most of our heading dogs were the 'plain-working' kind. They did not 'eye' the sheep or exercise any mesmerism, as is done by the present-day trial dog. **1985** [see 3 a above].

4. *Prison.* **Have you got eye-trouble?** 'Stop staring!'; or a warning to break eye-contact.
   1984 *Truth* 10 July 15 As I walked from the yard into the day room [at Lake Alice Mental Hospital] for the first time a young guy said to another: 'Have you got eye trouble?' 'Yeah,' he said. 'I'll fix it for you,' said the young guy—and smashed the other patient in the eyes with his fists. 'Eye trouble' is a common expression in Lake Alice and prisons. It 'afflicts' those who stare at others and it results in eyes being punched.

eyebright. [Spec. use of European *eyebright Euphrasia* spp.] Any of various native species of *Euphrasia* (fam. Scrophulariaceae), semi-parasitic herbs with opposite sessile leaves common in alpine grasslands; also with a modifier: **alpine eyebright** *E. monroi*, **New Zealand eyebright** *E. cuneata* and *E. zelandica*.
   1777 ANDERSON *Journal* Feb. in Cook *Journals* (1967) III. 805 Amongst the known kinds of plants [in Queen Charlotte Sound] were common and rough Bindweed..Eyebright [Original note: Euphrasia] and groundsel. **1838** POLACK *NZ* I. 295 *Brambles, eye-bright, groundsell,* and minor herbaceous vegetation,

supposed to be solely indigenous to New Zealand, abound throughout the country. **1888** HETLEY *Native Flowers of NZ* 27 [Heading] *Euphrasia monroi...* Eyebright. The Eyebrights are found in temperate regions of both hemispheres, about five being represented in the flora of New Zealand. **1896** *TrNZI* XXVIII. 497 The process would be closely analagous to that exhibited by..the 'eyebright' (*Euphrasia cuneata*). **1907** LAING & BLACKWELL *Plants NZ* 386 *Euphrasia [z]elandica* (*The New Zealand Eyebright*). A small herb, 1 in.–2 in. high,... in alpine situations. **1919** COCKAYNE *NZ Plants & Their Story* 101 The alpine eyebright (*Euphrasia Monroi*) has rather big flowers, considering the size of the plant, white with a yellow eye. **1961** *Merriam-Webster Third Internat. Dict.* 62 *Alpine eyebright n* : a showy New Zealand perennial herb (*Euphrasia monroi*) with yellow and white flowers. **1978** *Manawatu Tramping Club Jubilee* 89 Dotted in profusion amidst the tussock are magnificent Mt Cook lillies [*sic*], Eyebright and gentian all the way to the hut. **1989** PARKINSON *Travelling Naturalist* 139 Among these are the large mountain daisy..the New Zealand eyebright, or tutumako.

eye-clip, *v. Farming. trans.* To clip the wool growing over a sheep's eyes; to treat (sheep) in this way. See also EYE-WIG.
    1933 *Press* (Christchurch) (Acland Gloss.) 14 Oct. 15 *Eye-clip.*—To cut the wool away from round a sheep's eyes. If this is not done, the wool, especially on merinos is apt to grow over the and make the sheep *wool-blind*. Some people speak of eye-clipping as *Winking*. **1949** NEWTON *High Country Days* 195 Some of the finer woolled breeds of sheep at times grow too much wool on their heads. They become 'wool blind,' and it is necessary to 'eye clip' them. **1950** *NZJAg.* Oct. LXXXI. 349 Lambs..while ewes are being shorn..are being wigged or eye-clipped... Through eye clipping, wool blindness is avoided. **1968** TOMLINSON *Remembered Trails* 44 We had to eye clip the hoggets on the Station block, and it was getting into May. **1978** JARDINE *Shadows on Hill* 46 They are brought down to the station..and the wethers eyeclipped if this is required.

    Hence **eye-clipping** *vbl. n.* and *attrib.,* removing wool from around a sheep's eyes; **eye–clip** *n.,* see quot. 1982.
    1930 ACLAND *Early Canterbury Runs* First Series vi 18 Merino sheep..were not handled so often for **eye-clipping** and so on. **1947** NEWTON *Wayleggo* 46 I was wanted with my dogs for the spring eye-clipping. **1951** MCLEOD *NZ High Country* 40 Several years ago we mustered in a mob of wethers for eye-clipping in June. **1966** NEWTON *Boss's Story* 187 *Eye-clipping*: Sheep that become wool-blind (i.e. grow so much wool on their heads they cannot see) must periodically have the wool clipped away from around their eyes. **1968** TOMLINSON *Remembered Trails* 61 The Burchill musterers went home for a week's holiday and I was persuaded to help with the eye clipping muster, which started in May. **1978** PRESTON *Woolgatherers* 100 Mustering, drafting and eye-clipping kept all hands busy. **1982** *Agric. Gloss.* (MAF) 55 *Eye Clips*: Trade term for wool removed from the side of the face at crutching which though soft often contains a high proportion of kemps.

eye-drop. A marble-game in which the taw is (or can be) dropped from above.
    1972 SUTTON-SMITH *Folkgames Children* 175 There were..Eye-Drop, Knock-Backs, Leggings-Out (or Leggin's-Out), Span-'Em, and Backits. **1982** SUTTON-SMITH *Hist. Children's Play* 139 [c1870–85 at Grovetown] We played marbles, Ring, and Eye-drop with taws, glassies, stonies, and agots. **1995** *Independent* 8 Dec. 20 Eye drops were of no interest. But if you were going to play the rule was no bombies; no giant marbles called bomb squashers.

eye-wig, *v. trans.* EYE-CLIP. See also WIG *v.*
    1950 *NZJAg.* Apr. LXXX. 387 Each ewe..is eye-wigged if necessary. **1955** BOWEN *Wool Away* 64 Many of our sheep have become wool-blind, i.e. wool grows over their eyes so that they cannot see. These sheep are usually eye-wigged at crutching time.

    Hence **eye-wigging** *vbl. n.,* removing wool from around the eyes of a sheep.
    1955 BOWEN *Wool Away* 54 Sheep that require eye-wigging have the top-knot removed, and wool is also taken from below the eyes if required. **1982** *Agric. Gloss.* (MAF) 49 Removal of wool from the head (eye wigging) may be done at the same time [as crutching].

F

face. [Fig. or transf. uses of *face n.*]

1. [Cf. OED *face n.* 12 a.] **a.** An open hill slope. See also FACING, SIDELING 1 a.

  1857 *St. Leonard's Station Diary* in MacFarlane *Amuri* (1946) 126 Sheep seem all right as all on steep sunny faces which have partly cleared. **1865** CHUDLEIGH *Diary* 20 Oct. (1950) 201 We mustered about four miles of the fase [*sic*] of Ben McLeod. I went up some 7000 ft. **1887** PYKE *Hist. Early Gold Discoveries Otago* (1962) 141 Expensive lawsuits..have occurred, owing to the difficulty of exactly determining boundaries where the 'faces' are from 100 to 200 feet in height. **1924** *Otago Witness* (Dunedin) 17 June 68 We got past them..getting a close view of the big bare clay 'faces' on one side of the river, which look like cuttings. **1949** NEWTON *High Country Days* 137 The stag up in the face gave tongue again. **1975** DAVIES *Outback* 8 Those sounds meant a full day on the hills..climbing steep faces..to rescue trapped ewes. **1981** CHARLES *Black Billy Tea* 49 They chased that old boar... Through fern, face and gully and hills far away! **1992** *Dominion Sunday Times* (Wellington) 26 July 21 Vegetable sheep dot the most inhospitable faces.

b. *Farming.* With a modifier describing (a) the aspect of a face and whether it gets the (esp. winter) sun: **cold**, **dark**, **shady**, **sunny**; or (b) its surface features: **bush**, **ferny**, etc.

  1857 sunny face [see a above]. **1928** COCKAYNE *Vegetation of NZ* 231 This is seen on all sunny and shady slopes (the 'sunny' and 'dark faces' of the shepherds). **1937** AYSON *Thomas* 102 So up a pig track he started to the ferny face where the dogs were barking. **1938** *NZJST* XX. 232A Here it must be pointed out that what Cockayne described as *sunny* and *dark* faces are for the most part, and especially in Central Otago, essentially windward and leeward faces respectively. **1947** NEWTON *Wayleggo* 37 It was country of great open shingle faces. *Ibid* 110 bush faces [see BUSH C 2 b]. **1951** DUFF *Shepherd's Calendar* (1961) 41 No rabbit goes voluntarily to the cold faces when the warm ones are open. **1960** CRUMP *Good Keen Man* 32 All the bush faces were spotted with the dead branches of trees. **1960** SCRYMGEOUR *Memories Maoriland* 9 During the summer on these high altitudes, sheep throve, and had to be mustered to the sunny faces of the ridges where the snow first melted. **1978** PRESTON *Woolgatherers* 110 We could shift only those [sheep] caught on the dark faces, and bring them across to the sunny side. **1981** CHARLES *Black Billy Tea* 48 The dogs flushed the boar on a high ferny face. **1983** FRANCIS *Wildlife Ranger* 59 The dark faces of the spurs were now dangerous and it was easy to slip and fall disastrously. (The so-called dark faces were slopes and hillsides that got no sun during the winter and remained frozen.)

2. *Gumdigging.* [Fig. or transf. use of *face* (mining) the end of a tunnel, etc., at which work is progressing: cf. OED *face n.* 20 b.] **to work (gumland) on a face**, to trench and cut the land to extract gum.

  1970 THOMAS *Way Up North* 35 Instead of relying on a spear to locate gum in pockets or patches, they began working gum-bearing land 'on a face'.

3. Special Comb. **face brand** *v. farming obs. trans.*, to brand sheep on the face; **face-cut forestry** [transf. use of *face* surface: used elsewhere but recorded earliest in NZ], the first piece of timber sawn from a log on the breaking-down bench; **face fart**, to belch.

  1867 PHILLIPS *Point Jrnl.* 30 Jan. (Canterbury Pub. Lib. TS) 93 All hands **face branding** rams and then mustering Snowy Peak. **1868** *Marlborough Express* (Blenheim) 22 Feb. 5 All were face-branded U. **1874** BAINES *Edward Crewe* 180 After taking off a '**face' cut**, setting the gauger rollers, and placing the flitch in position, the man at the head starts the machinery [to cut boards]. **1950** WILSON *My First Eighty Yrs.* 105 So far we had asked for 'facecuts', the first slices off the logs with the bark adhering. **1982** in *Some Other Country* (1984) 237 'Arp barp,' went her husband. 'For God's sake stop that **face farting** all the time,' said Mrs Ransumeen.

4. [Var. of *off one's head* indicating craziness from drink, drugs, etc.] In the phr. **off one's face**, to be stupefied by drink or drugs; hence, mad, crazy.

  1984 BEATON *Outside In* 84 Di: No. Not mad. Sandy: Fucken off their faces, I reckon. Ma: Crazy. Plain Crazy! *Ibid.* 110 *Be off one's face*: To be 'stoned', stupefied by drugs; behave as if stoned. **1984** 16 F E30 Pakuranga Coll. 33 Off your face [F5] **1988** McGILL *Dict. Kiwi Slang* 78 *off one's face* stoned on marijuana, eg 'Only had a few puffs of that new stuff, eh. Off my face. Yeh.'

facial eczema. A contagious fungal condition commonly found in sheep, but also affecting cattle and fallow deer.

  1900 *Rep. Dept. Agric.* 8 July 200 [Heading] Acute Facial Eczema in Sheep. This disease, which is manifested by an eruption on the face and ears of lambs, is solely due to dietetic errors. **1913** *NZJAg.* Jan. VI. 578 Breeding-ewes have been at times heavy sufferers from facial eczema (or facial dermatitis), as this trouble of the skin of the head is termed. **1938** *NZJST* XX. 92A It was considered desirable to determine..the effect of the so-called 'facial eczema' on sheep-skins. **1941** *NZJST* XXII. 30A Outbreaks of facial eczema occurred..in 1916, 1917, 1928, 1929, and 1933. **1951** LEVY *Grasslands NZ* (1970) 60 Weather conditions..appear to have an intimate relationship with facial eczema outbreaks. **1971** *NZ Dairy Exporter* Dec. 20 Although the Facial Eczema Advisory Committee..had agreed that it could see no benefit from spending more money on research into facial eczema at this stage, it was proposed to maintain the same commitment of research staff.

facing. [f. FACE *n.* + SIDEL)ING.] FACE 1.

  1874 KENNAWAY *Crusts* 143 We saw the fire sweep away up the further sides of the range, and leave our unconscious sheep safe on the still grassed facings of their run. **1885** *NZJSc.* II. 481 It [kea] seeks as a nesting-place the shelter of almost inaccessible rocks or burrows its hole in steep facings. **1917** in Hosken *Life on Five Pound Note* (1964) 112 [Quoting a roadside stone erected in 1917, north of Burke's Pass township.] So shall your mountain facings and river flats be preserved to your children's children and for evermore. **1940** STUDHOLME *Te Waimate* (1954) 96 When sunny facings have been fired during hot dry weather, the roots of the grasses get badly scorched. **1952** BLAKISTON *My Yesteryears* 58 Mr. Tripp was particularly keen about burning but as far as the tussock land was concerned, especially the sunny facings.

factory. [Spec. use of *factory* a building used for manufacturing goods.]

1. In New Zealand very often *spec.* a *dairy factory* (DAIRY 4) manufacturing cheese, butter, and other milk products. Contrast the meat industry's use of WORKS for 'freezing works'.

  1892 MURPHY in *Settler's Handbook NZ* (1902) 102 The factory system is now fairly well established. *Ibid.* It is hardly necessary to point out that all butter and cheese intended for export will have to be factory-made. **1898** *Dairy Industry Act* in *Settler's Handbook NZ* (1902) 149 *Classification of Dairies.*—Dairies are registered as—'Factories' or 'creameries,' *i.e.*, milking at least fifty cows. **1928** *Free Lance* (Wellington) 25 July 42 The factory lorry comes swift and soon, Like hell down the road 'twixt midnight and noon. **1980** WOOLLASTON *Sage Tea* 56 The cows were dry and our fathers not going to the factory (called that [instead of 'creamery'] now that they made cheese there instead of butter).

2. Special Comb. **factory (creamery, shop) butter**, see BUTTER 2.

fadge. *Farming.* [f. Brit. dial.: cf. EDD 3; AND 1914.] An unpressed loosely-packed part-bale of wool, sewn up as it stands, and weighing less than 100 kg.

  1929 *NZJST* X. 326 A star bale sold at a crutching sale made 101^{1}/$_{4}$d., while a fadge of the same wool pooled later made 12^{1}/$_{4}$ pence. **1933** *Press* (Christchurch) (Acland Gloss.) 30 Dec. 13 *Wool bale* or *w[ool] pack.*—Becomes a *bale of wool* when filled and pressed and a *fadge* when loosely filled. **1940** MEEK 'Wool Commandeer' in Woodhouse *Farm and Station Verse* (1950) 153 There's baggy bales and shaggy bales, there's fadges, sacks and bags. **1978** REID *Centennial Hist. 1878–1978* 27 Most of the wool clips which the store received [c1890] were only three or four bales in total, usually 'spade-packed' and often in fadges or bags. **1982** *Agric. Gloss.* (MAF) 55 Fadge: Package of wool in a wool pack weighing less than 100 kg.

failing subject. *Obs.* See quot.

  1966 TURNER *Eng. Lang. Austral. & NZ* 173 Children often study one more subject than the minimum required to pass an examination; they call the extra subject their *failing subject*.

fair, *a.*

I. [Spec. or extended sense of *fair* equitable, reasonable: see OED *a.* 10.] See also *fair buck*, *fair burl*, etc. at BUCK *n.*^{2} 2, BURL *n.*^{1} 1, DINKUM A 1 a and C 1 c, SPIN *n.* 2 a. **1.** As **fair do** (occas. **fair**

doos) [f. Brit. dial. *fair dos* fair dealing: see EDD *fair* 7, and Suppl.], usu. an exclamation or asseveration indicating a request for fair play; or (ironically) expressing doubt at an exaggeration.

1891 CHAMIER *Philosopher Dick* 140 [Sailor Jack speaks] He cut right under me again. 'Fair doos! you hanimal!' says I. And with that, hup I jumps and goes for him straight. **c1940** Freq. among Marlborough schoolchildren. (Ed.) **1988** MCGILL *Dict. Kiwi Slang* 44 *fair do* yet another appeal, sometimes *fair dos*; eg 'Oh, fair dos, don't I get a turn?'

2. fair go! *int.* [The international English collocation *a fair go* equitable treatment, a 'fair deal', is recorded in NZ only from 1929: see AND *fair adj.*[1] 2 a, 1904; OED *go n.* 4 d.] As *exclam.*, orig. a two-up cry (cf. *fair spin*!), indicating the beginning of the spin or game; thence, a general exclamation or appeal 'Be fair!, be reasonable!', 'Is that true?', often used (from a speaker's point of view) to assert or reinforce the truth, etc. of a statement, or (from a hearer's) to express doubt, or ironic or mild disbelief.

1912 *Truth* 20 Jan. 7 Once upon a time the free and easy [two-up] 'school' with the 'ring-master', and his 'All set—a fair go' broke upon the stilly night. **1944** GASKELL *All Part of the Game* (1978) 26 No, fair go Bomb. This is dinkum. **1950** In *Some Other Country* (1984) 90 But Auntie, fair go, will he be here next year? **1961** CRUMP *Hang On a Minute Mate* 149 Fair go? asked Jack, scenting a yarn in Sam's tone. **1976** WILSON *Pacific Star* 8 Fair go. It really hurts. If you listen, I'll tell you why. **1980** MARSH *Photo-finish* 202 That vindictive, she is. Fair go—I wouldn't put it past her. **1992** SMITHYMAN *Auto/Biographies* 6 God, he was trying, trying to feel me up. I didn't know what to say, let alone do. Fair go.

3. In the phr. **fair suck of the sav (saveloy)**, an appeal for fair play.

1988 MCGILL *Dict. Kiwi Slang* 44 *fair suck of the sav/saveloy/sauce stick*..are some more appeals for fairness. **1992** *Dominion* Wellington) 27 Oct. 1 'All we want is a fair suck of the sav.' she said.

II. [A spec., often extended, use of Brit. dial. and slang *fair* expressing moderate commendation, thence 'absolute': cf. OED *a*. 11 c.] **4.** [AND *fair adj.*[2], 1903.] Absolute, complete, thoroughgoing; 'real'. See also DINKUM C 1 c.

1902 SATCHELL *Land of Lost* 26 While it held out it would be a fair pour. **1934** *Press* (Christchurch) (Acland Gloss.) 20 Jan. 15 *Fair*.—Absolute (in a bad sense): f[air] cow, f[air] knock out, etc. **1937** MARSH *Vintage Murder* 174 'A fair nark' or, more emphatically 'a fair cow', is anything inexpressibly tedious or baffling. **1944** *Short Guide NZ* 39 *Fair nark*—a very unpleasant person... *Fair treat*—denotes emphasis—eg, the boss went crook a fair treat. **1979** WILLIAMS *Skin Deep* 30 I just want it to be really good, that's all. I'm laying out a fair whack on all this, you know.

5. As **a fair cow** [AND 1904], used of a person, thing, situation, etc. displeasing, or apparently displeasing, to the speaker; occas. also as an exclamation. Cf. COW.

1933 SCANLAN *Tides of Youth* 52 'Did you have much trouble getting all this circus up from Tapuwai?'.. 'A fair cow,' drawled Potty Barker. *Ibid.* 59 Pat had only Potty Barker's 'a fair cow of a winter' to conjure scenes of dripping desolation. **1942** *NZEF Times* 21 Dec. 6 The Bedouin bint's a fair cow. **1944** *Short Guide to NZ* 38 'Cow' is a common word of abuse, not so surprising why so many of the people have to struggle with the beasts. If something is godawful, they'll say it's a 'fair cow,' or they'll call a bad day a 'cow of a

day.' *Ibid.* 39 *Cow*—may just mean cow, but may also mean an unpleasant man, woman, or situation. **1950** *Here & Now* Nov. 9 By and large..there is remarkably little difference in English here and in Britain. That is..after making due allowance for such atrocities as 'joker', 'it's a fair cow'.

fair *adv.* [f. Brit. dial. *fair adv.*, entirely, absolutely: see OED 9 c; AND 1888.] Completely; thoroughly; 'real' or 'really'.

1897 WRIGHT *Station Ballads* 38 I feel fair sick. **1904** LANCASTER *Sons o' Men* 88 It fair gets me down to see the poor brutes dying like flies. **1928** DEVANNY *Dawn Beloved* 190 I get fair sick of it. **1950** CHERRILL *NZ Sheep Farm* 183 I'm fair thrilled to bits.

fairy.

1. See quot.

1973 *Salient* (Wellington) 19 Sept. 11 A fairy and a butch are the female and male in a lesbian relationship.

2. In the phr. **away with the fairies**, said of a daydreamer or an impractical person.

1988 MCGILL *Dict. Kiwi Slang* 11 *away with the fairies* daydreaming or considered unsound in the head. **1990** *Matriarchs* 144 Some of them were 'away with the fairies' in a big way.

3. Special Comb. **fairy club**, a toadstool; **fairy flax**, ASTELIA 1; **fairy prion**, see PRION 3; **fairy tern**, see TERN 2 (4); **fairy trumpet**, a foxglove.

1988 *Dominion* (Wellington) 10 Dec. 3 Consider the Stinkhorn..the **Fairy Club** or the the Shaggy Parasol Mushroom. **1930** COWAN *The Maori* 213 The **fairy flax**, the *kowharawhara*, grew in great bunches of long leaves in the tree-forks. **1913** MANSFIELD in *Undiscovered Country* (1974) 299 And on to the great green shoulders of Mak[a]ra Hill. There they sat down on the blowing grass and pink '**fairy trumpets**'... 'Wot do you mean?' asked the little boy one day, sitting..making finger gloves of the fairy trumpets.

4. In the collocation: **fairy's closet**, FUNGUS 2 (1).

1927 *TrNZI* LVII. 923 fairy's closet *Clathrus cibarius*. Ver. [=Vernacular names heard by J.C. Andersen from sawyers, settlers, etc.] **c1940** *Fairy's closet* was a usual Marlborough term for a basket fungus. (Ed.)

fake *n. Obs.* Also **faik, fakement**. [See OED *fake, fakement* 1812 Vaux, a dodge.] A trick or dodge.

1862 THATCHER *Dunedin Songster I* 8 Sheenie boys [Jews]..up to a fakement. *Ibid.* 10 This little land fake didn't go down I'm told, For people have come to their senses, And I hear that the price for the lot's that are sold, Will only just cover expenses. **c1875?** THATCHER in *NZ Songster* V. 64 In all houses of amusement, Your nose of course you'll poke; At bowling places roll for drinks, And a short black pipe you'll smoke; Fakements pick up not a few. **1897** WRIGHT *Station Ballads* 33 Of course the fakement fizzled out, they had to knuckle down. **1907** *Truth* 21 Sept. 6 Simpson recognised two of the weather-protecting fakements as his, but couldn't recognise the third [in a court case about umbrella stealing]. **1914** GRACE *Tale Timber Town* 128 It's your faik, Dolphin, you planned it.

fake down, *v. Obs.* [Cf. AND 1888 applied to changing brands on stolen beasts.] To steal; ?to carry out a dishonesty.

1862 THATCHER *Dunedin Songster I* 3 And to let all the Londoners see How the new-comers here at night fake down; Three blankets from Jones and Bird's place, Constituting what's termed a shake-down.

fakement: see FAKE.

falcon. [Extended use of *falcon*, any of various birds of prey.] Also **bush (New Zealand, southern) falcon**. *Falco novaeseelandiae* (fam. Falconidae), a hunter preying mainly on birds. See also HAWK, KAIAIA, KAREAREA, SPARROWHAWK.

1773 FORSTER *Resolution Jrnl.* 3 Apr. (1982) II. 246 *Capt Cook* came very late..& brought 3 Seals, 3 Ducks, 10 Waterhens, a new Charadrius & a new Falcon. **1870** *TrNZI* II. 48 This bold little Falcon, which a few years since, was so frequently seen, is now of comparatively rare occurrence. **1882** POTTS *Out in Open* 37 [It] must be assigned to the falcon, which is commonly known by the name of the quail or sparrow hawk..*Falco Novae Zelandiae*..karewarewa of the Maoris, quail-hawk of the settlers. **1911** MORELAND *Through South Westland* 163 As I came back I saw a bush falcon in the beech before the door, dusky-black when he spread his wings, but speckled like a thrush below. **1927** GUTHRIE-SMITH *Birds* 122 The Falcon brooks no rival in his own domain, and will chase the Harrier out of his sky, hunt the shepherd's collies back to their master's heels, and attack even man himself. **1955** OLIVER *NZ Birds* 423 New Zealand Falcon. Bush Hawk. Karearea... The Bush Hawk was discovered in 1773..during Cook's second voyage. Latham called it the New Zealand Falcon which name was adopted by Gmelin when founding its present specific title. **1976** SOPER *NZ Birds* 30 To be attacked by a Falcon defending its nest is quite an experience, for these sturdy little predators, unlike most birds that stoop in anger at man, press home their attack with a determination and fearlessness and a sustained ferocity that is unnerving. **1981** New Zealand falcon [see SPARROWHAWK]. **1985** *Reader's Digest Book NZ Birds* 155 *Karearea, sparrowhawk, bush hawk, quail hawk, eastern falcon, southern falcon, bush falcon*... Since 1970 New Zealand falcons have had full legal protection but this has had little practical effect.

fall, *v.* [Brit. dial. *fall* to fell: see OED *fall v.* 51 c; EDD 10; AND 1793.] *trans.*

1. a. (*pa. ppl. fallen* or *falled, pres. ppl. falling*.) To fell (trees, bush).

1860 *Voices from Auckland* 67 Large quantities of bush have this season been 'fallen.' *Ibid.* 67 When to fall this bush? When to burn off? **1874** BAINES *Edward Crewe* 170 A bushman..entered into a contract with me to fall..200,000 feet of timber. **1882** HAY *Brighter Britain* I. 186 In felling bush, or 'falling' it, as we say out here, advantage is taken of the lay of the land. **1941** ALLEY & HALL *Farmer in NZ* 99 The bush was then felled, or 'falled'.

Hence **fallen** (occas. **falled**) *ppl. a.* [AND 1808], of trees or timber, cut down, felled; of bush land, cleared by the felling of trees.

1883 *Brett's Colonists' Guide* 18 Valuable trees..should..be..removed from the fallen bush before the fire. **1894** WILSON *Land of Tui* 93 Tonight we are to sleep true pioneer fashion, for this cottage is in the midst of a clearing, and the 'falled' timber is lying all round. **1915** MACDONALD *NZ Sheepfarming* 106 The fallen bush lands and some of the scrub lands have been surface sown in English grasses. **1986** RICHARDS *Off the Sheep's Back* 45 Each year after a new block of fallen bush had been burned off, we would have a wonderful harvest of cape gooseberries.

b. *transf.* To fell objects other than trees.

1911 *Truth* 22 July 6 Blue, Currie, and Littlecote were occupied in clearing the bricks away prior to removing the 'pins' to fall the wall.

2. To clear (land) by felling trees or bush.

1903 BAUGHAN *Reuben* 88 That bit o' bush paddock I falled myself. **1910** *Truth* 25 June 1 Can we not all admire the stout-hearted man who goes on to the bush, falls the land, and with sweat of his brow carves a home for himself and family out of the wilderness that's left?

FALL

fall, *n.*

1. [f. Brit. dial.: see OED *n.*¹ 14.] The process of felling trees; also, the trees or timber so cut down.

1849 in *Lett. from Otago* (1978) 13 Sept. 36 The trees are simply cut down... We have enclosed about 20 falls within the last two days, and will have all the area clear of wood tomorrow. **1899** BELL *In Shadow of Bush* 94 The axes had been ringing out cheerily from early morning, and the 'falls' had been frequent and far-sounding.

2. fall muster, the autumn muster, see MUSTER *n.* 2.

3. *Farming.* [AND *fall n.*² 1, 1888.] See quot. 1933. See also STOCKWHIP 1.

1933 *Press* (Christchurch) (Acland Gloss.) 14 Oct. 15 *Fall*... A plain strip of leather at the end of the lash of a whip to which the cracker is attached. **1940** [see CRACKER *n.*¹]. **1947** BEATTIE *Early Runholding* 42 The [bullock-driver's] whip was rawhide plaited sinnet, about six feet long, thick at the upper end..but tapering nearly to a point, to which was attached a narrow strip of rawhide, called 'the fall', finishing off with a twisted 'cracker' made of 'weetau' or dressed flax in place of whipcord.

4. *Gumdigging.* [Transf. from the usage of Brit. marl (*sc.* limey clay) diggers: see OED *n.*¹ 14 c.] A strip or wedge of gum-bearing ground split off in one piece by undermining the working face of an excavation.

1953 REED *Story of Kauri* 104 He purchased the land [c1900] and put a number of men on to it to take it down in 'falls' and remove the gum like a crop of potatoes.

falling, *vbl. n.* and *attrib.* [See *fall v.*1: AND 1792; US 1678.] (Pertaining to or used for) the felling of trees. Cf. BUSHFALLING *vbl. n.*

1819 MARSDEN *Lett. & Jrnls.* 4 Nov. (1932) 152 In consideration of Forty-eight Falling Axes to me [Hongi Hika] faithfully paid and delivered by The Reverend Samuel Marsden Clerke for and on behalf of the Church of England Missionary Society. **1866** MURRAY *Descr. Prov. Southland* 29 For the falling, splitting and cross-cutting of his posts and rails, he will find it again an advantage to get a mate. **1874** BAINES *Edward Crewe* 171 I am much amazed since my return to England to see 'woodmen' using such primitive and unserviceable 'falling-axes'. **1891** WALLACE *Rural Econ. Austral. & NZ* 232 Falling is done in winter, and burning off in the middle or end of summer.

faloose, falouse, varr. FELOOSE.

false bottom. *Mining.* [See OED *false a.* 17 a, 1881.] A bed of auriferous drift overlying a bed of non-auriferous drift which itself overlies a further auriferous drift layer immediately above bedrock. Cf. BOTTOM *n.*

1863 *AJHR D-6* 15 Referring to the existence of 'false bottoms', I attach a sectional diagram. **1896** MOFFATT *Adventures* (1979) 58 The wash was about six inches thick, lying on a false bottom, consisting of a thin layer of rusty cement, and under that thin white gravel [at Gabriel's Gully]. **1908** *NZGeol.SB (NS)* No.5 37 The basement rock is known to alluvial miners as 'reef bottom'; and the clays or other material interposed between the wash and the bed-rock as 'false bottom'. **1953** SUTHERLAND *Golden Bush* (1963) 84 In some places it was found that the original claims had been worked on a 'false' bottom of tough, stony clay. **1967** MAY *West Coast Gold Rushes* 195 False bottoms fooled even seasoned diggers, particularly at Kaniere. Claims considered worked out were frequently re-worked at a different level. **1983** NOLAN *Gold Fossicker's Handbook* 112 *False bottom*: a floor of compact clay or cemented material appearing to be the base of the alluvial deposit but beneath which lies a further, perhaps richer, deposit and the true bottom.

family. Special Comb. **family benefit** (also occas. **family allowance**) [see OED *family* 11: '*family-allowance*..in N.Z. called *family-benefit*', 1924], formerly, a payment made by the State to a parent or care-giver for the support of a child or children (see also DOMESTIC PURPOSES BENEFIT); **family court**, a court dealing with family law; **family po**, see FULL AS; **family shirker(s')** clause (section), see quots.

1950 JOSEPH *Imaginary Islands* 25 Live in a state house, raise forcibly-educated children Receive **family benefits**, and standard wages. **1959** SINCLAIR *Hist. NZ* 262 'Family benefits' were in 1938 paid only for the second and subsequent children of poor families; in 1946 they were given for the first child as well, in 1941 the means test was abolished and the—then—large sum of ten shillings was paid to the mother of every child under sixteen (or, in some cases, under eighteen) in the country. **1980** LELAND *Kiwi-Yankee Dict.* 39 Family Benefit. New Zealand pays its residents for having children. **1980** *Family Courts Act* s4 Establishment of **Family Courts**—Every District Court shall have a division, to be known as the Family Court. [**1916** *NZ Statutes* No.8 84 [Military Service Act] An Act to make Further Provision for the Raising and Maintenance of Expeditionary Forces during the Present War. *Ibid.* 96 [clause 35 (1)] If the Minister of Defence is satisfied with respect to any family that it consists of or includes two or more brothers who belong to the First Division of the Reserve, he may, at any time and from time to time after the enrolment of the First Division of the Reserve has been proclaimed and directed, give or cause to be given notice to all or any of those brothers to show cause before a Military Service Board why they should not be called up for service with the Expeditionary Force.] **1917** *Otago Witness* (Dunedin) 21 Mar. 38 The total number called up under the '**Family Shirker**' section (35) of the Military Service Act is 2851. **1919** *Hawera & Normanby Star* 14 July 8 Interesting details are available in reference to the operation of Clause 35 of the Expeditionary Force Act [see preceding quot.], popularly known as the '**Family Shirker**' Clause. When it was discovered that the clause was to come into operation, the Defence Department was flooded with names of alleged 'family shirkers'. **1939** BAXTER *We Will Not Cease* 10 Under the sub-clause in the Conscription Act, popularly known as the Family Shirkers' Clause, men belonging to families, no member of which had gone to the War, could be called up without having appeared in the ballot.

fan. [f. a resemblance in shape to that of a spread fan.]

1. *Geol.* [Used elsewhere but recorded first in NZ: see OED *n.*¹ 5 d.] A fan-shaped or cone-shaped deposit of alluvial shingle brought down when a river is in flood; a similar deposit or slip on a hillside (see quot. 1864). Cf. *shingle fan* (SHINGLE 3 b.)

1864 HAAST *Report on the Formation of the Canterbury Plains* 19 Dr Hector and myself..have adopted for the formation of those subaerial accumulations the expression 'Fan', for those of regular watercourses. **1874** *TrNZI* VI. 241 Extensive surveys.. made for railway and other purposes, have confirmed in a remarkable degree my views concerning the 'fan' character of the deposits of the principal rivers in every respect. **1885** *Ibid.* XVII. 352 Content with our day's walk, we camped on the large fan of Pass Creek. **1909** *Ibid.* XL. 38 [The Canterbury Plains] have been formed by the overlapping fans of great glacier streams. **1927** SPEIGHT *Natural History of Canterbury* 62 One word now universally accepted in geological literature, viz., 'fan', was first used by [Haast]. **1933** *Press* (Christchurch) (Acland Gloss.) 14 Oct. 15 *Fan.*—Hill creeks in Canterbury and Otago bring a lot of shingle down with them when they are in flood. On steep hillsides this shingle spreads on each side of the creek, narrow at the top and wide at the bottom. This natural feature is called a *f[an]*. **1988** DAWSON *Forest Vines to Snow Tussocks* 158 In the Cook Strait area the grey-leaved spaniard..is also a common plant on fans. **1992** SMITHYMAN *Auto/Biographies* 39 Ground water works out..gullies, to make a flat stream with fans.

2. A fan-shaped group of leaves, or clump, of the New Zealand flax, growing in the shape of a fan.

1930 *NZJST* XI. 274 During growth the young leaves arise from the centre of the [flax-]plants, so that the outer leaves of a 'fan' are the oldest. **1931** *Ibid.* XII. 165 Egg-laying is carried out during the night,... A favourite place is between the tree edges of leaves at the base of fans, where a single row may be inserted.

fancy-biscuit. [Spec. use of *fancy* 'ornamental' or 'fine' as distinct from 'plain'.] A superior kind of sweet biscuit.

c1940 at least, *fancy-biscuit* used in Marlborough and Wellington stores for the more elaborate and expensive 'sweet' biscuits. (Ed.) **1960** HILLIARD *Maori Girl* 76 She bought a bottle of soft-drink, tore the cake-bag down the seam and ate the fancy-biscuits for lunch.

fan mussel: see MUSSEL 2 (3).

fanny. [f. FAN(TAIL + -Y.] A familiar abbrev. and alteration of FANTAIL.

1875 *Richmond-Atkinson Papers* (1960) II. 399 I have also the mako-mako, silver-eye, riro-riro, miro-miro, fanny etc. **1967** NATUSCH *Animals NZ* 279 'Fanny'..is a well known and popular member of our bird fauna, flitting actively about with questing cries of 'tweet? tweet? tweet?', catching insects in mid air. **1994** LASENBY *Dead Man's Head* 130 I wonder if she'd [*sc.* a bantam] hatch out any eggs?.. Say a fanny's, or a grey warbler's.

fans. Also occas. **fangs.** [A var. of *fains*: see OED *fains*, 1879.] A children's truce or choosing word.

1966 TURNER *Eng. Lang. Austral. & NZ* 158 The way to ask for a truce in a game is to call *Pax*... At the school I went to, the word was *Fritz*, and the truce was terminated by the call *Fritz all over*, but we knew that some schools used *Fans* (from south-west English dialect *fainI* or *fainits*?). Apparently some New Zealand schools use or have used *baldy*, which sounds like a variant of English *barley*. **1983** *Listener* 5 Feb. 72 The commonest truce word in New Zealand seems to be 'fans' with a variant, 'fangs'.

fantail. [Poss. a shortened form of *fantail(ed) flycatcher*: AND 1827.]

[*Note*] North Island writers before c1840 prefer *piwaka(waka)* (Markham 1834, Yate 1835); early naturalists prefer FANTAILED (less often *fantail*) FLYCATCHER, or merely FLYCATCHER (q.v.); *fantail* as a popular name is attested from 1773 and was used by both Hutton (*Catalogue* 1871) and Buller (*Birds* 1873).

1. *Rhipidura fuliginosa* (fam. Muscicapidae) with subspecies in the North, South and Chatham Islands and black (mainly SI) and pied (mainly NI) phases, a small, friendly insectivorous bird of the bush and of domestic gardens, having a distinctive tail resembling a spread fan. See also FANNY, PIWAKAWAKA, TIWAKAWAKA.

1773 WALES *Journal* in Cook *Journals* (1961) II. 786 The last I shal [sic] mention is the Fan-Tail. Of these there are different sorts, but the body of the most remarkable one is scarce larger than a good Filbert, yet spreads a tail of most beautiful plumage full ¼ of a semi-circle, of, at least, 4 or 5 Inches radius. **1853** MACKIE *Traveller Under Concern* (1973) 96 The lively and elegant little fan tail was continually flitting about me spreading and erecting its tail. **1870** *TrNZI* II. 63 Piwakawaka. Fan-tail. The pied Flycatcher seems to prefer proximity to water in selecting its nesting-place. **1882** POTTS *Out in Open* 157 Towards autumn fantails frequent the verandahs, often enter the house, clearing the room of flies. **1910** GROSSMAN *Heart of Bush* 26 A dear little fantail, Piwakawaka, came fluttering from a ngaio tree. **1927** GUTHRIE-SMITH *Birds* 141 On calm July mornings parties of Fantails gather about their blossoming tops, fluttering and turning, diving and rising. **1948** *NZ Bird Notes* III. 3 We had an extraordinary visitation of fantails..when some 40 or 50 of them spent the day in a clump of gum trees near our stable. **1963** BAXTER *Collected Poems* (1980) 282 The trees rustle as October comes And fantails batter on the glass. **1985** *Readers' Digest Book NZ Birds* 280 By colonising man-made habitats the fantail may now be more abundant than when New Zealand was completely forested.

2. With a modifier: **black** (or **South Island**), **Chatham Island**, **pied** (or **North Island**).

(1) **black** (or **South Island**) **fantail**. *Rhipidura fuliginosa fuliginosa*, the black phase of the South Island fantail (see esp. quot. 1990).

1871 HUTTON *Catalogue Birds NZ* 15 Rhipidura tristis..Black Fantail. Tiwakawaka. **1885** *NZJSc.* II. 375 *Rhipidura fuliginosa...* Black Fantail, Black Flycatcher, Ti-waka-waka. **1904** HUTTON & DRUMMOND *Animals NZ* 79 *The Black Fantail. Tiwakawaka...* Found in both islands, but very rare in the North. **1923** *NZJST* VI. 91 Black Fantail. Remaining plentiful and widespread in the South Island, this species still occurs fairly frequently in the North Island. **1946** *JPS* LV. 156 *Pīwakawaka*, a bird (Rhipidura flabellifera), pied fantail: the so-called black fantail, which is chocolate-colour (R. fuliginosa), is tiwakawaka. The former is common throughout Newzealand [sic]; the latter is common in the South Island but rather rare in the North and is thought to be a mutant of the former. **1966** FALLA et al. *Birds NZ* 198 Fantail *Rhipidura fuliginosa...* Piwakawaka... Birds of normal colour pattern ('Pied Fantail') make up most of the population in North Island, but the 'Black Fantail' (i.e. dark phase) accounts for perhaps a quarter of the population of the South Island subspecies. **1985** *Reader's Digest Book NZ Birds* 280 *Fantail Rhipidura fuliginosa... Piwakawaka*, pied fantail, black fantail... South Island Fantail... R[hipidura] f. fuliginosa. **1990** *Checklist Birds NZ* 208 The species [*R. f. fuliginosa*] is dimorphic in the South Island, the proportion of the 'black' (melanistic) to 'pied' birds varying locally; melanism is rare in the North Island subspecies.

(2) **Chatham Island fantail**. *R. f. penita* (formerly *penitus*) of the Chatham, Pitt and South East Islands..

1955 OLIVER *NZ Birds* 494 *Chatham Island Pied Fantail...* The first record of the Pied Fantail in the Chatham Islands was that of H. H. Travers who lists it as being seen during his second visit to the group in 1868. **1985** *Reader's Digest Book NZ Birds* 280 *Chatham Island Fantail R. f. penitus*. **1990** *Checklist Birds NZ* 208 *Rhipidura fuliginosa penita..Chatham Island Fantail.*

(3) **pied** (or **North Island**) **fantail**. *R. f. placabilis*, the pied phase of the North Island fantail. See also PIWAKAWAKA and quot. 1990 of (1) above.

1871 HUTTON *Catalogue Birds NZ* 14 Rhipidura flabellifera... Pied Fantail. Piwakawaka. **1882** POTTS *Out in Open* 152 We find the flycatcher, of which there are here two species, namely, the pied fantail, *Rhipidura flabellifera*, called by the Maoris piwakawaka. **1895** ROBERTS *Southland in 1856* 53 The pied fantail, piwakawaka (Rhipidura flabellifera) is the best fly-catcher New Zealand possesses. **1904** HUTTON & DRUMMOND *Animals NZ* 77 *The Pied Fantail.—Tiwakawaka. Rhipidura flabellifera...* There are two species, and their habits are very much alike, so that what is said of the Pied Fantail may be applied to the Black Fantail. **1946** [see (1) above]. **1955** OLIVER *NZ Birds* 491 The North Island Pied Fantail was discovered at the Bay of Islands by Lesson, naturalist on the *Coquille* which visited New Zealand in 1824. **1966, 1985** [see (1) above].

3. a. *transf.* or *fig.* In Comb. **fantail crutch**, **fantail style**, applied to a method or style of crutching sheep.

1955 BOWEN *Wool Away* 53 The Fantail crutch, involving two positions, is physically harder, and in operation is slower. *Ibid.* One [method of crutching] is the old traditional method of coming in from the hock out to the tail, with the sheep turned the same way as in shearing. This is known as the Fantail style.

b. In the phr. **to have an appetite like a fantail**, to have a very slight appetite.

1964 HELMER *Stag Party* 83 I've got an appetite like a fantail, compared to some jokers I've seen.

fantailed flycatcher. *Obs.* Also **fantail flycatcher.** [AND 1841.] FANTAIL 1 (see also *Note*).

1773 FORSTER *Resolution Jrnl.* 28 Mar. (1982) II. 241 My Son had been on another party & had got the same Thrush & a little Fantailed Flycatcher likewise new. **1838** POLACK *NZ* I. 298 The *Piwaká-waká* is the Musicapa flabellifera, or fan-tailed fly-catcher. **1847** ANGAS *Savage Life* I. 326 Small birds, such as the fan-tailed fly-catcher..are also introduced into the [Maori] ear as ornaments. **1861** HAAST *Rep. Topogr. Explor. Nelson* 140 The fan-tailed flycatcher..and the New Zealand wren..both never tired of flying and hopping round the tents. **1879** *Auckland Weekly News* 5 July 15 Sydney Taiwhanga is a great humbug—or, as the Ngapuhi term him, *atiariraka* (the fantail flycatcher). **1883** *TrNZI* XV. 317 [The tui was] accompanied by a lively pair of fan-tail flycatchers. **1905** WHITE *My NZ Garden* 70 The tamest little bird we have is the Fantailed Fly-Catcher.

far, *a.* [Spec. use of *far* distant.] In special collocations, often with initial caps.: **the far north**, the (northern) north Auckland region; (northern) Northland; **the far south** the southernmost part of the South Island or the islands to the south of it.

1873 BULLER *Birds NZ* 59 The Red-fronted Parrakeet is..more plentiful in the southern portion of the North Island than in **the far north. 1889** WAKEFIELD *NZ after Fifty Years* 121 The far north of New Zealand, 'North of Auckland', as it is often familiarly called, even in official documents..is semi-tropical, and the people are like unto it. **1917** *Press* (Christchurch) 7 Feb. 8 The legend had long persisted in the South, and even near and in Auckland itself, that the Far North was more or less a waste of poor land, remarkable only for kauri gum, timber, Austrians, heat and roadlessness. **1924** *Free Lance* (Wellington) 28 May 13 They may take life more easily in our Far North..where frost seldom comes. **1939** GRIEVE *Sketches from Maoriland* (1961) 149 The people of the more frigid South have very little good to say for the almost tropical warmth of the 'Far North'. **1943** MARSH *Colour Scheme* 138 Of all the Maori clans living in this remote district of the far North, Rua's was the least sophisticated. **1957** GOLDBLATT *Democracy at Ease* 89 The writer spent his first night in New Zealand in a simple hotel in the Far North. **1970** THOMAS *Way Up North* 43 He told his audience that Houhora was in the far north where whales were caught in nets and oysters grew on trees. **1982** PEAT *Detours* 55 But the idea of the 'Far North' as a holiday destination, centering on Kaitaia, seems to have stuck. **1994** *Dominion* (Wellington) 24 Nov. 13 He was commenting..on a dispute between a Far North man and the department over a tangi grant. **1888** DOUGALL *Far South* [title page] **Far South**—Stewart Island, The Snares, Auckland, Campbell, Antipodes and Bounty Islands **1906** *TrNZI* XXXVIII. 340 A strange bird in Maori eyes is the *hakuai* of the off-shore islands in the far south. **1968** SEDDON *The Seddons* 177 Yes, these folk in the Far South were going to be dear friends of mine, and so they proved to be.

farewell, *v.* [Spec. use of *farewell* to take leave of, bid or say goodbye to: AND 1897.] *trans.* To formally honour (a person or group) on departure or retirement from a place, position, or organization.

1908 BARR *Brit. Rugby Team in Maoriland* 56 There were several..groups on..Dunedin's handsome railway station to 'farewell' the members of the British team. **1950** *NZ Post Office Eng. Course* (TS) 14 New Zealand has developed many phrases that depend on local interpretation: e.g. 'off the bitumen', 'motor camp', 'to farewell'. **1964** NORRIS *Settlers in Depression* 5 [He] was suitably farewelled when he left Hamilton a few months later. **1980** NEAVE *Land of Munros* 27 Mr Falloon spoke for those being farewelled. **1987** *Victoria Univ. Weekly Staff Circular* 13 Feb. On 22 February at 11 am the Victoria Child Care Centre is holding a party brunch at the Centre to farewell Maggie Haggerty... Please B.Y.O. and a plate of nibbles.

farewell, *n.* [f. FAREWELL *v.*: AND 1, 1880.] A formal gathering honouring a person's or group's departure or retirement.

1908 BARR *Brit. Rugby Team in Maoriland* 133 Dramatic Farewell Of Maoriland. **1968** SLATTER *Pagan Game* 172 The farewell under the stand, the half pies and the plates of tomato sauce, the jugs of beer. **1983** McELDOWNEY *Warm South* 38 Staff farewell and presentation..to Joy Smith, who leaves soon for a job in America.

farm.

1. a. [AND 1803.] As elsewhere, the term for an agricultural or 'mixed' landholding; in New Zealand use, a landholding smaller or less grand than that of a pastoral station.

1820 MARSDEN *Lett. & Jrnls.* 19 June (1932) 256 Some small farms were cultivated for potatoes, upon which the poor slaves were at work.

b. Used *attrib.* in special Comb. **farm bike**, a motor-cycle for farm use; **farm butter**, produced on or bought from a farm as distinct from factory-made, mass-produced, or shop-bought; **farm cadet**, see CADET *n.* 1 b; **farm yarder**, a wild or 'haymaker' punch.

1973 WHEELER *Hist. Sheep Stations NI* 92 But the happiest dog I saw on this trip was riding on the front of a **farm bike** with a shepherd. **1986** HULME *Windeater* 45 Two drovers behind the flock, one on a horse, the other on a farmbike, are pushing them hard. **1987** *Evening Post* (Wellington) 5 Aug. 24 *Farm bike 'obeys' whistle*... The Clinton farmer has an unusual problem with his Yamaha Bullfrog three-wheeled motorcycle.

FARMER

1951 Levy *Grasslands NZ* (1970) 337 There was no doubt about the unpleasantness of these feed flavours in the spring, particularly in home-made **farm butter**. 1966 Scott *Days That Have Been* 101 I would make beautiful yellow farm butter, for we had already purchased a churn. 1947 Brereton *No Roll of Drums* 136 Richards swung a **farm yarder** at him.

Hence **farmlet**, a small farm.
1962 Evans *Waikaka Saga* 175 Finally a large area [round Waikaka]..was declared a commonage... Between 1900 and 1914 this Commonage was cut up into farmlets varying from thirty to fifty acres. 1964 Morrieson *Came a Hot Friday* (1981) 51 Little wonder the dream of the farmlet still revisited him. 1979 *Otago Daily Times* (Dunedin) 28 Mar. 21 The new [Heinemann's] dictionary..does not contain..farmlet, fat (or sharp) sand, nor, amazingly, home-brew. 1986 Richards *Off the Sheep's Back* 108 Dolly's sister..had a small farmlet..where they milked a few cows.

2. *Spec.* an area where penguins gather.
1888 Dougall *Far South* 7 On the Snares the penguins are in what are called farms, that is to say in isolated groups, whereas on the Bounty Islands they are all over.

farmer.

1. [AND 1809.] In New Zealand usu. one following 'mixed' agricultural and pastoral farming, in earlier times often on a small holding. See also *mussel farmer* (mussel 3). Cf. cocky *n.*[1]
1814 Marsden *Lett. & Jrnls.* (1932) 122 He [Duaterra's half-brother] is every day at work either as a carpenter or farmer.

2. In special collocations: **farmer's butter**, *farm butter* (farm b); **farmers' jelly cake**, a 'custard' cake with no jelly in it.
1985 Hunt *I'm Ninety-five* 70 Factory butter was one and two a pound, separated **farmers' butter** one shilling a pound [c1910]. 1938 *Souvenir Book Cook. Recipes* 36 **Farmers' jelly cake**..eggs..milk..butter.. sugar..flour..soda..cream of tartar... Bake in meat dish.

far north, far south: see far *a.*

fart. Of the freq. various uses, the following, unrecorded elsewhere, may be locally distinctive.

1. In various phr.: **a. as low as** (or **lower than**) **a coal-miners' fart** (occas. **arsehole**), said of a contemptible person or behaviour.
1941 St. Patrick's College, Silverstream (Ed.). He's as low as a coalminer's fart—and that's underground.

b. to be worse than a (two-bob) fart in a bottle; **to be not worth a fart in a bottle**, etc., to be of no value.
1981 *Avondale College Slang Words* (Auckland) (Goldie Brown Collect.) *worse than a 2-bob fart in a bottle*: no good

c. pissed as a fart, very drunk.
1971 Shadbolt *Bullshit & Jellybeans* 85 Yah should seen him knocking back those half Gs. Pissed as a fart..spewed his ring out. 1985 *Landfall* 156 499 'Where's he?' 'Pissed as a fart on the kitchen floor!' said Phyllis coldly.

2. fart-arsing *vbl. n.*, messing around.
1982 Shadbolt *Once on Chunuk Bair* (1990) 49 You still fart-arsing? MAC: We're doing our best.

3. Special Comb. **fart-sack** (also **farter**), a trampers' or Army term for a sleeping-bag or (occas.) a bed.
1982 Holden *Wild Pig* 45 'What about that fart-sack of yours, huh?' 'What's wrong with my sleeping bag?' Stan retorted.

fast, *a.* and *adv.* Whaling. [OED *fast* 4 e, 1820.] In the phr. **to get (make) fast**, to make a successful harpoon strike of a whale; also *adj.*, of a whale, to be harpooned. See also fasten *v.*
1836 *Piraki Log* 14 May (1911) 35 2 mate got fast but was obliged to cut in consequence of receiving a blow from the whales flukes. 1968 Johnson *Turn of Tide* 23 Here the *Crescent* made fast and killed but the whale sank and the gunsman was forced to cut. 1982 Morton *Whale's Wake* 232 The Australians, like the British in the Arctic whaling industry, insisted that the whaleboat must be 'fast'. That is, if the harpoon struck a whale and remained there with the line attached to both the whale and the boat, the whale was immediately to be considered a 'fast fish' and the property of the party wich first secured it in that fashion.

fasten, *v.* Whaling. Also **fasten on** (or **to**). *quasi-trans.* and *absol.* To successfully harpoon (a whale).
1831 Bell *Let.* in McNab *Old Whaling Days* (1913) 10 It is a pity that it should often be necessary to fasten to the calf in order to secure the cow, but I do not apprehend that it will cause such a diminution of numbers as to injure the fishing. 1838 *Piraki Log* 28 Apr. (1911) 71 Two Boats were dispatched to a Whale the Iron drew and we lost her. *Ibid.* 21 May 73 Saw a large Whale which was in chase best part of the day, but she was so Galeyed we had no chance of fastening. 1905 Baucke *White Man Treads* 75 When the whale had been struck 'and fastened on', [the boat-steerer] went aft and steered the boat. 1982 Grady *Perano Whalers* 226 *Fasten*—To successfully harpoon a whale. 1982 Morton *Whale's Wake* 35 'Harpoon' was occasionally used in the logs and journals. See *Huntress*, 12 August 1836, for the use of the verb; 'the 2nd Mate harpooned one'. This is the only case encountered in logs which the word 'struck' or 'fastened' was replaced with 'harpooned', although *Rosalie*, 2 August 1827, had used the noun 'harpoons' and *Sharon*, 3 July 1843, used 'harpoon'.

fat, *a.*[1] [Spec. use of *fat* fattened (for slaughter).] [*Note*] The word 'prime' is now preferred in reference to the sale of stock.

1. a. Of stock, in prime condition and ready for slaughter.
1849 in Deans *Pioneers Canterbury* (1937) 159 We can import lean cattle..which would be fat and fit for the butcher by the time the settlers arrive. 1866 *Lyttelton Times* 28 June 2 A Fat Lot.—We hear that a sale of 2000 wethers..was made..the sheep averaging 62¼lbs in weight. c1875 Meredith *Adventuring in Maoriland* (1935) 95 Practically all the stock [*sc.* sheep] on the runs in New Zealand is fat; and, as there is an over-supply for consumption, squatters are forced to turn their fat stock into money by boiling them down for their tallow. 1902 *Settler's Handbook NZ* 94 If these sheep are well done to when hoggets they can be turned off fat, good weights and excellent mutton, at about twenty to twenty-two months. 1974 *NZ Agric.* 59 The products from this type of farm are wool, some store lambs, a few fat wether lambs..varying numbers of store or fat wethers.

b. In the phr. **as fat as mud** (also as **mud-fat**), applied to prime beasts in peak condition.
1947 Beattie *Early Runholding* 44 When the cattle were in prime condition they were described [in the 1860s] as being 'as fat as mud'. 1973 Wallace *Generation Gap* 197 Eight hundred [hoggets] were sold mud-fat and the rest were disposed of later on.

2. In collocations with the names of animals indicating prime condition: **fat cattle** (**sheep, stock**) [OED *fat a.* 14, 1880].
1847 in Deans *Pioneers Canterbury* (1937) 113 As soon as I get down to Port Cooper I have to take up

FAT

thirty head of **fat cattle**..to Port Nicholson. 1853 Deans *Pioneers* (1964) 82 I sold some fat cattle and bullocks for draught at £15 each. 1924 *Free Lance* (Wellington) 28 May 5 There was an exceptionally heavy yarding of fat cattle at Westfield yards last week. 1943 *NZJST* XXIV. 200A *Fattening-farms*.—Marketable products: Fat lambs, fat sheep, wool, fat cattle. 1902 *Settler's Handbook NZ* 96 There are other estates partly cultivated, and growing half-breds, where stores and **fat sheep** provide half the gross profits. 1848 Deans *Pioneers* (1964) 49 The prices for **fat stock** at Port Nicholson are falling fast. 1851 Weld *Hints to Intending Sheep-farmers* 6 He will be guided by the accessibility of some shipping port where he may dispose of his fat stock. c1875 [see 1 a above]. 1902 *Settler's Handbook NZ* 22 Year by year the imports of potatoes, fruits, butter, and fat stock are decreasing, owing to increased local production. 1914 Pfaff *Diggers' Story* 89 The fat stock of Westland is another adjunct to our pastoral wealth, and the district now turns out some of the primest beef. 1936 *Agric. Organiz. NZ* 427 Fat-stock farms of the highest efficiency are situated on land of high fertility.

3. fat lamb. a. A prime lamb ready for slaughter, usu. to be exported as frozen meat.
1891 Wallace *Rural Econ.* 369 Any of the various breeds and crosses now in the country will supply suitable mothers for fat lambs provided they are good milkers. 1894 *NZ Official Year-book* 304 It is to be hoped that before long the rearing of fat lambs will be looked upon as quite a distinct branch of sheep-farming. 1902 *Settler's Handbook NZ* 96 There are..highly cultivated properties within easy distances of the freezing-factories, where fat lambs are grown on rape, turnips, and clover. 1915 Macdonald *NZ Sheepfarming* 23 It..is a good breed where fat lambs are the aim. 1937 Ayson *Pioneering Otago* 101 The fat lambs brought about nine shillings per head. 1953 Scott *Breakfast at Six* 17 I don't go in for fat lambs right through. Like to breed my own ewe-hoggets. 1975 Newton *Sixty Thousand on the Hoof* 214 It [*sc.* Nokomai Station] is a fat-lamb proposition.

Hence, of lambs, **to go fat**, to achieve the status of 'fat lamb'.
1973 Newton *Big Country SI* (1977) 16 Over the last few years the lambing has averaged over 120 per cent..and half the surplus lambs go fat off the mothers at better than 30 pounds.

b. Used *attrib.* in Comb. **fat-lamb buyer, farm, farming, producer, raising, trade**.
1945 *NZJST* XXVI. 62 All lambs were picked for slaughter by a **fat-lamb buyer** as in normal commercial practice. 1943 *NZJST* XXIV. 201A On **fat-lamb farms** the bulk of the lambs are sold before the seasonal growth is fully advanced. 1962 Sharpe *Country Occasions* 43 [Heading] First Fat Drive... After long, anxious conversations with the local fat lamb buyer..the farmer fixes a day for the dispatch of a first draft to the works. 1950 Coop *Shearing Ewes before Lambing* 5 Shearing on fat-lamb farms is often delayed until the first draft of lambs is taken. 1974 *NZ Agric.* 15 [Caption] Right: *Fat-lamb farming on the flat land in western Otago* 1912 Rutherford *Impressions NZ Pastoralist on Tour* 83 If I may venture to offer a suggestion to our **fat lamb producers**, it is that they should dock their lambs shorter than they do now. c1927 Smith *Sheep & Wool Industry* 50 **Fat-lamb Raising**. The industry of raising lambs for the export trade and home consumption. 1951 Levy *Grasslands NZ* (1970) 205 In the summer irrigation could play a very much greater part in many dairying and fat-lamb-raising districts. 1913 *NZJAg.* Jan. VI. 275 For the purely early **fat-lamb trade** the Southdown is unsurpassed. 1936 *Agric. Organiz. NZ* 710 Lambs of the fine wool breeds of the South Island and lambs reared for the fat lamb trade are seldom shorn.

fat, *a.*² In the phr. **fat show**, always ironically used (cf. 'fat lot', 'fat chance': OED *fat a.* 10 c) implying no show or chance at all. Also as an interjection.
   1948 BALLANTYNE *Cunninghams* (1963) 63 It would be corker if he could go outside with Carole Plowman... Fat show! **1988** MCGILL *Dict. Kiwi Slang* 45 *fat show* little or no chance, or 'fat chance' (used in America too); eg 'Fat show we've got of making the finals.'

fat, *n.*¹ [AND 1888: also Brit. dial.: see EDD *fat n.*² 5, 1756.] Usu. *pl.* A prime lamb or cattle-beast ready for slaughter.
   1907 KOEBEL *Return of Joe* 20 The only different thing you'll see, I hope, will be a larger mob of fats. **1922** PERRY *Sheep Farming* 69 Under favourable conditions a good percentage of the lambs can be sold as fats off the mothers. **1948** SCOTTER *Run Estate & Farm* 36 [Prices] were reported [in the *Mail* 17 March 1909] as good; ten and sixpence..for stud..rams and lambs at 'fat' prices—8/- to 13/7. **1953** DUFF *Shepherd's Calendar* (1961) 116 For eight years I have done nothing but cook and wash up..listen to dull talk about fats and stores, or put up with being ignored. **1978** HAYES *Toss of a Coin* 111 Rape was now being grown, and lambs fattened on it could be sold as fats and not as stores. **1992** *Dominion* (Wellington) 11 Dec. 9 [Mangaweka sale] Fats:.. fat lambs $36–$43, fat ewes $30–$33..two-tooth cryptorchids $58–$60.

fat, *n.*² [f. *fat* affluent: AND 1906.] The wealthy section of the community, or a wealthy man, regarded as greedy and self-interested; occas. used as a name (**Mr Fat, Harry Fat, Fatman** [AND 1893] or **fat pigeon**) for a wealthy man.
   1904 *NZ Observer* 16 Jan. 16 He was one of the 'fat pigeons' whom the commercial law was not meant to protect. **1905** *Truth* 16 Sept. 1 At an Auckland Chamber of Commerce meeting a representative of fat proposed that he and his fellow fats [etc.]. **1909** *Ibid.* 29 May 7 They can't darn well help themselves, for shicker is as scarce as Fatmen in the heavenly orchestra. **1911** *Maoriland Worker* 15 Dec. 7 It was these same men who were called upon to give evidence on behalf of 'Fat'. **1912** *Dominion* (Wellington) 15 Mar. 2 These farmers are described by these 'gilded gentlemen', when speaking to other constituents, as the 'fat man', their born and natural enemy. **1956** BAXTER *Collected Poems* (1980) 161 Said Harry Fat, 'If you will take A business man's advice—Tell me a voter's income And I'll tell you his price.'

fat, *n.*³ [f. *fat* distended: AND 1967.] A (sexual) erection, esp. in the phr. **to crack a fat**, to have an erection.
   1985 O'SULLIVAN *Shuriken* 21 Like the stuff they put in your tea in the last one [*sc.* war]. Stop you cracking a fat at the front. **1988** MCGILL *Dict of Kiwi Slang* 31 *crack a fat*, a male erection and/or ejaculation. **1990** O'SULLIVAN *Snow in Spain* 71 [*sic*] she didn't know much else she said except taking her clothes off that was the trouble, grinding her bum so the wankeroos had themselves a free fat.

fat, *v.* Rabbiting. *trans.* and *intr.* To scrape the fat off (a rabbit skin).
   1959 MCLEOD *Tall Tussock* 107 One night we sat fatting skins by the fire. We'd had a good kill of rabbits that day. **1965** MACNICOL *Skippers Road* 48 After I would help to pick up and skin the rabbits. After tea..Archie would 'fat' while I wired. **1970** MCLEOD *Glorious Morning* 65 We..found quite a number of rabbits, which we skinned and then fatted and wired the skins... You had to scrape the fat off each skin with a pocket knife.

Hence **fatting** *vbl. n.*, the removing of fat from rabbit skins.
   1953 STRONACH *Musterer on Molesworth* 61 Here is done the most unpleasant part of the job—the 'fatting' of the skin. On the flanks beside the tail and under the 'armpits' are deposits of fat, and these must be removed. **1965** MACNICOL *Skippers Road* 48 Fatting, wiring, and packing [rabbit skins] were some of the jobs I took on.

fattening, *ppl. a.* Of land or country, used with reference to producing prime stock, esp. as **fattening country** or **farm**; of animals, denoting the ability to be fattened as prime stock.
   1915 MACDONALD *NZ Sheepfarming* 30 Supplying a good stamp of store sheep for the better and more fattening lowland country. **1943** *NZJST* XXIV. 200A *Fattening-farms*.—Marketable products: Fat lambs, fat sheep, wool, fat cattle. **1951** CRESSWELL *Canterbury Tales* 57 Crossed by the Leicester or Lincoln, the half-bred progeny was disappointing in size and fattening quality. **1960** SCRYMGEOUR *Memories Maoriland* 162 I leave to-morrow for Fielding [*sic*] to attend a sheep sale there, and may pick up some suitable fattening lambs. **1974** *NZ Agric.* 61 [Heading] Fattening Farms. These farms are on flat or undulating land that is highly fertile. *Ibid.* 63 Some large holdings contain both hill country and the lower 'fattening' type of land. **1993** *Dominion* (Wellington) 30 Apr. 11 Gisborne: Six sales, including three fattening farms that together fetched $2.8 million.

Hence **fattener**, a farmer who specializes in producing fat stock.
   1960 SCRYMGEOUR *Memories Maoriland* 160 Gradually introduced at the rival saleyards to many dealers, fatteners, lamb raisers, and other likeable 'sons of the soil'.

favourable country: see COUNTRY 2 d.

fear: see NO FEAR.

feather. [f. *feather* farthing.] In negative phrases **not to have a feather to fly with**, **not to have a feather left**, to be broke or penniless.
   1908 *Truth* 21 Nov. 5 If Sandow when he struck Hastings didn't have a flag to fly, he likewise didn't have a feather to fly with, and it is no doubt because of his deplorable state of impecuniosity that he contracted to pay 'Milky' a fiver a week. **1937** LEE *Civilian into Soldier* 101 I haven't a feather left.

feather-box. [f. a paraphrase of Ma. *waka (huia)*.] WAKA HUIA, a box for holding (huia) feathers.
   1963 *Dominion* (Wellington) 4 Sept. 1 A Maori treasure box perhaps a century old has been presented to the Dominion Museum in Wellington. 'Called a wakahuia, the box is a type commonly referred to as a "feather-box",' said Dr T. Barrow, keeper of the Maori and Pacific collection.

feather out, *v.* Goldmining. [f. *feather* to extend in feathery form + (*peter*) *out*: see OED *v.* 8.] Of a lead or vein, to extend in a feathery manner, growing wider and thinner, sometimes eventually petering out to nothing. Also as a *vbl. n.*
   1907 *NZGeol.SB (NS)* No.4 120 Throughout a distance of 800ft from the mouth of the drive these crosscuts show the vein to have an average width of 40ft, but from here southward a gradual 'feathering out' longitudinally is apparent. **1912** *Ibid.* No.15 79 It is noteworthy that the reefs did not persist up to the surface, but feathered out in the breccias.

Featherston Street farmer. *Wellington.* [f. *Featherston Street* in the Wellington business district.] A city businessman owning a farm as an investment. Cf. *Queen Street farmer* (QUEEN STREET 2).
   1972 *Dominion* (Wellington) 9 Aug. 1 Other people involved as 'Featherston Street farmers', in syndicates of more than six people in such things as farms and kiwifruit horticultural units, are also liable for big tax bills when they want to sell these properties. **1992** *Dominion Sunday Times* (Wellington) 27 Sept. 18 To others, such as the Queen, Featherston and Cashel St farmers of the late seventies and early eighties, [rural property] seemed to offer a gilt-edged investment propped up with taxpayer support.

feathery grass, tutu: see GRASS 2 (16), TUTU 2 (2).

federal: see RED FEDERAL.

feed, *n.*

1. [Spec. or transf. use of *feed* a meal; fodder.] A solid, heavy or satisfying meal. Cf. BINDER *n.*¹
   1840 BEST *Journal* Apr. (1966) 216 [Kororareka] boasts a very respectable club, who gave us a great feed. **1871** MONEY *Knocking About NZ* 40 After an astonishing feed on wood-hens and fern-root, they curled themselves up..and fell asleep. **1883** FERGUSON *Castle Gay* 177 And that by men [*sc.* shepherds] so much in need Was well pronounced 'a glorious feed'. **1905** *Truth* 26 Aug. 4 A weeks hard graft at the wash-tub..with three good feeds a day thrown in. **1936** HYDE *Passport to Hell* 49 Starkie provided his brother with a good feed: corn-cakes, fried vegetables mashed up with tinned salmon, floury scones, and the bacon crisp. **1949** *Here & Now* Oct. 31 I'll go up..and have some beers with the boys and talk about the footy and afterwards we'll have a bonzer feed at the Greek's on Seddon Street. **1953** SUTHERLAND *Golden Bush* (1963) 32 No, he didn't want a feed, he said; he's just got up from an 'almighty binder'. **1985** HUNT *I'm Ninety-five* 29 Those blokes were..a bit lazy when it came to cooking up a feed.

2. Farming. [f. Brit. dial. or provincial English *feed* (or *feed pasture*) fodder: cf. EDD 8 b; AND 1847.] Green grass as fodder for livestock.
   1853 ROCHFORT *Adventures of Surveyor* 24 We walked on..to Captain D—'s station, which is one of the best..a large open plain covered with good feed. **1860** BUTLER *Forest Creek MS* (1960) 48 There is no feed on this side of the creek at present—it was burnt..and the grass will not grow again till Spring. **1874** KENNAWAY *Crusts* 140 Though there was still feed for the stock, the whole face of the country was dried and parched. **1898** REEVES *Long White Cloud* 403 [On New Zealand speech.] Pasture is 'feed', herd and flock alike become 'mob'. **1939** BROWN *Farmer's Wife* 21 The 80 ewes and lambs appear to be making..no impression on the feed. **1950** *NZJAg.* Oct. LXXXI. 349 A wool-blind sheep is seriously hampered on run country in its search for feed. **1964** ANDERSON *Doctor in Mountains* (1974) 30 You may have been the last person out in a certain paddock, and may be asked, how's the feed? meaning, grass. **1984** MARSHALL *Day Hemingway Died* 20 'We could do with rain all right,' he said. 'I won't get a strike with any feed crops otherwise.'

3. Special Comb. **feed room** [OED *feed* 7 '*U.S.* and *N.Z.*', 1887], a room in which food for livestock is stored (occas. **feed-shed**, an outbuilding in which such food is stored).
   1907 *Levin & Co. Papers 1347* (ATLMS) 15 May in *Alfredton* (1987) 99 6 stalled stable, with feedroom and loosebox. **1939** MANSFIELD *Scrapbook* 2 Every morning I went across to the feed-room where he cleaned father's boots.

feed, v.

1. trans. To lay out non-poisonous bait on (a poison block) to accustom the target animal to bait-taking.
 1946 MILLER *There Was Gold* 130 One professional poacher I heard of used to watch a rabbiter 'feed' his block—that is, to cut up pieces of carrot along the intended poison lines so that the rabbits would get used to the feed before the strychnine was applied—and then, after two feeds, he would step in one night ahead of the rabbiter with his own poison and make a kill. 1953 STRONACH *Musterer on Molesworth* 60 The rabbits are then 'fed'. Carrots, cut with a knife, or minced, or even cut up in a box with a spade, are scattered along the furrow, or 'line'... The feeding is usually done three times, and the rabbits eat up the carrot each time. On the fourth night the poison is laid. 1973 NEWTON *Big Country SI* (1977) 56 The area to be poisoned is first 'fed' twice with straight oats and then poisoned.

2. *Farming*. As **feed out**, to distribute hay or other stock-food.
 1959 *NZ Dairy Exporter* July 39 He was convinced that..the best thing was 'to put on a lot of stock so the paddocks..would be eaten out, and then feed out..as soon as possible'.

feeder. [Spec. (and poss. obsolete) uses of *feeder* a person who feeds material to a machine, mill, etc.] **a.** *Goldmining*. One who feeds ore to the stampers.
 1875 *Official Handbook NZ* 259 [Wages on goldfields] bracemen..8/4, feeders..6/-.

b. *Farming*. One who feeds sheaves into a threshing mill.
 1962 EVANS *Waikaka Saga* 273 On this mill he worked as a straw-walloper on the straw-stack, forker on the sheaf-stack, feeder on the mill, and later as cook. 1971 [see CHAFFIE].

c. *Flaxmilling*. One who feeds flax blades to a stripper.
 1913 CARR *Country Work* 43 When the flax arrives at the mill it is weighed and credited to the cutter. The 'bench loader' then takes two or three bundles and puts them in a barrel (heavy end down). He then takes the longest leaves and places them on a bench convenient to the 'feeder'. *Ibid.* 44 The 'feeder' takes each blade separately and places the butt end into the 'stripper' which takes the green outer covering off.

feetou, feetow, varr. WHITAU.

feggie, var. WHEKE

feijoa. /fɪˈdʒuːə/, /ˈfiːˌdʒuːə/. [f. the name of João da Silva *Feijo* (1760–1824), a Brazilian engineer and naturalist: used elsewhere but of commercial significance in NZ; OED, 1898.] *Feijoa sellowiana* (fam. Myrtaceae), a South American evergreen shrub, widely cultivated commercially in New Zealand for its edible, greenish fruit; the fruit of the feijoa.
 1949 *Southern Cross* (Wellington) 20 May 8 Feijoas make very pretty specimen trees... You should not eat a feijoa until it falls on the ground of its own accord. 1954 WINKS *These New Zealanders* 80 [Excellent], too, are the wide variety of strange fruits which New Zealand gets from other members of the Commonwealth and which are rarely seen in America: Chinese gooseberries, feijoas..etc. 1965 GILLHAM *Naturalist in NZ* 237 There were guavas, figs, grapes, feijoas..and [the] fruit-salad plant. 1979 FRAME *Living in the Maniototo* 24 The kindly back garden with citrus trees and feijoas and guavas and the peach tree, let it [sc. a smell] be absorbed into the earth. 1982 BURTON *Two Hundred Yrs. NZ Food* 146 A native of South America, the feijoa is grown in many parts of the world only as an ornamental plant. Favourable conditions in New Zealand, however, produce sizeable fruit of considerable commercial and culinary potential. 1991 VIRTUE *Always the Islands of Memory* 135 She baked a banana cake and then a Pavlova and covered it with tinned feijoa slices and cream and sprinkled hundreds and thousands over that.

fella: see FELLOW.

fellow. In altered forms **fella** /ˈfelə/ (mainly among adolescents), and **fulla** (**ful**) /ˈfʌlə/ (/fʌl/) (often in representations of Maori or gang-related speech), a form of address or reference to peers (not, as OED, 'affected or vulgar', or necessarily or usually with derogatory connotations). Cf. YOUSE. **a.** As **fella**.
 1951 15 M 9 St Bede's, Chch 29 [M3] Fella 1953 13–15 M A1 Thames DHS 11 [M18] Fella 1978 MANTELL *Murder in Fancydress* 135 'Then got a blanket. Coupla books. By then all the fellas gone. Day-shift jokers, y'know. So goodoh to beaut there [sunbathing].' 1984 14–18 M E77 Pakuranga Coll. 28 [M4 F2] Fella

b. As **fulla**.
 1972 IHIMAERA in *Some Other Country* (1984) 161 Yes, I know you fullas, she [sc. a Maori grandmother] grumbled. 1985 *Women's Work* 223 'Howzat you fullas?' but the girls were already conferring and Charlotte [a Maori girl] was enraged. 1988 *More* (Auckland) Mar. 30 This sort of banter goes on all the time in shearing gangs..probably helps the young fullas from chucking it all in.

feloose /fəˈluːs/. WW1 & WW2 (Egypt). Also **faloose, falouse, filoose, fils.** [f. Arabic: cf. Partridge 8.] Money.
 1917 *Chron. NZEF* 5 Sept. 32 W.M.R. consoled themselves by securing the largest amount of 'filoose' through their win. 1918 *Kia Ora Coo-ee* 15 Oct. 13 I come now to a word which is among the first..that foreigners in Egypt learn—I mean *fils*, which is the Arabic word for money. 1942 *NZEF Times* 27 Oct. 6 [Heading] Johnny Enzed says..'Mafeesh Falouse'. *Ibid.* 7 Dec. 6 Just telling them about things... Explaining the shortness of faloose and all that. c1945 *Sixes & Sevens* (Troopship pub.) 7 'What are you going to use for feloose?'... 'I'll be living on my gratuity... Plus the odd acker from my grateful grandsons.'

fence, n.¹ [Not exclusively NZ, but of particular relevance to pioneer farming history ('Bad fences make bad neighbours'): cf. OED 5.]

1. a. A barrier of any of a variety of materials which either protects or demarcates (typically a *boundary fence*) or encloses an area of land. Often used or combined with a modifier which distinguishes the composition or purpose. For mainly pioneer New Zealand fence types (excluding straight-wire fences), see *boundary fence* (BOUNDARY 3), *bush-fence* (BUSH C 3 c), DITCH AND BANK, DOG-LEG, *pig-fence* (PIG n.¹ 4), POST-AND-RAIL, POST AND STAKE, RING FENCE, *scrub fence* (SCRUB n. 1 c), *snow-fence* (SNOW n.¹ 3), *sod fence* (SOD), STAB FENCE, STAKE FENCE, STONE FENCE, STUB FENCE, TAIEPA. See also RABBIT-PROOF *a*.
 1933 *Press* (Christchurch) (Acland Gloss.) 14 Oct. 15 *Fence*.—(1) I suppose a *f[ence]* is strictly a made *f[ence]* of wire or rails, and a hedge a growing *f[ence]*, but nine country people out of ten speak of a *gorse f[ence]*.

b. Special Comb. **fence-line**, the line along which a fence runs or may run; a boundary.
 1951 LEVY *Grasslands NZ* (1970) 245 Fencing was expensive, particularly where heavy timber had to be cleared from the fence line. 1984 BOYD *City of the Plains* 28 The fence line was somewhere near present day Charles Street.

2. In various phr. **a.** *Sheep-droving.* **between the fences**, on a road or highway (while droving).
 1949 NEWTON *High Country Days* 114 [The drovers] were now 'between the fences', and would travel by back roads.

b. to give the fence a run, to act as an aroused bull about to leap the fence into the heifer paddock to fulfil sexual urges (see also *fence-jumping* 3 below).
 1976 MCCLENAGHAN *Travelling Man* 21 'There's one or two good-looking housemaids here'... 'Thinking of giving the fence a run'... 'And so are you if I know anything.'

c. over the fence [AND 1918], shameless (of a person), scandalous; greedy, very unreasonable.
 1937 PARTRIDGE *Dict. Slang* 271 *fence, over the.* (Of a person) unashamed, scandalous; greedy; very unreasonable: New Zealanders' coll. variation (late C. 19-20) of S.E. *beyond the pale*. Perhaps ex local rules for cricket ['over the fence is six and out'].

3. Special Comb. **fence-breaker** [used elsewhere but recorded earliest in NZ], an animal which breaks through fences; **fence dog** *hist.*, *boundary dog* (BOUNDARY 3); **fence-jumping** (*transf.* from bull-paddock use), a fortuitous intermingling of gene-stock.
 1878 ELWELL *Boy Colonists* 218 He knew [where] Geddes' old horse, our old friend the **fence-breaker**, was feeding. 1904 *NZ Illustr. Mag.* July 278 With the ghost of a departed bark the old **fence dog** shambled out, as he became aware of my approach. 1992 *Dominion* (Wellington) 29 Aug. 9 The population..is mainly Inuit Greenlanders with mongoloid features, pale brown skin and black hair, but there has been much **fence-jumping** during the past 300 years and the resulting mix has produced attractive people.

fence, n.² [Poss. connected with EDD *fence* v.² (Cumberland) To mess about with water; to let it slop from side to side.] Ginger beer mixed with alcoholic liquor. Cf. *shandygaff.*
 1859 HIGGINS *Letters* (Hocken MS) 23 Feb. (6) Fence of any kind is ginger beer mixed with the other spirit so that [there] is port fence, Rum fence, sherry fence and stone fence, which is brandy and ginger beer.

fencer.

1. [Not exclusively NZ but of special significance in rural usage: recorded earliest in Australia; AND 1827.] A skilled workman employed to erect or mend (farm) fences. Often as **contract fencer**, one who works by contract.
 1850 *Rep. Auckland Agric. Society* 13 Apr. in Swainson *Auckland* (1853) 140 He is also a very good fencer, and an excellent helper in the garden. 1880 CHUDLEIGH *Diary* 12 Oct. (1950) 291 Took a final walk to the contract fencers and pointed out the lines of deposit to the carters and departed for Hamilton. 1909 THOMPSON *Ballads About Business* 62 Fossicker, fencer, rouseabout, and rabbiter he'd been, From Riversdale to Naseby every hamlet he had seen. 1933 *Press* (Christchurch) (Acland Gloss.) 14 Oct. 15 *Fencer.*—Man employed to erect and mend *f[ence]s*. 1982 HOLDEN *Wild Pig* 43 Sometimes they'd share [the hut] with a fencer or musterer. 1991 *Dominion* (Wellington) 9 Feb. 9 Men of their generation..now judge or coach younger contract fencers.

2. A sheep given to escaping through fences.
1951 Duff *Shepherd's Calendar* (1961) 23 I bought her [an old ewe] in the sale-yards with other odds and ends, and she was in charge in twenty-four hours. Fortunately she is not a fencer.

Fencibles. *Hist.* [Short for *defensible*: see OED A 5 'belonging to the corps called *Fencibles*', 1795; B 'a soldier liable only for defensive service at home'.]

a. Also **(Royal) New Zealand Fencibles**. See quot. 1922. See also pensioner, *military settler* (settler 1 c).
1846 Earl Grey to Governor Grey in La Roche *Hist. Howick & Pakuranga* 24 Nov. (1991) 56 In my Despatch No. 4 of this date, I have apprised you that Her Majesty's Government have determined upon raising for service in New Zealand a corps which will receive the designation of the Royal New Zealand Fencibles. *Ibid.* 58 The greater part at least of the Fencibles should..be established as near to Auckland as may be practicable. **1847** Grahame *Letter* 23 Nov. in Power *Sketches in NZ* (1849) 283 I have been compelled to employ [natives] at all kinds of work,—in rafting timber for the erection of cottages for the New Zealand Fencibles. **1848** Wakefield *Handbook NZ* 376 During the year 1847..about 500 veteran out-pensioners, constituted into a regiment of *New Zealand Fencibles*, have been sent to Auckland at public expense, with their wives and families. **1922** Cowan *NZ Wars* (1955) I. 450 The corps known as the Royal New Zealand Fencibles..was a body of veteran soldiers converted into military settlers, established through Governor Grey's efforts as a protection for the southern frontier of the Auckland Settlement. It consisted of discharged British soldiers, about three-fourths of them pensioners, and all men of approved character and physique. The corps was enrolled in England in 1847. The term of service in New Zealand was to be seven years (most of the soldiers became permanent settlers). On arrival in the colony each Fencible was given possession of a two-roomed cottage and an acre of land... The members of the corps were required to attend six days' drill in the spring and six in autumn, and to attend church parade every Sunday, fully armed, for inspection... The settlements in which the pensioners were established were Onehunga, Otahuhu, Panmure, and Howick; these places were practically founded as villages by the Fencibles. **1963** Norris *Armed Settlers* 36 After Hone Heke's rebellion..in 1845, military settlements to provide a bulwark between Auckland and the Maoris had been established, at Onehunga, Otahuhu, Howick and Panmure. These settlers were military pensioners, called 'Fencibles' and their villages were to form a ring of husbandmen trained to the use of arms; a self-supporting guard. **1983** Buckley *Of Toffs & Toilers* 143 The first families [of military settlers] reached Auckland in August 1847 on the *Ramilies* from Tilbury... Known as the 'Fencibles'—soldiers liable only for home service—they were provided with a house and land at the outpost settlements. **1991** *Dominion Sunday Times* (Wellington) 10 Nov. 24 If you ever wondered what NZ Fencibles meant, join the club. They were the British government's answer to Governor Grey's 1846 request to send a force here to defend Auckland from the Maoris.

b. Hence **fencible** (often init. cap.), used *attrib.* in Comb. or special Comb. **fencible cottage**, a cottage provided for a Fencible military settler; **Fencible ship**, one bringing Fencibles to New Zealand.
1976 Cresswell *MOTAT* 86 **Fencible Cottages**... A new regiment to be called the Royal New Zealand Fencibles was to be formed in 1846, and the conditions of enlistment were posted at every camp in Britain. Two of the cottages provided for these settler-soldiers are at Motat. **1983** Buckley *Of Toffs & Toilers* 143 The little fencible cottages built for the men and their families were at first double units of kauri weatherboards with newspapers pasted over the inside to keep out the draughts. **1991** La Roche *Hist. of Howick & Pakuranga* 62 Competition for berths on the **Fencible Ships** was very keen.

fencing, *vbl. n.*
1. [OED 1585.] The process or occupation of erecting or mending fences; fences collectively; fence material.
1828 Williams *Early Jrnls.* 21 June (1961) 135 Several natives on the beach from Waikari who had brought *Tacopa* for fencing. **1832** *Ibid.* 6 Nov. 263 Set two parties on getting posts for fencing, and some to saw fencing. **1868** Barker *Station Life* (1870) 216 There was quite an excitement in..seeing the changes the flood had made, and the mischief it had done to the fencing. **1991** *Dominion* (Wellington) 9 Feb. 9 Drake says wire was introduced to fencing in New Zealand in the 1860s.

2. Special Comb. **fencing contest**, a competition for fencers; **fencing contractor**, a professional fencer who works by contract; **fencing line**, *fence line* (fence 1 b).
1991 *Dominion* (Wellington) 9 Feb. 9 The [number eight] wire is likely to get its most professional handling if it is used in..the Golden Pliers **fencing contest** at the Mystery Creek Field-days near Hamilton. **1985** Hill *Moaville Magic* 10 The phone starts ringing at 5am most mornings as share-milkers, **fencing contractors**, milk-tanker drivers, and general purpose farmers with calving problems all try to get on the line at once. **1899** Bell *In Shadow of Bush* 10 He was ever forward..in taking the heaviest end of a log if a **fencing line** was being cleared.

fend off, *v. Obs.* To take, to steal.
1937 Partridge *Dict. Slang* 271 *fend off*. To take: New Zealand c[ant] (-1932). I.e., fend a thing off from another, i.e. for oneself. **1938** *Press* (Christchurch) (McNab Slang) 2 Apr. 18 [In local criminal slang]..'to clout,' 'to pole,' 'to fend off' are to steal.

fenwa, var. whenua.

fern.
1. Any of a large group of spore-producing vascular plants belonging to the class Filicopsida, of great practical significance (as a feature of the land and landscape, as a building material or for decoration, and esp. for the use of roots, rhizomes, and pith as a food of Maori and early European settlers), and often of symbolic significance. Freq. used *attrib.* in Comb. See also bracken, fern tree, para *n.*³, ponga, Prince of Wales feathers, spleenwort. Cf. *Land of Ferns* (land 2). **a.** The usual application of the simplex is to the main ferns of open lands, *Pteridium esculentum* (see also bracken) and similarly but less often to *Paesia scaberula* (see also *ring fern* 2 (15) below); and occas. to *Blechnum* spp. Cf. also pikopiko.
1769 Banks *Journal* (1962) 21 Oct. I. 416 Instead of bread they eat the roots of a kind of Fern *Pteris crenulata*, very like that which grows upon our commons in England. **1770** Cook *Journals* 31 Mar. (1955) I. 282 These firns are much alike if not the same as the Mountain ferns in England. **1807** Savage *Some Acc. of NZ* 8 The fern grows here in great abundance; the root..is held in great estimation by the natives. **1817** Nicholas *Voyage NZ* 142 The fern is an invaluable production to these people, who subsist in a great measure on the roots of it. **1834** Markham *NZ* (1963) 36 I believe there are Sixty different Species of Ferns in New Zealand, and whole Tracts of Country are covered with Fern. **1841** Bidwill *Rambles in NZ* (1952) 31 The country about Tawranga for about ten miles inland is almost a perfect level covered with fern. **1882** Potts *Out in Open* 80 *Pteris aquilina, var. esculenta,* for thus the botanist labels the New Zealand variety of the common fern or bracken. **1891** [see bracken]. **1933** *Press* (Christchurch) (Acland Gloss.) 14 Oct. 15 *Fern.*—This name covers any f[ern] growing outside the bush. The two chief kinds are bracken (Pteris) and the shiny-green kind (Blechnum). **1982** Woodhouse *Blue Cliffs* 7 He [sc. Mr Buchanan] remembered walking along a track made by wild pigs through tall fern and flax to the site of the present homestead. **1992** Park *Fence Around the Cuckoo* 223 Chimney stumps stood amongst the ragwort and tutu..and always the intractable fern..waiting outside the fence all the time.

b. *Fig.* in the phr. **fire in (the) fern** (with early variants), used *hist.* when describing the smouldering and eruptive nature of hostilities in the New Zealand Wars, esp. the Hauhau campaigns; and in modern use to describe discontent, a dispute, etc., which may smoulder and flare up from time to time.
1879 *Auckland Weekly News* 17 May 12 It was 'too late!'—a phrase which has been oft and mournfully repeated since 'the fern was set aflame' in 1860. **1883** Domett *Ranolf & Amohia* I. 250 Far as the *Reinga's* self erelong—down to those very dead, Like flames in fern when winds are strong, his widening glory spread. **1898** Reeves *Long White Cloud* 296 Spreading from point to point, dying down and then starting up, it was as hard to put out as a fire abroad in the fern. *Ibid.* 285 [Chapter heading: 1860s war] The Fire in the Fern. **1923** Cowan *NZ Wars* (1955) II. 3 When Pai-marire captured the impressionable and essentially religious Maori nature it spread like a fire in dry fern. **1936** Beaglehole *NZ—Short Hist.* 37 A 'fire in the fern', to use a vivid Maori metaphor. **1937** *King Country Chronicle* 11 Feb. 2 When the 'fire in the fern' died in the King Country, the Armed Constabulary was quartered in Hamilton. **1941** Baker *NZ Slang* 44 *Fire in the fern* for trouble or smouldering discontent. The expression *to spread like fire in the fern,* used of a rumour and even of an epidemic, is useful as well as alliterative. Dealing with the Maori Wars in the Sydney *Telegraph* as recently as February, 1940, a writer says: 'The fire in the fern has now gone out. Justice is being done to the Maori', which reveals that in Australia the phrase is linked with New Zealand. **1955** *BJ Cameron Collection* (TS July) fire in the fern (n) 1. The Maori wars, where fighting seemed to flare up in one place as soon as it was put down in another. (Historical). 2. Any fighting or dispute which drags on, blazing up here and there. **1959** Sinclair *Hist. NZ* 150 As the Maori wars, 'the fire in the fern', died down, life in the colony was at a very low ebb. **1995** *Evening Post* (Wellington) 27 Apr. 6 [Heading] The fire is in the fern. The consequences of the Government's non-intervention in the illegal occupation [by Maori activists] of Moutoa Gardens are piling up fast. Hardly a day passes without Maori protesters occupying a new tract of land.

c. *transf.* A rejected name for the unit of decimal currency; a shortened form of *Silver Fern* (fern 2 (18) b), a member of the national representative netball team.
1974 Muldoon *Rise & Fall of a Young Turk* 76 We [on the Decimal Currency Board] had had trouble with the name of the major unit... Other names [than dollar] flooded in: zealer, crown, royal, zeal, tui, fern, doubloon. **1995** *Sunday Star-Times* (Auckland) 13 Aug. B18

FERN

'With [majority of] [sic] the Ferns not being there it's sort of opened a lot of spaces for players,' said Colling of the nationals.

2. With a modifier: **climbing, comb, crape, crown, gully, hard, hen and chickens, horseshoe, hound's tongue, kidney, king, lace, pig, Prince of Wales, ring, scented, shield, silver, tangle, tree** (with the modifiers **black, rough, silver, slender**), **umbrella, velvet, water**. [*Note*] Over 100 main common names, many with numerous variations of modifier, were originally recorded. Those many which were idiosyncratic or merely book names translating (more or less expertly) generic and specific names have been omitted; as have the following which, though validly applying to native (and often also to adventive) species present in New Zealand, denote the same genera throughout the English-speaking community: adder's tongue (*Ophioglossum*), bladder fern (*Cystopteris*), bristle-fern (*Trichomanes*), filmy-fern (*Hymenophyllum*), maidenhair (*Adiantum*).

(1) **climbing fern**. *Blechnum filiforme* (fam. Blechnaceae), a native fern with creeping and high climbing rhizomes.

1910 COCKAYNE *NZ Plants & Their Story* 31 The Climbing Fern (*Blechnum filiforme*), showing the small early leaf-form. **1988** DAWSON *Forest Vines to Snow Tussocks* 49 Leaves of the climbing fern *Blechnum filiforme*.

(2) **comb fern**. Any of various terrestrial ferns of *Schizaea* spp. (fam. Schizaeaceae), having tufts of fertile pinnae (the 'comb') at the tips of the leaf stalk.

1909 *AJHR C-12* 15 *Schizaea fistulosa* var. *australis* (the slender comb-fern) has the habit of a small rush, and is a well-marked bog-xerophyte. **1982** WILSON *Stewart Is. Plants* 472 *Schizaea fistulosa* var. *australis Comb Fern*... Small tufts or clumps of stiffly erect, wiry, often wavy stalks, about 10-15 cm tall..each terminated by a comb-like cluster of brown fertile segments.

(3) **crape (crepe) fern**, occas. called **double** (or **single**) **crape fern**. PRINCE OF WALES FEATHERS (*Leptopteris superba*) and less commonly *L. hymenophylloides* (fam. Osmundaceae). See also HERUHERU.

1882 THOMSON *Ferns & Fern Allies NZ* 94 *Todea superba*... (Crape-fern). **1887** *Auckland Weekly News* 17 Dec. 8 By the streams I found some noble specimens of the crape fern, Todea Superba, of most delicate plumes. **1890** [see PRINCE OF WALES FEATHERS]. **1897** *Otago Witness* (Dunedin) 16 Dec. 7 Farther in the bush you will find the rare kidney fern, and the plumed fronds of the double crape, and the delicate leaflets of the maiden hair. **1910** *TrNZI* XLII. 17 In..dark places *Todea superba* (double crape-fern), were plentiful. **1951** DOBBIE *NZ Ferns* 20 *L[eptopteris] superba* (superb). 'Heru-heru.' The most beautiful fern in New Zealand; sometimes called 'Prince of Wales Feathers', or 'Crape Fern'. **1961** double crape fern [see PRINCE OF WALES FEATHERS]. **1982** SANSOM *In Grip of Island* 31 There's no better walk for seeing one of the Wonders of the World, the double crepe ferns or Prince of Wales Feathers, carpeted with umbrella mosses.

(4) **crown fern**. *Blechnum discolor* (fam. Blechnaceae), a common tufted forest fern, so called from its erect crown of fronds.

1948 MARTIN *NZ Nature Study* 119 On the ground in montane forest—crown fern (*Blechnum discolor*). **1964** HELMER *Stag Party* 42 In some places [in the Urewera] the crown fern completely obscured the path..and my legs were soon scratched and bleeding from the saw-toothed edges of the fronds. **1971** *VUWTC '71* 55 A jungle of pepperwood..rohutu..or the crown fern (*Blechnum discolor*) does not represent regeneration..but marks areas of extreme modification. **1982** WILSON *Stewart Is. Plants* 460 *Crown Fern*... Piupiu... Crowns of numerous, stiffly upright fronds up to a metre long. Crown fern dominates wide stretches of forest floor.

(5) **gully fern** (often **gully tree-fern**). Either of (a) *Cyathea cunninghamii* (fam. Cyatheaceae) (see also PUNUI 2), a tall slender tree-fern; or (b) *Pneumatopteris* (formerly *Cyclosorus*) *pennigera* (fam. Thelypteridaceae) (see also KOROKIO 3), a robust fern with a short trunk, common in damp gullies.

1921 DOBBIE *NZ Ferns* 108 *C[yathea] Cunninghamii*... 'Gully Fern.' A graceful tree-fern, very similar to *C. medullaris* but smaller, the trunk more slender—usually only half the diameter—the fronds less robust, wider in proportion to their length, more irregularly curved, not so drooping, more membranous. **1981** BROOKER et al. *NZ Medicinal Plants* 28 *Cyclosorus pennigera*... Common name: *Gully fern* Maori name: *Piupiu* This common fern is found in woods throughout New Zealand. **1989** BROWNSEY & SMITH-DODSWORTH *NZ Ferns* 85 *Cyathea cunninghamii*... Gully tree fern. *Ibid.* 91 *Pneumatopteris pennigera*... Gully fern.

(6) **hard fern**. [Extended use of *hard fern*, the European *Blechnum spicant*.] **a**. Any ferns of the genus *Blechnum* (fam. Blechnaceae), having thickish or hard-textured fronds, often with various modifiers, esp. **alpine hard-fern** *Blechnum penna-marina*.

1875 LOGAN *Ferns Which Grow in NZ* 44 [Heading] *L[omaria] alpina* The Alpine hard fern has a rhizome creeping, scaly, slender. **1882** POTTS *Out in Open* 85 Some species of *Lomaria* bear a very close resemblance to the 'hard ferns' of Great Britain, in fact, it may be said that the European genus *Blechnum* is here represented by that of *Lomaria*. *Ibid.* 261 Alpine hard-fern, *L. alpina*... Common in subalpine districts, forming large wide patches. **1910** COCKAYNE *NZ Plants & Their Story* 32 And the climbing hard-fern (*Blechnum filiforme*), with its two quite distinct forms of foliage-leaves on the one plant. **1948** MARTIN *NZ Nature Study* 119 Creek Hardfern and Lance-leaved Hardfern—these two ferns are usually found on stream margins at the edge of open forest. Both are exceedingly hardy. **1950** WODZICKI *Introduced Mammals* 219 Here [on the dry, rocky and under open spurs on Stewart Island] ferns were first slowly removed [by deer] except hard fern (*Blechnum discolor*). **1961** MARTIN *Flora NZ* 105 Those ferns having the generic name (*Blechnum*) are popularly known as hardferns by which is really meant hard ferns, as indeed most species are. **1969** long hard-fern [see KIOKIO]. **1972** [see (15) below]. **1982** WILSON *Stewart Is. Plants* 456 *Blechnum Hard Ferns*... They are easily recognized also by their hard texture and simply divided fronds.

b. *Paesia scaberula* (fam. Dennstaedtiaceae), a common weedy fern of cleared forest land. See also *lace fern*, *pig-fern*, *ring fern*, *scented fern*, *silver fern* (12), (13), (15), (16), (18) a (b) below.

1926 HILGENDORF *Weeds* 19 Hard Fern (*Paesia scaberula*), called also pig fern, and silver fern, is abundant in both islands. **1943** *NZJST* XXIII. 113B *Paesia scaberula* (hard fern, ring fern, scented fern, carpet fern) is considered one of the most troublesome weeds of the wetter hill farms of New Zealand. **1951** LEVY *Grasslands NZ* (1970) 15 Attuned to the geographical region were some particularly troublesome growths, and of these, the hard fern (or ring fern) became a special pest difficult to control and to guard against. **1972** [see (15) below].

(7) **hen and chickens**, or **hen and chicken(s) fern**. *Asplenium bulbiferum* (fam. Aspleniaceae), an Australasian fern bearing young plants on its old fronds.

1930 DEVANNY *Bushman Burke* 9 And watch the lesser forest folk; the cowtree and five-finger;.. the hen and chickens; all their brood, and the lawyer sneaking under. **1952** RICHARDS *Chatham Is.* 11 The broad spear-shaped fronds.. [of *A. bulbiferum*] have..leaflets which often produce bulblets near the top of the leaf on the upper surface which develop into young plants while still on the frond. Hen and Chickens. **1961** MARTIN *Flora NZ* 103 The Hen and Chicken Fern (*A[splenium] bulbiferum*) is a ubiquitous species in New Zealand forests... Under humid conditions, small plants may be observed growing from near the tips of the pinnae, whence popular name. **1982** WILSON *Stewart Is. Plants* 436 Hen and Chickens Fern..Mauku..most fronds sprouting tiny plants (bulbils) which drop off. **1992** ANDERSON *Portrait Artist's Wife* 169 She fingered the chip on the rim of the terracotta pot which housed a Hen and Chicken fern.

(8) **horseshoe fern**. PARA $n.^3$ (*Marattia salicina*).

1898 MORRIS *Austral-English* 203 *Horseshoe-Fern n.* name given in New Zealand to the fern *Marattia fraxinia* [sic].. called in Australia the *Potato-Fern*. **1904** TREGEAR *Maori Race* 99 The bulbs or large scaly bracts of roots at the base of the leaves of..the horseshoe fern (*para-reka*: Marattia salicina)..formed a delicious article of food. **1921** DOBBIE *NZ Ferns* 426 'Para', 'King fern', 'Horseshoe Fern'. The largest herbaceous fern in New Zealand; plentiful in the early days, now becoming scarce. The broad, glossy, dark-green fronds, and the little boat-shaped seed vessels are unmistakable. **1946** *JPS* LV. 149 *Para*, a large fern..horse-shoe fern, from the shape of the tuber. **1961** MARTIN *Flora NZ* 116 The Para or Horseshoe Fern (*Marattia salicina*) is often spoken of as the king fern, but this name belongs more appropriately to *Todea barbara*, a close relative of the British royal fern (*Osmunda*). **1981** BROOKER et al. *NZ Medicinal Plants* 29 *Marattia salicina*... Common names: *King fern, horseshoe fern* Maori name: *Para*... The 'horseshoes' cut from the rhizome were baked or boiled and were a good remedy for diarrhoea.

(9) **hound's tongue (fern)**. *Phymatosorus diversifolius* (fam. Polypodiaceae), an Australasian scrambling and climbing fern.

1959 STEVENSON *Book of Ferns* 151 *Phymatodes diversifolium* Hound's Tongue Fern or kowaowao. **1975** *Tane* 21 8 Polypodiaceae *P[hymatodes] diversifolium* hound's tongue. **1989** BROWNSEY & SMITH-DODSWORTH *NZ Ferns* 63 *Phymatosorus diversifolius* Hound's tongue, kowaowao.

(10) **kidney fern**. *Trichomanes* (or *Cardiomanes*) *reniforme* (fam. Hymenophyllaceae), a native fern with kidney-shaped fronds. See also KOPAKOPA a.

1867 HOCHSTETTER *NZ* 133 The singular form of the Kidney-fern (*Trichomanes reniforme*), the round, kidney-shaped leaves on the edges of which are bordered with seed pods. **1882** POTTS *Out in Open* 66 Let us suppose we wish to look on the 'kidney fern'..what a wide range of country lies before us! **1904** TREGEAR *Maori Race* 389 The badge of mourning was a wreath of green leaves or of lycopodium, or of the kidney fern..twisted in the hair. **1926** DEVANNY *Lenore Divine* 185 The kidney-fern was everywhere, sprawling over ground and trees in incredible profusion. **1951** FRAME *Lagoon* 7 My Picton grandmother..could..find kidney fern and make a track through the thickest part of the bush. **1978** MOORE & IRWIN *Oxford Book NZ Plants* 218 *Trichomanes* (*Cardiomanes*) *reniforme*... Kidney fern is common in damp forests but fronds are able to curl up and survive dry periods. A very peculiar fern, confined to New Zealand. **1988** DAWSON *Forest Vines to Snow Tussocks* 127 The forest floor has..masses of the translucent fans of the kidney fern.

FERN 259 FERN

(11) **king fern**. Also *obs.* **king's fern**. [f. Brit. *king fern Osmunda regalis*: cf. OED; AND *Todea* sp., c1910.] **a.** *Leptopteris* (formerly *Todea*) spp., PRINCE OF WALES FEATHERS; also occas. applied to *Todea barbara* (see quot. 1961).
　1882 POTTS *Out in Open* 108 *T[odea] superba*, 'the glory of the west'. Dr. Hooker's term for it is 'a most splendid fern'. How great the impression made by its marvellous beauty, may be assumed from the number of familiar names which have been bestowed upon it, as the Royal fern, the King's fern, Prince of Wales' feather, Velvet fern, Moss fern, Double Velvet fern. **1961** MARTIN *Flora NZ* 116 The true King Fern (*Todea barbara*) occurs only in the far north..though it is also native to Australia and South Africa.

b. *Cyathea* spp. MAMAKU, PONGA.
　1906 *NZGeol.SB (NS)* No.1 12 Settler's Name King-fern Maori name Mamauku [*sic*] Botanical Name *Cyathea medullaris*. **1963** PEARSON *Coal Flat* 420 kingfern: A local [Westland] name for the mamaku, *Cyathea medullaris*, the tall tree-fern with a wide frond-spread. **1987** [see PONGA 1 a].

c. PARA *n.*³ (*Marattia salicina*). See also *horseshoe fern* (8) above.
　1921 [see (8) above]. **1948** MARTIN *NZ Nature Study* 145 The roots or underground stems of bracken..kingfern (para)..and raupo. **1961**, **1981** [see (8) above].

(12) **lace fern**. See *hard fern* 6 b above, a fern having finely dissected fronds with the appearance of lace-work.
　1921 [see (16) below]. **1948** MARTIN *NZ Nature Study* 118 Forest clearings—cut-leaf bracken; lace fern (*Paesia*). **1961** MARTIN *Flora NZ* 110 The Silver Bracken or Lace Fern, also known in parts of Westland as the pig fern..is a slender and graceful plant. **1982** WILSON *Stewart Is. Plants* 428 *Paesia scaberula* Lace Fern..Ring fern..Scented fern... Fronds yellow-green..strongly scented in hot sunshine.

(13) **pig-fern**. See *hard fern* (6) b above. Occas. applied to BRACKEN (see quot. 1994).
　1926 [see (6) b above]. **1953** *Evening Post* (Wellington) 8 Oct. 7 The first plant to grip the ground after the burning on the southern slopes was bracken, known as 'pig-fern'. **1961** [see (12) above]. **1973** MCCARTHY *Listen...!* 36 Further investigation brought to light many pieces of totara posts in amongst the pig-fern! **1986** *Sunday News* (Auckland) 16 Nov. 5 Leaning back in a bed of pig fern the author was characteristically laconic. **1994** LASENBY *Dead Man's Head* 11 Denny closed his eyes and hung on to the pig-fern. *Ibid.* 158 *pig-fern* bracken fern.

(14) **Prince of Wales's fern**, see PRINCE OF WALES FEATHERS.

(15) **ring fern**. See *hard fern* (6) b above.
　1943, **1951** [see (6) b above]. **1967** HILGENDORF & CALDER *Weeds* 19 Hard Fern (*Paesia scaberula*), called also pig-fern, ring fern, and silver fern, is abundant in both islands. **1972** NEWTON *Wake of Axe* 112 One of the worst of the regrowth problems on this country [near Taumaranui] is the hard fern, or 'ring' fern as it is sometimes known... Ring fern..got the name because after burning the regrowth came up in the form of a circle outside the burnout area. **1982** [see (12) above].

(16) **scented fern**. See *hard fern* (6) b above.
　1921 DOBBIE *NZ Ferns* 166 *P[teris] scaberula*... A very fine-cut fern, rather harsh to the touch; sometimes called 'The Scented Fern', or 'The Lace Fern'. It gives forth a sweet aromatic perfume, especially in the hot sunshine. Fond of growing on sunny banks to the exclusion of other plants. **1943** [see (6) b above]. **1969** *Standard Common Names Weeds* 67 *scented fern* [=] *ring fern*. **1975** *Tane 21* 8 Pteridaceae *Paesia scaberula* scented fern. **1982** [see (12) above].

(17) **shield fern**, usu. with various modifiers, freq. with **prickly**. [Transf. use of European *shield-fern Aspidium* spp.: see quot. 1978.] **a.** *Polystichum* spp. (fam. Dryopteridaceae), a plant genus of tufted scaly ferns.
　1882 POTTS *Out in Open* 98 The shield ferns form a remarkable and noble group, at present comprising half a dozen species. *Ibid.* 269 Richard's or Black Shield Fern, *A[spidium] Richardi..* Abundant, especially near the sea. *Polystichum Richardi* black shield-fern. *Ibid.* 270 Snow or Alpine Shield Fern, *A. cystostegia..*. Habitat: On mountains 4000 to..5000 feet near the snow-line. *Ibid.* 271 Awned Shield Fern, *A[spidium] aristatum..*. Habitat: Kermadec Islands. **1909** *AJHR C-12* 14 All the ferns are evergreen, excepting..the alpine shield-fern (*Polystichum cystostegia*). **1915** *AJHR C-6* 11 *[Polystichum] Richardi*. Tutoki. Black shield-fern. Rock; forest. **1921** DOBBIE *NZ Ferns* 272 Aspidium (aspidos, of a shield—the covering of the seeds). 'Shield Fern'. A genus of about 70 species, with 5 well-authenticated species and 1 variety in New Zealand. **1973** MARK & ADAMS *Alpine Plants* (1979) 28 *Polystichum cystostegia..*. Mountain Shieldfern. **1978** MOORE & IRWIN *Oxford Book NZ Plants* 220 *Polystichum richardii..*. A stiff, hard fern, common on coasts and inland. The name, 'shield fern', comes from the shape of the indusium.

b. As **prickly shield fern**. *Polystichum vestitum*, a common native fern of montane and cool, wet places.
　1882 POTTS *Out in Open* 269 Prickly Shield Fern... Abundant in the mountain ranges of the South Island, less common in some parts of the North Island. **1890** FIELD *Ferns of NZ* 126 Aspidium Aculeatum 'Prickly Shield Fern'... This fern is found throughout New Zealand, and grows in both light and heavy bush, as well as among mere scrub... The New Zealand plant has also been called..'Polystichum vestitum'. **1915** *AJHR C-6* 11 *[Polystichum] vestitum*. Puniu. Prickly shield-fern. Forest. **1969** *Standard Common Names Weeds* 61 *prickly fern* [=] *prickly shield fern..*. *Polystichum vestitum*. **1982** WILSON *Stewart Is. Plants* 424 *Prickly Shield Fern..* Pūniu... Large spreading crowns of long, harsh-textured, glossy dark green fronds, a metre or more long on the largest plants.

(18) **silver fern** (occas. **silver king**). [f. the silver-white underside of fronds.] **a.** Usu. either of two ferns: (a) PONGA 2 (2) (see also *silver tree-fern* (20) b (c) below); (b) also as **silver king**, *Paesia scaberula*, see *hard fern* (6) b above.
　1883 DOMETT *Ranolf & Amohia* II. 336 Tree Fern... *O*. Filices; *G*. Cyathaea; *S. C.* dealbata or Silverfern and C. medullaris. **1921** DOBBIE *NZ Ferns* 98 *C[yathea] dealbata..*. 'Ponga,' 'Silver King.' There is no mistaking this noble tree-fern; the pure white underside of the fronds must attract the notice of the veriest tyro. **1926** HILGENDORF *Weeds* 19 Hard Fern (*Paesia scaberula*), called also pig-fern, ring fern, and silver fern, is abundant in both islands. **1979** MUNE *Mad Dog Gang* 65 It was like a tunnel up through the rotting pongas and spreading silver-ferns.

b. *fig.* and *transf.* Symbolic or characteristic of New Zealand: esp. in earlier use a New Zealand rugby union representative, and in later use a New Zealand netball representative (in *pl.* as *the Silver Ferns*, the national representative netball team), thence occas. connoting (aspiration to) any national representative sporting honour (see quot. 1995²); formerly also the name of a popular brand of cigarette tobacco, and the name of a passenger railcar running between Wellington and Auckland. Also in the phr. **to wear the Silver Fern**, to be a member of the national representative rugby union or netball team. See also FERNLEAF.
　1908 BARR *Brit. Rugby Team in Maoriland* 49 Britain was given more than a reasonable chance against the wearers of the silver fern. **c1938** A Marlborough (and other) schoolboys' obscene recitation of a play on tobacco and cigarette names including: They went behind the 'Silver Fern' and she showed him her 'Prize Crop'. 'Will you take "De Rezke",' she said. 'No' he replied. '"Craven, A?"' she said disgustedly. **1955** *BJ Cameron Collection* (TS July) silver fern (n) The emblem of NZ, worn by sporting representatives. **1965** [see (19) b (c) below]. **1975** HOWITT *NZ Rugby Greats* 37 Jarden was chosen straight from that Australia tour for the All Blacks. It took Clark another two years to win the silver fern. **1986** KNIGHT *Geriatrics* 82 [Greg Denholm] created a special niche..in All Black annals as the only man who has twice turned down an invitation to wear a silver fern. **1990** *Evening Post* (Wellington) 27 July 1 Tomorrow Paul Henderson will pull on an Otago rugby jumper and take on the touring Australians as he continues his quest to regain the silver fern. **1990** CHURCHMAN & HURST *Railways of NZ* 46 Three new twin-coach air-conditioned railcars for the Auckland to Wellington daylight run..were delivered from their Japanese builders in 1972 and were named 'Silver Fern' on account of their external finishing of ribbed stainless steel sheathing on a corrosion resistant carbon-steel frame. **1990** WILKINS *Veteran Perils* 22 O but didn't I have the full-blown misguided hatred of the Luddite, putting my five-cent coin on the tracks of the Silver Fern as it whistled north. **1991** *North & South* (Auckland) June 61 Late in June this year, the current New Zealand Netball Team, the Silver Ferns, will fly to Australia to defend the world championship title. **1991** *Evening Post* (Wellington) 6 Dec. 2 NZ Rail's Silver Fern passenger train is no longer running on the Wellington–Auckland route. **1993** *Evening Post* (Wellington) 7 Sept. 30 A Silver Fern since 1990, [she] is adamant the buzz of it all [*sc.* netball] has not gone. **1994** LASENBY *Dead Man's Head* 21 Polly took the Silver Fern tin from his pocket, rolled a cigarette..and stuck it in Tommy's mouth. **1995** *Sunday Star-Times* (Auckland) 13 Aug. B18 This 20-year-old scarfie could be wearing the Silver Fern in quick time... She was shooting star for Albion in this year's Caltex Cup. **1995** *Western News* (Wellington) 6 Oct. 20 The only way to score a silver fern this year was to switch codes, says..Skinnon after his selection in the Junior Kiwi under-19 rugby league team.

(19) **tangle-fern**. *Gleichenia dicarpa* (formerly *G. alpina* or *G. circinata*) (fam. Gleicheniaceae), having thin, spidery pinnae and forming dense thickets in light scrub. See also *swamp umbrella fern* (21) below. Cf. WAEWAEKAKA.
　1882 POTTS *Out in Open* 241 Tangle-fern... Wae-wae-kaka, matuka, matua-rarauke... Often found in swamps; [and] by the side of streams. **1909** *AJHR C-12* 47 Bog umbrella-fern, woolly tangle-fern. Southern forest, near outskirts; subalpine scrub. Very common. **1973** MARK & ADAMS *Alpine Plants* (1979) 22 Several species are virtually confined to peat-bogs—the wire rush..and the tangle fern (*Gleichenia alpina*). **1982** WILSON *Stewart Is. Plants* 432 *Gleichenia dicarpa* Tangle Fern..Spider fern..Swamp umbrella fern... Fronds wiry, forked..often forming extensive tangled thickets or cushion-like springy masses.

(20) **tree-fern**. **a.** Any of various large native ferns having a trunk-like stem with a crown of fronds, as PONGA (*Cyathea dealbata*), MAMAKU (*C. medullaris*), WHEKI (*Dicksonia squarrosa*).
　1826 SHEPHERD in Howard *Rakiura* (1940) 356 The Tree Fern is a very striking object in the woods, it grows from 20 to 40 feet in h[e]ight and from four to eight inches in diameter in its stem, which is of a spongy brittle nature. **1843** DIEFFENBACH *Travels in NZ*

I. 27 High tree-ferns, with the cabbage-palm, strike the eye as the most beautiful forms of New Zealand vegetation. **1859** Thomson *Story of NZ* II. 11 The room was decorated with the picturesque foliage of the tree fern [on the occasion of Sir George Grey's farewell dinner in Auckland 1853]. **1867** Hochstetter *NZ* 133 It is again ferns..that meet the eye, magnificent Tree ferns, their trunks as if coated with scales, and with neatly shaped crowns (*Dicksonia* and *Cyathea*). **1873** *TrNZI* V. 182 A bush-hand, living the life of a hermit in his little whare of tree-fern stems, up in the Waio river-bed. **1889** Prince *Diary of Trip* 10 The Beech Hut is built of slabs with a tree-fern roof, and contains eight sleeping berths. **1902** *Settler's Handbook NZ* 116 The nikau..is plentiful all through the district, and is everywhere accompanied by noble tree-ferns and palm-lilies. **1920** *Quick March* 10 Mar. 38 Some people speak and write of them as 'tree ferns'... The unobservant are apt to lump all fern-trees together, as pongas, or, in the vernacular, 'bungers'. **1965** Gillham *Naturalist in NZ* 23 Tree-ferns are plentiful in the New Zealand bush, coastal and mountain, northern and southern. **1979** [see spleenwort]. **1981** Locke *Student at the Gates* 73 There was a waterfall... Tree ferns and a cabbage tree grew between it and the still, deep pool.

b. With a modifier: **black, rough, silver (silvery), slender, white**.

(a) **black tree-fern**. mamaku.
1870 *TrNZI* II. 90 The Ponga Flat..owes its name to the large grove of Black Tree-ferns with which it was formerly covered. **1882** Potts *Out in Open* 18 Mamaku—this esculent appeared in junks of about a foot in length; it is the mucilaginous pith of the black tree-fern. **1890** Field *Ferns of NZ* 42 *Cyathea Medullaris* 'Black Tree Fern'. 'Mamaku' or 'Pitau' of the Maoris. This is the largest of our tree ferns, often attaining a height of sixty feet and occasionally more. **1906** Cheeseman *Manual NZ Flora* 949 [*Cyathea medullaris*]. *Korau; Mamaku; Black Tree-fern.* **1926** Crookes *Plant Life in Maoriland* 10 Take..the mamaku, or 'black tree fern' (Cyathea medullaris). This is one of the largest and most handsome of all our tree ferns. **1942** Andersen *Maori Place Names* 273 The great uncoiling fronds [of the mamaku] are thickly clothed with dark brown scales... It is these scales which gave the name black tree-fern. **1966** [see mamaku].

(b) **rough tree-fern**. weki.
1890 Field *Ferns of NZ* 50 Dicksonia squarrosa 'Slender Tree-Fern'. 'Rough Tree-Fern'. Maori Names, 'Weki' and 'Tuakura'. This is probably the commonest of our Dicksonias, as it is found all over the Colony. **1916** *Dunedin Field Club Catalogues of the Indigenous Plants* 28 Dicksonia squarrosa... Rough tree-fern. Weki. Common. **1952** Richards *Chatham Is.* 8 *D[icksonia] squarrosa*... Slender or Rough Tree-fern. Weki. **1969** *Standard Common Names Weeds* 65 *rough tree fern* [=] *wheki*. **1982** Wilson *Stewart Is. Plants* 420 *Dicksonia squarrosa* Whekī,.. Rough tree fern... Trunk dark brown or black, rough with persistent stalk bases.

(c) **silver tree-fern** (occas. **silvery tree-fern**, see quot. 1882). *silver ponga* (ponga 2 (2)). See also *silver fern* (18) a above.
1867 Hooker *Handbook* 768 Tree-fern, silver. *Cyathea dealbata*. **1875** Logan *Ferns* 16 [Heading] *C. dealbata*. This species is named 'ponga' by the Maoris, who strewed the fronds in the sitting and sleeping rooms of visitors of rank... This is called the silver tree fern, and is a very beautiful object. **1882** Potts *Out in Open* 56 As the spreading leaves are wafted aside, how lovely the contrast of the dark green top with its silvery-hued lining. This most characteristic feature of the silvery tree-fern is, by many, thought to confer the palm of beauty above its graceful rivals of the group. **1909** *AJHR C-11* 12 *Cyathea dealbata*. Ponga. Silver tree-fern. Forests of lowlands. **1924** Cockayne *Cultivation of New Zealand Plants* 106 Ferns requiring only the minimum amount of shade. *Cyathea dealbata* (ponga, silver tree-fern.). **1946** [see ponga 1 a]. **1965** Gillham *Naturalist in NZ* 23 It did not surprise me to find that the silver tree-fern had been adopted as the national emblem, alongside the kiwi. **1988** Dawson *Forest Vines to Snow Tussocks* 86 In the ponga or silver tree fern (*Cyathea dealbata*) the leaf bases decay more gradually and do not form well defined scars.

(d) **slender tree-fern**. *Obs.* wheki.
1890 [see *rough tree-fern* (b) above]. **1908** *AJHR C-14* 32 Dicksonia squarrosa. Wheki, weki. Slender tree-fern... Wet and upland forest. Slender tree-fern, with coriaceous fronds and persistent leaf-stalks on trunk. **1915** *AJHR C-6* 11 *Dicksonia squarrosa*... Weki. Slender tree-fern. Forest. **1966** *Encycl. NZ* III. 711 Ferns, tree... Slender.. tirawa, weki, wheki.. *Dicksonia squarrosa*.

(e) **white tree-fern**. *Cyathea dealbata*.
1922 *Auckland Weekly News* 15 June 60 Cyathea dealbata, the white tree fern, is harder than the medullaris or black.

(21) **umbrella fern**. Any of various ferns of the genus *Sticherus* (syn. *Gleichenia*) (fam. Gleicheniaceae), having fronds that take an umbrella-like form, esp. *Sticherus cunninghamii*. Also with a modifier: **alpine**, **swamp** (or **bog**).
1877 *NZ Country Jrnl.* 228 Now let us away..to the rapid waters of the Teremakau... There Cunningham's *Gleichenia* grows marvellously robust, its stiff many-branched fronds rise, tier above tier, in curved fan-like form—which habit, doubtless, induced settlers to call this species the 'umbrella fern'. **1885** *NZJSc.* II. 479 A well excavated (kakapo) home..was near the top of a..terrace on which..flourished a fine growth of the umbrella fern. **1890** Field *Ferns of NZ* 39 Gleichenia (Mertensia) Cunninghamii. The N.Z. 'Umbrella Fern'. Is only found in New Zealand. **1909** *AJHR C-12* 26 Where open, the sandy ground is covered with abundance of the alpine umbrella-fern (*Gleichenia alpina*), forming a close yellowish-green covering some 6 in. tall. **1910** Cockayne *NZ Plants & Their Story* 113 The bog umbrella-fern (*Gleichenia dicarpa*) frequently occupies large areas of boggy ground, its pale-green leaves and brown stems rendering it very conspicuous. *Ibid.* 163 Generally the leaf-surface [of *Blechnum*] is more or less vertical; but in *Gleichenia* it is horizontal, whence the species of that genus get the name of 'umbrella-ferns'. **1922** Mansfield *Stories* (1984) 475 Now they could see quite plainly dark bush. Even the shapes of the umbrella ferns showed, and those strange silvery withered trees that are like skeletons. **1948** Martin *NZ Nature Study* 119 Peat swamps—swamp umbrella fern (*Gleichenia dichotoma*). **1959** McLintock *Descr. Atlas* 30 Where the forest has been cleared and burnt, the resulting cover is all too often low scrub, rushes, and umbrella fern. **1982** Swamp umbrella fern [see (19) above]. **1991** *NZ Geographic* Apr.–June 112 Only a small cartel of particularly hardy plants could survive—titree, gorse, umbrella fern and small red carnivorous sundews are major components.

(22) **velvet fern**. *Lastreopsis* (formerly *Dryopteris* or *Ctenitis*) *velutina* (fam. Dryopteridaceae), having velvety fronds.
1921 Names in a list with letters (Nov. 1921) from H.B. Dobbie (Auckland) in **1927** *TrNZI* LVII. 966 (Andersen *Pop. Names*) *Dryopteris velutina* velvet fern. **1961** Martin *Flora NZ* 115 With smooth stems and reddish-brown, velvety fronds is the Velvet Fern. **1989** Brownsey & Smith-Dodsworth *NZ Ferns* 128 Lastreopsis velutina... Velvet fern.

(23) **water fern**. Either of two species found near or in water. **a.** *Histiopteris incisa* (fam. Dennstaedtiaceae), a widespread, tall, bracken-like fern, bluish-green when young.
1915 *AJHR C-6* 11 *Histiopteris incisa*... Matata. Water-fern. Forest. **1926** Hilgendorf *Weeds* 19 Water Fern (*Histiopteris incisa*), called also soft fern, grows around springs or in swamps, chiefly in the north. **1951** Levy *Grasslands NZ* (1970) 13 These gave protection to many secondary growths, including wineberry..bracken fern, water fern, and later, blackberry. **1982** Wilson *Stewart Is. Plants* 432 *Histiopteris incisa* Water Fern..Mātā. **1989** Brownsey & Smith-Dodsworth *NZ Ferns* 94 *Histiopteris incisa*... Water fern, Mata... Common everywhere from lowland to subalpine regions; in clearings, on forest margins..along stream banks, in thermal areas or in any disturbed habitats.

b. Occas. applied to *Azolla filiculoides* (formerly *A. rubra*) (fam. Salviniaceae), an aquatic free-floating fern; also with a modifier: **red water-fern**.
1910 Cockayne *NZ Plants & Their Story* 105 Take the case of the floating water-fern *Azolla rubra*. The red masses of this curious plant, covering still pools so thickly that one might think them dry land, must be known to all. **1926** Crookes *Plant Life in Maoriland* 137 Take..the water fern, Azolla rubra, which is so common on stagnant pools and slowly-moving streams. Certainly at the first glance there is nothing about it that even remotely resembles a fern. **1969** *Standard Common Names Weeds* 84 *water fern, red* [=] *azolla*. **1981** Brooker et al. *NZ Medicinal Plants* 26 *Azolla filiculoides* Lam. var. *rubra*... Common name: *Water fern* Maori name: *Karerarera*.

3. Used *attrib.* mainly in Comb. in the senses 'pertaining to, covered with, comprising, fern'.
a. As *attrib*.
1887 *Auckland Weekly News* 12 Feb. 8 The road lay over a number of fern ranges. **1905** White *My NZ Garden* 54 Fern-seekers would have little or no sport in the depths of the Bush, but just inside, it is deeply carpeted with Ferns. **c1920s** in Masters *Tales of the Mails* (1959) 47 We then had a stroll round until time to turn in to our fern bed under canvas. **1984** Holden *Razorback* 31 Razorback was still busily feeding in the fernbelt.

b. Comb. in the sense 'fern-covered': **fern-country, -flat, hill**.
1834 Markham *NZ* (1963) 62 We..got on an open plain, fine foot Path, through **fern country** undulating and quite pleasant for the Feet. **1847** Angas *Savage Life* II. 95 Many swamps had to be crossed, during our passage through an open fern country. **1896** [see fernbird 1]. **1907** Laing & Blackwell *Plants NZ* 6 Fern country is found throughout New Zealand but becomes more plentiful towards the North. Here there are large areas covered with the bracken. **1921** Guthrie-Smith *Tutira* (1926) 116 It was open fern country for the most part, extending from the foothills of the Ruahine and Kaweka ranges to the ocean. **1860** Donaldson *Bush Lays & Rhymes* 8 Away over the **fern-flats**. **1861** Haast *Rep. Topogr. Explor. Nelson* 13 He conducted us..through the bush, where we found a good blazed line, which brought us..to the open terraced fern flat. **1843** Selwyn in *NZ Part II* (Church in the Colonies VII) (1845) 12 Walked over **fern hills**, to a small village called Taupo; and on, through swampy plains, to Mangonui. **1864** Von Tempsky *Memoranda* (ATLTS) 73 The track we followed ran along a long valley lying behind high fern hills.

c. In Comb. or special Comb. forming adjectives: **fern-clad** [OED 1841], **fern-covered**, **fern-fringed** [OED 1842], **fern-girt**; **fern-spangled**, ornamented with the silver fern symbol.
1867 Hochstetter *NZ* 296 I did not dream then, that I should spend so many nights..in the bush or upon

the **fern-clad** hills of New Zealand. **1881** CAMPBELL *Poenamo* 99 On that morning the open country stretched away in vast fields of fern, and Nature reigned supreme. It is fern-clad now no longer, but green fields gladden the eye. **1905** BAUCKE *White Man Treads* 212 To the right..lie wave upon wave of manuka, gorse, and fern-clad hills. **1991** *NZ Geographic* Jan.–Mar. 108 Fern-clad gullies are the resting place for all manner of vehicles, from war-vintage saloons to four-wheel drive landrovers. **1876** *TrNZI* VIII. 423 Our **fern-covered** plains..do not yield readily to the efforts of the agriculturist. **1960** SCRYMGEOUR *Memories Maoriland* 160 Long were the hours spent in the saddle, through the **fern-fringed** roads, seeking stock, or properties for sale. **1909** THOMPSON *Ballads About Business* 103 Past **fern-girt** gully and gurgling creek, with a wealth of bush beside. **1910** FANNING *Players & Slayers* 36 A little bit of hard ground, a little bit of soft knee, a sudden meeting—and farewell the vision of the **fern-spangled** jersey of the All-Black.

d. *Special Comb.* **fern-burning**, *spec.* in the New Zealand wars, the burning of fern on open country to destroy enemy cover; **fern-crushed** *ppl. a.*, applied to pasture land on which intrusive bracken fern has been crushed; **fern-crusher**, an animal used to crush bracken fern; **fern-crushing** (also *ellipt.* **crushing**) *vbl. n.* (also as a *v. intr.*, quot. 1981), the agricultural practice of crushing fern, often prior to clearing it from the land, by overstocking esp. with cattle; **fern flower**, the sundew; **fern-grinding** *obs.*, see *fern-crushing* above; **fern-hook** [AND 1920], a special bill-hook for clearing fern; **fern-pounder** *hist.*, in former Maori society one who pounds fern-root to extract edible material, or the stone pestle with which fern-root is thus prepared; **fern-sparrow**, FERNBIRD; **ferntight**, a special sort of boot for wearing in the bush (see quots.).

1864? TEMPSKY *Memoranda* (ATLTS) 94 On the 13th of February Jackson and I had sent our two subalterns with 50 men **fern-burning** on the Pironghia. **1891** WALLACE *Rural Econ. Austral. & NZ* 231 In the New Zealand climate **fern-crushed** pasture-land of good medium quality will support one to three sheep per acre. **1916** *NZJAg.* June XII. 435 Cattle are often looked upon as more efficient **fern-crushers** than are sheep on land suitable for cattle. **1891** WALLACE *Rural Econ. Austral. & NZ* 230 **Fern crushing.** Of the fern country, that upon a limestone formation is the best and the least expensive to break in. **1921** GUTHRIE-SMITH *Tutira* 134 The first care of the settler was to increase his area of grass by the operation known through Hawke's Bay as 'fern-crushing' or 'fern-grinding',—words ominous of the part played by the unfortunate sheep, and which will be described later. It is sufficient now to state that after fire had cleared the tangled bracken growth, the ground was surface-sown and kept clear by browsing sheep. As the greatest growth of fern took place during late spring, it was then impossible to have too many sheep. Every squatter in Hawke's Bay was in the 'eighties 'fern-grinding', so that in those times sheep could not be bought at that season of the year. The result was that every sheep likely to survive the winter was kept, however old and however fleeced. It was at least a pair of jaws, a beast that could bite bracken. **1947** CLARK in Belshaw *NZ* (1947) 40 Beef-cattle are used for 'fern-crushing', that is, for keeping in check the undesirable second growth of bracken fern over large areas of the North Island hills. **1951** LEVY *Grasslands of NZ* (1970) 247 The exponents of crushing have many millions of acres to their credit, using cattle merely as an implement. **1967** RICKARD *Strangers in Wilderness* 47 An operation that seems to have been peculiar to the hill country of Hawke's Bay was the strenuous one known as fern-crushing. **1981** HUNT *Speaking a Silence* 46 But there were no cattle coming up to listen,... They'd been in there fern crushing, hundreds of acres of bracken. **1921** GUTHRIE-SMITH *Tutira* (1926) 169 The **Fern-flower** or Sundew (*Drosera binata*)..vacated the barren edges on which perforce they had been confined. **1972** SARGESON *Man of England Now* 29 As for the fern, it was up to him, he could please himself, although it was usually reckoned a **fern-hook** was the best; but he could see how he got on and stick to the slasher if he preferred. **1835** YATE *NZ* (1970) 218 Scarcely any other sound was heard, except that made by the **fern-pounder**, who was preparing this species of food. **1838** POLACK *NZ* I. 159 Among others of these sacred trifles, was a fern-pounder and a stone. **1882** POTTS *Out in Open* 83 It is possible that there may yet be heard the thud of the fern-pounder in some of the secluded valleys. **1888** BULLER *Birds NZ* II. 98 The melancholy note of the **Fern-Sparrow**, calling to his fellows among the rushes [at Lake Horowhenua], has grown languid and finally died away. **1969** NEWTON *Big Country NI* 245 [Musterers] wore what were known as **ferntights**, boots which, instead of the ordinary hobnails, had bush sprigs. **1986** RICHARDS *Off the Sheep's Back* 61 A bushman always wore a special type of boot known as 'ferntights', named because the upper part of the boot was sewn inside the lower leather, preventing sharp stakes from penetrating the seam and tearing the stitching.

fernbird.

1. *Bowdleria punctata* (fam. Sylviidae), a small brown bird of scrub and swamp, weak-flying, and having bedraggled fern-like tail feathers. See also *fern-sparrow* (FERN 3 d), *grass-bird* (GRASS 6), MATATA *n.*[1], REED SPARROW, *swamp-sparrow* (SWAMP 2 b), UTICK.

1888 BULLER *Birds NZ* I. 59 Sphenoeacus punctatus. (Fern-bird.)... *Native names.* Mata, Matata, Kotata, Nako, and Koroatito... It frequents the dense fern..of the open country. [HWO *Note* The 1873 edn. gives the English name as *common utick* only; changed to *fernbird* in the 1888 edn.] **1896** *TrNZI* XXVIII. 373 'Fern-bird' is rather a misnomer nowadays, for, whatever the habit of the utick may have been, I have never yet, though riding over hundreds of miles of fern-country..., observed the bird in this kind of herbage. **1904** HUTTON & DRUMMOND *Animals NZ* 88 The Fern-bird, as its name implies, frequents ferny lands. **1923** *NZJST* VI. 91 As with so many other species, the diminution in the numbers of the fern-bird is at first sight easily explicable. **1947** POWELL *Native Animals NZ* 86 Fern-bird... A small brownish striped and speckled bird with curious tail feathers... This bird has a curious double-note cry which sounds like 'U-tick'. **1967** NATUSCH *Animals NZ* 277 There are, or rather were, six races of fernbird... They are flimsy-feathered birds, living inconspicuously in manuka scrub or clumps of bracken. **1984** MORETON *Whirinaki* 39 The fernbird, an isolated relative of the warblers,... has been in New Zealand since before the first glaciers. **1991** *Dominion Sunday Times* (Wellington) 20 Oct. 25 They flew harmlessly by, as harmless as the fernbirds.

2. With a modifier identifying the provenance or locality of various species or sub-species of fernbirds: **Chatham Island(s)** *Bowdleria rufescens*, **Codfish Island** *B. punctata wilsoni*, **North Island** *B. punctata vealeae* and **South Island** *B. punctata punctata*, **Snares** *B. punctata caudata*, and **Stewart Island** *B. punctata stewartiana*.

1888 BULLER *Birds NZ* I. 62 Sphenoeacus rufescens. (Chatham-Island Fern-bird)... This well-marked species is confined to the Chatham Islands, where it was first discovered, in 1868. **1893** *TrNZI* XXV. 58 *Sphenaeacus rufescens...* (The Chatham Island Fernbird.) **1904** HUTTON & DRUMMOND *Animals NZ* 89 *The Chatham Island Fern-bird. Sphenaeacus rufescens. Ibid.* 90 It has a peculiar whistle, very like that which one uses in order to attract the attention of some other person at a distance. **1923** *NZJST* VI. 92 *Bowdleria rufescens*..Chatham Islands Fern-bird. Buller (1895)..stated that this species had been exterminated by wild cats and by the firing of low vegetation. **1936** GUTHRIE-SMITH *NZ Naturalist* 193 Within one minute of landing [on the Snares] I had spotted the Black Robin..and the Snares Fernbird. **1990** *Checklist Birds NZ* 203 *Bowdleria punctata vealeae*...North Island Fernbird (Matata)... *Bowdleria punctata punctata*... South Island Fernbird (Matata)... Now restricted as in the North Island to residual areas of suitable habitat. *Loc. cit. Bowdleria punctata stewartiana*... Stewart Island Fernbird...*Bowdleria punctata wilsoni*... Codfish Island Fernbird...*Bowdleria punctata caudata*... Snares Islands Fernbird. *Bowdleria rufescens*... Chatham Island Fernbird.

ferning, *vbl. complement.* The collecting of (native) ferns in the bush.

1886 BUTLER *Glimpses of Maori Land* 88 It was with the daughter of this lady that I went 'ferning'. **1897** *NZ Mail* 4 Feb. 34 *Ferns and Ferning* [title of a local news item] **1898** MANSFIELD in *Undiscovered Country* (1974) 3 The next day was very fine. Mrs Brown proposed that they should go ferning... The girls spent a very happy day, and got a great many nice ferns and some beautiful moss.

fernland. Orig. **fern land**.

1. a. Land covered, or once covered, with fern, mainly bracken *Pteridium esculentum*, or *Paesia scaberula*; in early use often contrasted with BUSH-LAND. See also *fern country* (FERN 3 b).

1840 June in Chambers *Samuel Ironside* (1982) 75 Our journey..has been over a large extent of fine fern land, watered by several splendid rivers. **1851** *Richmond-Atkinson Papers* (1960) I. 84 The forest we passed through was not continuous..so that every two or three miles we emerged into a little bit of open fern land. **1860** WILLOX *NZ Handbook* 80 The 'Bush' or forest land..becomes most speedily productive, but 'Fern' land, that is the land covered with fern and shrubby plants is..ultimately the most profitable. **1884** MARTIN *Our Maoris* 62 The grey scoria houses stood out on the bleak, high ground, unsheltered by a single tree, and all around was fern-land. **1911** *Truth* 22 Apr. 5 The search was a very strenuous ordeal, for the party were led through heavy bush, tangled scrub, flooded creeks, and rough fern land. **1935** STACK *More Maoriland Adventures* in Wily & Maunsell *Robert Maunsell* (1938) 136 The fern and manuka land refused to grow either corn, grass, or root crops, and most of our six hundred acres consisted of fern land. **1988** DAWSON *Forest Vines to Snow Tussocks* 152 Immediately after the destruction of the forests fernland established, but, with continued burning, grassland began to spread.

b. As **fernlands** *pl.*, areas of arable land once covered with fern.

1856 FITTON *NZ* 101 [Heading] Bush land as compared with fern. Almost all the crops..have been taken from what is called fern land... But..I know that when I left New Plymouth district..the bush land crops of wheat were deemed inferior..to those of open fern lands. **1859** FIRTH 6 Sept. in *Voices from Auckland* (1860) 67 [New comers] are puzzled by what is said about *fern-lands* and *bush-lands*.

2. *Obs.* [Cf. OED 2 b 'applied, esp. by Australians, to New Zealand'.] With init. cap., a name given to New Zealand by non-New Zealanders. See also LAND OF FERNS.

1926 GREY *Angler's Eldorado* 29 The hillside there

was covered with a wonderful growth of the tree ferns, which plant has given New Zealand the name Fernland.

Hence, **Fernlander**, an occas. journalistic name for an ALL BLACK.
1938 STONE *Rugby Players* 89 By defeating the Fernlanders the Springboks were justly proud in having gained for their country the Rugby supremacy.

fernleaf. [With reference to esp. the leaf of the *silver fern* (FERN 2 (18) a).]

1. A national emblem, esp. the silver fernleaf worn by national representative sporting teams, *spec.* those of rugby union and netball. See also FERN 2 (18) b, *Land of Ferns* (LAND 2).
1905 *Truth* 12 Aug. 2 [The British rugby team] will wear [their emblem] as the Maorilanders wear the fernleaf. **1938** *Weekly News* 26 Jan. [Caption] Wearing the Fern Leaf at the 1938 British Empire Games: Members of New Zealand's Team Sail for Sydney. **1946** SOLJAK *NZ* 8 The kiwi, like the fernleaf, is now a New Zealand national emblem and provided the name by which Dominion servicemen were popularly known during the war.

2. *Hist.* **a.** mainly *pl.*, also *attrib.* A New Zealander, esp. (from the fernleaf badge worn) a New Zealand soldier in WW1.
1916 *Chron. NZEF* 15 Nov. 127 Call them 'Overseas soldiers' or 'Down-under' men... Call them 'Cornstalks' or 'Fernleaves'—all out for a fight—But don't call them Anzacs, for that isn't right. **1917** *Chron. NZEF* 17 Jan. 223 What strikes me most about the Fernleaf crowd is their beautiful humility respecting the merits of their own country. **1917** *NZ at the Front* 134 First Fernleaf: 'I had a lot of trouble getting mine [*sc.* riding breeches] off a dead Ossie at Gallipoli.' Second Fernleaf: 'Dunno, Bill.' **1935** MITCHELL & STRONG in Partridge *Slang Today* (1935) 285 It [was] very generally believed by the New Zealand troops (*Fernleaves* or, as they preferred to call themselves, *Diggers*) that every English girl infallibly carried her return fare in case her soldier friend became *mad*. **1946** [see 1 above]. **1984** PUGSLEY *Gallipoli* 13 Indeed it was as New Zealanders that other nationalities identified us [in WW1], not as 'Otago' or the 'Canterbury boys' but as 'Fernleaves' or 'New Zealanders' and it made sense to do so ourselves. [1984 *Note*] 'Fernleaf' and 'Fernleaves'—the slang term for New Zealanders. **1990** LANGFORD *Newlands* 90 One third of all Fernleaves sent to luckdom come at Gallipoli died on Chunuk Bair.

b. Used *attrib.* in Comb., esp. **fernleaf badge**.
1917 *NZ at the Front* 106 It lay just off the crossroads—the little Fernleaf Cemetery. **1945** HENDERSON *Gunner Inglorious* 17 Onward, men of the Second New Zealand Expeditionary Force; onward, as our fernleaf badges say, on against the foe.

fern-root.

a. The root of the bracken, formerly commonly used, after treatment by pounding (with a fern-root pounder), as a food of the Maori and early European settlers. See also ARUHE, ROI.
1770 COOK *Journals* 31 Mar. (1955) I. 282 Firn [*sic*] roots they likewise heat..than [*sic*] beat them out flat. **1819** MARSDEN *Lett. & Jrnls.* (1932) 158 King George confirmed what she said, and lamented that he had no pork nor anything to give us for our supper but fern-root. **1830** CRAIK *New Zealanders* 96 Three women were employed in roasting fern root for us. **1849** TORLESSE *Papers* (1958) 72 Made fern-root cakes, &c. **1863** MANING *Old NZ* iii 65 I will carry fern root into my pa; I will *cure* those heads I have killed in war. **1881** CAMPBELL *Poenamo* 297 And what is the use of gold to me? Sovereigns put on Motu-Korea won't eat up fern-root and multiply—pigs would. **1905** BAUCKE *White Man Treads* 281 When..a large tangi or other party reduced his pataka or rua kumera contents, he..made shift with fern-root, berries, or mamaku (tree fern) until the next year's crop came in. **1915** *TrNZI* XLVII. 71 The staple food of the Taupo Maoris in pre-pakeha days was fern-root, the rhizome of *Pteris aquilina*. **1920** [see ARUHE]. **1939** BEATTIE *First White Boy Born Otago* 15 I have also eaten some native foods. I thought the kauru prepared from the cabbage tree was nice, but I did not like fernroot. **1946** [see ARUHE]. **1982** BURTON *Two Hundred Yrs. NZ Food* 3 Some Maori groups were forced to give up gardening altogether and to gather fernroot as their main source of starch.

b. Spec. Comb. **fern-root beater, fern-root pounder** *hist.*, *fern-pounder* (FERN 3 d), a stone pestle for preparing fern-root.
1875 *TrNZI* VII. 61 A patuaruhe, or **fernroot beater**, made of maire. **1947** BEATTIE *Early Runholding* 16 We came to the conclusion it [*sc.* the stone artefact] was a **fern-root pounder**.

Hence **fern-rooter**, a wild pig.
1922 *Northlander* 24 May (VUW Fildes Clippings 461a/262) There were numbers of wild porkers, all young and fat fern-rooters, how savoury!

fern tree. [AND 1793.]

a. *tree-fern* (FERN 2 (20)).
1773 FORSTER *Resolution Journal* 23 Apr. (1982) II. 263 The natives took the Stalks of the Ferntrees, broiled the whole & eat the inner-pulp. **1817** NICHOLAS *NZ* I. 232 The fern-tree, that ornament to the forest in these regions, was to be seen in many places growing with great luxuriance. **1839** TAYLOR *Journal* (ATLTS) 15 Mar. II. 74 We passed through several woods filled with fern trees and some very curious plants. **1847** JOHNSON *Notes from Jrnl.* in Taylor *Early Travellers* (1959) 121 The luxuriant beauty of the New Zealand forests almost equals that of the tropics, indeed the presence of the graceful fern-trees, and elegant nikau palms, gives them quite a tropical aspect. **1859** THOMSON *Story New Zealand* I. 156 The pith of the stem of the fern-tree..[is] eaten. **1861** *Otago Witness* (Dunedin) 19 Jan. 5 In the decoration of the [Otago Horticultural Society] show-room, the graceful young Red Pine, and the Ti and Fern Trees, ranked first among our native trees. **1881** CAMPBELL *Poenamo* 102 The palm fern-tree was there, with its crown of graceful bending fronds and black feathery-looking young shoots. **1903** *TrNZI* XXXV. 58 Mamaku (*Cyathea medullaris*). This is the black fern-tree of the settlers. **1922** COWAN *NZ Wars* (1955) I. 130 The slopes are black-pencilled with the stumps of the *wheki*, a fern-tree whose butt is as hard as ironbark and almost indestructible. **1953** DEWAR *Chaslands* 10 The principal building material used [on the Southland bush farms c1900] was fern-tree, known locally as bungie, upright on some walls, horizontal on others.

b. Used *attrib.* 'constructed of tree-fern trunks' in Comb. **fern-tree house**, **whare**.
1937 AYSON *Thomas* 130 A man named Adam Hunter built a fern-tree whare at Green Bushes. **1953** DEWAR *Chaslands* 10 They were to come to know every tree..within a radius of a mile of their fern-tree house there. **1967** McLATCHIE *Tang of Bush* 67 We could see that the ferntree house was now too small for our growing family.

fescue: see GRASS 2 (17).

fescue tussock: see TUSSOCK 3 (3) a.

few. [AND 1903: used elsewhere; recorded earliest in Austral.; see OED *few* 2 f.] Ellipt. for **a few beers**, an understatement for 'many' esp. in the phr. **to have (get) a few in**, to be drunk or tipsy.
1911 *Truth* 22 Apr. 6 The sub: 'But didn't 'Jimmie' shape up to Boys?' Witness: 'No, he couldn't he had a few in.' Jimmie grinned. The sub: 'Did you have a few in, too?' **1923** *Aussie (NZ Section)* 15 Aug. III Apart from a night at home after a few in..Slim Withers had never been what a professional man would call really 'crook'. **1946** SARGESON *That Summer* 63 The pair of us had a good few in. **1972** MITCHELL *Pavlova Paradise* 182 *'a few beers'*: 'I met Joe and we had a few beers' means probably that they drank solidly from Friday night to Sunday. **1984** MANTELL *Murder in Vain* 83 The landlady..said he had obviously been drinking. That was the way he behaved when he was half-cut. She insisted he was no trouble... Sometimes he did knock a few back.

fibrolite. Occas. erron. **fibrolight**. [f. a proprietary name.] A kind of asbestos cladding moulded into sheets and formerly used esp. as a cheap building material. Often *attrib.*
1916 *NZ Patent Office Jrnl.* [no number given] 6 July Fibrolite 13221 [filed] 6th June 1916 James Hardie and Co..Melbourne..Asbestos sheeting of all kinds. **1945** *NZ Dairy Exporter* 1 Nov. 40 You must get a permit from the Building Controller to use Fibrolite. **1972** GEE *My Father's Den* 75 Just beyond..are the huge fibrolite storage sheds of the Apple and Pear Marketing Board. **1988** LAY *Fools on Hill* 85 The second..related to several streets of look-alike fibrolite and tile houses. **1990** KIDMAN *True Stars* 85 In hot weather the fibrolite-clad walls overheated it [*sc.* a bach] until it was almost unbearable.

fiddle.

1. [f. the resemblance in shape to a fiddle.] A dressed mutton hindquarter.
[*Note*] In Australia, and occas. in rural New Zealand, also called a 'banjo'.
1937 AYSON *Thomas* 153 Jock Graham did a roaring trade in Dunedin by purchasing carrots in the Taieri and tying three of them to a hind leg of a sheep. This was known as a fiddle and he would hawk them through the streets and dispose of them for sixpence.

2. *Car-salesmen.* Fig. for a car radio.
1986 *NZ Herald* (Auckland) 22 Jan. sect. ii 1 Car dealers have a collection of jargon they use on the yard, so if you are thinking of taking up selling cars as a career, there are a few terms you should know... If you would like a car with a radio, ask if it has a 'harp' or a 'fiddle.'

fiddle, *v. Sawmilling.* [Prob. from fancied resemblance to the action of a fiddle bow.] *trans.* To crosscut logs, or to use a crosscut saw (on logs) singlehandedly.
1923 MALFROY *Small Sawmills* 8 Operation costs,.. Manufacture:—1. Sawmill—(a.) Fiddling or crosscutting logs at mill. **1953** REED *Story of Kauri* 163 His mate 'fiddled' the remaining wood—that is, sawed it single-handed.

Hence **fiddler**, one who cross-cuts logs into appropriate lengths; **fiddling** *vbl. n.*, cross-cutting (logs) into suitable milling lengths; **fiddling saw**.
1923 MALFROY *Small Sawmills* 28 The **fiddler** should be able to sharpen his own saw, and generally use his brains in the selection of lengths for current orders. *Ibid.* 31 It is the usual practice in this country to send logs to the mill in their full length, and have the cross cutting into merchantable length done at the mill skids. This is commonly called '**fiddling**', and a good fiddler can save a lot of waste. **1923** *Awards, etc.* 112

[Westland Timber Yards and Sawmill Employees] [Rates of wages] Slabby [£]0 13[s.] 0[d.] Fiddler, steam crosscut 0 11 0. **1951** *Awards, etc.* 453 [Westland Timber-Workers Award] [Rates of wages] Turner-down 3[s.] 11¾[d.] Fiddler, hand crosscut 4 0¼ Fiddler, power saw 4 0¼. **1928** *Free Lance* (Wellington) 25 July 7 When the loco arrives at the mill skids, the logs are hauled off by two winches, cut to the required length by the **fiddling saw**, then kicked to the Pacific bench which does the 'breaking down'.

fiddly-did. *Obs.* Also **fiddley**. [AND 1941.] Rhyming slang for 'quid', a one-pound note.
1964 Davis *Watersiders* 133 Remember asking a joker..if he'd shove a fiddly-did on the double for me. **1966** Turner *Eng. Lang. Austral. & NZ* 119 Baker lists a few examples of rhyming slang from Australia, among them..*fiddley did* for *quid*, whence *fiddley* 'profit'.

field.
[*Note*] *Field* as a landscape term has been replaced in New Zealand by *paddock*, except in sports use (e.g. football field), and as an abbreviation of GOLDFIELD, GUMFIELD (in which contexts *paddock* has a specific or restricted meaning).
1. [AND 1856.] GOLDFIELD. Also *fig.*
1853 Swainson *Auckland* 104 These regulations contain many stringent provisions with a view to prevent unauthorized intrusion, either on the gold field, or on adjoining land; and to secure orderly conduct on the field. **1896** O'Regan *Poems* 33 Life's claim is almost duffered..Swag, billy, and tin-dish I'll need no more In the new field that I'm off to. **1931** Coad *Such Is Life* 48 The two brothers..had forsaken their ordinary avocations..to try their luck on the newly discovered field. **1943** Hislop *Pure Gold* 22 The Otago fields were not so Kelly-gangish [as the Victorian]. **1953** Sutherland *Golden Bush* (1963) 152 They worked on different parts of the 'field but often met where the ale was flowing free and their taproom tales were a feature of the diggings.
2. GUMFIELD.
1882 Hay *Brighter Britain* II. 26 Often it is not necessary to move camp for months at a time, when the surrounding field is pretty rich in gum-holes. **1904** Patterson *Kauri-gum* 5 On arrival on a new field the nearest storekeeper is 'tapped' as to his willingness..to provide him [*sc.* the gumdigger] with a few weeks' provisions while he digs the necessary gum. **1913** Carr *Country Work* 42 It is estimated that there are 8,000 Croatians..on the fields. **1923** *NZJST* VI. 95 About thirty years ago the simplest form of contract on the fields was that under which the digger made..a payment. **1970** Thomas *Way Up North* 39 He carted sacked..gum from the fields to the wharf.

field mouse. Also occas. **bush mouse, wood mouse.** In New Zealand *field mouse* is applied to the common house-mouse, *Mus musculus* (fam. Muridae) when found out of doors.
[*Note*] The British field mouse is a vole.
1966 *Encycl. NZ* II. 680 The field mouse of England is a vole, not a true mouse, but here the common house mouse is called a field mouse when it occurs out of doors. **1986** Daniel & Baker *Mammals of NZ* 64 *House Mouse. Mus musculus Other names*: Field mouse, bush mouse. **1990** *Handbook NZ Mammals* 225 *House mouse Mus musculus* Linnaeus... Also called field mouse, wood mouse (English, popular usage only); kiore-iti (Maori). *Ibid.* 241 Feral house mice living independently in bush and farmland in New Zealand, and sometimes locally called 'field mice' or 'wood mice', are quite different from the rodents known by these names in the Northern Hemisphere.

Field's Express. *Hist.* [From the name of William Hughes *Field* (1861–1944), MHR for Otaki 1900–1911, 1914–35, who c1923 successfully advocated the service as a convenience for his constituents.] The familiar name of a rail passenger service (or services) formerly running daily between Wellington and Palmerston North, and stopping at all stations north of Paekakariki.
1924 *NZPD* CCV. 1217 Mr. Field (Otaki) asked the Minister of Railways, Whether the practice of taking off at Paekakariki the only comfortable first-class carriage attached to the train known as 'Field's express' leaving Thorndon at 5.55 p.m..may be discontinued. **1944** *Manawatu Evening Standard* (Palmerston North) 14 Dec. 4 To Mr. Field was due an improvement of the railway service between Palmerston North and Wellington, 'Field's Express' being named after him. **1972** Hoy *West of the Tararuas* 107 These three trains [*sc.* a Friday and Sunday Wellington–Palmerston North service] are all that is left of a twice-daily service which served the district from 1923 to 1958, and which was known as the Field's Express after the Member..for Otaki (Mr. Field) who campaigned for their introduction. **1991** *St Patrick's College Silverstream 1931–91 A Diamond Jubilee Magazine* 10 Trains played a significant part in Silverstream life between 1931 and 1956..the Limited from Auckland; Field's Express from the Manawatu.

fifths, *n. pl. Forestry.* See quot.
1952–53 *NZ Forest Service Gloss.* (TS) *Fifths.* Monies paid by the Forest service to County Councils for the express purpose of maintaining roads on which round or sawn timber is hauled. The amount is generally one fifth of the royalty value of the timber.

fifty acre. Denoting a standard size of allotment in early colonial days. Used *attrib.* in special Comb. **fifty-acre farmer**, a small farmer; **fifty-acre section**, a section of approx. 20.25 ha. Cf. FORTY-ACRE.
1850 Torlesse *Papers* (1958) 143 The only gentleman shop-keeper farmers are those who having a 50 acre section dabble in agriculture for pastime and to feed their horses, pigs, and poultry. **1894** Dowsing *He* 39 He's got a bit of land now, and calls himself a cockatoo (fifty acre farmer). **1940** Howard *Rakiura* 243 The land available for allotment he [*sc.* the Superintendent, c1872] divided into three classes: (i.) Free grants to each settler, consisting of a village allotment of a quarter-acre and a suburban allotment of twenty acres. (ii.) Fifty-acre sections at five shillings per acre. **1980** Yorke *Animals Came First* 59 There were eighteen fifty-acre farms allotted to men on relief in that district [in 1932]. It was known as the Te Karae Block.

fig, *n.*[1]
a. *Obs.* [Used elsewhere but of special significance in early colonial New Zealand.] A plug (of tobacco), in early colonial times often used as a unit of barter between Europeans and Maori. Cf. HEAD *n.*[1] 2.
1835 Yate *NZ* (1970) 127 Those [weapons] made of wood..may be purchased..sometimes for a mere trifle of a fig of negro-head tobacco. **1841** Bidwill *Rambles in NZ* (1952) 43 Thus, if you give a fig of tobacco, you may be sure they will ask for a pipe. **1851** *Richmond-Atkinson Papers* (1960) I. 83 We purchased a supply of potatoes with a few figs of tobacco which is the current coin in the interior. **1863** Moser *Mahoe Leaves* 9 I reward him for his hospitality with a few figs of tobacco, and pursue my way northward. **1881** Campbell *Poenamo* 165 Even sulky Te Hira would not grudge us that, in return, of course, for a fig of tobacco. **1940** Cowan *Sir Donald Maclean* 33 The payment..consisted of..100 figs of tobacco..two 'roundabouts'..and one axe.
b. Surviving in prison use, (a packet of) prison tobacco.
1973 Justin *Prisoner* 29 'A fig?' 'A packet of boob—prison, to you—tobacco. Haven't you learnt that yet?' **1980** Berry *First Offender* 152 'I got six figs for that load of rubbish'. Fig was a curious word, an Americanism that had some how filtered into N.Z. [*sic*] penal institutions and survived. It wasn't slang in the sense that screw and boob were. There was no other word for the cellophane packet that contained around fifty grammes of offcuts and substandard tobacco supplied by the companies. Nobody spoke of a packet of tobacco—it was always a fig. **1980** MacKenzie *While We Have Prisons* 96 *fig* an ounce of tobacco

fig, *n.*[2] *Obs.* As **native fig, New Zealand fig**, PATE, having digitate leaves resembling those of the fig-tree.
1907 *AJHR* C-8 20 *Schefflera digitata*..Pate. Native Fig. Forest. **1908** *AJHR* C-14 41 *Schefflera digitata*..Pate, patete. Native fig. Moist forest. Small tree, with digitate, thin leaves. **1915** *AJHR* C-6 14 *Schefflera digitata*..Pate. New Zealand Fig. Forest.

fight, *n. Hist.* A frequent early missionary-English translation of Maori TAUA q.v. 'war party'.
1827 Williams *Early Jrnls.* 23 Aug. (1961) 70 The natives came running, and exclaimed, *Ka puta te taua*, that is, the fight is in sight, or those for that purpose. **1831** *Ibid.* 25 Nov. 205 Went to Kororarika to see the Chiefs about the fight... [1961 *Note*] 'The fight' is a translation of *taua* much used by the missionaries and early settlers. Both the Maori word and the translation mean a 'war party' and are used whether the 'fight' is a mere local skirmish or a full-scale tribal war. **1838** *Piraki Log* 9 Jan. (1911) 64 this day we was put in suspense at dusk..five Boats came into the heads..we first took them for the fight coming from Cloudy Bay but they proved to be boats from Otago. **1847** Angas *Savage Life* II. 111 Great preparations are making [at Taupo] for the 'fight' from Paripari, which is expected here daily and the natives are busily engaged in preparing fire-arms and other weapons.

file. *Obs.* [Cf. OED *n.*[1] 3, fellow, esp. *old file*, 1812.] Fellow, chap, esp. **old file**, an 'old hand', an experienced person.
1845 Wakefield *Adventure NZ* I. 325 The 'old file' had guessed that the fish would alter its course a point or two. **1864** Thatcher *Invercargill Minstrel* 8 And get the [street] gratings properly laid down. Not in that curious gridiron style, To catch the heels of every poor file.

file fish. [See quot. 1956.] LEATHERJACKET 1.
1855 Taylor *Te Ika A Maui* 624 The *Pakirikiri*..file fish, is distinguished by two strong spines at the commencement of the dorsal fin, in shape like the letter V, both fronting the head, and standing out from the fin, these are elevated at pleasure, some fish have only one. **1898** Morris *Austral-English* 145 *File Fish.* Name given in New Zealand to the *Monacanthus rudis*..family *Sclerodermi*... The first of the spines of the dorsal fin is roughened in front like a file. **1938** [see TRIGGERFISH]. **1956** Graham *Treasury NZ Fishes* 374 Rough Leather Jacket, Trigger-fish or File-fish (Kokiri) *Parika scaber*... This interesting fish has a number of other vernacular names, such as File-fish, and all with a bearing on its construction. The name Leather-Jacket is due to the fancied resemblance to a North American lumber jacket, not unlike the dark brown coloured jumpers

fillet. *Sawmilling.* A lath inserted transversely between layers in stacks of sawn timber to allow air to circulate and to make the stack more stable. See also GLUT, STICKER *n.*², STRIP *n.*

1948 JEWELL *Accounting in Timber Industry* 128 *Fillets;* Sometimes called a 'sticker' or 'strip'. Is a strip of timber or board 1"x 1" or 2"x 1" placed between layers of boards in a pile and at right angles to the boards for the purpose of separating them and facilitating the circulation of air. **1952–53** *NZ Forest Service Gloss.* (TS) *Fillet.* A small dimension piece of timber placed at right angles to the boards in a pile of timber stacked for drying. syn. *Sticker, Strip.* **1987** MASSEY *Woodturning NZ* 93 *Fillet.* A wood spacer used to separate timber whilst air-drying.

Hence **fillet** *v. trans.*, to stack (timber) with laths between the layers of boards. Also **filleting** *vbl. n.*

1923 MALFROY *Small Sawmills* 38 *Filleting..*Stacking timber with strips or battens between the tiers to allow a free passage of air for seasoning. **1952** LYON *Faring South* 196 I also arranged the timber should be filletted or stacked with laths between and left to dry.

filoose, var. FELOOSE.

financial, *a.* [AND 1899.] In the phr. **to be financial,** *holding* (HOLD *v.*² 2). See also SILVERY *a.*

1935 STRONG in Partridge *Slang Today* (1938) 288 You never were a twister, because if you had been you could have denied being financial, and now you are going to shout for the boys. **1940** GILKISON *Peaks, Packs & Mountain Tracks* 104 In my 'varsity days, I dragged my old 'omnibus' over many a trail where, had I been more financial, I would surely have saved myself much trouble and toil by employing motor car or pack-horse. **1955** BJ Cameron Collection (TS July) financial (adj) Having some money. Cf. *holding.* **1968** *NZ Contemp. Dict. Suppl.* (Collins) 8 *financial adj.* and *adv.* possessing cash. **a1974** SYDER & HODGETTS *Aust. & NZ English* (TS) 343 *financial*: To have a supply of money to hand. 'Richie's shout, boys. Richie's financial, he had a good win today.'

finback: see WHALE 2 (5).

find. *Goldmining.* [Spec. use of *find* a discovery of treasure, etc.: AND 1851.] A discovery of gold.

1862 *Otago Goldfields & Resources* 19 Rich finds are constantly met with. **1879** HAAST *Geol. Canterbury & Westland* 101 They were bound for a creek..where some payable finds..had just been made by some prospecting party. **1887** PYKE *Hist. Early Gold Discoveries Otago* (1962) 15 The 'finds' were casual and inconsiderable. **1896** O'REGAN *Poems* 39 An' I trust on fairer diggins you have made a grander find.

finder. Also **finder-bailer, finding dog.** [Poss. a spec. use of Brit. dial. *finder, obs.* a dog trained to find and bring game that has been shot: cf. EDD.] A pig dog trained to find wild pigs. Cf. HOLDER.

1940 STUDHOLME *Te Waimate* (1954) 254 A good finding dog was frequently no good at holding, as he would probably simply run round and round the pig. **1951** finder-bailers [see BAILER]. **1962** *Listener* 19 Apr. 5 Could you describe the things a good pig dog's required to do?... There's two types of finders. There's the wind finder and the track finder. The wind finder will take a pig first... If you've got a good wind finder with you and you're working the right way into the wind, if there's a pig lying anywhere up to 1000 or 1500 yards away he'll be away like a shot... With a track finder the pig might be on the move and he'll leave a lot of scent on the undergrowth. The dog will immediately pick that up and he'll stick his nose on the ground... He'll tail off after the pig and stop him some way, nip him in the leg or somewhere else. **1971** BILLING *Statues* 97 Sark threw [the dog] half a sausage. 'That's my finder,' he said. 'He'll find a pig anywhere.' **1982** [see BAILER].

findon haddock. *Obs.* [Transf. use of Brit. *finnan* (or *findon*) *haddock,* smoke-cured haddock, named apparently from a place *Findhorn,* later confused with *Findon* a Scottish village.] In Otago, smoke-cured red cod (COD 2 (6), *Pseudophycis bacchus*).

1872 HUTTON & HECTOR *Fishes NZ* 115 Red Cod... Also called..the Haddock, (*Lotella bacchus*) is..the species that is cured and sold as the Findon Haddock at Port Chalmers. **1880** [see COD 2 (6)]. **1921** THOMSON & ANDERTON *History of Portobello* 74 When smoked as soon as possible after catching, it [*sc.* red cod] is the best approach to the celebrated Findon haddock.

fine, *a.*

1. As **fine gold,** gold in dust-like form or in small specks as distinct from coarse or nuggety gold. Contrast COARSE *a.*

1861 *McCrae to Provincial Council* 11 Nov. in Cowan *Down the Years in the Maniototo* (1948) 34 Found some nice prospects of fine gold. **1862** *Otago Goldfields & Resources* 20 The gold [from Waipori] is very fine, but very bright and pure. **1887** PYKE *Hist. Early Gold Discoveries Otago* (1962) 60 'Several specks of fine gold from the surface wash' on the Molyneux; 'several specks of fine gold' at the Bannockburn. **1918** [see COARSE *a.*]. **1925** BATHGATE *Random Recolls.* 28 It was surprisingly uniform in size [all bean-sized pieces] without any fine gold amongst it. **1976** [see COARSE *a.*]. **1983** NOLAN *Gold Fossicker's Handbook* 112 *Fine gold*: small specks of gold; also, refined gold of high purity.

2. As **fine art,** in the phr. **to have something down to a fine art,** to be very expert at (often something slightly illegal).

1941 *NZEF Times* V. 4 The boys had it down to a fine art. **1946** BRUNO *Maleesh George* 5 He had [it] down to a fine art.

fin fish. [f. *fin* the baleen of a whale: see OED *fin n.* 2 c.] WHALE 2 (14).

1823 ENDERBY 30 May in Morton *Whale's Wake* (1982) 27 Fin Fish..are never attacked as they are so powerful and mischievous that there is great danger in the attempt. **1875** *TrNZI* VII. 252 Whalers often speak of right whales as finners or fin-fish, from their yielding baleen or 'fin', as they term it.

finger. *Obs.* As **the old finger,** 'the old man', father.

1921 *Quick March* 11 July 15 The clever chap who wrote the epistle would have no hesitation in speaking to this effect: 'Dicken! I done me block right enough! I come home and the old finger hit the roof. Tike it from me, he's gotter rat.'

finner: see *finback* (WHALE 2 (5)).

fiord. Also **fjord.** [Spec. use of *fiord* a long, narrow, steep-sided sea-inlet.]

1. a. Applied (loosely) to the Marlborough Sounds.

1843 DIEFFENBACH *Travels in NZ* I. 122 In this fiord [*sc.* Queen Charlotte's Sound], as the Norwegians would call it, is a small island. **1926** COWAN *Travel in NZ* II. 2 Queen Charlotte Sound..is the chief maritime avenue; its deep waters, entered by a fine fiord, Tory Channel, are navigated by large steamers.

b. Applied to the South Island west-coast sounds.

1866 ANGAS *Polynesia* 93 The south-west coast is rugged and perpendicular, and intersected with numerous deep channels or 'fiords', running inland between stupendous precipices. **1868** LINDSAY *Contribs. NZ Bot.* 30 The *Fjords* of the West Coast rival, and probably surpass, those of Norway in the grandeur of their alpine scenery. **1872** *TrNZI* IV. 12 It is hoped that they will explore the glaciers and summits of mount Cook, together with the elsewhere unrivalled scenery of the neighbouring *fiords.* **1883** GREEN *High Alps* 70 Many spurs from these [Otago] ranges strike the coast, and inclose between them a number of fjords, or sounds, as they are usually called in New Zealand. **1902** *Settler's Handbook NZ* 30 *Fagus fusca* and other beeches predominate on the high lands between the lakes and the fiords on the west coast.

c. Applied to arms of Lake Te Anau.

1889 PRINCE *Diary of Trip* 19 Lake Te Anau... On this western side also there are three large arms or fiords. **1926** COWAN *Travel in NZ* II. 130 At least a dozen mapped mountain lakes send their waters into the lake-fiord [of Lake Te Anau], beside smaller tarns.

2. In *attrib.* in Comb. **Fiord Country, fiord district** *obs.*, FIORDLAND.

1892 *NZ Official Handbook* 220 In connection with the general subject [of the west coast sounds] a few words may be said of the Fiord Country, on the west coast of Otago, and which, as its name implies, is a country of fiords. **1903** *Otago Daily Times* (Dunedin) 4 Apr. (VUW Fildes Clippings 621/46) Prospecting the Fiord Country. By Wm. Wyllie... They then had to boat the provisions to the head of Edwardson Sound. **1913** GREGORY *Nature & Origin Fiords* 368 The fiord district of New Zealand is an ancient plateau which has undergone extreme oscillations in level. **1919** *TrNZI* LI. 222 It is pleasant to be able to record that the black weka is undoubtedly becoming more plentiful in the Fiord Country forest.

Fiordland. The area of fiord-like sounds on the southwest South Island coast, and its hinterland.

1892 MCHUTCHESON *Camp-life in Fiordland, New Zealand* [title: NZNB III. ii. 132, item M285] **1906** *TrNZI* XXXVIII. 338 The remnant [of Ngatimamoe was] driven into the vast forest wilderness of Fiordland. **1911** *TrNZI* XLIII. 451 The less important [is]..near the celebrated Milford Sound, in Fiordland. **1926** COWAN *Travel in NZ* II. 100 That is a typical bit of [Westland] scenery in a country that holds almost as wonderful a succession of landscapes as the Fiordland into which it merges. **1930** REISCHEK *Yesterdays in Maoriland* (1933) 237 Thereafter I remained alone in these Fjordland solitudes until October. **1951** HUNT *Confessions* 93 There are two factors which stimulate the forest growth in Fiordland. **1968** HALL-JONES *Early Fiordland* 15 The seaward aspect of Fiordland has long been known as 'The Sounds' or the 'West Coast Sounds'. The name 'Fiord' appears on three arms of Lake Te Anau, but nowhere on the coast. The sounds are, nevertheless, fiords in the true meaning of the word, hence the name 'Fiordland'. **1973** *Islands* 6 352 The mountain outline of Fiordland, all in snow and bush.

Hence **Fiordlander**, one born or resident in Fiordland.
 1992 *NZ Geographic* Jan.–Mar. 92 I find that the drowned trees had probably come from what the Fiordlanders call a tree avalanche.

fir. Also **fir-tree**. [Transf. use of northern hemisphere *fir Abies* spp. (fam. Pinaceae), a coniferous genus including important timber trees.]

1. *Obs.* Formerly applied to tall native conifers of the fam. Podocarpaceae, and occas. to other similar timber trees.
 1807 SAVAGE *Some Acc. of NZ* 8 The timber of which we have the most knowledge at the present is the fir, which grows here to an amazing height, and of such dimensions, as to admit being formed into a canoe capable of containing thirty persons. **1835** YATE *NZ* (1970) 9 The cocoa-nut tree..appears, in the distance, much like the mangroves, and the kahikatea, or white fir, of New Zealand. **1842** HEAPHY *NZ* 6 The Sydney merchants, who had bought land there [*sc.* at the Bay of Islands] on account of the valuable Kauri 'fir' that it produced..had endeavoured to dispose of it. *Ibid.* The red pines are the *Totara, Towa, Mahi*, and *Rata*... All these red firs make good spars for ships, and are frequently used by vessels visiting the settlements.

2. *Obs.* Once popularly applied to introduced *Pinus* spp. (fam. Pinaceae), esp. *P. radiata* RADIATA PINE. Also used *attrib.* in Comb. **fir-cone.**
 1866 BARKER *Station Life* (1870) 52 [We] ascend..to a large terrace-like meadow, sheltered from the north-west winds by a thick belt of firs, blue gums, and poplars. **1894** WILSON *Land of Tui* 262 Acres of wool-work covered the furniture [in an Arrowtown hotel parlour], beaded mats of grotesque design bestrewed the tables; upon the walls hung many coloured prints in fir-cone frames. **1932** CRESSWELL *Letters* 3 June (1971) 66 The white Alps in a great semi-circle around, the clump of fir-trees at the corner. **1951** FRAME in *The Lagoon* (1961) 46 When they set off down the fir-bordered road that led to the sound the sea kept making forever now in their ears. **1966** BAXTER *Collected Poems* (1980) 366 And round the next bend The fir trees with their pollen-bearing candles... Wooden motels and pine tree islands..[at Queenstown]. **1980** BENNETT *Canterbury Tale* 34 We had our games [c1907]. A favourite was 'Monkey', where the contestant climbed one of the fir trees along one side of the ground.

fire.

1. *Car-sales.* A car heater.
 1986 *NZ Herald* (Auckland) 22 Jan. sect. ii 1 Car dealers have a collection of jargon they use on the yard, so if you are thinking of taking up selling cars as a career, there are a few terms you should know... Nowadays most cars have 'fires', or heaters. **1989** MCGILL *Dinkum Kiwi Dict.* 31 *fire and flute* car heater and radio, from the days when they were not standard in our cars.

2. In the phr. **fire in (the) fern**, see FERN 1 b; **to light fires** (*whaling*), to use signal fires to communicate with whale-chasers.
 1982 GRADY *Perano Whalers* 227 Fires, to light—Signals to the whalers at sea in whale-chasers telling them in which direction to go to pursue whales sighted from shore vantage-points. The Peranos had a code of signal fires.

3. Special Comb. **fire-escape** *obs.* [f. a play on *hell-fire*], a nickname for a parson; **fire-fly**, a tent-fly used to keep the campfire and its environs dry in wet weather; **fireman** *West Coast* (a) a fish resembling a mullet; (b) *sealing* [f. the call reminiscent of an early fireman's wooden rattle], an obsolete name for the *great spotted kiwi* (KIWI 2 (2)); **fireship** *WW1*, a name for an established troop sport of disturbing an orderly evacuation by floating lighted paper down the running stream of water which flushes through a long, multi-seated lavatory; **fire-stick** [AND 1859], a burning stick used as a torch or as a fire-lighter; **fire-tree** *obs.* [f. the bright red of the blossom], POHUTUKAWA 1.
 1909 *Truth* 4 Sept. 1 An absent-minded old boy blew into a gospel foundry the other day and when the 'fire-escape' in charge said, 'Let us prey,' [*sic*] he gave as his response, 'On the people.' *Ibid.* A Porridgebyterian fire-escape called Millar has protested against Sunday concerts at Greymouth. **1918** *Quick March* 2 Sept. 1 A wowser-bird of the harp-and-halo variety (i.e., fire-escape, devil-dodger, hell-buster)..happened along and did a buttinski. **1889** PRINCE *Diary of Trip* 17 I was suddenly startled by the **fire-fly** which I had hung over the door space, being suddenly pulled to one side. **1897** WILMOT *Journal* in Reed & Reed *Farthest West* (1950) 140 We put up one of the tent flies for a firefly, the proper firefly being left at main camp for cook's use when baking tomorrow. **1904** *NZ Illustr. Mag.* Dec. 165 Our fire-fly was made of oiled calico, and proved of great service..as a nor'easter set in. **1930** DOBSON *Reminiscences* 91 When the tent was pitched and filled with brushwood, and a fire-fly at the end of the tent..a snug camp was made in a very short time. **1952** ORBELL *Comfort & Commonsense in Bush* 6 Fire Fly..you will be wise, very wise, to take another fly or large piece of canvas to cover that special area of ground in front of your fire place. **1870** WHITWORTH *Martin's Bay Settlement* 59 **Firemen**, [fish] somewhat resembling mullet. **1850** *NZ Jrnl.* X. 119 Mr.F. Strange, in a letter to Mr Gould says 'I am told that a second..species of Apteryx is to be found in the Middle Island, and that it stands about three feet high; it is called by the sealers the '**fireman.**' **1855** BONWICK *Geogr. Austral. & NZ* 180 The Fireman, a sort of a kiwi, stands three feet in height. **1866** ANGAS *Polynesia* 58 The *apteryx* is nocturnal in its habits... The largest species, the 'fireman' of the whalers, is from the Middle Island. **1867** HOCHSTETTER *NZ* 180 'The Fireman', Gould, *Birds of Australia, sub. tab.* 3., Vol. VI. Apteryx maxima, Bp. Compt. Rend. Acad. Sc. **1971** *New Zealand's Heritage* I. 11 Most of the birds, including kiwis, are recognisable from the descriptions [of the Foveaux Strait sealers], except one—a large bird they called the 'Fireman', because it made a noise like the wooden rattles which firemen of those days carried to give the alarm. **1917** in Miller *Camps, Tramps & Trenches* (1939) 42 Crook with dysentery all day... To cap it all some misguided clown let a '**fireship**' go sailing down the port 'wireless station'. This crude attempt at humour should be banned. **1819** MARSDEN *Lett. & Jrnls.* 27 Oct. (1932) 211 Before we left this village for the next I took a **fire-stick** into a shed, where our boxes stood with our provisions, and laid a little brimstone upon it to see what effect the fire would have. **1851** *McLean Papers* (ATLTS) IX. 167 He appeared with a fire-stick which he brandished about, apparently in search of something, and then lighted the remains of a candle. **1879** HAAST *Geol. Canterbury & Westland* 416 Now..the Moa-hunters disappear from the scene; but not without..leaving us..fragments of canoes, whares, and of wooden spears, fire sticks, and other objects. **1924** ANTHONY *Follow the Call* (1975) 30 I logged up about 10 acres... and had three blistering, heart-rending days burning it all at once. I went around every heap with a fire-stick first. **1936** BELSHAW et al. *Agric. Organiz. NZ* 358 With the coming of the European flora, and with the destructive agencies of man, with the firestick.., great modifications were made in the flora of the natural pastures. **1951** LEVY *Grasslands NZ* (1970) 273 It has taken only a few years of drastic treatment with the firestick, and with grazing animals..to turn this almost static tussock cover back to bare earth. **1975** KNIGHT *Poyntzfield* 41 We soon..played as friendly as before, quite willingly went to beg a 'fire stick' or do some little borrowing. **1860** BENNETT *Gatherings of Naturalist* 347 [The pohutukawa] is the New Zealand Oak and **Firetree** of the Europeans. **1966** *NZ Contemp. Dict.* (Aust.-NZ Suppl.) 616 *fire-tree n.* see pohutukawa

fireweed. [Orig. US: see Mathews, 1784; AND *Senecio* spp.] Any of various genera of plants which spring up after burns, most commonly *Senecio* spp. (formerly treated as *Erechtites*) (fam. Asteraceae), an erect daisy with lanceolate, often hairy leaves; also occas. WINEBERRY; and *Celmisia* spp. (fam. Asteraceae). As **Australian fireweed**, *Senecio bipinnatisectus* (formerly *Erechtites atkinsonii*).
 1907 LAING & BLACKWELL *Plants NZ* 246 *Aristotelia serrata* (The Wineberry)... In bush clearings, it is one of the first plants to come up, and would, on this account, be termed by the Americans a 'fireweed'. **1907** *AJHR* C-8 21 *Erechtites prenanthoides*. Common fireweed. Forest. **1910** COCKAYNE *NZ Plants & Their Story* 160 To the Elaeocarpaceae belongs the native currant (*Aristotelia racemosa*), one of the 'fire weeds' of New Zealand—i.e., a plant which comes up abundantly after a forest is burned. **1926** HILGENDORF *Weeds* 182 Fireweed (*Erechtites* spp.), occurs commonly all over the country as a wayside weed, and usually comes in great abundance after bush burns. **1933** *Press* (Christchurch) (Acland Gloss.) 30 Sept. 15 *Cotton plant.*—(Celmisia spectabilis). One of the few plants which shepherds can always identify. Sometimes called *fire weed*, as it flourishes after burns. **1940** LAING & BLACKWELL *Plants NZ* 470 *Erechtites prenanthoides*... A common 'fire weed' appearing in the bush after burning. **1969** *Standard Common Names Weeds* 3 *Australian fireweed* [s] *Erechtites atkinsoniae.* **1981** TAYLOR *Weeds of Lawns* 7 Australian Fireweed (*Erechtites atkinsoniae*) Perennial, introduced from Australia... Australian fireweed is common in many areas north of the Manawatu, but does not occur in the South Island.

Firm. *Hist.* As **the Firm** [Wilkes 1938], J.C. Williamson Ltd, theatrical entrepreneurs.
 1899 *Evening Post* (Wellington) 10 Jan. 3 'The Firm's' dramatic season.

first, *n.*

1. *Goldmining.* In the phr. **(the) first of (the)** prefixed to **gold, rush**, or the name of a goldfield, indicates the first influx of miners to, or the early days of, a new field.
 1874 BATHGATE *Col. Experiences* 86 In the early days of any gold-field, or at 'the first of the rush' as it is called, all is bustle and excitement. **1897** WRIGHT *Station Ballads* 64 When the bullockies came with their load, boys, The days of the first of the gold. **1914** PFAFF *Diggers' Story* 2 It was no uncommon thing at the first of the rush for [river-]bar tenders..to land 500 or 600 passengers a day at a pound a head. **1946** HARPER *Memories Mountains & Men* 113 In the early 90s there were still a number of real old diggers who came over 'at the first of the Coast', as they used to say, about 1865 or '66. **1967** MAY *West Coast Gold Rushes* 280 For impatient young men, anxious to be 'in the first of the rush'..every West Coast river was a likely grave.

2. *pl.* A term (often a cry) in marble playing indicating a claim to precedence in shooting.
 1953 SUTTON-SMITH *Unorganized Games NZ*

Primary School Children (VUWTS) II. 769 Action terms which refer to the shooting of the marbles are: Knuckle down..Slips, Firsts and Lasts and Forces. **1982** SUTTON-SMITH *Hist. Children's Play* 269 Here are some [marble] terms from Taranaki around 1880–90: firsts, lay-up, stakes, tips, sticking-taw.

first, *a*. [Spec. uses of *first* earliest in time or precedence.] In various special Comb. **first body**, the batch of immigrants to Canterbury who arrived on the FIRST FOUR SHIPS; **First Echelon**, see ECHELON; **first five-eighths**, see FIVE EIGHTH 2 a; **first ship** (usu. *pl.*), any one of the earliest emigrant ships bringing foundation settlers to any of the New Zealand settlements (see also FIRST FOUR SHIPS); in *attrib.* use often indicating social pre-eminence (see quot. 1976).

1851 *Lyttelton Times* 24 May 6 Your contemporary..attributes [the success of the colony] to the great advantages of the district, and the character of the **first body** of settlers... These particular privileges were assured only to that portion of the settlers who should form the first body,.. I am, Mr. Editor, Yours obediently, 'A Canterbury Colonist' of the First Body. **1898** HOCKEN *Contributions* 92 From the *Argo* to the *Mayflower*, from the *Arawa* to the *Tory*, a romantic story or a great repute has always attached to those 'first ships' and their sailors which left the shores of home for some obscure and distant land... Fifty years ago the *John Wickcliffe* and the *Philip Laing* of Otago, and the 'first four ships' of Canterbury, were invested with a halo which will always surround them. **1939** BEATTIE *First White Boy Born Otago* 67 The subject of these recollections was just seven years old when the 'first ships' came to Otago. **1942** GILBERT *Free to Laugh* 83 It was like being part of the real New Zealand, not as though we were the English arriving in the first ships.—our home was Hawaiki, our blood had reached Aotearoa sailing in the first great canoes. **1955** BJ *Cameron Collection* (TS July) first ships (n). The ships bringing the first settlers in the 1840s. In certain areas and circles, notably at New Plymouth, the descendants of those 'who came out in the first ships' are the centre of much snobbery. **1961** *Distance Looks Our Way* 2 Here is a list of the approximate number of days taken by a few of the 'first ships' of migrants to the early settlements. **1976** MCLEOD *A Girl Like I* 36 Seeing as most of Nigel's friends came from..wealthy first-ships families, we could all drive up to Taupo in their cars.

first fifteen.

a. Also **1st XV**. The premier rugby team of a secondary school or college.

1921 *Auckland Univ. College Carnival Souvenir* 14 Whether it's a matter of a place in the 1st XV. or a third in terms, it's a case of relying on your own efforts to attain it. **1934** MULGAN *Spur of Morning* 75 Free from Saturday afternoon work..he had long been one of the mainstays of the 'Varsity first fifteen. **1959** SHADBOLT *New Zealanders* (1986) 24 He was captain of the high school's first fifteen in his final year. **1967** ELLIOTT & ADSHEAD *Cowshed to Dog Collar* 20 The following year, 1933, I was selected for the First XV. **1987** SLIGO *Final Things* 37 It was over except for the trials for the first fifteen.

b. *transf.* Applied to an internationally significant 'team' or body, membership of which is an elitist symbol.

1992 *Sunday Star* (Auckland) 1 Nov. A6 [Heading] Show-off minnows prop up First XV... Yippee, we're back in the 'First XV of World Security,' fizzed McKinnon when news of New Zealand's election to the United Nations Security Council came through.

first four ships. Occas. init. caps. Also occas. as **the four ships**, the *Sir George Seymour*, *Charlotte Jane*, *Randolph*, and the *Cressy*, the fleet of emigrant ships bringing the founding settlers to Canterbury and making land in December 1850. Also used attributively to indicate social pre-eminence (see quot. 1959). See also *first ship* (FIRST).

1851 TORLESSE *Papers* (1958) 200 The class of people [among the first Canterbury settlers] is fair enough: there were more ladies in the first 4 ships than Nelson can boast of now, and there is an advertisement for a piano-tuner. **1876** KENNEDY *Colonial Travel* 203 Those who came out in the 'first four ships' were looked up to by later arrivals. To have 'come over with the Conqueror' bade fair to pale in face of having 'come over in one of the first four ships'. **1886** HART *Stray Leaves* 7 In the month of September [1850] the band of Canterbury Pilgrims.. set sail for Canterbury from Gravesend in four vessels, now known as the historical four ships, viz., *Sir George Seymour*, *Charlotte Jane*, *Randolph*, and the *Cressy*. **1935** GUTHRIE *Little Country* (1937) 5 There is a water-tight little community quietly proud of the fact that its people came out from the south of England in what are known as the First Four Ships. **1940** STUDHOLME *Te Waimate* (1954) 21 Canterbury had been chosen as the site, and the 'First Four Ships', carrying the settlers or 'Pilgrims', had arrived in Lyttelton at the close of the year 1850. **1959** SLATTER *Gun in My Hand* 77 They were not First Four Ships but they were gentry and they became squatter aristocracy as of right. **1966** *Encycl. NZ* I. 298 The main body of 780 immigrants, 106 of whom were land purchasers, arrived in four ships at Lyttelton in December 1850. **1975** ACLAND *Early Canterbury Runs* ix 270 Caverhill was one of the most remarkable of the pre-Adamite settlers (those who arrived before the first four ships) in Canterbury. **1986** BROWN *Weaver's Apprentice* 146 He earned the valuable support of those Women's Guild ladies who could trace their lineage back through the first four colonising ships.

fir-tree: see FIR.

fiscal envelope. A name given to a Government proposal to limit the total of Crown monetary compensation for past breaches of the Treaty of Waitangi to one billion (thousand million) dollars over ten years.

1994 *Evening Post* (Wellington) 9 Dec. 1 The Government's view is that once an iwi settles its claim and receives a payout from the fiscal envelope, set at $1 billion, that is the end of its claim. [**1994** *Dominion* (Wellington) 10 Dec. 2 Justice Minister Doug Graham remained adamant..that the Government's $1billion fiscal cap was not negotiable... Mr Graham said that, if at the end of the 10 years, five claims worth $100,000 each were left and the Government had $500,000 left in the envelope, it would not ask the five claimants to take less if unexpected additional claimants emerged.] **1994** *City Voice* (Wellington) 15 Dec. 1 The billion dollar 'fiscal envelope' should be rejected out of hand... The government's proposal to limit the total compensation for all historical breaches of the Treaty of Waitangi to $1 billion did not touch on issues of political control and authority 'which the treaty is all about'. **1995** *Dominion* (Wellington) 28 Mar. 6 From the start ministers were careful to avoid the words 'fiscal envelope', calling it instead the settlement envelope or the settlement package... The curious term first seeped out of Treasury briefing papers and made its way into the pulic arena in February 1993 as the 'envelope' in *The Dominion*, in an article discussing Government plans for a cap on all treaty claims. Later the term expanded to become the 'fiscal envelope'... 'Envelope' is a term which in Treasury jargon means a device for limiting and confining spending.

fish.

1. a. In early New Zealand often denoting a whale as an object of commercial pursuit.

1831 BELL *Let.* Nov. in McNab *Old Whaling Days* (1913) 9 The boats are sent out at daylight every morning, and when..they kill a fish it is towed ashore and flinched and boiled upon the beach. **1842** HEAPHY *Residence in NZ* 121 While [the whalers'] boats would be off the heads of the harbour, occasionally capturing 'fish' there. **1879** *TrNZI* XI. 33 The tide was not so strong as to draw in the 'fish' as they were termed [in Port Nicholson in 1839].

Hence **fish** *v*., to pursue and capture whales; **fisher**, a whaling vessel; **fishing** *vbl. n.*, whaling.

1802 Lieut.-Gov. King's *Queries to Whalers* 21 May in McNab *Hist. Records* (1908) I. 234 The example of ships fishing on this coast proves there is no material difference in time. **1913** MCNAB *Old Whaling Days* 1 Whalers had 'fished' off the northern coast from about 1794. **1831** *Let. from Cloudy Bay* 27 July in McNab *Old Whaling Days* (1913) 14 The following **fishers** are in Cloudy Bay:—The *Dragon*, full; *Courier*, 300 barrels *William Stoveld*, 300 barrels of black oil, and 400 of sperm. **1831** BELL *Let.* Nov. in McNab *Old Whaling Days* (1913) 9 If the **fishing** is to be carried on by a shore party, the try pots and huts are erected on the beach. **1842** HEAPHY *NZ* 38 Unfortunately for the New Zealand colonists..this trade [sc. whaling] is at present in the hands of the Sydney merchants, to whom most of the fishing stations belong.

b. In composition: **fishery**. *Obs*. (a) The business of catching and processing whales for oil, etc.

1802 Lieut.-Gov. King's *Queries to Whalers* 21 May in McNab *Hist. Records* (1908) I. 234 Do you think any advantage would attend the fishery by being allowed to go as far to the northward on this side [of] the Pacific as you are permitted to go on the east side? **1831** BELL *Let.* Nov. in McNab *Old Whaling Days* (1913) 3 The black whale fishery was tried in New Zealand some years ago, but it was abandoned until last year.

(b) A whaling-station.

1840 *Piraki Log* 27 Apr. (1911) 107 At 4 P.M. J.Robinson from Price's fishery and shipped two Hands. **1844** MONRO *Notes of a Journey* in Hocken *Contributions* (1898) 241 Most of the fisheries thereabouts [in Otago] are fitted out by him; and he [sc. John Jones] is the principal purchaser and exporter of the oil caught along the coast. **1851** WELD *Letter* Jan. in *NZGG* 21 Feb. (1851) 31 [We descended] upon the site of the old fishery of Amuri; there are no Europeans living there now, and the broken boats and deserted habitations told a melancholy tale of the decay of the whale fishery.

2. In the phr. **the fish of Maui** [a translation of Ma. *Te Ika ā Māui* with reference to the Maori myth of Maui's fishing up the North Island], the North Island.

c1963 BAXTER *Collected Poems* (1980) 280 Where the salt gush flowed in Hooking the fish of Maui on a pin.

3. Used *attrib.* in special Comb. in the names of plants and animals: **fish-bone tree** [f. the appearance of the leaves of the young plant], LANCEWOOD; **fish-eye** *Chatham Islands*, SILVEREYE; **fish-guts plant** [fanciful from the odour], *Chenopodium detestans* (fam. Chenopodiaceae), a fetid prostrate herb (see also *rotten fish plant* (ROTTEN *a*.)); **fish-hawk**, TERN 2 (3).

1860 BENNETT *Gatherings of Naturalist* 408 Europeans call the [Horoeka] the **'Fish-bone tree'**, from the peculiar appearance of its foliage. **1866** ANGAS *Polynesia* 36 The *Aralia crassifolia* or fish bone tree is a curious object in the New Zealand woods. It runs up with a slender stem to thirty feet, having tufts of leaves thrown out near the top, which are about a foot in length and an inch in breadth, of a thick, coriaceous texture, irregularly jagged at the edges and abrupt at the end. **1888** BULLER *Birds NZ* I. 242 Mr. T. Hunt, who has lived on Pitt Island for more than thirty years, in a letter to the press dated the 5th of September last, states that the *Zosterops* (to which he applies the name of **Fish-eye**) appeared there..about three weeks after the great Australian fire known in local history as Black Thursday. **1922** *Auckland Weekly News* 17 Aug. 17 Mr. R.W. Kerr..knew white-eyes on the Chathams, where they are known as fish-eyes. **1877** *TrNZI* IX. 550 It is the '**Fish-guts plant**' of the shepherds. [**1878** *TrNZI* X. 410 *Chenopodium detestans* [Fish-guts plant]... Cultivated land near the outlet of Lake Wanaka.] **1969** [see *rotten fish plant* (ROTTEN *a*.)]. **1988** WEBB et al. *Flora of NZ* IV. 429 *C[henopodium] detestans*..fish-guts plant. Very foetid prostrate herb..often reddish on exposed parts... Lowland to montane open tussock grassland..rare. (*Endemic*). **1870** *TrNZI* II. 76 Sterna caspia, Pall. **Fish-hawk**. This fine tern is content with merely a hollow scraped in the sand, just large enough to contain the eggs.

fit, *a*. In the word group **fit as** with some animal comparison, very fit and active, 'fit as a fiddle'.

a. fit as a buck rat.
1945 HENDERSON *Gunner Inglorious* 19 Grimy as a sweep, greasy as a butcher's pup manhandling ammunition, but oh I feel fine, fit as a buck rat. **1960** CRUMP *Good Keen Man* 13 He was about 45 and looked as fit as a buck rat. **1986** DAVIN *Salamander & the Fire* 76 Anyway it was a time when the chaps were so randy—death and the desert had something to do with it, I expect, and being young and fit as buck rats.

b. fit as a flea.
1969 MASON *Television Script* in *Solo* (1981) 210 Young Man: Deerstalker. Live in Hoky,... Up on the tops, all on my own. Fit as a flea, no beer, no gut, no birds, come down, cash my tails, live it up.

c. fit as a trout.
1980 LELAND *Kiwi-Yankee Dict.* 40 'Old Sam is as fit as a trout, he walked five miles yesterday just to sink a few with me.' Old Sam is in good shape.

fit, *n. Drug-users*. [A shortened form of *outfit*.] An outfit for injecting or using a drug; a hypodermic syringe.
1982 NEWBOLD *Big Huey* 13 I bought five more cans of morphine, and he threw in a fit as well so I could hit myself. *Ibid.* 248 Fit (n) Hypodermic syringe. Contraction of 'outfit'. **1983** *Dominion* (Wellington) 17 Feb. 4 I grabbed the fit and threw it out of the window. **1986** *Evening Post* (Wellington) 5 Apr. 19 Some addicts continue to..vomit at the thought of having a 'fit' in their hands, he says.

fit, *v. Criminals*. Also with **up**. To find or fabricate evidence to secure a conviction.
1938 *Press* (Christchurch) (McNab Slang) 2 Apr. 18 [In local criminal slang]..'to fit' is to find enough evidence to convict. **1949** PARTRIDGE *Dict. Slang Addenda* 1048 fit. v., corresponds to *fit*, n...: New Zealand and Australian c[ant]: since ca. 1930. **1982** NEWBOLD *Big Huey* 248 Fit up (v) See Dud Up [= 'Fabricate evidence to secure a conviction.].

Hence **fitted**.
1981 *Avondale College Slang Words* (Auckland) (Goldie Brown Collect.) *fitted*: framed

Hence **fit** *n*. [AND 1882], sufficient evidence for a conviction.
1937 PARTRIDGE *Dict. Slang* 279 *fit.* Sufficient evidence to convict (a wrongdoer): New Zealand c[ant] (–1932).

five. Used in various combinations and collocations where the number (of) *five* is of significance: **five-acre Tory**, a name for a politically conservative but very small land holder; **five-o'clock** in *attrib*. use, see *five to six* below; **man of fives** *obs.*, a pugilist (cf. modern *bunch of fives* 'fist'); **fivestones**, a variant of DUCKSTONE; **five to six** *obs.*, in the collocations: **five to six (five o'clock) rush** (or **swill**), describing the rush in the last hour of public bar drinking during the time of six-o'clock closing (see also SWILL).
1980 GLEN *Bush in Our Yard* 107 'Instant sheds, especially for that small cocky just establishing himself, or perhaps the **five-acre Tory**,'..the auctioneer presented the four buildings. **1871** MONEY *Knocking About NZ* 11 [He]..alighted on the road, and invited '**the man of fives**' to a speedy adjustment of their differences. **1953** SUTTON-SMITH *Unorganized Games NZ Primary School Children* (VUWTS) II. 740 **Fivestones** (Stoke—a remnant of Duckstones), Hayball (Brooklyn) [are throwing games mentioned today]. **1959** BOLLINGER *Grog's Own Country* 4 After the Second World War, a returned serviceman termed it the '**5 to 6** o'clock swill'. **1959** SLATTER *Gun in My Hand* 52 This land where Rugby is a religion and the race track a shrine and the five to six pub rush Communal Living. *Ibid.* 90 The bar is crowded for the five to six rush is in full swing. **1963** *Dominion* (Wellington) 23 July 1 New Zealander's liquor hours, notably the 'five to six swill' produced..debate and plenty of laughs at the National Party Conference yesterday. **1971** ARMFELT *Catching Up* 11 How do you like our Five O'clock swill? Not like the old country. All evening to drink your pint.

five eighth. Also **five eighths**. [See OED *five* C 2 '*Austral.* and *N.Z.*', 1905.]

1. In rugby football, one of the two players (first and second five-eighths) positioned between the halfback and the centre three-quarters.
1899 *Taranaki Herald* (New Plymouth) 21 Aug. 3 The following Auckland team has been selected..five-eighths Phelan, Riley; half-back Young. **1902** ELLISON *The Art of Rugby Football* 12 The backs, as played in New Zealand consist of a Full-back..the Five-eighth, who stands about midway between the forwards and the three-quarters, and the half-back, who generally plays close up to the forwards. **1908** BARR *Brit. Rugby Team in Maoriland* 165 The two half back system, which was afterwards to develop into the now well-known five-eighths, prevailed very largely about 1880. **1910** *Evening Post* (Wellington) 4 July 3 New Zealand.—Full-back, O'Leary; three-quarters, Stohr, Burns, Mitchell; five-eighths, Mitchinson, Mynott; half-back, Roberts. **1949** DAVIN *Roads from Home* 29 The two Star five-eighths would be too late to get back on side, however hard they ran. **1954** *Press* (Christchurch) 15 June 12 It is stated that in 1889 Alhambra came from Dunedin to play Merivale and played only one half-back instead of two. The man who would have been the second half-back 'stood between [the halfback] and the three-quarters line'. The Club had no name for the new position, and some discussion took place about it. The argument was ended when a Merivale player said that if the new position was between half and three-quarters, he must be five-eighths. The name was adopted. **1992** *Dominion Sunday Times* (Wellington) 13 Apr. 9 New Zealand has..introduced some distinctive features of its own—in a playing sense, there was the unique five-eighth system ('if he's not a half and he's not a three-quarter, he must be a five-eighth'). **1992** PALENSKI *Our National Game* 26 The pivot for most of Alhambra's attacks [in a game in Dunedin in 1890] was the extra player between the halfback and the three-quarter line. After the game..a Merivale back, one F. Childs, is credited with coming up with a new name, five-eighths... If the player was not a half and was not a threequarter, he said, he was between the two and therefore must be a five-eighth.

2. a. As **first five-eighths** (also *ellipt.* **first-five**), the rugby midfield back between the halfback and *second five-eighths*.
1968 SLATTER *Pagan Game* 186 No doubt their first five did hoist a good kick in the air but Pemberton should have been there to take the ball. **1978** GLOVER *Men of God* 14 I was an acolyte once, and later played first five for Marist. **1991** *Listener* 30 Sept. 17 In the backs, the Wallabies have an experienced halfback/first-five combination.

b. As **second five-eighths** (also *ellipt.* **second five**), the rugby midfield back between the *first five-eighths* and the centre three-quarters.
1917 *Free Lance* (Wellington) 10 Aug. 19 Tonks scored two fine tries that indicated a good movement was made in placing him the second five-eighths. **1935** *Free Lance* (Wellington) 15 May 51 A second five-eighth can deputise for a centre. **1958** MCCARTHY *Rugby in my Time* 65 They brought in John Tanner from Auckland at second five-eighth. **1968** SLATTER *Pagan Game* 126 From midfield scrums the first five goes one way yelling for the ball but the second five takes it from the half and goes the other way. **1985** PALENSKI *Loveridge Master Halfback* 238 More than any other backline position, except the halfback, the second-five is the player who calls the shots. **1991** *Dominion Sunday Times* (Wellington) 22 Sept. 29 Otago's second try came six minutes later, after some fine build-up play—especially by Hotton and classy second-five Steve Cottrell.

five-finger.

1. a. Also occas. **five-fingers.** (a) [f. the fingerlike shape of the palmate leaf.] Any of several small native trees of the genera *Pseudopanax* and *Schefflera* (fam. Araliaceae), having palmate leaves composed of 3–7 leaflets. See also FIG *n.*², HOUPARA, IVY-TREE, SEVENFINGER, *six-finger* (SIX), SNOTTY-GOB, *three-finger* (THREE), WHAUWHAU *a*, WHAUWHAUPAKU *a*.
1922 *Auckland Weekly News* 12 Oct. 17 Ivyworts..include..five-fingers, a small tree, particularly plentiful on the West Coast of the South Island, where cattle prefer it before any other plant in the forest. **1940** STUDHOLME *Te Waimate* (1954) 246 In this bush were..Ohau, (panax or five-finger),... koromiko and other shrubs. **1952** THOMSON *Deer Hunter* 161 Most of the greener type of shrubs, such as Whitewood and Five-finger, had almost disappeared. **1969** *Bull. Wellington Bot. Soc. No.36* 25 One of the key indicator species..is mountain five-finger (*Pseudopanax colensoi*), and this is extremely scarce. **1969** HARVEY & GODLEY *Botanical Paintings* 50 *Pseudopanax arboreum* Five-finger Whauwhaupaku Araliaceae... The name 'five-finger' is derived from the palmately compound leaves, and another name 'ivy-tree' reminds us that this species is in the ivy family. **1978** MOORE & IRWIN *Oxford Book NZ Plants* 98 *Pseudopanax arboreus*, *whauwhaupaku*. Five-finger is one of our commonest small trees. **1995** coastal five finger (*Pseudopanax lessonii* [see HOUPARA].

(b) [f. the finger-like shape of the fruit.] The fruit of the kiekie.
c**1920** BEATTIE *Trad. Lifeways Southern Maori* (1994) 525 What the Pakeha calls 'Five Fingers' grows

inside [the tawhara] and gets ripe in April and May, each being something like a banana in shape and very sweet to the taste. **1981** HENDERSON *Exiles Asbestos Cottage* 71 We are on safer ground when we come to the Asbestos Cottage speciality of five-finger juice. **1992** *Dominion Sunday Times* (Wellington) 26 July 21 Five-finger fruits ripen at the coldest part of the year, and it is odd to see silvereyes..gathering on the trees to feed.

b. As **five-fingered Jack** *obs.*, *Pseudopanax arboreus.*

1900 *Canterbury Old & New* 184 Broadleaf five-fingered Jack and the totara..jostle one another in the dense dry bush. **1940** LAING & BLACKWELL *Plants NZ* 324 *Nothopanax arboreum*... This is one of the most abundant trees on the fringes of the forest... It is known by a variety of names Five-fingered Jack (Canterbury), Snotty-gob (Taranaki), NZ Fig (Otago).

2. Also **five fingers**. Either of two grasses: doab *Cynodon dactylon*, or summer grass, *Digitaria sanguinalis*.

1926 HILGENDORF *Weeds* 25 Summer Grass..also called crab grass, finger grass, devil's fingers, five fingers and summer paspalum, is a weed of garden and cultivated lands. *Ibid.* 40 Doab (*Cynodon dactylon*), often called Indian doab or Doobj, Bermuda grass, five finger, and devil's finger, is a twitch very common in the North Island.

3. Also **fivefingers**. [f. the five or more rays of the pectoral fins.] *sea perch* (PERCH *n.* 2 (4)).

1938 *TrRSNZ* LXVIII. 416 *Helicolenus percoides*... Sea perch..(scroddie, fivefinger, soldier-fish, Jock Stuart, Highlander). **1956** GRAHAM *Treasury NZ Fishes* 344 Seaperch (Pohuiakaroa) Jock Stuart, Highlander, Fivefinger, Soldierfish or Scroddie... These names have a bearing on some distinguishing characteristic of the fish..while Fivefingers is given on account of the so-called five (really more) fingers (rays) of the pectoral fins, on which the fish has a habit of resting on the floor of the aquarium tank. **1966** DOOGUE & MORELAND *Sea Anglers' Guide* 287 Sea Perch... *Other names: Helicolenus papillosus;* Jock Stewart, scarpee, highlander, fivefinger, Maori chief, scrodie gurnard (Australia); pahuiakaroa (Maori). **1981** WILSON *Fisherman's Bible* 100 Five-finger: *see Sea Perch*

4. five finger, the five of the trump suit in the game of FORTY-FIVES q.v.

5. Also **five-fingered**. Used *attrib.* in collocations suggesting dishonesty: **five-finger discount** [Ayto & Simpson US 1966], shoplifting; **to use a five-fingered chequebook**, to shoplift or steal; **five-finger fly**, see quot.

1981 *Avondale College Slang Words* (Auckland) (Goldie Brown Collect.) *five-finger discount*: shoplifting **1990** *Ruby & Rata* (Film) I had to use my **five-fingered chequebook**. **1982** WOODHOUSE *Blue Cliffs* 279 **Five Finger Fly**: Hand when used for tickling fish.

five-fingered Jack: see FIVE-FINGER 1 b.

fix bayonets. Also **fixed bayonets**. [Prob. an extended use of WW1 term for home-brew spirit in POW camps from its sharp taste or effects: cf. Partridge.] Strong liquor, *spec.* a strong beer, or more recently, methylated spirits as a drink.

1906 ELKINGTON *Adrift in NZ* 241 We used to call the beer we bought in these [gum-]fields 'fixed bayonets', 'streaked lightning' and 'fire water'; they were the three brands, and the names were strangely suitable. **1984** Fix Bayonets [see JESSIE'S DREAM]. **1988** McGILL *Dict. Kiwi Slang* 45 *fix bayonets* methylated spirits..with ref. its sting.

fizz. Mainly *children*. Also **fizzy-drink**. A soft-drink; flavoured aerated water. Also in Comb. **fizz-bottle**, a (returnable) soft-drink bottle.

1938 FINLAYSON *Brown Man's Burden* 66 ('By the Calm Waters') The youngster cried, 'Atta boy!' as they raced to the store to buy bright red fizzy drinks and chocolate blocks. **1946** BEAGLEHOLE *Some Modern Maoris* 96 [A special dinner would] include:.. meat,.. cabbage, puha, raspberry drink, 'fizz', tea, and perhaps some beer. **1947** GASKELL *All Part of the Game* (1978) 86 Boxes of pies stood near..and rows of red and yellow fizz bottles along the wall. **1950** *Landfall* 16 310 There were mostly Maoris in the shop getting fizz and pies. **1951** FRAME in *Some Other Country* (1984) 101 O the train..and the bottle of fizzy drink that you could only half finish because you were too full. **1953** *Here & Now* June 22 Milk for the children or fruit drinks other than 'fizzies'. **1957** FRAME *Owls Do Cry* (1967) 146 The patients, toppling full of fizz and sky, climbed into the bus. **1982** PEAT *Detours* 226 Among fizz drinkers, those whose preference was Coke in cans had a lot to answer for.

fizz-boat. A small motorboat, usu. a fibre-glass hull driven by an outboard motor.

1977 *Daily Telegraph* (London) 24 Feb. 19 The water was like glass as the Royal barge came in, chased by speedboats, 'fizz boats'—the New Zealand name for outboards. **1987** GEE *Prowlers* 72 Phil..has an expensive boat: red and yellow fibreglass, a speedster, a real fizz-boat, with a floral plastic awning over the cabin and stainless-steel fittings everywhere. **1993** McCARROLL *Life Is So Complicated* 159 Yachties have a superior attitude to speedy power boats which they dismiss as fizz boats.

Hence **fizz-boater**, one who owns or drives a fizz-boat.

1993 *Evening Post* (Wellington) 8 Sept. 12 Fran Wilde..tackled the awful prospect of dear old Wellie town losing the Royal New Zealand Ballet to those fizz boaters, those backyard barbecuers, those plebs up north.

fizzer. *Children*. A cracker which does not explode, often broken in half and the powder ignited to make it 'fizz' (known to Ed. from c1938).

1983 STEWART *Springtime in Taranaki* (1991) 78 Next day, there was the curious..pleasure of searching for the crackers that had failed to explode, known [c1920s] as 'fizzers', and, holding a match to the black gunpowder as you bent them in two, duly fizzing them. **1984** TRAIL *Child of the Arrow* 45 A little lad had found a cracker without a wick in the grass near his gate and had coaxed his mother for a match to let the 'fizzer' off.

flag, *n. Obs.* [Spec. use of *flag* for plants with a bladed leaf, esp. iris: cf. OED *flag n.*¹]

1. Also occas. **flaggy grass**. RAUPO *n.* 1 a. See also COOPER'S FLAG.

1773 BAYLY *Journal* 17 Dec. in McNab *Hist. Records* (1914) II. 217 After breakfast the Surgeon & myself..& the Ships Cooper went in a small cutter..to get flags for the Coopers use. **1815** KING *Jrnl.* 15 Feb. in Elder *Marsden's Lieutenants* (1934) 97 Our house or hut is made with flags by the natives. **1817** NICHOLAS *Voyage NZ* II. 339 Flaggy grass Roupo. **1836** HEMPLEMAN *Let.* 17 Aug. in McNab *Old Whaling Days* (1913) 152 We wish you to procure for us..as many Flags [for caulking whale-oil casks] & Spars as possible. **1841** *Piraki Log* 17 Apr. (1911) 123 Men employed in bringing grass and flags from the creek. **1939** BEATTIE *First White Boy Born Otago* 29 What we used to call flags then [in the 1840s], but now known as bulrushes or by the Maoris called rapo (or raupo), were used by the coopers then. They were inserted between the joints and kept the oil casks as tight as a drum.

2. Either of FLAX 1 a or TOETOE.

1777 FORSTER *Voyage Round World* I. 201 On these they had laid the bark of trees, and covered the whole with the rough fibres of the flag, or New Zealand flax-plant. *Ibid.* 226 Many of their cloaks, made of the fibres of the New Zeeland flag (*phormium*), were new. **1780** SEWARD *Elegy on Capt. Cook* 12 In New Zealand is a flag of which the natives make their nets and cordage. **1834** MARKHAM *NZ* (1963) 35 The Thatch is the Toie Toie a kind of Flags that is used for the Huts, and an other one more like what our Coopers use for putting between the seams of a Cask, called Rappoo. **1853** ADAMS *Canterbury Settlement* 49 The 'warries'..are generally low, built of mud or reeds, and sometimes thatched with toē-toē a kind of grass or small flag which grows to the height of three or four feet.

flag, *v.* Also **flag away**. [Poss. reinforced by *flag off*, used of aircraft landings esp. on carriers.] *trans.* In rugby football, the action of linesmen indicating a miss at goal by waving lowered flags; hence, to dismiss; to put aside.

1968 SLATTER *Pagan Game* 115 He did not like radio commentaries because he did not have the type of mind that could readily visualise the game from such crescendic clichés:.. well and truly tackled, flagged away, favouring his leg, a flurry of fists, bundled into touch. **1980** *Listener* 6 Dec. 56 [I.A. Gordon] Confessing [my] ignorance of the origin of the verb 'to skull' (to drink quickly), the verb 'to flag' (to waive something, to put it aside, not to bother about it). **1986** *Evening Post* (Wellington) 5 Apr. 19 He doesn't take acid any more, but can never see himself flagging away marijuana. **1992** ANDERSON *Portrait Artist's Wife* 127 This was the man who had flagged away a half-share in Glenfrae, one of the sweetest holdings in the Bay. *Ibid.* Dora decided to flag away the Bay except for Grandpop.

flaggy grass: see FLAG 1.

flagon.

1. A large, usu. half-gallon (now 2.25 litres), bottle or container for draught beer or other drink; also its contents. See also *half-g* (HALF- 3 a (b)).

1956 *Dominion* (Wellington) 16 July 14 The association had not established that the cost of selling beer in flagons was greater than the cost of selling by other means. **1964** FRANCES *Johnny Rapana* 20 He reached for the flagon. Dinny always had a flagon about the house somewhere. **1976** JOHNSTON *New Zealanders* 148 As common are half-gallon flagons of draught beer (half-Gs), filled under pressure. **1982** [see HALF- 3 a (b)]. **1990** KIDMAN *True Stars* 8 One night, after a flagon, he elaborated, just the once.

2. Special Comb. **flagon beer**, beer provided in, or drunk out of, a flagon; **flagon-party**, a party where flagon beer is drunk; **flagon-wagon** (*joc.*), a truck carrying crates of flagons of beer.

1990 KIDMAN *True Stars* 8 They sang..on Saturday nights, drank flagon beer, brought a couple of dozen home. **1974** HILLIARD *Maori Woman* 110 The **flagon-parties**, the crates of half-gees on the sink, men in singlets queued up at the keg. **1973** WHEELER *Hist. Sheep Stations NI* 102 At this stage I remember..the '**flagon wagon**' arriving at Te Paki from Houhora, New Zealand's northernmost pub.

Flagstaff War. *Hist.* [The allusion is to Heke's cutting down of the British flagstaff at Kororareka.] The armed confrontation with Hone Heke in North Auckland beginning 8 July 1844. See also HEKE WAR, WAR 2 b.

1984 Barber *Red Coat to Jungle Green* 12 From 1844 to 1847 the 'red tribe' fought the first New Zealand war, against Hone Heke, and his allies. The 'Flagstaff War', as it is sometimes called, followed a build up of disappointment, frustration, and suspicion, amongst the northern tribes, in the years immediately following the signing of the Treaty of Waitangi.

flake. *gold flake* (GOLD 3).
1852 *NZGG* 10 Dec. V. 30(183) (Heaphy's Rep.) The greatest number of flakes in the prospecting dish, appeared upon washing some earth yesterday. **1852** *Gold Circular* in Swainson *Auckland* (1853) 109 One parcel of..[gold] consisting of large rich dust and flakes..was sold by auction..yesterday. **1969** Henderson *Open Country Calling* 110 I got gold out of twenty-five of them [*sc*. rivers]: not more than ten to twenty flakes in each case. **1991** *NZ Geographic* Apr.–June 106 Though erosion had long buried the gold-bearing gravels, nuggets and flakes could be recovered from some stream beds where water had cut down to the original deposits.

Hence **flaky**, of gold, existing as small flat scales.
1852 *Gold Circular* in Swainson *Auckland* (1853) 106 The dust consisted of flaky gold, of a pale lemon colour, largely intermixed with auriferous quartz. **1914** Pfaff *Diggers' Story* 123 On looking..shiny particles of flaky gold were revealed in unusually large quantities. **1924** *Grey River Argus* 9 Feb. 7 It is shotty, not flaky gold, that is the Diggers Delight.

flakers, *a.* [Cf. Partridge 8: Austral. and naval slang.] In the phr. **to be (get) flakers,** to be or become unconscious through drink, to become 'flaked out'.
1961 *Evening Post* (Wellington) 31 May 19 A 25 year old Maori pantrymaid reported as going to a party on the ship, 'and got flakers'. **1978** Hilliard *Glory & Dream* 166 'Anybody seen Charlie?' 'In the rubbity this arfto. He's probably flakers.' **1988** McGill *Dict. Kiwi Slang* 45 *flakers* drooping drunk and on the way out; eg 'For Pete's sake don't buy Beech another round. Can't you see he's flakers?'

flaky: see FLAKE.

flannel-leaf. The naturalized weed (*woolly) mullein Verbascum thapsus* (fam. Scrophulariaceae), having a large leaf flannel-like to the touch. See also *bushman's friend* (BUSHMAN 5), GOLDEN ROD, TOBACCO.
1926 Hilgendorf *Weeds* 155 Flannel Leaf..is commonly called mullein in England, and is frequently so called here as well. Its commonest local name is probably tobacco plant, or native tobacco, a name for which there is no justification in either appearance or use. Velvet mullein, woolly mullein, golden rod, and Aaron's rod are other appellations. **1974** *Dominion* (Wellington) 22 Nov. 5 Verbascum thapsus, a weed of poor land has many popular names. In New Zealand it is called native tobacco, velvet, flannel leaf and golden rod. **1983** Ell *Wildflowers & Weeds* 14 The Woolly Mullein is often known in New Zealand as flannel-leaf for its leaves have a woolly feel to them.

flap-jack, *n.*[1] Also early **flapper**. [f. Brit. dial.: also US *flapjack* a pancake.] A rough and ready pancake or fritter usu. of flour and water. Cf. FLIPPER (*flipperjack*), SLAP-JACK.
1863 Walker *Jrnl. & Lett.* (ATLTS) 4 May You ask if we had pan-cakes on Shrove Tuesday. I do not remember..but if there was no meat to be had, I think it very likely what are called here 'flappers' i.e. flour and water mixed up thin and fried in fat. They are very good with sugar. **c1872** in Meredith *Adventuring in Maoriland* (1935) 36 I am getting on better with my cooking. I will show you how to make 'flap-jacks' and 'johnny-cakes' when I come home. **1896** Harper *Pioneer Work* 196 [Comic bush menu.] Roti Roast Weka Entremets Flap-jack and Jam. **1914** Pfaff *Diggers' Story* 115 We made some flapjacks, and fried the bacon. **1921** Guthrie-Smith *Tutira* (1926) 151 Meantime..Stuart..was preparing the immediate luxury of flapjacks. **1936** *Cook. Book NZ Women's Inst.* 105 Flap Jacks. Three tablespoons oatmeal, 1 tablespoon flour, salt, small teaspoon baking soda. Mix dry ingredients, then moisten to a batter with buttermilk. Let stand for ten minutes in order to swell. Fry in bacon fat and serve round bacon for breakfast. **1945** Harper *Camping & Bushcraft in NZ* 11 To make a flapjack, mix some flour and baking powder into a thick paste.

flap-jack, *n.*[2] [See quot. 1961.] A seaweed of *Carpophyllum* spp.
1948 Martin *NZ Nature Study* 136 Rock Girdle or Flap-jack [illustrated] *Ibid.* 139 The rock tangles or tangleweeds have twisted zigzag stems and branches without leaves while the *Carpophyllums* or flap-jacks as a rule have flat stems and marginal branches. **1961** Martin *Flora NZ* 14 The commonest of the four species [of seaweed] is (*C. maschalocarpum*) which has been designated by the apt and appropriate name of flap-jack from the habit of the plant in swaying first in one direction and then the other as the water enters or recedes from the surge channels between tidal rocks. **1993** Gabites *Wellington's Living Cloak* 22 Beds of kelp lie offshore, but flapjack [*Carpophyllum maschalocarpum*] and *Champia* hug low-tide mark.

flapper: see FLAP-JACK *n.*[1]

flat, *n.*[1] [Spec. use of *flat* a piece of level ground: AND 1799.]

1. An area of level ground, often, in farming use, as distinct from hilly or broken country. Compare TERRACE 1 a.
1821 May *McCrae's Evidence before Commissioner Bigge* in McNab *Hist. Records* (1908) I. 535 In the interior of the country and along the east coast..there are extensive flats of rich alluvial land. **1839** Chaffers *Report* in Wakefield *Handbook NZ* (1848) 229 Between the bay and the valley at the back, spreads a flat, which contains between 200 and 300 acres of land. **1842** Mary F. Swainson let. in *William Swainson* 21 Aug. (1992) 90 The house that we are in is on one acre... We are on the Thorndon Flat. **1844** Deans *Pioneers Canterbury* (1937) 79 There are many miles of first rate soil in different places on the flat. **1852** Cook *Jrnl. Macquarie Is.* 1 The part joining the land is a flat about ¼ of a mile broad. **1860** in Butler *First Year* (1863) iv 60 We burnt the flats as we rode down, and made a smoke which was noticed fifty or sixty miles off. **1874** [see TERRACE 1 a]. **1882** Potts *Out in Open* 197 It was plentiful in the thickets that dotted the river bed flats. **1926** Cowan *Travel in NZ* II. 23 The decayed little *kainga* sits near the tip of a long flat stretching out southward from the peninsula. **1958** *Tararua* Sept. 48 Midday boil-up was at the end of the first long flat, after which our route lay over river boulders to a small flat. **1963** Pearson *Coal Flat* 53 'There's the Flat,' the young man said...'Flat?' she thought, 'I thought it would be a river-flat. That's a terrace.' **1982** *Agric. Gloss.* (MAF) 5 *Flat:* An area of level ground, usually near a river.

2. With various modifying prefixes. **a.** As **alluvial, fern, flax, pumice, toetoe flat.** See also *river flat.*
1840 *Rep. Martin from River Thames* Oct. in *GBPP (No.311)* (1841) 119 I have little doubt that..all these flax flats might be made available. **1843** *NZ Jrnl.* IV. 216 The natives showed me the point at which the water leaves the river, when the freshets come down, and crosses over the *toi-toi* flat. **1860** Donaldson *Bush Lays & Rhymes* 8 Away over the fern-flats. **c1875** Meredith *Adventuring in Maoriland* (1935) 45 On the way back..we found poor old Paitai stuck in one of those 'underground creeks' peculiar to the flax-flats of New Zealand. **1902** *Settler's Handbook NZ* 3 The soil is chiefly clay or light loam, with alluvial flats in the valleys, and all well watered. **1916** Cowan *Bush Explorers* (VUWTS) 4 We cantered over the fern and manuka-clothed pumice flats. **1934** Lee *Children of Poor* (1949) 11 Here and there beside the rivers were rich, alluvial flats and plains of country, easily broken by plough.

b. In place-names.
1842 Heaphy *NZ* 70 The town is chiefly built on what are called the 'Lambton' and 'Thorndon Flats', which are two pieces of flat or gently sloping ground, extending from the hills at the back of the town to the beach. Each of these flats is about a mile square. **c1875** Meredith *Adventuring in Maoriland* (1935) 62 I selected a tent-fly..and proceeded to a bare glade on the Kohiwai flat.

flat, *n.*[2] *Ellipt.* for FLATFISH 1.
1939 Brown *Farmer's Wife* 222 'No flats'..describing the goggle-eyed, square riggered flounders..and soles. **1986** Brown *Weaver's Apprentice* 93 In the [fishing-boat's] wheelhouse, the old army surplus radio was chattering. '..Nothin' but flats anyway.'

flat, *a.* and *adv.*

1. In collocations indicating 'at top speed', 'at full effort' 'to the limit of one's resources', 'flat out': **flat stick (sticks)** [origin uncertain: poss. an allusion to an accelerator lever]; **flat as a tack** [AND 1977: with a play on senses of *flat*], **flat tack** (occas. **flat tap**); **flat to the boards** [alluding to an accelerator being depressed flat to generate top speed: AND 1963].
1972 *Evening Post* (Wellington) 20 Aug. 'We are **flat stick** on Friday night and I refuse to turn this business away' he said. **1986** a US food-writer's comments on NZ English: p.c. Tui Flower *NZ Woman's Weekly* (14 Jan. 1987) Shearers stop for a *smoko* (coffee break), then work *flat stick* (at maximum effort). **1988** McGill *Dict. Kiwi Slang* 45 *flat stick* as fast as the vehicle will travel; eg 'He was going flat stick, but the cop was gaining on him.' **1990** Kidman *True Stars* 23 I'm flat sticks, can I talk to you later, lovey? **1971** Shadbolt *Bullshit & Jellybeans* 34 A gang..threw a bottle at the hotrod so we screwed **flat tap** into town to round up the boys. **a1974** Syder & Hodgetts *Aust. & NZ English* (TS) 354 Hard work. Under pressure. 'I'm **flat as a tack**, but don't worry—hard work never hurt anyone.' **1988** McGill *Dict. Kiwi Slang* 45 *flat tack* as fast as you can get yourself or your vehicle to go; eg 'She took the corner flat tack and somehow got round it on two screeching, smoking tyres.' **1991** *Evening Post* (Wellington) 9 Apr. 1 The Salvation Army is 'flat tack' with food calls in the city, which have doubled since Christmas. **1968** Slatter *Pagan Game* 150 I work **flat to the boards**, never even cough till ten, slogging me guts out to buy luxuries for the wife.

2. [AND 1911.] *Two-up.* Of spun coins, landing flat, not rolling on impact.
1917 *Chron. NZEF* 16 May 137 His hand was firm and sure his grip And two 'flat heads' they 'lob'!

flat, *v.* [f. *flat* a residential suite of rooms usu. on one floor: cf. NewSOD *flat v.*[2] '*Austral.*'.] *intr.* Also quasi-*trans.* **flat with** (a person). Esp. of

flatfish. [Local use of *flatfish*: cf. OED 1710.]

1. Any of a group of New Zealand fish having a flattened body and both eyes on one side of the head, esp. FLOUNDER *n.*, SOLE, and also BRILL, TURBOT; the group of such fishes collectively. See also FLAT *n.*²

1770 [see SOLE 1]. 1791 BELL *Jrnl. Voyage H.M.S. 'Chatham'* Nov. (Vancouver exped.) (ATLMS) 51 We never caught any Flat Fish. c1826–27 BOULTBEE *Journal* (1986) 110 flatfish—battik 1848 WAKEFIELD *Handbook NZ* 303 The habouka is taken..; flat fish and oysters in all the bays. 1855 TAYLOR *Te Ika A Maui* 624 The..(*patiki*,) or flat fish, is speared by torch-light. 1901 *TrNZI* XXXIII. 574 In two hours 48 dozen of flat-fish, brill, and other good fish were trawled. 1929–1930 *TrNZI* LX. 142 Practically no trawling has been done at the Chathams, so our knowledge of the flatfishes is rather meagre. 1956 GRAHAM *Treasury NZ Fishes* 210 The Lemon Sole, like the Common Sole, Flounder, Brill and Turbot... are known to fishermen, auctioneers, retailers and the public generally as Flatfish. 1986 *NZ Woman's Weekly* 30 June 45 I've always called them 'flatfish'. But I saw a big poster about NZ fish which declared they were called sole and never mentioned flatfish at all.

2. In the phr. **to lie like a flatfish**, to lie confidently and profusely.

1968 SLATTER *Pagan Game* 161 No warrant of fitness so I started lying like a flatfish—I'm not overstruck on that new cop.

flathead.

1. [AND 1790.] Any of various fish with a flattened head: see esp. MONKFISH *Kathetostoma giganteum*, and also GURNARD 1, 2 (1), MAORI CHIEF *n.*² 1, STARGAZER. See also CHINAMAN *n.*⁵, FRENCHMAN.

1872 HUTTON & HECTOR *Fishes NZ* 26 Notothenia coriiceps... Flat-head. 1886 SHERRIN *Handbook Fishes NZ* 301 Notothenia coriiceps... Flat-head, or Maori Chief. 1913 *TrNZI* XLV. 229 *Kathetostoma giganteum*... Anderton records one specimen of this fish—the 'flathead'—as taken about eight miles from Taiaroa Head. 1922 *Auckland Weekly News* 15 June 14 There is a flathead with grey and black and white spots, and with pale blue edges to his fins and tail. 1938, 1956 [see CHINAMAN *n.*⁵]. 1967 NATUSCH *Animals NZ* 224 The flathead, *Kathetostoma giganteum*..is usually found on its own, often burrowing in the sea bed with just the eyes and mouth showing... Some fishermen call it chinaman. 1970 SORENSEN *Nomenclature NZ Fish* 37 Monkfish..*Geniagnus monopterygius*.. [and] *Kathetostoma giganteum*... Other common names (both): Monkfish, Monks, Stargazer, Flathead (also applied at times to export gurnard); Churchills, Toebiters, Bulldogs, Spotted Stargazer, Maori Chief (Dunedin); Muddies. 1982 AYLING *Collins Guide* (1984) 198 *Deepsea Flathead Hoplichthys haswelli*... It is impossible to confuse this fish with any other; a huge flat head accounts for almost a third of the total length of the fish. 1986 [see MONKFISH].

2. [Cf. AND 1911–1950.] In the game of two-up, a coin thrown up flat without spinning so that it, will come down 'heads'. Cf. FLOAT *v.*

1917 *Chron. NZEF* 16 May 137 Two 'flat-heads' they 'lob.'

3. In full **flathead nail**. A nail with a wide, flat (rather than a rose-shaped, or cylindrical 'brad') head.

1986 *Listener* 26 Apr. 51 That [*sc*. a bach] strapped down a bit of paradise with corrugated iron and lead-head nails, fibrolite and flat-heads.

flattie.

1. Also **flatty**. [Used elsewhere but recorded earliest in NZ.] A small, flat-bottomed rowing-boat, simply built for use in shallow water.

1892 HOCKEN & FENWICK *Holiday Trip Catlins* 3 [We] accepted the use of a flat-bottomed boat, of the species known in the district as 'flatties'. 1903 *Otago Daily Times* (Dunedin) 19 Nov. 10 A hard-working boatman who goes fishing in a flattie and one or two net fishermen are pestered with requests for fish. 1928 *NZ Free Lance* (Wellington) 25 July 7 You have to get aboard the launch by means of a 'flatty' and that flatty has to do a bit of surf-riding. 1943 MANNERING *Eighty Years NZ* 160 One day a friend and I were blown out to sea in a flattie—not a nice experience. 1968 HALL-JONES *Early Fiordland* 112 Six years later, on 26 December 1898, Hall and Te Au set off from Snodgrass's hotel [Te Anau] in a 'flattie'. 1989 *Te Karanga* May 3 I have just finished an article..referring to flat bottomed boats (Flatties) used at Lake Ellesmere and Taumutu. In the early 1930s my Father bought a flattie which was used to go across to the Opihi mouth for whitebaiting season and also for eeling and floundering.

2. *WW2*. [f. *flat* (spin + -IE.] A state of fluster or confusion.

1944 *Coral Dust* Dec. Don't race round in a 'flattie' if you haven't finished your letter at 10.30, looking for candles.

3. [f. *flat* (tyre) + -IE.] A flat tyre.

1983 HENDERSON *Down from Marble Mountain* 184 Returning, I collect a flattie, rain begins, drenched I reach work. 1986 MCCAULEY *Then Again* 277 His own bike has a flattie. Maureen bought a new inner tube at Parenga, but though she's tried and Hennie's tried there seems to be no way of easing the wretched tyre off the rim. 1988 MCGILL *Dict. Kiwi Slang* 45 *flattie* a punctured tyre; eg 'She's given the old dunga too hard a time on the corners, she got a flattie on the back left and flapped to a stop.'

flax. [Transf. or extended use of *flax Linum* spp. (fam. Linaceae).]

I. *Phormium* spp. **1. a.** Either of two native species of *Phormium* (fam. Phormiaceae), *P. tenax* and, less frequently, *P. cookianum*, robust herbaceous plants with tough fibrous blade-like leaves arranged in fans forming large tussocks, the leaf and fibre being used as cordage, in rope-making, and in the manufacture of various plaited or woven articles. Often *attrib*. See also FLAG *n.* 2, *flax-lily* 5 c below, HARAKEKE, HEMP, *lily-flax* (LILY 3 a), PHORMIUM, WHARARIKI.

1773, 1783 [see *flax-plant* 5 b below]. 1793 *Capt. Raven to Lieut.-Governor King* 19 Nov. in McNab *Hist. Records* (1908) I. 179 The flax grows here [in Dusky Sound] in great abundance, from which our people made fishing-lines and kellick-ropes. 1804 [see HARAKEKE]. 1813 WILLIAMS *Rep. NZ Flax* Sept. in McNab *Murihiku* (1907) 131 The Flax of New Zealand, more properly called Hemp, has been an object of attention from most early knowledge of the Island. 1832 EARLE *Narrative Res. NZ* (1966) 64 Their food is always eaten out of little baskets, rudely woven of green flax. 1847 [see HARAKEKE]. 1851 *Lyttelton Times* 14 June 6 [These are in the Canterbury Block] *open grass* land..the *flax bottoms* and the *reclaimable swamp* land. 1860 27 Jan. in Butler *First Year* (1863) iii 28 How shall I describe everything..tussocks of brown grass—the huge wide-leaved flax. 1892 *NZ Official Handbook* 154 As a result of their investigations, the Committee urged that flax-owners should see that the flax is cut in such a manner as to leave the heart of the flax-fans uninjured. 1922 [see HARAKEKE]. 1930 PINFOLD *Fifty Yrs. Maoriland* 19 Good business was often done with New Zealand hemp, the world's best fibre for binder-twine. It belongs to the lily family and is popularly termed 'flax'. 1933 *Press* (Christchurch) (Acland Gloss.) 14 Oct. 15 *Flax*.—Phormium Tenax. 'The poor man's friend.' This plant, shaped like a giant tussock, was one of the most useful things that grew. The leaves or *blades* were ready-made straps and ropes for almost any purpose. The bush makes an excellent dog-kennel, and many a man has made a comfortable camp under one on a rough night. It is handy to tie a horse to and very good shelter for shorn sheep. The leaves are easily skinned; and the fibre was used for making crackers for stock- and bullock-whips. 1946 *JPS* LV. 160 *whararriki*, a plant (Phormium Cookianum) an inferior Maori flax. 1964 SARGESON *Collected Stories 1935–1963* 299 Flax: a plant that grows in clumps of tall sword-like leaves with strong fibres. Strips of the leaves can be used like twine, among other things, for tying tomato-plants to stakes. 1988 DAWSON *Forest Vines to Snow Tussocks* 181 The term 'flax' for the genus *Phormium*, although firmly established, is yet another inappropriate common name as *Phormium* and true linen flax (*Linum*) have in common only the possession of useful fibres. 1991 [see HARAKEKE].

b. Occas. as a distributive in senses *flax-blade* or *flax-bush*.

1879 BARR *Old Identities* 53 A Maori basketful [of flour] strapped with flaxes across his shoulder. 1924 LYSNAR *NZ* 100 Soon the monster bird came stalking Proudly through the waving flaxes.

2. With a modifier: **hill (mountain), native, New Zealand, scrub, swamp, variegated**.

(1) **hill (mountain) flax**. *Phormium cookianum* (formerly *P. colensoi*), a flax with blades shorter than those of *P. tenax* and inclined to droop, found on the coast, on dry hillsides and mountain slopes. See also WHARARIKI.

1834 MCDONNELL *Extracts Jrnl.* (1979) 18 The hill-flax is of a finer texture, whiter, and stronger, than that grown in the valleys, though the staple may not be quite so long. 1842 HEAPHY *NZ* 36 The hill flax is met with on the steepest and most exposed part of the coast. 1909 *AJHR* C-12 52 [*P.*] *Cookianum*..Whararriki..Hill-flax, mountain-flax... Coastal rocks, subalpine meadow.. Common on coastal rocks of Port Pegasus, but not noted in Paterson Inlet. 1919 COCKAYNE *NZ Plants &*

Their Story 40 Associations in which the yellow-flowered, drooping-leaved mountain-flax..is the leading plant occur at various points on coastal rocks. **1930** *NZJST* XI. 273 The first two are of importance to the flax-miller, while in the third is included the mountain-flax (*P. Cookianum*). **1953** SUTHERLAND *Golden Bush* (1963) 199 Under the lee of a rock outcrop, sheltered on two sides by clumps of mountain flax, we set up house. **1969** HARVEY & GODLEY *Botanical Paintings* 74 *Phormium colensoi* Mountain Flax Wharariki... is found throughout both main islands from sea level to about 4000 feet, and the name 'mountain flax', bestowed by Dr L. Cockayne in 1908, indicates only that it is more prominent in the higher parts of its range. **1988** DAWSON *Forest Vines to Snow Tussocks* 156 On the more sheltered aspects, so-called mountain flax (*Phormium cookianum*) may form a close cover.

(2) **native flax**. *Phormium tenax* and *P. cookianum*.
   1807 SAVAGE *Some Acc. of NZ* 50 The dress of the natives consists in a mat finely wove of the native flax. **1814** MARSDEN *Lett. & Jrnls.* 22 Sept. (1932) 133 New Zealand must be always considered as the great emporium of the South Seas, from its local situation..its rosin, native flax, etc. **1847** [see HARAKEKE]. **1857** ASKEW *Voyage Austral. & NZ* 347 The kits are made of native flax. **1898** MORRIS *Austral-English* 147 In New Zealand, the *Phormium* is called *Native Flax*. **1925** BATHGATE *Random Recolls.* 19 We passed through an area where grew the most luxuriant native flax I have ever seen. **1968** GRUNDY *Who'd Marry a Doctor?* 30 Our back yard rose steeply from the house to the fence line, where native flax had been planted as a wind break. **1974** *NZ Agric.* 153 In all, New Zealand has over 15 800 ha of self-sown native flax.

(3) **New Zealand flax** [AND 1789]. *Phormium tenax* and *P. cookianum*.
   1791 MENZIES *Journal* in McNab *Murihiku* (1907) 314 Indeed the only inducement I can at present discover [for clearing the land]..would be the establishment of a plantation of the New Zealand Flax which grows here spontaneous. **1821** *McCrae Evidence before Commissioner Bigge* May in McNab *Hist. Records* (1908) I. 536 I don't believe the New Zealand flax requires a very rich soil. **1839** WALTON *Twelve Months' Residence* 12 The most remarkable indigenous production of New Zealand, is the Phormium Tenax, or New Zealand flax. **1841** *Hobson Despatch* 4 Dec. in *GBPP House of Commons 1842 (No.569)* 179 The only exports from New Zealand are wood, phormium tenax, or New Zealand flax, pork, potatoes, maize, sulphur and oil. **1854** NOAH WEBSTER *Dict. Eng. Lang.* (5.edn.) 672 New Zealand Flax, *n*. A plant, the *phormium tenax*, having broad, stiff leaves, of extraordinary strength, whose fibres make excellent cordage. **1868** [see *flax-lily* 5 c below]. **c1875** [see HARAKEKE]. **1891** WALLACE *Rural Econ. Austral. & NZ* 249 New Zealand Flax or Phormium fibre, designated in the home-market [*sc.* British market] as New Zealand hemp. **1913** *NZJAg.* Jan. VI. 16 The refuse accumulates as a waste product in the process of producing the fibre variously known as New Zealand flax, New Zealand phormium, or New Zealand hemp. **1978** MOORE & IRWIN *Oxford Book NZ Plants* 180 Phormium tenax, New Zealand flax, harakeke. **1981** BROOKER et al. *NZ Medicinal Plants* 36 *Phormium tenax*... New Zealand flax, New Zealand hemp.

(4) **scrub flax**. A stunted variety of flax (prob. *hill flax* (1) above: cf. quot. 1823 (5) below), often forming a scrub.
   1851 CHAMBERS *Papers for People NZ* 15 Scrub-flax and fern occupy the wide plains. **1937** AYSON *Thomas* 159 But in the darkness Thomas could not see the difficulties in his way—the scrub flax and the almost precipitous side of the hill.

(5) **swamp flax**. A name for *Phormium tenax*, indicating a common habitat of lowland swamps and damp places.
   1823 KENT *Journal* in Begg *Port Preservation* (1973) 315 Examined every creek and cove..without seeing one acre of low ground or a plant of swamp flax; bush flax [*sc. mountain flax* (1) above, prob. from its bush-like form] appeared upon the sides of the mountains in every direction but upon cleaning some of the blades scarcely any flax was to be got from them. **1867** HOCHSTETTER *NZ* 152 We may distinguish..*Tuhara*, swamp flax, with a coarse, yellowish-white fibre; used especially for ropes, lines, etc. **1939** VAILE *Pioneering Pumice* 299 *swamp flax* Phormium tenax.

(6) **variegated flax**. A garden variety with an ornamental variegated leaf.
   1873 TINNE *Wonderland of Antipodes* 36 I tried very hard to send home..some plants of variegated flax (*Phormium Colensoii variegata*). **1990** *NZ Gardener* May 36 There are many variegated flaxes..but few are as reliable in the garden as *Phormium cookianum* 'Tricolor'.

3. The fibre or dressed blades of *Phormium*, often used *attrib*. in Comb. esp. with reference to Maori artifacts and articles of clothing.
   1777 ANDERSON *Journal* Feb. in Cook *Journals* (1967) III. 805 There is one [plant] which deserves particular notice, as the natives make their garments of it and it produces a fine silky flax superior in appearance to any thing we have and probably at least as strong. **1857** *Lyttelton Times* 12 Aug. 3 The Baron is requested to furnish these inquirers with estimates for the manufacture of *thirty* tons of gumless flax per week. **1866** ANGAS *Polynesia* 156 The 'topuni' consists of a large flax cloak, into which is fastened, with every thread, a portion of dog's hair.

4. Forming adjectives in combination with participles, etc.
   1856 FITTON *NZ* 204 Although New Zealand has long been celebrated as a flax producing country..very little New Zealand flax has found its way to this side of the world. **1883** DOMETT *Ranolf & Amohia* I. 183 That he the first might touch and taste, In flax-wov'n basket for a dish, A dainty pile of delicate fish. **1935** COWAN *Hero Stories NZ* 168 Half wading, half swimming, he went with the current, keeping close under the flax-bordered bank. **1964** MIDDLETON *Walk on Beach* 47 It seemed impossible that this..estuary, with its toe toe and flax-covered banks, was only half-an-hour's fast drive from the city. **1980** BENNETT *Canterbury Tale* 32 The first was swimming, which was learnt in our flax-girt creek meandering through its deep pools and rapid shallows.

5. In *attrib*. use. **a.** Pertaining to New Zealand flax or its processing; of articles, made from flax; of land, covered with flax.
   1867 HOCHSTETTER *NZ* 154 It is true [that up to 1859], there were some so-called flax factories, but their produce was inconsiderable as to quantity, and most deficient in quality. **1889** DAVIDSON *Stories NZ Life* 25 Rounding a large boulder on the side of a flax gully he came face to face with a large boar. **1892** *NZ Official Handbook* 154 The Committee urged that flax-owners should see that the flax is cut in such a manner as to leave the heart of the flax-fans uninjured. **1921** *NZJST* IV. 36 A number of possible uses of flax-waste were mentioned. **1922** COWAN *NZ Wars* (1955) II. 26 Boiled flax-root water poured on the wounds, and also dock-root..were our favourite remedies for gunshot and bayonet wounds. **1987** HUNT *Foxton 1888–1988* 117 The flax market remained depressed from 1890 to 1898... In this way Foxton was able to retain its identity as a 'flax town'. **1995** WINTER *All Ways Up Hill* 211 The big boys [at the backblocks school] ganged up and mustered the smaller ones with flax whips.

b. In Comb. **flax-blade, -fibre, field, flower, leaf, plant, stalk, -swamp**.
   1872 DOMETT *Ranolf & Amohia* 11 With **flax blades** binding to a tree The Maid who strove her limbs to free. **1889** BATHGATE *Far South Fancies* (1890) 151 Flax-blades: The plant known as NZ Flax has long ensiform [*i.e.* 'sword-shaped'] leaves commonly called blades. **1905** BAUCKE *White Man Treads* 256 He would lave any head with fermented herb-waters, and bandage it with split flax blades, according to an ancestral recipe. **1938** LANCASTER *Promenade* 44 He came pushing through the tall flax-blades and black koradi-sticks and found her sitting demure in her print gown. **c1875** MEREDITH *Adventuring in Maoriland* (1935) 43 These [eel bobs] are made by stringing worms on **flax-fibre**, which is attached in a loose lump by a cord to the end of a stick. **1882** HAY *Brighter Britain* II. 207 In the commercial world New Zealand flax-fibre was highly esteemed at one time, but has fallen out of favour. **1873** BULLER *Birds NZ* 49 When the korari-flower (*Phormium tenax*) is in season, the Kakas repair in flocks to the **flax-fields** to feast on the flower-honey. **c1835** BOULTBEE *Journal* (1986) 104 Some of the flowers here are both useful and ornamental, particularly the **flax-flower**, which abounds in a clear liquid honey. **1872** DOMETT *Ranolf & Amohia* 221 Little isles Where still the clinging flax-flower smiles. **1898** MORRIS *Austral-English* 148 *Flax-flower*..the flower of the *New Zealand flax*. **1978** FULLER *Maori Food & Cook.* 15 Bundles of kiekie and dried flax-flower stems were also used to carry fire. **1985** [see KORARI 2]. **1846** HEAPHY *Exped. S.W. Nelson* 12 Feb. in Taylor *Early Travellers* (1959) 197 The native..imitates, with a whistle made of a **flax-leaf**, the cry of the bird. **1851** *Richmond-Atkinson Papers* (1960) I. 82 [The Maori guides] tied up & slung [the pikaus] over their shoulders with strips of native flax leaf which serves for such purposes without any preparation. **1867** BARKER *Station Life* (1870) 127 That was one swag, and a very unwieldy one it was, strapped knapsack fashion, with straps of flax-leaves, on the back. **1873** PYKE *Wild Will Enderby* (1889,1974) III. iii 83 At first he cut a quantity of the broad flax-leaves, each five or six feet in length. **1884** BRACKEN *Lays of the Maori* 69 Zephyrs stirred the flax-leaves into tune. **1907** LAING & BLACKWELL *Plants NZ* 106 Love-tokens are said to have been made by the Maoris in the early days from strips of flax-leaves. **1935** COWAN *Hero Stories NZ* 253 Quite accidentally the fugitives discovered a pass between the Alps.., and toiling on..shod with *paraerae*, or sandals of flax-leaves, they crossed the divide. **1773** COOK *Journals* 11 May (1961) II. 136 The **flax plant** is as common here as in any other part of New Zealand. **1783** Aug. 23 James Matra's Proposal for Estab. of NSW in *Hist. Recs. NSW* I. pt.2 2 I mean the New Zealand hemp or flax-plant, an object equally of curiosity and utility. **1791** *Lieut.-Gov. King Descr. Norfolk Is.* 10 Jan. in McNab *Hist. Records* (1908) I. 120 The flax-plant of New Zealand grows spontaneously in many parts of the [Norfolk] island. **1829** ELLIS *Polynesian Researches* I. ii 27 The native flax-plant, *phormium tenax*..is by no means like the flax or hemp plants of England, but resembles, in its appearance and manner of growth, the flag or iris. **1840** POLACK *Manners & Customs* I. 12 By the aid of some flax-plants that grew indigenous on the sea-born isle, he formed some ropes which he attached to various stars. **1851** SHORTLAND *S. Dist. NZ* 168 Our natives soon constructed [a mokihi]..from the dry stalks of the flax plant.., a material as light as cork. **1871** MONEY *Knocking About NZ* 23 The roll of blankets was made as tight as could be, and tied with the blades of the flax plant. **1969** MEAD *Traditional Maori Clothing* 151 The outer decaying leaves of a flax plant were called pakawha, the mature leaves called muka. **1846** HEAPHY *Exped. to Kawatiri* 21 Apr. in Taylor *Early Travellers* (1959) 217 Constructed a raft of **flax-stalks**, or *korari*, in length about 22 feet. **1975** KNIGHT *Poyntzfield* 164

Suddenly into his mind popped the soft translucent jelly substance found at the base of the flax stalks in the swamps... Tumoti had gone to bed unwashed and unnoticed until the flax gum began to dry and contract. **1823** KENT *Journal* in Begg *Port Preservation* (1973) 327 It was scarcely possible for men to work in **flax swamps**, during hard gales. **1835** YATE *NZ* (1970) 206 The Puriri is everywhere surrounded with flax-swamps. **1844** in Shortland *S. Dist. NZ* (1851) 229 We lost sight of him in a flax swamp, and had to find our way out as best we could. **1867** BARKER *Station Life* (1870) 195 If the weather has been very dry..we attempt to burn a great flax swamp. **1881** BATEMAN *Colonist* 186 The tussock land abounds in the Middle Island, although the richest land was originally what are termed 'flax swamps'. **1907** MANSFIELD *Urewera Notebook* (1978) 39 Then the rain fell heavily drearily—on to the river and the flax swamp. **1921** *NZJST* IV. 36 In New Zealand the flax swamps could be easily converted into dairying-land. **1940** STUDHOLME *Te Waimate* (1954) 143 In some of the heavy flax swamps near the sea there were quite a number of really wild cattle. **1987** LANCASTER in *Happy Endings* 101 There was evil in the wild, sensuous smell of flax-swamp that rose to windward.

c. Special Comb. **flax agent** *hist.*, one acting as a collector of prepared flax-fibre for a (usu. Australian) principal; **flax basket**, any of various kinds or sizes of basket made from woven flax (see also KIT *n.*[1] 1 a, KETE, KONO); **flax-bush**, an individual clump of phormium; **flax-cutter** *hist.*, a worker who cuts flax in swamps for delivery to a flax-mill, hence **flax-cutting**; **flax-dresser**, a tradesman who prepares flax in a flax-mill (hence **flax-dressing**); **flax-grub**, either of the caterpillars *Orthoclydon praefactata* (fam. Geometridae) and *Tmetolophota steropastis* (fam. Noctuidae), the former eating strips of the leaf, the latter leaving notches in the edges of *Phormium tenax* blades; **flax honey**, the nectar of the flax-flower; the honey made by bees feeding on phormium flowers (see also *korari honey* (KORARI 4)); **flaxhook**, a flax-cutter's knife with a curved blade; **flax kit**, a large kit or basket made of woven flax (see also KIT *n.*[1] 1 a)); **flax land**, land on which flax is growing or has once grown; **flax-lily** *obs.* [f. the orig. classification of *Phormium* in fam. Liliaceae], the flax-plant, 1 above; **flax-line**, an extemporized rope of knotted flax-leaves; **flax-mat**, a piece of flax matting used for any of a variety of purposes (see MAT 1 and 2); **flax-matting**, matting woven from dressed flax; **flax-mill** *hist.*, a plant or factory for dressing New Zealand flax, hence **flax-miller**, **flax-milling** *vbl. n.*; **flax moth**, see MOTH 3; **flax-rope**, a rope plaited from flax; **flax sandal**, PARAERAE; **flax settlement**, a settlement formed to gather and trade in flax; **flax skirt**, PIUPIU *n.*[1]; **flax snail**, any of various species of the tall, spirally-shelled land univalves formerly of *Placostylus* spp. (fam. Bulimulidae), now esp. *Maoristylus hongii* (see also PUPUHARAKEKE); **flax-stick**, the flower-stem of *Phormium tenax*, esp. when dry (see KORARI 2); also *attrib.* or Comb. as **flax-stick boat**, **raft**, MOKI *n.*[2]; **flax trade** *hist.*, in early New Zealand, the trade in phormium between European and Maori entrepreneurs; **flax-trader** *hist.*, one carrying on such a trade; **flax tree** *obs.*, CABBAGE-TREE 1; **flax-works** *hist.*, *flax-mill* (above).

1833 WILLIAMS *Early Jrnls.* 15 Mar. (1961) 296 I also wrote a letter to some of the leading men of Tauranga..and one to a Mr. Scott [*sc.* a trader] who resided there as **flax agent**. **1938** WILY & MAUNSELL *Robert Maunsell* 37 Mr Tapsell, a flax agent at Maketu, had his premises burned down and all his property either destroyed or taken away. **1835** YATE *NZ* (1970) 31 Can Europeans be surprised that the New Zealanders should pay them in their own coin; that they should half fill their **flax baskets** with stones to increase the weight. **1847** ANGAS *Savage Life* I. 237 The woman, having the potatoes in a flax-basket or 'kit', with two handles, goes into the stream. **1922** COWAN *NZ Wars* (1955) I. 122 These Ngati-Mutunga..made up small casks of powder in flax-basket *pikaus* or back-loads. **1930** REISCHEK *Yesterdays in Maoriland* (1933) 154 It consisted of stewed eel and sweet potatoes, presented to us in little neatly woven, four-cornered flax-baskets. **1948** HENDERSON *Taina* 15 The *hangis* had just been uncovered and the food put into little freshly-made flax baskets called *kono*, one for each person. **1963** MASON *Pohutukawa Tree* 20 Aroha Mataira..wears a wide-brimmed straw hat. She carries a flax basket. **1978** FULLER *Maori Food & Cook.* 51 Place in a coarse kete (flax basket) and stand in fresh water..for two or three days. **1982** SANSOM *In Grip of Island* 136 The fresh fish were spread out on the grass for sale and housewives would be there with their woven flax baskets. **1844** MONRO *Notes of a Journey* in Hocken *Contributions* (1898) 246 It is a perfect sea of brown grass-tree tops, only relieved by the occasional green of a **flax bush**. **1860** in Butler *First Year* (1863) iii 29 It is volcanic, brown, and dry..then perhaps a flax bush, or, as we should have said, a flax plant. **1871** MONEY *Knocking About NZ* 134 An ambush was laid by the Maories behind some flax bushes. **1883** DOMETT *Ranolf & Amohia* I. 230 And the louder *flax-bushes* With their crowding and crossing. **1907** LAING & BLACKWELL *Plants NZ* 104 The settler [farmer] is never in want of a piece of twine with a flax bush growing near his home. **1922** COWAN *NZ Wars* (1955) II. 294 Suddenly a Hauhau sentry was surprised half asleep under a flax-bush. **1976** MASON in *Solo* (1981) 88 I first scooped a hole in the flaxbush and made a rough seat there. **1906** *Truth* 15 Sept. 3 A gang of **flax-cutters**..in Foxton. We finished the block of flax we were cutting in. **1913** *NZJAg.* Jan. VI. 256 I have about 100 acres of land in flax, and have always allowed the flax-cutters to cut it as they pleased. **1936** HYDE *Passport to Hell* 48 The duff boiled for three hours, and the rattle of tin plates was a newly invented song of the flax-cutters. **1973** FINLAYSON *Brown Man's Burden* (Pearson's Gloss.) 140 Until the depression flax mills and flax-cutters' camps... would be found near swamps where the flax grew. **1890** COX *Diaries 1888–1925* (ATLMS) 18 Mar. Fred..went flaxcutting yesterday and will work there now. **1936** HYDE *Passport to Hell* 47 Then he struck the rhythm of flax-cutting, and could do the job on his head. **1987** HARTLEY *Swagger on Doorstep* 58 A man told us he was not there but down in the swamp supervising flaxcutting. **1843** *Census New Plymouth* in *Establish. New Plymouth* (1940) 222 Other crafts and trades scheduled were, coopers, **flax-dressers**, gardeners, millers. **1894** *TrNZI* XXVI. 453 The blacksmith, the builder, the flax-dresser, and the farmer were soon busy. **1924** *Otago Witness* (Dunedin) 6 May 69 It was not until two years later that King obtained his New Zealand flax dressers. **1971** *New Zealand's Heritage* I. 277 However, one man named Williams, an expert flax-dresser..was rewarded by finding flax. **1892** *NZ Official Handbook* 153 A process of **flax-dressing** which will reduce the cost of production. **1971** *New Zealand's Heritage* I. 277 But the *Daedalus*..succeeded in taking two Maoris on board, a warrior and a tohunga [to teach flax-dressing]—rather unfortunate choices when it is considered that flax-dressing was neither toa nor tohunga work but wahine work. **1915** *NZJAg.* Jan. X. 5 Undoubtedly the most serious injury to flax swamps at the present day is caused by the larvae of a native moth called by millers the '**flax-grub**'. **1922** THOMSON *Naturalisation of Animals and Plants in NZ* 512 The two moths, whose larvae are known as 'flax-grubs'—*Xanthorhoe praefectata* and *Melanchra steropastis*—are both considered to be much more abundant now than they were formerly. **1930** *NZJST* XI. 280 The dry conditions and accumulation of dead leaves are favourable as well to the flax-grub. **1958** GILLESPIE *South Canterbury* (1971) 10 The ghost-like white moth..of the flax grub (*Orthoclydon praefectata*)..eats longitudinal slits on the surface of [flax] leaves. **c1920** BEATTIE *Trad. Lifeways Southern Maori* (1994) 124 Another old man corrected the statement that **flax honey** was dripped into the aruhe, which he said did not need it as it was sweet. **1945** BEATTIE *Maori Place-names Canterbury* 65 ['Taa-korari'] is to shake the flax-honey out of the flower cluster at the head of the stalk. This flax honey [*sic*] is sweet, and if there was not enough to make a drink it was sprinkled over certain foods. **1950** DEMPSEY *Wind from Sea* 20 There's plenty of flax-honey..the season has been too dry for clover honey. **1987** *Alfredton* 100 When cutting flax [c1911], the whole bush was cut with a sickle or **flaxhook**. **1987** RAIMONDO *Our Company Before* 397 One man stood in the middle of the [flax]bush and cut the blades in one stroke, using a sharp curved knife called a 'flaxhook'. **1877** PRATT *Colonial Experiences* 31 Potatoes were procurable from the Maoris in **flax kits**, at from one to five shillings the kit. **1882** POTTS *Out in Open* 17 Each damsel carrying a flax kit heavily laden with this favourite esculent. **1940** *Tales Pioneer Women* (1988) 33 She carried with her a flax kit of kumaras. **1959** SHADBOLT *New Zealanders* (1986) 22 We collected mussels and pipis in flax kits..and sunbathed the afternoon away. **1986** RICHARDS *Off the Sheep's Back* 101 An old flax kit, partly burned, contained the remains of a small child. **1848** WAKEFIELD *Handbook NZ* 258 The chief part of the land..yet cultivated near Nelson is **flax** or fern **land**. **1853** SWAINSON *Auckland* 38 About an equal quantity is dark-coloured, good, strong flaxland, suitable for wheat and potatoes. **1868** LINDSAY *Contribs. NZ Bot.* 80 Hence, next to bush and swamp-land proper..flax-land is regarded as the most desirable for agricultural purposes. **1872** *Phormium tenax as a Fibrous Plant* 2 On rich 'flax land' there are over 2,000 bunches of *Phormium* to the acre, or 100,000 leaves. **1868** LINDSAY *Contribs. NZ Bot.* 79 [*P. tenax*] is the long-familiar 'New Zealand Flax' plant or '**Flax Lily**'; terms which must now be held to include *P. Colensoi*. **1900** *Canterbury Old & New* 183 Here and there the monotony is relieved by clumps of native flax-lily with their broad sword-shaped leaves and tall flower-stalks. **1940** LAING & BLACKWELL *Plants NZ* 106 *Phormium tenax (The New Zealand Flax, or Flax-Lily).* **1873** PYKE *Wild Will Enderby* (1889, 1974) III. iii 83 Loosing the **flax-line**, he made a careful survey of the locality. **1922** COWAN *NZ Wars* (1955) II. 150 The end was fastened with a flax-line carried across the track. **1849** POWER *Sketches in NZ* 160 In the interior of the Pa the Wahinés, or matrons, are busy weaving **flax-mats**. *Ibid.* 172 The women were cooking, gossiping, or making flax-mats. **1864?** TEMPSKY *Memoranda* (ATLTS) 76 Whares with bullet proof flax mats for roofs, were built all along inside the rifle pits. **1908** GORST *NZ Revisited* 307 I felt a lingering longing for the old hospitality of former days, when the company sat on the ground, upon clean flax mats spread over the floor. **1945** BEATTIE *Maori Place-names Canterbury* 33 There was no roof on them [*sc.* Whatas], the food being covered with flax mats. **1982** MALCOLM *Where it all Began* 134 The women spent the morning making flax mats as plates for the guests. **1874** JOHNSTONE *Maoria* 2 The Maori cooks then place **flax-matting** upon the hot stones. **1848** WAKEFIELD *Handbook NZ* 265 **Flax-mill** and rope-walk in Suburban North [Nelson]. **1853** EARP *NZ* 96 The number of manufactuaries already established in the [Wellington] province is as follows:.. six cooperages, one flax-mill, four rope-walks, two sacking-looms. **1868** LUSH *Waikato Jrnls.* (1982) 148 Went to the Orchards' to see their new flax mill. **1873** TINNE *Wonderland of Antipodes* 4 We caught occasional glimpses on the bank of flax-mills, with their snowy fibre drying on the fern. **1889** KNOX *Boy Travellers* 210 Great quantities of flax are raised here nowadays, as you will understand when you know there are some forty and odd flax-mills in the colony. **1905** *NZ Illustr. Mag.* July 251 [Caption] Sunday Morning at a Flaxmill Camp. **1919** WAITE *New Zealanders at Gallipoli* 2 The flaxmill hand left swamp and mill and hurried to the nearest railway station. **1936** HYDE *Passport to Hell* 47 [The cut flax was] hauled by horses to the smoother ground where the waggons for Finnegan's flax-mill could pick it up. **1951** HUNT *Confessions* 23 The considerable fall in these many waterways made it possible to install waterwheels, which were freely used for power for flaxmills. **1978** SINCLAIR & HARREX *Looking Back* 166 Seiferts owned the seven-stripper 'Miranui' mill at Shannon in the Manawatu, the largest flaxmill ever operated in New Zealand. **1982** STUART *Satyrs of Southland* 15 [Caption] A flaxmill with waterwheel on William Stuart's property, Otapiri Gorge, before the turn of the century. **1894** *NZ Official Year-book* 268 Table showing the occupations of persons who insured in the government insurance department in 1893..**flaxmillers**..gumdiggers and sorters. **1921** *NZJST* Mar. IV. 36 Mr. Seifert had stated that the control of the disease was not the flax-millers' business. **1930** *NZJST* XI. 273 The first two [species] are of importance to the flax-miller. **1987** HUNT *Foxton 1888–1988* 122 A section of the Foxton community..felt the swamp should have been sold to a number of flaxmillers. **1892** *NZ Official Handbook* 158 Next to the saw-mill work as to the number of hands employed comes the occupation of **flax-milling**. **1913** CARR *Country Work* 10 Sheep-raising, flax-milling..and timber-milling are the main industries. **1936** BELSHAW et al. *Agric. Organiz. NZ* 56 A minor amount of flax-milling is carried on. **1951** HUNT *Confessions* 23 Flax had no value at that time. A year or so later..the flax-milling industry commenced. **1861** HAAST *Rep. Topogr. Explor. Nelson* 48 As we descended [the rope ladder], several of the steps..broke under our weight; but as Mr. Mackay had been kind enough some time before to replace the old **flax rope** by a new one, we had secure hand-hold. **1939** BEATTIE *First White Boy Born Otago* 15 A woman died and was lashed to a pole... The pole was placed on [the grave]..the flax ropes were undone, and let out slowly. **1898** HOCKEN *Contributions* 173 Boots were improvised of Maori **flax sandals** lined with a bit of red or blue blanket. **1832** HAY *Notices of NZ* (1979) 7 The **flax settlements** will rapidly assume a more permanent form, as the present desultory and speculative system progressively fails. *Ibid.* 10 Mascetu—a flax settlement; four Europeans here; likely to be permanent. **1964** FRANCES *Johnny Rapana* 183 A hundred years ago my people, your people, were running around in **flax skirts**. **1936** *Handbook for NZ* (ANZAAS) 63 [Caption] The **flax-snail**, *Placostylus hongii*.., a large herbivorous species, abounds on the island in the foreground. **1947** POWELL *Native Animals* 33 Pupuharakeke or Flax Snail (*Placostylus hongii*). A tall-spired solidly built chocolate to reddish-brown coloured snail about 3 inches in height. **1955** DELL *Native Shells* 58 The Flax Snails are only found in the northern part of the North Island, and even there they are only found close to the sea, often around flax bushes. **1966** *Encycl. NZ* III. 267 Snail, Flax or Pupuharakeke (*Placostylus hongii*)... Formerly these snails were abundant along the Northland East Coast... These snails..feed largely upon fallen karaka..leaves. They are found hidden..in flax..only when there is no other cover. **1980** LOCKLEY *House Above the Sea* 241 At the present time some light *Placostylus* flax snails, so called because they feed on the fallen leaves of karaka and other shrubs and den up in thick flax, are reduced to a few specimens in some northern localities. **1990** FOORD *NZ Descriptive Animal Dictionary* 151 Flax Snail... An elongated, plant-eating land snail up to 8cm long, on offshore islands in N. Auckland but almost extinct on the mainland. **1856** SEWELL *Journal* 2 Mar. (1980) II. 215 Got some dead **flax sticks** to boil a kettle with. **1861** HAAST *Rep. Topogr. Explor. Nelson* 29 The river fell, and by tying bundles of flax sticks together on each side of the canoe..we ventured down the stream with the flood. **1886** HART *Stray Leaves* 31 The most delicious honey in the world..was obtainable from the flax sticks. **1896** *TrNZI* XXVIII. 373 He will then..mount to the very top of the flax-stick..like a mouse or a house-fly. **1907** [see KORARI 2]. **1930** DOBSON *Reminiscences* 85 Just before the gorge began there were many acres of flax, the dead flower stalks (flax sticks) of which made excellent rafts. **1951** HUNT *Confessions* 37 As far as the eye could see over the country on the western bank was a vast sea of flax sticks. **c1962** BAXTER *Horse* (1985) 11 He had sailed **flax-stick boats** on it often enough, and gaffed eels. **1871** MONEY *Knocking About NZ* 52 [Moguey] Maori name for a raupo or **flax-stick raft**. **1904** *NZ Illustr. Mag.* Apr. 23 A suggestion to build a mokihi (flax stick raft) was quickly put into execution. **1832** WILLIAMS *Journal* 2 Dec. in Matthews *Matthews of Kaitaia* (1940) 30 They well know the difference between us and the Europeans living on shore who are connected with the **flax trade**. **1835** YATE *NZ* (1970) 31 The flax-trade, on the present system, cannot last long in New Zealand. The natives' wants are supplied; and their natural idleness will prevail over their desire for luxuries. **1843** DIEFFENBACH *Travels in NZ* I. 407 Tauranga was in former times an important place for the pig and flax trade... But from different causes the flax-trade has dwindled away. **1856** FITTON *NZ* 205 Nelson boasts an indefatigable advocate for the flax-trade in Mr. Natrass. **1863** MANING *Old NZ* xiv 211 Trading in flax in those days [1822–1826] was to be undertaken by a man who had his wits about him; an old **flax trader** of those days, with his 150 ton schooner 'out of Sydney', cruising all round the coast of New Zealand, picking up his five tons at one port. **1958** MILLER *Early Victorian NZ* 18 This concentration of power in the Cook Strait region and the acquisition of firearms from the whalers and flax-traders at Kapiti encouraged Te Rauparaha to embark on the conquest of the South Island. **1966** *Encycl. NZ* III. 522 The first European visitors to Wairoa..were flax traders. **1984** BOYD *City of the Plains* 4 European flax traders and whalers began to visit the Bay in the 1830s. **1847** BRUNNER *Exped. Middle Is.* 21 Oct. in Taylor *Early Travellers* (1959) 288 I can trudge along..with a pair of native sandals..made of the leaves of the flax, or, what is more durable, the leaves of the ti or **flax tree**. **1869** *TrNZI* I. (rev. edn.) 114 The capital hitherto employed in our local **flax-works**, has been too small.

II. *Linum* spp. **6.** Also **Chatham Island flax, linen (New Zealand linen) flax**. *Linum monogynum* (fam. Linaceae), a perennial native herb of mainly coastal habitats. See also RAUHUIA.
1777 ANDERSON *Journal* Feb. in Cook *Journals* (1967) III. 805 Amongst the known kinds of plants are common and rough Bindweed..rushes..Bullrushes, Flax. **1867** HOOKER *Handbook* 764 Flax, native. *Linum monogynum*. **1870** *TrNZI* II. 124 Linum monogynum. Flax [season of flowering] Nov.–Mar. **1889** FEATON *Art Album NZ Flora* 178 Rauhuia..Flax..Linum monogynum..Herb. **1900** *Canterbury Old & New* 183 A true flax [*Linum monogynum*] with handsome white flowers grows side by side with the usurper of its name. **1940** LAING & BLACKWELL *Plants NZ* 229 Linum monogynum (The true New Zealand Flax)... Native name *Rauhuia*. This is the true New Zealand flax; the plant which is usually so called being a lily. **1952** RICHARDS *Chatham Is.* 32 The Chatham Island flax is the same as that in New Zealand except the white blossom is here flaked with blue... Chatham Island Flax. Nau, Ra[u]huia. **1978** MOORE & IRWIN *Oxford Book NZ Plants* 54 Linum monogynum. The New Zealand linen flax is a plant of rocky outcrops..often with a profusion of white flowers. **1980** McGILL *Ghost Towns of NZ* 221 Rauhuia, New Zealand flax, or *Linum monogynum* was the country's first indigenous export, if you don't count dried heads.

7. Usu. with a modifier: **Australian, wild**. *Linum bienne*, the European pale flax, formerly treated as the Australian *L. marginale*, and often considered a weed.
1840 MATHEW *Journal* 7 Apr. in *Founding of NZ* (1940) 107 Not a flower did I see..but the little scarlet pimpernel twice and one little blue flower like the flax in New South Wales. **1926** HILGENDORF *Weeds* 117 Australian Linseed (*Linum marginale*), is also called wild linseed and wild or Australian flax. It is common all over the islands and is a twiggy and slightly branched perennial much like the cultivated variety. **1969** *Standard Common Names Weeds* 3 Australian flax *Linum marginale*. *Ibid.* 86 *wild flax* [=] *Australian flax*. **1981** TAYLOR *Weeds of Roadsides* 9 Australian Flax (*Linum marginale*)... An Australian plant widespread in New Zealand... This plant is now expertly identified as the European *L. bienne*.

III. *Astelia* spp. **8.** Usu. with a modifier as **bush-flax, tree-flax**, ASTELIA. See also KAHAKAHA, KOWHARAWHARA.
[*Note*] Some astelias are epiphytes on trees (hence the name *tree*-flax), many grow in the bush (hence the name *bush*-flax), as distinct from *Phormium*, a plant of open places.
1872 *TrNZI* IV. 243 The shaggy leaf-bases of A[stelia] Solandri, the 'tree-flax' of the settlers. **1874** [see KAHAKAHA]. **1908** *AJHR* C-11 36 [*Astelia nervosa*]..Bush-flax... *Astelia montana*. Alpine bush-flax. **1915** *AJHR* C-6 12 *Astelia nervosa*. Bush-flax. Forest. **1948** MARTIN *NZ Nature Study* 146 Various plants supplied fibres for the manufacture of mats and other clothing. Chief of these were the flax (*Phormium*), aute, kie-kie, cabbage-tree, toi..bush flax (*Astelia*). **1952** RICHARDS *Chatham Is.* 21 *Astelia..nervosa*... Bush Flax. Kakaha (strong). **1982** WILSON *Stewart Is. Plants* 300 *Astelia fragrans* Bush flax... Kakaha... Big fresh green tussocky clumps up to about 1 m tall... (=*A. nervosa* var. *sylvestris*). **1983** *Evening Post* (Wellington) 17 Dec. 8 Kaiwharawhara was the food of the bush flax, the edible young leaves and stems of a plant found growing in the forked branches of the puketea tree.

flaxie. *Obs.* [f. *flax*(-worker + -IE.]
1. A flax-cutter; a worker in a flax-mill.
1917 BROWN *Lay of Bantry Bay* 57 The Sporting 'Flaxie'. [Title] **1928** DEVANNY *Dawn Beloved* 29 No one came by but a young flaxie. **1995** WINTER *All Ways Up Hill* 208 Mick..ran across a crowd of flaxies playing two up, and never reached town.

2. As **flaxies' special** *obs.*, a train once used by flax-workers travelling between the Foxton flax-mills and Palmerston North.
1928 *NZ Free Lance* (Wellington) 19 Dec. 12 The roughest train in New Zealand..was the old time 'flaxies' special' running between Palmerston North and Foxton.

flea: see *kea flea* (KEA *n.* 2), MOUNT COOK FLEA, *turnip flea* (TURNIP FLY).

fleece. *Shearing*. In special Comb. **fleece boy, fleece-carrier**, FLEECE-PICKER; **fleece roller**, *wool roller* (WOOL 3).

FLEECE-O 274 **FLIMSY**

1889 CHUDLEIGH *Diary* 4 Nov. (1950) 368 I..put on my two station boys as **fleece boys**. The shed did not stop one minute. 1950 WOODHOUSE *Farm & Station Verse* 60 In the 90s..about 55 men were employed [on Benmore] in the shed: 28–30 shearers, 2 penners-up, 4 pickers-up, 2 broomies, 6 rollers, 1 classer, 1 **fleece-carrier**. 1868 *Puketoi Station Diary* Mar. in Beattie *Early Runholding* (1947) 104 Paid Wm. Gardiner, **fleece roller**, £11 7s 0d.

fleece-o. *Shearing.* Also **fleece-oh.** FLEECE-PICKER.
 1909 OWEN *Philip Loveluck* 173 A young Maori boy acted as '*Fleece-oh*!'—that is to say, he flicked the fleece up in his arms when it was cut from the sheep, grasped it by its four ends, and flung it out for Loveluck to fold. 1926 DEVANNY *Butcher Shop* (1981) 69 His 'fleeco', waiting his fleece, took hold and pulled gently. 1934 MILTON *Waimana* 195 Two male Maori experts..were engaged with the wife of Kuru..to act as 'Fleeco'. 1947 *NZ Observer* 15 Oct. 21 I watched in silent admiration as the 'fleeco' gathered up the fleece, took it to the table and, with a toss and a flip, laid it flat across its width. 1960 MILLS *Sheep-O* 27 Two shearers..were..acting as fleece-os—picking up the newly shorn fleeces and sweeping the board clear. 1974 HILLIARD *Maori Woman* 245 I remember last summer..we had a gang on our place and the fleeco was a girl of fifteen or sixteen. 1987 HUTCHINS *Tall Half-Backs* 79 Working in a wool store was my first encounter with the real working world. I was a fleeco boy Friday.
 Hence **fleeco** *v. intr.*, to work as a fleece-oh.
 1964 MIDDLETON *Walk on Beach* 204 Last time I heard of you you were fleecoing for Dad.

fleece-picker. *Shearing.* One who keeps the shearing board clear by picking up the freshly-shorn fleeces and throwing them on to the wool-table for sorting (but see also quot. 1989). Cf. *fleece-boy*, *fleece-carrier* (FLEECE), FLEECE-O, FLEECY, *picker-up* (PICK UP *v.* 1 b), *wool-handler*, *wool-picker* (WOOL 3).
 1861 HARPER *Lett. from NZ* (1914) 20 July 54 Shearing..is in full swing, so there are a number of extra men.., shearers, fleece-pickers, wool-sorters, and 'rouse-abouts'. 1892 SWANTON *Notes on NZ* 96 There are boys to pick up the fleeces; one fleece picker for every four or five shearers. 1913 CARR *Country Work* 14 The boss Maori undertakes to supply all the rouseabouts (as shed hands are termed) i.e., fleece pickers, wool rollers and 'Sheep oh!'. 1933 *Press* (Christchurch) (Acland Gloss.) 21 Oct. 15 *Fleece-picker.*—When a shearer finishes a sheep, the *f[leece]* is left lying on the *board*... It is *picked up* by a boy (the *f[leece]-p[icker]*), who carries it to a table throws it out flat to be skirted, rolled, and classed. The verb, to *f[leece]-pick*, means 'to be a fleece-picker'. 1940 STUDHOLME *Te Waimate* (1954) 130 [In 1882] fleece-pickers received 15/- a week, wool-rollers 25/- to 30/-. 1969 MCCASKILL *Molesworth* 81 In 1881, a boy of fourteen, he went to Tarndale as a fleece picker for the shearing. 1989 *NZ Eng. Newsletter* III. 24 *fleece picker*: This can be the person who picks the fleece off the floor and throws it on the wool table or the person who picks it over at the wool table.
 Hence **fleece-pick** *v. intr.* [a back-formation from *fleece-picker*], to do the work of a fleece-picker; **fleece-picking** *vbl. n.*, the work or occupation of picking up fleeces.
 1933 **fleece-pick** [see above]. 1913 CARR *Country Work* 14 **Fleece-picking**.—As soon as a shearer has taken the fleece off and let the sheep go through the port-hole to the counting-out pen, the picker gathers the fleece up in such a manner that she or he can on getting to the rolling table, throw it out with the breech part at the right end. 1968 JOHNSON *Turn of Tide* 68 Hilda soon learned the art of fleece picking. 1975 NEWTON *Sixty Thousand on the Hoof* 102 [A.H. Nordmeyer] was fleece-picking at Otematata as a boy.

fleecer. *Farming.* Usu. with a defining prefix **double**, **treble**, a sheep which has missed one or two shearings. See also *double-fleecer* (DOUBLE *a.*).
 1978 JARDINE *Shadows on Hill* 10 The big treble fleecer that had been caught away from his favourite bluff and ended up in the paddock.

fleecy. *Shearing.* [f. *fleec*(e + -Y.] FLEECE-PICKER.
 1894 WILSON *Land of Tui* 244 Meanwhile the shorn fleeces are carried to a large table in the wool-shed by a man appropriately named 'Fleecy', and are spread out by four wool-pickers. 1897 WRIGHT *Station Ballads* 100 They're going sheep and sheep,... And the fleecy boys are kept upon the run. 1904 LANCASTER *Sons o' Men* 78 The fleecies pattered the [shearing] lines unendingly, with feet that grew tender. 1933 *Press* (Christchurch) (Acland Gloss.) 21 Oct. 15 *Fleecy.*—Short name for f[*leece*]-*picker*. 1953 STRONACH *Musterer on Molesworth* 30 The 'fleecies', whose job was to pick up the fleeces, to sweep the board, and to apply tar to the cut sheep, clattered up and down. 1987 OGONOWSKA-COATES *Boards, Blades & Barebellies* 96 *Fleecy*. Shortened name for fleece picker; also known as 'fleece-oh'.

Fleet, *n.*[1] *Hist.*

1. a. Also **Great Fleet**, occas. **main Fleet**. Usu. init. caps. A fleet of eight founding canoes which brought, in concept or folk-legend rather than in reality, a 'main body' of Polynesian immigrants from Hawaiki to New Zealand c1350. Cf. MIGRATION.
 1924 LYSNAR *NZ* 20 The calabash, the kumara, the taro, and the yam, were carried in the fleet. 1933 in *Na To Hoa Aroha* (1988) III. 74 But I think a lot of mischief has been done by Percy Smith in giving the impression of a great fleet, that bore down on New Zealand in the fourteenth century. 1937 BUICK *Moa-Hunters NZ* 75 The accepted tradition is that the migration of 'the fleet'..took place about A.D. 1350, not A.D. 1524 as Mr. McKay assumes. *Ibid.* 226 That the glamour of migration continued down to historical times is suggested..by the coming, in approximately A.D. 1350, of what is known as 'the fleet' of eight canoes. 1949 BUCK *Coming of Maori* 8 It is thus five and a-half [*sic*] centuries ago or approximately A.D.1350 when the Fleet crossed the Great Ocean of Kiwa and made their landfall at Aotearoa. 1959 MCLINTOCK *Descr. Atlas* 1 The concept of a 'Great Fleet' is a post-European romanticisation and without traditional warrant. 1968 HALL-JONES *Early Fiordland* 22 Then, about 1350, the 'Great Fleet' arrived in New Zealand. 1977 DUFF *Moa-hunter Period* (3edn) x The fleet was a concept, not a convoy. 1979 SORRENSON *Maori Orig. & Migrations* 86 But as Anne Salmond has pointed out, at hui on maraes throughout the country, the Great Fleet lives on. 1983 LAMBERT *Illustr. hist. of Taranaki* 15 The myth of the 'Great Fleet' has pervaded New Zealand pre-history since late last century.

b. *attrib.* Pertaining to or descended from the founding immigrants of the 'Fleet'.
 1945 HALL-JONES *Hist. Southland* 64 The Ngaitahu were descendants of the Fleet Maoris. 1966 PHILLIPPS *Maori Life & Custom* 105 The evidence seems to indicate that the bow and arrow may have been known to our early Moa-hunter people and later rejected by the Fleet immigrants.

2. Hence **pre-Fleet** *attrib.*, a word formerly loosely used to describe the people (often wrongly considered as non-Maori) and culture, or the state of affairs existing in New Zealand, before the arrival of the 'Fleet' c1350. See also *pre-Maori* (MAORI B 6 b), MORIORI 3.
 1935 in *Na To Hoa Aroha* (1988) III. 200 The cave paintings in the South Island suggest some connection with the motifs of carvings recently dug up in the far North, and have to be re-examined in the light of a suggestion that such pre-Fleet peoples such as Waitaha..were responsible for the paintings. 1956 DUFF *Moahunter Period of Maori Culture* 18 The question now arises as to the date at which the Chathams had their last contact with New Zealand. It can be fairly confidently stated as pre-Fleet, since Moriori traditions include none of the well-known canoes of the Fleet. 1963 *NZ News* 2 Apr. 2 Pre-Fleet culture. 1966 PHILLIPPS *Maori Life & Custom* 30 It is possible that all whale hunting was done by the pre-Fleet people.

fleet, *n.*[2] *Logging.* A group of logs moved at the same time from the bush up on to the skids. Also as a verb **fleet up**, to jack or otherwise move a log up on to the skids to form part of a group or shipment.
 1953 REED *Story of Kauri* 171 Rolling roads were formed by laying three rickers or other small trees lengthwise to the line of road, and logs were placed crosswise on this road. There might be thirty or forty or more in a fleet [of logs]. Three men with timber jacks usually operated this job. 1969 MOORE *Forest to Farm* 38 Ofte[n] it [*sc.* a log] was 'fleeted up' on the skids ready for loading on to a bush tramway, the motive power for which was supplied either by draught animals or small steam locomotives.

flesher *Fellmongery.* One who removes any particles of flesh remaining on a pelt.
 1908 *Awards, etc.* 211 [Meat-workers award] [Rates of wages] Fellmongery hands, pullers, painters, fleshers, pelt-classers, curing-dolly, steam-drier, dollymen, scudders, skin-washers, wool scourers and trimmers, 8s. per day. 1951 *Awards, etc.* 329 [NZ Freezing-Workers Award] [Rates of wages] *Hidehouse*—Fleshers, when flaying hides and skins other than bobby calf skins, per hour [£]0 4[s.] 8½[d.].

flick, *v.*

1. In the phr. **to flick one's wick**, to hurry up, to 'shake it up'.
 1959 SLATTER *Gun in My Hand* 189 'Come on boy. Flick your wick. Can't waste it'. He pours me another.

2. To turn back or alter the odometer of a vehicle to make the mileage appear less.
 1991 *Motoring Today* (Automobile Assoc.) July 23 He would either transfer the speedo from the wreck or 'flick' the speedo of the stolen car to alter its reading.

flimsy.

1. *Obs.* [Survival of Brit. slang *flimsy* a bank-note: AND 1845–1930.] A one-pound note.
 1899 *Bulletin* (Sydney) 14 Jan. (Red Page) [Letter from *Loafer*, Tauranga.] Following are other local money-names:—1 pound note—*flimsy*, *rag* or *carpet*. 1977 *NZ Numismatic Jrnl.* Oct. 16 The pound note of pre-decimal days was variously known as a *quid*, *nicker*, *smacker*, *flimsy*, *rag*, and *carpet*.

2. *Philately. Hist.* [Extended use of *flimsy* a sheet of very thin writing paper.] The lightweight paper or form on which was written a message to be carried by pigeon mail service; the written message so carried.
 1929 *NZ Stamp Collector* X. 25 The letter which is

written on the 'flimsy' usual in pigeon posts, was dated Marotiri August 23rd 1899. **1931** COLLINS *Airmails & Pigeon Posts NZ* 10 One bird in particular was in the habit of reaching Auckland with its 'flimsies' in a damaged condition. **1968** WALKER *NZ Pigeon Post Stamps* 75 The Governor, The Earl of Ranfurly.. permitted [the agency] to display the Royal Arms on its flimsies and envelopes. **1984** PATERSON *Catalogue NZ Stamps* Perm. page UV.16 The above flimsy, shown in reduced size with its stamp superimposed, is the only used copy [of the stamp] known to exist on or off flimsy.

flinger. *sea perch* (PERCH *n*. 2 (4)); see quot.
1991 BRADSTOCK *Fishing* 21 *Sea perch*. Other names: scarpee, Jock Stewart, highlander, flinger, pohuiakaroa, *Helicolenus percoides*... Even small ones can take a big hook. This makes them a nuisance when you're fishing for something bigger, and explains why commercial long-line fishermen sometimes call them 'flingers'.

flinty. *Goldmining.* A vein of flinty quartz. Also as **flinty leader**, **flinty vein**, one indicating a gold-bearing reef.
1897 *AJHR* C-9 22 This country is..traversed by 'flinties' (small veins of cherty quartz). **1907** *NZGeol.SB (NS)* No.4 106 At the intersections of cross-veins, flinties, and 'flatheads', the mingling of waters that have come from different sources..has resulted in precipitation of the gold and its associated minerals. *Ibid*. 173 In the lower levels the patches of highly auriferous ore generally occurred at the intersections of 'flinties' with the vein. **1912** *NZGeol.SB (NS)* No.15 64 The nearest parallel to the 'flinties' or 'indicator' veins so common at Thames is seen in the Tairua Broken Hills Mine. Here a small flinty leader..intersected certain of the reefs. *Ibid*. 82 The richer material occurred..also..where 'cross-heads' or 'flinties' joined the main reef.

flip. *South Island*. A potato fritter.
1994 *Evening Post* (Wellington) 27 Dec. 13 Q. If you ordered a 'flip' in a South Island takeaway bar, what would you get? A. A potato fritter.

flip-flap. The *spotted shag* (SHAG 2 (16)).
1873 *TrNZI* V. 201 The spotted shag, or flip-flap, well known to our shore folk, is stated by ornithologists to be peculiar to New Zealand; its active movements enliven many a bluff headland or rocky inlet of our island coast line. **1985** *Reader's Digest Book NZ Birds* 125 *Spotted Shag*... Other names: *Parekareka, ocean shag, crested shag, flip-flap, blue shag*.

flipper. Also **flipperjack.** FLAP-JACK *n*.[1]
1911 FOSTON *Bell Bird's Lair* 47 He has now become a crack hand at making 'doe-boys' and 'Flipperjacks'. **1937** AYSON *Thomas* 108 Thomas tried his hand at baking flippers, with flour, water and a little salt for the ingredients, and treacle or sugar to sweeten the taste after the cooking was complete.

flitch. *Sawmilling*. [f. Brit. and US provincial use *flitch* a plank cut from the middle of a log.] A large slab, slice, or baulk cut from a log for later sawing into various sizes of timber; a roughly squared log for splitting into posts, etc.
1874 BAINES *Edward Crewe* 179 The frame of this saw was wide enough to admit the passage of a log six feet in diameter. By means of this we reduced the log to 'flitches'. **1892** *NZ Official Handbook* 158 The great round baulks of timber are 'broken down' being cut lengthwise (by saws moving up and down vertically) into 'flitches', which are passed over to the circular-saws to be ripped into boards and scantling. **1894** *NZ Official Year-book* 332 [Auckland mills] are fitted with vertical breaking-down saws, capable of dividing the largest logs into halves or flitches, as may be required. **1913** CARR *Country Work* 40 Old fashioned 'Breast' benches (where flitches from the breaking-down saw are cut into commercial sizes) are still used in many mills. **1920** MANDER *Story NZ River* (1974) 198 Halved and quartered, it [*sc*. the log] was then levered..on to greased rollers and rushed towards the big circulars, which turned it into flitches. **1961** CRUMP *Hang On a Minute Mate* 120 He could hit the flitches in exactly the right place to split out a post or batten. **1987** MASSEY *Woodturning NZ* 93 *Flitch*. A slab of wood sawn from a log.

Hence **flitcher**, the saw which cuts logs into flitches.
1981 MARRIOTT *Life in Gorge* 85 Face cuts, by the way, are the first boards to come off the flitcher.

float: see FLOATER 1 b.

float, *v*. *Two-up. trans.* To toss (coins) in such a way that they do not spin or spin infrequently while in the air.
1951 LAWSON *Gold in Their Hearts* 90 Well, everything was going well till..[he] spun two coins very high—trying to 'float' them—that means land them without spinning them more than twice.

floater. [Spec. uses of various senses of *floater* a thing or person that floats.]
1. *Goldmining*. **a.** [Orig. US: see OED *floater* 1 b.] A speck of gold thin or light enough to float in and out of the dish during panning-out.
1933 WASHBOURN *Reminiscences of Early Days* 4 The gold..[was] so much of a gold-leaf character... I have frequently seen large specks floating in and out of the dish when panning out there, and these in digging terms are 'floaters'.
b. Also **float, floatstone.** [OED 1881.] A fragment of ore (one of many) detached and carried away from a main reef.
1912 *NZGeol.SB (NS)* No.15 55 Such occurrences, however, are but analogous to the 'hard bars' or 'floaters' of the Thames mines. **1948** *NZGeol.SB (NS)* No.42 41 The loose auriferous rubble and 'floaters' of rich stone mined on the Lord Brassey claim were part of this great mass of slumped material. **1978** MCARA *Gold Mining Waihi* 322 *Float*: Loose pieces of quartz shed from a reef outcrop by weathering and found some distance away. **1983** NOLAN *Gold Fossicker's Handbook* 112 *Floatstone*: loose quartz in a river bed, usually remote from its parent lode.
2. A teacher without an allocated classroom.
1974 *Dominion* (Wellington) 13 Nov. 6 But classroom construction hasn't kept pace, so the teachers become 'floaters' or teachers without classrooms.
3. A floating voter.
1985 *Listener* 13 July 17 Socred..were also chewing away at the floaters so diligently they would give *anyone* a lift.
4. A fried scone (which floats on the surface of the cooking fat).
1990 p.c. Kiriwai Hilliard (Wellington). Flour..baking powder..salt..milk..dripping..make a scone dough ¼ inch thick..fry in dripping. Hinu Bread or Fry Bread. Some people call it floaters.

floatstone: see FLOATER 1 b.

float up. As **to float up to**, to approach (a person or group) casually.
1938 *Press* (Christchurch) (McNab Slang) 2 Apr. 18 'ducks' breakfast,' 'to float up to,' 'to blow up to,' 'to sleep in the Star Hotel' need no explanation.

Hence **float-up** *n*., a casual approach.
1937 PARTRIDGE *Dict. Slang* 287 *float-up*. A person's casual approach: New Zealanders': C. 20.

flock: see note at MOB *n*. 2.

flog, *v*. [Extended use of *flog* to sell, orig. illicitly: cf. OED 2 c.]
1. To steal, to take (without permission).
1939–45 *Expressions and Sayings 2NZEF (Nat. Archiv. TS WAII DA 420/1)* Flog—To sell or loot Army gear (or anything for that matter). **1959** SLATTER *Gun in My Hand* 96 You reckon I flogged those blankets. **1965** SHADBOLT *Among Cinders* 263 I flogged a fresh bottle from Jim's crate without him noticing. **1971** CRUMP *Bastards I Have Met* 19 And somehow he *still* went on flogging their diesel. They never found out how he was doing it. **1982** SHADBOLT *Once on Chunuk Bair* (1990) 54 I still haven't found the fucker... The fucker who flogged my shovel. **1995** CRUMP *Bushwoman* 22 I..traced the map on the wall through my tissue paper. Rivers, ridges and huts. Very poetic all this flogging [i.e., tracing other people's tramping maps without permission]! But it takes the love of creek-heads for me to flog anything.
2. As **flog off. a.** To depart hurriedly
1959 SLATTER *Gun in My Hand* 91 You'll go down the road if ya don't wake ya ideas up, I said. Was gonna give him a buncha five but I flogged off instead.
b. To sell, often in an unconventional way.
1976 MORRIESON *Pallet on Floor* 117 Flog off that section easy. No more scratching for a dollar. **1979** *Evening Post* (Wellington) 3 Apr. 5 Here is a man who took advantage of a school situation to flog off a narcotic. **1983** HALL *Hot Water* 17 It's been on the market for eight months. Every ex deer culler in the country's got a machine he's trying to flog off. **1985** BINNEY *Long Lives the King* 26 You're just suckholing 'cause he flogs off those cookers, or whatever they are, of yours.

floodgate. [f. Brit. dial.: see OED *gate* 2 b; EDD 2.] A gate designed to prevent stock movement along a creek bed, and for that purpose hung across a stream in such a way as to rise and fall with the water level.
1949 NEWTON *High Country Days* 120 Spanning a sizable creek where it burst from a deep and narrow gorge..it consisted of five-foot manuka poles..laced five or six inches apart on two wires—one at the top of the poles and the other three feet lower. The whole, known as a flood-gate, was suspended from a wire cable which was anchored to trees on either side..and so hung that the foot of the poles rested lightly on the shingle of the creek bed. The bottom, hanging free, could swing outwards in times of flooding and permit..debris to pass underneath. **1963** CASEY *As Short a Spring* 218 The wires are all undone, and the floodgate's wide open. **1973** WHEELER *Hist. Sheep Stations NI* 15 The 300-yard-long floodgate in the foreground is one of fourteen on White Rock [Station] rivers. 'The 'gate',' Jim explains, 'is really a batten-and-wire fence suspended from a heavy guy wire strained right across the riverbed. It is built this way to swing freely.' **1982** *Agric. Gloss.* (MAF) 28 *Flood [gate]*: Used across a stream so that it rises and falls with the water level.

flood-horse. A horse trained to cross rivers in flood.
1902 WALKER *Zealandia's Guerdon* 93 Two men were on the opposite bank..with the trained 'flood-horse.' It was a big leggy draught-horse..[to help people get across a flooded river in Canterbury].

FLOOR

floor. [Spec. or transf. uses of *floor* the lower surface of a room.]

1. The area of a woolshed on which shearing and ancillary wool-handling operations are carried out. Cf. BOARD *n.*[1] 1 a.

   1865 BARKER *Station Life* (1870) 32 After this repast..we set out for the wool-shed... After a moment or two I found it quite possible to proceed with Mr L— round the 'floor'. There were about twenty-five shearers at work.

2. *Goldmining*. A prepared surface for collecting alluvial gold from material washed over it.

   1882 HAY *Brighter Britain* II. 279 We see this liquid [*sc.* puddled ore] sent over 'beds', and 'floors', and 'ladders', and 'blanketings', and washed again and again.

flossie. [Prob. f. US slang *flossy* saucy, showy: AND 1899.] A prostitute.

   1910 *Truth* 31 Dec. 6 The evidence [at a prostitute's trial] of 'Tecs Gibson and Snow went to show that she was a common Flossie, and had been convicted within the past six months.

flounder, *n.*

1. Extended and transf. use of northern hemisphere *flounder* for various flatfish of the families Bothidae (left-eyed flounders) and (esp.) Pleuronectidae (right-eyed flounders, some of which are termed in New Zealand 'soles'). See also DAB *n.*[1], PATIKI 1.

   1777 ANDERSON *Journal* Feb. in Cook *Journals* (1967) III. 807 The principal fish caught by the seyne were Mullets and Elephant fish & a few soles and flounders. **1849** POWER *Sketches in NZ* 77 The flounders are a splendid fish, the finest of their tribe; spearing them by torchlight is an excellent sport. **1877** *TrNZI* IX. 487 Flounders are in the market all through the year. **1902** DRUMMOND & HUTTON *Nature in NZ* 73 Among the flat-fish, there are three or four different varieties of flounders, but they are usually all clubbed together. **1910** [see DAB *n.*[1]]. **1938** MAKERETI *Old-Time Maori* (1986) 243 The Maori sometimes caught the patiki or flounder with a spear. **1970** [see PATIKI 1]. **1983** KING *Whina* 38 The sea also brought them snapper, mullet, parore and flounder.

2. With a modifier: **black, common, diamond (diamondback), estuary, freshwater, greenback, Maori, mud, river, sand, square, yellow (yellow-belly)**.

(1) **black** (or **estuary, freshwater, Maori, mud, river**) **flounder**. *Rhombosolea retiaria* (fam. Pleuronectidae), an oval freshwater flatfish having an upper surface dark-black to olive marked with brick red spots and larger pale blotches, and an underside cream to yellow with black spots. See also *patiki-mohoao* (PATIKI 3 a).

   1911 *Rec. Canterbury Mus.* I. 197 Black Flounder— Patiki—*Rhombosolea retiaria*. **1913** *TrNZI* XLV. 232 *Rhombosolea retiaria...* I am not aware whether the black flounder is met with in the Otago Harbour..but it is found in brackish water. **1921** *NZJST* IV. 122 *Black Flounder; Patiki-mohoao*. This species, known generally as 'river-flounder', is occasionally taken at sea. **1938** *TrRSNZ* LXVIII. 408 *Rhombosolea retiaria...* River flounder (black flounder). **1956** GRAHAM *Treasury NZ Fishes* 204 New Zealand Black Flounder or River Flounder (Patiki-mohoao). *Ibid.* 205 It is known to fishermen..as the River Flounder as it is caught mostly inside or near the mouths of rivers and enters lakes where it lives chiefly among weeds. To some it is known as the Maori Flounder. **1969** POLLARD *Austral. & NZ Fishing* (1977) 211 *Rhombosolea retiaria*: Also known as mud flounder, river flounder, estuary flounder, patiki-mohoao..They are easily spotted by their balanced oval outline, the spots on top and by their fondness for estuaries. **1982** *Evening Post* (Wellington) 8 Dec. 37 Another rare species is the black flounder, which may be available in the lower North Island because a few are netted at Lake Onoke in the Wairarapa and sold locally. **1982** [see PATIKI 3 a]. **1990** MCDOWALL *NZ Freshwater Fishes* 322 The black flounder, sometimes known as the river or freshwater flounder, is a truly freshwater species, although its entire life is not spent in freshwater.

(2) **common flounder**, see *sand flounder* (9) below.

(3) **diamond (diamondback) flounder**, see *sand flounder* (9) below.

(4) **estuary flounder**, see *black flounder* (1) above.

(5) **freshwater flounder**, see *black flounder* (1) above.

(6) **greenback** (or **greenback flounder**). *Rhombosolea tapirina* (fam. Pleuronectidae), an oval coastal flatfish dark green above and white below, with a pointed snout.

   1913 *TrNZI* XLV. 232 *Rhombosolea tapirina...* The greenback flounder is also found in all the inlets along the coast. **1921** *NZJST* IV. 122 *Green-back Flounder*. Common around Dunedin. **1947** POWELL *Native Animals NZ* 66 The third common [flounder] species, the 'Green-back', *R[hombosolea] tapirina*..frequents both shallow and deep water either in harbours or off the open coast. **1960** PARROTT *Queer & Rare Fishes NZ* 108 There are four species of flounder recognised from New Zealand..they are the Sand Flounder, Yellowbelly, Black and Greenback Flounders. **1982** *Evening Post* (Wellington) 8 Dec. 37 The yellow-belly is a good table fish, although not in the same league as the superb but much less common greenback flounder. The flesh of this distinctive green coloured species is among the best, but unfortunately it is only found down the east coast of the South Island.

(7) **Maori** (or **mud**) **flounder**, see *black flounder* (1) above.

(8) **river-flounder**, see *black flounder* (1) above.

(9) **sand** (or **common, diamond (diamondback), square**) **flounder**. *Rhombosolea plebeia* (fam. Pleuronectidae), a diamond-shaped commercially important and predominantly coastal flatfish, greenish brown or greyish above and white below. See also DAB *n.*[1], PATIKI 1, SQUARE *n.* 2, *three-corner(s)* (THREE-), *tin-plate* (TIN *n.*[1] 1).

   1911 *Rec. Canterbury Mus.* I. 197 Sand Flounder New Zealand Flounder, Patiki, Three corner, Tinplate *Rhombosolea plebeia*. **1921** *NZJST* IV. 122 *Sand-flounder; Patiki*. One of the commonest flounders, frequenting deeper water than the yellow flounder, and never found in estuaries of rivers. **1936** *Handbook for NZ* (ANZAAS) 72 *Rhombosolea plebeia*: Dab or 'sand flounder'. **1947** POWELL *Native Animals NZ* 66 Sand Flounder..Patiki of the Maoris, is one of the three closely allied species of flat-fish marketed in New Zealand. **1956** [see PATIKI 1]. **1967** MORELAND *Marine Fishes* 32 Sand Flounder [*Rhombosolea plebeia*]... Other names are dab, diamond, tinplate, and square. The Maori name patiki, originally generic, is now loosely used for most flounders. **1982** *Evening Post* (Wellington) 8 Dec. 37 Many people claim that the flesh of the sand flounder is the best and sweetest of all flatfish... Otherwise known as the diamond or dab flounder, it is easily distinguished by its diamond shaped body.

(10) **square flounder**, see *sand flounder* (9) above. See also SQUARE *n.* 2.

(11) **yellow** (or **yellow-belly**) **flounder**, often ellipt. **yellow-belly**. *Rhombosolea leporina*, an oval, predominantly marine but often estuarine flounder, uniformly dark grey or grey-olive above and yellowish below. See also *patiki-totara* (PATIKI 3 c).

   1886 SHERRIN *Handbook Fishes NZ* 304 *Rhombosolea leporina* Gunther Yellow-belly. **1906** *TrNZI* XXXVIII. 551 Yellow-belly, not so common as the [common flounder]. **1913** *TrNZI* XLV. 232 The yellow-belly is the commonest flounder in the shallow lagoons and estuaries along the coast. **1921** *NZJST* IV. 122 *Yellow Flounder: Patiki-totara*. Found in abundance, Bay of Islands, Hauraki Gulf, and Bay of Plenty. **1938** *TrNZI* LXVIII. 407 *Rhombosolea leporina*... Yellow flounder (yellowbelly). **1947** POWELL *Native Animals NZ* 66 The common flounder with the yellow under-side is the 'Yellow-belly', *R[hombosolea] leporina*—it is commonly taken on mud-flats in harbours and in estuaries. **1956** GRAHAM *Treasury NZ Fishes* 201 New Zealand Yellow-belly Flounder (Patiki-totara) Has a dark grey uppersurface with darker markings on fins. The undersurface is yellowish with scattered black spots, sometimes small and numerous and sometimes without. It is from this decided yellow colouring..on the belly of the fish that it derives its common name yellow-belly. **1966** DOOGUE & MORELAND *Sea Anglers' Guide* 217 Yellowbelly Flounder... *Rhombosolea leporina*; patiki-totara (Maori). **1989** RICHARDS *Pioneer's Life* 32 One evening we speared 350 good-sized yellow bellied flounder.

flounder, *v.* To take flounder (usu. by net or spear). Often as a *vbl. n.*

   1967 HOLDEN *Empty Hills* 12 He's going floundering tonight—if he's lucky we might have a taste of fish for breakfast. **1968** GRUNDY *Who'd Marry a Doctor?* 73 Mr Harrington had long promised us a night of floundering in the lagoon. **1989** *Te Karanga* May 3 In the early 1930s my Father bought a flattie which was used to go across the Opihi mouth for the whitebaiting season and also for eeling and floundering.

   Hence **flounderer**, one who takes flounder.

   1968 GRUNDY *Who'd Marry a Doctor?* 75 There was a swishing as the flounderers, wading through the water, neared us. A line with more than a hundred flounders threaded on it was laid on the grass.

flour and blanket policy: see FLOUR AND SUGAR.

flour and sugar. *Hist.* Esp. as **flour and sugar policy** (also **sugar and flour, flour and blanket policy**, see quot. 1952), a 19th century Government policy of appeasing Maori demands by supplying food and clothing. See also SUGAR AND BLANKET.

   1848 SELWYN in *NZ Part V* (Church in the Colonies XX) 23 June (1849) 37 At first, there was an injudicious mixture of philanthropy and curiosity, which petted and pauperized the native people... The chiefs were invited to dinner,.. they were gratified with doles of flour and sugar, and presents of clothing. **1873** MATHEW *Autobiography* in *Founding of NZ* (1940) 205 Some [Maoris] were very threatening and unpleasant [at Porirua, in the 1840s], but they were soothed with fair words and presents of Flour and sugar and plenty of Tobacco. **1874** TROLLOPE *NZ* 156 The flour-and-sugar-policy is the nickname given to the practice by which the Government bribes the tribes into submission. **1898** HOCKEN *Contributions* 144 A bare-faced attempt was made to enrol the Maoris, who..were considered to be householders..within the meaning of the Act. To secure their votes the 'flour and sugar' policy was resorted to. **1903** *TrNZI* XXXV. 182 As for the 'special settlements' for natives, the plan is simply the old 'flour and sugar and blanket' system of the earlier history of the colonists. **1904** *NZ Observer* 6 Feb. 5 With Judge Butler..goes one more of the old school of native officials, the men who received their earlier training in the 'flour and sugar' days of Donald McLean. **1912** *NZ Free Lance Christmas Annual* (Wellington) 35 He had become the possessor of a fine new double-seated buggy, presented to him by the beneficent 'flour and sugar' Government. **1952** LYON *Faring South* 76 The [Maori] policy of that date [after seizure of Rauparaha] was called the 'Flour and Blanket policy'..and the wily savage..did not fail to exhibit a spirit of aggression. **1994** *Dominion* (Wellington) 25 Nov. 12 This [decimation of Whanganui people between 1840–1870s] was largely a result of the British government's 'sugar and flour policy', which supplied the river Maoris with goods laced with arsenic, Mr Tahuparae said.

flour bag. An empty linen bag orig. holding 50lb. or 100lb. flour, used (up to approx. WW2) as a container or as a useful household material for towels, clothing and underclothing, etc.

1873 PYKE *Wild Will Enderby* (1889,1974) III. iv 85 The bunks—rude structures of bush poles, with flour bag sacking—had been torn down. **1888** BARLOW *Kaipara* 102 They all brought their evening clothes with them, not in portmanteaus, but in *flour bags*. It is most surprising to a new chum to see the manifold uses to which flour bags are put to here. **1902** SATCHELL *Land of Lost* (1971) iv 16 In the corner lay his late visitor's luggage, consisting of a flour-bag and a haversack... The flour-bag..contained nothing but clothes. **1946** SARGESON *That Summer* 47 She'd tie a flour-bag over her head, get into gum-boots, and..do about twelve hours a day. **1973** MCELDOWNEY *Arguing with My Grandmother* 12 Gentility would have preferred lace table-mats; poverty was constrained to make do, for everyday use, with flourbags washed until the brand came out and then embroidered. **1980** YORKE *Animals Came First* 78 Flour bags became tea-towels or were used for lining little boys' pants or to make bloomers and other underwear for their mothers and sisters. **1992** GRACE *Cousins* 160 Mama had made you a skirt from a dress and a flour-bag blouse with a green button on it.

flouring, *vbl. n. Goldmining.* Of mercury, the losing of amalgamating properties (see quot.).

1876 *TrNZI* VIII. 334 While on an official visit to the Thames Goldfield I..[observed] the..effect of Cyanide of Potassium, in preventing the flouring of mercury used in working the blanketings. These blanketings I found have..a decidedly acid reaction, due..to the presence of ferric and ferrous salts.., and it is to the former..that what is commonly known as 'flouring', is mainly due, in the process cited above; such ferric salts being able to either oxidize or chloridize the surface of any mercury.., thus enfilming it with a compound, which being practically insoluble in water..prevents that metallic contact taking place between detached mercurial globules, which is necessary to amalgamation.

Hence **floured** *ppl. a.*, applied to mercury that has lost its amalgamating qualities.

1967 MAY *West Coast Gold Rushes* 238 The mercury plates were seldom perfect: the finest gold was lost by flotation while with cemented gold a thin coating of iron oxide ('rusty gold') often prevented amalgamation. The mercury itself became 'sick' or 'floured'; both sodium and nitric acid were employed to improve its amalgamating qualities. *Ibid.* 527 Floured mercury: mercury that has lost its amalgamating properties because of impurities in the ore or the wash. The mercury is then 'sick'.

fluff, *v.* [Cf. EDD *n.*² a slight explosion; a puff.]
1. As **fluff off** [poss. a transf. or euphemistic use of *fluff v.* to fart in a muted fashion; poss. a euphemism for *fuck off*], to depart rapidly, to 'scram', often used imperatively to unwanted company.

1944 FULLARTON *Troop Target* 121 [The two-pounders] darted in and out like scorpions and then fluffed off. **1953** SUTTON-SMITH *Unorganized Games NZ Primary School Children* (VUWTS) II. 677 Some of the [slang] expressions listed by children in two schools are:.. go bite your back, have a roll, fluff off, scram.

2. As **fluffing contest**, a farting contest, esp. among schoolboys.

1968 SLATTER *Pagan Game* 160 He always won the fluffing contest in the Prefects' room.

flume. [Used elsewhere but of special significance in early New Zealand goldmining: see OED *flume n.* 3.] In New Zealand applied esp. to an artificially constructed water race for (mainly) goldmining and (occas.) logging operations.

1871 MONEY *Knocking About NZ* 15 Our object was to make a 'flume', or aqueduct, which should carry the water of the creek above our heads, and allow us to work in the bed of it below. **1874** BAINES *Edward Crewe* 174 The stream at the [logging] dam was forty-five feet wide and at the centre of the structure I made a 'flume' sixteen feet wide, from the floor of which to the top was also sixteen feet. **1879** HINGSTON *Australian Abroad* 293 At these [West Coast] diggings..we could not but notice the use made of flumes—long gutters of wood, supported on sticks twenty feet or more in height, bringing and taking away water for dozens and dozens of miles. **1935** BLYTH ed. *Gold Mining Year Book* 11 *Flume*: Boxing or piping used to convey water from higher ground to a lower level. **1967** MAY *West Coast Gold Rushes* 527 Flumes: the more artificial portion of a water-race, consisting of piping, hose or wooden boxes; most commonly applied to wooden boxes used for conveying water to the claim. **1978** MCARA *Gold Mining Waihi* 322 *Flume*: An aqueduct. Several of these were used to carry water-races over streams and gullies. There were two large arch-supported flumes across the Ohinemuri River carrying the 12 ft by 4 ft low-pressure race.

Hence **fluming,** a system of flumes (occas. in modern use applied to the guttering and down-piping system used to channel rainwater from house-roofs); **flume off** *v.*, to carry excess water away from a claim by means of a flume.

1870 *TrNZI* II. 372 [The oldest drifts] can only be worked by bringing water to bear on them by a system of '**fluming**.' **1909** THOMPSON *Ballads About Business* 76 From the base of the fluming that makes a bridge To carry the head-race from ridge to ridge. **1976** VEITCH *Clyde on Dunstan* 47 By 1864 many races, some of them as long as 15 or 20 miles, were under construction, waters from distant creeks being carried in wooden troughs called fluming. **1871** MONEY *Knocking About NZ* 15 We worked on the Creek..getting very fair gold, though the great labour and expense necessitated in **fluming off** the water consumed more time and money than we could recover out of the claim.

flunks: see FUNK *n.*

fluting, *vbl. n. Obs.* [AND *v.* 1915, *n.* 1896.] 'Showing off' with words, 'holding the floor'.

1918 *Chron. NZEF* 10 May 158 An old hand won't write, and if a new one does he gets rubbed in for fluting.

fly, *n.*¹ Also **tent-fly**. Applied in New Zealand (and prob. elsewhere) in senses extended (beyond those of OED *fly n.*² 4 b) to a piece of canvas fitted (a) outside a tent to provide shelter for a specific purpose or at the entrance to form a door; (b) as an exterior sheet stretched over the ridge-pole so as to cover the ordinary tent roof with an air-space between; (c) occas., with one end fixed on two poles or other object, the other on the ground to form a rough, sloping shelter, or a wind or rain break. Often synonymous (as in quot. 1863) with *fly-tent*. Often with a modifier (as in **galley fly**, quot. 1949 or **skin fly**, quot. 1952) or forming combinations, *fire-fly* (FIRE 4).

1863 MARTIN *Diary* (Hocken MS) 26 Sept. Simon gave me two old pieces of Callico with which I tried to make a fly to sleep in going over the Mountains **1865** MUELLER *My Dear Bannie* (1958) 26 Sept. 49 I went to the Surveyors' houses—little houses of 10 x 15 ft., wooden framework, and green baize stretched over the rafters and side posts, and a large fly over the whole. **c1875** MEREDITH *Adventuring in Maoriland* (1935) 62 I selected a tent-fly (a twelve-foot square sheet of calico), rolled it up, threw it over my shoulder. **1881** BATHGATE *Waitaruna* 129 Diggers' tents by twos or threes..most of them being surrounded by a wall built of sods or turf, and protected by a weather-stained and patched 'fly'. **1896** HARPER *Pioneer Work* 50 Survey parties can have their loads packed on horseback, and carry tent and fly, with a second smaller fly to pitch at the end of the tent to shelter the fire. *Ibid.* 51 We therefore pitch an ordinary 6 ft. by 8 ft. canvas tent, on a ridge pole, with an 8 ft. by 10 ft. fly six inches above it. **1902** SATCHELL *Land of Lost* (1971) 25 The tent, with its fly to protect the roof from the direct beams of the sun, was soon in evidence. *Ibid.* 43 The fire, which must have otherwise been extinguished by the rain, was protected by a small fly of palm leaves, which the natives had given to Clifford for that purpose. **1913** BATHGATE *Sodger Sandy's Bairn* 113 Sod walls with flies of gunny-bags sewn together. **1949** NEWTON *High Country Days* 195 Galley fly. A shelter in which the packie or cook does his cooking when camping out, i.e., a tent fly erected handy to the fireplace. **1952** THOMSON *Deer Hunter* 177 We used the canvas canoe to bring ashore..a skin fly [sc. a fly made of skins] which we pitched to store dry wood for firing. *Ibid.* 178 The fly tent we used as sleeping quarters and the skin fly as a cooking galley. **1961** NOLAN *Bush Lore* 19 When it can be carried, and certainly for a base camp, a fly, long enough to provide a porch, makes camping much more comfortable.

fly, *n.*²

1. [AND 1911.] In the phr. **(to drink) with the flies,** (to drink) alone. Cf. JIMMY WOODSER.

1906 PICARD *Ups & Downs* 12 'What's yours? Ain't 'aving any, right oh, I'll have a Jimmy Wood's with the flies.' **1909** *Truth* 29 May 7 And was he on his ace, drinking with the flies, or did he shout for the boys like a toff? **1918** *Quick March* 2 Sept. 1 When last seen, the wowser-bird was fluttering off to have one with the flies. **1934** *Press* (Christchurch) (Acland Gloss.) 27 Jan. 15 *With the flies, to drink.*—To drink by oneself. **1959** DAVIN *No Remittance* 194 'Have you got a drink?' 'Sure there's a drink. You're welcome. I was just thinking of having one with the flies.' **1974** HILLIARD *Maori Woman* 166 He drank with the flies for twenty minutes and smoked a couple of cigarettes. The faces of the others in the bar did not interest him.

2. [Prob. orig. applied to active or moving cattle: AND 1845.] In the phr. **no flies on (about)** (a person), said of a clever or smart person (occas. evoking a smart reply about a freckled person 'But you can see where they've been.').

1892 Reeves *Homeward Bound* 23 A young man with a 'no flies about me' look on his face. **1896** Bracken *Tom Bracken's Annual* 38 There was no 'flies' on my chum. **1914** Thompson *The Sketcher* in Grant *Unauthorised Version* (1980) 86 [Cartoon caption—a clean-shaven Bill Massey pictured] Masseyite: 'Huh, too many cobwebs.' Wardite: 'No, there's no flies on Bill.' **1961** Crump *Hang On a Minute Mate* 92 We'll see if we can drop her off in a pub somewhere for a fiver. No flies on old Fred. eh! **1976** Sargeson *Sunset Village* 29 But you had to hand it to Trig, no flies on that old duchess.

3. See BLOW-FLY, TURNIP FLY.

fly, *n.*³ [f. *fly* an act or instance of flying: AND *have a fly*, 1915.] A spin, a go, an attempt, in the phr. **to give it a fly**, **to have a fly (at)**, to give it a go; a try; also in two-up **to have a fly**, to have a spin of the coins.
  1917 *NZ at the Front* 105 Come on, me lucky lads, you pick 'em an' I'll pay 'em. Hop right in, diggers, and have a fly with the old man. **1921** *Quick March* 10 Aug. 27 'Hop in, digs, and have a fly with the old man. Come on, thick and heavy, for I'm here today and gone tomorrow.' **a1974** Syder & Hodgetts *Austral. & NZ Eng.* (TS) 359 *Fly, to give it a fly* = to give it a go. 'We were just raw recruits, absolutely inexperienced. We often said we would like the experience of a big construction site. So anyway we gave it a fly.'

fly, *n.*⁴ *Flaxmilling.* [?Alluding to catching flax fibre from the stripping machine 'on the fly', i.e. before it touches ground as it emerges from the stripping machine.] Also as special Comb. **fly boy**. See quot. 1913.
  1889 Cox *Diaries 1888–1924* (ATLMS) 24 July We had a good run and put through a good bit of flax, Joe was fly today. **1913** Carr *Country Work* 44 The fibre as it leaves the stripper is caught by the 'fly boy', who collects enough to make into a hank, which he places convenient for the 'shaker'. The latter, with a motion like cracking a whip, gets rid of as much rubbish as possible.

fly a butterfly: see BUTTERFLY A 3.

fly-blown, *a.* [A transf. use and elaboration of *blown* of money, completely spent, with an allusion to *fly-blown* of meat, maggoty, useless: AND 1853.] Penniless, broke.
  1864 Thatcher *Songs of War* 20 When they know you're fly-blown You're then left alone. **1888** D'Avigdor *Antipodean Notes* 169 His [*sc.* a digger's] position [after he has cut out his cheque on drink] is then described by the very graphic adjective *fly-blown*. **1921** Foston *At The Front* 56 [The men] usually returned to the works fly-blown [after spending their cheques]. **1939** Beattie *First White Boy Born Otago* 170 It appeared that from October to Christmas he had made £2000 and he was now engaged in 'blowing it in'. He was reeling down the street ... and when he saw me he called out, 'Hey, Tom, I'm flyblown just now but come with me in a day or two and I will make your fortune for you.' *Ibid.* 171 You ask what the term 'flyblown' meant. It was a word used in those days [1860s] and meant a man had no money, but once I saw a man really flyblown. **1941** Baker *NZ Slang* 62 A person is *flyblown* when he is penniless.

fly-camp. [f. *flying-camp* (FLYING): cf. OED *n.*² 8, 1939.]. A temporary or makeshift camp or headquarters; a camp lying out and beyond a main camp; a bivouac or temporary shelter.
  1897 Wilmot *Journal* in Reed & Reed *Farthest West* (1950) 138 Mantle and Dan stayed in the fly camp—the rest of us came back... The men from the fly camp came down for tucker and stayed till 6 when they returned with swags. *Ibid.* 155 We shifted our camp today, and pushed on past our flycamp. **1952** Orbell *Comfort & Commonsense in Bush* 8 *Fly Camp or Bivvy.* This is the camp that needs to be of super-light equipment to go on your back to the high tops. **1968** Hall-Jones *Early Fiordland* 157 As the rain continued, they collected the rest of their provisions and packed them out to the various fly camps. **1990** Dawber *Floods, Slips, and Washouts* 31 Then when we'd got a bit further in, we took a fly camp into the bush... The fly camp was fairly primitive but we managed alright.
  Hence **fly-camp** *v. intr.*, to stay temporarily in a fly-camp. Often as a *vbl. n.*
  1952 Thomson *Deer Hunter* 32 The other four shooters were out on the job for a few more days fly-camping. *Ibid.* 89 Once when out fly-camping, we [were]..stranded several days without much in the way of food. **1960** Masters *Back-Country Tales* 57 I set off early one morning with the intention of fly camping and doing a few days' hunting along the tops.

flycatcher.
  1. *Obs.* [Spec. use of *flycatcher* for any of numerous kinds of small insect-eating birds: see OED *fly-catcher* 2.] In New Zealand usu. the FANTAIL *Rhipidura fuliginosa*, but also occas. ROBIN and TOMTIT.
  1773 Forster *Resolution Jrnl.* 2 Apr. (1982) II. 245 In the morning..I went..to the Indian Cove, & shot there..some new yellow headed Flycatchers, a fine large green and brown Pigeon. **1844** Stephens *Journal* (ATLTS) 251 The active little flycatchers..with their pretty fan like tails. **1847** Angas *Savage Life* II. 106 Among the smaller varieties [of birds], I observed..a black and yellow fly-catcher, and an extremely diminutive wren. **1855** Drury *Sailing Directions* 66 Birds met with in Pelorus... Flycatchers and Fantails. **1870** *TrNZI* II. 63 Fan-tail. The pied Flycatcher seems to prefer proximity to water in selecting its nesting place. **1888** Buller *Birds NZ* I. 14 Among the tangle of the underwood the ever-present Flycatcher displayed its pretty fan-like tail. **1892** Kelly *Journey Upper Waitara Valley* 7 The flycatcher also appeared in his familiar manner.

  2. [Transf. use of *flycatcher*, a plant which traps insects: see OED *fly-catcher* 3 b.] In New Zealand *Drosera* spp. (fam. Droseraceae), esp. *D. binata*, *D. rotundifolia*, fly-trap plants, native sundews; less commonly, a naturalized weed *Silene gallica* (fam. Caryophyllaceae) (see quot. 1926). See also *sticky weed* (STICKY *a.* 2).
  1881 *TrNZI* XIII. 261 All our species [of *Drosera*] catch and digest insects, and in fact are known in some districts by the name of 'Fly-catchers'. *Ibid.* 325 Insects are so frequently caught in the glandular hairs of [*Drosera* spp.] leaves that these herbs are known among the observant Southland settlers as 'fly-catchers'. **1889** Featon *Art Album NZ Flora* 141 Drosera... The Sundew... This extremely interesting genus is represented in New Zealand by six species, all of which are said to digest meats, and are known to the settlers as 'Fly-catchers'. **1926** Hilgendorf *Weeds* 74 Catchfly (*Silene* [*gallica*].). Varieties of this species have names *S. anglica* and *S. quinquevulnera*. Common names are spotted catchfly, flycatcher, sticky weed, and five wounds. It is common in cultivated land and waste places such as gravelly river-beds throughout both islands. **1952** Richards *Chatham Is.* 30 *Drosera..binata*... A fly-catcher, the handsomest of its species and the only one on the Chathams... Scented Sundew, Flycatcher. Wahu.

  3. *Goldmining. Hist.* [Transf. use of *flycatcher* birds or plants, or perh. from a resemblance in shape to contemporary kerosene-filled fly-catching troughs.] See quot. 1897.
  1897 McKay *Geol. SW Nelson* 52 As [the gold] progresses along different tail-race channels, it is gradually liberated from contact with the ironsands and, as free gold, is caught on tables called 'fly-catchers', placed in the channel to intercept the gold. **1952** Heinz *Prospecting for Gold* 34 And as free gold it was trapped on tables set across the streams, called 'fly-catchers'.

fly-cemetery. A pastry square with a mince-meat filling of currants, sultanas, etc.; also, a raisin biscuit. Cf. SQUASHED FLY BISCUIT.
  1939 Andrews in *Listener Short Stories* (1978) 1 Alec saw that there were fruit squares for afternoon tea and said hooray, fly cemeteries, and took one in each hand. **1960** 18C M B11 Nelson Boys College 22B fly cemetery for a biscuit with currants, etc. **1980** Leland *A Personal Kiwi-Yankee Dictionary* 41 Fly cemeteries—dead fly biscuits—raisin biscuits: a very thin flat cookie that comes in sheets and appears to be 90% fruit and 10% pastry—good but gooey. **1981** Gee *Meg* 11 She slipped an extra fruit square into my dozen. ('Fly cemeteries,' Lorna giggled, shocking me.)

fly door. Also **fly-proof door.** A metal-screen door, often on a self-shutting spring, placed outside a main door to prevent entry of flying insects.
  1979 *SANZ Gloss. Bldg. Terminol.* 41 *Door, fly-proof*—Partially or wholly fitted with a perforated fabric for the admission of air and the exclusion of flying insects. **1988** *Haeremai Hicks Bay* (Information Sheet, Hicks Bay Motel Lodge) Noise—... Please avoid banging of fly doors, and ensure that all fly doors and window screens are shut.

flyer. *Farming.* [Transf. f. *flier* that which moves quickly.] A sheep which can be quickly shorn.
  1955 Bowen *Wool Away* 156 Flyer. A very fast-shearing sheep; or the best in the mob. **1966** Turner *Eng. Lang. Austral. & NZ* 147 There are names for types of sheep, the *cot* with matted wool; the *cobbler*, a difficult sheep; the *flyer*, a fast one. **1989** *NZ Eng. Newsletter* III. 24 *flyer:* A fast sheep to shear.

flying, *ppl. a.* [Transf. from *flying* on the move; temporary: see OED *ppl. a.* 4.] In special collocations: **flying stock** *farming obs.* [cf. OED 4 f, 1837], stock bought in for temporary holding, conditioning, and prompt sale; **flying-camp.** [cf. OED 4, esp. d *Mil. flying-camp, flying column*], FLY-CAMP; **flying conductor** *obs.*, a tram conductor who moves from tram to tram collecting fares. (F.M. O'Brien, Wellington tramways p.c. 1951 notes a modern use: A *flier* is a temporary itinerant conductor who services crowded vehicles at rush-hour.)
  1891 Wallace *Rural Econ. Austral. & NZ* 259 The sheep kept [at Edendale estate, Southland] are largely a '**flying**' or bought-in **stock** for fattening and shearing. **1891** Douglas in *Mr Explorer Douglas* (1957) 153 I had a mental debate last night as to whether to shift all my Camp up as far as the foot of the Saddle, if there is one—or leave most of it here and take a **Flying Camp** and see what was a head [*sic*]. *Ibid.* 154 If bad weather comes on, it just becomes a matter of site [*sic* = 'sit'] up all night keeping the Fire warm, when a fellow has only a Flying Camp, a Fly and a single Blanket. **1897** Wilmot *Journal* in Reed & Reed *Farthest West* (1950) 179 From this main line I made several branch lines,

taking out flying-camps, and ascending a good many hill-tops, so as to obtain the best views of the country. **1946** *Tararua Story* 53 The 1939 party of 18..wanting to do more in the Kaimanawa Range itself, had a flying camp well up the Waipakihi. **1911** *Truth* 13 May 4 It is a remarkable fact that the [Tramway] Board has been taking on new men so liberally of late as 'students' and **'flying' conductors**, that the service is actually overstaffed.

flying fish: see MAROR0.

flying fox. Occas. ellipt. **fox**. [Fig. use of *flying-fox* a fruit eating bat: AND 1901.] An arrangement of cables whereby materials (or people) are carried across rivers, gorges, etc. by (a platform attached to) an overhead wire, often using gravity as the motive power; also applied to a similar smaller arrangement used as an item in a children's playground. Cf. CAGE.
1949 *Southern Cross* (Wellington) 2 Aug. 9 The Flying Fox, a cage which transports men and materials across the river, is directed by telephone. **1958** *Tararua* Sept. 31 *Miner's cage, chair*, or *cradle*. Any of these uses may be applied to the box on an endless rope used for crossing rivers. Trampers on the whole seem to prefer *cage*. The Australians use *flying fox*. **1982** *Agric. Gloss.* (MAF) 28 *Flying Fox*: Wire between two dead men used to carry fencing materials when laying out a line in steep hill country. **1988** RENNIE *Super Man* 118 [They] scrambled up the muddy bank to the high end of the flying fox. **1989** HINDLEY *Rotorua* 76 It leads to a much larger playground with a flying fox and climbing forms. **1995** CRUMP *Bushwoman* 54 The bottom of the river was no longer visible... A rusty old iron fox hung across it, but no need to use it.

fly-round. *Obs.* Also **fly round the clock.** A spree.
1897 WRIGHT *Station Ballads* 38 He went for a fly-round over to Sydney. **1911** *Truth* 11 Nov. 7 At the time McColl was perfectly sober, but he told witness that he had a 'fly round the clock' the night before, which witness understood to mean a bad night.

fly the garter. *Obs.* A children's game.
1953 MAGEE *Growing Up at the Diggings* in Heinz *Bright Fine Gold* (1974) 38 Some of the simple games played by the [West Coast] children [in the 1870s] were rounders, shinty, duckstone, tiggy touchwood, kiss in the ring, cockfighting, marbles, fly the garter and leapfrog. **1982** SUTTON-SMITH *Hist. Children's Play* 217 At school, however, there was little place for Duck Stones, with its dangerous stone-throwing... Cap On and Fly the Garter, also a danger on hard grounds and in crowded areas.

FOB /efʌu'bi/. *Derog.* Also **fob**. [An acronym of *Fresh Off the Boat(s)*.] A coloured immigrant newly arrived, esp. one from the Pacific Islands, often from Samoa.
1988 McGILL *Dict. Kiwi Slang* 46 *fob* Samoan; street talk. **1991** *Metro* (Auckland) Nov. 117 It's especially true if I'm with a group of New Zealand Chinese friends... They just assume that I'm one of the FOBs (fresh off the boats). **1995** *Dominion* (Wellington) 17 Apr. 23 A jaunty comedy based on the clash between traditional Samoan values and the New Zealand lifestyle, *Fresh off the Boat* portrays the effect an FOB (newly arrived immigrant) has on the lives of a New Zealand Samoan family. **1995** *Mana* 10 (Spring issue) 15 Like a lot of fobs—fresh-off-the-boat Islanders—we had problems adjusting.

folkie. [f. *folk*(singer or *folk*(song + -IE.] A folksinger or folk song.
1986 HULME *Windeater* 32 And now some treacly faded folkies coming up with We Shall Overcome. **1988** *Dominion* (Wellington) 31 Oct. 10 [Heading] Small death of a tragic old folkie. Buddy Holly's vital hit, Rave On, has been harnessed to the lucrative nostalgia treadmill.

fong. Occas. **fong-eye.** [Orig. unknown.] Strong liquor; occas., methylated spirits as a drink. Also with init. cap., a nickname for a reputed heavy drinker.
1939–45 *Expressions and Sayings 2NZEF* (Nat. Archiv. TS WAII DA 420/1) Fong—Fong-eye. Liquor of a dubious nature. **1967** MILLER *Ink on my Fingers* 177 The 'fong' experts were not encouraged by the genuine talent and were usually avoided. **1968** SLATTER *Pagan Game* 174 Everybody as full as a bull on the bus back from the game and they stopped for a leak..and Fong Needham fell down the bank. **1974** AGNEW *Loner* 39 It was so much easier [in the 1930s] to pay sixpence for a bottle of methylated spirits, commonly referred to as fong, drown your sorrows and lose yourself in a world of fantasy. **1979** GEBBIE & MCGREGOR *Incredible 8-Ounce Dream* 89 A group of regular drinkers set up a kitty to pay for taxis home... One of the farsighted drinkers threw a dollar to the 'fong fund' and made the comment, 'Tell me I'm not fit to drive and I'll use that to get a taxi home.' **1985** *Metro* (Auckland) Sept. 47 On the odd occasion he wouldn't front up in the morning. I always assumed it was because he'd attacked the fong (booze) the night before. **1988** MCGILL *Dict. Kiwi Slang* 46 *fong* methylated spirits. [*Jim Henderson*]

fonged, *a.* [See FONG.] Also **fonged up**, **half-fonged**. Drunk, tipsy.
1945 In freq. use by Wellington University students (Ed.) *Fonged* 'drunk' used; also *fong* or *fong-eye* for liquor. **1964** FRANCES *Johnny Rapana* 34 'Course, the boys had been stretching things a bit, and the old boy was pretty fonged up. **1965** WILSON *Outcasts* 50 It occurred to him that Harry was fonged already. The man scarcely showed it but for..a slight blurring of his words. **1974** AGNEW *Loner* 97 I watched three strangers, two of them already half-fonged, heating methylated spirits in a pan. **1988** McGILL *Dict. Kiwi Slang* 46 *fonged* drunk... *fonged up* drunk, cluttered, messed up, bewildered, stymied; combining fog and pong; eg 'He's all fonged up about whether or not she like him.'

foot, *n.*[1] *Fencing.* See quot. 1982.
1951 p.c. R. Gilberd (Okaihau). Posts in a dip are called 'foot-posts' because they require 'footing' to prevent their lifting as wires are strained. A 'foot' is a buried block of wood fastened either to the post or to the wires. **1962** SHARPE *Country Occasions* 157 In the gullies you have to attach a 'foot' to a post—a piece of timber or rock firmly slotted and wired into the bottom end. **1981** *Listener* 21 Mar. 67 Ross prepared a 'foot' to wedge into the base of the post. This was done with his well-used rammer. The 'foot' was a solid piece of totara with a length of No8 wire stapled to it. **1982** *Agric. Gloss.* (MAF) 28 *Foot*: A block of wood attached by wire to the post and buried with the post in the posthole, or some other device to stop the post being pulled out when the fence is strained. *Footing*: Same as foot. It may describe the material used for the foot.
Hence **foot** *v. trans.*, to attach a 'foot' to a fence-post.
1955 WILSON *Land of My Children* 177 They were scientific, too, these fences,.. six posts to the chain, six battens between each, strainers double footed and stayed. **1961** CRUMP *Hang on a Minute Mate* 126 Then for three weeks they dug post—and strainer—holes, ran out wires, footed posts, blocked and stayed the angles.

foot, *n.*[2] In full a *superficial foot*, as a measure of timber.
1848 WAKEFIELD *Handbook NZ* 265 This mill is capable of cutting 20,000 feet of timber per week. **1905** SATCHELL *Toll of Bush* (1985) 66 'About three-quarters of a million feet [of standing kauri]..easily got out.' **1964** DEMPSEY *Little World Stewart Is.* 16 He paid ten shillings per hundred feet for it, the best of heart rimu timber!

football. [Used elsewhere but of historical and social significance in NZ.]
1. Formerly almost exclusively the game of rugby union, now often also (as elsewhere), rugby league, but rarely 'association football' for which the usual term is 'soccer'. Often *attrib*. See also FOOTIE.
1870 *Colonist* (Nelson) 17 May in Swan *Hist. NZ Rugby Football* (1948) I. 1 Football Match—The College v. Town. **1870** [see INTERPROVINCIAL]. **1873** *Weekly News* (Auckland) 10 May 4 The football match, New Zealand against the World, which was postponed from the 29th ult., was played on Saturday at the Barracks. **1890** *Otago Witness* (Dunedin) 3 July 28 In the country districts, more interest is this year being taken in the game of football than has ever been the case before. **1905** *Truth* 24 June 7 [Heading] 'Football Column' [written by 'Pakeha']. **1917** INGRAM *Anzac Diary* (1987) 16 Sept. 44 The afternoon was spent in watching the 1st. and 2nd. Battalion football reps. in action against each other. **1920** football field [see TOWNSHIP 2]. **1936** ALLEN *Poor Scholar* 65 If he had been an English boy, he would have said 'Rugby' or 'Rugger', according to his status. In New Zealand you talk of 'Football' and you mean 'Rugby Football'. If you mean anything else you say 'association' or whatnot. **1960** SCRYMGEOUR *Memories Maoriland* 66 Football was in the ascendancy, for New Zealand players to the old Rugby Game, and hard training in spare time was the order of the day. **1981** KENNEDY *Straight from Shoulder* 23 There was a time when no end-of-year function of a local body, or A & P dinner or football club 'smoko' was complete without a toast to 'the press'. **1987** *MS Cellany* 16 Football posts teetered drunkenly in a passing field.
Hence **footballer**, one who plays rugby football; **footballing** *ppl. a.*, pertaining to rugby football.
1884 *Daily Telegraph* (Napier) 5 May in Swan *Hist. NZ Rugby Football* (1948) I. 92 A largely attended meeting of footballers was held at the Criterion Hotel on Saturday evening, when a Rugby Union for Hawke's Bay was formed. **1890** *Woodville Examiner* 23 Apr. in Swan *Hist. NZ Rugby Football* (1948) I. 107 It has long been felt that Masterton..and Palmerston North..are too far distant as footballing centres.

2. Special Comb. **football** (or **footie**) **brains**, an intuitive ability to master the skills of rugby football; **football ankle**, **football knee**, names for chronic ankle or knee injuries often caused by playing rugby football.
1940 GILKISON *Peaks, Packs & Mountain Tracks* 114 For some years my natural [climbing] mediocrity has been intensified by the particular handicap of a '**football ankle**'. **1959** SLATTER *Gun in My Hand* 99 'Yes, but it was Wilkinson who showed the **football brains** today...' 'Yeah, he's got the footie brains all right. He would have been an All Black if he'd played in a North Island union.' *Ibid*. 166 'Damned dirty play I call it...' 'Aw no, he was just using his head. Football brains, that's what it was.'

footie. Also **footy**. [f. *foot*(ball + -IE)]

1. a. Usu. formerly rugby union football, now often rugby league; as **the footie**, a football game or match.

   1900 *Auckland Weekly News* (Suppl.) 6 July 8 Failing anything more suitable, [a small boy] has a kick at his own hat or the headgear of the urchin across the road who has challenged him to a game of 'footy', as the youngsters call it. **1918** *Feilding Star* 4 Mar. 4 A chase or a game of 'footy' is a strenuous test for boys' clothes. **1948** BALLANTYNE *Cunninghams* (1976) 171 As in the old days when the footie was the only entertainment of the week. **1949** *Here & Now* Oct. 31 Cripes. I'll go up..and have some beers with the boys and talk about the footy. **1959** SLATTER *Gun in My Hand* 42 I remember you on that trip to Nelson for the footie. **1974** GIFFORD *Loosehead Len's Big Brown Book* 8 It seems to me they're takin' all the pleasure out of goin' to the footie these days. **1982** SHADBOLT *On Chunuk Bair* (1990) 55 Jesus, he that wild front row joker who plays footy for Wellington? **1994** LASENBY *Dead Man's Head* 12 Mr Welsh was refereeing a game of footy.

b. Used *attrib.* in Comb. as **footie boots, dance, -field, jersey, jumper, paddock, team**.

   1947 GASKELL *Big Game* 14 Afterwards I cleaned my **footy boots** and packed my gear. **1988** *Univ. Entr. Board Bursaries Eng. Exam.* 6 He bought new footy boots for my eldest brother too. **1963** ADSETT *Magpie Sings* 176 Last time I came to the **footy dance** a sheila told me to wipe the cow-muck out of me ears. **1953** *Listener* 17 Mar. Every Saturday afternoon Steerforth Smith steamed about the **footy field** while the crowd roared. **1959** SLATTER *Gun in My Hand* 229 It's a good job we fight our wars on the footie field. **1986** *Metro* (Auckland) July 133 You don't meet many women on the footie field do you? **1987** VIRTUE *Redemption of Elsdon Bird* (1988) 1 She wore **footy jerseys** and sometimes boots. **1979** *Loosehead Len's Gluepot Greats* in McLauchlan ed. *Acid Test* (1981) 153 A man dressed in a striped **footie jumper**..was calling..'bloody Aussie prawn tossers'. **1970** BALL *People Makers* 89 It is here, in the hard light of high noon on the **footy paddock**, where manly virtue is put to the test. **1945** HENDERSON *Gunner Inglorious* 116 I stuck it up on top of the photograph of the Old Boys' **footie team** I played for in 1935.

2. A rugby football.

   1953 *Listener* 17 Mar. He just happened..to be tenacious with a footy. **1984** EDMOND *High Country Weather* 100 Peter and Terry gobbled their porridge and went outside to kick the footy about.

foot-rot, *v. Farming*. [AND also *vbl. n.*, 1870.] *trans.* To treat (sheep) for foot-rot. Often as a *vbl. n.*

   1913 *Diary* in Studholme *Coldstream* (1985) 136 Jack was constantly on the farm..'foot-rotting the cull half-bred ewes', or 'shifting sheep'. **1940** STUDHOLME *Te Waimate* (1954) 116 Foot-rotting was a horribly monotonous job after one had been at it for weeks. **1956** DARE *Rouseabout Jane* 195 We did quite a lot of foot-rotting, which is a job I dislike as much as dagging. All lame sheep were driven into the woolshed for treatment..their hoofs pared down and the rot cut out. **1971** TAYLOR *Plekhov Place* 11 A little stock work..some help if foot-rotting or dipping was in progress. **1983** FRANCIS *Wildlife Ranger* 3 We were working in the sheep yards foot-rotting, an unpleasant job which involves trimming rotten and superfluous horn off the sheep's feet. **1986** OVENDEN *O.E.* 22 'Do? What do you do?.. You know the range of things: foottrotting to ocean racer crewing.'

   Hence **foot-rotter**, one employed to clean foot-rot from a sheep's feet; **foot-rotty** *a.*, of a sheep, suffering from foot-rot.

   1978 FISHER *Dolphins & Killer Whales* 45 Ralph's attitude towards the 'drifters'—gangs of scrubcutters, shearers, crutchers, **footrotters**, dippers, fencers and dockers was quite different. **1940** STUDHOLME *Te Waimate* (1954) 116 A lot of the infection is carried by **foot-rotty** sheep being put into saleyards and leaving the germ there ready to be carried away by the next mob that is put in the pen. **1981** CHARLES *Black Billy Tea* 75 It's not skittles and beer when you strike a wet year Following some foot-rotty flock.

footwall. *Mining*. [See OED *foot n.* 35, 1869 Austral.] The side or 'wall' of rock which is under a vein or lode.

   1868 *Thames Miner's Guide* 54 Foot-wall.—The under wall of an inclined vein. **1978** MCARA *Gold Mining Waihi* 322 *Footwall*: The underside wall of an inclined reef. **1983** NOLAN *Gold Fossicker's Handbook* 112 *Footwall*: the underneath wall of an inclined reef.

footy, var. FOOTIE.

Forbes parakeet: see PARAKEET 2 (4).

force, *n.* [Spec. use of *force* power to control.] Applied to the power of working-dogs to move sheep.

   1933 *Press* (Christchurch) (Acland Gloss.) 21 Oct. 15 *Force*.—The power of dogs to move sheep. It is different from *eye*, the dog's control of sheep by staring them in the face, and from *noise*, in that there are plenty of dogs which yap, yap continually and yet seem to make little or no impression on their sheep. Huntaways are sometimes spoken of as *forcing dogs*; but the term *f[orce]* is also applied to the ability of a heading dog to pull sheep.

force, *v.* [f. FORCE *n.*] *intr.* Of a sheep-dog, to move sheep in a required direction.

   1934 LILICO *Sheep Dog Memoirs* 27 [The dogs] would head, lead, hunt away, force and back, though of course, they were best at rouseabout work.

   Hence **forcer** *n.*, a sheep-dog able to move sheep in a required direction; **forcing** *vbl. n.*, the action of such a dog.

   1934 LILICO *Sheep Dog Memoirs* 1 These dogs had any amount of eye and style and yet they were powerful forcers with plenty of noise. *Ibid.* 5 [The dog] was no use in forcing but at shedding and control of a small lot, he was perfect.

forcing-pen. *Farming*. [AND 1935.] A small pen so constructed as to force stock in one direction, and usu. next to the race in a drafting or dipping yard. See also *crush-pen* (CRUSH).

   1922 PERRY *Sheep Farming* 16 [The sheep yards] should consist of receiving yards at each end, forcing pen, and drafting race. **1933** *Press* (Christchurch) (Acland Gloss.) 21 Oct. 15 *Forcing pen*.—Small pen next the race in a drafting or dip yard. **1955** BOWEN *Wool Away* 120 The *crush pens* or *forcing pens*..are usually one or two long pens that communicate by a two-way gate with the mouth of the *drafting race*. **1978** JARDINE *Shadows on Hill* 30 I was pushing them up in the forcing pen.

fordman. *Hist*. One responsible for guiding travellers across river-fords.

   1888 D'AVIGDOR *Antipodean Notes* 188 When rivers are at all high the 'pilot' horse is indispensable—a clever steady animal who spends his life in crossing and recrossing the river. It is interesting to watch the 'fordman' trying for a possible crossing on his horse. **1946** ACLAND *Early Canterbury Runs* 135 'Billy Gooseberry' afterwards became fordman at Coppin's Ford on the Rangitata.

forest.

1. Usu. replaces BUSH *n.* (q.v.) in technical, scientific, official (*spec.* as **State forest**) or other formal usage, esp. with reference to plantations of exotic trees.

   1958 *Tararua* Sept. 23 *Forest* is, of course, still in use, but it does not come as naturally to the tongue as *bush*, and there are no words derived from it in this part of the world. It is stiffer, more formal, more technical. We may speak of kauri forest or beech forest, but we get lost in the bush, fight bush fires, and climb above the bushline. The kauri forest, like the mixed podocarp forest, the sub-tropical rain forest..and such-like are terms that come from the botanist and forester, not from the layman—or from the bushman. **1966** TURNER *Eng. Lang. Austral. & NZ* 52 In New Zealand, *forest* usually refers to large tracts of introduced trees, usually pines grown for the paper industry... Officially the term 'indigenous forests' is used..for the native bush, at least in yearbooks and government reports, but *bush* is the standard term.

2. Special Comb. **forest level (limit, line)**, BUSHLINE.

   1884 *TrNZI* XVI. 87 High up the mountains, above the **forest-level**. **1907** *TrNZI* XXXIX. 298 Although frequently met with on the open alpine and subalpine hillside, I consider the bird essentially one of the **forest-limit**, where it maybe seen in numbers at the junction of the forest and subalpine meadows. **1959** *Tararua* Sept. 44 Those who have preferred *forest* have used *forest limit* and *forest level*. **1895** *TrNZI* XXVII. 274 The kea always lived high up the mountains a long distance above the **forest line**. **1912** *Ibid.* XLIV. 11 By defining the 'alpine flora' as that which prevailed above the forest-line. **1950** *Evening Post* (Wellington) 27 May 10 Dense forests of mountain beech cloak the hillsides up to 4,000 feet [in the Southern Alps] where the forest line thins out and gives way to tussocky subalpine scrub. **1966** TURNER *Eng. Lang. Austral. & NZ* 160 *Bush-line* or sometimes *forest-line* (for American *timber-line*, English *tree-line* and Australian *tree-line* or *forest-line*).

Forest Ranger, *n.*[1] *Hist.* A name given to a member of a volunteer corps of militia recruited to fight the Maori in the New Zealand Wars of the 1860s. As *pl.*, the body of troops formed from such volunteers. See also BUSHRANGER *n.*[1] 2, RANGER *n.*[1]

   [**1863** *Daily Southern Cross* (Auckland) Aug. in Bartlett *Emigrants* (1974) 72 In August 1863 an appeal for 'Active Young Men, having some experience of New Zealand Forests' to join 'a Corps of Forest Volunteers'.] **1863** MORGAN *Journal* 2 Sept. (1963) 74 The Forest Rangers, in command of Capt. Jackson, returned from Pukekohe this morning. **1873** ALEXANDER *Bush Fighting* 77 Forest Rangers (a body of settlers). **1922** COWAN *NZ Wars* (1955) I. 225 His [*sc.* Captain Harry Atkinson's] party of fifty men of No. 2 Company, Taranaki Rifles, was the first corps of forest rangers to take the field in New Zealand. The force, as the war went on, was increased to two companies, and was styled the Taranaki Bush Rangers. *Ibid.* I. 248 The inn was the headquarters of Jackson's Forest Rangers during the early part of the war. **1935** MAXWELL *Recollections* 73 During earlier Maori disturbances, besides troops from Home, there were many volunteer corps... There was also a force called the 'Forest Rangers' which saw much service in the wars of the eighteen-sixties. That force and the Colonial Defence Force merged into one that was known as the 'Armed Constabulary'. **1939** REED *Rewi's Last Stand* (1944) 82

'He's off to join the Forest Rangers,'... 'The Forest Rangers!' cried the Colonel. 'Pah! You should try and join a pukka regiment, my boy.' **1959** SINCLAIR *Hist. NZ* 136 A number of actions were fought along the road between the Waikato and Auckland. The settlers countered these tactics by forming a force of Forest Rangers, whose most famous commander was a flamboyant soldier of fortune, Gustavus Von Tempsky. **1992** SMITHYMAN *Auto/Biographies* 32 General Cameron's regulars have not yet crossed the Mangatawhiri line. Militia and Forest Rangers are eager to have a go.

Hence **forest-ranging** *ppl. a.*, having the skill to fight in the bush or in bush conditions.

1922 COWAN *NZ Wars* (1955) I. 211 Yet there were not only settler-soldiers but many of the veterans of the 65th which could have been formed into an excellent forest-ranging corps, competent to follow the Maori into the roughest country... But it was not until 1863 that the value of such bush-fighting companies was recognized.

forest ranger *n.*²: see RANGER *n.*³ 4.

forget-me-not. [Spec. use of *forget-me-not Myosotis* spp.] Species of *Myosotis* (fam. Boraginaceae), *spec.* and esp. (for its blue flower masses) *Myosotidium hortensia*, the **Chatham Island** (or **giant**) **forget-me-not**, popularly called *Chatham Island lily* (LILY 2 (3)).

1868 TAYLOR *Past & Present NZ* 225 The forget-me-not, Kopa-kopa Myosotis, with its fine bunches of flowers and large glossy leaves, is a native of these [Chatham] isles. **1891** *TrNZI* XXIII. 494 We found a few interesting plants [at the Snares]... A *Ligusticum* is found on the cliffs, and near it the pretty forget-me-not (*Myosotis capitata*). **1900** *Canterbury Old & New* 188 Presently we may emerge..upon some moor-like tableland in the heart of the ranges, where we again meet with a characteristic flora composed largely of..white gentians, blue ground-lilies, yellow forget-me-nots... *Myosotis australis*. **1910, 1943, 1952** giant forget-me-not [see LILY 2 (3)]. **1978** MOORE & IRWIN *Oxford Book NZ Plants* 168 *Myosotidium hortensia*, *Chatham Island forget-me-not*. **1991** *NZ Gardener* Aug. 29 Joyce Holmes hasn't forgotten to grow the beautiful Chatham Island forget-me-not..in her garden.

form, *v.* [AND 1865.] *trans.* To construct (a road).

1879 HAAST *Geol. Canterbury & Westland* 119 Mr. Greenlaw was in charge of the road party, which..had been sent up to form a bridle-path over the Pass. **1899** BELL *In Shadow of Bush* 109 [of a road] There is an unformed cross-road or street at the back of the township which leads on to our road... The timber is cleared off the centre, but it is not formed. **1901** *NZ Illustr. Mag.* V. 374 A track has to be formed over which logs can be jacked or dragged.

Hence **formed** *ppl. a.*, constructed, as of a road.

1899 BELL *In Shadow of Bush* 1 Roads, as the term is generally understood, were for a time unknown. At first, a pathway through the bush or along the felled road line..barely passable for a horse; then a formed clay track.

formation. The material or spoil forming the base of a road or track.

1885 'K' *Visit to Lake Rotoaira* 4 A great part of the way [the road is] formation only, through swamp unmetalled. **1906** [see MULLOCK *n.* 2].

forra, forry, varr. WHARE.

Forster's shearwater: see *fluttering shearwater* (SHEARWATER 2 (3)).

fort. [A transf. and weakened use of *fort* stronghold.] A child's place of refuge; a den.

1905 THOMSON *Bush Boys* 116 Two 'dens' or 'forts' were formed. **1919** *Quick March* 1 Dec. 73 'Come on I'll beat y'all to the fort,' shouts a ginger-headed boy... And what a fort it was!... Hollowed out of the sandy bank by the creek. **1953** SUTTON-SMITH *Unorganized Games NZ Primary School Children* (VUWTS) II. 631 Many pack games involve forts—the defence of forts and the attacking of forts. These forts may be much in the nature of 'cosy nooks'. They may also be a home away from home—to be defended to the last ditch—the symbol of the new independence. **1993** *Listener* 9 Jan. 30 Alison and her brothers liked the crib well enough when they were children, building forts in the macrocarpas, paddling in the warm waters.

forty-acre. *Hist.* [See OED *forty* C 2, US (1744) and NZ.] A section of land comprising forty acres (approx. 16.2 ha), esp. in special Comb. **forty-acre farmer, forty-acre man**, one who farms or receives a (free) forty-acre grant of land; **forty-acre paddock, forty-acre section**, a standard area of land esp. that offered under the forty-acre system; **forty-acre system**, a system of encouraging immigration by offering a grant of a forty-acre section of land. Cf. *paddock-farming* (PADDOCK *n.*¹ 6 a (b)).

1959 SINCLAIR *Hist. NZ* 100 In the eighteen-sixties the Auckland Provincial Council, for instance, promised each immigrant a 'free farm' of forty acres... As one of the '**forty acre farmers**' said in the House of Representatives thirty years later, he came out because he wanted 'a bit of land of his own'. **1860** *Voices from Auckland* 48 Will **Forty-acre men** ruin the country? **1869** MAY *May's Guide to Farming in NZ* 42 We were lately on the sections of two 'forty-acre men'. **1954** MILLER *Beyond the Blue Mountains* 71 Edie's big house stands on a *forty-acre paddock* known as the Wagon Reserve... Edie had 200 acres adjoining this block and he and a number of others were keen to get this *forty-acre section*. **1869** MAY *May's Guide to Farming in NZ* 42 The country was a dog-hole..the **forty-acre system** a most villainous take-in.

forty-fives. *West Coast.* Also **45's**. [Named from the scoring system: see also DARE, ne. US.]

[*Note*] Cf. *Encyclopedia Britannica* 11 ed. 1911 XXV. 713 for its origin as a variety of *spoil-five* 'an old game probably imported from Ireland where it is still very popular... The winning of all five tricks is called a "jink".'; OED *spoil-five* 1839, 1841 (Irish quots.), *jink n.*¹ 2 'The winning of a game of spoil-five, twenty-five, or forty-five, by taking all the tricks in one hand.'; see *Century Dict* (1900 edn.) *forty-five* for a concise description of the game; see for the modern game *The Official World Encyclopedia of Sports and Games* Paddington Press (1979) 89: 'Spoil five is similar to loo but has an unusual and complex ranking system. It is especially popular in the Republic of Ireland... Each person plays for himself...Note that the ace of hearts is always the third best trump, regardless of suit; the five of the trump suit is the highest; and the jack of the trump suit the second highest... Each player tries to win three tricks and to prevent anyone else from doing so... Each player puts..counters into a pool. It is won by the player taking three tricks in one hand... A player who wins three tricks may take the pool... Alternatively he may call "Jinx", implying that he will try to win the remaining two tricks... If he wins the extra two tricks he takes the pool, plus a sum from each player equal to his original contribution... If he does not..he loses the pool and the hand counts as a "spoil". *Spoil* is when nobody wins three tricks [and leads to a new hand with only the dealer contributing to the pool]. *Forty-five*. In this variant of spoil five only an even number of players can take part, divided into two equal and opposing sides. There is no pool.'

A card-game, a variety of spoil-five as explained above, traditionally played mainly in the Buller district and on the West Coast of the South Island, and prob. introduced by Irish immigrants (see esp. quots. 1958, 1979). See also JINK.

1872 *Inangahua Herald* 7 Feb. in Latham *Golden Reefs* 127 All [hotels] appeared to be doing a thriving trade and their customers appeared all as busy as 'the Devil in a gale of wind'—some were engaged in a little game of 'anti-up', others were trying their hand at 'blind hookey', 'forty-fives' and 'all fours', while a few were in the 'fifteen-two' business. **1875** WOOD & LAPHAM *Waiting for Mail* 32 I [the Otago Goldfields Commissioner] cannot describe how welcome that 'clay' [pipe] was to me..; the others having gathered round the rough table to enjoy the Irish game of 'Forty-fives'. **1914** PFAFF *Diggers' Story* 110 Consequently larger numbers grouped themselves outside [the Reefton Courthouse], where they passed the time in playing cards—the favourite game in those days [late 1860s] being 'forty-fives'. **1948** *Our Own Country* 99 In smoky little back parlours [in Westport] friendly little groups meet to play 'forty-fives' with uproarious oaths and much heavy thumping of the table... In this game the *five-fingers* (the five of the trump suit) beats all other cards. The trump suit order is five, jack, ace, king queen—all other suits begin with the king. Non-trump suits win high in red; low in black. The ace of diamonds is the lowest card in the pack unless diamonds are trumps, in which case it is the fourth best... The ace of hearts (the Maggy) is always the third best trump. It is credibly reported (*a*) that the game is of Irish origin (*b*) that there are no written rules (*c*) that the game can only be learned by playing it, and (*d*) it is as characteristic of Westport as whitebait or coal. **1959** HOBBS *Wild West Coast* 7 Even then there would be..that fabulous West Coast card game 'forty-fives'—a card game which suits the temperament of West Coasters and which, it is said, anyone but a true West Coaster finds difficulty in playing at all. **1962** LAWLOR *More Wellington Days* 38 Forty-fives was a popular card game introduced by Irish emigrants. There was a wealth of thumping and ejaculation as one scored a trick. **1979** CRUMPTON *Spencer: Gold Seeker* 41 The game played was called Forty-fives, and he could make neither head nor tail of the method of play. There was no money on the table, but a record of games played and won was made on a cribbage board by shifting a match about in the holes. At the conclusion of each game and [*sic*] a score of forty-five was reached, the losers shouted drinks for the other players... The sequence of the game is highest in red cards and lowest in black. The highest card in the pack is the five of whatever suit turns up, then comes the Jack, and the ace of hearts is always the third highest trump in the pack... They play four legs to a game which is called a 'horse.' Jim's playing a hundred pounds a game, twenty pounds a leg, and twenty pounds at the completion of the game. **1980** MCGILL *Ghost Towns NZ* 127 Gambling was poker or 45s, a diggers' card game from California involving legs, queer suits and Maggie, cries of 'Get Jinx!' [*sc.* jink(s)] and 'Go for the Doctor!'

forty-rod. *Obs.* [A play on its being warranted powerful enough to kill at 40 rods (201.16 m) distance: see DARE quoting 'killing forty rods around a corner' being an everyday Missouri remark (1856) about hard liquor; see OED C 1 US, 1863.] Hard (illicit) liquor (usu. bad whiskey). See also LIGHTNING-ROD.

Forty Thieves. *Hist.* In ironic or derogatory uses, mainly with reference to substantial rural land-owners. **a.** A name for a political group of land-owners in Nelson of the 1850s.

1940 McINTOSH *Marlborough* 137 In commenting on the fact that the power acquired by 'the Original Resident Land Purchasers' Association' was retained long after the [New Zealand] Company had ceased to exist, Saunders states [1857 Oct. in Nelson *Examiner*] 'It became a leading and bitter opponent, a dangerous and mischievous class combination, facetiously called 'The Nelson Supper Party' and more viciously called also 'The Forty Thieves'. This party was very ably led by Dr., afterwards Sir David, Monro, and retained all political power in their own hands until some time after the introduction of representative government into this country'.

b. An occasional name for the TWELVE APOSTLES (q.v., esp. quot. 1980 there), a group of 19th century Hawkes Bay land speculators.

forwarding yard. *Farming.* Also **forwarding pen**. A small pen or yard through which sheep move to the crush pen.

1950 *NZJAg.* July LXXXI. 7 *The forwarding yards or pens*, which are considerably smaller and consequently are useful for dealing with small mobs of sheep, as well as their function of leading up to *the crush or forcing pen(s)*. **1955** BOWEN *Wool Away* 120 *Receiving yards*. These must have the capacity to take incoming mobs. They communicate with the *forwarding yards*, or *diamond pens*, which are much smaller, and lead up to the *crush pens* or *forcing pens*.

fossick, *v.* [f. Brit. dial. (Cornwall) *fossick* obtain by asking, 'ferret out'; *fussick* bustle about: cf. also *fossack, fussock* a troublesome person; see EDD.]

1. *intr.* **a.** *Goldmining.* Also **fossick about**. [AND 1852.] To search about unsystematically for small amounts of alluvial gold.

1862 *Lyttelton Times* 22 Oct. in Haast *Julius Von Haast* (1948) 259 I've got a great geologist to look About for gold... And he's been fossicking in every nook, But nothing found. **1873** PYKE *Wild Will Enderby* (1889, 1974) III. ii 77 Do you think I can go fossicking in patience here, while you are running down the game? **1888** D'AVIGDOR *Antipodean Notes* 169 'To fossick about' meant, in the first instance, to search the chinks and crannies of a rocky watercourse for gold; it has now come to mean any searching at hap-hazard. **1958** *Whitcombe's Modern Jun. Dict.* (8edn.) 171 *fossick*. To dig or search for gold, especially on abandoned claims or 'tailings'; to hunt about or rummage for anything. **1960** MASTERS *Back-Country Tales* 23 That was the last trace found of those prospectors, and probable reason for the creek where they had camped and fossicked, becoming known as Gold Creek.

b. As **fossick about, fossick around**, to search about or to rummage for something other than alluvial gold; to potter about.

1873 *TrNZI* V. 189 The hind toes and claws help in maintaining the position of the [kiwi] when fossicking about the prostrate trunks. **c1875** MEREDITH *Adventuring in Maoriland* (1935) 159 One of the cadets, who had a private fowlyard, fossicked around and returned with between two and three dozen eggs. **1879** BARR *Old Identities* 102 He kept *fossicking* about, as scientific men are wont to do, stimulating enquiry and inducing others to enter with him upon researches. **1889** SKEY *Pirate Chief* 38 Not one of his [rabbit's] kindred is left to our whim To gamble [*sic*], to fossick, to hop out with him. **1896** HARPER *Pioneer Work* 59 When 'fossicking' for this route the week previous, our gymnastic feats were most interesting and amusing. **1905** *Truth* 24 June 1 The unsuspecting traveller leaves a swell hotel and plenty to fossick round for accommodation. **1917** *Great Adventure* (1988) 178 We spent a couple of hours fossicking about and picked up one or two useful bits of 'furniture' for our dugout. **1968** HALL-JONES *Early Fiordland* 33 In April 1967 Mr Evans was fossicking around Mary Island when he spotted a cave a few feet above the lake. **1980** LELAND *Kiwi-Yankee Dict.* 42 *Fossick (about).* To search for or look for something. 'I'll go fossick about in that rubbish heap I call an office, and see if I can can find those papers for you'.

2. *trans.* As **fossick out, fossick over**, to find (something) by searching or pottering about; to search (a place), often for signs of gold; to search out (a track or route).

1864 GRANT *Saturday Rev.* (Dunedin) X. 62 Another man, in a few hours, fossicked with his knife 10ozs [of gold]. **1870** WHITWORTH *Martin's Bay Settlement* 23 We caught some fish, and also fossicked out some potatoes. **1883** FERGUSON *Castle Gay* 72 All your grub you [*sc.* a horse] had to fossick Upon the dry and stringy tussock. **1888** DUNCAN *Wakatipians* 80 We fossacked our way through that grim collection of rocks, known to us by the name of the Devil's lumber box. **1896** BIGGAR *Diary* in Begg *Port Preservation* (1973) 348 I fossicked out a bit of string and fastening it round his [*sc.* the dog's] neck led him to the entrance of the track. **1914** GRACE *Tale Timber Town* 85 I shouldn't have left till I'd fossicked that gorge. **1931** LOVELL-SMITH *Old Coaching Days* 35 Lamps were taken from the coach, and Miles..began to fossick for traces of the right road. **1946** HARPER *Memories Mountains & Men* 88 One of [the dog's] accomplishments was to 'fossick' a route round a bluff.

Hence **fossicking** *vbl. n.* [AND 1852] and *ppl. a.* [AND 1859].

1862 *Otago Goldfields & Resources* 18 The progress will naturally be slow, particularly as the ground is so very patchy. As a 'fossicking' locality this is a favourite place. **1891** DOUGLAS in *Mr Explorer Douglas* (1957) 46 Fossicking up the Hope River gave no gold. **1913** CARR *Country Work* 37 Fossicking is carried on by Chinamen and old hands practically all over the province. **1960** MASTERS *Back-Country Tales* 23 Later, signs of where they had camped and done a bit of fossicking for gold were found on a creek. **1981** DENNIS *Paparoas Guide* 69 *Free fossicking area.* From Granite Creek..to Liverpool Creek (near the second swing-bridge on the track) as a free gold fossicking area where anyone can try their luck, and no long term licences will be granted.

fossick, *n.* [f. FOSSICK *v.*: AND 1904.] A search.

1898 VOGEL *Maori Maid* 332 Picking up the axe [she] followed her husband, not, however, until she had made a close fossick for any further gold there might be. **1907** STORER *Boy Settler* 127 I'll get into the boat and have a fossick around.

fossicker. [f. FOSSICK *v.* + -ER.]

1. [AND 1852.] One who fossicks for gold, often without having a miners' licence or a registered claim.

1855 *Nelson Examiner* 7 Nov. 2 I am happy to say that the fossickers and mica diggers have 'cut it'. **1872** *Otago Witness* (Dunedin) 13 Apr. 7 'Fossicker' in the digging vernacular means a miner generally working by himself in shallow ground, either old or new, but where he can overcome any difficulties by his own individual exertions without other assistance. **1894** O'REGAN *Voices Wave & Tree* 15 The gilded loafer 'does the block' and elevates his snout To see the rough-dressed fossicker, white haired and broken down Who strays from out the lonely wilds for his Christmas booze in town. **1909** THOMPSON *Ballads About Business* 62 Fossicker, fencer, rouseabout, and rabbiter he'd been, From Riversdale to Naseby every hamlet he had seen. **1967** MAY *West Coast Gold Rushes* 527 Fossicker: 'the fossicker is to the miner as the gleaner is to the reaper'. The fossicker picks out crevices or pockets but does not work the ground systematically. Often he did not hold a miner's right. **1981** CHARLES *Black Billy Tea* 61 The miners and fossickers did always agree.

2. *transf.* A forager.

1940 STUDHOLME *Te Waimate* (1954) 91 Some of these contract [station] cooks were great fossickers and managed to find quite a lot of green stuff for vegetables. **1970** THOMAS *Way Up North* 56 Of necessity our cattle became expert foragers and fossickers. **1971** TAYLOR *Plekhov Place* 111 The ghouls, the fossickers and the just plain inquisitive would be having a field day.

fossil gum: see GUM 2.

found a nail. *Shearing.* Rhyming slang for (shearing) 'round the tail'.

1933 *Press* (Christchurch) (Acland Gloss.) 25 Nov. 15 But [shearers] also use a rhyming slang sometimes among themselves; say, *found a nail* for *round the tail, hutch* for *crutch*, and so on. **1941** BAKER *NZ Slang* 42 *found a nail*, rhyming slang for 'round the tail'.

four. Used in various combinations and collocations where the number (of) *four* is of significance: **four-by-two** /ˌfobəˈtu/ [f. a transf. or fig. use of the common name of a standard, much-used pre-metric structural timber size, four inches wide by two deep], prison rhyming slang for 'screw', a prison officer; **four-figure man**, one of the first group of New Zealand volunteers in WW2, thus given a low Army identification number; hence, an experienced soldier, and attributively used to allude to the (often legendary) activities of such soldiers (cf. *grim dig* (GRIM *a.* b), *six-figure man* (SIX); THIRTY-NINER); **four main centres**, see MAIN CENTRE; **four-o'-clock**, Californian poppy (*Eschscholzia californica* fam. Papaveraceae), an introduced plant having a golden-yellow flower responsive to sunlight, and common on SI (esp. Marlborough) river-beds and other dry, stony places (see also JOHNNY-GO-TO-BED, SLEEPY JOE); **four-sider**, a wood-working machine formerly producing squared four-by-two timber; **four-tooth**, a sheep of 22 to 30 months old.

1982 NEWBOLD *Big Huey* 218 While somebody kept a lookout for **four-by-twos**, we'd boil up water or milk. *Ibid.* 248 Four-by-two. (n) Prison officer. Rhyming slang from Screw. **1944** FULLARTON *Troop Target* 63 We sent the wrong bloke. A **four-figure man** would have come back with the town clock. *Ibid.* 67 Hark at the four-figure man cracking hardy. *Ibid.* 103 That hardy four-figure myth—the regions of Bagush. **1959** SLATTER *Gun in My Hand* 94 His driver roared him away, away from the colonial rabble where an officer, a four-figure man who had shot paratroops hooked in the olive trees on Crete, could sit with his men in the last days of the war and be one of them. **1979** *Evening Post* (Wellington) 26 Sept. 2 There was no closer spirit than among the 'four-figure' men, as the First Echelon members were called, on account of their regimental numbers. **1982** *Evening Post* (Wellington) 18 Sept. 12 The forgotten legion, the thirty-niners, the four-figure man..all sound like mysterious titles. **1945** *NZ Dairy Exporter* 1 Dec. 90 It was the gay eschscholtzia, the '**four o'clocks**' or 'Sleepy Joes' (as we called them as children), that furnished me with my pen name. **1959** Slatter *Gun in My Hand* 171 The Taylor [River, Marlborough] river-fan glowing with *eschscholtzia*, the orange-yellow four-o'-clock, or bright with blue borage. **1988** p.c. Ted Reynolds (*NZ Herald*) 30 Mar. Eschscholtzia was called 'four o'clock' in Blenheim in the 1940s. **1944** *Korero* (AEWS Background Bulletin) 3 July 17 Rough-sawn timber is put through a machine known as a '**four-sider**'. This is an affair of whirling knives..which turns out four-by-twos, dressed smooth and squared on all sides. **1855** *Nelson Examiner* 7 Feb. 2 The sheep were two, **four**, and six-**tooth** ewes. **1860** *Puketoi Station Diary* (Hocken TS) 14 Mar. Ewe lambs 32 two tooth ewes 402 four & six tooth 638. **1899** Bell *In Shadow of Bush* 26 Has nobody a line of broken-mouthed ewes that could be palmed off to him as four-tooths. **1924** *Otago Witness* (Dunedin) 3 June 13 [Judgement in a case involving the definition of 'four-tooth'.] I have accordingly to settle the matter as follows—a ewe is correctly defined as a four-tooth until the fifth and sixth tooth reach maturity. **1981** Pinney *Early N. Otago Runs* 48 He objected to breeding halfbreds in order to sell them all as four-tooths; while older and older Merinos were retained. **1987** [see full-mouthed].

Foveaux Strait oyster: see oyster *n*. 2 (1).

fowl. Formerly the common New Zealand name for a domestic hen as an egg-layer or as food, since c1970 replaced esp. in the latter sense by 'chicken': poss. distinctively used in special Comb. **fowl house** [see DARE 1767, 'now esp. S[outh] C[arolina]'], a hen-house; **fowlyard**, a hen run.
  1889 Cox *Diaries 1888–1924* (ATLMS) 26 Mar. This afternoon I clipped the short hedge by the **fowl house** and cleaned up the clippings. c**1875** Meredith *Adventuring in Maoriland* (1935) 159 One of the cadets, who had a private **fowlyard**, fossicked around and returned with between two and three dozen eggs.

fox, *n*.: see flying fox.

fox, *v*. [f. obsolete Brit. slang *fox* to shadow a person.] *trans*. To stalk or spy on esp. amorous couples and usu. outdoors.
  1905 *Truth* 24 June 1 [In Christchurch] a bright young man was caught 'foxing' a couple in the park... It is pretty safe to say he has never 'foxed' since. **1909** *Ibid*. 30 Jan. 7 Bradley..entered the paddock before the amorous couple, and he also discovered two skunks secreted for the pleasant occupation of 'foxing' wicked couples. **1963** Pearson *Coal Flat* 153 'We're being followed,' he said. 'Peter Herlihy. He's foxing us.'
  Hence **foxer** *n. obs*., one who 'foxes' amorous couples; **foxing** *vbl. n*., see quot. 1916.
  1905 *Truth* 24 June 1 [Lovers in Hagley Park] soon became aware that they were being followed and watched by '**foxers**.' **1906** *Truth* 20 Jan. 5 The [larrikins'] practice of '**foxing**' couples who are taking a stroll in secluded spots..[in Christchurch] is a loathsome, lowdown game. These 'foxers' [etc.] **1916** *Stratford Evening Post* 30 Sept. 7 The practice known vulgarly as 'foxing' which consists in 'following up' or stalking persons (particularly couples) who frequent parks and reserves at night time, led to a prosecution. A 'foxer' is a person who makes a practice of following other people in parks—a prowler... [Counsel] The police seem to have been prowling... [Police] It is a case of the foxer foxed. **1968** Slatter *Pagan Game* 47 He had come up through all the grades [of sexual interest], progressing from foxing in the riverbed to the knotholes in the girls' dressing sheds at the baths.

foxglove. [Transf. use of *foxglove Digitalis purpurea* (fam. Scrophulariaceae).] Also **mountain foxglove.** Any of several native species of *Ourisia* (fam. Scrophulariaceae), herbs of mainly alpine habitats.
  1919 Cockayne *NZ Plants & Their Story* 101 The mountain-foxglove (*Ourisia macrophylla*) of the North Island and the snowy mountain-foxglove (*O. macrocarpa*) (and its variety *calycina*) of the South Island are the tallest of the New Zealand species, and exceedingly handsome plants. **1961** Martin *Flora NZ* 302 The Mountain Foxglove..is one of the main floral ornaments of the subalpine shrubberies of Mt. Egmont. **1988** Dawson *Forest Vines to Snow Tussocks* 178 The Ourisias are sometimes called mountain foxgloves. This is a common name with at least some validity since foxgloves and *Ourisia* belong to the same family.

foxie. [f. *fox* (terrier + -ie: AND 1906.] A fox terrier.
  1938 Hyde *Godwits Fly* (1970) 114 Wilson's foxie snapped at me, it nearly broke the skin. [**1963**] Anderson & Aitken *Speech & Idiom Maori Children* (1965) 41 It's a foxie (i.e. Here is a fox terrier [*sic*].) **1963** Audley *No Boots for Mr. Moehau* 111 Dave's foxie bitch..comes up fast with a shrill little yap-yap. **1985** O'Sullivan *Shuriken* 22 You know there are some jokers like that—sniff after anything. Proper little foxies.
  Hence **foxy** *a*., pertaining to the fox-terrier breed.
  1960 Scrymgeour *Memories Maoriland* 30 Jim developed [an interest in]..a foxy pup..and began to take an interest in Nature.

frame. Used *attrib*. in special Comb. **frame hut**, a hut built of boards over a timber frame; **frame pack**, a pack set on a frame which fits the contours of a tramper's back; **frame tent**, a timber frame covered with canvas.
  1891 Henty *Maori & Settler* 196 [Log-huts] are much cooler..in the heat of the summer than **frame-huts**... You can easily face them outside and in with matchboard. **1952** Orbell *Comfort & Commonsense in Bush* 16 In general a **frame pack** is the most comfortable to pack with provided it fits your body shape. **1958** *Tararua* Sept. 27 The two main varieties of packs are the *frame pack* and the *frameless pack*, sometimes called the *flat pack*. The frameless pack of course receives that name only on formal occasions, being more familiarly known by that elegant term *kidney rotter*. **1966** Turner *Eng. Lang. Austral. & NZ* 161 A pack may be a *frame pack* or *frameless pack*. **1986** *Sunday Star* (Auckland) 28 Dec. B1 She took the backpack off, put the framepack on, staggered a little. **1874** Bathgate *Col. Experiences* 134 We reached the township of Maori Point..consisting of a few '**frame-tents**', as fixed tents usually lined with green baize or druggetting are called. **1913** Bathgate *Sodger Sandy's Bairn* 78 The order of architecture known as a 'frame-tent'—that is, a frame consisting of posts let into the ground rising some six feet or a little more from its surface, and topped by a wall-plate from which sprang light rafters to a ridge pole. The whole was enclosed with stout calico.

freehold, *v. trans*. and *intr*. To buy out a lease; to make (a rural property) freehold.
  1933 *Press* (Christchurch) (Acland Gloss.) 21 Oct. 15 Freehold.—To make f[reehold], to buy the f[reehold] of run country. The past is *freeholded*. **1957** *NZ Farmer* 7 July 24 A reader..asks the question, 'Does it pay to freehold?' He is on a 486-acre section, with a 33-year lease in perpetuity, and has the right to freehold the section at Land and Survey Department valuation if he wishes. **1958** *NZ Farmer* 26 June 17 If we ever manage to freehold our farm, what would we pay in land tax?... There would be no change just because you freeholded the property.

freeze, *n*. In the phr. **do a freeze**, to miss out; to be left out or ignored; to lose out.
  c**1926** The Mixer *Transport Workers' Song Book* 110 For the foreman had me 'snouted', And I was doing a 'freeze'. He cared not if I was starving When he passed me by that day. **1955** BJ *Cameron Collection* (TS July) do a freeze (v) 1. To freeze. 2. To starve, go short, lose out. **1955** *Evening Post* (Wellington) 2 May The butchers will do a freeze this week when these shooters finish their plucking.

freeze, *v. Prison*. As **freeze (on)**, to refuse to share.
  1982 Newbold *Big Huey* 248 Freeze (on) (v) Refuse to share. **1989** Newbold *Punish. & Politics* 204 What they suspected was confirmed the next morning when Rangi's [bread] ration was found dumped into a rubbish bag. Roberts described his reaction:.. I felt bad because I felt, Stan'll be thinking 'Oh shit! This bastard's frozen on the scoff' [*sc*. did not pass the illicit food along].

freeze-out. [Orig. US 1856: see OED.] A variety of poker. See quot.
  1975 Anderson *Men of Milford Road* 54 Someone suggested we finish up with a 'freeze out'... The rules of this form of sport were simple. Each player had to have three threepenny pieces and on the first round all put in one threepence. An ordinary poker hand was then dealt and cards were bought as required. There was no betting as all hands were tabled face up and the man with the worst hand was 'frozen out'. All he had to do however, was to put in his second threepence and he was in again. After losing three threepences, however, he was frozen out for good. This went on until only two players remained and on the final game the winner took the whole kitty!

freezer.

1. a. [AND 1933.] As **the freezer**, the freezing works.
  1885 Acton-Adams *Letters* July in McCaskill *Molesworth* (1969) 56 Since then I have not put any sheep there except a mob of cull wethers on their way to the freezer at Picton. **1912** Rutherford *Impressions NZ Pastoralist on Tour* 147 Times were bad indeed [in the late 1860s]. The 'freezer' had not been put to a practical use. We didn't export dairy produce or meat. **1949** Davin *Roads from Home* 72 A turn at the shearing in the season, a few months with the freezer at Ocean Beach. **1989** Stirling *On Four Legs and Two* 12 My mate here works in the boning room in the freezer.

b. Also early **freezer room.** *freezing chamber* (freezing b).
  1918 let. 5 Jan. in *Boots, Belts* (1992) 59 You know I have worked in the freezer rooms lumping beef. **1982** *Agric. Gloss.* (MAF) 34 Freezer: Cold room with temperature below freezing.

c. One who works in the freezing-chamber at a freezing works; a cold-chamber hand or freezer hand.
  1901 *Awards, etc.* 438 [Canterbury Freezers Award] No freezers shall be asked to work outside at a lower rate of pay while work is going on in the chambers. **1908** *Awards, etc.* 637 [Canterbury Freezers] Any person..who may desire to work as a freezer..[can] become a member of the union. **1926** Devanny *Butcher*

Shop (1981) 28 It was the..temporary abode of the slaughtermen and freezers.

2. [AND 1897.] A farm animal (usu. a sheep) for slaughter and freezing, esp. for export.
   1889 WILLIAMS & REEVES *Colonial Couplets* 21 Be they [*sc.* sheep] freezers or crawlers or wethers or ewes. **1907** *NZ Official Year-book* 669 Sheep bred from merino ewes and longwool rams are the most suitable for the frozen meat trade, and are known as 'freezers.' **1951** *Awards, etc.* 324 [NZ Freezing-Workers Award] [Rates of wages] Cattle, per head— Boners [£]0 3[s.] 0[d.] Freezers 0 3 2¼ Chillers 0 3 8. **1968** *NZ Contemp. Dict. Suppl.* (Collins) 9 *freezer n.* sheep bred for export as frozen mutton.

3. A freezingly cold spell.
   1938 HYDE *Nor Yrs. Condemn* 169 Then, when it's sundown and a freezer, they get the damp into their chests.

freezing. In mainly *attrib.* use with reference to the freezing of meat for export. **a.** in collocations **freezing company, establishment, industry, wether.**.
   1894 *NZ Official Year-book* 312 Within the last few years several of the **freezing companies** in New Zealand have erected machinery for freezing by the compression..of ammonia. **1918** *NZJST* I. 164 Under normal conditions the freezing season is from about the middle of November to May or June. The fat stock— i.e., cattle, sheep, and lambs—are..bought outright from the farmer by the freezing company or meat-exporter. **1888** D'AVIGDOR *Antipodean Notes* 78 The flocks of sheep are consigned to the company owning the **freezing establishment**, which is erected in an open plain near the railway. **1951** CRESSWELL *Canterbury Tales* 56 You squatted, as the saying was, with mighty few sheep, and as the freezing industry was unknown, waited patiently for the natural increase to pile your sheep figures to astronomical heights. **1940** STUDHOLME *Te Waimate* (1954) 111 In 1887, skins off **freezing wethers** were worth 1/- each.

b. In special collocations: **freezing chamber,** the chamber in a freezing works where carcases are frozen, also *transf.* and *fig.* the Legislative Council, see quot. 1959; **freezing-factory, freezing-house** *obs.,* FREEZING WORKS.
   1887 *Auckland Weekly News* 1 Oct. 8 The storing capacity of the **freezing chambers** is equal to 30,000 carcases. **1900** *Taranaki Herald* (New Plymouth) 18 Jan. 2 Each of the six freezing chambers can accommodate 1000 sheep. **1949** COLE *It Was So Late* (1978) 49 Well, that's what Max used to call me—all full of self-righteousness after his vacation work in a freezing chamber or something. **1959** SINCLAIR *Hist. NZ* 168 In 1891 the [Legislative] Council passed the taxation bill and a bill, which both parties supported, to alter the tenure o[f] future appointments to the Legislative Council from life to seven years. It rejected every other important Liberal measure, thus earning the name of 'the freezing chamber'. **1989** PERRIAM *Where it all Began* 91 Off the cooling floor was a bank of six freezing chambers. **1902** *Settler's Handbook NZ* 96 And, again, there are the highly cultivated properties within easy distances of the **freezing-factories**, where fat lambs are grown on rape, turnips, and clover. **1888** D'AVIGDOR *Antipodean Notes* 84 These gentlemen [Messrs Nelson Brothers] have under their own control the many manufactures subsidiary to the slaughter and **freezing-houses**, and their work has increased enormously since they were first started a few years ago.

freezing works. [AND 1881.] *Pl.* An abattoir or factory where livestock are slaughtered and their carcasses frozen mainly for export; also occas. a factory where fish are processed (see quot. 1912). See also FREEZER 1 a, WORKS.
   1881 *Rep. Committee on Frozen Meat Trade* 21 Dec. in Macdonald *Canterbury Frozen Meat Company* (1957) 77 From experience of companies now working (in other countries), it is found that the operations can best be carried on by having the freezing works away from the port of shipment. **1892** *NZ Official Handbook* 138 The solution of all their difficulties..was found to lie in having freezing-works on shore, near to the place of shipment... In other cases..the freezing-works consist of a large building with a [freezing-]chamber, and powerful engines constantly at work. **1904** *NZ Observer* 19 Mar. 21 H L & R M were greatly interested with the boys at the freezing works wharf. **1912** CHUDLEIGH *Diary* 4 May (1950) 455 Miller brought some splendid frozen fish from Mr McLeans freezing works. **1936** BELSHAW et al. *Agric. Organiz. NZ* 629 Payment is made on freezing works killing sheets. **1948** BALLANTYNE *Cunninghams* (1976) 11 The..agents of overseas meat interests..had him first repair freezing works then pull them down. **1959** SLATTER *Gun in My Hand* 13 We live on slaughter in this country, butchery buys the cars..for those who know the freezing works only as a smell when the wind is in the south. **1992** *Metro* (Auckland) June 134 I would arrive on the bus in the dark, with the freezing works looming out of the mist like a Victorian prison.

Hence **freezing worker**, a person who works at a freezing works.
   1951 in *In Their Own Words* (1988) 131 The Wellington freezing-workers struck too. **1959** SLATTER *Gun in My Hand* 67 I'd like to see some of these people..who criticise freezing workers for going on strike. **1962** SHARPE *Country Occasions* 63 Presently a foreman appeared, one of those iron men who can manage freezing workers and to whom an enraged steer is a minor worry. **1979** TAYLOR *Eyes of Ruru* 15 My name is Tu the freezing worker. Ngati D.B. is my tribe. The pub is my Marae. My fist is my taiaha. **1986** *Metro* (Auckland) July 76 In 1932, wages were cut, and the freezing workers struck throughout the country.

frenchie. Also **frenchy.**

1. [f. *french*(-letter + -IE.] A condom.
   c**1930s** Taranaki schoolboys: p.c. Dr. D.E. Hurley. c**1945** Wellington University Students (Ed.). There was a young man of Cape Horn, Who wished that he'd never been born. He would never have been if his father had seen That the end of the frenchie was torn. **1963** FRAME *Reservoir* 8 Would he wear a frenchie? If he didn't wear a frenchie then she would start having a baby,... Frenchies, by the way, were for sale in Woolworths. Some said they were fingerstalls, but we knew they were frenchies. **1971** SHADBOLT *Bullshit & Jellybeans* 85 We don't know what they did in there but they left their frenchies lying around for the kids to play with on the way to church in the morning. **1987** SLIGO *Final Things* 71 'I've got a packet of frenchies,' said Karl.

2. Usu. *pl.* [f. *french* (fries + -IE.] Chips, french fries.
   1995 *Capital Times* (Wellington) 1–7 Mar. 16 Anyone notice how the quality of chips, french fries, Frenchies (as they're affectionately known to some) has really gone *downhill* in Wellington recently?

French ivy: see IVY 2 b.

French knitting: see RATSTAIL 2.

Frenchman. FLATHEAD 1.
   1956 GRAHAM *Treasury NZ Fishes* 286 Flathead *Kathetostoma giganteum*... Other names for the Flathead are Chinaman and Frenchman, but where these names originated and for what reason I do not know with certainty. **1981** [see CHINAMAN *n.*⁵].

French thistle: see THISTLE 2 (3).

fresh: see FRESHER.

fresh. [f. Brit. dial.: see EDD *fresh* 14.] A rush or sudden flood of water in a creek or river; a freshet.
   1843 DIEFFENBACH *Travels in NZ* I. 77 The river follows the western hills, and at its freshes overflows the left shore. **1853** ROCHFORT *Adventures of Surveyor* 26 During the freshes, which occur after heavy rains, the natives come down the river in their canoes by hundreds to see their friends. **1860** BUTLER *Forest Creek MS* (1960) 38 Having never crossed any of the rivers on horseback in a fresh, having never seen the Rangitata in a fresh..it may be imagined that I felt a certain amount of caution to be necessary. **1879** HAAST *Geol. Canterbury & Westland* 52 The river at our first crossing had been still in a state of fresh. **1889** KIRK *Forest Flora* 151 Taking advantage of the first 'fresh' caused by continuous rain, the sluices of the dams are opened. **1922** *Weekly News* 22 Mar. [Caption] When there are sufficient logs for a 'drive', the dam is 'tripped' during a 'fresh' or flood. **1930** PINFOLD *Fifty Yrs. Maoriland* 14 Heavy rain fell and a 'fresh' was the result. **1959** MASTERS *Tales of Mails* 119 At that time there was no bridge over the Waipawa river..and the crossing, especially if there was a fresh in the river, was a tricky one.

Hence **fresh out** *v.*, to move logs down a river by means of a fresh. Cf. DRIVE *v.*
   1953 REED *Story of Kauri* 263 The Kapowai Bush was finished about 1919, when the last of the logs were freshed out with the floods.

Hence **freshed** *ppl. a.*, of a river, in fresh.
   1863 BUTLER *First Year* viii 117 The Ashburton, however, was heavily freshed, and the night was pitch dark. *Ibid.* 118 The prospect was now brilliant, save that the Rakaia was said to be very heavily freshed.

fresher. *University slang.* [Prob. adopted f. Oxford Univ.: cf. OED *fresh n.*¹ 5, *fresher* 1882.]
a. Also early **fresh**. A first year student at a university.
   1893 *Canterbury College Diploma Day* 11 He's large is the 'Fresh' with the swilled [*sic*] head. **1938** *Salient* (Wellington) 9 Mar. 2 Fresher, we bid you welcome to Salamanca, the place where some of you will continue your education and others will begin it. **1945** *Salient* (Wellington) 2 Mar. 1 '45 Freshers may see Foundation Laid [*sc.* of Student Union Building]. **1968** SLATTER *Pagan Game* 81 The freshers' pyjamas slung around the neck of a pompous statue on the avenue. **1979** ASHTON-WARNER *I Passed This Way* (1980) 185 Gray had asked him to..see that I had a partner for the Freshers Ball [at Auckland, 1928]. **1988** LAY *Fools on Hill* 5 'Fresher?' 'Yes. What year are you?' 'Second. I'm going to the caff.'

b. In secondary school use, for a new pupil.
   1951 16–18 M 26 Marlborough C. 25 Freshers [M1 F4] **1951** 16–18 M 32 St Bede's, Chch 25 Freshers

freshwater. *a.* See CREEK 2; CRAYFISH 2 (1), FLOUNDER *n.* 2 (1), MUSSEL 2 (4).

Freyberg. [f. the name of General (Lord) B.C. *Freyberg* (1889–1963), Commander of the NZ Division in N. Africa and Europe during WW2.] In special collocations with reference to WW2: **Freyberg's butchers**, a name given by enemy propaganda to Maori soldiers on Crete;

Freyberg's circus, the Second New Zealand Division.

1944 REID *Turning Point* 44 The Maoris started to pick them out of their slit trenches on the ends of their bayonets. Hence the name of 'Freyberg's Butchers' by 'Lord Haw Haw'. **1986** *Dominion* (Wellington) 7 June 9 'Freyberg's Circus' (as the troops often called it) was maintained as much by rank-and-file laughter, horseplay, mischief, and the assertive, rumbunctious, enterprising spirits of autonomous man as it was by any subservience to conventional military organisation or to aspirations of professionalism.

fribby, *a.* [Of uncertain origin: cf. AND *frib* a small tuft of wool matted with grease, 1805; *fribby,* 1900.] Of locks of wool, small and short.

1915 MACDONALD *NZ Sheepfarming* 69 When the fleece is placed on the table, outside uppermost, the stained and fribby pieces should be taken off the edges. **1922** PERRY *Sheep Farming* 122 The fribby bits that fall on the board, when shaken from the fleece, should be swept under the table and left there until there is sufficient to make a bale. **1934** *Press* (Christchurch) (Acland Gloss.) 20 Jan. 15 *Fribby.*—Perhaps more a wool trade term than a station one. The yolky locks round the points taken off by the roller from a decently skirted fleece.

fried scones. Usu. *pl.*, a scone mixture divided into portions and fried in a pan; often regarded as a Maori dish. See also *buggers afloat* (BUGGER 2).

1915 MCCREDIE *Bungalow Recipe Book* 75 *fried scones..*flour..baking powder. Mix quickly with water. Fry. **1938** HYDE *Nor Yrs. Condemn* 48 When Susan came back, Starkie was eating fried scones in the kitchen. **1978** FULLER *Maori Food & Cook.* 27 fried scones (paraoa par[a]i—panakeke)(*Parai..*fry.)...Heat lard in pan and fry the scones until golden brown. **1989** *Broadsheet* May 31 They had fried scones for tea the last three nights.

friendly, *a.* and *n. Hist.*

A. *adj.* **a.** Applied to a Maori friendly to early European immigrants.

1816 HALL in Elder *Marsden's Lieutenants* (1934) 124 After Captain Graham returned to his vessel, my friendly natives being up the country in search of potatoes, a strange party came over from the other side of the Bay and got upon the sawyer's house-top. **1847** *Williams to Selwyn* 12 July in Carleton *Life of Henry Williams* (1874) II. 157 Waka and other friendly chiefs were perfectly confounded as to the intention of the Government. **1849** POWER *Sketches in NZ* 25 [He recommended me] not to attempt to ascend the mountain till the following day, when he..and Major Durie with the armed police, intended to join the friendly natives.

b. Applied to a Maori (or tribe) loyal to the Crown during the New Zealand Wars of the 19th century, often in the collocations **friendly Maori (native, party)**.

1854 *Richmond-Atkinson Papers* (1960) I. 151 The *friendly party* of natives (so it is stated) are sowing wheat and planting potatoes on the Waiwakaiho Block... It is feared by them that Henry Epuni would crop the land if the friendly natives did not. **1860** GRACE *Journal* 28 May in *Pioneer Missionary* (1928) 91 On my journey to and from Auckland, when I came in contact with both friendly and hostile Maoris. **1879** FEATON *Waikato War* 44 The so-called friendly natives in the stockade, as soon as the hostile natives opened fire, ran away into the bush. **1922** COWAN *NZ Wars* (1955) I. 50 Some of the friendly natives accompanied the white skirmishers. **1984** BARBER *Red Coat to Jungle Green* 15 An auxiliary force of 400 'friendly' Ngapuhi accompanied the Redcoats and provided them with intelligence of Hone Heke's movements.

B. *n.* [Ellipt. for *friendly Maori.*] Usu. *pl.*, often with init. cap. A Maori, or in *pl.*, a tribe, loyal to the Crown during the New Zealand Wars. Compare KUPAPA 1, QUEENITE.

1861 *Richmond-Atkinson Papers* (1960) I. 707 No natives about except the 'friendlies' at Poutoko and Hauranga. **1868** GRACE *Journal* 28 Nov. in *Pioneer Missionary* (1928) 204 Wherever we go now as Missionaries, whether amongst the Friendlies or Kingites. **1869** THATCHER *Wit & Humour* 14 This war is a terrible nuisance I vow. By foes and friendlies we have often been had. **1875** *Official Handbook NZ* 194 The service rendered by 'friendlies' is commemorated by this monument [at Wanganui]. **1882** POTTS *Out in Open* 13 On the steep path winding through the bracken we are met by a body of 'friendlies' of the Lower Waikato tribes. **1906** *Truth* 15 Sept. 7 One telegram stated that a body of 'friendlies' in the pay of the colonists, well-armed, well-drilled, and with plenty of ammunition had gone over to the enemy. **1959** SINCLAIR *Hist. NZ* 121 Instead, it urged, the Government should divide disputed land and buy whatever proportion belonged to the 'friendlies' or 'the progress party', as the settlers called the 'land sellers'. **1984** BARBER *Red Coat to Jungle Green* 38 The Maori troops who fought for the British queen were called 'friendlies'.

friendly road. Constr. with *the.*

1. *Obs.* Used fig. with reference to a worker, 'friendly' to the boss, who refused to support fellow-workers in industrial disputes.

1938 HYDE *Nor Yrs. Condemn* 171 'Righto, coming out [on strike].' Out of eighty quarry-men, three stayed on the friendly road, and had to take to the bush for the day.

2. *Hist.* Usu. init. caps. C.G. Scrimgeour's Auckland radio station 1ZB; also the programmes it ran in the early 1930s supportive of the poor and unemployed.

1937 *Truth* 20 Oct. 19 I am a 'Friendly Rodent'. Pardon, I mean 'Friendly Roadian'. Perhaps if I keep following the Friendly Road, I'll get a job worth £1500 some day. **1938** *Auckland Weekly News* 5 Oct. 10 The meeting was held under the auspices of the Friendly Road... This meeting..resolves that he be asked to advise the Friendly Road of his assurance that the hours and conditions of the Friendly Road sessions will remain undisturbed. **1959** SINCLAIR *Hist. NZ* 258 During the depth of the depression Labour Party Meetings were revivalist gatherings where bitterness against evil times mingled with the most pure visions of tomorrow. In Auckland a radio station known as 'The Friendly Road' run by the Reverend C.G. Scrimgeour ('Uncle Scrim'), broadcast the same evangelistic message in a programme called 'The Man in the Street'. **1974** MULDOON *Rise and Fall of a Young Turk* 6 She [*sc.* Muldoon's mother] was a devotee of Uncle Scrim and the Friendly Road movement on Station 1ZB.

frigate petrel: see PETREL 2 (9).

frilled shag: see SHAG 2 (8).

frog, *n.*[1]

1. Often **native** or **New Zealand frog.** Any of various tail-less, web-footed amphibians of the New Zealand family Leiopelmatidae, or of the introduced Australian family Ranidae.

1838 POLACK *NZ* I. 318 Toads, frogs, with their barometrical croak! croak! abound in the swamps. These subsultive reptiles do not differ from the species in Europe, each being animated with a similar determination to subjoin their remarks with open throat on approaching rain. **1870** *TrNZI* II. 87 [Title] On the New Zealand Frog (Leiopelma Hochstetteri), *with an account of its remarkable feature in the history of some species of Australian Frogs.* **1904** HUTTON & DRUMMOND *Animals NZ* 359 The New Zealand Frog. L[e]iopelma hochstetteri. *Ibid.* 360 This frog occurs only in hilly country, in the neighbourhood of streams. **1921** *NZJST* III. 308 The native frog is confined to the upper slopes of Mount Moehau, near the north end of the Hauraki Peninsula, and lives in the moss there so abundant... A second species of New Zealand native frog was recently discovered on Stephen Island. **1924** *JPS* XXXIII. 210 Whilst on these ranges [Moehau] we saw a number of the small native frogs (which old Hapi called 'kuripeke'), and said they were the 'mokai' or pets of the Patu-pai-arehe, and acted as sentries for their masters. **1930** REISCHEK *Yesterdays in Maoriland* (1933) 80 In this district I found the rare New Zealand frog (*pokopoko*) both in the creeks and deep down in the mines. **1947** POWELL *Native Animals* 76 Native frogs have a modified life history in which there is no free-swimming tadpole stage, but a minute tailed frog emerges straight from the egg. **1949** *Rec. Auck. Inst. Mus.* III. 374 New Zealand frogs, which proved to be *Leiopelma hochstetteri*, were discovered..near Warkworth. **1957** *TRSNZ* LXXXIV. 867 To A.S. Thomson, surgeon to the 58th Regiment, belongs the distinction of having written the first account of the New Zealand native frog. **1966** *Encycl. NZ* III. 66 The native frogs belong to a genus..restricted to New Zealand, which shows some of the most primitive skeletal and anatomical features of any known frog or toad. **1980** ROBB *NZ Amphibians & Reptiles in Colour* 17 The only amphibians native to New Zealand are those species of frogs belonging to the genus *Leiopelma* (family Leiopelmatidae). *Ibid.* 18 The first definite recorded finding of a native frog was in 1852, when some prospectors panning for gold in a mountain stream near Coromandel discovered a specimen under a large stone on a stream bank.

2. With a modifier: **Archey's, Hamilton's (golden, Stephens Island), Hochstetter's.**

(1) **Archey's frog.** [f. the name of Sir Gilbert *Archey* (1890–1974), Director, Auckland Institute and Museum.] *Leiopelma archeyi*, a nocturnal terrestrial frog often found on mist-shrouded ridges away from creeks. (In Coromandel also called **little red man** (see quots. 1952, 1966); cf. the Maori name *ngai kura* 'red tribe'.)

[**1952** REED *Coromandel Holiday* 76 The amiable mountain [Te Moehau] shelters..a strange race of diminutive men—the little Red Men of Te Moehau. These tiny people—the Patupaiarehe is their ancestral name—have had their home on the forested mountain for a long, long time. *Ibid.* 77 The little Red Men never suffer from thirst; they long ago made a pact of friendship with the little red frogs, who never fail in time of need to bring them water from the nearest spring.] **1966** SHARELL *The Tuatara, Lizards & Frogs of NZ* 62 Only in 1942 were these frogs on the Tokatea Ridge—first seen by Percy Smith in 1862, recognised..as a third species of native frog. They were named Archey's frog *Leiopelma archeyi*. *Ibid.* 64 The red tinge gave rise to the popular name of Little Red Man, under which the frog is known in the Coromandel district. **1990** FOORD *NZ Descriptive Animal Dictionary* 19 Archey's Frog. *Leiopelma archeyi*. A slender frog 4cm long, colour variable from green to brown, found high on Coromandel Pen... Other name: Little Red Man.

(2) **Hamilton's** [f. the name of Augustus *Hamilton* (1854–1913), Director, Dominion Museum] **(golden, Stephens Island) frog.** *Leiopelma hamiltoni*, a terrestrial frog found in coastal forest and damp but open scree, formerly esp. on Stephens Island in Cook Strait.

1954 *Bull. Wellington Bot. Soc.* No.27 5 The one

rare and unusual animal on the island is the Stephens Island frog. **1961** *Tuatara* VIII. 98 *Leiopelma hamiltoni*... Known as the 'Stephens Island Frog', it is also called by local inhabitants of the area 'the golden frog'. **1966** SHARELL *The Tuatara, Lizards & Frogs of NZ* 62 In 1918, H. Hamilton of the Dominion Museum discovered frogs under stones, deep in the boulder bank on top of Stephens Island. This frog was..named *Leiopelma hamiltoni*, the Stephens Island or Hamilton's frog. **1977** *Proc. NZ Ecol. Soc.* 46 There is now some evidence that tuataras may eat Hamilton's frogs. **1987** POWELL *Native Animals* (3edn.) 66 There are three species of native frogs: *L. hochstetteri* from several northern North Island mountain ranges; Archey's Frog *L. archeyi* from the Coromandel Range; and Hamilton's Frog *L. hamiltoni* from Stephens and Maud Island (Cook Strait area). **1990** FOORD *NZ Descriptive Animal Dictionary* 189 Hamilton's Frog... A small brown or yellow native frog with highly primitive features and no free tadpole stage, known only from Stephens I. and Maud I. Other name: Stephens Island Frog.

(3) **Hochstetter's frog**. [f. the name of Christian Gottlieb Ferdinand von *Hochstetter* (1829–84), geologist, who took the type specimens to Europe.] *Leiopelma hochstetteri*, a stocky, usu. brown, widely distributed North Island frog found in shaded creek edges in native forest up to about 800 m altitude.

1966 SHARELL *The Tuatara, Lizards & Frogs of NZ* 64 Hochstetter's Frog (*Leiopelma hochstetteri*)... Toes half-webbed. **1982** JACKSON *Wildlife NZ* 57 Hochstetter's frog..is chubby and dark to olive-brown with obvious webbing between its toes. **1990** FOORD *NZ Descr. Animal Dict.* 196 Hochstetter's Frog... A plump little brown frog to 44mm long, found in many places in northern NI... Other names: New Zealand Frog, Pokopoko.

3. Any of several species of Australian frogs of the family Ranidae introduced to New Zealand between 1868 and 1897, their names (poss. mainly 'book-names') often locally distinguished by the use of various modifiers: **green (great green, large green) tree frog** *Litoria* (formerly *Hyla*) *caerulea*; **golden** (or **green**) **bell frog**, *Litoria aurea* or *L. ramiformis*; **brown** (or **Australian, whistling**) **tree frog**, or **whistling (Tasmanian whistling) frog**. (*L. ewingi*).

1922 *Auckland Weekly News* 20 Apr. 15 The whistling frog..seems to be strictly nocturnal. **1933** *Canterbury Mountaineer* 32 Camped in the bush at Aickens to be disturbed only by whistling frogs. **1961** *Tuatara* VIII. 106 The three species that were successfully introduced are *Hyla aurera*, the Green Frog; *H. ewingi*, the Brown Tree Frog or Whistling Frog; and *H. caerulea*, the Great Green Tree Frog. **1966** SHARELL *The Tuatara, Lizards & Frogs of NZ* 66 So far, three species of Australian tree frogs of the genus *Hyla* have been introduced into New Zealand. *Ibid.* 67 Most commonly found throughout New Zealand is the *Golden Bell frog* (*Hyla aurea*)... The *Great Green Tree frog* (*Hyla caerulea*) found in the North Island is rather rare... The *Brown Tree* or *Whistling frog* (*Hyla ewingi*..), has been successfully introduced in Westland and has spread to Southland. **1986** HULME *Windeater* 39 A windless peace-filled night, the only sound that liquid continuous chirruping of tree-frogs. **1986** ROBB *NZ Amphibians & Reptiles* 26 The green tree frog, or golden bell frog... The first attempt to introduce them was apparently made in 1867... *Litoria ewingi*, the brown Australian tree frog, or Whistling frog..was introduced into New Zealand in a most casual manner. In 1875 Mr. W. Perkins brought some specimens from Tasmania in a bottle and liberated them in a drain in Alexandra Street, Greymouth... *Litoria caerulea*, the large green tree frog. A shipment of six dozen adults of this species was imported from Sydney by the Agricultural Department in 1897.

4. In the phr. **scarce as frog's feathers**, very scarce or infrequent.

1942 *NZEF Times* 7 Sept. 5 News this week is..scarce as frog's feathers.

frog, *n.*[2] *Obs.* [See Partridge 8 *frog* 8, a £1 note, from Austral. rhyming slang *frog skin* for *sovrin*.] A pound note.

1921 *Quick March* 10 Aug. 27 [The game is crown-and-anchor.] 'Murder on the old sergeant-major.' 'Ten frog half-way, cobber. Right, she's set.'

frog, *n.*[3] Also **froggy**. [A play on *Frog* Frenchman and FRENCHY: AND 1952.] A condom or 'french' letter.

1974 MORRIESON *Predicament* (1981) 95 'I love you, Ernie, but you will be careful, wontcha?' 'Sure I will baby... ' 'You got a froggy?' Maybelle said. **1987** NORGROVE *Shoestring Sailors* 50 'How do you ask a girl for a packet of frogs?'

Frogolia. [*Frog* Frenchman + *-olia* by analogy with PONGOLIA.] A jocular derogatory name for France. Also as **Frogolian**, a French national.

1976 GIFFORD *Loosehead Len's Bumper Thump Book* 12 We've certainly given Frogolia a fair go in the past. **1986** *Sunday Star* (Auckland) 29 June B1 But that joker was model for them statues on Easter Island compared with the poor old Frogolians by the end of the [rugby] test yesterday.

frogs' eggs. Also **frogs' eyes**. [Used elsewhere in boarding establishments: see Wilkes 1953.] Names applied to boiled sago or tapioca desserts as served in institutions.

c**1935** St Patrick's College, Silverstream: p.c. Fr Alex McDonald. 'Frogs' eyes' usu. for tapioca; 'frogs' eggs' for sago. **1960** 17C M B8 Wanganui Girls C.I 22B Frogs eyes—tapioca **1960** 17C F B10 Napier Girls H.S. 22B Frogs eggs (lemon sago) **1988** McGILL *Dict. Kiwi Slang* 46 *frog's eyes* boiled tapioca or sago, as usually inflicted on those in institutions. **1988** *Through the Looking Glass* 32 [I spent] a short time at Dio as a boarder, discovering the joys of..'frogs-eggs-and-snot'. **1992** GRACE *Cousins* 139 Have you heard of having frog's eggs and dead man's ears for pudding?

front, *a.* and *n.*[1] Mainly *SI*.

A. *adj.*

1. Of country in general, situated towards the coast away from the interior; of parts of a farm or run, situated near to a main road access or near the homestead.

1860 in Butler *First Year* (1863) iv 57 We had no difficulty getting through it [*sc*. a black-birch bush], for it had no under-growth, as the bushes on the front ranges have. **1874** KENNAWAY *Crusts* 216 The owner of a run, whose centre was about twenty miles from our station..had fitted up a rough out-station at our front and his back boundary. **1951** McLEOD *High Country* 5 On the first approach to the mountains they were met by great foothills... In many cases along these front hills there were large areas of forest or 'bush'. **1975** ACLAND *Early Canterbury Runs* (4edn.) 94 Run 17 of 10,000 acres, the front run, was taken up in November 1851. **1990** MARTIN *Forgotten Worker* 7 In 1854 a further ten large runs were established on the remainder of the plains between the Ashburton and the Rangitata Rivers; this meant that the entire plains and 'front hills' were taken up.

2. In special collocations: **front country**, *mainly* Canterbury, the country on the plains used for sheep-stations, as distinct from the BACK COUNTRY (q.v.) in the foothills of the Southern Alps (see also COUNTRY); **front paddock**, a paddock near the road access or homestead.

1860 BUTLER *Forest Creek MS* (1960) 54 Flax and cabbage trees belong more to the **front country**, they are not so characteristic of the back. **1933** JONES *Autobiogr. Early Settler* 72 No gardeners were kept except on the front country. **1940** STUDHOLME *Te Waimate* (1954) 104 Black pine (matai) was used [for fencing] on the front country. **1952** NEWTON *High Country Journey* 77 Mt. Somers station, a 'front' country block of about 16,000 acres, lies between Barossa and Winterslow. **1970** McLEOD *Glorious Morning* 24 These [Canterbury] ranges form a definite barrier between the 'front' and 'back' country and the inhabitants of each see little of each other. **1876** PEACHE *Journal* in Gray *Quiet with Hills* (1970) 49 **Front paddock** 80 acres/ Upper paddock 50 [do]/ Back paddock 10 [do]/ Middle paddock 20 [do] **1899** BELL *In Shadow of Bush* 149 I will come over tomorrow and help to shift the ewes and lambs into the front paddock—they want a change now. **1964** BACON *Along the Road* 52 Over Joe's front paddock we trekked, flushing pipits from clumps of grass. **1978** SUTHERLAND *Elver* 45 He'd either be in the front paddock, or in the cowbail. **1985** STEWART *Gumboots & Goalposts* 20 As I drove up his drive, I noticed a very large mare in the front paddock.

B. *n.*

1. Country, or parts of a farm, situated near to a main road access or to the homestead.

1985 LANGDALE-HUNT *Last Entail Male* 7 The Hunts successfully farmed the front of this block of land for over 20 years.

2. *Axemen*. The first 'scarf' or opening made in a log in a chopping contest.

1972 *Press* (Christchurch) 24 Oct. 3 But, as most experienced axemen knew, Hewitt had turned too soon. Lamberton took out a good 'front', meaning he had cut through more than half-way.

front, *v.*

1. As **front at** [AND 1968], to appear (at); to turn up (at).

1963 *Truth* 21 May 19 The ice hockey gives me one, so I front at the nanny goat and see that it's paying a spot. to front at..to go to

2. As **front up** [AND 1968], to appear before a court, etc.

1980 MACKENZIE *While We Have Prisons* 96 *front up* meet or appear before the parole board, superintendent, etc. **1982** NEWBOLD *Big Huey* 248 Front... (v) e.g.,—up. Appear, confront.

3. *Drug-users. trans.* To deal (in drugs) by supplying them for others to sell.

1982 NEWBOLD *Big Huey* 12 I began to sell to people I knew..and I soon began to find people to whom I could front my dope, according to a similar arrangement under which I had first entered the dealing circuit myself.

frontage claim. *Goldmining.* A mining claim on a river or creek frontage.

1892 PYKE *Gold-Miners' Guide* 7 Claims are classified as follows:—Alluvial deposits, and river- or creek-beds; Quartz lodes, reefs, and leaders; Sea-beach claims; Prospecting claims; and comprise ordinary claims, double ground, extended claims, frontage claims, special claims and dredging claims.

frost, frostie: see FROSTFISH.

frostbite. [Named f. US *frostbite sailing* or *boating* the sport of sailing in temperate latitudes during the winter despite cold weather: cf. Random House (1987); DARE *Frostbiter* 1934.] A sailing dinghy (see quots. 1966, 1989).

1948 CARTER *Little Ships* 129 These two classes, the Wakatere and Frostbite, both owe their existence to..the designer, Mr. J. Brooke, of Devonport, Auckland. *Ibid.* 131 Frostbite class dinghies have been raced in all parts of the North Island. **1955** *BJ Cameron Collection* (TS July) Frostbite (n) A type of small yacht. **1966** DYSON *Yachting the NZ Way* 155 The Frostbite is a clinker-built sailing dinghy with a single sail designed in 1938 by Mr. J.B. Brooke. **1978** TITCHENER *Little Ships of NZ* 71 Because of the multi-purpose use of the Frostbite, the class has survived to the present day... The Club had now introduced a fibreglass Frostbite. **1989** DAVIS *Kohimarama. A Collection of Fragments* 115 The Frostbite. In 1938 the Wakatere Boating Club decided to design and build a class similar to the American Frostbite Dinghy, a class in which very 'keen' American yachties raced in the winter.

frostfish. Also *ellipt.* **frost** or **frostie** (see quot. 1970). [Named from the silvery colour of the skin and the fish's reputation for stranding in cold weather.] *Lepidopus caudatus* (fam. Trichiuridae), a marine fish having a long thin silvery body, and occas. found stranded on beaches. See also *silver hake* (HAKE 2, note), HIKU, PARA *n.*², SUICIDE FISH, TIKATI.

1869 *AJHR* D-15 9 There is a fish called the 'frostfish' which throws itself on beaches during the winter months, usually during frosty weather with offshore winds; it is highly prized for its delicate flavour, and, as it comes in a season when fish is scarce, it commonly fetches a high price. **1877** *TrNZI* IX. 486 Frostfish only find their way to market in winter time, and are very irregular in supply. **1886** SHERRIN *Handbook Fishes NZ* 29 The frost-fish, or hiku of the Maoris, is esteemed the most delicious fish in New Zealand. **1894** WILSON *Land of Tui* 148 [Butter-fish] was certainly the first fish in the Colony..worth eating..excepting frost-fish. **1908** BAUGHAN *Shingle-Short* 186 As the plunge of the *Takapu*, straight is his speeding:—Frost-fish, we make for the shore! [1908 *Note*] The allusion is to the popular idea that the Frost-fish..comes ashore to die. **1927** SPEIGHT et al. *Nat. Hist. Canterbury* 199 The elongated, silvery-hued frost fish (*Lepidopus caudatus*) whose curious stranding habits can hardly yet be said to be satisfactorily explained. **1932** *NZJST* XIII. 232 *Frost-fish*...This is the para of most New Zealand Natives, and the tikati of Taranaki. **1947** [see PARA *n.*²]. **1956** GRAHAM *Treasury NZ Fishes* 307 It is said that the frostfish is never taken by hook and line or by nets and it is only cast ashore at places where there is a gentle slope and where the surf breaks some distance from the shore. **1967** NATUSCH *Animals NZ* 225 The frost fishes... have no scales. The 'silver' which rubs off like aluminium paint is the substance guanin, which gives many fishes their silvery sheen. **1970** SORENSEN *Nomenclature NZ Fish* 25 *Frostfish*... Other common names: Frosts or Frosties. **1986** PAUL *NZ Fishes* 123 *Frostfish Lepidopus caudatus*... A widespread species of temperate oceanic waters, generally simply called scabbard-fish, but known as frostfish in Australia and New Zealand (from the skin's colour which comes off when touched)... Frostfish (including freshly stranded specimens) are fine eating, with white delicate flesh.

frosty Friday: see THAT *pronoun* 2.

frozen, *ppl. a. Mining.* [Spec. use of *frozen* become fixed.] Of a mineral, fixed directly to a matrix without any apparent supervening layer.

1907 *NZGeol.SB (NS)* No.4 123 White crystalline quartz—this contains a considerable amount of gold in a very fine state of division, and is deposited directly on the wall-rock without any intervening selvage or parting—'frozen on', to use the expressive phrase of the miner. **1920** *NZJST* III. 174 Below the igneous rock and 'frozen' to it is 3 in. of stonycoke, passing downward with apparently unaltered coal.

fry. [f. Brit. dial. *fry* offal (often eaten fried); AND 1847.] Liver (freq. as **lamb's fry**, sheep-liver), often eaten fried.

1883 FERGUSON *Castle Gay* 177 And [Johnny-cake] went down with a relish high, With steaming tea and liver fry;—And that by men [*sc.* shepherds] so much in need Was well pronounced 'a glorious feed'. **1908** *Colonial Everyday Cookery* 84 Liver and Potato Pie. 1 lb. Sheep's Fry. **1912** *Otago Witness* (Dunedin) 17 July 31 I am frequently short of large numbers of sheep and lambs' fries, apart from allowing a percentage for what may be condemned. **1924** *Grey River Argus* 13 June 4 A counter lunch was put on consisting of baked potatoes, rissoles, sausage rolls or lamb's fry. **1947** *NZ Observer* 8 Jan. 25 For once, we began to enjoy sausages, savoury mince..lamb's fry and bacon. **1953** WEST *Drovers Road* 115 All Christmas days at Drovers Road seem to get mixed up in a sort of special excitement:.. lamb's fry for breakfast, and sitting round the table opening presents. **1982** BURTON *Two Hundred Years NZ Food* 114 For those who usually turn up their noses at 'liver', here is a simple..way to mask the flavour of lamb's fry. **1992** *Listener* 18 July 42 I guess it's our national squeamishness about eating offal that has led us to call lamb's liver, lamb's fry.

fuchsia. Also early **fuccer**; commonly misspelled *fuschia* (see quots. 1849, 1924). [Spec. use of *fuchsia*, derived from a latinized version of the name of a German botanist Leonhard Fuchs (1501–66).]

1. Occas. **Maori** or **native fuchsia**. Any of various endemic species of *Fuchsia* (fam. Onagraceae), deciduous plants with attractive flowers, edible fleshy berries and blue pollen. See also BUCKET-OF-WATER-WOOD a, KOHUTUHUTU, KONINI, KOTUKUTUKU.

1841 *NZ.Jrnl.* II. 238 Ground covered with..myrtles and Fuccer trees 40 foot hie. **1843** DIEFFENBACH *Travels NZ* I. 122 There are two fuchsias here: one, the Fuchsia excorticata, forms a moderate-sized tree, and is very common; the other..the Fuchsia procumbens, is very rare, and at present is met with only in Wangaroa Bay, to the northward of the Bay of Islands. **1849** *Notes on NZ* 31 The New Zealand *fuschia* grows to a height of 20 feet. **1853** MACKIE *Traveller under Concern* (1973) 117 Tho' this is midwinter the only plant which I observed casting its leaves was the Fuchsia. **1866** ANGAS *Polynesia* 51 The fuchsia is indigenous in New Zealand, the woods in many places being overgrown with an undergrowth of this elegant shrub. **1889** KIRK *Forest Flora* 53 The settlers sometimes term it kotukutuku or konini, but more generally fuchsia. **1890** *PWD Catalogue Timbers* (NZ & South Seas Exhib.) 11 Kohutuhutu (fuchsia)..Timber very strong, durable, and hard; used for house blocks and fencing posts; is almost indestructible by fire; grain prettily marked. **1900** *Canterbury Old & New* 184 The native fuchsia..and the fierce bush-nettle are conspicuous amongst the undergrowth. **1924** *Otago Witness* (Dunedin) 29 Jan. 69 Some big fuschias [*sic*]..embower a gurgling creek. **1926** *TrNZI* LVI. 670 'Kotukutuku' and 'kohutuhutu' have given way to 'fuchsia', or to the now less common misnomer 'konini-tree', unless used in the sense that 'pear-tree' is used. **1946** *JPS* LV. 14 The sitter [Wetini] is appropriately wearing a spray of kotukutuku (Maori fuchsia) flowers, usually red in colour, hence in the photo they come out white. **1966** [see KOTUKUTUKU]. **1970** JOHNSON *Life's Vagaries* 16 During the warm months there was a long season for koninis from the kotukutuku trees (native Fuchsia). **1980** MANTELL *Murder & Chips* 34 There were trees growing thick there—ngaio, taupata, native fuchsia.

2. Freq. as **tree-fuchsia**. *Fuchsia excorticata*, a small tree reaching 12 m in height. See also *fuchsia-tree* 3 below.

1842 HEAPHY *NZ* 45 The Tree Fuchsia (*Fuchsia excorticata*) is generally about thirty feet in height. **1853** SEWELL *Journal* 16 Feb. (1980) I. 149 The tree fuchsia not in flower, we are too late for the summer and too soon for Autumnal flowers. **1910** COCKAYNE *NZ Plants & Their Story* 29 *Fuchsia Colensoi*, a much more slender plant than the tree-fuchsia (*F. excorticata*), offers a transition to the scrambling habit, being frequently merely a shrub, and at other times a true liane. **1946** tree-fuchsia [see KOHUTUHUTU]. **1969** *Standard Common Names Weeds* 80 tree fuchsia *Fuchsia excorticata*. **1988** DAWSON *Forest Vines to Snow Tussocks* 35 The flowers of the tree fuchsia (*Fuchsia excorticata*) are mostly produced towards the ends of woody branches.

3. Special Comb. **fuchsia berry**, KONINI 2; **fuchsia-tree**, *Fuchsia excorticata*.

1850 LUSH *Auckland Jrnls.* 11 Nov. (1971) 36 After dinner we all went into a small wood near our house to gather **fuchsia berries**. **1849** ALLOM *Letter* in Earp *Handbook* (1852) 130 The *fuchsia* berry, or as it is called by the natives, *konini*, is also highly prized. **1937** AYSON *Pioneering Otago* 22 I remember the fuchsia berries were ripe and we had a good feed [in 1853]. **1940** *Tales Pioneer Women* (1988) 30 Fuchsia berries could be gathered for tarts. **1841** BIDWILL *Rambles in NZ* (1952) 91 I here saw some of the largest **Fuchsia trees**..I had met with in the country. **1853** ADAMS *Canterbury Settlement* 38 The wild fuchsia trees [were] clothed with many flowering parasites. **1883** DOMETT *Ranolf & Amohia* II. 48 The *King-pine* that grandly towers: The fuchsia-tree with its flowers. **1898** [see KOTUKUTUKU]. **1992** *NZ Geographic* Jan.–Mar. 91 I walk among a thicket of giant fuchsia trees, whose peach-pink bark hangs from the branches in loose braids.

fuck. As commonly used in NZ as elsewhere, but seldom distinctively. The following special combinations may poss. be New Zealandisms: **fuck-knuckle**, a term of abuse, or address to a peer; **fuckwit** [AND 1969], a complete fool or stupid person.

1983 *Salient* (Wellington) 21 Mar. 4 'How's tricks **fuck-knuckle**?' growled the leather lunged President, The Scab. 'Grouse,' replied Barf. **1984** 17 M E115 Pakuranga Coll. 1 Fucknuckle [M2] **1984** 14 F E120 Wgton Girls C. 24B Fuck knuckle **1988** MCGILL *Dict. Kiwi Slang* 46 *fuck-knuckle* idiot, often amiably applied; eg 'G'day, fuck-knuckle. How's it goin'?' **1973** *Salient* (Wellington) 26 Sept. 12 This group of pathetically understood pseudo shit-stirrers seem to have little else to do... For their benefit, and for that of Joseph Smith, another Puke **fuckwit**, I will interpret my letter. **1983** HULME *Bone People* 170 Whoever coined that was an unmitigated fuckwit, a bullshit artist supreme. **1984** BEATON *Outside In* 91 Kate: You're a fuckwit. **1986** *Evening Post* (Wellington) 4 Sept. 2 Referring to people who had made trouble for Mr Warren in his endeavours, she [Dame Cath Tizard, Mayor of Auckland] used the word 'f...wit'... 'It's a term frequently used to describe idiots,' she said.

full, *a.*

1. [Cf. Sc. *fou* drunk: AND c1848. Cf. c1875 MEREDITH *Adventuring in Maoriland* (1935) 81

FULLA

Mrs Dougal [a Dunedin Presbyterian]..gave her lawful spouse a particularly bad time if and when he returned home anyway fou'.] In the senses very drunk, or occas., stuffed with food and drink, usu. in various phrases with the form **(as) full as a** + noun: **(as) full as a boot**; **(as) full as a bull**, usu. '(roaring) drunk', but also occas. stuffed with food and drink; **(as) full as a butcher's dog**, very full (of food, etc.); **(as) full as the family po**; **(as) full as a goog (egg)**, very drunk; occas. stuffed with food; **(as) full as a lord**, **(as) full as a kite**, very drunk; **(as) full as a tick** [f. Brit. dial. 1892], very drunk; occas. stuffed with food, etc. See also DRUNK.

a1974 SYDER & HODGETTS *Aust. & NZ English* (TS) 367 **Full as a boot**. A state of intoxication. 'Hardie was as full as a boot! We put him on the stretcher and threw some blankets over him. The first time Hard's been well truly drunk since he got married.' **1987** ELDRED-GRIGG *Oracles & Miracles* 7 'Gitting himself full as a boot so he couldn't see the road to the dunny if it had red flags on it,' she'd say. **1947** NEWTON *Wayleggo* 103 By the time the dance was under way I was **'as full as a bull'** and ripe for anything. **1959** SLATTER *Gun in My Hand* 44 I spose ya'll get full as a bull at this reunion? **1964** HARVEY *Any Old Dollars Mister?* 22 They were nice and frothy [milkshakes]..and it took a heck of a long time to suck that thick stuff off the top with a straw. When Nuts finished his he..said, 'Jesus. I'm full as a bull.' **1974** BELL *Ballads of Racegoer* 21 As full as a bull they both got; And the owner's big loss was forgot. **1990** VIRTUE *In the Country of Salvation* 65 As she helped Seddon up the steps, he started shouting out.., slurring the words, 'Full as a bull's bum, Mum!' **1962** HORI *Half-gallon Jar* 2 I see the mother and father slug **as full as a butcher's dog** [with my plants and slug-killer]. **1968** SLATTER *Pagan Game* 164 **Full as the family poe** [*sic*]—The trouble with the game today. **1981** *Avondale College Slang Words* (Auckland) (Goldie Brown Collect.) *full as the family po*: drunk **1988** MCGILL *Dict. Kiwi Slang* 47 **full as a** boot/bull/Catholic school/**goog** (egg) very drunk. **1921** LORD *Ballads of Bung 'Stunology'* (1976) 10 'On the jag', 'juiced'..and oh, **'as full as a kite'**, 'Liquored'..**'as full as a Lord'** (get my meaning right?) *Ibid*. (1976) 11 Some will say you're **'as full as a tick'**, and some that your [*sic*] damned 'well tanked'. **1949** DAVIN *Roads from Home* 74 Full as a tick. **1970** COWLEY *Man of Straw* 108 'I'll shout you a Coke.' 'No thanks,' she said. 'I'm full as a tick.' **1973** *Islands* IV. 116 'Those dogs are full as ticks! Stuffed full on heifers dead of starvation!' **1981** HUNT *Speaking a Silence* 145 The old swagger was properly stunned when we left him; he was full as a tick with wine.

2. As **full of** (**full up of**) (occas. **full on**) [AND *a.*² 1871], fed up (with); weary (of); disgusted (with).

1881 NESFIELD *Chequered Career* 38 He bucked me off more times than I can remember and I began to get 'full' of him. **1881** BATHGATE *Waitaruna* 151 'This is no go, and we must give it best!... I'm full on this shooting racket.' 'You are adept at slang, Arthur, and no mistake.' **1892** REEVES *Homeward Bound* 33 I note the men have to do all the fielding and get tired, or as the colonial slang goes, 'full up', soonest. **c1930** *Whitcombe's Etym. Dict. Aust.-NZ Suppl.* 4 *full a.*— full up [of] a. sl. tired of. **1988** MCGILL *Dict. Kiwi Slang* 47 *full up* exasperated, weary, disgusted; eg 'I'm full up with this shower, Netty. Let's split.'

fulla: see FELLOW.

Fullers earth. *Obs. Theatrical.* Also **Fuller's earth**. [f. the name of the *Fuller* Brothers, esp. Benjamin John *Fuller*, governing director, entertainers and impresarios, who from c1911 to 1945 expanded the number of their theatres and cinemas in NZ to 64, and a play on *fuller's earth* an absorbent clay used (among other uses) for removing grease from cloth.] New Zealand, as a field for Fuller Brothers' theatrical enterprises. See esp. quot. 1966.

1937 PARTRIDGE *Dict. Slang* 307 *Fuller's earth...* New Zealand: theatrical and cinematic: from ca. 1912. Punning on the Fuller brothers, who, ca. 1910–30, owned a great number of N.Z. theatres and cinemas. (*The Daily Telegraph*, July 23, 1934.) **1938** *Press* (Christchurch) (McNab Slang) 2 Apr. 18 'Captain Cooker' is well known, better known than 'Fuller's Earth' as a synonym for New Zealand (from the theatrical family). **1966** *Encycl. NZ* I. 763 At one stage Dowling Street, Dunedin, where the [Fuller] 'firm' had two theatres running simultaneously, was jestingly known as 'Fuller's earth'.

full face queen. Also *ellipt*. **full face**, as a *n*. and *attrib*. The first New Zealand stamp, valid 1855–1873, featuring a 'full-face' portrait of Queen Victoria by the portraitist, A. E. Chalon. See also CHALON HEAD.

1922 *NZ Stamp Collector* III. 74 Mr H.L. Hayman showed us a very rare variety of the New Zealand 'full face Queen' issue the other night. **1923** *Ibid*. IV. 96 Of the New Zealand full faces I can only say I came away feeling smaller and more humble than I can ever remember feeling. **1930** *NZ Stamp Collector* XI. 22 Somebody at our Stamp Club meeting ventured to 'read a paper' at our last meeting—think of it! It was all about rouletted and serrated and full-face Queens. Heaven rest her royal bones! *Ibid*. 44 To find full-faces quoted at 9d. per dozen..makes one long for 'the good old days'. **1940** *NZ Stamp Collector* XXI. 5 The full-face collections of the Hon. Sir R. Heaton Rhodes and of Mr J.W. Grant are of world standard. **1977** FRANKS *All the Stamps of NZ* 18 These stamps are called full face Queens because they show a frontal view of Queen Victoria, whereas the later two sets showed a side view. **1984** *Catalogue NZ Stamps* Perm. page A5 More than any other New Zealand group, the 'Full-Faces' are subject to severe reduction in value on account of defects. **1990** *C.P.'s Newsletter* [Campbell Paterson Ltd] XLII. No.3 2 The Royal Collection display seemed very relevant with its concentration on Full face Queens.

full-mouthed, *a*. [AND 1855.] Of an adult sheep, having its full complement of eight incisors. See also *eight-tooth* (EIGHT).

1879 PEACHE *Journal* in Gray *Quiet with Hills* (1970) 58 Only about 2,500 being full-mouthed. **1933** *Press* (Christchurch) (Acland Gloss.) 9 Sept. 15 He [*sc.* a sheep] is full mouthed as long as his teeth remain perfect, and as they decline he becomes failing mouthed, broken mouthed, and finally a gummy. **1987** OGONOWSKA-COATES *Boards, Blades & Barebellies* 94 *Ages of sheep...* A sheep is a *lamb* until weaned. After weaning a lamb is called a *hogget* until shorn. A male lamb is a *ram lamb* until castrated, then a *wether*. A female lamb is a *ewe lamb*. After shearing, a ewe or ram lamb is usually called a *shorn hogget* until cutting the first two teeth. It is then called a *two-tooth*. Some use the term two-tooth as soon as the lamb is shorn. Next year the sheep is a *four-tooth*, then a *six-tooth* and then an *eight-tooth* or *full-mouthed* sheep. It is full-mouthed as long as the teeth remain perfect but then becomes broken-mouthed and gummy.

full pound. Also **full quid, full shilling**. In the phr. **not the full pound**, etc., see POUND *n.*¹ 2, QUID 1, SHILLING 1 a.

FUNGUS

fundie. [f. *fund*(amentalist + -IE.] One, usu. a Christian, who strictly maintains the traditional Protestant beliefs of literal interpretation of the scriptures and creeds.

1990 KIDMAN *True Stars* 39 Opposite to where the watcher stood was a Christian video shop... It was a temptation not to throw a rock through it, given what the kid thought of fundies.

fungus.

1. a. Also **bush-fungus** and (usu.) **Jew's ear fungus** (see also 2 (5) below). The edible fruiting body of *Auricularia* (formerly *Hirneola*) *polytricha* (fam. Auriculariaceae), commonly found as a tough, gelatinous, ear-shaped bracket on the dead branches and bark of esp. broad-leaved trees, and formerly collected, dried, and sold to Chinese merchants. See also HAKEKE, TARANAKI WOOL.

1882 HAY *Brighter Britain* II. 212 One fungus (*Hirneola, sp.*) is gathered here to a small extent for export to China. **1886** CHUDLEIGH *Diary* 8 June (1950) 345 I shipped 4 bales of fungus..for Piripi. **1891** *NZJSc.* (NS) I. 55 The fungus belongs to the same genus as the European Jews'-Ear (*Hirneola Auricula-judae*), a tough but gelatinous fungus formerly in reputation as an ingredient of gargles. The New Zealand fungus now under notice (*Hirneola polytricha*), is well described. **1902** *Settler's Handbook NZ* 42 The exports for 1899 were: Wool, 4,819 bales; fungus, 107 sacks. **1935**, **1940** [see TARANAKI WOOL]. **1963** CAMPBELL *Golden North* 29 Fungus grew only in damp places on rotten karaka trees,... Six sacks full would be worth about five pounds. **1970** JOHNSON *Life's Vagaries* 45 For pocket money Stella and I collected fungus, the velvety grey fungi that grows generally on dead and rotting wood in the bush. **1983** KING *Whina* 92 I used to collect and to buy fungus for selling to a Chinese merchant..in Auckland.

b. Used *attrib*. often in obsolete special Comb. as **fungus gatherer**, one who gathers fungus for sale, hence **fungus gathering**.

1935 MAXWELL *Recollections* 166 Taranaki certainly was in those days a land of fungus, and fungus picking and selling played a most important part for a long time. **a1937** COWAN *Pakeha & Maori* I. 6 He was close to the fungus-gatherers' camp. **1960** BOSWELL *Ernie* 137 Gum-digging and fungus-gathering went on at a furious rate. **1986** RICHARDS *Off the Sheep's Back* 46 Mum always sent us fungus gathering when she needed a few extra bob for the regatta or Christmas.

2. With a modifier: **basket, beech, bird-cage, birdsnest, Jew's ear, lattice, net, shepherd's basket, strawberry**. See also TOBACCO POUCH.

(1) basket fungus. *Ileodictyon cibarium* (formerly *Clathrus cibarius*) (fam. Clathraceae), a native fungus which expands to release a netted 'basket' from a white sphere. See also *devil's purse* (DEVIL 2) (or *stink-egg*), *fairy's closet* (FAIRY 4), PARUWHATITIRI, THUNDER-DIRT, *tutae kehua*, *tutae whetu* (TUTAE 2).

1922 *NZJST* V. 247 *Clathrus cibarius*, the 'bird-cage fungus'... This fungus, known variously as 'basket fungus', 'lattice fungus', 'Devil's purse', '*tutae whetu*', '*tutae kehua*'... It is found commonly throughout New Zealand during the late autumn and early spring. **1938** *Auckland Weekly News* 8 June 64 At one stage of its growth, the open-look basket-fungus..is edible. **1957** WILLIAMS *Dict. Maori Lang.* 188 *Matakupenga...3. Clathrus cibarium*, net or basket fungus. **1959** *Tararua Tramper* Oct. 10 The Maori treated unexpanded plants of the basket fungus as a great luxury. **1961** MARTIN *Flora NZ* 40 The Basket fungus or Lattice fungus spreads its globular latticed network a conspicuous white, slimy structure with an unpleasant odour, that never fails to amaze its beholders. Its miraculous and sudden appearance caused the ancient Maori to term it 'thunder dirt'. **1978** MOORE & IRWIN *Oxford Book NZ Plants* 12 *Clathrus cibarius, basket fungus*. **1983** *Land of Mist* 64 [Caption] Basket or lattice fungus. **1992** SMITHYMAN *Auto/Biographies* 72 A basket fungus occurred to her, that is what she would make of herself.

(2) **beech-fungus**, see *strawberry fungus* (9) below.
[**1988** DAWSON *Forest Vines to Snow Tussocks* 123 Silver beech is the only species attacked by a [beech] fungus, *Cytaria*, whose orangey, golf-ball-like fruiting bodies may be abundant on the branches of some trees.]

(3) **bird-cage fungus**, see *basket fungus* (1) above, quot. 1922.

(4) **birdsnest (birdnest, bird's nest) fungus**. The native genera of the fungal family Nidulariaceae whose spore bodies are borne in a cup or nest-like structure.
1978 MOORE & IRWIN *Oxford Book NZ Plants* 12 *Crucibulum vulgare*. Bird's nest fungus is found on dead twigs and old tree-fern debris on the forest floor. **1982** WILSON *Stewart Is. Plants* 490 *Nidula candida* Birdsnest fungus... Tiny cups on dead wood or twigs..with brown pellets of spore-bearing tissue nestling within, like eggs in a nest. **1984** *Hanmer Forest Park* 41 Some of the more common and interesting fungi found in the park are—flower fungus (*Aseroe rubra*), fly agaric (*Amanita muscaria*), woolly birdnest fungus (*Nidula candida*), and rainbow bracket fungus (*Trametes versicolor*).

(5) **Jew's ear fungus** (also *ellipt*. **Jew's ear**). [Spec. use of the European *Jew's ear fungus Auricularia auricula* (fam. Auriculariaceae).] See 1 a above. See also HAKEKE.
1882 POTTS *Out in Open* 18 Hakeke—the Jew's-ear fungus (*Hirneola auricula-Judae*); it is found rather plentifully in the forests of Pirongia; that which grows on the Karaka is most esteemed. **1924** *Otago Witness* (Dunedin) 17 June 66 The best-known [fungus]..which is quite common in Otago..is the Jew's ear Fungus. **1955** BOSWELL *Dim Horizons* 103 Fungus, the thick fungoid growth that we knew as 'Jews' ear', grew in abundance on the rotting karaka and mahoe logs left from the felling of the cows' feed. **1961** MARTIN *Flora NZ* 37 Finally, we have a group of fungi gelatinous when moist, but usually leathery when dry, of which the Jew's-ear Fungus..are typical members..the Jew's-ear fungus, so abundant on mahoe other forest trees, was formerly shipped by the ton to China for making soups. **1978** FULLER *Maori Food & Cook*. 85 Hakeke—Jew's ear fungus... Hakeke, Taranaki wool.

(6) **lattice fungus**, see *basket fungus* (1) above, quots. 1922, 1961, 1983.

(7) **net fungus**, see *basket fungus* (1) above, quot. 1957.

(8) **shepherd's basket fungus**. *basket fungus* (1) above.
1921 GUTHRIE-SMITH *Tutira* 27 [Caption] Shepherd's Basket Fungus. **1939** VAILE *Pioneering Pumice* 299 *Shepherd's Basket* Clathrus cibarius.

(9) **strawberry fungus**. *Cyttaria* spp. (fam. Cyttariaceae), a fungus parasitic on beech species, causing a gall fancifully resembling a strawberry. See also *beech strawberry* (BEECH 3).
1946 *Bull. Wellington Bot. Soc. No.14* 4 *Cyttaria gunnii*, the strawberry fungus, has been found in New Zealand only on silver beech. **1978** MOORE & IRWIN *Oxford Book NZ Plants* 10 *Cyttaria gunnii*. This strawberry fungus, also parasitic on silver beech, causes a rough globular gall... *Cyttaria nigra*. Black strawberry fungus grows on silver beech.., causing the wood to proliferate into a characteristically lumpy gall.

funk, *v*. [f. Brit. dial.: see EDD $v.^2$ and $n.^3$ 4, to cheat in marbles, to play without keeping the hand on the ground: Sc., East Anglia.] *intr*. To cheat at marbles by breaking a rule such as encroaching on a given mark.
1933 SCANLAN *Tides of Youth* 153 And once she tried to play with you, and you said she funked because her knuckle was inside the ring. **1972** SUTTON-SMITH *Folkgames Children* 176 [Waitara, Taranaki, 1899:] To fire a shot while holding the hand nearer to the ring than where the taw had lain, was to 'funk', an unforgiveable crime.

funk, *n*. Usu. *pl. funks*, also var. **flunks**, elaborated to **funnicks, funnigans**. A name for cribbing or cheating, or a cheating shot, in the game of marbles.
1953 SUTTON-SMITH *Unorganized Games NZ Primary School Children* (VUWTS) II. 769 Action terms which refer to the shooting of the marbles are: Knuckle down Stiff, Knee High, Funks [Flunks] [*sic*] or Funnicks. **1972** SUTTON-SMITH *Folkgames Children* 175 [Terms] related to ways of shooting marbles were cribbing, firsts, fudging, funks, funnicks, funnigans, flunks, forces, knee-high, knuckle-down-stiff.

funnicks, funnigans: see FUNK *n*.

funny, *a*. In various comparative phrases in the senses 'very funny', 'quite ridiculous': **(as) funny as a box of worms**; **(as) funny as a bit (piece) of string**.

1905 *Truth* 12 Aug. 3 The man in the street says 'it's as funny as a box of worms'. **1981** HUNT *Speaking a Silence* 144 That was funny as a bit of string. **1988** MCGILL *Dict. Kiwi Slang* 47 *funny (or silly) as a piece of string* very funny; often used ironically; eg 'That toddler with her eyebrow-raising is as funny as a piece of string.'

fun parlour. An amusement arcade.
[*Note*] In use much earlier than the recorded date: e.g. the amusement park in Manners Street in Wellington in the early 1940s was named the 'Fun Parlour'.
1983 MANTELL *Murder to Burn* 94 Only the dairy and the take-away still open. Down the other end usual crowd round the fun parlour but where I was, nobody else.

funs. [Cf. EDD *funny* n. 2, a game of marbles in Scotland, as in: 'In my time the game of "funny" was played in the same way as that of "earnest", except that in the former marbles lost during the game were restored at the close. "We were playing funny."'] A cry, when playing marbles for keeps, to indicate that the shot in progress is not for 'keeps', or that after the game the marbles won have to be handed back to the loser by the winner; the usual phrases are: 'funs or keeps', as an invitation at the beginning of a game; **to play funs**, when the game is not played seriously, 'for keeps', or to strictly agreed rules.
1950 SCANLAN *Confidence Corner* 58 If you ask me, she's making a beeline for Grant. Of course, she may be only 'playing funs' as the boys say, but I wouldn't put it past her to have a second go [at marriage]. **1951** FRAME *Lagoon* (1961) 116 I played ringie and holie. I played funs and keeps. **1972** SUTTON-SMITH *Folkgames Children* 175 Terms connected with the movement of the marbles were: cannons, clears, dead-stick, double-hits, fires, funs, gees. **1984** KEITH & MAIN *NZ Yesterdays* 288 [Caption] Marbles became 'in' or 'out' capriciously but someone always knew the rules of the various games—'holey,' 'liney' and, seen here, 'ringey'—which could be played for 'funs' or 'keeps'.

fur seal: see SEAL $n.^1$ 2 (1).

futta(h), futter, varr. WHATA.

FYO. [By analogy with BYO.] **Fill Your Own** *sc*. beer flagons.
1991 *Contact* (Wellington) 5 Dec. 4 [Advt] Dominion Tavern Bottlestore F.Y.O. 2 Ltr Flagons Lion Brown $4.70.

G

gadoa, var. KATOA.

gaga, var. KIE-KIE.

gala /ˈgalə/. Also **royal gala** (see quot. 1991). A variety of dessert apple with a thin skin and crisp flesh, found and developed in New Zealand.
   1966 *Orchardist NZ* May 106 A new hybrid apple, Gala,.. has been approved by the Apple and Pear Board. **1974** *Ibid*. Nov. 350 Gala is a uniquely New Zealand apple and at present is grown commercially only in New Zealand. **1987** GEE *Prowlers* 105 The Coxes and the Galas and the Golden and Red Delicious are harvested now and the pickers are working on the Granny Smiths. **1991** *New Zealand's Best Apple Recipes* 12 Gala. An apple with a pink blush on a yellow background, it was discovered by Mr Kidd of Greytown in the 1930's. A cross between Kidd's Orange Red and golden Delicious, it is a very sweet, crisp eating apple... Royal Gala. Discovered by Mr Ten Hove of Matamata in 1969. A red sport of the Gala variety. **1992** *Metro* (Auckland) Jan. 53 Let's put a green belt round the fertile valleys where the Galas, Granny Smiths and Albany Surprise grow so well. **1995** ANDERSON *House Guest* 12 Maureen's thumbnail was busy extracting a scrap of apple peel from between two molars. Royal Gala.

galatea /ˌgæləˈtiə/. *Hist.* [Cf. OED: from the name of HMS Galatea, 1882.] A blue-striped cotton material; also *ellipt*. for **galatea shirt**.
   1912 MANSFIELD *Stories* (1984) 109 Jo rode ahead. He wore a blue galatea shirt, corduroy trousers and riding boots. **1934** LEE *Children of Poor* (1949) 136 All the trousers were of serge or tweed. 'I like trousers of galatea.' 'Yes. But no one else does.' **1957** FRAME *Owls Do Cry* (1967) 136 There's pants for you, the maori [*sic*] nurse said. And a striped blue smock, galatea, and a grey jersey.

galaxias /gəˈlæksiəs/. [Often regarded as a *pl*. The Southern Hemisphere freshwater genus *Galaxias* was named by the French biologist Cuvier in 1812 from the resemblance of its spotted colour pattern to a galaxy of stars.] Any species of the genus *Galaxias* (fam. Galaxiidae). See also HIWI, INANGA *n*.¹, KOARO, KOKOPU, MINNOW, WHITEBAIT 1. In technical use often with a modifier: **alpine**, **common river**, **dwarf**, **longjawed**, and **lowland galaxias**.
   1872 GUNTHER in Hutton & Hector *Fishes NZ* (1872) 130 All *Galaxias* are extremely fat, so that it is impossible to handle them, even for a very short time, without the fat penetrating through the skin and soiling everything which comes into contact with them. **1940** PHILLIPPS *Fishes NZ* 14 Nearly every large lake in New Zealand tends to have its own distinctive types of Galaxias. **1955** STOKELL *Freshwater Fishes NZ* 19 In some localities attempts are being made to induce anglers and the public generally to use galaxias as a popular name. **1990** MCDOWALL *NZ Freshwater Fishes* 87 Many galaxias spend their whole lives in fresh water, but several diadromous species spend part of their lives at sea.

gallant soldier. A folk alteration of the name of the plant genus *Galinsoga*. Compare POOR PRETENCES.
   [**1980** TAYLOR *Weeds of Crops* 50 Galinsoga (*Galinsoga parviflora* and *G. quadriradiata*).. Galinsoga was found by botanists in Peru 200 years ago and taken to London and Paris. It later escaped to become a weed in Europe and other parts of the world. Although recorded in New Zealand in 1896, galinsoga has a limited distribution and is still spreading.] **1969** *Standard Common Names Weeds* 28 *gallant soldier* [=] *galinsoga*.

gallied: see GALLY *v*.

Gallipoli.
1. As a name symbolizing the Gallipoli peninsula and the Anzac operation which took place there during WW1. Cf. ANZAC A 2.
   1915 HARPER in *Lett. from Gunner* 7/516 27 Aug. (1978) 27 It is a very nice feeling to be leaving Gallipoli behind. **1918** MACGILL *An Anzac's Bride* 13 Dick had been through the hell-fire of Gallipoli, and was on seven days' leave. **1953** DUFF *Shepherd's Calendar* (1961) 149 Not to feel the importance of the occasion is like walking unmoved through a full cemetery or hearing nothing but the sea on Gallipoli beach. **1988** SHADBOLT *Voices of Gallipoli* 97 A sickening sideshow of World War I which is remembered, where recalled elsewhere at all, under the name of Gallipoli. For many New Zealanders, though, Gallipoli has remained as potent a placename as any in the outside world. **1990** *Dominion Sunday Times* (Wellington) 22 Apr. 8 It's 75 years ago on Wednesday that the human wastage that was Gallipoli began.

2. Used *attrib*. in Comb. and special Comb., esp. **Gallipoli Day**, an early ephemeral name for ANZAC DAY (see quot. 1918).
   1918 *Kia-ora Coo-ee* (1981) 15 May III. 8 [Heading] Gallipoli Day. The keeping of Gallipoli Day, originally called Anzac Day, is now an institution in Cairo. It was instituted by the Anzacs, but there were other heroes besides the Australian and New Zealand troops on Gallipoli; and it is in memory of all who fell on the spot, or who were later carried, after terrible sufferings, to their last resting place in Old Cairo, that we now keep the Day. **1964** MORRIESON *Came a Hot Friday* (1981) 23 Don's dad, a Gallipoli man, was sitting on the front veranda... His stump was giving him gyp. **1966** SCOTT *Days That Have Been* 154 Basil Champion is a Gallipoli veteran and his wife belongs to one of the pioneer New Zealand families. **1988** *Great Adventure* 130 As a Gallipoli veteran he found it difficult to relate to the majority of the R.S.A., who had joined up after 1915. **1990** *Dominion Sunday Times* (Wellington) 22 Apr. 8 [Heading] Reviving the Gallipoli effect.

gallops, *n. pl.* [Prob. formed on analogy of TROTS.] Often as **the gallops**. A race-meeting on a flat course in which the participating horses are gallopers as distinct from harness racers (trotters or pacers). In *sing*. a race for gallopers.
   1903 *Otago Witness* (Dunedin) 28 Jan. 68 My brother..rode his pony Rose in the gallop. **1909** *Truth* 9 Feb. 2 If the stiff-necked C.J.C. isn't careful it will find shortly that the..Trotting Clubs will wean the fickle public from the 'gallops'. **1931** *Dominion* (Wellington) 24 Sept. 13 [Heading] Avondale Gallops. **1964** HORI *Fill It Up Again* 5 I learned a lot about straps at the trots. I tell this coot I lose enough dough at the gallops. **1988** COSTELLO & FINNEGAN *Tapestry of Turf* 501 Clarkson called both trots and gallops in Canterbury. **1993** *Sunday Times* (Wellington) 21 Feb. 36 A consistent pattern will be established for the North Island gallops.

gallows. Also **meat-gallows**. [AND 1847.] A wooden frame, usu. of two uprights and a crosspiece, on which carcasses are hung to be dressed. See also *Spanish gallows* (SPANISH *a*.).
   1855 *St. Leonard's Jrnl.* 28 Feb. (ATLTS) Fisher and Loon returned bringing gallows posts. **1866** BARKER *Station Life* (1870) 64 I like to be removed from the immediate neighbourhood of all the work of the station, especially from that of the 'gallows',—a high wooden frame from which the carcases of the butchered sheep dangle. **1878** ELWELL *Boy Colonists* 82 The gallows [was] a pair of poles set upright with a third pole across the top, to which in the centre was fastened a hook. From this hook..there was suspended the carcase of a sheep. **1882** POTTS *Out in Open* 127 The second specimen was shot at dusk, on the meat-gallows of a secluded out-station. **1933** *Press* (Christchurch) (Acland Gloss.) 21 Oct. 15 *Gallows*.—Two upright posts, perhaps 10 feet high, with a strong rail across the top. When a sheep is half skinned it is pulled half way up until the skinning and dressing are finished. It is then pulled up to the top to hang out of the way of dogs. **1966** [see GAMBLE]. **1982** WHEELER *Hist. Sheep Stations NZ* 46 [Caption to a 4-pole, roofed structure] The gallows. [Lake Haupiri Station, Canterbury]

gally, *v. Whaling. Obs.* [f. Brit. dial. *gally* to frighten.] *trans*. To frighten or alarm (a whale). Often as a *ppl. a.* **gallied** (**galeyed, gallid**), occas. *transf*. to humans, frightened; unnerved, thrown into a nervous state.
   1838 *Piraki Log* 21 May (1911) 73 Saw a large Whale was in chase best part of the day, but she was so Galeyed we had no chance of fastening. **1878** JOLLIE *Reminiscences* (ATLTS) 25 He [Captain Toms] was a very old whaler..he had had most of the principal bones of his body broken by whales flukes but when I met him he was what the whalers called 'gallid' or afraid even of the sight of a whale. I expect his nerves were hurt when his bones were broken. **1913** MCNAB *Old Whaling Days* 288 They so gallied the poor brutes [of whales] that those which survived forsook their long established rendezvous to seek new grounds for food, and to bring forth their young in peace. **1982** GRADY *Perano Whalers* 227 *Gallied*—An alarmed or frightened whale. These often take off at high speed, or sound for extended lengths of time. Often gallied whales will adapt zig-zag swimming patterns under water. **1986** WEDDE *Symmes Hole* 203 It was like Joe Thoms gone gallied after getting thrashed against a stove boat by humpback flukes..and from then on couldn't set foot in a boat.

gam, *n. Ornithological.* [Transf. from an early whalers' use of *gam n.* a social meeting of whaling crews or whalers at sea, hence chiefly New England US dial., any sociable visit (DARE n[1] 1846, also v. 1849); poss. from a Scandinavian-influenced n. British dial. variant of *game* sport, festivity (so OED); DARE suggests a derivation from an abbrev. for obsolete British dial. *gammon* lively talk, chatter. The whaling use is recorded from NZ waters from 1850 (see DARE).] A lively sociable dancing or cavorting display on land, sea surface, or in the air by groups of young albatrosses. (Poss. used of other large sea birds: see quot. 1950.)

  1936 MURPHY *Oceanic Birds* 559 After the end of the breeding season, on March 26, 1913, I witnessed the same dance..hundreds of kilometres from any land... Scores of Wandering Albatrosses were about in the characteristic gams, and the whirlings, raising of wings, billing and squealing were in progress... Yearling young..were taking the same part as adult birds, which rules out any courtship connotation. *Ibid.* 560 Again, while I was on the South Georgian whaling banks on the occasion when the 'gamming' phenomenon was first noted, many groups of albatrosses were scrutinized through glasses. **1950** SORENSEN *Royal Albatross* 8 With the possible exception of the displays termed 'gams' (a word originating in the old whaling days meaning a talk together between various parties), the examples [of unusual behaviour] are usually performed by isolated individuals. *Ibid.* 9 Interesting features of albatross behaviour on land are the 'gams' or 'friendly meetings' (Fig. 1). These are defined as gatherings of two or more birds which go through the actions of courtship out of season. The majority of such birds are juveniles. [**1950** MATTHEWS *Wandering Albatross* 102 All round the [whaler] Jungfruen the sea was covered with blue mollies... They were not feeding much, but paddling about..; whenever two or three came close together they greeted with chesty brayings—*gamming* as the old whalers would say. In the old days when whalers met on the high seas they generally hove–to for a few hours and exchanged visits: they called such parties 'gams'.] **1962** BAILEY & SORENSEN *Subantarctic Campbell Island* 163 Conspicuous in the nesting colonies are little groups of albatrosses going through strange performances to which Sorensen..has applied the appropriate old sea-faring term 'gam'. *Ibid.* 168 Usually one albatross dominates the show..stepping awkwardly about, thrusting head and neck skyward with beak open as it gives a far-reaching neighing call —shaking the head vigorously—and culminating the performance with raised wings and a frenzy of calls.

gambel, gambol, varr. GAMBLE.

gamble. Also **gambel, gambol.** [f. Brit. dial. *gamble*, a var. of *gambrel*.] A bar of wood or iron, occas. with hooked ends, on which a carcass is hung by the hocks; a gambrel.

  1933 *Press* (Christchurch) (Acland Gloss.) 21 Oct. 15 *Gamble.*—When a sheep is pulled up on the *gallows* by a rope, the rope is tied to a g[amble], which is a piece of wood or iron, the ends of which are stuck through the sheep's hocks. The g[amble] also serves to keep the sheep's hind legs stretched. **1966** *Weekly News* (Auckland) 26 Jan. 39 My father already had the gallows ready, complete with ropes, pulleys and a 'gamble'. **1976** MORRIESON *Pallet on the Floor* 93 He strode briskly, a quarter-filled sack of skids and gambols over his shoulder. **1983** p.c. Dr. C. Corne (Auckland) 14 Oct. gamble, gambol, gambel—gambrel, for hanging carcasses on.

gang. [Spec. use of *gang* a group of people with a common purpose.] **a.** *Obs.* In a non-depreciatory or 'innocent' sense used (as elsewhere) for a group of children (usu. boys) with common interests who go about together and have a particular meeting-place (often a 'fort').

  1934 LEE *Children of Poor* (1949) 146 I stole a box. Soon I had a trolley. I stole boards from the timber yard and built a wooden hut for my gang in the backyard. **1982** SUTTON-SMITH *Hist. Children's Play* 78 In towns the same sort of group fighting was usually known as gang-fighting. Different gangs took different sides in the Paper Chase. (1900; Riwaka) **1992** *North & South* (Auckland) June 30 Our gang (believe me, the similarity between the handful of 10 and 12-year-olds and today's groups of the same name is nil) spent the summer swimming.

b. In current depreciatory use (as elsewhere), a close-knit hierarchical group held together under a leader by common interests, often perceived as anti-social, and often ethnic ('Maori gang') or particular ('bikie gang') and having a distinguishing name ('Black Power', 'Head-hunters', 'Mongrel Mob', 'Satan's Slaves'), a local headquarters, and an identifying 'patch'. As special Comb. **gang-bashing** *vbl. n.*, multiple or serial raping; **gang-splash** (occas. **gang-slash**), a 'gang' (or serial) rape.

  1968 *Dominion* (Wellington) 8 May 4 She..heard a boy..say: 'How about a gang splash?' She knew that this expression meant a number of boys having intercourse with a girl. **1971** [see GANGIE]. **1978** *Truth* 14 Feb. 3 I started pashing her up... Hutana who said he had been a Black Power boy for a month, said another gang member came up and told him there would be no gang-bashing in his garden.

gangie. Also **gangy**. A 'gang' or serial rape. Cf. LINE–UP.

  1968 *Dominion* (Wellington) 9 May 5 He explained he had heard the word 'gangy' called out as he returned to the clubhouse... He understood the word meant that 'a gang of boys was going out with one or two sheilas to have a group intercourse'. **1970** *Truth* 5 May 25 What is a 'gangie' or 'gangbang'?—A gang of jokers on to one girl. It could be rape, but might not be. I took it as rape. **1971** *Truth* 30 Mar. 7 Gary (Ngatai) said they wanted to have a 'gangie' on us [girls]... Sergeant: What is a 'gangie'?—It's a line-up. It's a group of males having intercourse with a girl or girls one after the other. Isn't that what happened?—Yes—but I wouldn't call that a gang splash.

gangster. A member of a GANG b. Compare MOBSTER.

  1971 *Truth* 20 July 14 An 11-man and one woman jury had found Jones guilty of the rape of a girl picked up from a city bus terminal on the night of Friday, April 23, and taken to a house on the Ellerslie Main Highway where she was forced to 'pull a train' of Hell's Angels and Storm Troopers gangsters. **1986** *More* (Auckland) May 26 It surprises me when she tells me how she met her gangster husband at a party when she was still in the 4th form. **1991** PAYNE *Staunch* 13 At least with the gangsters you knew where you stood;.. and once you had proved you could 'stand up', they accepted you.

gangy, var. GANGIE.

gannet.

1. The northern hemisphere name *gannet* for *Sula* spp. applied to the Australasian seabird of the same family, often recently as **Australian** or **Australasian gannet,** *Morus* (formerly *Sula*) *serrator* (fam. Sulidae). See also TAKAPU.

  1769 BANKS *Journal* 24 Dec. (1962) I. 449 Myself in a boat..killing chiefly Gannets or Solan Geese so like the European ones that they are hardly distinguishable from them. **1814** NICHOLAS *Voyage NZ* (1817) I. 76 Flocks of gannets and petrels flying round the ship in all directions. Hope to see New Zealand tomorrow. **1844** COLENSO *Excurs. Northern Is.* in Taylor *Early Travellers* (1959) 54 Several fine Gannets (*Sula,* sp.) attracted our attention... [The natives] call it Takupu. **1873** BULLER *Birds NZ* 323 Sula serrator. (Australian Gannet.)..Takapu. **1904** HUTTON & DRUMMOND *Animals NZ* 285 The Gannet is common in the northern parts of New Zealand, but is rarely seen south of Cook Strait. **1947** POWELL *Native Animals NZ* 79 Gannet (*Morus serrator*), Takapu of the Maoris, is common around the coasts of the North Island. *Ibid.* 80 The best known Gannet colony is at Cape Kidnappers, Hawkes Bay. **1966** *Encycl. NZ* I. 767 The gannet commonly seen in New Zealand seas is the Australasian gannet, *Sula bassana serrator.* **1985** *Readers Digest Book NZ Birds* 14 Takapu, Australian gannet, solan goose... Australasian gannets are on the increase in New Zealand. **1990** *Checklist Birds NZ* 79 *Morus serrator.. Australasian Gannet* (Takapu)... Adult birds range widely in New Zealand seas during winter.

2. *fig.* [f. nautical use: see OED *gannet* 2, 1929.] A selfish or greedy person; one who takes without asking.

  1922 *Evening Post* (Wellington) 1 Sept. 29 On being placed before me, this voluptuous creation was pounced upon by the gannets at my table. **1982** NEWBOLD *Big Huey* 248 Gannet (n) Selfish or greedy person. One who takes without asking.

gap, *v.* [Spec. use Brit. dial. *gap v.*: see OED; EDD 2.] *trans.* To make a (gap or notch) in the edge of a cutting implement. Cf. SHILLING 4.

  1934 *Press* (Christchurch) (Acland Gloss.) 27 Jan. 15 *Woolshed terms...* To *gap* shears is to make (accidentally) a g[ap] in the edge. **1958** *Straight Furrow* 6 Jan. 34 And from down in the shed vibrates Dad's angry voice 'Who's gapped my axe?'

Garden City. [Cf. OED: applied to Chicago (and other cities), 1841.] A nickname for Christchurch. See also CITY OF THE PLAINS.

  1906 PICARD *Ups & Downs* 34 Got loose in the garden city of Maoriland... Here's Cathedral Square, the centre of the City of the Plains. **1924** *Star* (Christchurch) 27 Dec. 6 It has become fashionable to refer to Christchurch as the City Beautiful and the Garden City, without doing very much to preserve..the boasted beauties of street and square and park. **1959** SLATTER *Gun in My Hand* 24 The city of Christchurch with its parks and avenues and the quiet Avon piddling through the town. The Garden City they call it. **1969** HASCOMBE *Down & Almost Under* 26 Was this the Garden City? Was this the place so very much like Home? **1976** JOHNSTON *New Zealanders* 163 The 'garden city' of Christchurch has a quiet charm which is excellently sampled in local bus tours. **1987** *Sunday News* (Auckland) 31 May 3 Mr Taylor said schoolgirls made sexual overtures to the garden city's bus drivers, but he didn't believe such behaviour was any more common than in the past.

Garden of New Zealand. *Obs.*

1. An early nickname for the settlement of Taranaki.

  1841 *Let. from Emigrant* in *Establish. New Plymouth* (1940) 148 I said [to Mr Ironside, Port Underwood Missionary], 'Do you know anything about Taranaki, New Plymouth Settlement?' 'Yes, well; I have travelled over it, and found it the garden of New Zealand.' **1856** FITTON *NZ* 145 The settlement of New Plymouth, or Taranaki..has been frequently spoken of as 'The Garden of New Zealand'. **1861** PAUL *NZ as It Was & Is* 34

GARFISH

Taranaki used to be called by its inhabitants 'The Garden of New Zealand'. **1911** *TrNZI* XLIII. 439 'We never used to have these heavy frosts before the emigrants came in,' said the old Taranaki settlers some twenty-five years ago, as they thought of the golden days, when the 'garden of New Zealand' was fenced off from the rest of the world by forty miles of standing bush. **1935** MAXWELL *Recollections* 165 'The Garden of New Zealand' was the earliest [name for Taranaki], and was certainly a very suitable one. For quite a long time it was known outside as 'The Land of Fungus'. **1943** MANNERING *Eighty Years NZ* 82 Taranaki had been justly called 'The Garden of New Zealand' from the early times of settlement.

2. *Obs.* Occas., the settlement of Nelson.

1864 HOCHSTETTER & PETERMAN *Geol. NZ* 112 The town of Nelson..enjoys..[a] climate the most agreeable and beautiful in New Zealand. With justice it may be called 'The Garden of New Zealand'.

garfish. [Transf. use of Brit. *garfish* the long-snouted fish *Belone vulgaris*: AND for fam. Hemirhamphidae, 1699.] *Hyporhamphus ihi* (fam. Hemirhamphidae, also called the *halfbeaks*), a slender elongate sea-fish with the lower jaw produced forwards in a long sharp beak. See also GUARDFISH, IHE, LONG TOM 3, PIPER, TAKEKE.

1844 COLENSO *Excurs. Northern Is.* in Taylor *Early Travellers* (1959) 54 A small but graceful species of Garfish..hastening away from its vivacious pursuers, flew, or rather sprung into my boat. **1868** PYKE *Province of Otago* 32 Many..varieties of sea-fish are caught round the coast, such as..flounders, soles, gar-fish, and others. **1879** *TrNZI* XI. 381 That no flounders should be sold under nine inches long..and no garfish under fourteen inches. **1886** SHERRIN *Handbook Fishes NZ* 34 This name [*sc.* garfish] is applied both to the skipper (*Scombresox Forsteri*) and to the ihi or half-beak, which are allied fishes representing those of the same names in the British seas... The half-beak, which is of rare occurrence in the British seas, is common all round New Zealand, and is the ordinary gar-fish that is so highly appreciated, especially in Auckland and Dunedin. **1898** MORRIS *Austral-English* 158 In Melbourne the *Garfish* is a true one, *Belone ferox*... In Tasmania, and New Zealand it is *Hemirhamphus intermedius*..Called..in Auckland the *Piper*. **1910** *NZ Free Lance* (Wellington) 10 Sept. 13 He sent..sixty dozen garfish to Wellington, and got only 6s 6d for them. **1927** SPEIGHT et al. *Nat. Hist. Canterbury* 198 The well-known garfish or piper..has the lower jaw protruding far beyond the upper, and uses it for grubbing among the seagrass in shallow bays. **1956** [see GUARDFISH]. **1960** DOOGUE & MORELAND *Sea Anglers' Guide* 195 Garfish... *Other names: Reporhamphus ihi;* piper, half-beak; ihe, takeke (Maori)... Medium fat fish with delicate flesh. Suitable for grilling or frying. **1972** *Press* (Christchurch) 21 Oct. 12 The garfish, or piper as it is called in Auckland, is a common fish along our coasts. **1982** AYLING *Collins Guide* (1984) 171 *Piper* (Garfish, ihi) *Hyporhamphus ihi*... The piper is an elongate fish with a long beak-like lower jaw.

Garibaldi shirt. *Obs.* [f. the name of *Garibaldi*, an Italian patriot (1807-82), leader of the 'Red Shirts': see OED, a kind of blouse worn by women, orig. of bright red stuff.] A usu. red flannel shirt, associated esp. with gold-diggers' costume.

1880 SENIOR *Travel & Trout* 196 The general [Maori] costume..was to put on a belltopper hat, garibaldi shirt, paper collar, and necktie, a pilot jacket..but French caps, deerstalkers, and wide-awakes were to be seen. **1927** BIDWILL & WOODHOUSE *Bidwill of Pihautea* 13 Garibaldi shirts [c1853] made of vivid red flannel. **1939** BEATTIE *First White Boy Born Otago* 170 Many of the diggers wore Garibaldi shirts, which had a red and black check.

gasper /ˈgaspə/. *Shearing.* A sheep which gasps for breath while being shorn, usu. from grass coming up into its throat.

1955 BOWEN *Wool Away* 156 Gasper. A sheep gasping for breath while being shorn. The trouble is usually caused by grass coming up into the sheep's throat. **1966** TURNER *Eng. Lang. Austral. & NZ* 147 There are names for types of sheep..the *sandyback* and the *gasper*, which gasps apparently because grass comes into its throat. **1982** *Agric. Gloss.* (MAF) 55 *Gasper:* Sheep gasping for breath while being shorn.

gate: see TARANAKI GATE; *swing the gate* (SWING *v.* 2); SWING GATE.

gate. [Cf. OED *n.*¹ 5 c, 1937.] The mouth.

1937 PARTRIDGE *Dict. Slang* 318 *gate*... The mouth: New Zealanders' (from ca. 1910), esp. soldiers' in G.W. **1938** *Press* (Christchurch) (McNab Slang) 2 Apr. 18 [In local criminal slang]..'moosh' or 'gate' is mouth. **1951** PARK *Witch's Thorn* 113 'Oh, shut yer big gate!' said his father shrilly. **1978** HILLIARD *Glory & Dream* 76 Not with a snuff-stick hanging out of their gates.

gaultheria /gɔlˈθɪrɪjə/, /gɒl-/. [Spec. use of *Gaultheria*, a genus of evergreen shrubs (fam. Ericaceae), f. the name (imperfectly latinized) of J.-F. *Gaultier* (1708–c1756), a French-Canadian physician and amateur botanist.] A native shrub of the genus *Gaultheria* (fam. Ericaceae) common in montane and subalpine habitats. See also SNOWBERRY 1.

1869 *TrNZI* I. (rev. edn.) 197 The Gaultherias cover large areas of ground on the mountains, the fruit being eaten by the Kaka parrots. **1900** *Canterbury Old & New* 188 Presently we may emerge from the forest upon some moor-like tableland in the heart of the ranges, where we again meet with a characteristic flora composed largely of heath-like Gaultherias. **1938** *Tararua Tramper* Feb. 15 Celmesias [*sic*] and ranunculus gave way to gaultheria and native broom, alpine scrub to ribbonwood.

gaw gaw, var. KAKA.

g'day, var. GIDDAY.

gear, *n.*¹ In various *spec.* uses of *gear* equipment.

1. *Prison.* A contrivance of flint and steel for lighting cigarettes.

c1941–45 p.c. 1951 members of the Riverside Community, Nelson: 'gear' was applied to flint lighting contrivances used in conscientious objector or detention camps where the allowance was only two matches a day. **1989** NEWBOLD *Punish. & Politics* 26 Another way of overcoming the match shortage [in prison] was by means of what was known as 'the gear'. Tinder would be made by burning a piece of rag and slapping it shut in a book. The tinder would then be kept in a small box of tin and ignited by striking a piece of flint or quartz from the quarry against a piece of steel to produce a spark.

2. *pl.* [Poss. from a Maori English pluralizing analogy with *clothes*.] Clothes. Occas. 'gear' in general.

1939-45 *Expressions and Sayings* 2NZEF (Nat. Archiv. TS WAII DA 420/1) Gears—Impedimenta. Skit on East coasters always using plurals. **1959** SLATTER

GECKO

Gun in My Hand 178 'We found a bricked-up room with a ton of good gears in it,' says a joker washing his hands of sin in the basin. 'Bags of loot.' **1986** *NZ Woman's Weekly* 30 June 76 [A 15-year-old writes] Finally, I don't turn up my nose at flash new clothes that my relations give me. As I said before, I'm not into some gears, so I just give them to Mum, who's my size too. **1989** TE AWEKOTUKU *Tahuri* 38 Only a big blond guy rifling through her bags. 'Don't worry, it's only me'... 'Hey!' she growled... 'Those are my gears.'

3. *Shearing.* The shears, or handpiece and its parts and attachments. See also COMB *n.*.

1955 [see COMB *n.*]. **1960** MILLS *Sheep-O* 163 He shore the amazingly high tally of 332 sheep with what is known as the 'narrow gear'. This is a handpiece with a comb and cutter not more than 2³⁄₈ inches in width.

4. With participial adjectives in jocular terms for body parts: **laughing gear**, mouth or teeth, esp. in the phr. **wrap your laughing gear round** (an item of food), to eat, start eating; **looking gear**, eyes.

1964 HELMER *Stag Party* 81 A joker no sooner gets comfortable than I looks up and smacks me lookin' gear fair at the rear end of a dirty big stag. *Ibid.* 82 'Crump, sometimes I think you're a damn liar,' I said. 'Here, wrap your laughin' gear round that lot,' Crump said, handing me a heaped plateful. **1976** GIFFORD *Loosehead Len's Bumper Thump Book* 40 Look for the joker who can't resist a bit of a Te Kuiti tickle to the laughin' gear of every bloke he tackles. **1988** McGILL *Dict. Kiwi Slang* 68 *laughing gear*; eg 'Wrap your laughing gear around this,', says Barry Crump, handing over a gutted fish in a TV ad, 1987.

gear, *n.*² [Transf. use of (*in*) *gear* a part of automotive, etc. transmission.] In the phr. **to get into gear**, get moving; **to find another gear**, to find extra speed or strength. Cf. A INTO G.

1986 *Marist Messenger* Dec. 36 Doom reckoned I should go because I could run the fastest. Before any of us could get into gear, Mrs Douglas came into the woolshed. **1988** McGILL *Dict. Kiwi Slang* 100 *she's/he's found another gear* sporting c[atch]/p[hrase] for horse or person accelerating, often when competition appears to be at full stretch.

Hence **geared up**, excited; ready to work at a high speed.

1985 BISHOP *Home & Abroad* 69 Most of the countries he [Dr Sutch] was arranging to visit were Communist-orientated and he appeared to be quite geared-up at the thought of these visits.

gecko, *n.*¹ A *spec.* use of *gecko* for any of various large-eyed baggy-skinned native lizards of the family Gekkonidae, either the drab grey-brown geckos (*Hoplodactylus* spp.) or the green tree-climbing geckos (*Naultinus* spp.) both having small scales which give them a dull-skinned appearance. The common book-names for these (mainly known as 'lizards' to non-discriminating local English-speakers) are: **common grey gecko** (*H. maculatus*), **forest gecko** (*H. granulatus*), **giant** (or **Duvaucel's**) **gecko** (*H. duvauceli*), **green** (or **green tree**) **gecko** (*Naultinus elegans*), **Stephens Island gecko** (*H. stephenseni*). See also KAKARIKI *n.*², MOKOMOKO.

1922 *Auckland Weekly News* 21 Dec. 17 New Zealand's green geckoes are absolutely harmless. **1947** POWELL *Native Animals* 74 Green Gecko (*Naultinus elegans*). A most handsome lizard, about six inches in length, and normally a velvety bright grass green. **1957** WILLIAMS *Dictionary of the Maori Language* 244 *Papa..Hoplodactylus pacificus, brown gecko* a lizard =

moko-papa. **1966** Sharell *The Tuatara Lizards & Frogs of NZ* 48 *Green tree gecko (Naultinus elegans..)*. The green tree geckos are very beautiful creatures. *Ibid.* 49 *Common brown or Pacific gecko (Hoplodactylus pacificus..)*. It is found all over New Zealand, often along the coast above high-water zone, at the edge of the bush and in the bush. **1966** *Encycl. NZ* III. 65 Geckos are nocturnal. The green gecko (*Naultinus elegans*) is an exception, for it shelters in foliage during the day... Duvaucel's gecko (*Hoplodactylus duvauceli*) which can attain 10 in. in length, is the largest species. **1979** *Forest & Bird 214* 34 Though not steeped in the antiquity of the tuatara, the New Zealand geckos are a unique group, comprising three endemic genera believed to have arisen from Miocene invasion. **1983** *Land of the Mist* 76 Geckos may be various shades of brown or grey, but the North Island green gecko, or kakariki, is the commonest in the Urewera. **1986** Gill *Collins Handguide to Frogs and Reptiles* 32 *Common Grey Gecko Hoplodactylus maculatus...* Probably the most widespread and abundant lizard in New Zealand. *Ibid.* 34 *Giant Gecko Hoplodactylus duvauceli... Size* Up to 160mm SV... The largest New Zealand lizard and one of the largest geckos in the world. *Ibid.* 40 *Stephens Island Gecko Hoplodactylus stephensi...* Known only from Stephens Island. **1986** Robb *NZ Amphibians & Reptiles* 54 *Hoplodactylus granulatus..* is often referred to as the 'forest gecko', which describes its normal habitat, but can lead to confusion with *H. pacificus*, which is also frequently found in forests. **1992** *Marlborough Express* (Blenheim) 31 Jan. 5 Chamois are there [at Puhi Peaks, Kaikoura].., black eyed geckos..the native weeping broom..and kea abound. **1995** Anderson *House Guest* 167 'You could get an accountant...' She looked at him as though he had been advocating the services of a gutless green gecko.

gecko, *n*.² Also **gekko**. [Prob. *g*(ink or *g*(ander + d)*ekko*, infl. by the form *gecko*; or perh. a variant of *geek* look.] In the phr. **to have a gecko at**, to have a look (or 'dekko') at.
 1979 p.c. G. McEwen (Auckland) *give us a gekko at*, etc. **1982** Prain *Seized* (Playmarket edn.) 5 Kate: Of course. Take your jacket off, I'll have a gecko at your guts.

gee, *v*.

1. [Used elsewhere but recorded earliest in NZ: see OED *v*.² 1 b.] *trans*. To urge (a horse, bullock, etc.) with a call of *gee*.
 1845 Wakefield *Adventure NZ* II. 133 He *geed* the bullocks and ploughed on.

2. *Obs*. [See OED *v*.² 1 c.] As **to gee for**, to support enthusiastically.
 1906 *Truth* 21 July 1 Pure-boy Bligh has denied on the platform that he is 'geeing' for the doctors. Anyhow, the doctors are geeing for Bligh.

3. [See OED *v*.² 1 c.] In the phr. **to make things gee**, to speed up, go with a bang.
 1909 Thompson *Ballads About Business* 10 Dat vouldn't affect us der least bit, he reckoned he'd make dings gee.

4. *Obs*. [Cf. OED *v*.¹ 1 a (archaic).] In the phr. **to not gee**, not to fit, suit.
 1911 *Truth* 13 May 6 He had been in the railway service, but hurt his hand, and they gave him only 12 months' work after that, when he had to go out and take on private enterprise. It didn't gee, and he wasn't able to pay 30s per week.

gege, gee-gee, gei-gei, varr. kiekie.

gekko, var. gecko *n*.²

gelly /ˈdʒeli/. Also **jelly**. **a.** [Used elsewhere but recorded earliest and of freq. use in NZ: see OED *jelly*, 1941.] An abbreviation of *gelignite*.
 1938 Hyde *Nor Yrs. Condemn* 152 All round..was the rattle..of sliding stones, with a sudden roar as a navvy pressed down on the battery touching off a plug of jelly. **1946** Sargeson *That Summer* 184 Once he struck rock, so brought some gelly home from the quarry and plugged a bit in and set it off. **1953** Hamilton *Till Human Voices Wake Us* 53 In the second, everything like Dets, Gelly, etc., has to be strictly accounted for to headquarters. **1967** McLatchie *Tang of Bush* 71 The bundle of 'jelly' sticks, with a detonator and fuse enclosed, was carefully placed in the bottom. **1985** *Listener* 2 Feb. 14 'Do you use dynamite or gelignite to blow up a safe?'.. 'You call it "gelly", don't you?' 'Yes.' 'Spelled with a g or a j?'.. 'G,' beamed the knowledgeable young man.

b. Used *attrib*. in special Comb. connoting the poisonous aspects of nitroglycerine: **gelly head** (also *transf*. a 'numbskull'), **gelly poisoning**, see quots.
 1978 McAra *Gold Mining Waihi* 274 Besides the smoke, the large quantities of explosives handled produced what were known as '**gelly heads**', which were severe headaches caused by absorption of nitroglycerine through the skin. **1986** Richards *Off the Sheep's Back* 5 The miners [at Martha Mine c1907] often suffered from severe headaches, known as 'gelly heads', caused by the fumes from blasting in confined spaces and from handling the 'gelly'... If [the nitroglycerine] came into contact with the miners' hands, and they then wiped the sweat from their foreheads, they would get a terrible headache. **1992** Park *Fence around the Cuckoo* 136 'A gang of jellyheads,' said Mera in a letter. 'We ought to line them [*sc*. Depression politicians] up and shoot them.' **1971** Bale *Maratoto Gold* 75 If you must roll the jelly to smaller or larger size do so with a piece of cardboard, paper or use gloves. If it does get on your hands, wash them immediately otherwise you will get **jelly poisoning**, and have a headache you won't forget in a hurry.

gem.

1. [Poss. a short form of an original *gem-cake, *gem scone*: but in *Colonial Everyday Cookery* (quoted below) *gems* are included in the 'bread' section, rather than in the 'scones' 'buns' or 'tea cakes' sections.] A sweet batter or scone mixture baked usu. in a gem-iron.
 c**1910** Beaton *Universal Cook. Book* 29 *Gems* self raising flour..eggs..sugar..warm milk..butter..salt... Have the gem iron at boiling heat..a tablespoon of the mixture..put into each. c**1930** *Electric Cookery—Hints Instruction & Recipes* 43 *Golden muffins or gems..* butter..castor sugar..eggs..marmalade..flour..soda. **1936** *Merry Meal Maker Cook. Book* 32 *Gems..* selfrising flour..butter..sugar..1 egg. Milk to mix a batter thicker than pikelets. **1963** Pearson *Coal Flat* 50 Mr O'Reilly having to take out his dentures to remove them from a treacle gem. **1982** Burton *Two Hundred Yrs. NZ Food* 157 Both gems and the gem irons they are made in are New Zealand inventions.

2. Special Comb. **gem iron** (also early **gem pan**), an orig. cast-iron tray, now also one of other metal or material, indented with two rows of rounded moulds, which is pre-heated to receive the gem mixture and then placed in a hot oven; **gem scone**, a scone-like mixture baked as a gem, or occas. in individual patty-pans.
 c**1910** **gem iron** [see 1]. **1982** Burton *Two Hundred Yrs. NZ Food* 157 If you are lucky enough to possess a set of the old heavy cast-iron gem irons..do not part with them. **1992** *Evening Post* (Wellington) 14 May 8 [Advt and illustration] At last! Genuine cast iron *gem irons* now available. Complete with recipes and instructions. $28. **1908** Col. *Everyday Cookery* 277 *White flour gems*..Flour..Milk..2 Eggs (whites only)..make a batter... Bake in hot **gem pans** in a quick oven. **1905** Brandon *'Ukneadit'* 69 **Gem scones**..Two Eggs..Sugar..Melted Butter..Flour..Cream of Tartar..Carbonate of Soda..Warm Milk..drop teaspoonful into greased patty pans. Bake..Split open and butter for afternoon tea. **1911** Tendall *Kirkcaldie & Stains Cook. Book* 10 *Gem scones* Put a little butter into each gem iron... Half fill them with mixture..quick oven. **1926** Futter *Home Cook. NZ* 203 *Gem scones*..put in..hot greased tins. Bake in quick oven.

gemfish. [A commercial name poss. developed from an abbrev. of the family name *Gem*(pylidae; AND (1974) suggests that the name *gemfish* was given by salespeople, as its former name *hake* was confused with *flake* the retail name for dogfish fillets.] A large, iridescent bluish, barracouta-like, deepwater food-fish, *Rexea* (formerly *Jordanidia*) *solandri* (fam. Gempylidae: snake mackerels). See also hake 1 c, king barracouta, kingfish b, tikati.
 1978 *Catch* Mar. 13 Gemfish *Rexea solandri—Jordanidia Solandri* Southern Kingfish, Silver Kingfish, hake. **1986** Paul *NZ Fishes* 121 *Gemfish Rexea solandri...* New Zealand names include silver or southern kingfish and hake (which is now easily confused with the true hake). The name gemfish, conveying family relationship as well as iridescence, is more appropriate.

gendarme. *Mountaineering*. [f. *gendarme* in French alpine use (1904), a pinnacle of rock, poss. from its upright, sentinel-like appearance reminiscent of a policeman on street duty.] A sharp, pointed rock or pinnacle.
 1926 Cowan *Travel in NZ* II. 57 Most savage of all is Mt. Blackburn..soaring nearly 8,000 feet into the sky, its razorback *arêtes* bristling with those jagged stony pinnacles which alpinists call *gendarmes*. **1959** McLeod *Tall Tussock* 23 Just above the sheep it ran on to the top of a small bluff with a big rock sticking up on it; what the mountaineers call a 'gendarme'. **1971** *Listener* 19 Apr. 56 They [Pete and Sam] got up the low scree, sidled across the first face..but they were getting bombed so they cramponed up to just below a gendarme.

General Assembly. *Hist*.

a. Occas. in shortened form as **Assembly**. [Spec. local use of *General Assembly*: see OED *assembly* 5 b.] The name applied, particularly in the nineteenth century, to the combined elective and appointive legislatures of the central government of New Zealand, and occas. loosely, to the House of Representatives alone (see quot. 1930); see also quot. 1987.
 1846 *Act to make further provision for Govt. NZ Islands* 28 Aug. (9 & 10 Vict. c. 103) in Rutherford *Sel. Documents* (1949) 20 VI... it shall be lawful for Her Majesty..to constitute..a General Assembly in and for the Islands of *New Zealand*, to be called the General Assembly of *New Zealand*, which said General Assembly shall consist of and be holden by the Governor..., and a Legislative Council, and a House of Representatives. **1856** *Richmond-Atkinson Papers* 18 May (1960) I. 222 Domett is my most particular friend in the Assembly... Next to him I see more of Stafford than of any other member. **1848** Earp *Handbook* 4 Under the new Constitution, the government of New Zealand is vested in a Governor appointed by the Crown, and a General Assembly, consisting of two

houses, one elected by the people, the other appointed by the Crown for life. **1877** *Richmond-Atkinson Papers* (1960) II. 440 Unconstitutionally, [Grey] started the provinces before the General Assembly—thus launching the constitution 'bottom upwards' as old Carleton used to say. **1898** [see LEGISLATIVE COUNCIL]. **1930** ACLAND *Early Canterbury Runs* 160 Poignedestre was a man of judgment and standing, and gave Francis Jollie a close run in the first South Canterbury election for a member of the General Assembly. **1948** LIPSON *Politics of Equality* 50 Ominous talk of separating the two islands into distinct jurisdictions was heard [in the 1860s] within the provinces and in the General Assembly itself. **1959** SINCLAIR *Hist. NZ* 87 It took Otago members over two months by sea to reach Auckland for the first session of the General Assembly. **1987** ROBERTS *Politicians, Public Servants & Public Enterprise* 12 The authority of the executive derives from the supremacy of Parliament, or, to apply the correct terminology for New Zealand, the General Assembly. That is the..'bipartite body consisting of the House of Representatives and the Governor-General', which exercises legislative function.

b. Formerly surviving (to the 1980s) in the name of the **General Assembly Library** (more frequently familiarly abbreviated to **the G.A.**), the library (now part of the National Library) attached to Parliament and housed as an adjunct to Parliament Buildings.

General Government. *Hist.* A name given in the 19th century to the government or administration responsible to the elected House of Representatives as distinct from the several provincial governments.

1854 *Richmond-Atkinson Papers* (1960) I. 156 We do not expect that the General Government will move in the affair. **1857** *Lyttelton Times* 1 July 2 The administration of our affairs [in the Province of Canterbury] is embarrassed by the great distance of the General Government from us. **1869** *Grey River Argus* 14 Jan. 2 The policy of self-reliance is being steadily pursued by the General Government. **1876** Reefton Petition in Latham *Golden Reefs* (1992) 284 We do not know what scheme of local self-government will be brought forward by the General Government.

general store. [Found elsewhere (recorded earliest in Australia: AND 1827) but of significance in, esp. rural, NZ.] The usual name for a store selling a wide range of merchandise (including groceries) for all home, farm and work needs: by 1980 confined mainly to rural use; STORE 1.

1843 *NZ Gaz.* Apr. in Gore *Levins* (1956) 9 *Wholesale & Retail General Store.* **1851** GODLEY *Let.* 27 Feb. in Carrington *Godley* (1950) 125 There are two 'general stores', three butchers, two bakers, etc. **1876** KENNEDY *Colonial Travel* 196 Two jolly old fellows..roamed into the 'general store' [at Temuka]..asking for a 'pund o' her best watter buskits'. **1888** BARLOW *Kaipara* 97 It boasts of..three general stores (or shops, as they would be called in England). **1939** GRIEVE *Sketches from Maoriland* (1961) 32 By far the most important building in the Pipiwai borough was the general store. **1948** *Our Own Country* 7 A general store, privately owned and complete with electric light and telephone, is still operated on the ground floor. **1959** SHADBOLT *New Zealanders* (1986) 204 Pub, post office, butcher..and general store. **1970** THOMAS *Way Up North* 73 Those old-time general stores were usually little more than cheaply constructed sheds with the longest side facing a main road. The primary needs, food, clothing and builders' equipment, were all catered for. **1985** BINNEY *Long Lives the King* 24 The Post Office [was] a newish building dating from the severance of this service from the General Store across the way.

Hence **general storekeeper** [AND 1840], see also STOREKEEPER 1.

1843 *NZ Gaz.* Apr. in Gore *Levins* (1856) 9 In consequence of the undersigned having to compete with so many General Storekeepers which are daily presenting themselves before the public, feels it is his duty to offer to the public a choice selection of Groceries.

Gene Tunney. [f. the name of James Joseph ('*Gene*') *Tunney* 1898–1978, heavyweight champion of the world 1926–28.] Rhyming slang for 'money'.

1963 *NZ Truth* 21 May 19 I was caster for Gene Tunney, so I took a slapsie maxie [=taxi] to the course.

gentian. [Spec. use of northern hemisphere *gentian Gentiana* spp.] A native herb of the plant genus *Gentiana* (fam. Gentianaceae), often with a modifier: **alpine** (or **bog**) **gentian**, *G. townsonii*, **Chatham gentian** *G. chathamica*.

1853 TAYLOR *Journal* 30 Jan. (ATLTS) VIII. 70 The chief plants I noticed [on Ruapehu] were a beautiful everlasting, the harebell, 2 kinds of gentian, a pretty speedwell, an epacris. **1863** BUTLER *First Year* ix 130 We have one very stupid white gentian; but it is, to say the least of it, uninteresting to the casual observer. **1933** *Press* (Christchurch) (Acland Gloss.) 21 Oct. 15 *Gentian*... This is another of the few plants most hill shepherds know. **1946** *Tararua Story* 7 And above the bush lies the alpine meadow,.. delicate gentians among the grass. **1952** RICHARDS *Chatham Is.* 39 *Gentiana..chathamica*... Chatham Gentian. **1978** *Manawatu Tramping Club Jubilee* 89 Dotted in profusion amidst the tussock are..Eyebright and gentian all the way to the hut. **1987** *Listener* 17 Jan. 30 Alpine gentians are hardly noticeable until their small, cup-like white flowers appear all over a mountain meadow towards the end of summer.

Gentle Annie. Occas. *ellipt.* **Annie**. [Poss. transf. from an allusion to or in a popular song 'When the springtime comes, Gentle Annie, And the wild flowers are scattered o'er the plain, Shall I never more behold thee, Never hear thy gentle voice again'.]

1. a. [AND 1913.] A name given to various hills or inclines (most, ironically, steep) on bridle-tracks and coach-roads and remaining as local names; occas. and locally a creek (cf. ROARING MEG).

1866 SMITH *Taranaki Jrnl.* 20 July in Cowan *NZ Wars* (1955) II. 529 Afterwards found good crossing and carried the road from the township to the top of 'Gentle Annie'. **1874** PYKE *George Washington Pratt* 15 There was naturally a desire to find a somewhat easier path [over hills in Otago] and so what was known as the 'Gentle Annie' track came into use and fashion. **1892** KELLY *Journey Upper Waitara Valley* 3 Our attention was concentrated in breasting those 'Gentle Annies' as the steep ridges are called [which] we are constantly ascending and descending on the greater portion of our route. **1924** WIN *The Win Family* 6 We have Gentle Annies in every district, a legacy of either incompetence or laziness [of surveyors]. **1971** LETHBRIDGE *Sunrise on Hills* 144 There are a number of so-called 'Gentle Annies' in New Zealand which I have negotiated from time to time, but this [at Ngaruroro] is one of the worst.

b. As a place-name in specific local use. (a) Waikaremoana.

1873 ST JOHN *Pakeha Rambles* in Taylor *Early Travellers* (1959) 573 It may be laid down as an axiom that whenever the tourist in New Zealand arrives at a hill christened 'Gentle Annie' he may prepare himself for a breather; there was no exception to the rule as far as concerned the 'Gentle Annie' of Waikarimoana [*sic*].

(b) Otago (also of a creek, see 2 below).

1891 A TRAMP ESQ. *Casual Ramblings* 108 A wondrous change all this since the days we 'swagged it'..up by the Molyneux, blessing 'Roaring Meg' and sweating over the 'Gentle Annie'. **1973** FERNANDEZ *Tussock Fever* 4 Not to worry..that a truck had broken down right on a bad bend of the Gentle Annie.

(c) Nelson.

1904 *NZ Illustr. Mag.* X. 100 Now you look out for this 'ere hill, it's called Gentle Annie, and lots o' blokes has come to grief on it. **1981** HENDERSON *Exiles Asbestos Cottage* 201 Two hours climb to get to Gentle Annie (the point where the power lines now cross the track).

(d) Auckland and Thames.

1874 LUSH *Thames Jrnls.* 21 July (1975) 150 Lucy told us that this morning all the upper part of 'Gentle Annie' (the hill at the foot of which their house is built) was covered with snow! **1934** MULGAN *Spur of Morning* 163 'Gentle Annie' was a hill they had to climb up to the bush uplands.

(e) Hawke's Bay.

1950 BARNS-GRAHAM *Sheep Station* 24 A long hill which bore the rather cynical name of 'Gentle Annie'.

(f) Taranaki.

1992 CONDON *Hurleyville* 80 One [delivery] was around the roads close to the township, the other went up to the Gentle Annie and beyond.

(g) Westland.

1953 MILLAR *High Noon* (1965) 146 He lived in a tiny hut [in Westland]..at the top of Gentle Annie. (One wonders how many Gentle Annies there must be in New Zealand!)

2. The name of a (sluggish) creek, *spec.* a tributary of the Kawarau River, Central Otago; also once the name of a former wayside inn or accommodation house in the Kawarau Gorge (see ROARING MEG a) supposedly commemorating a historical person named Annie. Also called 'Annie's Creek'.

1874 [see ROARING MEG a]. **1926** *NZ Observer* 8 Sept. 2 It has to be remembered that below the dam the Shotover River and the streams, 'Roaring Meg' and 'Gentle Annie' empty into the Kawerau [*sic*] River. **1939** BEATTIE *First White Boy Born Otago* 161 Amongst others who left [the Dunstan rush for Kawarau, c1862] were the members of a theatrical or concert party, and among them was a girl who sang a song called 'Gentle Annie' and this name was sometimes jokingly applied to her. Going over the hills some of the rest were grouching, but she tramped on lugging her swag..singing to cheer them on. The creek was called after her because of her brave spirit. That was said to be the reason of the name Gentle Annie. **1943** [see ROARING MEG a]. **1957** MCNEISH *Tavern in the Town* (1966) 28 Annie was quiet and pleasant and hence the nickname to [*sic*] her licensed premises, the Gentle Annie [in Kawarau Gorge]. **1984** *Listener* 3 Nov. 133 The name Gentle Annie evokes many things—rivers, mountain roads, hills—in all parts of the country. Gentle Annie is an elusive figure in our folklore; sometimes an object of tender love songs, she is also known, in the company of Roaring Meg, as a colourful figure in the bars of goldrush Queenstown.

3. *transf.* in various applications. As a type of a quiet, female goody-goody.

1950 WHITWORTH *Otago Interval* 8 [Mother] was no Gentle Annie but gallant and mettlesome.

gentleman.

1. As **gentleman of the road (swag)**, in ironic use, SWAGGER 1 a.
    1953 STRONACH *Musterer on Molesworth* 55 The homestead was full of people: two parties of deerstalkers, one party of trampers..and a gentleman of the road. **1947** BEATTIE *Early Runholding* 12 The class of wayfarers..were always called swaggers in Otago. These 'gentlemen of the swag' were not in evidence until after the gold diggings broke out.

2. Special Comb. **gentleman colonist, gentleman farmer**, ironically applied to a (usu. well-off and often inexperienced) person who was not seriously engaged in a 'hands-on' way in the pursuits of 'colonising', 'farming', etc.
    1853 ADAMS *Canterbury Settlement* 19 It could not be expected that a vast and uncultivated plain should present an inviting prospect to the unpractised eye of a 'gentleman colonist'. **1866** BARKER *Station Life* (1870) 74 He..and some other gentlemen..used to..ride twelve miles to Lake Ida..lunching at the solitary hut of a gentleman-farmer close by the lake.

3. As **Gentleman's Club**, commonly applied, often ironically, to any local private club thought (often in its own estimation) to be socially exclusive.
    1862 CHUDLEIGH *Diary* 3 Apr. (1950) 30 I drank tea and spent the evening with them at Laday's Club, a very nice house indeed. There is also a gentleman's club here [at Christchurch]. **1935** GUTHRIE *Little Country* (1937) 410 On the third corner was what was known to the citizens by the choice name of the Gentlemen's Club. **1990** SMITH *Will the Real Mr NZ Please Stand Up* 61 He also had a date with the Gentlemen's Club every night at five thirty and was home at six thirty.

geoduck /ˈɡuidʌk/. [Spec. use of *geoduck* (DARE 'Chinook jargon') a genus *Panope* of the N. American Pacific coast, esp. *P. generosa*.] Either of two species of *Panopea* (fam. Hiatellidae), esp. *P. zelandica* a large edible bivalve shellfish which burrows deeply into sand.
    1989 *Listener* 6 Nov. 33 Alick Shaw..uses up to 14 kilograms of geoduck in chowder weekly [in his Wellington restaurant]. **1990** *Southland Times* 10 Oct. Scores of Stewart Islanders are up in arms over geoduc [*sic*] (gooey duck) fishing in Paterson Inlet. **1991** *Dominion Sunday Times* (Wellington) 31 Mar. 21 [A] stall at the festival offered..sushi..and gooey duck salad. (The latter is a long tubular rather disgusting looking shellfish from Golden Bay.)

George. [f. a transf. use of the British royal name, esp. familiar in the early 19th, and early-mid 20th centuries, from the names and images on the heads of coins.] The name *George* was apparently once popular as an adopted English name for Maori males (cf. also HORI). It was also commonly used by New Zealand soldiers in Egypt during WW2 (probably as a part of wider military usage) as a dismissive or derogatory name, or mode of address, for an Egyptian.
    [**1823** CRUISE *Journal* 9 Apr. (1957) 77 He was accompanied by a person to whom the whalers had given the name of King George [Te Uru-ti or Kingi Hori]... As he and the celebrated George of Wangarooa will be frequently mentioned... [one] may caution the reader not to mistake the one for the other.] **1941** *NZEF Times* 18 Aug. 4 Talking about George (and one does a lot of it out here), it would be interesting to know why every New Zealander, irrespective of the wishes of his godfathers..should be honoured by his sovereign's patronymic. The NZEF, not to be out-done, describes every Abdul and Amid as 'George'. **1943** JACKSON *Passage to Tobruk* 95 George, the driver (all natives being christened George), pulled on the reins. **1945** MACDONALD *Away From Home* 13 [The ghari] carries eight Kiwis, one of whom dethrones 'George'... [These] chariot races..[are] highly dangerous to the 'georges'. **1983** HENDERSON *Down from Marble Mountain* 260 Everyone, soldier and Egyptian alike, is known as 'George', probably because our emperor is King George the Fifth or Sixth. He hasn't made much of an impact anywhere. 'How did that Wog know my name?' each perplexed quota asks in every new reinforcement.

geranium. [Spec. use of *Geranium* (fam. Geraniaceae) of Europe and Asia.] Endemic *Geranium* spp., usu. with a modifier: **Chatham Island (Chathams) geranium** *G. traversii* and **native geranium** *G. microphyllum*. See also CRANESBILL.
    1889 FEATON *Art Album NZ Flora* 178 Matuakumara [Maori name]..Geranium [Settlers' name]..Geranium dissectum..Herb. **1900** *Canterbury Old & New* 183 Amongst the host of introduced weeds it is difficult for anybody but a botanist to distinguish the smaller and less peculiar native plants, such as the..white-flowered native geranium [*Geranium microphyllum*]. **1922** *Auckland Weekly News* 19 Jan. 15 An Invercargill correspondent..has sent blooms of the Chatham Island geranium, which were grown in a Dunedin garden. **1926** soft geranium, wild geranium [SEE DOVE'S FOOT]. **1952** RICHARDS *Chatham Is.* 32 *Geranium..Traversii*..Chatham Island Geranium. **1971** *New Zealand's Heritage* I. 267 *Chatham Island Geranium, Geranium traversii*. Perennial herb with short silvery hairs densely covering the leaves and stems. Solitary flowers are produced in abundance. **1982** *Press* (Christchurch) 9 Oct. 15 For example, the Chathams geranium is Geranium traversii.

geri, var. GERRY.

German, *a.* As a modifier in various special collocations: often during WW1 and after changed (crypto-patriotically) to BELGIAN B q.v., or occas. to *English*. **German biscuit** or **cake**, a usu. spicy sweet biscuit, often filled with dried fruit (after WW1, usu. *Belgian* occas. *English biscuit*); **German collie**, see quot. 1933; **German doggies** *pl.*, stones rolled downhill to move sheep (cf. *Nelson huntaway* (NELSON 2)); **German ivy**, see IVY 2 b; **German owl**, see OWL 2 (2); **German sausage** [used elsewhere from 1837 (see OED *German* 4), previously in frequent use in New Zealand esp. before WW1, when *Belgian* (or *Dominion, luncheon*) *sausage* became usual], LUNCHEON SAUSAGE.
    1908 *Col. Everyday Cookery* 254 *German biscuits.*. Eggs..Sugar..Butter..Spice..Flour..Rice [ground].. Powder..Vanilla Essence..Salt..Mix with..milk..cut into rounds... While warm, place jam in between each two and ice the top one with white icing. Sprinkle pink sugar. **1911** TENDALL *Kirkcaldie & Stains Cook. Book* 15 *German biscuits* put two together..jam between. Ice either with pink or white icing. **1905** BRANDON *'UKNEADIT'* 63 *German cakes*..Flour [etc.] Sugar.. Butter..Egg..Milk... mix to a stiff paste; chop raisins, candied peel, figs, currants, almonds, apple, essence of lemon,.. sugar..Spread the mixture between. **1933** *Press* (Christchurch) (Acland Gloss.) 21 Oct. 15 *German Collie*.—A variety of sheep dog which is blue (black and white spots). He usually has one or both wall eyes. **1934** LILICO *Sheep Dog Memoirs* 3 She was what is known in New Zealand as a German collie but on the Borders they were called 'Bilton Blues'. **1875** PEACHE *Journal* in Gray *Quiet with Hills* (1970) 39 Towards the plain the sides of the mountain are steep and we sent some '**German doggies**' down to hurry the sheep. 'German doggies' are what the shepherds call the stones and rocks they roll down. **1988** PICKERING *Hills* 48 There is immense satisfaction in seeing the progress of a great boulder smashing its way downhill. In the high country such rock tumblings were referred to as 'german doggies', a cheap way, apparently, of persuading the sheep to head downhill. **1887** *Auckland Weekly News* 7 May 19 Many fatal results have occurred from eating **German sausage**, which, having been cooked, has remained for a long time thus protected before being eaten. **1899** MANSFIELD *Stories* (1984) 7 Sometimes, to make it more real, we had lunch together..and sharing the slice of German sausage and a bath bun with loaf sugar in it. **1917** *Wanganui Herald* 21 May 4 'I suppose you do not make German sausage now?' asked the chairman... 'We call it "luncheon", sir,' was the reply. **1938** HYDE *Godwits Fly* (1970) 65 And in all the butcher-shops, pink-rinded German sausage, with the delicious little triangles of bacon fat, had become 'Belgian sausage'. Belgium is brave little Belgium, one of our Allies.

gerry. Also **geri**. [Abbrev. of *geriatric*: AND 1977.] An elderly person.
    1982 MARSHALL *Master Big Jingles* 143 Lester Dipport despised the very old people of the party. He called them gerries. **1984** 14 F E122 Wgton Girls C. 31 Geri [a sick person]

get, *v.* In various phrasal verbs and phrases. **a. to get down on**, to take or appropriate; to steal.
    1949 PARTRIDGE *Dict. Slang* 324 *get down on*. To appropriate illicitly: New Zealanders': C. 20. **1980** LELAND *Kiwi-Yankee Dict.* 44 (to) *get down on*: does not mean 'to go down on', although there are similarities. 'I'm getting down on that tin of biscuits at the rate of knots.' I'm eating that jar of cookies very quickly. **1988** McGILL *Dict. Kiwi Slang* 48 *get down on* to steal; eg 'Let's get down on some of these stereos, eh?'

b. to get in behind, see BEHIND *adv.*

c. to get in on (someone) **for** (something), to deprive (someone) of (something).
    1911 *Truth* 21 Jan. 6 I've no doubt the old josser who got in on me for my 'print' makes a practice of getting his paper that way every day—it looked like it from what the other fellow in the carriage told me.

d. to get into, to attack vigorously (food, work, a problem, etc); to get 'stuck in'.
    1916 THORNTON *Wowser* 47 Watty's quick at the start—gets into his log quicker 'n Dave. **1917** in Miller *Camps, Tramps & Trenches* (1939) 11 We got into a feed at a boarding house.

e. to get it on (with), to have a (sexual) affair with.
    1984 BEATON *Outside In* 50 Helen:.. You know, I'm too scared to talk to half the women in here just in case I get mugged for gettin' it on with someone's girl. *Ibid.* 86 Sandy:.. Although, last year was grouse when the Virgin Mary got stuck into Joseph for tryin' to get it on with one of them Wise Kings. *Ibid.* Glossary 109 Get it on with: to have an affair with; fuck.

f. to get off, in various phrases. **to get off one's bike (horse, the grass)**, see BIKE 1 a, GRASS 5 b, HORSE *n.*[1] 2.

g. to get on (it), to instigate a drinking session; to take up or go on 'the booze'.
    1907 *Truth* 21 Sept. 5 He saw some of the barmaids at the Cri. 'get on' occasionally. On one occasion a bottle of cham was brought to his room, but the barmaid who called in was only there a couple of minutes. **1970** SLATTER *On the Ball* 134 I had shaken him off as soon as we arrived in London on the U.K. leave scheme from

Italy because, when he gets on it, he is likely to put a man in crook with the provosts. **1988** McGill *Dict. Kiwi Slang* 49 *get on it* dedicated drinking of alcohol; eg 'Is that you Colin? Hey, what d'ya say we get on it tonight?'

h. to get stuck into, see STICK *v.*

i. to get to (someone), to attack; to 'get stuck into'.
1911 *Truth* 26 Aug. 5 It was shown that another youth named William Thomas Turner followed the arrested one, yelling, 'Get to the cops!' 'Pull the coat off the cops!' etc.

j. to get up. [AND 1835; *getting up* 1845–80.] To prepare (wool) for sale. Also as *vbl. n.*
1851 WELD *Hints to Intending Sheep-farmers* 3 The 'sorting' and 'getting up' of the wools has not hitherto been sufficiently attended to. **1858** ACLAND *Notes Sheepfarming NZ* 6 For some time New Zealand wool was sent to this country very badly got up, partly from carelessness, partly from inexperience of the sheep-farmers. **c1927** SMITH *Sheep & Wool Industry* 80 On all large stations..a wool-classer is employed at shearing-time to 'get-up' the clip.

get, *n.* [f. verb *to get* to clear off: cf. OED *get n.*[1] 4; AND 1898.] **to do a get** (occas. **make a git**), to make a hasty departure, to do a 'bunk'.
1907 *Truth* 21 Sept. 5 Miss Taylor had been carrying on with a boarder, and he was told to do a polite get. **1910** *Ibid.* 15 Oct. 5 Bert Hicks also threatened to hit witness unless he 'did a get'. **1914** GRACE *Tale Timber Town* 32 I must make a git. So long. **1917** let. in *Boots, Belts* (1992) A day or two ago one of them [*sc.* conscientious objectors] escaped, [*sic*] a chap had taken him to the canteen, and he did a 'get' from there. **1988** McGILL *Dict. Kiwi Slang* 37 *do a get* hasty retreat; eg 'C'mon, youse jokers, let's do a get before old Musty catches us.'

G.G. /ˈdʒiˈdʒi/. [Abbrev. of *Governor-General*, used freq. in newspaper headlines.] As **the G.G.**, the Governor-General.
1933 in *Na To Hoa Aroha* (1988) III. 64 The G.G. is visiting Samoa and some of the islands of the Cook group. **1941** BAKER *NZ Slang* 62 The terms *His Ex* or *the G.G.* for our Governor-Generals have long since passed into colloquial speech. **1986** *Evening Post* (Wellington) 27 June 17 [Heading] G-G fears for SA. The Governor-General, Sir Paul Reeves, fears [etc.]. **1988** *Through the Looking Glass* 37 It was the twilight of deb balls, that female rite of passage..no longer to the G-G at G-H, but to the the Bishop of Auckland. **1996** *Sunday Star-Times* 31 Mar. C3 The GG-ship, of course, came as a 'complete surprise' to Sir Michael.

ghoa, ghoai, ghoi, varr. KOWHAI.

ghooparee, var. KUPARU.

ghoorea, var. KURI.

ghost shark: see SHARK 2 (8).

ghotarre, var. KOTARE.

giant. In the names of plants and animals, see: BULLY *n.*[1] 2 (4), CRAB 2 (3), EAGLE 1, FORGET-ME-NOT, PETREL 2 (10), SPANIARD 2 (2), SQUID 2 (3), WETA 2 (3).

giant disc, *v. trans.* To break up (land) using a disc-harrow with large discs. See also DISC *v.*
1951 *Landfall* 18 175 Billy's going to cut out that manuka so I can giant-disc it and put in a crop of turnips. **1963** *Weekly News* (Auckland) 3 July 37 We climbed a hill giant-disced to grey dust with chopped vegetation showing through.

gib. Also **gib board**.

1. a. As **gib**, *ellipt.* for GIBRALTAR BOARD.
1982 *Pacific Index Abbrev.* 134 *gib* gibraltar fibrous plaster board panels (NZ)

Hence **gib** *v. trans.* To line (a wall, room) with gibraltar board, usu. as **gibbed** *ppl. a.* lined with gibraltar board; **gibbing** *n.*, gibraltar-board lining.
1985 *More* (Auckland) Oct. 37 [The room] is 'awaiting decoration'. Right now it is in a bare **gibbed** state. **1985** McGILL *G'day Country* 123 'You know, not done up. This is the way it [*sc.* the old house] was 125 years ago. Apart from that bit of **gibbing**.'

b. Comb. **gib-stopping**, the filling with plaster of gaps, nail cavities, etc. in laid gibraltar board.
1987 *Karori News* (Wellington) 24 Mar. 18 [Advt] Gib Stopping Specialist **1989** *Dominion Sunday Times* (Wellington) 3 Sept. 3 Mr Reid says he picks his roles carefully and has recently completed a gib-stopping course for when the work dries up.

2. As **gib board**, a shortened form of GIBRALTAR BOARD.
1964 *NZ Patent Office Jrnl. No.1019* 12 June Gib-board 73200 [filed] 7 May 1963..wall board. N.Z. Wallboards Limited. **1988** MACRAE *Awful Childhoods* 59 The specifications mentioned only the foundations, framing timber, gib board and windows. **1990** *Dominion* (Wellington) 20 Dec. 12 The boy had been thrown across a room and at a wall so hard his head had passed through the gib-board.

gibraltar board. [A proprietary name for a gypsum plasterboard with a trademark or motto 'As solid as the Rock of Gibraltar'.] An interior building sheet consisting of gypsum held between two layers of cardboard. See also GIB.
1932 *NZ Patent Office Jrnl.* [no number given] 1 Dec. Gibraltar board 31346 [filed] 19th July, 1932. As solid as the Rock of Gibraltar..Registration of this trademark [etc.]. N.Z. Wallboards, Limited. **1940** *Otago Daily Times* (Dunedin) 10 Feb. 4 [Advt] Build Strength into your walls with Gibraltar Board. **1960** CROSS *Backward Sex* 14 Across a tarsealed yard was the New Wing, equal parts plywood, gibralter [*sic*] board, tin and glass.

gidday. Also **g'day**. [Elliptical and variant forms of *good day*: cf. OED *good a.* 10 c and *good day*; AND 1857.] A familiar (usu. male) greeting.
1919 *Quick March* 10 July 21 'G'day,' he said... 'Seen yer pickshers in the papers. Have a drink!' **1943** MARSH *Colour Scheme* 35 'Good evening, Mr. Smith,' said old Rua... 'G'day Rua.' **1957** FRAME *Owls Do Cry* (1967) 38 He stopped to talk to Francie.—Gidday, cutie. **1966** BRAMBLEY *Sea-cockies of Manukau* 75 My Bill called to them 'G'day! What you got in there?' **1979** MARSHALL *Supper Waltz Wilson* 21 'Gidday,' said a voice behind him and Deaker turned to find a grinning Maori boy in khaki shorts. **1985** McGILL *G'day Country* 151 'G'day,' he said. 'Howareys?' 'Fine.'

Hence **gidday** *n.* usu. *pl.*, greetings.
1990 *Dominion* (Wellington) 28 Apr. 6 Our first human in 24 hours trudged up the hill toward us. As we exchanged giddays, I felt a pang of sadness.

giegie, var. KIEKIE.

gift duty. A term for duty levied on gifts of money or property exceeding a certain amount in value (see quot. 1964).
1909 *NZ Statutes* No.10 47 [Death Duties Act] Gift duty shall constitute a debt due and payable by the donor to the Crown on the making of a gift. **1916** *NZ Law Reports* 937 [The District Land Registrar], having meantime ascertained that if the transfer was complete, the transaction would be liable for gift duty, refused to register the transfer until the amount of gift duty was paid. **1924** *Ibid.* 503 Gift duty would be payable only when the property should be transferred. **1964** *Mozley and Whiteley's Law Dict.* 168 *Gift Duty.* A duty chargeable (subject to certain exemptions) in respect of any disposition of property which is made otherwise than by will, whether with or without an instrument in writing, without fully adequate consideration in money or money's worth. See Part IV of the Estate and Gift Duties Act 1955.

giggie, var. KIEKIE.

giggle-factory. *Obs.* Also **gigglehouse**. [AND 1919.] A psychiatric hospital. Compare US *laughing academy*.
1943 MARSH *Colour Scheme* 71 When I've taken over this joint the resemblance to a giggle-house will fade out automatically. **1951** PARK *Witch's Thorn* 159 'Poor coot, oughta be in the gigglehouse,' said a loud whisper. **1966** TURNER *Eng. Lang. Austral. & NZ* 135 *Heading for the giggle-factory* recently noted in New Zealand may be a facetious nonce-expression [for *not all there*].

giggy, gigi, varr. KIEKIE.

ginger ale. *Prison.* Rhyming slang for 'bail', money as security against the release of one charged with an offence.
1963 *Truth* 21 May 19 Her pot and pan had smacked it for a blue with the ducks and geese, but was out on ginger ale. ginger ale..bail.

gink. [Poss. f. Brit. dial. *geek*, *keek* a peep: AND 1945.] A look, glimpse, esp. in the phr. **to get (have, give) (one) a gink at**. See also GECKO *n.*[2]
1961 *Home Life* Mar. V. 2 A pakeha joker from up the road has a gink at me and says. **1963** HILLIARD *Piece of Land* 24 'Give us a gink at your pictures, Bert,' Charlie invited. **1970** DAVIN *Not Here Not Now* 276 Didn't I see you when I was having a gink at your truck. **1984** WILSON *S. Pacific Street* 71 Later on we got a closer gink from the jury box at the Maori chap. **1991** ELDRED-GRIGG *Shining City* 105 'Let's have a gink,' Sissy said... I saw a male lying on a bed.

giraffe beetle. Also **giraffe weevil**. *Lasior(r)hynchus barbicornis* (Fam. Brenthidae), a mainly night-flying borer with an elongated rostrum fancifully resembling the neck of a giraffe. **a.** As **giraffe beetle**.
1925 MILLER *Forest & Timber Insects in NZ* 19 The first family is the Brenthidae, represented in New Zealand by at least two species, commonly known as the 'giraffe-beetles' on account of the extremely long auger-like snout or beak by means of which the female bores a hole in dead wood in order to lay her eggs. **1955** MILLER *Nature in NZ* 28 Giraffe Beetles (Brenthidae) are remarkable insects. The New Zealand species (*Lasiorrhynchus barbicornis*) is dark brown with lighter markings on the elytra. **1966** *Encycl. NZ* III. 705 Beetle, giraffe..tuwhaipapa..*Lasiorrhynchus barbicornis*. **1976** *NZ Entomologist* VI. 173 The rostrum of the male giraffe beetles, with antennae and mandibles at the extremity, is equal to the length of the body. **1982** SHARELL *NZ Insects* 104 The male giraffe beetle has

under its long rostrum a row of rather long hairs like a brush.
b. As **giraffe weevil**.
1925 MILLER *Forest & Timber Insects in NZ* 52 The Giraffe Weevil. (*Lasiorhynchus barbicornis* Fabr.) This is one of the leading insects associated with the decay of dead timber. It is a curious and distinct insect; the colour is blackish-brown with yellow markings on the back. **1947** POWELL *Native Animals* 49 Giraffe Weevil (Lasiorrhynchus barbicornis) as the common name indicates, has an extremely long neck or proboscis... The larvae are active borers of a great variety of our soft-wood trees, but the perfect insect is by no means common. **1952** *JPS* LXI. 50 Tuwhaipapa, Tuwhaitara. *Lasiorrhynchus barbicornis*, an insect..; the god of a new-made canoe... This giraffe-weevil bears a striking resemblance to a Maori canoe. **1971** MILLER *Common Insects* 79 A unique and conspicuous boring species is the Giraffe Weevil (*Lasiorhynchus barbicornis*), a narrow elongate insect with an unusually long fore thorax and snout; the Maori called it *tuwhaipapa*, or *tuwhaitara*, and considered it to represent the god of a newly-made canoe, to which it has some resemblance. **1982** SHARELL *NZ Insects* 104 New Zealand has one of the most grotesquely shaped weevils, the giraffe weevil *Lasiorrhynchus barbicornis*, which belongs to the group of primitive weevils, the family Brenthidae.

Girls' War. *Hist.* See quot. 1932.
1932 S. Percy Smith in Marsden *Lett. & Jrnls.* (1932) 451 'In 1830,' [S. Percy Smith] states, 'an occurrence took place at the Bay of Islands which is very illustrative of Maori customs and which led to further Nga-Puhi expeditions against the southern tribes. It has been called the 'Girls' War' for this reason: The captain of a whaler, then anchored off Kororareka..took to himself two Maori girls as wives. Tiring of these after a time he took two other and younger girls (sisters) and discarded the first pair. Not long after, the four girls were bathing on the beach at Kororareka and were sporting and chaffing one another... From chaff they got to abuse, and finally to cursing in the Maori sense. The mother of the first two girls rushed into the water and nearly succeeded in drowning the other two girls. The first two girls were said to have been connected with the family of Te Morenga, an influential chief of Kawakawa, whilst the [other]..were connected with Rewa's family, one of the most important of the Bay chiefs... Ururoa, a chief of Whangaroa..came to Kororareka with a large force and proceeded to plunder the *kumara* plantations of the local people, i.e., Te Morenga's and Pomare's tribes. This was on March 5th, 1830. The missionaries used their utmost persuasion to avert a conflict, for the two parties were now in close proximity; but on the following day, owing to the accidental discharge of a musket which killed a woman of the invading party, a general fight was brought on. **1961** ROGERS (ed.) in Williams *Early Jrnls.* 155 [1 Mar. 1830] Ururoa and the natives from Wangaroa, Matauri, &c., assembled at Rangihoua to come against Korararika. [1961 *Note*] This is the beginning of what became known as the 'Girls' War'. **1982** MORTON *Whale's Wake* 71 [Brind] is best known..for being the cause of the Girls War in which some Maori women quarrelled..thus causing their tribes to come to their support. **1993** *Defence Quarterly* No.1 12 In 1830, the Ngapuhi defeated the Ngati Manu in the so-called 'Girl's War' for the right to reap the economic benefits of the town and the five pounds sterling utu from each ship's master for anchorage.

Gisborne cockroach: see COCKROACH.

give, *v.* In various phrasal uses: see also **to give it a go**, see GO *n.* 1; **to give it to the Belgians**, see BELGIAN A; **to give one goss**, see GOSS *n.*[1]; **to give it jaro**, see JARO; **to give (one) rats**, see RAT *n.*[2] 1; **to give it a spin**, see SPIN *n.* 2 b.
1. to give (something **or the game**) **best**. [f. Brit. dial.: AND 1888.] To give up, abandon an occupation or activity; to acknowledge defeat.
1881 BATHGATE *Waitaruna* 151 'This is no go, and we must give it best!... I'm full on this shooting racket.' 'You are adept at slang, Arthur, and no mistake.' **1910** *Truth* 2 Apr. 4 The Borough Council..failed to get the City Council and the St Clair Borough Council to join the St. Kilda body in buying the sections, and it therefore gave the thing best. **c1930** *Whitcombe's Etym. Dict. Aust.-NZ Suppl.* 4 *give best v.*i..to acknowledge defeat; to give up. **1971** NEWTON *Ten Thousand Dogs* 87 He mustered on that class of country..until he finally gave the game best at Winterslow in 1958.
2. to give (an activity, a habit, etc.) **away**. [Fig. use of *give away* to give as a present: AND 1948.] To give up, abandon.
1962 SYDER AND HODGETTS *Aust & NZ English* (1974) (TS) 410 *To give the grog away.* To give the grog up. To stop 'drinking' altogether. 'While you're having one or two (drinks) you haven't 'given her up. To give the grog away you mustn't have any.' **1988** McGILL *Dict. Kiwi Slang* 50 *give it away* to abandon, often in exasperation; eg 'Give it away, Sean, it's just not worth it.'
3. to give it in, esp. in the construction **I give you that in** and occas. *ellipt.* **give it**. [Poss. a variant of *give in..that* to admit: see OED *give v.* 59 a.] To admit in argument or under pressure.
1935 Otago p.c. R. Mason (1953). I give you that in. 'I admit that.' **1968** SLATTER *Pagan Game* 85 You gotta givit, those boys get away with murder really. *Ibid.* 162 He'll give it a burl, that boy, I'll give him that in.

givor /ˈgaivə/, var. GYVER.

gladdy, var. KORARI.

glamour boys. *WW2.* [Orig. applied to RAF personnel: see OED *n.* 3.] A term applied to units or arms of the Armed Services other than the speaker's, whose situation was perceived as less dangerous or more pleasant than the speaker's own. **a.** Members of the Third New Zealand Division who were transferred to the Middle East after serving in the Islands.
1941 *NZEF Times* 22 Dec. 22 Dave rose to great heights—heights that would make the tales of the 'glamour boys' or 'cocoanut [*sic*] bombers' pale into comparative insignificance.
b. Those parts of the 2NZEF (North Africa) who travelled to (or via) Britain.
1945 WEBBER *Johnny Enzed in Middle East* [glossary] *Glamour boys*: Fair Causus Belli in 2NZEF. Title bestowed by the First and Third Contingents upon the Second Contingent after it got a blighty. **1946** FULLARTON *We Walked Alone* 89 The Fifth Brigade—the Glamour Boys—were still showing the flag in England. **1967** ELLIOTT & ADSHEAD *Cowshed to Dog Collar* 81 'Were you in the first Libyan campaign in 1940?' 'No. I was one of the "G-lamour Boys". We didn't come over until well after that.'

Glasgow lease: see LEASE 4.

glass alley: see GLASSIE.

glass arm. *Morse operators. Obs.* See quot.
1995 *Sunday Star-Times* (Auckland) C4 My 96-year-old uncle, who was a supervisor of a telegraph department for more than 40 years, could vouch for the fact that morse key operators developed a repetitive disorder, then referred to as 'glass arm'.

glass eel: see EEL 2 (3).

glass-eye. *Obs.* An occas. early Nelson name for SILVER-EYE.
c1920 BEATTIE *Trad. Lifeways Southern Maori* (1994) 507 The 'glass-eye' had a Maori name in Nelson... This 'glass-eye' is variously called white-eye, ringeye, waxeye and blight-bird.

glassie. Also occas. **glass alley.** [Cf. OED *n.*[2] 1887, a (prized) marble with coloured patterns.] A glass marble, usu. transparent, and often a BOTTLIE (q.v.) from a soft-drink bottle.
1932 *Tararua Tramper* Jan. 2 One or two items [in the old whalers' rubbish heaps] stimulated the imagination, as did an occasional marble of the glassy, ally, or stoney type, which hinted at small boys. However, marbles was a game the whalers indulged in during the many days of the off-season. **1933** SCANLAN *Tides of Youth* 153 Reverend Mother talks of when she used to give you marbles for being a good little boy—pee-wees and agates, and stonies and glassies and a big tor. **1959** LAWLOR *Old Wellington Days* 37 The marbles [c1900] ranged from the clay ('stinker') variety to the more elaborate coloured 'glassies', the agates and the larger varieties. *Ibid.* 130 In those days [c1906] a 'bottlee', was, if inferior to a 'glassee', some degrees above a 'stinker'. **1964** HOWE *Stamper Battery* 67 'Go on, Snowy!..Two glass alleys from lemonade bottles if you do it.' [c1880s] **1972** SUTTON-SMITH *Folkgames Children* 174 Then there were the terms referring to particular kinds of marbles: for example, agates, aggies.. bottlies..glassies..pewees, pisswees..stinkies, stonies, stripies. **1983** STEWART *Springtime in Taranaki* (1991) 100 Marbles..was played with those..beautifully named taws such as agaties, cat's-eyes and glassies (glassies were to be found in the tops of lemonade bottles) and with the small clay cannon-fodder called dakes. You knocked your opponent's dakes out of the ring with your taw, and then you could keep them. **1988** *Through the Looking Glass* 7 I could spin a top 'overarm' and shoot alleys, glassies and bottlies with the best of the boys.

glasswort /ˈglaswɜt/. [Extended use of *glasswort*, the northern hemisphere salt-tolerant species of *Salicornia* (fam. Chenopodiaceae), formerly used, for its mineral-rich ash, in glass-making.] *Sarcocornia quinqueflora* (formerly *Salicornia australis*) (fam. Chenopodiaceae), an Australasian salt-marsh herb with succulent leaves.
1869 *TrNZI* I. (rev. edn.) 207 Glasswort. Salicornia indica, Willd. **1969** *Standard Common Names Weeds* 29 glasswort Salicornia australis Sol. ex Benth. **1978** MOORE & IRWIN *Oxford Book NZ Plants* 52 *Salicornia australis*, glasswort. Also a maritime plant, growing in rock crevices. **1988** DAWSON *Forest Vines to Snow Tussocks* 155 In the most exposed situations low growing succulent plants predominate, including..the glasswort *Sarcocornia quinqueflora*.

glassy, var. GLASSIE.

glaxo /ˈglæksʌu/. [A transf. use of the proprietary name of a babyfood supplement ('Glaxo Builds Bonnie Babies') produced by the Glaxo Company which had a factory at or near Tauherenikau in the Wairarapa. Cf. 1915 *NZ Patent Office Jrnl.*

[no number given] 10 June Glaxo 11958 [filed] 27th April, 1914. Glaxo Builds Bonnie Babies... Manufacturers: The 'Glaxo' Co. Palmerston North..Infants' and invalids' food.] In special collocations: **a.** *WW1*. **Glaxo baby (Glaxo man)**, applied in WW1 to a military trainee at Tauherenikau Camp; **Glaxo camp**, a nickname for the Tauherenikau Training Camp, situated near the Glaxo factory (also *attrib.*).
1918 Bolitho *Book of C1 Camp Tauherenikau* 7 **Glaxo babies**. **1918** *Quick March* 2 Sept. 5 'What he saw in C1 Camp' Before I joined the 'Glaxo' **Camp** My spirits soared..I felt my age—just twenty! **1919** *Triad* 10 June 41 The other [candidate] was a young graduate of Wellington who is just commencing practice here, but who was a 'Glaxo' camp man who could not qualify in time to fight for his country. **1921** *Quick March* 10 Dec. 43 To the **Glaxo men** of Tauherenikau [Military Camp] (if they remember the events of their camp at all) this wee verse will be a precis.

b. As **Glaxo baby**, ironically applied in the Depression to a young ('baby') member of the special police recruited to control strikers in Auckland. Cf. special *n.* 2 b.
1992 Park *Fence around the Cuckoo* 207 University, Grammar, and King's College old boys all became 'specials', and paraded the streets wearing tin hats and white armbands and carrying batons. They were much heckled..and nicknamed Glaxo babies. (This refers to a baby food of the time that produced alarmingly obese infants.)

glide-clip. [New SOD labels the term '*Austral.*'] A frequent name for a paper-clip fashioned from bent wire.
c1953 *Glide-clip* a common office name in State departments for what was usually termed on the manufacturers' containers 'paper clip'. Known to informants, and still in use in 1994. (Ed.)

glide time. Flexible (or flexibility in) working hours allowing for varied starting and finishing times, introduced to the State Services in the 1970s.
1977 Hall *Glide Time* 14 You look as if you spent the night there... Isn't that carrying glide-time to excess? **1988** McGill *Dict. Kiwi Slang* 50 *glide time* an attempt by the Public Service to let staff work the 40-hour week that suited them became the title of Roger Hall's blockbuster play and ever since the concept has been informally viewed as an excuse for skiving or working for the government at a pace that would suit the most laid-back snail.

glimmer. A marble name, poss. applied to one with glimmering specks in it when held to the light.
1936 Hyde *Passport to Hell* 25 George Bennett's marbles were worth talking about, being composed in equal parts of alley tors and glimmers. *Ibid.* 26 The beautiful little sparkly lights in the hearts of the glimmers when he held them up one by one to the gas-jet atoned for all else. **1938** Hyde *Godwits Fly* (1970) 26 Once Curly Adams' bag of marbles, glimmers and chalkies, came up [from the street-sewer, c1912] on the shovel, and the drain-men gave them to Eliza.

glip. *Whaling.* [Origin unknown.] A smooth oily patch left on the surface of the sea by a swimming, or recently submerged, whale.
1982 Grady *Perano Whalers* 14 Every time a whale sounds there is a slick, known to the old-time whalers as glip, left on the sea's surface. It is a smooth patch, left by a fast swimming whale, that alerts any gunner of [*sic*] any changes of course. **1982** Morton *Whale's Wake* 37 When whales submerge they leave an oily smooth patch on the surface of the sea, called a 'glip', which sometimes also exists near surfaced whales.

globefish. [Transf. use of northern hemisphere *globefish*.] *Contusus* (formerly *Sphaeroides*) *richei* (and also a few from other less common genera) of fam. Tetrodontidae, a round-bodied pufferfish which inflates its body when alarmed. See also mousefish, publican-fish, pufferfish, toadfish, toado.
1872 Hutton & Hector *Fishes NZ* 72 Tetrodon richei... Globe Fish. **1897** *TrNZI* XXIX. 2443 Before proceeding with the descriptions of the two globe-fish, it may not be out of place to give a short epitome of the present varieties of the group Tetrodontina so far proved to inhabit the waters surrounding New Zealand. **1913** *TrNZI* XLV. 234 *Spheroides richei. (Amblyrhynchotus richei)...* The little globe-fish is occasionally met with in Otago Harbour. **1927** Speight et al. *Nat. Hist. Canterbury* 202 The Globe fishes (*Spheroides*) are small with large heads and the body studded with tubercles. **1938** *TrRSNZ* LXVIII. 418 *Sphaerodes richei*. Globe-fish (stink-fish). **1956** [see publican-fish]. **1972** Doak *Fishes* 110 In southern waters a more common species is the globefish, *Spheroides richei*, a much smaller fish up to 13cm in length, with less prominent spines which only become erect when it inflates. **1982** [see pufferfish].

globo /ˈɡlʌubʌu/. *Hist.*
a. From the name of *Globo* Bank of New Zealand Estates Co. Ltd, a subsidiary set up in 1890 to sell land assets of the Bank of New Zealand and quickly used as a term of opprobrium by political opponents.
1890 *NZ Observer* 12 July 1 Before rejoicing over the gobbling up of *globo*, I should like to know who constitute the Assets Company... The news that the *globo* assets are to be taken over by a syndicate of London capitalists..has sent the colonial press into ecstasies of delight. **1890** *Otago Witness* (Dunedin) 10 July 23 A company is being formed to take over the *globo* assets from the bank [of New Zealand]. **1890** *NZ Observer* 22 Nov. 4 What price *globo* white elephant shares? **1937** Partridge *Dict. Slang* 333 *globos*. Debenture shares in Bank of New Zealand Estates: Stock Exchange (–1895). A. J. Wilson *Stock Exchange Glossary*.

b. In *transf.* use, as a term of opprobrium.
1890 *NZ Observer* 13 Sept. 7 To talk of the *globo* Press of New Zealand as being unmuzzled is rank humbug. *Ibid.* 20 Sept. 7 The first symptom that the [Sailors'] Home was being worked on *globo* orders was seen in a notice that the charge for board was raised from 12s 6d to 15s per week.

glory box. [Poss. a play on *hope chest* and 'hope and glory': but cf. Brit. dial. *glory-hole*: OED 1 b, a receptacle (as a drawer, room, etc.) where things are heaped together without any attempt at order or tidiness; AND 1915.] **a.** A chest in which a woman stores linen, clothes, etc., and various treasured things, usu. against the time when she will be setting up her own household; the contents of such a chest.
1917 Brown *Lay of Bantry Bay* 59 Each girl her glory box must see And glimpse a future, gaily bright, When sweet hearts now will husbands be... (Levin, 1916). **1926** *NZ Dairy Produce Exporter* 30 Sept. 34 Dorothy had seized upon two beautiful boudoir caps, declaring that they should never again find their way into Lillie's 'Glory box'. **1938** Hyde *Godwits Fly* (1970) 114 At home in the evenings, Carly sews for her glory box,.. Doilies, table-centres, nightgown-tops..are..folded away. **1949** Davin *Roads From Home* 129 Seeing the neatly folded linen there, the carefully worked doilies and table spreads, the unworn silk nightdress, she knew she had blundered on Moira's hoard, her glory-box. **1956** Dare *Rouseabout Jane* 125 I was initiated into the wonders of her 'glory box'. This box contained all her greatest treasures, mostly in the linen line. **1972** Mitchell *Pavlova Paradise* 182 *glory box:* Bottom drawer with lid on... Some girls have glory boxes so big they live in them. **1984** Ebbett *When the Boys were Away* 28 [Advt] Treasure Chest Regent Glory Box. The ideal personal Treasure Chest and small ottoman 62/6 or 1/- per week. **1991** Eldred-Grigg *Shining City* 70 'This is where Mum kept her treasures,' Fag said, lifting the lid of a glory box.

b. *transf.* A 'treasure trove'; or, ironically, a 'mixed bag'.
1992 *Dominion* (Wellington) 10 Mar. 6 [Heading] A glory box of political exploits. Future generations will be able to look back at the great exploits of the last Labour and the present National governments with fond memory.

glory hole. [f. an ironic application of *glory* to an unpleasant place or situation.]
1. *Freezing works*. The entrance to the disposal chute where oddments of meat, etc. are conveyed to a processor.
1976 Morrieson *Pallet on Floor* 94 He strode briskly, a quarter-filled sack of skids and gambols over his shoulder, along the siding, stepping over the bright blotches of blood..outside the 'glory hole'. *Ibid.* 94 Chunks of wool-denuded meat [from the slipe master] were tossed into a barrow and, at intervals, wheeled to the 'glory-hole'.

2. *Flaxmilling*. *Obs.* A space on the underside of a flaxmilling machine, the work-place of the person responsible for removing the stripped fibres.
1951 Hunt *Confessions* 42 A Maori showed us where [the old flaxmill] was, and when we asked him if there were any signs he replied: 'Te glory hole and te garden'. We found the old 'glory hole' of the mill where once the catcher boy sat, covered with green pulp and flax gum as it dropped from the stripper rollers overhead.

glory of the hills: see hill glory.

glow-worm. [Transf. use of Brit. *glow-worm Lampyris* spp.] Also **New Zealand glow-worm**. The larva of a fungus gnat *Arachnocampa luminosa* (fam. Mycetophilidae), having luminous internal excretary tubules attached to the gut.
1848 Taylor *Journal* (ATLTS) 28 Feb. V. 187 We noticed many glow-worms and from the entrance took several specimens of stalactites. **1866** Oct. in Buller *Birds NZ* (1873) 360 The feeding of this bird [*sc*. kiwi] at night with the large glow-worm ('toke-tipa' of the natives) is a very interesting sight. **1889** *AJHR* H-18 2 Notwithstanding the lights carried by the party, the roof of this cavern about and beyond the Monsters is seen to be studded with thousands of glow-worms, giving the dark vault the appearance of a starlit sky. **1892** *TrNZI* XXIV. 164 During the early part of June a young friend of mine..informed me that he had found some pupae of the New Zealand glowworm.., attached to some rocks in the big gully of the Botanical Gardens, Wellington. **1924** *Otago Witness* (Dunedin) 30 Sept. 15 A radiance became manifest..the radiance of such a

massed body of glow-worms as cannot be found anywhere else in the world. **1933** *Proc. Linn. Soc. London* CXLVI. 3 One of the most remarkable insects in the New Zealand fauna is the luminous larva which has long been known as the New Zealand Glow-worm. **1960** *NZ Holiday* XVI. 18 The Waitomo Cave is the home of the New Zealand glow-worm, an insect which in its larval stage—and there is always the odd hundred thousand in the larval stage—transforms a vast grotto into a glow-worm-illuminated fairyland. The glow-worm grotto is reached through passage-ways, chambers and lime-encrusted walls. **1984** BRASCH *Collected Poems* 97 Glow-worm, pearl of night, By your own light The traveller must know you. **1990** *Regional Park News* (Auckland) Mar. 18 Glow worms are common in the ranges. They enjoy a moist environment and can be found in banks and caves.

glue. ?Mainly *racing. Obs.* [Orig. and mainly US: HDAS *glue* n. 1 1896, 1941 quots. only; Wentworth & Flexner 'Because it keeps body and soul together. Not common.'] Money, cash, 'hoot'.
    1917 BROWN *Lay of Bantry Bay* 57 In Shannon, Buckley, Kereru..The Sports are piling up their glue, And conning weights by slush-light blue.

gluepot. [AND 1875–1966.] A mud hole or similar place, usu. on a road or track, in which vehicles are likely to get stuck; also a local name.
    1865 CHUDLEIGH *Diary* 15 May (1950) 184 Poor Walker has lost five horses, one died..one sunk in the Glue Pot and though there were seven men with ropes they could not move it. **1912** WILSON *Reminisc. Early Settlement Dunedin* 240 Carefully straddling high ruts [in the badly constructed road]..he would dodge all the 'crab-holes and glue-pots' with a dexterity born of long experience. **c1930** *Whitcombe's Etym. Dict. Aust.-NZ Suppl.* 4 *gluepot n.* a bad place in a road where vehicles are liable to get stuck.

glut. *Southland sawmilling.* [f. Brit. (esp. Sc.) dial. *glut* a wooden wedge: cf. OED *n.*[6] *techn.* or *dial.* a wedge of wood or iron; EDD *n.*[1] 1.] FILLET.
    1948 *NZ Forest Service* (TS memo from Conservator Forests, Auckland) 9 Aug. The rate of loading loose timber might be increased if greater use were made of cross and upright battens (referred to as *gluts* in Southland).

gnai, gnaio, varr. NGAIO.

go, *v.*

1. *Mountaineering.* [Used elsewhere but recorded earliest in NZ: see OED *go v.* B 19 c.] *trans.* Of a route, to work, to be accomplishable.
    1883 GREEN *High Alps* (1976) 232 The route to the northern ridges of the peak..would not 'go'.

2. *trans.* **to go** (a person), **to go it.** [f. *go n.* a fight: OED *n.* 4 b; AND 1938.] *trans.* To fight; to argue with; to scold.
    1964 PEARSON *Glossary* to Sargeson *Collected Stories 1935–63* (1964) 300 *going: going it,* arguing; *get going about,* started talking volubly about. **1967** GROVER *Another Man's Role* 6 The nights he wasn't working she'd be going him for sitting around the house.

3. In various phrases. **a.** Indicating speed, enthusiasm, activity: **to go a roarer,** see ROARER; **to go eyes out,** see EYE 1; **to go for one's life** [cf. OED *go v.* 2 b], esp. as an exclamation of encouragement, orig. indicating a wholehearted effort.
    1953 STRONACH *Musterer on Molesworth* 32 Breakfast at half-past one, and as soon as we start to climb, go for your life. **1988** MCGILL *Dict. Kiwi Slang* 51 *go for one's life* give something your complete effort, or encouraged to do so ; eg 'Look, she's alone now, you wimp. Here's your chance. Go for your life.'

b. Indicating a move to a worse situation or state of affairs: **to go back to the bush (mat)**; **to go bush,** see BUSH A 3 b, c, MAT 3 a; **to go down,** [cf. OED *go v.* 78 *go down* m *slang* (orig. U.S.) to happen. (1946)], of a situation, to deteriorate, to end in violence, disaster, etc.; **to go down the road (track),** see DOWN *prep.* 3; **go to the pack,** see PACK *n.*[2] 2.
    1995 *Sunday Star-Times* (Auckland) 16 Apr. sect. A 5 We ended up in a blue over it. I thought we were going outside for a smoke... I just lost my rag. I realised what was happening. I just knew it was going to go down, you can't stop it, it just goes down.

c. to go for the doctor, see DOCTOR *n.*[3] 1.

4. a. to go off (at) (to go off pop (at)) [AND *pop,* 1904; see OED *go v.* 85 n], to 'explode' with anger, to lose one's temper with; to reprimand, to scold angrily. Occas. **to send** (one) **off pop,** to drive one to an angry outburst (see quot. 1936).
    1905 *Truth* 16 Sept. 1 [The editor] went off pop at the premeditated insult. **1933** PRUDENCE CADEY *Broken Pattern* 127 There's no need to go off pop quite like that. **1936** LEE *Not So Poor* 108 My Daughter called out that he [*sc.* her father] was Spoiling <u>her</u> plants, that sent <u>him</u> of pop and he called out to her to hurry up and Die. **1946** SARGESON *That Summer* 33 Every chance he got he'd pick on me and go off pop. **1982** NEWBOLD *Big Huey* 248 Go off (at) (v) Lose one's temper, go berserk, riot.

b. to go rude at, to insult angrily.
    1980 LELAND *Kiwi-Yankee Dict.* 47 *go rude at:* to exercise the fine art of the insult with respect to someone.

5. go on!, an exclam. expressing disbelief or doubt; occas. surprise.
    1904 MCMURRAN *New York to NZ* 143 [Slang phrases and colloquialisms] When one is relating a surprising incident the Maorilander exclaims dubiously 'Go on!' **1934** MULGAN *Spur of Morning* 24 'Why, there are only two boys over seventeen.' 'Go on. What's that native forward? Twenty, I'll bet.' **1976** WILSON *Pacific Star* 94 'I'm browned off, boy,' he replied... 'Go on, you piker,' Joe said

6. to go to the grass, to abscond, disappear.
    1909 *Truth* 29 May 7 But, alack and alas, Eady has once more gone to the grass. His miraculous 'cure' has been exploded like a pricked balloon, and great was the noise and fall thereof.

7. *Prison.* **to go under,** to be convicted.
    1982 NEWBOLD *Big Huey* 248 Go under (v) To be convicted.

8. a. *Chatham Islands.* **to go up,** see UP *adv.* 1 b. (Also **to go down,** see DOWN *adv.* 1.)

b. to go up as high as Baldwin, see BALDWIN.

9. to go out (to go out with) [cf. OED 68 *go with*], to keep company with; to 'walk out' as sweethearts.
    1984 16–17 F E3 Pakuranga Coll. 27 Going out [F13M5] (courting) **1984** 14 F E124 Wgton Girls C. 27 Going out [F3] **1984** 15–17 F E2 Pakuranga Coll. 27 Going out with [F9M5] **1984** 14 F E119 Wgton Girls C. 27 Going out with [F4] **1988** MCGILL *Dict. Kiwi Slang* 51 *go out with* keep company with; eg 'Peter has been going out with Beryl for yonks, must be at least eight months.'

10. *Obs.* **to go through** [AND *obs.* 1882, 1896], to rob (someone).
    1909 *Truth* 18 Dec. 6 Maggie McNeil, alias Linton, and Annie Maud Sales..made their second bow before Magistrate Widdowson..to answer the more serious charge of having 'gone through' Otto Hansen for his pocket-book. **1910** *Ibid.* 19 Feb. 7 He intended to give the money to Dagg, but on his way back he was drugged in a hotel and was 'gone through' for all the money he had.

go, *n.*

1. *Ellipt.* for **go-by** in the phr. **to give** (one) **the go.** To give up, to cut relations with (a person), to give (one) the brush-off.
    1904 LANCASTER *Sons o' Men* 231 Give yer the go, 'as she?.. Got some chap better? **1988** MCGILL *Dict. Kiwi Slang* 50 *give the go* to reject a suitor or abandon a place or job; short for 'give the go-by'; eg 'Why don't we give this game the go, eh?'

2. In the phr. **on the go,** in progress; occas., about to happen, 'in the wind'.
    1905 THOMSON *Bush Boys* 18 They learned that something was on the 'go'. **1964** PEARSON *Glossary* to Sargeson *Collected Stories 1935–63* (1964) 300 go: in *a few sidebets on the go as well,* in progress.

3. In the phr. **to give** (something) **a go** [OED *go* 2: used elsewhere and recorded earliest in Australia (1908)], to give (a job, a proposal, etc.) a try, to have a shot at.
    1910 *Truth* 13 Aug. 1 The most recent attempt was made by Jabez Wolffe... Before him 'Monty' Holbein 'gave it a go' every now and again, but has apparently got tired of the business and handed it over to Wolffe. **1918** *Chron. NZEF* 11 Oct. 130 An interesting competition. Give it a go! *Ibid.* 22 Nov. 264 It's a bit tight, but we'll give it a go. **1926** DEVANNY *Butcher Shop* (1981) 71 You'll have plenty of time to learn to waltz..if you start now. Shift the table back..and give it a go. **1960** MASTERS *Back-Country Tales* 59 Earlier on I had noticed a steep shingle chute running down from the top on the far side, so rather than turn back I decided to give it a go.

4. a go! *Exclam.* [Prob. from the call at cribbage: see OED 6 b.] Truce! Pax! Enough!
    1948 MUNDY *There's Gold* 32 I gave Sam a good dusting..and Sam suddenly cried 'a go'.

5. In the phr. **from go to whoa** [AND 1971], from start to finish.
    1958 *Listener* 25 July 30 Basie Viviers the skipper was the most delightful character..with a ton of guts from go to whoa even when he was crook. **1978** MANTELL *Murder in Fancydress* 55 And we didn't have much time. Ten days from go to whoa. **1987** *Dominion Sunday Times* (Wellington) 28 June 3 We were given only 12 months to organise the thing from go to whoa and trying to put in place significant sponsorship in less than 12 months was very difficult. **1989** RICHARDS *Pioneer's Life* 44 The next day it was a ding-dong battle from go to whoa. **1995** *Sunday Star-Times* (Auckland) 19 Feb. sect. B1 It was an opportunity for them to explain their understanding of the situation from go to whoa.

6. fair go, see FAIR *a.* 2.

goa, goai, varr. KOWHAI.

goashore /ˈɡʌuəˌʃo(ə)/. *Hist.*

1. Also with much variety of form as **goahore; go-ashore, go-a-shore, go on shore; go shore; goshore, koeshooa,** etc. [Ma. *kōhua* /ˈkoːhua/

adopted early from a Ma. dial. having a variety of /h/ which could be perceived by English speakers as /ʃ/, the whole further shaped by analogy with English *go-(a)shore* (cf. the early 'transitional' forms *koeshooa, goahore*; and compare *goai* for *kowhai*, *Showracky* for *Hauraki* (quot. 1834 below), *taisho* for TAIHOA): Williams 126 *kōhua*..1. *Maori oven.* 2. *A vessel used for boiling food by means of heated stones, a boiler. Kōhua is related to Maori kohu, kokohu 'hollow'.*] A three-legged iron pot, often with two lugs by which it could be suspended, used as a boiler or cooking utensil. See also KOHUA.

[**1815** KENDALL *New Zealanders' First Book* 46 Koeshooa A pot.] **1834** MARKHAM *NZ* (1963) 45 The Natives now begin to use Iron pots, known to them by the name of, 'Go on Shores', from the circumstance of Boats going up and down the Rivers, coming to an Anchor and going on Shore to Cook, but the Natives prefer the Old plan [*i.e.* coppre Mouries] and I think they are right. *Ibid.* 57 We went to Showracky [sc. Hauraki] to get some more 'Go ashores' or Iron pots. **1839** LANG *NZ in 1839* 15 The New Zealanders, for example, observing that the sailors on board the whaling vessels that touched at their ports uniformly carried an iron pot with them to cook their provisions when they went on shore, conceived the words *Go ashore*, which they were accustomed to hear when preparations were making for landing, was the proper name for an iron pot and they have accordingly been adopted as such in the New Zealand language. **1843** *NZ Jrnl.* IV. 177 [The Maoris] boil the [shark] in their 'go shores', or small iron pots. **1852** *Austral. & NZ Gaz.* 24 Dec. 528 I managed to get a glimpse of the meat, or rather bone, which was nearly two feet in length, having been doubled at the hock so that it might be put into the pot, or as they call it, goahore. **1870** PRENTICE *A Tale NZ* (GALMS) 32 Our domestic economy [on our Otago run] was at first unique, the cooking gear comprised a couple of three-legged iron pots called go-ashore's, ditto tin cans named billy's [*sic*]. **1880** CRAWFORD *Recoll. of Travel* 175 Our potatoes..were boiled and sodden from an iron pot, or goashore, as it is called. **1905** [see KOHUA]. **1911** *Piraki Log* Gloss. corrections 151f. 'Kohua' was the Maori name for an iron cooking-pot; 'goashore', the whalers' nearest attempt to pronounce it (Canon Stack). **1917** *Chron. NZEF* 12 Dec. 205 W'ats t'e stockpot, anyway? Is it like t'e goashore, t'e kohua pot wit' t'e t'ree legs t'at t'e old Maori sold t'e land for? **1921** GUTHRIE-SMITH *Tutira* (1926) 150 Camp ovens, go-ashores, and billies stood on the floor, or were slung from bars above the empty hearth. **1936** BEASLEY *Pioneering Days* 35 This [common utensil] was a round kettle-like pot of considerable dimensions with legs like a camp oven and with a handle to enable it to be hung over the fire. This was commonly called a 'go-ashore'. **1953** *Landfall* 27 13 Edwards had a whare with a roof of thatch, A Brown Bess, a go-ashore, ..Six fat grunters and a small spud patch. **1970** SANSOM *Stewart Islanders* 113 For although they [sc. the women on Stewart Island in 1872] had a camp oven, a 'go-ashore' or witch's pot, the round pot on legs..their homes required much else.

2. Any of several early anglicizations or re-formations of Maori proper names, possibly given as nicknames, with a play on English 'go ashore'.

1817 NICHOLAS *Voyage NZ* I. 210 Tarra, besides his head wife who was nearly as old as himself, had got another in the full bloom of youth, and extremely handsome. This lady, whose face was familiar to all the English sailors that happened to touch here [sc. North Auckland] went by one of those arbitrary names which they are so fond of assigning to women of her character; and was called by them Mrs. Goshore, a corruption, it would seem, of the words *go on shore*, and originating, perhaps, in some alluring request to that purpose on the part of the frail one herself. **1842** *NZ Jrnl.* III. 259 A small settlement belonging to Te Waukau (alias Goashore). **1878** HEBERLEY *Autobiogr.* (ATLTS) 27 The name of the Native that killed the man [c1834 near Cook Strait] was called goashore.

3. *South Island.* As **Go-ashore (Oashore, Oishew, Orsha)**, a southern whalers' early transliteration and re-formation of *Oi(o)h(o)a* or *Ohoa*, a place-name on Banks Peninsula (poss. attracted to the form *go-ashore* of 1 above), and later further anglicized to a more familiar *Horseshoe* (*Bay*).

1839 *Piraki Log* 31 Oct. (1911) 102 found it to be two Mowries from Bloody Jack, who was in Oashore Bay with fifteen boats. [**1911** Note in Glossary 162 Probably this bight, and the now-called 'Horseshoe Bay', were originally named 'Go-ashore'.] [**1840** *Stanley to Hobson* 17 Sept. in *GBPP House of Commons 1841 (No.311)* 82 [Akaroa table.] Occupation Piraki... Whaling station..Oishew... Whaling station..[Oioha] Rouncataki..Squatters.] **1841** *Piraki Log* 12 Apr. (1911) 123 In the afternoon went to Go'ashore in the boat. [Oahoa Bay s. from Piraki] [**1842** *Piraki Log* 30 Apr. (1911) 126 Brown from Orsha came and took off his bellows, nail-mould, and a loan of an anvil.] **1842** *Smith's Report* in Wakefield *Handbook NZ* (1848) 343 Cattle have been driven from Oihoa (or Go-ashore),.. to Akaroa in about eight hours.

goatfish. [Spec. use of *goat-fish*, a name given to several species of fish with chin barbels.] Any fish of the fam. Mullidae, esp. *Upeneichthys lineatus* (formerly *porosus*), *red mullet* (MULLET 2 (2)).

1922 *NZJST* May V. 93 Upeneus porosus... *Red Mullet*. Sold as 'goatfish' in Auckland, where it is fairly common. **1956** GRAHAM *Treasury NZ Fishes* 407 Goatfish *Barbupeneus signatus*. **1966** [see MULLET 2 (2)]. **1972** DOAK *Fishes* 43 Family: Mullidae Red mullet *Upeneichthys porosus*... Like all the Mullidae or goatfish family, the re[d] mullet frequents sandy bottom areas near rocks and reefs. Beneath its chin hangs a pair of long barbels, well provided with taste buds. **1982** [see MULLET 2 (2)]. **1986** PAUL *NZ Fishes* 95 *Goatfishes*. A family..of brightly coloured coastal fishes, all rather similar in shape. Their chin barbels are used for locating food.

goblin orange. [f. a resemblance of the fruit to tiny oranges.] The orange-coloured edible berry of the PATOTARA 1 q.v.]

1947 HUTCHINSON *At Omatua's Fireside* 127 The vernacular [name] varies in different districts... Leucopogon fraseri..heath, patotara, goblin orange.

gobstopper. [Used elsewhere (OED 1928) but recorded earliest in New Zealand.] A large (approx. 1 cm diam.) usu. spherical, hard lolly.

1906 *Evening Post* (Wellington) 28 Sept. 18 A penny 'gobstopper' a seemingly innocuous child's lolly, was the indirect cause of a spectacular fire..[at] Invercargill, last night. **1977** SUTHERLAND in *NZ Short Stories* (1984) 245 'Gob-stoppers in your mouth. *Two.*' **1988** *Univ. Entr. Board Bursaries Eng. Exam.* 6 I went to the milkbar and bought a gobstopper and some other lollies.

God's Own. Also **Godzone** (occas. **godzone**), **Gordzone**, **Gors Own**. In full **God's own country**.

1. a. As **God's own country** [orig. US *God's (own) country*, 1865: see OED *country* 2 b], New Zealand regarded, often ironically ('God's own country, and the devil's own mess'), as an earthly paradise, a catchphrase popularized during the political times of Richard John Seddon (Premier 1893–1906).

1892 *Star* (Auckland) in Bailey & Roth *Shanties* (1967) 82 Give me, give me God's own country (from a spieler's point of view), Where the scripper and the sharper conjugate the verb 'to do'. **1907** *Truth* 13 Apr. 4 A cool 'thou.' is not to be looked askance at at any time, and taxing Chows as they enter Gordzone Country is a profitable bit of business. **1926** DEVANNY *Lenore Divine* 20 [Richard John Seddon] the popularly acclaimed uncrowned king of the land he himself had named 'God's own Country'. **1939** CRESSWELL *Present Without Leave* 172 Their own country, which is an annex of the Neo-christian deity himself (God's Own Country, they call it, like 'The Queen's Own Rifles'). **1943** MARSH *Colour Scheme* 239 I venerate the British Commonwealth of Nations and the idea of a spy in God's Own Little Country gets my goat good and proper. **1957** GOLDBLATT *Democracy at Ease* 5 They were very soon to be assured that they inhabited 'God's Own Country'. **1969** MASON *Awatea* (1978) 110 'E te iwi pakeha! You God's-own-country scum!'

2. *Ellipt.* **God's own**, often in joc. form **Godzone** (**God-zone**, occas. **Gordzone**. **a.** New Zealand.

1916 *Shell-shocks* 66 He [sc. Bill Massey] is sure to have all his work cut out in suitably replying to all the nice things people..will say about him and his Army of Heroes from Gors Own, down under. **1917** *Great Adventure* (1988) 163 We are still approaching the last cape.., our last glimpse of God's own. **1926** TED WILDEY in *Aussie* XV 15 Sept. (1926) (NZ Section) xvi In the bad old days, this [far south] portion of 'God's own' had a reputation, sinister and sanguinary. **1964** REID *Book NZ* 25 Despite their smugness, too, about the felicities of 'God's Own Country' ('Godzone' simply, to the irreverent)..New Zealanders are not completely lacking in..self-criticism. **1972** MITCHELL *Pavlova Paradise* 63 In God-Zone you approach different topics with an adjustment of your volume control. **1985** SHERWOOD *Botanist at Bay* 45 'How long have you been in godzone?' 'Godzone. Is that a Maori expression?' 'Godzone country..is our proud name for..New bloody Zealand.' **1990** *Evening Post* (Wellington) 29 Dec. 4 [Heading] Whither God's Own in 1991?

b. *attrib.*

1979 *Listener* 7 Apr. 11 Out of the 'Godzone English' words on the *Listener* cover, all but two (kainga and kanuka) were already in the Hamlyn World Dictionary, published 1971. **1983** HULME *Bone People* 31 This godzone baby talk. Hottie lolly cardie nappy, crappy the lot of it, she snarls to herself. **1992** *Dominion* (Wellington) 17 Oct. 11 *Godzone Skies* is an excellent introduction to astronomy.

Hence **Godzoner**, a New Zealander.

1979 ASHTON-WARNER *I Passed This Way* (1980) 172 Norma's nine children..have as many good looks as any other Godzoners.

3. *Jocular variants.* **a. God's own paddock**, applied to gold-rich Waihi, with a play on PADDOCK *n*.² 1.

1906 *Truth* 20 Oct. 3 Way back at Waihi, where the gold comes from, things aren't too sudden and the pace that kills is an altogether unknown quantity in that benighted portion of 'God's own paddock'.

b. God's Loan Country, **Ward's Loan Country**, etc., two of various ironic variants (mainly in *Truth* weekly) critical of the contemporary Government borrowing policy under the Prime Minister (1906–12), Sir Joseph Ward (1856–1930).

1909 *Truth* 2 Oct. 6 He arrived in God's Loan Country from South Africa Boer War time, and industry

godwit.

a. Any of several migratory wading birds of the genus *Limosa* (fam. Scolopacidae) (but usu. the **eastern bar-tailed godwit** *L. lapponica baueri*) which breed in the northern hemisphere and summer in the southern. See also CURLEW 2, KUAKA a.

1835 YATE *NZ* (1970) 69 *Katatai*... [The banded rail] answers nearest to the godwit, of any I am acquainted with. **1841** BEST *Journal* 15 May (1966) 311 I also saw a fine Bittern, a small white Gull, a wader like a Godwit and shot a Pukako. **1844** COLENSO *Excurs. Northern Is.* in Taylor *Early Travellers* (1959) 44 Here..the Dusky Plover..and the Southern Godwit (*Limo*[*s*]*a*..) were in large flocks. The natives call..the latter, Kuaka. The Godwit is, when in season, very fat, and good eating. **1871** HUTTON *Catalogue Birds NZ* 28 Godwit. Curlew. Kuaka. *L. Novae Zealandiae*. **1888** BARLOW *Kaipara* 31 What are called curlew here are really godwit. **1901** *TrNZI* XXXIII. 217 About the end of November flocks of a..wading bird appear on the swamp—the godwit, or curlew as it is more commonly called. **1922** COWAN *NZ Wars* (1955) II. 314 Mr. Pitcairn..was killed on Uretara Island, where he was camped shooting *kuaka* (godwit). **1946** [see KUAKA 1]. **1951** HUNT *Confessions* 146 At the end of the [Farewell] spit we made acquaintance with the myriads of sea birds that abound there—godwits, or curlews, as they are sometimes called. **1955** OLIVER *NZ Birds* 286 *Eastern Bar-tailed Godwit. Kuaka Limosa lapponica baueri*. The Godwit, which is a well-known migrant to New Zealand, and whose long annual journeys never fail to excite wonder, was evidently the bird mentioned by Yate in 1835. **1966** BAXTER *Collected Poems* (1980) 336 Boulders interrupt the long jetty from whose black asphalt tongue the Godwits fly to their Siberian lakes. **1985** SHERWOOD *Botanist at Bay* 205 Parengarenga harbour..[was] normally deserted, except by bar-tailed godwits when they assembled there for the annual migration to Siberia and Alaska. **1991** *Evening Post* (Wellington) 15 Apr. 11 'Godwits are a striking wading bird..they are not a cheap dinner,' he said.

b. *fig.* with reference to the New Zealander's compulsion to travel 'home' to Britain.

1938 HYDE *Godwits Fly* (1970) xx Most of us here are human godwits; our north is mostly England. Our youth, our best, our intelligent, brave and beautiful, must make the long migration, under a compulsion they hardly understand; or else be dissatisfied all their lives long. They are the godwits.

godzone: see GOD'S OWN.

goey, gohi, goi, varr. KOWHAI.

gold. *Mining.* See also *drift-gold* (DRIFT *n.*²), *matrix gold* (MATRIX), *nest of gold* (NEST 1), *reef gold* (REEF 2).

1. In the phr. **to be on (upon) gold,** of a claim [AND 1871], to contain gold-bearing material; of a miner [AND 1893], to be working gold-bearing material.

1867 *West Coast Times* in Bromby *Eye Witness Hist.* (1985) 49 It was first stated that every claim was on gold; the poorest paying £40 per week. **1873** PYKE *Wild Will Enderby* (1889, 1974) III. i 75 They are on heavy gold, too, for I saw some of the stuff that they traded away. **1874** BATHGATE *Col. Experiences* 129 The Chinese, with their frugal habits when not 'on-gold'..were making [the claim] pay handsomely. **1888** PRESHAW *Banking Under Difficulties* 157 Nearly all were on gold, but no pile claims. **1946** MILLER *There Was Gold* 69 I was on gold all the time.

2. Used *attrib.* in Comb. **gold belt, days, -hunting** [AND 1851], **prospecting, -seeker** [AND 1852], **zone**.

1861 *Otago Witness* (Dunedin) 23 Mar. 10 Had the diggers, instead of going up Rolling river, crossed it at its junction with the Wangapeka river, opposite the saddle, and have gone westward up the Wangapeka to its source, they would..have got into the richest portion of the **gold-belt**. **1898** HOCKEN *Contributions* 108 At length the **gold days** and Cobb's coaches ended this uncertain travel. **1887** PYKE *Hist. Early Gold Discoveries Otago* (1962) 37 Peters had persuaded a man named Jenkins to accompany him in his **gold-hunting** expeditions, and for some time Jenkins 'fossicked' about the Woolshed. **1861** GABRIEL READ in *Handbook NZ Mines* (1887) 4 I take the liberty of troubling you with a short report on the result of a **gold-prospecting**..which occupied me about ten days. **1862** WEKEY *Otago As It Is* 51 The first detachment of **gold-seekers** gradually arrived [at Dunstan]. **1931** *NZJST* XII. 159 This non-discovery of payable auriferous ground was in great part due to the inexperience..of the gold-seekers. **1968** SEDDON *The Seddons* 37 In the bush near Jacksons..there are mounds which mark the place where three gold seekers died. **1971** GRIFFITHS *King Wakatip* 73 The Rees family barely had time to get settled again at their home station before the quiet pastoral barony..was invaded by a noisy..avalanche of gold-seekers. **1914** PFAFF *Diggers' Story* 42 We..did not locate payable gold. As a matter of fact we passed the **gold zone** as it is now recognised, as the alluvial only extends a certain distance back from the coast line.

3. Special Comb. **goldbag,** a (usu.) chamois bag used to hold alluvial gold; **gold-bed,** the auriferous layer immediately above bedrock; **gold box,** the receptacle in which auriferous material ('paydirt') is stored preparatory to being washed; **gold broker** [AND 1854], one who deals in gold; **gold buyer** [AND 1852], one who buys gold from miners, usu. on behalf of a bank; **gold-buying** *ppl. a.*; **gold circular,** a periodical official notice of information about a particular goldfield; **gold-coach,** the vehicle carrying gold from goldfields to a safe depository; **gold-combing** *vbl. n.*, searching or fossicking for gold (see COMB *v.*); **gold commissioner,** COMMISSIONER 1; **gold-crushing,** the crushing of auriferous quartz, etc. to allow extraction of gold; **gold-dish,** DISH *n.*¹, PAN *n.*¹; **gold-dredging** *ppl. a.*, pertaining to the collection of auriferous material by special dredges; **gold drift,** DRIFT *n.*²; **gold escort** [AND 1852], an armed party, usu. of mounted constabulary, responsible for guarding gold being transported from the diggings to a depository (see also ESCORT); **gold fever** [AND 1851; US 1847], an overwhelming urge to seek for gold and an associated state of irrational excitement; **gold flake,** gold whose particles take the shape of flakes (see also FLAKE); **gold-getter,** one who prospects for and obtains gold; **gold mania** [AND 1851; US 1849], see *gold fever* above; **goldpan,** DISH *n.*¹; **gold-panner,** a name applied to a modern amateur or 'weekend' gold-seeker; **gold receiver** *Otago*, an official accepting gold for safe-keeping; **gold-reefing** *ppl. a.*, pertaining to the mining of gold from quartz reefs; **gold-rush** [AND 1893; US 1876], a sudden influx of people to a newly-discovered goldfield (see also RUSH *n.*); **gold-saving,** action or process of recovering gold from auriferous material; **goldsaving cloth,** BLANKET 2; **gold saving table,** TABLE 1; **gold-tax** *hist.*, a tax levied by Provincial Governments on gold produced; **goldtown,** a town (often now a ghost-town) once famous for its gold production; **gold-wash,** the loose alluvial auriferous material washed down from an ancient lode; **gold-washing** *vbl. n.* (a) the process of forming *gold-wash* (b) [AND 1850; US 1832] the process of separating alluvial gold from *gold-wash*; **gold workings** [OED 1872], a place where gold-digging or gold-washing is carried out.

1864 BARRINGTON 20 July quoted in Taylor *Early Travellers* (1959) 419 He remembered seeing the **goldbag** at his feet but he was so cold and worn out that he never thought of picking it up. [Barrington, in desperate straits, had thrown away his swag and most of its contents.] **1907** DRUMMOND *Life & Work of Richard John Seddon* 12 At the Five-mile diggers carried the gold dust to Okarito to sell in billies, their ordinary chamois leather gold-bags being too small to contain their rich harvests. **1867** HOCHSTETTER *NZ* 113 They began 'deep sinkings', and after having dug to a depth of about 130 feet..struck a second **gold-bed**. **1905** *Otago Daily Times* (Dunedin) 25 Feb. in Evans *Waikaka Saga* (1962) 42 Cheyne then got a board and one of the plushes from the manager's office, laid the plush on the board, and fixed the board from the **gold box** to the streaming down pipe. Cheyne then took a quantity of sand out of the box, put it on the board, and turned the water on, and washed the sand back into the gold box. The gold remained on the plush. **1977** *Sunday Times* (Wellington) 27 Nov. 17 He shovels the black sand into the gold box, washes it through with water pumped from the lagoon on the other side of the sand hills. The gold falls on to the plush ('I just use an ordinary towel') which is then shaken into a baby's bath. **1852** *Gold Circular* 21 Dec. in Swainson *Auckland* (1853) 109 There can be no doubt that for good clean gold, ready market at fair prices will be found. Albert W.M. Hansard, **Gold Broker**. **1914** PFAFF *Diggers' Story* 43 The **gold buyer** from the Bank of New Zealand..rushed out to see the fun. **1930** DOBSON *Reminiscences* 123 They mistook George Dobson for a gold-buyer named Fox, who they heard was going to Greymouth with the gold he had bought. **1971** GRIFFITHS *King Wakatip* 83 He is carrier,... gold buyer, slaughterman..land agent, station-holder. **1925** BATHGATE *Random Recolls.* 27 Skinner..had been robbed when returning from a **gold-buying** expedition to the Nevis. **1853** SWAINSON *Auckland* 105 A few days after the sale [11 December 1852], the following **Gold Circular** was published, describing the quantity, character, and other particulars of the parcels of gold which had recently arrived from the [Thames] goldfield. **1949** SHAW & FARRANT *Taieri Plain* 36 It must have been impressive to see the **gold-coach** come swinging down the cutting accompanied by a mounted escort. **1938** HYDE *Nor Yrs. Condemn* 217 Once I was nearly going **gold-combing** with him, but I changed my mind and went to quod instead. **1867** HOCHSTETTER *NZ* 112 Mining statutes and digger licenses [*sic*] were issued, **gold commissioners** were installed, and escorts were established. **1859** THOMSON *Story NZ* (1974) II. 198 The gold was found both in quartz fragments and scattered through clay and sand;.. **Gold-crushing**, it was believed, would prove productive. **1967** MACNICOL *Echoes Skippers Canyon* 62 Had they carried a pick and shovel and a **gold-dish** they would have been welcomed. **1970** WOOD *Gold Trails Otago* 7 During prospecting the gold was separated from the dirt by hand panning in a gold-dish, but it was slow, tiring work. **1914** PFAFF *Diggers' Story* 123 The Okarito Gold Dredging Co. was one of the first..at the beginning of New Zealand's somewhat disastrous **gold-dredging**

boom. **1870** *TrNZI* II. 371 '**Gold drift**' consists of sand and gravel containing gold, and is formed by the action of running water in streams, or water in motion, as along a sea or lake beach. **1865** CHUDLEIGH *Diary* 18 July (1950) 194 Mr. Sherman the head of the Police and **Gold escort**. All police here are mounted and have pistols swords etc. **1881** NESFIELD *Chequered Career* 78 The gold escort was expected, and they agreed to murder all who came that road that day. **1914** PFAFF *Diggers' Story* 134 I once went to Charleston..in company with the Gold Escort, and it was a picture to see those fine troopers turn out, 'armed to the teeth'. **1925** BATHGATE *Random Recolls.* 15 Among other duties they formed the gold escort, and once a fortnight brought the gold to town [Dunedin]. **1949** REED *Story Canterbury* 265 A bank officer having been stuck up and robbed of some gold, the Provincial Council resolved to institute an armed gold escort. **1976** VEITCH *Clyde on Dunstan* 19 The first Gold Escort left Clyde for Dunedin on 3 October 1862, with 6031 oz. gold securely strapped on packhorses, under the supervision of Major Bracken and three troopers. **1857** *Lyttelton Times* 2 Sept. 4 The symptoms of the '**Gold Fever**' begin to be daily more distinct. **1862** CHUDLEIGH *Diary* 1 Sept. (1950) 56 The gold fever has taken every other man in the place. **1879** HAAST *Geol. Canterbury & Westland* 465 The gold said to have been obtained during the gold fever of 1865–70 in the Malvern Hills..proved to be either iron pyrites..or to put upon it a charitable construction..had been lost by accident. **1894** WILSON *Land of Tui* 109 For what, after all, is this gold-fever but gambling in its most incurable form. **1931** COAD *Such Is Life* 48 The two brothers Hitching had caught the gold-fever, and had forsaken their ordinary avocations..to try their luck on the newly discovered field. **1945** HALL-JONES *Hist. Southland* 108 Their station life was their main concern, and when the gold fever broke out not a one abandoned it for the fierce quest of sudden wealth. **1962** EVANS *Waikaka Saga* 85 But he had the gold fever really and truly, and though he got no gold he continued to work this claim till he was unable to walk the distance. **1976** VEITCH *Clyde on Dunstan* 12 Thousands were smitten with gold fever and it seemed that every man who could move was obsessed with the one aim. **1984** BOYD *City of the Plains* 23 Smitten with gold fever, he set off for diggings. **1853** SWAINSON *Auckland* 112 In the specimens of the gold-bearing veins of quartz of felspartick appearance, the **gold flakes** stand boldly out without any foreign substance between, and are easily bent or broken off. **1939** BEATTIE *First White Boy Born Otago* 169 During his sojourn on the diggings the narrator became acquainted with some **gold-getters** whose names are writ large on Otago's mining history. **1851** *Lyttelton Times* 12 July 5 The **gold-mania** at Sydney. **1853** ROCHFORT *Adventures Surveyor in NZ* 71 I find that the gold mania, though partially subsided, has not by any means worn off. **1940** *Tales Pioneer Women* (1988) 291 The original prospectors washed the gold-bearing soil in 'cradles' and '**gold-pans**'. **1981** HENDERSON *Exiles Asbestos Cottage* 115 Away up in the mists, hunting for minerals and wildflowers, then spiraling down into some sunless gorge, goldpan in hand or sluicebox shovelling. **1985** SHERWOOD *Botanist at Bay* 120 'This is the place,' said Moffat, looking round among the wreckage of the **gold-panners'** huts. **1970** WOOD *Gold Trails Otago* 5 This they lodged at Dunedin [in 1862] with the Chief **Gold Receiver** and, when granted a reward.., they revealed the location of their find. **1976** VEITCH *Clyde on Dunstan* 11 As it was now very likely that others would soon be arriving on the scene, Hartley and Reilly decided to go to the Gold Receiver in Dunedin with whom they lodged 87 pounds of gold. **1867** COOPER *Digger's Diary* (1978) 8 Men are working here with an energy..which I suppose can only be equalled..in other **gold-reefing** districts. **1931** COAD *Such Is Life* 48 This conversation took place on the Westland gold-field in the spacious days of the **gold-rush**. **1940** STUDHOLME *Te Waimate* (1954) 140 During the Gold Rush most of the fats went to the West Coast. **1965** McLAGLAN *Stethoscope & Saddlebags* 178 The laws of hospitality must be observed, and gold rush hospitality demanded that guests be given a drink. **1971** GRIFFITHS *King Wakatip* 112 The dancing rooms, prostitutes, billiard rooms, grog-shops..were among the inevitable facilities in gold-rush Queenstown. **1981** MARSH *Black Beech & Honeydew* 108 Ghost-towns with their shells of gold-rush pubs have not yet been smothered by bush or cleared to make roads. **1967** MAY *West Coast Gold Rushes* 526 Dead work: all preparatory work on a claim—sinking shafts, driving tunnels, constructing a race—before **gold-saving** commences. **1935** goldsaving cloth [see TABLE 1]. **1952** HEINZ *Prospecting for Gold* 48 A novel method of elevating in use in Westland was the 'Blow up'. The principle is similar to the hydraulic elevator, but in reverse... The water pressure forced the sands and gravels to the surface on to the **gold saving tables**. **1951** CRESSWELL *Canterbury Tales* 66 For a while, two million pounds worth of gold a year was recovered, and as Canterbury had jurisdiction over the whole area and collected the **gold-taxes**, the general prosperity may be imagined. **1980** McGILL *Ghost Towns NZ* 140 An epitaph surely for all bust **goldtowns**. **1908** *NZGeol.SB (NS)* No.5 38 We also find that the richest **gold-wash** always occurs on the inner or concave side of the curves in the course of a river. **1864** HOCHSTETTER & PETERMAN *Geol. NZ* 88 By the gradual wearing away of these rocks..large masses of debris have been formed, and nature itself has executed an operation of **gold-washing**, by collecting the heavier particles and depositing them in the gullies of streams, or in the conglomerates covering the slopes of the hills. **1887** PYKE *Hist. Early Gold Discoveries Otago* (1962) 15 I have nowhere yet known of any individual success at the occupation of gold-washing or digging as a business. **1931** LOVELL-SMITH *Old Coaching Days* 30 They despatched the late Mr. William Crawley..with a load of timber prepared for miners' cradles for gold-washing. **1873** PYKE *Wild Will Enderby* (1889, 1974) I. iv 17 The Dunstan **gold workings** were of two kinds—technically known as 'beach claims' and 'bank claims'. **1879** HAAST *Geol. Canterbury & Westland* 111 In order to visit the gold workings at and near Kanieri township, I crossed the river from Woodstock.

4. *fig.* or *transf.* **a.** Money.
1974 MORRIESON *Predicament* (1981) 98 The girl's under age... That's a twelve-month rap for carnal knowledge. I hope he's got plenty of gold.

b. See *good as gold* (GOOD *a.* 2 b). Also in the phr. of similar meaning **to be a gold watch** (or **she's a gold watch**), said to a person or of a thing giving satisfaction.
1987 Wellington taxi despatcher 10 Apr. 11.25 p.m. on the FM band. *T.D.* There? Cab six. *Cab six.* Yeah, I've got your Egmont Street. *T.D.* You're a gold watch, a gold watch.

c. As **gold top**, a kind of toadstool.
1991 *Dominion* (Wellington) 13 May 1 Invercargill police said..there had been an upsurge in the number of people out looking for the mushrooms, colloquially known as blue-meanies and gold tops.

Gold Coast.
a. [Prob. influenced by the name of the former West African colony, *Gold Coast*.] A former name for the SI WEST COAST, so-called from its rich goldfields. See also *Golden Coast* (GOLDEN 2).
1867 HOCHSTETTER *NZ* 115 The Wahi punamu of the Maoris (the greenstone coast) may now truly be called the New Zealand Gold-coast. **1868** DILKE *Greater Britain* I. 335 As there are no horses [in Hokitika] except those of the Gold-Coast Police, they cannot enjoy much riding.

b. *Golden Coast* (b) (see GOLDEN 2); the Wellington west coast.
1985 McGILL *G'day Country* 74 The Manawatu and the Gold Coast are very much the home leg for me, a route I could drive..in my sleep. **1986** *Contact* (Wellington) 11 July 2 Two Gold Coast residents have written to me complaining about this new scheme of dredging for pipis in-shore along the Paraparaumu beaches. **1987** KNOX *After Z-Hour* 208 We may have taken Mike's car up the Gold Coast at Anniversary Weekend, and cooled our wine in the rockpools of Pukerua Bay. **1994** *Contact* (Wellington) 20 Jan. 6 Our area [from Haywards turn-off to Waikanae] is known as the Kapiti Coast... It provokes annoyance to find the name Gold Coast still cropping up..since it was rejected several years ago as being inappropriate and confusing. **1994** *Dominion* (Wellington) 11 Aug. 12 [Advt] The Bishop Snedden Retirement Village Waikanae. The perfect retirement on Wellington's beautiful Gold Coast.

gold-digger. [AND 1852: US (Mathews), 1832.] A goldminer. See also DIGGER *n.*[1] 1.
1853 in *Canterbury Rhymes* (1866) 30 And a gold-digger's jumper to wear on pay-day. **1869** *AJHR* D-6 14 The roving..disposition, deeply ingrained in the character of the true 'gold digger', is one not easily overcome. **1879** HAAST *Geol. Canterbury & Westland* 66 Quite 8000 gold-diggers set out from Otago for the new Eldorado. **1896** HARPER *Pioneer Work* 30 Westland..was rushed by gold-diggers in the early sixties. **1914** PFAFF *Diggers' Story* 49 We left Nelson..with several gold diggers and a miscellaneous lot of cargo. **1930** DOBSON *Reminiscences* 141 A number of gold-diggers were working in the neighbourhood. **1949** SHAW & FARRANT *Taieri Plain* 36 When the gold-diggers began streaming up the ridge of Maungatua, above the school, they were regarded by the local people as somewhat of a menace.

gold-digging.

1. As *pl.* **gold diggings** (or **diggins**) [AND 1850; US (Mathews), 1849], a place where gold is found. See also DIGGING 1 a.
1852 *NZGG* 10 Dec. V. 30/182 I found Mr. Heaphy actively employed in superintending the Gold Diggings [on the Kapanga River]. **1853** ADAMS *Canterbury Settlement* 56 The newly discovered 'gold diggins' had at the period..greatly increased..the value of horses in Australia. **1879** HAAST *Geol. Canterbury & Westland* 85 We came to a broader road, which led to the gold-diggings situated higher up. **1887** HOPEFUL *Taken In* 135 If a man isn't 'up to the mark' he is called 'a regular shicer!' This phrase originated from the gold diggings. **1899** BELL *In Shadow of Bush* 13 This Harry..was one of those men who..spent most of their adult existence at the gold-diggings in one or other of the Colonies.

2. [AND 1851; US (Mathews), 1831.] Goldmining. Also *attrib.*
1859 BEGG *Diaries* 24 Sept. (1960) 20 I..walked out to the new gold diggings at Cape Saunders... I think gold digging leads to a great deal of evil. **1869** *AJHR* D-6 14 The contrast between a noisy gold digging town and the comparative solitude of a flax swamp would be too sudden and too great. **1874** KENNAWAY *Crusts* 229 A man, to be a good digger, must..learn *how* to be one; for gold-digging has become quite a recognised and separate department of labour. **1967** MAY *West Coast Gold Rushes* 274 Gold-digging was a hard game: the halt and the lame, the aged and infirm, had been weeded out long since. **1940** COWAN *Sir Donald Maclean* 112 It was 1874–75 before the old die-hards..became reconciled to the gold-digging invasion and consented to mining rights over their lands.

Hence by back-formation **gold-dig** v. intr.
1866 SMALL *NZ & Austral. Songster* (1970) 27 Bought a pick and a spade, and a-gold-digging went. **1914** PFAFF *Diggers' Story* 50 I then went to Waimangaroa, where I myself tried gold digging. **1930** DOBSON *Reminiscences* 152 Within a radius of some three miles about 12,000 men were gold-digging. **1981** HENDERSON *Exiles Asbestos Cottage* 111 In all, thirty would be gold-digging in widely scattered possies in the Tableland..in the 1930s Depression.

golden, a.

1. In the names of plants and animals, see: AKEAKE 2, FROG n.¹ 2 (2), LILY 2 (4), PLOVER 2 (3), SNAPPER n.¹ 2 (2), SPANIARD 2 (3), TAINUI 2, TAUHINU 3 (2).

2. Used to form special collocations connoting (often wished for) affluence or prestige: **Golden Coast** (a) obs. GOLD COAST a; (b) a promotional name for an area of the Wellington west coast from (roughly) Paremata north to Paraparaumu (see also GOLD COAST b); **Golden Coaster**, one who lives on Wellington's Golden Coast; **Golden Kiwi**, a national lottery, introduced in 1962, replacing the former *Art Union*, and itself replaced by a different gambling method, INSTANT KIWI q.v., in 1989; occas. a ticket in the Golden Kiwi lottery (see quot. 1977); **golden mile**, a name applied to a main city shopping street; **Golden Shears**, a New Zealand national shearing contest held annually since 1961; also the winner's award.
1884 REID *Rambles on Golden Coast* 122 This was the first recognition of 'the **Golden Coast**'. **1914** *The diggers' story, or, Tales & reminiscences of the Golden Coast, from Westland's earliest pioneers*. By Carl J. Pfaff. [Wellington 1914] [title: NZNB IV. 32, item P486] **1963** *Comment 17* Oct. 11 The **Golden Coast** has been dulled by leaden skies... At the end of the war the Golden Coast was scattered with baches where Wellington people spent summer weekends. **1986** REILLY *Deputy Head* 53 Sometimes on the weekends I drive out to the so-called Golden Coast—as far away as Peka Peka Beach sometimes.

Hence **Golden Coaster**, one who lives on Wellington's Golden Coast.
1963 *Comment 17* Oct. 11 Golden Coasters are not, by and large, keen gardeners. Perhaps the heavy clay deters them. More likely the Coast attracts..the open air fraternity which prefers boating and fishing. **1962** WEBBER *Look No Hands* 146 If I win the **Golden Kiwi**, we'll have a lash at economic growth. **1966** *Encycl. NZ* II. 347 In 1961 the Government decided to replace the art unions with the present Golden Kiwi lottery. **1977** SCOTT *Tom Scott's Life & Times* in McLauchlan *Acid Test* (1981) 180 He will gamble, allowing himself the odd Golden Kiwi. **1988** FRAME *Carpathians* 67 He'd spent the day like many other Pumaharians..searching through the Golden Kiwi results. **1957** GOLDBLATT *Democracy at Ease* 13 And thus we are jostled in the '**Golden Mile**' (for every town is bursting with prosperity) by a race of men & women. **1964** *Evening Post* (Wellington) 4 Jan. 9 A **Golden Shears** contest in the United Kingdom is to be staged in liaison with the Golden Shears International Shearing Championship Society in Masterton. **1988** *More* (Auckland) Mar. 28 I've even had the thrill of climbing onto the revered boards of the Golden Shears stage to collect a prize; second in the junior woolhandling. **1993** *Dominion* (Wellington) 6 Mar. 7 Entries for this year's Golden Shears championships in Masterton are 10 per cent up on last year.

golden rod. [Transf. use of *golden-rod Solidago* spp. (fam. Asteraceae), a European genus of herbaceous perennials with panicles of small yellow flower heads.] Occas. applied in New Zealand to introduced mullein *Verbascum* spp., which has yellow-gold erect flower heads; FLANNEL-LEAF.
1926 [see FLANNEL-LEAF]. **1969** *Standard Common Names Weeds* 29 *golden-rod* [=] *moth mullein*. **1974** *Dominion* (Wellington) 22 Nov. 5 Verbascum thapsus, a weed of poor land has many popular names. In New Zealand it is called native tobacco, velvet, flannel leaf and golden rod.

goldfield. Also pl. **goldfields.** [Recorded earliest in Australia: AND 1851.] A place where gold is mined.

1. a. In *sing.* form often with local modifier and init. cap.
1852 WYNYARD *Lieut.-Gov. Proclamation* 10 Nov. in Swainson *Auckland* (1853) 156 *Now, I*, the Lieutenant-Governor of the Province of New Ulster, *do hereby proclaim and declare* that..as soon as the necessary arrangements shall be completed, Licenses [sic] to work the said Gold Field will be granted by the Government on payment of a reasonable Fee. **1861** *NZ Goldfields 1861* (1976) 5 I know the importance which belongs to news of any kind from these gold-fields. **1873** PYKE *Wild Will Enderby* (1889, 1974) I. v 20 Commissioner was the title then given to the Goldfield's magistrates. **1898** HOCKEN *Contributions* 198 A petition was presented to the Council asking that a substantial reward should be offered for the discovery of a payable gold-field. **1914** PFAFF *Diggers' Story* 30 We had, since the days of the Dunstan Rush, been accustomed to paying gold-field prices. **1931** COAD *Such Is Life* 48 This conversation took place on the Westland gold-field in the spacious days of the gold-rush.

b. As a collective pl. **goldfields.**
1853 DEANS *Pioneers Port Cooper Plains* (1964) 85 Seeing the great attraction to emigrants that the gold fields hold out..I am afraid that we will soon suffer for want of labour. **1865** BARKER *Station Life* (1870) 16 The gold-fields on this coast were only discovered eight months ago. **1899** BELL *In Shadow of Bush* 85 [He] had tried his luck for a time on the gold-fields of the West Coast. **1968** SEDDON *The Seddons* 30 Along the..road that led from..the goldfields of Goldsborough to Kumara when old Fanny pulled the family buggy, those drives were a joy.

2. *Hist.* Special Comb. **goldfields agent**, one who advised on formal or legal matters on a goldfield (see also BUSH LAWYER n.² 1); **Goldfields Commissioner**, COMMISSIONER 1; **Goldfields Warden**, see WARDEN 1 a.
1911 BREMNER *Mt. Ida Goldfields* (1988) 32 Mr Brodie—who was acting as a sort of lawyer or **goldfields agent** there [at Clyde]—has my case in hand. **1861** *NZ Goldfields 1861* (1976) 38 The Tuapeka gold-field is under the charge, as I have said before, of Mr. Alfred Chetham Strode, **gold-fields commissioner**.

goldie, n.¹ *Hist.* A sovereign. Also as **little goldie**, a half-sovereign.
1899 *Bulletin* (Sydney) 14 Jan. (Red Page) [Letter from *Loafer*, Tauranga.] Following are other local money-names..half-sovereign—*half-thickun* or *little goldie*..sovereign—*thickun* or *goldie*. **1917** let. in *Boots, Belts* (1992) 36 I intend to take 5 pounds with me, the three goldies dad gave me and two notes. **1977** *NZ Numismatic Jrnl.* Oct. 16 Our nearness to Australia also resulted in our adoption of slang words in use there. Examples of these include *goldie* for sovereign, and *little goldie* for a half sovereign.

goldie, n.² [Prob. f. *(she's a) gold watch* (GOLD 4 b).] Usu. in the phr. **she's a goldie**, said of something valued; also as a catchphrase, everything's fine, 'good as gold'.
1982 May p.c. Neil Rowe (Wellington), 'She's a goldie' overheard from an old man, with the meaning of 'good as gold'. **1988** MCGILL *Dict. Kiwi Slang* 52 *goldie* an impressive or well-regarded object; used by Mrs Elsie Johns in NZ Oral History Unit, Martinborough study.

goldie, n.³

1. [f. *gold*(fish + -IE.] A familiar name for a goldfish.
1985 DUCKWORTH *Married Alive* 98 'Would a punch bowl do? A very big glass one?' Sidney asks. 'Not for the tropics. A couple of goldies—'. .'You said you wanted a goldfish.'

2. [f. Brit. dial.: see OED, EDD *goldy*.] *Carduelis elegans* (fam. Fringillidae), the introduced goldfinch.
1919 *Quick March* 1 Dec. 75 trapping goldfinches.. but finches brought a shilling a pair... The birds one snared in triumph brought their own punishment. The 'goldies' one put in the soap box..looked so small and helpless. **1966** FALLA et al. *Birds NZ* 225 Goldfinch *Carduelis carduelis..*Goldie.

golobeio ?/gɒˈlʌubijʌu/, var. KOROPIO.

gonce /gɒns/. *Obs.* [Origin unknown: AND (also *gons*) 1899–1941.] Money, cash.
1905 *Truth* 24 June 1 The typewriter girl has nothing to do with the gonce in her bosses [sic] safe, although she manipulates his keys. **1912** *NZ Free Lance* (Wellington) 21 Dec. 6 He may select rhino, cash, spondulicks, ready, oof, beans, brass, lucre, lift, dross, boodle, bunce, gonce, tin, or seventeen others that take too long to write. **1919** *Quick March* 10 Oct. 33 He was after land an' gonce an' boodle. **1921** *Quick March* 11 July 13 Everybody..must think every day of money, but although one may think 'money' he may call it 'gonce', 'oof', 'hoot', 'stuff', 'brass', 'ooftish', 'boodle', 'cash', 'gilt', 'kale', or a dozen other..things. **c1926** THE MIXER *Transport Workers' Song Book* 42 If the port is full of shipping I'm so anxious for the 'gonce'; But the Union will not let me Work all the ships at once.

Hence **goncing**, moneymaking. *ppl. a.*
1907 *Truth* 31 Aug. 6 The goncing game is getting far too strong, and this paper's representative was asked to spill a little ink on the place where the doctor wears his bell-topper.

gone a million: see MILLION.

gong, gonger, varr. GUNGER.

goob. Also **goobie.** [Var. of Brit. dial. *gob* a lump or clot of some slimy substance, phlegm: see OED *gob* n.¹ 1 a; also EDD *gob, gobby* or *gubby* (pron. also /gubi/).] A gob of spit, phlegm.
c1920s *goob* used on the West Coast for a lump of phlegm p.c. Bill Pearson. **1968** SLATTER *Pagan Game* 230 Tank's gang spent their desperate days..rocking the swing bridge, hoiking goobs smack into the river. **1985** MCGILL *G'day Country* 20 When I refired [sc. came to], Ken was on about gubies. I hadn't heard that word in years. Goobies? I had never seen it spelled. It meant spit. How could he know that word, he was too young? Why, it wasn't even in the *Heinemann New Zealand Dictionary*. Sometimes it meant something worse, vis-à-vis nose.

good, *a.*

1. [See OED *good a.* 1.] Of gold, plentiful.

1914 PFAFF *Diggers' Story* 56 There were over a thousand diggers..waiting to see the result of the prospect when we bottomed. We..struck very good gold. *Ibid.* 64 There was no ground to be got there... There was good gold there, but the claims were all taken up.

2. In various phrases or collocations indicating approval, assent, excellence, agreeableness, etc.
a. In the phr. **good on (you** etc.) /gʊdˈɒnjʌ/ etc. [prob. f. Brit. dial.: cf. EDD *good* 3 (13) 'A mild imprecation'; AND 1907], an exclamation of encouragement, agreement, etc.; 'good for you', 'well done'.

1905 THOMSON *Bush Boys* 44 First one and then another came up and congratulated in true British boys' style. 'Good on you, Dinkums, old man. Put it there, old feller.' **1948** FINLAYSON *Tidal Creek* (1979) 151 'Good on you, Uncle Ted,' says Jake. 'You're not too old yet.' **1959** *Listener* 21 Aug. 8 'Good on you!' said Dad, smacking my new leg approvingly, 'that's the spirit.' **1968** SEDDON *The Seddons* 60 My father's speech to his constituents was punctuated with shouts of 'Good on you!' 'Good on you!' 'Tell us some more!' **1970** *Dominion* (Wellington) 30 Jan. 1 He was delighted to hear that a Whangarei group was considering joining in on the beer strike. 'Good on them...,' he said. **1980** MARSH *Photo-Finish* 172 'Good *on* you, boy,' said Alleyn, displaying what he hoped was the correct idiom and the proper show of enthusiasm. **1991** PAYNE *Staunch* 48 If they can get away with it, good on them.

b. As **good as gold** affirming good will, approval, agreement in reply to a question or request; 'fine, good-oh, she's right'. Contrast the international English sense 'well-behaved' as in OED 9 a (1695).

1947 DAVIN *For Rest of Our Lives* 77 'The men get a good breakfast?' asked the Colonel. 'Good as gold, sir. I tried it myself.' **1968** SLATTER *Pagan Game* 52 Not stiff after yesterday's game are you? said the Coach solicitously. Good as gold, said the Captain. **1976** MCDERMOTT *Lost & Found NZ* 140 Again we had called ahead for accommodations..and got a 'good-as-gold' confirmation. **1980** MARSH *Photo-Finish* 36 'Meet Les Smith,' said the driver. 'Gidday,' said Les Smith. 'How's tricks, then, Bert? Good trip?' 'No trouble, Les.' 'Good as gold,' said the helmsman.

c. In the phr. **good ink** *obs.*, esp. **that's good ink**, something agreeable, pleasant.

1937 PARTRIDGE *Dict. Slang* 342 good ink(, that's). (That is) good, agreeable, pleasant: New Zealanders': from ca. 1910. **1938** *Press* (Christchurch) (McNab Slang) 2 Apr. 18 'good pup' and 'good ink' are terms of approval. **1941** BAKER *NZ Slang* 57 Twentieth century..expressions..include *good ink*, something pleasant or agreeable.

d. As **good pup** *obs.*, something fine, pleasant, successful.

1937 PARTRIDGE *Dict. Slang* 342 *good pup.* Anything good, e.g. a successful sale, a good bargain, a comfortable dug-out: New Zealanders': C. 20. Prob. at first a farmers' c[atch] p[hrase] of commendation. **1938** [see c above].

e. good oil, see OIL a.

3. In the phr. **good keen man** (also in variants **good keen bloke**, **good keen kiwi joker**), characterizing one who attacks a job, problem, situation enthusiastically but without thought of the consequences. (The catchphrase was popularized by Barry Crump's book title (1960), a regular catchphrase of the hero.) See also ORDINARY BLOKE.

1960 CRUMP *A Good Keen Man* [title: NZNB II. 310, item C1825] **1971** HOLDEN *Pack and Rifle* (1986) 69 You'll get used to Keith... I reckon he's the original good keen man. **1987** *Listener* 19 Sept. 31 After all, if your car broke down on the Desert Road, at least the Good Keen Man would stop and help you out. **1987** *Sunday News* (Auckland) 8 Nov. 21 A Canadian who was breaking her heart to meet a good keen Kiwi joker has broken her back in the attempt. **1989** VIRTUE *Upon Evil Season* 20 The tracts had been printed for nothing by a good keen bloke in Wellington. **1991** WOLFE *Kiwi* 53 The evolution of the Kiwi bloke has been one of rapprochement and training of the wild beast within—taking the 'hard' out of the good, keen, hard man. **1993** *Dominion* (Wellington) 16 Oct. 17 Even couch potatoes can sometimes still see themselves as a good keen man or woman.

goodbye.

1. In the phr. **goodbye and bugger you**, a jocular (often so called, 'sailor's') farewell; *hooray fuck* (HOORAY 2).

1949 THE SARGE *Excuse My Feet* 19 The familiar words 'Goodbye and—you !'

2. In the phr. **goodbye** (occas. **goodnight) McGinnis** [orig. unknown], an exclamation or expression of finality or ruination; 'that's the finish'.

1937 PARTRIDGE *Dict. Slang* 342 *good night, McGuinness!*..expressive of finality:.. New Zealand, from ca. 1910;.. ob. (1984 Partridge 8 487 id. NZ version of [good night! = That's finished it!] ca. 1910–35.) **1946** SARGESON *That Summer* 34 If you once went on the bust in a place like this it was good-bye McGinnis, he said. **1964** PEARSON *Glossary* to Sargeson *Collected Stories 1935–63* (1964) 300 goodbye McGinnis: the finish, ruination.

good night, McGuiness!: see GOODBYE 2.

good-oh /ˈgʊdʌʊ/. Also **good-o**.

1. *adj. in predicative use.* [AND 1914: cf. OED *a.* 4 c.] 'All right', very good.

1905 THOMSON *Bush Boys* 34 That was real good-o... We 'diddled' them properly that time. **c1930** *Whitcombe's Etym. Dict. Aust.-NZ Suppl.* 5 *good oh a.* fine, excellent, bonzer. [origin uncertain] **1959** SLATTER *Gun in My Hand* 13 They thought it was good-oh the first night, even the fish and chips was fun. **1964** HARVEY *Any Old Dollars Mister?* 110 I'll probably end up as a major or something good-o. Something with plenty of perks. That's me. **1978** MANTELL *Murder in Fancydress* 135 'Then got a blanket. Coupla books. By then all the fellas gone. Day-shift jokers, y'know. So goodoh to beaut there [sunbathing].'

2. *adv.* Often intensifying the action of the verb, 'like billy-oh'.

1916 ANZAC *On Anzac Trail* 34 We were told..that once in every three years or so, the rain came down good-oh. **1917** *Truth* 29 Dec. 6 The next thing Day saw was witness and her 'hubby' strafing each other 'good-o'. **1918** *Chron. NZEF* 27 Sept. 109 The wind rose and screeched and howled good-oh—a regular gale... Gorstruth! **1925** *NZ Tit-bits* 29 Apr. 6 The week-end boys from Trentham and Featherston [military camps]..were after these birds good O. **1937** MARSH *Vintage Murder* 49 We tried her [*sc.* the machine] out..and she worked corker every time. She worked good-oh, didn't she. **1948** FINLAYSON *Tidal Creek* (1979) 100 [The drummer] glares hard and bangs out the bumpy waltz time good-oh. **1978** HENDERSON *Soldier Country* 126 The little girl of Wadi Hanein started thriving goodoh. **1981** HENDERSON *Exiles Asbestos Cottage* 71 Took the pain away, antiseptic apparently, healed goodoh.

3. *Exclam.* Also occas. **goody-oh**. [AND 1918.] An exclamation or indication of assent or agreement; 'she's right'.

1926 PEACOCKE *His Kid Brother* 158 'Goodo,' said Dal. **1937** MARSH *Vintage Murder* 61 'Good-oh,.. get to it, you boys'. It is extraordinary how ubiquitous [New Zealanders] make that remark. It expresses anything from acquiescence to approbation. **1943** MARSH *Colour Scheme* 119 'Good-ow!' said Simon on a more enthusiastic inflection than he usually gave to this odious expression. 'Nice work, go on.' **1950** CHERRILL *NZ Sheep Farm* 42 'Good-o,' replied the other [New Zealander]. **1954** WINKS *These New Zealanders* (1956) 54 'Too right' especially common in North Auckland, and 'goody-oh' are two fascinating phrases [for Americans]. **1966** TURNER *Eng. Lang. Austral. & NZ* 135 The words *righto* and *goodo* are not confined to Australia and New Zealand but are so prevalent here that they deserve mention. **1988** MCGILL *Dict. Kiwi Slang* 52 *good-oh* exclamation of approval or agreement; variant of right-oh; eg 'Adds up, does it, Mr B? Yes? Good-oh, then. See you next week. Bye.'

goody-oh /ˈgʊdɪʌʊ/, var. GOOD-O.

gooey duck, var. GEODUCK.

goog /gʊg/. Also **googie**. [*Goog* (AND 1941) an abbrev. of *googie* (AND 1903) f. Sc. dial. *goggie* a child's name for an egg: see SND *googie*.]

1. An egg.

1941 *goog* 'egg' used at St Patrick's, Silverstream (Ed.). **1968** *NZ Contemp. Dict. Suppl.* (Collins) 9 *goog, googy n.* (*Coll.*) an egg; whence *full as a goog*, drunk. **1987** VIRTUE *Redemption of Elsdon Bird* (1988) 32 Mrs Daniels calls eggs googies. **1988** MCGILL *Dict. Kiwi Slang* 52 *goog* an antipodean egg, often a boiled one; probably from a toddler attempt, or a contraction of 'Good egg'.

2. *transf. Obs.* In full **golden goog (googie)** [f. a play on *golden egg*], a sovereign.

1909 *Truth* 27 Feb. 2 Mug is a humorous sort, and seen after the race in question, he remarked, 'She has cost me about 60 googs,' but I'll take my oath the squib will not cost me. *Ibid.* 24 July 1 Therefore, peace, be still; let Chapman and Co. gather up the sunbeams—in the shape of golden googies, silver and copper coins—scattered plentifully around their path, as Sankey and other Yankee-doodling hymn-howlers used to bawl when over here gathering in the gonce. **1917** *NZ Free Lance* (Wellington) 27 July 20 What would you think of our worthy Chief Justice..adjudicating on a case where the results of his verdict would put golden googies into his own pocket.

3. In the phr. **as full as a goog**, see FULL *a.* 1.

googie: see GOOG.

googly-eyed cod: see COD 3.

goolie /ˈguli/. Also **goulie**. [AND 'Prob. f. a N.S.W. Aboriginal language', 1924.] In New Zealand, usu. a large stone or boulder.

1955 *BJ Cameron Collection* (TS July) goolie (n) A big boulder. (Mainly used on the West Coast of the South I.) **1977** BURTON *South Wairarapa Workingmen's Club Centennial Book* 54. An Australian [Bruce Byrne]..resident locally for about 15 years... Introduced a new word into the [Greytown] District—'Goulie' for the large stones that abound in the local soil. **1982** 2YA Wellington 18 Oct. [A report of whitebait-selling in the Waikato, and putting a stone in to the container to increase the apparent amount.] 'I kept on pouring the whitebait into my containers and there was a dirty big goolie on the bottom.' **1989** RICHARDS *Pioneer's Life*

goomalla, var. KUMARA.

gooree, goori(e), goory, varr. KURI.

goose, *n.*[1]

1. Often as **extinct** or **flightless goose**. Either of two species of the extinct genus *Cnemiornis* (fam. Anatidae), large flightless geese having reduced wing-bones and long powerful legs.

1888 BULLER *Birds NZ* I. xxvi Following this [discovery] came the discovery by Sir James Hector of the remains of an extinct Goose, of very large if not gigantic proportions, and undoubtedly flightless. **1949** DUFF *Pyramid Valley* 23 Then there was a flightless goose (*Cnemiornis*) with wing-bones greatly reduced, and long and powerful legs developed for life on the ground. **1955** OLIVER *NZ Birds* 602 South Island Extinct Goose *Cnemiornis calcitrans*... North Island Extinct Goose *Cnemiornis septentrionalis*. **1977** DUFF *Moa-Hunter Period of Maori Culture* 362 Its faunal remains included moa (*Euryapteryx*), extinct goose (*Cnemiornis*) and extinct swan. **1988** STEVENS et al. *Prehistoric NZ* 74 The takahe, kakapo and extinct goose (*Cnemiornis*) are examples of late Cenozoic land-bird migrants that became large and flightless. **1990** HAYWARD *Trilobites, Dinosaurs & Moa Bones* 86 In addition to moas, other spectacular birds have disappeared including..a large flightless goose..and a laughing owl.

2. Canadian Goose. *Branta canadensis* (fam. Anatidae), the introduced Canada goose.

1922 THOMSON *Naturalisation Animals & Plants* 104 Canadian Goose; Maine Goose (*Branta canadensis*). The Wellington Society imported three in 1876, and 15 in 1879. **1952** THOMSON *Deer Hunter* 35 Canadian geese were in their thousands. **1987** *Dominion* (Wellington) 4 Apr. 8 Licensed bag limits have been announced for..Canadian Geese in the central North Island this hunting season.

3. *transf.* **a.** See COLONIAL GOOSE.

b. *Car-sales.* See quot.

1986 *NZ Herald* (Auckland) 22 Jan. sect. ii 1 Car dealers have a collection of jargon... That difficult customer with whom the salesman can never clinch the deal is known as a 'goose'.

4. In special Comb. **goose egg** *goldmining hist.* [f. the appearance], see quot.; **goose-neck binder** *obs. farming,* a type of harvesting machine.

1939 *NZGeol.SB (NS)* No.39 49 In most localities the basal bed is a quartz conglomerate containing well-rounded pebbles up to 4 in. in diameter—the '**goose eggs**' of the miners. **1940** STUDHOLME *Te Waimate* (1954) 169 The Woods was probably the first string binder tried here [c 1880s]. It was known as the '**Goose-neck**' **binder** because it had a long circular arm resembling the neck of a goose, which threw the sheaves away so effectively that in some cases when opening up a paddock, they went right over the fence.

goose, *n.*[2] *Sawmilling.* [For a conjectural origin see *goose-saw,* 2 below.]

1. *Ellipt.* for *goose-saw* (see 2 below).

1920 MANDER *Story NZ River* (1974) 198 They watched the progress of the log from the booms up the skids to the side of the breakdown platform... Then the small circulars, the drag, & the goose completed its metamorphosis into the regulation strips.

2. Special Comb. **gooseman** *sawmilling,* one who operates a goose-saw; **goose-saw** [prob. from the swinging-arm mechanism's fanciful resemblance to a goose's neck], a circular saw mounted on a swinging arm ('pendulum'), which docks the ends of sawn timber.

1943 BENNETT *English in NZ* in *Amer. Speech* XVIII. 85 [Timber-trade occupational terms include].. *goose man* ('drag' and 'goose' are various types of saw). **1957** *NZ Timber Jrnl.* July 49 Gooseman, the operator of a goose saw. **1901** *Awards, etc.* 8 [North Auckland Timber-Workers Award] Men in charge of main goose-saws, 7s... saw-doctor, £3 per week. **1908** *Awards, etc.* 337 [Wellington Sawmills Award] [Rates of wages] Men working at goose or swing saws [£]2 14[s.] 0[d.] Sawdust-men 2 11 0 Slabmen 2 14 0. **1920** MANDER *Story NZ River* (1974) 197 They went past the the **goose** and circular **saws** and the moving platform of the breakdowns to the skids. **1950** *Landfall 14* 125 The planer..spits out faced boards for the tailer-out to stack by the goose saw. **1951** *Awards, etc.* 519 [Marlborough Timber-Workers Award] [Rates of wages] Docking and sorting systems—Timber classer or grader, sorting table 4[s.] 1¼[d.] Goose-saw man who classes and/or docker who classes 4 0¾. **1967** GROVER *Another Man's Role* 34 Eighteen months later he graduated to the goose saw. About two feet across, it is used for docking the ends of sawn timber, and is fixed to the end of a beam that swings like a pendulum from a rafter.

gooseberry.

1. *Obs.* As **native gooseberry** [poss. named from a fancied resemblance to the Cape gooseberry berry], POROPORO.

1852 LUSH *Auckland Jrnls.* 3 Feb. (1971) 102 I have had promised me several plants of the Native gooseberry, the fruit with a smooth skin like a cherry and about that size, but a bright yellow when ripe... It bears two crops in the year, one in June—the other in March.

2. *WW1. fig.* [f. a resemblance to the thorny, tangled appearance of a leafless gooseberry bush.] See quot.

1921 STEWART *NZ Div.* 147 The slight losses sustained in the bombardment, and the energy with which the gaps in the wire were at once filled by ready-made circles of loose tangled wire known as 'gooseberries', all reflected the highest credit on the soldierly qualities of the defence.

3. See CHINESE GOOSEBERRY.

Gordon Hutter. [f. the name of *Gordon Hutter,* a well-known race-caller and wrestling commentator of the 1930s and 1940s.] Rhyming slang for 'butter'.

1939–45 *Expressions and Sayings 2NZEF (Nat. Archiv. TS WAII DA 420/1)* Gordon Hutter—Butter. **1949** p.c. Prof. P.S. Ardern. *Gordon Hutter* for 'butter' mainly heard in Auckland from the name of a well-known sports announcer involved in a high society sex-scandal (*Upper Hutter* became something of an ironic catchphrase).

goose-saw: GOOSE *n.*[2] 2.

Gordzone Country: see GOD'S OWN.

gorge. [Used elsewhere (see OED 7, 1769) but of frequent, and in Canterbury of distinctive, use in NZ as the word preferred over *ravine, canyon.*] A narrow opening in the hills, with high, steep, rocky sides and often with a river running through it; an upper river-catchment area (see quots. 1966, 1972).

1848 WAKEFIELD *Handbook NZ* 240 A series of narrow gorges, covered with flax, fern, and grass. **1860** in Butler *First Year* (1863) vi 82 But as we looked up the river-bed, we saw two large and gloomy gorges, at the end of each of which were huge glaciers. **1874** KENNAWAY *Crusts* 184 The hill-spurs get steeper, and the gorges get deeper. **1883** PARTINGTON *Random Rot* 325 The word 'gorge' hardly defines it. It is really a valley with most precipitous sides... The road is what is called a bluff road, that is, it is cut out of the side of the precipice. **1934** *Press* (Christchurch) (Acland Gloss.) 20 Jan. 15 *Gorge.*—A correspondent has been good enough to remind me of a usage of this word which I believe is peculiar to Canterbury; i.e., any main valley above the (technically correct) g*[orge]* of a river. For instance, musterers always speak of Hakatere, Mesopotamia, Manuka Point, Lake Heron, etc., etc., as being in the Ashburton, Rakaia or Rangitata G*[orge].* This usage goes back to at least 1894. **1950** CAMPBELL *Mine Eyes Dazzle* 20 All is new, and all strange, Terrible as a dusty gorge Where a great river sang. *Ibid.* 36 The hawk Hangs in a gem-hard sky. On motionless and lazy pinions It glides down the hot tired Corridor of the gorge. **1966** NEWTON *Boss's Story* 187 *Gorge*: A term common in Canterbury. Refers to the areas of hill country in the upper reaches of the main rivers, i.e. the Rakaia Gorge is the area of country from where the river disappears into the hills and up to its headworks. **1972** McLEOD *Mountain World* 310 *Gorge*: Used to describe a narrow river channel and also a whole river catchment. *e.g.* Rakaia Gorge.

Hence **gorge-bound,** encompassed by the sides of a gorge.

1960 *Over Whitcombe Pass* 10 The major obstacles lay in gorge-bound beds of the rivers and in the swiftness of the rivers themselves.

gorgy, *a.* [f. GORGE *n.* + -Y: used elsewhere, but first recorded in NZ.] Of a stream passing through, or country comprising, frequent gorges; having the characteristics of a gorge.

1891 DOUGLAS in *Mr Explorer Douglas* (1957) 130 Some very ugley [*sic*] gorgy looking gaps are looming up at the head of the flat. **1908** *NZGeol.SB (NS)* No.6 24 But largely owing to the difficulty of transporting stores up this extremely gorgy stream, the prospectors did not penetrate more than five or six miles. **1927** *The Spike* 49 A party followed down the Whakatiki river..only leaving the river when it became impassibly gorgy. **1933** *Tararua Tramper* Oct. 4 Descend into the gorgy headwaters of the Pakuratahi. **1946** *Tararua Story* 78 The creek was precipitous and gorgy and it was not until Monday afternoon that they reached the Waiohina. **1958** PASCOE *Great Days in NZ Mountaineering* 163 The innocent stream as seen from the light aircraft proved to be a bit gorgy with a waterfall leaping down. **1960** CRUMP *Good Keen Man* 135 We struck a few more small waterfalls and a lot of steep, gorgy places where the slippery rocks made travel slow and difficult.

gorry, var. KORRY.

gorse. [With reference to the introduced prickly shrub *Ulex europaeus* (fam. Fabaceae) recognized as a noxious weed in New Zealand from at least the 1870s, though still seen as a hedging plant in some areas; only occas. early called *furze*: a var. or Brit. dial. pron. /gɒs/ has also been used in NZ.]

1. Special Comb. **gorse-knife (gorse-slasher),** a short-handled slasher for clearing gorse.

1907 LANCASTER *Tracks We Tread* 80 Randal kicked aside his **gorse-knife**—he had been cutting brush in the gully beyond. **1962** SHARPE *Country Occasions* 132 'Give me two bob for it,' pleads the auctioneer. 'Well then, chuck in the saw and those two gorse knives as well. Now then a quid for the lot?' **1938** HYDE *Nor Yrs. Condemn* 253 [We were] given grubbers and **gorse-slashers**.

2. In the phr. **to have gorse in one's pocket**, to be tight-fisted, to be reluctant to pay one's share by putting one's hand in one's pocket to retrieve money.
  1985 Wellington. (Ed.) 'He's got gorse in his pocket', used by a woman of her tight-fisted husband. **1988** MCGILL *Dict. Kiwi Slang* 52 *gorsepocket* mean person; phr. *he's got gorse in his pocket*.

goshore, var. GOASHORE.

goss, *n.*[1] [From Brit. dial. or slang: see OED *goss*[3] (orig. unknown); EDD *n.*[3] Cornw., a fuss.] Usu. in the phr. **to give** (one) **goss**, to hurt or punish; to scold; to 'give one hell'.
  1874 BAINES *Edward Crewe* 43 We shall want his dog, for 'Smut' here might come to grief if we fell in with an old boar, and no one 'up' to give him 'goss'. **1914** GRACE *Tale Timber Town* 173 That's right, ole man, give 'em goss. **c1940** Used freq. in Marlborough (Ed.): *e.g.* My crook back's giving me goss this morning.

goss, *n.*[2] [A short form of *gossip*.] News.
  1985 *Salient* (Wellington) 9 Sept. 3 Student politicos who went to August Council didn't. Interesting goss from the 'Watch my manoeuvring' department? Well, 1983 Vic prez *Leighton Duley* stood for prez of NZUSA.

gossan /ˈgɒsən/. *Mining*. Also **gossen**. [f. Brit. (orig. Cornish) dial.: see OED, EDD *gossan*.] Decomposed rock of a reddish or ferruginous character forming part of an outcrop.
  1847 TAYLOR *Journal* (ATLTS) V. 135 A ferugineous [*sic*] porous mass which they [*sc.* at the copper mine, Kawau Island] styled gossand and which always overlies copper. **1862** CHUDLEIGH *Diary* 29 May (1950) 40 Took a spade and tin dish with us to look for gold, made a pit 6ft. deep and 4 by 3 keenly gossen. **1868** *Thames Miner's Guide* 54 Gossan.—A ferruginous condition of the top of a lode. **1938** *NZ Geol. Memoir* No.4 34 Early gold-seekers discovered a 'cupriferous [*sic*] gossan' when working along the floor of Reedy Creek [Otago]. **1983** NOLAN *Gold Fossicker's Handbook* 112 *Gossan*: rusty-looking rocks that often cap a lode containing sulphide minerals. Can be an indicator of gold, silver, copper, etc.

  Hence **gossanous** /ˈgɒsənəs/, of the appearance of, or containing, gossan.
  1907 *NZ Geol. SB (NS)* No.3 95 Below the gossanous portion a rich sulphide zone was met with. *Ibid.* No.4 105 At and in the vicinity of the vein-outcrops the ore, owing to oxidation of the pyrite and iron-bearing minerals generally assumes a rusty-brown colour and a gossanous appearance. **1911** *Ibid.* No.12 47 Where widest on the surface the gossanous rusty serpentine shows 4ft. 3in. across the dip.

go to whoa: see GO *n.* 5.

goulash. [Spec. joc. or contemptuous use of *goulash* a special kind of stew.] A rough stew, carelessly concocted.
  1946 JOHNSTON ed. *Twenty-one Yrs. with Boots & Pack* 38 Remember that goulash we used to turn out up at the hut. **1951** 14 M 10 Wellington H.S. 22B Goolash [M2] **1953** 15-16 M A24 Thames DHS 22B Goulash (goo-lash) [M3]

Gould's harrier: see HARRIER.

goulie, var. GOOLIE.

goure, var. KURI.

Government. Used *attrib.* (often with init. cap.) in special Comb. in senses of pertaining to, working for, controlled, funded or administered by the central government of New Zealand; in modern use, STATE q.v. **Government Agent** (also **(Government) land agent**) *hist.*, a Crown employee negotiating purchases of Maori land (see also *native agent* (NATIVE B 3 b), cf. *Land Purchase Commissioner* (LAND 1)); **Government Buildings**, see BUILDING; **Government Cut** *forestry*, see quot.; **Government head** *mining*, see HEAD *n.*[3] 2 a; **Government Life stamp** *philately*, any of various stamps issued solely for the use of the Government Life Insurance Department from 1891 to 1990; **Government rag** *hist.*, a paper currency note issued by Governor Fitzroy c1844 (see also SHIN PLASTER); **Government steamer** *hist.*, a coastal ship belonging to and run by the central government; **Government valuation**, the process (or result) of assessing the current value of land, and the improvements thereon, carried out by the Valuation Department (now 'Valuation New Zealand'); the resulting monetary value put upon a parcel of land, and/or the improvements thereon, by such a process.
  1851 in Grace *Pioneer Missionary* (1928) 10 The **Government land agent** had been here during my absence trying to convince them that it would be greatly to their advantage to sell. **1858** *Ibid.* 77 The war at Taranaki commenced by a land agent inducing a Chief to cut a boundary line (for the purpose of sale) through land of which he was, at most, a part owner only! **1940** COWAN *Sir Donald Maclean* 91 Mr. Maclean at this time was M.H.R. for Napier, and also **Government Agent** for the East Coast district. **1959** SINCLAIR *Hist. NZ* 109 In fact, according to a missionary and a government land purchase agent, who had early news of the meeting, no agreement [to form a Maori land league] was made. **1984** BOYD *City of the Plains* 12 It [movement for repudiation] originated in Maori aspirations to repossess land purchased by government agents in the 1850s and by private individuals under the 10-owner system, 1865–73. **1988** *Press* (Christchurch) 30 Aug. 6 He failed to fulfil the terms of the agreement reached between a previous agent, H.T. Kemp, and Ngai Tahu tribespeople at Akaroa in 1848. **1952–53** *NZ Forest Service Gloss.* (TS) **Government cut** A length of log, either at the stump or at the head of a tree which is left in the bush as a result of wasteful cutting. **1937** *NZ Stamp Collector* XVIII. 38 The 2d **Government Life Insurance** printed on thick Cowan paper in orange yellow, seems to have slipped out unnoticed. **1940** *NZ Stamp Collector* XXI. 4 One item.. which is possibly unique is a mint copy of the ½d Government Life Insurance perf. 14 x 11. **1950** *Postage Stamps of NZ* II. 187 The electrotype plates for surface printing from which the Government Life Insurance stamps of this period were produced were in use for over 30 years. **1963** *NZ Stamp Collector* XLIII. 130 The N.Z. Government Life stamps are printed on St Cuthbert's paper. **1970** *NZ Stamp Collector* L. 1 The first Government Life stamps were issued in 1891 and although they have never been available to the public as ordinary postage stamps they have always been an integral part of the New Zealand philatelic scene. **1988** BRODIE *History Government Life Postage Stamps* 85 On August 1935 the Director General of the Post Office G. McNamara made one more effort to get rid of the Government Life's stamps. **1941** SUTHERLAND *Numismatic Hist. NZ* 158 The Fitzroy notes were not issued for values below five shillings. The private paper notes were issued for small change, redeemable mostly in 'Five Shillings, in Government debentures'. Both the debentures and the private notes were issued on poor paper, and soon became known as '**Government Rags**' and 'Shinplasters' respectively. **1972** HARGREAVES *Beads to Banknotes* 41 The [Governor Fitzroy's (1844)] Debentures, popularly known as 'government rags', were given various nicknames. **1966** *Encycl. NZ* III. 332 *Sutherland, Donald* (1839–1919). Backwoodsman... Like so many more of his kind he became embroiled in the Maori Wars, and when fighting was finished he left the Armed Constabulary and took a job..on a **Government steamer**. **1896** *NZ Statutes* (60 Vict.) No.44 129 1. The Short Title of this Act is 'The Government Valuation of Land Act, 1896'. 2. For the Purposes of this Act the Governor may..Appoint a Valuer-General..and such District Valuers and other officers as are deemed necessary. **1896** *NZPD* XCVI. 116 If private individuals wish to avail themselves of the Government valuation of land throughout the colony they should have the opportunity of doing so by paying a fee. **1910** *NZPD* CXLIX, 418 When a man wanted to sell his property to the Government, the Government valuation was, as a rule, altogether too low. **1926** *NZPD* CCIX. 1008 There is no obligation upon local bodies to accept the Government valuations. **1954** *NZPD* CCCIV. 1513 Consideration should be given to Government valuations of land on an unimproved basis. **1986** *Press* (Christchurch) 22 Mar. 8 Government valuations were often conservative.

Government House.

1. An official residence (or former residence) of a Governor(-General) of New Zealand. **a.** Originally at Auckland, from time to time any of various buildings, one of which (occas. so called) presently houses the senior common room of the University of Auckland.
  1840 BEST *Journal* 5 June (1966) 226 I shall describe Govt House. Govt House is a Mauri built dwelling of Wattle & dab. **1856** SEWELL *Journal* 7 July (1980) II. 254 When we arrived [at Auckland] we found Government House far advanced, a large pretentious building, with a Palladian front, greatly disproportioned to the extent of the land around it, and above all, a sham, a wooden building affecting to look like stone..ill-contrived in its internal arrangements..altogether a thing to be ashamed of and disgusted at. **1864** NICHOLL *Journal* 6 Mar. (ATLMS) 152 We went by the Government House, the garden round it is rather well got up. **1974** BARTLETT *Emigrants* 37 Government House was a single storied wooden house, similar to one built at St Helena for Napoleon, pre-cut in London and erected for Governor Hobson.

b. At Wellington. (Now the major official residence.)
  1848 SELWYN in *NZ Part V* (Church in the Colonies XX) (1851) 91 At the temporary church near the Government House the usual English congregation assembled. **1851** *Lyttelton Times* 3 May 7 Given under my hand, and issued under the public seal of the Province of New Munster in the islands of New Zealand, at Government House, at Wellington. **1934** HYDE *Journalese* 107 Once having curtseyed at Government House, the fledglings are kept on exceedingly short commons. **1958** MILLER *Early Victorian NZ* 172 In 1850 a Grand Ball was held at Government House. All the beauty and fashion of Port Nicholson were there. **1986** *Evening Post* (Wellington) 31 Oct. 6 The entrance to Government House, Wellington, will soon have a Taranaki flavour.

2. *Hist. transf.* In occas. former use for the residence of a Provincial Superintendent.
  1898 HOCKEN *Contributions* 154 Messages were

sent down to the House [*sc.* the Otago Provincial Council], a gazette published, and one Proclamation at least issued from 'Government House', meaning, thereby, the pretty cottage of the Superintendent.

3. An early term for a *state house* (STATE).
   1941 *Lower Hutt Past & Present* 58 [Caption] Government Houses in a new street.

government stroke. [AND orig. of convict labour (1842), now freq. of public servants 1856–1979.]
a. A deliberately slow rate of work usu. by a Government workforce for fixed daily hours (usu. 8 a.m. to 5 p.m.).
   1874 TROLLOPE *NZ* 163 In colonial parlance the government stroke is that light and easy mode of labour—perhaps that semblance of labour—which no other master will endure, though government is forced to put up with it. **1898** HOCKEN *Contributions* 103 In [his reply] he showed..that..wages were 50 per cent. higher for 10 per cent. less work than in the old country. The result was unmeasured grumbling and the 'government stroke'. **1905** ACTON-ADAMS *Letters* 14 Aug. in McCaskill *Molesworth* (1969) 92 I want to know if the ordinary station hands work in the summer from 7.30 to 5.30 as they used to or whether you have dropped down to the Government stroke of 8 to 5. **1918** *Quick March* 2 Sept. 1 [The prying policeman] contentedly slithered back into the arms of Morpheus before continuing his—er—Government stroke [*sc.* on his beat]. **1935** *Star-Sun* (Christchurch) 19 Oct. 3 'Government stroke' is a phrase which has become part of New Zealand's language. It was in 1917, in the 'New Zealand Times', that the first article on the subject of 'Government stroke' appeared... Mr. Lawlor now recalls himself as the author. **1950** *PSA Jrnl* July 11 I had heard of 'The Government Stroke', but after my first job, I no longer believed in it. Even as a joke it has now gone out of fashion.

b. Loafing on the job.
   1873 TINNE *Wonderland of Antipodes* 63 On a wet day I have known the boat-men to.. leave us ourselves to carry the mails down to Mangawhare, whilst they did a 'government stroke', and lolled in their huts over a pipe.

c. Relief work or work subsidized by the State.
   1902 *NZ Illustr. Mag.* V. 379 You won't be the only one doing 'Govment stroke' in these parts [that is, free-selection men:- the Government finds them work while learning to farm and while paying off land.]

Hence **(Government) stroker** [AND 1892], one who works at a slow pace in Government or other work.
   1903 D'ESTERRE *Central Otago* 33 There are many 'strokers' in most cooperative labour gangs. **1912** *Evening Post* (Wellington) 21 Aug. 6 In the olden days the term 'Government stroke' was usually applied to the man with the pick or..shovel, but some of the most inveterate 'Government strokers' are armed with a pen.

Governor.
1. As a name for, and in the title of, the Sovereign's representative in New Zealand: as **Governor** 3 May 1841 to 31 Dec. 1847; **Governor-in-Chief** 1 Jan. 1848 to 7 Mar. 1853; **Governor of New Zealand** 7 Mar. 1853 to 27 June 1917; thence **Governor-General** 28 June 1917–. **a.** As **Governor**. *Hist.*
   1840 *Russell to Hobson* 9 Dec. in *GBPP House of Commons 1841 (No.311)* 24 I also transmit a commission under the Great Seal, by which Her Majesty has been pleased to appoint you to be the first governor of New Zealand. **1851** *Lyttelton Times* 12 Apr. 5 Is the Governor to make laws without consulting the people? **1868** *Interpretation Act 32 Vict. s* 12 The terms 'Governor' 'Governor-in-Chief' and 'Lieutenant-Governor' shall mean the person for the time being lawfully administering the Government of New Zealand. **1892** *NZ Official Handbook* 15 The Governor is appointed by the Queen. His salary is £5,000 a year, and is provided by the colony. **1909** [see NATIVE TITLE]. **1917** COX *Diaries 1888–1924* (ATLMS) 28 June It is reported today that the Governor of N.Z. is to be a Governor General.

b. As **Governor-in-Chief**. *Hist.* A title of the principal representative of the sovereign as distinct from the LIEUTENANT-GOVERNORS of the administrative divisions of New Munster, and New Ulster, or from any titular heads of proposed provincial councils.
   1851 *Lyttelton Times* 25 Jan. 3 Provincial Councils Bill... 24. No such Law or Ordinances shall be repugnant to the Law of England or to any ordinance to be made and enacted by the Governor-in-Chief, with the advice and consent of the Legislative Council of New Zealand, or by any General Assembly thereof. **1868** [see above].

c. As **Governor-General**. Occas. as a jocular abbrev. **Gov.-Gen**. See also G.G.
   1917 *Registration of Aliens Act 8 Geo.V* s11 The Governor-General may from time to time, by Order in Council gazetted, make regulations—(c) Prescribing the method in which particulars as to aliens shall be registered under this Act. **1972** *Dominion* (Wellington) 19 Oct. 4 'Yuk Yuk', of Wellington, suggests the story of Gov.-Gen's dogs would have made a good start. **1986** *Constitution Act* s2(2) The Governor-General appointed by the Sovereign is the Sovereign's representative in New Zealand.

2. As **Lieutenant-Governor**. *Hist.* The deputy of the Governor of New Zealand, and in the case of Hobson, a deputy of the then Governor of New South Wales; also later, while these divisions were extant, any of the chief administrators of the 'provinces' of New Munster and New Ulster (see quot. 1851).
   1840 *Gipps to Russell* 9 Feb. in *GBPP House of Commons 1841 (No.311)* 1 The Herald sailed for the Bay of Islands on the 19th ultimo, having on board Lieutenant-governor Hobson and his suite. **1846** *Constabulary Force Ordinance* [preamble] Be it enacted by the Lieutenant-Governor of New Zealand, with the advice of the Legislative Council thereof, as follows. **1848** WAKEFIELD *Handbook NZ* 85 Mr. E.J. Eyre was appointed Lieutenant-Governor, and arrived at Wellington in August, 1847. **1851** [see SUPERINTENDENT]. **1868** [see above]. **1986** *Illustr. Encycl. NZ* 847 Edward Eyre was appointed Lieutenant-Governor of New Munster and a Legislature and Executive Council was set up under the control of Governor-in-Chief Grey.

gow(h)ai, varr. KOWHAI.

grabbing, *vbl. n. Mustering*. The mustering and seizing of small groups of particular sheep, esp. strays or stragglers.
   1955 *NZ Farmer* 10 Oct. 20 The method [of killing wild sheep in Marlborough in 1921] was what was known to musterers as 'grabbing'. A small mob would be collected as conditions permitted with the heading dog... The dog then ran the sheep in behind a bank, fallen tree or boulder on the river bed where they were soon killed.

Hence **grabbing muster**, one undertaken to collect animals missed in a main muster.
   1968 TOMLINSON *Remembered Trails* 31 While one errant mob was being chased others would be getting away, so often they were left. A lot of grabbing musters had to be done after the main muster, but it was not by any means easy to find all the sheep.

graft, *n.* [f. Brit. dial. *graft* (hard) work of any kind: AND 1873.] Work of any kind, often as **hard graft**, demanding work, esp. hard manual or labouring work.
   1853 ROCHFORT *Adventures of Surveyor* 47 Afterwards I could have obtained an engagement in my own profession..but, finding that I could make more money by 'hard graft', as they call labour in the colonies, I would not take it. **c1875** MEREDITH *Adventuring in Maoriland* (1935) 61 After a spell of 'quill-driving' it takes one a week or so to get into one's stride of splitting, fencing, bullock-punching again. Meanwhile, one can make good money at hard graft. **1889** MITCHELL *Rhymes & Rambles* 47 Though the graft [*sc.* digging potatoes] is rather hard, Still industry has its own reward. **1906** PICARD *Ups & Downs* 34 Met a party from the sunny north looking for graft. **1912** FERGUSON *Castle Gay* 49 Aye! men were then, whate'r their craft, If work or skill or solid graft,... To social dictates unconformed. **a1924** ANTHONY *Me & Gus* (1977 Gus Tomlins) 21 It only gave us twenty-six bob for a day's graft. **1991** *Dominion* (Wellington) 26 Dec. 8 It's been hard graft [living and teaching on Pukapuka] —especially when one has been without one's mother tongue.

graft, *v.* [f. Brit. dial. *graft* to perform work: AND 1890; EDD 6 Yorkshire.] *intr.* **a.** To toil, to work hard.
   1889 [see *grafting vbl. n.* below]. **1908** KOEBEL *Anchorage* 78 He's been graftin' like a nigger all the morning. **1911** *Triad* 11 Sept. 45 The Premier's Private Secretary I was 'grafting' in the office long after the 'boss' had left. **1944** *Short Guide NZ* 37 To 'graft' means to work hard.

b. In Rugby Union, esp. of a forward, to play a hard and willing game.
   c1894 *Waikato Times (special edition)* in Norris *Settlers in Depression* (1964) 221 J.J. Sampson..centre forward grafted hard, splendid dribbler. J. Montgomery..worked hard in the pack, good at line play and always grafted hard. **1905** *Truth* 26 Aug. 2 The forwards shaped solidly and grafted well.

Hence **grafter**, occas. **hard grafter** *n.* [AND 1891], a hard (and willing) worker, a toiler; **grafting** *vbl. n.* and *ppl. a.* [AND *ppl. a.* 1980 (sport)], (hard-)working.
   1905 *Truth* 24 June 2 He was a hard **grafter**, was Murray. **1906** *Ibid.* 17 Feb. 8 The grafter has to pay his 2/6 first. **1930** *NZ Short Stories* 176 Actually Joe Tracy was not an idle man. He was a spasmodic grafter. **1946** SARGESON *That Summer* 162 The Williams were grafters. **1968** SEDDON *The Seddons* 295 In Australia and in New Zealand if you called a man 'a good grafter' you would mean he was a good worker. **1980** LELAND *Kiwi-Yankee Dict.* 51 *hard grafter:* The man you want to hire! Gung-ho all the way—this is the Stakhnovite [*sic*] of New Zealand. A hard worker. **1889** DAVIDSON *Stories NZ Life* 40 My brother Jim had to do the roughest of the '**grafting**'. He had to push his way up-country. **1907** KOEBEL *Return of Joe* 93 [He has] only seen us in our **graftin'** clothes. **1963** *Dominion* (Wellington) 23 Sept. 1 This solid grafting fellow may have won his position in the touring [rugby] team when it was found that the big..Aucklander was unable to pass the doctor.

grain-store. A large urban building for storing grain (esp. wheat, barley, oats) for sale.
   1874 *Oamaru Times* May in *Hist. N. Otago from 1853* (1978) 155 The space around the grain stores in Tyne street presents a busy appearance from day to

GRANDFATHER 308 **GRASS**

day. **1914** in *Hist. N. Otago from 1853* (1978) 90 On the Globe Hotel corner, was Mr Charles Traill's grain store. **1936** HYDE *Passport to Hell* 44 She was always down on the strip of beach behind the grain-stores on whose cobwebby, warm-smelling floor-space there were sometimes mass assaults with sacks and French chalk in preparation for dances.

grandfather, *attrib.* Used as an epithet suggesting size and age as in **grandfather hapuku**, see HAPUKU; **grandfather moth**, a large moth.
   1982 FRAME *To the Is-land* (1984) 56 We noted [at Oamaru]..the insects, bees, mason bees, night bees, butterflies, grandfather moths, spiders.

grandies, *n. pl.* [f. *grand*(parents + -IE + s.] A familiar or domestic term for grandparents.
   1995 ANDERSON *House Guest* 109 He sat in Margery's warm crowded flat filled with..snaps of her grandies and chairs with fat cushions.

granite. *Otago goldmining.* [Transf. use of *granite* a hard igneous rock.] Also as **granite wash**, unconsolidated superficial coarse quartz-rich alluvium washed out from an adjacent eroding granite ridge.
   1906 *NZGeol.SB (NS)* No.2 24 At River's claim the gold-wash..lies directly on the schist, and is followed by fine quartz sands and silts.., in turn followed by quartzose drifts—the 'granite wash' of the local miners [in Central Otago]. **1918** *NZGeol.SB (NS)* No.19 60 Quartz-grits..These fine gravels are locally [at Tuapeka] known by the strangely incorrect name 'granite'. **1933** *NZJST* XIV. 272 Areas of Maori Bottom and quartz conglomerates..the alluvial miners [of Central Otago] thought they were dealing with superficial alluvial deposits; they called the conglomerates the 'granite wash'.

granite trout. [f. the mottled black and slaty grey skin colour and pattern.] MARBLEFISH.
   1876 *TrNZI* VIII. 211 Haplodactylus meandratus. Granite Trout. **1906** *Ibid.* XXXVIII. 549 The granite trout is not infrequently met with in the harbour. **1917** WILLIAMS *Dict. Maori Lang.* 122 *Katirimu*, n. *haplodactylus meandratus*, granite trout; a sea-fish. = *kehe*. **1938, 1957** [see MARBLEFISH a]. **1966** DOOGUE & MORELAND *Sea Anglers' Guide* 246 Marblefish..granite trout; keke (Maori). **1986** PAUL *NZ Fishes* 111 Marblefish *Aplodactylus arctidens*. Also called marble trout, granite trout, Maori chief... Regularly seen by divers, sometimes speared or taken in shallow setnets... Poor eating.

granny, *attrib.* [AND 1, 1851: the *Sydney Morning Herald* as a type of an old-established, respectable newspaper given to conservative public advice.]
   1. *Obs.* The *Lyttelton Times* newspaper.
   1911 *Truth* 1 Apr. 4 Granny Lyttelton 'Times' wags her old womanish tongue in commenting on the 'secret' case as follows.
   2. As **Granny Herald**, the *New Zealand Herald*, Auckland.
   [**1910** *Truth* 30 July 4 The grandmother of the New Zealand press, the 'Auckland Herald', comes to light with an amazing story.] **1913** *NZ Observer* 29 Nov. 17 The tremendous and overwhelming unpopularity of Granny Herald..has been one of the most gingery developments of the big strike. **1964** MIDDLETON *Walk on Beach* 216 He would..unfold the morning paper and come out with: 'Let's see what Granny Herald's dishing out today.' **1986** *Metro* (Auckland) July 31 It's a genteel institution so established in Auckland, and so inescapable, that it has been personalised and familiarised and patronised as Granny. Does the name still fit? **1992** *Ibid.* Feb. 27 That was a very sympathetic article Granny Herald did about the launch of the McCahon Trust.

granny bonnet. [Cf. EDD (6) *granny-hood*, Yorkshire.] Species of *Aquilegia* (fam. Ranunculaceae), in New Zealand often called *aquilegia*, elsewhere *columbine*.
   1964 JEFFEREY *Mairangi* 9 The seeping dankness, the granny-bonnets and ladder ferns growing in unconventional places, the silent, entombed atmosphere. **1968** TURNER Review of *Pitcairnese Lang.* in *Anglia* LXXXVI. 360 Granny bonnet..is commonly used for the columbine in New Zealand. **1980** ADAMS *Wild Flowers* 22 Columbine and granny bonnet are popular names for an old-fashioned perennial flower now found in wayside places. Columbines seed freely and often hybridise... Botanical name: *Aquilegia vulgaris*, Europe. Family: Ranunculaceae. **1992** PARK *Fence around the Cuckoo* 12 When I knew..[Te Kuiti], it was a mid to late Victorian village, a town of corrugated-iron roofs:.. granny bonnets, larkspurs and cosmos in the gardens.

grapefruit. [Transf. use of *grapefruit*, the name of the fruit of the subtropical tree *Citrus paradisi* (fam. Rutaceae).] Usu. as **New Zealand grapefruit**, the plant and fruit of a hybrid cultivar of *Citrus maxima* and *C. aurantium*. See also *poorman's orange* (POOR MAN 2).
   1937, 1938[1], **1966** [see POOR MAN 2]. **1978** *Otago Daily Times* (Dunedin) 1 July 7 [Heading] N.Z. Grapefruit Wrongly Named. The export potential of New Zealand grapefruit could be enhanced if it was renamed, delegates to the annual conference of the New Zealand Citrus and Sub-tropical Council have been told... New Zealand grapefruit are not, in fact, grapefruit at all. They are a type of orangelo, and probably more accurately described by the nickname 'poor man's orange'. **1986** grapefruit [see POOR MAN 2].

grass.
   1. Any plant belonging to the family Poaceae (formerly Gramineae), or resembling members of that family in general appearance. See also ENGLISH GRASS, *native grass* (NATIVE B 2 a); and BAYONET GRASS, *cotton-grass* (COTTON PLANT, *Celmisia* sp.), CUTTING-GRASS or CUTTY-GRASS, *eel-grass* (EEL *n.* 4), HOOKGRASS, KARETU, PAMPAS GRASS, PORCUPINE GRASS, PURUA GRASS, SCURVY-GRASS, SILK GRASS, SPEARGRASS, SWORD-GRASS, TOETOE, TUSSOCK.

   2. Of the almost 200 common names of grasses collected, the following 46, many of them native grasses, are considered to have significant New Zealand reference (see further 1880 BUCHANAN *Manual of Indigenous Grasses*, 1992 Lambrechtsen *What Grass is That?* (4edn)). Their common names are usu. formed from *modifier + grass(-name)*: **avalanche, barley, bastard-, bay, blue-, New Zealand browntop, buffalo, bunch, bunny, carpet, Chilean (Chilian, Chili), coast, curly (curly snow), danthonia, elephant, feathery, fescue (Chewings, tall,** etc. **fescue), fortune, hair, hassock, hedgehog, holy, love, matua, mercer, needle (Chilian needle), oat, pincushion, plume, poa (common field, desert, tussock poa), rice (bush** or **meadow** or **New Zealand rice), rolling, salt, sand (sand-fescue), snow, snow patch, swamp, tinker, tree-, tuft (tufted), tumble, Vasey, wheat (blue wheat), white man's, wind.**

(1) **avalanche grass.** *Poa cockayniana*, a sward-forming grass of South Island alpine regions.
   1969 *Standard Common Names Weeds* 3 avalanche grass *Poa cockayniana* Petrie. **1978** WILSON *Wild Plants Mt. Cook National Park* 235 *Poa cockayniana* Avalanche grass.

(2) **barley grass.** [See OED *barley* 2; AND 1846.] Applied in New Zealand, and also in Britain (often as *meadow barley*), North America, and in Australia to various wild species of *Hordeum* (and occas., erroneously, of *Bromus*), the former use being recorded in New Zealand from 1891.

(3) **bastard-grass.** *Uncinia* spp. See also HOOKGRASS.
   1950 p.c. N.C.C. Small, W. Cameron; R. Mason (1953): used by Tararua trampers for a cutty-grass with little hooks on blades growing in small clumps. So-called, because 'it is a bastard to walk through'. North Island. **1988** PICKERING *Hills* 8 So to cope with the rituals of tramping, its pains and camaraderie, a slang language has developed to suit..[for example] 'bastard grass' and 'lawyer' (two unpleasant plants).

(4) **bay grass.** [Origin uncertain.] *Eragrostis brownii*, a perennial grass introduced from Australia. See also *love grass* (23) below.
   1951 LEVY *Grasslands NZ* (1970) 4 Associated with danthonia are baygrass, Heath grass, and ratstail. **1969** *Standard Common Names Weeds* 4 bay grass *Eragrostis brownii*..Nees. **1992** LAMBRECHTSEN *What Grass Is That?* 83 Bay grass... Common in waste places and poor pastures throughout North Island, especially in gumlands and on the East Coast.

(5) **blue-grass.** [Transf. use of *bluegrass* (Kentucky bluegrass) for *Poa* spp., esp. *P. pratensis*: see OED.] Applied in New Zealand to *Elymus rectisetus* (formerly *Agropyron scabrum*), a native grass with blue-green leaves; less commonly to other *Elymus* spp. See also *wheat-grass* (44) below.
[*Note*] *Poa pratensis* also is known in New Zealand as **Kentucky bluegrass**.
   1872 *TrNZI* IV. 303 *Triticum scabrum*... The blue-grass of settler; a valuable grass found in many countries. **1910** COCKAYNE *NZ Plants & Their Story* 87 Another grass of great importance is the blue-grass (*Agropyron scabrum*), still more or less abundant in some localities. **1921** GUTHRIE-SMITH *Tutira* (1926) 165 Here and there, too, on the rocks grew plants of blue grass (*Agropyr[on] scabrum*). **1933** *Press* (Christchurch) (Acland Gloss.) 16 Sept. 15 Blue-grass... A beautiful grass [blue wheat grass] on which horses are said to have worked as well as on oats. **1947** BEATTIE *Early Runholding* 152 Instead of conserving the native grasses..the early settlers burned them off..so that steep slopes that in the 'fifties were covered with rich 'blue grass' and anise are now quite bare. **1982** WILSON *Stewart Is. Plants* 406 *Agropyron scabrum* Bluegrass..Pātiti taranui... Bluish-green tufts of narrow leaves... Native to: N, S, St[ewart Islands]. Also Tasmania and Australia. (Now correctly called *Elymus rectisetus*).

(6) **browntop.** An early variant **New Zealand browntop** has been infrequently applied to *Agrostis capillaris* (formerly *A. tenuis*), a northern hemisphere grass of poor pasture land, distinguished in summer by its brownish-red flower heads.
   1936 BELSHAW et al. *Agric. Organiz. NZ* 358 The Danthonia tussock *D. Raoulii*, particularly of the

lowlands, is essentially potential grassland country, and in its natural state will support a sward of *Agrostis tenuis* (New Zealand Brown Top). [**1986** JOHNSON *Wildflowers Central Otago* 94 A lot of yarrow continues to flower into April and May, and browntop is the most persistent grass, catching the dews and frosts.]

(7) **buffalo grass**. [First noticed near Buffalo Creek, New South Wales: AND 1875.] *Stenotaphrum secundatum*, a coarse, springy lawn grass of usu. sandy soils, introduced from N. America (but not the *buffalo grass* of the North American prairies, *Buchloe dactyloides*).
1874 *TrNZI* VI. 48 *Stenotaphrum secundatum* buffalo grass. **1909** CHUDLEIGH *Diary* 17 Apr. (1950) 447 Then on to see J.J. Fougere where I got a sod of buffalo grass and another sod of native grass. **1951** LEVY *Grasslands NZ* (1970) 4 Kikuyu grass from Africa thrives well, whilst an old-timer, buffalo grass, holds its own in places. **1967** HILGENDORF & CALDER *Weeds* 55 Buffalo Grass..also called St. Augustine's grass. A perennial with stout creeping surface stems (stolons). **1981** TAYLOR *Weeds of Roadsides* 29 Buffalo Grass (*Stenotaphrum secundatum*). Low perennial with growth habit of Kikuyu grass.

(8) **bunch grass**. More commonly called 'short tussock', a tufted perennial grass, usually a *Festuca*, or a *Poa* species.
1959 MCLINTOCK *Descr. Atlas* 24 Tussock (bunch grass) grasslands, generally with species of *Poa* and *Festuca* dominant.

(9) **bunny grass**. *Lagarus ovatus*, the introduced hare's tail grass. Cf. *pussy-grass* (31) below.
1969 *Standard Common Names Weeds* 9 *bunnies* [=] *haretail*. **1980** LOCKLEY *House Above Sea* 199 One of the early colonisers of the bared shore above high tide..is the conspicuous, woolly-headed harestail (bunny) grass.

(10) **carpet grass**. [Spec. use of *carpet grass*, one which forms a close, smooth sward.] *Chionochloa* (formerly *Danthonia*) *australis*, a native alpine grass which forms extensive smooth swards on slopes. See also *hassock-grass* (20) below.
1906 CHEESEMAN *Manual NZ Flora* 888 *D[anthonia] australis*.. Forming extensive patches on alpine or subalpine slopes... 'Carpet-grass'; 'Hassock-grass'. A well-marked species, often covering acres on the higher mountains of Nelson and North Canterbury, usually affecting steep slopes. **1952** THOMSON *Deer Hunter* 99 A kind of carpet grass was also in abundance. It grows in a dense mass and when one walks across it, especially on a steep slope, caution has to be exercised. **1969** *Standard Common Names Weeds* 30 *grass, carpet Chionochloa australis*. **1988** DAWSON *Forest Vines to Snow Tussocks* 174 Among the smaller species of *Chionochloa*, which are found mostly at higher levels in herbfield, carpet grass (*C. australis*) is worth a special mention. As its common name indicates it does not have a tussock habit, but forms thick, extensive swards.

(11) **Chilean (Chilian, Chili) grass**. *Obs*. A local name for *Sporobolus africanus* (formerly *indicus*).
1872 *TrNZI* IV. 298 *Sporobolus elongatus* is generally known as 'Rat's-tail grass' as far south as Lake Taupo; but at Port Waikato it is called 'Chilean-grass,' as it is erroneously supposed to have been introduced with the so-called 'Chilian groundsel' *Erigeron canadensis*, a plant which appears to have been brought to this colony with grass seed from South America. **1883** *Brett's Colonists' Guide* 82 Rat-tail, or Chilian Grass (*sporobolus elongatus*) [*sic*]. This is a hard, wiry, tough grass, and affords good pasture for horses and cattle. **1892** *Auckland Weekly News* 26 Mar.

31 The botanical name of rat-tail or Chilian grass is..Sporobolus elongatus... Land full of rat-tail is a terror to plough, as too many settlers know. **1921** GUTHRIE-SMITH *Tutira* (1926) 179 Chilian grass or Rat's-tail (*Sporobolus indicus*), according to the late Bishop Williams, made its first appearance at the Bay of Islands in 1840, shortly after the arrival of a ship called the *Surabayo*, which, while on a voyage from Valparaiso to Sydney laden with horses and forage, put into the Bay of Islands in a disabled state, and was there condemned and her cargo sold. *Ibid*. 291 At present it carries a hirsute mat of Chili grass (*Sporobolus indicus*).

(12) **coast grass**. A local (Hawke's Bay) name for *Microlaena stipoides*, the native grass of coastal sand country. See also *meadow rice grass* (32) below.
1908 *TrNZI* XL. 516 This *Microlaena* [*M. stipoides*] goes by the local [Hawke's Bay] name of 'coast grass', but it grows freely sixteen miles inland at least, and at an elevation of over 3,000 ft. **1921** GUTHRIE-SMITH *Tutira* (1926) 291 When first known to me it still maintained what was probably its original vegetation—coast grass (*Microlaena stipoides*) and sparse spray-swept bracken.

(13) **curly (curly snow) grass**. *Chionochloa crassiuscula*, a moderately tall grass of alpine soils, distinguished by its thick curling leaf tips. Cf. TUSSOCK 3 (11).
1969 *Standard Common Names Weeds* 31 *grass, curly* [=] *curly snow tussock*. **1978** WILSON *Wild Plants of Mt. Cook National Park* 227 Chionochloa crassiuscula. Curled snow tussock, curly snowgrass.

(14) **danthonia (grass)**, see DANTHONIA.

(15) **elephant grass**. *Obs*. [Transf. use of *elephant grass* any of various tall robust tropical grasses.] *Paspalum urvillei*. See also *Vasey grass* (43) below.
1969 *Standard Common Names Weeds* 23 *elephant grass* [=] *Vasey grass*.

(16) **feathery grass**. [f. the appearance of the flower-head plumes.] TOETOE 1 a.
1905 *TrNZI* XXXVII. 119 *Arundo conspicua*. (Toetoe; Feathery-grass.) **1979** STARK *Maori Herbal Remedies* 101 *Cortaderia toetoe*, known as Feathery Grass, is a true grass found mainly near the coasts, around swampy places, or near streams.

(17) **fescue**. Any of many tufted native and introduced grasses of *Festuca* spp.; in New Zealand esp. **Chewings fescue** and **tall fescue**, and with other modifiers **Chatham Island, drooping, hard, sand, sandhill**.
[*Note*] In common names and reference *fescue* is often interchangeable with *tussock*.

a. Chatham Island fescue. *Festuca coxii*, a grass endemic to Chatham Island.
1911 *AJHR C-13* 35 *[Festuca Coxii]* Chatham Island fescue. Originally probably common, but now almost confined to ledges of rock covered with sand.

b. Chewings fescue; also *ellipt*. **Chewings**. Also erron. spelled -'*s*, -*s*'. [From the name of Charles Chewings (1859–1937); see quot. 1957.] A New Zealand cultivar of red fescue *Festuca nigrescens* (formerly *F. rubra*), a pasture grass.
1900 *TrNZI* XXXII. 237 The following grasses have done fairly well..: Prairie-grass, Chewing's fescue. **1912** *NZJAg*. Jan. IV. 21 Chewing's fescue: A few plants, but not doing well. Hard fescue: [ditto]. **1920** MACDONALD *Austral. & NZ Sheepfarming* 112 It is therefore necessary to sow only a small quantity of Chewing's, or preferably..have what might be called a 'Chewing's' paddock. **1936** BELSHAW et al. *Agric. Organiz. NZ* 81 The land is becoming gradually less

productive owing to the replacement of good by poor pasture plants such as redtop..Danthonia and Chewings fescue. **1957** *NZJAg*. Sept. XCV. 293 The history of the production of chewings fescue seed goes back to 1880, when a farmer in the Rimu district of Southland sowed down a 2-acre paddock in grass... The origin of the seed that was sown is obscure. *Ibid*. 295 The small paddock was harvested for seed, and later some, if not all, of this seed was used for sowing in some of the paddocks on 'Glenelg', a property in the Mossburn district of Southland. In 1887 that property was bought by Mr. George Chewings, and the first considerable quantity of seed, about 80 sacks, was harvested in 1890... Mr. Chewings went to the North Island on holiday [c1890], and during his visit advised various runholders to try some of his fescue seed... The result was that inquiries were received in Invercargill for samples of and quotes for 'Chewings' fescue', and the seed has been called chewings fescue since then. **1965** GILLHAM *Naturalist in NZ* 59 We passed through the famous chewings fescue pastures near Mossburn. **1985** BENTLEY & FRASER *Grand Limerick Tour* [No.] 67 On the drought-ridden Takapu Plain The sheep are most -ept, -ert, and -ane; All hail Chewings' Fescue That came to the rescue, Super grass, for a very brief rain.

c. drooping fescue. *Festuca multinodis*, a native grass distinguished by its sprawling habit and conspicuous nodes.
1915 *AJHR C-6* 11 *[Festuca multinodis]*. Drooping-fescue. Shaded rock.

d. hard fescue. *Festuca novae-zelandiae*, the common hard tussock of montane-subalpine grassland.
1880 BUCHANAN *Indigenous Grasses NZ* 159 *Festuca Duriuscula*..Hard fescue grass... A tall, slender, densely tufted grass. **1912** [see b above].

e. sand-fescue (sandhill fescue). *Poa triodioides* (also called *Austrofestuca littoralis*), a native grass of sand dunes.
1880 BUCHANAN *Indigenous Grasses NZ* 155 *Festuca littoralis*, var. *triticoides*..Sand Hill Fescue Grass... A tall, densely tufted littoral grass... Abundant on the coasts of New Zealand, where they are of great value in assisting to bind drifting sand. **1898** MORRIS *Austral-English* 169 Fescue G[rass].—Sandhill—*F. littoralis*..var. Triticoides. **1909** *AJHR C-12* 50 *Festuca littoralis*. Sandhill-fescue. Dunes. **1911** *AJHR C-13* 26 *Festuca littoralis* (the Sand Fescue-grass). *Ibid*. 35 *Festuca littoralis*. Sand-fescue. **1982** WILSON *Stewart Is. Plants* 380 *Poa triodioides* Sand Tussock..Sandhill fescue... Locally common, coastal sand dunes... Also Australia (=*Festuca littoralis*).

(18) **fortune grass**, see *tinker grass* (39) below.

(19) **hair grass**. [From its hair-like awns.] **a**. Usu. with a modifier: **southern (tufted, turfy) hairgrass**, *Deschampsia caespitosa*, or less commonly, *D. chapmanii*, a native tufted grass of damp sites.
1880 BUCHANAN *Indigenous Grasses NZ* 93 *Deschampsia Caespitosa*. Tufted Hair grass. **1898** MORRIS *Austral-English* 169 Hair G[rass].- Turfy—*Deschampsia caespitosa*. **1909** *AJHR C-12* 49 *Deschampsia caespitosa* tufted hair-grass. Semi salt meadow. Not common... *[Deschampsia] Chapmanni* southern hair grass. Subalpine meadow. **1936** BELSHAW et al. *Agric. Organiz. NZ* 365 This [Central Otago] country in its natural state carries a very poor type of vegetation, consisting of *Poa* and *Festuca* tussock..to depleted country, where scabweed..together with sorrel..storksbill..[and] hairgrass, may form the dominant cover. **1969** *Standard Common Names Weeds* 80 *tufted hair grass Deschampsia caespitosa*.

b. As elsewhere, applied to any of various introduced grasses of *Aira* or *Vulpia* spp.

1969 *Standard Common Names Weeds* 30 *grass, colonial hair* [=] *vulpia hair grass.* **1992** LAMBRECHTSEN *What Grass Is That?* 39 *Aira caryophyllea* L... Silvery hair grass.

(20) **hassock grass.** See *carpet grass* (10) above.
1906 CHEESEMAN *Manual NZ Flora* 888 *Danthonia australis.* Hassock-grass. **1961** ALLAN *Flora NZ* I. 479 [*Aciphylla* is found] in hassock grass of [Mt. Peel] summit ridge, 5000 ft. **1969** *Standard Common Names Weeds* 31 *grass, hassock* [=] *carpet grass.*

(21) **hedgehog grass.** *Echinopogon ovatus*, a shade-loving native annual grass having scabrous stems rough to the touch and bristly flower heads.
1969 *Standard Common Names Weeds* 31 *grass, hedgehog Echinopogon ovatus.*

(22) **holy grass.** [Local use of British *holy grass Hierochloe* spp.] A native grass of the genus *Hierochloe*. See also KARETU.
1880 BUCHANAN *Indigenous Grasses NZ* 13 *Hierochloe Alpina.* The Holy Grass... A slender subspecies will be valuable in the sub-alpine pastures of New Zealand as an early and nutritious food..for sheep. **1898** MORRIS *Austral-English* 169 Holy G[rass]. *Hierochloe alpina*..(Australasia, not endemic.) **1909** *AJHR C-12* 18 Here is a broad line of the stiff clubrush..with the holy-grass (*Hierochloe redolens*) growing through it. **1936, 1961, 1978** [see KARETU]. **1982** WILSON *Stewart Is. Plants* 410 *Hierochloe* [=holy grass] *redolens* [=sweet scented] Holy Grass... Kāretu.

(23) **love grass.** See *bay grass* (4) above.
1969 *Standard Common Names Weeds* 45 *love grass* [=] *bay grass.*

(24) **matua grass.** *Bromus unioloides*, a cultivar of prairie grass developed and named by the then New Zealand Department of Scientific and Industrial Research.
1986 *Press* (Christchurch) 24 Oct. The design was conceived..when he had problems last year drilling Matua prairie grass. **1990** *Dominion* (Wellington) 11 Jan. 7 Matua grass, a strain developed by the Department of Scientific and Industrial Research about 15 years ago, has performed well after two years of tests in Pennsylvania... Australia is the main foreign buyer of matua with European countries close behind.

(25) **mercer grass.** [Origin uncertain.] *Paspalum paspalodes* (formerly *P. distichum*), an introduced perennial grass with creeping stolons found in wet places in northern New Zealand.
1969 *Standard Common Names Weeds* 48 *Mercer grass Paspalum distichum.* **1992** LAMBRECHTSEN *What Grass Is That?* 113 *Paspalum distichum* L. (*P. paspalodes* (Michx.) Scribn.).. Mercer Grass... Common in wet pastures, swamps, and besides rivers and lakes throughout the North Island, especially the northern half.

(26) **needle grass.** [f. the needle-like appearance of the leaf.] A specific or local use for either of two grasses: **a.** *Rytidosperma* (formerly *Danthonia*) *setifolium*, a native grass with stiff, thin leaves.
1961 MARTIN *Flora NZ* 130 On the mountains of both islands the Wiry Danthonia (*D. setifolia*), so called because of the stiff, erect, acicular leaves, is the commoner species over wide areas. In Marlborough it is sometimes termed the Needle Grass.
b. Often as **Chilean needle grass**, an introduced grass of the genus *Stipa*.
1969 *Standard Common Names Weeds* 13 *Chilean needle grass Stipa neesiana. Ibid.* 52 *needle grass Stipa variabilis.* **1975** *Tane* 21 8 Gramineae *Stipa teretifolia* needle grass. **1981** TAYLOR *Weeds of Lawns* 30 Chilean Needle Grass (*Stipa neesiana*)... This South American grass is well established in dense patches on roadsides and in meadows at Blind River, 30km southeast of Blenheim. *Ibid.* 76 Needle Grass (*Stipa variabilis*)... This Australian grass is common in parts of Marlborough and Canterbury, and waves conspicuously in wind in the hills south of Blenheim and on Banks Peninsula from November.

(27) **oat grass.** A spec. use of the term for any of various native tufted grasses having flower heads with conspicuous oat-like awns; the simplex is usu. prefixed by one of many various modifiers.
a. *Obs.* A former name for the tussock grasses *Chionochloa* (formerly *Danthonia*) and *Rytidosperma* species. See also *oat tussock* (TUSSOCK 3 (7)).
c1857 GARVIE *Report* in Beattie *Early Runholding* (1947) 19 On the opposite side..the grass becomes rather thin, and consists almost entirely of one specie— a kind of oat grass, with a black seed. **1860** MURDOCH *Journal* Feb. in Beattie *Early Runholding* (1947) 116 The grass here [in Otago], called oat-grass, is very similar to, if not the same, as the kangaroo grass of Tasmania. **1880** BUCHANAN *Indigenous Grasses NZ* 83 *Danthonia semi-annularis.* New Zealand Oat Grass. *Ibid.* 85 *Danthonia semi-annularis.* Sheep Oat Grass. *Ibid.* 87 *Danthonia Buchanani.* Buchanan's oat grass... A tall, tufted, glabrous, perennial grass, found 1000–2000 feet altitude... It is a tall oat-like grass, the dark orange spikelets of which attract the attention very readily. **1898** MORRIS *Austral-English* 170 Oat G[rass].- Sheep—*Danthonia semi-annularis*..var. *gracilis*... Oat G[rass].- Hard—*D. pilosa*..var. *stricta*... Oat G[rass].- Alpine—*Danthonia semi-annularis*, var. *alpina*... Oat G[rass].- New Zealand—*D. Semi-annularis.* **1909** *AJHR C-12* 49 *Danthonia crassiuscula.* Alpine oat-grass. Subalpine meadow. **1911** *AJHR C-13* 34 *Danthonia semiannularis.* Common oat grass; Danthonia grass, medium, tufted. **1922** *NZJST* IV. 281 The gorge between Clyde and Cromwell, now bare and barren looking, when I was familiar with it in 1868 had an abundance of tussock and other grasses, including one known locally as oat-grass (*Danthonia*, species probably *flavescens*), which grew plentifully among the rocks on the lower slopes. **1939** BEATTIE *First White Boy Born Otago* 119 From this onward [in Central Otago c1860] two native grasses, known to the early stockmen as barley grass and oat grass respectively from a chance resemblance to those two cereals, were predominant.
b. A name for *Trisetum antarcticum*, a bluish-green tufted grass of montane-subalpine areas.
1872 *TrNZI* IV. 300 *Trisetum antarcticum.* Oat-grass.—A local grass, widely distributed; found from sea-level to 1,500 feet in dry soil; flowers October to January; useful in spring and summer; is affected by drought; a valuable grass. **1880** BUCHANAN *Indigenous Grasses NZ* 97 *Trisetum antarcticum.* Shining Oat Grass. **1909** *AJHR C-12* 49 *Trisetum antarcticum.* Shining oat-grass. Heath, subalpine meadow. **1939** *NZJST* XX. 233A The following species appear to merit thorough testing as to their nutritive quality..: native oat-grass *(Trisetum* spp.).. aniseed..and some species of *Anisotome*.
c. *Deyeuxia avenoides*, a small dark-green grass of alpine grasslands.
1969 *Standard Common Names Weeds* 50 *mountain oat grass Deyeuxia avenoides.*

(28) **pincushion grass.** *Agrostis muscosa*, a small, native blue-green grass forming soft patches, fancifully resembling pincushions.
1969 *Standard Common Names Weeds* 32 *grass, pincushion Agrostis muscosa.*

(29) **plume grass.** Either of *Dichelachne crinita* (**long-hair (-haired) plume grass**), a tall native grass with a shaggy flowering head having long awns; or *D. micrantha* (formerly *sciurea*) (**shorthair (-haired) plume grass**), a tall native grass with a spike-like flower head containing twisted awns.
1880 BUCHANAN *Indigenous Grasses NZ* 31 *Dichelachne crinita.* Long Hair Plume Grass. *Ibid.* 33 *Dichelachne sciurea.* Short Hair Plume Grass. **1898** MORRIS *Austral-English* 170 Plume G[rass].- Short-Haired *D. sciurea.* **1923** *NZJST* VI. 146 Dichelachne crinita..(plume-grass). Abundant, especially on the lower slopes, and even quite close to the sea. **1961** MARTIN *Flora NZ* 133 A common associate [of Danthonia] is the Plume Grass..., a tall, tufted annual grass with a long, terminal, dense spike with long projecting hair-like awns. **1969** *Standard Common Names Weeds* 69 *short-hair plume grass Dichelachne sciurea.* **1981** TAYLOR *Weeds of Roadsides* 111 *Long-hair Plume Grass* (*Dichelachne crinita*) Native, unimportant but very conspicuous when seeding in early summer... *Short-hair Plume Grass* (*Dichelachne sciurea*) Native, much more abundant and widespread than..[long-hair] but less conspicuous.

(30) **poa.** [f. the generic name *Poa*, species of meadow grass, transf. to New Zealand species.] Usu. with a modifier: **common field, desert, tussock. a. common field poa.** *Poa anceps.*
1880 BUCHANAN *Indigenous Grasses NZ* 119 *Poa anceps*, var. b., *foliosa.* Common Field Poa. **1923** *NZJST* VI. 146 *Poa anceps*..(common field poa). Mount Herbert, 2,800 ft., south and west sides.

b. desert poa. *Poa maniototo*, a tiny native grass of stony river flats of Otago and Canterbury.
1969 *Standard Common Names Weeds* 21 *desert poa* [=] *Poa maniototo.*

c. tussock poa. *Poa cita*, *silver tussock* (TUSSOCK 3 (10)).
1880 BUCHANAN *Indigenous Grasses NZ* 131 *Poa Intermedia*..Small Tussac Poa..A small tufted or tussac grass, from near sea level to 5000 feet altitude. **1898** MORRIS *Austral-English* 171 Poa G[rass].- Tussock— *P. caespitosa.* **1969** *Standard Common Names Weeds* 59 *poa, tussock* [=] *silver tussock.*

(31) **pussy-grass.** A grass with a long soft catkin, prob. the introduced hare's tail grass *Lagarus ovatus*. Cf. *bunny grass* (9) above.
1937 HYDE *Wednesday's Children* 75 Turning from the island's fauna to its flora, it had three kinds of grasses..a tawny twitch-grass.., pussy-grass, which was pale yellow and slender, furnished with a long catkin useful for tickling the neck of the person in front, and cutty grass. *Ibid.* 126 Pussy-grass grew through [the sand], thousands and thousands of whittled slender stalks, with nodding cream catkins at the ends of them.

(32) **rice grass.** [AND 1849.] Either of two species of *Microlaena*, *M. avenacea* (usu. as **bush rice grass**), a native grass of lowland forests; or *M. stipoides* (usu. as **meadow** or **New Zealand**) **rice grass**, a native grass with a creeping rhizome usu. found in shaded coastal woodland. See also *coast grass* (12) above.
1880 BUCHANAN *Indigenous Grasses NZ* 6 *Microlaena avenacea.* Bush Rice Grass. *Ibid.* 58 *Microlaena stipoides.* Meadow Rice Grass. **1892** *Auckland Weekly News* 30 Dec. 35 The fine-bladed grass is Microlena stipoides, or Rice grass, indigenous to the colony. **1898** MORRIS *Austral-English* 171 Rice G[rass].—Meadow—*M. stipoides*..Called also *Weeping Grass.* **1909** *AJHR C-12* 49 [*Microlaena avenacea*]. Bush rice-grass. Forests. Common. **1911** *AJHR C-13* 34 *Microlaena stipoides.* Meadow rice-grass. Grass dune. **1922** PERRY *Sheep Farming* 104 There are a few

other grasses used to a limited extent, such as Rice grass, Tall Oat grass, and Prairie grass, but they have a limited use, and need not be considered here. **1936** *Handbook NZ* (ANZAAS) 99 New Zealand rice-grass (*Microlaena stipoides*) is common in the warmer coastal areas. **1951** LEVY *Grasslands NZ* (1970) 30 Treading of stock led to a permanent perennial plant association, dominated by danthonia and including meadow rice-grass..and annual clovers such as suckling. **1969** *Standard Common Names Weeds* 64 *rice grass, bush Microlaena avenacea*. **1981** TAYLOR *Weeds of Lawns* 70 Meadow Rice Grass (*Microlaena stipoides*)... This low-growing native grass..is widespread in bush margins and in second-class pasture. **1982** WILSON *Stewart Is. Plants* 414 *Microlaena avenacea* Bush Rice Grass Dull blue-green tussock..completely unpalatable. **1992** SMITHYMAN *Auto/Biographies* 76 Small towns of our country, how many of them..want something which recalls their declared being as wind sighs through rice grass along the riverbank.

(33) **rolling-grass**. *Spinifex sericeus* (formerly *hirsutus*), a native grass of sand dunes having a bristly globular seed-head which falls off the plant and is blown along the dunes in the wind.

1880 BUCHANAN *Indigenous Grasses NZ* 15 *Spinifex hirsutus*. Spiny Rolling Grass. **1910** COCKAYNE *NZ Plants* 70 The spiny rolling-grass (*Spinifex hirsutus*), a native of Australia also, is another very important indigenous sand-binder.

(34) **salt grass**. Any of various species of the genus *Pucinellia* (formerly *Atropis*), introduced and native blue-green grasses of salt-marshes or coastal muds, esp. the native *P. stricta*.

1919 COCKAYNE *NZ Plants* 38 The chief species [in drying salt-swamps] are the southern water-pimpernel..the creeping selliera..and the salt-grass (*Atropis stricta*). **1969** *Standard Common Names Weeds* 67 *salt grass Puccinellia fasciculata... Puccinellia stricta... salt grass, reflexed Puccinellia distans*.

(35) **sand** (occas. **sand-fescue**) **grass**. **a.** *Desmoschoenus spiralis* syn. *Scirpus frondosus* (fam. Cyperaceae), PINGAO

[*Note*] Pingao is not a true grass.

1905 BAUCKE *White Man Treads* 2 White seashore sandhills..for..the wind..to pile into hillocks, until the wily pingau (native sand grass), creeping snakelike along... bound [them] into masses. **1911** *AJHR C-13* 35 [*Scirpus frondosus*]. Pingao. Sand-grass. Sedge-like, sand-binder.

b. Either of the native sand-binding grasses *Spinifex sericeus* (formerly *hirsutus*) (also **silvery sand-grass**), see *rolling grass* (33) above; or *Poa triodioides*, see *sand-fescue* (17) e above.

1874 *TrNZI* VI. 56 Other sedges and grasses might also be utilized, especially the curious sand-grass, *Spinifex hirsutus*, and sand-fescue grass, *Festuca littoralis*. **1888** CHUDLEIGH *Diary* 1 Aug. (1950) 363 I found..the Mairangi cattle got into the reserve and smashed up trees and sand grass. **1890** *Ibid*. 10 July 372 The various sand grasses are doing well where the stock can be kept away. They are all native grasses. **1911** *AJHR C-13* 34 *Spinifex hirsutus*...Silvery sand-grass..Grass, sand-binder. **1925–26** *NZJST* VIII. 200 Among the shore-plants..are the wild celery..with.. sand-grass (*Spinifex hirsutus*). **1959** MCLINTOCK *Descr. Atlas* 31 Planting of sand grass, lupins, and, in places, pines..is needed to protect farm land. **1995** CROWE *Which Coastal Plant?* 17 *Kōwhangatara Silvery Sand Grass Spinifex sericeus*... Silvery sand grass is an important native sand-binder, sending out a wide mat of long leafy runners... The common name comes from the long, soft hairs that cover the leaves, giving the plant a silvery sheen.

(36) **snowgrass** (or **snow tussock**, see TUSSOCK 3 (11)). **a.** Any one of several robust montane-alpine tussock grasses of the genus *Chionochloa* (formerly *Danthonia*). Also *attrib*.

1856 ROBERTS *Diary* in Beattie *Early Runholding* (1947) 18 The snowgrass was very rank and in flower, a greenish white, like rye grass. **1861** HAAST *Rep. Topogr. Explor. Nelson* 149 At a height of 4,200 to 4,300 feet, these sub-alpine shrubs..are succeeded by different kinds of snow grasses, so called by the settlers because they indicate the line at which, during the winter, the snow remains longest. **1872** *TrNZI* IV. 300 *Danthonia Cunninghamii*. Snow-grass.—A local grass, found at sea-level to 1,200 feet on moist land; affected by drought. **1906** CHEESEMAN *Manual NZ Flora* 886–887 *D*[*anthonia*] *Raoulii*... 'Snow-grass'. A most abundant plant in the hilly districts of the South Island. **1924** *Otago Witness* (Dunedin) 30 Sept. 67 We came out in the snow-grass country. **1933** *Press* (Christchurch) (Acland Gloss.) 2 Dec. 15 *Snowgrass* or *Snowtussock*.- (*Danthonia [flavescens]* and *D. [rubra].)* There are two kinds but shepherds do not distinguish between them. In Southland the kind they have there looks redder and is called locally *red tussock*. **1957** FRAME *Owls Do Cry* (1967) 24 As if there had been no Bible or Jesus going up to the mountain where the air is cool, tasting of snowgrass that grows all the way up. **1968** SLATTER *Pagan Game* 120 He loved to scramble through the maze of angled rock in a mountain gorge..that unrestrained world of rock and snow grass and astelia and mountain flax. **1984** BRASCH *Collected Poems* 87 Higher than birds climb from their marble forest The mountain lily nests In shade among scrawled rocks and snow-grass plumes.

b. *Obs.* **false snowgrass**. *Schoenus pauciflorus* (fam. Cyperaceae), a native sedge (but not a true grass) of damp tussock grasslands, having red or green culms.

1869 *TrNZI* I. (rev. edn.) 184 *Schoenus pauciflorus*, although strictly not a grass, forms grass-like tussocks, and is considered the true Snow-grass; it is Sub-Alpine. **1909** *AJHR C-12* 50 *Schoenus pauciflorus*. False snow-grass. Sub alpine meadow. **1919** COCKAYNE *NZ Plants* 127 Where streams flow through the montane low tussock-grassland sphagnum bog of a peculiar kind is common, its presence being at once recognized by the general grey colour given by its dominant species, a tussock-plant with reddish stems..the false snow-grass. **1969** *Standard Common Names Weeds* 71 *snow grass, false* [=] *bog-rush*.

(37) **snow patch grass**. *Chionochloa oreophila*, a native turf-forming grass of alpine grasslands.

1969 *Standard Common Names Weeds* 71 *snow-patch grass Chionochloa oreophila*. **1973** MARK & ADAMS *Alpine Plants* (1979) 254 *Chionochloa oreophila*..Snow-patch Grass. **1988** DAWSON *Forest Vines to Snow Tussocks* 191 Snowbank plants form a continuous sward, with the snow patch grass..usually predominating.

(38) **swamp grass**. Any of various swamp plants including the grasses KARETU (or *holy grass* (22) above) *Hierochloe redolens, swamp millet Isachne globosa*; and the non-grasses, RAUPO *Typha orientalis*, and *Carex* species.

1867 BARKER *Station Life* (1870) 110 The next step [after land purchase] is to build a sod hut with two rooms..thatching it with Tohi, or swamp grass. **1872** *TrNZI* IV. 298 *Hierochloe redolens*, and the more valuable *Isachne australis*, are alike called 'Swamp-grass' by the settlers. **1882** HAY *Brighter Britain* I. 210 The root of the raupo..the swamp-grass of which the Maori construct their warè, is edible. **1961** CRUMP *Hang On a Minute Mate* 135 You should have seen 'er [*sc.* a swamp]—half a mile round and all floating rushes and swamp-grass. **1988** MIKAERE *Te Maiharoa* 75 Turihuka being a legendary fisherman who was standing on a clump of swampgrass when a giant eel towed him out into the river, swampgrass and all.

(39) **tinker grass**. Also occas. **tinker-tailor**. [f. the counting-out rhyme 'Tinker, tailor, soldier, sailor' etc., thence Brit. dial. *tinker-tailor ryegrass*: see EDD *tinker* 1 n (5).] A mainly children's name for a ryegrass, *Lolium perenne*, whose seed-head, being formed of discrete seed-cases opposed on a stalk, can be used in counting out rhymes or games. See also *fortune grass* (18) above.

c1936 HYDE *Houses by Sea* (1952) 45 Fortune-grass, tinker-grass, Soldier-grass, rye, Cocksfoot and shivery-grass, Timothy, timothy. **1936** HYDE *Passport to Hell* 173 Tinker-grass on which New Zealand children tell their futures. **c1938** Wild ryegrass was used by Marlborough children for counting or reciting, under the name of 'tinker grass' or 'tinker-tailor' grass. (Ed.) **1963** FRAME *Reservoir* (1966) 139 The cutty grass and the tinkertailor were brushing against her black stockings.

(40) **tree-grass**. *Obs*. Any of various plants of tussock form, esp. NIGGERHEAD $n.^2$ *Carex secta*, and *snow tussock* (TUSSOCK 3 (11)) *Chionochloa* spp.

1844 TUCKETT *Diary* 13 May in Hocken *Contributions* (1898) 220 Beyond the bush land, that which is called grass land chiefly produces a very cutting wiry species, very similar to that which in swamps we call tree grass, but without the stem or trunk on which the former is elevated above the water surface.

(41) **tuft** (**tufted**) **grass**. *Obs. Poa cita*. See *tussock poa* (30) c above.

1851 LEE *Journal* Dec. in *Austral. & NZ Gaz*. 2 Oct. (1852) 393 The country is still very good..though there appears more tuft grass now. **1851** *Lyttelton Times* 28 June 6 The most conspicuous [grass] is the tufted grass.

(42) **tumble grass**. A native species of *Lachnagrostis*. See also *wind-grass* (46) below.

1982 WILSON *Stewart Is. Plants* 392 *Lachnagrostis* sp. or spp. *Tumble grass*... Heads contracted at first, then very open..the whole head often breaking free when ripe to roll in the wind.

(43) **Vasey grass**. *Paspalum urvillei*. See also *elephant grass* (15) above.

1984 *Standard Common Names Weeds* 113 *Vasey grass Paspalum urvillei*.

(44) **wheat (blue wheat) grass**. *Elymus rectisetus* (formerly *Agropyron scabrum*). See *blue-grass* (5) above.

1880 BUCHANAN *Manual Indigenous Grasses* 165 *Agropyron scabrum* blue wheat grass. **1898** MORRIS *Austral-English* 172 Wheat G[rass].—Blue— *Agropyrum scabrum*. **1969** *Standard Common Names Weeds* 6 *blue wheat grass Agropyron scabrum*. *Ibid*. 85 *wheat grass* [=] *blue wheat grass* **1981** TAYLOR *Weeds of Roadsides* 21 Blue Wheat Grass (*Agropyron scabrum*) Native perennial of low grazing value..occurs.. commonly in parts of Nelson, Marlborough north of East Cape or thereabouts. **1988** DAWSON *Forest Vines to Snow Tussocks* 149 Short tussock grassland..is characterised by the light brown tufts..of hard tussock..together with silver tussock... blue tussock..and blue wheat grass (*Elymus rectisetus*).

(45) **white man's grass**. *Poa annua*, an introduced annual grass.

1926 HILGENDORF *Weeds* 42 Annual Poa (*Poa annua*), is also called track grass and white man's grass, but its botanical name is most frequently used. An exceedingly common annual weed of road sides and garden paths all over the islands.

(46) **wind grass**. Any of several grasses with seed-heads able to be blown about in the wind, esp. *Deyeuxia billardieri*, a native tufted grass, and *Lachnagrostis filiformis*, a native perennial grass.

1961 MARTIN *Flora NZ* 133 Another common grass is the Wind Grass or Sand-bent *(Deyeuxia billardieri)* recognised at once by its erect, bushy habit and by its broad, lax, feathery panicles. **1969** *Standard Common Names Weeds* 33 *grass, sand wind Deyeuxia billardieri*. Ibid. 53 *New Zealand wind grass Lachnagrostis filiformis*. **1981** TAYLOR *Weeds of Roadsides* 105 New Zealand Wind Grass (*Lachnagrostis filiformis*) Short-lived perennial native with tall stems carrying very large, open heads containing fine seed.

3. The undigested herbaceous matter in an animal's intestines and stomach.

1951 May 17 Feilding Freezing Works terms p.c. Colin Gordon *Pelters open up* (that is, slit guts) and if not careful they cut the paunch and *grass* goes all over the place. **1991** *Dominion Sunday Times* (Wellington) 20 Oct. 21 He sliced the belly and grass spilled out greener than it ever grew, gassy as Brindle's cud.

4. [f. archaic Brit. slang: see OED *n*. 1 d.] A name often given to green vegetables served in institutions.

1982 NEWBOLD *Big Huey* 249 Grass (n) 3. Cabbage, lettuce, or silverbeet.

5. In various phrases. **a. stand off the grass**, an appeal not to encroach or interfere (cf. OED 9 a); or said to a person blocking one's view, also with elaborations such as **and let my wife (mother** see quot. 1965) **see the races**.

1951 HUNT *Confessions* 110 In effect we were told there was a city engineer to plan the city and would we please 'stand off the grass'. [**1965** WILSON *Outcasts* 161 'Righto. Righto.' The man motioned with his hand. But the curious townspeople who were pressing up against the truck moved back a mere half inch, so he spoke again with quiet, lazy authority. 'Come on. Let your mother see the races.'] **1980** *Views of English 2* 31 One regrets the passing of delightful expressions like 'Stand off the grass and let my wife see the races' said to a person blocking one's view.

b. In the phr. **get off the grass**, an exclamation expressing exasperated disbelief, disapproval or dismissal. (An elaboration of *get off* (with you).)

1984 16–17 F E3 Pakuranga Coll. 35B Get off the grass [F4M4]. **1988** *Sunday Star* (Auckland) 14 Aug. C1 [Heading] *Come on Gents, Get off the Grass*. John Stewart usually has talked so much sense..that it is hard to believe he uttered utter nonsense at the New Zealand Rugby Union council meeting. **1996** 17 Jan. TV1 *Shortland Street* (soap opera). A streetwise young female rejects another's advice with a dismissive 'Get off the grass!'

6. Used *attrib*. in special Comb. **grass-bird** *hist*., FERNBIRD; **grass caterpillar**, also **subterranean grass caterpillar**, PORINA; **grass fence**, a temporary 'break fence' for confining stock to a section of grazing (or 'break': cf. OED *n*.¹ 16) originally formed by two electric fence wires at the same height and one metre apart separating out a strip of herbage between the wires, the strip of unbrowsed grass so formed providing a sufficient barrier to stock when the power is switched off; **grasshopper** *transf*. or *fig*. (a) *hist*., a nickname for the Auckland Rifle Volunteers from the colour of their uniform; (b) a prison informer; (c) in the phr. **as big as a grasshopper's knee**, very small [perh. a variation of *stand knee-high to a grasshopper*]; **grass lily**, see LILY 2 (5); **grass-line**, the line or level on a mountain above which no grass grows; **grass-pheasant**, MATATA *n*.¹; **grassroots** (or **grass**) *goldmining*, the surface of the ground, esp. in the phr. **at the grassroots**, indicating surface gold; **grass-thief** *Canterbury hist*., a sheepowner deliberately grazing sheep on another's run.

1856 ROBERTS *Diary* June in Beattie *Early Runholding* (1947) 32 It [*sc*. Norway rat] also caught quail, ground larks, **grass birds**, and anything else that came its way. **1870** *TrNZI* II. 47 [It] was no rare occurrence..to hear the little Grass-bird utter its unchanging note u-tick, u-tick, as rising on feeble wings that just sustained it to the sheltering grass..beneath the..flax bush. **1884** [see MATATA *n*.¹]. c**1899** DOUGLAS in *Mr Explorer Douglas* (1957) 262 The Grassbird. [Heading] Bears some resemblance to a lark when on the ground, only it is slightly larger, and it can't sing and never soars, flying as little as possible [*sic*], preferring to run along the ground, or get a lift on a sheeps [*sic*] back. **1985** [see MATATA *n*.¹]. **1931** *NZJST* XII. 361 The havoc to farm pasture, lawns, and bowling-greens caused by the subterranean **grass-caterpillars** (*Porina* spp.) is well known. **1943** *NZJST* XXIII. 307A The true grass grub, *Odontria zealandica*, occurs in association with the subterranean grass caterpillar, *Oxycanus cervinata* (formerly called Porina). **1966** *Encycl. NZ* I. 319 The subterranean grass caterpillars have adapted themselves very successfully to the introduced grasses which now dominate the grasslands of New Zealand. **1982** *Agric. Gloss.* (MAF) 28 *Grass fence*: Fence made by two electric fence wires at the same height and 1 metre apart—where the herbage grows between. **1879** FEATON *Waikato War* 52 Their position..was defended mainly by a force composed of Wairoa Rifles, and of men from the different companies of the Auckland Rifle Volunteers, under the command of Captain J. McCosh Clark, No. 6 company..; this company some time afterwards, had a uniform of green cloth, and were dubbed the '**Grasshoppers**'. **1982** NEWBOLD *Big Huey* 73 Anybody who went to the screws over any matter like that related above was labelled a nark, a **grasshopper**, or a policeman. **1989** BIOLETTI *The Yanks Are Coming* 140 Jokingly I asked, 'Who's dead?' and was told, 'Oh, Private So-and-so...' Of course I felt as big as a **grasshopper's knee**. **1892** DOUGLAS in *Mr Explorer Douglas* (1957) 176 [A kind of heath] is very common all along the ranges close to the **grass line** and might be introduced as an ornamental tree in gardens or parks. **1899** *TrNZI* XXXI. 400 The subalpine scrub occurs..forming a distinct belt & barrier between the forest and the grassline. **1948** *Tararua 3* 50 On the following day three of us climbed in a strong northerly to the grassline of a ridge above the Henry River. **1958** *Tararua* 13 48 Silver-beech extended some hundreds of feet up the mountainside, then mountain [beech] came in again to the grassline. **1870** *TrNZI* II. 57 Sphenoeacus punctatus... Mata. Grass-bird, **Grass-pheasant**, Utick. **1967** MAY *West Coast Gold Rushes* 527 **Grass** or **Grass Roots**: the surface. **1974** HEINZ *Bright Fine Gold* 200 *At the grassroots*: Gold on the surface of the ground. **1992** LATHAM *Golden Reefs* 75 Fifty tons of stone..had already been 'brought to grass' from the leaders in the mine. Ibid. 132 It would start stamping the six hundred tons of quartz already 'to grass' before cleaning up. **1940** STUDHOLME *Te Waimate* (1954) 132 All told there were from 1,500 to 2,000 strangers [*sc*. sheep] each year, some 500 to 800 of these belonging to one or two men in the back country known to be '**grass thieves**,' that is men who deliberately turned sheep out on blocks of our country... The grass thieves thought we were hard on them, but after the Station disposed of the blocks adjoining them, they found our successors were far more severe, and this sort of thing quickly came to an end.

grass grub.

1. a. Also occas. **the Grub**. The larva of a cockchafer beetle, *Costelytra* (formerly *Odontria*) *zealandica* (fam. Scarabaeidae), which feeds on grass roots and hence is a major pasture pest.

1881 *NZ Country Jrnl*. V. 420 The grub.—Can any of the naturalists attached to your staff give our farmers an insight into the habits of that ruinous pest popularly called 'The Grub'? **1885** *AJHR* H-26 17 The roots of the olive as well as other fruit-trees are liable to the attacks of the grass-grub, which, although usually feeding upon the roots of grasses, has of late years developed a voracious taste for all kinds of roots. **1894** *NZ Country Jrnl*. XXVIII. 225 Grass Grub..is an indigenous insect, as the term implies. It is well known, but, unfortunately, little heeded. **1913** *NZJAg*. Jan. VI. 295 I was under the impression that the damage was occasioned by the ordinary grass-grub.., so well known in New Zealand on account of its very serious effect on pastures. **1934** MILLER *Garden Pests in NZ* 64 The grass grub is the larva of a native cockchafer beetle. This grub, by feeding upon roots, causes extensive damage to pastures and lawns. **1951** DUFF *Shepherd's Calendar* (1961) 19 I would gladly trade a thousand grains of wheat for two or three hundred grass grubs. **1966** *Encycl. NZ* I. 871 *Grass Grub* (*Costelytra zealandica*). The adult of this grub is a beetle which is commonly called the grass-grub beetle or the brown beetle. This species is the most serious insect pest in New Zealand. The larvae feed on roots of grasses. **1973** *NZ Entomologist* V. 222 Generally the vernacular names used are acceptable, but most New Zealand entomologists will take strong exception to the use of the name 'grass grub' for the subterranean grass caterpillars of *Wiseana* spp.—which are commonly known as Porina caterpillars. The term 'grass grub' should be restricted to Melolonthine larvae especially of the genus *Costelytra*. **1991** *North & South* (Auckland) May 91 His new grassgrub remedy uses bacteria in the grubs' stomachs to stop them eating.

b. grass-grub beetle. The adult flying beetle of the New Zealand grass-grub, *Costelytra zealandica*. See also *brown beetle* (BEETLE 2), TURNIP FLY.

1935 DIXON *Nature Study Notes* 33 [Heading] *The Grass Grub Beetle*... Also called the Copper-brown Beetle. **1943** *NZJST* XXIII. 306A There are twenty-eight native species belonging to the genus *Odontria*, but all observers agree that the principal grass grub is *Odontria zealandica*. In the larval stage this is known as 'grass grub', 'white grub', or 'curl grub', and the adult stage is known as 'grass grub beetle', 'brown beetle' or 'turnip fly'. **1955** MILLER *Nature in NZ* 25 But the more common Chafers are the Grass-grub Beetles which buzz about at dusk in the spring and summer, called *tutaeruru* by the Maori. **1967** NATUSCH *Animals NZ* 150 The various grass-grub beetles, such as the notorious *Costelytra* (formerly *Odontria*) *zealandica*, also belong [among the chafer beetles]. **1984** MILLER *Common Insects* 141 Grass grubs are the larvae of chafer beetles, of which there are many native species... The most abundant is the common Grass Grub Beetle..which creates a buzzing sound as it flies at dusk, often in great numbers from October to December.

2. Occas. the larvae of the PORINA q.v. (*Wiseana* spp.).

1925 TILLYARD *Insects in Relation to NZ* in *Mid-Pacific Magazine* XXIX. 669 Of the lower families, the Hepialidae are abundant, and their larvae, known as subterranean grass-grubs (genus *Porina*) do considerable damage to grass-lands, though not so much as the true grass-grubs or larvae of Melolonthinae. **1973** *NZ Entomologist* V. 222 The use of 'grass grub' for both *Wiseana* and Melolonthine larvae in a popular book can lead only to further confusion in the public mind. **1980** Leland *Kiwi-Yankee Dictionary* 48 *Grass grub* or *porina*... Grass grubs are Insect Larvae which can and do leave 50c sized bare spots all over a field.

3. *transf.* and *fig.* The nickname of a railcar.

1985 McGill *G'day Country* 171 He told me about the old Grassgrub railcar that used to travel this route, so called because it was green and slithered through these rich green market gardens south of Oamaru. **1988** McGill *Dict. of Kiwi Slang* 53 *Grassgrub, The* New Plymouth/Taumarunui and lower South Island railcar, from green colour of carriages.

grass-seeder. *Obs.*

1. *Banks Peninsula.* One who gathers grass-seed, usu. cocksfoot, for sale. See also COCKSFOOTER.

1910 *Truth* 24 Dec. 8 The industry will not give employment to half the usual number of men, and..a dead loss will be sustained by grass-seeders and croppers alike. **1922** Turner *Happy Wanderer* 211 The official issue of clothing [at the Rotoroa Island centre for alcoholics] is a wide-brimmed 'grass-seeder' straw hat. **1936** Allen *Poor Scholar* 202 The grass-seeder would entrust his cheque to the squatter.

2. One who sows grass-seed on cleared burns.

1913 Carr *Country Work* 31 Underscrubbers vary from 30s a week... Grass seeders 1s to 1s 6d an hour and tucker themselves.

Hence **grass-seeding** *vbl. n. obs.* (a) mainly *Banks Peninsula*, COCKSFOOTING.

1905 *Truth* 10 Oct. 1 The [Lyttelton] men..see the chance of making a few extra quid by crossing the harbour and indulging in a few weeks' grass-seeding. **1910** *Truth* 24 Dec. 8 The prolonged drought in Canterbury has ruined the cocksfoot crop on Banks Peninsula, and grass-seeding this year..will be an attenuated industry. **1928** *Na To Hoa Aroha* (1986) I. 95 Dairying in Taranaki, at Nuhaka, Ruatoki and in the far North..carpentering..grass-seeding, droving.. teaching, clerical & other work. **1936** Allen *Poor Scholar* 204 Grass-seeding is rather characteristic of these parts [Banks Peninsula].

(b) The sowing of grass-seed.

1990 Martin *Forgotten Worker* 45 [William Cox] decided to go back to Hastings where he took up bush-felling, shearing, grass-seeding and made good money.

grass-tree. Any of various native plants with long linear leaves.

1. *Obs.* CABBAGE TREE (*Cordyline* spp.).

1840 Mathew *Journal* in *Founding of NZ* (1940) 106 Lofty trees.., the graceful tree-fern and a sort of tufted reed-like grass tree of very bright vivid green. **1861** 27 Sept. in *NZ Goldfields 1861* (1976) 23 In charming variety were the elegant grass-tree, whose palm-like tufts of long rapier blade-shaped leaves hung gracefully over the tall slender stems. **1867** Hochstetter *NZ* 132 Here and there, in moist places, arises isolated the 'grass-tree' or 'cabbage tree' (Ti of the natives: *Cordyline australis*).

2. NEINEI, INANGA *n.*² (*Dracophyllum* spp.).

1869 *TrNZI* I. (rev. edn.) 206 Grass tree. Dracophyllum longifolium. **1870** Whitworth *Martin's Bay Settlement* 5 The hills rise very rapidly from the coast, being thickly wooded with hini-hini and other scrub, flax, grass-tree, cabbage-palm. **1889**, **1892** [see INANGA *n.*² a]. **1907** Broad-leaved Grass-tree [see NEINEI]. **c1920** Beattie *Trad. Lifeways Southern Maori* (1994) 192 Inaka is the name of a tree on the Titi Islands and some of my informants called it the grass tree. **1940** Laing & Blackwell *Plants NZ* 346 Plants belonging to [*Dracophyllum*] are generally known to colonists as grass-trees, though this term is also applied in Otago to the lancewood (*Pseudopanax*). The name is doubtless due to the long grass-like leaves of most of the species. **1958** *Tararua* Sept. 13 Tent space and firewood were some what scarce [here in the Ruahine range] but dry turpentine wood or grass tree (*Dracophyllum filifolium*) provided the welcome cuppa. **1961**, **1978** [see INANGA *n.*² b].

3. LANCEWOOD (*Pseudopanax crassifolius*).

1877 *TrNZI* IX. 151 *Grass Tree—Panax crassifolium*, is common everywhere throughout the province, and well known from its unique appearance. **1889** Kirk *Forest Flora* 59 It is commonly termed lancewood by the settlers in the North Island, and grass-tree by those in the South. **1890** grass [see HOROEKA]. **1898** Morris *Austral-English* 173 *Grass-tree*..(2) In New Zealand *Pseudopanax crassifolium*... When older, it grows more straight and is called *Lancewood*. **1909** *AJHR* C-12 58 *Pseudopanax crassifolium*. Horoheka, hohoeka. Lancewood, grass-tree (this name is common in Stewart Island and the south). **c1920** Beattie *Trad. Lifeways Southern Maori* (1994) 192 Kokoeka is what the bushman calls the grasstree. **1940** [see 2 above]. **1970** McNaughton *Tat* 74 He cut a grass tree with his pocket knife, took a rope from his saddle, fixed a loop on the end of the pole. **1982** [see LANCEWOOD].

graunch /grɒntʃ/, *v.* [f. Brit. dial *granch, graunch, craunch*, etc., to crush, to crunch between, or grind, the teeth: see OED *v.*, EDD.] *intr.* To make a grinding or scraping sound; to grate; to crunch. also *trans.*, to cause to graunch; to damage (esp. a mechanism or metal object).

c1946 Heard by Ed. from a passenger just after the interisland vessel *Tamahine* ran aground in Queen Charlotte Sound: 'The ship graunched over the rock bottom—the noise was terrific.' **1954** *Dominion* (Wellington) 1 July As far as I know 'to graunch' means to damage an engine, instrument, machine, etc., by using wrong tools and/or repair methods, and a 'graunch-artist' is 'a person who does that'. **1957** *Evening Post* (Wellington) 17 Apr. 8 [Heading] Graunch!—Bang goes more than the door. **1962** *Dominion* (Wellington) 13 Aug. 15 The plates were damaged when the 4,300 ton ship graunched its forward port side into the old Picton Ferry wharf. **1962** Crump *One of Us* 167 The van was graunching its way deafeningly up a gentle slope in second gear. **1979** Simons *Harper's Mother* 170 As I close the carriage door, the train graunches, stutters and moves forward. **1992** *Evening Post* (Wellington) 31 Aug. 5 She turned to see people scattering as the car graunched along in first gear. **1995** Anderson *House Guest* 167 She..sat massaging a shoulder she'd graunched last week.

Hence **graunch** *n.*, a grinding motion; **graunching** *vbl. n.*, a scraping, grinding (noise); as **self-graunching**, of machinery, (noisily) self-destroying; **graunchingly**, of a quality of being harsh or rough on the sensibilities; **graunchy**, tediously difficult or hard on the nerves.

1991 *NZ Books* Oct. 16 We've cheered every [rugby] score, every big 'hit'... Every surge, **graunch**, thud. **1986** Latham *WAAC Story* 84 Salutes got thrown to all and sundry, she pushed the right knob and the car started and with a lot of **graunching** as she got into gear. **1960** Muir *Word for Word* 233 'You bloody, rigid, **self-graunching**, non-adjustable, hunk of useless bloody scrap-iron,' Clarry said. **1979** *Dominion* (Wellington) 1 Oct. 4 [From a review by Bruce Mason] Thus we find ourselves in a **graunchingly** familiar hall equipped with a squalid kitchen and an excruciatingly painted backdrop of Mount Egmont. **1965** *Listener* 27 Aug. 9 John Pascoe himself knew that editing an encyclopedia would be a lengthy project. 'When I started I knew it was a **graunchy** job. But then I've always liked long graunchy jobs... I rather like long, slow patient plodding.'

grayling. [Transf. use of northern hemisphere *grayling*.] *Prototroctes oxyrhynchus* (fam. Prototroctidae), presumed extinct, a salmon-like, freshwater fish having a small adipose fin and comb-like teeth on the upper jaw. See also UPOKORORO.

1857 Hursthouse *NZ* I. 122 A sort of grayling is taken in a few of the clearest rivers. **1868** Harper *Lett. from NZ* 5 Feb. (1914) 120 Some miles back [from Kanieri] there is a lovely lake..its deep water..is full of a kind of grayling. **1872** Hutton & Hector *Fishes NZ* 123 Upokororo... The above is the native name of the Grayling..a fish that has been long familiar to settlers in certain districts, but..remained undescribed till last year. **1886** Sherrin *Handbook Fishes NZ* 135 Grayling (*Prototroctes oxyrhynchus*). Mr. Hursthouse, of Taranaki, writes: 'The upokororo, which you describe as a sea-visiting fish, is not such here'. **1892** Spackman *Trout in NZ* 6 Another is the native grayling, called by the Maoris upokororo... In 1888 a few of these graceful fish were captured, and placed in a pond, where they have become very tame... They are a mysterious fish, about whose habits little or nothing is known, found in one part of a stream to-day and disappearing no one knows where tomorrow. **1901** [see UPOKORORO]. **1924** *Otago Witness* (Dunedin) 8 July 9 The Upokororo [stream]..was undoubtedly named after that beautiful, but now almost extinct fish, the New Zealand grayling. **1937** Buick *Moa-Hunters NZ* 176 Grayling, too, must have come into the bill of fare [of the Canterbury moa-hunters]; but this fish..disappeared so quickly that the *upokororo* is only a far-off name to most of the elderly Maoris of to-day. **1956** Graham *Treasury NZ Fishes* 110 The grayling, now rarely seen, was common 50 years ago when I was a boy living at Brunnerton. **1978** McDowall *NZ Freshwater Fishes* 50 A specimen now in the British Museum in London was taken to England by scientists with the *Discovery* Expedition in the early 1930's... It could possibly be the last known Grayling caught and kept in a museum. **1990** *Listener* 17 Sept. 114 What a pity the people who are now saying no to catfish were not around when trout were first introduced to..New Zealand. If they had, they might know what a grayling (now extinct) was.

grazier. [Uncommon in British English, and usu. applied there to one who raises cattle for the market: AND 1804.] A (usu. large-scale) sheepfarmer. Cf. PASTORALIST.

1850 Torlesse *Papers* (1958) 132 We are so far in the country now, and consequently unable to procure fresh meat from graziers. **1861** *Butler to Marriott* 8 Aug. in Jones *Samuel Butler* (1919) I. 97 I am now a confirmed grazier; little enough, is it not, for all one's high aspirations to end in? **1882** Potts *Out in Open* 215 At length the grazier and sheep breeder had to give place to the agriculturalist. **1902** *Brett's Colonists' Guide* 156 At such times there is a good deal of notice given to the subject of 'irrigation by farmers and graziers'. **1920** Macdonald *Austral. & NZ Sheepfarming* 113 Cocksfoot is the sheet anchor of the New Zealand grazier. **1930** Davidson *Sketch of His life* 88 The lease expired in 1882, when government subdivided the property and released it to small graziers. **1952** *Here & Now* Dec. 50 The exceptions I mentioned are the graziers..who got into cropping at the instigation of the green-pea canners. **1970** McNeish *Mackenzie* 31 Talking to a grazier about the land question, he had used the phrase 'White Squattocracy'. He had said it casually and included himself in his usual derogatory way.

grazing. *Farming.* Pertaining to pastoral (esp. sheep) farming, or referring to the green-feeding of stock, esp. in the collocations: **grazing land**, **grazing property** [AND 1876], **grazing run**

[AND 1826].
1857 Hursthouse *NZ* II. 512 Pastoral lands are the wild **grazing lands**.. leased..for a term of years under a deed termed a 'run licence', to the emigrant. **1947** Newton *Wayleggo* 155 Station: large **grazing property**. **1982** *Agric. Gloss.* (MAF) 5 *Run:* an extensive grazing property usually in South Island tussock country. **1933** *Press* (Christchurch) (Acland Gloss.) 18 Nov. 15 *Run*... does. This usage [*sc.* 'station'] is now uncommon and *r[un]* in these contexts would probably mean *small grazing r[un]*. **1948** *Our Own Country* 135 [Regulations] legalized at that time [1856], allowed land outside the original Otago Block to be bought for grazing-runs at a low cost.

grease.
1. *Farming.* **a.** [OED 1863.] Wool grease; esp. in the phr. **in the grease**, of wool, not washed or scoured.
1863 Butler *First Year* x 160 If you wash them at all, you should do it thoroughly..otherwise you had better shear in the grease, i.e. not wash. Wool in the grease weighs about one-third heavier. **1880** Grant & Foster *NZ* 42 The weight of these [fleeces] in the grease seemed to average about 5½ or 6lbs., while that of the cross-breds were [*sic*] very little heavier. **1906** Stack *Through Canterbury* (1972) 27 The Bishop..took his part in the endless discussions about the..relative advantages of shipping wool scoured or in the grease. **1913** Carr *Country Work* 18 The bulk of the..wool clip is..sold..'in the grease', i.e., without being scoured.
b. Special Comb. **grease-boil**, a boil caused by contact with the grease in a sheep's wool.
1926 Devanny *Butcher Shop* (1981) 70 'What are grease boils?' asked Margaret. 'They are running sores, or ulcers which the shearers get on their legs and arms, usually through shearing wet sheep.' **1955** Bowen *Wool Away* 52 When a shearer does get grease boils he should rest with the legs up.
2. [Brit. dial.: see OED; EDD 2 rancid butter.] Butter.
1941 St Patrick's College Silverstream. A familiar name for butter (Ed.) **1937** Partridge *Dict. Slang* 350 *grease*... Butter: Australians' and New Zealanders' and Conway cadets': late C. 19–20. If inferior, *axle-grease.* **1967** McLatchie *Tang of Bush* 62 [The Howdie, the Scots midwife] went into the grocer's in Owaka and was heard to say, 'I wan a pun a grease to mak a haggis. I like the haggis better than the butter.'

greaser. A fall or setback, esp. in the phr. **to come a greaser**, to take a (literal or figurative) fall.
1951 14 M 14 St Bede's, Chch 16 Greaser [M2] **1951** 14 M 10 Wellington H.S. 16 Greaser [M6] **1953** 15–17 M A21 Thames DHS 16 Greaser [M17] **1980** Leland *Kiwi-Yankee Dict.* 27 *come a greaser:* (A) Have bad luck (of any kind) (B) To fall off as from a bike, skis, etc.

greasies, *n. pl.*
1. Takeaway fried food, esp. fish (etc.) and chips.
1968 *The Patler* (XVIII. 2) 11 Oct. 13 The only stop [for the rugby team] was at Woodville for pies and loads of 'greasies'. **1979** Williams *Skin Deep* 131 Across the road from Joe's [cafe]..a gang of callow youths eat their greasies and swig rudely from bottles of beer. **1987** *Dominion* (Wellington) 4 Sept. 7 *Kiwis go for greasies* Fish and chips still rates tops as New Zealanders' most popular takeaway meal. **1991** Eldred-Grigg *Shining City* 161 He called fish and chips 'greasies'.
Hence **greasy** (**greasey**) *n.*, a fast-food seller.
1978 *Manawatu Tramping Club Jubilee* 129 A hurried meal of fish and chips, grabbed hastily from a greasey's shop on the main road.
2. Shearing clothes.
1989 *NZ Eng. Newsletter* III. 24 *greasies:* Shearing clothes. This is an appropriate name for clothing which has become impregnated with grease from the wool.

greasy, *a.* In various phr. (**as**) **greasy** (**slippery**) **as a butcher's apron** (**pup**), said of anything very greasy (e.g. with oil, mud).
1945 Henderson *Gunner Inglorious* 19 Grimy as a sweep, greasy as a butcher's pup manhandling ammunition, but oh I feel fine, fit as a buck rat. **1964** Helmer *Stag Party* 82 I ups and hares over to the edge of the slip and starts down. Slippery as a butcher's apron it is, and I comes a gutser twice before I gets down to the stag.

great, *a.* In various uses in the sense 'large', occas. 'famous'.
1. In the names of plants and animals, see: *mountain buttercup* (buttercup 2 (3)), *crested grebe* (grebe 2 (1)), *spotted kiwi* (kiwi 2 (2)), *blue shark, white shark* (shark 2 (3) and (20)).
2. In special collocations: **Great Divide**, see Divide a; **great exodus** *hist.*, the emigration to Australia in the depression of the 1880s; **Great Migration**, see migration; **great New Zealand novel** (**The New Zealand Novel**), ironically referring to a yet to be written ideally famous local novel; **great stroke**, see stroke.
1951 Lawson *Gold in their Hearts* 93 [1893] was to be a memorable [year] for all New Zealand. The country was slowly recovering from the dreadful days of unemployment which led to the **Great Exodus**—a name given to the migration of thousands of people from New Zealand to Australia—in the late '80's. **1959** Slatter *Gun in My Hand* 125 What about your **Great New Zealand Novel**? Did you ever write it? You were always talking about doing it. **1966** Scott *Days That Have Been* 139 I had wonderful dreams of..eventually writing 'The New Zealand Novel' that people were always talking about.

grebe.
1. [Spec. local use of Brit. *grebe* a diving bird of fam. Podicipedidae.] Any of several small to medium-sized freshwater aquatic diving birds of the fam. Podicipedidae.
1856 Phillips *Rockwood Jrnl.* (Canterbury Pub. Lib. TS) 27 Dec. 60 John killed a couple of Grebe. **1870** *TrNZI* II. 47 The little Grebe with rosy breast, dived and sported with restless activity. **1879** Haast *Geol. Canterbury & Westland* 133 The water of the lake was perfectly clear..; a few grebes (*Podiceps rufipectus*), were swimming upon it, and gave life to the otherwise solitary and tranquil scenery. **c1899** Douglas in *Mr Explorer Douglas* (1957) 242 At one time the grebe was almost exterminated. Then a law was passed protecting them for all time. **1939** Beattie *First White Boy Born Otago* 121 I did not see the grebe.
2. With a modifier: **crested** (**great crested, Australasian crested**), **little**.
(1) **crested grebe** (**great** or **Australasian crested grebe**). *Podiceps cristatus australis*, a diving bird of South Island lakes, having dark brown upper and white lower plumage and blackish 'horns' or crests in summer. See also diver, pateketeke.
[**1773** Forster *Resolution Jrnl.* 9 Feb. (1982) II. 224 About 7 we saw a bird like a *crested Grebe* or like a *Loon*..which made a noise very near like a Goose.] **1861** Haast *Topogr. Exploration Nelson* 13 On the lakes..we found the crested grebe (Podiceps cristatus?), of which only very little is known. **1879** Haast *Geol. Canterbury & Westland* 138 The solitude [near Lake Ida] is enlivened by a great number of water-fowl..of which the Great Crested Grebe..is the most worthy of notice. **1883** Domett *Ranolf & Amohia* II. 103,338 O wild lake-bird! my Swift, my sweet, My lovely-crested Grebe! **1888** Great Crested Grebe [see pateketeke]. **1904** Hutton & Drummond *Animals NZ* 304 *The Crested Grebe*... Formerly, this bird was often seen on the larger lakes of the South Island, but the tourist traffic has disturbed them. It still haunts the smaller and less frequented lakes. **1926** Cowan *Travel in NZ* II. 126 Here too are to be seen wild ducks and that rare and beautiful bird the crested grebe. **1945** [see diver]. **1955** Oliver *NZ Birds* 88 Crested Grebe. Puteketeke... In 1844 Gould described a Crested Grebe which he stated came from Van Diemens Land, but which Mathews in his *Birds of Australia* says, according to the description, must have been from New Zealand. **1966** Falla et al. *Birds NZ* 27 Crested Grebe *Podiceps australis Maori name*: Puteketeke. **1983** Francis *Wildlife Ranger* 80 The first thing I spotted swimming and diving near the shore line was a pair of crested grebes, dark-plumaged birds with silvery white underbodies, the characteristic crests on their heads and swimming low in the water. **1990** *Checklist Birds NZ* 10 *Podiceps cristatus australis..Australasian Crested Grebe* (*Puteketeke*).

(2) **little grebe.** dabchick (*Poliocephalus* (formerly *Podiceps*) *rufopectus*).
[*Note*] The name *little grebe*, orig. applied to the endemic dabchick, is now also confusingly applied to the self-introduced *Australasian little grebe* (*Tachybaptus novaehollandiae* (fam. Podicipedidae).
1870 *TrNZI* II. 73 Totokipio. Dab-chick, Little Grebe. **1904** Hutton & Drummond *Animals NZ* 305 *The Little Grebe.—Totokipio*... The Little Grebe, or Dabchick, is fairly common in suitable localities in both Islands; but it is wary and is seldom seen. **1917** Williams *Dict. Maori Lang.* 565 *Weiweia,.. Podiceps rufopectus, little grebe.* **1922** [see dabchick]. **1921** Guthrie-Smith *Tutira* (1926) 214 Another lake bird to whom the future is secure is the Little Grebe.., whose nest is practically undiscoverable. **1930** Reischek *Yesterdays in Maoriland* (1933) 22 Paradise duck, grey duck, little grebe, and other water dwellers were enjoying life. **1957** Williams *Dict. Maori Lang.* 481 *Weiweia..Podiceps rufopectus, dabchick* (*little grebe*).

green, *a.* In special collocations: **greenback**, *greenback flounder* (flounder 2 (6)); **green beetle**, beetle 6 and 8; **green cart** [AND 1935], the legendary vehicle said to collect people for the lunatic asylum; **greenfeed** /ˈɡrinfid/ [AND 1876], grass, or fodder plants, grown for direct grazing by stock; **greenhood**, orchid 2; **green jade, jasper**, jade, jasper; **greenlip**, mussel 2 (5); **green-pickings**, see quot.; **green talc, talk**, talc; **green tobacco** [an elaboration of drug-users' use of *green* for 'marijuana'; poss. a local use in *Takaka*, a town in Nelson province within a former tobacco-growing area of NZ], marijuana.
1952 Thomson *Deer Hunter* 172 I don't know what anyone would have thought who could have watched us on the sly. Perhaps they would have thought we had been too long on our own acting as hermits, and were ready for the '**green cart**'. **1916** *NZJAg.* Sept. XIII. 190 The wise dairyman will produce sufficient soilage (**green-feed**-producing crops) & silage to make good all possible shortage of pastures in summer or winter. **1950** *NZJAg.* July LXXXI. 37 Maize for greenfeed is sown at the rate of 2 bushels per acre. **1985** Bremner *Woolscours NZ* (Glossary of old wool terms) 9 **Green-pickings** wool gathered from grass verges, fences,

trees at season's end. *Ibid.* 21 [Caption] Green pickings dot the paddock at Mount Somers, 1931. **1984** *Listener* 16 June 22 'A lot of **green tobacco**,' said the man. 'Marijuana. There's people in this town [Takaka] who've got money that shouldn't have money.'

green, *n.*

1. Woolscouring. Flax-milling. In full DRYING GREEN. A drying paddock, esp. in the phr. **on the green**, of scoured wool, or flax fibre, hung or spread out to sun-dry. Cf. PADDOCK *n.*¹ 2.

1985 BREMNER *Woolscours NZ* 9 *Green* paddock where wool was sun-dried. *Ibid.* 20 One day on the green at Murgatroyds in Auckland was sufficient for a newcomer from Yorkshire to hand in his notice protesting, 'If I'd have thought I'd have to work with arse higher than head, I'd never have left the Old Country'.

2. In the names **New Zealand green**, **Coromandel green** [f. the name of *Coromandel* a northern NI peninsula once associated with goldmining popular among those seeking alternative life-styles], locally grown marijuana.

1976 ROSE *New Zealand Green* [Title] **1982** PEAT *Detours* 98 I might happen on a gold nugget... I might fall not for Coromandel gold but Coromandel green, as renowned as the metal for its enslaving properties.

green-bird. *Obs.* KAKAPO.

c1826–27 BOULTBEE *Journal* (1986) 109 Greenbird—kòkabboo. **c1835** BOULTBEE *Journal* (1986) 37 Milford Haven [west coast sounds] is a wild romantic looking place,.. the woods are abundantly supplied with game, as woodhens, green birds, emus etc. **1844** MONRO in Hocken *Contributions* (1898) 261 Another bird, called by the whalers the 'green bird', by the natives the kakapo, is abundant on the west coast. **1866** MUELLER *My Dear Bannie* (1958) 100 Without a dog it is practically impossible to catch either kiwi or greenbird.

greenbone. [f. the greenish colour of the bones.] A name used esp. in the southern South Island. for the BUTTERFISH q.v. (*Odax pullus*)

c1920 BEATTIE *Trad. Lifeways Southern Maori* (1994) 501 The kelp fish of Canterbury is the Bluebone of Nelson and may be the Green-bone of Southland. **1921**, **1936** [see BUTTERFISH 1]. **1947** POWELL *Native Animals NZ* 69 An alternative name [for butterfish] is 'Greenbone' from the fact that the bones and the flesh in contact with them are stained bright bluish green. **1955** BAXTER *Collected Poems* (1980) 158 And feel below their ledge's roof The tugging greenbone flock. **1967** NATUSCH *Animals NZ* 224 Family Scaridae includes..the greenbone (if I may use its apt southern name), otherwise *Coridodax pullus*. **1970**, **1982** [see BUTTERFISH 1].

greenie. Usu. *pl.* [AND 1973.] A conservationist or environmentalist; as **the Greenies**, the environmental lobby, esp. as a political force.

1981 *Star* (Christchurch) 11 Feb. 7 Up in the Coromandel the conservationists or 'greenies', are locked with seven multi-national mining joints which are planning on turning over the peninsula. **1987** MOORE *Hard Labour* 82 I thought Bill Rowling's decision to give me responsibility for environmental concerns was one of his more humorous appointments. I care about the environment but the job requires someone who can relate to the 'Greenies'. **1988** *Listener* 20 Aug. 13 [Heading] *Black robin Budget*. Roger Douglas begins his Budget speech like a born-again latter-day greenie.

greenstone. [Spec. use of *greenstone* a hard green mineral: see OED.]

1. A nephrite rock of the s.w. South Island only, very hard and of the same chemical composition as jade but usu. of darker green than Chinese or Burmese jade; used for classical Maori ornaments, weapons, etc., and now commercially for general jewellery and ornaments. See also *axe-stone* (AXE 1), JADE, JADEITE, JASPER, NEPHRITE, POUNAMU 1, SERPENT STONE, TALC; and for varieties, INANGA *n.*³, TANGIWAI.

1769 PARKINSON *Journal* 15 Oct. (1773) 93 Several of them had pieces of green stone hung about their necks, which seemed to be pellucid, like an emerald. [1769 (?1773) *Note*] On examination it appears to be a fine sort of Nephritic stone. **1770** [see POUNAMU 1]. **1817** NICHOLAS *Voyage NZ* II. 339 The green-stone (jade) of which they make their axes, pattoo-pattoos, and ear ornaments Pooheenan [*sic*]. **1835** YATE *NZ* (1970) 151 'Manatungos', or remembrancers,.. are mostly made of the ponamu, the green stone found only in the Southern Island. **1853** SEWELL *Journal* 15 Mar. (1980) I. 208 She shewed us various articles..some manufactured of the peculiar Green-stone on which they set such value. **1864?** TEMPSKY *Memoranda* (ATLTS) 170 Loot.—We have had none of this either, except a few Maori weapons, mats and an odd greenstone here and there. **1883** DOMETT *Ranolf & Amohia* I. 138 And many a greenstone trinket had been given To get his chisel-flint so deftly driven. **1892** *TrNZI* XXIV. 480 In the Title of this paper the word 'greenstone' occurs, and this word is used throughout the text. I am quite conscious that the term is not geologically or mineralogically correct; but the stone of which I am writing is known by that name throughout New Zealand, and..here as elsewhere the scientific man employs that word to describe a totally different class of rock. **1917** WILLIAMS *Dict. Maori Lang.* 347 *Pounamu*, 1. Greenstone, jade. **1949** REED *Story Canterbury* 28 At the close of day he would take his precious greenstone with him to the..sleeping house, rub it till he fell asleep, and pick it up again at wakeful moments. **1951** CRESSWELL *Canterbury Tales* 9 This pah, the clearing station for New Zealand's greenstone traffic, was soon afterwards captured by Te Rauparaha. **1966** *Encycl. NZ* I. 875 Greenstone is the name commonly used for the predominantly greenish-coloured rock from which the Maori made many adzes and chisels.

Hence **greenstone** *v. intr.*, to prospect for greenstone.

1995 *Sunday Star-Times* (Auckland) 4 June sect. A 5 Mr Henderson still plans to go whitebaiting and greenstoning on the Arahura.

2. Used *attrib.* in Comb. in the names of highly-treasured Maori weapons or ornaments made from greenstone rather than from a less-prized material: **greenstone adze**, **axe**, **club**, **mere**, **pendant**.

1773 BAYLY *Journal* 9 Nov. in McNab *Hist. Records* (1914) II. 212 The Natives here behaved very friendly bringing everything they had to sell except the **green stone Ads's**. **1937** BUICK *Moa-Hunters NZ* 121 To begin with, we dug over a large extent..finding..a small greenstone chisel, a flake of a greenstone adze. **1769** PARKINSON *Journal* (1773) 22 Oct. 96 They had some **green stone axes** and ear-rings but they would not part with them. **1930** REISCHEK *Yesterdays in Maoriland* (1933) 69 He showed me..a patu-punamu, or greenstone axe. **1848** MCLEAN in Cowan *Sir Donald Maclean* (1940) 36 Some of them had their heads decorated with *huia* and *kotuku* feathers, not neglecting their *méré pounamu* (**greenstone clubs**), and every other ancient emblem of chieftainship. **1930** GUTHRIE *NZ Memories* 11 They..spent their time going either by water or through virgin bush (armed with spears and greenstone clubs)..to kill..their fellow tribes. **1863** MANING *Old NZ* iii. 57 No arms were to be seen..except the **greenstone mere** of the principal chiefs. **1897** CHUDLEIGH *Diary* 30 Oct. (1950) 396 I went to the pa early and saw Wi lying in state, the greenstone mere at his head and many greenstone ornaments. **1933** SCANLAN *Tides of Youth* 53 You might find some valuable greenstone Meres buried with the old chiefs. **1948** HENDERSON *Taina* 134 I was much impressed by these visitors..with *huia* feathers in their hair and **greenstone pendants** in their ears. **1968** SEDDON *The Seddons* 228 There was hardly time to thank the Native Affairs' Committee for their present of a greenstone pendant, there was little time even to say good-bye to the folks at home. **1970** MCNEISH *Mackenzie* 15 Wiremu gave him a greenstone pendant he was wearing and made the man bend down to touch noses.

greeny, var. GREENIE.

grenadier, *n.*¹ [Poss. f. its black cap reminiscent of a military fashion.] *white-fronted tern* (TERN 2 (10) *Sterna striata*), also called 'black cap'.

1966 FALLA et al. *Birds NZ* 164 White-fronted Tern *Sterna striata* Other names: Sea-swallow, Kahawai Bird, Tara, Blackcap, Grenadier, Swallowtail, Noddy (Chathams), Tikkitak (Stewart Is.). **1985** *Reader's Digest Book NZ Birds* 232 White-fronted Tern *Sterna striata*..black cap, grenadier.

grenadier, *n.*² Also **blue grenadier**. [Local use of *grenadier* applied to rattail fishes.] Any of various species of *Coelinchorus* spp., deep-water fish of the rattail family, Macrouridae. See also RATTAIL.

1985 *Evening Post* (Wellington) 18 May 56 The range [in a Wellington sea-food delicatessen includes] Blue grenadier, a deep water species which retails for about $7.49 a kilo. **1988** *Evening Post* (Wellington) 22 July 14 The fish, known as the 'rattail' or Coelinchorus, were caught off the coast of.. Taranaki, in the orange roughy grounds at a depth of 800m... The rattail also known as the grenadier is closely related to the codfish family, feeding on the bottom of the ocean.

grey, *a.* In the names of birds and fish, see: DUCK 2 (4), KIWI 2 (2) and 2 (3), MULLET 2 (1), TEAL *n.*¹ 2 (5), WARBLER 2 (3).

grey, *n.*¹

1. Also **gray**. [f. Brit. slang of uncertain origin: cf. OED *grey n.* 10; AND 1912, 1895 only.] A coin altered to have two heads or two tails; for the game of two up, esp. two tails and often in the phr. **to ring in a grey**, to surreptitiously introduce a two-tailed coin into the game.

1911 *Truth* 7 Oct. 7 Nelson had the kitty, and tossed, but Bradley caught the pennies in the air, and then discovered one of them was a double-headed coin, or in the language of the 'learned'—'a grey.' **1912** *Ibid.* 20 Jan. 7 Too often, he falls a ready victim to the crook and speiler [*sic*] who is adept in the art of 'ringing in a grey'; i.e., using a double-headed penny, and resorting to other devious, and dirty dodges. **1928** DEVANNY *Dawn Beloved* 163 A double-tailer is called a 'grey'. A double-header a 'nob'.

2. *Ellipt.* for *grey duck* (DUCK 2 (4)).

1904 CRADOCK *Sport in NZ* 60 The 'grey duck', ordinarily abbreviated into the one word 'greys'. *Ibid.* 203 The 'mob' of greys.

Grey, *n.*² *Hist.* [f. the name of Sir George *Grey* (1812–98), colonial governor (1845–53, 1861–68) and politician.] In composition, alluding to the political ideology or practice of

Sir George Grey, or to his followers: **Greyhound**, a 'Liberal' supporter of Sir George Grey in the General Assembly; **Greyism**, the political ideology of Grey and his supporters; **Greyite**, a supporter of Grey's political aims. See also *double G* (DOUBLE B).

1948 LIPSON *Politics of Equality* 125 In the opening days..of the new Parliament, Grey and his '**greyhounds**' (as his Liberal followers were called) found a weak spot to attack Vogel's ministry. 1879 *Auckland Weekly News* 6 Dec. 13 This is what comes of demagogues and **Greyism**. 1904 *NZ Observer* 16 July 5 But for his 'Greyism', Mr. Moss might very possibly have been a Cabinet Minister. 1879 *Auckland Weekly News* 4 Oct. 16 The young **Greyites** in the house reminded him much of the young greyhounds lately introduced into Canterbury. 1890 *NZ Observer* 20 Dec. 1 It ought also to carry out the Greyite 'plank' of taxing absentee bond-holders.

greyback. WW1. *Egypt.* [Brit. dial. and US: see OED 3; EDD 2 1 d.] A louse (esp. a head-louse) infesting human beings.

1917 *NZ At the Front* 16 Powder t' kill th' greybacks with [at Cairo]. 1918 *Kia-ora Coo-ee* (1981) 15 Apr. II. 5 Have a few words to say about old cobbers. There are two varieties of lice known to Billjim and his mates from Maoriland... The classification is difficult to an outsider, being governed by a minute colour scheme. First, there is the Transport Marine—a big grey chap with sooty markings; next come the Greybacks, which are too universal to deserve mention. 1918 *NZ at the Front* 132 The little greybacks are industrious and increase both night and day.

grey-backed mollymawk: see MOLLYMAWK 2 (5).

grey-backed storm petrel, grey-faced petrel: see PETREL 2 (19) b (b) and 2 (12).

grey-headed mollymawk: see MOLLYMAWK 2 (6).

greyhound. A thin rolled cigarette. See also RACEHORSE.

1970 DAVIN *Not Here Not Now* 107 On a chair was a tin full of sallow cigarette butts, rolled thin. Supplies must be running low if he was rolling himself greyhounds. 1988 MCGILL *Dict. Kiwi Slang* 53 *greyhound* thinly rolled cigarette.

grid. [Brit. slang: OED *n.* 7, 1922; AND 1927.] A bicycle (esp. if old).

c1938 *grid* for bicycle frequent among Marlborough boys (Ed.). 1948 BALLANTYNE *Cunninghams* (1976) 29 Back across the playground they met Mike Park who had some cricket gear resting on the crossbar of his grid. 1963 ADSETT *Magpie Sings* 177 She bucked us off! Bloody old grid bucked us off!..Take that, you piddling heap of scrap-iron. 1963 MORRIESON *Scarecrow* 63 'Hop on the bar of my grid,' said D'Arcy. 'I'll double you round to meet some pals of ours.' 1994 LASENBY *Dead Man's Head* 127 'We've got to go,' Bob said. 'We've only got two grids.'.. Denny trotted beside Joe who was doubling Polly.

gridiron, *n.*¹ *Canterbury Hist.* From the pattern of a *gridiron* (poss. esp. that used for contemporary street gutter or drain gratings), poss. influenced by a surveying term: cf. 1877 *TrNZI* IX. 97 The system of great triangulation cast over India is not that of 'net-work' as cast over the British Islands, but what is technically termed 'gridiron' or 'chain series'.] Usu. *attrib.* poss. passing into Comb. as **gridiron system**, pertaining to, or resulting from, the practice of gridironing (see GRIDIRON *v.*).

1876 PEACHE *Journal* in Gray *Quiet with Hills* (1970) 47 He had bought in as much land as he could afford to freehold and, as others were taking up the 'gridiron' leaseholds, he would have to have a great deal more capital to ensure this would not continue. 1883 REEVES in *Canterbury Rhymes* 127 Sir John Hall, then a squatter of squatters, and since reputed, although wrongly, to have been the originator of the 'gridiron' system of land buying. 1907 ALLOM *Note* July in Jollie *Reminiscences* (1878) (ATLTS) 39 [When he borrowed the MS from Jollie's wife, Allom wrote this comment on Jollie's account of buying the best parts out of a run in 1856.] This was probably about the beginning of the grid-iron process of picking the eyes out of the country, so much practised afterwards. 1946 ACLAND *Early Canterbury Runs* 82 [Sir John Hall] is erroneously supposed to have invented the 'grid-iron' system of land buying.

gridiron, *n.*² [f. the layout, and often the name *gridiron*, of the field on which American football is played.] A New Zealand name for American football. Also *attrib.*

1960 MCLEAN *Kings of Rugby* 61 American, or gridiron, football. 1980 LELAND *Kiwi-Yankee Dict.* 49 *gridiron*: In case the description doesn't ring any bells, this is the New Zealand name for the American version of football. 1989 *Sunday Star* (Auckland) 5 Nov. C10 [Caption] No comeback for this fallen gridiron player. 1992 *Evening Post* (Wellington) 20 Jan. 1 A Hutt Valley gridiron player..may face life-time suspension.

gridiron, *v.* [f. *n.*¹] *trans.*, occas. *absol.*, and often as a *vbl. n.* Usu. with reference to early Canterbury, to buy (strips of a run or pastoral leasehold) in such a way as to prevent any practical use of the intervening strips by another person. Cf. EYE 2, SPOT *v.*¹ 1.

1879 *Auckland Weekly News* 4 Oct. 16 He had inquired into the Canterbury gridironing system. *Ibid.* 4 Oct. 19 The quantity of land so gridironed did not exceed 5000 acres. 1882 STUART *Sir George Grey* 4 The greedy land-sharks..fain would they shark him, and gridiron too. 1883 PARTINGTON *Random Rot* 309 This run has been 'gridironed', that is, strips have been purchased to protect the owners against selectors. 1890 [see DUMMY *n.*¹]. 1890 *Otago Witness* (Dunedin) 21 Aug. 13 People ought to be compelled to take up the land according to the lay of the district..or we shall have the gridironing system of Canterbury repeated. 1898 MORRIS *Austral-English* 176 *Gridironing*..a term used in the province of Canterbury, New Zealand. A man purchased land in the shape of a gridiron, knowing that nobody would take the intermediate strips, which later he could purchase at his leisure. 1902 gridironing [see SPOT *v.*¹ 2]. 1904 *NZ Observer* 16 Apr. 2 The country has had quite enough of government by the Canterbury squatters, with their notorious gridironing system of land monopoly. 1912 *Truth* 27 Apr. 4 It was thought that the free-trade foolishness had..been buried with plural voting..land gridironing, and other swindles and unpleasantnesses. 1938 BURDON *High Country* 123 Some of the runholders now thought of two new devices to preserve their estates. The first consisted of buying a series of 20 acre sections fronting on a road, so spaced as to leave between them sections of 19 acres. Under the Waste Lands Regulations, none of less than 20 acres could be bought except by having it put up to auction. Few people would go to the trouble of having this done; and anyone who did was in all probability a man of small means, who stood little chance of outbidding the runholder. It usually happened, therefore, that all these 19-acre sections were retained without having to be purchased. This was known as 'gridironing.' 1958 MULGAN *Making of New Zealander* 104 Once when the *Press* was supporting the parliamentary candidature of a member of an old family, a friend said to me: 'The *Press* (Christchurch) forgets that that lot "grid-ironed" Canterbury.' 1960 gridironing [see SPOT *v.*¹ 2]. 1983 FRANCIS *Wildlife Ranger* 112 A powerful landowner..had for years dominated the Haast Valley and his cattle wandered and grazed rent-free over the lush valleys and river flats—rent-free because he had leased all the access. This practice, called grid-ironing, was not uncommon and was undertaken by numerous big landowners.

Hence **gridironed** *ppl. a.*

1980 MCLEOD *Down from Tussock Ranges* 169 In exchange for the freehold we surrendered round the lake, they [*sc.* the Lands Department] gave us an area of freehold land at Cora Lynn to fill in a gridironed area behind the old homestead.

Griffin's silverfish. [f. the name of L.C. *Griffin* a zoology assistant (1926–34) at the Auckland Museum.] BLUENOSE.

1957 PARROTT *Sea Angler's Fishes* 60 Griffin's silverfish *Seriolella amplus (Griffin)*... In 1928 the late L. T. Griffin, described and figured a new species of fish, very closely related to the Warehou (*Seriolella brama*) and Silverfish (*Seriolella punctata*), from specimens caught by hand lines in a rocky locality near Mayor Island, Bay of Plenty. This species probably replaces the Silverfish in our Northern waters. 1966 DOOGUE & MORELAND *Sea Anglers' Guide* 223 Griffin's silverfish... *Other names*..blue-jaw, bonito; matiri (Maori). 1986 [see BLUENOSE].

Griffin weed. Also **Griffin's weed.** [See quot. 1921.] A local name for the introduced European weed vervain *Verbena officinalis* (fam. Verbenaceae). See also *blue top* (BLUE *a.* 2 b).

1921 GUTHRIE-SMITH *Tutira* (1926) 299 Vervain (*Verbena officinalis*)..was first noticed on a station belonging to Mr Nairn; there it began to spread, and there it became known as Nairn's weed; the station then became the property of the late Mr Griffin. Now Mr Griffin, as chairman of the Wairoa County Council, touched the business and bosom of every up-country settler in the district. People knew him who did not know and had never known his predecessor; his office advertised the plant: presently, even in the immediate vicinity of its origin, the earlier designation was dropped, the later one assumed. It became known up and down the east coast as 'Griffin's Weed'. 1926 HILGENDORF *Weeds* 146 Vervain (*Verbena officinalis*), also called **blue top**, griffin weed, and missionary weed, is a slender tough-stemmed perennial 1 to 2 ft high, with a few opposite rough, cleft leaves, and small lilac flowers. 1969 *Standard Common Names Weeds* 34 *Griffin weed* [=] *vervain.*

grim, *a.* [f. *grim* forbidding, unrelenting.] **a.** Applied in WW2. and occas. after, often ironically or by meiosis, to dangerous or unpleasant conditions.

1944 *NZEF Times* 6 Mar. 2 'Been in a show?' 'And what a show!' said the bloke. 'Grim stuff.' 1945 HENDERSON *Gunner Inglorious* 91 Things are — grim. c1945 *Sixes & Sevens* (Troopship pub.) 7 'It's a grim show,' I said. 'You can't have a victory on one bot of Canadian.' 1950 *Evening Post* (Wellington) June 21 Cement supply 'pretty grim'.

b. WW2. As **grim dig**, a veteran soldier who has survived 'grim' conditions, *spec.* a surviving member of the First Echelon, 2NZEF, in the Middle East theatre. See also DIG *n.* 2, *four-figure man* (FOUR).

1943 *NZEF Times* 16 Oct. 5 The Grim Digs' doings Put me in a humour serene. **1945** *Victory Voyager* (Troopship pub.) 'Hi ya buddy. You soldiers have got some cute gab.' 'Grim old Digs ya know. Four years 'sa long time.' [Also humorously written *grymdygge*.] **1955** *Upper Hutt Leader* 4 June 5 [In a column 'Diggers Out of Uniform', in which the *Grim Dig* is the main character.] 'I'm an expert,' said the Grim Dig. 'Served a long, hard apprenticeship in some tough units.' **1963** *Dominion* (Wellington) 30 Jan. 8 As a Grim Dig I feel it is my duty to point out to the younger generation the origin and meaning of the expression 'she's right'... All Grim Digs should rise up in righteous wrath. **1977** HOLMES *Best of Homespun* 66 An extremely grim dig tramped up the stairs. and darted up to the kitchen to peer out the window. **1983** *Dominion* (Wellington) 5 Sept. 7 Noel Gardiner is an ex-Grim Dig in town to promote his second book... Who were the Grim Digs? They were the Kiwi soldiers of World War II. 'And they were grim when they came out of Greece and Crete,' Mr Gardiner said. **1992** ANDERSON *Portrait Artist's Wife* 8 He was not smiling; his face was grim. A grim dig.

grind, *v*. Shearing. *intr*. or *absol*. To sharpen handshears, or machine combs and cutters on a grindstone.
1934 *Press* (Christchurch) (Acland Gloss.) 27 Jan. 15 *Woolshed terms... To grind* (shears) is always used without the noun. A shearer never 'grinds his shears'. **1955** BOWEN *Wool Away* 156 Grind. To sharpen combs and cutters. **1987** OGONOWSKA-COATES *Boards, Blades & Barebellies* 96 Grind. To hold the shears to the grindstone in order to sharpen them.

grind, *n. Tramping*. [Spec. use of *grind* labour of a monotonous kind: see OED *n.*¹ 2 c.] A hard, tiring uphill tramp usu. with heavy packs.
1936 *Hills & Valleys* No.2 6 A tough grind under heavy packs brought us on to Neill. **1940** GILKISON *Peaks, Packs & Mountain Tracks* 79 They regard a walk over the hills to Silver Peak as a 'grind', and can take no pleasure in it. **1946** HARPER *Memories Mountains & Men* 189 The whole expedition was one which I should have looked upon as rather a 'grind' fifty years ago.

grinder. Usu. *pl*., a wild boar's upper tusks.
1940 STUDHOLME *Te Waimate* (1954) 255 Occasionally, old boars would lose their grinders, and the tusks would then grow right round in a circle. **1982** HOLDEN *Wild Pig* 132 [A boar's tusks] are sharpened by the grinding motion of rubbing them against the smaller, upper tusks that are called 'grinders'.

grog, *n*.
1. *grog* in the Brit. sense 'spirits, esp. rum, and water' is recorded from 1773, but is of distinctive historical significance only in special Comb.: **grog-den**, a low boozing place; **groghouse** *obs*., GROGSHOP; **grog-seller** *obs*. [AND 1827], one who sells spirits at a grog-shop; **grog-selling** [AND 1829], see quot. 1834; **grog-shanty** *hist*. [AND 1858], a grogshop (see also SHANTY 2), also, in 20th century use, an outlet for sly-grog in a dry district (see quot. 1937); hence **grog-shanty keeper**; **grog vendor** *obs*., see *grog-seller* above. See also GROGGERY.
1840 *NZ Jrnl*. I. 198 Where a year ago only three **grog-dens** warned the passer-by in the harbour not to land on the beach, a neat row of wooden houses..extends along the line of high water. **1836** ASHWELL *Lett. & Jrnls*. Dec. (ATLTS) I. 17 Six **groghouses** in the place. **1834** *NZ in the 1830s* 9 Aug. (1979) 30 Of the others, the most part are following the occupation of **grog-selling**;... but the **grog seller** has decidedly the most lucrative business. **1839** LANG *NZ in 1839* 7 The existence of a considerable European population..and the artificial wants of the natives, have..led..also to the settlement of a swarm of individuals..of a very different description, as retail dealers, grog-sellers, and panderers to the worst vices of the most abandoned of men. **1840** *NZ Jrnl*. I. 74 As for the grog-sellers described in the extract, we must observe that the Bay of Islands grog-seller is not one atom worse than the same class in our other Colonies. **1873** PYKE *Wild Will Enderby* (1889, 1974) III. xi 110 'Brandy Ben" was a notorious grog-seller, and was well known to the police. **1993** *Defence Quarterly* No.1 12 Estimates of the number of grogsellers [at Kororareka] range between 35 and 50. **1869** *Auckland Punch* 163 I..reached the **grog-shanty** in safety. **1872** *Otago Witness* (Dunedin) 13 Apr. 7 The word 'Loafer', as we use it upon the diggings, means a hanger-on of the grog shanties which we have here. **1890** *Ibid*. 23 Dec. 18 They..proceeded to 'knock down' their cheque in approved bush style at the first grog shanty. **1913** BATHGATE *Sodger Sandy's Bairn* 79 Men were engaged..in building..a store and a 'hotel', though both would in reality be 'grog shanties', and would retail liquor by the nobbler'. **1937** *King Country Chronicle* 20 Dec. 5 The man who does not permit overindulgence in many ways is doing a service..by keeping people away from 'grogshanties'. **1992** LATHAM *Golden Reefs* 156 Many of the [sly-grog] offenders were single women whose grog-shanties were associated also with prostitution and petty crime. **1980** ELDRED-GRIGG *Southern Gentry* 65 Gerit Alexander Chalmers..believed that those most likely to profit from land reform were 'the small publicans and **grog-shanty keepers** who gain a living out of the working people employed here'. **1836** ASHWELL *Lett. & Jrnls*. Dec. (ATLTS) I. 17 I also visit the **grog vendors** of Otuhio.

2. a. [A generalized use of Brit. *grog* spirits: AND 1832.] Any alcoholic liquor; booze.
1869 THATCHER *Local Songs* 32 Eicke's constitution, we hear, Was so delicate..That on the journey he'd be queer, Unless sustained by bottled beer; Simpson said pulling [*sc.* rowing] made him dry,... So of grog they took a good supply When they went to Ohinemuri. **1900** CHUDLEIGH *Diary* 14 Feb. (1950) 399 Edgar Clough left for S. Africa..and old Abner [Clough, a Chatham Island drunkard] has gone to Waitangi to see him off he says but I fear grog will be all he sees. **1919** CHUDLEIGH *Diary* 5 Jan. (1950) 465 The wage earners are bulging with money and spare time.... At any cost grog and sigerettes [*sic*] for all. **1921** *Quick March* 11 July 25 The slumbering form of the sleuth [*sc.* a King Country policeman] who set out to keep night-watch in the fern for a motor-load of illicit grog. **1956** WILSON *Sweet White Wine* 91 'I'll have some grog aboard too. I'll be a bit lit.'.. *grog*: alcohol **1962** HORI *Half-gallon Jar* 64 The Maori drink only two kinds of grog—the beer in the half-gallon jar and the beer in the bottle. **1983** HULME *Bone People* 28 Thin-fingered hands around the glass... Split chin upwards, and the dark grog [*sc.* stout] practically seen outside your skinny throat. **1993** O'SULLIVAN *Let the River Stand* 266 He preferred to stay at the hotel..rather than having to hit the grog out at the hydro camp every night.

b. Special Comb. **grog-artist**, see ARTIST; **grog-bar** *obs*., an unlicensed premises selling sly-grog; **grog-on**, a drinking bout; **grog-party**, a drinking party; **grog-tent**, a liquor tent at a showground, or at a sports gatherings, etc.
1905 *Truth* 24 June 1 Forty unlicensed **grog bars** in Ashburton. **1955** *BJ Cameron Collection* (TS July) **grog-on** (n) A drinking bout. **1936** HYDE *Passport to Hell* 90 At Christchurch, where the wet brigade had joined them and turned their progress into the first real grog party, a man yet fatter had repeated it. **c1972 grog-tent** applied to the 'refreshment tent' at the Cambridge (Waikato) local A & P show (Ed.).

c. In the phr. **on the grog** [AND 1959], on the booze.
1968 SLATTER *Pagan Game* 166 When he was on the grog his mind began to cast about for some excitement. **1981** CHARLES *Black Billy Tea* 75 I'd been on the grog and lost my best dog. **1988** *Dominion Sunday Times* (Wellington) 14 Feb. 19 We can't handle you because you run away & get on the grog.

grog, *v*. [AND 1 *v. intr.* to drink alcohol, 1959.] As **grog on**, to keep on drinking alcoholic liquor.
1968 GLEN *Holy Joe's People* 30 I stood with my back to the fire watching my cobbers grog on. **1976** MORRIESON *Pallet on Floor* 121 The driver, a Maori who threw the skins on the fellmongery paint-table where the skins were trimmed and sprayed with sodium sulphate, called out, 'Hey Tin-Whistle, the Eagle shat today. We're grogging on regardless.'
Hence **grogged up** *pa. ppl. a*. [AND 1956], drunk; **grogging** *vbl. n*. and *attrib*. [AND 1965], (pertaining to) the consumption of alcoholic liquor.
1962 WEBBER *Look No Hands* 124 You remember telling me you didn't want any of your **grogged-up** Old Dig friends giving her the lowdown on you? **1980** THOMPSON *All My Lives* 35 Her husband..had been banished to a hut behind the house where he held secret **grogging** sessions with supplies brought to him from the Henley pub. **1981** JOHNSTON *Fish Factory* 32 Committee work taking up too much of your grogging time, Dunstall? **1987** COX *Dirty Work* 21 Apparently they liked to watch TV in the dark, to cover illicit grogging.

groggery. *Obs*. Also **grogery**.
1. GROGSHOP.
1844 WILLIAMS *NZ Jrnl*. (1956) 69 I might say with propriety that six eighths of all the European houses are nothing more than grogeries. Here are in capital letters over the door 'Tap'. One in particular so-called Hotel, a man and his family the only occupants. **1959** SINCLAIR *Hist. NZ* 45 In the eighteen-twenties the debauchery natural to a whaling port took place mainly on board visiting ships. In the thirties it moved to numerous 'grogeries' ashore.

2. In modern occasional jocular use, a hotel, 'a pub'.
1905 *Truth* 19 Aug. 1 O'Shaunessy's Groggery.

grogshop. *Obs*. [Used elsewhere, but of historical significance in early New Zealand: see OED *grog n*. 4.] A low drinking-den selling alcoholic spirits.
1833 WILLIAMS *Early Jrnls*. 28 Apr. (1961) 309 After dinner went to Kororarika..; numbers of Europeans on the beach, indulging themselves in the grog shops which are now becoming general. **1837** RHODES *Jrnl. Barque 'Australian'* 29 Apr. (1954) 50 Through the detestable system of grog shops [at the Bay of Islands] the crew and officers were constantly in a state of drunkenness. **1840** POLACK *Manners & Customs* II. 280 To distinguish what are termed grog-shops and ship stores, the former is a small place where spirits reduced below proof are sold by the glass, whereas in the latter, spirits are never sold less than one fifth of a gallon, old measure. **1864** *Nelson Examiner* 17 May 2 There are many stores very fairly stocked, and one or two decent eating houses—grog-shops, of course, in plenty. **1908** *Truth* 8 Feb. 5 This general disregard for everything is not at all unlikely to make for the closing up of this glorified grog shop. **1921** *Quick March* 10

Sept. 11 [Fox River Settlement] had seventy-five public-houses—grog-shops, saloons, or what-not. **1959** BRUNO *Hellbuster* 10 Ashore, blue night mantled..the whaling station, veiling soft the haphazard settlement of weatherboard grogshops and general stores. **1963** CASEY *As Short a Spring* 276 The beauty times are when you get in with the mob and do the rounds of the brothels and grog-shops. **1971** GRIFFITHS *King Wakatip* 112 The dancing rooms, prostitutes, billiard rooms, grog-shops..were among the inevitable facilities in gold-rush Queenstown. **1993** *Defence Quarterly* No.1 12 The 'Duke of Marlborough' was the first grog shop to be licensed in 1840 [at Kororareka].

Hence **grog-shop keeper**.
1839 *Col. Gaz.* 28 Aug. 627 Grog-shop-keepers are to vie with the 'land-sharks' [from Sydney, in plundering the natives]. **1844** *NZ Co. Reports* XII. 77H Grog-shop keepers.

grommet, var. GRUMMET.

groper. Also occas. **grouper**. [Transf. use of *groper*, a var. of *grouper* a West Indian fish of fam. Serranidae.]
1. In the South Island the preferred name for HAPUKU q.v.; elsewhere in New Zealand occas. applied to other large-mouthed, good-eating fish. Cf. BASS.
1843 *NZ Jrnl.* IV. 263 The fish, which at Port Nicholson is known by the name of habooka, but which is called groper to the southward. **1868** PYKE *Province of Otago* 32 Many..varieties of sea-fish are caught round the coast, such as barracouta, groper, rock-cod. **1872** [see HAPUKU 1]. **1890** *Otago Witness* (Dunedin) 23 Jan. 18 It used to be the common practice of the early settlers of Otago to cure a good supply of groper for winter use, either pickled in barrels or smoked. **1902** [see HAPUKU 1]. **1918** *NZJST* I. 136 The class of fish supplied to this market before the war contained nothing so good as our groper (hapuku) or snapper. **1928** *Free Lance* (Wellington) 22 Feb. 8 Lady, did you say groper? Of course, here we are. The finest baby groper that ever came out of the sea. **1948** *Our own Country* 159 The groper with the dilated Eddie Cantor eyes. **1957** PARROTT *Sea Angler's Fishes* 70 The flesh of the Groper is well flavoured and finds a ready market. Unfortunately, both the Bass and Groper are sold under the one name 'Groper'. **1966** DOOGUE & MORELAND *Sea Anglers' Guide* 224 Groper or Hapuku... *Polyprion oxygeneios;* whapuku (Maori). Groper has a wide usage in the South Island, while hapuku is largely used in the North Island. **1972** BAXTER *Collected Poems* (1980) 545 Groper with throats like buckets. **1986** [see HAPUKU 1].

2. With a modifier: **spotted black, deep sea, grandaddy**.

(1) **spotted black groper**. *Epinephalus daemelii* (fam. Serranidae).
1977 FISHER *Angels Wear Black* 38 The Morepork..was a big fish—at least twelve pounds. They have a lot of meat on them and have been known to be mistaken by new chums for the Spotted Black Groper. **1982** AYLING *Collins Guide* (1984) 205 *Spotted Black Grouper Epinephalus daemeli*..Spotted black grouper..in New Zealand rarely reaches 80cm. **1986** PAUL *NZ Fishes* 84 Spotted black groper *Epinephalus daemelii*. Widespread in the Indo-Pacific region, including Australia, where it is known as saddled rock cod, and northern New Zealand.

(2) **deep sea groper**. A misleading retail or fish-shop name for a cardinal fish of the family Apogonidae, prob. the deepsea (or black) cardinal fish *Epigonus telescopus*, a deep water species found world-wide.
1991 *Evening Post* (Wellington) 18 June 4 Seafoods misled the public by advertising a fish called cardinal as deep sea groper, it has been alleged... Cardinal is a new fish species not well known to New Zealanders. There is no such fish as deep sea groper. **1991** *Dominion* (Wellington) 16 Aug. 13 A cardinal fish is not a groper, even when it is labelled deep sea groper, Judge Pat Keane ruled..today.

(3) **grandaddy groper**. A familiar term for and colloquial translation of MATUAWHAPUKU q.v., also *grandfather hapuku* (HAPUKU 3).
1991 BRADSTOCK *Fishing* 21 *Red scorpionfish*. Other names: grandfather hapuku, grandaddy [*sic*] groper, red rock cod, matuawhaapuku.

3. Special Comb. **groper throat**, the flaps below a groper's head as a table delicacy.
1945 *Korero* (AEWS Background Bulletin) 29 Jan. 16 Another was brimful of groper throats.

Groppi /'grɒpi/. WW2. (Egypt). [f. *Groppi's*, a Cairo tea-shop and hotel.]
1. As **Groppi mocker (mocka, mokka)**, a dress suit or dress clothes. See also MOCKER *n.*[2]
[**1919** WAITE *New Zealanders at Gallipoli* 38 The girls of Cairo were never treated more liberally and often to the daintiness of Sault's and Groppi's. **1959** *Upper Hutt Leader* 25 Mar. 5 'This,' said the Grim Dig. 'Please forward back sheesh.., also one overdue fare from Groppi's to Bab-el-Louk.'] **1939–45** Groppi mokka [see GROUSE]. **1949** THE SARGE *Excuse my Feet* 110 He went away in search of his *Groppi mokka*, which consisted of a freshly pressed..pair of slacks and a bush shirt. *Ibid*. 156 *Groppi mokka* (Kiwi & Ar.)—fine clothes: groppi being a posh restaurant. **1982** *Evening Post* (Wellington) 4 Oct. 41 The Groppi tea shop in the heart of the commercial centre [of Cairo] still does a thriving business, selling tea and ice cream to middle class Egyptians and occasional tourists. The tea house fashionable even during the war, insinuated itself into the language with 'groppi mocka' being the best clothes the Kiwis could muster for a day on the town. **1995** SLATTER *One More River* 90 Ewan, a natty dresser in groppi mokka, called it a mark eight soup plate.

2. As **Groppi's Light Horse**, a soldiers' name for the men and staff at base in Cairo.
1945 *NZEF Times* 5 Feb 4 [Caption] Haven't you ever heard of Groppi's Light Horse. **1988**. McGILL *Dict. Kiwi Slang* 53 *groppi mocker* dressing up, originally to visit Groppi's teashop/hotel in Cairo, WW2; *Groppi's Light Horse* was combatants' name for base troops at Cairo.

grot. [f. *grot*(to, with a rhyming play on *squat*: cf. also *grotty* foul, unclean.] A toilet (or toilet bowl); a defecation or its result.
1941 St Patrick's College Silverstream (Ed.) The grot(s) occas. used for the usual college word 'jakes' for toilets. **1980** *Lynfield College* (Goldie Brown Collect.) *grot*: toilet **1981** *NZ Police National Headquarters* (Staff Officer) (Goldie Brown Collect.) *grott*: slang term for a bowel movement; not considered polite; e.g., 'I'm just away for a grott.'

grouce, var. GROUSE.

ground, *n.*[1] Goldmining.
1. Rock or earth in which gold is found; occas., bedrock. See also GROUND-SLUICE *n.*.
1863 PYKE *Report in Handbook NZ Mines* (1887) 8 Three miners..discovered payable auriferous ground on the western watershed. **1868** *Thames Miner's Guide* 523 Country or ground.—Same as bed-rock. [*sc.* 'The mass of rock in which the veins or lodes occur']. **1871** MONEY *Knocking About NZ* 16 Our cradle was set,.. and we began to take up the ground in the bed of the creek to get down to the bottom where the heaviest gold always lies.

2. [AND 1851.] A goldfield; a piece of land being worked as a claim, or over which claims are or have been worked (see quot. 1967); an auriferous area which can support a given number of miners (see quots. 1868, 1869).
1868 *Thames Miner's Guide* 82 Description of claims... Anglo Maori, Waiotahi Creek. Six men's ground, taken up in April. **1869** *TrNZI* I. (rev. edn.) 479 He said that on many claims, a space as large as six men's ground at the Thames, was required for amalgamating ground. **1874** BATHGATE *Col. Experiences* 107 We had worked out the greater part of the grounds, and had sunk a couple of shafts in the claim, and had not used a stick of timber in either, for it was capital standing ground. **1914** PFAFF *Diggers' Story* 64 There was no ground to be got there... There was good gold there, but the claims were all taken up. **1967** MAY *West Coast Gold Rushes* 195 False bottoms fooled even seasoned diggers, particularly at Kaniere. Claims considered worked out were frequently re-worked at a different level. This explains the many small rushes which occurred on 'old ground'. *Ibid*. 527 Old ground: ground worked over or mined. **1992** LATHAM *Golden Reefs* 85 Westfield sues Hunt..and party..for holding illegal possession of four men's ground. [**1992** *Note*] Two hundred and forty feet.

ground, *n.*[2] *Obs*. [Spec. use of *ground* a space or area used for some special purpose (see OED 14 a): as 'whaling ground' used elsewhere but recorded earliest in NZ.] A whaling ground.
1836 *Let. from Port Cooper* 13 Sept. in McNab *Old Whaling Days* (1913) 153 The *Elizabeth* has taken 150 tuns, and she was late on the ground... The season is nearly over in the bays, and I consider the whale and shore parties to have taken this season about twenty thousand barrels. **1866** HUNT *Chatham Is.* 59 The busy [whaling] seasons lasted about five years; the ground then became pretty well cut up.

ground, *a*. In the names of animals, see: LARK 2 (1), PARROT 2 (4), PHEASANT, WETA 2 (4).

groundsel. Also **New Zealand groundsel**. [Extended use of *groundsel* the name of a northern hemisphere daisy *Senecio vulgaris* (fam. Asteraceae).] Any of various native herbs of genus *Senecio* (or *Brachyglottis*) (fam. Asteraceae).
1777 ANDERSON *Journal* Feb. in Cook *Journals* (1967) III. 805 Amongst the known kinds of plants are common and rough Bindweed..and groundsel. **1838** POLACK *NZ* I. 295 *Knot-grass, brambles, eye-bright, groundsell*, and minor herbaceous vegetation, supposed to be solely indigenous to New Zealand, abound throughout the country. **1844** TUCKETT *Diary* 16 Aug. in Hocken *Contributions* (1898) 224 Like the narrow plains of the Waikauroa, it grows only the wiry tree grass.., no aniseed, perennial groundsel, or milk thistle. **1867** HOOKER *Handbook* 764 Groundsel. *Senecio*, various sp. **1892** HUDSON *Elem. Manual NZ Entomology* 73 Its original food no doubt consisted of the 'New Zealand groundsel' (*Senecio bellidioides*). **1910** COCKAYNE *NZ Plants & Their Story* 43 Growing through these are certain shrubs or small trees, especially..kirk's groundsel (*Senecio kirkii*), bearing in its season white daisy-like blossoms. **1969** *Standard Common Names Weeds* 69 Shore groundsel *Senecio lautus*.

ground-sluice, *n.* Goldmining. [OED *ground* 18 a, 1869. A channel cut in the bottom or bedrock, into which the earth is conveyed by a stream of water.

1857 *Lyttelton Times* 4 July 5 There is every reason to believe that many other gullies that have not paid for tomming, will yield well to sluicing parties, especially for a ground sluice. 1863 LAUPER in *Over Whitcombe Pass* (1960) 43 He then asked me if it would pay to work; I answered perhaps it would, with a ground sluice, not in any other way, but we had not found the bottom, which is always best. 1865 *AJHR* C-4A 10 [Dunstan] Of the different methods of working, that of ground sluicing is most universally adopted—a ground sluice being nothing more than a rectangular drain cut for a depth of about a foot into the surface soil.

Hence **ground-sluice** *v. intr.*, to operate a ground-sluice; **ground-sluicer**, one who operates a ground-sluice; **ground-sluicing** *vbl. n.*, see quot. 1935.

1863 WALKER *Jrnl. & Lett.* (ATLTS) 12–13 Jan. On Saturday we went over into the other gully and watched a man **ground-sluicing**. Saw him wash out 2 dishes of dirt. 1875 WILBY *Diary* in Pfaff *Diggers' Story* (1914) 116 1875..I then went ground sluicing in Mosquito Creek, near Marsden. 1967 MAY *West Coast Gold Rushes* 195 A busy crowd of **ground-sluicers** soon parcelled up the whole of Kaniere Terrace amongst them. 1865 **ground sluicing** [see *ground-sluice n.* above]. 1874 BATHGATE *Col. Experiences* 91 In Otago, the principal kind of mining is ground sluicing similar to the method in Cornwall..[called] 'streaming'..the water is carried across gullies in wooden-boxes, or canvas hose, called fluming. 1887 *Handbook NZ Mines* 215 Ground-sluicing is now more generally adopted, unless where the ground is very deep. The sand is usually washed over the wide sluice-boxes, covered with different materials, such as plush, green baize, coir matting, and copper-plates coated with quicksilver, which catch the fine gold, while the lighter particles float away. 1890 *NZ & South Seas Exhibit.: Papers Read at Mining Conference* 64 The primitive mode of working, still extant, is 'ground sluicing' which means the running of water over and upon a face of alluvial drift. 1935 BLYTH ed. *Gold Mining Year Book* 11 *Ground Sluicing*: Washing by water under low pressure alluvial deposits in trenches cut out of the bed rock. 1967 MAY *West Coast Gold Rushes* 188 Neither the development of ground-sluicing nor the tunnel claims made Ross and Donoghue's distinctive.

grouper, var. GROPER.

grouse, *a*. Also **grouce**. [Origin unknown: poss. related to n. British dial. *crouse* 'pleased, happy, cheerful, lively', or poss. 'amorous' ('a crewse wench'): AND 1944.] Fine, excellent; 'beaut'; often as an exclamation of approval or delight.

1939–45 *Expressions and Sayings 2NZEF* (Nat. Archiv. TS WAII DA 420/1) Grouse mocker—Best clothes (also Groppi mokka). 1941 BAKER *NZ Slang* 51 In constant use by our youngsters..grouse. 1947 DAVIN *Gorse Blooms Pale* 200 An Iti bint, a real grouse brush she was, with bonzer black eyes and nice charlies. 1955 *BJ Cameron Collection* (TS July) grouse (adj) Marvellous. 1965 HILLIARD *Power of Joy* 266 Pat's with a grouse new girl again. Must be doing a line with her. 1974 MORRIESON *Predicament* (1981) 182 What a grouse looking brush. She's asking for it. I'd like to slam a length into that. 1983 *Salient* (Wellington) 21 Mar. 4 'How's tricks fuck-knuckle?'..'Grouse', replied Barf. 1991 *Listener* 4 Nov. 19 I ran, feeling the wind and rain washing over me. Man, it was grouse!

growl, *v*. To grumble. Also with **at**, to scold, to 'tell off'.

1869 *Grey River Argus* 23 Jan. 2 If the girls went to bed at twelve o'clock when [bar-room] dancing was over, they would be 'growled' at by Mrs Crawford if there were men about the bar 'shouting'. 1893 COX *Diaries 1888–1924* (ATLMS) 26 Mar. Bidwell was away [from Pahautea] when we arrived and the Mrs growled a good deal. 1904 LANCASTER *Sons o' Men* 159 Sereld..growled because someone had spilt tobacco-ash into his crib—which is bushman for dinner. 1948 in Pearson *Six Stories* (1991) 41 The big girl from Standard Six couldn't have kept us quiet; she just stared at us.., as if she didn't know whether to growl or grin. 1982 GILDERDALE *Sea Change* 241 *growl* Grumble. H.C. Storer's *The Boy Settler* (1907?): 'It's no use growling about the food.' 1990 *Evening Post* (Wellington) 19 Feb. 13 The accused once left a client bound in an upstairs bondage chamber while she went down the road to get lunch. The mistress said she had to 'growl' at Chignell for that. 1990 *Evening Post* (Wellington) 22 May 48 A woman customer he was attending to recently reprimanded her small child with..: 'Don't do that or the man will growl.'

grub: see GRASS GRUB, *white grub* (WHITE *a*. 1).

grubber.

1. *Obs.* [See OED *grubber* 2 (1598) which seems applied mainly to harrow-like agricultural implements.] In early New Zealand use applied to a kind of cultivator or harrow; later occas. to a stump-removing implement.

1861 *Otago Witness* (Dunedin) 6 Apr. 2 For Sale, at the stores of the undersigned, the following variety of agricultural implements, by Gray;... Grubbers. 1915 MACDONALD *NZ Sheepfarming* xix Stump grubbing... With a 'monkey' grubber you can quickly..clear Stumps Trees, etc., from your land.

2. a. In recent use a frequent word for a mattock or 'grub-hoe', 'grub-axe', a single adze-like head or a double-bladed head attached to a handle and used for removing strongly-rooted plants or for breaking the surface of soil.

1896 HARPER *Pioneer Work* 84 The first suggested they [*sc*. ice-axes] were 'grubbers which had been sent down for Ryan', another believed 'they were picks'. 1913 *Truth* 3 May 5 Constable Harvey was early on the scene, and he made a search and found outside the bedroom door the head of a heavy gorse grubber. 1938 HYDE *Nor Yrs. Condemn* 253 Well..the next morning we're taken out, lectured, and given grubbers and gorse-slashers, cutting blackberry. 1948 FINLAYSON *Tidal Creek* (1979) 124 And he picks up the grubber to go after the thistles that are everywhere over-running the place. 1966 SHARPE *Fiordland Muster* 90 At the hut Gunn found a mattock or what a Canterbury man would call a gorse grubber... 'You might be able to dig out a rabbit, too, with that grubber.' 1969 BAXTER *Collected Poems* (1980) 469 The beautiful loose earth..that crumbles to the blows Of the grubber. 1973 in *NZ Listener Short Stories* (1977) 147 'Grab hold of that bloody grubber,' I said. 'What's a grubber?' asked Mortimer [the Pom].

b. Special Comb. **grubber-pit** *n.*, a hole made with a grubber.

1903 *AJHR* C-1 93 During the coming season [in Otago] it is proposed to plant some 260,000 lined in trees, in what are termed 'grubber-pits'. These pits are prepared by removing the turf with a mattock.

grubber-kick. *Rugby football.* [Used elsewhere but apparently recorded earliest in NZ: see OED *grubber* 6, 1950.] A kick designed to drive the ball end over end along the ground, often with the prospect of a bounce favourable to the kicker.

1938 STONE *Rugby Players* 93 The time is well spent in practising the short overhead punt and the grubber kick.

grummet /ˈɡrʌmət/. Also **grommet** (/ˈɡrʌmət/ or /ˈɡrɒmət/), **grummit**. [Fig. use of *grummet* (var. *grommet*) (a rubber) washer on which to seat or tighten nuts, etc.: cf. Partridge: female pudend: low naut: ca 1860: cf. also *Surfin'ary* (1991) *grommet* 2 'A sixties Australian term for a [surfers' groupie] that has been adopted worldwide.'] **a.** A woman as a sexual object. As **shepherd's grummet**, a sheep as a sexual object.

1966 FAIRBURN *Collected Poems* 139 A bottomless lake, a loud wind-break, storms raging round the summit, a tailored cassock woven of tussock, a wiggle of shepherd's grummit. 1963 MORRIESON *Scarecrow* 146 A sexy little piece like you is wasted on these hoboes... Just wait till the boys see the class bit of grummit I've picked up for myself in the sticks.

b. A term among adolescents expressing dislike or contempt.

1984 16 M E93 Pakuranga Coll. 3 Gromet [something disliked] 1984 16 M E78 Pakuranga Coll. 25 Grommits [used for new kids] 1990 *Dominion Sunday Times* (Wellington) 22 Apr. 4 If you're called [by adolescents] a grommet (a surfing term)..you've been insulted.

grunds. *pl.* Occas. also **grundies**. [Orig. *grundies* rhyming slang for 'undies'.] A pair of (male) underpants.

1971 *VUWTC' 71* 49 Hey Colonel, you reckon..two grunds, two woollen shirts, long trou, bush singlet..will be enough [for a tramping trip]. 1980 LELAND *Kiwi-Yankee Dict.* 49 *grunds*: Male underwear, independent of its state of cleanliness. 1985 *National Business Review* 4 Nov. 27 He washed his bloody grunds [he had been carrying a freshly killed deer carcass] and I washed my grubby oddities. 1996 *North & South* Apr. 36 Do the washing. Shove in the grunds and a bit of powder.

grunt. [Cf. *Macquarie Dict. New Words grunt* torque, 1985.] Power; of a motor vehicle, power of acceleration.

1981 *Avondale College Slang Words* (Auckland) (Goldie Brown Collect.) *enough grunt*: power 1989 MCGILL *Dinkum Kiwi Dict.* 39 *grunt* power, often horsepower; eg 'Boy, has that souped-up Holden got some grunt!' 1995 *Dominion* (Wellington) 26 Aug. 15 [Advt] Real Grunt—XC340 Cordless Phone High Powered Extended Range.

grunter. [Spec. local use of *grunter* for a land animal or fish which grunts: see OED 1 and 2.]

1. A pig.

1837 BEST *Journal* 2 Sept. (1966) 106 [Voyage Out to Australia]..the sow was all right one of the sailors being there one of the baby grunters had however presumed to defunct. 1845 [see SPUD *n*. 1]. 1876 KENNEDY *Colonial Travel* 183 'Hurry up with them grunters!' roared the captain [of the Wakatip steamer]. 1953 *Landfall* 27 173 Edwards had a whare with a roof of thatch, A Brown Bess, a go-ashore,... Six fat grunters and a small spud patch.

2. GURNARD 1; cf. quot. 1957 below.

[1957 PARROTT *Sea Angler's Fishes* 168 The Gurnards often make a grunting or growling noise when taken out of the water, and in some countries they are called 'Growlers' on account of this peculiarity. The grunting noise is caused by the escape of air from the air-bladder through the pneumatic duct.] 1960 BAXTER *Collected Poems* (1980) 219 He's got no time for any man bludging. I owe him [*sc*. the publican] for a grunter and a bottle And he'll think I'm dodging.

GST /'dʒi 'es 'ti/. [f. the initials of *g*oods and *s*ervices *t*ax.] A single-rate tax on all goods and services.

1985 *Listener* 22 June 53 To New Zealand will go the doubtful distinction of being the only English-speaking nation to apply GST to the written word. **1985** *Listener* 13 July 17 Nine small businesses spent $1000 on a newspaper advertisement proclaiming..that GST stood for Gestapo Tax. **1986** *Sunday News* (Auckland) 20 July 21 Various stores have begun labelling their products with the retail price and the GST price marked in preparation for October 1. However, they aren't allowed to charge the GST price till October. **1986** *Listener* 25 Oct. 48 I read in the paper the other day of a man who was fined $100 with court costs $35, and was then donged $3.50 GST on the court costs.

guaranteed price. *Hist*. See quot. 1941.

[*Note*] The words 'Guaranteed Price' are not used in the Primary Produce Marketing Act 1936 which states that 'the general purpose shall be to assure to the producer a net return..equivalent to the return he would have received if such dairy-produce had been acquired by the Crown for export in accordance with the foregoing purposes of this Part of this Act'.

1936 *NZPD* CCXLIV. 683 [Nash] We shall set up machinery to fix the value of the land, from which the farmer gets his product, at a figure that is sustained by that guaranteed price. **1938** *Auckland Weekly News* 28 Sept. 78 Uppermost in the dairy-farmers' thoughts and conversations to-day are the recently announced guaranteed prices. **1941** ALLEY & HALL *Farmer in NZ* 113 The Primary Produce Marketing Act 1936..originated the principle of the guaranteed price, which may be summarised as the principle of a state guarantee of a definite price each season to dairy farmers for their butter and cheese and the taking over by the state of the responsibility for marketing these products overseas. **1959** SINCLAIR *Hist. NZ* 259 For the farmers there was to be a 'guaranteed price'. The state would purchase the farmer's produce, pay him a price based on average prices over a period—thus abolishing the element of speculation in his income—and sell it abroad. Sales in a good year might yield a reserve to be drawn on when prices fell. **1978** SUTHERLAND *Elver* 59 I'd have thought this guaranteed price proposal would have made you dairy farmers supporters of the Labour Party.

guardfish. Occas. *ellipt*. **guard**. GARFISH.

1773 WALES *Journal* in Cook *Journals* (1961) II. 787 There are not wanting Several Sorts [of fish] that are well known; such as Mullet, Cavallas, Guard-fish. **1840** MATHEW *Journal* 31 Mar. in *Founding of NZ* (1940) 101 On the way a guardfish jumped into the boat and was retained to help out a dish for the morning's breakfast. **1855** TAYLOR *Te Ika A Maui* 626 Hemiramphus marginatus, guard-fish, *heihe*, remarkable from its having a projection of the lower jaw one fifth of its entire length, which is from eight to ten inches. **1879** FEATON *Waikato War* 10 The Waikato Heads provided them with an abundance of fish from the schnapper to the dainty 'guard'. **1956** GRAHAM *Treasury NZ Fishes* 157 Garfish or Piper (Takeke) *Reporhamphus ihi*. This fish is known in Auckland as Piper, although in Otago it is called Garfish or Guard Fish. **1981** WILSON *Fisherman's Bible* 115 Guard-fish. *See Piper*.

gudgeon. *Obs*. [Transf. use of northern hemisphere *gudgeon Gobius* spp.]

1. KOARO.

1872 HUTTON & HECTOR *Fishes NZ* 59 Galaxias brevipinnis... Gudgeon. **1921** *NZJST* IV. 119 *Gudgeon*. The larval form is utilized for food in the spring and early summer months by the natives in the Thermal District... Known from lakes in the northern half of the South Island, the Waikato River, and thermal lakes. **1936** *Handbook for NZ* (ANZAAS) 73 *Galaxias brevipinnis*: [European Name] 'Gudgeon' [Maori Name] Taiwharu or kokopu. **1940** PHILLIPPS *Fishes NZ* 21 Gudgeon *Galaxias brevipinnis*...The gudgeon is a rather graceful fish, particularly when young.

2. Graham's gudgeon. [f. the name of David Henry Graham (1887–1965), naturalist and farmer, later a marine biologist at Portobello Marine Hatcheries.] *Grahamichthys radiata* (fam. Eleotrididae), a shallow marine bully whose transparent juveniles are sometimes mistaken for whitebait.

1956 GRAHAM *Treasury NZ Fishes* 320 Graham's Gudgeon..*Grahamichthys radiatus*. **1982** AYLING *Collins Guide* (1984) 286 Graham's gudgeon is a small goby-like fish. **1990** FOORD *NZ Descr. Animal Dict.* 169 *Graham's Gudgeon. Grahamichthys radiata.* A very small fish of shallow water.

guesser. [f. *guess v*. + -ER.]

1. *Obs*. A dishonest race-tipster.

1905 *Truth* 24 June 4 [They are] even more despicable than low-down spielers, all because they are not so well dressed as the shady individual 'guessers' who 'live on the game'. **1909** *Ibid*. 23 Oct. 7 What is a 'guesser'?—He is a man who frequents racecourses 'guessing' what horses are going to win... They are in touch with the bookmakers, get hold of the various fools who attend, and put them on to 'soft things'.

2. A nickname for a wool-classer.

1989 *NZ Eng. Newsletter* III. 23 *classer; wool classer*... He is colloquially known as the 'guesser' or 'conman'.

guest-house. [Spec. use of *guest-house*: see OED 3, a house of reception for paying guests.] An often stylish boarding house, frequently (or usually) for casual guests; a tourist house.

1933 *Press* (Christchurch) 2 Dec. 8 'Khartoum' Guest House, Cashmere Hills. Magnificent Situation overlooking Christchurch. **1970** *Evening Post* (Wellington) 17 Jan. 26 Sea View Guest House, Marine Pde, Napier, offers you a..cooked breakfast and TV.

guffy. [Poss. an adaptation and transf. use of Sc. *guffer*, a blenny: see OED.] SPOTTY 1 (*Pseudolabrus celidotus*).

1890 in Sutton-Smith *Hist. Children's Play* (1982) 133 As well, we went fishing for 'guffy' from the rocks. **1956** GRAHAM *Treasury NZ Fishes* 275 The name Spotty is derived from the presence of spots on each side of the fish... In Canterbury they are called Guffy. **1966** DOOGUE & MORELAND *Sea Anglers' Guide* 257 Spotty...*Pseudolabrus celidotus*; butterfish, kelpie, guffy. None is widely used. **1981** WILSON *Fisherman's Bible* 207 Spotty... Other names are kelpie, guffy, butterfish, pakirikiri and paketi (Maori). **1991** BRADSTOCK *Fishing* 17 Spotty. Other names paketi, butterfish, guffy.

guiver, var. GYVER.

gull.

1. Spec. use of *gull* for any of a family of long-winged seabirds, in distinctive local use only with modifiers. See also KARORO, *tarapunga* (TARA 4).

2. With a modifier: **black-backed (southern black-backed, kelp), black-billed, red-billed** (or **mackerel**), occas. **skua**.

(1) **black-backed** (occas. **southern black-backed, kelp**) **gull** (also *ellipt*. **blackback** (see quot. 1992)). *Larus dominicanus* (fam. Laridae), a large common coastal gull distinguished by its size and black and white colouring resembling the habit of the Dominican religious order, hence (as elsewhere) *Dominican gull*, **Dominican** (see quot. 1904). See also KARORO.

1870 *TrNZI* II. 75 Larus dominicanus... Kororo. Grey Gull, Black-backed Gull, Large Gull. **1873** BULLER *Birds NZ* 270 Larus dominicanus. (Southern Black-backed Gull)... Karoro... This fine Gull, which ranges over the whole Southern Hemisphere, is extremely plentiful. **1889** *TrNZI* XXI. 384 Among the other birds seen [on Auckland Islands] were the skua gull, the black-backed gull,... and the white-headed petrel. **1904** *NZ Illustr. Mag.* Mar. 482 The Karoro, or Black-backed Gull, in the wild and dreary solitudes of the Ocean Beach..named Larus Dominicanus (Dominican Gull) from his likeness to the mendicant brothers of that order... There was a luscious 'Paua' decaying on the beach, a great screaming of hungry Dominicans overhead. **1947** POWELL *Native Animals NZ* 80 Black-backed Gull..Karoro..is easily distinguished from either the Red or the Black-billed gulls by its much larger size. **1962** *Landfall Country* 327 An odd black-backed gull calls from the lake..and at night a boss grey duck will quack authoritatively to a few companions. **1986** BROWN *Weaver's Apprentice* 17 A lone black-backed gull..came to investigate. **1990** *Checklist Birds NZ* 160 *Larus dominicanus*... *Southern Black-backed Gull (Kelp Gull, Dominican Gull)*. Coasts and offshore islands of South America,.. Australia, New Zealand, subantarctic oceanic islands. **1992** SMITHYMAN *Auto/Biographies* 63 We watched a tired North Island muttonbird bullied by young blackbacks.

(2) **blackbilled gull.** *Larus bulleri* (fam. Laridae), a small slender inland gull with black legs and bill.

1871 HUTTON *Catalogue Birds NZ* 41 Larus bulleri... Black-billed Gull. **1872** *TrNZI* IV. 209 The Black-billed Gull breeds on the main river-bed. **1904** HUTTON & DRUMMOND *Animals NZ* 232 *The Black-billed Gull. Larus bulleri*... These birds pursue and capture various species of moths. **1923** *NZJST* VI. 75 Black-billed Gull. This species bred in 1907 on a South Island river-bed. **1936** GUTHRIE-SMITH *NZ Naturalist* 51 The birds breeding on [Bird Island, Nelson] were Caspian Tern..and Blackbilled Gulls..these in amity and friendship closely packed together. **1947** [see (1) above]. **1962** *Landfall Country* 326 The black-billed gulls had already departed. **1985** *Reader's Digest Book NZ Birds* 223 Middens show that the Maori ate black-billed gulls. **1990** *NZ Geographic* VII. 43 Most black-billed gulls now concentrate near the entrances and are highly predatory, taking most young of other birds.

(3) **red-billed** (formerly **mackerel**) **gull.** *Larus novaehollandiae scopulinus* (fam. Laridae), a common coastal gull with red bill and feet. See also JACKY *n.³*, *tarapunga* (TARA 4).

1871 HUTTON *Catalogue Birds NZ* 40 Larus scopulinus... Mackerel Gull. Tarapunga. **1888** BULLER *Birds NZ* II. 55 Larus scopulinus (Red-billed Gull). **1901** *TrNZI* XXXIII. 218 The mackerel gull is that dainty, cheerful little slate-backed sea-bird that congregates in such numbers on the..breakwater's end. **1922** *Auckland Weekly News* 17 Aug. 17 Small gulls, usually known as mackerel-gulls—they have white breasts, pearly grey backs, black marked wings, and crimson bills, legs and feet—were very plentiful on the banks abreast of the vessel. **1947** POWELL *Native Animals NZ* 80 Red-billed Gull... Tarapunga or Akiaki of the Maoris, is abundant throughout New Zealand, Australia, New Caledonia and South Africa. **1955** OLIVER *NZ Birds* 312 *Red-billed Gull Tarapunga, Akiaki. Ibid.*

GULLY

314 Red-billed Gulls are unmitigated robbers and are always to be seen in the breeding places of shags, gannets and terns. **1966** FALLA et al. *Birds NZ* 154 Red-billed Gull... A small gull closely related to the Silver Gull..of Australia. **1985** *Reader's Digest Book NZ Birds* 222 Large numbers of red-billed gulls scavenge at sewage outfalls, rubbish dumps, parks, playing fields, river banks and fishing ports. On arable land they follow the plough... Other names: *Silver gull, tarapunga, akiaki, mackerel gull, jackie.* **1990** *NZ Geographic* VII. 45 White-fronted terns and red-billed gulls still nest on islands off Mount Maunganui with some success.

(4) **skua gull.** SKUA.
1883 *TrNZI* XV. 401 *Lestris antarctica*, 'Sea Hen', 'Skua Gull'. **1891** *TrNZI* XXIII. 495 At the top of the hill we were attacked by sea-hawks or skua-gulls (*Stercorarius antarcticus*)... They are called skua-gulls from their resemblance to a northern species..and appear to be rare in New Zealand proper. **1904** HUTTON & DRUMMOND *Animals NZ* 220 The Skua Gull. *Stercorarius crepidatus.*

gully. Also **gulley.** [An extended use of *gully* ravine, eroded watercourse: see OED *n.*¹ 2 c; AND 1793.]

1. The usual New Zealand word for a small ravine; a small, deep and steeply-sided valley; an eroded watercourse. Often *attrib*.

1770 COOK *Journals* 30 May (1955) I. 332 I believe [*sic*] in the rainy seasons here are large land floods as we saw in many places gullies which seem'd to have been made by torrents of water coming from the adjacent hills. **1834** MARKHAM *NZ* (1963) 63 The Plains were covered with Fern.., in the Gullies high Timber remained. **1843** DIEFFENBACH *Travels in NZ* I. 378 We found a fine potato-ground in the gulley, and leeks and cabbages growing wild! **1853** ADAMS *Canterbury Settlement* 63 As we proceed northward, these gullies become deeper and more frequent. **1862** HODDER *Memories NZ Life* 56 Then there are hill and gully excursions [for picnics] **1866** BARKER *Station Life* (1870) 176 The hill-track was about as bad as..could be with..creeks at the bottom of the numerous deep ravines, or gullies as we call them. **1870** in Evans *Waikaka Saga* (1962) 18 These questions have reference to gulley workings. **1889** WILLIAMS & REEVES *Colonial Couplets* (1974) 3 Then there's what we call a *gully*, which of course we take to mean Just a small and narrow valley, in which bush is sometimes seen; You perchance, were you a new chum, might describe this as a dell, *Bushy gully* suits me better, serves my purpose just as well. **1896** HODGSON *Poems* 8 Vale, brook, and grove, to poet dear, Here changing name and dress, As *gully, creek,* and *scrub* appear, In conscious ugliness. **1909** THOMPSON *Ballads About Business* 103 Past fern-girt gully and gurgling creek, with a wealth of bush beside. **1922** COWAN *NZ Wars* (1955) II. 399 The Kapenga tableland..a gully-seamed broken plateau, is covered with a thick growth of *manuka*. **1933** *Press* (Christchurch) (Acland Gloss.) 21 Oct. 15 *Gulley.*—The depression between two spurs on a hill. A small valley. A depression on the flat caused by an old watercourse. **1959** MIDDLETON *The Stone* 56 Around and beneath us scrub-filled gulleys fell away to green flats. **1967** MAY *West Coast Gold Rushes* 198 While the energetic army of Waimea sluicers washed the terraces through the boxes and into the gully-beds, the Auckland Lead on the beach was all but duffered out. **1993** *North & South* (Auckland) Aug. 42 I'd said goodbye forever to the gulleys and the macrocarpa trees so familiar they had names.

2. A place where gold is found.

1857 *Lyttelton Times* 4 July 5 Every week tells us of some new gully being discovered. **1862** LINDSAY *Nat. Hist. in Coloniz.* 12 You may study the gneiss..in any of the holes of Gabriel's or Munroe's Gullies. **1863** WALKER *Jrnl. & Lett.* (ATLTS) (Central Otago) 11 Jan. Found ourselves in the evening on a high gulley where somebody had sunk a hole but found nothing.

3. Kauri logging. In the phr. **below in the gully**, a former cry to warn loggers of falling trees.

1914 *Weekly News* (Auckland) in Reed *Story of Kauri* (1953) 160 The stereotyped cry 'Below in the gully!' is sent forth, echoing from tree to tree. This is a timely warning for those working below to betake themselves to a spot of safety from flying limbs.

4. Special Comb. gully fern, see FERN 2 (5); **gully raker** goldmining obs. [cf. AND *gully-rake v.* 2 goldmining to search for surface gold, 1881], one who 'rakes over' or searches gullies for gold; **gully-raking** *vbl. n.*, searching gullies and awkward places for small groups of stock missed in a main muster.

1952 LYON *Faring South* 103 Indeed, I have known hatters or **gully rakers**, as men fossicking up back creeks were called, who relied very largely on..their dogs' hunting success. *Ibid.* 158 On all goldfields the hatter, the fossicker and the gully raker were a feature. The former might have an isolated claim which he worked without a mate... The two latter were generally to be found in out-of-the-way creeks and gullies where they often obtained a fair amount of gold. **1962** SHARPE *Country Occasions* 124 If no more than a couple of hundred sheep have been missed, two or more experienced musterers may be kept on to do some **gully-raking**—searching for small groups of sheep which can be brought in.

gum.

1. *Ellipt.* (and prob. the preferred usage) for KAURI-GUM, the resinous sap of the kauri usu. recovered in a hardened fossilized form. Often *attrib.* See also KAPIA, KAURI-GUM 1, KAURI RESIN.

1801 *Miss. Jrnl.* 'Royal Admiral' 19 June (ATLMS) Also we have purchased a quantity of rozinous gum taken from the root of some trees, it will burn like pitch or rozin. **1834** MARKHAM *NZ* (1963) 33 A great quantity of white Transparent Gum is found about the root of the Coudie. **1840** in Wilkes *US Exploring Exped.* (1852) I. 318 Potatoes and gum are also exported. **1851** ASHWELL *Lett. & Jrnls.* (ATLTS) II. 248 Wheat, gum..flax are in great demand. **1888** BARLOW *Kaipara* 153 Climbing this rope, the gum-seeker gains a footing on the branch, and with a tomahawk, hacks out the gum. **1889** KIRK *Forest Flora* 155 The digger pays no fee..: his only tools being a..'gum-spear' to test the ground, and a spade to dig out the 'gum' when found. **1892** *NZ Official Handbook* 155 Competent persons estimate that it will take fifty years at least..to exhaust the gum-deposits in the Auckland District. **1911** *Truth* 29 Apr. 5 Freeman asked him where he was going, to which he replied he was going to see him dig gum. **1951** HUNT *Confessions* 40 Armed with a long spear of rod iron, we 'diggers' tested these hillocks for gum. **1960** BOSWELL *Ernie* 104 The mill-hands at the little mill are having a binge in the Bluff gum-shed, at the store, tomorrow night. **1970** THOMAS *Way Up North* 35 Instead of relying on a spear to locate gum in pockets or patches, they began working gum-bearing land 'on a face'. **1987** WILLIAMS *Racing for Gold* 74 The gum market was experiencing a hitherto undreamed of upward trend.

2. With various modifiers indicating (a) source, as **fossil, old, range** (see quot. 1930), **swamp gum**, that found in the soil or in swampy ground, as distinct from **bush, crutch, tree**, the bled gum recovered from the live kauri tree by climbing (hence **tree-gummer**, one who climbs kauri trees to collect kauri gum, either solidified pieces lodged in forks of branches (**crutch**), or occas. 'tree-bled' gum); or (b) nature or quality of the gum, as **black, bold (bold East Coast)**, a class of superior kauri gum, **chalky, half-scraped** or **re-scraped**, etc. (see esp. quots. 1904, 1930, 1956). See also CHIP *n.*¹ 2, DUST 3, SEED 1; *black joe* (BLACK *a*² B 2).

1887 *Auckland Weekly News* 29 Jan. 24 **Black gum**, which at this season is in plentiful supply, continues dull of sale, as there is but little demand for this quality. **1937** BEALE *Seventy Yrs Auckland* 11 The pure translucent [kauri gum], known as '**Bold East Coast**'..was [in the 1850–60s] being used as a domestic fire-kindler. **1972** REED *Gumdiggers* 82 By the 1920s good quality 'bold' gum—the larger, hard pieces—had become increasingly scarce. **1902** *Cyclopedia NZ* II. 391 It often happens that cavities in the trees themselves become receptacles for the oozing sap. This is termed **bush gum**, and is obtained by climbing the trees, not by digging. **1930** *NZJST* XI. 303 The [kauri-gum] samples analysed were—(a) Resin recently secreted by the tree; (b) resin which had been a long time exposed to air or lying in store (bush gum); (c) fossil resin (range gum); (d) resin obtained from peat-bogs (swamp-gum). **1936** *NZJST* XVII. 370 The kauri Gum Commission of 1921 recommended a standard grading comprising some thirty different grades of fossil gum and four grades of bush gum. **1982** MALCOLM *Where it all Began* 27 Bush gum was obtained by climbing the trees..and one man would pull the other up into the tree where he used a hatchet to harvest the gum. **1936** *NZJST* XVII. 371 **Chalk**, or '**chalky gum**', is a particular grade recovered from swampy country and is characterized by its white or chalky appearance and large water content. **1956** [see *rescraped* below]. **1991** *NZ Geographic* Apr.–June 29 Gum seekers soon discovered that **crutch gum** could be recovered from the high forks [in kauri trees] by climbing for it. **1888** BARLOW *Kaipara* 153 All the gum dug out..belonged to Kauri trees of bygone ages, and is sometimes called **fossil gum**. **1890** *TrNZI* XXII. 82 A curious feature of gum-digging at the Barrier is that they get what is termed '**old gum**' in the forest as well as in the 'open'. **1904** PATTERSON *Kauri-gum* 7 If [the gum] is perfectly cleaned and of good quality, [the digger] sells it as '**rescraped**' or 'first-class gum', the proportionate value of which is nearly double that of ordinary—that is, 'half-scraped'. Then there is 'three-quarter scraped', a quality and value intermediate; 'inferior ordinary' and 'washed nuts' completing the list, be the gum white, black or bush. **1956** SUTHERLAND *Green Kiwi* (1960) 70 Some of the classifications under which gum was exported give an indication of the appearance of some of the grades: bright, rescraped bush, bright chips, black flour dust, chalk, bright seeds and black sugar are some of the names. **1988** p.c. Kendrick Smithyman (Auckland). An associated thing for **swamp gum** and *swamp kauri* is an 'oil', which I refer to as 'kauri gum oil' and which I must have seen talked about in print.. This is the *oil* which figures on northern maps extraordinarily, for instance, the L&S (1943) Provisional sheet N27 at map ref 601521, 'Old Oil Well'... This oil was (can I say?) a seep of sap (pre-solid kauri gum?) from buried kauri; as far as I know it was used in mixing paint. **1888** BARLOW *Kaipara* 154 **Tree gum** is not so valuable as ordinary gum found in the ground. *Ibid.* 149 [Caption] A Group of **Tree-gummers** under Kauri. **1982** MALCOLM *Where it all Began* 27 Commercially this 'tree gum' was not as valuable as that found on the ground.

3. a. Comb. gum-bag (see also PIKAU *n.* 3), **-box, -buyer, dust, hunting, -sack, -scraper, spade.**

1900 *NZ Illustr. Mag.* III. 209 His **gum-bag** was on his back. **1899** *TrNZI* XXXI. 478 And every available stick of rimu, totara black-pine, birch and puriri is being removed from the general bush to supply material for house and ship-building,..for **gum-boxes** and butter-kegs. **1900** *NZ Illustr. Mag.* III. 204 Storekeeper and **gum-buyer**. **1946** REED *Farthest North* 76 Hard workers,.. some [Dalmatians] became storekeepers and gum buyers. **1953** REED *Story of Kauri* 254 And Paul Juanavich, then the only gumbuyer in Gumtown, paid us five shillings per sack. **1961** REED *N. Cape to Bluff* 31 Mr. Joe Thomas..told me that he was a gum-buyer..; that there was still a market for good quality gum. **1970** THOMAS *Way Up North* 49 Storekeeper, gumbuyer, stockman and one-time whaler, no picture of Houhora's early days would be complete without him. **1963** CAMPBELL *Golden North* 116 I caught the train from Helensville..and shook the **gumdust**, sawdust and river mud out of my system. **1840** *NZ Jrnl.* I. 302 Smith, who has a turn for **gum hunting**, and I may say natural productions generally, is sanguine in the extreme about discoveries to be made. **1902** SATCHELL *Land of Lost* (1971) 45 Then Clifford buttoned his coat, threw a **gum sack** across his shoulders, and stepped out into the rain. **1925** MANDER *Allen Adair* (1971) 96 Allen stuffed the things into his gum-sack. **1963** CAMPBELL *Golden North* 19 The next morning my father took a gum sack..and, with the rest of the family holding the mouth of the sack open, each pig was caught. **1888** BARLOW *Kaipara* 152 [Caption] **Gum Scraper's** Knife, constructed so that the blade can be replaced when worn out. **1972** REED *Gumdiggers* 48 While in New Zealand he undertook to produce a spade suitable for use in the popular activity of gumdigging. The result of this undertaking was the Skelton Spade... Every store in the North stocked the '**gum spade**'... Mr O.Lee, Whitianga, tells me that his Skelton (No. 27221) has 'Kia Ora'..stamped on the back of the blade.

b. Special Comb. **gum-bleeder**, one incising a kauri tree to cause it to exude gum, hence **gum-bleeding**; **gum-carving**, an artifact carved from kauri-gum; **gum-climber**, one climbing kauri-trees in search of tree-gum; **gum-country**, GUMLAND; **gum-hair**, melted or softened kauri-gum spun out into hair-like masses; **gumhole**, a hole sunk by a gumdigger in search of gum; **gum-licence**, a licence to dig for kauri-gum on Crown land; **gum-man**, GUMDIGGER *n.*[1]; (**kauri-)gumnut**, NUT *n.*; **gum rush**, a rush to a gumfield; **gum-spear**, a spear or thin steel shaft, usu. on a wooden handle, used for probing the soil for kauri gum (see also SPEAR 2 a); **gum-store**, an establishment which purchases kauri-gum from diggers or stores it for them.

1972 REED *Gumdiggers* 30 Unfortunately many of these climbers were not content with removing the naturally shed gum, but accelerated the flow of resin by artificial means, adopting a plan by which they became known as **gum-bleeders**. **1973** ADAMS *Kauri* 23 Subsequently European gum bleeders devised a method of scaling the trunk using 12-inch long climbing hooks or hand spikes, and 1½ inch toe spikes fixed to wooden boots. **1972** REED *Gumdiggers* 31 Even Sir David Hutchins..believed that **gum-bleeding**, properly undertaken, would not injure the tree. **1973** ADAMS *Kauri* 25 The regrettable practice of gum bleeding was by no means confined to the Warawara Forest. **1888** BARLOW *Kaipara* 152 In most of the gumdiggers' huts..and in settlers' houses in gumdigging districts, are to be found specimens of amateur **gum-carving**, among which, hearts are by far the most popular subject. **1965** SHADBOLT *Among Cinders* 193 Almost every shelf in the hut was loaded with gum carvings. **1910** COCKAYNE *NZ Plants & Their Story* 40 '**Gum-Climber**' at work on trunk of a Kauri. **1897** *TrNZI* XXIX. 351 The road followed the watershed..passing over open '**gum**' **country** with a very monotonous vegetation. **1972** NEWTON *Wake of Axe* 199 Whatever the causes this burnt kauri country—known as 'gum country'—was considered to be of little value. **1960** BOSWELL *Ernie* 154 From both white and yellow gum he spun great tresses of '**gum hair**' that might have honoured any museum in the world. **1882** HAY *Brighter Britain* II. 17 Rich **gum-holes** here and there. *Ibid.* II. 26 Often it is not necessary to move camp for months at a time, when the surrounding field is pretty rich in gum-holes. **1900** *NZ Illustr. Mag.* III. 205 Each man sinks his own gumhole where he strikes the first gum. **1985** *Women's Work* 249 Animals often died bogged in a gum hole. **1902** *Cyclopaedia of NZ* II. 391 But most of the gum-bearing land is still owned by the Government, and may generally be worked by obtaining a **gum license** from the local body. **1965** SHADBOLT *Among Cinders* 190 Is it to an old **gum-man**, an old digger, that I speak? **1948 kauri-gum nut** [see GUMDIGGER *n.*[1]]. **1965** SHADBOLT *Among Cinders* 189 'We might be lucky if we keep our eyes open,' he said, 'and find a few nuts. Gum-nuts. There might be a few scattered round.' **1980** McGILL *Ghost Towns NZ* 176 [Caption] This Herekino store is a sign of the depressing Northland times after the **gumrush**. **1873** TINNE *Wonderland of Antipodes* 54 The first time I saw them at work with their **gum-spears**, they puzzled me... The 'spear' is simply a spike of iron, about a foot long, on the end of a pole. **1888** BARLOW *Kaipara* 147 The gum spear is a four-sided rod of steel, about four feet long, and pointed at one end. It looks very like a fencing foil, with a handle like a spade stuck in the end of it, instead of a hilt. **1913** *NZ Observer* 27 Sept. 17 The constable held the dangerous job of sole policeman at Hikurangi where the infuriated gum-digger holds sway and if necessary charges with a gum spear. **1920** MANDER *Story NZ River* (1974) 232 A gum spear and a spade leaned against the sack wall. **1943** *The Botany of Auckland* 22 Some fossilized resin still lies hidden from the gum-spear. **1965** SHADBOLT *Among Cinders* 112 'What's this?' I asked him. 'A gum-spear, boy. A gum-spear. Used to work with it on the gumfields.' **1972** REED *Gumdiggers* 49 The gum-spear, a slender, rapier-like instrument, fitted with an ordinary spade handle, varied in length from about three feet for use in shallow ground, to twenty-five or more for working deep swamps... An experienced digger could detect at once, by the feel, and the resistance met by the spear, whether he had struck timber, a stone or gum. **1988** [see JIGGER *n.*[3]]. **1884** *Maoriland An Illustrated Handbook* 196 Next to it is a large and remarkable two-storied blue-stone building, 40 by 30 feet, now used as a **gum store**. **1920** MANDER *Story NZ River* (1974) 230 Then driven by loneliness..he would 'go on the razzle-dazzle' at the public house that every gum-store ran as a sure getter of substantial profits. **1973** ADAMS *Kauri* 28 The Lichtenstein, Arnoldson and Company gum store, a building of four storeys, went up in flames.

gum: *ellipt.* for GUM TREE.

gumboot. Usu. *pl.* [Orig. US, made from *gum (arabic)* '(india) rubber', cf. OED *gum n.*[2] 9, 1850, then NZ 1875 as below: used elsewhere but of socio-economic and cultural significance, esp. as a commonplace or icon of NZ rural life.]

1. a. A waterproof rubber boot, reaching usu. to the knee, occas. to the thigh. See also GUMMY *n.*[4] Contrast British *wellington, welly.*

1875 WOOD & LAPHAM *Waiting for Mail* 13 Dick had presently laid aside his dripping oilskin and gum boots. **1889** PAULIN *Wild West Coast* 76 I put on oil skins and gum boots. **1892** *NZ Official Handbook* 298 [Table of Exemptions from Duties of Customs] 385. Gum-boots **1916** HEALEY, C.A. *MS Papers 2244* (ATLMS) 24 Oct. On fatigue repairing trenches front line. Issued with gumboots. **1926** *NZ Dairy Produce Exporter* 31 July 54 [Advt] Winter need not mean feet wet and cold if you are shod in a pair of Columbus Gum Boots. **1948** SCANLAN *Rusty Road* (1949) 68 At the back door, Roger pulled off his gum-boots and thrust his feet into slippers. **1959** *NZ Dairy Exporter* 10 Aug. 111 The trouble with farmers is the weather, old gumboots and lambing time. **1966** TURNER *Eng. Lang. Austral. & NZ* 172 *Wellingtons* and *plimsolls* are hardly known in New Zealand, *gumboots* and *sandshoes* being the words. **1986** *Dominion* (Wellington) 28 July 2 Prime Minister David Lange ran the gauntlet of gumboots at the Federated Farmers annual conference in Wellington last week and survived quite easily. **1995** gumboot throwing [see GUMMY *n.*[4]].

b. *fig. joc.* Stereotypically broad rural language.

1993 *Listener* 15 May 70 Kiwi comedians only have to master Gumboot, the language of roustabouts, fishermen and sportscasters, and they're away screaming.

2. In *attrib.* use, often *transf.* or *joc.*, with reference to farmers, or farming.

1985 *National Bus. Rev.* 27 May 1 Big-city trends may not go down too well in this neck of the woods [Hawke's Bay], where 'gumboot management' methods have been the norm around the boardrooms of companies in the down-to-earth business of servicing primary industry. **1986** *Metro* (Auckland) Aug. 8 What inspires writing, radio and television to wane (sic) on with his gumboot diplomacy image/fact? **1988** HILL *More from Moaville* 45 A ute boot sale, BYO gumboot throwing, raffles..[at School Gala day]. **1990** *Dominion* (Wellington) 1 Aug. 2 Manufacturers Federation president..said Federated Farmers' 'antics' over the policy betrayed unsophisticated 'gumboot politics'. **1991** *Evening Post* (Wellington) 24 May 4 I gained the impression that your source for this report [of a search for overdue trampers], a Mr Lance Cashell of Taihape, Search and Rescue Co-ordinator, is finding things a bit on the dull side up there in Gumboot Country.

Hence **gumbootette** *joc.*, a small gumboot.

1988 *Dominion* (Wellington) 24 Sept. 8 For the younger wearers, gumbootettes continue to appear in virtually every shade.

gumdigger, *n.*[1] *Hist.*

1. In full **kauri-gum digger**. One whose occupation is retrieving and selling fossil kauri gum. See also GUMMY *n.*[1]

c**1858** *Richmond-Atkinson Papers* (1960) I. 437 Of the kauri gum diggers 9/10ths are furnished by this tribe, & 2/3rds of the Auckland prostitutes. **1867** LUSH *Waikato Jrnls.* 4 Feb. (1982) 104 We passed through an encampment of Kauri gum diggers. **1873** TINNE *Wonderland of Antipodes* 53 Our nearest neighbours are a colony of gum-diggers, at the Kaiwaka swamp. **1888** BARLOW *Kaipara* 144 The sober-sided settler..hardly even has a good word for him; 'He's only a gumdigger', is an expression I have commonly heard used, to imply that the individual indicated was a person of no importance. The title 'gumdigger' itself may have something to do with the matter. It is not a nice word, and looks too much like 'gravedigger' at first sight. **1897** *TrNZI* XXIX. 496 So long as the gum-digger and bush-larrikin are allowed to put a match into anything that will burn, there is not much hope for either prevention or restoration. **1903** *NZ Illustr. Mag.* Oct. 17 Flannigan went there with a party of Maori gum-diggers. **1911** *Truth* 29 Apr. 5 He is described by those who had met him as a hard-working gum-digger, living the life of a recluse, perfectly inoffensive, and quiet. **1922** *NZJST* V. 189 Gum-diggers' camps are scattered over the whole area **1948** FINLAYSON *Tidal Creek* (1979) 55 The Hoppy Crummers are supposed to live on the sale of kauri-gum nuts—the dirty little nobs of kauri-gum that the gum-diggers wouldn't bother with. **1951** HUNT *Confessions* 40 The low rolling clay hills had..been the site of a vast kauri forest, and, being so remote, was still virgin country as far as gum diggers were concerned. **1972** REED *Gumdiggers* 141 Tucker—normally bread-and-butter, or cheese,.. wrapped in a piece of newspaper, gum-digger style.

2. As **gumdigger's dog** (or **bitch**), used in various phrases of derogatory comparison, **skinnier than a**, **as stupid (useless, mad) as a gumdigger's dog**.

1964 HELMER *Stag Party* 83 He'd rummage about in the tucker for something to take to bed with him. Peas, corned beef, it didn't matter... 'Musta been a pudgy individual.' 'Naw, skinnier'n a gum digger's dog, eh?' **1976** MCCLENAGHAN *Travelling Man* 133 That squint-eyed kid looked about as stupid as a gumdigger's dog. 'Made a Joe Hunt of yourself as usual.' **1984** *NZ Times* 28 Oct. 13 The lambs were breaking away everywhere, the accursed canine useless as a gumdigger's dog, and in fury this peppery Hawke's Bay cocky thrust clenched fists to the sky, yelling: 'O God! Send me a dog, send me a dog!'

3. In special collocations: **gumdigger's soap** *Northland* [f. the ability of the flower-heads to produce a lather], KUMARAHOU; **gumdigger's spear**, *gum-spear* (GUM 3 c); **gumdiggers' spud**, an orchid having an edible tuber used as a potato, MAORI POTATO 2.

1961 ALLAN *Flora NZ* I. 419 Dist.: N. On poor clay hills from Far North to Bay of Plenty and west of Te Kuiti. *Kumarahou*, **Gumdiggers' soap**. **1969** [see KUMARAHOU]. **1982** SALE *Four Seasons* 32 The kumerahou flowers also had the quality to crush into soapy lather. Hence the name, and presumably the use, of 'gumdiggers' soap'. **1911** *Truth* 3 June 5 The man then, according to prisoner, attacked him with a **gum-digger's spear**. **1967** HENDERSON *Return to Open Country* 207 The native orchids... We knew them as '**gumdiggers' spuds**' because of their bulbous roots.

gumdigger, *n.*² A dentist.

1913 *Truth* 7 June 7 Annie Pringle,... sued a dentist..for the maintenance of her illegitimate child. Lawyer R. Moody, of Auckland, appeared for the gum-digger. **1941** BAKER *NZ Slang* 52 A dentist is a *gumdigger*. **1953** 14 M A10 Thames DHS 24 Gum-digger (dentist). **1995** *Dominion* (Wellington) 28 Jan. 23 I'm even contemplating going to the dentist. Nothing like a bit of pain from a gumdigger to make you feel really alive.

Hence **gum-digging**, dentistry.

1932 BRUCE *Early Days Canterbury* 135 Purdie the dentist..was for many years among the leading practitioners in the somewhat primitive days of the art of 'gum digging'.

gum-digging, *vbl. n.*

1. As a quasi-participle in the phr. **to go gum-digging**, to take up the occupation of a kauri gumdigger.

1871 *McLean Papers* (ATLTS) XXXVII. 72 Paora Toki is gone gum digging up the Thames. **1879** GREY *His Island Home* 34 A great many of the natives abandoned their kaingas and went gum-digging, when that article brought a high price.

2. Also **kauri-gum-digging**. The occupation of retrieving and selling fossil kauri gum. Often *attrib*.

1879 GREY *His Island Home* 34 It is what is known as kauri-gum-land and indications of the gum-digging industry presented themselves the whole way through. **1882** HAY *Brighter Britain* II. 27 Gum-digging has often been a great assistance to settlers. **1890** *NZ Observer* 27 Mar. 9 The denizens of the Dead Kauri gumdigging Camp were five, all told. **1892** *NZ Official Handbook* 155 The cause of the increased output is..that a greater number of men now engaged in gum-digging. **1907** LAING & BLACKWELL *Plants NZ* 64 When the children of the settlers desire a little pocket money, they will often ask permission to go gum-digging in some newly ploughed paddock. **1911** *Truth* 29 Apr. 5 The last time he saw deceased alive was about 9 a.m. on April 5 going by the Wairakei bridge to follow his occupation of gum-digging. **1916** STALLWORTHY *Early N. Wairoa* 56 The gumdigging industry continued to drag along, giving the digger a poor remuneration for his work. **1920** MANDER *Story NZ River* (1974) 229 Ross had learned enough of the facts of the gum-digging life..to be..interested in its peculiar atmosphere. **1942** ANDERSEN *Maori Place Names* 273 Kauri-gum-digging settlement 10 m[iles] from Hokianga. **1974** BARTLETT *Emigrants* 102 It [*sc.* a piece of kauri gum] had probably been dug by Bob on his farm or on a gum-digging 'holiday'.

3. As **gum-diggings**, the locality or field in which kauri gum-digging takes place; a GUMFIELD q.v.

1924 *NZJST* VII. 98 The agitation spread throughout the gum-diggings, and at length the scope of the Act was broadened to this effect.

gumfield. *Hist*. Also often (collective) *pl*. **gumfields** on the analogy of *goldfields*. An area on the North Auckland peninsula containing fossil kauri gum.

1873 TINNE *Wonderland of Antipodes* 54 There is not a single kauri pine now standing on the gum-fields. **1882** HAY *Brighter Britain* II. 14 There are tracts of country, known as gum-fields, in which kauri-gum is to be dug up most plentifully. Gum-fields are poor lands usually, though some are adapted for settlement. **1888** BARLOW *Kaipara* 144 He lives an entirely isolated and a fearfully hard life out on the gumfield. **1892** BROOKES *Frontier Life* 190 A large gumfield 2 miles to the eastward of Wellsford. **1909** THOMPSON *Ballads About Business* 94 Among some foreign scum I am now upon a gumfield pokin' round for kauri gum! **1911** *Truth* 29 Apr. 5 A particularly atrocious murder was committed on the northern gumfields on April 8. **1920** MANDER *Story NZ River* (1974) 59 Bruce told them they could get a gum outfit at the Point Curtis pub,..and that they would be shown the way to the gum-field. **1935** *NZJST* XVII. 370 It is almost generally believed in New Zealand that the non-resinous impurities composed of sand, humus, vegetable fibres, charcoal, etc., from the gumfields..are desirable and even necessary ingredients for the manufacture of linoleum. **1943** WALL & CRANWELL *The Botany of Auckland* 22 And so north and east to the white 'gumfields' of the Henderson Riverhead and North Shore districts. **1947** *Reed's School Dict. Suppl.* 173 *gumfield*: area where kauri gum is found under ground. **1987** BATISTICH *Sing Vila* 24 With every shipload of Dalmatians coming to work on the gumfields that fear grew.

gumland. Often *pl.* as **gumlands**. Poor quality land, or areas of poor soil, once supporting kauri forests and containing or having contained fossil kauri gum. See also *gum country* (GUM 3 b).

1879 GREY *His Island Home* 34 The whole land lying between Whangaroa and Mangonui..[is] almost useless for grazing or agricultural purposes. It is what is known as kauri-gum-land and indications of the gum-digging industry presented themselves the whole way through. **1882** HAY *Brighter Britain* II. 16 On our farm and in the surrounding bush, although these are distinctly not gum-lands, there are little patches of ground..whence we have got a ton or two of gum at times. **1897** *TrNZI* XXIX. 350 Our road now led over open kauri-gum land with the usual sparse vegetation. **1900** *NZ Illustr. Mag.* III. 203 Here, then, on this gumland, is where the old Kauri forests grew. **1914** CHEESEMAN *Illustrations NZ Flora* plate 144 Clay hills..from the quantity of kauri-resin that has been dug from them, are locally known [in Northland] as 'gum-lands'. **1927** COCKAYNE *NZ Plants & Their Story* 102 Wherever the soil is extremely poor..as that sterile clay..which forms the Auckland gumlands, a more or less dense association of manuka occurs. **1934** *NZJST* XVII. 408 The gum-land soils of North Auckland are infertile grey to dark-grey compact silts, silt loams and clays usually containing kauri-resin. **1936** BELSHAW et al. *Agric. Organiz. NZ* 72 They were originally clothed with Kauri forest, and are fairly typical 'gumlands' soil. **1946** REED *Farthest North* 14 The father..had come down to the wharf to meet his boys, who were trudging after him to the recently purchased little gumland Government section three miles up in the hills. **1951** LEVY *Grasslands NZ* (1970) 3 Certain poor clay soils, popularly known as gum-lands, were dominated by the kauri and its associate the tawhero. *Ibid.* 5 Much arduous effort must be put into gum-land country before it will respond. **1969** MOORE *Forest to Farm* 57 Contiguous to my front boundary was an area of 'gumland', poverty stricken stuff covered in fern, scrub, and blackberry. **1978** MOORE & IRWIN *Oxford Book NZ Plants* 88 Kumarahou is at home in the gumlands of Auckland, those broad tracts of hungry country where great kauri forests once grew, leaving deposits of resin. **1988** DAWSON *Forest Vines to Snow Tussocks* 114 Another type of shrubland widespread in the north is found on terrain known as 'gumland'.

gummie, var. GUMMY.

gummy, *n.*¹ Also **gummie**. [f. (kauri) GUM + -Y.] GUMDIGGER. *n.*¹ 1.

1890 *NZ Observer* 19 Apr. 17 It is there that the gay and festive gummy and wife are found in their pristine loveliness. **1900** *Auckland Weekly News Xmas Number* 14 Hervey finally flung out to his own quarters with the Parthian shaft that a 'gummy' could fill our place better than its present occupant. **1906** *Macmillan's Mag.* Apr. 476 We soon were giving those gummies a hand to get some tucker ready.

gummy, *n.*² *Farming*. [Transf. use of *gummy a.* toothless: AND 1871.] An old sheep which has lost its teeth. Also *attrib*.

1908 *Truth* 16 May 1 Jerry Fail..attended the sale on the Culverden estate, and bought most of the 'gummies' for breeding purposes at as low a price as 1s 3d a-piece. A rumo[u]r that he is to have the barren ancients filled [*sic*] with false teeth is entirely without foundation. **1933** *Press* (Christchurch) (Acland Gloss.) 21 Oct. 15 *Gummy*.—An old sheep that has lost its teeth. Also used as an adjective, g[ummy] ewe, etc. **1952** *Straight Furrow* May 53 *gummy*, (farming) old ewes that have lost their teeth **1987** OGONOWSKA-COATES *Boards, Blades & Barebellies* 96 *Gummy*. An old sheep that has lost all its teeth and reached the end of its useful existence.

gummy, *n.*³ [f. its teeth being harmless to humans: AND 1893.] In New Zealand a name for the commercially important smoothhound dogfish, *Mustelus lenticulatus* (formerly *antarcticus*) (fam. Triakidae). See also DOGFISH 2, MANGA 2, MANGO 1, PIOKE, RIG *n.*¹, SHARK 2 (9), SMOOTH-HOUND; and LEMON FISH for the processed flesh.

1924 *NZJST* VI. 263 The smooth-hound, or gummy..is one of the small sharks commonly taken by trawlers around New Zealand, and popularly termed 'dogfish'. **1927** SPEIGHT et al. *Nat. Hist. Canterbury* 192 The smooth hound..is the small spotted dog-fish..often known as the Gummy on account of its flattened pavement-like teeth. **1938** *TrRSNZ* LXVIII. 400 *Mustelus antarcticus*... Smooth-hound (gummy,

GUMMY

dogfish). **1979** *Catch* May 16 Gummy Shark.. Smoothhound, pioke, rig, spotted dogfish. Family Triakidae (smooth dogfishes). N.Z. only, a similar species elsewhere. Pale golden brown above with many small white spots, white below. This colour pattern, and lack of spines, distinguishes the gummy from other N.Z. species.

gummy, *n.*[4] Also **gummie.** [f. GUM(BOOT + -Y.)] Usu. *pl.* GUMBOOT 1 a.
   1952 *Straight Furrow* May 53 *Gummies* (coll.) gumboots **1982** *Agric. Gloss.* (MAF) 50 *Gummies:*.. term used to describe gum boots, rubber boots, or wellington boots worn by farmers. **1988** *Dominion* (Wellington) 24 Sept. 8 The names of the 20-plus parts which make up your average gummie are descriptive and dramatic in themselves. **1995** *Dominion* (Wellington) 19 Apr. 1 Some people were paying money to biff gummies down the main street... Yesterday was Taihape Gumboot Day, the day when the world gumboot throwing record is annually under threat.

gummy-weed. *Southern SI.* [See quot. 1982.] Also **gummy.** *Splachnidium rugosum* (fam. Splachnidiaceae), a brown marine algae of sheltered coasts.
   1961 MARTIN *Flora NZ* 18 *Sea Cactus* or *Gummyweed (Splachnidium rugosum).* **1982** WILSON *Stewart Is. Plants* 314 *Splachnidium rugosum* Gummy..Fawn-brown tufts, darkest at base, the wrinkled branches filled with clear gummy liquid which exudes if the plant is broken.

gum tree.

1. Usu. as **New Zealand gum tree.** ORIHOU (*Pseudopanax colensoi*).
   1869 *TrNZI* I. (rev. edn.) 195 Gum tree (*Panax Colensoi*). A showy small tree, with large shining trifoliolate leaves in all stages of growth. **1890** *PWD Catalogue Timbers* (NZ & South Seas Exhib.) 9 Gum, New Zealand. **1909** THOMSON *NZ Naturalist's Calendar* 21 The most sombre hues are those of the..large-leaved Panax (sometimes erroneously called New Zealand gum tree).

2. In New Zealand usu. any one of the Australian *Eucalyptus* spp. (fam. Myrtaceae), or the wood, esp. those with a smooth bluish-grey bark, commonly grown for shelter or timber. Very often called **bluegum.**
   1834 MARKHAM *NZ* (1963) 34 He used Gum tree from Sydney for Keels, Coudy planks. **1851** *Lyttelton Times* 15 Nov. 1 To be sold in Lots... good dry Blue Gum at 15s. 6d. **1866** BARKER *Station Life* (1870) 84 The plantations about it..have grown up well, the willows, gum-trees, and poplars shelter it. **1882** POTTS *Out in Open* 33 Old settlers can doubtless recollect the rise, progress, and decay of the willow and poplar period, which was succeeded by a *furor* for the blue gum (Eucalyptus globulus). **1922** MANSFIELD *Stories* (1984) 458 She pulled up her gloves, hummed to herself and said to the distant gum-tree, 'Shan't be long now.' But that was hardly company.

3. a. In the phr. **to shoot up like a gumtree,** to grow rapidly.
   1891 CHAMIER *Philosopher Dick* 184 A youngster that has shot up like a gum tree.

b. In the phr. **up a gum-tree** [AND 1851], confused; in difficulties; in a predicament.
   1913 *NZ Bulletin* 8 Feb. 16 Not Understood! Oh, strike me up a gum tree. **1946** SIMPSON *If You'd Care to Know* 98 In Australia and New Zealand..a person up a gum tree is in some kind of trouble. **1955** *BJ Cameron Collection* (TS July) up a gumtree Up the pole, off the beam. **c1962** BAXTER *Horse* (1985) 70 He [*sc.* a priest] told me I [a homosexual] was up a gum tree. **1969** MASON *Awatea* (1978) 29 Gilhooly..Who you leading up a gum-tree? Why would Matt blow a safe?

c. In the phr. **to kid** (one) **up a gum-tree,** to thoroughly dupe.
   1938 HYDE *Nor Yrs. Condemn* 196 He had gone to Rotorua..for the King's birthday, and spent the day kidding the Maoris up gum trees, and cutting them down again. **1959** SLATTER *Gun in My Hand* 184 You could kid those Pongos up a gum tree. Told them I had a big cattle ranch back in Enzed.

gun, *n.*[1] [Ellipt., often spec., use of *great gun, big gun* a person of importance; one eminent in anything: see OED 7 b.]

1. *Farming.* Also **gun shearer.** [AND 1897.] An expert fast shearer. Often *attrib.* [AND 1916]. Cf. RINGER 1.
   1911 *Maoriland Worker* 6 Oct. 17 In contract sheds only fast men are welcomed by the 'boss'. Some men who are what we term 'guns,' are kept going all the season, and in many cases good honest shearers are cast off to make room for these 'guns'. **1934** *Press* (Christchurch) (Acland Gloss.) 20 Jan. 15 *Gun, big gun.*—A really fast shearer, one who could ring most sheds. E.g., 'So-and-So's a g[*un*] shearer.' The term is also applied to the several fastest shearers in a shed. **1947** NEWTON *Wayleggo* 39 There I saw some of our greatest gun (fast) shearers in action. *Ibid.* 128 That wonderful old gun..was no longer shearing there, but the ringer was Lew Aitken. **1955** BOWEN *Wool Away* 1 Balance, grace, rhythm, suppleness, with eye, brain and hand in smart co-ordination. All these are required to make a 'gun' shearer. **1963** *Dominion* (Wellington) 9 Sept. 6 Many of the North Island 'gun' shearers would compete in the [Golden Fleece] event at Alexandra on September 27–28. **1970** McLEOD *Glorious Morning* 254 *Gun shearer*: A very fast shearer who may be expected to 'ring the board', i.e. beat everyone else. **1986** RICHARDS *Off the Sheep's Back* 137 I often visited him on his coastal farm..long after our 'gun' days were over. **1990** MARTIN *Forgotten Worker* 86 By..[the 1860s] a skilled shearer could clip up to 100 sheep on a good day, and 'guns' could achieve up to 200.

2. a. [AND 1916.] A person expert at any activity, esp. at sport; a highly skilled person.
   1916 *Truth* 11 Mar. 6 A gun cutter [of flax], swamp lingo for a good man. **1951** CRESSWELL *Canterbury Tales* 90 All the 'guns' of the tennis world were there. **1975** HOWITT *NZ Rugby Greats* 102 The New Zealand forwards took control and, with Hill one of the guns in the rucks, pulled off a 17–10 victory. **1978** TUCKER *Thoroughbreds Are My Life* 56 Having produced my very first stud book in 1948, I was extremely pleased with my performance. I suppose I had begun to regard myself as a sort of 'gun guy' in the thoroughbred world. **1984** *Landfall 150* 131 I like 'Beginnings' because only the 'guns at Oakley' [Mental Hospital] suggest to us a setting and explanation for this meandering monologue.
   Hence **gunny** *a.,* expert.
   1980 *Lynfield College* (Goldie Brown Coll.) *gunny*: term of approval **1982** NEWBOLD *Big Huey* 104 I was a bit outclassed by all the gunny A grade players.

b. As **real gun,** expressing high approval, agreement, etc.; excellent.
   1966 *Dominion* (Wellington) 15 Oct. 3 Entries in the 'remarks' column of the visitors' book at the Aviemore power project [Otematata include]..real gun.

3. ?*Obs.* A person of importance.
   1917 let. in *Boots, Belts* (1992) 33 The [army] dentists were all having morning tea when [Sir James Allen] and all the big bugs came round... When they saw all the guns coming, they got back to work in a great hurry.

gun, *n.*[2] *Obs.* [Archaic or obs. in Brit. use: see OED *n.* 10, 1708, 1848.] A tobacco pipe.
   1930 DEVANNY *Bushman Burke* 164 Lighting up the pipe he had been smoking. 'Eating too many cigarettes so took to the old gun, Bert,' he explained. **c1940** *Gun* in use in Marlborough for a tobacco pipe (Ed.).

gun, *n.*[3] *Obs.* [A late use of *gun* thief, rascal: see OED *n.* 13; Partridge 8 5 'ob.: more Aus. than Eng.'.] A thief; a rogue; a spieler or confidence man.
   1904 *NZ Observer* 9 Jan. 7 The lost tribe of 'solid guns' and spielers visited the Thames for Christmas races. **1910** *Truth* 29 Oct. 2 Though there is no rule existing which debars fielders [*i.e.* bookmakers] from adopting such pointing tactics, the clubs could easily put a stop to it by refusing to license these guns when they apply the next time for registration.

gun, *n.*[4] [Prob. a transf. use of Brit. slang *in the gun* drunk: see OED *n.* 9; AND 1924.] In the phr. **to be in the gun,** to be out of favour; in line for punishment.
   1970 DUGGAN *O'Leary's Orchard* 27 Mrs Bernstein..was truly in the gun : with sums great or little..she had actually financed the bloody thing.

gundy. [Orig. unknown: AND 1906.] In the phr. **no good to Gundy,** no good at all.
   1918 *Quick March* 2 Sept. 1 This [interference] was no good to Gundy, so cobber the wood-chopper got busy swinging his axe. **1968** *NZ Contemp. Dict. Suppl.* (Collins) 10 *gundy, no good to* (Phr.) elaboration of phrase *not good enough for me.*

gunga /ˈɡʌŋɡə/. Also occas. **gonga** /ˈɡɒŋɡə/, **gunger.** [Cf. Partridge 8 *gonga* Anus. Services' C20.] The anus. (The form **gong** 'defecation' also heard (Ed.).)
   c1946 Nelson Boys' College p.c. J.H. Brownlee (Havelock, Marlborough) *gonga*, anus. [**1954** A Forest Service employee says: I had a good gong after lunch.] **1955** Wellington College p.c. HS Gajadhar *gunga*, anus; associated with corporal punishment and *Gunga Din* ('Though I've belted you and flayed you'). **1983** p.c. Dr. Chris Corne (Auckland) 14 Oct. gunga, gunger—anus, backside. **1985** O'SULLIVAN *Shuriken* 34 Oh, come on. He'd put a knife up your gunga quick as look at you, don't you worry. **1995** SLATTER *One More River* 119 I just sat on the gunga and looked at the idle cranes standing over the shipbuilding yards.

gunger, var. GUNGA.

gunner. *Whaling.* Also **gunsman.** [Spec. use of *gunner* an artilleryman.] The harpooner on a modern whale-chaser.
   1968 JOHNSON *Turn of Tide* 38 In the excitement of the chase the gunsmen seemed to fire at random for shot after shot missed. Irons were pulled in and guns reloaded with feverish haste. **1982** GRADY *Perano Whalers* 227 *Gunner*—Harpoon-gunner on a whale-chaser.

gunny bag. *Hist.* Also erron. **gulley bag.** [Transf. or fig. use of *gunny-bag*, a sack made from gunny, a coarse fabric.] A nickname for an early (Wellington) social set.
   c1875 MEREDITH *Adventuring in Maoriland* (1935) 58 Social distinctions here [in Wellington] are rather amusing. They have the 'Ice Creams,' the 'Jam Tarts,'

GURDY 325 GUTSFUL

and the 'Gunny Bags.' I have joined the Ice Creams [*sic*] assemblies, which have dances fairly often in the old provincial council room. **1968** JOHNSON *Turn of Tide* 28 There will be nothing improper: it will be very different from the assembly dances [in 1916] in your town where the cream-puffs, the jam-tarts and the gulley bags all gather for a fling.

gurdy: see HURDY-GURDY.

gurgler. [f. *gurgler* a name for a plug-hole of a sink, or the outflow of a water-closet, from the noise of the escaping water: Ayto & Simpson *Austral.* 1981.] In the phr. **(to go) down the gurgler**, (to be) ruined; (to go) 'down the drain'.

1986 *Bulletin* (Sydney) 3 June 32 Haines had previously worked for the New Zealand Dairy Board where he says he watched the Australian dairy industry go 'down the gurgler' while the New Zealand industry went ahead in leaps and bounds. **1988** *Evening Post* (Wellington) 7 July 6 [Cartoon caption] This country is really going down the gurgler, mate. Even the sheep are emigrating. **1989** *Dominion* (Wellington) 17 Aug. 2 Employment Minister Annette King opened Parliament's general debate with the accusation that National would be deservedly 'down the gurgler' because of its sexist attitude to women. **1992** TAYLOR *Fast Times at Greenhill High* 72 The high standards set for this newspaper..have gone down the gurgler and the tubes double quick.

guri, var. KURI.

gurnard. Also **gurnet**. [Spec. or transf. use of northern hemisphere *gurnard*: AND cites *gurnet* only (1828).]

1. Any of various shallow-water, bottom-dwelling fishes, esp. the *red gurnard Chelidonichthys kumu* (fam. Triglidae). See also FLATHEAD 1, GRUNTER 2, KUMUKUMU.

1777 ANDERSON *Journal* Feb. in Cook *Journals* (1967) III. 808 Sometimes we got a sort of small Salmon, Gurnards, Skate and Nurses. **1835** YATE *NZ* (1970) 71 Those saltwater fish most plentiful, and of greatest note, are, soles, mackarel..gurnards. **1840** POLACK *Manners & Customs* I. 202 Among the piscivorous tribes, are those well known in Europe under the appellations of snapper, tench, haddocks, pollock, salmon, gurnets. **1855** TAYLOR *Te Ika A Maui* 624 Of these the *Gurnard* (*kumu-kumu*) is most common, and the *Trigla Volitans* (*korama*) the most beautiful. **1880** SENIOR *Travel & Trout* 288 The snapper, mullet, and gurnet are only met with in the north. **1886** SHERRIN *Handbook Fishes NZ* 37 Tangaroa..by the aid of the fish, gained a great victory. To reward them for their heroism, he granted them any request they might make; and the gurnard, taking advantage of the offer, wished to be red, and to be able to grunt like a dying man; hence his colour, and the 'grunting noise'. **1901** *TrNZI* XXXIII. 574 In other parts king-fish..were found, and large numbers of elephant-fish, gurnard, and schnapper. **1905** *'Defiance' Cookery Recipes* 8 Oyster Soup..Oysters..Gurnet or Rock Cod..Carrot.. [etc.] Lemon Juice..Defiance butter. **1919** POATA *Maori as Fisherman* 14 Te Kumukumu (or Gurnett). **1947** REED *Dict. Suppl.* 173 *Gurnet*: edible fish. **1966** DOOGUE & MORELAND *Sea Anglers' Guide* 292 *Chelidonichthys kumu*; gurnard, common gurnard; kumukumu (Maori). **1970** SORENSEN *Nomenclature NZ Fish* 27 *Gurnard..Cheilodonichthys kumu*... Flathead, Shoal or Latchett. **1974** GLOVER *Wellington Harbour* 33 Sometimes snapper, groper..gurnet, cod, will grace it. **1986** PAUL *NZ Fishes* 80 *Gurnards*... They are good at producing sound and may grunt when captured. New Zealand has five species.

2. With a modifier: **mud (river, flathead), red, scaly, spotted**.

(1) **mud (river, flathead) gurnard**. STARGAZER 2 (2) (*Leptoscopus macropygus*).

1960 [see *mud grubber* (MUD 2)]. **1981** WILSON *Fisherman's Bible* 118 The Stargazer is sometimes known as the Mud Gurnard, River Gurnard or Mud-Grubber Gurnard but is in fact no relation. Similarly the Sea Perch is sometimes called a Rock Gurnard. **1986** mud, river, or flathead gurnard [see STARGAZER 2 (1)].

(2) **red gurnard**. The common brightly coloured food-fish *Chelidonichthys kumu* (fam. Triglidae). See also KUMUKUMU.

1773 FORSTER *Resolution Jrnl.* 21 Apr. (1982) II. 263 We found they had hauled in the Sein in the Indian Cove & got some Mullets..some red Gurnards (*Trigla Cuculus*). **1872** HUTTON & HECTOR *Fishes NZ* 113 Gurnard... The Red Gurnard or Kumukumu..is very abundant during the summer months in the harbours in the north,... and full nets are sometimes drawn near Wellington with no other fish in them. **1886** SHERRIN *Handbook Fishes NZ* 37 The best way to cook the red gurnard is to stuff with force-meat, and bake in a quick oven, in a pie-dish, covered with a few slices of fat bacon. **1913** *TrNZI* XLV. 230 The red gurnard is named *Trigla kumu* in the original list. **1921** *NZJST* IV. 122 *Red Gurnard*; *Kumukumu*. Commonly secured by trawlers up to 40 fathoms... Distribution: New Zealand coasts (rarer in the south). **1947** POWELL *Native Animals NZ* 72 Red Gurnard..Kumukumu of the Maoris, is easily recognised by its parchment-like side fins which resemble wings, and curious finger-like processes associated with these fins. **1956** GRAHAM *Treasury NZ Fishes* 359 It is a common statement that Red Gurnards surrounded by a net are able to fly over the top of a seine or trawl net to escape. I have not observed this. **1967** NATUSCH *Animals NZ* 231 Only the red gurnard is really common—a beautiful fish, with its pectoral fins coloured and burnished like great, filmy butterfly wings. **1970** [see KUMUKUMU]. **1982** AYLING *Collins Guide* (1984) 197 The red gurnard is a striking fish with a wedge-shaped head, and a rounded tapering body. Strong bony plates completely cover the head and gills. **1991** BRADSTOCK *Fishing* 3 Red gurnard and leatherjackets are fish that can make a 'grunting' noise. They make these kinds of noises underwater as a signal to each other.

(3) **scaly gurnard**. *Lepidotrigla brachyoptera* (fam. Triglidae).

1956 GRAHAM *Treasury NZ Fishes* 364 The generic name *Lepidotrigla* is from two Greek words, *Lepido*, scaly; and *trigla*, a gurnard. The name *brachyoptera* is from two Greek words, *brachy*, short; and *optera*, from pteron, a wing, a scaly Gurnard with short wings. **1982** AYLING *Collins Guide* (1984) 198 *Scaly Gurnard*... The body of this species is covered in large, obvious scales and is pink-red above and white beneath. **1986** PAUL *NZ Fishes* 81 Scaly gurnard *Lepidotrigla brachyoptera*. Restricted to New Zealand, but similar species occur elsewhere... Often mistaken for juveniles of the red gurnard.

(4) **spotted gurnard**. *Pterygotrigla picta* (fam. Triglidae).

1911 WAITE *Rec. Canterbury Mus.* I. 252 *Pterygotrigla picta*... Spotted Gurnard. **1921** *NZJST* IV. 123 *Spotted Gurnard*. A rare species in Auckland and Wellington markets. Examples noted in Wellington were received from Napier. **1956** GRAHAM *Treasury NZ Fishes* 365 Spotted Gurnard is not unlike the ordinary Gurnard but the colouration causes it to stand out as one of New Zealand's most exquisitely coloured fish. **1982** AYLING *Collins Guide* (1984) 197 The spotted gurnard is similar to the red gurnard in shape but has larger more protuberant eyes and is usually smaller... Body colour..is pink-yellow above with numerous small black spots, and white beneath.

gurnet, var. GURNARD.

gut. *Shearing*. [Transf. use of *gut*, innards, lining: see OED *n.* 2 g.] The flexible drive-shaft of a shearing machine encased in a downtube.

1955 BOWEN *Wool Away* 100 At times a gut will break. Every shed should have spare guts on hand so that such a mishap may not cause a long hold-up. New guts can be stored for protection in a piece of pipe, for rats have a special taste for new gut cores. **1982** *Agric. Gloss.* (MAF) 55 *Gut*: Flexible drive shaft of shearing machine which is encased in downtube.

gutbuster. *Tramping*. Also **guts buster**. See quots.

1955 *BJ Cameron Collection* (TS July) gutsbuster (n) 1. An extremely steep hill. 2. A road or track up such a hill. **1966** TURNER *Eng. Lang. Austral. & NZ* 120 A steep hill on the bush track to the Wellington student's tramping club hut is (or used to be) known as the G. B. or guts buster, and the name is used for other hills by trampers. **1988** McGILL *Dict. Kiwi Slang* 53 *gutbuster* a mountain likely to bust your gut because so difficult; mostly trampers' term.

guts: see *rough as guts* (ROUGH *a.* A 2 d).

gutser, *n.*[1] Also occas. **gutzer**. [AND 1918.] A heavy fall, esp. as **come a gutser**, to fall flat on one's guts, to come a cropper; also *fig.*, to fail significantly, to make a bad mistake.

1918 *Chron. NZEF* 10 Apr. 108 I reckon you've come a gutser, Digger. *Ibid.* 21 June 221 The tenderfoot..comes a 'gutzer' in those trenches. And is taught to take a rumble. *Ibid.* 19 July 274 In the colloquial parlance of the 'Digger', they came a gentle 'gutzer'. **c1926** THE MIXER *Transport Workers' Song Book* 28 You'll come 'gutzer' every time While you're on the 'fodder' wage. **1935** STRONG in Partridge *Slang Today* 287 He was a quean to look at, yet he produced; but when I tried to put the nips in for a franc he said he had been stung before, so you see I came a gutser. **1957** CROSS *God Boy* 98 The back wheel slid in some loose gravel. Down he went again in another beautiful gutzer. **1960** CRUMP *Good Keen Man* 111 I came one or two gutsers myself. **1973** *Sunday Times* (Wellington) 9 Dec. 49 Not for the first time, everyone associated with a taboo object came a gutser, including the film crew, who had the quickness of mind to film their own misfortune on a sinking boat. **1991** VIRTUE *Always the Islands of Memory* 30 She ran so fast Parnell was certain that her leg would come off and that Sister would have a gutzer.

gutser, *n.*[2] Also **gutzer**. [cf. EDD *gutsie*.] A greedyguts; also *fig.*, a TERROR.

1930 DEVANNY *Bushman Burke* 52 In his own vernacular that judgement was: 'A gutzer for women. Flash joker'. **1988** McGILL *Dict. Kiwi Slang* 53 *gutser* glutton.

gutsful. Also **gutful**. [Used elsewhere but esp. freq. in NZ: see OED *gutful* '*dial.* and *slang*'.] **a.** A bellyful; esp. in the phr. **to have a gutsful (of)**, to have had more than enough (of), to be fed up with (a person, situation, etc.).

1947 DAVIN *For Rest of Our Lives* The boys have had a gutful of this. You know what they thought of the last performance. **1959** SLATTER *Gun in My Hand* 67 I'd had a gutful. I was off home. **1965** SHADBOLT *Among the Cinders* 74 Don't talk to me about them bastards. I've had a gutsful of doctors in my time. **1972** *Dominion* (Wellington) 11 Sept. 4 The former Speaker Sir Roy Jack, was not to be mistaken for his meaning when he said he had had a 'gutsful' of demonstrations. **1991**

Press (Christchurch) 14 Oct. 14 I..have had a gutsful of rugby on TV.

b. In the phr. **not to be worth a gutsful of cold water**, to be worth very little.

   1959 SLATTER *Gun in My Hand* 207 No-one cares what happens to me. They're not worth a gutsful of cold water. To hell with the lot of them.

gutsing. *Shoplifters.* See quot.
   1994 *Dominion* (Wellington) 8 Aug. 9 A favoured method of stealing power tools and the like is 'gutsing'... Two bags are set under a bulky sweat top and trousers— It helps to have a bit of a gut too..—then a power tool gets put into each and the gut-laden thief walks out.

gutter. *Mining.* [AND 1853.] The lowest part of an old watercourse as a place where auriferous material is likely to be found.
   1863 WALKER *Jrnl. & Lett.* (ATLTS) 27 Jan. We found yesterday our next door neighbours had driven into our wall a good gutter and I believe got a good 9dwt. piece out while we were away on Saturday. **1890** *Evening Post* (Wellington) 10 Sept. 3 The Alice Fell Company are now working three shifts and hope soon to be on the gutter. **c1930** *Whitcombe's Etym. Dict. Aust.-NZ Suppl.* 5 *gutter n.* in mining, an ancient buried water-course containing gold-bearing material. **1946** MILLER *There Was Gold* 69 I..had struck the deepest part of the lead. It was a narrow gutter, no more than a foot wide at the most, and rich in heavy gold. **1962** WILSON *Linkwater* 95 This claim, with a gutter length of 1200 feet, was taken up in 1888. *Ibid*. 99 The gold was said to be clearly visible in the gutter as the water rushed in [from a collapsed shaft].

gutty. Also **gutty bait**. [f. *gut* intestines + -Y.] Whitebait at a stage where it has developed intestines.
   1982 HULME *Silences Between* 49 All my catch this season is glass-eels and cockabullies and bloody gutty bait. **1984** *Dominion* (Wellington) 3 Apr. 6 Gutty bait, fish that have developed intestines, are known as 'ngaruru'. **1989** *Dominion Sunday Times* (Wellington) 15 Oct. 13 'Gutty' bait which is darker than normal is rejected because it turns a bright unappetising green on freezing.

gutzer, var. GUTSER.

guyver, var. GYVER.

gypsy kettle. [See OED *kettle* 1 a, 'a pot or caldron (cf. *camp-, fish-, gipsy-kettle*)'.] A pot or cauldron used for boiling usu. over an open fire.
   c1846 WEEKES *My Island* in Rutherford & Skinner *Establish. New Plymouth* (1940) 118 Our cooking, as with most early settlers, was now an open-air affair with camp-oven and gypsy kettles.

gyver /'gaivə/. Also **givor, guiver, guyver**. [Orig. unknown: cf. EDD *guyvisome* soft, foolish; AND 1864.] Airs, affectation, 'side', excessive show, esp. in the phr. **to put on the gyver**.
   1897 WRIGHT *Station Ballads* 68 Oh, you ought to have heard him start to sing... He'd put on 'gyver' enough to last a full-bred actor a week. **1918** *Chron. NZEF* 5 July 253 The 'givor' that kid puts on, you would think he was a captain at least. **1919** *Ibid.* 24 Jan. 302 'Blimey! What's that guiver for, Tony?' Tony pointed to the flags and triumphal arches. **1928** DEVANNY *Dawn Beloved* 179 The guyver they put on [in speech]. It's sickening. **1975** DAVIN *Breathing Spaces* 46 'Sorry,' Wally called back in an extra-polite voice I hardly recognized, he could put on the gyver so well when he wanted to. **1982** STUART *Satyrs of Southland* 36 He's free and easy in his style, We hope he soon may make his pile, No pride with him or useless givor, A credit to the clan—McIvor.

H

haahow, ha-a-how, varr. KAKAHU n.[1]

Haast's eagle: see EAGLE 1.

habuka, var. HAPUKU.

haddock. [Transf. use of *haddock* a northern hemisphere codfish.] Applied in early New Zealand use to various marine fishes thought to resemble the Brit. haddock, esp. the HAKE 1 b (*Merluccius australis*, formerly *gayi*) and less frequently *red cod* (COD 2 (6) *Pseudophycis bachus*). Cf. FINDON HADDOCK.
 1838 POLACK *NZ* I. 322 Many other fish are equally numerous, answering to our *hakes, tench, bream, snapper, haddock*. 1842 GRAY *Fauna* in Dieffenbach *Travels in NZ* (1843) II. 222 Fam. Gadoideae *Lota baccha... Gadus bacchus...* Inhabits Murderer's Bay. It [*sc.* red cod] is probably the 'haddock' of the settlers: its native name in Queen Charlotte's Sound is 'Ehogoa'. 1872 HUTTON & HECTOR *Fishes NZ* 115 The fish to which the familiar name of Haddock has been applied (*Gadus australis*) is a new species, described by Captain Hutton from a few specimens that were cast up on the shore of Cook Strait... Also called the Yellow Tail and the Haddock, (*Lotella bacchus*) [*sc.* red cod] is a well known fish on some parts of the coast, being the species that is cured and sold as the Findon Haddock at Port Chalmers. 1886 SHERRIN *Handbook Fishes NZ* 37 Haddock (*Gadus Australis*)... Haddock..are caught by the trawl chiefly, though fish taken with the line are supposed to be preferable. 1892 *NZ Official Handbook* 167 Of the edible fishes..only the ling, hake and haddock..are among those of more southern types. 1906 *TrNZI* XXXVIII. 551 *Merluccius grayi*, [*sic*]. Locally known as 'haddock'. 1921 *NZJST* IV. 120 *Merluccius gayi. Whiting.* Sold as 'haddock' in Dunedin, but not common. Odd examples have been taken as far north as Hawke's Bay. 1957 PARROTT *Sea Angler's Fishes* 169 Hake Merlangius australis Whiting; Haddock.

had it, *a.* Also **haddit.** [f. a shortened form of the phrases *to have had it* to be ruined, useless, etc.., to have had enough (OED *have* v. 14 k), *and to have had* (a person, thing) to be fed up with (OED *have* v. 14 l) re-applied as an adjective.] Useless, etc.; unconscious, etc.; ruined (according to context); (poss., as in quot. 1972) exasperating.
 1972 IHIMAERA in *Some Other Country* (1984) 159 Anyway, she used to say, what with all my haddit kids and their haddit kids and all this haddit whanau being broke all the time..how can I afford to buy a new house? 1994 *Dominion* (Wellington) 2 Aug. 12 He saw..[X] hit Mr Maraki in the jaw... 'The man was had it. He was out' Mr Graham said.

ha-ea-ra-ka-he, var. HARAKEKE.

haere, *v.* [Ma. /ˈhaere/: Williams 30 *haere* (i) *1.* v. Come, go, depart... *Haere mai!* Welcome!.. *Haere ra!* Farewell! (Occas. *Haere mārie* 'Go in peace. Travel safely.')]

1. As **haere mai.** Anglicized pronunciation often /ˌhairiˈmai/. Also **haeremai,** and various early forms **hairemi, here moi, iremi,** etc. A greeting or expression of welcome; 'hullo'.
[Note] Distinguish from HARAMAI.
 [1804 Collins *Eng. Colony in NSW* (NZ Vocab.) 560 He-i-de-mai! Come here!] 1819 MARSDEN *Lett. & Jrnls.* (1932) 183 'Hairemi, hairemi, Atua!'—Come hither, come hither, thou God! 1823 KENT *Journal* in Begg *Port Preservation* (1973) 317 They received us with their usual friendly acclamation of Here moi, Here moi, come here, come here. 1832 WILLIAMS *Early Jrnls.* 13 Jan. (1961) 216 They were very glad to see us and gave us the usual welcome, *haere mai, haere mai,* Come, come. 1840 BEST *Journal* June (1966) 225 Were met by a large body of Mauries..who first sang the *Iremi*. 1863 MANING *Old NZ* i 16 Then, as the boat came nearer, another burst of *haere mai*! But unaccustomed as I was then to the Maori salute, I disliked the sound. 1883 RENWICK *Betrayed* 34 Haire mai ho! 'tis the welcome song Rings far on the summer air. 1898 MORRIS *Austral-English* 189 *Haeremai, interj*. Maori term of welcome, lit. come hither; *haere* is the verb. It has been colloquially adopted. 1908 *Auckland Weekly News* 13 Aug. 23 Peeping out from amongst the foliage is the device, in electric bulbs, 'Haere mai', and from the tip of the structure flies the American flag. 1938 FINLAYSON *Brown Man's Burden* (1973) 10 Huge old willow trees shaded one side of the marae which had a carved flagpole in its midst, and there fluttered a banner with the greeting, haere mai, on it. 1941 BAKER *NZ Slang* 42 *Kia ora*..was speedily anglicized, as was haeremai, welcome! as a loose term of greeting. 1960 HILLIARD *Maori Girl* 219 Worst of all [pakehas] were the amorous ones who knew only one or two words: *haeremai* or *e hoa*, or obscenities. 1983 HULME *Bone People* 467 Haere mai = as well as a greeting, this phrase means Come here. 1988 FRAME *The Carpathians* 30 These days you even say *tena koutou* or *haere mai* without saying *Hairy My* and looking nervous.

2. As **haere ra** [Ma. *ra adv.* there, yonder; or a particle denoting distance from the speaker], goodbye, farewell (to one departing). Also *ellipt.* **haere.** Hasten, with a play on English *hurry*.
 1881 CAMPBELL *Poenamo* 34 That is the native fashion of bidding goodbye... But meanwhile we must 'haere' along or we shall never get clear of Herekino. 1938 HYDE *Nor Yrs. Condemn* 169 [I say:] 'Haere ra, I'm going to Napier to get my divorce.' 1946 ZIMMERMAN *Where People Sing* 42 The crowd came with me, and instead of saying goodby or cheer-o, they said 'Haere ra' and I held them for it, for it means, 'Go, then.' 1983 HULME *Bone People* 131 'Haere ra, e Piri.' Simon didn't let go her hand, nor did he wave goodbye. 1994 *Tablet* (Dunedin) 18 Dec. 9 [Heading] Haere ra to a radiant New Zealander.

haeremai, *n.* Also occas. *ellipt.* **haere.** A cry of 'haere mai'; a welcome.
 1873 *Weekly News* (Auckland) 8 Mar. 14 Some 200 came down..in their canoes, and were..received with the usual 'haeremais' and 'tangis'. 1881 CAMPBELL *Poenamo* 142 [They] welcome you in woe-begone 'Haere mai's'. 1905 BAUCKE *White Man Treads* 175 But once the 'Haeremai' had been called, it meant that the best in the possession of the host shall be set before the newcomer. 1935 MAXWELL *Recollections* 43 The Maoris began to get very excited, and as the boathook grazed the steps, the 'haere mai' was very picturesque. 1938 LANCASTER *Promenade* 58 Having said the correct number of haere's and enoho's, Nene went off with the children. 1943 MARSH *Colour Scheme* 55 The Maori people of Wai-ata-tapu are glad that he has come here and would like to greet him with a cordial *haeremai*. 1970 THOMAS *Way Up North* 26 Visitors are being loudly welcomed with *haeremais* as they come within hearing distance. 1988 *Dominion Sunday Times* (Wellington) 14 Feb. 16 They do not share the tourist industry's pleasure that the many thousands of dollars this busload represents all go round the economy four or five times. The spirit of haere mai is noticeably lacking.

hag: see HAGFISH.

hagfish. Also as **hag.** [Spec. use of *hagfish* a general name for the fam. Myxinidae, primitive eel-like marine fishes exuding copious slime when captured: see OED *hag*[1] 5.] *Eptatretus* (also erron. *Heptatretus*) *cirrhatus* (fam. Myxinidae), a primitive semi-parasitic eel-like fish. See also *blind eel* (EEL 2 (1)), SLIMY n.1, SNOTTIE, TUERE.
 1872 HUTTON & HECTOR *Fishes NZ* 87 Bdellostoma cirrhatum. Hag. 1886 SHERRIN *Handbook Fishes NZ* 307 Bdellostoma cirrhatum. Hag. 1921 THOMSON & ANDERSON *Hist. Portobello* 76 Hag; Blind-eel. *Eptatretus cirrhatus*. Hags are never found far from the bottom, and their movements, when not disturbed, are rather slow. 1927 SPEIGHT et al. *Nat. Hist. Canterbury* 190 The Hag-fish (*Eptatretus cirrhatus*) is a marine form, with peculiar teeth capable of considerable protrusion. 1938 *TrRSNZ* LXVIII. 399 Hagfish (slime-eel, hag, slimy, borer). *Tuere...* Everywhere in and around Otago Harbour, 1–120 fathoms, over any type of bottom. 1947 POWELL *Native Animals NZ* 60 Hag fish... This grows to about 2 feet in length..even more revolting than the lamprey, to which it is closely allied. 1956 [see EEL 2 (1)]. 1957 WILLIAMS *Dict. Maori Lang.* 279 *Pia... Heptatretus cirrhatus*, hagfish or *blind eel*. 1965 GILLHAM *Naturalist in NZ* 135 The other bugbear was not a true fish at all but a 'hagfish', 'blind-eel', or 'slime-eel', first cousin to the lamprey. 1967 [see EEL 2 (1)]. 1982 GRADY *Perano Whalers* 111 Some of the whalers at Fishing Bay, especially the Maoris, enjoyed sea foods and found turi (blind eels or hagfish) a particular delicacy after they had been properly treated. 1991 BRADSTOCK *Fishing* 23 Hagfish. Other names: tuere, blind eel, snot-eel, snottie... Some very rude names are also used.

haggle. *Golf.* See quots.
 1987 p.c. David Norton (Wellington) 3 Dec. A haggle is a bet between the players on a round of golf, part of the money allocated to the winner(s) of the first nine holes, part to the second nine (this amount may be doubled by the losers of the first nine), and part to the overall winner(s). Currently on Karori Golf Course: 50c, 50c, $1. Sometimes money is played for on each hole, but I don't think this is part of a haggle. 1988 p.c.

M.J. Orsman (Wellington) Feb. 'Haggle' is used on Judgeford Golf Course (Pauatahanui) for playing for a small prize which all concerned share in but which the losing team pays for—the whole process is called a haggle. 'Are we going to have a wee haggle on the match.' **1993** *Metro* (Auckland) Dec. 60 'When I play [golf] with a group we like to have a bit of a haggle.' 'A haggle? 'A bet. There are any number of games you can play.'.. He tries to explain 'Atlanta' and 'Split Sixes', but loses me somewhere left of the rough.

hahunga. *Hist.* Also **haihunga, huhunga, uhunga.** [Ma. /ˈhahuŋa/: Williams 30 *Hahu, v. 1.* Disinter the bones of the dead before removing them to their final resting place.] A ceremonial disinterment and cleaning of the bones of a dead person before depositing them in a final private or secret resting-place.
[Note.] The ceremony was often called in English 'the lifting' or 'raising' (see quot. 1866), or 'scraping of the bones', and in post-European times was gradually replaced under missionary influence by conventional interment followed by the ceremony of 'unveiling'. Cf. *bone-scraper bone-scraping* (BONE 3), UNVEILING.
1828 WILLIAMS *Early Jrnls.* 23 May (1961) 130 Tekoke and most of the natives of the settlement had left to attend a *Hahunga* at Taeamai. **1835** YATE *NZ* (1970) 137 No further notice is taken of the deceased till the Hahunga, a grand annual feast; when the bones of all belonging to severaI united tribes are taken down, and removed to their last resting-place, in or near the sacred grove. **1840** POLACK *Manners & Customs* I. 75 These orations ended, the crowds depart, and the actions, &c. of the deceased only are spoken of until the exhumation (*haihunga*) takes place, about one year after the decease of the chief. **1856** SHORTLAND *Traditions & Superstitions* 147 A very curious ceremony, called *hahunga*, takes place when the skulls of the dead are exhibited to their living relations before being finally deposited in the secret family vault. **1863** MANING *Old NZ* 236 A *hahunga* was a funeral ceremony, at which the natives usually assembled in great numbers, and during which 'baked meats' were disposed of. [**1866** ANGAS *Polynesia* 150 The body is enclosed in a mausoleum of carved woodwork within the 'pah' for several months, and at the expiration of this period, the ceremony of 'lifting the bones' takes place, which is performed by the nearest relative of the deceased. The bones, after being well scraped and cleaned, are then deposited in a box, and buried.] **1873** TINNE *Wonderland of Antipodes* 66 The most..interesting ceremonial..was a 'huhunga,' or bone-scraping. **1882** POTTS *Out in Open* 105 Just opposite in the crevices of a beetling rock, red stained skulls and mouldering bones disclosed an ancient *uhunga*, a hidden place of sepulchre, as yet unravaged by irreverent collectors of Maori relics. **1895** *TrNZI* XXVII. 611 The *hahunga*, a feast attending the ceremonial raising of a chief's bones. **1963** KEENE *O te Raki* 190 *Hahunga*: ceremony of exhuming and scraping bones of the dead. **1973** OPPENHEIM *Maori Death Customs* 70 In the northern tradition the time lapse between the primary burial and *Hahunga* could be anything from a few months to several years.

haihunga, var. HAHUNGA.

haircut. *Car-salesmen.* In the phr. **to give a car a haircut,** to illegally wind back a used-car's odometer to show a false low mileage.
1987 *National Bus. Rev.* 3 Apr. 29 A number of prosecutions had involved used car dealers rewinding the odometers on vehicles—a practice known in the trade as giving a car a 'haircut'. **1990** *Motoring Today* Apr. 9 Normally, when speedos are illegally tampered with, the odometer is deftly wound back. In some shadier parts of the trade, this technique is known as 'giving the car a haircut'. **1995** *Sunday Star-Times* (Auckland) 2 Apr. A16 Create yet another definition of inflation called haircut inflation, so named for the odometer slice taken before Japanese used cars are exported to New Zealand—no matter what the total on the odometer before the haircut, the level afterwards is always rather low.

hair grass, seal: see GRASS 2 (19), SEAL *n.*¹ 2 (2).

hairy. A wild goat.
1982 HOLDEN *Wild Pig* 198 Peter was hunting a heavily bushed gorge, and came across three hairies; three white [wild] goats poised on a..spur.

hairy goat. [AND *goat* 2, 1941: a horse that performs badly in a race.] **a.** A racehorse, esp. in the phr. **to run like a hairy goat** (occas. **hairy dog**), orig. of a racehorse, to perform badly; occas., to run a fast race, to move quickly.
1954 JOURNET *Take My Tip* 77 Should Z [*sc.* a racehorse] lose his race..he is said to have *run like a hairy goat*, another foolish term as hairy goats are reputedly both agile and swift. **1959** SLATTER *Gun in My Hand* 23 An it ran like a hairy goat an I did me chips. *Ibid.* 127 I've just seen him running like a hairy dog all over Lancaster Park. **1964** MORRIESON *Came a Hot Friday* (1981) 69 Windsor Knot! What a hairy goat! What a divvy! **1971** LETHBRIDGE *Sunrise on Hills* 39 I'd been asleep. I went charging up that face like a hairy goat, just in time to see you jokers starting the muster. **1995** *Dominion* (Wellington) 20 May 19 The mare..ran like a hairy dog so..she was sprayed with a concoction which made all the chaps she raced with slow down to a heady saunter.

b. Occas. **to go** (**run**, etc.) **like a hairy goat,** of motors, etc., to 'run' roughly, unevenly.
1964 DAVIS *Watersiders* 137 Ever since [yesterday] she's [*sc.* a mo-ped] going like the one big hairy goat. Crook benzine, that's the story. **1973** FERNANDEZ *Tussock Fever* 33 'Damn thing's [*sc.* a shearing motor] running like a hairy goat.'.. 'I suppose it's worn out,' said Bessie.

haka /ˈhakə/. Also early **a'ka, ehaga, E'Haka** =he haka. [Ma. /ˈhaka/: Williams 31 *Haka* (i) *1. v.* Dance... *3. n.* Dance. *4.* Song accompanying a dance.]
1. a. In Maori contexts, a posture dance accompanied by a chant, usu. perceived by Europeans as a war-dance.
1777 SAMWELL *Account* 13 Feb. in Cook *Journals* (1967) III. 996 These War Songs they call Ehaga. [**1820** LEE & KENDALL *NZ Gram. & Vocab.* 133 A'ka. s... A war dance.] **1828** WILLIAMS *Early Jrnls.* 21 Mar. (1961) 113 They had several *'hakas* (dances), when the ground trembled beneath their feet. **1838** POLACK *NZ* I. 81 After each of my retinue were presented to the chief, partaking of the honour of the ongi, or salutation, the hákà, or dance of welcome, was performed... This dance, to a stranger witnessing it for the first time, is calculated to excite the most alarming fears. **1843** DIEFFENBACH *Travels in NZ* II. 57 E' Waiata is a song of a joyful nature; E' Haka, one accompanied by gestures or mimics. **1849** POWER *Sketches in NZ* 29 Aug 24th [1846].—The friendly natives..were busy..cleaning their arms, singing 'hakas', and making speeches. **1873** TINNE *Wonderland of Antipodes* 18 The young girls were dancing the voluptuous and disgusting 'haka'. **1896** *Otago Witness* (Dunedin) 23 Jan. 50 He also received a visit from three or four hostile Natives, who, with blood-curdling yells, duly performed the indispensable haka. **1908** GORST *NZ Revisited* 65 They danced what is called a 'haka', a dance of welcome; the contortions and gesticulations are most violent and quaint. **1917** *NZ at the Front* xiii Haka.—A Maori dance, with grotesque gesticulation and accompanied by a chant often as fierce as the dance. **c1920** BEATTIE *Trad. Lifeways Southern Maori* (1994) 484 The Maori dance most known to Europeans is the haka. It is generally, although erroneously, supposed to be a war-dance but (in Nelson at any rate) it was danced as an amusement. **1943** FINLAYSON *Brown Man's Burden* (1973) 88 It was a grand welcome; although the haka dancers unexpectedly faced the wrong way for the movie camera man. **1963** PEARSON *Coal Flat* 43 I'm a full Maori and proud, too... Old Mum she meant I'm still a savage, that's what she meant. Just quietly, eh? *Haka* and *tangi*. **1995** *Sunday Star-Times* (Auckland) 23 July C4 [Heading] ... [*sic*] but do we need a haka? Our footballers don't win the matches that count but excel at Maori war dances.

b. Applied to similar dances of other indigenous Pacific peoples.
1977 HOLMES *Best of Homespun* 36 Threatening hakas by spear-toting Fijian warriors.

2. In non-Maori contexts. A noisy posture dance usu. performed by males, accompanied by a chant (often in English or meaningless word forms) to encourage a sports team (esp. rugby union), to support a school (often as **school haka**) or community enterprise or rally; occas. presented as a welcome to visitors, etc.
[**c1900** St Patrick's College (Wellington) haka, traditionally performed since before the turn of the century: 'Boomeranga! Boomeranga! Bow-wow-wow!.. Boomeranga, boomeranga, Who are we, we are the boys of S.P.C.'] **1906** *Evening Post* (Wellington) 3 Jan. 5 [Edinburgh 20 Nov. 1905: Special Corresp.] A band of colonials assembled in strong force under the press box and by loud hakas..cheered the Blacks to battle. **1916** ANZAC *On the Anzac Trail* 27 We got to sleep at last [in military camp in Egypt], lulled by the dulcet strains of a Maori *haka* voiced by a home-coming band of late..revellers. **1927** *Glasgow Herald* 18 Mar. 13 [The Duke of York] was given an uproarious welcome by [Otago Univ.] undergraduates, who performed the vigorous 'Haka' and sang the University song. **1942** *Blue & White* (St Patricks College Annual Magazine) 54 Haka practice today was enlivened by a demonstration of the haka done by the First XV. **1959** SLATTER *Gun in My Hand* 78 Above the hubbub rises the distinct bom shikka bom of the visitors' haka. **1966** *Encycl. NZ* II. 679 Another [Maori loanword] is *haka*, now becoming well known wherever our football teams go. **1972** MITCHELL *Pavlova Paradise* 182 haka: Concession to race relations by NZ Rugby Union. **1983** HENDERSON *Down from Marble Mountain* 149 Someone starts the school haka. **1986** *Listener* 8 Nov. 8 Nor should we left-wing trendy feminist pooftah intellectuals forget that the ritual haka at the start of a rugby game antedates by many decades the perfunctory 'kia ora' with which we nowadays preface our performance. **1991** *Dominion* (Wellington) 3 Oct. 3 The haka before sports games was being used for racial abuse, Secondary Principals Association president Brother Pat Lynch said yesterday... Brother Lynch said the protocol of the haka before games needed to be reviewed.

3. *transf.* **a.** In the phr. **to dance (do) a haka,** to celebrate; to express glee.
1941 BAKER *NZ Slang* 42 By the 1890's the phrase *to dance a haka* had been adopted to describe an exhibition of pleasure. **1946** SOLJAK *NZ* 116 New Zealand colloquialisms which are of Maori origin include:.. *dance a haka:* to celebrate. **1955** *BJ Cameron Collection* (TS July) haka do a haka (v) To express glee.

b. A noisy fuss.
1960 ROGERS *Long White Cloud* 17 'When are you going back?' he asked of Hal. 'And don't give me a big *haka* about going to town.'

4. *Special Comb.* **haka party**, a group performing the haka, often formerly a non-Maori group performing imitation or weakened versions of the haka in support of sports or school teams, or at University revels.

1943 FINLAYSON *Brown Man's Burden* (1973) 89 The crowd rocked with laughter. 'Ake, ake, ake!' yelled the haka party. **1966** TURNER *Eng. Lang. Austral. & NZ* 169 The word *haka* 'a Maori war-dance' has become common as friendly hakas usually introduce a football match and haka parties associated with students' capping processions fix it in the minds of the leading citizens of tomorrow. **1991** *Victoria News* (Victoria University occasional publication) 16 Dec. 2 Victoria's kapa haka (haka party) recently won the Wellington regional competition.

Hence **haka** *v. intr.* (also early northern **shákka**), to perform or dance a haka.

[**1817** NICHOLAS *Voyage NZ* II. 340 To dance. Shákka.] **1828** WILLIAMS *Early Jrnls.* 23 Mar. (1961) 115 As soon as night had closed in the natives began to dance and after '*haka*ring for some time there was a general firing round, many fired ball. **1871** MEADE *Ride through Disturbed Dist.* in Taylor *Early Travellers* (1959) 444 We had not been in long, before one of the chiefs called on the girls to come and *haka* to the strangers.

hakari. Also **a'karii**, early northern **shackerie**. [Ma. /ˈhaːkari/: Williams 31 *Hākari 2.* Entertainment, feast...*3.* High wooden framework on which food was placed at a feast.]

1. A feast after a ceremonial funeral or other important occasion.

[**1820** LEE & KENDALL *NZ Gram. & Vocab.* 133 A'karii, *s.* A feast, where large presents of fish, potatoes, fern-root..are brought by the visitors to the party visited.] **1823** CRUISE *Journal* 21 Apr. (1957) 83 One of the gentlemen..was present at the shackerie, or harvest home (if it may be so called), of Shungie's people. It was celebrated in a wood, where a square space had been cleared of trees, in the centre of which three very tall posts, driven into the ground in the form of a triangle, supported an immense pile of baskets of koomeras. **1835** YATE *NZ* (1970) 139 There is another feast given at another period of the year, called the Hakari; but it is totally different from the Hahunga; the visiters [*sic*] bringing the cooked food, and receiving from their hosts an immense quantity, piled up in the form of a pyramid, eighty feet high, and twenty feet square at the base. **1847** ROSS *Voyage of Discovery* II. 99 These feasts, which are called 'Hakari' or feasts of peace, are now but rare occurrence. **1859** THOMSON *Story NZ* I. 189 The New Zealanders had another feast, called the hakari, very different from the hahunga. The hakari was a banquet given by nations to each other. **1863** *Richmond-Atkinson Papers* (1960) II. 34 Caught my poney [*sic*] & rode down to Mangaone..where there was said to be a great hakari (feast) going on, but it had not begun. **1904** TREGEAR *Maori Race* 113 The great festival of the Maoris was the *Hakari*. This name was sometimes applied to the building erected for the food as well as to the feast itself. **1963** KEENE *O te Raki* 190 *hakari:* great feast; large pyramid-shaped scaffolding, sometimes as high as 75 ft. to 80 ft. with platforms at about 10 ft. intervals from base.

2. In modern weakened use, a feast or spread (marking a special occasion).

1969 MASON *Awatea* (1978) Appendix II 115 Every penny gone, not a brass razoo left. Next day back to the wharf! What a *hakari*. **1970** JOHNSON *Life's Vagaries* 24 After the *hakari* the Maori hostess led her dark skinned one year old..to our table. **1980** *Listener* 22 Sept. 36 When all the intense intellectual activity was over for the day, the crafts people left for the Mihiroa marae for the hakari. Wine, beer, apple juice. Lots of splendid hot food. Speeches and songs.

hakari, var. HUCKERY.

hakawai, var. HAKUWAI.

hake. [Transf. use of *hake* a northern hemisphere gadoid fish, for various often unrelated marine fishes: AND 'gemfish', 1951.]

1. Any of various, often unrelated, marine fishes, the application of the name often varying from time to time and place to place. **a.** Applied to various genera.

1777 ANDERSON *Journal* Feb. in Cook *Journals* (1967) III. 808 The natives now and then brought Hake, Paracutas..and leather jackets. **1840** POLACK *Manners & Customs* I. 202 Among the piscivorous tribes, are those well known in Europe under the appellations of snapper, tench, haddocks..hakes. **1892** *NZ Official Handbook* 167 Of the edible [pelagic] fishes..only the ling, hake and haddock..are among those of more southern types. **1925** *NZJST* VII. 370 Another matter touching on the recurring annoyance of vernacular names is that up till 1891 *Lotella rhacinus* was universally accepted as the hake: then, in 1912, Waite, for no apparent reason, transfers this name to *Merluccius gayi*. **1957** PARROTT *Sea Angler's Fishes* 43 The application of the name 'Hake' to several distinct species of our fishes, is a good example of..confusion. In Blenheim, Nelson, Picton and Wellington, a very different fish, scientifically known as the *Rexea solandri* [*sc.* gemfish], and closely related to the Barracouta, with obviously no affinities to the Cod family, is called 'Hake' or 'Southern Kingfish'. The name Hake applied to this fish is entirely wrong. **1966** *Encycl. NZ* I. 898 *Hake* is a name applied to several quite different marine fish in different parts of the country. The whiting or haddock, *Merluccius australis*, is a true hake, very similar to the North Sea species; it is, actually, often called English hake... The southern kingfish, *Jordanidia solandri*, is also known as hake... The Cloudy Bay cod, *Lotella rhacinus*, is sometimes known as southern hake. **1970** SORENSEN *Nomenclature NZ Fish* 28 The position is further complicated by the almost indiscriminate use of the name hake, by fishermen, [for] other species of fish... The name Hake should not be applied to either Southern kingfish or the Whiptail although there can be little, if any, objection to the commercial name of Blue Hake for the latter species.

b. *Merluccius australis* (also listed as *M. gayi*, *Merlangius australis*, *Gadus australis*) (fam. Merlucciidae). Also less frequently **English hake**. A good food fish of moderately deep water. See also *English hake* 2 (2) below, HADDOCK, WHITING 1 b.

1911 WAITE *Rec. Canterbury Museum* I. 175 *Merluccius Gayi*..Hake, Whiting. **1927** SPEIGHT et al. *Nat. Hist. Canterbury* 200 Its close relative the Hake or Whiting (*Merluccius gayi*), is much less common. **1938** *TrRSNZ* LXVIII. 404 *Merluccius gayi*. Hake (whiting)... Vernacular: The name whiting, though more properly reserved for *Gadus*, is firmly rooted in Otago and Canterbury. *Merluccius* in England and America is called hake. **1957** PARROTT *Sea Angler's Fishes* 45 Hake *Merlangius australis*... This New Zealand species was for many years considered to be identical with a closely allied species originally described in 1847 from Chile, and is frequently referred to in the New Zealand literature as *Merluccius gayi*. **1966** DOOGUE & MORELAND *Sea Anglers' Guide* 209 English Hake... Other names: *Merluccius australis*; whiting. This is a true hake, very similar to the North Sea species. **1970** SORENSEN *Nomenclature NZ Fish* 28 *Hake... Merluccius australis*... Other common names: Whiting; English Hake. **1986** PAUL *NZ Fishes* 60 *Hake Merluccius australis*... Sometimes called English hake, from a similarity to a north-east Atlantic species... Quite different from the unrelated gemfish, but sometimes confused by the erroneous use of 'hake' for gemfish in some localities.

c. *Rexea* (formerly *Jordanidia*) *solandri*, GEMFISH. See also KINGFISH b.

1918 *NZJST* I. 269 Hake, or Southern Kingfish. *Rexea furcifera*. **1921** *NZJST* IV. 118 *Jordanidia solandri*. *Southern Kingfish*. Sold as 'hake' in Wellington... Large quantities are taken by the trawlers from Napier southward. Common, South Island. **1936** *Handbook for NZ* (ANZAAS) 72 *Jordanidia solandri*: Hake (Wellington), kingfish (Otago), barraconda (Auckland and Napier). **1957** PARROTT *Sea Angler's Fishes* 154 Southern Kingfish *Rexea solandri*... The Southern Kingfish is closely related to the Barracouta, and is known in the North Island as the 'hake' but this name is more accurately applied to a very different fish, *Merlangius australis*, which belongs to the true Cod family. **1966** DOOGUE & MORELAND *Sea Anglers' Guide* 280 Southern Kingfish... Other names: *Jordanidia solandri*; kingfish, hake, barraconda; king barracouta. **1986** [see GEMFISH].

d. *Lotella rhacinus*, **rock cod** (COD 2 (8) c). See also *southern hake* 2 (4) below.

1872 HUTTON & HECTOR *Fishes NZ* 116 *Lotella rhacinus*, a closely allied species [to *L. bacchus*, Red Cod]..has been termed the Hake, but is apparently a rare fish in these latitudes. **1892** *TrNZI* XXIV. 212 Hake (*Lotella rhacinus*). Only one specimen recorded, from Mokohinou, in August, 1887. **1957** PARROTT *Sea Angler's Fishes* 169 Rock Cod *Lotella rhacina* Southern Hake; Hake.

2. With a modifier: **blue** (or **whiptail**), **English, smoked, southern**. Also as **silver hake**, applied as a trade name to FROSTFISH in a Wellington fish-shop display 8 February 1995 (Ed.).

(1) **blue** (or **whiptail**) **hake**. HOKI (*Macruronus novaezealandiae*).

1970 SORENSEN *Nomenclature NZ Fish* 29 Hake, blue (a) Scientific name: *Macruronus novaezealandiae*. (b) Suggested commercial name[s]: Blue Hake. (c) Other common names: Whiptail; Rat-tail. **1986** blue hake [see HOKI 1].

(2) **English hake**. See 1 b above.

1936 *Handbook for NZ* (ANZAAS) 71 *Merluccius gayi*: The 'whiting' of Wellington fishmongers. **1970**, **1986** [see 1 b above].

(3) **smoked hake**. *Obs.* A name occas. given by the fish trade for smoked forms of less known or less desirable fish, esp. *conger eel* (EEL 2 (2)).

1918 *NZJST* I. 136 Conger-eel is occasionally smoked, and I have often met with it at Wellington hotel-tables under the name of 'smoked hake'.

(4) **southern hake**. **rock cod** (COD 2 (8) c).

1927 PHILLIPPS *Bibliogr. NZ Fishes* (1971) 23 *Lotella rhacinus*... Rock-cod or Southern Hake. **1956** GRAHAM *Treasury NZ Fishes* 172 Rock Cod or Southern Hake *Lotella rhacina*. Up to 1891 this fish was universally known to scientists and fishermen as Hake... The most common name among Otago fishermen was Rock Cod, because this fish favours a rocky habitat. **1966** [see COD 2 (4) b].

hakeke. Also **hakekakeka**. [Ma. /ˈhakeke/: Williams 31 *Hakeke*, and dial. var. *Hakeka*.] Jew's ear fungus (FUNGUS 1 a, 2 (5)).

1869 *TrNZI* I. (rev. edn.) 261 [Also eaten were] several *Fungi* [especially]..four..which grow on trees,— the Harori (*Agaricus adiposus*), the Hakeke, and the

Popoiahakeke (*Polyporus*) species, and the Pekepekekiore (*Hydnum clathroides*). **1881** *TrNZI* XIII. 30 Several fungi were also eaten..such as the two large terrestrial species called *pukurau*..; the *harore*..; the *hakekakeka*..; and the *paruwhatitiri*. **1882** [see FUNGUS 2 (5)]. **1922** COWAN *NZ Wars* (1955) II. 294 [The Hauhaus were reduced to existing upon] the *hakeke* or wood-fungus, and the *huhu*, the large white woodgrub. **a1937** COWAN *Pakeha & Maori* I. 4 They unloaded a packhorse and brought in a dozen bags of bush fungus, the hakeke of the Maori, which grows on old stumps and logs so plentifully. **1978** FULLER *Maori Food & Cook.* 85 Hakeke—Jew's ear fungus.

hakihaki. Also **akeake**. [Ma. /'hakihaki/: Williams 31 *Hakihaki*... *1*. Itch, skin disease.] A skin disease, *spec.* scabies. See also *Maori itch* (MAORI B 5 b).

1866 HUNT *Chatham Is.* 38 Of those diseases the *hakihaki*, as it is termed, is an aggravated form of itch, first arising in small pimples, which, becoming so many pustules, discharge an acrid fluid, which..spreads over the body. **1877** *TrNZI* IX. 25 Of such diseases, the *hakihaki*, as it is termed..is the most..disgusting. **1905** *Ibid.* XXXVII. 68 *Hakihaki* (scabies or the itch), a contagious animal-parasitic disease, a sort of eczema or dermatitis, caused by the presence of an animalcule, the itch-mite, in the skin, was one of the commonest and most troublesome complaints from which the Maoris suffered. **1918** *Kai Tiaki* XI. 155 The Opoutama school teacher reported an outbreak of ake, and to him I sent ointment, etc. **1952** LYON *Faring South* 171 The natives use the [Ngawha hot] springs largely for skin ailments, notably the akeake, or Maori itch. **1965** MCLAGLAN *Stethoscope & Saddlebags* 114 It *mustn't* be smallpox. It must be 'Aki Aki', a Maori name loosely applied to any rash but especially to scabies. **1983** KING *Whina* 100 I remember there was one family..that was covered in sores, like little buttons. Dr Smith said, 'Oh that's hakihaki. I can treat that.'

hakoakoa. Also **akoakoa**. [Ma. /ha:'koakoa/: Williams 32. *Hākoakoa* (ii) = *hākuakua n. 1*... fluttering shearwater. *2*... southern skua.]

1. MUTTONBIRD *n.* 1. See also RAINBIRD, SHEARWATER 2 (3).

1848 TAYLOR *Leaf from Nat. Hist.* 6 Hakoakoa, *sea bird.* **1869** *TrNZI* I. (rev. edn.) 105 Puffinus assimilis. Hakoakoa. Very numerous. **1871** [see LAUGHING JACKASS 2]. **1886** CHUDLEIGH *Diary* 9 Apr. (1950) 343 Some..Maoris went past us on horseback... They have collected 300 Akoakoa. **1888** BULLER *Birds NZ* II. 232 Puffinus griseus. (Sombre Shearwater)... Titi, Hakoakoa, and Totorore: 'Mutton-bird' of the colonists. *Ibid.* 233 Puffinus carneipes. (Flesh-footed Shearwater)... Hakoakoa. **1904** HUTTON & DRUMMOND *Animals NZ* 238 *The Shearwater.—Hakoakoa. Puffinus gavia*... The Shearwaters come on shore to clean out their burrows or make new ones in September. **1928** BAUCKE *Manuscript* (Bishop Museum Memoirs Vol. IX No.5 358) in Skinner & Baucke *Morioris* The most important [Chatham Island] edible sea-birds... hakoakoa hākōk' mutton bird.

2. SKUA.

1904 [see HAWK 2 (4)]. **1955** OLIVER *NZ Birds* 319 *Southern Skua. Sea Hawk. Hakoakoa Catharacta antarctica lonnbergi.* **1966** [see HAWK 2 (4)]. **1985** [see SKUA]. **1990** *Checklist Birds NZ* 158 Catharacta skua lonnbergi..Brown (Subantarctic) Skua (Hakoakoa)... In the New Zealand region, breeds on Macquarie, Campbell, Auckland, Antipodes, Snares, Chatham, Stewart, Solander Islands.

haku. [Ma. /'haku/: Williams 32 *Haku*... *1. Seriola grandis*, kingfish.] KINGFISH a. See also YELLOWTAIL 2 (3).

1849 *NZ Jrnl.* IX. 125 Yellow tail Haku. **1872** HUTTON & HECTOR *Fishes NZ* 111 The Haku of the natives is the King Fish (*Seriola lalandii*) of Wellington and the Yellow Tail of Australia. **1892** *TrNZI* XXIV. 209 King-fish, or Haku (*Seriola lalandii*), sometimes also called Yellow-tail. **1921** *NZJST* IV. 117 Seriola lalandi. *Kingfish; Haku...* Distribution: North Island and northern coasts of South Island (rarer farther south). **1947** POWELL *Native Animals NZ* 68 Kingfish..Haku of the Maoris, is an excellent sporting fish which readily takes the trolling hook or spinner. **1956** [see YELLOWTAIL 2 (3)]. **1964** MIDDLETON *Walk on Beach* 179 We caught several kahawai, some haku and a couple of small sharks.

hakuai, var. HAKUWAI.

hakuwai /'hakəwai/. Also **hakawai, hakuai, harkowhy**; also erron. **kakawai**. [Ma. /'ha:kuwai/: Williams 33 *Hākuwai = hākuai, hōkioi, n.* An extinct bird, heard at night.] A Maori legendary bird, heard at night but never seen; also the cry of the bird. See also BREAKSEA DEVIL, HOKIOI.

[*Note*] Suggested originals include *frigate bird* and *Haast's eagle*; the most probable being *snipe* in display flights.

1906 *TrNZI* XXXVIII. 340 A strange bird in Maori eyes is the *hakuai* of the off-shore islands in the far south... At night the fowlers gather round their campfires, and old songs are sung..and ghost-stories retold. In the darkness sometimes they hear the ghostbird screaming its '*Haku-ai, haku-ai, Ooh!*' and then a hair-raising swoosh of great wings... This bird, called the '*hakuai*' from its call, is spoken of as a spirit... The mystery of the *hakuai* may be dispelled by assuming it to be..the frigate-bird. **1912** [see HOKIOI]. **c1920** BEATTIE *Trad. Lifeways Southern Maori* (1994) 177 The hakuai is another mystery of the titi islands. At night this great bird shrieks 'hakuai' loudly three times in succession and then there follows a whirring noise like a hawser chain runing out. **1931** *Southland Times* 28 June 3 A heavy swishing sound passed over our heads, and within a few seconds called 'Hakuwai, Hakuwai'. Then followed a continuation of a sound as if a cable chain was lowered into a boat. **1953** *NZ Observer* 14 Oct. 16 The most incredible is the strange tale of the mystery bird—named, because of its call, the kakawai. **1954** BEATTIE *Our Southernmost Maori* 36 The Hakuai... Kaiporohu told Jas. Drummond the bird lived in the clouds over Foveaux Strait, hovering invisibly and crying piercingly 'Hakuwai, hakuwai, ho!' **1965** *Notornis* XII. 199 From this [diving] behaviour arose the legends of the Hakawai of the Southern Muttonbirders, a supernatural being variously described as being the father of the Mutton Birds, calling them away on their northern migration; or as a Maori Eagle, with joints on its wings. **1970** JENKIN *NZ Mysteries* 156 No one seems to have ever seen a *hakuwai*, but ask any muttonbirder and someone in the group will be sure to have heard the strange call of hakuwai, hakuwai, high in the midnight sky followed by the sound of a clanking chain. **1983** HENDERSON *Down from Marble Mountain* 142 He heard the harkowhy up in Canaan on the Takaka Hill, the ghost-bird never seen..crying like a chain rattling. **1987** MISKELLY in *Notornis* XXXIV. 96 The most popular description of the call of the hakawai was that it resembled 'a sound as if a cable chain was lowered into a boat'... Indeed many people still refer to the hakawai as if it were the chainbird. *Ibid.* 112 Many pieces of the hakawai puzzle are missing, probably forever, and other pieces have been shoe-horned into place, but all the available evidence indicates that the hakawai of the southern muttonbird islands was an aerial display of the Stewart Island Snipe. **1989** ANDERSON *Prodigious Birds* 92 It is a moot point whether the name *hakuwai* was derived from *hokioi* to explain the frightening sound of the mysterious *hakuwai* in flight (once the eagle was extinct), as Miskelly..suggests, or whether *hokioi* has been adopted, as an imperfect rendition of *hakuwai*, to provide a name for the eagle legend.

half-

1. In the names of coins or currency (all obsolete except *half-dollar* b): **half-bull** (**half-a-bull**), see BULL *n.* 1; **half-caser** [AND 1882: f. *caser* a five-shilling piece (f. Yiddish)], a half-crown; **half copper**, a half-penny; **half-dollar** (also **half-a-dollar**), formerly a half-crown; two shillings and sixpence (cf. DOLLAR 2); since the introduction of decimal coinage, fifty cents or a fifty-cent piece; **half-hundred**, a £50 note; **half-nicker** [f. Brit. dial.: see EDD *half* 6 (3) 1895], ten shillings or a ten-shilling note; **half note** (**half a note**), ten shillings or a ten-shilling note (see also NOTE *n.*[1]); **half quid**, a ten-shilling note; **half-thick** (**half-thickun**) [f. *thick' un* an obsolete term for a sovereign], a half-sovereign; **half-tiz** [f. Brit. slang *tiz* a sixpence], threepence (see also TIZZIE); **half-wheel**, a half-crown.

1887 *NZ Mail* (Wellington) 15 July 9, (NZ Slang) A half-crown [is] 'a half-a-caser'. **1899** *Bulletin* (Sydney) 14 Jan. (Red Page) [Letter from *Loafer*, Tauranga.] Following are other local money-names... 2.6d *half-bull, half-caser* or *two-and-a-buck*. **1906** *Truth* 5 May 5 Hubbub over Half-a-caser... Wrangle over sixpence. **1909** *Ibid.* 13 Mar. 4 The owner of the pocket-book, a man of means, sent along 2s 6d for the recovery of his pocket-book. He might have known that the reward would have gone to charity in any case, but half a dollar! Mother Mary Aubert is getting the half-caser, anyhow. **1977** [see DOLLAR 2]. **1972** HARGREAVES *Beads to Banknotes* 151 Half penny [:] **half copper**, brown, magpie, bawbee **1977** *NZ Numismatic Jrnl.* Oct. 16 The halfpenny was called a *half-copper* a *mag*, or a *rap*. **1908** *Truth* 15 Aug. 4 Now, to become a member of the League the sum of 2s 6d has to be planked down, and..quite a number of ardent Chow-haters have 'come to light' with their '**half-dollars**'. **1917** *Chron. NZEF* 2 May 110 One sporting sub wanted to be bet half a dollar to a gooseberry that the troop train would be snow-bound. **1946** SARGESON *That Summer* 57 One of the taxi-drivers asked me if I wanted to take a double, so I took a half-dollar one. **1956** CRESSWELL *Early NZ Families* 175 Father arrived there in 1884 with only half a crown, and..that half-dollar was all he had in the world! **1963** *Dominion* (Wellington) 8 Oct. 4 We use a colloquialism for a half-crown and five shillings and call them a half-dollar and a dollar even now. **1977** [see DOLLAR 2]. **1980** MACKENZIE *While We Have Prisons* 97 **half-a-hundred** fifty pounds (or dollars). **1937** PARTRIDGE *Dict. Slang* 368 **half-nicker**. Ten shillings; a 10s. note, half a sovereign: New Zealanders': C. 20. Ex dial. *half-a nicker* (1895: E.D.D). **1941** BAKER *NZ Slang* 52 We..describe a £1 note as a *nicker*, with *half-nicker* for ten shillings. **1977** *NZ Numismatic Jrnl.* Oct. 16 The ten shilling note, after its introduction into New Zealand in 1916, never gained a slang nickname of its own, but was generally 'half' something, as for example *half-quid*, or *half-nicker*. **1969** HASCOMBE *Down & Almost Under* 34 'What am I bid? What am I bid?..One note—one note—one note—one note.'..'**Half a note** then, if that's how you want it.' **1972** HARGREAVES *Beads to Banknotes* 151 Ten shillings [:] **half quid. 1910** *Truth* 7 May 7 In the evening he was bailed out in the sum of a sovereign, in place of the usual '**half-thick**' which is usually demanded of first-offending drunks. **1899** *Bulletin* (Sydney) 14 Jan. (Red Page) [Letter from *Loafer*, Tauranga.] Following are other local money-names...

HALF A SHAKE   331   **HALF-CASTE**

half-sovereign—**half-thickun** or *little goldie*. **1977** *NZ Numismatic Jrnl.* Oct. 15 The half sovereign was obviously a *half-thick 'un*, or sometimes *a thin 'un*. **1899** *Bulletin* 14 Jan. (Sydney) (Red Page) [Letter from *Loafer*, Tauranga] Following are other local money-names... 3d.—thrum, **half-tiz**, tray or tray-piece. **1977** *NZ Numismatic Jrnl.* Oct. 15 A *tray-bit*, or *trey, thrum*, or *half-tiz* are recorded for the threepence. **1963** GLOVER *Bedside Book* 20 'Five shillings,' said the woman in the telephone exchange... I tossed down two **half-wheels**.

2. As the first element in synonyms for 'tipsy': **half-rinsed**; also with FONGED, SHICKERED, SHOT *ppl. a.*

1937 PARTRIDGE *Dict. Slang* 368 *half-rinsed*. Slightly drunk: New Zealanders': from ca. 1912. **1989** MCGILL *Dinkum Kiwi Dict.* 42 *half-rinsed* fairly drunk.

3. In the names of containers for alcoholic liquor. See also FLAGON 1, JAR, PETER *n.*[2] **a.** With reference to glass containers, formerly of half-gallon (2.25 l) capacity and now often of plastic of 2 or 2.25 l capacity, used to hold draught beer (also occas. cheap wine) purchased for home consumption. (a) As **half-gallon**, or **half-gallon flagon**, occas. **half-gallon jar**.

1962 HORI *The half-gallon jar* [Title] **1965** SHADBOLT *Among Cinders* 190 He went into the hut and returned with a half-gallon flagon of wine and three glasses. **1974** GIFFORD *Loosehead Len's Big Brown Book* 8 A half-gallon flagon fits neatly in each [pocket].

(b) As **half-g (half-gee)** etc.

1964 *Evening Post* (Wellington) 3 Mar. 17 He was delighted to be offered a drink from what his host described as a 'half-G'. **1971** SHADBOLT *Bullshit & Jellybeans* 85 Real hard case that joker. Yah should have seen him knocking back those half Gs. **1972** MITCHELL *Pavlova Paradise* 182 *half-G:* Less than 50 per cent of a full-G. Also known in Dunedin as a peter, after the first missionary to land in that city, St Peter Speight. **1974** half-gees [see FLAGON 2]. **1982** *Dominion* (Wellington) 6 Oct. 3 New Zealand's traditional takeaway beer container—the flagon, also known as a 'jar', 'half-G' or 'peter'—was yesterday defended by its manufacturer. **1983** HULME *Bone People* 168 Could've been the couple of half g's I had though, or that hunk of pork. **1988** *Pacific Way* (Air NZ) July 50 Depending on regional expressions, [draught-beer containers] are variously known as a 'jar', 'peter', 'half-gee' (half-gallon) or the more modern 'pub pet' two-litre plastic bottle.

b. As **half-handle**, a reputed half-pint (285 ml) glass mug; also its contents (usu. beer). Cf. HANDLE 1.

1936 SARGESON *Conversation with Uncle* 10 And I drank two half-handles with the navvy. **1949** SARGESON *I Saw in My Dream* (1974) 191 You have the handle, Dave, he said. We got the one. Not more. The half-handle go better into the overcoat pocket, eh? **1965** SARGESON *Memoirs of Peon* 250 I had one forenoon invested in a half-handle of beer as an excuse for establishing myself in a public bar.

half a shake. [An elaboration of *a shake* a moment.] (Wait) a moment.

1909 THOMPSON *Ballads About Business* 43 I'll show you where they're wrong in half a shake. **1933** SCANLAN *Tides of Youth* 117 Half a shake—any more beer? **1953** 14-16 M A3 Thames DHS 15 Half a shake [M11]

halfback. *Rugby Union.* Also *ellipt.* **half.** [OED *half-* II a 1906.] The traditional and usu. term in New Zealand and elsewhere for British *scrum half*, in modern use the player behind the scrum forming the link between the forwards and the backs.

[*Note*] The early quots. refer to the time when teams played a full-back, three (centre-)three-quarters, and three halfbacks (so called) operating in the area behind the forwards.

1890 *NZ Observer* 2 Aug. 11 'Hooker' Conway played a really fine half-back game. *Ibid.* 13 Sept. 11 The half-backs were not up to much, C. Bayly being the best of the trio. **1902** [see FIVE EIGHTH 1]. **1904** *NZ Observer* 14 May 10 Mays was solid all through as half. **1906** GALLAHER & STEAD *Compl. Rugby Footballer* 71 The half-back as we know him in New Zealand is the donkey man of the team. **1913** *NZ Observer* 5 July 10 There are not many better halves in the competition than Ross. **1966** CLARKE & BOOTH *The Boot* 170 If the real test of a halfback is ability to play well behind a beaten pack, then..Briscoe would be among the first chosen. **1991** KNIGHT *They Led the All Blacks* 36 The..halfback..suffered especially from rulings against him for crooked scrum feeds.

half-bred, *a.* and *n.*

A. *adj.*

1. *rare.* Of people, HALF-CASTE a.

1844 TUCKETT *Diary* 22 May in Hocken *Contributions* (1898) 223 Since Dr. — visited this settlement, one of the residents, Mr. —, an educated man, has opened a school for half-bred or any other children.

2. *Farming.* **a.** [AND 1819.] Of a sheep, one resulting from a cross between two breeds, usu. between merino and another breed.

1876 PEACHE *Journal* in Gray *Quiet with Hills* (1970) 50 The half-bred ewes are looking well. **1894** *Otago Daily Times* (Dunedin) 17 Mar. in Evans *Waikaka Saga* (1962) 113 200 six and eight-tooth halfbred ewes at 10s. **1902** *Settler's Handbook NZ* 94 The first cross, or, as it is called, the half-bred sheep, has been found so suitable to the country that several attempts have been made to perpetuate or form a breed of pure half-breds, and with some success. **1915** [see B below]. **1933** *Press* (Christchurch) (Acland Gloss.) 21 Oct. 15 *Halfbred sheep.*—Originally only applied to a sheep by a longwool ram from a merino ewe, but now loosely applied to the type. Corriedale sheep were originally called *inbred h[alf]b[red].* Now *in-bred h[alf]b[red]* flocks are those which reintroduce merino or longwool blood, while the Corriedale flocks can only introduce Corriedale blood. **1938** BURDON *High Country* 110 Aug. 1869 Best wethers 11/- Sept. 23 2000 halfbred Romneys, mixed ages and sexes, 7/3. **1951** CRESSWELL *Canterbury Tales* 57 Crossed by the Leicester or Lincoln, the half-bred [merino] progeny was disappointing in size and fattening quality.

b. As **half-bred wool**, see quot.

1982 *Agric. Gloss.* (MAF) 55 *Halfbred wool:* Type of wool growth by either Corriedale, New Zealand Halfbred, or similar sheep containing between a quarter and three-quarters Merino blood.

B. *n. Farming.* A half-bred sheep.

1847 22 Oct. in Wakefield *Handbook NZ* (1848) 249 You must get a very considerable increase of price..for fine wool [from pure Merinos], to compensate for..want of the more prolific and hardy constitution of the half-bred. **1876** PEACHE *Journal* in Gray *Quiet with Hills* (1970) 52 We cut and tailed the lambs from..half-breds. **1892** SWANTON *Notes on NZ* 90 The class of sheep usually carried [on a sheep-farm] is what is called the 'half bred', a cross between a Merino ewe and a Leicester ram. **1915** MACDONALD *NZ Sheepfarming* 50 The half-bred is produced by the above crosses, and by placing the same kind of ram again to the half-bred ewes the cross-bred, so much prized for mutton-cum-wool, is obtained. **1922** PERRY *Sheep Farming* 38 The [Leicester] rams are extensively used..for mating with the Merino, for the production of the half-bred. **1930** ACLAND *Early Canterbury Runs* 7 Corriedales and Half-breds have displaced the Merinos except on the lightest and highest country. **1949** NEWTON *High Country Days* 195 Half-bred: A sheep which originates from a Merino–Leicester, Merino–Lincoln or Merino–Romney cross. They are used extensively in the high country and drier down country districts of the South Island. **1966** *Encycl. NZ* III. 236 The breed [*sc.* Lincoln] was used extensively for crossing with the merino to produce successive top-cross generations, colonial half-bred (wool 50s count), three-quarter bred (wool 46s), and crossbred (wool 40s to 44s count). **1980** MCLEOD *Down from Tussock Ranges* 219 For the uninitiated, the cross between a merino and a longwool sheep, usually Lincoln, Leicester or Romney, is called a half-bred.

halfbreed.

1. Of sheep, HALF-BRED B.

1878 CHUDLEIGH *Diary* 11 June (1950) 269 Sheep drafting, 4000, consisting of pure Leicester, pure Shropshire downs and halfbreeds of both sorts. **1922** PERRY *Sheep Farming* 33 Half Breeds..Other Breeds..Cross Breeds.

2. Of people, HALF-CASTE a.

1882 HAY *Brighter Britain* II. 135 Half-breeds, or Anglo-Maori men and women, form no inconsiderable section of the native community.

half-caste. Also **half-cast.** [Spec. use of *half-caste* (one) of mixed race.] Often *derog.*, implying that the race of one parent is superior to that of the other. See also HALF-BRED, *half-Maori* (MAORI A 7). **a.** One of mixed parentage, Maori and non-Maori; *spec.* having one parent a full Maori and the other a non-Maori.

1819 MARSDEN *Lett. & Jrnls.* (1932) 232 Whether the half-caste children will take to the woods remains to be ascertained. **1840** MATHEW *Journal* 28 Mar. in *Founding of NZ* (1940) 100 [The children are] much lighter in colour than I should have thought; it is probable..that those I have seen are half-caste. **1851** SHORTLAND *S. Dist. NZ* 77 The number of half-cast children is, as yet, very trifling; probably little more than three hundred. **1864** HEALE 15 Feb. in Wilson *Titi Heritage* (1979) 138 At Port Adventure there is a small settlement, now chiefly peopled by half-castes. **1879** HINGSTON *Australian Abroad* 367 It is only necessary to look at these half-castes in New Zealand to believe in the virtue and value of mixing blood—'miscegenation'. **1898** HOCKEN *Contributions* 165 With provisions and compass he followed the undoubted tracks of the [lost] party, those of Dr. Schmidt, a Maori boy, and a half-caste boy. **1905** BAUCKE *White Man Treads* 107 The other day a half-caste woman friend of Oparure..begged me..to lay before the public..the following distressing facts. **1913** *NZ Observer* 25 Jan. 3 Mr Thorpe was stopped by an attendant with the remark 'No Maoris or half-castes allowed here'. **1916** MANSFIELD *Journal* 12 Mar. (1954) 107 And further along [Tinakori Road] there lived an endless family of halfcastes who appeared to have planted their garden with empty jam tins and old sauce-pans and black iron kettles without lids. **1927** DONNE *Maori Past & Present* 270 Some of the Anglo-Maori half-castes are no more superstitious than is the average white man. **1943** MARSH *Colour Scheme* 230 Dikon fancied that a struggle was at work in the half-caste, between his European and his native impulses. **1959** SHADBOLT *New Zealanders* (1986) 16 I should have to share a tiny schoolroom..with some thirty other Maori, half-caste, and pakeha children. **1989** *Dominion* (Wellington) 14 Mar. 2 Describing himself as a half-caste, Judge Jurie said that there were many times he was tempted to publicly reject allegations of Maori bias.

b. *transf.* Of an English or Maori word the form of which has been affected by the other language.

1868 TAYLOR *Past & Present NZ* 134 *Rauna katoa* is a half-caste word, the English word round being here Maorified, and thus makes a more emphatic expression than any of their own.

half-g, half-gallon, half-handle: see HALF- 3.

half-hitch. [Poss. f. an alteration of *half-inch* rhyming slang for 'pinch' to steal; or poss. rhyming slang for 'snitch' to steal.] To steal.

1978 TUCKER *Thoroughbreds Are My Life* 35 There was no suggestion that John had deliberately half-hitched a bottle with no intention of replacing it.

halfpenny short of a shilling: see SHILLING 1 a.

half-pie, *a.* and *adv.*

A. *adj.* Also occas. **half-pai**, **half-pi**. [Poss. f. Maori *pai* good (cf. PIE ON).] Half-and-half; neither one thing nor the other; imperfect; incomplete or incompletely realized; unsatisfactory.

1911 *Maoriland Worker* 8 Dec. 13 The voting was of no 'half-pie' order, 205 in favour of the proposal, and 22 votes against. **c1926** THE MIXER *Transport Workers' Song Book* 11 I'd tell them what I think o'them... There's no half-pie about this kid. **1938** FINLAYSON *Brown Man's Burden* (1973) 67 They came to the settlement—just a few straggling houses and a half-pie store and a packing-shed hall. **1940** *Tararua Tramper* Feb. 6 Alarm 2.30 a.m., eventually left 7.50 on a half-pai day. **1949** WADMAN *Life Sentence* 8 New Zealanders who go home on scholarships and come back half-pi Englishmen. **1959** SLATTER *Gun in My Hand* 147 Got a half-pie farm out the north road. Doin well. **1963** PEARSON *Coal Flat* 71 I don't trust these half-pie good times. They can't last. **1974** HILLIARD *Maori Woman* 109 'Whereabouts do you live?' 'In a bed-sitter half-pie flat sort of thing.' **1989** DUDER *Alex in Winter* 120 His half-pie beard is surprisingly soft against my forehead. **1991** *Dominion Sunday Times* (Wellington) 17 Nov. 10 Should we not..concern ourselves with a third group—those of us who share values from several cultures, those who even use complex expressions like 'half-pai' and speak an evolving English language laced with Maori and Island words?

B. *adv.* In some way; partly; half-heartedly.

1949 *Dominion* (Wellington) Sept. 29 The gate was half-pie open. **1979** *Listener* 23 June 13 He never said much—even now he's half-pie invisible round town—but as a captain he led by example. **1982** NEWBOLD *Big Huey* 179 I'd half-pie suspected Jock because he'd been hanging around me a bit lately. **1990** *Listener* 6 Aug. 25 I could have gone to Invercargill but you'd have to get half-pie dressed up all the time.

half-time. [Spec. use of *half-time* the rest period during a game in some team sports.] Formerly, the refreshment break or interval between the 'shorts' and the feature film or between two feature films at the cinema.

1982 FRAME *To the Is-land* (1984) 108 We went to every film, watching through the news, the cartoon, the Pete Smith Novelties, the James Fitzpatrick travel talks, the serial, and, after halftime or interval, the 'big picture'. **1985** FRAME *Envoy from Mirror City* 25 During the interval [of the film-show] (which I, rugby-bred, knew as 'half-time'), Nigel, instead of rushing out to the foyer to smoke, bought ice creams. **1991** KEITH *Lovely Day Tomorrow* 67 Some theatre chains published their own magazines..and sold them along with the rock hard balls of ice cream at half time.

haliotis /ˌhæliˈʌutəs/. [f. the generic name *Haliotis* an adaptation of the Greek stems αλι- sea + ὠτ- the ear; OED 1752.] PAUA, *sea-ear* (SEA 1 b).

1851 WARD *Journal* 22 June (1951) 197 We tried the haliotis this evening boiled. **1904** TREGEAR *Maori Race* 92 The carved work of the gables was inlaid with haliotis (*paua*) shell. **1938** MAKERETI *The Old Time Maori* (1986) 234 When the strip of haliotis shell was cut to line a hook, the back had to be left in its original humpy state. **1952** LYON *Faring South* 77 The rocks leading to Houghton Bay and Terawhiti were a hunting ground for haliotis, or paua shellfish.

Hall's totara: see TOTARA *n.*¹ 2 (2).

hammer, *n.*¹ [Abbrev. of *hammer and tack* rhyming slang for 'back': AND 1942.] In the phr. **to have** (someone) **on** (one's) **hammer**, to have (someone) on (one's) back, to be under pressure from another.

1974 MORRIESON *Predicament* (1981) 197 This is just too hot to handle. I've got Huggins on my hammer and God knows what. **1984** WILSON *S. Pacific Street* 66 Well, you do get on my hammer a bit, Debby, the way you chase after anyone in long pants. **1989** RICHARDS *Pioneer's Life* 89 In a few days I was right 'on his hammer' [*i.e.* keeping up with his work pace].

hammer, *n.*² Drug users. [Poss. an abbrev. of *hammer and tack* rhyming slang for 'smack' heroin.] Heroin.

1982 NEWBOLD *Big Huey* 217 Craig..was doing eight for importing coke and hammer. *Ibid.* 249 Hammer (n) Heroin. Dates from mid 1970s, and coincides with the involvement of the criminal element in the drug trade. Cf. hammer-and-tack rhyming slang on 'smack'.

hammer and tack. [A variation on the black-smithing *hammer and tongs*.] In the phr. **to go hammer and tack**, to quarrel violently or noisily.

1960 HILLIARD *Maori Girl* 180 They were going hammer and tack all day.

hammerhead shark: see SHARK 2 (10).

Hancock's Half Hour. [Transf. use of the title *Hancock's Half Hour*, a popular BBC radio comedy programme.] A former name for the parliamentary adjournment debate. See quot. 1974.

1966 *Dominion* (Wellington) 15 June 7 Opening the first adjournment debate of the session, Mr. Kirk said the debate had become known to 'our lords and masters in the Press Gallery as Hancock's Half Hour'. **1974** MULDOON *Rise & Fall of a Young Turk* 66 In the House at this time [c1964] what was known as Hancock's Half Hour, after the BBC comedy programme, was instituted. At 10 pm on Tuesdays and Thursdays an Opposition member was entitled to move the adjournment of the House to launch an attack on any aspect of Government administration. Then followed five-minute speeches alternately from each side until the House rose at 10.30. *Ibid.* 67 The 'Hancocks' debates were abolished by mutual agreement.

hand, *n.*¹ In sense 'employee', often with a modifier, see: ALL HANDS AND THE COOK, *bush hand* (BUSH C 3 a), OLD HAND 2, *shed hand* (SHED *n.*¹ 2 e), *station hand* (STATION 5).

hand, *n.*²

1. a. As **in hand** *farming*, of a mob of sheep, under the control of a shepherd. See quot. 1933.

1930 ACLAND *Early Canterbury Runs* 5 Until wire fences were introduced about 1862, all sheep on the plains were kept more or less in hand. The practice was for a shepherd to go round the boundary once or twice a day. **1933** *Press* (Christchurch) (Acland Gloss.) 28 Oct. 17 *Hand, in, about.*—Sheep are *in h[and]* when you have them in a mob near you. A dog working close to you is working *about h[and]*. **1938** BURDON *High Country* 108 Difficulties arose..when a large mob was in hand and a steep, narrow gully had to be crossed; then there was always the danger of a 'smother'. **1953** STRONACH *Musterer on Molesworth* 12 Jack's instructions were short: 'You go down here. If you see any sheep, take them 'in hand, and down to the camp.' I didn't even know what 'in hand' meant. **1970** MCLEOD *Glorious Morning* 254 *In hand*: When sheep—usually a small number—are close to the musterer and under his firm control instead of stringing away ahead. Some musterers tend to get sheep in hand and slow the muster down.

b. As **about hand**, of a dog, at hand.

1933 [see a above]. **1949** NEWTON *High Country Days* 195 These [heading dogs]..are used for 'heading' and also for any quiet and careful work about hand, i.e., at close quarters.

2. As **in the hand**, said in reply to a request, query, etc., easily done, 'no trouble at all'.

c1977 p.c. Jane Godfrey (Wellington) 1982. In the Tawa–Porirua area of Wellington at least, the expression among teenagers (1977–82) *(a) piss in the hand* means with no trouble at all, no sweat. It is also conveyed by gestures, holding out the palm and tapping the centre of it with the forefinger of the other hand. **1980** LELAND *Kiwi-Yankee Dict.* 55 *in the hand*: 'You want me to talk that sheila into going to the party with us?' It's in the hand (easy). Just watch me.'

3. *Shearing.* Used *attrib.* in special Comb. **hand-piece,** [AND 1912], the hand-held clipping attachment of a shearing machine; **hand-shearing** *vbl. n.*, sheep-shearing using manually operated blade shears as distinct from machine shears; **hand-shears,** *blades* (BLADE *n.*¹ 1 a).

1915 MACDONALD *NZ Sheepfarming* xv [Advt] Cooper's Little Wonder Shearing Machine..The Shearing Attachments comprise..two *Latest Model Cooper Handpieces*... Cooper Combs and Cutters will fit any make of handpiece. **c1927** SMITH *Sheep & Wool Industry* 69 The handpiece used to get so hot as to blister the shearers' hands. **1949** SARGESON *I Saw in My Dream* (1974) 107 And as he got close [to the woolshed] he could hear the..whirring of the hand-pieces. **1955** BOWEN *Wool Away* 4 One hears some shearers called butchers. In fact it is not the shearer that does the butchering, it is the comb on his handpiece. **1960** [see HOT BOX]. **1973** FERNANDEZ *Tussock Fever* 3 On the board the noise changed. There was the high whirr of the shearing hand-pieces. **1986** IHIMAERA *Matriarch* 107 The drone of handpieces. The bustle of women on the board. **1936** BELSHAW et al. *Agric. Organiz. NZ* 434 **Hand-shearing** is still practised on many farms. **1986** RICHARDS *Off the Sheep's Back* 65 It had been built for hand or blade shearing, so was fairly cramped when converted to a three-stand machine shearing shed. **1933** *Press* (Christchurch) (Acland Gloss.) 28 Oct. 17 *Hand shears.* Sheep shears (as distinguished from machinery). Often called *blades*. **1987** OGONOWSKA-COATES *Boards, Blades & Barebellies* 96 *Hand shears*. Sheep shears, also called blades. **1989** *NZ Eng. Newsletter* III. 25 *handshears*: These are the tool of the blade shearer and usually called 'blades'. Also known as 'sheep shears', 'shears', 'tongs', 'swords', 'b-bows', 'bows', 'daggers', and 'Jingling Johnnies'.

hand, *v.* Usu. in the phr. **don't hand me that (stuff),** indicating disbelief, 'don't ask (me) to believe that!'

1951 *Landfall 17* 21 I tell him not to hand me that kind of stuff but he says there's no bull, it's fair dinkum.

handle.

1. [AND 1943, chiefly S. Austral. and N. Territory.] A glass beer mug (with a handle) formerly holding a reputed pint (568 ml), or (by synecdoche) its contents. See also *half-handle* (HALF- 3 b).

1909 *Truth* 29 May 7 What was 'Arry's lotion? Did he have 'a handle' of beer every time, or just a drop o' Scotch? **1913** MANSFIELD *Stories* (1984) 132 Behind the [bar] counter a big girl with red hair pulled the beer handles and cheeked the men. **1937** *Truth* 20 Oct. 22 Ale is not commonly served in 'pint' containers in this country, but in what is better known as a handle. **1941** [see MAIN CENTRE]. **1953** BAXTER in *Here & Now* Sept. 27 As I think in happy silence of the horrors I've escaped how I all but became R.C. how I was nearly raped by a sodomite gorilla once upon the bar I lean and drink another handle to the man I might have been. **1978** TUCKER *Thoroughbreds Are My Life* 16 He was told to produce a beer handle, which he did. **1980** LELAND *Kiwi-Yankee Dict.* 50 *handle*: Beer (or other beverage) served in a pint or half pint glass that has a mug style handle. **1990** *Dominion* (Wellington) 11 Nov. 4 Henman's revenge took the form of a 'king hit' on the forehead with a glass beer handle.

2. *Obs.* Usu. *pl.* The shafts of a horse-drawn vehicle.

c1900–20 in Henderson *Friends In Chains* (1961) 186 Handles: Slang term for waggon or other shafts. **1966** TURNER *Eng. Lang. Austral. & NZ* 142 A coach driver on the West Coast..who refers to the shafts of the coach as the *handles* on the principle that those words known even to a new chum require some disguise.

handy dog. *Farming.* A non-specialist or general-purpose working dog.

1933 *Press* (Christchurch) (Acland Gloss.) 25 Nov. 15 Some dogs will both h[ea]d and h[un]taway and are called *handy d[og]s*. They are not generally high-class heading dogs but very useful about hand and sometimes very useful mustering dogs. **1947** NEWTON *Wayleggo* 13 Occasionally one sees dogs that will both head and hunt equally well. They are known as handy dogs. **1951** McLEOD *NZ High Country* 46 Wait, the most wonderful dog I ever saw, a true 'handy' dog. He would bring sheep out of any place where dog or sheep could go. **1966** *Encycl. NZ* I. 493 *Handy Dog*: A dog which can do both heading and huntaway work. This 'all-round worker' is probably the most useful of all sheep dogs. **1982** *Agric. Gloss.* (MAF) 24 *Handy dog*: General-purpose dog that will head, hunt, back, and perform all the duties required in sheep yards and woolsheds.

hane, var. HANI.

hang, *v.*

1. In the phr. **to hang one on** (someone), to strike with the fist.

1970 SLATTER *On the Ball* 135 There is some discussion about hanging one on each other but the roar of the crowd diverts their attention to a Welsh forward.

2. As **hang out. a.** To be available, to exist.

c1926 THE MIXER *Transport Workers' Song Book* 69 When there is a job hanging out; If you ask him why he ain't he working, he's got the rheumatics and gout.

b. [See OED *hang v.* 26 d; AND 1890.] To last out, to hold out.

1944 FULLARTON *Troop Target* 87 I've been pretty crook for the last hour. But I wanted to hang out till we saw a house. **1953** Jan. Wellington. A typist says: 'I hope his ulcer hangs out, I'd hate to see him retire.' (Ed.)

c. *Drug users.* To crave for, to 'have one's tongue hanging out' for.

1982 NEWBOLD *Big Huey* 14 As the price of normally cheap local gear inflated, junkies began hanging out for their normal supplies. **1984** BEATON *Outside In* 64 Ginny *pours*... Come on, Ma. ... You know you're hanging out for a drop [of liquor]. *Ibid.* 110 *Hanging-out*: longing (for something). **1986** *Evening Post* (Wellington) 5 Apr. 19 This is how the methadone programme works. It..holds addicts, depending on their dosages, for about 24 hours, before they start hanging out. *Ibid.* Peter's early-days addiction routine started with a 'ping' in the morning and a cup of coffee... The time of the day he started 'hanging out' depended on a number of factors.

Hence **hanging out** *vbl. n.*, suffering from drug withdrawal or craving.

1986 *Evening Post* (Wellington) 5 Apr. 19 'Hanging out' means feeling like an old man who has been worked over with an electric cattle prod..going through hot and cold sweats, streaming eyes, nose runs.

hang, *n.* [Cf. OED *hang n.* 6 *(a)* hang of a 'an Austral. and N.Z. intensive phrase variously spelt'.] In mainly children's use, variations of **(a) hang of a,** (**hangava, hanguva; hangashin, hangashun, hangershun; heck (hack) of a, heckashin, heckashun**), euphemisms for *hell of a*; see also HELLISHING (f. *hellish*). With adverbial force, exceedingly; with adjectival, greatest, finest.

1941 BAKER *NZ Slang* 51 In constant use by our youngsters..hangava, hangashun. **1943** BENNETT *English in NZ* in *Amer. Speech* XVIII. 90 Equally meaningless.. are..the intensives *hanguva, hangershun*—modified forms of *helluva*. **1949** *Landfall 11* 145 Gosh, Dad's hangava crabby with you. **1950** SUTTON-SMITH *Our Street* 33 It's a hang of a wet day. **1955** BJ Cameron Collection (TS July) hangava (adv) Very. (Mainly children's slang). **1966** TURNER *Eng. Lang. Austral. & NZ* 159 Children are notable users of slang..and in these good old days [*sc.* 1930s] the most current included *hang of a, hangashun, hangashun* and *heckashun*, all intensives. **1978** GASKELL *All Part of the Game* 191 The more acceptable variations [of hellashin] were 'hangashin' and 'heckashin'. **1988** MCGILL *Dict. Kiwi Slang* 54 *hang of a/hanguva* intensive regarding something big or forceful; euphemistic version of 'helluva'; a fervent intensive favoured by juveniles; eg 'That was a hanguva good flick, eh?'

hangashin, hangashun: see HANG.

hangehange. Also **angeange, angi angi, hange hange.** [Ma. /ˈhaŋehaŋe/: Williams 34 *Hangehange* (ii)..*1.* Geniostoma [sp.].] *Geniostoma rupestre* (formerly *ligustrifolium*) (fam. Loganiaceae), a small native forest shrub. See also *pigwood* (PIG *n.*¹ 4), PRIVET.

[**1820** LEE & KENDALL *NZ Gram. & Vocab.* 134 A´ngi; Name of a certain tree.] **1853** HOOKER *II Flora Novae-Zelandiae I Flowering Plants* 177 *Geniostoma ligustrifolium*... 'Hange Hange'. **1867** HOOKER *Handbook* 764 Hange-hange... *Geniostoma ligustrifolium*. **1882** POTTS *Out in Open* 16 Women are bringing water in calabashes (taha), or boys riding in horses laden with fodder, consisting chiefly of leaves and boughs of the hange-hange. **1906** CHEESEMAN *Manual NZ Flora* 444 G[eniostoma] ligustrifolium... A perfectly glabrous much-branched shrub 4–12 ft. high. Hangehange. **1956** DAVIES *NZ Native Plant Studies* 148 *Geniostoma ligustrifolium* (Loganiaceae—strychnine family). Hangehange—N.Z. Privet. **1961** MARTIN *Flora NZ* 228 Amongst the shrubs that do not grow naturally in the southern part of the South Island we may note..the Hange-hange. **1978** MOORE & IRWIN *Oxford Book NZ Plants* 118 *Geniostoma ligustrifolium, hangehange*. A common, lightly branched shrub of lowland forest margins and track-sides in the North Island. **1988** DAWSON *Forest Vines to Snow Tussocks* 103 Other common shrubs are the thin-leaved hangehange (*Geniostoma rupestre*), kanono.

hangi /ˈhaŋi/, /ˈhaɲi/, /ˈhæŋi/. Also **angi, haangi, hanghi, hoangi, shangi** (early northern). [Ma. /ˈhaːŋi/: Williams 34 *Hāngī*... earth oven... *2.* Contents of the oven.]

1. A Maori earth oven consisting of a hole dug in the ground with the bottom lined with heated stones on which the raw food, suitably wrapped, is placed to be cooked by retained heat and steam when the hole is covered; the contents of such an oven; a communal meal cooked in an earth oven. See also COPPER MAORI 1; EARTH OVEN, KOHUA a, KOPA, MAORI OVEN 1, *native oven* (NATIVE B 3 a), UMU.

[**1820** LEE & KENDALL *NZ Gram. & Vocab.* 134 A´ngi; Name of a certain tree; a native oven.] **1824** KING 5 Aug. in Elder *Marsden's Lieutenants* (1934) 257 During the night a young chief dreamt he had killed all the people in one house and made the fire and cooked them in the shangi or oven. **1828** WILLIAMS *Early Jrnls.* 31 May (1961) 132 The *hangis* (ovens) were kept constantly supplied. **1838** angi maori [see COPPER MAORI 1 b]. **1843** SELWYN in *NZ Part II* (Church in the Colonies VII) 30 Oct. (1845) 32 Steam hanghis, or native ovens, always in readiness. **1873** ST JOHN *Pakeha Rambles* in Taylor *Early Travellers* (1959) 554 Good, nay delicious, as the *kora* is when boiled, or steamed in a *hangi* au naturel. **1881** CAMPBELL *Poenamo* 107 The steam was just arising from their hangis as these were being uncovered, and we were all soon served, each with a little freshly-plaited flax-leaf basket filled with most deliciously cooked kumeras, potatoes and peppies. **1894** *TrNZI* XXVI. 579 When the bodies placed in the *hangis* were cooked they were calabashed, and formally handed over to the Ngatitoa as payment for the children of Te Rauparaha. **1905** BAUCKE *White Man Treads* 103 Fine judgement, quick action, and having everything to hand, are necessary to be an accomplished haangi-builder. *Ibid.* 253 It was an appetising display..a mound of potatoes, haangi steamed. **1920** *Quick March* 10 June 38 The best camp oven..is the haangi, or earth oven of the Maoris. **1938** FINLAYSON *Brown Man's Burden* (1973) 10 From afar they could see rising smoke at the back of the whare manuhiri, or guest house, where haangi fires were being kindled. **1949** *Here & Now* Oct. 13 [Heading] Hangis and Hash-houses. Maori hangis are classed as 'eating-houses' in the new eating-house regulations. **1976** MORRIESON *Pallet on Floor* 52 They cooked pork and mutton *hangi-style*. **1986** *Contact* (Wellington) 14 Nov. 4 I heard about a hangi which was organised..last weekend..First one person climbing out of the hangi fell on the cinders..and had to be taken to hospital. **1991** *National Bus. Rev.* 21 May 10 Hangi cooking at the hotel is done by the Ngawha steam box method.

2. Food cooked in a hangi; a communal meal of such food; an occasion or party at which hangi food is served.

1908 *Souvenir All Nations Fair* 11 The hangi, or koopa maori..An hour is long enough for a moderate sized hangi..An uncooked hangi is considered by the Maori as a disgrace, a..sign of..disaster... It is not too much to hope that some day Hangi parties will become fashionable. **1926** Devanny *Butcher Shop* (1981) 61 They'll be having a hangi in the evening. **1948** *Our Own Country* 52 Here [on the Ruatoki *marae*] women organize monthly 'bring and buys' or *hangi* dinners at half-a-crown to collect parcels for Ruatoki boys overseas. **1963** Hilliard *Piece of Land* 9 It's a long time since I had a *hangi* chicken. **1979** Baxter *Collected Poems* 631 hangi *earth oven, or, by common usage, a feast*. **1986** *Victoria Univ. Weekly Staff Circular* 25 July A haangi is being held at the Quad Centre on Thursday 31st July at 12.00 noon. All tickets will be pre-sold at $5.00 each. **1991** *Evening Post* (Wellington) 3 Sept. 4 We do not lose our Maoriness by driving a Japanese car, smoking cigarettes made by a Pakeha New Zealander..heating up a frozen hangi in a microwave..made in Taiwan.

hanging bailey. [From William Alfred *Bailey*, hanged in 1934 for murder.] A children's game.

1981 Sutton-Smith *Hist. Children's Play* 259 Civilization is saved, for example, when instead of trying to torture a classmate a child says, 'Guess what happened to Bailey?' 'What?' 'This,' and the child pulls out the fold in a piece of paper on which Bailey has been drawn with his neck in a noose. When the fold is pulled out his neck suddenly appears as stretched several inches in length—a nice little game known as Hanging Bailey.

hangman. [A revival of a Brit. or fig. use of *hangman*, an archaic term of reprobation often used playfully: see OED 1 b.] A devil-may-care person; *hard case* (hard *a.* 1 a (a) (i)).

1944 *NZEF Times* 27 Mar. 7 A real hangman. That's what he was, I said. A real trouble-maker, a bad type. **1946** Webber *Johnny Enzed in Italy* 44 I've had you and your mob of hangmen around here. **1951** Young in *Listener Short Stories* (1978) 21 Frank lost his mellowness after a few drinks and became a terrible hangman. **1973** Leeming in *Islands* VI. 360 This would be a Barry Crump stereotype..Hangman of the country pubs, boxer.

hani. Also **hane**; early **hauni, hennee**. [Ma. /'hani/: Williams 34 *Hani* (i) a. A carved wooden weapon, used mainly by chiefs.] A carved wooden weapon having one end in the form of a halberd-like blade.

[**1817** Nicholas *Voyage NZ* II. 331 Halbert. Hennee **1820** Lee & Kendall *NZ Gram. & Vocab.* 152 Háne, *s.* A war instrument so called.] **1830** Craik *New Zealanders* 266 Lastly, they often carry an instrument somewhat like a sergeant's halberd... This they call a Hennee. **1838** Polack *NZ* I. 158 Three of the chiefs stood up erect in the canoe, brandishing a *háni* spear, or the tomahawk. **1840** Best *Journal* 29 Oct. (1966) 250 I bought a quantity of fishing hooks made of the Paua shell a mat and a Hauni. **1869** *TrNZI* I. (rev. edn.) 354 They carved handsome staves (*Hani* and *Taiaha*), out of the hard variegated wood of the *Ake*. **1890** Colenso *Treaty of Waitangi* 10 Here and there a *hani* (or *taiaha*, a chief's staff of rank, &c.) was seen erected, adorned with the long flowing white hair of the tails of the New Zealand dog and crimson cloth and red feathers. **1904** Tregear *Maori Race* 312 The quarter-staff or sword (*taiaha* or *hani*) was made of heavy hard wood.

happy, *a.* In various phrases of comparison: **(as) happy as a sick eel on a sand spit**, very unhappy; **(as) happy as a pig in shit**, very happy; **(as) happy as a flea at a dog show**, very happy; **(as) happy as Larry**, see Larry *n.*[1]

1947–48 Beattie *Pioneer Recolls.* (1956) 58 And so the seekers after 'Duncan' at length turned their faces homeward, looking about as happy as a sick eel on a sand spit. **1982** Shadbolt *Once on Chunuk Bair* (1990) 30 You ought to be as happy as a pig in shit up here. No other bugger's been this high. **1991** *Dominion* (Wellington) 9 Nov. 13 The troops mustered two dozen cans of Fosters, the chief (engineer) and I gave him [*sc.* a reporter] the rum we've been saving... He's as happy as a flea at a dog show.

hapu /'hapu/. Also **harpu**. [Ma. /ha'pu:/: Williams 36 *Hapū 3*. n. Section of a large tribe, clan.] A sub-tribe or extended family group; a clan. Cf. whanau.

1843 Shortland *Letter* 15 Aug. in Shortland *Traditions & Superstitions* (1856) 305 At the present day, these *Waka* are divided into many distinct *Iwi*; each of which is subdivided again into *Hapu*, or smaller communities. **1857** Hursthouse *NZ* I. 162 The 70,000 semi-civilised natives now in New Zealand are divided into some dozen chief tribes, and numerous sub-tribes and 'harpu'. **1861** *Memo. by Ministers on Gov. Grey's Proposed Institutions for Native Race* 1 Nov. in Rutherford *Sel. Documents* (1949) 112e The jurisdiction of the runanga should..be co-extensive with the lands of the hapu or hapus of which it consists. **1873** Tinne *Wonderland of Antipodes* 68 I was introduced as 'the most recent addition to the "hapu", or social circle of Kaihu Valley'. **1882** Potts *Out in Open* 21 The space in front of Hikurangi was crowded with an expectant audience seated in due order according to their respective hapus. **1904** *NZ Illustr. Mag.* Sept. 449 The evening kai was finished but the hapu sat on. **1920** *Quick March* 10 Jan. 13 The lonely little settlement of the Maori sheep-farming hapu was more than two thousand feet above the sea. **1930** *Na To Hoa Aroha* (1987) II. 30 And all this within the tribal or hapu limits, with an appeal to tribal sentiment and co-operation. **1949** [see tribe]. **1958, 1979** [see iwi a].

hapua. [Ma. /'ha:pua/: Williams 36 *Hāpua 2*. n. Pool, lagoon.] In mainly early South Island use, a lagoon.

1844 16 Jan. in Shortland *S. Dist. NZ* (1851) 219 Our path lay along a pebble ridge, with the sea on one side, and the lake Waihao on the other. This 'hapua', as all similar pieces of water are called, has no outlet to the sea except at times of floods... After leaving Waihao, which was nearly three miles long, we passed several small 'hapua' similar to it. **1906** Roberts in *Hist. N. Otago from 1853* (1937) 9 Both [flax and raupo]..grew plentifully round the Lagoon, or hapua, as the Maoris called it, which then contained nice clear water. **1945** Beattie *Maori Place-names Canterbury* 45 Waitarakao, a large 'hapua' or lagoon or sheet of water.

hapuka, var. hapuku.

hapuku /hʌ'pʊkə/, /hʌ'bʊkə/, /'hapʊkə/.
1. Commonly **hapuka**, and with much variety in the transliterations of the apparent Ma. variants (a) *hāpuku*; and (b) (mainly in early writings) *whāpuku*, wh- apparently representing a Ma. realization /w/ rather than /ɸ/: (a) **abouka, abouke, abuka, apuko; habooka, habouka, habuka, hahpuka, harboka, harbouker, horbocker, horpocker;** (b) **wabooka; wahpuka, wapuka, wapuku, whahpuka, whapuka, whapuku**. Spellings illustrate anglicized pronunciations of Maori variants with initial /h/, and /w/ (and poss. a zero initial consonant). Stress-patterns vary between the Maori (stress on initial syllable), and English (stress on second, or penult. syllable). *pl.* often with -s. [Ma. /'ha:puku/, /'fa:puku/: Williams 36 *Hāpuku, 1*... the groper... [also] *whāpuku, kapua, moeone*.] *Polyprion oxygeneios* (formerly *P. prognathus* and *Oligorus gigas*) (fam. Percichthyidae), a large fish of coastal and offshore reefs, a fine and valuable food fish. See also *New Zealand cod* (cod 2 (5)), *rock cod* (cod 2 (8) b), *codfish* (cod 1), groper.

[*Note*] Central and southern New Zealand usage has preferred *groper* to *hapuku*.

1820 Wapúku [see cod 1 a]. **1838** Polack *NZ* I. 322 Some deep banks lie off the east coast, on which the *kanai*, or mullet, *wapuka*, or cod-fish..abound. **1840** Best *Journal* (1966) 230 Port Nicholson abounds with fish the principal are the Kawa Kawa, Snapper, Harbouker, Barracouta. **1842** Heaphy *NZ* 48 Amongst those esteemed the most, the *Abuka* ranks first. It is generally of great size, but the flesh is of much delicacy of flavour. *Ibid.* 124 The great apuko, the snapper, and the crayfish, are very numerous [at the Chatham Islands]. **1843** *NZ Jrnl.* IV. 263 The fish, which at Port Nicholson is known by the name of habooka, but which is called groper to the southward. **1843** 4 Nov. in Shortland *S. Dist. NZ* (1851) 131 In the offing is..a celebrated fishing ground for the 'hapuku' or rock cod, as it is called by the whalers. **1844** *Piraki Log* 22 Jan. (1911) 147 Simson fishing: caught 18 horbockers—gave me one... [Jan. 25] Men out fishing:... Horpocker. **1845** Deans in *Pioneers* (1964) 42 One [fish] called Abouka grows to a very large size, I have seen them nearly as large as myself; they are as rich as the salmon and very fine flavoured. **1857** Cooper *NZ Settlers' Guide* 30 Hapuka, pronounced Habooka or wabooka. **1862** Carter *From the Black Rocks* 21 There is good fishing for a kind of codfish named by the natives Wahpuka or Hahpuka. **1872** Hutton & Hector *Fishes NZ* 102 The first on the list of marketable fishes is the Hapuka or Whapuka of the Maoris.., or Habuka, as the name is generally pronounced by Europeans, who in the South apply the name Groper to the same fish. **1882** Hay *Brighter Britain* II. 151 In the bays and tidal rivers are..the whapuka or rock-cod..and many others. **1902** Drummond & Hutton *Nature in NZ* 71 The kahawai, hapuka (the groper of Dunedin)..and the flat fish are found all round the coast. **1910** *Truth* 26 Mar. 8 'How big's the hapuka? As large as a schnapper?'... 'Why the 'arpooker comes in to eat the schnapper. He's the biggest deep water fish we have.' **1938** Hyde *Nor Yrs. Condemn* 234 Starkie never struck trouble but once, when he asked [on the transTasman boat] for some *hapuka* [?hə'bʊgə] at breakfast. A very young English steward commanded: 'You cut out that language in front of the women.' 'I asked for *hapuka*. Hapuka. Just plain *hapuka*.' 'There you are,' yelled the steward. 'He said it again. Said it three times.'.. 'For Christ's sake,' said the chief steward wearily: 'Get him some fried fish.' 'Fish? Is that all it means? I thought, in front of the women.' **1946** *JPS* LV. 150 *Hāpuku* is not the cod..: groper is the common name, or hapuka corrupted to harbuka. **1953** *Landfall* 27 175 Hapuka hooked like a rock on his line, Trumpeter barked like a sea-dog for his bone, When Antonio fished. **1986** Paul *NZ Fishes* 82 Widely known throughout New Zealand as either hapuku (often pronounced hapuka) or groper, the former generally in the North Island, the latter in the South.

2. Special Comb. **hapuku steak**, a slice cut at right-angles to the backbone.

c**1939** Basham *Aunt Daisy's Book of Recipes* 19 Hapuka steaks au gratin..sprinkle steaks with lemon juice, dip in flour..place in..piedish. Pour..milk..salt and pepper. Cover. Bake... Remove lid, sprinkle with grated cheese and breadcrumbs, bake. **1989** *Edmonds Microwave Cook. Book* 96 Hapuka steaks on a bed of vegetables.

3. As **grandfather hapuku (hapuku's grandfather)** [prob. f. a translation of the Maori

HARAKEKE

name for the scorpionfish, *matuawhāpuku*, with *matua-* = *kaumātua* 'adult; elder': see Williams 195 *matua* 7], SCORPIONFISH (*Scorpaena cardinalis*).

1927 SPEIGHT et al. *Nat. Hist. Canterbury* 201 The Soldier-fish (*Scorpaena cruenta*) and the variegated horror with the droll name of Hapuka's Grandfather (*Helicolenus percoides*) are members of the same order. **1928** *NZJST* IX. 290 A specimen of the 'hapuka's grandfather' (*Scorpaena cruenta*) contained digested seaweed or kelp. **1965** GILLHAM *Naturalist in NZ* 215 My useful catch had increased by two equally brilliant grandfather hapuka—fish with a fearsome line of stinging spines along their crested back. **1967** grandfather hapuku [see SCORPIONFISH]. **1972** DOAK *Fishes* 24 Our scorpion-fish or 'grandfather hapuku', *Scorpaena cardinalis*, is one such species, with its bristling spines, fleshy appendages and non-hydrodynamic body. **1982** grandfather hapuku [see SCORPIONFISH]. **1991** BRADSTOCK *Fishing* 21 Red scorpionfish. Other names: grandfather hapuku, grandaddy groper, red rock cod, matuawhaapuku.

harakeke. Also with much variety of early form as **arakeke**, **arikeki**, **ha-ea-ra-ka-he**, **harakike**, **harakiki**, **heregege**, **herekeke**; mod. erron. **harekeke**. [Ma. /ˈharakeke/: Williams 36 *Harakeke*, n. *1*. The general name for New Zealand flax... *2*. Flax plant: prob. cognate with Proto-Polyn. **fara* pandanus: see also Williams 488 *whara* (i) *1*. 'possibly applied to any plant with ensiform leaves'.] FLAX 1 a.

1773 FORSTER *Resolution Jrnl.* 8 June (1982) II. 300 A kind of sowing through small holes with strings of the Flaxplant or *Arākèke*. **1804** *Collins Eng. Colony in NSW* 343 On being promised that so soon as they had taught our [Norfolk] women 'emou-ha-ea-ra-ka-he', (i.e.) to work the flax, they should be sent home again, they readily consented. **1841** BEST *Journal* 18 May (1966) 314 For want of a proper string tied my shoes with some Heregege or green flax. **1847** JOHNSON *Notes from Jrnl.* 2 Jan. in Taylor *Early Travellers* (1959) 145 *Arikeki*, or native flax, again appeared. **1851** REES in *Irish Univ. Press Series GBPP NZ* IX. 1779 28 The blossoms of the herekeke (phormium tenax) afford a refreshing nectar in summer, very serviceable to the traveller. **1858** *Richmond-Atkinson Papers* (1960) I. 409 A *harakeke* line was then tied to them to signify the bond of love and union... (The flax line represent[ed] the bond of union between the Queen and [the Maori] King and both subject to God.) **1868** LINDSAY *Contribs. NZ Bot.* 83 In the North Island, the Flax-plant is also known as 'Harakeke', or 'Herekiakia',—its usual name there. **c1875** MEREDITH *Adventuring in Maoriland* (1935) 89 The whole [of the temporary Maori shelter] was then covered by layers of *toi-toi*..tied in position with the ubiquitous *harakiki* (New Zealand flax). **1882** HAY *Brighter Britain* II. 204 The Harakeke..is the justly celebrated New Zealand flax. **1904** TREGEAR *Maori Race* 222 [Flax] was as a general name spoken of as *harakeke*, but to the accurate speaker and observer there were over fifty varieties. **1922** COWAN *NZ Wars* (1955) I. 42 Large quantities of the native *harakeke*, or flax, were cut and tied in bundles. **1926** CROOKES *Plant Life in Maoriland* 99 But, alas, from her came no godlike son, but only the Hara-keke, the flax plants, the stalwart dwellers of the swamp lands and the stiff sentinels of the river banks. **1946** *JPS* LV. 151 *Harakeke*, general name for Maori flax. **1978** [see FLAX I 2 (3)]. **1991** *Dominion* (Wellington) 16 Apr. 7 If viewers leave this show saying harakeke instead of flax, that will have been a good achievement.

harakike, harakiki, varr. HARAKEKE.

haramai. *Rare or obs. in non-Maori contexts.* Also with much variety of early form as **haremai**, **haromai**, **heromai**, **herremi**, **horomai**, **hurramy**. [Ma. /ˈharamai/: Williams 37 *Haramai 1. v.* Come, arrive... *3*. As a shout of welcome.] A shout of welcome.

[*Note*] Distinguish from *haere mai* (HAERE 1) a greeting, often confused with *haramai* by English speakers, and difficult to distinguish (as poss. in quots. 1823, 1829 below).

1769 in Hawkesworth *Voyages* (1785) III. 229 When they came near enough to be heard, they waved their hands, and called out 'Horomai.' These ceremonies we were told were certain signs of their friendly disposition. **1770** BANKS *Journal* Mar. (1962) II. 35 Come here [Northern] Horomai [Southern] Horomai [Otahite] Harromai **1807** SAVAGE *Some Acc. of NZ* 76 Hurramy..Come here. **1817** NICHOLAS *Voyage NZ* I. 127 The moment we were perceived, one of their women..repeatedly cried out..in a loud and shrill voice, *haromai, haromai, haromai*, (come hither,) the customary salutation of friendship and hospitality. **1820** MCCRAE *Journal* (1928) 20 We were received with the greatest hospitality by his people who waving their mats called out to us—'Haromai, Harom[a]i', their welcome to strangers which means literally 'Come to us' 'Come to us'. **1823** CRUISE *Journal* (1957) 214 *Heromai*, or 'Come hither', is the salutation of peace and friendship. Where this word is not pronounced on the approach of the stranger the feelings of the people are not favourable towards him. **1829** ATKINS *Narrative* 2 Mar. in McNab *Hist. Records* (1908) I. 689 A number of natives collected at the place of our landing, and received us with the *herremi*, or 'salutations of friendship' (the principal of these are their joining noses). **1861** *Otago Witness* (Dunedin) 23 Mar. 10 Most joyful day when the Maories shall cry In true Christian love 'Haremai!' 'Haremai!'

hard, *a.*

I. In senses of 'hardened, tough' in special collocations with **case, doer, shot, thing**, describing a person (occas. a thing or situation) unconventional but likeable or amusing. **1. a.** As **hard case**. [Poss. originally a transferred or weakened use of *hard case* a hardened criminal, recorded in NZ from 1907 (see OED *hard* 7).] (a) (i) A brazen but likeable, amusing, shrewd, unconventional, often mischievous or adventurous, character; a 'good sport'; a 'dag'.

1897 WRIGHT *Station Ballads* (1945) 24 I thought of old tramps in the summer to stations far out at the back, When I met with the hardest of cases that live on the wallaby track—Men like him, full of tricks and devices. **1905** THOMSON *Bush Boys* 160 'E and 'is lot—there were 'alf-a-dozen on [*sic*] 'em—war the 'ardest cases I knowed of. **1911** KOEBEL *Maoriland Bush* 282 The term 'hard case'..is one of the most widely inclusive and general serviceable appellations imaginable. It may be employed in so many senses, from that of contemptuous pity, of ordinary condemnation, even to that of unwillingly extorted admiration. **1918** *NZ at The Front* 15 They had in their ranks a fair number of dare-devil 'hard cases'. **1924** *Otago Witness* (Dunedin) 17 June 71 My little brother is a very hard case. **1937** MARSH *Vintage Murder* 123 He's a hard case, that one..I reckon he's a real shrewdy. **1943** HISLOP *Pure Gold* 86 He was one of the hardest old cases I have ever had the pleasure of collecting a good cheque from. **1950** GASKELL in *Some Other Country* (1984) 78 Cliff was a hard case. He knew lots of yarns too. **1964** PEARSON *Glossary* to Sargeson *Collected Stories 1935-63* (1964) 300 hard case: *a hard-case joker*, a morally tough and irrepressible character who has had wide

HARD

experience of people and places; *a regular hard case to talk to*, an interesting and entertaining fellow; *a hard-case old sheila*, an amiable and amicable woman with experience of the world and of men. **1970** DAVIN *Not Here Not Now* 28 Geoff Dawson, the winger and a well-known hard case, was a bit tight. **1983** HULME *Bone People* 19 'And you keep on doing it? You're a bit of a bloody hard case, boy.'

(ii) Of a woman, sexually adventurous or willing.

1937 PARTRIDGE *Dict. Slang* 374 hard case... In Australia and New Zealand, a person morally tough but not necessarily incorrigible; also a witty or amusing dare-devil, one who loves fun and adventure; a girl ready for sexual escapades: all coll. from ca. 1880. **1938** HYDE *Godwits Fly* (1970) 24 John was encouraging Sandra to roll down the grass bank... Over and over flashed Sandra's fat legs... A lean man at John's elbow said, 'That's a proper little hard case you've got, Hannay,' and John laughed his best-pleased laugh. **1964** [see (i) above].

(b) In *attrib*. use. Also **hardcase**. Unorthodox, unconventional; odd-looking.

1916 TWIDLE *Diary* (MS) 23 May I. 37 Spent the day building Bivvies. They are hard case affairs. **1917** INGRAM *Anzac Diary* 2 Oct. (1987) 47 Stan Allan, my hardcase pal, who is forever prowling... came across a dead Jerry's leg sticking out from the side of a large shell hole. **1924** ANTHONY *Follow the Call* (1975) 55 After an inspection of our hard-case looking crockery..the ladies refused my tentative offer of afternoon tea. **1946** SARGESON *That Summer* 31 He was the hardest case bloke you ever came across. **1971** LETHBRIDGE *Sunrise on Hills* 50 A rattle of pebbles..announced the arrival of five or six hardcase-looking sheep. **1986** IHIMAERA *Matriarch* 40 This was my first night back in Gisborne and naturally my sisters were as hardcase as ever—the Maori version of the Three Stooges, Ko, To and Wo. **1991** PAYNE *Staunch* 48 It's [*sc.* a benefit fraud] quite hard case but if they can get away with it, good on them.

Hence **hard-casery**, unconventional or illegal but amusing behaviour.

1971 CRUMP *Bastards I Have Met* 59 One of the most remarkable attributes of the Hard-case Bastard is his memory for jokes, and when he's not actually engaged in some other kind of hard-casery he keeps up an almost continuous running patter of jokes from his seemingly inexhaustible fund of them.

b. As **hard doer**, see *hard case* a (a) above.

1916 ANZAC *On the Anzac Trail* 122 [The Australasian] is, as a rule, a 'hard doer'..often a hard, and fairly original, swearer. **1917** INGRAM *Anzac Diary* 29 Aug. (1987) 39 My companion is Stan Allen..a real hard 'doer', good pal and champion scrounger. **1918** *Quick March* 1 Oct. 13 Life was so simple when I was with the old Hard-Doers in Gallipoli and Armentieres. You carried on until you got a smack. **1925** WEBB *Miss Peters' Special* 49 So 'ee laughed and said I was a 'ard doer all right, and 'ee married us. **1948** BALLANTYNE *Cunninghams* (1976) 142 He believed her grandmother practically lived on the mat and her mother was something of a hard-doer. **1959** SLATTER *Gun in My Hand* 165 The younger one..looks like a hard doer and wears a tweed hat all squashed on his head. **1966** [see *hard shot* below]. **1988** MCGILL *Dict. Kiwi Slang* 55 *hard doer* incorrigible person, wag; eg 'Cliff's a hard doer, take my word for it. He's written off 15 stock cars, never won a race, no prize money. Now he's mortgaged his house to get another.'

c. As **hard shot** [cf. OED *shot* 22 b *dial. a queer shot* an 'odd customer'], see *hard case* a (a) above. Also *attrib*.

1938 HYDE *Nor Yrs. Condemn* 184 You get a divorce, Opal, eh? Fred's a hard shot, but he wouldn't stand in your way. **1946** SARGESON *That Summer* 66 I thought he looked a bit of a hard shot. **1959** SLATTER *Gun in My Hand* 91 He's a hard shot. Yeah, he's a woopkacker all right. **1966** TURNER *Eng. Lang. Austral. & NZ* 121 A *hard shot* is 'a hard case', 'a hard doer' or 'a hard nut', all these terms conveying an idea of eccentricity or lack of concern for conventions with a tone of tolerance or approval. **1968** SLATTER *Pagan Game* 231 He was the hard shot boy of the town. But all was forgiven when he became an All Black. **1981** HUNT *Speaking a Silence* 104 They were hard shots all right, tough as boots. **1991** DUFF *One Night Out Stealing* 17 It's only a lil ole fight. Men, as well as the hardshot women only to be found here.

d. As **hard thing**, see *hard case* a (a) above.
1918 *Chron. NZEF* 7 June 204 Without a smoke, he was a hard thing. **1935** MITCHELL & STRONG in Partridge *Slang Today* 286 [The] following [was] employed by those who served in the [Great] War..a *hard thing*, a man noted for his outspokenness, his hardihood, or his kindly if abrupt eccentricity, with which compare the more widely known *hard case*. **1976** MCCLENAGHAN *Travelling Man* 84 Hogan lay back on his bed..roaring with laughter. 'You're getting a bloody hard thing,' he said at last. **1988** MCGILL *Dict. Kiwi Slang* 55 *hard thing* resolute, outspoken or abrupt loner; eg 'Polt's been up in that old whare for years, never spoken to a soul, except to buy his provisions, when he has to. Hard thing, that Polt.'

2. In the phr. **(as) hard as nails**. **a.** [See OED *nail* 10, 1862.] In good condition. **b.** Physically or mentally very hard or tough; unyielding.
1865 CHUDLEIGH *Diary* 1 Nov. (1950) 203 Native grass is as good as oates and the open air in this climate keeps them [*sc*. horses] as harde as nails. **1888** D'AVIGDOR *Antipodean Notes* 112 Nine races out of ten are run on ground which we should call 'hard as nails'. **1952** *Landfall* 23 222 This lad prides himself as being 'hard as nails'... His first 'piss-up' is a landmark in his life.

II. In senses of 'composed of hard or tough material'. **3.** In the names of plants, see: BEECH 2 (5), FERN 2 (6).

III. In senses of 'physically demanding or exhausting'. **4.** As **hard graft**, **hard yacker**, see GRAFT *n.*, YACKER *n.*[1] 1.

hard, *n. Drug users*. A hard drug.
1982 NEWBOLD *Big Huey* 14 Because I was concerned about my health and didn't want a habit I made it a rule only to use 'hard' on the weekend. *Ibid.* 15 Once..the odd junkie confidante discovered I sometimes held hard, it was difficult..not to slip into the habit of selling a bit of peth; morph. opium tincture, and so on.

hard bar: see BAR *n.*[1] 2.

hard country.

1. *Goldmining*. Ground difficult to work for gold or unfavourable to recovery of payable ore. Contrast KINDLY *a*. a.
1896 *AJHR* C-3 51 The andesites occur in bars, varying from 20ft. [*sic*] to 300 ft. in width, and are termed by the [Thames] miners 'hard country', or 'blue bars'. **1898** [see KINDLY *a*. a].

2. *High-country Farming*. See quot. 1966.
1955 BOWEN *Wool Away* 3 The fact that fine-wool sheep are usually run on hard country is another reason why these sheep are slower to shear. They do not suit good country because their feet go quickly on heavy or wet land. **1966** NEWTON *Boss's Story* 187 *Hard country*: The harsher South Island high country—largely 'running' shingle and rock—is referred to as hard country.

hard-earned. As **the hard-earned**, a shortened form of *hard-earned cash*, cash money.
1962 HORI *Half-gallon Jar* 39 I have to separate myself from another couple of the hard-earned [*i.e.* pound notes] for these [cartridges]. **1979** WILLIAMS *Skin Deep* 6 Let's face it, in the present economic clime anybody who relieves you of the old hard-earned is worthy of notice.

hard-head. *Obs.* [Spec. use of *hardhead* the name of any of several fishes (see OED *hardhead*[1] 3) for a member of the fam. Uranoscopidae, the 'armourhead stargazers'.] *spotted stargazer* (STARGAZER 2 (5)).
1877 *TrNZI* IX. 486 *The Hardhead* (*Kathetostoma monopterygium*) is also seen occasionally, but its forbidding appearance is sufficient to prevent its being eaten, though wholesome enough. **1886** SHERRIN *Handbook Fishes NZ* 301 *Kathetostoma monopterygium*. Cat-fish, Hard-head, or Ngu. **1906** *TrNZI* XXXVIII. 549 *Genyagnus maculatus*. The cat-fish or hard-head.

hard-hitter. *Obs.* Also **hard-hitter hat**. [Poss. a play on BOXER (HAT); AND 1892.] A bowler hat. See also BOXER *n.*[1], HARD KNOCKER.
1895 ROBERTS *Diary of Jonathan Roberts* Jan. 7 My clothes were of the 'masher' type—white shirt, hard hitter, tight trousers etc. **1905** BAUCKE *White Man Treads* 121 His clothing consisted of..the remains of Joseph's coat on his back, and a rimless 'hard-hitter' on his head. **1914** in *Hist. N. Otago from 1853* (1978) 131 In the [18]90's the younger generation discarded their beards... The flat-topped hat gave place to the 'bun' or 'hard-hitter'. **1924** GIBSON *Gibbie Galoot* 1 I didn't mind so much when my former mates sat on my hard-hitter hat. **1932** SCANLAN *Pencarrow* 242 Then hats... Of course, they must have hard hitters... Black bowler hats—hard-hitters as they were usually called in the colony. **1952** LYON *Faring South* 98 Later [c1890s] came the 'hard hitter' or 'bowler' as I believe they call them now. **1982** JOHNSON *Coming & Going* 16 The old man in the hard-hitter hat walks his dog in the early morning sun.

hard knocker. *Obs.* Also **hard-knocker hat**. HARD-HITTER.
1936 SARGESON *Conversation with Uncle* 1 My uncle wears a hard knocker. **1948** FINLAYSON *Tidal Creek* (1979) 100 The drummer, who has lost his uniform cap [is] wearing a hard-knocker hat. **1964** SARGESON *Wrestling with the Angel* 70 [Stage direction—reference early 1880's] He takes off a squarish small-brimmed hard knocker, and hangs it on one of the pegs. **1973** FINLAYSON *Brown Man's Burden* (1973) 128 I saw one of those hansom cabs with the cabby perched up behind with his hardknocker hat on. **1986** RICHARDS *Off the Sheep's Back* 8 My father always wore a bowler hat, or hard knocker as they were called.

hard thinker. *WW1*. Usu. *pl*. The nickname for reinforcements who volunteered (reputedly after thinking hard and long) in the later stages of WW1. Contrast TOURIST.
1916 'The Hard Thinkers' [see TOURIST 1 b]. **1968** SEDDON *The Seddons* 232 The new arrivals in the 7th, the 8th and the 9th Reinforcements were not exactly despised, but were considered to be 'hard thinkers'. That was early in 1916. However the late-comers lived down this unjust imputation.

hard word. [AND 1918.] In the phr. **to put the hard word on**, to ask (someone) for a favour or a loan; esp. to proposition (usu. a woman) for sexual favours; occas. also to put pressure on (a person); or occas. as **to get the hard word**, to have pressure put on (one).
1927 DEVANNY *Old Savage* 144 If she shows the least evidence of refinement..to a man, he thinks she is putting the 'hard word' on him. **1951** PARK *Witch's Thorn* 24 What I calculate you oughta do, bo, is to see this Thrush of Erin when he drops into this burg, and put the hard word on him [to help you]. **1964** HORI *Fill It Up Again* 48 They are at me..trying to put the hard word on me for a few quid. **1970** *Listener* 21 Dec. 8 'Don't you think hitching's a little dangerous for females?' 'Well, some of the sheilas I know have had the hard word put on them.' **1972** *Truth* 17 Oct. 7 I put the hard word on the man I believed to be the father and he arranged to get some stuff to take. **1987** *Dominion* (Wellington) 24 Dec. 6 I hummed and haa-ed for a couple of weeks [about having a cancer operation], then I really got the hard word [from the doctor]. **1991** DUFF *One Night Out Stealing* 29 They were good guys...I thought we might put it on em. Put what, not the hard word surely? Ha-ha-ha.

harebell. [Transf. use of Brit. *harebell Campanula* spp. (fam. Campanulaceae).] Also **native (New Zealand,** occas. **Marlborough) harebell**. Any of several native species of *Wahlenbergia* (fam. Campanulaceae), a genus of small herbs of open dry habitats and possessing white or blue bell-shaped flowers.
1851 WELD *Letter* Jan. in *NZGG* 21 Feb. (1851) 34 Several veronicas of great beauty..harebell, a lily, and several varieties of ranunculus. **1869** *TrNZI* I. (rev. edn.) 205 Hare Bell. Wahlenbergia gracilis. **1900** *Canterbury Old & New* 183 Everywhere a graceful native harebell shows its blue or white flowers. **1952** RICHARDS *Chatham Is.* 44 *Wahlenbergia..gracilis*..Blue Harebell. **1961** MARTIN *Flora NZ* 254 Very choice rock-frequenting, floriferous herbs native to Marlborough..the Marlborough Hare-bell. **1969** *Standard Common Names Weeds* 52 New Zealand harebell *Wahlenbergia gracilis*. **1981** TAYLOR *Weeds of Roadsides* 103 New Zealand Harebell... Spindly but graceful native..with a few deep-blue bell-shaped flowers.

harekeke, harikiki, varr. HARAKEKE.

harore. Also **harori**. [Ma. /'harore/: Williams 38 *Harore*.] *Agaricus adiposus* (fam. Agaricaceae), an edible native mushroom.
1850 MCLEAN *Journal* in Cowan *Sir Donald Maclean* (1940) 52 The oven is being opened; it contains a large quantity of harore, or wild mushrooms. **1867** HOOKER *Handbook* 764 Harori... *Agariens adiposa*. **1869** *TrNZI* I. (rev. edn.) 261 [Also eaten were] several *Fungi* [especially]..four..which grow on trees,—the Harori (*Agaricus adiposus*), the Hakeke [etc.]. **1881** *TrNZI* XIII. 30 Several fungi were also eaten..such as the two large terrestrial species called *pukurau*..[and] the *harore* (*Agaricus adiposus*). **1990** CROWE *Native Edible Plants of NZ* 135 The cap of harore is orange-yellow, rusty-coloured at the centre becoming lighter towards the edges and covered with small brownish scales... This was one of the mushrooms eaten by the Maori, according to Colenso... Although Colenso refers here specifically to *Agaricus adiposus*, the Maori name harore can also be loosely applied to all mushrooms.

harrier. Also **harrier hawk**, occas. **Australasian harrier** (see quot. 1985) and formerly **Gould's**

harrier. *Circus approximans* (fam. Accipitridae), a slender, broad-winged brown bird of prey that hunts by quartering open ground. See also KAHU, *swamp-hawk* (HAWK 2 (6)).

1870 *TrNZI* II. 47 Amongst the..tohe tohe reeds, and saw-edged grass, a pair of Harriers had built their rough, flat-topped home. **1873** BULLER *Birds NZ* 11 Circus gouldi (Gould's Harrier)... Kahu and Manutahae. **1879** HAAST *Geol. Canterbury & Westland* 135 Its large size, more pointed wings, and dark colour distinguished it at once from the New Zealand Harrier.., so common all on our plains, but which I have never observed in the alpine regions. **1882** POTTS *Out in Open* 45 *Circus approximans*..the harrier; big swamp, or duck hawk, as it is indifferently called by many settlers; the kahu of the Maoris. **1898** MORRIS *Austral-English* 193 *Harrier*..assigned in New Zealand to *Circus gouldii*..(also called *Swamp-hawk*). **1904** HUTTON & DRUMMOND *Animals NZ* 154 *The Harrier.—Kahu*... In open low country, in both Islands, the Harrier is still common. **1914** GUTHRIE-SMITH *Mutton Birds & Other Birds* 15 We got a Harrier's nest composed entirely of the skeletons of the detached wings of Kuaka fledglings. **1930** *Evening Post* (Wellington) 6 Dec. 17 Not far away..in a thin growth of small flax and coprosma, a harrier had its nest. **1940** STUDHOLME *Te Waimate* (1954) 234 When the Harrier Hawk leaves its roosting place in the morning for the daily hunting ground, it travels fast and straight; during the day it circles round and round. **1955** CAMPBELL *By Reef & Range* 43 A harrier hawk flies past, accelerating as he sees [a sparrowhawk] so close. **1967** MIDDLETON in *NZ Short Stories III* (1975) 68 The harrier awoke to find herself tumbled among dusty leaves. **1985** *Reader's Digest Book NZ Birds* 152 *Australasian Harrier Circus approximans... Kahu, swamp harrier, marsh harrier*... When the Australasian harrier hunts, it flies slowly into the wind, alternately gliding and flapping up to nine metres above the vegetation.

Harry Pannell. Mainly *SI*.

1. Usu. *pl*. Also *ellipt*. **Pannells.** [f. the name of the boot-seller, *H. Pannell* and Co., Christchurch.] A stout boot favoured by musterers, trampers and other South Island hillmen. Cf. COOKHAMS.

[**1928** *Tararua Tramper* Nov. 4 [Advt] Tramping and Mountaineering Boots..Full supplies of Ice Nails, Clinkers and Swiss Tricouni... H. Pannell & Co. 105 Manchester Street Christchurch.] **1947** NEWTON *Wayleggo* 15 *Harry Pannells*: Boots, Pannell & Coy. being famous for their mustering boots. **1951** MCLEOD *NZ High Country* 43 At one time practically all the musterers in Canterbury got their boots from Pannells in Christchurch and even now I think the majority do; so much so that a Canterbury man will quite understand if you refer to boots simply as Pannells. **1969** MCCASKILL *Molesworth* 101 The best boots [c1907–14] came from Pannells in Christchurch and Ford in Rangiora, but even they might last only six weeks or seven [mustering].] **1971** NEWTON *Ten Thousand Dogs* 78 [The musterer] got to work on the dog with his 'Harry Pannells' (boots)... All Brandy [the dog] got for tea that night was another taste of Harry Pannell. [**1978** JARDINE *Shadows on Hill* 115 In rock-hoppers' slippers By Pannells made We'll tramp the peak Bluff, chutes and glade.]

2. In the phr. **to travel by (per) Harry Pannell**, to walk.

1947 NEWTON *Wayleggo* 35 It was all walking country..the musterers travelling either per 'Harry Pannell' (walking) or riding on the pack dray. **1973** NEWTON *Big Country* (1977) 112 In my mustering days we had to travel per 'Harry Pannell' (boots) and it was a two-day walk from the homestead to the Ada.

Hart. *Hist*. Occas. **HART**. The acronym of *Halt All Racist Tours*, an organization formed in 1969 to prevent rugby and other sporting connection with South Africa, thence broadly, to fight racism in New Zealand.

1971 *Otago Daily Times* (Dunedin) 23 Sept. 3 Anti-apartheid groups split last night over the controversial visit of the South African golf team. The Citizens Association of Racial Equality (Care) entered a pact not to disrupt the tourney featuring the South Africans in Auckland. But Halt All Racist Tours (Hart) pledged to go ahead with plans to disrupt the event. **1992** *Dominion* (Wellington) 3 Nov. 1 [Heading] Hart finally calls it a day after 23 vociferous years.

hash-.

1. [Spec. uses of *hash* cheap food.] Used *attrib.* in obsolete special Comb. **hash-foundry**, a cheap eating-house; **hash-house** [AND 'a cheap eating-house' 1896], a cheap boarding-house, reputedly serving hash as a usual meal.

1905 *Truth* 12 Aug. 1 A hungry 'dead beat' tried to strike one of Booth's [Salvation Army] **hash foundries** for a bit of tucker. *Ibid*. 9 Dec. 8 It has deserved the name of Hashburton ever since pubs gave way to hash-foundries. **1916** *Hutt Valley Independent* 6 May 4 Phil's hash foundry announced last week. **1905** *Truth* 24 June 2 *Hash-House Horrors* One considerate hash-house lady had no room vacant, but offered to make up a bed in the dining-room. *Ibid*. 7 Oct. 4 [Women's Column] There was a pretty hubbub in a Toney Wellington hash-house last week..because there are not enough men to go round and the bachelors in these dry-hash establishments are 'tapu' to the cousins..of the proprietress. **1911** *Triad* 11 Sept. 45 'I'm a private secretary, confidential secretary to —' 'A hash-house,' I said. **1918** *Chron. NZEF* 2 Aug. 11 The Froggies are complaining of losing eggs in the vicinity of Lou's hash-house.

2. In composition **hash-me-gandy** /ˌhæʃməˈɡændɪ/ (also **ashmegandy, hash-magandy**). [f. *hash* 'a dish made from chopped cooked meat, etc.; cheap food' poss. infl. by *salmagundi* 'a meat mixture', or by Sc. *gundie a.* 'greedy'; *n*. a sweetmeat made from treacle and spices: cf. EDD *gundie*; AND 1919.] A stew; also *transf.*, the residue from a boiling-down process (see quot. 1957); a second-rate mixture of items or ingredients (see quot. 1915).

1915 *Inglewood Record & Waitara Age* 3 Dec. 2 What [war correspondents] contribute to their newspapers is in the main a hashmagandi of second-hand stories. **1934** *Press* (Christchurch) (Acland Gloss.) 20 Jan. 15 *Hash-me-gandy.—Station stew*. **1941** BAKER *NZ Slang* 54 *Hash-me-gandy*, station stew (perhaps a sardonic reference to the meagre feeding requirements of Mahatma Gandhi). **1957** MACDONALD *Canterbury Frozen Meat Co.* 71 In the early eighteen-nineties digesters were installed for 'boiling down' the offals... This was essentially a stewing process which took four to six hours' cooking, and separated the fat by partial breakdown of the animal tissues. The residue, or 'ashmegandy', was dried in a machine for fertiliser material, as was the blood. **1987** OGONOWSKA-COATES *Boards, Blades & Barebellies* 96 *Hash-me-gandy*. Station stew.

hassock grass: see GRASS 2 (20).

hatchie. *Waterfront*. [f. *hatch*(man + -IE.] The watersider who directs the winchmen in loading and discharging operations.

c1926 THE MIXER *Transport Workers' Song Book* 112 The sling fell out, the hatchie said: 'You cow's son!' Then he landed me a 'beaut.' upon the chin. **1964** DAVIS *Watersiders* 28 'Hows it coming, hatchie?' asked Giant..breaking stride. Without turning his head..the hatchman replied, 'Just lifting the last of the plug, cocks.'

hatter. [Prob. f. *his hat covers his family* said of one alone in the world (see OED *hat* 5 c), infl. by *mad as a hatter*: AND 1853.] **a.** *Hist*. Orig. and usu. a goldminer, thence any rural or bush person, who prefers to work and live alone. Also occas. in collocations signifying something poor or small of its kind, large enough to serve only one person: **hatter's billy, diggings, tent** (see quots. 1906, 1933 below).

[**1853** ROCHFORT *Adventures Surveyor in NZ* 66 The Bendigo diggings are suitable for persons working singly, being generally very shallow sinking. Such persons are humorously called 'hatters'. They live alone, in a tent often not more than six feet long, three feet high, and three feet wide.] **1865** FARJEON *Shadows on Snow* 76 I was working as a 'hatter'. **1868** HARPER *Lett. from NZ* 10 July (1914) 143 Some of the men [are], in mining phraseology, 'Hatters', *i.e.* men who live and work by themselves, often old sailors and much travelled men, content with the solitude of well-kept huts... Whence the term 'hatter' I have never discovered; maybe because such solitaries are regarded as 'mad as a hatter'. **1876** KENNEDY *Colonial Travel* 189 These [holes] frequently form the grave of some unfortunate 'hatter', as a man who works alone and has all his property 'under his hat' is called [in Central Otago]. **1889** WAKEFIELD *NZ after Fifty Yrs.* 165 Miners who work alone are called 'hatters', one explanation of the term being that they frequently go mad from the solitude of their claim away in the bush, exemplifying the proverb 'as mad as a hatter.' **1890** *Otago Witness* (Dunedin) 23 Oct. 30 There was no doctor..within hail and no hospital handier than a 'hatters' 6 by 8 [ft] tent. **1899** *Auckland Weekly News* (Suppl.) 4 Aug. 4 Here I met a couple of 'hatters' working away in Maori Gully. **1906** *NZGeol.SB* (NS) No.2 26 The Waikerikeri goldfield [near Alexandra], where a good deal of ground has been turned over, was little better than a 'hatter's' diggings in its best days. **1911** MORELAND *Through South Westland* 19 They [*sc*. miners] dug and washed for gold in the creeks with the most primitive of outfits, amidst much toil and privation; and the solitaries came to be known as 'Hatters', the only explanation I ever got of the term being, that if they had nothing else to wash in, they washed in their hats! **1922** *Auckland Weekly News* 21 Sept. 19 In 1882 two claims..were taken by a well-known 'hatter'—solitary miner—named Edwards. **1933** *Press* (Christchurch) (Acland Gloss.) 28 Oct. 17 *Hatter.*—One who works and camps by himself. Originally a miner's expression, no doubt from the saying of a man without relations that he had 'all his family under his hat'... The word is in general use on stations. H[atter]'s *billy*, *tent*, etc., one just large enough for one man. **1946** HARPER *Memories Mountains & Men* 113 An old 'hatter' living [West Coast, 1890's] just above the beach, and looking out for patches of gold... I don't know the origin of the name, but some say it was because the man worked alone under his hat. **1952** [see *gully-raker* (GULLY 4)]. **1983** NOLAN *Gold Fossicker's Handbook* 112 *Hatter*: miner who works alone. Probably derived from the habit of such men of leaving their hats at the surface to indicate that they were working down the mine shaft. **1991** *NZ Geographic* Apr.–June 110 [Gold] Diggers (or 'hatters' as they were often termed) persisted, a few into the last decade.

b. A solitary person; one who prefers the company of self.

1909 *Truth* 13 Nov. 7 He has been living as a 'hatter'... But, tiring of playing a lone hand [etc.]. **1914**

GRACE *Tale Timber Town* 35 The game is to go mates with him—Scarlett, the 'hatter', and myself. **1924** GIBSON *Gibbie Galoot* 124 The skipper [of the Auckland timber-scow] I seldom saw, for he was a hatter and kept to his cabin and keg. **1980** ELDRED-GRIGG *Southern Gentry* 52 Shepherds watching the sheep on distant parts of an estate often went mad from loneliness or food poisoning—such men were known as 'hatters'.

hature, var. HAUTURE.

hauama. [Ma. /ˈhauama/: Williams 40 *Hauama = houama*, n. = *whau*: see also Williams 492 *Whauama*.] WHAU.
 1853 HOOKER *II Flora Novae-Zelandiae I Flowering Plants* 32 *Entelea arborescens*... 'Whau'..and 'Hauama', in the Middle Island. **1869** [see WHAU]. **1889** KIRK *Forest Flora* 45 The whau, or, as Mr. Colenso informs me it is sometimes termed by the Maoris, the hauama, is the only representative of its genus. **1889** FEATON *Art Album NZ Flora* 60 Entelea arborescens... The 'Whau', or 'Hauama'.—This very beautiful small tree is peculiar to the Northern Island of New Zealand, but is not common. **1907** LAING & BLACKWELL *Plants NZ* 242 *Genus Entelea*..Maori names *Whau, Hauama*.

Hauhau /ˈhæuˌhæu/, *n.*[1] and *a. Hist.* Also **How-How.** Usu. with init. cap. *pl.* **hauhau, hauhaus.** [Orig. f. Ma. *hau* used as a rallying cry *Hau! Hau!* (/ˈhau ˈhau/) or *Hauhau!* (/ˈhauhau/): cf. Williams 38 *Hau* (i), n. *1.* Wind, air... *2.* Breath; *Ibid.* 39 *Hau* (iv), n. *1.* Vitality of man, vital essence of land, etc., which was particularly susceptible to the attacks of witchcraft, etc.; *Ibid.* 39 *Hau* (vii), *hahau, hauhau,* v. *1.* Strike, smite, deal blows to.]

A. *n. a.* The Paimarire Maori religious sect or cult, founded by Te Ua in Taranaki in 1862, named by Europeans from the battle cry 'Hau! Hau!'; a member of the Paimarire sect, regarded esp. by Europeans as a fanatical fighter. Cf. PAI MARIRE.
 [**1864** *AJHR E-8* 2 Te Ua then made me [*sc.* Charles Broughton, 28 June 1864] a long speech, singing several Waiata's and 'Pai Marire' hymns. *Ibid.* 4 Atua Pai Marire, rire, Atua Pai Marire, haw!.. the 'Haw' is said to be a substitute for 'Amen'. **1884** MARTIN *Our Maoris* 173 He proclaimed a new religion, though indeed it was a mixture of wild applications of Old testament history with spells and incantations. A pole was set up in the pah, round which the people danced. They drew in their breaths all at once, somewhat in the way that paviours used to do. This deep groan at the end of each sentence, 'Hau', gave a name to the fanatical movement which lasts to this day.] **1865** *Richmond-Atkinson Papers* (1960) II. 171 The excitement among the Hau-hau and other hostile natives was reviving. **1865** *NZGG* 29 Apr. in Babbage *Hauhauism* (1937) 81 A fanatical sect, commonly called Pai Marire, or Hau Hau, has been for some time..engaged in practices subversive of all order and morality. **1868** TAYLOR *Past & Present NZ* 147 The new faith was called '*Pai marire*', but afterwards, from the noise the votaries made in their devotions, resembling the barking of dogs, they acquired the name of *Hauhaus*. **1873** *Weekly News* (Auckland) 10 May 20 The natives treated us with great kindness and hospitality, as indeed we invariably found the case with all the hauhaus we visited. **1889** KNOX *Boy Travellers* 239 Several tribes joined in this movement, and the new religion spread. It was called the Pai Marire by its adherents, who are known as Hau-Haus, or How-Hows, for the reason that they pronounce that sound in loud tones during the ceremonial worship or when engaged in battle. **1907** KOEBEL *Return of Joe* 310 Kirimata..a noted chief of the extinct How-Hows, was a formidable customer. **1912** WITTY *Colonial Songs* 3 In the month of October, '66, Sir Donald McLean was in a fix For the Hau Haus were going to fight like bricks At a place called Oamarunui. **1922** COWAN *NZ Wars* (1955) II. 6 The term 'Hauhau', by which the disciples of the new faith came to be known, had its origin in the exclamation 'Hau!' used at the end of the chorus chanted by the disciples. Literally it means 'wind'; but it has another and more esoteric significance, for it was the term applied to the life-principle of man, the vital spark. '*Anahera hau*', or 'wind angels', one of the curious phrases originating with Te Ua, was a reference to the fancy that the angels came to the Maoris on the winds of heaven, and that they ascended and descended by the ropes that were left dangling from the yardarms of the sacred mast, called the *niu*. 'Hau', 'hauhau', or 'whakahau', is also a battle-cry meaning 'Strike! Attack!' **1932** WILLIAMS *East Coast Hist. Rec.* 48 [1865] was the end of *Hauhauism* in these parts; for, though the name 'Hauhau' has been in use ever since to denote those who have been disaffected towards the Government or towards Christianity the peculiar quasi-religious practices prescribed by Patara were heard no more of. **1949** BUCK *Coming of Maori* (1950) 474 Possession was practised by the fanatical followers of the late post-European sect known as the *hauhau*, when dancing around a pole termed the *niu*. **1959** SINCLAIR *Hist. NZ* 138 Te Ua taught his followers that this divine service and a strict adherence to his instruction would make them impervious to bullets if, when under fire, they raised their right hand and cried '*Pai marire, hau! Hau!*' The *Hau hau*, as these fanatics were called after this incantation, at first showed incredible boldness in battle.

b. *transf.* In the phr. **to do one's hauhau**, see quot., a reference to the survival of hau-hau practices.
 1938 HYDE *Nor Yrs. Condemn* 189 Everything's Maori up there. Most of them are Christians now, but on a Sunday you can still see some of the old chaps doing their *hau-hau*, getting down and barking like dogs... That meeting-house is worth seeing.

B. *adj.* Pertaining to, describing, or characteristic of *Hauhau* or the behaviour of its adherents; occas. erron. applied to the Ringatu followers of Te Kooti (see quot. 1940).
 1868 LUSH *Thames Jrnls.* 21 Dec. (1975) 41 We disembarked on the side inhabited by the 'Queenites' (friendly natives) and then crossed over in boats to the Hauhau side of the river. **1881** NESFIELD *Chequered Career* 43 A large Hau Hau flag-staff stood in an enclosure. **1922** COWAN *NZ Wars* (1955) I. 366 He was a *tohunga* of the ancient Maori school; later he became a war-priest of the Hauhau fanaticism. **1934** HYDE *Journalese* 170 Witness the bloody devilment of the Hau-Hau creed, directly and simply developed from the Christian mystery of the Body and Blood of Christ. **1940** *Tales Pioneer Women* (1988) 56 When night came on the girls crouched in terror in the slab whare... In every shadow they saw the dark form of a Hau Hau warrior, for this was the Te Kooti Trail! **1968** SLATTER *Pagan Game* 173 Just rooking the Maoris for their land... No bloodshed, no massacre, no Hau Hau scare. Nothing for Technicolor.

Hence **Hauhauism**, the Pai-marire sect and beliefs.
 1868 TAYLOR *Past & Present NZ* 69 The worst of them [*sc.* Maori critics of Christianity] thought there could be no real good in our faith, when its professors could thus pay so little regard to its commands; they therefore invented another, and Hauhauism arose. **1873** ST JOHN *Pakeha Rambles* in Taylor *Early Travellers* (1959) 572 From the successes achieved in Wairoa in 1865..may be dated the first break-down of Hauhauism. **1899** GRACE *Sketch NZ War* 149 The national movement under Wiremu Tamihana, the King-maker, and the wave of religious enthusiasm called 'Hauhauism' which followed it. **1930** PINFOLD *Fifty Yrs. Maoriland* 102 Hauhauism may be regarded as the aftermath of the Maori War. **1966** *Encycl. NZ* II. 235 He averted a battle which would have cost the lives of many Ngati Porou converts to Hauhauism. **1983** LAMBERT *Illustr. Hist. of Taranaki* 47 Hauhauism was a cult which combined aspects of Biblical teaching with the traditional culture and priest-craft of the Maori.

hauhau, *n.*[2] [Ma. /ˈhauhau/: Williams 39 *Hau* (vii)... *hauhau* (i)..mud-fish.] MUDFISH 1.
 1923 *NZJST* VI. 62 [Heading] Note on the occurrence of the New Zealand Mudfish, or Hauhau (*Neochanna apoda*). **1929** BEST *Fishing Methods* 170 Kowaro, Hauhau... Given as names of the mud-fish. **1990** MCDOWALL *NZ Freshwater Fishes* 416 Phillipps..considered the brown mudfish (hauhau) to be a prized food amongst the Maori.

hauler. *Forestry.* [f. *haul* v. + -ER.] A stationary engine driving a cable-drum to the cable of which logs are attached to be hauled out of the bush. See also DONK *n.*[2] 1; *log-hauler* (LOG).
 [**1904** *TrNZI* XXXVI. 464 When the natural supply of water is not sufficient to float these [logs] they are forced along by driving-dams or hauled out of the bush, either by bullocks or steam-engines.] **1923** MALFROY *Small Sawmills* 13 A good snigger with a log is not jammed before signalling 'Right ahead' to the hauler. **1951** DUFF *Shepherd's Calendar* (1961) 42 As I stand today among the litter of logs waiting for the hauler to take them to the mill I wonder if my conduct has been civilized. **1952–53** [see DONKEY *n.*[1] 1]. **1966** BARRY *In Lee of Hokonuis* 45 (facing) [Caption of a picture of a stationary log-hauler] Halliday's Hauler at Waitane **1992** [see BREAK OUT *v.*[5]].

Hence **hauler-driver**, the workman controlling the hauler machinery.
 1951 *Awards, etc.* 520 [Marlborough Timber-Workers Award] [Rates of wages] Rail-tractor driver (other than steam) 4[s.] 2¼[d.] Hauler-driver or winchman requiring first-class ticket 4 4½ **1990** GEORGE *Ohakune* 95 Actually the bushmen, two cross-cutters, a ropey and a hauler-driver—these four men were expected to keep the mill going.

haul out. *n.* A non-breeding colony of fur seals.
 1995 *Contact* (Wellington) 29 June 1 The majority of New Zealand fur seals in the region are adult males, wintering over in non-breeding colonies known as 'haul outs', which are close to favoured feeding areas.

haumakoroa. Also **haumakaroa** (freq. in non-Maori use). [Ma. /ˈhaumakoːroa/: Williams 40 *Haumakōroa = haumangōroa.... Pseudopanax edgerleyi*.] *Pseudopanax* (formerly *Panax* or *Nothopanax*) *simplex* (fam. Araliaceae), a small native tree of lowland forests with compound lobed leaves when young and simple unlobed leaves when mature.
 1889 KIRK *Forest Flora* 211 *Panax simplex*... The Haumakoroa. **1890** *PWD Gen. Catalogue* (NZ & South Seas Exhib.) 31 Lithograph of haumakoroa foliage. **1910** COCKAYNE *NZ Plants & Their Story* 116 The other associated trees and shrubs [of the Auckland Islands] are the haumakaroa..[and] the inaka. **1950** WODZICKI *Introduced Mammals NZ* 164 Miss Mason identified the leaves of the following plants [Egmont National Park]:.. both leaves and fruit or seed of haumakaroa.. and broadleaf. **1961** MARTIN *Flora NZ* 165

HAUMATA

Haumakaroa..usually subalpine. **1982** WILSON *Stewart Is. Plants* 82 *Pseudopanax simplex* Haumakōroa... Small tree, sometimes a shrub.

haumata. [Ma. /ˈhaumata/: Williams 40 *Haumata*, n. Snow-grass.] The large tussock grass *Chionochloa*; and less commonly, a large sedge tussock of *Carex* spp. See also *snowgrass* (GRASS 2 (36)), *red tussock* (TUSSOCK 3 (9)).
1921 *TrNZI* LIII. 72 *Haumata* was the name of what are now called Maori-heads. **1969** *Standard Common Names Weeds* 36 *haumata* [=] *red tussock*. **1980** GIBBS *NZ Butterflies* 91 I have found larvae on *Chionochloa rubra* the large 'red tussock', or haumata so it is very likely that it utilises other species of snow tussock as well.

hauni, var. HANI.

haurangi, *a*. Also early **ourangi, showrangy**. [Ma. /ˈhauraŋi/: Williams 41 *Haurangi. 3.* Drunken.] Drunk. (Found mainly in Maori contexts.)
1834 MARKHAM *NZ* (1963) 45 Then I would give the Natives, a dram of Rum to wash it down... They like now to get Showrangy or drunk if they can. **1838** POLACK *NZ* I. 110 The natives, on perceiving me make use of this [tutu] berry, warned me not to swallow any of the seeds, as the doing so would make me *ourangi*, drunk, or mad. **1905** BAUCKE *White Man Treads* 97 In his absence [at the public house] the child died, and the stigma of the offence clung to him in 'Haurangi' (drunk). **1960** HILLIARD *Maori Girl* 101 She's getting around with a mob like this—haurangi half the time.

hauture. The spelling **hature** [Ma. /ˈhaːture/: Williams 38] has equal standing. [Ma. /ˈhauture/: Williams 42 *Hauture, n. Trachurus [sp.]*..horse-mackerel = hāture.] The *horse* or *jack mackerel* (MACKEREL 2 (3) and (2), *Trachurus* spp.).
1872 HUTTON & HECTOR *Fishes NZ* 110 Horse Mackerel... This is the Hauture of the natives, and the Scad of the northern hemisphere. **1890** [see MACKEREL 2 (2)]. **1921** *NZJST* IV. 117 *Horse-mackerel; Hature*. Commonly taken when trawling in Hauraki Gulf during the spring. **1956** GRAHAM *Treasury NZ Fishes* 237 Horse Mackerel (Hature) *Trachurus novae-zelandiae*. **1966** DOOGUE & MORELAND *Sea Anglers' Guide* 232 *Horse Mackerel*... mackerel; hauture (Maori). **1991** BRADSTOCK *Fishing* 18 *Jack mackerel.* Other names: yellowtail, horse mackerel, horsie, hauture, *Trachurus novaezelandiae*.

have on, *v*. [See OED *have v.* 14 n.]
1. To be prepared to accept (sexually).
1946 SARGESON *That Summer* 54 A girl came past that I thought might have me on. **1964** PEARSON *Glossary* to Sargeson *Collected Stories 1935–63* (1964) 300 have: *have (a woman) on*, take up a sexual opportunity with.
2. [AND 1941.] To (be prepared to) attack or fight (someone); to challenge (someone); to argue with (a person).
1955 *BJ Cameron Collection* (TS July) have someone on (v) To argue with or fight someone. **1983** *Dominion* (Wellington) 7 Apr. 7 'You get a lot of people who have you on in the street—sidewalk lawyers, we call them,' Pollock says. **1988** McGILL *Dict. Kiwi Slang* 55 *have on* to challenge or attack; WW2; eg 'Have him on about it, he'll back down for sure.'
3. In a negative phr., **not to have that** (or **it**) **on**, to want nothing to do with (it).
1957 p.c. Talbot *Letter* (Tauranga) 2 Dec. I'm not always understood when I say 'I'm having you on!'

meaning 'I'm pulling your leg'. Now I find that 'I'm not having that on' means 'I'm having no truck with that'. **1965** SARGESON *Memoirs of Peon* 252 I didn't see why we shouldn't introduce you... But John Morgan wouldn't have it on.

Hawaiki /haˈwaiki/. Also **Hawyjee, Heawye** (with /k/ elided or glottalized). [Ma. /haˈwaiki/.] The legendary homeland of Polynesian people, esp. the Maori. Also *transf*. (see quot. 1994).
1770 BANKS *Journal* 5 Feb. (1962) I. 463 He believed his ancestors were not from there but came originally from *Heawye* (the place from whence Tupia and the Islanders also derive their origin) which lay to the Northward where were many lands. **1777** in Ledyard *Journal* Feb. (1963) 15 After a labored enquiry on our part with regard to their ancestors.. the only information we obtained, is, 'That their forefathers at some very remote period..came from a far distant island called Hawyjee.' **1840** in Wilkes *US Exploring Exped.* Mar. (1852) I. 310 The first natives came from Hawaiki, situated towards the east, in several canoes. **1848** TAYLOR *Leaf from Nat. Hist.* xvii Whether Hawaiki, the island they came from, be one of the Sandwich islands or not it is difficult to say. **1856** SHORTLAND *Traditions & Superstitions* 2 We learn on such authority that the ancestors of the present race came from a distant island named Hawaiki, lying in a northerly or north-easterly direction from New Zealand, or from a group of islands, one of which bore that name. **1867** HOCHSTETTER *NZ* 204 All over New Zealand, the natives state that their ancestors migrated to the country from a place called Hawaiki. **1874** BAINES *Edward Crewe* 23 There is now no island in the Pacific Ocean known by the name of Hawaiki the mythical abode of the ancestors of the Maori. **1883** DOMETT *Ranolf & Amohia* I. 137 Since from *Hawaiki*, tempest-driven... Five hundred years ago had come. **1890** [see KOROTANGI]. **1904** TREGEAR *Maori Race* 441 Of these [myths] special mention may be made of the tales of migration to New Zealand from Hawaiki in the so-called historical canoes. **1921** GUTHRIE-SMITH *Tutira* 54 Descent is claimed by the Ngati-kahungunu from Rongo-kako, whose son Tamatea arrived in..one of the most famous canoes of the great *heke* or migration from the mythical Hawaiki. **1936** *NZJST* XVII. 465 When the 'fleet' of canoes 'Arawa', 'Tainui'. and others coming from Hawaike arrived at the East Cape about 1350 A.D. many of them came on to Hauraki. **1984** *Te Maori* 37 The Hawaiki of Nahe's text is a generic term for the last departure point of the ancestors. *Ibid*. 62 An associated view is that the Hawaiki of the canoe arrival traditions is a location inside New Zealand and that the voyages represent coastal migrations inside New Zealand rather than ocean crossings. **1994** *Community Voice: Wellington Access Radio Programme Guide* Dec. 1994–Mar. 1995 3 'Scotland is something of a Hawaiki for many Pakeha,' says Paterson. 'A spiritual homeland. Of the heart.'

Hence **Hawaikian** *a*., of Hawaiki.
1911 SHAND *Moriori People* 51 How is it, that, while showing so many points of agreement in their Hawaikian ancestry, there are so many generations between the dates of arrival in New Zealand and the Chatham islands. **1922** COWAN *NZ Wars* (1955) I. 185 Pekehawani, an ancient Hawaikian name, was here used by Potatau as an honorific term for the Puniu River. **1967** ASHTON-WARNER *Greenstone* 50 He can recite the list of his chieftain ancestors... Several lists, in fact, for there were collateral tables of names down through the generations from the far-back Hawaikian days.

hawk.
1. Transf. use of *hawk*, a member of the subfamily Accipitrinae for any New Zealand diurnal bird of prey mainly of families Falconidae (FALCON, *bush-*

HAWK

hawk or *quail hawk* and SPARROWHAWK); Accipitridae (HARRIER, *swamp-hawk*); Stercorariidae (*sea-hawk*). See also FALCON, HARRIER, KAHU, KAIAIA, KAREAREA, SPARROWHAWK. Cf. *fish-hawk* (FISH 3).
1773 BAYLY *Journal* 12 Apr. in McNab *Hist. Records* (1914) II. 206 I saw two kinds of small Hawkes, both being small. **1843** DIEFFENBACH *Travels in NZ* I. 77 Perhaps a hawk is seen watching the movements of a smaller bird. **1850** *Acheron Jrnl.* May in Howard *Rakiura* (1940) 391 Mr. Phillips' party bagged 20 wild duck—two wood hens and a small hawk. **1867** BARKER *Station Life* (1870) 147 Their greatest enemies are the hawks. **1883** DOMETT *Ranolf & Amohia* I. 305 Hawk..Falconidae. The most common species appears to be the Cercus [*sic*] Gouldi: or New Zealand Harrier. **1947** POWELL *Native Animals NZ* 82 [The Harrier] is commonly referred to as the hawk, but our true hawk or falcon is another species, *Falco novaeseelandiae*, which frequents the forested high country. **1966** FALLA et al. *Birds NZ* 98 Harrier *Circus approximans*... Hawk. **1989** [see KAHU].

2. With a modifier: **bush, harrier, quail, sea, sparrow, swamp**.

(1) **bush-hawk.** FALCON.
1873 [see KAREAREA]. **1882** [see *quail-hawk* (3) below]. **1904** HUTTON & DRUMMOND *Animals NZ* 153 The Bush-hawk, or Sparrow-hawk, lives in the mountains, where the forest is low and dense... Though smaller than the Quail-hawk, it is swifter and more savage and resolute. **1928** *NZJST* IX. 188 Quail-hawk..Bush-hawk... At one time both varieties of this hawk were fairly common in all the hill country, but only on rare occasions were they met with on the plains. **1938** [see KAREAREA]. **1949** *NZ Bird Notes* III. 85 About 2000 feet up near the edge of a strip of beech forest, [we] saw two bush hawks (*Falco novaeseelandiae*). **1955** OLIVER *NZ Birds* 423 The Bush Hawk was discovered in 1773 at Dusky Sound and Queen Charlotte Sound during Cook's second voyage. **1962** EVANS *Waikaka Saga* 129 Bush robins, parakeets, tomtits, grey warblers, riflemen, pigeons and the bush hawks are still to be seen. **1978** JARDINE *Shadows on Hill* 80 The kea shares the mastery..with another..rejoicing in the name of *Falco novaeseelandiae*, commonly called the sparrowhawk in the south, bush-hawk elsewhere. **1985** [see FALCON].

(2) **harrier hawk**, see HARRIER.

(3) **quail-hawk.** *Obs*. FALCON.
1867 PHILLIPS *Point Jrnl.* (Christchurch Pub. Lib. TS) 10 July 108 Shot 3 wekas and 13 rabbits and one quail hawk. **1870** *TrNZI* II. 51 *Falco novae zelandiae*..Ka rewa rewa-tara. Quail-hawk. In New Zealand..the head of the family [Raptores] must be fairly assigned to this bird, which is commonly known by the name of the Quail or Sparrow-hawk. **1882** *Encycl. Brit.* XIV. 54 No Kestrel is found in New Zealand, but an approach to the form is made by the very peculiar *Hieracidea..novae-zelandiae*..the 'Sparrow-Hawk', 'Quail-Hawk', and 'Bush-Hawk' of the colonists. **1930** REISCHEK *Yesterdays in Maoriland* (1933) 270 We saw a quail-hawk..dart down on a fully-grown young tui. **1966** FALLA et al. *Birds NZ* 99 New Zealand Falcon *Falco novaeseelandiae*... Bush Hawk, Sparrow Hawk, Quail Hawk, Karearea. **1985** [see FALCON].

(4) **sea hawk**. [Spec. use of *sea-hawk*: see OED 2.] SKUA.
1890 *Otago Witness* (Dunedin) 6 Mar. 11 A sea hawk had spiked my last sound albatross egg with his beak and was indulging in a deep booze in its delicious contents. **1904** HUTTON & DRUMMOND *Animals NZ* 221 *The Sea Hawk.—Hakoakoa. Megalestris antarctica. Ibid*. 222 [The Southern Skua] has been given the name of the Sea Hawk in account of its powerful beak and claws, and not on account of a ferocious disposition.

1914 GUTHRIE-SMITH *Mutton Birds & Other Birds* 40 I have watched the Sea Hawk poised for long like a Windhover in the air. 1917 WILLIAMS *Dict. Maori Lang.* 38 Hakoakoa (ii)... *Megalestris antarctica.* Sea hawk. 1925 GUTHRIE-SMITH *Bird Life on Island & Shore* 178 The Sea Hawk hates walking, and detests rapid walking. 1951 SORENSEN *Wild Life in Subantarctic* 11 Rapacious, bold, gluttonous, cannibalistic: all are adjectives descriptive of the southern skua gull, or sea-hawk as it is sometimes called. 1955 [see SKUA]. 1966 FALLA et al. *Birds NZ* 151 Southern Skua *Catharacta lonnbergi*... Sea-hawk, Hakoakoa. 1976 SOPER *NZ Birds* 177 Skuas are birds of prey, predatory sea birds, or sea hawks. 1986 FRASER *Beyond Roaring Forties* 24 The southern great skua..is an aggressive and powerful bird... If threatened, it attacks with swift aerial passes which justify its alternative name of sea hawk.

(5) **sparrow-hawk**, see SPARROWHAWK.

(6) **swamp hawk**. HARRIER.
1898 MORRIS *Austral-English* 449 *Swamp-hawk*..the New Zealand *Harrier.* 1930 REISCHEK *Yesterdays in Maoriland* (1933) 30 Besides these two varieties of birds I noticed the brown swamp-hawk..which is common everywhere and very destructive, slowly winging its way in wide circles over the Alps.

3. Comb. **hawk and pigeon** [cf. Partridge: *hawk and pigeon* Villain and victim: Society Coll: late C. 19–early 20], a children's game similar to 'bar-the-gate'.
1966 TURNER *Eng. Lang. Austral. & NZ* 159 Among the [children's] games that I remember [from Matamau school near Dannevirke in the 1930s] are two varieties of hide and seek, called *All Home* and *Fox and Hounds in Den,* and *Hawk and Pigeon,* a game sometimes known as *Bar the Gate.*

hawthorn. *Obs.* [Spec. use of Brit. *hawthorn* for unrelated but hawthorn-like plants.] Usu. **native (New Zealand) hawthorn. a.** From its thorns, MATAGOURI.
1867 HOOKER *Handbook* (List of Names) 764 Hawthorn, native. *Discaria Toumatou.*

b. From its blossom, PUTAPUTAWETA.
1907 *AJHR* C-8 19 *Carpodetus serratus*..New Zealand hawthorn. Upper forest. 1915 *AJHR* C-6 13 *Carpodetus serratus.* Putaputaweta. New Zealand hawthorn. Forest.

haymaking. *West Coast Goldmining.* [Perh. transf. from an allusion to the comparatively easy work of 'haymaking', or to the phr. 'make hay while the sun shines'.] Working rich goldbearing beach sand.

[1887 PYKE *Hist. Early Gold Discoveries Otago* (1962) 79 The miners, knowing the importance of 'making hay while the sun shines['], strained every effort to obtain the auriferous 'dirt', and stacking it on their claims, leaving the washing up and 'cradling' to be done when the getting of more dirt was impossible.] 1866 HARPER *Lett. from NZ* 6 Oct. (1914) 100 They give me a shovel, and with it nearly full of sand, direct me to shake it gently in the water till all the sand has gone, and then round its rim is a thin line of gold, fine as dust... This is the easiest way of getting gold, so easy, it is called 'Haymaking', but it will not last long, as the black sand brought down by the river, with its gold, from the mountains, and cast up on the beach, where it has lain for centuries, is of limited extent. 1868 HAAST in May *West Coast Gold Rushes* (1967) 222 When they come upon one of the rich spots, the fine particles of gold being often visible to the naked eye, they at once remove the black layer of sand out of reach of the tide, and wash it when convenient. [1967 *Note*] This method of working the beaches was also called 'haymaking' or 'beachcombing'. These terms were not applied to beach-workings above high-water mark. 1974 HEINZ *Bright Fine Gold* 21 The leads consisted of three types: those deposited between high and low water mark... This type of mining was called haymaking. 1967 MAY *West Coast Gold Rushes* 527 Haymaking: working a sea-beach claim below high-water.

hay-paddock. *Farming.* A farm paddock reserved (often for a set period) for hay production.
1960 HILLIARD *Maori Girl* 23 They gathered dry grass from the bottom wire of the hay-paddock where the sweep had missed it. 1966 *Te Reo* IX. 53 Is it not the case that [in New Zealand] wheat is grown in a wheatfield but hay is grown in a hay paddock? 1967 *Landfall* 21 127 The cock pheasant strutting in a hay-paddock.

he. Occas. early **e-, hi(-)**, the Ma. particle *he* /he/, often prefixed with the force of an indefinite article to early transliterations of Ma. words: *e.g.* **e-taboo** =he tapu, **hippah** =he pā.

head, *n.*[1]

1. *Hist.* [Spec. use of *head* the top or foremost part (of the body).] **a.** A preserved, tattooed Maori head as an article of commerce.
1829 ATKINS *Narrative* 2 Mar. in McNab *Hist. Records* (1908) I. 695 The practice of preserving heads is universal among the New Zealanders; they bring them as trophies from their wars, and in the event of peace restore them to their families, this interchange being necessary to their reconciliation. They now frequently barter them with Europeans for a little gunpowder. 1831 MARSDEN *Letter* 18 Apr. in McNab *Hist. Records* (1908) I. 716 When the chief who is with me went on board the Prince of Denmark he saw 14 heads of chiefs upon the table in the cabin... The chief knew the heads; they were his friends; when he retired he said, 'Farewell my people, farewell my people.' 1863 MANING *Old NZ* 59 We were always ready to deal with a man who had a 'real good head' and used to commission..men..to 'pick up heads' for them. 1906 *Truth* 14 July 7 Anyhow the trade in 'baked heads' is one that New Zealand may thank Governor Darling for having squelched.

b. head money, rental for grazing paid per head of stock.
1868 *McLean Papers* (ATLTS) XXVIII. 18 I think [the Maori owners] should be paid some small rental for the land in the first instance, with an additional sum as *head money* on all stock put on the run.

2. *Obs.* [Poss. a transf. use of *head* the rounded leafy top of a tree or shrub (cf. OED 9 a and b); or *ellipt.* for NEGROHEAD *n.*[1], NIGGERHEAD *n.*[1].] A stick of tobacco. Cf. FIG *n.*[1] a
1836 *Log 'Mary Mitchell'* 11 May in McNab *Old Whaling Days* (1913) 441 Paid Old Blucher the Chief 100 heads of tobacco for the house. 1838 POLACK *NZ* I. 64 This was carrying the jest too far; but I gave, as a tithe, a head of tobacco; which he, at last, admitted was compensation enough. 1841 BEST *Journal* 9 May (1966) 306 Te Tipa returned with a nice pig..at the same time giving us back three out of ten heads of Tobacco with which he had been intrusted.

3. [f. HEAD *v.* 1.] **a.** The result of a heading-dog's cast in its confronting, then halting or controlling, a mob or string of sheep.
1933 [see HEAD *v.* 1 c]. 1953 STRONACH *Musterer on Molesworth* 44 He [*sc.* a sheep-dog] made a beautiful head and flopped on his belly about ten yards from the sheep. 1971 NEWTON *Ten Thousand Dogs* 18 She has that hallmark of the real heading dog—a strong inherent instinct to keep out of sight of her sheep until she had completed her head.

b. Also with various modifiers, often indicating defined tasks at dog trials: **long head, short head.** See quot. 1966.
1959 MCLEOD *Tall Tussock* 124 *Long Head*: Long run for heading dog. 1966 *Encycl. NZ* I. 493 *Heading*. In the *long head* the competitor stands with his dog in a ring (1 chain in diameter) facing a hillside near the top of which three sheep are set loose. When time is called the dog is dispatched, either on a left-hand or a right-hand cast, up the hill for some 800 yards to a point behind the sheep. On command the dog 'lifts' the sheep and, keeping them together, 'pulls' them in a direct line back to his master in the ring. To allow the dog to show complete control over the sheep, the run ends with a 'hold in the ring'. This involves stopping the sheep in the ring and holding them there. The first stages of the *short head* are much the same, but over half the distance, 400 yards.

4. In various phrases. **a. head over turkey** [AND 1915], head over heels.
1953 14 M A17 Thames DHS 16 Head over turkey [M2] 1960 MASTERS *Back-Country Tales* 90 However, with..the rest of the party..hanging grimly onto a rope..to prevent the truck from sliding off the track and going head over turkey into gullies the wet, cold and risky job was eventually accomplished.

b. to sleep heads and tails (head and tail) [used elsewhere but recorded earliest in NZ], to sleep, one person's feet at the other's head; to double up in a bed in this manner.
1842 *Piraki Log* (1911) 143 Stopped at 'Tommy's' [a Maori's]... Slept on a Maori mat, wrapped in a blanket: 4 in a bed-place—heads and tails. 1851 WARD *Journal* 9 Jan. (1951) 109 All slept heads and tails in the kitchen. 1876 *Weekly Herald* 10 June in Scott *Seven Lives on Salt River* (1987) 52 On one Sunday, 18 bushmen and gumdiggers were lying 'heads and tails' in the deadhouse [sleeping off the effects of drink]. 1896 HARPER *Pioneer Work* 90 On turning in we lie 'heads and tails' in our blanket bags. 1945 HARPER *Camping & Bushcraft in NZ* 10 We slept 'heads and tails' in the half-tent.

head, *n.*[2] Usu. *pl.* as **the heads.** [Used elsewhere but of high frequency in NZ: see OED *head n.*[1] 22 the projecting point of the coast.] A promontory or headland, one of (usu.) two, marking or delimiting the entrance to a natural harbour.
1820 27 Nov. in Cruise *Journal* (1823) (1957) 175 Divine service having been read over the bodies..they were taken outside the heads, and committed to the deep. 1834 MARKHAM *NZ* (1963) 29 At 3 pm came to an Anchor at Parkinneigh a Village and had I suppose 150 Natives on board and a par of Fort about 12 miles from the Heads. 1840 BEST *Journal* June (1966) 229 All the land on the Eastern side [of Wellington harbour] is exceedingly steep and hilly down to the beach, from the Heads to the mouth of the river. 1898 HOCKEN *Contributions* 80 Otago..was appropriated to the whole block, but really relates to a small district within the Heads. 1942 GASKELL *All Part of the Game* (1978) 12 Once outside the heads, the long slow surge took hold of us. 1959 SHADBOLT *New Zealanders* (1986) 32 There the creeks became sea, and the sea swelled out to the harbour heads.

head, *n.*[3] *Goldmining.* [Spec. uses of OED *head* 17 a measure of water estimated in terms of pressure on a unit of area.]

1. a. In full **sluice-head.** [OED 1857.] The unit of measured volume of water sold to miners for washing auriferous alluvials from country, or for flushing auriferous matter through a sluice; see also quots. 1967, 1978, 1983.

1863 *AJHR* D-6 15 The length of the head races I estimate at about [120] miles representing about two hundred **sluice heads**. **1887** *Handbook NZ Mines* 18 A large paddock is excavated out of the bed-rock and into this the whole of the material is sluiced from the face... About 20 sluice-heads of water are required. **1892** PYKE *Gold-Miners' Guide* 33 *One sluice-head* must 'at all times' be allowed to flow in the natural bed of the stream, if required by the owner of the property through which such stream passes, or by the Warden of the district, or by any miner working in the bed of the stream. **1967** MAY *West Coast Gold Rushes* 249 Instructions were given for gauging a 'sluice-head' of water: one or two miners were permitted one sluice-head, and so on at the rate of one sluice-head for every additional two miners. **1978** MCARA *Gold Mining Waihi* 332 *Sluicehead*: Sixty cubic feet per minute. **1983** NOLAN *Gold Fossicker's Handbook* 112 *Head*: the unit of volume by which water was sold to alluvial miners.

b. *transf.* Applied to the flow of a natural spring.

c1870s MEREDITH *Adventures Maoriland* (1935) 145 The one [Tokomaru hot spring] we went to is just a boiling spring running about five 'sluice-heads' of boiling water.

2. *Hist.* With a modifier defining the particular kind or volume of any of various heads. **a.** As **Government head**, a standard measure of water supplied to a claim.

1870 *AJHR* D-40 7 Besides a number of smaller races, the..company supplies twenty Government heads of water. **1872** [see *Hogburn head* b below]. **1911** *TrNZI* XLIII. 470 The total length of all the races amounts to seventy miles, and the total carrying-capacity amounts to thirty-six Government heads of water.

b. As **Hogburn head** [f. *Hogburn* (now the town of Naseby) on the Otago goldfields], see quot. 1872.

1872 *AJHR* G-4 29 The 'Hogburn head' is a stream of water passing through an orifice sixteen inches by one inch, and running for the working day of eight hours... The Government head..is equal to two and a half times the Hogburn head..and..flows for 24 hours. **1911** BREMNER in *Mt. Ida Goldfields* (1988) 15 The water race proprietors were now masters of the position... They divided the Government head of water by three, and sold what was then called a Hogburn head for..£5 a week. It was some 16 inches by 2 inches with 6 inches of pressure on a dead level box. **1948** COWAN *Down the Years in the Maniototo* 43 From January 11 to March 11, 1870, the miners of Naseby went on strike, and finally induced the 'water squatters' to lower their rates from five pounds a 'Hogburn' head to two pounds.

head, *n.*⁴ [f. *head* (by synecdoche) a person.]

1. *Obs.* [AND 1918.] A rogue; a gambler or sharper.

1908 *Truth* 25 July 2 There were a few 'heads' up from Christchurch last Saturday and the Tommies [*sc.* bookmakers] could not understand their presence, but in the last race they explained why they were in attendance by the way they put the stuff on Cavatina. **1912** *Ibid.* 20 Jan. 7 Of course, there are [two-up] 'schools' here and there, and only a 'head', in other words 'a true sport', knows their locale.

2. A car-salesmen's term for a prospective customer, a 'john'.

1986 *NZ Herald* (Auckland) 22 Jan. sect. ii 1 Car dealers have a collection of jargon they use on the yard, so if you are thinking of taking up selling cars as a career, there are a few terms you should know. A

'plum' or a 'head' is a prospective customer, whom the salesman spies walking onto the yard.

head, *v.* [Spec. use of *head* to get ahead of: AND 1846.]

1. a. *trans.* To head off and stop, to turn back or guide (animals), an action now usu. performed by a HEADING DOG q.v.

1846 PHARAZYN *Journal* (ATLMS) 37 Finished flooring Kitchen... Afterwards heading home Sheep. *Ibid.* 38 Boys headed home Ewes in the afternoon Potatoe house finished. **1862** CHUDLEIGH *Diary* 17 Nov. (1950) 66 The sheep got out of the paddoc [*sic*] and we had some difficulty to head them. **1874** WILSON *Diary* 26 Apr. in Wierzbicka *Wilson Family* (1973) 184 Went for a good long walk..and found that 'Fop' was so fat and lazy that he would not head some sheep I sent him after. **1934** LILICO *Sheep Dog Memoirs* 6 He was a powerful dog to head or heel cattle.

b. *intr.* Usu. of a sheep-dog, to perform the work of heading.

1934 LILICO *Sheep Dog Memoirs* 27 [The dogs] would head, lead, hunt away, force and back, though, of course, they were best at rouseabout work. **1949** HARTLEY *Shepherd's Dogs* 2 The dog 'Trojan'..would head, hunt, lead, back, heel cattle..open and close gates. **1981** ANDERSON *Both Sides of River* 78 One of the musterers..gave him his first dog..who would hunt as well as head.

c. *transf.* As **head up**, to head off.

1891 *TrNZI* XXIII. 492 As we came out [of the Snares Islands], flocks of sea-birds flew and swam around us, and we headed up a great herd of nellies..and chased them awhile.

Hence **heading** *vbl. n.*, see quot. 1933.

1933 *Press* (Christchurch) (Acland Gloss.) 28 Oct. 17 *Head*... A dog goes round to the far side of a mob of sheep and stops them. This is called *heading*. Hence *heading dog*, one whose work this is. If he does it neatly he *makes a good h[ead]*... 3. The owner would say, 'I can *h[ead] with him*'. **1966** [see HEAD *n.*¹ 3 b].

2. *Canterbury.* [f. NOR'WESTER, a local strong, dry wind.] In the phr. **head a nor'wester (nor'west gale)**, said of a very good heading dog able to head the most difficult stock.

1947 NEWTON *Wayleggo* 52 This dog would 'head a nor' wester'. **1951** MCLEOD *NZ High Country* 22 He will catch a sheep no matter how fast they run or how rough the going—'Head a Nor' wester, that dog' as the saying goes. **1975** HARPER *Eight Daughters* 91 And dogs, what dogs the old men had—They'd head the wild nor'west gales And bring back fogs.

header. *Farming.* [f. HEAD *v.* + -ER.] HEADING DOG.

1938 BURDON *High Country* 107 Dogs are usually kept in the proportion of three or four huntaways to one header now. **1956** DARE *Rouseabout Jane* 161 Being a header he would run round the outside of any field and collect the sheep and drive them towards me. **1969** HASCOMBE *Down & Almost Under* 81 The one in the middle's a header, or an eye-dog he's sometimes called. **1970** MCNAUGHTON *Tat* 117 You should go [to the dog trials] and give your header a go, anyway. **1989** RICHARDS *Pioneer's Life* 26 A musterer always has two types of dogs, a noisy 'huntaway' and a silent 'header'.

heading dog. *Farming.* [f. HEAD *v.* 1.] A working dog trained to head off stock and drive them towards its master. See also HEADER.

1913 CARR *Country Work* 33 A new hand..is wise investing in a good huntaway or a heading dog. **1933** *Press* (Christchurch) (Acland Gloss.) 25 Nov. 15 The dogs that bring sheep are called *heading d[og]s*. **1949** NEWTON *High Country Days* 195 Heading dog: A dog

which has a natural instinct to cast out round sheep and bring them back to its owner. These are silent dogs; they are used for 'heading' and also any quiet and careful work about hand, i.e., at close quarters. **1960** MASTERS *Back-Country Tales* 203 Wag was a heeler..and Tot, a heading dog, small and as quick as lightning. **1978** JARDINE *Shadows on Hill* 7 Steve had told him to pull a small mob down to the flat 'to see what your heading dog is like'; she pulled too hard and nearly put them over a bluff. **1982** *Agric. Gloss.* (MAF) 24 *Heading dog*: Dog that goes around or heads off a group or an individual sheep.

heading 'em. [AND 1871.] The spinning of two coins in the game of two-up (to attempt) to have them fall heads-up; often, the game itself.

1907 *Truth* 18 May 1 'Heading 'em' as it [*sc.* two-up] is called, is carried on in a certain licensed billiard saloon. **1912** *Magpie* Mar. 'Two up' or 'Heading 'Em' **1912** *Truth* 20 Jan. 7 This is how the toiling and moiling son of the soil..loves to while away an idle and sometimes expensive hour in 'heading 'em'.

headings, *vbl. n. Goldmining.* [Spec. use of *heading* top layer: AND 1859.] Non-auriferous material overlying washdirt.

1869 *Auckland Punch* 163 [The shaft] had been partially filled up with 'headings', or refuse dirt from some of the claims close by. **1871** MONEY *Knocking About NZ* 18 I started them [the diggers] to cradle some 'headings', or dirt thrown out of deserted holes, which had not been considered worth washing by the lucky boys who had originally sunk them. **1881** BATHGATE *Waitaruna* 128 The white heaps of 'headings' marked the existence of holes clearly enough on the spurs.

headless chook: see CHOOK 3 a.

head log. *Sawmilling.* [f. *head* the leafy top of a tree: see OED *n.*¹ 9 b.] See quot. 1987.

1986 17 June TV2 *Country Calendar* [Of a kauri milling gang which cuts mainly old fallen trunks] We prefer to cut head logs and fallen logs—not standing timber. **1987** MASSEY *Woodturning NZ* 93 *Head-log* A saw log cut from the tree trunk above the first branch.

head-race. *Goldmining.* [Extended use of *head-race* the race or flume which brings water to a mill-wheel: OED 1846.] The race which brings water into a sluice. Contrast TAIL-RACE.

1863 *AJHR* D-6 15 The length of the head races I estimate at about [120] miles. **1877** WILBY *Diary* 3 Feb. in Pfaff *Diggers' Story* (1914) 116 Great flood.— dam, headrace, and tailrace swept clear away. **1884** REID *Rambles on Golden Coast* 151 Then a water-race is brought in to the claim from a higher level. This is termed the head-race. **1909** THOMPSON *Ballads About Business* 76 From the base of the fluming that makes a bridge To carry the head-race from ridge to ridge. **1953** SUTHERLAND *Golden Bush* (1963) 119 The job of building the new fluming to take place of the missing head-race wasn't simple. **1983** NOLAN *Gold Fossicker's Handbook* 112 *Head race*: a channel constructed to bring water to a mining site.

head shepherd. *Farming.* See quot. 1933.

1867 BARKER *Station Life* (1870) 152 Her husband is the head shepherd on the next station. **1907** KOEBEL *Return of Joe* 19 I used to be head-shepherd on Grant's station. **1933** *Press* (Christchurch) (Acland Gloss.) 28 Oct. 17 *Head shepherd.*—He takes charge of mustering, yards, and all sheep work when the manager is not present, and very often when he is. He cannot as a rule sack a man, but can send him in to the boss, who very soon will. **1946** ACLAND *Early Canterbury Runs* 121 In

1875 Crosbie left..and D. Oliver, the head shepherd, became manager. **1973** FERNANDEZ *Tussock Fever* 44 'I suppose Dad will make him head shepherd next season,' he mused.

head sherang: see SHERANG.

headsman. *Whaling.* [Used elsewhere but recorded earliest in NZ: see OED *headsman* 3, and *header* 4 b.] One in command of a whaleboat who, when a whale is sighted and harpooned, takes charge of the whale-lance at the boat's bow or 'head' for the final kill. (Occas. the headsman would also harpoon the whale.)
 1836 *Log 'Mary Mitchell'* 9 Aug. in McNab *Old Whaling Days* (1913) 453 I..found 4th mate had written a letter dated 31st July to John Guard requesting the employ in his service as a boat headsman. **1845** WAKEFIELD *Adventure NZ* I. 317 The [whalers] are enrolled under three denominations: *headsman, boat steerer* and common man. The headsman is..the commander of the boat; and his place is at the helm except during the moment of killing the whale, which task falls to his lot. **1856** FITTON *NZ* 13 [Natives] became skilful..also as 'headsmen' in managing the boats, and harpooning and killing the whale. **1898** HOCKEN *Contributions* 108 This Thomas was the headsman of the whaling party. **1905** BAUCKE *White Man Treads* 75 An old-time bay whaling station consisted..of at least two boats, with their crew of six men each. The headsman, or mate, four ordinary oarsmen, and the harpooner, or 'boat-steerer'. **1939** BEATTIE *First White Boy Born Otago* 53 Joe Millar was as good a headsman as ever. **1982** MORTON *Whale's Wake* 43 Deliberately learned and hard-won skill was thus one justification for the officer or headsman taking the place of the harpooner in the final kill.

head-station.

1. *Farming.* [f. *head a.* chief + STATION 3 b: AND 1835.] STATION 3 b, the homestead and main buildings of a stock station.
 1863 REES in Griffiths *King Wakatip* (1971) 97 It takes some time to work out the best sites for working a large run, and I have not been certain that the site of my head station would ultimately be permanent. **1881** SEALY *Are We Here to Stay* in Burdon *High Country* (1938) 150 You see scattered around the head stations little comfortable cottages, each with its neat garden. **1891** CHAMIER *Philosopher Dick* 6 A degree of civilisation which gained for the Marino head-station a widespread fame.

2. *Surveying.* The main or headquarters camp of a field-party.
 1878 JOLLIE *Reminiscences* (ATLTS) 14 These three Maories had been working for us..about 15 miles inland, when getting short of provisions we all returned to the head station.

health camp. A usu. summer (or short-stay) camp dedicated to the improvement of children's physical or emotional health.
 1920 *Auckland Weekly News* 29 Jan. [Caption] An experimental health camp for school children at Turakina, near Wanganui. The camp was established during the Christmas holidays [1919] by Dr. Elizabeth Gunn, medical inspector of schools, with the object of demonstrating that children suffering from malnutrition could be brought to a normal state of health by open-air treatment and proper feeding... Fifty-five children under 12 years of age went into camp. **1930** *Auckland Weekly News* 4 June [Caption] Caring for New Zealand's delicate children: Sunshine Club, Solarium, Community Club and Health Camp established in Auckland. **1949** BLANC *Money, Medicine & Masses* 155 Just as the milk-in-schools scheme was the first line of attack on malnutrition in children, so is the Health Camp a second line. **1958** ASHTON-WARNER *Spinster* 25 I'm going to write a letter to Mr Reardon when I go to Health Camp. **1966** *Encycl. NZ* II. 527 The originator of health camps was Dr Elizabeth Gunn who, as school medical officer at Wanganui, organised small summer camps for undernourished children in 1919. **1983** MCELDOWNEY *Warm South* 187 [1966 Sept. 8] I had a cup of tea at the Phys. Ed. School where Lilian..told me two riddles:.. 'Where would you take a sick fairy?' 'To an elf camp.' **1994** *Dominion* (Wellington) 24 Nov. 17 Much of the health camp therapy is based on restoring self-esteem, confidence and independence.

health stamp. Occas. *ellipt.* **health.** New Zealand stamps issued annually since 1929 carrying a surcharge on the postal rate for the support of health camps.
 1932 *NZ Stamp Collector* XIII. 81 Although the latest Health stamp for New Zealand created a very favourable impression in New Zealand it evidently has not met with the approval of our Australian confreres. **1938** *Postage Stamps of NZ* I. 400 The issue of Health Stamps in New Zealand had its origin in a suggestion made in 1926 by Mr. E. Nielsen, of Norsewood, Hawkes Bay, on behalf of his mother [Kirsten], that the system obtaining in Denmark and adopted in other countries of issuing Christmas seals should be followed in New Zealand, the proceeds..to be devoted to the upkeep of sanatoria or some deserving health object of the kind. **1942** *NZ Stamp Collector* XXXII. 4 The 1d of 1931 is actually the rarest of all the New Zealand healths. **1953** *NZ Observer* 18 Nov. 14 I sold Health Stamps—and we had fun from 11.30 a.m. to 1.30 p.m. **1966** *Encycl. NZ* II. 527 By 1929..summer health camps..[had been] held..funds being raised by voluntary subscriptions, supplemented by the sale of health stamps which first appeared in 1929. **1994** *Dominion* (Wellington) 24 Nov. 17 Health stamps..have become a distinctive and unique part of New Zealand culture.

healthy, *a.* [Spec. use of *healthy* with reference to qualities of land.] Of central North Island country, not bush-sick.
 1928 *TrNZI* LVIII. 539 The words 'healthy' and 'unhealthy' applied to Lands must be understood to refer respectively to those which are free from the disease [*sc.* bush sickness] and those on which it occurs. **1930** *NZJST* XII. 4 In the neighbouring healthy areas the sands are practically absent, and the ash is underlain by the upper Te Kuiti limestone with its attendant residual clay.

heaps. [Prob. ellipt. for *heaps of* (effort, praise, blame, etc.).] Esp. in the phr. **to give it** (or something) **heaps,** to give (something) a supreme effort; to work or make go at high speed; **to give** (a person) **heaps,** to blame, to scold; occas. **to get heaps,** to get (heaps of) praise or notice, occas. blame. Also as an intensifier 'very often', 'plenty'.
 1984 16 M E88 Pakuranga Coll. 13 Heaps: give it heaps **1987** 6 June TV1 Commentator on World Cup Rugby. He knew that — was looking over his shoulder. And he gave it heaps. **1988** MCGILL *Dict. Kiwi Slang* 56 *heaps*, phr. *give him/her/it heaps* give someone trouble or suggestion that you give something all your effort; eg 'Give her heaps, boy. Go on, that old dunga's used to it.' **1990** *Dominion* (Wellington) 19 June 20 If New Zealand beat Australia in tonight's..netball final, shooter Vicki Wilson will get 'heaps' from the Maori pupils at her school. **1994** *Dominion* (Wellington) 30 July 13 We ended up running away from there heaps. We kept getting a hiding because he was a pisshead.

heater. The usual New Zealand term for an electric bar-heater, elsewhere usu. 'electric fire'.
 1964 MIDDLETON *Walk on Beach* 235 Although the sun shone outside, an electric heater burned beside the desk. **1976** HILLIARD in *NZ Short Stories* (1984) 132 At home David made hmself a cup of cocoa and sat..warming his hands with the cup and staring at the electric heater. **1985** *Women's Work* 146 There was a coldness though,... so he..went to the kitchen to get the two-bar heater. **1992** *North & South* (Auckland) Jan. 87 I learned to wear jandals and say truck (not lorry)..chips..shift..footpath..heater (not fire).

heath. Also **native heath.** [Transf. use of Brit. *heath* (chiefly) *Erica* spp. (fam. Ericaceae) for heathlike plants of various plant families, esp. Epacridaceae.]

1. *Leucopogon* (formerly *Cyathodes*) *fraseri* (fam. Epacridaceae), PATOTARA 1.
 1867 HOOKER *Handbook* 764 Heath, native of Otago. *Leucopogon Frazeri* [*sic*]. **1900** *Canterbury Old & New* 183 Amongst the host of introduced weeds it is difficult for anybody but a botanist to distinguish the smaller and less peculiar native plants, such as the small white native heath [*Leucopogon fraseri*], and others too numerous to mention. **1969** *Standard Common Names Weeds* 23 dwarf heath [=] patotara.

2. *Dracophyllum* spp. (fam. Epacridaceae). See also INANGA *n.*[2], NEINEI.
 1879 HAAST *Geol. Canterbury & Westland* 115 Fortunately there were many shrubs of *Dracophyllum longifolium* growing in this locality... It is generally called a native heath by the Europeans. **1908** *AJHR* C-14 41 [*Dracophyllum Urvilleanum*]. Common needle-leaved heath. Erect shrub, with slender branches and almost vertical grass-like leaves.

3. *Gaultheria antipoda* (fam. Ericaceae), SNOWBERRY 1 a.
 1906 THOMSON *Intro. Classbook Bot.* 63 Native heath, or snowberry (*Gaultheria antipoda*). This is an extremely variable species, ranging from a low creeping shrub, with small lanceolate serrate leaves, to a tolerably large and erect bush, with much larger broad leaves.

4. Formerly as **prickly heath,** *Cyathodes juniperina* (formerly *Styphelia acerosa*) (fam. Epacridaceae) and *Leucopogon* (formerly *Cyathodes*) *fasciculatus,* MINGIMINGI.
 1908 *AJHR* C-11 39 *Styphelia acerosa* (prostrate variety). Mingimingi Sharp-leaved heath. Forest. [*Styphelia empetrifolia*]..(syn *Cyathodes empetrifolia*). **1915** *AJHR* C-6 14 *Styphelia acerosa.* Mingimingi. Sharp-leaved heath. Rock. **1953** GUTHRIE-SMITH *Tutira* 318 Prickly heath (*Leucopogon fasciculatus*).. sometimes appears within a few yards of thriving spreads of ryegrass. **1984** *Standard Common Names Weeds* 84 Prickly heath *Cyathodes juniperina.*

5. As **Australian heath,** *Epacris* spp. (fam. Epacridaceae); as **New Zealand heath,** *Epacris pauciflora,* a twiggy shrub having white flowers at the tips of erect branches.
 1969 *Standard Common Names Weeds* 3 Australian heath *Epacris* [spp.]. **1887** *Auckland Weekly News* 12 Nov. 8 On that high ridge..may be found the New Zealand heath, epacris pauciflora.

heather. Also **native heather.** [Transf. use of Brit. *heather Calluna vulgaris* (fam. Ericaceae).] *Cassinia* spp. (fam. Asteraceae). See also BOXWOOD.
 1868 PYKE *Province of Otago* 21 The modest gowan mingles with sweet-scented native heather; honey-suckles twine around cottage-porches. **1953** DEWAR *Chaslands* 19 The grass playing area [of the Southland school] was backed by a great area of 'boxwood' or native heather.

heavy, *a. Goldmining.*

1. Of water, at heavy pressure.
    1863 *AJHR* D-6 14 Where the water is heavy, and there are no means of cutting a tail-race, water-wheels have been erected.

2. [AND 1858.] Of gold, found in heavy particles.
    1866 *West Coast Times* in Pfaff *Diggers' Story* (1914) 127 On Saturday week..rumours were current in town..that heavy gold had been discovered at the back of the hospital. **1873** PYKE *Wild Will Enderby* (1889, 1974) III. i 75 They are on heavy gold, too, for I saw some of the stuff that they traded away.

heavy, *n.*

1. In the phr. **to do the heavy** [used elsewhere but recorded earliest in NZ: see OED *heavy* B 4], to make a fine show.
    1869 WHITWORTH *Grimshaw Comic Guide to Dunedin* 39 Shall we do the heavy, and expend 3/- to visit the dress-circle, like swells.

2. *Prison.* **a.** As **the heavies**, threats.
    1984 BEATON *Outside In* 40 They all have to come to you. The Boss! But you're startin' to be a bore. So piss off with the fuckin' heavies, 'cos you don't scare me.

Hence **heavy** *v. trans.*, to bring heavy (often violent) pressure upon (a person).
    1990 KIDMAN *True Stars* 149 Minna, I didn't give up seeing men to get heavied like I was.

b. In the phr. **to put** (someone) **on the heavy jacket**, to ostracize.
    1982 NEWBOLD *Big Huey* 198 Kapua..had been put on the heavy jacket by the Maoris in the can, and was sitting at a table all by himself.

heavy bush: see BUSH A 1 c.

hebe /ˈhibi/. Also with init. cap. A large genus of predominantly New Zealand evergreen shrubs (fam. Scrophulariaceae) named by the French botanist P. Commerson in 1789 (after *Hebe* the Greek goddess of youth and beauty), and formerly included in the genus VERONICA q.v. and often so called; KOROMIKO. See also KOKOMUKA.
    1927 *TrNZI* LVII. 13 A species usually is transferred to *Hebe* only when..we are pretty well convinced it is valid. **1951** HUNT *Confessions* 136 It has..speedwells or veronicas which in England are modest little blue flowers..but which here in New Zealand are not only an enormous family of numerous species with a range of colours varying from white to dark purple, but, in the form of shrubs and trees (known as Hebes), reach a height of forty feet. **1968** SLATTER *Pagan Game* 20 There were the scrublands of blackened second growth..the marginal land of bracken, hebe and flax, the reproachful columns of burnt-over bush. **1984** MANTELL *Murder in Vain* 68 He moved away, paused by a low-growing hebe.

hecacahoo, var. KAKAHU *n.*[1]

heckashin: see HANG *n.*

Hector's dolphin: see DOLPHIN 2 (4).

hedgehog grass: see GRASS 2 (21).

heel, *v. Farming.* Also **heel up**. *trans.* Of a cattle-dog, to bite at the heels of beasts to make them move.
    1918 *Hawkes Bay Herald* 11 July 3 He tied a rope around her nose and horns, got in the car, set it going, and had the dog 'heeling up' behind. **1889** REISCHEK *Wonderful Dog* 35 When the animal stops one [dog] will heel it up. **1934** LILICO *Sheep Dog Memoirs* 6 He was a powerful dog to head or heel cattle... I have often wondered how Teddy came to be such a fine natural heeler. **1940** STUDHOLME *Te Waimate* (1954) 138 Old Jim had two good dogs, one of which frightened the beasts by heeling them up (biting their heels), and the other by pulling their tails. **1982** *Agric. Gloss.* (MAF) 24 *Heel*: Bite (usually cattle) in the heel to make them move.

Hence **heeling** *vbl. n.*, esp. *attrib.* in **heeling dog** (also **heeler**), a dog trained to heel cattle.
    1934 [see above]. **1940** STUDHOLME *Te Waimate* (1954) 139 Some of the riders..went after the bullock...Two heeling dogs were also in the hunt. **1971** NEWTON *Ten Thousand Dogs* 168 *Heeling dog*: A dog which when working cattle will nip them in the fetlocks (heels) to shift them. There is a specific breed—the Australian blue heeler—which has a natural instinct to heel. **1985** RENNIE *Working Dogs* 39 *Heeling*. Most strains of Border Collie have plenty of eye and will also heel cattle.

heifer. [f. obsolete Brit. slang *heifer* a woman.]

1. *Obs.* In early whalers' or traders' parlance, a woman.
    1845 WAKEFIELD *Adventure NZ* I. 319 A chief was called a '*nob*'; a slave, a '*doctor*'; a woman, a '*heifer*'; a girl, a '*titter*'; and a child, a '*squeaker*'.

2. As **heifer station** *obs.* [AND 1839], a stock station running heifers after weaning.
    1851 WELD *Letter* Jan. in *NZGG* 21 Feb. (1851) 30 The track of downs and vallies between [the Hurunui]..and the Waiau-ua, now in the occupation of Mr. Caverhill as a heifer station, is the finest and richest cattle run I have seen in either island.

hei-tiki. Also early **e tiki**. [Ma. /ˈheitiki/: *hei* to wear around the neck + TIKI: Williams 44 *Heitiki*.] TIKI 1 a and note.
    [**1820** LEE & KENDALL *NZ Gram. & Vocab.* 153 Hei tíki; A miniature keep-sake, &c. worn in the bosom.] **1835** YATE *NZ* (1970) 151 The latter idea [that *heitiki*s represent the gods] was conceived from the *heitiki* being taken off the neck, laid down in the presence of a few friends meeting together, then wept or sung over. **1847** ANGAS *Savage Life* I. 327 Around the neck is worn a small and ludicrous figure, representing a man of grotesque proportions, with large red eyes, which is also formed out of green jade. These little images, termed *e tiki*, are regarded as amulets or charms; they pass as heirlooms from generation to generation, and are so greatly esteemed, that it is seldom a native can be persuaded to part with one. **1869** *TrNZI* I. (rev. edn.) 360 The quaintly carved greenstone *heitiki* suspended on their breasts. **1878** BULLER *Forty Yrs. NZ* 238 Around the neck was suspended the *heitiki*, a rude image..fashioned out of the precious green-stone. **1904** TREGEAR *Maori Race* 247 It has been sometimes thought that the *heitiki* was the image of a god, *hei* meaning 'to wear around the neck' and *Tiki* being the name of a god. Probably, however, the *heitiki* was only a memento of an ancestor. **1911** *Triad* 11 Dec. 25 'Then look at her *hei tiki*.' He picked up the flat greenstone image which hung from her neck by a string of flax. **c1920** BEATTIE *Trad. Lifeways Southern Maori* (1994) 57 Heitiki were usually made of greenstone and were objects of great veneration. **1932** ELDER in Marsden *Lett. & Jrnls.* (1932) 432 Maori amulets in the form of pendants were of many kinds, but the best-known is undoubtedly the *hei-tiki*. *Hei* means 'pendant,' while *tiki* means 'human.' The *hei-tiki* signified fertility and was appropriately worn by women. **1941** MYERS *Valiant Love* 15 Greenstone *hei-tiki*s suspended from their [*sc.* Maori women's] necks on strings of flax hung between their bare breasts. **1962** JOSEPH *Pound of Saffron* 113 'Hei-tiki,' he said. 'No one can tell what it is.'

heke. [Ma. /ˈheke/: Williams 44 *Heke*...7.] A party of travelling people; a migration; often used of the 'great migration' from Hawaiki, a Maori founding myth. Cf. HIKOI, MIGRATION.
    1864 *Richmond-Atkinson Papers* (1960) II. 117 Got a little consolation from Matiu te Huia, who declares that the supposed taua (or war party) is really a heke (or migration) of women & children. **1906** *TrNZI* XXXVIII. 3 Rauparaha..made preparations for his great *heke* or exodus from Kawhia to this district. **1913** MCNAB *Old Whaling Days* 39 Accordingly [Te Rauparaha] and the whole of his people set forth on that *heke* or migration. **1921** GUTHRIE-SMITH *Tutira* 54 Descent is claimed by the Ngati-kahungunu from Rongo-kako, whose son Tamatea arrived in..one of the most famous canoes of the great *heke* or migration from the mythical Hawaiki. **1933** 22 Mar. in *Na To Hoa Aroha* (1988) III. 73 Moriori traditions do not go very far back of the heke people. **1949** BUCK *Coming of Maori* 36 The great migration (*heke*) from Hawaiki is the most famous event in Maori history, because all the tribes trace their aristocratic lineages back to the chiefs of the voyaging canoes. **1970** JENKIN *NZ Mysteries* 102 They [*sc.* a Maori group] were going on an up-country heke or migration and in doing so had to cross a combined rail and road bridge over the river. **1988** MIKAERE *Te Maiharoa* 69 In the winter of 1877, with more than a hundred followers, the prophet set out for Omarama. The people of the heke (migration) called themselves Israelites,... Te Maiharoa's migration followed the coastal trail south to the Waitaki River... The heke moved at Te Maiharoa's pace and direction.

heketara. [Ma. /ˈheketara/: Williams 45 *heketara*..*Olearia rani*, a shrub.] *Olearia rani* (fam. Asteraceae or Compositae), a native shrub or small tree bearing panicles of white to yellowish flowers.
    1889 KIRK *Forest Flora* 225 Olea cunninghamii was discovered by Banks and Solander in 1769... I am indebted to..W.L. Williams for the Native name 'heketara'. **1910** COCKAYNE *NZ Plants & Their Story* 37 The heketara..produces multitudes of daisy-like flowers in the spring. **1934** *Tararua Tramper* Dec. 3 The Tauherenikau..looking very beautiful with the sweet-scented rangiora and heketara in bloom. **1961** ALLAN *Flora NZ* I. 669 N., S. Lowland forests and forest margins from near North Cape to lat. 42° *Heketara*... Type locality: 'Banks of rivers, Bay of Islands'. **1978** MOORE & IRWIN *Oxford Book NZ Plants* 130 *Olearia rani*, heketara. A tall, openly growing shrub or small tree with smooth hard trunk. **1986** SALMON *Field Guide Native Trees NZ* 314 [Caption] The bark of heketara, like that of most *Olearia* species, is thin and furrowed, peeling in narrow flakes.

Heke War /ˈheki ˈwɔə/. Also **(Hone) Heke's War**. The conflict in the 1840s between Hone Heke Pokai (1810?–50), a Ngapuhi leader, and British troops and Maori allies, also referred to as *the war in the north* (see WAR 2 b). See also FLAGSTAFF WAR.
    1890 *Otago Witness* (Dunedin) 6 Mar. 17 It will not perhaps be a serious departure..to spend a few minutes in inspection of the series of pictures collected..by Dr. Hocken, illustrative of Honi Heki's war. **1899** *Auckland Weekly News* (Suppl.) 29 Sept. 2 The 58th Regiment.. engaged in what is termed 'Heke's War', in 1845–46. **1900** *Auckland Weekly News Suppl.* 21 Dec. 6 The capture of Ruapekapeka Pa put an end to what was known as the Heke War. **1993** *Defence Quarterly* No. 1

hellishing, adv. Usu. as **hellashun, hellashing**. [An elaboration of *hellish*: see OED *hellishing*, 'Chiefly *Austral.* and *N.Z.*', 1931.] An intensifying adjective or adverb 'exceedingly'. See also HANG n.
   1950 GASKELL *All Part of the Game* (1978) 158 He thinks he's hung his clothes up and they fall down... It's hellashin funny. **1983** HULME *Bone People* 29 I'll be hellashing popular if I sent it home drunk. **1984** BEARDSLEY *Blackball 08* 62 Oh joy, oh boy, the lolly scramble, a hellashun big tin and Mr Stevens..hurling them in the air.

   17 Heke was wounded..in June 1845 and ceased to play an active part in Heke's War which was waged by Kawiti.

hells bells: see DAISY 2 (4) (*Helichrysum bellidiodes*).

hemp. *Obs.* Also **native** (or **New Zealand**) **hemp**. [Transf. use of hemp *Cannabis sativa* (fam. Cannabaceae), an annual plant once widely cultivated for its fibre, for NZ flax (*Phormium* spp.).] FLAX 1, the plant and the fibre derived from it. See also MUKA.
   1769 MONKHOUSE 11 Oct. in Cook *Journals* (1955) I. 573 The materials of this sort [of mat] thinks [*sic*] is of true hemp—it looked like it and had the proper smell. **1783** Aug. 23 James Matra's proposal for Estab. of NSW in *Hist. Recs. NSW* (1892) I. pt.2 2 I mean the New Zealand hemp or flax-plant, an object equally of curiosity and utility. **1814** MARSDEN in Elder *Marsden's Lieutenants* (1934) 55 I should wish you to bring as much hemp as you possibly can, and such spars and timber as you may..judge valuable. **1840** *NZ Jrnl.* I. 7 New Zealand Hemp (or Flax)... This product is commonly called New Zealand Flax. **1852** WILKES *US Exploring Exped.* I. 316 The native hemp (Phormium tenax) is a most useful plant. **1891** [see FLAX 2 (3)]. **1910** COCKAYNE *NZ Plants & Their Story* 109 The manufacture of fibre from phormium—'New Zealand hemp', as it is now called—has become one of the staple industries of the Dominion. **1930** [see FLAX 1 a]. **1955** *NZ Geogr. Soc. Rec.* July–Dec. 23 A change of name to 'hemp' in 1871 was of considerable advantage to the New Zealand flax industry in general. **1981** [see FLAX 2 (3)].

hen.
1. *Obs.* Also **native hen**. In early occas. use for MAORI HEN or WOODHEN, see WEKA.
   1773 WALES *Journal* in Cook *Journals* (1961) II. 787 The Hens, as we called them were a sort of *Rail*, which would stand & stare at us until we knocked them down with a stick. **1862** *Otago Goldfields & Resources* 34 Wild pigs, ducks, and the native hen, are abundant near some of the gold-fields.

2. As a suffix in the names of birds, see: *blue-hen* (BLUE *a.* 2 b), *bush hen* (BUSH C 4), MAORI HEN, *swamp-hen* (SWAMP 2 b), WATER-HEN.

3. In phrases of comparison. **a. (as) rare as hen's (hens') teeth, like hen's teeth,** very scarce. [Variants of the orig. US phr. (1858–) *scarce as hen's teeth* are also freq. in NZ: cf. OED *hen n.* 1 b.] Cf. *scarce as frog's feathers* (FROG n.¹).
   1956 DAVIN *Sullen Bell* 54 Flats are as rare as hen's teeth. **1988** *Sunday News* (Auckland) 27 Mar. 7 Baseball isn't played much in New Zealand—so the bats associated with the code are like hen's teeth.

b. (as) steep as the side of a hen's face, see STEEP *a*.

4. Special Comb. **hen and chickens,** see FERN 2

(7); **hencackle** (also occas. **cackle**) *mountaineering,* an easy climb, or expedition, usu. in the phr. **it's only a hencackle, it's not worth a hencackle (it's a mere hencackle),** dismissing a small or trivial thing (esp. a minor wound), a trifle.
   1934 *Canterbury Mountaineer* 9 In Switzerland the 'impossible' has graduated to the 'easy day for a lady ("hencackle" in our patois)'. **1935** *Ibid.* IV. 8 I must relate that it was on the winter slopes of the Blimit that the famous word 'hencackle' was coined by Evan Wilson... It was..suggested that [Mt] Oates was..too big an effort under such bad conditions to which Evan replied: 'Oates is a hencackle'. **1936** *Ibid.* V. 53 Went up and down that Baker Peak, as Barrer says a 'cackle', with indecent haste. **1939** PASCOE *Unclimbed NZ* 33 All the lasting alpine partnerships of Canterbury have been formed in the easy expeditions. 'Hencackles' we call these expeditions. **1941** BAKER *NZ Slang* 57 *Hencackle*..is applied by mountaineers to a mountain that is easy to climb. Doubtless there is a wider application of the term since *a mere hen cackle,* a trifle, seems to have been the origin of the application. **1988** MCGILL *Dict. Kiwi Slang* 56 *hen cackle* a mountain rated easy by climbers; any trifle.

Henare. *Obs.* [f. Ma. *Henare* /ˈhenare/, a common Maori name of the early 20th c., an adaptation of *Henry:* AND 1921.] A Maori; poss. in quot. *spec.,* a member of the Maori Pioneer Battalion. Cf. HORI.
   1918 *Chron. NZEF* 16 Aug. 32 As for Henare generally, his pride in Digger is unbounded... Henares all seek to outdo all other battalions engaged in the same duties as themselves. *Ibid.* 25 Oct. 151 One evening found all Henares wending their way to the local Y.M. Marquee.

hennee, var. HANI.

henrietta. *Hist.* Also **hinereta.** [f. the vessel *Elizabeth Henrietta* run aground early in 1824 on Ruapuke Island and credited with introducing mice to southern NZ.] Mainly in southern Maori use, a mouse.
   1920 *TrNZI* LII. 74 It is well known that the southern Maori call the mouse hinereta (henrietta) because a vessel of this name ('Elizabeth Henrietta' in 1823) introduced these little creatures to their notice. c**1920** BEATTIE *Trad. Lifeways Southern Maori* (1994) 190 Another old man said that the pekapeka raised an awful smell. It had a skin like a kiore..or like a hinereta (English mouse). **1922** THOMSON *Naturalisation Animals & Plants* 84 Pastor Wohlers, long a missionary working among the natives on Ruapuke in Foveaux Straits, states that mice were first brought to the island in the 'Elizabeth Henrietta', which was wrecked there in 1824, and that even as late as 1873 they continued to be known as 'henriettas'. **1993** EVISON *Te Wai Pounamu* 35 The mice which got ashore fron the ship ['Elizabeth Henrietta'] were the first seen on Ruapuke, and were called 'Henriettas'.

heppa(h): see PA.

herb.
1. *pl.* [Perh. an allusion to *feed a horse oats* to enliven it with hard feed: AND 1957.] Of motor vehicles, acceleration; of an engine, (horse)power, esp. in the phr. **to give** (occas. **feed**) **(her) the herbs,** give it throttle.
   1953 17 M A38 Thames DHS 6 Herbs: give her (giv' 'a) the herb(s) [M2] **1975** ANDERSON *Men of Milford Road* 152 He admitted that the car 'hadn't

quite got the herbs she used to have' but finished up by assuring me that 'she'll do us, boy—We'll get there.' **1984** 14 F E144 Wgton Girls C. 6 Rev up the herbs **1988** MCGILL *Dict. Kiwi Slang* 56 *herbs* power/speed/ratio, phr. *give him/her/it herbs* or *plenty of herbs* usually suggestion you depress car accelerator to the floor or its maximum; originally sluggish horses were given more herbs, or oats.

   Hence **herby** *a. transf.,* strong, powerful.
   1964 HELMER *Stag Party* 109 Good health, Ron... Say, that's a herby brew..does a joker good to get on the grog after a spell in the bush, eh?

herd-testing, *vbl. n.* and *attrib.* [Used elsewhere but recorded earliest in NZ: see OED *n.*¹ 4.] The testing of dairy herds usu. to estimate milk production in individual cows. Often *attrib.* Cf. also the early use of *cow-testing* (COW 6).
   1911 *NZJAg.* July III. 26 A striking case of the value of testing the individual members of a herd is reported from a district where a herd testing association has been established. **1920** POWDRELL *Dairy Farming* 46 It is strongly maintained that herd-testing—the periodical recording of the weight of each cow's produce together with a butter-fat test from which data the production of the cow for the period is calculated—is the surest way of distinguishing the drones. **1936** BELSHAW et al. *Agric. Organiz. NZ* 345 The major function of Herd Testing is primarily to determine the milk and butterfat producing ability of individual cows. *Ibid.* 346 Although herd testing and milk recording societies existed in Germany, Denmark, England and other countries many years earlier, systematic herd testing appears to have been first developed in New Zealand about the year 1920, when a model Herd Testing Association was established by the New Zealand Department of Agriculture in the Wairarapa. **1966** TURNER *Eng. Lang. Austral. & NZ* 45 About 1910 the practice arose of sampling milk from all the cows in a herd individually and testing the milk for its fat content. This process is called *herd-testing.* **1974** *NZ Agric.* 92 Herd testing helps farmers to maintain the standard of their herds—it shows up the lower producers so that they can be culled from the herd.

   Hence **herd-tester,** a person who visits farms testing milk samples to determine milk fat content and the productivity of the herd.
   1927 *NZ Dairy Produce Exporter* 22 Jan. 35 Most folks [get] the herd-tester to do their cows. **1960** CRUMP *Good Keen Man* 94 He told me..all about one of his sisters who was training to be a herd-tester. **1989** BIOLETTI *The Yanks Are Coming* 138 The girl herd-tester could well have gone to America as somebody's wife, but she resisted the temptation.

heregege, var. HARAKEKE.

hermit. [Transf. use of *hermit* a solitary.] In full **hermit sheep.** A sheep which lives alone, apart from the mob. See also *cabbage-tree sheep* (CABBAGE-TREE 4), PLACER *n.²* 1.
   1874 BATHGATE *Col. Experiences* 212 A sheep which has been badly tutued and recovers, loses its gregarious habits, and becomes what the shepherds call a 'hermit'. **1891** [see CABBAGE-TREE 4]. **1917** GLEN *Six Little New Zealanders* (1983) 70 Sometimes they brought in a 'hermit' sheep which lived by itself. **1925** BATHGATE *Random Recolls.* 20 The hermits were kept in a special paddock, and supplied the station mutton. **1933** *Press* (Christchurch) (Acland Gloss.) 28 Oct. 17 *Hermit.*—A single sheep which for some reason takes to living by himself, away from the mob. A *hatter* sheep, in fact. **1960** MILLS *Sheep-O* 124 A famous hermit sheep was successful in eluding all mustering activities for many years. **1970** SEVERINSEN *Hunt Far*

Mountain 25 It's mother, a double-decker fleeced hermit ewe, picked its way through the bush. **1981** HENDERSON *Exiles Asbestos Cottage* 80 Up in the mountains, young Roy Mytton so proudly succeeded in rounding up twenty-odd old hermits, defiant woolly sheep also known as 'double deckers', which had been wily enough to dodge last season's muster.

heron.

1. Usu. with a modifier, a spec. use of *heron* for any of several large wading birds of the family Ardeidae, having long necks and legs. See also CRANE, KOTUKU, MATUKU 1, MATUKU-MOANA.

1773 FORSTER *Resolution Jrnl.* 29 Mar. (1982) II. 243 We saw two shags & white bird which removed from tree to tree..it seemed to be a Heron. **1869** *TrNZI* I. (rev. edn.) 227 A small slate-colored [*sic*] Heron (*Ardea Matook*) inhabits our coasts.

2. With a modifier: **blue (blue reef, reef), white-faced** (occas. **white-fronted**), **white**.

(1) **blue (blue reef, reef) heron**. [AND as *reef heron*, 1848.] *Egretta sacra sacra*, a slaty-grey bird of coastal rocks, mudflats and the intertidal zone, usu. found solitary or in pairs. See also *blue crane* (CRANE 1), MATUKU 1 b, MATUKU-MOANA. [*Note*] The name *blue heron* is also occas. loosely applied to the *white-faced heron* of 2 (2) below leading to confusion in popular reference between it and the *blue (reef) heron* of 2 (1).

1777 ANDERSON *Journal* Feb. in Cook *Journals* (1967) III. 807 There is also about the shore a few sea gulls, some blue herons. **1838** POLACK *NZ* I. 306 *Blue herons, auks, sand larks, sand plovers, terns*..are met with in multitudes. **1868** PYKE *Province of Otago* 31 The noble white crane and blue heron are occasionally found. **1873** BULLER *Birds NZ* 229 The Blue Heron is not confined to New Zealand, but is found along the whole of the Australian coasts and throughout the Polynesian archipelago. **1885** *NZJSc.* II. 557 *Ardea sacra*,.. Blue, Purple, or Reef heron, Matuku.—May be observed alighting on reefs immediately on the ebb of the tide so that the birds stand in the water. **1899** DOUGLAS in *Mr Explorer Douglas* (1957) 247 The Blue Crane or Heron. This bird is much smaller than the white crane and in general appearance and habits it resembles the home heron to which species it no doubt belongs. **1904** HUTTON & DRUMMOND *Animals NZ* 192 The Blue Heron.—*Matuku. Demiegretta sacra*... Ibid. 193 This is a coast bird. It is much more common in the north than in the south. **1921** *Quick March* 10 Aug. 25 Along the western shore of Wellington Harbour there lives..a colony of blue herons. **1947** POWELL *Native Animals NZ* 83 Reef Heron (*Demigretta sacra*), Matuku-moana of the Maoris, is a graceful dark slaty grey bird with long beak and legs of bright yellow. **1985** *Reader's Digest Book NZ Birds* 132 Reef Heron *Egretta sacra sacra*.. Blue reef heron, eastern reef heron, blue crane, blue heron, matuku-moana... Reef herons in New Zealand are at the southeastern limit of their mostly tropical range, and for that reason alone may never be common. **1992** SMITHYMAN *Auto/Biographies* 62 At the edge of the tide one..native blue reef heron picks for what can be had.

(2) **white-faced heron**. (Occas. also called **blue crane** and (poss. erron. for *white-faced*) **white-fronted heron**.) *Ardea novaehollandiae novaehollandiae*, a grey-blue heron with a white face and throat, self-introduced from Australia and breeding in New Zealand from c1941; now the commonest heron in New Zealand. See also MATUKU 1 c, MATUKU-MOANA.

1885 *NZJSc.* II. 557 *Ardea novae-hollandiae*..Lath. White-fronted heron, Matuku. It is far from common in this district. **1904** [see MATUKU-MOANA]. **1955** OLIVER *NZ Birds* 388 *White-faced Heron. Matuku-moana*... First listed from New Zealand by Buller in 1865, several specimens having been obtained in the North Island. **1970** SANSOM *Stewart Islanders* 143 On the estuary white-faced herons feed with an occasional visit..of the kotuku or white herons. **1985** *Reader's Digest Book NZ Birds* 129 White-faced Heron *Ardea novaehollandiae novaehollandiae*... Blue crane... White-faced herons were occasionally sighted in New Zealand in the nineteenth century... Breeding was not however confirmed until 1941. **1992** SMITHYMAN *Auto/Biographies* 62 Across the flats..say half a dozen white faced heron stalk.

(3) **white heron**. *Egretta alba modesta*, a uniformly white, elegant bird, dispersing widely after the nesting season from the breeding colony at Okarito, south Westland; valuable to the Maori formerly for its feathers, and as a figure of a rare, welcome visitor. See also KOTUKU, *white crane* (CRANE 2).

1773 COOK *Journals* 25 Apr. (1961) II. 126 Lieut Pickersgill..shot a White Hern [*sic*] which answers exactly with Mr Pennants discription of the White Herns that either now are or were formerly in England. **1838** POLACK *NZ* I. 307 *Cormorants*, and *a white heron*, are found; said to have formerly existed in England, according to Pennant. **1846** [see KOTUKU 1]. **1873** BULLER *Birds NZ* 227 The White Heron occurs so sparingly in most parts of New Zealand, that 'rare as the Kotuku' has passed into a proverb among the Maoris. **1882** POTTS *Out in Open* 2 The white heron (often called the white crane) the kotuku..enjoys so extensive a range. **1904** TREGEAR *Maori Race* 180 The white crane or heron (*kotuku*: Ardea egretta) was kept for the sake of its feathers, which were plucked every five or six months. **1926** COWAN *Travel in NZ* II. 90 In its [*sc.* Okarito lagoon's] reed recesses there is a colony of that extremely rare and beautiful bird the *kotuku* or white heron. **1930** [see KOTUKU 1]. **1947** POWELL *Native Animals NZ* 83 White Heron (*Casmerodius albus*), Kotuku..is a stately white bird larger than the reef heron. **1958** [see CRANE 2]. **1985** *Reader's Digest Book NZ Birds* 131 *White Heron... Eastern great white egret, great white heron, white egret, large egret, kotuku...* White herons are birds of shallow wetlands. **1990** *Checklist Birds NZ* 89 *Egretta alba modesta*..White Heron (*White Egret, Kotuku*)... India, China and Japan to Australia and New Zealand.

3. In the proverbial **(white) heron of one (a single) flight**, said to a distinguished but rare visitor: a rendering of the Maori: *He kōtuku kai rerenga tahi i te tau.* 'A white heron whose flight is seen only once in the season.'

1940 *Otago Daily Times* (Dunedin) 10 Feb. 16 The Papal Legate..was described as 'the heron of one flight'. **1967** NATUSCH *Animals NZ* 269 'O rare white heron of a single flight'—seen rather oftener in New Zealand than Her Majesty the Queen of whom the poetic Maori phrase was used.

herring, *n.*[1]

1. Any of several mainly unrelated marine fish esp. *yellow-eyed mullet* (MULLET 2 (3)), and (occas.) PILCHARD.

1842 HEAPHY *NZ* 49 The bream, ling, gurnard, herring..are all in abundance, as are also many fish unknown elsewhere [than Wellington]. **1855** TAYLOR *Te Ika A Maui* 624 The *Aua*, herring..is plentiful in all the tidal rivers. **1877** *TrNZI* IX. 329 The herring or mullet is a very abundant fish in Otago Harbour and furnishes very good sport with a rod and line... The true herring was brought to market on one or two days during the summer. **1878** *TrNZI* X. 327 The herring (*Clupea sagax*) was brought to market in good quantity. **1883** *Ibid.* XV. 208 The same species was subsequently identified as the true Picton herring of commerce, of which the first received specimens were the *aua* or herring-mullet. **1902** DRUMMOND & HUTTON *Nature in NZ* 71 The little sea mullet, sometimes called the herring, and the flat fish are found all round the coast. **1921** THOMSON & ANDERTON *Hist. of Portobello* 32 The herring is represented in New Zealand waters by three or four more or less closely allied species, the nearest being the pilchard or sardine. **1947** [see AUA]. **1950** *Fisheries (Gen.) Regs.* (Reprint) 16 (2) 'Herring' means the yellow-eyed mullet (*Agonostomus forsteri*), but does not include the sardine or the species of *Mugil* known as mullet or kanae. **1963** *Commercial Fishing* Apr. 19 Picton's family whaling industry grew from herrings and a rumour. **1970** SORENSEN *Nomenclature NZ Fish* 40 *Pilchard*. Other common names: Sardine; Sprat; Anchovy; Herring. **1986** PAUL *NZ Fishes* 113 The yellow-eyed mullet is probably best known as the 'herring' taken by light-tackle wharf fishing.

2. With a modifier: **Picton, red**.

(1) *Obs.* **Picton herring**. [f. *Picton*, a port in the Marlborough Sounds.] A former local commercial name for a dried and smoked herring-like fish, usu. the PILCHARD (and later also used for the live pilchard), and occas. the *yellow-eyed mullet* (MULLET 2 (3)).

1872 HUTTON & HECTOR *Fishes NZ* 114 The Picton Herring, a dried fish commonly known throughout the Colony, is the Aua (sea mullet) preserved by smoking. **1883** [see 1 above]. **1898** MORRIS *Austral-English* 351 *Picton Herring*.. a name for several fishes when dried (like 'kipper'), especially for the *Sea Mullet*, or *Makawhiti* or *Aua*. **1918** *NZJST* I. 137 In Queen Charlotte Sound this fish is known as the 'Picton Herring', and is cured. **1921** *NZJST* IV. 118 *Sardinia neopilchardus. Pilchard; Mohimohi*. Sold in a smoked condition in Wellington as 'Picton herring'. **1940** PHILLIPPS *Fishes NZ* 7 In the case of Queen Charlotte Sound it has been suggested that the amount of decayed seaweed and black floating ooze is related to the non-appearance of the pilchard, or Picton herring as it is there named. **1956** [see PILCHARD]. **1970** SORENSEN *Nomenclature NZ Fish* 10 The Fisheries (General) Regulations 1950 (Reprint) defines 'Sardine' as the fish with the scientific name *Sardinops neopilchardus*, also known as the Picton Herring. **1986** PAUL *NZ Fishes* 40 In the 1880s a fishery in the Marlborough Sounds produced salted and smoked 'Picton Herring'... The Marlborough fishery was revived..in the 1940's but ceased in 1950.

(2) **red herring**. *Emmelichthys nitidus*, often called 'red bait', having pink fins and a red tail, a mid-water fish frequently found swimming with pilchards.

1921 *NZJST* IV. 115 *Emmelichthys nitidus*. *Red bait-fish*. Rare, and only occasionally utilized as a food fish. Taken in seine among mackerel, and commonly known as 'red herring'. **1981** WILSON *Fisherman's Bible* 35 *Baitfish, red*... Grow up to about 16 inches and known also as..red herring. Colours light pink to dark red.

herring, *n.*[2] *Hist.* Also **hereni, heringi**. [f. a Ma. adaptation *hereni* (/ˈhereni/) of English *shilling* attracted to the English form *herring*.] A shilling, apparently a standard Maori charge for work done for or goods sold to the early settlers.

1842 *Lett. from Settlers* (1843) 81 The [natives] ask one herring..that is one shilling. **1857** ASKEW *Voyage Austral. & NZ* 346 The 'herring', for shilling, is doubtless derived..from the sailors, and others settled in the island from the metropolis. **1862** HODDER *Memories NZ Life* 68 The chief wanted three herren (shillings). **1866** HUNT *Twenty-five Yrs. Experience* 11 'Hereni' shilling..herring is the..white man's corruption.

1873 TINNE *Wonderland of Antipodes* 23 My Maori landlord..charged me only 'five heringi' (shillings) for my tea, bed, and breakfast. **1887** *NZ Mail* (Wellington) 15 July 9 (NZ Slang) A shilling [is] 'a peg', or 'a denah', or 'a herring'.

herringbone cowshed: SHED *n.*¹ 4 b.

herring scad. [Spec. use of *herring scad* for either of two local spp. of jack mackerel.]

1. KOHERU.
    1875 *TrNZI* VII. 247 Caranx koheru. sp. nov. Native name—Koheru... The Herring Scad. **1886** [see KOHERU]. **1971** WILLIAMS *Dict. Maori Lang.* 125 *Kōheru = kōheriheri*, n. *Decapterus koheru*, herring-scad.

2. Occas. applied erron. (poss. following Whitley 1955) to any of the *Trachurus* spp., the *jack* or *horse mackerels* (MACKEREL 2 (2) and (3)).
    1955 WHITLEY *Namelist* in Graham *Treasury NZ Fishes* (1956) 406 Herring scad *Trachurus declivis* (Jenyns). **1957** PARROTT *Sea Angler's Fishes* 86 The Herring Scad *Trachurus declivis*... The herring scad is very similar to the Horse Mackerel in the shape of the body and the arrangement of the fins. **1981** WILSON *Fisherman's Bible* 120 Herring-scad. A species similar to, and often confused with, the Horse Mackerel.

heruheru. [Ma./'heruheru/: Williams 46: for *Leptopteris* spp.]

1. *crape fern* (FERN 2 (3) *Leptopteris hymenophylloides*).
    1867 HOOKER *Handbook* 764 Heru-heru... *Leptopteris hymenophylloides*. **1870** *TrNZI* II. 128 Leptopteris hymenophylloides. Heru heru. **1982** WILSON *Stewart Is. Plants* 436 *Leptopteris hymenophylloides* Crape fern... Heruheru... (=*Todea hymenophylloides*). **1984** MORETON *Whirinaki* 26 Bottle-green with heruheru or crepe fern (*Leptopteris hymenophylloides*).

2. PRINCE OF WALES FEATHER (*Leptopteris superba*).
    1909 [see PRINCE OF WALES FEATHER]. **1975** *Tane 21* 8 Osmundaceae *Todea hymenophylloides*. **1982** WILSON *Stewart Is. Plants* 436 *Leptopteris superba* Prince of Wales Feathers... Heruheru... Double crape fern..(=*Todea superba*).

hewai, var. WAI, WHAI.

hibiscus.

1. Also **starry** (occas. **native**), **Spirits Bay hibiscus**. *Hibiscus trionum* (fam. Malvaceae), a commonly cultivated introduced herb of coastal habitats (incl. Spirits Bay near the far northern tip of New Zealand), once thought to be indigenous.
    1889 FEATON *Art Album NZ Flora* 57 [Heading] Hibiscus Trionum... The Native Hibiscus. The 'Hibiscus trionum'.—This very beautiful tender annual, is indigenous to both Islands. **1907** LAING & BLACKWELL *Plants NZ* 260 *Hibiscus trionum (The Starry Hibiscus)*. **1981** BROOKER et al. *NZ Medicinal Plants* 64 *Hibiscus trionum* L. Common name: Starry hibiscus. Maori name: Puarangi... Mr A.H. Watt obtained the Maori name from older people at Te Kao, when the New Zealand Post Ofice wished to use an illustration of *Hibiscus* on a postage stamp. **1982** SALE *Four Seasons* 48 We already have..in the garden the..rengarenga lily..and the Spirits Bay hibiscus, a primrose yellow bloom with a deep purple-brown centre.

2. As **Hibiscus Coast**, a promotional name for an indeterminate area of the east coast north of Auckland with its hinterland, centering on the Whangaparaoa Peninsula; also the name of a Telecom calling area in that general locality.

    1968 SLATTER *Pagan Game* 23 He knew the winterless north was a tourist gimmick, the Hibiscus Coast hallucinatory, winter was winter anywhere in the land. **1987** *Sunday News* (Auckland) 24 May 3 The Hibiscus Coast resident said this week he went on the domestic purposes benefit..because of a wrangle with customs officers. **1993** *NZ Tablet* (Dunedin) 3 Feb. 5 A few years ago on the Hibiscus Coast we were greeted to a rock Mass of the theatrical scores of Andrew Lloyd Webber. **1993** *Dominion* (Wellington) 3 Feb. 2 The late Sir Robert Muldoon, pictured..outside his Hatfields Beach bach which Hibiscus Coast historians have begun a fundraising drive to save.

hickapenny. *Hist.* [An early Ma. adaptation of 'sixpence': cf. Duval II. 80 *hikipene*, 1842.] A sixpenny piece.
    1879 *Auckland Weekly News* 10 May 16 A young Maori has started as a shoe-black, and as he only charges a 'hickapenny', I have no doubt that he will be largely patronised. **1879** *Auckland Weekly News* 27 Sept. 15 The necessary hickapennies made their appearance. **1887** *NZ Mail* (Wellington) 15 July 9 (NZ Slang) A sixpence [is] 'a sprat', 'a tanner' or (a Maori term) 'hick-a-penny'.

hickety-pips. *Hist.* Also **Hicketi-Pift, Hickety-fifth (Pipth)**. [From *hikitipipi*, a Ma. adaptation of *Sixty-fifth*.] The 65th Regiment, the Royal Tigers.
    1887 *Auckland Weekly News* 23 Apr. 18 Dr. Neill will be remembered..as the well-known staff-surgeon of the 'Tigers' or 'Hickety-fifth' as their Maori foes were accustomed to call them. **1899** GRACE *Sketch NZ War* 95 The Maori replied, 'Kapai te Hickety Pipth' (65th). 'Good, it is the sixty-fifth regiment.' **1910** *NZ Free Lance* (Wellington) 31 Dec. 5 His father was a sergeant in the 65th Regiment—the old 'Hiketi-Pift', as the Maoris called them. **1979** *Evening Post* (Wellington) 29 Mar. 23 The ghosts of the 'Royal Tigers' or 'Hickety-pips' will soon be left on their own on Wellington's Mt. Cook as the last soldiers leave the disbanded Home Command HQ at Buckle St. next month. They acquired another nick-name, the 'Hickety-pips', from the Maori pronunciation of 65th as 'hikitipipi.' **1981** *Evening Post* (Wellington) 14 Oct. 22 Joined [in Wellington] about 1846 by the 65th... They got their nickname of Hickety-pips from the nearest the Maoris could approximate the name of their regiment—'hikitipipi'.

hickory. As **New Zealand hickory**, *mountain toatoa* (TOATOA 1 b *Phyllocladus alpinus*).
    1889 KIRK *Forest Flora* 199 *Phyllocladus alpinus*... The Mountain Toatoa... This species is most plentiful in mountain districts, and is most generally known in the South Island as 'toatoa'..; by settlers and bushmen it is called 'celery-pine'..and in Southland 'New Zealand hickory'.

high country.

1. Often as **the high country**, mountainous (usu. SI tussock) country, esp. mountain foothills when used for sheep farming. Compare HILL COUNTRY.
    1874 BATHGATE *Col. Experiences* 212 Squatters whose runs include high country. **1874** KENNAWAY *Crusts* 138 At the head of one of the lakes [*sc*. Tekapo]..a Scotchman had taken up some high country for sheep, and..was quite content with the short fine summers. **1894** *NZ Official Year-book* ii [The Land for Settlements Act, 1894] also allows of the exchange of high pastoral country belonging to the Crown for agricultural land suitable for small holdings. **1900** SCOTT *Colonial Turf* 166 Little wonder that... so many of the lonely out-shepherds in the high country of Otago have gone

dotty. **1919** *TrNZI* LI. 224 In Stewart Island it [*sc*. the dotterel] occurs in fair numbers..visiting the bare tops of the high country. **1922** PERRY *Sheep Farming* 8 Besides the kea, which destroys a certain number of sheep in the high country of the South Island, there are no predatory animals. **1934** MULGAN *Spur of Morning* 236 I Mark felt a real sympathy for some of the men and women out back in the high country—where runs ran right up to the glaciers. **1963** WALLIS *Point of Origin* 10 The station Dad manages is owned by a bloke named Dent. Thirty thousand acres, most of it high country. **1980** MCLEOD *Down from Tussock Ranges* 9 In the last thirty years or so a great deal has been written about the New Zealand high country and it might be thought that the term 'high country' might apply to almost any part of so mountainous a land. In fact, what is meant is really a type of life rather than a definable area, though it is of course confined to a rather narrow strip of land on the eastern side of the Southern Alps from Marlborough to Southland. When the High Country Advisory Committee was formed in 1940 we sought fruitlessly for some definition which would determine what was eligible as a high-country property. Was it altitude? There were lots of areas in New Zealand of similar height but having no sort of common problems.

2. In *attrib.* use pertaining to or characteristic of the mountainous parts of (mainly) the South Island, esp. in respect of their use for pastoral farming and of the life-style associated with such farming.
    1930 ACLAND *Early Canterbury Runs* 8 The severe snow storms..used up several years profits of the high country runholders. **1945** BAXTER *Collected Poems* (1980) 34 [Title] *High Country Weather* Alone we are born And die alone; Yet see the red-gold cirrus Over snow-mountain shine. **1950** *NZJAg.* Oct. LXXXI. 293 The high-country tussock grassland of Marlborough has been occupied for pastoral purposes for almost 100 years. **1960** MASTERS *Back-Country Tales* 28 The Kaweka..was the first of several high-country huts that have been erected by the..Heretaunga Tramping Club. **1974** *NZ Agric.* 57 The high-country farms are all in the South Island... The stock on these high-country farms may graze in altitudes as high as about 1500 to 1800 metres, though most of the 'runs' utilise areas up to about 900 m only. **1989** RICHARDS *Pioneer's Life* 44 It took some getting used to these high country sheep. **1992** *Marlborough Express* 31 Jan. 5 Born and raised in the high country.., Don has developed an inherent love of high country life.

    Hence **high-countryman**, one born, resident, or working on a high-country farm.
    1922 TURNER *Happy Wanderer* 51 The high-countryman may drink his cheque. **1989** CAMPBELL *Frigate Bird* 112 Tell me of a high-countryman who's not attached to his bit of rock.

highlander. [see quot. 1956] Any of several kinds of reddish scorpionfish esp. *sea perch* (PERCH *n.* 2 (4) *Helicolenus percoides*). Cf. JOCK STEWART.
    1938 *TrRSNZ* LXVIII. 416 *Helicolenus percoides*. Sea perch, so called John Dory (scroddie, fivefinger, soldier-fish, Jock Stuart, Highlander). **1956** GRAHAM *Treasury NZ Fishes* 344 Seaperch (Pohuiakaroa) Jock Stuart, Highlander, Fivefinger, Soldierfish or Scroddie... [The names Jock Stuart and Highlander] are supposed to be given on account of the colouring of the fish resembling, in some ways, the tartan of a Scot. **1966** [see FIVE-FINGER 3]. **1991** BRADSTOCK *Fishing* 21 Sea perch. Other names: scarpee, Jock Stewart, highlander, flinger, pohuiakaroa, *Helicolenus percoides*.

hihi. Also **ihi**. [Ma. /'hihi/: Williams 48 *Hihi* (i) 9..stitch-bird.] STITCHBIRD.

1842 GRAY *Fauna* in Dieffenbach *Travels in NZ* (1843) II. 187 *Ptilotis cincta*... Kotihe of the natives... Ihi of the natives of Taranaki. **1873** [see STITCHBIRD]. **1886** *TrNZI* XVIII. 112 *Pogonornis cincta*.—Hihi, Matakiore, Stitchbird. **1904**, **1917** [see STITCHBIRD]. **1929** DUGGAN *NZ Bird Songs* 42 'For the down of the Hihi,' said Topine Te Mamaku, 'Is as yellow as the comb of the bee.' **1955** [see STITCHBIRD]. **1967** NATUSCH *Animals NZ* 285 The Maori knew [the stitchbird] as hi-hi, from its call. **1970** [see STITCHBIRD]. **1985** *Reader's Digest Book NZ Birds* 289 Stitchbird *Notiomystis cincta*... Hihi.

hiker. *Obs. Ellipt.* for *hiker's biscuit*, a hard sustaining biscuit.
1937 *Tararua Tramper* Nov. 6 Exchanged last few hiker fragments and lurid tales for cakes and tea. **1940** *Ibid.* Mar. 10 For strenuous trips..sustaining foods..such as: Pemmican,.. hikers or plasman biscuits. *Ibid.* Nov. 4 As a supplement to the breakfast and evening meal, there should be available cabin bread or hikers, with butter, honey or cheese.

hikoi. [Ma. /'hi:koi/: Williams 50 *Hīkoi*, v. Step; P.M. Ryan *New Dict. of Modern Māori*, *hikoi* to step out; march; walk.] A communal march or walk in support of a cause, popularized by the protest march by a Maori group to Waitangi for Waitangi Day celebrations, 6 February, 1984. Compare LAND MARCH (LAND 1).
1984 *Evening Post* (Wellington) 4 Feb. 2 'Give me an "H", give me an "I", give me a "K", give me an "O", give me an "I". What have we got?' 'Hikoi (walk),' they yelled as they entered the Taitokerau Maori district. **1984** *Ibid.* 7 Feb. 2 Those on the hikoi or peace walk under the Kotahitanga banner of Maori unity, had decided before they reached the Waitangi Treaty grounds that they would not be divided. **1987** *Listener* 8 Aug. 31 The Taranaki tribes..organised a commemorative hikoi (expedition) to Dunedin. **1989** *New Zealandia* Nov. 10 A hikoi or pilgrimage 'in support of the sacredness of all life' is expected to draw Catholic youth from all over the country. **1995** *Evening Post* (Wellington) 13 Jan. 14 The traditional prelude to the Treaty of Waitangi commemorations, a Maori protest movement march to Waitangi, will leave Cape Reinga this year on February 1. Te Hikoi ki Waitangi will make its 10th annual pilgrimage in stages... Hikoi organiser Hilda Harawira said today each stage would be led by team leaders.

hiku. [Ma. /'hiku/: Williams 50 *Hiku* (ii) n... frost-fish = *pāra*.] FROSTFISH.
1872 HUTTON & HECTOR *Fishes NZ* 109 The Frost Fish, or Hiku of the Maoris..is esteemed the most delicious fish in New Zealand. **1886** SHERRIN *Handbook Fishes NZ* 300 *Lepidopus caudatus*... Frost-fish, Hiku, or Para. **1890** *Otago Witness* (Dunedin) 30 Jan. 17 A much longer and more delicate fish is the hiku of the Maori, or frost fish. **1929–30** *TrNZI* LX. 147 Frost Fish. Maori: Hiku, Para. **1966** DOOGUE & MORELAND *Sea Anglers' Guide* 277 Frostfish... Other names: para, hiku, taharangi (Maori).

hill.
1. a. As **the hill**, a high-country mustering beat; occas. the high country itself; hence in the phr. **to be on the hill**, to be out mustering; **to be off the hill**, to be finished mustering.
1933 *Press* (Christchurch) (Acland Gloss.) 28 Oct. 17 No shepherd or musterer speaks of mountains. He may be mustering the side of Mount Cook, but he is, still *on the h[ill]*. **1941** CURNOW *Island and Time* 2 The cowman home from the shed went drinking with the rabbiter home from the hill. **1953** STRONACH *Musterer on Molesworth* 18 We got off 'the hill' quite early, put the sheep across Cat Creek at Tarndale, and raced for the homestead. *Ibid.* 29 But we got our mail, and were glad to be for a day or so 'off the hill'. **1962** SHARPE *Country Occasions* 123 That is typical of what a high-country man calls a good day on the hill. **1968** TOMLINSON *Remembered Trails* 37 Watty took my swag and I went up to meet the musterers as they came off the hill. **1971** NEWTON *Ten Thousand Dogs* 20 Old Jack Halliday often used to talk of his days 'on the hill'. I used to lap up these stories of mustering and droving.

b. *attrib.* Situated in, characteristic of or pertaining to high country.
1862 *Richmond-Atkinson Papers* (1960) I. 807 Duppa tells me the buying mania will spread into the [Canterbury] hill runs even to the snowy country. **1934** LILICO *Sheep Dog Memoirs* 15 He was a great hill dog. *Ibid.* 17 This Hemp was an ideal type [of dog] for hill work. **1934** *Press* (Christchurch) (Acland Gloss.) 27 Jan. 15 There is a most interesting footnote on..[placer sheep in] 'Tutira'..which everyone who is interested in hill sheep should read. **1967** MACNICOL *Skippers Canyon* 129 The playful pup grew to a large..dog. He proved too easy-going and too much of a 'sundowner' for hill work.

c. Special Comb. **hill-bag**, a musterer's bag holding tucker and other necessities (cf. TUCKER BAG); **hill station**, a high-country sheep-station; **hill-stick**, mustering stick (MUSTERING 2).
1967 MACNICOL *Echoes Skippers Canyon* 151 Jack's **hill-bag**, with his liquor and less-important personal odds and ends, had given way under strain. **1978** JARDINE *Shadows on Hill* 76 I took off the hill-bag and started in to my lunch. **1987** HALL & WRIGHT *Shepherd's Year* 15 We [musterers] all carry a hill bag which will contain a parka, lunch, binoculrs. **1950** *NZJAg.* Oct. LXXXI. 292 **Hill Stations**..Cull run cows not required for breeding. **1960** MILLS *Sheep-O* 95 On smaller flat-land farms it is..easy to muster sheep back into the shelter..., but on the bigger hill-stations..the task can be almost hopeless. **1967** MACNICOL *Skippers Canyon* 41 The men wade into the melee [*sc.* dogfight] with **hill-sticks** and hobnailed boots. **1969** MCCASKILL *Molesworth* 101 A musterer's stick would then be pushed through the hamstrings and the carcase lifted... Apart from his dogs the musterer's most used piece of equipment was his hill stick, a six-foot piece of manuka with a ferrule fitted at the end to reduce wear. **1978** JARDINE *Shadows on Hill* 4 With the two dogs beside him he leaned on his hillstick and watched..the other musterer. **1990** MARTIN *Forgotten Worker* 63 The mustering stick, known as a 'hillstick' or 'nibbie', was usually made from manuka and had a metal ferrule.

2. As **the Hill** [spec. use of *hill* alluding to Mount Eden, Auckland], Mount Eden Prison.
1950 *Here & Now* Nov. 15 The Hill is just about permanently short of screws, which incidentally shows what sort of place it is. **1953** *Here & Now* Nov.–Dec. 41 It's typical of the prison system that the clothes at The Hill, where there are plenty of visitors, are passable, and you'll even get into trouble up there for not reporting a tear in your coat.

3. As **the Hill** [f. the location of Parliament on a rise in Wellington], Parliament (Buildings).
1980 LELAND *Kiwi-Yankee Dict.* 18 *boys on the hill*: Not usually the boys in the band. This phrase refers to the Members of Parliament, New Zealand's unicameral legislature. **1981** KENNEDY *Straight from Shoulder* 99 Some pretty hard things were said about the way Journalists were digging into the business affairs of the Fitzgeralds [relations of a Government Minister]. Quite plainly the men on the 'hill' regarded it as prying. **1986** *Contact* (Wellington) 14 Nov. 7 Numerous battles with Greenies have obviously made someone on the Hill acutely aware of the dangers of tangling with tree lovers. **1989** *Landfall 171* 374 There are two 'The Hills' in Wellington, University and Parliament, both taking in their fair share of fools. **1993** *Evening Post* (Wellington) 21 Aug. 2 Election day speculation is the trendy sport up on the hill.

4. In the phr. **over the hill. a.** *Christchurch.* (a) Over the Port Hills to Christchurch from Lyttelton, and vice versa.
1853 SEWELL *Journal* 3 Feb. (1980) I. 123 Many houses to let in consequence of some persons having gone to the diggings—others over the hill (as they call it) into the Plains. **1889** MITCHELL *Rhymes & Rambles* 19 I got over the hill to Port Lyttelton, and got a job. **1934** *Press* (Christchurch) (Acland Gloss.) 27 Jan. 15 *Over the hill*.—In the earliest days *to go o[ver] t[he] h[ill]* simply meant to go to Lyttelton; but in later years it meant 'to be sent to gaol' at Lyttelton. **1967** MAY *West Coast Gold Rushes* 114 Vessels arriving at Lyttelton from Dunedin added their quota, the diggers 'proceeding immediately over the Hill upon landing at the jetty'. **1985** LANGDALE-HUNT *Last Entail Male* 72 I eventually rode over the hill to Lyttelton and the ship after dinner on Monday. **1991** *Dominion Sunday Times* (Wellington) 31 Mar. 21 I used to know a number of people who had never been to Christchurch, never been over the hill, but that doesn't apply now.

(b) *Obs.* In the phr. **to go over the hill**, to be sent from Christchurch to Lyttelton gaol.
1934 [see (a) above]. **1936** BAUGHAN *People in Prison* 211 Going over the hill for the umpteenth time on the same old charge.

b. *West Coast.* Across the Southern Alps to (or occas., from) Canterbury.
1963 PEARSON *Coal Flat* 421 *over the hill*: West Coast expression for 'across the Southern Alps', that is, in Canterbury province. **1974** HULME in *Listener Short Stories* (1977) 118 One thing everybody does know about the Coast is bait. White bait... Tons..are railed and flown over the hill, weekly. **1989** *Aspects Society of Mary in NZ* 15 O'Donnell had too popular a following in Westland to risk sending him back [from Canterbury] 'over the hill' again to Ahaura.

c. Across the Rimutaka hill between Wairarapa and Wellington.
1992 *Dominion* (Wellington) 3 Sept. 7 [Advt] Over The Hill? If your business is based in the Wairarapa but you want to promote it over the hill, call..Wellington Newspapers.

hill-country. *Farming.* [Spec. use of *hill-country* a district composed of hills.]
1. Mainly North Island hilly or steep land esp. that used for pastoral farming. Often *attrib.* Compare HIGH COUNTRY.
1783 LEDYARD *Journal* (1963) 18 When he came to understand she was about to sail [he] went up into the hill country and invited the warriors to come down and kill the strangers. **1842** HEAPHY *NZ* 26 The hill country in New Zealand is..far from being useless; it is always preferred by the natives for their plantations of potatoe and maize. **1870** *TrNZI* II. 73 In the hill-country, a few years since, this [widgeon] was sufficiently common. **1897** *TrNZI* XXIX. 513 Looking to the right is seen perhaps the most extended stretch of hill-country in the whole of New Zealand. **1905** BAUCKE *White Man Treads* 147 We had now reached the hill country, winding about [in the train] with many a cunning turn. **1915** MACDONALD *NZ Sheepfarming* 106 A great part of the hill country in New Zealand under pasture is devoted..to the grazing of sheep. **1922** PERRY *Sheep Farming* 90 The writer will content himself with noting here a few..points in the management of sheep..on this type [*sc.* tussock high country]..as differing from the..grassed hill country such as that found in the North

Island, which is heavily stocked. **1936** Belshaw et al. *Agric. Organiz. NZ* 281 The unavoidable deterioration of some of the hill country pastures has affected wool quality in several ways. **1949** Sargeson *I Saw in My Dream* (1974) 111 You know, Andy reckons someday the Government'll decide to shut up all this hill country. **1956** Dare *Rouseabout Jane* 160 I had known only hill country shephering hitherto. **1966** *Encycl. NZ* I. 135 There has been rural depopulation in remoter hill-country areas. **1974** *NZ Agric.* 40 The fertility and the carrying capacity of much of this 'hill country' have been increased through aerial topdressing. **1982** *Agric. Gloss.* (MAF) 5 *Hill country*: Steep to rolling country, usually with only a small proportion accessible by wheeled tractor. In New Zealand usually it had previously been covered in bush.

2. Special Comb. **hill-country farm**, a farm comprising mainly hilly or steep land, usu. in the North Island.

1936 Belshaw et al. *Agric. Organiz. NZ* 710 'Lamb's Wool' comes mostly from cross-bred lambs on hill country farms. **1943** *NZJST* XXIV. 201A The ewe flocks are maintained by annual drafts..drawn largely from the hill-country farms. **1974** *NZ Agric.* 59 The lower hill-country farms are a very important section of sheep farming in both the North and South Islands. **1987** Hartley *Swagger on Doorstep* 79 Fagan's hill-country farm went as far as the bushline of the Paeroa Range.

hill-flax: see FLAX 2 (1).

hill glory. Also **glory of the hills** *Olearia arborescens* (fam. Compositae), a shrub-daisy.

1961 Martin *Flora NZ* 212 Fig. 60 Glory of the Hills (*Olearia arborescens*), a common shrub of lowland hills & stream banks. *Ibid.* 213 What is perhaps the most variable of all the shrub-daisies..is that known as the 'hill glory' (*O. arborescens*). In summer its panicles of pure white blossom are conspicuous in montane shrubberies.

hillman. [f. HILL 1 a.]

1. A high-country musterer.

1947 Newton *Wayleggo* 109 Jock was what is known among hill men as a Sunday dog—normally a damning description. **1973** Newton *Big Country* (1977) 205 This wild rockbound country..became almost a Mecca for high-country musterers and the Algidus gangs have included the names of many of our best-known hillmen.

2. *Tramping.* A tramper-mountaineer, esp. one expert at or preferring mountain tramping.

1951 *Tararua Tramper* Apr. 3 No detail of what a hillman should know is omitted. **1958** Mason *Tararua* Sept. 28 The Maori *whare* has never really caught on with hillmen, who prefer to call their erections huts. **1981** Henderson *Exiles Asbestos Cottage* 23 In the belief..that you'd be shot at if you disobeyed [the proprietary owners], everyone yelled out..even the most distinguished visitors..or the occasional semi-familiar hillman passing through.

hinahina. Mainly *SI.* Also **hinihini**, **ina-ina**, **inihina**, **ini-ini**. [Ma. /'hinahina/: Williams 50 *Hinahina..= māhoe.*] MAHOE.

1867 Hooker *Handbook* 765 Hinahina, *Geolog. Surv. Melycitus ramiflorus...* Ini-ini... *Melycitus ramiflorus*. **1869** *TrNZI* I. (rev. edn.) 190 Hinahina or Mahoe (*Melicytus ramiflorus*). **1870** *TrNZI* II. 122 Melicytus ramiflorus. Hina hina. **1889**, **1890** [see MAHOE]. **1907** Laing & Blackwell *Plants NZ* 266 In the South the plant is generally known as the *Ina-ina*, in the North it is called the Mahoe. **1911** Shand *Moriori People* 8 Inihina—Hinahina or Mahoe, in Maori—was considered [by Moriori] the best wood for the rubber [in firemaking]. **1922** *NZJST* IV. 280 Besides the broadleaf..fuchsia..hinahina..and other widely distributed trees, an occasional pokaka..were to be found. **1940** Studholme *Te Waimate* (1954) 123 Underscrub dense... Matipo, Ini-ini, Konini, Pokaka. **1961** Martin *Flora NZ* 180 Still another associate is the Mahoe or Whitey-wood, likewise known in Otago as Hina hina, a name often corrupted to 'eenee-eenee'. **1980** Brasch *Indirections* 26 We shot with bows and arrows; bows of cherry, arrows of bamboo or of hine hine (we pronounced it [in Dunedin c1918] henny-henny), the whitey wood that grew in the Belt just outside the back gate.

hinaki.

1. Also **inacke**. [Ma. /'hi:naki/: Williams 51 *Hīnaki*, n. Wicker eel-pot.] A Maori wickerwork (later often wire) eel basket or eel-trap.

1844 Taylor *Journal* 2 Oct. (ATLTS) III. 26 They went to the hinaki and found it almost full they took about 2 doz. [eels]. **1905** Baucke *White Man Treads* 256 My father and his younger brother went to lift a 'hinaki' (eel basket) into the canoe. **1918** *TrNZI* L. 297 Although the *hinaki*, or eel-pot, is a common object in most Maori villages... I do not remember ever having seen it described. **1937** Buick *Moa-Hunters NZ* 175 By January the eels were on the move..to become victims to the cunningly made *hinaki tuna*, or eel-traps, set at the openings of the weirs. **1945** Beattie *Maori Place-names Canterbury* 34 I..saw him put a hinaki in the river, and next morning it was full of silver bellies. **1956** Graham *Treasury NZ Fishes* 61 As a youth, in 1905–09, I made eel nets 'hinaki' from half-inch wire netting to catch eels as food. **1964** Middleton *Walk on Beach* 47 I dumped the hinaki in tall grass by a culvert and clumped onto the bridge. **1978** Sutherland *Elver* 63 They soon went off up the river to clear the eels from the hinaki they had set under the bridge. **1987** Wilson *Past Today* 59 Eel weirs..were built to facilitate the taking of large quantities of eel, the weirs guiding the eel into hinaki suspended on them.

2. *transf.* and *fig.* [f. Ma. *hīnaki* in modern use, 'prison'.] A lockup or prison.

1945 *NZEF Times* 5 Feb. 4 When jokers go out the monk on vodka they have to build an inacke around them before they wake up. **1981** Johnston *Fish Factory* 93 If a joker turned up at Court..surely he deserved more than..the judgement of a visiting magistrate to decide he should go into the *hinaki*. **1993** *North & South* (Auckland) Feb. 89 You know what a hinaki is? It's a thing that catches eels, eh. They also use that word for prison.

hinanga, var. INANGA.

hinau /'hinæu/. Also with much variety of early form as **enou**, **henou**, **henow**, **hinou**, **whinau**, etc. [Ma. /'hi:nau/: Williams 51 *Hīnau*, n. *Elaeocarpus dentatus*.] *Elaeocarpus dentatus* (fam. Elaeocarpaceae), a tall forest tree (and also its wood), producing masses of white flowers, edible berries the pounded kernels of which form a meal from which **hinau bread** is baked, and a useful bark the source of black dye. See also LILY-OF-THE-VALLEY, OLIVE 2, POKAKA.

[*Note*] The name has been occas. mistakenly applied to the related POKAKA (*E. hookerianus*).

1817 Nicholas *Voyage NZ* I. 340 Steeping bark of tree *enou* from which [the natives] extract a black dye. *Ibid.* II. 245 The trees which the natives chiefly make subservient to their purposes, are [besides the pines]..the henow, from which they extract a black dye. **1835** Yate *NZ* (1970) 49 Hinau... This tree is also partial to a rich alluvial soil. **1838** Polack *NZ* I. 162 Handsome mats of silken white, or glossy jet, dyed by an infusion of the bark of the henou-tree. **1844** Williams *NZ Jrnl.* (1956) 105 The Hinau is also a handsome tree, the bark is of a bright purple, it dyes a beautiful permanent black. **1850** McLean *Diary* May in Cowan *Sir Donald Maclean* (1940) 52 Hinau berries are most plentiful. **1866** Angas *Polynesia* 46 Of these [fibres] they manufacture their finest articles of dress..dyeing their borders black and red..with the juices of the 'tanehaka' and the 'hinau' tree. **1889** Featon *Art Album NZ Flora* 178 Whinau [Maori name]..Hinau [Settlers' name]..Eleocarpus dentatus..Tree. **1899** Bell *In Shadow of Bush* 239 And afterwards..as he sat on a hinaú log outside the door and smoked his pipe. **1922** *Auckland Weekly News* 16 Mar. 15 The hinaus' creamy raceme resembled [a] spray of lilies-of-the-valley. **1940** Laing & Blackwell *Plants NZ* 261 The bark of the Hinau makes an excellent blue-black dye. **1982** Burton *Two Hundred Yrs. NZ Food* 6 Hinau (Elaeocarpus dentatus) is a tall forest tree with purple berries about 15 millimetres in length... The berries were pounded and then sifted... The meal was then kneaded into a paste with a little water and formed into dark brown, oily cakes. **1995** *Evening Post* (Wellington) 30 Nov. 15 The [hinau] berry flesh was removed by soaking in water, then rubbing or pounding off the flesh. The remains were sieved and the powdery meal would then be shaped into cakes and cooked in a hangi... Hinau bread probably wouldn't be a favourite today and has been likened to a coarse, bitter custard powder!

hinihini, var. HINAHINA.

hino: see HINU.

hinu. Also early **eènoo**, **e-he nue**, **enu**, **henu**, **hino**, **inu**. [Ma. /'hinu/: Williams 51 *Hinu* n. *1.* Oil, fat.]

1. a. Fat, oil; whale-oil.

[**1804** *Collins Eng. Colony in NSW* 561 E-he nue, *Whale oil, or any other fat*. **1817** Nicholas *Voyage NZ* II. 329 Oil. Enu **1820** Lee & Kendall *NZ Gram. & Vocab.* 139 Inu, *s...* Oil. **c1826–27** Boultbee *Journal* (1986) 112 fat (sub)—eènoo] **1922** Cowan *NZ Wars* (1955) II. 219 The hands [of the white soldier] were laid [in the hangi] with the palms uppermost, because when they were cooked they curled up, and the hollow palm was full of *hinu* or gravy, which was a great delicacy to the olden Maori. **1939** Beattie *First White Boy Born Otago* 23 The [Otago] Maoris used to rub hinu-titi or muttonbird oil on their heads and into their hair.

b. Body fat(ness).

1969 Hilliard *Green River* 10 Gong-Gong patted his belly. 'Plenty butterfat in me, man! All this hinu—here.' **1976** Harrison *Broken October* 46 Complete feeling for the fat man,.. for his comic fatness and his Maori knowing and feeling this thing of hinu.

2. Special Comb. **hinu-bread**, a flour and water dough fried in hot fat, the result resembling fried scones.

1969 Hilliard *Green River* 14 He filled the glasses again and passed around the tin of buttered hinu-bread that his wife Roimata had baked fresh in the morning. **1990** recipe p.c. Kiriwai Hilliard. *Hinu Bread* or *Fry Bread*. Some people call it *floaters*. Flour..baking powder..salt..milk..dripping..make a scone dough ¼ inch thick..fry in dripping.

3. it's there te hinu! ('there is the oil') /is 'tɜ tə 'hinu/, a catchphrase (mainly used by Maori speakers) of delight, enthusiasm.

1950 p.c. R. Gilberd (Okaihau) 18 June It's there te hinu. Origin in Okaihau, Northland and has penetrated to Whangarei. Outside Maori territory it will be meaningless and so its scope is limited. **1950** p.c. J.

Richards: heard in the English use of East Coast Maori speakers. *Is there te hinu.* Expression of enthusiastic delight, especially among Maori children (for example, at the pictures). Often shortened to '*is-s-s there!*' with [s] drawn out and loudly hissed. **1952** *Here & Now* Jan. 21 'D'ere d'hino,' said the Maori boy at the pool table... 'D'ere d'hino' means literally 'there is the oil'. It was originally used to describe orgasm. Now it just means anything that's good.

hioi. [Ma. /'hi:oi/: Williams 52 *Hīoi* (i), n. *1*... native mint.] MINT (see quots. at MINT).

hippah: see PA.

hippies, *n. pl. Obs.* Men's brief swimming trunks.
1943 BENNETT *English in NZ* in *Amer. Speech* XVIII. 92 *togs*, used of bathing suits than of clothes in general; *hippies*, bathing trunks. **c1988** p.c. P. Ranby, Auckland. Used during 1940–50s for men's short or brief swimming togs; later 'trunks'.

His Ex. A familiar shortened form of 'His Excellency the Governor(-General)'.
1840 MATHEW *Journal* 16 Feb. in *Founding of NZ* (1940) 50 We six of us slept very comfortably—his Ex. in a bed, of course, and his officers on sofas and mattresses on the floor around him. **1910** *Truth* 2 Apr. 4 Governor Plunket has been farewelling in the South Island... Ashburton..did itself proud, when His Ex. happened along to say 'Ta-ta'. **1934** HYDE *Journalese* 223 'Blo,' otherwise the Observer's veteran cartoonist, W. H. Blomfield, made a practice of portraying His Ex. with the vice-regal monocle firmly affixed in his eye. **1941** BAKER *NZ Slang* 62 The terms [shared with Australia] *His Ex* or the *G.G.* for our Governor-Generals have long since passed into colloquial speech. **1973** LEE *Political Notebooks* 37 'Do you mean,' enquired Bill Parry, 'that the po has to be hawked to Auckland and back each time His Ex travels?' 'Yes. And breakages are costly,' replied Bob.

hiss, *v. Wellington tramping.* [Transf. use of *hiss v.* suggesting the sound of high-speed movement.] *intr.* To tramp at a fast pace.
1933 *Tararua Tramper* Dec. 2 Just 58 seconds later Stan Reid 'hissed' round the manuka bushes and up the straight to run an extremely creditable second in a gruelling race. **1938** Ibid. May 4 The harrier traffic hissed past on the return through the 5 mile. **1958** *Ibid.* Sept. 29 Visitors to Wellington comment on the brisk pace of the pedestrians, and Wellington trampers have achieved a certain notoriety for the speed with which some of them travel in the hills. It is not surprising, therefore, that its hillmen and hillwomen should *hiss* along, that *hissers* and *little hissers* should flourish, and that *little hisser* should sometimes be used as a term of approbation—'stew a hisser', 'a real hisser of a day'. *The Tramper* first gives to *hiss* in 1934, and *hisser* with reference to a stew appears on 1940, but to a person not until 1943, though it must have been so used long before. **1988** McGILL *Dict. Kiwi Slang* 56 *hiss* to tramp rapidly, in phr. *hiss along*; mostly among trampers.

Hence **hisser**, a fast or very fit tramper; thence, something or someone excellent of its kind.
1939 *Tararua Tramper* Jan. 4 The limit men on 18 minutes are near the first saddle by now, with 'hissers'..on scratch sucking Glucose D and consolation in their fitness. **1945** *Ibid.* July 15 The hissers pitched camp at 4,000 ft on the west bank, in a pleasant grove of ribbonwood and totara. **1958** [see above].

hit, *v.* Of the various phrases, phrasal verbs, etc. formed with *hit v.* (often marked by OED 'Chiefly *U.S.*') the following have been retained as in some way distinctive in New Zealand use.

1. *trans.* [See OED *hit v.* 11 to go upon (a course), e.g. 'hit the trail, road'.] In the phr. **to hit the breeze**, to take to the open air; **to hit the toe** *drug-users*, to decamp, to run away; **to hit one's straps**, to decamp.
1974 AGNEW *Loner* 70 But I dared not sleep. I stayed wide awake until the first crack of dawn, when I hit the breeze, never to return. **1982** NEWBOLD *Big Huey* 20 That's if he hasn't already switched the whole lot with icing sugar and hit the toe. **1988** McGILL *Dict. Kiwi Slang* 56 *hit your straps* to take off quickly; possibly from earlier meaning of looking for one's swag-straps, meaning to consider looking for another job.

2. to hit out (after, for) [cf. OED 19 a 'Now *dial.* and *U.S.*'], to go, to start out or strike out (after).
1947 NEWTON *Wayleggo* 62 She [*sc.* a sheep-dog] caught the original mob..recast, and was hitting out after another lot [of sheep]. **1953** STRONACH *Musterer on Molesworth* 22 Then he washes up the dishes, packs his gear, saddles and loads his horses and hits out for the next camp—anything from two to twenty-five miles away.

3. As **to hit up. a.** In the phr. **to hit** (someone) **up (for)** [see OED 27 c], to ask for, to importune (esp. for money).
1917 *Chron. NZEF* 5 Sept. 28 We hit him up for a loan for weeks afterwards and he always came to light too. **1955** *BJ Cameron Collection* (TS July) hit up (v) To ask for a loan or a favour. **1957** CROSS *God Boy* 98 'I'll have to hit my old man up for a new bike,' he said.

b. As **to hit up** *drug-users*, also *absol.* [see OED 8 g], to inject (with) drugs.
1972 BAXTER in *Islands* 1 29 The junkies hit up whenever they felt like it. They stayed smashed out of their skulls for days on end. **1979** *Dominion* (Wellington) 29 Aug. 3 'Dave asked me to hit him up,' Adams said. 'Dave said that they had some gear.' Adams said he took this to mean hard drugs. **1982** NEWBOLD *Big Huey* 12 It's really good shit, man. Pharmaceutical... It's real good shit. Pure shit. I'll hit you up if you like. **1986** *Evening Post* (Wellington) 5 Apr. 19 Most addicts 'hit up' in the arm because it is convenient.

hitch. *Mining.* [See OED *n.* 2 *Mining.* a slight fault or dislocation of the strata.] A natural fissure in rock (strata) caused by displacement; an artificial fissure or recess.
1868 *Thames Miner's Guide* 54 Fault.—A fissure, accompanied by a displacement of the strata, same as a slide, heave, hitch, throw, and trouble. **1978** McARA *Gold Mining Waihi* 324 *Hitch*: A recess usually cut in the solid rock as a socket for a timber leg or stull.

hiwi. The small fish *Galaxias maculatus*; WHITEBAIT.
1927 PHILLIPPS *Bibliogr. NZ Fishes* (1971) 13 *Galaxias attenuatus*. Minnow; Hiwi or Inanga. **1929** BEST *Fishing Methods* 171 When the parent [*inanga*]..return to the rivers they are termed *karaha, hiwi,* and *pahore*. **1956** GRAHAM *Treasury NZ Fishes* 118 Our New Zealand Whitebait is the young of a native freshwater fish commonly known as Minnow, or Inanga or Hiwi to the Maori, and erroneously called a Trout.

hiwihiwi. [Ma. /'hiwihiwi/: Williams 54 *Hiwi* (iii)..*4. Chironemus marmoratus.*] *Chironemus marmoratus* (syn. *C. fergussoni*) (fam. Chironemidae), a marine fish of esp. northern shallow reefs and weed beds. See also KELPFISH 3, ROCKFISH.

1875 *TrNZI* VII. 243 Haplodactylus fergussoni. sp. nov. Native name—Hiwihiwi. **1886** SHERRIN *Handbook Fishes NZ* 45 Hiwi Hiwi... It is highly prized by the Natives as a food fish, who say it is principally caught about the East Cape and Tologa [*sic*] Bay... They describe it as a 'rock fish', freckled, with white spots. **1892** *TrNZI* XXIV. 206 Hiwihiwi—*Chironemus fergussoni.* This fish is only once recorded, a single specimen having been taken at Mokohinou in September, 1887. **1927** [see KELPFISH 3]. **1967** NATUSCH *Animals NZ* 222 [The]..hiwihiwi or northern kelp fish..an olive-brown fish brindled with green, red or brown, is commonest in the far north. **1982** AYLING *Collins Guide* (1984) 239 *Hiwihiwi* (Kelpfish) *Chironemus marmoratus. Ibid.* 240 Hiwihiwi are most abundant on the north-east coast of the North Island between North Cape and East Cape but stragglers are found as far south as Cook Strait. **1991** BRADSTOCK *Fishing* 20 *Hiwihiwi.* Other names: kelpfish, rockcod... A pretty fish, easily recognised by its mosaic pattern of light and dark colours and white spots.

Hobart. *Obs.* Esp. in phr. such as **We communicate (correspond) with (post to) Hobart (Melbourne)**, a euphemism for 'Tatt(ersall')s lottery tickets sold here', alluding to Tattersall's Tasmanian Lottery, with bases in Hobart or Melbourne. See also CONSULTATION, TATTS 1.
[*Note*] The selling of overseas lottery tickets was once illegal; thus ticket-sellers for Tattersall's Tasmanian lottery advertised with such discreet notices in their shop windows that tickets bought would be posted direct to the customer from Hobart.
1951 *Here & Now* Jan.–Feb. 25 [Heading] We communicate with Hobart every week. **1952** *Here & Now* Jan. 31 Their realisation staked on the still intangible ticket from Hobart. **1966** TURNER *Eng. Lang. Austral. & NZ* 175 It was illegal to sell tickets in Tatt's in New Zealand but many barbers' shops displayed a notice, 'We communicate with Hobart', which was universally understood... It was clear that in the context of a barber's shop window the notice *meant* 'we sell tickets in Tatt's', but legally a man can announce that he writes to Tasmania. **1976** JOHNSTON *New Zealanders* 144 [Tatts] was euphemistically known as..an 'overseas consultation'. Tickets were sold fairly widely; a few tobacconists still discreetly advertise 'We post to Hobart'. **1980** BRASCH *Indirections* 408 A little newsagent's window on Plimmer Steps [in the 1940s]..bore the same message in its oracular pronouncement that *We Communicate Weekly with Hobart*.

hobnail. [Transf. use of *hobnail* a metal stud fastened to the sole of boots.]

1. In the phr. **to put on hobnailed boots**, to ride roughshod over opposition.
1898 HOCKEN *Contributions* 181 The Superintendent appointed his own son-in-law, Mr. Cutten, to the vacant post, which was in the gift of the Executive and should have been filled by them. In his opening speech to the Council he justified this action, or rather rode roughshod over any objections to it. 'Now,' he said, 'I would have Mr. Cutten and all others to know that I am in no degree to be swayed from doing what I have a right to do—to put the right man into the right place—whether that man happens to be my son-in-law or any one else'—a mode of speech now known amongst politicians as 'putting on hobnailed boots'.

2. In the comb. **hobnail express**, travel(ling) by foot, esp. in the phr. **to go on the (by) hobnail express**, to go on foot.
1952 THOMSON *Deer Hunter* 173 We set off via hobnail express down the road. We had walked from seven to eight miles when our friend returned to take us

home. **1981** PINNEY *Early N. Otago Runs* 38 Into every corner the shepherds had to go on the hobnail express, often under conditions where a slip meant death. **1995** CRUMP *Bushwoman* 18 It's Landrover and horse country, not fit for the hobnail express.

hobo. *Obs.* [Spec. or transf. use of US *hobo* a shiftless, wandering workman or tramp.] A rough-and-ready fellow; occas., a lout.

1933 EADDY *Hull Down* 103 There's a hobo up there who cant lay out a yard. *Ibid.* 116 Wilhelm, the German hobo, had been disrated to boy for bad steering. **1937** PARTRIDGE *Dict. Slang* 394 *hobo, pl hoboes...* In New Zealand and Australia, in post-G.W. days, it is often applied to a rough-and-ready fellow. **1960** SCRYMGEOUR *Memories Maoriland* 189 Sitting opposite [c1920s] were several typical Fielding [*sic*] hobos, each perhaps but certainly not in the studbook... One of the hobos gurgled, and said, 'Want to make an impression on that pretty icicle..'. Jim quietly replied 'Thanks for your advice, but I do not want any information from 'hobos' nor even from 'quadroons'.' *Ibid.* 195 Dad is very taken with you, and with the fact that you skittled those Maori hobos has tremendously advanced your stocks.

Hobson's Choice. *Hist.* Occas. also **Hobson's folly**. [Applied ironically by NZ Company settlers to various sites chosen by Lieut.-Governor William *Hobson* (1793-1842) for settlement, with an allusion to the expression *Hobson's choice* being no choice at all.]

1. Orig. the choice of Auckland as the site of the capital, over the Bay of Islands or Wellington.

1840 *NZ Jrnl.* I. 292 If Captain Hobson should neglect the central position of Port Nicholson, and fix the site of the Government city—capital it never will be—at the Thames, 'the Hobsons folly' must necessarily be mocked on one side by the growing capital of Port Nicholson,.. and on the others by the flourishing shipping harbour of the Bay of Islands. **1841** *NZ Jrnl.* II. 237 [Col. Gazette heading] 'Hobson's Choice' **1843** WOOD *Twelve Months in Wellington* 17 The entrances and exits to 'Hobson's Choice' are not circumscribed. **1845** WAKEFIELD *Adventure NZ* II. 28 'Hobson's Choice' as Auckland was very generally called.

2. Applied to the choice of Nelson rather than Canterbury as a site for the first South Island New Zealand Company settlement.

1877 PRATT *Colonial Experiences* 254 When Colonel Wakefield was apprised of..an expedition..to found the settlement of Nelson, and was desirous that..[the leader, Captain Wakefield] should proceed to Port Cooper plains..Governor Hobson peremptorily forbade his going south, and limited the choice for the new settlement to the shores of Blind Bay, hence Nelson has always been called 'Hobson's Choice'. **1900** *Canterbury Old & New* 67 Hobson..limited the choice for the [New Zealand Company] settlement to Blind Bay... Hence Nelson was for years [from 1841] known as 'Hobson's Choice'.

hock, *v.* [Extended use of *hock* to pawn.] *trans.*
a. To sell (something) under duress, or illegally.
1949 THE SARGE *Excuse My Feet* (Gloss.) *Hock* (Army): to sell something illegally..on the black market.
b. To gain, to 'come by'; to 'score' (something).
1962 CRUMP *One of Us* 99 'Do you reckon this is any bloody better than a bloody desert?'... 'We might just hock a feed here, if we're lucky'.

hockey club. *WW1.* See quot. Cf. HOCKEY STICK 2.

1937 PARTRIDGE *Dict. Slang* 394 *hockey club, the.* A, the, venereal hospital: New Zealand soldiers': in G.W. Ex. a hockey-club-shaped instrument used in the treatment of the disease.

hockey stick. [Fig. for various things shaped like a hockey stick.]
1. *pl.* Mutton chops.
1941 p.c. W. Brownlee (Marlborough). Used by Nelson College Boarders for mutton chops. **1947** NEWTON *Wayleggo* 114 Mutton chops, or hockey sticks as they are generally known, are the back country man's breakfast. **1953** STRONACH *Musterer on Molesworth* 4 Watty [the Tarndale cook] fed us again, chops and more chops. He called them 'hockey-sticks'. **1972** MCLEOD *Mountain World* 310 *Hockey Sticks*: Musterers' name for mutton chops. **1987** OGONOWSKA-COATES *Boards, Blades & Barebellies* 96 *Hockey Stick*. Mutton rib chops popular for breakfast.

2. *WW2.* An instrument used in the treatment of VD. Cf. HOCKEY CLUB (WW1).
1968 SLATTER *Pagan Game* 68 He had listened to Jock, who had the grave misfortune to contract V.D. on final leave, giving his celebrated account of how the MO had thrust an instrument nicknamed the hockey stick into him.

hoe in(to), *v.* [Transf. use of *hoe v.* to break up soil, to attack (weeds, etc.) with a hoe: AND 1935.] To attack vigorously (esp. an opponent, or food), to 'get stuck in' (to a task). See also *dig in* (DIG *v.* 3).
1918 BOLITHO *C1 Camp Tauherenikau* 9 I was 'hoeing in' [to tucker]. **1963** AUDLEY *No Boots for Mr. Moehau* 16 But everybody put theirs [*sc.* food offerings] into a pile..to make a beaut feast, girls too; everyone hoeing in with plenty of laughing and chiack. **1968** SLATTER *Pagan Game* 115 I'm taking the [rugby team] for some road work. They didn't hoe in enough last night so I'm taking them on a good long run. *Ibid.* 161 He gives me the tat-tas so I hoed into him. **1969** MOORE *Forest to Farm* 117 Rationing..did not make things easier [during WW2], but everyone 'hoed in' as we say, and made the best of it. **1993** *Salient* (Wellington) 16 Aug. 4 VUWSA President..hoed into the rest of Exec at one of the longest Exec meetings of the year.

hog. *Obs.* Often also **og, ogg, 'ogg**. [f. obsolete Brit. slang *hog* a shilling (see OED *n.*¹ 8): prob. orig. f. the figure of a hog on a small silver coin.] A shilling (piece).
1908 *Truth* 18 Apr. 2 Larst Wellington meetin', we wus orl stoomed right out, bar 16 ogg. *Ibid.* 28 Nov. 7 Aschoo, or Asher, or whatever he answers to when invited to cumanavadrink, was charged with 'mischief'—smashing a window and doing damage to the extent of eight 'hog'. **1917** *Chron. NZEF* 19 Sept. 63 Yours (bar the two ogg) disgustedly. **1918** *Ibid.* 2 Aug. 13 Ginger Dick..has taken to knitting d'oyleys, which he retails..at two 'ogg a time. **1937** PARTRIDGE *Dict. Slang* 580 *ogg or og.* A shilling: New Zealanders': C. 20. A corruption of *hog* (a shilling). **1951** p.c. a Wellington barber (who had used the term *two-ogg* for a florin.) *Two-hog, two-ogg* once commonly used for two shillings or a two-shilling piece. **1964** MORRIESON *Came a Hot Friday* (1981) 84 'Lend us a quid, shag.' 'You go to hell! You're into me for ten hog now.'

hog(g): see HOGGET 1 a.

hogback.
1. See HOGSBACK.
2. A kind of Maori adze shaped like a hog's back.
1937 BUICK *Moa-Hunters NZ* 204 The larger of the adzes, 9½ inches long, was made of a hard, fine-grained black stone commonly used for this purpose... In shape it was what is known as the 'hog-back' type, and had been brought to a high degree of finish.

Hogburn head: see HEAD *n.*³ 2 b.

hogget. [Widespread extended use of *hogget* a yearling sheep: also in occas. early southern NZ farming use *hog(g)* f. Sc. or Brit. dial.]

1. a. Also occas. early **hog, hogg**. A young sheep between weaning (4 months) and (approx.) first shearing (14–16 months).
1848 PHARAZYN *Journal* (ATLMS) 183 Hog Ewes. **1859** *Puketoi Station Diary* (Hocken TS) 11 Nov. Finished drafting wethers which were put accross [*sic*] Wedderburn... Number including hogs about 1540. **1860** *Puketoi Station Diary* (Hocken TS) 30 Aug. Cut and tailed 130 Ewe..lambs drafted off Hoggits—tally of whole flock..1813. **1894** CHUDLEIGH *Diary* 8 June (1950) 386 Daging and doseing 530 hoggets. **1937** AYSON *Pioneering Otago* 41 The wethers were out on the Waiwera hills, and the hoggets ran near the homestead. **1947** BEATTIE *Early Runholding* 85 Names. —Some of the words used to define the sheep [c1858–69] were different then, and we read of 'hogs' or 'wedder hogs', and 'hoggets' or 'ewe hoggets'. A hog (or hogg) was a yearling wether, a hogget a yearling ewe. **1960** MASTERS *Back-Country Tales* 35 This in turn led to a dearth of suitable winter pasture country for hoggets. **1982** *Agric. Gloss.* (MAF) 50 *Hogget*: Young sheep between weaning (4 months old) and 14–16 months of age. The hogget stage usually ends when the animals are shorn (around 14 months old). There are ram hoggets, ewe hoggets and wether hoggets. **1987** [see LICK *n.*²].

Hence **hoggethood** *joc.*, the state of being a hogget.
1953 SUTHERLAND *Golden Bush* (1963) 193 By the time Peter reached hoggethood it was clear that he was going to be an immense animal.

b. Meat from the carcass of a sheep between 12 and 24 months old; often loosely for sheep-meat from animals obviously 'older' than lamb but not yet 'mutton'.
1953 LINKLATER *Year of Space* (1954) 207 I have seen their admirable mutton brought upon the table in such miserable shape that the hogget—so they call a sheep of uncertain age—appeared to have been killed by a bomb. **1979** SIMONS *Harper's Mother* 155 Kitty fusses, taking a leg of hogget out of the freezer for tonight's dinner. **1982** BURTON *Two Hundred Yrs. NZ Food* 104 New Zealanders are alone in distinguishing hogget from lamb or mutton. Lamb is the meat of any animal from six weeks until it grows its first two teeth, from which time it becomes hogget. When a full set of teeth is grown, the meat from the sheep becomes mutton.

2. A young goat.
1986 *Dominion* (Wellington) 11 Aug. 14 The purchase included 421 goats—105 bucks and the rest does carrying kids and hoggets.

hogsback. Also **hog-back, hog's back**. [Prob. transf. f. *hogback* a ridge so shaped.] A cloud shaped like a hog's back; esp. in Canterbury, one heralding a northwest storm.
[*Note*] As applied to a sharply outlined ridge or spur (OED 2, 1834), in freq. use in New Zealand since at least 1849; also *hog-backed ppl. a.* (OED 1862) in occas. use since 1849.
1933 *NZ Alpine Jrnl.* V. 180 Dark clouds... a bevy of 'hog-backs' *Ibid.* 235 A 'hog's back' warned that further storms were brewing. **1945** HARPER *Camping & Bushcraft in NZ* 39 The most infallible warnings of a

nor'wester are the very high clouds of a peculiar torpedo shape, with a hard, rounded upperside like a whale's back—'hog backs' is the usual name among alpine men. **1958** *Tararua 12* 27 It is scarcely necessary to mention the well-known *hogsbacks*, those torpedo-shaped clouds which form on the east side of the Southern Alps during a nor'wester and presage bad weather in the ranges. **1971** *Listener* 19 Apr. 56 In the end they saw some hogsbacks up above the col so they tossed it in and glissaded down back to their bivvy.

hoha /ˈhʌuˌhaː/, *a.* and *n.* Also **hoohaa**.
A. *adj.* [Ma. /ˈhoːhaː/: Williams 55 *hōhā*, a. *1*. Wearied with expectation, importunity, anxiety... *2*. Wearisome.] Bored; fed up, annoyed; tired; tiresome.
  1834 WILLIAMS *Early Jrnls.* 3 Sept. (1961) 388 After breakfast felt so extremely *hoha* that I accompanied Mr. Baker up the river for an airing. **1972** GRACE in *NZ Short Stories III* (1975) 186 What a waste of a good house for those two nuisance things. I hope when I have kids they won't be so hoha. **1978** HILLIARD *Glory & Dream* 190 'Why didn't Tuku come for it?' 'How do I know? too hoha I suppose.' **1985** MITCALFE *Hey Hey Hey* 82 Riki..was tripping and pushing..'Why you so hoha!' said Gary, mildly, when Riki punched him on the arm. **1989** TE AWEKOTUKU *Tahuri* 26 She was lonesome, and hoohaa, and bored. *Ibid.* 101 hoohaa: pron. 'haw-hah' fed up, bored, impatient. **1990** *Listener* 1 Oct. 109 I was gettin' a bit hoha with the shivery yodel-lin' sobs they was both makin'.
B. *n.* A person who is a nuisance.
  1974 GRACE in *Some Other Country* (1984) 173 Think she'd be pleased after that neat ride we gave her. Look at the little hoha. God can she scream.

hohere, var. HOUHERE.

hoheria. [A generic name, formed from Ma. *houhere*, used as a common name.] HOUHERE.
  1947 REED *Dict. Suppl.* 174 *hoheria*: tree, modification of houhere, lacebark, ribbonwood. **1985** SHERWOOD *Botanist at Bay* 120 They had barely time to hide in the undergrowth behind a hoheria before Ed..appeared.

hohoeka. *Obs.* Also **ohoeka**. [Ma. /hoˈhoeka/: Williams 56 = *horoeka*.] LANCEWOOD. Cf. HOROEKA.
  1853 [see HOROEKA]. **1867** HOOKER *Handbook* 765 Hohoeka, Middle Island... *Panax crassifolia. Ibid.* 766 Ohoeka... *Panax crassifolia.* **1882** HAY *Brighter Britain* II. 195 The Ohoeka (*Panax crassifolium*) is a small shrub-like tree. **1889** KIRK *Forest Flora* 59 Mr. Colenso informs me that this tree is termed horoeka by the Maoris; and I learn..that it is also known as hohoeka, a name which is stated by Dr. Lyall to be used in the South Island.

hoick, *v.* Also **hoik**. [f. Brit. dial. var. of *hawk v.*: see OED *v.*²] To (clear one's throat and) spit. Also as a noun, a gob of phlegm.
  1968 SLATTER *Pagan Game* 230 Tank's gang spent their desperate days..rocking the swing bridge, hoiking goobs smack into the river. **1969** MCINNES *Castle on Run* 161 Listening to [the men] yarning, joking, teasing; watching them hoick. **1969** BAXTER *Collected Poems* (1980) 439 I had the job of hosing down The hoick and sludge and grit **1988** MCGILL *Dict. Kiwi Slang* 56 *hoick* to spit, possibly from its sound.
  Hence **hoicking** *vbl. n.*, hawking; clearing the throat and spitting.
  1983 *National Bus. Rev.* 4 July 37 And cut out the hoiking and scratching yourselves.

hoihere, var. HOUHERE.

hoiho. [Ma. /ˈhoiho/: Williams 56 *hoiho*..the yellow-eyed penguin.] *yellow-eyed penguin* (PENGUIN 2 (9)). (The *hoiho* appears on the New Zealand five-dollar banknote.)
  1842 GRAY *Fauna* in Dieffenbach *Travels in NZ* (1843) II. 199 *Eudyptes antipodes*... Auckland's Island. M. Lesson refers to a species of this family under the native name of Ho-i-ho. **1859** THOMSON *Story NZ* I. 24 Two Divers, the Korora and the Hoiho, are met with, the famous wingless penguins of sailors. **1871** HUTTON *Catalogue Birds NZ* 53 Great Penguin. Hoiho. **1904**, [see PENGUIN 2 (9)]. **1989** *NZ Geographic* I. 15 Known in Maori as the Hoiho, or 'noise-shouter', the yellow-eyed penguin grows to about 60 cm and is the largest of New Zealand's five native penguins.

hoka. Also early **ehogoa** (=e hoka). [Ma. /ˈhoka/: Williams 56 *Hoka* (iii), n. *1*...red cod.] *red cod* (COD 2 (6)).
  1842 GRAY *Fauna* in Dieffenbach *Travels NZ* (1843) II. 222 Fam. Gadoideae *Lota baccha*... Inhabits Murderer's Bay. It is probably the 'haddock' of the settlers: its native name in Queen Charlotte's Sound is 'Ehogoa'. **1855** TAYLOR *Te Ika A Maui* 628 The *Hoka* is a fish with thick lips and very prominent eyes, small scales, having long dorsal and ventral fins, in addition to its pectoral and caudal ones, it is a foot long, and is found in Queen Charlotte's Sound. **c1920** BEATTIE *Trad. Lifeways Southern Maori* (1994) 315 You would catch hoka (red cod) in winter—short, thick fellows. **1937** BUICK *Moa-Hunters NZ* 176 Next in progression came the shoals of red cod—the *hoka* of the Maori—chased from the [Waitaki] river-mouth by the assaults of the voracious kahawai. **1956** GRAHAM *Treasury NZ Fishes* 166 Red Cod (Hoka) *Physiculus* (*Pseudophycis*) *bachus*. The Maori name for Red Cod is Hoka, a very appropriate name as it is said to mean 'to eat anything'. **1966** DOOGUE & MORELAND *Sea Anglers' Guide* 208 Red Cod... *Other names:*.. hoka (Maori)... Little fat, a flaky rather flavourless fish. Unsuitable for frying. **1982** [see COD 2 (6)].

hokarari. [Ma. /ˈhokarari/: Williams 56 *Hokarari*, n... the ling.] LING.
  1921 *NZJST* IV. 123 Genypterus blacodes. *Ling*; *Hokarari*. A deep-water fish, to be secured during all months of the year. Common around Stewart Island and the South Island generally. **1947** [see LING]. **1967** MORELAND *Marine Fishes* 36 Ling... Also known as..hokarari and hoka (Maori). **1982** BURTON *Two Hundred Yrs. NZ Food* 77 An offshore species which is most abundant from Cook Strait southwards, ling (or *hokarari*) is a long, slender fish which weighs up to 14 kilograms.

hokey-pokey. Also occas. **hoky poky**. [Prob. transf. f. *hokey-pokey* the name of a cheap yellowish ice-cream once sold (in Britain) by street vendors often in the form of wrapped cubes: see OED *n.* 2.]
1. A brittle porous toffee often sold in (chocolate-coated) lumps.
  1899 MANSFIELD *Stories* (1984) 6 We always gave him the same presents—three sticks of Juno tobacco and three cakes of hokey-pokey. **1959** LAWLOR *Old Wellington Days* 111 A favourite of the day [c1900–1905] was hokey-pokey in spite of the fact that it caused more toothache than any other lolly. **c1964** *Atlas Cook. Book* 52 Hoky Poky. 2 oz. sugar, 4 oz. butter, 1 cup flour, 1 dessertspoon golden syrup, 1 dessertspoon milk, 1 level teaspoon soda. Heat milk and syrup. Stir in the butter until melted. Add the soda and when frothing add the dry ingredients. Roll into balls and flatten with a fork on a cold tray. Bake at 375° for 10–15 minutes. **1965** HILLIARD *Power of Joy* 95 He wished now he'd put his hand out too, perhaps they'd have given him some [money], enough for a hokey-pokey and a jigsaw. **1982** BURTON *Two Hundred Yrs. NZ Food* 150 [Heading] Hokey pokey biscuits. These biscuits and the related confectionery..are apparently a New Zealand specialty. **1988** *Through the Looking Glass* 6 There was always [early 1930s] a ha'penny..for a chew bar, a 'lamp post', a little bag of aniseed balls or a hokeypokey bar. **1990** *North & South* (Auckland) Oct. 37 On certain days when the wind was blowing in the right direction we could smell the peppermint or hokey pokey or chocolate.

2. In *transf.* use as (a) an obsolete humorous re-shaping of a Maori place-name; (b) a re-shaping of *hokey-tokey* (see OED *hokey-cokey*), the name of a dance.
  1878 JOLLIE *Reminiscences* (ATLTS) 5 Started farming operations at 'Wakapouaka'—or as called in vulgar English 'Hokey-pokey'. **1984** KEITH & MAIN *NZ Yesterdays* 289 Baloo baloo balight, All on a Saturday night, Put your right hand in, Put your right hand out, Shake it a little a little And turn right about. This curious song had a revival in another form as the boisterous dance-hall craze of World War II, the hoki toki, or as many South Islanders called it, the hokey pokey.

hoki /ˈhʌuki/. [Ma. /ˈhoki/: Williams 57 *Hoki* (iii)..the whiptail.] *Macruronus novaezelandiae* (formerly *Coryphaenoides novae-zelandiae*) (fam. Merlucciidae, hakes), a large silvery sea-fish of moderately deep New Zealand and s. Australian waters; a good food fish, of great commercial importance. See also WHIPTAIL, WHITING 1 c (*obs.*); and the trade name *blue hake* (HAKE 2 (1)).
  1872 HUTTON & HECTOR *Fishes NZ* 49 Coryphaenoides novae zelandiae. Hoki... Thrown up in large quantities on the shores of Cook Straits after heavy gales. **1898** MORRIS *Austral-English* 197 *Hoki, n.* a New Zealand fish, *Coryphaenoides novae-zelandiae*. **1938** *TrRSNZ* LXVIII. 404 *Macruronus novae-zelandiae*. Whip-tail. Hoki. **1956** GRAHAM *Treasury NZ Fishes* 163 Whiptail (Hoki)... A fifty-inch Hoki was caught by Captain W. Durry while trawling in twenty fathoms off Otago Heads, 18th May, 1933. **1979** *Dominion* (Wellington) 3 Aug. 2 While New Zealand deep-sea trawlers are rushing to the West Coast to catch the latest export winner—hoki—some foreign boats are dumping the species. **1986** PAUL *NZ Fishes* 61 Hoki *Macruronus novaezelandiae*... Alternative names include blue hake, whiting (wrongly), and whiptail... The fillets flake easily..; they are excellent for forming into fish block for reprocessing and are now the mainstay of the value-added product..segment of the..market. **1991** *Contact* (Wellington) 21 Feb. 1 We didn't eat hoki five years ago, but we do now.

hokioi. Also **Hokioe**. [Ma. /ˈhoːkioi/: Williams 57 *Hōkioi* = *hākuai, hōkiwai*, n. An extinct bird of nocturnal habits, held in superstitious regard by the Maori, said never to be seen.] HAKUWAI; the cry of the hakuwai.
  1864 *Otago Witness* (Dunedin) 12 Feb. 2 A newspaper called 'The Hokioi', the name being derived from a semi fabulous bird of evil omen had been started at Ngaruawahia... 'The Hokioi' would brook no rival in its nest in the rearing of its cantankerous brood. **1873** BULLER *Birds NZ* 340 He stated..that a similar bird [to the Great Frigate Bird, *Fregata aquila*] had been killed by the natives at Ihuraua..and that all who had seen it pronounced this the true 'Hokioi' of Maori tradition—a long-winged bird that is supposed to soar in the

heavens, far above the range of human vision, and to descend to the shore at night to feed upon shell-fish. **1874** *TrNZI* VI. 64 Dr. Hector suggested to me that the *Harpagornis* might possibly be the Hokioi of the Maoris, which..according to Buller, is the Great Frigate Bird (*Fregata aquila*). **1879** Hokioe [see MOA 1 a]. **1890** *Otago Witness* (Dunedin) 18 Sept. 31 There is an Hokioi above there, an Hokioi above there, Hark, the rustling as he shakes his wings! **1912** *Otago Witness* (Dunedin) 11 Sept. 76 Many legends are associated with the mythical bird 'hokioi'... In the South and in some parts of the North Island it is identical, apparently, with the 'hakuwai' which has seven joints in its wing, lives in the sky, and presages trouble... Its cry was 'Hokioi! Hokioi! Hu!' The last word represented the whizzing sound made by the bird in flight. **1936** LAMBERT *Pioneering Reminisc. Old Wairoa* 51 The *hokioi* is described as a bird with wings two fathoms long, and that as it flies it makes a swishing noise or booming sound. **1949** DUFF *Pyramid Valley* 23 *Harpagornis* has come down in Maori legend as the hokioi. **1953** *Landfall* 27 177 Edward Edwards, stay at home with your children, Far in the bush the *hokioi* is calling And whets his beak on the sound of death. **1961** REED *Myths & Legends of the Maori* 193 There is nothing to be seen but you hear a cry, a dreadful laughter floating down from the heights. 'Hokioi—Hokioi' is the cry, and as it ceases you hear that eerie whistle as a bird swoops down and up again into the blackness and silence of the night sky. **1983** HULME *Bone People* 262 The clouds are long and black and ragged, like the wings of stormbattered dragons. Or of hokioi...huge birds. **1989** [see HAKUWAI].

Hokitika swindle. [f. *Hokitika* (/ˌhʌukiˈtɪkə/) a West Coast town + *swindle*.] A hotel bar game involving the guessing of a sequence of numbers or numbers in a sequence, orig. popularized on the West Coast as 'Hokitika Swindle' or 'Hokitika', but played throughout New Zealand.
    1941 BAKER *NZ Slang* 57 The Hokitika Swindle is an hotel bar game played in order to create a jackpot from which payment of drinks may be made. It is based on a method of counting, whereby the person who calls a certain number in sequence pays a specified sum into the jackpot [or shouts the round]. **1953** *Evening Post* (Wellington) 23 Sept. 16 '*Hokitika*' Game Led To Fight. A fight outside a hotel in Lower Hutt follow[ed] a game of 'Hokitika.'... In a statement to the Police Parascuk said that 'Hokitika' consisted of guessing the numbers on a £1 note. He lost 15/- this way and accused Cloake of cheating.

hokka, var. AKA.

Hokonui /ˈhɒkəˈnui/. *Hist.*
1. *Also erron.* **Hokanui.** [Named from the Hokonui Hills, Southland, once notorious for illicit distilling.] A name for, or applied to, illicitly distilled liquor, or its distilling.
    1930 *Auckland Weekly News* 1 Jan. [Caption] Customs officials at Invercargill destroying a quantity of illicit whisky (Hokonui brew) recently confiscated by the authorities. The whisky is illegally brewed at 'stills' erected in isolated parts of the province. **a1935** Court verbatim evidence in Stuart *Satyrs of Southland* (1982) 89 Mr Macalister, 'You do know of the existence of Hokonui in the district?' Mr Findlay, 'Not at Hedgehope. Hedgehope is not Hokonui.' Mr Macalister, 'Have you ever tasted Hokonui whisky?' Mr Findlay, 'Not for many years.' **1942** *NZEF Times* 30 Nov. 6 Now they've got down to the Hokonui moonshine, they're meeting a different class of people. **1944** MARSH *Died in the Wool* 185 Hokanui..the local equivalent of potheen. **1959** DAVIN *No Remittance* 66 'What is it?' 'It's the best Hokonui.' 'And what's Hokonui?' 'It's the poteen they make up in the Hokonui Hills that you can see from the door there.' **1963** *Dominion* (Wellington) 14 Sept. 12 A man now living in quiet retirement..once tried to control the wild Hokonui brewers in the hills of Southland... Mr Abel still has a bottle of genuine Hokonui. It carries the label, 'Awarua Special, 85 per cent proof'. **1971** WATT *Centenary Invercargill* 1 Another former whaler, McShane, also settled at Sandy Point and became Southland's first '*Hokonui*' manufacturer. He distilled spirits from the edible part of the cabbage tree. **1984** WILSON *S. Pacific Street* 9 Some kids reckoned he had a secret whisky still hidden in the bush, where he made hokonui to slygrog to the local people.

2. *Comb.* **Hokonui swindle** [prob. a confusion or erroneous association of *Hokitika swindle* a bar-game and *Hokonui* illicit liquor], a drinking game in which the ability to hold liquor and perform complicated physical or intellectual tasks is tested.
    1985 HODGES *Drinking Vernacular* in *Sites* (1985) XI. 18 In an earlier paper..I have included discussion of a drinking game called Hokonui Swindle where failure to perform a complicated intellectual exercise leads to an individual being made to drink repeatedly.

hoky poky, var. HOKEY-POKEY.

hold, *v.*[1] [Spec. use of *hold v.* to prevent the escape of.]
1. *trans.* Of a sheep-dog, to keep (sheep) together in a mob or group; esp. at dog trials, in the phr. **to hold in a ring**. Cf. HOLDING DOG.
    1933 *Press* (Christchurch) (Acland Gloss.) 28 Oct. 17 *Hold*.—To h[old] sheep is keep them together, or to h[old] them where they are.

2. Of a pig-dog, to hold (a wild pig) usu. by the ear. Also as a noun in the verbal phr. **to get hold**. Cf. HOLDER.
    1848 WAKEFIELD *Handbook NZ* 166 Many kinds of dogs..go under the general name of *pig-dogs*, and combine courage with speed, being used chiefly to hunt the wild hog, and taught to hold him, when caught, by ear or jowl, until the hunter comes up. **1874** BAINES *Edward Crewe* 46 When we got 'up' the first pig was keeping the dogs at bay, and as yet they had failed to 'get hold', and no wonder, for..he had lost his ears. **c1875** MEREDITH *Adventuring in Maoriland* (1935) 64 If the bulldog were released before reaching the quarry, he would 'go in' at once, and would probably be exhausted with holding the pig before we could get there. **1989** STIRLING *On Four Legs and Two* 8 We put the dawgs in and they held him [sc. a wild pig] good while we moved in to finish him off, but just as we did, the dawg on his nose let go and he got round at the other dawg that had him by the hind leg.

hold, *v.*[2]
1. *Obs. trans.* To have (money or valuables) in one's possession.
    1866 BURGESS *Confessions* (1983) 117 He's a bloody artful old cove: I think he holds it, for I noticed something pretty bulky in his trouser's pockets.

2. *Usu. in the phr.* **to be holding** [AND 1924], to be in funds, to have ready cash. See also FINANCIAL *a.*, SILVERY *a.*
    c1926 THE MIXER *Transport Workers' Song Book* 11 *In the Pub*: 'What ho, Jerry, how yer holding?' 'Blime, can't you see I'm bent? I haven't made enough this week For to pay the bloomin' rent.' **1935** MITCHELL & STRONG in Partridge *Slang Today* 286 [The] following [was] employed by those who served in the [Great] War..*how are you holding?*, how much money have you; **1943** HISLOP *Pure Gold* 34 As I was holding very well on the day, I did not mind [losing out on a winning dividend]. **1955** *BJ Cameron Collection* (TS July) holding (adj) Having some money. Cf. *financial*. He had only been in the car for a few moments when Bishop asked how he was holding financially. **1962** CRUMP *One of Us* 169 'Tell you what, we'll split up what [money] we've got left between us—are you holding okay, Scrubby?' 'Yeah, I've got plenty, thanks.' **1983** COOPER *Wag's Tales* 9 It took me quite a while when I went out into the grown up world to get used to hearing the greeting 'Gooday, Howy're holding?'

holder. *Pig-hunting.* [f. HOLD *v.*[1] 2 + -ER.]
a. A hunting dog trained to hold wild pigs with its teeth. See also HOLDING DOG 2.
    1935 ROBERTS *NZ Land of My Choice* 89 When the dogs had worried [the pig] for some time we let the 'holders' go. **1951** [see BAILER]. **1965** WATSON *Stand in Rain* 132 Tony gave Abungus a bull terrier bitch called Tuki. 'She'll be a good holder,' Abungus said. **1982** [see BAILER].

b. As **holder-bailer,** a dog trained to bail and/or hold a wild pig. See also BAILER quot. 1951.
    1960 CRUMP *Good Keen Man* 107 Wait till you see my dogs Crump... Picked up a champion holder-bailer down country.

holding dog. [f. HOLD *v.*[1]]
1. *Farming.* A dog trained to hold sheep in a group or mob.
    1952 DUFF *Shepherd's Calendar* (1961) 74 Jim..who has a holding dog, missed a ewe two or three days before he dipped. **1971** NEWTON *Ten Thousand Dogs* 168 *Holding dog*: A dog which will catch and hold [sheep].

2. *Pig-hunting.* HOLDER a.
    1940 STUDHOLME *Te Waimate* (1954) 255 When out mustering, the sheepdogs would bail up a pig, and as the shepherds would have no proper holding dog,.. it was not an easy matter to finish it off. **1943** MANNERING *Eighty Years NZ* 45 With two good holding dogs, one on each ear, we would tackle any boar with spears, or knives only. **1955** CAMPBELL *By Reef & Range* 10 At the end of two days' hunting, aided by a large holding dog..Jim still knew nothing of Red Boar's whereabouts.

holding paddock.
1. [AND 1934.] A paddock where stock are assembled and held (for shearing, moving, killing, etc., occas. for winter feeding); also a paddock on a stock-route where travelling stock can rest overnight. See also obsolete ACCOMMODATION PADDOCK. Cf. *night paddock* (NIGHT 1).
    1918 *NZJST* I. 342 To reduce this excitement [in cattle] holding-paddocks are necessary. **1933** *Press* (Christchurch) (Acland Gloss.) 28 Oct. 17 *Holding paddock*.—A small p[addock] close to yards, woolshed, or mustering hut, for holding (not feeding) sheep. **1951** McLEOD *NZ High Country* 12 In the neighbourhood of the station there must be several holding paddocks varying from 50–500 acres, for holding mobs of sheep during shearing and other times. **1956** DARE *Rouseabout Jane* 189 There were holding paddocks at convenient intervals all the way [to the freezing works]... No-one ever kept their stock in these paddocks longer than twenty-four hours, as there was no feed in them: they were just for convenience in holding animals overnight. **1964** DICK *High Country Family* 25 This fencing of suitable areas for winter holding paddocks..made the working of winter months much more practical and sensible. **1986** RICHARDS *Off the Sheep's Back* 53 Before leaving home for the sale Dad would have

arranged for a holding paddock reasonably close to the saleyards where the mustered sheep could have a feed and a rest for the night.

2. *transf.* Special housing for the elderly; an old people's home. See also HOLDING PEN 2.

1988 McGILL *Dict. Kiwi Slang* 57 *holding paddock*: Pensioners' flats or old-age housing settlement. **1994** *Tablet* 5 June 18 *Waiting for God's* writers are running out of ideas credible within the setting, a home for old people, a holding paddock as I have heard it described.

holding pen.

1. A pen near or attached to a woolshed where sheep are held prior to shearing.

1922 PERRY *Sheep Farming* 16 The shearing board should be of good width, and be separated from the holding pens by a solid wall, so as to facilitate penning up. **1987** OGONOWSKA-COATES *Boards, Blades & Barebellies* 96 *Holding pen*. Small pen close to the woolshed for holding the sheep.

2. *transf.* A prison; an old people's home.

1985 *Listener* 5 Oct. 19 If you are in Parry you understand those jokers who came back from the war and stayed all stuffed up... Parry is just a holding pen. **1988** LAY *Fools on Hill* 38 And he would always think that it wasn't much of an end for a man..living out his last days in a geriatric holding pen, picking up other people's rubbish.

holding yard. [AND 1929.] A yard close to a woolshed or cowshed for holding stock about to be shorn, docked, milked, etc. Cf YARD *n.* 1.

1950 *NZJ Ag.* July LXXXI. 7 The check pens in turn usually open into much larger holding yards, which correspond in size to the receiving yards. **1955** [see *drafting pen* (DRAFTING 2)]. **1969** McCASKILL *Molesworth* 99 The hessian, supported by standards, was used for the holding yard, the lambs never charging it as they do with netting. **1978** SUTHERLAND *Elver* 36 Audrey and Peggy wet down the concrete of the bails..with..water from the trough in the corner of the holding yard. **1986** RICHARDS *Off the Sheep's Back* 65 There were holding and drafting yards at the back of the shed, but the 'counting out' pens opened out directly into a 100 acre paddock.

hold the belt: see BELT *n.*²

hole, *n.*¹ [AND 1851–1960.]

1. *Goldmining.* **a.** A miner's excavation in the ground; esp. in the phr. **to bottom (open, sink) a hole**.

1852 *NZGG* V. 26:165 (Rep. Gold Discovery in Coromandel) They reached a bend of the Creek, where they found Ring's party at work, sinking into the bed of it... Your Committee had a quantity of the stuff taken out of this hole, and washed. **1853** ROCHFORT *Adventures of Surveyor* 66 Now, by law, if you are away from your hole twenty-four hours you cannot reclaim it. **1863** WALKER *Jrnl. & Lett.* (ATLTS) 8 Jan. 9 Monday,.. prospected about 2 miles down the bank of the river, opened a hole. Tuesday 9th bottomed the hole, found colour. **1887** CHUDLEIGH *Diary* 23 July (1950) 356 Got samples [of quartz] from several holes to take away and have assayed. **1909** THOMPSON *Ballads About Business* 66 Comes a miner treasure seeking,.. Sinks a hole with pick and shovel. **1914** PFAFF *Diggers' Story* 115 Got a 3½ oz. nugget from the bottom of a hole that had been left. **1946** MILLER *There Was Gold* 69 I had sunk my first prospect hole at the lower end of a shallow depression.

b. A dredge paddock or pond.

1900 KITTO *Pract. Dredgeman's Manual* 18 If you are working a bank claim it is important that you keep the hole or paddock wide... This can only be done by taking out the corners every time you move ahead, and..to do this it is necessary to keep the stern of the dredge out towards the centre of the paddock.

2. *Kauri-gum-digging.* An excavation to recover kauri gum.

1970 THOMAS *Way Up North* 30 To see a fit and experienced gumdigger sinking a hole large enough to allow freedom of action, deep enough to get the gum..was to see something special as a test of competence, fitness and endurance.

hole, *n.*² *Canterbury.* [Spec. local use of *hole n.* for a railway tunnel.] In the phr. **(the) hole in (through) the hill**, the Lyttelton railway tunnel. Cf. HILL 4 a.

1856 WARD in *Canterbury Rhymes* (1883) 38 For thy precious zig-zags are too steep for a cart, And we're hopeless of holes in thy hill. **1885** MOSLEY *Illustr. Guide Christchurch* 27 Until the 'hole through the hill' was decided upon. **1932** BRUCE *Early Days Canterbury* 175 The [Lyttelton–Christchurch] tunnel was..thrown open to the public for inspection on June 10, 1867... On that auspicious day two thousand people passed through the 'hole in the hill'. **1959** SLATTER *Gun in My Hand* 18 The unreality of the tunnel, of this half-carriage..drawn by an electric locomotive which would have astounded the pioneers who dug this hole through the hill.

holes. *pl.* Also in altered form as sing. **holey, holie, holesy**. A marble game involving propelling marbles into holes.

[**a1946**] *Alfredton* (1987) 75 Colin Houlbrooke recalled [from the period 1927–46] the two main areas for battle with marbles as being the sealed area for 'rings' and the dirt area behind the shed for 'holes'. **1951** FRAME *Lagoon* (1961) 116 I played ringie and holie. I played funs and keeps. **1953** SUTTON-SMITH *Unorganized Games NZ Primary School Children* (VUWTS) II. 719 There is only one record of a New Zealand game in which a formal penalty element entered. This was a game of marbles called Dumps and was played at Wakefield in 1875. In this game the loser, in a marble game of Holey, was required to hold his marble partially exposed between the fingers of his closed fist [for others to shoot at]. **1966** TURNER *Eng. Lang. Austral. & NZ* 159 Marble games..included.. *holes*, in which one had to roll a marble into the last of a series of holes, called *poison*, before attacking an opponent's taw. **1989** McGILL *Kiwi Baby Boomers* 43 At the orphanage we played holesy... You had four holes in a row about a metre apart... The first to get his marble into all four holes became a killer. **1995** *Independent* 8 Dec. 20 Liney was the game the big [Dunedin] boys played when they were intent on quickly taking all the marbles from the little kids. I preferred holey and ringey.

holesy, holey, holie: see HOLES.

holly. *Obs.* [Transf. use of European *Holly, Ilex aquifolium* (fam. Aquifoliaceae).] Usu. with a modifier: **Maori (mountain, native, New Zealand) holly**. *Olearia ilicifolia* (fam. Asteraceae), a mainly subalpine shrub daisy with sharply serrated leaves.

1863 HECTOR *Geol. Exped. Otago* 459 New Zealand Holly is also very common along the shore. **1892** DOUGLAS in *Mr Explorer Douglas* (1957) 176 Holly one foot in diameter are [*sic*] comparatively common [on the West Coast] and the Mountain Heaths grow into small trees.

hollywood. Mainly *sporting.* [Fig. or transf. use of *Hollywood* as a famous home of acting.] A feigned injury orig. during a team game, esp. football, and often in the phr. **to do (pull, throw) a hollywood**, to feign or exaggerate the seriousness of an injury during a game to gain some advantage (or respite) for a player or the team.

1964 McLEAN *Willie Away* 115 Welsh players nearby were soon telling the All Blacks not to worry about the incident..because 'Clive is only "throwing a Hollywood"'. **1971** *Sunday Times* (Wellington) 18 July 22 A 'Hollywood' is, of course, a performance by a player feigning injury. 'Hollywoods' happen on defence but never on attack. **1980** LELAND *Kiwi-Yankee Dict.* 32 *do a Hollywood:*... This term means to exaggerate. It usually refers to the histrionic exaggeration of an injury on the playing field. **1981** *Evening Post* (Wellington) 9 Mar. 5 The accused..shouted and argued with police for the benefit of his friends. 'In other words, you did a Hollywood,' said Judge Gilbert. **1988** *Ibid.* 23 Nov. 37 Recently I found myself dealing, in a relatively public place, with a young man who, in the words of the immortals, was 'throwing a Hollywood'. **1991** *Sunday Star* (Auckland) 15 Sept. B1 I think he pulled a Hollywood and I'm not blaming him for it.

holt. [f. *holt*, and a var. of Brit. dial. *in holds* a wrestling term: see OED *hold n.* 2 b; AND 1902.] Often as *pl.*

1. A wrestling hold.

c1940 *holt* for wrestling hold in common use among Marlborough boys (Ed.). **1968** SEDDON *The Seddons* 22 The boys learnt a form of wrestling called 'Collar and elbow' brought by miners from Lancashire... In 'Collar and elbow' the opponents clutched one another in strange 'holts'.

2. In the phr. **to come (get) into (to) holts with, to get a holt on**, to come or get to grips with (a person, problem, etc.).

1909 *Truth* 3 July 8 Mr Lundon cross-examined witness at length and with determination, and as a result got into holts with Beak Kettle, more than once. **1910** *Ibid.* 7 May 7 Then the Madigan Bros. came along and Lottie loosed her tongue and turned the vials of her wrath on Charlie Madigan, with the result that they got into 'holts'. Though the constable separated them several times they fought like tigers. **1916** CHURCH *Tonks* 267 When we get to holts with the Germans it will be a close thing. **1964** *Sports Post* (Wellington) 1 Aug. 6 Last week there came a new development, when the New Zealand Rugby League council came into holts with the corporation. **1964** McLEAN *Willie Away* 45 When one got into holts with 'Mickey'..he would retreat.

holy grass: see GRASS 2 (22).

homai /ˈhʌumai/. [Poss. related to Ma. /ˈhoːmai/: *Hōmai, homai v.* to give, to bring to the person speaking; poss. related to HOMAICKY.] A children's game.

1982 SUTTON-SMITH *Hist. Children's Play* 230 I remember two essentially Maori games, Cat's Cradle and Homai, but the others were all traditional English games I think,... (1912–20; Ohau) *Ibid.* 231 There are games recorded in this period for which there is no record before 1900 though they may well have existed under other names... *Hawkes Bay*: Wolf Wolf Go Home, Homai.

homaiacky ?/ˌhʌumaiˈjæki/. [Poss. related to HOMAI; poss. from *Home my Jacky*, in the game of Bedlam.] A former children's game. See entry for KICK-THE-TIN.

home, *n.*[1] *Hist.* [Used elsewhere by Britons abroad for 'England', or for the 'British Isles'.]

1. Often with init. cap. **a.** [AND 1808.] Usu. and mainly England, later the British Isles. See also *Old Country*, *Old Dart* (OLD 1 a and b).

1815 KENDALL 19 Oct. in Elder *Marsden's Lieutenants* (1934) 112 I have in my last letter..written Home for assistance. **1824** MARSDEN *Lett. & Jrnls.* 13 Jan. (1932) 412 I have this day suspended the Rev. J. Butler from all connection with the Church Missionary Society until the pleasure of the committee is known at Home. **1834** BENNET *Wanderings* 331 And it is easy to recognise a person from *home*, or one born in the colony, no matter what class of society, from [the pure English of the colonials]. **1842** DEANS *Pioneers* (1964) 9 I may take a trip Home in a few years hence—see my friends, get married and come back again. **1862** HODDER *Memories NZ Life* 51 All are emigrants [at Nelson]; all have reminiscences about the mother-country, which is invariably designated *home*. **1864** HARPER *Lett. from NZ* 20 Dec. (1914) 78 I stayed with friends in Melbourne, awaiting a passage Home in one of Money Wigram's monthly sailing ships. **1887** *Auckland Weekly News* 10 Sept. 2 Everyone in New Zealand speaks of England as 'Home', even those who were born in the colony and have never visited the old country. **1895** *TrNZI* XXVII. 240 Take..the land which we New-Zealanders still speak of under the familiar term of 'Home'. though many of us have never lived there. **1902** IRVINE & ALPERS *Progress of NZ* 429 The New Zealanders have so far remained more distinctly English than, perhaps, is the case in some of the larger colonies... all classes, whether immigrant or native-born, habitually speak of the United Kingdom as 'Home'. **1927** MULGAN *Home: New Zealander's Adventure* 3 As far back as I can remember, it was 'Home'. In the little New Zealand country community in which we lived, it was as natural to talk of England and Ireland as 'Home' as it was to call New Zealand a colony. **1929** *Na To Hoa Aroha* (1986) I. 163 With that generation also had largely passed the pakeha who was wedded to the idea of England being 'Home'. The native born New Zealand pakeha is looking nearer to his native heath for objects of study, literary effort and missionary care. **1934** LEE *Children of Poor* (1949) 121 New Zealand has never established its own culture except of material things. For decades it has called Britain Home, a term that is finally being discarded. **1949** SARGESON *I Saw in My Dream* (1974) 247 She looked like a real old-timer, but they said she was married to a toff before she came out from Home. **1952** *NZ Geogr.* Apr. 5 The colonists endeavoured to reproduce..features of the country that many New Zealanders still, anachronistically, call 'home'. **1959** SLATTER *Gun in My Hand* 53 How typical of Christchurch that there should be a New Brighton and a Pier too! An attempt of the marooned to remind them of Home. Why can't we forget Home and make a country of our own? **1962** CURNOW *Four Plays* (1972) 106 His *men* friends call him plain Mandragora—the way they do at Home. Bob: Home? Where's that? Gillian: Oh, you know what I mean. **1970** JOHNSON *Life's Vagaries* 64 The principal, a stickler for British teachers, asked her where she was educated and she replied quite honestly, 'At home'. He understood her to mean England, so she was given the position. **1987** *Metro* (Auckland) May 52 People talked of England as 'Home' [in the 1950s] but there was a growing Americanism in the movies.

b. As used by servicemen serving overseas during WW1, New Zealand. (See also quot. 1934, 2 below.)

1918 *Kia-ora Coo-ee* (1981) 15 Dec. VI. 13 She was an 'Aussie' boat and had just come from home. **1919** *Quick March* 1 Dec. 67 The soldier who has come home is not glad because there is so much to remember... 'Home' was a glad place to look forward to, but now that home is reached it does not shine in contrast to the light of other days.

2. In quasi-adverbial use in the phr. **to go home**, to visit, or return to, Britain; also *transf.* of clothes, to wear out.

1857 LUSH *Auckland Jrnls.* 12 June (1971) 188 Mr. Abraham said: 'I suppose you know we are going almost immediately to England?'... He told me his journey via Suez would cost him £400 .. So 'going home' is rather expensive. **1879** HINGSTON *Australian Abroad* 295 Colonists and emigrants are always going to go somewhere or other. We know several who have been 'going home' as they call it, for ten years past. **1907** CHUDLEIGH *Diary* 15 Jan. (1950) 438 I have arranged for wife and self to go home..via Australia, New York, Liverpool. **1927** *NZ Tablet* (Dunedin) 7 Sept. 29 Miss Nelle Scanlan, a vivid reporter and journalist..is going home to when her sphere of work. **1929** DEVANNY *Riven* 41 I want to go Home, Mother. To London. To Paris. I *must* go Home, Mother. **1934** MULGAN *Spur of Morning* 19 'I hope to go Home some day,' said Philip... 'You mean England, I suppose?' asked Mark. 'Yes, of course,' replied Philip. He really meant the British Isles with England predominant. 'Well, I don't think of England as Home,' said Mark... 'If there's any "Home" for me in that sense, it's Ireland. But this country is our real home.' **1941** BAKER *NZ Slang* 43 When an article of clothes, etc., becomes worn and ceases to be of service it is said colloquially *to have gone home*. This use is probably derived from the fact that many New Zealanders *go Home*—visit Britain—when they are old.

3. *attrib.* passing into adjective. [AND 1858.] English or British; from Britain.

1844 STEPHENS *Journal* (ATLTS) 358 [My] land around me is beginning to have a 'home' look. **1857** *Lyttelton Times* 12 Aug. 4 In the home country a very large percentage of children die within twelve months after their birth. **1892** *NZ Official Handbook* 123 Merino mutton was not suitable for the Home markets. **1902** *Settler's Handbook NZ* 42 Home steamers can enter the roadstead and pick up cargo without difficulty. **1912** *Truth* 1 June 4 Now, I think if you leave England alone, and just look after your own country, you will find plenty of matter in it to fill your paper, including immorality. You seem to have a derry on the Home people. **1929** DEVANNY *Riven* 92 Sometimes Marigold found Home mail days not quite enough. **1955** *Landfall* 34 132 In the early nineties, however, Auckland seldom saw those Home-going steamers.

4. Special Comb. **home boat** *obs.*, a ship plying between Britain and New Zealand; **Home Government** [AND 1830], the government of Great Britain; **home papers**, newspapers from Britain.

1912 *NZJAg.* Jan. IV. 273 The fruit was shipped from Motueka and Nelson in small coastal steamers, which transferred the fruit into the **Home Boat** at Wellington. **c1926** THE MIXER *Transport Workers' Song Book* 104 You might get on a Home boat, Dad, But that is not the worst. **1959** MIDDLETON *The Stone* 12 Two home boats and at least two coasters! Good eh? **1967** BAXTER *Man on a Horse* 146 Further out lay a Home boat, riding on the water. **1983** HENDERSON *Down from Marble Mountain* 35 They left behind the two canvas deck-chairs in which they'd sat, side by side on the 'Home' boat's long journey halfway round the world. **1842** HEAPHY *NZ* 11 In making known to the deputation [of Wellington settlers] the arrangements and plans he [*sc.* Sir George Gipps] would propose for them to the **home Government**, he assured them of the interest which he took in the welfare of the colony. **1864** *Richmond-Atkinson Papers* (1960) II. 117 But anything more treacherous than the Home Govt. [*sic*] in luring on the Colony to such..expenditure for the final settlement of this Maori question..I never heard of. **1872** 'J.H.K.' *Henry Ancrum* 55 He exchanged to [a regiment] in N.Z., where what are called colonial allowances, though paid by the Home government, would enable him to to support himself. **1889** KNOX *Boy Travellers* 241 [The Maori War] very often was a matter of much perplexity to the Home Government of Great Britain. **1874** WILSON *Diary* 21 Apr. in Wierzbicka *Wilson Family* (1973) 179 Got my letters from Victoria but not my home letters, which is strange especially as I got **home papers**. **1939** BEATTIE *First White Boy Born Otago* 125 The *Otago Witness* (Dunedin) made a welcome if irregular appearance, and Home papers occasionally came.

home, *n.*[2] [Spec. or transf. uses of *home* an abode.]

1. [AND 1848.] A (dwelling) house; a house to live in and its material surroundings.

1908 *Dominion* (Wellington) 15 July 3 A large number of our most successful present-day farmers were fairly well-to-do, and had nice homes even when they were on the 'boards'. **1948** *Our Own Country* 30 [You] see instead pleasant bungalows with lawns and flower beds and trees, all very tidy and peaceful... The homes are modern and sit comfortably on large sections.

Hence **homette**, a small or temporary house.

1958 *NZ Farmer* 6 Mar. 4 More accommodation in the shape of houses, homettes and caravans was provided by the [rabbit] boards.

2. WW1. A dug-out in the front trenches.

1937 PARTRIDGE *Dict. Slang* 399 home... A dug-out in the front trench: New Zealand soldiers': 1915–18.

3. As **home unit** [AND 1949], any one of a group of similar small dwellings which may be bought or rented (see also UNIT *n.*[2] 1).

1987 *Metro* (Auckland) May 70 That was what her home unit in Onehunga was worth shared among her four siblings. **1987** *Te Reo* 38 132 A *townhouse* is emphatically upmarket from a *home unit*.

4. In various phr. in which *home* represents a place of security, a goal to be reached. **a.** In the phr. **home and dried** [AND 1918], a var. of *home and dry* (see OED *adv.* 2 b), certain to succeed or win.

1949 SARGESON *I Saw in My Dream* (1974) 34 You only need to take your shirt off like me, and we'll be home and dried [*sc.* win the tennis game].

b. home and hosed [AND 1959], certain to succeed or win; safe and sound.

1958 *Political Science* Sept. 90 You see my secret is to lull managers and workers into believing that 'she'll be right'. If somebody relaxes for a minute I'm home and hosed. **1962** CURNOW *Four Plays* (1972) 108 Here we are, home and hosed. **1968** SLATTER *Pagan Game* 206 Then you'll be jake. Pile on a coupla tries and you'll be home and hosed. **1970** SLATTER *On the Ball* 139 'Home and hosed,' said Spandau. 'Don't be so cocky,' I tell him. **1985** O'SULLIVAN *Shuriken* 60 Of course once you do have the respect of these fellows you're virtually home and hosed.

c. home on the pig's back [AND 1948], see PIG *n.*[1] 2 c.

d. to get home on (a person or thing) *obs.*, to land a telling blow on, to score off successfully.

1910 *Maoriland Worker* 3 Some months ago I wrote the 'Lone Hand' I would not renew my subscription if they published fraud advertisements, and specified Kugalman's soap and a hair restorer. They replied, in the 'Bulletin', that both articles were good, and said I would not use them because I was 'incurably bald and hopelessly unclean'. Now see me get home on them. **1911** *Truth* 17 June 1 Queen Mary

home, *n.*³ [Spec. use of *home* 'dwelling-house' for a main farm-house.] Used *attrib.* in special Comb. to denote proximity to the *home station* or farm homestead: **home-block**, the block or area immediately surrounding the home-station; **home paddock** [AND 1872], the paddock nearest to or surrounding a station homestead; **home-run**, the run adjacent to the home-station; **home station** (cf. STATION 3 b) [AND 1827], the homestead and out-buildings of a stock station.

1888 CHUDLEIGH *Diary* 23 Apr. (1950) 361 I never saw the country so bare of food... The view deteriorates as fast as the plough improves the **home blocks**. **1904** LANCASTER *Sons o' Men* 3 Lane's out-station was twelve rough miles from the home-block, and much sheep–country lay beyond that. **1866** BARKER *Station Life* (1870) 66 The country outside the **home paddock** is too rough for thin material. **1874** KENNAWAY *Crusts* 208 One evening, I remember a neighbouring back-station holder, after a long day's journey, rode up late along the fence-side of our home-paddocks, amidst a chorus of challenge from the sheep-dogs. **1888** CHUDLEIGH *Diary* 28 Apr. (1950) 361 There is no food to be seen on the run outside the home paddocks. **1901** *Ibid.* 20 Sept. (1950) 407 The action..in driving my stock from Mairangi and so overcrowding the home paddocks cuts into me in every way. **1925** *Aussie (NZ Section)* 15 Dec. III We reach the home paddock without further trouble. **1953** SUTHERLAND *Golden Bush* (1963) 194 Sometimes he would be lured temporarily into an adjoining paddock for a time, but before long he'd be back in the home paddock. **1971** TAYLOR *Plekhov Place* 54 I left the house, crossed the home paddocks. **1992** GRACE *Cousins* 106 The horses are in the home paddock ready to take us to the train. **1868** CHUDLEIGH *Diary* 18 Feb. (1950) 216 I rode the length and breadth of the **Home run** but could not find a sheep. **1853** ADAMS *Canterbury Settlement* 69 The station..was a large sheep farm, extending over twelve square miles of pasture land... The **home-station** was situated at the mouth of the river Motunau. **1865** BARKER *Station Life* (1870) 31 By the time we had reached the Home Station we were quite ready for luncheon... The manager has a nice house; and the wool-shed, men's huts, dip &c., are near each other. **1870** PRENTICE *A Tale NZ* (GALMS) 30 There was one outlying shepherd who slept three or four miles from the Home-Station. **1888** DUNCAN *Wakatipians* 22 The buildings of the home-station were represented by a 'futter' and a long narrow hut. **1947** BEATTIE *Early Runholding* 11 On a big property you could find several 'stations', and the principal one was called 'the home station', while the others were 'out-stations'. **1971** GRIFFITHS *King Wakatip* 73 The Rees family barely had time to get settled again at their home station before the quiet pastoral barony..was invaded by a noisy and often drunken avalanche of gold-seekers.

home alone, *a.* Of incidents or situations of child neglect in which children are left alone in the home while their caregiver goes about business or pleasure.

1994 *Listener* 1 Oct. 24 In August, Social Welfare discovered 22 home alone cases in the lower North island. **1995** *Dominion* (Wellington) 8 Apr. 6 [Heading] Home-alone charge expected. Police expect to charge a Rotorua woman they said left her two young daughters home alone with only breakfast cereal to eat.

homebake. *Drug-users.* [f. HOME *n.*² + *bake*.] Home-made morphine or heroin extracted from (mainly) codeine phosphate by a process involving heat. Also *attrib.* See also BAKE *v.*²

1984 *Truth* 4 Dec. 6 Addicts shooting home bake are 'dicing with death'. *Ibid.* The druggies use them [*sc.* codeine tablets] to make heroin or morphine. They call their home made drugs 'home bake'. **1985** *Press* (Christchurch) 25 May 22 'Homebake manufacture appeared to be widespread partly because of the shortage of illegally imported morphine and heroin,' he said. **1986** *Evening Post* (Wellington) 5 Apr. 19 Homebake's popularity has also declined with the influx of bakers and subsequent plummet in quality. **1989** *Dominion* (Wellington) 15 Apr. 3 Before going to the supermarket to rob it, Ward injected herself with a homebake drug.

Hence **home-bake** *v. trans.*, to manufacture (morphine or heroin) from codeine phosphate in home surroundings, esp. by applying heat (quot. 1985, 27 May); **homebaker**, one who manufactures homebake; **homebaking** *vbl.n.*, see quot.

1985 *Press* (Christchurch) 27 May 22 'We think it must be made clear that imprisonment will be the normal penalty for "**homebaking**" morphine or heroin,' said his Honour. **1985** *Press* (Christchurch) 25 May 22 [Heading] Jail Promised All '**Homebakers**'. **1986** *Evening Post* (Wellington) 5 Apr. 19 Homebakers usually sell by the millilitre. That amount is considered to be a 'hit'. **1995** *Dominion* (Wellington) 5 Apr. 3 The extent of New Zealand's **homebaking** problem has forced one drug manufacturer to reformulate.. Panadeine... Police say homebaking—the process of extracting codeine from codeine compounds to produce heroin and morphine—is a distinctively New Zealand problem due largely to immigration controls restricting the availability of hard drugs.

home of gold. [Prob. a var. of Cornish dial. *house of ore* an accumulation of rich ore: EDD *house* 2 4.] A place or claim rich in alluvial gold.

1867 BARKER *Station Life* (1870) 186 One of them had been a digger, and was pronouncing an opinion that this creek was very likely to prove a 'home of gold' some day.

homer, *n.*¹ WW2.

a. [AND 1945.] A wound bad enough to send one home to New Zealand.

1939-45 *Expressions & Sayings 2NZEF (TS N.A. WAII DA 420/1)* Homer—Wound that gets a soldier home. **1942** *NZEF Times* 5 Oct. 5 He wagged his stumps at me. 'Look at me..I've got a homer.' **1944** FULLARTON *Troop Target* 27 He..collected a nasty thigh wound. 'A homer,' said several gunners enviously. **1959** DAVIN *No Remittance* 151 [WW1] He looked at my hand [which had been injured]. 'I heard you'd got a homer,' he said. **1970** SLATTER *On the Ball* 153 One of the injured hopefully hobbled to the M.O. and asked anxiously, 'Do you think she's a homer, Doc?'

b. A trip home to New Zealand, usu. occasioned by a wound.

1945 WEBBER *Johnny Enzed in Middle East* 11 He ought to get a homer out of that. **1951** WILSON *Brave Company* 93 'Everyone does [crack up sometime],' agrees Cadman briefly. Cryptically he adds, 'Some get homers. Others get base jobs. The rest?'

homer, *n.*² An illicit installation of a telephone in someone's home.

1987 *Sunday Star* (Auckland) 20 Dec. M1 Some Telecom linesmen are stealing push-button telephones from their employers and illegally installing them in the homes of friends..for a $50 fee. Most of the jobs, which Telecom linesmen call 'homers', involve replacing an old dial telephone with two push-button models, one on an extension.

home science. [f. HOME *n.*²: OED 'Term not used in Britain.', quotations suggest it was orig. and chiefly NZ (so NewSOD); cf. 1963 F.F. Laidler *Gloss. Home Econ. Educ.* 46 The term 'Home Science' as used in New Zealand is, in general comparable with the terms 'Domestic Science' in the U.K. and 'Home Economics' in the U.S.A.] The study or science of domestic economy.

1912 *Univ. Otago Calendar* 79 The Home Science Department (opened in April, 1911) has been housed for the present in part of the old Mining School. **1932** BUTCHERS *Education System* 182 The School of Home Science followed [in Otago] in 1911, in consequence of a generous gift of Mr. John Studholme. **1943** MURDOCH *High Schools NZ* 362 Home science students may substitute arithmetic for mathematics. **1992** *NZ Encyclop.* 370 Otago is the only NZ university which confers degrees in dentistry, home science, physical education.

homestead, *n.*¹ [Spec. use of *homestead* a farmstead with its dependent buildings: see OED *n.* 2.]

1. STATION 3 b; *home station* (HOME *n.*³), the station headquarters including the owner's residence and the ancillary buildings.

1849 *Handbook Suburban & Rural Dists. Otago* 6 Sheep or cattle owners, who, establishing their temporary homesteads or stations, near or in the bush, might run their flocks and herds amongst the hills. **1854** RICHARDSON *Summer's Excursion* 27 There are equitable arrangements for the purchase or sale of homesteads built on such runs if not exceeding 80 acres. **1866** BARKER *Station Life* (1870) 64 I am glad we have chosen to build our house here instead of at the homestead two miles off; for I like to be removed from the immediate neighbourhood of all the work of the station. **1870** PRENTICE *A Tale NZ* (GALMS) 29 Add to [the Whata] a small brush sheep-pen and you have the homestead or station complete. **1891** PRICE *Through Uriwera Country* 61 As an out-station is to the homestead of a sheep run so is this little fort to Te Teko. **1909** *Truth* 13 Nov. 7 It [*sc.* gum-digging territory] is a wild country. There are no promenades. Settlers usually stay on their own homesteads. **1912** [see STATION 3 b]. **1940** STUDHOLME *Te Waimate* (1954) 103 They returned to the Homestead only when it was necessary to get fresh stores. **1947** NEWTON *Waylego* 12 The musterer's job is to muster the sheep off such [high] country into the respective homesteads. **1947** BEATTIE *Early Runholding* 11 The custom in the old days was to call the buildings on a run 'the station', and the land that went with it was 'the run'... Gradually the signification was altered by loosely calling the whole run a station, and then the real station became a homestead and the out-stations became shepherds' huts.

2. [AND 1822.] The owner's residence, or main house on a rural property, as distinct from other out-buildings or employees' housing. See also *big house* (BIG *a.*).

1851 *Lyttelton Times* 1 Jan. 6 Picturesque crags and wooded gullies, among which Messrs. Rhodes's homestead and farm-buildings are perched. **1853** ADAMS *Canterbury Settlement* 70 This homestead much resembles a small English farm-house save that the sleeping loft had seldom fewer than ten occupants. **1866** ANGAS *Polynesia* 111 This [Wairarapa] is one of the finest pastoral districts in New Zealand, now exhibiting several little village-towns, and the homesteads and stock-stations of numbers of thriving settlers. **1881** CAMPBELL *Poenamo* 99 The white gleam of the farmer's homestead dots the landscape. **1907** MANSFIELD *Urewera Notebook* (1978) 51 Here we drive in and ask for a paddock. Past the shearing shed—past the homestead to a beautiful place with a little patch of bush. **1926** [see *big house* (BIG)]. **1934** MULGAN *Spur of Morning* 261 In this high country he met some of the original selectors..had seen tent give way to mud or stone hut, and that replaced by the long, low wooden homestead, with its deep verandah, its big, comfortably furnished rooms. **1943** HISLOP *Pure Gold* 129 Travellers are coming and going as in the old homestead days, and very seldom does one pass without a cup of tea and many a time a meal. **1946** ACLAND *Early Canterbury Runs* 19 When an old-fashioned squatter..used the word 'homestead' he generally used it to signify the owner's residence, as opposed to the men's quarters and other station buildings, and then only when the residence was at some distance from the working buildings, otherwise he called it the 'Big House'. **1973** FERNANDEZ *Tussock Fever* 1 Barbara..dawdled across the horse paddock by the homestead heading for the dusty, noisy, drafting yards. **1981** ANDERSON *Both Sides of River* 9 The homestead is situated..at the foot of a bush-clad mountain after which the station is named.

homestead, *n.*² *Hist.* [Cf. US *homestead* an allotment of rural land sufficient for the maintenance of a family: AND 1832.]

1. A small rural land-holding.
  1961 REED *N. Cape to Bluff* 107 My father..saved enough to buy a homestead of twenty-nine acres of unimproved Crown land.

2. Special Comb. in the main sense of 'an area of rural land dedicated to the erection of a farm house and buildings': **Homestead Act**, a familiar term applied to the various Land Acts (see note at *homestead system* below) permitting the purchase of land for a farm homestead and buildings; **homestead block**, a section of rural Crown land (of varying size according to locality) sold or leased on condition that a residence or station be established on it; **homestead pre-emptive right** *hist.*, see quot. 1981; **homestead settler**, one who is established on a homestead block; **homestead system**, see quot. 1892; cf. also 1877 *NZ Statutes* No.29 185 [Land Act 1877] It shall be lawful for the Board to permit the original holder of a pastoral license..to apply for and purchase in one block..an allotment of land not exceeding three hundred and twenty acres on which to erect buildings, yards, or such other improvements as may be necessary for working the run. [Marginal note] Licensee may purchase land on run for homestead. [Similar arrangements are continued in the 1885, 1892, 1894 Acts.]
  1887 *Auckland Weekly News* 5 Mar. 8 I am quite convinced that the **Homestead Act** is a very practicable and wise measure. **1879** *Auckland Weekly News* 15 Mar. 14 It will also open up another '**homestead**' **block**. **1948** *Our Own Country* 135 [Regulations] legalized at that time [1856], allowed land outside the original Otago Block to be bought for grazing-runs at a low cost. (Runholders were allowed 80 acres for the homestead block with 10 acres for each outstation.) **1948** SCOTTER *Run Estate & Farm* 65 Edward Menlove died in 1903. His homestead block of 1,241 acres was then entered in the roll under the name of his son-in-law. **1984** BOYD *City of the Plains* 28 On his homestead block of 8 acres he erected a family residence. **1981** in Crawford *Station Years* 246 Runholders were able to register with the Provincial Council improvements such as buildings, plantations, fencing, and yards, for which they were granted an improvement pre-emptive right (I.P.R.) covering fifty acres of land surrounding the improvement. A **homestead pre-emptive right** (H.P.R.), which afforded protection for 250 acres, could also be registered... One H.P.R. could be taken out for each property and it was only businesslike that each runholder should use this right to secure 250 acres around his homestead against purchase by an outsider. An H.P.R. was initially intended to cover the owner's or manager's home, but, in the case of runs of over 5,000 acres, could be extended to cover an outstation. **1887** *Auckland Weekly News* 5 Mar. 8 The **homestead settler** earns nothing for the first two years. **1879** *Auckland Weekly News* 15 Mar. 13 The '**homestead**' **system** means a peculiar mode of dealing with lands open for selection without payment, but subject to provisions for cultivation and residence. **1892** *NZ Official Handbook* 284 [Heading] Homestead system. Under this system the settler makes no payment for the land, the only cost to him being the expenses of survey. On the fulfilment of conditions, which are five years' residence, the erection of a house, and the cultivation of one-third of the selection if open land, and one-fifth if bush-land, the Crown grant is issued.

Hence **homestead** *v.*, to be a tenant on (part of) the land belonging to a large stock station; **homesteader**, a tenant on a large stock station.
  1926 DEVANNY *Lenore Divine* 161 I've already got quite a number of my men, our own colour, you know, **homesteading** at a merely nominal rent. **[1876]** MCCASKILL *Molesworth* (1969) 45 The Jack Fitch mentioned in the story has been identified as a '**homesteader**' on Tarndale [Station] in 1876. **1887** *Auckland Weekly News* 5 Mar. 8 I met one settler amongst these homesteaders who had previously been employed as a manager.

homeward bounder. *Goldmining. Hist.* [f. HOME *n.*¹ 1 a.] A claim or strike rich enough to allow a return to Britain.
  1967 MAY *West Coast Gold Rushes* 275 The richest claim was always a 'homeward-bounder'. A Nelson digger recalled how at work his mates talked of 'trips to Europe, going back for a week, and astonishing the Natives generally'. *Ibid.* 329 J. F. Byrne & Co. showed off their wares by the light of six kerosene chandeliers and advertised. The real homeward bounder! An ounce to the Dish can be Saved by buying your clothing and boots at the Corinthian hall.

homey. *Obs.* Also freq. **homie.** Often with init. cap. [f. HOME *n.*¹ 1 a + -Y.] A native-born Briton, esp. as an immigrant to New Zealand. Often *attrib.*
  [Note] Homey was the predominant colloquial use up to WW2, after which *Pom(my)* gained ground.
  1926 FAIRBURN *Letters* (1981) 15 He is a 'homey' who came out to Australia, buggered up a grocer's shop, and came on to Norfolk. **1937** LEE *Diaries* 10 Dec. (1981) 50 10 *December*... I have been referring to a Homie attitude. Is New Zealand to stand on its own feet or become a dependency of Britain? **1938** HYDE *Nor Yrs Condemn* 165 Don't mind if you're called a Homie. After all, what does it mean? Somebody from Home. A bit sissy, but it could be worse. **1948** BALLANTYNE *Cunninghams* (1976) 21 But this homey Simmons was a loudmouth with a big opinion of himself. **1950** [see PONGO A b]. **1953** *Truth* 8 Apr. 9 I have never felt any hostility towards any 'homie' or 'pommie' until recently. **1960** MUIR *Word for Word* 181 He knew the men still regarded him as a Homey, though it was well over thirty years since he'd left the Old Country. **1986** OWEN & PERKINS *Speaking for Ourselves* 78 [The immigrants] were 'Homeys'—the word 'Pommy' wasn't in use then [in the early 1930s depression], and we called them 'Homeys', and this was used in a derogatory manner..as if it was something contemptible. **1993** SINCLAIR *Halfway Round the Harbour* 101 'Homies', as my parents called 'Poms', were extremely unpopular at No. 33.

Hone Heke's War: see HEKE WAR.

honey.

1. a. As **wild honey**, honey made by honey bees not owned or controlled by an apiarist. Also *fig.*, see quot. 1964.
  1867 BARKER *Station Life* (1870) 181 The mistress of this charming 'bush-hut' insisted on our having some hot coffee and scones and wild honey. **1894** *TrNZI* XXVI. 221 Some four or five bushmen had proceeded to Kerikeri..for the purpose of collecting wild honey. **1910** GROSSMAN *Heart of Bush* 20 Wild honey and clotted cream..tea-cakes in piles and preserves. **1934** HYDE *Journalese* 109 And perhaps the heavy sweetness of wild honey. **1958** GILLESPIE *S. Canterbury* 341 The early surveyors in South Canterbury often obtained wild honey. **1964** CAMPBELL *Wild Honey* 28 These things: gallantry, passion, solitude, and loveliness – how they glow!.. .. *Wild honey.* **1986** RICHARDS *Off the Sheep's Back* 27 We always had plenty of wild honey. The bees would build their hives in hollow trees.

b. See *flax honey* (FLAX 5 c), *korari honey* (KORARI 4), *manuka honey* (MANUKA 3).

2. *transf.* Special Comb. **honey-pot**, a children's name for a jump into water with one's hands clasped around the knees, landing noisily on one's backside.
  1953 SUTTON-SMITH *Unorganized Games NZ Primary School Children* (VUWTS) II. 744 The athletic games of strength include Bull in the Ring, Buck Jumping, Cock-Fighting, Honey Pots. **1980** LELAND *Kiwi-Yankee Dict.* 52 *honey pot/bomb:* [In New Zealand] it is the name of that swimming pool spectacular, spectator drenching dive, you [Americans] know as a cannonball dive. **1992** *Landfall* 183 313 It's been..high dives and honeypots into these piscine deeps.

honeymoon shear. A humorous name for the crutching or cleaning of a ewe's rear preparatory to tupping.
  1986 RICHARDS *Off the Sheep's Back* 148 As tupping season was approaching I also gave them a light ringcrutch (a honeymoon shear) before turning them out into a larger paddock.

honey mushroom. [Extended use of *honey mushroom*, *Armillaria mellea*, a destructive tree parasite.] *Armillariella novae-zelandiae* (fam. Tricholomataceae), a large fungus with honey-coloured caps found growing in groups on dead broadleaved trees.
  1970 TAYLOR *Mushrooms & Toadstools NZ* 3 [Caption] Armillariella novae-zelandiae. *Honey mushroom.* **1982** WILSON *Stewart Is. Plants* 492 Honey Mushroom... Honey coloured toadstools... Common on dead wood in forest and scrub. Not known to be edible. **1983** *Land of Mist* 64 [Caption] (1) Honey mushroom (2) Red tobacco pouch fungus (3) Violet tobacco pouch fungi.

honeysuckle. [Transf. use of *honeysuckle Leycesteria periclymenum* (fam. Caprifoliaceae) for unrelated NZ species of *Knightia* (fam. Proteaceae) having nectar-rich flowers.] Also as **Maori (native, New Zealand) honeysuckle.** REWAREWA.
  1839 WAKEFIELD *Journal* (ATLMS) A tree, called by the English here, the honeysuckle furnishes excellent wood for boat-building. **1842** *Lett. from New Plymouth* (1968) 27 Nov. 58 There is also rata, tawa, honeysuckle &c., which, though of harder nature, may hereafter be

applied to many useful purposes. **1889** KIRK *Forest Flora* 50 The rewarewa is often termed 'honeysuckle' by the settlers, but it is not easy to imagine any reason for the application of the name. **1890** *PWD Catalogue Timbers* (NZ & South Seas Exhib.) 14 Rewarewa (honey-suckle)... Soft wood, straight grained, prettily mottled, and used largely for ornamental purposes of all descriptions. **1910**, **1926** native honey-suckle [see REWAREWA]. **1936** *Handbook for NZ* (ANZAAS) 32 The dull-red flowers [of rewarewa], laden with nectar (hence the misleading settlers' name 'honeysuckle'), appear in dense racemes. **1940** LAING & BLACKWELL *Plants NZ* 150 *Knightia excelsa* (Maori honeysuckle) A tree, sometimes reaching the height of 100ft...found only in the North Island and on the southern shores of Cook Strait. **1969** *Standard Common Names Weeds* 53 New Zealand honeysuckle [=] rewarewa. **1989** [see REWAREWA].

hongi /ˈhɒŋi/, *n*. Also early **ehonge**, **e-hon-gi** (=he hongi), **ongi**. [Ma. /hoŋi/: Williams 58 *Hongi* 3. Salute by pressing the noses together.]

1. A Maori greeting or salutation made by pressing or touching (freq. erroneously 'rubbing') noses. See also NOSE *n*.¹

1793 KING *Journal* Nov. in McNab *Hist. Records* (1914) II. 547 After the ceremony of Ehonge (*i.e.*, joining noses) he took off his how, how, [*sic*] or mantle, and put it on my shoulders. **1804** *Collins Eng. Colony in NSW* (NZ Vocab.) 558 E-hon-gi, *The ceremony of joining noses as a salute*. **1838** POLACK *NZ* I. 47 The ongi, or native salute of touching noses..immediately proved they were of New Zealand origin. **1841** WAKEFIELD *Journal* 20 Feb. in Heaphy *NZ* (1842) 58 Were these missionaries, who shook hands and gave the *hongi* to my people, and then put them to death? **1859** THOMSON *Story NZ* I. 200 At meeting men and women pressed their noses together... This salutation is called hongi, and is defined as a smelling... During the hongi the lips never met, there was no kissing. **1882** POTTS *Out in Open* 23 The hongi, a method of salutation by rubbing noses together, we saw frequently performed. **1904** TREGEAR *Maori Race* 142 The Maori salutation (*hongi*) was to press the nose against the nose of the person greeted; sometimes with a low crooning song of welcome or lament. **1911** [see NOSE *n*.¹ e]. **1951** HUNT *Confessions* 38 On the day appointed hundreds of Maoris..assembled at the tapu plot, and, with much hongi and wailing, set about digging. **1985** ROSIER-JONES *Cast Two Shadows* 88 Tui presses noses with the old lady, then Maude... 'Whenever I'm out here in the wop-wops with youse jokers, the hori comes out in me. Kapai and hongi.'

2. In the phr. **to have a hongi with**, to greet with a hongi.

1983 *Evening Post* (Wellington) 1 July 14 Sir Graham has a hongi with Mr Alan Napier, a member of the Wellington Mongrel Mob who works at Tapu Te Ranga.

hongi, *v*. [See HONGI *n*.] *trans*. and *intr*. To press noses in greeting (someone) in the Maori manner.

1853 GRACE *Letter* 29 Dec. in *Pioneer Missionary* (1928) 35 They should shake hands and 'hongi' (press noses) in the presence of all, be good friends and neighbours. **1877** GRACE *Journal* Aug. in *Pioneer Missionary* (1928) 264 Immediately jumping up he hongied (touched noses) with me, and saluted me as 'the face of Te Heuheu'. **1914** *Hawera & Normanby Star* 31 Jan. 4 Then all shook hands and hongied (rubbed noses) and so concluded a very interesting meeting. **1945** *JPS* LIV. 97 As each arrives, she goes through the bus, shaking hands and hongi-ing everyone. There is a set pattern for the hongi—clasp hands, briefly press together the tips of the noses, make a wailing sound, press noses briefly for a second time... Close relatives hongi for a longer period than the formal brief nose-press. **1983** *Evening Post* (Wellington) 1 July 14 Today he 'hongi-ed' (pressed noses) with all those at the marae and looked at the new meeting house being built. **1988** *Sunday Star* (Auckland) 9 Oct. A1 The Tainui elder said they had just hongied when Hineware Harawira (34) came up beside Mr Curtis and punched him in the head.

honking, *vbl. n. Caving*. Abseiling into caves at speed.

1992 *Evening Post* (Wellington) 19 Dec. 1 The name Haggas Honking Holes is a combination of the speed at which cavers abseil down into the caves (honking) and the Haggas farm the caves lie under.

hoodackie, var. HOODICKY.

hoodicky. Also **hoodackie** and other spoken variants. A mainly young people's name for a thingamebob. (The following variants have been noted from c1940 to c1951: **doodacky, doohickey, hoodle-lacky, hoojacky, hoojah, hoojit, howdzacky**.)

c**1945** *Sixes & Sevens* (Troopship pub.) 7 'My oath,' I said. 'Many a Jap binjie is going to get a hoodickey stuck in it before sparrow-hiccough.' **1955** *BJ Cameron Collection* (TS July) hoojacky (n) Thingummy. **1988** McGILL *Dict. Kiwi Slang* 57 *hoodackie* thingummygig; variant of 'doodackie'.

hooer /ˈhuə/. Also **hua**, **whoo-er**, **whoo-whaa**. [A dial. or variant pronunciation of *whore*, common in 18th–19th century English, and represented in editions of John Walker's *A Critical Pronouncing Dictionary* [etc.] (1845 edn.) as the primary polite pronunciation used (among others) by 'the Stage'; also freq. in the familiar speech of modern New Zealanders but rarely associated with *whore*, and often thought to be of Maori origin (hence the form **hua**): AND 1937.] Used in opprobrious address or reference; also in a weakened sense, in familiar reference to people and things.

c**1940** In common use among Marlborough boys, esp. as 'You dirty hooer.' (Ed.) **1960** MUIR *Word for Word* 184 'About this Stevens book. I thought I'd mention it now though it's not due out for a while yet.' 'Is that the fat hooer?' 'Yes, it'll be fairly thick.' **1971** *Listener* 22 Mar. 12 The dirty hua didn't even take a shower before he shot through. **1979** *Islands* 27 462 All right, you hori hooer! Send us one [frozen carcass] down for a try... If I get one of them big hooers up my arse, you'll get one of my size nine kadoodies up yours! **1981** JOHNSTON *Fish Factory* 65 Spalpeen! Dirty little whoo-whaa! Oh, my God! The shame you've brought on your family... Dirty little slut! **1983** KIDMAN *Paddy's Puzzle* 81 Mrs Mawson called her a whore then. Only she said it 'whoo-er' the way the children did at school, or over at the [Frankton] Junction. **1986** *Salient* (Wellington) 29 Sept. 15 [Letter signed] Yours in Madity Mal the boozy Hua. **1991** *Dominion Sunday Times* (Wellington) 20 Oct. 21 'Mr Katene has crossbreds like that,' I said, seeing the earmark plain as day. 'What'll the Katenes say?' 'That hooa's got no comeback. Should fix his fences, I'd say.'

hoohaa, var. HOHA.

hoojacky, var. HOODICKY.

hook, *n. Gumdigging*. A hooked implement for retrieving buried kauri-gum (see quot. 1972).

1900 *NZ Illustr. Mag.* III. 208 The tools used by the digger are the spade, the spear and the hook... The hook is used for raising the gum from the deeper and wetter swamps. It is a rod of iron perhaps twelve feet long, looped at one end for a handle, and with the last three feet of the other turned off at right angles and given its own peculiar shape. **1972** REED *Gumdiggers* 50 The hook was used for drawing up nuggets of gum from the depths of swamps, after location by the spear. The hook consisted of a galvanised pipe an inch or so in diameter, equipped at one end with a spade handle, and at the other end with a steel 'toe', about an inch and a half in length, welded to the pipe, and forming the 'hook'. It is said that expert diggers could bring up with ease gum of various sizes from great depths.

Hence **hooker**, one who uses a hook to retrieve kauri-gum; **hooking** *vbl. n.*

1900 *NZ Illustr. Mag.* III. 208 When the swamps are dry the **hooker** has to open up the hardened surface with a spade. **1904** PATTERSON *Kauri-Gum* 6 In former times, even in winter, '**hooking**' has been practised in the swamps... The necessary tools were a long spear and a long hook—a long iron rod with a curved end. The gum..found by the spear..[was] worked up through the slime with the hook. **1913** CARR *Country Work* 42 Another method of getting the gum is by 'hooking'. **1916** STALLWORTHY *Early N. Wairoa* 53 In the swamps, the method of securing the gum was by spearing or hooking or, in shallow ground, by groping.

hook, *v.*¹ *Racing slang*. [Wilkes 1949.] *trans*. To ride (a horse) to lose.

1910 *Truth* 14 May 2 His owner was not satisfied with his display on the second day, and he interrogated young Cress, who stood on his 'dig.' and asked owner McDonald if he thought he hooked him. Of course McDonald thought nothing of the sort, but wanted some explanation of his horse's poor showing. *Ibid.* 21 May 2 [Unfashionable jockeys] are compelled to 'hook 'em' as they get so little kudos that four quid is often very handy to them. **1962** HORI *Half-gallon Jar* 24 That horse has got no show. He is dead... He is going to be hooked, pulled and run into the ground.

hook, *v.*² [Transf. use of *hook* a swinging blow made by a boxer.] *trans*. To punch (someone).

1963 *Truth* 30 July 5 Talk of 'demons' and 'jokers' being 'hooked' proved too much for Mr L.G.M. Sinclair, S.M., in Auckland Court. ... Te Atatu mussel curer, Benjamin Patrick Nathan, 28, explained. '"Demons"' he said, were detectives. 'To be "hooked" was to be "punched".'

hook, *v.*³ [Spec. use of *hook (up)* to make fast by a hook.] *trans*. To tow away (a repossessed vehicle).

1987 *Sunday Star* (Auckland) 5 July B1 Doing repos won't make you rich. Hooking a car pays $75 to $80 plus GST and maybe another $50 if tracking it has taken a lot of work.

hook, *v.*⁴ [Various elaborations of *hook* to make off: see OED *v*. 3.] In the phr. **to hook one's bait (mutton, muttons)**, **to hook off**, to make off (quickly), to clear out; also **to hook one's mutton** *transf*. (with a play on fixing a carcass on a gambrel, or catching a sheep with a crooked stick), to take one's partner for a dance (see quot. 1929).

1929 MILTON *Love and Chiffon* 233 Look slippy, buddies. Hook your muttons for an extra. **1938** ANTHONY in Davin *NZ Short Stories* (1953) 219 I hooked off on my own and rambled aimlessly about. **1940** SARGESON *Man & Wife* (1944) 75 If Ted saw her coming up the road he'd hook off if he could before she got near. And if he couldn't I'd hook off while they had their barney. **1941** BAKER *NZ Slang* 53 To *hook one's bait* or *mutton*, to depart (a variant of the English *sling one's hook*). **1966** TURNER *Eng. Lang. Austral. & NZ* 177 Some expressions that have been claimed for New Zealand are *at the rate of knots* 'very fast', *hook your mutton* 'clear out'. **1988** MCGILL *Dict. Kiwi Slang* 57 *hook your mutton* clear out, similar to 'slinging your hook'; eg 'Let's hook our mutton, there's no welcome here, fellas.'

Hooker's sea lion: see *sea lion* (SEA 1 b).

hookgrass. Any one of various native sedges (not true grasses) belonging to the genus *Uncinia* (fam. Cyperaceae) and distinguished by their hooked fruits which stick to clothing, fur, and hairy legs. See also *bastard-grass* (GRASS 2 (3)).
 1946 *Bull. Wellington Bot. Soc. No.14* 8 Here are some [vernacular names]..: *Uncinia australis*, hook grass; *Earina* spp., bamboo orchid. **1949** *Tararua Tramper* Aug. 6 Also noted were horopito, water fern and stinko... Further down we struck lawyer..and hookgrass. **1966** *NZ Farmer* 28 Apr. 37 Hook-grass is a different kettle of fish. **1982** WILSON *Stewart Is. Plants* 340 *Uncinia* Hooked Sedges... Hookgrasses... These grass-like plants are characterised by ripe seed heads which readily attach their seeds to hairy legs and clothing by means of tiny projecting hooks. **1992** *Dominion Sunday Times* (Wellington) 26 July 21 In the valleys you will gather..the seeds of hookgrass in your socks, as you become the unwitting spreader of cunning plant progeny.

hool, *v.* [Poss. a var. of *hurl* or a portmanteau of *hurl* and HOOP *v.*: cf. EDD *hull v.* 3 hurl.] *intr.* To move vigorously or at speed. Cf. HOOP *v.*
 1944 FULLARTON *Troop Target* 41 Better get a wriggle on, Kori. There's 4 or 5 Jerry armoured cars hooling along the road. **1970** SLATTER *On the Ball* 138 From the kick-off the Welsh forwards hool into a loose ruck.

hoon. [Of unknown origin.]
 1. *WW2.* A term used by conscientious objectors in detention camp for a person whose objection to military service was based on other than religious convictions; a political or humanitarian objector.
 c1941 p.c. A.C. Barrington, Riverside Community, Nelson (1951): also Professor J. McCreary, Victoria University (1985): *hoon* was used among detained conscientious objectors for a non- religious objector to military service. **1953** HAMILTON *Till Human Voices Wake Us* 154 I hadn't been in detention long when I heard his name mentioned... He hadn't gone to jail with the first group... They reckoned he'd stuck to his religion all through and the Hoons* [*non-religious groups*] gave me the impression that he took his religion seriously... You couldn't take much notice of the Hoons of course, not about a thing like that. Most of them just lumped the religoes together. *Ibid.* 164 There was a sort of line drawn in the [detention] camps between the Hoons and the religoes. **1982** SANDYS *Love & War* 244 'I'm lucky to be here [in a detention camp for conscientious objectors]. Reckon they must have got me mixed up with the Hoons. I'd be much worse off in a regular gaol.'.. The majority are Hoons—military defaulters. Against war for reasons of sanity and humanity, not out of religious conviction.

Hence **hoonism**, the belief system of a non-religious objector.
 1953 HAMILTON *Till Human Voices Wake Us* 208 True Hoonism, God be praised, was rare in the camps and most of those who approached the standard..were political or union men.

2. A fool; a stupid person.
 c1951 p.c. F.M. O'Brien. *Hoon* in K-force yakker was a fool or clot: the word is used in Wellington at least among tramwaymen. **1980** LELAND *Kiwi-Yankee Dict.* 52 *hoon*: Turkey (human variety). This expression is largely confined to the southernmost part of the South Island.

3. a. [AND 1938.] A lout; a boisterous or noisy exhibitionist.
 1980 *Dominion* (Wellington) 11 Dec. 6 Just inside the door at Flanagans' and the police radio operator Paul Curtis races in, 'Boss, there's a crowd of hoons fighting... ' The 'hoons'—anyone who is not a police officer. **1983** *Dominion* (Wellington) 24 Mar. 1 To a hoon, the gully is the place behind the embankment, aclank with discarded beer cans, where you propel your fellow hoons when you all get drunk, and where you relieve yourself in the process of getting drunk. **1988** *Evening Post* (Wellington) 9 Nov. 2 [Heading] Waterfront race hoons on agenda. The 'hoon effect' caused by the Nissan Mobil 500 is one area that could be looked at in a major review. **1990** *Dominion* (Wellington) 18 Jan. 6 [Heading] Kea 'hoons' plague beachgoers. Hoons who make life miserable at beach resorts are usually the loud, human variety, not a native alpine parrot with a beak like a Swiss army knife.

b. A 'hoonish' escapade.
 1986 *Metro* (Auckland) Mar. 27 Golden haired boy,.. head motor salesperson..'borrowed' *Aunty Astle's* Roller for a bit of a hoon..and roared away to a Parnell pizzeria.

4. Special Comb. **hoon bin** [formed on rugby league, etc. *sin bin*], a place where (drunken) louts misbehaving at sporting fixtures can be confined to 'cool off'; **hoonchaser**, a traffic cop; **hoon-ethos**, a name for an attitude of moral and social insensitivity.
 1986 *Metro* (Auckland) Sept. 70 [Heading] Cops Three nights on the road with the **hoonchasers**. **1986** *Listener* 20 Dec. 13 The best-known primer for this kind of activity, and indeed an integral part of the **hoon-ethos** itself, is the drinking game.

5. In jocular composition: **hoondom**, hoons as a group; **hoonery**, loutish behaviour; **hoonish** *a.*, loutish; **hoonmobile**, a vehicle driven by a hoon.
 1983 *Dominion* (Wellington) 24 Mar. 1 On display was a wide range of these Wellingtonians—louts, larrikins, lunks, lummoxes, yahoos—the creme de la creme of **hoondom**. **1987** *Dominion* (Wellington) 21 Sept. 3 The chief executive of the Hotel Association, Tom Sheehy, said last night that students contained elements of '**hoonery**', just as did other groups of society. **1983** *Listener* 5 Nov. 70 A lot of **hoonish** summer behaviour may be the very result of biorhythmical and biochemical imbalances. **1986** *Salient* (Wellington) 5 May 3 According to Professor Taylor the capping band came in acting 'loutish and hoonish' whilst dropping beer cans. **1993** *Evening Post* (Wellington) 10 June 29 Market research had shown the rock-oriented Windy [Radio] was not retailer-friendly. It had young, hoonish connotations. **1993** *Dominion* (Wellington) 16 Jan. 10 I wasn't sure whether to be flattered or outraged by the stares from the rear windows of the hoonmobiles.

hoon, *v.* [f. HOON *n.*] *intr.* **a.** Usu. as **hoon around**, to do things in an irresponsible way.
 1983 p.c. Mr Nixon (Palmerston North), letter on adolescent & school slang 21 Oct. *hoon*—as verb. He likes to hoon round on his bike. Also hoonery. **1987** MOORE *Hard Labour* 19 One [life] in the city, being political; the other at weekends, hooning around up north, though music, new friends in Auckland and the Vietnam protests were slowly combining to give my life more direction. **1988** *Evening Post* (Wellington) 9 Nov. 2 Former deputy Mayor..said after the race she had noticed people 'hooning around' Ohariu Valley.

b. As **hoon it up**, to party in a noisy drunken way.
 1983 *Listener* 25 June 13 The Young Nats hooned it up [at the Party Conference] until the small hours of the morning.

Hence **hooning** *vbl. n.*, noisy loutish behaviour.
 1986 *Listener* 20 Dec. 13 There is an entire substratum of what we might call 'part-time hoons', 'weekend hoons' or 'holiday hoons'. The sons (and daughters) of the middle classes, they are less professional in their hooning. **1990** *Listener* 13 Aug. 14 [The Mk 2 Zephyr's] chunky..features are redolent of the halcyon days of hooning, when dropping patches and sitting three-up in front were codes of cool.

hoop, *v.* [Poss. Brit. dial. var. of *whoop*: cf. EDD *hoop* 11 (*Fig*?) 'to speed, hurry' Sc. 1766. *e.g.* My lord wants a coach; now he may get an Anstruther bark and hoop o'er to Versailles.] To move at speed; often as **hoop along**, to rush, to speed. Cf. HOOL *v.*
 1945 *Johnny Enzed in Middle East* 31 Pious injunctions [to the gharry driver] to 'yella', 'igri', 'hoop it along' and 'set it alight'. **1955** *BJ Cameron Collection* (TS July) hoop (v) To rush or tear. **1973** *Dominion* (Wellington) 14 Dec. 3 'But these blokes who are breaking the law come hooping in pick out about eight or nine well-grown animals [*sc.* wapiti], many of them pure-breds,' he said. **1975** NEWTON *Sixty Thousand on Hoof* 57 Harry..is a very capable and experienced pilot and on these 'spotting' trips he hooped in and out of gullies with the wing tips..only feet clear of the slopes. **1992** GRAHAM *Breaking the Habit* 14 We would tiptoe and whisper round the house until we could whoop off to school with great shouts of relief.

hooped, *a.* [Poss. f. *as tight as a (barrel) hoop*.] Also **hoopsy-coopsy** [f. *hoo*)ped + ti(*psy*). Drunk.
 1941 in Reid *Book NZ* (1964) 288 But Adolph one night when 'hooped' Decided to send his paratroops. **1962** HORI *Half-gallon Jar* 27 And this plonk have the real kick alright and soon the coot get very hoopsy-coopsy. **1988** MCGILL *Dict. Kiwi Slang* 58 *hooped* drunk.

hooray /hʌˈræɪ/, /hʊˈræɪ/.

1. Also occas. **hurrah**. [*Transf.* use of a var. of (the cry) *hurrah*: AND 1898.] Goodbye!, cheerio!
 1918 let. 1 Dec. in *Boots, Belts* (1992) 144 Well Mum, I have very little news of any sort. Hurrah just now. Trusting you are all well. Willie. **1924** ANTHONY *Follow the Call* (1975) 65 When he said good-bye to his mother on going to the war I expect old Clive just..said 'Hooray, Ma!'. **1935** GUTHRIE *Little Country* 66 'Allo' 'Fine day' 'Yair' pause. 'Going far?' 'Aw, no. Up along'. Long Pause. 'Aw well, hooray!' 'Hooray!' **1943** BENNETT *English in NZ* in *Amer. Speech* XVIII. 91 'See you some more' is the common phrase of casual farewell, the alternative being 'hooray' (the New Zealand modification of 'hurrah'). **1959** SLATTER *Gun in My Hand* 152 'Cheeri,' he calls. I don't like these new slangs. Hooray is the word. Everybody in the Div said hooray. **1969** HASCOMBE *Down & Almost Under* 108 We learnt that at midday exactly..the salutation is always 'good-afternoon', and that either 'Cheery' or 'Hooray' is the colloquial way of saying goodbye. **1973** WILSON *NZ Jack* 116 'Well I've got to go now. See you later,' Tina said..'Cheerio,' Lorna said. 'Hooray,' I said. **1983** HULME *Bone People* 103

HOOT

'Hooray,' says the postie, cheerfully. 'Hooray to you too.' **1990** VIRTUE *In the Country of Salvation* 5 Mrs Whiti came out to wave hooray.

2. Often in extended and dismissive form, **hooray fuck**, often said as an insult to someone who has offended the speaker (perh. suggested by *Goodbye and bugger you* (GOODBYE), the so-called sailor's farewell). See also *strike me bloody hooray* (STRIKE *v.*).

1951 May 17 Feilding Freezing Works terms p.c. Colin Gordon. When the whistle goes there are cries of 'Hooray fuck!'. **1988** MCGILL *Dict. Kiwi Slang* 58 *hooray fuck!* WW2 army exclamation, modified to *hooray f-f-forget it*, undoubtedly unmodified again at news of war's end.

hoot: in the sense 'money' see UTU 3 for discussion and quotations.

hooter. [Prob. a play on the noise of farting or flushing.] The toilet.

1968 SLATTER *Pagan Game* 162 Went to the hooter to shake hands with an old friend—Shot through on the inner coming into the straight.

hop, *v.* Various phr. or uses of *hop v.* to jump; hence, to move quickly. **a.** As **hop across**, to make a quick or sudden journey or trip.

1865 *McLean Papers* (ATLTS) XXVIII. 226 Little Whitmore [said] that then he would hop across to Wairoa and settle that business. **1950** *Landfall 16* 30 He hopped across by the swing bridge.

b. As **hop in**, to make a vigorous entry or start.

1917 *Chron. NZEF* 5 Sept. 28 The boys [were] having a bit of a spin up, and he hopped into the ring and did a trot for seven hundred frames. **1917** *NZ at the Front* 105 Come on, me lucky lads, you pick 'em an' I'll pay 'em. Hop right in, diggers, and have a fly with the old man.

c. In the phr. **to hop one's frame** *imp.*, 'shake it up!', 'get a move on'; also, to make a sudden trip.

1918 *Battle Cl Camp Tauherenikau* Shake it up, Bill: hop your frame my lad! **1918** BOLITHO *Book of the Cl Camp* 35 Not so much lead-swinging, come on, hop your frames. **1947** DAVIN *For Rest of Our Lives* 209 Got fed up..so hopped my frame to Cairo for a spell.

d. In the phr. **to hop the bags**, see BAG 2.

hop, *n.* [Transf. use of *hop(s)* an ingredient in beer, for beer or liquor: used elsewhere but chiefly in NZ and Australia.]

1. *pl.* Usu. as **the hops**, intoxicating liquor, esp. beer.

1906 PICARD *Ups & Downs* 9 She [sc. a barmaid] simply made the hops flow... I was passing the snake juice on to the Merican. **1946** SARGESON *That Summer* 34 He was keeping strictly off the hops. **1960** SCRYMGEOUR *Memories Maoriland* 112 The 'Bosun'.. was a real trick, partial to 'hops', always clean and spruce. **1979** WILLIAMS *Skin Deep* 146 They're a bit on the emotional side, this being a side effect of the hops, and..they could go either way.

2. Special Comb. **hop beer**, a mild (often 'ginger') beer made from hops and other ingredients; **hophead**, a regular drinker, a person fond or overfond of alcoholic liquor; **hop-spree** *Nelson obs.*, an occasion marking the end of the hop-picking season.

1873 WILSON *Diary* 30 Jan. in Wierzbicka *Wilson Family* (1973) 158 We are very much interested by the [diggers'] process..our visit being enhanced by a good swig of **hop beer** as they call it made of hops, sugar, ginger and water. **1901** in Lawlor *More Wellington Days* (1962) 21 May 12..Mama made some hop beer. **1962** LAWLOR *More Wellington Days* 21 This was not the home brew we know today. It was mild inoffensive stuff... The making of the hop beer interested me, particularly the calico bag crammed with hops and later the yeast welling lazily over the tops of the bottles or from the hole in the small wooden keg. **1942** *NZEF Times* 17 Aug. 16 Private Harry **Hophead**. **1948** BALLANTYNE *Cunninghams* (1976) 166 It's Betty that can't hold the liquor... She's a real lily of a hophead. **1952** *Landfall 23* 208 Among young people greetings like 'Hophead', 'Ram', 'Burglar', 'Sheik', 'Stopout', are accepted as flattery: 'burglar' I heard only in the army. **1966** TURNER *Eng. Lang. Austral. & NZ* 132 The term *hophead* is (or was) used in convivial greetings, 'Hello, hophead,' the implication that the person addressed was a persistent drinker being equivalent to calling him a decent joker. **1974** MORRIESON *Predicament* (1981) 73 He was a dead-beat old hophead. **1980** MACKENZIE *While We Have Prisons* 97 *hop-head* an alcoholic. **1989** RICHARDS *Pioneer's Life* 44 He was a very efficient and quiet man but a 'hop-head' whenever he had the opportunity. **1982** SUTTON-SMITH *Hist. Children's Play* 168 In the first decades of this century, when I was a boy in Waimea, not a school tea party (an all-district event) went by without playing Bingo and/or Drop the Handkerchief. These were also the usual games at '**hop-sprees**' and end-of-picking payouts where there was ginger-pop or better. [Waimea West: 1910]

hoppy. [f. *hop*(scotch + -Y.] A children's familiar name for hopscotch.

c1930–35 p.c. R.B. McLuskie. *Hoppy* for hopscotch used by West Coast children. **1982** FRAME *To the Island* (1984) 83 Marbles came and went, and hopscotch was in, and I spent my time searching for smooth, round 'hoppy' stones... Dots and Chicks and I played hoppy out on the footpath.

Horgan's weed. [f. *Horgan* the name of a Marlborough farming family.] CURNOW'S CURSE.

1926 HILGENDORF *Weeds* 236 Horgan's weed (*Calandrinia caulescens*), common near Blenheim. Purple flower, also called Portulaca and Curnow's Curse. **1967** HILGENDORF & CALDER *Weeds* 78 Curnow's Curse (*Calandrinia ciliata* var. *caulescens*) is also called portulaca, horgan's weed, and purple calandrinia. It has spreading fleshly stems and somewhat fleshy leaves. **1969** *Standard Common Names Weeds* 38 *Horgan's weed* [=] calandrinia.

Hori /ˈhori/, occas. /ˈhɒri/. *Offensive in non-Maori use.* Also **horri**, **horry**; *pl.* often *hories*, *horries*. [f. Ma. *Hōri* (/hoːri/), an alteration of George: AND a nickname for a Maori, 1922.] See also GEORGE. Cf. HENARE, JACK *n.*[1]

1. Without an article. **a.** Apparently favoured as a name for Maori males from the early 19th century (prob. from the 'royal' Georges on coins and in freq. official reference), developing in the 20th century in non-Maori use as a collective name for non-individualized Maori people.

1921 *Quick March* 11 July 26 In the matter of deep water diving Hori has little in common with his relations in the South Sea Islands. **1952** *Here & Now* Sept. 29 Civility costs nothing, but you mustn't let Hori think you're soft, or he'll try to put one over you.

b. In non-Maori use, a general term of address or reference to a Maori not known to the speaker.

1933 BAUME *Half–caste* 26 The driver of the mail car felt a warmth towards mankind. 'Hori,' he said to Paul (as a negro is 'Sambo', a Maori is 'Hori' to the poor white). 'You like a drink, eh?' **1936** LAMBERT

HORI

Pioneering Reminisc. Old Wairoa 112 The 'Digger': 'One pair, Hori?' 'No, by korry, just the one trouser I want.' **1943** JACKSON *Passage to Tobruk* 23 'You fight Nazis, too, eh Hori?' 'Py corrie, yes.' **1959** SLATTER *Gun in My Hand* 99 Detective: I'd like to speak to you outside, Hori. **1964** FRANCES *Johnny Rapana* 84 Some of them called him Johnny, others called him Hori. They called him Hori because they did not know what else to call him : impersonally, without malice, in the same way they called each Chinaman John. **1982** HOLDEN *Wild Pig* 89 Clarry bristled, 'Don't lay odds on that one, Hori!' 'Aw, you're full of Pakeha bullshit,' said a heavily built Maori.

2. a. Often *pl.* as **the horis**, also with init. cap. (A) stereotypical Maori.

1938 FINLAYSON *Brown Man's Burden* (1973) 24 The overheard remark still rankled: 'The horis, they can live on pipis.' **1947** DAVIN *For Rest of Our Lives* 252 But I dare say, there'll be some left over for us and the Horis [sc. the Maori Battalion]. **1952** *Landfall 23* 220 The New Zealand soldier had his 'Wogs' and 'Ities' and 'Teds', at home there are the 'Chinks' and 'Ikes' and 'Dallies' and even the 'Horis'. **1960** MUIR *Word for Word* 42 You've got to drag the Horrys into a New Zealand book these days. People expect it. **1972** *Truth* 26 Sept. 6 What has happened to that open-handed, good natured, tolerant fellow so well-known here and overseas as the happy hori. **1982** SANDYS *Love & War* 23 'Wiri! You lazy horrie! It's gone 3. Get your ass into gear.' **1982** O'SULLIVAN *Rose Ballroom* 28 Skull worked with the Hories who were O.K. so long as their tight-arse worries over land rights and such didn't throw them in flurries. **1986** *Metro* (Auckland) Sept. 34 Is this genuine or is he just giving me the dumb 'I'm just an ignorant hori' act? **1990** WILKINS *Veteran Perils* 38 And the biggest plus for our Horis was that the most popular teacher was this Hori., who actually made you forget this about him.

b. Used by a Maori, of a Maori.

1960 HILLIARD *Maori Girl* 219 'He's off a farm, your husband?' 'Him and me both. All horis come off the farm, I think.' **1964** FRANCES *Johnny Rapana* 41 'What's being a Maori got to do with it?' Taku demanded loudly. 'We're all horis. Whether we're up there or down here, we're still horis. What difference does that make?' **1983** HULME *Bone People* 241 He laughs bitterly. 'I'm a typical hori after all, made to work on the chain, or be a factory hand, not try for high places.' **1988** *Dominion* (Wellington) 1 July 10 Brown and white there were no differences between the colours then [in WW2]. The happy members of the 28th Battalion referred to themselves as 'horis'.

c. As **the hori**, 'the Maori', Maori characteristics or features.

1985 ROSIER-JONES *Cast Two Shadows* 44 'Same father, different mother,' Tui tells Emma. 'That must be the hori coming out in me,' Tui laughs up at Uncle Whetu. *Ibid.* 88 Tui presses noses with the old lady, then Maude... 'Whenever I'm out here in the wop-wops with youse jokers, the hori comes out in me. Kapai and hongi.'

3. Used of a non-Maori. **a.** Of other Polynesians.

1964 BOOTH *Footsteps in Sea* 124 What a terrible time they are having with those island horis up north.

b. In joc. *transf.* use, a white person.

1964 HELMER *Stag Party* 80 'This little hori's damned hungry,' Crump said, lifting the tea billy from the dingle stick. 'I could scoff a real binder, just quietly.'

4. In *attrib*. use. Also as a special collocation **hori story**, an anecdote or story involving Maori stereotypes.

1974 BELL *Ballads of Racegoer* 9 Along the Desert Road that Hori horse he never stop; Only once, to get some *kai*. **1970** SARGESON in *Landfall 93 or 94* p. You know the resistance to, and contempt that has been poured on, the Hori stories. But Hori stories are still going on all of the time. It's only that what is the basis of the Hori story is badly used or is a fatigued artistic form. **1974** HILLIARD *Maori Woman* 246 He's been telling hori-stories for as long as I can remember. Heh Hori, you been out of the district a year and now your wife's expecting them again, how's that Hori? **1986** *Listener* 6 Dec. 21 I'm getting that sick of being ripped off by blimmin' hori boys. **1993** O'SULLIVAN *Let the River Stand* 253 And Pai Weston lying out there now with his hori outfit at Matangi.

horn. *Obs.* In the phr. **to go round the horn**, a drinking game.
1866 *Narr. Maungatapu Murders* 51 'We were doing what is generally called "going round the horn" for drinks'. *Judge* 'That is a game of chance, of course; by which it was decided who should pay for refreshments.'

horny. [f. its spines.] THORNFISH.
1938 *TrRSNZ* LXVIII. 414 *Bovichthys variegatus*... Thornfish (horny). **1956** GRAHAM *Treasury NZ Fishes* 299 Thornfish or Horny... This beautifully marked and coloured fish is sometimes called Horny by boys. Both the common names are derived from the sharp spines which puncture the flesh of one's hands when taking the Thornfish from a net. **1982** AYLING *Collins Guide* (1984) 274 *Thornfish* (Horny, dragonet)... The thornfish is a small, cylindrical fish with scaleless body... There is a distinctive strong spine directed upward and backward on each gill cover behind the eyes... Thornfish are common in tidepools..from the Wellington area southwards. **1986** PAUL *NZ Fishes* 117 *Thornfish Bovichthys variegatus* Family Bovichthyidae (thornfishes). Sometimes called horny, or dragonet (which is the name of a similar but unrelated fish).

horoeka. Also early **hayroiicar.** [Ma. /'ho'roeka/: Williams 61 *Horoeka = hohoeka*, n. *Pseudopanax* [sp.].] LANCEWOOD (*Pseudopanax crassifolius*). Cf. HOHOEKA.
1831 BENNETT in *London Med. Gaz.* 5 Nov. 150 The Horoeka Tree of New Zealand. This tree..has not yet been observed by botanists in flower or fructification. **1834** MARKHAM *NZ* (1963) 35 There is a yellow wood called Hayroiicar I have a walking stick of this wood, Twists like a Creeper. **1853** HOOKER *II Flora Novae-Zelandiae I Flowering Plants* 96 *Aralia crassifolia*... Nat. names, 'Horoeka', *Cunn.*; 'Hohoeka', Middle Island. **1869** *TrNZI* I. (rev. edn.) 195 Horoeka... A singular-looking plant in all stages of its growth. **1884** *Ibid.* XVII. 216 Amongst smaller trees and shrubs the most prominent are the horoeka. **1890** *PWD Catalogue Timbers* (NZ & South Seas Exhib.) 9 Horoeka (grass tree)... Timber dense and compact, and has been used for piles and fencing posts; suitable for ornamental work. **1915** [see LANCEWOOD]. **1926** CROOKES *Plant Life in Maoriland* 14 We could hunt through the bush all day for a young tree similar in growth and appearance to the full-grown horoeka, but never a one would we find. **c1937** HYDE *Selected Poems* (1984) 37 They cut the yellow twisted horoeka For sticks. **1946** *JPS* LV. 151 *horoeka*, a small tree..lancewood. In young trees long, thick, stiff leaves turned down like ribs of an umbrella. **1966, 1982** [see LANCEWOOD].

horokaka. [Ma. /'horokaka/: Williams 61 *Horokaka* (i) n. *Disphyma australe*, ice-plant.] ICE-PLANT (*Disphyma australe*).
1906 CHEESEMAN *Manual NZ Flora* 191 *M[esembryanthemum] australe...Horokaka*. **1910** [see ICE-PLANT]. **1940** LAING & BLACKWELL *Plants NZ* 167 *Mesembryanthemum australe* (*The Southern Mesembryanthemum*)... *Horokaka*. **1952** [see ICE-PLANT]. **1978** MOORE & IRWIN *Oxford Book NZ Plants* 44 Horokaka, like many 'ice plants', has plump three-angled leaves. **1981** [see ICE-PLANT].

horomai, var. HARAMAI.

horopito. Also **horapito**.
1. [Ma. /'horopito/: Williams 61 *Horopito*, n. *1. Pseudowintera axillaris*.] Either of two shrubs or small trees of the genus *Pseudowintera* (formerly *Drimys*) (fam. Winteraceae), *P. axillaris* or *P. colorata*, having pungent-tasting leaves. See also NUTMEG-TREE, *bush-painkiller* (PAINKILLER 2), PEPPER-TREE 2, PEPPERWOOD 1.
1847 ANGAS *Savage Life* II. 23 The air in the neighbouring woods was rendered quite fragrant with the *horopito*. **1853** HOOKER *II Flora Novae-Zelandiae I Flowering Plants* 12 *Drimys axillaris*..Nat. name 'Horopito'. **1889** KIRK *Forest Flora* 1 The horopito, or pepper-tree of the settlers, is an ornamental shrub or small tree occurring in woods. **1890** *PWD Gen. Catalogue* (NZ & South Seas Exhib.) 16 Lithograph of horopito (pepper tree) foliage. **1907** LAING & BLACKWELL *Plants NZ* 172 *Drimys axillaris*... Called by the settlers the Pepper Tree. Maori name *Horopito*. **1915** Horapito [see PEPPER-TREE 2]. **1923** [see PEPPERWOOD]. **1949** *Tararua Tramper* Aug. 6 Also noted were horopito, water fern and stinko. **1951** in Pearson *Six Stories* (1991) 63 Round his head was a mad red garland of horopito and quintinia leaves. **1961** ALLAN *Flora NZ* I. 135 Lowland to higher montane forest..often forming thickets after destruction of forest. *Horopito*. **1988** DAWSON *Forest Vines to Snow Tussocks* 103 Horopito (*Pseudowintera axillaris*) with its dark green shiny leaves has also been termed 'pepper tree' for the same reason [of hot tasting leaves].

2. As **red horopito**, the shrub *Pseudowintera colorata*.
1909 *AJHR* C-11 6 Another very plentiful plant in the bush is the red horopito..the bright-red leaves of which serve as compensation for the general absence of coloured flowers. **1978** MOORE & IRWIN *Oxford Book NZ Plants* 34 *Pseudowintera colorata*, red horopito. On bush edges from about Rotorua southwards, this shrub is easily recognized by its strongly blotched red leaves. **1982** HARRIS *Field Guide Common NZ Trees & Shrubs* 5 Red Horopito Small tree up to 3m. Branchlets and leaf stalks reddish. Leaves..blotched with red.

horror house. *Children*. [Transf. use of *horror house* a place of synthetic 'horrors' at a fun-fair.] MURDER HOUSE.
1953 SUTTON-SMITH *Unorganized Games NZ Primary School Children* (VUWTS) I. 382 There is a tendency to refer to the game-dentist (and to the real school dentist) in an exaggerated manner. 'Here's for the butcher shop', or 'I'm off to the horror house', (Waddington [19]49) or 'Here's my grave number.' (Forbury), These games are reported mainly by children of mid-primary years.

horrors, *n. pl. Obs.* As **the horrors**, the DT's, delirium tremens; but widened often to a bad attack of 'the shakes'. See also DINGBAT 1 b; *dry horrors* (DRY *a.* 3) a more freq. modern use.
1851 SHORTLAND *S. Dist. NZ* 111 [The whalers] frequently became a prey to delirium tremens, or 'the horrors', as they aptly call that disease. **1880** *TrNZI* XII. 434 No old Maori ever had delirium tremens; no old Rangatira ever had the 'horrors'—not even 'hot coppers'. **1890** PHILIPS *Reminisc. Early Days.* 6. One day, our [ship's] doctor, who always took a tumbler of rum..got the horrors. **1895** CHAMIER *South Sea Siren* 85 That awful condition called the horrors. **1900** SCOTT *Colonial Turf* 50 We heard he was in the horrors.

horse, *n.*[1]

1. The four legs of a game of FORTY-FIVES (q.v. for quotation).

2. In the phr. **to get off one's horse** [var. of *get off one's bike*], to become angry; do one's block.
1943 JACKSON *Passage to Tobruk* 68 We duly told [the drunken, irritable soldier] not to get off his horse.

3. In the phr. **to sell a horse**, a gambling game, see SELL *v.* 2.

4. In the phr. **horses in the stable**, a play in the game of knuckle-bones.
1982 MARSHALL *Master Big Jingles* 55 Creamy was even better with the aluminium ones [*sc.* knuckle bones]. Cutting cabbages, camels, swatting flies, clicks, little jingles, through the arch, goliath, horses in the stable; Creamy mastered them all.

5. Special Comb. **horse-bite**, a sudden harsh squeezing of the leg just above the knee; **horse-collar swag** [AND 1888], see *horse-shoe swag* below; **horse-dray**, a shafted dray drawn by a horse; **horse-paddock** [AND 1839], a paddock close to a homestead, hotel, school, etc. where horses may be enclosed until needed; **horse-rake** *obs.*, a hay-rake drawn by a horse; **horse-shoe**, any one of the growths resembling horse-shoes in shape found on a *horseshoe fern* (FERN 2 (8)); **horse-shoe swag** [AND 1880], a swag rolled in the shape of a horse-shoe (cf. *horse-collar swag* above); **horse's mane weed**, either of two aquatic plants of the genus *Ruppia* (fam. Ruppiaceae), *R. megacarpa* of brackish coastal waters, or *R. polycarpa* of fresh and brackish waters, both resembling a horse's mane in appearance.
1949 SARGESON *I Saw in My Dream* (1974) 109 Aw Len darling, Jack said with a grin, take it easy. And he brought his hand down smartly on Len's leg, giving him a **horse-bite** that made him jump and spill his tea. **1953** SUTTON-SMITH *Unorganized Games NZ Primary School Children* (VUWTS) II. 685 [Of schoolboy 'tortures'.] 'Chinese burns, full nelsons and hamalocks [*sic*]' (Karori),.. 'Squeezing knuckles, horse bight [*sic*], ... punch in the chocolate which is called the paralyse' (the chocolate is the thigh) (Stockton). **1873** PYKE *Wild Will Enderby* (1889, 1974) I. i 6 [He] then proceeded forthwith to arrange his blankets, in the form known to the initiated as '**horse-collar swag**'. [**1881** BATHGATE *Waitaruna* 170 Gilbert saw him..with his blankets rolled up into the form of a most gigantic horse-collar, after the most approved fashion among swaggers.] **1864?** TEMPSKY *Memoranda* (ATLTS) 83 Along the banks of the Waikato we met now the endless trains of bullock carts, pack-horses and **horse drays** going to the front for transport service during the grand move of the General. **1874** KENNAWAY *Crusts* 219 Three hours later we brought down a horse-dray, and took him and all his remaining goods and chattels to our house. **1857** PAUL *Lett. from Canterbury* 90 [Make] a **horse-paddock**, ram-paddock,.. oats or wheat-paddock, and a good, permanent washing-place. **1878** KIERNAN *Diary* 4 Jan. in Guthrie-Smith *Tutira* (1926) 122 Kite and C.H.S. sledged posts from Tylee's spur and cut some Kohi posts for the horse paddock. **1925** MANDER *Allen Adair* (1971) 52 He and Jim had fenced in a yard enclosing the stable, and were now fencing a larger area for a horse paddock. **1939** GRIEVE *Sketches from Maoriland* (1961) 60 His well-feigned astonishment that the familiar rails of the horse-paddock were not in that particular corner, placed him in the front rank of equine actors. **1948** FINLAYSON *Tidal Creek* (1979) 100 They put the gig in the shade of the trees in the hotel paddock and let the pony go in the horse paddock adjoining. **1966** TURNER *Eng. Lang. Austral. & NZ* 144

Before the school bus was common, country schools normally provided a *horse-paddock* for children who rode to school. **1973** FERNANDEZ *Tussock Fever* 1 Barbara..dawdled across the horse paddock by the homestead heading for the dusty, noisy, drafting yards. **1987** CHRISTIE *Candles & Canvas* 79 It [Tarawera Hotel] nestled on a flat piece of ground..devoid of any growth except for a thin line of exotic pines between the hotel and the horse paddock. **1991** *Dominion Sunday Times* (Wellington) 20 Oct. 25 I took the boulder through the yards..through the horse paddock into the bridle track. **1913** CARR *Country Work* 11 Haymaking... The jobs to look for are 'cocking up' (with a two or three pronged fork), driving the **horse rake** (no handrakes are used nowadays)..loading the drays or sledges when ready. **1981** BROOKER et al. *NZ Medicinal Plants* 29 *Marattia salicina*... Common names: *King fern, horseshoe fern* Maori name: *Para*... The '**horseshoes**' cut from the rhizome were baked or boiled and were a good remedy for diarrhoea. **1892** MCHUTCHESON *Camp Life Fiordland* 46 He laid it down dogmatically that for comfort and convenience nothing equalled the '**horse-shoe**' **swag**... The horse-shoe won't do in the bush. **1969** *Standard Common Names Weeds* 39 **horse's mane weed** *Ruppia megacarpa* Mason *Ruppia polycarpa* Mason. **1978** MOORE & IRWIN *Oxford Book NZ Plants* 202 *Ruppia megacarpa, horse's mane weed*. In Lake Ellesmere hundreds of hectares of shallow, slightly brackish water are suited to this species... The dark fibrous stems..are compared to horsehair but the stems are coarser and up to a metre long.

horse, *n.*[2] See quot.
1979 *SANZ Gloss. Bldg. Terminol.* 64 *Horse*. Slipper or board carrying the template of the various members of a moulding for running plaster cornices and mouldings.

horse, *a.* In the names of plants and animals often indicating greater size or coarseness, see: MACKEREL 2 (2), MUSSEL 2 (6).

horsie. A familiar name for *horse mackerel* (MACKEREL 2 (2)).
1991 BRADSTOCK *Fishing* 18 *Jack mackerel*. Other names: yellowtail, horse mackerel, horsie, hauture, *Trachurus novaezelandiae*.

horseshoe fern: see FERN 2 (8); see also PARA, *n.*[3]

hose, *v.*

1. *trans*. To fill (a vessel) with beer from a nozzle attached to a plastic hose-pipe.
1968 SLATTER *Pagan Game* 155 He got up to go to the bar for a refill. While his jug was being hosed he looked about the crowded clubroom and waved at the men he knew.

2. As a phrasal verb in various transferred uses: **hose down**, to rain heavily; **hose in**, to win easily or by a wide margin; **hose off** (prob. a. var. of *piss off*), to thoroughly displease (as **hosed off** *ppl. a.*, disgruntled); **hose out**, to overcome completely (in a contest, game, etc.).
1979 WILLIAMS *Skin Deep* 63 It's been absolutely **hosing down** all morning and out on the expansive blank field not even a dicky bird ventures. **1995** CRUMP *Bushwoman* 18 By nightfall it was hosing down... No fire tonight, no billy-tea. **1988** MCGILL *Dict. Kiwi Slang* 58 *hose in* win easily; eg 'Free 'n' Easy **hosed in**, fulfilling the faith of all those punters who had made her odds on favourite for the cup.' **1959** SLATTER *Gun in My Hand* 98 People in those damned cloth caps waving rattles and saying innit smashing Charlie. Couldn't go it at all. **Hosed me off** completely.

1987 *Sunday News* (Auckland) 22 Feb. 7 Hosed off firemen are fuming over reports that Members of Parliament could soon be picking up a massive 20 per cent pay hike. **1988** MCGILL *Dict. Kiwi Slang* 58 *hosed off* fed up; perhaps from being hosed with water... Current usage would be: 'Was I hosed off when the first decent shower of rain brought down the wooden retaining wall I'd spent a whole day building.' **1975** HOWITT *NZ Rugby Greats* 134 He **hosed me out** completely. It was my first and last game as lock at that level!

hospital pass. *Rugby Football*. **a.** A rugby pass to a player about to be (heavily) tackled, and thus liable to be injured. Occas. called a 'Hail Mary' pass, from a prayer needed to make it successful.
1981 *Avondale College Slang Words* (Auckland) (Goldie Brown Collect.) Feb. *hospital pass*: a slow pass at rugby which causes injury (rugby union) **1988** MCGILL *Dict. Kiwi Slang* 59 *hospital pass* rugby passing of ball to player about to be heavily tackled; eg 'When Gary threw Barry a hospital pass with two dirty big Wallaby flankers converging on him, you could hear the collective gasp of 42,000 spectators over the anguished voice of TV commentator Keith Quinn.'

b. Transferred to situations, appointments, events over which a participant has no control.
1988 *Dominion* (Wellington) 3 Oct. 21 Mr Hulme described his seven-week stint as general manager as a 'corporate hospital pass' and wants to quell speculation that he should carry the can for Imageering's problems [leading to large losses]. **1991** *Sunday Star* (Auckland) 22 Sept. A7 Paul East called it a 'hospital pass'—and sure enough, the Beehive wounded these days could fill a casualty ward.

hostie: see *air hostie* (AIR).

hostile, *a.* and *n*. *Hist*. [Spec. use of *hostile* unfriendly.]

A. *adj.*

1. *Hist*. Of Maori, or tribes, hostile to the Crown during the New Zealand Wars.
1842 *Dawson to Colonial Secretary* 11 Jan. in *GBPP 1842 (No.569)* 194 [E.J. Wakefield] who has lately resided..amongst the Taupos and other hostile tribes, informed me..that it was his intention to proceed to Auckland. **1860** GRACE *Letter* 28 May in *Pioneer Missionary* (1928) 91 On my journey to and from Auckland, when I came in contact with both friendly and hostile Maoris, I found one opinion only, namely, that the war had begun hastily. **1879** FEATON *Waikato War* 44 The so-called friendly natives in the stockade, as soon as the hostile natives opened fire, ran away into the bush. **1940** COWAN *Sir Donald Maclean* 93 Maclean was kept well informed as to the movements of the hostile natives.

2. In the phr. **to go hostile (at)** [AND 1941], to become angry (with), to go off (at), to express annoyance (at).
1935 STRONG in Partridge *Slang Today* 287 When I done all my sugar and never even had the makings, he went very hostile because I never told him I was swept. **1941** HAYDON *NZ Soldiers in England* 17 Wouldn't he go hostile if he knew who pinched his bacon. **1962** CRUMP *One of Us* 51 I'll see if I can get the dog for you and if your missus goes hostile about it I'll take it myself. **1978** HENDERSON *Soldier Country* 17 That afternoon the troops again went hostile, the grub was worse, just plain stinking. **1988** MCGILL *Dict. Kiwi Slang* 51 *go hostile* act angrily; eg 'If he says one more word to her, I'll really go hostile.'

B. *n*. *Hist*. A hostile Maori. See also *Jack Maori* (JACK *n.*[1]), KINGITE, REBEL.

1921 *TrNZI* LIII. 24 Young McKillop..mounted a gun on the long-boat of the 'Tyne'..and strolled up and down the harbour bombarding hapless hostiles. **1922** COWAN *NZ Wars* (1955) I. 225 Day after day Atkinson led out his war-party of practised bushmen-settlers..and soon had the country free from hostiles for a radius of many a mile from New Plymouth.

hot, *a.*

1. In special collocations of *hot* 'heated' (also *fig.*): **hot box** *shearing obs.* [f. *hotbox* (railways) an overheated axle-box], a nickname for an early shearing-machine handpiece; **hot dog** [transf. use of US *hot dog* a hot sausage wrapped in a bread roll], a sausage (or saveloy) pre-cooked, battered and served on a stick; **hot fence, hot line** *farming*, an electric or electrified fence(-line); **hot pea** *racing obs.*, a heavily-backed favourite; **hot rice**, a children's game; **hotwater-bottle** *railways*, see quot.; **hotwater-cupboard**, an airing cupboard usu. containing the hotwater cylinder.
1960 MILLS *Sheep-O* 19 The handpieces of these earlier machines, resembling somewhat those of modern barbers, caused much dissatisfaction. Through overheating and blistering the shearer's hand they were labelled '**Hot Boxes**', 'Smokers' and similar uncomplimentary terms. **1979** *Heinemann NZ Dict.* 525 **hot dog** 1. a sausage fried in batter on a stick. **1982** *Evening Post* (Wellington) 8 Mar. 11 [Advt] Hot dogs Pre-cooked Battered and on Sticks. **1995** *Dominion* (Wellington) 17 Mar. 9 New Zealand rail boss..and Ed Burkhardt chairman of the board..sometimes prefer..battered fish and hot dogs on sticks. **1982** *Agric. Gloss.* (MAF) 28 **Hot fence**: An electric fence or a traditional fence that has been electrified. **1985** *Farming Session* (King Country) 22 Nov. [Farmer says] I've got them [cows] behind a **hot line**. **1908** *Truth* 8 Apr. 2 The ruse was successful, and the horse just beat the '**hot pea**' in the race. **1982** SUTTON-SMITH *Hist. Children's Play* 264 Other games are Humpty Dumpty (known as Dunk and Davey in the 1920s), Kick the Tin, and **Hot Rice**. **1972** LEITCH *Railways of NZ* 200 Train-heating vans have been used in the North Island to provide steam heating in conjunction with diesel haulage. Known to rail-fans as 'the **hotwater bottles**', the six vans are fitted with an oil-fired Stone Vapor steam generator. **1981** HOOPER *Goat Paddock* 19 He reached into the **hot-water cupboard** and yanked out his rifle.

2. In special collocations of *hot* '(geo)thermal' (cf. THERMAL *a.*): **hot lake** (usu. *pl.*), any of the warm thermal lakes of esp. the central North Island; also as **the hot-lake(s) district** (contrast COLD LAKE); **hot pool**, a thermal spring.
1872 *TrNZI* IV. 6 My visit to the **Hot lakes** was made in company with the Duke of Edinburgh. **1880** SENIOR *Travel & Trout* 207 We must..prepare for our journey to the hot lakes. **1883** *Auckland Weekly News* 27 Oct. 15 The want of some place of worship has been a standing subject of complaint with invalids and visitors in the Hot Lake District. **1898** HUDSON *NZ Moths & Butterflies* 100 During the summer of 1879 I came across *S. convolvuli*..near Ohinemutu, in the Hot Lake District. **1902** *Settler's Handbook NZ* 38 [Rotorua] is the chief township in the hot-lakes district. **1924, 1934** [see COLD LAKE]. **1908** *AJHR* C-11 31 The **hot pools** themselves contain abundance of a blue-green alga. **1940** *Evening Post* (Wellington) 7 Aug. 7 While playing outside St. Faith's Church, Ohinemutu,.. a Maori child..fell into one of the small hot pools guarded by a railing. **1952** *Evening Star* (Dunedin) 26 Feb. 4 A Maori child..was fatally scalded as the result of a fall into a hot pool at Whakarewarewa last night. **1968** DENNAN *Guide Rangi* 82 Tragedies in the hot pools go far back into history. **1989** RICHARDS *Pioneer's Life* 80

They too followed in the footsteps of their parents by frolicking in the hot pools. **1990** *Motoring Today* July 36 Today..there are hot pools and mineral baths throughout the North Island and in..Hanmer Springs in the South Island.

hotel.

1. Used elsewhere (cf. OED *hotel* 3) but of significance in New Zealand in extended but standard use as the usual term until the 1970s for a public house or licensed premises offering accommodation as well as bar-trade in liquor. Cf. ACCOMMODATION-HOUSE 2, PRIVATE HOTEL (unlicensed); and now in standard use *tavern* (offering bar-trade, often meals, but no accommodation).

[*Note*] *Inn* is rarely used in general reference, but is now found in the names (occas. tonally 'twee') of particular premises.

1844 WILLIAMS *NZ Jrnl.* (1956) 69 I might say with propriety that six eighths of all the European houses are nothing more than grogeries... One in particular so-called Hotel, a man and his family the only occupants, over the door a large sign one third as large as the front, with bold letters 'Victoria Hotel'. **1850** *Emigrants' Lett. from British Colonies* 83 Men, when in [Nelson] town, after having transacted their business, have nothing to do but lounge about the 'hotel', as it is called. **1869** *Auckland Punch* 138 Landlords, as a rule, object to 'public house', and prefer the more pretentious title 'hotel'. **1874** PYKE *George Washington Pratt* 89 For already there was an hotel (there are no inns in the colonies). **1879** CLAYDEN *England of Pacific* 50 Hotels are quite a feature of colonial life. They are mostly well-fitted up, and altogether unlike the average English public-house. They are in fact public boarding-houses. **1887** HOPEFUL *Taken In* 71 The town [Lyttelton] was hilly.., and for so small a place there seemed no end of 'Pubs', or *Hotels* as they are called here. **1899** BELL *In Shadow of Bush* 21 The hotels..were large, pretentious buildings of their class, with verandah and balcony to each, and were well-conducted inns, the accommodation afforded to travellers being all that could be expected— equal, indeed, to that of some of the best hotels in the larger centres. **1948** FINLAYSON *Tidal Creek* (1979) 100 They put the gig in the shade of the trees in the hotel paddock and let the pony go in the horse paddock adjoining.

Hence **hotelkeeper**, a publican.

1867 COOPER *Digger's Diary* 2 Nov. (1978) 7 There is very little respect paid here to..the Sabbath, at least among the store-keepers and hotel-keepers. The stores are almost all open; hotels have their doors closed but not fastened. **1888** D'AVIGDOR *Antipodean Notes* 76 I..[relate] what a New Zealand hill hotel-keeper and butcher told me. **1899** *NZ Times* (Wellington) 30 Dec. 2 Hotel-keepers report crowded houses still.

2. Comb. **Hotel de Garvey** or **Garvie** *obs.* [f. the name of the Superintendent, *Garvey*], the Wellington Gaol.

1906 *Truth* 13 Jan. 5 'Hotel de Garvey' [the Wellington Gaol]. **1959** LAWLOR *Old Wellington Days* 137 Dwan [editor, Weekly Herald] was originator of the term 'Hotel de garvie' (The Terrace gaol).

hotete. *Obs. in English use.* Also **hotte**. [Ma. /'ho:tete/: Williams 62 *Hōtete* n.] Either of two genera of caterpillars. **a.** *Wiseana* spp., the VEGETABLE CATERPILLAR. See also AWHATO 1.

1843 DIEFFENBACH *Travels in NZ* I. 422 To the fungi, also belongs a very curious plant, parasitical on a caterpillar, viz. the Sphaeria Robertii, called hotete by the natives. **1847** ANGAS *Savage Life* I. 292 Amongst the damp moss at the root of the *rata* trees, in the shady forests not far from Auckland, and also in various parts of the Northern Island, are found those extraordinary productions called vegetable caterpillars—the *hotete* of the natives. **1867** [see AWHATO 1]. **1878** BULLER *Forty Yrs. NZ* 499 The vegetating caterpillar (*Hotete*) is a singular production. **1882** HAY *Brighter Britain* II. 229 The Hotete is the so-called 'vegetating caterpillar'.

b. *Agrius* spp. AWHATO 2.

1856, **1904**, **1931** [see AWHATO 2]. **1935** DIXON *Nature Study Notes* 22 The caterpillar can be distinguished from other large caterpillars by the curved horn on the top of the last segment of its body. The Maoris consider it as one of their worst enemies and call it 'ho-te-te'.

hotte, var. HOTETE.

hottie. [f. *hot*(shot + -IE: AND *Obs.* 1910.] A skilful and successful person; a 'hotshot'.

1910 *Truth* 15 Jan. 5 The Chow is a hottie on gold, and is fairly numerous on pan-worked claims, but quartz mining looks a little bit harder work than Chows usually take on.

houhere. Also early **oe ére**; **hohere, houhere, houheria, howhere.** [Ma. /'houhere/: Williams 63 *Houhere* (i), *houhi*, or *houī*, n *Hoheria populnea*, the lacebark: PPN **fau* =?hibiscus underlies Ma. *whau, hou.*] *Hoheria* spp., esp. *H. populnea*, and often *H. angustifolia* and *H. lyallii*, small, white-flowered, graceful trees with fibrous many-layered underbark; LACEBARK 1 a. See also HOHERIA, HOUI, WHAUWHI.

[**1820** LEE & KENDALL *NZ Gram. & Vocab.* 141 O'e, ére [*sc.* hoihere] Name of a certain shrub.] **1853** HOOKER *II Flora Novae-Zelandiae I Flowering Plants* 30 *Hoheria populnea...* Nat. name, 'Houheria'. **1867** HOOKER *Handbook* 765 Hohere... Houhere... *Hoheria populnea*. **1869** *TrNZI* I. (rev. edn.) 264 For net-ropes the tough stringy bark of the Houhere, and also of the Whauwhi or Houi (*Hoheria populnea*, and of its varieties,) was plaited together. **1882** HAY *Brighter Britain* II. 198 The Howhere..is a fine large tree of the linden kind. **1889** FEATON *Art Album NZ Flora* 54 'The Hohere'.—This very handsome tree is found in the mountainous districts of the Middle Island... Owing to the flowering habit of the tree, and its fruit being a depressed sphere, hanging on a long..stalk, it is commonly known by the settlers as the 'Wild Cherry'. **1890** *PWD Gen. Catalogue* (NZ & South Seas Exhib.) 19 Houhere (lacebark or ribbonwood) head piece. **1906** CHEESEMAN *Manual NZ Flora* 79 The Maoris apply the names *hoihere* or *houhere* to varieties [of *Hoheria populnea*] indifferently; the European settlers usually call all the forms 'ribbon-wood' or 'lacebark'. **1946** SOLJAK *NZ* 12 Few forest trees surpass in loveliness the white flowering houhere, from whose lacy bark the Maori made a kind of tapa cloth. **1968** *Landfall* 22 255 White edge of the sea White as the flower Of lacebark, Te houhere, White edge of the sea Eating the land. **1983** MATTHEWS *Trees NZ* 32 The lacebark, *Hoheria populnea*, known to the Maori as houhere, is a fast growing slim-trunked tree.

houheria, var. HOUHERE.

houi. Also **houhi, houia, howi.** [Ma. /'houhi/, /'houi/: Williams 63 *Houhi* = houhere... *Houi* = *houhi.*] HOUHERE, LACEBARK 1 a and b (*Hoheria* or *Plagianthus* spp.).

1867 HOOKER *Handbook* 765 Houi, Col[enso]. *Hoheria populnea*. **1886** KIRK in *Settler's Handbook NZ* (1902) 121 [Native name] Houi..[Settlers' name] Ribbonwood..[Family] Malvaceae. **1889** FEATON *Art Album NZ Flora* 55 The 'Houi' or 'Whau-whi'..grow abundantly in both Islands. **1889** KIRK *Forest Flora* 207 Plagianthus betulinus is an attractive tree..Mr. Traill informs me that it is termed 'houi' by the Stewart Island Natives, and by those on the Chatham islands. I believe that the name is applied in other parts of the colony. **1890** *PWD Catalogue Timbers* (NZ & South Seas Exhib.) 9 Houi (ribbonwood)..Plagianthus betulinus..Timber white and straight grained; suitable for manufacturing paper **1897** *Otago Witness* (Dunedin) 4 Nov. 53 I have been told some of the houia (lacebark) trees shed their leaves. **1898** MORRIS *Austral-English* 205 *Houi*, n. Maori name for New Zealand tree, *Ribbonwood..*, N.O. Malvaceae, kindred to *Hoheria*, *Plagianthus Betulinus*, sometimes called *Howi*. **1907** LAING & BLACKWELL *Plants NZ* 250 *Hoheria* is a modification of the native name. Maori names *Houi, Whauwhi, Houhere.* **c1920** BEATTIE *Trad. Lifeways Southern Maori* (1994) Houi is the common ribbonwood. **1949** BUCK *Coming of Maori* 156 Some change in the appearance of small fancy satchels was obtained by using thin layers of bark from the *houhi* or ribbon-wood.

houia, var. HOUI.

hound's tongue: see FERN 2 (9).

houpara. [Ma. /'houpara/: Williams 63 *Houpara*, *houparapara* = *parapara.. Pseudopanax lessonii.*] *Pseudopanax lessonii* (fam. Araliaceae), a shrub or small tree of northern New Zealand coastal associations. See also FIVE-FINGER.

1936 *NZJST* XVII. 725 The flax..and the houpara..form a dense..thicket [on Little Barrier]. **1961** MARTIN *Flora NZ* 159 Houpara (*Pseudopanax lessonii*) 3-5 leaflets. **1978** MOORE & IRWIN *Oxford Book NZ Plants* 100 *Pseudopanax lessonii*, houpara, from northern coasts has light green, compound leaves. **1995** CROWE *Which Coastal Plant?* 36 *Houpara Coastal Five Finger...* In the wild, houpara is often seen as an understorey shrub..and is valued in conservation planting as a colonising plant in damaged coastal areas.

house.

I. In the names of the New Zealand legislative assemblies. **1.** *Hist.* **Houses of Assembly**, a former name of the two legislative houses forming the New Zealand parliament.

1854 *Richmond-Atkinson Papers* (1960) I. 156 At the opening of the session of the General Assembly the Lower House with a single dissentient voice, voted it desirable..to introduce the English practice of government by filling the chief offices of government with persons possessing the confidence of the Houses of Assembly. **1882** POTTS *Out in Open* 32 Interesting documents which have at various periods been laid before the Houses of Assembly. **1995** CROWE *Which Coastal Plant?* 36 *Houpara Coastal Five Finger...* In the wild, houpara is often seen as an understorey shrub..and is valued in conservation planting as a colonising plant in damaged coastal areas.

2. House of Mummies, an obsolete jocular nickname for the former appointive Legislative Council. Cf. *freezing chamber* (FREEZING).

1890 *Evening Post* (Wellington) 9 Nov. 2 The Legislative Council, Mr. Buckland said..was generally known in Wellington as the 'House of Mummies', in fact it was 'A Museum of Fossils'.

3. *transf.* **house of parliament**, a privy, esp. one outdoors.

1944 *Short Guide NZ* 38 A 'john' means a cop, not a toilet, and the latter is sometimes called (between men only) a 'dyke' or 'house of parliament'. **1964** ANDERSON *Doctor in Mountains* (1974) 90 His entire shearing was held up because all his men had 'the backdoor trot'. He said, 'We have only two "houses of parliament" down here, and there has been a queue for both all night.'

4. House of Representatives, formerly the elected lower legislative chamber, now the sole legislative chamber, in the New Zealand Parliament.

1846 *Act to make further provision for Govt. NZ Islands* 28 Aug. (9 & 10 Vict. c. 103) in Rutherford *Sel. Documents* (1949) 20 It shall be lawful for Her Majesty..to constitute..a General Assembly in and for the Islands of *New Zealand*, to be called the General Assembly of *New Zealand*, which said General Assembly shall consist of and be holden by the Governor..., and a Legislative Council, and a House of Representatives. **1888** BARLOW *Kaipara* 177 Then we have a House of Representatives, consisting of a Speaker, Chairman of Committees, Clerk of Committees..and ninety members. The M.H.R.'s are elected for three years. **1959** SINCLAIR *Hist. NZ* 87 The 1852 constitution was extremely democratic, more so than those then in force in the Australian colonies. The six Provincial Councils, the House of Representatives, and the Superintendents of the Provinces were all elective, though the members of the Legislative Council (the Upper House) were nominated for life by the Governor. **1987** ROBERTS *Politicians, Public Servants & Public Enterprise* 12 The authority of the executive derives from the supremacy of Parliament, or, to employ the correct terminology for New Zealand, the General Assembly. That is the '... bipartite body consisting of the House of Representatives and the Governor-General', which exercises legislative function.

II. In senses of *house* residence. **5. Special Comb. house-block**, PILE *n.*²; **house cow**, a cow kept for milk for a household; **house paddock**, a paddock close to a house or homestead where a milch cow, family horse, or other animals may be kept; **house-trashing**, a party during which the interior of the house or flat is vandalized (see also DEMOLITION PARTY).

1875 KIRK *Durability NZ Timbers* 14 House blocks..rarely continue in good condition for more than ten years. **1906** CHEESEMAN *Manual NZ Flora* 161 Easily distinguished from [manuka] by its greater size,... wood durable; [kanuka is] much used for piles, house-blocks, posts and rails, &c. **1925** MANDER *Allen Adair* (1971) 61 He forgot any doubts..when the first load of timber arrived, nor had anything the power to damp his spirits the night the houseblocks were all in. **1966** TURNER *Eng. Lang. Austral. & NZ* 150 In winter, one or two *house cows* might be milked *by hand*. **1976** VANCE *Bush, Bullocks & Boulders* 240 When Betty and I first came here [*sc.* to Ashburton], everyone milked a house cow and most people kept a few chooks. **1983** HENDERSON *Down from Marble Mountain* 50 She emphatically..refused to learn to milk the two or three depraved housecows, well aware if she did so she was trapped for life. **1986** RICHARDS *Off the Sheep's Back* 66 We unharnessed the horses and turned them loose in the '*house paddock*'. *Ibid.* 148 I allowed my new flock to rest..in the house paddock before mustering then into the yards for earmarking. **1989** STIRLING *On Four Legs and Two* 40 She might get Milk Fever and that's why I kept her handy in the house paddock. **1987** *Sunday Star* (Auckland) 18 Oct. A6 Anger at high rents is mainly to blame for '**house-trashing**' in this country, says the Tenants Protection Association.

how, *adv*. In various phrases of greeting, mainly in male use. **a. How are you going?** (**How ya going?**, **How's it going?**, occas. **Howsit?**) [AND 1930].

1984 17 M E97 Pakuranga Coll. 11 How are your going love? **1984** 14 F E139Wgton Girls C. 11 How ya going [F2] **1984** 16 M E84 Pakuranga Coll. 11 How's it going [M4F3] **1984** 17 M E103Pakuranga Coll. 11 Howzit **1988** MCGILL *Dict. Kiwi Slang* 59 *how's it goin', mate?* Kiwi greeting; quintessentially so... *how ya goin', mate?* Kiwi greeting, fairly quintessential.

b. How would you be? (**How'd you be?**, **Howja be?**)

1947 in Pearson *Six Stories* (1991) 28 But first he sized the situation up: 'Well, how'd you be? You've got a free hand now.' **1960** KEINZLY *Tangahano* 150 A man came down the road behind them, whistling... 'Howja be, Mrs Pilgrim?' **1963** CASEY *As Short a Spring* 271 'And how would you be?' 'All right'. **1969** MCINNES *Castle on Run* 124 Talk. A man's voice.—G'day kiddo! How'd y'be? **1974** AGNEW *Loner* 178 'How'd you be?' I greeted them cheerfully. 'We're the civil police, Joe,' one of them said. **1978** BALLANTYNE *Talkback Man* 164 'Good morning, Phil. How are you, today?' 'Box of birds, Miss. How would you be yourself?' **1987** DUDER *Alex* 42 'How'd ya be?' he muttered.

c. How are the bots biting, see BOT *n.*¹ 1 b.

d. *Obs.* **How's the way?**

1935 MITCHELL & STRONG in Partridge *Slang Today* (1935) 286 [The] following [was] employed by those who served in the [Great] War... *how's the way?*, how are you (faring). *Ibid.* 287 How's the way, Joe?

e. How's tricks? [See OED *how adv.* A 2 a.]

1949 DAVIN *Roads from Home* 49 How's things?..How's tricks with you? **1980** MARSH *Photo-Finish* 36 'Meet Les Smith,' said the driver. 'Gidday,' said Les Smith. 'How's tricks, then, Bert? Good trip?' 'No trouble, Les.' 'Good as gold,' said the helmsman.

howdie. *Otago Scottish.* [f. Sc. and n. Brit. dial.] A midwife.

1949 SHAW & FARRANT *Taieri Plain* 192 In each district certain women excelled as nurses, particularly in maternity work, and in time they became the recognised 'howdies' or midwives of the neighbourhood. **1967** MCLATCHIE *Tang of Bush* 62 The local midwife [at Owaka, Southland, c1898] ('Howdie'—in Scottish) arrived and shared Ethel's room, while I was turned out into the 'lean-to'.

howhere, var. HOUHERE.

hua, var. HOOER.

huahua. [Ma. /'huahua/: Williams 64 *Huahua*. *1*. n. Birds, etc., captured for food, game... Applied particularly to game preserved in its own fat.] Birds preserved in their own fat.

1851 SHORTLAND *S. Dist. NZ* 70 There was..'huahua' or potted birds, besides preserved eels, and a variety of other dainties. **1908** *Souvenir All Nations Fair, Gisbourne* 13 Huahua, or Preserved Pigeons... Snare your pigeons when the kahikatea berry is ripe, and the birds..fat... Roast... The huahua should be brought in and served with much ceremony.

huckery /'hʌkəri/, *a.* Also **hakari, huckory**; occas. **huck**. [Origin uncertain: see Smithyman's article quoted below for a derivational conjecture that it is an adaptation of Ma. *Hakurara* and/or *hakirara* slovenly; trifling.] Unpleasant; 'off-putting'; unwell; or as an exclamation expressing dislike, esp. as **huckery moll**, a dirty, slovenly, or sexually promiscuous woman.

1972 SMITHYMAN in *Te Reo 15* 31 [Title] The 'Huckery Mole'. A script produced this year [1972] by an Auckland university student... referred to 'a huckery mole', which context showed was animate, animal, female, and held in derogation... The local (even, according to some [students], their own spontaneous) contracting of *huckery* to *huck* was volunteered. *Ibid.* 32 Its age is uncertain, suggested by some to be about five years... *Ibid.* 35 The structure 'X is huckery' seems more narrowly, positively, held [by students] than a flexible or variable 'a huckery X'. **1982** MCCAULEY *Other Halves* 23 'I'd have thought Audrey was a very sexy lady?' 'Huckery moll. was her idea [to screw].' **1988** HINEIRA in *New Women's Fiction* 110 The waiting kids danced and shrieked. Ya! Ya! Ugly hakari bus! Ugly hakari bus! **1988** MCGILL *Dict. Kiwi Slang* 59 *huckery* unwell, jaundiced. **1991** PAYNE *Staunch* 12 There's a party going on. Huckory-looking biker girls wander back and forth, swigging beer from the bottle and raging to the music. **1993** *Dominion* (Wellington) 25 Mar. 27 Jools looking pretty huckery in dun frock and plastic sandals.

hue. Also early **U´e**. [Ma. /'hue/: Williams 66 *Hue* (i), n... calabash, gourd.] CALABASH; and poss. other (and edible) gourd-like fruits.

[**1820** LEE & KENDALL *NZ Gram. & Vocab.* 146 U´e, *s.* A melon, cucumber, or anything that matures upon the ground.] **1843** DIEFFENBACH *Travels in NZ* II. 49 The calabashes (hue) were, according to their traditions, the next addition to their stock of eatables. *Ibid.* II. 363 Hue, *or* ue—a gourd, calabash, cucumber. **1869** *TrNZI* I. (rev. edn.) 259 These were—two roots, and one gourd-like fruit; the Kumara, or sweet potato..the Taro..., and the Hue, a large kind of gourd. **1905** BAUCKE *White Man Treads* 12 The staple cultivated foods of the ancient Maori..were: Kumara, taro, and hue. **1963** KEENE *O te Raki* 191 *hue:* gourd plant, the hard shell of which was used for water jars. **1978** FULLER *Maori Food & Cook.* 7 The gourd, hue, which was brought to New Zealand and cultivated, was eaten when young. **1982** BURTON *Two Hundred Yrs. NZ Food* 4 [Title] Hue (gourds) Young fruit of the gourd plant were cooked in the hangi and eaten, but their main use was as eating and drinking vessels.

Huey, var. HUGHIE.

Hughie. Also **Huey**. [Of uncertain origin: poss. an alteration of *send it down David* (or *Davy*), a soldiers' greeting to a shower of rain likely to postpone a parade (Fraser & Gibbons *Soldier & Sailor Words* 72): AND 1912 (shearers', to invite rain).] The ironically fancied weather-god of trampers and other out-door people, esp. in the exclamation **Send her down Hughie!**, an invitation to rain, or a defiance of bad weather.

1944 *NZEF Times* 27 Mar. 7 Send down some at your very earliest, Hughie. **1945** *Tararua Tramper* Nov. 4 If our trip could have been taken as a precedent for the club's ski activities this winter then 'Old Hughie' would have been working overtime. **1950** *Canterbury Mountaineer* 51 Easter, when the proposer proposes and 'Hughie' disposes. **1958** *Tararua* Sept. 27 The derisive phrases, 'Send it down, Hughie' and 'Let it come down, Hughie', go back to early in this century and are variants of the British military catch-phrase 'Send it down, David'. 'Send her down, Hughie', common in Australia's droughty climate, may not be so derisive. Judging by a verse attached to Dekker's *Shoemaker's Holiday*, St. Hugh has long been associated with rain. **1959** SLATTER *Gun in My Hand* 147 Wife says send her down hughie but I says cut it out. Can't rain for the footie. **1971** *Listener* 19 Apr. 57 Well, that night Hughie sent it down, a nor' wester followed by a southerly buster. **1988** PICKERING *Hills* 46 New Zealand weather, sometimes called 'Huey', is fast and fickle, with abrupt and noisy changes of mood. **1992** *Listener* 2 Mar. 28 Send her down, Hughie, cried Iris... Any murmur against it I certainly didn't hear above the rain that Hughie sent down.

huhu /'huhu/. Also **hou-hou**, **u´hu**. [Ma. /'huhu/: Williams 66 *Huhu* 6. n. Larva of the beetle *Prionoplus reticularis*.] Also as **huhu grub**, the edible larva of the native flying beetle *Prionoplus reticularis* (fam. Cerambycidae), found in decaying wood, a Maori delicacy; also as **huhu beetle**, **huhu bug**, the beetle itself. See also *matai beetle* (BEETLE 9).

[**1820** LEE AND KENDALL *Grammar and Vocabulary* 146 U´hu, *s*. A certain worm. **1843** DIEFFENBACH *Travels in NZ* II. 363 Huhu—moth, grub.] **1844** COLENSO *Excurs. Northern Is.* in Taylor *Early Travellers* (1959) 51 I have..several of the *Larvae*, which are large, wrinkled, and of a dirty-white colour, with a black head... The natives call them Huhu, and consider them a great delicacy! **1873** BULLER *Birds NZ* 65 It was amusing to see [the huia's] treatment of the huhu. This grub, the larva of a large nocturnal beetle..infests all decayed timber, attaining at maturity the size of a man's little finger. **1888** BULLER *Birds NZ* I. 14 Its food consists largely..of the huhu grub. **1889** *TrNZI* XXI. 219 I found a saddleback busily digging in the decayed timber for the larvae of the huhu beetle. **1902** *Ibid.* XXV. 64 The wood-boring grub found in logs or dead trees..and known as *huhu*, is eaten, either raw or roasted, in its first two stages of growth. **1922** *Auckland Weekly News* 14 Dec. 17 I will turn you into a Huhu Bug..a nasty wriggly, common Huhu Bug that lives in a rotten log. **1925** *NZ State Forest Service Bulletin* No.2. 44 *The Huhu Beetle*..is perhaps the largest native beetle, and its grub or huhu is conspicuous for its size and its presence in many a dead log in the forest. **1938** HYDE *Nor Yrs Condemn* 147 He walked back to..where two little brown men were still fiddling with the earth-oven. 'Looks like maggots to me,' he said... '*Hou-hou* grub. Pretty good, eh?' **1949** SARGESON *I Saw in My Dream* (1974) 44 The children had gathered ferns and learned their names, and the names of the trees, and looked for wetas and huhus. **1960** CRUMP *Good Keen Man* 45 When I filled in the Day Book I'd ask Mori for his tally and he'd reply, 'Found a beauty huhu log, boy.' **1967** NATUSCH *Animals NZ* 150 The huhu, *Prionoplus reticularis*, also known as 'horny bug,' 'crusty back' and 'hum-bug' in adult life, is said to be a toothsome morsel in the grub stage—but should not be washed down with alcohol as its tissues already carry a fair amount from the wood it consumes. **1981** *Islands* 8 14 Huhu moths batter the screen on the kitchen door. **1986** GEE *Fire-raiser* 44 'What would she be like with nothing on?'..'Like a huhu grub.' **1995** *Sunday Star-Times* (Auckland) 10 Sept. A4 Trixie Gibson is flat out at her Tolaga Bay farm dipping huhu grubs into chocolate sauce and free-flow freezing them.

hui /'huwi/, *n.*[1] Occas. early **hui hui**. [Ma. /'hui/: Williams 66 *Hui* (i), *huihui*... 5. n. Assembly, group.]

1. A meeting on a marae for social, business, or religious purposes; a meeting anywhere of Maori people, or less often of Maori and non-Maori, to discuss Maori matters.

1846 TAYLOR *Journal* 23 Dec. (ATLTS) IV. 153 A number of worthless natives came to the Hui like the people who followed Jesus for the sake of the loaves. **1847** ANGAS *Savage Life* II. 152 Most of the Otawhao natives are now..planting *kumeras* for the great *hui hui*, or feast, to be given by old Te Whero Whero during the next season. **1858** *Richmond-Atkinson Papers* (1960) I. 408 The *hui* at Rangiaohia to promote the Maori King movement broke up on Friday last. **1863** MOSER *Mahoe Leaves* 58 The term 'Hui'..though strictly meaning a feast, is used commonly by the West Coast natives, for a sacramental gathering. **1908** *TrNZI* XL. 164 A *hui* is a gathering of the tribe, the *hapu*, or the family, and may be held for any purpose of common interest. **1938** HYDE *Nor Yrs. Condemn* 131 They had a dance coming on, a real *hui*, with an orchestra and a strange *pakeha* drink called claret cup. **1948** *Our Own Country* 52 You may be lucky enough to see a *hui* in progress. Perhaps a welcome home to one of the many Ruatoki boys who are serving with the Maori Battalion. **1959** SHADBOLT *New Zealanders* (1986) 20 I mean it's common knowledge what happens at the pa when there's a big hui. **1963** HENDERSON *Ratana* (1972) 45 During the Christmas *hui* of 1924..Morehu were gathered on the *marae*, Ratana made a last effort to cooperate with the recognised churches. **1986** *Contact* (Wellington) 2 May 6 Great excitement among computer behaviourists about the third Unix users conference coming up in the second week of May in Rotorua. It is, in fact, a hui and will be opened by the Governor General Sir Paul Reeves. **1990** *Listener* 6 Aug. 22 Take her approach when invited to address the theme of a high-level hui on the 'Role of Museums in Interpreting Maori Culture'.

2. In special Comb. **hui-hopper**, one who participates in one hui after another; **hui-worker**, one who helps with the preparations for a hui.

1989 *Evening Post* (Wellington) 21 Jan. 7 Peter Tapsell..is tired of '**hui-hoppers**' and wants no more State-funded huis. The goal may be laudable, but why does Stan Rodger announce a forestry hui the very same day? **1961** HILLIARD in *Listener Short Stories* (1977) 59 The **hui-workers** had been busy..carrying water, sorting out gear, cutting wood, slicing meat for the ovens.

hui, *n.*[2] [Ma. /'hui/: Williams 67 *Hui* (iv) *n*...the sweep.] A name applied to the SWEEP (*Scorpis lineolatus*), and occas. to the very similar and commoner *blue maomao* (MAOMAO 2 (1) *Scorpis violaceus*).

[*Note*] The common and scientific names for these two species are often confused.

1927 PHILLIPPS *Bibliogr. NZ Fishes* (1971) 37 *Scorpis aequipinnis*... Sweep; Hui. **1966** [see MAOMAO 2 (1)]. **1967** NATUSCH *Animals NZ* 221 Family Scorpididae. This group includes two species of *Scorpis*, the maomao..and the hui (both northern fish). **1981** WILSON *Fisherman's Bible* 128 Hui Maori name for Blue Maomao **1991** BRADSTOCK *Fishing* 19 A sweep is blue-grey and never has any yellow fins [as has maomao]. It is also called hui and *Scorpis lineolatus*.

huia /'huijə/. Also occas. early **uia**. [Ma. ´*huia*: Williams 67 *Huia*, n. 1.]

1. *Heteralocha acutirostris* (fam. Callaeidae), a glossy, black, orange-wattled bird, once prized by the Maori for its white-tipped tail feathers, now extinct.

[**1820** LEE & KENDALL *NZ Gram. & Vocab.* 146 U´ia, *s*. A certain bird.] **1835** YATE *NZ* (1970) 60 *Huia*—This bird is found only in the mountainous districts of Taranaki, and farther south than Waiapu or the East Cape. **1843** DIEFFENBACH *Travels in NZ* I. 90 The continued loud and shrill whistling of my guide, *uia, uia, uia*, in imitation of the note of the birds, had attracted four, which alighted on the lower branches of the trees near him. **1845** WAKEFIELD *Adventure NZ* I. 91 The huia is a black bird about as large as a thrush, with long thin legs and a slender semi-circular beak, which he uses in seeking in holes in trees for the insects on which he feeds. In the tail are four long black feathers tipt with white..much valued by the natives as ornaments for the hair on great occasions... The natives attracted the birds by imitating the peculiar whistle, from which it takes the name of huia. **1866** ANGAS *Polynesia* 70 The 'huia'..is an elegant bird..about the size of a crow. **1876** *TrNZI* VIII. 192 It will be gratifying to lovers of natural history to hear of the recent discovery of a nest of the Huia in the Orongorongo Ranges, near Wellington. **1882** POTTS *Out in Open* 23 As on state occasions he wears a headdress composed of the skins of the much-prized huia. **1892** *TrNZI* XXIV. 453 Those two birds kept for their feathers were the *huia* (*Heteralocha acutirostris*) and the *kotuku*. **1912** *NZ Free Lance* (Wellington) 21 Dec. 4 Mr Jack Stevens..is once more on the job in the huia-hunting crusade. **1938** MAKERETI *Old-Time Maori* 269 I was always told by my old people that a pair of huia lived on most affectionate terms. **1940** *Tales of Pioneer Women* (1988) 137 Fifty years ago the Huia was plentiful in the Woodville-Kumaroa district. **1985** *Reader's Digest Book NZ Birds* 308 Presumed extinct since 1907, the huia belongs to the same ancient wattlebird family as the saddleback and the kokako. **1990** *Checklist Birds NZ* 226 *Heteralocha acutirostris*...*Huia*... Recorded historically only from forests of the eastern and southern North Island... Last generally accepted record 1907, but quite credible reports up to c.1920.

2. Special Comb. **huia feather**, a prized Maori ornament and later a general fashion element. Cf. WAKA HUIA.

1848 MCLEAN *Diary* 26 May in Cowan *Sir Donald Maclean* (1940) 36 The elder men were dressed in their best dogskin and *kaitaka* mats, some of them had their heads decorated with *huia* and *kotuku* feathers. **1883** RENWICK *Betrayed* 36 One snow-tipped huia feather graced his hair. **1897** CHUDLEIGH *Diary* 30 Oct. (1950) 396 I went to the pa early and saw Wi lying in state... His head had huia feathers on either side, flowers on his chest. **1907** MANSFIELD *Urewera Notebook* (1978) 52 In the shearing sheds—the yellow dress with huia feathers on the coat jacket with scarlet rata blossom. **1920** BOLITHO *With the Prince in NZ* 39 A huia feather and a carved pipe inlaid with pawa shell were added to the gifts. **1930** GUTHRIE *NZ Memories* 37 Being very tall, [the Maori guests] presented a dignified appearance clad only in their silky white *Kaitakas* with huia feathers in their hair. **1963** PHILLIPPS *Book of the Huia* 39 During the visit of the Duke and Duchess of York to Rotorua..one of the guides removed the huia feather from her own hair and placed it in the band of the bowler hat the Duke was wearing. This simple act increased the demand for huia feathers a hundredfold. **1990** *Dominion* Suppl. (Wellington) 22 July 25 At the turn of the century huia tail feathers became popular in fashion garments.

hump, *v*. [Transf. use of *hump* to make humped: AND *hump it*, 1891, *hump carry*, 1851.]

1. a. *trans*. To carry (a tiring load) usu. on the back or shoulders.

1855 *Nelson Examiner* 7 Nov. 2 Mr. Kealy met them 'humping' their toms, they having found a good prospect, so they are now upon their own 'hook'. **1860** BUTLER *Forest Creek MS* (1960) 50 Oh! what fires we made—..then we humped in three stones for seats. **1871** MONEY *Knocking About NZ* 93 Having cut a sufficient quantity, we 'humped' it out of the bush and packed it beside our new home. **1882** HAY *Brighter Britain* II. 25 He must hump all his belongings on his own back over..forest and morass. **1898** HOCKEN *Contributions* 78 The provisions for the distant stations were..'humped' over the intervening land portion of the journey. **1933** *Press* (Christchurch) (Acland Gloss.) 28 Oct. 17 *Hump*.—To carry, especially a tiring load. **1964** DAVIS *Watersiders* 129 A lot of men who've been humping meat for the last ten years started like you [as a watersider]. **1971** *Listener* 19 Apr. 56 He was fair-

HUMP

dinkum bushed... So he got on a blaze and humped his pack up towards the cage.

Hence **humping** *vbl. n.*, a carrying or shifting as a back-load.
1882 HAY *Brighter Britain* I. 117 It was too far from the river, he said, and would necessitate such an amount of 'humping'. Bosh about humping! returned the majority.

b. *quasi-intr.* As **to hump it**, to travel carrying a swag or load.
1865 FARJEON *Shadows on Snow* 66 The best thing we [diggers] can do..is to try and hump it back again tomorrow. **1899** BELL *In Shadow of Bush* 30 And here I am,.. but dead broke—without a cent—had to hump it all the way on foot.

2. In various phr. with reference to carrying a swag on one's back or shoulders. **a.** As **to hump** (one's) **swag**. Cf. SWAG *n.*¹ 1 a.
1863 GOLDIE in Beattie *Pioneers Explore Otago* (1947) 136 Digger custom, we humped our swag. **1873** WILSON *Diary* 30 Jan. in Wierzbicka *Wilson Family* (1973) 158 Humping our swags again we start very much refreshed to climb the hills. **1909** THOMPSON *Ballads About Business* 63 O'er the dreary Maniototo many a time he'd 'humped' his swag. **1941** MYERS *Valiant Love* 37 Joe 'humped' his swag, and Daniel sent him off to catch the train. **1986** OWEN & PERKINS *Speaking for Ourselves* 68 There was I, on my Pat Malone, starting off on my first experience at humping a swag.

b. As **to hump** (one's) **bluey**. Cf. *bluey-humper* (BLUEY *n.*¹ 1 a).
1897 WRIGHT *Station Ballads* 30 I'd best hump my bluey on. **1909** *Truth* 6 Nov. 1 Go home thou wowser on the wallaby; hump bluey, carry Matilda, pad the hoof, thou parsonical howler. **1918** *Chron. NZEF* 5 July 251 We 'umped our blueys for about three miles through the mud to Terrynikow. **1934** SCANLAN *Winds of Heaven* 290 Swaggers were met on the country roads, 'humping their bluey', a billy..tied to their rolled-up blanket. **1955** WILSON *Land of My Children* 115 Stella..encouraged him to..go to Auckland by train. 'No, I'll hump bluey there, but coming back..well I mightn't own a bluey by then.' **1970** JOHNSON *Life's Vagaries* 73 If folks were reduced to walking and humping the bluey the least one could do was to give a lift.

c. As **to hump** (one's) **drum**. Cf. DRUM *n.* 1.
1909 THOMPSON *Ballads About Business* 73 'Twas somewhere up near Timaru—That town whose Celtic-sounding name Suggests to me a wild 'Hurroo!' To make a rhyme to fit the same—That many years ago began To 'hump his drum' an Irishman.

d. As **to hump Matilda**. Cf. MATILDA a.
c1875 MEREDITH *Adventuring in Maoriland* (1935) 173 Not relishing the prospect of 'humping Matilda' round the country, looking for a job, I decided to get back home.

hump, *n.* Obs. [AND 1890 only.] An arduous walk or tramp carrying a load (on the back).
1863 WALKER *Jrnl. & Lett.* (ATLTS) 27 Jan. On Saturday we started over the hill for provisions and brought over 120 lbs. principally flour. It was a precious hump, but we hope to hire a horse in the course of a day or two.

humpback (whale): see *humpback* (WHALE 2 (7 a)).

humpie, *n.*¹ Also **humpy**. [AAW ad. Aboriginal Jagara language (Brisbane region) ŋumbi 'temporary shelter'; AND a temporary shelter of Aborigines 1846, thence any makeshift dwelling.]

1. a. A rough, make-shift shelter; (later) a rough shack.
1906 *Red Funnel* I. No.1 42. Seated on an empty Kerosene-case outside his bark humpy, a man was sorting and scraping..gum. **1915** ADAMS *Grocer Greatheart* 73 We'll run up a sort of 'humpy' for the ladies tomorrow [wrecked on desert island]. **c1926** THE MIXER *Transport Workers' Song Book* 123 I gaze on the moon through the holes in the roof, Which shows that the 'humpie' is not weatherproof... Some calls it a 'lean-to', a 'humpie', a 'shack'. **1991** *NZ Geographic* Apr.-June 22 When I was digging you had to get a licence, and that entitled you to dig anywhere and to put up a humpy (shack).

b. Transf. to an animal shelter.
1936 GUTHRIE-SMITH *NZ Naturalist* 186 The perturbed bird [snipe] would merely emerge with full spread pinions from its isolated humpie of manuka. **1963** RAWLINSON *Clouds & Pebbles* 12 Like a hermit crab among the winding roots, his humpy's two shaky walls of tin propped between the rockface and a sack.

2. Any cramped quarters.
1979 ADCOCK *Butter in Lordly Dish* 104 Had his own quarters, the two-roomed shop... The *humpy*, as we called it, was lighted only by a lamp. **1986** HALEY *Settlement* 60 Then again a modest bach or humpy on the edge of the mere would be ideal.

humpie, *n.*² [f. HUMP(BACK + -Y.] A humpback whale (WHALE 2 (7 a)).
1982 GRADY *Perano Whalers* 227 Humpies—Humpback whales. A species of whalebone or baleen whale, the *Megaptera longimana*. It is distinguishable by its low rounded dorsal fin and its humps.

humpy, var. HUMPIE.

hunchback: see *humpback* (WHALE 2 (7) a).

hundred. *Hist.* [f. *hundred*: in England (subsequently Ireland), a subdivision of a county or shire, having its own court: thence, an administrative division of a county in British American colonies: see OED *hundred* 5.]

1. A subdivision, used esp. in the provinces of Otago and Southland, comprising lands set aside for settlement.
1848 WAKEFIELD *Handbook NZ* 317 ['Terms of Purchase of Land in the Settlement of Otago' agreed on by the 'Otago Association' and the Company] 11. Reservations to be made.. of the Sites of Villages and Towns..in the Several Parishes and Hundreds. **1858** *Otago Witness* (Dunedin) 4 Dec. 5 We hesitate not to confess ourselves admirers of the Hundred system and of agriculture rather than of runholding. **1863** HEYWOOD *Vacation Tour Antipodes* 224 In Otago no land can be bought unless within the boundary of some *hundred* as it is called... The Government of the Province proclaim *hundreds* when they deem necessary. **1873** WILSON *Diary* 9 Feb. in Wierzbicka *Wilson Family* (1973) 173 The Provincial Government have the power of declaring any portion or the whole of a run into 'hundreds' as they are called, the land in this hundred can be bought by any person at £1 per acre for the cheapest price. **1898** HOCKEN *Contributions* 167 The old Otago Block had already been divided into Hundreds, at first three in number, but was now subdivided for greater convenience into eight. **1937** AYSON *Thomas* 94 He had to find rent of ground to give him the right to run cattle on 'the hundred,' and had to pay two and sixpence assessment a head to the Wardens to be spent on road-making. **1948** SCOTTER *Run Estate & Farm* 15 In 1869,.. the administration of the hundreds was centralized in Dunedin (Times June 18, 1869). **1952-53** *NZ Forest Service Gloss.* (TS) Hundred Under the old land-subdivision system in New Zealand, a subdivision of a County. Still used in parts of Southland in the place of Survey District. **1977** MARKS *Hammer & Tap* 510 Under the 1856 land regulations, the settled areas [of Otago] were divided, for purposes of better government, into eight districts, called 'hundreds', within which land was for sale at ten shillings per acre with a forty shilling per acre improvement clause. **1980** ELDRED-GRIGG *Southern Gentry* 66 The [Otago] provincial government also empowered itself to confiscate grants and create small farming settlements called 'hundreds'.

2. A proposed subdivision of the North Island for purpose of defence against expected Maori protest.
1861 SIR GEORGE GREY *Memorandum* 2 Nov. in Rutherford *Sel. Documents* (1949) 112a Each district [of the proposed Maori portion of the North Island] to be divided into about six hundreds from the runangas of each of which will be selected two persons to represent such hundred in the runanga of the district. **1922** COWAN *NZ Wars* (1955) I. 233 Grey and his Ministers introduced also a system of local government; under this plan the Maori country was to be divided into districts and 'hundreds', over each of which a Civil Commissioner was to be placed to grapple with the task of governing the natives in his zone of influence. **1991** LA ROCHE *Hist. of Howick & Pakuranga* 213 The early colonial administrators had perpetuated the curious old English land subdivisions of 'Hundreds'... Thus the County of Eden was divided into the hundreds of Howick, Onehunga... Each Fencible settlement and the surrounding countryside constituted a Hundred.

hune. [Ma. /'hune/ Williams 69 *Hune* 2. Pappus of seeds of *raupō*.] The pappus or down extracted from the seed-heads of raupo.
1867 HOOKER *Handbook* (List of Names) 765 Hune... Pappus of the seeds of *Typha angustifolia*. **1869** *TrNZI* I. (rev. edn.) 267 As a cataplasm..they used..the Hune, or *Pappus* down of the large Bulrush. **1935** JACKSON *Annals NZ Family* 86 Mattresses were made [c1860] from the down on the seed of the raupo, *hune*, thoroughly dried in the sun.

hungry, *a.*¹ Goldmining. Also **hungry-looking**. [AND 1853: see OED *hungry* 6 c.] Of quartz or other potentially auriferous material, non-auriferous, or of low gold content.
1868 *Thames Miner's Guide* 78 A glance will convince the experienced miner that [the reef] is free from the peculiar appearance there is about non-auriferous quartz, which is denominated by miners as 'hungry-looking stuff'. **1875** *AJHR* H-3 39 At the eastern face..the good looking quartz is only from 5 to 12 inches in thickness, the remainder being hungry-looking. **1909** *TrNZI* XLI. 81 Barren Reefs, or Buck Reefs... In Otago they consist of very wide, massive, bold outcrops of 'hungry' glassy quartz. **1910** *NZGeol.SB (NS)* No.9 45 Small pieces of quartz are included in the conglomerate bands which have already been described, but such as were seen by the writer of this report are of a decidedly 'hungry' appearance. **1953** SUTHERLAND *Golden Bush* (1963) 63 It was encouraging to think of Bluey's nugget when working a block of 'hungry' wash. **1978** MCARA *Gold Mining Waihi* 29 It may have been that the white 'hungry' appearance of much of the quartz on the surface discouraged earlier prospectors. **1983** NOLAN *Gold Fossicker's Handbook* 112 *Hungry*: of quartz or a mining site, barren or barely payable.

hungry, *a.*² [AND 1855.] Mean, niggardly.
1973 WHEELER *Hist. Sheep Stations NI* 97 Doug still remembers the hungry stations where they ate old ewe, potatoes, rice pudding and, at the weekend, one pound of 'brownie' per man.

hunt, *v. Farming.* [Various spec. uses of *hunt* to drive (stock).]

1. a. *trans.* Of a person, to drive (stock) from behind; to send (a dog) to hunt stock; to clear (an area) of stock by driving. Also as a *vbl. n.* (see quot. 1978).

1907 *TrNZI* XXXIX. 284 While in the act of hunting a dog for the sheep a kea flew down to the back of a sheep. **1953** Stronach *Musterer on Molesworth* 14 The next day we spent hunting the sheep on towards Boundary Creek. **1970** McNaughton *Tat* 25 'You go ahead and take the gate, and I'll hunt them up the race,' Mike said... 'You're hunting them through too fast!' Legge shouted back... Legge and Ustice hunted the sheep forward, and they ran nicely for a while. **1978** Jardine *Shadows on Hill* 5 We'll hunt the basin back out to you, so keep quiet. *Ibid.* 6 [The sheep] had soon passed and needed no hunting to keep them moving.

b. *intr.* Of a dog, to drive sheep from behind.
1949 Hartley *Shepherd's Dogs* 2 I taught him to hunt correctly and to back sheep and finally disposed of him for £22. **1981** Anderson *Both Sides of River* 78 One of the musterers..gave him his first dog..who would hunt as well as head.

2. As **hunt away. a.** Of a dog, to drive (sheep) away from the shepherd, or from a given spot.
1933 *Press* (Christchurch) (Acland Gloss.) 28 Oct. 17 *Huntaway.*—A dog whose work is to drive sheep forward when mustering. As a verb the word is used in two senses, illustrated by the sentences: 'That dog hunts away well' and 'I hunt away with that dog'. **1934** Lilico *Sheep Dog Memoirs* 27 [The dogs] would head, lead, hunt away, force and back. **1970** McNaughton *Tat* 101 He could hunt a mob away, as well as pull, and he was also a champion yard dog, barking when commanded.

b. *trans.* As **hunt**, in *transf.* use, to drive (a person or animal) away.
1904 *NZ Illustr. Mag.* Oct. 25 February 25th.— Loafer called; dirty loafer, hunted him; found my largest apple had fallen off the tree.

3. As **hunt down**, see quots.
1933 *Press* (Christchurch) (Acland Gloss.) 28 Oct. 17 *Hunt down.*—To hunt the sheep of[f] the higher parts of their winter country on to lower, safer spurs when snow is expected, e.g., 'We hunted down every day for a week, but no snow came.' This is a very common expression in the Lakes district of Otago. I cannot remember hearing it in Canterbury, though the job is done often enough. **1934** Harper *Windy Island* 232 Viper had turned her mob neatly over to Rough, who was hunting them away down the mountainside. **1966** Newton *Boss's Story* 188 *Hunting down*: Where sheep are wintered on high unfenced country subject to snow it is a common practice to keep them hunted down from the higher, more dangerous snow levels.

4. As **hunt up**, to periodically muster sheep into a mob. Also as *vbl. n.*
1966 Newton *Boss's Story* 48 Many sheepmen advocate 'hunting up' (periodically mustering them up, *Huperei*. **1978** Fuller *Maori Food & Cook.* 85 during tupping but it is my belief that ewes..are best left alone at that time.

hunt, *n. Farming.* The ability of a dog to drive or hunt stock away from the handler; also, to back on command while doing this.
1982 *Agric. Gloss.* (MAF) 24 *Hunt*: Ability of a dog to drive or hunt stock away from the handler, also to back on command while doing this. It can do a 'straight' or 'zig-zag' hunt.

huntaway. *Farming.* [f. *v.* to hunt away.]

1. A noisy sheepdog trained to bark on command and drive sheep forward from behind. See also *Nelson huntaway* (Nelson 2).

1912 *Otago Witness* (Dunedin) 11 Sept. 35 A huntaway should be a free-running dog, noisy and under good command, and should lose points for not taking directions readily, insufficient noise, being too rash or too slow, and not keeping sheep on a good course. **1934** Lilico *Sheep Dog Memoirs* 26 So far as I have heard and read, there is no other part of the world which has strains of natural huntaways, so we must accept the idea that huntaways are entirely a New Zealand product. **1949** Newton *High Country Days* 195 Huntaway: A noisy dog whose natural instinct is to hunt or chase sheep away. On account of their noise they are used for forcing mobs, work in the drafting yards, and for clearing or 'hunting' sheep off tracts of country. **1951** McLeod *NZ High Country* 5 The shepherds soon bred dogs which had more the characteristics of the Old English sheepdogs—bouncing barking dogs which..drive..sheep... They called them huntaways and this word is now so well known in New Zealand that it is part of the language. **1966** *Encycl. NZ* I. 493 The huntaway sheep dog is a New Zealand development. **1984** Rennie *Working Dogs* 12 The Beardie was developed as a barking dog because in some parts of Scotland, particularly in the Western Highlands, much of the ground is covered with bracken, which combined with the deep gullies known as corries, makes it impossible for a heading dog to see his sheep. Here the shepherd has to get out above the sheep and more or less chase them out of the thick cover. These dogs were known as hunters, and it is presumably an adaptation of this name which led to the designation, huntaway.

2. The name of a class of test at a sheep-dog trial.
1966 *Encycl. NZ* I. 493 *Huntaway.* In both huntaway classes three sheep are set loose at the foot of the hill. While the shepherd remains at the bottom, his dog, working and barking to command, hunts the sheep upwards on a defined line away from his master. In the zig-zag hunt, the sheep are directed through three sets of flags 1 chain apart and spaced equally up the hill on a zig-zag course of approximately 440 yards. The course for the straight hunt is about the same length, from the foot of the hill up to and through a set of flags 1 chain apart.

hunter. In special Comb. or collocations: **hunter shepherd**, one who hunts sheep down from dangerous high-country and keeps them within a boundary; **hunters' pie**, see quot. 1936.
1960 Masters *Back-Country Tales* 103 It was built to house the **hunter shepherd**, whose job it was to keep sheep from straying over the unfenced Kereru boundary, and on to the Ruahine tops, and hunt down the wild dogs and pigs that infested the area. **1936** *Hills & Valleys* II. 10 I attended the making of a **hunters' pie**. First I laid the [newly taken] skin on the ground, cutting up the meat into small pieces, not forgetting the kidney and a small piece of bacon..salted and added a little water and then folded carefully. When the fire was well burnt down I scraped the sticks and embers away, placing the pie with the folded side on top.

huperei. [Ma. /ˈhuːperei/: Williams 70 *Hūperei = perei... Gastrodia cunninghamii.*] *Gastrodia cunninghamii* (fam. Orchidaceae), a native saprophytic orchid, having an edible tuber formerly eaten by the Maori.
1940 Laing & Blackwell *Plants NZ* 126 *Gastrodia Cunninghamii (Cunningham's Gastrodia)...* Maori name, *Huperei*. **1978** Fuller *Maori Food & Cook.* 85 Huperei—*Gastrodia cunninghamii*. **1982** Wilson *Stewart Is. Plants* 294 Black Orchid... Hūperei... Flowers numerous, white within, dark brown without.

hupiro. [Ma. /ˈhuːpiro/: Williams 70 *Hūpirauriki*, n. *Coprosma foetidissima...* = *hūpiro*.: Ma. *piro* stinking.] stinkwood.
1918 *NZJST* I. 266 *Coprosma foetidissima* (the hupiro of the Maori and the 'stinkwood' of the settler)..has proved a disappointment. **1940** Laing & Blackwell *Plants NZ* 425 *Coprosma foetidissima (The Foetid Coprosma). Ibid.* 427 Maori name *Hupiro*. **1952** [see stinkwood]. **1982** Wilson *Stewart Is. Plants* 61 Stinkwood... Hūpiro... Shrub or small tree... Leaves strong-smelling when crushed.

hurdy-gurdy. *Hist.* [Transf. use of *hurdy-gurdy* a barrel-organ turned by a crank.]

1. *Gumdigging.* A gum-washing machine turned by a hand crank.
1948 Reed *Gumdigger* 45 This, then, was the simplest form of gum-washing machine—the 'hurdy-gurdy' as I had heard it called. **1972** Reed *Gumdiggers* 82 The machine age on the gumfield appears to have been heralded as early as 1915 when an ingenious digger, whose name has unfortunately been forgotten, introduced what came to be known as the 'hurdy-gurdy' or 'gurdy'. *Ibid.* 83 In its simplest form it was a tub, or a section of a small galvanised iron tank, the bottom perforated with small holes. In the centre stood a strong, revolving, upright shaft, to the lower part of which was attached a wooden paddle, extending on both sides of the shaft, almost to the sides of the tank. The top of the revolving shaft was fitted with a horizontal handle, enabling the paddle to be swung to and fro in a half-circle. This simple machine was usually operated by two men; a supply of gum-bearing dirt having been put into the tank, buckets of water were thrown in by one man while the other vigorously turned the shaft handle this way and that, stirring up the soil while the muddy water flowed out through the perforations. **1991** *NZ Geographic* Apr.–June 22 The golf course—we dug all that for gum with a spade, a spear, a kerosene tin and a hurdy-gurdy.

2. A kind of threshing mill.
1990 Martin *Forgotten Worker* 127 The mechanisation of threshing came early. The first machine was the 'Peg-Drum' threshing mill, also known as the 'Hurdy Gurdy'. This was a great advance on hand-threshing, and consisted of 'a revolving drum within a concave of bars. To the drum were fitted a large number of small iron pegs..and these passed closely between the pegs of the concave. The drum revolved at high speed, and the grain was "threshed" from the ears of corn as it passed between the two sets of pegs.'

hurrah, hurray, varr. hooray.

hustler. The name of a patent drag-harrow.
c1918 in Ogilvie *Moonshine Country* (1971) 74 In August 1918 Hugh McCully of Waitohi showed a gathering of local farmers what his new drag harrow was capable of doing. This cultivator, which he called a 'hustler', had a width of 6ft 9½ ins and was fitted with fifteen tines. Hustlers are commonplace nowadays. **1934** *NZJST* XV. 289 *Preparation Cost...* Two grubbings with hustler (one for irrigation): one man and six horses for twelve hours.

hut.

1. In early European pre-settlement use, a Maori dwelling.
1773 Forster *Resolution Jrnl.* 9 Apr. (1982) II. 250 Afternoon we returned to our new Friend the natives..; we therefore landed & went up to their hut. **1801** *Miss. Jrnl. 'Royal Admiral'* (ATLMS) 24 Apr. We saw only one settlement of actives..we saw a few huts.

2. [AND 1816.] **a.** In early colonial use, a rough living quarters of a newly-established farm or station, usu. comprising a single room; then, the living quarters of farm hands as distinct from the homestead (MEN'S HUT q.v.); also used esp. in mountain or hill country as the name for a shelter or temporary living quarters for itinerant trampers, hunters, etc. (as *shepherd's hut* (SHEPHERD), *trampers' hut* (TRAMPER 2). Cf. CRIB *n.*¹ 1 a, WHARE 4.

1851 *Lyttelton Times* 1 Feb. 3 At the end of the bush an alarming fire occurred, the high wind blowing the sparks of an open air fire against a neighbouring hut, built of dried fern and wattles. **1857** PAUL *Lett. from Canterbury* 90 You are fairly entitled to something better than a warré, say a two-roomed hut for yourself. **1861** BUTLER *Note* Apr. in Jones *Samuel Butler* (1919) I. 87 *April, 1861*—It is Sunday... There are five men sleeping in the hut. I sleep in a bunk on one side of the fire. **1935** ODELL *Handbook Arthur's Pass National Park* 20 They will no doubt be ultimately opened up by the formation of tracks and the erection of huts, and will then allow of the fullest exploitation of the winter sports attractions of the Park. **1947** BEATTIE *Early Runholding* 33 He [*sc.* the pioneer pastoralist] has built a domicile of some sort, be it of canvas, calico, bagging, sticks, ferntrees, grass, slabs, mud, clay, stone, or wattle and daub. He may call it various names according to its materials, but three names would not enter his head—i.e., crib, bach, or shack. He may call it a cabin, a shanty, a cottage, a warrie, but probably he would use the commonest term of all—hut. **1987** OGONOWSKA-COATES *Boards, Blades & Barebellies* 96 *Hut.* House where the station hands or shearers live. Some call it a whare. Until the 1930s and 40s the men usually ate, cooked and slept in a one-roomed hut with a fireplace at one end and bunks in tiers around the walls. Often there were no facilities for washing other than the creek. Today most huts are quite comfortable, with separate rooms for eating and sleeping, showers and toilets.

b. A trampers' or hillmen's hut, often given an identifying name.

1889 PRINCE *Diary of Trip* 10 The Beech Hut is built of slabs with a tree-fern roof, and contains eight sleeping berths. **1907** *TrNZI* XXXIX. 198 The accommodation at the Routeburn Hut, although plain, is quite satisfactory. The hut consists of three rooms furnished with wooden bunks, tables, shelves, and forms.

3. Special Comb. **hut-ground** *goldmining hist.*, an area on which a claim-holder may build a hut; **hut-keeper** *obs.* [AND 1826], a person who manages the cooking, cleaning, etc. of esp. a men's hut on a farm or station.

1892 PYKE *Gold-Miners' Guide* 7 Every holder of a miners' right is entitled... To occupy for residence an area of 24ft. frontage by 48ft. depth, as '**hut**- or tent-ground', without registration; but 'tent-ground' must not be taken up on any known auriferous or argentiferous ground, nor in the line of, or adjacent to any gold-workings. **1847** ANGAS *Savage Life* II. 167 On the opposite side of the island..was a hut belonging to the superintendent of the mine,...and it was intimated that the '**hut-keeper**' would provide for our temporal necessities. **1851** *Col. Church Chron.* VI. 293 Got the stock-man and hut-keeper, the only men on the station, to come to me. **1861** BUTLER *Letter* Apr. in Jones *Samuel Butler* (1919) I. 87 My bullock-driver and hut-keeper have two bunks at the far end of the hut, along the wall. **1870** PRENTICE *A Tale NZ* (GALMS) 37 The [out-]shepherd had no hut-keeper for a companion and assistant as in Australia. **1882** HAY *Brighter Britain* I. 140 The Little'un was one day detailed as hut-keeper. It so happened that he had our entire stock of crockery to wash up. **1912** BOOTH *Five Years NZ* 73 The station hands [c1861] comprised a shepherd, bullock driver, hut-keeper.

Hence **hut-keep** *v. intr.*, see quot.

c1930 *Whitcombe's Etym. Dict. Aust.-NZ Suppl.* 6 *hut n.* the building on the sheep station where the shearers live, often a large stone building. *hut-keep* v. trans. to look after the hut of a miner, shepherd, etc.

hutiwai. Also with much variety of form as **atwai, hatiwai, hutuwai, otiwai, utiwai, utuwai**. [Ma. /'hutuwai/: Williams 72 *Hutiwai, n.*... the bidibidi.] BIDDY-BID *n.* 1 a; also used in, or as the name of, a patent remedy, poss. from its early use, infused, as a 'tea' and as a folk or Maori remedy (see quots. 1889, 1936, 1946).

1848 WAKEFIELD *Handbook NZ* 123 Another advantage is to be found in the absence of *burrs* in the New Zealand runs... In some parts of New Zealand there does exist a small *burr*, called *otiwai*. **1853** [see PIRIPIRI 1 a]. **1868** [see BIDDY-BID 1 a]. **1889** FEATON *Art Album NZ Flora* 125 Acaena sanguisorbae... The Native Burr... The 'Hutiwai', or 'Piripiri'..an infusion of the leaves is said to afford a substitute for tea, but it is the opinion of the writer that the results are not commensurate with the trouble of brewing. **1891** WALLACE *Rural Econ. Austral. & NZ* 301 Unlike the New Zealand bur Atwai or Pidi-pidi, [Australian, bur-clover] cannot be easily broken up in working. **1913** *NZJAg.* Jan. VI. 87 [Query from] 'Utuwai', Colyton:—Will you please let me know if there is any way of destroying utuwai, or bidabid as it is more commonly called? **1922** PERRY *Sheep Farming* 138 It is a mistake to think that seed (hatiwai or bidi-bidi) in wool is crushed to dust in the dumping. **1936** *NZ Railways Mag.* June 29 For digestive troubles there is virtue in an infusion of the *piripiri* or *hutuwai*, the stickfast plant popularly known as the 'biddibid'. **1946** BEAGLEHOLE *Some Modern Maoris* 222 These [herbs in a Maori pharmacopeia] range from boiled hutiwai (*Acaena sanguisorbae*) for general stomach disorders. **1959** MIDDLETON *The Stone* 42 Sheep fed among rotting logs and patches of hutuwai. **1986** RICHARDS *Off the Sheep's Back* 82 The farm itself was very poor and covered with hutiwai (biddy bids), so the sheep were fairly slow cutting.

Hutton's rail, shearwater: see RAIL 2 (3), SHEARWATER 2 (4).

hutu, var. UTU.

hutu. Also early **utuhutu**. (?=**hutuhutu**). [Ma. /'hutu/: Williams 73 *Hutu* (i)... 1. *Ascarina lucida*: prob. PPN **futu* applied to various trees in various places, e.g. po*hutu*kawa.] *Ascarina lucida* (fam. Chloranthaceae), a small native tree of lowland and lower montane forests.

1838 POLACK *NZ* II. 400 There are many other woods of much service to Europeans, differing in quality, among others..the *Kaikamoko*..*Utuhutu*. **1867** HOOKER *Handbook* 765 Hutu, *Geolog. Surv. Ascarina lucida*. **1889** KIRK *Forest Flora* 269 Ascarina lucida is the hutu of the Maoris. **1939** COCKAYNE & TURNER *Trees NZ* 28 Ascarina lucida (Chloranthaceae). Hutu. **1961** MARTIN *Flora NZ* 165 Hutu..leaves in opposite pairs, coarsely serrate. **1978** MOORE & IRWIN *Oxford Book NZ Plants* 38 Hutu is common in places on the west coast of the South Island and in parts of the Coromandel Range. **1989** PARKINSON *Travelling Naturalist* 104 Trees that would seem more at home on the..West Coast..kaikawaka, mountain toatoa, sweet hutu, and southern rata.

hydro /'haidrʌu/. [Ellipt. for *hydro-electric* referring to the generation of electricity by water power.] Esp. as **the hydro**, a (usu. formerly State) hydro-electric scheme, works, dam, or the headquarters of a hydro project or works. Often *attrib.*

1938 HYDE *Nor Yrs. Condemn* 117 There was a sort of virtue in that, especially in the expensive hydros. Bede Collins, who visited the father of them all, the giant dam at Arapuni, for which the Waikato River had been backed miles out of its course. *Ibid.* 200 Did I ever tell you about that hydro..I was on a bit south. **1960** KEINZLY *Tangahano* 78 I went to school here. I was born in a hydro camp. **1965** LEE *Rhetoric at Red Dawn* 158 Gordon Coates could be interesting on the Mangahao hydro or the duplication of a railway. **1965** WEBBER *Try Again Friday* 164 Limited fishing will probably be permitted in State hydro-controlled rivers and lakes. **1971** CRUMP *Bastards I Have Met* 14 That's why I turned down Gordon's suggestion that he and I apply for jobs on the hydro together. **1984** BRASCH *Collected Poems* 57 Labourer at the hydro scheme, bookie's tout, Billiard-room marker. **1993** O'SULLIVAN *Let the River Stand* 266 He preferred to stay at the hotel..rather than having to hit the grog out at the hydro camp every night.

I

ice-block. [AND 1948.] An artificially coloured and flavoured ice-water confection sold frozen on a stick. (Known to informants from at least the mid-1950s.)
1989 McGill *Baby Boomers* 24 Before iceblocks came on the scene, we used to buy frozen oranges for threepence. **1993** Barnett & Wolfe *At the Beach* 9 We grow up with rich, ingrained memories of summer at the beach..dusty metalled roads..ice blocks and ice cream.

ice-plant. [Transf. use of *ice plant* South African *Mesembryanthemum* spp. (fam. Aizoaceae), succulent herbs with expanded fleshy leaves.] Also **Maori (native, New Zealand) ice-plant**. *Disphyma* (also early *Mesembryanthemum*) *australe* (fam. Aizoaceae). See also HOROKAKA, *pig's face* (PIG n.¹ 2 b).
1867 Hooker *Handbook* 765 Ice-plant, native, *Tetragonia expansa* and *Mesembryanthemum australe*. **1888** *TrNZI* XX. 142 The first plants noticed after leaving the beach were well-known maritime species, such as the ice-plant. **1910** Cockayne *NZ Plants & Their Story* 63 The ice-plant.., (pig's-face, horokaka), which so frequently drapes the coastal cliffs with its pale-green leaves, and bears rather large rose-coloured flowers, is a pleasing and familiar example. **1923** Cockayne *Cultivation NZ Plants* 87 Horokaka, ice-plant..has pink, or white (in one var.) *fls*. **1940** [see PIG n.¹ 2 b]. **1952** Richards *Chatham Is.* 27 *Mesembryanthemum..australe*..Ice Plant. Horo-kaka. **1971** *New Zealand's Heritage* I. 266 *Maori Ice Plant, Disphyma australe*. Seaside plant which trails over rocks and cliff faces often only a few feet from the sea. Flowers are either creamy-white or pink. **1981** Brooker et al. *NZ Medicinal Plants* 54 *Disphyma australe... New Zealand ice plant*, round-leaved pigface. Maori names: *Horokaka, ruerueke*. **1988** Dawson *Forest Vines to Snow Tussocks* 155 In the most exposed situations low growing succulent plants predominate, including the native ice plant. **1995** *City Voice* (Wellington) 11 May 14 There'll be a mix of coastal natives, including wild celery, sand convolvulus, Maori ice plant, and even NZ spinach.

I-class: see IDLEALONG.

identity: see OLD IDENTITY.

idlealong /ˈaidələˌlɒŋ/. Also **Idle Along**. [See quot. 1964.] A class of small centreboard yacht (see quot. 1948); also (except in Auckland) classified as *I-class* (see quot. 1991).
1935 *Dominion* (Wellington) 26 Sept. 11 Rules for the 'Idle Along' class Championships of New Zealand were approved by the Wellington Provincial Yacht and Motor-Boat Association at its meeting last night. **1935** in **1991** Harrison *Ebb and Flow* 63 It was decided to leave the Idlealong championship in the hands of A.T. Round. **1948** Carter *Little Ships* 131 Less than ten years ago Mr. Alf Harvey, of Wellington, conducted a series of experiments in an effort to evolve a suitable small class racer, and the results of his efforts are seen today in the ever-increasing fleet of Idle Along craft. *Ibid.* 132 The boats are of a restricted type and measure 12.8 feet (approx. 3.90 m) overall, and have a beam of approximately 6 feet (1.83 m). They are built on the square chine principle, with a good rise in floor forward of amidships, which flattens out to a broad tuck stern. The original model was gunter rigged, but it was found..the boats perform better with a Bermudian rig. **1955** *BJ Cameron Collection* (TS July) Idlealong (n) A type of small yacht. **1964** Mander & O'Neill *Give a Man a Boat* 21 A chap called Alf Harvey, from Petone, came along in the early 1930s and built a boat he named *Idle Along* which, because of its beam and stability and roominess, appealed to a great number of people. Here was the middleman's boat. *Ibid.* 62 The Idle Along was hard-chined like the Z class and much bigger than the two inches difference in length would lead one to imagine. **1966** Dyson *Yachting the NZ Way* 159 The Idle Along was designed before World War II to suit the blustery conditions of Wellington. **1978** Tichener *Little Ships of NZ* 72 The Idle Along class thrived in the late 1940s and 1950s, but in common with other classes such as the Z and X, the change to plywood construction was left too late. The class slowly declined and finally died in the late 1960s. **1991** Harrison *Ebb and Flow* 77 In September 1948 the Club appointed measurers to the dinghy racing classes as follows: Peter Lamb to the I Class (Idlealong).

-ie, *suffix*.

1. Also **-y**; the *-ie* form is usually preferred for nouns. As a suffix constantly giving rise to new formations it is esp. frequent in New Zealand English not only (as elsewhere) in creating diminutive or hypocoristic forms, but also in creating familiar, often shortened, forms of the names of many common objects, creatures and people. Its local frequency may possibly be due to influence from northern English or Scottish dialects (cf. *postie*), or possibly as a general feature of working-class or occupational language imbedded in New Zealand English. (The suffix -o is less frequent in NZ English than in Australian.) The -IE feature is often remarked on:
1983 Hulme *Bone People* 31 This godzone baby talk. Hottie lolly cardie nappy, crappy the lot of it, she snarls to herself. **1984** *Listener* 14 Apr. 13 Smoko was held in the donko, where we'd adjourn after working like billyo. (The old tendency for working argot to end words in 'o' appears to have been displaced by modern tendencies to end it in 'ie' like 'bikkie' and 'prezzie'.) **1988** *North & South* (Auckland) Sept. 41 Where else are they so big on hypocorisms?.. They're those dinky little words we make up, like these: kiddies (children), cardies (cardigans) [etc.]. **1989** *Pacific Way* Jan. 10 One feature of New Zealand speech that is often commented on by visitors is our inordinate fondness for abbreviations which end in 'ie' or 'y'. *Ibid.* 11 In summer we buy aerosols to ward off the mossies and blowies. **1991** Duff *One Night Out Stealing* 32 Man, them possies're sure suckers for death. Hedgies, though, ya gotta watch for the hedgehogs their prickles don't puncture your tyre. *Ibid.* 110 She might be funny, but weren't no-one gonna step in bat for her, not a tranny [transvestite]. **1995** *Dominion* (Wellington) 27 May 23 The cameras stuck like glue to [America's Cup yachtsmen] Blakie and Couttsie (one gives our sporting heroes an -ie at the end of the name when they reach Olympian heights).

2. Examples recorded include:
air hostie, an air hostess.
Aussie, Australia; an Australian.
bantie, a bantam.
blightie, a blightbird.
brickie, a bricklayer.
carbie, a carburettor.
cardie, a cardigan.
cashie, a used car bought and sold for cash.
chaffie, one on the chaff-hole of a chaffcutter.
chalkie, *obs.*, a Stock Exchange employee who, before computerization, chalked up price changes.
clubbie, a surf life-saving club member.
crookie, a bad or broken person or thing.
cuzzy, a cousin.
diffy, a differential.
dredgie, a dredge-worker.
droppie, a dropped goal.
dustie, a rubbishman.
Dutchie, a Dutch person.
flattie, a flat tire.
fleecy/fleecie, a fleece-picker.
folkie, folksinger.
fundie, a (religious) fundamentalist.
goldie, a goldfinch.
googie, (*obs.*) an egg.
greenie, a conservationist.
gummy, **gummie**, a gumboot.
hatchie, a hatchman.
homey, a person from England.
hoppy, hopscotch (children's).
horsie, horse mackerel.
hottie, a 'hotshot', expert.
humpie, a humpback whale.
jointie, a sideshow worker.
kelpie, a kelp-fish.
leggie, a leg break.
lippy, lipstick.
littlie, a small child (?poss. f. Sc. dial.).
loosie, a loose (rugby) forward.
milkie, an opaque, milky marble.
mullety, a mullet boat.
parrie, a paradise duck.
pinnie, a pinball machine.
planny, a plantation (children's).
probie, a probation officer.
pulpie, a pulp-and-paper worker.
rellie, a relative.
ridie, a sideshow worker.
ringie, a ring-keeper (two-up).
roadie, a roadman; a road-service operator.
roughie, a wild-mannered cattle beast; a rough sheep.
roughy, a rough-mannered person.
sammie, a sandwich.
shortie, an undersized crayfish.

shottie, a shotgun.
shrewdie, a shrewd person.
sickie, (a period of) sick-leave.
slittie, a slit-trench.
soapie, a soap-opera.
soddie, sod cottage.
spacies, space-invader arcade games.
sparkie, an electrician.
sparklie, a sparkling marble.
speccie, a specification.
spoonie, a spoonbill.
stackie, a stackman (on haystack work).
steamie, a steam engine.
steelie, a steel ball-bearing marble.
Steinie, a bottle of Steinlager beer.
stiffie, an erection.
stinkie, an unfavoured marble.
stockie, a stock bowler (cricket); a stock-car owner or driver.
subbie, a sub-contractor.
sunnies, sunglasses.
swaggie, a swagger.
swampie, a swamp-hen (pukeko).
swiftie, a shrewd play or ploy.
swordie, a swordfish.
tankie, a member of a military tank group.
towie, a tow-truck operator.
trammie, a tram-car driver or conductor.
truckie, a truck driver.
Vinnie, a member of the St Vincent De Paul Society.
Westie, one from the western suburbs of Auckland.
wettie, a wet suit.
windie, a wind-surfer.
yachtie, a yachtsman.
zeddy, a Z-class sailing boat..

ignimbrite. [f. Latin *ign*(is fire + *imber* shower (of rain, etc.) + *-ite* (a mineral-name formant): a name introduced in 1932 by a geologist, Patrick Marshall, for rocks widespread in the Taupo Volcanic Zone, and now used world-wide: cf. OED.] A rock formed from fragmented fast-flowing volcanic lava whose incompletely solidified fragments may weld together when it comes to rest. See also WILSONITE.
[*Note*] Formerly called *welded tuff*, incorrectly, as tuff is by definition water-laid.
1932 *NZJST* XIII. 200 (P. Marshall) The type of rocks formed in this way varies greatly, but it is suggested that they should all be included in a separate group, for which the name Ignimbrite seems satisfactory. **1951** *NZ Geogr.* Oct. VII. 77 In New Zealand it was he [Patrick Marshall] who proposed the name 'ignimbrite' for the rhyolitic welded tuffs so characteristic of the Volcanic Plateau. **1993** *Evening Post* (Wellington) 5 Apr. 13 The ground floor [of the Rotorua thermal area] is mainly made up of ignimbrite, a rock peculiar to New Zealand. A specific type of volcanic matter..it leaves veins of iron oxide scoring the ground like pink and orange streamers.

ihe. Also **heihe** (=he ihe), **ihi**. [Ma. /ˈihe/: Williams 74 *Ihe*... the garfish.] GARFISH.
1844 COLENSO *Excurs. Northern Is.* in Taylor *Early Travellers* (1959) 55 Here [near Bay of Islands, the natives] call them [*sc.* garfish] Takeke; but among the southern tribes, Ihe. **1855** TAYLOR *Te Ika A Maui* 626 *Hemiramphus marginatus*, guard-fish, *heihe*, remarkable from its having a projection of the lower jaw one fifth of its entire length, which is from eight to ten inches. **1886**, **1960**, **1982** [see GARFISH].

ihi, varr. HIHI (STITCH-BIRD); IHE.

illegal tegel /-ˈtigəl/. [f. a rhyming play on *Tegel* a registered proprietary name for a brand of dressed poultry.] Any protected or restricted bird taken illegally for food.
1972 *Forest & Bird* 185 7 To add insult to injury, it is the boast of many Chatham Islanders that 'illegal tegels' (their phrase for the slaughtered albatrosses) have been served to all visiting dignitaries over recent years (no doubt unbeknown to some). It is to be hoped that the nickname does not become an epitaph. **1980** GLEN *Bush in Our Yard* 85 Commenting on the large number of native wood pigeons about the area, Viv laughingly called them '[il]legal Tegel', and in the next breath reminded me of the fine for taking one. **1989** PARKINSON *Travelling Naturalist* 28 The kereru is sometimes called kuku in the north and sometimes by the name 'illegal Tegel'.

immigrant. See also EMIGRANT.
1. a. A person, often a member of a managed immigration scheme, who migrates to New Zealand as an intending settler. Often *attrib*. See also *assisted-immigrant* (ASSISTED), and the fanciful rhyming variant JIMMYGRANT.
[*Note*] Since c1980 the word *migrant* has tended to replace *immigrant*.
1844 MONRO *Notes of Journey* in Hocken *Contributions* (1898) 231 The New Zealand Company was..on the point of landing a large body of immigrants on a part of New Zealand, with regard to the nature..of which neither it nor any of its agents had anything like accurate information. **1853** DEANS *Pioneers* (1964) 85 Seeing the great attraction to emigrants that the [Australian] gold fields hold out, and that we have now no funds for immigrants, I am afraid that we will soon suffer for want of labour. **1867** BARKER *Station Life* (1870) 110 When..the better class of immigrant arrives with a little capital, the favourite investment is in freehold land. **1877** *TrNZI* IX. 43 Though intensely interesting are all questions connected with the immigrant; of equal, if not greater interest are those concerning their offspring. **1883** *Ibid.* XV. 499 When gout does appear it is always in the person of the immigrant. **1900** *Canterbury Old & New* 134 Some of these were free immigrants, some were assisted, and some paid their own passages. **1920** *NZ Free Lance* (Wellington) Dec. 18 The newly-arrived male immigrant is a familiar sight in Wellington these days..noticeable at once by his tweed cap, soft collar, turned-up trouser hem, the thick soles of his boots and the apple-red of his cheeks. **1953** *NZ Herald* (Auckland) 12 Oct. 8 The Dutch plane brought 64 immigrants, who received a great reception from hundreds of Dutch settlers. **1963** NORRIS *Armed Settlers* 211 The immigrant officer [c1870s] sent the immigrants up country [from Auckland] in batches. **1972** MITCHELL *Pavlova Paradise* 177 The soprano section of the chorus of complaint is manned almost entirely by disgruntled immigrants. **1980** HALL *Prisoners of Mother England* v I'd always looked on immigrants as a bunch of whinging Poms, but now I realise we treated them like shit! **1992** SCHOUTEN *Tasman's Legacy* 120 Not all immigrants settled. Some never got over their homesickness, while others suffered marital problems.

b. Applied to a Polynesian founding migrant.
1924 LYSNAR *NZ* 69 There is a plant the Maoris call 'Tainui'. It is interesting because of its association with a tradition that a specimen in the North Island sprang from a green timber used in the building of the 'Tainui', a canoe which brought some of the Maori immigrants to New Zealand between five and six hundred years ago.

2. Special Comb. immigrant (immigrants) barracks, temporary quarters or communal housing for newly-arrived immigrants (see also BARRACKS 1, *emigration barracks* (EMIGRATION 2); **immigrant ship,** one bringing immigrants to New Zealand.
1914 in *Hist. N. Otago from 1853* (1978) 48 In the autumn of 1874..Mr M. Grenfell was busy..erecting the **Immigrants Barracks** for the Government [for imported railway workers]. **1940** HOWARD *Rakiura* 317 In 1884, Mr. T. Kirk..examined the immigrant barracks mouldering to ruin at Port William. **1898** MEREDITH *Reminisc. & Experiences* 14 I think the fifth **immigrant ship** had just arrived, and most of the immigrants were clustered about the shore of Lyttelton Harbour. **1980** HALL *Prisoners of Mother England* iv I arrived in Wellington in April 1958 after a six-week [holiday on an] immigrant ship, the 'Captain Cook'. **1983** FRANCIS *Wildlife Ranger* 1 These two distinct groups and the conventional paying passengers made up the passenger list of many immigrant ships sailing to the Antipodes [in the 1920s].

immigration. See also EMIGRATION.
1. The action or process of coming to New Zealand as an intending settler. Often *attrib*.
1861 *NZ Goldfields 1861* 20 Sept. (1976) 31 The largely increasing immigration to this province from adjacent colonies..makes it imperative on the part of the Government..to come forward with an authoritative declaration. **1875** *Official Handbook NZ* 76 As it was found..that the required money payments seriously checked the flow of a very desirable class of immigration, the Government decided upon making immigration absolutely free. **1889** MITCHELL *Rhymes & Rambles* 39 He'll vote against free immigration, Look after land sharks in the north, Break up every sheep run and Station. **1938** HYDE *Nor Yrs. Condemn* 117 This joined effect with the immigration schemes, particularly those which were determined to keep New Zealand middle-class. **1952** *Dominion* (Wellington) 10 Oct. 6 The Association may have done the Government an injustice by reading into the recently announced cut..a Government intention to make a major departure from the established immigration policy. **1963** NORRIS *Armed Settlers* 210 The policy of immigration and public works, originating from Julius Vogel in 1870, was popular and began to help the town and district to recover quickly from the slump. **1980** HALL *Prisoners of Mother England* iv Certainly immigration itself has fascinated me for a long time, not only immigration to New Zealand but to countries such as USA and Australia. **1992** SCHOUTEN *Tasman's Legacy* 140 A senior immigration official came out to the ship on a pilot boat.

2. Special Comb. Immigration Agent *hist.*, one employed by the NZ Company to assist in its immigration schemes; **immigration barrack** *hist., emigration barracks* (EMIGRATION 2), see also BARRACKS; **Immigration Commissioner** *hist.*, a public official with responsibilities for immigration.
1849 in Cutten *Cutten Lett.* (1979) 34 Owing to the pressure of business as **Immigration Agent** to the N.Z.C..I have been unable to examine the goods with the invoice. **1898** HOCKEN *Contributions* 161 Mr. Allan had charge of the Port Chalmers School, and upon his retirement..was appointed Immigration Agent. **1848** WAKEFIELD *Handbook NZ* 271 The Company's **Immigration Barracks,** excellently adapted for soldiers, [was] built [in Nelson] round three sides of a square. **1851** *Lyttelton Times* 5 Apr. 5 The immigration barracks which have been thoroughly cleaned and whitewashed for their occupation are again filled. **1951** CRESSWELL *Canterbury Tales* 23 By then there were the best part of a thousand people in Port, some in the immigration barracks, some camping out of doors.

IMPROVE

1976 HOLCROFT *Old Invercargill* 70 [Caption] This building in Tay Street [Invercargill] was at first a storehouse... It became the town's immigration barracks after the original barracks..were demolished in 1875; and in 1891 it housed the Fire Brigade. 1988 SOMERSET *Sunshine & Shadow* 139 In the early days of the Canterbury settlement all foreigners or any persons with an odd sounding name were sent to the immigration barracks at Carlton near Oxford. 1861 *NZ Goldfields 1861* 20 Sept. (1976) 5 Her decks were cleared, to allow for a search for stowaways, and of those other processes known to Custom-house officers and **immigration commissioners**.

improve, *v.* [Spec. use of (US and archaic English) *improve* to bring land into cultivation: see OED *v.*² 2. b; AND 1834.] *trans.* and *intr.* To increase the value of (land) by clearing, cultivation, fencing, building, etc.

1875 *Southland Times* July in Howard *Rakiura* (1940) 309 Here have I been for years squatting on a bit of land I can't get surveyed, and don't care to fence and improve. 1899 BELL *In Shadow of Bush* 19 A plantation of pines and macrocarpa had already attained forward growth, and showed that this farm must have been one of the first in the locality to be cleared and improved. 1905 THOMSON *Bush Boys* 71 Some hundred acres of the bush..had been felled, burned, and stumped... Another hundred acres or more had been 'improved' into the condition of a 'log clearing'. 1916 STALLWORTHY *Early N. Wairoa* 39 Mr. H.T. Smith, an enterprising bush contractor, purchased and improved land at Arapohue. 1981 CRAWFORD *Station Years* 245 Some protection for runholders was essential, for they could not be expected to improve their runs if the land and improvements were in danger of being freeholded without warning by an outside buyer.

Hence **improved** *ppl. a.*, of land, made more valuable by clearing, fencing, etc. Contrast UNIMPROVED *ppl. a.*

1882 POTTS *Out in Open* 42 As they [sc. quail-hawks] approach the confines of cultivation and improved lands, a large proportion of them are shot. 1893 CHUDLEIGH *Diary* 28 Feb. (1950) 383 The fern and manuka is [sic] covering up the improved land. 1933 SCANLAN *Tides of Youth* 41 I can't afford to buy improved land, so I must take up a block of bush, and..clear it. 1986 RICHARDS *Off the Sheep's Back* 64 The farm was poor and only partially improved, the majority being in its original state of scrubby tea tree.

improve, *n.* [AND 1959.] In the phr. **on the improve**, improving in health, wealth, efficiency, etc.; 'on the mend'.

1906 Cox Diaries 1888–1925 7 Sept. I think my cold is on the improve now. 1995 Rugby league commentator 15 July The team's on the improve.

improvement. [US: see OED 2.] Often *pl.* Those items of permanent value added to land through clearing, cultivation, pasture and soil management, the erection of buildings, fences, etc.

1841 DEANS *Letter* in Deans *Pioneers Canterbury* (1937) 33 Mr Molesworth let a town acre of his for £240..for 14 years, buildings and improvements to remain at the end of the lease. 1856 FITTON *NZ* 223 The necessary building for the residence of the stock-owner..together with the garden, paddocks, &c., and the sheds for shearing and preparing the wool, are all included in the sale of a run under the general name of 'Improvements'. 1861 *Butler to Tripp* 13 Oct. in Maling *Samuel Butler* (1960) 56 I said the improvements [sc. an unfinished hut] are not worth mentioning, you may have the lot & section for £40 cash. 1891 WALLACE *Rural Econ. Austral. & NZ* xv 225 Many [New Zealand] settlers naturally prefer the lease, as..it leaves a settler free to to invest his capital in improvements. 1902 *Settler's Handbook NZ* 67 Every lessee must, within one year from the date of his lease, put on substantial improvements to a value equal to 10 per cent. of the price of the land. 1912 *NZJAg.* Jan. IV. 475 But when the £100 spent in repairing and renewing rabbit-proof fences is considered as improvements to the property the total account should only be debited with £241. 1930 ACLAND *Early Canterbury Runs* 180 The Studholmes had the Terrace station... When they sold it about 1862..the only improvements on it were a shepherd's hut and a set of sheep yards. 1949 REED *Story Canterbury* 128 The pre-emptive right of purchase of fifty acres around any improvement..led to abuses. 1963 WALLIS *Point of Origin* 11 All the money Dad had set aside for improvements and stock went down the drain. 1981 [see IMPROVE *v.*].

imshi /ˈɪmʃi/. Mainly *WW1*. Also **imisi, imshee**. [f. colloq. Egyptian Arabic.] Go away!

1916 'Men of Anzac' in *Anzac Bk.* 135 Imshee is the Arabic for 'go away'. The Australasian Corps, which had so far employed it only to street hawkers in Cairo, used this war cry on April 25. 1917 THORNTON *With the Anzacs in Cairo* 32 'Too much; *imshi*' (go away). 1918 *Chron. NZEF* 8 Nov. 175 Van Oomptenburg..has to impshee rapidly nowadays from a country..he was willing to wager..he was forever in full possession of. 1919 *Quick March* 10 July 33 'Igri wallah, imshi Y'allah.' Jackos, jackals, 'gala gala'. 1942 *NZEF Times* 15 June 6 He'd better buzz off, waddle, imshi or fly. *Ibid.* 15 Feb. 6 Anyway, he's imshied. 1953 16 M A32 Thames DHS 6 Imshi 1990 DAWBER *Floods, Slips, and Washouts* 54 I also learnt a few words of Arabic, just enough to bargain a bit in the bazaars. I still remember some of the words most commonly used, like..'imisi yalla', 'go away', or 'clear out'.

in. In the phr. **(to) be in**.

1. With prepositional function. [Poss. a shortened form of *be in to win*, or *be in for one's chop* (i.e. 'share'), or *be in on* (an understanding, secret), to be privy to, to be an active participant in: cf. OED *in prep.* 11, 28.] **a.** Often as an exclam. (also heard as **be in to win**), expressing an intention or invitation to participate in an activity, etc.

1941 *Evening Post* (Wellington) 16 Nov. 6 Temptation was placed in their way and they decided, to use a colloquialism, to 'be in' [sc. on a two-up school]. 1946 SARGESON *That Summer* 85 We got Maggie to come and be in as well [sc. on a party]. 1959 SLATTER *Gun in My Hand* 90 One for Herbie... Be in, it's ya birthday Herbie. 1960 HILLIARD *Maori Girl* 73 'The old girl just brought in the famous tray,' the girl said. 'Come on, you better be in or the rest of them'll clean it up.' 1981 HOOPER *Goat Paddock* 19 'Yeah, I'll come,' I said casually. 'Might as well be in.'

b. To pay one's full share of a round of drinks.

1948 *NZ Geogr.* 166 Drinking on the West Coast has an etiquette of its own... 'Be in or be out', you will be told, is the motto on the Coast.

2. With adverbial function. [See OED *in adv.* 6 j, Sc. and NZ.] Of a school, with teachers and pupils present and classes in progress.

1949 SARGESON *I Saw in My Dream* 40 But I don't remember nothing about when school was in. 1989 *Sunday Star* (Auckland) 16 July C3 [Heading] School's In.

inacke, var. HINAKI.

ina-ina, var. HINAHINA.

INANGA

inaka, var. INANGA.

inanga /ˈɪnʌŋ(g)ə/, /ɪnˈnʌŋə/, *n.*¹ Also **enaki** (occas.), **inaka** (freq.), SI forms from Ngai Tahu Ma. dial.; **hinanga, inonga, inunga**. [Ma. /ˈi(ː)naŋa, ˈinaka/: Williams 77 *Inaka*. [=] *inanga*. ([Ngai] Tahu.); *Īnanga, inanga* n. *1* . Whitebait.] *Galaxias maculatus* (fam. Galaxiidae), a small slender-bodied freshwater fish, the adult of the common whitebait; also the young of the smelt, *Retropinna retropinna*. See also COWFISH, GALAXIAS, WHITEBAIT.

1843 SELWYN *Journal* in *NZ Part II* (Church in the Colonies VII) 30 Oct. (1845) 33 Here we found the natives engaged in cooking white fish (Inanga), a small fish the size of a minnow, caught in great abundance in Taupo and Rotorua Lakes. 1845 WAKEFIELD *Adventure NZ* II. 100 This fish is called *hinanga* [sic], and resembles Blackwall white-bait in size and flavour. Its colour is a pinkish white, spotted with black. 1851 *Lyttelton Times* 5 July 7 The young of the enaki, very much like the white-bait, are a delicacy, and much prized by the natives. 1859 ROCHFORT *Jrnl. Two Expeds.* 301 The inonga or whitebait. 1867 [see WHITEBAIT 1]. 1872 HUTTON & HECTOR *Fishes NZ* 129 At Taupo Lake and other places in the interior small fish which the Maoris collectively term Inanga, but which are chiefly of the species now referred to [*Galaxias*], form the food of the natives for many months in the year. 1881 NESFIELD *Chequered Career* 34 There is a wretched little fish called the Inunga..that is generally found in small creeks. 1899 *TrNZI* XXXI. 79 I have frequently, and at several places, seen large shoals of the 'inanga' at sea. 1906 *Truth* 17 Mar. 1 He used to fish for inungas with a bent pin. 1922 *Auckland Weekly News* 22 July 17 The water was alive with shoals of small fish, three or four inches long—the inaka of the Maoris. 1930 *NZ Fishing & Shooting Gaz.* 1 Feb. 10 The large size inanga, smelt or silvery make a delicious table fish (with a cucumber smell and flavour). The natives used to net large numbers, and early settlers often netted quantities and preserved them in bottles with weak vinegar and cloves. 1943 MANNERING *Eighty Years NZ* 158 Maori names for these indigenous fish are interesting—whitebait is 'inanga tutuna'—that is round like an eel. Smelt is 'inanga papa'—flat-sided like a smelt. 1968 GRUNDY *Who'd Marry a Doctor?* 51 Floured and fried in boiling fat, inanga was a delicious treat, with a flavour all its own. In appearance inanga resembled a sardine. 1986 PAUL *NZ Fishes* 48 Inanga are shoaling fishes, usually found in pools, backwaters, swamps and lagoons a short distance inland from direct tidal influence, as well as in tidal estuaries. 1990 MCDOWALL *NZ Freshwater Fishes* 123 Because of the milkiness of the milt and the way it discolours the water,.. the adult inanga are sometimes called cowfish.

inanga, *n.*² Also **enak(i)** (occas.), **inaka** (freq.), SI forms from Ngai Tahu Ma. dial. [Ma. /ˈi(ː)naŋa, ˈinaka/: Williams 77 *Inaka*. [=] *inanga* ([Ngai] Tahu); *Īnanga, inanga* n... *3. Dracophyllum longifolium*, grass tree.] *Dracophyllum longifolium* (includes *D. filifolium*) (fam. Epacridaceae), a shrub or small tree. See also DRACOPHYLLUM, GRASS-TREE 2, HEATH 2, TURPENTINE 2. **a.** As **inaka**, the form commonly used in the South Island.

[c1826–27 BOULTBEE *Journal* (1986) 110 oak—enak]. 1870 *TrNZI* II. 177 There is no Rata [on Campbell Island], and the Enaki is of a smaller and finer species than that of the Aucklands, and bears a small white bell-shaped flower, with a strong perfume, as of hawthorn. 1889 KIRK *Forest Flora* 215 Mr. Traill informs me that [*Dracophyllum longifolium*] is termed 'inaka' by the Maoris on Stewart island: it is one of several trees termed 'grass-tree' by the settlers in the South Island. **1892** CARRICK *NZ's Lone Lands* 23 The inaka—so named by the Maoris but known amongst the settlers of southern New Zealand as the grass-tree—likewise grows abundantly, near the sea, in both [Auckland and Campbell] islands. It is not an uncommon tree in..the Middle Island of New Zealand. **1919** COCKAYNE *NZ Plants & Their Story* 41 In similar situations the inaka..and the mountain-flax..are common. **1964** DEMPSEY *Little World Stewart Is.* 24 The vegetation there is mainly manuka, koromiko and the short-leaved inaka, the grass-tree. **1982** WILSON *Stewart Is. Plants* 80 *Dracophyllum longifolium* Inaka..Turpentine scrub... Erect shrub or small tree.

b. As **inanga**, the form commonly used in the North Island.

1906 CHEESEMAN *Manual NZ Flora* 423 *D[racophyllum] longifolium*... Very variable in stature,.. a shrub from 4 to 8 ft. high,... a small tree 12 to 25 ft... *Inanga; Grass-tree*. **1940** LAING & BLACKWELL *Plants NZ* 351 *Dracophyllum longifolium* (*The Long-leaved Grass-tree*). A shrub or tree, 3 ft.–30 ft. high..Maori name, *Inanga*. **1961** MARTIN *Flora NZ* 192 The Grass-tree or Inanga..is yet another species of Dracophyllum. **1978** MOORE & IRWIN *Oxford Book NZ Plants* 114 *Dracophyllum filifolium* is one of the group of 'grass trees' or needle-leaved species with few-flowered racemes..known generally as 'inanga' in the north, 'inaka' in the south, and 'turpentine bush' to those who use the twigs to make a quick fire.

inanga, *n.*[3] Also **inaka.** [Ma. /'i(:)naŋa/: Williams 77 *Īnanga, inanga*..2. A whitish variety of greenstone.] A pale variety of GREENSTONE q.v.

1915 ROBLEY *Pounamu* 16 *Auhunga* is slightly paler than *kawakawa*. *Inanga* has a colour paler still, so that in parts it approaches grey or creamy white. **c1920** BEATTIE *Trad. Lifeways Southern Maori* (1994) 522 Inanga, inaka, or ina' (as it was sometimes called shortly in hurried pronunciation) was a whitish-coloured greenstone and was regarded as the best of the lot. **1932** ELDER in Marsden *Lett. & Jrnls.* (1932) 432 One of these [lighter] varieties [of greenstone] resembled in shade and translucency the fish called whitebait, and was in consequence called *inanga*. **1946** ZIMMERMAN *Where People Sing* 149 Each variety has its own Maori name, but the two most prized are *inanga*, which is heavily flecked with white, and *tangiwai*, the deep, clear kind. **1972** BAXTER *Collected Poems* (1980) 537 To you my love is a pendant Of inanga greenstone.

incorporation. Often with init. cap. [Spec. use of *incorporation* from *incorporate* to form into a legal corporation.] A legal method of consolidating the customary titles of the numerous Maori owners of a block of land into one legal title; esp. as **land incorporation**, the corporate entity resulting from such a consolidation.

1909 *NZ Statutes* No.15 234 [Native Land Act] When two or more areas of Native freehold land each of which is owned in manner aforesaid by more than five owners (whether the owners are the same or different persons), and are so situated as to form a single continuous area, the Court may make a single order of incorporation in respect of the whole or part of that continuous area. *Ibid.* No.15 235 On an order of the incorporation being made..the legal owners of the land..shall become a body corporate with perpetual succession under the named of 'The Proprietors of [Naming the land in accordance with the order of incorporation].' **1953** *NZ Statutes* II. 1196 [Maori Affairs Act, s.269] When any area of Maori freehold land is owned for a legal estate in fee simple by more than three persons as tenants in common thereof..those owners may be incorporated by an order of incorporation made by the Court in accordance with the following provisions of this Act... An order of incorporation may be made to enable the body corporate of owners established thereby: (a) To occupy and manage as far as the land or any portion of the land proposed to be vested in the body corporate, and to carry on any agricultural or pastoral business thereon: (b) To use the land or any part thereof for the growing of timber. **1982** *Dominion* (Wellington) 17 Feb. 9 Incorporations are almost a Maori concept. They do away with the individualisation of land... Incorporations give people their own turangawaewae. They bring people together—keep alive with whakapapa, the blood-lines, the stories about people, the language. **1987** *National Bus. Rev.* 30 Jan. 1 Representatives of Maori land incorporations which have land leased to the forest service are understood to be studying their options on land that is to be transferred..on April 1.

Indian, *n.* and *a. Obs.* [Prob. an application of the name *Indian* American Indian; Cook and his company also applied the name to Tierra del Fuegans and Australian Aborigines.]

A. *n.* An early European term for a Maori. Cf. NEW ZEALANDER 1, SQUAW.

1769 COOK *Journals* 9 Oct. (1955) I. 168 Seeing some of the natives on the other side of the river..I order'd the yaul in... In the mean time the Indians made off. **1770** PARKINSON *Journal* 8 Feb. (1773) 119 We observed a great difference betwixt the inhabitants on this side of the land, north of Cook's Straits, and those of the south... The latter..seem to want the spirit or sprightliness of the northern Indians. **1791** *Jrnl. 'Chatham'* 22 Nov. in McNab *Hist. Records* (1914) II. 499 When Captain Cook was here he only saw three families of Indians.

B. *adj.* MAORI B 1 a.

1769 COOK *Journals* 19 Oct. (1955) I. 181 At 7 AM brought too under Cape Table and set away the Indian Canoe. **1777** EDGAR *Log 'Discovery'* 12 Feb. in McNab *Hist. Records* (1914) II. 225 The Country about Charlotte Sound abounds in Hills..& these Hills exceedingly difficult of access except by Indian Paths of which there are very few. **1817** NICHOLAS *Voyage NZ* I. 113 The singular prospect of an Indian village, and of natives paddling to the ship in their canoes. **1836** *Log 'Mary Mitchell'* 28 Apr. in McNab *Old Whaling Days* (1908) 436 Indian Cunning was plainly to be seen and as far as regards White men I fear their honesty will prove Something Equivocal.

informal. Applied to a vote or voting paper not executed in correct form, hence invalid or spoilt, esp. as **informal vote**, a vote rejected because of a formal error made by the voter in registering the vote.

1890 *Otago Witness* (Dunedin) 11 Dec. 16 Majority for Dawson 419. Informal votes, 18. **1899** *Hawera & Normanby Star* 15 Sept. 2 Municipal Elections... W. Adamson 120, E. Fake 115, A.C. Atkinson 109... Informal 7. **1935** *NZ Free Lance* (Wellington) 11 Dec. 68 Number of votes rejected as informal... 213. **1957** *Wanganui Herald* 2 Dec. 5 [Tabulation] Cotterill 6121 Mrs Maclean 4262 Marks 3167 There were 39 informal votes on the preliminary count. **1990** *Victoria University of Wellington Council Elections Statute 1990* in *Calendar* (1993) 604 (c) all informal voting papers shall be rejected. 23. *Informal votes* A voting paper will be rejected as informal—(a) if..[there follows a list of conditions]. **1991** ELDRED-GRIGG *Shining City* 12 'Two votes for Ash. One vote for me... One informal vote,' she said.

ini-ini, var. HINAHINA.

ink. *Obs.* Rhyming slang for 'drink'; liquor, 'booze'. Contrast *good ink* (GOOD *a.* 2 c).

1909 *Truth* 11 Dec. 7 Alfred drifted to the hall of the Thespians 'full of ink'..and started to interpolate gratuitous and unnecessary remarks into the play. **1911** *Ibid.* 1 Apr. 6 Lawyer Hoban, for the two accused, who were charged with supplying 'ink' to infants, emphasised the liability of a barman being deceived by the elderly influence of the Uniform, and mentioned that many of our police officers..might be mistaken for schoolboys. **1912** *Poem* in Scott *Seven Lives on Salt River* (1987) 55 When full of ink, to walk unable, Don't hesitate but try the stable.

Hence **inked**, **inky** *a.* [AND 1898], tipsy, drunk.

1909 *Truth* 11 Dec. 1 He made quite a stir by alleging that a man who wanted to see Harding's footballers play in Masterton was much 'inked'. **1910** *Truth* 30 July 7 He was going by train to Palmerston, being decently inky at the time, & happened to ask one of the passengers if he knew the family with whom his wife was living. **1921** LORD *Ballads of Bung 'Stunology'* 10 Again 'inebriated', 'inked', and, ah, 'intoxicated' too Mean quite the same as 'jamboreed'.

inkberry. BLUEBERRY (*Dianella nigra*).

1970 MOORE & EDGAR *Flora NZ* II. 41 N[orth], S. [Islands] Forest floor, banks and track edges. *Turutu*; *blue-berry; ink-berry*. **1978** MOORE & IRWIN *Oxford Book NZ Plants* 182 *Dianella nigra*. Turutu, blueberry, inkberry, or whistles thrives in lowland scrub, on clay banks, and along bush tracks... Shining berries, ranging from palest grey to almost purple, or clean blue and white like old china, ripen in great numbers but they drop at a touch. **1990** WEBB et al. *Flowering Plants NZ* 124 Our only native is *D[ianella] nigra*, inkberry or turutu, found under dry forest or scrub, but sometimes in swampy ground... The berries are obvious, violet-blue and glossy with inky juice. *Ibid.* 125 The inky berries fall off readily when ripe, and are eaten by birds.

ink-plant.

1. *Obs.* TUTU 1 a.

1898 MORRIS *Austral-English* 211 Ink-plant, *n*. another name for the 'toot,' a New Zealand shrub... Called Ink-plant on account of its juice, which soon turns to black. There is also an European Ink-plant, *Coriaria myrtifolia*, so that this is only a different species.

2. Also **red ink plant**. INKWEED.

1906 CHEESEMAN *Manual NZ Flora* 1085 *Phytolacca octandra*... Ink-plant; Poke-weed. **1926** [see INKWEED]. **1969** *Standard Common Names Weeds* 63 *red ink plant* [=] *inkweed* [*Phytolacca octandra*].

inkweed. Also **pheasant weed** (see quots. 1926, 1969). *Phytolacca* sp., an introduced perennial herb having black berries containing a reddish juice. See also *red ink plant* (INK-PLANT 2).

1913 *NZJAg.* Oct. VII. 369 Inkweed, or pokeweed (*Phytolacca octandra*), is a poisonous plant. **1924** *NZJST* VII. 187 There [is] also..an alien plant, *Phytolacca octandra*, the 'inkweed' of the settlers. **1926** HILGENDORF *Weeds* 70 Inkweed (*Phytolacca octandra*) is also called poke weed, red ink plant, and pheasant weed. It is found on waste land and new pastures from Wanganui northwards, but is commonest in Auckland. **1951** LEVY *Grasslands NZ* (1970) 4 Many introduced weeds typical of subtropical climates are present, the more common ones being wild portulaca, inkweed, redroot, thorn apple. **1969** *Standard Common Names Weeds* 40 *inkweed* [=] *pokeweed... Phytolacca octandra*. **1981** TAYLOR *Weeds of Roadsides* 73 Inkweed (*Phytolacca octandra*)... In late autumn purple berries..capable of staining strongly... This Central American plant is distributed accordingly to its limited tolerance to frost.

inky: see INK.

inland pohutukawa: see POHUTUKAWA 2 (1).

inner, *n*. Two-up. An 'in-better'; see entry for OUTER *n*. 1.

insignis: see PINE 4.

Inspector of Sheep: see *Sheep Inspector* (SHEEP 2).

instant kiwi. [A var. of *Golden Kiwi* (GOLDEN 2) the name of a national lottery.] A lottery in which a winner uncovers the amount of any cash prize by scratching or rubbing off the removable surface of a lottery ticket. See also SCRATCHIE.
  1989 *New Zealandia* Nov. 3 The schoolgirls are flocking to the corner store to scratch away at the Instant Kiwis. **1990** *Dominion* (Wellington) 19 Sept. 3 He had spent the whole of his benefit on 'scratchies' like Instant Kiwi, the first week they were available, 'but he hasn't bought one since'.

integrate. [Transf. use of US *integrate v.*, *integrated* with reference to schools having multi-racial rolls.] Of an independent (non-State) school, to become part of the State system of education.
  1969 *Labour Party Manifesto* Labour would encourage any independent schools that wish to integrate themselves into the State system and would safeguard salaries and conditions of any teachers at these schools. **1990** *Dominion* (Wellington) 20 May 3 The schools—formerly private schools, mainly Catholic, which have been integrated into the state system—are being granted roll increases while state schools rolls are falling.

  Hence **integration**, the process of integrating non-State schools into the State education system; **integrated school**, a non-State school which has become part of the State system.
  1975 *Private Schools Conditional Integration Act* [Title] **1989** *Dominion* (Wellington) 26 Aug. 11 His school turned around its falling rolls by becoming one of the first integrated schools.

intercolonial, *a. Obs.* Applied to shipping, trade, etc., plying, conducted, etc. between the Australian colonies or states and New Zealand.
  1904 LANCASTER *Sons o' Men* 1 He knew very well that the thread of mouse-colour sighted seaward..was cast by the smoke of a passing inter-colonial boat.

interior. *Obs.* In early use, esp. of the North Island, the New Zealand hinterland away from the coast.
  1815 *Deeds ceding land to Missionaries* 24 Feb. in Nicholas *NZ* (1817) II. 194 All that piece and parcel of land situate in the district of Hoshee, in the Island of New Zealand, bounded on the south side by the bay of Tippoona.., on the north side by a creek of fresh water, and on the west by a public road into the interior. **1830** MARSDEN *Lett. & Jrnls.* (1932) 491 On asking Mrs. Hamlin who she [a young native girl] was, she informed me that she came out of the interior and had formerly lived with her. **1851** *Richmond-Atkinson Papers* (1960) I. 83 We purchased a supply of potatoes with a few figs of tobacco which is the current coin in the interior. **1872** HUTTON & HECTOR *Fishes NZ* 129 At Taupo Lake and other places in the interior small fish which the Maoris collectively term Inanga..form the food of the natives for many months in the year. **1874** KENNAWAY *Crusts* 83 As the value of back runs began to be proved, explorers pushed back in greater numbers into the interior to look for them. **1889** *TrNZI* XXI. 32 In those good old times the interior was occupied, they say, by Turehu or Patupaiarehe, a race short in stature and of fair skin. **1898** HOCKEN *Contributions* 55 It was upon this expedition that the first information was given by the natives of the existence in the interior of certain animals, concluded from the description to be beavers. **1948** COWAN *Down the Yrs. in the Maniototo* 2 The term Central Otago, which some fifty years ago referred only to the limited area of the Maniototo Plain..now embraces also the much greater mountainous area beyond the Dunstan Range, which formerly was known vaguely as 'the interior'. **1974** MULDOON *Rise & Fall of a Young Turk* 56 The old railway from Nelson into the interior..had been closed by the Holland Government. **1986** BELICH *NZ Wars* 29 The basic pattern of military operations..was a series of British forays into the hilly and bush-clad interior.

interisland, *a.*

1. Existing or conducted between the North and South Islands.
  1929 *Tararua Tramper* July 3 An old Maori burial ground.., the point where the inter-Island [*sic*] cable is supposed to touch the North Island..were all viewed. **1983** MANTELL *Murder to Burn* 84 Elsewhere [in Wellington Harbour]..the inter-island scow made its weekly trip to Petone wharf. **1983** MCINTYRE & FIELD *Cook's Wild Strait: The Interisland Story* [Title].

2. In special collocations: **interisland ferry**, a ferry, or ferry-service, plying between the North and South Islands; **interisland match**, a sporting contest between teams (usu. rugby union) representative of the North and South Islands (first contest 1897).
  1966 TURNER *Eng. Lang. Austral. & NZ* 136 A young English woman who had just arrived in New Zealand shared a cabin on the **inter-island ferry**. **1976** JOHNSTON *New Zealanders* 116 The railways dominate..with focus on the Cook Strait inter-island ferries. **1980** MANTELL *Murder & Chips* 62 Further over, the inter-island ferry was making its turn towards the entrance on the way to the South Island. **1948** SWAN *Hist. NZ Rugby Football* I. 725 An attempt to play an **Inter-Island match** was made sixteen years before the first fixture was actually contested. In 1881 the Secretary of the Wellington Union..was unable to interest Otago and Canterbury Unions in his proposal. **1959** SLATTER *Gun in My Hand* 75 Before the war you'd see three tries scored by one wing three-quarter in an inter-island match on Athletic Park. **1966** *Encycl. NZ* III. 153 Next to the international [rugby union] engagements the Inter-Island match perhaps holds most interest. In all, 57 such matches have been played [since 1897]. **1982** LAMBERT & PALENSKI *NZ Almanac* 385 The Plunket Shield..is now at stake in the intermittent interisland match.

  Hence **Interislander**, a name adopted in 1989 to identify the inter-island rail ferries and ferry service.

intermediate school. Often in shortened form **intermediate**. A school accepting only forms one and two pupils being those approximately 11 to 13 years old.
  [*Note*] The name JUNIOR HIGH SCHOOL q.v., a concept imported from the US, was found less satisfactory than *intermediate* to describe the development within the NZ educational system. The latter name has been used variously in other educational systems (see OED *intermediate adj.* A 1 d 1893, 1945; Webster (1961) 2 a).
  1922 *AJHR* E-11 5 The junior high school or 'intermediate school' as it is sometimes called, is being very rapidly developed in the United States. **1933** *Education Amendment Act 1932–33* s.3(1) 'Inter-mediate School' means a public school to which are admitted from one or more public or native schools pupils who belong to the senior division. *Ibid.* s.3(6) The Kowhai Junior High School shall hereafter be deemed to be an intermediate school. **1966** *Encycl. NZ* I. 540 The majority of children have all their primary schooling from Primer 1 to Form II in one school. In a number of places, however (mainly in large centres), pupils who have completed the work of Standard 4 are transferred to central two-year institutions known as intermediate schools... As intermediates are consolidated schools, it is possible to provide them with a library, an assembly hall, [etc.] **1994** *The Telephone Directory Wellington* 163 Evans Bay Intermediate School Kemp St Klbni.

internal assessment. [Cf. OED *assessment* 5 b.] The assessment of a student's level of educational attainment by performance within the institution or course attended rather than by external examination. (Applied also to the assessment of courses from work done within the course, rather than by an end-of-year examination.)
  1972 *NZ News* 26 Jan. 3 The Post Primary Teachers' Association is pressing for internal assessment in place of the examination at fifth form level. **1972** ELLEY *External Exam. & Internal Assessments* 77 Internal assessment may enable teachers to evaluate a variety of qualities with more validity than a single public examination can do.

interpreter. Usu. in New Zealand, an official Maori Interpreter, licensed after proficiency examinations, to interpret between Maori and English.
  1909 *NZ Statutes* No.15 256 [Native Land Act] A judge of the Native Land Court may suspend an Interpreter. **1912** *Free Lance* (Wellington) 6 Jan. 10 [Advt] Parata & Co... Land and Estate Agents, Native Interpreters, Native Agents. **1938** FINLAYSON *Brown Man's Burden* (1973) 77 Tacked to the wall was a notice done in faded ink: REGISTERED MAORI INTERPRETER. **1973** WALLACE *Generation Gap* 155 I and two other interpreters had been engaged by the [Provincial] Council to accompany some of them into a wayback pa.

interprovincial. Existing, conducted, travelling, etc. between any of the New Zealand provinces or provincial districts.
  1857 *Richmond-Atkinson Papers* 15 June (1960) I. 276 But..the [shipping] service is not to commence for two years and even then would not supply interprovincial communication. **1869** *AJHR* D-6 18 Every assistance should be given to inter-provincial trade. **1870** *Colonist* (Nelson) 6 Sept. in Swan *Hist. NZ Rugby Football* (1948) I. 3 A challenge for a match at football, sent by fifteen of Nelson to fifteen of Wellington, has been accepted... Advantage will then be taken of witnessing the first large 'Inter-Provincial' match of football, an amusement which appears to be threatening to assume extensive proportions. **1894** *NZ Official Year-book* 67 There are no records of interprovincial arrivals and departures. **1906** DIXON *Triumphant Tour of the NZ Footballers 1905* 6 A fifteen from the Auckland Football Club made the first journey through the colony, inaugurating a system of interprovincial tours. **1976** JOHNSTON *New Zealanders* 87 The high point of inter-provincial rugby is the Ranfurly Shield. **1989** *Heinemann NZ Dict.* 1049 'Plunket *Shield*' (a former interprovincial cricket trophy).

invasion: see AMERICAN INVASION, AUSTRALIAN 3.

inverteds: see DINK *n.* 1 b.

investment. *Horseracing.* [Cf. OED *invest v.* 9 c, 1951 to lay out money on betting.] A euphemism for a bet, or for betting, on horse-races.

  1944 WOOD *Understanding NZ* 252 Bets made on the 'Tote' are called investments. **1966** TURNER *Eng. Lang. Austral. & NZ* 174 The respectability of racing is enhanced by the use, even in official publications such as the *Yearbook*, of the term *investments* for bets and *dividends* (popularly *divvies*) for money won.

Invincibles. Usu. as a collective *pl.* **the Invincibles**, the nickname of the 1924 New Zealand rugby union team touring Britain, France and Canada, and winning all games played.

  1938 STONE *Rugby Players Who Have Made NZ Famous* 62 Freddie [Lucas] toured with Cliff Porter's 1924 'Invincibles'. **1948** SWAN *Hist. NZ Rugby Football* I. 206 The 29 players [of the 1924 team] have been styled 'the Invincibles'—and justly so. **1993** *Dominion* (Wellington) 18 Aug. 3 The 1920s All Black Invincibles feature on a NZ Post stamp that has won an award in Italy.

iris. As **native** or **New Zealand iris**, *Libertia ixioides* (fam. Iridaceae), occas. *L. grandiflora*. See also MIKOIKOI, TURUTU 2.

  1900 *Canterbury Old & New* 183 Everywhere..a tuft of the grassy-leaved small-flowered native iris [Libertia ixioides]. **1952** RICHARDS *Chatham Is.* 21 *Libertia ixioides*..New Zealand Iris. Mikoikoi. **1982** WILSON *Stewart Is. Plants* 296 *Libertia ixioides* Mikoikoi..Native iris..Tūkāuki. **1987** *Bull. Wellington Bot. Soc. No.43* 69 *Libertia grandiflora* (NZ iris)..Forest. **1990** WEBB et al. *Flowering Plants NZ* 114 Flowers of native irises are simple compared with those of their relatives overseas. Both sets of petal-like parts are white... Although small, flowers are produced freely and form an attractive display in a wild or garden setting. *Ibid.* 115 [Caption] *Libertia ixioides*, often called native iris, shows many features typical of the family. Leaves are sword-like in flattened tufts. Flower parts are in threes.

Irish, *a.* Various derogatory or belittling uses (now rare) of *Irish* in the collocations: **Irish combine**, a flail; **Irish confetti**, gravel (cf. Partridge 8: 'brickbats'); **Irish curtains**, cobwebs; **Irish king** in the phr. **buggered for the want of an Irish king**, an often jocular elaboration of *buggered* 'ruined; frustrated'.

  1913 CARR *Country Work* 12 After the [cocksfoot] is all cut..it is collected in sheets, carried to a floor, and threshed out with an '**Irish Combine**', or, in other words, a flail. **1940** STUDHOLME *Te Waimate* (1954) 167 The only implements available [c 1850–60] were spades, shovels, picks, hoes, scythes, sickles, and flails, the last named commonly known as 'The Irish Combine'. **1961** MACKAY *Puborama* 70 Promptly Fred picked up a handful of gravel and..scattered the **Irish confetti** somewhere in its [*sc.* the top floor window's] vicinity. **1987** ELDRED-GRIGG *Oracles & Miracles* 47 And if the sight of a cobweb caught Mum's eyes as she shot quick glances of inspection into the windows of neighbouring houses she'd toss her head. 'Hmph,' she'd say. '**Irish curtains** in her window.' **1968** SLATTER *Pagan Game* 161 Trouble was she was a Mickey Doo—**Buggered for the want of an Irish king**.

Irishman.

1. *Hist.* A Maori Catholic.

  1893 MACKENZIE *Overland* 20 We halted [c1853] at a house, which our men said belonged to an 'Irishman' (i.e. a Maori Roman Catholic).

2. See WILD IRISHMAN.

iron. [AND 1859.] Often *attrib.* (Built of) corrugated iron.

  1851 *Lyttelton Times* 15 Nov. 1 To Be Sold, An Iron House. [**1876** *TrNZI* VIII. 166 On the goldfields, timber is preceded by calico and corrugated iron.] **1885** *Wairarapa Daily* 9 Apr. 2 The walls and roof are of iron. **1891** *NZJSc.* (NS) I. 151 Mr. Garry had also 21 holes made in his iron roof by the hail. **c1890s** DOUGLAS in *Mr Explorer Douglas* (1957) 15 In the second period [of architecture (c1860s, Westland)], weather board, and iron distinguish the Archetectures [*sic*]..and bottles are now only to be seen stacked round the Pubs. **1924** ANTHONY *Follow the Call* (1975) 6 Before I could live in that shack I had to put some new sheets of iron on the outside. **1943** *Tararua Tramper* Nov. 4 It was snug enough inside the hut with its..walls packed with tussock between iron and scrim. **1955** BOWEN *Wool Away* 115 Building paper should be used under the iron above the shearing board. **1966** TURNER *Eng. Lang. Austral. & NZ* 172 The word *iron* alone is very often used for roofing iron. **1981** GEE *Meg* 48 I came to Robert's iron shack... Its corrugated walls were green.

ironbark. southern rata (RATA 2 (3)). Cf. IRONHEART, IRONWOOD a.

  1875 KIRK *Durability NZ Timbers* 18 Ironbark—Rata.—(*Metrosideros lucida*).

ironheart. *Obs.* Also **downy ironheart**. [f. the hardness of its wood, *downy ironheart* prob. coined by Domett also from the whitish or 'downy' appearance of the flower buds immediately before flowering.] POHUTUKAWA. Cf. IRONWOOD a.

  1872 DOMETT *Ranolf & Amohia* 311 It was the 'downy ironheart' That from the cliffs o'erhanging grew. **1898** MORRIS *Austral-English* 212 *Ironheart* a New Zealand tree, *Metrosideros tomentosa*... native name, *Pohutukawa*. **1968** *NZ Contemp. Dict. Suppl.* (Collins) 10 *ironheart n.* magnificent N.Z. tree, the *pohutukawa*.

ironsand. [Used elsewhere but of special significance in NZ: see OED *iron n.*[1], 1805.] A sand rich in particles of iron ore found on many west coast beaches, particularly those of Taranaki northwards (often as **Taranaki iron sand**), or (usu. as **black sand**) those of the South Island West Coast.

  1769 COOK *Journals* 15 Nov. (1955) I. 203 We found thrown upon the Shore..in this [Mercury] Bay quantities of Iron Sand. **1830** CRAIK *New Zealanders* 184 Captain Cook remarked..the great quantities of iron-sand which were brought down to the shore by every little rivulet of fresh water from the interior. **1848** WAKEFIELD *Handbook NZ* 281 The 'Titanic iron sand'..is found all along the sea-beach between Sugarloaf Point and the mouth of the Waitera. **1852** LUSH *Auckland Jrnls.* 2 Dec. (1971) 126 One boy..gave me a sample of the iron sand found in various spots along our beach, from which gold can be washed. **1862** *Richmond-Atkinson Papers* (1960) I. 801 The iron sand question is still in a state of 'embranglement'. **1879** *Auckland Weekly News* 1 Nov. 6 I have just witnessed a copious stream of the Taranaki iron sand pouring like water from a temporary furnace. **1904** *NZ Observer* 2 July 7 The plant for the Taranaki Ironsand Company will be on the ground in three months. **1923** *NZJST* VI. 140 Taranaki ironsand consists principally of magnetite (magnetic oxide of iron), ilmenite (titanate of iron), ferro-magnesian minerals such as augite and hornblende, some olivine and quartz. **1991** STEWART *Springtime in Taranaki* (1991) 84 The beach was of the famous Taranaki iron-sand, grey in the heat where we sunbaked, gleaming black where it stretched out far and flat to meet the water.

ironwood. [Spec. use of *ironwood* (the very hard wood of) any of various trees.] **a.** Esp. in the South Island, either of two trees, *Metrosideros robusta* or *M. umbellata*, RATA 1.

  c1826–27 BOULTBEE *Journal* (1986) 110 Ironwood—lāhtah **c1835** BOULTBEE *Journal* (1986) 103 The trees are easily cleared away, being either pine or other soft wood; except the iron wood, which grows to a large size, the wood of this tree is a dark red colour. **1858** THOMSON *Reconn. Survey S. Dist. Otago* in Taylor *Early Travellers* (1959) 328 Pine and ironwood were..plentiful in the woods of Forest Hill. **1869** *TrNZI* I. (rev. edn.) 158 The Rata (called ironwood in the South). **1871** DOCHERTY in Haast *Julius Von Haast* (1948) 550 The Ka-ka-po..gather a few dry leaves..in the heart of a rotten rata which is the Ironwood tree. **1889** KIRK *Forest Flora* 99 Although the two plants [*M. lucida* and *M. robusta*] are easily distinguished..it may be advisable to term this species the southern rata, and *M. robusta* the northern rata... Both species are called 'ironwood' by the bushmen. **1892** CARRICK *NZ's Lone Lands* 22 The rata, or ironwood, of New Zealand,.. was getting into colour..in these parts. **1909** [see RATA 2 (1)]. **1936** GUTHRIE-SMITH *NZ Naturalist* 179 From amongst them [on Kaipara Island]..rise..small Ironwood (*Metrosideros lucida*). **1940** LAING & BLACKWELL *Plants NZ* 296 The rata, as its common name, iron-wood, suggests, produces an extremely hard timber. **1967** [see RATA 1]. **1982** WILSON *Stewart Is. Plants* 72 *Metrosideros umbellata* Southern Rātā Ironwood.

b. *Obs.* Occas. in the North Island, PURIRI.

  1847 *McLean Papers* (ATLTS) I. 37 I must endeavour to get them of puriri or ironwood, so as to be durable. **1849** HURSTHOUSE *New Plymouth* 16 The Puriri, or Iron Wood. **1868**, **1882** [see TEAK]. **1883** [see OAK].

Island, *n.*[1]

1. As **the Islands** *pl.*, usu. with init. cap. [Spec. use of *island*: cf. OED 1 d; prob. orig. ellipt. for *Pacific Islands* or *South Sea Islands*.] The South Pacific Islands, that is, the 'Polynesian' South Sea Islands (esp. those east of Fiji), often having special associations for New Zealanders.

  1769 BANKS *Endeavour Jrnl.* I. (1962) 444 After this they shewd us a great rarity 6 plants of what they called *Aouta* from whence they made cloth like the Otahite cloth; the plant proved exactly the same, as the name is the same, as is usd in the Islands. **1850** SELWYN *Letters* (ATLTS) IV. 772 'The Islands'—as the groups [Selwyn] has visited are called now, by the Sailors and Clergy. **1877** *TrNZI* IX. 87 Ladies and children will find it of the utmost advantage to annually leave the islands for a couple of months, in order to escape the summer heat. **1911** *Truth* 9 Sept. 4 Up Auckland way the crusade in favor [*sic*] of cheap domestic labor has resulted in a scheme for the importation of a number of black 'boys' from the islands. **1933** EADDY *Hull Down* 99 Standing there at the wheel..all sorts of thoughts kept coming and going; thoughts of trips to the Islands, and round the New Zealand and Australian Coasts. **1957** FRAME *Owls Do Cry* (1967) 26 The man next door belonged to the Church, a missionary, who had been to the Islands. **1976** WILSON *Pacific Star* 134 I really liked the flavour of it, after the Australian and American plonk we'd drunk up in the Islands. **1991** *Dominion* (Wellington) 27 Sept. 9 A woman called her new neighbours 'coconuts' and told them to go back to the Islands.

ISLAND

2. a. *Hist.* Orig. the North Island as a gloss for New Zealand.

1816 KENDALL 12 Nov. in Elder *Marsden's Lieutenants* (1934) 132 The natives, instead of taking his part against us, encourage him to leave the island. **1821** *Sugden to Earl of Bathurst* 18 Jan. in McNab *Hist. Records* (1908) I. 516 A party about emigrating [*sic*] to New Zealand begs most respectfully to solicit the assistance of Government in their undertaking. I am (with several who have resided on the island) convinced an English colony would soon become flourishing and happy.

b. *pl.*, often with a modifier, as **these Islands, the New Zealand islands**, New Zealand.

1847 *Spectator* Jan. 2 (Wellington) in Miller *Early Victorian NZ* (1958) 149 [The 1846 Constitution Act] sweeps away the whole system of official machinery..—all the 'Treaty of Waitangi' nonsense, and all the past Downing-Street plans for hindering the settlement of the islands. **1849** *Gov. Grey to Earl Grey* 30 Nov. in Rutherford *Sel. Documents* (1949) 39 The state of tranquillity which has continued to prevail in these Islands, has altogether surpassed my expectations. **1863** MOSER *Mahoe Leaves* 10 [You] have anathematised the settlers of these Islands as the source of much mischief in the minds of the New Zealanders. **1940** LAING & BLACKWELL *Plants NZ* 136 We might at least expect some consistent nomenclature [for beech species] to be adopted through the islands.

3. *pl.* The Chatham Islands.

1848 SELWYN in *NZ Part V* (Church in the Colonies XX) 30 Aug. (184) 100 Among the rest were several men and women of the aboriginal race of the Islands..—Their name, as spoken by themselves, is Tangata Maori*ori*. **1865** CHUDLEIGH *Diary* 14 Nov. (1950) 204 At that time the oldest and principal resident of the Chatham Islands was in his house... [He] charters a small ship to take down stores to the island... By means of this ship I propose to reach and return from the Islands. **1866** HUNT *Chatham Is.* 60 The old bay whaling parties have long since ceased to trouble the Islands. **1995** *Dominion* (Wellington) 17 Oct. 3 A team of 19 Wellington police were in the islands at the weekend to back up the sole constable.

Island, *n.*² *Hist.* As **the Island**, the Salvation Army establishment for the rehabilitation of addicts (alcoholic and others) on Rotoroa Island in the Hauraki Gulf. Occas. in the phr. **to go (be sent) to the Island; to get the Island**.

1922 TURNER *Happy Wanderer* 219 He says the desire [for drugs] has gone altogether, that 'the Island' has made him fit and allowed him to get natural sleep. **1945** BURTON *In Prison* 19 [The drunk's] record is a very long one but as this is his first offence since his return from the Salvation Army 'Island' the magistrate only mumbles—'Ten shillings and costs!' *Ibid.* 115 As he has had several [drunken] offences lately he will certainly get three months, and very possibly the 'Island'. **1960** CRUMP *Good Keen Man* 77 There were rumours..he'd gone on the booze and ended up on 'the island'.

Island, *a.*¹

1. Occas. as **Islands**, of or pertaining to the South Pacific Islands and their people, esp. to their culture and produce. See also ISLAND ORANGE.

1882 *TrNZI* XIV. 406 The position of Auckland with respect to the Island trade..points to a successful industry in the manufacture of citric acid in this city. **1905** *Truth* 28 Oct. 8 The Island fruit trade. **1929** *Evening Post* (Wellington) 3 Sept. 16 The standard of living of the Cook Islander is much lower than that of the New Zealand workman; the pick of Island labour can be obtained for 15s a week. **1945** TEXIDOR *In Fifteen Minutes* (1987) 172 Mr Withers' eyes were burrowing into a red flower on Roy's island shirt. **1955** *BJ Cameron Collection* (TS July) island basket (n) a basket of coconut fibre made in the Islands and commonly used in NZ. **1958** *Public Service Official Circular No.1958/3* 29 Jan. 19 *Inspector of Islands Schools.* Duties:.. to assist in the general development of education in the Pacific islands, to inspect island schools, to supervise island students. **1976** WILSON *Pacific Star* 129 'This is better than island beer, eh?' Doc said. **1982** BURTON *Two Hundred Yrs. NZ Food* 3 These [Maori food] plants were the island yam..the bottle gourd,.. and the kumara. **1987** *Metro Fiction* 13 She ridiculously overpaid an Island woman to do her cleaning. **1991** *Metro* (Auckland) Jan. 88 Nootu (45), shambling Island walk..frizzy black hair pulled back into ponytail..dominates the family.

2. Of or pertaining to the Chatham Islands.

1880 CHUDLEIGH *Diary* 28 Mar. (1950) 285 Went to Bishops Court and talked with the Bishop about Island matters. *Ibid.* 26 Nov. 449 William Bauc[k]e came to see me [at Waikato] and have an Island talk. He gave me a copy of his book. **1968** GRUNDY *Who'd Marry a Doctor?* 42 On New Year's Day the annual race meeting was held. Local youths..competed on island-bred horses.

Islander. [f. ISLAND *n.*¹ 1 + -ER.]

1. Also *obs.* **South Sea Islander** (OED *south-sea* 5 c, 1832 Earle). A native or inhabitant of one of the (usu. Polynesian) Pacific Islands, esp. those (Cook Islands, Niue, Samoa, Tonga, etc.) having close ties with or providing immigrants to New Zealand; a New Zealander of Pacific Island birth or descent; freq. *spec.* **Cook Islander**, a Polynesian born or resident in the Cook Islands, or descended from such a person (see quot. 1989). See also PACIFIC ISLANDER.

1770 COOK *Journals* 31 Mar. (1955) I. 288 What is meant by the South Sea Islands are those Islands we our selves touch'd at, but I gave it that title because we have a[l]ways been told that the same Language is Universally spoke by all the Islanders. **1817** NICHOLAS *Voyage NZ* I. 16 Contrasting..the genius and habits of this people [*sc.* New Zealanders] with those of the other Islanders in this immense Ocean, he [Marsden] found them much more prepared for cultivation than the generality of savage tribes. **1832** EARLE *NZ* (1966) 58 I am persuaded that these South Sea Islanders, though so nearly of the same complexion, still are not of the same race. **1869** *TrNZI* I. (rev. edn.) 341 In Colour the New Zealanders varied more than those of any other of the Polynesian islanders. **1873** *TrNZI* V. 33 Cook learnt that..the natives had plenty of excellent vegetables.. which they ate like the South Sea Islanders. **1893** *Ibid.* XXV. 441 The 'bad memory' of the civilised man is like colour-blindness or myopia, a defect largely due to his artificial habits, and from which the unlettered islander is exempt. **1905** *Truth* 28 Oct. 8 No inducement for the Islanders to ship to Auckland. **1921** STEWART *NZ Div.* 9 In the formation of each company the 2 leading platoons were composed of Maoris or Islanders in tribes, and the other two of Pakehas. **1933** in *Na To Hoa Aroha* (1988) III. 88 This will inaugurate a deliberate attempt to bring the Cook Islander closer to his New Zealand relative. **1964** MIDDLETON *Walk on Beach* 192 There were many single rooms to let. Some of the advertisements said: Europeans only need apply or no Maoris or Islanders. **1985** MCGILL *G'day Country* 174 Despite that, readers were assured, folk were friendly and you could find Maori and Islander values here parallel to the strong clan-like traditions of the Presbyterians. **1989** CAMPBELL *Frigate Bird* 71 'Are you a Maori?' 'No—a Cook Islander.' 'Ah—a Coconut.'

2. *Obs.* Occas. formerly a Maori.

1815 MARSDEN *Lett. & Jrnls.* (1932) 130 When I take into consideration what I saw of these islanders,.. I am strongly inclined to believe that they will soon be ranked among civilized nations. **1823** CRUISE *Journal* 20 Mar. (1957) 59 A message was immediately sent to the captain [of the whaler]..to request that he would not issue powder and muskets to the islanders. **1830** CRAIK *New Zealanders* 47 While thus employed, and with numbers of the islanders mixed with them, in one moment each was fallen upon by..barbarians. **1838** POLACK *NZ* I. iii Many of the details regarding the sayings and doings of the islanders may be accounted as being of too simple a nature for record.

3. *Obs.* Occas. a native of the Melanesian islands.

1851 LUSH *Auckland Jrnls.* Oct. (1971) 89 Poor Blanche was rather upset at the intelligence of [Bishop Selwyn's] bringing so many as 13 South Sea Islanders... After Hall the Bishop called the 13 Islanders to him and introduced me to them. **1856** FITTON *NZ* 4 It is probably at least two hundred years, since a party of islanders from some of the numerous group near Torres' Strait..arrived on the northernmost of the three islands, forming the group now called New Zealand.

4. One born or resident on the Chatham Islands; occas. a MORIORI 1 a (see quot. 1923).

1868 CHUDLEIGH *Diary* (1950) 28 Jan. 214 Mr Rolleston has called a general meeting of the native islanders to talk to them about the survey. *Ibid.* 24 Mar. 235 The Islanders are much as they were. The Island appears more dead than ever. **1923** SKINNER *Morioris Chatham Is.* 20 Whataroho's informants say that the name Moriori was given to the natives of the Chatham Islands by the Taranaki invaders and that the islanders called themselves Mouriuri. **1951** *NZ Geogr.* Apr. 97 The Chatham Islands are legally part of New Zealand but are not of it. Islanders speak in their soft dialect of 'going up to New Zealand'. **1968** GRUNDY *Who'd Marry a Doctor?* 41 Many islanders were versatile with musical instruments. **1985** LANGDALE-HUNT *Last Entail Male* 61 I remember a young islander..telling me how he used to gallop through the sheep in the holding paddock at Flower Pot..just to annoy Gabriel. **1995** *Dominion* (Wellington) 17 Oct. 3 The inside of a Wellington fishing boat was smashed..after clashes between islanders and 'New Zealanders' over fishing rights.

5. One born or resident on Stewart Island.

1940 HOWARD *Rakiura* xii There has gathered about the adventurous lives of the Islanders a rich store of popular local history. *Ibid.* 230 The islanders found a ready market for limited quantities of the shell in Germany. **1970** SANSOM *Stewart Islanders* 125 Islanders always considered they had taught him some of his tricks. *Ibid.* 138 Two escaped Borstal boys, one an Islander..pulled across from Bluff. **1981** ALLAN *See Our Island* 19 It is, to the Islanders a plain fact... Those whose ancestry digs deep into the past are Stewart Islanders. The rest of us are New Zealanders.

island lily: see LILY 2 (6).

Island orange. Occas. **Cook Island orange.** A yellowish, thin-skinned, juicy variety of orange grown in the Pacific Islands, formerly exported to New Zealand, but now used mainly as a source of juice.

1887 *Auckland Weekly News* 23 July 28 Island oranges were sold in..Gisborne last Saturday, at 8s a case. **1919** *Hawera & Normanby Star* 12 July 7 The bad condition of a recent large shipment of Island oranges was the subject of..comment at the city market. **1932** *Oamaru Mail* 9 June 6 Island oranges..are selling cheaply in the markets at present. **1933** NGATA *Let.* 23 Jan. in *Na To Hoa Aroha* III. 58 It should go a long way to re-establishing the Rarotonga and Cook Island orange. **1946** *NZJST* XXVII. 281 Island sweet orange (*Citrus sinensis* Osbeck) and citronelle (syn. rough lemon, *C. limonia* Osbeck) are the rootstocks on which New Zealand citrus groves have been almost exclusively established. **1948** *Our Own Country* 42 To the side of them were Island orange trees which had been grown from seedlings. **1951** *NZ Geogr.* Oct. 124 In past years wild oranges—the common 'island' oranges—constituted almost all the citrus exports [from Rarotonga]. **1963** *Evening Post* (Wellington) 5 Sept. 14 As one who is more partial to Island oranges than any others, I was pleasantly surprised when, earlier this year, they were available at 8d a lb.

itinerant teacher. *Hist.* See quot. 1921; also later applied to a teacher visiting schools to provide instruction in special subjects, e.g., music.
  1921 *Regs. for Employment & Payment of Itinerant Teachers* In cases where the establishment of full-time or part-time schools is impracticable, itinerant teachers may..be appointed by an Education Board to give house-to-house instruction to pupils of school age in isolated districts. **1987** *Dept. Educ. Circular 1987/72* 20 Nov. The existing Itinerant Teachers of Maori positions..will be disestablished.

ivy. [Transf. use of northern hemisphere *ivy Hedera* spp. (fam. Araliaceae).] See also IVY-TREE.

1. Maori (native) ivy, any of several plants, esp. PATE (*Schefflera digitata*).
  1838 POLACK *NZ* I. 294 The *barks* of trees are covered with *liands* and flowering *convolvuluses*... the *Lilium perennae*, or common ray-grass; *hedera*, or native ivy, are often met with. **1922** *Auckland Weekly News* 8 June 15 Beneath willows..near Nile Street, Nelson, there is a mass of the plant popularly known as native ivy. **1946** *JPS* LV. 155 Maori ivy, a tree (*Schefflera digitata*), a five-fingered Maori ivy (the fruit only being similar).

2. Any of several naturalized South African plants of *Senecio* spp. (fam. Asteraceae). **a.** As **Cape ivy**, *Senecio angulatus*, a perennial herb of coastal places, having yellow flowerheads in autumn and winter.
  1969 *Standard Common Names Weeds* 40 Ivy, Cape. *Senecio angulatus*. **1981** TAYLOR *Weeds of Roadsides* 33 Cape Ivy... South Africa perennial tending to sprawl... Less common than German ivy. **1990** *Listener* 16 July 116 Those of us who have spent hours trying to contain this pest (it seems impossible to eradicate it) would prefer to see a campaign to make cape 'ivy' a noxious weed, rather than one to promote it as a desirable ground cover.

b. As **African (French, German, native) ivy**, *Senecio mikanioides* (formerly *scandens*), a perennial climber with ivy-shaped leaves.
  1898 HUDSON *NZ Moths & Butterflies* 140 *Senecio scandens* (called by settlers French Ivy). A common climbing plant having a superficial resemblance to ivy, but with much brighter green leaves, and yellow berries. **1922** *NZJST* V. 58 Just below the Nile Street Bridge [Nelson] (over the Marton River) there a steep bank covered with the so-called 'native ivy' (*Senecio mikanioides*). **1953** STRONACH *Musterer on Molesworth* 28 There was a lot of native ivy growing in them and it looked well, above the lake—but I found it not very dependable as an aid to rock climbing. **1969** *Standard Common Names Weeds* 1 African ivy [=] German ivy... *Ibid.* 28 German ivy *Senecio mikanioides*. **1981** TAYLOR *Weeds of Roadsides* 61 German Ivy (*Senecio mikanioides*) Perennial climber. **1988** WEBB, SYKES, GARNOCK-JONES *Flora NZ* IV. 275 German ivy is similar to *S. angulatus* in being a scrambling plant of coastal sites.

ivy-tree. Any of several native trees of the genus *Pseudopanax* (fam. Araliaceae), esp. LANCEWOOD q.v. (*Pseudopanax crassifolius*), and mountain ivy-tree (*Pseudopanax colensoi*). See also FIVE-FINGER 1.
  1867 HOOKER *Handbook* 765 Ivy-tree, *Panax Colensoi*. **1870** *TrNZI* II. 121 *Panax crassifolium*, the Ivy tree. **1883** HECTOR *Handbook NZ* 127 Horoeka, ivy-tree. An ornamental, slender, and sparingly-branched tree. Wood close-grained and tough. **1889** *TrNZI* XXI. 382 There is also [on Auckland Islands] the ivy tree (*Panax simplex*), [and] the stink-wood. **1908** *AJHR* C-11 39 [*Nothopanax arboreum*]. Whauwhaupaku. Common ivy-tree. Forest. **1930** REISCHEK *Yesterdays in Maoriland* (1933) 273 The low-lying parts [were] overgrown with rata, ivy-tree (*Panax simplex*), and the so-called stink-wood. **1939** COCKAYNE & TURNER *Trees NZ* 89 *Nothopanax Colensoi*... Orihau, Mountain Ivy-tree. **1961** MARTIN *Flora NZ* 183 The three-finger or Mountain Ivy-tree has as a rule three sessile leaflets. **1969** [see FIVE-FINGER 1].

iwi. [Ma. /ˈiwi/: Williams 80 *Iwi, n... 4*. Nation, people.] **a.** Also *pl*. A Maori tribe; a people recognizing a common eponymous ancestor. See also TRIBE.
  [*Note*] From the 1980s freq. in official and popular reference.
  [**1820** LEE & KENDALL *NZ Gram. & Vocab.* 140 I'wi, *s.* A tribe; a family.] **1843** *Letter* 15 Aug. in Shortland *Traditions & Superstitions* (1856) 305 At the present day, these *Waka* are divided into many distinct *Iwi*; each of which is subdivided again into *Hapu*, or smaller communities. **1856** SHORTLAND *Traditions & Superstitions* 223 The term *Iwi*, commonly translated Tribe, applies also to those primary divisions, but more generally to their larger subdivisions. **1863** MANING *Old NZ* xiv 215 [He was the] recognised war chief of almost all the sections of the *hapu* of a very numerous and warlike *iwi* or tribe. **1904** TREGEAR *Maori Race* 161 Names of tribes (*iwi*) were generally denoted by the prefix Ngati, meaning 'descendants of', as Ngati-Raukawa the descendants of Raukawa. **1922** *Auckland Weekly News* 12 Jan. 14 Iwi means more than merely a tribe, or a people, or a nation. It means a group of beings that, having the same physical shape and attributes, have also the same mental or instinctive qualities and a common all-pervading unity of disposition. **1949** [see TRIBE]. **1958** MILLER *Early Victorian NZ* 13 Later the tribes (*iwi*) and subtribes (*hapu*) spread out, proceeding up river-valleys and their tributaries. **1969** MASON *Awatea* (1978) 90 And the tree cracks, splits, falls, the iwi scattered like leaves. **1979** WEBSTER *Rua* 85 The Tuhoe tribe (iwi)..was divided into a number of sub-tribes known as hapu which were thought to be connected by descent from common ancestors. **1986** *Evening Post* (Wellington) 15 Dec. 17 The newspaper advertisement says the person must be acceptable to iwi (people, tribe) of the Porirua to Otaki area. **1991** *Evening Post* (Wellington) 5 Mar. 1 Maori belonging to the two local iwi within the West Coast District have access to appropriate health care services to some extent whilst non iwi Maori have very few culturally appropriate services.

b. In *attrib.* use passing into Comb.
  1988 *Dominion* (Wellington) 6 Oct. 1 Most Maori iwi (tribal) authorities will this year spend..funds on administration costs. **1989** *Evening Post* (Wellington) 2 Oct. 3 [Caption] 300 staff dropped in transition to iwi agency. Staff numbers have been reduced..in the transition from the Department of Maori Affairs to the Iwi Transition Agency, which took over from today. The agency will maintain the department's existing programmes and services until they can be transferred to iwi authorities. **1989** *Principles for Crown Action on the Treaty of Waitangi* 10 The second article of the Treaty guarantees to iwi Maori the control and enjoyment of those resources and taonga which it is their wish to retain. **1990** *Dominion* (Wellington) 17 July 28 Mr Durie said the mood of the weekend hui was that the congress should never move from being iwi-driven. **1996** *Sunday Star-Times* 3 Feb. A2 Detective Constable Brett Watene, the Tokoroa police iwi liaison officer, said beating and taking the patch of a rival gang member is known as scalping.

J

Jack, *n.*[1] *Hist.* Also **Jack Maori**. [See OED *jack n.*[1] 1 d a form of address to an unknown person, 1889.] Formerly applied familiarly to Maori opponents in the New Zealand Wars. Cf. HORI, HOSTILE B.

1864 ASHWELL *Lett. & Jrnls.* (ATLTS) IV. 487 The Soldiers said well Jack Maori how do you do. **1922** COWAN *NZ Wars* (1955) I. 209 A good-natured soldier..hearing him moaning something which sounded like '*wai*' (water), was trying to make him drink..saying, 'Here, Jack, here's *wai* for you.' The soldiers always addressed the Maoris as 'Jack', and the Maoris the soldiers as 'Tiaki' also.

jack, *n.*[2] [Cf. *jack* a young or male animal or bird: see OED *n.*[1]] In the names of various animals. Cf. JACKBIRD. **a.** Occas. the KOKAKO.

1866 *Report on Stewart Island* 26 Dec. in *NZ Govt. Gaz. Prov. of Southland* (1867, 21 Jan.) V. No.1 (Griffiths Collect.) Here for the first time, I saw a pretty little bird called the Jack, with red wattles and burnished red feathers on the back and wings. This bird is, I understand, peculiar to the southern part of the Island. Its note is melodious, nearly equal to that of the tui, or parson bird. **1884** REID *Rambles on Golden Coast* 29 This was not so..with a more attractive little bird—'a crow' or a 'jack'.

b. The *blue penguin* (PENGUIN 2 (1)). Cf. JACKASS 2.

c1899 DOUGLAS in *Mr Explorer Douglas* (1957) 286 There a[re] two varities [*sic*] of this preadamite looking bird, the king or crested penguin which is the largest, and the jack which is much smaller and far more numerous.

c. An adult male turkey.

1982 *Agric. Gloss.* (MAF) 48 *Stag (or Jack)*: Adult male turkey.

jack, *n.*[3] In the phr. **to have (take) a jack**, to take a look. Cf. JACK NOHI.

1976 GIFFORD *Loosehead Len's Bumper Thump Book* 7 The Bok fullback Buchler takes a jack at the pill. **1984** BEATON *Outside In* 74 Ginny: Look who's talkin'. Yous should have a jack at her diary. *Ibid.* 110 *have a jack at*: to take a look at. **1989** TE AWEKOTUKU *Tahuri* 26 Sometimes she'd have a sneaky jack... 'Sina that fucken kid's watchin' us again.'

jackaroo, var. JACKEROO.

jackass. [f. its braying cry.]

1. See LAUGHING JACKASS 1 (WHEKAU).

2. *Obs.* As **jackass bird**, a species of penguin.

1851 STEPHENS *Journal* (ATLTS) 495 A species of penguin, which is called by the sailors the 'Jackass Bird' from its [screaming] note somewhat resembling the bray of that animal.

jackbird. *Obs.* Also occas. **jack**. [Prob. f. JACK *n.*[2] a name for a young bird + *bird*, influenced in some cases by back-formation from TIEKE the Ma. name for *saddleback* and also (with *Tiaki*) a transliteration into Maori of English *Jack*(y).] A uniformly brown starling-like bird, the juvenile stage of the *South Island saddleback* (SADDLEBACK).

1873 BULLER *Birds NZ* 23 It has become the habit to speak of this bird as the Brown Saddle-back; but as this is a misnomer, inasmuch as the absence of the saddle is its distinguishing feature. I have accordingly adopted the name of Jack-bird, by which it is known among the settlers of the South Island. Why it should be so-called I cannot say, unless this an adaptation of the native name 'Tieke'..equivalent in the Maori vernacular, to our 'Jack'. **1885** *NZJSc.* II. 377 *Creadion carunculatus*... Saddle-back, Jackbird, Tieke. **1898** MORRIS *Austral-English* 218 *Jack-bird, n.* a bird of the South Island of New Zealand. **c1920** BEATTIE *Trad. Lifeways Southern Maori* 335 He [*sc.* a Maori informant] had never heard how the Maoris caught..the tieke [often called 'the jack' by young Maoris as Tieke is [a] southern form of pakeha name Jack. H.B.] (saddleback). **1927–28** *NZJST* IX. 235 We think we have seen the supposed 'jackbird' fed by the adult saddleback under conditions which establish the fact [that they are the same species] beyond any question of doubt. **1936** GUTHRIE-SMITH *NZ Naturalist* 178 Native birds on Kaipara [Island south of Stewart Island] included Tui, Bellbird, Saddleback, Jackbird—if indeed it be a species at all. **1965** *Notornis* XII. 192 It was my first sighting of the immature S.I. saddleback, the Jackbird of Buller..and a beautiful bird it is, with its warm brown plumage and chestnut tail coverts.

jacker. *Sawmilling*. Also **jack-hand, jackman**. [Spec. use of *jacker* one who jacks.] One who works a timber-jack in the bush or at a sawmill.

1906 *Red Funnel* II. 13 Drivers, axemen, rafters, jackers—all were represented. [1906 *Note*] *Jacker*: A man who rolls heavy logs by means of a screw-jack. **1908** *Awards, etc.* 339 [Wellington Sawmills Award] [Rates of wages] Jackman [£]3 0[s.] 0[d.] Skidman 2 14 0. **1924** GIBSON *Gibbie Galoot* 66 In the bush, a man's joy or misery depends upon his attitude towards his mates, just as his life depends upon the skill of his fellow axemen, the dexterity of his fellow jack-hands. **1936** RUST *Whangarei & Dist.* 163 Timber was being got..along its immense stretch of foreshore. Hundreds of bushmen, loggers, jackers, bullock-drivers, cross-cutters and rafters were employed. **1947** *Forest & Bird 155* 15 The men operating the jacks, called jackers, became very expert, and on level ground could keep a log continually on the move.

jackeroo. Also **jackaroo**. [Orig. unknown (so AAW): AND first applied (1845) in Queensland to a white man living beyond the bounds of close settlement, thence, to a station cadet, 1870.]

1. CADET *n.* 1.

c1870s MEREDITH *Adventuring in Maoriland* (1935) 61 Here I am, back at the station again doing jackeroo work until the next [Parliamentary] session starts. **1898** VOGEL *Maori Maid* 147 A jackeroo is a cadet. **1904** CRADOCK *Sport in NZ* 149] At the homestead when we had fossicked out a bit of mutton..I found a confounded 'jackaroo' (Anglicé 'mud student') who had only arrived from the Old Country today, 'dossed' down on my bed. **1910** *Truth* 2 July 6 Take the 'jackaroos' on a station... They get a remittance which keeps them in clothes, l[e]ggings and riding breeches, and an occasional trip to town... They are practically banished from the old country to save the family from being disgraced, and this place is being made a dumping ground for these wastrels. **1960** SCRYMGEOUR *Memories of Maoriland* 127 One after another seasoned stockmen, jackeroos alike, were chased up the stockyard rails. **1981** CHARLES *Black Billy Tea* 11 Open up the gate now and let the bucker go, And see another jackaroo come down covered in snow!

2. A learner or tyro at any occupation, sport, etc.

1961 HENDERSON *Friends in Chains* 43 Playing jokes was not uncommon among us, and, as a new-chum, or jackaroo, I took my share from the men [at the sawmill] until my turn came.

jack-hand: see JACKER.

Jackie, var. JACKY.

Jackie Howe. *Shearing*. Also **Jacky Howe**. [f. the name of *John* Robert (*Jacky*) *Howe* (?1861–1920), a champion Australian shearer of the 1890s: AND 1930.] A sleeveless black singlet worn esp. by shearers and other rural workers.

1934 *Press* (Christchurch) (Acland Gloss.) 20 Jan. 15 *Jacky Howe*.—Sleeveless singlet, cut nearly to the waist under the arms. Named after the famous *J[acky] H[owe]* who rang many of the South Island sheds in the 'nineties. **1953** STRONACH *Musterer on Molesworth* 30 The long line of shearers, attired usually in..a 'Jackie Howe', which is a flannel vest affair, were quiet. **1960** MILLS *Sheep-O* 169 To this day if you walk into a clothing store of the right kind and ask for 'a couple of Jackie Howes' you will be given the black or blue sleeveless woollen singlets so favoured by shearers and bushmen in Australia and New Zealand. **1980** *Star* (Christchurch) 11 Mar. 10 The contestants [*sc.* women weight-lifters] wore costumes rather like one-piece Jackie Howe singlets with T-shirts underneath. **1986** RICHARDS *Off the Sheep's Back* 97 The mornings were so cold it was necessary to put on extra 'Jackie Howes' and cardigans. **1987** *Alfredton* 167 One day a lucky swagger was given two Jackie-Howe singlets which the farmer's wife didn't think her husband would miss.

Jack jumper. Any of various beetles of the fam. Elateridae (click or jumping beetles).

1922 *Auckland Weekly News* 16 Mar. 15 When he was a boy his mates and he knew members of that beetle's [*sc.* a native elator's] family as Jack Jumpers.

jack mackerel: see MACKEREL 2 (3).

jackman: see JACKER.

Jack Maori: see JACK *n.*[1]

Jack Nohi. [Poss. f. *jack* look + *nohi* prob. a Ma. adaptation of *nosy*.]

JACKO

1. A nosey parker. See also NOSY *n.* a.
 c1940–50 North Auckland, p.c. Barry Mitcalfe. He was a regular Jack Nohi. **1988** McGILL *Dict. Kiwi Slang* 76 *nohi* nosey person, often *Jack nohi*; from Maori 'kanohi', the face; eg 'You bloody nohi, why don't you get on with your own work and leave me to do mine in peace and quiet.'

2. A look-round; a peek. See also JACK *n.*³
 1973 *Reflections: Voices from Paremoremo* 32 Everytime his in-laws come around, if it wasn't for a Jack Nohi then it was for something else. **1987** p.c. Peter Janssen: heard at Huntly (and also at other North Island places); known also to P. Ranby, from Auckland (p.c. 1987). What are you doing? I'm having a Jack nohi (meaning: I'm having a look, a poke round; being nosey). What's that over there. Let's go and have a Jack nohi.

Jacko. WW1. [Prob. f. JACK(Y *n.*¹ 2 + *-o*: AND 1916.] A Turk(ish soldier).
 1915 *Rangitikei Advocate & Manawatu Argus* 17 Sept. 3 Jacko by the way is the latest name for the Turk. What the origin of it is I could not say. **1918** *Kia-ora Coo-ee* (1981) Aug. 5 A certain New Zealand Regiment camped on the Jordan flats, recently came under the eagle eye of brother 'Jacko', who immediately went 'butcher's hook' or 'ram's horn' and launched forth much frightfulness. **1919** *Quick March* 10 July 33 'Igri wallah, imshi Y'allah.' Jackos, jackals, 'gala gala'. **1982** SGT. GASPARICH on *Helles attack May 1915* in Pugsley *Gallipoli* (1984) 194 Every time we threw earth up [digging in on Gallipoli] we got a shower of bullets because Jacko, we found out afterwards was lined up along a ridge well above us.

Jack Stewart, var. JOCK STEWART.

jackstraw. ANIMATED STRAW, the stick insect.
 1913 STOWELL *Maori–English Tutor* 109 Rō—mantis, jackstraw. **1989** p.c. Wendy Pond. 'Jackstraw' is widely used for stick insect by Northland Maori when speaking in English.

jack up, *v.* [Prob. a transf. or fig. use of *jack up* to raise with a jack: contrast Brit. dial. and slang *jack up* to ruin; to give up.]

1. To arrange (for), to engineer; to wangle.
 [*Note*] The verb poss. originated among NZ troops in North Africa during WW2.
 1939–45 *Expressions & Sayings 2NZEF* (TS N.A. WAII DA 420/1) Jack up—Prepare anything. **1942** *NZEF Times* 7 Sept. 5 In recent weeks NCO's have had a trying time 'jacking up' all sorts of things, 'Jack up a fatigue party', or 'jack up a list of this or that' could be heard all over the lines. *Ibid.* 12 Oct. 6 *Jack up*: A term meaning to achieve the apparently impossible or to bring order out of chaos; to arrange, inveigle, wangle or bolster up (a) Any transport (b) any alibi (c) leave (d) ED Pay—usually without the prior knowledge or consent of authority. **1949** COLE *It Was So Late* (1978) 74 For I remember he went on to say, 'The old man had it all jacked up. I was to be made a junior partner when I had taken my degree'. **1950** FAIRBURN *Letters* 10 June (1981) 196 You can surely jack up some pretext for flying north. **1962** CRUMP *One of Us* 90 He helped Toddy down to his ''ut'.., sat him on the bed, jacked him up a meal of sorts. **1985** STEWART *Gumboots & Goalposts* 50 'I'll jack-up someone to referee,' Walton volunteered.

2. In various contextual senses: to rebuild, fix up; to re-organize; to raise (one's) spirits.
 1942 *NZEF Times* 16 Aug. 6 Some of the pubs could do with a jacking up... Not enough service and civility. **1945** WEBBER *Johnny Enzed in Middle East* 13 May take a year to jack it up again. **1986** DAVIN *Salamander & Fire* 52 I knew I was too tired for any amount of gin to jack me up.

3. As **jack** (oneself) **up**, to get settled in, to settle (oneself) down; to make (someone) at home. Also in the phr. **to get jacked up**.
 1946 WEBBER *Johnny Enzed in Italy* 44 'All happy in the service..?' 'Of course they're not.' 'They've had plenty of time to jack themselves up by now.' **1970** SLATTER *On the Ball* 137 'And chapel three times on Sunday was a bit much for a colonial troop.' 'Come back to London with me and I'll jack you up,' says Spandau. **1971** *Listener* 22 Mar. 13 I'll see you right at a boardin' place until you get jacked up.

 Hence **jacked-up** *ppl. a.,* arranged, wangled, contrived; **jacking-up** *vbl. n.,* a fixing-up; an arranging.
 1962 *Dominion* (Wellington) 9 Nov. 6 Full on *Jacks*. This has been **jacked-up** question week in the House. This old, simple device deceives no one... The method is for a Government member to ask a Minister a question, the reply to which will embarrass the Opposition. **1971** CRUMP *Bastards I Have Met* 92 Apparently they'd recruited him to play the part of 'the other man' in a jacked-up divorce case. **1942** *NZEF Times* 7 Sept. 5 This business of '**jacking up**' now. **1944** *Hospitiki* (Troopship pub.) Vol.3 14 The gentle art of Jacking-up. **1965** HILLIARD *Power of Joy* 266 She's done all her jacking-up of partners and promising of dances beforehand.

jack-up, *n.* [f. JACK UP *v.*]

1. A trick, a wangle, an underhand deal done to produce a dishonest result.
 1945 WEBBER *Johnny Enzed in Middle East* (Gloss.) *jack-up*: a dirty plot **1968** SLATTER *Pagan Game* 70 He had a genius for the jack-up, always got his platoon billets. **1979** *Otago Daily Times* (Dunedin) 28 Mar. 21 It is a great pity that sharp differences of meaning explained in the publisher's publicity for such Anglo-New Zealand words as mall, docket, jack-up, social studies etc. were not included in the dictionary proper. **1985** STEWART *Gumboots & Goalposts* 50 'That competition was a jack-up, Hendy' he answered, 'because only the sixth and seventh forms were in.' **1993** *Evening Post* (Wellington) 12 Mar. 8 Surely this is a jack-up; they sounded as though they'd been preparing for a day.

2. Special Comb. **jack-up parade,** a smartening-up parade.
 1945 WEBBER *Johnny Enzed in Middle East* 36 [The chickens] started cheeping during a jack-up parade.

Jacky, *n.*¹ *Obs.* Also **Jackie.** [Perh. f. a general Services' application of *Jack(y)* to opponents.]

1. *Boer War.* A Boer.
 1900 *Let. from Trooper Ditely* 8 Mar. in Hawdon *New Zealanders & Boer War* (1907) 140 Up rushed a Jackie and pointed his rifle at me... By this time the jackies were round us like a swarm of bees.

2. *WW1* (Gallipoli). A Turk. See also JACKO. Cf. *Johnny Turk* (JOHNNY 2 a).
 1918 *Quick March* 1 Nov. 33 Occasionally a Maxim rattled off a few rounds, but it was all for the sake of 'normality', and without murderous intent. If 'Jacky' would only keep on working we were quite content to have it so.

Jacky, *n.*² [AND *Jacky n.*³ 2 , 1941: abbrev. of *Jacky Jacky* 'the typical Aboriginal'.] In the phr. **to sit (sit up) like Jacky,** to sit up straight or with confidence (often an impertinent or ingenuous confidence).
 1947 NEWTON *Wayleggo* 106 To sit there like Jacky in front of a mob of grinning, barracking station hands..made me feel a perfect fool. **1955** BJ Cameron *Collection* (TS July) sit up like Jacky (v) To put on one's best party manners. **1959** SLATTER *Gun in My Hand* 45 Can't go these [bar] stools. Sitting up here like Jacky. I like the old style. **1978** SUTHERLAND *Elver* 24 So there they were..sitting up like jackie in the back of the 1930 model Austin Sixteen. **1981** MARRIOTT *Life in Gorge* 49 The sight of Avery, sitting up like Jackie, trundling up the road..without a clue how close to death he had been, didn't seem to make us feel any better. **1987** *Province New Nelson Writing* 13 Ron sat like jacky behind the wheel. You'd have thought he was driving a Rolls he looked so pleased with himself. **1996** *Dominion* (Wellington) 2 Mar. 23 Warren [the instigator of *Coronation Street*] sat up like Jackie in the Rovers Return positively vibrating in every fibre of his being with..interviewee eagerness.

jacky, *n.*³ Mainly *Chatham Islands.* Also **jackie.** [An adaptation of Ma. *tiaki(-aki).*] red-billed gull (GULL 2 (3)).
 1952 RICHARDS *Chatham Is.* 83 *L[arus] novae hollandiae*... Red-billed Gull, Jacky. Tiaki-aki. **1966** FALLA et al. *Birds NZ* 154 Red-billed Gull *Larus scopulinus*... Tarapunga, Mackerel Gull, Jackie (Chathams). **1985** [see GULL 2 (3)]. **1995** RYAN *Reed Dict. Mod. Maori* 244 *tarapunga* gull-jackie..red-billed gull.

jade. Often as **green** (or **New Zealand**) **jade,** formerly commonly, now occas., applied to varieties of GREENSTONE 1, esp. in its use for Maori artefacts, and occas. for modern jewellery. Cf. JADEITE.
 1777 FORSTER *Voyage Round World* I. 161 [He] presented the captain with a piece of green nephritic stone, or *jadde*, which was formed into the blade of a hatchet. **1817** [see GREENSTONE 1]. **1839** TAYLOR *Journal* 28 Apr. (ATLTS) II. 120 Their Tikis or green jade ornaments are becoming so scarce that I could not procure one without paying an exorbitant price, they are only made in the South Island where the stone is found. **1840** POLACK *Manners & Customs* II. 30 The Meri is..formed of the green talc, jade, serpent-stone, and jasper (for it has been called by all these names). **1868** PYKE *Province of Otago* 39 Jade—ordinarily known as Maori Greenstone (*Poenamu*) occurs *in situ* on several parts of the West Coast. **1874** BAINES *Edward Crewe* 84 To hew a canoe into shape..is no small undertaking..but what a labour! with nothing save..hard wood wedges, and tools of 'jade'. **1892** [see POUNAMU 1]. **1904** TREGEAR *Maori Race* 248 The Maori greenstone (*pounamu*) called jade, jadeite, nephrite, etc., by Europeans, is a mineral very restricted in its deposits. **1917** [see GREENSTONE 1]. **1927** DONNE *Maori Past & Present* 31 The jade *hei-tiki* was suspended on the neck. **1946** ABBERLEY *Chase Me a Kiwi* 165 The substance is popularly known as 'greenstone' but it has been variously called 'jade', 'jadeite' and 'nephrite' by Europeans. **1959** MCLINTOCK *Descr. Atlas* 2 The only sources of greenstone (jade)..lay in this region. **1965** CAMERON *NZ* 33 Te Waipounamu (greenstone, or New Zealand jade) is a more common name for the South Island. **1986** BELICH *NZ Wars* 337 *mere* short club, sometimes of greenstone (New Zealand jade).

jadeite. Occas. used for GREENSTONE 1. Cf. JADE.
 1892 [see POUNAMU 1]. **1904** [see JADE]. **1926** COWAN *Travel in NZ* II. 84 Here is an appropriate moment to tell the story of the jadeite or *pounamu* which first won celebrity for the West Coast. **1946** [see JADE].

jaffa /'dʒæfə/. [A proprietary name (see quot. 1951) recalling the colour of a *Jaffa orange* f. *Jaffa*, a port in Israel.] A round sweet having a hard bright-orange coating or shell enclosing a soft chocolate centre; once often popular among children for rolling down the sloping floors of picture theatres during matinees.

1951 *Patent Office Jrnl* 29 Mar. [Registration] No. 49713 [of] 11 October 1950. *Jaffas*. James Stedman Henderson's Sweets Limited, of Sweetacres, Roseberry, Sydney, N.S.W., Australia, and of Victoria and Graham Streets, Auckland, New Zealand, confectioners and chocolatiers. **1953** SUTTON-SMITH *Unorganized Games NZ Primary School Children* (VUWTS) I. 407 [Play with sweets and natural food includes] making pepper pots and paper boats with lolly papers; playing marbles with jaffas. **1980** HALL *Prisoners of Mother England* 20 Almost instantly..a packet of jaffas [goes up] in front of every female face [at half-time]. **1983** HENDERSON *Down from Marble Mountain* 203 Princess and Shorts [picture theatres] on the corner and magnificent Jaffa-rolling. **1987** *Chosen Place* 104 Jaffas. Orange candy coated chocolate **1991** *Cuisine* June/July 18 Many readers will remember when chocolate and orange first collided. It was on the floorboards under the ninepennies at the Majestic. Years later, Jaffa rollers can enjoy the same flavour combination but at a more sophisticated dress circle level.

jake, *a.* Also early **jakes**. [f. *jake* orig. US, but see also EDD Suppl. *jake-easy*. Sc. 1895 Oh, buy't if ye like; I'm jake-easy on't; see OED.] All right, 'O.K.', esp. in the phr. **she'll be (she's) jake**, expressing confidence in a happy outcome; reassurance, agreement, etc. See also JAKELOO.

1918 *Chron. NZEF* 2 Aug. 11 I'm jakes now with the levers up, as they say. **1919** *Ibid.* 24 Jan. 302 To the old hands everything was 'jake, an' no whizz-bangs'. **1934** *Press* (Christchurch) (Acland Gloss.) 20 Jan. 15 *Jakerloo, Jake.*—All right, comfortably placed. (Since 1918?) **1943** *NZEF Times* 10 May 5 He won't worry about a plate... She'll be Jake on the counter. **1948** MARTIN *Voices I* 7 'You'll miss the boat...' 'She's jake,' he told me. **1957** GOLDBLATT *Democracy at Ease* 6 Perhaps the most common and characteristic cry of the Kiwi is 'She's jake!' **1965** GILLHAM *Naturalist in NZ* 147 'Up there she's jake.' Which was just another way, I discovered, of saying all's right with the world. The feminine personal pronoun is used exclusively on these occasions—such a nice gesture. **1970** DAVIN *Not Here Not Now* 108 'Are you all right for money ?'..'She's jake, thanks.' **1970** *Listener* 12 Oct. 12 Long as there's plenty of beer, she'll be jake. **1978** HENDERSON *Soldier Country* 141 'Right,' promised the Collie and the Scotch Terrier. 'She's jake, boss,' and off they trotted.

jakeloo /ˈdʒæikəˈlu/, *a. Obs.* Also **jakealoo, jakerloo.** [An elaboration of *jake*: AND 1919.] All right, 'O.K.' Occas. as an adverb. Cf. JAKE.

1934 [see JAKE]. **1936** HYDE *Passport to Hell* 174 Jakeloo, Starkie; she's [*sc.* a wound] a little beauty, clean through my arm! **1944** *Short Guide NZ* 39 *Jake, jakealoo*—good, okay. **1955** BJ Cameron Collection (TS July) jakealoo (adv) All right, all in order. **1964** HOSKEN *Life on Five Pound Note* 36 In a letter to his mother [the seven-year-old] wrote: 'I thought I was omesick, but Aunty said I was just ungry, and after I et tu bitates and three elpins of apple by I felt jakeloo.'

Jamie Woodser, var. **Jimmy Woodser.**

jandal /ˈdʒændəl/. [A proprietary name, prob. f. *j*(apanese s)*andal*.] A simple sandal (often of rubber or plastic) held to the foot by two straps joined across the arch to the sides and to a single strap fitted between two toes. (In Britain often termed *flip-flop(s)*, in Austral. and also now occas. NZ, *thong(s)*.)

1958 *NZ Patent Office Jrnl. No.29* Apr. 946 Jandals 60683 [filed] 4 October 1957..footwear and all types of hosiery. J. Yock and Company Limited. **1966** *Listener* 29 Apr. 6 Her jandals made a pleasing crunchy sound on the tiny cockle shells. **1976** HILLIARD *Send Somebody Nice* 171 The [hippie] boys in denim jackets and jeans and jandals, the girls in heavy jackets..and skirts..and jandals. **1979** GEBBIE & MCGREGOR *Incredible 8-Ounce Dream* 63 Eventually Charlie Brown's trundler..sliced over Bob's jandal-clad foot, leaving us with a hobbling barman. **1986** *Listener* 26 Apr. 46 *Jandal*... I am told it [*sc.* jandal] is a portmanteau word from *Japanese sandals*. **1994** *NZ Herald* (Auckland) 19 Apr. [correspondence page] [Letter from Michael Yock and P. Yock] Jandals (Japanese sandals) were first manufactured by Anthony Yock of Jandals Ltd in Onehunga, and the name was the invention of Morris Yock.

janker /ˈdʒæŋkə/. *Logging. Hist.* Also occas. **jenker, junker**; freq. later **jinker** /ˈdʒɪŋkə/. [f. Sc. dial.: EDD *janker* a long pole on two wheels used for carrying wood, the log being fixed to it by strong clasps (1832); SND A carriage adapted to the easy loading and conveyance of timber; AND *jinker* only, 1889.] Two wheels connected to an arched axle fitted with a tow-bar, under which the front end of the log (or long load) to be towed was raised off the ground and fastened by chains, the apparatus being moved by bullocks. Cf. CATAMARAN 2, *timber-wheel* (TIMBER *n.*¹). (The modern equivalent is called a *logging arch*.)

1885 *Wairarapa Daily* 17 Mar. 2 He will be able to fetch the logs right in to the mill by means of a tram without using junkers at all. **1923** *Awards, etc.* 111 [Westland Timber Yards and Sawmill Employees] [Rates of wages] Waggon-drivers [£]4 5 [s.] 0[d.] Lorrie and jenker drivers 4 5 0 Dray-drivers 4 0 0. **1940** *Tales Pioneer Women* (1988) 199 Here the material had to be unloaded and jinkered across a 2000-acre paddock to Inchbonnie... A jinker is a two- or four-wheeled contrivance used for transporting logs out of the bush. **1961** HENDERSON *Friends in Chains* 87 Then upward from the wilderness, with heavy props and beams, In waggons, drays and jinkers crept the panting timber teams. *Ibid.* 187 Jinker: Two large wheels and hooped axle used for logging in the bush. **1981** HUNT *Speaking a Silence* 10 I can even remember way back to seeing the bullock jankers go by here, taking the logs to the mill. *Ibid.* 34 The old bullock janker; it was just two big wheels with a long pole and two bullocks, one each side, hooked on with great big yolks [*sic*] around their necks. **1985** HAWKE & SCOTT *Early Farm Machinery in NZ* 134 Jinkers were another form of transport for logs, and other long loads. **1988** Museum, Northland p.c. Kendrick Smithyman [Notice on exhibit] Logging jinker. Often referred to as a logging arch, it was occasionally used as another method [besides the catamaran] of moving logs but was not popular on steep grades having a tendency to overrun the bullock team. On flat land however this method was quite satisfactory as the rear end of the log dragged along the ground and acted as a brake... Jinker restored by Mr Reg Poyner. **1992** PARK *Fence around the Cuckoo* 12 The old people of Te Kuiti competed against each other with mud stories. 'Remember the time a bullock team and jinker sank in the main street?'

Hence **jinker** *v. trans.*, to transport (esp. timber) by jinker.

1940 [see above]. **1985** HAWKE & SCOTT *Early Farm Machinery in NZ* 134 During the building of the West Coast to Otira railway, material was brought up..to Mitchell's where it was unloaded and jinkered across a 2000 acre paddock to Inchbonnie.

japara /dʒəˈpɑrə/. Also **japarra, jhapara**. [Found recorded elsewhere only as quot. 1930 below, and in *The Macquarie Dictionary* (1981): origin uncertain (cf. quot. 1930); cf. also *Japara* in the 17c. the chief port of the kingdom of Mataram in Java then the Dutch East Indies.] A light-weight, tightly-woven, often waterproofed cotton material used for making tents, oilskins, etc.

[**1930** *Mercury Dict. of Textile Terms* 287 *jhapara*—A native Indian woven muslin cloth, made from Indian cotton and embroidered with floral designs in silk. About 48 ends and 42 picks per inch. 40's T., 40's W. The yarns generally are of a brown tint.] **1910** *TrNZI* XLII. 14 The material is that of which the fine top-sails of yachts are made, technically known as japarra—an Egyptian fabric. **1917** *NZ Free Lance* (Wellington) 19 Jan. 11 At night time the adventurers would paddle ashore, pitch their Japara tent, citronella themselves, boil the billy, and settle down to a night of slaughtering mosquitoes and sand-flies. **1948** GILKINSON & HAMILTON *Moir's Guide Book* (2edn.) 81 The most suitable material is light-weight japara, which is a strong closely-woven cotton, and this is usually proofed with a linseed oil or similar preparation. **1952** THOMSON *Deer Hunter* 20 Sleeping bags are fairly straight forward, the only stipulation being that they should weigh no more than 4lbs, including a waterproof cover of japara (aeroplane cloth). **1961** NOLAN *Handbook for Trampers* 18 There are many different tents on the market but the standard four-man 6ft x 8ft or three-man 5ft x 7ft japara tents with 1-ft walls are adequate. **1973** *Consumer* 92 27 A heavy quality coated nylon parka or the familiar oiled japara are suitable for heavy rain. **1991** *NZ Woman's Day* 1 May 53 [Advt] They're back! And even better than ever! Oily Japara Parka. They've always been unbeatable weather beaters, now they're even better than before, in the latest dark green shade of fabric from overseas.

jar. In New Zealand, usu. a 2.25 l FLAGON, formerly a *half-gallon* (HALF- 3).

[*Note*] Contrast Brit. (and occas. NZ) use of *jar*, a glass of beer.

1911 *Truth* 16 Dec. 5 He tried to humo[u]r her by first getting her home, and then getting a jar and two riggers of beer from the hotel. **1952** *Here & Now* Oct. [back cover] 1/2 gallon Jars of wine for only 8/9..only 8/9 for a half-gallon jar. **1959** SLATTER *Gun in my Hand* 14 Blokes coming up the drive every night, some lumping cartons of beer, some carrying jars of draught. **1982, 1988** [see *half-gallon* (HALF- 3 a (b))].

Hence, **jargozzled** [f. *jar* + *gozzled* a fanciful alteration of *guzzled*.] Very drunk.

1921 LORD *Ballads of Bung 'Stunology'* (1976) [10] 'On the jag', 'juiced', 'joyed', 'jargozzled', and oh, 'as full as a kite'.

jaro /ˈdʒærʌu/. [Origin unknown.] In the phr. **to give** (one) **jaro, to give jaro to** (someone), to scold, to abuse; to 'give (one) hell'.

1904 LANCASTER *Sons o' Men* 42 Cookie'll give yer jaro 'f yur late fur supper. **1937** PARTRIDGE *Dict. Slang* 434 *jaro*, give (a person). To scold, vituperate: New Zealand: C. 20. **1988** McGILL *Dict. Kiwi Slang* 50 *give jaro* to scold (Maori 'whauraura', to scold); eg 'If that kid doesn't pipe down soon I'll give it jaro, by crikey.'

jasmine. [Transf. use of *jasmine Jasminum* spp., a plant having fragrant white flowers.] Also **Maori (native, New Zealand) jasmine.** Either of the two New Zealand climbing plants of the genus *Parsonsia* (fam. Apocynaceae), *P. heterophylla* bearing fragrant flowers (see also KAIHUA), or *P. capsularis* bearing fragrant white

flowers, often flushed reddish in bud (see also AKAKIORE, KAIKU). See also PERIWINKLE n.²
1922 *Auckland Weekly News* 28 Sept. 17 The flowers of the New Zealand jasmine, small, white, and sweetly scented, are displayed chiefly on the outskirts of the forest. **1929** *Tararua Tramper* Oct. 2 Another pretty climbing plant now is Parsonsia heterophylla. This has large panicles of scented creamy white flowers, and is sometimes called N.Z. jasmine. **1940** LAING & BLACKWELL *Plants NZ* 360 Parsonsia heterophylla (*The Varied-leaved Parsonsia*)... Flowers white, scented. (Maori Jasmine). **1966** *Encycl. NZ* III. 478 [Caption] Parsonsia heterophylla, *Maori jasmine, a shrub which climbs by twining stems. Ibid.* III. 711 Jasmine, New Zealand..akakiore..*Parsonsia capsularis*. **1982** WILSON *Stewart Is. Plants* 44 *Parsonsia capsularis* Native Jasmine... Akakiore... Kaikuu... Slender, many-branched climber... Flowers small, clustered, creamy, flushed reddish in bud. **1983** *Land of Mist* 65 You might identify the common liane, kaihua, also known as Maori jasmine because of its small, white, scented flowers. **1988** DAWSON *Forest Vines to Snow Tussocks* 57 The two species of *Parsonsia*, sometimes known as native jasmine, are found in lowland forest and shrubland throughout the country.

jasper. *Obs.* Occas. as **green jasper**. Formerly used for varieties of GREENSTONE 1. Cf. JADE.
1769 MONKHOUSE 18 Oct. in Cook *Journals* (1955) I. 581 He had a narrow slip of Jasper talk [=talc] formed somewhat like a french bean, hanging to his ear. **1777** ANDERSON *Journal* 25 Feb. in Cook *Journals* (1967) III. 809 Neither is there any mineral worth notice but a green jasper or serpent stone of which the natives make their tools and ornaments. **1830** [see TALC]. **1840** [see JADE].

javelin-fish. [See quot. 1956; AND 1896.] Any of several rat-tail fish of fam. Macrouridae, esp. *Coelorinchus* (formerly *Coelorhynchus*) *australis* an abundant food fish, and *Lepidorhynchus denticulatus*. See also RATTAIL.
1921 *NZJST* IV. 120 Coelorhynchus australis... Javelin-fish. Occasionally taken by trawlers in Golden Bay. Highly esteemed as a food fish. Distribution: Known from South Island coasts and Wellington Harbour. **1938** *TrRSNZ* LXVIII. 404 *Coelorhynchus australis...* Javelin-fish (rat-tail). **1956** GRAHAM *Treasury NZ Fishes* 161 Javelin-fish... The common name javelin is bestowed on this fish [*C. australis*] from the sharply-pointed snout like the sharp end of a javelin used in olden times in warfare. **1967** NATUSCH *Animals NZ* 214 Whiptails and javelin fish are less common members of the [true codfish] group. **1989** PAULIN et al. *NZ Fish* 124 *Lepidorhynchus denticulatus* javelinfish. **1990** FOORD *Descr. Animal Dict.* 350 RUGOSE RATTAIL *Coelorinchus australis*. A large fish with tapering tail and with rows of spines on the body scales found..off central NZ... OTHER NAME: Javelin-fish.

Jay-force, var. J-FORCE.

J.C. bird: see JESUS CHRIST BIRD.

jellie, jelly, varr. GELLY.

jenker, var. JANKER.

Jenny. [From a fanciful resemblance to the action of a spinning jenny.]
1. *Fencing.* Also **spinning Jenny**. A device for paying out rolls of wire along a fence line. See also wire spinner (WIRE *n.* 2).
1951 ACLAND *Early Canterbury Runs* 372 *Jenny.* Four spokes at right angles, revolving on a block. Coils of wire are unwound from it when fences are erected. **1981** *Listener* 21 Mar. 67 The coil, 650 metres long, was heavy stuff. Ross placed it over a spinning Jenny, an ingenious device which simply unwound as the wire was pulled. He then set off down the fencing line. I watched Jenny do her stuff without fault until 200 metres of wire had unwound. **1984** *Dominion* (Wellington) 5 Jan. 5 [I learned how to] use a spinning jenny for running out new wire... All the skills of the fencer were shown to me. **1982** *Agric. Gloss.* (MAF) 28 *Jenny*: Device for unrolling rolls of wire along a fence line. May be called a spinning jenny or a wire spinner.

2. Jenny-wheel. *Mining.* See quot.
1961 HENDERSON *Friends In Chains* 187 Jenny-wheel: Winding rope which passes round wheel on top of poppet-head.

jerry, *v.*
1. [f. US slang *jerry a.*, in the phr. *to be jerry to* to be 'wise' to: see OED *a.²*; AND 1894.] To understand; to catch on (to); to tumble to. Cf. JERRYRUMBLE.
1917 *Digger Transport Mag.* 4 May The excuse was so full of Mer(r)it that the officer failed to 'jerry' to it. **1924** SCANLON *Digger Stories* 10 No; no;..you don't jerry. **1938** *Press* (Christchurch) (McNab Slang) 2 Apr. 18 'To be a dag at,' 'to put across a beaut,' 'to jerry to'..need no explanation. **1959** SLATTER *Gun in My Hand* 91 Tried to cut me out with me sheila. Hadn't jerried to it before. Put the kybosh on that smartly. **1968** SLATTER *Pagan Game* 174 Ted Wallis will never jerry to what is wrong with the game today. **1978** MANTELL *Murder in Fancydress* 154 Soon as Stroud jerried to what I was getting at he couldn't get out from under fast enough. **1982** NEWBOLD *Big Huey* 250 Jerry (v) Catch on, understand.

2. Also as a *n.*, esp. in the phr. **to take a jerry to**, to understand, to discover.
1937 PARTRIDGE *Dict. Slang* 437 *jerry*,... a recognition, discovery, 'tumble'. **1969** *Landfall* 92 328 It was time this country—ah! Took a jerry to itself.

jerryrumble, *v. Obs.* [f. JERRY *v.* + *rumble* to understand, poss. rhyming slang for 'tumble' to suddenly discover.] *intr.* To discover, to understand; to 'tumble to'. Cf. JERRY.
1906 *Truth* 25 Aug. 5 Mary played up to the sky and fought hard, but O'Connor clinched, and soon Mary jerryrumbled that ju-jitsu was not her long suit. **1906** *Truth* 1 Sept. 8 Now he jerryrumbles that the fact of the matter is that he was half-cock when he waxed so eloquent.

Jessies's dream. Rhyming slang for 'STEAM' q.v., methylated spirits (as a drink).
1984 *NZ Times* 10 June 10 Round the World for Ninepence, Jessies's Dream, Fix Bayonets, devotees called methylated spirits, recommending orange juice as a dilutant. **1988** McGILL *Dict. of Kiwi Slang* 63 *Jessie's dream* methylated spirits; Isaiah 11:1 'And there shall come forth a rod out of the stem of Jesse'; WWII army.

Jesus Christ bird. Also **J.C. Bird**. Any of various seabirds, from their apparent ability to 'walk' on water, skimming the water lightly with moving feet, esp. the *white-faced storm petrel* (PETREL 2 (19) b (e)). Compare DANCING DOLLY, SKIPJACK 2.
1966 FALLA et al. *Birds NZ* 55 White-faced Storm Petrel *Pelagodroma marina*. *Other names*: Takahikare-moana, Skipjack, Jesus Christ Bird (shortened to 'J.C. Bird'). **1979** [see PETREL 2 (19) b (e)]. **1982** *SALE Four Seasons* 38 From this apparent walking on water derives the name petrel—from St Peter. By the same analogy, [the storm petrel] is sometimes called the Jesus Christ bird.

jetboat. A motor-boat usu. of shallow draft propelled by a jet of water pumped forcefully out from below the stern waterline (see quot. 1983); also *spec.* **Hamilton jet (jetboat)**, a boat propelled by a Hamilton jet unit designed by Charles William ('Bill') Feilden *Hamilton* (1899–1978).
1963 HAMILTON *White water, the Colorado jet boat expedition, 1960.* [Title] [**1968** *NZ Patent Office Jrnl. No.1062* 9 Feb. Buehler Jet B82686 [filed] 14 November 1966..jet boats, parts and accessories thereof. The Buehler Corporation. Indiana.] **1970** *Listener* 27 Feb. 1 [Caption] The experimental jetboat on the Waimakariri River, 1951. **1971** *NZ Patent Office Jrnl. No.1098* 20 Jan. Hamilton Jet 92680 [filed] 4 February 1970..jet propelled boats and parts and accessories therefor in this class. C.W.F. Hamilton & Co. Limited. **1972** *Evening Post* (Wellington) 29 Feb. 38 Twenty one feet long, weighing two and a half tons, made in NZ, and only drawing 7 inches of water when cruising at 35 miles per hour, two $12,000 jet boats daily ply the Wanganui River. **1975** *NZ News* 8 Jan. 9 Another development of consequence in New Zealand has been the invention of the jet boat... Propelled and steered by its water jet, the Hamilton jet boat can make 180-degree turns in its own length. **1983** BLOXHAM *Jet Boat* 1 A jet boat is a standard boat fitted with a car engine to drive a sophisticated pump or 'jet unit'. This draws water in through an intake in the bottom of the hull and forces it out at high pressure, jet-like, through a nozzle in the rear. Unlike a conventional boat, the jet boat has neither propeller nor rudder. Instead, it is pushed along, and steered, simply by the thrust of the jet stream. *Ibid.* 23 It was addressed simply: 'Hamilton Jet Boat Inventor, New Zealand'. *Ibid.* 64 In 1967 a Wanganui-based operator..began the longest commercial jet-boat run in the Southern Hemisphere.

jetboating, *vbl. n.* and *ppl. a.*
a. The use of jetboats for transport or sightseeing; the sport of racing jetboats.
1976 JOHNSTON *New Zealanders* 87 A watersport available to only a few is jetboating. **1983** BLOXHAM *Jet Boat* 1 In 30 short years New Zealand has become the home of the jet boat and New Zealanders the undisputed masters of the art of jet boating.

Hence **jet boater**.
1983 BLOXHAM *Jet Boat* 82 New Zealand and Canadian jet boaters regard each other with a mixture of awe and envy.

b. *ppl. a.* Pertaining to, or using, jet boats.
1977 *Dominion* (Wellington) 15 Sept. 4 The marathon is the longest and toughest jet boating event in the world—appropriately enough, as New Zealand is the original home of the sport. **1986** *Listener* 16 Aug. 82 Squadrons of jet-boating crayfishers make their way..to the fast refrigerator trucks which will take the delicacy out of town.

jewel bird. *Obs.* SILVEREYE.
1905 THOMSON *Bush Boys* 176 Jewel birds, with tiny silver eyes, green as emerald, whirr in a flock from out a bushy tree.

jeweller's shop. *Goldmining.* [AND 1853.] A very rich gold deposit or claim.
1879 *Herald* (Reefton) in Latham *Golden Reefs* (1992) 306 Bill once more appeared upon the scene at Westport, dressed out in new togs, and talked mysteriously about his new 'jeweller's shop'. **1880** BATHGATE *NZ* 60 Occasionally a mine apparently barren

takes a capricious turn and becomes what the miners term 'a jeweller's shop'. **1967** MAY *West Coast Gold Rushes* 527 Jeweller's shop:..(Australia) A claim of exceptional richness. **1968** *NZ Contemp. Dict. Suppl.* (Collins) 11 *jeweller's shop n.* quartz glittering with ore; very rich ore.

jew's ear: see FUNGUS 2 (5).

J-force. *Hist.* Also **Jayforce, Jay Force.** [f. *J(apan + force.*] The New Zealand contingent of the British Commonwealth occupation force in Japan.
  1945 *Freyberg to Prime Minister* 9 Oct. in *Documents Relating to Second World War* (1951) II. 445 Jayforce is coming into being on or about 15 October... In view of your desire for leave to England for Jayforce personnel, we are arranging to send about 100 officers and men of all earlier reinforcement drafts posted to Jayforce with the first leave party. **1947** *Tararua Tramper* July 20 Ray Babbage has returned with the first draft of the J-Force. **1951** *Here & Now* Mar. 9 The New Zealand contingent in Korea is not large... And if it were mainly serving, as J-Force did, as occupation and police troops, it would not matter much to us. **1984** BARBER *Red Coat to Jungle Green* 126 Before the close of August 1945 the New Zealand Government had accepted Britain's invitation to contribute to the Commonwealth [occupation] force... This was to be Jayforce. *Ibid.* 127 Jayforce was to be reduced to 4000 all ranks—to be mainly military, with an artillery, engineer, medical, ordinance, signals and provost support. **1986** LATHAM *WAAC Story* 44 Thirty six WAAC posted to 6GH went to Japan with 'J' Force on 15 December 1945 as part of the Occupational Force there. *Ibid.* 188 Some of the Sisters and Nurses from there came on with us to Florence where Jay Force was formed.

jigger, *n.*¹ [Spec. or extended use of Brit. dial. *jigger*: see OED *n.*¹ 5 q, and the use of *jig* for various mechanical reciprocating devices; DCan 3 a hand-car, 1934.]
  1. *Railways.* **a.** A small railway hand-car or trolley for carrying workmen, orig. propelled by hand-worked levers, later by a petrol engine.
  1904 LANCASTER *Sons o' Men* 158 Two men sat on the little iron jigger that straddled the wooden tram-line. **1913** *NZ Observer* 14 June 5 You had better go on the first jigger. **1926** PEACOCKE *His Kid Brother* 162 The jigger's a bit down the line. **1953** *Evening Post* (Wellington) 25 Mar. 14 A surfaceman..was killed..when a train overtook him as he was travelling between Wiri and Homai on a jigger. **1963** MORRIESON *Scarecrow* 64 It seemed like pain was the express and hatred was a little puffing billy and they met full on. Me, I was sitting on a jigger between them. **1980** MCLEOD *Down from Tussock Ranges* 233 The old days, when maintenance of the line was carried out by small gangs of surfacemen..travelling up and down the track on hand-pulled jiggers, were dead. **1992** SMITHYMAN *Auto/Biographies* 15 a great black tomcat squats..on the flat top of a motorised jigger.
  b. *Special Comb.* **jiggerman,** a railway surfaceman who travels by jigger.
  1981 *Climate* 32 Oct–Nov. 34 On tracks running nowhere to nowhere jiggermen search embankments for clues to missing trains.
  2. [Any of various frames on wheels: cf. EDD *n.* 4.] Cf. JANKER, (*jinker*). **a.** *WW1.* A frame on wheels to carry wounded.
  1918 *Chron. NZEF* 8 Nov. 179 At last I commenced the second stage—this time on a 'jigger', a frame on two rubber-tyred wheels which holds the stretcher—a journey of about half a mile, to the Collecting Station.
  b. Humorously applied to an old motorbike and sidecar.
  c1924 ANTHONY *Me & Gus* (1977 Gus Tomlins) 15 All he wanted me to do was to go into town with him in the jigger, and drop in there casually by myself and ask if Mr Tomlins had been in.
  c. *Logging.* [Prob. f. Brit. dial.: see EDD *n.* 4 Kent.] Poss. JIGGER 1 a conflated with *jinker* (JANKER).
  1949 DE MAUNY *Huntsman in Career* 162 Chancey..went off on the jigger down the narrow track into the bush each morning. **1972** NEWTON *Wake of Axe* 193 This involved snigging the [kauri] logs to the tramline terminus, loading them on the jiggers, and snigging them from the line to the river's edge.
  d. *Stevedoring.* A hand-truck, balanced on one pair of wheels. Cf. SAMSON.
  1964 DAVIS *Watersiders* 36 That's the tally-clerk. He's counting the number of carcases the boys load on the jigger.

jigger, *n.*² *Axemen.* [Poss. f. the springy ('jigging') movement of the board in use.]
  1. Also **jigger-board, jigger-stick.** A board fashioned to fit into a slot cut in the trunk of a standing tree (or in axemen's competitions, a high block) on which the axeman or sawyer stands to put in a scarf or cut (see quots. 1952, 1971); occas. applied to a framework erected at the base of a tree to be felled (see quot. 1953).
  1944 GILBERD in *NZ New Writing 3* 55 We would have given you..nerves to stand the narrow insecurity of the jigger-board. **1952** LYON *Faring South* 177 A jigger was simply a slab of white pine or rimu, axe-trimmed to a diameter of about six inches by three inches deep, and slightly thinner toward the extremity. In the end nearest the tree was bolted a forked piece of steel..which had a point or boss on the upper side... The bushman commonly cut a neat hole in the tree about level with his breast, or even higher. Into this little chamber the bushman pushed the steel head of the jigger..and aided by vines climbed up till he stood upright on the jigger. **1953** REED *Story of Kauri* 161 In earlier days a jigger (rough frame to provide a foothold) was erected for the crosscutter to stand on. **1961** CRUMP *Hang On a Minute Mate* 11 How long is it since a man stood on a jigger-board or boiled his billy over a manuka fire. *Ibid.* 42 During the next two weeks Jack learned about scarfing..jigger-boards..and axe sharpening. **1971** FORD-ROBERTSON *Terminol. Forest Sci.* 252 *Jigger(-board)* (New Zealand)..a short board or plank, its end notched into the bole, on which the cutter stands so as to enable him to fell the tree at a level not reachable from the ground. **1973** WALLACE *Generation Gap* 204 Two were standing on jiggers three feet from the ground, chopping rhythmically. **1978** *Manawatu Tramping Club Jubilee* 86 The big stumps with the jigger-stick cuts were a help in track-finding. **1983** LAMBERT *Illustr. Hist. of Taranaki* 83 [Caption] Here, two axemen chopping from jiggers, have begun to scarf a large tawa. **1994** ARNOLD *New Zealand's Burning* 28 By the late 1870s contract bush felling gangs were becoming common... Where a trunk was large..bushmen became adept at cutting further up, working from a stage of pieces of wood and ponga. In the later 1880s the stage gave way to the jigger-board, which fixed into a notch in the trunk.
  2. *Special Comb.* **jigger-chop, jigger-board chop,** an axemen's standing chopping contest involving the use of jigger-boards to reach the log to be chopped through.
  1952 *National Geographic Mag.* Apr. 452 Hamilton's Agricultural and Pastoral Show included a 'jigger chop'. **1963** HILLIARD *Piece of Land* 176 The best thing of the day to watch, the three-tier jigger-board chop. **1966** *Wanganui Photo News* 4 June 43 [Caption] Champion axeman Sonny Bolstad is watched by the Queen Mother as he competes in a jigger chop.

jigger, *n.*³ *Gumdigging.* JOKER *n.*²
  1988 p.c. Kendrick Smithyman (Auckland) 7 June *jigger* or alternatively *joker*, the top section of a gumspear... Source: historic photograph caption on information board at an archival gumfields site cared for by Lands and Survey.

Jimmy, *n.*¹ *Obs.* [AND 1859.] Abbrev. of JIMMYGRANT; an immigrant; a new chum.
  1850 W. Halse let. 6 Oct. in *McLean Papers* (ATLTS) VIII (July–Dec.). 177 I am glad it [*sc.* the farm] has not, as usual, fallen into the hands of the 'Jimmies' usurpers of the soil, but into those of a man who intends to surpass in improvements, anyone in the place. **1968** *NZ Contemp. Dict. Suppl.* (Collins) 11 *jimmy n.* immigrant. See *pommy.*

jimmy, *n.*² *s. South Island.* [Origin unknown.] Used by southern Maori with reference to things of ill-omen: **jimmy bird,** an albino muttonbird; **jimmy-work,** sorcery, TOHUNGAISM q.v. Cf. TAIPO 1.
  1918 *TrNZI* L. 145 On the 14th June, 1916, I had an interview with Mrs. Sidney Ladbrook..who had just then returned from a birding expedition to Evening Island... Mrs. Ladbrook informed me also that such a specimen [*sc.* a pure white muttonbird] is called a '**jimmy bird**' if it has white or pink eyes, but if the eyes are black it is known as a 'queen bird'. **c1920** BEATTIE *Trad. Lifeways Southern Maori* (1994) 179 The present-day Maoris call a white muttonbird a 'jimmy-bird' but the collector [*sc.* Beattie] could get no reason for this name, although his informants admitted it was given through a lingering superstitious dread of directly naming a thing of ill-omen. *Ibid.* 183 The white titi (an atua or 'jimmy-bird') was an evil omen. *Ibid.* 413 In one long house thatched with reeds and which stood at Rapaki till thirty years ago '**Jimmy-work**' was said to go on. 'This was just tohungaism'—but none of those present could say how the name 'Jimmy' originated in this connection. They considered it probable, however, that those who first used the term did so because it was uncanny to say the real name.

Jimmy Allen's art union: see ART UNION 1 b.

jimmy-grant. *Obs.* [AND 1859.] Rhyming slang for 'emigrant' or 'immigrant'.
  [*Note*] The only substantial NZ record is Wakefield's in *Adventure in NZ*, repeated in his *Handbook* of 1848, and the short form JIMMY *n.*¹ q.v. Later quotations merely recall or record Wakefield's use.
  1845 WAKEFIELD *Adventure NZ* I. 337 The profound contempt which the whaler expresses for the 'lubber of a *jimmy-grant*' as he calls the emigrant. *Ibid.* II. 180 Some of these [beach-combing] whalers seemed curiously divided between contempt for the inexperience of 'jimmy-grants', as they called the emigrants, and surprise at the general industry. **1941** BAKER *NZ Slang* 23 Another term..was *jimmygrant*... It has hitherto been supposed that this example of rhyming slang was of Australian origin. **1948** IRVINE-SMITH *Streets of My City* 32 At the close of 1840, there were 2,500 settlers, or in whaler parlance, 'Jimmy Grants', upon its shores. **1985** MCGILL *G'day Country* 123 A whaler would surely have dismissed me as one of those landlubberly 'jimmygrants'.

Jimmy nipper. *Obs.* Prob. the *tree weta* (WETA 2 (5)) which has obvious biting jaws.

1888 BARLOW *Kaipara* 187 Another insect very commonly found in soft wood..is called by the natives the 'Weta', but by vulgar little boys '*The Jimmy Nipper*'. *Ibid.* 188 [I asked] a settler, an old [Irish] soldier what they were called. 'Jimmy Nippers to be shure, sir!'

Jimmy Wood's, var. JIMMY WOODSER.

Jimmy Woodser. Also (rarely) **Jamie Woodser, Jimmy Wood's.** [Cf. AND, f. *Jimmy Wood*, the name of a character in the poem of that name by Barcroft Boake in the *Bulletin*, and perh. the name of an actual person, 1892.] Cf. FLY *n.*², *Johnny Woodser* (JOHNNY 2 b).

1. An alcoholic drink taken alone when company is present; occas. a drink taken privately to avoid 'shouting' for others (see quot. 1975).
1906 *Truth* 8 Sept. 1 Adams..had sneaked in [to the hotel] surreptitiously to enjoy a 'Jimmy Woodser'. **1906** PICARD *Ups & Downs* 12 'What's yours?' 'Ain't 'aving any, right oh, I'll have a Jimmy Wood's with the flies.' **1916** *Wairarapa Daily Times* 6 Sept. 4 A 'Jamie Woodser' is the exact equivalent of a 'Parnell Shout' which is the only kind of 'shout' now permitted. **1933** *Press* (Christchurch) (Acland Gloss.) 28 Oct. 17 *Jimmy* or *Johnny Woodser*.—Slang. A drink by yourself. It is a common expression up-country in New Zealand, but may be also common in England for all I know. **1934** *Press* (Christchurch) (Acland Gloss.) 20 Jan. 15 *Jimmy Woodser*.—A correspondent tells me that James Woods was a shearer on the Darling River, New South Wales, in the 'eighties. He spent the off season in Bourke. He was fond of a glass of beer but was never known to shout. He always drank on his own, so that when the shearers saw any one go to the bar by himself they always said he was having a J[immy] W[oodser]. Hence the saying. **1975** ANDERSON *Men of Milford Road* 52 I picked up the rum bottle off the counter and poured each of us a 'Jimmy Woodser' which we downed very quickly. **1985** BINNEY *Long Lives the King* 42 Pour herself a Jimmy Woodser to keep pace with him while out of his eyeline—? She thought better of that.

2. A person who prefers to drink alone, or apart from a 'school'.
1908 *Truth* 25 July 4 Knowing not when he will get another, he drinks deep of what he lays his hands on, and deteriorates into a Jimmy Woodser and absorbs his liquid with the flies, and sheds any small remnant of rectitude that he might have had about his clothes. A new species of Jimmy Woodser has been reported as having blossomed at a Clutha *dry district* benefit football match. **1910** *NZ Free Lance* (Wellington) 19 Nov. 10 The bracing ozone, the green hills..are supposed to work a complete change for the better in the Jimmy Woodsers who graduate from the bar to the police court. **1942** *NZEF Times* 21 Dec. 17 You'll find me lonesome in a Naafi, a-drinkin' to me sins, A-sippin' like a Jimmy Woodser.

Hence **Jimmy Woodsering (Woodsing)** *vbl.n.*, drinking alcoholic liquor alone.
1916 *Stratford Evening Post* 8 Sept. 4 A shocking example of 'Jimmy Woodsering' was brought under the notice of the Wellington police... A man was so palpably under the influence of drink that, to use a colloquialism, he was dead to the world. **1928** DEVANNY *Dawn Beloved* 307 Duke preferred to drink alone..'Jimmy Woods-ing', as the [West Coast] miners called it.

jingle. *Hist.* [Prob. f. Brit. dial.: AND *Hist.* 1862.] A covered two-wheeled carriage.
1865 BARKER *Station Life* (1870) 12 I gave F— no peace until he took me for a drive in a vehicle which was quite new to me—a sort of light car with a canopy and curtains, holding four, two on each seat, *dos-à-dos*, and called a 'jingle',—of American parentage, I fancy. **1925** BATHGATE *Random Recolls.* 16 (Griffiths Collect.) The public used to go there [Vauxhall Gardens] either by boat or round the head of the bay by 'jingle', as the omnibus cabs then [c1860s] plying in Dunedin were called.

jingle box. *Obs.* A sovereign. (No other record of this use.)
1972 HARGREAVES *Beads to Banknotes* 151 Sovereign[:] nicker, jingle box **1977** *NZ Numismatic Jrnl.* Oct. 15 British nicknames that have been current at some time in New Zealand's history include the following. A Sovereign was variously known as a *jingle box*, and *a thick 'un*.

Jingling Johnny. *Obs.* [AND 1941.] A blade-shearer; also a SWAGGER 1 a.
1934 *Press* (Christchurch) (Acland Gloss.) 20 Jan. 15 *Jingling Johnnies*.—Old time slang term for hand shearers. **1987** OGONOWSKA-COATES *Boards, Blades & Barebellies* 96 *Jingling johnnies*. Early colonial slang term for hand shearers. **1989** *NZ Eng. Newsletter* III. 25 *Jingling Johnny:* Originally a swagman but also another name for a hand shearer. Many of the old shearers carried their swags from shed to shed and no doubt their shears and billycans jingled as they walked.

jink. [See FORTY-FIVES for discussion.] A play in the game of forty-fives.
1980 MCGILL *Ghost Towns NZ* 127 Old Calamity was an early one-man band of fiddle, horn, cymbals and kettledrums. Gambling was poker or 45s, a diggers' card game from California involving legs, queer suits and Maggie, cries of 'Get Jinx!' and 'Go for the Doctor!'

jinker, var. JANKER.

jinner. [Alteration of *ginger.*] A nickname for a red-headed person.
1965 HILLIARD *Power of Joy* 266 Silk stockings; and Jinner's strides are half-mast. Here and there a hint of lipstick.

jockey.
1. *Shearing.* See quots. 1989, 1996.
1951 MCLEOD *NZ High Country* 26 The shearers buy their shears from the station and then proceed to cut them and bend them, and embellish them with 'drivers', 'knockers', 'jockeys' and 'cockspurs' until their makers would hardly recognise them. **1978** [see KNOCKER *n.*³]. **1989** *NZ Eng. Newsletter* III. 25 *Jockey:* A piece of flax stick fitted to the bow to build up the grip on a pair of shears. **1996** p.c. Dr S.R. Pennycook. The various stages of setting up shears include..optionally, fitting a *jockey* and (or) a *monkey* (shaped blocks of wood whipped on to one or both handles with seaming twine, to customise them to the grasp of a shearer with big hands; a jockey sits on the top handle, and a monkey hangs under the bottom handle).

2. *Obs. Logging.* A sawyer in a two-man team who does not pull his weight, but 'rides' on the saw and his companion's strength.
1986 OWEN & PERKINS *Speaking for Ourselves* 62 If he wasn't a good man at the end of a saw—some blokes were 'jockeys', they rode it—well, he wouldn't last long in the bush as far as his work was concerned.

3. As **jockey cap**, any of the *Tigridia* spp., garden plants of the iris family noted for their flamboyant flowers.
1985 *Press* (Christchurch) 25 Jan. 8 Known as 'peacock flowers' or 'tiger flowers' in the Northern Hemisphere, the tigridias lurk in New Zealand behind the absurd name 'jockey caps', presumably because of the shape and brilliant colours of their large, six-petalled flowers.

Jock McKenzie: see JOCK STEWART.

Jock Stewart. Also **Jack Stewart, Jock McKenzie** (see quot. 1965), **Jock Stuart,** usu. with init. caps. [A Scottish allusion from its tartan-like coloration.] Any of various scorpionfishes (fam. Scorpaenidae) but esp. *sea perch* (PERCH *n.* 2 (4) *Helicolenus percoides*). Cf. HIGHLANDER.
1922 *Auckland Weekly News* 9 Mar. 15 Jack Stewart has earned this local name because its dominating tints are those of the Stewart tartan. **1938** *TrRSNZ* LXVIII. 416 *Helicolenus percoides*... Sea perch, so called John Dory (scroddie, fivefinger, soldier-fish, Jock Stuart, Highlander). **1956** [see FIVE-FINGER 3]. **1965** *Evening Post* (Wellington) 20 Aug. 29 The scorpion fish, variously known as red rock cod, grandfather hapuku, Jock McKenzie or scarpee is not good to eat and its spines are capable of inflicting painful cuts. **1966** MCCLENAGHAN *Fiordland* 149 Hardly had the heavy sinker hit [the bottom] than the first Jock Stewart was on the way up... An ugly fellow with big eyes and spiny fins, and with the general appearance of a piece of tartan, he is called 'Jock Stewart' along the Fiordland coast. **1967** NATUSCH *Animals NZ* 231 Family Scorpaenidae includes the seaperch, *Helicolenus percoides*, better known as Jock Stuart..an ugly, spiny customer related to the dangerous stone fish and scorpion fish of tropical reefs. **1986** PAUL *NZ Fishes* 78 *Scarpee Helicolenus percoides*... Known from New Zealand and southern Australia. These fishes, known variously as scarpees, sea perches, jock stewarts, etc. were once thought to comprise a single species. **1991** BRADSTOCK *Fishing* 21 *Sea perch.* Other names: scarpee, Jock Stewart, highlander, flinger, pohuiakaroa, *Helicolenus percoides*.

Joe, *n.*¹ *Obs.* [Prob. Brit. dial.: see EDD *Joe n.*¹ northern dial. in the phr. *to be Joe*, to be master; AND 1854 'Prob. from the name of Charles Joseph La Trobe (1801–75), Lieutenant-Governor of Victoria'.] A cry, often **Joe! Joe!**, used to greet, 'barrack', or give notice of newcomers or strangers to a diggings; used especially as cry warning of the approach of authorities; an example or occurrence of this cry.
1861 *NZ Goldfields 1861* 4 Oct. (1976) 35 Not ten minutes ago, hearing a roar of 'Joe'—and this old Ballarat appellation, used as a term of ridicule, is in constant use in Dunedin and on the goldfields—from many voices. **1861** *Letter to Lyttelton Times* 16 Dec. in **1862** *Otago Witness* (Dunedin) 18 Jan. 7 (Griffiths Collect.) The cry of 'Joe' is purely a digger's word and is invariably used on the diggings as a greeting to new chums. **1863** HEYWOOD *Vacation Tour Antipodes* 165 In the early days of the Australian diggings 'Joe!' was the warning word shouted out when the Police or Gold Commissioners were seen approaching, but it is now the chaff for the new chums [in Dunedin]. *Ibid.* 188 Several men working on the roads [in Taranaki] shouted 'Joe' after us; but as we knew the meaning of this joke they did not get a rise out of us. **1871** MONEY *Knocking About NZ* 103 I had to undergo a tremendous fire of 'Joes' from every chum I passed. The word 'Joe' expresses the derision usually bestowed on new chums on the diggings, or any man acting, or dressing, or speaking in any way considered as *outré* by the diggers themselves. **1937** AYSON *Thomas* 31 No sooner had he left the store than the diggers caught sight of his bell-

topper and began greeting him with cries of 'Joe, Joe'. **1967** MAY *West Coast Gold Rushes* 527 'Joe! Joe!' was the old Australian warning-cry signalling the approach of 'the traps' (the police) or of commissioners checking for gold-digging licences.

Joe, *n.*²

1. The usual shortened form of *Joe Hunt* rhyming slang for 'cunt' in the sense of 'complete fool', esp. as **to make a Joe of (oneself)**, to make an ass of (oneself).

1960 16C F B4 Wanganui Girls C. 1 Joe **1963** *Dominion* (Wellington) 30 Sept. 4 [Heading] Player makes big 'joe' of himself. The [Wellington] club awards its Joey emblem to the player who, in the judgement of the reserves, makes the biggest 'Joe' of himself during the match. **1969** HILLIARD *Green River* 58 And anyway, what a joe they'd think he was, ringing to ask the name of his nearest neighbour. **1988** MCGILL *Dict. Kiwi Slang* 63 joe a fool, or acting foolishly, in phr. *make a joe of yourself.*

2. [From a familiar shortening of the name of the religious community (the Sisters of St) *Joseph.*] Also **Joey**. A nickname for a nun of the teaching Order of St Joseph; in pl. as **the Joes**, the Order collectively; often as **Black Joes** or **Brown Joes** according to the colour of the habit.

1992 PARK *Fence Around the Cuckoo* 28 In 1979 the Sisters of St Joseph were withdrawn from that school... Many of the Joeys, as we called them, were Australian women who suffered greatly in the deathly winters. **1996** *Wel-Com* (Wellington) Aug. 8 Many who read the..newsletter were educated by the 'Brown (or Black) Joeys'.

Joe, *n.*³ [?f. *Joe Blake* rhyming slang for 'flake'; or poss. f. *Joe Hunt* a partial rhyme on 'out the monk'.] In the phr. **out the Joe**, completely drunk; out cold (through drink).

1964 MORRIESON *Came a Hot Friday* (1981) 122 He's out the monk. Really out the Joe. He's made a fair dinkum job of himself [with drink] today.

joe, *v. Goldfields hist.* [f. JOE *n.*¹: AND 1854.] To cry 'joe!' to indicate the approach of, or to express disapproval of, an official, a policeman, or a newcomer or stranger.

1863 *Otago Colonist* 25 July in Lovell-Smith *Old Coaching Days* (1931) 35 Seating himself on the axle in a comical position, he was 'Joe'd' by a chorus of lookers-on. Replying that those who had nothing better to do than 'Joe' him were a set of 'tarnation fools', he drove off at top speed. **1871** MONEY *Knocking About NZ* 103 I was joined one by one by many others, several of whom had been among the first to 'Joe' me at the beginning. **c1875?** THATCHER in *NZ Songster No.3* 87 The swell that in London rides through Rotten-row, Is admired and bowed to by many, you know; But if he were to ride down our country roads, I rather think he would be pretty well 'joed'. **1966** TURNER *Eng. Lang. Austral. & NZ* 153 A correspondent to the Press, 24 May 1864, reported: You may form some idea of the estimate in which the escort is held by the miners, when I tell you that it was 'joed' yesterday for a distance of a quarter of a mile.

Hence **joeing** *vbl. n.*

1861 *NZ Goldfields 1861* 4 Oct. (1976) 38 The Tuapeka gold-field is under the charge..of Mr. Alfred Chetham Strode, gold-fields commissioner, a gentleman who appears to be highly popular among the miners, a feeling demonstrated somewhat by his uniform exemption from the 'joe'-ing with which everyone else clad in decent apparel is greeted.

Joe Blakes. Rhyming slang for the 'shakes', a fit of nervous shaking brought on by fright, breakdown, or alcoholic excess.

1942 *NZEF Times* 6 Apr. 6 He had rejected..the possibility of rain, leaking pipes, or a sudden call by that ubiquitous family, the Joe Blakes. **1945** *Ibid.* 19 Feb. 5 He was a noted sufferer from..'the Joe Blakes'. **1959** [*RSA*] *Review* Dec. 17 [Heading] Non-Alcoholic Joe Blakes... He was operated on by an Aussie doctor, without anaesthetic... When the orderlies let him go he nearly jittered off the table with a dose of joe-blake reaction. **1961** CRUMP *Hang On a Minute Mate* 27 I tell you, Jack me boy, it gave a man the Joe Blakes just to look at it. **1964** MCLEAN *Willie Away* 159 Marked cases of Joe Blakes, or taa-taas, developing..at prospect of further hellish flashes and cracks. **1978** JARDINE *Shadows on Hill* 76 I..carefully edged well back until it was safe to stand up, then went and sat down with my back to a rock and had a fit of Joe Blakes.

Joe Burke. *WW1.* Rhyming slang for 'Turk'. See also *Joe Turk* (JOHNNY 2 a).

1917 *Chron. NZEF* 13 June 185 The Gaza battle revealed..that 'Joe Burke' (as Johnny Turk is now called by our mounted boys) is in considerable strength. **1963** 'Joe Burke' [see *Johnny Turk* (JOHNNY 2 a)].

Joe McNab. *Prison.* Rhyming slang for 'stab'.

1982 NEWBOLD *Big Huey* 250 Joe McNab (v) Stab.

Joe Morgan. *Obs.* [Origin unknown.] Usu. *pl.* as **the Joe Morgans**, the horrors, the DTs.

1928 SMYTH *Jean of Tussock Country* 87 You would give anybody the Joe Morgans.

Joe Turk: see *Johnny Turk* (JOHNNY 2 a).

joey: see (*wood and*) *water joey* (WATER 2 b).

joey, *n.*¹ *Hist.* [Origin unknown.] A 'bottle' lantern made from a candle placed in the neck of an inverted bottle the bottom of which has been knocked or cut off. (See also LANTERN for a list of synonyms.)

1947 HOWITT *Pioneer Looks Back Again* 19 When we wanted to go out at night in our country house [c1883] we used a 'Joey' bottle lantern, or a slush lamp.

joey, *n.*² [Poss. f. JOE *n.*² 1.] A mistake.

1959 LAWLOR *Old Wellington Days* 139 I'll never forget the Cockney clarinet player [who].. made a 'Joey' on the top note of a cadenza, looked sadly at me and whispered 'there goes me job'.

jog. *Obs.* [f. Brit. dial. *jag, jog* a small cart-load of hay, wood, etc.: see OED *jag n.*² 1 a '*dial.* and *U.S.*'; EDD *jag(g). jog n.*¹] A small (often loosely tied) bale or truss of hay.

1991 LA ROCHE *Hist. of Howick & Pakuranga* 148 [Caption] Dufty Bell with a load of jogs in the 1947 Howick Centennial Parade. Jogs of hay were a major Howick export last century. *Ibid.* 184 'Jogs' or trusses of hay were cut from stacks, tied with flax and sold in Auckland [c1867–].

jogger. Mainly *Chatham Islands.* Also occas. **jogger cart**. A horse-drawn farm cart with pneumatic tyres used mainly on the Chatham Islands, but also associated with stock-droving in mainland New Zealand. Cf. SULKY.

1950 SIMPSON *Chatham Exiles* 109 [Caption] Mud-trained horses have no trouble hauling these Chatham Islands joggers over the boggy countryside. *Ibid.* 145 Horse and ox are still the principal means of haulage, and the islanders have invented a conveyance that overcomes the worse features of the bog—the so-called jogger. **1956** BLAIR *Life & Work at Canterbury Agric. College* 204 E.R.H. took two others with him to the near Selwyn waters..travelling by College jogger and horse. *Ibid.* 342 The day of the horse for farm work was definitely over at Lincoln, except for the jogger carts which still served the shepherd, stockman and the farm overseer. **1957** *DSIR Newsletter* July 31 Travel on the main island [of the Chathams] was by horse or 'jogger'. **1959** SLATTER *Gun in My Hand* 227 [The tourists] never see a mob of sheep coming in a gravel road out Te Wharau way with the jogger behind and the friendly wave from the drover. **1984** HOLMES *Chatham Is.* 59 Also in use was the 'jogger' a cartlike vehicle with two pneumatic-tyred wheels, seating about three people and drawn by two horses attached to a shaft... Tom McClurg of Te Whakuru made the first 'jogger' in Chathams, about 1940. **1991** DALLAS *Curved Horizon* 78 [In 1942] we were told that we..must relinquish our cars and travel from farm to farm by horse-drawn rubber-tyred joggers.

John.

1. [Poss. short for *John Hop*; but cf. AND 'abbrev. of *johndarm*', ad. French *gendarme*; 'used elsewhere but recorded earliest in Aust.', 1898.] Often *pl.* as **the Johns**. A policeman (incl. a military or traffic policeman), a 'cop'.

1905 *Truth* 28 Oct. 6 The Johns had a bad time of it keeping their sleepy eyes on suspicious customers. **1910** *Truth* 2 Apr. 1 Magistrate: 'The language is very bad—it is the most profane I have seen for some time. What is meant by the reference to '— — Johns'? Is 'John' a profane term?' Sergeant: 'No, your Worship, 'Johns' means policemen.' **1918** *Chron. NZEF* 22 Nov. 206 'Never mind about that,' said the John—and dumped him in the cell. **c1926** THE MIXER *Transport Workers' Song Book* 30 Quick, on with your coats—here's the 'John'. **1942** *NZEF Times* 31 Aug. 6 These poor soldiers, having nowhere to go, went into the old Bull and Bush..and were nabbed by the Johns. **1959** SLATTER *Gun in My Hand* 213 Nah, we don't want the cops... We don't want trouble with the bloody johns. **1964** HARVEY *Any Old Dollars Mister?* 24 We stopped and waited to see if this traffic john got squashed between the trams. **1983** MANTELL *Murder to Burn* 115 Coupla young johns wanted to move into the room pronto.

2. Special Comb. **John Dunn** *obs.* [ad. French *gendarme*: AND 1905], a policeman; **John Hop, john hop**, occas. ?journalistic **Johnop** [rhyming slang for 'cop': AND 1907], a policeman or military policeman.

1905 *Truth* 28 Oct. 5 A man..said he had never known a policeman to tell a lie. In future, a copper will not be nicknamed **John Dunn** or Moses. He will be called George Washington. **1906** *Ibid.* 14 July 1 I do not speak of so-called indecent postcards, most of which are only indecent in the eyes of a stupid John Dunn, but of downright horrors in lust. **1905** *Truth* 14 Oct. 1 The local [Taihape] **John Hop** went out into the bush..to arrest him. **1916** *Chron. NZEF* 15 Nov. 134 We formed up to march..headed by a red-capped John Hop' from the Coldstream Guards. **1920** *NZ Free Lance* (Wellington) 11 Aug. 9 The Johnops total 719, of whom five are Maoris. **1938** *Press* (Christchurch) (McNab Slang) 2 Apr. 18 The New Zealander might advise him [the traveller] to beware of 'the John Hops'. **1965** GEE *Special Flower* 121 'It must have been a shock to you too... Have you seen the johnhops?' **1976** MCCLENAGHAN *Travelling Man* 27 Well, the John hops are determined to get us. **1984** BEARDSLEY *Blackball 08* 244 John hop rhyming slang for 'cop' or policeman.

John Dory. *Zeus faber* (fam. Zeidae), a fish common in New Zealand waters and considered identical with the northern hemisphere *john dory* (see OED). See also KUPARU.

1769 PARKINSON *Journal* 9 Nov. (1773) 104 Native..brought us a large quantity of fish, mostly of the mackrel kind, with a few John Dories. **1960** BAXTER *Collected Poems* (1980) 218 The John Dory printed with God's thumbmark?

Johnnie, var. JOHNNY.

Johnny. Also **Johnnie.**

1. a. As **English Johnny** [a specific defined use of *Johnny* fellow: cf. OED 1], an Englishman.

[**1925** MANDER *Allen Adair* (1971) 5 Come along and see the johnny. He's an Englishman. Going back Home. A queer duck.] **1874** 'Hermul' in Heinz *Bright Fine Gold* (1974) 141 After the roaring days had passed away, there arrived at Hokitika a typical English 'Johnnie'. **1913** MANSFIELD *Stories* (1984) 134 He had ridden over..to help hunt down the young fellow who'd murdered Mr Williamson... They found him [the murdered Mr Williamson] in the barn, shot bang through the head, the young English 'johnny' who'd been on the station learning farming—disappeared. *Ibid.* 136 He was the English johnny who'd killed Mr Williamson.

b. In *ellipt.* uses: for JOHNNY CAKE q.v.; *John(ny) Norton obs.* [f. the name of *John Norton* (1862–1916) editor and part-owner of the *Truth* weekly in Australia and founder of the New Zealand *Truth*], a nickname for the *Truth* weekly; *Johnny Turk* (2 a below); JOHN DORY.

1946 HOGAN *Roads That Go Up & Down* 8 We threw our swags beneath the swaying trees, Then cooked our evening 'Johnnies' on the coals. **1908** *Truth* 25 Apr. 1 A Christchurch resident rushed hurriedly into Prohib. Isitt's tract emporium Colombo-street t'other day and asked for Norton's 'Truth'. 'Give us a "Johnny",' he said, producing three coppers. [*Ibid.* 20 June 6 [quoting Canterbury College 'Capping Mag.'] 'John Norton's' itself better taste would display Than these two rags.] **1919** WAITE *New Zealanders at Gallipoli* 290 The soldiers bore no malice [against the Turks]. 'Goodbye Johnnie, see you soon in the Suez Canal.' **1970** MIDDLETON in *Some Other Country* (1984) 156 'Oh that's a johnny: a john dory. Best eating fish in the sea'... 'We've got any amount with the johnny. You take the snapper'.

2. Used in weakened senses of *Johnny* 'fellow' as a prefix in the formation of familiar names of persons (often with patronizing or contemptuous allusion) or things. (Cf. also a similar general use of *Jack* or *John*.) **a.** Of persons: **Johnny-come-lately**, a newly-arrived immigrant or farm-hand; **Johnny raw** [f. Brit. dial.: AND 1840], NEW CHUM; **Johnny squatter**, SQUATTER 3; **Johnny (Joe) Turk** *WW1* [AND 1916], a Turk (see also JACKO, JACKY *n.*¹ 2, JOE BURKE).

1933 *Press* (Christchurch) (Acland Gloss.) 28 Oct. 17 *Johnny-come-lately*.—Nickname [c1890–1910] for a cowboy or any newly-joined hand or recent immigrant. **1900** SCOTT *Colonial Turf* 116 [Two card-sharping spielers speak.] They were **Johnny Raws** and got at them properly [*i.e.*, swindled them]. **1911** *Maoriland Worker* 7 July 11 I think you would do more good for the cause if you took the above-mentioned officials [of the Shearers' Union] under your wing and gave them some advice and not let them play into the hands of **Johnnie Squatter** the way they are by fighting among themselves. **1916** HARPER 14 June in *Letters from Gunner 7/516* (1978) 42 There is always something new to expect from **Johnny Turk**, and he fights square too, which can hardly be said for some of the forces which have been sent out against him. **1919** WAITE *New Zealanders at Gallipoli* 93 Johnny Turk had been caught napping, and the initiative of the New Zealand private soldier had sealed his fate. **1921** *Quick March* 10 Sept. 27 Woe betide the Johnny Turk surprised by the modern Maori. **1963** AITKEN *Gallipoli to the Somme* 34 I further found that I bore the Turk no trace of enmity—nor for that matter did any of us; he was to us 'Johnny Turk' or 'Joe Burke', almost a fellow sufferer. **1990** LANGFORD *Newlands* 69 Johnny Turk shot the waterbag and I watched the water trickle away.

b. Of things: **Johnny-all-sorts**, applied to something made up of or displaying a mixture of things; **Johnny Gee** *obs.* [origin unknown], methylated spirits (as a drink); **Johnny-go-to-bed**, *Eschscholzia californica* (fam. Papaveraceae), the Californian poppy whose golden-yellow flower is responsive to sunlight (see also *four-o'clock* (FOUR); **Johnny Woodser** *obs.* [AND 1895], a variant of JIMMY WOODSER.

1866 *Lyttelton Times* 11 Aug. 2 These villains were camped on O'Donoghue's diggings, and..professed great anxiety to obtain a stand in the street whereon to erect a '**Johnny-all-sorts**' store. **1917** MILLER *Econ. Tech. Cook. Book* 289 *Johnny All Sorts*..Butter..Sugar.. Eggs..Flour..Milk..Fruit..Powder... Bake in small pans, or as one cake. **1938** HYDE *Nor Yrs. Condemn* 152 The first few nights [at Waikaremoana hydro camp], Starkie was out of tune with his bedmates, for two of them were drinking methylated spirits, which they called 'metha' and '**Johnny Gee**'. **1926** HILGENDORF *Weeds* 86 Californian Poppy (*Eschscholzia californica*), often called eschscholtzia [*sic*], and sometimes **Johnny-go-to-bed**, on account perhaps of its nightcap-like calyces, is found in profusion on the shingly river-beds of the South Island. **1933 Johnny Woodser** [see JIMMY WOODSER 1]. **1941** BAKER *NZ Slang* 46 Terms..recorded during the closing twenty years of last century [include].. *Johnny Woodser*, a drink taken alone 'with the flies' (this is a New Zealand version of the Australian *Jimmy Woodser*).

Johnny cake. Also **Johnnie cake**. [Transf. use of a US term for a variety of cornbread usu. cooked flat on a griddle or pan: AND 1827.] A small damper baked in hot ashes or a sweetened scone-like mixture cooked in a frying pan or oven. See also JOHNNY 1 b.

c1859 in Beattie *Pioneers Otago* (1947) 53 My supply of flour..was eked out in one 'Johnny cake'. **c1875** MEREDITH *Adventuring in Maoriland* (1935) 36 I will show you how to make 'flap-jacks' and 'johnny-cakes' when I come home. **1883** FERGUSON *Castle Gay* 177 And he in less than half-an-hour Had such a pile of Johnnie-cake, That on the embers he did bake. **1890** *Otago Witness* (Dunedin) 16 Oct. 30 And this, too, to colonials who had known most of them what it was to hunger and thirst after 'damper' or 'johnnycake' warranted to stay by a man for three days at a stretch! **1896** MOFFATT *Adventures* (1979) 60 I was sitting on a log [at Tutaki, Nelson] attending to some Johnny cakes that were baking in the frying-pan. **1919** *Quick March* 1 Dec. 43 The unsentimental travellers made their Christmas meal from the odd pannikin of flour kneaded into Johnny cakes, and cooked in the ashes. **1922** MANSFIELD *Stories* (1984) 458 Tea was laid on the parlour table—ham, sardines, a whole pound of butter, and such a large johnny cake that it looked like an advertisement for somebody's baking-powder. *Ibid.* 503 The little girls sat under the pines eating their thick mutton sandwiches and big slabs of johnny cake spread with butter. **1936** *Cook. Book NZ Women's Inst.* 119 Johnny Cake. One and a-half cups flour, 1½ cups bran, 1 cup milk, 2 tablespoons sugar, 1 egg, 1 teaspoon soda, ½ teaspoon cream of tartar, 2 tablespoons butter, 2 tablespoons golden syrup. **1995** WINTER *All Ways Up Hill* 173 As well as his stories he [*sc.* a bush settler, c1880s] would give them a 'Johnny Cake' to eat. They were heavy and unusual, and quite different from anything their mothers made.

join noses: see NOSE *n.*¹ b.

joint. *Obs.* [AND 1897: recorded by Partridge as chiefly Cockney.] A fellow, 'joker'.

1909 *Truth* 21 Aug. 4 Witness had oysters, whereupon a 'joint' named Mahony, who was with accused, made insulting remarks. **1918** let. 28 Oct. in *Boots, Belts* (1992) 137 A big Dink came strolling along and this joint [*sc.* a Tommy officer] hauled him up and asked him why he did not salute. **1919** *Quick March* 10 Oct. 33 The bald-headed joint representin' Ostrigia.

joint family home. A family house and land settled jointly on the spouses giving them limited protection from creditors, and to the surviving spouse the right of inheritance.

1950 *NZPD* CCXCII. 3490 The idea of a joint family home was given legislative form back in 1895 [by the Family Homes Protection Act, 1895 (1895 *NZ Statutes* No.20 66)], but the Act has been practically a dead-letter. **1950** *NZ Statutes* No.43 527 An Act [Joint Family Homes Act] to Provide for Joint Family Homes. *Ibid.* 528 A husband and wife or either of them may settle any land on the husband and wife as a joint family home..where—(a) The husband and wife reside and have their home in a dwellinghouse erected on the land. **1964** *Mozley and Whiteley's Law Dict.* 202 The effect of settling any land as a joint family home is that, subject to the Joint Family Homes Act 1950, the husband and wife on whom the land is settled become the legal and beneficial owners of the land as joint tenants subject to all mortgages, etc. then affecting the land. **1985** GORDON & DEVERSON *NZ Eng.* 41 Some longer phrases..joint family home..warrant of fitness..road user charges.

jointie. *Show people.* [*joint* + -IE.] One who sets up and dismantles a sideshow booth and its appropiate paraphernalia.

1996 *Dominion* (Wellington) 4 Mar. 27 The 'ridies and jointies' who travel round setting up rides and sideshows were less than enthusiastic when first approached about the [TV] show.

jo jo weed: see ONEHUNGA WEED.

joker, *n.*¹ [f. Brit. slang *joker* merry fellow: AND 1810, then 1887–; now mainly, but not exclusively in NZ and Austral. use.]

1. A usu. male fellow, chap, bloke, cove. See also ORDINARY JOKER.

1868 *Auckland Punch* II. 7 If Louis Napoleon could be prevailed upon to bring over his Zouaves, and join the mounted marines, together with some Indian *Jokers*. **1888** A TRAMP, ESQ. *Ramblings* 92 The driver of this coach was the joker that wanted to charge me a shilling. **1897** WRIGHT *Station Ballads* 34 But he dodged them—how he done it, not a bloke as seen it knows! And the other joker maddened when he couldn't touch his man, While we coves all laughed and shouted, and the barracking began. **1905** *Truth* 4 Nov. 8 The police seldom run these jokers in, but they did so a few days back when a worthless shanty-keeper..was caged on two charges. **1938** HYDE *Nor Yrs. Condemn* 189 'They aren't bad. They're good jokers when you get to know them, only they don't go much on work. **1943** BENNETT *English in NZ* in *Amer. Speech* XVIII. 88 Joker, for 'chap', 'guy', goes back to early nineteenth-century

English, but still persists strongly in New Zealand. **1959** MIDDLETON *The Stone* 35 Aw he goes out after sheilas in the park with those jokers from Central. **1962** HORI *Half-gallon Jar* 3 The pakeha joker from up the road tells me that [the tomatoes] have got the borer. **1971** SHADBOLT *Bullshit & Jellybeans* 85 A real shithot bloke... Real hard case that joker. **1981** MCLEOD *Bedside Book* 8 I sleep with my friends' jokers because I don't think anyone should want to own anyone else. **1987** GRAY *Stepping Out* 59 'Giving you your bit is she, then?'... Simon blushed... 'She's all right,' he said gruffly. 'She's a good joker.' **1989** BIOLETTI *The Yanks Are Coming* 87 Something else the Americans latched on to was the term 'joker', referring to a New Zealand man. They found this hilarious. **1989** *Listener* 7 Jan. 13 'You don't want to go in there [*sc*. a strip joint], mate.' 'Why not?' I asked. 'They're all jokers, eh?'.. 'Transvestites..jokers who dress up as women.'

2. *transf.* or *fig.* for various animals or objects.
1962 *Listener* 19 Apr. 5 The first pig he ever saw... It was only a little joker, admittedly. **1979** SIMONS *Harper's Mother* 15 'But I'm taking it off now so that I can fit this joker here on instead.' As he speaks he takes an enormous metal 'V' from the bench, fits it onto the place where the skid had been. **1985** HUNT *I'm Ninety-five* 30 Then if you wanted morning..tea..you got tea and scones, big yellow jokers with eggs in them. **1986** *Sunday Star* (Auckland) 13 July C12 There'd been a nest of bees in an old totara log there for years, little black jokers with evil tempers and fearsome weaponry.

joker, *n.*² Gumfields. See quot. 1972.
1948 REED *Gumdigger* 50 After that chance discovery every spear was equipped, at a few inches from the point, with a coil of fine wire, known as 'the joker', securely fixed. **1972** REED *Gumdiggers* 49 Some time after its introduction, the [gum] spear came to be fitted with what was called the 'joker,' or 'toggle'. This was a coil of fine wire, bound round the spear a few inches from the point. It allowed the spear to be thrust into the ground with the minimum of resistance, there being no 'drag' on the shaft. **1988** joker [see JIGGER *n.*³].

journo. [f. *journ*(alist + -O: AND 1967.] A journalist.
1978 BALLANTYNE *Talkback Man* 58 'Ivan Downs. Used to be on the Herald.' 'Thought you looked like a journo.' **1986** *Woman's Weekly* 14 July 12 The Baha'i faith's the most important thing on earth. I've been tellin' journos that for ten years, and the buggers won't listen. **1990** O'SULLIVAN *Snow in Spain* 30 Which of course a good journo would never do, because he would not seem one of the team.

Judas sheep. *Freezing works.* Also **Judas.** [Spec. use of *Judas* a betrayer.] A trained sheep used to lead others into a slaughterhouse. Also *transf.*
1953 SUTHERLAND *Golden Bush* (1963) 196 It has often been suggested that a career awaited Peter at the freezing works where, as a Judas sheep, he could end his days decoying his apprehensive fellows to their deaths in the killing pens. **1971** TAYLOR *Plekhov Place* 57 She laughed and led the way, the Judas-sheep leading her flock of one to the slaughter. **1980** *Evening Post* (Wellington) 6 May 16 'Sheep naturally following a "Judas" animal are simply behaving like sheep,' writes Dr Holmes. 'The "Judas" is cheap to buy and maintain... Fortunately the "Judas" sheep is on the way back, and the new meat works..are training up animals for the job.'

judder-bar. [f. *judder* a violent shaking + *bar n.*] A low tranverse ridge in a roadway to limit speed. Also *transf.* **judder-bar disease,** a humorously conceived imaginary disease said to result from driving (at speed) over judder-bars.
1984 *Listener* 21 Jan. 30 Thongs and *speed bumps* are there [in *The Macquarie Dictionary*] but not *jandals* or *judder bars*. **1991** *Dominion* (Wellington) 4 Dec. 15 The only unusual aspect of the past year has been the Government quietly accepting the role of judder bar to a media steamroller. **1996** *Independent* 26 Jan. 25 The third ad has a photo of a street with judder bars, along which are painted 'Experience the excitement of a ribbed condom'.

jug.
1. A (litre) jug, or its contents (usu. beer), filled and sold to customers at the bar.
1968 SLATTER *Pagan Game* 162 And the jugs came..and still the words came pouring out like bubbles. **1976** JOHNSTON *New Zealanders* 87 [Beer] is served through pistol-like nozzles at the end of plastic hoses; the usual receptacle is a jug, containing about 32 fluid ounces. **1977** *Truth* Sept. 11 'I had had eight or nine jugs of beer,' Ward is alleged to have told police. **1983** MANTELL *Murder to Burn* 47 Anyway, we looked up around half-past nine, went along the pub for a jug.
Hence **jug** *v. trans.*, to slash or attack (with a beer jug). Cf. BOTTLE *v.*²
1977 *Truth* 6 Sept. 11 I was with the Momo boys, one had just been jugged in the toilets.

2. A jug-like container in which water is boiled by an electric element.
c1940 (*electric*) *jug* known to the editor as a usual and frequent Marlborough use. **1979** SIMONS *Harper's Mother* 159 'Time for a cuppa,' he says. 'I'll put the jug on.'

jumbuck. Also with much variety of form as **jambuck, jimbok, jims buckes, jumbuk.** [AND 'Of unknown origin: used orig. in *Austral. pidgin* and poss. an alteration of an English word' e.g. *jump up* (so also AAW): 1824.]
1. A sheep.
1858 in *Canterbury Rhymes* (1866) 60 And refuse to wet their fleeces; Till one bolder than the others, Jumbuck of a forward nature, Takes the stream. **1867** PHILLIPS *Point Jrnl.* (Canterbury Pub. Lib. TS) 9 Aug. 112 Hastily collecting a small but heroic band of attendants..she [*sc.* Lady Barker] sallied forth and mustered the Hills in person—reporting fewer casualities [*sic* in TS] among the 'jambucks' [*sic* in TS] who were camped there than she had dared to hope. **1879** BARRY *Up & Down* 137 This was the first mob of 'jimboks' I had seen driven since I left Australia. **1888** DUNCAN *Wakatipians* 87 I had never expected to get gentlemen..to come and shear our commonplace 'Jumbucks'. **1896** TICHBORNE *Noqu Talanoa* 95 Our girls very often possess fathers who own considerable stretches of 'jumbuk' property. **1909** MEEK in Woodhouse *Farm & Station verse* (1950) 59 So, with jims buckes wet or dry, the billy will have to boil. **1913** CARR *Country Work* 17 Sheep are the backbone of New Zealand, and by learning work in connection with 'Jumbuck' (a favorite [*sic*] name for the animal) one can travel all over New Zealand. **1924** *Otago Witness* (Dunedin) 30 Sept. 67 At last we reached the packtrack..thence to the chilly ranges and the silly 'jambucks' that were to be our spoil. **1933** *Press* (Christchurch) (Acland Gloss.) 28 Oct. 17 *Jumbuck.*—Slang for sheep. The word was imported by the *shagroons* from Australia, but has always been in common use here. **1966** NEWTON *Boss's Story* 188 *Jumbuck*: A merino wether. **1987** OGONOWSKA-COATES *Boards, Blades & Barebellies* 96 *Jumbuck.* Slang for sheep.

2. *transf.* A silly fellow; a 'silly sheep' of a person.
1917 *Hutt Valley Independent* 14 Apr. 4 An asinine Base Record jumbuck.

3. *pl.* A children's game of trying to buck a 'rider' off the 'back' (i.e. a chain of people forming a long 'back' by each placing the head between the knees of the person in front), often within a certain time; or also, of trying to leapfrog over such a chain.
1951 SUTTON-SMITH 'NZ Variants of the Game "Buck Buck" ' in *Folk-Lore* June LXII. 332 A version [of Buck Buck, a children's game of bucking a rider off the back]..under the name 'Jumbucks' is played today by one of New Zealand's tramping clubs in its haunts near the snow line.

jump, *v.*¹ [f. US mining: AND 1852.]
1. *Goldmining. trans.* To seize, or take over (a claim) without colour of legal right.
1862 HODDER *Memories NZ Life* 82 The new rush..had been made by some men to tempt people to give up their claims in [the Gully] into which they might 'jump' immediately the ambitious occupants left to better themselves. **1867** COOPER *Digger's Diary* 8 Nov. (1978) 10 The whole day taken up in pegging off, an important and essential operation, as till that is done we are not safe, being liable to the unpleasant visits of any who are inclined to jump our claim. **1871** MONEY *Knocking About NZ* 73 He is the man who will..smash up a store, jump a claim, rob a church..with equal zest. **1881** NESFIELD *Chequered Career* 75 What the blazes d'ye mean, yer young cuss, by jumping our claim. **1911** BREMNER in *Mt. Ida Goldfields* (1988) 9 I..made Hamiltons [goldfield] in time to save my site from being jumped.

2. *trans.* To steal, to take over (something) without colour of right.
1891 A TRAMP, ESQ. *Casual Ramblings* 124 When a [railway] seat is known to be occupied—although for the moment vacated—it is not to be 'jumped'. **1968** SEDDON *The Seddons* 20 One of our friends comes to us with the news that whitebait are running in the Teremakau River and that the rills or runways we made last week with large stones on the bank of the river may be 'jumped' by early comers.
Hence **jumper** [AND 1854], a claim jumper; **jumping** *vbl. n.* and *attrib.*, claim-jumping; **jumped** *ppl. a.*, also *transf.* unlawfully occupied.
1873 PYKE *Wild Will Enderby* (1889, 1974) I. v 22 The assembled miners, in their own interests naturally averse to '**jumpers**', backed up the official. **1896** MOFFATT *Adventures* (1979) 75 One man went down to the claim,.. and gave the jumpers five minutes to clear out. **1864** AJHR C-4 25 **Jumping** Forbidden. **1867** COOPER *Digger's Diary* 8 Nov. (1978) 10 There is a great deal of jumping going on in all directions. *Ibid.* [The preacher is the leader of a claim-jumping gang.] How would [the text 'Do unto others'] be treated by this jumping preacher? **1873** PYKE *Wild Will Enderby* (1889, 1974) I. v 20 The rowdies were generally detested for their jumping propensities. **1914** PFAFF *Diggers' Story* 20 'Jumping' was not unknown, nor always unsuccessful, failing clear proof of actual occupation by the former owner. **1967** MAY *West Coast Gold Rushes* 527 Jumping: to get possession of a claim (or business section) by force, dishonesty or some sharp trick. **1910** *Truth* 5 Feb. 4 The finance committee of the Auckland City Council has at last taken action with regard to the '**jumped**' street in that city, on a portion of which has been built the premises known as Cochrane's auction mart.

jump, *v.*² In the phr. **to jump the broomstick** [EDD *jump* 3. *jump over the besom;—the broom* to cohabit without marriage, Lincoln, Somerset],

of a man and woman, to live together before (or without) marriage.
   1913 Bathgate *Sodger Sandy's Bairn* 153 There was no parson or anybody hereabouts who could marry us, so Brown and I just jumped the broomstick. **1939** Beattie *First White Boy Born Otago* 25 The taking of a Maori wife by a whaler was mostly a case of 'jumping the broomstick'.

jumper. *Hist.* [Spec. use of *jumper* a loose, shirt-like outer garment worn by sailors, workmen, etc.: see OED *n.*², 1853; EDD.] A loose-fitting outer garment reaching to the knees, a kind of 'bush-shirt' or strong cardigan, of serge, canvas, or calico and usu. blue, part of the 'costume' of 19th century goldminers and also of mounted police and bush-fighters. Cf. LAMMIE, SWANNDRI. [*Note*] The use of *jumper* for a short, usu. knitted, 'pullover' or 'jersey' is a later development: see OED *n.*² 2 1908.
   1852 *Richmond-Atkinson Papers* (1960) I. 112 All the family..enter into the preparations of the emigrants with immense zest, and the most jovial rehearsals of hats..'jumpers' 'jerseys' fustian..and in short every imaginable species of colonial garment continually goes forward. **1853** in *Canterbury Rhymes* (1866) 30 A gold digger's jumper to wear on pay-day. **1868** Dilke *Greater Britain* I. 335 I saw conspicuous among their [*sc.* diggers'] red shirts and 'jumpers', the blue-and-white uniform of the mounted police. **1874** Bathgate *Col. Experiences* 165 [The Police] wore a short loose coat, or jumper, of fine cloth, with a double-peaked glazed shako. **c1875** Meredith *Adventuring in Maoriland* (1935) 78 On that occasion [*sc.* a fancy-dress ball] he appeared as a stockrider, dressed in scarlet jumper, corduroy pants, and top-boots. **1885** Forbes *Souvenirs of Some Continents* in *NZ Reader* (1895) 260 There emerged from the bar of a public house a man who wore the long boots and the woollen jumper of a miner. **1899** Grace *Sketch NZ War* 120 Dressed in a blue jumper, with a pair of brown tweed trousers on tucked into digger's knee-boots, I wore a forage cap with the Army Medical Staff badge. **1922** Cowan *NZ Wars* (1955) II. 342 [The Maori scouts] marched barefoot. Steve's bush uniform consisted of a blue jumper and a pair of trousers cut short at the knees.

jumping, *ppl. a.*

1. As a modifier in the names of insects: **jumping jack,** weta 2 (4); **jumping spider,** *cave weta* (weta 2 (1)).
   1929 Martin *NZ Nature Book I* 104 The most common weta of the South Island is that commonly known as the **Jumping Jack** (*Onosandrus pallitarsis*). It lives in the ground. **1948** Martin *NZ Nature Study* 203 The commonest are the Tree Weta, Jumping Jack, and Cave Weta. *Ibid.* 204 [see *ground weta* weta 2 (4)]. **1935 jumping spider** [see Mount Cook flea].

2. As **jumping jack,** a firework making multiple explosions which causes it to 'jump'.
   1972 *Sports Post* (Wellington) 21 Oct. 9 For the past two weeks I have been startled..by 'bangers' and 'jumping jacks' let off by Wellington youngsters.

jumpmaster. [Transf. from parachute-jumping.] The person in charge of a bungy-jumping operation.
   1990 *Dominion* (Wellington) 10 May 15 A woman was asked to sign a form clearing a bungy-jump firm of liability minutes after watching her boy-friend fall to his death... The jumpmaster in charge..appeared at a depositions hearing charged with manslaughter. *Ibid.* 20 Nov. 9 [He] was jumpmaster for Heavy Rubber Company Bungi Jumpers at Rainbow's End amusement park on February 10.

junction, *n.* [Spec. use of *junction* the point or place where two things join.] The meeting-point of two rivers or two river-branches.
   1846 Brunner *Exped. Middle Is.* 12 Dec. in *Early Travellers* (1959) 261 Walked about two miles up the river, past the junction of the Mapu and the end of the surveyed country. **1861** Haast *Rep. Topogr. & Geol. Exploration Nelson* 11 From the bearings taken here, it was evident that it lay at the south-western side, near the junction of the Roto-iti and Rotoroa, which together form the Kaiwatire, or Buller river. **1862** *Otago Witness* (Dunedin) 23 Aug. 7 About twelve or fifteen miles below the junction..we first obtained payable prospects. **1885** *TrNZI* XVII. 353 We proceeded up the right-hand branch some two miles above the junction, and turning to the right began the ascent of the mountain. **1937** *NZJST* XIX. 123 Looking south-west from the junction of Maruia and Buller rivers. **1946** *Tararua Tramper* July 16 The river was quite wide and open to the..junction, then on up the Hodder, which is narrow and gorgy.

junction, *v.*

1. As **junction with,** of two rivers, to join.
   1907 *TrNZI* XXXIX. 383 Between these two rivers, some miles from where they junction with the Buller.
1912 *Ibid.* LII. 13 The Totara Creek, a small tributary of the Mokau River, junctioning with it about eighteen miles above its mouth.

2. Of two veins or reefs, to join.
   1907 *NZGeol.SB (NS)* No.3 98 A quartz-sample submitted by a prospector in the area [was] said to come from a point where several small veins junctioned. **1912** *Ibid.* No.15 79 The localities where two reefs junctioned. **1922** *NZJST* V. 118 At or about 2,000ft the Martha may also be expected to junction with the Royal lode.

jungle juice. Mainly *WW2* (Pacific). [AND 1942 Armed Services.] Strong (often rough or crude) liquor.
   1946 Soljak *NZ* 115 Following are examples of colloquialisms..*jungle juice*: strong liquor (Pacific war vintage). **1976** Wilson *Pacific Star* 182 Unfortunately, I think jungle juice sent us silly even more quickly than morbid thinking did. **1981** Stewart *Hot & Copper Sky* 156 Something comes over him when he gets on the old jungle juice.

junior high school. *Obs.* A school which formerly provided a three-year course for 12 to 14 year olds. Cf. also INTERMEDIATE SCHOOL.
   1922 *NZ Gaz.* 7 Sept. 2389 For the purposes of these regulations a 'junior high school' means a school established to provide a three-year course of instruction. **1924** *Educ. Amendment Act* S9 A 'junior high school' means a school providing courses of instruction occupying normally three years and, in general, covering the higher stages of the course of primary instruction and the earlier stages of the secondary course. **1932–33** *Educ. Amendment Act* S3(6) The Kowhai Junior High School shall hereafter be deemed to be an intermediate school.

junk. *Whaling. Hist.* [Cf. OED 4, 1850.] The soft part of a sperm-whale's head.
   1837 Rhodes *Jrnl. Barque 'Australian'* 7 Apr. (1954) 47 Watch employed boiling out the junk. *Ibid.* 59 At 6pm got one case baled and the junk cut up. Hung the other head astern.

junker, var. JANKER.

just quietly: see QUIETLY.

K

k: see KATH.

kaa–kaa, var. KAKA.

kaakahu, var. KAKAHU.

kaanga, var. KANGA.

káawai, var. KAHAWAI.

kadi, var. CADY.

kaeaea, var. KAIAIA.

kaeo /'kaiʌu/. Also **kaio.** [Ma. /'kaːeo/: Williams 82 *Kāeo,* n,.. *3... sea squirt.*] *sea-tulip* (SEA 1 b). See also *sea potato* (SEA 1 b).
　c1920 BEATTIE *Trad. Lifeways Southern Maori* (1994) 330 An intelligent middle-aged Maori said the kaio or 'sea nut' was cut open, then soaked in freshwater [*sic*] and eaten raw. It tasted like oysters. **1947, 1952** [see *sea tulip* (SEA 1 b)]. **1967** NATUSCH *Animals NZ* 187 Kaeo and Sea Potatoes subclass Ascidiacea The stalked [sea] squirt *Pyura..*is common in the south. The Maori knows it as kaeo, and eats the inner part which has a good briny taste, slightly iodiny... But a northern Maori..said he did not eat kaeo. 'Not Taranaki food—only Southland Maori food.' **1972, 1983** [see *sea tulip* (SEA 1 b)].

kaetatowa, var. KAHIKATOA.

kagháá, var. KAKA.

kahakaha. [Ma. /'kahakaha/: Williams 82 *Kaha* (ii)..*kahakaha. Astelia* [sp]. ASTELIA (esp. *A. solandri*). Cf. KAKAHA.
　1844 WILLIAMS *NZ Jrnl.* (1956) 111 [No New Zealand flowers are] remarkable for either beauty or fragrance except Kaha Kaha, Wara Wara and the Papapa (or the Parpuppa). The Kahakahas are fragrant and oderous [*sic*]; it varies in colors [*sic*] sometimes being dark and sometimes of a light pink and yellow. **1869** [see KOWHARAWHARA]. **1874** *TrNZI* VI. 55 Kahakaha, *Astelia solandri.*—The tree-flax of the settlers; abundant on lofty trees and rocks throughout the Colony. **1889** *Ibid.* XXI. 37 Kahakaha (*Astelia solandri*) grow[s] luxuriantly in the upper parts of the branches. **1904** TREGEAR *Maori Race* 238 Sometimes..the soft leaves of *kahakaha* (Astelia banksii) were also taken into the service of mat-makers. **1910** COCKAYNE *NZ Plants & Their Story* 27 Perched high up..in the forks of the branches are bird-nest-like masses, several feet in circumference, of a plant of the lily family (kahakaha, *Astelia Solandri*). **1926** CROOKES *Plant Life in Maoriland* 6 But of all the perching plants none is so striking or decorative as the kahakaha and the kowharawhara, both members of the Astelia family.

kahawai /'kawai/. Also with much variety of form as **carwai, carwhy, káawai, kahuwai, karwi, kauwhai, kawai, kawhai.** [Ma. /'kahawai/: Williams 83 *Kahawai.*]

1. *Arripis trutta* (fam. Arripidae), a greenish-blue to silvery-white Australasian sea fish, valued as food and as a game fish. See also KOPAPA, SALMON, *sea trout* (TROUT 2 (7)).
　[**1820** LEE & KENDALL *NZ Gram. & Vocab.* 154 Káawai, A certain fish.] **1833** WILLIAMS *Early Jrnls.* 24 Oct. (1961) 335 Dined at 6 o'clock on kahawai, which was exceedingly fine. **1841** BIDWILL *Rambles in NZ* (1952) 115 The Salmon of the English, or Carwai (Carwhy), is a most excellent fish, the best I have tasted in the Southern Hemisphere. **1849** POWER *Sketches in NZ* 77 He, in New Zealand, who has never seen the Kawai fishing, has nothing seen. **1853** SEWELL *Journal* 2 Apr. (1980) I. 227 I think they call it Karwi or some such name but it is an inferior sort of bass, watery and flavourless. **1874** BAINES *Edward Crewe* 236 Presently we let out a line astern and caught some kahuwai and two baracuta. **1887** MURDOCH *Dainties* 17 Stewed Kawhai..butter..add..flour..salt..cayenne..two glasses of claret..juice of a lemon. When it boils lay in the fish, cut in nice pieces, and stew. **1906** BULLEN *Cruise 'Cachalot'* 299 Fish swarmed about us of many sorts, but principally of the 'kauwhai', a kind of mullet very plentiful about Auckland. **1918** *NZJST* I. 271 Small quantities of kahawai may be seen exposed for sale during the summer months. **1926** GREY *Angler's Eldorado* 56 Suddenly there was a white splash across the school, swift as light, and then a crash of water as thousands of *kahawai* leaped to escape some prowling enemy. **1956** GRAHAM *Treasury NZ Fishes* 242 There was a small demand for them over the counters when they were termed Sea Trout, but not under the name of Kahawai. **1978** [see SALMON 2]. **1983** *Freshwater Catch 18* 16 Kahawai fishery in the Motu..Fishing for kahawai is mainly carried out from the river banks and from the sides of the braids. The preferred method is casting.

2. Special Comb. **kahawai hook (-spinner)**, a piece of bright shell or metal to which a hook is attached for catching kahawai by trolling.
　1842 BEST *Journal* (1966) 362 The **Kawai hook** is formed of a piece of oblong Pearl let into a bit of wood of the same shape to the extremity of which a *bone* hook is usually attached. **1986** WEDDE *Symmes Hole* 71 The miscellaneous refuse of affluent boredom..a mislaid **kahawai spinner.**

kahawai bird. [Usu. considered to be named in English from its habit of following and thus indicating schools of kahawai: but poss. more immediately f. Ma. *kāhawai,* Williams 82 n. *Hydroprogne caspia,* Caspian tern.] *white-fronted tern* (TERN 2 (10) *Sterna striata*).
　1908 BAUGHAN *Shingle-Short* 53 *Kahawai-bird*: A species of tern. **1934** *Feilding Star* 22 Feb. 4 Skimming the water were thousands of kahawai birds. **1947** POWELL *Native Animals NZ* 80 White Fronted Tern (*Sterna striata*), Tara... This is the graceful little 'Kahawai-bird' or 'Sea-swallow', which pursues schools of small surface fish, wheeling, darting and dipping to the water, in its energetic quest of food. **1966** [see TERN 2 (10)]. **1982** SALE *Four Seasons* 105 These white-fronted terns are better known by another title here. They are the kahawai birds, of the wheeling, diving flocks, which off-shore tell the trolling fisherman where to trail his line. **1990** *NZ Geographic* VII. 45 [Caption] Flock of white-fronted terns (also known as kahawai birds) nests on a shellbank.

kahika. Also early **kaíka.** [Ma. /'kahika/: Williams 83 *Kahika,* n. *1... = kahikatea.*] KAHIKATEA.
　[**1820** LEE & KENDALL *NZ Gram. & Vocab.* 156 Kaíka. Name of a certain tree.] **1838** POLACK *NZ* II. 397 The *Kahika* is a useful wood, but little known. **1851** SHORTLAND *S. Dist. NZ* 307 Kahika, Syn. kahikatea..a lofty tree of the order Taxaciae, acquiring sometimes a height of 200 feet. **1921** GUTHRIE-SMITH *Tutira* 71 Close to this orchard grew..three tall white pines, survivors of the kahika grove, from which the flat had probably taken its name. **1944** BEATTIE *Maori Place-names Otago* 39 Do not confuse this name [*sc.* kahikatoa] with 'kahikatea,' which is the North Island name for the white pine, a tall tree which the southerners call 'kahika.'

kahikatea /ka‚hıkə'tiə/, /‚kaikə'tiə/. Also with much variety of early form as **kahikatera, kahikatia, kaihikatia, kaikatea, kaikaterre, kaikotia, kakaterra, kikatea, kikatee, kikitea, kycata,** etc. [Ma. /'kahikatea/: Williams 83 *Kahikatea* [=] *kahika..*white pine.: *tea* white, clear.]

1. *Dacrycarpus* (formerly *Podocarpus*) *dacrydioides* (fam. Podocarpaceae), a tall coniferous timber tree of mainly swampy ground; also the timber. See also CYPRESS (*rare*), KAHIKA, KIKE, KOROI, *sugar-loaf, swamp, white pine* (PINE 2 (16), (17), (19) a).
　[*Note*] Modern usage prefers *kahikatea* to *white pine*.
　1817 NICHOLAS *Voyage NZ* II. 245 The trees which the natives chiefly make subservient to their purposes, are..a large tree named eckoha, and another named kycata, a tall and beautiful tree. **1823** CRUISE *Journal* (1957) 20 The one [tree fit for masts] is called by the natives Kaikaterre, the other *Cowry* or *Cowdy.* **1835** YATE *NZ* (1970) 39 Kahikatea... This tree only flourishes in low, swampy, or alluvial soils. **1841** HODGSKIN *Narr. Eight Months Sojourn NZ* 26 The kahikatera may be ranked next to the kourie for size and beauty. **1855** TAYLOR *Te Ika A Maui* 439 White-pine..kahikatea, kahika, koroi... This tree is generally called white pine from the colour of its wood. **1863** MORGAN *Journal* 17 Nov. (1963) 118 Lawless..was charged with having..stolen two Kaihikatia boards from some timber. **1875** LASLETT *Timber & Trees* 304 The kahikatea or kakaterra-tree. **1876** *TrNZI* IX. 160 [White pine] timber is known in all the provinces except Otago by the native name of 'kahikatea'. **1889** KIRK *Forest Flora* 41 The kahikatea or 'white pine' of the timber merchants is a noble tree, often forming dense forests in swampy districts. **1896** *AJHR* H-24 5 (*Interim Report No.3 Of Timber Conference, July 17*) The Committee recommends the disuse of the terms 'red-pine', 'white-pine', and 'black-pine', in favour of rimu, kahikatea and matai, in order to prevent their being confused with timbers having similar names in Europe. **1908** BAUGHAN *Shingle-Short* 188 Tall and erect as a *Kahikatea,* Princely, well-tatoo'd, a terror to

foemen. **1920** MANDER *Story NZ River* (1974) 9 Hard blackish kahikateas brooded over the oak-like ti-koti [*sic*] with its lovely scarlet berry. **1936** BELSHAW et al. *Agric. Organiz. NZ* 578 The chief indigenous trees of commercial value are: Kauri..Kahikatea or white pine. **1954** *Listener* 21 May 22 'Is that a white pine you have there?'.. 'Him? He's a kike.' 'Kike?' 'Yes. It's really ki-katee, but we leave out the tee.' **1960** HILLIARD *Maori Girl* 11 Sometimes Haki looks at the stumps of the kahikateas he felled for the first house. **1987** WILSON *Past Today* 101 Known as King's Mill, it had been built in the early 1920s by Bay of Islands interests and cut all useful timbers, but specialised in the manufacture of kahikatea-veneered butter boxes for dairy companies in the north and elsewhere.

2. In *attrib.* use as Comb. **kahikatea berry, bush, pine, swamp, tree.**
1849 ALLOM *Letter* in Earp *Handbook* (1852) 130 The **kaikatea berry** is another favourite fruit with the natives. **1882** HAY *Brighter Britain* II. 189 **Kahikatea bush** often occupies marshy ground, and..has a somewhat bare and spectral aspect. **1840** Mar. in Wilkes *US Exploring Exped.* (1852) I. 317 The Kaurie and **Kaikotia pines** yield spars which for large ships are not surpassed by any in the world. **1853** HOOKER *II Flora Novae-Zelandiae I Flowering Plants* xxix With the exception of the groves of the Kaikatea Pine on the swampy river banks..there is little to arrest the botanist's first glance. **1864?** VON TEMPSKY *Memoranda* (ATLTS) 36 European readers will not be the wiser when I say it was a **Kahikatea swamp**—New Zealanders, who have been up to their waist in it..will appreciate our work. **1888** BULLER *Birds NZ* II. 259 For many miles along the low banks of the Manawatu and other tidal rivers in the North Island there are what the settlers term 'kahikatea swamps', extending often considerable distances inland. **1841** BIDWILL *Rambles in NZ* (1952) 121 Scattered at intervals are small groves of tall **Kaikatea trees**. **1904** *NZ Observer* 24 Sept. 16 The Wellington *Mail* inserts a large photograph of a group of kahikatea trees and labels it 'kikitea' trees.

kahikatera, kahikatia, varr. KAHIKATEA.

kahikatoa /ˌkaikəˈtʌuə/, /ˌkaikəˈtoə/. Also with much variety of early form as **kaetatowa, kaikatoa, kaikatua, kicaitore, kikatore, koi katoa**. [Ma. /kahiˈka:toa/: Williams 83 *Kahikātoa, 1.* n... [=] red *mānuka*.] Usu. MANUKA, but also often KANUKA, KATOA.
1821 McDonald *Evidence before Commissioner Bigge* May in McNab *Hist. Records* (1908) I. 559 Q. Of what sort [of wood]? A. Of white and red pine and a wood called 'black oak'. Q. Is it of the species called 'kaikatua'? A. It is. **1832** BENNETT in *London Med. Gaz.* 18 Feb. 750 This tree..is probably a species of Leptospermum. It is found abundantly at New Zealand..and is named Kaetatowa, or Manuka, by the natives. **1834** MARKHAM *NZ* (1963) 33 Kicaitore is a Shrub with a strong Aromatic smell, a small leaf with a hard berry. **1835** YATE *NZ* (1970) 5 [It] is covered with..a species of tree named Kahikatoa (*Leptospermum scoparium*), bearing a white blossom and a hard round berry. **1838** POLACK *NZ* I. 105 The..plain was covered with..the ever-flowering kaikátoa which emitted a fragrant odour. **1840** CAMPBELL *Present State NZ* 6 Hills covered with fern, 'kikatore', and other small shrubs. **1853** HOOKER *II Flora Novae-Zelandiae I Flowering Plants* 70 Leptospermum *scoparium*..'Kahi katoa' and 'Manuka'. **1867** HOCHSTETTER *NZ* 158 Kahikatoa, Manuka (*Leptospermum scoparium*); the leaves of this shrub are a very common substitute for tea. **1889** KIRK *Forest Flora* 235 The manuka, or, as it is less frequently termed, the 'kahikatoa', is the most common plant in the colony. **1898** MORRIS *Austral-English* 226 *Kahikátoa* [kahi' katoa] Maori name for

New Zealand shrub, but no longer used by the settlers. **1907** LAING & BLACKWELL *Plants NZ* 272 *Leptospermum scoparium* (*The Manuka*)... Maori names *Manuka, Kahikatoa*. Colonists' [English] name, Tea-Tree. **1944** BEATTIE *Maori Place-names Otago* 39 When in a hurry, or feeling orthographically tired, he [*sc.* the southerner] calls the big manuka [*sc.* kanuka] 'kaikatoa'.

kahinghee, var. KAINGA.

kahu. [Ma. /ˈka:hu/: Williams 84 *Kāhu*. n. *1*... hawk, harrier.] HARRIER. See also HAWK.
[*Note*] Occas. applied erroneously to the New Zealand falcon.
[**1820** LEE & KENDALL *NZ Gram. & Vocab.* 155 *Káhu, s.* Name of a certain bird.] **1835** YATE *NZ* (1970) 60 *Kahu*—A large and powerful bird, of the hawk species. **1859** THOMSON *Story NZ* I. 23 Of the *Falcon* family, there are two species in New Zealand; one, called Kahu, is about the size of a Pigeon. **1869** *TrNZI* I. (rev. edn) 218 Owing to the misapplication of the native names, Kahu and Karearea, in Mr. Gray's first list [in Dieffenbach], writers in this country have inevitably fallen into the error of considering our large brown hawk the *Falco harpe*, and our 'Sparrow-hawk' the *Falco brunnea*, of that author. **1870** *TrNZI* II. 52 Circus assimilis..Kahu. Harrier. One of the commonest large birds met with on 'the plains'. c**1875** MEREDITH *Adventuring in Maoriland* (1935) 56 When comparing the two governors, Sir George Grey and Sir George Bowen, [the Maori MPs] compared the former to a *kahu* (hawk) which flies overhead—one can always tell what it is doing; while they likened Sir George Bowen to a *kiori* (rat) which burrows underground—one never knows where it is coming up. **1882**, **1904** [see HARRIER]. **1947** POWELL *Native Animals NZ* 82 Harrier (*Circus approximans*), Kahu..is the common bird of prey of the countryside. **1952** RICHARDS *Chatham Is.* 77 *Circus approximans Gouldii*..Harrier Hawk. Kahu. **1968** SLATTER *Pagan Game* 20 They could watch a hawk wheeling in the sky. Kahu the Harrier, Circus Approximans, his wife, who had Zoology in her degree, had told him. **1989** PARKINSON *Travelling Naturalist* 50 [This is] an abbreviation of Pirongia-te-Aroaro o Kahu (the fragrant presence of Kahu), not Kahu the hawk, but Kahupeka the wife of Ue.

kahuwai, var. KAHAWAI.

kai /kai/. [Ma. /ˈkai/: Williams 85 *Kai* (i) ... 2. Eat. ... 5. Food.] Food; a meal. See also KAIKAI.

1. a. In Maori contexts.
1840 WAKEFIELD *Diary* (ATLMS) 15 Mar. My boys set off..for a native settlement, where they could get some kai. **1870** *TrNZI* II. 172 The Maoris said that..they often cook their potatoes and other kai, quite easily in it. **1882** POTTS *Out in Open* 24 At the door two men are entering with a huge vessel of kai, made of flour, sugar and water. **1898** MORRIS *Austral-English* 226 *Kai* Maori word for *food*; used also in the South Sea islands. *Kai-kai* is an English adaptation for feasting. **1904** *NZ Illustr. Mag.* Sept. 449 The evening kai was finished but the hapu sat on. **1912** *Poem* in Scott *Seven Lives on Salt River* (1987) 55 The spree was at the Pahi pub..Te kai, kapai, waipiro plenty. **1917** *NZ at the Front* [frontispiece] *Private Puripeef* 'Plenty Kai up there!' **1938** LANCASTER *Promenade* 115 He looked very ruddy and English among the fat Maori women.. plaiting little green-flax baskets for kai. **1960** HILLIARD *Maori Girl* 143 They only want you there to cook their kai and wash their clothes. **1988** *Dominion* (Wellington) 12 Nov. 3 After the speeches were completed an invitation was made to rub noses, shake hands and have kai.

b. As **a kai**, a meal.
1972 BAXTER *Collected Poems* (1980) 589 To have

a body Means to get cold feet on a road, To need a kai, to need friends. **1985** MITCALFE *Hey Hey Hey* 117 What say me and the girls come round, make a proper kai for you, tomorrow night? **1985** *Landfall* 156 453 And don't cook. You come down the marae after and have a kai down there you hear me [*sic*].

Hence **kai** v., to eat. (KAIKAI v. is more frequent in English contexts, esp. in early use.)
[**1778** FORSTER *Observations* 284 A Comparative Table of the Various Languages in the Isles of the South-Sea. [English] *To eat*..[New-Zeeland] e kāi **1851** *Richmond-Atkinson Papers* (1960) I. 102 He has sent his 52 ewes & 56 lambs to 'kai' our grass. **1880** in Sutton-Smith *Hist. Children's Play* (1981) 117 Any fairly long silence might mean that a boy was 'kai-ing' or 'scoffing,' and occasionally warnings were given very righteously against any such meal.

2. a. In non-Maori contexts.
1856 in *Richmond-Atkinson Papers* (1960) I. 244 Pitcairn is also with me working for his kai. **1898** VOGEL *Maori Maid* 274 We might have 'kai' at the Maungaiti bush. **1910** *Truth* 16 Apr. 4 It is horrid to contemplate a young lady, who regards the beach as sacred to the uses of a Lovers' Paradise, coming home from church and seeing a surf-bather's bare feet as he toddled home to kai. **1915** *Hutt Valley Independent* 3 July 3 Our boys growled at the amount of sand they had to eat with the kai at Zeitoun. **1918** *Chron. NZEF* 16 Aug. 31 When his usual cheery 'Kai-oh!' reached our ears the diggers rushed forward..to get their eating utensils. **1936** LEE *Hunted* 22 'Do you want the kai?' 'Kai', the Maori word for food, was the [reform] school term for slices of inch-thick bread. **1948** FINLAYSON *Tidal Creek* (1979) 30 'This is what pays for the kai,' [Uncle Ted] says. 'Look at the nice little drop [of cream] in the can already.' **1959** SLATTER *Gun in My Hand* 224 The Maoris must smile at the pakeha going all Maori when he's overseas. People on the ship to England wearing tikis and saying good kai this morning. **1986** *Landfall* 160 491 The Works closed at four, which meant at least two hours before Danny could expect..'kai'—greasies probably, and his stomach sent out signals. **1994** *City Voice* (Wellington) 15 Dec. 25 [Heading] Barbie kai for vegetarians... Whack another sausie on the Barbie, mate!

b. Special Comb. **kai cart (kai kart)** [a play on PIE-CART], **kai stall, kai wagon**, a pie-cart or roadside stall selling fast foods.
1957 MCNEISH *Tavern in the Town* (1984) 150 You've got the pie-cart, known as the **kai-cart**, on the left. **1986** *Listener* 16 Aug. 82 And in Ruatoria the kai kart opposite the pub has to compete with the spectacle of 20 horse-riding, flag-waving Rastafarians galloping through the town. **1990** *Dominion* (Wellington) 12 July 3 Maori Battalion veteran..shows some of the pork and puha battalion members are serving up in their Maori **kai stall** at the touring expo New Zealand 1990. **1987** *NZ Outlook* Mar. 18 Now one side [of the Ruatoria main street] is near empty, the only new-looking addition being a mobile takeaway **kai wagon**.

kaiaia. Also **kaeaea**. [Ma. /ka:ˈiaia/: Williams 86 *Kāiaia* = *kārearea, kāeaea*.] FALCON.
1844 [see SPARROWHAWK]. **1871** HUTTON *Catalogue Birds NZ* 1 Quail Hawk. Sparrow Hawk. Kaiaia. **1882** HAY *Brighter Britain* II. 221 The Kaiaia..is a sparrowhawk, smaller than the Kahu. **1888** BULLER *Birds NZ* I. 213 Harpa novae zealandiae. (Quail-hawk)... Karearea, Kaiaia, Kaeaea, Kakarapiti, Karewarewa, and Tawaka.

kaianga, var. KAINGA.

kaieo, var. KEA.

kaihikatia, var. KAHIKATEA.

kaihua. Also **kaihu**. [Ma. /ˈkaihua/: Williams 87 *Kaihua* (ii), n. *Parsonsia heterophylla*.] JASMINE (*Parsonsia heterophylla*).

1951 LEVY *Grasslands NZ* (1970) 93 Kaihu, a long narrow-leaved climber, changes its leaf form considerably in the adult. **1961** ALLAN *Flora NZ* I. 550 Coastal to lowland and lower montane forests throughout, especially marginal. *Kaihua*. **1978** MOORE & IRWIN *Oxford Book NZ Plants* 120 *Parsonsia heterophylla*, *kaihua*. A twining woody liane that climbs high on forest trees. **1983** DENNIS *Land of Mist* 65 You might identify the common liane, kaihua, also known as Maori jasmine because of its small, white, scented flowers.

kaik, var. KAIKA.

kaika /ˈkaikə/, /kaik/. *South Island*. Also with much variety of early form as **kaik**, **kaik'**, **keike**, **kike**, **kipe**, **kyack**. [Ma. *kāika* /ˈkaːika/ southern (Ngai Tahu) dial. form of *kāinga*: *kaik* develops in English from a pronunciation with an unvocalized final /a/ often imperceptible to English speakers.] KAINGA. **a.** As **kaika**.

[**c1826–27** BOULTBEE *Journal* (1986) 113 settlement—*káika*. **c1835** BOULTBEE *Journal* (1986) 62 During the few days we remained at the Kaika Totoe (Totoe's Settlement) we lived on fernroot, cockles, and small dried eels. **1848** MANTELL *Diary* 24 Oct. in Stevenson *Maori & Pakeha* (1947) 128 Arrived at the Kaika, Wahinei searched the wata and among a quantity of putrid fish..found 2 kits of potatoes. **1854** in Studholme *Te Waimate* 11 Feb. (1954) 23 The village is situated..at the Western extremity of the Bluff Peninsula, and contains about a dozen of Maori houses. It is a 'Kaika'. **1878** ELWELL *Boy Colonists* 108 He and the [horse] breaker then rode to Waikoura, from thence to the Maori keike..and then home again. **1906** ROBERTS in *Hist. N. Otago from 1853* (1978) 4 The land was consequently uninhabited, with the exception of small kaikas at Waitaki mouth..and Omarama. **1949** ECCLES & REED *John Jones of Otago* 63 A week or two later Watkin..took possession of a hut nearer the Maori kaika. **1978** NATUSCH *Acheron* 103 March 29 was spent..on the way to the Waimakariri kaika. **1995** *Otago Daily Times* (Dunedin) 6 Apr. 8 The Maoris from Canterbury kaikas..were said to intend to settle on the Benmore run in order to assert ownership.

b. As **kaik**.

1842 *Piraki Log* 20 May (1911) 130 The two boats (one from Mr. Duvachelle) stopped at the Mawrie Kipe. **1851** WARD *Journal* 13 Jan. (1951) 109 We reached a Maori kyack, or fishing village. **1862** CHUDLEIGH *Diary* 21 Apr. (1950) 33 There are mourays here and two kikes or villages. **1877** PRATT *Col. Experiences* 169 We strained our eyes..to discover..some faint vestige of the Maori kaik. **1890** ROBERTS *Oamaru* 9 We had to get wheat from the Maoris at the Kaik. **1937** AYSON *Thomas* 17 Immediately realizing the dreadful mistake he had made, he rushed to the Maori kaik which was quite near and cried out for milk. **1949** SHAW & FARRANT *Taieri Plain* 3 One of his party..returned with two boats manned by natives from the Maori kaik beyond the gorge. **1983** HULME *Bone People* 97 They used to say, Find the kaik' road take the kaika road, the glimmering road of the past into Te Ao Hou. **1992** FARRELL *Skinny Louie Book* 35 Some had married into families up the kaik.

kaika, var. KAHIKA, KAIKU.

kaikai /ˈkaikai/, *v*. *Obs*. Also **kiki**. [Early European writers often use a reduplicated form *kaikai* to replace KAI, esp. as a verbal form 'to eat', or 'to feast', the latter poss. a reflex of the frequentative *kakai* 'to eat frequently', or poss. adopted from a Polynesian pidgin.] *trans*. and *intr*. To eat. See also KAI 1 b.

[**1817** NICHOLAS *Voyage NZ* I. 139 Many of them had never before..beheld an European, and to see *packa[h]â kiki* (the white man eat,) was a novelty of so curious a nature, that they gazed on it with wonder and delight. **c1826–27** BOULTBEE *Journal* (1986) 113 eat–kai kai] **1834** MARKHAM *NZ* (1963) 54 And some seem to think that the Missionaries pray to the Attuah 'Spirit or God', to Kiki or 'eat up' the people, as they seem to be a fast decreasing People. **1842** *Piraki Log* 15 Aug. (1911) 143 Stopped at 'Tommy's' [*sc*. a Maori]. Kikied the 'tivers' and the fish. **1847** ANGAS *Savage Life* II. 130 Before I took leave of Te Heuheu..he made me 'kai kai', or eat with him. **1851** *Richmond-Atkinson Papers* (1960) I. 103 One cannot look at some of the ancient grey headed cannibals who tell..[*sic*] with gusto of the days when they 'kaikai' (eat) conquered enemies or slaves, who discriminate the saltness of the 'pakeha' from the sweetness of the maori, & the superiority of both to 'poaka' pork.

kaikai /ˈkaikai/, *n*. Also **kiki**. [See KAIKAI *v*.]

1. (An abundance of) food; feasting.

[**1807** SAVAGE *Some Acc. of NZ* 75 Kiki..Food.] **1817** NICHOLAS *Voyage NZ* I. 267 [Our New Zealand companions]..were not a little surprised that we could not relish such fine *kiki*, (food,) as well as themselves. **1842** BEST *Journal* 12 Apr. (1966) 346 A still better [excuse for not proceeding] might have been found in the pigs and abundance of other Kaikai steaming in the Hangis. **1845** WAKEFIELD *Adventure NZ* I. 29 He explained to us that everyone would cry very much, and then there would be very much kai-kai or feasting. **1866** HUNT *Chatham Is*. 19 [Rauparaha said] 'We shall have lots of kai-kai.' **1879** FEATON *Waikato War* 7 Then came the general body of Natives, women laden with kai kai and baggage bringing up the rear. **1930** GUTHRIE *NZ Memories* 31 *Kai-kai*, or feasting, was an institution with the Maoris. **1985** MITCALFE *Hey Hey Hey* 122 [Samoan speaks] 'You know, book up the kai-kai. Didn't I give you enough?' [1985 *Note*] kai-kai: big feast

2. *transf*. or *fig*. **a.** Referring to horse food.

1842 *NZ Herald & Auckland Gaz*. 12 Jan. in Best *Journal* (1966) 417 When just within a few yards of the winning post, they both had a spill, *Bobby* [a racehorse] bidding us adieu for the day went home for, as we suppose, some 'ki ki'.

b. As a jocular name for a private house.

1859 *Richmond-Atkinson Papers* (1960) I. 452 James's new mansion is known as 'The Palace of Art'. Harry's house is distinguished as 'Kai kai Lodge' (in reference to the uniform abundance of meat & drink) whilst Henry's mansion is named 'Damper Hall'.

c. As a cry of hungry welcome, or an exclamation over food.

1863 MOSER *Mahoe Leaves* 34 A roar of 'kai-kai! haeremai', created a sudden sensation amongst the outsiders. **1939** BEATTIE *First White Boy Born Otago* 62 Mother fried some [mushrooms] and I boldly tried one, but 'O kaikai!' I soon got rid of it.

kaikamako, var. KAIKOMAKO.

kaikatea, kaikaterre, varr. KAHIKATEA.

kaikatoa, kaikatua, varr. KAHIKATOA.

kaikawaka. [Ma. /ˈkaikawaka/: Williams 88 *Kaikawaka*.., *Libocedrus plumosa*.. = *kawaka*.] Either of two forest trees of the cypress family (Cupressaceae), esp. the high-altitude species *Libocedrus bidwillii* (see PAHAUTEA), and less commonly *L. plumosa* (see KAWAKA). See also CEDAR.

1889 KIRK *Forest Flora* 157 Mr. Colenso informs me that this fine tree [*Libocedrus doniana*] is termed kawaka and kaikawaka by the Maoris: it is sometimes unfortunate that the latter name is generally applied to the next species, *Libocedrus Bidwillii* [pahautea], by surveyors and bushmen, especially in the central and southern parts of the North Island. **1909, 1936** [see CEDAR 2 (1)]. **1980** ADAMS *NZ Native Trees 1* 17 Kaikawaka is a small tree reaching 16m (50 ft). At high altitudes it is often much shorter, very stunted, gnarled or contorted by the wind. **1981** DENNIS *Paparoas Guide* 162 Special mention could be made here of the New Zealand cedar pahautea (*Libocedrus bidwillii*—sometimes called kaikawaka, although that name should probably be confined to *L. plumosa* which does not extend this far south). **1983** MATTHEWS *Trees NZ* 26 The kaikawaka..is a tree of high country forest.

kaikomako /ˌkaikəˈmakʌu/. Also **kaikamako**. [Ma. /ka(h)iˈkoːmako/: Williams 88 *Kaikōmako* = *kahikōmako*, *Pennantia corymbosa*.] *Pennantia corymbosa* (fam. Icacinaceae), a small tree of lowland forests having a divaricating juvenile form and bearing panicles of fragrant white flowers. See also BRIDAL-TREE.

1832 BENNETT in *London Med. Gaz*. 22 Sept. 794 [Heading] Kaiko-mako tree of the natives of New Zealand... This tree..attains the elevation of twenty-five to thirty feet. **1838** POLACK *NZ* II. 400 There are many other woods of much service to Europeans, differing in quality, among others: the..*Kaikamako*. **1853** HOOKER *II Flora Novae-Zelandiae I Flowering Plants* 35 *Pennantia Corymbosa*... Nat. name, 'Kaikomako'. **1869** *TrNZI* I. (rev. edn.) 265 Fire, by friction, was obtained from several woods; the Kaikomako..was..the one most prized. **1882** HAY *Brighter Britain* II. 198 The Kaikomako..will be much cultivated as a garden ornament. **1890** *PWD Catalogue Timbers* (NZ & South Seas Exhib.) 10 Kaikomako..Timber light coloured and straight in grain, suitable for tool handles and turning. **1910** COCKAYNE *NZ Plants & Their Story* 37 *Pennantia corymbosa* (the kaikomako) vies in its purity with any bridal flower. **1946** [see BRIDAL-TREE]. **1959** SINCLAIR *Hist. NZ* 21 Fortunately, before all her fires were extinguished, the goddess threw a few sparks into the *kaikomako* tree from which mankind were able to make fire by rubbing two sticks together. **1961** MARTIN *Flora NZ* 178 The kaikomako, also known as Cheesewood and Bridal Tree, commences life as a bushy shrub. **1987** EVANS *NZ in Flower* 57 Kaikomako's profuse panicles of sweetly fragrant, small white flowers appear from November to February.

kaikotia, var. KAHIKATEA.

kaikou, var. KAIKU.

Kaikoura buttercup: see BUTTERCUP 2 (2).

kaiku. Also **kaika**, **kaikou**. [Ma. /kaiˈkuː/: Williams 88 *Kaikū* = *kaikūkū*, n. *Parsonsia capsularis*.] JASMINE (*Parsonsia* spp.).

1853 HOOKER *II Flora Novae-Zelandiae I Flowering Plants* 181 Parsonsia *heterophylla*..Nat. name, 'Kai Ku'. **1869** *TrNZI* I. (rev. edn.) 206 Kaikou. Parsonsia albiflora. **1870** *TrNZI* II. 124 Parsonsia albiflora Kaika. **1906** CHEESEMAN *Manual NZ Flora* 440 *P[arsonsia] heterophylla*... A tall and slender branching climber. *Kaiku*; *Kaiwhiria*. **1951** LEVY *Grasslands NZ* (1970) 93 Kai[k]u, a long narrow-leaved climber, changes its leaf form considerably in the adult. **1961** [see PERIWINKLE *n*.²]. **1982** [see JASMINE].

Kaimanawa wild horses. A surviving population of free-ranging horses once spread over much of the central North Island but now restricted to the south-western area of the Kaimanawa Mountains. Cf. BRUMBY.
1981 *NZ Statutory Regulations* 1981/239 1100 Horse (*Equus*), except those horses known as Kaimanawa wild horses. **1989** *NZ Geographic* Jan.–Mar. 53 Once hunted to the point of extinction, the Kaimanawa wild horses now thrive in the harsh high country of the Desert Road. **1996** *Evening Post* (Wellington) 7 June 2 Opponents of the plan to cull the Kaimanawa wild horses are investigating legal action to save the herd. *Loc. cit.* The Kaimanawa wild horse working party decided the herd should be culled to 800 horses.

kai moana. [Ma. /'kai 'moana/ *kai* food + *moana* sea, lake.] Seafood in wide variety, including shellfish, fish, crustaceans, seaweeds and other sea plants.
1963 *Kai Moana* 1 May 1 The title, 'Kai Moana'—Food of the Water, is appropriate. **1974** HILLIARD *Maori Woman* 186 He might have had a deep-freeze for the kai moana. **1983** HULME *Bone People* 110 There was really only cods' eyes there..unless you count the scallop's...[*sic*] but there truly was fourteen different kai moana. **1991** *More* (Auckland) Jan. 56 We eat organic food from our gardens and orchard areas, along with organic meat, kai moana (seafood), eggs from our own chooks and locally made cheese. **1992** ANDERSON *Portrait Artist's Wife* 20 He leant across Sarah who was puddling about with her avocado and kai moana.

kainga. Also with much variety of early form as **kahingha, kahinghee, kaianga, kanga, kanger, kyhinga.** [Ma. /'ka:iŋa/: Williams 81 *Kā* (i), v. intr. Take fire... *kāinga* n. (deriv. from *kā*, and so, properly, place where fire has burnt; hence) *1*. Place of abode... *2*. Unfortified place of residence, whether consisting of one or more huts.] See also KAIKA. **a.** Also early **kainga Maori.** A Maori village.
1814 KENDALL 19 June in Elder *Marsden's Lieutenants* (1934) 63 In the afternoon I visited the kahinghee or place of Whittohee in company with Mr. Hall. [**1815** KENDALL *New Zealanders' First Book* 46 Kahingha A residence. **1817** NICHOLAS *Voyage NZ* II. 334 A residence. Kyhinga.] **1834** MARKHAM *NZ* (1963) 30 All the Village (Kanger Mourie) turned out to see the Horse rode. *Ibid.* 45 I have many times made a grand Meal in a Kanga Mouri or Native Village on Pippies. **1840** in Chambers *Samuel Ironside* (1982) 76 The chiefs on both sides made speeches..with the invitations to their respective kaingas. **1847** ANGAS *Savage Life* I. 332 The New Zealander..resides in his pah, which is a fortified stockade; or in *Kainga Maori*, or native settlement, which is not enclosed, where the houses are scattered about as in a village. **1851** *Richmond-Atkinson Papers* (1960) I. 80 You see many native dwellings & many canoes for they are a most locomotive people, few as ignorant of all but their own kainga as our British Hodge. **1882** HAY *Brighter Britain* II. 284 She rules a large kainga, situated on the Ohinemuri creek. **1896** *Otago Witness* (Dunedin) 23 Jan. 50 We are abreast of Atene (Athens), a cosy-looking kainga located on the bank of a picturesque bend of the river. **1910** *Kai Tiaki* July 103 It is a much-debated question in every kainga or village, whether the European civilisation has fulfilled its expectation. **1938** FINLAYSON *Brown Man's Burden* (1973) 26 Only Maoris were there, and one or two rough-looking Pakehas, the kind that cadge from any kainga. **1945** *Maori Social Welfare & Advancements Act 1945* in *Speeches & Documents* (1971) 417 A Tribal Committee may..define the boundaries of any kainga, village, or pa. **1970** THOMAS *Way Up North* 4 The meeting house, situated in the centre of the kainga, was the usual type of those days. **1986** BELICH *NZ Wars* 247 Te Ngutu was a *kainga* or village rather than a purpose-built *pa*.

b. Occas. *transf.* to a European house.
1851 *Richmond-Atkinson Papers* (1960) I. 90 It is about 3 furlongs from the kainga Hursthouse. *Ibid.* I. 735 As a Taranaki settler... [*sic*] I wished to know if it was safe for us to return to our kaingas.

kaio, var. NGAIO.

kaipa maori, var. COPPER MAORI.

kaitaka. Also **ki tuck-er.** [Ma. /'kaitaka/: Williams 90 *Kaitaka* (i), n. Cloak made of the finest flax.] A fine cloak or cape woven from bleached flax fibre, and having a taniko border. Compare KOROWAI, PARAWAI.
[**1820** LEE & KENDALL *NZ Gram. & Vocab.* 157 Kai táka; A mat so called.] **1834** MARKHAM *NZ* (1963) 40 Cacahows are now getting very scarce and a Ki tuck-er or Mat Cacahow, [with] ornamented borders, is rarely to be seen in the present day. **1835** YATE *NZ* (1970) 157 The process is most tedious, requiring from three to four months close sitting to complete one of their kaitakas—the finest sort of mat which they make. **1847** ANGAS *Savage Life* I. 239 This gay [Maori] damsel..knew how to set off her charms to advantage; for, over a European dress, she had..wrapped herself coquettishly in a beautiful kaitaka. **1863** MOSER *Mahoe Leaves* 34 I should have difficulty in individualising the groups..in every kind of dress from the most select slop fashions..to the normal kaitaka (bordered mat). **1882** HAY *Brighter Britain* II. 205 The kaitaka..made from a choice variety of flax, has a gloss like silk or satin, and, though thick, is perfectly soft and flexible. **1904** TREGEAR *Maori Race* 235 Only chiefs of good position wore the *kaitaka*. **1922** COWAN *NZ Wars* (1955) I. 134 A commanding figure he was..draped in a finely woven and beautifully patterned *parawai* or *kaitaka* cloak. **1930** GUTHRIE *NZ Memories* 37 Being very tall, [the Maori guests] presented a dignified appearance clad only in their silky white *Kaitakas* with huia feathers in their hair. **1978** NATUSCH *Acheron* 142 The coffin, covered with a beautiful kaitaka, was..rowed across to a Maori burial ground [at Stewart Island].

kaitiaki. Occas. also **kai tiaki.** [Ma. /kai'tiaki/: f. *kai* an agentive prefix to the transitive verb *tiaki*; cf. P.M. Ryan *Dict. Modern Māori* (1995) 75 *kaitiaki* guard, caretaker, manager, trustee.] Guardian; steward. Also **kaitiakitanga,** see quot. 1991.
1908 [Masthead Title] *Kai Tiaki (The Watcher—The Guardian) The Journal of the Nurses of New Zealand* I. No.4 1 The title of our paper is a word taken from the language of the native race..and means 'The Watcher'—'The Guardian', the guardian of the helpless, the watcher over the sick and suffering. **1985** *Report of the Waitangi Tribunal on the Manukau Claim* (WAI–8) 79 To restore the mana of the tribes and to protect their particular interests, one set of Guardians, the Kaitiaki o Manukau should be appointed by the Minister of Maori Affairs to seek the well-being and preservation of the traditional status of the tribes in the harbour and environs... The leaders selected as kaitiaki would be vested with mana, and theior role would be to uphold the mana of the people. **1991** *NZ Statutes* 606 [Resources management Act] 'Kaitiakitanga' means the exercise of guardianship; and, in relation to a resource, includes the ethic of stewardship based on the nature of the resource itself. **1993** *NZ Statutes* 129 [Maori Land Act] The court may..constitute a kai tiaki trust in respect of any interests in Maori land or General land..or any shares in a Maori incorporation, or any personal property, to which any person under disability is beneficially entitled. **1995** *NewsVuw* (Wellington) 20 Mar. 17 An 8-bed house has been set up [at Victoria University] with a kaitiaki (house mother) to provide accommodation which is less alienating for Maori students.

kaiwhiria. [Ma. /'kaifiria/: Williams 90 *Kaiwhiria,* n. *1. Parsonsia capsularis...* 2. *Hedycarya arborea...* = *pōporo-kaiwhiri*.] Any of several plant genera.

1. *Hedycarya arborea,* PIGEONWOOD.
1867 HOOKER *Handbook* 765 Kaiwhiria, Col[enso]. *Hedycarya dentata.* **1882** HAY *Brighter Britain* II. 198 The Kaiwhiria (*Hedycarya dentata*) is remarkable [for its handsome foliage]. **1898** MORRIS *Austral-English* 227 Kaiwhiria, *n.* Maori name for New Zealand tree [*sic*]... Porokaiwhiri is the fuller name of the tree. **1904** TREGEAR *Maori Race* 67 The sticks were generally made of *matai* or *kaiwhiria*. **1927** GUTHRIE-SMITH *Birds* 2 The limestone range east of the lake [Tutira] at one time grew..fuchsia, rama rama, ngaio, kaiwhiria, etc., etc.

2. *Pseudopanax simplex,* HAUMAKOROA.
1867 HOOKER *Handbook* 765 Kaiwiria, *Geolog. Surv. Panax simplex.* **1869** *TrNZI* I. (rev. edn.) 194 Kaiwhiria (*Panax simplex*). A small, dark-foliaged, 1-foliolate shrub-tree.

3. *Parsonsia* spp., JASMINE.
1873 BULLER *Birds NZ* 154 I have sometimes found its crop distended..with the berries of the kaiwiria (*Parsonsia albiflora*). **1906** CHEESEMAN *Manual NZ Flora* 440 *P[arsonsia] heterophylla*... A tall and slender branching climber..*Kaiku; Kaiwhiria*.

kaka /'kaka/, /'koko/. Also with much variety of form (often reflecting the freq. pronunciation /'koko/) as **caca, caw-caw, gaw-gaw, kaakaa, kagháá, kau kau, kaw-kaw.** [Ma. /'ka:ka:/: Williams 81 *Kā* (ii) v. Screech,.. *kākā Nestor meridionalis*.]

1. a. *Nestor meridionalis* (fam. Psittacidae, sub-family Nestorinae), a large olive-brown forest parrot, having red underwing feathers formerly used by the Maori as ornament. See also PARROT 2 (1), (2) and (7), TOMAHAWK 2.
1774 FORSTER (Newton) [OED] Kagháá. **1835** YATE *NZ* (1970) 162 On the image, placed at the nose of the canoe, is fixed a large wig of the feathers of the kaka, or New-Zealand parrot. **1842** *Piraki Log* 20 June (1911) 134 I was shooting on top of the hill: got 2 pigeons and a 'Kau Kau'. **1843** DILLON *Letters* 16 Jan. (1954) 18 The birds are caw-caw, a kind of parrot very good to eat. **1853** MACKIE *Traveller under Concern* 4 Mar (1973) 85 A brown parrot which we often see in confinement being kept for the Maoris as a decoy for others is excellent eating, its native name is 'kaw-kaw'. **1865** HAYNES *Ramble in NZ Bush* 31 The gaw-gaw—a handsome parrot. **1873** BULLER *Birds NZ* 49 When the korari-flower..is in season, the Kakas repair in flocks to the flax-fields to feast on the flower-honey. **1884** BRACKEN *Lays of the Maori* 38 I heard mocking Kakas wail and cry above thy corse. **c1899** DOUGLAS in *Mr Explorer Douglas* (1957) 184 We were camped on a hill side [*sic*] in a regular roosting place for Caw Caws. **1905** WHITE *My NZ Garden* 68 Our introduction to the 'Ka Ka', so called from its cry, or, rather, his introduction to us (for we eat him), was with mixed feelings. **1917** *NZ at the Front* xiii Kaka.—A New Zealand parrot, the scarlet feathers from the under wing of which were prized by the Maoris for ornamentation, and especially in the manufacture of their feather mats or cloaks. **1936**

[see PARROT 2 (7)]. **1936** *Canterbury Mountaineer* 37 Caw-caws were fairly plentiful. **1947** SMITH *N to Z* 38 Prior to each election the parties hold what is called a Caucus... It seems reasonable to suggest that this word was originally spelt 'Kakas', the sound made at a meeting of Kakas or native parrots. **1966** DURRELL *Two in the Bush* 49 This Kaka tea party had started off with just two or three birds. **1990** *New Scientist* (Britain)16 June 23 Kaka chicks are covered with thick down—to keep them warm in the cool New Zealand climate.

b. Used *attrib.* in Comb. **kaka-hunting (taking), pasty, pie.**

1888 BULLER *Birds NZ* I. 163 The Kaka is particularly abundant in the Urewera country, and during the short season the rata is in bloom the whole Maori population..are out **Kaka-hunting**. **1905** BAUCKE *White Man Treads* 20 To the Maori, kaka-taking was keen sport, and to be successful demanded first-class mimicry. **1866** *Lake Wakatip Mail* 28 July 2 Few things are better appreciated by travellers than a **caw-caw 'pasty'**. **1856** HEPBURN *Let. from Otago* 28 June in *Journal* (1934) 161 The supper consisted of roast beef, boiled mutton, steak and **kaka pies**, fowls, tongues, plum puddings..etc.

Hence **kah-kah** *v. intr.*, to make a noise like a kaka.

1915 *Hutt Valley Independent* 25 Sept. The egg-bound mob are merely kah-kah-ing on the kerbstone again.

2. With a modifier distinguishing a brown **North Island kaka** (*Nestor meridionalis septentrionalis*) from a dull green **South Island kaka** (*N. m. meridionalis*).

1955 OLIVER *NZ Birds* 547 It was early noticed that the North Island Kaka differed from the common one in the South Island. *Ibid.* 549 The South Island Kaka was first discovered at Dusky Sound in 1773 during Cook's second voyage. **1957** MONCRIEFF *NZ Birds* 55 North Island Brown Kaka... Smaller and browner than the South Island Kaka. *Ibid.* 57 South Island Green Kaka... Distinguished from Brown Kaka by top of head being nearly white, back and wings brownish green. **1990** *Checklist Birds NZ* 175 *Nestor meridionalis septentrionalis*..North Island Kaka... *Nestor meridionalis meridionalis*..South Island Kaka.

kaka-beak. [f. a similarity in the shape of its flower to a kaka's beak.]

1. Also **kaka's beak**. *Clianthus puniceus* (fam. Papilionaceae), a shrub with bright red beak-like flowers, now rare in the wild. See also CLIANTHUS, KAKA-BILL, *red kowhai* (KOWHAI 2 (1)), KOWHAI NGUTUKAKA, PARROT'S-BEAK, PARROT'S-BILL.

1885 *Wairarapa Daily* 15 Jan. 2 It is not unlike the bloom known as the 'Ka Ka's beak'. It..is known to Victorians as the 'desert pea' of Australia. **1892** *Otago Witness* (Dunedin) 24 Nov. 5 A plantation of a shrub which is in great demand in England and on the Continent, and is greatly neglected here—the Clianthus puniceus, or scarlet glory pea of New Zealand, locally known as kaka beak. **1907** LAING & BLACKWELL *Plants NZ* 210 *Clianthus puniceus* (The Scarlet Clianthus)... This tree is known as the *Red Kowhai, Parrot's Bill*, or *Kaka's Beak*. Native name *Kowhai-ngutu-kaka*, signifying the *Parrot-beaked kowhai*. It is also called in the Urewera Country *Ngutu-Kakariki*, the *Parroquet's Beak*. **1943** MATTHEWS *NZ Garden Dict.* (3edn.) 43 *Clianthus* (Red Kowhai, Parrot's Beak or Kaka Beak). **1971** *New Zealand's Heritage* I. 267 *Kaka Beak...* Coastal plant sometimes known as the red kowhai. **1985** GRACE in *Landfall 156* 454 But over here it's all from the old place—kaka beak, gladdies, gerbera, hydrangea—it's my mother's flowers from the old place. **1989** PARKINSON *Travelling Naturalist* 84 The kakabeak shrub..in the wild is a rare plant indeed. **1993** *Evening Post* (Wellington) 11 Oct. 14 A new strain of the endangered kakabeak plant has been found in the Kopua Forest.

2. *Mitella spinosa*, a stalked barnacle.

1967 NATUSCH *Animals NZ* 116 *Mitella*..is one of the rugged stalked barnacles of exposed coasts; known as kaka-beak, it is edible.

kaka-bill. KAKA-BEAK 1.

1898 MORRIS *Austral-English* 228 *Kaka-bill n.* a New Zealand plant, the *Clianthus*.., so called from the supposed resemblance of the flower to the bill of the *Kaka*... Called also *Parrot-bill, Glory-Pea*, and *Kowhai*. **1923** COCKAYNE *Cultivation NZ Plants* 97 *Clianthus puniceus* (kaka-bill, red kowhai..) has green pinnate *lvs*..and brilliant bright-scarlet *fls*... Amongst wild plants various forms differing in size of flower and colour..can be seen. **1968** *NZ Contemp. Dict. Suppl.* (Collins) 11 *Kaka-bill*..*n*. N.Z. shrub with showy red flowers resembling a parrot's bill.

kakaha. [Ma. /ˈka:kaha/: Williams 82 *Kaha* (ii), n,.. *kakaha*... 2. *Astelia nervosa*.] ASTELIA 1. Cf. KAHAKAHA.

1867 HOOKER *Handbook* 765 Kakaha, Hector. *Astelia nervosa*. **1952** [see FLAX 8]. **1978** *Manawatu Tramping Club Jubilee* 100 [Ruahines] the large clusters of berries of the kakaha (astelia) glow bright red among the green. This leads us up to about the 3000 foot contour. **1982** [see FLAX 8].

kakahi. [Ma. /ˈka:kahi/: Williams 83 *Kahi* (i) ... *kākahi. 1. Hyridella menziesi*, a fresh-water bivalve mollusc.] Any of various *Hyridella* spp. (fam. Unionidae), freshwater mussels, MUSSEL 2 (4).

1870 TAYLOR *Te Ika a Maui* 635 The *Unio*, or fresh-water mussel, *kakahi*, inhabits nearly all our streams and lakes. **1904** TREGEAR *Maori Race* 108 Fresh water mussels (*kakahi*) were gathered with a large rake used in the lakes. **1921** *TrNZI* LIII. 445 It is curious that the *kakahi*, or fresh-water mussel, whilst the least appetizing of the lake food-supplies, is the most important in story, song and proverb. **1938** MAKERETI *Old-Time Maori* (1986) 243 Kakahi, the fresh-water mussel, was a food liked by the old Maori, but I did not care for it myself, as I missed the tang of the salt-water mussels. **1949** BUCK *Coming of Maori* (1950) II. 235 The rake was lowered from a canoe on to the shoals with beds of the freshwater clam termed *kakahi*. **1955** DELL *Native Shells* (1957) 59 Fresh Water Mussel (*Hyridella menziesi*, Maori Kakahi, size 3 inches..). **1977** *Maori Cookbook* 37 Kakahi is a black fresh water mussel... Kakahi Soup 2 cups kakahi... Boil kakahi until well cooked and strain, using the juice for soup. **1987** POWELL *Native Animals* 31 Fresh Water Mussel (Kākahi) *Hyridella menziesi*. This, or related species or subspecies, are found buried in mud in most of our lakes, rivers and streams. **1990** [see MUSSEL 2 (4)].

kakaho. [Ma. /ˈka:kaho/: Williams 83–84 *Kaho*, n,.. *kākaho*, n. Culm of the toetoe.] TOETOE; or (usu.) its reed-like stem.

1843 TAYLOR *Journal* (ATLTS) Aug. 51 Kakaho/Toetoe a tall grass the stem used in place of reeds. **1843** *An Ordinance for imposing a tax on Raupo Houses, Session II. No..xvii. of the former Legislative Council of New Zealand* [From A. Domett's collection of Ordinances, 1850.] Section 2..there shall be levied in respect of every building constructed wholly or in part of *raupo, nikau, toitoi, wiwi, kakaho*, straw or thatch of any description [..£20]. **1853** HOOKER *II Flora Novae-Zelandiae I Flowering Plants* 299 *Arundo conspicua*..Nat. name, 'Kakaho'. **1869** *TrNZI* I. (rev. edn.) 263 Kakaho reeds..were often used for the same purpose. **a1876** WILLIAMS *East Coast Hist. Rec.* (1932) 88 The huts were always well constructed... The interior was lined with reeds of the toe-toe, kakaho or arundo conspicua. **1924** *Free Lance* (Wellington) 28 May 24 The 'tukutuku' work for the walls and 'kakaho' for the ceiling had to be supplied from New Zealand. **1931** *Na To Hoa Aroha* (1987) II. 120 We have assembled a lot of kakaho at Rotorua, material much cheaper than mock kakaho, but a little more difficult to handle. **1940** COWAN *Sir Donald Maclean* 146 And along the river bank the *kakaho*, the *toetoe* or pampas grass, once waved its plumes abundantly. **1981** BROOKER et al. *NZ Medicinal Plants* 58 *Cortaderia fulvida*... Toetoe, *kakaho*.

ka-kahoo, kak'ahoo, kakahou, varr. KAKAHU.

kakahu. *Hist.* Also with much variety of early form as **cacahow, cacarhow, cackakoo, cockahoo, eka-ka-how** (=he kakahu); **haahow, ha-a-how, hecacahoo** (=he kakahu); **kaakahu, ka-kahoo, kakahou, kakkahow**. [Ma. /ˈka:kahu/: Williams 84 *Kahu* ... *kākahu*. *1. n.* Garment..strictly only those of fine texture.] A finely-textured, woven flax cloak. Cf. MAT 1 a.

1769 COOK *Journals* 9 Nov. (1955) I. 195 One Man offer'd to sale an Haāhow, that is a square piece of cloth such as they wear. **1770** PARKINSON *Journal* (1773) 127 Hecacahoo, *A garment*. **1777** ANDERSON *Journal* 25 Feb. in Cook *Journals* (1967) III. 817 Kak'ahoo..Cloth. **1793** *Lieut.-Gov. King to Henry Dundas* 19 Nov. in McNab *Hist. Records* (1908) I. 172 He took off his ha-a-how..& put it on my shoulders. In return, I made him a present of an ha-a-how made of green baize decorated with broad arrows. [**1804** COLLINS *Eng. Colony in NSW* 561 Eka-ka-how, *Cloth wove from the flax*. **1807** SAVAGE *Some Acc. of NZ* 75 Kakahow..A mat, or clothing.] **1814** MARSDEN *Lett. & Jrnls.* 20 Dec. (1932) 89 Some of them [the natives] put out their heads from under the top of their kakkahows, which are like a beehive, and spoke to me. **1826** SHEPHERD *Journal* 25 Mar. in Howard *Rakiura* (1940) 365 The sailors here..rolls themselves up in a blanket or New Zealand cackakoo or Matt and sleeps upon the Fern. **1832** EARLE *Narr. Residence NZ* (1966) 59 They were clothed in mats, called Ka-kahoos. **1834** MARKHAM *NZ* (1963) 30 Moyterra..sent back two large Pigs, and a Cacahow mat... He covered himself with his Cacarhow or Native Cloak. **c1835** BOULTBEE *Journal* (1986) 46 The natives had evidently been confused, for their cockahoos, and spears were scattered about on the beach. **1847** ANGAS *Savage Life* I. 262 He wore a very coarse flax cloak of the kind called *kakahu*. **1890** *Otago Witness* (Dunedin) 23 Oct. 27 The two were confined in a whare and were put to making kakahus. **1897** *TrNZI* XXIX. 174 Two small mats, just commenced (*kakahu*). **1969** MEAD *Traditional Maori Clothing* 196 Where special cloaks are used, such as kahu tukutuku, a cloak which is circulated around members of the whaanau and brought out whenever a death occurs..or kaakahu whakamahana, a warming cloak..there is a clear preference for cloaks which have kiwi feathers. *Ibid.* 209 Some whaanau have their own cloaks which they use to cover their own dead. In the North such cloaks are called kaakahu tukutuku (circulating cloaks) and they circulate around member families.

kakako, var. KOKAKO.

kakapo /ˈkakəˌpʌu/, /ˈkækəˌpʌu/, early /ˈkɒkəˌpʌu/. Also early **cocyps** (poss. typographical error =*cocypo*), **kòkabboo**. [Ma. *kākā* parrot + *pō* night /ˈka:ka:po:/: Williams 91 Kākāpō.]

KAKARAMU 391 KAMAI

a. *Strigops habroptilus* (fam. Psittacidae, subfamily Strigopinae), a large, green, nocturnal, flightless parrot. See also GREEN-BIRD, *ground* (*night, owl*) *parrot* (PARROT 2, (4) a, (8), (9)), TARAPO.

[**c1826–27** BOULTBEE *Journal* (1986) 109 Greenbird—kòkabboo.] **1843** DIEFFENBACH *Travels in NZ* II. 45 In former times the birds called..kakapos..formed part of the food of the natives, but now these birds have become nearly extinct in the northern island. **1851** WELD *Letter* Jan. in *NZGG* 21 Feb. (1851) 31 [The Maori] said that formerly he had often been there to catch kakapos (green night parrots) in a black birch wood above the Awatere pass. **1861** HAAST *Rep. Topogr. Explor. Nelson* 57 During the night we heard for the first time the cry of the kakapo... I was much interested here on observing the tracks of numerous kakapos, or night parrots. **1870** DOCHERTY in von Haast *Life and Times of Sir Julius von Haast* (1948) 550 The year that the Kie-Kie has three cobbs the Kakapo have three eggs and the year that the Kie-Kie has four cobbs the Kakapo has four eggs, but stranger still the year that the Kie-Kie has three cobbs and a little abortive one that never ripens, that very year the Kakapo has three eggs and one more she never brings out. **1889** SKEY *Pirate Chief* 17 On pipis he lives—on cockles and eels, And lobsters so fine and so red;.. And kakapos stewed for desert [sic]. **1893** NEWTON *Dict. Birds* (Britain) 475 In captivity the Kakapo is said to show much intelligence, as well as an affectionate and playful disposition. **1914** HOWE in Pfaff *Diggers' Story* 112 When Jemmy the Warrigal and I..stopped at the Big Grey River, [we] saw a lot of men looking at a big green bird, a Cocyps, and they could not make out what sort of bird it was. At last a Geordie..came up and settled the question for us by exclaiming, 'Why, he is a hawk, kill the ——, kill the ——!' **1918** *NZ at the Front* 84 The Kakapo Is somewhat slow And usually half asleep. **1926** COWAN *Travel in NZ* II. 122 These men in their young days made periodical expeditions up into the lakes region, hunting for the *kakapo* or ground parrot. **1930** *Wanderlust Magazine* I. 35 My Maori mate told me that the kakapo's crop, when freshly killed, makes a capital poultice, drawing poison quickly and effectively. **1955** OLIVER *NZ Birds* 553 The Kakapo is a ground bird which runs at a good pace and when pressed sometimes opens its wings. **1966** DURRELL *Two in the Bush* 107,108 'What is a Kakaporium?' 'It is a place..where one keeps kakapos'... The Kakapo's other name is Owl Parrot, and this is singularly apt for even a professional ornithologist could be pardoned for mistaking it for an owl at first glance. **1989** *Illustr. Encycl. NZ* 629 Because it is nocturnal, the kakapo is hard to observe but its unusual mode of life leaves visible traces.

b. *attrib.*
1851 *Lyttelton Times* 8 Mar. 7 The black birch kakapo bush between the Clarence and the Awatere..must be to the east of 'Barefell's Pass'. **1864** BARRINGTON *Diary* 27 Mar. in Taylor *Early Travellers* (1959) 404 Continued through the forest, alongside the kakapo range till we came to a swamp. **1869** *TrNZI* I. (rev. edn.) 223 There can be little doubt that as colonization spreads into Kakapo country, this species..will rapidly disappear. **1891** *TrNZI* XXIII. 115 At Martin's Bay I met..an old settler..who spent much time..collecting kakapo-skins. **1903** HENRY *Flightless Birds of NZ* 21 There are considerable areas in the bottoms of valleys..where berries are produced in great plenty, and such places are called 'kakapo gardens'. **1981** HENDERSON *Exiles Asbestos Cottage* 114 Kakapo tracks were very distinct, a foot wide and clearcut, through the tussock and passing clearly under the logs of occasional fallen trees. **1990** *New Scientist* (Britain) 16 June 21 'We can't leave them to their own devices with all the problems we have given them,' says..a kakapo biologist.

kakaramu, var. KARAMU.

kakareao, var. KAREAO.

kakariki /ˌkakəˈriki/, /ˌkɒkəˈriki/, *n.*[1] [Ma. /ˈkaːkaːriki/: Williams 91 *Kākāriki*.] Any of several (usu. green) parakeets of the genus *Cyanoramphus* (fam. Psittacidae, sub-family Platycercinae); PARAKEET.

1841 BEST *Journal* 23 Apr. (1966) 292 I shot by the way two very beautiful Paroquets (Kakarekas). **1849** POWER *Sketches in NZ* 72 There are some pot-shooters, who are brutes enough to kill the gaily coloured little parrot, the 'Kaka-riki'. **1853** POWER *Recollections* 345 The little parroquet, 'the kaka-riki', with green jacket and red vest, is too much of a dandy to make himself otherwise agreeable. **1869** [see PARAKEET a]. **1870** *TrNZI* II. 64 *Platycercus auriceps*... Kakariki... The smaller Parroquet is a beautiful object, as with merry note it darts across the forest glade, with its bright green plumage glinting in the sunshine. **1905** THOMSON *Bush Boys* 177 The Kakariki, our little green paroquet, screeches from high up in the trees. **1937** *King Country Chronicle* 15 Nov. 4 The threatened extinction of the green New Zealand parrot, the kakariki, is causing naturalists considerable concern. **1946** *JPS* LV. 143 *Kākāriki*.., red-headed parakeet (riki, little; whence little kaka). **1966** FALLA et al. *Birds NZ* 175 Yellow-crowned Parakeet *Cyanoramphus auriceps* Maori name: Kakariki. **1970** *Evening Post* (Wellington) 17 Jan. 19 A colourful feast of red, orange and purple berries attracted..the..kakariki. **1990** *Listener* 16 July 15 Three kakariki circle above us in the forest canopy, calling loudly.

kakariki, *n.*[2] [Ma. /ˈkaːkaːriki/: Williams 91 *Kākāriki*.. 2. *Naultinus elegans*, green lizard.] A small green GECKO q.v. (*Naultinus elegans*), *manuka lizard* (MANUKA 3).

1842 GRAY *Fauna* in Dieffenbach *Travels in NZ* (1843) II. 203 *Naultinus elegans*... Northern Island, amongst decayed trees, and running about between the fern. Called *Kakariki*. **1843** DIEFFENBACH *Travels in NZ* II. 117 A beautiful green lizard, called kakariki, is especially dreaded, as being a metamorphosed Atua. **1878** BULLER *Forty Yrs. NZ* 498 Two sorts of lizards are to be met with, the *Tuatara* and the *Kakariki*..the latter eight inches long. **1879** *Auckland Weekly News* 5 Apr. 16 Who has seen the *kakariki* (death lizard) crawl down the open throats of the tribes? **1895** *TrNZI* XXVII. 95 The name *Kakarika* (indicative of colour) is applied alike to the green lizard and to the green Parrakeet of our woods. **1904** HUTTON & DRUMMOND *Animals NZ* 347 *The Spotted Lizard.—Kakariki. Naultinus elegans... The Green Lizard.—Kakariki. Naultinus grayi*. Upper surface green, sometimes with minute black dots... North Island only. Common... A yellow variety has been found at Maketu, Taranaki, and the Kaipara. **1922** *Auckland Weekly News* 7 Dec. 17 The ngarurapapa..was not..so terribly fearsome a thing as was the kakariki, or green tree-lizard. **1949** BUCK *Coming of the Maori* 61 The reptiles..were lizards (*mokomoko*) of the following species: *tuatara, teretere*..and *moko-kakariki*. **1983** [see GECKO].

kakaterra, var. KAHIKATEA.

kakawai: see HAKUWAI.

kakeno, var. KEKENO.

kaki. [Ma. /ˈkaːki/: Williams 94 *Kakī* (ii), n.] *black stilt* (STILT 2 (1)).

1873 BULLER *Birds NZ* 205 *Himantopus novae zealandiae*. (Black Stilt)... Kaki. **1904** [see STILT 2 (1)]. **1955** OLIVER *NZ Birds* 304 Black Stilt. Kaki... The first..of this species to be brought under the notice of ornithologists were collected in Wellington Harbour. **1989** PARKINSON *Travelling Naturalist* 136 The black stilt, or kaki, was once our most common stilt, but predation, combined with the opening up of the country..has meant a sharp drop in numbers. **1990** *Checklist Birds NZ* 131 *Himantopus novaezealandiae.. Black Stilt* (*Kaki*)... Formerly the dominant and probably the only stilt in New Zealand... Now much reduced and breeding apparently only within the Waitaki river-system.

kakkahow, var. KAKAHU.

kakorimaka, var. KOKORIMAKO.

kaladdie, kaladi, varr. KORARI.

kale. [f. N. Amer. slang: cf. OED 2, 1912.] Money, cash.

1921 *Quick March* 11 July 13 Everybody..must think every day of money, but although one may think 'money' he may call it 'gonce', 'oof', 'hoot'..'kale', or a dozen other..things. **1946** COOZE *Ten Bob Each Way* 8 If you want to make kale. **1947** DAVIN *For Rest of Our Lives* 147 A man would get very meskeen too, losing his kale on Two-up. **1955** *Truth* 9 Mar. 4 I might give you a hand to knock off some of that kale. **c1962** BAXTER *Horse* (1985) 43 Tony would have the kale. But he did not like putting the bite on Tony.

kamahi /ˈkamai/. Also **kamai, karmahi, karmai**. [Ma. /ˈkaːmahi/: Williams 92 *Kāmahi*, n. *Weinmannia racemosa*... = *tawhero*.]

1. (Usu.) the common forest tree *Weinmannia racemosa* (fam. Cunoniaceae), bearing racemes of small, cream flowers; also the timber. See also TAWHERO 1.

[*Note*] *Kamahi* is often confusingly applied to *W. silvicola* (see b below); and even more confusingly termed 'birch' locally (see BIRCH 2, 3 (1), (2) b (a), 3 (9) b, *black birch* (BIRCH 3 (2) b).

1867 HOOKER *Handbook* 765 Karmahi... *Weinmannia silvicola* and *racemosa*. **1869** *TrNZI* I. (rev. edn.) 199 Towai, or Karmai (*Weinmannia racemosa*). A beautiful large tree, especially when in flower. **1889** [see BIRCH 2]. **1890** *PWD Catalogue Timbers* (NZ & South Seas Exhib.) 10 Kamahi.. *Weinmannia racemosa*..Wood hard, strong, and firm, liable to twist when exposed..grain prettily marked. **1910** COCKAYNE *NZ Plants & Their Story* 41 The towai or kamahi (*Weinmannia racemosa*), yielding an excellent bark for tanning, and a wood both ornamental and strong. **1925–26** *NZJST* VIII. 96 In the rain-forest..young kamahis are very rarely found germinating on the ground. **1940** LAING & BLACKWELL *Plants NZ* 197 *Weinmannia racemosa* (*The Kamahi*). A tree from 70 ft.–90 ft. in height, with larger leaves and flowers than those of *W. sylvicola*. **1984** MORTON *Whirinaki* 18 Spring, summer and autumn see kamahi smothered in bloom with racemes of pinkish-white flowers, followed by the small reddish fruit capsules, giving the tree its unmistakable reddish glow.

2. Less commonly applied to a related species, *Weinmannia silvicola*, TOWAI 1 b (or TAWHERO 2), a forest tree restricted to the northern North Island.

1889 FEATON *Art Album NZ Flora* 136 This tree [*W. silvicola*, 'towai'] is sometimes called Tawhero, or Kamai, and is not unusually confounded with *W. racemosa*, the Tawhero or Kamai proper. **1953** *Landfall* 26 122 He had played his violin under a kamahi tree.

kamai, var. KAMAHI.

kamokamo /ˈkʌmɪkʌm/, /ˈkʌmɪ ˌkʌmɪ/, /ˈkʌmʌu ˌkʌmʌu/. Also with much variety of form as **cooma-cooma**, **cumicumi**, **kamukamu**, **kumakuma**, **kumi-kum(i)** (freq.), **kummy kum**, **kumukumu**. [Ma. /ˈkamokamo/: Williams 92 *Kamokamo* (ii)... Fruit of the gourd. (Possibly from *cucumber*, and restricted to imported gourds.); Duval II. 209 records *kukama* 'cucumber' from 1844. See also quot. 1867.] **a.** In modern use *Cucurbita pepo* (fam. Cucurbitaceae), a stubby green marrow having when mature a yellowish skin deeply ribbed and extremely hard.
    [**1871** WILLIAMS *Dict. NZ Lang.* 43 *Kamokamo*, n. *vegetable marrow.* **1867** HOCHSTETTER *NZ* 298 They conducted me through the plats [*sic*] surrounding the huts, upon which turnips (Tonapi), melons (Hue), cucumbers (Kumokuma) [*sic*], maize (Kaanga), potatoes (Rapana)..were thriving exceedingly well.] **1890** *NZ Observer* 1 Nov. 18 That trifle..published in the *Observer*..caused ructions..in the land of cumicumi [*sc.* Taranaki], and milk and pumpkin squash. **1915** HAY *Reminisc. Early Canterbury* 19 The juice was strained from the berries..and the liquor fermented and bottled in the shell of a kuma-kuma. This was a gourd resembling a vegetable marrow. *Ibid.* 33 The Maoris grew..a kind of gourd they called 'Cooma-Cooma'. **c1920** BEATTIE *Trad. Lifeways Southern Maori* (1994) 461 The only item [of introduced plants]..that was mentioned by the principal informant was that the kamukamu (marrow) was introduced by the white people. **1935** MAXWELL *Recollections* 96 The provisions [near Parihaka, 1881] consisted of potatoes, kumaras, kumi-kumis (a sort of hard long pumpkin, with the skin deeply ribbed—kumi-kumi is the Maori name for pumpkin). **1944** *Westport News* 30 June 5 The crop subsidy scheme..provides for a subsidy to be paid on..kumikumi. **1955** BOSWELL *Dim Horizons* 151 They grew corn and kumaras..and the wonderful iron-barked ridged marrows that they called [c1890s, Northland] 'kumikumi'. (I have never ascertained whether it is really a Maori name or not.) **1978** HILLIARD *Glory & Dream* 17 'We should put in some kamokamo too.' 'You mean kumi kumi.' 'No, I don't. I mean kamokamo. Stupid pakeha saying, come-ee, come-ee.' **1983** KIDMAN *Paddy's Puzzle* 91 I give little Billy a shillin' to get me some kummy kum for dinner and some cig'rettes. **1983** *Evening Post* (Wellington) 8 Feb. 26 It is called kamokamo, sometimes spelled kumukumu, less often kumakuma, cooma-cooma or kumi-kumi, and very often sloppily pronounced 'cum-cum' for short... By 1936 (at the very latest) the kamokamo was recognised as a commercial variety of squash, since it was listed as such in a book 'Vegetable Growing in New Zealand' published that year. **1985** *Listener* 6 Apr. 52 To start with there was an antipasto platter. This was followed by an entrée of whole kumikumis (a type of squash) filled with a puffy soufflé.
b. Apparently a dish comprising kamokamo shoots. (Not otherwise recorded.)
    1946 ZIMMERMAN *Where People Sing* 75 For to season the large lump of home cured corned beef, she had picked a heap of the tender end-shoots of a squash vine and had boiled them as she would *puha*—and the result was *kamokamo*, and it was good.

kanae. Also early **kanai**, **kani**. [Ma. /ˈkanae/: Williams 93 *Kanae*..grey mullet.] grey mullet (MULLET 2 (1) *Mugil cephalus*).
    [**1820** LEE & KENDALL *NZ Gram. & Vocab.* 158 Kanáe, *s.* The mullet fish.] **1838** POLACK *NZ* I. 322 Some deep banks lie off the east coast, on which the *kanai*, or mullet..abound. **1847** ANGAS *Savage Life* II. 42 The fresh-water lake of Waikari..is remarkable for having a salt stream running through it, in which the sea-fish called *kani* are caught. **1855** TAYLOR *Te Ika A Maui* 624 *Kanae*..is a delicious fish, it frequents the mouths of rivers, but it is not usual to find it beyond the influence of the tide. **1860** *Richmond-Atkinson Papers* (1960) I. 671 Tu 25 Dec Mosquitoes rather worse than usual... [*sic*] Magnificent breakfast of kanae & oysters. **1872** HUTTON & HECTOR *Fishes NZ* 113 Kanae... The Grey Mullet is a very familiar fish to residents in the northern ports of the colony, where it forms a staple article of food among the natives at certain seasons, and is the commonest fish sold in Auckland. **1888** *Order in Council, Regs. under Fisheries Conservation Act* 10 Jan. The months of December, January, and February in each year are here prescribed a close season for the fish of the species of the mugil known as mullet or kanae. **1904** [see MULLET 2 (1)]. **1921** *NZJST* IV. 120 Grey Mullet; *Kanae*... I have recorded this species as far south as D'Urville Island. **1947** POWELL *Native Animals NZ* 67 Grey Mullet.., Kanae of the Maoris, is an excellent food fish, rich in fat and protein. **1966** [see MULLET 2 (1)]. **1987** SCOTT *Seven Lives on Salt River* 18 The harbour is celebrated for its fish. Among these are mullet or kanae, a jumping fish. **1990** McDOWALL *NZ Freshwater Fishes* 420 The grey mullet (kanae) was well known to the Maori.

kanai, var. KANAE.

Kanaka. *Obs.* [ad. Hawaiian *kanaka*: used elsewhere but recorded early in NZ: AND 1836.] A Pacific Islander, esp. one working on whaling and other ships.
    1836 *Log 'Mary Mitchell'* (Whaler) 14 July in Manson *Story NZ Family* (1974) 50 14 July:.. [*sic*] a Kanaka drunk. Flog him..4th mate sick. **1853** ADAMS *Canterbury Settlement* 79 The Kanakas (the natives of the Sandwich Islands) still call them brothers. **1868** CHUDLEIGH *Diary* 11 Feb. (1950) 215 We had one Maori and two Kanakas in the boat, and one Maori and one Negrow on shore with one Moriore and two Maori women to cook. **1946** *JPS* LV. 152 *kanaka*, the equivalent of the tangata in New Zealand, where kanaka is never used for a Maori.

kanakana. Also **kunakuna**, **kunekune**, **kùnna kùnna**. [Ma. /ˈkanakana/: Williams 93 *kanakana*... 3...lamprey.] LAMPREY.
    [c1826–27 in Boultbee *Journal* (1986) 113 small eels—kùnna kùnna] **1878** JOLLIE *Reminiscences* (ATLTS) 14 [In 1846, the Maoris] used to visit Molineux to exchange mutton birds for 'kune kunes' or lampreys. **c1920** BEATTIE *Trad. Lifeways Southern Maori* (1994) 151 The kanakana has no stomach and no bones, and it is better than eels to eat but he [*sc.* a Maori informant] had never heard of anyone dying from a surfeit of them. **1936** *Handbook for NZ* (ANZAAS) 73 *Geotria australis*: [European Name] Lamprey [Maori Name] Korokoro or kunakuna. **1949** SHAW & FARRANT *Taieri Plain* 77 Pigs were plentiful in the hills and certain streams harboured the choice kana kana. **1989** HULME & MORRISON *Homeplaces* 9 There is an abundance of fish here, eel and kanakana.

kanga. Also **kaanga (pirau)**. [Ma. /ˈkaːŋa ˈpirau/: *kānga* perh. a Maori adaptation of English *corn* (so Duval II. 131 *kanga*, 1833); Williams 283 *Pirau a.* Rotten.] Usu. as **kanga pirau** (occas. **kanga wai**, **kanga kopiro**) fermented or 'rotten' corn, a Maori delicacy. See quots. 1963, 1992. See also *rotten corn* (ROTTEN *a.*).
    1843 DIEFFENBACH *Travels in NZ* II. 366 *Kanga*—corn, maize. **1847** ANGAS *Savage Life* II. 64 Before we entered the court-yard..we were almost suffocated by the violent stench of kaanga, or stinking corn, arising from a large pot. **1867** *Richmond-Atkinson Papers* (1960) II. 228 I found the owner of the shawl, the bag of bullets & the kaanga pirau—a young fellow named Te Horo. **c1875** MEREDITH *Adventuring in Maoriland* (1935) 146 I sampled a new Maori dish on this trip—*kanga kopirau* (rotten corn). It has a bouquet just about as potent as the dead whale I mentioned in my last [letter]. **1905** BAUCKE *Where White Man Treads* 2 Plantations of..Kaanga (Indian corn). **1917** *Chron. NZEF* 18 Apr. 79 Kaanga Kopiro—Maize steeped in water until the odour makes it a delicious item of diet. **1949** BUCK *Coming of Maori* (1950) II. 111 Indian corn..received the name of *Kanga*, the Maori form of the word corn. **1951** KOHERE *Autobiography of a Maori* 127 Both my wife and I occasionally enjoy a dish of kaanga wai, as the Maoris of Rotorua call it. **1960** HILLIARD *Maori Girl* 16 She knew he would never use a stagnant drain to prepare such a table-delicacy as kanga pirau... Corn left for months in running water to rot; highly-prized [Maori] food. **1983** *Listener* 9 July 76 Kaanga is a traditional corn dish. Old maize cobs are thrown into a sack and left in running water for two months... Kaanga is also called stink corn. **1992** *Dominion* (Wellington) 11 Feb. 3 Kaanga wai was a method of preserving corn and keeping it in a partially processed state for convenient use. It had become a traditional food since the introduction of corn more than 200 years ago and the flavour was highly prized. As a cold custard it is refreshing and tangy... Also known as kaanga kopiro or kaanga pirau in some parts of New Zealand, the food was traditionally made by sinking bags of corn in a stream for months. **1992** *NZ Skeptic* Dec. 8 Perhaps..the 14th century originators of this pious fraud did not use sausage skin..but stripped a blood-filled vein from the saint's leg, say, and piously washed it in a mountain stream, like *kaanga pirau*.

kanga, var. KAINGA.

kangaroo.
1. *WWI.* [AND 1883.] An Australian soldier.
    1916 IVORY in *Anzac Book* 129 The stream [of people] ebbs before your [Alexandrian] 'garry-driver's' long-drawn 'Haasib' (mind out), to let pass some official dignitary or some riotous party of Kangaroos. **1918** *Chron. NZEF* 30 Jan. 286 Tommies and overseas Kangaroos and Diggers enter into conversation with peasants.

2. In the phr. **land of the kangaroo**, a journalistic name for Australia.
    1960 SCRYMGEOUR *Memories Maoriland* 48 26 men on the board, mostly Australians, who came over in the off-season making a good cheque on the soft cutting New Zealand flocks, then hired their professional ability back to the land of the kangaroo.

3. Special Comb. **kangaroo dog (hound)** *obs.* [AND 1805] (also *ellipt.* **kangaroo**), an Australian breed developed for kangaroo hunting from the Scottish deerhound and the greyhound, introduced to New Zealand and often used for hunting wild dogs.
    c1835 BOULTBEE *Journal* (1986) 45 Our kangaroo dog, timid as he was, partook of his share of the action, running in amongst, and biting the naked bodies of the natives. **1848** WAKEFIELD *Handbook NZ* 166 Many kinds of dogs have been introduced by the Colonists; including *Bull-dogs*, by the whalers, [and] *Kangaroo-dogs*, (a mixture of greyhound and mastiff) from New South Wales. **1853** MACKIE *Traveller under Concern* (1973) 109 A kangaroo dog will stalk up to the table which from his great height he is able to overlook. **c1864** in *Puketoi Station Diary* Sept. in Beattie *Early Runholding* (1947) 81 In September 1864 the diggers' dogs were such a menace to the flocks that Murisons sent over to Hamilton's run for the loan of a 'kangaroo hound'. These big dogs of a boarhound type were

KANGER

imported from Australia to Otago in the 'fifties to aid in the extinction of the real wild dogs then so common in the backblocks. **1865** BARKER *Station Life* (1870) 28 Mr. L— brought a large dog with him, a kangaroo-hound (not unlike a lurcher in appearance), to hunt the wekas. **1878** *TrNZI* X. 323 He advised us to get kangaroo dogs for the purpose of keeping them [wild dogs] down... He [*sc.* a wild dog] was soon brought down by one of the kangaroos.

kanger, var. KAINGA.

kani, var. KANAE.

kanono. [Ma. /ˈkanono/, /ˈkaːnono/: Williams 94 *Kanono, kānono,* n. *Coprosma australis.*] *Coprosma grandifolia* (formerly *australis*) (fam. Rubiaceae), a small tree of lowland forests with large opposite leaves. See also MANONO; PAPAUMA 2, RAUREKAU.

  1923 COCKAYNE *Cultivation NZ Plants* 45 *C[oprosma] grandifolia* (kanono) 15ft. has very large, broad *lves*; *drupes*, reddish-orange, showy. **1951** LEVY *Grasslands NZ* (1970) 87 Such species as lancewood, karamu..kanono..with tree ferns, weki, and mamuku. **1966** PHILLIPPS *Maori Life & Custom* 28 Joined leaves of the kanono or manono..were wrapped around the bodies of eels which were being prepared for the oven. **1978** MOORE & IRWIN *Oxford Book NZ Plants* 122 Kanono, the largest-leaved New Zealand *Coprosma*, is a small tree of lowland forests of the North Island and northern South Island. **1982** WILSON *Stewart Is. Plants* 108 *Coprosma grandifolia* Kanono..Shrub or small tree..(=*C. australis*).

kanuka /ˈkanukə/. Also early **kanuku.** [Ma. /ˈkaːnuka/: Williams 94 *Kānuka. White manuka, rauriki.*: AND 1914 'tea-tree'.] *Kunzea* (formerly *Leptospermum*) *ericoides* (fam. Myrtaceae), a small, white-flowered, evergreen tree common in regenerating scrub. See also KAHIKATOA, *tree manuka, white manuka* (MANUKA 2 (3) and (4)), MANUKA-RAURIKI, MYRTLE a, RAWIRI.

  [*Note*] (*fide* Wendy Pond, 1990) Taitokerau (Northland) Maori usage reverses the usual perception, treating *kanuka* as 'red' manuka (*Leptospermum*), and *manuka* as 'white' (*Kunzea*); some Maori dialects apply *kanuka* to both *Leptospermum* and *Kunzea* species: cf. 1889 and 1940 quots. below.

  [**1871** WILLIAMS *Dict. NZ Lang.* (3edn.) 44 *Kānuka,* n. *leptospermum ericoides*; a tree.] **1886** KIRK in *Settler's Handbook NZ* (1902) 121 [Native name] Kanuku..[Settlers' name] Tea-tree..[Family] Myrtaceae **1889** KIRK *Forest Flora* 123 This species [*L. ericoides*] is one of the plants commonly called manuka by the bushmen... It is known as 'kanuka' and 'maru' in the East Coast district. **1910** COCKAYNE *NZ Plants & Their Story* 147 There are at least two other species in New Zealand—one, the tree-manuka or kanuka, a common plant enough. **1940** LAING & BLACKWELL *Plants NZ* 289 *Leptospermum ericoides* (The Tree Manuka)... Maori name *Manuka-rauriki*, but now very often called the *kanuka*. Both islands. **1959** [see MANUKA 2 (2)]. **1960** MASTERS *Back-Country Tales* 160 Jack twigged a sturdy kanuka down the track a bit. He made a dive for it. **1970** SEVERINSEN *Hunt Far Mountain* 70 Half a dozen wild sheep appeared quite close, grazing in dense kanuka. **1985** MARSHALL *Nest of Cuckoos* 164 I'll..move into an own-your-own... No garden to worry about. No kanukas lying across the lawn.

kaokao, var. KOUKOU.

kapai /ˈkaˈpai/, *a.*, *adv.*, and *int.* Also **ka pai,** and with much variety of early form as **capai, capi,**

cawpie, ka-pi, kaupai, kaupi, etc. [Ma. /kaːˈpai/: Williams 249 *Pai,* (i) (pl. *papai*). 1. a. Good, excellent.: *ka* (verbal particle).]

A. *adj.*

1. In Maori contexts, 'that's good', 'well done'; fine, 'O.K.'.

  [**1817** NICHOLAS *Voyage NZ* II. 332 Good. Ka-pi.] **1848** *Lett. from Otago* (1978) 16 He takes a tune on the trump; different natives can play, they say it is *capi,* that is, good. **1853** ROCHFORT *Adventures of Surveyor* 18 [The chief] deliberately turned the ornamented portion of his person [*sc.* his tattooed behind] round for her examination, at the same time shouting *Kaupi!! Kaupi!!!* (good!! good!!!). **1866** *Canterbury Rhymes* 85 You like hapuku drying; Kapai the smelt, the duck, the eel, And shark when putrifying. **1905** BAUCKE *White Man Treads* 235 Two highly-educated half-caste women, both married to honest European gentlemen; whose children and grandchildren understand of Maori 'kapai' and no more. **1912** *Poem* in Scott *Seven Lives on Salt River* (1987) 55 The spree was at the Pahi pub..Te kai, kapai, waipiro plenty. **1959** SHADBOLT *New Zealanders* (1986) 147 'More music,' Tom insisted. '*Kapai te* music.' **1983** HULME *Bone People* 110 Ka pai, but you let me get tea on say, Friday though? **1985** ROSIER-JONES *Cast Two Shadows* 88 Maude turns to Tui. 'How are you?' 'Kapai. Kei te pai.'.. 'Whenever I'm out here in the wop-wops with youse jokers, the hori comes out in me. Kapai and hongi.'

Hence **kapai-ing** *vbl. n.*, the interchanging of 'kapai' indicating a pleasant meeting.

  1843 BARNICOAT *Journal* (ATLTS) 3 June 110 There is great kaupai-ing. After this we [*sc.* Barnicoat and Te Rauparaha] parted excellently pleased with one another.

2. In non-Maori attributive and predicative use: (very) good, 'O.K.'.

  1849 MCKILLOP *Reminiscences* 132 We had learned how to sleep in the bush with a blanket round us..build a waré or hut..and say Cawpie the maori, 'very good the native!' **1860** *Taranaki Punch* VI. 2 The pudding turned out kapai until we came to cut it. **1889** WILLIAMS *Colonial Couplets* 12 I replied she was '*Kapai*' (excessively good), Though I doubt if she always behaved as she should. **1896** *NZ Herald* (Auckland) 14 Feb. [Leader] The Maori word which passed most familiarly into the speech of Europeans was 'kapai,' 'this is good.' **1906** *Truth* 19 May 2 As far as defensive work [in football] was concerned, one can only say that it was 'kapai'. **1917** *Chron. NZEF* 31 Jan. 246 The Trooper's first impression of Turkey left nothing to be desired, and the bathing especially looked 'kapai'. **1918** *Chron. NZEF* 13 Mar. 62 The New Contingent Association is opening..a fine big recreation room in the hospital for the Blue Boys... It is to be known as the Kapai Club. **1933** BAUME *Half Caste* 55 You're looking kapai, Ngaire. **1941** MYERS *Valiant Love* 33 Uncle Alec says your pastry is ka-pai. You won his heart with that cherry pie. **1962** HORI *Half-gallon Jar* 34 It's a kapai morning, the sun is shining, the birds are singing. **1988** *Through the Looking Glass* 126 I remember..many that..were corruptions of Maori words. I spell them here as they sounded to me then: *ehoa, harka, kupai, kure, munga munga typo, markuta, pooku, tangy.*

3. In names of served foods.

  1913 *Australasian Cook. Book* 117 Kapai mutton steaks..butter..grated horseradish..cayenne pepper.. Worcester sauce..juice of half a lemon..spread over the steaks..dip in egg and breadcrumbs. Fry carefully. **1982** BURTON *Two Hundred Yrs. NZ Food* 127 [Title] Kapai salad (...) Very typical of the old school of New Zealand salad making, this one, so no wonder that it has been dubbed kapai, or 'OK'.

KARAKA

B. *int.* That's good, 'well done'.

  1836 MARSHALL *Narr. Two Visits NZ* II. 256 'Kapai! Good!' being the only vocable by which satisfaction at the receipt of kindness is communicable. **1840** *Bunbury's Rep.* 28 June in *GBPP House of Commons 1841* (*No.311*) 109 To which he [the chief] replied 'Capai! capai!—Good! good!' apparently much satisfied. **1851** LUSH *Auckland Jrnls.* 8 Aug. (1971) 84 At which he grinned again, and..said, '*Kapai-Kapai.* It is good—it is good.' **1930** GUTHRIE *NZ Memories* 49 [She] accepted them with pleasure crying, 'Kapai, Kapai'. **1960** HILLIARD *Maori Girl* 153 Afterwards they lolled back on the beds, the tray piled high with dirty dishes... 'Kapai!' shouted Henry.

kapa, kapa-maori, var. COPPER MAORI.

kapeta. [Ma. /kapeˈtaː/: Williams 96 *kapetā... Dogfish.*] Probably school shark *Galeorhinus galeus* (fam. Triakidae, see SHARK 2 (15)), occas. (poss. in error) the spiny dogfish *Squalus acanthias* (fam. Squalidae, see DOGFISH 1).

  1911 *TrNZI* XLIII. 598 The season for fishing the *kapeta* (dogfish) was restricted to two days only in each year. **1929** *NZJST* XI. 223 The spiny dogfish (*Squalus fernandinus*) is one of those species of shark which has attained importance as an economic species... It is generally called oke-oke, or kapeta, by [Maori]. **1963** KEENE *O te Raki* 191 *Kapeta:* school shark, grows to length of 7 ft.

ka-pi, var. KAPAI.

kapia. [Ma. /ˈkaːpia/: Williams 96 *Kāpia,* n. Kauri gum.] KAURI-GUM, GUM.

  [**1820** LEE & KENDALL *NZ Gram. & Vocab.* 159 *Kapía, s.* A hard resinous substance from a tree; gum.] **1838** POLACK *NZ* I. 109 The base of these [kouri-]trees and the earth around, was covered with the *kápia*, or gum, that exudes in large quantities from their trunks. **1861** *Richmond-Atkinson Papers* (1960) I. 685 Very much interested in a large stratum of lignite to be seen under the sandcliffs [at Moiatoa], kapia still in. **1869** *TrNZI* I. (rev. edn.) 267 The black pigment for [tattooing was] obtained from the soot of..Kapia, or Kauri resin, dug out of the earth. **1882** HAY *Brighter Britain* II. 14 Kauri-gum—or Kapia, as the Maoris call it..is another peculiar product of this northern extremity of New Zealand. **1922** COWAN *NZ Wars* (1955) I. 55 In the larger of the semi-subterranean huts are fires burning, fed with *manuka* branches and heaps of *Kapia*, or kauri-gum.

kapuka. Also **kapook.** [Ma. /ˈkaːpuka/: Williams 97 *Kāpuka,* n. *Griselinia littoralis...* = *pāpāuma.*] BROADLEAF 1. Cf. PAPAUMA 1.

  1844 [see BROADLEAF 1]. **1867** HOOKER *Handbook* 765 Kapook, Hector. *Griselinia lucida.* **1889** KIRK *Forest Flora* 69 This handsome tree [*Griselinia littoralis*] is known as the puka in many districts... Mr. C. Traill states that it is called kapuka on Stewart Island, and I have heard that name applied in Southland. **1906** [see BROADLEAF 1]. **c1920** BEATTIE *Trad. Lifeways Southern Maori* (1994) 67 [Maori] tops were..usually made of kapuka (broadleaf). **1963** POOLE & ADAMS *Trees and Shrubs NZ* 146 *G. littoralis...* Kapuka, broadleaf. Shrub or tree reaching 17 m. Leaves..leathery. Flowers in small panicles, minute, greenish. Berry 6mm long, black.

kapura maori, var. COPPER MAORI.

karaka /kəˈrækə/, /ˈkrækə/. Also with much variety of form as **caraceer, cracker, karoaka, karooka, karraka, koraka, kraka.** [Ma.

KARAKAHIA

/ˈkaraka/: Williams 98 *Karaka*, n. 1... a tree; and fruit of same.]

1. a. *Corynocarpus laevigatus* (fam. Corynocarpaceae), a spreading tree common in coastal areas, having glossy, dark-green leaves and fleshy orange-yellow ovoid berries with a poisonous kernel. See also COW-TREE 1, KOPI, *New Zealand laurel* (LAUREL a). Often *attrib*.

1777 ANDERSON *Journal* 25 Feb. in Cook *Journals* (1967) III. 804 Two [trees] that bear a sort of plumb of the size of prunes, the one yellow and the other black... These are call'd Karraka by the natives. **1833** WILLIAMS *Early Jrnls.* 13 Feb. (1961) 282 At daybreak we landed in a quiet bay, where the boys immediately commenced to explore the neighbourhood for *Karakas*. **1834** MARKHAM *NZ* (1963) 47 Some of their Woods stink very much in burning for instance the Caraceer or Cracker as we call it. **1840** WAKEFIELD *Diary* (ATLMS) Mar. 55 We climbed up to the pah, thro' a fine grove of *Krakas*, which encircles its base. **1853** SWAINSON *Auckland* 38 The deep-green, glittering-leaved karaka, clustering, in unusual profusion, around the tall stems of the statelier forest trees. **1874** BAINES *Edward Crewe* 144 On either side [of the harbour] much of the land was covered with a growth of manuka..karaka, and other smaller kinds of timber. **1882** HAY *Brighter Britain* II. 193 The Koraka [*sic*]..was brought to New Zealand by the Maori. **1908** BAUGHAN *Shingle-Short* 65 Once again comes the glitter of light on the glossy Karaka?.. [1908 *Note*] *Karaka* (kah-rakk-ah): New Zealand laurel. **1910** COCKAYNE *NZ Plants & Their Story* 153 Some English names are corruptions of Maori ones, as biddy-biddy for piripiri, cracker for karaka, maple for mapou. **1926** *TrNZI* LVI. 670 In some instances the Maori name has been adopted but corrupted:.. 'bunger' (now fortunately seldom heard) for 'ponga'; 'cracker' (also falling into disuse) for 'karaka'. **1963** KEENE *O te Raki* 191 *karaka*: New Zealand laurel tree; grows to 30 to 50 ft. in height; has large, orange, fleshy berry 1 in. to 2 in. long. **1986** DEVANNY *Point of Departure* 46 Along this depthless silky sand [towards Cape Farewell] we would ride..and climb huge sandhills crowned with groves of shining cracker trees. **1982** BURTON *Two Hundred Yrs. NZ Food* 6 A handsome tree with dark green, glossy leaves, the karaka..yields a bountiful crop of oval-shaped berries... The outer flesh is tasty but the bulk of the food value is in the inside kernel.

b. Applied to the *karaka-berry* (2 b below).

1837 WAKEFIELD *Brit. Colonization* 324 [Quoting Sydney *Herald* 17 April 1837] The kraka, a fruit of oblong shape. **1840** POLACK *Manners & Customs* I. 91 A long lane was formed on an extensive level plain, fifty feet in width, by two high walls, formed by perhaps upwards of ten thousand baskets of potatoes, kumeras, Indian corn..steamed kernels of the native fruit, (*káráká*).

c. As a place-name, the quot. indicating a common pronunciation with a play on *cracker* 'first rate'.

1993 *Dominion* (Wellington) 27 Jan. 1 [Heading] Colt makes a Karaka of a profit. Dannevirke farmer..matched the big guns at the national yearling sale at Karaka yesterday.

2. a. *attrib*. passing into Comb. esp. **karaka-tree**.

1838 POLACK *NZ* I. 92 This was situated amid a cluster of the *káráká* fruit-trees, whose poracious appearance produced a pleasing effect. **1841** BIDWILL *Rambles in NZ* (1952) 55 We..then could only get a few stunted Karoaka or Karooka bushes to make a fire with. **1854** *Richmond-Atkinson Papers* (1960) I. 143 The wide placid river and beautiful groups of karaka trees... [*sic*] on the banks are the attraction. We dined in the karaka grove. **1863** MOSER *Mahoe Leaves* 22 Small potatoes, termed 'kotero', and the berries of the karaka tree..are both..considered great delicacies. **1911** *Truth* 10 June 6 Edith and Harry Hodges, of Christchurch, have been married 13 years, and there was a time when domestic felicity flourished like the green karaka tree. **1922** MANSFIELD *Stories* (1984) 488 Then the karaka-trees would be hidden. **1951** HUNT *Confessions* 20 Our chief source of revenue was to gather in the bush fungus, which usually grew upon the dead and partly decayed stems of karaka and mahoe trees. **1957** FRAME *Owls Do Cry* (1967) 53 Small buttons like pearl green as karaka leaf are sewn to sleep. **1987** WILSON *Past Today* 61 His [*sc*. James Crawford's] party passed the deserted Pukehika, an unfinished church 'embowered in a lovely grove of karaka trees'.

b. Special Comb. **karaka-berry (karaka-date)**, the orange-yellow fleshy berry of the karaka; **karaka-nut**, the poisonous kernel of the karaka-berry, formerly used by the Maori as a food after it had been treated by lengthy soaking and cooking to remove the karakin poison.

1842 HEAPHY *NZ* 43 The *Towa* and *Kraka* berries also yield an useful oil. *Ibid.* 94 Canoes [loaded with] water-melons, and baskets full of the kernel of the krakaberry. **1852** *Austral. & NZ Gaz.* 16 Oct. 407 The elder girl got up a high tree to get me what one called cracker (*karaka*) berries. **1872** [see KARAKIN.] **1904** *TrNZI* XXXVI. 11 One of the earliest of these traditions..is..that Maruroa and Kauanga brought the karaka-berry from Hawaiki. **1913** *NZ Observer* 7 June 24 Your interesting note about the Waiotahi family of boys who lived on Karaka berries, and all became dissenting parsons, is not believed. **1926** CROOKES *Plant Life in Maoriland* 56 We find that the karaka berries so much beloved by the native pigeon stand out in quite startling contrast to their dark green background. **1974** HILLIARD *Maori Woman* 177 She would go to the creek..to look for koura under the stones..; or to the bush to gather karaka-berries. **1883** DOMETT *Ranolf & Amohia* II. 16 Hard violet drupes of the great *laurel-tree* And gold **karaka-dates**. **1911** SHAND *Moriori People* 5 For variety they had Fernroot (*Eruhè*) and **Karaka nuts** (of which latter, in good seasons, they preserved very large quantities). **1928** BAUCKE *Manuscript* (Bishop Museum Memoirs Vol.IX No.5 343–382) in Skinner & Baucke *The Moriois* 359 The most relied upon as food to be preserved for winter use was the karaka nut. **1981** karaka nut [see KARAKINE].

karakahia. [Ma. /kaˈrakahia/: Williams 98 *Karakahia*.] *white-eyed* (earlier *white-winged*) *duck* (DUCK 2 (9)).

1886 *TrNZI* XVIII. 117 *Nyroca australis.*—Karakahia, White-winged Duck. Both Islands; Australia. **1904** HUTTON & DRUMMOND *Animals NZ* 315 *The White-winged Duck.—Karakahia. Nyroca australis.* **1955** [see DUCK 2 (9)]. **1985** *Reader's Digest Book NZ Birds* 151 White-eyed Duck *Aythya australis*... Karakahia.

karakia, *n*. Also early **crackee crackee**. [Ma. /ˈkarakia/: Williams 98 *karakia 1*. n. Charm, spell, incantation..2 v. intr. Repeat a form of words as a charm or spell,.. v. trans. Repeat an incantation over (a person or thing).]

1. In traditional Maori contexts, a ceremonial incantation.

[1820 LEE & KENDALL *NZ Gram. & Vocab.* 159 Karakía. s... A religious ceremony; a calling, as upon God; a prayer.] **1833** WILLIAMS *Early Jrnls.* 14 Mar. (1961) 294 The party assembled naked..the Priest an old greybearded man..stood up in front with outstretched arms..and repeated over his *karakia*, or prayer, to Tu, the God of War. **1843** DIEFFENBACH *Travels in NZ* II. 57 E' Karakia is a prayer or an incantation, used on certain occasions. **1851** SHORTLAND *S. Dist. NZ* 68 While the priest chants a 'karakia' or incantation in measure, the 'taua' keep time by leaping together. **1871** MEADE *Ride through Disturbed Dist.* in Taylor *Early Travellers* (1959) 491 He therefore announced..that there must first be a great *karakia*, or ceremony of worship, to induce the great *Atua* (spirit) to inspire them rightly as to what was to be done with the pakeha. **1879** *Auckland Weekly News* 17 May 8 It would not surprise us if Te Kooti..were to on the first celebration of the Hauhau *karakia*, turn the tables. **1910** *Kai Tiaki* July 104 The first and most urgent remedy in a Maori sickness is the appropriate 'karakia'. **1937** BABBAGE *Hauhauism* 58 At the meeting..there was to be a grand performance of the Pai Marire Karakia (incantation) in the hope of drawing over the Poverty Bay natives. **1959** SINCLAIR *Hist. NZ* 23 The higher class of *tohunga* had many functions. They could recite the *karakia* (prayers, incantations, spells) with greater efficacy than the layman. **1983** HULME *Bone People* 393 Old karakia he mentioned to make stones float, and find halfdead people cluttering up his beaches. **1990** *Listener* 17 Dec. 76 The karakia really contain all the protocols of conservation, safety and renewal.

2. In Christian contexts, a prayer or prayers; a service of worship; a sermon.

1817 NICHOLAS *Voyage NZ* I. 274 [The New Zealander] replied, that it [*sc*. tapu] was no gammon at all; 'New Zealand man,' said he, 'say that Mr. Marsden's *crackee crackee* (preaching) of a Sunday, is all *gammon*.' 'No, no,' I rejoined, 'that is not *gammon*, that is *miti*,' (good.) 'Well then,' retorted the tenacious reasoner, 'if your *crackee crackee* is no gammon, our taboo taboo is no gammon.' **1833** WILLIAMS *Early Jrnls.* 31 Mar. (1961) 303 In the evening we held *karakia*, and delivered our message in the name of the Lord. **1847** ANGAS *Savage Life* II. 13 At sunset, the natives went through their *karakia*, or worship, which is performed by the Christians every night and morning. **1866** HUNT *Chatham Is.* 50 The morrow was the Sabbath. He would then attend the *karakia*, or church, and during the morning service I determined to search his *whare*. **1985** HOWE *Towards 'Taha Maori'* in *English* (NZATE) 19 Karakia—'prayer'. This word refers to both the church service, and the prayer or special chant performed at the opening and close of meetings **1989** *A New Zealand Prayer Book, He Karakia Mihinare o Aotearoa* [Title of the NZ Anglican Prayer Book]

karakia, *v*. Also early **keakea**. [See *n*.] *trans*. and *intr*. To chant (a ceremonial incantation) over (a person or thing); in Christian contexts, to pray (for).

[1814 KENDALL 6 Sept. in Elder *Marsden's Lieutenants* (1934) 59 Six days men were allowed to work, and every seventh day was appointed as a day of rest from labour, and to *keakea atua*; for this was the only term which we could then make use of in order to convey to their ideas our worshipping the Supreme Being.] **1832** WILLIAMS *Early Jrnls.* 6 Jan. (1961) 213 If they should be in a situation that they cannot land, everyone immediately ceases talkg., and they commence 'Karakia' their incantations. **1844** WILLIAMS *NZ Jrnl.* (1956) 95 A poor dying native is..drawn into the open air, to [be] karakiaed or prayed for by the priest. **1874** CARLETON *Henry Williams* (1948) 69 The natives said he had *Karakia'd* us—a term they apply to our religious worship. **c1920** BEATTIE *Trad. Lifeways Southern Maori* (1994) 413 A boy hurt his leg..[and] was carried to Taki who karakia'd it and the boy ran home. **1930** COWAN *The Maori* 184 When the people gathered at the *maara*, the cultivation plot, the priest *karakia*'d the field, chanting his incantations to Maru and the gods of the *kumara*. **1948** HENDERSON *Taina* 26 That was the only tree that wasn't *karakiaed*.

karakin. Also early **karakine**, erron. **korakine**. [f. Ma. *karak*(a + *-in*.] The poisonous principle of the karaka kernel.

1872 *TrNZI* IV. 363 The author [W. Skey] announced that he had succeeded in isolating the bitter principle of the Karaka berry, and had found it to be a crystallizable resin... Mr. Skey proposed to name the new resin 'Karakine'. **1882** HAY *Brighter Britain* II. 193 The Koraka [*sic*] (*Corynocarpus laevigata*) was brought to New Zealand by the Maori... The fruit is edible; the kernel contains 'korakine' [*sic*], a narcotic poison. **1889** KIRK *Forest Flora* 171 [Skey] has appropriately named this bitter principle of the karaka 'karakine'. **1946** *JPS* LV. 148 *karakin* is an English word derived from a Maori word, karaka: had the Maori given the name it would no doubt have been karakino (kino, bad). **1981** BROOKER et al. *NZ Medicinal Plants* 13 Karakin, the poisonous principle of the karaka nut, has been found by Carter to contain several nitro groups.

karamu /kəˈramu/. Also occas. **kakaramu**. [Ma. /karaˈmuː/: Williams 98 *Karamū*, *kāramuramu*, *kākaramū*, n. *Coprosma*.]

1. Any of several native plants of the genus *Coprosma* (fam. Rubiaceae), esp. *C. lucida*, a small tree or shrub having pale bark and leathery leaves, and *C. robusta*, having pliable glossy leaves and frequently used as a hedge-plant. Often *attrib*. See also COFFEE, COPROSMA, KARANGU, *orange-leaf*, *orange-wood* (ORANGE 1 a), *yellow-wood* (YELLOW 2).

1848 BRUNNER *Exped. Middle Is.* 14 Mar. in Taylor *Early Travellers* (1959) 308 When..[wekas] feed on the berry of the karamu, they get very fat. **1853** HOOKER *II Flora Novae-Zelandiae I Flowering Plants* 104 *Coprosma lucida*... Nat. names, 'Karamu' and 'Karangu'. **1868** [see KARANGU]. **1874** WHITE *Te Rou* 221 Then they tied a few Karamu branches in front of them and went towards the settlement. **1883** DOMETT *Ranolf & Amohia* I. 302 Coffee-bush (*Karamu*)... Several species. Fruit and seeds like small coffee berries, in scarlet colour, arrangement, and taste. **1898** [see COFFEE]. **1935** STACK *More Maoriland Adventures* in Wily & Maunsell *Robert Maunsell* 139 The rays of the rising sun first struck the glistening leaves of the flax..and karamu shrubs in the swamps adjoining the river. **1940** LAING & BLACKWELL *Plants NZ* 423 *Coprosma robusta*... A stout shrub, 2 ft.–12ft. in height... Maori name, *Kakaramu* or *Karamu*. **1952** RICHARDS *Chatham Is.* 60 Maoris do not use any of the karamus as firewood as heat makes the odour worse than ever. **1988** DAWSON *Forest Vines to Snow Tussocks* 103 Accompanying species may be the two common larger-leaved coprosmas both known as karamu: *C. robusta* and *C. lucida*.

2. As **tree karamu**, *Coprosma arborea*, a small tree. See also MAMANGI.

1886 KIRK in *Settler's Handbook NZ* (1902) 122 [Native name] Karamu..[Settlers' name] Tree-karamu. **1889** KIRK *Forest Flora* 275 'Karamu' is applied by the Maoris to several species of *Coprosma*, among which, I believe this [*C. arborea*] is included, but it is commonly termed 'tree-karamu' by bushmen and settlers in the North. **1890** PWD *Gen. Catalogue* (NZ & South Seas Exhib.) 29 Tree karamu slab.

karanga. [Ma. /ˈkaraŋa/: Williams 98 *Karanga*. *1.* v. Call, summon,.. *2.* Welcome.] A Maori ceremonial call of welcome. Also as **karanga caller**, a female member of a group performing a karanga.

1905 BAUCKE *White Man Treads* 253 Now it was part of [Maori] festal ceremonies to chant a 'Karanga' (call of welcome), when he brought food to set before the stranger guests. **1974** *N.Z. Listener* 20 July 10 All of a sudden I was jolted..the karanga, the shrill haeremai, haeremai coming down the marae. **1986** *Evening Post* (Wellington) 26 Aug. 34 Mrs Harata Solomon..performs the karanga (call) at the start of the PPTA conference in Wellington today. **1986** IHIMAERA *Matriarch* 28 To one side, a special group of elders was sitting, ready to give their speeches of welcome once the karanga of the women had been completed. **1987** *Listener* 21 Feb. 10 'Come on, Bolger,' mutters an impatient karanga caller by the meeting house door.

Hence **karanga** *v. intr.*, to call in welcome.

1986 HULME *Windeater* 95 Waina shivers. Her voice rises in a beautiful quaver, controlled keening, as she karangas in return.

karangu. *Obs. in English use.* Also **karanghu**. [Ma. /karaˈŋuː/: Williams 98 *Karangū* = *karamū*..*Coprosma* [sp.].] KARAMU 1.

[**1820** LEE & KENDALL *NZ Gram. & Vocab.* 160 Karángu; Name of a certain tree.] **1838** POLACK *NZ* II. 400 There are many other woods of much service to Europeans, differing in quality, among others: the..*Warangai*..*Karanghu*..&c. **1853** [see KARAMU 1]. **1868** LINDSAY *Contribs. NZ Bot.* 71 [*Coprosma lucida*] is also known to the Otago natives as 'Kalamou'..; and to the North Island Maoris as 'Karamu'..'Kakaramu', or 'Karangu'. **1869** *TrNZI* I. (rev. edn.) 204 Karangu. Coprosma foetidissima.

karawa, var. KAREAO.

kare, var. KORRY.

kareao. Also with much variety of early form as **calawar, kakareao, karawa, karea(u), karehao, karewa(o), kuri-wao, kuriwau.** [Ma. /ˈkareao/: Williams 100 *Kareao, kakareao, karewao, kakarewao*, n. *1...* supplejack.] SUPPLEJACK 1 a.

1840 TAYLOR *Journal* (ATLTS) 10 Jan. II. 179 I had a narrow escape of being strangled a kareao (souple jack) got round my neck. **1840** *NZ Jrnl.* I. 232 Creepers..as the calawars, rendering the forest impenetrable. **1848** WAKEFIELD *Handbook NZ* 144 The woods are almost impenetrably interwoven with lianes, or supple-jacks, called Kareau by the natives. **1848** SELWYN in *NZ Part V* (Church in the Colonies XX) (1849) 76 We then resorted to the usual expedient of torches made of 'karehao' (supple Jack) or 'katoa'. **1852** *Wellington Gazette* in Earp *Hand-Book for Intending Emigrants* 230 Thick underbrush of *konine* (fuchsia)..&c. [is] entwined with kuriwau or supple-jack. **1855** DRURY *Sailing Directions* 67 Trees [met with in Pelorus]. Ti—Ti palm or Ti bush, common everywhere. Supplejacks—Karea of natives. **1867** HOOKER *Handbook* 765 Kareao, *Rhipogonum scandens*. Ibid. 766 Kuri-wao, *Hector*. **1882** [see SUPPLEJACK 1 a]. **1888** CHUDLEIGH *Diary* 25 June (1950) 362 All hands at bush fencing and all very tired. Karawas as thick as a cloud, every tree hung together like wax. **1908** BAUGHAN *Shingle-Short* 189 Now the *Kareao* snaps, now the kiékié is brown'd and wind-eaten... [1908 *Note*] *Kareao* (*Karry-ow*): The supple-jack; a liana. **1930** GUTHRIE *NZ Memories* 47 Two native boys were..working on the pattern of a whaler's or maori house, [and] first made a framework of *kareau* or supplejack. **1939** BEATTIE *First White Boy Born Otago* 98 To make a log fence you drove in two stakes here and there..and filled up with sticks lying flat and lashed with karewao vine. **1946** *JPS* LV. 143 *Kareao*, a vine..., supplejack; tough thin black vine. **1952** LYON *Faring South* 156 From the bush [near Buller River] plaited two cables of the karewa, or as we call it, supplejack vine. **1966** kakarewao [see SUPPLEJACK 1 a]. **1986** RICHARDS *Off the Sheep's Back* 87 The sharp end of a kareao (supplejack) sprang back and pierced the corner of my eye.

karearea /kʌˈræiəræi/. Also freq. **karewarewa**, early occas. **kari-area**. [Ma. /kaːˈrearea/: Williams 100 *Kārearea*. *1. n. Falco novae-seelandiae...* = *kāeaea, kāiaia, kārewarewa*.] FALCON.

1842 GRAY *Fauna* in Dieffenbach *Travels in NZ* (1843) II. 186 *Falco brunnea*..Kauaua..Kari-area of the natives of Queen Charlotte's Sound. **1847** TAYLOR *Journal* (ATLTS) 18 Apr. V. 33 As we went we heard a karewarewa (the sparrow hawk) screaming. **1859** karewarewa [see SPARROWHAWK]. **1867** *Richmond-Atkinson Papers* (1960) II. 234 I asked [one of the new hands] what the bird was at the top of the niu? and without prompting he said 'a karearea' & the reason was as I supposed that Kapariera (Gabriel) had first appeared in the form of that bird. **1873** BULLER *Birds NZ* 1 Hieracidea novae zealandiae. (Quail Hawk)... Karearea, Kaiaia, Kaeaea, Kakarapiti, Karewarewa, and Tawaka. *Ibid.* 6 Hieracidea brunnea. (Bush-hawk)..Karearea, Kaiaia, Kaeaea, Kakarapiti, Karewarewa, and Tawaka... 'Sparrow-Hawk' of the colonists. **1882** [see FALCON]. **1904** HUTTON & DRUMMOND *Animals NZ* 149 The Quail-hawk.—Kare-wa-rewa. **1938** *Auckland Weekly News* 28 Sept. 11 If the karearea, or bush-hawk, screamed in rainy weather, it was an accurate sign of a change [*sc.* of weather]. **1955** [see FALCON]. **1967** NATUSCH *Animals NZ* 274 *Falco novaeseelandieae*, the Karearea..is a handsome bird, swift flying, and full of fight. **1989** PARKINSON *Travelling Naturalist* 141 The scarce falcon, or karearea, can also sometimes be seen, its piercing whistle or scream often betraying its presence before it comes into sight.

kareau, karehao, varr. KAREAO.

kareko, var. KARENGO.

karengo(rengo). Also **kareko** (SI variant from Ngai Tahu Ma. dial.). [Ma. /ˈkareŋo/: Williams 100 *Karengo*. *2. n...*an edible seaweed.] *Porphyra columbina* (fam. Bangiaceae), a common edible red seaweed. See also PARENGO.

1844 [see PARENGO]. **1848** TAYLOR *Leaf from Nat. Hist.* 32 Karengo, a green sea weed, edible. **1869** *TrNZI* I. (rev. edn.) 262 A few also of the sea-weeds were eaten; such as, the Karengo, (A tidal species of *Laminaria* found plentifully from the East Cape to Cape Turnagain). **1881** *TrNZI* XIII. 29 Another peculiar plant was the *karengo* (*Laminaria* sp.), a sea-weed. **1904** TREGEAR *Maori Race* 102 A few varieties of seaweed were also cooked..the principal of these was a species of Laminaria (*karengo*). **1912** *Otago Witness* (Dunedin) 25 Dec. 80 Sustaining herself by shellfish and 'karengo' (edible seaweed), she continued her weary way. **c1920** BEATTIE *Trad. Lifeways Southern Maori* (1994) 126 If any North Island people come down to Otago..and go to the seashore they get quite excited over the amount of kareko going to waste. *Ibid.* 304 Karengo, which is fine seaweed of red, pink and green colors [*sic*], is still eaten here [in Canterbury] boiled and dried or fried in fat—it is very good. **1938** *Auckland Weekly News* 2 Mar. 42 There is the reef which is the seasonal gathering ground of the edible seaweed, karengo, a favourite article of diet of the Maori. **1966** *Encycl. NZ* III. 214 Upper intertidal levels are occupied by species such as *Porphyra columbina*, the karengo. **1978** FULLER *Maori Food & Cook.* 37 Edible Seaweed (Parengo or Karengo) Parengo (*Porphyra columbina*) is found at intertidal levels and was used by the Maori as a sort of relish. **1983** HULME *Bone People* 113 I also look after a stand of mushrooms..and my karengo beds are very carefully tended. **1989** HULME & MORRISON *Homeplaces* 60 Kareko (also known, in the north, as parengo) is a kind of laver. **1996** *Evening Post* (Wellington) 1 Feb. 21 Karengo (Porphyra columbina) is a green seaweed with a silky texture to the frond. It looks like a small crumpled salad lettuce..and darkens to a purply-brown when it dries. All parts of this plant can be eaten.

karetu. [Ma. /ˈkaːretu/: Williams 101 *Kāretu*, n. *Hierochloe*.] *Hierochloe redolens* (fam. Poaceae), a robust sweet-scented native grass. See also *holy grass* (GRASS 2 (22)).

[**1820** LEE & KENDALL *NZ Gram. & Vocab.* 160 Karétu, *s.* A plant so called.] **1843** TAYLOR *Journal* (ATLTS) Aug. 51 Karetu a sweet scented grass. **1869** *TrNZI* I. (rev. edn) 266 The daisy like flowers of the Roniu.. and the flowering tops of the sweet-scented grass Karetu (*Hierchloe redolens*), were worn around the neck. **1870** *TrNZI* II. 102 *Hierochloe redolens...* 'Karetu.' Common in wet places and swamps, of rather stout habit but sweet and succulent. **1882** HAY *Brighter Britain* II. 199 The Karetu.., which is not a shrub exactly, but a grass, renowned for its delicious scent. **1904** TREGEAR *Maori Race* 14 The sweet-scented grass *karetu*..was spread in the sleeping houses of chiefs, as in Germany the same plant [*i.e.* holy grass] is strewed on festival days before the doors of churches. **1936** ALLAN *Intro. to Grasses of NZ* (DSIR Bulletin 49) 118 *H(ierochloe) redolens* (karetu: Holy-grass). A large grass forming extensive tufts or patches. **1949** BUCK *Coming of Maori* 174, 289 Women wore belts (tu) formed of braided strands of fragrant *Karetu* grass. **1961** MARTIN *Flora NZ* 132 Moist soils both on coastal cliffs and in subalpine valleys are the usual station of the Karetu or Scented Holy Grass. **1978** *Bull. Wellington Bot. Soc. No.40* 48 Frequently the sachet was woven of holy grass *Hierochloe redolens* or karetu, which was itself sweetly scented. **1982** Kāretu [see GRASS 2 (22)].

karewa(o), varr. KAREAO.

karewarewa: see KAREAREA.

kari-area, var. KAREAREA.

Karitane /kærəˈtɑni/, *attrib.* [f. *Karitane*, a place-name in the South Island associated with Sir F. Truby King (1858–1938).]

1. Used *attrib.*, often passing into Comb., of or pertaining to the system of ante- and post-natal care for mothers and babies initiated by Sir F. Truby King; applied specifically to the first hospital established by King to give such care, thence to the nursing headquarters of the Plunket Society, Society hospitals and family support units, and later as a brand-name for infant-food products manufactured by or for the Society. See also PLUNKET.

1913 [see 2 below]. **1917** WRENCH *Let.* in *King Truby King* (1948) 234 I am convinced that our greatest need in this country is a Training Centre on Karitane lines. **1948** KING *Truby King* 107 The word 'Karitane' has become famous in connection with Truby King Mothercraft work; but its origin is far removed from babies. The Huriawa or Karitane Peninsula lies at the south end of the wide Waikouati Bay. **1955** *BJ Cameron Collection* (TS July) karitane baby (n) A baby being reared under the plunket system of infant care originated by Sir Truby King. **1960** SCRYMGEOUR *Memories Maoriland* 153 Always a leader in the van of social welfare, the Dominion had given much thought and practical expression in the methods of 'Karitane' and 'Plunket' care of babies. **1984** BOYD *City of the Plains* 217 The Society..faced three major problems: finance,

finding a suitable nurse, giving her a Karitane training and retaining her services, and objections from doctors.

2. Special Comb. **a. Karitane Home**, a Karitane hospital; **Karitane hospital**, a hospital for babies and nursing mothers applying Truby King's principles; **Karitane nurse**, a nurse trained at a Karitane Hospital esp. in the care of babies and nursing mothers, and young children; often *ellipt.* **Karitane** (see quots. 1968, 1990, 1991), occas. *transf.* (see quot. 1954); **Karitane nursing**, specialist child-and-mother-care nursing usu. done in the patient's home.

1944 *Korero* (AEWS Background Bulletin) 6 Nov. 12 On a terrace below the **Karitane Home**, there is a small but well-equipped laboratory. **1955** *BJ Cameron Collection* (TS July) karitane home (n) A hospital for babies based on the principles of the plunket system. The first such hospital was at Karitane, near Dunedin. **1958** *NZ News* 11 Mar. 3 As an example, he [*sc.* Sir Truby King] successfuly treated thirteen neglected infants in his own home [at Karitane], and ultimately six model 'Karitane' homes were founded throughout the Dominion. **c1962** BAXTER *Horse* (1985) 7 The misunderstanding between them..stretched right back to the cotton wool and enemas and foreskin-clipping doctors of a Karitane nursing home. **1913** KING *Feeding & Care of Baby* 43 What has been achieved..on a relatively small scale at the **Karitane Hospital** is reflected enormously magnified in the district work. **1965** McLAGLAN *Stethoscope & Saddlebags* 78 Other delicate babies followed them and so his beach cottage at Karitane became the first Karitane baby hospital. All the Plunket Society's baby hospitals are called 'Karitane' hospitals and Plunket nurses are trained in them. **1990** *Matriarchs* 140 Mothers came into the Karitane Hospital if they were having trouble nursing their children, or if the babies were not well. **1924** *Otago Witness* (Dunedin) 1 Apr. 61 Here girls..learn how to qualify as baby nurses in private homes, with the certificate of a **Karitane nurse**. **1938** *Auckland Weekly News* 16 Feb. 11 Nurses trained only in baby management are called Karitane Nurses, so called because the first children so cared for came under [Dr King's] personal supervision at his home in Karitane. **1938** *NZ Observer* 28 July 7 I saw a bunch of young kickers on my rounds, in charge of a cheerful Karitane nurse. **1947** GASKELL *All Part of the Game* (1978) 121 Margaret had started training as a Karitane nurse. **1954** MACFARLANE *Te Raka* 36 A Karitane nurse in the shape of a man in dingy blue dungarees or a cow girl in jodhpurs takes charge of [the calf] immediately [it is born]. **1965** MACNICOL *Skippers Road* 45 None of the children..ever saw a Karitane nurse or was weighed after leaving the nursing home. **1968** SLATTER *Pagan Game* 167 Erik was mightily puzzled by the boy's strange conduct. Was he training to be a Karitane or what? **1980** HALL *Prisoners of Mother England* 21 Raelene had this Karitane who went straight to town, bought a few knick knacks for her glory box. **1987** *Dominion* (Wellington) 27 July 9 These were the days when a Karitane nurse could be hired for three guineas a week. **1990** *Matriarchs* 142 I went round to various houses as a Karitane... It was something quite special to be a Karitane and we honoured the name, but oh, it was hard work. **1992** *North & South* (Auckland) Nov. 108 The distinction between a Plunket nurse and a Karitane is an important one. Plunket nurses must be registered nurses before they embark on the 17-week Plunket training course and they often have additional midwifery or nursing qualifications. Karitanes have basic child-care training with no nursing qualification required. **1990** *Matriarchs* 142 **Karitane nursing** in England was a different experience from working here.

b. *fig.* and *transf.* As **karitane gold (yellow)**, applied attributively (and jocularly) to yellow or

yellowish colours, suggestive of infants' faeces.

1964 p.c. G.L. Gabites Wellington *Karitane*. Used esp. by servicemen c1940 for scrambled eggs made from egg-powder. Also (from their yellow shoulder-patches) as a name for a member of the NZ Tank Brigade. **1968** SLATTER *Pagan Game* 173 Green Band, Red Band, Gold Top, Double Brown, Nut Brown..all the colours of purge. Karitane yellow. What was he babysitting for on Friday night? **1973** HAYWARD *Diary Kirk Years* (1981) 112 At Parliament our offices have been repainted, and deep pile carpet of an unfortunate 'Karitane' gold has been laid.

Hence **karitane-ing** *vbl. n.*, Karitane-style nursing.

1990 *Matriarchs* 144 Once back in London I did a certain amount of Karitane-ing.

karmahi, karmai, varr. KAMAHI.

karo. [Ma. /ˈkaro/: Williams 102 *Karo* (iii), n. *1. Pittosporum* [spp.].] Any of several small native trees of the genus *Pittosporum* (fam. Pittosporaceae), esp. the coastal tree *P. crassifolium*. See also TURPENTINE TREE 1.

1842 BEST *Journal* 10 Apr. (1966) 365 Picked up a pretty shrub 'Te Karo' from which the Maories extract an oil which they highly esteem. **1853** HOOKER *II Flora Novae-Zelandiae I Flowering Plants* 23 Pittosporum *cornifolium...* Hab. Northern Island..Nat. name, 'Karo'. **1889** [see TURPENTINE 1 a]. **1890** *PWD Gen. Catalogue* (NZ & South Seas Exhib.) 20 Lithograph of karo foliage. **1910** COCKAYNE *NZ Plants & Their Story* 79 Other common coastal trees in the north are the karo (*Pittosporum crassifolium*)..and the whau. **1951** LEVY *Grasslands NZ* (1970) 87 Such species as lancewood..kamahi, mahoe, tarata, karo. **1963** MOORE & ADAMS *Plants NZ Coast* 94 Karo and pohutukawa grow together and both belong naturally only to the Auckland province.

karoaka, karooka, varr. KARAKA.

karoro. Also **korora** (erron.). [Ma. /ˈkaroro/: Williams 102 *Karoro*, n. *1.*] The *black-backed gull* (GULL 2 (1)).

[**1820** LEE & KENDALL *NZ Gram. & Vocab.* 160 Károro, *s.* Name of a certain bird.] **1859** THOMSON *Story NZ* I. 23 The Korora, a sea-bird, carries up into the air living shell-fish, which it breaks by letting fall on hard rocks. **1861** *Richmond-Atkinson Papers* (1960) I. 680 Saw another noteworthy sight... [*sic*] a young karoro just out of the nest, running along in a curious human way all by himself. **1873** BULLER *Birds NZ* 270 Larus dominicanus. (Southern Black-backed Gull)... Karoro; the young bird distinguished as Ngoiro. **1898** MORRIS *Austral-English* 242 *Karoro...* Black-backed Gull, *Larus dominicanus.* **1904**, **1947** [see GULL 2 (1)]. **1966** FALLA et al. *Birds NZ* 154 Southern black-backed Gull *Larus dominicanus...* Karoro, Ngoiro. **1985** GRACE in *Landfall 186* 450 One of them is eyeing the bait, head of the soldier, and is following... It's dead meat, hooked, Krazy Karoro.

karowai, var. KOROWAI.

karraka, var. KARAKA.

karrea(u), var. KAREAO.

karuhiruhi. [Ma. /kaːˈruhiruhi/: Williams 102 *Kāruhiruhi.*] *pied shag* (SHAG 2 (13)).

[**1820** LEE & KENDALL *NZ Gram. & Vocab.* 154 Ka dúi dúi. Name of a certain bird.] **1844** WILLIAMS *NZ Jrnl.* (1956) 115 The Kauau or common diver, the

KARWAI

[K]aruhiruhi, the first name is generally used, the Black Shagg or diver and the latter to the smaller diver, with white brest [sic]. **1873** BULLER *Birds NZ* 328 Phalacrocorax varius. (Pied Shag)... Karuhiruhi. **1947** POWELL *Native Animals NZ* 79 Pied Shag (*Phalacrocorax varius*), Karuhiruhi..is a common coastal species from North Cape to Stewart Island. **1955** OLIVER *NZ Birds* 207 *Pied Shag Karuhiruhi...* The Pied Shag is found in both Australia and New Zealand but it was first described from New Zealand. **1985** *Reader's Digest Book NZ Birds* 116 *Pied Cormorant... Karuhiruhi, pied shag.* **1990** *Checklist Birds NZ* 81 *Phalacrocorax varius varius..Pied Shag (Pied Cormorant, Karuhiruhi).*

karwai, var. KAHAWAI.

kataitai. Also erron. **katata.** [Ma. /kaːˈtaitai/: Williams 103 *Kātaitai*, n... 2. *Anthus novaeseelandiae... = pīhoihoi.*] PIPIT.
   1842 GRAY *Fauna* in Dieffenbach *Travels in NZ* (1843) II. 192 *Alauda Novae Seelandiae...* Kataitai of the natives of Cook's Straits... A 'Ground Lark' is given under the name of Pihoihoi, by Mr Yate. **1859** [see LARK 2 (1)]. **1930** REISCHEK *Yesterdays in Maoriland* (1933) 63 On August 12 I went to the swamp to look for larks (*katata*).

katero, var. KATIPO.

Kath. *Obs.* Also **K.** *Ellipt.* for KATHLEEN MAVOURNEEN 1 (see also quot. 1937 below).
   1928 ALPERS *Cheerful Yesterdays* 274 I had never heard this name for the indeterminate sentence, which is now well established in prison slang, 'Kath', videlicet, 'Kathleen Mavourneen' because: 'It may be for years, and it may be for ever'. **1937** PARTRIDGE *Dict. Slang* 449 *kath (or K)*. An indefinitely long term of imprisonment: New Zealand c[ant] (–1914). —2. Hence, 'the duration'..: New Zealand military: 1915–18. **1941** BAKER *NZ Slang* 53 [Underworld slang includes]..*kath*, a prison sentence of indefinite length. **1958** WALL *Queen's English* 127 A rare example of real..wit in the criminal class is 'Kathleen Mavourneen' or 'kath' for an indeterminate sentence. This dates from about 1910 and originated either in New Zealand or in Australia.

Kathleen Mavourneen. [f. the title of the song, *Kathleen Mavourneen* with reference to the line 'It may be for years and it may be forever': AND 1910.]
   1. *Obs.* Formerly, an indeterminate prison sentence (esp. under the Habitual Criminals and Offenders Act, 6 Edw. VII s 2(1)(a) 1906, absorbed into the 1908 Crimes Act, providing for such a sentence for any person declared a 'Habitual Criminal' by the Court, and now replaced in practice by preventive detention). Occas. a prisoner undergoing such a sentence. See also ACT, COLLAR 1, KATH, KEY *n.*[1]
   1907 *Red Funnel* IV. 21 New Zealand has now introduced 'habitual criminals' legislation... The criminal classes, with caustic wit, christened the obnoxious measure the 'Kathleen Mavourneen' Act, the allusion being to a familiar line in that most pathetic and charming ballad—'It may be for years, and it may be for ever'. **1910** *Truth* 10 Dec. 4 Amy..has been transferred to New Plymouth, there to undergo detention as a 'Kathleen Mavourneen'. **1928**, **1958** [see KATH]. **1980** MACKENZIE *While We Have Prisons* 9 In prison language they had been given the 'collar', the 'key', the Kathleen Mavourneen sentence—'It may be for years and it may be for ever'. *Ibid.* 97 *Kathleen Mavourneen* indeterminate sentence.

   2. *transf.* Applied, often as an *attrib.*, to anything which may extend into the undefined or distant future, the 'never-never'; occas. a long delay.
   1905 *Truth* 19 Aug. 1 A Kathleen Mavourneen loan is one that may be for years and it may be for ever. **1934** SCANLAN *Winds of Heaven* 298 I hate these Kathleen Mavourneen engagements..it may be for years and it may be forever. **1949** SULLIVAN in *The Standard* May (1952) 31 [In answer to a question on when the Government intended to proceed with new works] Hon. W. Sullivan said 'There will be no Kathleen Mavourneen as far as we are concerned' in an election address on 22 November 1949. **1981** LOCKE *Student at the Gates* 53 She earned extra money when she could and in her third year had a 'Kathleen Mavourneen' loan arranged through the registrar.

   3. As **Kathleen Mavourneen stakes**, the allusion is to the former declaration of a person to be a 'Habitual Criminal'.
   1910 *Truth* 21 May 8 A candidate for the 'Kathleen Mavourneen Stakes,'.. appeared..in Wellington's Magistrate's Court on Saturday and Monday last. *Ibid.* 4 June 7 [Heading] Kathleen Mavourneen Stakes. Sheehan did not exhibit any intention of worrying, and when sentenced to twelve months and labelled as an habitual criminal, which at his age (63) means life, he passed down the trap feeling apparently relieved.

katipo /ˈkæti,pʌu/, /ˈkʌt-/. Also **katepo.** [Ma. /katiˈpoː/: Williams 103 *Katipō*, n. *1*..a venomous spider.] Also as **katipo spider**, *Latrodectus katipo* (fam. Theridiidae), a venomous native spider.
   1841 *Best Journal* 10 Apr. (1966) 286 We procured Specimens of the Katipo a Spider held in great awe by the Mauries it [sic] is an ugly insect with a round black body about the size of a pea its bite is said to be venomous. **1851** REES in *GBPP NZ* (Irish Univ. Press Series) IX. 1779 28 Of arachnidae, two, called by the natives katipo, are poisonous. **1867** HOCHSTETTER *NZ* 440 We were cautioned by the natives against a small, black spider with a red stripe on its back, which they call Katipo or Katepo. **1879** *Auckland Weekly News* 11 Oct. 8 Mrs. Bettis..was bitten by a poisonous spider, the Katipo, last week, and suffered excruciating agony in consequence. **1885** *TrNZI* XVII. 419 The common locust and grasshopper were seen, and the poisonous katipo spider is also to be found. **1905** WHITE *My NZ Garden* 75 We have one small venomous Spider, the 'Katipo', but as it is not in the least aggressive, and is branded on the back with a red stripe, it is easily avoided. **1910** *School Journal* Part II Nov. 164 Maoris state that their children have often died from katipo-bites. **1924** LYSNAR *New Zealand* 104 There are hundreds of kinds of spiders..but the katipo is the only one whose bite is very poisonous and dangerous. **1938** HYDE *Godwits Fly* (1970) 4 The katipo, a tiny black spider with a red spot on his back, is almost the only poisonous thing in the country. **1954** BEATTIE *Our Southernmost Maoris* 66 The katipo, the spider with the red band, they declared was a native. **1968** BAXTER *Collected Plays* (1982) 39 If there's a katipo under a stone, its better not to lift it. **1977** HALL *Glide Time* (1984) 15 Watch out for the katipos. **1984** *The Weta* VII. 60 The inflamed area of her leg showed two small 'pin pricks' about 1mm apart, consistent with a spider bite. (The chelicerae of a katipo spider will inflict such a wound).

katoa. *Obs.* in English use. Also early **gadoa**. [Ma. /ˈkaːtoa/: Williams 104 *Kātoa*, n. *Leptospermum scoparium... = kahikātoa, mānuka.*] KAHIKATOA.
   1841 *NZ Jrnl.* II. 51 This tree [Totarra]..does not grow on the lowest banks, which are generally covered with gadoa trees. **1844** *House of Commons Rep. from Sel. Committee on NZ* 29 Jul 611 The kahikatoa, also

KAUPAPA

called gadoa, or manuko, a philadelphus with a very hard and brown wood. **1848** SELWYN in *NZ Part V* (Church in the Colonies XX) 30 Aug. (1849) 76 We then resorted to the usual expedient of torches made of 'karehao' (supple Jack) or 'katoa'..it was [agreed].. that we should light a fire and bivouac for the night.

katote. [Ma. /ˈkaːtote/: Williams 104 *Kātote, katote* (i), n. *1*... a tree-fern.] *Cyathea smithii* (fam. Cyatheaceae), a native tree fern having a persistent skirt of dead fronds.
   1885 *TrNZI* XVII. 217 The most common species are the poka (*Dicksonia squarrosa*) and the katote..; the stem and fronds of the latter are sometimes used as food for cows. **1920** *Quick March* 10 Mar. 38 A peculiarity of another kind [of fern], the katote, is that its fronds..all incline sharply upwards. **1984** MORTON *Whirinaki* 51 [Caption] The katote (*Cyathea smithii*) can be distinguished from other tree-fern species by its hanging skirt of dead leaf-stalks or stipes.

kaua kaua, var. KAWAKAWA *n.*[1]

kauau, var. KAWAU.

kaudi, var. KAURI.

kauka: see *ti-kauka* (TI *n.*[1] 3 (2)).

kau kau, var. KAKA.

kaumatua. [Ma. /kauˈmaːtua/: Williams 106 *Kaumātua. 1*. n. Adult. *2*. Old man or woman.] *Pl.* often **kaumatuas**. A Maori elder; occas. *transf.* to a non-Maori (see quot. 1989). See also ELDER.
   [**1820** LEE & KENDALL *NZ Gram. & Vocab.* 161 Kau mátua; A grown-up person.] **1835** WILLIAMS *Early Jrnls.* 22 Feb. (1961) 414 We..assembled..for English service, where we mustered twelve *kaumatuas* besides children. **1846** TAYLOR *Journal* (ATLTS) 4 June IV. 34 He said they were like a widow feeble having lost their kaumatua, (his father). **1863** *Richmond-Atkinson Papers* (1960) II. 25 Komene & others..recommended them to turn back as they would not see the kaumatuas if they went on. **1879** *TrNZI* XI. 72 Many a deliberation of the *Kaumatuas* or elders took place over the prepared model, ere the shape was finally settled. **1900** *Auckland Weekly News Xmas Number* 12 The *kaumatua*, or senior chief, headed the procession. **1929** *Na To Hoa Aroha* (1986) I. 168 The trouble is that there are too many babus..& no kaumatuas to steady them. **1936** LAMBERT *Pioneering Reminisc. Old Wairoa* 58 Nightly the *kaumatuas*, or learned men of the tribe, make the flesh of little children creep with tales of dread *taniwhas*. **1946** ZIMMERMAN *Where People Sing* 165 Kingi Tahiwi, the *kaumatua*, the old leader, was one of the wisest and most adroit handlers of young people that I have ever seen. **1960** HILLIARD *Maori Girl* 36 The kaumatuas sit on apple-boxes, in their dungarees, braces over their shirts, boots covered with dust. **1989** QEII *Arts Council Arts Times No.15* (Autumn) Pat Macaskill [a pakeha interested in the arts] is a kaumatua with a special philosophy. **1990** *Evening Post* (Wellington) 29 Sept. 1 A kaumatua with the group..placed a pouwhenua (marker denoting possession) on the pa site.

kaupai, var. KAPAI.

kaupapa. [Ma. /ˈkaupapa/: Williams 107 *Kaupapa... 12..Plan, scheme, proposal.*] Used in English contexts in senses of 'private agenda', '(personal) philosophy'. As *attrib.*, based on Maori principles. Often in the special Comb. (and occas. absolutely as a familiar shortening

KAUPI

of) **kaupapa Maori school**, **kura kaupapa Maori**, a primary school with teaching methods based on Maori language and culture;

1989 *Educ. Amendment Act* s14 The notice establishing a Kura Kaupapa Maori shall specify the aims, purposes, and objectives that (together with the use of te reo Maori as the principal language of instruction) constitute its different character. **1990** *Dominion* (Wellington) 25 July 5 To raise Maori educational achievement and to promote the survival of the Maori language a further five kura kaupapa Maori schools will be funded. **1991** *Dominion Sunday Times* (Wellington) 10 Nov. 13 Two new kura kaupapa Maori (Maori language schools) are being established and more could be set up next year. **1991** *Dominion* (Wellington) 30 Mar. 12 The value we bring to our music is that it is kaupapa music, it has a cause, it is meaningful, and we don't just do it to entertain, though of course it can be entertaining. **1993** *Contact* (Wellington) 11 Feb. 8 We're talking about community pride. The kaupapa is providing a community centre. It's a stand tall concept. **1994** *Evening Post* (Wellington) 21 May 12 For someone with Riwia Brown's kaupapa it was a challenge to work with a novel written by Alan Duff. **1996** *Dominion* (Wellington) 8 Mar. 8 New Zealand's 36 kura kaupapa Maori schools teach children using only the Maori language. Their underlying philosophy (kaupapa) is based on Maori values.

kaupi, var. KAPAI.

kaurehe. Also erron. **kaureke**. [Ma. /'kaurehe/: Williams 108 *Kaurehe*..2. n. Monster.] A land creature in Maori legend. Cf. WAITOREKE.

1848 in Mantell *Petrifactions* (1851) 105 About ten miles inland of Arowhenua Bush there is a lake where an indigenous terrestrial quadruped called Kaurehe is said to exist... Maopo, headman at Te Taumutu, states that the Kaurehe lays eggs as large as those of a duck! **1870** TAYLOR *Te Ika a Maui* 604 It is probable..that there is another [quadruped], which is known to the natives by the name of *kaurehe*, but it is of a very retired character, and extremely rare. **c1920** BEATTIE *Trad. Lifeways Southern Maori* (1994) 354 [From a Temuka informant] The kaurehe is a big lizard or reptile sometimes on the land and sometimes in the water. Some were said to be of great size. He had not seen any of them although he had heard of them. **1956** DUFF *Moahunter Period Maori Culture* 289 The Maoris informed [Mantell] that about ten miles inland there was 'a quadruped which they called Kaureke [*sic*], and that it was formerly abundant, and often kept by their ancestors in a domestic state as a pet animal!' **1960** *Rec. Canterbury Mus.* 7 180 The Maori certainly acknowledged a large fauna of completely mythical beasts, monsters and man-like creatures with supernatural powers, of which the *kaurehe*, some sort of man-eating dragon, was one; but the same word was used by Mantell's informants for a very different sort of creature, and had this 'otter' been a purely imaginary beast it would surely have had more remarkable characters than were attributed to it. **1986** [see WAITOREKE].

kauri /'kæuri/. Also with much variety of early form as **cawdi(e)**, **coudie**, **courie**, **cowdee**, **cowdi(e)**, **cowdy**, **cowree**, **cowri(e)**, **cowry**, **kaudi**, **kaurie**, **kawdie**, **koude**, **koudi**, **kouri**, **kowree**, **kowri**, etc. [Ma. /'kauri/: Williams 108 *Kauri*, n. *1*.]

1. a. *Agathis* (formerly *Dammara*) *australis* (fam. Araucariaceae), a massive coniferous tree of the northern NI rain forests, and its valuable straight-grained timber. Often *attrib*. See also *king pine*, *New Zealand pine*, and occas. *mountain pine* (PINE 2 (6), (9), (8) a).

1817 NICHOLAS *Voyage NZ* I. 233 Mountain pine, called by natives cowrie. *Ibid*. 305 The pine, called by the natives *cowree* abounds with resin. **1820** McCRAE *Journal* (1928) 21 [We] came to a very fine forest of Koude fit for our purpose..conveying it when felled to the water. **1823** CRUISE *Journal* (1957) 20 The one [tree fit for masts] is called by the natives Kaikaterre, the other *Cowry* or *Cowdy*,... Some of the Cowry trees..rose one hundred feet without a single branch. **1834** MARKHAM *NZ* (1963) 33 The Coudie or Courie, as it is called, the New Zealand Pine, growing 80 or 90 feet without a branch. **1834** WILLIAMS *Early Jrnls.* 28 Jan. (1961) 359 Went with the Sawyers up to Waikino; felled one *Kauri* and one *Tanakaha*. **1853** HOOKER *II Flora Novae-Zelandiae I Flowering Plants* 231 The Kawdi, Cowri, Kaudi, Kowri, or Cowdi Pine of New Zealand, as it is indifferently spelt or mis-spelt and pronounced, is too well-known a tree to require a detailed description for its identification. **1881** CAMPBELL *Poenamo* 73 Waiheki had many a stately kouri growing on it. **1889** KIRK *Forest Flora* 144 The Native name 'kauri' is the only common name in general use. When the timber was first introduced into Britain it was termed 'cowrie-' or 'kowdie-pine'; but the name speedily fell into disuse. **1893** *TrNZI* XXV. 439 The fires..originate among..the old kauri-workings. **1913** *NZ Observer* 12 July 3 Half the 'party' walls in the flimsy buildings that do duty as shops or dwellings are no more fire resistant than painted kauri. **1959** SHADBOLT *New Zealanders* (1986) 101 I grew to awareness rejecting as alien our scrubby backblocks farm, the thick bush of tall kauri, rimu and kahikatea. **1989** PARKINSON *Travelling Naturalist* 105 The largest tree recorded in New Zealand was a giant Kauri known as 'Father of the Forest', which stood near the head of hill creek, near Mercury Bay.

b. As **kauri pine**; also *attrib*.

1838 POLACK *NZ* II. 388 Few of the Kauri pine spars were procured by these vessels. **1847** ANGAS *Savage Life* II. 166 Up a small ravine in the dense forest, we came to a saw-pit, close to which were growing some magnificent *cowdie* pines. **1851** *Lyttelton Times* 15 Feb. 1 On sale..a quantity of well-seasoned Kauri Pine Timber and Shingles, just imported. **1867** HOCHSTETTER *NZ* 140 The Kauri-pine is justly styled the Queen of the New Zealand forest. **1873** TINNE *Wonderland of Antipodes* 54 There is not a single kauri pine now standing on the gum-fields. **1889** [see 1 a above]. **1946** SOLJAK *NZ* 11 The towering kauri pine, which is found as far north as the Fiji Islands, grows only in the warmer parts of New Zealand.

2. In early use occas. applied loosely to any large timber-tree, thought (perh. often wishfully) to resemble kauri, esp. KAHIKATEA (*Dacrycarpus dacrydioides*).

1834 McDONNELL *Observations on New Zealand* 10 Mar. in Howard *Rakiura* (1940) 366 Seals are numerous in the season, and the [Stewart] Island abounds in flax and splendid resorts of 'Cawdie'. [**1940** *Note*] In common with other early commentators on the South, McDonnell uses 'kawdie' (kauri) loosely for any large forest tree, it seems. **1839** WALTON *Twelve Months' Residence* 15 Another species [apart from the Koudi pine], called the cowdie by the natives, the *dammara excelsa* of botanists, is no less remarkable for its strength and useful properties.

3. In occas. early use, a shortened form of KAURI-GUM.

[**1820** LEE & KENDALL *NZ Gram. & Vocab.* 161 Kaudi, *s*. A species of fir-tree; resin.] **1845** *Clarke to Mair* 20 Dec. in Reed *Gumdiggers* (1972) 105 I arrived here [at Kaitaia] on the *Fly*. I now send her back with about ¾ tons of Kowrie and four bales wool... I think the Kowrie sent is very good and clean... The natives are going now to dig for me on some land you formerly purchased.

KAURI

4. Comb. **kauri bush**, **forest**, **-spar**, **timber**, **trade**, **-tree**.

1882 HAY *Brighter Britain* II. 9 The Whangapoua **kauri bush** extends over some 30,000 acres. **1897** *TrNZI* XXIX. 493 The tufts of the toe-kiwi..which are a feature of the kauri bush, are set in a blaze. **1905** SATCHELL *Toll of Bush* 91 There is one note from a man called Wadham, who has a kauri bush for sale. **1834** MARKHAM *NZ* (1963) 41 The **Coudie Forests** is [*sic*] on the tops of the Hills all the way up and down the River. **1843** DIEFFENBACH *Travels in NZ* I. 228 [I have] many times seen kauri-forest burning, not fired for the purpose of clearing the land, but in order to get a dozen or two of logs. **1883** HECTOR *Handbook NZ* 122 The kauri forests are largely composed of other trees as well as their characteristic tree. **1907** LAING & BLACKWELL *Plants NZ* 62 A kauri forest is a wonderful sight, with the clean, erect stems rising like grey columns to a height of from 80 to 100 feet—sometimes to 60 or 70 feet without throwing out a branch. **1951** HUNT *Confessions* 40 The low rolling clay hills had..been the site of a vast kauri forest. **1978** MOORE & IRWIN *Oxford Book NZ Plants* 90 *Mairehau*. A small shrubby tree typical of dry ridges in kauri forest and not extending further south. **1986** HALKETT & SALE *World of the Kauri* 29 The kauri forest is really a multitude of 'mini-forests' or stands of trees. **1820** MARSDEN *Lett. & Jrnls.* May (1932) 87 He was anxious if possible to get **kowree spars**, as that wood was deemed of a much superior quality to the kikatea. **1841** BIDWILL *Rambles in NZ* (1952) 28 It will be seen, from what I have said, that people have been greatly deceived in England with regard to the supply of cowry spars, &c., to be derived from New Zealand. **1986** HALKETT & SALE *World of the Kauri* 46 The trade in kauri spars between New Zealand and Australia grew rapidly. **1842** *Hobson Despatch* in *GBPP 1842 (No.569)* 12 Mar. 193 A notice respecting **Kauri timber**..was converted into the means of exciting the most alarming apprehensions. **1842** HEAPHY *NZ* 41 The **Kauri trade** has been for a long time a source of great profit. **1986** HALKETT & SALE *World of the Kauri* 54 One use of kauri timber..was that of street paving. **1835** YATE *NZ* (1970) 36 It will scar[c]ely be believed by an English timber-merchant, that I have measured a **Kauri-tree** whose circumference was forty feet. **1838** POLACK *NZ* I. 109 The almost impervious forest of Pámáki..was densely studded with splendid kouri-trees. **1973** ADAMS *Kauri* 12 The existence of the kauri tree..was first noticed by early explorers.

5. Special Comb. **kauri-bug**, *black beetle* (BEETLE 1); **kauri-burr**, an ingrown knot in a piece of kauri timber having a distinctive pattern; **kauri bushman**, a feller, logger, etc. with experience of kauri bush; **kauri-butanol-value**, see quot.; **kauri grub**, PUPURANGI, the KAURI SNAIL; **kauri land**, usu. land of poor fertility on which kauri forest grows, or has grown (cf. GUMLAND); **kauri-like** *a.*, resembling the kauri; **kauri-line**, the line of latitude (approx. 38° S) below which the kauri does not produce viable seed; **kauri ricker**, RICKER 2; **kauri silk**, see quot.; **kauri-swamp moss**, a moss found in kauri country and often cultivated in gardens.

1882 HAY *Brighter Britain* I. 151 That malignant thing we call a **Kauri-bug**... [**1882** *Note*] Species of *Blatta* or cockroach,.. called Polyzosteria novaezelandiae. **1888** BARLOW *Kaipara* 182 The Kauri bug (called by the Maoris the Kekereru), with its power of emitting a terrible..smell when alarmed, has been..fully dealt with by writers. **1960** *NZ Junior Encycl.* I. 351 (Miller) It has been said that the term [Maori bug] is a corruption of the original and inoffensive European name of 'kauri bug'. **1890** *PWD Gen. Catalogue* (NZ & South Seas Exhib.) 16 **Kauri burr**, veneered. *Ibid*. 22 Centre-piece, kauri burr. **1958**

MASON *Tararua* Sept. 23 It is interesting to note that, however freely we may talk about the bush, most of us do not speak about *a bush*, *bushes*, or *the bushes* in the way we do about *a forest*, *forests*, or *the forests*, although the **kauri bushmen** do so. **1991** MCKAY *Working the Kauri* 1 The kauri bushmen's labours were important for the development of northern New Zealand in the last century. **1961** *Merriam-Webster Third Internat. Dict.* 1234 **kauri-butanol value** *n* : a measure of the solvent power of a petroleum thinner for paints and varnishes that is determined as the number of milliliters of the thinner just causing turbidity in a standard solution of a hard kauri in normal butyl alcohol **1930** REISCHEK *Yesterdays in Maoriland* (1933) 63 On August 12 I went to the swamp to look for larks..and also found the **kauri grub** (*Helix busby[i]*), only to be seen in the kauri area. *Ibid.* 70 I remained in this forest till the 20th, finding many kauri grubs. **1841** BIDWILL *Rambles in NZ* (1952) 28 In most of what is here called '**Cowrie land**' the trees are often a quarter of a mile asunder, and rarely closer than a hundred yards. **1843** DIEFFENBACH *Travels in NZ* I. 228 It is utterly impossible ever to make good the damage thus done [by clearing forests]..as the kauri-land is so exhausted that scarcely anything will grow on it but fern and manuka. **1990** *Listener* 8 Oct. 106 Descriptions of browsing dinosaurs pushing over **kauri-like** trees or the atmosphere of a moa barbecue at Shag Point are vibrant. **1959** MCLINTOCK *Descr. Atlas* 24 In the forests of the far north, to the north of the '**kauri line**', kauri..occurred frequently, or was locally dominant. **1963** AUDLEY *No Boots for Mr. Moehau* 89 This farm hasn't no use for a coot that doesn't know a swingletree from a **kauri rika**. **1973** ADAMS *Kauri* 16 Kauri rickers made up the first cargoes. **1972** MOSHEIM in Reed *Gumdiggers* 25 '**Kauri Silk**', generally in the form of plaited strands representing the long tresses of blonde hair often seen on young girls of the period, appeared during this time... When a plait was made, often up to five feet long in finished form, it was tied with a ribbon and bow, top and bottom, and coiled in a suitable box, and offered for sale, or entered in any suitable exhibition competitions... To produce a nice specimen it is essential to have a good piece of gum. It would require to weigh about two pounds, so that it could be firmly gripped, and should be pale and clear, and free from ruptures and defects. This seems to be difficult to acquire in these days. The lump must be scraped and cleaned and dried... With an old metal frypan or an old metal plate on the hot range, moved about to get just the right temperature, the lump of gum was pressed on to the plate until the surface melted, and was then slowly drawn out to arm's length or further, and as this was done, the melted surface miraculously came away in these beautiful drawn fibres, which were placed on the nearby table. The operation was completed [*sic*: ? repeated] until the required three bundles of strands were produced. These were plaited with a standard three-plait. The conditions of the old-time warm and humid kitchen were very necessary for the success of this process, as the gum fibres when cold are very fragile. **1961** MARTIN *Flora NZ* 79 The **Kauri-swamp Moss** (*Eucamtodon inflatus*) when well grown is one of our most handsome mosses. Though found in the South Island, it is much more common in the northern part of Auckland province, especially on..kauri-country.

6. *fig.* In the phr. **in the kauri**, in the backblocks, in the remote country districts, with orig. reference to the North Auckland peninsula.

1974 BELL *Ballads of Racegoer* 9 Now he lived in the kauri, and a place called Hare-Kare And he owned a big red Maori horse, used to call him Harry.

kauri-grass. *Astelia trinervia* (fam. Asphodelaceae), a robust plant with a tussock habit common in the undergrowth of kauri forests. See also *bush-flax* (FLAX 8).

1872 *TrNZI* IV. 242 *Astelia trinervia* kauri-grass..forms a large portion of the forest undergrowth from the extreme north to the upper Waikato. *Ibid.* 246 The 'Kauri-grass' of the settlers, ascends from the sea level to 2,000 ft. **1910** COCKAYNE *NZ Plants & Their Story* 43 The kauri trees themselves are some distance apart, and the spaces between are filled up with a close growth of huge tussocks of the kauri-grass (*Astelia trinervia*)—which, of course, is not a grass at all, but belongs to the lily family. **1961** MARTIN *Flora NZ* 245 Lilies are represented by two perching *Astelias*..these being the tall Kauri-grass (*A. trinervia*) of kauri forests and the common Bush-flax (*A. nervosa*). **1970** JOHNSON *Life's Vagaries* 81 A variety of ferns including the lovely climbing *Lygodium* mingled with the graceful kauri grass which is really a species of *Astelia*. **1982** SALE *Four Seasons* 33 We find [toropapa] in a kauri grove..beneath the tufted neinei, or spiderwood, amid the smooth kauri grass.

kauri-gum.

1. GUM. See also KAURI RESIN. Often *attrib.*

1834 MARKHAM *NZ* (1963) 63 One of the Boys set fire to the dry Fern..and we saw lumps of Clear Coudy Gum which is always to be found about the roots of the Coudy. **1837** *Sydney Colonist* 8 Feb. in McKenzie *Gael Fares Forth* (1935) 182 Sailed from Bay of Islands, Feb. 8 1837..with 45 bags of cowdie gum. **1847** ANGAS *Savage Life* II. 166 The *cowdie* gum is a clear resin, having a very strong aromatic flavour. It is chewed by the northern natives. **1857** ASKEW *Voyage Austral. & NZ* 362 The cargo consisted of..wool, flax, sperm-oil, and kaurie gum. **1869** THATCHER *Local Songs* 11 Where Maories are swarming, in vessels they come, And for powder and shot they exchange kauri gum. **1872** WARD *Life Among Maories* 48 A resin exudes from [the Kauri] and is exported from Auckland under the name of Kauri Gum. **1882** HAY *Brighter Britain* II. 14 Kauri-gum—or Kapia, as the Maoris call it..is another peculiar product of this northern extremity of New Zealand. **1889** KIRK *Forest Flora* 155 Sometimes a storekeeper will lease a block of kauri-gum land. **1894** *NZ Official Year-book* 338 Although a true resin, this is usually miscalled kauri-gum. **1900** *Auckland Weekly News Xmas Number* 27 Stanton had to boil his billy of tea with a few lumps of kauri gum. **1909** THOMPSON *Ballads About Business* 94 Among some foreign scum I am now upon a gumfield pokin' round for kauri gum! **1922** COWAN *NZ Wars* (1955 I. 55 In the larger of the semi-subterranean huts are fires burning, fed with *manuka* branches and heaps of *Kapia*, or kauri-gum. **1949** SARGESON *I Saw in My Dream* (1974) 273 Kauri gum: gum deposits from the enormous kauri of Northland, formerly collected by gumdiggers and exported for use in the paint and varnish industry. **1986** HALKETT & SALE *World of the Kauri* 60 Kauri gum was used in fires by settlers and by soldiers to heat their rations during early campaigns.

2. Comb. **kauri-gum digger, kauri-gum-digging, kauri gumland**, see GUM-DIGGER, GUM-DIGGING, GUMLAND.

kauri pine: see KAURI 1 b.

kauri resin. GUM. See also KAURI-GUM 1.

1839 TAYLOR *Journal* 5 Nov. (ATLTS) II. 162 Poor sterile pipe clay land..with great abundance of the cowry resin evidently proving these plains [Wangaroa] were once cowry forests. **1847** ANGAS *Savage Life* I. 316 These incisions [for Maori women]..are cut with sharp shells, and dyed..with a mixture of carbonized Kauri resin. **1869** *TrNZI* I. (rev. edn.) 267 The black pigment for [tattooing was] obtained from the soot of..Kapia, or Kauri resin, dug out of the earth. **1889** KIRK *Forest Flora* 154 The price of kauri-resin varies to a great extent: the digger sometimes receives as low as £20 per ton. **1924** *NZJST* VI. 7 The exports of gold, scheelite, and kauri-resin are not likely to increase beyond their pre-war volume. **1934** *Ibid.* XV. 409 The gum-land soils of North Auckland are infertile..usually containing kauri-resin, or, as it is usually called, kauri-gum.

kauri snail. PUPURANGI. See also *bush snail* (BUSH C 4), *kauri grub* (KAURI 5).

1937 POWELL *Shellfish NZ* 41 The best known member of this group is the *Pupurangi*, or kauri snail known scientifically as *Paryphanta busbyi*. **1946** *Rec. Auck. Inst.* III. 101 The well-known North Auckland Kauri snail still exists in scattered forest reserves from the Kaipara district to the vicinity of Kaitaia. **1950** *NZJAg.* Sept. LXXXI. 285 The shell exhibits ranged from the humble pupurangi or kauri snail (which numbers nearly 50 varieties in New Zealand alone) and lays white-shelled eggs in a leafy nest on the floor of the forest.. to the proud argonaut. **1966** *Encyclopedia NZ* III. 267 Snail, Kauri or Pupurangi (*Paryphanta busbyi*). This is a North Auckland representative of a group of large carnivorous snails found only in New Zealand... The animal feeds on earthworms and slugs. **1975** *NZ Nature Heritage* LXVII. 1863 The large native land snails belong to two families, the Paryphantidae (of which the northern Kauri Snail, Pupu-rangi, is an example) and the Bulimulidae (the Flax snails). **1989** *NZ Geographic* II. 110 The kauri snail..lives among decaying vegetation in the kauri forests, though not specifically in kauri litter. **1990** [see PUPURANGI].

kauru. [Ma. /'ka:uru/: Williams 108 *Kāuru* = *kōuru*, n... 2. Edible stem of *tī-para* (Cordyline).] The interior of the stem or root of a cabbage-tree, cooked as a Maori delicacy.

1844 Jan. in Shortland *S. Dist. NZ* (1851) 234 Te Rehe brought us a basket of 'kauru', or baked root of the 'ti' for which Waiateruati is celebrated. **1851** SHORTLAND *S. Dist. NZ* 308 Kauru, the root of the Ti or Whanake after it has been baked in the native oven. **1897** *TrNZI* XXIX. 175 Small bundle of the vascular part of the cabbage tree stem or root (*kauru*). **1939** BEATTIE *First White Boy Born Otago* 15 I thought the kauru prepared from the cabbage tree was nice, but I did not like fernroot. **1947** STEVENSON *Maori & Pakeha* 80 Other writers have stated that this food was known as kauru, and that it was allowed to remain in the ovens for at least 12 hours. **1988** MIKAERE *Te Maiharoa* 29 The carrot-shaped roots and the young stems of the cabbage tree were the source of the delicacy known as kauru... The kauru was gathered just before the trees flowered, when the plants were at their sweetest. Roots and stems were steamed in large ovens to crystallise their sugar content. The cooked kauru was then pulled apart, dipped in water and chewed.

kauta. Also early **kouta**, **couter**. [Ma. /'ka:uta/: Williams 108 *Kāuta*, n. Cooking shed.] A building housing a hangi; COOKHOUSE.

1834 MARKHAM *NZ* (1963) 57 We found we could cook much better in the House than in cook house (Couter). **1840** POLACK *Manners & Customs* I. 214 *Koutas*, or cooking-houses, are merely small sheds to protect the *artistes* from the inclemency of the weather. **1843** DIEFFENBACH *Travels in NZ* II. 43 The native oven..is situated either in the open air or in a house (te-kauta) constructed of logs at a small distance from each other. **1882** POTTS *Out in Open* 20 In the forest clearing..is a taikawa, on which is thrown the unused food from the kauta of our little camp. **1982** BURTON *Two Hundred Yrs. NZ Food* 3 On a permanent marae, hangis were dug out of the floor of a cookhouse (*kauta*),

kauwau, var. KAWAU.

kauwhai, var. KAHAWAI.

kavakava, var. KAWAKAWA n.¹

kawa. [Ma. /ˈkawa/: Williams 109 *Kawa* (i)... 6. A class of *karakia*, or ceremonies in connection with a new house or canoe, the birth of a child, a battle, etc.] The protocol or etiquette accepted on a marae. (Often used to refer to the order of speakers or speaking.)
    1983 OLIVER *Baxter* 155 It was a meeting of many separate mournings, held together by respect and affection for the..figure in the open coffin, and by the capacity of Maori kawa to unify and dignify even such disparate elements. **1985** *NZ Times* 12 May 5 In A Block [Paremoremo Prison] [mainly Maori] residents analysed, discussed, settled differences, produced their own kawa and democratically decided on standards. **1987** *NZJH* Apr. 176 Judge Durie transformed the Tribunal..henceforth it met on the marae of the claimants, and observed their kawa in its hearings.

kawai, var. KAHAWAI.

kawaka. Also **kawhaka.** [Ma. /ˈkawaka/: Williams 110 *Kawaka* (i), n. *Libocedrus plumosa*.] *Libocedrus plumosa* (fam. Cupressaceae), a tall tree of mainly lowland forests, yielding a dark red, even-grained timber. See also ARBOR VITAE, CEDAR 2 (2), CYPRESS, KAIKAWAKA.
    1832 BENNETT in *London Med. Gaz.* 7 Jan. 506 A tree of Natural Family *Coniferae*, collected without.. flower or fruit; it is named Káwaka by the natives of New Zealand, attaining the height of from 60 to 70 feet..The natives informed me that it derived the name Káwaka from the branches growing out regularly on each side. **1835** YATE *NZ* (1970) 45 Kawaka..is a tree growing about thirty feet high. **1843** DIEFFENBACH *Travels in NZ* I. 323 I have not seen the fructification of the kawaka. **1869** *TrNZI* I. (rev. edn.) 236 The graceful fern-plumaged Kawaka. **1872** *TrNZI* IV. 249 The kawaka..or arbor vitae, recognised at a distance by its bark hanging in broad ribbon-like flakes..showing how apposite was its old trivial name 'plumosum'. **1889** KNOX *Boy Travellers* 201 Then there is the Kawaka, which has a remarkable kind of a durable wood. **1890** [see CEDAR 1]. **1902** *Settler's Handbook NZ* 19 The timber on the western side consists of red- and white-pine, matai (or black-pine), totara, kawhaka (or cedar). **1935** *Canterbury Mountaineer* 125 The building timber is all totara and kawhaka, cut out of the bush close by. **1966** *Encycl. NZ* II. 208 Kawaka occurs in lowland forest from Northland to the centre of the North Island and again in the north-west tip of the South Island. **1986** SALMON *Native Trees NZ* 91 [Caption] Kawaka foliage showing compressed adult leaves arranged in four rows around the branchlets.

kawakawa, n.¹ Also **kaua kaua, kavakava.** [Ma. /ˈkawakawa/: Williams 109 *Kawa* (i) *1.* Unpleasant to the taste, bitter. *Ibid.* 110 *kawakawa..1*..a shrub.: the form *kawakawa* derives from PPN **kawa* 'kava, *Piper methysticum*', the Pacific plant (and drink) (Walsh & Biggs 30).]

1. *Macropiper excelsum* (fam. Piperaceae), a native shrub or small tree with aromatic leaves. See also *bush painkiller* (PAINKILLER 2), PEPPER 1, PEPPER-TREE 1, PEPPERWOOD 2.
    [**1820** LEE AND KENDALL *NZ Grammar and Vocabulary* 161 Kaua kaua; A certain tree; and the fruit of the same tree.] **1838** POLACK *NZ* I. 295 To the southward a species of *long pepper* is found, of little value; the *kauá kauá*, or *kává* (bitter), of the Friendly Islands, is also abundant. **1842** HEAPHY *Residence in NZ* 46 A cane, the *Kawa-kawa*, or pepper-tree, similar to the Otaheitan *Kara*, is also occasionally used in place of tea: the taste is pleasant and very aromatic. **1855** DRURY *Sailing Directions* 67 Trees [met with in the Pelorus] Kawa-Kawa. **1870** *TrNZI* II. 123 Piper excelsum Kawakawa. **1882** HAY *Brighter Britain* II. 191 The Kawa-kawa (*Piper excelsum*) is a large shrub of the pepper tribe, allied to kava and cubebs. **1898** MORRIS *Austral-English* 245 Kawa-kawa, n. Maori name for an ornamental shrub of New Zealand, *Macropiper excelsum*... The missionaries used to make small beer out of the *Kawa-kawa*. **1907** LAING & BLACKWELL *Plants of NZ* 128 *Macropiper excelsum* (*The Lofty Pepper*)..Maori name *Kawakawa*. **1938** FINLAYSON *Brown Man's Burden* (1973) 39 The wreaths of bitter kawakawa around their heads were not more bitter than their tears of grief. **1946** *JPS* LV. 149 *kawakawa*, small tree..related to the tree whose roots provide the kava drink: wood has no rings, but radiating rays; stem knotted like bamboo. **1982** BURTON *Two Hundred Years of NZ Food* 4 Smoking branches of kawakawa (pepper tree) kept insects at bay. **1991** *NZ Geographic* Apr.–June 116 More recently, he launched tea made from kawakawa (native pepper) and horopito—both labelled as 'organically grown in nuclear-free New Zealand'.

2. Special Comb. **kawakawa tea**, a potable infusion of kawakawa leaves. See also quots. 1842, 1898, 1991 above.
    1866 HUNT *Chatham Is.* 31 Then I made some *kaua-kaua* tea, and that, with molasses and biscuit, refreshed us exceedingly.

kawakawa, n.² [Ma. /ˈkawakawa/: Williams 110 *kawakawa..4*.] A dark variety of greenstone.
    1915 ROBLEY *Pounamu* 16 *Kawakawa* is stone of a pure rich green colour, and is not spotted or veined with dark or light markings. *Auhunga* is slightly paler than *kawakawa*. **1929** FIRTH *Primitive Econ. NZ Maori* 389 Most prized was the *kahurangi* stone..; the *inanga* variety perhaps comes next,.. followed by the *kawakawa*, dark olive-green, dull and opaque. **1962** JOSEPH *Pound of Saffron* 113 'See this one'—he held the heavy red-mottled adze in his palm—'that's the red kind, totoweka, woodhen's blood. The deep green, that's kawakawa.'

kawana. [Ma. /ˈkaːwana/: Williams Appendix *Kāwana* Governor: a Maori adaptation of *governor*.] The Governor(-General) of New Zealand.
    1845 SELWYN in Drummond *Married & Gone to NZ* (1960) 121 [Willie] was to play with the children [at Government House] and I talk to Mata [*i.e.* Mother] Kawana, which I always like to do she is so ladylike and good and cultivated. **1871** MEADE *Ride through Disturbed Dist.* in Taylor *Early Travellers* (1959) 432 We received visits from a number of the heads of families, bringing 'salutations to the people from "Te Kawana" (the Governor)'. **1873** *Weekly News* (Auckland) 29 Mar. 7 The women all wore green wreaths of willow, expressive of their regret at the departure of the 'Kawana'. **1912** *Free Lance* (Wellington) 10 Aug. 4 The bewildered old Maori stood there watching the retreating cloud of dust that contained the 'Kawana'. **1928** *Free Lance* (Wellington) 25 Apr. 42 The feeling of the Maoris was ably expressed by one native who, clad in a blanket, rose to address the 'Kawana' after other speakers had spoken.

kawanatanga. [Ma. /ˈkaːwanaˌtaŋa/ *Kawana* + *-tanga* one of a number of suffixes forming abstract nouns from common nouns.] A Governor's or government authority or sovereignty. Also *attrib.*, supportive of government authority.
[*Note*] The word occurs in the text of the Treaty of Waitangi and is translated 'governorship of the Queen', 'Her Majesty's authority'.
    1864 SEWELL *NZ Native Rebellion* 9 As to the former, it is true they surrendered to the Queen the 'Kawanatanga'—the governorship—or sovereignty. **1922** COWAN *NZ Wars* (1955) II. v My thanks go forth to my old warrior friends, both Kawanatanga and Hauhau. **1986** BELICH *NZ Wars* (Maori Gloss.) 337 *kawanatanga* Governor's sphere, Governor's authority **1989** *Principles for Crown Action on the Treaty of Waitangi* 7 The Principle of Government. The Kawanatanga Principle. The Government has the right to govern and to make laws. *Ibid.* 11 '[Rangatiratanga] means the wise administration of all the assets possessed by a group for that group's benefit:.. *Kawanatanga* is subject to a promise to protect *Rangatiratanga*. *Rangatiratanga* is subject to an acknowledgment of *Kawanatanga*... It is the *right* of all citizens, Maori, Pakeha, and other New Zealanders, that there be effective Government or *Kawanatanga* in such matters.

kawau. Also **kauau, kauwau.** [Ma. *ka'wau*: Williams 110 *Kawau* (i), *kōau*, n... shag.] Any of several shags, esp. *black shag* (SHAG 2 (2) *Phalacrocorax carbo novaehollandiae*).
    [**c1826–27** BOULTBEE *Journal* (1986) 109 Shag—kàh.] **1841** COLENSO in Buller *Birds NZ* (1888) 152 Two species [of Cormorant] inhabit these shores; one, with entirely black plumage, which the natives call Kawau. **1843** DIEFFENBACH *Travels in NZ* I. 77 The cormorants themselves have something solemn in their aspect, and are called by the New Zealanders kauwau, or the preachers. **1844** WILLIAMS *NZ Jrnl.* (1956) 115 The Kauau or common diver. **1855** DRURY *Sailing Directions* 66 Cormorants—several kinds..all kinds are called Kauwau by the natives. **1871** HUTTON *Catalogue Birds NZ* 50 Graculus carbo... Cormorant. Black Shag. Kawau. *Ibid.* 51 Graculus varius... Pied Shag. Kawau. **1882** HAY *Brighter Britain* II. 222 The Kawau..is one of the commonest birds... They build in trees, in large 'shaggeries'. **1904** HUTTON & DRUMMOND *Animals NZ* 295 The Black Shag.—Kawau. Phalacrocorax carbo. **1946** *JPS* LV. 152 *Kawau*, a water-bird..cormorant; shag: the various species distinguished by the Maori with a suffix. **1952** RICHARDS *Chatham Is.* 89 *Phalacrocorax..carbo*... Black Shag or Cormorant. Kawau. **1990** *Checklist Birds NZ* 81 *Phalacrocorax carbo novaehollandiae*..Black Shag (Black Cormorant, *Kawau*)... Breeds throughout the main islands of New Zealand and on the Chatham Islands.

kawaupaka. [Ma. /ˈkawauˈpaka/: Williams 110 *Kawau* (i) *kawau paka*..little pied shag.] *little pied* (or *white-throated*) *shag* (SHAG 2 (11) and 2 (18)).
    1873 BULLER *Birds NZ* 330 Phalacrocorax brevirostris. (White-throated Shag)... Native name.—Kawau-paka...The White-throated Shag, which appears

to be confined to New Zealand and the Chatham Islands, frequents the freshwater rivers and lagoons in all parts of the country. **1955** OLIVER *NZ Birds* 202 White-throated Shag. *Kawau-paka Phalacrocorax brevirostris.* **1966** [see SHAG 2 (18)]. **1985** [see SHAG 2 (18)]. **1990** *Checklist Birds NZ* 82 *Phalacrocorax melanoleucos brevirostris..Little Shag (Kawaupaka).*

kawdi, var. KAURI.

kawe. *Hist.* Also **covey, kawa** (erron.). [Ma. /ˈkawe/: Williams 111 *Kawe,.. 6.* Straps by which a bundle is carried on the back.] A *swag-strap* (SWAG *n.*[1] 4 a).
 1862 HODDER *Memories NZ Life* 137 Our knapsacks, or swags, as they are more generally called,.. were fastened to our back with a pair of slings called 'coveys' which are made by the natives of dressed flax. **1924** *Otago Witness* (Dunedin) 17 June 6 The balance pole..was abandoned in favour of the kawa [*sic*], which corresponds to the bushman's swag straps and to the soldier's knapsack. **1930** DOBSON *Reminiscences* 157 We carried all our loads with the Maori *kawe*, two long flat bands of plaited flax, the ends of which, dressed and narrowed down, were connected or joined together with a flat band about ten inches in length.

kawekawea. [Ma. /kawekaweˈaː/: Williams 111 *Kawekaweā = koekoeā.*] The *long-tailed cuckoo* (CUCKOO 2 (2)).
 1867 *Richmond-Atkinson Papers* (1960) II. 228 There is a flagstaff here [*sc.* Waimate Plains], fenced in & surmounted by the figure of a bird, probably a kawekawea as it was a great *niu* or Pai Mariire pole at one time. **1873** BULLER *Birds NZ* 73 Eudynamis taitensis. (Long-tailed Cuckoo)... Koekoea, Kawekawea, and Koheperoa. **1966** FALLA et al. *Birds NZ* 181 Long-tailed Cuckoo *Eudynamis taitensis*... Koekoea, Kawekawea, Kohoperoa.

kawhai, var. KAHAWAI.

kawhaka, var. KAWAKA.

kaw-kaw, var. KAKA.

Kay force, var. K-FORCE.

kea /ˈkiə/, /ˈkæiə/, *n.* Also **kaieo, keha, keo, kia.** [Ma. /ˈkeɑ/: Williams 112 *Kea* (i) *keha, n. Nestor notabilis..*probably so called from its screech; 116 *kia* (iii), *n.* An onomatopoeic name of..the mountain parrot. = *kea.*]
 1. a. *Nestor notabilis* (fam. Psittacidae, subfamily Nestorinae), a large, inquisitive, often destructive, dark-green, mountain parrot. See also *green parrot, mountain parrot, Mount Cook parrot* (PARROT 2 (3), (5), (6)), *sheep-killer* (SHEEP 2).
 1862 HAAST in *Julius Von Haast* (1948) 215 What gave still greater interest..was the presence of large green alpine parrots (*Nestor notabilis*), the Kea of the Natives, which visited constantly the small groves of beech trees near our camp. **1873** BULLER *Birds NZ* 52 (Kea Parrot)... 'Kea' of the Maoris; 'Mountain-Parrot' of the colonists. **1885** *NZJSc.* II. 481 *Nestor notabilis...* Mountain or Green parrot, Sheep-killer, Kea, Kia, Keha, Keo, Kaieo.—By all these names is this troublesome bird known by the highland shepherds and sheep musterers in alpine districts from Lakes Wanaka and Hawea to the river Rangitata. **c1899** DOUGLAS in *Mr Explorer Douglas* (1957) 254 Unlike the Kakas, who have a dozen different cries, the Kea has just one, weird Key-a-Key-a, hence its name. **1911** MORELAND *Through South Westland* 80 The kakas..have smaller beaks than their relative, the sheep-killing kea of the eastern slopes. **1933** *Press* (Christchurch) (Acland Gloss.) 28 Oct. 17 I am told by the greatest living authority on native birds that no recognised naturalist any longer denies that keas kill sheep. **1958** PASCOE *Great Days in NZ Mountaineering* 156 They dug out a platform for the tent..and got stuck into another kea stew. **1966** DURRELL *Two in the Bush* 115 Five keas appeared... Their strutting, pompous walk, their general attitude of being the lords of all they surveyed, combined with this oft-repeated and never varying cry, make them remind me irresistably of a small group of Fascists. **1976** SOPER *NZ Birds* 21 Provided one is on hand to protect one's belongings, Keas by their comical antics, their capacity for play and their utter fearlessness, can provide much entertainment. **1990** *Dominion* (Wellington) 18 Jan. 6 [Heading] Kea 'hoons' plague beachgoers. Hoons who make life miserable at beach resorts are usually the loud, human variety, not a native alpine parrot with a beak like a Swiss army knife.
 b. (Representing) the cry of the kea.
 1883 GREEN *High Alps* 216 Ere I could catch him he recovered..and, flying to a boulder about 200 yards away, gave forth a volley of 'keas' which surpassed anything I had ever heard before. **c1899** [see a above]. **1905** *Evening Post* (Wellington) 2 Nov. 6 The keas uttered their own cry—'Kea, Kea'—to which the turkey-cocks responded, and for the rest of the afternoon the parrots amused themselves by setting the turkeys gobbling.
 Hence **kea** *v. intr.*, to cry 'kea'; **kea'd** *passive* or *ppl. a.*, of a sheep, attacked by a kea.
 1883 GREEN *High Alps* 215 Pitching on a boulder, near my head, he 'kea'd' at me with renewed vigour. **1952** NEWTON *High Country Journey* 97 I never saw a single sheep which had been 'kea'd'. **1955** *BJ Cameron Collection* (TS July) kea'd (adj) Attacked by a kea. **1973** NEWTON *Big Country SI* (1977) 197 Although the birds were far more plentiful back on the latter place the only kea'd sheep I saw were in the vicinity of Red Hills.
 2. Special Comb. **kea beak**, the beak of a kea as a token of proof for payment of a bounty on birds killed; **kea flea**, the flea *Parapsyllus nestoris nestoris* (fam. Siphonaptera), having the kea as a primary host; **kea gun (pistol)**, a modified shotgun used for killing keas (see quots.); **kea hunter**, one employed to hunt keas; **kea louse**, any of various chewing lice (fam. Mallophaga), including *Heteromenopon kea* and *Neopsittaconirmus kea*, having the kea as a primary host; **kea pistol**, see *kea gun* above; **kea smuggler**, one who smuggles kea out of New Zealand as part of an illicit trade in protected bird species.
 1923 *Dominion* (Wellington) 12 Jan. 2 **Kea beaks** are purchased by the Mackenzie County Council but not by the Waitaki County Council. **1967** NATUSCH *Animals NZ* 160 The **kea flea** (*Parapsyllus nestoris*), another 'very nice new flea' (*P. lynnae*, host unknown)..are..new species. **1969** BILLING *Alpha Trip* 122 Nailed tramping boots, plimsolls, binoculars, a 12-gauge shotgun and a .410 **kea gun**—a locally designed hand-gun made from a Spanish .410 shotgun breech and hammer, with a flintlock style pistol grip and a sixteen-inch barrel. It was designed for high-country shepherds who wanted to shoot from the saddle the..keas. **1970** MCLEOD *Glorious Morning* 75 Some of the men carried 'kea guns'—usually a folding 410-bore shotgun with a single barrel which would fit in a haversack. **1995** *Dominion* (Wellington) 30 Nov. 7 He became a gun-collector through buying an old kea gun. **1888** BULLER *Birds NZ* I. 169 So destructive..have they become on some of the sheep-runs that the aid of Parliament has been invoked to abate the nuisance by offering a subsidy to **Kea-hunters**. **1978** *Manawatu Tramping Club Jubilee* 79 The stories we had been told of **kea lice** seemed only too true. **1992** *Dominion* (Wellington) 29 Sept. 3 The two men..were armed with a sawnoff shotgun and what appeared to be a **kea pistol**—a smallbore shotgun with a long barrel. **1990** *Evening Post* (Wellington) 31 Aug. 1 [Heading] **Kea smuggler** sentenced.

keakea, var. KARAKIA *v.*

kea-kea, kee-kee, varr. KIEKIE.

keeney-seeney, keeny-seeny, varr. KINGY-SEENY.

keeps. [Prob. a shortened form of *for keeps* indicating indefinite possession: cf. *finders, keeps; losers, weeps.*] A name (often a cry) for a (phase of a) marble game where marbles won are kept by the winner.
 1951 FRAME *Lagoon* (1961) 116 I played funs and keeps... [The kids] came for miles to play marbles with me. **1953** SUTTON-SMITH *Unorganized Games NZ Primary School Children* (VUWTS) II. 770 It is important to distinguish these 'Action-Terms' of marbles..such as Ringer,... Keeps, Pink. **1984** KEITH & MAIN *NZ Yesterdays* 288 [Caption] Marbles became 'in' or 'out' capriciously but someone always knew the rules of the various games..'liney' and, seen here, 'ringey'—which could be played for 'funs' or 'keeps.'

keg.
 1. [Spec. use of *keg* small barrel or cask: AND 1896.] A barrel of beer esp. as the source of supply for a private drinking party.
 1917 *Chron. NZEF* 16 May 137 He shunned the liquor from the keg, And spurned his dusty mouth. **1943** *NZEF Times* 27 Sept. 10 You can't see the keg... This big joker is standing in front of it. **1959** SHADBOLT *New Zealanders* (1986) 108 Sandy..sometimes took her off to his wild proletarian parties..where kegs flowed and fights flared. **1964** REID *Book NZ* 259 I had a beer from the keg on the cream-truck, And the cop had one, too, you can bet your life. **1974** HILLIARD *Maori Woman* 110 The flagon-parties, the crates of half-gees on the sink, men in singlets queued up at the keg. **1981** HENDERSON *Exiles Asbestos Cottage* 14 Plenty of garrulous half-shot but willing hands..had all the wool stacked..by 1 am, when they turned to even more willingly and cut the keg. **1995** *Dominion* (Wellington) 12 Sept. 1 'We were having church for Ivan followed by a barbecue and a keg or two at my place,' she said.
 Hence **keg** *v. intr.*, esp. as **to keg it up**, to take part in a heavy beer-drinking session; **kegger** *n.*, one who takes part in a keg-party (in quot. 1911 prob. an allusion to illegal drinking, Invercargill being then 'dry'); **kegging** *vbl. n.*, formerly in Invercargill, and in other 'dry' or no-licence districts, the purchasing of a keg of beer in a licensed district and bringing it home to a no-licence district for consumption; later, taking part in a keg-party.
 1995 *Dominion* (Wellington) 12 Sept. 1 Most of the group on the bus..had been '**kegging it up**' since Friday celebrating the birthday of a one-year-old girl. **1911** *Truth* 12 Aug. 1 The prosecution of '**keggers**' in and around Invercargill has led to the adoption of the saying, 'No rest for the beery.' **1967** MILLER *Ink on my Fingers* 174 The police kept a tolerant, if suspicious, eye on the 'keggers'. **1910** *Truth* 14 May 5 '**Kegging**,' i.e., that beastly habit of boozing out of a keg, is peculiarly a New Zealand habit. **1976** HOLCROFT *Old Invercargill* 112 In August [1906, two months after no-

license had been carried] a new social phenomenon made its appearance. Two parties of young men..bought a keg of beer from the depot outside the town boundary 'and straightaway consumed its contents'... This may have been the first recorded instance of 'kegging', a form of public drinking which for a long time seemed to be peculiar to Invercargill.
2. In special Comb. **keg-party** [AND 1950], a drinking party with a beer-keg as the main source of supply of liquor; **keg race**, a drinking contest among university students.
1948 *Our Own Country* 17 The people who had rented his basement flat in Auckland took advantage of his absence to hold noisy **keg parties**. **1955** BJ Cameron *Collection* (TS July) keg party (n) A party built around one or more kegs of beer; a drinking party. **1976** HOLCROFT *Old Invercargill* 113 This [stricter regulation in 1880] did not mean the end of kegging [in Invercargill]. Although the climate was not ideal for alfresco drinking, keg parties were held frequently in gardens and reserves. **1986** *Salient* (Wellington) 11 Aug. 15 Firstly, if more people had been moderate in their drinking and went to the Ball for a formal evening instead of a **Keg Race**, then the alcohol would have lasted past 12pm.

keha, var. KEA.

kehe. Also **kehei**; **ngehe**. [Ma. /'kehe/: Williams 112 *Kehe* (i), n. *1*... granite trout: also *ngehe* 232.] MARBLEFISH. Cf. KEKE.
1855 TAYLOR *Te Ika A Maui* 628 The *Ngehe* is a rock fish, curiously spotted, white and brown. **1875** *TrNZI* VII. 241 Haplodactylus meandratus..Native name—Kehei. **1886** SHERRIN *Handbook Fishes NZ* 36 It [sc. granite trout] is called by the Natives kehei. **1908** HAMILTON *Fishing & Seafoods* 63 Sometimes kehe are caught, seized with the hands, and lifted quickly out of the water. **1926** *TrNZI* LVI. 599 Poles of manuka are also used to make the framework of the trap-net for the *kehe* fish. **1949** BUCK *Coming of Maori* 215 However, a scoop net termed *kupenga koko kehe* was used in rocky channels on the East Coast to catch *kehe*. **1951** KOHERE *Autobiography of a Maori* 127 Here at East Cape, kehe [sc. granite trout] is tender and fat in autumn.

kehua. [Ma. /'ke:hua/: Williams 112 *Kēhua*, n. Ghost, spirit.] A ghost. (Hyde's *kehu* (quot. 1934) prob. derives from an English user's not uncommon non-hearing of Maori devocalized [a] final.)
1869 *TrNZI* I. (rev. edn) 384 This haunting spirit, or phantom, (*Kehua*,) which haunted its former place of residence, when in the body..differed widely from the sensible intellectual spirit (*Wairua*), which had departed to the *reinga* and which was not feared. **1904** TREGEAR *Maori Race* 426 If one met a *kehua* (ghost) you had only to offer it some cooked food and it would instantly disappear, for ghosts, like all supernatural beings, dislike cooked food. **1934** HYDE *Journalese* 169 I met one little nun who quite definitely believed in the 'kehu'—an agile sort of Maori banshee, who is seen perching on the gateposts immediately before a death. **1946** *JPS* LV. 152 *kēhua*, ghost; particularly baneful if it is one of yourself. **1970** [SEE WAIRUA]. **1989** TE AWEKOTUKU *Tahuri* 55 He told spooky kehua stories that made your skin tingle. **1990** *Listener* 1 Oct. 108 I made water regardless, shuddering aside all the bad dreams and the kehuas of the night.

keike, var. KAHIKATEA.

keke. [*Keke* is not recorded by Williams, and may poss. be an error for KEHE, copied from Phillipps (1921 below, repeated in a 1927 publication); it may poss. be a Ma. dial. variant known to Phillipps and adopted by later writers: Strickland in *Nga tini a Tangaroa* (1990) includes both *kehe* and *keke* as names for *Aplodactylus arctidens*, marblefish.] MARBLEFISH. Cf. KEHE.
1921 *NZJST* IV. 115 (Phillipps) Aplodactylus meandratus... *Marble-fish*; *Keke*. **1956** GRAHAM *Treasury NZ Fishes* 248 Granite Trout or Marble Fish (Keke) The common names of this fish are derived from the resemblance of the skin to marble or granite. **1967** [see MARBLEFISH]. **1982** AYLING *Collins Guide* (1984) 240 *Marblefish* (Keke) *Aplodactylus arctidens*.

kekeno. Also early **cakenno**, **kekino**. [Ma. /'kekeno/: Williams 114 *Keno*... *kekeno*... 2... sea-lion; and *A. forsteri*, seal.] A seal, esp. the New Zealand fur seal (SEAL *n*.[1] 2 (1)).
[**1817** NICHOLAS *NZ* II. 329 Phoca, or seal Cakenno **1820** LEE AND KENDALL *NZ Grammar and Vocabulary* Kekéno, *s*. A seal fish.] **1842** GRAY *Fauna* in Dieffenbach *Travels in NZ* (1843) II. 183 The Fur-seal of commerce..was formerly hunted in great numbers, especially on the western coast of the middle island... Kekino is their native name. **1867** HOCHSTETTER *NZ* a162 The sea-bear (*Kekeno*) has probably ceased to select the North Island for its home; or it is only the rugged and uninhabited Southwest Coast of South Island, that still continues to afford it sufficient solitude for cubbing. **1904** HUTTON & DRUMMOND *Animals NZ* 38 *The Fur Seal*.—Kekeno. *Arctocephalus forsteri.*) c**1920** BEATTIE *Trad. Lifeways Southern Maori* (1994) 156 Kekeno is the name of the fur seal. The white sealers called the males 'wigs' and the females 'clapmatches'. **1989** PARKINSON *Travelling Naturalist* 147 That these animals had Maori names is significant as it indicates their regular occurrence on our coastline. Fur seals are known variously as kekeno or pakeke.

kekerengu. Also with freq. adaptations of Ma. (dial.) variants, **kéke réhu**, **kekereru**, **kekeriru**, **kikárá ru**, **kikereru**. [Ma. /'ke:kereŋu:/ /'ke:kereru:/: Williams 113 *kēkerengū* = *kēkereū*, n. *Platyzosteria novae-seelandiae*.] The *black beetle* (BEETLE 1).
[**1820** LEE AND KENDALL *NZ Grammar and Vocab.* 162 Kéke rehu; A beetle.] **1838** POLACK *NZ* I. 320 The most disgusting insects in nature exist among the spear-grass..; it is called the *kikáráru*. Its odour is disgustingly offensive, and it is often found in rush or other dwelling-houses. **1844** Kekerere [see BEETLE 1]. **1848** TAYLOR *Leaf from Nat. Hist.* 5 *Kekeriru*, large black wood-bug. (*Cimex memoralis*). **1855** LUSH *Auckland Journals* (1971) 29 May 157 Raupo cottages always with Kekeriru, a large black wood bug, larger than the English black beetle..which when crushed emits a most horrid stench. **1867** HOCHSTETTER *NZ* 171 This Blatta is doubtless the same insect named by the natives Kikararu, which was erroneously taken for a bug. **1873** BULLER *Birds NZ* 75 The Kekereru or fetid bug, the large bush *Cicada*..all contribute to the support of this bird. **1888** [see *kauri bug* (KAURI 5)]. **1904** TREGEAR *Maori Race* 181 The centipede (*were*), the caterpillar (*whe*), the Maori-bug (*kekerengu*)..were all supposed to have been brought in the canoes. **1916** GASCOYNE *Soldiering in NZ* 115 The Maori's name for these horrible insects [*sc.* Maori bugs] is *kekerengu*. **1924** kikereru [see *black-bug* (BLACK B 2)]. **1955** MILLER *Nature in NZ* 48 So why not the rather pleasing Maori name *kekerengu* (kay-kerenoo)? but if this has to become 'kickerang' as the place Kekerengu, north of Kaikoura is now called, then let us have 'black stink-roach'! **1974** *NZ Nature Heritage* XXIII. 635 Only the largest received a name: *kekerengu*, the large black stink-roach.

kekerewai, var. KEREWAI.

kekeriru, var. KEKERENGU.

keketerehe. *Chatham Islands.* [Not recorded in Williams: Ma. /'keketerehe/.] *Olearia chathamica* (now considered a variety of *O. oporina*) (fam. Asteraceae), a shrub or small tree daisy with showy purple flowers confined to coastal forest margins in the Chatham Islands.
1906 CHEESEMAN *Manual NZ Flora* 281 [*Olearia chathamica*] Chatham Islands: In swampy places on higher parts of the island... *Keketerehe*. **1952** RICHARDS *Chatham Is*. 67 *Olearia chathamica*,.. Chatham Tree-daisy. Keketerehe. **1978** MOORE & IRWIN *Oxford Book NZ Plants* 130 *Olearia chathamica, keketerehe*. A few species of *Olearia* have purple disc florets..in the Chathams..*O. chathamica* on drier ridges.

kekino, var. KEKENO.

kekogop, var. KOKOPU.

Kelly. [f. a proprietary name (see quot. 1921): AND 1909.] A brand of axe favoured by axemen. Cf. PLUMB.
1913 CARR *Country Work* 29 For many years to come the 'whoof' of the bushman, as he sinks the 'Kelly', or the 'Plumb' (two favourite brands of American axes, the latter especially) into..rimu..will be heard. **1921** *NZ Patent Office Jrnl.* [no number given] 22 Sept. W.C. Kelly perfect axe 16188 [filed] 16th December, 1919. Kelly Axe Manufacturing Co [now the True Temper Corporation, from 1949.].. Axes, hatchets, and the like included in this class. **1968** *NZ Contemp. Dict. Suppl.* (Collins) 11 *kelly n*. (*Sl.*) axe; *on the kelly*, engaged in axe work. **1975** NEWTON *Sixty Thousand on the Hoof* 71 This has been a story of the axe and the Condon boys were literally brought up with a 'Kelly' in their hands.

Kelly gang. [f. the name of Ned *Kelly* (1857–80), an Australian bushranger and gang leader.] In various *transf.* uses.
1. *Hist.* The name given to a group of powerful politically manipulative businessmen.
1948 LIPSON *Politics of Equality* 222 There had existed for some years [in the 1920s] in the city of Auckland a small but powerful ring which possessed the controlling interests in various breweries, insurance companies, and industrial ventures... [1948 *Note*] Opponents have called this clique 'the Kelly gang' after the name of Ned Kelly, a notorious Australian gangster. **1955** BJ Cameron *Collection* (TS July) Kelly gang (n) Any powerful and supposedly unscrupulous group of businessmen or others. **1986** GUSTAFSON *Cradle to Grave* 168 The major protagonists at the 1935 election, however, were Labour and the United–Reform coalition, which had merged formally in May 1935 into a National Political Federation, becoming in 1936, after the election, the New Zealand National Party. The 'Kelly Gang' of Eliot and Ernest Davis and Oliver Nicholson in Auckland worked hard to prevent conservative notables from defecting from National to the Democrats, even to the extent of offering jobs and directorships.

2. *Freezing works.* A gang of workmen engaged in miscellaneous work.
1981 *Press* (Christchurch) 17 Nov. 1 Of the 66 meat workers employed [at Petone]..only 17 will stay..six in the freezing chambers, two in the kelly gang, one in the rendering department, and eight watchmen. **1983** *Evening Post* (Wellington) 10 Feb. 26 Savings..had been made by a drop in overtime pay and

putting 22 men on a 'Kelly gang' late last year. They were taken off the killing chain and given other jobs around the [Wellington City] abattoir and they lost all overtime.

3. As **kelly-gangish** *a.*, having the characteristics of robbery with violence associated with the Australian Kelly gang.
1943 Hislop *Pure Gold* 22 The Otago fields were not so Kelly-gangish [as the Victorian], although a few rough necks did get the rope in the finish.

kelp. [Transf. use of *kelp*, North American *Nereocystis* spp. for New Zealand *Durvillaea* spp.]

1. BULL KELP 1 and 2.
c1826–27 Boultbee *Journal* (1986) 113 kelp—limmoo. **1911** [see BULL KELP 1]. **c1920** [see RIMU 1 a].

2. Special Comb. **kelp bag**, see quot. 1844. See also *bull-kelp bag* (BULL KELP 2), POHA.
1844 in Shortland *S. Dist. NZ* 18 Jan. (1851) 224 A kelp bag—the air bladder of a fucus—is easily found of the size required, made by nature. In this the young 'titi' are packed, after being cooked, and the oil which has escaped in the cooking is poured on them. Over the exterior of the bag is then laid the bark of the 'totara' tree. **1921** *Auckland Weekly News* 14 July [Caption] 4. Mutton bird islands off the coast of Stewart Island... 6. Filling a kelp bag with the preserved birds. **1952** [see POWHA]. **1965** Gillham *Naturalist in NZ* 35 They repack the [muttonbird] carcasses in kelp bags, where they may last for years. **1989** Hulme & Morrison *Homeplaces* 61 Rimurapa is probably best known, among Maori, for its use in making poha-rimu, the big kelpbags that helped store muttonbirds between seasons.

kelpfish. Any of various smaller coastal fishes associated with kelp, including greenish wrasses of the fam. Labridae, occas. (esp. in early use) the BUTTERFISH (1, *Odax pullus*), and some species of fam. Chironemidae.

1. Also **southern kelpfish.** BUTTERFISH 1.
1871 *TrNZI* III. 131 *Coridodax pullus.* A large quantity of the Kelp-fish were offered for sale in and about Wellington..The fish..are covered with a slimy mucus, like that of the eel. **1872, 1886** [see BUTTERFISH 1]. **1906** *TrNZI* XXXVIII. 551 *Odax vittatus...* Kelp-fish. Otago heads and inside the harbour occasionally. **1913** [see BUTTERFISH 1]. **c1920** Beattie *Trad. Lifeways Southern Maori* (1994) 501 The kelp fish of Canterbury is the Blue-bone of Nelson and may be the Green-bone of Southland. **1927** Phillipps *Bibliogr. NZ Fishes* (1971) 40 *Odax vittatus...* Kelp-fish; Tarao... *Coridodax pullus...* Butterfish, Southern Kelp-fish; Marari. **1936, 1945, 1957, 1970** [see BUTTERFISH 1]. **1982** Ayling *Collins Guide* (1984) 265 Butterfish (Greenbone, Marari) *Odax pullus...* Small individuals have a markedly different colour pattern from that of the adults and until recently were thought to belong to a separate species named the kelpfish, *Odax vittatus.*

2. Any of several species of wrasse (fam. Labridae) esp. *Notolabrus fucicola*, *banded parrotfish* (PARROTFISH 2 (1)) and *N. celidotus* SPOTTY 1. See also KELPIE *n.*[1] 2 and 3, *old maid* (OLD 3).
1879 *TrNZI* XI. 384 The Wrasse and Parrotfish are mostly caught outside among the kelp, and with the Spotty are indiscriminately named Kelp-fish by the [Otago] fishermen, though the term Butterfish is also given to the smaller sorts. **1922** [see PARROTFISH 2 (1)]. **1967** Natusch *Animals NZ* 224 Family Labridae (wrasses). Large-scaled fishes with rather silly faces, wrasses..are known by various local names: spotties, soldiers, kelp fish, parrot fish, etc. **1981** Wilson *Fisherman's Bible* 140 Kelpie. A name given variously to the Spotty, Banded Parrotfish, Kelpfish, Butterfish and Greenbone. Generally regarded as the other proper name for Butterfish. **1991** Bradstock *Fishing* 18 *Banded parrotfish.* Other names: kelpfish, kelpie.

3. Any of several fishes of the fam. Chironemidae esp. *Chironemus marmoratus* (also called **northern kelpfish**). HIWIHIWI.
1927 Phillipps *Bibliogr. NZ Fishes* (1971) 38 *Chironemus marmoratus...* Kelpfish; Hiwihiwi. **1967** Moreland *Marine Fishes* 26 Kelpfish [*Chironemus marmoratus*]... Other names include the Maori hiwihiwi and ngakoikoi. **1967** [see HIWIHIWI]. **1986** Paul *NZ Fishes* 111 *Kelpfish Chironemus marmoratus* Family Chironemidae (kelpfishes), a small group restricted to Australasia.

kelp-fly. Also **kelpie**. Any of several flies (fam. Helcomyzidae and Coelopidae) commonly found in swarms near the seashore, and whose larvae develop in kelp.
1926 Tillyard *Insects of Austral. and NZ* 371 *Phycodromiidae* (Kelp-flies). Usually fairly large flies, found on kelp on sea-beaches, and particularly abundant in higher latitudes. **1968** Grundy *Who'd Marry a Doctor?* 72 Unfortunately he had forgotten to shut the windows and the floors in some rooms were strewn with kelp flies. (They normally inhabit the seaweed on the beaches, but when lights shine at night they fly noisily at the windows like hordes of moths.) **1974** Hayward *Diary of the Kirk Years* 15 Feb. (1981) 217 The light attracts thousands of tiny moths—kelpies, they're called [here on the Chathams]—which cling like a heavy curtain to the window and the porch wall outside. **1984** Miller *Common Insects* 92 A number of different flies breed in heaps of decaying kelp on the seashore. Among them is the native Small Blue Blowfly (*Calliphora hortona*), but the more interesting are the chocolate-brown kelp flies.

kelp-hen. *Obs.* Prob. the *western weka* (WEKA 2 (6) *Gallirallus australis australis*).
1874 *TrNZI* VI. 152 Kelp-hen, Black wood hen. As soon as the tide begins to recede these dusky Rails come out on the shore to feed amongst the kelp. **1882** Potts *Out in Open* 218 There was gotten a goodly number of the kelp-hen (*Ocydromus fuscus*). **1961** *Merriam-Webster Third Internat. Dict.* 1236 *Kelp hen...* a weka of South Island of New Zealand that feeds on marine animals.

kelpie, *n.*[1] Also **kelpi**. [f. KELP(FISH + -IE.]

1. BUTTERFISH 1 (*Odax pullus*).
1956 Graham *Treasury NZ Fishes* 261 Greenbone, Butterfish, Kelp Salmon, or Kelpie (Marari) *Coridodax pullus...* The name Kelpie, of course, is derived from its habit of living amidst kelp and it is easily understood how the 'ie' was tacked on by fishermen. **1957** Parrott *Sea Angler's Fishes* 169 Kelpi *Coridodax pullus* Greenbone; Kelp Salmon; Kelpi; Kelpfish. **1972** Doak *Fishes* 97 Skindivers and fishermen call the juvenile butterfish a 'goldie' or 'kelpie'. Many people will be surprised to learn that these two fishes are beyond doubt the same species.

2. *banded parrotfish* (PARROTFISH 2 (1) *Notolabrus fucicola*).
1966 Doogue & Moreland *Sea Anglers' Guide* 259 Banded Parrotfish... Kelpfish, kelpie. **1967** Moreland *Marine Fishes* 22 Banded Parrotfish... Also called kelpie, kelpfish, and sometimes butterfish. **1991** Bradstock *Fishing* 18 *Banded parrotfish.* Other names: kelpfish, kelpie, *Pseudolabrus fucicola*.

3. SPOTTY 1 (*Notolabrus celidotus*).
1966 Doogue & Moreland *Sea Anglers' Guide* 257 Spotty... *Pseudolabrus celidotus;* butterfish, kelpie, guffy. None is widely used. **1982** Malcolm *Where It All Began* 105 He and Ted would spend hours..fishing for 'spotties', other names are butterfish or kelpie or..Pakirikiri. **1986** Paul *NZ Fishes* 107 *Spotty. Pseudolabrus celidotus.* Alternative names include paketi, kelpie, and butterfish (the last two being misleading).

kelpie, *n.*[2] [Cf. AND 1895, f. the name of an individual bitch, *Kelpie* (c1872), a progenitor of the breed.] A working dog used for both sheep and cattle.
c1875 Meredith *Adventuring in Maoriland* (1935) 46 An old shepherd..happened along with this particular dog, a rough-haired Kelpie. **1934** Lilico *Sheep Dog Memoirs* 8 [In 1902] Mr. A.E. McLeod, of..New South Wales, who bred kelpies, called on me. **1970** Porter *Nor'west Arch* 90 The coin could be hidden..but still the shrewd kelpie would find it and put it at Bob's feet. **1984** Rennie *Working Dogs* 13 The Kelpie is a 'handy' dog capable of working both sheep and cattle.

kelpie: see KELP-FLY.

kelp-salmon. BUTTERFISH 1 (*Odax pullus*).
1913 *TrNZI* XLV. 231 The butter-fish, kelp-fish or kelp-salmon, as it is variously called, is very common in Otago Harbour. **1921** [see BUTTERFISH 1]. **1938** *TrRSNZ* LXVIII. 412 *Coridodax pullus...* Greenbone (butterfish, kelp-fish, kelp-salmon). **1956** Graham *Treasury NZ Fishes* 261 *Coridodax pullus...* The name kelp-fish is given on account of its habit of feeding on kelp or seaweed... Kelp-salmon is given for two reasons. The first part, kelp, is explained in the last paragraph, while..salmon, is because the fish is not unlike a Salmon in shape, so much so that new chums who caught this fish have been under the impression they had caught the protected introduced salmon.

keo, var. KEA.

keouree, var. KIORE.

kerbstone.

1. As **kerbstone language** *obs.*, coarse, 'gutter' language.
1905 *Truth* 11 Nov. 5 Tongue-murdering..was [a term] used during the hearing of an assault case at Lyttelton..using..kerbstone language with much emphasis [he said].

2. Special Comb. **kerbstone jockey** WW1, a soldier in the Army Service Corps transport section.
1935 Mitchell & Strong in Partridge *Slang Today* 286 [The] following [was] employed by those who served in the [Great] War.. kerb-stone jockey, the rider of a fully harnessed horse of the transport section of the Army Service Corps, for the animal was so laden that the man was as safe as on the ground. **1937** Partridge *Dict. Slang* 451 *kerbstone jockey.* A soldier in the Transport (A.S.C.): New Zealand soldiers'; in G.W. A safe job, comparatively; esp. as the horses were heavily harnessed. **1938** *Press* (Christchurch) (McNab Slang) 2 Apr. 18 [Slang of the N.Z.E.F.] A 'kerbstone jockey' served in the A.S.C.

kereru. Also early **hagarrèroo** (=he kereru). [Ma. /kere'ru:/; Williams 114 *Kererū.* n... wood pigeon... = *kūkū, kūkūpa.*] PIGEON 1.
1842 Gray *Fauna* in Dieffenbach *Travels in NZ* (1843) II. 194 *Carpophaga Novae Seelandiae...* Hagarrèroo of the natives of Dusky Bay... Koukoupa... Kukupa... Kuku. **1855** [see PIGEON 2 (5)]. **1873** [see

PIGEON 2 (3)]. **1898** [see KUKU]. **1904** TREGEAR *Maori Race* 105 The fine New Zealand pigeon (*kukupa* or *kereru..*) was snared or speared in great quantity. **c1920** *South Island Maori Lists 'Wahi Mahika Kai'* in Beattie *Maori Place-names Canterbury* (1945) 64 Kereru—the beautiful native pigeon..good to eat. **1946** *JPS* LV. 152 *Kererū*, a bird..pigeon; the echoic kūkū and kūkupa less commonly used. **1952** LYON *Faring South* 104 So very fat were the kereru at this stage that if they struck a root in falling the bird burst at the side of the breast. **1970** *Evening Post* (Wellington) 17 Jan. 19 A colourful feast of red, orange and purple berries attracted..the plum-plumaged Kereru (wood pigeon). **1992** *NZ Geographic* 13 Jan.–Mar. 113 Kereru are eating monkey apple seeds and spreading this species far and wide.

kerewai. Also **kekerewai**, **kiriwai.** [Ma. /'kerewai/, /ke:'kerewai/: Williams 114 *kerewai*, *kēkerewai*. a small green beetle.] *manuka beetle* (BEETLE 8).

1848 TAYLOR *Leaf from Nat. Hist.* 15 *Kekerewai*, a little green beetle eaten by the natives. **1855** TAYLOR *Te Ika a Maui* 421 *Kiri wai manuka*, a small green beetle, abounding in the summer amongst the manuka trees..it is striped with green and red. **1870** TAYLOR *Te Ika a Maui* 641 The *kiriwai*, a very beautiful metallic green one, with red streaks, visits the Manuka trees. **1904** TREGEAR *Maori Race* 109 [The Maori] esteemed as food the small green beetle (*kekerewai*) found on the tea-tree (*manuka*) shrub. **1955** MILLER *Nature in NZ* 25 Other very common forms are the Green Manuka-beetles, the *kekerewai* of the Maori, who included them in his diet. **1971** MILLER *Common Insects* 143 The small green Manuka Beetles were *kekerewai*, or simply *kerewai* (*kere* to float, and *wai*, water), *kerewai manuka* (which is self-explanatory). **1982** BURTON *Two Hundred Years of NZ Food* 10 The small green manuka beetle, known as *kekerewai*, was mashed up with raupo pollen and steamed in small baskets as a type of bread.

keriberry. [f. a name suggested by a horticulturalist, Roy Hansen.] *Rubus rugosus* (var. *thwaitesii*) (fam. Rosaceae), an evergreen having as a fruit a black waxy drupelet, broadly conical in shape.

[*Note*] The plant, also called 'Himalaya blackberry', is thought to have been introduced in 1820 by a CMS missionary, James Shepherd, probably from India but possibly from Fiji or self-introduced from Indonesia. The fruit was 're-discovered' in Whangarei in 1935.

1985 *NZ Gardener* Sept. 13 Since 1972, Mr Roy Hansen..has had an interest in an evergreen berry he has named the keribery. **1988** WEBB et al. *Flora NZ* IV. 1134 *R[ubus] rugosus* has been recently introduced into horticulture under the name keriberry with the suggestion that it may have been deliberately brought to N.Z. as early as 1820.

Kermadec. In the names of plants and birds, see: PARAKEET 2 (5), PETREL 2 (13) and 2 (19) b (c), POHUTUKAWA 2 (2).

kero. [AND 1930.] Abbrev. of KEROSENE.

1941 *Tararua Tramper* Oct. 2 All but two days' eats and most of the kero were left at Heath's to be brought up next day. **1968** *Listener* 15 Mar. 6 Just picture us flicking on lights (no candles and kero to mess with). **1974** in *Listener Short Stories* (1977) 121 There was the risk of..having the breath thumped from one by a carelessly swung kero tin. **1987** SLIGO *Final Things* 63 Natalia approached with the tin of kero.

keropia, var. KOROPIO.

kerosene.

[*Note*] *kerosene*, the orig. spelling of a proprietary name, is in common use; *kerosine* is the generally preferred mod. technical and commercial spelling.

1. In New Zealand (as in Australia and US) *kerosene* is the usual equivalent of British English *paraffin (oil)* (see OED note), and has been recorded from c1860 (the *McLean Papers* mention a 'Kerosine creek' c1863). The main, distinctive New Zealand uses, now often obsolete or obsolescent, are combinatory.

1868 *Marlborough Express* (Blenheim) 9 May 6 Just received..15 cases Kerosene Oil..American Brooms, Tubs, and Buckets. **1966** TURNER *Eng. Lang. Austral. & NZ* 22 Trade has given currency to such words as *kerosene*: an English lady surprised a New Zealand chemist by asking for four gallons of 'paraffin' and he surprised her by supplying four gallons of 'liquid paraffin'.

2. Special Comb. with the second element usu. designating a container for storing or transporting kerosene, and subsequently used to improvise a utensil, article of furniture, or a building material: **kerosene-case** [AND 1903], a former standard wooden case holding two 4-gallon tins of kerosene, subsequently used as a makeshift seat, a cupboard, etc.; **kerosene lamp** [OED 1869], a lamp burning kerosene; **kerosene tin** [AND 1896], the name for a former standard 4-gallon square-topped tin (often orig. holding kerosene) and subsequently to c1940 altered to form a container (with a swinging wire handle attached), a boiler, a (4-gallon) measure; or, cut and flattened, for use as a building material.

1872 in Meredith *Adventuring in Maoriland* (1935) 29 Two **kerosene-cases** nailed together, with a bag for a coverlet and door, accommodate my wearing apparel. **1905** BAUCKE *White Man Treads* 278 Or, maybe, a slatternly unpainted board house..its furniture a single kerosene case nailed to the wall for a cupboard. *Ibid.* 304 He invited me to his whare, and seated me in the seat of honour—the slab bunk—while he made shift with the ubiquitous kerosene case store-all. **1874** *TrNZI* VI. 257 A portion of this oil [from Poverty Bay,..] was tested for illuminating purposes in an ordinary **kerosene lamp**. **1872** in Meredith *Adventuring in Maoriland* (1935) 29 For a mirror there is a **kerosene-tin** filled with clean water. **1890** *Otago Witness* (Dunedin) 16 Oct. 30 And this, too, to colonials who had known most of them what..it had been to partake of 'Sunday duff' boiled in a kerosene tin. **1897** *AJHR H-10* 6 [Official list of applicants for patents.] Buckley, J.W., Wellington, N.Z. Making use of disused kerosene tins as boilers..8223 29 Jan. **1905** SATCHELL *Toll of Bush* 46 There were no evidences of any attempt having been made to utilise this compensation..beyond what were furnished by a hut roofed with kerosene tin and a small enclosure. **1916** MANSFIELD *Aloe* (1982) 109 Two spoon fulls of this will be enough..in a kerosene tin of water to kill thousands of fleas. **1922** *NZJST* V. 37 The Nolan amphora, or vessel for storing oil (how much more satisfying aesthetically than a kerosene-tin!) may be described as a theme in root-two. **1944** TEXIDOR in *In Fifteen Minutes* (1987) 167 The soft drinks were mixed in two kerosine tins. **1963** PEARSON *Coal Flat* 375 Now Mrs Torere brought out..a half-kerosene tin of cooked mutton-birds preserved in fat. **1986** RICHARDS *Off the Sheep's Back* 31 The water for making the tea was always boiled in kerosene tins over an open fire. **1988** GIBBONS *Recollections* 14 Kerosene tins cut lengthwise made excellent roasting dishes. **1991** O'REGAN *Aunts and Windmills* 100 All petrol [in the 1920s] was bought in what we chose to call a kerosene tin. These tins were later put to a wide variety of uses, most notably as milk buckets. **1994** LASENBY *Dead Man's Head* 64 He led into a shed covered with flattened-out kerosene tins.

3. In the names of plants, with reference to a facility for burning easily or well: **kerosene plant** *Dracophyllum uniflorum* (see quot. c1957), or the introduced woolly nightshade *Solanum mauritianum* (fam. Solanaceae); **kerosene wood**, occas. and locally BROADLEAF q.v.

c1957 p.c. R. Mason, heard in Christchurch. **Kerosene plant** *Dracophyllum uniflorum*, so called from its ability to burn wet and green. **1992** *Listener* 3 Feb. 25 Woolly nightshade, also known as the kerosene plant or tobacco weed, is more common in the North Island. **1981** HENDERSON *Exiles Asbestos Cottage* 60 Broadleaf for sustained blaze, called '**kerosene wood**' down south, 'kapama' we called it.

ket, var. KIT *n.*[1]

kete. Also early **kétta**, **kête** [?=/ket/]. [Ma. /'kete/: Williams 115 *Kete*, n. *1*. Basket made of strips of flax, etc.] A flax basket woven Maori-fashion from strips of flax or similar leaves (see discussion at KIT *n.*[1]).

[**1815** KENDALL *New Zealanders' First Book* 16 Kétta A basket. **1820** LEE & KENDALL *NZ Gram. & Vocab.* 162 Kéte, *s.* A basket.] **1827** WILLIAMS *Early Jrnls.* 28 Dec. (1961) 94 He presented 5 *ketes* of potatoes which I received with much pleasure. **1845** SELWYN 23 Jan. in Drummond *Married & Gone to NZ* (1960) 114 I mounted Mr Hadfield's nice horse.., little Willie in a large potato kete (basket) affixed to poles and carried by two men. **1884** MARTIN *Our Maoris* 44 They might have said, as an old Maori woman long afterwards said to me, 'Mother, my heart is like an old kête (*i.e.*, a coarsely-woven basket). The words go in, but they fall through.' **1897** *TrNZI* XXIX. 174 The *kete* was a large one, laced up with a long attached cord. **1927** *NZ Tablet* (Dunedin) 21 Sept. 39 Last year all the senior girls made ketes and tatuas. **1946** *JPS* LV. 152 *kete*, flat basket made of strips of flax: a basket of like shape but made of prepared flax dyed with cross-pattern in black called Maori-kit. **1969** MASON *Awatea* (1978) Appendix II 114 Mirinia will open up her huge flax *kete* and waddle off to my kitchen. **1979** *Star* (Christchurch) 9 Apr. 13 But no doubt as schools continue to appreciate the art of Maoridom children will one day be taught to make such kete for themselves. **1990** *Listener* 17 Dec. 76 The kete..were made especially to collect pipi. **1995** ANDERSON *House Guest* 39 She came beating on his door at one a.m...an unravelling kete in her hand.

kettler: see *tin-kettler* (TIN-KETTLE *v.*).

key, *n.*[1] Prison. [f. an allusion to *lock and key.*] KATHLEEN MAVOURNEEN 1.

1980 MACKENZIE *While We Have Prisons* 9 In prison language they had been given the 'collar', the 'key', the Kathleen Mavourneen sentence—'It may be for years and it may be for ever'.

key, *n.*[2] [Spec. use of *key*, that which holds other parts together: see OED *n.*[1] a.]

1. *Obs.* A piece which locks the bow into the yoke of a bullock harness. Cf. BOW 1.

1940 *Tales Pioneer Women* (1988) 151 They were returning [in a bullock dray]..when a carelessly tied 'key' that held the 'bow' into the 'yoke' dropped out and let one bullock free.

2. *Logging*. The tree in a timber drive which when felled will set the other heavily scarfed trees falling in succession; *king-tree* (KING *n.*[2] 2).

1986 [see DRIVE *n.*[2] 2].

Keystone Brigade. *WW1. Hist.* The Rifle Brigade, prob. from an ironic allusion to Mack Sennett's bumbling 'Keystone Cops'.

1915 GRAY, Norman *MS Papers 4134* (ATLMS) 19 Nov. The NZ Rifle Brigade, alias the 'Trents' is now known as the Keystone Brigade.

K-force. *Hist.* Also **Kayforce.** [f. *K*(orea) *force*.] The name given to the New Zealand contingent sent as part of the United Nations force to Korea in December 1950. Also *attrib*.

1950 *Dominion* (Wellington) 29 July 8 Throughout New Zealand yesterday more than 1500 volunteers answered the call for service in the K-Force, New Zealand component of the United Nations forces in Korea. **1951** *Evening Post* (Wellington) 30 Jan. 7 [Heading] K Force Lines Up with Famous Unit. **1964** BOOTH *Footsteps in Sea* 54 Some of Jim's K-force cobbers..had known Dick since before Seoul. **1987** *Those Were the Days* V. 25 New Zealand sent to Korea a contingent known as Kayforce comprising an artillery regiment, a signals troop, a transport platoon, a light aid detachment..a total strength of 1044. **1990** *Evening Post* (Wellington) 2 June 27 On July 26 [1950], the Government announced the raising of K Force, a ground force to join the UN contingent in Korea.

khaki, *a. WW1.* [Transf. use of *khaki* the brownish colour of the NZ army uniform, to suggest patriotism.] In cooking, esp. *khaki cake*, of coffee-colour, to suggest khaki, and often decorated with red, white and blue trimmings.

1915 *Our Boys Cook. Book* 107 *Khaki Cake* butter..sugar..egg..flour..desiccated cocoanut..vanilla.. cream of tartar..carbonate of soda. **1915** MCCREDIE *Patriotic Fete..Bungalow Recipe Book* 58 *Khaki Pudding*..flour..breadcrumbs..suet..sugar..raisins..eggs.. allspice..lemon peel. Mix with beer and boil 4 hours. **1917** MILLER *Econ. Tech. Cook. Book* 281 *Khaki Cakes*..Butter..Sugar..Eggs..Milk..Flour... Soda..Cream of Tartar..powdered Cinnamon... Cover tops with white icing, and ornament with red and blue sugar. **1924** *Help the Babies Cook. Book* 111 *Khaki Cake*..butter..sugar.. flour..cocoa..almonds..cocoanut..milk..eggs..baking powder. **1936** *Home of Compassion Recipes* 81 *Khaki Cake*..sugar..butter..eggs..flour..cocoa..baking powder..vanilla..put together with butter icing and ice the top. **1938** *Souvenir Book Cook. Recipes* 31 *Khaki Sponge*..flour..butter..sugar..eggs..cocoa..desiccated cocoanut..milk..baking powder... Bake.

kia, var. KEA.

kiakia, var. KIEKIE.

kia ora /ki(ə)'orə/. [Ma. /ki'ora/: Williams 116 *Kia* + Williams 240 *Ora* (i)... 2. Well, in health: Williams 116 does not illustrate the use of *kia* as an optative verbal particle which, when followed by certain stative verbs, has the force of an imperative.] **a.** *interj.* A greeting or farewell ('May you be well'); 'hello', 'goodbye'; (as a toast) good health.
[*Note*] Freq. in non-Maori use from c1890 to c1940, then revived in the 1980s.

1898 MORRIS *Austral-English* 247 *Kia ora, interj.* Maori phrase used by English in the North Island of New Zealand, and meaning 'Health to you!' A private letter (1896) says 'You will hear any day at a Melbourne bar the first man say *Keora ta-u*, while the other says *Keora tatu*, so replacing 'Here's to you!' These expressions are corruptions of the Maori, *Kia ora taua*, 'Health to us [two]!' and *Kia ora tatou*, 'Health to all of us!' **1905** BAUCKE *White Man Treads* 273 That soulless braggarts might pose as almoners, and call from the highway, 'Kia ora oh coloured brother!' and go on their way. **1914** ALGIE, Colvin *MS Papers 1374* (ATLMS) 28 Oct. This afternoon our two friends HMS Pyramus and Philomel left us on their way back to New Zealand... They both had the signal 'Kia ora' while we returned it with 'Goodbye Good luck'. **1920** BOLITHO *With the Prince in NZ* 33 One displayed large sheets of tin on his machine with the words 'Welcome' and 'Kia Ora' painted on them. **1930** *NZ Short Stories* 145 'What is it you say when you drink in your country?' 'Kia Ora!' explained a Maoriland trooper. Piet reverentially said 'Kia Ora!' and sucked the mouth of the bottle. **1945** HENDERSON *Gunner Inglorious* 52 '*Kia Ora*' said the Italian [P.O.W.] guards... Politeness indeed..the Maori Battalion must have passed this way... '*Kia Ora*.' This didn't seem to satisfy the guards, however... We soon found out they were saying '*Che ora*?' (What is the time?) **1964** DAVIS *Watersiders* 123 'Kia ora,' we said [drinking up]. **1973** PEARSON in Finlayson *Brown Man's Burden* 137 'And they smiled sweetly and said, "Kia ora" '. Literally the phrase means 'Be well', but to these pakehas it is one of the few phrases of Maori they know and they probably think it means 'Good luck' or 'Hullo'. **1984** *Evening Post* (Wellington) 25 May 1 On Monday the 'Post' was first to report the plight of Mrs Naida Povey, an Auckland Maori tolls operator who was ordered to stop greeting callers with 'kia ora'. **1993** *Dominion* (Wellington) 27 Mar. 20 Why should New Zealanders adopt 'kia ora' as a national greeting?

b. As a noun, an instance of the use of *kia ora* as an expression of welcome.

1904 *Grey River Argus* 20 Feb. 2 In the evening His Lordship will be greeted with further 'Kia-Oras' in the shape of a banquet.

kick, *n. Obs.* [A survival of obs. Brit. slang.] A sixpence, esp. in the phr. **two-and-a-kick,** poss. rhyming slang for 'two-and-six', a half-crown piece. Cf. BUCK *n.*³ 1.

1917 *Truth* 6 Oct. 6 He told how the wool growers could get four and a 'kick' for their wool. **1919** *Quick March* Mar. 51 Nice 'namel paint—five an' a kick (5s 6d) the tin. **1977** two-and-a-kick [see BUCK *n*³ 1].

kick, *v.* In the phr. **to kick up bobsy-die,** see BOBSY-DIE a; **to kick with the left foot,** see LEFT-FOOTER.

kicker. *Shearing.* [Spec. use of *kicker*, an animal that kicks.] A sheep that struggles and kicks while being shorn.

c1875? *NZ Songster* III. 63 Thinks I, this here's a kicker, But started off again; And I found a second sticker, For no Bells could I obtain. **1955** BOWEN *Wool Away* 156 Kicker. A sheep that keeps on struggling and kicking while being shorn. **1982** *Agric. Gloss.* (MAF) 56 *Kicker*: Sheep that struggles and kicks while being shorn.

kick-the-tin. *obs.* Also **kick-the-block (boot).** A (usu.) boys' game or pastime, also known as HOMAIACKY q.v.

1904 in Lawlor *More Wellington Days* (1962) 68 Played kick the tin on the reclaimed land. Corker fun. **1937** ALLEN *Hedge-sparrow* 30 He had in his time named her in a game of kick-the-tin. **1953** SUTTON-SMITH *Unorganized Games NZ Primary School Children* (VUWTS) II. 513 Of the Help-He games, Kick the Tin, is the most widely known. A tin is placed in the centre of a circle. One He is in charge of the tin. He can only tag the other players when his tin is in the centre of the circle. Any players he catches must stay in the circle. Any non-caught player can help and free the other caught players by running through the circle and kicking the tin out of it. Other names for this game are: Kick the Boot (Gisborne [18]90), Knock the Block or Homaiacky (Nelson [18]95), Kick the football or Piacky (Mangatainoka). **1972** SUTTON-SMITH *Folkgames Children* 80 More popular were those [tagging] games in which the players helped one another to fight the He, and of these the most widespread was the game known as *Kick the Tin* (e-3), Kick the Boot, Kick the Block, or Homaiacky. In this game the He was put on guard of a jam tin placed inside a small circle marked on the ground. [Other players hid: those He could see he named and tapped the tin three times and 'captured': other hiders waited till they had chance to kick tin out of circle: then all were free again.]

kid-fucker. *Prison.* A sexual abuser of children.

1973 *Salient* (Wellington) 19 Sept. 15 After my first month at Wi Tako I was not classed as a 'kid-fucker' by any of the inmates..and I found that any 'kid-fucker' who was victim of any assault invariably brought it upon himself. **1980** BERRY *First Offender* 27 All child sex-offenders were generally known as kidfuckers by the other inmates **1991** STEWART *Broken Arse* 40 This is for setting me up. *Thump*. This is for being a kid-fucker. *Thump*.

kidney. *Tramping.* In special Comb. **kidney-bruiser (buster, -crusher, -rider, rotter)**, a name for a frameless tramping pack, from its habit of riding low on the back.

c1940 p.c. Les Cleveland (Wellington), 1964. *Kidney-sweater*, and occ. *kidney-rotter*; terms for a haversack of the kind which does not have a metal frame. When the wearer begins to sweat under the exertion of carrying a load, a patch of sweat appears on his clothes where his back chafes against the pack. In general use in mountaineering and tramping circles throughout New Zealand. **1943** *Tararua Tramper* Dec. 5 Has anybody used loofahs on a kidney-rotter pack as mentioned in 'Kamet Conquered', to keep the pack from touching the back? **1958** *Tararua* Sept. 27 The frameless pack..receives that name only on formal occasions, being more familiarly known by that elegant term, *kidney-rotter*, or less frequently as *kidney-buster*, *kidney-crusher*, *kidney-sweater* or *kidney-rider*. **1971** *Listener* 19 Apr. 56 Out of the boo-ai comes three trampers... One had..clinkered boots and an old kidney-rotter. **1988** PICKERING *Hills* 78 For instance [a past generation's] packs (or swags as some would have been calling them) would be A-frame 'kidney-bruiser, kidney-rotter, kidney-crusher' types with billies dangling off the back and tents lashed to the outside.

kidney fern: see FERN 2 (10).

kidney pie. *Obs.* [An elaboration of or play on Brit. slang *kid* humbug: see OED *n*.⁵] Insincere praise, flattery.

1935 MITCHELL & STRONG in Partridge *Slang Today* 286 [The] following [was] employed by those who served in the [Great] War..*kidney pie*, insincere praise or what the Americans call *bull*. *Ibid.* 287 His offsider said 'Give a man a fair go', so I gave him a bit of kidney pie and there was nothing lousy about him. **1941** BAKER *NZ Slang* 57 [Twentieth century expressions include] *kidney pie* humbug or deceit. **1955** *BJ Cameron Collection* (TS July) kidney-pie (n) Soft talk, humbug.

kidstakes. Also **kidsteaks.** [Prob. joc. formation on Brit. slang *kid* humbug + *stakes* as in horseracing feature races ('The [x] Stakes'): AND 1912.] Nonsense, humbug.

1943 MARSH *Colour Scheme* 25 'I'll tell my great-grandfather..and he'll *makutu* you.' 'Kid-stakes!

KIEKIE

Nobody's going to put a jinx on me.' **1949** SARGESON *I Saw in My Dream* 154 But it looked as if it was all kidsteaks. **1964** PEARSON Glossary in SARGESON *Collected Stories 1935–63* 301 kidsteaks: *all kidsteaks*, full of blarney.

kiekie /ˈkiki/, /ˈkiəkiə/, /ˈgɪgi/, /ˈgæiˌgæi/. Also with much variety of transliterated form, often indicating a perceived lengthening of the orig. Ma. vowels, and falling by provenance roughly into (a) mainly NI, from a perceived root-form **kiekie** (/ˈkiekie/), **kea-kea**, **kee-kee**, **kiakia**, **kihikihi**, and only occas., from **giegie*; and (b) mainly SI, from **giegie* /ˈgiegie/, **ga-ga**, **gege**, **gee-gee**, **gei-gei**, **gigi**, **giggi**, **giggy**; and only occas. from **kiekie** as **kiakia**, **kihi-ki**. [Ma. /ˈkiekie/: Williams 117 *Kiekie*, n.]

1. The climbing plant *Freycinetia baueriana* (formerly *banksii*) (fam. Pandanaceae), its long, narrow leaves (formerly used as a clothing or building material), and the edible flower-bracts (tawhara) or fruit (ureure, i.e. 'penis-like', or five-fingers); also formerly in Westland **summer** and **winter kiekie** (see quots. 1905, 1930). See also FIVE-FINGER 1 a (b), PINEAPPLE 1, SCREWPINE, TAWHARA, UREURE.

[**1820** LEE & KENDALL *NZ Gram. & Vocab.* 163 Kíekíe; Name of a certain plant.] **1838** POLACK *NZ* I. 392 As a preservative against rain, many large garments are worn..made of the *kiakia*, spear-grass, which is impervious to the element. *Ibid.* II. 23 The sail is made of raupo leaves or kiákiá, grass, etc., of triangular shape. **1842** HEAPHY *NZ* 44 The first of the indigenous esculent fruits is the *Kia-kia*. It grows on a parasitical plant of the same name; and in form much resembles the pineapple. Its taste is very agreeable and cool. **1854** GOLDER *Pigeons' Parliament* 77 The trees were..covered with a kind of parasite plant, called a kee-kee, having a thick cabbage-like stock. **1863** MARTIN *Diary* (Hocken MS) 26 Sept. A hill..covered with bush supple jacks Lawyers and Kea-Kea with innumerable land slips. **c1875** MEREDITH *Adventuring in Maoriland* (1935) 135 We went out into the bush after *tawharas* this week. This is the fruit of the *kia kia*, a parasite which climbs and adheres to the dead trees. The Maoris make excellent hats resembling the celebrated 'cabbage-tree' hats, from the fibre of the leaves. **1889** PAULIN *Wild West Coast* 100 Gee-gee and supple jack. **c1890s** DOUGLAS in *Mr Explorer Douglas* (1957) 14 He can learn how to make rafts..or rig up a lean-too [*sic*] with flax or gei-gei. **1896** HARPER *Pioneer Work* 33 The kihi-ki..which grows on the lower hills near the sea [is] also eatable. **1898** MORRIS *Austral-English* 247 *Kie-kie*..frequently pronounced *ghi-ghi* in the North Island of New Zealand, and *gay-gie* in the South Island. **1905** THOMSON *Bush Boys* 179 'I vote for a day among the "Summer Giggies",' said Denis. (Giggies is the bush boy corruption of 'Kie-kie,' a large sweet luscious fruit, or more strictly flower, found in our bush.) **1930** DEVANNY *Bushman Burke* 254 The gagas were past the budding stage... This is what we [in the South Island] call a summer gaga with yellow forks. Then there are what we call winter gagas. The forks are green. **1940** *Tales Pioneer Women* (1988) 155 One day the boy..went..to look for kie-kie, or gi-gis, as they called them [at Karamea]. **1952** LYON *Faring South* 104 One source of food supply was derived from the all pervading kihikihi, or as the settlers called it, the gigi. **1979** [see SCREWPINE]. **1981** CHARLES *Black Billy Tea* 25 Lawyer and geigei and blackberry root, Biddy-bid burrs, matagouri and toot!

2. Special Comb. **kiekie basket**, **kiekie hat**, one made of the leaves of the kiekie (see also quot. 1875 in 1 above).

1882 POTTS *Out in Open* 20 In the forest clearing..is a taikawa, on which is thrown the unused food from the kauta of our little camp, together with the empty kie-kie baskets. **1912** BAUGHAN *Brown Bread* 132 [With an] untrimmed *gege* hat tilted back upon her head *Ibid.* 136 Soft shirts with turned-down collars, blue dungarees, belts, and great *gege* hats make up [the haymakers'] 'rig'. **1926** *NZ Observer* 2 Jan. 6 A kie-kie hat is one of the most comfortable makes of headpieces.

kievi-kievi: see KIWI.

kihi-ki, var. KIEKIE.

kihikihi, var. KIEKIE, KOHEKOHE.

kikatea, var. KAHIKATEA.

kike /kaik/. Abbrev. of an anglicized pronunciation /ˌkaikəˈtiə/ of KAHIKATEA 1. Also *attrib*.

1954 *Listener* 21 May 22 'Is that a white pine you have there?'.. 'Him? He's a kike.' 'Kike?' 'Yes. It's really ki-katee, but we leave out the tee.' **1969** MOORE *Forest to Farm* 43 This meant that on a fairly large log of kahikatea—always referred to as 'kike'..I would ultimately receive 15s. **1974** HILLIARD *Maori Woman* 259 It would be worth it just for those kike-trees he's got at the side.

kike, var. KAIKA.

kikereru, var. KEKERENGU.

kiki, var. KAI.

kikiararu, var. KEKERENGU.

kikitea, var. KAHIKATEA.

kilikiti: see *Samoan cricket* (SAMOAN 1).

kill, *v.* [Spec. use of *kill* to perform an act of killing.] *intr.* To slaughter (an animal) for meat; of stock, to produce a carcase.

1862 CHUDLEIGH *Diary* 8 July (1950) 47 Put furse [*sic*] over the yard we are going to kill in, the mud being about two feet deep. **1940** [see FAT *n.*¹ a]. **1946** ACLAND *Early Canterbury Runs* 191 At three years old, the steers used to kill about 900 lb. off grass. **1947** GASKELL *Big Game* 53 'Your turn to kill, you know...' 'You out of meat?' **1950** CHERRILL *NZ Sheep Farm* 67 No need to fash about feeding them people. I killed a couple o'days since, so there's plenty o'meat.

Hence **kill** *n.*, the process of commercial slaughtering of animals for meat and other products; the number of animals so killed within a certain period; **killable** *a.*, of stock, in good or prime condition for slaughter.

1963 *Dominion* (Wellington) 23 Mar. 15 Another point was that the freezing companies were interested in establishing a continual **kill**..in the interests of economy, rather than a seasonal kill just for export. **1982** *Collins Concise Eng. Dict.* 618 *kill... 16. N.Z.* a seasonal tally of the number of stock killed at a meatworks. **1983** *Marlborough Express* (Blenheim) 13 Jan. 3 **Killable** stock has been sent off to freezing works at Picton, Nelson and points south.

killer, *n.*¹ Farming. [AND 1914.] Also **killer sheep**. A sheep or cattle-beast intended to be killed for meat, usu. for prompt consumption on the farm. See also MUTTON 1. Cf. FREEZER 2.

KILLING

1897 SCOTT *How I Stole 10,000 Sheep* 9 'Well, you know the killers, don't you?' 'Yes,' I replied, (*sc.* the sheep that the boss used for his own mutton at the house). **1907** KOEBEL *Return of Joe* 294 We were to be treated to a portion of valuable stud ram for supper in place of the ordinary 'killer'. **1913** BATHGATE *Sodger Sandy's Bairn* 158 He had just brought in some sheep for 'killers'. **1930** DAVIDSON *Sketch of His Life* 30 The bulls..when fat, were worth an extra £1 per head..as they were such good 'killers'. **1949** HARTLEY *Shepherd's Dogs* 32 We have seen the 'dud' dog on a station that is capable of yarding 'killers' in first class style, because he was always used for this job. **1962** SHARPE *Country Occasions* 68 If you show an experienced dog a butcher's knife..he will..round up a mob of killers (sheep to be used as mutton for the homestead) without any further word of command. **1969** MCCASKILL *Molesworth* 248 The livestock on Molesworth are not confined to the thousands of cattle, two dozen horses, a few killer sheep, and Miss Ann's tame pig. **1970** MCNAUGHTON *Tat* 98 Young Charlie [a station hand] didn't close the gate properly..and all the killers got out yesterday.

killer, *n.*² In special Comb. with reference to the extermination of noxious animals, esp. rabbits and opossums: **Killer Board**, a Rabbit Board charged with the local extermination of rabbits; **killer policy**, a policy of extermination of noxious animals.

1952 NEWTON *High Country Journey* 38 The Mackenzie Country has recently come under the control of the **Killer Board** and it yet remains to be seen how effective their [rabbit control] measures will be. **1948** *Our Own Country* 46 There are few rabbits [around Gisborne]; a vigorous '**killer**' **policy** has seen to that. **1954** MILLER *Beyond the Blue Mountains* 89 The war against the rabbit was..to take various forms before the present-day killer policy was put into operation. **1963** *NZ Geogr.* Oct. 166 Since the national adoption of the 'killer policy' by rabbit boards in 1947..a greater measure of control has been achieved.

killing, *vbl. n.*

1. Used of the butchering of animals, on farms and in freezing works and abattoirs. **a.** As a noun, the total number of animals killed within a particular time, season, etc.

1956 *NZ Meat Producer* Oct. 5 The 1955–56 season was a most difficult one, especially in dealing with the abnormal killings occasioned by the drought in the South Island. **1966** *Encycl. NZ* II. 257 Killings at works for export and for home consumption were 951,000 wethers and 4,600,000 ewes.

b. As an *attrib.* Of stock (usu. sheep) butchered for food on the farm, or in freezing works for export.

1970 MCNAUGHTON *Tat* 95 Charlie left a gate open and a hundred wethers—the [station] killing mob—escaped through it. **1980** *The Nation* 27 Nov. 6 Although the industry will have to invest a lot of capital in new machinery, it will be a lot less than the massive amounts spent..on meeting..killing requirements... The money saved will be passed on to farmers in the form of reduced killing charges.

2. Special Comb. **killing house**, a slaughter-house on a sheep-station; **killing paddock** [AND 1922], the paddock where sheep for farm consumption are held; **killing pen**, a pen where sheep for farm consumption are held before slaughter; **killing season** *freezing works* [AND 1939], the late spring and summer when most export stock is slaughtered; **killing-shed**, a shed in which stock is slaughtered; **killing sheep**

[AND 1901], KILLER n.¹; **killing sheet**, the record of the number and ownership of sheep killed in a freezing works.
   1933 *Press* (Christchurch) (Acland Gloss.) 4 Nov. 15 *Killing House.*—Slaughter house on station. **1951** MCLEOD *High Country* 18 They..tell [the newcomer musterer] where the killing house is to get some dog tucker. **1987** OGONOWSKA-COATES *Boards, Blades & Barebellies* 96 *Killing House.* Slaughterhouse on the station. **1907** KOEBEL *Return of Joe* 281 I see'd [the dog] after some sheep in the **killing paddock**. **1919** WILSON in Wierzbicka *Wilson Family* (1973) 126 The killing paddock was the first fence put up. **1961** CRUMP *Hang On a Minute Mate* 162 He killed and dressed the fattest wether in the killing paddock when it was his turn. **1975** HARPER *Eight Daughters* 30 As soon as he could afford it George spread lime, starting in the killing paddock. **1953** STRONACH *Musterer on Molesworth* 45 My first attempt [to pen killing sheep] was at Molesworth. The **killing pen** is pretty difficult there. **1918** *NZJST* I. 20 They also have a general day motor load of 100 to 200 kilowats during the **killing season**, falling off very much during the slack season. **1936** BELSHAW et al. *Agric. Organiz. NZ* 630 The normal killing season [in the North Island] lasts from November to June, the heaviest months being from January to April. **1979** FRAME *Living in Maniototo* 52 Lance had never had such a holiday job [in the freezing works]. He'd never been part of the Killing Season. **1980** *The Nation* 27 Nov. 32 A loadout ban during an otherwise peaceful-looking killing season would have been a sad affair. **1957** *NZ Meat Producer* Feb. 9 Davidson wrote to him [Thomas Brydone, the Land Company's superintendent] in April, 1881, telling him to erect a **killing shed**. **1933** *Press* (Christchurch) (Acland Gloss.) 4 Nov. 15 *Killers, killing sheep.*—Sheep for station mutton. **1953** STRONACH *Musterer on Molesworth* 45 The most trying ordeal for a new-chum musterer is getting in the killing sheep. **1936** BELSHAW et al. *Agric. Organiz. NZ* 629 Payment is made on freezing works **killing sheets**.

kilt, *v. Farming. Obs.* [f. the resemblance to a *kilt* of a long double-fleece hanging in folds.] To shear the legs and belly wool of a double-fleeced sheep.
   1934 *Press* (Christchurch) (Acland Gloss.) 20 Jan. 15 *Kilt, to.*—To shear the legs and belly wool of a double fleecer in the autumn. Another verb for the process is *to trace high*.

kina /ˈkinə/. [Ma. /ˈkina/: Williams 118 *Kina*, n. *1*...sea-urchin, sea-egg.] *Evechinus chloroticus* (fam. Echinometridae), a common green sea-urchin or sea-egg esp. in its use as a sea-food.
   [**1820** LEE & KENDALL *NZ Gram. & Vocab.* 164 *Kína s.* A sea egg:] **1848** TAYLOR *Leaf from Nat. Hist.* 17 Kina, *sea egg.* **1908** WILLIAMS *Souvenir All Nations Fair, Gisbourne* 6 *Kina, or Sea Urchin...* Cut the shell in half..leaving only the yellow pulp which may be scooped out..and taken raw as a relish... Another method is to..roast, and serve hot. **c1920** *South Island Maori Lists 'Wahi Mahika Kai'* in Beattie *Maori Place-names Canterbury* (1945) 62 Kina—the sea-urchin or sea-egg. **1938** MAKERETI *The Old-Time Maori* 237 Kina (Echinus) commonly called the sea egg, has a prickly shell, and the inside is generally eaten raw. **1954** BEATTIE *Our Southernmost Maori* 63 In Bluff Harbour we used to get the kina (sea egg). **1960** HILLIARD *Maori Girl* 153 Netta took the tongues from the kinas and put them into a dish with vinegar. **1972** BAXTER *Collected Poems* (1980) 538 A whare by the seashore Where you can look for crabs and kina. **1985** MCGILL *G'day Country* 56 A fishshop was selling dabs (baby flounder) and crab sticks..and pots of ex-Chatham Islands kina roe. **1986** PAUL *NZ Fishes* 172 *Sea urchin...* Alternatively sea egg or kina. Restricted to New Zealand, but similar sea urchins occur in most seas. **1992** *Cuisine* (Auckland) June/July 4 The festival is a celebration of strictly local taste treats, ranging from Marlborough's renowned Sauvignon Blanc to stuffed mussels, sea eggs (kina).

kinaki. [Ma. /ˈkiːnaki/: Williams 118 *Kīnaki.*] Mainly in Maori contexts, a relish; food which is eaten to enliven other food. Also *attrib.*
   [**1820** LEE & KENDALL *NZ Gram. & Vocab.* 164 Kínaki, *s.* Victuals added for variety's sake.] **1846** COTTON *Letter* in MacMorran *Octavius Hadfield* (1969) 77 I send you by Henry a pot of English blackcurrant jam—as a *kinaki*. **1873** *AJHR G-1* 5 If it be a Maori who is taken by me, he will also be made into a *kinaki* for my cabbage. **1898** MORRIS *Austral-English* 248 *Kinaki*, n. a Maori word for food eaten with another kind to give it a relish. **1903** *TrNZI* XXXV. 23 The kumara..with any food..as birds, fish, or other *kinaki* (relish), are piled on the stones. **1921** GUTHRIE-SMITH *Tutira* 70 This man's body..was eaten as a relish—*kinaki*—with the fern root. **1930** *Na To Hoa Aroha* (1987) II. 21 They could have satisfied most of the 'kinaki' wants from the coast, but preferred forest products. **1949** REED *Story Canterbury* 67 To the water, fern-root and damper brought with them was added as *kinaki*, or relish, a fat young *titi*, or mutton-bird. **1982** BURTON *Two Hundred Yrs. NZ Food* 6 After a time, the [tutu] juice would set and was eaten as a relish (*kinaki*) or with fernroot or fungus.

kindly, *a.* Also **kind**. [Prob. f. Brit. dial. *kindly* of country which repays cultivation: see EDD.] See also COUNTRY. **a.** *Farming.* Of country, favourable to stock-raising.
   1973 NEWTON *Big Country SI* (1977) 3 This country is green all the year round. All lambs go fat... This is 'kind' country, which has that something about it that takes a stockman's eye.

b. *Goldmining.* Of country, favouring good returns of ore. Contrast HARD COUNTRY.
   1897 *AJHR C-9* 38 The decomposed andesites generally possess a characteristic yellowish-brown or grey colour, and form the 'kindly country' of the local miners; while the solid andesites and tuffs possess a greenish or dark-blue or purple colour and are generally known as 'hard country'. **1912** *NZGeol.SB (NS)* No.15 63 The favourable or 'kindly' country of the miner is a completely propilitized andesite or dacite. **1913** [see DEAD *a.*¹ 2]. **1922** *NZJST* V. 115 The miner, quickly recognizing these characters, uses them in his search for ore-bodies, and calls any rock exhibiting them 'favourable' or 'kindly' country. **1992** LATHAM *Golden Reefs* 430 *Kindly*: A tract of country or a reef was said to be kindly-looking when it gave promise of carrying gold.

kindy. [f. *kind*(ergarten + -Y: AND 1973.] A familiar name for kindergarten.
   1959 SLATTER *Gun in My Hand* 146 Two kids at school now and the little joker's at kindy. **1962** *Hataitai Herald* (Wellington) 15 June [Caption] *Kindy Open House*: Hataitai Kindergarten. **1979** SIMONS *Harper's Mother* 134 You don't have to do a thing except collect her from kindy and keep an eye on her until I get home.

king, *n.*¹
1. See MAORI KING.
2. a. With init. cap. Used *attrib.* in Comb. (often *hist.*), with reference to the Maori King movement, **King-Maori, -meeting, native, tribe**. See also KING COUNTRY, KING-MAKER, KING MOVEMENT, KING PARTY.
   1864 NICHOLL *Journal* (ATLMS) 19 July 267 We then went up to the villages..which we found cram full of **King Maoris** who have given themselves up. **1879** GUDGEON *Reminisc. War in NZ* 18 The [friendly Maories]..as a rule, disliked us quite as much as the King Maories did. **1879** CHUDLEIGH *Diary* 28 Apr. (1950) 279 I went to Allexandria en rout to Kopua to see the great **King meeting**. **1862** *Otago Witness* (Dunedin) 23 Aug. 2 The **King Native** was intended now to act as a bar to colonization. **c1864** TEMPSKY *Memoranda* (ATLTS) 127 There were tribes in that neighbourhood, as the Arawas for instance who hated the King natives worse than the whites. **1878** BULLER *Forty Yrs. NZ* 134 No communication with any white person was permitted, by the 'King' natives. **1862** *Otago Witness* (Dunedin) 23 Aug. 8 The most important feature is, the state of destitution to which a variety of causes have reduced most of the unsettled or **King tribes** in this neighbourhood.

b. In composition **kingship**, the office and mana of the Maori king.
   1966 *Encycl. NZ* III. 648 [Mahuta] was succeeded in the 'Kingship' by his eldest son, Te Rata.

king, *n.*²
1. WW1, occas. WW2. [Spec. uses of suffixed *king* one pre-eminent in an activity, etc.: see OED 6.] As a suffix connoting an accomplished practitioner or expert in a trade, sport, etc., often in a derog. sense, occas. in absolute use (see quot. 1994). Cf. -ARTIST.
   1906 *Truth* 21 July 7 [Of a politician] The 'Yes-no' king. **1917** *Chron. NZEF* 5 Sept. 28 He [Sergeant Jones] was the greatest 'swi-up' king in the 'Inverteds'. *Ibid.* 28 Sept. 28 Two..[sergeants] were universally known as 'C.B. Kings' [*sc.* NCOs given to ordering soldiers confined to barracks]. **1918** *Ibid.* 30 Aug. 65 Our first halt's made on the journey round, With the bull-ring Bayonet Kings. **1936** TREADWELL *Recolls. Amateur Soldier* 31 One of the Crown and Anchor 'kings' was reported to have said, 'That damned sergeant has skinned all the schools!' **1941** HAWDON *NZ Soldiers in England* 7 Voices of the 'two-up' and 'housie' kings. **1943** *NZEF Times* 26 July 8 Described by the police as the 'Borer King'..a salesman pleaded guilty [to misrepresenting napthalene as a borer cure]. **1968** SLATTER *Pagan Game* 70 Tank Tarrant, the loot king, cracking open a German paymaster's safe. **1974** MORRIESON *Predicament* (1981) 30 No one wants to pal with a guy who's [*sic*] old man's a metho king. **1994** GRANT *On a Roll* 119 Every fighting unit [in WW2] had its 'two-up king', a skilled organiser who would arrange a game in a matter of minutes... The kings were 'ringies' and in charge of the money. They covered bets that were too big for other players to cover..and ensured the game ran smoothly... The bets complete, [the ringie] yelled 'Come in Spinner' and the designated gambler tossed the pennies.

2. *attrib.* as a prefix connoting the large size, superiority, etc., or special importance of the item described. **a. king cobber**, a great or close friend; **king fleece**, *double fleece* (DOUBLE *a.*) or by synecdoche, a double-fleeced sheep; **king hit** [AND 1917], a knock-out punch or blow, (occas. as a *v.*); **king table**, the first or top table of a euchre party; **king tide**, a high spring tide; **king tree**, the 'key' tree which when felled sets off a timber drive (see also KEY *n.*² 2).
   1984 WILSON S. *Pacific Street* 6 It was as if we were **king cobbers**, engaged on some secret project together. **1975** DAVIES *Outback* 82 These **king fleeces** are crafty old ewes who have been too shrewd to be caught in the muster... Having missed the shearing, they carried enormous fleeces—hence the name, **king fleeces**. **1961**

CRUMP *Hang On a Minute Mate* 164 There were some tough rags in that little bunch [of belligerent bushwhackers]. One **king-hit** and I was a goner. **1975** ANDERSON *Men of Milford Road* 101 (Griffiths Collect.) During the evening someone or other was alleged to have administered a king hit, because he laid his opponent out cold. **1980** MACKENZIE *While We Have Prisons* 97 *king hit* an unexpected and crushing blow usually causing severe injury. **1990** *Dominion* (Wellington) 3 Nov. 4 Henman's revenge took the form of a 'king hit' on the forehead with a glass beer handle. **1993** *Dominion* (Wellington) 25 May 13 He 'kinghit' and 'decked' Danny Sekona and then stabbed him. **1980** WOOLLASTON *Sage Tea* 41 The table [in the Huinga public hall c1915] they used as the **King table** at the Wednesday night euchre parties became an altar. **1987** SCOTT *Seven Lives on Salt River* 53 [Caption] The tide rules. *Tui* caught on the Otamatea, and Pahi Motel marooned in 1938 by a **king tide** and strong south-westerlies. **1972** NEWTON *Wake of Axe* 155 A gang would sometimes scarf for a full week before they let the '**King**' tree go... Each tree in that area would have a scarf cut in it to the point where it was about to fall, and when the whole of that particular area was completed the 'King' tree would be felled [and set the others falling].

b. In the names of plants and animals, see: CRAB 2 (1), FERN 2 (11), PENGUIN 2 (4), PINE 2 (6), SHAG 2 (9), TARAKIHI 2. See also KING BARRACOUTA, KINGFISH, KINGFISHER.

king: see *day for a king* (DAY 2); *not to call the king one's uncle* (CALL *v*. 3).

kingaseeny, var. KINGY-SEENY.

king barracouta. Also **king couta**. [Prob. f KING(FISH + BARRACOUTA.] GEMFISH.
 1927 SPEIGHT et al. *Nat. Hist. Canterbury* 199 A related family includes..the King Barracouta, *Jordanidia solandrii* (often known locally as Kingfish, but not to be confused with the North Island Kingfish which is a form or Yellowtail). **1966** DOOGUE & MORELAND *Sea Anglers' Guide* 280 Southern Kingfish..: *Jordanidia solandri*; kingfish, hake, barraconda; king barracouta, Tasmanian kingfish (Australia); tikati. **1981** WILSON *Fisherman's Bible* 30 King Barracouta: See Southern Kingfish and Hake, the two names the King Couta goes under in New Zealand.

King Country.

1. *Hist*. Also occas. early **King's country**, occas. **King's territory**. An area in the central North Island roughly between Te Awamutu and Taupo, a territory which for a time in the 19th century was under the Maori King's control, and susceptible to his mana and authority. Often *attrib*. Cf. KING *n*.¹ 2, MAORI KING.
 1859 *McLean Papers* (ATLTS) V. 201 The natives of the 'King Party' have intimated to Mr Cheltham their intention of preventing him from bringing spirits into the 'King's Territory'. **1873** TINNE *Wonderland of Antipodes* 6 Behind us rose the mountain of Pironghia, on the border of the 'King's country'. **1874** TROLLOPE *NZ* 157 Alexandra..is so near the 'King' country that a moderate walk would place you in his Majesty's dominions. **1887** *Auckland Weekly News* 26 Mar. 8 The so-called King Country is rapidly undergoing development. **1900** *TrNZI* XXXII. 365 The Maru-iwi lived contiguous to the east coast, in a district till lately known as 'the King-country'. **1910** COWAN *Maoris of NZ* 294 The men..finally faced death..in the famous redoubt at Orakau, on the borders of what afterwards came to be known as the King Country. **1944** MULGAN *From Track to Highway* 58 In the end he took refuge in the King Country. **1964** NORRIS *Settlers in Depression* 1 These military settlements were formed with the object of stopping the Maoris, who had retreated to what is now called the King Country.

2. In modern use (/ˈkɪŋˌkʌntri/), the North Island region roughly contiguous with the former territory of the Maori King, until recent times a 'dry' area within which alcoholic liquor could not be sold.
 1885 *Wairarapa Daily* 28 Feb. 2 Hitherto, the attention of these three places, during the present attack, has been directed towards the Tuhua District, or as it is more vaguely termed, the King Country. **1893** *TrNZI* XXV. 353 Mr. Max von Bernewitz..showed me..some fragments of rocks which had been forwarded from the King-country. **1905** BAUCKE *White Man Treads* 188 What a refutation of the outcry—'Drunken King Country! Debauched King Country! Sly-grog selling King Country!' till one sickens of the sound. **1916** *Chron. NZEF* 27 Dec. 201 The latter is making me rapidly forget my poor old girl of the king country [*sic*]. **1920** MACDONALD *Austral. & NZ Sheepfarming* 123 The King country (New Zealand) method of breaking in fern lands is well worth recording. **1926** DEVANNY *Butcher Shop* (1981) 28 It lay right on the borderline of the King Country, wherein prohibition reigned. **1959** MIDDLETON *The Stone* 33 There was not another man like him anywhere in the King Country. **1973** SARGESON *Once Is Enough* 13 By that time one of my sisters had been to stay with another King Country relative, on a farm even more remote than my uncle's. **1989** PARKINSON *Travelling Naturalist* 48 The King Country is named after the movement King Tawhiao led last century to resist alienation of Maori land.

3. In special Comb. poss. alluding to the preoccupation with liquor of the European community in an area previously 'dry': **King Country spanner**, a bottle-opener, often with the crest of the town of Taumarunui on it.
 1958 *Truth* 27 May 14 There are those who nostalgically look back on the days of no-licence and sly grog and wonder where the move to have the King Country union discard the traditional 'King Country spanner' as its emblem originated... The King Country spanner was more than just a bottle-opener—it was a symbol of stout-hearted refusal to submit meekly to a 'dry' regime that King Country thought was unjustly imposed on it. **1959** *Weekly News* (Auckland) 4 Mar. 22 After all, up to last year King Country stalwarts went out to Rugby battle bearing a magnificent 'King Country spanner'—a replica of a bottle opener. **1968** *NZ Contemp. Dict. Suppl.* (Collins) 11 *King Country spanner n.* bottle opener.

king couta: see KING BARRACOUTA.

king crab: see CRAB 2 (1).

King Dick. *Hist*.

1. The familiar nickname of Richard John Seddon (1845–1906), an impressively authoritarian Prime Minister of New Zealand (1893–1906), current to c1914, then a freq. historical use.
 1902 HARPER *Lett. from NZ* 1 Feb. (1914) 302 Richard Seddon, known as 'King Dick'. **1921** BRYCE *Modern Democracies* (1929) II. 300 Richard Seddon, or King Dick as he was commonly and affectionately called, was born at St. Helens in Lancashire in 1845. **1948** LIPSON *Politics of Equality* 366 Neither Seddon in his 'King Dick' era nor Ward..displayed after 1900 the initiative he had shown before. **1959** SINCLAIR *Hist. NZ* 186 From the late nineties until 1906 New Zealand was ruled by a benevolent despot known as 'King Dick'. **1962** LAWLOR *More Wellington Days* 117 And then 'King Dick' himself, an imposing figure. **1974** MULDOON *Rise and Fall of a Young Turk* 7 Her [*sc*. Muldoon's mother's] hero..was Seddon, and I too grew to regard 'King Dick' as New Zealand's greatest politician. **1986** RICHARDS *Off the Sheep's Back* 7 It was a monument to 'King Dick', New Zealand Prime Minister Richard John Seddon. **1992** *Dominion Sunday Times* (Wellington) 9 Aug. 9 He [*sc*. R. E. Muldoon] was the most active Prime Minister since his idol, King Dick Seddon.

2. Applied to persons or animals as a name or nickname.
 1905 *TrNZI* XXXVII. 35 Riki Tatahunga, better known as 'King Dick', died recently at Tauranga... His illness was ascribed to witchcraft, brought on because he appeared as advocate against his own tribe in a Land Court case. **1920** *Otago Witness* (Dunedin) 28 Dec. 1 The lion at Wellington Zoo, known as King Dick, is suffering from paralysis of the legs.

3. [With a play on the *king*-prefix] *Obs. fig*. KINGFISHER.
 1905 THOMSON *Bush Boys* 59 'There's no other place a patch on it for King-dick's nests...' 'King-dick' is the colonial boys' name for the native Kingfisher.

4. A children's prisoners'-base game. [Prob. f. KINGY-SEENY, *king caesar*, etc. influenced by *King Dick* 1.]
 1971 SHADBOLT *Bullshit & Jellybeans* 25 It was [at Blockhouse Bay school c1950s] Kingaseeny (or Bulldog, King Dick or Bar-the-Door for those outside Auckland) at lunchtime, rugby on Wednesday, the gang after school. **1972** [see KINGY-SEENY].

kingey, var. KINGI.

kingfish. [Spec. use of *kingfish*, any of various fish noted for size or value as food: AND 1825.] Either of two unrelated and very different fishes of families Carangidae 'northern kingfish', or Gempylidae 'southern kingfish'. **a.** *Seriola lalandi* (fam. Carangidae), a recognized gamefish of mainly North Island open waters, distinctively coloured blue-green often with a pale bronze sheen above and silvery-white below, and having a pale yellow to brass-coloured strip extending along the flank from the eye to the tail. Also called **yellowtail kingfish**, **northern (North Island) kingfish**. See also HAKU, KINGIE, YELLOWTAIL 2 (3).
 1872 HUTTON & HECTOR *Fishes NZ* 111 The Haku of the natives is the King Fish (*Seriola lalandii*) of Wellington and the Yellow Tail of Australia. **1898** MORRIS *Austral-English* 248 *King-fish, n*. In New Zealand a sea-fish..(Maori, *Haku*), sometimes called the *Yellow Tail*. **1912** *Dominion* (Wellington) 19 Jan. 4 A large king-fish, weighing 37 lb, was caught off the Onehunga wharf on Tuesday. **1921** THOMSON & ANDERTON *Hist. Portobello* 78 North Island Kingfish; Yellowtail *Seriola lalandii*... This fish is occasionally met with on this coast, but only during the summer months. **1926** GREY *Angler's Eldorado* 41 I saw a huge kingfish, so the boatman called it..If he was not a regular old yellowtail, belonging to the family *seriola*, then I missed my classification. The boatmen call this species kingfish; but kingfish belong to the mackerel family, and there was no mackerel about this fish. **1936** *Handbook for NZ* (ANZAAS) 72 *Seriola grandis* (=*S. lalandi* of earlier authors): Kingfish (of North Island), yellow-tail. **1943** MANNERING *Eighty Years NZ* 175 The 'kingfish' of the northern waters is not the kingfish of the Christchurch market (which is akin to the barracouda)... His scientific name is Seriola Lalandii and his Maori appellation 'haku'. **1953** *Landfall* 27 177

KINGFISHER

Her lover was a kingfish hung in the moonlight. **1967** MORELAND *Marine Fishes* 50 Yellowtail or Northern Kingfish... The Maori name haku is still in use. **1979** *Commercial Fishing* Nov. 29 The two species beyond any doubt with the best prospects for fishing in Northern New Zealand waters are snapper and northern Kingfish (Yellow-tail). **1986** PAUL *NZ Fishes* 88 Yellowtail Kingfish *Seriola lalandi*... The name yellowtail is widely used internationally, and Southern Yellowtail is recommended for New Zealand fish. However, the name kingfish is well established and unlikely to be discarded, being also applied to a number of related and unrelated species in different countries. Yellowtail Kingfish is perhaps a reasonable compromise. **1990** *Evening Post* (Wellington) 26 Sept. 46 Kingfish especially, are creatures of habit, they will generally feed at particular times of the day.

b. *Rexea* (formerly *Jordanidia*) *solandri* (fam. Gempylidae) GEMFISH. Also called the **silver (southern, South Island) kingfish**. See also HAKE 1 c.

1911 WAITE *Rec. Canterbury Museum* I. 236 *Rexea Furcifera*..King fish. **1921** THOMPSON & ANDERTON *Hist. Portobello* 78 Southern Kingfish *Rexea furcifera*... This fish is very common in the Dunedin shops, being taken nearly all the year round both by the trawlers and the line fishermen. **1936** *Handbook for NZ* (ANZAAS) 72 *Jordanidia solandri*: Hake (Wellington), kingfish (Otago), barraconda (Auckland and Napier). **1936, 1957** [see HAKE 1 c]. **1957** WILLIAMS *Dict. Maori Lang.* 417 *Tikati*... *Jordanidia solandri* hake, South Island kingfish. **1967** NATUSCH *Animals NZ* 226 Family Gempylidae. The barracouta..and the bright, blue-backed, silver-sided southern Kingfish..both grow to about five-feet long. **1970** SORENSEN *Nomenclature NZ Fish* 32 *Kingfish, silver*..: *Rexea solandri*..Suggested commercial name[s]: Silver Kingfish; Silver King..Other common names: Southern Kingfish. **1978, 1982, 1986** [see GEMFISH].

kingfisher. [Transf. use of northern hemisphere kingfisher *Alcedo atthis* (fam. Alcedinidae).] *Halcyon sancta vagans* (fam. Alcedinidae), a small dumpy fish- and insect-eating bird with large head, heavy bill and iridescent blue and green plumage. Also with modifiers indicating a New Zealand provenance (**Maori, New Zealand**). See also KING DICK 3, KOTARETARE.

1773 FORSTER *Resolution Jrnl.* 2 Apr. (1982) II. 245 In the morning..I went..to the Indian Cove, & shot there two new Kingfishers. **1834** MARKHAM *NZ* (1963) 41 Shot some King fishers and a Duck or two. **1843** DIEFFENBACH *Travels in NZ* I. 59 Kingfishers, oystercatchers, tuis, and cormorants enlivened the trees on its shores. **1857** HURSTHOUSE *NZ* I. 120 The kingfisher, the chiming bell-bird, black robin, flycatcher..are common round every homestead. **1870** *TrNZI* II. 52 We have counted as many as eight of our Kingfishers sitting in company; after a heavy rain we have observed, on our lawn, several of the croquet hoops occupied at one time by these striking-looking birds. **1883** DOMETT *Ranolf & Amohia* I. 154 Let some *kingfisher* Slip darting from the post. **1897** *TrNZI* XXIX. 140 Take, for instance, the common Maori kingfisher (*Halcyon vagans* = Kotaretare). **1905** WHITE *My NZ Garden* 69 The native Kingfisher is a very conspicuous-looking bird, much larger than the English species. **1920** MANSFIELD *Stories* (1984) 233 A lovely kingfisher perched on the paddock fence preening his rich beauty. **1957** FRAME *Owls Do Cry* (1967) 19 And a kingfisher, colour-fast, will sit on a telegraph wire and be stroked. **1964** [see KOTARETARE]. **1989** PARKINSON *Travelling Naturalist* 100 Kingfishers were considered by the Maori to be unlucky and if a war party came across one, the battle would be called off. **1990** *Checklist Birds NZ* 191 *Halcyon sancta vagans*..New Zealand Kingfisher (*Kotare*).

kingie. Also **kingey, kingi.** [AND 1936.] KINGFISH a.

1920 *Quick March* 10 Feb. 38 The island received its name from the myriads of kingfish there... To fish there requires..a few hundred fathoms of spare line if you want to haul in the biggest old 'kingeys' of them all. **1968** [see COUTA]. **1984** WILSON S. *Pacific Street* 44 'Won't it be terrific,' Martha said. 'Mayor Island's supposed to be fantastic for kingies and bronzies and black coral and all that.' **1985** *NZ Outdoor* Oct–Nov. 3 Harbour Kingfish—When the kingis are running the action can be fast and furious. **1991** BRADSTOCK *Fishing* 20 *Kingfish*. Other names: kingie, yellowtail kingfish, haku, *Seriola lalandi*.

kingism. *Hist.* [f. KING n.¹ + -ism.] KINGITANGA. See also MAORI KING.

1862 *AJHR* E-7 9 With many Natives the idea of kingism is of a very vague and indefinite character. **1863** MORGAN *Journal* July (1963) 49 It [Moketu] was a hot bed of kingism—the pa where plans were concocted and bloody resolves made. **1871** MEADE *Ride through Disturbed Dist.* in Taylor *Early Travellers* (1959) 480 It [sc. a comet] appears to hang directly over Taranaki, the hotbed of Kingism and rebellion, and its presence is interpreted by the Maories in very different modes. **1878** BULLER *Forty Yrs. NZ* 134 Here [at Ngaruawahia], in the heart of 'Kingism'..no communication with any white person was permitted, by the 'King' natives.

kingitanga. With init. cap. [Ma. /ˈkiːŋitaŋa/: Williams Appendix *Kīngi*: f. Ma. *kīngi* (ad. English *king*) + *-tanga*, one of a number of suffixes forming abstract nouns from common nouns; Duval II. 179 *kingitanga* = 'reign' 1830, = 'Maori kingship', 1860.] Belief in and support for the idea of a Maori king or Maori kingship.

1860 *Richmond-Atkinson Papers* (1960) I. 540 Ta Kerei publicly acknowledged his adhesion to the Kingitanga. **1922** COWAN *NZ Wars* I. 233 But the Kingitanga was the stumbling-block. **1985** HOWE *Towards 'Taha Maori'* in *English* (NZATE) 20 Kingitanga—this word refers to the King movement and all it stands for. Belief in the kingitanga rests strongly with the Tainui people and the Waikato Maniapoto, and is being increasingly accepted as a positive force for all Maoridom by other tribes and regions. **1986** IHIMAERA *Matriarch* 212 She wanted him to be an emissary between her people and the Kingitanga movement.

Kingite. *Hist.* [f. KING n.¹ + -ite.] **a.** A supporter of the Maori King and kingitanga. Cf. QUEENITE.

1857 ASHWELL *Lett. & Jrnl.* (ATLTS) II. 290 The other party, the Kingites, anxious for the entire independence of their country. **1860** BUDDLE *Maori King Movement* 14 The great body of the Waikatos returned home, and the Kingites proceeded to Rangiaohia to complete the installation of their sovereign. **1879** FEATON *Waikato War* 6 The Kingites, as the Waikatos styled themselves, were so called on account of their having set up for themselves a King. **1882** POTTS *Out in Open* 10 Messages arrive that it would suit the Kingites to postpone..the progress to Hikurangi. **1910** COWAN *Maoris of NZ* 289 All might have gone well had the Kingites been able to restrain their more turbulent spirits. **1938** WILY & MAUNSELL *Robert Maunsell* 130 The Kingites resolved to thoroughly investigate the matter, and for that purpose a large party of them set out for Patumahoe. **1959** SINCLAIR *Hist. NZ* 112 The Kingites were not merely copying the settlers' political organization.

b. *attrib.* (1965 quot. prob. represents a *transf.* use.)

KING MOVEMENT

1860 *Richmond-Atkinson Papers* (1960) I. 600 One of the Kingite chiefs here..returned not long ago from Waikato. **1871** MEADE *Ride through Disturbed Dist.* in Taylor *Early Travellers* (1959) 427 Amongst the whole of the 'Queenites' (in contradistinction to the 'Kingite' followers of the so-styled Maori king) Poihipi is probably the most influential chief. **1882** POTTS *Out in Open* 27 So ended this great meeting of Kingite natives. **1908** STEWART *My Simple Life* 84 This Te Kooti..maintained a guerilla resistance..for many years after our 'Kingite' neighbours had accepted British authority. **1938** WILY & MAUNSELL *Robert Maunsell* 22 He knew that a trial of force was the inevitable corollary of the kingite movement. **1941** SUTHERLAND *Numismatic Hist. NZ* 176 Two Kingite chiefs visited Vienna. **1965** *Dominion* (Wellington) 2 Sept. 2 Te Rauparaha retaliated when the people east and west of the Waikato cared not to join his kingite movement by a campaign of slaughter in these areas.

King-maker. *Hist.* [Spec. use of *the Kingmaker* the popular designation of the Earl of Warwick (1420–71) for his part in securing the accession of Edward IV and the restoration of Henry VI.] Formerly one who supported the idea of and helped to establish a Maori king, usu. or specifically (with **the** and init. cap.) applied to Wiremu Tamihana Tarapipipi Te Waharoa (William Thompson) (?–1866), 'Ngati Haua leader, teacher, diplomat' (DNZB), and also to his descendants.

1857 *Richmond-Atkinson Papers* 2 June (1960) I. 271 The actual business to be done at the meeting [of the Waikato Maori] is of less moment than the meeting itself. For the Native Doctors seem to argue that it is necessary that the British Government should oppose to the King Makers something of greater eclat..than the village circuit. **1879** FEATON *Waikato War* 6 The idea of having a king, or the king movement, was started by Wiremu Thompson one of the leading Waikato chiefs, who was afterwards called 'The King-maker'. **1899** GRACE *Sketch NZ War* 148 The national movement under Wiremu Tamihana, the King-maker, and the wave of religious enthusiasm called 'Hau-hauism' which followed it. **1922** COWAN *NZ Wars* I. 154 The kingmaker's appeals to the *pakeha* Administration read pathetically. **1938** WILY & MAUNSELL *Robert Maunsell* 46 At Te Akau..lived Wiremu Tamehana (William Thompson), who must not be confused with the much greater personage..who, a few years later, came to be known as 'The Kingmaker'. **1946** BEAGLEHOLE *Some Modern Maoris* 290 It is true that two of the early king-makers were associated with local Maoris. **1968** SLATTER *Pagan Game* 108 Kevin [a teacher] was rambling on about a television quiz he had seen the previous evening and when a contestant was asked who was the Kingmaker he had promptly replied Warwick. Kevin held that any patriotic New Zealander should have said Wiremu Tamihana. **1986** BELICH *NZ Wars* 76 The contemporary misnomers 'moderates' and 'extremists' have stuck to the two major parties [of the King Movement], represented by Wiremu Tamehana ('The Kingmaker') and Rewi Maniapoto respectively. **1990** *DNZB* I. 516 During the late 1850s Tamihana became involved in the establishment of a Maori king. For this he was given the title 'Kingmaker' by Pakeha.

Hence **king-making** *vbl. n.*

1860 BUDDLE *Maori King Movement* 4 [The party] went forth..ostensibly for the purpose of exhorting the chiefs..to submit to the authority of the Governor, but really on a mission of King-making.

King movement. *Hist.* Also **Maori King movement.** A Maori attempt from the late 1850s to achieve unity of purpose and action under the guidance of a single leader, the Maori King.

1858 *Richmond-Atkinson Papers* 21 June (1960) I. 408 The *hui* at Rangiaohia to promote the Maori King movement broke up. **1864** GORST *Maori King* 39 If we had educated the natives in civilisation..as British subjects..nothing would have been heard of 'land-leagues' and 'king-movements'. **1879** [see KING-MAKER]. **1884** KERRY-NICHOLLS *King Country* 6 In 1854..Te Heuheu..summoned a native council in Taupo, when the King movement began in earnest. **1892** *NZ Official Handbook* 275 He [*sc.* King Tawhio] has..quite recently..accepted a pension from the present Native Minister... It is hoped that it will lead to the end of the 'King movement'. **1908** *AJHR C-11* 3 During the first half of the last century, before the 'King' movement shut up so much of the centre of the North Island from the colonist, more than one traveller..had managed to evade the Native guardians of the place. **1959** SINCLAIR in Gorst *Maori King* xiii The King movement survives today, though its followers are less numerous than a century ago. **1977** KING *Te Puea* 38 [The Mercer and Ngati Tipa people] initiated the 'whitebait tribute' by which commercial buyers from Maori fishermen paid a tax that went towards expenses for King Movement practices.

king-o-sene, var. KINGY-SEENY.

king party. *Hist.* [f. KING *n.*¹ + *party*.] The party or supporters of the Maori King as distinct from the KUPAPA or party 'friendly' to Europeans.

1859 [see KING COUNTRY 1]. **1860** BUDDLE *Maori King Movement* 72 It becomes..the duty of those entrusted with native interests..to enter promptly into negotiations [*sic*] with the king party. **1868** TAYLOR *Past & Present NZ* 116 He indignantly threw down the Crown grant and left, to become a leader of the king party.

King's country: see KING COUNTRY 1.

king seenie, var. KINGY-SEENY.

King's territory: see KING COUNTRY 1.

kingy-seeny. Also with much variety of form as **keeney-seeney, keeny-seeny, kingaseeny, King-o-sene, King Seenie**, etc. (see esp. quot. 1972). [Alterations of *King Caesar*, a children's tagging game (often with a crowning or 'kinging' ceremony of patting on the head or back), widespread in most English-speaking communities under this and many other names: see OED, EDD.] A children's tagging game. See also KING DICK 4.

1905 THOMSON *Bush Boys* 84 Others wanted [to play] 'Prisoners' Base' or 'Chivvy', 'Brewer', 'Egg-in-the hat', 'Duck-stone', 'Red Rover', or 'Kingy-seeny'... Kingy-seeny' it was to them and they did not care whether that had a meaning or not. *Ibid.* 125 [The game is described.] **1928** *Free Lance* (Wellington) 15 Aug. 35 Beyond that ceremony came trials at 'Kingaseenie' which were essentially tests for discovering speed, swerving and collaring material for the football team. **1953** SUTTON-SMITH *Unorganized Games NZ Primary School Children* (VUWTS) II. 508 The best example of a crowning ceremony is one that was called Kinging. In this ceremony the captive was patted on the head while he lay flat on the ground with other players astride him. If he managed to move during the ceremony, then the rhyme must begin again. 'King-seeny, one two three, You're the very man for me.' **1965** HILLIARD *Power of Joy* 133 He liked nearly all the boys [at primary school in early 1930s]... They played cock-fighting and keeny-seeny. **1971** Kingaseeny [see KING DICK 4]. **1972** SUTTON-SMITH *Folkgames Children* 81 The most widely known and most popular tagging game in all historical periods— in fact, the most popular game in New Zealand—was undoubtedly the game known variously as *Bar the Door* (E-8)..Julius Caesar; King Caesar; King's Den; King Dick; King O'Seenie; King O'Weenie; King Seenie; King Seize-Her; King-a-Sene. **1978** King-a-sene [see BULLRUSH]. **1984** LOCKE *The Kauri & the Willow* 80 If he caught a runner, the King would pat his head three times and say, 'King of Seni, one two three, you're the only man for me. King, king, king!' **1988** *Back Then—Volume Two* (Oral History Birkenhead) 89 We played [at Northcote school c1908] what they used to call King-o-sene (*sp*?). **1992** CONDON *Hurleyville* 25 A popular game was what we in Hurleyville called Keeney-Seeney. It has a variety of other names. One person would call a boy's name out of the whole group and try an catch him and pat three times on his back before he got to the other end. If not caught the whole school would go to the other end—any caught would form part of the catching team.

'kin oath: see OATH c (b).

kio, var. NGAIO.

kiokio. [Ma. /ˈkiokio/: Williams 118 *Kiokio*, n. *1. Blechnum capense*.] *Blechnum* sp. (formerly treated as *B. capense*) (fam. Blechnaceae), a robust native fern with long drooping fronds commonly found on damp road banks and alongside forest streams. See also *hard fern* (FERN 2 (6)).

1922 COWAN *NZ Wars* (1955) II. 355 A large body of Hauhaus was in concealment behind a thick bank of the drooping *kiokio* ferns. **1952** RICHARDS *Chatham Is.* 13 *B[lechnum] capense*... Long Hard-fern. Kio Kio. **1969** HARVEY & GODLEY *Botanical Paintings* 10 *Blechnum capense* Long Hard-fern: Kiokio Blechnaceae. Kiokio is one of our commonest ferns, and..is widespread and adaptable. **1983** *Whakarewarewa Forest Park* 50 Fronds of the kiokio usually cover the banks of streams or the sides of roads.

kiore. Also early **E-keré** (=He kiore), **keuree**. [Ma. /kiore/: Williams 119 *Kiore*, n. *1*. Rat, mouse.] **a.** The Polynesian rat (*Rattus exulans*), RAT *n.*¹ 1

[*Note*] Polack (quot. 1838) is apparently applying the name to an introduced ship rat.

[**1804** *Collins English Colony in NSW* 561 E-keré, A rat. **1815** KENDALL *New Zealanders' First Book* 16 Keuree A rat. **1820** LEE AND KENDALL *NZ Grammar and Vocabulary* 164 Kí re; A mouse, rat &c.] **1838** POLACK *NZ* I. 314 The *kiore*, or rat, has been introduced at an early period by European vessels. **1849** STRANGE *Journal* 7 Mar in *Canterbury Papers* (1851) 79 [The Norway rat] destroys the *kiore*, or native rat. **1865** HURSTHOUSE *England's New Zealand War* 38 The Native Rat (Kioré) not larger than the English Water-Rat, is the only indigenous four-footed creature found in New Zealand... The Kioré is now..scarce. **1904** TREGEAR *Maori Race* 106 The small frugivorous rat (*kiore*) was an article of food highly esteemed... When cooked they were like large juicy sausages. **1911** SHAND *Moriori People* 6 Native Rats, called *Kiore*, were common to the [Chatham] island: but it is believed they were not eaten by the Morioris. **1938** *Auckland Weekly News* 21 Aug. 31 The native rat, kiore, was also particularly fond of this flower as food. **1973** *Proc. NZ Ecol. Soc.* XX. 120 Failure to find a single island where kiore have established which also supports a clearly self-maintaining population of tuataras strongly suggests that the species cannot persist in the presence of this rat. **1980** LOCKLEY *House Above the Sea* 168 In camp at White Island in the Bay of Plenty,... we watched kiore scampering around our feet at meal times. **1990** *Handbook NZ Mammals* 175 The kiore is the smallest of the three species of rats in New Zealand, but similar in appearance to the ship rat.

b. As **kiore Maori**, 'native rat', distinguished from *kiore pakeha*, the 'European' (English or Norway) 'rat'.

1843 DIEFFENBACH *Travels in NZ* II. 45 The *kiore maori*, or native rat, and the guana, were once favourite dishes, but they have met with the same fate. **1848** WAKEFIELD *Handbook for NZ* 167 The smaller kind is supposed to have been introduced first, and is called *kiore maori*, or *native rat*. **1866** ANGAS *Polynesia* 55 In New Zealand there exists a frugivorous native rat, called 'kiore maori' by the aborigines, which they distinguish from the European species,... called 'kiore pakeha,' or the stranger rat. **1871** *TrNZI* III. 1 A small rat recently caught..at Wangaehu..has been identified by the Maoris of this district (where it was formerly very abundant) as the veritable Kiore Maori. **1885** *Ibid.* XVII. 205 About one thing [the Maori] are perfectly agreed; the Kiore Maori was good to eat; 'bettern rabbit.' **1986** [see RAT *n.*¹ 1].

kip. Occas. **kippie**. [Perh. f. Brit. dial. *kep v.* to catch; to throw up in the air: see EDD *n.* and *v.* 1; AND 1887.]

1. A small, flat piece of wood used for tossing pennies in two up. See also BAT *n.*²

1909 [see 2 below]. **1912** *Truth* 8 June 1 One James Holt..had on him when arrested two double-headed pennies and three kips, one genuine and two that are known as 'swindling kips', with a hole at the palm into which the good and the bad pennies can..be worked in a way to easily deceive the unwary. **1928** DEVANNY *Dawn Beloved* 162 One man takes the kip and places two pennies on it... He hands [his bet] to the ring-keeper. **1934** *Fielding Star* 6 Feb. 5 Six two-up kips, a crown and anchor board, and a number of double-headed pennies were exhibited in the Police Court at Rotorua. **1976** HILLIARD *Send Somebody Nice* 75 In the centre stood the spinner with his kip and two pennies. **1978** TAYLOR *Twilight Hour* 106 The loss of an arm or a leg did not stop them playing two-up... Hopping around on one leg, tossing the kippie, and then arguing the toss. **1992** COSTELLO *Howard* 50 At the same camp..I was caught running the two-up school; a carry-over from the days when I used to put the pennies on the kip at the Whakatu freezing works.

Hence **kipper** *n. obs.*, a two-up player who holds the kip.

1906 *Truth* 12 May 1 When the 'two-up' school is raided it is a mix-up between 'copper' and 'kipper'.

2. *Fig.* In the phr. **to rush the kip**, to be keen to achieve a hasty decision; to rush into things without due consideration or consultation.

1909 *Truth* 31 July 6 He..aspired to fame..when..he..'rushed the kip', as it were, with Sir Joseph Ward, and asked him to suppress gross and licentious books and literature. **1913** *NZ Bulletin* 8 Feb. 16 It kinder gives a bloke the bloomin' pip to find his efforts all knocked 'umpty dumpty by other blokes what allers rush the kip.

3. *Obs.* The name for a stick in a children's game.

1972 SUTTON-SMITH *Folkgames Children* 159 In this game the cat [a thin 6-inch stick with pointed ends] was sometimes called the Cunning Joe stick (Waikouaiti, Otago, 1900) or the kip (Dunedin, 1895). It was a game for four players.

kipper. [f. the popular association of *kipper* 'a cured herring' with Britons: AND *n.*² 1946, 'A sailor in the Royal Navy; an English person'.] A name for an Englishman or English sailor.

c1951 May p.c. Pugh-Williams An Englishman as opposed to a 'Kiwi'. I have heard this term mainly in the New Zealand Navy. The NZ (Naval) Division was formed in 1921 and it may have been used from this year. **1971** Glover *Poetry NZ*('The Vial') 44 Up in Butler's country I came across it (Butler the young clever Kipper chap, not old Hudibras).

Hence **Kipperland**, Britain.

1963 Glover *Bedside Book* 147 I was trying to explain that this fellow came from England. 'You know—Angleterre, Pomerania, Kipperland.'

kippie: see KIP.

kirikiti: see *Samoan cricket* (SAMOAN 1).

kirimoko. *s South Island*. Also in southern SI (with Ma. /r/ being represented by /l/, and often /k/ being represented by /g/, and final vowel unvoiced) **kilimoko, Killmogue, Kilmog**. [Ma. /'kirimoko/: Williams 119 *Kirimoko*... 2. A tree name ([Ngai] Tahu.).] MANUKA 2 (2); also as an Otago and Southland place-name.

1892 Osborn in Richards *Foveaux Whaling Yarns* (1995) 42 The eleven miles through Killmogue swamp [some miles from the Bluff] was only a narrow footpath made by the natives... The leaves of this bush, or Killmogue, makes [*sic*] excellent tea, and both the whites and natives use it for that purpose. The bush is about ten feet in height and the brush part is very fine. **c1920** Beattie *Trad. Lifeways Southern Maori* (1994) 191 The kilimoko or kirimoko, a kind of small manuka, comes out in white flowers and later in berries. **1995** *Dominion* (Wellington) 21 Aug. 1 [He] had crossed the centre line while driving over the Kilmog hill [20 km north of Dunedin].

kiriwai, var. KEREWAI.

kiss, *n.*[1] [f. the two sections 'kissing' after being pressed together: the 1883 quot. illustrates the orig. Brit. sense (OED *n.* 3, 1825) a small sweetmeat, a sugar plum; *New SOD* (1993) 4 'A small cake..; a sweet, a chocolate.'] A small cake usu. of an upper and lower part joined together with icing or jam; and with cocoa added, **Maori kiss**.

[**1883** *Brett's Colonists' Guide* 619 Kisses.—Whisk the whites of 8 eggs to a stiff, solid froth, then stir gently in by degrees 1 pound of finest powdered sugar... Lay the mass out in shape of small half-eggs... sieve fine sugar over the top, and then bake them in a moderate oven.] **1936** *Cook. Book NZ Women's Inst.* (4edn.) 143 Kisses. Quarter lb butter, $\frac{1}{4}$ lb sugar, 2 eggs..flour..1 cup ground rice (small), 1 good teaspoon baking powder, essence to taste. Beat butter and sugar to cream. Add eggs, then flour with powder and ground rice, and lastly essence. Bake in hot oven in small teaspoon lots, then fasten together with butter icing or jam. **c1945** *Tui's Commonsense Cook.* 248 *Kiss.* What you need:— 2 oz. butter. 1 teacup sugar. 2 eggs. $\frac{3}{4}$ cup flour. $\frac{1}{2}$ teacup cornflour. 1 heaped teaspoon b. powder. [etc.] **1955** *New Home Cook. Book* 146 Maori kisses (*Very Nice*) Two..tablespoons of sugar, 4 tablespoons of butter, $\frac{1}{2}$ cup shelled walnuts, 1 cup chopped dates, 1 cup of flour, 1 tablespoon cocoa, $\frac{1}{4}$ teaspoon vanilla..[etc.] **1961** *Edmonds Sure to Rise Cook. Book* 18 Kisses..drop in teaspoon lots on cold oven shelf and bake in quick oven (400° F.); when cold, put together with jam and sprinkle with icing sugar. **1989** McGill *Dinkum Kiwi Dict.* 66 *Maori kisses* old-fashioned Kiwi biscuits using cocoa, milk, butter, flour, sugar and baking powder.

kiss, *n.*[2] [Transf. use of a similar term in the game of billiards: see OED *n.* 2 b.] A play in a marble game where one marble strikes another lightly and stops.

1953 Sutton-Smith *Unorganized Games NZ Primary School Children* (VUWTS) II. 769 Action terms related to the movements of the marbles are, Throughs and No Throughs, Tracks and Clears, Stops and Rolls, Lay-Up, Manyies, Kiss, Ons.

kit, *n.*[1] Occas. early **ket** (*pl. kets*) and **kite**. [In most uses ad. Ma. *kete* /'kete/, poss. from an anglicized form *kite* (/'kɪte/), later reinforced in early settlement by Brit. dialect (and possibly US) *kit*: see OED *kit* 1 b a kind of basket, esp. one made of straw and rushes for holding fish, 1847–48.] In general use, KETE, a basket woven from strips of flax.

1. a. In Maori contexts, representing Ma. *kete*, often as a container for fruit, vegetables or shellfish, esp. kumara and potatoes. (a) **kit** forms (see also *flax kit* FLAX 5 c).

1834 Markham *NZ* (1963) 46 They make Baskets or Kits as we call them for Potatoes. **1841** Bidwill *Rambles in NZ* (1952) 79 Taking a kit in my own hand, [I] set off in the direction of the water-course in order to botanise. **1854** *Richmond-Atkinson Papers* (1960) I. 155 I find it quite impossible to get any kits for Mrs Blundell. The natives here are too profitably occupied in agriculture to give any time to the making of kits. **1863** Moser *Mahoe leaves* 34 Things..were got ready at last, and served up in baskets made of flax, known as kits. **1881** Campbell *Poenamo* 107 The [native] oven is a simple contrivance whereby a kit of kumeras or an entire Maori can be cooked with equal convenience. **1898** Morris *Austral-English* 249 Kit, *n.* a flexible Maori basket; not the English *kit* used by soldiers, but the Maori word *kete*, a basket. **1903** *TrNZI* XXXV. 22 On these were piled about half a dozen kits (flax baskets) of kumara. **1930** Reischek *Yesterdays in Maoriland* (1933) 204 And a piece of uncooked meat in a flax-basket (*kit*) to take with him. **1958** Ashton-Warner *Spinster* 41 'When I comes to this word "basket" in my book I never says "basket".' 'Oh?' 'I allays says "kit".' 'Why?' ''Cause "basket" it's too much like swearing so I says "kit".' **1961** in *Listener Short Stories* (1977) 56 On the back of a truck, guarding a kit of soft-drinks between her knees, a kuia..sat smoking.

(b) **kite** forms (*obs.*).

1845 Meurant *Diary* (TS) 10 A native of this place..complained of the soldier stealing 43 Kites of potatoes and 24 fowls and wished to be paid. **1845** Taylor *Journal* (ATLTS) III. 47 50 kites of potatoes. **1858** Smith *Notes of Journey* 13 Jan. in Taylor *Early Travellers* (1959) 360 We..were enlivened by a good hour's *tangi* between our guide and the woman..at the end of which our guide.. knocked off, and fell upon a *kite* of potatoes.

(c) **ket** forms (*obs.*).

1850 *Church Missionary Intelligence* I. 17/408 Enormous kets of taro. **1861** *Richmond-Atkinson Papers* (1960) I. 705 You are summoned to appear before me..for having entered [Nopera's] premises and from there pulled without his leave one Ket of Corn. **1865** Carter *Life NZ* 432 He returned with two kets or baskets of plantains. **1872** Ward *Life Among Maories* 52 The Maori baskets, still in general use among both races, are called *Kets*.

b. In non-Maori contexts. (a) A Maori kit in general use as a basket.

1868 Chudleigh *Diary* 25 Feb. (1950) 216 I found a kit of apples most uncomfortable to carry. **1875** *Evening Post* (Wellington) 30 Jan. 2 The accused offered to carry her kit. **1886** Butler *Glimpses Maoriland* 85 We took with us kits—New Zealand bags made of flax. **1922** Mansfield *Journal* (1954) 305 'There, mother, let me take him!' said the young woman anxiously, quietly. She tossed the kit away. **1949** *Here & Now* Oct. 18 The nightmarish business of struggling on and off vehicles with a folding push-chair, a heavy baby, a kit of napkins. **1973** Finlayson *Brown Man's Burden* (Pearson's Gloss.) 141 kit: hand bag or basket made of flax

(b) Often as **string kit**, a (string) shopping-bag or basket.

1941 Baker *NZ Slang* 55 We have also put into wide use the term *kit* for a shopping basket. **1946** Soljak *NZ* 116 New Zealand colloquialisms which are of Maori origin include:.. *kit:* shopping bag; from Maori *kete* (flax basket). **1960** Hilliard *Maori Girl* 210 On Friday nights they went shopping together..Arthur carrying the string kits. **1975** *Islands* XI. 33 She had categories. Briefcase/toolbag/string kit. **1981** Anderson *Both Sides of River* 21 They walked nearly four kilometres [to school c1882, Canterbury]..their books and lunch packed in a 'Maori-kit' (coarse string bag) slung over their backs. **1986** O'Sullivan *Pilate Tapes* 59 Put her shoes in the string kit and the kit under a big gum. **1989** [see 2 below].

2. As **Maori kit**, a KETE.

1856 Fitton *NZ* 68 The natives generally bring their produce to market in neatly made baskets, plaited from flax and known by the name of 'Maori kits'. **1873** Barker *Station Amusements* 7 I give my few simple orders to the cook, and prepare, to pack a 'Maori kit', or flat basket made of flax, which could be fastened to my side-saddle. **1893** Ferguson *Bush Life* 287 She was evidently obtaining supplies of necessary stores; and the various parcels..though placed in a Maori kit, seemed to weigh considerably. **1907** Mansfield *Urewera Notebook* (1978) 62 I got a Maori kit. **1914** in *Hist. N. Otago from 1853* (1978) 117 Waving a Maori kit which contained her supper in a 'Blue Peter', she [*sc.* a tipsy woman] chased them down the platform. **1934** Lee *Children of Poor* (1949) 88 Mother would come home with a scrag end of meat..a fragment of this or a portion of that, all wrapped in newspaper and carried in a Maori kit. **1946** [see KETE]. **1959** Taylor *Early Travellers* 360 [1959 Note explaining the form *kite*.] A bag-shaped basket woven of flax, cabbage-tree leaves, &c.; frequently called a 'Maori kit'. **1972** Baxter *Collected Poems* (1980) 585 We can go out with Maori kits to gather Watercress. **1989** *Pacific Way* Jan. 10 A Maori kit, or kete, is actually a string shopping bag.

3. Applied to a Melanesian woven bag.

1856 Patteson in Yonge *Life John Coleridge Patteson* (1874) I. 247 Walking about in the hot sun, with a Melanesian kit, as we call them, slung around the neck, with clothes and books, is really fatiguing.

4. In composition **kitful (kit-full)**, the amount of a full kit, often as a measure.

c1872 in Meredith *Adventuring in Maoriland* (c1875) (1935) 36 In this hole they [*sc.* Maori hangi-builders] put some kindling..[and] put a kitful of stones..on top of the faggots, and light the kindling. **1879** *Auckland Weekly News* 6 Dec. 8 So far the natives have been very successful, one old woman getting a large kitful every day. **1882** Hay *Brighter Britain* II. 175 As proof of the re-establishment of cordial relations, kitsful of peaches, melons, kumera, taro, and other gifts were carried by the party. **1902** Satchell *Land of Lost* 161 I will give you a kitful when you go away. **1935** Maxwell *Recollections* 28 A large kit-full of peaches could at that time be purchased for a shilling. **1951** Kohere *Autobiography of a Maori* 127 One could always expect to bring home a kitful of kehe. **1975**

SUMMERS *Anna of Strathallan* 24 You're positively reeking of beer. I can only suspect that Barney, as usual, had a kitful of bottles.

5. In the phr. **to carry the kit**, to run errands for family household needs, etc.
 1911 FOSTON *Bell Bird's Lair* 12 The lad hesitated. He was tired of carrying the kit and said so.

kit, *n.*² *Obs.* [f. various senses and uses of *kit* an assembly of articles.]
1. See quot.
 1933 *Press* (Christchurch) (Acland Gloss.) 4 Nov. 15 *Kit* or *Kitt.*—A bundle of (usually flax) sticks with a coat or blanket over them, strapped on the pommel of a saddle to help a rider to stick to a bucking horse.
2. A 'pack' of liquor.
 1905 *Truth* 19 Aug. 1 In prohibition districts eight bottles of tanglefoot are known as a 'kit', and two kits are described as a drunk.

kitchen. In special Comb. [cf. OED *kitchen* 7] **kitchen evening**, **kitchen party** (*obs.*), **kitchen tea** [AND 1934], a pre-wedding party (or shower) to which guests bring gifts of kitchen-ware for a bride-to-be.
 1931 *Star* (Auckland) 22 Mar. 7 A **kitchen evening** was given by Mr. and Mrs. A.R. Gillett at their residence..in honour of Miss Sabina Gardner, whose marriage..takes place shortly. **1937** *King Country Chronicle* 21 Aug. 5 The parish hall was well filled..when a kitchen evening was tendered to Miss M. Ansell and Mr. Schou, who are to be married shortly. **1945** *NZ Dairy Exporter* 1 Mar. 89 Friends..rallied around when I returned home just prior to our marriage and gave us a marvellous kitchen evening. **1919** *Otago Witness* (Dunedin) 18 June 27 A number of young ladies of the district met..the object being a 'kitchen party' to Miss Lawrence, prior to her marriage. **1922** *Auckland Weekly News* 16 Feb. 57 [They] gave a delightful '**kitchen tea**' recently in honour of [their guest] whose marriage is to take place shortly. **1948** SCANLAN *Rusty Road* (1949) 179 Trixie gave a 'linen tea' for the bride-elect, and a 'kitchen tea' and a 'china tea' followed, each making some contribution to the household equipment. **1980** WILLIAMS *Wedded Bliss* in McLauchlan *Acid Test* (1981) 188 The Stag Night has no educative role, as does its female counterpart, the Kitchen Tea. **1988** MCGILL *Dict. Kiwi Slang* 66 *kitchen tea* female version of stag party on eve of wedding, usually not especially alcoholic and usually where sensible kitchen or unusually presents are given to the bride-to-be.

kite, *n.*¹
1. [f. Brit. dial. *kite* stomach: see EDD.] The stomach.
 1864–67 *Saturday Rev.* II. 7 We should have men go forth, with well-filled kites, at the sound of the 8' o'clock bell, joyfully to their appointed tasks.
2. In the phr. **arse over kite**, see ARSE 2; **full as a kite** [poss. also a play on *kite* a carrion bird], see FULL 1.

kite, *n.*² *Obs.* [f. *kite* a soaring toy controlled by a long string.]
1. In phrases alluding figuratively to a 'high' emotional state: **to be knocked (driven) kite high**, to be driven, etc. as far as possible, to the end of one's tether, 'sky high'.
 1897 *Tom Bracken's Annual* II. 48 He is sure to bang in upon you with some beastly earthly concern which simply knocks you 'kite high'. **1906** *Truth* 9 June 5 But I [*sc.* 'Jim the Milker'] must tell you that the cocky that I work for ain't a bad sort of chap, but he is driven kite-high by a joker that comes around..to collect his intrest [*sic*]. **1909** *Ibid.* 13 Mar. 4 He was knocked kite high, however, when the owner of the pocket-book, a man of means, sent along 2s 6d for the recovery of his pocket-book.
2. As **kite-high** [related to the phr. **high as a kite** drunk, not recorded until 1939: see OED *high* 16 b], very drunk. See also *full as a kite* (FULL 1).
 1906 *Truth* 13 Oct. 4 A moral wreck if ever there was one. A drink or two sends him kite high.
3. Special Comb. **kite-string**, 'apron string' in the phr. **to have** (one) **on a kite-string**, to have (one) attached by close ties.
 [*Note*] The reference perh. also contains a play on umbilical cord (*kite* =stomach).
 1971 *Listener* 22 Mar. 13 Get seen around with a good woman on your kite-string and no-one bothers you regardless.

kite: see KIT *n.*¹ 1 a (b).

kitset. The package of components from which a complete article (often a model) can be built; elsewhere usu. called a *kit*. Often *attrib.*
 1963 *Weekly News* (Auckland) 8 May 56 *Transistor Radio Kitsets* **1968** SLATTER *Pagan Game* 22 He shunned plastic kitsets as being far too small for the detail he craved. **1970** DUGGAN *O'Leary's Orchard* 137 I've a sense of myself, kitset man, assembled in a jiffy. **1979** *Commercial Fishing* Dec. 39 [Heading] Scampi [boat] available in kitset form. **1986** BROWN *Weaver's Apprentice* 122 Chester wrapped the kit set Lancaster bomber with a tube of model cement, then pushed the parcel across the counter. **1986** *Listener* 15 Nov. 5 A kit-set confessional ready for removal—could make a good shed or cupboard for tools & implements.

ki tucker, var. KAITAKA.

kivi(kivi), varr. KIWI.

kiwakiwa. Also **kiwikiwi**. [Ma. /ˈkiwakiwa/: Williams 120 *Kiwa,.. kiwakiwa,.. 3. n. Blechnum* [sp.], a fern. = *kawakawa, kiwikiwi.*] *Blechnum fluviatile* (fam. Blechnaceae), a native fern of damp, shaded sites, commonly found beside streams, hence its occasional name *creek fern.*
 1979 STARK *Maori Herbal Remedies* 38 Kiwi Kiwi *Blechnum fluviatile*. This herb is found in damp, rather hilly woodlands of New Zealand. **1981** BROOKER et al. *NZ Medicinal Plants* 26 *Blechnum fluviatile*... Maori name: *Kiwikiwi*. Found throughout New Zealand in damp hilly forest. **1982** WILSON *Stewart Is. Plants* 464 *Blechnum fluviatile* Kiwakiwa... Rosettes of olive-green fronds..Common..on banks, streamsides and in gullies.

kiwano /kɪˈwanʌu/. [A registered trademark f. *kiw*(i) + (ban)*an*(a) + -o invented by a grower, Sharyn Morris, to combine *kiwi*, a suggestion of its delicate banana-like flavour, and the suffix *-o* of other exotic fruits as *pepino, babaco, tamarillo.*] *Cucumis metuliferus* (fam. Cucurbitaceae), a trailing vine with orange-yellow edible fruit, a native of the Kalahari Desert introduced to New Zealand from Africa c1920 and recently developed as a crop plant of subtropical Northland; also elsewhere variously named (*African*) *horned cucumber* or *melon, jelly melon, Mexican fruit salad, spiny cucumber.*
 1985 *NZ Gardener* Sept. 15 For each horned bump on its attractive football-shaped skin, the kiwano has almost as many names. **1986** *Evening Post* (Wellington) 23 July 30 *Cucumis metuliferus* is the botanical name for a relatively new development in New Zealand horticulture. It is the kiwano, sometimes known as horned melon, African horned cucumber, or jelly melon, and is thought to have originated in tropical Africa. **1995** *Evening Post* (Wellington) 9 May 19 Kiwanos are a recent introduction to New Zealand horticulture. John Morris started growing them on his Kaukapakapa property in 1981.

kiwi. Also early **kivi**, occas. reduplicated **kievi-kievi, kivi-kivi, kiwikiwi**. [Ma. /ˈkiwi/: Williams 120 *kiwi*: Proto-Polynesian *kiwi* a bird species: see Walsh & Biggs 35 Tuamotuan *kivi* 'a curlew'; see also the discussion in *Notornis* 28 (1981) 216–217 which equates Cook Islands *kivi* with the bristle-thighed curlew (*Numenius tahitiensis*), a well-known, hen-sized, brown migratory wader with a down-curved bill; it is not improbable that early Maori settlers associated the similar New Zealand land bird with the known Pacific Island *kivi*, and applied the Island name to the former.] Often *attrib.*

1. Any of the three species of flightless nocturnal birds of the New Zealand genus *Apteryx* (fam. Apterygidae), having rudimentary wings, no tail, a long probing bill and primitive feathers. See also APTERYX, *blue-hen* (BLUE *a.* 2 b), EMU 1, ROA, ROWI, TOKOEKA.
 [**1820** LEE & KENDALL *NZ Gram. & Vocab.* 164 Kíwi, *s.* Name of a certain bird.] **1835** YATE *NZ* (1970) 58 *Kiwi*—The most remarkable and curious bird in New Zealand. **1840** BEST *Journal* May (1966) 222 I was however so lucky as to get..a specimen of the Kivi-Kivi. **1840** POLACK *Manners & Customs* I. 96 A small garment of the feathers of the Kievi-kievi bird was sported with great pride and state by the wearer. **1844** MONRO *Notes of a Journey* in Hocken *Contributions* (1898) 261 It seems likely that there are two species of kivi, one much larger than the other. **1852** *Zoologist* X. 3409 [Title] On the habits of the Kiwi-kiwi **1863** [see APTERYX]. **1883** DOMETT *Ranolf & Amohia* II. 11 'Twas nothing but that wing-less, tail-less bird Some furry three-legged thing without a head, Fixed to the ground—a tripod'... Boring for worms—less feathered too than furred—The *kiwi*—strange brown-speckled would-be beast. **1888** BULLER *Birds NZ* I. 237 Last Sunday I dined on stewed Kiwi at the hut of a lonely gold-digger. **c1899** DOUGLAS in *Mr Explorer Douglas* (1957) 228 The Mountain Kiwi. I have very little to say regarding this bird, as I have only seen two of them, and being pushed with hunger, I ate the pair of them, under the circumstances I would have eaten the last of the Dodos. **1905** [see APTERYX]. **1914** *Lyttelton Times* 3 Jan. 8 The bird had a long bill, thick legs, no wings, and peculiar feathers. It was, of course, a kiwi. **1922** *Auckland Weekly News* 23 Mar. 15 I felled bush in the best kiwi country in New Zealand—at Ranana, on the Wanganui River. **1929** DUGGAN *NZ Bird Songs* 34 Under the roots of a tree, Hidden, oh hidden deep, Safe from the prying sun, Huddled the kiwis sleep. **1935** JACKSON *Annals NZ Family* 136 I once had a kiwi given me in Alexandra, Waikato. He was not an interesting pet at all, wouldn't make friends, and was difficult to feed. **1940** *Press* (Christchurch) 23 July 8 'When I came to New Zealand first, I had no idea what a kiwi was', he added 'I thought it was something they made boot polish out of.' **1957** GLOVER *Since Then* 30 Confronted by the swamp on every side The moa gave its country up and died; The kiwi stretched its stunted wings in vain, But took no flight, and sank to earth again. **1989** *NZ Prayer Book* 64 Rabbits and cattle, moths and dogs, Kiwi and sparrow and tui and hawk: Give to our God your thanks and praise.

2. The three species of *kiwi* are indicated by various modifiers comprising, either singly or in combinations, the colour epithets (**brown, grey** or **spotted**), those of size (**big, giant, large, small**), of locality (**North (South, Stewart) Island, southern**), or of appearance (**straight-billed**). For ease of reference, the species have been made the basis of division, and the many various common names indicated for each.

(1) *Apteryx australis*, **brown kiwi** found in three sub-species (but see now also TOKOEKA 2): *A. australis mantelli* **North Island** (or **North Island brown**) **kiwi**, see esp. quots. 1904, 1947; *A. australis australis* **South Island** (or **South Island brown, southern, big**) **kiwi**, see esp. quot. 1985, see also ROWI, TOKOEKA; *A. australis lawryi* **Stewart Island** (or **Stewart Island brown, giant**) **kiwi**, see esp. quot. 1985. See also TOKOEKA.

1871 HUTTON *Catalogue Birds NZ* 23 Apteryx mantelli... Brown Kiwi. **1873** South-Island Kiwi [see TOKOEKA 1]. **1884** *TrNZI* XVII. 191 *Apteryx australis*. Roa. South Island Kiwi. **1885** *NZJSc*. II. 505 North Island Kiwi, Brown Kiwi.—Still to be found in many parts of the North Island, it is also met with on some adjacent islands. **1885** Big Kiwi [see ROWI]. **1893** *TrNZI* XXV. 85 *Apteryx australis*... (*The South Island Kiwi*)... In disposition this bird differs entirely from my other captive Kiwis—*Apteryx maxima, Apteryx haasti*, and *Apteryx oweni*—being far more fierce and aggressive. **1897** *Ibid.* XXIX. 185 I have since been able to procure..two rough skeletons of the Giant Kiwi (*Apteryx lawryi*) from Stewart Island. *Ibid.* 204 *Apteryx lawryi*... (Stewart Island Kiwi.) **1904** Southern Kiwi [see ROWI]. **1904** HUTTON & DRUMMOND *Animals NZ* 326 *The Brown Kiwi.. Apteryx mantelli*... The northern species, the Kiwi-nui of the Maoris, is now rare. Its plumage is darkest on the back, and the feathers on its back differ from those of other species by being harsh to touch. **1914** GUTHRIE-SMITH *Mutton Birds* 96 During day-time the Stewart Island Kiwi not infrequently moves abroad. **1923** *NZJST* VI. 81 The brown kiwi is one of the species which Guthrie-Smith considers will always maintain itself in the broken country on his run in Hawke's Bay. **1940** HOWARD *Rakiura* 323 The Stewart Island Kiwi..is of the spotted variety, and is the largest known species. **1947** POWELL *Native Animals NZ* 76 The North Island Kiwi stands about 12 inches in height and its plumage is largely dark reddish-brown streaked with black... South Island Kiwi (*Apteryx australis*), Tokoeka of the Maoris, is larger and more robust than the North Island species, but similar in appearance, coloration and habits. **1955** OLIVER *NZ Birds* 47 *North Island Kiwi. Apteryx australis mantelli*. In 1827 the North Island Kiwi was met with at Tolaga Bay, in the East Cape district by d'Urville. *Ibid.* 51 *South Island Kiwi. Tokoeka. Rowi. Apteryx australis australis*. **1966** FALLA et al. *Birds NZ* 19 The North Island Brown Kiwi..differs from..Stewart Island Brown Kiwi..in the stiffened tips of the feathers (harsher to the touch). **1973** MARSHALL et al. *Common Birds* (1978) 15 Brown Kiwi... *Apteryx australis* Field Characters..size of large domestic fowl..loose, coarse bristly feathers..long thin bill with nostrils at tip. **1985** *Reader's Digest Book NZ Birds* 38 The South Island brown kiwi has grey-brown plumage, with a rufous tinge and black streaks. This kiwi is found mainly on the Fiordland and Westland coasts south of 43° S... The Stewart Island brown kiwi is the largest [brown kiwi]. It has grey-brown upper parts streaked with black and rufous; and grey underparts streaked with brown. **1990** *Dominion Sunday Times* (Wellington) 9 Dec. 30 The zoo's senior keeper..recently accompanied a brown kiwi to West Berlin zoo.

(2) *Apteryx haastii*, **great (large) grey**, or **great (large) spotted kiwi**. See esp. quot. 1947. See also *fireman* (FIRE 3), ROA.

1873 BULLER *Birds NZ* 371 Apteryx haasti. (Large Grey Kiwi)... Roa or Roaroa. **1893** *TrNZI* XXV. 87 *Apteryx haasti*... (The Large Spotted Kiwi). Lovers of natural history will be glad to learn that this very rare species of Kiwi from the South Island..has been successfully introduced into the North Island. **1904** HUTTON & DRUMMOND *Animals NZ* 332 *The Great Spotted Kiwi.*—*Roa-Roa*... This is a large bird. It was named [*haastii*] as a compliment to the late Sir Julius von Haast. **1923** *NZJST* VI. 82 Great Grey Kiwi; Roa. Judging from the scanty reports, this is still the rarest of the three species of *Apteryx*. **1947** POWELL *Native Animals NZ* 76 Large Grey Kiwi (*Apteryx haastii*), Roa..is almost as large as *australis* but is greyish brown, mottled and cross banded with brownish black. **1959** WILSON *Bird Is. of NZ* 93 He was camped in a tent in Dusky Sound in January 1957 and a big roa (the large grey kiwi) came and sat on a pile of leaves by the tent every night from 9 p.m. to daylight. **1966** FALLA et al. *Birds NZ* 20 Great Spotted Kiwi *Apteryx haasti*..Roa. **1990** *Checklist Birds NZ* 9 *Apteryx haasti..Great Spotted Kiwi (Roa)*... Original distribution probably throughout Westland..and northwest Nelson. Now common and widespread only in forests of northwest Nelson and Paparoa Range.

(3) *Apteryx owenii*, **grey (little grey), little spotted**, occas. **straight-billed kiwi**. See esp. quots. 1966, 1990. See also *blue-hen* (BLUE *a*. 2 b).

1871 HUTTON *Catalogue Birds NZ* 23 Apteryx oweni... Grey Kiwi. **1873** *TrNZI* V. 188 Straight-billed kiwi, Grey Kiwi, Blue-hen of the [West Coast] diggers. **1873** BULLER *Birds NZ* 368 Apteryx oweni. (Little Grey Kiwi)... Kiwi-pukupuku... The Grey Kiwi is distributed over a great portion of the South Island, and in some of the remote districts is still very abundant. **1885** [see *blue-hen* (BLUE *a*. 2 b)]. **1896** HARPER *Pioneer Work* 42 The enormous egg produced by such a small bird as the grey kiwi. **1904** HUTTON & DRUMMOND *Animals NZ* 329 *The Grey Kiwi*... which is sometimes called the Straight-billed Kiwi, and the Little Grey Kiwi by diggers. **1923** MYERS *Endemic Birds in NZJST* VI. 82 Little Grey Kiwi... Three localities are reported in the South Island where this small species still occurs. **1947** POWELL *Native Animals NZ* 76 Little Grey Kiwi (*Apteryx owenii*), Kiwi-pukupuku..is the smallest of the..species. It is yellowish grey, mottled and irregularly cross banded with blackish-brown. **1990** *Checklist Birds NZ* 8 *Apteryx oweni..Little Spotted Kiwi (Kiwi-pukupuku)*... On European settlement rare in the North Island..; in South Island throughout forest areas of Marlborough, Nelson, Westland and Fiordland. **1990** *Listener* 16 July 15 These people think nothing of sitting in the bush on some remote ridge, in pitch darkness counting little spotted kiwi calls.

3. As an emblem of New Zealand.

1898 *AJHR* F-1 v Sixpence (*Sap-green*) [postage stamp]—Representation of Kiwi *regardant*, surrounded by semicircular band of solid colour, bearing the words 'New Zealand' in white letters, and supported by oblique labels, 'Postage', 'Revenue', on left and right respectively. **c1899** DOUGLAS in *Mr Explorer Douglas* (1957) 225 From the fact that bank notes, postage stamps and advertisement chromos, [*sic*] generally have a portrait of this unholy looking bird on them, it is evident that the kiwi is the accepted national bird of New Zealand. **1905** WHITE *My NZ Garden* 68 I suppose the Apteryx (Kiwi) ought to lead the van; for a bird that cannot fly sounds almost as uncommon as a pig that can. **1908** BARR *Brit. Rugby Team in Maoriland* 54 [A poem *What 'Kiwi' Means*.] *Said Leo*: 'What's this..that's broke my blessed head? It's called out here 'The Kiwi''—alluding to N.Z. **1946** SOLJAK *NZ* 8 The kiwi, like the fernleaf, is now a NZ national emblem and provided the name by which Dominion servicemen were popularly known during the war... Appropriately enough, the nickname 'kiwi' has also been applied to grounded airmen throughout the Allied air forces. **1959** *Dominion* (Wellington) 24 Oct. 14 Our familiar emblem is a rare bird—the kiwi... .Almost as rare as the kiwi is the toheroa soup we talk about but seldom sip. **1966** *Encycl. NZ* I. 571 The kiwi..as a national emblem is of comparatively recent date. It was used after 1911 in the badge of the 2nd South Canterbury (Territorial) Regiment and became widely known from the giant kiwi carved on the chalk hill above Sling Camp, England, during the First World War. After 1940 the kiwi became synonymous with New Zealand servicemen overseas. The Kiwi Concert Party, which toured many battle areas during the Second World War, and the Kiwi (New Zealand Army) Football Team, which toured the British Isles, France, and Germany in 1945–46, greatly enhanced the emblem's popularity... More recently, the kiwi has become the emblem used by New Zealand rugby league representative teams. **1980** GRANT *Unauthorized Version* 96 [Lloyd of the New Zealand Herald was the first cartoonist to widely use the kiwi to symbolise New Zealand, illustrated in cartoons of 1910, 1915 in Grant's book.] **1991** *Dominion Sunday Times* (Wellington) 3 Nov. 12 I think that was what was behind the fuss over the kiwi card... The Kiwi is the bird for all New Zealanders and they were going to divide it up, make it a divisive symbol.

4. Usu. *pl.* as **the Kiwis**, in names of troupes, (touring) teams, etc., or in *sing*. as the name of an individual member of such a group. **a.** A women's hockey team in Wellington c1908.

1908 *The Spike* (Victoria College) VII. No.1 June 44 V.C. v Kiwis. Win 3–0. At last the pride of the victorious Kiwis has been humbled in the dust [by the Victoria College women's hockey team].

b. WW1. A (pierrot) troupe of NZ Expeditionary Force entertainers; a NZ Divisional concert party.

1917 24 Aug. in *Camps, Tramps & Trenches* (1939) 123 The 'Kiwis', the New Zealand Pierrots. **1917** WILLIAMS *New Zealander's Diary* 15 Sept. (c1922) 260 The same evening the 'Kiwis' (our Pierrots) gave a highly entertaining performance in front of our billets. **1918** *Chron. NZEF* 2 Aug. 10 The existing pierrot troupes, 'The Kiwis', 'Tuis' and others have reached..a high standard of excellence. *Ibid.* 5 July 248 'The Kiwis' are the best known company of amusement purveyors with the Division, and they were the first on the field as N.Z. Divisional entertainers. **1939** MCKINLEY, ERNEST *Ways and by-ways of a singing Kiwi: with the N.Z. divisional entertainers in France* [title: NZNB III. 140, item M423] **1971** MCKEON *Fruitful Yrs.* 129 It was..[in 1917] that we first made contact with the 'Kiwis', the divisional concert party... We were to see the 'Kiwis' in many other settings before the war ended. **1979** DOWNES *Top of the Bill* 53 At the height of the bitter and tragic battles of Ypres and Passchendale..the Kiwis and their now well camouflaged canvas theatre could be found..at the nearby town of Dickebusche. *Ibid.* 54 The next production put together by the Kiwis was a musical revue called *Y Go Crook*. **1991** WOLFE *Kiwi* 34 Also to come out of the First World War was a remarkable line-up of performing servicemen, the best known of whom were the Kiwis, who first trod the boards in northern France. *Ibid.* 35 [Caption] The Kiwi Concert Party photographed upon its return from entertaining the troops in the trenches of France in 1917.

c. WW2. The familiar name of the Kiwi Concert Party, during WW2 and after.

[**1941** *NZEF Times* 18 Aug. 8 A recent visit to the rehearsal room of the Kiwi Concert Party revealed that a bigger and better show is in the course of production.] **1950** *Programme 'The Kiwis Revue Company'* (printed

Wellington 1950) To have shepherded the now famous all-soldier 'Kiwis Revue' through an Australian tour which began in April, 1946, and to finish up with the company smiling, successful and intact in 1950 is no mean achievement. This responsiblity has been that of Terry Vaughan, the Kiwis Producer and Musical Director... [who has] been with the Kiwis ever since their inception in the Middle East in 1941 when the 2nd N.Z.E.F. formed its own Entertainment Unit with men of the Division. Sir Bernard Freyberg, V.C...has always kept a paternal eye on his 'Kiwi Concert Party'. **1952** *Evening Post* (Wellington) 30 Apr. 15 Wally Prictor, the female impersonator who left the Kiwis to go into business..had since..rejoined the party.

d. *WW2.* The 2NZEF rugby union football team during WW2, and briefly after.

1946 *JPS* LV. 148 Kiwi is now a common name of the footballing Newzealander [*sic*]. **1948** SWAN *Hist. NZ Rugby Football* I. 728 The 2nd N.Z.E.F. Team, popularly designated 'The Kiwis', undertook a strenuous tour, playing matches in England, Wales, Ireland, Scotland, Germany and France. **1947** MCCARTHY *Broadcasting with the Kiwis* 55 Scott made it complete by kicking two 45-yard penalties to give the 'Kiwis' a victory (11–3), and the honour of being the first New Zealand victors over Wales at Cardiff. **1959** SLATTER *Gun in My Hand* 75 I haven't seen a decent game [of rugby] since the Kiwis played on this ground in 1946. They were soldiers and they brought to the game something of the spirit of daring that we never see today. **1975** HOWITT *NZ Rugby Greats* 264 It is generally conceded that J.B. Smith played his greatest Rugby with the 2nd NZEF team, the Kiwis, in Great Britain and France in 1945–46. **1982** *Press* (Christchurch) 18 Dec. 64 Ron Stewart was one of the men who chose the celebrated New Zealand Army team, the Kiwis, in 1945. **1993** SINCLAIR *Halfway Round the Harbour* 73 I watched him play for the Kiwi (army) rugby team against England at Twickenham. The Kiwis won.

e. The NZ representative rugby league team (as distinct from rugby union **All Blacks**).

1966 [see 3 above]. **1978** DRYDEN *Out of the Red* 159 The fullback who made the team was Aucklander Jack Fagan, the surest goal-kicker..ever to play for the Kiwis. **1986** *Sunday Star* (Auckland) 13 July B1 Newcastle.—The Kiwis hope a big crowd at the opening match of their rugby league tour here today will help their cash flow problems.

5. Frequently in proprietary or brand-names, or trademarks. **a.** Various examples.

1905 BRANDON *'Ukneadit'* [back pages] [Advt] 'Kiwi' Brand. Lemon, Vanilla, etc. **1964** NORRIS *Settlers in Depression* 6 He [G.B. Beere] called his [flour] mill, situated south of Hamilton West, the Kiwi Mill, and, by 1878, had installed new and improved machinery. **1991** WOLFE *Kiwi* 41 The very first kiwi trademark registration dates from 1877, and was used by Kempthorne Prosser & Co. of Auckland and Dunedin for household drugs and chemicals.

b. As **Kiwi (boot, shoe) Polish.** [AND 1910 (patent).]

1919 WAITE *New Zealanders at Gallipoli* 40 The most ubiquitous person [in Egypt in WW1] was easily the bootblack..'Bootsa clean, sir! no good, no money; Kiwi polish, sir!' **c1950** *Story of the Kiwi* 7 Most of these newly-enlightened individuals first learned about the Kiwi when soldiers of New Zealand, Australia and Britain, carried this shoe polish with them to all parts of the world. In sharing their polish with allies, they also shared information. *Ibid.* 10 In 1906, John Ramsay's son, William, had developed [in Melbourne] an unusually fine bootpolish to which he gave the name 'Kiwi'.

6. As a pseudonym in authorship: the first two uses recorded in the *NZ National Bibliography* are in Vol. 3, pp. 228 and 60–61.

1896 [Moffatt, S.] A Nelson Digger: some incidents of his life. By 'Kiwi' [*pseud.*]. **1911** KIWI On the Swag Sketches of station life in Hawke's Bay.

7. Occas. in *WW1*, but mainly in *WW2*. **a.** A New Zealand soldier. (Often humorously pronounced /ˈkaiwai/, perhaps in imitative guying of the pronunciations of US servicemen.) (a) *WW1*.

1918 *Chron. NZEF* 21 June 225 We christened the Adjutant 'Kiwi'—the symbol of En-Zed. **1919** *Quick March* 11 Aug. 19 [In an estaminet a French girl] ran about pouring beer, and calling every New Zealander 'Kiwi', and each Australian 'Kangaroo', sometimes prefaced by an adjective. **1936** HYDE *Passport to Hell* 136 [In] Lemnos—drill broken by trials of prowess between the New Zealanders and the Second, First, and Fourth Australians. The Kiwis took the Kangaroos on at Rugby football.

(b) *WW2* and later.

1941 HAWDON *NZ Soldiers in England* 8 Watch the antics of the 'Aussies' and 'Kiwis'. **1944** *Hutt & Petone Chronicle* 20 Dec. 12 We..pulled up to announce our arrival to a rather officious-looking officer who wasn't very impressed by a few Kiwi Diggers. **c1950** *Story of the Kiwi* 2 In World War II, in fact, New Zealanders were generally labelled Kiwis by their allies. This nickname was accepted quite happily by all but the young airmen. **1959** SLATTER *Gun in My Hand* 56 Mick..told me to get the bren mags from the pouches of the Kiwi lying [dead] outside... I said sorry Dig... I took the mags from his pouches. **1984** BOYD *City of the Plains* 312 The way in which the executive committee of 'diggers' [*i.e.* WW1 veterans] immediately opened its ranks to 'kiwis' and gradually made way for them ensured the RSA strong, continuing support.

b. As a form of address, occas. to a woman (see quot. 1947).

1918 *Chron. NZEF* 10 Apr. 101 [Caption] 'Say Kiwi, some coot told me you were a wingless bird.' 'Dicken Yank, yer gotter have arms when there's a war on.' **1943** JACKSON *Passage to Tobruk* 93 Me clean shoes, Kiwi, very good [Cairo] shoe shine boy, half acca! **1947** *Sports Post* (Wellington) 16 Aug. 9 She was surprised to hear a bus-driver hail her, 'Hello, Kiwi'. **1949** COLE *It Was So Late* (1978) 43 Then, recognizing the..heavy uncertainty of a soldier just out of uniform, his voice changed. 'Haven't got all day, Kiwi!' **1956** WILSON *Sweet White Wine* 138 The Maori [running a two-up board on a troopship] did not twitch a muscle of his face... I said, 'This is a raid. Fold up your board, Kiwi, for half an hour.' **1964** MIDDLETON *Walk on Beach* 43 They saved our lives, eh Kiwi, these Square-heads? **1976** WILSON *Pacific Star* 7 'Let's get airborne, Kiwi,' my [RZNAF] mate Ted would say to me.

c. As /ˈkiːˈiːwiː/, a chant or call of encouragement to a New Zealander or New Zealand team at an international sports meeting, test match, etc.

1992 *North & South* (Auckland) Jan. 71 When I was going through the last 3 metres of my race, I could hear all these people chanting 'ki-wi! ki-wi!'.

8. Usu. with init. cap., a New Zealander, prob. orig. applied to a white male. Cf. ORDINARY BLOKE for stereotypical phrases (as *ordinary, real Kiwi,* etc.).

1916 *Wairarapa Daily Times* 20 Nov. 3 [A poem 'The Cry of Your Child' about 'couldn't care less' attitudes, by G.M. Woodford, Masterton, Nov, 5th.] Now this is the song of the flash trip home and the courteous 'cordiale' Of the casual young kiwi who took a fat rook for a pal, And went on a high and lordly drunk... It's the syren song of the shiftless crew that sail in the ship 'Don't Care'. **1949** PARTRIDGE *Dict. Slang*

Addenda 1093 *Kiwi.* 2. A New Zealander: Australian coll.: C. 20. **1954** WINKS *These New Zealanders* (1956) 47 The Kiwis—I hope I am on friendly terms to use the word by now—often begin a sentence with a long, aspirated 'Well'. **1960** *Penguin Book NZ Verse* 64 In every New Zealand poet, almost, there is a streak of the 'Kiwi'—our word for patriotic common man—who disapproves, distrusts, or despises the personal voice. And the 'Kiwi'..is a bird of some social ancestry. **1971** LETHBRIDGE *Sunrise on Hills* 82 He was a typical 'kiwi'. That is, if the chief characteristic of a kiwi is his refusal to be pushed around. **1983** *Dominion* (Wellington) 15 Sept. 1 One possible alternative name [to New Zealander] is 'Kiwi', he [the Race Relations Conciliator] says. 'Already to many people overseas we are identified as Kiwis...We are the Kiwis an assortment of peoples living and contributing to New Zealand.' **1988** MACRAE *Awful Childhoods* 48 She assumed Dunc already knew Gaz's mother was a Kiwi of Maori descent. **1990** *Dominion Sunday Times* (Wellington) 22 Apr. 8 I am not an Enzedder, or a Kiwi, or an Antipodean, or an Anzac... I am a New Zealander, of northern European descent, as it happens. **1993** *Listener* 10 Apr. 12 The term Kiwi suggests that we are all culturally bereft hicks from Hicksville.

9. *Transf.* The name of a coin, or of the New Zealand currency unit. **a.** *Obs.* A New Zealand florin.

1946 *JPS* LV. 148 *Kiwi*..has also become the name of the New Zealand florin, because of the kiwi on the obverse.

b. (a) *Hist.* A name formerly suggested for the New Zealand pound.

1941 SUTHERLAND *Numismatic Hist. NZ* 181 The [Government Bank Note] Designs Committee [1933] decided to give prominence to the *kiwi*..firstly because it was distinctive of the country, and secondly because of a suggestion that the overworked term 'pound' did not accurately describe the New Zealand measure of value in relation to [other pounds]. It was suggested that an appropriate substitute would be the term *kiwi* which was in line with a current official proposal to use 'rand' for the South African unit, and an unofficial proposal to use 'roo' for the Australian unit. *Ibid.* 274 In view of the then active advocacy of a decimal system of coinage, and the fact that the florin was a 'decimal coin' introduced in Great Britain in 1849.. the [1933] Coinage designs Committee decided that the kiwi should be associated with this coin, firstly because the term 'kiwi' had been suggested as a possible name for the new decimal unit of value for New Zealand, and secondly because coins are frequently described colloquially by the designs they carry.

(b) A familiar name among foreign exchange dealers for the New Zealand dollar.

1985 *National Bus. Rev.* 11 Mar. 1 Last week..the 'kiwi' went up to 47 United States cents on Wednesday morning... The demand for the 'kiwi' last week was created by exporters, who had held funds offshore and had to bring them back, said a dealer. **1985** *NZ Times* 19 May 18 The market's starting to warm up... The dealer trading the aussie is now constantly on the phone..Kiwi trading is slow. **1991** *National Bus. Rev.* 27 Sept. 48 As the cries from exporters echoed around Beehive corridors, the Kiwi's strength was of distinct embarrassment to the government.

10. A familiar name for distinctive *New Zealand English* (NEW ZEALAND B 4 b (a)).

1981 MARSH *Black Beech & Honeydew* 202 It is good honest kiwi to kick the English language into the gutter. **1983** *Landfall* 147 277 We generally laughed as he practised his Kiwi..or spoke Cockney. **1988** *Pacific Way* June 27 Names..are supplied, as is what the author calls 'A Crash Course in Kiwi', a linguistic guide for the unwary. **1992** *Onslow Parish Newsletter* 26 July 1 We've now translated it into 'Kiwi'.

11. *Golden Kiwi* (GOLDEN 2).
1962 *Evening Post* (Wellington) 17 Oct. 23 *Changes Possible in Kiwi Lottery* Thought was being given to changing the Golden Kiwi lottery prizes. **1977** HALL *Glide Time* 40 And we each put in fifty cents towards Kiwi and Jackpot tickets. **1988** *Listener* 27 Feb. 65 First there are those New Zealand words [in Collins English Dictionary, 2nd ed.]..for example..*kiwi* (as in Golden Kiwi).

12. Mainly in non-New Zealand use, KIWIFRUIT.
1972 *Daily Colonist* (Victoria, B.C.) 2 Aug. 19 Have you noticed a small brown fruit called kiwi in local markets lately?..Sometimes called a Chinese gooseberry. **1973** *Sat. Rev. Soc.* (US) Mar. 53 Twenty-six different crops, most of them fruit—almonds, apples.. kiwis, nectarines, olives. **1982** BURTON *Two Hundred Yrs. NZ Food* 138 'Kiwifruit' is an embarrassingly contrived name, but..it seems here to stay. Thankfully, however, the name has been shortened to plain 'Kiwi' in our major markets in the United States and Germany.

13. In the phr. **as hard to catch as a kiwi**, very elusive.
1953 REED *Story of Kauri* 251 He is a very busy man, and often from home, and we were told that he was 'as hard to catch as a kiwi'.

14. *attrib.* in a sense 'characteristic of or pertaining to New Zealand or New Zealanders', passing into adjectival use, usu. with init. cap., and often forming the second element of an adjectival Comb. (for example, **part-kiwi**). See also NEW ZEALAND B 2 a, ORDINARY BLOKE for esp. stereotypical uses. **a.** WW2. In various Armed Services applications, *spec.* applied to the 2NZEF rugby union football team, or any of its members (see quot. 1973).
1941 *NZEF Times* 22 Sept. 13 Brave Kiwi soldier **1943** JACKSON *Passage to Tobruk* 114 The Kiwi gun crews command the respect of their comrades. **1946** SOLJAK *NZ* 126 The first Kiwi echelon landed in Egypt in February, 1940. **1973** MCCARTHY *Listen..!* 10 In a book I wrote after the [1945] tour I had this to say..: 'This day the Kiwi forwards went for the doctor.' **1976** WILSON *Pacific Star* 181 'Oh, but they were tough, Kiwi fliers in those days, Nora,' I went on.

b. In general use.
1957 GOLDBLATT *Democracy at Ease* 6 But exactly this was the life of the Kiwi farmer. **1960** MUIR *Word for Word* 181 'Some of you jokers could do with a stir-up,' Fred said in his slow, part-Midlands, part-Kiwi accent. **1966** *Encycl. NZ* II. 678 Men often tend to regard 'good' speech as effeminate or 'cissy' and are apt to cultivate a manner of speech which is sometimes described as 'kiwi'. **1977** HALL *Glide Time* 10 A typical Kiwi who has found himself in a clerical job. Fairly uncouth, and has a Kiwi accent. **1988** *Evening Post* (Wellington) 14 July 37 The great Kiwi clobbering machine does not exist in the bookworld. **1992** *Salient* (Wellington) 7 Dept. 16 The lawnmower is a great Kiwi icon. It's the ideal Kiwi zombie killing machine.

15. Special Comb. **kiwi bear**, a suggested trade-name for possum meat; **kiwi berry**, an obsolete trade-name for KIWIFRUIT; **Kiwi-country**, a jocular name for New Zealand as the native haunt of New Zealanders; **kiwi disease** *obs.*, the institution of a 'nuclear free' policy, esp. in respect of visits of US warships; **kiwi feather**, the feather of the kiwi as a component or ornament of prized Maori clothing or coverings, and occas. of European; **kiwi grace**, see quot.; **kiwi green**, a variety of New Zealand-grown cannabis; **kiwi haircut**, see quot.; **kiwi-hunting**, the hunting of kiwis for food or taxidermy; **kiwi rose** (an Austral. use), see quot.; **kiwi's friend** *obs.*, WEKA; **kiwi share** (a term prob. used from 13 Apr. 1989 when the Government sold its shares in Air New Zealand Ltd), a company share with special rights attached (such as the need to gain the consent of the holder before certain numbers of shares can be sold to overseas interests, or before varying the basis of charging for services offered by the company) issued, at the time of privatization of a State Owned Enterprise or publicly owned organization, to the Minister of Finance to be held on behalf of the Crown; **kiwi-skin**, the skin of a kiwi with feathers attached, esp. with reference to the composition of fine Maori cloaks; **Kiwispeak**, broad New Zealand speech; **kiwi suspension**, an illegal or *de facto* suspension from school of a student difficult to discipline usu. by persuading parents to remove the offender.

1988 *Star* (Auckland) 28 June 1 Possum stew exporters are trying to win acceptance for '**Kiwi bear**' in Oriental restaurants. **1966** TURNER *Eng. Lang. Austral. & NZ* 172 When Chinese gooseberries were introduced to the United States recently, and apparently needed to be renamed, they were called *giant* **kiwi berries**. **1974** *NZ Agric.* 126 There is an increasing emphasis on exporting horticultural produce—especially strawberries and Chinese gooseberries ('kiwi fruit' or 'kiwi berries'). **1963** CASEY *As Short a Spring* 22 A fellow that's come all the way from Pommieland to have a quick look at **Kiwi-Country**..at least ought to have an overcoat to put on himself. **1985** *Dominion* (Wellington) 20 May 1 Mr Mack said the United States did not particularly care about New Zealand but was worried by the nuclear warships ban because it might result in a spread of 'the **Kiwi disease**' to other areas. **1990** *NZ Geographic* VII. 33 'Spread "Kiwi disease"—nuclear-free seas' reads a protest banner hung from [Auckland Harbour] bridge by intrepid Greenpeace volunteers in 1987. **1869** *TrNZI* I. (rev. edn.) 344 [The Maori men returned to the making] of their prized dog-skin, or **Kiwi-feather**, clothing mats. **1905** *Daily Chron.* 7 July VI. 7 The presents included..a rug of kiwi feathers from New Zealand. **1937** *King Country Chronicle* 6 Apr. 4 In the 'seventies, kiwi-feather muffs and boas and even coats came into vogue. **1938** FINLAYSON *Brown Man's Burden* (1973) 39 They had covered his shrunken body with fine kiwi-feather cloaks. **1980** LELAND *Kiwi-Yankee Dict.* 58 **kiwi grace**: (before meals): '2, 4, 6, 8, bog in, don't wait.' **1976** ROSE *NZ Green* 5 Cannabis Sativa..is better known to us by its Spanish-Mexican name, Marijuana. Or pot, grass, weed, dope, gear, **Kiwi green**. **1967** BAILEY & ROTH *Shanties* 148 I got a real **Kiwi haircut**, Bit off the top and short back and sides. **1867** HOCHSTETTER *NZ* 181 Dogs are also used in **kiwi-hunting**. **1990** *Canberra Times* (Aust.) 4 July VIII. 5 Australia's waratah, the emblem of NSW, is gaining fame elsewhere as the **kiwi rose**. **1859** THOMSON *Story NZ* I. 27 [T]he Weka, is about the size of a pheasant; it is called the **Kiwi's friend**, from associating with that bird, and resembling it in its habits. **1990** *NZPD* DVII. 2040 The Government will continue to hold its **Kiwi share**, controlling the maximum shareholding of any single foreign party and transfers of blocks of shares among parties. It will also ensure that Telecom's commitment with respect to residential services will remain in place. *Ibid.* 2054 The law would state that the Kiwi share could not be terminated except by an Act of Parliament. **1990** *Annual Report of Air New Zealand Ltd* 50 [On 13 April 1989, the Authorised and Issued Capital was increased to $280,000,001 by the issue of one fully paid special rights convertible share of $1.00 to the Government.] *Ibid.* 60 The Crown retains one special rights convertible preference share ('Kiwi Share') in Air New Zealand. **1992** *Dominion* (Wellington) 23 Dec. 1 The Government has agreed to sell half of Trans Power..keeping a single 'Kiwi share' for itself and the other half in state-owned Electricorp. **1995** *Dominion* (Wellington) 12 Apr. 18 Telecom's 'politically untouchable' Kiwi share obligations, ensuring free local calls and below inflation rate price rises, have come under attack at an international telecommunications conference. **1879** *Auckland Weekly News* 11 Oct. 7 He wears a **kiwi-skin** cap like one worn by the Maori King. **1990** *Dominion Sunday Times* (Wellington) 25 Feb. 24 [Heading] **Kiwispeak** gets a raw deal... But there's nary a sign of lurgy, surely just as valid in Kiwispeak. **1992** *Dominion* (Wellington) 21 Apr. 8 He overlooks the worst aspect of kiwispeak, namely, the nasalisation of the means of (voice) production. **1991** *Dominion Sunday Times* (Wellington) 14 Apr. 15 The Maori education authority has welcomed the Education Ministry's plan to revise suspension and expulsion guidelines and hopes it will stop '**Kiwi**' **suspensions** and expulsions. Chief executive Hemi Flavell said 'Kiwi' suspensions and expulsions were ones which were not recorded officially but brought about the same outcome. Schools were required to notify the ministry of any suspensions or expulsions in their schools, but Mr Flavell said principals often used subtle language to disguise them. **1995** *Dominion* (Wellington) 15 Mar. 1 The report recommends action against 'kiwi' suspensions, where parents are asked to withdraw a child from school rather than the child being excluded formally.

16. a. In Comb. prefixed to words and particles to form adjectives: **Kiwi-born**, **Kiwi-fashion**, **Kiwi-like** (also *transf.*), **Kiwi-style**.
1987 *MS Cellany* 6 The mother was sure her son, **Kiwi-born**, would have a sense of belonging. **1959** SLATTER *Gun in My Hand* 235 Each moving in his own little world, each following instinctively his cobber ten paces in front..the jolting of the water-bottle swung on the rear, **Kiwi-fashion**. **1867** HOCHSTETTER *NZ* 188 [Caption] **Kiwi-like** Moa. **1984** *National Bus. Rev.* 15 Oct. 7 PS: Don't let your scepticism show while making your obeisance to these guardians of public morals. That would be most un-Kiwilike. **1990** *Sunday Mag.* 23 Sept. 6 Now he..has plans to launch aerobics **Kiwi-style** in Japan.

b. In composition **Kiwian**, a New Zealander; **Kiwiana**, any of many 'collectibles', items redolent of New Zealand life and culture (see also *New Zealandiana* (NEW ZEALAND C)); **kiwi-afy**, **kiwicization**, **kiwification**, to make (the making of) a person or thing New Zealand in character; **Kiwidom**, the body of New Zealand culture and ideology regarded as a stereotypical whole; **Kiwified**, given a New Zealand appearance or character; **kiwihood** *ironic*, the state of being a stereotypical New Zealander; **kiwi-ish**, suggestive of loyal but stereotypical New Zealand interests; **kiwiness**, the state or condition of being a stereotypical New Zealander.

1918 *Chron. NZEF* 16 Aug. 31 It could not be contradicted that the **Kiwians** were now making a step or two forward in the war. **1989** BARNETT & WOLFE *New Zealand! New Zealand! In Praise of Kiwiana* [Title] **1990** *Listener* 3 Aug. 12 It follows that the icons of *Kiwiana*, so many of them drawn from advertising's rose-coloured world, amount to a fairly one-sided view of New Zealand. **1992** *Evening Post* (Wellington) 7 Aug. 5 The numerous little jokes about the sacred cows of Kiwiana are as sharp and telling as the strands of a barbed wire fence. **1996** *Evening Post* (Wellington) 27 Jan. 11 '[Dame Cath Tizard] **Kiwi-afied** the position,' says old friend and former colleague..Phil Warren. **1986** *Dominion* (Wellington) 6 June 8 NZPOD [Pocket

KIWIFRUIT

Oxford Dictionary]..is..a somewhat careless cosmetic **kiwicisation** of a British prototype, Allen's 'POD of Current English'. **1984** *National Bus. Rev.* 30 July 15 It could well have been said—again—last week that Sir Robert cut across the prevailing mood of **Kiwidom**. **1985** *National Bus. Rev.* 29 Apr. 15 Sundry pan-African organisations which don't seem to have any sort of independent existence other than pronouncing curses upon Kiwidom in times of rugby controversy went through their rituals, threatening bans that would prevent Kiwi sportsfolk from playing anywhere on planet Earth. **1986** *Dominion* (Wellington) 26 Apr. 7 It is the first that is the true test of **Kiwification**; of how deeply the editor has delved into the base test to transform it from something alien into something indigenous. **1993** *Dominion* (Wellington) 25 May 22 But with its imaginative, more **Kiwified** set..it is very much a New Zealand show. **1987** *Dominion Sunday Times* (Wellington) 27 Dec. 6 Sportsmen like Sir Edmund Hillary and Colin Meads become archetypes of sainted **Kiwihood**. **1986** *Listener* 8 Nov. 8 Apologists for modern journalese and **Kiwi-ish** claim that ours is a living language and in good health. **1985** *Rip It Up* (Auckland) Nov. 28 Apart from the indefinable '**kiwiness**' of it all, I would have to say the difference lies in the strength of the songs. **1991** *Sunday Star* (Auckland) 6 Oct. D1 'We're all about kiwiness,' announces the 43-year-old high roller.

kiwifruit. *Actinidia deliciosa* (fam. Actinidiaceae), a vigorous vine from South China, and its small, brownish, hairy fruit with tender green flesh, formerly called CHINESE GOOSEBERRY. See also KIWI 12, *kiwi berry* (KIWI 15). Also **kiwifruiter**, a commercial grower of kiwifruit (see quot. 1993).
   1973 *NZ Patent Office Jrnl. No.1129* 6 Sept. Pacific Kiwi fruit B102913 [filed] 15 January 1973..canned kiwi fruit (Chinese gooseberries). Auckland Export Limited. **1974** *NZ Agric.* 126 There is an increasing emphasis on exporting horticultural produce—especially..Chinese gooseberries ('kiwi fruit' or 'kiwi berries'). **1982** BURTON *Two Hundred Yrs. NZ Food* 138 The kiwifruit, or Chinese gooseberry as it was once known, is a native of China... A Mr James McGregor brought the seeds back to New Zealand from a trip to China soon after the turn of the century... It was not until 1940 that commercial plantings came into production. **1982** *Listener* 3 July 32 There's a display of kiwifruit products—kiwifruit toothpaste, kiwifruit soap, cheesecake..and kiwifruit-flavoured vitamin C tablets for constipation. **1990** *Gramophone* Feb. 1437 Many people have put metronome markings before everything else. It's become the kiwi fruit of modern musicology. **1993** *Metro* (Auckland) Feb. 105 There are mixed emotions in Te Puke for the plight of the kiwifruiters.

kiwi-ism. Also **kiwism**. **a.** A distinctive item of New Zealand speech or language, a New Zealandism.
   1944 FULLARTON *Troop Target* 29 'Which way did you come?' 'Through Larissa, eh?' The final 'eh?' spoken on a rising inflection, is a meaningless Kiwi-ism common to many North Islanders. **1971** ARMFELT *Catching Up* 56 The Kiwisms were slightly accentuated, betraying that they had been popped in for the Englishman's education. **1989** *Listener* 7 Jan. 13 And it's anybody's guess what Japanese tourists make of such Kiwisms as 'She's apples' 'put the nips in'. **1989** *Dominion Sunday Times* (Wellington) 16 Apr. 24 [Heading] Kiwi-isms without the metaphor. **1991** *Contact* (Wellington) 24 Oct. 2 J G Wilson has collected some more examples of Kiwi-isms. A loaf of 'brad', The 'Labbanon', the Social Welfare 'bannufut' and the New Zealand-invented 'jatboat'.

b. The state or condition of being a (stereotypical) New Zealander.
   1984 *NZ Times* 38 Oct. 12 Sargeson's views on insularity, true Kiwi-ism, puritanism, and the craft of writing are to be found in each of the 30 pieces here.

kiwikiwi, var. KIWI; KIWAKIWA.

Kiwiland. New Zealand. Cf. MAORILAND 3.
   1947 DAVIN *For Rest of Our Lives* 396 I'll be going back to good old Kiwiland when the ship pulls out. **1964** DAVIS *Watersiders* 47 This is Kiwiland, see. And we have gentleman's agreement here. **1986** *National Bus. Rev.* 21 Feb. 19 At the end of the twentieth century the opportunities for civilised dining in Kiwiland are greater then ever. **1989** CAMPBELL *Frigate Bird* 42 You were the local boy who'd made good in Kiwiland.

kiwism, var. KIWI-ISM.

kladdy, var. KORARI.

knifehand. A freezing works employee who trims or otherwise dresses carcasses.
   1974 HILLIARD *Maori Woman* 53 He'd had eight months as a knife-hand in a bacon factory. **1982** NEWBOLD *Big Huey* 12 When exams finished..one of my new friends got me a job as a knifehand at the freezing works.

knife depot. WWI. A (field or base) hospital.
   1915 *Rangitikei Advocate & Manawatu Argus* 1 July 4 When one leaves the 'Knife Depot', or the hospital, as it is sometimes called, we all get a new rig out.

knifey. [Cf. OED 'Chiefly Sc.'.] A (usu.) boys' game. See also STAGKNIFE.
   1901 *NZ Illustr. Mag.* IV. 852 The younger children here finished so they leave ceremoniously, and play 'knifey' in the yard. **1939** COMBS *Harrowed Toad* 90 Another fieldsman..may have seen the ball but has been indulging spasmodically in 'knifey'. **1972** [see STAGKNIFE].

knock, *v.* [f. *knock trans.* hit.]
1. In various phr. **a. to knock** (something) **into a mish** *obs.* [*mish* poss. ellipt. for *mish-mash* a pulp], to be vastly superior to.
   1865 THATCHER *Col. Songster* 17 When no one's looking, fill your dish, and you may wash out what you wish, Puddling mullock's knocked into a 'mish', Hard work will but annoy.
b. to knock the corners off (someone), to punish violently.
   1906 *Truth* 14 July 1 The wife is a healthy, hale woman and after knocking corners off both hubby and the girl, she fired the pair into the street.
c. to knock the wool out of (one's) head, to wake (one) up, to make (one) think clearly.
   1907 KOEBEL *Return of Joe* 40 Seems to have knocked some of the wool out of my head already.
d. to knock (something) **humpty dumpty**, to demolish completely.
   1913 *NZ Bull.* 8 Feb. 16 It kinder gives a bloke the bloomin' pip to find his efforts all knocked 'umpty dumpty' by other blokes.
e. to knock (one) **all to the pack**, to have a bad effect on.
   1938 HYDE *Nor Yrs. Condemn* 190 [Liquor] knocks them all to the pack.
f. to knock (one) **for a row of ash-cans**, to impress greatly; to astound.

KNOCK

   1946 WEBBER *Johnny Enzed in Italy* 12 I suppose you're going to get a shampoo & a permanent wave too... You'll knock her for a row of ash-cans.
g. to knock the drawing room out of (someone), to harden or toughen physically.
   1952 BLAKISTON *My Yesteryears* 16 It [the horse] was not fit to ride, and I was not going to ride it again. Mr Tripp smacked his thigh, clapped his hands and laughed. 'That will knock the drawing room out of you!' said he.
2. In various phrasal verbs. **a. to knock across**, to meet; to come across, to run across.
   1897 WRIGHT *Station Ballads* 38 For all my looking I could never knock across his track.

b. to knock back. (a) [f. Brit. dial.: see OED *knock v.* 7 b.] To check, to retard.
   1945 *NZ Geogr.* 27 An early winter will knock his flock back. **1946** SARGESON *That Summer* 85 The two sprees had knocked me back considerably [financially].

(b) [AND 1918.] To refuse or reject.
   1955 BJ Cameron *Collection* (TS July) knock back (v) To refuse or reject. (The English slang meaning of to consume is also current in NZ). **1988** McGILL *Dict. Kiwi Slang* 66 *knock back* rejection or refusal, often of sex; eg 'He systematically propositioned every woman at the party, and was knocked back every time.'

c. to knock off. (a) **to knock** (a person) **off**, to sack, to discharge (a person).
   1881 BATHGATE *Waituruna* 172 Mr. Ramshorn.. would growl at the offending shearer and make use of some vague threat of 'knocking him off.'

(b) to dispose of; to sell.
   1955 *Truth* 9 Mar. 4 I might give you a hand to knock off some of that kale. **1985** O'SULLIVAN *Shuriken* 28 They make those trinket affairs for him... Then he takes them and knocks them off in town.

d. to knock out. (a) [AND 1853.] To recover (payable gold).
   1857 *Lyttelton Times* 5 Aug. 5 It has now been cleared up, and we think for some time, when we expect to knock out 7ozs a-day. **1863** WALKER *Jrnl. & Lett.* (ATLTS) 4 Jan. It is very jolly to live in one's own house..because we can knock out enough to live upon at any time. **1871** MONEY *Knocking About NZ* 18 They knocked out in this day as much gold as sufficed to make them afterwards two rings.

(b) [AND 1881.] To earn, esp. in the phr. **to knock out tucker**, to recover enough (gold) to pay for food.
   1873 PYKE *Wild Will Enderby* (1889, 1974) I. xiv 47 By most of the neighbouring miners, they were regarded as two industrious young men, who worked very hard for a bare living—'just knocking out tucker', as the phrase went. **1874** PYKE *George Washington Pratt* 24 I can knock out tucker enough for the pair of us.

e. to knock over *logging*, to fell (a tree) (see also KNOCK DOWN 2).
   1882 HAY *Brighter Britain* 184 A single bushman could have knocked that tree over before dinner time.

f. to knock under [prob. an extended use of *knock under* to submit, to yield: see OED *knock v.* 15] in absolute use, to die.
   1870 *McLean Papers* (ATLTS) XXXII. 168 I am trying, by dint of resolution, to pull through all [my sickness] and hope a change for the better, but fear I shall have, some of these days, to knock under. **1898** VOGEL *Maori Maid* 158 When father knocks under, me and my brother we'll come into the business.

knock about, *v.*

1. Also **knock around**. [Used elsewhere but recorded earliest in NZ: see OED *knock v*. 7 d.] Of a thing, etc., to lie around somewhere, to be at hand or available.

1866 HUNT *Twenty-five Yrs. Experience* 45 My carpet bag I left knocking about amongst them with utmost carelessness. **1874** PYKE *George Washington Pratt* 27 It seems there's a joke knocking around somewhere. **1897** PHILIPS *Memories of Past* 21 When we did have them they were generally pretty severe [fires], such as..W.S. Grahame's in Fort Street (any amount of drink knocking about). **1908** KOEBEL *Anchorage* 45 Do you know of a billet knockin' about anywhere that 'ud suit him, boss? **1948** FINLAYSON *Tidal Creek* 17 I'll just see about a box that ought to be knocking about.

2. To do knockabout or rouseabout work esp. on a farm; to do odd jobs.

1891 CHAMIER *Philosopher Dick* 314 He was an 'old hand' who was employed to 'knock about'.

knockabout, *n.* [AND 1867.] Often as **knockabout hand**, one who can turn a hand to any kind of, esp. farm, work.

1885 *Ida Valley Station Letterbook* 26 Oct. in Martin *Forgotten Worker* (1990) 27 I think *yearly* wages will have to come down, before any great reduction can justly be made in wages of tablemen & knockabouts at shearing. **1891** CHAMIER *Philosopher Dick* 7 Two cadets..[gave] their services as knockabout hands. **1968** *NZ Contemp. Dict. Suppl.* (Collins) 11 *knockabout n.* man of all work on a station, rouseabout. **1981** PINNEY *Early N. Otago Runs* 37 He [Middleton] commented [1885]:'Knockabouts are plentiful enough but three-fourths of them are not worth their salt in a woolshed.' **1988** MCGILL *Dict. Kiwi Slang* 66 *knockabout* handyman, or station hand.

knock-back.

1. [AND 1915.] A refusal, a snub.

1939–45 *Expressions & Sayings 2NZEF* (TS N.A. WAII DA 420/1) Knock back—A refusal. **1943** SARGESON in *Penguin New Writing 17* 56 And I said to myself, well, a knock-back from one of yous isn't going to make me lose any sleep. **1959** MASTERS *Tales of Mails* 36 The knockback the men had got from the lady..made those fellows come to the conclusion that what they had just come through, was one of the worst accidents ever to happen in those parts. **1960** HILLIARD *Maori Girl* 161 She had mentioned the knock-back from the Tallahassee Milk Bar. **1970** DAVIN *Not Here Not Now* 231 'Well,' [said Martin] 'it was a bit of a knockback all right but it was always on the cards, of course.'

2. A marble game.

1972 SUTTON-SMITH *Folkgames Children* 175 In the nineteenth century the ring game seems to have been the most popular marble game... There were Little Ring..Knock-Backs.

knock down, *v.*

1. [f. *knock down* to fell, dispose of: AND 1845.] To spend quickly (esp. a cheque or wages) on a drinking bout, esp. in the phr. **to knock down a cheque**.

1853 in *Canterbury Rhymes* (1866) 19 The breath Of the Royal Hotel in town; A prime *Manilla* in my mouth, Whilst I knock my earnings down! **1861** HARPER *Lett. from NZ* 20 July (1914) 65 [Station hands] draw a considerable amount for wages, and travelling to some shanty of a public house..proceed to 'knock down their cheque', giving it to the landlord, and bidding him treat all comers as long as it lasts. **1879** GREY *His Island Home* 32 They were 'knocking down' their cheques and living at the rate of 10,000 a year. **1881** BATHGATE *Waitaruna* 248 There were several shearers on the spree knocking down their cheques. **1904** CRADOCK *Sport in NZ* 10 Their rabbit cheques generally find their way to the nearest public house, to be 'knocked down' as soon as received. **1925** BATHGATE *Random Recolls.* 28 A lengthy 'spree'..did not stop till he had spent, or as it was then [c1860s] called 'knocked down', about a hundred pounds. **1933** *Press* (Christchurch) (Acland Gloss.) 4 Nov. 15 *Knock Down...* Spend (wages) lavishly or quickly, usually on drink. **1953** REED *Story of Kauri* 121 Two old-timers..after 'knocking down a cheque', left the public house late one dark night.

Hence **knocking down** *vbl. n.* and *attrib.* [AND 1873], free-spending.

1879 GREY *His Island Home* 32 They seemed to derive intense satisfaction from the knocking-down process until their resources were exhausted.

2. [f. Brit. dial. *knock down* to reap: see EDD.] **a.** To cut down or fell (a tree, scrub etc.); to reap (a crop).

1882 HAY *Brighter Britain* I. 187 A bushman..ought to knock down an acre of stuff in from five to ten days. **1949** SARGESON *I Saw in My Dream* (1974) 123 The only other thing he's good for is knocking down a bit of scrub. **1961** CRUMP *Hang On a Minute Mate* 31 Can you knock a tree down?.. Can we knock a tree down..scoffed Sam... If you'd seen us a week ago you'd know whether or not we could knock a tree down. **1969** MOORE *Forest to Farm* 47 We came to a big kahikatea tree not less than four feet in diameter and I recall his query was 'knock him down boss?'.. He was duly 'knocked down' later entirely by axe work.

b. *fig.* Esp. in the passive, to be felled by death.

1910 *Truth* 28 May 5 Recently deceased Charles Knox, of Westland, who was 'knocked down' at 97, was another old New Zealand pioneer.

3. To dispose of or 'knock back' (a drink).

1947 DAVIN *For Rest of Our Lives* 51 'Give us a beer'. So he knocks down a beer. **1988** MCGILL *Dict. Kiwi Slang* 66 *knock down* to drain a glass of a beverage, usually alcoholic, mostly beer; eg 'He knocked down the yard of ale and called for another.'

knockdown, *n.* [Orig. US 1865: see OED B 5; AND 1915.] An introduction (to a person).

1911 *Truth* 6 May 4 A man always wants a 'knock down' to hop off with when he's breaking a bit of fresh ground with the women. **1930** *National Educ.* May 197 I heard one young fellow ask another to 'give him a knockdown to that tart in the green skirt'. I gathered that he was asking for an introduction to a young lady. **1946** SARGESON *That Summer* He had his girl with him... He called me over and gave me a knock-down. **1950** *Listener* 3 Mar. 8 He took an age giving me a knockdown to Mum.

knocker, *n.*[1] [Of unknown origin: AND 1891.] Impudence, the 'hide'.

1907 *Truth* 4 May 3 The holes and lumps which studded the field were similar to the crude entrenchments of a Maori battlefield, and how the Rugby Union can have the 'knocker' to send senior teams to play on such a ground is beyond my understanding.

knocker, *n.*[2] *Mining.*

1. In full **knocker-line**. See quot. 1978.

1911 *Maoriland Worker* 3 Nov. 5 I think levers should be placed on all levels, so that he [*sc.* a mine engine-driver] could pull the knocker, instead of at the present time he has to put his head out in the shaft and perhaps have to pull about 100–1500 [*sic*] feet of line... I think there should be a stiff penalty as to anyone being allowed to handle the knocker line except the person in charge, as it tends to confuse the enginedriver. **1978** MCARA *Gold Mining Waihi* 183 Two 'knocker-lines' of half-inch-diameter wire-rope were installed in each hoisting compartment so that they could easily be reached from any point in the shaft and signals transmitted to the winding-engine driver. *Ibid.* 325 *Knocker-lines*: Half-inch-diameter wire-ropes suspended in the shaft and used to signal the winding-engine driver. **1986** RICHARDS *Off the Sheep's Back* 5 The only other means of communication with the surface [above the goldmine] was primitive. A long wire, known as the 'knocker line', extended down the shaft and was accessible at each level. Each pull rang a bell in the winding house.

2. A large block of wood, part of the mechanism for tripping a timber dam.

1991 *Historic Places* Sept. 29 The dam was tripped by pulling a wire at the end of which was a large block of wood usually made of rata called a knocker.

knocker, *n.*[3] *Shearing.* [Spec. use of *knocker* that which knocks: AND 1895.] See quots. 1933, 1987.

1933 *Press* (Christchurch) (Acland Gloss.) 4 Nov. 15 *Knocker.*—A small leather pad fixed near the heel of shears to keep the blades from closing too far. **1938** BURDON *High Country* 84 A piece of raw hide known as a knocker is now used to prevent the shears clashing when closed, but before this was introduced the clack and snap of steel meeting steel was a noise inseparable from any busy shearing shed. **1951** MCLEOD *NZ High Country* 28 The knockers on the shears silence the sound of steel on steel and all you hear is a faint tap-tap as the shears close. **1978** JARDINE *Shadows on Hill* 130 They had received their two free pairs of blades..and had spent many hours..attaching drivers, jockeys, spurs and knockers. **1987** OGONOWSKA-COATES *Boards, Blades & Barebellies* 96 *Knocker*. Small pad of leather, flax or binding, usually attached to a spike cut near the heel of the shears to keep the blades from clicking when closing. **1990** MARTIN *Forgotten Worker* 84 Rawhide 'knockers' made the work [of blade shearing] almost silent.

knocker, *n.*[4] [AND 1962.] In the phr. **on the knocker**, promptly; esp. of a bill or invoice, immediately payable or paid promptly.

1949 Marlborough store: 'No tick; cash on the knocker.' **1988** MCGILL *Dict. Kiwi Slang* 66 *knocker*, phr. *on the knocker* punctual; originally 'cash on the knocker', meaning cash on demand, prompt payment required; eg 'Crombie is invariably here on the knocker for council meetings, no matter how busy he might be.'

knocker: see HARD KNOCKER.

knuckle-up. A bout of fisticuffs; a punch-up.

1961 CRUMP *Hang On a Minute Mate* 165 And remember, Jack me boy, there's no winners in a fight,... A real mate isn't going to judge you on how good you are in a knuckle-up. **1984** PARTRIDGE *Dict. Slang.* 658 *knuckle-up.* A fight, esp. with bare fists: NZ: since late 1940s. (Harold Griffiths, 1970.) Cf. Brit. *punch-up.*

ko. Also **koko**. [Ma. /ko/: Williams 120 *Kō* (i), A wooden implement for digging or planting.] A Maori digging implement.

1819 MARSDEN *Lett. & Jrnls.* (1932) 165 They have another wooden tool about seven feet long, pointed like a hedge stake, and a piece of wood lashed on about two feet from the ground to place the foot upon to aid in thrusting the instrument into the ground. They call the tool koko. **1847** ANGAS *Savage Life* I. 290 We passed through a native plantation..where the inhabitants... were using the *ko*, a wooden instrument something resembling a spade, with which they root up the matted fibres of the fern below the surface of the soil. **1869** *TrNZI* I. (rev. edn.) 352 A *ko*, a rude kind of narrow and pointed spade with a very long handle, to which, at about 18 inches or more from the point, they fitted a small crooked bit of carved wood, as a rest for the foot. **1879** *TrNZI* XI. 89 This implement (called a *ko*) might be just as well termed a lance, or pick. **1904** TREGEAR *Maori Race* 321 The principal agricultural tool was the digging-stick (*ko*), this being a pole or shaft of hard wood from seven to ten feet in length, with a step or foot-rest (*hamaruru*) lashed on about a foot from the end that entered the ground, this end being pointed or with an edge at foot and sides. **1911** *TrNZI* XLIII. 597 The ditch..still showed perfectly clearly the gouge-like impressions of the wooden *ko* with which it had been dug. **1926** COWAN *Travel in NZ* II. 112 [As Rakaihaitu] went from place to place he hollowed out with his magical *ko*, or wooden sharp-pointed digging implement, the beds of those great lakes. **1930** COWAN *The Maori* 186 The *ko*-men worked across from the corner, gradually extending their front as the field opened out. **1941** ALLEY & HALL *Farmer in NZ* 3 His [*sc.* the Maori's] instant casting aside of his poor crude *ko* and *timo* (or grubbing stick) in favour of European spades and hoes. **1955** PHILLIPPS *Maori Carving Illustr.* 16 Designs carved on the upper ends of ko or digging stick. **1984** MARSHALL *Day Hemingway Died* 126 'There's an artefact down there,' he said firmly. 'A ko I think, or perhaps a spear.'

Hence **ko-ing** *ppl. a.*, digging.
1930 COWAN *The Maori* 186 The white man Kimble Bent worked with these *ko*-ing parties every season.

koa, var. KOWHAI.

koara, var. KOARO.

koarea. Early **Rauwarea**, poss. erron. MS reading for *Kauwarea*. [Ma. /ˈkoarea/: Williams 122 *Koarea*, n... golden snapper.] *Centroberyx* (formerly *Trachichthodes*) *affinis*, occas. *Austroberyx affinis*. See also *golden snapper*, *red snapper* (SNAPPER *n.*[1] 2 (2) and (4)).
1843 WILLIAMS *NZ Jrnl.* (1956) 41 The whole of the long range of the New Zealand Coast is abundantly supplied with beautiful fish. Of this variety of 78 species I will name a part, viz..Rauwarea, a snapper. **1921** [see SNAPPER *n.*[1] 2 (2)]. **1956** GRAHAM *Treasury NZ Fishes* 175 Golden Snapper (Koarea) *Centroberyx affinis*... This is one of the most beautiful fish ever seen by me. **1967** NATUSCH *Animals NZ* 215 Rocky and sandy grounds, in the north, are the home of *Trachichthodes*..a golden fish known variously as golden snapper, koarea, and (in Australia) nannygai. **1982** [see SNAPPER *n.*[1] 2 (4)].

koaro. Also **koara**, **kowaro**. [Ma. /ˈkoːaro/: Williams 122 *Kōaro*, *kōwaro*,.. 5. *Galaxias huttoni*, a fresh-water fish found in Lakes Rotoaira and Rotopounamu.] The name, orig. restricted to *Galaxias* from the Taupo area, is now adopted for the widespread freshwater *Galaxias brevipinnis* (fam. Galaxiidae). See also GALAXIAS, GUDGEON, *mountain trout* (TROUT 2 (4)).
1855 TAYLOR *Te Ika A Maui* 414 *Koaro*, a small fresh-water fish, three inches long, much esteemed; this is found in most rivers and lakes. **1872** HUTTON & HECTOR *Fishes NZ* 129 It may be useful to give a list of the different fishes the Maoris distinguish in the Taupo district... Koaro.—Not found in Taupo Lake, but only in Rotoaira. **1886** SHERRIN *Handbook Fishes NZ* 142 The Koara [*sic*] is a small spotted fish from 1½ in. to 2½ in. in length, found only in Lake Rotoaira, south of Taupo. It is said by the Natives to resemble the koara of the sea in shape. **1919** *TrNZI* LI. 263 *Koaro* is the Maori name of a small fish obtained under peculiar conditions from Roto-a-Ira. **1926** *NZPD* CCXI. 289 The Tuwharetoa Tribe had a little lake called Rotoaira, and they had native fish there called the kowaro. **1940** PHILLIPPS *Fishes NZ* 36 The koaro is known only from Lakes Roto-pounamu and Rotoaira. Maori efforts to acclimatize the species in Taupo have failed over many generations. **1963** WOODS *Freshwater Fishes* 31 The Koaro is readily identified by locality. It is the only fish of its general appearance known from the thermal lakes area. **1990** MCDOWALL *NZ Freshwater Fishes* 110 Young koaro..are expert climbers and seem to have little difficulty negotiating damp, vertical rocky faces to reach habitats above falls... Because of this..the koaro is sometimes known as climbing galaxias.

koatuku, var. KOTUKU.

koauau. [Ma. /koːˈauau/: Williams 122 *Kōau... kōauau*, n. *1*. A kind of musical instrument played with the nose; also a flute for mouth.] A flute-like Maori instrument.
1917 *NZ at the Front* 164 He [*sc.* bagpipes] sound like one t'ousand koauau, Maori flute. **1930** *NZ Short Stories* 35 He proceeded toward the edge of the cliff, slowly, breathing into his *koauau*, to warm it into a sweet tone. **1993** *Sunday Times* (Wellington) 28 Feb. 26 After dinner [c 1920] the old man produced his flute; it was not a koauau: it was a piece of gaspipe about 10 inches long.

kodero, var. KORERO.

kodi maka, var. KORIMAKO.

koekoea. Also early **koe-koea**, **koekoia**. [Ma. /koekoeˈaː/: Williams 123 *Koekoeā*, n.] *long-tailed cuckoo* (CUCKOO 2 (2)).
1843 DIEFFENBACH *Travels in NZ* II. 123 Two migratory cuckoos..called kohaperoa, or koekoia..mark the period of the first potato-harvest. **1857** HURSTHOUSE *NZ* I. 115 The koekoea, second cuckoo, arrives. **1873** [see CUCKOO 2 (2)]. **1907** MANSFIELD *Urewera Notebook* (1978) 61 The small boy is raggedly dressed in brown—he wears a brown felt hat with a 'koe-koea' feather placed rakishly to the side. **1922** *Auckland Weekly News* 7 Dec. 19 This cuckoo, the koekoea, is not to be confused with the bronze or shining cuckoo, called by the Maoris pipiwharauroa. **1955** OLIVER *NZ Birds* 538 Long-tailed Cuckoo. Koekoea *Eudynamis taitensis*. **1966** FALLA et al. *Birds NZ* 181 Long-tailed Cuckoo *Eudynamis taitensis*... Koekoea, Kawekawea, Kohoperoa. **1985** [see CUCKOO 2 (2)]. **1990** *Checklist Birds NZ* 183 *Eudynamys taitensis*... Long-tailed Cuckoo (*Koekoea*).

koekohe, var. KOHIKOHI.

koekoia, var. KOEKOEA.

ko(e)teedo, varr. KOTIRO.

kogohooe, var. KOHIKOHI.

kogop, var. KOKOPU.

koha. [Ma. /ˈkoha/: Williams 123 *Koha* (i). *3*. Present, gift.] A gift; a donation, a contribution.
1982 *Evening Post* (Wellington) 23 Mar. 5 A $15 weekly charge [at the language nursery] has been suggested, but not finalised. Payment might be made by way of the traditional Maori koha (contribution). **1983** HULME *Bone People* 293 We were on our way to you with this koha. **1986** *New Outlook* Sept.–Oct. 10 The gift of money had been left [by the TV crew] as a koha for food. **1992** *Capital Times* (Wellington) 9–16 Sept. 1 The late night atmosphere will be laid back and entry by koha.

kohai, var. KOWHAI.

kohanga reo. Also in a shortened form **kohanga**. [Ma. /ˈkohaŋa ˈreo/: Williams 124 *Kōhanga* = *kōwhanga*, n. *1*. Nest; Williams 336 *Reo* (i)... *4*. Language, dialect.] A pre-school educational institution at which the Maori language is the medium of instruction; a 'language nursery' or 'language nest' where (esp. urban) Maori pre-school children can learn and enjoy their language and culture; the building housing a kohanga reo. See also LANGUAGE NEST.
1982 *Evening Post* (Wellington) 23 Mar. 5 The nga kohanga reo (language nurseries) will open now in Wellington and Wainuiomata. **1983** *AJHR* E-1 19 Early in 1982 the Department of Maori Affairs received approval to set up 5 official Te Kohanga Reo centres for pre-school children...to provide an environment where Maori language is fostered. **1988** MACRAE *Awful Childhoods* 142 He said he needed it for kohanga business... The kohanga were getting a grant of twelve thou a year. **1990** *Evening Post* (Wellington) 11 July 8 Maori children continue to do poorly in the classroom, except those attending Kohanga Reo, or pre-school Maori language nests. **1993** *Dominion* (Wellington) 12 June 3 Approval to build a kohanga reo on a council park in Miramar..has been granted despite objections by neighbours.

kohaperoa, kohapiroa, varr. KOHOPEROA.

kohekohe /ˈkʌuwiˌkʌuwi/. Also early **eckoha** (=he kohe); **kohikohi**. [Ma. /ˈkohekohe/: Williams 124 *Kohe* (ii)... *kohekohe*, n... a tree.] *Dysoxylum spectabile* (fam. Meliaceae), a tall tree of the North Island and Marlborough Sounds, having a reddish wood, large glossy pinnate leaves and conspicuous panicles of white flowers in winter. See also *native cedar*, *New Zealand cedar* (CEDAR 2 (2)), *native mahogany* (MAHOGANY 1).
1817 NICHOLAS *Voyage NZ* II. 245 The trees which the natives chiefly make subservient to their purposes, are a large tree named eckoha, [etc.]. **1835** YATE *NZ* (1970) 48 Kohekohe... A fine handsome tree, with a trunk free of branches, to a height of forty feet. **1838** POLACK *NZ* II. 398 The *Kohikohi* another of the many laurel trees of the soil, grows to a height [*sic*] of fifty feet. **1848** TAYLOR *Leaf from Nat. Hist.* 20 *Kohekohe, tree*;.. wood red; the New Zealand mahogany or cedar. **1851** *Richmond-Atkinson Papers* (1960) I. 99 We had our blocks at work today pulling down some stiff stumps of Kohikohi (a red wood used for fencing and roof-shingles). **1875** [see CEDAR 1]. **1883** HECTOR *Handbook NZ* 127 Kohekohe.—A large tree, 40–50 feet high. Its leaves are bitter, and used to make a stomachic infusion; wood tough but splits. **1890** [see CEDAR 1]. **1907** LAING & BLACKWELL *Plants NZ* 222 *Dysoxylum spectabile* (*The Kohekohe*). A tree, often 50 ft. in height... This tree is known to settlers as the *New Zealand Cedar*. **1922** [see CEDAR 2 (2)]. **1936** GUTHRIE-SMITH *NZ Naturalist* 97 Of the primeval growth that once covered [Stephen Island, Marlborough], little or nothing remains—only here and there an inconsiderable grove of cedar—kohekohe—a species difficult to burn. **1946** *JPS* LV. 152 *Kohekohe*, a

KOHEPEROA 419 **KOHUTUHUTU**

tree..fragrant flowers hanging from stems and bole in mid-winter. **1983** LAMBERT *Illustr. Hist. of Taranaki* 35 The predominance of small wooden buildings with vertical cladding and kohekohe shingles were [*sic*] a distinctive feature of the town.

koheperoa, var. KOHOPEROA.

kohepiro. [Ma. /ˈkohepiro/: Williams 124 *Kohepiro*, n.: Ibid. 125 *Koheriki 1: Angelica rosaefolia.*] (Usu.) *Scandia rosifolia* (formerly *Angelica rosaefolia*) (fam. Apiaceae), a native herb of the northern North Island; occas. also ANISEED.
    1867 HOOKER *Handbook* 765 Koheriki... *Angelica rosaefolia.* Koherika; Kohepiro. **1906** CHEESEMAN *Manual NZ Flora* 225 [*Angelica rosaefolia*] *Koherika; Kohepiro.* **1930** *NZJST* XI. 152 Where the slopes are broken..the following shrubby trees grow abundantly: Kohepiro (*Angelica rosaefolia*) [etc.]. **1979** STARK *Maori Herbal Remedies* 41 Kohepiro, Koheriki (Maori Anise) *Gingida montana.* **1981** BROOKER et al. *NZ Medicinal Plants* 95 *Angelica rosaefolia,* Koheriki, *kohepiro.*

koheru. Also **kohédu.** [Ma. /ˈkoːheru/: Williams 125 *Kōheru, kōheriheri,* n. *Decapterus koheru.*] *Decapterus koheru* (fam. Carangidae), a smallish elongated sea-fish of north-eastern coastal waters, electric blue on the back, silver-white on the belly. See also HERRING SCAD 1, YELLOWTAIL 2 (6).
    [**1820** LEE & KENDALL *NZ Gram. & Vocab.* 165 Kohédu, *s.* A certain fish.] **1875** *TrNZI* VII. 247 Caranx koheru... Koheru... The Herring Scad. **1886** SHERRIN *Handbook Fishes NZ* 100 There is an allied species [to the trevalli] called the koheru, or the herring scad, which is without doubt edible. **1921** *NZJST* IV. 117 *Yellowtail; Koheru.* Common around North Auckland Peninsula during the early summer months. **1957** PARROTT *Sea Angler's Fishes* 81 The Koheru has a robust, elongate body, nearly four times as long as its greatest depth, and covered with very small scales which entirely cover the breast. **1966** DOOGUE & MORELAND *Sea Anglers' Guide* 233 Koheru... *Other names:*.. horse mackerel, scad. Food qualities: Quite reasonable if soused in vinegar—the best bait for marlin. **1972** DOAK *Fishes* 38 As a school of large koheru wheeled around me in a tight circle I was amazed to hear an electric buzzing in the water. **1982** AYLING *Collins Guide* (1984) 216 [Koheru] sometimes sweep in close to the rock faces on the offshore islands and, pose briefly, bodies twitching, for the parasite-picking crimson cleaners, milling around for a few minutes before streaming back out into open water. Koheru are found between North Cape and East Cape.

kohi, var. COO-EE, KOHIKOHI, KOWHAI.

kohia. Also **kowia.** [Ma. /ˈkoːhia/: Williams 125 *Kōhia, Tetrapathaea repanda.*] *New Zealand passionfruit* (PASSIONFRUIT 1).
    1848 TAYLOR *Leaf from Nat. Hist.* 30 Kowia, *passion flower.* **1867** HOOKER *Handbook* 765 Kohia... *Passiflora tetrandra.* Mantle of kohia, kareao, and other epiphytic plants. **1889** *TrNZI* XXI. 37 The kohia (*Passiflora tetrandra*) is very abundant. **1902** *Brett's Colonists' Guide* 743 Ko-hia... The seeds are bruised into pulp, and heated in a Maori oven. **1940** [see PASSION-FLOWER]. **1965** HILLIARD *Power of Joy* 179 From the grass a ponga was trying to find the sun through a thicket of kohia. **1978, 1982** [see PASSIONFLOWER 1]. **1992** *NZ Gardener* Jan. 37 There is one species of passion flower native to New Zealand—this is sometimes called the New Zealand passionfruit or Kohia and is *Passiflora (syn. Tetrapathaea) tetrandra.*

kohikohi. Also **koekohe, kogohooe, kohi, kohikoi.** [Ma. /ˈkohikohi/: Williams 125 *Kohikohi* (ii) n. *1. Hemerocoetes acanthorhynchus... 2. Latridopsis lineata,* trumpeter.] Any of various species of Opalfish, *Hemerocoetes* spp. (fam. Percophidae), or the common trumpeter, *Latris lineata* (fam. Latrididae) (TRUMPETER 1).
    1842 GRAY *Fauna* in Dieffenbach *Travels in NZ* (1843) II. 213 The New Zealand name of this fish [*sc. Haemerocaetes acanthorhynchus*] is written 'Kogohooe' by G. Forster, and 'Kohikoi' by Dr Dieffenbach. **1872** HUTTON & HECTOR *Fishes NZ* 107 The Trumpeter..which..the natives call Kohikohi, is the best flavoured of any of our fishes. **1878** *TrNZI* X. 326 [Maori or Settlers' Name] Kohi, Trumpeter.. [Scientific Name] *Latris hecateia.* **1885** *TrNZI* XVII. 419 The fishing off the island is very good, there being abundance of hapuku, kohikohi, maumau, schnapper, kahawai, tarakihi. **1927** PHILLIPPS *Bibliogr. NZ Fishes* (1971) 39 *Latris lineata...* Trumpeter; Kohikohi. **1945** koekohe [see TRUMPETER 1]. **1966** DOOGUE & MORELAND *Sea Anglers' Guide* 253 Trumpeter... A large, strong-swimming fish of rough ground... *Other names: Latris lineata;* trumpeter (Australia); kohikohi. **1988** FRANCIS *Coastal Fishes NZ* 40 Trumpeter (Kohikoi) *Latris lineata...* Trumpeter are usually seen singly or in small groups over shallow reefs.

kohikohi, var. KOHEKOHE.

kohikoi, var. KOHIKOHI.

kohoa, var. KOHUA.

kohoperoa. Also freq. early **kohaperoa,** occas. **kohapiroa, koheperoa.** [Ma. /ˈkoːhoperoa/: Williams 124 *Kōhaperoa.* = *kōhoperoa;* 126 *Kōhoperoa.*] *long-tailed cuckoo* (CUCKOO 2 (2)).
    1835 YATE *NZ* (1970) 65 *Kohaperoa*—This bird is remarkable for its long body, and short cock's beak. **1838** POLACK *NZ* I. 300 The *kohapiroa* : this little fellow is remarkable for taking particular care of itself... It fills the bushes with melodious notes, only equalled by musical bells. **1843** [see KOEKOEA]. **1859** THOMSON *Story NZ* I. 26 The Kohoperoa..is about the size and colour of the sparrow-hawk. **1869** [see CUCKOO 2 (2)]. **1873** BULLER *Birds NZ* 108 [The Grey Warbler] is the willing victim of our two migrating Cuckoos, the Warauroa and Koheperoa. **1882** HAY *Brighter Britain* II. 223 The Koheperoa (*Eudynamis Taitensis*) is a long-tailed, brown-plumaged cuckoo. **1904** *TrNZI* XXXVI. 113 *The Kohoperoa or Koekoea, Long-tailed Cuckoo.* **1926** [see CUCKOO 2 (2)]. **1946** *JPS* LV. 152 koekoea, kohoperoa, a migratory bird.., long-tailed cuckoo, screamer; winters in Samoa group. **1966** [see KOEKOEA]. **1985** [see CUCKOO 2 (2)].

kohorimako, var. KORIMAKO.

kohua. *Hist.* Also with Ma. variant **kohue:** also **kohoa,** and the early anglicized GOASHORE q.v., **kohoa.** [Ma. /ˈkoːhua/, /ˈkoːhue/: Williams 126 *kōhua 1.* Maori oven..*kohu* (ii). *2..*boiler; 126 *Kōhue* = *kōhua,* n. Boiler.] **a.** HANGI 1.
    1843 DIEFFENBACH *Travels in NZ* II. 43 The native oven, *hangi* or *kohua,* made in the well-known manner with heated stones. **1898** MORRIS *Austral-English* 251 *Kohua, n.* Maori word, for (1) a Maori oven; (2) a boiler.
    b. An iron pot (or pan) for cooking; GOASHORE 1.
    1845 WILLIAMS *Journal* in Drummond *Married & Gone to NZ* (1960) 44 A kohue full of water for washing our late visitors' sheets had to be emptied out to mix flour for the natives. **c1853** CHALMERS *Otago Reminisc.* in Beattie *Pioneers Explore Otago* (1947) 35 [The Maori] should show me the country and in payment..I should give him a '*kohoa*' (that is, a three-legged iron pot). **1862** CARTER *From the Black Rocks* (1950) 38 We found the women already up, a fire lighted, and some potatoes and fish being cooked in an iron pot, or kohua. **1905** BAUCKE *White Man Treads* 72 The last day of all he [*sc.* Captain Cook] gave Toia another pot, and..with much pointing at it, said 'Now go ashore.' So we took that to be its name; for do we not call it at this distant day a 'kohua'? **1921** *Quick March* 11 Apr. 29 The [gambling] stakes were usually thrown into a three-legged iron pot—the 'kohua' of the old-timers. **1940** MATTHEWS *Matthews of Kaitaia* 66 The plate was placed on the embers, and a large three-legged pot known as a *kohue* was turned over it, and a fire built over the pot. **1982** BURTON *Two Hundred Yrs. NZ Food* 1 The third method, boiling (or *kohua*), seems to have been used more rarely.

kohuda, var. KOURA.

kohuhu. [Ma. /koːˈhuːhu/: Williams 126 *Kōhūhū, Pittosporum tenuifolium.*] *Pittosporum tenuifolium* (fam. Pittosporaceae), a small black-barked tree of lowland forest and scrub, having light green leaves with a wavy margin, pungent when crushed; commonly cultivated for hedges. See also BUCKET-OF-WATER-WOOD c, KOHUKOHU 2, *black mapau* (MAPAU 2 (1)), *black matipo* (MATIPO 2 (1)), TAWHIRI, TIPAU 2.
    [**1820** LEE & KENDALL *NZ Gram. & Vocab.* 165 Kohúhu, *s.* A shrub so called.] **1853** HOOKER *II Flora Novae-Zelandiae I Flowering Plants* 21 *Pittosporum tenuifolium...* Common as far south as Akaroa... Nat. names, 'Mapauriki', *Cunn.*; 'Kohuhu', *Col.*; 'Karo' of Middle Island, **1867** HOOKER *Handbook* 765 Kohuhu... *Pittosporum tenuifolium.* **1939** [see MATIPO 2 (1)]. **1940** LAING & BLACKWELL *Plants NZ* 199 *P. tenuifolium* was called by [the Maori] the *Tawhiwhi* or *Kohuhu.* **1951** LEVY *Grasslands NZ* (1970) 87 Such species as lancewood, karamu..kohuhu..with tree ferns, weki, and mamuku. **1978** MOORE & IRWIN *Oxford Book NZ Plants* 66 *Pittosporum tenuifolium.* Kohuhu is another small tree that grows naturally in both North and South Islands. **1982** [see MATIPO 2 (1)].

kohukohu. [Ma. /ˈkohukohu/: Williams 126 *Kohu* (iii) *Kohukohu 1. Stellaria* [spp.]... *4. Pittosporum tenuifolium... 5. Scleranthus biflorus.*] Any of various plants.
    1. *Scleranthus biflorus* (fam. Caryophyllaceae), a small mat-forming herb common on coastal rocks, sometimes found on mountain screes and rocks.
    1853 HOOKER *II Flora Novae-Zelandiae I Flowering Plants* 74 Scleranthus *biflorus...* Nat. names, Northern Island, 'Kohu-Kohu'. **1869** *TrNZI* I. (rev. edn.) 207 Kohukohu. Scleranthus biflorus. **1870** *TrNZI* II. 126 Scleranthus biflorus Kohu kohu.

    2. KOHUHU.
    1889 FEATON *Art Album NZ Flora* 177 Kohukohu [Maori name]..Kohukohu [Settlers' name]..[*P.*] obcordatum..Small tree. **1981** BROOKER et al. *NZ Medicinal Plants* 16 Best specially mentions kohukohu (*Pittosporum tenuifolium*) as important for raising the 'tapu' on sick people.

kohutuhutu. Also early **koutu utu.** [Ma. /koːˈhutuhutu/: Williams 127 *Kōhutuhutu,* n. *Fuchsia excorticata..= kōtukutuku.*] FUCHSIA 1 and 2. Cf. KOTUKUTUKU.
    1835 YATE *NZ* (1970) 111 The fruit of the Kohutuhutu, *Fuchsia excorticata.* **1838** POLACK *NZ* I.

288 The *korai, koutu utu, miro,* and *putuhutu,* are wild forest fruits, prized only by the elder natives. **1867** HOOKER *Handbook* 765 Kohutuhutu, *Col[enso]. Fuchsia excorticata.* **1886** KIRK in *Settler's Handbook NZ* (1902) 122 [Native name] Kohutuhutu..[Settlers' name] Fuchsia. **1890** [see FUCHSIA 1]. **1907** LAING & BLACKWELL *Plants NZ* 294 *Fuchsia excorticata* (*The Tree Fuchsia*)... Maori name *Kotukutuku* or *Kohutuhutu,* and of the fruit, *Konini.* **1946** *JPS* LV. 152 *Kōhutuhutu,* an irregularly-growing tree (Fuchsia excorticata), tree-fuchsia: more commonly kōtukutuku, but kōhutuhutu adopted to avoid possible confusion with kōtuku, white-heron.

koi katoa, var. KAHIKATOA.

koinga. [Ma. /'koiŋa/: Williams 128 *Koinga* (i), n... shark.] Any of several small sharks or dogfish, esp. *Squalus acanthias* (fam. Squalidae). See also DOGFISH 1.
 1924 *NZJST* VI. 262 Smooth-hound, *Mustelus antarcticus...* This shark was known to the Maoris as 'koinga'. **1927** [see OKEOKE]. **1956** GRAHAM *Treasury NZ Fishes* 80 Spined Dogfish (Koinga or Okeoke) *Koinga lebruni...* The generic name *Koinga* is from a Maori word which means 'a sharp point' in allusion to the sharp spine in front of each dorsal fin. **1963** KEENE *O te Raki* 192 *Koinga:* spine shark; grows to 2 ft. in length. **1982** AYLING *Collins Guide* (1984) 64 *Spotted Spiny Dogfish..Squalus acanthias* (Spotted dog, southern dogfish, koinga). **1991** [see DOGFISH 1].

koiro: see NGOIRO.

koitareke. Also early **koitareki.** [Ma. /'koitareke/: Williams 128 *Koitareke...* 2. *Porzana pusilla,* marsh crake.] CRAKE a.
 1871 HUTTON *Catalogue Birds NZ* 33 Ortygometra affinis... Spotted Rail. Koitareki **1873, 1886** [see CRAKE a]. **1904** [see RAIL 2 (8)]. **1955** [see CRAKE a]. **1966** FALLA et al. *Birds NZ* 106 Marsh Crake *Porzana pusilla* Other name: Koitareke. **1985, 1990** [see CRAKE a].

kokako. Also early **kakáko, koukaato** (prob. a transcription error). [Ma. /'ko:kako/: Williams 129 *Kōkako,* n... New Zealand crow.]
 1. *Callaeas cineria* (fam. Callaeidae), a large bluish-grey forest bird of limited flight, having bright blue (North Island subspecies) or orange (South Island subspecies) fleshy wattles. See also BELLBIRD 1 b, CROW n.[1] I, JACK n.[2] a, WATTLE BIRD.
 [**1820** LEE & KENDALL *NZ Gram. & Vocab.* 166 Kókako; Name of a certain bird.] **1835** YATE *NZ* (1970) 64 *Kokako*; called, by some, the New-Zealand crow... It has a strong black beak..and a small brilliant light-blue flap hanging down on each side, from the ear. **1838** POLACK *NZ* I. 301 The *kakáko* is a species of crow, not unlike its European counterpart. **1844** WILLIAMS *NZ Jrnl.* (1956) 102 The green koukaato fluttering among [the pohutukawa's] blossoms, singing its lively and melodious notes. **1855** DRURY *Sailing Directions* 66 Birds met with in Pelorus... New Zealand Crow—Kokako. **1861** HAAST *Rep. Topogr. Explor. Nelson* 139 The first is the kakako.., the New Zealand crow. **1874** *TrNZI* VI. 146 The Kokoka loving a moist temperature will probably soon entirely forsake its ancient places of resort. **1882** HAY *Brighter Britain* II. 224 The Kokako..is a crow, and is not uncommon in the Kaipara. It has blue wattles on the beak. Its note is peculiar, being sometimes a low, hollow boom, and at others a shrill and somewhat bell-like tone. **1890** *Otago Witness* (Dunedin) 6 Mar. 35 Melody awoke us all..tuis, mokos, kokakos or crow..all piping forth. **1929** DUGGAN *NZ Bird Songs* 31 Little heart, be proud of the Kokako... May it Ko for ever on the ridges. May it Ko until the sun turns cold. **1946** *JPS* LV. 144 *kōkako,* two birds (Callaeas wilsoni—North Island, and C. cinereous [*sic*]—South Island), blue-wattled crow and orange-wattled crow, the colour of the wattles being the only difference; nearly if not quite extinct: this is the bird to which the echoic name bell-bird was first applied. **1966** [see *bluegill* (a) (BLUE a. 2 b)]. **1988** MORRIS & SMITH *Wild South* 206 In Maori legend [its] long legs are said to be a gift to the kokako from the demi-god Maui when the bird brought him water after his long battle with the sun.
 2. With a modifier: **North Island** (or **blue wattled**), **South Island** (or **orange-wattled**).
 (1) **North Island** (or **blue-wattled**) **kokako**. *Callaeas cinerea wilsoni.* See also *bluegill* (a) (BLUE *a.* 2 b).
 1955 OLIVER *NZ Birds* 520 *North Island Kokako...* The first mention of the North Island Kokako that I can trace is that of Yate in 1835. **1966** *Encycl. NZ* II. 235 There are two races of kokako, *Callaeas cinerea wilsoni,* the blue-wattled kokako, which occurs in the North Island, and *Callaeas cinerea cinerea,* the orange-wattled kokako, inhabiting the South Island and Stewart Island. **1989** MORRIS & SMITH *Wild South* 204 The North Island kokako survives in the dense podocarp forests of the North, but there are only small pockets of forest today. **1990** *Dominion* (Wellington) 6 Nov. 10 The North Island kokako or blue wattle crow is endangered and about 1500 survivors are confined mainly to the Bay of Plenty and King Country.
 (2) **South Island** (or **orange-wattled**) **kokako**. *Callaeas cinerea cinerea.*
 1955 OLIVER *NZ Birds* 523 *South Island Kokako Callaeas cinerea.* This is the Wattle-bird of Captain Cook and was discovered at Dusky Sound in 1773. **1966** *Encycl. NZ* II. 235 The South Island kokako, though once locally common, is now very rare. [*op. cit.* orange-wattled kokako, see (1) above.] **1988** MORRIS & SMITH *Wild South* 203 The South Island kokako, which had orange wattles (sometimes almost vermilion) with a touch of blue at the base, has become so rare (because of deer and predators in the beech forests where it lived) that it is now believed to be extinct. **1990** *Dominion* (Wellington) 6 Nov. 10 The only evidence that the South Island kokako may have survived was a feather found on Stewart Island in 1986.

kokidi, var. KOKIRI n.[1]

kokihi. [Ma. /'ko:kihi/: Williams 130 *Kōkihi* (i),.. 2. n. *Tetragonia expansa.*] SPINACH.
 1867 HOOKER *Handbook* 765 Kokihi... *Tetragonia trigyna.* **1869** *TrNZI* I. (rev. edn.) 267 On the New Zealanders learning to write, they used..the crimson juice of the berry of the Kokihi, (a species of *Tetragonia*). **1906** [see SPINACH]. c**1920** BEATTIE *Trad. Lifeways Southern Maori* (1994) 118 Kokihi is a seaside plant with red berries and these could be eaten as they were harmless. **1952** RICHARDS *Chatham Is.* 27 *Tetragonia..trigyna...* Beach Spinach. Kokihi. **1982** BURTON *Two Hundred Yrs. NZ Food* 16 Another New Zealand native, New Zealand spinach, or kokihi, so impressed the ship's botanist, Sir Joseph Banks, that he took it back to England and grew it in his own garden.

kokiri, n.[1] Also early **cokiddie, kokídi; kokori** (prob. erron.). [Ma. /'ko:kiri/: Williams 130 *Kōkiri...* 4. n. Spear... 6... leather-jacket; a fish.] LEATHERJACKET 1 (*Parika scaber*). See also SPEARFISH.
 1817 NICHOLAS *Voyage NZ* II. 22 I observed in one of the canoes a very singular fish, which the natives call *cokiddie,* or the spear-fish. It was about the size of a perch, and shaped very like it, except the head, which was rather oblong, than of a pig; its skin was quite rough, and behind its head nature had armed it with a sharp bone, about two inches long, which it could extrude and draw in at pleasure. It was from this bone that the natives gave it the name of cokiddie, which signifies *spear* in their language, and therefore appropriate enough. [**1820** LEE & KENDALL *NZ Gram. & Vocab.* 166 Kokídi, s,.. also a certain fish.] **1844** COLENSO *Excurs. Northern Is.* in Taylor *Early Travellers* (1959) 52 The natives..had taken several very fine Kokori (*Balistes* sp...)... Its skin is of a dirty-olive colour, and rough, resembling shagreen. **1921** [see CREAMFISH]. **1947** [see LEATHERJACKET 1]. **1949** BUCK *Coming of Maori* 215 Various fish were caught but the most satisfactory was the leather jacket (*kokiri..*) which is the plague of line fishermen owing to their small mouths removing the bait. **1956** GRAHAM *Treasury NZ Fishes* 374 Rough Leather Jacket, Trigger-fish or File-fish (Kokiri) *Parika scaber.* **1963** KEENE *O te Raki* 192 *Kokiri:* leather jacket (a kind of fish). **1982** [see LEATHERJACKET 1].

kokiri, n.[2] [Ma. /'ko:kiri/: Williams 130 *Kōkiri* 2. *v.* Dart, rush forward, charge.] Used of a Maori community group aiming to expedite Maori interests or to advance the solution of difficulties facing Maori people. Mainly *attrib.,* esp. in **kokiri unit**.
 1981 *Evening Post* (Wellington) 3 Feb. 16 Kokiri (to advance) units will consist of department staff who will provide a full-time support service to community action programmes. **1982** *Evening Post* (Wellington) 14 July 10 The proposal to establish a kokiri basic skills centre in Porirua as an alternative way of learning for young Maoris and Islanders has been virtually abandoned.

koko. *Obs. in English use.* [Ma. /'ko:ko:/: Williams 130 *Kōkō = Tūī:* ad. Ma. kō to sing, as birds.] TUI 1.
 1839 TAYLOR *Journal* (ATLTS) II. 109 They ornament their canoes with the same [feathers] the natives call the bird *koko* or tui. **1847** ANGAS *Savage Life* II. 6 The lone cry of the *ko ko,* (a species of a goatsucker) echoed plaintively from amongst the dense copse-like underwood. **1851** *Lyttelton Times* 25 Jan. 6 The sooner these apt pioneers of civilization [*i.e.* the shepherd and the herdsman] arrive to 'disturb the ancient solitary reign' of the wild pig, and the koko, the sooner will this fine district be ready for whole villages of Englishmen. **1873** BULLER *Birds NZ* 87 Tui and Koko; the young bird distinguished as Pi-tui or Pikari. **1884** *NZJSc.* II. 276 *Prosthemadera Novae Zealandiae...* Parson-bird, Poe-bird, Tui, Koko. **1897** *TrNZI* XXIX. 165 'Koko' is the name given to the bird tui, the parson-bird..by the Moriori, and also used by the Maori in the south of New Zealand. c**1920** *South Island Maori Lists* 'Wahi Mahika Kai' in Beattie *Maori Place-names Canterbury* (1945) 64 Koko—the tui (also spelt kokoo to show the accent is on long second vowel).

kokobula, var. COCKABULLY.

kokoai, var. KOKOWAI.

kokomuka. [Ma. /'ko:ko:muka/: Williams 130 *Kōkōmuka,* n. *Hebe salicifolia,* etc.] Any of several species of *Hebe* (fam. Scrophulariaceae), esp. the coastal shrub *H. elliptica,* distinguished by its attractive clusters of mauve flowers. See also HEBE.
 1867 HOOKER *Handbook* 765 Kokomuka. *Veronica* sp. **1870** *TrNZI* II. 176 [The Snares are] almost entirely covered with scrub and trees of stunted growth, the Tupari, Akeake, and Kokomuka. **1889** *TrNZI* XXI. 380

KOKOPARA

The island [sc. Snares] is mostly covered with bush, the akeake (*Olearia* sp.) and kokomuka (*Veronica elliptica*) being the commonest trees. **1982** WILSON *Stewart Is. Plants* 68 *Hebe elliptica* Kōkōmuka... Bushy shrub.

kokopara. Also **kokopuru** (not recorded by Williams). [Ma. /ˈkokopara/: Williams 130 *Kokopara*..Small freshwater fish (Whang[anui dial.]), variety of *Galaxias* ([Ngai] Tahu.) (also 130 *Kōkopuruao*..Large variety of *Galaxias fasciatus*); Williams 151 *Koukoupara*, n. A fish.] COCKABULLY 1, KOKOPU 1.

c1920, **1920** [see COCKABULLY]. **1940** STUDHOLME *Te Waimate* (1954) 249 Fifty years ago the Waimate Creek was full of native trout, or Kokopuru; in fact the Maoris called the creek Waikokopuru... The Kokopuru was rather a pretty fish; it had a slimy skin like an eel, with large golden spots all over it. **1942** ANDERSEN *Maori Place Names* 300 The Waimate creek, flowing through the town of Waimate in South Canterbury, was formerly, and still is locally, known as the Waikokopuru, not Waikokopu, and some of the Pakehas thought that when the Maori used the name kokopuru he was trying to say 'cock-a-bully'. **1945** BEATTIE *Maori Place-names Canterbury* 63 The panako is the rock trout, and is nearly extinct. It looks like the kokopara in shape, but is black in colour. **1989** HULME & MORRISON *Homeplaces* 10 Not to mention the whitebait called kokopara, that somehow transmogrified to be the cockabully.

kokopu. Also early **kekogop** [=?he kogopu], **kogop** (the final devoiced Ma. /u/ not perceived by the interlocutor). [Ma. /ˈko:kopu/: Williams 138 *Kopu* (i), *kōkopu* n. *1. Galaxias fasciatus... 3. Gobiomorphus gobioides*, bully, a freshwater fish.]

1. Any of several small freshwater fish of *Galaxias* spp. (fam. Galaxiidae). See also BULLY n.¹, COCKABULLY 1, GALAXIAS, KOKOPARA, PARA n.¹, *Maori trout, mountain trout, native trout* (TROUT 2 (3), (4), (5)).

[**1820** LEE & KENDALL *NZ Gram. & Vocab.* 166 *Kokópu*,.. Name of a certain fish.] **1842** GRAY *Fauna* in Dieffenbach *Travels in NZ* (1843) II. 211–212 *Clinus littoreus*... Named 'Kogop' by the natives of Queen Charlotte's Sound.. *Tripterygion varium*... Named 'Kekogop' by the... natives of Queen Charlotte's Sound. **1845** TAYLOR *Journal* 19 Nov. (ATLTS) III. 176 [Near Taupo in a lake]..it was surprising what a number of kokopu we picked up... It is of a dark yellow color [*sic*]. **1857** HURSTHOUSE *NZ* I. 122 The spotted Kokopu, called trout..abounds in every brook. **1872** HUTTON & HECTOR *Fishes NZ* 128 *G. fasciatus*..is the Kokopu proper... [It is] a fat sluggish fish found lurking under stones and rotten logs in all the streams in the colony. **1886** SHERRIN *Handbook Fishes NZ* 138 The Natives..say there is the kokopu of the stream and the kokopu of the lake, which are quite distinct from each other. **1892** *AJHR* H-45 3 In the earlier days there were no edible fish of any size in the streams of the colony if we except..the wretched kokopu (*Galaxias fasciatus*). **1903** *TrNZI* XXXV. 318 The kokopu proper..afford very tame sport, but are fair eating, resembling the eel in flavour. **1922** THOMSON *Naturalisation Animals & Plants* 187 The kokopu, a name corrupted in the south of the South Island to cock-a-bully (*Galaxias kokopu*), was sometimes popularly called trout. **1938** MAKERETI *Old-Time Maori* 243 Taupo Lake was full of kokopu when I was a child... The kokopu was generally taken on dark nights in summer and autumn and was 5 to 12 inches long and sometimes more. Its flavour was not unlike whiting, and there were about six varieties. **1956** GRAHAM *Treasury NZ Fishes* 116 While I was farming..in the Bay of Plenty,... small streams, no more than a trickle in the summer months, had numerous Kokopu living in small holes and in good condition. **1978** FULLER *Maori Food & Cook.* 13 Kokopu (*Galaxias fasciatus*) was good but bony eating—the Maori knew three varieties, rauinahehe, reretawa and para.

2. With a modifier: **banded (barred)**, **giant** (occas. **black**).

(1) **banded (barred) kokopu**. *Galaxias fasciatus*.

1963 WOODS *Freshwater Fishes* 27 The pattern is the most certain means of identifying the Banded Kokopu which has light bands on a darker ground. **1978** MCDOWALL *NZ Freshwater Fishes* 57 *Galaxias fasciatus*..Banded Kokopu Like the Giant Kokopu, the Banded Kokopu is sometimes known as Maori Trout or Native Trout. **1980** *Freshwater Catch* VI. 6 The banded kokopu is a small whitebait—often only up to about 45mm long—which is a distinct amber colour, and is often referred to as 'golden bait' by whitebaiters. **1983** *Land of Mist* 72 The banded kokopu is another whitebait species reaching 26 cm. Its habitat is a pool in a small bush-covered stream which may be a considerable altitude and distance from the sea.

(2) **giant** (occas. **black**) **kokopu**. *Galaxias argenteus* (fam. Galaxiidae). See also BULL TROUT.

1939 Black Kokopu [see TROUT 2 (4)]. **1963** WOODS *Freshwater Fishes* 25 The Giant Kokopu was the first native freshwater fish to be recognised scientifically; this was in 1789. **1979** *Freshwater Catch* V. 8 Christchurch FRD recently received a kilogram of line-caught whitebait from the Chatham Islands... It was an adult giant kokopu (*Galaxias argenteus*), with what explorer Douglas described as the 'Hebrew alphabet' displayed on its back and sides. **1980** *Freshwater Catch* VI. 7 That the giant Kokopu is an 'adult' whitebait is perhaps the most extraordinary, since the adult is a large bulky fish... Known to reach nearly 600mm and 3kg. **1990** MCDOWALL *NZ Freshwater Fishes* 89 The giant kokopu is the biggest species of *Galaxias*, not only in New Zealand, but also in the whole family. It was the first galaxiid discovered, being collected by naturalists visiting New Zealand with Captain James Cook in 1773.

kokopuru: see KOKOPARA. See also COCKABULLY, KOKOPU.

kokori, var. KOKIRI *n.*¹

kokorimako, kokoromaka, varr. KORIMAKO.

kokowai. Also **cocoi**, **kokó ai**. [Ma. /ˈko:ko:wai/: Williams 131 *Kōkōwai*, n... red ochre.] Red ochre, a pigment used in Maori decoration or the earth burnt to produce it; occas. applied to the paint produced by mixing red ochre with shark oil.

[**1820** LEE & KENDALL *NZ Gram. & Vocab.* 166 *Kokó, ai, s.* Red ochre; red paint for the skin.] **1836** WILSON *Jrnl.* in *Missionary Life & Work NZ* (1889) III. 43 Two large totara posts..daubed with *kokowai*. **1840** *NZ Jrnl.* I. 202 On the banks of the Wai wakaio..he found an extensive layer of the yellow ochre, which when baked, forms the *Kokoai* or red paint of the natives. **1841** BIDWILL *Rambles in NZ* (1952) 61 The natives are very fond of daubing their heads with a sort of red paint which they call 'cocoi'. **1866** HUNT *Chatham Is.* 16 Rubbing *kokoai*, or ochre, over my face, and sticking feathers in my hair, he [Rauparaha] declared that I should be his *Pakeha-Maori* forever. **1879** *TrNZI* XI. 75 *Kokowai* is a kind of pigment, burnt, dried, and mixed with shark-liver oil. **1898** MORRIS *Austral-English* 251 *Kokowai*, n. Maori name for Red Ochre, an oxide of iron deposited in certain rivers, used by the Maoris for painting. **1905** BAUCKE *White Man Treads* 7 The monstrosities which decorated his whare runanga (meeting-house) posts..and the rafters painted with kokowai (iron-ore rust)..sighed an adoring, admiring content at the sight of his highest standard in art. **1922** COWAN *NZ Wars* (1955) I. 119 His naked body was as slippery as an eel's, coated with a mixture of *kokowai*, or red ochre and shark-oil. **1963** BARROW *Life & Work of Maori Carver* 28 The red clay or haematite used by the Maori was first burnt, then powdered, when it became *kokowai*.

KONAKI

kollady, kolladdie, varr. KORARI.

kolly, var. KORRY.

komate /ˈkɒmati/, *a.* WW1. Also **komaty**. [ad. Ma. *ka* (verbal particle) + *mate* dead: the form has been made familiar to English speakers from the opening words of a well-known haka *Ka mate, ka mate! Ka ora, ka ora!* 'It is death, death! It is life, life!'] Dead. Occas as a *noun*, see quot. 1937.

1918 *Shell-Shocks* 27 Fifteen 'ploomin' Maori komate. **1935** MITCHELL & STRONG in Partridge *Slang Today* (1935) 286 [The] following [was] employed by those who served in the [Great] War.. *komaty*, dead, from Maori *ka mate*. **1937** PARTRIDGE *Dict. Slang* 464 *komate*. A dead or a wounded soldier: a sick horse: New Zealand soldiers': 1915–18. Ex Maori *ka mate* dead. **1968** *NZ Contemp. Dict. Suppl.* (Collins) 12 *komate adj.* dead.

komaty, var. KOMATE.

konaki /kʌuˈnæki/, /ˈkʌunæki/. *NI* and *Chatham Is.* Also **konake, koneka, koneke**. [ad. Ma. *kōneke* /ˈko:neke/: Williams 133 *Kōneke*, n. sledge.]

1. Also **konaki sledge**. A farmer's or timberman's sledge, often with runners in front and wheels at the back. See also SLEDGE *n*. Cf. CATAMARAN 2.

[**1820** LEE & KENDALL *NZ Gram. & Vocab.* 167 *Konáke, s.* A slip with the foot. **1871** WILLIAMS *Dict. NZ Lang.* (3edn.) 59 *Koneke*, n. *sledge*.] **1914** HALL *Woman in Antipodes* 86 I also got some insight into up-country life [in King Country]..noting..the primitive Maori 'koneka' or sledge. **1915** [see SLEDGE *n*.]. **1937** *NZ Railways Mag.* Dec. 11 The sledgers would haul them [sc. piles of firewood] on their *konekes* down a short cut on the mountain side. **1942** *NZJAg.* Apr. LXIV. 270 The konaki is a partly wheeled and partly runnered vehicle... The name konaki is apparently derived from the Maori 'Ko neke', meaning to slide, crawl or move from one place to another. **1952–53** *NZ Forest Service Gloss.* (TS) Konaki A sledge, with or without wheels, for extracting split forest produce. Originally the term referred to a rough wheelless sledge made from the fork of a tree. **1963** BACON *In the Sticks* 64 I saw Jacob come home, trudging slowly across the paddock beside a koneke loaded with branches, drawn by an old grey horse. **1978** SUTHERLAND *Elver* 36 This pile was built on a konaki sledge. **1981** MARRIOTT *Life in Gorge* 20 Joe..explained that a konake is like a sledge, only it has two wide wheels almost at the back and when the horse pulls it lifts the front and the load runs on the wheels. **1981** SUTHERLAND & TAYLOR *Sunrise* 60 It was a rich compost which would be later carted away in the konaki sledge.

2. *Chatham Islands.* See quots. See also *Chatham Island truck* (CHATHAM ISLAND 2).

1950 SIMPSON *Chatham Exiles* 145 [The jogger's] rival is the konake, akin to the jogger, but with iron or wooden wheels and a sledge runner in front, and it may be drawn by oxen instead of horses. **1984** HOLMES *Chatham Is.* 59 Before the coming of motorised transport, the mode of transportation was the 'Chatham Island Truck' (Konake), a wooden flat-decked horse or bullock-drawn vehicle, with iron or wooden wheels at the back and sledge runners on the front.

koneka, koneke, var. KONAKI.

konini /kʌu'nɪnɪ/. Also occas. **konine, koniny**. [Ma. /'ko:nini/: Williams 134 *Kōnini*, n. Fruit of *Fuchsia excorticata*.]
 [*Note*] *Konini* is strictly the fuchsia-berry, but is often erroneously used for the tree itself (more properly *kotukutuku*), an error perhaps reinforced by the entry for *konini* on page 68 of Williams *Dict. NZ Lang*. 4edn. 1892 (corrected in the 5edn. 1917) '*Konini, n. fuchsia excorticata*; a tree'. The attributive use *konini-tree* is acceptable; *konini-berry* is tautologous.

1. Erron. FUCHSIA 1, KOTUKUTUKU.
 1844 *NZ Jrnl*. IV. 595 A thick underbrush of konine (fusia) [*sic*]. **1852** *Wellington Gazette* in Earp *Hand-Book for Intending Emigrants* 230 [The alluvial bush land] is wooded chiefly with *pukateas, kaikateas..rata* trees, and thick underbrush of *konine* (fuchsia). **1871** *Evening Post* (Wellington) 2 Jan. 2 We have been shown a sample of jam made from the berries of the 'koniny' or wild fuchsia. **1882** POTTS *Out in Open* 114 The berries of the konini, of various species of coprosma, ripening early, furnish some part of its food supply. **1907** MANSFIELD *Letters* (1984) I. 31 We got great sprays of clematis—and konini. **1940** STUDHOLME *Te Waimate* (1954) 242 The under-scrub was very dense, Matipo, Ini-Ini, Konini, Pokaka..and others. **1967** HARPER *Kettle on Fuchsia* 12 A sweeping drive skirted by rhododendrons and azaleas, growing beside cabbage-trees, totaras, and koninis. **1975** KNIGHT *Poyntzfield* 18 Many trees stood about—mostly Konini, just then full of flowers at their best.

2. The fuchsia-berry, the small purplish fruit of the *Fuchsia excorticata*.
 1847, 1853 [see KOTUKUTUKU]. **1883** HECTOR *Handbook NZ* 127 *Fuchsia excorticata... kotukutuku*. The fruit is called Konini. **1898** MORRIS *Austral-English* 251 *Konini, n*. Maori name for..the fruit of the New Zealand fuchsia, *Fuchsia excorticata*. **1907** [see KOHUTUHUTU]. **1942** ANDERSEN *Maori Place Names* 282 The konini is so well known that the tree itself is called konini more often than kotukutuku. **1970** [see FUCHSIA 1]. **1982** BURTON *Two Hundred Yrs. NZ Food* 7 Other berries popular as delicacies were..the small, sweet berries (known as *konini*) of the kotukutuku or tree fuchsia.

3. In Comb. **konini berry, konini tree**.
 1861 MOORE *Reminiscences* (ATLMS) 1 **Konini Berries**. **1914** PFAFF *Diggers' Story* 109 We used to pick fern and cook it, and konini berries [on the West Coast c1860]. **1926** *NZ Observer Xmas Annual* 27 Nov. 26 They had feasted on Konini berries until they were 'fed up' beyond the bounds of politeness. **1978** NATUSCH *Acheron* 88 Conversely, the French housewives used konini berries [from Akaroa] in their conserves—and *très bon* too. **1981** HENDERSON *Exiles Asbestos Cottage* 187 Has anyone ever eaten enough konini berries? **1926 konini-tree** [see FUCHSIA 1]. **1983** HENDERSON *Down from Marble Mountain* 39 A konini tree all brown papered and black with berries to be eaten by the handful.

kono. Also **konu**. [Ma. /'kono/: Williams 134 *Kono* n,.. 3. Small basket for cooked food.] A small woven flax basket for holding cooked food.
 1860 BUDDLE *Maori King Movement* 47 Look here, this is mine holding a food-basket (kono) in his hand, which he buried in the earth. **1905** BAUCKE *White Man Treads* 253 The food-bearers advanced in a compact body, each carrying a 'kono' (small food basket). **1923** *Northlander* 11 Jan. (VUW Fildes Clippings 461a:130) When we [youngsters] received our little flax-baskets (kono) of vegetables, we scuttled off. **1930** *NZ Short Stories* 31 The welcoming over—aha!—the grace of the young women bearing their *kono*, the little baskets of food. **1948** HENDERSON *Taina* 15 The *hangis* had just been uncovered and the food put into little freshly-made flax baskets called *kono*, one for each person. **1972** BAXTER *Collected Poems* (1980) 537 To others my love is a plaited kono Full or empty, With chunks of riwai, Meat that stuck to the stones. **1982** BREAM *Island of Fear* 72 She's going to show me how to weave a foodbasket, a *konu*.

kon-tiki. [f. the name of the raft used by Thor Heyerdahl (b. 1914) for a drift voyage in the Pacific Ocean.] See quot. 1963.
 1963 *Evening Post* (Wellington) 23 Jan. 14 The central Bay of Plenty 'mystery ship'..could very well be a very large 'Kon-Tiki' fishing device... [**1963** *Note*] A 'kon-tiki' is a small raft used by fishermen to drift their lines out well beyond the breakers using wind assistance. They are controlled by a line from the shore. **1972** *Press* (Christchurch) 25 Oct. 2 Two children suffered injuries at Waihi Beach on Saturday morning when a speeding bikie swept up a Kon Tiki line which dragged them into the tide.

konu, var. KONO.

koohakka, var. KUAKA.

kookoo, var. KUKU *n.*[1]

kookoopa, var. KUKUPA.

koomar(r)a, koomera, varr. KUMARA.

koorooroo, var. KORERO.

koota, kooter, kooti(e), varr. KUTU.

kooura, var. KOURA.

kopa. *Obs. in English use*. Also **koppah** (?/'kɒpa/), perh. influenced by English *copper*. [Ma. /'kopa/: Williams 135 *Kopa* (i) 5. Native oven... (R[arawa]).] HANGI 1. See also COPPER MAORI 1.
 1882 HAY *Brighter Britain* II. 153 Fish and meat were frequently roasted..but the great national culinary institution was the earth-oven, the kopa or hangi. **1913** ROBERTS *Place Names* 24 Food was cooked by steaming in a hangi or kopa (an oven dug out in the ground). **1915** HAY *Reminisc. Earliest Canterbury* 32 He [a pig] was then placed in the koppah, which was made as follows:- A hole was firstly dug in the ground and then partially filled with stones. **1923** *NZJST* VI. 54 One name for these food-steaming pits is *kopa*, a much ill-used term, for it has been corrupted into 'copper' by the intrusive *pakeha*, who discourses of 'copper mouree' with glib assurance.

kopakopa. [Ma. /'kopakopa/: Williams 135 *Kopa* (i)... *kopakopa*... 2. n. *Myosotidium hortense*... 3. *Trichomanes reniforme*, kidney fern.] Any of several unrelated plants. **a**. *kidney fern* (FERN 2 (10)).
 1857 HURSTHOUSE *NZ* I. 134 The Underwood, consists of..the delicate lady's hair, the Kopakopa, an elegant plumy fern. **1981** BROOKER et al. *NZ Medicinal Plants* 27 *Cardiomanes reniforme... Kidney fern... Kopakopa*.

b. Native and introduced species of plantain, *Plantago* spp.
 1867 HOOKER *Handbook* 765 Kopa-kopa... *Plantago* sp. **1905** *TrNZI* XXXVII. 67 They also used..a lotion prepared by boiling the leaves of the plant *kopakopa* (*Plantago major*). **1981** BROOKER et al. *NZ Medicinal Plants* 79 *Plantago* sp. Common name: *Plantain* Maori names: *Kopakopa, parerarera*. **1992** EDWARDS *Mihipeka* 56 You now use another type of leaf—kopakopa... This heals and closes the wound.

c. *Chatham Island lily* (LILY 2 (3)).
 1868 TAYLOR *Past and Present of NZ* 225 The forget-me-not, Kopa-kopa Myosotis, with its fine bunches of flowers and large glossy leaves, is a native of these [Chatham] isles.

kopapa. [Ma. /'kopapa/: not recorded in Williams.] A small or young KAHAWAI 1.
 1967 MORELAND *Marine Fishes* 50 Kahawai... Small examples are known as kopapa in northern New Zealand. **1970** SORENSEN *Nomenclature NZ Fish* 30 *Kahawai* Other common names: Kahawai; Kopapa (juveniles). **1986** PAUL *NZ Fishes* 92 *Kahawai Arripis trutta*... The name kopapa is sometimes given to the barred or spotted juveniles.

kopa maori, var. COPPER MAORI.

kopata. [Ma. /'ko:pata/: Williams 136 *Kōpata*, n,.. *Kōpatapata* 3. n. *Pelargonium inodorum* and *Geum urbanum*, plants.]

1. *Pelargonium inodorum* (fam. Geraniaceae), an inconspicuous native herb of open grassland and other open habitats.
 1853 HOOKER II *Flora Novae-Zelandiae* I *Flowering Plants* 41 Pelargonium clandestinum... Nat. name, 'Kopata', Middle Island. **1867** HOOKER *Handbook* 765 Kopata, Lyall. Pelargonium clandestinum. **1889** FEATON *Art Album NZ Flora* 75 The 'Kopata'.—This pretty perennial herb is abundant throughout both Islands. Kopata springs up indigenously upon nearly all newly-cultivated soil, and becomes a hardy weed. **1905** *TrNZI* XXXVII. 67 They also used the ashes of burnt 'tussac' grass, and a lotion prepared..from the bruised leaves of the *kopata*. **1952** RICHARDS *Chatham Is*. 32 *Pelargonium..inodorum*... Scentless Pelargonium. Kopata, Puku-puku. **1980** TAYLOR *Weeds of Crops* 63 Kopata..is widespread in New Zealand, frequent after fires or bush clearing and in some districts in field crops.

2. The introduced herb, wood avens *Geum urbanum*, or the related species *G. allepicum* (fam. Rosaceae).
 1867 HOOKER *Handbook* 765 Kopata... *Geum urbanum* var. *strictum*. **1889** FEATON *Art Album NZ Flora* 123 Geum urbanum..var. *strictum*. The Common Avens or Herb Bennet. The 'Kopata'. **1981** BROOKER et al. *NZ Medicinal Plants* 85 *Geum urbanum* L. Common names: *Common avens, herb-bennett* Maori name: *Kopata*. The variety of this widespread species which occurs in New Zealand and Australia is known as var. *strictum*.

kopi. Mainly *Chatham Islands*. [Ma. /'ko:pi/: Williams 137 *Kōpī*, n. *1*...= karaka. 2. The berry.] KARAKA 1 a. Often *attrib*.
 1838 POLACK *NZ* I. 287 The [karaka] seed is said to be poisonous in its crude state, but is much esteemed by the natives, when cooked after their method. The seeds in this state taste of oil only, and are called *kopi*. **1878** CHUDLEIGH *Diary* 10 Mar. (1950) 267 The ground..[was] covered with fallen branches of kopi nuts. **1884** *Ibid*. 329 Felled a nest of large kopi trees. **1910** COCKAYNE *NZ Plants & Their Story* 121 The commonest of the

forest-trees is the karaka, here [on the Chathams] called kopi.., whose smooth bark was frequently adorned with a figure or a three-fingered man by the Maori artists. **1923** SKINNER *Morioris Chatham Is.* 4 I was able to see the two surviving Morioris..to study the carvings on the *kopi* trees. **1940** LAING & BLACKWELL *Plants NZ* 247 It also grows in the Chatham Islands, where it is known to the natives as *Kopi. Karaka* is by far the commonest name. **1952** RICHARDS *Chatham Is.* 63 *Corynocarpus..laevigata...* Kopi (for both tree and fruit).

koppa, koppah maori, varr. COPPER MAORI, KOPA.

kopukapuka. Also **kopuko-puko.** [Ma. /ko:'pukapuka/: Williams 138 *Kōpukapuka,* n. *1*... Chatham Island lily... *2. Ranunculus hirtus.*] Either of two unrelated plants *Chatham Island lily* (LILY 2 (3)), or *Ranunculus hirtus* (fam. Ranunculaceae), a buttercup.

1882 CHUDLEIGH *Diary* 1 Nov. (1950) 313 West went round the place and planted Kopuko-puko, arums and sweet peas in the afternoon. **1952, 1966** [see LILY 2 (3)]. **1981** BROOKER et al. *NZ Medicinal Plants* 82 *Ranunculus hirtus...* Maori names: *Kopukapuka, maruru...* This buttercup is abundant and variable and occurs throughout New Zealand in wet places.

koputotara. Also **kopuwai-totara.** [Ma. /ko:pu:'to:tara/: Williams 139 *Kōpūtōtara, = kōpūwaitōtara,* n... porcupine fish.] PORCUPINE-FISH.

1886 SHERRIN *Handbook Fishes NZ* 306 *Chilomycterus jaculiferus...* Porcupine-fish, or Kopuwai-totara. **1927** PHILLIPPS *Bibliogr. NZ Fishes* (1971) 57 *Allomycterus jaculiferus...* Porcupine-fish; Koputotara. **1956** [see PORCUPINE-FISH]. **1966** DOOGUE & MORELAND *Sea Anglers' Guide* 295 Porcupinefish... *Other names: Allomycterus jaculiferus;* koputotara. **1982** [see PORCUPINE-FISH].

kora, var. KOURA.

koraddee, korad(d)i(e), varr. KORARI.

korai, var. KOROI.

koraie, var. KORAU.

korali, var. KORARI.

koramika, var. KOROMIKO.

korara, var. KORORA.

korari /kə'rari/, /kə'rædi/, /kə'lædi/, /'klædi/. Also with much variety of transliterated form, esp. in the South Island, poss. partly from Ma. dialectal variation, but mainly from various non-Maori perceptions of Ma. /k/ as English [k] often spelt *c*; Ma. /o:/ as [ɒ], [ə], or [zero]; Ma. /r/ as [r] or [l] or [d]; and Ma. /i/ final as a variety of Brit. or NZ English *-i* final: **clad(d)y, colladdy, colladie, co(o)rad(d)i(e), coradé, courad, craddie, gladdy, kaladi(e), kaladdy, kauradi, kladdy, koladdy, kolladie, koraddee, korad(d)ie), koraddy, korali, korati, korori, kouradi, kraddy.** [Ma. /'ko:rari/: Williams 140 *Kōrari... 3...* flower stem of flax... *4.* The plant itself (in the north).]

1. Mainly *NI. flax-plant* or (occas.) *flax-blade* (FLAX 5 b).

1814 KENDALL in Elder *Marsden's Lieutenants* (1934) 64 Duaterra and a party of friends were actively employed in cutting koraddee (or flax in the growing state) on the other side of the bay. **1820** MCCRAE *Journal* (1928) 22 The hill was covered completely with the flax plant which is called Coradé Mauvre, and which grew in great luxuriance. **1838** POLACK *NZ* I. 104 We descended into a deep flat valley, covered with the korari, or flax plant. **1840** *NZ Jrnl.* I. 82 Portions of flax are to be seen adjoining almost every village; it is of incalculable service to the natives. In its natural state it is called *korari* or *korali.* **1843** *Ibid.* IV. 177 Kauradi or Flax. **1868** LINDSAY *Contribs. NZ Bot.* 82 In Otago the general name of the [flax] plant, as a whole, is 'Korari,'—or as metamorphosed by the settler, pronounced and spelt 'Kourādi,' or 'Corādi'. The same term is applied in the North Island equally to the whole plant, and to the dried flower-stem when cut for rafts or other purposes; or exclusively to the flower-stalk. **1882** HAY *Brighter Britain* II. 204 The Harakeke or Korati [*sic*] (*Phormium tenax*) is the justly celebrated New Zealand flax. **1988** *Through The Looking glass* 117 A strict discipline in relation to schoolwork..was balanced by total freedom..fight with craddie sticks.

2. Mainly *SI.* The tall flower stem of the native flax; *flax-stick* (FLAX 5 c).

1844 MONRO *Notes of a Journey* in Hocken *Contributions* (1898) 240 A mogi..is a floating body..made of bundles of bulrushes tied together, and strengthened by the flowering stem of the flax, called koradi. **1879** BARR *Old Identities* 53 A Kolladie (the flower-stalk of the flax: about seven feet long) was carried by each as a balancing pole. **1888** DUNCAN *Wakatipians* 9 We collected all the dried *cooraddies* (flower stalks of the flax-bush). **1893** FROBISHER *Sketches of Gossipton* 75 Through bush and fern and flax koladdy,...no more will follow me poor Paddy. **1907** LAING & BLACKWELL *Plants NZ* 106 A flax-stick, or dried flower stem, is known to colonists as a korari, koradi, or kaladi. The first name is of course, the correct one. **1914** in *Hist. N. Otago from 1853* (1978) 43 These koraddi were in great demand as firewood. **1927** *NZ Dairy Produce Exporter* 26 Feb. 39 She grabbed something between a dropper and a post and I a Koradi. **1939** BEATTIE *First White Boy Born Otago* 12 The [Maori] tops would be whipped by means of a lash of flax tied to a bit of koradi (flax stick). **c1942** p.c. R. Mason 7 June 1952. Cladies were used at Foxton flaxmill instead of laths to make a house for raising seedlings. It was called the clady house. **1953** DEWAR *Chaslands* 40 The largest circle possible was marked out with koraris thrust into the turf [to mark out a race in Southland c1900]. **1976** 'Kaladdies' [see BUFFALO CHIPS]. **1978** MOOR & IRWIN *Oxford Book NZ Plants* 180 Leaves come off in two rows, their bases overlapping in a flat fan from which emerges the stout flower stalk (korari, corrupted to 'claddy'). **1985** GOWANS *Heart of High Country* 35 Her dirty fingers poked into the embers her flax flowers, dead grass and dung, which she called her 'yellow pine' or 'buffalo chips' or the melodic-sounding 'Kaladdies'.

3. *attrib.* in senses 1 and 2 above, passing into an adjective, of or pertaining to, made of flax or flax-sticks.

1834 MARKHAM *NZ* (1963) 62 My Traps went inside, and in an hour some Pork and Potatoes from a 'Coppre Mourie' came in Smoking with the Koraddie Baskets, and at it we went. **1843** TAYLOR *Journal* 10 July (ATLTS) 48 we had to ascend by an almost perpendicular path in one place having a Koradi rope to lay hold of. **1873** BULLER *Birds NZ* 49 When the korari-flower..is in season, the Kakas repair in flocks to the flax-fields to feast on the flower-honey. **1898** HOCKEN *Contributions* 38 He enjoyed more peaceful slumbers than under the miserable shelter of the korari breakwind at Kuri Bush. **1922** *Auckland Weekly News* 20 Apr. 15 The only passage was by flax korori raft or mokihi. **1926** COWAN *Travel in NZ* II. 28 The tall *korari* stalks of the flax-bushes..[bear] abundant promise of honey liquor for the summer birds. **1938** LANCASTER *Promenade* 44 He came pushing through the tall flax-blades and black koradi-sticks and found her sitting demure in her print gown.

4. Special Comb. **korari honey** (occas. *ellipt.* **korari**), the abundant nectar of korari flowers or the honey derived from it (see also *flax-honey* (FLAX 5 c)); **korari stick,** *flax-stick* (FLAX 5 c).

1848 BRUNNER *Exped. Middle Is.* in Taylor *Early Travellers* (1959) 293 The honey of the flax blossom is also in season, called **korari**, and, when mixed with fern root, also makes a species of confectionery. **1849** ALLOM *Letter* in Earp *Handbook* (1852) 131 Whilst enumerating the fruits of New Zealand, the honey (*korari*) of the *Phormium tenax*, or flax plant, must not be forgotten. **1860** SCOTT *Rough Notes on Travels* 42 One of our party had taken eight hundred pounds..of 'Korari honey' last season. **1888** BULLER *Birds NZ* I. 98 In December and January..[Tuis] leave the forest and repair to the flax-fields to feast on the korari honey. **1898** HOCKEN *Contributions* 37 Accordingly a raft, constructed with bundles of **korari sticks** tied together..was launched with the next flood tide. **1904** LANCASTER *Sons o' Men* 279 He whistled the evening hymn monotonously.., beating time with a koradi stick against the raupo and flax leaves. **1922** COWAN *NZ Wars* (1955) II. 470 The heart..was carried up country, stuck on the end of a *korari* stick (flax-stalk), and was taken to the Kuiti district. **1933** *Press* (Christchurch) (Acland Gloss.) 14 Oct. 15 The dried reed stalks [of flax] (which Maoris and children tied into bundles to make rafts) are called *f[lax]-sticks, koradi s[tic]ks* or *kraddy s[tic]ks.* **1952** LYON *Faring South* 69 [He]..obtained a stout korari stick from a neighbouring swamp. **1975** NEWTON *Sixty Thousand on the Hoof* 182 The first man to navigate the lake [*sc.* Wakatipu] was Donald Hay and he did so in 1859 on a raft made of koradi sticks. **1981** HOOPER *Goat Paddock* 111 'I'll show you how I used to make claddy-stick canoes.'.. Soon he had cut and hollowed a ten-inch length of claddy-stick, pointed a bow.

5. As **kaladdy,** a rounders bat.

1972 SUTTON-SMITH *Folkgames Children* 154 'A common bat [for rounders] was the stem of the Korari, from the flax bush. It had to be still wet because it was brittle when dry. We called it a Kaladdy' (South Clutha, Otago, 1875).

ko-raro, var. KORERO.

korati, var. KORARI.

korau. Also **koraie, korou.** [Ma. /'ko:rau: Williams 140 *Kōrau,* n. *1. Cyathea medullaris* a large tree fern. = *mamaku. 2.* Young shoots of ferns. *3.* Turnip or similar roots (mod.).]

1. MAMAKU, or its edible shoots.

[**1820** LEE & KENDALL *NZ Gram. & Vocab.* 168 *Kórau, s.* A glutinous plant so called.] **1838** POLACK *NZ* I. 287 The *korou*, which the branches of another of these umbelliferous trees afford is equally prized, together with the saccharine roots of the ti, cabbage-tree. **1844** WILLIAMS *NZ Jrnl.* (1956) 109 The most remarkable [fern] is koraie which grows from ten to fifteen feet high. The stem and stalk are dark or black. **1855** [see MAMAKU]. **1867** HOCHSTETTER *NZ* 158 Mamakau, Pitau, Korau..an arborescent fern; the entire stem being peeled is eaten and when cooked is very good; it is a favourite dish of the natives. **1877** GRACE *Journal* Aug. in Grace *Pioneer Missionary* (1928) 273 A gigantic tree lay by the road, against the trunk of which a number of fronds of a beautiful korau were leaning. **1894** *TrNZI* XXVI. 620 The lovely nikau palm..with the stately koraus growing beside it, is slaughtered to furnish cheap decoration for a country ball-room. **1922** *Auckland Weekly News* 11 May 15 That monarch is not as well known as its cousin, the mamuku korau or black tree-fern. **1946** *JPS* LV. 152 *korau*, edible young shoots of mamaku.

2. The tops of the wild turnip eaten as greens.
1851 SHORTLAND *S. Dist. NZ* 170 These fish [*sc.* eels], 'korau' or wild turnip tops, and fern root, were just now the natives' only food. **1867** HOOKER *Handbook* 765 Korau, Lindsay. *Brassica Rapa*. **1992** PARK *Fence around the Cuckoo* 220 I took her advice and every day gathered half a sugarbag full of puha..and korau, the wild turnip.

koreka, var. KOREKE.

koreke. Also **koreka, koreko.** [Ma. /ˈkoreke/: Williams 141 *Koreke* (i) n. *1.*] New Zealand quail (QUAIL 1).
1870 *TrNZI* II. 66 Coturnix novae zelandiae... Koreka. Quail. This excellent game bird is almost extinct. **1885** *NZJSc.* II. 484 Quail. Koreke. At this early date of the settlement of the country it is painful to have to write of a species as a thing of the past. **1904** TREGEAR *Maori Race* 105 The quail (*koreke*: Coturnix N.Z.), the rail..and many other land-birds were cooked or potted down. **1922** *NZJST* IV. 275 Quail (or koreke) shooting was delightful sport. They were round my station [in the 1850's] in thousands. **1946** [see QUAIL 1]. **1955** OLIVER *NZ Birds* 438 *New Zealand Quail. Koreke Coturnix novaezealandiae.* **1989** PARKINSON *Travelling Naturalist* 64 The..extinction of the native quail (koreke) was accelerated by the introduction of these birds [*sc.* finches] and their competition for food.

koreko, var. KOREKE.

korero, *n.* Also with much variety of early form as **corero, corrirow, kodero, koorooroo, koraro, korerro, kororo, korrero, orero** (?with init. glottal stop = ˀorero). [Ma. /ˈko:rero/: Williams 141 *Kōrero*. *1.* v. Tell, say. *2.* Address. *3.* v. Speak, talk. *4.* n. Conversation. *5.* News. *6.* Story, narrative, discussion: cf. PPN *kooLeLo 'talk', Walsh & Biggs 37.]

1. In Maori contexts, talk, discussion; a public meeting for discussion; a parley.
[**1770** PARKINSON *Journal* (1773) 127 *Orero*, To speak, or a speech. **1807** SAVAGE *Some Acc. of NZ* 75 Corero..Speaking.] **1834** MARKHAM *NZ* (1963) 30 A very Original set of Tattooed Gentlemen cam[e] aft and there was a grand Corrirow or Talk on the occasion. **1840** BEST *Journal* (1966) 218 A Korero took place in which the Mauries were found very tractable. *Ibid.* 223 The Koorooroo commenced afresh. **1851** WARD *Journal* 3 Feb. (1951) 121 A korerro, or native counsel. **1866** HUNT *Chatham Is.* 17 The usual amount of shaking hands and rubbing noses being over, a long *korero*, or talk, ensued. **1871** MONEY *Knocking About NZ* 131 They [the Colonel and the Maori party] had a corero or parley for some time, while we..looked to our carbines in case of a row. **1881** CAMPBELL *Poenamo* 146 It was arranged we were to have a grand consultation *korero* next morning. **1938** HYDE *Nor Yrs. Condemn* 169 [I say:] '*Haere ra*, I'm going to Napier to get my divorce.' You never hear such a *korero*. They don't like a divorce. **1940** COWAN *Sir Donald Maclean* 41 It was a very long drawn out argumentative *korero*. **1966** MEAD *Richard Taylor* 24 Next morning he had a long friendly korero with the Maoris, after which he started..with his party and a local guide. **1971** *Listener* 22 Mar. 7 The korero..would let the Maoris tell the pakehas what they couldn't so easily tell them in a setting shaped by European conventions. **1984** *Te Maori* 22 In the popular sense a taonga is a highly prized possession to which is attached korero (text or story).

2. In non-Maori contexts. **a.** Often /kɒˈriːrʌu/. Discussion, a talk; thence, a meeting, get-together.
1855 *Richmond-Atkinson Papers* (1960) I. 176 [Dr. Montgomery and C.W. Richmond] had a long korero about New Zealand and the Bay. **1866** LUSH *Waikato Jrnls.* 11 Apr. (1982) 81 As I called in at some of the houses and had long *koreros* with the inmates my progress was so slow. **1909** *Truth* 3 Apr. 6 After a lengthy korero their Worships said they wouldn't undertake the responsibility of dismissing the case. **1917** INGRAM *Anzac Diary* (1987) 76 Met several Whakatane boys to-day and had a great korero, swapping experiences and information about friends. **1920** *NZ Free Lance* (Wellington) 7 July 4 [Heading] At the Korero House... There is evidently some good virile stuff amongst the new members of the House [of Representatives]. **1930** WHITE *Mystery Island* 27 Remington could drop me anywhere before the 'korero' was over. [**1930** *Note*] 'talk'. **1943** *NZEF Times* 4 Oct. 1 After many koreros..it was decided to hit Perrett in the way it would hurt him most. **1953** SUTTON-SMITH *Unorganized Games NZ Primary School Children* (VUWTS) II. 606 The fort was used for Koreros, toymaking (tops, whips, bows and arrows etc.) and feasts. **1962** HORI *Half-gallon Jar* 9 Those M.P. jokers make the entertaining korero. **1982** HUNN *Not Only Affairs of State* 116 I conferred with Ambassador Foss Shanahan who had come up from Singapore. It was no striped pants session..simply a casual Kiwi korero in the open air.

b. *spec.* A Savage Club meeting or get-together.
1905 *Truth* 23 Sept. 4 Last Saturday evening the Savage Club concluded their season with a 'korero'. **1913** *NZ Observer* 1 Feb. 4 The von Haast has some mild celebrity as a scribbler of topical verse and local allusion which is useful at Savage Club koreros and students' yells. **1957** *Star-Sun* (Christchurch) 12 Aug. 3 Savage Cliff Milne was installed as Chief Savage at the..korero of the Christchurch Savage Club on Saturday evening. **1971** McKEON *Fruitful Yrs.* 224 In 1923..I became a member of the Wellington Savage Club... The koreros (meetings) were held, as they still are, on every second Saturday night..from May to October.

c. *Hist.* A name given to a former left-wing faction in the Public Service Association national body.
1964 *Dominion* (Wellington) 18 Aug. 2 The [Public Service Association] meeting is expected to elect Mr Sorrell who will probably have the backing of the ruling 'korero', a factional organisation which supports Left-wing policies and has introduced the association to the foreign policy field. **1987** *Dominion* (Wellington) 26 Sept. 8 More could have been said by Roth about the Korero, the left-wing group that led the PSA from the end of the war up to the mid 1960s.

korero, *v. Obs.* [See *n.*] *intr.* To talk, to hold a discussion. (Rare in non-Maori contexts.)
[**1804** COLLINS *Eng. Col. in NSW* 560 E-ko-re-roo, *To converse.* **1817** NICHOLAS *Voyage NZ* II. 331 Language, or to speak Ko-raro.] **1839** WAKEFIELD *Journal* 26 Sept. in *GBPP House of Commons 1841 (No.311)* 145 He spoke amidst repeated cries of 'Korrero, korrero' or, speak, speak, which were sometimes used seriously. **1840** BEST *Journal* June (1966) 222 Here was a pretty dilemma! The Chiefs ran up and down and koorooroed. **1843** TAYLOR *Journal* 8 July (1842-43) (ATLTS) 47 Here I preached and koreroed with y [*sic*] natives **1912** *NZ Free Lance Christmas Annual* (Wellington) 35 The older Queens..korero'd long and earnestly.

Hence **korero-ing** *vbl. n.*, talking; discussion.
1845 *NZ Jrnl.* V. 284 When the psalm-singing was ended, it was succeeded by an equally fervent kororoing (talking). **1881** CAMPBELL *Poenamo* 108 We..left Waipeha to do some trade 'koreroing' with the natives and follow after us along with the chiefs. **1890** *Otago Witness* (Dunedin) 28 Aug. 36 We concluded it was safest to do our koreroing with half a mile of water between.

korerro, var. KORERO.

kori, var. KORRY.

korikori. [Ma. /ˈkorikori/: Williams 142 *Kori* (i) n... *korikori* n... a large buttercup.] mountain buttercup (BUTTERCUP 2 (3)).
1867 HOOKER *Handbook* 765 Korikori, Lindsay. *Ranunculus*, various sp. **1870** *TrNZI* II. 124 Ranunculus pinguis Kori kori. **1889** FEATON *Art Album NZ Flora* 7 Ranunculus insignis... The 'Korikori'.—This fine plant is a native to the Northern Island, and a portion of the Nelson district... [It] is probably the largest buttercup in the world. **1968** SALMON *Alpine Plants NZ* 213 [Caption] Korikori plant in flower, Mt. Ruapehu, 1,550m (5,000ft) (January). *Ibid.* 212 *Korikori Ranunculus insignis* A branching hairy herb up to 90cm high found in alpine grasslands, herbfields, and rock crevices from East Cape to the Kaikoura Mountains. **1978** *Manawatu Tramping Club Jubilee* 99 Nesting under an inclined rock face [in the Ruahines] is a bed of kori-kori, the mountain buttercup (Ranunculus insignis).

korimako /kɒrəˈmakʌu/. Also with much variety of early form as **kódi máka, korimáku, koromoko, kurimako; kokorimako, kokoromaka.** [Ma. /ˈkorimako/,/ko:ˈkorimako/: Williams 142 *Korimako* n. *Anthornis melanura* [with 13 variants and synonyms]; 131 *Kōkorimako, kōkoromako.*] BELLBIRD 1 a. See also MAKOMAKO *n.*[1] 1. **a. korimako** forms.
[**1820** LEE & KENDALL *NZ Gram. & Vocab.* 165 Kódi máka; Name of a certain bird.] **1838** POLACK *NZ* I. 299 The *korimáku* is about the size of a thrush, covered with dark-coloured feathers. **1842** TAYLOR *Journal* 23 Nov. (ATLTS) 7 The koromoko its solitary song in the still night sounded inexpressibly sweet. **1855** TAYLOR *Te Ika A Maui* 75 In the first oven..a korimako was cooked. **1873** BULLER *Birds NZ* 91 Anthornis melanura. (Bell-bird).— Mako, Makomako, Komako, Kokomako, Korimako, Kohimako..Titimako, and Kopara. Of the above names, Korimako is most generally used by northern and Makomako by southern tribes. **1882** HAY *Brighter Britain* II. 220 The Kurimako or Ko[k]orimako (*Anthornis melanura*) is a bird about the size of a thrush. **1906** *TrNZI* XXXVIII. 339 A beautiful bush-musician in the South Island..is the bellbird (*korimako* or *makomako*). **1932** STEAD *Life Histories NZ Birds* 145 In the early days, many people called Anthornis 'Mockie', a derivation of its Maori name 'mako' or 'Korimako', but that name is dying out. **1946** *JPS* LV. 149 *Korimako*, a bird (Anthornis melanura), the bell-bird: in some places makomako, but korimako adopted to avoid confusion with the tree makomako. **1966** FALLA et al. *Birds NZ* 218 Bellbird *Anthornis melanura*... Korimako, Makomako, Mockie. **1970** *Evening Post* (Wellington) 17 Jan. 19 A colourful feast of..berries attracted..native birds whose songs rang through the crisp, clear air—the bell-like notes of the korimako [*sic*] (bell bird), the throaty call of the tui. **1986** HULME *Windeater* 44 Plenty of gulls and oyster catchers, treefrogs, a morepork or two, and a cynical korimako.

b. kokorimako forms.
1835 YATE *NZ* (1970) 55 The *Kokorimako* is about the size of the sparrow, with a small, oblong, dark

KORIMAKU — KOROTANGI

eye..has a remarkably shrill quick cry, *Te te te te*, which it keeps up for some minutes. **1849** TAYLOR *Journal* 16 June (ATLTS) VI. 112 Formerly when they received their name from the parent a kokorimako was eaten in the feast..that the child might be an orator and renowned for the sweetness of his voice, as the kokorimako is for his singing. **1859** THOMSON *Story NZ* I. 24 It is the Kokoromaka of the natives, and the Bell-bird of the settlers. **1882** [see a above].

korimaku, var. KORIMAKO.

korimiko, korimuka, varr. KOROMIKO.

kormera, var. KUMARA.

koro. [Ma. /'koro/: Williams 143 *Koro* (iii) n. *1*. Old man...*3*. A term of friendly address to an adult male.] (A term of friendly address ('uncle') or reference to) an elderly Maori man.

[**1820** LEE & KENDALL *NZ Gram. & Vocab.* 168 Kóro, *s*. A growing–up person.] **a1873** TAYLOR in *Some Poems of the Maori* transl. by Richard Taylor (1805–73) (no date, unpaged, printed for Unity Books and their friends at the Wai-Te-Ata Press, Wellington [?c1970]) [Title] 'Taunt Sung to the Impaled Head of an Enemy Chief'. Bare your lips, koro. Well may you grin. **1967** ASHTON-WARNER *Greenstone* 54 On occasion she glances at the severe old face of her great-grandfather, her koro. **1972** BAXTER *Collected Poems* (1980) 567 One by one the girls Come in to visit their old hairy koro. **1987** *Dominion* (Wellington) 7 Apr. [Title of poem by Apirana Taylor] 'Feelings and Memories of a Koro and Kuia'. **1989** *Saturday Express* (Marlborough) 13 May 1 [Caption] A brief ceremony in Maori and English saw koro Len Nukunuku blessing this fine trophy won by Vivienne Hewson. **1994** *Reach Out* 35 *Taha Maori*. To know and understand the Maori perspective on the 'take' [= 'central concern'] by korero with kuia and koro.

koroai, var. KOROWAI.

koroi. *Obs.* in non–Maori use. Also early **korai**. [Ma. /koro'i:/: Williams 144 *Koroī*, n. *1*. Fruit of the white pine..*2*. The tree itself.] The swollen fruit receptacle of the KAHIKATEA 1; applied (rarely) to the tree itself, occas. as **koroi pine**.

[**1820** LEE & KENDALL *NZ Gram. & Vocab.* 168 Kóroi; Fruit so called.] **1838** POLACK *NZ* I. 288 The *korai, koutu utu, miro*, and *putuhutu*, are wild forest fruits, prized only by the elder natives. **1843** BEST *Journal* 4 May (1966) 302 Our people collected great quantities of 'Koroi' the berry of the Kahikatea a very paletable [*sic*] fruit. **1850** ANGAS *Savage Life* II. 19 The Rimu and the koroi pine, seventy or eighty feet in height. **1869** *TrNZI* I. (rev. edn.) 261 The Kahikatea..,—the fruit of which was called Koroi. **1874** WHITE *Te Rou* 154 The koroi is a white pine which bears fruits plentifully only once in 7 years. **1990** CROWE *Native Edible Plants* 25 The swollen red stalk, or 'berry', [of the kahikatea] was eaten raw by the Maori and called 'koroi'.

korokia, var. KOROKIO.

korokio. Also **korokia**. [Ma./'korokio/: Williams 144 *Korokio*, n. *1. Hebe salicifolia*... *2. Corokia buddleioides.*] Any of several unrelated plants.

1. a. A shrub or small tree of the endemic genus *Corokia* (fam. Cornaceae), named by the pioneer botanist Allan Cunningham in 1839 from an altered form of *korokio*. See also *wire-netting bush* (WIRE 2).

1860 *Puketoi Station Diary* 17 July in Beattie *Early Runholding* (1947) 91 Went for firewood and brought home a load of Korokio. **1910** COCKAYNE *NZ Plants & Their Story* 120 [In the Chatham Islands] the korokia is named *Corokia macrocarpa*, and in its larger fruit and broader leaves is distinct from *C. buddleioides* of the North Island. **1939** BEATTIE *First White Boy Born Otago* 119 Up round the Manuherikia there were clumps of korokio (pronounced 'koroki-o', not 'koro-kio'). **1963** KEENE *O te Raki* 192 korokio shrub with wiry, tough, hard wood. **1969** *Standard Common Names Weeds* 42 korokio *Corokia cotoneaster* Raoul. **1978** MOORE & IRWIN *Oxford Book NZ Plants* 102 *Corokia cotoneaster*, korokio. A shrub a metre or two high, common in lowland and montane scrub.

b. As **korokio-taranga**. [Ma. /'korokio 'ta:raŋa/.] *Corokia buddleioides* (fam. Cornaceae), a much-branched shrub of coastal and lowland forest of the northern North Island.

1853 HOOKER *II Flora Novae-Zelandiae I Flowering Plants* 98 *Corokia buddleioides*... Nat. name, 'Korokia-taranga'. **1867** HOOKER *Handbook* 765 Korokio-taranga... *Corokia buddleioides*. **1906** CHEESEMAN *Manual NZ Flora* 237 *C[orokia] buddleioides*... Korokia-taranga. **1961** MARTIN *Flora NZ* 227 There are several fine shrubs from the Auckland province that would grace any garden. In this group we would include The Korokia-taranga (*Corokia buddleioides*).

2. A large-leaved *Hebe* species; KOROMIKO.

1867 HOOKER *Handbook* 765 Korokio, Lindsay. *Veronica* sp. **1961** ALLAN *Flora NZ* I. 887 The name *koromiko* (*korokio* in the Far North) is commonly used for the larger willow-lvd [*Hebe*] spp. In the high country the name 'boxwood' refers to some small-lvd *Hebe*.

3. *Chatham Islands*. The fern *Pneumatopteris pennigera*, gully fern (FERN 2 (5)).

1952 RICHARDS *Chatham Is.* 10 *A[spidium] pennigerum*... Korokio.

korokoro. [Ma. /'korokoro/: Williams 143 *Koro* (i)... *korokoro*... lamprey.] LAMPREY.

1858 BEETHAM *Diary* 13 Oct. in Rickard *Strangers in Wilderness* (1967) 98 Oct.13th... Went fishing in the evening got one korokoro by the tail. **1922** *NZJST* May V. 97 *Geotria australis*. *Lamprey*. Called 'piharu' and 'korokoro' by the Maoris. **1936** *Handbook for NZ* (ANZAAS) 73 *Geotria australis*:... Lamprey..Korokoro or kunakuna. **1956** GRAHAM *Treasury NZ Fishes* 58 Lamprey (Korokoro) *Geotria australis*.

korokoro-pounamou. [Ma. /'korokoro-'pounamu/: Williams 144 *Korokoropounamu* n. *Girella cyanea*.] bluefish (BLUE *a.* 2 b).

1892 *TrNZI* XXIV. 215 Again, from Mokohinou Mr. Sandager records, in September, 1888, the capture of a fish which he calls 'korokoro-pounamou'. The specimen weighed 6 lb... I do not know what fish is referred to. **1921, 1957** [see BLUEFISH]. **1966** DOOGUE & MORELAND *Sea Anglers' Guide* 243 Bluefish... Other names: *Girella cyanea*; korokoropounamu (Maori). **1981** WILSON *Fisherman's Bible* 34 Bluefish *Girella cyanea*..inhabits our more northern waters... The Maori name of 'korokoropounamou' is still heard in some remote areas.

korolah, var. KORORA.

koromiko. Also with much variety of early form as **coarimika, coramico, coromica, koramika, korimiko, korimuka, koromika, korumeek** (see also a Ma. variant *koromuka*, Williams 145). [Ma. /'koromiko/: Williams 144 *Koromiko*... *Hebe salicifolia*, etc.] **a.** A member of a large genus of evergreen shrubs *Hebe* (fam. Scrophulariaceae), mostly native to New Zealand and formerly included in the genus *Veronica*, esp. *H. salicifolia* the willow-leaved species, and *H. stricta*. See also BOX *n.*[3], BOXWOOD, HEBE, KOROKIO 2, VERONICA, WILLOW 2.

1842 SELWYN *Journal* 10 Dec. in *NZ Part I* (The Church in the Colonies) (1844) 81 As we descended, the bed of the river began to expand into wider spaces..clothed with Koromiko and Tutu trees. **1858** BEETHAM *Diary* 15 Oct. in Rickard *Strangers in Wilderness* (1967) 99 The third pig was a good sow which we steamed with green koromiko in first rate style. **1863** CHUDLEIGH *Diary* 1 Aug. (1950) 97 [I] got some Coramicos a nice little shrub. There are innumerable varieties. **1868** LINDSAY *Contribs. NZ Bot.* 68 *V[eronica] Salicifolia*... The Otago settlers also call it 'Korimuka', (Martin,)—'Korumeek,' (Hector,)—properly spelled 'Koromiko'—a term also applied to *V. parviflora*, Vahl... and perhaps in general, to all *shrubby* species of the genus. **1869** WAITE *West Coast Goldfields* 25 A shrub called 'coarimika' [is a cure for diarrhoea.] **1871** MONEY *Knocking About NZ* 77 We had found the whole of the ranges above almost bare of bush, patches of the manuka and coromica alone affording shelter and firewood for a camp. **1875** HOGG *Lays & Rhymes* 43 The meek manuka and the korimiko, Adorn the rugged banks of Motupiko. **1885** *Wairarapa Daily* 28 Feb. 2 [Advt] Heilbron's German Worm Cakes and Fitzgerald's Koromiko Extract are Patented. **1898** koramika [see VERONICA]. **1904** TREGEAR *Maori Race* 21 Sometimes invalids were taken to a stream by the priest who sprinkled the sufferer..with a sprig of veronica (*koromiko*). **1927** GUTHRIE-SMITH *Birds* 2 The limestone range east of the lake [Tutira] at one time grew..dense fern, high tutu, koromiko. **1964** TUWHARE *No Ordinary Sun* (1977) 10 Bearing leaves of koromiko and black cauldron aswirl with the mangled roots of flax or lawyer vine. **1983** HULME *Bone People* 466 Koromiko = useful tree if you've got a crook stomach or diarrhea [*sic*].

b. *Special Comb*. **koromiko tea**, an infusion of koromiko leaves as a remedy for diarrhoea and various stomach complaints.

1884 COX in Woodhouse *Blue Cliffs* (1982) 47 Dose 300 lambs with turpentine, oil, and koromiko tea.

koromoko, var. KORIMAKO.

korora. Also early **korara, korolah**. [Ma. /koro'ra:/: Williams 145 *Kororā 1.* n.] *little blue penguin* (PENGUIN 2 (1)).

[**1815** KENDALL *New Zealanders' First Book* 46 Korolah A penguin. **1820** LEE & KENDALL *NZ Gram. & Vocab.* 168 Kórora, *n*. A penguin.] **1842** GRAY *Fauna* in Dieffenbach *Travels in NZ* (1843) II. 199 *Spheniscus minor*... Koróra. **1857** HURSTHOUSE *NZ* I. 121 The Korora, a small green penguin, is the craftiest little fisherman of all coast birds. **1870** Korara [see PENGUIN 2 (1)]. **1882** POTTS *Out in Open* 213 Another common sea-bird is the grey plumaged little penguin, (*Spheniscus minor*)... *Korora*. **1898** MORRIS *Austral-English* 254 *Korora, n.* Maori name for a *Blue Penguin*, *Spheniscus minor*. **1905** BAUCKE *White Man Treads* 62 A smaller canoe..some working strange paddles; others firm in their seats like 'korora' (penguins) awaiting the tide. **1952** RICHARDS *Chatham Is.* 92 *Eudyptula..minor*... Blue Penguin. Korora. **1990** *Checklist Birds NZ* 69 *Eudyptula minor*... Blue Penguin (*Korora*).

korori, var. KORARI.

kororo, var. KARORO, KORERO.

korotangi. [Ma. /'korotaŋi/: not recorded in Williams.] A stone bird of reputed symbolic significance among the Maori but of doubtful provenance.

1882 *TrNZI* XIV. 103 The Carved Stone Bird, named korotangi. *Ibid.* 104 Mr Sheenan tells me that Rewi Maniapoto was greatly pleased to see the Korotangi on his visit to the Waikato, and kept it on the table near his bed, waking up at intervals to *tangi* over it. **1890** *TrNZI* XXII. 499 The Korotangi is the name given to a stone bird said by the Maoris to have been brought from Hawaiki by them in their canoe Tainui. *Ibid.* 500 The Korotangi was found in a hole, in which was growing a large kahikatoa-tree (manuka) very old. **1904** *NZ Illustr. Mag.* Sept. 442 Korotangi is the name given by the Maoris to a curiously-carved stone bird. **1917** *JPS* XXVI. 138 A version of the *waiata* for Korotangi was sung for me by..an aged man of the Awataha settlement in Shoal Bay, Auckland. **1929** *Ibid.* XXXVIII. 56 It is clear that the song refers to a living bird, and that there is nothing to connect it with the stone bird we know as the Korotangi. **1930** REISCHEK *Yesterdays in Maoriland* (1933) 198 Traditions lead only these few centuries back, but the holy bird, Korotangi, about which learned argument was raging when I left New Zealand, may perhaps prove a link with a still more distant past. The Korotangi is the figure of a small sea-gull carved out of dark green serpentine. **1947** *The Spike* 16 Antiquity is new to us: There's little But Korotangi and the Tamil bell. **1950** *Southern Cross* (Wellington) 20 May 8 Korotangi is made of a kind of dark green serpentine... It somewhat resembles a prion; but the nostrils are those of a duck. **1973** *Dom. Mus. Rec. Ethnol.* II. 108 The artistic features of Korotangi are clearly unusual in the context of Maori art. *Ibid.* 109 Albert Walker..gave an astounding version of the provenance of Korotangi. He claimed that he purchased it on board a New Zealand coaster. *Ibid.* 111 Korotangi is probably made with metal tools and of a stone which does not occur in Central and Eastern Polynesia. **1984** *Listener* 14 July 74 What we don't know is whether the stone bird in the National Museum is *the* Korotangi of the Tainui canoe. **1990** *Dominion* (Wellington) 14 Nov. 42 In its return home the exhibition has some important additions..with the inclusion of the canoe Teremoe, Raharuhi Rukupo's great 1842 meeting house, and the mysterious stone bird Korotangi.

korou, var. KORAU.

korowai. Also early **kóro ai.** [Ma. /ˈkorowai/: Williams 146 *Korowai, korokorowai,* n. Cloak.] A Maori cloak decorated with black twisted tags or thrums. Compare KAITAKA, PARAWAI.

[**1820** LEE & KENDALL *NZ Gram. & Vocab.* 168 Kóro ai; A certain garment.] **1835** YATE *NZ* (1970) 158 The *korowai* and *tatata* are two garments nearly alike in texture; they both have a number of loose strings hanging outside, which gives them a neat and comfortable appearance. **1840** WAKEFIELD *Diary* (ATLMS) (1840) 27 Mar. [43] I bought..a black string mat or *korowai*. **1866** ANGAS *Polynesia* 156 The mat most generally worn is the black-string mat called 'e koroai,' a flax dress thickly ornamented with black strings or filaments, about a foot long, which have a very graceful appearance as they hang over the folds of the drapery. **1882** POTTS *Out in Open* 23 Robes of piu piu, korowai, or pihepihe, contributed a great variety of costume. **1904** TREGEAR *Maori Race* 234 The *korowai* was of fine flax beaten out with a club to make it soft. It was generally worn by women and girls. **1922** COWAN *NZ Wars* (1955) II. 13 She was dressed only in a beautiful *korowai*, a white cloak of fine dressed flax. **1938** FINLAYSON *Brown Man's Burden* (1973) 10 Old Tamarua is delivering a speech of welcome, mere in hand, korowai cloak swishing as he paces to and fro. **1941** SUTHERLAND *Numismatic Hist. NZ* 15 The most valuable gifts that can be bestowed include the dogskin cloak, the *korowai* cloak with black edges, and the kiwi feather cloak. **1969** MEAD *Traditional Maori Clothing* 215 Fundamental to formal ceremonial costume is the korowai or feather cloak and it is around this garment that a costume complex is built. **1992** *Landfall 183* 259 Years earlier, a much younger self Lay face down in hot dry sand... Summer a korowai Around bare shoulders.

korrero, var. KORERO.

korry. Also with much variety of form as **corry**, **gorry**, **gorrie**, **kare**, **kolly**, **kori**, **korri**. [*Korry*, *gorry*, a form representing an alteration in spoken Maori of *God* (occas. poss. *golly*), used as a substitute in oaths: see also OED *gorry*.] **a.** In the phr. **by (pai, py) korry** (**gorry**, occas. **kare**), often as a euphemism for *by God*, and formerly freq. as an indicator of a stereotypical or 'stage Maori' mode of humour now usu. considered improper or otiose (see quot. 1938). Cf. PLURRY.

1892 in Gibson *Gibbie Galoot* (1924) (Frontispiece) [Facsimile letter from Maori Girl of 16 in 1892, in 'pidgin', ending:] My sister say you fond of little boys and girls well py gorry bimeby I give you plenty I send you xx Hohepa. **1898** VOGEL *Maori Maid* 41 Py Kolly..which represents the Maori's 'By Golly'. **1911** *Truth* 27 May 4 The recent Christchurch sittings of the Supreme Court found an astonished Maori charged with an offence against a half-caste girl of sixteen, but the defence put up by Lawyer Donnelly..so impressed the jury that they returned a verdict of not guilty. Py Korry! **1927** DONNE *Maori Past & Present* 214 The Maoris opened wide their eyes and said, 'Py korry!' **1935** MAXWELL *Recollections* 158 The Maori exclaimed, 'You think he dead, by gorry that the first time he ever do that.' **1938** FINLAYSON *Brown Man's Burden* 32 'Py korry, that right!' Wi admitted to himself. [*Py korry* omitted in the 1973 edition p. 31: elsewhere (29, 31) 'by golly' used.] **1941** MYERS *Valiant Love* 45 'By corry!' shouted Huoto. **1943** JACKSON *Passage to Tobruk* 23 'You fight Nazis, too, eh Hori?' 'Py corrie, yes.' **1956** GRAHAM *Treasury NZ Fishes* 355 The Maori women..would exclaim with great vehemence: 'By gorry, Mister, I never seen him go in.' **1960** HILLIARD *Maori Girl* 158 Netta, you're not a fool, but pai kare! you talk like one sometimes. **1964** HARVEY *Any Old Dollars Mister?* 41 The huge Maori put the Yank down..'By Kori,' he said with a kind smile. 'That was a cracker yarn, mate.' **1969** MOORE *Forest to Farm* 43 This appealed to the Maori, who..bawled, 'By Korri—the blurry good sulky eh?!!' **1982** SANDYS *Love & War* 153 'By gorrie,' Wiri muttered.

b. In *fig.* use as a noun. A Maori.

1947 *NZ Woman's Weekly* 22 May 17 Come on, Dad, the Pai Korry's are on again.

koru. [Ma. /ˈkoru/: Williams 147 *Koru* (i)... 3. A bulbed motif in carving and scroll painting.] The stylized fern scroll pattern used in Maori decoration; also used commercially, e.g. as a logo by Air New Zealand (see quot. 1994).

1938 PHILLIPPS *Maori Carving* 205 The *koru*, or *pikopiko*, which today rarely appears in carving, but is used in the construction of composite patterns for rafters. **1947** *The Spike* 18 The *koru* is the spiral design used in Maori art. **1964** BARROW *Decorative Arts NZ Maori* 64 Their elaborate curvilinear designs are usually based on a small bulb-like motif (*koru*) shaped like the looped top of an uncurling fern frond. **1981** *Dominion* (Wellington) 26 Nov. 17 McLeavey said 'Gordon Walters invented the koru'. He knows and I know that the koru has its origin in ancient Maori folk art... If popular usage annexes new words to a language, we will allow Walters the distinction of being the inventor of the koru in the language of contemporary New Zealand art. **1988** *Pacific Way* Nov. 47 The description..fails to mention..the striking koru pattern she used to decorate the waistline. **1994** *Dominion* (Wellington) 16 June 22 How did the gannets in the latest Air New Zealand television commercial learn to fly in koru formation?

korumeek, var. KOROMIKO.

koruru. [Ma. /ˈkoruru/: Williams 147 *Koruru*.] A carved figure placed on the gable of a Maori meeting-house.

[**1871** WILLIAMS *Dict. NZ Lang.* (3edn.) 64 *Kōrūrū*..figure placed on the gable of a house.] **1897** HAMILTON *Maori Art* (1901) Pt.2 85 The junction of the barge-boards was covered by a carved flat face, the *koruru*, which was adorned with feathers, and sometimes surmounted by a full-length figure, the *tekoteko*. The *koruru* was kept in place by a boss at the back. **1904** [see TEKOTEKO]. **1916** BEST *Maori Storehouses* 3 The carvings thereof were of the *koruru*..type. *Ibid.* 25 Such minor adornments as a carved head (*koruru*) on the gable. **1949** BUCK *Coming of Maori* 129 A carved head (*koruru*) was placed over the vertical join of the two barge-boards forming the gable apex... Sometimes a complete human figure (*tekoteko*) was used instead of a *koruru* type. **1966** PHILLIPPS *Maori Life & Custom* 123 A group of carved heads, koruru, illustrating a variety of presentation. **1979** *Islands* Nov. 5 The face of the Koruru figure on the ridge-pole of the Meeting House, staring blindly at its past.

kotahitanga. [Ma. *kotahi* 'one' (Williams 147 *Kotahi*) + *-tanga*, one of a number of suffixes forming abstract nouns from common nouns.] A movement for national unity among Maori tribes; 'one-ness', unity. Cf. KINGITANGA.

1935 *Let.* 24 Aug. in *Na To Hoa Aroha* (1988) III. 200 A minor victory of the kotahitanga movement. **1959** SINCLAIR *Hist. NZ* 112 The *kotahitanga* or 'unity' movement took shape at innumerable tribal or inter-tribal meetings, like that at Manawapou. **1991** *Evening Post* (Wellington) 26 Sept. 2 Mrs Hura paved the way to Kotahitanga (Maori unity) by joining the National Maori Congress, sharing the presidency with Maori Queen Dame Te Atairangikaahu and Sir Hepi Te HeuHeu.

kotare, var. KOTARETARE.

kotaretare. Freq. as **kotare**; and also early **ghotarre**, **kotaritari**. [Ma. /ˈkoːtare/, /koːˈtaretare/: Williams 148 *Kōtare, kōtaretare*,.. kingfisher.] KINGFISHER.

1835 YATE *NZ* (1970) 67 *Kotaretare*—This bird is a species of the kingfisher; but it is much smaller, and not so beautiful in its plumage as birds of that class found in England. **1838** POLACK *NZ* I. 298 The *kotáritári*, an alcedo, or kingfisher, supposed to feed on worms. **1842** GRAY *Fauna* in Dieffenbach *Travels in NZ* (1843) II. 187 *Halcyon vagans*... Ghotarre of the natives of Dusky Bay... Kotaretare Kotaritari... Kotare popo. **1859** THOMSON *Story NZ* I. 24 The Alcedinidae family has only one species, the Kotaretare or kingfisher. It..possesses the habits of the English bird, although its plumage is not so bright. **1873** BULLER *Birds NZ* 69 Halcyon vagans. (New-Zealand Kingfisher)... Kotare and Kotaretare; 'Kingfisher' of the colonists. **1897** [see KINGFISHER]. **1904** HUTTON & DRUMMOND *Animals NZ* 115 *The Kingfisher.—Kotare. Halcyon vagans*. **1930** *NZJST* XI. 154 Birds seen occasionally [on Three Kings included] kingfishers—kotaretare (*Halcyon*

KOTARITARI

sanctus). **1947** POWELL *Native Animals NZ* 86 On the whole kingfishers are most useful birds to the agriculturalist, for they consume large quantities of grubs and insects. The Maori name is Kotare. **1964** HINTZ *Trout at Taupo* 3 Kotare, the kingfisher, will make his darting flight—a flash of electric blue against the paler blue of the sky. **1989** PARKINSON *Travelling Naturalist* 102 The kingfisher (kotare) favours the cliff for nesting sites and they sit on the power lines looking for lunch along the roadside verges.

kotaritari, var. KOTARETARE.

koteedo, kotero, varr. KOTIRO.

kotero. Also **kotiro.** [Ma. /ˈkoːtero/: Williams 148 *Kōtero*, n. Potatoes steeped in water.] Preserved (or small) potatoes; in later use, preserved kumara.

1847 BRUNNER *Exped. Middle Is.* in Taylor *Early Travellers* (1959) 285 Tipia and party..were also fed..each having a kit of potatoes and taro, a large quantity of the *kotiro*, or preserved potato, and garnished well with different sorts of fish. **1863** MOSER *Mahoe Leaves* 22 Small potatoes, termed 'kotero', and the berries of the karaka tree..are both..considered great delicacies. **1982** BURTON *Two Hundred Yrs. NZ Food* 4 [Title] Kumara kotero (cured kumara). Kotero may be fried or, as in the traditional recipe, cooked in hot embers.

kotiro, var. KOTERO.

kotiro. *Obs.* in English use. Also **ko(e)teedo, kotero.** [Ma. /ˈkoːtiro/: Williams 149 *kōtiro* n. Girl.] A girl.

1814 MARSDEN in Elder *Marsden's Lieutenants* 9 Mar. (1934) 58 I told you when you were at Parramatta I would send you a gentleman to teach your tameheekes (tamarikis) and ko[e]te[e]dos (kotiros) to read. [**1815** KENDALL *New Zealanders' First Book* 45 koteedo; A girl. **1820** LEE & KENDALL *NZ Gram. & Vocab.* 169 Kotíro, *s.* A young girl.] **1863** MOSER *Mahoe Leaves* 34 My friend Harry..had fraternized with a bevy of Kotiros (or young girls) with whom he was flirting prodigiously. **1905** SATCHELL *Toll of Bush* 71 The Mallons..belonged to the earlier pioneers, the family having been established in the days when the white man came alone into the native settlement and picked his wife from the bright-eyed kotiros of the hapu. **1906** *Truth* 15 Sept. 6 Maori Tangata and Pakeha Kotero. At Tauranga Police court..a Maori and a white girl were charged.

kotuku. Also early **koatuku.** [Ma. /ˈkoːtuku/: Williams 150 *kōtuku,* n. *1.*]

1. *white heron* (HERON 2 (3)).

[**1820** LEE & KENDALL *NZ Gram. & Vocab.* 169 Kotúku, *s.* Name of a certain bird.] **1846** HEAPHY *Exped. to Kawatiri* in Taylor *Early Travellers* (1959) 219 Shot a very fine *koatuku*, or white heron. **1851** SHORTLAND *S. Dist. NZ* 169 As we pulled up the river, we saw several 'kotuku', a species of heron with white plumage, hovering over the cliffs. **1861** HAAST *Rep. Topogr. Explor. Nelson* 137 It was admirable to behold the kotuku (white crane) with his head laid back, darting his pointed beak at his foes. **1882** HAY *Brighter Britain* II. 225 The Kotuku, or crane.., must just be mentioned, though none of us ever saw one. But the Maori have a proverb—'as rare as the kotuku'. **1904** TREGEAR *Maori Race* 40 If the feathers seen in the dream were those of the white crane (*kotuku*) the child would be a boy. **1929** DUGGAN *NZ Bird Songs* 16 Haeremai the Heron, The White Crane, the lost bird, Home is the Heron, home, home the Kotuku. **1930** *Taranaki Herald* 5 May 6 The Ngati-Ruanui tribesfolk camped there [in the Ngaere swamp]..snaring ducks and that now almost extinct beautiful bird, the kotuku, or white heron. **1946** *JPS* LV. 153 *Kōtuku*, a bird (Egretta alba), white heron or egret, always rare even in Maori regard, whence the proverb: He kōtuku rerenga tahi (A heron of one flight)—applied to a distinguished visitor. **1975** *New Zealand's Heritage* LXVI. 1849 White Heron... Known as the kotuku, it took a very prominent place in Maori folk-lore. It became in turn a symbol for anything rare, or for anything beautiful. **1985** *Reader's Digest Book NZ Birds* 131 In Maori oratory, the most exquisite compliment is to liken someone to the kotuku. **1990** *Checklist Birds NZ* 89 Egretta alba modesta... White Heron (White Egret, *Kotuku*).

2. *Special Comb.* **kotuku feathers.**

1848 MCLEAN *Diary* 26 May in Cowan *Sir Donald Maclean* (1940) 36 The elder men were dressed in their best dogskin and *kaitaka* mats, some of them had their heads decorated with *huia* and *kotuku* feathers. **1989** PARKINSON *Travelling Naturalist* 166 When the Pakeha arrived they had already been reduced to one small colony..and a demand for kotuku feathers for the millinery trade reduced them still further from 25 pairs in 1871 to about four in 1940.

kotuku-ngutupapa. [Ma. /ˈkoːtukuˈŋutupapa/: Williams 150 *Kōtuku-ngutupapa*..royal spoonbill.] *royal spoonbill* (SPOONBILL 2).

1955 OLIVER *NZ Birds* 400 Royal Spoonbill. Kotuku-ngutupapa Platalea regia An Australian species recorded on six occasions between 1861 and 1932, and continuously since 1942. **1985** *Reader's Digest Book NZ Birds* 137 Royal Spoonbill Platalea regia Gould, 1838... Other name: *Kotuku-ngutupapa*... Known to the Maori as kotuku-ngutupapa, the royal spoonbill must have reached New Zealand from Australia many times before European settlement. **1990** *Checklist Birds NZ* 95 Platalea regia... Royal Spoonbill (*Kotuku-ngutupapa*).

kotukutuk, var. KOTUKUTUKU.

kotukutuku. Also **kotukutuk, tookytooky.** [Ma. /koːˈtukutuku/: Williams 150 *Kōtukutuku*, n. *1.*] *tree fuchsia* (FUCHSIA 2). See also KOHUTUHUTU.

1847 BRUNNER *Exped. Middle Is.* 17 Feb. in Taylor *Early Travellers* (1959) 267 The fruit of the kotukutuku, called konini, is a pleasant tasted berry, and is ripe about this month. **1853** HOOKER *II Flora Novae-Zelandiae I Flowering Plants* 56 Fuchsia *excorticata*, Linn. fil... Nat. name, 'Kotuku-tuku', *Cunn*.; of the berry 'Konini', *Lyall*. **1882** HAY *Brighter Britain* II. 194 The Kotukutuku..is akin to the fuchsia seen in the gardens at home. **1898** MORRIS *Austral-English* 475 *Tookytook, n.* a corruption of *Kotukutuku*.., a Maori name equivalent to *Konini*, the fruit of the *Fuchsia*-tree. **1907** [see KOHUTUHUTU]. **1926** COWAN *Travel in NZ* II. 32 Here and there a little watercourse..arboured over by a matted roofing of *kotukutuku*. **1939** BEATTIE *First White Boy Born Otago* 13 I never tasted a drink made of kotukutuk (fuchsia berries), but I once helped to eat a pie made of them and it was very sweet. **1966** TURNER *Eng. Lang. Austral. & NZ* 168 The *konini* or native fuchsia is called *kotukutuku* in Maori, and has been called *tookytook* in English. **1970** [see FUCHSIA 1]. **1986** OWEN & PERKINS *Speaking for Ourselves* 67 He said, 'Well, there's a swarm on a kotukutuku by the track—how about taking them?'

koude, koudi(e), var. KAURI.

kouka: see *ti-kauka* (TI *n.*¹ 3 (2)).

koukaato, var. KOKAKO.

KOURA

koukou. Also **káokáo, roukou** (prob. a misreading of MS *K* as *R*). [Echoic on one of the bird's cries: Ma. /ˈkoukou/: Williams 151 *Kou* (ii) *koukou*. *1*. v. intr. onomatopoetic [*sic*]. Hoot. *2*...more-pork.] **a.** MOREPORK 1 a.

1835 YATE *NZ* (1970) 53 *Koukou*—The bird so called is a small owl, a native of New Zealand; and partakes of all the character of the common British owl... Its name has been given to it as an imitation of its cry. **1838** POLACK *NZ* I. 300 Hawks, or..the mournful *káokáo, or owl*. **1844** WILLIAMS *NZ Jrnl.* (1956) 115 The Roukou is the screech owl, abounding in New Zealand fern forests, and its cries are considered ominous at times by the natives or aborigines. **1859** [see RURU]. **1873** BULLER *Birds NZ* 20 This note resembles the syllables *kou-kou*, uttered from the chest; and among the northern tribes the bird is usually called by a name resembling that cry. It is, however, more generally known as the 'Ruru', and in some districts as the 'Peho'. **1889** *TrNZI* XXI. 200 [Title] *A few stray Notes on the New Zealand Owl*, Athene novae-zealandiae... *Ruru and Koukou of the Maoris, and Morepork of the Settlers*. **1946** [see RURU]. **1983** KING *Whina* 134 We called that bird a koukou, that was the Hokianga name for it. Other places call it ruru.

b. A call of the morepork.

1888 [see MOREPORK 1 b]. **1916** COWAN *Bush Explorers* (VUWTS) 15 The mournful ruru calls his 'kou-kou', 'kia toa' from a branch. **1920** *Quick March* 10 Apr. 13 We made shift to lighten this inevitable infliction of the Maori bush with the yarns that go best to the accompaniment of a crackling log, the 'Koukou' of the Morepork.

koukoupara, var. KOKOPARA.

koumara, var. KUMARA.

koura. Also with much variety of early form as **gora(u), goura, kahouda, kaura, kohuda, kooura, kora.** [Ma. /ˈkoːura/: Williams 151 *Kōura* [for saltwater and freshwater crayfish spp.].] CRAYFISH. **a.** The saltwater crayfish (*Jasus* spp.).

[**1770** COOK *Journals* 31 Mar. (1955) I. 287 [*English*] A Lobster [*New Zeland*] Kooura [*South-sea Islands*] Tooura. **1815** KENDALL *New Zealanders' First Book* 46 Kahouda Crayfish. **1820** LEE & KENDALL *NZ Gram. & Vocab.* 169 Kóura, *s.* The crayfish.] **1839** WALTON *Twelve Months' Residence* 30 Of the crustaceous genus there is the kohuda, or crayfish, about the size of our lobster, and resembling it in flavour. **1842** GRAY *Fauna* in Dieffenbach *Travels in NZ* (1843) II. 266 Palinurus sp. 'Lobster, or Sea Cray-fish.'..'Kohuda or cray-fish', Kohura. **1843** WILLIAMS *NZ Jrnl.* (1956) 41 Of this variety of 78 species [of fish] I will name a part, viz... Gora, crawfish, similar to lobster. **1851** SHORTLAND *S. Dist. NZ* 70 There was the 'mango' or shark, the 'koura' or cray fish..and a variety of other dainties. **1875** CHUDLEIGH *Diary* 15 Sept. (1950) 241 At the beach I got a few potatoes and some koura crayfish. **1885** *TrNZI* XVII. 419 The fishing off the island is very good, there being..plenty of shell-fish such as koura or crayfish. c**1920** *South Island Maori Lists* 'Wahi Mahika Kai' in Beattie *Maori Place-names Canterbury* (1945) 62 Koura—this is the crayfish, the same name applying both to the big sea ones, and the small river ones found far inland.

b. *freshwater crayfish* (CRAYFISH 2 (1), *Paranephrops* spp.). See also CRAWLER 2, CRAWLIE.

1847 JOHNSON *Notes from Jrnl.* 5 Jan. in Taylor *Early Travellers* (1959) 152 *gorau*, a species of cray-fish, or rather fresh water lobster for they more resemble the latter. **1855** TAYLOR *Te Ika A Maui* 414 Amongst the Crustacea is the *koura*, which is the general name for both the sea cray fish and the fresh water..the latter is from four to eight inches long. **1873** St John *Pakeha Rambles* in Taylor *Early Travellers* (1959) 554 Rotorua has its *kora*, a large prawn, or diminutive fresh water lobster. **1929** goura [see CRAYFISH 2 (1)]. **1937** Hyde *Wednesday's Children* (1989) 135 Small fresh-water lobsters, known as koras, shared a like view. **1974** Hilliard *Maori Woman* 177 She would go to the creek..to look for koura under the stones. **1984** Wilson *S. Pacific Street* 5 Sometimes..we'd go down to the creek..to catch koura, those small freshwater crayfish we called crawlies. **1992** *North & South* (Auckland) May 71 When KAL drains the pond, along with..'Cran's Bully', a number of good-sized native koura will also be destroyed.

kouradi, var. KORARI.

kouri, var. KAURI.

koutu utu, var. KOHUTUHUTU.

kowai, var. KOWHAI.

kowarawara, var. KOWHARAWHARA.

kowdie, var. KAURI.

kowhai /ˈkʌuwai/, /ˈkʌufai/. Spelling evidence suggests two basic Ma. forms of initial /k/ underlying transliterations: a mainly NI form realized with initial [k], and a mainly SI form realized with initial [g] both with variations (bilabial /ɸ/, or /h/, or in recent times /f/) of the medial consonant: thus (NI) **kowhai** (var. **kowhy**), **kowai, kohai** (varr. **koa, kohi** etc.); and (SI) **gowhai, gowai, *gohai (ghoa, ghoai, ghoi, goa, goai, goey, gohi)**, suggesting mainly SI anglicized pronunciations /ˈgʌuwai/, /ˈgʌu(h)ai/, /ˈgʌuə/. Transliterations of the shape ***kofai, *gofai** have not been found. [Ma. /ˈkoːfai/, /ˈkoːhai/: Williams 152 *Kōwhai, kōhai*. n. *1. Sophora* [spp.]: cf. Walsh & Biggs 37 PPN **koofai* 'tree sp.'.]

1. The native trees *Sophora* (formerly *Edwardsia*) *tetraptera* and *S. microphylla* (fam. Fabaceae), common along river banks and forest margins, and distinguished in early spring by masses of golden-yellow flowers (cf. *yellow kowhai* 2 (2) below). See also ACACIA 1, LABURNUM, LOCUST TREE. **a. kowhai** forms. (a) As **kowhai** (occas. **kowhy**).

1831 Bennett in *London Med. Gaz.* 12 Nov. 182 *Sophora tetraptera*... This tree is the Kowhy, or Kongia, of the natives, and attains the height of from forty to fifty feet. **1847** Angas *Savage Life* II. 10 The yellow *kowhai* tree, at this season of spring, covered with a profusion of golden blossoms, ornamented the banks of streams. **1853** Hooker *II Flora Novae-Zelandiae I Flowering Plants* 52 *Edwardsia grandiflora*... Nat. name, 'Kowhai'. **1868** Lindsay *Contribs. NZ Bot.* 73 *S. tetraptera*..var. *microphylla*... The 'Kowhai' of the North Island Maori; the 'Kowai' of settlers,—or as the word is variously corrupted and spelt by them,— 'Goai' or 'Ghoai', 'Goa' or 'Ghoa'. According to Hector, the type is known to Otago Maoris as 'Houma'; while the term 'Kowhai' is applied to var. *grandiflora* in common with its other varieties. Var. *microphylla* is also sometimes designated by the colonists the Native 'Laburnum' or 'Mimosa', from the similarity of its foliage, in the arboreous condition, to that of these familiar..European trees. **1898** Morris *Austral-English* 254 *Kowhai, n.* Maori name given to (1) Locust-tree, Yellow Kowhai (*Sophora tetraptera*..N.O. Leguminosae). **1900** *Canterbury Old & New* 184 The pea-flowered kowhai attracts the melodious tui to its honey-laden blossoms. **1910** [see LABURNUM]. **1920** Mander *Story NZ River* (1974) 9 There was a riotous spring colour in the forest, voluptuous gold and red in the clumps of yellow Kowhai and crimson Rata. **1946** *JPS* LV. 144 *Kōwhai*, a tree (*Sophora tetraptera*), the yellow-flowering tree, first to blossom in spring, and adopted as the national flower of New Zealand. **1969** *Standard Common Names Weeds* 42 *kowhai Sophora microphylla*. **1983** Hulme *Bone People* 133 The kowhai is a tall thin tree, with greybrown bark... Anyway, co-eye English pronunciation, kor-fie Maori pronunciation, alla same tree, get it?

(b) As **kowai**.

1833 Williams *Early Jrnls.* 13 Nov. (1961) 346 The *Kowai* was very conspicuous whose tender boughs hung elegantly over the stream. **1848** Taylor *Leaf from Nat. Hist.* 20 Kowai, acacia bearing a yellow flower. (Edwardsia microphylla) **1851** *Lyttelton Times* 28 June 6 The timber in [the groves] is chiefly Kaikatea..Remu, (red pine), Pokaka, Kowai, and Totara. **1868** kowai [see (a) above]. **1884** Martin *Our Maoris* 94 It was spring-time, and..the yellow kowai blossoms hung over the brim of the river in masses of gold.

(c) As **kohai** (var. **koa, kohi**).

1844 Monro *Notes of a Journey* in Hocken *Contributions* (1898) 242 The kohai is also a very common tree in the woods [in Otago], and grows to a large size. **1851** in *Otago Jrnl.* 8 (1852) Aug. 126 White and black pines, koas etc. **1878** Kiernan *Diary* 4 Jan. in Guthrie-Smith *Tutira* (1926) 122 Kite and C.H.S. sledged posts from Tylee's spur and cut some Kohi posts for the horse paddock. **1882** Potts *Out in Open* 186 The small leaved kohai..contrast[s] well with the dusky hue of the dark-leaved fagus.

b. Mainly South Island variants of **gowhai, gowai** and ***gohai (ghoa, ghoai, ghoi, goa, goai, goey, gohi, goi)**, usu. anglicized as /ˈgʌu(w)ai/.

1856 Tancred *Nat. Hist. Canterbury* 20 Another valuable tree is the goi or yellow clianthus. **1860** in Butler *First Year* (1863) vii 104 I remember nothing but a rather curiously shaped gowai-tree. **1866** Barker *Station Life* (1870) 94 I can give you no idea of the variety among the shrubs..the mappo, the gohi, and many others. **1868** ghoa(i), goa(i) [see a (a) above]. **1869** *TrNZI* I. (rev. edn.) 171 I refer to the kowhai, or as it is called in the south the gowhai. **1889** Blair *Lays of the Old Identities* 36 The land of the goi tree, mapu and pine, The stately totara, and blooming wild vine. c**1920** Beattie *Trad. Lifeways Southern Maori* 174 The birds were just then keeping low in the goai bushes. **1926** *TrNZI* L. 670 'Kowhai' went through many stages—'goa', 'gohi' &c. before settling to the two forms 'kowhai' in the North and 'gowhai' or 'gowai' in the South. **1933** *Press* (Christchurch) (Acland Gloss.) 21 Oct. 15 Gowai.—A common spelling and pronunciation of *kowhai* (Sophora). It was from this tree that many bullock-yokes were made. **1954** *Listener* 21 May 22 'What about kowhai?'.. 'Co-eye? Oh, go-eye!.. Funny the way you call him.' **1957** *Dominion* (Wellington) 12 Aug. [corresp. col.] Bushmen usually called a puketea, buckyteer; a kowhai, goey.

2. With a modifier: **red (scarlet), yellow**.

(1) **red (scarlet) kowhai**. KAKA-BEAK (*Clianthus* sp.). See also KOWHAI NGUTUKAKA.

1850 Stephens *Journal* (ATLTS) 472 The Scarlet Kowhai (a native of the Northern Island). **1884** Bracken *Lays of the Maori* 21 The dazzling points Of morning's lances pierced the bursting hearts..And waked the red kowhai's drops from sleep. **1906** Cheeseman *Manual NZ Flora* 121 *Kowhai-ngutu-kaka*..it is now commonly cultivated in gardens throughout the colony under the name of 'red kowhai'. **1922** *Auckland Weekly News* 16 Feb. 15 The scarlet kowhai brightens thousands of gardens. **1943** Matthews *NZ Garden Dict.* 43 *Clianthus* (Red Kowhai, Parrot's Beak or Kaka Beak). **1971** *New Zealand's Heritage* I. 267 Kaka Beak... Coastal plant sometimes known as the red kowhai. **1991** *Hist. Howick & Pakuranga* 33 She is wearing a garland of red kowhai, or kaka beak.

(2) *Obs.* **yellow kowhai** (*Sophora* spp.).

1858 Smith *Notes of Journey* 14 Jan. in Taylor *Early Travellers* (1959) 361 Between the two is a pretty grove of yellow kowai. **1889** Featon *Art Album NZ Flora* 117 The 'Yellow Kowhai'... The wood of the 'Kowhai' closely resembles the European 'Laburnum', and possesses great strength. **1897** Courage *Lights & Shadows* 237 Yellow Goi, as the men called it, or 'Kowhai', as the Maories called it. **1905** [see LABURNUM].

3. *Special Comb.* **kowhai moth**, see MOTH 4.

kowhai ngutukaka. [Ma. /ˈkoːfai ˈŋutukaːkaː/: Williams 152 *Kōwhai ngutukākā*.] KAKA-BEAK 1. See also *red kowhai* (KOWHAI 2 (1)).

1835 *Transactions of Horticultural Soc. London* in *TrNZI* (1886) XVIII. 293 This drawing..was taken from a fresh specimen of the plant 'raised in England from seed gathered by the missionaries in New Zealand, where it is said to be called 'Kowhaingutu-kaka', or Parrot's-bill. **1842** Wade *Journey in Nthn Is.* 196 Kowai ngutukaka [parrot-bill kowai] [*sic*]; the most elegant flowering shrub of the country. **1853** Hooker *II Flora Novae-Zelandiae I Flowering Plants* 49 *Clianthus puniceus*... Nat. name, 'Kowhaingutu kaka', a parrot's bill. **1869** *TrNZI* I. (rev. edn.) 369 The red *Clianthus puniceus*..[was] called.. *Kowhai-ngutu-kaakaa*.. Parrot's-bill Kowhai. **1889** Featon *Art Album NZ Flora* 177 Kowhai-ngutu-kaka [Maori name]..Crimson Kowhai [Settlers' name]..*Clianthus puniceus*..Shrub. **1907** [see KAKA-BEAK 1]. **1946** *JPS* LV. 153 *kōwhai-ngutukaka*, a shrubby tree (*Clianthus puniceus*), red-flowering kowhai (kākā-beak), parrots-bill. **1960** [on the 2d. stamp definitive issue] in *Catalogue NZ Stamps* (Campbell Paterson, 1978) permanent page O2 2d Kaka Beak (Kowhai-Ngutu-Kaka). Commonly called 'Kaka beak' from the resemblance of the flowers to the beak of the Kaka parrot, (see 1/- 1898 Pictorial). The plant is a low shrub and rare in a wild state. **1989** Parkinson *Travelling Naturalist* 84 Of particular interest to botanists at Lake Waikaremoana..the kaka-beak shrub, the kowhai-ngutu-kaka of the Maori.

kowhaiwhai. [Ma. /koːˈfaifai/: Williams 152 *Kōwhaiwhai* n. Painted scroll ornamentation.] Painted scroll-work or ornamentation in Maori art.

1946 Zimmerman *Where People Sing* 122 Overhead, the beams were painted with the lovely intricate *kowhaiwhai* pattern in black, white, and brick red. **1950** *NZJAg.* Aug. LXXXI. 187 The tuku tuku or kowhaiwhai (coloured scroll work) and the tukutuku (decorative reed panels) are admirable examples of Maori art. **1986** Ihimaera *Matriarch* 191 The gravity and reverence for the past were evident on all the rafters, painted in the typical designs of the kowhaiwhai, bold red, white and black curvilinear designs. **1986** Hulme *Windeater* 93 They've got their fancy cardigans on, natural wool with kowhaiwhai patterns across the chest.

kowharawhara. Also early **kowarawara**. [Ma. /koːˈfarafara/: Williams 152 *Kōwharawhara*. *1.* n. *Astelia* [spp.].] Epiphytic species of ASTELIA q.v., usu. *Astelia solandri* (formerly *cunninghamii*). See also WHARAWHARA.

1849 Taylor *Journal* 16 June (ATLTS) VI. 113 On its being remarked that he [*sc.* Mamaku of Otaki] was

KOWHY

going gray he said, yes, you don't see the kowarawara (an epiphyte) growing on the ngaio or mahoe, a tree which is of no value. **1853** HOOKER *II Flora Novae-Zelandiae I Flowering Plants* 259 Astelia *Cunninghamii*... Nat. name, 'Kowhara-whara'. **1869** *TrNZI* I. (rev. edn.) 266 Sometimes the snow-white downy fibres from the under side of the leaves of the Kowharawhara, and the Kahakaha, (*Astelia Cunninghamii*, and *Solandri*,)..were also used..to ornament..the head. **1874** *TrNZI* VI. 55 Kowharawhara, *Astelia banksii* and *A. cunninghamii*, have the habit of the [tree-flax]. **1881** *TrNZI* XIII. 62 The waving of the long leaves of the kowharawhara. **1926** [see KAHAKAHA]. **1970** MOORE & EDGAR *Flora NZ* II. 27 The Maori name, *Kowharawhara*, originally recorded for *A. solandri* by Cunningham, was probably used in a generic sense. **1995** CROWE *Which Coastal Plant?* 40 *Coastal Astelia*... Kōwharawhara [*Astelia banksii*] is related to the lilies commonly seen perching in the forks of forest trees, but this astelia is one of those that grow on the ground or on rocks.

kowhy, var. KOWHAI.

kowia, var. KOHIA.

kowri, kowry, varr. KAURI.

kowshore, var. KAUHOA.

kraddy, var. KORARI.

kraka, var. KARAKA.

kuaka. Also **koohákka**. [Ma. /ˈkuːaka/,/ˈkuaka/: Williams 154 *Kūaka, Kuaka*, n... eastern bartailed godwit.] Any of various birds but esp. the *eastern bar-tailed godwit*; and, in the South Island, the common *diving petrel Pelecanoides urinatrix*. **a.** GODWIT a. (Also used of similar birds.)

 [**1815** KENDALL *New Zealanders' First Book* 47 Koohákka A bird like a woodcock. **1820** LEE & KENDALL *NZ Gram. & Vocab.* 170 Kuáka, *s.* Name of a certain bird.] **1844** [see GODWIT a]. **1873** BULLER *Birds NZ* 198 Limosa baueri. (Barred-rumped Godwit)..*Native name*.—Kuaka. **1882** [see CURLEW 1]. **c1890** BUCKLAND in Parkinson *Travelling Naturalist* (1989) 31 The beach was covered with kuaka ..thousands hovering overhead to find a footing. **1905** BAUCKE *White Man Treads* 250 These thoughts flew through my brain like a covey of kuaka (snipe). **1911** SHAND *Moriori People* 6 The young of many sea birds..were used as food [on the Chathams], such as *Kuaka* (plover), young gulls (*Ngoiro*), shags. **1922** [see GODWIT a]. **1946** *JPS* LV. 153 *kūaka*, a migratory bird (Limosa novae zealandiae), godwit; nests in Siberia. **1982** KEENE *Myrtle & Sophia* 32 On his return a week later, I cooked him a kuaka pie and invited Eva to join us. **1991** *Evening Post* (Wellington) 15 Apr. 11 But godwits—kuaka—are being used by Mr Rata to make a point. He said most young Maori would prefer Kentucky Fried Chicken.

b. *Southern South Island. diving petrel* (PETREL 2 (7)), a muttonbird.

 1914 GUTHRIE-SMITH *Mutton Birds* 201 *Pelecanoides urinatrix*—Diving Petrel—Kuaka. Kuaka is also in the North Island a name given to the Southern Godwit. **1940** HOWARD *Rakiura* 205 These are the names used by the southern Maori... Kuaka: *Pelicanoides Urinatrix*, or Diving Petrel. **1955**, **1966**, **1982**, **1990** [see PETREL 2 (7)].

kudi, var. KURI.

kuhi. var. COO-EE.

kuia. [Ma. /ˈkuia/: Williams 154 *Kuia* (i) *1*. Old woman.] An old, or senior, woman, respected because of age or seniority within a family group; often used in address or reference (see quot. 1989) Also familiarly as **kui**, 'granny, Nana' esp. when used by a child (see quot. 1992).

 [**1820** LEE & KENDALL *NZ Gram. & Vocab.* 170 Kúia, *s.* A kind term for mother.] **1871** MEADE *Ride through Disturbed Dist.* in Taylor *Early Travellers* (1959) 455 [He] told the messenger that his friend was a *kuia* (a not very complimentary term for an old woman). [1959 *Note*] *Kuia* merely means old lady. **1948** HENDERSON *Taina* 24 A shrivelled-up *kuia*, well hidden among the crowd, called out. **1958** ASHTON-WARNER *Spinster* 156 I ask Nanny when the tattooed wrinkled barefooted old Maori Kuia comes over in person at noon. **1965** CAMERON *NZ* 93 A mundane example of a description of the present situation was recently offered in impromptu fashion by a *kuia* (translate 'old woman,' but without the harsh connotations of 'old'). **1972** *Listener* 10 July XI. 2 A tribute to the last of the *kuia* or old Maori women with the tattooed chins. **1985** McGILL *G'day Country* 62 I approached Lees' General Store. The kuia no longer sit against the corrugated iron fence alongside..dribbling on their moko. **1989** TE AWEKOTUKU *Tahuri* 20 Now Kuia will get mad at me... Kuia was a quietly snoring hump on the other side of the room. **1992** *Dominion* Wellington) 14 Nov. 11 Like her revered kui (her nanny), who knows immediately when a close relation has died, the depth of..[her] Maoritanga..also gives her prescience.

kuki, var. COOKEE.

kuku, *n.*[1] Also **kookoo**. [Walsh & Biggs 39 PPN *kUkU*[2] 'pigeon' (poss. also echoic from the cooing sound of the pigeon): Ma. /ˈkuːkuː/: Williams 153 *Kū* (iii) *1*...Coo... *Kūkū*, n. *Hemiphaga novaeseelandiae*.] PIGEON 1; also its cry. See also KUKUPA.

 [**1820** LEE & KENDALL *NZ Gram. & Vocab.* 170 Kúku... The cry of a pigeon.] **1841** BEST *Journal* 4 Apr. (1966) 284 In the Evening I shot a pair of Kookoos and by moonlight a pair of Owls. **1855** TAYLOR *Te Ika A Maui* 406 The pigeon bears two names—the kuka and kukupa, which are common to the isles. **1871** MEADE *Ride through Disturbed Dist.* in Taylor *Early Travellers* (1959) 461 A brace of *kuku*, or *kukupa*, had been snared for our breakfast..; the *kuku* is the name of the New Zealand pigeon. **1882** POTTS *Out in Open* (1976) 45 Less fleet on the wing than the blue rock pigeon, the heavy fruit-consuming kuku..urges its sounding pinions vainly in its efforts to escape. **1898** MORRIS *Austral-English* 255 *Kuku*, or *Kukupa*..Maori name for the New Zealand *Fruit-pigeon*... Called also *Kereru*. The name is the bird's note. **1905** BAUCKE *White Man Treads* 19 First in his [Maori] catalogue, for flavour and bulk, the plentiful kereru, or kuku (pigeon) headed the list. **1936** [see PIGEON 2 (4)]. **1946** [see KERERU]. **1955** [see PIGEON 2 (2)].

kuku, *n.*[2] [Ma. /ˈkuku/: Williams 155 *Kuku*... *6*. *Mytilus*..and other species of mussel.] MUSSEL 1.

 [**1820** LEE AND KENDALL *NZ Grammar and Vocabulary* 170 Kukúku, *s.* A shell-fish so called.] **1861** [see MUSSEL 1]. **1870** TAYLOR *Te Ika a Maui* 633 Fam. Mytilidae has many representatives, *powhe, kutai, kuku*. **1894** *TrNZI* XXVI. 433 For general purposes the shells of both the *pipi* and the *kuku*, or mussel, were constantly in request. **1905** BAUCKE *White Man Treads* 2 White seashore sandhills, representing the accumulated deaths of ages of pipi, pupu, kuku, and

KUMARA

other molluscs. **1912** *NZ Free Lance* (Wellington) 13 Apr. 5 They dropped their kuku-shells and embraced themselves tightly. **1929** BEST *Fishing Methods* 63 An old folk-tale describes a quarrel that arose in remote times between the Kuku and Pipi families at Waikaru—that is, between mussels and cockles. **1938** MAKERETI *The Old-Time Maori* (1986) 237 Kuku, mussels, were taken from the rocks by hand and collected in baskets. **1963** HILLIARD *A Piece of Land* 55 'Where's those kukus?' 'In the washhouse.' **1978**, **1990** [see KUTAI].

kukupa. Also early **coo couper, kookoopa**. [Ma. /ˈkuːkupa/: Williams 157 *Kupa* (i)... *2*. v. intr. Soar... *Kūkupa... Hemiphaga novaeseelandiae*.] PIGEON 1. Cf. KUKU *n.*[1]

 [**1815** KENDALL *New Zealanders' First Book* 47 Kookoopa A pigeon.] **1817** NICHOLAS *Voyage NZ* I. 351-352 Shunghi..shot a bird called the *kookoopa*, of a blue plumage, and somewhat larger than our pigeon. [**1820** LEE & KENDALL *NZ Gram. & Vocab.* 171 Kukúpa, *s.* Pigeon.] **1834** MARKHAM *NZ* (1963) 56 When in the Woods she looked out for the (Coo Coupers) or Pigeons, and had a sharp eye. **1840** [see PIGEON 1]. **1851** LUSH *Auckland Jrnls.* 16 Dec. (1971) 14 Searles amused himself with shooting a Kukupa one of the most beautiful birds the country pos[s]esses. **1873** [see PIGEON 2 (3)]. **1881** CAMPBELL *Poenamo* 115 The kukupa..was just the bird created expressly for the true cockney sportsman. **1894** *Richmond-Atkinson Papers* (1960) II. 597 They were stewing the two birds when a kukupa (bush pigeon) flew up and perched. Bob shot it. **1926** [see PIGEON 2 (5)]. **1949** BUCK *Coming of Maori* 93 The principal forest birds sought for food were the wood pigeon (*kereru, kukupa, kuku*). **1986** WEDDE *Symmes Hole* 200 'How's what called?..' 'Those pigeons...' 'Kukupa.'

kukuruatu. [Ma. /ˈkuːkuruatu/: Williams 155 *Kūkuruatu*.] Usu. *shore plover* (PLOVER 2 (6)); occas. *sand plover* (PLOVER 2 (5)).

 1869 *TrNZI* I. (rev. edn.) 105 Thinornis Novae Zelandiae. Kukuruatu. At Whangapoua. **1871**, **1904** [see PLOVER 2 (5)].

kumakuma, var. KAMOKAMO.

kumara /ˈkum(ə)rə/, /ˈkʊm(ə)rə/. The spelling **kumera** has equal standing. Also with much variety of early form as **coom(e)ra, c(o)umal(l)a, cumera, goomālla, koomar(r)a, koomera, kormera, koumara, kumera, kummura, kuumara, kymoura**. [Ma. /ˈkuːmara/,/ˈkuːmera/: Williams 155 *Kūmara, kūmera... Ipomoea batatas*: Walsh & Biggs 40 PPN *kumala 'sweet potato'*.]

1. a. The sweet potato *Ipomoea batatas* (fam. Convolvulaceae) as it is known in Polynesia. See also *sweet potato* (SWEET *a*. 3).

 1769 PARKINSON *Journal* 22 Oct. (1773) 97 Adjoining to their houses are plantations of Koomarra... A sweet potatoe, which the Otaheiteans call Oomara. **1773** COOK *Journal* 29 May (1961) II. 168 I call'd them Coumalla a root common in many parts of *Eahei nomauwe* [the North Island] and is as I could find from this man not unknown to the Inhabitents [sic] of *Tavai-poenammoo*. **1778** FORSTER *Observations* 284 A Comparative Table of the Various Languages in the Isles of the South-Sea.. [English] *Potatoes* (sweet)..[New-Zeeland] Goomälla. **1814** KENDALL in Elder *Marsden's Lieutenants* 5 July (1934) 64 I was presented with six baskets of sweet potatoes or kymoura ready cooked for my dinner. **1817** NICHOLAS *Voyage NZ* I. 110 These gardens were planted with turnips, *coomeras*, or the sweet potatoe, and the common potatoe. **1827** Williams *Early Jrnls.* 23 Mar. (1961) 46 Her wish [was] to go up the Kawakawa to assist in takg. up of the *Kumaras.* **1828** *Ibid.* 20 Mar. 112 Six large baskets of *kumera* were immediately turned out for our part. **1834** Markham *NZ* (1963) 42 We had to go through Cultivation mostly all the way. Indian Corn, potatoes and Cumeras or Sweet potatoes. **1841** Bidwill *Rambles in NZ* (1952) 48 These level spots are carefully planted with kormeras, corn, &c. **1851** *Richmond-Atkinson Papers* (1960) I. 88 There was nothing else to help ourselves to except kumara or sweet potato, in appearance like long thin potatoes, in taste like boiled chestnuts [*sic*]. **1863** Maning *Old NZ* 55 Behind the pigs was placed..a heap of potatoes and *kumera*..so there was no want of the raw material for a feast. **1884** Martin *Our Maoris* 26 After this we came to a long row of poles, on which was hung an immense supply of dried shark (the dogfish split in two), besides baskets of ku-me-ras (sweet potatoes). **1891** Wallace *Rural Econ. Austral. & NZ* 108 Sweet potatoes or coomras are extensively grown on shingly land by the Maori population. **1904** *NZ Free Lance* (Wellington) 12 Mar. 13 The sound of..falling kumeras made life unbearable. **1907** Mansfield *Urewera Notebook* (1978) 53 We came to the pah... The built place for koumara and potato. **1946** *JPS* LV. 148 *kūmara* is the spelling of the name of this tuber, and this has been the spelling in the *Journal of the Polynesian Society*,...from its first volume in 1892 to the present day. It has more than once been suggested that the tuber first came from Peru, and this is fully discussed in *Journal of the Polynesian Society*, vol. 54 (1945), 175, where the point is made that the northern Quichua-speaking people of Peru and Ecuador have the sweet potato and know it under the names kumar, komal, and kumal. **1963** Pearson *Coal Flat* 375 Now Mrs Torere brought out a kit of kuumaras, some pipis, and a half-kerosene tin of cooked mutton-birds. **1971** *Listener* 16 Aug. 54 Be careful with the kumara... Its energy value is twice that of the potato.

b. In European cookery, esp. as recent 'takeaway' food, **kumara chips**, deep-fried chipped kumara.

1913 *Australasian Cook. Book* 121 Kumara Pie (usually called 'Mock Apple') **1932** *St. Andrew's Cook. Book* 48 *Kumara, Glazed*... Wash and pare..kumaras. Cook..put in a buttered pan..boiling ½ cup sugar..water.. butter. Brush kumaras with syrup and bake. **1936** *Home of Compassion Recipes* 47 *Mashed Kumara*... Boil kumaras in salted water until tender and mash them..add..butter..salt..hot milk. Beat until light. **1991** *Cuisine* Aug.–Sept. 9 Canterbury Tales won their section with..kumara gateau and a mushroom sausage. **1992** *Metro* (Auckland) Feb. 81 Hot dishes like..kumara pie and rigatoni with asparagus sound promising but sadly don't measure up to expectations. **1992** *Listener* 8 June 23 Chicken, Bacon and Kumara Hot Pot. **1992** *Salient* (Wellington) 27 July 14 The rest of what we're doing is very top secret, but I can tell you we will be needing an awful lot of kumara chips.

2. Special Comb. **kumara-bird**, *long-tailed cuckoo* (cuckoo 2 (2)); **kumara pit**, rua *n.*[1] 1.

1904 *TrNZI* XXXVI. 134 Like the Cuckoos in other parts of the world, they appear before rainy weather or coincident with it, and have thus come to be known in many widely different localities as 'Rainbirds' and 'Storm-birds'. In many parts of Otago and Canterbury they were called by the early settlers 'Potato-birds', as they invariably came on the scene as the potato-planting was going on; similarly, in the North Island they got the name of '**Kumara-birds**'. **1912** *Otago Witness* (Dunedin) 18 Sept. 16 An old friend..took me to see some shallow holes on the side of a ridge, which he spoke of as being old Maori **kumara pits**. **1951** Kohere *Autobiography of a Maori* 114 The pakehas..telling the Maoris that it [*sc.* a building problem] was beyond them as it was not a kumara pit. **1970** [see rua *n.*[1] 1]. **1989** Richards *Pioneer's Life* 32 Many of the ridges are fortified..while on the main spurs and flats are the remains of kumara pits.

3. *transf.* or *joc.* use. See also *stiff kumara* (stiff *a.* 3 b). **a.** In the phr. **to suck the kumara**, to fail; to lose out.

1984 16 M E69 Pakuranga Coll. 9 You Sucked a Kumera **1986** p.c. R. J. Edney to Professor I. A. Gordon. 28 Apr. I am writing to ask whether you know the origin and meaning of the phrase 'sucked the kumera'. The phrase has come into use among a group that I associate with. One member thinks that he may have read the phrase in a NZ Listener article that described either a broken down or crashed rally car as having 'sucked the kumera'. It would appear to mean 'broken' or in equivalently colloquial terms 'come a cropper'. **1995** *Metro* (Auckland) July 130 She must really, really want to be mayor if she's willing to risk losing a fourth time. Still, if the worst comes to the worst and she sucks the kumara again, I believe the good folk of Invercargill are looking for a new mayor.

b. A nickname for Maori.

1913 *Auckland Univ. College Students Carnival Programme* 27 The spike Hapu—A Tribe Kumera—A sweet Spud **1985** Mitcalfe *Hey Hey Hey* 16 'Samoa, eh? Another coconut, eh? We got to crack these coconuts, eh Gary, else there be no room for us kumaras, what you reckon?' So they were Maoris.

c. As **couch kumara** [transf. use on analogy of *couch potato*], one who 'grows' immobile on a couch watching TV, etc.

1991 *Evening Post* (Wellington) 15 July 8 Those couch kumaras and junk TV addicts among you probably weren't even aware that there's a film festival going on... In an effort to shame you out of your apathy before you become a permanent growth on the furniture, I shall now examine some of the..titles.

4. In composition as **kumaraphile** *joc.*, one who is devoted to kumara as a food.

1988 *Sunday Star* (Auckland) 30 Oct. B2 One suspects if a new strain of puha appeared in Inner Mongolia tomorrow we'd have an instant gang of puhaologists zapping off with due ceremony..to the land of Ghengis Khan... Now a message to kumaraphiles of all shapes, sizes and persuasions.

kumarahou. Also **kumarahau.** [Ma. /ˈkuːmarahou/: Williams 158 *Kūmarahou*, n. *1. Pomaderris* [sp.], a shrub. *2. Quintinia serrata*, a tree.]

1. *Pomaderris kumeraho* (fam. Rhamnaceae), a common shrub of northern New Zealand, having compact showy heads of bright yellow flowers which create a lather when rubbed between wet hands. See also *golden tainui* (tainui 2), *gumdigger's soap* (gumdigger *n.*[1] 3), poverty plant.

1853 Hooker *II Flora Novae-Zelandiae I Flowering Plants* 46 *Pomaderris elliptica*... Hab. Northern Island... Nat. name, 'Kumarahou'. **1867** Hochstetter *NZ* 132 Only Manuka and Rawiri bushes..or Kumaharau (*Pomaderris*) and Koromiko..are intermixed with *Pteris*. **1872** *TrNZI* IV. 271 I well remember seeing..the hill sides [at Titirangi] yellow from..the blossoms of the kumarahou. **1889** Kirk *Forest Flora* 255 For the native name [of *Quintinia serrata*] 'kumarahou' I am indebted to..W.L. Williams, who informs me that it is applied to this plant in the East Cape district: it is also commonly applied to *Pomaderris elliptica* by the Maoris living to the north of the Auckland Isthmus. **1910** Cockayne *NZ Plants & Their Story* 52 Smaller shrubs are *Pomaderris elliptica* (kumarahou), *P. phylicaefolia* (tauhinu). **1934** Kumerahau [see poverty plant]. **1953** *Here & Now* Aug. 20 I got a better med[i]cine. Maori med[i]cine. I got it from a bush in the north. *Kumarahou.* **1969** Harvey & Godley *Botanical Paintings* 48 *Pomaderris kumeraho* Kumarahou Rhamnaceae... The attractive yellow flowers are produced in spring, and when rubbed with a little water produce a slight lather, which has led to the local name of 'gumdigger's soap'... The specific name, which was given by Allan Cunningham in 1839, is his spelling of the Maori name, and is said to mean 'kumara planting time'. **1981** Locke *Student at Gates* 73 I shan't forget the first time I saw [near Auckland]..masses of kumarahou adorning a barren outcrop of white clay. (A cultivated variety is now sold as golden tainui.)

2. (Less commonly) *Quintinia serrata*, New Zealand lilac (lilac 1); or a tree of same family (Escalloniaceae) *Ixerba brexioides*, tawari.

1844 Williams *NZ Jrnl.* (1956) 106 The Kumarahou is a common tree and bears a small berry and a white flower which is very fragrant and handsome and not unpleasant to the taste. *Ibid.* 119 [1956 Note] Name given to several shrubs and trees seems here to refer to *Ixerba brexioides*. **1889** [see 1 above]. **1890** *PWD Catalogue Timbers* (NZ & South Seas Exhib.) 11 Kumarahou (N.Z. lilac) ..*Quintinia serrata* ..Timber a light red colour, and principally used for firewood.

kumi. [Ma. /ˈkumi/: Williams 156 *Kumi*..*2.* A huge, fabulous reptile.] A Maori mythical monster taking the form of a huge reptile.

1899 *NZ Times* (Wellington) 28 Oct. 3 'Dummy'..is the only living man who has seen a kumi... Most people in Gisborne are inclined to doubt the whole story, and think the native might have seen anything but a real kumi. So now, when anyone tells a story of any kind, the truth of which seems open to doubt, people say, 'Ah, that's a kumi.' **1924** Lysnar *New Zealand* 5 By this route..came the Tuatara, or Kumi, one of the oldest creatures that inhabit the earth. **1926** *Press* (Christchurch) 28 Aug. 13 This [indigenous arboreal] animal was supposed to be known to the Maori, who called it 'Kumi'. **1944** *Korero* (AEWS Background Bulletin) 31 July 13 The Kumi, seen for the first time in three generations, used to live in trees and among boulders, grew to 12 ft. long, had huge jaws with curved teeth (like the one seen) and used to lie in wait for its prey. **1953** Guthrie-Smith *Tutira* (3edn.) 77 The *tohunga* recited further incantations, which had the effect of making the *kumi* visibly grow... He saw with his own eyes the reptile increasing into a formidable monster. **1966** *Encycl. NZ* I. 48 In all probability..tales of water-dwelling monsters and other huge reptiles known as *kumi* were nothing more than distorted folk memories of the crocodile of the western Pacific or Asia. *Ibid.* 49 A more precise sighting of a *kumi* was allegedly made in September 1898 on W.D. Lysnar's East Coast station, Arowhana. A Maori bushman was startled by the sight of a huge lizard some 5 ft long advancing towards him.

kumi-kumi, var. kamokamo.

kummura, var. kumara.

kummy kum, kumokumo, varr. kamokamo.

kumu, var. kumukumu.

kumukumu. Also **cuma, kumu.** [Ma. /ˈkumu/, /ˈkumukumu/: Williams 156 *Kumu*..*kumukumu*. *1.* n. *Chelidonicthys kumu*, gurnard.] *red gurnard.* (gurnard 2 (2)).

[**1820** Lee & Kendall *NZ Gram. & Vocab.* 171 Kúmu kúmu; Name of a certain fish.] **1843** Dieffenbach *Travels in NZ* I. 65 A fish was often caught which is nearly allied..to one described by Cuvier under the name of Trigla papilionacea: the natives called it kumu

kumu. It is of bright orange-colour... Taken out of its element, and in expiring [it] lose[s] its vivid colours. **1843** WILLIAMS *NZ Jrnl.* (1956) 41 Of this variety of 78 species [of fish] I will name a part, viz... Cuma, a red fish similar in form to a catfish in the US. **1855, 1872** [see GURNARD 2 (2)]. **1886** SHERRIN *Handbook Fishes NZ* 37 The red gurnard, or kumukumu, is very abundant... The grunting noise which this beautifully-coloured fish makes when caught is a great source of amusement to amateur fishermen. **1919** [see GURNARD 1 b]. **1921, 1947** [see GURNARD 2 (2)]. **1957** PARROTT *Sea Angler's Fishes* 168 The Maori name [for Red Gurnard, *Corrupiscis kumu*] kumukumu is often shortened by Europeans to 'Kumu'. **1966** [see GURNARD 1 a]. **1970** *NZ Boating World* July 71 The red gurnard, known to the Maoris as kumu-kumu (meaning wriggling tail), is the subject of this month's recipe.

kumukumu, var. KAMOKAMO.

kunakuna, var. KANAKANA.

kune-kune. [Ma. /ˈkunekune/: Williams 156 *kunekune*, a. Appearing round.] *Sus scrofa* (fam. Suidae), a small fat short-legged breed of feral pig. Often *attrib.* as **kune-kune pig.**
  [**1778** FORSTER *Observations* 188 The hogs [of the Marquesas, Friendly Isles and New-Hebrides] are of that breed which we call the Chinese, having a short body, short legs, belly hanging down almost to the ground, ears erect, and very few thin hairs on the body.] **1982** HOLDEN *Wild Pig* 24 The kune-kune pig [a smaller type], with its short characteristic beads (or dewlaps) hanging from his lower jaw, possessed a remarkable ability to fatten quickly. **1986** *Press* (Christchurch) 21 May 20 If animals had their pop. charts, New Zealand's kune kune pig would have to find a high place among the list of unusual animals... It's surprising, therefore, that..so few are aware of how close kune kune pigs are to becoming extinct. **1990** *Handbook NZ Mammals* 360 There is another type of pig in New Zealand (sometimes called the 'Maori pig' or kune-kune, meaning 'fat and round') which was, at least at one stage, semiferal... Contrary to popular belief, they definitely did not arrive with the Maori.

kupadu, var. KUPARU.

kupae. Also **kupai.** [Ma. /ˈkupae/: Williams 157 *Kupae..Clupea antipoda*, sprat.] SPRAT; poss. also applied to a small freshwater fish (see quot. 1986).
  1886 SHERRIN *Handbook Fishes NZ* 94 Sprats are called kupai by the Natives at the Thames, and are found in great abundance..in the Kaipara waters. **1921** *NZJST* IV. 118 Clupea antipoda... *Sprat; Kupae.* **1956** GRAHAM *Treasury NZ Fishes* 102 Sprat (Kupae) *Maugeclupea antipodum.* **1986** RICHARDS *Off the Sheep's Back* 22 They taught me how to catch eels, kupai, and koura (crawlies) out of nearby streams.

kupai, var. KUPAE.

kupapa. [Ma. /ˈkuːpapa/: Williams 157 *Kūpapa...* 5. Be neutral in a quarrel.]

1. The Maori force supporting the Crown in the New Zealand Wars, or any of its members. Often *attrib.* Cf. FRIENDLY *n.* B; contrast KING PARTY.
  1866 SMITH *Taranaki Jrnl.* 21 Oct. in Cowan *NZ Wars* (1955) II. 532 Ten *kupapas*, or allies, arrived in camp today from Wanganui. **1882** POTTS *Out in Open* 15 At sundown barriers were placed at each end of the terrace, ingress or egress only permitted to the pakeha party and their numerous escort of Kupapas. **1922** COWAN *NZ Wars* (1955) II. 1 It was in fact only the help of these loyalist or Kupapa tribes..that turned the scale and brought lasting peace to the old frontier. **1960** *Richmond-Atkinson Papers* (1960) II. 138 He was on the point of leaving the Colony when Colonial and kupapa troops..carried an outwork at Weraroa..without loss. **1978** SINCLAIR & HARREX *Looking Back* 35 Some of the main tribes fought alongside the settlers during the Anglo-Maori wars, and became known as the *kupapa* or 'friendlies'. **1984** BARBER *Red Coat to Jungle Green* 44 How did they regard the Queen's Maori soldiers? They had a name for them—Kupapa, a derisive term used by Kingite and Hauhau to identify those they believed to be crawling on their bellies to the Pakeha. *Ibid.* 48 The Field Force divisions, augmented by kupapa units, were a select force kept at full strength until the mid-1870s. **1986** BELICH *NZ Wars* 211 The *kupapa*, Maoris fighting on the British side, were variously known as 'loyalists', 'Queenites', and 'the friendly natives'.

2. In modern applications, a Maori supporting Pakeha or Crown initiatives; occas. an 'Uncle Tom'.
  1928 NGATA *Let.* 9 Feb. in *Na To Hoa Aroha* (1986) I. 70 The Kingite part of the Maniapoto are all right and so are those we may call the 'Kupapa'. **1988** *Dominion Sunday Times* (Wellington) 1 May 10 A class of people was created—we [Maori activists] call them kupapa—from the first time the Pakeha arrived. These are collaborators or 'crouchers' who serve white needs and white interests and prop up the colonial system.

kuparu. Also early **ghooparee, kupádu.** [Ma. /ˈkuparu/: Williams 157 *Kuparu*, n...John Dory.] *Zeus faber* (fam. Zeidae), JOHN DORY.
  [**1820** LEE & KENDALL *NZ Gram. & Vocab.* 171 *Kupádu, s.* Name of a certain fish.] **1842** GRAY *Fauna* in Dieffenbach *Travels in NZ* (1843) II. 209 *Pagrus latus*.—..Taken in the sea..in Queen Charlotte's Sound. In the latter locality its native name is 'Ghooparee.' **1921** *NZJST* IV. 121 Zeus faber Linnaeus. *John-dory; Kuparu...* Distribution: Odd examples have been secured as far south as D'Urville Island and French Pass. **1956** GRAHAM *Treasury NZ Fishes* 178 John Dory (Kuparu) *Zeus australis.* **1966** DOOGUE & MORELAND *Sea Anglers' Guide* 214 John Dory... St. Peter's fish; kuparu (Maori)... Flaky but firm flesh with delicate flavour. **1982** AYLING *Collins Guide* (1984) 180 *John Dory* (Kuparu)... John Dory are often seen swimming partly on their side..a prelude to one of their fish mimicking tricks.

kura kaupapa (Maori): see KAUPAPA.

kuri /ˈkuri/,/ˈguri/. Also with much variety of form as **gh-òrea** (Forster 1778), **(E)gooree** [=he kuri], **goori(e), goory, goure, kúdi;** in 20th century use the *goori* forms are often derogatory. [Ma. /kuːri/: Williams 159 *Kurī*, n. *1*. Dog... *2*. Any quadruped: Walsh & Biggs 39 PPN *kulii 'dog'.]

1. Also occas. **kuri dog,** DOG *n.* 1.
  1770 PARKINSON *Journal* (1773) 127 [A Vocabulary of the Language of New Zealand.] *Egooree*, A dog. **1773** COOK *Journal* 3 June (1961) II. 170 [A native who had been butted by a goat] told a very lamentable story against Goure the great Dog, for so they call all the quadrepeds [*sic*] we have aboard. [**1820** LEE AND KENDALL *NZ Grammar and Vocabulary* 170 *Kúdi, s.* A young dog, pig, &c. **c1826–27** BOULTBEE *Journal* (1986) 111 dog—goòree] **1838** POLACK *NZ* I. 308 The *karáráhé* [= kararehe], or dog (Canis Australis), which, when young, is known as *kuri*, has been an inhabitant some two or three centuries. **1843** DIEFFENBACH *Travels in NZ* II. 46 The native name is kuri, the general name for the dog amongst the Polynesian race; but it is very curious that the Spanish word 'pero' is also known to them. **1861** [see DOG 1]. **1892** *TrNZI* XXIV. 15 The dog (*Canis familiaris*) or kuri, the only domesticated animal of the Maori, has attracted suprisingly little archeological attention. **1920** *Quick March* 10 Jan. 15 Those kuris..have not vanished yet. They were the ancestors of the wild dogs that used to be plentiful in all this Taupo country. **1938** HYDE *Nor Yrs Condemn* 136 He left the door open, the firelight near her, a crouching golden dog; not rough-coated dirty white, like poor old *kuri*, the Maori dog, who has died out. **1946** [see DOG 1]. **1981** *NZ Jrnl. Archaeology* III. 18 Osteological evidence..could be employed to argue that some South Island kuri were used to bail and hold moas, if only the small and medium-sized species. **1990** [see DOG 1].

2. The European dog, often of ill-thrift, early associated with Maori ownership or Maori settlements, esp. (*pl.*) such dogs running wild in packs. Often (*derog.*) as **goory (dog),** and as *Maori dog, native dog* (see DOG 2), such a dog in Maori ownership.
  1913 *Auckland University College Students Carnival Programme* 27 Warriors, Wahines, Kuri, Poaka, Tamariki, Kumeras, Karos, Interpreters (1st, 2nd and 3rd grade), Poets Laureate, Poi Dancers, Guides, &c. on application to the Registrar. **1916** COWAN *Bush Explorers* (VUWTS) 19 We had a couple of pig dogs with us, Maori kuris, which Hursthouse had borrowed from an old wahine at Te Kuiti. **1920** *Quick March* 10 Apr. 27 'Alexa' contributes a note on the modern Maori Kuri... the Maori tykes that roam the wilds of Ohinemutu. **1930** GUTHRIE *NZ Memories* 77 At this time—June, 1841—the colonists..were constantly overlooking annoyances..such as..the perpetual worries caused by the half-starved and abominable *kuri* or dog. **1976** FINLAYSON *Other Lovers* 90 As he neared the [Maori] houses dogs ran out to sniff at him, slinky half-snarling, half-cowering goories. **1940** *Tales of Pioneer Women* (1988) 51 The [shearing] gang of twenty or so Maori men, women, and children, with the inevitable kuri..would come stringing into the station. **1944** FINLAYSON in *Listener Short Stories* (1977) 17 Everywhere you looked there were squalling kiddies and goory dogs and grey-headed old men with carved pipes. **1945** HALL-JONES *Historical Southland* 108 They [*sc.* early runholders] had good sport together among the native game and the wild cattle and the hunting of the kuri.

3. a. Hence, any mongrel or unruly dog.
  1900 SCOTT *Colonial Turf* 180 It was a sort of poodle... As long as he remained in the room, no one would think of asking who owned the kuri. **1935** MITCHELL & STRONG in Partridge *Slang Today* 286 [The following was employed by those who served in the Great War:] *goori*, a dog, from Maori *kuri.* **1943** BENNETT *English in NZ* in *Amer. Speech* XVIII. 93 *goory*, a mongrel dog, from Maori *kuri.* **1955** *BJ Cameron Collection* (TS July) goory, goory dog (n) A native or ownerless dog of nondescript appearance. **1964** CAPE 'Down the Hall on Saturday Night' in Reid *Book of NZ* (1964) 258 As soon as I've tied up the guri, As soon as I've broomed out the yard, As soon as I've hosed down my gumboots, I'll be living it high and living it hard. **1983** HENDERSON *Down from Marble Mountain* 122 Never forget the toitoi plumes of the dogs' tails leading on, the *kuri's* ecstasy and exit when detecting a stinking burned barbecued possum *cordon bleu.*

b. *transf.* Usu. as **goorie,** a poorly performing racehorse.
  c1920 p.c. Mr T. O'Sullivan (Auckland 1967): 'That goorie would have its work cut out to come last.' **1949** p.c. W.H. Mabbett: 'That thing's [*sc.* a racehorse] only a goorie.' **1995** p.c. Peter Haines (Auckland): 'a

poorly performed racehorse. In widespread use on the racecourse. I have not encountered the term in print': 'You've put your money on Jim's Hope? That goori will be lucky to finish last.'

c. *transf.* A contemptible person, a mongrel, a 'ratbag'.

1965. WILSON *Outcasts* 37 Where is that Jimmy? Dog of a child. Kuri. Feed me, woman, I'm done for. **1970** *Listener* 12 Oct. 13 'Are you going to marry her?' I said. 'Why should I? Let go of me, you goorie,' he said. **1975** CLEARY *Pocketful of Years* 23 [A Maori speaks] 'You kuris better tell your mates that any more rowdiness..and we bottle you all up with no escape.'

kurikuri. *Obs.* [Ma. /ˈkurikuri/: Williams 159 *Kuri, kurikuri...* 2. *Aciphylla squarrosa*.] SPANIARD 1.

1853 HOOKER *II Flora Novae-Zelandiae I Flowering Plants* 88 *Aciphylla squarrosa*... Nat. name, 'Kuri Kuri', Middle Island. **1868** LINDSAY *Contribs. NZ Bot.* 50 *A. squarrosa*... The 'Papaii' of the North Island Maoris..; the 'Kuri-kuri' of those of the South Island. **1906** CHEESEMAN *Manual NZ Flora* 209 *A[ciphylla] squarrosa*... *Taramea; Kurikuri; Spear-grass.* **1940** LAING & BLACKWELL *Plants NZ* 339 *Aciphylla squarrosa* (*The Spaniard*)... Maori name *Kuri-Kuri*; local name, *Spaniard* or *Wild Spaniard*.

kurimako, var. KORIMAKO.

kuri-wao, kuriwau, varr. KAREAO.

kuriwhengi, var. KURUWHENGI.

kuruwhengi. Also **kuriwhengi.** [Ma. /ˈkurufeŋi/: Williams 160 *Kuruwhengi, kuruwhengu* (i) n.] SHOVELLER.

1873 BULLER *Birds NZ* 252 *Spatula variegata.* (New-Zealand Shoveller.)... *Native name. Tete, Putaitai, Kuruwhengi, Kahoho*, and *Wetawetangu*, 'Spoon-bill Duck' of the colonists. **1904, 1955, 1966, 1985** [see SHOVELLER]. **1990** *Checklist Birds NZ* 104 *Anas rhynchotis variegata*... New Zealand Shoveler (*Kuruwhengi*)... New Zealand. Throughout both main islands.

kuta, var. KUTU.

kutai. Also **kuutai.** [Ma. /ˈkuːtai/: Williams 160 *Kūtai...* Mussel... = *kuku*.] MUSSEL 1.

1870 [see KUKU *n.*^{2}]. **1879** [see TAKEKE]. **1910** *Otago Witness* (Dunedin) 25 May 89 The mussel, *Myrtilus* [*sic*] *latus*, the Maori *kutai*, makes excellent eating and is much sought after by the Natives. **1978** FULLER *Maori Food & Cookery* 52 The common North Island mussel (*Perna canaliculus*) is greenish and larger than the blue-black South Island mussel (*Mytilus edulis*). Kuku and kutai are the Maori names applied to both species. **1989** RICHARDS *Pioneer's Life* 32 Mounds of pipi, kutai and pupu shells mark their camp sites. **1990** STRICKLAND *Nga tini a Tangaroa* (unpaged) Kuutai: mollusc, mussel; *Perna canaliculus* and others; kuku.

kuti, var. KUTU.

kutu /ˈkutə/, /ˈkuti/. Also with much variety of form as **cootie, cootoo, koòta, kooter, kooti(e), kootoo, kuta, kuti.** [Ma. /ˈkutu/: Williams 160 *Kutu..1.* Louse.. *2.* Vermin of any kind infesting human beings: PPN *kutu 'louse', Walsh & Biggs 41: in modern NZ English use, esp. since WW1, reinforced by gen. English *cootie*, a (head-)louse, poss. ad. Malay *kutu* (see OED *cootie*).]

1. a. A body-louse, esp. a head-louse.

[**1771** BANKS *Journal* (1962) Jan. 240 Specimens of Language South Sea Outou Malay Coutou a louse. **1815** KENDALL *New Zealanders' First Book* 47 Kootoo A louse.] **1817** NICHOLAS *NZ* I. 87 These vermin, which are too well known among us to require their name being repeated, are in their [*sc.* New Zealanders'] language called *cootoos*, and the inhabitants in general are equally full of them. [**c1826–27** BOULTBEE *Journal* (1986) 114 Louse—koòta.] **1831** WILLIAMS *Early Journals* 20 Apr. (1961) 176 Every prospect of being over run with fleas and *kutus*. **1843** DIEFFENBACH *Travels in NZ* II. 370 Kuta—a louse Kutu *id*. **1939** GRIEVE *Sketches from Maoriland* (1961) 45 In the earlier days when Mr. Bird inspected the Native Schools himself, word of his coming was the signal for..a feverishly waged war upon the wily *kutu*. **1941** BAKER *NZ Slang* 50 Terms originated in the first Great War [include]..*chatty*..a louse (the versions koota and kooti from the Maori *kutu*, a louse, had been in use much earlier). **1958** ASHTON-WARNER *Spinster* 112 That was Rita's kootie. It jumped out of her hair into mine last week. **1964** BACON *Along the Road* 24 Did you see that hotel? I'm sure you would have woken up..with your head full of cooties. All sorts of people stay there!.. There's a few Maoris [at school]... John has to do a cootie hunt about once a month. **1965** *Dominion* (Wellington) 2 July 7 Mr. Kirk said that Mr. Hanan, while in opposition, had inflamed the passions of the people against apartheid, but we were now saying those people protesting against it were 'kooters on a kuri'—fleas on a dog. **1986** *New Outlook* XXI. 49 All of them got kutus... Even if a Whistler manages to get his head clean he soon catches them again.

b. As a nickname.

1939 BEATTIE *First White Boy Born in Otago* 13 The Maori wife of Steve Smith, a whaler, was named Kuti. The word 'tuiau' means a flea in Maori and according to us youngsters [c1840s] 'kuti' meant lousy.

2. Special Comb. **kootie comb**, a fine-tooth comb for removing head lice and their eggs.

1958 ASHTON-WARNER *Spinster* 123 I'll just find out for myself about the lice... So [we] buy a tooth-comb, but what we call in the *pa*..a 'kootie comb.'

Hence **kootiest, kutieish**.

1958 ASHTON-WARNER *Spinster* 125 When things at the school are looking their kootiest I cheer up and think there'll be a change soon. **1986** MACRAE in *New Outlook* XXI. 49 The Whistler kid would scratch his head then rub kutieish hands all over Caleb.

3. *v.* **de-kutu** *trans.*, to de-louse.

1978 NATUSCH *Acheron* 103 March 29 was spent.. on the way to the Waimakariri kaika,.. A pretty girl sat de-kutuing the head of her handsome admirer, popping the proceeds into her mouth.

kuumara, var. KUMARA.

kuutai, var. KUTAI.

kyack, var. KAIK(A).

kygata, var. KAHIKATEA.

kyhinga, var. KAINGA.

kyka kara, var. KAHIKATEA.

kyke, var. KAIK(A).

kymoura, var. KUMARA.

L

Labour. Also, in early 20th century trade union and party-political use, **Labor**. [Spec. use of *labour* the general body of wage-earners viewed with regard to its political interests and claims.]
1. With init. cap. In pre-1916 use often a short form of reference to the 'Labour Party' reformed in 1910 from the Independent Political Labour League and reorganized in 1912 as the United Labour Party; in later use usu. with reference to the (New Zealand) Labour Party founded July 1916.
   1910 *Truth* 20 Aug. 4 The presence in Parliament of a Labor Party will have a steadying influence on those politicians who have so far chiefly sought to use Labor. **1966** *NZ Encycl.* II. 799 Labour interpreted the 'slump' as less a crisis of overproduction than of under–consumption. **1994** *Dominion* (Wellington) 4 June 2 The continued low ranking of Labour leader Helen Clark..will worry Labour strategists.
2. Special Comb. **Labour Day** [orig. US: cf. OED *labour* n. 8, 1886; see also quot. 1995 below], a statutory holiday observed until 1910 on the 2nd Wednesday in October (Labour Day Act 1899), changed by the Public Holidays Act (1910) to the 4th Monday in October (often *attrib.*); **Labour Weekend**, orig. short for *Labour Day weekend* (see quot. 1929 below), the long weekend in October which includes the Monday Labour Day holiday.
   1899 *NZ Statutes* No.17 50 An Act to constitute a public Holiday to be known as **Labour Day**... 1. The Short Title of this Act is 'The Labour Day Act, 1899'... s2. The second Wednesday in the month of October in each year shall be known as 'Labour' Day. **1910** *NZ Statutes* No.71 363 [Public Holidays Act] Where in any Act..reference is made—(a) To Labour Day, such reference shall hereinafter be deemed to be to the fourth Monday in October, and not to the second Wednesday in October. **1929** *Tararua Tramper* Nov. 1 It was not until the recent Labour Day week-end that an official Club trip..was made. **1947** *Evening Post* (Wellington) 28 Oct. 8 Tomato plants for planting over the Labour Day weekend had been sold in numbers... The Labour Day weekend is traditionally the time when tomato plants may first be planted. **1962** JOSEPH *Pound of Saffron* 31 Waiting to be loaded with gear, liquor and groceries he would need for the long week-end holiday. For Monday would be Labour Day. **1988** MACRAE *Awful Childhoods* 49 But it was still Labour day. **1939** *Tararua Tramper* Nov. 1 Merely impressions of a **Labour Week-end** that found itself at Mount Egmont. **1948** *Evening Post* (Wellington) 22 Oct. 6 If the tradition of wet Labour weekends is not maintained in Wellington this year sportsmen..should..enjoy themselves. **1962** *Ibid.* 22 Oct. 12 Labour weekend was still death-free..up to late this morning. **1988** *Dominion* (Wellington) 7 Oct. 1 Up to 400 Mongrel Mob members are expected to converge on Wellington for a Labour Weekend convention in Owhiro Bay. **1995** *Sunday Star-Times* (Auckland) 22 Oct. C7 The first Labour Day in New Zealand was celebrated in 1890, originally as a commemoration of the eight–hour working days.

labouring emigrant: see EMIGRANT 1.

Labourite. Also **Laborite**. [Spec. use of *Labourite*: cf. OED 1903.] A member or supporter of the political Labour movement, or, *spec.*, of the Labour Party of New Zealand and its policies.
   1905 *Truth* 16 Dec. 4 Supporting the Laborites [*sic*]. **1948** LIPSON *Politics of Equality* 219 Under charges of sedition various Laborites were given prison sentences [during WW1]. *Ibid.* 239 Of eleven secondary urban centers, six returned a Laborite and five a Nationalist [in 1946].

laburnum. *Obs.* [f. the resemblance of the yellow flowers to those of northern hemisphere *Laburnum* spp.] Also **native** (or **New Zealand**) **laburnum**. KOWHAI 1.
   1866 ANGAS *Polynesia* 51 Along the banks of the rivers, the 'kowai' or 'native laburnum', displays its profusion of golden blossom. **1868** [see KOWHAI 1 a (a)]. **1905** WHITE *My NZ Garden* 92 The New Zealand Laburnum (*Sophora tetraptera*), (Yellow Kowhai) is a splendid deep yellow, with much larger flowers and calix than the English Laburnum. **1907** LAING & BLACKWELL *Plants NZ* 214 The [kowhai] tree is sometimes called the *New Zealand Laburnum*. **1910** COCKAYNE *NZ Plants & Their Story* 37 The yellow kowhai (*Sophora grandiflora* and *S. microphylla*) has been fitly termed the New Zealand laburnum. **1917** *NZ at the Front* xiii Kowhai Tree.—New Zealand laburnum tree.

lacebark.
1. Any of several trees of the family Malvaceae having fibrous, layered, lace-like inner bark. See also RIBBONWOOD, THOUSAND-JACKET. **a.** *Hoheria* spp., esp. *H. populnea*. See also HOHERIA, HOUHERE, HOUI, *orange blossom* (ORANGE 1 b).
   1848 *NZ.Jrnl.* VIII. 71 The whole of this is of a very rich soil, well timbered with Totara, Maihi..and a beautiful lace-bark tree, the bark of which is dressed and made into mats by the natives. **1889** FEATON *Art Album NZ Flora* 55 The inner bark [of *Hoheria*] is peculiar, and consists of layer upon layer of laced fibre... From this peculiarity it is called by the settlers the 'Thousand Jacket', 'Lace-bark', or 'Ribbon-wood'. **1890** [see HOUHERE]. **1905** WHITE *My NZ Garden* 90 Its vernacular names are 'Ribbon Wood' and 'Lace Bark', for when the bark is pulled off and cut into strips it reminds one of insertion lace. **1910** COCKAYNE *NZ Plants & Their Story* 37 The various species of trees known as lacebark (*Hoheria*..[spp.]), are, in their season, dense masses of snowy flowers. **1920** MANSFIELD *Stories* (1984) 232 In the garden some tiny owls, perched on the branches of a lace-bark tree, called: 'More pork; more pork.' **1940** LAING & BLACKWELL *Plants NZ* 264 The settlers name it [*sc. Hoheria*] lacebark, ribbonwood, or thousand-jacket. This inner fibre is remarkably tough, and is, therefore, often used for cordage. **1966** *Encycl. NZ* II. 254 *Lacebark, Houhere... Hoheria* is an endemic representative of the almost cosmopolitan Mallow family. The genus has five species carrying the common name of lacebarks because of the lace-like network of the inner bark fibres. **1980** WOOLLASTON *Sage Tea* 43 When I told Eddie..about our three trees and their names as I knew them, he said lacebark was incorrect, it should be ribbonwood... [My parents] would have none of it. Lacebark it was and would ever be. **1988** [see RIBBONWOOD].
b. *Plagianthus* spp. See also MANATU, RIBBON-TREE, RIBBONWOOD 2 (1) and (3), WHAUWHI.
   1869 *TrNZI* I. (rev. edn.) 159 The woods are skirted by a..growth of the handsome Lace-bark tree (*Plagianthus Lyallii*). **1877** *TrNZI* IX. 175 Ribbonwood, P. betulinus,.. Whauwhi, Maori name, according to Hector; lace-bark tree, settlers' name according to Buchanan. **1889** KIRK *Forest Flora* 279 The whau-whi [*P. lyallii*], or 'lace-bark' as it is usually termed by settlers, is one of the most graceful and beautiful flowering trees in the New Zealand flora.
2. Special Comb. **lacebark bonnet** *hist.*, a bonnet made from or trimmed with the lacy fibrous inner bark of a lacebark tree.
   [**1879** *Auckland Weekly News* 11 Oct. 7 The curiosity which attracts a great deal of attention is a hat or bonnet made from the 'lace-bark tree'.] **1889** FEATON *Art Album NZ Flora* 55 The inner bark is peculiar, and consists of layer upon layer of laced fibre... The idea of utilising this natural network has been accepted by persons in the Nelson district..and many pretty little ornamental articles have been produced from it. A favourite use to which it has been put is that of bonnet construction, and it is asserted that at one time 'Lace-bark' bonnets were quite fashionable in Nelson. **1907** LAING & BLACKWELL *Plants of NZ* 252 It is also beautifully perforated, and has been employed for many ornamental purposes, such as trimming for ladies' hats, basket work, etc. Lace-bark bonnets are said to have been at one time fashionable in Nelson. **1948** IRVINE-SMITH *Streets of My City* 33 For women, lace-bark bonnets became fashionable [c1840s].

lace fern: see FERN 2 (12).

ladder. *Dredging*. The continuously revolving bucket-mechanism of a gold-dredge together with the boom which carries it.
   1882 HAY *Brighter Britain* II. 279 We see this liquid [*sc.* puddled ore] sent over 'beds', and 'floors', and 'ladders', and 'blanketings', and washed again and again. **1900** KITTO *Pract. Dredgeman's Manual* 16 Before letting down the ladder you should examine the bottom tumbler and hangers to see [if] they are all right. **1962** EVANS *Waikaka Saga* 48 They let the ladder (the dredge buckets) down during two night shifts, and immediately the returns of gold rose. **1963** PEARSON *Coal Flat* 421 ladder: The continuous line of excavating buckets carried on an oblique endless chain on a gold-dredge.

ladies (a plate): see LADY 1.

lady.
1. Usu. in *pl.*, often with init. cap., in various formulaic phrases of the form **ladies (bring) a plate** (**basket, dish, supper-dish**) or **ladies** [price stated] **and a basket**, etc., with reference to providing a contribution of food to a social occasion, often with remission of (part of) the

full entrance fee paid by males (see quots.). Cf. BASKET SOCIAL. **a.** As **(a) basket**.
   1920 *Otago Witness* (Dunedin) 21 Dec. 1 The part that needs clearing up is..'Gents 1s; ladies, 1s, and basket'. **1935** COWAN *Hero Stories NZ* 158 'A dance will be held in Paewhenua Hall on.. Good music. Good floor. Gents, 2/6; Ladies, 1/6 or Basket. Otorohanga Patrons—Metalled road to the door.' That was the notice the other day in a King Country paper. 'Ladies, a basket' is a customary dance-night formula in the outback, and a convenient arrangement it is. Those liberal baskets of home-made dainties outdo anything you can buy for the money in your town shops. **1943** BENNETT *English in NZ* in *Amer. Speech* XVIII. 86 Visitors reading notices in New Zealand papers, might be puzzled by phrases like 'Rooms with tray' and 'Ladies bring basket'; in both cases the container stands for the thing contained—breakfast and afternoon tea delicacies respectively. **1956** DARE *Rouseabout Jane* 44 Admission was generally 'gentlemen 2s. 6d., ladies a basket', which puzzled me considerably at first, until I found that ladies took a basket of refreshments..and this exempted them from paying.

b. As **a plate**.
   1935 *Tararua Tramper* Oct. 1 Free Ambulance dance... Ladies 6d. and a plate; gentlemen, 2/-. **1939** *Tararua Tramper* Mar. 4 Dance... Subs. Ladies 6d. and a plate of supper, or 1/6. Gents 2/6. **1949** *Tararua Tramper* June 12 A dance will be held in the Clubroom..Gentlemen, 2/6. Ladies, A Plate. **1953** SCOTT *Breakfast at Six* 70 'Didn't you see the notice? "Gents half-a-crown, ladies a plate".'... Larry explained what 'a plate' meant in the backblocks. **1963** KINROSS *Please to Remember* 31 Give me a concert in the Druids' Hall with dance to follow (Gents 2/6; Ladies a plate). **1972** MITCHELL *Pavlova Paradise* 16 When going to social functions make your wife take a plate. Every immigrant will assure you that his wife did this in response to the 'ladies a plate' instruction. **1979** TOOGOOD *Out of the Bag* 108 'Ladies a plate' suppers were always given for us after the show. **1988** *North & South* (Auckland) Nov. 45 In reality, the boys abandoned you at the door of the supper room [in the 1940s]..and rushed to the tables to cram themselves with the sumptuous spread the 'Ladies A Plate' had provided.

c. As **please bring a plate**.
   1992 *NewsVUW* (Victoria University) 3 Nov. 11 *Lesbians on Campus*: Late afternoon gathering;... video *Post Vatican II*. Tea and coffee, please bring a plate.

d. As **a supper dish**.
   1929 *Tararua Tramper* Sept. 4 Our next dance. Make it as successful as the last. Ladies a supper dish; gentlemen 2/6. **1933** *Ibid.* Oct. 4 Grand novelty dance (in the new clubroom)... Ladies, 6d. and a supper dish; gentlemen 2/-.

2. As **ladies and escorts**, formerly applied to a women's bar where men were permitted entry only if they were escorting wemen. (The phr. is of much earlier use (at least from mid 1920s) than the quots. suggest.)
   1980 LELAND *Kiwi-Yankee Dict.* 61 *lounge bar*: This used to be, and still is in some places, the 'Ladies and Escorts Bar'. Unlike the public bar, genteel ladies can drink here and unlike the public bar, seats are provided. **1985** BINNEY *Long Lives the King* 24 The smaller pub, the Criterion, was less favoured by the townsfolk; its beer garden served wayfarers..; its lounge bar, Ladies and Escorts Only.

3. As the first element in phrases or special Comb.: **Lady Astor** [origin uncertain, but prob. includes... a play on late Latin *aster* (f. Greek) 'star'], the Africa Star medal or medal ribbon; **the** (or **Our**) **Lady of October** [f. its blooming in spring], CLEMATIS a; **ladies on bicycles**, see TWO;

lady's slipper orchid, see ORCHID 3; **lady's waist** [AND 1934], a small (5 oz, occas. 7oz, i.e. 150 or 200 ml), slender beer-glass having a brim wider than than the base and a vertical silhouette usu. concave in shape; the liquor contained therein.
   1939–45 *Expressions & Sayings 2NZEF (TS N.A. WAII DA 420/1)* **Lady Astor**—Africa Star. Also called Berka 8 and Zib-bib Star. **1981** HENDERSON *Exiles of Asbestos Cottage* 86 Surely, the possibility of sneaking in just one more flower, **The Lady of October** as Golden Bay housewives call our native clematis, from the earth to the stars. **1985** *NZ Times* 3 Feb. 12 Up to 10 years after such a bushfire..some stumps were soothed with a brief cool bandage of white native clematis, which is called, charmingly, Our Lady of October over The Hill in Takaka. **c1920** p.c. W.H.B. Orsman, **lady's waist** heard from at least WW1: Ed. recalls it in freq. use from c1945–55 for a standard 5oz or 7oz slender beer-glass.

lager phone. [Prob. f. *lager* (with reference to the beer-bottle tops employed) + xylo)*phone*: AND 1956.] See quot.
   1990 *Dominion Sunday Times* (Wellington) 4 Mar. 19 The lager phone, a broom handle with beer bottle tops nailed on, thumped the floor and rattled, for that home-made feeling, is the only instrument not going through an amp.

lagoon. [In Brit. use, an area of salt or brackish water.] A shallow freshwater lake; a large pond.
   1836 RHODES *Jrnl. Barque 'Australian'* (1954) 35 He has located himself on the margin of a freshwater lagoon about a quarter of a mile from the beach [Of Sunday Island]. **1849** WAKEFIELD *Colonial Surveying* 59 Lagoons differ from lakes in being generally formed by surface water gathering in low grounds during the winter, from which there is no outlet. **1856** PHILLIPS *Rockwood Jrnl.* 27 Dec. (Canterbury Pub. Lib. TS) 60 Dec. 27 Paradise Flapper on a Lagoon. **1862** CHUDLEIGH *Diary* 8 Feb. (1950) 76 [At Butler's Mesopotamia Station on the Rangitata] there is fine undulating country spotted with small lakes or lagoons and streams. **1879** HAAST *Geol. Canterbury & Westland* 121 Next morning..after passing a succession of lagoons and ponds, [we] reached at last the upper end of Lake Coleridge. **1884** *TrNZI* XVI. 65 In the grassy bed of a dry lagoon near Lake Guyon. **1885** *TrNZI* XVII. 188 In August I measured the ice in one of the lagoons on top of the Alps. **1898** REEVES *Long White Cloud* 403 'Lagoon' has replaced the English 'pond', except in the case of artificial water. **1915** *TrNZI* XLVII. 121 Many of them [sc. ridges] are covered with extensive peat bogs, dotted over with numerous lagoons. **1933** *Press* (Christchurch) (Acland Gloss.) 4 Nov. 15 Lagoon.— Any tarn, pond, or open water too small to be called a lake. **1958** *Better Business* July 75 The summit of Maunga-Pohatu is an eerie, desolate place, with its three lagoons.

lahtah, var. RATA.

lair: see LAIRY.

lairy, *a*. Also **leary**, **leery**. [Orig. Cockney *lairy* knowing: AND 1898.] Socially unacceptable; rowdy.
   1905 *Truth* 2 Sept. 7 Lounging Leary Larrikins Lashed. **1906** *Ibid.* 21 July 4 The larks of the leary larrikin are becoming a menace to the peace and comfort of citizens and a source of annoyance and loss to city restaurant keepers. **1987** *Metro* (Auckland) May 114 Would that Autalavou..take over management of Eden Park's leery chaos.

   Hence **lair (lare)** *n*. [AND 1923], a vulgar or

flashy show-off; **lair off** *v*., to speed off in a vulgar, flashy fashion.
   1965 HILLIARD *Power of Joy* 292 God! there she stands talking to two **lares** on bikes. I could kill them. **1952** *Landfall 23* 216 The youth **leering off** to his first booze-up drinks as if he had been initiated into the mysteries of manhood.

lake: see COLD LAKE, *hot lake* (HOT *a*. 2).

lambburger, var. LAMBURGER.

lamb down, *v*.

1. [AND 1848.] *intr*. To help with or oversee the birth of lambs.
   1860 in Butler *First Year* 28 Jan. (1863) iii 32 Most marvellous of all, it is not his sheep which lamb, but he [*sc*. a runholder] 'lambs down' himself.

2. *Obs. fig*. [AND 2, 1850.] To encourage (esp. a station-hand) to spend earnings on liquor.
   1880 [see *vbl. n*. below]. **1917** *Chron. NZEF* 25 July 251 A Maori Pioneer was 'lambed down' last week. **1952** LYON *Faring South* 161 The result was always the same, and the guileless one went back [to the bar] to be duly lambed down which, in common parlance, meant he was allowed to shout for all hands, was soon moneyless and found himself on the verge, if not quite in the delirium tremens stage.

   Hence **lamber down** *n. obs*. [AND 1880], one who encourages workmen to spend earnings on liquor; **lambing down** *vbl. n*., see quot. 1908.
   1952 LYON *Faring South* 161 The main body of [West Coast] diggers were noted as a very hard-drinking group, and had possibly one of the most notorious '**lambers-down**' existent to help them in their folly. **1880** *Evening Post* (Wellington) 9 June 3 [Heading] '**Lambing down**' in Invercargill [i.e., a Publican's cashing in on a drunk shearer's cheque]. **1890** MOORE *NZ for Emigrant* 217 The little process by which the publican is fattened and the bushman skinned is facetiously called 'lambing down'. **1899** BELL *In Shadow of Bush* 23 And if a good deal of 'lambing down' was done in his house [*sc*. a rough and rowdy hotel] and he were charged with it, he would say, with his foreign accent, 'If a fellow vill knock down his cheque and spendt his moneys in drink, vy, he may as vell and betters do it in mine house as in anoder man's'. **1908** *Truth* 3 Oct. 4 A specific charge was laid against Burke of what is classically known as 'lambing down,' a common enough business in the olden days but little heard of now, except in the backblocks of Australia after shearing. The process is simplicity itself. A shearer comes along with a cheque for 80 or 100 [pounds], gives it to the publican, gets rapidly drunk, and then drunker, and then D.T.'s and then wakes up and goes back into the never-never to rake up another cheque. For a publican in these enlightened days to be accused of this kind of business is a very serious thing. **1918** *Chron. NZEF* 7 June 200 I hope to hear of fewer 'lambing-down' cases in future. **1921** FOSTON *At The Front* 150 'Lambing down' was a frequent occurrence. **1961** MACKAY *Puborama* 12 In these modern times, 'lambing down', a term that passed for good Australian slang, has become a little out of date. It was born of the experience of the average bushman or shearer, accustomed to an annual..spree at the nearest shanty hotel. Over the counter went his hard-earned cheque and, when that cheque was 'cut out'..the celebrant was kicked out.

lambie, var. LAMMIE.

lambing, *vbl. n. Farming*.

1. [In Brit. use rare as a non-attributive: see

OED.] Of a ewe, producing a lamb or lambs; also of a flock, the collective result of lambings.
1845 DEANS *Pioneers* (1964) 45 Our nearest neighbours, Messrs Greenwood at Port Cooper, will have about 1,500 this lambing season. **1851** *Lyttelton Times* 12 July 1 The Undersigned desires to rent..sufficient pasturage for 2,000 Sheep after landing, till after lambing and shearing time. **1873** BARKER *Station Amusements* 9 There were too many lambs belonging to a summer lambing.

2. Special Comb. **lambing paddock**, a paddock reserved for ewes about to lamb; **lambing percentage**, a measure of the number of lambs produced from the ewes in a flock.
1882 *TrNZI* XIV. 271 Most stock-owners wean their lambs on their best feed..**Lambing paddocks** should be virgin pasture. **1960** SCRYMGEOUR *Memories Maoriland* 112 Gradually both sons were allotted lambing paddocks, during the lambing season. **1968** GRUNDY *Who'd Marry a Doctor?* 39 It was too bad if [the stock] had drawn their dying breaths..in a lambing paddock. **1943** *NZJST* XXIV. 201A A **lambing percentage** of about 100 is obtained. **1953** SUTHERLAND *Golden Bush* (1963) 178 He seldom spoke and when he did it was usually to call down the wrath of heaven on the wild pigs that ignored his boundary fences and slashed his lambing percentages every spring.

lamb marking: see MARK *v.*

lamb's fry: see FRY.

lamb sheet. *Farming*. A device to prevent lambs 'breaking' or stampeding from a mob (see quot.).
1951 MCLEOD *NZ High Country* 25 In some districts things called 'lamb sheets' are used. These are long strips of scrim or calico about three feet wide and twenty yards long with a cord through the top. When the sheep approach the yard and the danger of a break begins, three or four of these sheets are run out between the men, making a sort of false yard of flapping white sheets which frightens the lambs back into the mob and enables the pressure to be put on to force them into the yard.

lamb's quarters. Transf. use of Brit. *lamb's quarters* 'fat-hen' for New Zealand salad herbs of the genera *Atriplex*, *Chenopodium* (fam. Chenopodiaceae) and *Tetragonia* (fam. Aizoaceae).
1773 FORSTER *Resolution Jrnl.* 8 June (1982) II. 297 The common *Sow-thistle* is likewise in great plenty..together with a kind of *Lamb's-Quarters*. **1777** FORSTER *Voyage Round World* I. 200 We also found [at Queen Charlotte Sound] a..kind of plant which our people called lamb's quarters (*tetragonia cornuta*,) which we frequently used as sallads. **1983** HULME *Bone People* 110 So Kerewin's next meal featured a salad with fourteen different greens in it, all plucked within a one-mile radius of the Tower. Sorrel, wild turnip, lambsquarters, dandelions, pikopiko curls, puha.

lamburger. Also **lambburger.** [f. *lamb n.* + ham)*burger*.] Ground lean mutton used as a hamburger-type filling.
1969 SCHULTZ *Busy Cook's Look-It-Up Bk.* 42 Neck or shank meat is good for grinding into 'lamburgers'. **1984** *Star* (Auckland) 2 Mar. A1 [Caption] Meet the lamburger—New Zealand's answer to the hamburger and hot dog. **1986** *Salient* (Wellington) 14 July 13 Lange is doing for New Zealand humour what Mike Moore is doing for the lamburger. **1989** CHURCHMAN *Route of the Coastal Express* 16 This [menu] includes such choices as Canterbury Lamburger.

lamington /ˈlæmɪŋtən/, /ˈlemɪŋtən/. Also **le(a)mington, lemmington.** [AND 1909, 'Prob. f. the name of Charles Wallace Baillie, Baron *Lamington* (1860–1940) Governor of Queensland (1895–1901)'.] In early use **lamington cake**, a sponge shape covered with chocolate icing and coconut, later occas. with jelly and coconut, and possibly earlier used of the whole sponge itself.
1916 *Celebrated Amuri Cook. Book* (1927) 67 *Leamington Cakes*. One cup butter, 1-1/2 cups sugar, 1 cup milk, 3 cups flour..4 eggs, essence vanilla... Bake in flat tin... When cold cut into squares. [Ice with cocoa icing; cover with desiccated coconut.] **1924** *Help the Babies Cook. Book* 133 *Lemmington Cakes*..roll in desiccated cocoanut. **1926** FUTTER *Home Cook. NZ* 217 *Lamington Cakes*..when cold cut in small cakes, ice..[with chocolate icing] sprinkle with desiccated cocoanut [*sic*]. **1928** *Everybody's Cook. Book Tested Recipes* 28 *Lemingtons*... When cake is quite set cut into blocks and roll in cocoanut [*sic*]. **1929** MCKAY *Pract. Home Cook.* 164 *Leamingtons* when cooked..cut into small pieces, and ice with thin chocolate icing. **c1939** BASHAM *Aunt Daisy's Book of Recipes* 135 *Lamingtons*... Dip cake squares into [chocolate] icing... Roll in desiccated cocoanut [*sic*]. **1943** *NZEF Times* 12 July 5 What he really wanted was thirty dozen leamingtons. **1984** BEARDSLEY *Blackball 08* 244 lamington: cube of sponge cake coated in chocolate icing or jelly, and dried coconut. **1992** *Salient* (Wellington) 17 Aug. 32 The lemmingtons in the cafe aren't made of real lemmings (something should be done about this).

lammie. *West Coast*. Also **lambie, lamby, llamy**. [Spec. use of Brit. dial. *lammie* a thick quilted woollen overgarment worn by sailors: see OED: perhaps f. *lammie* 'a little lamb'.] A waterproof flannel coat, usu. sleeveless, worn for work in the open. Cf. JUMPER, SWANNDRI.
1924 *Grey River Argus* 20 Feb. 7 [Advt] 26/-; Men's Heavy Double Kaiapoi LAMMIES. **1929** *Ibid.* 18 Jan. 3 [Advt] Men's Navy Lammies, double throughout, guaranteed rainproof; riding and walking styles—39/6 each. **1938** *Grey River Argus* 9 July 2 [Advt] The Workers' Friend. *Llamys*. I have pleasure announcing that I am the sole agent for Westland's famous LLAMYS—the garment used by Miners, Stockmen, Farmers, Roadmen and Railway Workers. A warm, weatherproof pure wool garment to work in... Their Character and General Excellence remain unchanged after 50 years of unprecedented popularity and widespread demand... H. Hamer, Kumara. **1952** *Evening Post* (Wellington) 12 May 9 The fame of the West Coaster's 'own' garment for outdoor workers—the ubiquitous miner's 'lammie'—has spread far afield... But what is a lammie? In the first place it is a strictly utilitarian garment with no claims to attractiveness in appearance. The original type—still in use after 70 years—was a loose-fitting almost shapeless shirt buttoned in front and with elbow-length sleeves made of flannel and water-proofed. It is this proofing quality which has established the popularity of the lammie. It was an ideal garment for outdoor workers on the West Coast climate, enabling them to keep dry without the encumbrance of an overcoat and it was soon in general use on the gold fields, later to be adopted by bushworkers, navvies and many farmers. At first the lammie was made of moleskin, then grey flannel and over the past 20 years of navy flannel, but the proofing formula has remained unchanged. In recent years there has also been developed a modified style, double breasted Coast fashion, but the original shirt style is still popular... The story of its origin has been lost. It is thought, however, that it was probably brought to the goldfields by the first Welsh diggers and that it may have been spelt 'Llamy'. **1952** *Ibid.* 16 May 6 In reference to your article on the West Coast shirt called a 'lammie', when a girl over 58 years ago [c1894] I used to visit a couple named Tait who lived in Dillmanstown... A draper named Todd used to get special flannel by the bolt for Mrs. Tait, and she made these 'lammies'. She waterproofed them by dipping them in a special solution two or three times and hanging them on a line dripping wet, to dry each time... I'm sure she never sold one to a Chinaman. It was Mrs. Tait's own invention I am sure. **1952** *Grey River Argus* 8 Aug. [For Sale Column] Llamys, double breasted all sizes... Hamer's Drapery Kumara. **1956** *Weekly News* (Auckland) 28 Jan. 44 From Taylor's Hill I could see the miners in their lambies—those long waterproof smock-like overshirts—working at the claim face. **1981** HUNT *Speaking a Silence* 29 Our favourite overcoat those days was a lambie. It was made of wool and really turned the water. It had no shape..just the armholes; it fitted anyone. **1993** *NZ Outdoor* June/July 36 [Advt] The 'Lamby' Bushshirt. A legend throughout the land. Made from quality 100% wool weave, wool lined, lined hood and lace-up front... Lamby bushshirt $139.00.

lamprey. [Spec. use of *lamprey* a fish of the genus *Petromyzon*.] *Geotria australis* (fam. Geotriidae), a primitive eel-like (but finless), sea-going freshwater animal. See also KANAKANA, KOROKORO, PIHAPIHARAU, PIPIHARAU.
1773 FORSTER *Resolution Jrnl.* 8 Apr. (1982) II. 250 We got some other new fish,..besides in the Evening a Lamprey..was caught. **1843** TAYLOR *Journal* (ATLTS) 10 June 30 The lamprey I find is a sea fish wh[ich] comes up the river, it is like an eel except the head which is more like a leech but very ugly & forbidding. **1855** TAYLOR *Te Ika A Maui* 383 The lamprey is taken in the same way as the eel... From its being very oily, it is highly prized... So extremely fond are the natives of the lamprey, that deaths from it are far from being uncommon. **1867** THOMSON *Rambles with Philosopher* 89 The lamprey, I may mention for the benefit of those who have not seen it, is not unlike a huge leech. It holds on to the rocks by a sucker, and by this means ascends the perpendicular rocks. Its colour and shape otherwise are not unlike the eel. **1878** [see KANAKANA]. **1882** [see PIPIHARAU]. **1904** TREGEAR *Maori Race* 108 Lampreys (*piharau*) were caught in loose mats of fern laid in small streams. **1927** SPEIGHT et al. *Nat. Hist. Canterbury* 191 There are three stages in the life history of the river-lamprey..which is known from practically all the Canterbury rivers. **1956** GRAHAM *Treasury NZ Fishes* 62 Lampreys have been so abundant that, on occasions, they have stopped the large water wheel that drives the paper mill at Mataura (Otago). **1966** *Encycl. NZ* II. 258 Maoris esteemed the lamprey as food and formerly captured large numbers of them during the seasonal migration or 'runs', which normally occur at night. **1990** MCDOWALL *NZ Freshwater Fishes* 38 Lampreys are the most primitive and peculiar fish-like animals found in New Zealand's fresh waters, and are the survivors of a very ancient group of aquatic animals that first populated the waters of the earth at least 300 million years ago.

lancewood. [Poss. a transf. use of *lancewood* a West Indian wood (cf. OED 1); prob. from the lance-like shape of its juvenile form.] *Pseudopanax crassifolius* (fam. Araliaceae), a native tree or shrub having in its juvenile form long, toothed leaves pointing downwards from a usu. slender, erect stem. See also GRASS-TREE 3, HOHOEKA, HOROEKA, IVY-TREE, UMBRELLA-TREE.
1866 BARKER *Station Life* (1870) 94 The lancewood [is] a tall, slender stem..with a few long leaves at the top, turned downwards like the barb of a spear, and looking exactly like a lance stuck into the ground. **1872** *TrNZI* IV. 250 The lance-wood..[is at first] only a

LAND 436 LAND

straight rod, perhaps, ten feet high, with linear, toothed, and mottled leaves eighteen inches long, growing *downwards* at an acute angle with the stem. **1888** D'AVIGDOR *Antipodean Notes* 152 Slender lance-wood emerges..from the convolvulus-leaved but thorny 'lawyers' and the low manuca scrub. **1900** DENDY in *Canterbury Old & New* 186 Here also we find a characteristic New Zealand tree in the lancewood, most remarkable in the half-grown state, with its tall straight stem and long stiff drooping leaves with saw-like edges. **1915** *AJHR* C-6 14 *Pseudopanax crassifolium*..var. *unifoliatum* T. Kirk. Horoeka. Lancewood. Forest. **1922** *Auckland Weekly News* 12 Oct. 17 Ivyworts..include the lancewood, cultivated in many New Zealand gardens. **1966** *Encycl. NZ* II. 258 *Lancewood, Horoeka*... Heteroblasty, or the character of having two or more distinct kinds of shoots, especially where the juvenile differ from the adult, occurs in many New Zealand plants... No plant possesses it more markedly than lancewood. **1982** WILSON *Stewart Is. Plants* 82 *Pseudopanax crassifolius* Lancewood... Horoeka... Grass tree (local name for juveniles).

land.

1. In special Comb. connoting Maori land(s) or Crown land(s) in respect of alienation (by purchase or lease), or of management: **Land Board** *hist.*, a local or regional State-appointed board set up to investigate and register claims to Crown land; **land claim** [orig. US: cf. OED 12, 1812], a claim to have purchased Maori land; **Land (Purchase) Commissioner** *hist.* [AND 1828], a Government agent officially overseeing or authorizing the purchase of Maori land, or arbitrating disputes over such land (see also *Native Commissioner* (NATIVE B 3 b), cf. *Government Agent* (GOVERNMENT)); **Land Court**, see MAORI LAND COURT; **Land District**, see quot.; **land fever**, the rush to buy or claim unsettled land, usu. that in Maori ownership; **land-grabber** [spec. use of *land-grabber*: see OED 1872], LAND-SHARK 1; **land-grabbing**; **Land Incorporation**, see INCORPORATION; **land-jobber** *hist.* [used elsewhere, but of special significance in relation to early private acquisition of Maori land: AND 1835], one speculating in the private acquisition and further sale of Maori land (cf. LAND SHARK 1); **land-jobbing** *ppl. a.* and *vbl. n.* [AND 1809], (pertaining to) such speculation in Maori land; **land march** (also **land rights march**, **Maori land march**), a march from Te Hapua, Northland, to Parliament Buildings, Wellington, made in 1975 by Maori people led by (Dame) Whina Cooper to draw attention to long-held grievances over confiscation of Maori land (see also HIKOI), hence **land marcher**; **land-office** *hist.* [spec. use of *land-office* an office dealing with the sale, etc. of unsettled lands], a Provincial (later Central) Government official registry for land-claims, land-sales, etc.; **land-order** *hist.* [AND 1838], in early settlement, a written authorization of ownership, or of the right to ballot for ownership, of a section or sections of land, part of the New Zealand Company purchases; **land question** *hist.*, also **native land question**, an overall view or general perception of the alienation (or confiscation) of Maori lands based variously on a European or a Maori viewpoint on such matters; **land rights** [AND 1964], the rights of the Maori to ownership of (originally) Maori land; **Land Sales** [spec. use with reference to provisions of the Land Sales Act during WW2], the regulating of the sale and purchase of land instituted as a stabilization measure during WW2; **Land Wars**, occas. with init. caps., used by some modern writers for NEW ZEALAND WARS q.v.

1890 *NZ Mail* 14 Nov. 25 The first case of alleged dummyism was ventilated at the **Land Board** on Wednesday. **1924** *Otago Witness* (Dunedin) 9 Dec. 18 We would have the matter investigated through the Land Board and the head office [of the Lands Department]. **1842** RETTER in Manson *Take Up My Pen* (1971) 26 There is much distress in the Colony on account of non-settlement of **land claims** and a great deal through drink. **1898** HOCKEN *Contributions* 45 Perfect specimens [of moa bones] were sent home by the latter [*sc.* Mantell]..to his father..in 1849, whilst engaged as commissioner for the settlement of native land claims. **1949** REED *Story Canterbury* 183 He had further aroused the hostility of the leaders of the settlement by his decisions on certain complicated 'pre-Adamite' Banks Peninsula land claims. **1844** TUCKETT *Diary* 28 Apr. in Hocken *Contributions* (1898) 213 There are nearly twenty other Europeans residing here [at Molyneux], most of whom have enclosures of cultivated land... If any claim has been advanced by any of these squatters, none has been approved by the **Land Commissioners**; yet they will consider themselves aggrieved if ejected from their dwellings without compensation. **1845** *Parliamentary Debates* (G.B.) Vol. LXXXI col. 947 in Rutherford *Selected Documents* (1949) 14A page 2 He had also the opportunity of personal communication with Mr. Spain upon the duties of a Land Commissioner. **1860** MARJOURAM *Diary* 3 Feb. in *Sergeant, Sinner* (1990) 35 I accompanied (in disguise) the Assistant-Native Land Commissioner to the river Waitara, to spy out the adjacent country. **1887** *Auckland Weekly News* 21 May 28 Land Purchase Commissioners were appointed. **1957** *NZ Timber Jrnl.* Oct. 73 **Land District**: A major land division of New Zealand used for both survey and land administration purposes. **1940** WAITE *Port Molyneux* 15 This **land fever** [after 1840] has been described as 'sharking' or 'grabbing', and 'bona fide speculation'. **1905** BAUCKE *White Man Treads* 238 The Crown itself has become that obnoxious person, the **land-grabber**! and a ruin to the Maori—ye gods, a most cruel, domineering land-shark! **1917** *Truth* 1 Dec. 3 There are many thousands of acres still in the grip of the land-grabber. **1944** BEATTIE *Maori Place-names Otago* 73 Long after the time of the 'land-grabbers' of the 'thirties and 'forties of last century, we have pioneer documents giving Maori names. **1986** BELICH *NZ Wars* 77 Selwyn and Williams make particularly unconvincing land-grabbers. **1977** MARKS *Hammer & Tap* 510 To prevent '**land-grabbing**', a runholder [in Otago] was bound to place a certain number of sheep and cattle on every thousand acres and have it fully stocked six months after taking out the lease. **1839** *Instructions Secretary of State to Captain Hobson, C.O.* 14 Aug. 209/4 251–81 in *Speeches & Documents* (1971) 13 Having by these methods obviated the dangers of the acquisition of large tracts of Country by mere **Landjobbers**, it will be your duty to obtain, by fair and equal contracts with the Natives, the Cession to the Crown of such Waste Lands as may be progressively required for the occupation of Settlers resorting to New Zealand. **1839** LANG *NZ in 1839* 22 A matter of question as well as of considerable interest among the land jobbers of the Bay of Islands to whom Barrier Island belonged. **1843** DIEFFENBACH *Travels in NZ* I. 11 A few land-jobbers raised the price thus high, having bought the ground in all the best situations. **1839** LANG *NZ in 1839* 45 Whether the New Zealanders remain in that unconverted and heathen state, or adopt such a mere nominal profession of Christianity as they are likely to arrive at under the influence of **land-jobbing** missionaries, the prospect for that unfortunate people is gloomy in the extreme. **1840** *Hobson to Normanby* 20 Feb. in *GBPP House of Commons 1841 (No.311)* 12 This mania for land-jobbing is by no means confined to Europeans, but has extended to the natives. **1843** CHAPMAN *NZ Portfolio* 40 A considerable quantity of the capital imported into New Zealand from the Australian colonies..is invested in land,— 'speculating in the real estate', as the Americans call it, or 'land jobbing', as its enemies designate it, being a favourite occupation with the Sydney folk. **1853** SEWELL *Journal* 8 Mar. (1980) I. 184 All the valuable spots will be jobbed away. River banks will be seized on. In short all the Land-jobbing Vultures will be down upon their prey. **1862** THATCHER *Dunedin Songster 3* 10 This wonderful township belongs, you must know, To some grasping land-jobbing faker, And the price that he gave for it some time ago, Was about twenty shillings an acre. **1975** *Evening Post* (Wellington) 29 July 1 Organisers of the **Maori land rights march** from Northland to Wellington hope to complete the more than 700-mile trek in about a month. **1975** *NZ Herald* (Auckland) 15 Oct. i 6 At best opinion among Maori land marchers seems to be divided on the result of the 700-mile long trek to Parliament Buildings. **1987** *Nelson Evening Mail* 16 Sept. 6 Maori people need to cooperate more if they are to consolidate the gains of the Maori land march, Dame Whina Cooper says. **1992** GRACE *Cousins* 206 She was talking about the Maori people assembling at Te Hapua to begin the Land March that would bring them from the top of the North Island to Parliament with their Memorial of Rights. **1851** TORLESSE *Papers* (1958) 206 I slept in Cass's bed at the **Land Office**, he having been unable to return from Lyttelton. **1886** HART *Stray Leaves* 29 At the Land Office [in Christchurch in 1852], which was really the Government Office, all the settlers were congregated. **1902** *Settler's Handbook NZ* 63 The Commissioner's office is known as the principal land office, and in some of the larger districts there are one or more local offices. It is with these land offices the selector has to transact all business. **1930** ACLAND *Early Canterbury Runs* 114 A man applied at the Land Office for a likely piece of country which he had seen on his travels... If no one else established a prior claim the Waste Lands Board gave him the run. **1939** BEATTIE *First White Boy Born Otago* 118 Some of the Central runs had been applied for at the Dunedin Land Office late in 1857 and others during 1858. **1970** MCNEISH *Mackenzie* 16 It was only a race with a missionary to reach the Land Office. **1839** Let. in *William Swainson* 4 July (1992) 62 L/- [*sc.* pounds sterling] New Zealand Land Company's Office, 1 Adam Street, Adelphi. July 4, 1839... These are to certify that I have this day registered the Application of William Swainson Esq. for five **Land Orders** according to the printed Terms of Purchase... John Ward Secretary. **1843** WOOD *Twelve Months in Wellington* 61 A Company's land-order is a clog to freedom of action. **1848** WAKEFIELD *Handbook NZ* 175 The purchasers then received [in London] land-orders entitling them to choose one Town-section and one rural section for each land-order, in the rotation governed by the number drawn for it; and the native reserves took their chance with the rest. **1868** TAYLOR *Past & Present NZ* 275 The holders of the company's land orders were called, in the infancy of the colony, 'sectionists', and regarded as great men, being the only possessors of land. **1930** GUTHRIE *NZ Memories* 76 This [being beaten for good land] had already happened more than once, for his 'land order' (drawn by ballot) being a high number he was obliged to wait till those with lower ones had made their first choice. **1848** SELWYN in *NZ Part V* (Church in the Colonies XX) 23 June (1849) 38 The events at the Wairau, and the **Land Question** had made a breach between the two races. **1852** *Saunders' Monthly Mag.* in *Canterbury Colony* (1976) I. 20 The next step of Sir George was to place the 'land question' on a satisfactory footing, then no easy job. **1860** SWAINSON *Memo. to Gov. Gore Browne* 7 May in Rutherford *Sel. Documents* (1949) 108 The native land question remains to be considered, and on its satisfactory solution the ultimate fate of the Maori race..materially depends. **1874** BAINES *Edward Crewe* 77 Ah! 'that land question' was always a source of trouble in New Zealand, like anything else when the ownership is uncertain. **1880** SENIOR *Travel & Trout* 236 Old colonists in New Zealand..are divided amongst themselves upon the land question. **1958** MILLER *Early Victorian NZ* 149 A struggle for control of the land, and the land question involved the native question and the system of precarious military alliances established by Fitzroy. **1982** O'SULLIVAN *Rose Ballroom* 28 Skull worked with the Hories who were O.K. so long as their tight-arse worries over **land rights** and such didn't throw them in flurries. **1951** *Here & Now* July 6 Much of the 50% rise since **Land Sales** control was lifted is due to this [*sc.* the remunerative private enterprise of buying houses for speculative resale]. **1971** BAXTER *Collected Poems* (1980) 517 The river..swollen..with weeping from the hills For what was lost in the **Land Wars**. **1973** PEARSON in Finlayson *Brown Man's Burden* 134 Kapi is probably referring to the land wars between Maoris and European Troops in the 1860s. **1986** BELICH *NZ Wars* 77 The idea that the seizure of Maori land was the main British political and military objective has been so widely adopted that the conflicts are often called 'The Land Wars'. **1992** *NZ Tablet* (Dunedin) 13 May 14 The land wars ruined any prospect of a Maori mission.

2. In phr. referring, often emblematically, to New Zealand (occas. to Maori New Zealand) or to districts within New Zealand: **Land of Ferns**, New Zealand (cf. FERNLEAF); **land of the lost** *hist.* [f. *Land of the Lost*, the title of a novel of the northern gumfields by William Satchell (1902)], the relatively infertile Northland gumfields country perceived as attracting mainly the desperately poor or disadvantaged; see also LAND OF THE LONG WHITE CLOUD.

[**1835** YATE *NZ* (1970) 15 One of the most peculiar features in the character of this country is the fern, which everywhere flourishes most luxuriantly.] **1910** COCKAYNE *NZ Plants & Their Story* 1 To be sure, New Zealand is known as the **land of ferns**, and not without truth. **1940** LAING & BLACKWELL *Plants NZ* 7 The ferns form such a prominent feature in the Flora, that New Zealand is often termed 'The Land of Ferns', and a fern frond has been taken as its emblem. **1913** CARR *Country Work* 42 The tussock plains round Lake Taupo..are gardens of Eden in comparison. No wonder [the northern gumfield country] is christened 'The **Land of the Lost**'.

3. *WW1*. In the phr. **land of the three S's** [f. the initial letters of *S*ergeants, *S*cabies and *S*yphilis], a soldiers' name for Egypt.

1936 HYDE *Passport to Hell* 149 Say '**Land of Three S's**' to any New Zealander or Aussie and he'll get you all right.

land league. *Hist*. Also (**Anti-land-selling**) **League**, and usu. with init. cap. A name given by the settlers of the 1850–60s to a suppositional Maori organization, based on the notion that a firm agreement had been made among some NI Maori tribes, and an actual organization set up, to prevent the further sale of Maori land to Europeans. See esp. quot. 1959.

1855 *Richmond-Atkinson Papers* (1960) I. 177 Of late there has been formed a League amongst various of the tribes on Cook's Straits for resisting further alienations of land to the Europeans... The Church of England missionaries labour under a strong suspicion of fostering and even originating this Land League... People feel certain that [Bishop Selwyn] will do his best to patch up a hollow truce and to shield the murderous Land-Leaguers. **1859** THOMSON *Story NZ* (1974) II. 225 To keep this spirit alive, an Anti-landselling League was formed among some of the Taranaki tribes... One tribe, not belonging to this League, was induced..to offer a quantity of land for sale in 1854. **1860** SELWYN *Memo. to Gov. Gore Browne* 8 May in Rutherford *Sel. Documents* (1949) 108g Land Leagues are the reasonable protest of an unrepresented majority against an aggressive minority. **1899** *Richmond-Atkinson Papers* (1960) II. 615 His court of appeal was at first the Land League, after 1860 the [Maori] King. **c1910** MACDONALD *Reminiscences* (VUWTS) 65 The 'Maori Land League' and the 'Maori King Movement' were growing into consistency and power. **1922** COWAN *NZ Wars* (1955) I. 147 If we could view the question from a national Maori point of view we should find much to approve of in the principle of the League. **1938** LANCASTER *Promenade* 194 The Taranaki Maoris were likely to require some facing presently, having established their own Land League. **1940** COWAN *Sir Donald Maclean* 11 This growing feeling culminated in 1852 in the formation of a confederation of tribes which came to be called the Land League, binding themselves, so far as Taranaki was concerned, to put a stop to all sales of land northward of the Bell Block. **1959** SINCLAIR *Hist. NZ* 109 In later years the settlers came to believe that a conspiracy was hatched against them at Manawapou; that the Maoris formed a 'land-league..a *war league*, a league of blood and death'. In fact, according to a missionary and a government land purchase agent, who had early news of the meeting, no agreement was made. **1970** MCNEISH *Mackenzie* 20 A month before, Matthew Whitehouse, the Superintendent, had told Polson in a letter that the natives of the north were forming land leagues. **1990** BARBER et al. in *Sergeant, Sinner* 6 In Taranaki [in 1856], settler insistence that they must have more land was met by resistance from a Maori Land League that prohibited sale. The Land League had its genesis at a large inter-tribal meeting or hui instigated by Wiremu Kingi and held at Manawapou in 1856.

Hence **Land-Leaguer** (**leaguer**), a member or supporter of a 'Land League'.

1855 [see above]. **1899** *Richmond-Atkinson Papers* (1960) II. 615 Of the state of things around New Plymouth..from the active interference of the Land-leaguers with the Taranaki land question to W. Kingi's taking it up the only competent historian is Mr Parris. **1922** COWAN *NZ Wars* (1955) I. 151 This suggestion is said to have led to an offer to the chief named to become king of the federated tribes, but here again the leaguers met with a refusal. **1959** SINCLAIR *Hist. NZ* 123 The Government had come to the conclusion that the Taranaki feuds, the shortage of lands for settlement, and therefore the danger of war, were all due to the illegitimate interference of non-owners, whether kingites, land leaguers, or chiefs, in land sales.

Land of the Long White Cloud.

1. Also **Great White Cloud**, and in various shortened forms. Occas. with lower case initials. The most popular of several translations of *Aotearoa*, adopted, often ironically, as a romantic appellation for New Zealand. See also AOTEAROA.

[**1898** REEVES *The Long White Cloud—Ao Tea Roa* [Title]] **1903** *TrNZI* XXXV. 180 The home of the Maori in the 'Land of the Great White Cloud' may, perhaps, be long continued. **1917** *NZ at the Front* 54 You, too, in the Land of the Long White Cloud, will have a thought for us. **1918** *Chron. NZEF* 13 Feb. 4 May you return soon to the 'long white cloud'. **1929** DUGGAN *NZ Bird Songs* 24 Spring was in the South lands, Trees with blossoms bowed, When they on the water Found the Long White Cloud. **1936** HYDE *Passport to Hell* 286 Land was in sight, just a faint blue line..above it floating the band of silver which made the old Maori canoe-explorers call New Zealand *Ao-Te-Aroa*—Land of the Long White Cloud. **1942** *NZEF Times* 21 Dec. 11 In the Land of the Long White Cloud thou shalt study the Dole. **1944** *Ibid.* 23 Dec. 5 Mail from the Long White Cloud quite upsetting. **1957** GOLDBLATT *Democracy at Ease* 12 The milk bars, the rendezvous of the 'Land of the Long White Cloud', are interspersed and barnacled to the Picture House. **1961** [see AOTEAROA 2]. **1966** [AOTEAROA 1]. **1968** *Evening Post* (Wellington) 5 Aug. 13 Right now the land of the long white cloud is broke and the people are bitter. **1983** HENDERSON *Down from Marble Mountain* 275 Fifteen grammes [of WW2 soldiers' airletter] wing home to the long white cloud for nine pence. **1986** OVENDEN *O.E.* 67 Then it's no trouble for Intelligence to..push him off to a new life, lost in the land of the long white cloud. **1989** *A NZ Prayerbook* 64 You Maori and Pakeha, women and men, all who inhabit the long white cloud: give to our God your thanks and praise.

2. In jocular or ironic variations: (**land of the**) **long white shroud, land of the wrong white crowd, land of the long black cloud**.

1943 JACKSON *Passage to Tobruk* 23 In due course more men arrived from the **Land of the Long White Shroud**. **1956** DAVIN *Sullen Bell* 20 Last I heard of you was that you had wangled yourself a plane back to the land of the long white shroud. **1982** *Dominion* (Wellington) 17 Feb. 12 New Zealand was beginning to look like the Land of the Long White Shroud for the Australian cricket team. **1992** *Listener* 11 July 20 I cannot understand whinging Kiwis who insist that the long white shroud still reigns, this is a boring or unsophisticated place. **1988** MCGILL *Dict. Kiwi Slang* 68 **land of the wrong white crowd** New Zealand perceived as dominated by Pakehas, backlash c/p variant of translation of Maori name for New Zealand. **1992** *Evening Post* (Wellington) 3 Aug. 1 Prime Minister Jim Bolger is refusing to be dragged into a row about Australian election advertising which paints New Zealand as '**the land of the long black cloud**'.

land shark. *Hist.* [AND 1836.]

1. A greedy and unscrupulous speculator in the purchase of (esp.) Maori land. Cf. *land-jobber* (LAND 1).

1839 LAING *NZ in 1839* 14 A class of persons in that colony [*sc.* New South Wales] who were known by the name of Land Sharks..have turned their eyes all at once to New Zealand. **1841** JAMESON *NZ, S. Austral. & NSW* 265 The missionaries have been stigmatised under the name of land-sharks, a term of reproach in common use throughout the Australian Colonies. In New Zealand, the flattering cognomen was bestowed on those who had purchased immense tracts of territory at a very cheap rate; it therefore designated another variety of the *squalus* family. **1859** THOMSON *Story NZ* (1974) II. 31 Out of this scramble [for land] sprang up the 'landsharks', a class of men who bought land from savages, and took advantage of their childish ignorance regarding its value. **1865** HURSTHOUSE *England's NZ War* 79 *Land-sharks*: Twenty years ago this was a term rife in Australia and New Zealand. **1874** WILSON *Diary* 28 May in Wierzbicka *Wilson Family* (1973) 195 Found Jackson who introduced me to Walker, one of the Canterbury speculators or Land Sharks as the newspapers rejoice to call them. **1889** MITCHELL *Rhymes & Rambles* 39 He'll vote against free immigration, Look after land sharks in the north, Break up every sheep run and Station. **1905** [see *land-grabber* (LAND 1)]. **1945** *People's Voice* 21 Nov. 3 [Heading] Land Sharks Remembered. **1986** *Listener* 12 Apr. 36 The

LAND-SHARKING

conflicting viewpoints..that the Maori should accept the Queen's protection against the French and land sharks..were most interesting to hear.

2. *transf.* An unscrupulous business person.

1881 BATHGATE *Waitaruna* 271 The way some of these land-sharks [*sc.* publicans] will keep an unfortunate man in a state of intoxication for weeks, so long as he has any money..then when his money is done they will kick him out remorselessly. **1988** *Through the Looking Glass* 127 Land agents who were also house agents (always called 'landsharks' by my parents, perhaps partly because we couldn't afford to buy a house and rent was a regular hurdle)..varied.

land-sharking, *vbl. n. Hist.* [AND 1840.] Unscrupulous speculation in the purchase of (esp.) Maori land. See also SHARKING *vbl. n.*

1839 *Colonial Gaz.* 28 Aug. 627/2 Land-sharking means pretending to purchase, but really obtaining somehow, land from the natives. **1848** WAKEFIELD *Handbook NZ* 54 This mode of acquiring land from savages [*sc.* by fraudulent blank contract forms] is now well known as *land-sharking*; a name which implies preying on the weakness of childish ignorance. **1851** *NZ* in *Chambers Papers for People* 4 The signatures of the chiefs were purchased for the merest trifle and sailors, with the earnings of a year, became mighty landlords. The system grew into disrepute among the conscientious settlers, and has become famous as land-sharking. **1904** *NZ Observer* 10 Sept. 4 He [*sc.* Tom Russell] had a finger in most land-sharking pies. **1913** *NZ Observer* 25 Jan. 2 The most strenuous regulations were made against land sharking and speculative builders. **1945** *People's Voice* 21 Nov. 3 I would tell the honourable gentleman to have a good look, and see whether some of his relatives were not amongst the champions who outlawed 'land-sharking' from the Maoris.

language nest. Also **language nursery.** [Translations of Ma. *kohanga reo.*] Usu. KOHANGA REO; also applied to other Polynesian pre-school language-learning cultural groups.

1983 *Dominion* (Wellington) 29 July 2 Maori Affairs Minister Ben Couch is thrilled that Maori language nurseries will get $500,000 to take on unemployed people as temporary extra staff. **1984** DAVIES *Bread & Roses* 145 It is good to know that now, in a number of areas, Maori pre-schools, Te Kohanga Reo (Language Nests), are providing that confidence within Maori culture. **1988** *Dominion* (Wellington) 7 Oct. 6 [Heading] Extension to house Cook Islands language nest. A hall is to be extended on Wellington's town belt land so a Cook Islands language nest can be established. **1988** FRAME *The Carpathians* 83 We have our language nests now. Kohanga reo. **1995** *Dominion* (Wellington) 12 Apr. 3 A Samoan..will oversee reviews of Pacific Island language nurseries.

lantern: see BALLARAT, BOTTLE *n.* 2, BUSH C 3 d, COLONIAL A 5, DIGGER *n.*[1] 3 c, JOEY *n.*[1], MANROPE, MINER, WEST COAST B 3.

lantern fish. [Named from its phosphorescent light spots.]

1. A usu. small midwater fish of the fam. Myctophidae, esp. *Lampanyctodes hectori.*

1911 WAITE *Rec. Canterbury Museum* I. 166 *Myctophum Humboldti*... Lantern Fish. **1927** PHILLIPPS *Bibliogr. NZ Fishes* (1971) 16 *Myctophum humboldti*... Lantern-fish. **1981** WILSON *Fisherman's Bible* 142 The pretty little Lanternfish comes in about 40 varieties in our waters but is usually only ever found when it is dead and washed ashore. It..gets its name from the fact that it has rows of phosphorescent light spots along its undersides. **1986** PAUL *NZ Fishes* 54 *Lanternfish Lampanyctodes hectoris.* Family Myctophidae.. probably the most common New Zealand lanternfish.

2. [Prob. from Brit. dial., alluding to its transparency: see OED *lantern* 9 'the smooth sole'.] WITCH.

1921 [see MEGRIM]. **1956** GRAHAM *Treasury NZ Fishes* 186 In Napier [*Caulopsetta scaphus*] is known as Lantern-fish, but for what reason I am unable to say, unless it is from the peculiar transparency when it is held up to a strong light. **1981** WILSON *Fisherman's Bible* 74 Megrim... Sometimes called Lantern-fish (because a lantern could be easily shone through it) and known to the Maoris as 'mahue'—the fish that is left behind.

lare: see LAIRY.

larickin, var. LARRIKIN.

lark. [Transf. use of Brit. *lark* 'skylark' (fam. Alaudidae) for the NZ species *Anthus novaeseelandiae* (fam. Motacillidae) 'ground-lark'.]

[*Note*] The prefixed *ground-* and *sand-* (the latter used occas. by early writers) were not generated as specific epithets to describe the New Zealand bird but transf. as compounds, the first prob. (poss. by Yate) directly from Brit. dialectal *ground-lark* the meadow pipit (see EDD *ground n.*[3] 3 (5)).

1. As **lark** (or **native** or **New Zealand lark**), the *ground-lark* of 2 (1) below, PIPIT.

1841 BEST *Journal* 20 May (1966) 315 The only signs of life we saw all day long was an occasional lark. **1847** ANGAS *Savage Life* II. 132 Larks..are abundant here [at Omurua]. **1860** BUTLER *Forest Creek MS* (1960) 43 Save an ubiquitous lark exactly like our English lark except that it does not sing and has two white feathers in the tail, one sees no birds at all. **1861** *NZ Goldfields 1861* (1976) 38 In fact the only wild birds..were one or two..New Zealand larks—who, alas! only break through their customary muteness to give utterance to a harsh unpleasant squeak. **1882** HAY *Brighter Britain* II. 224 The Pihoi (*Anthus N.Z.*) is the so-called native 'lark'. It is a ground pipit, and may often be seen fluttering and chirping about a bush road. **1890** *Otago Witness* (Dunedin) 11 Dec. 41 The eggs of the native lark..are so marked as to be well concealed in the tussock..where they are laid. **1940** STUDHOLME *Te Waimate* (1954) 235 [Caption] *Native Lark*, dipping and rising. **1966** *Encycl. NZ* II. 776 The New Zealand pipit, sometimes inaccurately called ground lark or native lark, is a local race..of a very widely distributed species. **1985** [see 2 (1) below].

2. With a modifier: **ground, sand.**

(1) ground-lark. PIPIT.

1835 YATE *NZ* (1970) 58 *Pihoihoi*—This bird resembles the canary in shape and size... It might not be improperly designated the ground-lark, which it very much resembles. **1843** DIEFFENBACH *Travels in NZ* I. 325 Of animal life nothing was visible, with the exception of..a brown ground-lark very common in New Zealand. **1859** THOMSON *Story NZ* I. 25 The Kataitai or ground-lark, is the most numerous bird in the country. It rarely sings unless its nest is approached, when it rises in the air a short distance and sings, evidently for the purpose of drawing off the danger. **1869** *TrNZI*I. (rev. edn.) 109 The other birds..were..the Fan-tail.. the Ground-lark..the New Zealand Titmouse. **1873** [see PIPIT]. **1898** MORRIS *Austral-English* 176 *Ground-Lark*... In New Zealand, a bird also called by the Maori names, *Pihoihoi* and *Hioi*. **1904** TREGEAR *Maori Race* 181 The centipede..the Maori bug..and the ground lark (*hioi..*), a sacred bird, were all supposed to have been brought in the canoes. **1914** in *Hist. N. Otago from 1853* (1978) 43 Occasionally a ground lark makes a short flight over the tussocks. **1923** *NZJST* VI. 96 Ground-lark; Pipit. This engaging little bird is so well adapted to open country and native tussock associations that with the spread of pastoral areas it is more than maintaining its numbers. **1939** BEATTIE *First White Boy Born Otago* 121 I saw [in Central Otago in the 1860s] the sparrow-hawk, the rock wren, and plenty of hawks and pihoihoi (ground larks). **1947** POWELL *Native Animals NZ* 86 New Zealand Pipit (*Anthus novae-seelandiae*), also called the ground lark, is a common bird throughout the country. **1971** WILLIAMS *Dict. Maori Lang.* 280 *Pīhoihoi,... Anthus novaeseelandiae*, ground-lark. **1976** [see PIPIT]. **1985** *Reader's Digest Book NZ Birds* 270 *Pipit Anthus novaeseelandiae..New Zealand Pipit A. n. novaeseelandiae*... Other Names: *Pihoihoi, groundlark, native lark.*

(2) sand lark. In early (also in recent Chatham Island) reference, usu. *ground lark* (1) above; occas. applied to other limicoline birds.

1773 FORSTER *Resolution Jrnl.* 30 May (1982) II. 289 I shot a Shag, my Son two Sand Larks. **1777** ANDERSON *Journal* Feb. in Cook *Journals* (1967) III. 807 A small sandy colour'd plover, & some sand larks; and a small Penguin. **1838** POLACK *NZ* I. 306 Blue herons, auks, sand larks, sand plovers, terns. **1885** [see PLOVER 2 (1)]. **1966** FALLA et al. *Birds NZ* 216 New Zealand Pipit..*Pihoihoi, Sandlark* (Chathams).

larrikin. Also **larickin, larrkan.** [f. Brit. dial. *larrikin* a mischievous and frolicsome youth: see EDD Suppl.; AND 1868.] Cf. LARRY *n.*[2]

1. A street rowdy or a young urban hoodlum; an irresponsible vandal.

1866 *Canterbury Rhymes* (1883) 102 A local inspector..told Constable E. [to go] down to a nursery garden, whose owner complained that the larickins..ne'er left him an apple. **1868** HARPER *Lett. from NZ* 5 Feb. (1914) 123 We are beset with larrikins [in Hokitika] who lurk about in the darkness and deliver every sort of attack on the walls and roof with stones and sticks. **1875** *Otago Daily Times* (Dunedin) 17 July (Editorial) The people of Otago have no intention whatever of spending their revenue in educating Auckland larrikans or supporting indolent officials in Wellington. **1883** *Educ. Monthly* 4 Aug. 7 Though everybody speaks and writes about the 'larrikin', what is he?.. I presume, I may say, he is of the male sex and that his age ranges from 12 to 21. He is of town origin. His amusements are various. He likes to be in the streets, and rather prefers to be about theatres. Smoking is his pastime. As to his actions the larrikins may be classed under two headings: 1) The mischievous larrikin 2) the criminal larrikin. **1896** HODGSON *Poems* 6 But a stranger bird haunts our streets at night, Bred of civilisation and sin—..We call him Larrikin. **1905** *Truth* 2 Sept. 7 Lounging Leary Larrikins Lashed—the Decay in British Manhood. Have you ever made a study of the hooligan of the Antipodes, our own binging, leary, larrikin. **1910** *Truth* 18 June 1 A larrikin is not necessarily a loafer or a criminal, though he is often, if not invariably, a member of a push which may, and usually does, contain a certain criminal element, and a still larger element verging towards criminality. **1922** MANSFIELD *Stories* (1984) 457 She supposed Alice had picked up some horrible common larrikin and they'd go off into the bush together. **1951** PARK *Witch's Thorn* 43 The white larrikins jammed on their flat hats and scurried out of there like Maori-bugs. **1975** CLEARY *Pocketful Years* 22 But what can one old woman do with night coming down and nobody to protect her from these larrikins [*sc.* bikies]. **1980** MANTELL *Murder or Three* 78 Lucky we found it [*sc.* an abandoned car] first... Before some larrikins commandeered it for a joy riding spree.

2. a. A high-spirited often socially unconventional young person; a lively adolescent, a 'young devil'; often applied humorously to lively children.

1884 BAKER *Daughter of the King* 194 The sound of children's voices..not the melodious voices of angelic children..but the voices of Colonial 'larrikins', healthy, loud, and penetrating. **1897** DUCHESS OF BUCKINGHAM *Glimpses Four Continents* 130 The 'larrikins', as we called the young and giddy portion of this crew [who had landed to explore the creeks], found the bush impenetrable. **1934** LEE *Children of Poor* (1949) 202 Everything conspired to render me happy, even a pretty girl called Mona. She was no larrikin, neither did she hold aloof. **1972** MITCHELL *Pavlova Paradise* 183 *larrikin*: Young people of whom you happen not to approve. **1985** MARSHALL *Secret Diary Telephonist* 10 He said it was vicious interference from that cheeky young larrikin in the Labelling Department.

b. *transf.* A lively or rowdy animal; also the name of a racehorse.

1876 *Saturday Advertiser* (Dunedin) 19 Aug. 5 After racing together..Larrikin drew gradually away, the mare falling again at the last fence, the race was over. **1901** *TrNZI* XXXIII. 218 The big Caspian tern is a bird of much dignity, and somewhat shier than his lesser relative the common tern, or sea-swallow, who is a jeering noisy fellow, a 'larrikin' of birds. **1904** CRADOCK *Sport in NZ* 152 A desperate young larrikin of a trout.

3. *attrib.* passing into *adj.* and *Comb.* esp. *larrikin element*. Rowdy and socially irresponsible. (In later use often humorously applied in a weakened sense.)

1885 *Wairarapa Daily* 28 Dec. 2 What few pranks there were played are due entirely to the young larrikin element of the town. **1888** PAYTON *Round About NZ* 186 I cannot help remembering the remonstrance of a big burly 'officer' [of the Salvation Army] to two young men of the larrikin element who persisted in interrupting continually. **1892** BROOKES *Frontier Life* 27 Some of the most larrikin elements it would be possible to conceive. **1895** GRACE *Maoriland Stories* 168 [A woman says:] Why didn't you dance [the Polka] the larrikin way. **1900** *Egmont Star* (Hawera) 27 Oct. 2 'Larrikin heel' in men's, youth's, boy's, women's, and maid's boots, is an item that appears on the Unionists' 'statement' in the bootmakers' dispute now before the Conciliation Board. **1926** *Press* (Christchurch) in Bailey & Roth *Shanties* (1967) 72 Now all you larrikin volunteers, [from Kumara, Westland c1885]. **1956** *Street Society Christchurch* 5 Larrikin groups, though not common, were also observed [in Cathedral Square, Christchurch, 20 Apr. 1956]. Numbers of noisy youths and girls congregated for short periods and engaged in loud conversation and laughter. **1960** SCRYMGEOUR *Memories Maoriland* 30 She fished, waded in the creeks..or with the larrikin elder brother Jim, following him round the rabbit traps in the evenings. **1985** JONES *Gilmore's Dairy* 33 Gilmore worried that they were..frightening off custom with their larrikin presence.

4. In composition: **larrikina, larrikiness** [AND *larrikiness*, 1871], a female larrikin; **larrikinish**, characteristic of a *larrikin* 1.

1883 PARTINGTON *Random Rot* 82 Girls who are fast and assume the airs and ways of men, are called 'larrikinas'. **1907** *Truth* 26 Jan. 3 Their language is often that of the larrikiness; and their manners still oftener, both in public and private, would disgrace a demi-rep. Many of them are demi-reps, masquerading under cover of a marriage licence. **1879** *Auckland Weekly News* 19 Apr. 7 Much indignation is felt at their larrikinish behaviour.

larrikinism. [AND 1870.] Behaviour characteristic of a LARRIKIN (1 or 2 a).

1871 *Evening Post* (Wellington) 27 Apr. 2 [Heading] Larrikinism v. Public Entertainments **1882** HAY *Brighter Britain* I. 39 Sometimes the youth finds himself in the police court, charged with 'larrikinism', an offence that is sure to be severely punished... He is not altogether bad—not so frequently thieving and breaking the law, as intent on simple mischief and practical jokes of the coarsest and roughest sort. **1897** *AJHR* H-16 6 There is also a decrease in the number of offences that might be classed as the acts of larrikins, and larrikinism..is not so prevalent. **1902** WALKER *Zealandia's Guerdon* 23 The out-of-doors behaviour of certain people... [which] I think you term 'larrikinism' in your funny language. **1914** in *Hist. N. Otago from 1853* (1978) 92 Feeling often ran very high at local elections and the declarations of the result was [*sic*] usually accompanied by a good deal of larrikinism. **1926** DEVANNY *Butcher Shop* (1981) 34 Drink, and the well-bred larrikinism of the idle younger set. **1939** BEATTIE *First White Boy Born Otago* 181 The horseplay became so rough that Andrew was chased into a cabin where he..escaped the worst of the larrikinism. **1942** *NZEF Times* 2 Feb. 2 There was no undue larrikinism. **1963** *Evening Post* (Wellington) 10 Sept. 16 For 'irresponsible larrikinism', two 17-year-old workmen were placed on probation for 12 months... At a previous hearing the youths,.. pleaded guilty to breaking into an implement shed at the Shandon Golf Club, removing a tractor, and driving it round the grounds. 'This is not an ordinary case of burglary, but rather irresponsible larrikinism,' the Magistrate told the youths. **1980** LELAND *Kiwi-Yankee Dict.* 59 *larrikin—larrikinism*: A larrikin is a wild young man. Larrikinism is what such a young fellow *might* engage in: vandalism. (see: *yahoo, yob-yobbo*) **1992** *Evening Post* (Wellington) 19 Dec. 4 In actuality, it is the day when..the boss searches for and finds his latent larrikinism just under the skin.

Larry, *n.*¹ [Used elsewhere (e.g. 1993 on the Brit. TV programme 'Coronation Street') but recorded earliest in NZ: poss. related to Brit. dial. *larrie*: see EDD *larrie* joking, jesting; a practical joke; a lark; AND 1905.] In the phr. **(as) happy as Larry (larry)**, very happy.

c1875 MEREDITH *Adventuring in Maoriland* (1935) 133 We would be happy as Larry if it were not for the rats. **c1910** MACDONALD *Reminiscences* (VUWTS) 21 We did not vex ourselves..with wailing or complaint..on the contrary we were as 'happy as Larry'. **1948** FINLAYSON *Tidal Creek* (1979) 91 Is he still in the asylum?' 'Oh, he's as happy as Larry,' says Uncle Ted. **1950** WHITWORTH *Otago Interval* 29 I was a regular tomboy, happy as larry with my brothers. **1966** NEWTON *Boss's Story* 110 Although too big and heavy to be a good walker he was happy as Larry on that job. **1981** GEE *Meg* 136 She sort of forgets. But that's the way things go. She's as happy as Larry.

larry, *n.*² [AND 1891.] A short form of LARRIKIN.

1937 ALLEN *Hedge-Sparrow* 18 Nicholas was set on by a lot of larries because his father's a Morrowite. **1954** Oct. p.c. R.Mason who heard a Christ's College, Christchurch, boy call to another: 'You're a larry, that's all you are.'

lash, *n.*¹ In various *transf.* or *fig.* senses of *lash* a hit, a go, an attempt, esp. in the phr. **to have a lash (at)**; and also **to give** (something) **a lash to leg** [f. cricketing slang], to undertake an action vigorously; to give something a good go.

1906 *Truth* 1 Sept. 4 Have a lash at a man. [**1908** *Ibid.* 28 Nov. 5 Thereupon Smith caught him by the right arm and yelled to his mate. 'Lash' he cried. And the other person 'lashed!' Troon got it on the countenance and went down like a log.] **1917** *Chron. NZEF* 5 Sept. 28 Said Martin of the Dinks, 'Why, he was the greatest 'swi-up' king in the 'Inverteds', and he used to give the vin rouge a boscar lash to leg. **1945** *NZ Geogr.* 28 A few may spend their cheque in a glorious lash at the beer. **1948** BALLANTYNE *Cunninghams* (1963) 38 Hoping to get a lash at the Huns. **1986** RICHARDS *Off the Sheep's Back* 75 As the weeks went by I became like a young colt straining at the bit. I was rearing and longing to have a 'lash'.

lash, *n.*² The part of the thong of a stockwhip to which the cracker is attached. See BELLY 2, quots. 1933, 1940.

lash, *v. Criminal slang.* [f. English legal *laches* negligence in the performance of a legal duty: see OED *laches n* 2.] To fail to honour a debt or obligation. Hence **lasher**, one who fails to honour a debt, etc.

1982 NEWBOLD *Big Huey* 250 Lash (v) Fail to honour a debt or obligation. From the English legal term *laches* (negligence). *Ibid.* 118 Brian..was spewing on them for it and all morning was calling out across the compound, saying they were eggrolls and lashers and weaklings, for failing to stick fat.

last ditcher. *WW1.* Any one of those choosing to be evacuated last from Gallipoli in order to help conceal the evacuation from the Turks. See also DIEHARD.

1918 *Quick March* 1 Nov. 31 So soon as the men heard what was afoot there was a rush to be included in what they were pleased to call the 'last ditchers'.

last shower. [Cf. Partridge: Austral. C20.] In the phr. **not to have come down in the last shower**, indicating experienced awareness on the part of the speaker.

1988 McGILL *Dict. Kiwi Slang* 60 *I didn't come down in the last shower* I am not a fool; to which the reply is: 'You mightn't have come down in the last shower, but you're pretty wet all the same.'

late night. Also occas. **late-night shopping**. A week-night (after WW2 until the 1980s, usu. Friday) when most retail shops open beyond, say, 5.30 p.m. until, say, 9.00 p.m. .

1899 *NZ Times* (Wellington) 26 Oct. 5 The suggestion is that the Wednesday night early closing be abolished, that Friday be the late night for shopping, and that shops should close at one on Saturday afternoons. **1917** *Wanganui Herald* 2 May 4 The law provided for Friday being the late night when Saturday was the half-holiday. **1963** *Comment* 17 Oct. 13 Perhaps this might be the beginning of the end for Friday late-night shopping! **1985** McGILL *My Brilliant Suburb* 29 Down the bay [*sc.* Island Bay, Wellington] on the late night—bright buttery lights. **1993** *Hutt News* (Lower Hutt) 6 Apr. 21 [Advt] Hours: Two late nights Tuesday and Friday.

latrine intelligence: see LATRINOGRAM.

latrinogram. Mainly *WW1* and *WW2*. Also **latrine gram**, occas. **latrine intelligence**; occas. **craptogram** (see quot. 1940). [f. *latrine* + (-*o*-) +tele)*gram*: see OED, 'Services' 1944.] A latrine rumour (supposedly overheard when two or three men are gathered together defecating).

1915–19 HOLMDEN in Boyack *Behind the Lines* (1989) 3 This ignorance naturally led to the invention of rumours, which generally went under the name

Latinograms so named from their probable place of origin. **1940–41** HM Transports 23 and 23A (Troopship pub.) 12 X the Unknown to where we're on the way A craptogram solves it fresh every day. **1944** BRUNO *Desert Daze* 12 Beautiful spies..make such a fuss of Field Officers to gain the latest latrine intelligence. **1944** FULLARTON *Troop Target* 18 Anyway there's no dinkum oil. Only latrinograms..it may be all hooey. *Ibid.* 24 He was a mine of information—both 'latrinograms' and the 'dinkum oil'. **1983** HENDERSON *Down from Marble Mountain* 263 Base camps, such as Maadi, really mushroom rumours which are called with every justification 'latrinegrams'. **1984** *Islands* 34 110 And, though I didn't know it at the time except for latrinograms which you could never really trust, we really were already making preliminary plans for a transfer.

laugh. In the phr. **to be away laughing**, often as an exclamation, to be off to a good start; to be in the lead; to be well on the way to success.

1965 WATSON *Stand in Rain* 72 Wait till the insurance for the truck comes through. Then we're away laughing. **1974** HILLIARD *Maori Woman* 11 Once you get the *feel* of it you're away laughing as they say but it's not..easy at the start. **1980** MANTELL *Murder or Three* 76 As far as Mrs King was concerned, it simply meant teaching her a few tricks with the computer and she was away laughing.

laughing gear: see GEAR *n.*[1] 4.

laughing jackass. *Obs.* [Named from a distinctively 'braying' cry.]

1. WHEKAU. Cf. *laughing owl* (OWL 2 (1)).

1860 BUTLER *Forest Creek MS* (1960) 45 The laughing jackass is unlike the well behaved boy inasmuch as the latter is seen and not heard—the former is heard but has never yet been seen. **1871** *TrNZI* III. 63 Why [the whekau] should share with one of our petrels and the great *Dacelo* of Australia the trivial name of 'laughing jackass' we know not; if its cry resembles laughter at all it is the uncontrollable outburst, the convulsive shout of insanity. **1882** POTTS *Out in Open* 122 A larger species [of owl] is less well known; it is *Athene albifacies*, wekau of the Maoris, also it is known by some up-country settlers as the big owl or laughing jackass, at times it is confused with a petrel. **1898** MORRIS *Austral-English* 215 There is another bird called a *Laughing Jackass* in New Zealand which is not a *Kingfisher*, but an *Owl, Sceloglaux albifacies*... (Maori name, *Whekau*).

2. [Wilkes 1827.] Any of several petrels and shearwaters. Cf. HAKOAKOA.

1871 HUTTON *Catalogue Birds NZ* 45 Puffinus gavius... Rain-bird or Wet-bird. Shearwater, Laughing Jackass(?). Hakoakoa... *Ibid.* 48 Prion Turtur. Soland. Whale-bird. Laughing Jackass(?). **1874** POTTS *On Recent Changes in Fauna* 8 Laughing Jackass is one of the names conferred on the wekau... This distinction is shared by an Australian bird as well as by some of our seabirds amongst the petrels or Procellaridae. **1939** BEATTIE *First White Boy Born Otago* 121 A bird we called [c1860s] the Laughing Jackass could also be heard screeching at night near the [Otago] coast. **1940** STUDHOLME *Te Waimate* (1954) 250 On foggy evenings the laughing petrels, or laughing jackasses, as some people called them, would come rushing in from the sea, making for their nesting places in the hills, and start their hair-raising clatter close overhead.

laughing owl: see OWL 2 (1).

laurel. [Transf. use of (*bay*) *laurel Laurus nobilis* (fam. Lauraceae).] Also **laurel tree**, applied in New Zealand, usu. with a modifier, as **hedge (native, New Zealand) laurel**, (a) to trees and shrubs of habit similar to the laurel and with glossy leaves, esp. KARAKA and PUKATEA, and occas. NGAIO, BROADLEAF (fam. Cornaceae), and MAPAU *Pittosporum tenuifolium* (fam. Pittosporaceae); and (b) to trees of *Beilschmiedia* spp. (fam. Lauraceae), TARAIRE, TAWA. **a.** Laurel-like plants.

1857 [see NGAIO]. **1867** THOMSON *Twelve Yrs. Canterbury* 29 Gnaio shrubs (the native laurel). **1874** PYKE *George Washington Pratt* 42 The native laurel (the 'broadleaf' of the colonists). **1898** MORRIS *Austral-English* 195 *Hedge-Laurel, n.* a name given to the tree *Mapau..*, an evergreen shrub of New Zealand, of the genus *Pittosporum*... It has dark glossy foliage and handsome flowers, and is planted and cultivated in the form of tall garden hedges. *Ibid.* 263 *Laurel, n.* The English tree-name is applied in Australia to various trees, viz.. The New Zealand Laurel is *Laurelia novae-zelandiae*; called also *Sassafras*. **1905** WHITE *My NZ Garden* 90 Karaka, sometimes called the 'New Zealand Laurel', makes a fine large evergreen tree 40 feet high. **1908** [see KARAKA 1 a]. **1940** LAING & BLACKWELL *Plants NZ* 247 A handsome tree with laurel-like foliage [*sc.* karaka]... This tree is often called by settlers the 'New Zealand Laurel'.

b. *Beilschmiedia* spp. of the laurel family.

1883 DOMETT *Ranolf & Amohia* II. 16 Hard violet drupes of the great *laurel-tree* And gold karaka-dates. *Ibid.* II. 336 Laurel-tree (Tarairi)... *O.* Lauriniae; *G.* Neodaphne; *S. N.* Tairairi. **1966** *Encycl. NZ* III. 711 Laurel, New Zealand.. taraire.. *Beilschmiedia taraire*... tawa . . *B. tawa.*

lawsoniana. [f. a popular use of the specific name.] *Chamaecyparis lawsoniana* (fam. Cupressaceae), *Lawson's cypress*, a tall pyramidal tree commonly planted in gardens and used for hedges and windbreaks. Often *attrib.*

1945 *NZ Dairy Exporter* 1 Oct 75 The hedge surrounding the house is a lawsoniana, and already has reached a height of five feet. **1959** 29 June in Barry *In Lee of Hokonuis* (1966) 227 Applications were made to the Board for 50 Lawsoniana trees and for subsidy of £20 on Giant Stride. **1960** ASHTON-WARNER *Incense to Idols* 237 Stoned fruit..all tucked away securely behind the poplar and lawsoniana breakwinds. **1965** SARGESON *Memoirs of Peon* 270 We sat in the shade of a lawsoniana hedge. **1978** SUTHERLAND *Elver* 7 Danny..that afternoon hid in the lawsoniana hedge at the doctor's. **1988** JACKSON *Rainshadow* 61 Crouched under the lawsonianas by the Dental Clinic, a sense of loss..seized me. **1994** LASENBY *Dead Man's Head* 12 He pushed through the lawsoniana hedge around the school horse paddock.

lawyer. [AND *lawyer vine*, 1878.]

1. Also occas. **leafless (Maori, swamp) lawyer**. BUSH LAWYER *n.*[1]

1861 HAAST *Rep. Topogr. Explor. Nelson* 6 [We had] to scramble through a dense growth of wild irishmen, lawyers, and other prickly plants. **1862** GOLDIE in Beattie *Pioneers Explore Otago* (1947) 94 That plague to man in all New Zealand bush—'Maori Lawyers'. **1868** LINDSAY *Contribs. NZ Bot.* 54 In this condition [*Rubus australis*] forms one of the most..troublesome 'Lawyers,' or 'Supple-Jacks,' of the forest. **c1871** MASTERS *Autobiography* (ATLMS) 36 Also a vine called by the settlers, 'Lawyers', owing to the difficulty you have to extricate yourself from them, are hanging over your head. **1888** D'AVIGDOR *Antipodean Notes* 152 Slender lance-wood emerges..from the convolvulus-leaved but thorny 'lawyers'. **1896** HARPER *Pioneer Work* 34 It may be explained that a 'lawyer' is a bramble which grows in very dense masses, and is covered with small thorns. It is so named because, when once a man is unfortunate enough to get into its clutches, he finds it hard to free himself. **1905** THOMSON *Bush Boys* 36 It was a tangled thicket of branches and creepers in front of him, and the cruel 'Tataramoa' or 'Lawyer' (significant name—a wretched creeper of the bramble species with a superabundance of barb-like hooks that catch and tear one most grievously), had made its way all among them. **1949** SARGESON *I Saw in My Dream* (1974) 164 There was kidney fern but no more lawyer thank God. **1952** THOMSON *Deer Hunter* 129 Going became fairly difficult, broken rocks retarding our progress, not to mention a mass of lawyer (a type of native rambling rose if it could be so called). **1966** NEWTON *Boss's Story* 29 A 'lawyer', perhaps I should explain, is a dense bushy plant characterised by thousands and thousands of hooklike barbs along..its creeper-like brambles and tentacles. **1981** TAYLOR *Weeds of Roadsides* 85 Leafless Lawyer (*Rubus squarrosus*) Native perennial carrying many rearward facing spines and usually only small remnants of leaves. **1988** DAWSON *Forest Vines to Snow Tussocks* 64 *Rubus australis* is most common in swamp forest and is sometimes referred to as 'swamp lawyer'.

2. *attrib.* passing into Comb., esp. **lawyer berry**, **bush**, **vine**.

1886 *TrNZI* XVIII. 79 The patch of scrub..contains a few mapau..and 'lawyer'..bushes. **1893** FERGUSON *Bush Life Austral. & NZ* 250 Lawyer bushes, significantly so termed, from the clinging pertinacity of their nature. **1899** BELL *In Shadow of Bush* 186 Where a soft, yielding mass of the prickly, fast-clinging, flesh-scoring 'lawyer' vines..received and enveloped him. **1910** *Truth* 16 Apr. 1 A slim tendril of a lawyer vine had apparently pierced the stem of the young tree. **1933** *Press* (Christchurch) (Acland Gloss.) 4 Nov. 15 *Lawyer.*—Various species of Rubus. A briar-like plant which is a nuisance to men in the bush... When growing in the open it is often called a *l[awyer]-bush*. **1953** DEWAR *Chaslands* 12 Fern and moki and fuchsia, laced through with lawyer bramble, grew dense..at their feet. **1964** TUWHARE *No Ordinary Sun* (1977) 10 Bearing leaves of koromiko and black cauldron aswirl with the mangled roots of flax or lawyer vine. **1982** SUTTON-SMITH *Hist. Children's Play* 94 We roamed through the tracks in it and in season enjoyed the lawyer berries. **1986** DEVANNY *Point of Departure* 19 One Saturday morning, for the purpose of gathering lawyer berries from the bush I had discovered, my mother..crossed the mudflats.

lawyer's wig. [f. a fancied resemblance to a lawyer's wig.] The toadstool *Coprinus comatus*.

1978 FULLER *Maori Food & Cook.* 85 Lawyer's wig... *Coprinus comatus.* **1979** NATUSCH *Wild Fare for Wilderness Foragers* 31 Marie Taylor recommends the Shaggy Ink Cap or Lawyer's Wig, *Coprinus comatus*, as good eating.

lay. *Whaling.* [Used elsewhere but recorded early on the NZ coast: see OED *lay n.*[7] 8, 1850.] The share of the proceeds of a venture allotted to each participant. Also in the phr. **to sail upon the lay**, of a crew member, to ship out in expectation of a share in the proceeds of a whaling venture. Also *transf.*

1840 JOHNSON *Plain Truths* 61 The whalers all sail upon the lay..or, every person on board receives, according to a graduated scale, a portion of oil which is to be given up as per agreement, to the employers at a certain price, not above half the amount they would obtain for it, were they to sell it themselves at Sydney. **1893** JACOBSON *Tales of Banks Peninsula* 207 We were all on a 'lay'... If you are on 1/100th when 100 tons are got, you get one, and when you are on a 'lay' they find you—that's the difference between a lay and going shares. If you are on shares you find yourself. **1902** SATCHELL *Land of Lost* 27 Ain't there a lay of any kind? If so, I'm on it.

lay-by, *n.*[1] *Coalmining.* [Cf. Webster (1961) *Mining* a siding for empty cars.] A siding on an (underground) mine tramway-system.
   1901 *NZ Illustr. Mag.* IV. 614 The driver takes the trucks through the mine races, and deposits them in lay-bys, places similar to..railway sidings. **1912** *NZ Geol. SB (NS)* No. 15 18 In the Grand Junction Mine..electrically driven fans, placed in 'lay-bys' in the underground road ways, have been found effective. **1928** DEVANNY *Dawn Beloved* 170 At the point where the bord left the dip a 'lay-by' was put in. This was a double road about two chains long, one side of which received the full trucks as they were run out from the mine, and the other took the empties coming in from the surface. **1963** PEARSON *Coal Flat* 28 The four of them walked along the tunnel, past the main lay-by where another trucker was sending off the last boxes. **1980** THOMPSON *All My Lives* 40 Two shifts a day she [*sc.* the mine-horse] would drag upwards of 200 half-tonne boxes, six at a time, into the lay-by, where Frank..would jig them down to the next level.

layby, *n.*[2] [AND *n.* 1926: *v.* 1969.] The reservation of an intended retail purchase by paying a deposit to 'lay it by' against later full payment and collection.
   1943 BENNETT *English in NZ* in *Amer. Speech* XVIII. 95 A systems of hire-purchase called the 'Lay-by' has resulted in the verb 'layby', pronounced and written as one word. **1955** *BJ Cameron Collection* (TS July) lay-by (n) A method of buying articles where by a deposit is paid and the article put aside for handing over if the balance of the price is paid within a limited time. **1966** TURNER *Eng. Lang. Austral. & NZ* 172 Goods may be bought on a *layby* system. **1986** WATSON *Address to a King* 63 I can remember putting one [skirt] on layby and paying it off over the weeks.
   Hence **layby** *v. trans.* and *intr.*
   1943 [see quot. above]. **1986** *Sunday Star* (Auckland) 13 July D14 [Heading] Layby Now. We all want to beat GST, but with money invested we all want to wait until September 30... By paying a deposit now, we will set up your boat motor, dinghy, etc, for delivery on or near September 30. **1992** *Metro* (Auckland) June 110 We went and lay-byed a fridge-freezer and a Gentle Annie automatic washing machine.

lay on, *v.* [Cf. Partridge: *obs.* Austral. colloq. ca. 1860.] In the phr. **to lay** (one) **on to** (something), to put somebody on to, or in the way of (an advantage, etc.).
   1862 WEKEY *Otago As It Is* 51 Unreasonable demands were made by some [Dunstan gold-seekers] to *lay them on* to some spot where they could *make tucker*. **1863** WALKER *Jrnl. & Lett.* (ATLTS) 4 Jan. We were talking to a man..who says he knows of a good creek for gold... He talks about packing stores over there and wintering in it and has offered to lay us on. **1891** COTTLE *Frank Melton's Luck* 25 The..friends..were always 'laying him on' to these good things. **1943** HISLOP *Pure Gold* 32 I am feeling pretty crook today, Jimmy, and I am going to get a tooth out. Can you lay me on to a good dentist? **1992** LATHAM *Golden Reefs* 105 Further prospecting revealed gold-bearing stone and the happy discoverers 'scattered themselves to hunt up old mates and, as the saying is, 'lay them on'.
   Hence **lay-on** *n.*, ?advantageous information or share; ?a stake-out.
   1872 *Inangahua Herald* 7 Feb. in Latham *Golden Reefs* (1992) 127 Rumour was afloat that a number of gentlemen..of a speculative turn of mind were expected to arrive, of course, to get a lay-on [1992 *Note*] a stake-out.

lay-up. A play in a game of marbles wherein one's taw may be brought up close to the target marble.
   1953 SUTTON-SMITH *Unorganized Games NZ Primary School Children* (VUWTS) II. 769 Action terms related to the movements of the marbles are, Throughs and No Throughs, Tracks and Clears, Stops and Rolls, Lay-Up, Manyies, Kiss. **1982** SUTTON-SMITH *Hist. Children's Play* 269 Here are some [marble] terms from Taranaki around 1880-90: firsts, lay-up, stakes, tips, sticking-taw, nothings.

lazy stick. A test of comparative strength, often a bar-room contest, in which two competitors sit facing each other on the floor with knees drawn up and each, firmly grasping a stick or broom handle placed between them horizontally at right-angles to them, at a given signal try to draw or drag the opponent off the floor out of the sitting position. See also SINGLE STICK.
   1937 AYSON *Thomas* 166 He used to enter into competition with other heavyweights in the district pulling at the 'lazy stick'. **1953** SUTTON-SMITH *Unorganized Games NZ Primary School Children* (VUWTS) II. 744 The athletic games of strength include Bull in the Ring, Buck Jumping, Cock-Fighting, Honey Pots, Heave-Ho..and Lazy Stick. **1959** HOBBS *Wild West Coast* 92 In his young days Beban had excelled at lazystick. A good stout piece of wood—the handle of a long-handled shovel will do—is grasped by the two opponents who sit down facing each other, soles of their boots pressed together and the lazystick between them. **1959** DAVIN *No Remittance* 110 So the next thing he was he'd got Mark Hogan into an argument about strength and then they were hard at it with the lazy-stick on the floor. **1962** EVANS *Waikaka Saga* 163 The lazy stick was also another event contested [at Waikaka] but little is heard of it now... How many broom handles they broke or crowbars they bent pulling the lazy-stick does not bear mention. **1979** CRUMPTON *Spencer* 38 Charlie's the best lazy stick puller in the [Hokitika] district, but this young bloke looks good and he's keeping off the drink.... Bets were quickly settled... One of the barmen produced a broomstick and..said, 'Are you ready? Hold it... [*sic*] take the strain... [*sic*] right?'

lead /liːd/, *n.*[1] *Farming.* [Spec. use of *lead* a path, alley: see OED *lead n.* 2 c.] A kind of cattle-race.
   1865 CHUDLEIGH *Diary* 11 Apr. (1950) 173 The lead from the yards is circular and uphill just before entering the dip which is like a 60 ft. washing tray. **1878** ELWELL *Boy Colonists* 214 They made a 'lead' in the stockyard for branding the cattle. This was something like a 'race' for branding sheep with a swing gate... It had a wide entrance gradually getting narrower and narrower till it became a lane only just wide enough for one beast at a time to squeeze through... Five or six would be jammed in at one time..the gate at each end being closed..in a few minutes each lot could be branded.

lead /liːd/, *n.*[2] *Farming.* [Spec. use of *lead* the front or leading place: AND 1904.] See quot. 1933.
   1933 *Press* (Christchurch) (Acland Gloss.) 4 Nov. 15 *Lead...* The front part of a mob of sheep. **1960** SCRYMGEOUR *Memories Maoriland* 11 When the bailiffs arrived, with the bleating flock of sheep, she turned the lead, placed herself..between the ford and the sheep.

lead, *v. Farming.* [f. *lead n.*[2]] *intr.* Of a sheep-dog, to run ahead of a mob to keep them steady. Cf. LEAD *n.*[2]
   1934 LILICO *Sheep Dog Memoirs* 27 [The dogs] would head, lead, hunt away, force and back. **1949** HARTLEY *Shepherd's Dogs* 2 The dog 'Trojan'..would head, hunt, lead, back, heel cattle.

leader. [Transf. use of *leader* the front horse of a team: AND 1843.] One of the front two bullocks of a team.
   1860 in Butler *First Year* (1863) vii 105 In the small river Ashburton..we had a little misunderstanding with the bullocks; the leaders..slewed sharply round, and tied themselves into an inextricable knot with the polars [*sic*]. **1874** WILSON *Diary* 13 May in Wierzbicka *Wilson Family* (1973) 190 They yoked up the Bullocks today, after some trouble they got the leaders and two behind them. **1891** CHAMIER *Philosopher Dick* 9 He could [with a whip]..tickle the ear of the leader, or flip a fly from off the rump of a poler. **1905** CHUDLEIGH *Diary* 20 Nov. (1950) 430 My ploughman upset his dray... The leaders got away leaving the shafter on his back. **1933** *Press* (Christchurch) (Acland Gloss.) 4 Nov. 15 *Leaders.*—The two front bullocks of a team, which had to be specially broken in for this work. **1986** OWEN & PERKINS *Speaking for Ourselves* 160 The pair in front were the leaders; they answered commands immediately... At the back of the team were the 'chainers'.

lead-head /'lɛd,hɛd/. A shortened form of **lead-head(ed) nail**, one capped with lead and used to fasten (corrugated) roofing iron in a weatherproof fashion. (Known to Ed. since at least 1940.)
   1994 LASENBY *Dead Man's Head* 158 lead-heads lead-capped nails for fastening iron roofs.

leading dog. [f. *lead n.*[2] and *v.*] *Farming.* A dog sent to the 'lead' or front of a mob to control its speed and stop it breaking or stampeding.
   1897 SCOTT *How I Stole 10,000 Sheep* 9 We had no 'leading' dog. **1933** *Press* (Christchurch) (Acland Gloss.) 4 Nov. 15 *Leading-dog.*—A dog trained to run ahead of a mob of sheep to keep them steady. Sheep drivers always use them; but hill shepherds do not like their dogs to learn to lead, as it is supposed to make them slack in *pulling* sheep. **1960** MASTERS *Back-Country Tales* 219 Once all were in, Athol would give a low whistle; the leading dogs would vanish. **1966** *Encycl. NZ* I. 493 *Leading Dog:* Some 'heading' dogs have a natural aptitude for leading sheep. They are trained to work at the head of a mob of sheep and keep them in check. This is a most useful dog when droving sheep. **1982** *Agric. Gloss.* (MAF) 24 *Leading dog:* Dog used to go in front of a mob to control its speed and stop it breaking or stampeding.

leaf. *Obs.* A one-pound note.
   1964 MORRIESON *Came a Hot Friday* (1981) 87 'I don't want to play on this,' he said 'But if you could trust me for a leaf.'

league: see LAND LEAGUE.

leamington, varr. LAMINGTON.

leaner. [f. *lean* to rest on a surface + -ER.] A small, high table or built-out shelf in a hotel bar, for 'stand-up' drinkers to lean their elbows and rest their glasses on.
   1976 MORRIESON *Pallet on Floor* 16 Sam..was about to drink his beer when he caught sight..of..Joe Voot leaving one of the jug tables known as 'leaners'

and heading for the back door. **1979** *Evening Post* (Wellington) 24 Nov. 12 They had noticed a group of persons against a leaner at the rear of the bar. **1995** *Evening Post* (Wellington) 25 Feb. 14 The drinking [in six o'clock swill days] was done standing up, at long bars and chest-high upright tables known as 'leaners'.

lean-to. [Transf. use of *lean-to* a building whose rafters pitch against another, or against a wall.] A rough or temporary shelter built against a tree, or against posts, etc.; a flat-roofed shack or shanty.
1851 WARD *Journal* 25 Jan. (1951) 116 I found Torlesse camped in a tohe-tohe lean-to with four men. **1859** *Puketoi Station Diary* (Hocken TS) 4 Nov. Posts of lean-to put up. [Nov. 9] lean to put up for shearing. **1880** BERRY *Farming North NZ* 24 Sometimes the first erection is a 'lean-to'—the back part only of that which will one day be a permanent residence. **1889** WAKEFIELD *NZ After Fifty Yrs.* 159 'Cockatoos', or cottage farmers,.. each..living in a humble 'lean-to'. **1891** WILLIAMS & REEVES *In Double Harness* 20 Their lovely leanto's aspect shocked them. **c1926** THE MIXER *Transport Workers' Song Book* 123 I gaze on the moon through the holes in the roof, Which shows that the 'humpie' is not weatherproof..some calls it a 'lean-to', a 'humpie', a 'shack'.

learners' chain: see CHAIN *n.*[1] 1 b.

leary, var. LAIRY.

lease. See also *pastoral lease* (PASTORAL 3).
1. [AND 1897.] A piece of rural land leased for farming.
1987 *National Radio Rural Programme* 18 July Erewhon is part of a 15,000 hectare lease. **1992** *Jrnl. NZ Lit.* 10 53 Wright removed to a Crown Lease in the Baton Valley near Nelson, and constructed a cabin for himself.
2. As **lease in perpetuity**, occas. familiarly **everlasting lease**, a lease of Crown land for 999 years at a fixed rental.
1892 *NZ Statutes* No.37 227 [Land Act] Every lease or transfer of lands made under the perpetual-lease system, or the lease-in-perpetuity system..shall be made in manner provided in section eighty-one. *Ibid.* 244 Lease-in-Perpetuity Lands... No lessee in perpetuity shall be capable of becoming the lessee under more than one lease. **1894** *NZ Official Year-book* 201 In New Zealand, this tendency to State-ownership has taken a more pronounced form than in any other of the Australasian Colonies, and the duration of the leases has become so extended as to warrant the name, frequently given to the system, of 'everlasting leases'... Since all lands held under the Crown 'by lease in perpetuity' are subject to land-tax, the necessity for the periodical revaluations under the perpetual-lease system is done away with. *Ibid.* 202 In addition to the many advantages offered by the 'lease-in-perpetuity' system, the Land Act provides others to meet the wants of different classes. **1924** *Land Act* s2 'Lease in perpetuity' means a lease of land granted under the Land Act, 1892, for a term of nine hundred and ninety-nine years. **1959** SINCLAIR *Hist. NZ* 177 In the place of Rolleston's perpetual lease, which gave Crown tenants a right of purchase, they [McKenzie and Ballance] introduced a 'lease-in-perpetuity', a tenure which carried no right of purchase, but abandoned the periodical revaluations. For a low rental, state tenants were to receive a 999-year lease. **1983** *NZ Valuer* XXV. 369 It is regrettable that there should also exist the 'Lease in Perpetuity'..deriving from the Land Act 1892. Since it is a lease for 999 years it is clearly not in in perpetuity... There is still an expiry date.
3. As **perpetual lease.** *Hist.* **a.** A lease of Crown land with the right of renewal (thus 'perpetual') consequent on residence on and improvement of the land, with rental revaluations at set recurring periods of various duration, and often with right of purchase. See quot. 1898.
1892 [see 2 above]. **1894** *NZ Official Year-book* 202 The features of the system were, originally, the possession of a small farm, not exceeding 50 acres in extent, held under a perpetual lease for terms of thirty years, with recurring valuations at the end of each terms... Residence and improvement of the soil were compulsory. **1898** MORRIS *Austral-English* 347 *Perpetual Lease,* though a misnomer, is a statutory expression in New Zealand. Under the former Land Acts, the grantee of a perpetual lease took a term of thirty years, with a right of renewal at a revalued rent, subject to conditions as to improvement and cultivation, with a right to purchase the freehold after six years' occupation. **1902** *Settler's Handbook NZ* (Lands Dept.) 24 3. Lands held on perpetual lease..120 [holders] 13,008 [acres] 4. Lands held as leaseholds in perpetuity..1,000 [holders] 191,150 [acres] **1905** BAUCKE *White Man Treads* 295 I asked a farthest outback his tenure : 'Well,' and he lingered on the 'well,' 'mine is a perpetual lease.' **1953** *Evening Post* (Wellington) 24 Mar. 3 [Advt] No. 8 Cleremont Terrace... To be sold at our rooms..on Tuesday March 31, At 2.30 pm... Title is Perpetual Lease in 21 year periods from January 1, 1953. **1959** SINCLAIR *Hist. NZ* 161 In 1882 he [*sc.* William Rolleston] introduced legislation to stop the further sale of public lands and to establish a 'perpetual lease' at a low rental, though with periodic revaluations; but the Legislative Council..frustrated his purpose by giving lessees a right of purchase at a cheap rate.
b. Comb. **perpetual-lease system**.
1892 *NZ Official Handbook* 92 The operation of what is called the perpetual-lease system with right of purchase, which became part of the land-law of the colony in 1882, has had the effect of lessening the demand for land under deferred payments. **1894** [see 2 above].
4. As **Glasgow lease** [origin uncertain: the evidence of W.K.S. Christiansen in the article quoted below (1983) rules out connection with Glasgow city; present evidence (including the time lapse) suggests no direct connection with the name of the Rt. Hon. the Earl of *Glasgow*, Governor of New Zealand 1892–97], a form of ground lease which is perpetually renewable, the land tenure being equivalent to freehold thus facilitating the raising of loans.
1958 *NZ Valuer* XVI. 13 The advantages and disadvantages of leasehold tenure to the lessee are detailed in all textbooks on the subject and, confining my remarks to perpetually renewable or 'Glasgow' types of lease concerned with sites only and not buildings which are the ones generally met with in Wellington City, these are, in the main, as follows. **1969** *NZ Valuer* XX. 449 Glasgow leases usually have provision for rental review at set intervals. **1971** *Ibid.* XXI. 338 It is a lease known in New Zealand as the Glasgow lease, that is it is a lease for 21 years and is perpetually renewable. **1983** *Ibid.* XXV. 369 The references quoted indicate a general familiarity among valuers with what a 'Glasgow' lease is understood to be... It is generally recognised the name 'Glasgow' is of New Zealand provenance and most probably used exclusively in New Zealand. **1983** *NZ Law Jrnl.* Nov. 348 (W.K.S. Christiansen) On the evidence available to the writer there is neither any connection between the origin of the lease and the city of Glasgow, nor is what we here generally recognise as a Glasgow type of lease known in Glasgow or elsewhere in Scotland... A Glasgow lease is apparently a lease of land only and not buildings; the term is for 5, 7, 10½, 14, 21 or 22 years; it is renewable in perpetuity; the rent is reviewable at regular intervals; the lessee owns the improvements and is entitled to compensation for them if he does not renew the ground lease. **1992** *Metro* (Auckland) June 14 The board of the trust acknowledges Glasgow leases may no longer be a particularly satisfactory form of land tenure.

leatherjacket. [AND 1770.]
1. Any of various rough-skinned fishes of the fam. Monacanthidae esp. *Parika scaber.* See also CREAMFISH, FILE FISH, KOKIRI *n.*[1], TRIGGERFISH. [*Note*] A variety of scientific and popular names, often confusing to the lay observer, have been applied to 'leatherjackets' of this family.
1777 ANDERSON *Journal* 3 Feb. in Cook *Journals* (1967) 808 The natives now and then brought..a small sort of Mackarel, parrot fish and leather jackets. **1838** POLACK *NZ* I. 323 Many other fish are equally numerous, answering to our *hakes, tench..leather-jackets.* **1872** HUTTON & HECTOR *Fishes NZ* 120 Leather Jacket... This remarkably shaped fish (*Monacanthus convexirostris*) is very common in Wellington Harbour... The Maori name for this fish is Kiriri. **1886** SHERRIN *Handbook Fishes NZ* 58 Leather Jacket (*Monacanthus convexirostris*)... In other countries, members of this genus are called trigger fishes. *Ibid.* 59 The leather-jacket is not known in the Auckland market, but is common enough outside the harbour. **1911** WAITE *Rec. Canterbury Museum* I. 256 *Pseudomonacanthus Scaber*... Rough Leather Jacket... *Pseudomonacanthus convexirostris*... Smooth Leather Jacket. **1921** [see CREAMFISH]. **1938** [see TRIGGERFISH]. **1947** POWELL *Native Animals NZ* 72 Leather-jacket.., Kokiri of the Maoris, is a curious rough-skinned fish with..a trigger-like spine on the back which can be locked into a vertical position at will. This fish resembles brown suede leather except for the fins, which are bright yellow. **1956** GRAHAM *Treasury NZ Fishes* 372 Smooth leather Jacket or Trigger-fish *Allomonacanthus convexirostris* (Gunther). The Smooth Leather Jacket, sometimes known as Spotted Leather Jacket, like the..Rough Leather Jacket, belongs to the Family of Trigger-fishes, so named from the large trigger-like spine on the back. *Ibid.* 374 Rough Leather Jacket, Trigger-fish or File-fish (Kokiri) *Parika scaber*... This interesting fish has a number of other vernacular names, such as File-fish, and all with a bearing on its construction. The name Leather-Jacket is due to the fancied resemblance to a North American lumber jacket, not unlike the dark brown coloured jumpers used by hikers. The word rough is attached to the name Leather Jacket by fishermen, because the scales are furnished with sharp points which make the skin so rough that one's fingers cannot be rubbed freely in a direction from tail to head without losing part of one's skin, hence the name File-fish. **1970** SORENSEN *Nomenclature NZ Fish* 33 Leatherjacket..*Navodon scaber*... Creamfish (fillets); Leatherjacket... Other common names: Triggerfish; Filefish. **1982** BURTON *Two Hundred Yrs. NZ Food* 76 [Title] Leatherjacket. This cheeky little thick-skinned fish, also known as creamfish, triggerfish or *kokiri* in Maori, is widespread around the rocky coast of New Zealand.
2. Occas., esp. in Otago, *Congiopodus leucopaecilus* (fam. Congiopodidae), PIGFISH 2 (2).
1877 *TrNZI* IX. 486 There is another fish, termed the *Agriopus leucopoecilus* (Leather Jacket, or Pigfish), quite different from the fish of that name in the North, which is very palatable..but it is very seldom eaten. **1886** SHERRIN *Handbook Fishes NZ* 59 The leather-jacket is not known in the Auckland market... The fish called by that name in Dunedin (*Agriopus leucopoecilus*) is a different fish altogether, belonging

LEATHERLEAF 443 LEGISLATIVE COUNCIL

to a different family, and though palatable, with white firm flesh.. is seldom eaten. **1892** [see PIGFISH 1]. **1906** *TrNZI* XXXVIII. 545 *Congiopodus leucopoecilus*... The fish is popularly known as 'pig-fish'... It is sometimes called 'leather-jacket', a name which, however, is more correctly applied to [*Parika*] *scaber*, another very common fish in Otago Harbour. **1936** *Handbook for NZ* (ANZAAS) 72 *Cantherines scaber*: and *C. convexirostris*: Leather jackets. **1956** GRAHAM *Treasury NZ Fishes* 351 This fish [Pigfish *Congiopodus leucopaecilus*] is sometimes called Leatherjacket by many fishermen, probably on account of its leathery skin, but this name is misleading as the proper and popular Leather Jacket is a smaller fish.

leatherleaf: see LEATHERWOOD.

leather-plant. [f. the texture of leaf.] COTTON PLANT (*Celmisia* spp.). See also *mountain daisy* (DAISY 2 (7)).

1867 HOOKER *Handbook* 766 Leather-plant. *Celmisia*, various sp. **1868** LINDSAY *Contribs. NZ Bot.* 53 The extreme toughness of the leaf and the presence of this cottony material [on the under surface] have given rise to the popular colonial name applied to the more familiar species [of *Celmisia*],—the 'Leather' or 'Cotton' plant. **1874** *TrNZI* VI. 56 The various species of *Celmisia*, chiefly known by the settlers as cotton-grass or leather-plant, appear well adapted for our purpose. **1898** *TrNZI* XXX. 419 The trig. station lies at the south end of the [Hikurangi] mountain-top... At the foot of these rocks the ground is soft with patches of leather-plant (*Celmisia spectabilis*). **1906** CHEESEMAN *Manual NZ Flora* 310 *C*[*elmisia*] *coriacea*... Cotton-plant; *Leather-plant*. **1961** MARTIN *Flora NZ* 263 What is regarded by many as the finest and noblest species is that sometimes termed the Cotton plant (*C*[*elmisia*] *coriacea*) or Leather Plant, in several of its numerous forms.

leatherwood. Also occas. **leatherleaf**, **leatherwood tree.** Any of various hardy branching tree daisies of fam. Asteraceae with thick leathery leaves, esp. *Olearia colensoi* and occas. *Brachyglottis* (formerly *Senecio*) *eleagnifolia* and *B. rotundifolia*. See also *brown backs* (BROWN *a.* 2 b), MUTTONBIRD SCRUB, TUPARE.

1961 MARTIN *Flora NZ* 210 Another daisy shrub growing in great abundance round the coasts of Stewart Island is that known as the Leatherwood or Muttonbird shrub (*S*[*enecio*] *puffini*), the leaves of which were at one time frequently used as postcards. **1962** SEVERINSON *Hunter Climb High* 21 Above 3000 feet [in the Ruahine Mountains] the black beech becomes much more stunted, giving way to belts of the despised leatherwood scrub. **1970** SEVERINSEN *Hunt Far Mountain* 151 Once I had fought up through the leatherwood out of the chasm the travelling [in Fiordland] was excellent. **1971** *VUWTC'71* 54 Strictly, there has not been a 'leatherwood tree' on the top of Mt. Alpha in living memory, but in the 1930's the alpine shrub zone (consisting principally of Olearia colensoi 'leatherwood trees')..was in the process of being modified by red deer. **1979** WEBSTER *Rua* 188 Paneera..said it could be recognised by a large rock on which grew leatherwood (Olearia Colensoi). **1981** DENNIS *Paparoas Guide* 164 It is frequently made difficult by thick patches of hardy leatherwood and turpentine scrub. **1988** PICKERING *Hills* 40 [Caption] A closely grown mat of leafs from a high alpine shrub known as 'leatherwood' or 'leatherleaf'. Ruahines.

leer, leery: see LAIRY.

left-footer. [Orig. N. Ireland dial. *dig with the left* (or *wrong*) *foot*, to be a (Roman) Catholic; in NZ associated with rugby football as one who kicks, or a kick executed, with the left foot.] A (Roman) Catholic.

1944 FULLARTON *Troop Target* 26 What about the R.C.'s [for the Anzac service]? Oh, Yes. Leave the left-footers behind you as gun-picquets. **1959** SLATTER *Gun in My Hand* 234 For Mick would have been with the left-footers down at the R.C. cathedral. **1983** HENDERSON *Down from Marble Mountain* 170 The left-footers, the R.C.'s and a Jew or two came into college assembly each morning after the Lord's Prayer. **1995** *Metro* (Auckland) June 26 Left-footers, read on. The new Catholic Bishop of Auckland..has a brother Chris.

Hence **to kick with the left foot**, to be a (Roman) Catholic (commonly heard but not found in writing).

c1930 p.c. Tom Dennehy: *kick with the left foot* used on the West Coast and elsewhere, esp. among Catholics. **c1935** p.c. A. Campbell: *kick with the left foot* used in Dunedin c1935. **c1942** p.c. S. Webber (Wellington, 1956) 'He kicks with the left foot.'.

leg, *n.*

1. *Horseracing.* Either of the two races (the **first leg** or **second leg**) on the horses in which a cumulative 'doubles' bet has been placed.

1917 *Free Lance* (Wellington) 21 Dec. 21 The second leg of the double, the Railway, also affords food for reflection. **1941** *Sports Post* (Wellington) 4 Jan. 4 He completed the 'double' by piloting the promoted hack Chief Lord to victory in the New Plymouth Handicap, the second leg. **1959** SLATTER *Gun in My Hand* 146 Did you jokers get on to the big double today? I only got the first leg in but I made a packet on the last race. **1991** *Dominion* (Wellington) 20 Mar. 11 Manhire recites a poem to the packed auditorium in Kuala Lumpur's city hall, wonders at the passionate simultaneous translation by a young Malaysian woman, and notes that the reading 'ends with what must be an impenetrable reference to the second leg at Trentham'.

2. A section of a game of forty-fives, see FORTY-FIVES q.v. (quot. 1979).

3. In the phr. **to have legs on one's belly**, to be a sycophant or crawler; **to talk the leg off an iron pot**, see TALK 3.

1943 BENNETT *English in NZ* in *Amer. Speech* XVIII. 92 'You've got legs on your belly' would be addressed to a sponger or sycophant. **a1974** SYDER & HODGETTS *Austral. & NZ English* (TS) 485 *To have legs on his belly*. Very derogatory. To seek the favour of the boss at the cost of one's self-respect. 'He never supports us if we have an argument with the boss. He's not liked among us, because he's got legs on his belly, that's why.'

leg, *v.*

1. *Shearing. trans.* See quot. 1934.

1934 *Press* (Christchurch) (Acland Gloss.) 20 Jan. 15 *Leg* (3).—To *l*[*eg*] a sheep is to haul him from the pen to the board by his hind leg, a practice much objected to, especially by owners of heavy sheep. **1955** BOWEN *Wool Away* 19 There are several ways of catching sheep:.. Legging the sheep out on the board. The sheep is caught by the hind leg, and, with the other hand on the back of the sheep, it is dragged backwards.

2. *Freezing works. intr.* To skin the leg of an animal; to release the pelt from the legs.

1910 *Awards, etc.* 388 Gut hands may be allowed to learn on the boards, provided they leg for slaughtermen equally and in rotation. **1960** SCRYMGEOUR *Memories Maoriland* 39 The trappers brought on pack-horse their 'catch' [of rabbits] of the previous night, slit down the belly line, freed of inside then legged to hamstring and hock.

Hence **legger** *n.* [OED 1905], one who slits the pelt on the back legs preparatory to skinning an animal; **legging** *vbl. n.*, see quot.; also as special Comb. **legging-table**, the area in a freezing works where legging is done.

1949 STRONACH in Woodhouse *Farm & Station Verse* (1950) 188 The **legger** slits as a surgeon does, And the puncher strips the pelt. **1966** *Mate* Aug. 42 Adrian was a legger and a legger's working life practically depended on the sharpness of his knife. **1951** 17 May Feilding Freezing Works terms p.c. Colin Gordon *Legging*: slitting back legs. **1951** *Awards, etc.* 323 [NZ Freezing-Workers Award] In the event of a cut-out on any board and slaughtermen are required to wait ten minutes or more, they shall be paid at the rate of 5s. 4¹/₂d. per hour from the time the last sheep leaves legging-table to go on the chain. **1982** *Dominion* (Wellington) 12 Mar. 11 It was [in 1956] the solo butchers who were given the tougher jobs like legging and pelt punching.

leggie. *Cricket.* [f. *leg*(break + -IE.] A leg break.

1984 *Listener* 10 Mar. 26 Chris Smith asked Billy Ibadulla how to play leg spin. Ibadulla..did what he could, including bowling him some leggies. **1991** *Sunday Star* (Auckland) 17 Nov. B2 [Caption] One-dayers spin leggies out of test contention.

leggings, *n. pl.* Inferior wool from the legs of sheep.

1950 *NZJAg.* Oct. LXXXI. 313 Pick over the lambs' wool. Pick out stained wool, face pieces, leggings, and top-knots, as these wools make the buyer suspicious. **1957** *Ibid.* Nov. XCV. 327 On the question of leggings or leg pads from below the hocks, there is often more discussion than is warranted.

leg-in section. [f. the resemblance of the map view of the driveway and section to a leg and foot, as viewed on a ground-plan.] An urban back-section reached by a narrow driveway.

1964 SUMMERS *Smoke & Fire* 8 This new house, high on its hill [in Dunedin], stood behind the other houses that once had had bigger gardens but had sold their back sections. They called them leg-in sections because they had narrow steep drives running up between the houses to the garages built under the homes, with steps beside the drive for the walkers. **1979** *Otago Daily Times* (Dunedin) 28 Mar. 21 The new [Heinemann's] dictionary..does not contain..leg-in, woolly (as a noun), farmlet.

Legislative Council. [AND 1823.] A council appointed in the Crown Colony period to advise the Governor on matters of administration and policy; later, until the institution was abolished in 1950, applied to the second chamber (the Upper House) of a bi-cameral General Assembly until 1892, having members appointed for life, after 1892, for a 7-year term. Cf. SUICIDE SQUAD.

1840 *Charter for Erecting the Colony of NZ* 16 Nov. in Rutherford *Sel. Documents* (1949) 8 And whereas..it is further enacted, that in case we shall by any letters patent as aforesaid establish any such new colony or colonies as aforesaid, it shall be lawful for us..to authorize any number of persons, not less than seven, including the governor or lieutenant-governor of any such new colony or colonies, to constitute a Legislative Council or Legislative Councils for the same, and that every such Legislative Council shall be composed of such persons as shall from time to time be named or designated by us for that purpose, and shall hold their places therein at our pleasure, and that it shall be lawful for such Legislative Council to make and ordain all such laws and ordinances as may be required

LEG-ROPE

for the peace, order, and good government of any such colony as aforesaid, for which such Legislative Council may be so appointed. **1843** CHAPMAN *NZ Portfolio* 128 The legislative council of New Zealand is composed entirely of men interested in one single settlement, that of Auckland. **1846** [see GENERAL ASSEMBLY a]. **1854** *Nelson Examiner* 6 Sept. in Jackson *NZ Legislative Council* 34 The Legislative Council is acknowledged to have fairly won for itself the appellation of the 'Council of Old Ladies'. **a1856** SEWELL *Journal* (1980) I. 72 Under the 1852 Constitution Act a House of Representatives of thirty-seven members, elected on a broad franchise, and a Legislative Council of sixteen nominated members, were summoned to meet at the seat of government in Auckland by Colonel Wynyard, the senior military officer. **1865** *Richmond-Atkinson Papers* (1960) II. 168 It gives me quite a chilly sensation,—the thought of you taking a seat in that quiet, sleepy, unknown Legislative Council. **1888** BARLOW *Kaipara* 177 A Legislative Council, consisting at present..of a Speaker..and forty-six members, each member being appointed *for life*... [1888 *Note*] The Legislative Council is supposed to correspond with the House of Lords at home, but it is called out here by the irreverent, the Old Man's Refuge. **1898** HOCKEN *Contributions* 140 For the government of the Colony as a whole there were constituted the two Houses which at present exist—the Legislative Council and the House of Representatives, together constituting the General Assembly. The councillors were nominated by the Governor, in this respect resembling the old nominee system. They held their seats for life. **1903** *NZPD* CXXVII. 61 I think it is time we should make the Legislative Council a more useful body or else wipe it out altogether. **1948** LIPSON *Politics of Equality* 360 Such is the record of the New Zealand Legislative Council over the last forty years that..this must be considered one of the most futile and ineffective second chambers in the world. **1950** *NZPD* CCLXXXIX. 282 I say now that it is a policy of the Government to abolish the Legislative Council as we have it today. **1972** JACKSON *NZ Legislative Council* 212 The record of the Legislative Council is not one which is likely to inspire confidence in the role of nominated second chambers, particularly in small states. **1987** MCLINTOCK & WOOD *Upper House in Colonial NZ* 16 The late Legislative Council was the second of that name.. [The Governor in 1841] had a few officials.., an Executive Council..and a Legislative Council, consisting of the same officials together with three hand-picked settlers. **1992** *Dominion* (Wellington) 28 Sept. 8 From the outset our legislative Council was fashioned on the British House of Lords.

Hence **Legislative Councillor**.
1992 [see SUICIDE SQUAD].

leg-rope, *n*. *Farming*.

1. [AND 1849.] A rope used to fasten a back-leg of a bailed cow to prevent it kicking during milking.
1862 BUTLER in Maling *Samuel Butler* (1960) 58 She [*sc.* the cow] was so quiet that we milked her there and then with no leg rope. **1878** ELWELL *Boy Colonists* 235 [The cow] kicked out at Ernest, who was trying to get the leg-rope on. **1952** WILSON *Julien Ware* 6 After placing his pail outside the yard he returned and untied the leg rope that secured the brown Jersey. **1963** DUGGAN *Collected Stories* (1981) 199 Dried off all four tits and let the cow out into the race where, taking the legrope with her, she squittered off wild in the eyes. **1972** *NZ Dairy Exporter* Jan. 39 Those were times of six sets of cups in a walk-through shed; back chains, legropes—those filthy things. **1987** CHRISTIE *Candles & Canvas* 9 He rose, set the bucket aside, untied the leg-rope, and let the cow out.

2. Special Comb. **leg-rope hitch**, an easily-released hitch used to fasten a leg-rope.

1978 SUTHERLAND *Elver* 37 [A cow named] Only moved into the bail and stood quietly while John hooked the holding chain round her backside, and pinned her tail to the bent nail in the wall. Only gave him her leg and John made a leg-rope hitch first time.

leg-rope, *v*.

1. *trans*. To temporarily disable (a beast) by roping its legs. Also *transf.*
1856 ROBERTS in Beattie *Early Runholding* (1947) 43 At Macfarlane's the men saddled fresh horses and rode in some cattle... We had to head rope those requiring branding, and after hauling them up to a corner post, leg-roped and threw them on their side. **1983** HENDERSON *Down from Marble Mountain* 153 I would have defied to the death Correspondence School lessons, even had I been leg-roped.

2. *trans*. **a.** To apply a leg-rope to (a dairy cow) to facilitate milking.
1895 *Ann. Rep. Dept. Agric.* III. 88 When the milker has bailed-up and leg-roped the cow..he should..wash the cow's udder and teats and his hands. **1911** FOSTON *Bell Bird's Lair* 36 Each cow was to be carefully leg-roped. *Ibid*. 37 Ted was shown how to 'leg-rope' a cow and bail up. **1930** GUTHRIE *NZ Memories* 110 They first of all leg-roped her. **1948** FINLAYSON *Tidal Creek* (1979) 28 He drives each cow in her accustomed turn from the yard into the bail, leg-ropes her..and settles himself on a stool to milk. **1969** SARGESON *Joy of Worm* 243 A reluctant dairy-cow, one that persisted in refusing to be bailed-up and leg-roped for the milking. **1986** OWEN & PERKINS *Speaking for Ourselves* 172 I'd been allowed to leg-rope her—I was a bit nervous about the leg-rope thing—and I got a *lovely* froth on the milk. **1991** *More Earlier Days on the Coast* 18 The first cow-shed was a walk-through type, and each cow had to be leg-roped.

Hence **leg-roping** *vbl. n.*, the restraining of a dairy cow's hind leg(s) to facilitate milking.
1912 BAUGHAN *Brown Bread* 142 Much to my surprise, there was no leg-roping, and hardly any bailing-up. **1990** EDWARDS *AWOL* 55 I had enough know-how..to do the baling up and leg roping.

b. *fig*. To tie (someone) into a relationship.
1956 WILSON *Sweet White Wine* 63 'You don't see much of women, Sim, do you?'.. 'You want to start picking them over for years before you leg-rope one of them. They're like any other possession.'

lemmington, var. LAMINGTON.

lemon: see LEMONFISH.

lemonfish. Also *ellipt*. **lemon** (see quot. 1970). A trade-name for shark flesh (usu. spotted dogfish, *Mustelus lenticulatus*) used as food, esp. in fish and chips; but also occas. used for other unfavoured food fish such as hake. Cf. DOGFISH, GUMMY *n*.[3], *gummy shark, school shark* (SHARK 2 (9) and (15)).
[**1921** *NZJST* IV. 118 *Southern Kingfish*. Sold as 'hake' in Wellington and 'lemon-fish' in Auckland. **1957** PARROTT *Sea Angler's Fishes* 155 It [*sc*. Southern Kingfish, *Rexea solandri*] is also known as 'Hake' in Auckland and sometimes sold as 'lemon-fish'. **1964** MORRIESON *Came a Hot Friday* (1981) 34 'Could I have a little lemon to go with with this lemon fish?' said Cyril... 'Don't be sharkastic.' **1970** SORENSEN *Nomenclature NZ Fish* 44 *Smoothhound* (a) Scientific name: *Mustelus antarcticus*... Other common names: Kini; Pioke; Lemons; Lemonfish. **1977** *Dominion* (Wellington) Nov. I. 6 A mercury level seven times the legal limit has been found in a sample of shark destined for Wellington fish shops... The samples would normally have ended up in someone's fish and chip parcel, or would have appeared behind a fish-shop window as 'lemon-fish'. **1986** PAUL *NZ Fishes* 30 Rig *Mustelus lenticulatus*... The flesh is white, firm textured and boneless, suited to most cooking methods; usually sold as lemonfish. **1991** [see DOGFISH 1].

lemon honey. A filling or spread made from lemon, butter and egg, occas. (and elsewhere, usually) called *lemon cheese* or *lemon curd*.
1936 *Cookery Book of the NZ Women's Institutes* 151 *Lemon Honey* Half lb. sugar, grated rind and juice of 2 lemons, 2 ozs butter, 2 eggs. Strain the juice, beat the eggs, put all ingredients into a saucepan and cook gently till thick and smooth. Do not let boil. **1955** *New Home Cookery Book* 153 *Lemon Honey* Half lb. sugar, grated rind and juice of 2 lemons, 2 oz. butter, 2 eggs. **1993** *Dominion* (Wellington) 26 June 15 Lemon honey (or lemon curd) somehow captures the essential 'sunniness' of lemons.

lemon squeezer. *WW1*. [f. the shape.] A peaked and straight-brimmed felt hat formerly worn by New Zealand soldiers and now occas. worn in ceremonial parades.
[*Note*] The lemon-squeezer replaced an earlier wide-brimmed slouch hat with a longitudinal crease, termed (from South African usage) a 'smasher hat': cf. 1921 STEWART *NZ Div*. 64 It may be noted that during this period of training [about August 1916] the Division formally adopted the method of wearing their felt hats with brim horizontal and crown peaked. 1924 AUSTIN *Official Hist. NZ Rifle Brigade* 67 The felt hats, officially known as 'smasher' hats, were still worn with the longitudinal crease in the top [up to the 7th September, 1914, when the peaked arrangement was ordered].
1948 *Southern Cross* (Wellington) 3 May 3 The Lemon Squeezer style..was formerly worn by the Territorials... This type of hat came into being at a Territorial camp held at Takapau in May 1914, when all units wore the slouch hat turned up at the left side... [Colonel Malone said] 'You have a hat that..resembles the peak in your district... You will now carry the badge of Mt. Egmont on your collar and hat and a replica of the peak on your head. **1953** *Truth* 28 Jan. 19 K-Force are disgusted with the changing of the lemon-squeezer hat. The hat is solely New Zealand's own. **1957** *[RSA] Review* May 15 The first photograph is one taken at an annual territorial camp of the 11th Taranaki Rifles Regiment at Hawera about 1912 and shows the C.O...Lieut.-Colonel W.G. Malone wearing the peaked slouch hat with the four dents in it. This was our headdress on special occasions... We certainly entered Awapuni Camp wearing the Lemon Squeezer... [Malone] stated at Awapuni that all units of the Wellington Infantry Regiment were to wear their slouch hats after the style of his prior regiment. **1959** SLATTER *Gun in My Hand* 48 'You get all sorts,' says the young soldier with the neatly-pressed uniform and the level brim on his lemon-squeezer. **1965** CAMERON *NZ* 1 In the more opulent..towns, the [war] monument is frequently a warlike, pensive, or courageous figure in the uniform of the World War of 1914–18, with a characteristic 'lemon-squeezer' hat. **1977** *Dominion* (Wellington) 19 July 1 There were lemon squeezers, high ostrich feather busbies..one horse hair wig and peaked hats. **1984** PUGSLEY *Gallipoli* 56 Malone's Wellington Battalion wore their brimmed felt hats with four distinctive dents, later known as the 'Lemon Squeezer'. Malone instituted this headdress in his Territorial Battalion, the 11th Taranaki Rifles, and on his appointment to command the Wellington Battalion of the NZEF made this the headdress in the battalion. In 1916 this was adopted by the New Zealand Division. It is still worn in the NZ Army on ceremonial occasions. **1991** *Evening Post* (Wellington) 13 May 6 At one [Anzac Day]

parade I attended there was an Australian representative in true Australian gear—on the heads of all the fine young New Zealanders there was not one lemon squeezer.

lemon-tree borer. *Oemona hirta* (fam. Cerambycidae), a native long-horn beetle, a pest of orchard trees.

1885 AJHR H-26 13 He has observed the beetle [*Aemona* sp.] for several years in connection with the fertilization of the Yucca, but its identity with the lemon-tree borer has not hitherto been suspected. **1896** *Dept. Agric. Fourth Rep.* 157 The Lemon-tree Borer. This is another native insect, a beetle called *Oemona humilis*... In the early days of the colony it used to bore into tea-tree (*Leptospermum*), and it still continues doing so; but of late years, as its original haunts were cleared for cultivation, it has betaken itself to trees that we prize more highly. **1925** MILLER *Forest & Timber Insects: Forest Service Bull.* No.2 48 The Lemon Tree Borer... This longhorn breeds normally in several living native trees, such as red-teatree and wineberry, but frequently attacks poplar, Chatham Islands akeake. **1965** MANSON *Nature in NZ* 29 The lemon tree borer varies considerably in size, some specimens being only half an inch long, while others may measure more than one inch. **1971** SHARELL *NZ Insects* 101 Another longicorn beetle, narrow-bodied, and whose length varies from 17 to 25mm., is the common lemon-tree borer. **1982** CHAPMAN & PENMAN *Garden Pest Book* 36 [Caption] Lemon tree borer damage. The branch has been spilt to reveal the tunnel and exit hole. **1986** ANDREWS *Southern Ark* 40 New Zealand Insects collected on Cook's Voyages..Lemon Tree Borer.

lemonwood. [f. the lemon-like fragrance of the crushed leaves.] TARATA 1.

1889 FEATON *Art Album NZ Flora* 35 The 'Tarata'... is known to the settlers in some parts as 'Lemon Wood'. **1898** MORRIS *Austral-English* 267 Lemon-wood, n. one of the names given by settlers to the New Zealand tree called by Maoris Tarata.., or Mapau. **1907** [see TARATA 1]. **1942** ANDERSEN *Maori Place Names* 287 The tarata was sometimes called lemon-wood because of the fragrance of the crushed young leaves. **1987** EVANS *NZ in Flower* 58 Its English common name, 'lemonwood', alludes to the lemon-like smell emitted by its leaves when crushed or bruised. **1991** ELDRED-GRIGG *Shining City* 75 Holding Mummy's hand, walking along the lemonwood hedges of Cirencester Terrace, I felt confused.

lepto. Abbrev. of *leptospirosis*. See quot. 1981.

1968 *Straight Furrow* 21 Feb. 3 No 'Lepto' Vaccine. Vaccine for humans against leptospirosis is now unobtainable in New Zealand. **1981** 2YA Wellington radio programme 31 Jan. Lepto—a flu-like disease recently associated with milking cows—a growing concern among farmers and families for increased production. **1984** *Marlborough Express* (Blenheim) 20 Jan. 22 Lepto prevention in farmer's hands

lettuce. With a modifier: **acrid lettuce**, *Lactuca virosa* (fam. Asteraceae), an introduced annual or biennial herb naturalized in both the North and South Islands; **miner's lettuce**, *Claytonia perfoliata* (fam. Portulacaceae), an introduced annual herb naturalized in the Wellington region and parts of the South Island.

1969 *Standard Common Names Weeds* 44 Lettuce, acrid *Lactuca virosa*... Lettuce, miner's *Montia perfoliata* (Willd.) Howell. **1985** PARHAM & HEALY *Common Weeds NZ* 66 Miner's lettuce *Claytonia perfoliata*..Gardens, sandy waste land.

Lib-Lab. *Hist.* [Spec. use of *Lib-lab* f. *lib*(eral + *lab*(our, in Britain applied to British Liberal-Labour party alliance of c1915–22.] A shortened and often familiar form of *Liberal and Labour Federation*, set up in the 1890s by Seddon to forestall the establishment of a Labour Party in New Zealand; also previously applied to Liberal members of Parliament having 'labour' sympathies.

1910 *Truth* 26 Mar. 4 His position..has no doubt convinced him that a bad second to..the chairman of the Lib-Lab Federation, does not indicate a successful result to a mayoral campaign. **1911** *Maoriland Worker* 20 Oct. 17 I want to belong to something that has grit and can fight boldly for its rights, not a Lab-Lib., Lib-Lab., half-and-half concern that allows it self to be tied up bound hand and foot by the employers' C. and A. Act. **1947** BELSHAW *NZ* 92 Ballance's leadership of the 'Lib-Labs', as the party was popularly known, until his death in 1893. **1959** SINCLAIR *Hist. NZ* 197 It [the United Labour Party] comprised a group of Trades and Labour Council officials and ex-'Lib-Labs' (Liberal-Labour supporters). *Ibid.* 303 Lib-Lab. Member of Liberal-Labour Federation, 1899 (A term also used in England).

Hence **Lib-Labism**, Liberal-Labour sympathies.

1911 *Maoriland Worker* 30 Oct. 17 As to Mack's platform, it is a nauseous mixture of Lib.-Labism and Cold Tea.

licence.

1. See DEPASTURAGE LICENCE.

2. [AND 1851.] A gold-licence or permit to take gold, superseded by the MINER'S RIGHT.

1852 WYNYARD *Lieut.-Gov. Proclamation* 10 Nov. in Swainson *Auckland* (1853) 156 Now, *I*, the Lieutenant-Governor of the Province of New Ulster, *do hereby proclaim and declare* that measures are now being taken with a view to that object, and that, as soon as the necessary arrangements shall be completed, Licenses to work the said Gold Field will be granted by the Government on payment of a reasonable Fee.

licensed interpreter. One trained and licensed to translate spoken and written Maori into English (and vice-versa), esp. in respect of official or legal documents and occasions.

[**1900** *NZ Statutes* No.6 13 [Native Interpreters Classification Act] The Governor is hereby empowered to classify as interpreters of the first or second grade all persons licensed.] **1909** *NZ Statutes* No.15 256 [Native Land Act] Every such licensed Interpreter shall, in accordance with the terms of his license, be either an Interpreter of the first grade or an Interpreter of the second grade. **c1910** MACDONALD *Reminiscences* (VUWTS) 39 I have been..in intimate contact..with Maoris, and I have for many years been a licensed Interpreter. **1958** *Statutory Regulations* 22/98 Every Interpreter who signs any document in his official capacity shall add after his signature the words 'Licensed Interpreter'. **1984** BOYD *City of the Plains* 10 Storekeepers and licensed interpreters were willing to work for Stuart, Tanner and other Europeans for a commission.

licensing, *ppl. a.* As elsewhere used frequently in special collocations with specific reference to controlling the sale of alcoholic liquor, as in *licensing committee, licensing district, licensing poll.* For **licensing trust**, see TRUST 1.

lichen moth: see MOTH 5.

lick, *n.*[1]

1. [f. Brit. dial. and US *lick* a spurt at racing, a short brisk run: see OED *lick n.* 6.] As **full lick**, at full speed.

1948 BALLANTYNE *Cunninghams* (1963) 203 Clive ran..full lick into the sea.

2. [AND 1915.] In the phr. **to go for the lick of one's life**, to depart quickly, run off at top speed; to work at a forced pace.

1944 FULLARTON *Troop Target* 46 'Go for the lick of your life down the lane', commanded Rangi. **1946** SARGESON *That Summer* 84 With all of us going for the lick of our lives, there's only be time for a wisecrack now and then.

3. As **licks**, a large amount, esp. in the phr. **(to go in for) big licks**, to proceed in an ambitious or vigorous way, to 'go great guns'. (The connection with 1 and 2 above is not clear.)

1865 *Dunedin Punch* 30 Sept. 128 [He] went in for bigger licks. **1960** CROSS *Backward Sex* 8 There were licks of flat country.

lick, *n.*[2] *Farming.* [f. *lick* a mineral deposit (orig. natural) licked by stock; also (often in a slightly different sense) N. Amer., Austral.: see OED *lick n.* 2 b.] Also as **salt-lick**, a block of mineral dietary supplement, often formerly of rock salt, placed in the paddock for the animals to lick, or in a granular form in, for example, a drum with a rotating ball that the animals lick. See also *cattle-lick* (CATTLE 3).

1915 MACDONALD *NZ Sheepfarming* 120 [Sheep] should..be given a regular supply of salt or a lick. *Ibid.* 121 A salt lick, consisting of 40lb. Liverpool salt, 1lb. sulphated iron, is useful. *Ibid.* 122 Several licks are recommended as being effective for worms. Thirty parts of Liverpool salt, 3 parts lime, 3 parts flowers of sulphur, and 1 part powdered bluestone, is good. **1920** POWDRELL *Dairy Farming* 38 A lick of rock-salt should be provided. **1928** STAPLEDON *Tour Austral. & NZ* 84 It is the belief of the animal nutritionists that extreme mineral deficiencies may be made good by providing 'licks' containing the ingredients missing. **1936** BELSHAW et al. *Agric. Organiz. NZ* 82 'Bush sickness' is now combated entirely successfully by giving the animals a lick of limonite (hydrated oxide of iron) ground to the finest powder and mixed with salt. **1938** *NZJST* XX. 192A The use of cobaltized salt-lick kept ewes healthy for two breeding-seasons. **1948** FINLAYSON *Tidal Creek* (1979) 135 Perhaps the cows need a bit of lick, Jake. See how they're chewing sticks and other trash lately. **1951** LEVY *Grasslands NZ* (1970) 336 It has always been a source of wonderment to me that specialists in animal nutrition frown on proprietary mineral licks. **1982** *Agric. Gloss.* (MAF) 5 A lick is a block of material containing minerals or dietary supplement that is placed in the paddock for the animals to lick. It may be in the form of a drum with a rotating ball that the animals lick. **1987** GEE *Prowlers* 105 Already I'd set up an experiment to control bush sickness in sheep, using controlled groups of hoggets and different licks and drenches.

Lieutenant-Governor: see GOVERNOR 2.

life. *Whaling.* [f. *life* life-spot, vital point: found elsewhere but recorded earliest on the NZ coast: see OED 3 e.] Usu. as **the life**, the vital spot (of a whale).

1838 POLACK *NZ* II. 421 Whales have been killed at the first blow, when successfully struck under the fin, termed the life. **1845** WAKEFIELD *Adventure NZ* I. 328 The lance flies a good foot into the spot below where the 'life' is said to be.

lift. *Farming.* [Used elsewhere, esp. in sheep-dog trialling: cf. OED 5 i.] The action of a heading dog in moving sheep towards the shepherd from a standing position after heading and stopping a mob or group.

1949 HARTLEY *Shepherd's Dogs* 20 A nice steady 'lift' with the huntaway standing head-on to his sheep. **1971** NEWTON *Ten Thousand Dogs* 168 When a dog has completed his head his next job is quietly to start them on the 'pull'. This, the first movement in the pull, is known as the lift. To pull is to bring the sheep back to the man. **1982** *Agric. Gloss.* (MAF) 25 *Lift:* Action of a dog to move sheep from a standing position.

Hence **lift** *v. trans.* and *intr.*, of a sheep-dog, to move (sheep) from a standing position.

1949 HARTLEY *Shepherd's Dogs* 3 The system..gives the trainer greater command where there is likelihood of the dog 'setting' sheep and failing to lift or pull. *Ibid.* 33 Much will depend upon the manner in which the sheep are lifted... Allow the dog to stand a few moments to familiarize the sheep with his presence before being brought on to lift. **1966** [see HEAD *n.*¹ 3 b].

lifter. *Quarrying.* An explosive charge to break up and 'lift' material into a convenient position.

1965 *Evening Post* (Wellington) 17 Feb. 18 Seven shots were laid—four lifters and three easers—and 150 lb. of gelignite was used. **1978** MCARA *Gold Mining Waihi* 326 *Lifters*: The bottom holes of a round, drilled close to the floor and pointing slightly downwards. Lifters were timed to fire last and threw the heap of rock up into a convenient pile.

lifting the bones: see HAHUNGA.

light bush: see BUSH A 1 c.

lighthouse. *Hist.* A sly-grogger (see quot. 1910).

1908 *Truth* 8 Aug. 1 The 'lighthouse' so familiar in prohibited districts is becoming quite common in Christchurch. **1910** *Ibid.* 15 Jan. 5 The illicit dealer in shypoo and chain-lightning sets himself up as a 'light-house'... The 'light-house', in short, is an individual who carries round a bottle with him and personally canvasses customers. *Ibid.* 19 Mar. 6 Arrested as a 'lighthouse', or moveable pub, for overnight beer-chewers seeking a hair of the dog, he was also set down as an idle and disorderly person.

light-mantled sooty albatross: see ALBATROSS.

lightning-rod. *Obs.* [f. mainly US *lightning* low quality spirits: see OED 2 a.] Adulterated, often illicit, spirits. Cf. CHAIN LIGHTNING, FORTY-ROD.

1916 THORNTON *Wowser* 26 Bill had had some lightning-rod last night. [1916 *Note*] Adulterated spirits.

light-wood. [Poss. because it springs up in the light, that is, when heavy bush is cleared: AND *Acacia* sp., 1803.] WINEBERRY 1.

1899 *TrNZI* XXXI. 475 The makomako, or settlers' '*light-wood*', springs up over the clearings on the Mount Egmont slope.

lignum vitae. *Obs.* [Spec. use of *lignum vitae* a tree having very hard wood: AND 1803.] A tree yielding hard, heavy wood, usu. *Dodonaea viscosa* (AKEAKE), or *Metrosideros* spp. (RATA I, also IRONWOOD a).

[**1773** WALES *Journal* 10 May in Cook *Journals* (1961) II. 785 One in particular whose wood is almost as hard as Lignum Vitae and as beautiful as Cedar. **1807** SAVAGE *Some Acc. of NZ* 8 Their weapons of war prove the existence of a hard wood somewhat similar to lignum vitae growing in this country.] **1835** YATE *NZ* (1970) 47 Aki—called the *Lignum vitae* of New Zealand, from its hardness, weight, and colour: is useless for all common purposes, and is very difficult to work. **1840** *NZ Jrnl.* I. 139 The Aki, called, though without much reason, except from its hardness, the *lignum vitae* of New Zealand, except from its hardness, is fit only for small ornamental work. **1848** WAKEFIELD *Handbook NZ* 143 Ake-ake... This is a variety of the Rata. It is often called the *Lignum vitae* of New Zealand, and resembles that wood in hardness, weight, and colour. **1869** *TrNZI* I. (rev. edn.) 276 The Ake, or New Zealand Lignum Vitae, (*Dodonaea viscosa*), is a small tree or large shrub. **1889** FEATON *Art Album NZ Flora* 96 The 'Ake-ake'..is abundant in dry woods throughout the Islands... By the settlers it is sometimes called 'Lignum Vitae' on account of its density and weight, being the heaviest of New Zealand woods.

lilac. [Transf. use of *lilac*, a shrub or small tree of *Syringa* spp. (fam. Oleaceae).]

1. As **native (New Zealand) lilac**, the tree *Quintinia serrata* (fam. Escalloniaceae), KUMARAHOU 2, TAWHEOWHEO.

1889 FEATON *Art Album NZ Flora* 131 Quintinia serrata... The 'Native Lilac'... The typical form of this tree is confined to the kauri district, about Auckland, where it varies from a shrub with lilac-coloured flowers, to a tree forty feet high. **1889** KIRK *Forest Flora* 255 For the native name [of *Quintinia serrata*] 'kumarahou' I am indebted to..W.L. Williams... The settlers frequently term this plant the 'New Zealand lilac'. **1890** [see KUMARAHOU 2]. **1940** [see TAWHEOWHEO].

2. As **Marlborough** (or **New Zealand**) **lilac**, *Hebe hulkeana* (fam. Scrophulariaceae), a small shrub endemic to the north-eastern South Island and noted for its showy panicles of lilac-coloured flowers.

1910 COCKAYNE *NZ Plants & Their Story* 80 The delightful Veronica Hulkeana, with varnished green leaves, whose masses of delicate lilac flowers have earned for it the name of New Zealand lilac. **1961** MARTIN *Flora NZ* 199 These Marlborough shrubs include..the New Zealand Lilac (*Hebe hulkeana*). **1978** MOORE & IRWIN *Oxford Book NZ Plants* 174 *Hebe hulkeana*. The 'Marlborough lilac' grows on limestone bluffs from the Conway River northwards as a bush half to one metre tall..and flowers range from pinkish lavender to white. **1987** EVANS *NZ in Flower* 74 *Hebe hulkeana* Marlborough lilac.

lilipi /'lɪlɪpi/. *Hist.* Also with much variety of form as **lilipee**, **lilipu**, **lillipe**, **lillip(p)ee**, **lillipy**; **rerepe**, **rerepi**, **riripi** (Maori); shortened form **lipi**. [Poss. from Ma., though *rerepe*, and *rerepi* are only recently recorded (but not in Williams) for recipes using native NZ ingredients (see quots. 1956, 1978, 1982 below); *riripi* is attested early, but is prob. a Ma. adaptation of *lilipi*.] A porridge or gruel made of flour (occas. with sugar added), or of grain boiled; also as **rerepe**, with native ingredients. Cf. DOUGHBOY 1 b, STIRABOUT.

1850 TORLESSE *Papers* (1958) 122 The Poatini [Poutini] (West Coast) natives arrived. Feasted them on Lilipee. **1860** *Taranaki Punch* 5 Dec. 8 They..treat certain not over-respectable [Maori] people with lilipi. **1861** HAAST *Rep. Topogr. Explor. Nelson* 22 I found that [our provisions] would only last us ten days by confining ourselves to a small pot of lillipe (or boiled flour) twice a day. **1874** KENNAWAY *Crusts* 147 The poor children, who lived principally on heavy bread and 'lillippee' (a mixture containing nothing more nor less than paper-hanging paste) cried at intervals. **1880** CRAWFORD *Recoll. of Travel* 99 One old lady..presented us with a dish of lillipee, which is simply flour and water. **1900** *Canterbury Old & New* 116 The fare [of the Maori feast c1885] was to consist of Lipi, dried shark and potatoes. Upon arriving at the Pah I found the 'Lipi' mixed in a canoe. It consisted of flour, sugar, and water. The men were sitting round, helping themselves by means of pannikins, mussel shells, and their hands. **1912** *Free Lance* (Wellington) 13 Apr. 5 One day the native cooks opened the bag of lime, thinking it was flour, and proceeded to mix it with water and sugar, in order to provide 'stirabout' or 'lillipee,' dear to the palate of the Maori. **1915** HAY *Reminisc. Earliest Canterbury* 34 [The Maori] were also [fond] of wheat and sugar boiled together, to which they gave the name of 'Lilipu'. **c1920** BEATTIE *Trad. Lifeways Southern Maori* (1994) 460 She had made a sort of white syrup of flour, sugar and water. The collector asked what this was and she said rerepi. **1948** HENDERSON *Taina* 111 The most important dish..was a kind of gruel made out of flour, sugar, and water, mixed in a canoe, and called *lilipi*. **1956** BOSWELL *Dim Horizons* 129 She made what we called 'lillipy', a corruption of the Maori rerepe, a dish made by boiling the pollen of the raupo in water to a porridge. Mother's 'lillipy' was made by stirring plain flour into boiling milk to a thick porridge, when it was poured out on to a huge meat plate and dotted and dabbed with butter and sugar, with a good sprinkling of nutmeg. It also was a fine lunch on a cold day. **1957** McNEISH *Tavern in the Town* (1984) 156 He ladled his *lipi* from a three-legged pot in the kitchen. **1966** CARKEEK *Kapiti Coast* 52 Hadfield in his 1839 diary mentions eating a meal which included boiled flour. This is probably the same food which became known to the Maoris later as riripi. It consisted of flour and water, with sugar to sweeten, boiled and served up as a kind of porridge. In the early whaling days it was often served up to a whole village community from a canoe set up like a trough from which the villagers scooped their requirements in large bowls or paua shells. Many of the Ngati Raukawa of Otaki have vivid recollections of having eaten riripi in their childhood. **1975** KNIGHT *Pointzfield* 18 We got a 'fiery stick' from some Maoris..who were waiting for a 'Goashore' of 'Riripi' to cool... The mess was in time cool enough, when they all surrounded the great pot, some with pewter spoons,... but most with shells from the beach [at Wellington in the 1850s]. **1982** BURTON *Two Hundred Yrs. NZ Food* 6 A kind of gruel (rerepi) was also made of the [hinau] meal by mixing with water and placing hot stones in the bowl. *Ibid.* 17 Stirabout, otherwise known as lillipee, consisted simply of flour and sugar mixed together with a little boiled water.

lilliput cards. [f. a proprietary name.] Small or miniature playing cards.

c1941 Used freq. at St Patricks College, Silverstream in the 1940s (Ed.). **1984** BEATON *Outside In* 59 Sandy produces some lilliput cards.

lillipy, var. LILIPI.

lily.

1. [An extended or transf. use of *lily* a bulbous plant of the genus *Lilium* for any of various mainly native plants of the lily family, or thought (often fancifully) to resemble members of that family, thus: fam. Liliaceae: *bog, bush, golden (golden star), grass, island, Mabel Island, New Zealand, Poor Knights, renga, rock, sky, swamp, Taranaki*; fam. Boraginaceae: *Chatham (Chatham Island)*; fam. Iridaceae: *Minnie Dean's*; fam. Ranunculaceae: *mountain, Mount Cook, Rockwood, shepherd's, water.* Cf. RENGARENGA 1.

2. With a modifier: **bog, bush, Chatham (Chatham Island), golden (golden star), grass** (occas. **sky**), **island, Mabel Island, Minnie Dean('s), mountain, Mount Cook, New Zealand, Poor Knights, renga** (occas. **Taranaki**), **rock, Rockwood, shepherd's, swamp, water.**

(1) **bog lily**. Any of various robust tufted herbs of *Bulbinella* (formerly *Chrysobactron*) spp. (fam. Liliaceae); *Maori onion* (ONION 2). See also *swamp lily* (17) below.

1933 *Canterbury Mountaineer* 44 The stream banks..were covered with the brilliant yellow tapering flower stems of the bog lily Chrysobactron Hookeri. **1969** *Standard Common Names Weeds* 7 bog lily [=] Maori onion. **1982** WILSON *Stewart Is. Plants* 296 *Bulbinella gibbsii* var. *gibbsii* Bog Lily... Maori onion... Native to: St[ewart Island] (var. *balanifera* occurs in N. and S. [Islands]). **1987** EVANS *NZ in Flower* 99 *Bulbinella hookeri* Maori onion, bog lily.

(2) **bush lily**. [That is a lily-like plant found in the bush.] ASTELIA 1, esp. *A. fragrans, A. grandis*, and *A. nervosa* (fam. Liliaceae). See also *bush-flax* (FLAX 8).

1900 *Canterbury Old & New* 184 The native fuchsia..and the fierce bush-nettle..are conspicuous amongst the undergrowth, together with the bush-lily... Astelia nervosa. **1978** MOORE & IRWIN *Oxford Book NZ Plants* 182 *Astelia fragrans*. Bush lily grows rather like flax in lowland to montane forest from about the latitude of Thames southwards. **1990** WEBB et al. *Flowering Plants NZ* 111 Orange fruits and tufts of sword-like leaves on *Astelia grandis*, one of the bush lilies, that grows in swamps and wet lowland forest.

(3) **Chatham Island (Chatham Islands, Chatham) lily**. *Myosotidium hortensia* (fam. Boraginaceae), a robust native mega-herb with striking foliage and blue flower masses, once common around the coasts of Chatham Islands, now rare in nature but frequently cultivated as a garden plant. See also FORGET-ME-NOT, KOPAKOPA C, KOPUKAPUKA.

1864 MUELLER *Vegetation of the Chatham Islands* 34 One of the most singular and beautiful of the few endemic plants of the Chatham-Islands. Without flowers it resembles more a Funkia than any co-ordinal species, and hence it may be that it passes under the strangely inappropriate name Chatham Islands Lily. **1907** LAING & BLACKWELL *Plants NZ* 348 The plant..is much cultivated in gardens in New Zealand, and is then known as the Chatham Island Lily. **1910** COCKAYNE *NZ Plants & Their Story* 123 The most famous of all the Chatham Island plants is the giant forget-me-not..frequently called by the absurd name of the Chatham Island lily, or, what is worse, Macquarie cabbage! **1940** LAING & BLACKWELL *Plants NZ* 368 *The Chatham Island Lily*... Leaves thick and shining, bright green. Flowers in dense head, 2 in.–5 in. across... azure blue, with purple eye. **1943** MATTHEWS *NZ Garden Dict.* (3edn.) 124 *Chatham Island Lily*—Sometime referred to as the Giant Forget-Me-Not. **1952** RICHARDS *Chatham Is.* 41 The Chatham Island Lily or Giant Forget-me-not, as it is now more suitably called, is a huge plant... Giant Forget-me-not. Ko-puka-puka. **1966** *Encycl. NZ* III. 711 Chatham Islands lily . . kopakopa, kopukapuka . . *Myosotidium hortensia* **1984** *Landfall* 150 177 *The Chatham lily*... [I]t has pink and blue flowers in the the spring. It used to cover the islands. Now it is rare.

(4) **golden (golden star) lily**. *Bulbinella rossii, Maori onion* (ONION 2).

1889 *TrNZI* XXI. 382 Another handsome plant is called golden lily (*Anthericum rossi*) by the sealers, on account of the bright-yellow blossoms. **1930** REISCHEK *Yesterdays in Maoriland* (1933) 273 I noticed..the so-called golden lily (*Anthericum rossi*) grew in patches over a wide area. **1970** golden star lily [see ONION 2].

(5) **grass lily** (occas. **sky lily**). *Herpolirion novae-zelandiae* (fam. Liliaceae), a grass-like swamp plant having narrow leaves and white or pale blue flowers.

1919 COCKAYNE *NZ Plants & Their Story* 91 The grass-lily (*Herpolirion novae-zelandiae*), [is] a summer-green herb with short grass-like leaves an inch or two long, and, for the size of the plant, a rather large bluish flower. *Ibid.* 127 Perhaps the prettiest denizen of these Southland bogs is the pale-blue grass-lily..which, when not in flower, may be mistaken for a grass. **1940** LAING & BLACKWELL *Plants NZ* 111 *Herpolirion novae-zelandiae* (*The Grass-lily*). This little plant is found in elevated swamps in Nelson and Canterbury, on the Taupo plains, and in lowland swamps in Otago and Stewart Island. **1964** DEMPSEY *Little World Stewart Is.* 73 We found a small patch of a tiny white grass-lily. **1973** MARK & ADAMS *Alpine Plants* (1979) 224 *Herpolirion novae-zelandiae*... Grass Lily **1982** WILSON *Stewart Is. Plants* 302 *Herpolirion novae-zelandiae* Sky Lily... Grass lily... Tiny tufts of blue-green, rather stiff, grass-like leaves... Flowers conspicuous..pale to sky blue.

(6) **island lily**. [Named from *Poor Knights* and other offshore islands.] See *Poor Knights lily* (12) below.

1978 MOORE & IRWIN *Oxford Book NZ Plants* 180 *Xeronema callistemon*, island lily, raupo-taranga. A spectacular plant known only on islands of the Poor Knights and Hen and Chickens groups of the eastern coast of north Auckland.

(7) **Mabel Island lily**. *Marlborough*. [Named from an island in Picton harbour.] RENGARENGA.

1919 COCKAYNE *NZ Plants & Their Story* 39 In the north of the North island and the Marlborough Sounds the rock-lily (*Arthropodium cirratum*), called in the latter locality the 'Mabel Island lily'..forms pure colonies. **1948** MARTIN *NZ Nature Study* 145 The roots or underground stems of bracken, Mabel Island lily (rengarenga), cabbage-tree, kingfern. **1969** HARVEY & GODLEY *Botanical Paintings* 68 *Arthropodium cirratum* Renga Lily: Rengarenga... In Picton it is advertised to launch trippers as the 'Mabel Island lily'. **1983** GUNSON *Collins Guide to Seashore* 121 Found on the mainland and offshore islands from Marlborough northwards is the rengarenga, or rock lily..also known as Mabel Island lily.

(8) **Minnie Dean's Lily**. [f. *Minnie* (Williamina) *Dean* (1847–95), a notorious Winton (Southland) baby farmer executed 1895: see quot.] A naturalized plant, montbretia (*Crocosmia* x *crocosmiiflora*) (fam. Iridaceae), often a rampant garden pest.

1965 MCLAGLAN *Stethoscope & Saddlebags* 77 She'd smothered or overdosed with laudanum ever so many infants, and buried them in her garden. Over their graves she planted montbretias, which some Southland people still call 'Minnie Dean's lilies'. **1994** *Sunday Star Times* 22 May A7 A tiny lily called Minnie Dean is greeted with horror whenever its sprays of orange flowers blossom in a flower bed. 'If it comes up in your garden..you rip it out and burn it.' **1996** *Dominion* (Wellington) 8 Mar. 13 As a child in Southland my mother knew montbretias as Minnie Deans because it was said they grew wherever the notorious baby farmer buried her victims.

(9) **mountain lily**. *Ranunculus lyalli* (fam. Ranunculaceae), a tufted herb of alpine and subalpine southern New Zealand, having large glossy leaves and white flowers with a yellow centre. See also *mountain buttercup* (BUTTERCUP 2 (3)); *Mount Cook lily* (10) and *shepherd's lily* (16) below.

1880 *TrNZI* XII. 331 The zone of herbaceous plants ascends to 6000 feet... Prominent..are the numerous species of *Celmisia*..the well-known mountain lily (*Ranunculus lyalli*), and many other species of the same genus. **1888** HETLEY *Native Flowers NZ* II. 6 In the valley we had passed through by the side of the stream, there were numerous plants of Ranunculus Lyalli, or Mountain Lily, as it is called. **1889** [see (16) below]. **1896** HARPER *Pioneer Work* 265 The most beautiful is the now well-known Mountain Lily (*Ranunculus Lyalli*). **1910** GROSSMAN *Heart of Bush* 30 Mountain lilies and daisies and the Alps themselves were too delightful to be resisted. **1921** TANNOCK *Manual of Gardening* 142 The mountain lily, when well grown, is very beautiful, and it thrives in some gardens. **1947** *Reed's Dict. Suppl.* 175 mountain lily: large white buttercup. **1951** HUNT *Confessions* 136 It has in the erroneously called..Mountain Lily..the largest buttercup in the world. **1966** *Encycl. NZ* II. 680 English names of animals and plants are sometimes mistakenly applied... The great buttercup of the alps, *Ranunculus lyalli*, is called the mountain lily. **1984** BRASCH *Collected Poems* 87 Higher than birds climb from their marble forest The mountain lily nests In shade among scrawled rocks and snow-grass plumes.

(10) **Mount Cook lily**. See *mountain lily* (9) above.

1866 HARPER *Lett. from NZ* 15 Oct. (1914) 96 The Mount Cook Lily, with its plate-like leaves. **1883** GREEN *High Alps* 173 Of the smaller plants the great *Ranunculus Lyallii*, or Mount Cook lily as it is called by the colonists, was especially interesting. **1907** LAING & BLACKWELL *Plants NZ* 166 *Ranunculus Lyallii*... The plant is known to colonists as the Mountain, Shepherd's, or Mount Cook Lily. The name is most inappropriate, as the plant is not a lily, but a large white buttercup. However, any large-leaved herbaceous native plant is called by the colonists a lily, especially if it has white flowers. **1970** SEVERINSEN *Hunt Far Mountain* 20 Noteworthy of the Upper Branch [Canterbury] is a profusion of the lovely Mt. Cook Lily. **1981** PINNEY *Early N. Otago Runs* 33 In 1879 he sent down to Campbell at Otekaieke 'a few roots and seeds of the Mount Cook Lily'. **1989** PARKINSON *Travelling Naturalist* 139 The Mount Cook lily, actually a buttercup, is well known and deservedly acclaimed.

(11) *Obs*. **New Zealand lily**. RENGARENGA.

1848 *NZ Jrnl.* VIII. 69 Rengarenga, *Arthropodium cirratum*.—[This] is the New Zealand lily, and is one of its most beautiful flowers, the root is large and fleshy, and is eaten. **1881** *TrNZI* XIII. 30 The thick fleshy roots of the New Zealand lily, rengarenga.., were also formerly eaten. **1904** TREGEAR *Maori Race* 99 The roots of the New Zealand lily (rengarenga..) had to be cooked in the oven before becoming fit for food.

(12) **Poor Knights lily**. [Named from Poor Knights Islands.] *Xeronema callistemon* (fam. Liliaceae), a robust, tufted herb of iris-like habit endemic to Poor Knights Islands and Hen (Taranga) Island off the east coast of North Auckland. See also *island lily* (6) above.

1973 *Dominion* (Wellington) 10 May 5 The [cliff-hanging] plants chosen were the poor knights lily (*Xeronema callistemon*) and ringaringa, also called the New Zealand rock lily. **1982** HOLDEN *Wild Pig* 40 The Poor Knights lily, a flax-like plant which grew in great clumps and had sharp-edged points. **1984** *Evening Post* (Wellington) 4 Feb. 12 The Poor Knights lily is a member of the larger lily order, but the flower spikes look more like a scarlet bottlebrush, with leaves like a bearded iris. **1985** *Forest & Bird* 199 35 The Poor

Knights Lily..was discovered in 1924 by a scientific party visiting the Poor Knights Islands 25 km off the east coast of Northland. **1990** WEBB et al. *Flowering Plants NZ* 125 Poor Knights lily, *Xeronema callistemon* comes from two island groups off the Northland coast and its only close relative grows in New Caledonia.

(13) **renga lily**, occas. locally **Taranaki lily**. RENGARENGA.
1922 *Auckland Weekly News* 2 Mar. 15 The section has one native representative in New Zealand, the very much larger, but otherwise similar, 'Taranaki lily'. **1940** LAING & BLACKWELL *Plants NZ* 104 Usually known as the Rock-lily. ([preferred name] *Renga-lily*). **1969** [see *Mabel Island lily* (7) above]. **1979** NATUSCH *Wild Fare for Wilderness Foragers* 35 And the tubers of the renga lily..are supposedly as edible in wild New Zealand as the onion and garlic bulbs of civilised old Europe.

(14) **rock lily (New Zealand rock lily)**. RENGARENGA; also occas. applied as **New Zealand rock lily** to the *Poor Knights lily* (see (12) above quot 1973).
1907 LAING & BLACKWELL *Plants NZ* 102 [*Arthropodium cirratum*] Usually known as the Rock-lily. **1919** [see (7) above]. **1924** [see RENGARENGA]. **1983** [see (7) above].

(15) **Rockwood lily**. *Obs. Local.* [from Rockwood Station, Canterbury.] See *mountain lily* (9) above.
1868 DILKE *Greater Britain* I. 341 Upon its [*sc.* Lake Misery's] banks there grows a plant, unknown, they say, except at this lonely spot—the Rockwood lily—a bushy plant, with a round, polished concave leaf, and a cup-shaped flower of virgin white. **1882** POTTS *Out in Open* 76 Years ago in one charming spot amongst the Malvern Hills, the *ranunculus Lyallii* [*sic*] or Rockwood lily kept company with our *hypolepis*. **1988** *Press* (Christchurch) 11 Feb. 10 During Victorian times *Ranunculus lyalli*, the Mt Cook or Mountain Buttercup, was known in England as the 'Rockwood Lily'... Rockwood Station, owned by Henry Phillips, was one of the earliest established homesteads... However, the precise connection with Rockwood..has yet to be discovered.

(16) **shepherd's lily**. See *mountain lily* (9) above.
1889 FEATON *Art Album NZ Flora* 6 Ranunculus Lyalli... The 'Shepherds' or 'Mountain Lily'..is indigenous to the Middle Island..at an elevation of 2000 to 3000 feet. **1895** *Pictorial NZ* 242 The Mount Cook, or Shepherds' Lily—no lily at all, but a buttercup. **1906** CHEESEMAN *Manual NZ Flora* 10 [*R. Lyallii*] has received many local names, as the 'mountain lily', 'shepherds lily', 'Mount Cook lily'. **1907** [see (9) above].

(17) **swamp lily**. **a.** *Maori onion* (ONION 2). See also *bog lily* (1) above.
1919 COCKAYNE in McCaskill *Molesworth* (1969) 201 Burning is indefensible..where there is a chance of greatly increasing an unpalatable plant, especially the swamp-lily (*Chrysobactron hookeri*). **1970** [see ONION 2].

b. Any of several lily-like introduced plants of wet places: esp. *Ottelia* sp. and flag-iris.
1969 *Standard Common Names Weeds* 76 *swamp lily Ottelia ovalifolia* (R.Br.) L. C. Rich. **1980** HEALY & EDGAR *Flora NZ* III. 31 [Caption] *Ottelia ovalifolia*, swamp lily. **1984** FRAME *Angel at My Table* 14 The 'flag-stations' which I still ignorantly supposed to be named after the flag-lilies or swamp lilies, dark blue with pale white-blue throats specked with yellow, growing in the many swamps along the line.

(18) **water lily**. *Obs.* See *mountain lily* (9) above.
1867 HOOKER *Handbook* 769 Water-lily, New Zealand. *Ranunculus Lyalli*. **1872** *TrNZI* IV. 254 Conspicuous among the sub-alpine plants are the magnificent *Ranunculi*..the 'water lilies' of the shepherds. **1889** FEATON *Art Album NZ Flora* 6 Ranunculus lyalli... It has been named by the shepherds of Otago the 'Water Lily' on account of its fancied resemblance to that plant.

3. a. Prefixed to the names of plants: **lily-flax**, FLAX 1 a; **lily-palm**, CABBAGE-TREE 1.
1930 REISCHEK *Yesterdays in Maoriland* (1933) 228 Of the cabbage-like plants the most important is the lily-flax (*Phormium tenax*). **1942** ANDERSEN *Maori Place Names* 1 It is known that the ti (cabbage tree or lily palm) was very abundant [in Canterbury].

b. Suffixed to the names of plants, see: *flax-lily* (FLAX 5 c), PALM-LILY.

lily-of-the-valley. In the names of plants with flowers resembling those of the common garden *lily-of-the-valley*: **lily-of-the-valley tree**, HINAU; **lily of the valley vine**, *Salpichroa origanifolia* (fam. Solanaceae), a scrambling herbaceous South American vine having white flowers.
1946 *JPS* LV. 149 *hinau*, a forest tree (Elaeocarpus dentatus), *lily-of-the-valley tree* (because of the appearance of its white flowers). **1969** *Standard Common Names Weeds* 44 lily of the valley vine *Salpichroa origanifolia*. **1988** *Flora NZ* IV. 1236 Lily of the valley vine is an escape from cultivation... It is regarded as a serious weed because of its rampant growth which smothers other plants.

limby. *WW1, WW2.* [f. *limb* + -Y.] A man who has lost a leg.
1918 *Chron. NZEF* 13 Mar. 61 One of our brightest 'Limbies' lately went to town with 15s. in his pocket. **1919** *Great Adventure* (1988) 250 This is in direct contradiction of a promise..that limbies would be accommodated in specially fitted vessels. *Ibid.* 255 We hear that after the next limby boat goes..there will be none until August. **1920** *Quick March* 10 July 17 In connection with the recent meeting of 'limbies' of the Wellington R.S.A., two instances were quoted of tramway officials behaving in such a manner towards men who had lost legs. **1937** PARTRIDGE *Dict. Slang* 484 *limby*. A man that has lost a leg: New Zealanders': in G.W. **1945** HENDERSON *Gunner Inglorious* 75 Ray and I were 'limbies', both having lost the left leg. **1955** *Truth* 22 June 14 [Heading] Limbies' Leaders. **1978** TAYLOR *Twilight Hour* 106 There were eight hundred men on the ship including a number of limbies.

lime-juice. *Obs.* [f. *lime-juice* used as an antiscorbutic on immigrant ships: AND *obs.* 1855.] In references suggesting that newly arrived, thus colonially inexperienced, immigrants could be identified by lingering traces of limejuice.
1881 BATHGATE *Waitaruna* 151 And yet a fellow told me the other day, he could tell at once that I had not been long in the country, or, as he phrased it, 'that I had not got the lime-juice out of me yet;' so it can't be colonial slang that I speak. **1884** TREGEAR *S. Parables* 10 I see that you are a new arrival and if you will kindly stand on one side (for the smell of limejuice is unpleasant) I will tell you. **1889** DAVIDSON *Stories NZ Life* 41 Jim had a mate..who looked with contempt upon my brother as being quite a new chum, and savouring strongly of lime juice.

Limited. [Cf. OED *limited express* or *mail* (*U.S.*), a train carrying a limited number of passengers.] Usu. as **the Limited**, often with modifiers (see quot. 1928), and in full the **Limited Express**, an express train formerly running between Auckland and Wellington; occas. applied to a South Island 'main trunk' train (see quot. 1990). See also MAIN TRUNK 3 a.
[*Note*] At times (e.g. c1940–50) when two express trains were running between Wellington and Auckland the term 'Limited' was popularly confined to that leaving in the early evening, and the term 'Express' to the train leaving in the mid-afternoon.
1924 *Otago Witness* (Dunedin) 2 Dec. 34 The night 'limited' from Wellington can collect passengers from the afternoon Wairarapa train. **1926** *NZ Observer* 22 May 6 According to the Star the country will be bankrupt if the Daylight Limited is kept on. **1928** *Free Lance* (Wellington) 18 July 35 The introduction of the Limited train between Auckland and Wellington made an immediate appeal to the popular imagination... The introduction of a summer running train, which took advantage of the daylight, was also 'limited in its accommodation'... It brought about a desire for more specific titles, so 'Daylight Limited' and 'Night Limited' became the terms commonly used in referring to them. **1947** SMITH *N to Z* 81 The 'Limited' is the train which runs daily between Wellington and Auckland (and vice versa). It leaves Wellington at 7.10 p.m. **1957** FRAME *Owls Do Cry* (1967) 34 The chocolate biscuits were for Aunty Nettie passing through on the Limited. **1964** CAPE *'Taumarunui'* in Reid *Book of NZ* (1964) 223 Well, they took me on as fireman on the Limited Express, And I thought that she'd be jake but now it's just a flaming mess. **1973** WILSON *NZ Jack* 178 I got all packed up and went off on the Limited express from Frankton Junction one night at ten o'clock. **1989** RICHARDS *Pioneer's Life* 43 We finally arrived in Ngaruawahia it was just in time to see the *Limited* roar past on its way to Frankton. **1990** CHURCHMAN & HURST *Railways of NZ* 179 [Caption] In school holidays, the number of cars on the 'South Island Limited' required double heading of JA's.

limmoo, var. RIMU *n.*[2]

limpet. [Spec. use of northern hemisphere *limpet.*]

1. Any of various cap-shaped univalve molluscs.
1777 ANDERSON *Journal* in Cook *Journals* (1967) III. 808 Of other shellfish there are ten or twelve sorts such as periwinkles, wilks, limpets, and some very beautiful sea Ears. **1791** BELL *Journal of Voyage in H.M.S. 'Chatham'* (ATLMS) 51 We never caught any Flat Fish—and the only Shellfish besides small Musells and Limpets were Cray-fish. **1834** McDONNELL *Extracts from Journal* (1979) 15 There are abundance of lobsters..limpets, and cockles. **1840** POLACK *Manners and Customs* I. 202 Among the piscivorous tribes, are those well known in Europe..besides a great variety of testaceous and crustaceous fishes..such as clams..limpets, wilks..mutton-fish, &c.

2. With a modifier forming mainly 'book-names' as: **black-edged, encrusted, fragile, golden, grooved, keyhole, ornate, radiate, siphon (false, large siphon), slit**.

(1) **black-edged limpet**. *Notoacmea pileopsis* (fam. Lottiidae), a dark-bordered species.
1947 POWELL *Native Animals* 26 Black-edged Limpet (*Notoacmea pileopsis*). Lives on exposed rocks towards high tide. **1955** DELL *Native Shells* (1957) 17 Black-edged Limpet... *Notoacmea pileopsis*... It may be recognised by the characteristic dark border inside the shell, and the shape of the central area. **1990** FOORD *NZ Descriptive Animal Dict.* 48 Black-edged Limpet *Notoacmea pileopsis*. A limpet living towards high tide level, 2–3 cm long, mottled greenish-white, the interior with a black margin.

(2) **encrusted limpet**. *Patelloida corticata* (fam. Lottiidae), a small limpet.

1947 Powell *Native Animals* 26 Encrusted Limpet (*Patelloida corticata corallina*). A small flat limpet, more or less star-shaped, which is found at extreme low tide on the open rocky coast. **1955** Dell *Native Shells* (1957) 17 Encrusted Limpet... *Patelloida corticata*... This small limpet lives near low tide mark where its shell is often coated with a living seaweed, which makes it very hard to distinguish from the rock beneath. **1990** Foord *NZ Descriptive Animal Dict.* 136 Encrusted Limpet. *Patelloida corticata*. An abundant intertidal limpet..with strong radial ridges giving the margin a crenulation.

(3) **fragile limpet**. *Atalacmea fragilis* (fam. Lottiidae), having concentric rings on the shell.

1947 Powell *Native Animals* 26 Fragile Limpet (*Atalacmea fragilis*)... It..has a pattern of concentric brown rings on a green ground. **1970** Penniket *NZ Seashells in Colour* 12 Fragile Limpet (*Atalacmea fragilis*)... An extremely thin shell aptly named *fragilis*. It is difficult to collect intact, the thinnest of blades being necessary to remove it without damage. **1983** Gunson *Collins Guide to Seashore* 88 The fragile limpet *Atalacmea fragilis* (15mm) is aptly named, for empty shells are very rare; once the animal has died the extremely thin shell is quickly damaged and broken. **1990** Foord *NZ Descriptive Animal Dict.* 153 Fragile Limpet. *Atalacmea fragilis*. A small, nearly flat limpet with a very thin shell marked with regular concentric strips of olive-brown.

(4) **golden limpet**. *Cellana flava* (fam. Nacellidae), a handsome yellow limpet.

1970 Penniket *NZ Seashells in Colour* 12 Golden Limpet (*Cellana radians flava*)... Certainly our most beautiful limpet, this subspecies lives on limestone rocks..from East Cape to Kaikoura. **1983** Gunson *Collins Guide to Seashore* 88 The golden limpet *C. flava* (50mm)..is a beautiful golden yellow when young, sometimes marked with black radial lines, and growing dull with age. **1990** Foord *NZ Descriptive Animal Dictionary* 167 Golden Limpet. *Cellana flava*. A solid, tall limpet, smooth except for low radial ribs, white to bright orange.

(5) **grooved limpet**. *Tugali elegans* (fam. Fissurellidae), having a shallow groove on the smooth inner side of the shell.

1947 Powell *Native Animals* 24 Grooved Limpet. (*Tugali elegans*). Not a true limpet but another relative of the slit-limpets. **1970** Penniket *NZ Seashells in Colour* 10 Grooved Limpet. (*Tugali elegans*)... The inside edge is finely toothed with small raised lines and at one end it has the shallow groove from which it takes its name. **1983** Gunson *Collins Guide to Seashore* 87 Smaller [than the shield shell] is the grooved limpet *Tugali elegans* (35mm), its shell a finely-ridged white or pale blue and the animal coloured a dull yellow. **1990** Foord *NZ Descr. Animal Dict.* 184 Grooved Limpet. *Tugali elegans*. A large limpet from northern NI.

(6) **keyhole limpet**. *Monodilepas monilifera* (fam. Fissurellidae), having a distinctive 'keyhole' opening at top of shell.

1937 Powell *Shellfish NZ* 30 Allied to *Haliotis* is..the keyhole limpet, *Monodilepas*... *Monodilepas*, a small deep-water shell, has a large opening in the top. **1947** Powell *Native Animals* 24 Key-hole Limpet (*Monodilepas monilifera*). Grows up to ¾ of an inch in diameter and is conspicuous on account of the key-hole shaped opening in the apex of the shell. **1970** Penniket *NZ Seashells in Colour* 10 Keyhole Limpet... As in the slit limpet, the small 'keyhole' in the apex of the shell is used for expulsion of water, from which the animal has extracted its oxygen. **1983** Gunson *Collins Guide to Seashore* 87 Two scarcer shells are the keyhole limpet *Monodilepas monilifera* (20mm) and the slightly larger slit limpet *Emarginula striatula*. **1990** Foord *NZ Descr. Animal Dict.* 213 Key-hole Limpet. *Monodilepas monilifera*. A small gastropod..with numerous radial ribs and concentric ridges, and a very large opening at top of the shell.

(7) **ornate limpet**. *Cellana ornata* (fam. Nacellidae), a handsome, upper–tidal limpet.

1970 Penniket *NZ Seashells in Colour* 12 Ornate Limpet (*Cellana ornata*)... The upper surface has an attractive pattern of raised lines and dots. **1983** Gunson *Collins Guide to Seashore* 88 The slightly smaller ornate limpet *Cellana ornata* (40mm)..actually wears away a depression in the rock to gain a better seal, and will return to the same position after foraging for food on the nearby rocks. **1990** Foord *NZ Descr. Animal Dict.* 293 Ornate Limpet. *Cellana ornata*. A distinctive limpet 3–4 cm long, with about 11 sharp radial ribs and weaker ribs between these, generally brown or black with white dots.

(8) **radiate limpet**. *Cellana radians* (fam. Nacellidae), the common large limpet.

1947 Powell *Native Animals* 26 Radiate Limpet (*Cellana radians*). The common northern limpet. It grows up to two inches in length and has a great variety of colour markings. **1955** Dell *Native Shells* (1957) 17 Radiate Limpet... *Cellana radians*, Maori *Ngakihi*... Several large limpets occur on practically all rocky coasts throughout New Zealand. The Radiate Limpet is the commonest in most places. **1970** Penniket *NZ Seashells in Colour* 12 Radiate Limpet... Young shells have a bold pattern of spots and blotches which tend to disappear with age. **1983** Gunson *Collins Guide to Seashore* 87 Some twenty species and subspecies of limpet live around the coast... The most common is the radiate limpet *Cellana radians* (50mm). **1990** Foord *NZ Descr. Animal Dict.* 329 Radiate Limpet. *Cellana radians*. An extremely valuable limpet, greenish-grey, normally with 20–25 low radial ribs marked in dark brown; 3–4 cm long.

(9) **siphon limpet**. Any of various highly developed air-breathing shellfish of the fam. Siphonariidae which have reverted to the limpet shape for protection, including the **large siphon limpet** *Benhamina obliquata*, and species of *Siphonaria*.

1947 Powell *Animals NZ* 30 Siphon Limpet (*Siphonaria zelandica*)... These false limpets are distinguished by a deep internal groove at one side of the shell which leads to the opening of the lung. **1955** Dell *Native Shells* (1957) 32 Large Siphon Limpet... *Benhamina obliquata*... Siphon limpets may be recognised by a raised groove that runs down one side of the shell... The large siphon limpet lives towards high tide mark where it is found sheltering under ledges and in cracks. **1990** Foord *NZ Descr. Animal Dict.* 377 Siphon Limpets. Inter-tidal air-breathing gastropods resembling limpets but with a groove on one side, inside the shell.

(10) **slit limpet**. Any of various members of fam. Fissurellidae having a characteristic deep slit in shell margin, esp. *Emarginula striatula*.

1937 Powell *Shellfish NZ* 30 Allied to *Haliotis* is the slit limpet, *Emarginula*... Instead of the row of holes along the back, *Emarginula*..has a slit extending some distance in from the posterior margin of the shell. **1970** Penniket *NZ Seashells in Colour* 10 Slit Limpet (*Emarginula striatula*)... A curious little shell widely distributed throughout our waters. **1983** Gunson *Collins Guide to Seashore* 87 Two scarcer shells are the keyhole limpet *Monodilepas monilifera* (20mm) and the slightly larger slit limpet *Emarginula striata*. **1990** Foord *NZ Descr. Animal Dict.* 383 Slit Limpet *Emarginula striatula*. A white or pale green gastropod 1–2cm long, with numerous radial ribs, and with a long, narrow anterior slit.

line, *n.*[1] [A development of *survey line*, one fixed by instrument, marked or cut across country to establish boundaries, the line of roads, etc.: see OED *line n.*[2] 26 e; AND 'line of road', 1828.]

1. a. A cut or otherwise marked survey line or road line used as a bush track; often *ellipt.*, a bush track or road. Cf. *road-line* (ROAD 4).

1841 *NZ Jrnl.* II. 224 Col. Wakefield is also about to direct a line or bridle road (the basis of the future road) to be cut. **1853** *Richmond-Atkinson Papers* (1960) I. 133 There is what we call a *good* bush road to Rata Nui but beyond it there are two miles of bush walking along what is called 'a line'; a line is made by cutting the supple jacks and small shrubs with a bill-hook. **1861** Haast *Rep. Topogr. Explor. Nelson* 13 He conducted us..through the bush, where we found a good blazed line, which brought us..to the open terraced fern flat. **1864** Marshman *Canterbury 1862* 24 As the population spreads, and the country becomes enclosed, and vehicles are confined to the reserved lines of roads, it becomes necessary to form them and lay on metal. There are several trunk lines through the settled districts. **1879** *Auckland Weekly News* 13 Sept. 7 The line is surveyed, and it would be a great convenience to Tauhoa. **1890** Grossman *Angela* 2 This track was known to the neighbourhood as 'Mount's Line'. **1899** Bell *In Shadow of Bush* 1 Roads, as the term is generally understood, were for a time unknown. At first, a pathway through the bush or along the felled road line..and barely passable for a horse; then a formed clay track.

Hence **line-cutter**.

1879 *Auckland Weekly News* 20 Dec. 19 Mr. Triphook and his staff of line-cutters have completed the surveys.

b. A formed road, often extant in modern street or road names (see quot. 1943). Cf. LINESMAN.

1864 *Press* (Christchurch) 22 Sept. in Turner *Eng. Lang. Austral. & NZ* (1966) 194 I mean by the Purau line the road from Akaroa to Purau. **1943** Bennett *English in NZ* in *Amer. Speech* XVIII. 87 In some country districts (the Manawatu, for example) the roads are named *lines*..Richardson's Line, Union Line—presumably from early boundary or surveyors' lines. **1972** in Wisniowski *Tikera* (1877) (trans. Podstolski 1972) 95 At last we stopped in a place where I felt hard ground and wheel-ruts under my feet. 'That's a line,' said Tikera. 'I knew that 'lines' were the guideways cut by European surveyors. I was back in white man's country. *Ibid.* 302 [1972 *Note*] This idiomatic use of 'line' is in the Polish *linia*. In New Zealand it still survives in place names. Country roads are often 'lines' and even in the heart of Lower Hutt City there is a 'White's Line'.

Hence **line** *v.*, to mark out (land) with surveyors' lines.

1976 Brown *Difficult Country* 47 The land at the junction of the Matakitaki and Buller which was not heavily bushed was lined and later surveyed in sections.

2. [A development of *railway line*.] **a.** The Main Trunk Line, esp. in the phr. **down the** (or **up the**) **line**, for travel south or north in New Zealand. Cf. MAIN TRUNK.

1906 Picard *Ups & Downs* 26 No thanks to this party who had been smoodging to a clina up the line instead of slinging the roaring lion his hash. **1964** Davis *Watersiders* 108 Remember me telling you I went up to my uncle's place [near Taihape] but she wasn't a roaring success. Well, after I shot through I headed down the line to Palmerston and got me a job as postie.

b. [Poss. f. Brit. slang *up the line* to prison: see Partridge *line*.] **down the (up the) line**, used as euphemisms for admission to a psychiatric

hospital depending on its position north or south relative to the speaker.
1949 p.c. R. Mason. *up the line* in Porirua Mental Hospital, Wellington only; e.g. He has been up the line. **1963** Adsett *Magpie Sings* 64 Once Mrs Baker had gone away and Mrs Tonkin hinted that she knew where to. It was a place nobody mentioned much and was called 'down the line'. **1984** Frame *Angel at My Table* 15 The train drew into the station. Yes, the loonies were there; everyone looked out at the loonies, known in Oamaru as those who were sent 'down the line', and in Dunedin, 'up the line'.

3. A fence-line.
1973 Wallace *Generation Gap* 224 This is the time to ring-fence the lot [*sc*. bush farm]. It'll be rough cutting the line. Yes..the roughest timber will be left lying across the plurry line.

4. *West Coast. Obs.* [A development of *line* boundary.] In the phr. **over the line**, over the boundary of a no-licence (prohibitionist) licensing district.
1937 Scott *Barbara Prospers* 76 The first hotel 'over the line'.

line, *n.*[2] [AND *line* 5, 1933: a poss. transf. use of *line* a department of activity; see OED *n.*[2] 13 d.] In the phr. **to do a line with (somebody)**, to make up to, to act amorously toward.
1944 Fullarton *Troop Target* 63 He was doing a heavy line with the saddler's daughter. **1947** Gaskell *Big Game* 88 She was trying to do a line with George. **1965** Hilliard *Power of Joy* 266 Pat's with a grouse new girl again. Must be doing a line with her.

line, *n.*[3] [Spec. use of *line* a set of goods for sale: see OED *n.*[2] 30.] **a.** A mob of sheep for sale.
1899 Bell *In Shadow of Bush* 26 Has nobody a line of broken-mouthed ewes that could be palmed off to him as four-tooths. **1933** *Press* (Christchurch) (Acland Gloss.) 4 Nov. 15 *Line.*—A mob of sheep when sold, or offered for sale. 'Will you take the l[*ine*], or a *run off*?' asks the auctioneer, meaning, 'Will you take them all, or part of them?' **1977** Bruce *Life in Hinterland* 47 I could easily have refused to take them..but seeing that I had never refused a line yet, we counted them out and handed them to the drover. **1992** *Dominion* (Wellington) 11 Dec. 9 Two-tooth male sheep topped the sale at Mangaweka..with a line supplied by Mike Valentine fetching from $42.50.

b. A number of bales of the same sort of wool for sale.
1922 Perry *Sheep Farming* 121 The hogget, wether, and wet ewe fleeces are best made into separate lines, provided..at least three bales of each can be made. **1936** Belshaw et al. *Agric. Organiz. NZ* 710 In large clips of 100 bales or more each of these lines would usually be subdivided into two lots. **1950** *NZJAg.* Oct. LXXXI. 313 The broker has a good binning system and can handle most of the oddments. If a line of four bales cannot be made, send the wool in for binning.

linen flax: see flax II.

linesman. [f. line 1 b, a line of road.] One who sees to the upkeep of road surfaces and clears drains and culverts, etc. at road edges; a roadman. See also roadie 1. Cf. surfaceman.
1888 Willis *Geysers & Gazers* 7 When we had cleared one slip away another came into view. I asked the driver why the linesmen had not attended to the matter. **1938** Hyde *Godwits Fly* (1970) 129 The linesmen lived in tents with a board cookhouse.

line-up. [Cf. OED *line-up*, 1973 Glasgow.] A gang-rape, or the queue forming to take part in a gang-rape. (In Austral. usu. termed *queue*.) Cf. gangie.
1970 *Truth* 3 Feb. 39 Murray said she was familiar with the term 'line-up'. Mr Bennetts: So this rape was in fact a line-up? Murray: Yes. It was against my will. You have been a party to line-ups on several occasions? I probably have, but if so I was under the influence of alcohol and I can't remember them. **1971** [see gangie].

liney /'laini/. A marble game in which marbles are shot at targets from behind a line rather than from outside a ring.
1972 Sutton-Smith *Folkgames Children* 174 There were Little Ring, Liney, Follows, Follow the Taw, Holey. **1984** Keith & Main *NZ Yesterdays* 288 [Caption] Marbles became 'in' or 'out' capriciously but someone always knew the rules of the various games—'holey', 'liney' and, seen here, 'ringey'. **1995** *Independent* 8 Dec. 20 Liney was the game the big [Dunedin] boys played when they were intent on quickly taking all the marbles from the little kids. I preferred holey and ringey.

ling. [Transf. use of *ling* a northern hemisphere fish usu. of fam. Gadidae.] *Genypterus blacodes* (fam. Ophidiidae), a large, eel-shaped deepwater fish of commercial importance. See also *Cloudy Bay cod* (cod 2 (4)), hokarari, rari *n.*[2]
1841 Weekes *Journal* 24 Mar. in Rutherford & Skinner *Establish. New Plymouth* (1940) 39 The emigrants have been engaged in fishing over the vessels side [in Cloudy Bay] with a hook and line, catching a number of ling and rockcod. **1855** Drury *Sailing Directions* 67 Fish [met with in Pelorus]. Ling—about four feet long, resembling the European fish of the same name. **1868** Pyke *Province of Otago* 32 Many..varieties of sea-fish are caught round the coasts, such as barracouta, groper, rock-cod, ling. **1877** *TrNZI* IX. 487 Ling has a sickly look about it which keeps people from fancying much; but it is, nevertheless, a most palatable article of food, and, moreover, can be salted down with great ease. **1886** Sherrin *Handbook Fishes NZ* 59 Ling (*Genypterus blacodes*)... This fish is also known as the Cloudy Bay cod, and is exceedingly common in Cook Strait and on other parts of the coast to the southward... It must be remembered that the European ling belongs to quite a different family. **1892** *NZ Official Handbook* 167 Of the edible [pelagic] fishes..only the ling, hake and haddock..are among those of more southern types. **1902** Drummond & Hutton *Nature in NZ* 71 The snapper..and the trevally are essentially northern; while the trumpeter, the red cod, and the ling are just as essentially southern. **c1920** Beattie *Trad. Lifeways Southern Maori* (1994) 392 They went fishing and caught good fish such as moki, trumpeter and groper for their mother, while poor fish such as ling and mako they gave to Maui's mother. **1947** Powell *Native Animals NZ* 72 Ling..Hokarari of the Maoris, grows up to 4 feet in length, with a weight of 30 lbs, and looks just like a giant tadpole. **1956** Graham *Treasury NZ Fishes* 337 The crayfish had been swallowed head first and had apparently caused the death of the Ling through perforation of the stomach wall. **1966** Doogue & Moreland *Sea Anglers' Guide* 285 Ling... Other names: *Genypterus blacodes;* rock ling (Australia); hokarari, hoka... An undesirable by-product of fishing on rocky locations for more desirable species. **1978** *Catch* Nov. 31 Little was known of its biology but it was feared that ling might be long-lived so that present high catch rates would not be sustained. **1980** *Catch* Apr. 11 In the light of greatly improved airfreight services between New Zealand and Japan the marketing of fresh chilled sashimi quality ling may warrant further investigation.

linga, var. linger.

linger /'lɪŋgə/, *n. West Coast whitebaiting.* Also **linga.** [Poss. joc. from *linger* (*longer*) to remain in a place.] A whitebaiter's shelter.
1979 Peat *Cascade on the Run* 33 If stand and gear conform to regulations and established practice, the design of the whitebaiter's shelter does not. It is set up—built would be too lavish a term—on the bank near the stand, a place where a whitebaiter can keep his sandwiches dry. Corrugated iron and the long stumps of the black tree fern are favourite materials in the construction of the 'linga'. (The word comes from 'linga-longa', where a man may linger longer.) **1989** *Dominion Sunday Times* (Wellington) 15 Oct. 13 Like most stand holders Betty Eggeling has a 'linger' where she can linger longer in wet weather. The shelter is a spartan corrugated iron box. Others are more palatial with carpet, wood burning stoves, and battery-powered television.

linnet. *Obs.* [Transf. use of *linnet* for any of several native bush birds resembling the European linnet (fam. Fringillidae) in size, shape, or song.] *brown creeper* (creeper *n.*[1]); or poss. bellbird.
c1835 Boultbee *Journal* (1986) 104 The birds [in West Southland] are not remarkably musical—the linnets are rather so. [1986 *Note*] The linnet, brown creeper (*Finschia novaeseelandiae*), was occasionally called brown linnet in earlier days. **1863** Butler *First Year* ix 137 Our linnet is a little larger than the English, with a clear bell-like voice, as of a blacksmith's hammer on an anvil. Indeed, we might call him the harmonious blacksmith. **1871** Brown Linnet [see creeper *n.*[1]].

lipi, var. lilipi.

lippy. [f. *lip*(stick + -y: AND 1955.] A lipstick.
1993 *Dominion* (Wellington) 26 Mar. 8 Your diarist hauled out the gladrags, dusted down the jewels, bought a new lippy and joined the glitterati.

little. In the names of birds, see: bittern 2 (2), diver, grebe 2 (2), owl 2 (2), penguin 2 (1), shag 2 (10) and (11), tern 2 (6) and (9).

little enemy. *Otago. Hist.* [Prob. f. an adaptation or transf. (joc.) use of (*great*) *Enemy* the Devil: cf. OED *enemy* A 1 b.] The Scottish majority's name for a non-Scottish or non-Presbyterian faction in early Otago politics and society.
1874 Bathgate *Col. Experiences* 31 The few Englishmen who had the hardihood to 'locate' themselves in Otago in those days [c 1853] were united together for purposes of self-defence [against the intolerant 'Cameronian' spirit] and were known as the 'little enemy'. **1879** Barr *Old Identities* 89 Not that there was entire unanimity [at the meeting]. The noisy and always ridiculous 'little enemy' [*sc.* the English minority] was there. **1898** Hocken *Contributions* 119 It was at this time [c 1851], that the smart and appropriate sobriquet of the 'Little Enemy' was affixed to a small but obstructive body of gentlemen in the community, mostly of standing and intelligence, and supporters of Sir George Grey. English and Episcopalian, they were viewed as intruders..and reciprocated by seeing in the special scheme of the settlement and its leaders all that was narrow and intolerant. In a superior way they stood aloof from the rest, and their attitude was one of opposition... No quarter was given, no consideration shown on either side. The advent of the beneficent constitution finally ended these bickerings, and..though the term 'Little Enemy' clung long, it was rather as a memory than a badge. **1978** Locke *The Gaoler* 25 The 'Little Enemy' made use of the first newspaper, the

Otago News, to attack and ridicule Captain Cargill. **1979** in Cutten *Cutten Lett.* 16 Another was the advent of that English faction known as the little Enemy, exacerbated by Grey who persisted in sending down, unasked for, Englishmen to fill administrative posts, at the expense of the finances, religious ideals and aspirations of the Scottish colony.

little goldie: see GOLDIE *n.*¹

little house. [f. Brit. dial., esp. Sc.: SND 1764; AND 1886.] A euphemistic name for a privy, esp. one out doors. (In freq. conversational use; also recorded in a jocular Maori translation, WHARE-ITI.)
    1941 Baker *NZ Slang* 53 *Little house*, a privy [Baker curiously glosses this as underworld slang.] **1955** *BJ Cameron Collection* (TS July) little house (n) A lavatory. (This term is stated to have been obsolete in England since 1850). **1968** *NZ Contemp. Dict. Suppl.* (Collins) 12 *little house n.* privy. **1988** McGill *Dict. Kiwi Slang* 70 *little house, the* toilet.

little red man: see FROG 2 (1).

littlie. [f. *little* + -IE: AND 1965.] An infant; a child.
    1974 *Sunday Times* (Wellington) 3 Feb. 48 Play dough: Littlies will play for hours with moulding dough—like plasticine. **1985** Mitcalfe *Hey Hey Hey* 102 It's the [electronic] game the littlies play. And Jumbo Bug. **1988** *North & South* (Auckland) Sept. 41 Where else are they so big on hypocorisms?.. They're those dinky little words we make up, like these: kiddies (children)..littlies (children).

live, *v.*

1. In various phr. implying bare, frugal, or miserable subsistence. **a. to live on birdseed**, to live frugally.
    1962 Hori *Half-gallon Jar* 72 This coot is about five feet high and very pale. He looks as if he had been living on bird seed or had spent the winter up a burnt gully.
b. live on (occas. **off**) **the smell** (occas. **odour**) **of an oily** (**oil**) **rag**, to live meanly (esp. as regards food), to live (or eat) most frugally; to live on next to nothing,
    1867 Thomson *Rambles with a Philosopher* 133 He himself had lived on the odour of an oiled rag for six weeks. **1889** Davidson *Stories NZ Life* 48 Dennis O'Brien had scrubbed along for many years, a miserable kind of existence... living on the 'smell of an oil rag'. **1898** *NZPD* cv.554 [Gumdiggers] live on the smell of an oil-rag. **1946** Sargeson *That Summer* She got the pension, but people said she saved every penny of it and lived on the smell of an oil rag. **1959** Slatter *Gun in My Hand* 147 Makin more money now. No more livin on the smell of an oily rag. Dirty big roast at the weekend. **1973** Newton *Big Country SI* (1977) 87 They [*sc.* mules] can live on the smell of an oily rag..and are as tough as old boots. **1987** *Dominion* (Wellington) 23 July 9 Our living [in Christchurch in 1940s] was superb. Lashings of fruit and those wonderful vegetables. We lived like kings on the smell of an oily rag. **1991** *Dominion* (Wellington) 5 Nov. 12 In the 95 pages of How to Live off the Smell of an Oily Rag, the Whangarei-based Newmans also pack entertainment and a host of suggestions that would not make a down-at-heel former yuppie too embarrassed. **1992** *North & South* (Auckland) May 33 At mealtimes..they [*sc.* members of a Catholic teaching order] used to pass around an oily rag, taking turns to smell it, and that is what they lived on.

2. In the phr. **to live in a good paddock**, to live well.
    1959 Slatter *Gun in My Hand* 147 You can shove the bully beef. Livin in a good paddock. Never had it better. On the box seat.

lizard.

1. See GECKO *n.*¹, KAKARIKI *n.*², *manuka lizard* (MANUKA 3), MOKOMOKO, SKINK, TUATARA 1.
[*Note*] Most monolingual English-speakers in New Zealand recognize only *tuatara* as a specific common vernacular name for a native reptile; *geckos* and *skinks* are most often referred to in common speech merely as 'lizards'. Dated references to the use of the name *lizard* in or with reference to New Zealand are fully given in the author index of Whitaker & Thomas *NZ Lizards, an annotated bibliography* (Lower Hutt, 1989).
    1777 *Anderson's Jrnl.* Feb. in Cook *Journals* (1967) III. 808 No reptile is found here except two or three sorts of small harmless Lizards. **1815** Kendall *New Zealanders' First Book* 22 Nárrara A lizard or reptile. **c1920** Beattie *Trad. Lifeways Southern Maori* (1994) 187 The tree lizard was described as black, ugly and sluggish and its Maori name was given as mokopapa... In the Otago Museum an old Maori saw the Spotted Lizard (*Lygosoma grande*)... The Green Lizard (*Naultinus elegans*) he called a karara-moko-huruhuru.

2. *fig. Farming.* [See quot. 1913: AND 1897.] A nickname for a shepherd or musterer.
    1913 Carr *Country Work* 33 Shepherds are frequently known as 'Lizards'—the other station hands declare that all the work they do is to crawl over the hills and go to sleep in the sun. **1933** *Press* (Christchurch) (Acland Gloss.) 4 Nov. 15 *Lizard.*—Slang for *musterer*, I suppose because they both crawl over the hills. **1969** Moore *Forest to Farm* 19 The active stock work was carried out by men..there to gain experience and earn money. They were known as 'the lizards' (because they were rock-crawlers I suppose).

llamy, var. LAMMIE.

loaming, *vbl. n. Goldmining.* [f. *loam n.* a kind of soil: AND 1896.] Searching an area for gold by washing.
    1952 Heinz *Prospecting for Gold* 20 Frequently he may find on hill slopes quartz fragments intermingled with soil or clay... the wise man will wash the attached soil and if a tail of gold is obtained proceed to prospect the area systematically. This method is called 'loaming'.

lobster.

1. [Transf. use of *lobster*, a large marine decapod crustacean of the genus *Homarus*: AND 1826.] Applied esp. in early texts to CRAYFISH.
    1769 Cook *Journals* 1 Nov. (1955) I. 189 [Natives] sold us some Lobster Mussels and two Conger ells [*sic*]. **1834** McDonnell *Extracts Jrnl.* (1979) 15 There are abundance of lobsters, crawfish, oysters, prawns, and shrimps.
2. a. As **rock lobster**, now the preferred tradename, comprising two *Jasus* spp. (fam. Palinuridae).
    1969 *Rock Lobster Regs.* 1969/250 1894 The Rock Lobster Regulations 1969... 'Rock lobster' or 'lobster', means any spiny crayfish or packhorse crayfish; and includes the tail or any other part of any such crayfish. **1978** *Catch* Aug. 16 To many Europeans and Americans crayfish (or crawfish) live in freshwater while lobsters all live in the sea. That is why the name of our marine crayfish was changed to rock lobster. **1982** Burton *Two Hundred Yrs. NZ Food* 66 New Zealand crayfish are usually marketed in the United States as 'rock lobster'. **1991** *Dominion* (Wellington) 12 Mar. 6 Rock lobster was the biggest fishery earner after orange roughy.
b. As **packhorse rock lobster**, *Jasus verreauxi. packhorse crayfish* (CRAYFISH 2 (2)).
    1972 *AJHR H-15* 51 Some of the larval stages of the 'packhorse' rock lobster have also been described. **1981** *Catch* Dec. 31 Packhorse or green rock lobsters (*Jasus verreauxi*) occur around mainland New Zealand, the Kermadec Islands and parts of eastern New Zealand. **1991** *Dominion* (Wellington) 12 Mar. 6 The quota for packhorse lobsters, a separate species found mainly in the north, has been confirmed at 22 tonnes.
c. As **red rock lobster**, *Jasus edwardsii*. CRAYFISH 1 a.
    1972 *AJHR H-15* 51 The early life history of the principal species, the red rock lobster, *Jasus edwardsii* has now been worked out. **1983** *Catch* Feb. 12 There has been little research published on the Chathams rock lobster fishery. Only the red rock lobster, *Jasus edwardsii* occurs there. **1986** [see CRAYFISH 1 a].

local.

1. In special Comb. defining various political institutions or options: **local body**, the usual New Zealand term for *Local Authority*, an elected organ of local government; **local government** *hist.*, a specific use of the term formerly applied to Provincial as distinct from Central Government; **local option** [OED 1878], the option given to voters of an electorate or licensing district to decide whether alcoholic liquor should or should not be sold within its boundaries.
    1935 Guthrie *Little Country* 15 'Taxes for this and taxes for that, and borough rates, and nothing in return...' 'Too much borrowing by **local bodies**'. **1842** Heaphy *NZ* 9 ['Bushrangers,'—patrolling Wellington], with fetters in their hands, for the intimidation of the inhabitants, served but to prepare them [the Company settlers] for the still harsher usage they were to meet from **local government**. **1848** Wakefield *Handbook NZ* 75 At his [Fitzroy's] first visit to Cook's Strait, he took advantage of his position to make insulting public attacks on gentlemen who had opposed the Missionary views, and the preceding acts of Local Government. **1851** *Lyttelton Times* 16 Aug. 5 The great event of the week is the unmistakeable demonstration of public feeling on Thursday, in favour of local government for Canterbury. **1904** *Free Lance* (Wellington) 16 Apr. 12 **Local Option** is, and always has been, a help to iniquity. **1944** *NZEF Times* 7 Feb. 4 The decision of the recount in the Invercargill local option issue has been announced. **1959** Sinclair *Hist. NZ* 182 Since it was distinctly possible that Stout might split the Liberal Party over this issue [temperance], Seddon was in 1893 obliged to forestall him by introducing a 'local option'. This gave the voters the right to decide on the continuation or reduction of liquor licences in their electorates; a three-fifths majority could prohibit the sale of liquor altogether.

2. As **local and general**, a name applied to a column or page of mixed news paragraphs formerly in newspapers under a heading 'Local and General (News)'.
    1952 *Landfall* 23 (Pearson 'Fretful Sleepers') 217 'As usual, nothing in it,' he says and reads the Local and General and the sports page.

locate, *v. Obs.*

1. [Spec. use of *locate* to take up one's abode.] *v. intr.* or *reflexive.* [AND 1827.] To establish (oneself) (as a settler).
    1838 Symonds *Notes on Cloudy Bay* 417 Three or four Europeans have lately located there. **1848**

WAKEFIELD *Handbook NZ* 12 At no period of a settler's progress are roads so essential to his convenience..as when he first proceeds to locate himself in the bush. **1860** *Voices from Auckland* 47 Form yourselves into communities to locate in the bush... Don't locate yourself on bad land. **1874** BATHGATE *Col. Experiences* 31 The few Englishmen who had the hardihood to 'locate' themselves in Otago in those days were united together.

Hence **location** *n*. [AND 1813], a (homestead) block of land.
1871 MONEY *Knocking About NZ* 120 The owners refused to sell their 'location'.

2. *v. trans*. To place or settle (a person).
1841 *NZ Gaz. & Spectator* 6 Mar. (Wellington) in Richards *Whaling & Sealing Chatham Is*. (1982) 22 A person calling himself Captain Richards, of the schooner *Cheerful*, has beguiled and smuggled from the [Wellington] beach, four to five young females to carry with him to the Chatham Islands, to locate them..amongst the reckless set who form the members of a whaling gang.

3. *v. trans*. *Hist*. To take up (a mining claim) permanently.
1873 PYKE *Wild Will Enderby* (1889, 1974) I. iv 17 Mr George W. Pratt concluded to *locate* a beach claim.

locey, var. LOCI.

loci. Also **locey**, **lokey**, occas. **loco**. [f. an alteration of *loco* (f. *loco*(motive): cf. OED *loco*.] A small locomotive engine, esp. for hauling logs from the bush on private tram-lines, or trucks on a light-rail system in a mine, freezing works, etc.
[**1854** Richmond *Letters* I. 313 The speed of a bullock approaches that of a locomotive railway.] **c1900** *loci* was the usual name in the Pelorus Valley for the steam-engines of the rail-system used to transport logs from the bush to mill (Ed.). **1908** *Awards, etc.* 339 [Wellington Sawmills Award] [Rates of wages] Tram repairers and layers [£]2 14[s.]0[d.] Engine-drivers for loco. or traction 3 3 0 Ropeman who splices his own ropes 3 0 0. **1923** *Awards, etc.* 112 [Westland Timber Yards and Sawmill Employees] [Rates of wages] Loco.-drivers [£]0 15[s.]0[d.] Traction-engine drivers 0 16 8. **1924** *Otago Witness* (Dunedin) 22 Jan. 72 The timber is taken to the nearest station in trucks drawn by horses or an engine called a 'locey'. **1947** GASKELL *All Part of the Game* (1978) 84 She often saw wisps of smoke rising against the bush... Sometimes she heard a lokey puffing. **1950** loci tracks [see CHAMBER 2]. **1953** REED *Story of Kauri* 194 A tram line or..operated by a locomotive (shortened to 'loco' in bush parlance). **1974** HILLIARD *Maori Woman* 25 Through gaps..she could see the railway yards..locis were hauling rakes of trucks. **1982** *Listener* 14 Aug. 60 [Caption] Bill Oats with his lokey, which provides cheap and reliable transport over boggy ground. The first task was construction of a small 'lokey'... Oats already had a set of wheels suitable for wooden rails, and the engine from an old Ford 100E was at hand. It took 2½ days to build, and with half a 44-gallon drum as a bonnet and a coat of green paint, was soon looking a picture. An old four-wheel railway trolley coupled on behind completed the rolling stock. **1984** BEARDSLEY *Blackball 08* 12 On to the wharf..a lokey with a rake of coal trucks.

lock. Usu. *pl.* Also **lox**. [Spec. use of *locks* used by wool dealers for the lowest class of remnants.] The short fleece-wool which has either fallen between the slats of the wool table or been swept from the shearing board. Cf. PIECE 1.
1856 FITTON *NZ* 234 New Zealand.—Scoured fleece, 1s. 8-1/2d... pieces and locks, 1s. 1d. **1901** *TrNZI* XXXIII. 196 White wool divides, when skirted by the roller at the wool-table, thus: Belly pieces, say, 6d. per pound..fragments or locks, 4d. per pound. **1915** MACDONALD *NZ Sheepfarming* 69 The wool table, about 7ft. x 5ft., is made of battens about 1½in. wide..to permit the locks or second cuts to fall through. **1920** MACDONALD *Austral. & NZ Sheepfarming* 148 The belly wool and the pieces or locks are kept separate from the fleece when rolling it. **1936** BELSHAW et al. *Agric. Organiz. NZ* 710 'Locks' consist mainly of short pieces of wool such as second cuts, sweepings and short wool that falls on to the table during handling. **1950** *NZJAg.* Oct. LXXXI. 310 Boards which fit between cleats on opposite legs of the [wool] table keep the locks from being trampled on. **1973** FERNANDEZ *Tussock Fever* 166 'Lox?' 'Oh, that's floor sweepings.' **1982** *Agric. Gloss*. (MAF) 56 *Locks*: Short wool which has either fallen through the wool table or been swept from the shearing board (also spelt lox).

Hence **locky** *a.*, of the inferior nature of locks.
1955 BOWEN *Wool Away* 142 The wool on the legs and head [of the English Leicester], however, is locky and open, and does not retard shearing, in that it combs very well.

Lockwood. [f. a proprietary name.] A building constructed mainly of pre-cut tongue-and-groove wooden timber, designed to interlock when fitted together. Usu. *attrib*.
1985 McGILL *G'day Country* 82 On a dark wet night a Lockwood home is cheering. **1987** *Evening Post* (Wellington) 12 Dec. 6 The members who came from high-flying private sector jobs are still getting over the shock of Parliament's squalid offices, either in the bowels of the old building or in Siberia, the tacked-on Lockwood annex out the back. **1988** PICKERING *Hills* 66 The big, sanitised Lockwood huts of the national parks have never looked comfortable in their surroundings. **1994** *Dominion* (Wellington) 17 June 7 Construction began in August 1989 and was completed the following year, though only eight Lockwoods were built against the 14 stipulated.

locky: see LOCK.

loco, var. LOCI.

locust.

1. Also **singing locust**. [Transf. use of *locust* for fam. Cicadidae: AND 1834.] A cicada.
[*Note*] Cicadas were unknown to many early settlers who transferred to them known names (e.g. *locust*) or used descriptive names (e.g. SINGER, SCORPION FLY q.v.).
1848 TAYLOR *Leaf Nat. Hist.* 16 Tarakihi, *locust*. Tatarakihi, *locust*. Syn. with Tarakihi. **1855** TAYLOR *Te Ika A Maui* 419 *Cicada Zeal:*—There are four varieties of the *tarakihi* (locust); these lively and noisy insects are only heard in summer. **1855** *Maori Mementos* 188 *Song of the locust and the ant*. **1900** *TrNZI* XXXII. 5 In New Zealand we have a second species [of parasitic fungi] attacking the larva of the singing locust (*cicada*). **1902** DRUMMOND & HUTTON *Nature in NZ* 61 The cicada, which in summer fills the air with chirping, is very common in almost all parts of the colony. Sometimes it is called a locust, though it does not belong to that family. **1909** *TrNZI* XLI. 240 The *kikihi*, or *kihikihi*, or *kikihitara*, is the cicada or singing locust. **1929** MARTIN *NZ Nature Book I* 113 *Cicadas* or *Singers*.—Much the commonest name for the chirping insects one hears on sunny, summer days is that of Cricket or Locust, but as this is quite the wrong name, originating doubtless from the similarity of their chirping songs to those of the true cricket, we refrain from using it. **1968** *NZ Contemp. Dict. Supp*. (Collins) 12 locust *n.* erroneously applied to a cicada.

2. Any of various species of WETA.
1883 DOMETT *Ranolf and Amohia* I. 152 As the great wingless *locust* bare, That scrapes from rotting trees his pithy fare. **1895** *TrNZI* XXVII. 174 Captain Fairchild collected..[on Bounty Island] specimens of one of those wingless locusts called weta by the Maoris—by which name they are known to all New-Zealanders. **1913** *Lore of the Whare-Wananga* 132 Wēta (wingless Locust). **1926** TILLYARD *Insects of Austral. and NZ* 96 The subfamily *Rhaphidophoridae* contains the Cave Locusts, also called Cave Wetas in New Zealand, where they are, much more abundant than in Australia. **1971** MILLER *Common Insects in NZ* 136 Weta are often incorrectly called locusts.

locust-tree. *Obs*. Also **locust**. [Transf. use of *locust-tree*, applied to a number of trees of the legume family Fabaceae, for the native tree *Sophora tetraptera* of the same family.] In occas. use for KOWHAI 1.
1883 DOMETT *Ranolf & Amohia* I. 161 Where feathery *locust-trees* o'earched A little plot... Their yellow-blossomed branches laid In luxury of emerald shade. **1898** [see KOWHAI 1 (a)].

log, *n*.[1] Special Comb. in senses connected with logging or clearing bush: **log-clearing**, a bush-clearing which has not been logged up; **log-hauler**, a stationary engine and winch used to haul logs by a 'rope', a steel logging line, from bush to the skids (cf. HAULER); **log-skids**, see SKID 1; **log stain** *woolgrowing*, discoloration of wool with charcoal from bush burns (see also *bush stain* (BUSH C 3 c)); **log whare**, a bush hut made of logs.
1905 THOMSON *Bush Boys* 26 This was a typical '**log-clearing**,' but the latter term is misleading in regard to such a place. The 'Bush' had indeed been 'felled', and the fire sent through it, burning up the scrub and branches and small wood, but great charred logs and stumps still covered the ground so thickly, lying one across another in all directions, or piled in great heaps, that, at little distances, scarce a patch of bare earth was visible... These 'log-clearings' formed grand places for games of 'hide-and-seek'. **1913** CARR *Country Work* 40 **Log-haulers**, worked from an engine, are used in some mills. Hooking the winding rope on to suitable trees..demands..quickness of judgment. **1930** SMYTH *Wooden Rails* 35 They saw the oil-driven winch, or log-hauler, as it is called. **1948** *Our Own Country* 26 One shop [at Thames] specialized in the manufacture of sawmilling and bush-working machinery, log-haulers in particular. **1983** KING *Whina* 84 He went into the bush and found a job operating a log hauler at Tapuwae. *Ibid.* 85 [Caption] Richard Gilbert working his log hauler. **1923** MALFROY *Small Sawmills* 6 Advantage can be taken of placing the **log-skids** and breakdown bench on a higher level. **1951** *Awards, etc.* 529 [Marlborough Timber-Workers Award] All mills, excluding log-skids, shall be suitably roofed to afford workers protection from wet weather. **1969** MOORE *Forest to Farm* 65 [Caption] Sheep in a new clearing—note the tangle of timber which will cause '**logstain**' in their wool. **1982** *Agric. Gloss*. (MAF) 56 *Log stain*: Discoloration of wool with charcoal from bush burn. Also called bush or charcoal stain. **1905** THOMSON *Bush Boys* 47 Mr. MacLean could see the little **log whare** from the kitchen window. It was a small hut about 20 feet long by 12 feet broad, built of logs roughly fashioned with the axe, and smeared with earth and clay. *Ibid.* 48 Such is the typical log-whare in which the pioneer bush-settler and family..have to spend years of a rough, bush life.

log, *n*.[2] A marijuana cigarette.
1987 COX *Dirty Work* 43 'Best dope right here in my pocket. You smoke?'... The log Bill produced was a fat one. He set it alight, had a quick blow then passed.

log: see LOG OF WOOD.

logging, *vbl. n.*

1. See *logging-up* (LOG UP *v.*).
   1844 *Molesworth* to *House of Commons Committee on NZ Matters* in Wakefield *Handbook NZ* (1848) 177 The expense of clearing was as follows: felling and lopping, logging and burning, at 5*l.* an acre. **c1871** MASTERS *Autobiography* (ATLMS) 50 On fine nights we used to work late, loging [*sic*], that is rolling larger trees together, to burn them out of the way, to get rid of them.

2. Special Comb. **logging-bank**, see quot.; **logging line**, the steel-rope line of a log-hauler; **logging-pan** or **logging-shoe**, a moulded steel plate on which the front of a log to be hauled rests to prevent it digging into the ground.
   1923 MALFROY *Small Sawmills* 39 **Logging-bank**..A raised platform for landing logs with the hauling-rope to facilitate loading same on trucks, &c. **1930** SMYTH *Wooden Rails* 50 A **logging line** could be put in. **1973** WHEELER *Hist. Sheep Stations NI* 34 [Caption] **Logging pan** for dragging logs, bullock tie (or wishbone) used on the yoke, and in front a logging dog that grips the log to prevent it from falling off the logging pan. **1923** MALFROY *Small Sawmills* 15 This **logging-shoe** is made out of 7/16 in. mild steel plate, 4ft. by 3ft. The nose is cut in a circular shape, and the edges are curved up like the bow of a river-boat.

log of wood.

1. Also *ellipt.* **log**. A familiar nickname for the *Ranfurly Shield* (SHIELD 1 a).
   1935 *Free Lance* (Wellington) 11 Sept. 19 [Caption] The captains in last Saturday's Ranfurly Shield match... Between them is the 'log of wood'. **1953** *Evening Post* (Wellington) 3 Aug. 14 [Heading] After Twenty-Two Years... 'Log of Wood' comes back to Wellington. **1963** *Ibid.* 2 Sept. 12 Wellington will field the same team in its first defence of the Ranfurly Shield..as lifted the 'log of wood' from Auckland. **1973** WILSON *NZ Jack* 82 We..won the Ranfurly Shield from Auckland. But Auckland's team might have been weakened..the Saturday we took that Log of Wood off them. **1975** HOWITT *NZ Rugby Greats* 20 The following week they defended the log against Wanganui. **1986** MCMENAMIN *Glory Days* 13 'The log of wood', or simply 'the log', as the shield [*sc.* the Ranfurly Shield] became affectionately known, has provided some of the most glorious chapters in the history of New Zealand rugby.

2. As **log holder**, the provincial rugby union for the time being holding the Ranfurly Shield.
   1974 *Sunday Times* (Wellington) 14 Apr. 19 And the log holders are becoming accustomed to Tayler's cross country course.

log up. *v.*

a. *trans.* Usu. in passive use. In bush-clearing, to pile up (logs) for burning; to clear (ground) by piling up unburnt logs. Also *fig.*
   1883 *Brett's Colonists' Guide* 18 They [*sc.* trees] can be felled and logged up or used for firewood. **1891** WALLACE *Rural Econ. Austral. & NZ* 232 When the [bush] burning is badly done..the rubbish lies thick over the ground and the whole has to be gone over again and 'logged-up'. **1905** THOMSON *Bush Boys* 32 These [big unburned trees] are 'logged up' afterwards, that is rolled together and piled round the stumps, so as to dry thoroughly preparatory to 'firing' them again. **1908** BAUGHAN *Shingle-Short* 84 The Stars are its shining logs; Here, sparse and single, but yonder, as logg'd-up for burning, Close in a cluster of light. **1913** *NZ Geol. SB (NS)* No. 16 27 When the milling-timber has been removed the undergrowth is cut down and..burned... Later the unburned wood is 'logged up' and burnt. **1924** ANTHONY *Follow the Call* (1975) 30 I logged up about 10 acres..and had three blistering, heart-rending days burning it all at once.

b. Also *v. intr.* or *absol.*
   1924 ANTHONY *Follow the Call* (1975) 7 Sam used to hook his horse on to big trees when he was logging up. **1955** WILSON *Land of My Children* 80 He..put in the..morning and evening on his own land, and 'logged up' by the light of his fires half the night. **1977** MULINDER *Pioneer Family* 39 [A. Anderson's Reminiscences of the Wairarapa 1870's] After tea [Dad] was at work logging up and burning to clear the ground.

   Hence **logging-up** *vbl. n.* and *ppl. a.*, piling up logs for burning.
   1860 MORGAN *Journal* 21 Apr. (1963) 18 Finished fencing on Wednesday, and since then have been busy at the occupation of 'logging up'. **1889** *Collinson's Colonial Mag.* I. 1. 26 Logging-up is generally done in the autumn, when there are strong gales of wind blowing. The bush which has been felled in winter, is set fire to, and in a day or two, when the ground is sufficiently cool for walking on, the still-burning logs are rolled together and piled up with rubbish, so that they may be burnt clear away. **1902** *Brett's Colonists' Guide* 21 There is very little logging-up done now-a-days, and with a good burn it is quite unnecessary... Two or three chains around the site should be logged up and burnt. **1951** LEVY *Grasslands NZ* (1970) 250 Following the initial primary forest burn, secondary scrub fires and logging-up burns continue the breaking-in process. **1978** SINCLAIR & HARREX *Looking Back* 102 The commonest method of clearing bush..was simply to burn it off... The subsequent process of 'stumping' and 'logging up' could be prolonged. **1989** RICHARDS *Pioneer's Life* 49 Farm work, scrub cutting, logging up and burning went on as usual.

lokey, var. LOCI.

loll: see LOLLY.

lolly. Also *occas.* **lollie**, and in a familiar short form **loll** (see quots. 1984, 1988). [f. Brit. dial., a shortened form of *lollipop*: see EDD 1.]

1. The usual word in New Zealand for any sweetmeat. Cf. BOILED LOLLY, CONVERSATION (LOLLY), *paper lolly* (PAPER 3 b).
   [**1860** CARGILL *Otago* 18 The importation of lolly-pops (sweeties) is enormous, and a maker of these juvenile joys has commenced the manufacturing of them in Dunedin, and not only sells largely in the settlement, but exports them to other parts of New Zealand.] **1862** HOBHOUSE *Selected Let.* 9 Sept. (1992) 95 'Mrs 'obhouse are you fond of conversation lollies?' was a question with wh [*sic*] she [*sc.* a badly-spoken Nelson servant] mystified me one day. **1864** LUSH *Waikato Jrnls.* 16 Nov. (1982) 34 Tui gave me a lolly and in biting it I broke one of my false *front* teeth. **1879** *Pol. Ballads from Free Lance* 8 [Give him] 'baccy and lollies, and plenty of prog. And prime the old beggar with lashions of grog. **1884** BLAIR *Industries NZ* 16 It does not follow that the taste for lollies in the rising generation is dying out. **1898** 'H.' *Grain of Gold* 4 [A child] would get a pat on the head and a 'lollie'. **1915** *Great Adventure* (1988) 76 They kissed us and handed us lollies and fruit. **1925** MANDER *Allen Adair* (1971) 49 One afternoon a country girl had hailed him from her horse. 'I want some lollies', she called. **1934** LEE *Children of Poor* (1949) 131 'Hullo, Milly.' 'Hullo.' 'Have a lollie?' he had a poke of sweets. **1940** STUDHOLME *Te Waimate* (1954) 138 [The drover] always had lollies (sweets) in his pockets which he gave to any kids who happened along. **1984** 14 F E 144 Wgton Girls C. 22 A Lols **1986** *Wellington Write Price Supermarket* 19 Feb. (Ed.). Checkout woman: Don't forget your lolls. [*sc.* packets of winegums]. **1991** *National Business Review* 27 Sept. 53 Cadburys..worked on designs for two buses, one covered in lollies and the other a total Cadburys chocolate bus.

2. a. Comb. **lolly bag, maker, shop** [AND 1854].
   1906 PICARD *Ups & Downs* 3 [A] pale consumptive comp..who couldn't fight his way out of a **lollie bag**. **1932** BRUCE *Early Days Canterbury* 121 And there was old Hill the **lolly-maker**, whose specialty was bulls-eyes of a minty flavour. **1985** *Islands* 34 157 What is Murdock's occupation?..latrine attendant, caddy, lollymaker, editor, paperboy, bellhop. **1879** *Auckland Weekly News* 19 Apr. 17 The prisoners kept a fruit and **lolly shop** at the top of Shortland-street. **1906** in Lawlor *Old Wellington Days* (1959) 111 July 22... Bought some Bulgarian Rock from Nickel's..lolly shop. **1913** *Truth* 31 May 5 Subsequently, respondent returned to Wellington, and petitioner discovered her in a lolly-shop in Willis-Street. **a1927** ANTHONY *Gus Tomlins* (1977) 102 During the next couple of hours I got interested in a dear little flapper who worked in a lolly shop in Stratford. **1936** LAWLOR *Murphy's Moa* 66 The lolly shop still existed. **1951** PARK *Witch's Thorn* 78 And Mrs Bedding, the lolly-shop lady, poured out all the wonders she had stored..in the back of the shop. **1982** FRAME *To the Is-land* (1984) 65 In Thames Street my chief place of call was the lolly shop with its notice *High Class Confectionery* which I read as High *Glass* confectionery. **1991** *North & South* (Auckland) June 33 Opposite the Club hotel there used to be a lolly shop where they made delicious ice cream.

b. Special Comb. **lolly bottle, lolly jar**, a large bottle or jar in which shopkeepers displayed lollies for sale, esp. in the phr. **to be caught with (one's) hand in the lolly jar**, to be caught red-handed in something underhand; **lolly paper** [AND 1968], the paper wrapping on a sweet, esp. a toffee; **lolly-stick** [AND 1911], a lollipop, a boiled sweet on a stick (or poss. one shaped like a stick); **lolly water** [AND 1905], a non-alcoholic, sweetened soft drink.
   1888 BARLOW *Kaipara* 163 This lollipop-sucking bushranger for several weeks completely baffled all efforts..leaving behind him..jam tins, **lolly bottles**, pie dishes,.. and rural policemen. **1988** *Dominion Sunday Times* (Wellington) 27 Mar. 2 In the resulting confusion..Mr O'Flynn did a fair imitation of a kid with his hand caught in a **lolly jar**. **1994** *Dominion* (Wellington) 4 Oct. 6 Who got caught with their hand in the lolly jar? Why, none other than [the] associate health minister. **1938** *Tararua Tramper* Aug. 9 Why shouldn't 100 people paying sixpence each amount to one pound eighteen and seven pence halfpenny and a couple of **lolly-papers**? **1958** ASHTON-WARNER *Spinster* 6 If you don't lock it you'll find apple-juice on the precious keys and crumbs of biscuit and lolly papers. **1960** HILLIARD *Maori Girl* 201 Screwed-up lolly-papers, a bar of chocolate as yet unopened. **1980** MANTELL *Murder or Three* 14 The small clearing..had so much accumulated debris—ice-cream wrappers, lolly papers. **1992** *North & South* (Auckland) May 41 They also had to endure the manager..stalking up the aisle..if ever he heard any kids..rattling lolly papers during the screening. **1883** *Auckland Weekly News* 2 June 6 They would be the minute after [quarrelling] 'licking the same **lolly-stick**'. **1965** *Dominion* (Wellington) 5 July 2 But when it comes to soft drinks, lemonade and squash and stuff, they can't get enough of it. To think they actually prefer **lolly-water**. **1978** BALLANTYNE *Talkback Man* 59 A warning from the barman, Phil. He says lolly water can be as dangerous as booze. **1982** GEE *Halfmen of O* 66 Wish I 'ad some whisky. Or else a cuppa tea. This blackberry juice yer feedin' me tastes like lolly water. **1991** ELDRED-GRIGG *Shining City* 154 It's ouzo...It's a kind of lolly water.

3. a. In the phr. **to chuck (lose, toss) one's lollies** [f. the vari-coloured nature of regurgitated individual pieces], to vomit.

1988 McGill *Dict. Kiwi Slang* 70 *lolly* any sweets, short for lollipop...—*chuck* or *lose your lollies* to spew.—*do one's lolly* lose one's temper.

Hence **lolly-tosser**, one who is given to vomiting or who has vomited.

1988 *Metro* (Auckland) June 27 And while this was going on, what was the lolly tosser doing?..maybe she was just looking for somewhere to dematerialise as her company had done the minute they saw the beginnings of a very long and loud psychedelic yawn.

b. In the phr. **to do one's lolly**, to 'do one's block', to become excited or angry.

1955 *BJ Cameron Collection* (TS July) do one's block, do one's bun, do one's lolly (v). To get excited, lose one's head.

4. In the phr. **to give (someone his/her) lollies**, to give someone his/her deserts.

1977 *Evening Post* (Wellington) 19 Mar. 3 When spoken to by police Julian admitted injuring the boy, who, he said, had tried to 'worm in' on Julian's girlfriend. So Julian 'gave him his lollies'.

lolly scramble. [f. LOLLY + *scramble*.]

1. The scattering of lollies for children to scramble for.

[**1885** *Wairarapa Daily* 7 Jan. 2 After lollies had been scrambled with a liberal hand..the teacher addressed the children.] **1929** *Northern Advocate* (Whangarei) 7 Jan. 7 The usual lolly scramble..served to add to the enjoyment of the kiddies. **1961** Frame *Faces in the Water* 97 The lolly scramble..was held both for the amusement of the staff..and for the pleasure of the patients. **1972** Anderson *Let. from James* 144 The afternoon [of the picnic] was spent in treasure hunts, paper trails and lollie scrambles. **1984** Beardsley *Blackball 08* 62 Oh joy, oh boy, the lolly scramble, a hellashun big tin and Mr Stevens..hurling them in the air, a great coloured fan, plop, plop, plop into the grass.

2. a. *fig.* An undignified or childish scramble for money, power, glory, etc.

1962 Webber *Look No Hands* 69 In an effort to sustain this difficult role, it [*sc.* the State] attempts the exercise of conducting a lolly scramble with one hand and snatching back the lolly with the other. **1978** *NZPD* CCCCXVIII. 1246 The Leader of the Opposition called it a lolly-scramble budget. There were not many lollies, but there were a few of them for the farmer who does not really want them. **1985** *National Bus. Rev.* 26 Aug. 28 [Heading] Business outlook: no lolly-scramble. Those still hoping the finance minister would be master of ceremonies at the sort of sectoral lolly-scramble which has characterised many New Zealand budgets were disappointed. **1991** *NZ PC World* Dec.–Jan. 9 But behind all the gimmicks to make you view their wares—an elaborate multimedia demonstration, a lolly scramble for giveaways..some vendors do have interesting products. **1992** *Sunday Star* (Auckland) 25 Oct. A10 [Heading] Political Lotto lolly scramble sordid fray.

b. *attrib.* Suggestive of the vigorously competitive nature and kaleidoscopic appearance of a lolly scramble.

1983 Henderson *Down from Marble Mountain* 30 My first visit to the swirling and lolly-scramble atmosphere of the A & P Show at Richmond.

long, *a.* Alluding to a public highway, specifically the grass or grazing along public road-sides. [Cf. Brit. dial. *long meadow, long pasture* (EDD).]

1. a. As **long acre**, esp. in the phr. **to graze** (occas. **farm**) **the long acre**, (to turn stock out to graze) the grass beside a public road.

1966 p.c. I. Davey (Whangarei) 29 July Long acre, the long narrow roadside strip of grass illegally grazed by farmers. **1978** *Dominion* (Wellington) 27 June 7 Cattle reared on East Coast hill country are driven on hoof to Waikato for fattening, feeding on grass growing on roadsides. Farmers call it 'grazing the long acre'. **1981** Charles *Black Billy Tea* 45 A big flock of sheep and no blooming hay! I have tried to sell 'em and I can't get a taker, So I am goin' to go grazing on the long, long acre! **1986** Owen & Perkins *Speaking for Ourselves* 77 And also, there was a bit of living off the 'long acre' [in the early 1930s]. The long acre was the roadside..but you seemed to think that if there was too many sheep wandering the long acre, one wouldn't be missed.

b. As **long meadow**, in occas. New Zealand use for *long paddock*.

1971 Armfelt *Catching Up* 55 Overgrazed, the bastards! No wonder the poor girl [*sc.* a ewe] sought the long meadow.

c. As **long paddock** [AND 1929], the preferred New Zealand use for roadside grazing.

1933 *Press* (Christchurch) (Acland Gloss.) 4 Nov. 15 *Long paddock, the.*—Slang for the road. People turn stock out on it, or travel them on it, to get cheap grazing. **1949** *Rep. Royal Comm. Sheep-farming Industry* 87 The time must come when New Zealand will have to give consideration to what has become known as 'the long paddock'—that is to say the long acres of land which flank either side of the roads and railway lines of New Zealand. **1950** Cherrill *NZ Sheep Farm* 113 Cooper has let out all his stock into the long paddock. Rachel had learnt by now that the 'long paddock' was the ample grass verge on either side of the back country roads. **1961** Reed *N. Cape to Bluff* 198 I saw, almost for the first time on this journey, cows grazing in 'the long paddock'. **1984** Boyd *City of the Plains* 84 As more land was occupied, more horses and cows were turned out into 'the long paddock', especially at night when gates were deliberately left open. **1993** Bertram *Capes of China* 20 Fruit-picking and the gathering of cocksfoot seed from the 'long paddock' on the verges of country roads were our commonest source of extra pocket-money.

2. As **long road**, see ROAD 1 b.

long: see SO LONG.

long blow: see BLOW *n.*¹

long drop. An outdoor privy built over a hole in the ground. [Beale (ed.) in Partridge 8. 'I met it in Cyprus, later 1950s'.]

1972 *Truth* 26 Sept. 25 Featherston County Council..forces are out to preserve privies and 'long drops' for the relief of Ning Nong locals. **1981** Johnston *Fish Factory* 175 'Dunny box for a new long drop,' Hec grunted and continued with his work. **1992** *Dominion* (Wellington) 26 Jan. 6 'Rob's mob' was a figment of a warped imagination. This mythical horde of rabid adherents could have held a meeting in a Taranaki long drop. **1993** *Press* (Christchurch) 22 Jan. A Lincoln University student lives with the..knowledge that her workplace was formerly a long-drop toilet... The [park toll-]booth..had been acquired by a bach-owner and installed atop a deeply-dug hole for the convenience of bach-users.

longfin. *pink maomao* (MAOMAO 2 (2) *Caprodon longimanus*).

1927 Phillipps *Bibliogr. NZ Fishes* (1971) 33 *Caprodon longimanus*...Longfin; Mata. **1957** Parrott *Sea Angler's Fishes* 75 The Longfin *Caprodon longimanus*... The Longfin, so called on account of the long pectoral fins, has a rather interesting distribution, being found in New Zealand, Australia and Chile. This is not a common species in New Zealand, but it is occasionally caught in moderately deep water off the North Island. **1957** Williams *Dict. Maori Lang.* 185 *Mata*, (iii)... 2... *Caprodon longimanus, longfin*. **1966** Doogue & Moreland *Sea Anglers' Guide* 212 Pink Maomao or Longfin... Although commonly called pink maomao, particularly in the far north, this species is a member of the groper and butterfly perch family (Serranidae), so is not strictly a maomao. *Other names: Caprodon longimanus;* mata (Maori). **1981** Wilson *Fisherman's Bible* 143 Longfin Alternate name for Pink Maomao.

long john. A long narrow loaf baked in a squared enclosed tin.

1972 *Marlborough Express* (Blenheim) 29 Sept. 6 Long John loaves, which will sell at the same price, 14c, will take the place of barracoutas. **1988** McGill *Dict. Kiwi Slang* 70 *long john* oblong loaf of bread baked in tin container.

long pig. *Hist.* [f. *long* suggesting upright stance: found elsewhere but recorded earliest from New Zealand.] Human flesh as food.

1857 Mundy *Our Antipodes* (4edn.) 181 No more 'long pig' for [the Maori]. **1905** *Truth* 19 Aug. 5 'Waimate Witness' records that an old Native, Tiki..still smacks his lips in recollection of the joyous feasts he used to have chewing long pig. **1905** Brandon *'Ukneadit'* 104 *Baked warrior (also called 'long pig'.)* Select a well-tattooed warrior..lay him with..supply of green leaves, in the oven... Bake for six hours... Seasonable after a battle. **1926** *Aussie* (NZ Section p. xvi) 15 Sept. This portion of 'God's own' had a reputation, sinister and sanguinary. The Maoris were exceedingly fierce, with an abnormal taste for 'long pig' (human flesh). **1936** Lambert *Pioneering Reminisc. Old Wairoa* 31 Then Old Wairoa was a land of savages and in war-time 'long pig' was not disdained as an article of diet.

long pull: see PULL *n.* b.

long sleever. [AND 1877.] A tall beer glass; a tall glass of beer. See also SLEEVER 1.

1887 *Auckland Weekly News* 1 Oct. 7 Boss, gimme a long sleever. **1897** A Tramp, Esq. *Casual Ramblings* 95 He [*sc.* a publican] just took a 'long sleever' of his own beer to cool his choler. **1950** In Marlborough c1950 *long sleever* was applied to a 12oz. glass (of beer) (Ed.).

long-snouted pipefish: see PIPEFISH 2.

long-tailed.

1. In the names of animals, see: CUCKOO 2 (2); SKATE *n.*¹ 2 (2), *stingray* (RAY 2 (3)).

2. Special Comb. **long-tailed griffin** *obs.* [poss. f. a trade name], a pit-saw; **long tailed one** *obs. criminal slang* [Partridge, cant: ca1835], a banknote; **long-tailed sheep**, or **long-tailer**, a sheep which has escaped docking.

1929 Win *Early Hist. Dovedale Valley* 1 The circular saw..was a great advance on the **long-tailed Griffin** (as we called the pit-saw) [c1860–70s at Nelson]. **1866** *Lyttelton Times* Aug. 6 [Burgess, Maungatapu bushranger] made use of a cant expression that he had seen '**long tailed ones**' the cant phrase for notes. **1863** Chudleigh *Diary* 26 Dec. (1950) 115 We did not see one pig but got 7 **long-tailed sheep**. **1965** Macnicol *Skippers Road* 18 I'd tell them where the maid went—where no dog had ever been And brought out some **long-tailers** that no man had ever seen,

long time. *Obs.* In the phr. **on the long time**, on credit, on the 'never-never'.
  1896 MOFFATT *Adventures* (1979) 50 We were strongly advised by..[the storekeeper's wife at Washbourn's Flat, Collingwood] to go and set up in Manrope Gully and, if we wanted a start, we could have tools and tucker on the long time.

long tom. As the name of devices or implements.
1. *Goldmining.* Also with init. caps. [AND 1852.] A gold-washing sluice-box; see quot. 1862. See also TOM *n.*¹
  1852 *NZGG* 10 Dec. V. 30:183 (Heaphy's Rep.)The implement most effectual in economising labour is the 'Long Tom', or trough strainer, cradles are but of little comparative service. **1862** HODDER *Memories NZ Life* 75 A 'long-tom'—a kind of trough, about ten feet long, with a sheet of perforated iron at the end, through which the gold and small substances drop into a riddle-box below. **1874** BATHGATE *Col. Experiences* 130 Removing auriferous dirt from the paddock to the 'long tom' or sluice-box. **1937** AYSON *Thomas* 23 He made a cradle and 'long tom' from a pattern given him by an old digger from Australia. **1970** WOOD *Gold Trails Otago* 81 More elaborate methods of winning gold include cradling, crevicing, setting up a sluicebox or 'Long Tom'.

2. [f. the length of its shaft.] **a.** A long-handled shovel.
  1909 THOMPSON *Ballads About Business* 70 Just below the elevator there's a fellow on the watch, Fishing with a 'long tom' shovel; now and then he makes a catch,

b. *Railways.* See quot.
  1986 *Listener* 1 Mar. 11 Not for me the noisy proline but the quiet of the auger and fang-spanner—long tom and jim crow, strumming on the old banjo. [**1986** *Note*] long tom: long blade used for placing measured amount of gravel under sleepers.

3. *transf.* [Poss. f. its long, shovel-like snout.] GARFISH.
  1981 WILSON *Fisherman's Bible* 142 Long-tom *see* Garfish.

Long White Cloud, var. LAND OF THE LONG WHITE CLOUD.

look, *v.*

1. *Farming. Obs.* [f. Sc. or northern Brit. dial.: cf. EDD 4.] *trans.* To look over, inspect (country, land, stock, etc).
  1933 *Press* (Christchurch) (Acland Gloss.) 4 Nov. 15 *Look.*—I am told that on some South Canterbury stations they l[ook] the sheep or paddocks, i.e., go and see that they are all right. I have never heard the word used myself. **1940** STUDHOLME *Te Waimate* (1954) 133 This sort of thing [*sc.* grass-thieving, by running on another's country] quickly came to an end, one old Scot looking his country with a catching dog and a sharp knife. Dead sheep, like dead men, tell no tales.

2. In the phr. **to look (out) for one's swag-straps**, see *swag-strap* (SWAG *n.*¹ 4 a).

looking gear: see GEAR *n.*¹ 4.

lookout. *Whaling.* [Spec. use of *lookout* a station from which a look-out can be kept: see OED 2 a.] A place or point of vantage on land from which a watch for whales may be kept; occas., one keeping 'lookout' at such a place. Also *attrib.*
  1836 GREENE in McNab *Old Whaling Days* (1913) 155 When the spout of a whale would casually come within the scope of vision from the 'look out point' [in Cloudy Bay], no less than seventy to eighty boats would put off in pursuit. [**1843** DIEFFENBACH *Travels in NZ* I. 49 They pull to the entrance of Tory Channel, where a view opens over Cook's Straits and Cloudy Bay from the southern headland, where they keep a 'look-out' for the spouting of a whale.] **1851** LUCETT *Rovings in the Pacific* I. 136 Kapiti..is used, in the season, for a 'look out', or whaling station. **1905** BAUCKE *White Man Treads* 75 On the highest point on the land, looking seaward, a 'lookout' was stationed to signal that whales were in sight. **1968** JOHNSON *Turn of Tide* 16 The lookout at the Heads, where the whalers in their long boats had kept their vigil for years, was no longer the watch-tower. **1982** GRADY *Perano Whalers* 227 *Lookout*—Lookout Hill [Tory Channel], from where many whales were spotted.

loopie. Mainly *SI.* Also **loopy.** [Of uncertain origin.] A tourist; occas. a prying visitor (see quot. 1993). Cf. ASPHALT.
  1975 *Press* (Christchurch) 28 July 30 (Griffiths Collect.) [In Aug. 1975 *loopie* was used on TV1 without explanation.] A television news item about the visit to Stewart Island by the Prime Minister (Mr Rowling) referred to the islanders' word for tourists, 'loopys.' An islander has told the 'Southland Times' that the word originated in another corner of Southland, Milford Sound, about 1970. 'The name was coined by hotel staff who appeared to have a great contempt for "loopys"', said the islander. 'It refers to the peculiar looping motion of the hand while swatting sandflies and to the 'loopy' questions they ask.' **1982** PEAT *Detours* 199 I was 'another bloody loopy' and God knows the town [*sc.* Fox Glacier, West Coast] was full of them—tourists on a loop of the South Island via the Coast. **1984** *Listener* 16 June 23 Loopies: the local [Golden Bay] word for tourists. I didn't understand it. **1984** *Ibid.* 30 June 44 Aucklander Geoff Chapple..wondered why the South Island word for tourists is 'loopies'... We thought it must have come from 'loopy', meaning wrong in the head, but sources in the southern heartland assure us that the term almost certainly derives from tourists' propensity for taking the loop road in any given area, with the general idea of seeing more of the countryside. How diverting. **1991** *Metro* (Auckland) Aug. 116 Though the Q[ueenstown] P[romotion] B[ureau] insists on calling tourists 'visitors', the townsfolk call them 'loopies'. **1993** *Sunday Times* (Wellington) 18 Apr. 7 Stewart Islanders don't particularly like tourists. They call them loopies. **1993** *City Voice* (Wellington) 30 Sept. 22 Since..Rose's article..I have been plagued by all sorts of people stamping around my garden and hillside looking for marijuana... If any of the *City Voice* readers are being 'loopies' in our neighbourhood and do find any marijuana..tell us where.

loose, *a. Rugby union.*

1. Of a forward, not bound to the scrum.
  1916 CHURCH *Tonks* 233 He's a grand forward in a scrum or on the loose.

2. Hence **loosie** /ˈluːsi/ [f. *loos*(e forward + -IE], a loose forward, i.e. one not binding as part of the TIGHT FIVE q.v.
  1977 *Dominion* (Wellington) 12 Sept. 18 'We are strong in our loosies but we are still short of locks and props, particularly at loosehead,' he said. **1981** *NZ Times* 2 Aug. 19 Though not lacking fighting spirit, the Otago team was continually unsettled by..the fiery loosies. **1989** ROMANOS *Famous Fullbacks* 133 A fullback who can crash into the line, hold up play and wait for the loosies is a huge bonus for his team. **1995** *Sunday Star-Times* (Auckland) 9 Apr. sect. B 4 It's murder out there as a loosie when the other pack gets on top.

loot flash. *WW2.* [f. a supposed propensity of NZ troops for looting.] A jocular name for the Italy Star.
  1959 SLATTER *Gun in My Hand* 192 The chap with the ribbons up..the 39–45 Star and the Italy Star, the Spam Medal and the Loot Flash we called them. **1968** SLATTER *Pagan Game* 71 Follow me, Ape Platoon, he used to say, and you'll win the V.D. and Scar. Or the Dysentery medal. The Loot Flash.

loppy. [AND (1897) suggests Brit. dial. *lop* to hang about, to idle; see EDD *v.*²; OED *v.*², but see also OED *loppy n.* which suggests a derivation f. *loppy, a.* flea-ridden.] A station or farm rouseabout.
  1960 SCRYMGEOUR *Memories Maoriland* 49 More frequently application of the loppies galloping down the board, to the ever increasing cry of 'Tar'. The cut was becoming rougher. *Ibid.* 49 When sunlight decreed 'wet sheep'..the shearers would declare a break, whilst the 'loppies', paid wet or fine, would be put on varying jobs to fill in the time until the Lords and Masters of the situation agreed to work.

lost tribe. Used with reference to a recurrent myth which supposes that Ngati-mamoe (or Waitaha) Maori tribal remnants escaping from aggressors formed a 'lost tribe' in the remote south-western South Island. Cf. MAEROERO.
  1938 *Auckland Weekly News* 5 Jan. 9 In South Westland there still live settlers who can recall meeting men who claimed to have come across definite signs of the existence of the 'lost tribe', and old records of Riverton..also contain many references to the same early belief. **1968** HALL-JONES *Early Fiordland* 23 Let us take a closer look at what became known as the 'lost tribe', but let us be quite clear that they were not the 'last of the Ngati-mamoe' as is so often stated. **1989** PARKINSON *Travelling Naturalist* 154 [Ngatimamoe] survivors fled into the wilderness of Fiordland and this flight has led to many fanciful stories of their survival here as a 'lost tribe'. **1992** *NZ Geographic* Jan.–Mar. 80 These fleeting ghostly glimpses of human life in harsh territory gave birth to the story of the Lost Tribe, said to have been remnants of Kati Mamoe driven west by tribal warfare into exile. **1992** *Metro* (Auckland) June 73 They produced evidence that..they were, in fact, members of a 'lost tribe'—the Pakakohi.

lot. *Hist.* [Prob. OED *lot* 6 a 'now chiefly US', 'a plot or portion of land assigned by the state to a particular owner', influenced by OED *lot* 7 'an article offered separately at a general sale'.] A town lot or allotment; in early New Zealand use, a section or allotment of town land subject to auction; or occas., a subdivision of a country section. Cf. *town allotment, town lot, town section* (TOWN 2).
  1841 D. Sinclair & others, Wellington to Sir George Gipps 10 Feb. in *GBPP 1842 (No.569)* 131 By the Government advertisement for the sale of town lands at Auckland, it was stated that sections..would be exposed to sale by auction, but we have since learned that several allotments, comprising some of the most valuable lands in the township, have been reserved from such sale..and that these sections are to be paid for, not according to the price..of the less valuable lots in their vicinity..but at the average price of half the town sections. **1843** CHAPMAN *NZ Portfolio* 108 Each country section disposed of in small lots may be regarded as a section withdrawn from the supply on hand, for immediate use. **1859** THOMSON *Story NZ* II. 60 At Auckland the people were living on the government expenditure, and awaited the arrival of immigrants to occupy the houses they had built, and re-purchase the town lots they had bought.

Lotto. *transf.* [Spec. use of *lotto* (OED ad. Italian *lotto*, 1778) a game played with cards divided into numbered squares and numbered disks drawn on a lottery principle: prob. in NZ also reinforced by association with *lott*(ery + -o.] A national lottery wherein individuals, seeking a prize, mark numbers on a 'housie'-like card, or buy a ready-marked sheet, (a 'lotto ticket') in an attempt to match those eventually drawn at random by the organizers. Often used *attrib.* in special Comb. **Lotto shop**, an authorized selling-point for Lotto tickets; **Lotto ticket**.

1988 *Sunday News* (Auckland) 21 Feb. 2 At a lotto shop in Takapuna, Auckland, on a Monday morning one nice old lady said to another: 'I like to get in early before they sell out.' *Ibid.* 3 Apr. 2 Graham of New Lynn was caught in heavy rain after buying his Lotto ticket. *Ibid.* 3 Apr. 11 Soon there'll be something worse than reading about some tinny person who's just won Lotto. 1988 *Sunday Star* (Auckland) 27 Mar. B1 In the lotto game of life, it may seem unfair that some blokes always crop up with the winning numbers. 1990 *Dominion* (Wellington) 1 Aug. 13 Writers may be playing for smaller stakes than those who buy their weekly fix of Lotto tickets but many of them regard..book awards as a lottery, a game of chance, a literary All Blacks. 1991 *Sunday Star* (Auckland) 4 Aug. A3 Residents believe the men who robbed the Lotto shop..killed Steel... Police say the Lotto burglary is only one of many leads.

lousy head. *little black shag* (SHAG 2 (10)).
1952 RICHARDS *Chatham Is.* 89 P[halacrocorax] *sulcirostris*... In the breeding season it wears a number of white plumes on its head and neck... Little Black Shag. Lousy Head.

love grass: see GRASS 2 (23).

low country. Farmland on a plain or in lower foothills. Contrast HIGH (or HILL) COUNTRY.
1952 BLAKISTON *My Yesteryears* 19 By 8a.m., we had our 14,000 wethers across the Waihi on to what was then called the 'low country' now Ben Hope. 1952 *NZ Geogr.* Oct. 131 The bulk of fertiliser is still used on the low country, but increasing quantities are now being applied to the hill country. 1977 BRUCE *Life in Hinterland* 65 A man should either have a low country block and use this in summer only, or he should have enough money not to worry when the snow comes.

lowland galaxias, ribbonwood: see GALAXIAS, RIBBONWOOD 2 (1).

lox: see LOCK.

loyalist. *Hist.* FRIENDLY B.
1986 BELICH *NZ Wars* 211 The *kupapa*, Maoris fighting on the British side, were variously known as 'loyalists', 'Queenites', and 'the friendly natives'.

luck, *v. trans.* In the phr. **to luck** (something) **through**, to trust to luck.
1986 *Evening Post* (Wellington) 9 Oct. 1 Mr Wilson said he thinks the reason for the delay is that 'either they thought they'd luck it through or we would forget. It just doesn't happen like that.'

lucky spot. Also occas. **spot waltz**. A dance in which a prize eventually goes to the couple standing in a pre-selected spot on the dance floor when the music stops.
1943 Lucky Spot [see SUPPER 2]. 1944 *Ellesmere Guardian* 22 Dec. 6 A Monte Carlo was won by Miss M. Allen and Mr. P. Abbott, a lucky spot by Miss. M. Moorhead and Mr. A. Duff. 1944 *Taihape Times* 24 Dec. 1 Annual Xmas Eve Dance... New Series Monte Carlo. Spot Waltz. 1944 *North Wairarapa Herald* 30 Dec. 4 Included in the varied programme..were a number of novelty dances, winners of which were: Lucky Spot one-stop, Miss S. Ransy and Mr. H. Morrison; Monte Carlo, Miss E. Davie and Mr. W. Graham. 1992 FARRELL *Skinny Louie Book* 128 The music stops. 'Cra-zee!' says Andrew... 'It's a Lucky Spot!'

lug-biter. *Obs.* Also occas. **lugger.** [AND 1911.] One who 'bites' one's lug for money or favours; a persistent bludger or borrower of money. Cf. *chew (one's) lug* (CHEW *v.* a).
1905 *Truth* 9 Sept. 5 He looked so much more like a low-down lug biter than a wool-king. 1906 *Ibid.* 27 Jan. 1 The lug-biter is so persistent..that you can't ask a friend for a bob without him growing..coldly irresponsive. *Ibid.* 12 May 1 Half a dozen luggers, Waiting for a shout.

lugger: see LUG-BITER.

lumber, *v.* [Transf. use of Brit. slang *lumber* to place (property) in pawn: used elsewhere but apparently (see OED *v.*³ quots.) chiefly Austral.: cf. AND 1812.] *trans.* To arrest and charge (someone) with (or impose a sentence) for an offence; to catch (someone) out in some illicit or underhand act.
1905 *Truth* 26 Aug. 1 Do sometimes lumber a 'prominent resident'. 1942 *NZEF Times* 16 Nov. 15 You're lumbered at last. 1957 WILSON *Strip Jack Naked* 29 'I can lumber you, Jack, any time I want to... I can pot yer like a sitting duck.' 1961 CRUMP *Hang On a Minute Mate* 136 We were sneaking into the church to bunk down last night when the johns lumbered us. 1971 BAXTER *Collected Poems* (1980) 533 The magistrate said, 'This..Can't go on!' He lumbered me With six months in Mount Crawford. 1982 NEWBOLD *Big Huey* 23 Being silent is doing you no good at all because when the shit hits the fan, boy, it's *you* who's going to get lumbered.

lump-fish. [The name derives from the general lumpish appearance of the fish.] Any of *Trachelochismus* spp. (fam. Gobiesocidae), small fish which cling to rocks with suction discs formed from their ventral fins.
1773 FORSTER *Resolution Jrnl.* 8 Apr. (1982) II. 250 We got some other new fish, viz. a small Lumpfish. 1927 PHILLIPPS *Bibliogr. NZ Fishes* (1971) 55 *Trachelochismus pinnulatus* (Forster). Lump-Fish. 1956 GRAHAM *Treasury NZ Fishes* 370 I have found Lump-fish..always at or below low tide mark holding on to the surf-beaten rocks with their adhesive suckers. 1967 NATUSCH *Animals NZ* 233 [The cling fish's] relative *Trachelochismus*, the lump fish, has a rather more pointed snout and no incisors. The lump fish lives in slightly less exposed parts of [rocky coasts]. 1983 GUNSON *Collins Guide to Seashore* 174 The clingfish..and the lumpfish *Trachelochismus melobesia* can both be found clinging with their sucker-like discs to the undersides of rocks, where they feed on small animals brought to them by wave action.

luncheon sausage. Occas. *ellipt.* **luncheon**. A general name (popularised patriotically to obviate the use of the then usual *German sausage*) during WW1 for a kind of pre-cooked spiced meat in the form of a large, pink, often red-skinned sausage usu. sold sliced in portions by weight. See also BELGIAN B, DOMINION 2, *German sausage* (GERMAN *a.*).

1917 *Wanganui Herald* 21 May 4 'I suppose you do not make German sausage now?' asked the chairman... 'We call it "luncheon", sir,' was the reply. 1936 *Cookery Book NZ Women's Inst.* (4edn.) 29 *Luncheon Sausage*... Mince steak and bacon, add breadcrumbs and nutmeg, salt and pepper, break in eggs and mix all together and steam in a basin for 3 hours. 1938 *Grey River Argus* 4 Feb. 12 [Advt] Luncheon Sausage Swan 10d. lb. 1987 CHRISTIE *Candles & Canvas* 93 Vera also cooked the meals, which consisted monotonously of porridge for breakfast, Belgium (luncheon) sausage with rice and curry sauce. 1992 *Marlborough Express* (Blenheim) 30 Jan. 10 [Advt] Venison & Goats Make excellent sausages, saveloys, luncheon and patties.

lurk. [f. general slang *lurk* a method of fraud: see OED *n.*¹ 2; EDD *v.*¹; AND 1891.]

1. a. A cunning scheme (to avoid work, make money, etc.); a cunning dodge; a racket.
c1926 THE MIXER *Transport Workers' Song Book* 87 If he doesn't break away from [the conditions] Through some underhanded 'lurk'. 1949 THE SARGE *Excuse My Feet* (Gloss.) *Lurk*—(Army slang) A scheme for dodging work or duty.

b. The 'tricks of the trade'.
1946 COOZE *Ten Bob Each Way* 8 After years of hard work He had learnt all the lerk [*sic*] And prayed hard for a chance to get rich.

2. Esp. in the phr. **(to be on to) a good lurk**, an easy or soft job; a profitable enterprise or business.
1959 SLATTER *Gun in My Hand* 20 Stamping was a good lurk. 1960 HILLIARD *Maori Girl* 238 Yet unless he got into some 'lurk' like that he'd be a casual labourer, a wage-worker for the rest of his days. 1961 *Listener* 15 Sept. 29 I suspect Barry Crump found he was on a good advertising lurk when he was interviewed for Book Shop. 1988 MCGILL *Dict. Kiwi Slang* 70 A frequent example: 'You're on to a good lurk', meaning a cushy job.

lux, *v.* [f. the proprietary name Electro)*lux* a brand of vacuum cleaner.] To clean by vacuum cleaner. Occas. as a noun, a vacuum cleaner.
1980 HALL *Prisoners of Mother England* 21 Refused to 'lux the venetians. 1980 LELAND *Kiwi-Yankee Dict.* 61 *lux*: (A) to vacuum one's carpet (B) a vacuum cleaner. This, like hoover, is a corruption of a brand name. In this case, Electrolux, which appears to be the most widely used vacuum cleaner in New Zealand. 1986 *More* (Auckland) May 134 I jiffed the bath, handbasin and loo, polished the mirrors..then luxed the carpet. 1988 MCGILL *Dict. Kiwi Slang* 70 *lux* to vacuum; short for electrolux. 1992 *NZ English Newsletter* 6 11 (Bartlett *Regional Variation: Southland*) [Other items which may be diagnostic of Southland English are:] *lux* (vacuum cleaner). 1996 *Tablet* (Dunedin) 21 Jan. 8 Shifting from the South Island to the North—from Invercargill all the way up to Morrinsville... Things that stick out most is we roll our R's, we call 'luncheon' 'belgium' and we call 'vacuum cleaning' luxing.

lympho. *Farming.* [*lymph*(adenitis + -o.] Lymphadenitis, an inflammation of the lymph nodes of a farm animal.
1950 *NZJAg.* Oct. LXXXI. 345 *Caseous lymphadenitis* is referred to as 'C.L.A.' or 'lympho' in the works killing sheets... There is substantial economic loss. 1980 NEAVE *Land of Munros* 123 [Colin Hercus's] achievements..in such matters as feeding sheep on oats in the winter, the control of lympho..these..are part of New Zealand's Agricultural History.

M

maaleesh, maaleish, varr. MALEESH.

maanawa, var. MANAWA.

Mabel Island lily: see LILY 2 (7).

mac: see MACROCARPA.

macarell, var. MACKEREL.

machine.

1. *Horseracing.* As **the machine**, the mechanical or electric (now electronic) on-course totalizator.
1889 REEVES in Woodhouse *Farm & Station Verse* (1950) 22 What a lot [of money] you left behind in the 'machine'. **1891** WILLIAMS & REEVES *In Double Harness* 8 When racing was developed by the aid of the 'machine'. **1904** *NZ Observer* 30 July 3 Honest bookmakers..are in some respect preferable to the machine. **1939** *Taranaki Herald* (New Plymouth) 23 Aug. 3 An electric machine has a tremendous advantage over the old manual totalisator. **1949** *Southern Cross* (Wellington) 15 Aug. 9 Each paid more than £25 on the win machine.

2. *Farming.* **a.** Often *pl.* Among dairy farmers, a milking machine.
1913 CARR *Country Work* 38 Owing to the difficulty in getting efficient 'teat pullers' (as milkers are familiarly known) machines are being largely brought into use. **1918** COX *Diaries 1888–1924* (ATLMS) W. Renall? came..and put the machine so [*sic*] that it is doing the milking this evening. **1966** TURNER *Eng. Lang. Austral. & NZ* 149 The *milking machines*, normally simply called the *machines*, always in the plural.

b. (a) *shearing machine* (SHEARING B 3).
1906 *Awards, etc.* 626 In sheds where machines are used..the shearers to pay for combs and cutters at cost price. **1913** CARR *Country Work* 14 The owner or manager generally gets his own pressers and expert (where machines are run). *Ibid.* 16 We were not sorry when the whistle blew (it is a machine shed) all the same. **1917** *NZJAg.* Sept. XV. 134 The majority of the larger sheepowners..have come to recognize the advantages of 'machines' over 'blades'. **1945** *Korero* (AEWS Background Bulletin) 23 Apr. 23 Generally speaking, machines are used on the plains and blades in the back country. **1955** BOWEN *Wool Away* 9 Relative quality of workmanship between blades and machines is a debatable point. **1960** MILLS *Sheep-O* 19 This establishes the date [Nov. 17, 1900] of the change-over from blades to machines. **1975** NEWTON *Sixty Thousand on the Hoof* 213 Nokomai is another of the high-country stations which have recently changed over to the machines. **1986** *Marist Messenger* Dec. 34 There's nothing spooking the sheep. They're quiet enough. It could be one of the boys setting up machines.

(b) Used *attrib.* in special Comb. with reference to machine-shearing as distinct from blade-shearing: **machine man**, a machine-shearer; **machine shear**, *shearing machine* (SHEARING B 3); **machine shearer** (also **machine man**), a shearer who works with a shearing machine rather than with blades; **machine shearing** *vbl. n.*; **machine (shearing) shed**, a shearing shed equipped with and using shearing machines.
1955 BOWEN *Wool Away* 9 **Machine men** only stop a few times a run to change cutters, compared with blade men giving their shears several wipes in a run. **1975** NEWTON *Sixty Thousand on the Hoof* 213 It [*sc.* a woolshed] holds 1800 woolly sheep—barely sufficient for eight fast machine-men. **1900** *Acton-Adams Let.* 22 May in McCaskill *Molesworth* (1969) 83 *Shearing:* I have arranged with the Smoko Shearing Company of Wellington, to erect 10 **machine shears** on the western board of the shed. **1912** *The Sheepowners' Handbook* 11 Shearing Classes have been well attended by students..in order to qualify as **machine shearers**. **1905** *Weekly Press* (Christchurch) 25 Jan. 13 [Advt] 'Wolseley' sheep-shearing machines... Pioneers of **machine shearing**. **1912** *The Sheepowners' Handbook* 11 Satisfactory arrangements were made for..classes in both Machine-Shearing and Wool-Classing at Glenmark Station. **1950** *NZJAg.* Oct. LXXXI. 351 Until the outbreak of the Second World War all shearing at Glenaray was done with blades, but owing to the acute shortage of blade shearers..the owners were forced to change to machine shearing. **1913 machine shed** [see 2 b (a) above]. **1986** RICHARDS *Off the Sheep's Back* 65 It had been built for hand or blade shearing, so was fairly cramped when converted to a three-stand machine shearing shed.

mackerel. Also early **macarell, mackrel**. [Transf. use of *mackerel* the marine fish *Scomber scomber* and other similar fish of the fam. Scombridae.]

1. Any of several commercially important pelagic schooling fish of families Scombridae (mackerels, tunas) or Carangidae (jack or horse mackerels).
1769 COOK *Journals* 8 Nov. (1955) I. 194 The natives..sold us..as much fish as served all hands, they were of the Mackarel kind and as good as ever was eat. **1835** YATE *NZ* (1970) 71 In the mackerel-season, when several tribes go together to the little creeks where these fish frequent, and always succeed in capturing some hundreds of thousands. **1842** in *Lett. from New Plymouth* (1843) (1968) 10 Feb. 3 There are plenty of mackerel here, but no nets to catch them, and there are pilchards. **1851** SHORTLAND *S. Dist. NZ* 143 Mackerel were playing around us in large shoals, and were taken in great numbers by the crew... This fish was much larger than its namesake known on the shores of the West of England, and had not its delicate flavour. **1872** HUTTON & HECTOR *Fishes NZ* 112 Mackerel. This valuable fish (*Scomber australasicus*) is only known to me from two large hauls..made in Wellington Harbour about the 15th December, 1870, but it appears to be the fish..called by the natives Tawa-tawa. **1886** SHERRIN *Handbook Fishes NZ* 61 Mackerel (*Scomber Australasicus*)... In colour, size, and form it closely approaches the common mackerel of England, and is very superior in delicacy to the scad or horse-mackerel, which is commonly called the mackerel in New Zealand. **1904** TREGEAR *Maori Race* 107 Mackerel were prepared by being cleaned inside and washed with salt water, then half-cooked in the oven. **1936** HYDE *Passport to Hell* 15 Or in the evening..a one-armed man solemnly proffers a large and gleaming mackerel, caught off the edge of the Auckland wharves. **1958** PARROTT *Big Game Fishes* 25 The..Mackerels are clearly distinguished by their general shape and colouration, and by the series of detached finlets behind the dorsal and anal fins. **1986** PAUL *NZ Fishes* 124 The names 'tuna' and 'mackerel' are themselves not clearly defined and do not always indicate true relationships.

2. With a modifier: **blue** (or **Australian, common, English, Pacific, slimy, southern**), **horse, jack.**

(1) **blue** (or **Australian, common, English, Pacific, slimy, southern**) **mackerel**. *Scomber australasicus* (fam. Scombridae). See also SLIMY 2, TAWATAWA.
1922 *NZJST* V. 93 *Southern Mackerel.* Except during the months June to October, small numbers of these mackerel are received continuously in Auckland throughout the year. Sold as 'Australian mackerel'. **1947** POWELL *Native Animals NZ* 70 Southern Mackerel... This closely resembles the well-known English Mackerel. It is shining bluish-green on the back with spots and meandering bars of dark colour. **1966** DOOGUE & MORELAND *Sea Anglers' Guide* 267 Common Mackerel... *Other names:*.. southern mackerel, English mackerel..tawatawa (Maori). **1977** *Catch* May 13 The blue mackerel..is another member of the group of relatively unexploited but potentially important commercial species common in North Island and northern South Island waters, as well as along the South Australian coast. **1986** PAUL *NZ Fishes* 124 Blue mackerel *Scomber australasicus*... An Indo-Pacific species... In New Zealand it has often been called English mackerel and Pacific mackerel, but it is becoming more widely and appropriately known now as blue mackerel. **1991** BRADSTOCK *Fishing* 20 *Blue mackerel.* Other names: slimy mackerel, English mackerel, common mackerel, Pacific mackerel, *Scomber australasicus.*

(2) **horse mackerel**. [Transf. use of *horse-mackerel* any of several fish allied to the mackerel: cf. AND.] See *jack mackerel* (3) below. See also HAUTURE, HERRING SCAD 2, HORSIE, YELLOWTAIL 2 (1).
1769 *An 'Endeavour' Log* 9 Nov. in McNab *Hist. Records* (1914) II. 147 A large Body of Indians came off in their Canoes and brought great quantities of horse Macarell. **1773** FORSTER *Resolution Jrnl.* 2 May (1982) II. 268 Capt. Cook..found the fish..which proved a *Horse-Mackrel*, a kind of fish we had never caught before. **1841** HODGSKIN *Narr. Eight Months Sojourn NZ* 33 Large quantities of the horse mackerel are annually caught, and dried by the natives. **1872** [see HAUTURE]. **1880** SENIOR *Travel & Trout* 288 Amongst the sea-fishes fit for food there are..a number of periodical fishes..and these include..horse-mackerel. **1890** *Otago Witness* (Dunedin) 23 Jan. 18 The horse mackerel (*Trachurus trachurus*) or hauture of the Maori, is a fish..common to the seas of Britain and New Zealand. **1906** *TrNZI* XXXVIII. 550 *Trachurus trachurus...* The horse-mackerel or scad. **1922** *NZJST* V. 93 Horse-mackerel. Large numbers are smoked and sold in Auckland. In a smoked condition horse-mackerel

is considered to resemble the Yarmouth bloater in flavour. **1957** PARROTT *Sea Angler's Fishes* 183 The Horse Mackerel..may be at once recognised by the bony plates, called scutes, which entirely cover the lateral line along each side of the body. **1970** MIDDLETON in *Some Other Country* (1984) 150 Luke was still out of work..when the mackerel began to come in... One day, the other [fishermen]..hauled in a fine 'horse mackerel'. **1986** [see (3) below]. **1990** FOORD *NZ Descr. Animal Dict.* 216 Koheru... *Decapterus koheru*..Horse mackerel..Scad.

(3) **jack mackerel**. The trade-name preferred (esp. to *horse mackerel* (2) above, and the synonyms given there) for either of *Trachurus novaezelandiae* and *T. declivis* (fam. Carangidae), or the closely related *Decapterus koheru* (KOHERU).

1970 SORENSEN *Nomenclature NZ Fish* 34 Mackerel...*Trachurus declivis*... Suggested commercial name[s]:..Jack mackerel. **1986** PAUL *NZ Fishes* 90 *Jack mackerels Trachurus novaezelandiae, T. declivis*... Commonly called horse mackerel. The name jack mackerel is more appropriate and is applied to a number of related species of *Trachurus* throughout the world.

mackerel gull: see GULL 2 (3).

mackrel, var. MACKEREL.

Macquarie cabbage. Also freq. **Macquarie Island cabbage.** [f. the name of the subantarctic *Macquarie* Island, and the plant's use as greens.]
1. *Stilbocarpa polaris* (fam. Araliaceae), a herb of the subantarctic islands bearing large hairy corrugated leaves, used by early sealers as an anti-scorbutic. Cf. PUNUI.

1870 *TrNZI* II. 176 [The Snares are] almost entirely covered with scrub... Of M'Quarrie cabbage there is abundance, and of fine growth, some of the leaves measuring two feet in diameter. **1883** *TrNZI* XV. 448 *Stilbocarpa polaris*, 'Macquarie Island Cabbage' of the sealers, in flower and fruit [on Macquarie Island]. **1909** *Subantarctic Is. NZ* I. xxi A translation..contains references to..some of the more conspicuous plants, among the latter being the *Stilbocarpa polaris*, which he speaks of as the Macquarie Island 'cabbage' and which was used..as a vegetable. **1965** GILLHAM *Naturalist in NZ* 32 The same story can be told of the 'Macquarie Island cabbage'..which is found..on that island..but there, at 54° 30´, retreating before the depredations of introduced rabbits. **1978** MOORE & IRWIN *Oxford Book NZ Plants* 96 *Stilbocarpa polaris*... Early whalers and sealers used the plant as an antiscorbutic, hence the old name 'Macquarie Island cabbage'. According to experience in 1950–51, 'The petioles taste like celery when cooked; pickled rhizomes taste like turnips; and leaves when cooked like wet blotting paper'.

2. Erroneously applied to *Chatham Island lily* (LILY 2 (3)).

1910 COCKAYNE *NZ Plants & Their Story* 123 The most famous of all the Chatham Island plants is the giant forget-me-not (*Myosotidium nobile*)..frequently called by the absurd name of Chatham Island lily, or, what is worse, Macquarie cabbage!

macrocarpa /mækrə'kapə/, /maikrə'kapə/. Occas. abbrev. **mac** (see quot. 1991); also **makrakapa**, **microcarpa**. [From the specific epithet of *Cupressus macrocarpa*.] *Cupressus macrocarpa* (fam. Cupressaceae), a medium-sized tree introduced from California and now very common in lowland areas of New Zealand as a hedge and shelter-belt plant, or a plantation timber tree; also its wood and timber. Also *attrib*.

1879 *Auckland Weekly News* 1 Mar. 13 They [*sc.* nurserymen] consider the *Macrocarpa* more suitable for shelter, and a quicker grower. **1899** BELL *In Shadow of Bush* 19 A plantation of pines and macrocarpa had already attained forward growth, and showed that this farm must have been one of the first in the locality. **1905** SATCHELL *Toll of Bush* 5 In the centre of the green plain was a group of white buildings, surrounded by a hedge of macrocarpa. **1928** *Free Lance* (Wellington) 11 Jan. 18 His Worship was up on his roof trying his hand at being his own chimney sweep, and..hauled a macrocarpa branch up and down the flue, till it stuck there. **1947** DAVIN *For Rest of Our Lives* 385 They were in a quiet high place on the crown of the gebel, sitting under a broad macrocarpa. **1951** FRAME *Lagoon* (1961) 60 Oh how lovely..to have a macrocarpa hedge instead of African Thorn. **1960** SCRYMGEOUR *Memories Maoriland* 113 Originally..sheltered by thick microcarpa hedges..was a beautiful site of a previous homestead. **1982** *Karori News* (Wellington) Apr. [Advt] For Sale Firewood Makrakapa, good loads, $55, delivered. **1991** *Western News* (Wellington) 17 June 15 [Advt] Dry Firewood Manuka, Native, Pine, Mac. Bag or Bulk

mad, *a*. [f. *mad* usu. 'angry'; but often 'mentally unbalanced'.] In the formula **(as) mad as (a)** + noun or noun phrase introducing various phr. signifying 'very angry' or 'most eccentric'.
a. mad as a maggot. (a) Very angry. Cf. MAGGOTY *a*.

1943 BENNETT *English in NZ* in *Amer. Speech* XVIII. 90 The verbs *to go snaky, to go maggoty* (cf. U.S. *maggoty*, whimsical) [mean to show anger or annoyance]. Phrases like 'mad as a maggot', 'mad as a meat-axe' are obviously linked with these expressions..; whether *mad* in the sense of angry is a survival of an English provincialism, or has been introduced from America, is not clear.

(b) [Cf. OED *maggot* whimsical fancy, a capricious person.] Most capricious; silly; eccentric.

1956 SUTHERLAND *Green Kiwi* (1960) 121 'Good bloke,' said Bailey, 'Mad as a maggot, of course'. **1968** BAXTER *Collected Plays* (1982) 24 Young Jack Skully, mad as a maggot, singing out in the dark. **1988** McGILL *Dict. Kiwi Slang* 71 *mad as a maggot* very mad, very silly, very angry, very eccentric;.. eg 'Old Millie's mad as a maggot, you know, hosing the lawn when it's raining, that sort of thing.'

b. mad as a gumdigger's dog, see *gumdigger's dog* (GUMDIGGER *n*.[1] 2).

c. mad as a meat-axe. (a) [AND 1946: cf. OED *mad adj.* 8, 1855.] (a) Very angry. Occas. **as wild as a meat-axe**, very wild.

a**1927** ANTHONY *Gus Tomlins* (1977) 172 Sally and Ann came in again with the tea. They looked as mad as meat-axes, thinking about the cat, but neither had the nerve to say anything. **1947** DAVIN *For Rest of Our Lives* 76 We're just about worn out with it..and the Colonel had come out, mad as a meat-axe, and saying there's your Labour Government for you. **1970** SANSOM *Stewart Islanders* 145 Although sold to him as 'bullocks broken in to the harness' they were 'as wild as meat-axes'. **1988** McGILL *Dict. Kiwi Slang* 71 *mad as a meataxe* very mad, very angry.

(b) Most eccentric. Occas. *ellipt*. **meat-axe** a crazy person.

1943 MARSH *Colour Scheme* 105 You're dopey... Gee whiz, you're mad... Aw, hell, you're as mad as a meat axe. **1959** SLATTER *Gun in My Hand* 231 He went mad and they shot him mad as a meat-axe in Oamaru. **1960** MUIR *Word for Word* 55 Blue. The blue of your eyes. Copenhagen china, gentian smoke, sky, Reckitts. Henderson, you're as mad as a meat-axe. **1986** HULME *Windeater* 177 She's as mad as a meat-axe, they say. Why do they say that? A meat-axe is a razor weapon. **1993** *Dominion* (Wellington) 27 Sept. 10 Assorted meat axes and wombats like Gilbert Miles..will provide supporting sideshows.

d. mad as a snake [AND 1917], most eccentric.

1955 *BJ Cameron Collection* (TS July) mad as a snake Very mad. **1966** TURNER *Eng. Lang. Austral. & NZ* 115 There is simile: 'as mad as a snake', 'as bald as a bandicoot'. **1974** MASON *Hand on Rail* (TS 1987) 27 *Roar of rage from Drinker. Rangi runs off, stands a moment.* Rangi: Thomas à Becket! Fuck! *He gives the fingers*,... Drinker 1: Mad as a bloody snake. They all are! **1990** O'SULLIVAN *Snow in Spain* 71 [*sic*] see that's the puzzle about you mitch, steady like that and mad as a snake.

e. mad as a wet hen, see WET HEN a.

mad dog. In the phr. **to go mad dog**, to act in a vigorously strange or eccentric fashion.

1916 MANSFIELD *Aloe* (1982) 75 For three days she laid the table and took the mending basket on to the verandah in the afternoon but after that she 'went mad-dog again' as her father expressed it and there was no holding her.

maemae, var. MAIMAI.

maeroero. Also **maero**, **maeroro**, **mairoero**. [Ma. ?/'maeroero/: cf. Williams 164 *Maero (i) 1.* n. A fabulous monster.] A supposed or legendary 'wildman of the woods' or member of a LOST TRIBE q.v., or of a supposed savage pre-Maori race.

1844 MONRO *Notes of a Journey* in Hocken *Contributions* (1898) 262 Behind Toutuki, [the prospective Otago settler] may explore the mountain dreaded by the natives, on account of its being the favourite residence of the mairoero. This is a wild man of the woods, strong, cunning, and mischievous, and addicted to running off with young people and damsels. His body is covered with coarse and long hair, which also flows down from the back of his head nearly to his heels. To compensate for this excessive quantity behind, his forehead is said to be bald. He was vividly described to us by a Maori who had seen one long ago, when he was a little boy, and was of opinion that 'there is not a more fearful wild-fowl than your *mairoero* living.' **1867** HOCHSTETTER *NZ* 211 The inhabitants of the North Island..tell of savages with long hair, long fingers and nails, who eat their food raw and who are supposed to live in the most inaccessible ravines and forests of the Tararua range. These savages who are supposed to be the last of the aborigines of New Zealand, are called Maeros. In like manner the natives of South Island tell of the Ngatimamoes, as savages living in the mountains. However both the Maeros and Ngatimamoes are probably degenerated Maori tribes, which have been driven back into the mountains. **1875** *TrNZI* VII. 144 I have to record..a trace of human life on this island..reaching back beyond history, and supporting the Maori tradition that this island was inhabited before their arrival here, and that the Maeros of the North Island and the Ngatimamaeros of the South Island, may yet be found to be real aborigines, and not degenerate wild Maoris, as has been supposed by many. c**1920** BEATTIE *Trad. Lifeways Southern Maori* 214 The Maeroero were wild men of the woods, a kind of uncouth fairies... They are not recorded in the Waitaki region, but down the east coast of Otago and most frequent in the Tautuku forests. They are described as wild hairy creatures but strange to say they play the flute beautifully. **1934** HYDE *Journalese* 169 In the forest depths, beyond the slopes where the red deer show themselves on the skyline, still roam the woman and man maeroro, the huge ogres of Maori legend. **1989** ANDERSON *Prodigious Birds* 104 At the end of 1874 Haast argued that..the Moa-hunters were probably Melanesians known as Maero or Mohoao.

mafia: see *New Zealand mafia* (NEW ZEALAND B 4 b).

mafish /maˈfiʃ/. *WW1* and *WW2*. Also **mafeesh**. [Cf. OED ad. colloq. Eastern Arabic *māfī-sh* 'there is nothing'.] Dead; finished.
 1916 ROSS *Light & Shade* 16 'Mafeesh', [the dying soldier] said quaintly. **1918** *Kia Ora Coo-ee* 15 Oct. 13 When you wish to state that you have no money, you must say *Ma fish fils*... Literally, it means 'There is no money'. **1918** *Shell-Shocks* 24 Jack Brown's mafish (finished), stopped one in his 'bivvy', knocked half his head off. **1986** DAVIN *Salamander & the Fire* 50 But it's mafish for Reading. The high jump. Of course, no one could prove anything.

mag, *v.* [f. Brit. dial. (see EDD) *mag v.* to prattle, to scold; *n.* chatter, incessant talk; a chatterer: AND 1895.] *trans.* and *intr.* To chatter (about); occas. to 'fast-talk' (a person), to spiel.
 1908 *Truth* 18 Apr. 2 The graft was as follows: The owners of the horse thought their boy could mag pretty well, so they cross-kidded to him, by explaining that it would be folly to back the horse here. *Ibid.* 11 July 2 It is their flow of language that catches the mug, just as the guesser 'mags' his pigeon into backing a stumer. **1935** MITCHELL & STRONG in Partridge *Slang Today* 285 [The] following [was] employed by those who served in the [Great] War. *mag*, to talk, generally in an aimless manner. **1980** MANTELL *Murder Or Three* 70 I mean, every time she talked about some man it was a different name. But lately the name she's been magging is Price.
 Hence **mag** *n.* A talk, chat; a chatterer.
 1935 STRONG *WW1 scene* in Partridge *Slang Today* 287 In London, for preference; there I can have a mag to a tabby. **1943** SARGESON *NZ New Writing* I. 6 She was a mag.

maga, var. MANGA.

Maggie. [Origin unknown.] Also **Maggy**. The ace of hearts in the card-game of FORTY-FIVES.
 1948 *Our Own Country* 100 In smoky little back parlours [in Westport] friendly little groups meet to play 'forty-fives'... The ace of hearts (the Maggy) is always the third best trump. **1980** MCGILL *Ghost Towns NZ* 127 Gambling was poker or 45s, a diggers' card game from California involving legs, queer suits and Maggie, cries of 'Get Jinx!' and 'Go for the Doctor!'

maggot: In the phr. *as mad as a maggot*, see MAD *a*. a.

maggoty, *a.* [Brit. dial. *maggotty* queer tempered; irritable: cf. EDD *maggot n.*¹ 2 (3)] Angry, annoyed; esp. in the phr. **to go maggoty**, to become angry. Cf. *mad as a maggot* (MAD *a*. a).
 1915 let. 14 July in *Wanganui Herald* 10 Sept. 8 Don't tell him I asked you to, as he would go maggetty [*sic*]. **1916** INGLIS 18 Dec. in Boyack *Behind the Lines* (1989) 114 [To his fiancee:] So I gave her your address. Don't go maggoty missus. I won't do it no more. **1936** SARGESON *Conversation with Uncle* 24 There was a shearer who used to go maggoty if a lamb wouldn't sit still. **1943** [see MAD *a*. 1 a]. **1984** BEARDSLEY *Blackball 08* 66 Bad news, Bob? You look down in the mouth— a bit maggoty? *Ibid.* 244 maggoty: annoyed, angry

Maggy, var. MAGGIE.

magho, var. MANGO.

Magna Carta: see *Maori Magna Charta* (MAORI B 5 a).

magnoon. *WW1*. and *WW2*. *Egypt*. Also **magnoun, magnune, maknoon**. [f. colloq. (Egyptian) Arabic: AND 1917.] Crazy, silly, mad.
 1918 *Kia-ora Coo-ee* (Cairo) (1981) 15 Apr. II. 18 Yes, poor Bob Gordon's gone magnune. Last I saw of him, he was in a sand cart..and humming in tune with its maddening melody. **1941** *NZEF Times* 1 Sept. 7 Some magnoun gentleman..put forward the brilliant suggestion of going out to the Pyramids. **1945** HENDERSON *Gunner Inglorious* 170 Don't think I'm magnoon (crazy), but I've got the wind up over those knives. **1946** BRUNO *Maleesh George* 53 He's gone crazy... Absolutely maknoon with the heat.

magpie.
 1. [f. the magpie's thieving habits.] One who borrows without permission.
 1944 FULLARTON *Troop Target* 34 You bloody magpie, what have you done with my tobacco.
 2. [An emblem of Hawke's Bay taken from the Australian magpie, a black and white bird acclimatized in great numbers in the province.] Often *pl.* The Hawke's Bay Rugby Union representative team, from the colours of the playing jersey, banded black and white.
 1952 FRASER *Ungrateful People* 9 [In 1926] All Blacks Cooke, Mill, Johnson and Grenside played for the 'Magpies' who retained the Shield that year. **1986** *Sunday News* (Auckland) 13 July 57 [Heading] Mistakes feast costs Magpies. There was little merit in a Bay of Plenty 23–18 win over Hawke's Bay. **1992** *Dominion Sunday Times* (Wellington) 9 Aug. 29 [Heading] Magpies swoop on woeful Wellington... The Magpie forwards were dynamic in the second half.
 3. Special Comb. **magpie moth**, see MOTH 6; **magpie ore** *goldmining*, see quot.
 1906 *NZ Geol. SB* (NS) No.1 52 The black and often shining argillite cemented in the white quartz presents a marked contrast, and this variety is termed by the miners 'magpie' ore.

mahi, var. MAI.

mahoa, var. MAHUE.

mahoe /ˈmahoi/, /ˌmaˈhʌui/. Also occas. **mahoi**. [Ma. /ˈmaːhoe/: Williams 164 *Māhoe* (i).. = *hinahina*.] *Melicytus ramiflorus* (fam. Violaceae), a small tree having pale whitish bark and commonly found near the coast or in second-growth bush. See also COWTREE 1, HINAHINA, WHITEWOOD 1 a.
 [**1820** LEE & KENDALL *NZ Gram. & Vocab.* 172 Má e óe; Name of a certain tree.] **1835** YATE *NZ* (1970) 49 Mahoe (*Melicytus ramiflorus*) has a thin, spiral and elegant leaf... The bark is smooth and light. **1849** [see NGAIO]. **1854** *Richmond-Atkinson Papers* 6 Jan. (1960) I. 141 I found a pigeon on its nest in a mahoi. **1863** MOSER *Mahoe Leaves* 5 [T]he graceful ko-whai..droops over the banks of a small creek..intermingled with..the fresh leaved Mahoe. **1889** KIRK *Forest Flora* 3 This tree is called by the natives mahoe in the North, hinahina in the South. **1890** *PWD Catalogue Timbers* (NZ & S. Seas Exhib.) 11 Mahoe (whitewood)... The 'hinahina' of South Island; timber white, soft, used for gunpowder charcoal. **1912** [see COWTREE]. **1926** COWAN *Travel in NZ* II. 32 Here and there a little watercourse..arboured over by a matted roofing of..*mahoe* or whitewood. **1940** LAING & BLACKWELL *Plants NZ* 280 In the South the plant is generally known as the *Ina-ina*, in the North it is called the *Mahoe*. **1951** HUNT *Confessions* 20 Our chief source of revenue was to gather in the bush fungus, which usually grew upon the dead and partly decayed stems of karaka and mahoe trees. **1961** [see HINAHINA]. **1988** DAWSON *Forest Vines to Snow Tussocks* 102 Other species which tend to be more wide ranging are mahoe..pigeonwood..toro.

mahogany. [Transf. use of *mahogany* for a similar NZ wood.]
 1. Also **native** (or **New Zealand**) **mahogany**. KOHEKOHE.
 1848 TAYLOR *Leaf from Nat. Hist.* 20 *Kohekohe, tree*;.. wood red; the New Zealand mahogany or cedar. **1935** *Tararua Tramper* June 4 This month the native mahogany, Dysoxylum spectabile, the kohekohe, is festooned with its beautiful greenish white flowers... The timber from this tree takes a fine polish.
 2. See *mahogany pine* (PINE 2 (7), TOTARA).

mahoi, var. MAHOE.

mahou, var. MAHUE.

mahrie, var. MAORI.

mahue. Also erron. **mahoa**. [Ma. /ˈmahue/: cf. Williams 165 *mahue* (i) pt. *1*. left (behind).] WITCH; as the Maori name suggests, a fish of little value.
 1911 Mahoa [see WITCH]. **1929–30** *TrNZI* LX. 142 *Caulopsetta scapha*... Megrim or Witch. Maori: Mahoa. **1956** GRAHAM *Treasury NZ Fishes* 186 The Maori name Mahue, according to my Maori friends means 'to be left behind', so the Maori too knew it was a valueless fish for food—and left it behind.

mai. *Obs. in English use.* Also occas. **mahi, maii, moy**. [Ma. /ˈmaːiː/: Williams 166 *Māi* (ii), n... = *mataī*.] a. MATAI 1.
 1831 BENNETT in *London Med. Gaz.* 12 Nov. 184 *Podocarpus Species*... This tree, the Mai or Matai of the natives of New Zealand, is an unpublished species of Podocarpus. **1841** *NZ Jrnl.* II. 152 We came to a beautiful plateau..covered with the finest spars I have seen..chiefly kikatea and moy, or the white and red pine of the sawyers. **1851** *Lyttelton Times* 28 June 6 The timber in [the groves] is chiefly..Mahi, (black pine)..and Totara. **1869** *TrNZI* I. (rev. edn.) 165 On drier ground [in Marlborough Sounds] he would find the Mai..festooned with parasites. **1870** *Ibid.* II. 122 [Podocarpus] spicata. Mai [season of flowering] Nov.–Dec. **1883** HECTOR *Handbook NZ* 124 *Podocarpus spicata*... Matai, Mai, Black-pine of Otago.—A large tree, 80 feet high; trunk 2–4 feet in diameter. **1898** MORRIS *Austral-English* 279 Mai or *Matai*, *n.* New Zealand tree, now called *Podocarpus spicata*. **1946** *JPS* LV. 145 *Matai*, a tree (Podocarpus spicatus), black-pine: often shortened to māi.
 b. As **maiberry**, the edible fleshy black berry of the matai.
 1849 ALLOM *Letter* in Earp *Handbook* (1852) 130 *Maiberry*, or *Mataki*, is a small round fruit of the same colour as the *tawa* berry.

maide, var. MAIRE.

maiden, *a*.

1. *Goldmining.* [Spec. use of *maiden*: see OED B II 5 c *maiden ground*, unworked ground.] Applied to country, or on the West Coast a black-sand beach, not yet worked for gold.
  1906 GALVIN *NZ Mining Handbook* 124 Where what is called the 'maiden beach' has all been cut away, it is hopeless to expect a repetition of the 'good old times' [of easy gold]. **1914** PFAFF *Diggers' Story* 43 We went up the creek to prospect... We pushed on into maiden country, i.e. the Right Hand Branch, and got very good prospects.

2. *Sawmilling.* As **maiden heart**, see quot.
  1952–53 *NZ Forest Gloss.* (TS) *Maiden Heart.* A term used in Westland to denote the innermost part of the intermediate heart zone in rimu and miro.

maidi, var. MAIRE.

maihi. [Ma. /ˈmaihi/: Williams 166 *Maihi* (i) *1*.] The facing boards on the gable of a house, often ornamented with carving on the lower ends.
  1838 POLACK *NZ* I. 138 It was surmounted with a *maihi*, or frontispiece, which was decorated with feathers. **1895** *TrNZI* XXVII. 674 The *maihi*, or gable-boards, have carvings of the mythological animal known as the *manaia*—probably a kind of taniwha. **1955** PHILLIPPS *Carved Maori Houses* 107 From this we may conclude that the maihi were cut and prepared in a timber-factory in Whanganui on order from the builders. *Ibid.* 135 On the other side we find a human figure near the lower maihi end. **1961** MEAD *Art of Maori Carving* 12 Besides the very ornate maihi, amo and pae..it was not unusual for the complete front wall to be a mass of carvings. **1969** BARROW *Maori Wood Sculpture* 116 [Caption] A vertical panel, one of a pair supporting the left bargeboard (*maihi*) of the Arawa storehouse named Puwai-o-te-Arawa. **1995** *Evening Post* (Wellington) 13 Mar. 19 A five-metre-long, heart totara maihi, or gable board, has been installed at the Museum of New Zealand.

maii, var. MAI.

maikaika. Also **makaika**. [Ma. /maːˈikaika/: Williams 167 *Māika* (iii) *māikaika, māmāika*, n. *Orthoceras strictum*, an orchid the tuber of which was eaten... Said to be applied also to *Thelymitra pulchella*, a similar plant.]

1. *Orthoceras strictum* (formerly *O. solandri*) (fam. Orchidaceae), a native terrestrial orchid with an edible tuber.
  1853 HOOKER *II Flora Novae-Zelandiae I Flowering Plants* 243 Orthoceras *Solandri*... Nat. name, 'Makaika'. **1867** HOOKER *Handbook* 766 Maikaika, *Col[enso]*. Orthoceras Solandri. **1978** FULLER *Maori Food & Cook.* 7 Perei and maikaika, types of orchis, were sought after.

2. Also ?**maikuku**, **Mai Kuku**. [Cf. Williams 167 *Maikuku*... 2. Claw, hoof: it is uncertain whether *maikuku* is a valid modern variant of *maikaika*, or a descriptive term, which Richards (1952) glosses.] The sun orchids, *Thelymitra longifolia* and *T. pulchella*, (fam. Orchidaceae). See also MAORI POTATO 2.
  1853 HOOKER *II Flora Novae-Zelandiae I Flowering Plants* 244 Thelymitra *pulchella,*... Nat. name, 'Makaika'. **1867** HOOKER *Handbook* 766 Maikaika... Thelymitra *pulchella*. **1906** CHEESEMAN *Manual NZ Flora* 670 [Thelymitra longifolia] Makaika. **1952** RICHARDS *Chatham Is.* 23 Thelymitra... longifolia... A ground orchid having a fleshy leaf... Common thelymitra, Maori Potato. Mai Kuku (claw). **1961** MARTIN *Flora NZ* 311 The flowers of the Maikuku (T[helymitra] longifolia) vary much in colour. **1982** BURTON *Two Hundred Yrs. NZ Food* 8 Types of rare orchids known as perei (*Gastrodia cunninghamii*) and maikuku (*Thelymitra longifolia*) were greatly prized for their masses of thick edible tubers.

maika ka. Also **maikai ka**, **maikaika**. [Ma. /ˈmaːikaˈka/ Williams 167 *Māika* (iii)..*māika ka*, n... = *rengarenga*.] RENGARENGA 1.
  1853 HOOKER *II Flora Novae-Zelandiae I Flowering Plants* 254 Arthropodium *cirratum*... Nat. name, 'Renga Renga', in Northern Districts, and 'Maikai Ka', in Southern. **1869** *TrNZI* I. (rev. edn.) 267 The blanched bases of the leaves of the harakeke (*Phormium*), and the roots of the Rengarenga or Maikaika (*Arthropodium cirratum*), were sometimes roasted and beaten to a pulp and applied warm to..abcesses. **1981** BROOKER et al. *NZ Medicinal Plants* 63 Arthropodium *cirratum*... Common name: *Rock lily* Maori names: *Rengarenga, maikaika, maika ka.*

maikuku, var. MAIKAIKA 2.

mail. Special Comb. **mail-car** [AND 1945], a passenger service vehicle which collects and delivers mail-bags from and to rural post offices from a central post office, or a car which delivers rural household mail (and parcels, etc); **mail cart** *obs*. [OED 1837], a cart in which rural or farm mail was delivered and collected; **mail launch**, a launch which delivers household mail, goods, passengers, etc. on a regular basis to water-bound localities; **mail-run**, the rural delivery run of a mail car (or mail boat).
  1915 COX *Diaries 1888–1924* (ATLMS) 24 Apr. I..walked to the post office..and came into Carterton by the **mail car** with five others. **1919** *Quick March* 10 July 22 Now watch..the Rosebud mail-car comin' down the zig-zag. **1920** *Weekly News* 8 Apr. [Caption] Washing down the mail car after the completion of the journey from Rotorua to Taupo. **1933** [see HORI 1]. **1947** GASKELL *Big Game* 48 She had returned from town at midday in the mailcar. **1969** MASON *Awatea* (1978) 24 Pera. What time's the mail car? **1973** WALLACE *Generation Gap* 209 But surely you know the uses a country mailcar is put to, Edna? **1980** NEAVE *Land of Munros* 46 I was sometimes called upon [c1920s] to drive a mail car to Omarama and Benmore Station on mail days to take surplus passengers and small goods to relieve the bus load. **1863** CHUDLEIGH *Diary* 6 Mar. (1950) 80 Reached Young's early from having one man taken 12 miles in the **mail-cart**. **1868** DILKE *Greater Britain* I. 340 Bumping and tumbling in the mail-cart through the rushing..waters of the Taramakao, I found myself within the mountains of the Snowy Range. **1937** HYDE *A Home in This World* (1984) 47 I was always getting letters by the weekly **mail launch**. **1994** mail launch [see DRAY *n.* 1]. **1961** CRUMP *Hang On a Minute Mate* 88 He'd still be putting up fences..instead of doing the Whenuaroa **mail-run** in a flash new truck.

maimai /ˈmaiˌmai/. Also **maemae**, **mia-mia**, **mimi**. [Often mistakenly considered of Maori origin: see AND *mia-mia* 1 1839 Aboriginal shelter, 2 1855 A traveller's temporary shelter; AAW 'It appears to have originated as *maya* or *maya-maya* in Nyungar, the language of the Perth-Albany region of Australia'.]

1. *Hist.* Mainly *SI*. **a.** A makeshift or temporary bush shelter quickly put together from materials at hand.
  1860 in Butler *First Year* (1863) May v 72 The few Maories that inhabit this settlement travel to the west coast by way of this river... We saw several traces of their encampments—little *mimis*, as they are called—a few light sticks thrown together, and covered with grass, affording a sort of half-and-half shelter for a single individual. **1861** *NZ Goldfields 1861* (1976) 27 Sept. 23 A dreary swamp next succeeded, beside which were a few *kaiks*, the mia-mias of the Maoris, who were here for the eeling season. **1873** ST. JOHN *Pakeha Rambles* in Taylor *Early Travellers* (1959) 555 In the days of bush fighting it used to be a common occurrence at the end of a day's march, when the *maemaes* had been knocked up by the side of a stream, to see..men..set to work with pannikin..and 'wash' for a prospect. [**1873** *Note*] A low hut worked up with sticks and interlaced raupo or fern, open in front, with roof reaching to the ground on the windward side. **1896** HARPER *Pioneer Work* 35 It is always possible to build a good 'wharé' or 'mai-mai' with bark stripped from the rata..totara..or cedar. **1914** *Hist. of N. Otago* (1978) 43 Other evidence that the Maoris camped in this locality was the remains of what I believed were called mai-mais. These were shelters made by plaiting the tips of the leaves of a large flax bush in such a manner as to form an arched canopy. **1915** MALONE 12 May in Phillips *Great Adventure* (1988) 47 I found [on Gallipoli] a little mimi of boards and sacks and felt and found only one man in it. **c1920** BEATTIE *Trad. Lifeways Southern Maori* (1994) 42 This name pahuri rightfully denotes a shelter of branches, rushes, flax, grass, etc., run up in the bush or on river banks when travelling about birding or fishing... The Maoris nowadays usually call such shelters 'maimai' but my aged friends consider that this is a 'foreign word'. **1945** HALL-JONES *Hist. Southland* 107 Many a pioneer camped under a tree... The next stage was a maimai, a crude shelter of boughs still used by duckshooters. **1972** MCLEOD *High Country Anthol.* 276 At the junction of the Wills I built myself a 'mimi' and stopped for the night. **1981** HUNT *Speaking a Silence* 104 First of all they just built a maimai: we stopped in it first night we went there.

b. *attrib*. Constructed like a maimai out of materials at hand.
  1979 WILSON *Titi Heritage* 98 Perhaps it was this [*sc.* the Ring of God's blessing] which kept the old mai-mai church intact for such a long time.

2. *transf.* uses. **a.** A permanent hut; occas. *joc.* for a home.
  1906 *Red Funnel* II. 12 When I'm sitting in my mi-mi Where the log-fire brightly burns. **1924** *Otago Witness* (Dunedin) 22 Apr. 65 We encamped for the night in an old maimai. **1945** WRIGHT *Station Ballads* 63 'Maimai'..the name for an out of way hut; there was one on the Dunstan Range many years ago and another is on Benmore Station. **1979** WILSON *Titi Heritage* 86 The biggest thatched house (Mai Mai) ever built was at Solomon's Point and was still standing in 1934.

b. Applied to a dog-kennel.
  1982 SANSOM *In Grip of Island* 152 These small fern-tree mai-mais were Frank Woodrow's dog kennels.

c. As a West Coast place-name.
  1985 MCGILL *G'day Country* 149 Ruatapu has a sawmill, New Forest has, appropriately, red pine for prefabs..Maimai is logs, Reefton coal.

3. (The usual modern sense.) A duckshooter's shelter or hide, usu. made of brushwood, raupo, etc.; occas. applied to similar structures such as a Maori-built hide for bird-snaring (see quot. 1920).
  1913 *NZ Observer* 17 May 17 The gallant Aucklander who returns with a large bunch of ducks has paid 30s for his mia mia and 12s per day for his Maori 'guide'. **c1920** BEATTIE *Trad. Lifeways Southern Maori* 174 To catch kakas..you could select a forked

tree, one with two or more branches..and build a..'maimai' on a stage under them. **1939** VAILE *Pioneering the Pumice* 299 *Mai-mai* a covert. **1945** [see 1 above]. **1959** SLATTER *Gun in My Hand* 224 Bert looking out the porthole at the wide Pacific and saying not a duck to be seen, what a helluva mai-mai this is. **c1961** BAXTER *Collected Poems* (1980) 304 More than a shroud He needs the maimai's breast of shade... when loud On ragged flights the shotguns played. **1972** MCLEOD *Mountain World* 310 *Mimi*: Corruption of Maori word for a hide or shelter. **1980** LELAND *Kiwi-Yankee Dict.* 61 *Maimai*. There you are, crouching, cold, wet(?), and expectant in your little hut among the reeds next to your favorite lake. Duck season is about to open and you await the sunrise and the game in your Duck Blind.

main, *n. West Coast. Obs.* [Of local significance in NZ: cf. OED *main n.³*, 1688.] Usu. *pl.* A cockfight, often with several cocks engaged at once.

c1880s in Seddon *The Seddons* (1968) 16 Cock fighting was a favoured sport on the goldfields and some very gallant birds were bred for this old English pastime. At Marsden, a secluded mining township in the bush some distance from Kumara, many cock fights were fought and a lot of money changed hands over the fate of these fights called 'mains.' **1968** SEDDON *The Seddons* 348 The clamorous challenges of the old English game cocks melted the hearts of some of the committee-men but cock fights were not part of the popularity of the [Greymouth] Poultry Show and mains did not materialise.

main body.

1. *Hist.* Occas. used of early immigrants into Canterbury settlement.

1851 GODLEY *Selection from the Writings* 3 June 204 I will not abandon hope that..with the arrival of the 'main Body' I shall receive an intimation that my services as the agent of a central governing body in England will no longer be required.

2. *WW1.* **a.** The first large contingent of the New Zealand Expeditionary Force which left on 16 October 1914 eventually for Egypt, to be followed during the war by a series of 'reinforcements'; but see also quot. 1989.

1916 *Letter* 2 Apr. in Malthus *ANZAC* (1965) 158 It rather gave me the blues to think of the happy times we had at the same place in the Main Body. **1918** *NZ At the Front* (Digger's Dict.) 32 *Main Body*.—Two magic words. If these be whispered into the ear of a sympathetic M.O., they produce excellent results. **1937** *Truth* 13 Oct. 13 The second reunion of the Main Body men is to be held..on..October 16. **1950** *RSA Review* Feb. 7 All those men who sailed with the Main Body, 1st N.Z.E.F., on October 16, 1914..were invited to attend. **1966** *Encycl. NZ* III. 560 With supporting troops and reinforcements 8,427 men embarked, with 3,815 horses... The Main Body, as it was later called, under Major-General Godley..was the largest single body of New Zealand troops ever to leave these shores. **1978** HENDERSON *Soldier Country* 21 3,817 horses no less, sailed away with the Main Body (the first mass of soldiers to leave New Zealand in War I for Egypt). **1989** in Boyack *Behind the Lines* ix Main Body. The New Zealand troops who sailed before 1916, but sometimes used to mean only the soldiers who sailed with the first convoy in October 1914.

b. Used *attrib.* in special Comb. **Main Body man (boy)**, a member of the Main Body, an experienced soldier. (Also *joc.* **mainbodyite**.)

1916 *Chron. NZEF* 16 Oct. 83 On the medical staff are quite a number of 'mainbodyites'. **1917** *Ibid.* 31 Jan. 257 Still, they drop one stripe on landing here, to give the mainbodyites a chance. **1918** let. 26 July in *Boots, Belts* (1992) 113 Last night one of our corporals, a main body boy[,] was told he would have a good chance to get back to N.Z. **1918** *Quick March* 25 May 16 Of course, it is well known that many of the Main Body men and certain Reinforcements..learned some of the geography of France. **1918** *NZ at the Front* 32 There are two great primary classes [of diggers] a) Aucklanders b) others. They may be further subdivided into: 1) Nat Goulds 2) Dinks 3) Stokers 4) Main Bodymen. **1963** AITKEN *Gallipoli to the Somme* 99 On making a rapid tour I felt that Sergeant Bree (a Main Body man with a very early number, 8/13) on the right had his men too near the trees.

main centre. (Usu.) as **(the) four main centres**, see quot. 1966; also *attrib.* pertaining to or characteristic of the four main centres.

1941 *NZEF Times* 15 Dec. 4 Sixpence has been fixed as the price for a 12 ounce handle of beer in the four main centres. **1946** SOLJAK *NZ* 82 Despite their difference in size, these four 'main centres' have preserved a marked individuality. **1951** KOHERE *Autobiog. of a Maori* 53 I have visited all four main centres of New Zealand, as well as other towns. **1966** TURNER *Eng. Lang. Austral. & NZ* 193 The *Four Main Centres*, as the four cities which for a long time were of a quite different order of magnitude from other places in New Zealand are called, are named Auckland, Wellington, Christchurch and Dunedin. **1972** MITCHELL *Pavlova Paradise* 42 Lacking main centre status [the thirteen smaller centres] clamour for the outward and visible signs of city stature—a university, a new airport, a Government Life building, a railway, a piecart. **1985** MCGILL *G'day Country* 162 Our four main centres have fine railway stations and foul areas around. **1986** BROWN *Weaver's Apprentice* 221 They were amazed to find demonstrations going on so far from a main centre.

main divide: see DIVIDE b.

mainland.

1. From the point of view of offshore islands, esp. the Chatham Islands and Stewart Island, either of the two main islands of New Zealand.

1774 FORSTER *Resolution Jrnl.* 1 Nov. (1982) IV. 678 The Capt. intends to try to get the boar & set him with a pregnant Sow, somewhere on the Mainland ashore. **1891** *NZJSc.* (NS) I. 161 Several interesting land birds inhabit the [Snares] island... The grass bird..although now rare on the mainland, was frequent on this little island. **1968** GRUNDY *Who'd Marry A Doctor?* 41 As freight was much too expensive to return bottles to the mainland the piles grew year by year as blots on the [Chatham Island] landscape. **1984** KIDMAN *Going to the Chathams* in *Landfall* 150 177 Yes the mainland is 800 kms away & mainlanders from the north whisper. **1985** HUNT *I'm Ninety-five* 270 What I missed, from the mainland and that?... One old man at Ruapuke used to say, 'It's looking bad weather over there at New Zealand'... We [Stewart Islanders] say 'mainland', and we do know what's going on over there. We say 'over there at New Zealand' as a joke nowadays. **1992** [see PIGEON 2 (2)].

2. Usu. as **the Mainland**, the South Island; orig. by South Islanders, but now in general ironic or joc. use.

1949 *Journeys 34* 56 I'm sure South Islanders are right in claiming that they live on the 'mainland'. **1954** WINKS *These New Zealanders* (1956) 55 One last warning: We Americans promise not to confuse the South Island with The Glorious Mainland. **1965** CAMERON *NZ* 33 The South Island is sometimes called Te Waka o Maui (the Canoe of Maui) which suits South Islanders' sense of pride in being on the 'mainland'. **1973** WILSON *NZ Jack* 106 Well, so Otago won... A victory for the good old Mainland. **1988** *Dominion* (Wellington) 24 Sept. 8 In the deepest recesses of the mainland, they're [*sc.* gumboots] supposedly called Southland Slippers.

Mainlander. [MAINLAND + -ER.]

1. *Chatham Islands.* A person from mainland New Zealand.

1950 SIMPSON *Chatham Exiles* 149 Mainlanders are immune from this phenomenon [of influenza] for the first two years of their stay, but after that they fall victim along with island-born people. **1989** *Listener* 13 Nov. 110 Passage to the Chathams..was uncertain... Not easily deterred..he and a fellow mainlander slipped unobserved down..in the forward hold.

2. SOUTH ISLANDER a.

1955 *Truth* 21 Dec. 4 You Mainlanders haven't got any sense, or you wouldn't have come north at this time of the year. **1962** WEBBER *Look No Hands* 93 'You *are* a Mainlander, though,' said the Bloke, 'and that makes it just as hard.' **1978** HENDERSON *Soldier Country* 135 A Mainlander, Christchurch-born..he became a farm valuer. **1985** STEWART *Gumboots & Goalposts* 14 'We're right behind you all the way,' and 'Get stuck in to these mainlanders.' **1992** *Press* (Christchurch) 1 Feb. 2 The happy disposition of Mainlanders has made an unforgettable impression on two English visitors.

main range: see RANGE *n.* 1 c

mainstreaming. The educational process of placing children with special needs (for example, through handicap, disability, or brilliance) in ordinary ('mainstream') school classes.

[*Note*] The equivalent term used in the US is 'inclusive education'.

1993 *Evening Post* (Wellington) 16 Mar. 6 CCS [Crippled Children's Society] believes in inclusive education or mainstreaming which ensures that children with special needs and their parents have the right to choose mainstreaming as a first option.

main trunk.

1. Also often *attrib.* as **main trunk line**, **main trunk railway**. Often init. caps. The principal railway line between **a.** Wellington and Auckland; and **b.** (less freq.) between Picton and Dunedin (or Invercargill).

[*Note*] Cf. **1863** The/ Waikato and Ngaruawahia,/ the Proposed/ New Capital/ of/ New Zealand;/ with/ a Railway from Auckland to the Proposed New Capital, and Thence/ to Wellington, with Branches to Hawke's Bay and Taranaki,/ to Be Called/ the Great Trunk Railway of New Zealand,/ by/ A Settler... 1863 [title page: *NZNB* I. ii. plate facing 912].

a. *North Island.* Often *attrib.*

1887 *Auckland Weekly News* 14 May 8 The Main Trunk railway runs within a few miles of this proposed National Park. **1897** *TrNZI* XXIX. 284 Taken from one of the cuttings on the main trunk line near Hunterville. **1917** *Free Lance* (Wellington) 14 Sept. 13 She was down from up the Main Trunk now visiting her married daughter. **1934** HYDE *Journalese* 224 It has been unofficially recorded that Lord Jellicoe was one of the few to use the communication cord on the Main Trunk. **1951** PARK *Witch's Thorn* 36 All the way along the Main Trunk became a positive, virulent thing. **1964** CAPE 'Taumarunui' in Reid *Book of NZ* (1964) 223 I'm an ordinary joker getting old before my time For my heart's in Taumarunui on the Main Trunk Line. **1985** MCGILL *G'day Country* 80 There was trouble out of Palmerston North with the electrification of the Main Trunk. **1991** *Evening Post* (Wellington) 7 Nov. 3

Repair crews had worked through the night and it was hoped to have the Main Trunk reopened today.

b. *South Island.*

1902 *Settler's Handbook of NZ* (Lands Department) 52 The main trunk railway-line is constructed to Culverden, twelve miles north of the Hurunui, the southern boundary of the district. **1951** FRAME *Lagoon* (1961) 9 The Main Trunk Line brings more tourists [to Picton], my aunt said.

2. Any of the trains plying the main trunk lines. Cf. LIMITED.

1955 MACLEOD *Voice on the Wind* 22 But best of all was when they caught [c1870s] the Main Trunk ('Vogel's train') to Rangitata.

3. a. In *attrib.* use as Comb. **main trunk express, route, train**.

1913 *NZ Observer* 23 Aug. 3 The Railway Department certainly made a bad blunder in taking off the second **Main Trunk express** during the winter months. **1916** COWAN *Bush Explorers* (VUWTS) 14 He was made prisoner...while surveying the **Main Trunk route**, and was..kept chained up..in a whare at Te Kumi. **1912** *Auckland University Capping Carnival Programme* 6 June 46 There was a Tournament held in a Southern town: We sent our annual team as usual to win renown, They kissed their mothers... And left by the **Main Trunk Train**. **1985** BINNEY *Long Lives the King* 13 Above the mud of the embankment the Main Trunk train sat, dirty silver, idle.

b. Special Comb. **main trunk gothic**, joc. used of the architectural style found at Taihape on the Main Trunk line.

1959 MCCORMICK *Inland Eye* 9 [The] styles [of Taihape public buildings] showed a surprising diversity, ranging from the classical severity of the bank to the pinnacled romanticism of the Anglican church, an exceptionally fine example of Main Trunk Gothic.

Hence **main-trunk** *v. absol.*, to travel on a main trunk train.

1910 *Truth* 17 Sept. 4 He sold the pub., came to Wellington, saw this 'Tottie' off to Sydney, then Main-Trunked it to Auckland.

maioriori, var. MORIORI.

maire /ˈmairi/. Also early **maide, maidi, mairi, maree**. [Ma. /ˈmaire/: Williams 168 *Maire* (ii) *1.* n. *Olea cunninghamii* and other species of *Olea.*]

1. a. A forest tree of the genus *Nestegis* (formerly *Olea*) (fam. Oleaceae) of the North Island and northern South Island, esp. as **black maire** *N. cunninghamii,* a tall tree with a dark brown wood valued as firewood. See also MAIRE-RAUNUI, *New Zealand olive* (OLIVE 1).

[**1820** LEE & KENDALL *NZ Gram. & Vocab.* 173 Maide; Name of a certain tree.] **1838** POLACK *NZ* II. 397 *Mairi* or *maidi, (cedrus Zelandicae,)* is the closest grained and toughest of woods in the country. **1841** HODGSKIN *Narr. Eight Months Sojourn NZ* 27 Maree, a fine large tree, produces a mohogany-coloured [*sic*] wood. **1856** SHORTLAND *Traditions & Superstitions* 184 Maire is a species of yew; its wood is one of the hardest in New Zealand. **1875** KIRK *Durability NZ Timbers* 21 Maire.—(*Olea cunninghamii* and *O. lanceolata*)... Black Maire.—(*Olea apetala*). **1883** HECTOR *Handbook NZ* 132 Maire—a small tree ten to fifteen feet high, six to eight inches in diameter; wood hard, close-grained, heavy, used by Maoris in the manufacture of war implements. **1898** [see OLIVE 1]. **1908** BAUGHAN *Shingle-Short* 13 *Maire* (*my-ray*): A native timber. **1946** *JPS* LV. 144 *Maire*, a tree (Olea cunninghamii). **1986** SALMON *Native Trees* 287 In our fireplace maire burned slowly with great heat and without sparking.

b. [Cf. Williams 168 *Maire* (ii)... *Maire taiki, Mida salicifolia.*] *Mida* (formerly *Santalum* or *Fusanus*) *salicifolia* (fam. Santalaceae), a slender forest tree having glossy leathery leaves. See also SANDALWOOD 1.

[*Note*] The generic name *Mida* is an adaptation of an early *maide* form of *maire.*

1853 HOOKER *II Flora Novae-Zelandiae I Flowering Plants* 224 *Santalum Cunninghamii...* Nat. name, 'Maire'... This plant is not the 'Mida' of the New Zealander, as Mr Colenso assures me, but the 'Maire', and closely resembles *Eugenia Maire*, the 'Maire Tawake'. **1869** *TrNZI* I. (rev. edn.) 275 The Maire:- Two, or more, very distinct genera, containing several trees, (*Santalum*..and *Olea* sp.), are confounded under this Native name; although the natives themselves generally distinguish them pretty clearly,—calling the *Olea,* Maire-rau-nui. Both were by them called maire, from the fact of both being hard-wooded. **1889** KIRK *Forest Flora* 137 *Fusanus cunninghamii...* The maire... It is frequently termed 'New Zealand sandal-wood' by settlers. **1906** CHEESEMAN *Manual NZ Flora* 624 A small slender tree 10–25 ft. high... *Maire*; *New Zealand Sandalwood.* **1939** [see SANDALWOOD 1]. **1961** MARTIN *Flora NZ* 164 Maire or sandalwood (*Mida myrtifolia*) leaves alternate or opposite, 2–3 in.

c. MAIRE TAWAKE (*Syzygium maire*).

1843 DIEFFENBACH *Travels in NZ* II. 123 It is made of the hard wood of the maire (Eugenia maire). **1843** TAYLOR *Journal* Aug. (ATLSS) 52 Maidi a tree bearing red berries like the bay wood very hard the natives make their clubs of it. **1973** SARGESON *Once Is Enough* 63 Miles promised to take me to a part of the bush where the trees were nearly all maire, and there were pigeons feeding in hundreds on the maire berries.

2. With a modifier: **black, white.**

(1) **black maire**. Any of several trees known also as *maire* or MAIRE-RAUNUI, esp. *Nestegis* (formerly *Olea*) *cunninghamii* (see 1 a above), and the wood of these trees.

1875 KIRK *Durability NZ Timbers* 21 Black maire..is sometimes 40 feet high or more. **1885** *Wairarapa Daily* 24 Apr. 2 It is said that black maire is much sought for at Home for machine bearings. **1890** *PWD Catalogue Timbers* (NZ & South Seas Exhib.) 11 Maire-rau-nui (black maire)..Olea Cunninghamii... One of the strongest of New Zealand timbers; it is hard, dense, and very heavy; the grain handsome and nicely marked. **1904** *TrNZI* XXXVI. 460 Two clubs of black-maire (*Olea cunninghamii*)—the kind used by the natives in crushing fern-root—were found. **1938** HYDE *Nor Yrs. Condemn* 117 Underneath, in silt, the workers found a buried forest of black *marae* [*sic*] trees. **1986** [see (2) below].

(2) **white maire** [f. the colour of the bark]. Formerly but rarely MAIRE TAWAKE; usu. the tree *Nestegis lanceolata* of the North Island and northern South Island (see 1 a above).

1882 HAY *Brighter Britain* II. 193 The Maire-Tawhake (*Eugenia Maire*), or 'White Maire'. **1889** KIRK *Forest Flora* 107 This species [*Olea lanceolata*], which is usually termed 'white-maire' by the Auckland woodmen, in its most developed state forms a round bushy-headed tree with dark bark, and rarely exceeds 50ft. in height. **1890** *PWD Catalogue Timbers* (NZ & South Seas Exhib.) 11 Maire, white..Olea lanceolata... Timber very even in grain, hard, and shrinks little; used for wood engraving, machine-bearings, fencing-posts, rails, &c. **1910** *TrNZI* XLII. 477 The white maire..is here [among Tuhoe] known as *maire-rau-nui* and *maire-roro.* **1940** LAING & BLACKWELL *Plants NZ* 355 *O. lanceolata* (*The White Maire*)... Bark white... Timber similar to that of the Maire. **1961** MARTIN *Flora NZ* 164 White maire... Bark whitish; leaves narrow, opposite. **1975** *Tane* 21 8 Oleaceae *Nestegis lanceolata* white maire. **1986** SALMON *Native Trees NZ* 290 The wood of white maire is tough and durable, like that of black maire.

mairehau. [Ma. /ˈmaireˈhau/: Williams 168 *Maire* (ii) *1.* n... *Maire hau, Phebalium nudum.*] *Phebalium nudum* (fam. Rutaceae), an aromatic shrub of the North Island, having gland-dotted leaves.

1867 HOOKER *Handbook* 766 Mairehau... *Phebalium nudum.* **1869** *TrNZI* I. (rev. edn.) 236 Of our shrubs and smaller timber trees, several are of strikingly beautiful growth..(e.g.) the Houhere..the Mairehau, *Phebalium nudum.* **1889** FEATON *Art Album NZ Flora* 80 Phebalium nudum..The 'Mairehau'.—This shrub is peculiar to the northern portion of the Northern Island. **1907** LAING & BLACKWELL *Plants NZ* 220 *Phebalium nudum* (*The Naked Phebalium*)... Maori name *Mairehau.* **1961** MARTIN *Flora NZ* 227 There are several fine shrubs from the Auckland Province that would grace any garden. In this group we would include..the Mairehau (*Phebalium nudum*). **1978** MOORE & IRWIN *Oxford Book NZ Plants* 90 Mairehau. A small shrubby tree typical of dry ridges in kauri forest and not extending further south. No bush scent is sweeter than that of the dull reddish leaves. **1981** LOCKE *Student at Gates* 73 Kath and I were so entranced by the dainty shrub mairehau that we vowed we'd call our first daughters by that name.

maire-raunui. [Ma. /ˈmaireˈrauˈnui/: Williams 168 *Maire* (ii) *1.* n... *Maire rau nui, O. cunninghamii.*] MAIRE 1 a and *black maire* 2 (1) (*Nestegis cunninghamii*).

1853 HOOKER *II Flora Novae-Zelandiae I Flowering Plants* 175 *Olea Cunninghamii...* Nat. name, 'Maire raunui', Col. A tree about 50 feet high, unbranched below. **1869** *TrNZI* I. (rev. edn.) 275 The natives themselves generally distinguish them [*sc. Santalum* and *Olea*] pretty clearly,—calling the *Olea,* Maire-rau-nui. **1889** KIRK *Forest Flora* 103 The maire-rau-nui is one of several trees to which the name 'maire' is commonly applied by settlers and the younger Maoris; the older Maoris..distinguish it as the maire-rau-nui. It is often called 'black-maire' by the bushmen. **1910** COCKAYNE *NZ Plants & Their Story* 41 The maire-rau-nui (*Olea Cunninghamii*), an extremely strong timber.

maire tawake. Also **maire-tawhake, maire tawhaki**. [Ma. /ˈmaire ˈtawake/: Williams 168 *Maire* (ii) *1.* n...*Maire tawake.*] *Syzygium* (formerly *Eugenia*) *maire* (fam. Myrtaceae), a tree of swampy or boggy land, having edible red berries. Also called **swamp maire**.

1853 HOOKER *II Flora Novae-Zelandiae I Flowering Plants* 71 Eugenia *Maire...* Nat. name, 'Maire tawake'. **1869** *TrNZI* I. (rev. edn.) 263 The *hard-wooded* Maire-tawhake, *Eugenia Maire*, was..used by the Northern tribes (among whom it alone grew) for husbandry implements. **1872** *TrNZI* IV. 249 Near it the maire-tawhake.., clothed from base to summit with white myrtle-like flowers and leaves. **1889** FEATON *Art Album NZ Flora* 169 The 'Maire-tawhake'..is almost wholly confined to the Northern Island, on swampy land, and principally in the northern districts. **1907** LAING & BLACKWELL *Plants NZ* 288 *Eugenia Maire* (*The Maire*)... Maori name, *Maire[-]tawhaki.* The timber makes the best of firewood. **1989** PARKINSON *Travelling Naturalist* 30 The lower and more swampy areas are dominated by kahikatea and maire-tawake, the swamp maire. **1993** GABITES *Wellington's Living Cloak* 48 The round-crowned swamp maire has specialised roots also. It sends up small fingers that absorb air through spongy tips.

mairi, var. MAIRE.

mairoero, var. MAEROERO.

maka, var. MANGA.

makaika, var. MAIKAIKA.

makaka. [Ma. /'maːkaka/: Williams 168 *Mākaka* (i)... *3. Carmichaelia* of several species, shrubs.] A native broom *Carmichaelia arborea* (formerly *australis*) (fam. Fabaceae), a much-branched, usually leafless, shrub of open habitats having sweet-scented flowers. See also BROOM 1.
 1867 HOOKER *Handbook* 766 Makaka, *Geolog. Surv. Carmichaelia australis*. **1872** *TrNZI* IV. 252 These are dotted with bushes of makaka..with its leafless branches, the representative of the yellow broom of Europe. **1889** FEATON *Art Album NZ Flora* 177 Makaka [Maori name]..Broom [Settlers' name]..Carmichaelia Australis..Shrub. **1897** [see BROOM 1]. **1966** *Encycl. NZ* III. 710 Broom, New Zealand . . makaka, tainoka, taunoka . . *Carmichaelia* spp.

maka-maka, var. MAKOMAKO.

makamaka. [Ma. /'makamaka/: Williams 168 *Maka* (i)..*makamaka*... 5. n. *Ackama rosaefolia*.] *Ackama rosaefolia* (fam. Cunoniaceae), a small tree of northern North Island kauri forests, having compound leaves and showy panicles of cream flowers.
 1853 HOOKER *II Flora Novae-Zelandiae I Flowering Plants* 79 Ackama rosaefolia... Nat. name, 'Maka Maka'. **1867** HOOKER *Handbook* 766 Maka-maka... *Ackama rosaefolia*. **1889** KIRK *Forest Flora* 113 The makamaka is one of the fine plants first discovered by Allan Cunningham. Being confined to a small district in the most northern portion of the colony it is but little known. **1910** COCKAYNE *NZ Plants & Their Story* 46 Confined to the north are..the makamaka... and some other trees and shrubs. **1939** COCKAYNE & TURNER *Trees NZ* 24 Makamaka. A small, bushy tree, 15–40 ft. high, or a shrub... *Distribution*.—Northern Auckland. **1944** *Bull. Wellington Bot. Soc. No.8* 1 He would like to show me a patch of Makamaka. **1951** LEVY *Grasslands NZ* (1970) 87 In the far north the kauri and its associates, taraire, mangeao, makamaka.. predominate. **1978** MOORE & IRWIN *Oxford Book NZ Plants* 76 Makamaka is a small tree with light green foliage set off by brownish stems and twigs.

make, *v.*
 1. *Goldmining*. [See OED *make v.*[1] 73 b to extend in a certain direction; AND 1850.] *intr*. Of auriferous (esp. black-sand) material, to build up.
 1908 *NZGeol.SB (NS)* No.6 25 On the sea-beaches the 'black-sanders' often have to wait many weeks or months before a payable patch of black-sand 'makes'. *Ibid.* 153 Though a rich patch of black-sand often makes in a single tide it is evident that the first working of the beaches makes a noticeable inroad on the store of gold available.
 Hence **make** *n.*, a build-up (of auriferous material).
 1875 *AJHR H-3* 53 The quartz..changes in character from crystalline and brown ferruginous in the higher to dense and bluish-grey in the lower parts of the workings—in fact the latter quality represents a so-called 'new', or 'second make'.

2. [See OED *make v.*[1] 65 to accomplish a distance by travelling.] *intr.* and *trans.* To travel.

 1934 *Press* (Christchurch) (Acland Gloss.) 20 Jan. 15 *Make.*—(1) (Of sheep) to travel; making up, making back, etc.; (2) (of men) arrive at, get to; e.g., *m[ake]* the station. **1952** THOMSON *Deer Hunter* 184 We had only found and skinned twelve before we reckoned it was time to make homewards if we wanted to reach camp before dark.

3. *trans.* Of a sheep-dog, to make (sheep) docile or amenable; of sheep, to be made amenable to handling or guiding.
 1971 NEWTON *Ten Thousand Dogs* 66 I'd picked up a young heading dog..which..was the greatest dog I've ever seen at getting on good terms with—or 'making'—sheep. *Ibid.* 80 The sheep were big, strong, touchy Merino wethers, easily upset, and when Boy finally walked them into the ring they were like three pets... When those sheep entered the ring they were really 'made', and Bill could have done anything with them.

4. In various phrases **to make a smoke**, see SMOKE *n.*[1] 1; **to make a sale**, see SELL OUT; **to make one's marble good**, see MARBLE 1; **to make wages** *goldmining*, see WAGES 1.

makings, *n. pl.* [Cf. OED *makings* 8 b 'N. Amer., Austral. and N.Z. colloq.'.] Tobacco and a tissue paper for rolling a cigarette.
 1930 DEVANNY *Bushman Burke* 26 He grinned and took out the 'makings'. **1939** *Dominion* (Wellington) 15 Sept. 13 I hand 'em on the makings, gentlemen, I hand 'em on the makings. **1949** LLEWELLYN *Troopships* 7 The normal Kiwi..his clothes in a heap beside him, the 'makings' handy. **1963** PEARSON *Coal Flat* 70 Rogers offered him a cigarette but McKenzie shook his head and pulled out the makings in a way that seemed to suggest that tailor-mades were a stigma of middle-class ideology. **1992** ANDERSON *Portrait Artist's Wife* 63 He..reached in a trouser pocket for the makings and rolled a cigarette.

maknoon, var. MAGNOON.

mako /'makʌu/, *n.*[1] [Ma. /'mako/: Williams 170 *Mako* (i) n. *1*..mako shark...2. Tooth of the same, worn as an ear ornament: OED derives *mako* from Maori; Walsh and Biggs *mako[2] 'shark sp.' gives only Maori and Marquesan *mako* as the extant descendants of PPN *mako. (Any Japanese form is prob. a borrowing of the Pacific word: the 1727 quot. below is suspect in its application as far exaggerating the length of the *mako*.)]

1. a. As **mako**. Pl. *makos*. Often (wrongly) regarded by English speakers as *ellipt*. for *mako shark*, *Isurus oxyrinchus* (fam. Lamnidae), a prized game fish, blue above, lighter or white below, esp. valued by the Maori for its teeth as ornaments. Cf. *blue pointer shark*, *mackerel shark*, *porbeagle shark* (SHARK 2 (4), (11), (14)).
 [**1727** J.G. SCHEUCHZER tr. *Kaempfer's Hist. Japan* I. 1. 133 [OED] *Mako* never exceeds three or four fathom in length. **1820** LEE & KENDALL *NZ Gram. & Vocab.* 173 Máko; A certain fish.] **1848** TAYLOR *Leaf from Nat. Hist.* xiii Mako, the shark which has the tooth so highly prized by the Maoris. **1872** HUTTON & HECTOR *Fishes NZ* 77 Lamna Glauca... Tiger Shark. *Mako*... The shark from which the Maoris obtain the teeth with which they decorate their ears. **1885** *TrNZI* XVII. 21 The mako, a small shark much prized by the natives for its teeth. **1892** *TrNZI* XXIV. 416 Fifty years ago..a Maori chief would be known by wearing certain emblems or insignia indicative of rank, one of which was the tooth of the *mako* as an ear-pendant. **1908** HAMILTON *Fishing & Sea-Foods* 29 The teeth of the mako (*Lamna nasus*) were held in great esteem as ornaments for the ear. **1926** GREY *Angler's Eldorado* 178 A cream-white torrent of water burst nearer to us, and out of it whirled the mako going up sidewise then rolling, so his whole underside, white as snow, with the immense pectoral fins black against the horizon, shone clearly to my distended eyes. **1937** HYDE *Wednesday's Children* (1989) 75 There are few sharks around New Zealand but makos, and..the Maoris wear mako teeth in the holes of their ears as proof of valour. **1958** PARROTT *Big Game Fishes* 100 In life the mako is deep blue above and lighter along the sides... It feeds on smaller fishes..and has been known to attack Swordfishes. **1980** BERRY *First Offender* 57 He'd eaten fish and chips happily for years until he found out that mako was the Maori name for shark.

b. As **mako shark**.
 1928 *Free Lance* (Wellington) 8 Feb. 17 Lord Grimthorpe, the English banker..exceeded all his expectations by landing the world's record mako-shark off Cape Brett. **1946** *Dom. Mus. Rec. Zool.* I. 8 During my first visit to the Bay of Islands, I questioned older natives about the truth of the story..that the ancient Maori was accustomed to lasso the mako shark for the sake of its teeth, and several said it was true. **1957** WILLIAMS *Dict. Maori Lang.* 170 *Mako* (i), n. *1. Isurus glaucus*, *mako shark*. **1966** DOOGUE & MORELAND *Sea Anglers' Guide* 184 Mako Shark... *Isurus oxyrhinchus*; sharp-nosed mackerel shark, blue pointer. **1982** AYLING *Collins Guide* (1984) 51 *Mako Shark*..*Isurus oxyrinchus* (Blue pointer, mackerel shark, bonito shark). The mako has been described as the quintessential shark. It is probably the most graceful, the most beautifully coloured, and the fastest swimming of all the sharks.

2. In full **mako tooth**. A (mako) shark tooth worn esp. as an ear ornament or as part of a necklace.
 1840 POLACK *Manners & Customs* II. 177 Mako, or tooth of the ground-shark. **1847** ANGAS *Savage Life* I. 267 She was dressed in the European fashion..but retained the *mako*, or shark's teeth, in her ears. **1882** POTTS *Out in Open* 10 From one ear depends the glistening máko. **1936** HYDE *Check to Your King* (1960) 117 They wore pieces of *mako* tooth in the lobe of the ear. **1957** BAXTER *Collected Poems* (1980) 185 A girl with a necklace of mako teeth They dug from a sandcliff facing south. **1962** JOSEPH *Pound of Saffron* 113 This is for the ear, too—the mako, like a shark's tooth.

mako, *n.*[2] and *n.*[3]: see MAKOMAKO *n.*[1] and *n.*[2]

makomako /'makʌuˌmakʌu/, /'mɒkəˌmɒk/, /'mɒkiˌmɒk/, etc., *n.*[1] Also unreduplicated MAKO *n.*[2]; **maka-maka**, **mako-mak(')**; and developments of a perceived form **moko** or **mokomoko**, often reflecting a folk-etymological reshaping under the mistaken belief that the bellbird is (like the tui) a *mocking*-bird: **mock-a-mock**, **mockie**, **mocki mock**, **mockymock**, **moke-mok**, **moki(-mok)**, **mokimoki**, **mokky**. [Ma. /'makomako/: Williams 170 *Mako* (iii), *makomako*, n... bell-bird. = *korimako*.] Cf. MOCKER *n.*[1], MOCKIE *n.*[1], MOCKING-BIRD.

1. BELLBIRD 1 a (*Anthornis melanura*). Cf. KORIMAKO. **a.** Forms from **mako, makomako**.
 1840 DIEFFENBACH *Acc. Chatham Islands* in *Jrnl. Royal Geogr. Society* XI. 195–215 in Holmes *Chatham Is.* (1984) 95 The mako-mako, the finest songster in New Zealand, is also found here. **1841** *NZ Jrnl.* II. 51 Here and there a hawk follows its prey..or the mako interrupts the silence with his melodious notes. **1873** [see KORIMAKO]. **1894** WILSON *Land of Tui* 161 What musician has evoked a strain that echoes the..Maka-maka trills from his exultant little throat? **1908** BAUGHAN *Shingle-Short* 126 The *Mako-mak'* pull'd and gave to

them Green feathers from her wing. **1914** Pfaff *Diggers' Story* 11 The singing of the Makos (bell birds) and Tuis in the morning was exquisitely beautiful. **1928** Baucke *Manuscript* (Bishop Museum Memoirs Vol.IX No.5 343–382) in Skinner & Baucke *Morioris* 362 Tui and mako (bell birds) were killed by the birder hutching beneath a cone of fern fronds. **1932** mako [see korimako]. **1950** Beattie *Far Famed Fiordland* 49 Tuis, mokimokis, makomako, canaries and robins were common. **1966** Falla et al. *Birds NZ* 218 Bellbird *Anthornis melanura*... Korimako, Makomako, Mockie. **1978** Preston *From Rocks to Roses* 21 To coax the makomaks and tuis—Those hearty honey-eating birds —To sing arpeggios and thirds I'd even go without drambuies. **1985** *Reader's Digest Book NZ Birds* 290 Bellbird *Anthornis melanura... Korimako, makomako, mockie*. **1990** *Checklist Birds NZ* 214 *Anthornis melanura melanura... Bellbird (Korimako, Makomako)*.

b. Forms from **moko, mokomoko** (see also 1950, 1966, 1985 a above).

1871 Hutton *Catalogue Birds NZ* 6 Anthornis melanura... Bell-bird. Mocker. Korimako. Moko-moko. **1884** *NZJSc.* II. 277 Anthornis melanura... Bell bird, Korimako, Makomako, which last name seldom often render into mockymock. **1889** Blair *Lay of the Old Identities* 51 She sings her simple lays Like moko on the tree. **1896** *TrNZI* XXVIII. 51 In November, kakas, tuis, and mokos were here in great numbers feeding on the honey of the rata-blossoms. **1898** Morris *Austral-English* 299 *Moko-moko, n.* (1) Maori name for the Bell-bird. **1904** Lancaster *Sons o' Men* 136 The mock-a-mocks woke there to answer most sweetly. **a1917** Effie Studholme 'The Song of the Native Born' in Studholme *Te Waimate* (1954) 307 Then the Moki's sweet song peals out like a bell. **1933** mako-mako, moki-mok, mokky [see bellbird 1 a]. **1977** Bruce *Life in Hinterland* 73 But for the Mocki Mock's liquid music..I was alone with the Creator's handiwork.

2. ?tui.

1941 Marsh *Surfeit of Lampreys* (1951) xiv 218 She found herself describing the New Zealand Deepacres..how English trees grew into the fringes of the native bush, and how English birdsong, there, was pierced by the..notes of bell-birds and mok-e-moks.

makomako /ˈmakʌuˌmakʌu/, /ˈmɒkəˌmɒk/, /ˈmɒkiˌmɒk/, etc., *n.*² Also as unreduplicated mako *n.*³; **maku, mockamock, moki, moko, moko-mok**. [Ma. /ˈmakomako/: Williams 170 *Mako* (ii), *makomako, n. Aristotelia serrata*.] wineberry 1.

1848 Taylor *Leaf from Nat. Hist.* 20 *Mako*, a tree; the bark used as a black dye. *Makomako*, a tree. **1848** Brunner *Exped. Middle Is.* 21 May in Taylor *Early Travellers* (1959) 310 Tried a new species of fruit, the berry of the *moko*, and found it very palatable. **1861** *Richmond-Atkinson Papers* 24 Mar. (1960) I. 696 Just before the fireplace were a few makos which they [*sc.* marauding Maori bands] had been sleeping on. **1885** *TrNZI* XVII. 216 Amongst smaller trees and shrubs the most prominent are the horoeka..and the mako. **1890** makomako [see currant]. **1901** *NZJE* III. 86 The large membranous leaves of our moko scrub.., afford a very good example of this phenomenon. **1939** Beattie *First White Boy Born Otago* 13 The mako or native willow has a little blue-black berry full of seeds which you spit out when eating. **1940** moko-mok [see currant]. **1959** Taylor *Early Travellers* 402 [1959 Note] In Otago it [*sc. Aristotelia*] is called New Zealand currant or 'Moko-mok'; and is otherwise known as Mako-mako or wineberry. **1963** Pearson *Coal Flat* 421 mockamock: The wineberry, a small fast-growing tree often the first to establish itself after bush has been felled or cleared. **1967** McLatchie *Tang of Bush* 59 Taking the axe [c1900]..I searched the bush for a moki. **1975** Knight *Poyntzfield* (1975) 58 Haura was able to fill his sugar bag with berries from the maku trees that grew plentifully and so beautifully by the edge of the bush [near Rangitikei c1850s]. **1982** Burton *Two Hundred Yrs. NZ Food* 7 Other berries popular as delicacies were..the ripe, black berries of the makomako or wineberry.

mako-mak('), var. makomako *n.*¹

makootoo, var. makutu *v.*

makrakapa, var. macrocarpa.

maku, var. mako *n.*³

makutu, *n.* and *a*. Also **makuta**. [Ma. /ˈmaːkutu/: Williams 171 *Mākutu*. 1. v. trans. Bewitch... 2. n. Spell, incantation.]

A. *n.*

1. Sorcery, witchcraft; a spell.

[**1820** Lee & Kendall *NZ Gram. & Vocab.* 174 *Mákutu,... s.* Witchcraft.] **1830** Marsden *Lett. & Jrnls.* (1932) 478 The New Zealanders have a strong belief in witchcraft, which they call *makutu*, and think that those persons who have the power to *makutu* can kill any person they choose by this art. **1843** Dieffenbach *Travels in NZ* II. 16 The belief in witchcraft (makuta) [*sic*], to which many [natives] have fallen victims. **1863** Moser *Mahoe Leaves* 65 There were old men—firm believers in Makutu (witchcraft). **1905** *TrNZI* XXXVII. 35 By means of *makutu* a person could be made to offend against some law of *tapu* without his being aware of it, and in such case illness or death was sent by atua who had been insulted... This *makutu* business was the dangerous part of a *tohunga's* profession. **1936** Lambert *Pioneering Reminisc. Old Wairoa* 77 Tohungaism, and the practice of *makutu*..are all practically dead. **1944** Finlayson *Brown Man's Burden* (1973) 16 The school-kids were boasting about old Tupara putting a makutu curse on Monday. **1953** *Here & Now* Aug. 21 Hinewaka, he speaks, died from *makutu*, the death-magic! **1969** Mason *Awatea* (1978) 46 Tina. You go and chase yourself. Don't you come any of your old makutu over me, Irapeta. **1972** Baxter *Collected Poems* (1980) 590 And like a wave of black water The makutu hits me. **1986** Sorrenson in *Na To Hoa Aroha* I. 32 Their deaths led some Ngatiporou, even Ngata himself at times of despair, to conclude that Waikato had put a makutu on them. **1992** Edwards *Mihipeka* 55 My mother had a makutu placed on her when she married our father.

2. mate *n.*¹, *Maori sickness* (Maori B 5 a).

1988 *Dominion* (Wellington) 30 Mar. 12 A bus driver was struck on the head..by a man who claimed he suffered from Makutu [*sic*], a Maori sickness, the High Court at Auckland was told yesterday... He was not insane..yet he was mentally unstable... He had suffered from makutu, a form of mental illness peculiar to Maoris, and its associated personality disorder.

B. *adj.* Pertaining to sorcery: in predicative use, put under a spell, bewitched.

1820 Marsden *Lett. & Jrnls.* 13 June (1932) 253 The alleged cause was that a near relation of Koro Koro's had been poisoned (bewitched—*makutu*) when on a visit to the Thames. **1847** Johnson *Notes from Jrnl.* 7 Jan. in Taylor *Early Travellers* (1959) 169 Others again more credulous impute it, to the malevolent influence of an *Atua* or evil spirit, or to the individual being *makutu* or struck by an *evil eye*. **1856** Grace *Rep. Taupo Dist.* 31 Dec. in *Pioneer Missionary* (1928) 6 No doubt, had any of our people been taken ill and died, the belief would have been that they were 'makutu' (bewitched), that is, that the god of their great Chief had entered the sick person and devoured him for violating his 'tapu'. **1872** *Weekly News* (Auckland) 7 Dec. 5 The natives here indulged in a little makutu humbug last week. **1905** *NZ Herald* (Auckland) 11 Feb. Suppl. 1 This woman..tried to induce Paki to cease his makutu practices. **1987** *NZJH* XXI. No.1 19 She was a makutu old lady.

makutu, *v.* Also **makootoo**. [See *n.*] *trans.* To bewitch (a person).

1825 Hall 10 Jan. in Elder *Marsden's Lieutenants* (1934) 235 We were told by the natives there that the dead bodies were three slaves that were killed for makootooing a chief, that is bewitching or praying evil prayers against him that caused his death. **1828** Williams *Early Jrnls.* 25 Mar. (1961) 117 It is generally current that Pango..had *makutu*d (bewitched) 'Hongi and caused his death. **1830** [see *n.* 1 a]. **1840** Polack *Manners & Customs* I. 74 That they bewitched (mákutu) his enemies and strengthened the hearts of his friends. **1873** Tinne *Wonderland of Antipodes* 34 The father took down his tomahawk, and creeping up cautiously, lest he himself should be makutu-ed by a look, brained his parent. **1892** *Star* (Auckland) 15 June in Bailey & Roth *Shanties* (1967) 83 Heaven itself would be *makutu*ed by some fellows that I know. **1905** Baucke *White Man Treads* 263 'Good,' she replied, 'then it is you and I; I will makutu you and kill you!' **1913** *NZ Observer* 26 July 10 The opposing hapu..had made sure of victory by carefully makutu-ing the playing-ground beforehand. **1943** Marsh *Colour Scheme* 25 'I'll tell my great-grandfather..and he'll *makutu* you.' 'Kid-stakes! Nobody's going to put a jinx on me.' **1966** Meredith *A Long Brief* 208 'I am going to makutu you.' In my boyhood in the Waikato I have known several instances where people died, their relations claiming they were makutued.

maleesh /ˌmaˈliʃ/. *WW1* and *WW2*. Also with much variety of form as **maaleesh, maaleish, ma'lêsh, malesh, marleesh**. [f. Egyptian Arabic 'no matter': AND *mahleesh*, 1918.] Often as **maleesh the**, indicating dismissal of or indifference to the idea or thing indicated; but occas. as an adjective (see quot. 1947).

1918 *Kia Ora Coo-ee* 15 Oct. 13 Ma'lêsh is not simple. It means 'It does not matter', or 'Never mind', and is really two words. **1942** *NZEF Times* 6 Apr. 6 Maleesh all the impersonal pronouns, said the bloke. *Ibid.* 21 Dec. 20 After a while he adopted the 'maleesh' attitude. **1943** *Ibid.* 6 Sept. 5 Maleesh the lingo. **c1944** in Cleveland *Great NZ Songbook* (1991) 115 When in conversation you're bound to say *maaleish*; Traces of Egypt linger still. **1947** *NZ Observer* 2 July 16 I have been attended..by 'maleesh' and mediocre dentists, and by downright butchers. **1971** Newton *Ten Thousand Dogs* 142 There was a local horse running that day and when that race came up it was '*maleesh*' the dog trials. **1981** Gee *Meg* 172 He spoke to his men in their Middle East slang: shufti and maleesh and *bint*. **1992** Farrell *Skinny Louie Book* 64 'Maleesh,' said Martin, 'Forget it. I'm on civvy street now.'

malthoid /ˈmælθoɪd/. [OED f. *malth*(a bitumen + *-oid*.] The proprietary name of a bituminous material mixed with wood fibre and used as a roof- or floor-covering or for other surfaces. Often *attrib*.

1909 *Otago Daily Times* (Dunedin) 31 Dec. 10 [Advt] 'MALTHOID'—As a floorcloth is cheaper and will outlast the most expensive linoleum. **1918** *Chron. NZEF* 8 Nov. 175 The rumour has it that the bath-house was a decent affair..until some thoughtless sapper climbed it to lay the malthoid roofing, whereupon the building incontinently collapsed. **1936** *NZ Patent Office Jrnl.* [no number given] 3 Dec. Malthoid 33927 [filed] 28th May, 1935. Pabco Products (Australia)

Limited..Asphalt roof roofing, damp-course, weatherproof building-paper or sheathing-felt, pipe-covering, floor-covering, sarking-felt and lining-materials made of paper and/or felt containing protecting and preserving compositions saturated and/or coated with mineral substances and/or asphalt, all the foregoing goods being goods included in Class 17. **1939** *Tararua Tramper* Aug. 8 Three care-free youths were having a marvellous time up on the roof, trying to fix Malthoid on to nothing. **1946** *Tararua Tramper* July 19 Waikamaka Hut, situated right at the main forks of the river, is stoutly built of malthoid and corrugated iron. **1960** MASTERS *Back-Country Tales* 29 The hut is a malthoid construction, with beech pole framework. **1973** FERNANDEZ *Tussock Fever* 39 As David lifted the latch to enter the malthoid hut a putrid stench sent him gasping back. **1986** RICHARDS *Off the Sheep's Back* 35 The roof was closely timbered, then covered by strips of Malthoid paper.

mamagu, mamakau, mamako, varr. MAMAKU.

mamaku. Also with much variety of early form as **Māmāgu, mamakau, mamako, mammok, mamuk', mamuka, mummock, mummuke, mumoki.** [Ma. /ˈmamaku/: Williams 171 *mamaku. 1.* n...an edible tree-fern.] *Cyathea medullaris* (fam. Cyatheaceae), the black tree fern; also occas. its edible pith prepared as food (see PITAU 1). See also *king fern* (FERN 2 (11) b), *black tree fern* (FERN 2 (20) b (a)), *black ponga* (PONGA 2 (1)), KORAU 1.

 1773 *Mā[m]āgu* [see PONGA 1 a]. [**c1826–27** BOULTBEE *Journal* (1986) 110 Cassada—kartto and mammok.] **1837** WAKEFIELD & WARD *Brit. Colonization* 324 Mumoki, called by the Europeans cassada. **1841** BIDWILL *Rambles in NZ* (1952) 100 I also saw here for the first time the gigantic tree fern (Mummuke), the young fronds of which are eaten by the natives, as well as the soft part of the head of the trunk, corresponding to the cabbage of the palm. **1846** HEAPHY *Exped. to Kawatiri* 16 May in Taylor *Early Travellers* (1959) 232 *Mamaku*, when mixed with wine, sugar, and spice in a tart, might be mistaken for baked apple. **1855** HOOKER *II Flora Novae-Zelandiae II Flowerless Plants* 7 Cyathea *medullaris*... Nat. name, 'Korau' of the northern tribes, 'Mamaku' of the southern, *Col*. **1867** HOCHSTETTER *NZ* 158 Mamakau, Pitau, Korau..an arborescent fern. **1874** BAINES *Edward Crewe* 198 Then there were the magnificent tree-ferns, one kind..called punga by the natives; another sort..they call mamaku. **1882** POTTS *Out in Open* 15 The thick syrup (mamuka) prepared from the pith of the great treefern..was deliciously cool, of a pleasant bittersweet flavour. **1889** PAULIN *Wild West Coast* 107 Pieces of mummock were brought away for cooking purposes. **1890, 1926** [see FERN 2 (20) b (a)]. **1938** HYDE *Godwits Fly* (1970) 116 When they have passed the mamuk' tree-fern..they know the Day's Bay fetish has been properly observed. **1957** *Dominion* (Wellington) 12 Aug. [corresp. col] The kaponga or brown tree fern is not nearly so handsome as the mamaku, or black tree fern. **1965** GILLHAM *Naturalist NZ* 24 The black ponga is a giant among ferns, reaching heights of 60 feet with fronds nearly 18 feet long... The Maoris refer to the black tree-fern as mamaku and formerly cleaned their new-born babes with the soft mass of black scales brushed from the young uncurling fronds. **1982** BURTON *Two Hundred Yrs. NZ Food* 7 [Heading] Mamaku (tree fern) In springtime, the rough outer bark of selected tree ferns (Cyathea medullaris) was chipped with a sharp instrument to allow the sometimes bitter juices to trickle out.

mamangi. [Ma. /ˈmaːmaːŋi/: Williams 172 *Māmāngi,* n. *Coprosma repens* and other species..= *angiangi, taupata.*] Any of several native plants of the genus *Coprosma* (fam. Rubiaceae), esp. the small tree *C. arborea*, also known as *tree karamu* (KARAMU 2).

 1867 HOOKER *Handbook* 766 Mamangi..*Coprosma spathulata*. **1889** KIRK *Forest Flora* 109 *Coprosma Baueriana* is a handsome evergreen shrub or small tree exclusively restricted to maritime situations... Williams states that it is the 'mamangi' of the East Cape Natives: it does not appear to have received any distinctive appellation from the settlers. **1939** COCKAYNE & TURNER *Trees NZ* 34 *Coprosma arborea* (Rubiaceae). Mamangi. **1966** *Encycl. NZ* I. 399 The largest growing species [of *Coprosma*] is..mamangi..a small tree 15–25 ft high common in the open, lowland forest from near the north to about the centre of the North Island. **1975** *Tane* 21 8 Rubiaceae C[oprosma] arborea mamangi.

mammok, mamuk', mamuka, varr. MAMAKU.

mana /ˈmanə/. [Ma. /ˈmana/: Williams 172 *Mana* (i) *1.* n. Authority, control... *2.* Influence, prestige, power... *3.* Psychic force.]

1. In Maori contexts, authority; prestige; influence; power or control.

 1843 DIEFFENBACH *Travels in NZ* II. 371 Mana—command, authority, power. **1848** TAYLOR *Journal* (ATLTS) 4 June V. 219 He replied it was true he should not be able to understand what was said but still the 'mana' or efficacy of the prayers there offered up would be of as much avail to him as to the rest of the congregation. **1858** *Richmond-Atkinson Papers* (1960) I. 460 At Whanganui they object to the form of deed conveying the 'mana' or power over the land to the Queen. **1860** BUDDLE *Maori King Movement* 17 Another object aimed at is the preservation of what they call the 'mana' of the Chiefs. This word means authority, power, influence. *Ibid*. 18 'Kia mau te mana o te whenua' is another expression now in frequent use, i.e., 'hold fast the mana of the land'... This is altogether a new application of the term; perhaps it has been adopted in consequence of the Queen's Sovereignty over the Island having been translated as the Queen's mana. But it certainly did not originally mean that which is now claimed for it, viz., a Chief's 'manorial right'. This use of the word was not heard until this Maori King movement originated it. **1881** CAMPBELL *Poenamo* 166 Should the future, unhappily, foment squabbles between the two races, the time might come when we should be glad to shelter ourselves under the 'mana' (the protection) of good old Kanini. **1893** *TrNZI* XXV. 485 But as soon as that deadly invention, gunpowder, came in use both knight & chief rapidly lost their mana or reputation for doughty deeds. **1904** TREGEAR *Maori Race* 317 The word *mana* itself has no English equivalent, but it may be best rendered in this connection as 'prestige', that is, 'influence derived from former achievements and from a confident expectation of future success'. **1929** BUCK *Coming of Maori* 17 Some tribes openly stated that *mana* and prestige came from the canoes. **1938** HYDE *Nor Yrs. Condemn* 169 When I come back [to the pa] they treat me as if I'm not there, and my husband, he's the big fellow—got the big *mana*, eh? **1959** SINCLAIR *History NZ* 21 Nevertheless they possessed considerable power by the virtue of *mana* (a word meaning something more than 'prestige') which resulted from exalted descent and past achievements. **1987** *Dominion* (Wellington) 9 Sept. 8 She said the difference in mana from the traditional whanau to the Mongrel Mob was that, with the mob, mana was not based on family links and members were accountable only to themselves.

2. In 19th c. use, also with quotation marks or in italics. In non-Maori contexts, prestige, or the authority of people, movements or things, esp. of public figures.

 1856 *McLean Papers* (ATLTS) III. 53 The old man is anxious to have the 'mana' of the undertaking and so far I am quite willing to humour him. **1898** REEVES *Long White Cloud* 403 Very few words have been adopted from the vigorous and expressive Maori. The convenient 'mana'..covers prestige, authority, and personal magnetism. **1907** DRUMMOND *Life of Seddon* 54 The liberal leader's 'mana' was gone. **1934** HYDE *Journalese* 21 The mana of the Bulletin was great, and had its awkward moments for its many imitators over here in New Zealand. **1950** WILSON *My First 80 Yrs.* 44 Archdeacon Harper..was a great personality and had a *mana* all of his own. **1965** LEE *Rhetoric at the Red Dawn* 117 Clever organiser Bert Davy knew that Ward was a shadow of the man who had done great things in Seddon's day, but he knew that the Ward mana persisted. **1984** HOLCROFT *Way of Writer* 171 My mana rose locally, and the serial brought almost as much satisfaction to the Dales..as it did to me.

manaia, n.[1] [Ma. /maˈnaia/: Williams 173 *manaia 1.* n.] A grotesque beaked figure, a birdlike head on a human body, often seen in Maori wood carving.

 1895 *TrNZI* XXVII. 674 The *maihi*, or gableboards, have carvings of the mythological animal known as the *manaia*—probably a kind of taniwha. **1910** COWAN *Maoris of NZ* 165 Some of the wall slabs are carved into fantastic figures of fabulous water-monsters..others represent the mythical creatures known as the *manaia* and *wheku* with bird-like beaks and snaky tails all coiled in endless spirals. **1924** BEST *The Maori* II. 574 A common design in the carved work of superior houses and elevated storehouses is that known as the *manaia*..a figure composed of a long, slim body, a birdlike head, and an indefinite number of legs. **1966** *Encycl. NZ* II. 410 Apart from the naturalistic figure, every type of full-faced figure has a *manaia* to match... The head of the *manaia* can, in each case, be recognised as half of the head of the appropriate matching figure divided down the middle of the face.

manaia, /məˈnaiə/, n.[2] [Ma. /maˈnaia/: Williams 173 *Manaia 3*...seahorse.] *Hippocampus abdominalis* (fam. Syngnathidae), the sea-horse.

 1927 PHILLIPPS *Bibliogr. NZ Fishes* (1971) 20 *Hippocampus abdominalis*... Sea-horse; Manaia. **1956** GRAHAM *Treasury NZ Fishes* 149 Seahorse (Manaia) *Hippocampus (Macleayina) abdominalis*. **1967** MORELAND *Marine Fishes* 16 The Maori name manaia refers to the spiral tail [of the seahorse]. **1982** AYLING *Collins Guide* (1984) 195 Seahorse (Manaia) *Hippocampus abdominalis*.

man alone. [f. the title of a NZ novel (pub. 1939) by John Mulgan (1911–45).] A type (or stereotype) of the independent, outdoors New Zealander.

 1983 FRANCIS *Wildlife Ranger* 72 [Chapter heading] Man Alone **1987** *Dominion Sunday Times* (Wellington) 27 Dec. 6 Kiwis make myths of 'man alone' type efforts against the juggernaut of state authority, but cringe weekly when it comes to doing something for themselves. **1989** BIOLETTI *The Yanks Are Coming* 16 The silent 'Man Alone' New Zealand male, suspicious of language, talk and books, contrasted strongly with the fast-talking servicemen from bustling American cities.

manaoa, var. MANOAO.

manatu. [Ma. /ˈmaːnatu/: Williams 173 *Mānatu,* n. *Plagianthus betulinus.*] LACEBARK 1 b, RIBBONWOOD 1 (*Plagianthus* spp., esp. *regius*).

 1906 CHEESEMAN *Manual NZ Flora* 78 [*Plagianthus*

betulinus] Ribbon-wood of Europeans; manatu of the Maoris. **1915** [see RIBBONWOOD 2 (1)]. **1952** RICHARDS Chatham Is. 64 P[lagianthus] chathamicus..Manatu. **1978** MOORE & IRWIN Oxford Book NZ Plants 72 Plagianthus betulinus, manatu. The riverbank ribbonwood is considered by some botanists to be more correctly known as Plagianthus regius. **1986** SALMON Native Trees NZ 184 Manatu is the largest of the New Zealand deciduous trees.

manawa. Also **maanawa.** [Ma. /ˈmaːnawa/: Williams 174 Mānawa (i) n...mangrove.] MANGROVE 1.

[**1820** LEE & KENDALL NZ Gram. & Vocab. 174 Manáwa s.... Also the name of a certain tree.] **1838** POLACK NZ II. 398 Manawa and Tuputupu, two varieties of the well-known mangrove, cover the mud banks of the rivers and creeks of the country in which they flourish. **1843** DIEFFENBACH Travels in NZ I. 204 The arms of the Parenga-renga inlet..generally terminate in swamps, grown over with what is called the New Zealand mangrove (Avicennia tomentosa), named manawa by the natives. **1853** HOOKER II Flora Novae-Zelandiae I Flowering Plants 204 Avicennia tomentosa... Nat. name, 'Manawa'. **1888** COLENSO Fifty Years 43 We also noticed the absence of..the shore-loving Maanawa. **1906** CHEESEMAN Manual NZ Flora 567 Muddy creeks and estuaries from North Cape to Opotiki and Kawhia on the west. Manawa; Mangrove. **1946** JPS LV. 153 Mānawa, an amphibolic tree..mangrove. **1964** NORRIS Settlers in Depression 201 When the peat had been burnt [at Rukuhia Swamp, Hamilton] there would be a network of manawa branches.

manawau, VAR. MANOAO.

Manchester. [Ellipt. and transf. use of Manchester wares cotton goods manufactured at Manchester (England): AND 1907.] Usu. attrib. passing into special Comb. **Manchester department,** the department in a general or other store which sells Manchester goods; **Manchester goods,** cotton goods, esp. sheets, pillowcases, towels, orig. manufactured mainly in Manchester.

[**1859** FOWLER Southern Lights & Shadows (1975) 13 In fact at Maitland, a country town, nearly one hundred miles from Sydney, I went over a drapery and general store larger and more lavishly appointed, incredible as the assertion may appear, than the great Manchester warehouses of St. Paul's Churchyard.] **1879** Auckland Weekly News 26 Apr. 14 [Advt] Drapery, Manchester Goods, Men's and Boys' Clothing. **1905** Evening Post (Wellington) 5 Jan. 7 [Heading] Manchester Department White, pure linen Table Damask. Ready made Table Cloths... Unbleached Twill Sheeting. **1911** Evening Post (Wellington) 3 Jan. 11 [Advt for Cole's Cash Drapery Company] unequalled bargains in sterling Manchester lines Special New Year sheeting bargain... Irish Linens. **1922** Evening Post (Wellington) 2 Oct. 11 [Advt] Manchester Department. Just arrived, new shipment of white counterpanes, coloured quilts, and printed bedspreads. **1933** Ibid. 16 Nov. 21 Black's for bargains. We're giving up Manchester and cotton and silk dress goods..the balance of our Manchester and napery Clearing at Half price. **1972** MITCHELL Pavlova Paradise 183 Manchester: Japanese cotton goods. **1980** LELAND Kiwi-Yankee Dict. 62 manchester: In the industrial revolution the city of Manchester specialized in the mass production of things made of cloth. As a result the manchester department of your local New Zealand department store sells the sheets, towels, etc.

manga, VAR. MUNGA (food).

manga. Also SI variants **maga, maka, mòkka.** [Ma. /maŋˈaː/: Williams 177 Mangā, n. 1. Thyrsites atun... 2. Mustelus antarcticus, gummy shark.] Either of two unrelated sea-fish.

1. BARRACOUTA 1 (Thyrsites atun).

[**c1826–27** BOULTBEE Journal (1986) 113 Boracoota—mòkka.] **1842** GRAY Fauna in Dieffenbach Travels in NZ (1843) II. 210 Thyrsites atun... This fish is named 'Maga' by the natives of Queen Charlotte's Sound, where it was seen by the Forsters. **1872** HUTTON & HECTOR Fishes NZ 109 This fish [sc. barracouta] is a favourite with the Maoris, who call it the Manga or Maka. **1929** BEST Fishing Methods 45 Worser amused us by an exhibition of his skill in catching manga. This is a long fish without scales, exceedingly voracious. **1947** POWELL Native Animals NZ 71 Barracouta.., Manga of the Maoris, is a long narrow fish attaining a length of almost 4 feet. **1966** DOOGUE & MORELAND Sea Anglers' Guide 279 Baracouta... Other names: Thyrsites atun; manga (Maori).

2. A small shark or dogfish, GUMMY n.³

1927 PHILLIPPS Bibliogr. NZ Fishes (1971) 7 Mustelus antarcticus... Gummy; Manga. **1947** [see SHARK 2 (9)]. **1956** GRAHAM Treasury NZ Fishes 71 Smoothhound Dogfish (Manga) Emissola antarctica... The name Smoothhound is given to one of the two New Zealand species of Dogfish.

mangamanga, VAR. MANGEMANGE.

mangeao. Also **mangeo, mangiao, mangio.** [Ma. /ˈmaŋeao/: Williams 177 mangeao, mangeo... Litsaea calicaris... = tangeao.] Litsea calicaris (fam. Lauraceae), a small dioecious tree of the northern North Island; also its useful wood. See also TANGEAO.

1848 TAYLOR Leaf from Nat. Hist. 20 Mangiao, a tree; the ash of this country. **1869** TrNZI I. (rev. edn.) 274 The Tangeao or Mangeao..is a small tree, also confined to the Northernmost parts of the Island. **1874** BAINES Edward Crewe 127 I was fortunate in getting some mangio-boards to build her with, from my friends out the sawmill. **1887** Auckland Weekly News 27 Aug. 10 Mr. Tremain..showed us some screwdrivers which he had fitted with handles of mangiao, a native wood, which, from its toughness and lightness, is admirably adapted for such a purpose. **c1890** BODELL Soldier's View Empire (1982) 214 That fine Timber Mangeao got scarce, I closed the Mill. **1905** TrNZI XXXVII. 118 Mangeo, Mangeao. Used in the vapour bath by lying-in women to promote the lochial discharge. **1950** WODZICKI Introduced Mammals 163 [Turbott found on Three Kings] wharangi..mangeao (Litsaea calicaris). **1961** ALLAN Flora NZ I. 137 Dist.: N. Lowland forest from near North Cape to lat. 38° Mangeao.

mangemange. Also with much variety of form as **mangamanga, manghee manghee, mangi-mangi, maunga-maunga, monga monga, mongi-mongi, mongo mongo, mongu-mongu, mounga-mounga, mungamunga, mungi-mungi,** reflecting a variety of early anglicised pronunciations and poss. of Ma. dial. variants. [Ma. /ˈmaŋemaŋe/: Williams 177 Mangemange... a climbing fern.] Lygodium articulatum (fam. Schizaeaceae), a twisting, climbing forest fern of the northern North Island.

1817 NICHOLAS NZ I. 343 These [sc. fish-catching baskets] were made of the bark of a tree called manghee manghee, and were ingeniously contrived. **1842** BEST Journal 20 Apr. (1966) 354 They now made a basket like an Eel Pot which they wove of Mongu-mongu. **1843** DIEFFENBACH Travels in NZ I. 426 They tie [bundles of raupo] together with the mangi-mangi, a climbing fern, the Lygodium articulatum of Achille Richard. **1847** ANGAS Savage Life II. 30 We passed several primitive landmarks..one being composed of three upright posts, with balls of mange mange—a dried creeper—fastened on top. **1874** BAINES Edward Crewe 42 [He] passed the night on the table in the 'living-room' [of the bushman's hut], a couch he mightily improved by an extemporary mattrass [sic] of Mongo Mongo vines. **1882** HAY Brighter Britain II. 201 The Mounga-mounga..is the delight of persons camping out. It has a stem like small twine... Bunches of it make capital bedding. **1888** BARLOW Kaipara 139 A couple of sacks [on stakes]..[form] the bed, on which is laid either dried ferns or Mongi-mongi as a mattress. **1900** Auckland Weekly News Xmas Number 27 Stanton Delland lay on his mungamunga bed in his whare by the Auckland Harbour. **1925** TRACY Piriki's Princess 88 With a mungi-mungi vine for our line. **1930** REISCHEK Yesterdays in Maoriland (1933) 88 We travelled..to the top of a high, narrow range of precipices, overgrown with short, thick scrub and manga-manga. **1955** BOSWELL Dim Horizons 39 Our mattresses were of mange-mange, a bush creeper of dense tangled growth, sufficiently springy if not very soft when green. **1978** MOORE & IRWIN Oxford NZ Plants 216 The strangest thing about mangemange is that the true stem is very short but the leaf goes on growing at its tip and may be many metres long. **1986** RICHARDS Off the Sheep's Back 44 The bedding and mange-mange mattress would be neatly rolled and stacked along one end.

mangeo, VAR. MANGEAO.

Mangere /ˈmaŋəri/, /ˈmʌŋɡəri/. [f. Mangere (Ma. /ˈmaːŋere/) a locality (now a city) in s. Auckland.] Special Comb. **Mangere clover,** a New Zealand name for an introduced clover Trifolium subterraneum (fam. Fabaceae), common throughout most of New Zealand, but first recorded from Mangere; **Mangere pole,** a climbing French bean.

1926 HILGENDORF Weeds 107 [Subterranean Clover] is a small clover growing on rather rich land in scattered localities in both islands... It has become the dominant weed in many pastures near Auckland so that it is sometimes called 'Mangere clover', and has spread to most or all districts where ploughing is practised. **1956** NZJAg. June XCII. 518 Subterranean clover was first recorded in New Zealand in this district [Mangere] and was known for many years as Mangere clover. **1986** MATTHEWS NZ Garden Book 199 Among climbing French beans the stringless varieties 'Shiny Fardenlosa' and 'Mangere Pole' are popular. **1987** Yates Garden Guide 63 Varieties of Climbing beans are:... Mangere Pole: an excellent late-season cultivar... Pods are long, shiny dark green, stringless, flat and very attractive. **1992** NZ Gardener Apr. 25 Grown in the same way as Mangere pole, but in the warmer areas here, they [sc. yard-long beans] can be very vigorous and highly productive annual climbers.

Mangere rail: see RAIL 2 (7).

manghee manghee, VAR. MANGEMANGE.

mangiao, VAR. MANGEAO.

mangi-mangi, VAR. MANGEMANGE.

mangio, VAR. MANGEAO.

mango /ˈmʌŋɡʌu/. Also **mágho.** [Ma. /ˈmaːŋ oː/: Williams 178 Mangō n. Shark, dogfish; a general name but applied also to Mustelus antarcticus, gummy shark (= makō [Ngai Tahu]).]

MANGROVE

1. Any of various sharks and dogfish, esp. *Mustelus antarcticus*, GUMMY *n.*³ Compare and contrast MANGA 2 and 1.
 [**1815** KENDALL *New Zealanders' First Book* 9 Mágho. A shark.] **1838** POLACK *NZ* I. 101 My companion eyed it much..and observed, that the mango, or shark, was a rich treat to the New Zealanders. **1844** COLENSO *Excurs. Northern Is.* in Taylor *Early Travellers* (1959) 50 This bay..is a favourite resort of several species of *Squalus* in the summer season; at which time the natives..take them in great numbers. They call them Mango. **1851** SHORTLAND *S. Dist. NZ* 70 There was the 'mango' or shark..and a variety of other dainties. **1860** *Richmond-Atkinson Papers* 19 Dec. (1960) I. 669 Tasted tupakihi & mango for first time... Mango rather like putrid leather. **1882** HAY *Brighter Britain* II. 151 In the bays and tidal rivers are the mango or sharks—the most highly-prized food-fish. **1898** MORRIS *Austral-English* 282 *Mango, n.* Maori name for the *Dog-fish*.., a species of shark. **1946** *JPS* LV. 153 *mangō*, a sea-fish, shark, or dog-fish; a general name, adopted by Pakeha for shark, with erratic pronunciation, including manggo. **1977** *Glenfield College Maori Cookbook* 57 Mango Maroke (Cured or Dried Shark). Cut fresh shark into strips, hang out to dry and store for winter use. **1981** [see DOGFISH 2].

2. With a suffixed Maori modifier.

(1) **mangopare, mango-pare**. [Ma. /maˈŋoːˈpare/: Williams 178 *Mango... Mangō-pare*.., hammerhead shark.] *hammerhead shark* (SHARK 2 (10) *Sphyrna zygaena*).
 1855 [see SHARK 2 (10)]. **1886** SHERRIN *Handbook Fishes NZ* 118 Mango, it should be remembered, seems almost a generic name for shark in the North, as there is the mango-taniwha, a large variety; the mango-pare, the hammerheaded shark; the mango-reremai, the common dog-fish; the mango-pekepeke, and the mango-aruroa. **1924** *NZJST* VI. 262 Synonyms: *Squalus zygaena; Zygaena malleus; Cestracion zygaena*. The hammer-headed shark, or mango pare (*Sphyrna zygaena*), appears for the most part to live in the open sea. **1951** POWELL *Native Animals NZ* (1959) 60 Hammerhead Shark (*Sphyrna lewini*), Mangopare of the Maoris. **1967** MORELAND *Marine Fishes* 12 Hammerhead Shark... The Maori name mango-pare is still in use but is met with only rarely.

(2) **mango-ripi**. [Ma. /maˈŋoːˈripi/: Williams 178 *Mangō.. Mangō-ripi, Alopias vulpinus*, thresher shark.] *thresher shark* (SHARK 2 (18) *Alopias vulpinus*).
 1947, 1956, 1966 [see SHARK 2 (18)]. **1987** POWELL *Native Animals NZ* 55 Thresher Shark (*Mango Ripi*) *Alopias superciliosus*.

mangrove. [Specific use of *mangrove*, a tree of the plant family Avicenniaceae.]

1. Also occas. **white mangrove**. *Avicennia marina* (formerly *A. officinalis, A. resinifera*) (fam. Avicenniaceae), a small native tree found on tidal mudflats of the northern North Island. See also MANAWA.
 1769 COOK *Journals* 11 Nov. (1955) I. 196 Very low flat Islands all cover'd with a sort of Mangrove trees and several places of the Shores of both sides of the River were cover'd with the same sort of wood. **1817** NICHOLAS *NZ* I. 231 the *mangrove* is found in the low and marshy shores in great abundance, and is likewise considerably larger than in New South Wales. **1838, 1843** [see MANAWA]. **1869** *TrNZI* I. (rev. edn.) 235 North of the Thames..he will be struck with the appearance of the White mangrove..growing within the range of the tide. **1889** KIRK *Forest Flora* 271 This littoral tree is well known to settlers as the 'mangrove' or 'white mangrove', and is found in estuaries or muddy tidal rivers. **1906, 1946** [see MANAWA]. **1986** STEVENSON *Wetlands* 74 Tall mangroves may be found in almost all the estuaries that indent the coast of Northland.

2. In *attrib.* use.
 1769 COOK *Journals* 16 Nov. (1955) I. 204 In speaking of Mercury Bay I had forgot to mention that the Mangrove trees found there produce a resinous substance very much like rosin [the (erron.) reference is to kauri-gum]. **1840** MATHEW *Journal* 2 Apr. in *Founding of NZ* (1940) 103 We walked round the little valley..shut in on one side by a mangrove flat covered with water at high tide. **1882** HAY *Brighter Britain* I. 117 Half a mile in front is a mangrove swamp, beyond which flows the river. **1906** *TrNZI* XXXVIII. 354 I learn..of a still more anomalous station for this shrub—viz., on mangrove islands in the Rangaumu Estuary. **1948** FINLAYSON *Tidal Creek* (1979) 41 She glides along with half her hull..above the level of the mangrove flats or the bare tussocky shores.

 Hence **mangroved** *ppl. a.*
 1959 SHADBOLT *The New Zealanders* (1986) 10 I grew to awareness rejecting as alien our scrubby backblocks farm, the mangroved tidal creek.

3. Special Comb. **mangrove fish**, PARORE.
 1875 *TrNZI* VII. 245 Parore, or Mangrove Fish. **1886** [see PARORE]. **1899** *TrNZI* XXXI. 96 Notes on Parore (the Mangrove fish). **1921** [see PARORE]. **1957** WILLIAMS *Dict. Maori Lang.* 268 Parore, n. *Girella tricuspidata*, mangrove-fish. **1986** PAUL *NZ Fishes* 101 *Parore. Girella tricuspidata*... Known variously as blackfish, black snapper, black bream, and mangrove fish.

mangu mangu taipo: see TAIPO 7.

manoa, var. MANOAO.

manoao /ˈmʌnəwæu/, /ˈmæn-/. Also erron. **manaoa, manoa, manoua;** early **manawau**. [Ma. /ˈmanoao/: Williams 176 *Manoao, n. 1. Dacrydium colensoi*, mountain pine. *2. Dacrydium kirkii*, Barrier pine.] Any of three members of fam. Podocarpaceae.

1. Either of *Lagarostrobos* (formerly *Dacrydium*) *colensoi*, a moderate-sized coniferous tree of wet forests; or less freq. *Lepidothamnus* (formerly *Dacrydium*) *laxifolius*, a sprawling coniferous shrub. See also *mountain pine, silver pine, Westland pine, yellow pine* (PINE 2 (8) d, (15), (18), (20) b), TAR-WOOD 1.
 1867 HOOKER *Handbook* 766 Manawau, *Geolog. Surv. Dacrydium Colensoi*... Manoao... *Dacrydium Colensoi.* **1869** *TrNZI* I. (rev. edn.) 192 Manoua (*Dacrydium Colensoi*). A small tree, found at an altitude of 1000 to 2000 feet, at Dunedin, and at the sea level on the west coast. Leaves of two kinds, spreading and imbricate. **1875** KIRK *Durability NZ Timbers* 22 Manoao.—(*Dacrydium colensoi.*) **1883** HECTOR *Handbook NZ* 124 *Dacrydium colensoi*... Manoao, Yellow-pine.—A very ornamental tree, 20–80 feet high. Wood light yellow. **1889** *Canterbury Resources & Progress* 52 Silver or Westland Pine, Manoao, (*D. Westlandium*). **1889** KIRK *Forest Flora* 189 *Dacrydium colensoi*... The manoao... This remarkable mountain-pine was originally discovered in Dusky Bay by Dr. Menzies in 1791..the present species is termed 'yellow-pine' and 'tar-wood' by the Otago bushmen. *Ibid.* 191 *Dacrydium kirkii*... The manoao. **1908, 1918** [see PINE 2 (15) a]. **1961** ALLAN *Flora NZ* I. 1001 *Manoao:* Dacrydium colensoi, D. kirkii.

2. *Halocarpus* (formerly *Dacrydium*) *kirkii*, a handsome coniferous tree of the northern North Island, having distinctive juvenile foliage. See also *barrier pine* (PINE 2 (1)).
 [*Note*] Similarity of verbal form occas. leads to a confusion of *manoao* (*Halocarpus kirkii*) with MONOAO (*Dracophyllum subulatum*), a line of error poss. beginning with the 1906 Cheeseman *Manual*, thence to 1961 (1982) Allan *Flora of NZ* (Vol. I), and 1963 Poole and Adams *Trees and Shrubs* (pp. 26, 247 but not 160), thence to OED.
 1889 KIRK *Forest Flora* 191 The Manoao... The wood of the manaoa [*sic*] is of a light-brown colour. **1905** SATCHELL *Toll of Bush* (1985) 41 The founder of the family slept in the graveyard, beneath the manoa [*sic*] trees on the summit of the hill. **1906** CHEESEMAN *Manual NZ Flora* 656 *Silver-pine; Monoao* [*sic* for *Manoao*]. Very close to [*Dacrydium intermedium*]. **1961** ALLAN *Flora NZ* I. 109 *D. kirkii*... Dist.: N. Lowland forest, occ., from lat. 35° to 37° *Monoao* [*sic* for *Manoao*]. Type locality. **1963** POOLE & ADAMS *Trees & Shrubs* 26 *D[acrydium] kirkii*... Monoao [*sic* for *Manoao*]. Tree reaching 25 m. Bark light brown... L[owland], M[ontane]. Hokianga to Auckland, local. **1978** MOORE & IRWIN *Oxford Book NZ Plants* 210 *Dacrydium kirkii*. Manoao occurs only in north Auckland. **1988** DAWSON *Forest Vines to Snow Tussocks* 40 A group of conifers formerly included in *Dacrydium*; silver pine..bog pine..*H. biformis* and manoao (*H. kirkii*).

manono. [Ma. /ˈmanono/: Williams 176 *Manono... Coprosma australis*... = *kanono*.] KANONO.
 1905 *TrNZI* XXXVII. 116 *Coprosma grandifolia. (Manono)* The sap obtained from the inner bark is applied in cases of *hakihaki*—scabies (Best). **1966** [see KANONO]. **1981** BROOKER et al. *NZ Medicinal Plants* 86 *Coprosma australis*... Maori names: *Manono, papauma*.

manook, var. MANUKA.

manool /ˈmænʌu(w)ɒl/. [f. MANO(AO + -*ol*.] A bicyclic diterpenoid alcohol $C_{20}H_{34}O$, derived from the wood of the manoao (*Halocarpus kirkii*) and used as an ambergris substitute in perfumery.
 1935 *Chem. Abstr.* XXIX. 6591 The red resin extd. with alc. from *D. biforme* yields..a neutral light yellow viscous oil.., giving on fractional distn. about 90% of a very viscous colorless liquid (II) solidifying to crystals of the compn. C20H34O... II is therefore a bicyclic diterpene alc. with 2 double bonds, for which the name *manoōl* is proposed. **1968** *NZ News* 2 Oct. 15 Manool, an ambergris-like product which is extracted from trees that take hundreds of years to grow, may provide New Zealand with a new export market. **1988** BROOKER, CAMBIE, COOPER *Economic Native Plants NZ* 59 A number of commercial firms within New Zealand have attempted to export manool or its relatives to perfumery companies.

manoua, var. MANOAO.

manouka, var. MANUKA.

manpower, *n.* WW2. [Spec. use of *manpower* the number of people available for (esp. military) service: see OED *man n.*¹ 20.] Often familiarly **the manpower**, the name given to the authority set up during WW2 to direct people into occupations or work essential to the war effort. Usu. *attrib.*
 1942 *Statutory Regulations* 5/19 The National Service Emergency Regulations 1940, Amendment No.8: There shall from time to time be appointed..such number of District Man-power Officers as may be required. *Ibid.* 21 In any essential undertaking.. (a)

MANPOWER

Except with the permission in writing of the District Man-power Officer, the employer shall not terminate..the employment of any person for the time being employed therein..except in case of emergency... (b) Except with the permission in writing of the District Man-power Officer, no person for the time being employed in the undertaking shall leave his employment. *Ibid.* 24 The Minister may..direct all persons of any specified classes..to register for employment with the District Man-power Office. **1963** HILLIARD *Piece of Land* 81 Anyway, I wrote to the Manpower (they had the Manpower then, this was during the war)... I wrote and asked them if they could let me have a man to give a hand on the place. **1989** BIOLETTI *The Yanks Are Coming* 84 The 'Manpower Authorities' were responsible for directing labour to essential industries... If we stayed away from work without due cause we had to go before the manpower officer and he could fine us for absenteeism.

manpower, *v. WW2.* [f. *n.*] *trans.* Usu. in passive construction. To direct (a person) into non-military work essential to the war-effort.

1952 THOMSON *Deer Hunter* 122 A few months later I was 'manpowered' out of the Army by the Director of Deer Operations for six months in the upper Waitaki country. **1963** KINROSS *Please to Remember* 169 Daddy's been manpowered or something, and they've made him join the Home Guard! **1974** MULDOON *Rise and Fall of a Young Turk* 16 Some [of the Division] were 'manpowered' out to preferred civilian jobs and the rest of us sailed to reinforce the Division in Italy. **1989** BIOLETTI *The Yanks Are Coming* 84 Girls were manpowered from all over New Zealand to work in centres far from home.

Manrope. *Nelson goldfields. Hist.* [f. the nickname of a gold-digging party, see quot. 1933: cf. OED *n.*[1] 20 a *manrope* a ship's gangway or ladder.] Used in Comb. (or as **the Manrope**) as a place-name in the Slate River area of nw. Nelson, and as **manrope lantern** for a 'bottle' lantern (see quot., see also LANTERN).

1896 MOFFATT *Adventures* (1979) 50 We were strongly advised by her [*sc.* the storekeeper's wife at Washbourn's Flat, about 8 miles from Collingwood, Nelson] to go and set up in Manrope Gully. **1896** MACKAY *Narrative of the Opening of the Hauraki Dist.* 17 A run on the 'Manrope' at Slate River. **1933** WASHBOURNE *Reminisc. Early Days* 5. The 'manrope' party were so called because they had to descend to their claim by means of man ropes in the Gorge of Slate River... Lanterns were an unknown luxury on the diggings and one of the party invented [one] by breaking the bottom out of an 'Old Tom' bottle, and this was carried upside down with a candle dropped into the neck of it. This has always since been known as a 'manrope lantern' [on the Nelson goldfields, c1857–59]

manuca, var. MANUKA.

manuhiri. The spelling **manuwhiri** has equal standing. [Ma. /ˈmanuhiri/ /ˈmanufiri/: Williams 176 *Manuhiri, manuwhiri,* n. Visitor, guest.] A visitor to a marae.

[**1820** LEE & KENDALL *Grammar* 175 Mánu wídi; Person from a distant part.] **1843** DIEFFENBACH *Travels in NZ* II. 371 Manuwiri—a stranger, a traveller..Manuhiri—*id*[*em*]. **1863** MOSER *Mahoe Leaves* 34 Harry and I, as manuwhiri's, (strangers) were not forgotten. **1884** MARTIN *Our Maoris* 4 As soon as the weather cleared after my arrival, all the Maoris..came up..to inspect the Mà-nu-hi-ri, *i.e.,* the stranger. **1917** *NZ at the Front* 162 He werry kind to t'e Manuhiri, t'e visitor. **1927** DONNE *Maori Past & Present* 272 In this home one may meet the Maori and the white *manuhiri* (guest), as it is open house to visitors. **1973** FINLAYSON *Brown Man's Burden* (1973) 142 whare manuhiri: the hall for accommodating guests at huis on the marae. **1985** HOWE *Towards 'Taha Maori' in English* (NZATE) 20 Manuhiri—visitors. The manuhiri are those visitors to a marae who come from outside it. Though manuhiri may be related to the hosts, they are usually not close family. **1986** *PSA Jrnl.* 19 July 12 [Heading] *Sponsoring the manuhiri* Have you ever thought about what is involved in sponsoring a refugee?... The theme for this year's refugee Sunday is 'many manuhiri'. The manuhiri are the 'people coming in', and New Zealand has a tradition of welcoming strangers that goes back to the very first people who settled here.

manuka /ˈmanəkə/, /məˈnukə/, /məˈnjukə/. Also with much variety of early form as **mánook, manouka, manuca, manukau, marnaka, menuka, minuka,** etc., often representing varying pronunciations; occas. abbrev. in speech to **nuka** /ˈnukə/ or /ˈnʊkə/. [Ma. /ˈmaːnuka/: Williams 176 *Mānuka* (i), n. *1. Leptospermum scoparium* and *L. ericoides.*]

1. a. *Leptospermum scoparium* (fam. Myrtaceae), a common native scrub bush (occas. as **manuka bush**) or small tree; also its wood, esp. when used as firewood (see also *tea-broom* (BROOM 4), KAHIKATOA, TEA-TREE 1); and also less freq. *Kunzea* (formerly *Leptospermum*) *ericoides* (fam. Myrtaceae), a small tree (KANUKA, see also *tree manuka* 2 (3) and *white manuka* 2 (4) below), MYRTLE a. Occas. used collectively for the thick scrub composed of these plants (see quot. 1888).

[c**1826–27** BOULTBEE *Journal* (1986) 110 tea tree bush—mánook.] **1838** POLACK *NZ* II. 395 This wood [kaikatoa], called to the southward, Mánuka, is remarkably hard and durable. **1842** WADE *Journey in Nthn Is.* 75 The Manuka, or, as it is called in the Northern part of the island, Kahikatoa,.. is a mysterious plant, known in Van Diemen's Land as the tea tree. **1849** in *Lett. from Otago* 13 Sept. (1978) 33 A great deal [of the wood] is merely a kind of scrub very much like your shrubbery wood or minuka, a sort of little use but for firewood. **1853** ADAMS *Canterbury Settlement* 14 Though we must have been at least eighty miles distant from the land, the scent of manuca, a beautiful heath which grows to a considerable size, was like the perfume of a hayfield. **1857** HURSTHOUSE *NZ* II. 365 The perfumed manuka, the scarlet myrtle and giant fuchsia. **1861** *NZ Goldfields 1861* (1976) 23 Here [at Taeri] was..the manukau, a shrub like the [Victorian] tea-tree scrub, only more greenly leaved. **1873** BARKER *Station Amusements* 257 I found..a heap of dry Menuka bushes, which make the best touchwood for lighting fires. **1888** PAYTON *Round About NZ* 128 I..retired into the *manuka* to dress. **1898** MORRIS *Austral-English* 283 Manuka *n*. the Maori name for *Tea-tree*... Properly, the accent is on the first syllable with broad *a*. Vulgarly, the accent is placed on the second syllable. **1908** BAUGHAN *Shingle-Short* 75 *Manuka: (Mah-noo-kah):* Here pronounced, as often by the settlers, with the stress on the second syllable. A shrub with small aromatic tea-like leaves. **1926** HILGENDORF *Weeds* 126 Manuka (*Leptospermum scoparium*), also called tea tree (of which titri is an inverted corruption), or scrub, *tout court*. **1933** *Press* (Christchurch) (Acland Gloss.) 4 Nov. 15 Manuka.—Usually pronounced ma-*nu*-ka or ma-*noo*-ka in Canterbury and Otago and the West Coast, not ma-nuka as in the North Island. **1948** MACFARLANE *This NZ* 39 Great hillsides of flowering manuka—North Islanders call this plant 'marnaka', South Islanders 'manooka', while the New Zealand farmers refer to it as a 'bloody nuisance'. **1961** FRANCE *Ice Cold River* 99 Sometimes they..were lost in the manuka forest. Forest it was, for here the manuka was not scrub, but trees six to ten feet tall. **1981** HENDERSON *Exiles Asbestos Cottage* 18 The little blue ornament remained very dear to her, very close and comforting, among the scrub, manuka, and the ancient remembering cries from the stalking brown woodhens.

b. Used *attrib.* or as an adjective, made of, comprising, covered with or surrounded by manuka wood or scrub.

1841 BEST *Journal* 21 May (1966) 315 In consequence I travelled untill after dark and then lay down under a few Manouka bushes. **1857** *Lyttelton Times* 1 July 1 On Sale. Stout Manuka posts and rails, any quantity. **1874** BAINES *Edward Crewe* 156 We then cut ten 'manuka' pins, two feet long, sharpening one end..into a thin wedge. **1879** HAAST *Geol. Canterbury & Westland* 429 Thus we obtained several portions..of totara piles..and a fork made of manuka wood. **1907** MANSFIELD *Urewera Notebook* (1978) 39 The manuka and sheep country—very steep and bare. **1916** COWAN *Bush Explorers* (VUWTS) 4 We cantered over the fern and manuka-clothed pumice flats. **1922** MANSFIELD *Stories* (1984) 452 In a steamer chair, under a manuka tree that grew in the middle of the front grass patch, Linda Burnell dreamed the morning away. **1938** LANCASTER *Promenade* 19 A heavy hasty step sounded up the manuka-track from the Beach. **1957** FRAME *Owls Do Cry* (1967) 53 I will make you, Toby, a salt shirt with small buttons like pearl white as manuka bud. **1985** FRAME *Envoy from Mirror City* 170 I hoisted the [clothes] line further in the air with the old manuka-stick prop. **1991** *NZ Gardener* Aug. 11 Manuka cultivars are available from most garden centres.

2. With a modifier: **bush, red, tree, white**.

(1) **bush manuka.** KANUKA. See also *tree manuka* (3) below.

1871 *TrNZI* III. 187 The Bush Manuka, as it is called, attains a considerable size.

(2) **red manuka.** *Leptospermum scoparium,* having a reddish wood and underbark; also applied to horticultural varieties with red flowers (e.g. *Leptospermum scoparium* variety 'Nichollsii') which are often also called 'crimson manuka'.

1877 *TrNZI* IX. 174 Manuka..Hooker..Botanical name..Kahikatoa..Maoris.. According to Colenso..Tea or ti tree..Settlers..Red manuka..Settlers. **1921** TANNOCK *Manual of Gardening in NZ* 135 The popularity of native plants has increased greatly since the red manuka (*Leptospermum Nichollsii*) received the gold medal..at the International Horticultural Exhibition..a few years ago. **1936** *NZJST* XVII. 724 Red manuka (*Leptospermum scoparium*) becomes co-dominant with the [*L. ericoides*]. **1940** *NZJAg.* Jan. LX. 5 Red or stunted manuka. (*Leptospermum scoparium*)... Inadequate pasture cover..cannot check manuka aggression. **1959** *Tararua Tramper* Oct. 7 The insect is found associated with both red manuka (*Leptospermum scoparium*) and white manuka or kanuka. **1975** DAVIES *Outback* 75 Red manuka is heavy wood. **1981** BROOKER et al. *NZ Medicinal Plants* 71 *Leptospermum scoparium*... Common names: *Tea tree, red manuka.*

(3) **tree manuka.** KANUKA (*Kunzea ericoides*).

1910 COCKAYNE *NZ Plants & Their Story* 37 The tree-manuka (*Leptospermum ericoides*), with its multitude of white or pinkish flowers. **1922** *NZJST* IV. 280 Towards the head of the North-east Valley a considerable quantity of tree-manuka (*Leptospermum ericoides*) grew. **1940** [see KANUKA]. **1981** BROOKER et al. *NZ Medicinal Plants* 71 *Leptospermum ericoides*... Common names: *Tree manuka, white manuka* Maori name: *Kanuka.*

(4) **white manuka**. KANUKA (*Kunzea ericoides*). See also *white tea-tree* (TEA-TREE 2 (2)).

1877 *TrNZI* IX. 144 This is the variety known as white manuka. **1883** HECTOR in *Handbook NZ Mines* (1887) 28 White manuka L. ericoides. **c1920** BEATTIE *Trad. Lifeways Southern Maori* (1994) 512 There are two kinds of manuka, viz. manuka-pouri (black manuka) and a 'white manuka' the kiripapa. **1953** SUTHERLAND *Golden Bush* (1963) 41 The call of a Californian quail..came from a shelter-clump of white manuka. **1966** BRAMBLEY *Sea-cockies of Manukau* 27 A half-dozen magpies whirled up the slope to settle in a big white manuka. **1981** [see (3) above].

3. Special Comb. manuka beetle, see BEETLE 8; **manuka blight**, a sooty mould *Capnodium* spp. formed on honey-dew exuded by a scale insect *Eriococcus orariensis*, infesting red manuka and (to lesser extent) kanuka; **manuka broom**, a broom made of manuka twigs; **manuka honey**, a dark honey from the nectar of manuka flowers, reputed to have special medicinal or health-promoting qualities; **manuka lizard**, *Naultinus elegans*, a green lizard (see also KAKARIKI *n*.²); **manuka manna**, a white sugary exudation from manuka (see also PIA MANUKA); **manuka scrub**, a common scrub of stunted *L. scoparium*; **manuka tea**, also called **manuka brew**, an infusion of manuka leaves drunk as tea.

1950 *NZJAg.* Apr. LXXX. 337 [Heading] Danger Seen in Propagation of **Manuka Blight**. Publicity now being given to the so-called 'manuka blight' and to its use in destroying manuka on pasture land merits very careful examination. **1954** *NZ Geographer* Oct. 110 The manuka blight was first introduced into the [Hawke's Bay] region in 1945... [1954 Note] The blight is caused by the action of a small sucking insect which feeds on the sap of the manuka and which secretes large quantities of a clear sticky substance known as 'honey-dew'. A black sooty mould forms on this secretion. A combination of sap loss and mould slowly kills the plant. **1971** MILLER *Common Insects* 116 Manuka Blight. About 1937 isolated areas of red manuka..in the upper Orari Gorge, South Canterbury, were found to be attacked by a blight. **1981** TAYLOR *Weeds of Roadsides* 91 Manuka blight is caused by a scale insect *Eriococcus orariensis*, which is native to Australia where manuka has long been adapted to it. [**1769** COOK *Journals* 28 Oct. (1955) I. 184 Employ'd Wooding, cuting [*sic*] of Broom stuff and making of Brooms, there being a shrub here very fit for that purpose.] **1907** LAING & BLACKWELL *Plants NZ* 274 The Maoris made use of [manuka] for their paddles and spears, and a bunch of twigs makes an excellent broom. *Ibid.* 449 [Index entry.] **Manuka broom**, 274. **1940** *Tales Pioneer Women* (1988) 153 Mother would draw out the embers with a long scraper, and brush out the oven with a big manuka broom dipped in cold water. **1948** HENDERSON *Taina* 29 It was forenoon, and Kara had..swept the mud floors of the two houses with a home-made *manuka* broom when two visitors came to see her. **1983** COOPER *Wag's Tales* 7 We used to sweep the [dirt] floor with a manuka brush broom and play away there for hours. **1902** WALKER *Zealandia's Guerdon* 57 '**Manuka**' and eucalyptus **honey**. **1934** HYDE *Journalese* 110 Manuka honey..dark, sweet, gathered by the droning wild bees whose nests are high up in rimu or manuka..is the best of all. **1992** *Dominion* (Wellington) 21 Oct. 7 Manuka honey is unusually effective as an antiseptic dressing for wounds, burns, and ulcers, research at Waikato University has shown. **1994** *Dominion* (Wellington) 26 July 13 Stomach ulcer sufferers continue to empty supermarket shelves of manuka honey hoping for a simple cure that has already been debunked. **1947** HUTCHINSON *At Omatua's Fireside* 124 [A lizard] called 'ka[ka]riki' by the Maoris, and 'manuka lizard' [c1909] by the settlers. **1940** LAING & BLACKWELL *Plants NZ* 289 As a result of injuries caused by sap-sucking insects the leaves are sometimes covered with a white crystalline substance, known as **manuka manna**. The substance is probably a complex sugar, but so far has not been thoroughly investigated. **1981** BROOKER et al. *NZ Medicinal Plants* 72 Pia (or manuka manna) is composed of mannitol. **1851** SHORTLAND *S. Dist. NZ* 167 We were unable to find any fire-wood, but some low blackened '**manuka**' scrub which had been burnt the year before. **1864** HOCHSTETTER & PETERMAN *Geol. NZ* 65 Clover fields contrasting strongly with the fern and manuka scrub..of the clay soil. **1876** CHUDLEIGH *Diary* 21 June (1950) 250 It is, further, covered with manuka scrub fern and tutu. **1881** BATHGATE *Waitaruna* 275 The other [gully] was in some parts overgrown with manuka scrub. **1940** HOWARD *Rakiura* xviii From about 900 feet upward the forest merges into a manuka scrub. **1981** MARSH *Black Beech & Honeydew* 86 'Here you are, old fellow,' said my father coming through the stunted manuka scrub with a billy-ful of spring water. **1863** MARTIN *Diary* (Hocken MS) 30 Sept. We cannot say it is high living that is the cause [of our skin complaint] so we have concluded it is the **Manuka Tea**. I am determined not to drink any more. **1866** MUELLER *My Dear Bannie* (1958) 110 The last of our tea and sugar we shall have tomorrow.., and after that 'bidy-bidy' tea, or 'Manukau' tea, without sugar. [**1908** BAUGHAN *Shingle-Short* 75 An' wasn't she a picture! pouring good an' hot, Tea (not *manuka*-brew, but Tea!) from the pot.]

manuka-rauriki. [Ma. /'maːnuka/ /'rauriki/: Williams 176 *Mānuka rauriki*, [*Kunzea*] *ericoides*.] KANUKA.

1867 HOOKER *Handbook* 766 Manuka-rau-riki, *Col[enso]. Leptospermum ericoides*. **1869** *TrNZI* I. (rev. edn.) 236 Of our shrubs and smaller timber trees, several are of strikingly beautiful growth..(*e.g.*)..the Manuka-rau-riki, *Leptospermum ericoides*. **1889** KIRK *Forest Flora* 124 Mr. Colenso informs me that 'rawiri', as it [*sc. Kunzea ericoides*] sometimes called in the North Island, is erroneous, and that the proper name is manuka-rauriki. **1890** *PWD Catalogue Timbers* (NZ & South Seas Exhib.) 12 Manuka-rau-riki..Timber dense, heavy, and of great strength and toughness; used for house blocks, fencing rails, wheelwrights' purposes, and firewood. **1924** *NZJST* VII. 381 The principal trees are the manuka rauriki. **1930** *NZJST* XI. 152 [Three Kings] is clothed principally with white tea-tree—manuka rauriki.

manukau, var. MANUKA.

manuwhiri, var. MANUHIRI.

maodi, var. MAORI.

maoia, var. MOA.

maomao. Also **maumau**. [Ma. /'maomao/: Williams 178 *Mao* (iii) *maomao... Scorpis violaceus*.]

1. Any of various reef-fish, but esp. *Scorpis violaceus* (fam. Kyphosidae), the *blue maomao* (see 2 (1) below).

[**1820** LEE & KENDALL *NZ Gram. & Vocab.* 179 Maumau, *s*. Fish so called.] **1873** *TrNZI* V. 153 Rurima is famous for its fish; hapuka.. barracoota..mackerel..and the delicious little maomao. **1892** *Ibid.* XXIV. 209 Maomao (*Ditrema violacea*)... Mokohinou and Portland Island. **1922** *NZJST* V. 93 Scorpis violaceus. *Maomao*. Mr. Griffin, of the Auckland Museum, informs us that both this species and the sweep (*Scorpis aequipinnis*) are sold as 'maomao' in Auckland. **1936** *Handbook for NZ* (ANZAAS) 72 Scorpis violaceus: Maomao. **1947** POWELL *Native Animals NZ* 69 Maomao is an excellent food fish, but as it frequents rocky ground, hook and line is the only satisfactory means of capture, hence it is seldom seen in the markets. **1959** MIDDLETON *The Stone* 13 Around the wharf piles where barnacles and mussels clung..flitted the little pakirikiri and maomao. **1963** *Evening Post* (Wellington) 4 Apr. 29 'Mao-Mao,' he said. Within seconds a beautiful blue gamester was threshing in the bottom of the boat. **1988** *Through the Looking Glass* 21 The piper we caught at Cornwallis [Manukau] were superb, but still not a patch on the mau-mau we caught off a single rock.

2. With a modifier: **blue**, **pink**.

(1) blue maomao. *Scorpis violaceus* (fam. Kyphosidae), an iridescent-blue, good-eating fish of northern NI (esp. ne. coastal) waters. See also HUI *n*.²

1966 DOOGUE & MORELAND *Sea Anglers' Guide* 244 Blue Maomao... *Other names: Scorpis aequipinnis*; hardbelly (Australia); maomao, hui (Maori). **1972** DOAK *Fishes* 49 A group of blue maomao will often divebomb a patch of sand among the rocks, skimming off it on their sides and ascending for another turn. **1986** PAUL *NZ Fishes* 101 *Blue maomao Scorpis violaceus*... Also occurs off southern Australia... A smaller and duller coloured species, known as sweep, *S. aequipinnis*, is also present in our waters.

(2) pink maomao. *Caprodon longimanus* (fam. Serranidae), a bright pink schooling fish of mainly northern New Zealand and se. Australian waters. See also LONGFIN.

1921 *NZJST* IV. 114 Two fishes, one, from the Bay of Islands, known popularly as 'pink maomao'..are omitted from the list. **1966** [see LONGFIN]. **1972** DOAK *Fishes* 29 Very large Koheru..would select a pink maomao and rub their bodies against it. **1982** AYLING *Collins Guide* (1984) 207 The pink maomao is a relatively large sea perch.

Maori /'mæuri/, /'maori/, /'mari/, /'mɒəri/ and a variety of other modern pronunciations some of which, esp. in attempting to replicate the sound of Maori intervocalic /r/, approach that of RP *mouldy* spoken quickly, *n*. and *a*. Also with much variety of early form as **Mahrie**, **Máodi**, **Maoude**, **Maouri**, **Mauri**, **Maury**, **Mauvre**, **Mawrie**, **Mourai**, **Mouray**, **Mouri(e)**, **Moury**, **Mowree**, **Mowrey**, **Mowrie**. [Ma. /'maːori/ Williams 179 *Māori* (i) *1*. a. Normal, usual, ordinary *2*. Native, or belonging to New Zealand, Maori (a comparatively modern use...) *3*. n. Person of the native race, New Zealander, Maori.] Cf. *buck Maori* (BUCK *n*.¹ 2), COPPER MAORI, PAKEHA MAORI, TAHA MAORI. Compare TANGATA MAORI, TANGATA WHENUA. Contrast PAKEHA.

[*Note*] *Origin*. The modern Māori noun *Māori* prob. developed from the adjective) after the arrival of Europeans to fill a need to distinguish the 'usual' or 'ordinary' *tangata māori* from the 'extraordinary' or 'unusual' *tangata mā* (white) *tangata pora* (strange or extraordinary (boat) people), *tangata tupua* (foreign or demonic or goblin people), or *Pākehā*.

Modern spelling forms. Maori was the spelling of the Williams *Dictionary* from 1844 (and presumably the standard form in Maori) until the 7edn. 1971 when *Māori* was introduced (*maori* as in *tangata maori* is the spelling of the Treaty of Waitangi). *Maori* has been the standard form in English since c1850.

Plural forms. The plural of the countable noun in English has usu. been *Maoris*; with also a generic 'collective' *the Maori* (occas. also, collocatively, *Maori people*, etc.) used when referring to the Maori as a race. A zero-inflection plural (spelt usu. *Maori*, but also *Māori*, or

Maaori) has become increasingly common from the 1980s being generally insisted upon by central educational and public service authorities and most of the electronic and print media, and preferred by modern Maori users of English, though sounding odd and perhaps somewhat patronizing to many native speakers of idiomatic New Zealand and other forms of English whose traditional practice allows only a few names of food or game animals to always (*sheep, deer, cod*) or usually (*bison, grouse, quail, salmon, swine*) take a zero plural, as distinct from names (including certain nationality and tribal names as *Navaho(s), Hopi(s)*) which may have both zero and *-s* forms. (See QUIRKE, R. *et al. A Comprehensive Grammar of the English Language* (1985) pp. 307–8: see also 2 a below quot. 1952, and the quotations in 2 b below.) The plurals *Maories* and its variants, freq. until c1870, are still found in informal writing but are now regarded as erroneous in both Maori and English use.

A. *n.*

I. In early Maori and non-Maori contexts. **1.** Usu. as **tangata maori**, with *maori* regarded primarily as an adjective ('usual, normal') suffixed to a noun (usu. *tangata* 'human being') as in Maori usage. See TANGATA MAORI for quots. **1815, 1820, c1826–27, 1834, 1836, 1840, 1843**, etc., and remarks there.
[*Note*] The assumption of English-speakers that the post-positioned adjective *maori* functioned as a noun was perh. a significant factor giving rise to the sense (and use) 2 below.

II. In non-Maori contexts.
[*Note*] In English use **Maori** has now replaced as preferred usage the 18th c. **Indian**, the 18th c. and early 19th c. **New Zealander**, the **aborigine** common in early writing associated with 'imperial' agencies such as the Colonial Office and the Church Missionary Society (a use possibly reinforced by the title **Protector of Aborigines**), and the longlasting **native** (1769–1947). In the 1840s **Maori** (often previously found in Whaling logs and journals of the 1830s—see further 1982 Morton *The Whale's Wake* 118) came into more frequent use, often with an explanatory gloss 'native', presumably mainly for British readers, and possibly indicating that the word was confirmed in local but not in British usage. (Schnackenberg's hypothesis in quot. 1945 below is not in complete agreement with the evidence.) It did not replace **Native** in official use until 1947 when, among other changes, the name of the Department of Native Affairs was changed to Department of Maori Affairs (see *Native Affairs, Native Minister* (NATIVE B 3 b, esp. quot. 1947). A spelling with an initial capital has been the predominant form from earliest times.

2. a. (a) A member of the Polynesian race who first peopled New Zealand; a person whose ancestry includes one member of that race. See also ABORIGINAL B, ABORIGINE a, NATIVE A 1 a, TANGATA WHENUA 3 a (a).
1834 MARKHAM *NZ* (1963) 66 The old people believe that the (Atua) God of the Parkiars Strangers is killing or eating the Mouries or Natives. *Ibid.* 117 Europeans are not considered so good eating as the Mouries as they are too salt. **1836** *Piraki Log* 20 Apr. (1911) 33 Spare hands and Mouries building a house. [Native is not used in the *Log.*] **1836** *Log 'Mary Mitchell'* 22 May in McNab *Old Whaling Days* (1913) 443 Latter part fine weather 5 boats out by means of 3 Mowrees. **1839** TAYLOR *Journal* (ATLTS) 29 Mar. II. 78 This Maori's house and property were left untouched, he is now like the maniac. [*native* is the preferred use in Taylor's 1839–49 *Journal*: this is the first occurrence of *Maori*.] **1840** *NZ Journal* I. 202 [The Missionaries] tried all they could to dissuade the people from selling their land, instancing the way in which the *maories* had been driven off the land. [1840 *Note*] 'natives'. *Ibid.* I. 222 I sent a maury (native), as they call themselves. *Ibid.* I. 293 [Dicky Barrett's] house is always full of cast-away sailors, and flat-bellied Mauris (natives). **1841** WEEKES *Journal* 13 Apr. in Rutherford & Skinner *Establish. New Plymouth* (1940) 47 A 'Mourai' or native thatched the house with a long grass called *toi-toi*. **1841** BIDWILL *Rambles in NZ* (1952) 85 I said that a Pakiha could do no harm in going up [the mountain], as..the taboo only applied to Mowries. **1842** GRAY *Fauna* in Dieffenbach *Travels in NZ* (1843) II. 281 The Deinacrida, according to the Maouries, generally keeps high up on the trunk. **1845** WHISKER *Memo. Book* in Barthorp *To Face the Daring Maoris* (1979) 71 The Blacks or Mowreys acted very well... The Natives ware [*sic*] no clothes at all. **1859** THOMSON *Story NZ* I. 59 No light is thrown on the origin of the New Zealanders from the name Maori which they call themselves. This word rendered, by linguists 'native', is used in contradistinction to pakeha, or stranger. **1862** CHUDLEIGH *Diary* 21 Apr. (1950) 33 There are mourays here and two kikes or villages. **1878** BULLER *Forty Yrs. NZ* 163 The word *Maori*, means whatever is native or indigenous. By the English plural of the word, *Maories*, we understand the aborigines, or natives. **1898** MORRIS *Austral-English* 284 *Maori, n.* (pronounced so as to rhyme with *Dowry*)... The form of the plural varies. The form *Maoris* is considered the more correct, but the form *Maories* is frequently used by good writers. **1904** TREGEAR *Maori Race* 114 Many of the canoes (*waka*) of the Maoris are still in evidence. **1917** WILLIAMS *Dict. Maori Lang.* 425 Taipo... This word is used by Maoris believing it English, and by Europeans believing it Maori, it being apparently neither. Colenso suggests *tae-po*, but this is not used by the Maori. **1930** *Na To Hoa Aroha* (1987) II. 12 Our progress resolves into two periods, the transition of Polynesian into Maori and the transition of Maori into New Zealander. **1945** *JPS* LIV. 233 (E.H. Schnackenberg) The frequent use [following the Treaty of Waitangi] of the expression *nga Rangatira me nga Tangata maori* (with a small m) *o Niu Tireni* (the chiefs and people of New Zealand) appears to have been too cumbersome for official records and was quickly abbreviated to the one word Maori. **1949** SARGESON *I Saw in My Dream* (1974) 117 He's part maori for sure though, because once he got me to witness a paper and it was about maori land. **1952** *NZ Geographer* Oct. 104 (Metge) A distinction may be made between 'Maori' and 'Maoris' as plural forms. The former refers to the Maori people as a whole and as an ethnic and cultural entity; the latter designates individuals of this people (cf. *The Coming of the Maori* and *Some Modern Maoris*). **1953** *NZ Statutes* No.94 1078 'Maori' means a person belonging to the aboriginal race of New Zealand; and includes a half-caste and a person intermediate in blood between half-castes and persons of pure descent from that race. **1971** WILLIAMS *Dict. Maori Lang.* 77 Maoris distinguish between *inanga papa*..and *inanga tūtuna*. **1977** DUFF *Moahunter* 12 This raises the question of what we mean by the term Maori. Why should Kupe be termed a Maori, if (according to Maori tradition) he was a Society Islands voyager?.. Every immigrant from tropical Polynesia did not become a Maori the moment he stepped ashore in New Zealand... The use of the term Maori (lit. normal, ordinary or proper) to distinguish the Polynesian inhabitants of New Zealand from the intrusive European is even more clearly a late development and certainly post-European. **1983** HULME *Bone People* 304 What's wrong with war songs, tit? What do you ignorant young grab-arses know what's better? Yahhh..they get round with bloody Mahries and behave worse than they do. **1993** *NZ Statutes* No.4 10 [Te Ture Whenua Maori—Maori Land Act] 'Maori' means a person of the Maori race of New Zealand; and includes a descendant of any such person.

(b) In often contemptuous non-Maori use, **the Maori**, Maori 'blood' or Maori ancestry.
1967 SARGESON *Hangover* (1984) 30 Perhaps it *was* the Maori in him. He was unique.

b. Main variations from *-s plural* forms. (See the general introductory note to the entry.) (a) As **the Maori**, usu. collective taking a singular verb. The Maori people as an ethnic or cultural entity.
1841 *NZ Journal* II. 292 [The natives] sometimes say 'the mouri no like much work'. **1856** SHORTLAND *Traditions & Superstitions* 73 The New Zealanders have given the locality of New Zealand to events recorded in ancient tales; which are probably exaggerated accounts of what may have occurred in the countries from which the *Maori* came formerly. **1868** LINDSAY *Contribs. NZ Botany* 62 *G[eranium] dissectum*... The 'Matuakumera' of the North Island Maori. **1882** HAY *Brighter Britain* II. 210 The root of the raupo.., the swamp-grass of which the Maori construct their wharè, is edible. **1899** GRACE *Sketch NZ War* 44 As soon as the Maori saw our object, they opened fire. **1917** GRAY, Norman *MS Papers 4134* (ATLMS) 9 Sept. As you know, the Maori is an ugly customer when he gets a few in. **1929** BEST *Fishing Methods* 43 The kehe..are believed by the Maori to live on vegetable matter. **1940** HOWARD *Rakiura* xi It was at last purchased from the Maori in 1864 by an unwilling Government. **1959** McLINTOCK *Descr. Atlas* 72 In the country proper the Maori has retained his traditional mode of life which is symbolised in the *marae*. **1984** BOYD *City of the Plains* 4 The Maori ran pigs in the swamp and grazed horses, sheep and cattle on the few rough patches of native grass.

(b) As **Maori**, a zero termination plural without a prefixed **the** and used with an English plural verb form.
1875 *TrNZI* VII. 3 This paper has been compiled from..tales collected..when there were still a few Maori alive who were acquainted with their ancient lore. **1928** ANDERSEN et al. in McCrae *Journal* 29 Tooi (Tuai) and Teeterree.., two young Maori who had visited London. **1979** WEBSTER *Rua* 212 Maori who remembered Rua at the time, but were not followers, had very differing opinions about the prophet. **1984** BOYD *City of the Plains* 5 Maori began to realise that they had been pushed into selling by government agents. **1992** *Dominion* (Wellington) 24 Mar. 6 I would very much like to see The Dominion refrain from further use of the word 'Maoris' and in future replace it with 'Maori'.

(c) Occas. **nga Maori**, the Maori plural form with a preceding plural article.
1851 LUCETT *Rovings in the Pacific* I. 118 Nga Maori are keenly alive to the degradation of exposure.

3. The Maori language, occas. widened in spoken reference to include Maori society and culture as a field of study (= 'Maori Studies' as in 'To take Maori at University'). Also as **dog Maori** [formed on *dog Latin* a corrupt form of Latin], barbarously-formed or corruptly incorrect Maori as spoken by one badly taught, or one wishing to insult the hearer (see quots. 1943, 1976); **standard Maori**, a putative reference variety (see quot. 1928). See also NATIVE A 2, NEW ZEALAND A 3. Cf. PIDGIN-MAORI 1.
[**1817** NICHOLAS *Voyage NZ* II. 347 It is good to read the language of New Zealand Kapi ta karakea a koraro no New Zealand.] **1828** WILLIAMS *Early Jrnls.* 17 Aug. (1961) 141 The Service very pleasant and as all the natives assembled and part of it is held in *Maori*, which keeps up their attention. **1834** MARKHAM *NZ* (1963) 42 One [copy] translated into Mowrie. **1841** BIDWILL *Rambles in NZ* (1952) 40 In Mowrie (New Zealand language) it is not difficult to express the sound by desiring the experimenter to say 'na' (nah) without

moving his tongue. **1858** *Richmond-Atkinson Papers* 19 Sept. (1960) I. 429 Consulted with Maria whether it would be well to go among the Negroes for six months to learn Maori. **1869** *TrNZI* I. (rev. edn.) 392 Several Europeans now speak the New Zealand language... They have never thought..in *Maori*; hence, while many of them are ready to speak of the meagreness of the New Zealand tongue, the leanness is entirely on their own side. **1874** [see PIDGIN-MAORI 1]. **1881** CAMPBELL *Poenamo* 129 He did not now require a sleeping dictionary to learn Maori from. **1894** *TrNZI* XXVI. 537 In Maori, it means 'to count'; in Moriori, 'to calculate'. **1905** BAUCKE *White Man Treads* 177 I brought no introduction—except [if] a knowledge of Maori be called such. **1928** CHAPMAN in McCrae *Journal* 5 What I call 'standard Maori' is spoken in the Waikato valley. The matter of dialect is unimportant outside New Zealand. **1939** BEATTIE *First White Boy Born Otago* 20 We did not get very far with our Maori, but I used to go to Maori services with Taipo (Joe Benson) and picked up quite a lot of it. **1943** MARSH *Colour Scheme* 26 'Tell him yourself,' said Huia. She added, in dog Maori, an extremely pointed insult. **1976** MASON in *Bruce Mason Solo* (1981) 183 I will call it, in dog-Maori, pukutangi, weeping gut. **1986** *Evening Post* (Wellington) 21 June Paul Temm feels essentially unchanged by his experience on the tribunal..listening to the elders vent their frustrations in Maori.

4. A Cook Islands Polynesian; the Polynesian language of the Cook Islands.

1904 TREGEAR *Maori Race* 555 The natives of Rarotonga and Tahiti call themselves 'Maori', as the New Zealander does. **1911** *Pooh-Bah of the Pacific* 15 No efforts made to train the Maoris for self-government. [**1969** *NZ Statutes* No.127 834 [Maori Purposes Act] *Housing assistance for Polynesians*. The Maori Housing Act 1935 is hereby amended by inserting after section 2..."(2A). For the purposes of this Act, the term 'Maori' shall be deemed to include any Polynesian who is a native of any island of the South Pacific Ocean and any person who is a descendant of such a Polynesian if.."(a) He is a New Zealand citizen; or "(b) He has lived in New Zealand for 5 [amended 1977 to '3'] years and is permanently resident in New Zealand."] **1991** *Metro* (Auckland) Jan. 88 The youngsters..have practically no Cook Island Maori.

5. *Obs.* In various transf. uses. **a.** *Ellipt.* for ?MAORIHEAD.

1870 in Trask *Elizabeth of Lavington* (1976) 47 As I happened to be out getting 'Maoris' for the fire and saw the stars.

b. Maori (Maori and Pakeha), a children's game.

1972 SUTTON-SMITH *Folkgames of Children* 56 Occasionally these relationships became the subject matter for children's play, as in Maoris..or Pakehas and Maoris. **1984** KEITH & MAIN *NZ Yesterdays* 288 Oddly enough, there does not seem to have been a Maori and pakeha variant [of Cowboys and Indians], although a stalking game called 'Maori' is recorded as being played in the 19th century. **1987** PARKER *Not to Yield* 128 [Taranaki, 1870–80s] Before Buffalo Bill gave the children of the world the game of Cowboys and Indians..., my brothers and I had found a much more imaginative outlet for our youthful exuberance. We played Maori and Pakeha.

6. With prefixed modifiers indicating colour or race. **a. white Maori**. (a) *Mining*. *Obs*. In *transf*. use, a heavy whitish cement-stone, esp. tungstate of lime; scheelite. See also CHINAMAN *n.*[1]

1868 PYKE *Province of Otago* 39 [Scheelite] generally occurs as a coarse white heavy sand, difficult to pan off when washing gold, and is called 'White Maori' by the miners. **1883** BATHGATE *Illustr. Guide Dunedin* 169 Tungstate of lime occurs plentifully in the Wakatipu district, where from its weight and colour it is called *White Maori* by the miners. **1897** [see CHINAMAN *n.*[1]]. **1941** BAKER *NZ Slang* 46 The following New Zealand terms, recorded in the closing twenty years of the last century, are also worthy of comment:.. *white Maori*, tungstate of lime (New Zealand miners' use). **1965** [see *black Maori* b below].

(b) *Derog*. A Maori who has adopted European ways.

1988 MCGILL *Dict. Kiwi Slang* 122 *white Maori*..a Maori who has adopted Pakeha name and/or ways, as quoted in New Zealand Oral History Unit study of Martinborough.

b. black Maori (or **Maori**). *Goldmining*. Dark pebbles composed of iron and manganese oxides. See also *Maori stone* B 5 a below.

1890 *Otago Witness* (Dunedin) 6 Mar. 12 There are no less than some five or six of these bottoms..the intervening layers between each bottom being composed of white quartz and conglomerate boulders, intermixed with 'Maoris', black sand, and scheelite detritus. **1919** *NZJST* II. 116 The 'black Maoris' of the Otago gold-diggers consist in most cases of rolled pebbles formed of a mixture of iron and manganese oxides. **1965** WILLIAMS *Econ. Geol. NZ* 190 This hard ferro-manganese material forms the pebbles known to the early alluvial miners as 'black Maori' (as contrasted with 'white Maori'—scheelite).

7. As a second element in Comb. and special Comb.: **half-Maori** (also used *attrib.*), HALF-CASTE; **mallowpuff Maori** [f. *mallowpuff* the proprietary name of a chocolate-coated marshmallow biscuit], an abusive epithet for one who is brown on the outside but white-centred (or soft-centred) about things truly Maori; **town Maori**, **urban Maori**, a Maori who has lost contact with rural-based tribal roots as distinct from a member of an iwi.

1881 CAMPBELL *Poenamo* 286 That old 'Pakeha Maori'—the name by which such of our countrymen as married Maori maidens and became **half-Maories** were known. **1989** *Press* (Christchurch) 14 Feb. 19 The great brown clobbering machine is a major obstacle to Maori achievement at school, say two researchers... Achievers are labelled '**mallowpuff Maoris**' and, in some cases, deliberately break from their Maori friends to escape negative peer pressure. **1978** BROWNING *Watch Your Language* 28 'Blay stuck-up bish, blay *pakeha*... Her'n that other one, o' there. Blay **town Maori** things she's good, eh?' **1996** *Sunday Star-Times* (Auckland) 12 May A7 If **urban Maori** do unite..the pan-tribal movement is set to become a major commericial and social force.

B. *adj.* Usu. with init. cap.

1. [A new formation from English usage rather than a continuation of the orig. Maori adjectival use of *māori* 'indigenous', 'native'.] **a.** Of, characteristic of, or pertaining to, the Maori race, its culture and society. See also ABORIGINAL A 1, INDIAN B, NATIVE B 1 a, NEW ZEALAND B 1 a.

[*Note*] Early adjectives *Indian* and *aboriginal* were commonly replaced first by *New Zealand* and *native*; the former as it widened its reference to include things pakeha, was itself further progressively replaced by *native* in its denotation 'Maori'. *Native* itself (poss. as it widened its popular senses to include at first flora and fauna, then the non-Maori native-born) was gradually replaced by *Maori* in specific reference to the Maori and to things Maori, to be finally replaced by *Maori* in official use in 1947.

1834 MARKHAM *NZ* (1963) 51 One of them read the Translation of Colonel Arthurs letter..in the Mourie language. **1842** *Piraki Log* 1 May (1911) 126 Pinney, cook, signed articles; also William Brown and three Mawrie boys. **1848** TORLESSE *Papers* (1958) 41 Plenty of timber upon the hills on the west side of the bay from the maori station at Raupaki. **1859** THOMSON *Story NZ* I. 280 Between 1810 and 1838 many Maori men visited Sydney, Europe and America; but no New Zealand woman had yet seen the civilised world. **1863** MOSER *Mahoe Leaves* 58 It merely represented what my early impressions were on the moral condition of the Natives, and..closer intimacy with the Maori race has considerably shaken the opinions I then formed. **1873** TINNE *Wonderland of Antipodes* 33 My host..entertained me..with an inexhaustible repertoire of Maori lore and legend. **1929** BUCK *Coming of Maori* 28 The *taniko* in the embroidered borders of cloaks, is from the point of technique the latest development in Maori weaving. **1933** *Press* (Christchurch) (Acland Gloss.) 4 Nov. 15 *Maori*.—Used as an adjective synonymous with *native*, except that it seems slightly contemptuous. We admire native bush, pasture, or game; but M[*aori*] hens (woodhens), M[*aori*] cabbage..are caricatures of their English namesakes. **1945** *JPS* LIV. 115 We may say first that the tangi indicates clearly the Maori attitude to death and shows us this attitude contrasting strongly with the customary Pakeha attitude. **1947** *NZ Statutes* No.59 653 [Maori Purposes Act, 147] Wherever the term 'Native' appears in any Act, regulation, rule..that term shall..be hereafter read as the term 'Maori'. **1983** KING *Whina* 40 'Maori' explanations were invariably invoked to explain catastrophes. When boats were lost on the Hokianga bar, for example, it was because something had been done to offend the taniwha.

b. Pertaining to the Maori language, often including Maori society and culture as a subject or field of study. See also NATIVE B 1 b.

1851 SHORTLAND *S. Dist. NZ* 305 In the 'Maori' version of the Testament, thus saith the Lord, has been rendered 'e ai ta te Atua'. As the words in 'Maori', however, do not convey the sense..of a command,.. we should prefer as a translation [..etc.] **1891** *NZJSc.* (NS) I. 103 The Maori student..will welcome the opportunity now afforded to him of comparing the forms and equivalent values of cognate words in the great Polynesian area.

2. In mainly 20th century non-Maori *attrib.* use, often with stereotypical, pejorative, derogatory, or offensive reference, applied to anything inferior or 'uncivilized' in construction, appearance or style; or connoting (low) cunning, or other odious comparison (see also 5 b below). Some uses by Maori speakers of English can be ironic or self-deprecating (see quots. 1946, 1960).

1857 *Richmond-Atkinson Papers* 23 Jun. (1960) I. 279 June and July being mid winter and the road being in its Maori state, we could not depend on getting in to Ahuriri or Auckland on the fixed day. **1857** *Lyttelton Times* 5 Sept. 5 A gaunt shaggy scarecrow of a Maori porker, with legs as long as your arm and a savage snout as long as his legs! c**1875** MEREDITH *Adventuring in Maoriland* (1935) 103 He (Wi) [a blind Maori] told me that..he rode from Mawhia to Gisborne..on a mere Maori bridle track, by himself. **1934** HYDE *Journalese* 125 Maori pigs are the only inhabitants. **1941** BAKER *NZ Slang* 44 *Maori*..[in] its slightly contemptuous adjectival use, as in *a Maori dog*, *a Maori garden*, *Maori manners*. Here the term is employed to signify something unkempt, rather disordered or wild, something a little 'uncivilized'. **1943** BENNETT *English in NZ* in *Amer. Speech* XVIII. 93 The word *Maori* itself is occasionally used as a term of contempt—as in 'That's a Maori..' (of a thing). **1946** BEAGLEHOLE *Some Modern Maoris* 295 Again, the word Maori for these [Otaki Maori] people has taken on a secondary meaning when it is used as an adjective referring to any object that is broken, dilapidated, hard to use, or about which people are so casual that it does not function efficiently.

Thus a 'Maori' door is one on which the catch is broken or which fits so badly that it blows open in the wind... A 'Maori' gate is always a weird contraption made of bits of wire, string, parts of an old iron bedstead—something so complicated that it defies the ingenuity of the non-expert either to open or close. The owner of the gate jokes about his 'Maori' gate. **1960** HILLIARD *Maori Girl* 218 They kidded each other in a way that would have been offensive with *pakehas*. When Shirley put a cigarette-butt down the sink..Netta would say, 'That's a real Maori trick, that one! Real East Coast!' **1963** DUGGAN *Collected Stories* (1981) 200 Maori girls, Maori farms, Maori housing: you'd only to hear my father put tongue to any or all of that to know where he stood, solid for intolerance, mac, but solid. **1970** DAVIN *Not Here Not Now* 194 'What time is Bill [Rangata] coming to pick us up for the dance?' 'About half-past seven, he said. But he's a bit Maori about time.' **1972** *Sunday Times* (Wellington) 24 Sept. 47 It's [*sc.* a cartoon strip] perpetuating the idea people have of something as being a real Maori trick, or a real Maori way of doing things. It's derogatory.

3. Pertaining to Cook Islands Maori.
   1905 *Truth* 10 Oct. 5 Indeed we almost doubt if King Ned knows of the existence of the Cook Islands. Still so long as the Maori inhabitants swear allegiance to him, it's all Sir Garnett. **1951** *NZ Geogr.* Oct. 127 (Johnston 'Citrus Industry of the Cook Islands') The occupier was confirmed as the owner under Maori custom and became capable of pledging the freehold to the administration as security for financial and material advances.

4. In the names of plants and animals. **a.** NATIVE B 2, NEW ZEALAND B 3.
   1860 SCOTT *Rough Notes of Travels* 32 The red, white and blue 'maori' trees (maori, as already intimated, is the name of the aborigines of New Zealand; but the word is also conventionally used to describe anything that is good, beautiful, or superior) look handsome. **1889** *TrNZI* XXI. 198 On [the nettle leaves] being used up I tried the hungry creatures [*sc.* larvae] with several other leaves of Maori plants, but none would they touch. **1897** *TrNZI* XXIX. 140 Take, for instance, the common Maori kingfisher. **1946** *JPS* LV. 149 *houhere*, a tree (Hoheria populnea), ribbonwood, lacebark, thousand-jacket. One of the three or four deciduous Maori trees.
   b. In special collocations in the names of plants and animals, usu. with an English common name as a second element, in the senses (a) 'indigenous, native, New Zealand', less often (b) 'growing or running wild; non-domesticated', occas. with derog. connotations 'as used by Maoris; fit only for Maori use': (a) see ANISE, BLOWFLY 1, CROW *n.*[1] I 3, DAPHNE, DOCK 1, FLOUNDER *n.* 2 (1), FUCHSIA 1, HOLLY, HONEYSUCKLE, ICE-PLANT, IVY 1, JASMINE, LAWYER 1, MAORI-BUG, MAORI CHIEF[2], MAORIHEAD, MAORI HEN, MAORI POTATO, MINT, MISTLETOE 1, ONION 2, PAINKILLER 2, PARSNIP, PRIVET, RAT *n.*[1] 1, SALMON 1, SANDALWOOD 1, SPURGE, TOBACCO, TROUT 2 (3), TURNIP 1, VINE; (b) see CABBAGE 1, CELERY 2 (1), DOG *n.* 2 b, also CUNNING *a.* (*cunning as a Maori dog*), ONION 2, PARSNIP. See also below **Maori chicken** *obs.*, (roast) WEKA: **Maori devil** *obs.* [poss. from the nickname TAIPO], WETA 2 (5); **Maori fire**, KAIKOMAKO (*Pennantia corymbosa*: see 1940 Laing & Blackwell *Plants of NZ* 244ff. for an account of the kaikomako in Maori lore and its subsequent use in the making of fire); **Maori gooseberry**, POROPORO; **Maori lemon**, a cross between an orange and a lemon (poss. *poorman's orange* (POOR MAN 2)); **Maori melon**, a gourd grown by the Maori; **Maori peach**, a wild peach; **Maori pony**, a brumby, or a broken-in wild horse mainly from the King Country or the central North Island; **Maori rabbit** *Otago obs.*, a rat (poss. the KIORE) as food.
   1857 *St Leonard's Station Diary* in Macfarlane *Amuri* (1946) 125 Must [kill] soon, as getting tired of **maori chiken** [*sic*]. **1907** LAING & BLACKWELL *Plants of NZ* 188 The weta, or **Maori Devil**, is a large orthopterous insect of the genus Deinacrida. **1927** *TrNZI* LVII. 934 **Maori fire** *Pennantia corymbosa* [Vernacular names heard by Andersen at Stony Bay, Banks Peninsula] [1927 *Note*] So called because used for Maori fire-sticks; the tree is also personified as Hine-kaikomako. **1946** *JPS* LV. 151 *kaikomako*, a small tree.., bridal-tree, Maori fire... The softer of the two woods used by the Maori for producing fire by friction: he can get the blaze in under a minute and a half. c**1920** BEATTIE *Trad. Lifeways Southern Maori* (1994) 118 Poroporo grew on the Otago Peninsula... The fruit was yellow and sweet and were about the size of a gooseberry and hence the settlers often referred to them as **Maori gooseberries**. **1972** RAFTER *Never let Go!* 57 In winter they had '**Maori lemons**', a cross between a lemon and an orange; curiously enough, the children ate the skin of the 'Maori lemons' and threw the juicy pulp away. **1844** SARAH GREENWOOD 10 Nov. in Drummond *Married and Gone to NZ* (1960) 78 We have now in the garden [at Motueka]..**Maori melons**, spinach. **1920** *Quick March* 10 Apr. 37 Do you know the Korako peach?... The Korako (meaning white) is the old **Maori peach**, as it is called, the big white honey-sweet fruit the natives received from the missionaries. **1946** *NZ Geogr.* 247 Trees were first raised from stones brought to New Zealand by missionaries and early settlers; they were subsequently grown so widely by the Maori that they became known as the 'Maori' peach. None survives today. **1925** *NZ Dairy Produce Exporter* 31 Oct. 35 I never did think anythin' o' those **Maori ponies** that yer drive into the sale from the tussock country 'yond Rotorua. **1938** WINTER *King Country* 41 Mr. H. Bromley, mounted on a Maori pony. **1948** DOUGLAS in Woodhouse *Farm & Station Verse* (1950) 173 Still in the going is old Bill Bennett On the Maori pony he bought from the Pound. **1863** PYKE *Report* in *AJHR* D-6 7 Driven back by the want of provisions, which compelled him to feed on '**Maori rabbits**' (*Anglice*, rats), Caples made a second attempt. **1872** *TrNZI* IV. 140 In the early days of the gold rush, they [*sc.* kiore] were not uncommon in the interior, used to be caught and eaten by the diggers under the name of Maori rabbits. **1968** HALL-JONES *Early Fiordland* 78 [Caples] then retreated up the Hollyford, ravenously hungry, to eat every 'Maori rabbit' (rat) he could catch.

5. In special collocations. **a.** In non-derog. applications, see MAORI BATTALION, MAORI CHIEF[1], MAORI KING, MAORILAND 1 and 2, MAORI LAND COURT, MAORI MISSION, MAORI PAKEHA, MAORI SCHOOL, MAORI WAR. See also below: **Maori Affairs**, see *Native Affairs* NATIVE B 3 b; **Maori All Black** (*pl.* Maori All Blacks), a member of a NZ rugby union Maori-only representative team chosen on racial criteria: in *pl.*, the team itself; **Maori assessor**, see ASSESSOR; **Maori axe**, a pre-European stone adze, AXE; **Maori basket**, a basket plaited from NZ flax, also KETE or KIT *n.*[1]; **Maori belly wool**, describing a type of shearing stroke or method of efficiently clipping belly wool; **Maori Bible**, the Maori-language translation of the King James Bible; **Maori bottom** *Central Otago goldmining* [from its brown colour], BOTTOM *n.* 1, composed of brownish gravel (cf. also CHINAMAN *n.*[1]); **Maori bread**, an unleavened bread, or one made from potato yeast (also called *paraoa rewena*: see also PARAOA *n.*[2]); occas. PUNGAPUNGA, a bread made from raupo pollen (see quot. 1890); **Maori burn**, a children's 'torture' (cf. *Chinese burn* (CHINESE 2)); **Maori calendar**, a Maori-devised calendar based variously on lunar, seasonal, etc. cycles; **Maori chain**, a method of crossing a river safely by forming a human chain by holding hands; **Maori church**, a church designed and built by Maori for a Maori congregation and worship, and usu. featuring Maori decoration and motifs; in modern use, often (collectively) the Maori bishops and people of the Anglican communion; **Maori concert**, a concert comprising mainly Maori songs, poi dances, hakas, etc.; **Maori concert party**, a Maori entertainment troupe, now usu. termed a '(Maori) cultural group', performing traditional and contemporary Maori items; **Maori Congress**, a group of Maori tribal representatives come together to discuss Maori concerns and present to the Government and the public a concerted view on such matters; **Maori Contingent** *WW1*, the Pioneer battalion of Maori volunteers (see quot. 1917); **Maori copper** [prob. an inversion of COPPER MAORI], COPPER MAORI 1, HANGI 1; **Maori Council**, a local council supported by the State to discuss and advise on things Maori; also a national body of eminent Maori formed to bring Maori matters to the notice of the authorities; **Maori death**, a former name for pneumonia, once prevalent and fatal among the Maori population; **Maori difficulty**, *native difficulty*, *native problem* (NATIVE B 3 b); **Maori doctor**, see quots.; **Maori English**, varieties of English typical of, but not exclusive to, Maori speakers, typically perceived from its lack of -*s* plurals, a confusion between countable and non-countable nouns, phonemic interchanges (esp. c/g, p/b, r/d generating forms like *py korry* 'by God'), and an elliptical syntax (see also PIDGIN-MAORI 2): in former times poss. equated with the 'stage Maori' of e.g., the *Hone Tiki Dialogues* of A.A. Grace (1910), or W.N. McCallum ('Hori') *The Half-gallon Jar* (1962), and often associated with working-class Maori and Maori entertainers; **Maori fence**, TAIEPA; **Maori flute**, a usu. bone flute, often called 'nose flute'; **Maori grave** *transf. obs.*, a former local Otago name for a CRAB-HOLE q.v.; **Maori gravel**, dark gravel used by early Maori to warm the soil for kumara-growing in areas of marginal soil temperature; **Maori hole** (mainly *Nelson–Marlborough*) (a) RUA; (b) holes formed by the removal of gravel by early Maori (cf. *Maori gravel*); **Maori hut** (occas. **house**) *hist.*, one built or made in former Maori fashion usu. of raupo, nikau, etc., and often built as temporary accommodation by (or for) early Pakeha settlers (see also *raupo hut* (RAUPO 3 a)); **Maori Interpreter**, see INTERPRETER; **Maori kilt**, PIUPIU *n.*[1]; **Maori kiss**[1], HONGI *n.*; **Maori kiss**[2], KISS *n.*[1]; **Maori kit**, see KIT *n.*[1] 2; **Maori language**, *attrib.* used, alluding to the preferential or institutional use of Maori rather than English, often in the collocation **Maori language nest**, KOHANGA REO; **Maori Magna Carta (Charta)** [transf. use of Brit. hist. *Magna Carta*], the Treaty of Waitangi; **Maori mat**, see MAT 1 b and 2; **Maori nut** *obs.*, a karaka berry or kernel prepared (i.e., detoxified) by soaking, steaming and drying; **Maori Parliament** *hist.*, a council formed to advise the Maori King; **Maori path**, see *Maori track* below; **Maori pioneer** *WW1*, a member of the Maori Pioneer Battalion; **the Maori problem (question)** *hist., native question* (NATIVE B 3 b), a pakeha term for the Maori–Pakeha differences over sovereignty, political, social, and economic (esp. land-sale) rights (cf. *native difficulty* NATIVE B 3 b); **Maori renaissance**, a name applied to the resurgence in the later 20th century of Maori interest and endeavour in things Maori; **Maori reserve**, see RESERVE 2; **Maori sandal**, usu. *pl.*, PARAERAE; **Maori scare** *hist.*, a fear of Maori attack common among European settlers c1840–1870, a state of rural mind induced by rumour, press reports and the occasional killing of a settler; **Maori scent**, see quot.; **Maori scone**, FRIED SCONE; **Maori seat**, one of the four parliamentary seats reserved to Maori representation; **Maori shoe**, see *Maori sandal* above; **Maori sickness**, *mate Maori* (MATE *n*.¹); **Maori skirt** (also *transf.*), PIUPIU; **Maori sore**, HAKIHAKI; **Maori spade**, the KO, a Maori digging implement; **Maori spear**, TAIAHA; **Maori stone**, *black Maori* (see A 6 b above); **Maori summer**, a humorous coinage on 'Indian summer' for unexpectedly fine, gentle weather; **Maori swing** (Ma. *morere*), see quot. 1847; **Maori tea**, an infusion of tea-tree or biddy-bid leaves; **Maori time**, a reputedly less rigorous view of time and time schedules than that of the European; **Maori township**, see TOWNSHIP 2 b; **Maori track**, a well-trodden route taken by past generations of Maori travellers; usu. referring to an ancient or traditional Maori 'highway' (as, for example, the 'greenstone' tracks between the South Island east and west coasts: see also *Maori path* above); **Maori Trustee**, a statutory official with special responsibility for trustee and estate matters for any person of Maori descent (see also quot. 1964); **Maori village**, see VILLAGE 1; **Maori warden**, a semi-official, uniformed volunteer who patrols public places, bars, etc. in ways helpful to Maori people and the general community; **Maori way** [f. a translation of *taha Maori*], a mode of action governed by a Maori ideology; **Maori welcome**, POWHIRI, a formal ceremonial welcome given to visitors to a marae.

1986 *Dominion* (Wellington) 23 May 14 Surely Mr Hirs[c]h should have a look at **Maori All Blacks**, Maori golf tournaments, Maori tennis tournaments etc., which discriminate against white people. **1986** SORRENSON in *Na To Hoa Aroha* I. 33 Thus he [*sc.* Ngata] was an active supporter of Maori rugby, both on a tribal level, through the competition for the Prince of Wales trophy, and on a national level, through the Maori All Blacks. **1992** COSTELLO *Howard* 46 That's why Ray Keepa was a Maori All Black and should have been an All Black. **1937** AYSON *Thomas* 82 Lying near the ovens were a good many **Maori axes** and spear heads in a perfect state of preservation. **1986** OWEN & PERKINS *Speaking for Ourselves* 26 He came home..bringing exotic things back like little gold nuggets in bottles and Maori axes and kea feathers. **1853** SEWELL *Journal* 22 Aug. (1980) I. 367 Our ball attire sent over in **Maori Baskets**. **1874** HAYTER *Notes of a Tour in NZ* 12 The common way [of cooking is] to suspend a Maori basket, or 'kit', as it is termed, containing the article to be cooked, in a boiling pool. **1930** GUTHRIE *NZ Memories* 162 He produced a Maori basket with a day-old *kuri* (dog) inside! **1975** KNIGHT *Poyntzfield* 30 Father went over his beloved books..putting what he must leave in a Maori basket, sent two of us to carry the basket to Miss Cowper. **1990** MARTIN *Forgotten Worker* 90 Two changes of technique in the early twentieth century revolutionised shearing—the 'long blow' and the '**Maori belly wool**'... The Maori downward belly-wool technique, which was developed in Hawke's Bay, avoided the time-consuming and arduous blade technique of sitting the sheep upright and opening out the belly with a series of short strokes around the sheep. **1860** MARJOURAM *Diary* 1 Feb. in *Sergeant, Sinner* (1990) 32 I took a **Maori Bible** down from one of the shelves, and asked him if I should read a little; but, on seeing the book, he replied that he would not listen to me unless I used Kawirois's Bible. **1897** MCKAY *Older Auriferous Drifts Central Otago* 25 These [sandstone gravels] are decomposed so far as to assume the usual light-brown colour of what is known in the Upper Manuherikia and Naseby districts as '**Maori bottom**'. **1908** *NZGeol.SB (NS)* No.5 42 These consist of yellowish brown sandstone gravels, well rounded and fairly uniform in size... The gravels form the well-known 'Maori bottom' of the Maniototo and Manuherikia basins. **1939** *NZGeol.SB (NS)* No.39 108 The brownish quartz-sandstone gravels, locally [at Naseby] known as Maori Bottom, are seldom payably auriferous. **1962** *NZGeol. Surv. Map* Sheet 22 Early Pleistocene gravels were deposited in fault-angle basins in Central Otago and became deformed by the continuing fault movements that led to their formation; these gravels, termed 'Maori Bottom' by the gold-miners, were deeply weathered to a rusty-brown colour during the later Pleistocene. **1890** *Otago Witness* (Dunedin) 9 Jan. 17 Here we have a cake of **Maori bread**, called punga punga. **1960** CRUMP *Good Keen Man* 46 On a wet Sunday Mori baked a few rounds of Maori bread. They were about the same shape as the wooden cart-wheels in old drawings, and I doubt if they tasted much better. **1971** BAXTER *Collected Poems* (1980) 517 [J]ust a knife to cut open the loaf of Maori bread. **1989** CRANNA *Visitors* 38 Tamati was..slowly eating the big maori-bread sandwiches he brought every day. **1994** *Dominion* (Wellington) She showed the kids [at primary school] how to make Maori bread. **1963** FRAME *Reservoir* 49 And she twisted my arm once more, and caught at my wrist, giving me a vicious Chinese and **Maori burn** combined. **1868** LINDSAY *Contribs. NZ Botany* 73 The flowering of [the *Kowhai*] and the *Fuchsia* tree are two of the diagnostic features of [September] in the **Maori calendar**. **1890** *Otago Witness* (Dunedin) 18 Sept. 31 We had to ford rivers sometimes a quarter of a mile wide, with the ice-cold water reaching to our armpits, which we did by forming a **Maori chain**—that is, hand in hand, with the strongest man up-stream. **1851** GRACE *Rep. Turanga Dist.* 31 Dec. in *Pioneer Missionary* (1928) 16 It is a **Maori Church** of comparatively small pretensions, but is..the first Native-built Church in this land which has a chancel. **1943** MARSH *Colour Scheme* 81 It was on that same evening..nine days before the **Maori concert**. **1974** PRESTON *Lady Doctor* 113 I was fortunate to attend more than one Maori concert while in Rotorua [in the 1920s]. **1965** GILLHAM *Naturalist in NZ* 200 In the evenings there were **Maori concert parties**. **1971** *New Zealand's Heritage* I. 74 [Caption] Maori child wearing a piupiu, typical costume worn nowadays by Maori concert parties. **1992** *North & South* (Auckland) Jan. 83 Something which makes me feel very New Zealand is when I'm overseas and there's a Maori concert party performing songs about the arrival in the land of the long white cloud. **1993** *Evening Post* (Wellington) 23 Feb. 4 This Maori Congress carry-on serves the rest of us Maori..on a silver platter. **1917** *Chron. NZEF* 18 Apr. 78 Unfortunately, though we could fight like the Infantry, the Infantry could not dig like us. So the Powers that be made us Pioneers. [1917 *Note*] The Pioneer battalion was formed from the Otago Mounted Rifles and the **Maori Contingent**. **1963** HENDERSON *Ratana* (1972) 16 When the [Great] War was over, men of the Maori Contingent were still landless despite their war service. **1983** *Land of the Mist* 33 After 1914, Rua's lack of enthusiasm towards Tuhoe recruitment for the Maori Contingent started rumours which believed him to be an ally of the Germans. **1864** CHUDLEIGH *Diary* 7 Oct. (1950) 147 We roasted half a sheep in a **Maori copper**, that is first dig a hole in the ground in proportion to the thing you want to cook. Line the bottom and sides with stones as big as a breakfast cup then light a fire over them [etc.]. **1878** HEBERLEY *Autobiog.* (ATLTS) 31 The Natives took a cask of lime, and thought it was a cask of flour, they went to work and made dumplings of it and baked them in what is termed a Maori Copper. **1919** POATA *Maori as Fisherman* 10 They must be cooked off a tapu ground in the Maori copper only, custom forbidding any other method. **1903** *TrNZI* XXXV. 180 The passing of the **Maori Councils** Act of 1900... The Maori Council is a step forward in the direction of progress. **1905** BAUCKE *White Man Treads* 273 Besides, who will take leases for 21 years with a Maori council title? **1986** SORRENSON *Na To Hoa Aroha* I. 27 Ngata replied..by saying that he could not leave New Zealand because of political commitments... 'You wouldn't have the heart to entice me away from a prospect so alluring! Compare washing up bills with banana groves, Maori Councils with your lotus-eaters!' **1938** *NZ Observer* 10 Nov. 6 One of her favourite grandchildren succumbed to pneumonia ('the **Maori death**'). **1863** MANING *Old NZ* (vii) 105 Here I am..within a hairbreadth of settling 'the **Maori difficulty**' without having been paid for it. **1880** CRAWFORD *Recoll. of Travel* 314 By a '**Maori doctor**' I mean a person who professes, from knowledge of the language and customs of the Maoris, and from personal influence among them, to have exclusive power of managing them [*e.g.* Grey, Donald McLean]. **1989** GALBREATH *Walter Buller* 135 Clearly Buller was not always trusted by the Maori people he dealt with..but his evident ease among them sometimes brought him the labels of 'Maori man' or 'Maori doctor' from colonists. There was a subtle difference in meaning between the two. A 'Maori doctor' was one of those experts, especially in politics, who were thought to understand Maori ways, and how to manage Maori people... Buller could accept that label as a mark of respect for his professional skill and knowledge. But 'Maori man' (meaning a Maori sympathiser) was a term of disparagement or denigration. **1926** LAWLOR *Maori Tales* 9 The reader should be warned that the apparently phonetic spelling of English as it is commonly supposed to be spoken by Hori is not to be accepted as authentic '**Maori English**'. **1971** *Maori Children & Teacher* (Dept of Education) 42 It is sometimes stated that a Maori child's spoken vocabulary often lacks idiom. It is true that he has limited access to the wide range of expressions that enrich the English language, but 'Maori English' is perhaps excessively idiomatic in its use of colloquial phrases, slang, and short, pithy expressions that convey more meaning than is in bare words. **1972** HAWKINS in *NZ Jrnl. Educ. Studies* May 68 [Title] Restricted Codes and Maori English. I hope to have shown, in this review, that we should not accept uncritically the assumption that Maori English constitutes a restricted code or that Maori children are cognitively deficient. We know that Maori English is different from Standard English and we are aware of some of the factors that make it so. **1993** Tony Deverson in *Of Pavlovas, Poetry and Paradigms* (1993) 205 Esmeralda..in *Came a Hot Friday*, uses some constructions which are or have been thought to be markers of Maori English: 'You just an animal like all those other peoples.' **1849** TAYLOR *Journal* (ATBTS) 20 May VI. 93 A neat **Maori fence** surrounds the grave [of Mr Millar]. **1917** *NZ At the Front* 164 He [*sc.* bagpipes] sound like one t'ousand koauau, *Maori flute*. **1890** *Otago Witness* (Dunedin) 25 Sept. 18 We will find a quantity of small mounds with a depression on one side giving a miner the idea that someone has been sinking a prospecting hole in some localities. These are called **Maori graves** (from their resemblance to a grave not filled in). *Ibid.* 9 Oct. 20 Eastward of Te Anau and Manapouri lakes there are large areas of crabholes or 'Maori graves' caused by falling trees. **1929** BUCK *Coming of the Maori* (Cawthron Lecture) 3 In the Waimea Plains, an area of soil, known as **Maori gravel**, was shown to be very rich in available phosphoric acid and potash. This area is an old Maori pre-European cultivation. Pits had been dug to obtain sand and gravel, which, after having the larger stones removed, were spread over the natural loam top soil to render it more suitable for the cultivation of the kumara. **1936** *Agricultural Organization in NZ* 810 Rigg, T., and Bruce, J.A.: The Maori Gravel Soil of Waimea West, Nelson. *New Zealand Cawthron Institute Bulletin* (1923). **1894** *JPS* IV. 221 When the Nelson settlement was founded, whole sections of land in the Waimea were almost entirely worthless owing to the many large irregular-shaped pits, or '**Maori Holes**' from which the gravel had been taken by some former inhabitants. **1903** *TrNZI* XXXV. 21 The enormous number of these *ruas* on the volcanic plains of Taranaki..shows the extent of former plantations. They are called 'Maori holes' by the settlers; and before the country was thoroughly reclaimed they caused the loss of a good many horses and cattle. **1954** p.c. R. Mason I always use the term 'Maori-hole' [for a shallow pit], which I learnt from my mother, ex-Wanganui district. **1839** *Piraki Log* 24 June (1911) 90 At 6 P.M. the **moury House**..took fire, and with great difficulty the flames were extinguish'd. **1841** *NZ Journal* II. 162 I retired to a **Mauri hut**, which I had purchased as a private residence temporarily, till the sections should be given out. **1842** WICKSTEAD in *Lett. from New Plymouth* 23 Nov. (1968) 68 The Maori or Raupo huts are daily losing their occupants and falling into decay, being replaced by substantial *cob*, or mud-walled dwellings, but oftenest by neat wooden buildings. **1880** SENIOR *Travel & Trout* 214 The recurrence of Maori huts warned us that we were in Maori Country. **1876** KENNEDY *Colonial Travel* 232 The native who had not risen to the supposed dignity of a full suit appeared in a **Maori kilt**—a mat tied round his waist giving free-play to his bare legs and feet. **1924** LYSNAR *NZ* 79 [Maori hunters] are often seen returning from the chase with their fierce-looking dogs, great-limbed men, wearing the Maori kilt or shawl (a piece of coloured blanket or flax mat wrapped round their loins). **1944** ROBACK *Dict. International Slurs* (1979) 53 **Maori kiss**: a greeting consists of rubbing noses. **c1940s** TS Index to Baucke *Where the White Man Treads* (1928) Victoria University Library: Fildes collection copy no. 1788 *Maori Kiss*, see Hongi **1988** *Press* (Christchurch) 29 Aug. 20 **Maori-language** primary schools must eventually lead to demands for Maori-language secondary schools and tertiary education. **1990** *Evening Post* (Wellington) 15 Aug. 3 Mr Puketapu's Tangata programme of the early 1980s introduced kohanga reo, or Maori language nests. [**1841** *Report of George Clarke, Protector of Aborigines in GBPP 1842* (No.569) 4 Jan. 98 They had, I said, in their hands the magna carta of the country, securing to them everything which could make them respected. Their land and everything they had was their own.] **1936** BUICK *Treaty of Waitangi* 98ff [Title of chapter iv] The **Maori Magna Charta**. **1940** MATTHEWS *Matthews of Kaitaia* 128 T. Lindsay Buick, in his book on the Maori Magna Charta, gives a full and interesting account of the proceedings. **1955** *BJ Cameron Collection* (TS July) Maori magna charta (n) The Treaty of Waitangi 1840. (Historical). **c1920** BEATTIE *Trad. Lifeways Southern Maori* (1994) 302 Karaka berries could be eaten after they had been prepared by steaming for twenty-four hours in a Maori oven and then dried. This converts them into '**Maori nuts**'... They were like nuts and were up to two inches long... You took off the kiri (skin or husk) and ate the kernel. **1879** *Auckland Weekly News* 19 Apr. 6 The **Maori Parliament** strongly opposed it [*sc.* a land survey]. **1840** MATHEW *Journal* 5 Oct. in *Founding of NZ* (1940) 194 There is a **Maori path** winding through the copse up the hill to the Flag staff, and thus far is our usual evening walk. **1858** *Richmond Atkinson Papers* (1960) I. 339 He [*sc.* a native] said that there was an old Maori path from Puapua over the Papakauri mountain to Tawariki on the Mokau river. **1978** TAYLOR *Twilight Hour* 54 I think it was the **Maori Pioneers** who dug most of that bloody communications sap. **1933** in *Na To Hoa Aroha* (1988) III. 90 But the figures will convince you more than any Parliamentary report of the change that has come over the official..attitude of the responsible people here towards the **Maori problem**. **1961** *Comment 8* 8 The report is a vigorous European attempt to present an over-all picture of the 'Maori problem'. **1860** *McLean to F.E. Maning* 3 Nov. in Cowan *Sir Donald Maclean* (1940) 77 However, every well-wisher of the Maori race must hail with satisfaction a spirit of enquiry among the Europeans, as to the **Maori question**, which must lead to a more full appreciation and just recognition of their social and political rights. **1902** KELLY *Heather & Fern* 91 [Verse title] 'The Maori Question'—'Debit and credit'. **1910** *Kai Tiaki* July 103 To draw attention of the nursing world to this aspect [*sc.* health] of the Maori question, I have put together..a few notes. **1936** *Handbook for NZ* (ANZAAS) 10 The history of New Zealand since 1840 can be summarized under three heads: (1) English colonization involving land questions which interlocked with (2) the Maori question. **1965** CAMERON *NZ* 95 A second **Maori renaissance** seems to be under way, aided by this all-embracing term [*Maoritanga*]. **1991** *Landfall 179* Sept. 368 Even supposing that the Maori Renaissance could reverse structural inequalities in society..such atavistic ethnic revivals..have not always the happiest results. **1861, 1896 Maori sandals** [see PARAERAE]. **1928** *NZ Free Lance* (Wellington) 7 Mar. 35 They were just skin and bones; their clothes were trousers frayed away till they were only ragged knee-breeches..and Maori sandals of plaited cabbage-tree leaves on their feet. **1939** BEATTIE *First White Boy Born Otago* 178 He would walk down to Dunedin wearing pararas (Maori sandals) and carrying his boots. **1948** HAAST *Julius Von Haast* 201 On the beaches and in river-beds they [Haast and Dobson c1862] wore Maori sandals. **1940** *Tales of Pioneer Women* (1988) vii They have told of '**Maori scares**,' when they had to flee for their lives from hostile natives, and of other 'Maori scares,' which proved to be merely neighbourly visits. **c1920** BEATTIE *Trad. Lifeways Southern Maori* (1994) 64 The shepherds on the sheep-runs call sweet-smelling leaves 'Maori scent', but my informants could not name the plants which gave to those [Central Otago] mountains their particular fragrance. **1966** FINLAYSON *Brown Man's Burden* (1973) 119 Mum baked the bread and **Maori scones** there. **1966** *Arena 65* June 4 Mum baked real white bread, Pakeha bread, and you know those Maori scones fried golden brown all over? **1985** *Listener* 15 June 79 The **Maori seats** had their genesis in the political system established under the New Zealand Constitution Act, 1852... Initially, it was intended that the Maori seats be held by Pakehas. **1939** BEATTIE *First White Boy Born Otago* 32 The narrator says the second line should read 'Old Jack Hughes had **Maori shoes**', according to the way he heard it as a child. These Maori shoes were flax or cabbage-tree sandals and many a white man wore them. **1946** BEAGLEHOLE *Some Modern Maoris* 205 He thinks of sickness..particularly that kind of sickness which he calls **Maori sickness**, as very often caused by spirits as a punishment for the violation of tapu or custom. **1981** BROOKER et al. *NZ Medicinal Plants* 74 The inner bark [of *M. fulgens*] was also boiled and the liquid was drunk for 'Maori sickness'. **1985** *Press* (Christchurch) 30 Jan. 32 week to the psychiatric hospital to diagnose and treat 'Maori sickness', break tapu and sometimes hold Church services in Maori. **1987** [see MATE *n.*[1]]. **1965** GILLHAM *Naturalist in NZ* 24 The most common kind in [Stewart Island] is Smith's tree-fern, easily recognisable by the '**Maori skirt**' of old leaves which dangles from its 'waist'. **1984** MIHAKA *Whakapohane* 46 I kind of suspected that [*sc.* ignorance of things Maori] when you referred to the so-called Maori skirt as consisting of beads. **1960** HILLIARD *Maori Girl* 48 Netta anointed and dressed their ringworm and '**Maori sores**'—angry red patches which grew bigger each day and seemed to eat away the flesh. Little Rangi had them in the crook of his arms. **1842** *Best Journal* (1966) 20 Apr. 354 Warriors armed with seven long spears having a rest for the foot on them like a **mauri spade**. **1866** HUNT *Chatham Is.* 17 [Rauparaha] took down a **Maori spear**, highly ornamented with feathers, and placed it in my hand. **1906** *NZGeol.SB (NS)* No.1 89 Small concretions popularly known as '**Maori stones**' on account of their high specific gravity, are frequently met with in the concentrates derived from [Humphrey's Gully] gravels [Hokitika]. **1983** HULME *Bone People* 251 The weather has held fine and windless; ('**Maori summer**,' he says. 'In the middle of winter?' 'When better to get a bit of brown in?') **1847** ANGAS *Savage Life* II. 118 The **Maori** or native **swing** is an amusement amongst the Taupo people which is obsolete upon the coast. A pole, generally the trunk of a *kaikatea* pine, is erected in the centre of an open space adjoining the village; flax ropes are suspended from the top, and, holding on to these, the natives swing round and round, in a manner similar to that which is practised in gymnasia and at country fairs in Europe. **1984** LOCKE *The Kauri & the Willow* 79 The boys swung round and round the pole, as with the Maori swing or morere. It was known as the Giant's Stride. **1866** MUELLER *My Dear Bannie* (1958) 15 Jan. 114 Before leaving for my shingle-bed, they got a couple of eels roasted, and some **Mauri tea** boiled for breakfast. **1903** *TrNZI* XXXV. 179 I believe it would prove a great boon..warning the natives of the dangers of inordinate use of tobacco, sleeping on the ground, and drinking Maori tea. **1946** BEAGLEHOLE *Some Modern Maoris* 295 Take '**Maori' time**. The modern Maori adapts himself to two concepts of time. One is the pakeha concept: time is something solid, fixed, definite, to which other activities must be geared... 'Maori' time, on the other hand, is a plastic medium that flows round and adapts itself to the activities of the day. The 'Maori' time for anything is when you are ready to do it... It is this 'Maori' time then that rules the casual life of the Maori. Pakeha time is a sort of necessary nuisance to which you adapt yourself so as to be able to do other desirable things. **1951** KOHERE *Autobiography of a Maori* 70 Recently..my cousin and I divided time into two categories—pakeha time and Maori time. We have found that there is something to be said for Maori time which really means any time. **1983** *Evening Post* (Wellington) 20 Aug. 44 'Maori time' has been described as a concept in which people and not the clock are the deciding factors in dictating the course of events. **1983** *Dominion* (Wellington) 25 Aug. 3 The term 'Maori time' could be used in an insulting way, but frequently no disparagement was either intended or taken, Race Relations Conciliator Hiwi Tauroa said yesterday. Mr Tauroa..said Maori people frequently used the expression 'Maori time'. **1990** CHAVASSE *Integrity* 53 Now, boss, we've been on Maori time for an hour or two. We'd better get on to pakeha time. What did you come here for. **1843** *NZ Jrnl.* IV. 216 My men walked round the river by a **Mauri track**. **1892** *TrNZI* XXIV. 607 This mountain..over which passes the Maori track from Tokaanu, appears to have a gentle slope. **1911** *Ibid.* XLIII. 605 One occasion..I travelled..to Mangamuka by the old Maori track crossing the western shoulder of Maungataniwha. **1930** *Tararua Tramper*

May 2 Here a Maori track commences, and leads through the bush to Maungapohatu. **1940** COWAN *Sir Donald Maclean* 53 The olden maori tracks often kept to the high ridges, a precaution against surprise by enemies. **1950** RICHARDS in Chudleigh *Diary* (1950) 212 There were well defined foot tracks from one [Chatham Island] pa to another but as the Maoris walk with their feet turned inwards, a Maori track is too narrow for Europeans or for a horse to walk on in comfort, and is only just wide enough for one sheep at a time. **1986** RICHARDS *Off the Sheep's Back* 64 In those days [in the Raglan district] it was possible to travel along any of the main ridges, as they were recognised as old Maori tracks and could not be fenced off. **1963** AUDLEY *No Boots for Mr. Moehau* 118 There will be a long delay before the Court's decision is made absolute and the money is placed with the **Maori Trustee**. **1964** *Mozley and Whiteley's Law Dict.* 233 By s. 6 of the Maori Trustee Act 1953 the Maori Trustee is constituted a corporation sole with perpetual succession and a common seal. The Maori Trustee may accept special trusts for Maoris or the descendants of Maoris (s. 11) and may accept appointment as the executor, administrator or trustee of any Maori.., or as the agent or attorney of any Maori [etc.]. **1961** REED *N. Cape to Bluff* 27 This is to certify that during his stay in Te Kao he did not disturb the peace. K. Wiki, No. 19, **Maori** District **Warden**, Te Kao. **1986** *Evening Post* (Wellington) 2 July 10 —, a trainee Maori warden of Wellington, had earlier pleaded guilty to a charge of assault with intent to injure. **1988** *Sunday Star* (Auckland) 5 June A9 Maori Warden Eb Hauraki says he hasn't been called out once..in the past six months. **1934** in KING *Whina* (1983) 261 When you say that supervisors must work in the **Maori way**, what you mean is that they must work having proper regard to the Maori customs and usage? **1987** *Sunday Star* (Auckland) 12 Apr. A3 [A prominent Maori teacher] says placing the curse [on a burglar] is 'the Maori way' of dealing with such matters, as the police hold little hope of recovering his belongings. **1988** *Sunday Star* (Auckland) 23 Oct. A12 Lack of rosters or records of work justified as the 'Maori way' was 'ridiculous' said Mr Tauroa. **1920** BOLITHO *With the Prince in NZ* 36 Arrangements were made to transport the natives..to Rotorua, where the great **Maori welcome** was extended to the Prince.

b. In dismissive, derogatory, belittling, or offensive applications of *Maori*: **Maori bed**, MAORI BUNK; **Maori boy**, an adult male Maori (cf. BOY); **Maori cannon**, a blunder at billiards; **Maori car**, an old or decrepit vehicle; **Maori chrome**, see quot.; **Maori day off**, absenteeism from the workplace; **Maori ear**, an ear infection (usu. 'glue ear') reputedly prevalent among Maori children; **Maori fallow**, of cultivated land, allowed to revert to its original state of fern, scrub, etc.; **Maori half-crown** *obs.*, a penny piece; **Maori holiday**, see quots.; **Maori huntaway**, a stone rolled down hill to move sheep (see also HUNTAWAY 3, *Nelson huntaway* (NELSON 2)); **Maori itch**, formerly applied to irritations or itchy eruptions of the skin blamed on louse-infestations or kinds of scabies commonly thought to be prevalent among Maori people (see also HAKIHAKI); **Maori marriage**, a marriage according to Maori custom, regarded as a common-law marriage by Pakeha (see also *Maori wedding* below); **Maori mustang** [f. *Mustang* a trade-name for a high-powered car], the Mark II Ford Zephyr; **Maori oats** *obs.*, see quot.; **Maori overdrive**, see quot.; **Maori porridge**, boiling mud (a Maori joke on gullible tourists); **Maori pot**, HANGI 1; **Maori pox**, see *Maori itch* above, HAKIHAKI; **Maori roast**, fish and chips (occas. other takeway foods) as a main meal; **Maori season**, a notional open season for Maori trout poachers; **Maori sidestep**, see quot. 1979; **Maori tackle**, see quot.; **Maori wedding**, see quot.; **Maori weed**, a BRUMBY q.v., esp. one from the central North Island; **Maori wife**, a mistress for bush living, a Maori woman married in traditional Maori fashion to a Pakeha male (see also *Maori wedding* above).

1969 HENDERSON *Open Country Calling* 224 The rest of the hut was taken up by a platform, known as a '**Maori bed**', to hold four men. **1944** FINLAYSON *Brown Man's Burden* (1973) 14 'Eh, goody-goody all right for the pakeha,' said Monday. 'This **Maori boy** means to have a good time.' **1959** SLATTER *Gun in My Hand* 99 I've seen some very good Maori boys on the paddock. Real good boys. Winnin or losin. They got a flair for the game. **1986** LATHAM *WAAC Story* 27 When the U.S. came into the war, there was a small influx sometime late in 1942. They made a few bloomers at first, but the old hands soon put them on the right track about..the way they addressed the Maori boys. **1991** DUFF *One Night Out Stealing* 13 Oh but you Maori boys are sure prudes. **1948** p.c. R. Mason (1953) A **Maori cannon** is where the striker's white hits (say) the red and knocks it against the other white, or where, in making a cannon, one opponent's white is sunk. **1983** *Listener* 24 Sept. 59 The complaint to the [Race Relations Conciliator] was in one sense rightly made because 'Maori time' belongs to a whole genre of derogatory sayings which include such negative ones as 'Maori day off', 'Maori PT', '**Maori car**', etc. **1983** p.c. Herb Wilford. Hastings. **Maori chrome** a second-hand car dealer's term for spotting chrome work with silver or other paint. **1983 Maori day off** [see *Maori car* above]. **1988** MCGILL *Dict. Kiwi Slang* 72 *MDO* Maori day off; a sickie, or a day absent from work with pretended illness; offensive. **1965** *Dominion* (Wellington) 2 Sept. 2 For more than half a century the '**Maori ear**' had been regarded in medical practice as a most unrewarding condition to treat in more ways than one and by both parties concerned, the report said. If future generations of Maori children retained their greater susceptibility to ear disease, every year would add to the size of the problem till it might become too big ever to be solved. **1887** *Auckland Weekly News* 24 Sept. 29 Some of the enclosures have been allowed to take a **Maori fallow**— i.e. have gone back to flax bush and milk weed. **1899** *Bulletin* (Sydney) 14 Jan. (Red Page) [Letter from *Loafer*, Tauranga.] Following are other local money-names... 1d.—***Maori half-crown***, *brownie* or *copper*. **1955** *BJ Cameron Collection* (TS July) maori half-crown (n) A penny. **1980** LELAND *Kiwi-Yankee Dict.* 62 **Maori holiday**: Like other socioeconomically disadvantaged groups, the Maori is the butt of a number of jokes... A Maori holiday is the day after payday. **1981** *Avondale College Slang Words in Use* (Auckland) (Goldie Brown Collection) Feb. *sickie*: a Maori holiday **1985** GORDON & DEVERSON *NZ Eng.* 42 Similar [derogatory] expressions include *Maori holiday* = the day after pay-day. **1978** JARDINE *Shadows on Hill* 61 First he would try a couple of '**Maori huntaways**' so, selecting a good-sized round rock and going to the edge of the bluff he was on, he rolled it over, on a line that would pass close to the sheep. **c1920** BEATTIE *Trad. Lifeways Southern Maori* (1994) 84 Itch, often called The **Maori Itch** [[scabies]] [*sic*] by Europeans nowadays, was a troublesome complaint of the olden Maori. It was called hakihaki in Murihiku. **1938** HYDE *Nor Yrs. Condemn* 148 The last one [*sc.* Maori hut] he struck had been full of fleas, and these thin lads..were the ones to have Maori itch. When you struck that you were sorry for yourself. **1952** LYON *Faring South* 171 The natives use the [Ngawha hot] springs largely for skin ailments, notably the akeake, or Maori itch. **1939** BELTON *Outside the Law* 98 **Maori 'marriages'** are still observed among the Maoris. **1990** *Listener* 13 Aug. 14 The Mk 1 Zephyr [corrected later to Mk 2] (once commonly referred to as the **Maori Mustang**) has a special place in local mythology. *Ibid.* 9 Sept. 115 The 'Maori Mustang' was the Mark II Zephyr..not the Mk I as stated in the text [of Kiwiana article 13 Aug.]. **1908** *Truth* 1 Feb. 2 The term, '**Maori Oats**', has long since lost its significance; its present meaning is no more or less than a small country meeting registered under the governing rules of racing. **1981** *Avondale College Slang Words in Use* (Auckland) (Goldie Brown Collection) Feb. ***Maori overdrive***: neutral **1988** MCGILL *Dict. Kiwi Slang* 72 *Maori overdrive* sliding your car in neutral downhill; offensive. **1908** STEWART *My Simple Life* 71 We were shown hot mud-holes [at Tarawera, c1882], steam bursting out of bottomless pits, **Maori 'porridge'**, which Sophia [a Maori guide] made us taste off the end of a stick, assuring us we 'could live on it'. We preferred to reserve our appetites for lunch. **1853** in Mackenzie *Overland Auckland to Wellington* (1893) 23 Soon the **Maori pot** was steaming... The Maori pot consists of a hole in the ground etc. **1913** *NZ Observer* 2 Aug. 4 His Worship investigated and came forth with the positive verdict of Haki Haki or **Maori pox**. *Ibid.* 2 Aug. 16 The disease was not chicken pock or small pock or Maori pock—but just plain kapok. **1984** 17 M E109 Pakuranga Coll. 22B **Maori roast**: fish and chips. **1986** *Metro* (Auckland) Aug. 194 This delicacy of the English-speaking world is referred to in other circles as 'shark and taties', 'Maori roast', or 'greasies'. **1988** MCGILL *Dict. Kiwi Slang* 72 *Maori roast* a pie and a jug; offensive. **1989** MCGILL *Dinkum Kiwi Dict.* 66 *Maori roast* fish and chips; possibly offensive. **1964** HINTZ *Trout at Taupo* 220 When winter comes, the '**Maori season**' begins and, the law and the activities of rangers notwithstanding, they [*sc.* Maori poachers] consider themselves entitled to take trout when they want them. **1979** ZAVOS *After the Final Whistle* 193 A '**Maori sidestep**' is [a] term frequently used by rugby men..to describe the tactic of putting the shoulder down and charging through and over an opponent rather than actually side-stepping him. **1984** *Dominion* (Wellington) 21 Aug. 3 The term 'Maori sidestep' was made during the instant re-play of Stone's first-half try, which ended with a powerful, barging dive at the line. Mr Wallace complained that commentator Grant Nisbett described it as 'the famous Maori sidestep'. **1994** *Evening Post* (Wellington) 13 June 4 Maoris do not appear offended, indeed many have mentioned this colloquialism, like 'Maori side-step', is most commonly used by Maoris. **1986** TV1 interview with George Nepia referring to Welsh game of 30 Aug. 1924. I'd have to do a **Maori tackle**—eh— I'd bang on to two or three of them without the ball. **1986** OWEN & PERKINS *Speaking for Ourselves* 109 In those days [c1890s] they had what was known as the '**Maori wedding**', which was not legal to the Pakeha, but was a binding thing among the Maori people themselves. A young couple would decide that they wanted to become man and wife, and they would have to tell their parents they wanted this. Well, at night-time everyone would congregate in the meetinghouse [the matter would be discussed, the boy and girl would be asked whether they wanted to marry, and they would take each other in front of all their people]. **1904** *NZ Observer* 6 Feb. 7 They say... That a lot of '**Maori weeds**' and other horseflesh are wide-eyed with surprise at the extra feeds they are getting. Japan wants re-mounts. **1918** *Chron. NZEF* 5 July 251 It takes Bill and I two hours to catch that old roany Maori weed we used for packing tucker. **1920** *Kai Tiaki* XIII. 176 The horse looked very sad, and I had my doubts about it reaching the settlement, but one can never tell what these Maori 'weeds' are capable of. **1960** SCRYMGEOUR *Memories of Maoriland* 165 Once at a horse sale at Palmerston North, Mr. Bob Waller was selling a draft of what might be termed 'Maori Weeds', or rather stunted, but nice condition nags, from the Sandy Country towards Foxton. **1963** *Dominion* (Wellington) 31 Aug. 7 Undoubtedly there was good blood among these horses [on Kaingaroa Plain, c1910], though the great majority would come into the somewhat elastic classification of 'Maori weed.' In actual fact, there was no reproach in the term. Born and reared on the inhospitable plains, a horse developed a stamina that no finely-bred animal possessed. **1847** CHAPMAN *Let. to His Father* 24 Nov. in Miller *Early Victorian NZ* (1958) 24 Unable to bear the solitary life, not a few acquired '**Maori wives**', which was 'the conventional name for a Maori mistress'. **1849** in *Lett. from Otago* (1978) 14 Apr. 27 Eight white men are living among the natives, and have married Maori wives.

6. Forming adjectival collocations. **a.** With a suffixed element, usu. a participle: (a) esp. **Maori-bred**, **Maori-owned**.

1854 MALONE *Three Yrs. Cruise* 118 An impromptu race of **Maori-bred** horses, ridden by Maories, added much to the amusement of the day. **1916** COWAN *Bush Explorers* (VUWTS) 2 Each..picked out a horse from the little mob of Maori-bred animals that the packer brought along. **1963** *NZ Geog* Apr. 58 No doubt much of the pork exported [from Taranaki c1850] had been derived from Maori-bred pigs, and it was possible that some of the flour was from..Maori-owned flour mills. **1936** *Agricultural Organization in NZ* 575 Sales of timber from **Maori-owned** forests are not subject to any operational restrictions beyond regular felling and prevention of fire. **1963** *NZ Geog* Apr. 56 What was a growing evil common to sheep owners throughout the North Island at this time [c1850], namely the frequent killings (especially of lambs) by half-wild Maori-owned dogs. **1987** *National Business Review* 30 Jan. 1 And the government's stance..is understood to have nudged others into..reviewing forest service leases of Maori-owned land.

(b) With various other suffixes.

1843 *Letters from Settlers* 6 *Mauri* grown potatoes Ibid. 54 Six maori built houses. **1851** *Richmond-Atkinson Papers* (1960) I. 103 This fear of spoiling their 'happy valleys' has been epidemic on the ministry here, and has made the missionaries oppose colonization and led them to vamp up all the nauseous maudlin maori fancying stuff that has caused disaster..here. **1879** GUDGEON *Reminisc. War in NZ* 42 Maori-like, ever suspicious, they expressed a belief that his house had been built opposite the mouth of the river..to guide man-o-war boats to surprise them at night. **1879** SIMMONS *Old England & NZ* 21 If you can muster up sufficient courage, fondle in your arms a dirty little black cherub and kiss it Maori-wise. **1881** CAMPBELL *Poenamo* 152 For the pork of those days was not as these days, for it was Maori-fed—in other words, the pigs were free to roam and get fat how and where they could, or remain lean. **1986** *Dominion* (Wellington) 29 Sept. 12 Congratulations to Mr Norman Jones, MP..on his open protests against Maori-led racism in this country. **1989** *Evening Post* (Wellington) 19 Jan. 2 Secondly, the commission sought a Maori-speaking secretary... Maori-only advertisements did not preclude non-Maori from applying for the job. **1990** *Dominion* (Wellington) 18 July 12 The National Museum is aiming to become 'Maori-centric' instead of Eurocentric.

b. With various prefixes forming adjectives and nouns: **anti-Maori**, **half-Maori**, **non-Maori**, **pan-Maori**; **philo-Maori** *a*. and *n*., showing (or one who shows) sympathy with Maori causes, esp. during the New Zealand Wars; **pre-Maori**, with reference to a supposed *tangata whenua* pre-dating the Maori, a theory now discredited (see quot., see also MORIORI 3); **pro-Maori**, **un-Maori**.

1946 BEAGLEHOLE *Some Modern Maoris* 30 The pakehas in the district are definitely **anti-Maori**. **1991** *Evening Post* (Wellington) 28 Nov. 5 Alan Duff's article..is so..anti-Maori and downright derogatory that I have trouble..what I should comment on first. **1881** CAMPBELL *Poenamo* 68 This was my first experience of a native crew and of their songs, but many were the songs I had heard both in boat and in canoe ere the **half-Maori**, half-Pakeha settling of the 'early days' had passed away, and became exchanged for purely Saxon manners and customs. **1953** DUFF *Shepherd's Calendar* 5 Nov. (1961) 150 I heard the other day that my half-Maori grandchildren, aged six, four, and three stand up solemnly and salute the radio set when they hear 'God Save the Queen'. **1989** *Evening Post* (Wellington) 19 Jan. 2 There were many **non-Maori** people who did have adequate Maori language skills. **1990** *Listener* 9 July 100 There, **pan-Maori** organisations such as the Maori Women's Welfare League, Maori Council,.. emerged to promote self-determination. **1995** *Dominion* (Wellington) 24 Apr. 8 Jim Bolger has stated that he is receptive to the idea of a pan–Maori spokesperson. **1864?** VON TEMPSKY *Memoranda* (ATLTS) 77 I have elicited a correct view of an action on which many aspersions have been cast in this country, by the **Philo-Maori** party. **1865** *Punch in Canterbury* 5 Aug. 82 Exclaimed the philo-Maori chaps with admiration, then, of the noble Maori savage. **1878** BULLER *Forty Yrs. NZ* 416 Those who knew the natives could say that war and ruin were convertible terms; but they were denounced as 'philo-Maories'. **1887** *Auckland Weekly News* 8 Oct. 7 Bishop Hadfield was absent from Wellington..the mere mention of whose name, and commendation of whose Philo-Maori sentiments..was quite sufficient to make the 'vigorous prosecution of the war' men clear out of the sanctuary. **1948** HENDERSON *Taina* ix Often the facts and events it records are brutal, and there is nothing philo-Maori about the book. **1984** BOYD *City of the Plains* 10 A genuine philo-Maori, who objected to settler arrogance and injustice, he was nevertheless interested in the Heretaunga himself. **1986** BELICH *NZ Wars* 79 But 'philo-Maori' writers such as Octavius Hadfield and William Martin expended a great deal of ingenuity in doing just that. **1984** *Te Maori* 61 Outside this sequential linkage of ancestor to successive descendant cultures, there is no evidence for any pre-Maori element in New Zealand. The supposed **pre-Maori** and non-Maori Moriori of mainland New Zealand as depicted by earlier writers are simply the early Maori. **1989** ANDERSON *Prodigious Birds* 100 Colenso..in 1864, had already argued that other traditional and mythological evidence spoke of a pre-Maori colonisation. **1948** LIPSON *Politics of equality* 107 Honest, direct, and trusting in character, of democratic sympathies..**pro-Maori** in policy, Fox entered a coalition in which Whitaker secured most of the advantages. **1983** KING *Whina* 128 As a judge [F.O.V. Acheson] was decidedly pro-Maori..which resulted eventually in his being relieved of his judicial appointment. **1946** BEAGLEHOLE *Some Modern Maoris* 123 He is, of course, **un-Maori** in this respect. **1951** KOHERE *Autobiography of a Maori* 107 It was so un-Maori to urge a visitor to pass on instead of inviting him inside.

7. In composition: **Maoria** *obs*., things Maori collectively; **Maoriana**, materials relevant to Maori culture, history, society, etc.; **Maorihood**, the state of being Maori; **Maori-ish**, *a*., tending towards Maori attitudes, outlook, vision, etc.; **Maori-ism**, anything characteristic of or peculiar to Maoridom.

1874 JOHNSTONE *Maoria. A sketch of the manners and customs of the aboriginal inhabitants of New Zealand*. [Title] (Preface) Perhaps the principal reason which has 'tapued' **Maoria** to the writer of fiction is the difficulty of depicting a Maori heroine. **1918** *Feilding Star* 1 Aug. 2 A welcome addition to this desired collection [of books using Maori material] is '**Maoriana**', by Elan Westerwood..a well sustained poetic romance. **1946** SOLJAK *NZ* 44 [Sir James Carroll's] watchword, 'Hold fast to your **Maorihood**', inspired one of the most remarkable racial revivals in history. **1986** *Metro* (Auckland) Sept. 35 The sort of **Maori-ish** character I do works because they can identify it. **1881** CAMPBELL *Poenamo* 119 Was our day to have been spent in vain? Saints of **Maori-ism** forbid! **1995** *Dominion* (Wellington) 26 June 8 In his appraisal of..*The Travesty of Waitangi*, Professor Bill Oliver uses the old trick of associating dissent (in this case against Maorism) with unbalanced minds.

Maori, *adv*. In English use as an occas. quasi-adverb in 'in Maori fashion', implying something less than Pakeha standards, or 'into Maori ancestry', as in the phr. **to marry Maori**.

1974 MASON *Hand on Rail* (1981 TS) 18 Hingawaru: Wish she'd have married Maori, though.

Maori Battalion.

1. *WW1*. The Maori Pioneer Battalion of the New Zealand Expeditionary Force.

1921 *Quick March* 10 Sept. 23 [Title] *The August of 1915. A Story of the Maori Battalion* By Major F. Waite, D.S.O., N.Z.E. **1986** SORRENSON in *Na To Hoa Aroha* I. 29 When the Maori Battalion was sent to the Western Front in 1916 Buck was granted his request to transfer to combat duty; he was promoted to second-in-command of the Battalion with the rank of major.

2. *WW2*. The 28th (Maori) Battalion, the Maori unit of the Second New Zealand Expeditionary Force.

1943 JACKSON *Passage to Tobruk* 54 The Maori Battalion staged their never-to-be-forgotten raid on the enemy. **1952** FINLAYSON in *Brown Man's Burden* (1973) 112 'The big land scheme for the Maori Battalion men,' a friendly chap told Harry. **1960** HILLIARD *Maori Girl* 44 War was declared. Several Matiti men volunteered for service with the Maori Battalion. **1973** PEARSON in Finlayson *Brown Man's Burden* (1973) 138 In the second world war Maoris served willingly, without the distrust that marked their attitude to fighting for the pakeha in the first world war. Maori soldiers served in the 28th Battalion ('the Maori Battalion') in North Africa, Crete, and Italy. **1990** *Listener* 4 June 50 Second, it is mischievous to suggest that the Government insisted on the Maori Battalion being initially led by Pakeha.

Maori-bug.

a. *black beetle* (BEETLE 1).

1873 TINNE *Wonderland of the Antipodes* 52 Fleas, Maori bugs, sand-flies and mosquitoes were bad enough. **1885** *AJHR* H-26 9 In the North it [*sc*. kauri bug] was spoken of as the 'Maori bug', but this name is misleading, being commonly applied to the *karamu* [*sic* ?=kekerengu], so well known on account of the unpleasant odour which it emits when touched. **1907** HULL *College Songs* 46 Generally speaking, a township [in North Auckland] consists of a 'pub', a store, half-a-dozen scattered homesteads, and about thirty-nine million Maori bugs. The Maori bug is about half an inch by an inch, but his influence extends over about half an acre. **1917** WILLIAMS *Dict. Maori Lang.* 133 *Kekerengu*, = kekereru, n. *Periplaneta fortipes*, black wood-bug, Maori bug. **1928** *NZ Free Lance* (Wellington) 22 Feb. 37 [Caption] A memorial is to be erected to the brave scientist who lost his life in an endeavour to discover something able to overpower the notorious Maori bug. **1938** HYDE *Nor the Years Condemn* 156 The unlined walls of his shack..let out neat dark-brown streams of Maori bugs. **1951** PARK

Witch's Thorn 43 The white larrikins jammed on their flat hats and scurried out of there like Maori-bugs. **1966** *Encycl. NZ* I. 269 *Bug, Maori (Platyzosteria novaezelandiae)*. Maori bug is the commonly accepted name for the largest endemic cockroach of New Zealand... All stages of the Maori bug are shining black. **1972** *Evening Post* (Wellington) 31 Oct. 33 Platyzosteria soror looks rather like the native black cockroach, Platyzosteria novaeseelandiae, formerly known as the 'Maori bug.' **1989** McGill *Baby Boomers* 56 We used squashed Maori bugs as poison tips on arrows. **1993** Sinclair *Halfway Round the Harbour* 68 I used to lie on my bunk watching hundreds of black beetles—'maori bugs'—crawling above my head.

b. *fig.* An offensive name for a Maori.

1992 *Evening Post* (Wellington) 7 Mar. 6 I am a New Zealander, Maori and female, and I object to being called a 'Maori bug, tarpot, nigger, and black bastard'.

Maori bunk. *Tramping.* [Alluding to the Maori custom of sleeping communally on the floor of a wharepuni.] A communal sleeping place in a tramping hut, or tent; a large bunk sleeping several people at once. See also *Maori bed* (Maori B 5 b).

1938 *Tararua Tramper* May 4 Home is where the body is, and the Maori bunk is comfortable. **1945** *Tararua Tramper* June 6 One main room about 16ft x 16ft, space for 16 people, entrance through small porch, Maori bunk 8ft wide full length of hut and if necessary another 8ft x 8ft at one end. **1958** Pascoe *Great Days in NZ Mountaineering* 156 They dug out a platform for the tent, lined the floor with rocks as a sleeping-bench or Maori bunk, and got stuck into another kea stew. **1978** *Manawatu Tramping Club Jubilee* 17 Design for a hut [c1932]..to have a large open fire place and a bench type bunk (known in tramping circles as a Maori bunk), was approved. [**1978** Note on *bunk*] A large mattress or bunk base on which many people could sleep. **1988** McGill *Dict. Kiwi Slang* 72 *Maori bunk* common bed for several people, usually trampers; not intended to be insulting.

Maori chief.[1] [Spec. use of *chief* a tribal leader.]
1. Often init. cap. An early name for a Maori tribal leader. See also chief, chieftain. Cf. ariki, rangatira.

1858 Grace *Letter* 24 Mar. in *Pioneer Missionary* (1928) 77 There is little doubt but that, with a few official leaders appointed direct from Home as protectors, the Maori Chiefs would be found quite able to take their full share in the representation. **1884** Martin *Our Maoris* iii Great interest was excited in England in many quarters by the arrival..of three Maori Chiefs from New Zealand. **1958** Miller *Early Victorian NZ* 9 The English settlers were to receive the bulk of the land; the Maori Chiefs were to receive private properties..and the 'inferior' natives were to become a landless proletariat.

2. *Obs.* Transferred (prob. after the commercial name *Arran chief*) as the name of a former variety of table potato.

1916 *Wairarapa Daily Times* 6 Sept. 1 [Advt] Seed Potatoes... Maori Chief (a great blight resister and a heavy cropper).

Maori chief.[2] [From an external colour pattern suggesting a Maori chief's moko.]

1. Any of several species of the family Nototheniidae (ice-cods) esp. *Paranotothenia* (formerly *Notothenia*) *angustata*; *black cod* (cod 2 (2)). See also flathead 1.

1878 *TrNZI* X. 330 Some odd fishes now and then turn up in the market, such as the Maori-chief, cat-fish etc. **1879** *TrNZI* XI. 381 That very dark-skinned fish, the Maori-chief, *Notothenia maoriensis* of Dr. Haast, is not uncommon but is rarely seen more than one at a time. **1886** [see flathead 1]. **1896** *The Australasian* 28 Aug. 407 At first it would seem improbable that a fish could be like a man, but in Dunedin a fish was shown to me called Maori Chief, and with the exercise of a little imagination it was not difficult to perceive the likeness. **1906** *TrNZI* XXXVIII. 550 *Notothenia maoriensis*... Commonly known as 'Maori Chief'. **1921** Thomson & Anderton *Hist. Portobello* 94 The Maori-Chief is not a pretty fish, but it is very good for the table. **1938** *TrRSNZ* LXVIII. 414 *Notothenia macrocephala*... Maori chief. **1956** Graham *Treasury NZ Fishes* 294 Some have said that the Maori Chief is not a pretty fish but those who have studied art agree with me that despite its dark colourings and tattooed-like head, there is a beauty in this fish which fascinates the lover of colour blendings. **1967** Natusch *Animals NZ* 224 *N[otothenia] macrocephala*, sometimes called Maori chief..is handsomely 'tattooed' in black and olive. **1982** Ayling *Collins Guide* (1984) 275 The maori chief, often named the black cod, is a large bottom-living fish similar in shape to the blue cod. **1986** Paul *NZ Fishes* 117 *Maori chief Paranotothenia angustata* Family Notothenidae (southern cods, ice cods). Sometimes called black cod.

2. marblefish (*Aplodactylus arctidens*).

1922 *NZJST* V. 92 *Aplodactylus meandratus. Marble-fish.* Generally known as 'Maori chief' in Auckland... During the winter of 1921 June specimens were received in Wellington from the Marlborough Sounds and sold as 'Maori chief'. **1956** Graham *Treasury NZ Fishes* 248 At one time this fish was sold in Auckland and Wellington as Maori Chief but I do not know why this should be, as the true Maori Chief is quite different and not at all like the Granite Trout. **1986** Paul *NZ Fishes* 111 *Marblefish Aplodactylus arctidens*. Also called..Maori chief.

3. *sea-perch* (perch *n.* 2 (4) *Helicolenus* spp.).

1966 Doogue & Moreland *Sea Anglers' Guide* 287 Sea Perch... Reddish brown with blotches and spots on most of body and fins. *Other names: Helicolenus papillosus;* Jock Stewart, scarpee..Maori chief. **1967** Moreland *Marine Fishes* 26 Sea Perch [*Helicolenus percoides*]... Scarpie, Maori Chief, fivefinger, and scrodie, are some of the many names in use.

Maoricize, *v.* Also **Maori-ize, Maorize.** *trans.* Usu. as a *past ppl. a.*, esp. of a word, given a Maori form or character. Cf. maorify *v.*

1859 Thomson *Story NZ* I. 199 All the English week-days have been Maorised except Sunday, which is known as the Ratapu, or sacred day. **1893** *TrNZI* XXV. 410 In writing a Maori-ised English word there is no attempt to spell it English fashion. **1913** Roberts *Place Names* 5 It is only the English word Maoricised. **1945** Beattie *Maori Place-names Canterbury* 66 A European told me this last word ['paaka' for a division of land] was the word 'block' Maoricised, but an ancient meaning of paka was a fence or enclosure.

Hence **Maori-ization, Maorization** *n.*, the process or result of making (a word) Maori in form or character.

1928 Andersen in McCrae *Journal* (1820) 29 But *b* finds no place in the vocabulary, and *būka būka* was evidently regarded as a Maorization of the word 'book' though *pukapuka* is genuine Maori. **1935** Odell *Handbook Arthur Pass National Park* 67 On one map it appears as Koeti Stream which looks like a Maori-ization of 'Goat.'

Maori dictionary. *Hist.* [Prob. a variant of *sleeping dictionary* a woman from whom a man learns a foreign language during a sexual relationship, recorded earliest in NZ (quot. 1881 below): see OED *sleeping vbl. n.* 2 b, 1928.] A Maori concubine from whom an English speaker learns Maori.

[**1881** Campbell *Poenamo* 129 He did not now require a sleeping dictionary to learn Maori from.] **1972** MacIntosh *Hist. of Fortrose* 16 Most of these 'retired whalers' had Maori wives and families. The old saying for this union was, 'I've bought a Maori dictionary'.

Maoridom. The Maori people collectively; occas., their cultural and spiritual heritage (see quot. 1958). Occas. *attrib.*

1860 *Richmond-Atkinson Papers* (1960) 12 May I. 580 I am afraid it is not possible to believe that anything but a sharp physical lesson will go home to young Maoridom. **1874** Baines *Edward Crewe* 87 It is the great unwritten creed in all 'Maoridom' that nothing is wrong unless found out. **1883** *Canterbury Rhymes* 116 Gleamed all their muskets bare, Frightening the children there, Heroes to do and dare, Charging a village [*sc.* Parihaka], while Maoridom wondered. **1893** *TrNZI* XXV. 411 The word 'Devil,' *Rewera*, and the name 'Satan'..have been naturalised in Maoridom. **1901** *NZ Illustrated Magazine* IV. 785 [Heading] Some Aspects of Maoridom **1922** Cowan *NZ Wars* (1955) II. 37 It was a kind of advanced frontier post, beyond which the chiefs of old Maoridom held undisputed rule. **1930** *Na To Hoa Aroha* (1987) II. 51 A gathering representative of the Crown, Parliament..the Press and Pakeha public and all sections of Maoridom, gathered together all the elements that constitute the New Zealand community of to-day. **1948** Bagnall & Petersen *Colenso* 51 The native teacher..became a power in Maoridom. **1958** *Press* (Christchurch) 29 Mar. 8 They are a new breed, leaving their Maoridom behind them. **1979** Taylor *Eyes of Ruru* 13 I am the taiaha left among people who dance and twirl poi in gaudy halls of plastic Maoridom. **1988** *Sunday Star* (Auckland) 23 Oct. A12 Pakehadom, as controllers of media, choose and create the so-called spokespersons for Maoridom. **1994** *Dominion* (Wellington) 5 Oct. 11 The Maoridom use of restorative justice is a possible option [for dealing with domestic violence].

Maori fashion. In the phr. **in Maori fashion,** in the manner of Maori practice or tradition; from or belonging to Maori society, culture, and tradition.

1851 Grace *Journal* Mar. in *Pioneer Missionary* (1928) 10 We had not been long here before my boys had dressed the pig in the Maori fashion. **c1867** Maunsell in Wily & Maunsell *Robert Maunsell* (1938) 188 A very large party of the tribe were assembled on the lawn..who, as the coffin approached, commenced firing off their guns and yelling and shouting in true Maori fashion. **1881** Campbell *Poenamo* 172 He well knew the martyrdom he had to go through whilst others only wept—Maori fashion—and feasted. **1920** *Quick March* 10 Apr. 13 A bushmanlike figure was the Boss, for he cannily packed his trousers in his swag and travelled bare-legged, Maori fashion. **1939** Beattie *First White Boy Born Otago* 15 I have also seen a burial carried out in Maori style... I have caught wekas in the Maori fashion. **1945** *JPS* LIV. 112 Piri was only adopted in the Maori fashion—raised by Rata and never legally 'adopted'. **1963** Campbell *Golden North* 33 Huge meals of pigs, kumaras, potatoes and eels were cooked Maori fashion.

maorify, *v.* Also with init. cap. *trans.* To make (words, ideas, customs, etc.) Maori in form or character. Cf. maoricize *v.*

1868 Taylor *Past & Present NZ* 134 *Rauna katoa* is a half-caste word, the English word round being here Maorified. **1878** Buller *Forty Yrs. NZ* 295 They took the name of Pikopo. This no doubt was maorified from the Latin word *episcopos*. **1889** *TrNZI* XXI. 205 These words are ludicrously Maorified from the owls' common note of *kōu, kōu!*..by a kind of onomatopeia. **1922** Cowan *NZ Wars* (1955) II. 4 He had taken a Scriptural name, Zerubbabel (maorified into Horopapera). **1945** *JPS* LIV. 231 (S.J. Baker) *To Maorify*, to infuse with or influence by Maori elements. **1988** *Dominion* (Wellington) 24 Dec. 8 I am a white New Zealander, not a Pakeha..and I am bewildered and angered by incessant demands and efforts to Maorify everything.

Hence **maorified** *ppl. a.*, made Maori in form or character; **maorification**, a familiarization in or adoption of Maori attitudes.

1840–41 *Ironside's Journal* in MacDonald *Pages from Past* (1933) 130 In conversing with [Maoris] I was often puzzled with these **Maorified**-English expressions that fell so glibly from their lips. **1863** Maning *Old NZ* iii 52 At last the war-dance ended; and then my tribe (I find I am already beginning to get Maorified)..endeavoured to out-do even their amiable friends' exhibition. **1910** *NZ Free Lance* (Wellington) 3 Sept. 4 The other Morioris and the Maorified Maoris are early expecting a shoal of blackfish on the beach. **1922** Cowan *NZ Wars* (1955) II. 12 A maorified version of the Benediction was chanted with one voice. **1940** Cowan *Sir Donald Maclean* 85 Round them [*sc.* niu poles] marched the half-crazed people..chanting..the prayers of the '*Kororia*', Maorified English phrases and scraps of English and Roman Catholic church services. **1948** Henderson *Taina* 24 Another reason was that he was a 'Maorified' *pakeha*, and therefore one on whom you could play a joke without offence. **1990** *Contact* (Wellington) 24 Aug. 2 When the Electricorp bosses checked into Huka lodge for their **Maorification** course, it reminded me of a group of foreigners trying to find out how everyday Kiwis live.

maorihead. [Prob. a local transformation of *niggerhead* a tall swampgrass: but cf. *toetoe-upoko-tangata* 'toetoe-head-human' =?'Maori–head' toetoe.] Often with init. cap. niggerhead *n.*[2]

[**1906** Cheeseman *Manual NZ Flora* 767 *M[ariscus] ustulatus*... Abundant in lowland districts throughout... *Toetoe-upoko-tangata*, *Toetoe-whatu-manu*.] **1856** Roberts *Diary* in Beattie *Early Runholding* (1947) 18 Maori-heads, a kind of grass tree about three feet high, abounded in the swamps [of the Waimea Plain c1856]. **1861** *NZ Goldfields 1861* (1976) 24 To the village succeeded a swamp full of 'Maori heads', which plant I can only liken to our own Victorian grass tree, except that it is a greener and thicker tuft. **1878** Elwell *Boy Colonists* 67 'Niggerheads', you know, are what you in New Zealand call 'Maori-heads'. **1889** Paulin *Wild West Coast* 31 Maori-head is the name given to a kind of grass which grows in tufts..often several feet long. It is always found on swampy ground. When the swamp is drained the Maoriheads disappear. **1891** Douglas *Report to G.J. Roberts* in *Mr Explorer Douglas* (1957) 148 Down where the drunken Woman's Creek Flows past the Cranky Man There sitting on a Moarie [*sic*] head I first espied my Nan. **1920** *TrNZI* LII. 72 *Haumata* [a snow grass tussock] was the name of what are now called Maori-heads. **1956** Beattie *Pioneer Recolls.* 44 She rapidly crossed by jumping from one Maorihead to another and being complimented on her agility and skill, laughingly exclaimed, 'A rush bush never deceived an Irishman.'

Maori hen. *Obs.* Mainly *SI.* [*Maori* = 'native', 'New Zealand'.] weka 1. Cf. *Maori chicken* (Maori B 4 b).

1863 Barrington *Diary* 25 Dec. in Taylor *Early Travellers* (1959) 393 We had a plum duff boiling..cooked four Maori hens, and had a jolly afternoon. **1870** Whitworth *Martin's Bay Settlement* 49 I roasted a Maori hen which Don had captured for his supper. **1889** Williams *Colonial Couplets* 26 Come to me when evening falls, And the oily weka calls... [**1889** *Note*] Called 'maori hens' by the early settlers, probably because all were of the *weka* sex. **1890** *Otago Witness* (Dunedin) 16 Oct. 30 And this, too, to colonials who had known most of them what it was..to long vehemently for Maori hen only three removes from a watertight boot soaked in hair oil! **1904** Hutton & Drummond *Animals NZ* 178 Unfortunately, the Wekas, the Wood Hens, or Maori Hens, as they are sometimes called, are becoming rare. **1914** in *Hist. N. Otago from 1853* (1978) 88 Maoris used the [Oamaru] site as a camp, and..kept up a big fire for cooking eels and Maori hens. **1926** Cowan *Travel in NZ* II. 63 The *weka*..is often called the wood-hen, or 'Maori-hen'. **1933** *Press* (Christchurch) (Acland Gloss.) 4 Nov. 15 *Maori*... We admire native bush, pasture, or game; but *M[aori]* hens (woodhens)..are caricatures of their English namesakes. **1946** [see weka 1]. **1952** *Landfall* 24 304 The harsh cry of a Maori-hen rose..and ebbed into silence again. **1963** Campbell *Golden North* 43 They claimed the right to the birds..weka and Maori hen that teemed in their thousands in the swamp land. **1991** O'Regan *Aunts and Windmills* 65 [West Coast drovers in the 1920s] would recount where they heard the tui..and spotted a Maori hen (they still used the colonial term for a weka) scuttling across the road.

Maori-ize: see Maoricize.

Maori King.

1. Usu. with init. caps. The acknowledged leader of an orig. 19th century Maori independence ('king') movement, a confederation of several NI tribal groups. See also King *n.*[1], Maori Queen. Cf. King Country.

1858 Grace *Letter* 24 Mar. in *Pioneer Missionary* (1928) 75 The moment I heard that it was intended to discuss the propriety of making a Maori King, I refused to be present. **1859** *Richmond-Atkinson Papers* 10 May (1960) I. 456 There is probably not a single village of any size in which all belong to the king's party and hence I think that the Government..might override the law-giving party of the maori king. **1878** Buller *Forty Yrs. NZ* 412 The 'Maori King' had now become a fact. **1922** Cowan *NZ Wars* (1955) I. 148 At this meeting [in 1854], too, the idea of a Maori king for the Maori people was discussed and fervently approved. **1938** Wily & Maunsell *Robert Maunsell* 69 Of the two non-signing chiefs referred to in Maunsell's report, one was the great Potatau Te Whero-whero, the first Maori King. **1959** Sinclair *History NZ* 110 it was the first of a series of great inter-tribal meetings which marked the rise of a Maori national movement and led, in 1858, to the election of a Maori king. **1960** Masters *Back-Country Tales* 199 A fitting close it seemed to a grand day's sport with grand companions, in an untamed and beautiful corner of the land of the Maori King.

Hence **Maori kingship**.

1933 in *Na To Hoa Aroha* (1988) III. 111 It is too early to say what course the Maori 'kingship' will now take.

2. Comb. Maori-King flag, movement, party.

1860 Marjouram *Diary* 15 May in *Sergeant, Sinner* (1990) 50 Telegraphic news from Bell Block that the natives are displaying the **Maori-king flag**. **1857** *Richmond-Atkinson Papers* 9 Dec. (1960) I. 328 The natives..interested in the **Maori King movement** [are] generally speaking opposed to the opening of the road until the Maori King has given his consent. **c1910** Macdonald *Reminiscences* (VUWTS) 65 The 'Maori Land League' and the 'Maori King Movement' were growing into consistency and power. **1983** Lambert *Illustr. Hist. of Taranaki* 34 The idea of the Maori King Movement was mooted. **1859** *Richmond-Atkinson Papers* 23 May (1960) I. 460 If..the **maori king party** as a rule should continue to demand payment from the carrier as a maori, it must be taken up. **1860** Buddle *Maori King Movement* 18 The disputed land at Waitara is claimed by the Maori King party because the King's mana has reached it.

Maoriland. Also **Maori land**. [Orig. Maori *a.* with *land n.*, thence to a combined form *Maoriland*, in *transf.* use.]

1. Usu. as two words, applied concretely to land for which Maori customary or legal title is recognized as valid; land in Maori ownership and control.

1857 *Richmond-Atkinson Papers* 17 June (1960) I. 278 A European squats down on Maori land and the Government grant[s] him a license [*sic*]. The natives object to it and protest against it but in vain. **1863** Carberry *Journal* 18 Nov. (ATLTS) At Taranaki also Maori Land will be confiscated and military settlements formed. **1886** Cheeseman *A Rolling Stone* I. 7 A wealthy man had bought the Maori-land. **1887** *Auckland Weekly News* 21 May 28 All four classes dealt with Maori lands in much the same manner—paying for large areas with goods and articles of small value. **1900** Scott *Colonial Turf* 113 I've lost the rent money for the Maori land my father has leased. **1912** Chudleigh *Diary* 10 Oct. (1950) 461 Tripp held that I could not buy or lease any more Maori land but I could let my stock on it and pay Inia when he asked for it. **1949** Sargeson *I Saw in My Dream* (1974) 117 He's part maori for sure though, because once he got me to witness a paper and it was about maori land. **1950** *Noxious Weeds Act* (preamble) 'Maori Land' means Maori land within the meaning of the Maori Land Act, 1931. **1960** Hilliard *Maori Girl* 9 The best of the cow-country is owned by the *pakehas* and every inch of the occupied Maoriland is mortgaged to them. **1984** Marshall *Day Hemingway Died* 21 There was bush on the Maori land beyond the estuary, but most of the hills were brown in the summer. **1991** *Dominion* (Wellington) 6 Sept. 2 Maori Affairs Minister Winston Peters has appointed a three-person review team to look at low rentals on Maori land.

2. a. In early use occas. as two words, New Zealand as the land of the Maori; pre-Pakeha New Zealand. Cf. Tuhoeland.

1863 Maning *Old NZ* i 3 It was..from the deck of a small trading schooner..that I first cast eyes on Maori land. It *was* Maori land then; but, alas! what is it now? *Ibid.* vii 105 There were in the old times two great institutions, which reigned with iron rod in Maori land—the *Tapu* and the *Muru*. **1881** Nesfield *Chequered Career* 45 Spiritism is a very old institution in Maori-land, and conversations with departed spirits, through the medium of the 'tohunga', were held..prior to the arrival of the Pakeha. **1903** *TrNZI* XXXV. 46 In Maoriland seeds were planted at the full of the moon. **1920** *TrNZI* LII. 48 Kai-Tahu, who belonged to the conquering strain, whose achievements in Maoriland were analogous to the Norman Conquest. **1936** Lambert *Pioneering Reminisc. Old Wairoa* 58 But while it may not be possible to claim for Tuhoeland a monopoly of fairy-folk, it is true that nowhere in Maoriland are there such varieties of legends. **1958** *Better Business* XXI. No.219 75 Moa bones found in a cave while excavating for the foundations of a new Auckland hospital have been identified as the remains of the ancient birds of Maoriland.

b. *Hist.* In the phr. **the heart of Maoriland**, the King Country.

1888 RINGLAND *In Southern Seas* 96 You are away from the beaten track of travel, and far into the heart of Maoriland [*sc.* the King Country]. **1930** REISCHEK *Yesterdays in Maoriland* (1933) 113 A fortunate accident made it possible for me to enter the King Country, the heart of Maoriland.

3. [AND 1859.] **a.** Orig. or mainly a journalistic name for New Zealand as a whole (esp. freq. after the adoption of the term by the Sydney *Bulletin* in the 1880s), now infrequently used.

1865 CARTER *Life in NZ* 428 In the first expedition I ever undertook in Maori-land I was accompanied by two gentlemen. **1874** BAINES *Edward Crewe* 286 [I] would like again, if ever I got back to Maoriland, to have another turn in my old boat. **1884** KERRY NICHOLLS *Maoriland: an Illustrated Handbook to New Zealand* [Title] **1890** BRACKEN *Musings in Maoriland* [Title] **1894** *Argus and Newtown Chronicle* 10 Aug. 3 The Sydney Bulletin in writing of New Zealand, styles it Maoriland; Queensland, though, it dubs Bananaland. **1907** *Red Funnel* IV. 33 Have we not drawn our sins of advertisement to a head by tamely adopting the foreign [*sc.* Australian] label of 'Maoriland' for our country? As a foreign label it is melodious and inoffensive... As adopted and ratified by ourselves, it is as appropos and dignified as a sale-board at the front gate. **1919** WAITE *New Zealanders at Gallipoli* 184 Smoking the ration cigarette after tea, the New Zealander..would see the sheep..cropping the sweet green grass of Maoriland. **1922** *Quick March* 10 June 7 As New Zealand the world knows us, for better or for worse, and the title will stick... As for Zealandia, Maoriland, and the like, we may safely leave them to the poets. **1938** *Labour pamphlet for Northern Maori* in Gustafson *Cradle to Grave* (1986) [facing 232] Maui our Ancestor fished up this Aotearoa of ours from the dark waters of Kiwa. Today it is our Rangatira Savage who is fishing up this Maoriland of ours from the gloom and slime of depression. **1947** STEVENSON *Maori & Pakeha* 156 Apparently some time during the early part of the 19th century, the continuity of this ancient form of life was finally broken and Moaland became Maoriland. **1976** WILSON *Pacific Star* 129 When we flew home we sang songs... Our green and brown Maoriland below looked wonderfully bright, as we came in over the coast.

b. *attrib*. NEW ZEALAND B 2.

1905 *Truth* 12 Aug. 7 Casualness is asserted to be a Maoriland characteristic. **1916** *Chron. NZEF* 30 Aug. 1 The four Maoriland Parliamentarians have had a good time..and have greatly enjoyed their stay in the old Dart. **1930** JEWELL in *NZ Short Stories* 145 [Piet] dived into his sack and produced a bottle of 'dop'. 'What is it you say when you drink in your country?' 'Kia Ora!' explained a Maoriland trooper. **1955** CAMPBELL *By Reef & Range* 22 Joints of cold roast hogget mutton and a bottle..of..apple cider. It was a Maoriland man's picnic. **a1967** *Where There's an Egg in the House* 23 Maoriland Croquettes 1 cup chopped cooked Fowl.. chopped Celery..1 pint Oysters..thick white Sauce... Breadcrumbs 1 Egg... Fry until golden brown. Serve with brown bread and butter.

Hence **Maorilander** *obs.* [AND 1892: prob. orig. Australian], a New Zealand-born white; a New Zealander; also in *pl.* usu. as **the Maorilanders**, a name for early New Zealand representative rugby union teams.

1893 BRACKEN *Lays & Lyrics* 5 A recent arrival from New Zealand walking along Collins St, Melbourne, a short time since encountered another Maorilander. **1898** MORRIS *Austral-English* 286 *Maorilander, n.* modern name for a white man born in New Zealand. **1905** *Truth* 24 June 1 At the present gait of going the Maorilander of the future will have an oval-shaped head [like a rugby ball]. **1912** RUTHERFORD *Impressions NZ Pastoralist on Tour* 139 We ate our Christmas dinner in company with a small party of other Maorilanders. **1960** SCRYMGEOUR *Memories of Maoriland* 26 For two years the youthful Maorilanders walked to school and back. **1966** *Encycl. NZ* I. 33 When the 1905 tour of Britain began..the players were referred to as the New Zealand Football Team, or, more simply, the New Zealanders, though occasionally terms such as 'Maorilanders' and 'Colonials' did service. **1992** *Metro* (Auckland) Jan. 79 The 1884 team and other New Zealand teams through to the 1930s were invariably described as 'Maorilanders'.

Maori Land Court. Orig. **Native Land Court**, also *ellipt.* **Land Court.** A judicial authority set up in 1865 to settle legal and customary questions about the title and disposition of Maori-owned land and related matters; an instance of the holding of such a Court. **a.** *Hist.* As **Native Land** (occas. early or informal **Lands**) **Court.**

1865 *Native Rights Act* s5 In any action in which the title to or any interest in any such land is involved the Judge before whom the same shall be tried shall order that any issue or issues in such action in which such title or interest is involved whether they be issues of fact or of Maori Custom or Usage shall be tried in the Native Lands Court. **1868** CHUDLEIGH *Diary* 22 Apr. (1950) 220 Saw Rolleston who is holding a Native Land Court [at Christchurch]. **1876** *TrNZI* VIII. 422 The Native Land Courts, in the eyes of the present generation of colonists, are chiefly interesting as the means of investigating Maori titles to land, and as the agency for peacefully transferring, by consent of the Maori proprietors, these lands to European owners. **1886** *The Native Land Court Act 50 Vict.* s5 There shall be within the Colony of New Zealand a Court of Record, to be called 'The Native Land Court', for the investigation and determination of titles to Native land and for several other purposes hereinafter set forth. **1892** *NZ Official Handbook* 274 The institution, above all others, in which the Natives take a lively interest is the Native land court. **1904** *NZ Observer* 25 June 23 Any European is considered more likely to do justice in the Native Land Court than a native expert, however learned in the lore of his race. **1924** *Otago Daily Times* (Dunedin) 5 Feb. 1 A peculiar position was mentioned at a sitting of the Native Land Court at Greymouth. **1941** SUTHERLAND *Numismatic Hist. NZ* 14 A debt of this nature contracted some twelve generations ago was recently recognized by the Native land court.

b. *Ellipt.* As **Land** (occas. **Lands**) **Court.** [AND 1877.]

1887 *Auckland Weekly News* 26 Feb. 8 It is a little noisy when the Maoris collect here to a Land Court. **1905** *TrNZI* XXXVII. 35 His [*sc.* Riki Tatahunga's] illness was ascribed to witchcraft, brought on because he appeared as advocate against his own tribe in a Land Court case. **1934** MULGAN *Spur of Morning* 44 There were always a few natives about... Some of them were in town on land court business. **1959** SINCLAIR *Hist. NZ* 143 The war having broken the Maoris' will to resist, the Land Courts then quietly separated them from their lands. The function of the courts was to ascertain Maori title and to issue a Crown freehold title to the owners who, now that Crown pre-emption was abolished, were free to sell either to settlers or to the Government. **1960** HILLIARD in *Mate* 5 14 When we get home, you write to the Land Court, find out about that land.

c. As **Maori Land Court.**

1931 *NZ Statutes* No.31 166 [Native Land Act] There shall continue to be a Court of record called as heretofore the Maori Land Court. **1964** *Mozley and Whiteley's Law Dict.* 232 The Maori Land Court is constituted under Part IV of the Maori Affairs Act 1953... The Maori Land Court exercises extensive jurisdiction in relation to Maori land and in relation to the affairs of the Maori people. **1973** WALLACE *Generation Gap* 176 In no time, Bert, and two..partners..found themselves outside the Maori Land Court in Wanganui to attend the auction of a particular block that had taken their fancy. **1988** *Dominion* (Wellington) 29 June 2 The Maori Land Court will then be asked to vest the reservation in a body corporate, which will include representation from the tangata whenua (local people), appointed by the court in trust for the community.

Maori Mission.

1. Any of various organizations established to advance Christian religious, educational or charitable work amongst the Maori. Often *attrib*.

1887 *Auckland Weekly News* 8 Oct. 7 The sermon was of course on [Anglican] Maori Mission work... My attention was attracted by..one of the old mission crosses of the Catholic Maori Mission. **1916** MANSFIELD *Journal* (1954) 115 We are making cheap flannelette chemises for the Maori Mission... Those poor Maoris! they can't all be as fat as these chemises. **1937** *Marist Messenger* Feb. 6 Fit instruments have brought the Maori Mission to the heights. **1946** *Ibid.* May 1 In 1878 the Bishop of Wellington provided for the restoration of the Maori Mission in his diocese by sending to the natives Father Soulas S.M. **1955** *Ibid.* Jan. 25 She was a missionary of many years standing as a member of the Maori Mission League of St. Teresa. **1989** *Aspects of the Apostolates of the Society of Mary in NZ* 99 Some of the Mission Areas changed the name of this Apostolate from 'Maori Mission' to 'Maori Pastoral Area'. **1992** *NZ Tablet* (Dunedin) 13 May 14 The land wars ruined any prospect of a Maori mission.

2. In composition: **Maori missioner**, **Maori missionary**, a clergyman or evangelist who attends to the Christian conversion and spiritual needs of the Maori.

1865 CARBERRY *Journal* (ATBMS) 3 Jan. A messenger in the shape of a **Maori Missioner** came into Raglan in great haste. **1946** *Marist Messenger* Mar. 21 The Maori Missioners would like to record their thanks to all who supplied holy pictures. **1955** *Ibid.* June 15 This trip with a Maori Missioner had been an object lesson. **1989** *Aspects of the Apostolates of the Society of Mary in NZ* 98 This was something of the scene when I joined these Maori Missioners in May 1970. **1990** *NZ Historic Places* June 17 By 1860 the early vernacular churches were falling into decay. With the appointment of Rev. J.W. Stack as Maori Missioner to the people of Canterbury and Otago, the kaiks were encouraged to rebuild their churches in more permanent materials. **1936** *Marist Messenger* Feb. 21 Shortly before the sudden illness which took this great **Maori Missionary** from earth we met a young man from Hamilton.

Maoriness. The quality or state of being Maori; the possession of perceptible Maori characteristics.

1877 MARTIN *Letter* in Grace *Journal* in *Pioneer Missionary* (1928) 258 Let it not be said that the Maoriness of a man unfits him to be a Bishop! **1969** HILLIARD *Green River* 73 What, after all, was wrong? It was his Pakehaness... What is wrong with the Negroes is their Negroness... What is wrong with me is my Maoriness. **1973** *Islands* 6 357 The Maoriness of the North Island is what is best about it—to this Southerner, at least. **1983** HULME *Bone People* 238 I think he was ashamed, secretly ashamed, of my Nana and her Maoriness. **1991** *Evening Post* (Wellington) 3 Sept. 4 We do not lose our Maoriness by driving a Japanese car, smoking cigarettes made by a Pakeha New Zealander..heating up a frozen hangi in a microwave.

Maoriori, var. MORIORI.

Maori oven.

1. HANGI 1. Cf. EARTH OVEN, *native oven* (NATIVE B 3 a), OVEN 1.
[*Note*] *hangi* is now the preferred use; earlier preferences were *native oven* giving way to *Maori oven*, thence to *earth oven*.
   1840 *Best Journal* (1966) 12 Dec. 265 A Mauri oven deserves that a few lines should be devoted to it. **1847** BRUNNER *Exped. Middle Is.* 30 May in Taylor *Early Travellers* (1959) 278 The natives searching for food found a recently-made Maori oven and a *wari*. **1863** HARPER *Lett. from NZ* 1 Oct. (1914) 75 Then followed dinner, served *al fresco* in Maori style; fish, potatoes and cabbage, perfectly cooked, all steamed in Maori ovens. **1871** WILLIAMS *Dict. NZ Lang.* (3edn.) 56 *Koohua*, n. 1. *Maori oven*; 2. *boiler*. **1881** BATHGATE *Waitaruna* 144 Not long since Ramshorn discovered some Maori ovens with Moa bones in them. **1905** [see HANGI 1]. **1926** CROOKES *Plant Life Maoriland* 10 This would be cut into small slabs..afterwards being baked in the 'hangi', or Maori oven. **1946** BAXTER *Collected Poems* (1980) 45 And by the bay itself were cliffs with carved names And a hut on the shore beside the Maori ovens. **1970** MCLEOD *Glorious Morning* 37 When you come to think of it, this [brick bread-oven] is only the European version of the Maori oven.

2. *Canterbury and Otago.* A hole in the ground found on the Canterbury Plains, the remains of an old Maori oven, or which resembles such remains (e.g., former Maori gravel-pits). Cf. *Maori hole* (MAORI B 5 a).
   1878 ELWELL *Boy Colonists* 28 The plain..was..frequently broken by what are known as 'Maori Ovens', that is large holes, almost round, with sloping sides about four feet deep. **1914** *History of North Otago* (1978) 43 Close by this whare there were three depressions, each six feet across and 2 feet 6 inches deep. These were Maori ovens. **1937** AYSON *Thomas* 115 He was riding Frank full tilt down a ridge when the pony went bang into a Maori oven covered with rubbish. **1966** BARRY *In the Lee of the Hokonuis* 372 If he came to a maori oven or swampy patch, he would lift the lantern above his head, as a signal to stop.

Maori Pakeha, *n.* and *a.*

A. *n.* A non-Maori whose outlook or accomplishments are thought to be Maori. Contrast PAKEHA MAORI 1.
   1867 HOCHSTETTER *NZ* 293 The helm [of the canoe] was managed by Captain Drummond Hay, whom the Maoris jestingly styled a 'Maori Pakeha', because he had acquired certain Maori-accomplishments to perfection. **1964** FRANCES *Johnny Rapana* 37 And when he walked towards the silent men, he walked not as a Maori-pakeha or pakeha-Maori, but as a Maori and a pakeha, possessed now of a rare thing that made him equal to all men. **1985** HOWE *Towards 'Taha Maori'* in *English* (NZATE) 4 New Zealander—combinations of the above? A Pakeha? A Maori? A Maori Pakeha? A Pakeha Maori? And what of all the other important racial and cultural groups in New Zealand?

B. *adj.* Usu. with init. caps. Shared by Maori and Pakeha.
   1941 SUTHERLAND *Numismatic Hist. NZ* 1 Every phase of the early Maori–Pakeha history of New Zealand has been associated with barter. **1953** *Here & Now* June 28 I believe it's a long way from being typical of maori–pakeha relationships. **1974** MASON *Swan Song* (TS 1987) 41 Isobel: How Maori are you?... Half? Three-quarters? Smithson: I'm not sure. I think, half. You see: I was a piece of flotsam, thrown up on the beach of Maori–pakeha relations... Brought up pakeha. **1992** *Dominion* (Wellington) 7 Mar. 2 It fell short of guaranteeing Maori–Pakeha equality principles in the Treaty of Waitangi.

Maori-phile.
A lover of things Maori, a supporter of Maori causes; as an adjective, characteristic, or pertaining to such an attitude. Also *attrib.* Cf. *philo-Maori* (MAORI B 6 b).
   1927 MARAIS *Colonisation of NZ* ix 'Native policy' had a great deal to do with this disastrous state of affairs. It was a 'Maori-phile' policy administered by the aid of missionaries according to the principles of the Aborigines Committee of 1837. **1928** *Na To Hoa Aroha* (1986) I. 140 For this we owe a great debt to Coates. The danger is that some day they will accuse him of being ultra Maori-phile. **1966** *Encycl. NZ* II. 88 Recent research appears to confirm that the 'Great Fleet' of Maori tradition is a myth coined by European Maori-phil[e]s in the generation after the Maori Wars.

Maori potato.

1. Any of several varieties of mealy potatoes with reddish or purple skins and some interior coloration, grown orig. and traditionally by the Maori, the present varieties poss. descended from stock introduced in late 18th or early 19th centuries. See also RIWAI, TAEWA.
   [**1820** LEE & KENDALL *NZ Gram. & Vocab.* 203 Róke róke; A species of the potatoe. [Prob. so-called from its shape: *roke* 'excrement'.] **1857** ASKEW *Voyage Austral. & NZ* 347 They [*sc*. potatoes] have darkish coloured, thin skins, and when cooked are mealy, and have a good flavour. **1887** *Auckland Weekly News* 29 Jan. 17 If the newly-located settlers made an effort to get a supply of seed of the uwhi, a winter potato generally grown by the Maoris in the north, they would find this much to their advantage... The uwhi, a large round pink potato, is a far more abundant cropper than the ordinary kidney potato.] **1959** MASTERS *Tales of Mails* 134 Jeff and his companion ran out of food, and for 6 weeks after their arrival at Herbertville [in 1856], had to live on shell fish and Maori potatoes. Captain Cook had left seed potatoes with the Maoris, hence the Maori potatoes. **1969** HILLIARD *Green River* 13 'You got any Maori potatoes this year?' 'How you mean Maori potatoes?' 'You can tell a real Maori potato by you cut it and it's got a design right through.' **1971** *New Zealand's Heritage* I. 253 The first permanent European introduction of real consequence to the Bay of Islands was a type of potato, brought by Marion du Fresne's expedition of 1772 and called by the New Zealanders uwhi—the name of one of their own yams. The uwhi potato and other early introduced varieties—known collectively today as 'Maori potatoes' although each has its own distinctive name—are still found growing in some home gardens, more especially in the rural areas of the north. **1982** BURTON *Two Hundred Yrs. NZ Food* 14 These early varieties of Irish potato came to be known as 'Maori potatoes' and are still found in country areas of Northland. **1983** *Botany Div. Newsletter* (DSIR) No. 85 11 (Thomson) [Title] *The Maori Potato*. The ancient potato cultivars commonly referred to as Maori potatoes may be descended from tubers given to the Maori by early explorers, or they may have come direct from South America with the early colonisation of the Pacific. Doug Yen..now at the Bishop Museum appears to have been the first to collect and study these early potatoes (*The Potato Journal Summer 1961/61*: 2–5) and he refers to the introductions by de Surville in 1769 and 1772 and by Cook in 1773. Yen also refers to the possible introduction direct from South America, since Callao in Peru and Acapulco in Mexico were provisioning ports for whaling vessels. **1991** *NZ Gardener* Aug. 30 American whalers brought what are now called Maori potatoes and one called 'Nga oto outi' with deep eyes and a purple skin was dug for me.

2. The tubers of a ground orchid. See also *gumdigger's spud* (GUMDIGGER 3). Cf. PEREI.
   1952 RICHARDS *Chatham Is.* 23 Thelymitra... *longifolia*... A ground orchid having a fleshy leaf... Common thelymitra, Maori Potato. Mai Kuku (claw). **1969** *Standard Common Names Weeds* 46 *Maori potato* [=] *microtis*: sun orchid.

Maori PT.
orig. WW2. *derog.* Also occas. **white man's PT**. [f. *Maori* (as stereotypically 'lazy') + *PT* physical training.] Resting, loafing. (Also elsewhere known as *Egyptian P.T.*)
   1939–45 *Expressions & Sayings 2NZEF* (TS N.A. WAII DA 420/1) Maori PT—Lying on bed (or anywhere) dozing. **1943** JACKSON *Passage to Tobruk* 105 Maori Physical Training, or Maori P.T..meant no more and no less strenuous exercise than lying on the flat of his back on his bed. **1943** *NZEF Times* 5 July 6 Back to the only position they know, To what Maoris call—white man's PT. **1946** *Tararua Tramper* June 8 The party ended with the dawn and people amused themselves variously from then on. 'Maori P.T.' was a very popular exercise. **1959** SLATTER *Gun My Hand* 43 Come on pakeha she would say. Get up from there. None of that Maori P.T. **1965** WILSON *Outcasts* 149 Doing a bit of Maori P.T., eh, Jim? Come on. We need your help to win this game of poker. **1986** DAVIN *Salamander & the Fire* 166 He was off to have his cup of char..before he did anything else. I thought I'd do the same and have a bit of Maori PT as well. **1994** *Dominion* (Wellington) 23 May 1 A Race Relations letter demanding Tourist Minister John Banks explain his 'Maori PT' comment may not be the hoax he thinks it is. Mr Banks used the expression in Parliament in reference to Winston Peters, who was asleep. He also used it to describe police who were sleeping when they should have been watching a suspect. **1994** *Sunday Star-Times* 29 May C4 [From Douglas Wall, Kaitaia] Maori PT... I first heard this expression for 'taking a rest' from soldiers of the No. 28 Maori battalion at Northern Military District Training School at Narrow Neck, Auckland, in 1941. **1994** *Evening Post* (Wellington) 2 June 15 Mr Tapsell [Parliament's Maori Speaker] said he found nothing wrong with using the term 'Maori PT'. 'I and friends of mine, both Maori and pakeha, often use it,' Mr Tapsell said.

Maori Queen.
A female leader in the line of succession of the MAORI KING.
   1922 COWAN *NZ Wars* (1955) II. 470 The slayers of Timoti..intended to lay the heart before Tepaea, or Tiaho, the Maori Queen, but she disapproved of their actions, so the trophy was not presented to her. **1986** MILLER *Getting Around NZ's North Island* 59 The Maori Queen, Dame Te Atairangikaahu, lives at Waahi Marae in Huntly. Her ceremonial headquarters are at Turangawaewae Marae in Ngaruawahia. **1990** *NZ Herald* (Auckland) 7 Feb. sect. i 2 Prayers were presented by the Archbishop of New Zealand..the Maori Queen..and the Bishop of Auckland.

Maori school.
Hist. An institution established, orig. by Christian missionaries, then by the State, to provide primary education for Maori children. Orig., and until 1948 officially, styled *Native School* (NATIVE B 3 a).
   1853 GRACE *Letter* 29 Apr. in *Pioneer Missionary* (1928) 24 Maori Schools in or near to colonial towns are absolutely foolish. **1867** HOCHSTETTER *NZ* [facing] 306 [Caption] The Maori-school of the Rev. Mr. Ashwell at Taupiri. **1912** *Kai Tiaki* Oct. 99 Nurse Lewis..has been giving a series of lectures..to the pupils of a Maori school. **1935** *Star Sun* (Christchurch) 17 Dec. 12 Life moves with a certain zest in a Maori school. **1948** *NZ Educ. Gaz.* Vol. XXVII No. 3 1 In pursuance of the Maori Purposes Act 1947..in future Native Schools are to be referred to as Maori Schools. **1956** *AJHR E-1* 31 Formerly the Maori School was the focal point in the Maori community. **1968** *Ibid.* 27

During 1968 the Maori Schools Service was preparing for the transfer of administration of Maori schools to education boards. **1988** *Dominion* (Wellington) 29 June 10 *Maori Schools...* The Maori state primary schools (called 'native schools' until 1947) were established after 1867 usually in remote, rural, and predominantly Maori communities. The official policy was one of assimilation. The schools provided an English-type education and special instruction in English for Maori children, the majority of whom still spoke Maori as their first language.

maoritanga. Often with init. cap. [Ma. *Māoritanga*: f. *Māori* + *-tanga* one of a number of suffixes forming abstract nouns from common nouns.] A general name for traditions, practices and beliefs which are Maori as distinct from non-Maori; 'Maoriness'.
 1843 DIEFFENBACH *Travels in NZ* II. 370 Maoritanga—native custom, natural use. **1933** in *Na To Hoa Aroha* (1988) III. 85 There is no doubt that more than the spirit which pervades our people on development work... What impressed the Tokerau delegates last year when they visited those districts was the 'maoritanga' of the tribes inhabiting that part of the Eastern Maori electorate. It was not a maoritanga of the lips as among the Waikato, but was manifested in persistent cultural traits, carvings, plaiting, marae ceremonial, poetry and song, speech and so forth. **1946** ZIMMERMAN *Where People Sing* 59 Immediately she came in, however, something within her made her incline to the *maoritanga* of her companions, and I believe it was at her request that the girls began to speak only Maori in their free hours. **1957** BAGNALL in Introduction to Cruise *Journal* 9 Only less astonishing than the number of chiefs who went overseas..during this time was the contrast between their general bearing while away and the resumption of their Maoritanga on their return. **1963** HENDERSON *Ratana* (1972) 4 [King Tawhiao] withdrew across the Puniu River to bear the standard of *Maoritanga* in isolation from missionaries. **1972** BAXTER *Collected Poems* (1980) 556 You might stay well if you learnt Maoritanga. **1983** HULME *Bone People* 64 My father's father was English so I'm not yer 100% pure. But I'm Maori. And that's the way I feel too, the way you said, that the Maoritanga has got lost in the way I live. **1988** MACRAE *Awful Childhoods* 88 'I'm not interested in any maoritanga shit,' Lillian said.

Maori title. Also **Maori customary title**, and orig. until 1947 **Native (customary) title**, also **Native (land) title**. Often constructed without an article. [Mathews cites for the US a similar *Indian title*, 1660.] The legal right to the possession of land deriving from original Maori ownership and custom, and confirmed by the Treaty of Waitangi.
 1847 in HAAST *NZ Privy Council Cases* (1938) 390 The practice of extinguishing Native titles by fair purchases is certainly more than two centuries old... It is now part of the law of the land, and although the Courts of the United States, in suits between their own subjects, will not allow a grant to be impeached under pretext that the Native title has not been extinguished, yet they would certainly not hesitate to do so in a suit of one of the Native Indians... In solemnly guaranteeing the Native title, and in securing what is called the Queen's pre-emptive right, the Treaty of Waitangi, confirmed by the Charter of the Colony, does not assert either in doctrine, or in practice, anything new and unsettled... The right which resides in the Crown is..the exclusive right of extinguishing the Native title. **1856** *NZPD* (1858–60) 2 May 49 The 73rd clause of the Constitution Act..enables Her Majesty to delegate the power of negotiating for the extinction of the Native title. **1858** in **1860–61** *AJHR* E-1 7 The Grants to individual Natives will effect a gratuitous transmutation of the Native Title of occupancy into an English fee-simple. **1860** *NZPD* (1858–60) 10 Aug. 283 The measures ought to be framed..for effecting..the following objects:- The individualization of Native title. **1873** *NZ Statutes* No.60 279 [Native Reserves Act] Any notification..stating that the Native title over any land being a Native reserve therein described was extinguished previously to a date therein specified, shall for all purposes be conclusive proof that the Native title over the land described in such notice was extinguished at some time previously to the date therein specified. **1876** *TrNZI* VIII. 422 The Native Land Courts, in the eyes of the present generation of colonists, are chiefly interesting as the means of investigating Maori titles to land, and as the agency for peacefully transferring, by consent of the Maori proprietors, these lands to European owners. **1909** *NZ Statutes* No.15 181 A Proclamation by the Governor that any land vested in His Majesty the King is free from the Native customary title shall in all courts and in all proceedings be accepted as conclusive proof of the fact so proclaimed. **1909** in Salmond *Public Acts of NZ 1908–1931* (1932) VI. 87 The customary Native title to the land of New Zealand has now for the most part been extinguished. **1909** *NZPD* CXLVIII. 1273 To declare..that the situation of the Native-land difficulty is to individualise every Native-land title, and allow the Native to sell his land and become landless, is counsel not only of folly but also of weakness. **1953** *NZ Statutes* No.94 1143 [Maori Affairs Act] The Maori customary title shall be deemed to have been lawfully extinguished in respect of all land which..was continuously in the possession of the Crown. **1959** SINCLAIR *Hist. NZ* 143 The function of the [Land] courts was to ascertain Maori title and to issue a Crown freehold title to the owners who, now that Crown pre-emption was abolished, were free to sell either to settlers or to the Government. **1986** HINDE, MCMORLAND & SIM *Introd. to Land Law* 18 [Heading] Maori customary title and the Maori Land Court. Upon the assumption of sovereignty over New Zealand the Crown acquired not only title to all land in New Zealand, but also the exclusive right of extinguishing Maori title, either by the free conquest of the Maori occupiers or by legislation. **1994** *Sunday Star* (Auckland) 23 Jan. A9 That seemed..to pose a more widespread threat to any land, now privately owned, which had been under Maori title.

Maori War.
1. Often init. caps., usu. *pl*. A European-oriented term for the wars of the 1860s; NEW ZEALAND WAR. **a.** As **Maori War**.
 1860 PICKMERE in Matthews *Matthews of Kaitaia* (1940) 209 And some hen-hearted people leaving in fright of the Maori war. **c1875** MEREDITH *Adventuring in Maoriland* (1935) 83 There is a good story told of an incident which occurred near Wanganui during the Maori War. **1899** GRACE *Sketch NZ War* i This sketch of the Maori War is not intended to have any merit except spontaneity. **1925** BATHGATE *Random Recolls.* 18 There was a good deal of discontent in the Old Country about the Maori War. **1940** *Tales of Pioneer Women* (1988) 37 The Maori War was in progress at this time [1864], and father joined the Fourth Waikato Militia Regiment. **1961** REED *N. Cape to Bluff* 82 Captain Gilbert Mair and Major William G. Mair, Maori War heroes.

b. As **Maori wars**. (A common present use.)
 1918 *Kia-ora Coo-ee Second Series* (Cairo) (1981) 15 Aug. II. 16 Sir Harry Atkinson, formed the settler-riflemen into a mounted force of a nature demanded by the topographical and tactical conditions of the fiercely-contested Maori wars. **1922** COWAN *NZ Wars* (1955) II. 462 This was the last time Te Kooti was seen over a gun-sight, and it was the final engagement in the Maori wars. **1935** GUTHRIE *Little Country* 411 Down in the arena, half a dozen veterans of the forgotten Maori wars..tilted their old beards up towards the sky. **1945** BURTON *In Prison* 123 There has been a deepseated inferiority among the Maori people ever since the conclusion of the Maori wars. **1957** FRAME *Owls Do Cry* (1967) 12 There had been Maori Wars and the white people had taken a block of land—how big is a block of land, Toby wondered. **1960** OLIVER *Story NZ* 87 A small piece of fertile land at Waitara..precipitated that protracted frontier engagement called the Maori Wars. **1983** *Listener* 24 Sept. 10 There should be no place in New Zealand for the expression 'the Maori wars'. They could possibly be called 'the land wars' but 'te riri Pakeha' (white man's anger) would be more accurate.

2. In various phrases **a. it will (all) come right after the Maori war**, an expression of optimism.
 1916 MANSFIELD *Aloe* (1982) 71 He had one saying with which he met all difficulties. 'Depend upon it, it will all come right after the Maori war.'

b. since the Maori wars, an expression of long duration of past time.
 1959 MIDDLETON *The Stone* 76 I think it was the first real excitement there had been in the area since the Maori Wars. **1962** CURNOW *Four Plays* (1972) 101 They've been at it since the Maori Wars. **1970** LEE *Mussolinis Millions* 102 There had never been a local mobilisation of civilians since the days of the Maori Wars.

3. Special Comb. **Maori War Medal**, a medal issued to veterans of the New Zealand Wars.
 1912 *NZ Free Lance* (Wellington) 10 Aug. 4 There were Crimean decorations there..as well as the more plentiful Maori War medal. **1920** BOLITHO *With the Prince in NZ* 103 There was an 1866 Maori War medal on one tunic, and one veteran..wore the medal of the Afghanistan war.

Maorize: see MAORICIZE.

Maoude, Maouri, varr. MAORI.

mapau /'mapæu/, /'mapʌu/. The spelling **mapou** has equal standing. Also **mappo**, **mapua**. [Ma. /'ma:pau/, /'ma:pou/: Williams 179 *Māpau, māpou... Myrsine australis...* = *matipou, tīpau.*] See also MAPLE.

1. Any of a group of unrelated shrubs or small trees of roughly similar general appearance having leaves often aromatic when crushed and usu. with undulate margins; commonly used as hedge plants or ornamentals. See also MAPLE. **a.** *Myrsine* spp. (fam. Myrsinaceae), esp. *M. australis* red *matipo* (MATIPO 2 (2)) having reddish bark; less commonly, usu. as **weeping mapou**, *M. divaricata*, a divaricating shrub with drooping branchlets. See also LAUREL a, TIPAU 1.
 1853 HOOKER II *Flora Novae-Zelandiae* I *Flowering Plants* 173 Suttonia *australis*, A.Rich... Nat. names, 'Mapau', 'Sipau', and 'Matipo', Middle Island, *Lyall*. 'Tipau', north of the Thames river, and 'Mapua', south of that river, *Colenso*... A small leafy tree, very closely resembling *Pittosporum undulatum* in appearance. **1866** BARKER *Station Life* (1870) 94 I can give you no idea of the variety among the shrubs..the varieties of matapo..the mappo, the gohi, and many others. **1882** HAY *Brighter Britain* II. 198 The Mapau (*Myrsine Urvillei*) affords good material for fencing. **1898** [see LEMONWOOD]. **1907** [see 2 (3) a below]. **1939** BEATTIE *First White Boy Born Otago* 30 The Maori went to the bush and cut down a mapou—not matapo, which is

MAPAURIKI

neither Maori nor English. **1940** [see MATIPO 2 (2)].
1978 MOORE & IRWIN *Oxford Book NZ Plants* 116 *Myrsine australis, mapau*. A tall shrub widespread..recognized by its dull red stems. **1982** WILSON *Stewart Is. Plants* 64 *Myrsine divaricata* Weeping Māpou... Shrub, or small tree up to 4 m, with stiffly weeping, more or less interlacing branchlets. **1984** HOLMES *Chatham Is.* 93 *Myrsine Coxii* (Mapou)—a small swamp-forest tree.

b. Loosely used for some *Pittosporum* species (fam. Pittosporaceae), usu. with a colour modifier (see 2 below), and esp. *P. tenuifolium* (see *black mapau* 2 (1) below) and *P. eugenioides* (see *white mapau* 2 (3) below).

1868 PYKE *Province of Otago* 34 There are several varieties of Pittosporum (*Mapau*) in Otago. **1869** *TrNZI* I. (rev. edn.) 200 Mapau Pittosporum tenuifolium, Banks and Sol.

c. *South Island. Obs. Carpodetus serratus*, see *white mapau* 2 (3) b below.

2. With a modifier: **black, red, white**.

(1) **black mapau**, also occas. as **mapauriki**. Usu. *Pittosporum* spp., esp. *P. tenuifolium*, KOHUHU. See also *black matipo* (MATIPO 2 (1)).

1853 HOOKER *II Flora Novae-Zelandiae I Flowering Plants* 21 Pittosporum *tenuifolium*..common as far south as Akaroa,... Nat. names, 'Mapauriki', *Cunn.*; 'Kohuhu', *Col.*; 'Karo' of Middle Island. **1869** *TrNZI* I. (rev. edn.) 194 Black Mapau, or Tipau (*Pittosporum Colensoi*). A shrub tree, very ornamental in contrast with the last [sc. white mapau], the whole tree very dark coloured. **1882** HAY *Brighter Britain* II. 198 The mapauriki (*Pittosporum tenuifolium*) has handsome foliage..and can be grown as a shelter tree. **1889** KIRK *Forest Flora* 75 The tawhiwhi of the Maoris [*Pittosporum tenuifolium*] was discovered during Cook's first voyage by Banks and Solander... By the settlers it is frequently called 'black mapou' on account of the colour of the bark. **1891** [see (3) a below].

(2) **red mapau**. *red matipo* (MATIPO 2 (2)). See also 1 a above.

1869 *TrNZI* I. (rev. edn.) 199 Red Mapau (*Myrsine Urvillei*). A small tree common at Dunedin... Wood dark-red, very astringent, used as fence stuff, but subject to the attack of a boring beetle. **1877** *TrNZI* IX. 143 *Red mapau—Myrsine urvillei*. This is a small tree, well known to everyone from its conical shape and dark foliage. **1892** *NZ Official Handbook* 150 Mapau, red-mapau, or red-birch (*Myrsine urvillei*) **1909** *AJHR* C-12 59 Rapanea Urvillei. Mapau, tipau. Red mapau, matipo or maple. **1982** WILSON *Stewart Is. Plants* 104 *Myrsine australis* Red Māpou..Matipou..Small tree, sometimes reduced to a shrub.

(3) **white mapau. a.** *Pittosporum eugenioides*, TARATA 1.

1869 *TrNZI* I. (rev. edn.) 194 White Mapau; Tarata (*Pittosporum eugenioides*) One of the most beautiful trees in New Zealand, grows to a comparatively large size in Otago, with a trunk 18 inches to 2 feet in diameter... The leaves when bruised and mixed with fat, are used by the Maories, as a perfume. **1889** KIRK *Forest Flora* 81 The tarata is the largest of the New Zealand species of *Pittosporum*, and, although most commonly known by its proper Native name, is also called by the settlers 'white mapau,' 'turpentine,' and 'maple'. **1891** *NZJSc.* (NS) I. 71 In the neighbourhood of Dunedin:.. White mapau—*Pittosporum eugenioides*; Black Mapau—*Pittosporum tenuifolium*. **1907** LAING & BLACKWELL *Plants NZ* 195 [*Pittosporum eugenioides*] is known by a variety of names amongst the colonists, such as *Mapau, White Mapau*, and even *Maple*, and *Lemon-tree*.

b. *Obs. Carpodetus serratus*, PUTAPUTAWETA.

1869 *TrNZI* I. (rev. edn.) 199 White Mapau, or Piripiriwhata (*Carpodetus serratus*). An ornamental shrub-tree, with mottled-green leaves, and large cymose panicles of white flowers. **1877** *TrNZI* IX. 144 *White mapau—Carpodetus serratus*. A small tree like the black mapau... It has mottled green leaves, and large white flowers; the wood is white and fibrous. **1883** HECTOR *Handbook NZ* 132 *Carpodetus serratus*... Tawiri, White Mapau... A small tree, 10–30 feet high, trunk unusually slender. **1889** KIRK *Forest Flora* 77 Settlers..also term it [sc. *Carpodetus serratus*] 'mapau', 'white mapau', 'white maple', and 'white birch'. **1892** *NZ Official Handbook* 150 Tawiri-kohu-kohu, or white-mapau (*Carpodetus serratus*).

mapauriki: see MAPAU 2 (1).

maple. [An alteration of *mapou* or *mapau*, the spelling *-ou* becoming *-le* final poss. perceived as indicating an Otago Scottish dial. realization of ('dark') /l/ final (cf. 'fu' the noo'): the form was esp. freq. in Otago.] Any of various species of *Myrsine, Pittosporum, Carpodetus* to which MAPAU (q.v.) is applied. Also as **black maple, white maple** (see quot. c1920).

[**1769** COOK *Journals* 29 Oct. (1955) I. 186 The tree which we cut for fireing was something like Maple and yielded a whitish Gum. [Prob. Tarata, *Pittosporum eugenioides*.]] **1858** *Otago Witness* (Dunedin) 1 May 3 For Sale, A Quantity of Scantling, pit sawn. 250 Round Maple Posts and Rails..30,000 Shingles. 200 Feet Good Goi and Black Pine Piles, at 9d per foot. **1875** *Official Handbook NZ* 107 Goi, rata, bokako, birch, maple [*Pittosporum*]. **1885** *The Adelaide Observer* 6 June 41 in Hill *Richard Henry of Resolution Island* (1987) 88 Maple trees..all entangled by a dense undergrowth of ferns & parasitic creepers. **1889** [see MAPAU 2 (3) a]. **1898** MORRIS *Austral-English* 287 *Maple, n.* In New Zealand, a common settlers' corruption for any tree called *Mapau*. **1907** [see MAPAU 2 (3) a]. **c1920** BEATTIE *Trad. Lifeways Southern Maori* (1994) 191 Rau tawhiri [=black mapau *P. tenuifolium*] = black maple of the settlers. Tarata [*P. eugenioides*] = white maple of the settlers. **1939** BEATTIE *First White Boy Born Otago* 151 A saleyard had been newly made of green maple [in Central Otago c1860s], and as the logs had been recently hauled out of the bush they were still thick with clay and mud. **1967** MCLATCHIE *Tang of Bush* 34 [Otago] The maples—red, white and black—were there, and ribbonwood or lace bark.

mapou, mappo, mapua, varr. MAPAU.

marae /ˈmʌrai/, /mʌˈrai/.

1. a. Also early **morie**. [Ma. /ˈmarae/ or /maˈrae/: Williams 180 *marae 1*. n. Enclosed space in front of a house; courtyard; village common.] The courtyard (usu. grassed) of a Maori meeting-house, the centre of tribal life; often now used of the whole complex of courtyard, meeting-house, and ancillary buildings and grounds. Also in modern use as **urban marae**, a marae complex designed to serve Maori townspeople of mixed iwi affiliation who have moved away from their tribal areas.

[*Note*] Maori meeting-houses as such are post-European: the Maori marae as a ceremonial gathering place must be distinguished from the larger ritualistic Tahitian marae, an application probably (erroneously) reflected by Cook's Tahitian interpreter and recorded in the 1769 quot.

[**1769** COOK *Journals* 2 Nov. (1955) I. 191 We have before now observed on several parts of the Coast small Villages inclosed with Pallisades, and Works of this kind built on eminences and ridges of hills, but Tupia hath all along told us that they were Mories or places of Worship, but I rather think that they are places of retreat or Stronghold. **1820** LEE & KENDALL *NZ Gram. & Vocab.* 176 Maráe, *s.* A court-yard.] **1868** TAYLOR *Past & Present NZ* 12 The young chief..led him to the *marae*, and there surrounded by all the inhabitants of the pa, he related all the circumstances of the case. **1888** BULLER *Birds NZ* II. 64 [The skua] came into the possession of the Hon. Wi Parata, who kept it in [sic] his *marae* until it became quite tame. **1908** GORST *NZ Revisited* 303 We walked up..to the 'Mar[a]e', the wide open space in the centre of the town, where a great assembly of Waikato Maories was waiting for us. **1933** in *Na To Hoa Aroha* (1988) 11 June III. 85 The feature of his visit was the display afforded in the ceremonial receptions at fourteen maraes. **1940** COWAN *Sir Donald Maclean* 146 The *marae*, or village assembly ground, the square among the houses, was the gathering-place of tribe or *hapu*. **1959** MCLINTOCK *Descr. Atlas* 72 In the country proper the Maori has retained his traditional mode of life which is symbolised in the *marae*. In a literal sense the term means the open courtyard in front of the communal meeting house; today..it embraces all aspects of community life—community buildings, tribal gatherings, church activities, and recreation. **1979** TAYLOR *Eyes of Ruru* 15 My name is Tu the freezing worker. Ngati D.B. is my tribe. The pub is my Marae. My fist is my taiaha. **1986** IHIMAERA *Matriarch* 116 The marae as we know it today is taken to mean a complex comprising a meeting house, courtyard and dining hall, although this is a relatively modern innovation. Originally the marae was the earthen courtyard in the village, and it was situated immediately outside the chief's house. **1988** *Listener* 5 Mar. 16 The gate across the road into the Nga Hau e Wha Christchurch National marae is chained and double-padlocked. **1993** *Contact* (Wellington) 11 Feb. 8 Wellington Regional Council has approved the lease of a two hectare site..to the Ngai Hau E Wha O Papa-ra-rangi Society for their urban marae (papakainga).

b. *Transf.* in non-Maori use, a communal gathering-place.

1969 BAXTER *Collected Poems* (1980) 471 This is a kind of pakeha marae; I'm only a lodger. **1979** GEBBIE & MCGREGOR *Incredible 8-Ounce Dream* 11 The bar is the Pakeha marae.

2 a. *attrib.* passing into adjectival use.

1933 in *Na To Hoa Aroha* (1988) III. 85 It was not a maoritanga of the lips as among the Waikato, but was manifested in persistent cultural traits, carvings, plaiting, marae ceremonial, poetry and song, speech and so forth. **1986** *Landfall* 160 492 It was hoped that the hour's bus ride into town each day would be a broadening experience for a sheltered 'marae' kid. **1988** *Dominion* (Wellington) 22 Nov. 10 Members of many other marae committees throughout New Zealand share the vision of Whakaruruhau, of young people being trained and employed to grow trees and other plants from marae-based nurseries.

b. Special Comb. **marae** (or **marae-based**) **justice**, a proposed system (often arising from the wishes of a local people) of judging Maori wrongdoing on the marae rather than within the State judicial system; **marae language**, a term coined to identify the state of a language which, having no wide community support, becomes used only ceremonially or on special occasions by a specialist group of Maori speakers; **marae pudding**, a plain steamed pudding of sufficient size or quantity to feed a crowd of guests.

1989 *Evening Post* (Wellington) 6 May 1 The woman who led a protest in the Porirua District Court on Wednesday demanding **marae-based justice** for her brother says there is growing support..for the idea.

1991 *Dominion* (Wellington) 16 May 9 [The remit] said the desire to return to marae justice and the dignity of the student should be considered. **1993** *Dominion* (Wellington) 9 Oct. 13 With reference to the recent comments on 'marae justice', it is regrettable that the justice authorities and the police so peremptorily closed off consideration of a recognised role for Maori authorities in policing certain categories of crime. **1992** *Dominion* (Wellington) 14 July 9 Without tangible benefits from facility in Maori, the language is likely to fossilise into '**marae**' **language**..used only symbolically. **1978** FULLER *Maori Food & Cookery* 29 Steamed **Marae Pudding** for 260. 6 kilos (13 lbs) flour..3 doz. eggs... Grease with butter 1 doz large fruit or milk-powder tins. **1986** *From the Kitchens of the World* 200 *Marae Pudding Supreme.* There is one thing Maori ladies share with diplomatic wives. They often prepare food in large quantities... This pudding recipe..is sufficient to cater for 250 people!

marae, var. MAIRE.

marare(e), varr. MARARI.

marari. Also **marare**, **mararee**, **mararii**. [Ma. /mara'ri:/: Williams 181 *Mararī*, n...butterfish.] BUTTERFISH (*Odax pullus*). Cf. RARI *n.*[1]

1842 GRAY *Fauna* in Dieffenbach *Travels in NZ* (1843) II. 218 *Odax pullus...* Named 'Mararee' by the inhabitants of Queen Charlotte's Sound. **1872** [see BUTTERFISH 1]. **1886** SHERRIN *Handbook Fishes NZ* 14 Dr. Knox..gives the following interesting details of the marare of the Natives. **1898** *TrNZI* XXX. 556 The New Zealand butter-fish was called 'marare'. **1921** Marari [see BUTTERFISH 1]. **1945** [see BUTTERFISH 1]. **1957** PARROTT *Sea Angler's Fishes* 130 The Butterfish was known to the Maoris as Marari, and was captured by using basket traps close inshore. **1967** [see RARI *n.*[1]]. **1982** [see BUTTERFISH 1]. **1988** FRANCIS *Coastal Fishes* 46 Butterfish (Greenbone, Mararii, Kooeaea) *Odax pullus*.

marble.

1. [Prob. f. a game of marbles; poss. f. the drawing of marbles in Art Unions or lotteries: AND 1928.] In the phr. **to make one's marble** (occas. **marbles**) **good** (with somebody), to ingratiate oneself with, to improve one's position with; see quot. 1918 for a slightly different use. See also ALLEY.

1898 ANDERSON *Bushfalling Reminisc.* (1947) in Mulinder *A Pioneer Family* (1977) 41 I always made my marbles good with Cookie [the cook at the bush camp] by cutting up firewood. **1909** *Truth* 15 May 7 He 'made his marble good', he alleged, by paying up a score he owed. **1918** *Quick March* 1 Oct. 13 You knew [in WW1] that [Death] would miss you if your marble was good. **c1926** THE MIXER *Transport Workers' Song Book* 31 Some tap the boss before they join, And their record clearly shows By this they make their marble good. **1944** FULLARTON *Troop Target* 26 I was making my marble good [*sc.* with a woman]. **1968** SLATTER *Pagan Game* 163 Making his marble good with the missus.

2. Special Comb. **marble clock** [a 'marble clock' was an expensive clock with reliable works encased in a carved marble body], in the phr. **to go like a marble clock**, to run or go well; **marble-top**, a name for an old-fashioned aerated-water bottle having a patent stopper in the form of a (usu.) glass marble.

1947 DAVIN *For the Rest of Our Lives* 101 'If I didn't..I wouldn't have any excuse to ask you how they're doing.' 'Going like a **marble clock**, Smithy.' They're through the first line.' **1973** *Meanjin Quarterly* June 133 'Morning boss. Still raining. How are the Russkies?' 'Going like a marble clock, Smithy.' 'Good on them.' **1971** *Bottle News* No.2 (Christmas) [3] One theory..for the extinction of the marble stopper bottle is that the bottles were all being smashed for the marble, by children... Readers will be interested to know that some of the old **marble tops** had earthenware marbles.

marblefish. Also **marbletrout**. [f. the mottled ('marbled') colouring of the skin.] *Aplodactylus arctidens* (fam. Aplodactylidae), a large, heavy-bodied seaweed-eating fish, having a mottled ('marbled') skin pattern. See also GRANITE TROUT, KEHE, KEKE, MAORI CHIEF *n.*[2] 2.

1921 *NZJST* IV. 115 *Marble-fish; Keke.* Secured in deep water in the vicinity of kelp, and is sometimes taken in mullet-nets. **1938** *TrRSNZ* LXVIII. 411 *Haplodactylus meandratus* (Richardson). Marble-fish (granite trout). **1957** PARROTT *Sea Angler's Fishes* 112 The Marble fish, or Granite trout as it is sometimes called, derives its name from the colour, which is black, mottled with slaty grey, resembling the markings of granite or marble. **1967** MORELAND *Marine Fishes* 28 Marblefish... Another name is marbletrout, while the Maori keke is still in use in some northern areas. **1967** NATUSCH *Animals NZ* 222 Family Aplodactylidae. The marble-fish or keke..grows to thirty inches, and is found throughout New Zealand. **1972** DOAK *Fishes* 65 One of the few fishes that feed largely on seaweeds, the Marble fish has the small mouth of a weed-eater; its coloration is suited to the background of rocks and kelp in which it lurks, lighter or darker in tone according to the surroundings. **1981** WILSON *Fisherman's Bible* 161 Marblefish... Other names commonly used in the southern waters where it is found are Marbletrout and Granitetrout. **1986** [see GRANITE TROUT].

marble-leaf. [f. the 'marbled' pattern of the leaf surface.] PUTAPUTAWETA.

1961 MARTIN *Flora NZ* 180 Sole representative of the endemic and monotypic genus *Carpodetus* is Putaputaweta or Marble-leaf. **1978** MOORE & IRWIN *Oxford Book of NZ Plants* 78 *Carpodetus serratus, putaputaweta, marble-leaf...* It is one of the species grouped by foresters under the slightly opprobrious term 'scrub hardwoods'. **1981** HARRIS *Field Guide to Common NZ Trees and Shrubs* 14 Putaputaweta (Marble Leaf) *Carpodetus serratus...* Leaves have a marbled effect.

marching, *attrib.* Special Comb. **marching competition**, a competitive event among marching teams to establish the team best at formation marching; **marching girl** (often *pl.*), a girl or woman trained to march in formation; **marching team**, a team of such women as a unit or entry in the sport of competitive formation marching.

1934 *Dominion* (Wellington) 24 Mar. 6 The Inter-house girls' **marching competition**, which is on a bigger scale than last year, will be one of the main attractions tonight. **1952** *Here & Now* July 9 (A.R.D. Fairburn) Not for a long time have I observed such an odd symptom of our *malaise* as the business of '**marching girls**'. This cult has not only established itself firmly in New Zealand: it is even being exported... Enquiries I have made as to the origin of this astonishing sport, or prank..have so far been fruitless. **1961** *Listener* 24 Nov. 36 Visitors from America say that as a major attraction, our marching girls are much superior to their Drum Majorettes. **1980** LELAND *Kiwi-Yankee Dict.* 63 *marching girls:* One of New Zealand's less comprehensible phenomena. Imagine teams of 10 to 50 pre-pubescent (and early post) little and middle-sized girls, dressed like the baton-twirlers that accompany High School bands, wearing busbies like the guards at Buckingham Palace. Now remove the batons and train them to march and countermarch like a crack military drill team. **1987** *Listener* 24 Oct. 21 Fiona Samuel, *The Marching Girls* writer, has always thought marching girls are 'neat'. **1990** KIDMAN *True Stars* 15 He went off with a driving school instructor who used to be a marching girl. **1941** *Dominion* (Wellington) 31 Mar. 5 [Caption] The Governor-General..as he passed between the lines of the guard of honour from the girls' **marching teams** at Athletic Park on Saturday. **1968** SLATTER *Pagan Game* 176 The pureep of the marching team whistle.

mare(e), varr. MAIRE, MARAE, MERE.

mari(e), varr. MAIRE, MERE.

marigold: see MARSH-MARIGOLD.

Marion. *Hist.* [f. the name of *Marion* du Fresne (1729–1772) a French sea captain killed, with his crew, in a Maori revenge attack in 1772.] An early Maori nickname for 'Frenchman' esp. as **the tribe of Marion**; in *pl.*, the French. Cf. WI-WI *n.*[2]

1831 *Petition of Chiefs to King William* 16 Nov. in Buick *Treaty of Waitangi* (1936) 11 We have heard that the tribe of Marion is at hand coming to take away our land... [1936 *Note*] The French were called by the natives 'the tribe of Marion' after Captain Marion du Fresne, who met his untimely death at their hands in 1772. **1839** LANG *NZ in 1839* 16 One of the natives..perceived that M. Lacoste was not an Englishman, and asked Mr. Mair 'if he were not a Marion' to which Mr Mair replied in the affirmative. Marion['s]..name has ever since [c1800] been the synonym for 'Frenchman' in New Zealand. **1840** POLACK *Manners & Customs* II. 121 The French are known only, to this day, to the New Zealanders as *Te heveh no Mariou*, or the tribe of Marion.

Marist /'mærəst/, /'marəst/, *a.* [f. *Marist* (ad. French *Mariste* f. *Marie*), of the Society of Mary, its missionary and teaching members, schools, etc.] Used *ellipt.* for a Marist Brothers Old Boys rugby team; or for a Marist Brothers school (e.g. The boys go to Marist, the girls to a State school).

1953 *Landfall* 28 252 You reckon if Marist win the toss They'll win the game as well?

mark, *n.* In the phr. **up to the mark**, meeting expectations; in good health or spirits, usu. as **not to feel (be) up to the mark**.

1887 HOPEFUL *Taken In* 135 If a man isn't 'up to the mark' he is called 'a regular shicer!' **1916** THORNTON *Wowser* 51 He ain't feelin' just up to the mark today.

2. In the phr. **a good mark** [AND 1845], applied to a reliable, honest, trustworthy or creditworthy person.

1914 GRACE *Tale Timber Town* 121 He's one of the best-marks in Timber Town. **c1930** *Whitcombe's Etym. Dict. Aust.–NZ Suppl.* 7 *mark n.*—a good mark sl. an honest or trustworthy person. **1949** Havelock (Marlborough) store. 'He's OK. A good mark for up to about 50 quid.' (Ed.) **1968** *NZ Contemp. Dict. Supp.* (Collins) 13 *mark, a good n. (Sl.)* reliable, honest, trustworthy person.

mark, *v.* *Farming.* [AND 1883, of earmarking and other processes, including castration.] *trans.*
a. Orig. to mark the ear of (a lamb, less freq. a calf), completing at the same time other processes,

MARKET

as the castration of male lambs, docking; now often a familiar rural term for 'castrate'. Cf. CUT AND TAIL.

c1875 MEREDITH *Adventuring in Maoriland* (1935) 145 These [East Coast Maori] sheep are all long-tailed, and have never been marked, except on their ears. **1883** FERGUSON *Castle Gay* 168 But by-and-bye the overseer Rode out to learn the shepherds' cheer. It now was time to mark the lambs. **1906** CHUDLEIGH *Diary* 28 Sept. (1950) 436 I commenced marking lambs today. **1922** PERRY *Sheep Farming* 79 [Caption] Temporary yards for marking lambs. **1951** MCLEOD *NZ High Country* 19 800 lambs to catch and mark. **1968** GRUNDY *Who'd Marry a Doctor?* 66 The cattle are sorted out, and the bulls are marked. **1973** NEWTON *Big Country SI* (1977) 65 I was interested to find that all the calves—marked in March and fairly sizable—are done in the bail.

b. *Obs.* To earmark.

1912 BOOTH *Five Years NZ* 26 A good hand can cut and mark two thousand lambs per day. **1933** *Press* (Chistchurch) (Acland Gloss.) 4 Nov. 15 *Mark*.—To *ear-m[ark]*. Now a frequent euphemism for *cut and tail*.

Hence **marking** (also **lamb marking**, occas. **calf-marking**) *vbl. n.*, the operation of castration; the process of castrating a group of lambs, etc.

1891 WALLACE *Rural Econ. Austral. and NZ* 43 Lamb-tailing and marking were on at this time—the end of June. **1922** PERRY *Sheep Farming* 79 *Lamb Marking*.—The castration and docking of lambs is best carried out when the lambs are from four to six weeks old. *Ibid.* 94 *Lamb Marking*... Once the operation of earmarking, tailing, and castrating is commenced. **1937** AYSON *Pioneering Otago* 94 Mr. Shaw took on what was called thirds at lamb marking time, and put his own earmark on every third lamb [of Brugh's flock running with his]. **1950** *NZJAg.* Sept. LXXXI. 197 Lamb marking consists of three different operations: the placing of a distinguishing mark in one or both ears, the amputation of tails, and the castration of male lambs. **1973** NEWTON *Big Country SI* (1977) 65 Calf marking is another major job that is done in Bush Gully yards... All the calves..are done in the bail... The marking cradle was tried but did not find favour. **1978** JARDINE *Shadows on Hill* 108 Of all the jobs..on a high-country property that of lamb-marking provides the greatest scope for the occurrence of unforeseen events.

market. In the phr. **to go to market** [AND 1870], to become angry, upset, disturbed; of a horse, to buck furiously; also heard as a mild interjection **Oh go to market!** expressing exasperation (Ed.).

1918 *Kia Ora Coo-ee* July 4 Later on, in the mess, a brother officer 'going to market' because he had been rebuked. **1924** ANTHONY *Follow the Call* (1975) 7 Peter came home drunk every once a week and made his poor wife milk 24 cows by herself while he slept it off.., then woke up at about 8 p.m. and went to market because she didn't have a hot tea cooked. **1947** NEWTON *Wayleggo* 153 *Go to market*: A horse bucking. **1992** PARK *Fence around the Cuckoo* 206 Did I go to market! A fur coat! Where did he think I was going to wear a fur coat.

Marlborough. In the names of plants and animals: see DAISY 2 (6), HAREBELL, LILAC 2, SHAG 2 (9).

marleesh, var. MALEESH.

marnaka, var. MANUKA.

maroro. [Ma. /'maroro/: Williams 184 *Maroro, 1. n...species of flying fish*.] *Cypselurus lineatus* (fam. Exocoetidae), a large flying-fish.

1855 TAYLOR *Te Ika A Maui* 624 Of the Fam. Esocidoe may be noticed the *Maroro*, or flying fish... This singular fish in New Zealand attains the length of eighteen inches. **1886** SHERRIN *Handbook Fishes NZ* 305 *Exocaetus speculiga*... Flying-fish, or Maroro. **1927** PHILLIPPS *Bibliogr. NZ Fishes* (1971) 21 *Evolantia microptera*... Flying-fish; Maroro. **1966** DOOGUE & MORELAND *Sea Anglers' Guide* 207 Flyingfish... *Other names*: *Cypselurus lineatus;* maroro (Maori)... There are at least three kinds of flyingfish present in our northern waters, but only the above species is at all common. **1987** POWELL *Native Animals NZ* (3edn.) 59 *Flying Fish* (*Maroro*) *Cypselurus lineatus*. This grows up to 400mm long, and is generally distributed in east coast waters from the Bay of Plenty northwards.

marre(e), varr. MERE.

marsh. In the names of plants and birds, see: CRAKE a, CRESS, RAIL 2 (8), RIBBONWOOD 2 (3). See also MARSH-MARIGOLD.

marsh-marigold. Also **marsh marygold**. [Transf. use of northern hemisphere *marsh-marigold Caltha palustris* for NZ *Psychrophila* (formerly *Caltha*) spp.] Either of *Psychrophila novae-zelandiae* or *P. obtusata* (fam. Ranunculaceae), small creeping herbs of wet places and creek-sides, having heart-shaped leaves.

1869 *TrNZI* I. (rev. edn.) 200 Marsh Marygold. Caltha novae-zelandiae. **1909** *AJHR* C-12 54 *Caltha novae-zelandiae*..New Zealand caltha or marsh marigold... Occurs from almost sea-level at Port Pegasus to the summits almost of the mountains. **1982** WILSON *Stewart Is. Plants* 274 *Caltha novae-zelandiae*..Yellow Caltha..New Zealand marsh marigold... Small, hairless rosettes... Flowers pale yellow.

maru. [Ma. /'ma:ru:/: Williams 184 *Mārū*... 5...a water plant.] *Sparganium subglobosum* (fam. Sparganiaceae), an aquatic plant having flowers in spherical heads, and beaked fruits.

1853 HOOKER *II Flora Novae-Zelandiae I Flowering Plants* 238 Sparganium *simplex*... Nat. name, 'Maru'. **1867** HOOKER *Handbook* 766 Maru, *Col[enso]. Sparganium simplex*. **1906** CHEESEMAN *Manual NZ Flora* 744 *S[parganium] antipodum*... Maru. **1961** MARTIN *Flora NZ* 141 Mention should be made of the Maori Burr Reed or Maru (*Sparganium*), a common rush-like marsh plant in parts of the North Island with flat, strongly-keeled leaves and erect stems. **1991** CLARKSON et al. *Botany of Rotorua* 61 [Caption] The star-shaped burrs (seedheads) of maru, a member of the burr-reed family, restricted to a few swamps in this district.

maruiwi, var. MORIORI.

mary, var. MERE.

Mary Ann. *Obs.* A domestic servant.

1910 *Truth* 16 Apr. 6 Magistrate Bishop commented strongly upon the foolishness of Margaret toiling for such a wage when she could command something decent as a domestic with her keep thrown in. The case was adjourned to enable Margaret to become a Mary Ann at a more remunerative screw. **1911** *Ibid.* 19 Aug. 1 Canterbury wool kings have formed a 'Domestic syndicate' to take advantage of the cheap fares of British Mary Anns to New Zealand brought about by the Government.

Hence *v. intr.*, to work as a domestic.

1911 *Truth* 19 Aug. 5 At sixteen she met the usual betrayer, and drank of the cup of bitterness and experience, but subsequently, until she was twenty-two, she Mary-Anned with industry at various places and lived a chaste and virtuous life.

mash, *v. Obs.* [Used elsewhere, but poss. more frequently and to a later date in NZ: see OED *mash v.*² 2 1883–93; *masher* 1882–89 'common in 1882 and a few years after'.] *trans.* and *intr.* Also in the phr. **to be mashed on**, to fall deeply in love with, to have a 'crush' on; to pay heavily amorous, but often unwanted, attention to.

1887 *Auckland Weekly News* 28 May 20 'The gods' love her, but she still lives to mash the boys. **1893** *NZ Observer* 19 Aug. 21 W.P. and E.M. were doing more mashing than dancing on Friday night. **1893** *Ibid.* 30 Sept. 21 Someone is much mashed on Miss M.K. **1907** *Truth* 5 Jan. 5 She and 'Curly' generally got their meals at certain tearooms in Bathurst-street where one of the girls got so 'mashed' on her [*sc.* a woman living as a man] as to be positively embarrassing.

Hence **masher** *n.*, a man who fancies himself as a 'lady-killer'; **mashing** *vbl. n.*, amorous attention.

1879 *Auckland Weekly News* 11 June 7 As for those who belong to the noble army of the **masher** and the dude, everyone knows that they like barmaids. **1885** *Wairarapa Daily* 13 June 2 He was a new chum just out from England, and..he was the first masher we ever saw. He wore a curly brimmed hat and had curly brown hair... He never came out without a flower in his buttonhole... All down our street, they called him 'the beautiful mashah'. **1893** FROBISHER *Sketches of Gossiptown* 78 The first appeared like one self-pleased, And somewhat of a flash-air, With bushy whiskers, black-avised, A dapper little masher. **1906** *Truth* 14 July 5 [It was] unsafe for any girl to wait abroad for her legitimate lover or any wife for her husband. She was almost invariably to be accosted by some prowling 'masher'—a word that was in much more common use then [20 years before] than it is now—and cases of condign punishment for such audacity, at the hands of lover or husband, were so frequent as hardly to excite comment. **1885** *Wairarapa Daily* 10 Dec. 2 At Dunedin recently they gave a 'masher' concert for a charitable purpose and..a net balance..was handed over. The balance is supposed to have been spent in **mashing**. **1904** *NZ Observer* 13 Aug. 22 Mashing seemed to be carried out in great style.

Hence also by back-formation **mash (-up)**, *n.*, a passionate bout of amorous affection, a 'pash'.

1887 *Auckland Weekly News* 12 Mar. 14 When in Feilding I did as Feilding did, even to a mash with the solitary barmaid Feilding possesses. *Ibid.* 15 July 21 Was that D.G. doing a big mash-up by the church on Sunday night. **1893** *Ibid.* 9 Sept. 21 Miss K.C. of Whangarei was doing a heavy mash with G.B. last Sunday. **1904** *Ibid.* 17 Sept. 21 R.M. and B.H. were doing a great mash..last Sunday.

mason-bee, mason-fly: see MASON-WASP.

mason-wasp. Also **mason-bee**, occas. **mason-fly**. [Transf. use of *mason wasp* a solitary wasp *Odynenus murarius*: see OED *mason n.*¹: AND *mason-wasp* 1894, *mason-fly* 1896.] *Pison spinolae* (fam. Sphecidae), a native solitary wasp which constructs a nest of mud cells.

1888 BARLOW *Kaipara* 190 One other insect, called the Mason bee, I must mention. This fly builds a nest of a kind of white mortar, stocks it with small spiders, and lives in solitary state. **1902** DRUMMOND & HUTTON *Nature in NZ* 61 The insect known here as the mason bee is really a wild kind of wasp, named Pison. **1913** *School Journal* I. 56 Mason wasps had built their nests between the maps and the wall! **1926** Tillyard *Insects of Austral. and N.Z.* 207 In New Zealand those species which construct clay nests in cracks and crannies are called 'Mason Wasps', but this name is elsewhere more generally used for the Eumenidae. [**1926** *Note*] Or, quite incorrectly, 'Mason Bees'. **1935** Dixon *Nature Study Notes* 14 [Heading] The Mason Wasp Description—It is not a wasp, but a large black fly with body shaped like that of a wasp... It also has a sting. **1948** Finlayson *Tidal Creek* (1979) 56 Jake stares hard at a mason-bee that's building its clay nest in the sleeve of Mr Crummer's coat. **1955** Miller *Nature in NZ* 36 The Mud-dauber, or 'Mason-bee'..., is also a spider hunter; it is black with narrow white markings on the abdomen. It creates a loud buzzing as it builds its nest of mud under loose bark, in crevices of buildings, in key holes, and even unused tobacco pipes and folds of garments. **1964** Bacon *Along the Road* 123 A mason wasp landed on the stump at my shoulder, and made quick, jerky runs from crevice to crevice of the bark. **1971** Miller *Common Insects* 25 A well known solitary wasp is the Mason Wasp..which also occurs in Australia and elsewhere in the Pacific. It is usually, but quite incorrectly, called a mason bee. **1982** Frame *Is-land* (1984) 56 We noted [at Oamaru]..the insects, bees, mason bees, night bees.

Massey. [f. the name of William Ferguson *Massey* (1856–1925), a supporter of small-farmers' interests; Prime Minister, 1912–25.]

1. *Obs.* WW1. Usu. *pl.* Army issue boots; Bill Massey 1.
 1917 *The Digger* (Troopship pub.) 26 Tiny looked his very best in his 'Massey's'. **1919** *Quick March* 10 Oct. 33 Tom knocked the tea-leaves out of his otherwise empty pannikin, against the heel of his 'Masseys', and gravely spat. [**1939** Mulgan *First With the Sun* 119 Mr Massey, however, gave his name to the army boot.]

2. Special Comb. **Massey's Cossacks** (usu. *pl.*, occas. *ellipt.* **Cossack**) *hist.*, a name given by their opponents to the mounted special constables recruited in 1913 to control strikers (see SPECIAL *n.* 2 a); also (quot. 1993) occas. misapplied (or transferred) to the special constables recruited to control unemployed protesters in the Depression of the 1930s (see SPECIAL *n.* 2 b).
 1946 Soljak *NZ* 62 The Government [of 1913], the employers and the farmers retaliated by organizing special constables and vigilante groups, known to unionists as 'Massey's Cossacks' to work the ports and break the strike. **1959** Sinclair *History NZ* 206 The Farmers' Union organized its effort on military lines and enrolled mounted farmers as 'specials' and others to form 'arbitrationist' unions to work the wharves and even to man ships... In Wellington there was some fighting between the strikers and 'Massey's Cossacks'. **1989** Barber *NZ* 94 In Wellington 'Massey's Cossacks' with Bernard Freyberg (later Commander of the Second New Zealand Expeditionary Force) amongst them, charged wildly up Bolton Street and into Post Office Square, firing their revolvers and batoning all in or near their paths. The port was opened by force. **1989** *Those Were the Days* 17 Whether 'scab' or 'Cossack' or plain looker-on, New Zealanders could say 'Aye' to that. **1993** Bertram *Capes of China* 48 The only serious clashes [in Auckland in 1932] took place in Karangahape Road; most of them were provoked by the reckless behaviour of 'Massey's Cossacks', territorials from the Waikato Mounted Rifles who had been drafted up from the farm with their horses, and armed with those longer wooden batons that were so awkward to handle for unskilled riders.

3. In composition **Masseyism** *hist.*, the (collective) policies of the Massey government; **Masseyite** *hist.*, a supporter of these policies.
 1905 *Truth* 24 June 2 Coquetting with the Masseyites. **1906** *Ibid.* 28 Apr. 3 Masseyism is dead.

mat. *Hist.*

1. a. Formerly the name given by Europeans (poss. first by seamen: see 1770 quot.) to any of various Maori outer garments, or other coverings, that usually were, or appeared to be, flat pieces of woven material (usu. of New Zealand flax) and very often decorated with thrums; a Maori cloak or garment. See also *flax mat* (FLAX 5 c), KAKAHU.
 [**1770** Cook *Journals* 31 Mar. (1955) I. 279 Their common clothing are very much like square thrum'd matts that are made of rope yarns &c. to lay at the doors or passages into houses to clean one [*sic*] shoes upon, these they tye round their necks the thrum'd side out and are generally large enough to cover the body as low as the knee; they are made with very little preparation of the broad grass plant before meantioned.] **1773** Forster *Resolution Jrnl.* 28 Mar. (1982) II. 242 The oldest man..had a redbrown Matt on his back; The rest..had likewise Matts, but of a whiter hue, than the old Mans. **1791** Bell *Jrnl. Voyage H.M.S. 'Chatham'* (Vancouver exped.) (ATLMS) Nov. 6 Most of them [*sc.* Chatham Islanders] were cover'd with Matts and Seal Skins hung loosely over their Shoulders, which reach'd down to about the Hip. **1807** Savage *Some Acc. of NZ* 50 The dress of the natives consists in a mat finely woven of the native flax..with a fringe all round. **1817** Nicholas *Voyage NZ* 13 Dec. I. 75 The dress he [*sc.* Duaterra] put on consisted of a large mat made of flax, which descended below his waist, and was fastened round it by a belt of the same material. **1830** Craik *New Zealanders* 177 We mean the plant from which the natives fabricate..the cloaks, or mats, as they have been somewhat improperly called, which form their clothing. **1849** Torlesse *Papers* (1958) 72 He gave me a dogskin mat by the Ngaticahounas [Ngatikahungunu]. **1859** Thomson *Story NZ* II. 249 [Tamihana] rose with the sun, shook the fleas out of his mat, and joined the consistent Christians in prayer and praise. **1866** Angas *Polynesia* 155 Before the introduction of blankets, the clothing of the New Zealanders consisted entirely of garments manufactured from the fibres of the native flax. These garments, or 'mats,' as they are generally termed, display great ingenuity and taste in their fabrication. **1883** Domett *Ranolf & Amohia* II. 4 Some extra mats for tent-roofs against rain. **1913** Adams *Collected Verses* 30 Then the impatient chiefs Of Awhita, flinging their mats aside And grasping *meres*, to the war-dance sprang. **1940** *Tales of Pioneer Women* (1988) 252 The high class women..stayed at home and made mats—piupiu from the fibre of flax, pokeka, rain mats from dried flax.

b. As **Maori mat, native mat.**
 1827 Williams *NZ Jrnl.* (1961) 7 Jan. 36 On their landing, many of them were stripped and furnished with native mats. **1846** Johnson *Notes from Jrnl.* 22 Dec. in Taylor *Early Travellers* (1959) 119 [This]..with two good blankets wrapped up in a Maori mat, is the personal baggage. **1874** Baines *Edward Crewe* 231 But in days gone by..the above style of house was almost a necessity, Maori mats [were] quite an insufficient barrier against the cold during the winter nights. **1890** *Otago Witness* (Dunedin) 31 July 31 The bride wore a lovely Maori mat, and Tamatoa the Salvation Army uniform. **1906** *Truth* 27 Jan. 5 Second-hand Maori mats. **1938** Hyde *Nor Yrs. Condemn* 116 They had carried Massey through packed streets in Wellington, in..a coffin draped with the Union Jack and a fine Maori mat. **1984** *Metro* (Auckland) May 124 The coffin was covered with a Maori mat and borne by Cabinet ministers.

2. Also **bed mat, Maori mat.** A (sleeping) mat laid on the floor or used as a covering.
 1834 Markham *NZ* (1963) 41 The Chief..gave me a small mat to sleep in and cut fresh Palm leaves, and a clean Mat for me to sleep on. **1842** *Piraki Log* 15 Aug. (1911) 143 Slept on a Maori mat, wrapped in a blanket. **1871** Grace *Journal* 28 Oct. in *Pioneer Missionary* (1928) 237 He took out a box and placed on the floor three of the finest sleeping-mats I have ever seen, and quite new. **1881** Campbell *Poenamo* 155 After rolling yourself in your blanket, horse-rug, or Maori mat, you could sleep most comfortably. **c1920** Beattie *Trad. Lifeways Southern Maori* (1994) The bed coverings were several mats of the softest whitau... These bed mats were called kakahu, the same as the mats worn by persons, but were larger..than the ones for personal wear. **1936** in *Na To Hoa Aroha* (1988) III. 212 The arts and crafts section comprised..rough kits and floor mats. **1940** Cowan *Sir Donald Maclean* 109 He addressed his speech to a lone white man who sat before him on a mat in the meeting house. **1953** *Here & Now* Aug. 21 Beneath the carven counterparts of their ancestors..the Maoris lament on their mats. **1986** *Evening Post* (Wellington) 31 Oct. 6 Te Atiawa women are still plaiting the mat to be laid at the main door.

3. Allusively referring to the Maori way of life in various phrases. **a.** Esp. in phr. **to go (back) to the mat**, **to return to the mat**, of a Europeanized Maori, to return to Maori customs and way of life as though resuming the old Maori dress; to 'go native'. Cf. BLANKET 1.
 1933 Scanlan *Tides of Youth* 109 Some of the Maoris, educated in youth and brought up in British ways, returned in later life 'to the mat'. **1947** Gaskell *All Part of the Game* (1978) 88 She spoke so pleasantly that Miss Brown decided she must have been somewhere to a Maori High School and then come back to the mat. **1951** Kohere *Autobiography of a Maori* 102 Many a Te Aute boy has been said to have 'gone to the mat', or to have answered 'the call of the wilds', because, after receiving a college education he has gone back to the pa, making little or no use of his education. **1965** Sargeson *Memoirs of Peon* 17 But eventually Aramati left us ('to go back to the mat', my grandmother said). **1976** Morrieson *Pallet on Floor* 49 They all go back to the mat in the end. What's bred in the bone comes out in the flesh... Eating dried shark and sleeping on the mat... Back to the mat. I've seen it time and again. **1988** *Through the Looking Glass* 128 Even an educated 'Pakeha-fied' Maori would end by going 'back to the mat'. **1994** Lasenby *Dead Man's Head* 15 Her mother had more than a touch of the tar brush, and the girl will end up going back to the mat, I'll be bound.

b. In the phr. **to come under (a person's) mat**, to accept as a protector, or as a betrothed.
 1938 Lancaster *Promenade* 235 'Perhaps it's better,' said Tiffany with youth's cruelty towards an unwanted lover. 'Hemi is always asking me to come under his mat.'

c. In the phr. **to wear the mat**, to assume a Maori way of life.
 1938 Lancaster *Promenade* 117 One day I think all Maoris will wear the mat again.

d. In the phr. **to live on the mat**, to live in Maori fashion.
 1948 Ballantyne *Cunninghams* (1976) 142 He believed her grandmother practically lived on the mat and her mother was something of a hard-doer.

4. Comb. **mat pin**.
 1903 *TrNZI* XXXV. 112 The more common things to be found in the neighbourhood of old settlements are bone mat-pins, bone barbs of fish-hooks.

mata: see MATATA *n.*[1]

matagauri, matagory, varr. MATAGOURI.

matagouri /mætəˈguri/, /mætəˈgæuri/, /mætəˈgori/. [An alteration of Ma. *tūmatakuru*.] Also with much variety of form following various pronunciations: the preferred modern spelling **matagouri** (with **matagowry, matagory**) represent forms where the last element rhymes with 'goori', 'cowrie', 'gory' respectively. Early spellings fall into three groups: (a) a **tumatakuru** group: *tomata-guru, tomatagorra* (see TUMATAKURU for further variants); (b) a **matakuru** group: *matakura, matakuri; matakauri, matakouri, matakoura, matakowri;* (c) a **matagouri/ matagory** group: *matagauri, matagowri(e). Discaria toumatou* (fam. Rhamnaceae), a thorny native bush or small tree forming thickets in open country, esp. in the South Island. See also HAWTHORN a, *scrub-thorn* (SCRUB *n.* 1 c), TUMATAKURU, WILD IRISHMAN.

c1857 GARVIE (Rep. on Otago) in Beattie *Early Runholding* (1947) 19 Towards the Manuherikia only a few patches of matakaru, and a dark small-leaved shrub are to be met with. **1859** *Otago Gaz.* 22 Sept. 280 Much of it is encumbered with matakura scrub. **1890** *Zealandia* I. 613 A few stunted matakuri (or Wild Irishman). **1896** *Otago Witness* (Dunedin) 7 May 48 The tea generally tastes of birch or matagouri. **1897** *Tom Bracken's Annual* No.2 37 That matagauri ridge beyond was called the camping ground. **1898** MORRIS *Austral-English* 289 *Matagory, n.* a prickly shrub of New Zealand... also called *Wild Irishman*... The Maori name is *Tumatakuru*, of which *Matagory*, with various spellings, is a corruption, much used by rabbiters and swagmen. **1909** THOMPSON *Ballads About Business* 43 By the mountain creeks that murmur where the matagauri grows. **1914** in *Hist. N. Otago from 1853* (1978) 42 Continuing our walk we find it impeded by a tangle of tussock, bracken, flax, matakouri, spear grass,..all of which has vanished today. **c1919** COCKAYNE in McCaskill *Molesworth* (1969) 154 On the rather loose soil of the gentle slopes [of the Upper Awatere Valley] where there are thickets of wild Irishman or matagouri (*Discaria toumatou*) are many rabbit warrens. **1924** *Otago Witness* (Dunedin) 11 Nov. 66 The thief had disappeared—lost among the spear-pointed matakowri. **1925** BATHGATE *Random Recolls.* 27 I saw that the supposed bushranger was a compact bush of matakoura or wild Irishman. **1939** BRASCH *Collected Poems* (1984) 5 Only the thorn Alone on the parched rise, inhuman matakauri Dry-green and fibrous, sorrowing. **1945** *NZ Geogr.* 154 The steppe was originally burned to get rid of the matagowrie and spear grass. **1953** *Landfall 28* 253 I—who would have gladly gone Barefoot a thousand miles across Matagouri, so we were one. **1966** *Encycl. NZ* II. 680 Many native plants have Maori names more or less mutilated such as *matagowri, goai* (kowhai), and *biddy bid* (piri piri). **1978** MOORE & IRWIN *Oxford Book NZ Plants* 88 *Discaria toumatou*, matagouri, tumatu-kuru, wild Irishman. **1988** MIKAERE *Te Maiharoa* 78 There was the little thing..playing about quite happily amongst the matagouri and the taramea.

matagowri(e), matagowry, varr. MATAGOURI.

matai /ˈmætai/. Also early **mataihi**. [Ma. /mataˈiːˌ/: Williams 187 *Mataī, n.*]

1. *Prumnopitys taxifolia* (formerly *Podocarpus spicatus*) (fam. Podocarpaceae), a robust, long-lived coniferous tree of lowland forests, much prized for its heavy and durable timber; also the wood or timber. See also *black pine* (PINE 2 (2) a), MAI a.

1831 [see MAI a]. **1835** YATE *NZ* (1970) 50 Matai..a plant with a small yew-tree leaf, a strong smell, and a rough bark. **1843** *NZ Jrnl.* IV. 217 We crossed a small stream..and entered the bush, which consists principally of totara, rimu and mataihi. **1853** EARP *NZ* 113 Of the [Wairarapa] plain, about 100,000 acres is covered with fine timber, chiefly totara, matai..&c., all highly valuable for..cabinet work and carpentry. **1877** *TrNZI* IX. 159 I have in this paper adhered to the popular [Canterbury, Otago] name of black-pine for this timber, but the native name matai is always used in the North. **1890** *PWD Catalogue Timbers* (NZ & South Seas Exhib.) 12 Matai (black pine)... A useful wood, heavy, close grained, easily worked, shrinking little. **1910** COCKAYNE *NZ Plants & Their Story* 41 The matai..is a fine wood for resisting weather. **1954** DUFF *Shepherd's Calendar* (1961) 202 The boys have cut down rimu, totara, matai, and pinus growing on the property. **1984** MORTON *Whirinaki* 83 [Caption] Matai growth is very slow, annual rings averaging only about 0.7 mm.

2. Special Comb. **matai beer** (see also *pine-beer* (PINE 3)), the sap, or a mixture of sap and water, taken from certain matai trees (possibly later fermented) and drunk as a 'beer' (according to informants the term was used from at least c1900 by Marlborough bushmen); **matai beetle,** see BEETLE 8.

1920 *Quick March* 10 Dec. 11 I dimly remember as a youngster in the days when the Forty-Mile Bush was still standing, such a drink as 'matai beer' was sometimes spoken of amongst bushmen. Apparently it was made from the sap of the matai tree, extracted by the simple process of boring an auger-hole in the trunk. **1921** *Ibid.* 10 Feb. 13 In Carterton..in the 'sixties, when there was little else than bush there..I have frequently drunk the matai beer which gushes out of the centre of the tree when the axemen get to the heart. The flavour varies, but always has something of the tang of resin about it, though it is not at all a bad drink... I never heard of this matai beer being intoxicating. **1961** MACKAY *Puborama* 95 In the rip-roaring times of the King Country, Matai beer was a favourite with those who were strong enough and tough enough to drink it. It went out of favour when 'cruisers' for the various timber mills complained that much good yellow pine was being ruined through the number of deep axe cuts and even auger holes in the standing trees, made to let the potent juice run into waiting pannikins or buckets. The favourite recipe for this form of wood alcohol represented the addition of three or four cupsful of the sap to each gallon of 'ordinary' liquid refreshment. That the resultant mixture had a pretty hefty kick to it may be judged from this description handed in to the Taihape newspaper (1912): 'Matai beer is the term used to describe a certain brand or grade of alcoholic brew. It may be identified easily. It smells like an ancient bar room the morning after. It tastes like used machine oil, only a very low grade of machine oil.' **1978** FULLER *Maori Food & Cook.* 83 [Heading] Matai Beer. I have been told by old bushmen and Maoris about making beer from the sap of the matai tree... Apparently when the tree was being cut down the watery sap was collected, more water was added and also some ordinary beer, or yeast. It was left to ferment and was reputed to be quite strong though I have not been able to find any written evidence of this. **1990** CROWE *Native Edible Plants of NZ* 32 Early bushmen drank the sap and called it matai beer. To collect this, a tree which had a black stain running up the trunk would be drilled at its base with an auger, then plugged and tapped as a barrel. Kirk points out that the young trees rarely contain much of this beer, and that very old trees produce sap of 'a sour, acrid and unpleasant flavour'. Taken from the right trees, however, the newly collected sap is 'brisk and refreshing; but, like many other beverages, speedily becomes 'flat' when exposed to the air'. Easterfield and McDowell describe the liquid as 'light-brown', and say that its taste is 'styptic and sweetish, followed by a bitter after-taste'. Matai beer was regarded as effective against tuberculosis (Brooker & Cooper).

mataitai. [Ma. /maːˈtaitai/: Williams 187 *Mātai (ii). Sea... mātaitai... n.* Fish or other foodstuffs obtained from the sea or from lakes.] As **mataitai reserve,** an area of water over which Maori people have exclusive fishing rights.

1992 *Dominion* (Wellington) 7 Dec. 2 Alarm about mataitai reserves, where only Maori people could fish, could put the Sealord's settlement at risk. **1992** *Evening Post* (Wellington) 12 Dec. 5 Proposed mahinga mataitai (sea-food gathering) reserves will be set aside for exclusive use by particular Maori tribes.

matakauri, var. MATAGOURI.

matakite. [Ma. /ˈmatakite/: Williams 188 *Matakite. 1. n.* Seer, one who foresees an event; also the vision.] A Maori seer; the power of second sight.

1856 SHORTLAND *Traditions & Superstitions* 125 In the first place, his father goes to consult the *matakite*, or seer of the family, to learn the cause of the illness. **1878** BULLER *Forty Yrs. NZ* 202 The *Matakite*, or seers, were analogous to the clairvoyant. **1922** COWAN *NZ Wars* (1955) I. 294 In our party was an old *tohunga*..; he was gifted with the power of *matakite*, or second sight. **1983** KING *Whina* 58 It was while Whina was at school..that she received the first intimation that she had the gift of matakite or second sight.

matakoura, matakouri, matakura, matakuri, matakuru, varr. MATAGOURI.

matapo, var. MATIPO.

matata, *n.*¹ Also **mata.** [Ma. /ˈmaːtaːtaː/: Williams 185 *Mātā (iii), mātātā, n...*fern-bird. = *kōtātā.*] FERNBIRD.

[**1820** LEE & KENDALL *NZ Gram. & Vocab.* 177 *Máta, s.* Name of a certain bird.] **1835** YATE *NZ* (1970) 60 *Matata*—A small dusky-coloured bird, with a white and brown spotted breast. **1842** GRAY *Fauna* in Dieffenbach *Travels in NZ* (1843) II. 189 *Sphenaeacus punctatus...* Mata of the natives of Tasman Bay... Matata... Lives in the Typha swamps and amongst fern. **1859** THOMSON *Story NZ* I. 25 The Matata, a small low-flying bird with a shrill cry..has four long and four short tail feathers, similar in texture to those of the Kiwi. **1863** *Richmond-Atkinson Papers* 29 Sept. (1960) II. 63 The korimakos in full chorus in the bush and the larks and matatas in the open land about us. **1873** BULLER *Birds NZ* 128 Mata, Matata, Kotata, Nako, and Koroaitito... It frequents the dense fern..of the open country. **1884** *NZJSc.* II. 283 Utick, Grass-bird, Matata.—At one time very commonly met with about the swamps and round the edges of lagoons where the coarse water grasses grew rankly. **1904** TREGEAR *Maori Race* 329 Some little swamp-birds (*matata*) were caught and torn to pieces. **c1920** BEATTIE *Trad. Lifeways Southern Maori* (1994) 166 There is still a bird called mataa to be found in the swamps. It is about the size of a sparrow. **1947** POWELL *Native Animals NZ* 86 Fern-bird (*Bowdleria punctata*)... It is the Matata of the Maoris. **1952** RICHARDS *Chatham Is.* 72 *Spheneacus.. rufescens.*.Chatham Island Fern Bird. Matata. **1985** *Reader's Digest Book NZ Birds* 274 Fernbird *Bowdleria punctata...* Swamp thrush, grass bird, matata. **1990** *Checklist Birds NZ* 203 *Bowdleria punctata punctata...* North Island Fernbird (*Matata*)... South Island Fernbird (*Matata*).

matata, *n.*² [Ma. /ˈmaːtaːtaː/: Williams 185 *Mātātā..1. Rhabdothamnus solandri.*] *Rhabdothamnus solandri* (fam. Gesneriaceae), a small shrub of North Island coastal and lowland forest, having soft hairy leaves and attractive orange tubular flowers.

1867 HOOKER *Handbook* 766 Matata, *Geolog. Surv. Rhabdothamnus Solandri*. **1961** MARTIN *Flora NZ* 228 In North Island forests the Matata is a common shrub distinguished at once by its handsome red-striped, pendulous, orange blossoms. **1978** MOORE & IRWIN *Oxford Book NZ Plants* 158 *Matata*. A slender branching shrub up to 2m tall.

match.

1. *pl.* Also **matchsticks**. A bar-room game played with matches.

1979 *Dominion* (Wellington) 12 Dec. 1 At one stage during the party she was Mr Reid sitting..playing 'matchsticks'... The game involved trying to throw a match into the other person's drink. If this happened, the loser had to drink a full glass of whisky. **1985** *Sites* XI. 18 (Hodges 'Drinking Vernacular') Even a simple game like matches requires that to avoid drinking a person must be able to skilfully toss a matchstick into a distant glass. **1988** *Dominion Sunday Times* (Wellington) 13 Mar. 16 Other well-known [drinking] games are Hokonui Swindle, Bottles..Cardinal Huff, All Blacks, Matches, and The Amazing Grimaldi Brothers.

2. In special Comb. **match-farming**, the habitual clearing of land by burning-off; **match-happy**, a farmer or farm-hand keen on habitual burning-off as a farming technique.

1950 *Evening Post* (Wellington) 8 May 8 The burning this year is threefold in origin: '**Match-farming**', to take advantage of the occasional season when fern will fire; fire from 'over the hill'..; and fire due to carelessness. **1969** MCCASKILL *Molesworth* 201 On Molesworth itself burning had ceased to be a major management practice but there was still the '**match-happy**' musterer.

matchsticks: see MATCH 1.

mate /ˈmate/, *n.*¹ [Ma. /ˈmate/: Williams 192 *mate. 1. Dead... 13.* sickness, injury, wound.] Sickness; injury. Esp. as **mate Maori**, ill health or death coming to one who has broken a tapu. See also MAKUTU A 2, *Maori sickness* (MAORI B 5 a).

[**1804** *Collins English Colony in NSW* 559 E-mattee, *means also* death. *Sick*. **1820** LEE & KENDALL *NZ Gram. & Vocab.* 178 *Máte... s.* Sickness. *a.* Sick.] **1851** *McLean Papers* (ATLTS) IX. 196 My 'mate' [*sc.* wound] detained me twelve days at one place. **1946** BEAGLEHOLE *Some Modern Maoris* 219 The sign most often taken to indicate this sort of sickness is that the sickness does not appear to be yielding readily to ordinary Maori or to pakeha methods of treatment. It is then considered to be a Maori sickness—a 'mate Maori' as the phrase is commonly used—and for sure, safe, and quick results, treatment should be referred to a Maori expert, a tohunga, either male or female, who will use a combination of religious prayer, seance-possession, and magic to restore the sick person to health. **1963** HENDERSON *Ratana* (1972) 9 To break the law of *tapu* was to die of *mate Maori*, the sickness caused by an uneasy Maori conscience or the influx of demons. **1979** BINNEY et al. *Mihaia* 25 Inexplicable sickness, *mate Maori*, is often attributed to evil forces living in the human body; their extraction, possible only by faith in the healer, is a major part of the role of a tohunga. **1987** *Metro* (Auckland) May 100 If a Maori is genuinely disturbed, in Maori terms, the answer again is to restore their mauri (life force), as for physical illness. This is particularly true for *mate* Maori, Maori sickness, which arises from spiritual and social causes, not physical ones (Pakehas would call it psychosomatic).

Hence in occas. early use **mate (matty)** *v.*, to kill.

1777 *Bayly's Journal* 15 Feb. in McNab *Historical Records* (1908) II. 220 [The New Zealanders] cry'd out he was Mattied, viz. kill'd; which made him & his other men rise up & attack our People.

mate /mæit/, *n.*² [Spec. use of Brit. *mate* habitual companion, an associate, fellow, comrade; a fellow-worker or partner: OED *mate n.*² 1 'Now only *colloq.*'.]

[*Note*] The most popular name for a friend or acquaintance (poss. also as a term of address) among esp. male adolescents (14–17 years) between 1951 and 1984 according to questionnaires given to college students: 74 male and 23 female noted it as a friendship term.

1. a. [AND 1834.] An equal partner in an enterprise.

1855 *Lyttelton Times* 18 Apr. 6 He [*sc.* McKenzie, the sheep stealer] stated that he had no mates with him, although traces of other men could be seen. **1869** *AJHR* D-6 3 True as steel to his mates, the digger's sympathies are reported to go no further. **1874** BAINES *Edward Crewe* 188 These men usually have 'mates' and are hired in pairs. **1899** BELL *In Shadow of Bush* 14 Harry and his mate had now been working in the bush districts of the North Island [on contract bushfalling] for two or three seasons. **1905** *Truth* 12 Aug. 5 His mate would look after him.

b. In the phr. **to be (go) mates (with)** [AND 1876], to work as an equal partner with.

1866 FARJEON *Grif* 162 It isn't a very gentlemanly thing..for you to have to go mates with an old lag. **1887** PYKE *Hist. Early Gold Discoveries Otago* (1962) 40 Both of us worked hard for a week or so, and got a few ounces with a tin dish. Read stayed with me during the time. He wanted me go 'mates' with him and find him in 'tucker'. **1898** *NZ Times Extra* Hawthorne and Philpotts went 'mates' as sleeper-getters.

c. As **dividing mate** *goldmining*, see quot.

1914 PFAFF *Diggers' Story* 79 The custom, which was quite common, of a party becoming dividing mates. This was a sort of partnership entered into..by which the men, before separating, agreed to share, in case any of them struck gold, with the others... Here are two instances—Joe had four dividing mates who were prospecting in various parts of the Coast.

2. [AND 1841.] An acquaintance or companion through circumstance, esp. one engaged in the same activity as oneself; occas. used by or of females.

1862 HODDER *Memories NZ Life* 71 My mates, or 'chums', [among the diggers] were a queer set. **1874** WILSON *Diary* in Wierzbicka *Wilson Family* (1973) 197 Joint is my mate [in a two-berth cabin] from Christchurch. **1881** NESFIELD *Chequered Career* 36 The out-station that I went to was about seventeen miles from the head-station... I was particularly fortunate in having a very decent companion for a 'mate'. **1964** MIDDLETON *Walk on Beach* 212 'I like your mate,' I said, meaning Marion. **1967** GROVER *Another Man's Role* 6 He'd go out with his mates and come home drunk. **1989** TE AWEKOTUKU *Tahuri* 13 The basketball Girls... Going to meet their mates. Going to play the game.

3. a. [AND 1891.] A loyal or 'sworn' (usu. male) friend; one whose loyalty is real and constant.

1866 BARKER *Station Life* (1870) 104 The pride and delight of his *mate* was much greater than my [dancing] partner's; he stood near his friend prompting him through the mazes of the most extraordinary quadrille. **1904** LANCASTER *Sons o' Men* 176 [A distraught back-country farmer's wife to her husband's friend.] 'Take me away! Take me where he can't find me! You're strong. You wouldn't let him have me back—' 'He's ma mate. He is ma mate, I tell ye. I canna dae him wrang. Ye dinna ken what ye say. He is ma mate.' 'Don't I know? Don't I?' **1939** CRESSWELL *Present Without Leave* 189 New Zealanders make the most reliable and dauntless companions there are, and in dangerous situations..will never leave a mate, as they call one another, for a moment. **1978** TAYLOR *Twilight Hour* 16 I never asked him any more questions either then or any other time... He was a great mate. **1987** VIRTUE *Redemption of Elsdon Bird* (1988) 16 Uncle Bryce..went to his best mate's house..and got shickered on beer.

b. As **old mate**, often as **me (my) old mate** /mi ˌjaʊl ˈmæit/ (often *joc.*). A bosom companion; a longtime close friend; also used in address.

1864 *Gold Digger's Notes* (1950) 50 I went to visit some old mates seven or eight miles off. *Ibid.* 51 I went digging again, with my old mate, of course. **1879** *Auckland Weekly News* 26 Apr. 6 Maynes had passed himself off..as an old mate of McLennan's. **1897** WRIGHT *Station Ballads* 16 'Look here, old mate,' says he, 'I'll cook the spuds... And you can build a duff!' 'All right, old mate,' says he, 'And good enough.' **1909** THOMPSON *Ballads About Business* 91 'Come along with me to Southland,' said my old mate then to me, 'You'll be sure to get some yacker.' **1952** *VUC First Yr. Eng. Class* 6 May I would include among New Zealand English words: *me ol' mate*. **1985** O'SULLIVAN *Shuriken* 21 It's the Army, my old mate. Your privilege is to serve. To defend. **1993** *Dominion* (Wellington) 20 Sept. 6 I have a niece..who gets on the blower..and rings up all her old mates in outer Pongolia or wherever.

4. [AND 1843; see also EDD 3 (Yorkshire, Notts.).] As a casual form of (usu.) friendly address mainly to a stranger. Cf. COBBER 2, DIGGER *n.*¹ 7, SPORT.

1865 CHUDLEIGH *Diary* 30 Apr. (1950) 179 Half the township would have shouted for me if I would have drank..and I was asked all down the river if I was the man that lost a fine horse saying Well mate, I am sorry for you. **1873** PYKE *Wild Will Enderby* (1889, 1974) III. i 77 See here, mate, I'll tell you what I conclude to do. **1897** WRIGHT *Station Ballads* 103 Sings out, 'Are you ready to go, Jack?' 'You can cast her adrift, mate,' I said. **1909** THOMPSON *Ballads About Business* 62 For he [*sc.* a swagger] was fairly well informed, although he called me 'Mate'. **1938** HYDE *Godwits Fly* (1970) 123 He was disappointed when the tramp called him 'Sir', instead of 'Digger' or 'Mate'. **1962** HORI *Half-gallon Jar* 24 This big joker say to me, 'Listen, mate, my horse has got no show.' **1979** HULME in *Islands* 25 240 'I said, your ticket mate.' He doesnt mean friend. **1980** MARSH *Photo-Finish* 201 'Are you thinking of Maria?' 'Too bloody right I am, mate.'

5. In the special collocation **mates' rates**, reduced preferential rates of payment for friends or acquaintance. Cf. 1660–63 *A Beggar I'll Be*, a black-letter broadside ballad in John S. Farmer *Musa Pedestris* (Cooper Square Publishers, N.Y.) (1964) 29 We bill all our Mates at very low rates, While some keep their Quarters as high as the fates.

1980 LELAND *Kiwi-Yankee Dict.* 64 *mates rates:* If you happen to be a plumber, storekeeper, paperhanger, etc. Mates rates is what you charge your friends, considerably discounted from what you charge the general public. **1991** MCCARTEN *Modest Apocalypse*

mate, v.

1. *Whaling.* As **to mate with**, of whale-ships, to sail together for a time. Also **mating** *vbl. n.* See also *keep* or *join company* (COMPANY *n.*²).

1836 *Log 'Mary Mitchell'* 27 Aug. in McNab *Old Whaling Days* (1913) 456 Mated with *South Boston* Butler. **1913** McNab *Old Whaling Days* 247 'Mating', or 'la pêche par association' was common to the French as well as the Americans, but no mention of it is made among the Australians.

2. To join another as a mate (MATE *n.*² 1).

1875 Whitworth *Cobb's Box* 5 How the other two ever got to mate with him I never could make out.

matepo, var. MATIPO.

mateship. [The NZ use was prob. derived from the Australian, being esp. freq. post-1960 as a term of social commentary: AND 1864.] Male comradeship, often regarded as an ideal.

1913 *NZ Observer* 25 Jan. 2 Mateship during a common danger or a common struggle is in most cases mateship of the best kind throughout life. **1921** *Quick March* 10 Sept. 13 When I married and started on my own, forty men came to help me fell the first bush... That is the true spirit of clanship and mateship. **1967** May *West Coast Gold Rushes* 301 Mateship among the diggers to some degree mitigated the hardships of gold-digging in a rough country. **1979** Gebbie & McGregor *Incredible 8-Ounce Dream* 46 One small city pub I worked in was living proof that mateship was integral to after-hours imbibing. **1986** Richards *Off the Sheep's Back* 64 At home I became more of a loner. I longed for the mateship and solidarity I had experienced when working in the bush. **1990** *Dominion* (Wellington) 17 Oct. 38 The play also looks at the New Zealand notion of 'mateship'. 'We have this notion of ourselves as valuing mateship, which is fine, but under the guise of mateship people can behave fairly disagreeably to each other,' he says.

matey. [f. MATE *n.*² + -Y: AND 1854.] An occas. term of friendly address.

1865 Chudleigh *Diary* 30 Apr. (1950) 179 One man exclaimed So help me there lies the finest horse that ever crossed the Terahmacow and all echoed him. Another said Matey never own a good horse, another said, Justly you might as well tell an overlander to drown himself at once as ride a bad horse. **1922** Mansfield *Stories* (1984) 489 Some one [*sic*] whistled, some one sang out, 'Are you right there, matey?' 'Matey!' The friendliness of it, the—the—Just to prove how happy she was, just to show the tall fellow how at home she felt, and how she despised stupid conventions... She felt just like a work-girl. **1951** 15 M 23 Wellington H.S. 29 Matey [M3]. **1951** 15 F 3 Marlborough College 29 Matey. **1995** Anderson *House Guest* 37 Emmeline laughed, 'I might get stuck, matey.'.. 'Don't you like being called matey?' He took off his glasses... 'I don't mind.'

Matilda. *Hist.* [AND 'Transf. but unexplained use of the female name', 1892.] **a.** SWAG *n.*¹ 1 a, esp. in phr. **to carry matilda, to give matilda a roll** (or **ride**), to go on the swag.

1906 *Truth* 17 Feb. 8 The poor devil [of a worker] is on the rocks, and has got to give Matilda a roll again, 68 [He] had decided to take a different route..so he could call in on his brother-in-law, who was repairing his motor mower at mates' rates. **1996** *Evening Post* (Wellington) 6 June 3 His job with NZ First was not full time and he was being employed on 'mates rates', he said. and swing her on to his hungry frame. **1906** Picard *Ups & Downs* 7 Put my bag of tricks in the hall—haden't [*sic*] formed acquaintance with dear Matilda or Miss Bluey in them days. *Ibid.* 8 [I] may some day have to give Matilda another ride through this spot they call God's own country. **1909** *Truth* 6 Nov. 1 Therefore, Woollcombe, get thee hence; go home thou wowser on the wallaby; hump bluey, carry Matilda, pad the hoof, thou parsonical howler. c**1926** The Mixer *Transport Workers' Song Book* 139 That night he packed up his 'Matilda'. **1937** Partridge *Dict. Slang* 512 *Matilda.* See *waltz Matilda.* Among New Zealanders (–1932), gen. *carry Matilda.*

b. *fig.* or *transf.* A burden.

1911 *Maoriland Worker* 9 June 2 Every [NZ] child born owes to the money lords of England £80! That's a nice little 'Matilda' for a million people to carry, isn't it?

matipo /ˈmætɪˌpʌu/. Also occas. **matapo, matepo, matipou.** [Ma. /ˈmatipou/: Williams 194 *Matipou..Myrsine australis...* = *māpou, tīpau.*]

1. Usu. with a modifier, one of a group of unrelated shrubs or small trees of roughly similar general appearance. See also MAPAU. **a.** *Pittosporum* spp., esp. *P. tenuifolium* (see *black matipo* 2 (1) below), and *P. eugenioides* (see *white matipo* 2 (5) below).

1853 [see MAPAU 1 a]. **1858** Smith *Notes of Journey* in Taylor *Early Travellers* (1959) 383 On most of the rivers about here [upper Waikato], grows a tree quite new to us; it is something like the matepo, and very graceful. **1866** Barker *Station Life* (1870) 94 Varieties of matapo..each leaf a study, with its delicate tracery of black veins on a yellow-green ground. **1880** *TrNZI* XII. 329 The tipau, or matipo (Pittosporum tenuifolium), makes the best ornamental hedge I know of. **1883** Chudleigh *Diary* 21 Apr. (1950) 321 Let Abner the fencing contract 4 miles..600 matipo posts per mile. **1903** *TrNZI* XXXV. 305 About the beginning of 1902 a branch of the so-called matipo (*Pittosporum tenuifolium*)..was sent to me. c**1920** Beattie *Trad. Lifeways Southern Maori* (1994) Rautawhiri, the black maple of the bushman, is often seen in hedge-form when it is called matipo by townspeople, the real matipo being a smaller shrub. **1939** [see MAPAU 1 a]. **1940** Studholme *Te Waimate* (1954) 242 The under-scrub was very dense, Matipo, Ini-Ini..Lemonwood and others. **1969** Hascombe *Down & Almost Under* 148 Sweet smelling matipo trees.

b. *Myrsine* spp., esp. *M. australis* (see *red matipo* 2 (2) below).

1853 [see MAPAU 1 a]. **1867** Hooker *Handbook* 766 Matipo, Middle Island... *Myrsine Urvillei.* **1889** Kirk *Forest Flora* 25 The mapau [*Myrsine urvillei*] is also known as the tipau and matipou. **1907** Laing & Blackwell *Plants NZ* 332 The name Matipo is generally applied by Europeans to *Pittosporum tenuifolium*, but this [*Myrsine australis*] is apparently the plant to which the Maoris attached it. **1946** *JPS* LV. 153 *Matipou*, a tree (Myrsine [sp.]), commonly mispronounced matipo, the 'o' with the non-Maori sound of the English diphthongal 'o'..or matapo: the Maori shortening of the word is mapou. **1960** Hilliard *Maori Girl* 152 Henry commented on the legs of the girls: 'Too thin! Like matipo.' 'Too much hino at the top!' **1975** *Evening Post* (Wellington) 19 Sept. 2 The only true Matipo has red stems and is also named Mapou (Myrsine australis). **1982** Matipou [see MAPAU 2 (2)].

2. With a modifier: **black, red, swamp, weeping, white.**

(1) black matipo. KOHUHU, esp. when used as a hedge-plant. See also *black mapau* (MAPAU 2 (1)).

1939 Cockayne & Turner *Trees NZ* 107 *Pittosporum tenuifolium* (Pittosporaceae). Kohuhu, Black Matipo. **1966** *Encycl. NZ* III. 711 Matipo, black.. matipo..*Pittosporum tenuifolium.* **1981** Harris *Field Guide Common NZ Trees & Shrubs* 8 *Kohuhu* (Black Matipo) *Pittosporum tenuifolium* Tree up to 10m. with black bark.

(2) red matipo. *Myrsine* (formerly *Suttonia*) *australis* (fam. Myrsinaceae), a shrub or small tree up to 6 m, having red bark on younger branches and branchlets, and leaves with very wavy margins. See also MAPAU 2 (2).

1900 *Canterbury Old and New* 184 matipo [**1900** *Note Pittosporum*].., red matipo [**1900** *Note*] *Myrsine urvillei*]. **1909** [see MAPAU 2 (2)]. **1940** Laing & Blackwell *Plants of NZ* 353 *Suttonia australis* (The Red Matipo). **1965** Gillham *Naturalist in NZ* 31 Scattered among the rest stood the broadleaf, the red matipo..and the wheki tree-fern.

(3) swamp matipo. *Myrsine* (formerly *Suttonia*) *coxii* (fam. Myrsinaceae), a shrub of swamp forest on the Chatham Islands.

1910 Cockayne *NZ Plants & Their Story* 124 The swamp-matipo, *Suttonia Coxii* [of the Chathams], with its pretty mauve varieties. **1952** Richards *Chatham Is.* 65 *Suttonia..chathamica..*Swamp Matipo. Mataira.

(4) weeping matipo. *Myrsine divaricata,* a shrub with drooping branchlets; *weeping mapou* (MAPAU 1).

1908 *AJHR* C-11 39 *Suttonia divaricata.* Weeping matipo. Forest, sub-alpine scrub. **1910** Cockayne *NZ Plants & Their Story* 60 The weeping-matipo (*Suttonia divaricata*)..the mountain-currant..the wauwaupaku. **1978** Moore & Irwin *Oxford Book NZ Plants* 116 Weeping or wiry matipo is widespread from lowland to subalpine levels.

(5) white matipo. TARATA.

1886 Kirk in *Settler's Handbook NZ* (1902) 121 [Native name] Kowhiwhi..[Settlers' name] White-matipo. **1940** Studholme *Te Waimate* (1954) 246 In this bush were..konini, white and red matipo.

matook, matou cou, varr. MATUKU.

Matric /maˈtrɪk/. *Hist.* A once-common abbrev. of MATRICULATION.

1929 *Na To Hoa Aroha* (1986) I. 182 The incentive to obtain licensed interpreters' certificates and Maori being made a subject for the Civil Service Entrance Exams formed the first outside step. Then followed the Matric. **1947** *NZ Observer* 3 Dec. 21 Once in every one and a-half years, on an average, there was a row about one or more 'Matric' papers. **1952** Thomson *Deer Hunter* 21 I've heard young men cursing the day they left the city to come to the back-country, wondering why they didn't work harder at school in their matric. year. **1962** Glover *Hot Water Sailor* (1981) 45 I got my Matric..at the age of fifteen [in the 1920s]. **1974** Morrieson *Predicament* (1981) 18 [He] was in the lower fifth form [in the 1930–40s]..which entitled him to have a tilt at the University Entrance examination known generally and erroneously in those days as 'Matric'. **1986** Crane *I Can Do No Other* 212 He found life very full..two hours' teaching a 'matric' (University Entrance) Evening Class in English. **1995** Slatter *One More River* 51 I had passed, to everybody's surprise..the University Entrance Examination known to us as Matric.

matriculation. *Obs.* [Transf. use of *matriculation* formal entry into a university.] The common former name for the University Entrance public examination, largely replaced by accrediting; esp. in the phr. **to get one's matriculation,** to pass the university entrance examination. See also MATRIC.

1875 *TrNZI* VII. 160 [Heading] *Subjects of Examination for Matriculation.* **1901** *NZJE* III. 89 If the matriculation sufficeth, why go to the expense and trouble of having a 'D' examination [*sc.* a teaching-certificate examination] at all? Or again, why does the Matriculated student receive his partial 'D', while the candidate who has passed..is denied Matriculation privileges. **1924** [see PUBLIC SERVICE 2]. **1933** SCANLAN *Tides of Youth* 163 Peter was making a final attempt to get his matriculation, his previous failure having greatly incensed his father. **1934** *Feilding Star* 12 Apr. 4 'This will be the business man's matriculation certificate,' declared..[the] Minister of Education, when the regulations were published of the School Certificate Examination. **1938** HYDE *Godwits Fly* (1970) 98 Carly hadn't to sit for matriculation, which would have frightened her out of her life. **1980** BENNETT *Canterbury Tale* 72 I had just passed Matriculation and the time seemed suitable.

Hence **matriculate** *v. intr.*, to pass or complete one's matriculation examination; often as **matriculated** *ppl. a.*, having passed the matriculation examination (see also quot. 1901 above).

1953 *Here & Now* June 29 *Peter*, survey chainman, matriculated, rep-footballer. **1956** *Landfall 40* 286 When he matriculated, he hadn't done as everyone expected and gone to the city to enrol at university. **1986** OWEN & PERKINS *Speaking for Ourselves* 176 My sister Dorothy went to Nelson College for Girls and matriculated and came home, and she passed what was called a 'D' certificate, the first of the teaching certificates.

matrix. As **matrix gold**, gold embedded in a matrix of quartz, etc. regarded as the main source of a find of alluvial gold (cf. OED *matrix* 3 a).

1852 *Coromandel Gold Field. Provisional Regulations* in Swainson *Auckland* (1853) 159 Regulations for the working of matrix Gold combined with Quartz or any other rock, remaining in its original place of deposit, will be published as soon as conveniently may be, and as occasion may require... All alluvial or matrix Gold procured without due authority..will be liable to be seized. **1853** *NZGG* 12 Jan. VI. 1:2 (Heaphy's Report) The parties..are continuing..with every prospect of finding eventually the matrix Gold, which the nuggets now obtained indicate to be in the vicinity of the workings. **1890** *TrNZI* XXII. 403 This would point to the mammillated appearance being caused by a certain amount of attrition on the rough, pointed, matrix gold.

matua grass: see GRASS 2 (24).

matuawhapuku. [Ma. /'matua 'fa:puku/: Williams 195 *Matuawhāpuku*..red rock cod.] *red rock cod* (COD 2 (7)). See also *grandfather hapuku* (HAPUKU 3), *grandaddy groper* (GROPER 2 (3)).

1921 [see COD 2 (7)]. **1957** PARROTT *Sea Angler's Fishes* 163 Scientific name: *Ruboralga cardinalis*. Common name: Red Rock Cod. Maori name: Matuawhapuku. **1966** DOOGUE & MORELAND *Sea Anglers' Guide* 289 Red Scorpionfish... *Scorpaena cardinalis;* red rock cod, scarpee, grandfather hapuku, cobbler; red rock cod (Australia); matua-whapuku (Maori). **1982** AYLING *Collins Guide* (1984) 196 Sea Perch (Jock Stewart, Matua-whapuku) *Helicolenus percoides*..(*Helicolenus papilosus*). **1991** BRADSTOCK *Fishing* 21 *Red scorpionfish.* Other names: grandfather hapuku, grandaddy [*sic*] groper, red rock cod, matuawhaapuku.

matuhi. Also **matuhituhi**. [Ma. /'ma:tuhi/, /ma:'tuhituhi/: Williams 195 *Mātuhi*... *mātuhituhi*..*Xenicus longipes*, bush wren.] WREN 2 (1) (*Xenicus longipes*).

1873 BULLER *Birds NZ* 115 Xenicus longipes. (Bush-wren)... Matuhituhi, Piwauwau..and Huru-pounamu. **1947**, **1955**, **1966** [see WREN 2 (1)]. **1985** *Reader's Digest Book NZ Birds* 265 Bush Wren *Xenicus longipes*... This tiny, inconspicuous bird may be extinct... Other Names: Matuhituhi, green wren, Tom Thumb bird. **1989** PARKINSON *Travelling Naturalist* 74 Here..examples of the bush wren or matuhi were taken about 1850.

matuka, var. MATUKU.

matuku /mʌ'toku/. Also early **matook, matou cou, matuka**. [Ma. /'matuku/: Williams 195 *Matuku*.]

1. Any of several wading birds of the fam. Ardeidae. [Cf. 1820 LEE & KENDALL *NZ Gram. & Vocab.* 178 Matúku, *s.* A bird so called.] **a.** [Ma. Williams 195 *Matuku*, n. *1*... Brown bittern, = *matuku-hurepo*.] BITTERN 2 (1) (*Botaurus poiciloptilus*). See also MATUKU-HUREPO.

1847 *NZ Journal* VII. 218 At dawn, I heard the voices of the natives..in a village, from which I had been separated only by a Raupo swamp below me..the favourite haunt of the Matuka, or bittern. **1859** THOMSON *Story NZ* I. 27 Three of the *Heron* family live on the land. The Matuku, or bittern, has the cry of a bull. **1867** HOCHSTETTER *NZ* 293 The New Zealand bittern or Matuku (*Botaurus melanotus*), and the wild-duck. **1882** HAY *Brighter Britain* II. 221 The Matuku..is a bittern, long-legged and billed... The Maori are expert at catching them but I cannot say that bittern meat is good. **1907** DRUMMOND *Life & Work of Richard John Seddon* 374 Listen to the sullen matuku, The bittern that bellows in the swamp. **1945** BEATTIE *Maori Place-names Canterbury* 64 The matuku, or bittern, once common enough is not mentioned [in Maori food lists]. **1966** [see BITTERN 2 (1)]. **1990** *Checklist Birds NZ* 93 *Botaurus poiciloptilus*... Australasian Bittern (*Matuku*).

b. Also **matukutuku**. [Ma. /'ma:tukutuku/: Williams 195 *Matuku*, n... *2*. *Demigretta matook*, blue heron..*matuku-moana*..*mātukutuku*.] HERON 2 (1). Cf. MATUKU-MOANA.

1842 GRAY *Fauna* in Dieffenbach *Travels in NZ* (1843) II. 196 *Herodias matook*... Matook of the natives of Queen Charlotte's Sound... Matou cou. **1844** [see CRANE 1]. **1862** *Richmond-Atkinson Papers* 23 Nov. (1960) I. 803 In the afn. while we [were] sitting on the beach..a matuku, a small blue heron, came down near us. I have not seen one for several years. **1888** BULLER *Birds NZ* II. 129 Ardea sacra. (Blue Heron)... Matuku-tai, Matuku-nuia, and Matukutuku. **1904** [see HERON 2 (1)]. **1946** *JPS* LV. 153 *matuku*, two birds, 1, Botaurus poeciloptilus, bittern, and 2, Demigretta sacra, blue-heron; the Maori distinguished these two according to their habitat: 1, matuku-hurepo (swamp matuku) and 2, matuku-moana (sea-matuku). When the Pakeha mentions the matuku he always refers to the bittern; the other he always calls blue-heron. **1971** mātukutuku [see HERON 2 (1)].

c. [Ma. Williams 195 *Matuku*, n... *3*. *Notophoyx novaehollandiae*, white-faced heron.] HERON 2 (2). Cf. MATUKU-MOANA.

1885 [see HERON 2 (2)].

2. *Fishermen*. A wet fly (poss. orig. made from bittern's feathers).

1950 *Landfall 16* 306 I quickly put on a matuku; the largest wet fly in the box.

matuku-hurepo. Also **matuku urepo**. [Ma. /'matuku 'hurepo/ = 'swamp-matuku': cf. Williams 195 *Matuku 1*.] BITTERN 2 (1). See also MATUKU 1 a.

[**1820** LEE & KENDALL *NZ Gram. & Vocab.* 178 Matúku Urepo; [A bird so called.]] **1835** YATE *NZ* (1970) 67 *Matuku urepo*—This bird is a species of crane. **1844** COLENSO *Excurs. Northern Is.* in Taylor *Early Travellers* (1959) 54 This bird is very shy... Its plumage has a very elegant appearance, being of light colour underneath, and reddish-brown on the back and wings, dappled with black... The native name for this bird is, Matukuhurepo. **1870** *TrNZI* II. 69 Botaurus poicilopterus... Matukuhurepo. Bittern. Not so frequently met with as before such an extensive breadth of swamp-land had been drained and cultivated. **1888** [see BITTERN 2 (1)]. **1904** HUTTON & DRUMMOND *Animals NZ* 195 *The Bittern.—Matuku-hurepo*. **1947**, **1966**, **1985** [see BITTERN 2 (1)].

matuku-moana. [Ma. /'matuku 'moana/ = 'sea/lake matuku': cf. Williams 195 *Matuku 2*.] Either of the *reef heron* or *white-faced heron* (HERON 2 (1) or (2)). Cf. MATUKU 1 b and c.

1904 HUTTON & DRUMMOND *Animals NZ* 192 *The White-fronted Heron.—Matuku-moana. Notophoyx novae-hollandiae*. **1947** [see HERON 2 (1)]. **1955** [see HERON 2 (2)]. **1966** [see CRANE 1]. **1987** POWELL *Native Animals NZ* 74 Reef Heron (Matuku Moana) *Egretta sacra*. This is a graceful slaty-grey bird with long beak and legs of bright yellow.

matukutuku: see MATUKU 1 b.

matuku urepo, var. MATUKU-HUREPO.

mauku. [Ma. /'mauku/: Williams 197 *Mauku*..*1*. *Asplenium bulbiferum* and *Hymenophyllum* spp.] Either *Asplenium bulbiferum*, *hen and chicken fern* (FERN 2 (7)); or less commonly, the filmy ferns *Hymenophyllum* spp., or other ferns.

1922 COWAN *NZ Wars* (1955) II. 219 'It was usual, too,' added the old *pakeha-Maori*, 'to cook some *pikopiko*, the young curly fronds of the *mauku* or ground-fern, with the [human] meat'. *Ibid.* II. 428 A rather good bush vegetable is the *pikopiko*, the curled shoots of the *mauku* fern. The natives have long given up the use of these bush foods. **1929** FIRTH *Primitive Econ. NZ Maori* 51 The young fronds of the *mauku*..also furnished vegetable food. **1952** RICHARDS *Chatham Is.* 5 *Hymenophyllum*..*rarum*..Filmy Fern. Mauku (for all the filmy ferns). **1981** BROOKER et al. *NZ Medicinal Plants* 25 *Asplenium bulbiferum*... Hen and chickens fern Maori names: *Mauku, mouku* 'Mauku' has been identified as *Asplenium bulbiferum*, *Cordyline pumilio*, and *Hymenophyllum* spp. by Williams and as *Asplenium bulbiferum* by Best. 'Mouku' has been identified as *Asplenium bulbiferum* by Williams and as *Marattia salicina* by Tregear. **1982** WILSON *Stewart Is. Plants* 36 *Asplenium bulbiferum* Hen and Chickens Fern... Mauku..most fronds sprouting tiny plants (bulbils) which drop off.

maunga-maunga, var. MANGEMANGE.

mauri. [Ma. /'mauri/: Williams 197 *Mauri* (i) *mouri*..*1*. Life principle, thymos of man...*2*. Source of the emotions..*3*. Talisman, a material symbol of the hidden principle protecting vitality, *mana*, fruitfulness, etc. of people, lands, forests, etc.] The life force or principle.

1910 *Kai Tiaki* July 104 The mind of every Maori is well stored with those different 'karakia'..to protect the life principle (Mauri) of man. **1936** in *Na To Hoa Aroha* (1988) III. 227 No doubt the face presented by the ensemble of marae and camp organisation...together with the mauri of the meeting of diverse, scattered

MAURI

tribal elements, might be characterised as excellent. **1983** *Dominion* (Wellington) 6 July 4 He also held the title of mauri, 'life and soul' of those tribes and of the Ringatu Church. **1985** HOWE *Towards 'Taha Maori'* in *English* (NZATE) 21 Maoris strongly believe in mauri, and just as a life force may wax or wane depending on a person's health or status, so can his or her 'mauri'. Lack of mauri can cause a person to die. **1987** *Metro* (Auckland) May 100 If a Maori is genuinely disturbed, in Maori terms, the answer again is to restore their mauri (life force), as for physical illness.

mauri, maury, mauvre, varr. MAORI.

mawhai. [Ma. /'ma:fai/: Williams 198 *Māwhai* (i)..*1*...a plant.] *Sicyos australis* (formerly *angulata*) (fam. Cucurbitaceae), a native scrambling plant of the northern North Island having spinose gourd-like fruits.
 1853 HOOKER *II Flora Novae-Zelandiae I Flowering Plants* 72 *Sicyos angulatus*... Nat. name, 'Mawhai'. **1867** HOOKER *Handbook* 766 Mawhai, Col[enso]. *Sicyos angulatus.* **1906** CHEESEMAN *Manual NZ Flora* 190 *S[icyos] angulata, Linn.* Mawhai. **1924** *NZJST* VII. 382 The mawhai..is a trailing plant belonging to the pumpkin and gourd family... The fruits are armed with barbed spines. **1961** ALLAN *Flora NZ* I. 319 Dist.: K., Three Kings, N. Coastal to lat. 39° 30´, now mainly on islands *Mawhai.*

mawree, mawry, varr. MAORI.

maxi. [f. *maxi*(mum security prison.] (Paremoremo) maximum security prison. Cf. PARRIE.
 1995 *New Zealandia* (Auckland) July 48 I was also touched by..[the prison ministry team member's] kindness in maxi (Paremoremo maximum security prison). Now I am in the medium prison.

McGuiness, M(a)cGinnis: see GOODBYE 2.

mearee, var. MERE.

meat-axe. In the phr. **(as) mad as a meat-axe**, very angry or eccentric, see MAD *a*., c.

meat works. [AND 1895.] A FREEZING WORKS or abattoir.
 1950 *Landfall 14* 125 As I get off the bus this morning and sniff the first cloying smells from the meat works I don't mind. **1959** MCLINTOCK *Descr. Atlas* 57 A further meat export works being erected near Invercargill should commence killing in 1960. **1960** CRUMP *Good Keen Man* 46 The hut stank like a meat works.

meccano set. *Obs. Prison.* A jocular or euphemistic name for a hangman's movable scaffold.
 1980 MACKENZIE *While We Have Prisons* 44 At this time it was decided to have a movable scaffold capable of being transported to wherever required... A later version of this contraption became known as the Meccano Set—a term used in official telegrams— 'Meccano Set arrived safely and erected'. *Ibid.* 73 Suitable secrecy surrounded the arrival of the completed scaffold and a telegram went to Head Office, Justice Department, that the 'Meccano Set' had arrived safely. **1993** YSKA *All Shook Up* 168 The sack filled with sand..could be used [at Mt Eden prison in 1955] on dry-run hangings on the silver-painted steel gallows, known as the 'Meccano Set'.

medal: see COOK MEDAL.

meero, var. MIRO *n.*¹

meeting house. The central large building on a marae, usu. decorated, and used as a place of assembly for discussion, and for a communal sleeping-quarters for visitors. See also *wharenui, wharepuni, whare runanga* (WHARE 2).
 [*Note*] The concept is post-European. The earlier CARVED HOUSE q.v. often seemed to be a chief's dwelling or used for a special purpose.
 1873 TINNE *Wonderland of Antipodes* 9 Enjoying dry..quarters at the great 'whare-puna', or meeting-house, of the tribe. **1891** WALLACE *Rural Econ. Austral. & NZ* 218 [Caption] Maori Whare-Pani [*sic*], or Meeting House. **1904** TREGEAR *Maori Race* 277 There are still some beautifully carved specimens of tribal meeting-houses to be seen, but almost all have been spoilt by the introduction of European doors and windows. **1924** *TrNZI* LV. 367 In many places, the tribal meeting-house stands alone or flanked by a solitary cook-house, patiently awaiting until a death or some object of great moment shall for a brief period draw its people together under its sheltering roof. **1937** *Tararua Tramper* Feb. 6 Having spent the night in a meeting-house, we continued on our way. **1946** ZIMMERMAN *Where People Sing* 93 It took me the time spent in walking two squares to figure out that *whare runanga* probably meant meeting house. **1952** FINLAYSON *Brown Man's Burden* (1973) 112 Just across the courtyard was the meeting-house with its splendidly carved posts and panels. **1967** BAXTER *Collected Poems* (1980) 400 On the concrete path to the meeting house It was the women who cried out. **1976** FINLAYSON *Other Lovers* 100 'You're our visitor and you sleep tonight in the whare runanga – you know, the meeting-house...' Johnny took Jim over the paddock to the carved house. **1989** HOGG *Angel Gear* 26 Boy guides us through the meeting house and its carved figures.

megrim /'megrəm/. [Transf. use of Brit. (Cornish and Sc.) dial. *megrim* a sole-like fish of lowish value: see OED *megrim*².] WITCH.
 1911, 1913 [see WITCH]. **1921** *NZJST* IV. 121 *Caulopsetta scapha. Megrim.* Known as 'witch' or 'lantern-fish' at Napier. Taken by trawlers in sandy localities as far north as Hauraki Gulf. **1938** [see WITCH]. **1947** POWELL *Native Animals NZ* 67 Thirteen species of flat-fishes are known from New Zealand waters, including..the Megrim, *Caulopsetta scapha*, which is not popular as a food fish as it is usually very thin. **1956** [see WITCH]. **1967** NATUSCH *Animals NZ* 217 All [flatfish] but the megrim..have the right (as opposed to the left) side uppermost... All are excellent food fish—again with the exception of the megrim. **1982** *Evening Post* (Wellington) 8 Dec. 37 Ironically, the most abundant of all New Zealand flounders, the witch or megrim, is useless for eating because of its multitude of long thin hair-like bones and thin watery flesh.

melon. *Obs.*

1. See *Maori melon* (MAORI B 4 b (a)).

2. A simpleton, fool.
 1937 PARTRIDGE *Dict. Slang* 516 *melon.* A new cadet: Royal Military Academy: from ca. 1870: ob. Ex his greenness, as is 2, the Australian and New Zealand sense (late C. 19–20), a simpleton, a fool. **1938** *Press* (Christchurch) (McNab slang) 2 Apr. 18 [The traveller to New Zealand] might be..told ..that he was 'a melon' to have come out and 'given it a pop'.

3. In the phr. **to do one's melon**, to lose one's head; to become angry or excited.
 a1974 SYDER & HODGETTS *Aust. & NZ Engl.* (TS)

MERCURY BAY WEED

266 *To do the melon,* or *to do one's melon* mean the same thing [as *to do one's block*].

melt, *v. Obs.* [AND *Obs.* 1869.] *trans.* To squander (one's pay-cheque) on drink.
 1873 HOLLOWAY *Jrnl. of a Visit 1873–75* (ATLMS) 22 Apr. 56 Shearers..draw..a 40 to 50 check, and taking it to the nearest Public House, would hand it over to the landlord, saying, just let me know when that's melted. **1889** LANGTON *Mark Anderson* 31 A shepherd from an up-country station..who had come to Dunstan..to 'melt' his cheque.

men's hut. *Rural.* Also **men's quarters, men's whare.** A bunkhouse or bunkhouse-dining building for housing shearing, farm or station hands. See also *shearers' hut* (SHEARER 2), WHARE 4 b. **a.** As **men's hut.**
 1864 [see SHEARER 2]. **1865** BARKER *Station Life* (1870) 34 We peeped in at the men's hut—a long, low wooden building, with two rows of 'bunks' (berths, I should call them) in one compartment, and a table with forms around it in the other, and piles of tin plates and pannikins all about. **c1875** MEREDITH *Adventuring in Maoriland* (1935) 39 So I invited him to come into the men's hut, and have it out, which challenge he gleefully accepted. **1883** PASH *Report on NZ* 6 Farm labourers are generally housed in a tolerably sized building called the men's hut. **1933** *Press* (Chistchurch) (Acland Gloss.) 4 Nov. 15 *Men's hut.*—House where the station hands live. On some stations it is called the *station house,* and now often the *whare*, which word was, I suppose, brought from the North Island stations. Originally the men cooked, ate, and slept in a one-roomed hut, with a fireplace and colonial oven at one end and bunks in two or three tiers round the walls. Nowadays most *m[en's] h[ut]s* are reasonably comfortable houses with separate rooms. **1940** [see CUDDY 2 b].

b. As **men's quarters.**
 1926 DEVANNY *Butcher Shop* (1981) 33 Tutaki passed to the men's quarters where dinner was awaiting them. **1978** JARDINE *Shadows on Hill* 173 Halfway..was sited the working centre of the station—men's quarters, cookshop, stables. **1983** FRANCIS *Wildlife Ranger* 2 The men's quarters in those days differed little from station to station. The roof and walls were corrugated iron, usually unlined.

c. As **men's whare.**
 1910 GROSSMAN *Heart of Bush* 260 Johnnie, who looked after the Haeremai cattle..slept in a bunk in one of the men's whares near the yards and woolsheds.

menuka, var. MANUKA.

mercer grass: see GRASS 2 (25).

Mercury Bay weed. [Named f. *Mercury Bay,* Coromandel Peninsula.] *Dichondra repens* (fam. Convolvulaceae), a small creeping native herb with kidney-shaped leaves common in grasslands and used as a lawn-grass substitute in warm districts.
 1947 *NZ Observer* 9 Apr. 19 I shall try that Mercury Bay weed for a lawn. **1950** *NZJAg.* Aug. LXXXI. 109 The perennial *Dichondra repens,* a member of the convolvulus family, has some merit as an alternative to the better-known lawn grasses... Mercury Bay weed is not a grass but a small, low-growing, creeping plant which roots at the nodes and has small kidney-shaped leaves. **1969** *Standard Common Names Weeds* 48 Mercury Bay weed [=] dichondra. **1975** *Tane* XXI. 8 Convolvulaceae *Dichondra repens* Mercury Bay weed. **1987** *Bull. Wellington Bot. Soc. No.43* 71 *Dichondra repens* (Mercury Bay weed).

mere /ˈmeri/. Also with much variety of early form as **mar(r)e**, **ma(r)ree**, **marie**, **mary** (freq. in early use), **mearee**, **meri** (freq.), **mery**; occas. redupl. **meremere**, **meri meri**. [Ma. /ˈmere/: Williams 201 *Mere* (i), n.] Cf. **patu** a.

1. A short flat Maori war-club of bone, stone, or greenstone (see 2 below); see esp. quot. 1904. See also BATTLE-AXE. **a.** As **mere**.

[**1820** LEE & KENDALL *NZ Gram. & Vocab.* 180 Mére, *s.* A war-club.] **1820** MARSDEN *Lett. & Jrnls.* Aug. (1932) 277 He informed me that when he was at the Thames on a former occasion a chief had given him a maree, one of their war instruments, to sell for him for an axe. **1823** CRUISE *Journal* 2 Mar. (1957) 45 The existence of the sufferer is terminated by a blow on the head, struck with a stone club called a mearée. **1830** CRAIK *New Zealanders* 94 [They] struck them on the head with their merys. **1830** LANG *Poems* (1873) 116 Beneath his shaggy flaxen mat The dreadful marree hangs concealed. **1833** SHERIDAN *Letter from 'Sydney Monitor'* in McNab *Old Whaling Days* (1913) 48 In former days when in battle..[they had] an instrument made out of beautiful blue or green marble stone, which they call a Mary. **1834** MARKHAM *NZ* (1963) 84 Then the Chief with his Marré gives him a Clip on the Pipkin and he is speedily cut up, and so ends the life and begins the feast. **1836** WISHART 2 Apr. in McNab *Old Whaling Days* (1913) 146 Warepowre..laid aside his marie (hatchet of green stone). **1840** MATHEW *Journal* 6 Feb. in *Founding of NZ* (1940) 41 [Patamouri] presented the Governor with one of their splendid Green Talc Hatchets or 'Mares' expressly for Queen 'Wikitoria'. **1841** BIDWILL *Rambles in NZ* (1952) 93 I had an instance to-day of the great value the natives sometimes set on their ornaments of green stone maries (meri), as the whites call them. **1864?** TEMPSKY *Memoranda* (ATLTS) 167 There was not the slightest degree of shilly shallying—the tomahawk and the mere going to it with true New Zealand zest. [1864 *Note*] A short flat hand club, of stone or whalebone, with edges, a scull-cracker of the most approved shape. **1878** [see PATU]. **1898** MORRIS *Austral-English* 290 *Mere*, (pronounced *merry*), a Maori war-club..made of any suitable hard material—stone, hard wood, whalebone. To many people out of New Zealand the word is only known as the name of a little trinket of *greenstone*..made in imitation of the New Zealand weapon in miniature, mounted in gold or silver, and used as a brooch, locket, ear-ring, or other article of jewelry. **1904** TREGEAR *Maori Race* 310 The most beautiful of all Maori arms was the battledore shaped weapon (*mere*), somewhat resembling a flat club, but which was not handled in the usual manner of a club. **1946** *JPS* LV. 153 *mere*, battledore-shaped weapon of greenstone; a most valued weapon, both to Maori user and Pakeha collector. A very commonly-used word, and almost invariably mispronounced like Mary. **1957** *Listener* 22 Nov. 4 We know what a 'mere'..or a 'hangi' is, but they remain essentially Maori in idea. **1986** BELICH *NZ Wars* 337 *mere* short club, sometimes of greenstone (New Zealand jade)

b. Reduplicated **meremere**.

1861 *Otago Witness* (Dunedin) 6 Apr. 6 They commenced a war dance..armed with guns, spears, *taiahas*, *meri meri*, &c. **1882** POTTS *Out in Open* 13 Amongst the chiefs..towered Ahipena Kaikau, taiaha in hand, and..a big man with a heavy whalebone mere-mere. **1913** *NZ Observer* 8 Nov. 20 Down in the Hawke's Bay District the other day someone found a Maori meremere of such a size that one strong man could handle it only with difficulty. **1935** MAXWELL *Recollections* 56 I asked a young Maori..how long it would take to finish the *mere mere*.

2. mere pounamu [Ma. /ˈmere ˈpounamu/], the finest kind of greenstone mere.

1846 HEAPHY *Exped. to Kawatiri* 25 May in Taylor *Early Travellers* (1959) 237 The inmates of each house were engaged in making *meri poenamu*..for 'trade' or presents northward. **1851** SHORTLAND *S. Dist. NZ* 34 In the northern island [the rakau-pounamu] is called a 'patu-pounamu' or 'meri-pounamu'. **1863** MANING *Old NZ* ii 26 I would not give one of your locks, my dear, for all the gold, silver, pearls, diamonds, *mere pounamus*—stop, let me think,—a good *mere pounamu* would be a temptation. **1882** POTTS *Out in Open* 13 In the..armament might be seen..the prized mere pounamu chipped from its bed of jade. **1899** *Richmond-Atkinson Papers* (1960) II. 618 Two elderly natives..brought to my house a very handsome mere pounamu (greenstone club).

meri, merimeri, varr. MERE.

merino /məˈriːnʌu/, *a.* and *n.* [Spec. uses of *merino* (pertaining to) merino sheep, or their fine wool.]

1. Special Comb. **merino dog**, of a sheep-dog, trained to work merino sheep; **merino fence**, one constructed to contain merino sheep.

1978 PRESTON *Woolgatherers* 112 They were Romneys, we had **merino dogs**, and the sheep took no notice whatever of them. **1982** WOODHOUSE *Blue Cliffs* 23 Some of the fences were of the old **Merino type**—five thick wires, no barb, iron standards and posts, generally of broadleaf from nearby bush.

2. *Obs. fig.* As **pure merino** [AND a non-convict settler; hence one having social pretensions, 1826], a person of fine breeding.

1907 *Truth* 23 Mar. 5 It is more than probable that Black has not a good character, and if one may imagine from what has been said, the Missioners don't look on Black as being a good, fond, loving spouse, that his domestic relations are not all pure merino.

mermaid. Applied to various sea plants or animals. **a.** As **mermaid's purse (pinbox)**, a capsule containing a skate's egg.

1956 GRAHAM *Treasury NZ Fishes* 98 These [skate's] eggs are passed off in horny, oblong capsules and are known to fishermen and others as Skate Barrows, Sailors' Purses, Mermaid's Purses and Mermaid's Pinboxes, and are often picked up on the shore after storms. Each capsule contains one egg. The shape is like a miniature pillow, with four horns (one at each corner).

b. As **mermaid's beads** pl., *Chaetomorpha darwinii* (fam. Cladophoraceae), a green alga that resembles a string of bright green beads, occas. known elsewhere as 'sea emeralds'.

1961 MARTIN *Flora NZ* 9 The largest of several forms is *Chaetomorpha darwinii* [an epiphytic seaweed] sometimes designated Mermaids' Beads or Sea Emeralds.

c. As **mermaid's toenails**: see TOENAIL.

message. [f. Sc. dial.: see SND *message* Sc. usage: a visit to the shop to make purchases, most commonly in the *pl.* of the purchases made, one's shopping (1788).] In the phr. **to run (go) messages**, to run shopping errands, to do small shopping for another.

1950 SUTTON-SMITH *Our Street* (1975) 17 You went for the messages this morning. *Ibid.* 33 Most Saturday mornings after messages had been done..Brian and Smitty..would go along to the park. **1965** MACNICOL *Skippers Road* 144 I..went on to do the weekly shopping for both families. When I returned to the car after the last message it was in an uproar. **1987** *Listener* 29 Aug. 44 Aunt Mag had a nasty habit of asking you to go to the grocer's or the butcher's on some message or other, just when you were planning to do something quite different. **1992** *NZ English Newsletter* 6 11 (Bartlett *Regional Variation: Southland*) [Other items which may be diagnostic of Southland English are:] *messages* (shopping; e.g. *I'm off to do the messages*).

messenger. *Obs.* A false die.

1880 *Evening Post* (Wellington) 15 Apr. 2 Other implements of gambling. Among them was a false die or, in the 'speelers' slang, a 'messenger'.

metha, var. METHO.

metho.

1. Also **metha.** [f. *meth*(ylated spirits + -O: AND 1933.] Methylated spirits as an alcoholic drink.

1938 HYDE *Nor Yrs. Condemn* 152 Two of them [sc. workers at a hydro camp] were drinking methylated spirits, which they called 'metha'... 'I knew a joker went blind drinking that metha.' **1945** BURTON *In Prison* 116 Poor Paddy is a dreadful wreck now, and probably never will be anything more than a half-crazed sponge for absorbing 'metho'. **1959** LAWLOR *Old Wellington Days* 134 'Metho' was a popular beverage in these days [c1906]... Not a 'metho' fiend and with no criminal tendencies was Oliver Chittle.

2. [AND 1933.] Also **metho king**. A methylated-spirits addict.

1947 *NZ Observer* 7 May 11 Dealing with the 'Methos'... Commander Campion knows just about every 'metho' and no-good in Auckland. **1974** AGNEW *Loner* 31 Despite the frequent abuse of European drunks and methos, I had never seen a Chinese react unpleasantly. **1974** MORRIESON *Predicament* (1981) 30 No one wants to pal with a guy who's [sic] old man's a metho king. **1986** CRANE *I Can Do No Other* 99 The 'methos', the drinkers of methylated spirits, were considered the lowest of the low.

Meyer lemon. /ˈmaɪə/. [f. the name of Frank N. *Meyer*, a botanical explorer of the US Dept. of Agriculture, who obtained the variety at Fengtai, near Beijing, China, where it was used as an ornamental pot plant, and introduced it into the US in 1908.] The name, commonly used in New Zealand and in areas of the US, of a medium-sized variety of hardy lemon having a smooth, thin golden-yellow skin and copious juice of mild flavour.

1926 *NZJAg.* XXXIII. 392 *Citrus-fruits*... Lemons..[Varieties recommended for planting] Lisbon, Eureka..[Varieties recommended for future trial] Genoa, Meyer. **1939** *NZJST* XX. 56A Varietal infection [by citrus-canker] occurred roughly in the following order..: Ponderosa lemon; Eureka, Lisbon, and Meyer lemons; grapefruit. **1949** *NZJAg.* LXXIX. 245 A citrus fruit which in recent years has gained much favour with the New Zealand home gardener and commercial citrus orchadist is the Meyer lemon. It is a sweet orange-lemon hybrid that comes into early fruiting and for its size bears a profuse crop of useful attractive fruit... It has been so commonly referred to in citrus districts of the United States as the Meyer lemon that this name has come to be generally recognised as its proper designation... Until 1940 commercial planting in New Zealand was not extensive. **1966** *Encycl. NZ* I. 758 The main kinds of citrus grown commercially in New Zealand include 'Lisbon' and 'Eureka' type lemons, 'Meyer' lemons.

mia-mia, var. MAIMAI.

mic-a-mic, michi michi, varr. MIKI-MIKI.

mice. *Quartzmining.* Also **mice-eaten.** Of quartz, full of holes.
   1871 *Grey River Argus* June in Latham *Golden Reefs* (1992) 114 Let them not listen to the public-house yarn, 'It was all mice', or 'It was all picked stone'...let them come and look for themselves. **1992** LATHAM *Golden Reefs* 431 *Mice-eaten*: Quartz full of holes.

Mick. [Of unknown origin: AND 1918.] The tail of a coin (in two up). (Also heard (Ed.) as *Michael*, used by three men playing pitch and toss at Woodbourne Aerodrome, Marlborough 17 Apr. 1957.)
   1938 ROBERTSON *Cameliers in Palestine* 198 The priest places two coins on a short piece of polished wood which he calls a kip, and raising his eyes to the sky, he throws up the coins as an offering to Allah. All the worshippers raise their eyes also to the sky, and then bow solemnly over the mat, and say together, 'God Almighty', and the priest answers, 'A pair of Micks', which means that the offerings are not accepted.

mick-a-mick, var. MIKI-MIKI.

Mick Dooley: see MICKY DOOLAN.

mickey, mickeymick, micky, varr. MIKI-MIKI.

Micky Doo: see MICKY DOOLAN.

Micky Doolan. Also early **Mick (Mickey) Dooley**, and in shortened form **Micky (Mickey) Do(o); Mickey Doolan, Micky Doolin.** [f. *Mick*, a freq. Irish familiar forename, and surname *Doolan*, in transf. use for both 'Irishman' and 'Catholic' (cf. OED *mick*[1]).] An (Irish) Catholic. See also DOOLAN a.
   1905 *Truth* 9 Sept. 1 A Mick Dooley asked a Wellington barmaid for 'some of that new Frinch drink'. *Ibid.* 23 Sept. 1 Where Mickey Doos have always been. [**c1935**] CAMPBELL *Island to Island* (1984) 87 We'd gang up on kids who chucked off at us—like the boys from the Catholic home. They'd call us [from the Presbyterian Boys' Home in Dunedin] 'Pressbuttons'; we'd call them 'doolans', 'doolies', 'Mickey Doolans'—or worse. **1965** MCELDOWNEY *Warm South* (1983) 123 When she came in from shopping she found that Michael Hickey had the gym full of 'little Micky Doos'—Holy Name children. **1972** *Salient* (Wellington) 5 July 5 However the fact that Mike only polled 529 votes against 434 for a wog, 409 for a micky doolan and 253 for Professor Liley's stand in shows. **1982** *National Business Review* 2 Aug. 32 And it [*sc.* boxing] was something Catholic kids (Mickey Doos) were forced to do that gave us another excuse for avoiding them. **1987** *Landfall* 162 163 And this time I promised Dad that I'd never play with that little Micky Doolin bastard again. **1995** *Dominion* (Wellington) 1 Apr. 21 It's enough to start a horrid little internecine scrap – them Mickey Dos trying to flog the Protty Dog [=Anglican] nuns for their turgid little doco.

micky-mick, var. MIKI-MIKI.

Middle Island. Also occas. early **Midland Island.** Usu. collocated with the def. art., an old name for the South Island which gave prominence (esp. in pre-colonization whaling times) to Stewart Island as the third, southernmost, island. *Middle Island* begins to be discarded in favour of SOUTH(ERN) ISLAND q.v. from c1855, and is finally replaced by SOUTH ISLAND q.v. on maps, c1905.
   1820 MARSDEN *Lett. & Jrnls.* Nov. (1932) 323 They..informed me that they had crossed Cook Straits and landed on the Middle Island. **1832** *Deed* 9 Nov. in McNab *Old Whaling Days* (1913) 90 In Witness whereof I have this day set my hand and Seal in my Tatto likeness Opposite. Middle Island or Tavai Poenammoo. **1840** [see NEW LEINSTER]. **1843** DIEFFENBACH *Travels in NZ* I. 195 [In a table showing the names of Native tribes of Cook's Straits] Shores of the Midland Island. Massacre Bay. **1859** WILSON *Rambles at Antipodes* 103 Southern Island (or as it is usually most absurdly called, the 'Middle Island', on account of a third little island existing still further to the south). **1867** HOCHSTETTER *NZ* 36 The usual denominations of the three Islands were North, Middle and South Islands. It is certainly more proper to distinguish only the two principal Islands as North Island and South Island, and to allow the third small Island to pass by the exclusive name of Stewart's Island. **1868** [see SOUTH ISLAND 1 a.]. **1872** *Evening Post* (Wellington) 21 May [Leader] The half-holiday movement is spreading rapidly through the Middle Island, and particularly in that money-making go ahead province Otago. **1888** PAYTON *Round about NZ* 173 I get a good deal mixed up as to which is the Middle Island and which is the South Island, and the term Middle Island is scarcely ever used. **1902** *Settler's Handbook of NZ* 18 The Nelson Land District comprises the north and north-western portion of the Middle Island. **1924** LYSNAR *NZ* 15 The South or Middle Island of New Zealand is a land of beautiful rivers, lakes and forests. **1943** *St. Michael's Anglican Church A Century of Christian Witness* 3 The Church at Waimea West was probably the first Anglican Church built in the 'Middle Island'. **1957** CRESSWELL *The Case for the South Island* (VUW:TS) Sept. 1 Our Island has already had six namings—By Tasman—Staten Land. By the Dutch Parliament or States General—Nieu Zeeland. By Sir George Grey or the Crown—New Munster. By the Central Government—The Middle Island. Since 1905—The South Island. **1980** ELDRED-GRIGG *Southern Gentry* 68 By 1865 public men were referring to the South as a distinct economic and social unit—'the civilization of the Middle Island'.

midgic /'mɪdʒɪk/. *Obs.* [Origin uncertain: poss. from Sc. dial. *midgeck, midjick* varr. of *midge* something small.] A shilling.
   1937 PARTRIDGE *Dict. Slang* 519 *midgic*. A shilling: New Zealand c[ant](–1932). Prob. ex *mejoge* [a shilling: c1750–1780]. **1938** *Press* (Christchurch) (McNab Slang) 2 Apr. 18 New Zealanders have their curiously sounding slang. 'Prejagarnint',... 'midgic' (one shilling). **1941** BAKER *NZ Slang* 52 We use *midgic* for a shilling, where the Australian habitually uses *deener*.

Midland Island, var. MIDDLE ISLAND.

miggles, *n. pl.* Also **migs, mikles.** [Cf. Wentworth & Flexner *mig* (1) c.1890–c.1925; *Miggle(s)* the game of marbles.] A marble-game.
   1976 *Evening Post* (Wellington) 29 June 14 miggles = marbles [examples of]..words and sayings sent in by 'Tuesdate' readers—things their parents said when they were at school. **1951** 14 M 10 Wellington H.S. 21 Miggles, mikles [games out of school] [M5] **1951** 14 M 10 Wellington H.S. 21 Migs **1951** 15 M 9 St Bede's, Chch 20 Migs

mighty, *a.* Excellent, fine; also as an expression of approval or agreement.
   1973 WILSON *NZ Jack* 90 Though I was only sixteen, I was tall for my age and Gil reckoned we could get away from it. 'Good idea,' I said. 'Mighty. We've got to drink to our glorious victory.' **1978** BALLANTYNE *Talkback Man* 116 'Grandpop was 82 this week.' 'That's mighty,' Stan told Grandpop... 'What do you think of the slippers, Stan?' 'Mighty,' Stan said. *Ibid.* 120 '[The racehorse'll] do it easy',... 'He's a mighty nag.'

migration. As **the Great Migration**, with reference to an out-dated theory of a Polynesian founding migration in the 14th century from Hawaiki to New Zealand in a single fleet of canoes. See also FLEET *n.*[1] 1 a; HEKE.
   1904 TREGEAR *Maori Race* 560 It has proved (in my opinion) conclusively that the Maoris from whom the leading tribes claim descent, those ancestors said to have arrived in the Arawa, Tainui, Aotea, and other canoes of the Great Migration, were certainly not aborigines of New Zealand, even if there were other Maoris or other inhabitants resident on these islands when the Hawaiki canoes arrived. **1924** LYSNAR *NZ* 20 [Heading] The Great Migration about A.D. 1350. **1949** BUCK *Coming of Maori* 36 The great migration (*heke*) from Hawaiki is the most famous event in Maori history, because all the tribes trace their aristocratic lineages back to the chiefs of the voyaging canoes. **1995** *Sunday Star-Times* (Auckland) 1 Oct. A7 Tanya Rogers said Moriori of the [Gisborne] area consider themselves distinct from Maori, though intermarriage has clouded the lines between them. 'All of our ancestors have been on the land at least 700 years before the great migration came along.'

migs: see MIGGLES.

miha. [Ma. /'miha/: Williams 201 *Miha* (i), *n*... 2. Young fronds of fern.] An immature fern frond (a 'fiddle-head' frond) often used as a logo.
   1985 *Listener* 1 June 10 By all means let us have the miha as our national symbol; that is, if we want to be perceived as a snail in its shell—or curled up in the foetal position. **1986** *NZ Times* 6 Apr. 1 The symbolic fern frond which created controversy when selected as a new national and 'emotional' symbol for New Zealand's exports is officially a failure. Launched less than a year ago, the miha, which is a young ponga frond, is to be let to wither and die.

mihanere, *n. Hist.* Also with some variety of early form as **mihinare, mihorari; mitanari, mitonere.** [Ma. /'mihinere/, /'mihinare/: an adaptation of English *missionary*, a Protestant missionary: see Williams Appendix *Mihinare, mihingara,* missionary; 'Anglican'; Duval III. 237 *mihanere*, etc. 'missionary', 1830.] A Maori Christian convert. Cf. MISSIONARY 1 *n.* and *a.*, PIKOPO 2.
   1841 *Joseph Somes to Lord John Russell* in GBPP *House of Commons 1841* (No.311) 19 Apr. 129 [Henry Williams] had not given them [*sc.* Maori owners, for land] even a fish-hook or a head of tobacco, except..to those who became converts to the mihanere (missionary) creed. **1841** WAKEFIELD *Journal* 20 Feb. in Heaphy *NZ* (1842) 58 Others [*sc.* Maori converts] again said that they had turned 'Mitanari'..and that the white Mitanaris said the 'Pukapuka' would be strong against the heathen. **1842** HEAPHY *NZ* 54 It was to the effect, that should he turn 'mitonere' his father would return and see him. **1847** ANGAS *Savage Life* II. 153 Hongi Hongi..in answer to my inquiry as to whether he was a 'mihorari' or a 'pikopo' (Catholic), confessed with evident delight that he was a 'devil' [*sc.* heathen]. **1898** HOCKEN *Contributions* 56 Altogether, there were..not less than 150 natives, who, according to their custom, being *mihanere* or Christianised, assembled twice a day for religious service. **1928** *Na To Hoa Aroha* (1986) 17 Dec. I. 160 The Ringatus, a strong factor on this side, are prepared to arrive at a modus vivendi with the mihinare.

mihi. [Ma. /'mihi/: Williams 201 *Mihi*... 2. Greet.] A formal Maori greeting.
1945 *JPS* LIV. 106 [Speeches] consisted of greetings and references to Rata [the deceased whose tangi it was] (what the Maori calls a mihi), then welcomes to the visitors. **1969** MASON *Awatea* (1978) 95 Werihe... Now we just send him our mihi, our aroha, and our warmth. He will need them. **1986** SORRENSON in *Na To Hoa Aroha* I. 16 He [Buck] had the equally chastening experience of being unable to reply in Maori to the formal mihi on the Rangitukia marae near Ruatoria. **1990** *Listener* 6 Aug. 22 Take her approach when invited to address the theme of a high-level hui... After the mihi Kirby gets down to business.

Also **mihi** *v. trans.*, to greet, to welcome.
1985 MITCALFE *Hey Hey Hey* 159 It might be a good idea to have the parents along on the first Club afternoon, fine way of getting them to feel at home here in the school, you could mihi them in.

mihinare, mihorari, varr. MIHANERE.

miki-miki /'mɪkəmɪk/, /'mɪki͵mɪk/, *mainly SI.* Also with much variety of early form as **mic-a-mic, michimichi, mick-a-mick, mickey, mickeymick, micky, mickymick, miki, miki-mik, mikkimik**: with **mick-a-mick** and **mickymick, miki-mik** forms being esp. frequent. [Ma. /'mikimiki/: Williams 202 *Miki..mikimiki = mingimingi.*] Mainly applied to the shrub *Cyathodes juniperina* or to the small-leaved *Coprosma* spp. *C. propinqua* and *C. linariifolia*; MINGIMINGI. Also *attrib.*

1. *Cyathodes* sp. (fam. Epacridaceae).
1858 THOMSON *Reconn. Survey S. Dist. Otago* in Taylor *Early Travellers* (1959) 342 Thus, spear grass, and scrub called *tomataguru*, and *michimichi* grow on hard ground. **1890** *Otago Witness* (Dunedin) 30 Oct. 20 I know that the starlings feast on the native miki-miki berries while they are in season. **1898** MORRIS *Austral-English* 292 *Mickey, n.* In New Zealand, a corruption of *Mingi... Ibid.* 294 *Mingi,..* In south New Zealand it [Cyathodes] is often called *Micky.* **1900** *NZ Illustr. Mag.* III. 254 A patch of mic-a-mic gave out onto open ground. **1939** BEATTIE *First White Boy Born Otago* 12–13 The Maori boys would eat the blue mikimiki [Cyathodes] but not the yellow mikimiki [prob. Coprosma], which they said was poisonous. **1940** STUDHOLME *Te Waimate* (1954) 242 The underscrub was very dense, Matipo, Ini-Ini, Konini, Pokaka, Mick-A-Mick..and others. **1949** NEWTON *High Country Days* 98 In the shade of a clump of miki-mik they boiled the billy. **1970** MCNEISH *Mackenzie* 14 The smoke rose in spirals, carrying with it the..odours of the bush..mikimiki and liverwort and the woody fragrance of manuka. **1986** HULME *Windeater* 167 It already has rats and shags and the mikkimik. **1989** PARKINSON *Travelling Naturalist* 73 This coast gets the full blast of Wellington's famous winds, resulting in..ground-hugging plants typified by such rugged species as..mikimiki and tauhinu.

2. COPROSMA, *Coprosma* spp. (fam. Rubiaceae).
1868 LINDSAY *Contribs. NZ Bot.* 72 The 'Mikimik' or 'Yellow Wood' of the Otago settler. A tall shrub. **1885** *Adelaide Observer* 6 June 41 in Hill *Richard Henry of Resolution Island* (1987) 88 Maple trees, totara, miki miki..all entangled by a dense undergrowth of ferns and parasitic creepers. **1918** [see YELLOW-WOOD]. **1933** *Press* (Christchurch) (Acland Gloss.) 4 Nov. 15 *Mickymick.*—A native shrub from which sticks are cut. **1961** MARTIN *Flora NZ* 215 A majority of small bushy shrubs with twiggy branches and small opposite leaves are Coprosmas, colloquially known as 'wiggy bushes' or 'miki-miks', this name being a corruption of the Southern Maori miki-miki. **1963** PEARSON *Coal Flat* 421 Mickeymick: A compact twiggy scrub with small leaves of the genus *Coprosma*. (From Maori *mingimingi*).

mikkimik, var. MIKI-MIKI.

mikles, var. MIGGLES.

mikoikoi. [Ma. /mi'koikoi/: Williams 202 *Mikoikoi, n. Libertia* [spp.].] *Libertia ixioides* (fam. Iridaceae), a native iris possessing tufts of sword-like leaves and attractive white flowers. See also IRIS, TURUTU 2.
1940 LAING & BLACKWELL *Plants NZ* 113 *Libertia ixioides* (*The Ixia-like Libertia*)... Maori name, *Mikoikoi.* **1952**, **1982** [see IRIS].

military, *a.* Special Comb. **military John** WW2, a military policeman (cf. JOHN 1); **military settler,** see SETTLER 1 b (c).
1946 BRUNO *Maleesh George* 5. A well lit chaplain's batman lick[s] three military johns.

milk. Used *attrib.* in special Comb. **Milk Authority** *obs.*, a local authority set up by statute to ensure an adequate supply of good quality milk within its jurisdiction; **milk billy** [AND 1935], see BILLY *n.*¹ 4); **milk cheque,** see quots.; **milk-in-schools scheme** *hist.*, the former daily provision of State-funded milk to school children; **milk-line,** the main pipe or tube of a milking machine which carries the milk from the bails to the holding tank; **milk monitor** *obs.*, a school pupil appointed to help distribute the milk provided by the milk-in-schools scheme; **milk shed,** MILKING SHED; **milk-stand** *obs.*, formerly a structure, of convenient height for loading and unloading, and situated near a dairy-farm's road entrance, on which a farmer's milk-cans were placed for collection (see also quot. 1950); **milkstone** [see OED 2 b, 1949], a scaly deposit precipitated on the inside of the metal pipes of a milking machine; **milk-supplier,** a dairy farmer, usu. a shareholder, supplying milk to a cooperative dairy factory; also one supplying milk to a town-milk scheme; **milk token,** also *ellipt.* **token** [spec. use of *token* a stamped piece of metal or plastic serving as a medium of exchange: see OED *n.*¹ 11 a], usu. a plastic (formerly metal) disc bought from a milk-vendor and placed in an empty milk-bottle on a house frontage as payment for milk delivered; **milk-treatment station,** a central plant for treating milk (for example, by pasteurization), and bottling or otherwise encasing it, esp. for town consumption; **milk vendor,** a formal name for a milkman.

1944 *NZ Statutes* No.30 320 '**Milk Authority**'..means the Metropolitan Milk Board or..the Borough Council prescribed by Order in Council under this Act [Milk Act] as the Milk Authority for the district. *Ibid.* 340 The principal function of each Milk Authority under the Act shall be to ensure for the inhabitants of the milk district an adequate supply of milk of a standard not less than the standard prescribed under the Sales of Food and Drugs Act, 1908. **1950** *NZJAg.* Feb. LXXX. 163 A committee of supply..arranges with the local milk authority to supply all the milk for that district. **1924** ANTHONY *Follow the Call* (1975) 12 Every month my **milk cheque** would come to hand. **1988** WARR *Bush-burn to Butter* 56 There was now [by 1900] a regular monthly milk cheque from the local dairy factory. **1938** *AJHR H-31* 25 In 1936 the Government inaugurated the **Milk-in-schools Scheme**, the object of which is to make available to every child attending public and private primary schools and kindergartens, and, where desired, every child attending post-primary schools, a half-pint of milk each school-day. **1949** BLANC *Money, Medicine & Masses* 155 Just as the milk-in-schools scheme was the first line of attack on malnutrition in children, so is the Health Camp a second line. **1987** *Those Were the Days (1930s)* 24 [Caption] Milk in schools: Introduced in 1937 the scheme continued for 30 years. **1950** *NZJAg.* Feb. LXXX. 113 In dry weather dust is..drawn into the **milk line** through the teat cups before these are adjusted on the cow. **1978** SUTHERLAND *Elver* 40 They shot a bottle brush on a long line through the main milk line, and they scrubbed the main line with that. **1990** *NBR Weekly Magazine* 9 Feb. 36 This baby boomer finally became price sensitive to milk, ending a lifetime association with dairy products that had included distinguished service as a **milk monitor** for one term in Standard 2. **1980** LELAND *Kiwi-Yankee Dict.* 66 **milk shed**: the place where one of New Zealand's foremost primary products passes from bovine to man. **1988** WARR *Bush-burn to Butter* 119 One of the first efforts to improve the handling of milk on the farms was to raise the standard of hygiene in both the milking process and in the milkshed. **1920** POWDRELL *Dairy Farming* 100 Don't place your **milk-stand** near evil-smelling drains or manure heaps. **1950** *NZJAg.* Oct. LXXXI. 369 *milkstand* (a) where the milk cans stand to collect the flow from the machine. (b) where they stand overnight, only one collection in 24 hours. (c) where they wait to be collected by milk lorry. **1960** CROSS *Backward Sex* 14 Between Albertville and the sea is a strip of untidy dairy land..carrying..boxthorn hedges, ricketty milk-stands. **1988** JACKSON *Rainshadow* 60 We passed a ruined milkstand, dri[f]toes across a cattle-stop made of railway lines. **1949** *NZJAg.* Nov. LXXIX. 487 **Milkstone** is the casein of milk which has become attached to metal in the form of encrustations. **1950** *NZJAg.* Mar. LXXX. 267 All metal pipes must be brushed..to avoid the development of milkstone. **1892** *NZ Official Handbook* 128 The success which has attended the erection of certain factories on the co-operative principle. viz.., that the **milk-suppliers** shall largely be the share-holders—is bearing good fruit. **1945** *NZEF Times* 22 Oct. 5 The Department cannot deliver without **milk tokens**. **1952** *Dominion* (Wellington) 11 Oct. 10 Most of the city's grocery shops will stop selling milk tokens after the end of the month. **1954** WINKS *These New Zealanders* (1956) 69 Milk tokens are not used in the States. **1960** HILLIARD *Maori Girl* 236 From the front of the house came the jangle of metal tokens in milk bottles. **1976** MCDERMOTT *Lost & Found NZ* 145 What are milk tokens? They are metal or plastic tokens you put in your empty milk bottle for the milkman to replace with full bottles. **1950** *NZJAg.* Oct. LXXXI. 303 When the Milk Commission sat in 1943 the standard of many **milk-treatment stations** in New Zealand was regrettably low. **1980** LELAND *Kiwi-Yankee Dict.* 66 *milk treatment station*: The milk comes from the milk shed on individual farms and is then collected..and taken to a..Milk Processing Plant where it is pasteurized. **1946** *Evening Post* (Wellington) 29 Oct. 8 The Hutt Valley **Milk Vendors'** Association has, through its member vendors, advised consumers.. that after November 1 summer prices will be charged. **1957** *Evening Post* (Wellington) 1 Nov. 12 Milk Vendors' Vehicles Let Sun Shine In **1987** *Dominion* (Wellington) 25 May 6 Wellington's milk vendors have decided to take their concerns about the fate of home deliveries to the streets next month with a truck parade to Parliament.

milk bar. Also occas. **milk-shake bar.** [OED *milk n.*[1] 10 a, 1935 Austral. quot.]

1. Not confined to New Zealand but a significant part of a local sub-culture in the 1940s and 1950s: a shop with seating (often in booths) selling milk-shakes, soft-drinks, confectionery, and also light snacks.

   1938 *NZ Observer* 23 Aug. 14 Funny things happen in these here milk bars. **1945** HENDERSON *Gunner Inglorious* 116 And the kid sister—gee, she must be about seventeen now and working in a Sunshine milk-shake bar—she et six on end and spewed 'em all up. **1948** BALLANTYNE *Cunninghams* (1976) 123 Outside Barry suggested a milkshake, so you went into a milk bar and you sat in a booth sucking raspberry shakes through straws. **1954** WINKS *These New Zealanders* (1956) 62 Milk bars do not exist in America—ice cream, 'pop'..are obtained at..a drug store. **1960** KEINZLY *Tangahano* 43 The milk bar sold sausages, it sold vegetables, it sold groceries but it didn't sell disinfectant. **1966** *Weekly News* (Auckland) 6 Apr. 41 I would lead the reluctant child at lunchtime towards the same milk-bar. **1982** BURTON *Two Hundred Yrs. NZ Food* 33 Milk bars, mostly rather pale imitations of their American counterparts, appeared in the 1950s, and these were soon replaced by coffee houses. **1988** *Univ. Entr. Eng. Exam. Commentary* 3 *milkbar* (forerunner of dairy with more limited stock). *Ibid.* 6 He gave me some extra money, so I went to the milkbar and bought a gobstopper and some other lollies.

2. Special Comb. **milkbar cowboy** [cf. OED *cowboy* 3 b, *drugstore-cowboy*], a motor-cyclist youth who with others congregated at town milk bars.

   1951 *Truth* 22 Mar. 4 New Zealand was plagued with the noisy, untidy nuisance of milkbar cowboys—motorbike gangs often bent on trouble. **1952** *Ibid.* 14 May 5 'Milk bar cowboys' (also described as youthful motorcyclists with a smattering of square dance fever who nightly mob juke boxes) were warned that they would have to behave themselves. **1956** [see BODGIE a]. **1957** FRAME *Owls Do Cry* (1967) 60 And the brazen milk-bar with the new class, the milk-bar cowboy, the teddy-boy hanging around the door. **1967** BAXTER *The Man on the Horse* 122 An alcoholic grave-robbing friend said to me the other day, as we sat and watched the milkbar cowboys come and go. **1972** MITCHELL *Pavlova Paradise* 183 Expressions still used [for people one does not approve of] are 'milk-bar cowboy', 'flagon wagon gang' and even occasionally 'Teddy boy'. **1988** JACKSON *Rainshadow* 113 We usually ended up at the Centreway, ordering sundaes or sodas and watching the milkbar cowboys revving their motorbikes.

milkie. [f. *milk*(-coloured + -IE; AND 1908.] An opaque playing marble of milk-like colouring or appearance.

   1951 14 M 14 St Bede's, Chch 21 Milkies [=marbles] **1959** LAWLOR *Old Wellington Days* 37 The marbles [c1900] ranged from the clay ('stinker') variety to the more elaborate coloured 'glassies'... Some of them were beautifully made—the 'milkies' and 'sparklies'. **1972** SUTTON-SMITH *Folkgames Children* 174 Then there were the terms referring to particular kinds of marbles: for example..milkies, molly-bars.

milking-bail: see BAIL *n.* 1.

milking cow. *Mining.* A method of mining by collapsing large areas of countryside and drawing off the broken-up ore through chutes.

   1978 MCARA *Gold Mining Waihi* 314 *Caving method*: Also known as the 'milking cow'; it applied to an area of several acres where the Mine Lake is now. The method started with the collapse of the large arches on the Martha reef about No. 1 shaft, and was later systematically developed by a series of sub-levels on Nos 7, 8 and 9 levels which were used to weaken this section of country and cause it to run so that it could be drawn off through chutes. It operated for a quarter-century and is conservatively estimated to have yielded over a million tons of good run-of-mine grade ore. *Ibid.* 327 *Milking Cow or Caving Block*: (See also caving method). A block of country between Nos 1 and 6 shafts and Junction Road.

milking shed. COWSHED. See SHED *n.*[1] 4 b for the various types of cowshed, *angle-park*, *tandem*, *walk-through*, etc.

   1849 ALLOM *Letter* in Earp *Handbook* (1852) 123 The [stock] yard is generally divided into..a large yard for the whole herd, a drafting yard, and a milking yard, at one end of which is placed the milking shed, cow bails, and calf house. **1863** MOSER *Mahoe Leaves* 23 We..came upon a stock-yard belonging to an outsettler, and in the milking shed, we put up for the night. **1910** CHUDLEIGH *Diary* 21 May (1950) 450 I have decided to..put up one new milkmens house and milking shed. **1921** *NZJST* IV. 113 Additional important advantages are available from the supply of electrical power in the milking-shed. **1935** GUTHRIE *Little Country* (1937) 281 The cows huddled outside the milking-shed that night with swollen udders. **1949** *Here & Now* Oct. 17 Power lines to the cow-shed don't necessarily mean electric stoves..plenty [of women] still help in the milking sheds. **1959** DAVIN *No Remittance* 95 The more I saw of the house, the milking-shed, the pigsty, the hen-run..the less I was impressed. **1963** HILLIARD *Piece of Land* 82 The milking shed was a sight to see: as spick and span as a doctor's surgery. **1971** CURNOW in *Nowhere Far from the Sea* 124 She's all of eighty said the cowman, Down at the milking-shed. **1988** FRAME *The Carpathians* 194 He walked..to..where houses alternated with fields of black-and-white cattle with..full udders and swishing tails, congregated by the gates to the milking sheds.

milkman. *Farming.* [Recorded earliest in NZ: OED 2, 1902.] One who milks cows on a sheep station or sheep farm. See also COWMAN.

   1868 *Puketoi Station Diary* 10 Aug. in Beattie *Early Runholding* (1947) 104 Wm. Raby, men's cook, and Peter Bisset, milkman, etc., commenced work. **1910** [see MILKING SHED].

milko. Also **milk-oh.** [f. the call 'milk-o': found elsewhere but recorded earliest in NZ: AND (the call) 1865; the person, 1907.] A milkman.

   1906 *Truth* 28 July 1 A Newtown housekeeper got a shock t'other morning when quite woman-like she asked the milk-oh if the morning's supply of lacteal fluid was quite pure. 'Oh yes,' replied milk-oh, 'it has been paralysed by the public anarchist.' **1949** *Southern Cross* (Wellington) 28 June 2 She had told 'Milko', in future, to leave her only brown bottles. **1987** ELDRED-GRIGG *Oracles & Miracles* 40 The milko would rattle past with his cart of a morning..cause we was getting milk through the Charitable Aid Board [c1930].

milkshake, *n.* Also abbrev. **shake.** (The illegal use of) bicarbonate of soda solution to improve the performance of a racehorse.

   1990 *Dominion* (Wellington) 2 May 1 'Milkshakes'—the use of stomach tubing to give a horse a mixture believed by some to enhance performance—came to a head early in March when the [Harness Racing] conference issued a statement outlawing the practice on racedays. **1990** *Sunday Star* (Auckland) 23 Dec. 12 The New Zealand Harness Racing Conference is only weeks away from introducing new testing, which it hopes will also kill off another wave of rumours about milkshakes and drugs in the game. The testing is designed to detect bicarbonate of soda or baking soda, the prime ingredient of the milkshake. **1991** *Sunday Star* (Auckland) 15 Dec. B8 [Heading] Fed-up trainer ready to quit over shake 'shambles'. *Ibid.* 15 Dec. B8 The New Zealand Harness Racing Conference..is facing legal action from yet another trainer questioning the accuracy of its milkshake detection programme.

Hence **milkshake** *v. trans.*, to administer a 'milkshake' to (a racehorse). Also as a *vbl. n.* and *attrib.*

   1990 *Sunday Star* (Auckland) 23 Dec. B12 Cups winning trainer John Langdon, who has been investigated for allegedly milkshaking horses, says drug rumours in harness racing have gone too far. **1991** *Evening Post* (Wellington) 22 Feb. 28 Milkshaking is the common term for administering a large dose of bicarbonate of soda..mixture to a horse which harness racing officials say enhances stamina. **1992** *North & South* (Auckland) Jan. 20 The milkshaking debate still goes on in the trotting industry. **1992** *Sunday Star* (Auckland) 26 Jan. B6 [The trainer] arranged for racecourse inspector Norm Scott to keep the filly under surveillance..to prove he was not milkshaking her.

milk-tree. A small native tree of the genus *Streblus* (formerly *Paratrophis*) (fam. Moraceae), esp. *S. heterophyllus* (formerly *P. microphylla*), a tree of lowland and coastal forest exuding thick, sweet milky juice when the bark is cut. With a modifier: **coastal milk-tree** *S. banksii*, and **Three Kings milk-tree** *S. smithii*. See also COWTREE, MILKWOOD, TAWAPOU 2, TOWAI 2, TUREPO.

   1853 HOOKER *II Flora Novae-Zelandiae I Flowering Plants* 224 The 'Milk-tree' of the Nelson and Wellington colonists is described by Mr. Bidwill and Dr. Sinclair as producing a milk which is used with tea and is equally suitable for the purpose with that of the cow. A large tree, 60 feet high..often extremely like *Carpodetus Serratus*... Nat. name 'Towai'. **1869** [see TAWAPOU 2]. **1873** *Catalogue Vienna Exhib.* (Morris) Milk-tree..a tall slender tree exuding a milky sap: wood white and very brittle. **1886, 1906** [see TUREPO]. **1924** *NZJST* VII. 379 The coast milk-tree..is one of those species which is now found mainly on islands. **1935** *Tararua Tramper* July 2 The juices of the lawyer, the rata, and the milk tree are drinkable. **1940** LAING & BLACKWELL *Plants NZ* 141 *Paratrophis microphylla* (The Milk-tree). Tree, sometimes 30–40 ft. in height. If a slit is cut in the bark of this tree, a thick, sweet, milky juice will flow from it. **1950** WODZICKI *Introduced Mammals NZ* 163 [Turbott found in 1948 on Great Island, Three Kings] wharangi..mangeao..Three Kings' milk-tree (*Paratrophis smithii*). **1961, 1982** [see TUREPO]. **1992** *North & South* (Auckland) Apr. 17 [Scientists] have done a thorough job explaining the milk tree cannot regenerate because kiore are eating its seeds.

milkwood. MILK-TREE.

   1890 *PWD Catalogue of Timbers* (NZ and South Seas Exhibition) 12 Milkwood (waiuatua)..*Epicarpurus microphyllus*..A very light white wood. [Waiū-atua = milk of the gods]. **1919** July 29 Vernacular names supplied to J.C. Andersen by W. Best, Otaki in *TrNZI* (1927) LVII. 935 Milkwood *Paratrophis microphylla*. **1924** *NZJST* VII. 186 In *Paratrophis Banksii* there is an example of a large-leaf form of the turepo, or 'milkwood' of the bushman.

mill. [Various spec. uses of *mill*, used elsewhere but of significance in (esp.) the rural NZ community.]

1. A threshing-machine, a threshing mill. See also *tin mill* (TIN *n.*[1] 1).

1853 in Deans *Pioneers of Canterbury* 6 July (1937) 254 I have had a good deal of trouble in damming the river for the thrashing mill. **1871** in Evans *Waikaka Saga* (1962) 273 On this mill he worked as a straw-walloper on the straw-stack, forker on the sheaf-stack, feeder on the mill, and later as cook. **1888** BRADSHAW *NZ of Today* 180. Why are you tying, or stooking..this harvest? I thought I'd wait till the mill started. [**1888** *Note*] 'threshing machine' **1944** LEE *Shining with the Shiner* 41 He could fork from a stack to a mill with any man on earth when he was in the mood. **1978** HAYES *Toss of Coin* 112 When the time came to thresh the grain a traction-engine usually pulled the mill between stacks, and ten men were required. **1982** LYNN *Lynnwood Tree* 92 Their father was working on a mill, (a mill in Ashburton in those days [c1925] meant a threshing mill). **1990** [see *tin mill* (TIN *n.*[1] 1)].

2. *Goldmining*. [Spec. use of OED *mill n.*[1] 2 a.] The processing or stamping works of a quartz mine.

1868 *Thames Miner's Guide* 93 The first mill erected on the Thames Gold Field was called Great Expectations. It commenced working about November, 1867, and consisted of four wooden stampers, shod with plates of iron, the whole worked by a donkey-engine. **1882** POTTS *Out in Open* At the Thames Goldfields we have noticed it in abundance..within sound of the clang and din of the stampers in the busy crushing mills. **1983** NOLAN *Gold Fossicker's Handbook* 113 *Mill*: the processing works of a mine.

3. A sawmill.

1891 *TrNZI* XXIII. 488 These logs are then rolled on to a kind of sleigh or tram-cart by the help of screw-jacks, and conveyed up by horses to the mill. **1913** CARR *Country Work* 40 Old fashioned 'Breast' benches..are still used in many mills. **1969** MOORE *Forest to Farm* 38 Sometimes it was milled in a bush mill at that point [*sc.* at the hauler stand].

4. A flax-mill for processing New Zealand flax (see FLAX 5 c).

1888 COX *Diaries 1888–1925* (ATLMS) 23 Nov. A good deal of Flax is out and dressed in the neighbourhood and I hope to get some work at some of the Mills. **1919** WAITE *New Zealanders at Gallipoli* 2 The flaxmill hand left swamp and mill and hurried to the nearest railway station. **1951** HUNT *Confessions* 37 As far as the eye could see over the country on the western bank was a vast sea of flax sticks. The *Lily* tied up at the bank within a few yards of the mill.

5. Special Comb. **mill boss**, the foreman or manager of a sawmill; **mill feeder**, one who feeds a threshing mill with sheaves; **millhand**, in New Zealand usu. a sawmill worker, occas. formerly a worker in a flax-mill; **mill road**, the track from a sawmill to its bush workings, or from the mill to a formed road; **mill-skids**, SKID 1; **mill timber**, millable timber; **mill time**, see quot.

1933 EADDY *Hull Down* 42 The **mill boss** jumped aboard. **1936** LEE in *Some Other Country* (1984) 32 He stood on the stack and looked down upon the **mill feeder** who, knowing the Shiner held the fork would have for him a measure of contempt. **1936** RUST *Whangarei and Dist.* 163 Hundreds of bushmen, loggers, jackers..were employed besides stackers, saw doctors, benchmen and **mill-hands** in the different sawmills [at Maungakaramea]. **1981** MARSH *Black Beech & Honeydew* 103 'Too Bloody Big'..was what the mill-hands said repeatedly of the giant we had seen felled. **1981** HOOPER *Goat Paddock* 20 She's a bit rough along here, but we'll take it easy along the old **mill road**. **1923** MALFROY *Small Sawmills* 7 The best conditions..are an easy falling grade from bush to **mill-skids**. **1953** SUTHERLAND *Golden Bush* (1963) 35 From this contract resulted another to supply logs for delivery at the mill skids. **1934** HARPER *Windy Island* 193 Open up immense bodies of **mill timber**. **1966** TURNER *Eng. Lang. Aus. & NZ* 153 Some [saw]mill terms have died out. One is **mill time**. This was a setting of the clocks an hour early so that the working day, eight to five by mill time, was really seven to four. It was a kind of localized summer time to allow the saw sharpeners to work in daylight after working hours.

millable, *a*. Of a tree or forest, worth milling for timber.

1946 *Bull. Wellington Bot. Soc. No.14* 4 Trees are killed by the hundred, though they are millable if killed from above. **1951** CRESSWELL *Canterbury Tales* 142 Isn't it more likely that they listened to Torlesse saying 'the country's easy and roadable, there are 3,500 acres of millable bush.'

million. In the phr. **gone a million** [AND 1913], done for; finished.

1908 *Truth* 28 Nov. 8 He left him and remarked to another 'screw', 'Paddy's gone a million', and in two days Paddy did join the millions, for through the timely intervention of a priest, Paddy was taken to the Public Hospital on a Thursday night..on the following Sunday..he was dead. **1918** *Quick March* 1 Nov. 15 It is well known how the Turkish word 'mafish' is commonly used now in place of old slang, such as 'gone a million', 'blown out', 'snuffed it'. **1958** *Listener* 23 May 6 We scraped in in that game, only because Elvidge scored his usual try... Otherwise, we were gone a million. **1974** MORRIESON *Predicament* (1981) 190 You're my biggest worry. If father smells a rat we're gone a million. You've got to get yourself home fast.

millionaire's salad. The edible heart of the nikau; *nikau heart* (NIKAU 2).

1982 BURTON *Two Hundred Yrs. NZ Food* 7 Succulent and sweet to the taste, nikau heart later became known as 'millionaire's salad' because the tree dies when the heart is removed. **1985** *Evening Post* (Wellington) 4 Jan. 9 A favourite food of the settlers was the pith of the nikau palm which was edible raw as a green vegetable. It was nicknamed 'millionaire's salad' because if the pith was taken the palm died. **1995** *Evening Post* (Wellington) 30 Nov. 15 The tip or heart of the [nikau] palm has been called the 'millionaire's salad' as the entire plant dies for this one small meal.

mimi /ˈmimi/. Also early **mimme, mimmi**. [Ma. /ˈmimi/: Williams 202 *Mimi. 1.* v. intr. Make water... *2.* n. Urine.] Usu. as a noun, urine, or urination (occas. as a verb.); also in the phr. **to have a mimi**.

[**1804** *Collins English Colony in NSW* (NZ Vocabulary) 559 E-ma-mi, *To go to make water*. **1817** NICHOLAS *Voyage NZ* II. 336 Urine. Mimme. **1820** LEE & KENDALL *NZ Gram. & Vocab.* 180 Mímí,... *s.* Urine... *v.n.* Making water. **c1826–27** BOULTBEE *Journal* (1986) 283 urine, mimmi]. **1983** HULME *Bone People* 260 Have a mimi, grab a couple of half g's, and walk back. **1986** mimi pot [see POTAE]. **1988** MCGILL *Dict. Kiwi Slang* 73 *mimi hill* comfort stop; from Maori 'mimi', to urinate; eg 'Coming up to mimi hill, chief?' **1992** GRACE *Cousins* 15 The girl behind him said, 'Bubba done mimi, Bubba done tutae,' and Aunty stamped her foot.

mimi, mi-mi, var. MAIMAI.

mimosa. *Obs.* Also occas. **native mimosa**. [Transf. use of *mimosa* Australian *wattle*, for *kowhai* from the yellow colour of their flowers: see also 1868 quot.] KOWHAI 1.

1838 POLACK *NZ* I. 294 Many species of the *laurel* (laurus) exist..and a species of the retiring *mimosa*, or sensitive plant. **1848** WAKEFIELD *Handbook NZ* 144 Everywhere to be seen..the beautiful mimosa, called Kohai, covered with clusters of yellow flowers. **1868** LINDSAY *Contribs. NZ Bot.* 73 *S. tetraptera*, Aiton, var. *microphylla*, Jacq... Var. *microphylla* is also sometimes designated by the colonists the Native 'Laburnum' or 'Mimosa', from the similarity of its foliage, in the arboreous condition, to that of these familiar..European trees.

mince, *v*.

1. As a *vbl. n.*, a ship-girl's expression for working several boats.

1982 *Truth* 19 Jan. 7 And the Napier girls talked about 'mincing'. That means when they hop from one ship in port to another.

2. As **to mince about**, to hang about.

1984 BEATON *Outside In* 25 Sandy:... I've been up to the [prison] office eh? Runnin' messages for cowface, eh? Ma: You'll mince about once too often, lady. *Ibid.* 110 *Mince* to hang about where one shouldn't be.

mine. *Mountaineering*. [Transf. use of *mine*, a deep hole in the earth.] A crevasse. Also *v. intr.*, to slip into a crevasse.

1939 PASCOE *Unclimbed NZ* 143 Our party took over the lead, and we plunged across the slopes alive with new snow. Tom in front went 'mining' down crevasses twice, but luckily the 'mines' were little ones and the rope was conveniently taut. **1950** *Canterbury Mountaineer* 78 He was carefully inched over the side. About half the rope was out when it suddenly slackened. Had he encountered a 'mine', or one of the many little lakes to be found on the glacier?

miner. In special collocations: **miner's cage (chair, cradle)**, CAGE q.v., or a box-like structure or platform suspended on a wire, for crossing rivers, steep gullies, etc.; **miner's code**, see quot.; **miner's cress**, *Lepidium* sp.; **miner's lantern**, a 'bottle' lantern (see quot., see also LANTERN); **miner's lettuce**, *Montia* sp.; **miners' train**, see quot.

1943 HISLOP *Pure Gold* 49 [Caption] **Miner's chair** Over Cromwell Gorge. [The picture shows a platform on an iron frame hanging by pulleys on a wire across a gorge.] **1958** *Tararua* Sept. 31 **Miner's cage**, *chair*, or *cradle*. Any of these uses may be applied to the box on an endless rope used for crossing rivers. Trampers on the whole seem to prefer *cage*. The Australians use *flying fox*. **1959** MILLAR *Westland's Golden 'Sixties* 28 The rules that meeting [at Collingwood in 1857] drew up became known as the **Miners' Code**, and it formed the basis of the Mining Act of 1859, the first of its kind in New Zealand. **1969** *Standard Common Names Weeds* 49 **miner's cress** *Lepidium densiflorum* Schrad. **1872** HARPER *Letts from NZ* (1914) 10 Nov. 172 My host had given me a **miners' lantern**... It is made of a clear glass bottle, the bottom of which is cut off by means of a worsted thread, soaked in paraffin oil, tied around it, and set alight. In the neck of the bottle, inside, a piece of candle is lit, the bottle carried by its neck upright, and, provided there is no rain, no lantern is more effective, and, if needs be, it can be stuck upright in the ground. **1969** *Standard Common Names Weeds* 49 **miner's lettuce** *Montia perfoliata* (Willd.) Howell. **1990** CHURCHMAN & HURST *Railways of NZ* 196 The 6.35 am from Greymouth was the '**Miners' Train**', while the return working, the 7.35 am from Rewanui was the 'Fannie Train', as the women from Dunollie and Rewanui used it to go to work in Greymouth.

miner's right. Also **miners right**, occas. init. cap. [AND 1855.] A licence to dig for gold on public or private land. Cf. *prospectors' right* (PROSPECTOR).

1858 *NZ Statutes*, No.74 358 [Gold Fields Act] It shall be lawful for the governor to cause documents to be issued, each of which shall be called 'The Miner's Right' and shall be granted to any person applying for the same upon payment of the sum of One Pound. **1862** WALKER *Jrnl. & Lett.* (ATBTS) 15 Jan. Two Germans made 40lbs weight of gold out of one hole, but somebody found out they were working without a 'Miners' Right' and so turned them out and went in themselves. **1875** WOOD & LAPHAM *Waiting for Mail* 26 No sin-born cloud its lustre dim, no vice or folly blight, But Heaven's blessing ever rest upon our 'Miner's Right'. **1882** HAY *Brighter Britain* II. 289 Everyone rushes at the clerk's table, and..dumps down his note (£1) for the 'Miner's Right', which is his license and authority to dig for gold within the limits of the field. **1892** PYKE *Guide* 4 [s.18] *Miners' rights* are issued to any person not under the age of *fourteen* years, are in force throughout the colony for twelve months from the date of issue, and are not transferable. Miners' rights authorising mining on Crown lands are charged *ten shillings* each; and for mining on Native lands *twenty shillings* each, or such other sum as the Governor may have agreed to pay to the owners of Native lands. **1976** NOLAN *Hist. Gold Trails Nelson & Marlborough* 12 The Miner's Right, used on the goldfields from the earliest days until replaced by the Prospectors' Right in 1971.

mingie /ˈmɪndʒi/ *n.* [f. *mingy a.* mean, stingy.] A mean or stingy person; a meanie.

1919 MANSFIELD *Letters* 15 Nov. (1993) 95 By the way, Re Jeanne. She has been sending hampers of fruit even to *Kay*. Didn't you get one? Aren't they prize mingies?

mingimingi /ˈmɪŋiˌmɪŋi/. Also **mingi**. [Ma. /ˈmiŋimiŋi/: Williams 202 *Mingi, mingimingi.* n. *1. Cyathodes juniperina... 2. Leucopogon fasciculatus...3. Coprosma propinqua... [=] miki*: cf. **1820** LEE & KENDALL *NZ Gram. & Vocab.* 180 Míngi, *s.* A shrub so called.] Any of several native shrubs with small and often sharp-tipped leaves belonging to the families Epacridaceae and Rubiaceae. See also **miki–miki**.

1. Epacridaceae, esp. *Leucopogon* (formerly *Cyathodes*) *fasciculatus* and *Cyathodes juniperina*. See also HEATH 4.

1867 HOOKER *Handbook* 766 Mingimingi.. *Leucopogon fasciculatus...* Mingi.. *Cyathodes acerosa*. **1889** KIRK *Forest Flora* 213 The mingi... *Cyathodes acerosa* is a shrub or, rarely, a small tree, 18ft. high, with pungent leaves and minute white flowers. **1906** CHEESEMAN *Manual NZ Flora* 411 *C[yathodes] acerosa...* An erect or rarely decumbent branching shrub 4–15 ft. high.. *Mingimingi. Ibid.* 415 *L[eucopogon] fasciculatus...* A branching shrub or small tree 5–15 ft. high.. *Mingi*. **1910** COCKAYNE *NZ Plants & Their Story* 51 The large bushes of the mingimingi (*Styphelia acerosa*), some with abundance of white and others with pink drupes. **1926** CROOKES *Plant Life Maoriland* 104 First of all we have [in the heath family] the mingi mingis (the various members of the family Cyathodes), which can easily be recognised owing to their close resemblance to manuka. **1936** *Manuka Blossoms* 9 The mingi-mingi in her berried dress. **1964** DEMPSEY *Little World Stewart Is.* 73 At the edge of the bush, slim trunks of kamahi formed a background for prickly bushes of mingi-mingi, with their slightly flattened white drupes reminiscent of old-fashioned linen buttons, stitched in the middle. **1978** MOORE & IRWIN *Oxford Book NZ Plants* 112 *Cyathodes* (*Styphelia*) *fasciculata*. This mingimingi (a Maori name given to various small- or narrow-leaved plants) is common..as a shrub up to 2m tall. **1981** BROOKER et al. *NZ Medicinal Plants* 51 *Cyathodes juniperina*... Maori names: *Taumingi, tumingi, mingimingi...* This small-leaved shrub, formerly known as *C. acerosa*..is common and variable. *Ibid.* 52 *Leucopogon fasciculatus...* Maori name: *Mingimingi...* Allan has transferred this species to *Cyathodes*, as *C. fasciculata*.

2. Rubiaceae, esp. the genus *Coprosma* (and occas. its wood), esp. *C. propinqua*. See also COPROSMA 2, *yellow-wood* (YELLOW 2).

1867 HOOKER *Handbook* 766 Mingi, *Lindsay. Coprosma myrtillifolia*. **1868** LINDSAY *Contribs. NZ Bot.* 72 The 'Mingi-mingi' [*Coprosma parviflora*] of the Otago settler. The commonest form of the plant on exposed uplands is a smallish, stout, erect shrub. **1889** KIRK *Forest Flora* 187 Although the yellow-wood [*Coprosma linariifolia*] is widely distributed, its Native name is unknown to settlers, even to those versed in Maori lore. In Otago it is known as 'miki-miki', but this name is applied to *C. foetidissima* on Stewart Island: by woodmen it is frequently termed 'mingi', which is..the Native name of *Cyathodes acerosa*: the same name is applied to *Coprosma Colensoi*, but I am unable to say whether correctly or not. **1890** *PWD Catalogue Timbers* (NZ & South Seas Exhib.) 12 Mingi..Coprosma linariifolia..Wood even grained and yellowish in colour. *Ibid.* 28 Mingi (mikimiki) slab. **1918** *NZJST* I. 143 *Coprosma Cunninghamii...* Mingimingi, yellow-wood. **1952** RICHARDS *Chatham Is.* 60 [*C.*] *propinqua*.. Common Coprosma. Mingi-mingi.. *C. Cunninghamii*.. Mingi-mingi (twisted in grain). **1962** EVANS *Waikaka Saga* 239 The whole [Waikaka] valley and the..ridges were covered [in 1876] with luxurious white tussocks.. diversified with..trees and shrubs comprising.. matagouri and mingimingi (*Coprosma propinqua*). **1982** WILSON *Stewart Is. Plants* 60 *Coprosma propinqua* Mingimingi... Bushy dark shrub about 1–5 m tall. **1992** *Dominion Sunday Times* 26 July 21 There may be mingimingi showing blue or white fruit.

mini- [Abbrev. of *miniature*.] Special Comb. **minibin**, a small skip, or portable hired rubbish bin; **mini golf course** (also **minnie golf course**), a miniature golf-course; **mini-tanker**, a small beer-tanker, or mobile beer-tank, hired to service large gatherings.

1986 *National Bus. Rev.* 1 Aug. 56 The New Zealand listing follows the signing of franchising agreements by Miniskips New Zealand to establish operations here based on the rapid acceptance in Australia of its waste disposal concept using small, on-call collection vehicles and **minibins**, known in Australia as 'skips'. **1934** HYDE *Journalese* 24 For a while, when the '**minnie golf course**' was all the rage and you couldn't step into a public building without treading on a 'minnie', there was one in the top floor of this old building. **1977** HALL *Glide Time* 14 John. Must have been some party. Jim. Great..[*sic*] until someone drove off with the **mini-tanker**.

mining, *ppl. a.* In special collocations: **mining advocate**, **mining agent** *hist.*, a person permitted to plead causes before Goldfields Commissioners; **mining right**, a popular variant of MINER'S RIGHT q.v.

1888 PRESHAW. *Banking Under Difficulties* 154 In the early days of the goldfields,.. if there were not two full-blown lawyers to be had, **mining advocates** (as they were termed) were allowed to appear and plead the cause of their clients. **c1880s** in Seddon *The Seddons* (1968) 17 As a buggy mare Daisy was ideal. My father's work as a mining advocate took him to outlying places in the goldfields. **1925** BATHGATE *Random Recolls.* 30 Very often some of the litigants were represented by an ex-policeman..who combined the practice of **mining agent** (as such bush lawyers were called) with keeping a public house. **1992** LATHAM *Golden Reefs* 114 An occasional round was fired by a Reefton mining agent..who published a long report in the Greymouth paper in June 1871. **1948** *Our Own Country* (from Korero, AEWS magazine) 23 [On] the first few days prospectors returned from the territory which has since made fortunes, wanted back the pound they had paid for their **mining rights**.

minke whale: see WHALE 2 (9).

Minnie Dean's lily: see LILY 2 (8).

minnow. Also **New Zealand minnow**. [Transf. use of English *minnow* a small fish.] *Galaxias maculatus* (fam. Galaxidae), a small coastal and freshwater fish. See also COWFISH 1, WHITEBAIT 1.

1872 HUTTON & HECTOR *Fishes NZ* 129 The other species (*G. attenuatus*)..it is proposed to distinguish as the New Zealand Minnow. It is a little fish constantly seen in most lakes and clear running streams, with much the same habits as the English minnow. **1886** SHERRIN *Handbook Fishes NZ* 141 Whitebait, or Minnow... At Taupo Lake and other places in the interior, small fish, which the Maoris collectively term inanga.. are obtained in..abundance. **1892** SPACKMAN *Trout NZ* 25 The bait used is..the New Zealand minnow (*Galaxias attenuatus*). **1921** THOMSON & ANDERTON *Hist. Portobello* 71 Minnow. *Galaxias attenuatus*..is common in streams on the east coast; it is the only species which enters the sea. **1947** POWELL *Native Animals NZ* 63 As the result of intensive investigation by Captain Hayes, the complete life history of *Galaxias attenuatus* or the New Zealand Minnow, as it is often termed, was made known. **1956** GRAHAM *Treasury NZ Fishes* 119 Today, with the advance of agriculture things have changed for the worse for Whitebait, since horses, cattle, not to mention human beings, destroy enormous numbers of eggs by tramping down the vegetation on the banks of the rivers, where the Minnow deposits her eggs. **1978** [see COWFISH 1]. **1990** MCDOWALL *NZ Freshwater Fishes* 117 *Galaxias maculatus*..Inanga... Various common names are used for the adult, including cowfish and minnow, but the name inanga is in wide and general use.

mint. Usu. as **Maori (native, New Zealand) mint, wild mint**, *Mentha cunninghamii* (fam. Lamiaceae). See also HIOI.

1867 HOOKER *Handbook* 766 Mint. *Mentha. Mentha Cunninghamii*. **1870** *TrNZI* II. 126 *Mentha Cunninghamii* Mint. **1909** *AJHR* C-12 60 *Mentha Cunninghamii*. New Zealand mint. Heath. Moderately common. **1940** LAING & BLACKWELL *Plants NZ* 387 *Mentha Cunninghamii* (*Cunningham's Mint*)... A small endemic species. (Maori mint). **1952** RICHARDS *Chatham Is.* 43 *Mentha..Cunninghamii*. A minute, fragrant perennial... The whole plant has a delicious smell... New Zealand Mint. Hioi. **1957** WILLIAMS *Dict. Maori Lang.* 52 *Hioi... 1. Mentha cunninghamii*, a plant, native mint. **1979** STARK *Maori Herbal Remedies* 18 *Hioi* (*Maori Mint*) *mentha cunninghamii* This slender prostrate herb may be found in both the North and the South Islands. **1981** BROOKER et al. *NZ Medicinal Plants* 60 *Mentha cunninghamii* Benth. Common name: *Maori mint* Maori name: *Hioi* **1982** SALE *Four Seasons* 103 But I have also discovered that New Zealand has its own wild mint—hioi of the Maori—which is flowering now.

minuka, var. MANUKA.

miro /'mirʌu/, /'mirʌu/, n.¹ Also early **meero**. [Ma. /'miro/: Williams 203 *Miro* (i).] **a.** *Prumnopitys ferruginea* (formerly *Podocarpus ferrugineus*) (fam. Podocarpaceae), a robust coniferous tree of lowland forest with hard, straight-grained timber; also the timber. Often *attrib.* See also *black pine* (PINE 2 (2) b), CHERRY.

[1820 LEE & KENDALL *NZ Gram. & Vocab.* 181 Míro, *s.* A fruit-tree so called; also the fruit of the *Míro.*] 1820 MCCRAE *Journal* (1928) 26 Next day went to Wy Whero a fine tract of cultivated land—Peaches—Taroo Flax, Meero—return to house. 1835 YATE *NZ* (1970) 45 Miro... This plant grows to the height of from forty to sixty feet. 1841 BIDWILL *Rambles in NZ* (1952) 36 Next in abundance is the Miro..a tree exactly like the English yew, but bearing sweet berries about the size of horse-beans, with an internal seed. 1853 MACKIE *Traveller under Concern* (1973) 78 The 'miro'..is also excellent timber, but too scarce for general use. 1875 LASLETT *Timber & Timber Trees* 308 The miro-tree..is found in many of the forests in New Zealand. 1896 HARPER *Pioneer Work* 34 For external use, we have the gum of the miro pine.., the finest healing ointment for an open wound that I have ever used, and a sure cure for warts. 1939 BEATTIE *First White Boy Born Otago* 13 Rimu is the red pine, and for the miro I never heard an English name. 1963 KEENE *O te Raki* 193 *miro:* tree 50 ft. to 80 ft. high; has reddish-purple berries ³/₄ in. long; favourite food of native pigeon. 1984 MORTON *Whirinaki* 75 Miro fruits are..up to 2 cm long, and are eagerly sought by pigeons.

b. The miro-berry, the deep red, swollen seed receptacle of the miro (see also quot. 1963, 1984 a above).

1838 POLACK *NZ* I. 288 The *korai, koutu utu, miro,* and *putuhutu,* are wild forest fruits, prized only by the elder natives. 1957 FRAME *Owls Do Cry* (1967) 17 And sometimes she called herself, if she were writing about bush, Miro, the little red berry.

miro, n.² [Ma. /'miro/: Williams 203 *Miro* (ii).] *Petroica macrocephala* (fam. Eopsaltriidae), the tomtit (MIROMIRO); occas. erron. for the New Zealand robin (ROBIN 1 *Petroica australis*) or the black robin (ROBIN 2 (1) *P. traversi*).

1898 MORRIS *Austral-English* 295 Miro (1) Maori name for a *Robin*..adopted as the scientific name of a genus of New Zealand Robins. The word is shortened form of *Miro-miro.* 1952 RICHARDS *Chatham Is.* 71 *Miro Traversi...* Found now only on Little Mangere Island.. Black Wood Robin. Tou-tou-wai, Miro.

miromiro. Also **mirro mirro.** [Ma. /'miromiro/: Williams 203 *Miro* (ii).] TOMTIT (*Petroica macrocephala*) Cf. *butcher-bird* (BUTCHER n. 2), MIRO n.², NGIRUNGIRU, TIT n.¹, WHEEDLER.

1842 GRAY *Fauna* in Dieffenbach *Travels in NZ* (1843) II. 190,191 *Miro longipes...* Gha toitoi of the natives of Dusky Bay... Miro miro... *Miro Forsterorum.*—Turdus minutus... Deep-shining black, with the breast and abdomen pale yellow;.. Mirro mirro of the natives of Queen Charlotte's Sound. 1855 TAYLOR *Te Ika A Maui* 403 Miro-miro (*Miro alibifrons*). A little black-and-white bird with a large head; it is very tame, and has a short melancholy song. The miro toi-toi (*muscicapa toi-toi*) is a bird not larger than the tom-tit. Its plumage is black and white, having a white breast and some of the near feathers of each wing tinged with white. 1873 BULLER *Birds NZ* 124 Myiomoira toitoi. (Pied Tit)... Miromiro, Komiromiro, Ngirunguru. 1884 [see TIT 1 a]. 1904 TREGEAR *Maori Race* 436 He visited the wood-fairies..in the form of a tiny bird, the *miromiro.* 1946 [see TIT 1 a]. 1955 OLIVER *NZ Birds* 478 White-breasted Tomtit. Pied Tit. *Miromiro Petroica toitoi.* 1964 [see TIT 1 a]. 1990 *Checklist Birds NZ* 209 *Petroica macrocephala toitoi...* North Island Tomtit (*Miromiro*).

mirro mirro, var. MIROMIRO.

mirror dory: see DORY 2 (1).

miserable, a. In phr. in senses 'bedraggled', or 'parsimonious': **as miserable as a bandicoot, shag (on a rock),** see BANDICOOT n., SHAG 3.

mis-mother, v. Farming. Usu. *passive.* Of a lamb, to be separated from its mother. Freq. as a *vbl. n.* or *ppl. a.* Contrast MOTHERING *vbl. n.*

1922 PERRY *Sheep Farming* 94 Any undue disturbance of the [Merino] ewes at this time will result in much mis-mothering of lambs. 1936 *NZJST* XVIII. 895 As soon as they could be handled without fear of mismothering the lambs were weighed. 1940 STUDHOLME *Te Waimate* (1954) 114 Then they let the ewes and lambs out on to a big block..the result being that fully 500 lambs were mis-mothered. 1947 NEWTON *Wayleggo* 153 As the mob is bunched on the approach to the yard, the lambs become mis-mothered. 1951 *Duff Shepherd's Calendar* (1961) 2 Jan. 9 If sight were the only method by which lambs can identify their mothers, or the chief method, mis-mothering after shearing would be a far more serious problem than it is now. 1966 NEWTON *Boss's Story* 140 The whole aim in mustering ewes and lambs is to avoid mis-mothering.

mission. Denoting the 19th century Christian (usu. Protestant) evangelistic missions to Maori. In special Comb. **mission-boy,** a Maori servant, or attendant at a mission, under Christian instruction (cf. BOY 1); **mission house** *hist.,* the residence of a missionary at a MISSION STATION.

1841 BIDWILL *Rambles in NZ* (1952) 43 The **mission-boys** were very attentive to their prayers and hymns every evening and morning, and commenced them always without my reminding them, which I had been desired to do by their masters in case of their omission. 1840 MATHEW *Journal* 16 Feb. in *Founding of NZ* (1940) 50 The [Wesleyan] **Mission House** and Chapel are built on elevated ground..back from the Shore. 1853 ROCHFORT *Adventures of Surveyor* 27 Two quaint bridges connect the town; and the neat little whares of the natives, with the mission-house, church, parsonage, and schools, contribute to render the place a little paradise. 1898 HOCKEN *Contributions* 107 No vestige whatever of this [whaling establishment at Waikouaiti] remains save the broken-down fence and overgrown graves of the little cemetery, which was close by Mr. Watkin's mission house.

missionary, n. *Hist.*

1. a. [An anglicization of Ma. *mihanere,* itself a Maori adaptation of *missionary.*] A (usu. Protestant) Maori Christian convert. Contrast PIKOPO (a Catholic convert). Also *attrib.*

1834 MARKHAM *NZ* (1963) 41 The Native Settlements become thicker. They are all Missionaries as they call the Christians. 1841 BIDWILL *Rambles in NZ* (1952) 44 It sounds rather curious to hear a native, in answer to a question as to whether he is a missionary or not, reply quite coolly, 'No, I'm a devil!' 1854 MALONE *Three Yrs. Cruise* 22 Mihaneri (missionaries, the universal name, in New Zealand, for Protestant Christians).

b. Special Comb. **missionary settler,** see SETTLER 1 b (a); **missionary station,** see MISSION STATION.

2. In names of plants. **a.** *North Island Hist.* [f. its introduction by early missionary families.] The introduced sweet briar, *Rosa rubiginosa* (fam. Rosaceae).

1881 LARKWORTHY *NZ Revisited* 30 The sweet briar, which [in Tarawera] goes by the name of 'Missionary' blocking the roads and vacant spaces. 1898 REEVES *Long White Cloud* 17 Sweet briar..covers whole hillsides to the ruin of pasture. Introduced, innocently enough by the missionaries, it goes by their name in some districts. 1912 BAUGHAN *Brown Bread* 48 'Missionary', in the North Island is frequently an alternative spelling for 'sweet-brier', which is a pest. 1921 GUTHRIE-SMITH *Tutira* (1926) 274 Sweet-briar (*Rosa rubiginosa*), 'Missionary' as it is still called, has been spread abroad by the horse... As its local name—'Missionary'—implies, sweet-briar too is a child of the Church of England.

b. missionary weed. *blue top* (BLUE a. 2 b), a vervain.

1926 HILGENDORF *Weeds* 146 Vervain (*Verbena officinalis*), also called **blue top,** griffin weed, and missionary weed, is a slender tough-stemmed perenial 1 to 2 ft high, with a few opposite rough, cleft leaves, and small lilac flowers.

missionary, a. *Hist.*

1. (Protestant) Christian. Cf. MIHANERE.

1843 STEPHENS *Letters* 145 The Missionary natives, as they are called. 1847 ANGAS *Savage Life* I. 242 At sunset, the people of this settlement being 'missionary' natives, a bell was struck, and they went through their evening devotions. 1849 POWER *Sketches in NZ* 63 In some of the missionary Pas there is a little more pretension [among the unmarried girls] to prudery and reserve.

2. With reference to a viewpoint supporting a Maori and Crown stance on the sale of Maori land.

1848 WAKEFIELD *Handbook NZ* 75 At his [Fitzroy's] first visit to Cook's Strait, he took advantage of his position to make insulting public attacks on gentlemen who had opposed the Missionary views, and the preceding acts of Local Government.

3. Of a horse's pace, slow, steady, careful and ambling, as would befit the dignity of a stereotypical 19th century clergyman.

1899 BERTHA *Cameron In Fair NZ* 26 A broken-down crock that will go along at a missionary pace.

mission station. *Hist.* Also occas. **missionary station.** [AND 1841; see OED 10 *U.S.,* 1828.] A headquarters, often at first primitive, from which a resident missionary can undertake the Christian evangelization of the local Maori people. Cf. STATION 1.

1835 YATE *NZ* (1970) 11 Waianiwaniwa..is a fine fall of the waters of the Kerikeri, about two miles from the Mission station. 1842 HEAPHY *NZ* 6 A small commercial community had thus grown up around the missionary station, dependent entirely upon trading. 1851 *Richmond-Atkinson Papers* 23 Feb. (1960) I. 84 We succeeded in hiring a small canoe..to take us up the rivers Waikato & Waipa as far as..Mr Buttle's missionary station. 1860 BUDDLE *Maori King Movement* 26 Was the note of alarm that sounded from the mission station at Waipa a false alarm? 1884 MARTIN *Our Maoris* 30 As we approached the Mission station, we rejoiced to see fenced fields with cattle grazing, white houses embowered in trees, and beyond a church. 1903 HUXLEY *Life & Lett. Thomas Huxley* I. 76 He utilised a week's stay here characteristically enough in an expedition to Waimate, the chief missionary station. 1938 *Auckland Weekly News* 16 Feb. 26 One of the interesting features will be the Maori camp at the Show Grounds, where 330 Catholic Maoris chosen from

Maori mission stations will assemble. **1949** Eccles & Reed *John Jones of Otago* 59 The thought of the masterful man, so free with his fists, setting up a mission station, must have caused many tongues to wag. **1973** Wallace *Generation Gap* 142 [The minister and his wife] lived on his mission station, a 100-acre block of land which was presented to him by..the local paramount chief. **1981** *AA Guide to NZ* 247 In 1835, a missionary called Chapman established a mission station at Rotorua.

mistletoe. [Transf. use of European *mistletoe Viscum album* (fam. Viscaceae) for related NZ species of parasitic shrubs: AND chiefly fam. Loranthaceae or Viscaceae, 1862 (yellow).]

1. Also occas. **Maori (native) mistletoe.** Any of several genera of parasitic shrubs belonging to the plant families Loranthaceae and Viscaceae; esp. *Ileostylus micranthus* (formerly *Loranthus micranthus*) with greenish-yellow flowers, *Peraxilla* spp. (formerly *Elytranthe*) with scarlet flowers, parasitic shrubs of southern beeches (*Nothofagus* spp.), and *Tupeia antarctica* (see also PIRITA 2) (all fam. Loranthaceae).

1853 Mackie *Traveller under Concern* (1973) 105 On one tree saw a fine bunch of a species of Mistletoe [prob. Tupaeia] with white berries. **1861** Haast *Rep. Topogr. Explor. Nelson* 146 Several species of Loranthus (misletoe) [*sic*] also adorn the woods, growing principally upon the evergreen..black and white birch. **1888** Buller *Birds NZ* I. 233 [The nest] is placed on the lateral fork of a branch of totara, supported underneath by an epiphytic growth of native mistletoe (*Loranthus micranthus*). **1891** *NZJSc.* (NS) I. 202 Our first excursion was through..beech forest in which we noted..the gorgeous crimson mistletoe. **1900** *Canterbury Old & New* 186 On the whole the beech forest is dark and gloomy, but here and there it may be lighted up by a tuft of scarlet or yellow native mistletoe [1900 *Note*] Species of *Loranthus*. **1910** Cockayne *NZ Plants & Their Story* 47 Parasitic on the beech—trees are two mistletoes, the one, *Elytranthe tetrapetala*, having the most showy scarlet flowers, and the other, *E. flavida*, having yellow flowers. **1917** Williams *Dict. Maori Lang.* 148 Kohuorangi,.. 3. *Tupeia antarctica* mistletoe. **1922** *Auckland Weekly News* 26 Jan. 19 The magnificent beech forests of the South Island, now aflame with the scarlet flower of the native mistletoe. **1940** Laing & Blackwell *Plants NZ* 148 *L. micranthus*, Maori mistletoe. **1959** Masters *Tales of the Mails* 49 The track..leads through a lovely piece of bush where again native mistletoe..and other lovely shrubs were in bloom. **1978** Moore & Irwin *Oxford Book NZ Plants* 80 Some stems [of the silver birch] become malformed through infestations of mistletoe, *Elytranthe colensoi*. **1988** Dawson *Forest Vines to Snow Tussocks* 123 More brilliant splashes of colour..may be provided by certain mistletoes which commonly parasitise the beeches. *Peraxilla colensoi*, usually found on silver beech, and *P. tetrapetala* have bright red flowers. *Alepis flavida* with orange-yellow to yellow flowers used to be common, but has now been depleted by opossums.

2. With a modifier: **scarlet, yellow**.

(1) **scarlet mistletoe.** *Peraxilla colensoi* and *P. tetrapetala* (fam. Loranthaceae).

1888 Hetley *Native Flowers NZ* III. 30 [Heading] Loranthus Colensoi Scarlet Mistletoe Native Name: Pirita This is a most beautiful plant, growing principally in the forests near Nelson in Spring, when it blossoms. **1908** *AJHR C-11* 37 *Elytranthe tetrapetala*. Scarlet mistletoe. **1940** Laing & Blackwell *Plants NZ* 148 *Elytranthe tetrapetala* (The Scarlet Mistletoe)... Both islands. Common on *Nothofagus Solandri*. Fl. Jan. Feb. **1960** Masters *Back-Country Tales* 81 I doubt if any more pleasing sight could have been met up with along the whole length of the ranges at Christmas time than the old whare, when that most beautiful of our native flowers, the scarlet mistletoe, is hanging in festoons from the sombre beeches that encircle the glade.

(2) **yellow mistletoe.** *Alepis flavida* (fam. Loranthaceae).

1908 *AJHR C-11* 37 [*Elytranthe flavida*]. Yellow mistletoe. Forest. **1940** Laing & Blackwell *Plants NZ* 148 *Elytranthe flavida* (The Yellow Mistletoe). **1961** Martin *Flora NZ* 152 A yellow or orange-flowered species (*E[lytranthe] flavida*) known as Yellow Mistletoe is abundant in beech forest south from East Cape.

mitanari, mitonere: see MIHANERE.

mo /mʌu/. Also occas. **mou.** [AND 1894.] Abbrev. of moustache.

1915 *Hutt Valley Independent* 6 Nov. 4 Takes the curl out of the literateur's mo. **1938** Hyde *Nor Yrs. Condemn* 29 The plum-coloured lady has a better mo than yours. **1950** *Landfall* 13 20 She came out all dressed up in Dad's clothes..with a wee mou drawn with chalk.

moa /'mʌuə/, /'moə/.

1. Also early occas. **moia, moe, movie** (prob. erron., see quot. 1989). [Ma. /'moa/: Williams 203 *Moa* (i) n. *1. Dinornis*..and other species, extinct birds: see quot. 1949 1 a below: Walsh and Biggs 66 PPN **moa* 'fowl'.] **a.** Any of several genera and species of large extinct flightless ratite birds of the order Dinornithiformes, browsing herbivores ranging in head height from almost 1 m, 20 kg weight (e.g. *Euryapteryx curtus*), to 3 m, 240 kg (e.g. *Dinornis giganteus*).

1839 Taylor *Journal* 26 Apr. (ATLTS) II. 117 Here [near Tokomaru] a valley was pointed out in which the great bird moa was said to exist, the natives say they dread to hear its cry as it is a certain portend [*sic*] of death. **1841** Best *Journal* 20 Apr. (1966) 291 Te Warru amused us with accounts of..the Moia a species of Ostrich supposed to be extinct. **1842** Gray *Fauna* in Dieffenbach *Travels in NZ* (1843) II. 195 To this order [Fam. Struthionidae] probably belongs a bird, now extinct, called Moa (or Movie) by the natives. The evidences are, a bone very little fossilized, which was brought from New Zealand by Mr. Rule to Mr. Gray, and by him sent to Professor Richard Owen. **1844** Barnicoat *Journal* (ATLTS) 5 May 170 The native[s] report that the gigantic Moe Bird still inhabits the interior [of Otago]. **1844** Williams *NZ Jrnl.* (1956) 114 The Moa, a most powerful and tremendous large bird (called Moa from More) but very few of these birds have been seen of late years. **1851** Shortland *S. Dist. NZ* 137 This he..mistook for a human bone; but on bringing it to the village, it was recognized by the natives as that of a bird now extinct, called by them a 'Moa'. **1860** in Butler *First Year* (1863) iii 35 The moa, as you doubtless know, was an enormous bird, which must have stood some fifteen feet high. **1876** Kennedy *Colonial Travel* 201 The skeleton of a moa, through the limbs being set far back and the breast overhanging, resembles that of a giraffe with the front legs lopped off. **1879** Haast *Geol. Canterbury & Westland* 449 At the same time it is possible, that the large bird of prey met with in the heart of the Alps..may be the Movie or Hokioe of the Maoris, or even the *Harpagornis* of which the bones were first obtained in the..deposits of Glenmark. **1880** *TrNZI* XII. 64 It was called a Moa... It was attended and guarded by two immense *Tuataras*, who, Argus-like kept incessant watch while the *Moa* slept. **1890** *NZ Observer* 1 Feb. 6 In the deepest grot of this secret spot Does the Moa choose to dwell. **1896** *Otago Witness* (Dunedin) 23 Jan. 51 In the scrimmage.. one of the eggs, which was a yard in circumference, rolled into the river and was immediately swallowed by the hungry shark, which so enraged the moa that it sprang into the water and, after a severe tustle [*sic*], killed the shark. **1929** Duggan *NZ Bird Songs* 24 Said God to the Moa: 'Now for many springs I have watched you walking, I will take your wings!' **1937** Buick *Moa-Hunters NZ* 185 The kick of the Moa is said to have been a forward one, and it is narrated that the ruse was to place a hunter in front of a bailed-up bird, his duty being to make feints to attack, and, as soon as the threatened bird lifted its foot to kick in defence, an enemy lurking in the rear would bring a long pole into play and with it strike the bird on its rigid leg, causing it to lose balance, and before it could regain its feet it was set upon and killed. **1949** Buck *Coming of Maori* 19 The name *moa* was applied to the domestic fowl throughout Polynesia... From the presence of the word moa in even a few Maori references, it seemed evident that the first settlers, having no introduced moa, applied the spare name to a local bird which appealed to them as furnishing an even better supply of food than the domesticated fowl which they knew in their homeland. **1974** *NZ Nature Heritage* III. 63 It thus seems probable that the ancestors of moas and kiwis walked into New Zealand before the break-up of Gondwanaland. **1989** Anderson *Prodigious Birds* 11 The word 'moa' first came to light in January 1838 when the missionary William Williams, accompanied by a mission printer, William Colenso, travelled to the East Coast. *Ibid.* 92 Rule called it 'A Movie', but his own paper (Rule 1843) unwittingly demonstrates that this was no more than a misunderstood reference to a common Maori name for the North Island, *Ika na Maui* (or 'Movie'), meaning the Fish of Maui. **1990** *Dominion Sunday Times* (Wellington) 23 Dec. 15 First the Maoris came, burning out the moa and forcing back the beech forests.

b. With a modifier: with the exception of **bush moa**, and poss. **giant moa**, most of the common names given in quot. 1988 are book names or common names confined to the ornithological community.

1955 *BJ Cameron Collection* (TS July) bush-moa (n) The smallest known species of moa, which seems to have lingered in Fiordland until the early 19th century. **1966** *Encycl. NZ* II. 575 Giant moas were probably extinct about A.D. 1500; the smaller bush moas may have lingered on in remote parts of the South Island until the early nineteenth century. **1974** *NZ Nature Heritage* III. 73 It is probable that at least one of the smaller [moas], the South Island bush moa (*Megalapteryx*) survived until early in the 19th century. **1988** Worthy *An Illustrated Key* (Nat. Mus. Misc. Series No.17) 4 [List of moa species, vernacular names, and distribution.] ANOMALOPTERYGIDAE *Anomalopteryx didiformis* (Owen) Little bush moa... *Megalapteryx didinus* (Owen) Upland moa... *Emeus crassus* (Owen) Eastern moa... *Euryapteryx curtus* (Owen) Coastal moa... *Euryapteryx geranoides* Stout-legged moa... *Pachyirnis mappini* (Archey) Mappin's moa... *Pachyornis australis* (Oliver) Crested moa.... *Pachyornis elephantopus* (Owen) Heavy-footed moa... DINORNITHIDAE *Dinornis struthoides* (Owen) Slender bush moa...*Dinornis novaezealandiae* (Owen) Large bush moa...*Dinornis giganteus* (Owen) Giant moa.

2. a. In *attrib.* use.

1988 Dawson *Forest Vines to Snow Tussocks* 144 The 'moa theory' has a science fiction ring to it, just as would a 'dodo theory'... Essentially, [the authors] propose that the divaricating shrub habit is probably unique to New Zealand and results from an environmental factor that was unique to New Zealand, namely the moas. **1989** Anderson *Prodigious Birds* 52

The moa skeletons were found in small clusters of individuals which Duff (1941) thought might reflect load-bearing variations in the surface peat. **1990** *Listener* 8 Oct. 106 Descriptions of browsing dinosaurs pushing over kauri-like trees or the atmosphere of a moa barbecue at Shag Point are vibrant. **1990** *Listener* 20 Aug. 27 The egg recovered by Eyles and Duff was placed reverently in Canterbury Museum to take its place among the last survivors of a breed: the world's only intact moa egg water-bottle.

b. As an adjectival Comb. **moa-grey** *fig.*

1964 BAXTER *Collected Poems* (1980) 292 Three moa-grey professors in a row Most ably represent the status quo.

3. Special Comb. **moa bed**, an area or cache of moa fossils, bones, or other remains; **moa bone**, the bone of the extinct moa; **Moaland** [a joc. formation recalling MAORILAND], New Zealand.

1873 *TrNZI* V. 94 *On Moa Beds.* By W.B.D. Mantell, F.G.S. **1888** BULLER *Birds NZ* I. xxx As the first explorer of the artificial Moa-beds, his opinion is entitled to great weight. **1843** TAYLOR *Diary* 17 July in Mead *Richard Taylor* (1966) 40 'And there discovered a complete Valley filled with **moa bones** not far short of elephant's in point of size.' **1858** THOMSON *Reconn. Survey S. Dist. Otago* in Taylor *Early Travellers* (1959) 333 Moa bones are found here in abundance... He and his tribe feasted on the moa in his younger years. **1860** in Butler *First Year* Jan. (1863) iii 35 They showed me some moa bones which they had ploughed up. **1879** HINGSTON *Australian Abroad* 329 We wanted a moa-bone as a relic, and a tattooed Maori's head also, if they could be got; but no such good fortune happened to us. **1888** BULLER *Birds NZ* I. xviii The first Moa-bone of which we have any record was a mere fragment of a femur..which was brought to England in 1839. *Ibid.* I. xxii In 1852-55 it fell the lot of Mr. Walter Mantell..to explore the Moa-bone deposits. **1895** *TrNZI* XXVII. 237 A little further on were groups of Maori ovens, and quantities of small fragments of moa-bones. **1920** *Otago Witness* (Dunedin) 2 Nov. 54 We often came across moa bones on the surface. **1957** FRAME *Owls Do Cry* (1967) 50 Toby, when you get better we will go to the rubbish dump and find things. A diamond. A lump of gold. A moa bone. **1989** ANDERSON *Prodigious Birds* 51 In 1891 Forbes collected numerous moa bones from ploughed land at Enfield, and estimated that 800–900 moa skeletons had been deposited there. **1905** *Truth* 12 Aug. 2 On a dirty, windy day Athletic Park is probably the very bleakest spot in **Moaland**. **1947** STEVENSON *Maori & Pakeha* 156 Apparently some time during the early part of the 19th century, the continuity of this ancient form of life was finally broken and Moaland became Maoriland.

moa-hunter.

a. A term first used by Haast c1870 to denote a person who hunted moas; later (from quot. 1922) used to describe a member of an early stage of New Zealand Maori culture, associated with hunting of the moa and use of its bones and eggs for artefacts. Also *attrib.*

1870 HAAST in *Proc. Zool. Soc.* 53 I have been so fortunate as to find a large Moa-hunters' encampment, with their cooking-places and kitchen-middens. **1872** *TrNZI* IV. 66 [Title] *Moas and Moa Hunters.* Mr Davie was of the opinion that the author [*sc.* Haast] had not by any means clearly established that the Moa-hunters were a distinct race from the Maoris. **1884** *NZJSc.* II. 295 The Moa hunters were more favoured..in this district [*sc.* Canterbury] with a supply of food. **1893** *TrNZI* XXV. 34 [Dr Haast] persists in denying the ethnical identity of the moa-hunters and the Maoris. **1922** *Auckland Weekly News* 22 July 16 [Mr Skinner] thought the moa hunters could be placed at a period antecedent to 1000 years ago. **1933** *Na To Hoa Aroha* (1988) III. 73 The work done by Skinner and others in investigating the moa-hunters does not reveal any other than Eastern Polynesian stock. **1951** CRESSWELL *Canterbury Tales* 7 Whether or not you believe this, it is certainly true that about 1066 the Moa-hunters and Morioris arrived in Canterbury. **1959** SINCLAIR *History* 15 Excavations in both islands have uncovered something of the life of an almost forgotten people, perhaps the first inhabitants of New Zealand, who are called the moa-hunters because of the association in their graves and middens of their characteristic tools or ornaments and the bones and eggs of the moa. **1963** *NZ Geog* Apr. 96 By using a small 'm' for 'moahunters' Dr Cumberland skilfully avoids entanglement in the current controversy among New Zealand prehistorians over the respective claims of 'Moa-hunter Maori' or 'Archaic East Polynesian' to designate the early phase. **1977** DUFF *Moa-hunter* xii Because this hunting economy and imported artifact styles coincided with the then unknown period of the extermination of the Moa in particular, Skinner, Duff and Buck revived the term *Moa-hunter Maori* to distinguish the first phase of ecological adaptation from the climax Classic Maori phase of the eighteenth century... The term Moa-hunter is preferred here to the longer 'Archaic Phase of New Zealand East Polynesian', too easily corrupted to 'Archaic Maori', with 'Archaic' meaning only 'early'. **1989** ANDERSON *Prodigious Birds* 6 A substantial consensus on these matters [of ancestry of *moa-hunter* and application of the term], not achieved until the 1950s, was that the moa-hunters were exclusively east Polynesian by ancestry (and Maori by retrospective ascription), and had arrived about 1200 years ago, bringing with them a distinctive aceramic, neolithic material culture... For the early assemblage Duff revived Haast's term 'Moa-hunter' which, by implication, inverted the proposition that people who hunted moas had a certain kind of material culture. *Ibid.* 109 As for the term 'Moa-hunter' it has, in my view, outlived its usefulness. Even in the lower-case it implies something about cultural typology to which it is quite inappropriate.

b. *Joc.* One who pursues reputed moa sightings, usu. during the summer journalistic 'silly season'.

1993 *Evening Post* (Wellington) 4 Feb. 4 [Advt] The modern day moa hunter is recognisable by a circular emblem containing a bird form and the words The Original Swanndri, generally worn on the left breast of the outer garment.

Hence **moa-hunting** *vbl. n.* and *ppl. a.*

1872 *TrNZI* IV. 78 Proceeding now to the traces left by the moa-hunting population. **1905** WHITE *My NZ Garden* 109 Moa-hunting might afford good sport, and their joints give variety to the butchers' shops. **1933** in *Na To Hoa Aroha* (1988) III. 73 A push by conquering tribes in the North or the call of adventure—greenstone and moa-hunting—would force or attract from the North to the South. **1937** BUICK *Moa-Hunters NZ* 231 Consistent with this spirit of precaution, might it not..have been considered indiscreet to become communicative regarding their Moa-hunting exploits? **1948** COWAN *Down the Years in the Maniototo* 5 The greenstone and the moa-hunting expeditions would halt wherever food was available. **1963** *NZ Geogr.* Apr. 95 The importance of this essay is the convincing case presented for the wholesale devastation of forest as early as the thirteenth century..when the pivot of the early fishing and fowling economy appears to have been moa-hunting. **1989** ANDERSON *Prodigious Birds* 157 Moa-hunting was very probably an individual or small group activity in which snares, dogs and wooden spears were used.

Moari(e), var. MAORI.

moa stone. Also occas. **moa gizzard stone.** [In some uses poss. from Ma. *moa* a kind of stone: cf. Williams 203 *Moa* a stone often found in spherical masses, some compound of iron; also called *moamoa.*] Usu. *pl.* A round stone, one of many found in groups or masses, and reputed to be a moa gizzard or crop stone. See also *bird-stone* (BIRD *n.* 4).

[**1820** LEE & KENDALL *NZ Gram. & Vocab.* 181 *Móa s.* A stone, also the name of a person, and of a place.] **1856** TANCRED *Nat. Hist. Canterbury* 13 There are found on parts of the plains little heaps of rounded agate or quartz pebbles (far distant from any rocks of that nature) which are popularly called 'moa stones', and are supposed to be the contents of the gizzards of those birds which have died at the places where these heaps are found. **1863** BUTLER *First Year* ix 139 I do not remember finding a single sandstone specimen of a moa gizzard stone. **1872** *TrNZI* IV. 71 The testimony that Moa bones have been found lying loose amongst the grass on the shingle of the [Canterbury] plains, together with small heaps of so-called Moa stones where probably a bird died & decayed, is too strong to be set aside altogether. **1888** BULLER *Birds NZ* I. xxviii With many of these buried skeletons are found little heaps of crop-stones... I have in my possession a very interesting collection of these 'gizzard-stones', consisting of quartz-pebbles, carnelians, and pieces of chert, all worn and polished by attrition... [**1888** *Note*] Mr. Frederick Chapman (to whom I am indebted for these 'Moa-stones') writes [etc.]. **1893** *TrNZI* XXV. 27 To aid in the digestion of this food, the moa, like many other birds, swallowed little pebbles, which, rounded & polished by the friction of their stomach, assumed a peculiar form, and are called to this day 'moa-stones' by the natives, who are familiar with them. **1925–26** *NZJST* VIII. 65 [Australian] settlers called them [*sc.* australites] 'gum-stones,' as we in New Zealand say 'moa-stones.' **1970** MCNEISH *Mackenzie* 29 Polson rummaged in a bag and brought out some tiny pebbles. 'And these,' he went on, 'are moa stones.' As he rolled them on the table, the surface radiated with a chameleon intensity. **1985** STUDHOLME *Coldstream* xiii These bones were not, as one would expect them to be, near the moa stones, but scattered generally over the run. [**1990** *Dominion* (Wellington) 19 Oct. 9 In a rare prosecution under the Antiquities Act, Masao Yamakawa, 39, admitted in Christchurch District Court attempting to take two moa gizzard stones and a moa toe bone.]

mob, *n.* [Transf. use of *mob* a disorderly or riotous crowd, a rabble: see OED *mob n.*[1]]

1. a. *Hist.* [AND 1828 applied to Aborigines.] Often in the phr. **a mob of natives**, a crowd or party of (potentially hostile) Maori.

1834 in McNab *Old Whaling Days* (1913) 424 A mob of natives came running into the hut where we stopped. **1845** WAKEFIELD *Adventure NZ* I. 437 The 'mob' of natives, having rushed in upon their fallen foe. **1849** TORLESSE *Papers* (1958) 63 We all went..to Goashore by 4p.m., meeting a mob of Moeraki natives at Kai-tiri-tiri. **1886** BURROWS *Heke's War* 32 A considerable mob of Heke's people passed through our settlement. [The word *party* replaces 'mob' in the 1845 MS, Tues 27 May 1845.] **1991** *Press* (Christchurch) 16 Oct. 20 Mr O'Regan has vanquished the northerners before the Waitangi, the media and the courts and now intends to have pakeha legislation confirm his claim that Te Rauparaha's mob were driven out of 'Ngai Tahu' lands.

b. In modern use in the name of a Maori-organized gang **Mongrel Mob**, reputedly deriving from a magistrate's derogatory reference to a group before his court. Cf. MOBSTER, MONGREL 3.

1984 WILSON *S. Pacific Street* 4 He said he was a mongrel. Then in the police station, according to the constable's evidence, he broke down and said he wanted to leave the mob. **1986** *National Radio* 'Morning Report' 17 Dec. [George Mamfredos, Leader of the Mongrel Mob speaks:] Whatever cause the mob sets itself every mobster is required to adhere to it.

2. Applied to an assembly of originally large animals often considered in some way wild or needing control, esp. farm animals, usu. sheep or cattle. **a.** A flock or drove of sheep; a herd or drove of cattle, including milking cows to which *herd* would now usu. be applied.

[*Note*] *Flock*, recorded in New Zealand from 1841, is now a formal term which does not usu. connote a *drove* of sheep as *mob* can, being defined for the purposes of official statistics as a 'group of two or more sheep with a single owner'. It is in freq. use in Comb. such as *flock-master*, *flock-owner* (both recorded from 1844).

1842 *NZ Journal* III. 22 A herd [of cattle], or mob as we call it. **1853** DEANS *Letters* (1937) 24 Sept. 295 I should like to put all the calvers in one mob. **1856** SEWELL *Journal* (1980) II. 215 How to get your Sheep out of a mixed mob—that's a trial for human patience. **1860** DONALDSON *Bush Lays & Rhymes* 14 Now to the stockyard crowds the mob, 'twill soon be milking-time. **1867** BARKER *Station Life* (1870) 169 It was more horrible to see the drowning..huddled-up 'mob' (as sheep *en masse* are technically called). **1874** KENNAWAY *Crusts* 46 It needs incessant care to prevent stragglers breaking away from the head and sides of the mob, and the rear of the flock, made up of the weaker sheep, requires an equally constant lookout. **1882** POTTS *Out in Open* 72 The gang of musterers is actively engaged in collecting the straggling sheep into large mobs. **1928** *Weekly News* 12 Jan. [Caption] A mob of nearly three thousand cattle was mustered and yarded for branding and drafting. **1950** *NZJAg.* July LXXXI. 7 Its purpose is to divide a mixed flock..into any required number of smaller mobs. **1967** DIBBLE *A Way of Love* in *NZ Short Stories III* (1975) 151 The farmer walked his horse behind the mob. **1982** *Agric. Gloss.* (MAF) 5 *Mob*: [Used of] Sheep Cattle Goats Horses. Usually smaller group within a flock or herd.

b. Extended to animals other than sheep and cattle.

c1846 WEEKES *My Island* in Rutherford & Skinner *Establish. New Plymouth* (1940) 130 After a little quiet watching I observed a mob of some fifty pigs hunt down a lamb, and then gobble it up. **1856** ROBERTS *Diary* June in Beattie *Early Runholding* (1947) 34 We now had quite a large mob of breeding mares on the run. **1868** BARKER *Station Life* (1870) 234 At the entrance of the gorge is a large stockyard, and near to it..a large mob of horses is generally to be found feeding. **1875** *TrNZI* VII. 130. For about 400 birds of this large size [*sc.* Moas] to have been roasted in so small a compass in one mob would be a physical impossibility. **c1875** MEREDITH *Adventuring in Maoriland* (1935) 97 In the morning our dogs stuck up a mob of pigs on a small, clear-topped rise. **1904** CRADOCK *Sport in NZ* 57 A bevy, or 'mob' [of pheasants] (as every collection of any living thing is called in New Zealand). **1933** *Press* (Chistchurch) (Acland Gloss.) 4 Nov. 15 *Mob*.—Any number of sheep, cattle, or horses together. The words *herd* and *flock*..are not used in this sense in New Zealand. *M*[*ob*] is also applied to birds and wild animals; e.g., ducks, quail, deer, or pigs. **1943** HISLOP *Pure Gold* 49 I pointed to a mob of paradise ducks in his turnip field. **1960** CRUMP *Good Keen Man* 21 We saw nine deer in one mob and had no rifle. **1986** RICHARDS *Off the Sheep's Back* 31 Sometimes an acre would have to be resown owing to large mobs of quail eating the seed.

3. [AND 1848.] A group of people (esp. workmen) with common work or social interests or a common identity. Cf. ROB'S MOB.

1845 WAKEFIELD *Adventure NZ* I. 309 He was most pleased with the eccentricities of the 'Whaling mob' he had to rule. **1852** *Austral. & NZ Gaz.* 10 Jan. 11 In Major Hornbrook's words, 'the *Steadfast's* mob is a much jollier mob than that of the *Duke of Bronte*'. (The word 'mob' in colonial diction only means a 'set of people'.) **1861** DUPPA *Diary* in Crawford *Sheep & Sheepmen Canterbury* (1949) 48 Commence shearing with a strong mob of shearers. **1907** KOEBEL *Return of Joe* 257 [He] had but a few hours ago formed one of their 'mob,' and [was] the most skilful bushwhacker in the district. **1916** *Chron. NZEF* 16 Oct. 87 It was good to see the splendid eagerness of the 'mob' generally for work. **1960** ASHTON-WARNER *Incense to Idols* 23 I know one girl from another, course you do in my mob anyway.

mob, *v*. *Farming*. [f. MOB *n*. 2: AND 1856.] Also **mob up. a.** *trans*. To muster or collect (stock) into a (or one) mob.

1863 BUTLER *First Year* viii 126 The sheep being mobbed up together near the spot where they are intended to enter the water, the best plan is to split off a small number. **1922** PERRY *Sheep Farming* 92 It is essential to see that the rams get well amongst the ewes, which should be well 'mobbed up' if not mustered. **1947** NEWTON *Wayleggo* 85 Little mobs everywhere, all of which had to be caught and mobbed up. **1958** *Auckland Weekly News* 10 Sept. 3 By mobbing stock, Ruakura experts showed that sheep could be kept free from facial eczema if the farmer acted quickly enough. **1960** *Proc. 10th Lincoln College Farmers' Conference* 98 The Bush Gully cows are mobbed up and on 15 January the first bulls..are put with the cows. **1970** MCNAUGHTON *Tat* 61 They found the dogs had about one hundred and fifty ewes mobbed against a boundary fence. **1980** *Evening Post* (Wellington) 6 May 16 Dogs are efficient in wide open spaces for mobbing and driving sheep but they should be chained up on reaching yards. **1981** *Star* (Christchurch) 30 May 7 We are starting to mob up the ewes.

b. *intr*. Of sheep (and occas. of other animals), to gather (or join) in a mob.

1878 CHUDLEIGH *Diary* 10 Mar. (1950) 267 Spent some hours driving the main mob of sheep from the fence where they mob day and night. **1953** STRONACH *Musterer on Molesworth* 31 Thus the sheep missed previously have the opportunity to 'mob up' and join in with the shorn sheep. **1958** *The NZ Young Farmer* X. No.14 114 When the shepherd is riding round the ewes they tend to move in front of him and mob up in a corner of the paddock near a gateway. **1960** MASTERS *Back-Country Tales* 185 They mobbed, then with tails and manes flying took off full gallop up the valley. **1981** ANDERSON *Both Sides of River* 78 When the strings of sheep were mobbing on Jack's Flat, the end of the muster was in sight.

mob grazing: see MOB STOCKING.

mobster. [f. (MONGREL) MOB + gang)*ster*, with a play on US *mobster*.] A member of the Mongrel Mob Maori gang. See also MONGIE. Cf. GANGSTER, MOB *n*. 1 b, MONGREL 3.

1986 *National Radio* 'Morning Report' 17 Dec. [George Mamfredos, Leader of the Mongrel Mob speaks:] Whatever cause the mob sets itself every mobster is required to adhere to it. **1991** *Sunday Star* (Auckland) 4 Aug. A3 [Heading] Mobsters grilled over vet killing. The police see Mongrel Mob members as prime suspects for the killing. **1994** *North & South* (Auckland) Dec. 84 Fotu claimed to have been at a mobster (Mongrel Mob) party..and to have gone from there to the dairy.

mob-stock *v*.: see MOB STOCKING.

mob stocking, *vbl*. *n*. *Farming*. Also **mob grazing**. The moving of a mob of grazing livestock from paddock to paddock, often called 'intensive' or 'rotational' grazing; the placing of a large mob of cattle in a confined area of land to clear it of scrub or roughage.

1951 LEVY *Grasslands NZ* (1970) 303 Both hard fern and piripiri decline and disappear if the pasture is stimulated by topdressing and by the adoption of an off-and-on mob grazing system. **1953** *NZ Farmer* 8 Oct. 47 Mr Lockhart says the greatest improvement in hill country will come from adoption in some farm or another of the policy found successful on flat farm lands—rotational grazing or, better termed 'mob stocking'. **1959** *Ibid*. 2 Apr. 15 Mob stocking is similar [to rotation grazing] but more aptly describes the practice of using a large mob of stock confined to a restricted area for the particular purpose of clearing away unwanted roughage or rubbish.

Hence **mob-stock** *v*. *trans*. and *intr*., to graze intensively, to move (a mob) from paddock to paddock at short intervals.

1960 *Proc. of 10th Lincoln College Farmers Conference* 69 The stud ewes are mob-stocked during the six weeks on the tussock. **1982** *Agric. Gloss.* (MAF) 7 *Mob Stock*: To move herd or flock from paddock to paddock at short intervals (also called 'intensive grazing' or 'rotational grazing').

moca, var. MUKA.

moccasin. Also as a familiar short form **moc**. Usu. *pl*. [Prob. transf. f. N. Amer. (Indian) *moccasin*: cf. also Brit. dial. *mokins* garters made of coarse sacking; *moggins* clogs.] Shearers' temporary sacking footwear usu. cut from a wool-pack (see quot. 1966).

c1927 SMITH *Sheep & Wool Industry* 75 The shearers at the pen gates arrayed in their working clothes, with bowyangs..and moccasins on (a kind of shoe made out of wool-pack, after the style of the foot-covering of the Red Indian). **1934** *Press* (Christchurch) (Acland Gloss.) 27 Jan. 15 *Moccasins* are the sacking slippers which most shearers make to work in. **1959** MIDDLETON *The Stone* 53 The shearers would be back in the whare... They would make new pairs of jute moccasins. **1964** MIDDLETON *Walk on Beach* 243 Have they taken their handpieces and mocs and gone to chase better money elsewhere? **1966** *Encyclopedia NZ* III. 229 Shearers nearly all wear..home-made sacking 'moccasins', which are soft on the feet and nonslippery on the greasy shearing board. **1978** JARDINE *Shadows on Hill* 131 They [*sc*. shearers] were all dressed in the recognised style, blue sleeveless bush singlets..white moleskin trousers supported by bowyangs below the knees, and moccasins made from woollen caps. **1981** SUTHERLAND & TAYLOR *Sunrise* 44 He found the cap of a woolbale and cut his shearing moccasins from it with a pair of blades.

mock, *a*. [See OED *mock a*. 2.] In culinary preparations, 'imitation' as in special Comb. **mock cream**, an imitation cream filling for cakes and sponges; **mock whitebait**, see WHITEBAIT 2 b.

c1929 *Nelson Cookery Book* 80 **Mock Cream**... ³/₄ cup milk, 1 dessertspoon cornflour, 1 tablespoon butter, a small ¹/₂ cup flour. **1961** *'Sure to Rise' Cook. Book* 35 Mock Cream... Mix cornflour and milk together smoothly, boil for 3 or 4 minutes. Mix butter and sugar to a cream, add cooked cornflour when cold, beat well. Mock Cream Filling 3 oz. butter, 2 oz. sugar, ¹/₂ teaspoon gelatine softened in 1 tablespoon cold water... 2 tablespoons boiling water. **1986** *Listener* 12 July 52 As far as I know, 'mock cream' cake fillings are indigenous to this country. There are no similar recipes

mockamock, var. MAKOMAKO *n.*[1] and *n.*[2]

mocker, *n.*[1] [f. MAKO *n.*[2]: see comment at MOCKING-BIRD: for variant forms see MAKOMAKO *n.*[1] 1 b, MOCKIE *n.*[1]] BELLBIRD 1.

1871 [see MAKOMAKO[1] 1 b]. **1872** *Appendix Proc. Otago Prov. Council* 39 The following is a list of the birds shot..*Anthornis melanura*, bell bird or mocker [etc.]. **1896** *TrNZI* XXVIII. 361 The bell-bird, familiarly called the 'mocker'. **1904** *TrNZI* XXXVI. 129 The cuckoo had a full-grown mocker..in its claws. **1934** HARPER *Windy Island* 307 Mako-mako New Zealand 'bell-bird', popularly known as the 'mocker' or 'mockie'.

mocker, *n.*[2] [Origin unknown: AND 1953.] Clothes, attire; 'clobber', 'gear'. See also *Groppi mocker* (GROPPI 1).

1947 NEWTON *Wayleggo* 154 We needed a pretty useful sense of humour to see the fun in climbing out of bed and donning clammy, greasy shearing mocker. *Ibid.* 154 *Mocker*: clothes. **1959** SLATTER *Gun in My Hand* 51 Gets into his old mocker and gets stuck in. Just one of the boys. *Ibid.* 205 Say, have you seen that trol in the blue mocker?

Hence **mockered** *ppl. a.*, dressed up.
1965 SHADBOLT *Among the Cinders* 250 She was mockered up to the nines.

mockie, *n.*[1] Also **mocky**, **moki**, **mokky**. [f. MAKO *n.*[2]] BELLBIRD 1 a and b, occas. early, TUI (see quot. 1946). Cf. MAKOMAKO *n.*[1] 1 b, MOCKER *n.*[1]

1903 *NZ Illustr. Mag.* VIII. 355 As the first sun-ray tipped the hill, the mocky's call sounded. **1903** *Otago Witness* (Dunedin) 18 Nov. 68 I can hear the mokis and other birds singing outside on the trees. **1933** mokky [see BELLBIRD 1 a]. **1934** 'mockie' [see MOCKER *n.*[1]]. **1946** *JPS* LV. 147 *tui*..an excellent mimic, and so by the settlers called the mocking-bird, shortened to mockie... Then, because some folk thought mockie was short for makomako, a name of the bell-bird (korimako) in some parts, some thought it was the korimako which was the mimic. **1966** FALLA et al. *Birds NZ* 218 Bellbird *Anthornis melanura*.. Korimako, Makomako, Mockie. **1970** MCLEOD *Glorious Morning* (Gloss.) 255 '*Mockie*' (makomako): The little green bellbird. **1974** ANDERSON *Mary-Lou* 47 The bellbirds sometimes called Mockie, (which is a corruption of their Maori name *mako*) that visit our garden are ridiculously tame.

mockie, *n.*[2] Mainly *Otago–Southland.* Also **moki**. [f. MAKO *n.*[3]] WINEBERRY 1.

1967 MCLATCHIE *Tang of Bush* 59 Taking the axe [c1900]..I searched the bush for a moki (mako-mako) tree with a slight bend. *Ibid.* 66 Moki sticks were burnt in the fire until just right for charcoal [c1900].

mocki mock, var. MAKOMAKO *n.*[1]

mocking-bird. [Transf. use of northern hemisphere *mocking-bird* for TUI, a mimic: occas. as an adaptation of MAKO *n.*[1] (see also MOCKER *n.*[1], MOCKIE *n.*[1]), the bell-bird, which is not, as it is often thought to be, a mimic or mocking-bird.] TUI 1; occas. also erron. BELLBIRD 1 (see quot. 1853).

1773 FORSTER *Resolution Jrnl.* (1982) II. 278 Mocking birds, Yellowheads & various other birds inhabit these impenetrable Forests. **1830** CRAIK *New Zealanders* 187 The most remarkable bird is one to which Cook's people gave the name of mocking-bird, from the extraordinary variety of its notes. **1838** POLACK *NZ* I. 296 The *tui*, or mocking-bird, is best known to the stranger in the country. The natives vend these birds, in wicker cages, to their transient visitors: it is called tui, from the resemblance of its note to that sound. **1845** DEANS *Pioneers* (1964) 44 The most remarkable bird of the singing species is the tui, mocking bird or parson bird, by all which names it is called. Mocking bird because it tries to imitate a great many others. **1853** MACKIE *Traveller under Concern* (1973) 90 I was struck by the clear melodious notes of a bird which our [Nelson] party called the mocking bird, it was of an olive green colour about the size of a thrush [*sc.* a bellbird]. **1859** THOMSON *Story NZ* I. 24 [One honeysucker], well known among the settlers and the natives by the name of Tui, is the Parson or Mocking-bird of navigators. **1867** THOMSON *Twelve Yrs. Canterbury* 15 Several kinds of birds are indigenous to the woods and waters; among them the oyster-catcher, bittern..mocking or parson bird. **1883** DOMETT *Ranolf & Amohia* II. 338 Mocking-bird or Tui..and 'Parsonbird', by Captain Cook. **1899** DOUGLAS in *Mr Explorer Douglas* (1957) 267 As for there [*sic*] being called the mocking bird, I never heard such a name applied to them... [I] never once heard the Tui imitate anything. **1912** FERGUSON *Castle Gay* 60 See here are met... The robin's chirp and lintie's trill, And mocking bird, with fantail heard, And parroquet's green clamouring shrill. **1946** [see MOCKIE *n.*[1]].

mocky, var. MOCKIE *n.*[1]

moeone. [Ma. /ˈmoeone/: Williams 204 *Moeone..3...* bass.] BASS.

1921 *NZJST* IV. 114 Polyprion... *Bass; Moeone.* Generally to be secured in deeper water than the groper. **1956** GRAHAM *Treasury NZ Fishes* 224 Bass Groper (Moeone)... This large fish was at one time thought to be the well-known Groper or Hapuku but it is now known to be specifically different. It is wider and deeper in the body. It also has larger eyes and bigger scales. **1966** DOOGUE & MORELAND *Sea Anglers' Guide* 226 Bass... Other names: *Polyprion moeone*; bass-groper; moeone, toti (Maori)... This fish is very similar to the hapuku (grouper) and should be fished for in exactly the same manner. **1981** WILSON *Fisherman's Bible* 32 The Maori name 'Moeone' is frequently used for this fish [Bass] which can grow up to almost two metres.

Moeraki boulder. [f. Ma. (Ngai Tahu dial.) *Moeraki* /ˈmoeraki/, the name of a north Otago beach area.] Any of variously sized (up to 2 m in diameter) spherical boulders formed by crystalization around an organic core or seed and found on beaches near Moeraki (see esp. quot. 1966).

[**1844** SELWYN *Journal* 19 Jan. *NZ Part III* (Church in the Colonies VIII) (1851) 15 After breakfast we walked on to Moerangi whaling station, passing on the way..some most remarkable boulders, which appear to have been formed not by rolling but by crystallization.] **1879** *Auckland Weekly News* 4 Oct. 15 The irregularity in composition of the Moeraki boulders is so great that it would be practically impossible to manufacture cement from them of uniform quality. **1903** *TrNZI* XXXV. 193 They appear to be of a dense black basalt, many of them round in shape, and..somewhat of the look of Moeraki boulders. **1940** MCCLYMONT *Exploration of NZ* (1959) 49 [Mantell] studied the Moeraki boulders and remarked that the whalers called them 'Ninepins' and the spot itself 'Vulcan's Foundry'. **1966** *Encycl. NZ* II. 575 The Moeraki Boulders are situated..midway between Hampden and Moeraki townships in North Otago... The boulders are grey-coloured septarian concretions, which have been eroded out by wave action from the cliffs of soft, black mudstone that back the beach. **1985** *Listener* 6 Apr. 91 Along the way she [*sc.* Shona McFarlane] also looks at natural art. 'Sculptures' like the Moeraki boulders. **1991** *Dominion Sunday Times* (Wellington) 28 Apr. 2 They [*sc.* the Maori community] planned to take sightseers to the mammals..and flora in the area, and the famous Moeraki boulders.

moeriki. [Ma. /ˈmoeriki/: Williams 205 *Moeriki..* a species of rail.] The extinct *Dieffenbach's rail* (RAIL 2 (4), *Rallus philippensis dieffenbachii*) of the Chatham Islands.

1842 GRAY *Fauna* in Dieffenbach *Travels in NZ* (1843) II. 197 *Rallus Dieffenbachii...* Moeriki of the natives of Chatham Island. **1869** *TrNZI* I. (rev. edn.) 228 The only member of the new genus *Hypotaenidia* is the Moeriki..an extremely beautiful Rail, restricted in range to the Chatham Islands. **1873** [see RAIL 2 (4)]. **1886** *TrNZI* XVIII. 113 *Rallus dieffenbachii.*—Moeriki. Chatham Islands. Extremely rare, if not extinct. **1955** [see RAIL 2 (4)].

mogey, mogge, moggy, moghee, mogi(e), mogihi, moguey, varr. MOKI *n.*[1] or *n.*[2], or MOKIHI *n.*

mohimohi. [Ma. /ˈmohimohi/: Williams 205 *Mohi* (i)..A sea fish. *mohimohi...* 2..pilchard.] PILCHARD (*Sardinops neopilchardus*).

1903 *TrNZI* XXXV. 319 About 60 lb..weight of pilchard or mohimohi. **1921** *NZJST* IV. 118 *Pilchard; Mohimohi.* Sold in a smoked condition in Wellington as 'Picton herring'. **1938** [see PILCHARD]. **1956** GRAHAM *Treasury NZ Fishes* 104 Pilchard (Mohimohi)... The Pilchard is known from the northern end of the South Island as the Picton Herring.

moho. [Ma. /ˈmoho/: Williams 205 *Moho* (i) *1. Notornis.*] TAKAHE.

1848 R. TAYLOR in *Proc. Zool. Soc.* (1850) XVIII. 211 [OED] *Moho* Rail, colour black, said to be a wingless bird as large as a fowl..; it is nearly exterminated by the cat. **1851, 1873** [see TAKAHE]. **1898** STACK *South Island Maoris* 87 When told that they had killed [their prisoner], he said 'You have done foolishly, for not a soul of you will now be spared; you will be banished to the haunts of the moho..and in the depths of the forest will be your only place of safety.' **1966** FALLA et al. *Birds NZ* 109 Takahe: *Notornis mantelli...* Moho. **1985** *Reader's Digest Book NZ Birds* 170 Takahe *Notornis mantelli...* Moho.

moho-pereru. [Ma. /ˈmohopeˈru/: cf. Williams 206 *moho pererū* banded rail.] *banded rail* (RAIL 2 (2) *Rallus philippensis*).

1871 HUTTON *Catalogue Birds NZ* 32 Striped Rail. Mohopereru. **1873** BULLER *Birds NZ* 176 *Rallus philippensis.* (Striped Rail)... Patatai, Popotai, Mohotatai, Moho-patatai, Moho-pereru. **1886** *TrNZI* XVIII. 117 *Rallus philippensis.*—Mohopereru, Striped Rail. **1904, 1955** [see RAIL 2 (2)]. **1966** [see RAIL 2 (9)]. **1990** *Checklist Birds NZ* 118 *Rallus philippensis assimilis...Banded Rail* (Moho-pereru)... Main islands of New Zealand.

mohoua, var. MOHUA.

mohua. Also **mohoua.** [Ma. /ˈmohua/: Williams 206 *Mohua...* yellowhead.] YELLOWHEAD.

1842 GRAY *Fauna* in Dieffenbach *Travels in NZ* (1843) II. 189 *Mohoua ochrocephala...* Mohoua houa of the natives of Tasman Bay... Popokatea, natives of Cook's Straits. **1870** *TrNZI* II. 57 Mohoua ochrocephala..Mohoua. Canary. **1904, 1966** [see CANARY *n*.¹ 1]. **1990** *Checklist Birds NZ* 205 Yellowhead (*Mohua*)... Formerly widespread in South and Stewart Island forests, now well established only in Fiordland and at Arthur's Pass National Park.

moia, var. MOA.

moit. *Woolgrowing*. [f. Brit. dial. *moit* (a variant form of *mote*) a particle of wood, stick, etc. caught in the wool of sheep: see OED; AND 1899.] Light vegetable matter contaminating fleece-wool.
1982 *Agric. Gloss.* (MAF) 57 *Moit*: Light vegetable matter contamination (also called shive). **1985** BREMNER *Woolscours NZ* 9 *Moit* vegetable matter—leaves, fern, hay (but not seeds or burr)—in wool.

Hence **moity** (also **morty**) *a*. [AND 1878]. Of wool, contaminated with moit.
c1927 SMITH *Sheep & Wool Industry* 115 Topknot—consisting of very light, short, moity, and inferior wool. **1955** BOWEN *Wool Away* 32 [One blow is made]..with the comb on the side to cut the morty [*sic*, prob. from pronunciation] neck wool (the first few inches up the neck) that is always a bit cotty and is the hardest to break.

mokapuna, var. MOKOPUNA.

moke. [Transf. use of *moke* a donkey: AND 1863.]
1. A horse, often used light-heartedly or with connotations of inferiority.
1880 LAPHAM *We Four* 31 I caught my moke. **1898** HOCKEN *Contributions* 193 Frankton was called [by W.G. Rees] after Mrs. Rees' Christian name, Frances..and Moke Creek [c1860] after old Donald, the first horse which fed upon its grassy banks. **1906** *Truth* 3 Mar. 6 A bush horse-owner [was] hauled up to explain the running of his moke. **c1924** ANTHONY *Gus Tomlins* (1977) 17 As I pointed out to him, what's the use of shooting a good moke like that just because he's high-spirited? **1934** mud mokes [see DUB *n*. 1]. **1955** *BJ Cameron Collection* (TS July) moke (n) A horse. **1960** BOSWELL *Ernie* 105 Seems they swapped over the bridles and saddles of the horses..and hitched the mokes to different posts. **1981** CHARLES *Black Billy Tea* 17 Where are the boys they used to breed, That liked their horses rough? A moke that couldn't buck them off They thought was ladies' stuff.
2. As **the Mokes**, a nickname of the Colonial Transport Corps during the New Zealand Wars.
1863 MORGAN *Journal* (1963) Dec. 135 By-the-bye, let no gentleman or lady, if sending a letter to any person in this corps, address it to 'the Mokes'. Such a derogatory title will not be recognised... The communication..must be addressed to the 'Colonial Transport Corps', or what is very much shorter, to the 'C.T.C.'

mok-e-mok, var. MAKOMAKO *n*.¹

moki: see MOCKIE *n*.²; MOKIMOKI *a*.

moki, var. MAKO *n*.³

moki /ˈmʌuki/, *n*.¹ Also early **mogge, moghee**. [Ma. /ˈmoki/: Williams 207 *Moki* (i)...*Latridopsis ciliaris*.]
1. Sea-fishes of either of the families Latrididae which includes the main central and southern New Zealand blue-grey species (see *blue moki* 2 (1) below); or Cheilodactylidae which includes the main NI species (see *red moki* 2 (4) below). (The unmodified form *moki* usu. denotes the *blue moki*.)
1777 ANDERSON *Journal* Feb. in Cook *Journals* (1967) III. 807 We observ'd already that the principal fish caught by the seyne were Mullets..and a fish in shape much like the Bream but so large as to weigh five, six or seven pounds. It is blackish with thick lips and calld Mogge by the natives. **1840** BEST *Journal* 4 Nov. (1966) 261 12'00 weight of Rays were taken..in Evans's Bay besides Moki and other fish. **1842** GRAY *Fauna* in Dieffenbach *Travels in NZ* (1843) II. 209 *Latris ciliaris*... This fish is named 'Moghee' by the natives of Dusky Bay. It is also an inhabitant of Queen Charlotte's Sound. **1858** SHAW *Gallop to Antipodes* 135 Besides cod, there are seals, trumpeter, moki, barracouta, flounders, skate and warihou. **1872** HUTTON & HECTOR *Fishes NZ* 108 The Moki..is an abundant fish in the Wellington market. **1882** POTTS *Out in Open* 204 [The spotted shag's] take of fish must be astonishingly great, as a half-pound moki is soon engulfed in its capacious throat. **1896** *TrNZI* XXVIII. 54 Even the moki and butter-fish join the hunt. **1902** DRUMMOND & HUTTON *Nature in NZ* 73 Neither it [*sc*. butterfish] nor the moki takes bait freely. **1922** *Auckland Weekly News* 15 June 14 The moki in the next tank is encased in soft blue velvet with fins of electric blue. **1956** GRAHAM *Treasury NZ Fishes* 255 Moki *Latridopsis ciliaris*... This is one of our popular commercial fish and ideal for either roasting, baking, boiling or frying. **1982** BURTON *Two Hundred Yrs. NZ Food* 78 Moki is an attractive blue-grey and silver fish of shallow coastal waters south of the Bay of Plenty.
2. With a modifier: **blue, copper, painted, red**.
(1) **blue moki**. *Latridopsis ciliaris* (fam. Latrididae), a large bottom-living deep-bodied olive-green (juvenile) to blue-grey (adult) sea-fish.
1972 DOAK *Fishes* 73 While blue moki, especially juveniles, occasionally lurk beneath ledges and in caves, they are more commonly seen swimming over the sand in groups or schools near rocks in deeper water beyond 30 feet. **1982** AYLING *Collins Guide* (1984) 246 The blue moki is a large bottom-living fish, common in southern New Zealand, that attains a maximum length of around 1m and a weight of over 10kg.
(2) **copper moki**. *Latridopsis forsteri* (fam. Latrididae), a silvery pink-striped, black fringed sea-fish, often found with blue moki. See also *bastard trumpeter* (TRUMPETER *n*.¹ 2 (1)).
1913 *TrNZI* XLV. 228 *Latris aerosa*... It is called by Hutton 'the copper moki'. **1972** DOAK *Fishes* 74 The bastard trumpeter, *Latridopsis forsteri*, is a common reef fish in Tasmania... Also called the copper moki, the bastard trumpeter is thinly distributed throughout New Zealand. **1988** FRANCIS *Coastal Fishes* 39 Copper moki often occur in association with blue moki, but are much less abundant.
(3) **painted moki**. *Cheilodactylus ephippium* (fam. Cheilodactylidae), a strikingly patterned sea-fish distinguished from the red moki by two pairs of small protuberances on the forehead.
1972 DOAK *Fishes* 69 Painted moki *Cheilodactylus ephippium*... Close relative of the red moki but more strikingly patterned, the painted moki was discovered in northern waters only in recent years. **1982** AYLING *Collins Guide* (1984) 245 Painted Moki *Cheilodactylus ephippium*... The painted moki is similar in shape and size to the red moki... It may be distinguished..by its elaborate colour pattern. **1986** PAUL *NZ Fishes* 104 Painted moki *Cheilodactylus ephippium*... A member of the colourful reef fauna seen, photographed and unfortunately sometimes speared by divers. **1988** FRANCIS *Coastal Fishes* 37 Painted moki are often seen in caves or crevices by day, but they also move around on the reef.
(4) **red moki**. **a.** *Cheilodactylus spectabilis* (fam. Cheilodactylidae), a large, deep-bodied sea-fish, red-brown with whitish vertical stripes and associated with reefs. See also NANUA.
1938 *TrRSNZ* LXVIII. 411 *Chironemus spectabilis*... Red moki. **1956** GRAHAM *Treasury NZ Fishes* 254 During 1919–24, several Red Moki were seen among catches of a line fisherman of Opotiki. **1967** MORELAND *Marine Fishes* 40 Red Moki..known as banded morwong in Australia and by the Maori name nanua in some of New Zealand's northern areas. **1972** DOAK *Fishes* 66 The red moki is a home-ranging fish and lives in small groups or tribes of about two to eight. **1982** AYLING *Collins Guide* (1984) 243 Coloration of the red moki is particularly distinctive, with eight red-brown vertical stripes on the body and fins set on a whitish background.
b. Used, apparently in error, for the *copper moki* (2) above.
1921 *NZJST* IV. 115 *Latridopsis aerosa*... *Red Moki*. Received occasionally in Wellington from the vicinity of D'Urville Island and the Marlborough Sounds. Distribution: Known only from the waters of the South Island.
3. Special Comb. **moki kelp**, a type of kelp providing a feeding ground for moki.
1971 *New Zealand's Heritage* I. 116 By the same token, a New Zealander wandering along any circumpolar coast on the island of South Georgia in the South Atlantic, Kerguelen in the Southern Indian Ocean, and Tierra del Fuego might not catch a moki, but he would have a good chance of finding moki kelp.

moki /ˈmʌuki/, /ˈmʌugi/, *n*.² *Hist*. The spelling **mokihi** has equal standing. Also (esp. in the southern South Island) **maggy, mogey, mogi(e), mogihi, moguey** from a Ma. variant perceived as */ˈmo:gi(hi)/. [Ma. /ˈmo:ki:/ /ˈmo:kihi/: Williams 207 *Mōkī, mōkihi*... *1*. n. Bundle..2. Raft made of a bundle of flags, rushes, or dry flower stalks of flax.] A raft, usu. of bundles of dry flax-sticks or raupo reeds. **a.** In NI use.
1835 WILSON *Jrnl*. 25 Aug. in *Missionary Life and Work in NZ* (1889) ii 25 The moki only carries one person at a time. You sit as on horseback. **1838** POLACK *NZ* I. 218 A bundle of these rushes are often tied together, to enable a person to cross a stream. These..are called mokis, are very buoyant, and resist saturation for some time. **1844** SELWYN *Journal* 17 Jan. *NZ Part III* (Church in the Colonies VIII) (1851) 14 The *mokihi* is formed of bundles of rushes, bound tightly together in the form of a boat. **1858** *AJHR* C-3 18 We crossed the river on mokis... He will effect by means of large mokis carrying upwards of a ton. **1871** MONEY *Knocking About in New Zealand* 52 Moguey, a Maori name for a raupo of flax-stick raft. **1889** WILSON *Missionary Life & Work* 26 The river we had passed on our *mokies*. **1904** *NZ Illustrated Magazine* Apr. 23 A suggestion to build a mokihi (flax stick raft) was quickly put into execution. **1936** LAMBERT *Pioneering Reminisc. Old Wairoa* 178 He..sent..his men over the hill to cut *raupo* wherewith they made *mokihis*.
b. In SI use.
1844 MONRO *Notes of a Journey* in Hocken *Contributions* (1898) 240 The method of crossing [the Waitaki] is upon a mogi, which is a floating body, somewhat in the shape of a boat, made of bundles of bulrushes tied together, and strengthened by the flowering stem of the flax. **1849** TORLESSE *Papers* (1958) 73 Went to look at a mogihi of the Moeraki

natives. **1858** THOMSON *Reconn. Survey S. Dist. Otago* in Taylor *Early Travellers* (1959) 340 They ventured upon [the Waiau River] in maggies or rafts of flax stalks. **1863** Lauper in *Over Whitcombe Pass* (1960) 50 It would take too long to make a mogie. **1871** MONEY *Knocking About NZ* 52 We began..carrying them in bundles to..where the *mogueys* or rafts were to be launched when completed. **1884** REID *Rambles on Golden Coast.* 53 It had been used by the diggers as the keel of their 'mogey'. **c1899** DOUGLAS in *Mr Explorer Douglas* (1957) 218 There are five different kinds of rafts... They are the Oblong raft, the A shaped, the Moki, the half Moki and the catamaran. **1940** STUDHOLME *Te Waimate* (1954) 128 He..would return home by means of a raupo mokihi (raft), floating down the Waitaki to Glenavy. **1952** HEINZ *Prospecting for Gold* 6 His party..floated down stream on a 'mo[kih]i', or raft built of flax sticks. **1988** MIKAERE *Te Maiharoa* 75 He would help travellers on the lake [Tekapo] by sending a fair wind to push their mokihi (reed boats) in the right direction.

mokihi *n.*: see MOKI *n.*[2]

Mokikinui spud: see SPUD 2.

moki(-mok), mokimoki, varr. MAKOMAKO.

mokimoki. [Ma. /ˈmoki/, /ˈmokimoki/: Williams 207 *Moki* (ii), *mokimoki*... a plant used for scenting oil. Cf. 1820 LEE & KENDALL *NZ Gram. & Vocab.* 182 Móki móki; A plant so called.]

1. Also **moki.** *Phymatosorus scandens* (fam. Polypodiaceae), a fern formerly used by the Maori for scenting oil.

1844 WILLIAMS *NZ Jrnl.* (1956) 110 Mokimoki a species of fern grows profusely on trees, near streams or moist places, it is a pretty little fern. **c1920** BEATTIE *Trad. Lifeways Southern Maori* (1994) 480 The mokimoki is a sort of fern which has a pleasant scent... Its fine tendrils or leaves are boiled in..woodhen oil..as a perfume. **1946** *JPS* LV. 154 *mokimoki* or *moki*, a fern (Polypodium pustulatum), used by the Maori for scenting oil, and highly valued for this purpose. **1953** DEWAR *Chaslands* 12 Fern and moki and fuchsia, laced through with lawyer bramble, grew dense and hopeless at their feet. But beyond was the native bush [in Southland]. **1989** BROWNSEY & SMITH-DODSWORTH *NZ Ferns* 65 Phymatosorus scandens..Fragrant fern, Mokimoki.

2. *Doodia mollis* (formerly *D. caudata*) (fam. Blechnaceae), a fern.

1907 LAING & BLACKWELL *Plants NZ* 322 The gum of the taramea was collected at early dawn; and with it were mixed the fronds of moki-moki (the fern *Doodia caudata*) and of the piri-piri. **1989** BROWNSEY & SMITH-DODSWORTH *NZ Ferns* 152 Doodia mollis... Mokimoki.

mokky, var. MAKOMAKO *n.*[1], MOCKIE *n.*[1]

moko, var. MAKO *n.*[3], MOKOMOKO.

moko, *n.*[1] Also early **amoco, amoko, emaho** (=he moko); erron. **moki.** [Ma. /ˈmoko/: Williams 207 *Moko.* n. *1.*]

1. a. Tattooing on the face or body, in early times incised with a special implement, in modern times applied with a tattooing needle or drawn on the surface of the skin. See also TATTOO.

1769 BANKS *Journal* 26 Nov. (1962) I. 439 They had a much larger quantity of Amoco or black stains upon their bodys and faces. [**1770** PARKINSON *Journal* (1773) 127 A Vocabulary of the Language of New Zealand... Emaho, *Tataow.* Hewaca, *A canoe.*] **1793** KING *Journal* Nov. in McNab *Hist. Records* (1914) II. 546 One or two Chiefs..were distinguished by the marks (Amoko) on their face. **1807** SAVAGE *Some Acc. of NZ* 46 The operation of tattooing, which the natives call amoco, is usually performed in the following manner. **1819** MARSDEN *Lett. & Jrnls.* (1932) 172 The chisel was constantly dipped in a liquid made of soot from a particular tree, and afterwards mixed with water, which communicates the blackness or, as they call it, the amoko. **1838** POLACK *NZ* I. 171 He was entirely marked with the *moko*, or tattoo. **1843** DIEFFENBACH *Travels in NZ* II. 33 The tattoo, or '*moko*', which is the native name, is done either with the sharp bone of a bird, or with a small chisel. **1851** SHORTLAND *S. Dist. NZ* 16 It may not be out of place here to observe, that the tattoo or 'moko', as it is termed in native language, is neither intended to constitute a distinctive mark between different tribes, nor to denote rank, as has been variously stated. **1894** *TrNZI* XXVI. 436 It only so far denotes rank as showing that the possessor of a handsome *moko* must have had the wherewithal to well remunerate the artist. **1904** TREGEAR *Maori Race* 257 The tattooing (*moko*) of a man's face in late times followed a pattern almost invariable. **1959** SLATTER *Gun in My Hand* 226 Bloody students...Drunken boys in grass skirts with cork tattoo moki but they woudn't know that and the Procesh Day lorry decorated with fernery. **1960** HILLIARD *Maori Girl* 36 She eyed the lipstick with deep suspicion and rubbed the moko on her chin. **1985** MCGILL *G'day Country* 62 I approached Lees' General Store. The kuia no longer sit against the corrugated iron fence alongside..dribbling on their moko. **1995** *National Geographic* Oct.–Dec. 40 'You coming back to see us for ta moko, Hone?' Chiefy [a Rastafarian gang member] jested, asking me..if I wanted a tattoo.

b. *transf.* and *fig.* (a) A moko pattern as a signature.

1838 POLACK *NZ* II. 92 He stoutly denied [the theft], saying he had bought it from a store up the river, but I showed him my moko or signature on the linen. **1940** WAITE *Port Molyneux* 37 'I, Toawick, are now become Rangatera or Chief of these Southern territories', and he affixed his moko (the tattoo marks on his face) to the deed. **1941** SUTHERLAND *Numismatic Hist. NZ* 81 Nias also sailed around New Zealand to secure signatures or 'moko marks' of the different Maori chiefs.

(b) *fig.* A pattern of lines on the face.

1979 MARSHALL *Supper Waltz Wilson* 39 In the dull glow of the heater she began to undress. 'Let's go away then,' he said, and the glowing element caught the lines of his face in a pattern, a *moko* almost, of resignation. **1982** SANSOM *In Grip of Island* 21 Their [*sc.* old people's] lines and wrinkles were their own and no one else's, as if, without any effort, they had grown their own personal moko.

2. Special Comb. **moko-artist**, an expert in engraving moko.

1921 *Quick March* 11 July 26 It is more than half-a-century since a 'moko' artist plied his trade among the warriors. **1935** COWAN *Hero Stories NZ* 161 Hauauru, a splendid old chieftain with a face deeply engraved by the *moko*-artist's chisel.

Hence **moko** *v. trans. fig.*, to adorn with wrinkles as though with a moko; also as a *ppl. a.* **moko'd, mokoed**, adorned with a moko or tattoo.

1973 *NZ Gaz.* Nov. No.91 33 With a smile that moko'd her aged face and warm gentle lines she weaved her plaintive fingers through my hair. **1952** BRUNO *The Hellbuster* 14 Mr. M'Fergus watched blankly as three heavily-built well-*moko'd* Maoris..climbed lightly up the ship's ladder. *Ibid.* 15 A little group apart, the *moko'd* warriors conferred. **1962** BAXTER *Collected Poems* (1980) 250 The moko'd elders Caught the message—'Clothes are what count most'. **1995** *National Geographic* Oct.–Dec. 40 Looking at the mokoed, laughing faces of Hone, Whare and Chiefy..it was hard to see them as arsonists.

moko, *n.*[2] *Ellipt.* for MOKOPUNA.

1989 *Listener* 20 Nov. 34 She won't kick the bucket till her favourite moko gets home, Mrs Pippin. **1991** *Evening Post* (Wellington) 16 Feb. 2 [Heading] Home is where the mokos are.

moko-mok, var. MAKOMAKO *n.*[2]

mokomoko. Also **moko, mokopapa.** [Ma. /ˈmoko/, /ˈmokomoko/: Williams 207 *Moko... 3.* A general term for lizards (skinks and geckos) used with various epithets. *Moko-moko, Leiolopisma* (formerly *Lygosoma*) spp., skink.] Also with various Maori qualifying suffixes, any of various small lizards, both skinks and geckos. See also GECKO *n.*[1], SKINK.

[**1820** LEE & KENDALL *NZ Gram. & Vocab.* 182 Móko móko; A small lizard.] **1842** GRAY *Fauna* in Dieffenbach *Travels in NZ* (1843) II. 202 Tiliqua Zelandica. Harmless Lizard... 'Is called *Moko-Moko* by the natives of Cook's Strait.' **1867** HOCHSTETTER *NZ* 340 I..could observe only the little Moko-Moko (*Mocoa Zelandia*..or *Lampropholis moco*). **1898** MORRIS *Austral-English* 299 Moko-moko... Maori name for the lizard, *Lygosoma ornatum*,...or *Lygosoma moko*. **1904** TREGEAR *The Maori Race* 182 A mottled and speckled lizard (*moko tapiri*) was supposed to bring forth the New Zealand cuckoo. *Ibid.* 213 [An evil omen.] If one heard the chirp of the small house-lizard (*moko-ta*). *Ibid.* 217 A certain kind of lizard (*moko-tapiri* or *moko-papa*) that lives in hollow trees. *Ibid.* 349 *The Tree Lizard.*—Moko-papa. Dactylocnemis pacificus... The Tree Lizard lives on trees and is very sluggish in its movements. It is common in the Auckland district. *Ibid.* 352 *The Common Lizard.*—Mokomoko. Lygosoma moco... The Mokomoko is found under stones and logs, both in the bush and in the open country. The colours are very variable. **1922** *Auckland Weekly News* 7 Dec 17 The universal belief amongst [the Maori] is that the bird is a transmutation of the mokopapa or ngarura-papa, the brown tree-lizard of settlers. **1928** *NZJST* IX. 288 Gecko (*Dactylocnemis* sp.): Mokopapa.—Two varieties of small nocturnal gecko inhabit the offshore [Alderman] islands. **1948** HENDERSON *Taina* 139 I also showed him a remarkable lizard called a *mokomoko* that lived in a hole in the rocks near the beach. **1966** SHARELL *The Tuatara, Lizards & Frogs of NZ* 57 The fact that in the Western Pacific the name for crocodile is Moko-tolo, and that the Maori uses the same word Moko for all lizards and also for the huge legendary saurians, the Taniwhas, suggests that it is an old belief. **1983** *Land of Mist* 76 The commonest skink is the mokomoko which may reach 18 cm in length.

mokopapa: see MOKOMOKO.

mokopuna. Also early **mokapuna, mokopoona.** [Ma. /ˈmokopuna/: Williams 208 *Mokopuna..1.* Grandchild.] In mainly Maori use until the 1980s, a (Maori) grandchild, great-niece or great-nephew. See also MOKO *n.*[2]

[**1817** NICHOLAS *Voyage NZ* II. 335 A grandson Mokopoona.] **1824** KING 29 Feb. in Elder *Marsden's Lieutenants* (1934) 256 The old grandfather was sitting by and listened with great attention and was much pleased in encouraging his mokapunas to pay attention to instruction. **1928** *Na To Hoa Aroha* (1986) I. 91 Tai has presented the House with its second 'mokopuna' also a male & descendant on his sire's side of Te Rangimatemoana. **1931** *Na To Hoa Aroha* (1987) II.

MOLE

138 Tai has a family of three. Purewa has a family of one. There are now six mokopuna. **1949** BUCK *Coming of Maori* (1950) III. 342 Though one [of two people] may be *mokopuna* to the other on the lineage count, he may also be *tuakana* [elder brother] from family descent. **1958** ASHTON-WARNER *Spinster* 58 He trusted me to care for his 'mokopuna'. **1973** FERNANDEZ *Tussock Fever* 17 The old women cared eagerly for their mokopuna—were upset if they were not given some to bring up. **1983** *Metro* (Auckland) Nov. 144 Years ago..the old Maori women would come to playcentre and teach their mokopuna the skills of Maoridom. **1992** *Metro* (Auckland) June 99 She sits in a glamorous black trouser suit, hot-pink earrings swinging wildly, intermittently answering her relentless cell phone, 'kia ora, kia ora, my dear'—asks after 'the baby, er the mokopuna' in her husky melodious voice.

mole, var. MOLL.

moles, *n. pl.* [Abbrev. of MOLESKINS: AND 1879.] MOLESKIN 1 and 2.
1881 NESFIELD *Chequered Career* 75 We spent many jolly evenings in the claims, and met men in rough flannels and dirty soil-stained moles. **1900** *Otago Witness* (Dunedin) 18 Jan. 26 [Advt] Men's Working Trousers... Coloured Moles. **1974** WOOD *Victorian New Zealanders* 32 Corduroy working trousers were commonly worn, as well as the popular off-white moleskins which, a Riverton man recalled..: 'I remember when coloured moles came in for Sunday wear, they looked fancy enough but had an awful smell.' **1989** *NZ English Newsletter* III. 25 *moles, moleskins*: Shearing trousers though not common today.

moleskin. [Spec. use of *moleskin* a strong, cotton cloth: see OED 2 & 3.]
1. As moleskin trousers [Used elsewhere but of historical significance as a regular part of early colonial male outdoor clothing: AND 1839], trousers made of moleskin fabric, the distinctive wear of colonial rural workers (esp. shearers), diggers, and later, prisoners.
1848 WAKEFIELD *Handbook NZ* 375 [List of prices]..flush trousers, 7s. to 10s. [per] pair. moleskin do., 8s. to 10s. **1871** MONEY *Knocking About NZ* 18 In a place [*sc.* the diggings] where open shirts, moleskin trousers tucked into long boots, crimson sashes tied round the waist, and tall American wide-awakes, were the prevailing attire. **1898** HOCKEN *Contributions* 130 The customary dress of the settlers was a blue woollen shirt or blouse, moleskin or cord trousers, strong boots and felt hat. **1928** *Free Lance* (Wellington) 28 Mar. 42 The grey-beards of today can recall when moleskin trousers were not out of place for the average man in Wellington. **1930** DOBSON *Reminiscences* 156 During the exploring days the clothes worn were the strongest procurable, moleskin trousers, very thick and heavy, either brown or white (moleskin is a thick twilled cotton material, and when wet it is almost waterproof and like soft leather), stout flannels, and a flannel shirt.
2. Usu. *pl.* as **moleskins**, *ellipt.* for *moleskin trousers* (see 1 above).
1905 THOMSON *Bush Boys* 164 'E [*sc.* the parson] didn't stand on no confounded ceremony, but soon appeared in the moleskins and jersey of the bushmen, and..made 'isself quite at 'ome among 'em. **1913** CARR *Country Work* 6 Don't bring out [to New Zealand] moleskins..they are as out-of-date as the `Moa'. **1934** LEE *Children of the Poor* (1949) 21 I can shut my eyes and see that shuffling parade of men in broad-arrowed moleskins. **1989** [see MOLES].
3. Special Comb. **moleskin squatter** *obs.*, see quot. 1934.

1934 *Press* (Christchurch) (Acland Gloss.) 20 Jan. 15 *Moleskin squatter*.—Working man who had come to own a small sheep run. A correspondent writes: 'The last time I heard it was when the Government cut up Cheviot in 1893... Since then m[oleskin] s[quatter]s have become too numerous to attract attention, or perhaps the term could not survive the end of the fashion for wearing m[oleskin]s.' **1941** BAKER *NZ Slang* 40 Among other terms we have derived from farm life and sheep stations are *moleskin squatter*.

molimawk, molimork, varr. MOLLYMAWK.

moll /mʌul/. [f. *moll* a prostitute, rhyming in NZ English with *mole*, and often so spelt.]
1. Also **mole**. Mainly in the speech of adolescents, a derogatory or dismissive name for any girl or young woman.
1953 SUTTON-SMITH *Unorganized Games NZ Primary School Children (VUWTS)* II. 677 Some of the [slang] expressions listed by children in two schools are: 'Up the shoot..blast it, mole, balls to you, shut your face.' [In pub. 1972 *Folkgames of Children* 138 misinterpreted as 'Mole balls to you'.] c**1962** BAXTER *Horse* (1985) 66 That bloody moll up the road just about killed me. She tore the skin off my back with her nails. **1973** *Islands* 6 385 The girls lose their self-confidence [in adolescence], boys become assertive and loud. The Female becomes an Object of Abuse (Mot, Mole). **1984** BEATON *Outside In* 72 Ginny: Watch your fucken language, you stuck up li'l moll [in the author's TS *mole*]. Ibid. 110 *Moll*, an abusive term for a woman. **1989** TE AWEKOTUKU *Tahuri* 35 What! You stupid moll! Look, you're sixteen, I'm eighteen, see.
2. Approaching the sense of 'prostitute', in various phrases. **a.** As **ship-moll**, see SHIP-GIRL; **Asian** (or **Jap**) **moll**, a prostitute catering for Asian fishermen.
1973 *Salient* (Wellington) 19 Sept. 11 The other main regulars of the bistro are the ship molls and the hillybins (lesbians). **1982** *Truth* 19 Jan. 7 Those who specialise in Japanese are called 'Jap molls', then there are 'Asian molls', Scannies, for those who go with Scandinavians.
b. In the phr. **like old molls at a christening**, descriptive of loud, indiscriminate chatter.
1968 SLATTER *Pagan Game* 103 All this hooha about a new school, everyone talking at once like old molls at a christening. All that natter natter.

molly; molly-bar: see *black molly* (BLACK *a.*[2] B 2); MULLIBAR.

mollyhawk, var. MOLLYMAWK.

mollymawk. Also **mollyhawk**; **molimawk**, **molimork**, **molymawk**. [Transf. use of northern hemisphere *mollymawk, mallemuck,* ad. Dutch *mallemok*: see OED.] Cf. *black molly* (BLACK *a.*[2] B 2). See also TOROA.
1. Any of several smaller species of albatross of the genus *Diomedea* (fam. Diomedeidae).
1851 KENNAWAY *Biscuit & Butter* (1973) 91 Today..a large bird called molymawk was caught by means of a fish hook and bait. **1853** ADAMS *Canterbury Settlement* 8 Among these may be noticed the albatross, the molimawk, the Cape pigeon, and several varieties of tern and petrel. **1863** BUTLER *First Year* i 12 Huge albatrosses, molimorks (a smaller albatross)..and many more, wheel continually about the ship's stern. **1871** HUTTON *Catalogue Birds NZ* 44 Diomedea melanophrys... Molly-mawk. **1888** DOUGALL *Far South* 19 The penguins, mollyhawks, and ice-birds, make the

MOLLYMAWK

[Bounty] islands their breeding place. **1904** LANCASTER *Sons o' Men* 123 A knot of molly-hawks spilt, clutching and shrieking, into the surf. **1922** *Auckland Weekly News* 3 Aug. 17 [Sailors] usually use the name albatross for large species with white backs, and mollymawk for smaller species with dark backs. **1911** ESCOTT-INMAN *Castaways Disappointment Island* (1980) 101 Think of the food—the tough, fishy mollymawk, badly cooked at the best, and the seaweed and the grass. **1983** HULME *Bone People* 247 It was the kind of bird Kerewin called a mollymawk, and Joe, toroa.

2. With a modifier: **black-browed** (**New Zealand black-browed**), **Bounty Island**, **Buller's**, **Chatham Island**, **grey-backed**, **grey-headed**, **Salvin's**, **shy**, **white-capped**.

(1) **black-browed** (**New Zealand black-browed**) **mollymawk**. *Diomedea melanophrys* (with two subspecies), having a white head and yellow bill. See also TOROA.
1955 OLIVER *NZ Birds* 178 *Black-browed Mollymawk*... This beautiful and common species was early known to voyagers in the southern hemisphere and is the species usually known as the Mollymawk. **1966** FALLA et al. *Birds NZ* 31 *Black-browed Mollymawk*... Adult plumage is pure white except for black wings and mantle, dark grey tail and a smudge of smoky grey about the eye. **1985** *Reader's Digest Book NZ Birds* 61 Black-browed mollymawks pair for life and usually breed in large colonies on cliffs or hills near the shore. **1990** *Checklist Birds NZ* 17 *Diomedea melanophrys impavida*... New Zealand Black-browed Mollymawk... Breeds only on the northern coasts of Campbell Island... Ranges widely in New Zealand seas.

(2) **Bounty Island mollymawk**, see *Salvin's mollymawk* (7) below.

(3) **Buller's mollymawk**. [Named after W.L. Buller (1838–1906) ornithologist, lawyer, and judge of the Native Land Court.] *Diomedea bulleri* (with two subspecies), having a white-crowned grey head and black-sided yellow bill.
1948 *NZ Bird Notes* III. 73 The main island of Snares is one of the chief breeding places of Buller's mollymawk. **1966** FALLA et al. *Birds NZ* 32 Buller's Mollymawk... Superficially it resembles the Grey-headed with a central dark band separating the yellow of the upper and lower surfaces of the bill. **1985** *Reader's Digest Book NZ Birds* 64 *Buller's Mollymawk Diomedea bulleri*... Buller's Mollymawk breeds in New Zealand, on small outlying islands.

(4) **Chatham Island mollymawk**. *Diomedea cauta eremita*, a subspecies of the *shy mollymawk* ((8) below), having a dark-grey head.
1955 OLIVER *NZ Birds* 174 *Chatham Island Mollymawk Thalassarche cauta eremita* The Chatham Island Mollymawk was one of the discoveries of the Whitney South Seas Expedition..which visited New Zealand in 1926. **1984** HOLMES *Chatham Is.* 100 Chatham Island Mollymawk..confined to a colony on Pyramid Rock. **1990** *Checklist Birds NZ* 18 *Diomedea cauta eremita*..Chatham Island Mollymawk.

(5) **grey-backed mollymawk**, see *Salvin's mollymawk* (7) below.

(6) **grey-headed mollymawk**. *Diomedea chrysostoma*, a circumpolar species freq. wrecked on New Zealand coasts, but otherwise not often seen off the mainland.
1904 HUTTON & DRUMMOND *Animals NZ* 265 The *Grey-headed Mollymawk*. Ibid. 266 It is not uncommon on the coasts of New Zealand, but its breeding place has not yet been ascertained. **1922** [see (9) below]. **1955** OLIVER *NZ Birds* 170 The Grey-headed and Black-browed Mollymawks breed in the same colonies

on Campbell Island. **1966** FALLA et al. *Birds NZ* 31 Grey-headed Mollymawk *Diomedea chrysostoma. Ibid.* 32 The adult bird has a dark grey head and neck, well defined from the white plumage of the rest of the underparts. **1985** *Reader's Digest Book NZ Birds* 62 Unlike the vociferous black-browed mollymawk, with which it shares its breeding grounds, the grey-headed mollymawk is generally a quiet and undemonstrative bird. **1990** *Checklist Birds NZ* 18 *Diomedea chrysostoma..Grey-headed Mollymawk.*

(7) **Salvin's (Bounty Island, grey-backed) mollymawk.** [Named after Osbert *Salvin* (1835–98) British naturalist and ornithologist.] *Diomedea cauta salvini*, a subspecies of the *shy mollymawk* ((8) below).
 1904 HUTTON & DRUMMOND *Animals NZ* 263 The Grey-backed Mollymawk. *Thalassarche salvini.* White, with a pale grey head, except the forehead and crown, which are white. **1955** OLIVER *NZ Birds* 172 Bounty Island Mollymawk *Thalassarche cauta salvini* Before the Subantarctic Islands of New Zealand were explored a few specimens only of the Bounty Islands Mollymawk were obtained on the New Zealand coast. **1966** FALLA et al. *Birds NZ* 34 Grey-backed (Bounty Island) Mollymawk... *Diomedea salvini*... Usually regarded as a subspecies of the Shy Mollymawk. **1990** *Checklist Birds NZ* 17 *Diomedea cauta salvini*... Salvin's Mollymawk.

(8) **shy (white-capped) mollymawk.** *Diomedia cauta cauta*, having three sub-species **Chatham Island** ((4) above), **Salvin's** ((7) above) and **New Zealand white-capped** ((9) below, quot. 1990). See also quot. 1985.
 1910 *Proceedings in TrNZI* XLI. 28 *Thalassogeron cautus*... (Shy Mollymawk). **1966** FALLA et al. *Birds NZ* 34 Shy (White-capped) Mollymawk *Diomedea cauta.* **1985** *Reader's Digest Book NZ Birds* 65 *Shy Mollymawk Diomedea cauta*... In New Zealand, there are three subspecies of the shy mollymawk: the white-capped mollymawk, Salvin's mollymawk, and the Chatham Island mollymawk.

(9) **(New Zealand) white-capped mollymawk.** See *shy mollymawk* (8) above.
 1904 HUTTON & DRUMMOND *Animals NZ* 265 The White-capped Mollymawk. *Thalassarche bulleri.* **1922** *Auckland Weekly News* 3 Aug. 17 The common mollymawk should not be confused with its cousins, the white-capped mollymawk, the grey-headed mollymawk, the yellow-nosed mollymawk, and the grey-backed mollymawk. **1955** OLIVER *NZ Birds* 170 White-capped Mollymawk... The White-capped Mollymawk was first collected in Bass Strait. **1985** *Reader's Digest Book NZ Birds* 65 *White-capped mollymawk*: About 64,000 pairs breed on Disappointment, Auckland and Adams Islands in the Auckland Islands. **1990** *Checklist Birds NZ* 17 *Diomedia cauta steadi...New Zealand White-capped (Shy) Mollymawk.*

3. *fig.* As **mollyhawking**, a trawlermen's term for poaching fish from an area already being worked by another boat, from the mollymawk's practice of following fishing-boats on the chance of seizing fish.
 1989 *NZ Geographic* III. 64 The vessel is clearly towing across our patch—'mollyhawking' as the practice is known.

molymawk, var. MOLLYMAWK.

momley peg: see STAGKNIFE.

momo boy: see MONGIE.

Mondayized, *ppl. a.* Of public holidays the celebration of which is held on or transferred to the Monday of the week in which they occur in order to provide a long 'holiday-weekend'.
 1964 *Dominion* (Wellington) 17 June 7 This was the real Anzac Day, and not a mondayized day which may have to be adopted, he [the Chief Justice] said. **1966** TURNER *Eng. Lang. Austral. & NZ* 156 To extend [the weekend] further, holidays are arranged to fall on Monday when possible, or are *Mondayized.* Occasionally such decisions are reversed and the word *demondayized* is heard, so that a writer of humorous verses..once protested that he was an *antidemondayizationist.* **1974** *Evening Star* (Dunedin) 17 Jan. The holiday [*sc.* New Zealand Day] must be observed on February 6 and cannot be 'Mondayised'. **1993** *Sunday Times* (Wellington) 25 Apr. 8 Anzac day is not yet Mondayised.

Hence **Mondayizing** *vbl. n.*
 1955 *Evening Post* (Wellington) 28 Oct. 13 One result of 'Mondayising' of Christmas and New Year's Day will be no 'Evening Post' on Monday, December 26, and Monday, January 2.

money gold. *Obs. Pidgin.* A sovereign; sovereigns as money.
 1841 *NZ Jrnl.* II. 92 Natives talk about money-gold. *Ibid.* II. 213 There is an ornament in general wear, made from the Poenama, a green stone..the answer I have on asking for it is 'all the same as money gold to the Pauaha (the mauri money,) and rangatira wear it.' **1842** *Letters from New Plymouth* (1843) (1968) 8 We can get them from the natives for blankets or for 'money gold' as they call it, which we call sovereigns.

money side. *Shearing.* Also **money-making side.** See quot. 1949. See also WHIPPING SIDE.
 1949 NEWTON *High Country Days* 196 Money Side: A shearer calls the last side of the sheep to be shorn the 'money' side. It is the side on which he finished the job, and is also to collect the money for doing the job. **1951** McLEOD *NZ High Country* 29 Some young shearer has stolen a march on his faster mates and got onto the 'money-side' first, and a bit of an ironic cheer goes up as he whips over the last hind leg and kicks his sheep out of the porthole. **1989** money-making side [see WHIPPING SIDE].

mong /mʌŋ/. [Abbrev. of MONGREL.]

1. Also **mung.** A mongrel (dog).
 1938 HYDE *Nor Yrs. Condemn* 162 What do we want a dog for, 'specially a mong like that? **1980** SMITHYMAN in *Te Reo* 22-23 107 *Gooree*, synonymous with *mong/mung..*('a dog of no pedigree') reportedly survives in rural New Zealand. **1979** MITCALFE *Pighunter* 11 'That bloody mong, Shiloh, no sooner off the chain than away.'

2. A term of abuse for a person.
 1988 McGILL *Dict. Kiwi Slang* 73 *mong* mongrel; also popular as a mild term of abuse. **1990** *Dominion Sunday Times* (Wellington) 22 Apr. 4 If you're called [by adolescents] a..mong..you've been insulted.

mongamonga, mongi-mongi, varr. MANGEMANGE.

Mongie, /mʌɲi/. Also **Momo boy, Mongo.** [f. MONG(REL 3 + -IE.] A member of the Mongrel Mob gang.
 1977 *Truth* 6 Sept. 11 I was with the Momo boys, one being had just been jugged in the toilets. **1982** NEWBOLD *Big Huey* 220 The Black Power gang were sworn enemies of both the Heads and the Mongies. *Ibid.* 251 Mongie (n) Member of the Mongrel Mob gang. **1983** *Dominion* (Wellington) 16 Aug. 3 Mr Toogood: What did you hear Tangitutu say?—If it was him, 'Don't — us mongies around.' **1990** O'SULLIVAN *Snow in Spain* 12 When Betty cry and her friends say don't Betty, everyone your friend, even the mongoes standing up you get on the bus, want to carry your bag.

mongo mongo, var. MANGEMANGE.

mongrel. [A survival of an obs. Brit. use as a term of contempt: see OED *mongrel* 1 b; AND 1919.]

1. A term of abuse or contempt for a person, animal, or thing. Also *attrib.* Cf. DOG *n.* 6 b, MONG.
 [**1906** PICARD *Ups & Downs* 47 Saw a mob of mongrel-bred hoodlums bashing an old man about [at Bluff].] **1910** *Truth* 23 July 2 The owner neither swore nor raised his voice as he replied, 'The horse is in the stall; just go and take him, too, saddle and all, you mongrel.' **1961** CRUMP *Hang On a Minute Mate* 88 Number seven in the second leg was a bit of a mongrel. **1962** CRUMP *One of Us* 140 Proper mongrel of a bloke he turned out to be. **1981** HENDERSON *Exiles Asbestos Cottage* 62 Apples and several stone fruits are hardy enough for high and frosty places—it's a pretty mongrel spot in New Zealand where they won't grow. *Ibid.* 129 'Some mongrel's firing at me!' cried dad, justifiably on the alert, poised to take cover and defend himself. **1991** *Dominion Sunday Times* (Wellington) 20 Oct. 3 He said his brother was 'a bit of a mongrel' but the family was motivated by misgivings about the police case.

2. With some racial, often offensive, connotation implying mixed Maori and European or other ancestry. See also HALF-CASTE, QUARTER-CASTE.
 1946 BEAGLEHOLE *Some Modern Maoris* 299 Skin colour and the mixture of blood which is responsible for it [*sc.* high visibility in a white world] are often commented on by one Maori to another. The terms 'mongrel', 'black mongrel', 'dago', or 'black nigger', for instance, are often used by Maoris either in referring to themselves or to other Maoris in the neighbourhood. Thus one informant, in introducing herself, remarked: 'I'm only a mongrel'—meaning only a mixed-blood Maori. **1984** WILSON *S. Pacific Street* 47 The trouble with me wasn't so much that I was poor as that I was half Maori. I was just a bloody mongrel to some of them.

3. Usu. with init. cap. A member of the *Mongrel Mob* (MOB *n.* 1 b). See also MONGIE.
 1984 [see MOB *n.* 1 b]. **1987** *Dominion* (Wellington) 7 Jan. 6 [Heading] Two more Mongrels arrested... Ten Mongrel Mob gang members have now been charged.

Hence **Mongrelism,** the ideology or lifestyle of the Mongrel Mob gang.
 1991 PAYNE *Staunch* 19 Those policeman, prison officers, social workers and members of the public I spoke with who described the Mongrel Mob as rabble, loose cannons and social disasters were missing the whole point of 'Mongrelism'.

mongu-mongu, var. MANGEMANGE.

monk: see MONKFISH.

monk /mʌŋk/. WW2. [Origin uncertain: poss. orig. rhyming slang for 'drunk'. The association with the gambling game of *two up* seems coincidental.] In the phr. **out the monk,** disabled in various senses. **a.** Done for, 'had it'.
 1939–45 *Expressions & Sayings 2NZEF* (TS N.A. WAII DA 420/1) Out the Monk—Finished—had it etc. Popularised in Syria at two-up. **1944** *NZEF Times* 21 Aug. 5 Our water-bottles had had it (what's known as 'out the monk'). *Ibid.* 4 Sept. 4 They tell me [the Bulgarians] are out the monk, too [*sc.* out of the war].

Ibid. 30 Oct. 5 Without a [flit-gun] you're out the monk. **1944** [see SPRUIKER 2]. **1994** CLEVELAND *Dark Laughter* 116 For most World War 2 soldiers the concept of death was masked by euphemisms like bowled, hit..and out the monk. This last metaphor (derived from the gambling game of two-up) was used by New Zealanders to describe either death or states of insensibility or unconsciousness that were not necessarily brought about by violence (e.g., sleep or drunkenness).

b. Unconscious, often through drink; asleep.

1945 *NZEF Times* 5 Feb. 4 When jokers go out the monk on vodka they have to build an inacke around them before they wake up. *Ibid.* 24 Dec. 8 Every time it was necessary to put..[the pig] in the box for a move he was put 'out the monk' by a hyp[o]dermic injection of morphia. **1959** SLATTER *Gun My Hand* 135 And those drunken sprees helped the others to forget. But no-one ever saw him out the monk. No-one ever saw Mick paralytic. **1964** MORRIESON *Came a Hot Friday* (1981) 122 He's out the monk. Really out the Joe. He's made a fair dinkum job of himself [with drink] today. **1965** WATSON *Stand in Rain* 135 Tony saw Dick and Fred out the monk under them pine trees by the lake yesterday. **1970** SLATTER *On the Ball* 136 Play is stopped when one of the forwards is seen to be out the monk but they soon bring him round and down goes the scrum again. **1976** MORRIESON *Pallet on Floor* 69 It's Jack Voot, real shickered. Looks like he's out the monk. **1994** [see a above].

c. Disabled through illness or lack of some essential.

1946 WEBBER *Johnny Enzed Italy* Glossary *Thirteen List*: Army medical list showing personnel stricken by palsy, out the monk, or otherwise sick and ailing. **1947** DAVIN *For Rest of Our Lives* 331 Let Jerry plug away till he's sick of it and out the monk for petrol. **1995** SLATTER *One More River* 112 We rolled on..without a check except for a platoon truck put out the monk by a mine.

d. In the phr. **to be out the monk with**, to be offside with, to have fallen out with.

1946 WEBBER *Johnny Enzed in Italy* 54 I'm out the monk with the O.C.

monkey.

1. a. *Obs.* The cover of the 'box' of a patent wool-press, levered down to compress the wool.

1913 CARR *Country Work* 16 Pressing.—When there is sufficient wool in one bin, the pressers (generally two) get to work. One gets into the 'box' as the lower portion of the patent presses is called, while his mate..hands him..the fleeces. These are placed in tiers, and tramped down until the lower box is full. An upper box is then swung..or lowered on to the lower one, and the process repeated. When full, the 'monkey' or cover is put into position, the spears (wire rope) affixed, and the two men lever the cover down until the top box is clear.

b. (a) [AND 1911]. In full **monkey-strap** (see quot. 1933).

1929 SMYTH *Bonzer Jones* 14 Virginia gripped the reins and mane tightly in her left hand, then seizing the monkey-strap in her right she vaulted quickly into the big Colonial saddle... She clung to the monkey-strap and pressed her legs tightly against the heaving bosy. **1933** *Press* (Christchurch) (Acland Gloss.) 4 Nov. 15 *Monkey*.—A handle made by putting a strap between two dees on a saddle and rolling it round itself. It is to hold on to when riding a bucking horse. **1944** *Korero* (AEWS Background Bulletin) 9 Oct. 28 A 'monkey', a strap looped several times through the dees on the pommel of the saddle, is fitted on. **1969** NEWTON *Big Country NI* 51 I take my hat off to the man who can ride bareback. I couldn't ride a rocking horse without a 'monkey'—a leather strap attached to the saddle for the rider to hold on to.

(b) A strap to hold hand-shears steady on the hand; also a shaped block attached to the bottom handle of a handshears to provide a better grip for large hands (compare JOCKEY 1).

1989 [see DRIVER]. **1996** [see JOCKEY 1].

2. *Obs.* A boys' climbing game.

1980 BENNETT *Canterbury Tale* 34 We had our games [c1907]. A favourite was 'Monkey', where the contestant climbed one of the fir trees along one side of the ground..and did a grand traverse of as many trees as possible. It was characterized by noise, boasting, cheating and an occasional sprained wrist.

3. Special Comb. **Monkey Grubber** [a proprietary name registered to Trewhella Bros. Pty Ltd, Trentham, Victoria, Australia], a mechanical stumper; **monkey jumping** [suggestive of a monkey's leaps], see quot.; **monkey-man** [f. slang *monkey* a mortgage], one who provides a mortgage; **monkey oyster**, an Auckland *rock-oyster* (OYSTER 2 (4)); **monkey shaft** *mining* [AND 1869], a vertical shaft in a mine; **monkey tree**, a monkey-puzzle tree, *Araucaria araucana* (fam. Pinaceae) whose densely arranged leaves make climbing difficult.

1915 MACDONALD *NZ Sheepfarming* xix Stump grubbing—..With a '**Monkey**' **Grubber** you can quickly..clear Stumps, Trees, etc., from your land. **1920** *Otago Witness* (Dunedin) 2 Nov. 10 [Advt] Stump-Grubbing does not now mean a lot of hard back-breaking work with pick, shovel, and axe; it means just a few minutes' work with the 'Monkey' Grubber and you have the stump or tree right out, roots intact. **1972** *Marlborough Express* (Blenheim) 1 Nov. 2 He had been seen by a traffic officer travelling slowly and veering to the wrong side of Waikawa Road, stopping in the middle of it then '**monkey-jumping**' to the side. **1953** FAIRBURN in Bailey and Roth *Shanties* (1967) 158 The good times are over, The **monkey-man** has foreclosed. **1983** KING *Whina* 38 We [sc. a Hokianga Maori family c1890s] called the oysters '**monkey oysters**', because they stuck to the mangroves and looked as if they were climbing trees when the tide went out. **1880** SUTHERLAND *Tales of Goldfields* 69 They began to think they might be already too deep for it, and a small '**monkey**'-**shaft** was therefore driven upwards from the end of the tunnel. **1941** BAKER *NZ Slang* 28 Gold-fields brought the *reefer*, the *deep lead*, the *gutter*, the *monkey shaft*. **1920** MANSFIELD *Stories* (1984) 245 They lived about a mile away in a house called **Monkey Tree** Cottage. *Ibid.* 246 I can walk round the monkey tree on my head at our place.

monkfish. Also *ellipt.* **monk**. [Transf. use of northern hemisphere *monkfish*: named from the head shape fancifully resembling a monk's cowl.] Either of two larger stargazers, *Kathetostoma giganteum* or, occas., *Genyagnus monopterygius* (fam. Uranoscopidae). See also BOOF, BULLDOG, FLATHEAD 1, MUDDY 2, *giant stargazer, spotted stargazer* (STARGAZER 2 (3) and (5)). Occas. sold retail as *deep sea cod* (COD 6), see quot. 1993.

1960 monk [see STARGAZER 2 (5)]. **1967** MORELAND *Marine Fishes* 20 Spotted Stargazer [Genyagnus monopterygius]... Other names include monkfish, catfish, dogfish, and flathead. **1970** SORENSEN *Nomenclature NZ Fish* 37 Monkfish..Geniagnus monopterygius..[and] Kathetostoma giganteum... Other common names (both): Monkfish, Monks, Stargazer, Flathead (also applied at times to export gurnard); Churchills, Toebiters, Bulldogs, Spotted Stargazer, Maori Chief (Dunedin); Muddies. **1986** PAUL *NZ Fishes* 118 Monkfish *Kathetostoma giganteum*... Known by a number of local names: giant stargazer, flathead, bulldog, boof, etc. The name monkfish is well established for this species in New Zealand, whereas overseas it is used for similarly shaped but unrelated anglerfishes. **1993** *Evening Post* (Wellington) 10 Feb. 52 [Advt] Export Quality Boneless Monkfish (Deep Sea Cod) Fillets.

monoao. Also early **manoa**; occas. **monowa**, **monowai**. [Ma. /ˈmonoao/: Williams 209 *Monoao... Dracophyllum subulatum*, a shrub.] *Dracophyllum subulatum* (fam. Epacridaceae), a scrub plant having slender, rigid leaves, found esp. on the NI volcanic plateau.

[*Note*] The name is occas. confused with MANOAO.

1847 TAYLOR *Journal* 28 Apr. (ATLTS) V. 51 The mountains here [central North Island] are very lofty and covered with an ochreous soil, the manoa principally grows on them. It is a sacred shrub not used [by the Maori] as fuel for cooking. **1906** CHEESEMAN *Manual NZ Flora* 426 D[racophyllum] subulatum... North Island: From Rotorua..to..Ruahine Mountains. 350 to 3500 ft. *Monoao.* **1922** *Auckland Weekly News* 23 Mar. 15 Here and there a clump of koromiko..a patch of celmesia [*sic*] and the little heath-like flower of the shrub called monowa. **1936** BELSHAW et al. *Agric. Organiz. NZ* 365 They [pumice soils] support in their natural state a cover of stunted manuka and monoao (*Dracophyllum subulatum*). **1945** BEATTIE *Maori Place-names Canterbury* 28 Beyond Mackenzie Pass the name of a shrub, Te Monoao, denotes the Snow River. **1951** LEVY *Grasslands NZ* (1970) 10 Poa tussock, danthonia tussock, stunted bracken, stunted manuka, monoao..and *Pimeleas* were the more dominant plants of the poorer areas. **1963** POOLE & ADAMS *Trees & Shrubs* 160 D[racophyllum] subulatum... Monoao. Shrub reaching 2 m. Branchlets long, slender... Flowers in short racemes. L[owland], M[ontane]. Shrub land; especially on so-called 'frost flats' of the volcanic plateau. **1971** monowai [see DAISY 2 (7)]. **1981** TAYLOR *Weeds of Roadsides* 99 Monoao (*Dracophyllum subulatum*) Native shrub resembling manuka but more spindly, rather smaller and reddish. Common in frost pockets and other small areas on the elevated pumice land in the Taupo region.

monowa, monowai, varr. MONOAO.

monsoon bucket. A device in the form of a container carried by helicopter from which water can be released to control bush and scrub fires.

1972 *NZ Patent Office Jrnl. No.1115* 19 June Midland Monsoon 94915 [filed] 22 September 1970..fire extinguishing apparatus. Midland Steel Works Limited. **1985** *Dominion* (Wellington) 3 Apr. 1 Mr Girling-Butcher returned to New Zealand and in association with the Auckland firm Tru-Test developed the monsoon bucket.

monte. Also **monty**. [transf. f. the card game *Monte*, or the card-trick 'three-card monte'.] Also in the phr. **for a monte**. A certainty; a sure thing. Also occas. as an adjective 'fine' (see quot. 1963).

[**1861** *Gabriel's Gully* 22 Oct. in Manson *I Take up My Pen* (1971) 87 The population of Tuapeka has been increased if not honoured, by a visit from a select party of eye-openers from the other colonies, who practice the lucrative game of the thimble, fleecing the green ones to the tune of £5 a bet and, failing custom at that, Monte for a change.] **1906** *Truth* 17 Mar. 7 They said it was a 'monte'—You'd be winning £60. **c1945** SIXES & SEVENS (Troopship pub.) 7 It's a monty they're sucking a couple of yens' worth of saki right now. **1947**

DAVIN *For the Rest of Our Lives* 297 'How d'you do.' From Christchurch, this chap Sloan, for a monty, with that particular brand of New Zealand English. **1955** *BJ Cameron Collection* (TS July) monty (n) A cert. **1963** *Salient* (Wellington) 23 July 2 What a monty trip. Rolleston House put on over 60 gallons of grog and females. **1968** SLATTER *Pagan Game* 163 I'm a monty for the big double Saturday. I got me contacts. **1970** *Listener* 12 Oct. 12 Old Jerry wouldn't think of looking for me over this way. That's for a monty. To keep going's the right thing. **1972** *Truth* 31 Oct. 19 Publican Brian Malin, whose big Alsatian Monte makes it a monty for him to get to the bank on time.

Monte Carlo. [Poss. a fig. use of *Monte Carlo* the name of the gaming centre, suggesting the element of chance involved in winning the prize.] A dance variation on musical chairs in which the dancers are gradually eliminated by cutting cards or various other selection processes (e.g. colour of dress) to leave a prize-winning couple on the dance-floor.
1943 [see SUPPER 2]. **1944** *Waiuku News* 30 June 3 The winners of the monte carlo were Miss Nancy Torpey and Private R. Tane. **1944** *Hauraki Plains Gazette* 22 Dec. 2 The school children's Monte Carlo was won by Marie Coxhead and John Crosbie. **1948** BALLANTYNE *Cunninghams* (1976) 78 Next they shuffled around in a fox-trot, then there was a Monte Carlo, but she didn't win it and she didn't expect to.

monty, var. MONTE.

mooca, mooka, varr. MUKA.

Mooloo /ˈmuluː/. [The name (an elaboration of *moo*) of a representation of a *cow*.] The mascot of the Waikato representative rugby union team.
1956 *NZ Herald* (Auckland) 11 June in McLean *The Best of McLean* 41 The game itself began with all the customary exertions of a very funny 'Mooloo', the so-called cow, which kept smart time to an extremely smart pipe band. **1977** MCLEAN *Winter of Discontent* 144 The fine old spirit of the 1950s, typified by that egregious old creature of the cowyard, 'Mooloo', began to shine. **1986** KNIGHT *Shield Fever* 82 A supporters' club [*sc.* for Waikato in 1951] was formed and, in keeping with the animal on which so much of Waikato's affluence was based, a famous mascot, 'Mooloo' was born. Rance Hawkins, a sign-writer at Booth and Chapman, the department store in downtown Hamilton..was the man who conceived the cow which would quickly become New Zealand's most famous.
 Hence **Mooloo Club**, the Waikato rugby union supporters' group.
1986 KNIGHT *Shield Fever* 82 The Mooloo Club was now in full stride [*sc.* in 1952] and it launched itself into organising an all-embracing invasion of Auckland.

moonfish. [See OED *moonfish* (16c.; also *opah* 17c.): from its shape and appearance.] *Lampris guttatus* (fam. Lampridae), a fish of middle depths, blue and red with silver spots occurring throughout almost all warm oceans, and caught in small numbers off the New Zealand coast. Also called **opah**.
1911 WAITE *Rec. Canterbury Museum* I. 186 *Lampris Pelagicus..*Opah. **1922** *NZJST* IV. 316 *On the Occurrence of the Opah, or Moonfish, in New Zealand Waters...* The only record I can find of the occurrence of this rare pelagic fish..is that by Hector in 1884. **1929-30** *TrNZI* LX. 146 The Opah, Moon Fish, or Red Fish. *Ibid.* 146 This handsome species, the Opah or Moon Fish, is known to the Maoris as *Aro kura*. **1956** GRAHAM *Treasury NZ Fishes* 410 Moonfish *Lampris regius*. **1967** NATUSCH *Animals NZ* 224 Family Lampridae: The rare and gorgeously-tinted moonfish.. belongs here—black blue or green, sides opalescent, under parts rose—pink, fins and jaws scarlet, the whole sprinkled with silver spots. **1982** AYLING *Collins Guide* (1984) 187 *Moonfish* (Opah) *Lampris guttatus...* The moonfish is a huge, almost disc-shaped fish ranging in size from 1m to over 1.8m... It is interesting to note that the Maoris considered these fishes good eating.

moonwort. Transf. uses of European *moonwort, Botrychium lunaria* for New Zealand ferns of *Botrychium* spp. (fam. Ophioglossaceae).
1875 LOGAN *Ferns* 61 [Heading] B. ternatum. This species, known as Moonwort, includes the *B[otrychium] cicutarium* and the varieties *A.* and *B.* of Dr. Hooker's Handbook. **1915** *AJHR* C-6 11 *Botrychium australe..*Moonwort..Tussock pasture. **1961** MARTIN *Flora NZ* 118 The related Moonwort (*Botrychium lunaria*) is one of the two species met with in New Zealand.

mooriori, var. MORIORI.

mopoke. *Obs.* Also **mopork.** [AND *mopoke*, 1825.] Formerly occas. used for MOREPORK 1 a.
1899 BELL *In Shadow of Bush* 241 As Old Dan turned and walked towards the wharé a 'mopoke' owl..shrieked and flew away. **1904** *NZ Illustr. Mag.* Sept. 403 A mopoke hooted eerily from the shadows behind the tent. **1911** BOREHAM *Selwyn* 68 Night after night, when the *mopoke* was shouting his strange cry down the wooded valleys, the party would paddle ashore. **1921** *Quick March* 11 July 19 The moon is hid as the evening skies cloud o'er at the mopoke's plaintive shriek. **1938** HYDE *Nor Yrs. Condemn* 273 I think maybe he's hungry in the nights, 'cos when I come in he's wide awake as the *mopoke* under the sacks. **1947** *NZ Woman's Weekly* 9 Jan. 1 Only..the hoot of an owl and the plaintive cry of a mopork ripped that silence.

moral. [f. Brit. slang *moral,* abbrev. of *moral certainty:* see OED 9 'Now chiefly *Austral.*'; AND 1878.] A certainty; a sure winner.
1891 A TRAMP, ESQ. *Casual Ramblings* 36 He tipped him [*sc.* a racehorse] for a moral for the Newmarket Handicap. **1896** EYTON *Rugby Football* 31 It looked a moral for England. **1908** *Truth* 30 May 3 It's a moral you never took a university course. That undecipherable scrawl suggests you manipulate a rimu log instead of a pen. **1918** *Chron. NZEF* 5 July 243 He wants to make a moral of a place at Mangere He's had in mind for nearly twenty years. **1959** SLATTER *Gun in My Hand* 166 We'll get our own back, that's a moral. **1968** SLATTER *Pagan Game* 164 He's a moral to get potted.

moray. [Transf. use of *moray*: (OED '*U.S.*') for local species of the fam. Muraenidae.] Any of various eel-like fishes of fam. Muraenidae, of which the following main species are distinguished in the technical literature (selected quots. only are given below): **grey moray**, *Gymnothorax nubilus*; **mosaic**, *Enchelycore ramosus*; **mottled**, *G. prionodon*; **speckled**, *G. obesus*; **yellow**, *G. prasinus* (see quots. at PUHARAKEKE).
1982 AYLING *Collins Guide* (1984) 92 The grey moray is the smallest and most slender of the New Zealand morays... Grey morays are common around the off-shore islands of Northland and the Bay of Plenty... *Mottled Moray* (spotted moray, saw-toothed moray)... It is dark brown with a mottled arrangement of white spots... This species is common around the offshore islands from the Bay of Islands north. *Speckled Moray Gymnothorax obesus...* The speckled moray is the largest of the species found in New Zealand waters... It is dark brown in colour with closely spaced fawn speckles over the entire body. *Ibid.* 93 The mosaic moray..is the most spectacular of the morays... The body colour is white or pale grey with mosaic patterning of olive green or brown... Mosaic morays are common around the Poor Knights Islands. **1986** PAUL *NZ Fishes* 47 Grey Moray *Gymnothorax nubilus*. Blue-grey with irregular darker markings... The smallest and most slender New Zealand moray, averaging 40–60cm, reaching about 100cm... *Speckled moray Gymnothorax obesus...* The head is noticeably short and blunt... Mottled Moray *Gymnothorax prionodon*.. Brown with a mottled arrangement of light spots, variably spaced... Mosaic Moray *Enchelycore ramosus*. Blue-grey to pale-brown, flecked with dark brown, and overlaid by a broad network of darker brown. **1988** FRANCIS *Coastal Fishes* 19 *Speckled moray Gymnothorax obesus...* Speckled morays behave aggressively towards each other, so they are presumably territorial.

more-ore, var. MORIORI.

morepork /ˈmɔːpɔk/. Also occas. **more porke**. [Imitative of its main call.]

1. a. *Ninox novaeseelandiae novaeseelandiae* (fam. Strigidae), a small brown native owl. See also KOUKOU, MOPOKE, *New Zealand owl* (OWL 1), *night-hawk* (NIGHT 1), RURU.
1849 POWER *Sketches in NZ* 74 Amongst the commonest birds which frequent the forests is a small owl, generally known to the settlers by the denomination of 'More pork', from a habit it has of pertinaciously reiterating this phrase for about half an hour before daylight. **1853** SEWELL *Journal* (1980) I. 326 He had sat for three hours listening for the cry of the 'Morepork'. **1860** BUTLER *Forest Creek MS* (1960) 45 I should add the 'More pork', a night bird which is supposed to say these words. **1873** BULLER *Birds NZ* 17 (New-Zealand Owl, or Morepork). Ruru, Koukou, and Peho. **c1899** DOUGLAS in *Mr Explorer Douglas* (1957) 258 The Owl or Morepork... It[s] cry is a very distinct more-pork which must have been unpleasantly suggestive to a boats crew when landing on a cannibal coast. **1905** WHITE *My NZ Garden* 70 A small Owl flies about the garden towards night; it is commonly called the 'Morepork', owing to its distinct pronunciation of those two words. **1916** [see KOUKOU b]. **1928** *Free Lance* (Wellington) 34 Moreporks can't expect a monopoly of the bush at night. **1934** HYDE *Journalese* 16 In a tree by a little dark pool sits a morepork, blinking at you out of cynical amber eyes. **1966** *Encycl. NZ* II. 583 The morepork is one of a number of native species that have to some extent, at least, adapted themselves to environments that have been greatly changed since settlement. **1976** SOPER *NZ Birds* 63 Moreporks have a variety of other calls, the most common of which is a vibrating 'cree-cree' heard usually during the breeding season. **1984** BRASCH *Collected Poems* 97 Morepork, shrewd sentry owl, Watching night pass, Sleepless, censorial. **1990** *Listener* 16 July 15 One uninvited guest [at an outdoor dinner], a morepork, swoops within centimetres of us.

b. (Representing) the call of the morepork.
1847 *NZ Jrnl.* VII. 219 The Rura rura, a small owl, kept up its incessant monotonous cry of 'More porke, more porke'. **1888** BULLER *Birds NZ* I. 13 As the night closed in upon us we heard all round the solemn notes of the New-Zealand Owl: first, a distinct *kou-kou, kou-kou;..* and then, in alternation, the alarm note and ever familiar cry of 'more-pork'. **1905** THOMSON *Bush Boys* 59 More-porks is the small New Zealand owl, so-called from its peculiar guttural cry, which imagination easily converts into 'morepork' with a liberal roll on the *r*.

1920 MANSFIELD *Stories* (1984) 232 In the garden some tiny owls, perched on the branches of a lace-bark tree, called: 'More pork; more pork'. **1944** *Korero* (AEWS Background Bulletin) 23 Oct. 24 In the early spring the answering calls of 'more pork; more pork; more pork' are alternated by husky crooning notes and screech-like cries of mating birds. **1964** DEMPSEY *Little World Stewart Is.* 74 We all heard the moreporks calling in the dark, 'More *pork!* More *pork!*' **1985** *Reader's Digest Book NZ Birds* 257 Voice *more-pork, boo-book, quor-coo* or *ru-ru,* sometimes repeated in quick succession.

2. *transf.* and *fig.* A slowcoach; a dawdler; a stay-at-home.

1874 POTTS *On Recent Changes in Fauna* 8 The name at least, if not the appearance, of the morepork..is well-known throughout the colony... Whence the colonial epithet (whether of Australian or New Zealand origin is uncertain) applied to a dawdling person, who is often described as 'a regular old morepork'. **1959** MASTERS *Tales of Mails* 91 One of his theories was that farming couldn't be made to pay nohow, and that it would be better for him and his neighbour..to cease chopping away at the bush, clearing fern and perching up at the head of the valley like a couple of moreporks.

3. *transf.* [Poss. f. the dark and mottled colouring.] Any of various marine fishes. See quots.

1921 *NZJST* IV. 123 Notothenia macrocephala... *Maori Chief.* Known to Wellington fishermen as 'morepork.' Secured off Island Bay during the autumn... Distribution: South Island and southern coasts of North Island. **1970** SORENSEN *Nomenclature NZ Fish* 18 *Cod, Rock... Lotella rhacinus...* Other common names: Parrotfish; Soldiers, Kelp, Kelpies, Moreporks, Marblefish, Maori Chief, Wrasse, Bourbon, Guffy, Cloudy Bay Cod, Rasp. **1977** FISHER *Angels Wear Black* 37 Even the Morepork (sometimes called the Kelpfish) thought that the only way out was to go past my ear.

Moriori /ˈmoriori/, /ˈmɒriɒri/, /ˈmɒriori/. Also with much variety of early form as **Maioriori, Maoriori, Maruiwi, Mooriori, Moraori, More-ore, Moriore, Mouriuri, Muriuri, tchakat mai-hor-r** (see esp. quot. 1923). [Ma. /ˈmo:riori/: Williams 209 *Mooriori,* n. A name given to the people of Chatham Island; as late as 1857 they called themselves *tangata maiorori. Ibid.* 167 *maiorori,* a. Native. The inhabitants of the Chatham Island until recent years described themselves as *tangata maioriori.*] For pronunciations, see also H. D. Skinner in 1946 *JPS* LV. 172. (See esp. quot. 1977 at 3 below.)

1. a. The original Polynesian people of the Chatham Islands. See also ABORIGINE b, CHATHAM ISLANDER 1, NATIVE A 1 b.

1865 *Richmond-Atkinson Papers* (1960) II. 145 While waiting on the beach..I had a long talk with a genuine Moriori (qu[er]y. Moriri?) or real aboriginal of the Chatham islands & some of the southern parts of New Zealand. I shall try & get some account of their language out of him but it will soon be extinct in Wharekauri. **1865** HURSTHOUSE *England's NZ War* 81 I have conversed with a very intelligent old Native who was one of these [Ngatiawa] emigrants to the Chathams. He described the Morioris as being rather smaller and darker than the New Zealanders but still delicate eating; while eels were found in great profusion. **1866** ANGAS *Polynesia* 138 [Journal of the Linnean Society, London.] The remnant of the More-ores (the name given to the aboriginal inhabitants), exclusive of the few who are still retained in slavery, is settled at Ohangi, on the south-east side of the [Chatham] island. **1866** HUNT *Chatham Is.* 29 The aborigines term themselves Moriori, their conquerors still call them *paraiwharas,* or blackfellows—not from their complexions..but, in their ideas, the term is synonymous with slavery. **1868** TAYLOR *Past & Present NZ* 225 There was a singular aboriginal race there [at the Chatham Islands] when they were first discovered, called the Muriuri, or Kiri Waka Papa, but more generally known as the Parakiwara, black fellow, a name of reproach given by the Maori on account of their dark color. **1877** *TrNZI* IX. 15 *Notes of the Traditions and Customs of the Mori-oris.* By W.T.L. Travers **1897** *TrNZI* XXIX. 151 The total population, including the Maoris and Morioris of the Chathams, was 39,805 persons. **1919** *TrNZI* LI. 415 Chatham Island..was peopled by a branch of the Polynesian race known variously as Maioriori, Mouriuri, and Mooriori (generally spelled 'Moriori'). [1919 *Note*] This is probably not a tribal or race name, but, like the word 'Maori', an adjective meaning 'native'. Bishop Selwyn, who visited the island in 1848, says that they called themselves 'tangata maoriori'. **c1920** BEATTIE *Trad. Lifeways Southern Maori* (1994) 446 Te karaka said that the old Maoriori stock on the Chathams came from the South Island of New Zealand. **1923** SKINNER *Morioris Chatham Is.* 20 Whatahoro's informants say that the name Moriori was given to the natives of the Chatham Islands by the Taranaki invaders and that the islanders called themselves Mouriuri. But it is impossible to believe that this is the truth. *Ibid.* 34 The designation usually applied to the natives of the Chatham Islands, and the form used by all the older observers who worked among them, is Moriori. This is the form used by Hunt, Shand, Welch, Deighton, and S.Percy Smith. Travers also used it in his paper of 1870, but in 1876 he used Mori-ori, a form which is without authority but in which he has been followed by several later writers. Of the other variants 'Maioriori' appears to be supported by the greatest weight of authority. This form appears to have been published first by Mair..who speaks of 'the Chatham Islanders, or Moriois, or, more correctly, Maiorioris.' I am informed by Archdeacon Herbert Williams that his father, who visited the Chathams with Bishop Selwyn in 1857, recorded that the natives called themselves *tangata Maioriori,* and Archdeacon Williams says that this form had the support of the late Robert Shand. Bishop Selwyn..speaking of his visit in 1848, says the islanders called themselves *tangata Maoriori,* 'differing from the name of the New Zealanders only in the reduplication of the last syllables.' The three forms noted—Moriori, Maioriori, and Maoriori—are reported on the authority of the islanders themselves... The form Mouriuri is not recorded by any person who has worked among the islanders. After consideration of these facts, the form Moriori has been adopted in this work. **1928** BAUCKE *Manuscript* (Bishop Museum Memoirs Vol. IX No.5 343–382) in Skinner & Baucke *Morioris* 357 Unlike the Maori, the Moriori had no name for his race. When questioned, he answered: 'tchakat Mai-hor-r.' This not having the assonance of Maori speech, [the] purist changed it to 'tangata Moriori' (Moriori man); by which name the race became known to common use. **1950** SIMPSON *Chatham Exiles* 26 Meanwhile at Chatham Island the *tangata whenua*—or Morioris as we now call them—found that their new home boasted no timber. **1982** *Oxford Bk. of Contemporary NZ Poetry* 28 Reputedly last of his kind, quite surely one of the last not crossbred but (as They said) pure as pure goes, a Chatham Island Moriori taken for a slave when a boy, taken again in some other raiding. **1993** *Dominion* (Wellington) 1 June 10 Chatham Island Morioris have joined the chorus of discontent at the Government's selection of the Treaty of Waitangi Fisheries Commission.

b. *attrib.* passing into adjective. (Characteristic) of the Chatham Islands Moriori.

1866 HUNT *Chatham Is.* 32 She had been a Moriori belle, sighed for by many a dusky swain. **1877** *TrNZI* IX. 16 The manners and customs of the Mori-ori people. **1898** CHUDLEIGH *Diary* 10 Feb. (1950) 397 He has ridden 35 miles and carried a kit of Moriori stone adzes on his back. **1933** in *Na To Hoa Aroha* (1988) III. 73 Moriori traditions do not go very far back of the heke people. **1947** STEVENSON *Maori & Pakeha* 144 Indeed, without the knowledge of the Moriori maro it would have been rash to speculate on its original form. **1968** GRUNDY *Who'd Marry a Doctor?* 52 Back in Moriori times there was no cultivation of the land or planting of any food crops. **1987** *Dominion* (Wellington) 14 Dec. 1987 Half the inhabitants are Maori or Moriori descendants.

c. Special Comb. **Moriori flax**, an astelia of the Chatham Islands.

1984 HOLMES *Chatham Is.* 93 *Astelia chathamica...* It has long silvery sword-like leaves with flower heads like the cabbage tree and in the autumn berries are produced. (Locally called Moriori flax.)

2. The language of the Chatham Island Moriori.

1865 *Richmond-Atkinson Papers* (1960) II. 145 Maori & Moriori are mutually unintelligible but no doubt they are only two dialects of one tongue. **1894** *TrNZI* XXVI. 537 In Maori, it means 'to count'; in Moriori, 'to calculate'. **1919** *TrNZI* LI. 415 Moriori appears to be farther removed from Maori than the dialects of many islands of the Pacific. **1947** FAIRBURN *Letters* (1981) 178 I'll support just about anything short of a proposal to translate 'Lyttelton Harbour' [a poem by D'Arcy Cresswell] into Moriori.

Hence **Moriorize** *v. trans.,* to transliterate into a Moriori form.

1866 HUNT *Chatham Is.* 33 My name Frederick they had Moriorized into Pererika, and by that name they ever afterwards addressed me.

3. A name misapplied to the earliest immigrants to New Zealand, who have been variously described or labelled as 'pre-Fleet', 'Melanesian' (or 'dark-skinned'), 'pre-Maori', and thought to have been part of a separate 'pre-Maori' migration, but now recognized as an earlier part of the general Polynesian migration. Also, with their culture, freq. termed *Moa-hunter.* Often *attrib.* Cf. *pre-Fleet* (FLEET *n.*[1] 2), *pre-Maori* (MAORI B 6 b).

1873 TINNE *Wonderland of Antipodes* 34 It..is probably true that the Hawaiians or Samoans immigrated here in olden times; but in all probability they murdered the weaker race of Morioris. **1898** *TrNZI* XXX. 32 The editors have pointed out that I laid too much stress on the Melanesian affinities of the Morioris. **1901** *Ibid.* XXXIII. 325 The abandoned pit-dwellings of the ancient Moriori inhabitants..prove beyond question that much of the bush on the shores of the Pelorus Sound was a regrowth. **1949** REED *Story Canterbury* 24 The first inhabitants of whom we have any knowledge were the Morioris, whose origin is somewhat obscure. They were a people already established here when the Polynesian pilgrims of the Great Migration arrived. **1952** TAYLOR *Lore and History of the South Island Maori* 11 The *Ngati Mamoe* and the second *Waitaha Tribe* have been loosely referred to as Morioris. The Morioris who went from the South Island to the Chatham Islands over 1000 years ago were actually more Polynesian than the Maori, so we must look further back than the days of Toi in New Zealand to pick up the Melanesian tar brush. **1961** *Distance Looks Our Way* 20 According to the traditions, when Toi arrived the country was well inhabited... These people are the *tangata whenua* of the traditions and they were divided into a number of groups... By an unfortunate and unjustified identification these people have become known in New Zealand by the name 'Moriori' which rightly belongs only to the prehistoric inhabitants of the Chatham Islands. **1977** DUFF *Moa-hunter* 14 There are also the strongest objections to using the term

Moriori, which to the man in the street has come to mean the tribes immediately preceding the Fleet, but almost invariably with the implication that they were an inferior Melanesian people who thoroughly deserved their fate in being driven away to the Chatham Islands by the superior Polynesians from Hawaiki. **1989** ANDERSON *Prodigious Birds* 107 The Lore of the Whare-Wananga..held that the original inhabitants of New Zealand were a dark-skinned, lazy and primitive people known as Maruiwi (or Mouriuri) who were either exterminated by, or married into, the Polynesian Maori, except for those who departed to the Chatham Islands and became Moriori. **1993** *Dominion* (Wellington) 29 May 14 But do we give the title *indigenous* to the Maoris or the Moriors who preceded them? **1995** *Sunday Star-Times* (Auckland) 1 Oct. A7 Tanya Rogers said Moriori of the area [near Gisborne] consider themselves distinct from Maori.

b. Special Comb. **Moriori myth**, see quots.
1957 *Here & Now* Apr. 19 I refer of course to the persistent Moriori myth still sedulously fostered in the primary schools of this country. **1972** ed. note in WISNIOWSKI *Tikera* (trans. Podstolski) 301 This passage embodies an early version of what has become known as the 'Moriori myth'. Except for the name Moriori, which was borrowed from the Chatham Islands and applied by 1880 to supposed pre-Maori inhabitants of New Zealand, the theory is all here in a book published in 1877, based on material collected in the mid-1860s. A black-skinned, curly-headed people with timid dispositions, presumably negroid or Melanesian, were supposed to have been found in possession of New Zealand by the first Polynesian settlers and exterminated by them except for a few with whom they intermarried, so that their racial traits appeared from time to time among the Maoris. **1979** SORRENSON *Maori Orig. & Migrations* 53 referring to Williams writing in *JPS* (1937) XLVI. 105–122 Then in 1937 he [*sc.* Williams] published an essay called 'The Maruiwi myth'. This was concerned largely with the first part of the legend of the coming of the Maori—'that the first Polynesian settlers who arrived with Toi..found the North Island—possibly both islands—inhabited by a non-Polynesian race, known as Maruiwi or Mouriuri, whom they subsequently exterminated; a small remnant alone escaping to colonize the Chatham Islands'.

morning star. *Tawera spissa* (fam. Veneridae), a small bivalve abundant on sandy beaches in northern New Zealand.
1947 POWELL *Native Animals NZ* 22 Morning star (*Tawera spissa*). A small Venerid about an inch in length, very abundant on most of our northern sandy beaches. **1966** *Encycl. NZ* II. 585 *Morning Star* (*Tawera spissa*). This fish has a small venus shell; it is very abundant on most open sandy beaches. It is easily recognised by its colour pattern of brown zigzag markings.

morning tea: see TEA 3 c.

morning wood. Also **morning's wood.** Kindling set aside to fire up domestic stoves each morning.
c1920s p.c. R. Mason. *Morningwood* is kindling for lighting the fire in the morning. **1959** ANDERSON in Heinz *Bright Fine Gold* (1974) 16 Dad used to split thin wood and place it up the chimney to dry for morning's wood and often that wood caught fire. **1964** HOWE *Stamper Battery* 107 Then I asked Wockie to carry in some morning wood, got the stove going and put the dinner back..to heat. **1981** SUTHERLAND & TAYLOR *Sunrise* 50 Bill's last job was to get the morning wood and kindling. **1982** HUNN *Only Affairs of State* 35 If you were week-ending with him in a bach at Waiheke, he'd wash his share of the dishes, and cut his share of the morning wood.

Morton Mains disease. [f. *Morton Mains* a township in Southland.] A local Southland sheep disease.
1935 *NZJST* XVII. 600 In certain parts of Southland a sheep sickness occurs during the late spring and summer months. The ailment has been loosely called 'Morton Mains disease' because of its prevalence in that district.

morty: see MOIT.

Moscow. *Obs.* [An attraction to a familiar form *Moscow* of Brit. slang *mosker* a pawner, or of *moskeneer* to pawn something for more than it is worth: OED 1874, ad. Yiddish: AND 1941.] As **Moscow ticket**, pawn ticket; and in the phr. **in Moscow**, in pawn, in hock.
1908 *Truth* 18 Apr. 2. 'E interdooces er Moscow ticket fer 12 ogg two razors 'n two pipes it sez on the paper, an mentions ther fact that arf-er-doller 'ull part 'im an ther ticket. **1939** *Press* (Christchurch) 19 Oct. 7 Thomson asked if he had a 'spark' [*sc.* 'a diamond (ring)'] for sale, and at noon Wilson returned to the bar with the ring... When interviewed..Thomson told [the detective] that some mug in the bar of the St George Hotel [Wellington] said he had a 'spark in Moscow' (meaning in pawn).

Moses. *Obs.* [Poss. a play on Moses 'the lawgiver' of the Old Testament.] A policeman; *pl.*, the police.
1905 *Truth* 28 Oct. 5 A man..said he had never known a policeman to tell a lie. In future, a copper will not be nicknamed John Dunn or Moses. He will be called George Washington. *Ibid.* 4 Nov. 4 Embryo policemen he [wants] to push into the force. More Moses' are not required.

mossie: see MOZZIE.

moth. [In locally significant use only with a defining word.]
1. astelia moth. *Charixena iridoxa* (fam. Yponomeutidae), a leaf-miner associated with the plant genus *Astelia*.
1924 *TrNZI* LV. 327 Charixena iridoxa... The Astelia-moth... This, one of the most striking of the endemic moths, has an extremely interesting life-history, and amongst leaf-mining insects its mine is the largest, the most conspicuous, and most interesting of all. **1971** SHARELL *NZ Insects* 61 Among the numerous leaf-miners, the Astelia moth..is outstanding. **1986** HULME *Windeater* 219 We have many splendid and curious small creatures, from giraffe-weevils to astelia moths.

2. cabbage-tree (occas. **cabbage-palm** or **palm lily**) **moth**. *Epiphryne* (formerly *Venusia*) *verriculata* (fam. Geometridae), a moth associated with the cabbage-tree.
1929 MARTIN *NZ Nature Book I* 142 The *Cabbage Tree Moth*..has the wings marked with lines that match perfectly the veins of the dry leaf of the common cabbage-tree (Cordyline). **1934** MILLER *Garden Pests NZ* 56 The foliage of the cabbage-tree is frequently holed on the surface and notched along the edges—this is the work of the cabbage tree moth caterpillars. **1947** POWELL *Native Animals* 55 Cabbage-tree Moth... The moth always rests lengthwise on the dead leaves of the cabbage-tree. **1955** MILLER *Nature in NZ* 13 A very common looper eats holes in cabbage-tree leaves; it is greenish and flattened and lives in the unopened leaves of the tree. The moth is the Cabbage-tree Moth. **1966** GASKIN *Butterflies and Common Moths* 130 The Cabbage Palm Moth... It is very common in the Wellington area. It can be beaten from the leaves of the cabbage tree palm. **1971** SHARELL *NZ Insects* 66 The little Cabbage tree or Palm lily moth..is one of the most remarkable examples of an insect simulating its background. **1986** COOK *Small World of Roadside* 94 These trees play host to a beautiful native moth..usually called the cabbage-tree moth.

3. flax moth. Any of several moths (associated with FLAX 1) of the families Geometridae (esp. *Orthoclydon praefactata* (formerly *praefectata*), also called **flax looper moth**) and Noctuidae (*Tmetolophota steropastis*, also called **flax notcher moth**). Cf. *flax grub* (FLAX 5 c).
1918 *NZJST* I. 320 I believe that the larva of..the northern flax-moth, also conceals itself during the day. **1926** TILLYARD *Insects of Austral. and NZ* 452 The genus *Venusia* includes the well-known Native Flax Moth of New Zealand, *V. praefactata*.., a pale coloured species, whose larva is a pest on Native Flax..attacking the undersides of the leaves and exposing the fibres, causing them to decay. **1930** *NZJST* XI. 278 [Caption] Graph illustrating the..life-cycle of the New Zealand flax-moth (*Orthoclydon praefactata*). **1955** MILLER *Nature in NZ* 13 One often sees narrow strips removed from the lower surface of *Phormium* leaves, the work of a greenish looper with red lines along the body; it is nocturnal and shelters in the curled-up dead fibres during the day. The moth is the white Flax Moth..which has faint brownish lines and dots on the wings; this flitting, ghost-like nocturnal moth adds to the eeriness of a flax swamp after dark. **1966** GASKIN *Butterflies and Common Moths* 103 Persectania steropastis..The Flax-notcher Moth. **1984** MILLER *Common Insects* 60 Most flax bushes have a few..leafblades damaged by the caterpillars of two species of moths—the Flax Looper Moth (*Orthoclydon praefactata*) and the Flax Notcher Moth (*Tmetolophota steropastis*), the former being peculiar to flax, but the latter also attacking the foliage of toetoe grass.

4. kowhai moth. *Uresiphita polygonalis maorialis* (fam. Geometridae), see quot. 1934.
1934 MILLER *Garden Pests in NZ* 52 Kowhai Moth... The caterpillar of this native moth sometimes becomes epidemic, when it does considerable damage to kowhai, broom, lupins, and sometimes clover... The moth is comparatively small, the fore wings being yellowish-brown with darker markings, and the hind wings orange-yellow with a blackish border. **1971** SHARELL *NZ Insects* 61 When, towards the end of summer you are sitting at the edge of sand dunes, your picnic place may be invaded by numbers of..caterpillars of the Kowhai moth. **1984** MILLER *Common Insects* 16 Kowhai Moth. When the caterpillars of this native moth (*Uresiphita polygonalis*) become epidemic they defoliate kowhai trees. **1991** *Evening Post* (Wellington) 7 Mar. 17 [Heading] A feathered foe of the kowhai moth... These [hairy green caterpillars] are the caterpillars of the kowhai moth, identified by greyish brown forewings and orange hind wings. They have co-existed with kowhai trees for aeons, without doing them lasting damage.

5. lichen moth. Any of several native moths of *Declana* and *Izatha* spp. (fam. Geometridae), white with black or green markings, camouflaged to lichen. See also *zebra moth* 9 below.
1929 MARTIN *NZ Nature Book I* 144 A number of beautiful *Lichen-moths* have green wings marked with white or black blotches, in close imitation of the lichens amongst which they must be sought. **1965** MANSON *Nature in NZ* 51 The Lichen Moth—*Izatha peroneanella*. Even though this moth is comparatively small it is one of the most striking species seen in New Zealand. **1974** *NZ's Nature Heritage* XVI. 447 Many insects use camouflage as a means of protection. This lichen moth blends in well with its surroundings. **1989**

LESSITER *Butterflies and Moths* 3 *Lichen or Zebra Moth (Declana atronivea).* The caterpillar feeds on blackberry, lichen, lancewood and five finger.

6. magpie moth. [Transf. use of Brit. *magpie moth Abraxas grossulariata* (fam. Hypsidae), named from a resemblance to the coloration of the European magpie.] *Nyctemera annulata* (fam. Arctiidae), a day-flying moth having black wings patched with white or yellow spots.

1922 THOMSON *Naturalisation of Animals and Plants in NZ* 512 The common magpie-moth (*Nyctemera annulata*) has certainly become extremely abundant wherever the introduced ragwort..has become a common pest. 1923 *N.Z. School Journal Part III* Aug. 217 The magpie-moth of New Zealand is more like a butterfly, and is at first mistaken for one. 1934 MILLER *Garden Pests* 24 One of the..commonest in any part of the country from spring to autumn, is the magpie moth (*Nyctemera annulata*) and its caterpillar, the 'woolly bear'. 1943 MCPHERSON *Complete NZ Gardener* 281 *Magpie Moth*: This common black moth with white spots on the wings is usually seen about gardens in day time. 1955 MILLER *Nature in NZ* 17 The day-flying Magpie Moth..has black wings with two cream, or white spots on the fore pair and one on the hind pair, and the black body banded with yellow. 1966 GASKIN *Butterflies and Common Moths of NZ* 98 The Magpie moth, with its velvety black wings marked with white and abdomen banded with orange, is very common throughout the country. 1972 *Press* (Christchurch) 16 Sept. 11 Magpie Moth (*Nyctemera annulata*) 1970 2½c [stamp]: Definitive issue. (Later overprinted 4c.).. The second moth is the common and conspicuous Magpie Moth. 1986 ANDREWS *The Southern Ark* 88 Specimens collected by Quoy and Gaimard and others on Dumont d'Urville's second voyage to New Zealand..Magpie Moth.

7. porina moth: see PORINA.

8. puriri moth. [f. PURIRI a tree whose wood is a favoured host of the larvae.] *Aenetus virescens* (fam. Hepialidae), a large green ghost moth (i.e. one whose colour harmonizes so well with the background as to be almost invisible when at rest).

1907 LAING & BLACKWELL *Plants of NZ* 350 These holes [in the puriri logs] are made by a soft-bodied grub, which develops into the puriri moth. 1935 DIXON *Nature Study Notes* 22 *The Puriri Moth*.... Also called the 'Giant Swift Moth' and the 'Ghost Moth'. 1947 POWELL *Native Animals of New Zealand* 56 Ghost Moth..often called the Puriri Moth. This is the largest of our native moths, and it is confined to the North Island. 1955 MILLER *Nature in NZ* 20 With its wing expanse of up to six inches, the Puriri Ghost Moth..is the giant among New Zealand moths. 1964 BACON *Along the Road* 53 Alfie spied a puriri moth almost concealed among lichen growth... The youngsters were all familiar with these great moths.., but they were intrigued by the cunning way its lime green wings with their pale yellow marbling dissolved into the tufted tree trunk. 1983 *Land of the Mist* 71 [Caption] The puriri moth, or ghost moth, is a swift and powerful flier.

9. zebra moth. [f. the zebra-like wing-markings.] See *lichen moth* 5 above.

1966 GASKIN *Butterflies and Common Moths* 153 *Declana atronivea*... The North Island Zebra Moth. *Ibid.* 154 *Declana egregia*... The South Island Zebra Moth. 1972 *Press (Christchurch)* 16 Sept. 11 S.I. Zebra Moth (*Declana egregia*) 1970: 3c [stamp]: definitive issue. (Named Lichen Moth on stamp.) The first is the South Island Zebra Moth, also known as the Lichen Moth, a member of the family selidosemidae. This is one of several families of moths whose caterpillars are popularly known as 'loopers'. *Ibid.* 16 Sept. 11 A closely related moth, the North Island Zebra Moth, which is confined to the North Island, has the forewings ornamented with broken black lines, giving the wings a more or less speckled or spotted appearance. 1982 SHARELL *NZ Insects* 68 A strikingly beautiful moth is *Declana atronivea* of the North Island, and the species *D. egregia*, of nearly similar colouring which occurs in the South Island. Its satiny white wings have an intricate pattern of black markings. Its common names are Black speckled moth and Zebra moth.

Mother Cameron's weed. Also **mother-of-cameron weed**. [Origin unknown.] *Hypericum perforatum* (fam. Clusiaceae), the introduced toxic weed, St John's wort.

1946 *Bull. Wellington Bot. Soc.* 14 Aug. 8 There are some popular names..which seem to have hitherto escaped print and are only known locally... Here are some to start with.. *Hypericum perforatum*, Mother Cameron's weed (Central Otago). 1965 MACNICOL *Skippers Road* 159 Mother-of-Cameron weed, perhaps better known as St John's wort, was troublesome on both the Aurum and The Branches stations in our time. 1969 *Standard Common Names Weeds* 50 *Mother Cameron's weed* [=] *St. John's wort*.

mother country. Also **mother land**. Usu. with init. caps. and def. art. [AND 1832–1986.] England, later Britain, in its early relationship with New Zealand. Cf. HOME *n.*¹ 1, *Old Country, Old Dart* (OLD 1 a and b).

1820 MCCRAE *Journal* (1928) 10 Inducements to a Great Nation..to establish a Colony..more likely to repay the fostering care of the Mother Country. 1834 MCDONNELL *Extracts Jrnl.* (1979) 18 I can have no hesitation in asserting, that thousands of tons of this valuable article of commerce may be shipped off annually from New Zealand to the mother-country. 1851 *Lyttelton Times* 10 May 7 'Tis not that..my mother-country's soil Will not support her child. 1864 *Cardwell to Grey* in Rutherford *Select Documents* 26 Sept. (1949) 152 New Zealand must be regarded..as owning no dependence on the Mother-Country. 1905 *Truth* 24 June I. 7 To send Jimmy Duncan to the Mother Country as a coach to the New Zealand team. 1919 WAITE *New Zealanders at Gallipoli* 1 The pioneer settlers of New Zealand left the Mother Country for many reasons, but primarily because they wished for a freer existence... A few weeks after the dreadful tragedy of Serajevo..New Zealand placed all her resources at the disposal of the Mother Land.

mothering, *vbl. n. Farming.* [f. *mother v.* to find a mother for a lamb or calf: see OED *mother v.* 5.] Contrast MIS-MOTHER *v.*

1. Usu. as **mothering up**, matching up a motherless lamb with a ewe whose lamb has died.

1922 PERRY *Sheep Farming* 79 Working in an open paddock also allows the subsequent mothering 'up' to be carried out more expeditiously. 1969 MOORE *Forest to Farm* 80 This 'mothering-up' of odd lambs [to ewes who have lost their lambs] takes quite a lot of the shepherd's time. 1971 TAYLOR *Plekhov Place* 15 'At long last a dryer for the clothes. Bliss at lambing time.' 'Don't tell me you use it for mothering-up.' 1982 *Agric. Gloss.* (MAF) 13 *Mothering*: Same as fostering. *Ibid.* 12 *Fostering*: Making a dam accept an offspring other than its own, or giving an offspring to another dam. 1985 STEWART *Gumboots & Goalposts* 91 None of the recognised mothering on techniques of sheep husbandry would work with goats and we had a lot of orphans.

Hence **mother up** *v. intr.*, of a ewe, to become attached to her lamb.

1956 *Weekly News* (Auckland) 8 Feb. 45 I was to keep them [*sc.* sheep] there until dark to 'mother-up'.

2. Special Comb. **mothering-box**, a warm box where orphan lambs are first placed to survive and strengthen; **mothering-paddock**, **mothering-pen**, a special paddock or pen in which a ewe which has lost its lamb and a lamb which has lost its mother can be brought together.

1980 *Evening Post* (Wellington) 10 Sept. 40 (Footrot Flats) [Cartoon] I love watching the ewes accept the little orphaned lambs. I wonder if there is anything in the **mothering box** at the moment? 1952 BLAKISTON *My Yesteryears* 21 As every ewe block had a set of yards and a **mothering paddock**, ewes and lambs were mustered in sections, with very early starts to avoid the summer heat. 1959 *NZ Dairy Exporter* 10 Aug. 115 All that was left over from the previous day was a ewe and lamb in the Bush Paddock **mothering pens**. 1969 MOORE *Forest to Farm* 69 Picking up the orphan [lamb] I locate the bereaved mother [sheep], and, collecting her dead lamb, work her quietly into a mothering pen in the corner of the block. 1984 *Dominion* (Wellington) 6 Jan. 5 In strategic places we built roofed mothering-up pens from wooden car cases for ewes and orphan lambs.

mother land: see MOTHER COUNTRY.

mother-of-cameron weed, var. MOTHER CAMERON'S WEED.

mother whitebait: see WHITEBAIT 1 c.

mottled. Applied to valued varieties of kauri (occas. of totara and other) timber that presents a mottled appearance.

1874 BAINES *Edward Crewe* 169 Beautifully mottled logs are sometimes met with, and are frequently made into furniture. It is a question with bushmen whether this mottled or bird's-eye appearance is a disease of the tree or another variety. 1882 HAY *Brighter Britain* II. 189 Mottled totara is as much esteemed for cabinet work as mottled kauri. 1883 HECTOR *Handbook NZ* 122 Some of the largest and soundest kauri timber has richly mottled shading, which appears to be an abnormal growth, due to the bark being entangled in the ligneous growth, causing shaded parts, broad and narrow, according as the timber is cut relative to their planes. This makes a rich and valuable furniture wood, and in the market is known as 'mottled kauri'. 1888 BARLOW *Kaipara* 113 Mottled Kauri trees are usually found in rocky situations. 1925 MANDER *Allen Adair* (1971) 61 Besides this, Peter picked out as a gift mottled kauri for the front room and the ceiling and some fine bits of bird's-eye totara for the doors and cupboards.

Hence **mottling** *vbl. n.*, see quot.

1987 MASSEY *Woodturning NZ* 93 *Mottling* Broken striped figuring that reveals horizontal waves in wood grain.

mou, var. MO.

mouku, var. MAUKU.

mounga-mounga, var. MANGEMANGE.

mountain.

1. a. In the names of plants (often merely translating the specifics *alpinus, montana*), see: AKEAKE 2, BEECH 2 (6), BIRCH 3 (8), BUTTERCUP 2 (3), CABBAGE-TREE 2, CEDAR 2 (1), COTTONWOOD 2, CURRANT, DAISY 2 (7), FLAX 2 (1), FOXGLOVE, HOLLY, IVY-TREE, LILY 2 (9), MUSK b, NEINEI, PALM 2, PINE 2 (8), RATA 2 (1), RIBBONWOOD 2 (2), TOETOE

2 (1), TOTARA *n.*¹ 2 (2), TUTU 2 (2), WINEBERRY 3. See also *mountain mop* 2 below.

b. Of animals, see: DUCK 2 (2) a, PARROT 2 (5), TROUT 2 (4).

2. Special Comb. **mountain goat**, in various *transf.* or *fig.* senses, of a person or vehicle that climbs hills or steep places as well as a mountain goat; *spec.*, also as **goat**, a name for a four-wheel-drive vehicle (formerly) used to take skiers from the Chateau Tongariro up to the Mount Ruapehu ski-fields; **mountain mop** [f. the tufts of leaves at the end of its bare branches resembling a mop], NEINEI; **mountain mutton** *obs.*, a cryptic name for venison in the days when any commercialization of deer or venison was a punishable offence; **mountain oyster**, usu. *pl.*, sheep's testicles as a rural gourmet delicacy; **mountain-wash** *Otago goldmining obs.*, see quot.; **mountain wind** *Taranaki hist.*, a wind seemingly blowing from Mount Taranaki.

1952 *Evening Post* (Wellington) 1 July 11 Of streets that only a **mountain goat** or a resident of Hataitai could love. **1952** *Tararua* 36 Like a lot of mountain goats. **1952** July p.c. H.S. Gajadhar *Mountain goat* is the name given to the four-wheel drive vehicle at the Chateau Tongariro, used to take skiers by a narrow often snowbound Bruce road up to the skiing grounds on Mount Ruapehu. **1965** GILLHAM *Naturalist in NZ* 188 The last few miles to the ski huts [beyond Chateau Tongariro] would be in a 'mountain goat'—a navy blue Landrover which drove gamely up. **1978** *Manawatu Tramping Club Jubilee* 68 After the bus trip [c1950s] to the Chateau we stayed the night in the bunk-house before catching the goat up the Bruce road. **1946** *Bull. Wellington Bot. Soc.* 14 Aug. 8 There are some popular names, including those of introduced species, which seem to have hitherto escaped print and are only known locally... Here are some to start with..*Dracophyllum traversii*, candelabra tree, **mountain mop**. **1958** *Tararua* Sept. 30 The mountain mop is *Dracophyllum traversii*, and gets its name, given to it by Canterbury mountaineers apparently, from the tufts of leaves at the ends of the branches. **1961** MARTIN *Flora NZ* 227 This might be described as a miniature of the Mountain Mop or Nei-nei. **1988** MCGILL *Dict. Kiwi Slang* 74 *mountain mop Dracophyllum traversii* plants used by trampers in Canterbury area as cleaner for pots and billies. **1953** ELVY *Reminiscences* in Millar *High Noon* (1965) 88 It pulled up at the Pelorus Hotel, Canvastown [c1900], and..the travellers went to the dining room... 'What'll you have, beef or **mountain mutton**?' he [*sc.* the publican] asked... The young man gave his order..and was served with slices of juicy, tender venison. In those days deer were protected, to be shot only in season, and under licence, so what the travellers ate was poached. It was a feature of the hotel, under mountain mutton. **1980** LELAND *Kiwi-Yankee Dict.* 68 **mountain oyster**: Unlike the beautiful Bluff oysters, these do not come in shells. They are the gonads of rams. **1989** RICHARDS *Pioneer's Life* 91 But I have known people who will travel miles with a basin to collect these delicacies [*sc.* lambs' testicles]. Fried in breadcrumbs they are known as mountain oysters and I believe they resemble brains or whitebait. **1995** *National Geographic* Oct.–Dec. 38 On many stations docking is still done by the faster cut-and-bite method... It also produces 'mountain oysters'—a local [East Coast] delicacy fetching $50 for an ice cream container full. **1897** MCKAY *Older Auriferous Drifts Central Otago* 28 At higher levels, under and surrounding the upper township, there is what is called the '**mountain-wash**', a thick deposit of coarse gravels evidently derived from the eastern slopes of the northern part of the Carrick Range. **1854** *Richmond-Atkinson Papers* (1960) I. 141 The houses in this neighbourhood have been in some danger from bush firings... Then just as several people had lighted their clearings a strong gale from the south-east, what is called here 'the **mountain wind**', sprang up. In a few hours all the dead trees and stumps in the neighbourhood were on fire.

Mount Cook flea. [f. the name of *Mount Cook*, New Zealand's highest mountain.] *Pharmacus montanus* (fam. Rhaphidophoridae), a cave weta restricted to the Southern Alps; *cave weta* (WETA 2 (1)). See also *jumping spider* (JUMPING 1).

1929 MARTIN *NZ Nature Book I* 104 The Hooker Valley at Mount Cook is the home of a moderately large weta, facetiously termed the *Mount Cook Flea*.., which congregates sometimes in considerable numbers under the morainic boulders in the herb-field. **1935** *NZ Alpine Journal* VI. 22(172) The scientific name of the insect is *P. montanus*. It appears to be variously referred to as 'Mount Cook Flea,' 'Jumping Spider' etc., but as the insect is allied to the weta, a more correct name would be *Alpine Weta*. **1971** MILLER *Common Insects in NZ* 139 A mountain species..called the 'Mount Cook Flea,' lives in rock crevices above the snowline and leaps up in showers if disturbed. **1978** JARDINE *Shadows on the Hill* 84 Many of the high sunny faces support scattered colonies of mountain wetas..the 'Mount Cook Flea'. **1982** SHARELL *New Zealand Insects and Their Story* 135 One species popularly named Mt. Cook flea..lives in great numbers above the snow line (about 7,000 ft.) on the Southern Alps. **1990** MEADS *The Weta Book* 35 This jumping behaviour has resulted in one particularly active mountain species (*Pharmacus montanus*) being given the name 'Mount Cook Flea,' from its habit of leaping madly about when disturbed.

Mount Cook lily: see LILY 2 (10).

Mounteds. WW1 (Egypt). *pl.* Usu. as **the Mounteds**, any of the various New Zealand contingents of *Mounted Rifles* to WW1. See quot.

1918 *Kia-ora Coo-ee Second Series* (1981) 15 Aug. II. 16 New Zealanders in these regions [*sc.* Egypt] are popularly referred to, in their Homeland, as 'The Mounteds'; and as being indicative of their peculiarities in method of warfare, the term has its value.

Mount Egmont buttercup: see BUTTERCUP 2 (4).

Mouray, Mouree, Mouri(e), varr. MAORI.

Mouriuri, var. MORIORI.

Moury, var. MAORI.

mouse: see FIELD MOUSE. Cf. HENRIETTA.

mousefish. [See quot. 1956.] GLOBEFISH (*Contusus richei*).

1956 GRAHAM *Treasury NZ Fishes* 378 Globe-fish *Contusus richei*... It has several other popular names such as Balloon-fish and Mouse-fish... The mouse-fish is the most popular among some fishermen and when the fish is distended it does present a striking resemblance to a mouse, with its cunning looking face. **1981** WILSON *Fisherman's Bible* 115 [Globe-fish]... Other names include Toado, Balloon-fish, Mouse-fish, (N.Z.)... Gives off an offensive odour when handled.

mouth, *n.* In various phrases.

1. *Obs.* **to have a mouth on one**, to be thirsty for alcoholic drink.

c**1875** MEREDITH *Adventuring in Maoriland* (1935) 74 You need not be afraid of my sobriety, for although many of the thirsty crowd that come into my office ask me if I have 'a mouth on me', I invariably refuse. *Ibid.* 151 Mac a [squatter]..asked us all 'if we had a mouth on us', which of course we had... Mac asked us all round to nominate our poisons.

2. *farming* **full mouth**, of a sheep, to have the full complement of 8 teeth; **to be gone in the mouth**, see quot. See also MOUTH *v.*

1974 ANDERSON *Mary-Lou* 42 Each year..[a sheep] cuts two more teeth until it has eight teeth, which is a 'full' mouth. **1949** NEWTON *High Country Days* 195 Gone in the mouth: Sheep whose teeth are broken and uneven with age are 'gone in the mouth'.

3. to talk out of the side of one's mouth, see quot.

1989 NEWBOLD *Punish. & Politics* 27 Evidence of this communication restriction is visible today among the older criminals, some of whom still habitually talk out of the sides of their mouths, without moving their lips. The habit is said to have originated in the days when prisoners were often forbidden to speak to one another. Today, to describe a person in gaol as one 'who talks out of the side of his mouth' is to say that the person is an 'old lag' or an 'old boobhead'.

mouth, *v. Farming.* [AND 1870.] *trans.*, occas. *intr.* To estimate the ages (of sheep) by examining the teeth.

1863 CHUDLEIGH *Diary* 1 Oct. (1950) 105 [We] began mouthing sheep. Polhill who has bought the run and the sheep took down the mouths on paper as the sheep are to be paid for according to their ages... You catch a sheep in your arms, carry it to the gate where the mouther stands, hold the mouth open for him to look at and you at the same time call out two, four, six, full or whatever it may be... So you know the number age sex etc. of your whole mob. **1913** STUDHOLME *Coldstream* (1985) 136 Jack was constantly on the farm, 'mouthing ewes in the yards'. **1956** DARE *Rouseabout Jane* 8 They were 'mouthing the dry sheep'—whatever that meant... I would be able to tell the grannies by looking at their teeth. **1972** NEWTON *Sheep Thief* 74 I found the opportunity to mouth several of those double fork sheep—and one was only a four tooth. **1982** *Agric. Gloss.* (MAF) 49 *Ageing*: Sheep, like all ruminants have no top teeth. They have a hard dental pad. Lambs are born with eight small temporary milk incisors (front teeth) and these are replaced in pairs, from the centre outwards, at certain ages. Hence you can 'mouth' or age a sheep and estimate its age

Hence **mouther** *n. obs.*, one who mouths a sheep for age; **mouthing** *vbl. n.*, checking the teeth of sheep for age, etc.

1863 mouther [see above]. **1951** ACLAND *Early Canterbury Runs* (1975) 375 *Mouthing*.—Determining the age of sheep by examining their teeth.

movie, var. (prob. erron. for) MOA.

Mowree, Mowri(e), Mowry, varr. MAORI.

mozzie. Also **mossie.** [AND 1936.] A mosquito. See also WAEROA.

1943 *Fourth Generalities* (Army Magazine) 39 The 'mozzies' are not a great deal worse than flies. **1969** MASON *Awatea* (1978) 20 Last year, Matt was eaten alive with mozzies. **1986** *Sunday Star* (Auckland) 15 June A5 Their weapon: A 45-cent bar of soap that keeps the mosquitos away for 12 hours by blocking the mozzies' sensory organs. **1987** *Alfredton* 70 The first night the mossies got at us and we were all in a real mess.

Mr Cutts: see THEY'RE OFF, MR. CUTTS.

Mrs. *Women's Prison.* A name for a lesbian partner.
  1968 Taylor in *Genetic Psychology Monographs* (1970) LXXXI. 92 Female offenders of all ages were tattooed almost exclusively with tattoos that marked homosexual relationships they had with their young 'Mrs.', teenage 'Darls', or adult 'Dollies'.

Mrs Green. As a name or symbol for the open countryside, the green grass of the roadside, esp. in the phr. **to sleep with Mrs Green**, to sleep in the open air; also, perh. *transf.*, SWAG. Cf. STAR HOTEL.
  1937 PARTRIDGE *Dict. Slang* 781 *sleep with Mrs Green.* To sleep in the open: New Zealand tramps' c[ant] (–1932). I.e. on the green grass. 1941 [see STAR HOTEL]. 1958 *NZ Herald* (Auckland) 29 Nov. 14 If Scandinavia and Arctic Canada fathered the formal pack, it was New Zealand and Australia which invented the pack's poor cousin, personified as 'Mrs Green' in the former land, and famously as Matilda in the latter.

Mrs Potts iron. *Hist.* [Origin unknown: AND 1907.] A superior kind of smoothing iron, usu. nickel plated.
  1963 BACON *In the Sticks* 181 *Mrs Potts irons*— Solid, boat-shaped laundry smoothing irons, having clip-on handles which enabled them to be placed on the side of a stove or hearth to be heated. Usually used in pairs, one heating while the other was used.

mud.
1. mud-fat, as fat as mud, see FAT *a.*[1] 1 b.
2. Special Comb. **mud flounder**, see FLOUNDER 2 (7); **mud-grubber**, see STARGAZER 2 (2); **mud-gurnard**, see GURNARD 2 (1); **mud pigeon**, see quot.; **mud-pool**, usu. a boiling or hot mud-pool (cf. also PORRIDGE POT); **mud volcano** [poss. transf. f. US *mud volcano* a name for the Mississippi phenomenon of *mud lump*: cf. OED *mud n.*[1] 5 a], a boiling mud-pool.
  1960 DOOGUE & MORELAND *Sea Anglers' Guide* 262 Stargazer... Other names: *Leptoscopus macropygus*; river gurnard, **mud gurnard**, flat-head gurnard, **mud grubber**. 1981 WILSON *Fisherman's Bible* 118 The Stargazer is sometimes known as the Mud Gurnard, River Gurnard or Mud-Grubber Gurnard but is in fact no relation. 1966 FALLA et al. *Birds NZ* 119 Northern (Variable) Oystercatcher *Haematopus reischeki* Local name: **Mud Pigeon.** 1986 *The Age* (Melbourne) 28 Apr. 11 Bottles of pre-boiled water are a regular feature of hotel rooms. Not, of course, in New Zealand. If the water is not flowing cleanly across tourist advertisements, it is preboiled in geysers and **mud-pools**. 1841 BIDWILL *Rambles in NZ* (1952) 50 About a mile from the Pa, are a number of **mud volcanoes** (if they may be so called), consisting of hollows varying from fifty to one hundred and fifty feet across, filled with mud.

muddy, *n.* and *a.*
1. *Northland.* As **muddy fish**, *grey mullet* (MULLET 2 (1)).
  1897 *AJHR* H-17 2 The other variety [of mullet] [which stays in the harbour] is known to the fishermen as the 'settler' or 'muddy fish'. When opened they are not clean and bright..but full of slimy mud.
2. MONKFISH.
  1970 SORENSEN *Nomenclature NZ Fish* 37 *Monkfish* (a) Scientific name: (i) *Geniagnus monopterygius* (ii) *Kathetostoma giganteum*... Other common names: (both) Monkfish, Monks..Muddies.

mudfish. [Spec. use of *mudfish* a fish which inhabits mud.]
1. Any of various species of the freshwater fish *Neochanna* (fam. Galaxiidae), esp. *N. apoda*, able to survive in the mud or debris of swamps and small water bodies that may dry up in the summer. See also HAUHAU *n.*[2], *spring eel* (EEL 2 (9)).
  1872 HUTTON & HECTOR *Fishes NZ* 130 A most curious fish, allied to the [*Galaxias*], is the Mud Fish (*Neochanna apoda*). 1873 BULLER *Birds NZ* 237 He produced a dish of water containing some 'mudfish'... This singular fish..is very common in the Hokitika district, being found in all the creeks and surface-ponds in the woods... On the pools becoming dry these mudfish burrow into the moist soil or clay..remaining there for an indefinite time, or until the return of the rainy weather rendered their pools habitable again. 1884 REID *Rambles on Golden Coast* 175 A peculiar fresh-water fish..[which] has attracted attention..is the 'West Coast Mud Fish', a fish which was once supposed to take to and reside in the mud from choice. 1912 *Otago Witness* (Dunedin) 25 Sept. 76 The fish is the New Zealand mud-fish (Neochanna apoda). It is usually found in clay, in places which are overflowed by rivers when they are in flood. 1929 BEST *Fishing Methods* 104 The name *kowaro* seems to be also applied to the 'mudfish' as it is termed—some form of fish found in mud near springs, and also by men engaged in excavating drains. 1936 *Handbook for NZ* (ANZAAS) 73 *Neochanna apoda*: Mudfish Hauhau or waikaka. 1940 PHILLIPPS *Fishes NZ* 41 The mud-fish is also a member of the family Galaxiidae; but differs from members of the genus Galaxias in that it has no ventral fin. 1957 WILLIAMS *Dict. Maori Lang.* 39 *Hauhau* (i) n. *Neochanna apoda*, mud-fish = waikaka. 1980 *Freshwater Catch* VIII. 14 Mudfishes were discovered early in the colonisation of New Zealand, the first ones being found when the settlers were digging stumps out of the land to prepare garden plots. There is an early story that settlers wrote back to England that when digging their potatoes they encountered these small mudfish and so their gardens were prolific, producing both fish and chips! 1990 MCDOWALL *NZ Freshwater Fishes* 138 The mudfishes form a group of closely related species that have become specialised to life in a distinctive type of habitat—swamps, creeks and drains that tend to dry up in the summer.
2. With a modifier: **black, brown, Canterbury**.
(1) **black mudfish**. *Neochanna diversus*.
  1956 GRAHAM *Treasury NZ Fishes* 400 Black Mudfish *Neochanna diversa*. 1981 *Freshwater Catch* XII. 9 The Whangamarino Swamp is one of the few viable habitats left for the endangered black mudfish. 1990 MCDOWALL *NZ Freshwater Fishes* 150 *Neochanna diversus*... The black mudfish occurs most abundantly in swamps and wetlands, in still and gently flowing waters, and often in areas that are heavily overgrown with scrub or filled with twigs, leaves and other litter.
(2) **brown mudfish**. *Neochanna apoda*. See also *spring eel* (EEL 2 (9)).
  1956 GRAHAM *Treasury NZ Fishes* 400 Brown Mudfish *Neochanna apoda*. 1963 WOODS *Native Introduced Fishes* 37 The Wairarapa is the best known area for the Brown Mudfish, but it occurs in other scattered localities, including parts of the South Island. 1978 MCDOWALL *NZ Freshwater Fishes* 82 The Brown Mudfish was the first of the New Zealand mudfishes to be discovered, and was originally described more than 100 years ago... It is sometimes known as Mud Eel or Spring Eel. 1980 *Freshwater Catch* VIII. 14 The brown mudfish is the best known species... It is found in diverse habitats from small gravelly, spring-fed streams, to overgrown roadside and farm drains and creeks, swamps, water lying around the floor of podocarp forests and pakihi bogs.
(3) **Canterbury mudfish**. *Neochanna burrowsius*.
  1927 PHILLIPPS *Bibliogr. NZ Fishes* (1971) 14 *Galaxias burrowsii*... Canterbury Mudfish. 1936 *Handbook for NZ* (ANZAAS) 73 *Galaxias burrowsii*: Canterbury mud-fish. 1940 PHILLIPPS *Fishes NZ* 39 Canterbury Mud-fish... This is one of the most degenerate species of Galaxias and has been placed in a separate genus. 1956 GRAHAM *Treasury NZ Fishes* 400 Canterbury Mudfish or Mud Galaxias *Saxilaga* (*Lixagasa*) *burrowsius*. 1979 *NZJMFR* XIII. 111 This research was done because the Nature Conservation Council wished to create reserves for preservation of the Canterbury Mudfish, *N. burrowsius*. 1986 *Woman's Weekly* 28 July quoted in *Listener* 4 Oct. (1986) 5 Although many of the creatures are exotic, they are now concentrating on New Zealand natives, including the extinct Canterbury mudfish, which looks like thriving. 1990 MCDOWALL *NZ Freshwater Fishes* 140 Populations of the Canterbury mudfish still persist as small pockets in those habitats that remain.

mudflat. As **mudflats**, a high-country man's nickname for lowland or down country flats or farms.
  1947 NEWTON *Wayleggo* 154 *Mud-flats*: A high country man's name for down country flats. Heavy land. 1951 MCLEOD *NZ High Country* 46 Some of the men go back to spend the winter on the stations; some to the 'mud flats' and some to such jobs as rabbiting and deer shooting. 1952 NEWTON *High Country Journey* 21 He duly took a job down country... Six months later he was back again... He'd got footrot down on the 'mud flats' and had to come back to the hard country.
  Hence **mudflat-man**, a down-country farmer.
  1971 NEWTON *Ten Thousand Dogs* 29 Ray, a mudflat-man, was just another 'cockie' as far as dogs went.

mud snail. Also **mudflat snail.** *Amphibola crenata* (fam. Amphibolidae), an air-breathing univalve found abundantly on mudflats. See also PERIWINKLE *n.*[1]
  1947 POWELL *Native Animals* 30 Mud Snail... The Maoris of old esteemed this shellfish as a food and called it Titiko. 1955 DELL *Native Shells* 32 Mud Snail... Titiko, Takarepo or Whetiko... Mud Snails are found in enormous numbers on the mud banks in tidal estuaries. 1966 *Encycl. NZ* III. 267 Snail, Mud... About the size of a garden snail, this is the shellfish seen scattered in thousands over upper tidal mud flats. 1974 CHILD *NZ Shells* 84 Mudflat Snail (*Amphibola crenata*)... For the hours when it is covered by the incoming tide, the Mudflat Snail takes in a bubble of air, closes its aperture, and waits quietly for the tide to ebb again. 1983 GUNSON *Collins Guide to Seashore* 91 Here too, in the quiet waters of estuaries and mudflats, is the mud snail *Amphibola crenata* (25mm), its shell a strongly-ridged and box-like structure.

muehlenbeckia /mjuːlənˈbekijə/. Also **mühlenbeckia.** [Named for Dr H.G. Muehlenbeck (1798–1845), a naturalist interested in the mosses and fungi of Alsatia.] POHUE b.
  1900 *Canterbury Old & New* 183 Occasionally one sees a scrubby bush of *Muehlenbeckia*, covered with its curious white berries. 1951 in PEARSON *Six Stories* (1991) 70 They..found a copse of fuchsia and maahoe, overgrown with a solid mass of muehlenbeckia, windproof. 1963 PEARSON *Coal Flat* 421 mühlenbeckia: A rambling climber which often strangles its host tree under its dense masses of leaves and stems. 1980 BRASCH *Indirections* 19 Thick growths of muehlenbeckia creeper here and there formed small cave shelters against the rock. 1981 TAYLOR *Weeds of Roadsides* 101 Large-leaved Muehlenbeckia (*Muehlenbeckia australis*). Perennial native climber.

mufti. [Spec. use of *mufti* plain clothes worn by any one who has the right to wear a uniform.] 'Civilian' clothes worn by secondary school students on days when they would normally be required to wear a school uniform. Also as a special Comb. **mufti day**, a day when the wearing of school uniform is optional.
 1974 Bream *I'm Sorry Amanda* 147 The following Friday was 'mufti day'. On one school day each year our pupils are permitted to wear clothes of their choice instead of uniform, a concession for which they pay a minimum of ten cents towards the Corso fund. 1977 Peddie *Christchurch Girls' High School* 191 Perhaps the ultimate 'uniform change' has been for the Seventh Formers. They can now go into mufti for the third term, anticipating their emancipation from school rules by a few months. 1989 Dashfield *To the Stars* 203 Mufti, the mini-skirt, co-ed, community service..going to the pictures were the order of the day.

muka /'mukə/. Also early **e-mu-ka** (=he muka), **mo(o)ca**, **mooka**. [Ma. /'muka/: Williams 213 *Muka... 1*. Prepared fibre of flax.] The (prepared) fibre of flax. See also hemp.
 [1804 Collins *English Colony in NSW* 561 E-mu-ka, *The flax plant when dressed.* 1807 Savage *Some Acc. of NZ* 76 Mooca..Thread, cord, rope.] 1814 Marsden 9 Mar. in Elder *Marsden's Lieutenants* (1934) 58 You will send the *Active* full of moca..fish, and nets. 1830 Craik *New Zealanders* 181 In this prepared state it is..called mooka. 1840 *NZ Jrnl.* I. 82 Portions of flax are to be seen adjoining almost every village; it is of incalculable service to the natives... When scraped or dressed the common or inferior is called *mooka*. 1869 *TrNZI* I. (rev. edn.) 276 Muka of the natives, as the dressed fibre of the Harakeke, or Flax Plant. 1904 Tregear *Maori Race* 222 The fibre (*muka*) was then steeped for three or four days in running water, taken out and pounded with a stone beater. 1930 Pinfold *Fifty Yrs. Maoriland* 25 As the blood oozes from the wound, it is dexterously wiped away with the 'muka', a small bunch of finely prepared flax. 1946 *JPS* LV. 154 *muka*, prepared fibre of flax (harakeke). 1953 Reed *Story of Kauri* 141 At other times we would sit down amongst some flax bushes, and make 'muka' for whip-lashes. 1960 Boswell *Ernie* 143 Beautiful, compactly plaited whips complete with handle, leather thong and muka lash. Muka is the Maori name for the flax fibre after the green has been scraped from the fibrous skeleton. 1982 Hulme *Silences Between* 16 I was playing, making knots in the muka in the sun and I dropped the tangle, forgot it. 1991 *More Earlier Days on the Coast* 12 This [marae] building was constructed without any nails. It was tied together with muka (the fibre from flax).

mulabar, var. mullibar.

mulberry /'mʌlbri/. *Hist.* [Transf. use of *mulberry Morus* spp. (fam. Moraceae).]

1. As **paper mulberry**, aute (*Broussonetia papyrifera*).
 1869 *TrNZI* I. (rev. edn.) 262 [One only fibre-yielding plant] was generally cultivated, and that..was not indigenous;.. the aute, or paper-mulberry tree (*Broussonetia papyrifera*);.. It has long been nearly, if not quite, extinct. 1905 [see aute]. 1917 Williams *Dict. Maori Lang.* 28 Aute, n... *paper-mulberry*, formerly cultivated by the Natives in New Zealand. 1924 *Otago Witness* (Dunedin) 17 June 6 Dr. P.H. Buck..believes that early Maori navigators brought paper mulberry plants to New Zealand from their homes in the tropics.

2. As **native (New Zealand) mulberry**, whau, having large heart-shaped leaves resembling those of the English mulberry (*Morus nigra*).
 1870 *TrNZI* III. 185 *Entelea arborescens*... The Whau, or native Mulberry, is remarkable for its immense cordate leaves; it is impatient of cold exposure. 1940 Laing & Blackwell *Plants NZ* 257 In some places this tree is called the New Zealand Mulberry, on account of the shape of the leaves.

Muldoon /mʌl'dun/.
 a. As a formant in composition: **Muldoonery**, **Muldoonian**, **Muldoonism**, alluding to the political, financial and economic policies, or to the aggressive and vindictive personal style and authoritarian manner characteristic of (Sir) Robert David *Muldoon* (1921–92), Minister of Finance (1967–72, 1975–84) and Prime Minister (1975-84) in National Party administrations. Cf. *think big* (think v. 2); Rob's mob.
 1986 *National Business Review* 12 Sept. 10 Are we then to presume that in sensing imminent economic disaster, plagues of Rogernomics and a famine from **Muldoonery**, the bay's good people have turned to more mighty beings than the present government. 1988 *Contact* (Wellington) 29 July 7 Not only that, the Burmese have abandoned 'Muldoonery' after decades of controls. 1992 *Dominion Sunday Times* (Wellington) 2 Nov. 19 Despite the party's protests..that's essentially more 'Muldoonery' at a time when New Zealand already has abundant superstructure. 1992 *Metro* (Auckland) Feb. 8 [He] is displaying the worst type of residual **Muldoonian** thinking. 1973 *Dominion* (Wellington) 14 Feb. 7 The epithet '**Muldoonism**', used by politicians, schoolchildren and businessmen alike, has become a familiar word in the Kiwi vocabulary. 1974 Muldoon *Rise & Fall of a Young Turk* 104 Muldoonism in education was simply the same approach that I tried to use with other problems. 1986 *Listener* 9 Aug. 39 *The Rose* was topical, they said, because it dealt with Muldoonism at its height... The play was just as much a comment on the political reactions of New Zealanders as it was about Muldoonism. 1992 *Dominion Sunday Times* (Wellington) 9 Aug. 10 It was a long and strange journey for New Zealand into Muldoonism.
 b. In *transf.* uses for other situations or political policies.
 1987 *Metro* (Auckland) Jan. 118 For the majority of men—and increasing number of women—it is at present simply Muldoonism brought into the sphere of personal and professional relations. Deny your most tender feelings, destroy those who reveal themselves as vulnerable or sensitive, put down the opposition like dogs, polarise everybody in sight, create plausible scapegoats..and hate..with all the venom you can muster.
 Hence **Muldoonist** *a.*, characteristic of Muldoon or Muldoonism.
 1989 *Dominion* (Wellington) 15 Apr. 2 The combative Winston Peters and former prime minister Sir Robert Muldoon took it as a compliment when Mr Caygill scoffed at them as being 'the Batman and Robin of failed Muldoonist policies'.

mullet. [Spec. use of *mullet* marine fishes of families Mullidae (goat fishes) and Mugilidae (true mullets).]

1. Usu. with a modifier, any of various fish of the family Mugilidae, mainly pelagic but also including the reef-loving *Upeneichthys lineatus* (fam. Mullidae) (see *red mullet* 2 (2) below).
 1769 Parkinson *Journal* (1773) 5 Nov. 104 We sent the pinnace to haul the seine, and caught a large draught of mullets, and other kind of fish. 1894 *Auckland Weekly News* 6 Jan. 34 If a settler in the Kaipara feels inclined for a dish of mullet, he takes his boat and paddles it up a shady creek near a bank, suddenly drops his paddles on the water, when lo and behold, a few mullet are sure to jump into his boat. 1929 Best *Fishing methods* 180 Karaka Tarawhiti..told me that mullet was one of the fish taken by natives in the river as far up as Rangiriri. 1971 Holmes *Century of Sail* 149 Where there's mud and mangroves, there's mullet. 1985 Orbell *Natural World of Maori* 30 On the day before the sharks were to be caught, one of the camps presented a busy and animated scene, with some of the men..bringing in mullet they had netted for bait.

2. With a modifier: **grey** (**Auckland, deep-sea, jumping, river, sea, striped**), **red, yellow-eye(d)** or **sea**.

(1) **grey** (**Auckland, deep-sea, jumping, river, sea, striped**) **mullet**. *Mugil cephalus* (fam. Mugilidae), a cosmopolitan species, olive-green above and grey below. See also kanae, *muddy fish* (muddy n. and a.).
 1844 Colenso *Excursion Northern Is.* in Taylor *Early Travellers* (1959) 53 This salt-water inlet is famous for a species of Grey Mullet. 1886 Sherrin *Handbook Fishes NZ* 52 The grey-mullet is a very familiar fish to residents in the northern parts of the Colony, where it forms a staple article of food among the Natives at certain seasons, and is one of the commonest fish sold in Auckland. 1892 *TrNZI* XXIV. 211 Sea mullet... Such numbers of these fish were taken from time to time by netting that no attempt was in many cases made to state them in figures. 1904 Tregear *Maori Race* 188 The sea-mullet (*kanae:*..) often ascends tidal rivers in great numbers. 1922 *NZJST* V. 94 Grey Mullet. Common in the Auckland market from midwinter to October. Variously sold as 'deep-sea' or 'Auckland' mullet. 1936 *Handbook for NZ* (ANZAAS) 72 *Mugil cephalus*: Mullet, Auckland mullet. 1966 Doogue & Moreland *Sea Anglers' Guide* 207 Grey Mullet... *Other names: Mugil cephalus;* mullet, river mullet; sea mullet, mangrove mullet (Australia); kanae (Maori). 1986 Paul *NZ Fishes* 112 *Grey mullet Mugil cephalus*... Alternatively sea mullet, striped mullet. Widespread, particularly in tropical and subtropical seas. 1990 McDowall *NZ Freshwater Fishes* 282 In some rivers the grey mullet can be seen moving upstream in great shoals, the fish leaping repeatedly from the water as they travel (hence the local common name of jumping mullet).

(2) **red mullet**. *Upeneichthys lineatus* (formerly *porosus*) (fam. Mullidae), a reef-loving fish, variably coloured, but usu. pink with blue head stripes and blue body spots and having well developed chin barbels. See also ahuru, goatfish.
 1922 [see goatfish]. 1957 Parrot *Sea Anglers' Fishes* 96 The Red Mullet *Upeneichthys porosus*... This species belongs to the Red Mullet family (*Mullidae*) and must not be confused with the Grey Mullets of the family *Mugilidae*. The Red Mullet of New Zealand is closely related to the European Mullet. 1966 Doogue & Moreland *Sea Anglers' Guide* 238 Red Mullet..; goatfish; ahuruhuru (Maori). 1979 *Catch '79* June 27 Red Mullet... Two chin barbels; large loose scales. 1982 Ayling *Collins Guide* (1984) 225 Goatfish (*Upeneichthys porosus*)... (Red mullet, ahuruhuru)... The goatfish is an elongate, bottom-living fish of inshore waters.

(3) **yellow-eye(d)** or **sea mullet**. *Aldrichetta forsteri* (fam. Mugilidae), a small fish of estuaries and harbours, blue-green above and silver below and noted for its bright-yellow iris, much fished for sport by children and others under its popular name 'herring'. See also aua, herring n.[1] 1, sprat.

1872 Hutton & Hector *Fishes NZ* 114 Sea Mullet... The Makawhiti or Aua of the Maoris..is a common fish... It is commonly called Herring, from its general resemblance in size..to that fish. **1886** Sherrin *Handbook Fishes NZ* 65 Makawhiti... Called the sea-mullet in other places, but the makawhiti or aua by the Maoris. **1921** *NZJST* IV. 120 *Common Mullet; Aua.* Common in the estuaries of all tidal rivers, often entering fresh water in the summer. **1927** Phillipps *Bibliogr. NZ Fishes* (1971) 30 *Agnostomus forsteri*... Yellow-eyed Mullet, Herring. **1947** Powell *Native Animals NZ* 67 Yellow-eyed Mullet..is usually called the Herring, but it is not related to the English fish of that name. **1956** Graham *Treasury NZ Fishes* 214 The common name Yellow-eyed Mullet has been given..in allusion to the conspicuous and bright yellow iris of the eye. **1957** Parrott *Sea Angler's Fishes* 170 Yellow-Eyed Mullet... Skipper; Herring; Sea Mullet. **1967** Moreland *Marine Fishes* 48 Yelloweye Mullet... Other names are herring, common mullet, and sprat. **1970** Sorensen *Nomenclature NZ Fish* 39 *Mullet, Yellow-eyed..Aldrichetta forsteri...* Suggested commercial name[s]: Sea Mullet; New Zealand Kipper (smoked). **1987** *Listener* 8 Aug. 62 Up the creek was a small bridge where gangs of boys, a few known from school, but mostly wild boys, not tribal members, hunted for large sprats and yellow-eyed mullet. **1990** McDowall *NZ Freshwater Fishes* 278 The yelloweyed mullet is one of New Zealand's best known fishes, being especially familiar to fishermen on wharves, river estuaries and harbours.

3. *transf.* and *fig.* **stunned mullet** [AND 1953], as the type of complete amazement or stupefaction.
  1989 *Dominion* (Wellington) 9 Aug. 9 Mr Lange's farewell speech to a Parliament still somewhat in stunned mullet mode brought out the finest qualities in some. **1992** *Evening Post* (Wellington) 11 Apr. 2 The 1500 staff [under notice] were 'shellshocked' and behaving like 'stunned mullets' because of the confusion. **1995** *Dominion* (Wellington) 20 May 19 Mune staggered around in gifted-stunned-mullet-silent-movie acting style before conking out on the floor.

4. a. Spec. Comb. **mullet boat**, a class of broad-beamed small sailing boat having a movable centreboard orig. to allow its use for (mullet-)fishing in shallow tidal waters. See also MULLETY.
  1921 *Star* (Auckland) 14 May 18 An addition was made to the rules governing ballast in the mullet boat class. **1944** Carter *Little Ships* (1948) 101 The name of mullet-boats dates back to the very early days of New Zealand's colonization, and although there is no record for the first boat which was built in Auckland, there is sufficient evidence to say the type was evolved somewhere about the year 1880. The boats were designed for a specific purpose, the netting of mullet which abound in the shallow tidal reaches, creeks and estuaries of the Hauraki Gulf, and its environs. **1964** Mander & O'Neill *Give a Man a Boat* 19 Our own mullet boats raced on length, too, from twenty to twenty-eight feet, which would appear..to have been the ideal length for boats fishing out of Auckland in an earlier age. **1971** Holmes *Century of Sail* 150 The mullet boat is peculiar to Auckland. **1992** *Metro* (Auckland) Feb. 90 Mullet boats don't have keels, only centreplates that can be raised and lowered, like dinghies.

b. In *attrib.* use often as Comb. **mullet-boat boys, mullet boatie; mullet yachtie**, with a connotation of belonging to a high-spirited boating group.
  1992 *Metro* (Auckland) Feb. 90 They are the **mullet-boat boys**, the present bearers of the torch for a class that developed in the middle of last century. *Ibid.* 99 For all their larrikin streak, the **mullet boaties** have a strong sense of history in an era of throwaway fibreglass yachts... It was a **mullet yachtie** who dropped a wallaby through the window of the Mansion House ballroom on Kawau Island during a New Year's dance.

mullety /ˈmʌləti/. Mainly *Auckland.* A *mullet-boat* (MULLET 4); occas. (esp. in *pl.*) one who sails a mullet boat.
  1959 *Sea Spray* Apr. 38 [Heading] *P.C.C. and Mullet Boats.* Of interest to mulletties was the recent launching of the E class *Shiralee*. **1961–62** *Ibid.* Dec.–Jan. 70 Who said mulleties were a dying class. **1970** Smithyman in *Te Reo* 16 9 Local [Auckland] variations on yacht-design abounded, and local namings (*patiki, mullety, fourteen-footer, zeddy*) were coinages. **1971** Holmes *Century of Sail* 153 Perhaps the most popular type of mullety has been the twenty-two-footers. **1992** *Metro* (Auckland) Feb. 90 The perverse appeal of the 'mullety' is that she was never designed as a yacht, but as a cheap and small cargo boat... The mullety started life in the 1860s as a fishing boat with a broad beam for carrying the catch, and a shallow draught for sailing up the creeks and mudflats of the Waitemata and the gulf.

mullibar /ˈmʌliˌbɑ/, /ˈmɒliˌbɑ/. Also **molly-bar** (and *ellipt.* **molly**), **mulley-bar, mulabar**. [Origin unknown.] A large marble.
  1934 Marks *Memories* 22 [Charles Skerrett who had migrated with his parents from India] introduced what we then called the 'mulabar' [c1870s]. It was a stone marble about one inch in diameter that was impelled by the middle finger of the right hand, assisted by the thumb and finger of the other hand, into the ring. **1972** Sutton-Smith *Folkgames Children* 174 Then there were the terms referring to particular kinds of marbles: for example, agates, aggies..milkies, molly-bars, mulley-bars [mullibars: large marbles]. **1984** Keith & Main *NZ Yesterdays* 288 There were agates, aggies, American alleys..mollies.

mullock, *n.* [Spec. use of Brit. dial *mullock* rubbish, refuse matter: see OED *n.* 1 a.]

1. a. *Goldmining.* [AND 1855.] Non-gold-bearing rock or earth regarded as rubbish; the tailings of auriferous material from which the gold has been taken.
  1868 *Thames Miner's Guide* 55 Mullock.— Rubbish. **c1875** Thatcher *The Leary Boy* in *NZ Songster No.5* 64 When no one's looking fill your dish, And you may wash out what you wish, Puddling mullock's knocked into a 'mish,' Hard work will but annoy. **1889** Paulin *Wild West Coast* 104 We sunk a shaft..and got into a drift of mullock and iron stained earth and granite boulders. **1900** *NZ Mines Record* 16 July 496 On looking around he saw the mullock falling from the hanging-wall on deceased. **1914** Grace *Tale of Timber Town* 152 Across the scarred, disfigured valley, over the mullock heaps,.. bearded men..collect in Canvas Town's one ramshackle street. **1935** *NZJST* XVI. 111 The gangue is whitish quartz, with a mullock layer in places on the walls. **1964** Howe *Stamper Battery* 105 Much of the mullock or mine tailings was sand. **1992** Park *Fence Around the Cuckoo* 224 Somewhere under the pastures must be the long-rotted sawdust heaps that littered the valley like mullock dumps.

b. *Coalmining.* Non-coal-bearing material.
  1904 *Awards, etc.* 8 [Hikurangi Coal-Miners Agreement] For all unsaleable coal and mullock filled in or thrown back 11d per skip shall be paid. **1911** *Maoriland Worker* 15 Sept. 6 The height of stopes should not exceed 8ft. or 9ft. from the mullock. *Ibid.* 3 Nov. 5 I think the old signal of three and one much better than the present four, as he [*sc.* the mine enginedriver] is likely to get confused with a straight three to raise mullock.

c. *transf.* Worthless material or rubbish dredged up with oysters. Cf. CULCH.
  1973 *NZ Heritage* XCIX. 2771 Large clumps of animal life which come up in the culch in the dredge are known as 'mullock'. **1979** Robjohns *Bluff Oyster Industry* 11 A term widely used by oystermen to describe certain fauna very unpopular with them is 'mulloch'. [*sic*]... Mulloch is a smelly mattered-up conglomeration of bryozoans..etc. **1990** *Listener* 24 Sept. 19 In my opinion the mulloch [*sic*] was put there [on the oyster beds] by nature and there must have been a reason for it.

2. Spoil, earth filling.
  1879 *Auckland Weekly News* 1 Mar. 14 The majority of the corpses wear a peaceful appearance, and were only disfigured by mud and mullock. **1883** *Auckland Weekly News* 3 Nov. 23 The little hillocks along its course contained a mullock which, when spread on the road in a puddly state, dried, and set like concrete. **1906** *Truth* 24 Feb. 5 Parties [of Main Trunk navvies] are often wheeling with wheelbarrows mullock to make up formation five or six chains from the 'gullet' of the cutting.

3. *fig.* **a.** Rubbish; nonsense; 'muck'.
  1866 Burgess *Life of Richard Burgess* (ATLTS) 127 (46) He said, 'No bloody fear. I should know it was a lot of mullock they were telling[,] for you are not like this Jew. **1908** *Truth* 18 July 6 A lot of mullock in the city dailies on 'How to go on the Land' would be more appropriately labelled, 'How to go Broke on the Soil'. **1911** *Triad* XVIII. No.9 11 We have a lot of trash and maudlin mullock in these days. **1982** Newbold *Big Huey* 153 'What do you reckon about this stale bread, Greg?'... 'Fucking mullock.' *Ibid.* 251 Mullock (adj) Bad, of poor quality. **1984** Trail *Child of the Arrow* 51 I remember we had 'bubble and squeak' for breakfast that morning. 'Mullock' my father called it. I'd often heard the term used by the miners and I imagined they meant rubbish or muck when they spoke of it, but I understood that my father was only teasing when he referred to our favourite breakfast as 'mullock'. **1990** Wilkins *Veteran Perils* 103 Brad, you heap of mullock, you're giving me a bad case of the mulligrabs [*sic*].

b. In the phr. **to sling (poke) mullock at** [AND 1916], to ridicule or mock.
  1887 *NZ Mail* (Wellington) 15 July 9 (NZ Slang) 'To sling mullock', is to throw mud. **1968** *NZ Contemp. Dict. Supp.* (Collins) 13 *mullock at, to poke v.* to ridicule, make fun of.

4. Special Comb. **mullock band**, see quots.; **mullock reef**, one with a high proportion of mullock to gold-bearing ore; **mullock rocks**, see quot.; **mullock-tip**, a place where mullock from a mine is dumped.
  1868 *Thames Miner's Guide* 55 Mullock.— Rubbish; a vein filled with various kinds of stone is called a **mullock band**. **1900** *NZ Mines Record* 16 Mar. 305 The miner took the naming of rocks into his own hands, and pronounced the softer country 'sandstone', where this had not to be called 'puddingstone', '**mullock-bands**', or 'hard-bars'. **1875** *AJHR* H-3 29 The reefs of the Carrick Range..are peculiar clayey ferruginous '**mullock reefs**' or rather 'quartz-mullock reefs'. **1961** Henderson *Friends In Chains* 187 **Mullock Rocks**: Waste material from quartz mines. **1966** Turner *Eng. Lang. Austral. & NZ* 152 *Mullock* is less frequent and retains a specialist sense of 'rubbish from a mine'. It is not common in general New Zealand English, but *mullock rocks*, 'waste material from quartz mines', occurs in a West Coast context. **1896** *AJHR* I-4A 36 Reserving to the company..rights-of-way and passage..**mullock-tips**, races and other rights and privileges acquired for mining purposes.

mullock, v. Goldmining
1. [AND 1940.] trans. To cover or litter (a locality) with mullock.
1861 *NZ Goldfields 1861* (1976) 4 Oct. 36 It is very probable that many portions of Gabriel's Gully will pay for reworking, for the place has been terribly 'mullocked' by the original workers.
2. As **mullock over, mullock through.** To search worked-over ground for gold.
1897 WRIGHT *Station Ballads* 60 For the country as far as I've seen it's as chock full of holes as a sieve. With the Chinkies a-mullocking through it and yet those coves manage to live.
Hence **mullocker** [AND 1905], one who clears away the refuse in a mine.
1910 *Awards, etc.* 47 [Wages: in or about a mine] Chambermen 8[s.] 6[d.] Bracemen 8 6 Mullockers 8 0.

mullocked, ppl. a. Dead drunk; useless.
1986 *Salient* (Wellington) 28 Apr. 5 By nine o'clock everybody is absolutely mullocked. The combination of the alcohol, the soothing paint, the aggressive bar staff who get the adrenalin going everytime you go up to the bar and the boring conversation is enough to make any person a babbling drooling uncontrolled mess.

mullocky, a. [AND 1862.] Containing much mullock; rubbishy.
1876 *TrNZI* VIII. 177 [Quartz-crushing] is accomplished thus [on the Thames goldfield]... The quantity of water varies according to the material operated upon, whether it be mullocky or not. 1878 *TrNZI* X. 502 *Antimonite.*—Union Jack Reef, Mullocky Gully. 1897 A TRAMP, ESQ. *Casual Ramblings* 116 It presents itself to me as a 'buckreefy' 'mullocky leadery' sort of country. 1909 [see COUNTRY 2 b].

multiple-unit: cf. UNIT *n.*¹

multy, a. Obs. Theatrical. [A short form of Parlyaree *multi cattivo* ad. Italian *molto cattivo* very bad: cf. Partridge 8 *multee kertever*; AND 1880.] No good, very bad.
c1872 WHITWORTH *Spangles & Sawdust* 5 I got a place at a livery stable, but although that kep' me in grub, and I slep' in a spare stall, the billet was very multy, and I kep' on the kivvy for something better... [1872 *Note*] 9. [multy] No good. 10. [kivvy] Look out (qui vive.) 1907 *Truth* 21 Sept. 5 This was the multy show that was so roughly dealt with in 'Truth' some months ago.

mummock, mummuke, mumoki, varr. MAMAKU.

mung, var. MONG.

munga /mʌŋgə/, WW2.
1. Also occas **manga; mangare.** [Abbrev. of Brit. tramp and Services slang *mungaree* food, ad. It. *mangiare* to eat: AND 1918.] Food, a meal. Also *attrib.*
1943 *NZEF Times* 25 Oct. 11 We argued quite a lot until munga time. [*Ibid.* 24 May 6 Meanwhile it is time for mungaree. 1944 *Ibid.* 19 June 4 I can also see a couple of bags of mangare there.] c1945 SIXES & SEVENS (Troopship pub.) 15 F. stands for F-deck, where munga queues wait. 1947 DAVIN *For Rest of Our Lives* 75 [The cook] swore he'd give them some good manga to go off with. *Ibid.* 344 We'd been topping our liquor off with a bit of manga, a bloody good feed of steak and three eggs each. 1955 *Upper Hutt Leader* 5 June 4 'Munga,' said the Grim Dig. 'Tucker. All the best moaners work on the munga.' 1970 *Listener* 12 Oct. 12 Or a rich, smoking mutton chop? A man has to eat. White or brown, everyone scoffs the same munga.
2. Special Comb. **munga party,** the rations detachment.
1959 SLATTER *Gun in My Hand* 55 Then he posted the picket and we sat in the stable resting up and waiting for the *munga* party to come up.

mungamunga, mungi-mungi, varr. MANGE-MANGE.

mungimungi taipo, tarpot: see TAIPO 7.

murder house. A children's name for a school dental clinic. See also earlier HORROR HOUSE.
1964 BULLOCK in Reid *Book NZ* 240 'Missed writing to-day. Had to go to the Murder House instead.' 'The Murder House?' My hand falters to my throat. 'You mean the Headmaster's Study?' 'No, the Dental Clinic. See?' 1980 LELAND *Kiwi-Yankee Dict.* 68 *murder house*: At most large schools, and for each collection of small ones, there is a small prefabricated building set slightly apart... The children..consider a visit to the school dental clinic an unpleasant necessity, at best. Hence the name. 1989 *Dominion Sunday Times* (Wellington) 7 May 14 [Heading] Murderhouse. 'One kid was drilled so long she [*sc.* the dental nurse] got through to the wooden headrest.' 1991 KEITH *Lovely Day Tomorrow* 24 She has an appointment that day at the school's 'Murder House'—the dental clinic, with its treadle drill ably wielded by the dental nurse.

Muriuri, var. MORIORI.

Murrumbidgee whaler: see WHALER 2 b.

muru, *n.* Hist.
1. [Ma. /'muru/: Williams 215 *Muru,* v. trans... 5. Plunder... 6. Wipe out, forgive.] A Maori compensatory plundering or property-stripping expedition against one who has offended in some way against the community; the institution or custom of muru.
[*Note*] Williams does not record in Maori use a noun form as such, the main or prior form recorded in quasi–English use.
1836 WILSON *Jrnl.* 24 Aug. in *Missionary Life and Work in NZ* (1889) III. 48 We were told the events which led to the burning of the mission station, and the *muru* which followed. 1860 BUDDLE *Maori King Movement* 24 Now there is to be no 'muru', *i.e.* no plundering to obtain *utu* for insult or wrong. 1863 MANING *Old NZ* (vii) 105 There were in the old times two great institutions, which reigned with iron rod in Maori land—the *Tapu* and the *Muru.* Pakehas who knew no better called the *muru* simply 'robbery', because the word *Muru,* in its common signification, means to plunder. But I speak of the regular legalized and established system of plundering as penalty for offences, which in a rough way resembled our law by which a man is obliged to pay 'damages'. 1878 BULLER *Forty Yrs. NZ* 85 I heard that a *muru,* or robbery, had been perpetrated. 1889 KNOX *Boy Travellers* 205 Another curious custom of the Maoris was the *muru*; the word means 'plunder'—and some folks might call it robbery. 1900 *Canterbury Old and New* 151 Death was not always the punishment that followed a violation of the law of tapu, sometimes a violation was visited by temporal punishment, in accordance with the institution of muru... [The sick or unfortunate were] plundered of their worldly goods. 1904 TREGEAR *Maori Race* 139 A remarkable custom was that of 'plunder' (*muru*)..a method by which an offence was expiated. It consisted of a band of persons (*taua*) visiting the offender and stripping him of all his movable property... If a man allowed one of his boy children to get hurt, the tribe would *muru* the father for the loss..since the boy probably would have been a future warrior. *Ibid.* 141 Perhaps 'damages' rather than 'plunder' is the best translation of *muru.* 1921 GUTHRIE-SMITH *Tutira* 267 Neither..was *muru* an institution likely..to foster foresight. 1932 ELDER in Marsden *Lett. & Jrnls.* (1932) 157 This plundering [in Aug. 1819] of those who had committed an offence against the community was called *muru.* 1949 BUCK *Coming of the Maori* 421 The custom of *muru* (raiding) was sometimes employed by visitors if a death was due to accident. 1961 in WILLIAMS *Early Jrnls.* 20 Altogether the year was a very troubled one, with many rumours of the death of Hongi, who had been wounded at Whangaroa, and consequent threats of *muru.* 1995 *Sunday Star–Times* (Auckland) 24 Dec. C6 Traditionally, compensation or muru was demanded from Maori who committed any form of offence against the community. Today, Maori society should do the same – within the legal system.
Hence **muru** v. trans., to strip (someone) of property. See also STRIP *v.*
1843 DIEFFENBACH *Travels in NZ* II. 374 Muru—forgive, spoil, rob, bruise. 1904 [see 1 above]. c1920 BEATTIE *Trad. Lifeways Southern Maori* (1994) 275 So the people went there and muru'd him (but there was not much to take, gravely added the narrator). 1948 HENDERSON *Taina* 33 'If you give her what she deserves, her family come and *muru* you'... 'They would come and seize everything you had..and leave you stripped and destitute, and all for not looking after your wife better'... 'I have been twice *murued* by my wife's relations.'
2. Special Comb. **muru party,** a Maori customary plundering party enforcing muru (see also *stripping party* (STRIP *v.*).
1904 TREGEAR *Maori Race* 103 The plantations were far apart, for fear that either an enemy's war party or a friendly plundering (*muru*) party might ruin the results. 1905 BAUCKE *White Man Treads* 29 I should first sneak away such valuables as I could conveniently hide, and stolidly awaiting the muru party, console my dejection with the comfort that the fates had not forgotten me, had singled me..out for the distinguished honour of a muru raid! 1948 HENDERSON *Taina* 177 He lingered on for two days and died. His father was *murued.* The *muru* party assembled at Rangi's house and awaited the signal.

muscle, var. MUSSEL.

mushy, a. Woolgrowing. [Spec. use of *mushy* soft, pulpy: AND 1901.] Of wool, lacking character. See quots.
1915 MACDONALD *NZ Sheepfarming* 87 *Mushy Wool*—Shows no pronounced staple; from badly bred or old sheep. 1982 *Agric. Gloss.* (MAF) 57 *Mushy*: Wool which is lacking character. Usually a sign of low fleece weight.

musk. [Spec. use of *musk Mimulus* spp.] Any of several unrelated native shrubs or herbs. **a.** Also **Maori** or **New Zealand musk.** A native or introduced herb belonging to the musk genus *Mimulus* (fam. Scrophulariaceae).
1910 COCKAYNE *NZ Plants & Their Story* 38 *Mimulus repens* musk. In some places, but by no means everywhere, growing in the pools or streams, is the beautiful New Zealand musk. 1926 HILGENDORF *Weeds* 157 Musk (*M[imulus] moschatus*), called also scented musk, is a small creeping, hairy-leaved, often scented yellow-flowered species, often forming masses a yard or so across, in damp places or on stream beds. 1961 MARTIN *Flora NZ* 243 Commonly on the margin of the

stream itself grows the New Zealand Musk (*Mimulus repens*), a leafy herb with lilac-tinted flowers internally yellow. **1969** *Standard Common Names Weeds* 51 *musk Mimulus moschatus* Dougl. **1993** GABITES *Wellington's Living Cloak* 40 Also rare around Wellington, the sweet scented Maori musk [*Mimulus repens*] grows in the Makara estuary..but not in abundance. This ground-hugging herb bears pretty mauve flowers.

b. Also **mountain musk**. Any of various aromatic herbs or shrubs belonging to either *Celmisia* or *Olearia* genera (fam. Asteraceae).

1896 HARPER *Pioneer Work* 218 This shelter [on the Karangarua River, s. Westland] we named 'Musk Camp', because here our only firewood was mountain musk, as it is generally called. **1900** *Canterbury Old & New* 209 Did not want of space forbid I could tell..of grassy glades carpeted with Celmisia, whose aromatic scent fills the air. This plant the shepherds call the Mountain Musk, and smoke it mingled with tobacco for the fragrance it affords. [**1900** *Note*] *Celmisia discolor*, *Cel. incana* and *Cel. Sinclairii*. **1908** *AJHR* C-11 40 *Celmisia incana*. Mountain musk. Shrub-steppe, south and west. **1919** COCKAYNE *NZ Plants & Their Story* 109 There will be numerous circular mats of different kinds of mountain musk—e.g., *Celmisia discolor*, *C. intermedia*, and *C. Sinclairii*. **1933** *Press* (Christchurch) (Acland Gloss.) 4 Nov. 15 M[ountain] musk, used for flavouring tobacco, is Celmisia novae-zelandiae. **1940** LAING & BLACKWELL *Plants NZ* 446 *Olearia moschata* (*The Musky Olearia*)... South Island: sub-alpine scrub... Mountain musk, Incense-plant.

Musket War. Usu. *pl*. A name given by modern historians to the inter-tribal conflicts among northern NI Maori tribes c1818–33 after the introduction of the musket to New Zealand. Also occas. *native war* (NATIVE B 3 b), or NEW ZEALAND WAR 1.

1983 KING *Whina* 18 When [the northern tribes] move out of the [Northland] area as a group, as they did during the musket wars, they are known generically as Ngapuhi. **1986** BELICH *NZ Wars* 20 From 1818, parts of the North Island were convulsed by increased tribal warfare. These conflicts continued in full force until about 1833, and are known as the Musket Wars.

muso /'mjuzʌu/. [f. *mus*(ician + -o: AND 1967.] A musician.

1970 *In Touch* (Wellington) May 7 Besides astounding local musos and setting the bizz in a buzz, Lewis produced a creditable future single. **1986** *Metro* (Auckland) Oct. 13 Another poor tortured soul whose other half shot through with a muso. **1988** SCOTT *Glory Days* 141 We all knew being a third-rate muso didn't pay that well and Cash did a bit of receiving on the side. **1992** *Cuisine* (Auckland) June–July 4 Even the entertainment was mostly from local musos.

mussel. Also early **muscle**. [Spec. use of the northern hemisphere name *mussel* for bivalves of the fam. Mytilidae.]

1. Any of various mostly edible bivalve molluscs of the marine family Mytilidae, usually attached to rocks or substrate by a byssus of tough threads; also members of the mud-dwelling families Pinnidae, and Solemyidae, or of the freshwater family Unionidae. See also KAKAHI, KUKU *n*.[2], KUTAI.

1769 PARKINSON *Journal* (1773) 1 Nov. 101 We..traded with them for cloth, crayfish, and muscles. **1777** ANDERSON *Journal* Feb. in Cook *Journals* (1967) III. 808 The rocks are abundantly furnish'd with great quantitys [sic] of excellent muscles, one sort of which that is not very common measures above a foot in length. **1791** BELL *Jrnl. Voyage H.M.S. 'Chatham'* Nov. (Vancouver exped.) (ATLMS) 51 The only Shellfish besides small Musells [sic] and Limpets were Cray-fish. **1807** SAVAGE *Some Acc. of NZ* 11 To such as are fond of cockles, muscles, and all the varieties of small shell-fish, the bay of islands [sic] must prove a most desirable place to visit. **1826** SHEPHERD *Journal* in Howard *Rakiura* (1940) 357 Cockles Mussels & oisters are plentiful and excellent. **1839** WALTON *Twelve Months' Residence* 29 The mussels produced on our coasts are Lilliputians, compared with those of New Zealand, some of which expand to a foot in length. **1848** WAKEFIELD *Handbook NZ* 161 Mussels, cockles, and *clams* also resemble our English sorts. **1861** HAAST *Rep. Topogr. Explor. Nelson* 141 The kuku (Mytilus canaliculatus), the mussel, is also very abundant. **1879** HAAST *Geol. Canterbury & Westland* 416 Then follows a series of shell beds, consisting of the remains of the following species, now still inhabiting the estuary;... Cockle..Pipi.. Periwinkle..and *Mytilus smaragdinus* (Mussel). **1929** [see KUKU *n*.[2]]. **1937** POWELL *NZ Shellfish* 22 Mussels contain iodine, a substance in which New Zealand foodstuffs generally are very deficient. **1970** THOMAS *Way Up North* 54 Mussels, paua, sea eggs and the whole range of their near and distant cousins were there for the taking.

2. With a modifier: **blue (black), date, fan, freshwater, green (green-lipped), horse (pinna), nesting (nestling), razor, ribbed**.

(1) **blue** (occas. **black**) **mussel**. *Mytilus edulis aoteanus* (fam. Mytilidae), a dark blue-black mussel common from East Cape southwards and averaging 4–7 cm in length. See also PIPI 1 d.

c1920 BEATTIE *Trad. Lifeways Southern Maori* (1994) 503 The blue mussel was..called kuku the same as in the North Island. **1949** BAXTER *Collected Poems* (1980) 80 Morning finds him on his daily round Stripping black mussels on a tide-swept ledge. **1955** DELL *Native Shells* (1957) 37 The Ribbed Mussel is smaller than either the Green mussel or the Black Mussel. **1978** *Catch '78* Mar. 21 Research is still going on into mainly the green-lipped (*Perna canaliculus*) and blue mussel (*Mytilus edulis*). **1988** *Back Then—Volume Two* (Oral History Birkenhead) 68 They grow on piles, the black mussels. Gee whiz! **1990** FOORD *NZ Descr. Animal Dict.* 53 Blue Mussel. *Mytilus edulis*. A dark blue to black bivalve 10cm long with one edge more rounded than the other.

(2) **date mussel** (or **date shell**). [f. a resemblance to a date-stone.] *Lithophaga* (formerly *Zelithophaga*) *truncata* (fam. Mytilidae), a rock-boring mussel.

1924 BUCKNILL *Sea Shells NZ* 90 Lithophaga truncata... Commonly known as the Date shell, this species is a rock-borer. **1947** POWELL *Native Animals* 20 Date Mussel (*Zelithophaga truncata*)... This mussel bores into soft mudstone, aided by an acid secretion which does not dissolve the shell because of the thick horny outer covering. **1955** DELL *Native Shells* 37 The Date Mussel owes its name to its general resemblance to a date stone. **1967** NATUSCH *Animals NZ* 80 A third borer, the date mussel.., excavates hard rocks by means of an acid secretion. **1971** POWRALL *NZ Shells & Shellfish* 50 The Date Mussel..lives in its hole in the rocks, with only a tiny mark to show where it is hidden. **1983** GUNSON *Collins Guide to Seashore* 76 The boring or date mussel *Lithophaga truncata* (35mm) attaches itself to low tide rocks by boring into them using an acid secretion and securing itself within the hole with the byssus threads.

(3) **fan mussel**. See *horse mussel* (6) below.

1917 WILLIAMS *Dict. Maori Lang.* 181 Kukuku... *Atrina zelandica*, *fan mussel*. **1924** BUCKNILL *Sea Shells NZ* 94 Atrina zelandica... The Fan mussel. A long, large, wedge-shaped, fragile bivalve. **1948** MARTIN *NZ Nature Study* 230 Typical Bivalve Shells... Kupa or Fan mussel. **1968** [see (6) below].

(4) **freshwater mussel**. A mussel of *Hyridella* spp. (fam. Unionidae) of up to 10 cm length, with dark leathery coating and found throughout New Zealand in rivers, streams and lakes. See also KAKAHI.

1859 THOMSON *Story NZ* I. 30 The fresh-water mussel and the crayfish are plentiful in some places. **1861** HAAST *Rep. Topogr. Explor. Nelson* 9 I found..one of Mr. Brunner's old camps, near which were plenty of freshwater mussel-shells (unio), and some felled trees. **1870, 1904, 1921, 1938** [see KAKAHI]. **1947** POWELL *Native Animals NZ* 34 Fresh-water Mussel... This or related species or subspecies are found buried in mud in most of our lakes, rivers and streams. They grow from 2 to 4 inches in length, and are covered with a thick dark green horny epidermis. **1955** [see KAKAHI]. **1967** NATUSCH *Animals NZ* 80 The freshwater bivalve *Hyridella*..is found in many of our lakes, rivers and creeks, where it lives buried beneath the mud. **1990** FOORD *NZ Descr. Animal Dict.* 154 Freshwater Mussel... A robust bivalve, the shell is smooth with a black covering..the larvae disperse by hooking on to a small fish... Other Names: Kaeo..Kakahi.

(5) **green (green-lipped) mussel**. Also *ellipt.* **greenlip**. *Perna canaliculus* (fam. Mytilidae), a large greenish mussel reaching at least 23 cm and averaging 10–15 cm in length, commercially farmed for local and export markets. Also occas. called **perna**.

1966 *Encycl. NZ* III. 710 Mussel, large green . . kuku, kutai . . *Perna canaliculus* **1979** *Catch '79* June 21 It was thought that the green-lipped mussel contained elements—or a hormone—lacking in arthritis sufferers. **1981** *Marlborough Sounds* 8 [Advt] World famous Marlbourough Sounds seafood delicacy Green Lipped Mussels. **1986** PAUL *NZ Fishes* 169 Also called green-lipped mussel... Green mussels have a long history of exploitation in New Zealand. **1989** *Marlborough Express* (Blenheim) 10 May 20 Blues are farmed prolifically along the coast of Galicia, Spain's Atlantic seaboard... That region produces 240,000 tonnes..worth $150 million, less than half the value of greenlips. **1990** FOORD *NZ Descr. Animal Dict.* 176 Green Mussel. *Perna canaliculus*. A very large, thick bivalve, up to 15cm long, more curved than Blue Mussel. **1990** DUFF *Once Were Warriors* 19 Mussels. Dozens of the sweet little creatures. Greenlips, the farmed jobs.

(6) **horse** (occas. early **pinna**) **mussel**. *Atrina zelandica* (fam. Pinnidae), a large (40 cm) fragile-shelled mussel found offshore almost completely buried in fine sediment and harvested commercially in small quantities. See also *fan mussel* (3) above.

[**1842** GRAY *Fauna* in Dieffenbach *Travels in NZ* (1843) II. 259 *Pinna Zelandica*... The gigantic mussels,... are probably *Pinnae*, as they have the habit he describes.] **1847** ANGAS *Savage Life* I. 246 The *pinna mussel* (*Pinna Zealandica*) was found in considerable abundance, sticking in the mud at the mouth of a small river that discharged itself into the [Wellington] harbour. **1917** WILLIAMS *Dict. Maori Lang.* 85 Hururoa..horse-mussel, a shell-fish. **1947** POWELL *Native Animals* 20 Horse Mussel (*Atrina zelandica*). **1955** DELL *Native Shells* 40 Horse Mussel... *Atrina zelandica*, Maori *Hururoa* or *Kupa*, size 7 inches... This is our largest bivalve shellfish. **1968** MORTON & MILLER *NZ Sea Shore* 518 The fan mussel or horse mussel,... though much less common..is a familiar mollusc of harbour flats, and may also frequent relatively clean, sandy grounds, close offshore. Our largest New Zealand bivalve, *Atrina*, may reach more than a foot in length. **1970** PENNIKET *NZ Seashells in Colour* 74 Horse Mussel

(*Atrina zelandica*)... A shell that is found at low tide in mudflats throughout New Zealand, lodged upright with only an inch or so of the broad end showing. **1987** POWELL *Native Animals NZ* (3edn.) 19 Horse Mussel (Hururoa) *Atrina Zelandica*. Like a half-closed fan, grows to 300–450mm long. The shell is thin, covered with hollow spines.

(7) **nesting (nestling) mussel**. *Modiolaria impacta* (fam. Mytilidae), a small (3–5 cm) mussel which forms a nest of fibrous threads completely covering clusters of shells.

1947 POWELL *Native Animals* 20 Nesting Mussel (*Modiolaria impacta*). An oval, rather inflated mussel from 1 to 1½ inches in length, found under stones at low tide, throughout New Zealand. **1955** DELL *Native Shells* 38 Nesting Mussel... This shell has the habit of spinning a cocoon-like covering made up of fine byssus threads inside which the shells live. **1968** MORTON & MILLER *NZ Sea Shore* 131 We may notice first the small nestling mussel.., which has a plump, nutlike shell an inch or more long, olive green to polished brown in colour, sculptured with radial ribs in front and behind but not at the middle of the valve. **1973** *NZ Heritage* XCIX. 2771 Components of mullock are mainly clumps of nesting mussels, the strongly tangled colonies of thin-shelled oval bivalves matted together with fibrous byssus threads. **1981** WILSON *Fisherman's Bible* 169 Nesting Mussel..gets its name from the fact that it 'spins' a nest of byssus thread and lives communally in a large matt-like group. **1990** FOORD *NZ Descr. Animal Dict.* 271 Nesting Mussel... It lives under stones and in kelp holdfasts, hidden in a nest of fibres spun from a gland in its foot.

(8) **razor mussel**. *Solemya parkinsoni* (fam. Solemyidae), a chestnut-coloured thin-shelled mussel found buried deep in mudflats below low tide.

1947 POWELL *Native Animals NZ* 19 Razor Mussel (*Solemya parkinsoni*). A thin-shelled bivalve about 2 inches long covered with a dark chestnut coloured shining epidermis which extends beyond the edge of the shell as a scallop fringe. **1955** DELL *Native Shells* 35 The Razor Mussel lives buried deep in sandy mud and is usually only seen when it is washed ashore. **1970** PENNIKET *NZ Seashells in Colour* 70 Razor Mussel (*Solemya parkinsoni*)... In spite of its common name it is not a mussel. **1990** FOORD *NZ Descr. Animal Dict.* 332 Razor Mussel *Solemya parkinsoni*. A thin-shelled bivalve 4–5cm long, covered with a thick, shining coating which splits into a fringe of squarish pieces.

(9) **ribbed mussel**. *Aulacomya (ater) maoriana* (fam. Mytilidae). See quot. 1970.

1955 DELL *Native Shells* (1957) 37 The Ribbed Mussel is smaller than either the Green mussel or the Black Mussel. **1968** MORTON & MILLER *NZ Sea Shore* 304 The blue mussel, *Mytilus edulis aoteanus* and the ribbed mussel, *Aulacomya maoriana*..establish themselves only in scattered tufts on fully exposed shores. **1970** PENNIKET *NZ Seashells in Colour* 72 Ribbed Mussel..Found from Cook Strait southwards this shell is easily recognised by its sharply pointed triangular shape and heavily ribbed surface. **1990** FOORD *NZ Descr. Animal Dict.* 340 Ribbed Mussel... A small mussel, seldom more than 5cm long, with numerous flexuous ribs on the surface.

3. Special Comb. **mussel barge (boat)**, a flat-bottomed barge or other boat specially designed for the harvesting (or also transport) of cultivated mussels; **mussel farm**, licensed stretch of coastal water, with the raft, ropes, buoys, etc. required for cultivating mussels; **mussel farmer**, one who works a mussel farm; **mussel-farming**, the commercial cultivation of mainly green-lipped mussels, *Perna* sp., usu. from ropes attached usu. to rafts anchored close to shore (or stakes driven into the sea-bed) in a designated licensed patch of coastal water; **mussel-rope**, a special 'hairy' rope (hanging vertically in the water from lines or rafts) on which mussel spat are attached to develop. (see also *Christmas-tree rope* (CHRISTMAS TREE 2).

1991 COWLEY *Bow Down Shadrach* 91 She had never driven a boat as big as the **mussel barge** and the thrill of getting it out of the Havelock channel, made her sing inside herself again. *Ibid.* 90 This flat-bottomed boat was heavier in the steering than their own **mussel boat**. *Ibid.* 8 That's our **mussel farm**. See those black buoys halfway across the Sounds? **1977** *Catch* '77 Oct. 23 If this unexpected source of help had not been forthcoming, the formation of a **mussel farmers'** cooperative would have, at best, been delayed. **1989** CRANNA *Visitors* 18 Some Island fella—said he was a mussel farmer from up north. **1979** *Catch* '79 Sept. 11 The Fishing Industry Board has held the last of its annual **mussel-farming** workshops. **1983** *Catch* '83 Dec. 13 As soon as mussel farming became established in different parts of the Sounds, it was obvious that the growth rate..differed from area to area... These differences are apparent to the mussel farmer through the variation in meat yield. **1981** *Catch* '81 Dec. 11 [Heading] Mussel mesh versus **mussel rope**.

4. In the names of plants and animals: **mussel's beard**, see quot.; **mussel-picker**, TOREA 1.

1947 POWELL *Native Animals NZ* 6 **Mussel's Beard** (*Sertularia bispinosa*). A yellowish-brown, fine, hair-like mass which grows commonly amongst low tidal sea-weeds, in rock pools and especially upon the shells of living mussels. **1980** LOCKLEY *House Above Sea* 180 There is also the plain, all-black torea (known as the 'variable oystercatcher') locally [in Hauraki Gulf] called '**mussel-picker**,' a solitary bird which haunts the rocky shore where mussels grow.

muster, *n*. Farming. [Transf. use of *muster* an assembling of soldiers, sailors etc. for inspection: see OED *n.*¹ 3 a, *v.*¹ 2 a; AND 1844.]

1. Also occas. **general muster**. The rounding up and bringing together of livestock in one place for any of various farming purposes.

1841 REVANS *Lett. to Chapman* (ATLTS) 90 I am not yet confident of the mode in which flock and stock musters will be dealt with by the natives. **1858** ACLAND *Notes Sheepfarming NZ* 12 The great difficulty in cleaning the sheep consists..in getting a clean muster. **1862** WEKEY *Otago As It Is* 11 The difficulties of shepherding here must always be great..; a full muster at shearing time is never obtained. **1867** BARKER *Station Life* (1870) 173 It is impossible to estimate our loss until the grand muster at shearing. **1878** ELWELL *Boy Colonists* 172 The mode of mustering adopted by Ernest was this. He..made a separate muster of each part [of the run]. **1882** POTTS *Out in Open* 39 It may be mentioned that during a cattle muster on the Haketere..a female quail-hawk was observed with a tui, trussed in her talons. **1892** SWANTON *Notes on NZ* 97 Previous to shearing those is the general muster, which means the rounding up and bringing in of all the sheep, good and bad, on the 'run'. **1899** BELL *In Shadow of Bush* 79 It was expected that a few of Morton's sheep might have got through the dividing fence since the last muster. **1934** *Press* (Christchurch) (Acland Gloss.) 27 Jan. 15 Muster... The usual..[names of high country musters] are (beginning in spring): the cutting and tailing *m[uster]*; shearing *m[uster]*; straggle *m[uster]* (in old days the shorn sheep were always turned out before the country was straggled, so that they would lead the woollies in); dipping or weaning *m[uster]* (to wean the lambs and dip the ewes); fall (or autumn) *m[uster]*; straggle again; then scratch *m[uster]* or 'look over' to get the last of the sheep off the summer country before winter. This last is an undress sort of *m[uster]*, the men catching what stragglers they can in the basins. **1966** SHARPE *Fiordland Muster* 54 How long would we spend on the actual muster? **1978** JARDINE *Shadows on Hill* 34 It was the weaning and dipping muster in the height of summer.

2. With modifier indicating the kind of muster performed (see also quot. 1934 1 above, and MUSTERING *vbl. n.*): **fall (or autumn) muster** *Sl farming* [f. *fall* autumn], one undertaken to bring sheep down from high country likely to be snow-covered in winter; **scratch muster**, see *straggle-muster*; **shearing muster**, the main muster to bring sheep in for shearing, drafting, and other farm operations; **straggle-muster** (also **straggler(s) muster**), a muster directed at rounding up stragglers missed at the main muster (see also MUSTER *v.*, and STRAGGLER).

1975 HARPER *Eight Daughters* 97 Near the end of the **autumn muster** when the sheep were being brought off the snow country, he would ride to the Bush Hut. **1981** [see *mustering stick* (MUSTERING 2)]. **1933** *Press* (Christchurch) (Acland Gloss.) 14 Oct. 15 Fall.—(1) Autumn. For some reason station people usually speak of *f[all]* and *f[all]-muster*, though so far as I know the word is not in common use elsewhere in New Zealand. **1947** NEWTON *Wayleggo* 118 They were in dangerous snow country, where every sheep left in the fall muster could be written off. **1950** *NZJAg*. Oct. LXXXI. 356 *April*: Fall muster commences [on Glenaray, Canterbury]. **1962** SHARPE *Country Occasions* 118 The fall muster is one of the big occasions in a high-country year. It is..one of the few occasions on which New Zealanders use the word 'fall' instead of autumn. **1975** HARPER *Eight Daughters* 110 Jack Sinclair's wife wrote: In 1933 the musterers started the fall muster from Jack Mac's on 8 April and landed the 18,000-odd, the first mob, on the station on 18 April. **1982** WHEELER *Hist. Sheep Stations NZ* 5 [Caption] Horses were being shod, some quite unwillingly, for the fall muster. **1953** STRONACH *Musterer on Molesworth* 9 Usually it is mustered by two gangs, one of six and one of four men... But this was a **scratch muster** and we were all together. **1904** *NZ Illustr. Mag.* Apr. 48 It was away back where roads were unknown..and where a few hundred sheep annually evaded the **shearing muster**. **1950** COOP *Shearing Ewes before Lambing* 20 On fat lamb farms..the shearing muster cannot be considered a muster at all. **1964** DICK *High Country Family* 11 The weeks of spring had so far been short, and too busy—and now the shearing muster was upon us. **1978** JARDINE *Shadows on Hill* 115 The shearing muster was the easiest muster—some of the true summer blocks were not yet stocked. **1982** WOODHOUSE *Blue Cliffs* 50 During the shearing muster of 1889 there was a disastrous smother when mustering off from the Back Country. **1933** *Press* (Christchurch) (Acland Gloss.) 16 Dec. 31 Straggler... Sheep that has been left on the country at a muster... It is usual to go over the country again to pick them up, hence **straggle muster** and verb to straggle. **1934** [see 1 above]. **1940** STUDHOLME *Te Waimate* (1954) 119 Frequently the blind sheep were left behind and had to take their chance with the stragglers [*sic*] muster. **1962** SHARPE *Country Occasions* 123 Sheep which act like that stay out on the summer country until they are either found in a 'straggler muster' or buried by snow. **1969** McCASKILL *Molesworth* 53 The first sheep shorn at Tarndale were from the straggle muster of the autumn of 1881. **1970** McNAUGHTON *Tat* 62 This three thousand acre block was supposed to have been mustered, but the straggler muster hadn't been carried out. **1973** FERNANDEZ *Tussock Fever* 171 They were mustered in December and there was a straggle muster about March. **1989** RICHARDS *Pioneer's Life* 47 I had been asked if we would return in three weeks to shear the 'straggle muster'.

muster, *v. Farming.*

1. *trans.* **a.** [AND 1813.] To round up and bring together (livestock, including occas. birds) for various purposes including, for dairy cows, milking.
 1846 Pharazyn *Journal* (ATLMS) 23 June 45 Assisted in mustering Ewes and Lambs into Stockyard. **1852** *Homebush Jrnl.* 27 Mar. in Deans *Pioneers* (1964) 154 27th.—Mustered them and all were correct; 280 young and old. **1862** Chudleigh *Diary* 25 Sept. (1950) 60 We had breakfast by 6 and started to muster the cattle. **1878** Elwell *Boy Colonists* 172 The sheep had to be mustered..in the latter part of the spring for cutting and tailing. **1888** D'Avigdor *Antipodean Notes* 74 They are more easily 'mustered' than the sheep of the Australian plains, as they are more afraid of dogs. **1895** *TrNZI* XXVII. 278 After a number of years, when sheep were mustered in from the back ranges, it was noticed that several would die in the yards. **1924** Anthony *Follow the Call* (1975) 10 I still whistled as I mustered the cows into the yard determined not to let..a leaky can put me out. **1933** *Press* (Christchurch) (Acland Gloss.) 4 Nov. 15 *Muster*.—To collect the sheep together on a block of country, for shearing, drafting, or moving them. **1947** Newton *Wayleggo* 12 The musterer's job is to muster the sheep off such [high] country into the respective homesteads. **1985** *NZ Outdoor* (Koro Wetere letter) Oct.–Nov. 6 As part of the [geese culling] operation the station's light plane was used to 'muster' the geese to enable them to be shot more easily.

b. [AND 1886.] Also as **muster out**, to clear (country) of livestock; to gather together (livestock) in a place.
 1863 Chudleigh *Diary* 27 Sept. (1950) 104 [We] go to Lake Heron on Monday to help Mellish muster his run. **1867** Barker *Station Life* (1870) 122 But it is very difficult to 'muster' these ranges. **1879** Kiernan *Diary* 24 Mar. in Guthrie-Smith *Tutira* (1921) 130 All hands mustered 'Rocky Range'. Got 62 woolly sheep. Total mustered to date 6630. **1891** Chudleigh *Diary* 28 Mar. (1950) 374 Mustering Korako. One horse left in bog. **1953** Stronach *Musterer on Molesworth* 15 We spent three days in camp at Boundary Gully, mustering out the head of the creek. **1973** Newton *Big Country SI* (1977) 12 The lease was for 2500 acres but as sheep could wander at will a big stretch of country had to be mustered.

2. *intr.* or *absol.* **a.** To make a muster (of livestock).
 1861 *Puketoi Station Diary* (Hocken TS) 3 Apr. Worthington..stayed all night going to muster to morrow. **1862** Chudleigh *Diary* 22 July (1950) 49 Misty in the morning soon cleared off. Mustering all day. **1878** Elwell *Boy Colonists* 173 Walker's men never mustered beyond the 'Saddle'. **1881** Nesfield *Chequered Career* 37 We generally dispensed with horses when mustering. **1891** Cottle *Frank Melton's Luck* 33 We're mustering and branding. **1952** Blakiston *My Yesteryears* 18 Starting at dawn, we climbed up the Clayton side of the range, leaving men at intervals to muster along the side. **1968** Tomlinson *Remembered Trails* 40 I have mustered on most rough country and always found four dogs sufficient.

b. Of animals, to be susceptible of mustering.
 1938 Burdon *High Country* 108 The sheep that were run on the hills in the seventies were..Merinos, and they mustered far more easily than the coarser-woolled sheep that are run today.

3. As **muster off** *trans.* and *intr.*, to complete a high-country muster; to bring (a completed muster of animals) off the hill; to complete a final muster (of a property). Also as a noun **muster-off**.
 1878 Elwell *Boy Colonists* 208 They all started from the hut to muster off 'Nob' mountain. **1953** Stronach *Musterer on Molesworth* 17 Later, when we mustered off, I examined the ewe; she had only one wound—just beside the backbone. *Ibid.* 53 Sheep ran off the hill; walking became easier, the drifts of snow were fewer, and we mustered off. **1971** Newton *Ten Thousand Dogs* 17 From the muster-off we took the mob down the road and past the homestead to a holding paddock a mile or so distant. *Ibid.* 71 The country was open right to the bottom. It was here that I mustered off.

4. As **straggle (scratch) muster**, to muster (country) for stragglers missed at a main muster; to make a straggle muster. See also straggle *v.*, and **straggle-mustering** (see mustering *vbl. n.*).
 1953 Stronach *Musterer on Molesworth* 25 For the rest of us, fifteen long days, if the weather kept fine, and then fifteen more days to straggle muster the same block. **1969** McCaskill *Molesworth* 105 Mowat says that once when straggle mustering, Boddington contended that Travellers Valley should really be 'Travers' after the botanist.

5. *fig.* or *transf.* In the phr. **to muster an easy beat**, to have an easy job.
 1988 McGill *Dict. Kiwi Slang* 74 *muster an easy beat* a comfy job (Jim Henderson); eg 'Here's me pulling night patrols and you're pen pushing. You mustered an easy beat, mate.'

musterer. *Farming.*

1. [AND 1889.] A person paid to muster livestock.
 1863 Chudleigh *Diary* 19 Dec. (1950) 114 All the musterers dogs have come home. **1872** Barker *Christmas Cake* chapter 1 Tired musterers sit down under the shadow of a great rock..and have a ten-minutes 'spell' and half a pipe. **1882** Potts *Out in Open* 188 The agile musterer, clambering amongst those rocky fastnesses. **1892** Swanton *Notes on NZ* 97 To accomplish this [muster] on large 'runs', additional hands called 'musterers' have to be engaged. **1911** *Maoriland Worker* 8 Dec. 14 The musterers on this place are all of the right sort. **1938** Burdon *High Country* 105 Thus the work [of shepherds], from being permanent, became seasonal, and gangs of men would go from station to station as they were wanted... They were called musterers. **1942** *NZEF Times* 31 Aug. 5 You might easily have become the best fly-musterer in that part of the world [*sc.* Egypt]. **1978** Jardine *Shadows on Hill* 4 With the two dogs beside him he leaned on his hillstick and watched..the other musterer. **1981** Anderson *Both Sides of River* 78 One of the musterers..gave him his first dog..who would hunt as well as head.

2. In special collocations: **musterer's stick**, *mustering stick* (mustering 2); **musterer's hut**, a hut on a station or large farm for the use of musterers (cf. *shepherd's hut* (shepherd *n.*); **musterer's sponge** *joc.*, see quot. 1978.
 1969 McCaskill *Molesworth* 101 A **musterer's stick** would then be pushed through the hamstrings and the carcase lifted... Apart from his dogs the musterer's most used piece of equipment was his hill stick, a six-foot piece of manuka with a ferrule fitted at the end to reduce wear. **1940** *Tararua Tramper* Feb. 1 A **musterer's hut**, clean cured sheepskins hung from the rafters; seven bunks for nine, so one used the table and another the hearth. **1950** *NZJAg.* Oct. LXXXI. 346 Bush Hut, one of the 14 musterers' huts on Glenaray station. **1978** Jardine *Shadows on Hill* 32 A good big damp fruitcake made a welcome change from cold duff or '**musterer's sponge**' (ginger cake).

3. In the phr. **all cock and ribs, like a musterer's dog**, said of a thin, lanky person.
 1986 Hulme *Windeater* 122 He prowls around the flat..a tall skinny fella in tight jeans, all cock and ribs like a musterer's dog.

mustering, *vbl. n. Farming.* [AND 1847.]

1. The act or process of rounding up and bringing scattered livestock together, or this regarded as an event or season. Also *attrib.*
 1860 Duppa Sept. in Crawford *Sheep & Sheepmen Canterbury* (1949) 47 To collect stragglers for a second mustering. **1863** Chudleigh *Diary* 19 Dec. (1950) 114 It always rains at mustering. **1873** Pyke *Wild Will Enderby* (1889, 1974) II. iii 56 Never was he happier than..when, as at mustering seasons, madly galloping over the plains, he chased the wild cattle. **1891** *NZJSc.* (NS) I. 173 The result..was that at nearly every mustering these short-winded sheep used to be left behind. **1928** *Weekly News* 12 Jan. [Caption] A remarkable sight during the mustering. **1959** *TrRSNZ* LXXXVII. 13 The first certain evidence of stocking is the record of the mustering of the main range and Blowhard in September, 1873. **1960** Scrymgeour *Memories of Maoriland* 8 Long mustering days, mostly on foot.

2. Special Comb. **mustering billy**, one carried by a musterer for making tea on the hill; **mustering boots** *pl.*, *Pannells* (Harry Pannell 1); **mustering camp** [AND 1911], a field headquarters for a general muster; **mustering dog** [AND 1937], see quot.; **mustering hut**, see quot. (see also *shepherd's hut* (shepherd *n.*)); **mustering stick**, a long, stout stick as a useful aid in negotiating steep or rough country (see also *hill-stick* (hill 1 c), *musterer's stick* (musterer 2), nibbie); **mustering time**, the season or time for a muster (see also *fall muster* (muster *n.* 2)); **mustering yard**, a yard built to allow sheep recently mustered to be held, drafted, or otherwise processed.
 1953 Stronach *Musterer on Molesworth* 8 We halted at the Saxon for a 'boil'. Each filled his small **mustering billy** and held it over the fire on the end of the mustering stick. **1980** McLeod *Down from Tussock Ranges* 203 The reward was to get your name on the silver replica of a mustering billy, the old-fashioned wide-bottomed pot with a mug which fitted inside to form a lid, and was boiled, when time permitted, hanging from the end of a mustering stick over a hastily-lit fire. **1985** Langdale-Hunt *Last Entail Male* 25 Some of the oil (black fish or bottle-nosed grampus) was still in the workshop in my time, until my brother, Reg tried it out on his **mustering boots** one day and was begged..to leave them outside because they made her feel ill. **1930** Acland *Early Canterbury Runs* 138 More stories were told of him in shearers' huts and **mustering camps** than of any other runholder. **1933** *Press* (Christchurch) (Acland Gloss.) 25 Nov. 15 Some dogs will both h[ea]d and h[un]t[a]w[a]y and are called *handy d[og]s*. They are not generally high-class heading dogs but very useful about hand and sometimes very useful **mustering dogs**. **1933** *Press* (Christchurch) (Acland Gloss.) 4 Nov. 15 *Mustering hut*.—More often simply *hut*. Built out on a run for men to camp in, it is usually of one room with a fire-place, table, bench, and bunks round the sides. **1939** Cresswell *Present Without Leave* 188 The next night we reached one of the mustering-huts near the head waters of the Rangitata. **1975** Harper *Eight Daughters* 77 Paul Thomson was sent in from a mustering hut one day to collect more cheese. **1981** Pinney *Early N. Otago Runs* 68 The old mustering and boundary huts were of stone and the fences were rabbit-netted. **1951** McLeod *NZ High Country* 24 With his long **mustering stick** in his hand, he has a walking beat... Mustering sticks are usually nearly shoulder high and must be strong and tough and not too heavy. They are hard to get in some districts and a good one is carefully kept. Manuka is the commonest wood, but Miki-miki and Hazel are sometimes used. **1966** Newton *Boss's Story* 188 *Mustering Stick*: When on the hill, high-country musterers carry a long walking-

stick. Usually of manuka, it is about five feet long and is used for vaulting creeks etc. and as an aid to keeping balance when sidling sheep country. Also referred to as a nibby or pole. **1977** ANDERSON *Life in Hinterland* 100 To test [the ice] out he sent his mustering stick down to see if it would stop in this lip or cup. **1981** ANDERSON *Both Sides of River* 78 In April 1921 Ron was taken out to help with the autumn muster... Davis also gave him a stout mustering-stick and showed him how to make the best use of it when sidling across a steep face. **1881** NESFIELD *Chequered Career* 36 The sheep on our run in Hawkes Bay were never disturbed except at **mustering-times**. **1889** *Zealandia* (July 1889–June 1890) I. 30 When mustering time came, I got the usual notice. **1953** MIDDLETON in *NZ Short Stories* (1966, 1976 repr.) 186 Never saw such a great pack in all the King Country, as old Charlie's. See him coming in from the back country at mustering-time with a mob. **1879** KIERNAN *Diary* 9 Jan. in Guthrie-Smith *Tutira* (1921) 123 T.C.K..went to the back country to erect **mustering-yards** at the 'Burnt Bush'.

3. With modifier indicating the kind of mustering: **scratch** (or **straggle**) **mustering**, the rounding up of stragglers missed at a main muster.

1947 NEWTON *Wayleggo* 155 Scratching: Straggle mustering, i.e., looking for sheep that have been missed in the main musters. **1966** NEWTON *Boss's Story* 38 This straggle-mustering after the autumn muster had never been practised at Mount White to my knowledge. *Ibid.* 84 It was a job I aways liked—scratch mustering or 'scratching' as it was called—but you've got to have a good heading dog.

mutton.

1. [A survival of a Brit. use: see OED *mutton* 2 a.] A sheep (to be) killed to provide meat for farm consumption. See also KILLER *n.*[1]

1890 *Otago Witness* (Dunedin) 23 Jan. 43 The favourite morsel of the unhappy mutton which attracts the kea most strongly is the fat on the kidneys. **1956** DARE *Rouseabout Jane* 171 It was not long before I was promoted to killing three muttons each week. **1964** DICK *High Country Family* 86 The shepherd sallied forth to slaughter a mutton, aided only by a waning moon and his instinct. **1968** TOMLINSON *Remembered Trails* 28 I could kill a mutton sheep, and I learned to use an axe. **1988** *Univ. Entr. Board Bursaries Exam. Eng.* 6 He gave her a mutton once or twice a year for looking after me.

2. In *transf.* and *fig.* uses, see *mountain mutton* (MOUNTAIN 2), UNDERGROUND MUTTON.

3. *n. pl.* As **muttons**, in various phrases. **a. to be one's muttons**, to be what one likes; to be one's strong point.

1940 *National Education* (Wellington) Feb. 16 Milk, however, is small Charlie's muttons. **1941** BAKER *NZ Slang* 54 When we speak of something being *our muttons* or *a person's muttons* we mean that it is regarded with particular favour, that we like it especially well. **1955** *BJ Cameron Collection* (TS July) muttons (n) Something desired.

b. to hook one's muttons, see HOOK *v.*[4]

4. Special Comb. **muttonbag**, a bag or cloth formerly used to protect frozen sheep carcasses, esp. for export; **mutton board**, the part of the freezing works where mutton-sheep are killed and processed; **mutton chain**, the processing chain of a freezing works devoted to sheepmeat, see CHAIN *n.*[1] a; **mutton-flap**, often shortened to **flap**, the belly flesh of a side of mutton as a cheap cut of meat; also *fig.* or *transf.*, see quots.; **mutton lord**, SQUATTER 3 a or 'sheep-king'; **mutton track**, in the phr. **to walk the mutton track**, of a swagger, to follow a route or 'beat' from one sheep station to another.

c1930 *Whitcombe's Etym. Dict. Aust.-NZ Suppl.* 8 **mutton-bag** n. cloth used to protect frozen mutton. **1981** *Evening Post* (Wellington) 11 Mar. IV. 4 The dispute began after the union had applied restrictions to the work of members in the lamb cutting room and labourers on the **mutton board** in an attempt to improve pay and conditions. **c1920** p.c. W.H.B. Orsman. **Mutton-flap** used in Marlborough from at least WW1, and often cooked outdoors at picnics on wire-netting over embers. **1964** PEARSON *Glossary* to Sargeson *Collected Stories 1935–63* (1964) 301 mutton flap: a cheap cut of meat. **1960** HILLIARD *Maori Girl* 235 He slapped the roll of flesh around her belly. 'You've got a fair sort of **mutton-flap** there, old girl.' **1891** A TRAMP, ESQ. *Casual Ramblings* 59 The **mutton lords** live on roast duck and green peas. **1891** CHAMIER *Philosopher Dick* 42 Our 'mutton lords', as we call them, prosper and grow fat. **1974** AGNEW *Loner* 69 For several months I explored the North Island, walking the **mutton track** of the sheep stations and never once being refused a shakedown. *Ibid.* 78 [The swagger's] name was Hank and he wanted to know which were the best mutton tracks to follow, which station owners were the most generous and who had the best cooks.

muttonbird, *n.* [Poss. f. its use, like mutton, as a standard early Australasian flesh food, or from the smell of its roasting flesh (see quot. c1840): AND 1790.]

1. The young of any of various seabirds taken for food, usu. of the genus *Puffinus* (fam. Procellariidae), esp. the sooty shearwater or titi *P. griseus*, and in the North Island, the grey-faced petrel or oi *Pterodroma macroptera*. See also BIRD *n.* 1, HAKOAKOA 1, OI, PETREL 2 (12), SHEARWATER 2 (6), TITI 1. Also *attrib.*

1823 KENT *Journal* in Begg *Port Preservation* (1973) 321 We were visited this day by Tyeroa a chief belonging to a native settlement about Molyneux harbour, he had been..on the east side of Stewarts island..procuring seal and Mutton birds for the winter. **1836** RHODES *Jrnl. Barque 'Australian'* (1954) 35 The six sailors..had entirely subsisted on an aquatic bird they called a mutton bird, and cabbage tree. [**c1840** STOKES in Howard *Rakiura* (1940) 209 [Muttonbirds] are the most disgusting objects; with a rank, rammish odour sufficient to deter any but the coarsest appetites.] **1844** MONRO *Notes of a Journey* in Hocken *Contributions* (1898) 254 The cottages in Stewart's Island are all well garnished with a luxury of the southward—the mutton bird. This I take to be the bird which is sometimes called the sheerwater, or the sooty petrel. **1857** HURSTHOUSE *NZ* I. 121 The young titi (mutton-bird), a species of puffin, is caught by the natives in great quantities, potted in its own fat, and sent as a sort of 'pâté de foie gras' to inland friends. **1863** HEYWOOD *Vacation Tour Antipodes* 232 The natives in the South [of Stewart's Island] trade largely with their brethren in the North, in supplies of the mutton-bird. **1871** [see OI]. **1882** POTTS *Out in Open* 162 They draw from deep burrows the tender nestlings of the mutton bird. **1904** HUTTON & DRUMMOND *Animals NZ* 247 *The Kermadec Island Mutton Bird. Oestrelata neglecta*... This species does not form burrows, like the other members of the genus, but breeds in the open. **1906** BULLEN *Cruise 'Cachalot'* 353 They [*sc.* Maori traders] brought us potatoes..cabbages, onions, and 'mutton birds'. This latter delicacy is a great staple of their flesh food... When it is being cooked in the usual way, *i.e.* by grilling, it smells exactly like a piece of roasting mutton, but it tastes..like..a kippered herring. **1922** *Quick March* V. No.5 15 The tuatara lives in the same burrows as are used by the oii, the titi the toanui. All three of these petrels are included in the term mutton-birds. **1937** HYDE *Wednesday's Children* 74 Sometimes she would insist on cooking mutton-birds, from whose enormous breasts spouted streams of oil. **1947** POWELL *Native Animals NZ* 79 Mutton Bird (*Puffinus griseus*), Titi or Oi..was and still is in the South an important item in the diet of the Maori people. **1952** RICHARDS *Chatham Is.* 84 Muttonbirds were so called from their fancied flavour of mutton. **1963** PEARSON *Coal Flat* 375 Now Mrs Torere brought out a kit of kuumaras..and a half-kerosene tin of cooked mutton-birds preserved in fat. **1974** HILLIARD *Maori Woman* 126 In the end what they wanted was..a muttonbird, pork-bones-and-puha Maori. **1982** BURTON *Two Hundred Yrs. NZ Food* 9 On the southern coasts and in the Bay of Plenty, the greatest delicacy was the muttonbird or sooty shearwater, a type of seabird known to the Maori as *titi*. **1992** SMITHYMAN *Auto/Biographies* 63 We watched a tired North Island muttonbird bullied by young blackbacks.

2. In names of plants associated with muttonbirds or muttonbird habitats: **muttonbird leaf**, see *muttonbird tree* below; **muttonbird plant** *Chatham Is.*, *Leptinella* (or *Cotula*) *featherstonii* (fam. Asteraceae), a robust feathery-leaved herb confined to peaty ground in the Chatham Islands; **muttonbird shrub**, PUHERETAIKO (see also MUTTONBIRD SCRUB); **muttonbird sedge**, see quot.; **muttonbird tree** *Stewart Island*, mainly TUPARE; (see also MUTTONBIRD SCRUB, MUTTONWOOD); **muttonbird tussock grass**, see quot.; **muttonbird wood**, MUTTONWOOD (see also MUTTONBIRD SCRUB).

1980 GLEN *Bush in Our Yard* 150 Biddy came back from Stewart Island with a **mutton bird leaf** tree. **1910** COCKAYNE *NZ Plants & Their Story* 124 Other interesting Chatham Island plants are the **mutton-bird plant** (*Cotula Featherstonii*), which grows only near the holes of the petrels. **1984** HOLMES *Chatham Is.* 94 *Cotula featherstoni* (Mutton-bird Plant)—a perennial grey-coloured plant of 10–15 cm... It is associated with petrels and other burrowing birds. **1965** GILLHAM *Naturalist in NZ* 32 These [two species] are so closely associated with the bird rookeries that they bear the respective names of **muttonbird tussock grass**, *Poa foliosa*, and **muttonbird sedge**, *Carex trifida*. **1923** COCKAYNE *Cultivation NZ Plants* 60 *S. rotundifolius* (**mutton-bird shrub**..) is finally a small tree..admirable for shelter, not damaged by heavy sea gales. **1891** muttonbird shrub [see LEATHERWOOD]. **1891** *TrNZI* XXIII. 494 This tree [*Olearia*] is known in Stewart Island as the **mutton-bird tree**; and we soon found the reason, for the whole of the ground..is honey-combed with mutton-bird holes. **1898** MORRIS *Austral-English* 310 *Mutton-bird tree*, a tree..: so called because the mutton-birds, especially in Foveaux Straits, New Zealand, are fond of sitting under it. **1903** *NZ Illustr. Mag.* Nov. 115 Kai..is a..somewhat uninteresting island, as the sombre-coloured mutton bird tree is almost the only vegetation. **1930** *Wanderlust Magazine* II No.1 55 The birds prepare the old nesting holes..in the loose black soil under the Tupare—or mutton-bird trees. **1979** WILSON *Titi Heritage* 64 The 'muttonbird trees' (Olearias) have a very limited life. **1988** SMITH *Southlanders at Heart* 121 So I found a tree—the 'Mutton Bird'—and wrote upon a leaf.

3. Special Comb. **muttonbird island**, in general any one of many islands off the coast of Stewart Island, the nesting places of mutton birds; *spec.* with init. caps., a group of islands, so-named, off the ne. and sw. coasts of Stewart Island; **muttonbird oil** [AND 1872], the abundant oil from fat muttonbirds; **muttonbird season**, see (quot. at) BIRDING 2.

1858 THOMSON *Reconn. Survey S. Dist. Otago* in Taylor *Early Travellers* (1959) 339 Bates informs me, that before he started from Jacob River on the 6th [March 1857]..the natives were preparing to proceed to the **Mutton-Bird Islands**. **1910** *Truth* 19 Feb. 1 The Maoris were gathered together..for the purpose of being present at the sitting of the Native Land Court to deal with the mutton-bird islands. **1921** *Weekly News* 14 July Mutton bird islands off the coast of Stewart Island. **1939** *Taranaki Herald* (New Plymouth) 4 May 6 The first big drafts of mutton-birds from the Muttonbird Islands have reached the market. **1987** [see HAKUWAI]. **1890** *Otago Witness* (Dunedin) 17 Apr. 19 They tore up every piece of linen and rag they could find and bound up and dressed them with **mutton bird oil**. **1938** LANCASTER *Promenade* 253 Split fish drying everywhere in the sun,.. rancid odours of whale-oil, mutton-bird-oil, berry-oil, smells of pungent fern-root being scraped for food. **1939** BEATTIE *First White Boy Born Otago* 23 The [Otago] Maoris used to rub hinutiti or muttonbird oil on their heads and into their hair.

muttonbird, *v*. [AND 1945 (1872 as *vbl. n.*).] *intr*. To take the young of muttonbirds for food or sale.
 1918 *TrNZI* L. 144 This most interesting specimen was captured..where Mr. Smith was mutton-birding. **1944** BEATTIE *Maori Place-names Otago* 84 A taua (grandmother) narrated:- 'I have been muttonbirding on Horo-mamae (Owen Island)... I have also gone muttonbirding on Potoma (Evening Island).

muttonbirder. [AND 1881.] One who takes the young of muttonbirds for food or sale. Cf. BIRDER.
 1890 *Otago Witness* (Dunedin) 17 Apr. 19 The occupants of the boat were..mutton birders. **1914** GUTHRIE-SMITH *Mutton Birds & Other Birds* 19 Even then Leask pressed fish hooks on us..for the last lot of mutton-birders had..nearly starved. **1917** *TrNZI* XLIX. 168 There has been some clearing round the muttonbirders' huts. **1921** *Weekly News* 14 July [Caption] A typical camp of the muttonbirders. **1937** BUICK *Moa-Hunters NZ* 194 This method of preserving the flesh of birds is closely akin to that followed to-day by the mutton-birders on the southern islands. **1940** HOWARD *Rakiura* 211 The mutton-birders remain for but six or eight weeks. **1965**, **1970** [see HAKUWAI].

muttonbirding, *vbl. n*. [AND 1872.] The taking of the young of muttonbirds for food or sale. Often *attrib*. See also BIRDING 1.
 1850 *Acheron's Jrnl.* 28 Apr. in Howard *Rakiura* (1940) 386 Nearly all the residents [of Stewart Island were] off 'mutton-birding'. **1898** HOCKEN *Contributions* 37 Arrived here [at Taieri], they found the few huts deserted, the natives having gone on a mutton birding expedition. **1903** *NZ Illustrated Magazine* Nov. 117 We now induced the Captain to tell us something of his mutton-birding experiences. **1940** HOWARD *Rakiura* 207 The natives and half-castes of Stewart Island..the descendants of those nominated in the Deed of Sale as sole proprietors of the mutton-birding rights, betake themselves to the islets. **1978** FULLER *Maori Food & Cookery* 14 Torches (rama) were used extensively for night travel, for muttonbirding and other nocturnal hunting. **1985** *Reader's Digest Book NZ Birds* 97 Muttonbirding begins on 1 April.

muttonbird scrub. Stewart Island. As a general name, applied to the coastal scrub of Stewart Island dominated by the tree daisies TETEAWAKA, TUPARE, and PUHERETAIKO. See also MUTTONBIRD.
 1889 *Zealandia* I. No.33 149 The last pinch up the mountain [*sc*. Lee's Knob] is very steep, and leads through a dense scrub composed almost entirely of *Olearia colensoi*, which, in common with another large-leaved plant (*Senecio rotundifolius*) bears the name of Mutton Bird scrub, from the fact that growing, as they commonly do, on sandy ground near the beach, these bushes are favourite hiding-places for muttonbirds. **1910** COCKAYNE *NZ Plants & Their Story* 76 Where the coastal scrub of Stewart Island is densest, it has received the name of 'mutton-bird scrub'. This consists largely of the puheritaiko. **1914** GUTHRIE-SMITH *Mutton Birds & Other Birds* 13 Amongst this bracken's miserable short fronds..grow groundsel trees scattered in park-like isolation. Mutton Bird scrub is its island name. **1940** LAING & BLACKWELL *Plants NZ* 477 S. rotundifolius [puheretaiko] is the mutton-bird scrub of Stewart Island. **1940** [see TETEAWAKA]. **1953** LINKLATER *Year of Space* (1954) 203 There is muttonbird scrub [on Stewart Island] with thick green leaves that have white undersides, there are, perhaps, a dozen others. **1964** DEMPSEY *Little World Stewart Is.* 47 The familiar mutton-bird scrub, tupare, covers much of the ground and there is a handsome relative, also called tupare, which grows only on a few of the islands in Foveaux Strait and on the Snares. **1965** GILLHAM *Naturalist in NZ* 21 Trees belonging to the daisy family often don a protective coat of woolly hairs, colourful Stewart Island examples being the mauve-flowered daisy trees..and the yellow-flowered muttonbird scrub (*Senecio reinoldii*). **1982** WILSON *Stewart Is. Plants* 102 The term 'muttonbird scrub' is often used generally for coastal scrub dominated by any of the tree daisies, frequently mixed with inaka. **1982** [see PUHERETAIKO].

mutton-fish. *Hist*. Also *occas. ellipt*. **mutton**. [Poss. f. the resemblance of the texture of the cooked flesh to tough, dark mutton: AND 1830.] PAUA.
 c1826–27 BOULTBEE *Journal* (1986) 110 muttonfish—pàhiwah. **1838** PALMER *Trial Evidence* 16 May in McNab *Old Whaling Days* (1913) 209 [James Davidson's evidence.] I know a fish called mutton fish, which is much eaten by the men, but I never heard of its being unwholesome or producing worms. **1838** [see PAUA-SHELL 1]. **1842** GRAY *Fauna* in Dieffenbach *Travels in NZ* (1843) II. 239 *Haliotis Iris*... The foot black when alive. The 'mutton-fish' of the colonists; eaten boiled, but very tough. **1853** MACKIE *Traveller under Concern* (1973) 113 The beautiful pearly shell of the mutton fish is also common. **1859** THOMSON *Story NZ* I. 31 The finest shells [include]..the *Haliotis iris* mutton shell. **1861** HAAST *Rep. Topogr. Explor. Nelson* 141 In the pools on the rocky shores, the Haliotis Iris (mutton fish) is the principal inhabitant. **1882** HAY *Brighter Britain* II. 151 On the shores are oysters, mussels, cockles, mutton-fish, crabs, and other shell-fish in profuse abundance. **1890** *Otago Witness* (Dunedin) 25 Sept. 35 On landing [at Bluff] we noticed some fishermen..selling handsome mutton fish shells, of which the prismatic colours are so beautiful that very pretty ornaments and jewellery are fashioned out of them. **1904** *NZ Illustr. Mag.* Mar. 482 There was a luscious 'Paua' or Mutton-fish decaying on the beach. **1917** WILLIAMS *Dict. Maori Lang.* 170 *Kororiwha.. Haliotis australis*, sea-ear, *mutton-fish*; a univalve mollusc. **1935** *NZJST* XVI. 297 The paua..also called mutton-fish by settlers, was first brought to England by Captain Cook. **1951** KOHERE *Autobiog. of a Maori* 50 We were given *kumaras* and *paua*... [*1951 Note*] A shell-fish, or mutton-fish. MCCLYMONT *Explor. NZ* 42 They lived on mutton fish.

muttonwood. Also **muttonbird wood**. Either of the shrubs PUHERETAIKO or TUPARE. See also MUTTONBIRD SCRUB.
 1889 KIRK *Forest Flora* 205 *Olearia Colensoi* mutton-wood. Mr Traill informs me that it is the tupari of the Stewart island Natives; it is, however, generally termed 'mutton-bird wood', or 'mutton-wood' by settlers, on account of its growing on outlying islands frequented by mutton-birds. **1897** *TrNZI* XXIX. 205 In hunting his plan was to..intercept them [*sc*. Stewart Islands kiwis] on their way from their open feedinggrounds to the shelter of the 'mutton-bird woods'. **1898** *Merriam-Webster Internat. Dict.* 2027 *Mut′tonwood′..n. (Bot.)* A composite tree of New Zealand (*Olearia Colensoi*) so called because it grows on islands frequented by mutton birds. [*Local, N. Z.*] **c1930** *Whitcombe's Etym. Dict. Aust.-NZ Suppl.* 8 *mutton-wood n.* a shrub found in coastal areas visited by mutton-birds. **1982** [see PUHERETAIKO].

my oath, my bloody (or) **colonial oath**: see OATH.

myrtle. *Obs*. [AND 1825.] Also **New Zealand myrtle**. Any of various native plants of the Myrtle family (Myrtaceae), esp. *Leptospermum scoparium*, but also *Lophomyrtus* spp. and *Metrosideros* spp. **a**. *Leptospermum* or *Kunzea* spp., MANUKA or KANUKA.
 1773 FORSTER *Resolution Jrnl.* 30 Mar. (1982) II. 244 We..found a fine Myrtle tree, the Leaves of which made good Tea... The next morning we tried all the three different Teas; viz: the Myrtle, the Spruce & the New Zealand one of which the first seems the most palatable. **1796** MURRY *Jrnl. 'Britannia'* Jan. in McNab *Hist Recs.* (1908) II. 534 The Myrtle is not so large, it grows near the water, has a red bark, and is known by the smell of its leaf which very much resembles the smell of the leaf from which its [*sic*] takes its name, it is of use for turners or Cabinet makers. **1817** NICHOLAS *NZ* II. 246 There is here also a species of the myrtle similar to that found in various parts of New South Wales. Another part of it grows in the country about Dusky Bay, an infusion of which was drank [*sic*] by the crew of the Endeavour, as a substitute for tea. **1834** MARKHAM *NZ* (1963) 33 Hattay [crossed out by Markham] or Ettay is a Tea tree, quite different to the Tea tree bush, a sort of myrtle.

b. *Lophomyrtus* spp. and *Neomyrtus* (formerly *Myrtus*) *pedunculata*, RAMARAMA, ROHUTU.
 1843 DIEFFENBACH *Travels in NZ* I. 26 Near the beach appear shrublike veronicas, myrtles [1843 *Note* Myrtus bullata.]..and flax. **1848** [see RAMARAMA]. **1869** *TrNZI* I. (rev. edn.) 193 Myrtles (*Myrtus Obcordata* and *pedunculata*). Two handsome shrub trees, common near Dunedin. **1870** *TrNZI* II. 122 Myrtus obcordata Myrtle. **1889** KIRK *Forest Flora* 127 *Myrtus obcordata* myrtle. This charming myrtle is a much-branched evergreen shrub or small tree, 6ft. to 15ft. high, producing its white flowers and red berries in great profusion. **1908** *AJHR* C-11 38 *Myrtus pedunculata*... Rohutu. Small-leaved myrtle. Forest. **1910** GROSSMAN *Heart of Bush* 16 'Why, it's the myrtle.' 'Yes, it is myrtle—rama-rama,' the man answered unnecessarily. **1966** *Encycl. NZ* III. 711 Myrtle, New Zealand . . ramarama, rohutu . . *Myrtus* spp. **1981** BROOKER et al. *NZ Medicinal Plants* 72 *Lophomyrtus bullata* (A. Cunn.) Burr. Common name: *Native myrtle* Maori name: *Ramarama*... It was known as *Myrtus bullata*. **1982** *Field Guide Common NZ Trees & Shrubs* 10 Myrtle *Myrtus obcordata* Shrub reaching 5m.

c. *Metrosideros* spp., RATA I.
 1851 *Richmond-Atkinson Papers* 25 Mar. (1960) I. 79 One of these parasites [on the stems of timber trees], the red myrtle, winding in & out of its patron becomes itself an enormous tree stifling the original growth... It is covered in season with lovely scarlet & gold flowers in shape like those of the English myrtle. **1857** [see MANUKA 1]. **1889** FEATON *Art Album NZ Flora* 177 Aka [Maori name]..Myrtle [Settlers'

name]..Metrosideros scandens..Climber. **1930** GUTHRIE *NZ Memories* 170 Further on [was] the rata, or scarlet myrtle, New Zealand's crimson glory, coloured mountain-side and gorge.

d. Comb. **myrtle-tea**, an infusion of manuka leaves. Cf. TEA-TREE 1 a.

1777 FORSTER *Voyage Round World* I. 143 But the constant supply of fresh fish..together with the spruce-beer and the myrtle-tea, contributed to keep us healthy..even in this damp climate.

N

nahui. [Ma. /ˈnahui/: Williams 217 *nahui.. Alternanthera sessilis.*] *Alternanthera sessilis* (formerly *A. denticulata*) (fam. Amaranthaceae), a trailing herb of damp sites with clusters of papery flowers.
   1969 *Standard Common Names Weeds* 51 *nahui Alternanthera denticulata.* **1981** TAYLOR *Weeds of Roadsides* 103 Nahui (*Alternanthera denticulata*) Small introduced herb... It is scattered throughout the North Island in damp places. **1988** WEBB et al. *Flora NZ* IV. 102 Nahui is described as indigenous in N.Z. Floras but its habitats are always artificial or greatly modified. Thus, it may have been introduced by Polynesian settlers. It has almost certainly spread southwards in N.Z. during the past century.

nail: see FOUND A NAIL.

nailrod. *Obs.* [Transf. use of *nailrod* a strip or rod of iron from which nails are cut: AND 1890.] A dark tobacco sold in a tight roll.
   c1875 MEREDITH *Adventuring in Maoriland* (1935) 125 Well, the fact is..I want to enjoy the aroma as well as the smoke [of the cigar], and if it gets mixed with that of the nail-rod you fellows are smoking I shall miss it. **1886** *NZ Herald* (Auckland) 8 Nov. 7 Nailrod and 1lb bars..with a full assortment of havana.. Cigars. **c1930** *Whitcombe's Etym. Dict. Aust.-NZ Suppl.* 8 nailrod *n.* coarse, dark tobacco smoked by bushmen. [from shape of plug] **1938** *Press* (Christchurch) (McNab Slang) 2 Apr. 18 A 'nailrod' was a double finger of tobacco.

nammoo, nammoui, varr. NAMU.

namu. Also **nammoo, nammoui, ngamu.** [Ma. /ˈnamu/: Williams 217 *Namu..sandfly.*] SANDFLY.
   [**1815** KENDALL *New Zealanders' First Book* 10 Nammoo A sand fly. **c1826–27** BOULTBEE *Journal* (1986) 109 sandflies—nammoo.] **1833** WILLIAMS *Early Jrnls.* 24 Oct. (1961) 335—*Namus* and moschettos trying and vexatious. **1834** MARKHAM *NZ* (1963) 46 Fine and Moon light Nights I go and sleep in the Bush as the House is full of Fleas, Mosquitoes and Sand flys or Nammouies. **1843** DIEFFENBACH *Travels in NZ* I. 145 During the day a sandfly (ngamu), a tipula, is very troublesome in New Zealand, especially near the seashore. **1867** HOCHSTETTER *NZ* 287 The sandflies..the Ngamu of the natives, small midges (*Simulium*), are most frequent on the sea-coast. **1922** COWAN *NZ Wars* (1955) II. 13 Their bare legs and arms might be covered with *namu* (sandflies), but they apparently did not feel their bites. **1946** *JPS* LV. 154 *namu,* a gregarious insect (Simulia australiensis), sandfly, a most pertinacious suicidal little bloodsucker which will suffer death rather than relinquish the feast. **1955** MILLER *Nature in NZ* 30 Sandflies (*Simuliidae*), the Maori *namu,* breed either in mountain torrents or in sluggish streams according to the species. **1984** MILLER *Common Insects in NZ* 52 So it was that *namu,* the sand fly, and *waeroa,* the mosquito, veterans in the art of war, claimed the right of feud; and as..warriors passed through the opened gates of war, the more daring and silent *namu* chanted her famous vaunt which has passed into history: 'What matter if I be slain, so long as I draw forth the blood of the Maori people of the world?'

nanua. [Ma. /ˈnanua/: Williams 218 *Nanua..Chironemus spectabilis.*] red moki (MOKI *n.*[1] 2 (4)).
   1886 SHERRIN *Handbook Fishes NZ* 19 Dr. Hector says it is common near the East Cape, and is called by the Natives ehouhounamu [?=e nanua pounamu] or nanua. **1921** *NZJST* IV. 116 Chironemus spectabilis. *Maratea*; *Nanua.* A fish common in the Auckland market. **1957** PARROTT *Sea Angler's Fishes* 118 The Red Moki *Chironemus spectabilis*... Maori name: Nanua. **1967** [see MOKI *n.*[1] 2 (4)]. **1988** FRANCIS *Coastal Fishes* 37 Red Moki (*Nanua*) *Cheilodactylus spectabilis*.

nap. [Abbrev. of *nappy* or *napkin.*] A baby's napkin.
   c1940 p.c. R. Mason (1953) heard *nap* for napkin in Dunedin. **1959** SLATTER *Gun in My Hand* 104 Keeping kids off the flowers. Wiping up the pee on the floor. The stink of naps in the laundry. **1988** LAY *Fools on Hill* 87 She shook her head, hugging the child to her... 'Get me a dry nap, will you?' she said. **1989** *Evening Post* (Wellington) 18 Oct. 33 We 'special people' had a good night out. We found that old-fashioned naps are better than throwaways—and a two-pinner is still more watertight than a one-pinner.

Napier beetle: see BEETLE 10.

nappy valley. [f. *nappy* a familiar form of (baby's) napkin, with an ironic play on *Happy Valley.*] Applied to any of various (valley) dormitory suburbs where young couples with children are (or were) the predominant householders; in Wellington *spec.* Wainuiomata.
   1972 MITCHELL *Pavlova Paradise* 34 [Wellington's suburbs] are all thoughtfully hidden away..in the isolation ward of the Hutt Valley and its satellites such as Wainuiomata (or Nappy Valley as the locals have it). **1986** *Salient* (Wellington) 6 Oct. 7 Known as Nappy Valley during the '60s, Wainui preceeded Porirua as the haven of young couples who could just scrape up mortgage deposits. **1987** TV2 News 9 Apr. Time has seen [the Auckland suburb] Glenfield change from a nappy valley to a middle-class housing area. **1991** *Evening Post* (Wellington) 2 Nov. 10 Wainuiomata is not the crime-ridden 'nappy valley' often depicted. **1991** SMITH *Twist & Shout: NZ in the 1960s* 8 For women, it was the kitchen and child-rearing in Nappy Valley with other mothers.

narara, var. NGARARA.

nardoo berry: see SNOWBERRY 1 a.

nark, *n.* [f. Brit. slang and dial.: see OED *nark n.* 2 and *v.* 2. 'Freq. in *Austral.* and *N.Z.*'; also EDD *v.*] Someone or something that irritates or annoys one; a vexatious person or a vexation.
   1918 let. 14 Jan. in *Boots, Belts* (1992) 65 It is a nark being placed in Auckland [Regiment] rather than Otago. **1929** MILTON *Love & Chiffon* 178 'That Rooster narks me,' said Henare. The word rather intrigued Valerie. 'Nark seems a very accommodating word, Henare... You can say "a nark" (noun)... "He narks me" (verb), "a 'narked' expression" (adj) and "He looked 'narked'" (adverb), also, Oh nark it! (an exclamation). **1937** MARSH *Vintage Murder* 114 It's a blooming nark, dinkum it is. **1944** *Short Guide NZ* 39 Nark—an unpleasant person. **1959** SLATTER *Gun in My Hand* 167 What a bloody nark you turned out to be. A joker oughta bash ya. **1960** MUIR *Word for Word* 255 You're bloody lucky I don't do you over just for being such a nark. **c1980** BENNETT *Canterbury Tale* 83 There you go, lad, picking on a fellow again, the moment you see him. Bloody little nark you are. Can you lend me a quid? **1991** ELDRED-GRIGG *Shining City* 17 'He's a nark when he's had one too many,' Ginnie said.

nark, *v.* [See *n.*] *trans.* To annoy, irritate; freq. as a *ppl. a.* annoyed, irritated.
   1907 STORER *Boy Settler* 122 'I tell you I am as good a man as you.' 'Don't get narked, mate,' interposed the cool..voice of John Parker. **1929** [see NARK *n.*]. **1946** SARGESON *That Summer* 32 I'd feel it sort of put me in the wrong, and I'd feel a bit narked with Fred. **1948** BALLANTYNE *Cunninghams* (1976) 58 [He] wanted to kiss her..but she wouldn't let him because Gil would be narked. **1968** GRUNDY *Who'd Marry a Doctor?* 96 That day..she was a bit narked to see me sitting beside the driver, and, not looking too pleased about it, she got into the back on the hard metal seat. **1989** VIRTUE *Upon Evil Season* 22 Effie was more narked than Adin at first at how she and her two battlers were looked on by others in Whangarei. **1993** MILNER *Intersecting Lines* 43 Hughie..had an animal liking but little respect for his elder brother, whom he delighted in narking.

narrow comb: see COMB *n.*

nashi. [f. Japanese *nashi* (oriental) pear: cf. *Macquarie Dict. New Words* (1990) nashi (also *kiwi star*) 1988.] A cultivar of the wild *Pyrus pyrifolia* (fam. Rosaceae), an Asian, pear-flavoured, russet-skinned pip-fruit of oblate shape. Also *attrib.*
   1981 BOLLARD *Prospects for Horticulture* 111 The nashi, or oriental pear (*Pyrus serotina*) is a pip fruit which essentially has not been tried in New Zealand. **1988** YEREX *Best of Both Worlds* 108 Asian pear (nashi) is not really a sub-tropical at all as it will, in the main, grow in most area where apples and ordinary pears grow. **1990** WHITE *Nashi* 2 The word 'nashi' is Japanese for pear and, in New Zealand, is now used to describe pear cultivars that have been introduced from Japan... Nashi cultivars have been selected from the wild pear *Pyrus pyrifolia* Nakai (*P. serotina* Rehder), which is endemic to Japan and the southern parts of China and Korea. **1991** *North & South* (Auckland) Mar. 57 Canned nashis are another recent new line. **1993** *Dominion* (Wellington) 5 Mar. 11 A good week for buying..the nashi with both the hosui and kosui (brown russet skins) the best varieties.

nassella tussock: see TUSSOCK 3 (5).

Nat. *Derog. Ellipt.* for NATIONALIST, NATIONAL A 2. Often as **the Nats,** the National party, a New Zealand conservative political party, its members

or supporters, or a government formed from its members. See also NATIONAL.
 1939 LEE *Diaries* 18 Mar. (1981) 138 18 *March*..At the same time the Nats circulate my scarlet letter. **1975** *Listener* 10 May 8 Bona fide Nats who spend their childhood on horseback are not expected to ever walk properly. **1987** MOORE *Hard Labour* 29 I used to joke that it was quality not quantity that mattered: the Lord only had a dozen workers and one of them was a Nat! **1990** *Evening Post* (Wellington) 29 Sept. 1 [Heading] Nats' inflation target laudable goal—Peters.

Nat Goulds, *n. pl.* WW1. [f. an ironic play on *Nat*(haniel) *Gould* (1857–1919), and the name of his best-seller *Landed at Last* London, G. Routledge 1899.] A jocular nickname for later reinforcements comprising mainly conscripted men or those slow to enlist.
 1918 *NZ at the Front* 32 There are two great primary classes [of diggers] a) Aucklanders b) others. They may be further subdivided into. 1) Nat Goulds 2) Dinks 3) Stokers 4) Main Bodymen. **1918** INGRAM *Anzac Diary* 23 Feb. (1987) 87 The 32nds. [Reinforcements] are nicknamed the 'Half Minutes', and all reinforcements now arriving, being conscripted men, come under the general name of 'Nat Goulds'. This from the fact that Nat Gould was the author of a book titled 'Landed at Last'. **1918** *Chron. NZEF* 16 Aug. 34 Mac's face wore a Nat Gould smile—'Landed at Last'.

nati: see NGATI.

national, *a.* and *n.*

A. *adj.*

1. a *Hist.* Of New Zealand as a Maori country; MAORI B 1 a
 1851 GRACE *Rep. Turanga Dist.* in *Pioneer Missionary* (1928) 16 This Church will be, if finished according to Maori architecture, the greatest monument of national art that New Zealand contains, and which the present race is likely ever to execute. **1890** COLENSO *Treaty of Waitangi* 15 Nearly in the midst stood Hakitara, a tall Native of the Rarawa Tribe, dressed in a very large and handsome silky white *kaitaka* mat (finest and best kind of garment, only worn by superior chiefs),.. the whole of Native (I might truly say of national) design and manufacture. **1932** ELDER in Marsden *Lett. & Jrnls.* (1932) 427 The Ngati-Whatua, Uri-o-Hau, and Roroa met him [in Feb. 1825] on the banks of the Waimako with over 1,000 men, but these were armed only with the old national weapons and had but two muskets among them.

b. NEW ZEALAND B 2, connoting New Zealand as an independent nation of mixed race as distinct from a colony.
 1890 COLENSO *Treaty of Waitangi* 6 He [sc. the author] applied to the Government of the colony to publish his MSS., deeming them, though brief, to be not merely interesting, but also of a colonial, if not of a national, importance, especially in days to come.

2. Usu. init. cap. Pertaining to the New Zealand National Party, a conservative political party. See also NATIONALIST.
 [**1935** *Dominion* (Wellington) 17 Sept. 12 Nothing has yet been decided about calling a caucus of the National Party to discuss the Budget.] **1949** *JPS* Mar. 12 National candidates *tend* to be wealthier than Labour. **1953** *JPS* Sept. 43 National party candidates in more than half the electorates obtained more than the average National vote. **1977** DOUGHTY *Holyoake Years* 62 The New Zealand National Party came into official being in May, 1936... The nineteen National members began a long struggle to convince the country of their philosophy. **1983** MARSHALL *Memoirs* I. 93 There was in fact a former general manager of Railways already in Parliament as a National member.

3. In the special collocation **national station** (also often formerly **YA (station)**), a member of the 'National' radio network of non-commercial stations broadcasting usu. light music, programmes of general public interest, and news.
 [**1933** *NZ Tablet* (Dunedin) 15 Mar. 4 There is no doubt the B stations were extremely popular among the listeners, many of whom preferred their programmes to the average broadcast from the YA stations.] **1935** *Star Sun* (Christchurch) 23 Nov. 24 3ZM started the breakfast sessions. These were copied by the National Stations. **1955** *BJ Cameron Collection* (TS July) national station (n) A radio broadcasting station over which advertising is not allowed. **1988** FRAME *Carpathians* 68 He even smiled amusedly, noting that the 'old' national station that once kept strictly to 'Where E'er You Walk'..and brass band music, now played a 'musak' selection.

B. *n.* A conservative political party.

a. A name attached to elements of the Liberal Party in the late 1920s, subsequently (1927) joining with others to form the 'United' Party; also NATIONALIST 1.
 [**1925** *Evening Post* (Wellington) 4 June 6 [Heading] A National Party. Why it is Necessary... Mr. Harry Atmore, Independent member for Nelson, said there were unmistakable indications of an overwhelming desire..for a National Government. He believed that a large number of candidates for the next election would be announced as Nationalists. **1948** LIPSON *Politics of Equality* 222 In desperation at their successive defeats [from 1922] the Liberals had sought an elixir of political life under new slogans and labels, calling themselves first Liberal, then Liberal-Labor, then National, and eventually rising as the United party.

b. The name chosen in 1936 for the political party arising out of an amalgamation of the United and Reform parties in 1935, and since then the main conservative party in New Zealand politics. See also NAT.
 1938 *Dominion* (Wellington) 10 Oct. 8 [Advt] Will she have to pay poll tax? Under Labour... Yes! Boys and girls will have to pay... Under National... No!.. Vote National. **1948** LIPSON *Politics of Equality* 230 The coalition, which now presented itself as the National party, received 260,000 votes. **1962** MITCHELL *Waitaki Votes* 9 The workers..tend to support the Labour Party, while the business and professional people in the 'better' parts of town..support National. **1983** GEE *Sole Survivor* 22 His parents—'my old Mum and Dad'—had switched their vote to National. **1990** *Evening Post* (Wellington) 29 Sept. 1 National would inherit an economy in crisis..Mr Peters said.

national death: see *New Zealand death* (NEW ZEALAND B 4 b).

Nationalist. *Hist.* Usu. cap.

1. A name in the 1920s for a member or supporter of 'National Reform' or 'National Liberal' party policies. Cf. NATIONAL B a.
 1925 *Evening Post* (Wellington) 27 Oct. 6 There will be 39 straight-out contests..15 between Reform and Nationalist party; 6 between Nationalists and Labour. *Ibid.* 9 Mr. Forbes said the Liberals had been criticised for changing their name to Nationalists.

2. Also occas. early **Nationalistic.** Pertaining to the National Party (NATIONAL B b), often in absolute use as a noun.
 1935 *Dominion* (Wellington) 19 Sept. 10 [Heading] Nationalist Views... That was the opinion of a Nationalist member of the House, who apparently had hoped for a more persuasive programme for the election campaign. **1935** *Na To Hoa Aroha* (1988) III. 197 Reform and United agreed virtually to amalgamate. Throughout the electorates..the two parties have been getting together and forming local Nationalist committees. *Ibid.* III. 198 The Nationalists should win, and it may happen..that the Maori vote will be the decisive factor. **1948** LIPSON *Politics of Equality* 229 Of eleven secondary urban centers [*sic*], six returned a Laborite and five a Nationalist. **1949** *JPS* Mar. 9 Certainly, in 1946, a Nationalist candidate was returned for Mt. Victoria. **1958** WOOD *This NZ* 96 At the general election of 1938..the detailed means by which the Nationalists proposed to preserve the existing society were almost identical with those by which Labour hoped to lead the country..toward..socialism. **1966** MILNE *Political Parties NZ* 62 The Nationalists..had promised that, once they were elected, they would stop prices from rising. **1989** BARBER *NZ A Short Hist.* ix 136 In May [1935] the United and Reform parties announced a name change, declaring that they would henceforth call themselves 'Nationalists', and that they were supported by a new political body, the National Political Federation. (The National Party was not formed until May 1936, later to become a mass party for all who opposed Labour.)

national superannuation. Also familiarly **national super.** A tax-funded State pension for New Zealanders aged over 60 introduced in 1977 to replace both the former income-tested 'age benefit' (also known as '(old-)age pension') and the 'superannuation benefit' (more popularly known as 'universal super(annuation)') and in its early stages of formulation by the Labour Party often called 'national superannuation' (see quots. 1935, 1938)). See also SUPER *n.*³
 [*Note*] National superannuation was at first from 1977 paid 'universally' without income test, but from 1985 the amount was reduced in proportion to the amount of other income; from 1990–92 it was temporarily renamed 'guaranteed retirement income' ('GRI').
 1935 *NZ Labour Party Election Manifesto* in Hanson *Politics of Social Security* (1980) 37 (c) A National Health and Superannuation Scheme... Superannuation to all persons at the age of sixty years. **1938** *Evening Post* (Wellington) 26 Feb. 10 The Government does not propose to proceed with its national superannuation and health insurance proposals during the coming part of the session, according to an announcement made by the Prime Minister. **1976** *Social Security Amendment Act* s13 National Superannuation—Subject to the provisions of this Part of this Act, every person who has attained the age of 60 years shall be entitled to receive National Superannuation under this Part of this Act. **1986** OVENDEN *O.E.* 111 Grog..early retirement and ten years getting fat on National Super. **1987** *Social Security Amendment Act* s8 No person shall be entitled to National Superannuation unless the person is ordinarily resident in New Zealand. **1991** *North & South* (Auckland) June 45 Politicians both National and Labour dug the hole they are in with national superannuation, or 'guaranteed retirement income' as Labour curiously renamed it despite knowing it is not guaranteed at all. **1994** *Dominion* (Wellington) 22 June 27 The Income Tax Act is cluttered with 144 references to New Zealand Superannuation, previously known as Guaranteed Retirement Income and, before that, National Superannuation.

native, *n.* and *a.* [Spec. use of *native* indigenous (person).]

A. *n.*

1. *Obs.* Often init. cap. **a.** MAORI A 2 a (a).

NATIVE

[*Note*] *Native* n. preceded *Maori* in common use, replacing earlier *New Zealander* and the quasi-official *aborigine* (see note at MAORI A 2). In official use (e.g. in statutes and other documents, *NZ Parliamentary Debates* or 'Hansard'), *Native* (with init. cap.) was the main spelling of both the noun and adjective until replaced by *Maori*.

1769 COOK *Journals* 9 Oct. (1955) I. 168 Seeing some of the natives on the other side of the river..I order'd the yaul in... In the mean time the Indians made off. **1773** COOK *Journals* 23 May (1961) II. 167 Towards noon we were visited for the first time by some of the Natives, they stayed and dined with us and it was not a little they devoured. **1807** SAVAGE *Some Acc. of NZ* 6 It is advisable not to suffer any natives to come on board until the ship is brought to an anchor. **1828** WILLIAMS *Early Jrnls.* 24 Aug. (1961) 142 At four we assembled for evening service in the chapel, when all the natives attended: we commenced with a native hymn, and after the church service we sang an english [*sic*] hymn, native prayer, after which I then addressed the natives from John 1.29. **1835** YATE *NZ* (1970) 258 The following are Letters from some of the baptized Natives, expressive of their desire to be admitted to the Holy Communion. **1840** [see ABORIGINAL A 2]. **1842** in Wily & Maunsell *Robert Maunsell* (1938) 76 I am thankful to say that things are going on amicably between the colonists and natives... The aborigines have lost a real friend in our poor late Governor. **1865** *NZ Statutes* No.71 264 [Native land Act] 'Native' shall mean an aboriginal Native of the Colony of New Zealand and shall include all half-castes and their descendants by natives. **1888** PAYTON *Round About NZ* viii It is always the custom in New Zealand, especially in the North Island, to use Maori words frequently in referring to the natives and their doings. **1890** COLENSO *Treaty of Waitangi* 15 Nearly in the midst stood Hakitara, a tall Native of the Rarawa Tribe. **1902** *Settler's Handbook NZ* 6 The Natives still own about 20,000 acres, but not much of it is fit for settlement. **1921** *NZJST* IV. 88 A Colac Bay native narrated that the late Rawiri te Awha had been one of a party of Maoris living on the shores of Te Anau. **1921** GUTHRIE-SMITH *Tutira* (1926) 386 *Pakeha* and natives alike..were eager to come to terms. **1935** *NZ Statutes* No.34 212 [Native Housing Act] 'Native' means a person belonging to the aboriginal race of New Zealand, and includes a person descended from a Native. **1946** BEAGLEHOLE *Some Modern Maoris* 300 Many Maoris resent the fact that they are called 'natives' by the pakehas. Joking among themselves, they may call each other natives, but the use of the word in this connection becomes a joke just because of the resentment at its use by the pakeha. One informant expressed the matter thus: 'We're not natives, we're Maori. A native is an aborigine, a savage, while we are three or more generations away from that... We like to be called Maori. We're proud of being Maori, not natives.' **1951** KOHERE *Autobiog. of a Maori* 54 I don't wonder why a wealthy sheep-farmer a few years ago tried..to persuade the natives to alienate the island to him. **1975** WILLIAMS *Dict. Maori Lang.* 23 Aute, n. 1..paper mulberry, formerly cultivated by the natives in New Zealand.

b. MORIORI 1 a.

1791 *Jrnl. 'Chatham'* 29 Nov. in McNab *Hist. Records* (1914) II. 504 The Natives who had quitted their station as soon as they saw us land [on 'Chatham' Island] now advanced hastily. **1791** BELL *Journal Voyage H.M.S. 'Chatham'* (Vancouver expedition) (ATLMS) 6 Nov. 62 We had proceeded but a little way when we first observed the Natives forming rather hastily into a Body by the edge of the wood abreast of us.

2. *Obs.* The Maori language; MAORI A 3.

1842 in Wily & Maunsell *Robert Maunsell* (1938) 76 He has rapidly advanced in native, and can preach with some fluency. **1849** TAYLOR *Journal* 20 Feb. (ATLTS) VI. 27 [Mr. Laurie] alluded to the complaint made by some of the writers on New Zealand that we taught the natives the Christian faith in native instead of English.

3. [AND an Australian-born white, 1806.] A white person born in New Zealand.

1900 *Canterbury Old & New* 6 The Committee of the Christchurch Branch of the N.Z. Natives' Association wishes to record its hearty thanks to the contributors of papers and photographs. **1918** *Quick March* 1 Aug. 29 Among the little bodies with a big name in this Dominion is the New Zealand Natives' Association, Wellington... The N.Z.N.A. had the benefit of a very enthusiastic secretary.

4. [AND 1793.] An indigenous plant or animal. See also NEW ZEALANDER 4.

1921 GUTHRIE-SMITH *Tutira* (1926) 204 Another reason assigned for the disappearance of the natives is ability to compete with alien breeds in regard to food-supply. **1959** MIDDLETON *The Stone* 65 'The kumara is a curious plant,' he said... 'But it's a native, Dan, isn't it?' **1985** HUNT *I'm Ninety-five* 261 No, my father didn't mind us shanghaiing thrushes and that, but he always said don't touch the natives. We did, though—pigeons and tomtits and tuis. **1986** *NZ Woman's Weekly* 28 July quoted in *Listener* 4 Oct. (1986) 5 Although many of the creatures are exotic, they are now concentrating on New Zealand natives, including the extinct Canterbury mudfish.

B. *adj.*

1. *Obs.* **a.** Occas. also **native Maori**. MAORI B 1 a (see note there) as distinct from 'European' or 'Pakeha'. See also NEW ZEALAND B 1 a.

1814 KENDALL 6 Sept. in Elder *Marsden's Lieutenants* (1934) 59 We were presently surrounded by many native men, women, and children. **1820** MARSDEN *Lett. & Jrnls.* (1932) 251 For this purpose we took two native guides and set off on our journey... We arrived at a native village just at dark. **1834** MARKHAM *NZ* (1963) 29 When the Bar was crossed Canoes or in the Native Mourie Tongue, Walker Mouries, or Native Boats, boarded us. **1841** *Gov. Hobson's Proclamation* 3 May in Rutherford *Sel. Documents* (1949) 11(a) The Governor avails himself of this occasion to appeal to the good feelings of the colonists generally in favour of their fellow-subjects of the native race, who require only instruction and good example to become equal to Europeans in moral, as they already are in physical attainments. **1851** *Lyttelton Times* 27 Sept. 5 Every man, woman, and child in the colony shall be taxed to pay it [*sc.* the debt of the New Zealand Company], not only *English*, but *Native*. **1853** ROCHFORT *Adventures of Surveyor* 14 Maorie, native name of the aborigines. **1872** *TrNZI* IV. 298 I regret my inability to give either native or settler's names of the native grasses. **1889** KIRK *Forest Flora* 144 The Native name 'kauri' is the only common name in general use. **1921** GUTHRIE-SMITH *Tutira* (1926) 117 Tutira was leased by forty native owners to T.K. Newton. **1938** HYDE *Godwits Fly* (1970) 128 People, white and native, lived in the landscape, though you didn't see them... It was Maori country. **1940** HOWARD *Rakiura* 210 Mutton-birding is the only modern survival of native enterprise. **1984** MARSHALL & STARTUP *From the Bay to the Bush* 44 Government..replaced the Armed Constabulary mail service by a native contractor, fortnightly, by horse, with a subsidy of £126 a year.

b. In the Maori language; MAORI (B 1 b) as distinct from 'English'.

1828 native hymn [see A 1 a above].

2. Applied to plants and animals and their products. Contrast ENGLISH *a.* 3. **a.** MAORI B 4, NEW ZEALAND B 3, in the sense 'indigenous to New Zealand', and often forming general and special collocations as **native bird** [AND 1860], **native bush**, **native forest** [AND 1831], **native grass** (often *pl.*), any of various indigenous grasses as distinct from ENGLISH GRASS, **native tree**.

1870 *TrNZI* II. 49 If..it should be deemed impossible to avert the impending fate which threatens the existence of many species of our **native birds**, we must endeavour to find some compensation for so great a misfortune, in..the introduction of foreign birds. **c1899** DOUGLAS in Pascoe *Mr Explorer Douglas* (1957) 222 The Canterbury plains and open parts of Otago have few native birds. **1906** CHUDLEIGH *Diary* 1 Mar. (1950) 431 The Acts of 1880 protection of native birds and imported game is in force in Chathams. **1927** GUTHRIE-SMITH *Birds* 9 The Dominion was to be transformed into a sixth rate Britain; our own native plants and native birds were unworthy of us. **1967** NATUSCH *Animals NZ* 249 Some 250 species of native birds, including odd stragglers from their places, have been recorded. **1984** MARSHALL *Day Hemingway Died* 7 I could hear the native birds in the bush, and the waves on the beach. **1853** SEWELL *Journal* (1980) I. 429 After surveying our Estates rode home with Mr Raven through the **Native Bush**—not so picturesque by half as the Wellington Woods, but striking. **1873** PYKE *Wild Will Enderby* (1889, 1974) IV. iii 122 On the left side arose a succession of grassy bluffs surmounted by native 'bush'. **1899** BELL *In Shadow of Bush* 2 Thickly strewn with blackened logs and branches..these clearings stand out in ugly contrast with the virgin native bush. **1919** WAITE *New Zealanders at Gallipoli* 9 The clean blue sky, the waving toi toi on the fringe of native bush..made an ineffaceable impression. **1920** BOLITHO *With the Prince in NZ* 20 The Domain is a far spreading park land, with undisturbed native bush, botanical gardens, and recreation grounds. **1950** CHERRILL *NZ Sheep Farm* 53 Oh, that's just Native Bush. **1964** HINTZ *Trout at Taupo* 36 It is scrub-clad, with some lovely remnants of native bush. **1985** FRAME *Envoy from Mirror City* 160 At last we entered the Hauraki Gulf sailing slowly past the Bays with their unexpectedly colourful houses..set against..the darker green where stands of native bush remained. **1838** POLACK *NZ* I. 347 The trees in the **native forests** are full of similar resins, which often exudes even from the tops of the leaves. **1902** *Settler's Handbook NZ* 274 The southern portion of the county was originally covered with native forest. **1915** CHUDLEIGH *Diary* 24 Jan. (1950) 464 The Island is much as it was but Wharekauri [i.e. Chudleigh's station] is returning to its native forest. **1946** SOLJAK *NZ* 11 These exotic forest resources are being expanded to..facilitate preservation of the native forests, which the early settlers wastefully reduced. **1835** YATE *NZ* (1970) 75 The **native grasses** flourish throughout the year... All English grasses flourish well; but the white clover never seeds. **1849** ALLOM *Letter* in Earp *Handbook* (1852) 125 A few words on the native grasses will not be out of place. **1872** *TrNZI* IV. 292 To facilitate the collection of such information, they prepared a printed list of such native grasses as appeared to them most valuable (33 in number). **1884** BLAIR *Industries NZ* 59 In the olden times it was an accepted theory in Otago, that..the milk of cows fed on native grass would not make butter. **1902** *Settler's Handbook NZ* 11 The extent of land in sown grasses was, in November, 1899, no less than 2,320,505 acres, while 2,042,789 acres were in tussock or native grass. **1922** PERRY *Sheep Farming* 50 Change of pasture from Native to English grasses..has driven the Merino back to the high country. **c1938** HYDE *Selected Poems* (1984) 85 But the native grass stands back, Uncouth and alone. **1951** [see ENGLISH GRASS]. **1982** WHEELER *Hist. Sheep Stations NZ* 12 Unless you walk over this country [*sc.* Central Otago] you'll miss the native grasses, like danthonia and the blue tussock. **1841** in Rutherford & Skinner *Establish. New Plymouth* (1940) 78 But the **native trees** and shrubs are as thickly coated as ever with their green leaves. **1873** MATHEW *Autobiography* in *Founding of NZ* (1940) 205 A sloping lawn with flower beds and then a belt of..partly native trees. **1964** DAVIS *Watersiders* 111 Did you notice anything about that big native tree we just passed?

b. In special collocations formed mainly from *native* + (usu.) *Brit. English common name*, in the names of indigenous plants and animals, see: ANISE, ANISEED, ASH, BAMBOO 1, BEE 1 b, BEECH 1, BEGONIA FERN, BLUEBELL, BRAMBLE, BROOM 1, BURR *n*.¹ 1, CARROT 1 b, CEDAR 2 (2), CELERY 2 (1), CURRANT, DAISY 2 (8), DAPHNE, DOCK 1, DOG 1, FIG *n*.², FLAX 2 (2), FUCHSIA 1, GERANIUM, HAREBELL, HEATH, HEATHER, HEMP, HOLLY, HONEYSUCKLE, ICE-PLANT, IRIS, IVY 1, LABURNUM, LARK 1, LAUREL, LILAC 1, MIMOSA, MINT, MISTLETOE 1, MULBERRY 2, PARSLEY, PASSION-FLOWER 1, PASSIONFRUIT 1, PEPPER 1, QUAIL 1, RAT *n*.¹ 1, SANDALWOOD 1, SCABWEED, SCREWPINE, TEAK, THORN, THYME 1, TOBACCO, TROUT 2 (5), VIOLET.

c. As **native guano**, local human excrement as a garden booster.

1964 NORRIS *Settlers in Depression* 185 Unfortunately, I cannot say whether the author of the following advertisement [in the 1880s] was successful in his enterprise: 'New Patent Manure Native Guano Made from nightsoil, is a most valuable manure and is guaranteed to contain more than 42 per cent of phosphates of lime..£5.10.0. per ton net.'

3. In special collocations. **a.** In the sense MAORI B 1 a. **native bishop**, a Maori bishop; **native chapel**, a chapel dedicated to Christian services in Maori; **native chewing-gum**, see quot.; **native chief**, see CHIEF; **native church**, an independent Maori Christian church under the control of Maori bishops; **native mat**, see MAT 1 b; **native oven** [AND 1834], HANGI (see also MAORI OVEN 1); **native party** *hist.*, a term applied by those Europeans sympathetic to New Zealand Company land claims to those supporting Maori land rights; **native path**, see *Maori track* (MAORI B 5 a); **native sandal**, PARAERAE; **native school** *hist.*, (a) a school set up by Church missions for the Christian instruction of Maori; (b) often *pl.*, a secular school(-system) for the instruction of Maori set up by the State (see MAORI SCHOOL); **native school-teacher**, a teacher in a native school; **native settlement**, see SETTLEMENT 1 b; **native teacher** *hist.*, an ethnic Maori teacher usu. of religion in a mission or native school; **Native Team**, a privately-promoted Maori rugby union team which toured Britain and Australia in 1888–89; **native township**, see TOWNSHIP 2 b; **native track**, *Maori track* (MAORI B 5 a); **native village**, see VILLAGE 1; **native wine**, a liquor made from the juice of the tutu berry.

1877 GRACE *Letter* 19 July in Grace *Pioneer Missionary* (1928) 256 I hope the C.M.S. will persevere steadily on this point. We ought to give Native Churches **Native Bishops**. **1848** SELWYN in *NZ Part V* (Church in the Colonies XX) 23 June (1849) 7 On the next hill to the eastward a wooden chapel is now rising, intended chiefly for native services;.. Beyond the **native chapel**..stands the ruined chapel of St. Stephen, built four years ago of unsound stone. **1988** MCGILL *Dict. Kiwi Slang* 75 **native chewing gum** puha stalk used for chewing, bitter at first, good mixed with resin from tarata or lemonwood. **1877** [see *native bishop* above]. **1820** LEE & KENDALL *NZ Gram. & Vocab.* 134 A´ngi; Name of a certain tree; a **native oven**. **1834** MARKHAM *NZ* (1963) 44 Coppre Mourie, or the Native Ovens are described I rather think in Captain Cookes Voyages. **1841** BIDWILL *Rambles in NZ* (1952) 30 And when I visited it, I saw all the native ovens (copper mowries, according to English pronunciation) in which the cooking had been performed, and a portion of the entrails, etc., were strewed about. **1853** SWAINSON *Auckland* 145 Two long lines of native ovens mark the spot where the bodies were cooked; and a smaller oven with a wreath around its edge. **1863** MOSER *Mahoe Leaves* 6 I am regaled with some potatoes and a bit of fish, admirably cooked in a native oven. **1871** WILLIAMS *Dict. NZ Lang.* 19 *Hapii*, n. *native oven* or *cooking pit*; *haangi*. **1881** CAMPBELL *Poenamo* 61 Cannibal feasts did come off now and again on the sly, but the Pakeha was too dear a morsel, and moreover, was far too salt to be put into a Hangi (native oven) for epicurean Maories. **1903** *TrNZI* XXXV. 23 It..is generally known among European settlers as the 'native oven', though the term 'steaming-pit' would be a more exact description. **1938** *Tararua Tramper* Nov. 4 Where occupations were situated, native ovens have been discovered. **1957** WILLIAMS *Dict. Maori Lang.* 34 *Hangi*, n. *1. Native oven*, consisting of a circular hole in the ground, in which the food was cooked by heated stones. *2.* Contents of the oven. **1848** WAKEFIELD *Handbook for NZ* 72 The missionaries..by the appointment of one of their number to be Protector of Aborigines, were identified with the **native party**. **1841** in Rutherford & Skinner *Establish. New Plymouth* (1940) 78 Until within a late period we had been unable to penetrate the interior of the country to any distance from the coast, but we now by means of a **native path** or two, recently discovered by the sawyers, can get to the forest. **1847 native sandals** [see PARAERAE]. **1839** TAYLOR *Journal* 27 Apr. (ATLTS) II. 118 This morning I attended the **native school** men women and children there were about 200 present arranged in circles the women apart around the female teachers some writing some learning their letters others repeating the catechism [*sic*]. **1847** *Annals of the Diocese of NZ* in Wakefield *Handbook NZ* (1848) 378 This is the work of our native schools, and has occupied forty spades, great and small—the older [men] digging, the younger.. pulverizing the soil. **1858** *Native Schools Act* [Title] Act to grant... in aid of schools for the education of the Aboriginal Native Race. Short title Native Schools Act. **1867** *Ibid.* [Title] Act to regulate..Maori Schools—short title Native Schools Act. **1879** *Auckland Weekly News* 4 Jan. 18 The Peria native school was examined..on Friday. **1884** HARPER *Lett. from NZ* 14 Jan. (1914) 214 At Arahura there is a Native School, attended also by a few European children. **1892** [see COLLEGE a]. **1908** *TrNZI* XL. 171 Tried by another standard..the Native-school system is not so satisfactory. In the first place, the school is a 'Native school'; the race-distinction is emphasized from the start. **1914** *Educ. Act* S56 569 A native school shall be deemed to be a public school. **1932** BUTCHERS *Education System* 84 In the Native Schools the wife of the head teacher is commonly the first assistant. **1948** *NZ Educ. Gaz.* Vol.XXVII No.3 1 In pursuance of the Maori Purposes Act, 1947..in future native Schools are to be referred to as Maori Schools. **1968** *Crime in NZ* 43 He [*sc.* a three-quarter caste Maori] was educated at a native school. **1993** *Sunday Times* (Wellington) 31 Jan. 15 It is 30 years since the state-funded system of Native Schools (later called Maori Schools) ceased to exist. **1949** *Auckland Weekly News* 5 Jan. 22 The heavy expenses incurred by many of the **native school teachers** in travelling..from remote backblock stations affords an illuminating commentary on the sacrifices that are made by so many teachers. **1832** WILLIAMS *Journal* 4 Dec. in Matthews *Matthews of Kaitaia* (1940) 33 They seemed pleased with the proposal, and I told them that if a European should come we would supply them with **native teachers**, which we shall, at all events, have in our power. **1848** SELWYN in *NZ Part V* (Church in the Colonies XX) 30 Aug. (1849) 101 A small class of candidates were confirmed..but I could not satisfy myself with those who were presented by the native teachers for baptism. **1851** GRACE *Rep. Turanga Dist.* 31 Dec. in *Pioneer Missionary* (1928) 17 I am unable to report very favourably of Native Teachers. **1860** BUDDLE *Maori King Movement* 14 A Native Teacher then read a portion of Scripture, sang a Hymn, and engaged in prayer, after which Te Heuheu chanted a song of welcome. **1884** MARTIN *Our Maoris* 48 One of the native teachers said: 'Though the heavens are black around us, this is the bright spot of blue sky, which gives hope that the storm will soon pass away.' **1904** *NZ Observer* 8 Oct. 5 The mortality amongst the **Native team** that journeyed to the Old Country has been remarkable. **1905** *Evening Post* (Wellington) 1 Nov. 2 An ex-member of the Native team which toured Great Britain and Ireland emphasised this in a letter to the press a week or two ago. **1948** SWAN *Hist. NZ Rugby Football* I. 268 The next [*sc.* after 1884] team to leave our shores was the 1888–89 New Zealand Native Team, which played in the British Isles and Australia; this team was privately promoted. **1992** *Metro* (Auckland) Jan. 78 Joe Warbrick..was appointed captain of the New Zealand Native team that toured the United Kingdom in 1888/89, even though the team included four Maori players. **1848** *NZ Jrnl.* VIII. 71 There is at the present time a good **native track** through the valley to Manawatu. **1869** *Memo. from Native Minister* 29 Oct. in Cowan *Sir Donald Maclean* (1940) 106 Native tracks, as a rule, follow the best lines of the country, but are generally capable of being improved in detail. **1882** POTTS *Out in Open* 82 Its magnificent growth is pre-eminently displayed, as for instance, by the native track from Roti-iti towards Maketu. **1930** REISCHEK *Yesterdays in Maoriland* (1933) 155 I sent Caesar after him, but because the native track was exceedingly narrow, the dog could not get ahead of the horse. **1867** HOCHSTETTER *NZ* 139 The natives express from the [tutu] berries an agreeable violet juice..called **native wine**.—When boiled with Rimu, a seaweed, forms a jelly which is very palatable.

b. In special collocations in the sense MAORI B 1 a alluding to the (often past) administration of Maori affairs by local, State or statutory authorities or officials and their political or ministerial superiors: **native affairs** (also init. cap.), Maori matters, *spec.* as **the Department (Minister, Secretary) of Native Affairs** (now **Maori Affairs**), the State department, and its administrative and political heads, dealing with Maori matters; **native agent**, *Government Agent* (GOVERNMENT); **Native Assessor**, see ASSESSOR; **Native Commissioner** *hist.*, one appointed to arbitrate disputes (usu. land disputes) between Maori and Pakeha; **Native Department**, the former name of the department of State admininstering Maori affairs; **native difficulty**, a European name for the disputes between Europeans and the Maori, usu. over land (see also *native question* below, and *Maori problem* MAORI B 5 a); **Native Interpreter**, see INTERPRETER; **native land a** (also occas. **Native Lands**), land under Maori ownership or control, MAORILAND 1, also *attrib.* (see also *Native title* below), **b** *hist.* as **Native Land(s) Court**, see MAORI LAND COURT; **Native Magistrate** *hist.*, a Maori appointed to deal with minor judicial matters arising among the Maori; **Native Minister** *hist.*, formerly the Minister of the Crown, from 1858 responsible for Maori affairs; **Native Office** (see also *Native Department* above) *hist.*, an early name for the office of Central government responsible for Maori affairs; **native problem**, see *native difficulty* above; **Native Protector** *hist.* [AND 1842], an official appointed to look after Maori interests, a PROTECTOR OF ABORIGINES q.v.; **native question** *hist.* [spec. use of a general English collocation: cf. OED *a*. 15], a European view of interaction between whites and Maoris, esp. over land ownership (cf. also *native difficulty* above); **Native reserve**, see RESERVE 2; **Native Secretary** *hist.*, an early name for the permanent official head of the Native Department (also (see quot. 1848) the term used for the political head before the adoption of 'Native Minister' in 1858); **Native (customary) title** (also **Native land title**), see MAORI TITLE; **native war** *hist.*, NEW ZEALAND WAR, rarely, Maori inter-tribal conflict (see quot. 1843; see also MUSKET WAR).

[Note] A search of the *NZPD*, the *Wellington Almanack* and other sources between 1822 and 1890 reveals a varied nomenclature for the political and bureaucratic offices, often loosely applied: from a first use in 1851, *Native Secretary* or *Native Secretary's Department* (*Office* June 1858) are preferred until 1861 when *Minister for Native Affairs* (C.W. Richmond) appears, 1863 *Native Minister* (F.D. Bell), 1866 *Native Department*, (1870) 1879 *Native and Defence Office*, 1880 *Minister for Native Affairs* controlling a *Native Office*. In official publications *Native* invariably takes an init. capital.

1856 *NZPD* (1856–58) 2 May 49 I gather that the administration of **Native affairs** is not to be intrusted to Ministers, but to the Governor alone. **1860** *NZPD* (1858–60) 3 Aug. 187 I desire to thank the Minister for Native Affairs for his very able statement. *Ibid.* 10 Aug. 281 The substance of that arrangement [founded on the departmental memorandum of May, 1856] was this: Ministers were to consult the Native Affairs Department in the ordinary way. **1934–35** *NZ Statutes* No.44 445 [Title] [*Board of Native Affairs Act*] An Act to establish a Board of Native Affairs and to provide for the Setting-up of District Native Committees. **1943** MARSH *Colour Scheme* 228 I shall go to the Minister of Native Affairs. **1946** *NZPD* CCLXXIII. 786 The Hon. Mr. Mason (Minister of Native Affairs) replied. **1947** see quots. *Native Minister* below. **1966** *Encycl. NZ* II. 816 As a member of Parliament he [*sc.* Pomare] used his influence to secure the setting up of two Royal Commissions on Native Affairs. **1912** *Free Lance* (Wellington) 6 Jan. 10 [Advt] Parata & Co... Land & Estate Agents, Native Interpreters, **Native Agents**, Insurance & Financial Agents. **1924** *Otago Witness* (Dunedin) 5 Feb. 1 A Native Agent..said there was a song composed by the defeated foe for ownership which told what they would do if opportunity arose. **1940** COWAN *Sir Donald Maclean* 91 Maclean's position as Native Agent on the East Coast was one peculiar responsibility in that era of turmoil in the Maori world. **1984** BOYD *City of the Plains* 162 The Liberal candidate in 1896 was A.L.D. Fraser, a Hastings land and native agent. **1860** MARJOURAM *Diary* 3 Feb. in *Sergeant, Sinner* (1990) 35 I mounted Colonel Murray's horse, and..rode along the beach, until I overtook the **Native Commissioner**. **1869** THATCHER *Wit & Humour* 14 When our troops get a slant these same wretches to slay, A Native Commissioner steps in the way. **1879** *Auckland Weekly News* 29 Mar. 18 Mr. Williams, Native Lands Purchase Commissioner, arrived at Parihaka. **1940** COWAN *Sir Donald Maclean* 34 The next responsibility devolving on the young Native Commissioner was..settling the..dispute between *pakeha* settlers and Maori land-owners at Wanganui. **1858** *NZPD* (1856–58) 5 July 581 Hence the need of a permanent Native Department, with the Governor at its head, not responsible to the Assembly, but bound to supply it with every information sought for. **1860** *NZPD* (1858–60) 3 Aug. 190 [The Governor] has no knowledge of their language, and hence is entirely in the hands of the officials of the Native Department. **1912** RUTHERFORD *Impressions NZ Pastoralist on Tour* 162 We talk of 'taihoa' in connection with our Native Department. The real home of unadulterated 'taihoa' is Italy. **1932** *Na To Hoa Aroha* (1988) 17 Sept. III. 20 The activities of the Native Department have reached the stage when the pakeha, who had been strenuous in his advocacy of the proper utilisation of native lands, was due to look for weaknesses. **1948** LIPSON *Politics of Equality* 411 In general, the Maoris have viewed the Native Department with some suspicion and reserve... Sensitive to the superiority of Europeans in matters of material technique, they are irritated by such a *faux pas* as the very title 'Native Department', implying, in the English language, that the Maoris are a 'native', and hence an inferior, race. **1863** MANING *Old NZ* xiv 211 Talk to me of the '**native difficulty**'—pooh! I think it was in 1822 that an old friend of mine bought, at Kawhia, a woman who was just going to be baked. **1863** MORGAN *Journal* 27 May (1963) 41 Were this native difficulty settled, the country would go ahead with amazing stride. **1881** *NZPD* XXXIX. 550 My own impression with regard to the Native difficulties in the past is that there has scarcely been a difficulty—there has scarcely been a single war in this colony—in which the Europeans have not been more to blame than the Natives. **1936** LAMBERT *Pioneering Reminisc. Old Wairoa* 20 When Dr. F.F. Ormond purchased the Orangitirohia block..not all the Natives had been satisfactorily dealt with, and a 'Native difficulty' of the first grade soon arose. **1892** PYKE *Gold-Miners' Guide* 4 *Miners' rights* are issued..for mining on **Native lands** *twenty shillings* each, or such other sum as the Governor may have agreed to pay to the owners of Native lands. **1902** *Settler's Handbook NZ* (Lands Department) 11 Of the Native lands in this district, a very considerable portion has been leased to Europeans, but there still remains in the hands of the Maoris a valuable estate. **1912** RUTHERFORD *Impressions NZ Pastoralist on Tour* 162 The manner in which he has handled the Native Land Question on behalf of the Maoris has been admirable. **1934–35** *AJHR* G-11 32 For the purpose of rendering any Native land or any land owned by Natives fit for settlement, the Native Land Settlement Board (formerly the Native Minister) may decide to apply the provisions of section 522 to that land. **1948** *Our Own Country* 49 This [Ruatoki] valley is Native land and is being farmed by the Maori owners with the assistance and supervision of the Native Department. It is only one of the many Native-land-development schemes scattered throughout New Zealand. **1887** *Auckland Weekly News* 16 Apr. 8 There was unveiled..a monument in memory of Reihana Kiriwi, who was for many years **native magistrate** in this district. **1858** *NZPD* (1856–58) 5 July 581 Why should there not be a permanent **Native Minister** as His Excellency's Adviser on Native Affairs? **1860** *NZPD* (1858–60) 3 Aug. 187 He had listened attentively to the statement of the Native Minister; it opened no new ground. **1879** *Auckland Weekly News* 15 Mar. 8 The police will not serve it [*sc.* an information] till they receive direct instructions from the Native Minister. **1892** *NZ Official Handbook* 275 [Tawhiao, the Maori King] has..quite recently..accepted a pension from the present Native Minister. **1913** *NZ Observer* 11 Jan. 3 We cannot believe that either the Native Land Court or the Native Minister, any Native Minister, would not be particularly careful before approving an application. **1932** *Na To Hoa Aroha* (1988) 17 Sept. III. 20 The hectic career of the Native Minister should be stayed. **1947** *NZPD* CCXVI. 269 When I first entered this House I said that the word 'Native' should be abolished and the word 'Maori' be used instead whenever it applied to Maori people. Since then the fruits are beginning to be seen because there used to be a..Native Affairs Committee..which is now called the Maori Affairs Committee and I understand that the Prime Minister..is our Native Minister... Why not Maori Minister?.. I think he will eventually be called the Minister in charge of Maori Affairs. **1947** *NZ Statutes* No.56 653 [Maori Purposes Act, 1947] All references to the Native Minister in any Act, regulation..shall be hereafter read as references to the Minister of Maori Affairs. **1953** p. c. R. Mason *fide* her father the Hon. H.G.R. Mason, a Cabinet minister at the time. The term 'Native' in 'Native Minister', 'Native Department' etc. was dropped during the war in favour of 'Maori', in deference, I understand, to the opinion of B.B.C. who found *native* a term much disliked in India, etc., and wished to avoid it in broadcasts. **1858** *NZPD* (1856–58) 18 May 448 I might go on multiplying proofs from the extraordinary correspondence the **Native Office** carries on with the aborigines. **1860** *Richmond-Atkinson Papers* (1960) I. 563 This letter..I had intended to send in to the Native Office in order that it might be..published. **1879** *Auckland Weekly News* 5 July 12 It had been one of the traditions of the Native Office since its institution, that no European, out of its pale, should ever say anything to a native, and that all who did so were enemies of the Government and of their own race. **1937** *Tomorrow* 3 Mar. 275 As lately as January 14th, a Christchurch paper printed a leader congratulating you and me once more on there being no **native problem** in New Zealand. **1846** *Wakefield to Gladstone* 20 Jan. in Rutherford *Sel. Documents* (1949) 15(A) There should be no exceptional law for natives within the municipalities, **Native Protectors**, for example, are an exceptional class of officers, whose very appointment suggests the idea of a natural hostility between the colonists and the Natives. **1848** WAKEFIELD *Handbook for NZ* 81 Among other useful ameliorations, [Grey] abolished the office of Native Protector. **1857** *Lyttelton Times* 4 July 5 I [Mackay, Jnr.] have been requested by several of them [*sc.* natives] to act as native protector... As the natives become more numerous on the diggings, it will be essential to appoint a person for this purpose. **1887** *Auckland Weekly News* 17 Sept. 8 After receiving a good bullying from the Native Protector..for swearing to my own goods, the native was fined double the value of the hat. **1843** WOOD *Twelve Months in Wellington* 16 The Company's agent promises roads, and the settlement of the **native question**. **1846** *Gladstone to Grey* 26 May in Rutherford *Sel. Documents* (1949) 18 What is called the Native Question, presents greater difficulties. **1858** *Memo. by Native Secretary* 13 Oct. in Rutherford *Sel. Documents* (1949) 105.1 The tenor of this [Ministers' memorandum on Native Affairs] would lead a person unacquainted with the past history and present condition of this Colony to suppose that now, for the first time, the difficulties of the native question have been properly appreciated and successfully grappled with. **1863** MORGAN *Journal* 5 July (1963) 42 The native question is still absorbing the attention of the people of this colony. **1892** *NZ Official Handbook* 275 The Native question now has lost much of the importance it once possessed. **1958** MILLER *Early Victorian NZ* 82 While the smugglers erased the customs along the coast, the native question was becoming progressively more complicated. **1970** MCNEISH *Mackenzie* 23 It's the native question, you see, and this stupid new Governor. **1848** *NZ Gov. Gazette* (Prov. New Munster) I. No.19 10 Aug. 1 For the future, the duties of the **Native Secretary** will be performed by..the Civil Secretary. **1857** *Lyttelton Times* 26 Aug. 3 Mr. MacLean (the **Native Secretary**), is reported to have arrived at Hawke's Bay. **1884** MARTIN *Our Maoris* 61 He..threw out dark hints to the Native Secretary that, if favour was shown to the prisoner, it might become unsafe for travellers to pass through his district. **1843** DIEFFENBACH

Travels in NZ I. 395 **Native wars** [Used as a page heading describing conflicts between the Rotorua tribes and esp. Ngapuhi.] **1860** BUDDLE *Maori King Movement* 6 Thus commenced the **Native War** at Taranaki, which has continued from that day [c1854] to this. **1874** KENNAWAY *Crusts* 225 Though checked somewhat by the cost of the native war..which is now happily at an end,—the Southern Island..has still..many years of prosperous days before her. **1890** *Otago Witness* (Dunedin) 6 Mar. 18 [Governor Fitzroy] brought on the first Native war with the Crown. **1913** MCNAB *Old Whaling Days* 118 The lessons which had not been learned in the 'sixties', after several Native wars had taken place. **1934** MULGAN *Spur of Morning* 239 Some of the officers, especially veterans of the native wars..are quite good.

4. Of country, in its aboriginal state, virgin.

1933 *Press* (Christchurch) (Acland Gloss.) 14 Oct. 15 On native country *f[lax]* is always a sign of good land.

5. In collocations forming adjectives in the sense of MAORI B 1 a. **native-built, native-fashion**.

1851 GRACE *Rep. Turanga Dist.* 31 Dec. in *Pioneer Missionary* (1928) 16 It is a Maori Church of comparatively small pretensions, but is, I believe, the first **Native-built** Church in this land which has a chancel. **1864** CAMPBELL *Martin Tobin* I. 102 'That's **native fashion**; the Maoris know how to live, bless 'em!' **1941** SUTHERLAND *Numismatic Hist. NZ* 37 When clad in a shoulder mat, Native fashion, or when stripped to the waist with the haft of a tomahawk in his flax-cord belt, which supported his kilt-like *piupiu*.

6. Pertaining to or characteristic of a non-Maori person born in New Zealand as distinct from a first-generation 'immigrant'. **a.** As **native**.

1986 DEVANNY *Point of Departure* 57 In one respect no distinction could be made between the migrant and the native women; all were open and discursive about the intimate details of domestic and family life.

b. As **native-born** [AND (of a non-aboriginal) 1820]. Also in early use, one of Maori or mixed race born in New Zealand (see quot. 1836).

1836 MARSHALL *Narr. Two Visits* 46 Twenty seven infants present, of whom seventeen were native born, and three of these Anglo-New Zealanders. **1890** *NZ Alpine Jrnl.* II. 157 He was..not a native born West Coaster. **1894** *TrNZI* XXVI. 621 In fact, there are many native-born New-Zealanders who could not distinguish between a rimu and a kauri. **1902** IRVINE & ALPERS *Progress of NZ* 429 The New Zealanders have so far remained more distinctly English than, perhaps, is the case in some of the larger colonies... All classes, whether immigrant or native-born, habitually speak of the United Kingdom as 'Home'. **1929** *Na To Hoa Aroha* (1986) I. 163 With that generation also had largely passed the pakeha who was wedded to the idea of England being 'Home'. The native born New Zealand pakeha is looking nearer to his native heath for objects of study, literary effort and missionary care. **1939** BEATTIE *First White Boy Born Otago* 77 The great bulk of the children came from overseas and only a few belonged to families..who had been settled in Otago for years, and hence had native-born children. **1943** MARSH *Colour Scheme* 45 They [*sc.* English-born upper-class misfits] used to be called remittance men, and in this extraordinary country received a good deal of entirely misguided sympathy from native-born fools.

naughty. [AND 1959; Ayto Simpson 'mainly Austral. and NZ'.] Often in the phr. **to have a naughty**, an act of sexual intercourse. (In borstal or prison argot often coded for tattooing, etc., as '0E' = *nought + ee*.)

1963 *Times Lit. Sup.* 12 Oct. 793 [Letter from..Auckland] Would you please whisper in the ear of the young lady who reviewed *The Stuart Case* in your issue of August 10 that 'to have naughty' is not crude Northern Territory English. It is throughout the South Seas the polite and strict analogue of 'to have sexual intercourse'. **1968** TAYLOR 'Tattooing...' in *Genetic Psychology Monographs* (1970) No.81 92. Some [borstal boys] had tattooed the code 'O410E' ('Oh for one naughty') to evoke the response 'O410E2' from girls. **1973** HILLIARD in *NZ Short Stories* (1975) 82 Dear Marcia, I got your illegle [*sic*] note and I have hid it... Henny 0410E **1977** HALL *Glide Time* 22 Hugh. That really sums up New Zealanders' attitude to sex, doesn't it..'a naughty'. Or that charming abbreviation..'a naught'. **1988** RENNIE *Super Man* 116 One of the officer cadets..wanted me to ring his sheila to say he wouldn't be home for a naughty. **1990** *Evening Post* (Wellington) 21 Nov. 20 When last seen she was being carried with a strange, far-away look in her eyes to a night of naughties with the Sultan.

Hence **naughty** *v. trans.* [AND 1977], to have sexual intercourse with (someone).

1968 SLATTER *Pagan Game* 219 And the Thomas girl says he tried to naughty her. Well it hasn't affected his play [at rugby] any. **1980** LELAND *Kiwi-Yankee Dict.* 69 *naughty*: To have carnal knowledge of a member of the opposite sex.

ne?: see EH?

neck. *Farming.*

1. *pl.* Also **neck wool**. [AND 1928.] The often matted wool shorn from a sheep's neck.

1936 BELSHAW et al. *Agric. Organiz. NZ* 710 'Necks', which are generally removed when skirting, are baled separately in the case of large clips. **1950** *NZJAg.* Oct. LXXXI. 311 Frames hinged to a wall [of a shearing-shed] can be very useful to support a wool pack for bellies, necks, etc. **1973** FERNANDEZ *Tussock Fever* 3 Erina had gathered up Mutu's last fleece and thrown it expertly on the table before the classer. A few random wrist movements removed the necks and edging pieces. **1982** *Agric. Gloss.* (MAF) 57 *Neck wool*: Matted collar of wool from around the neck of a sheep.

2. In the phr. **going up the neck**, with reference to a shearing stroke; see quot.

1989 *NZ Eng. Newsletter* III. 24 *going up the neck*: This expression refers to the blows on a sheep from the brisket towards the head. 'Opening up the neck' or 'going up the spout' mean the same thing.

necklace. In the names of plants and animals, see quots. See also NEPTUNE'S NECKLACE, *Venus' necklace* (VENUS 2).

1947 POWELL *Native Animals NZ* 27 Necklace Shell (*Tanea zelandica*). About an inch in diameter, and has a beautiful pattern of reddish-brown markings on a light brown to white polished surface. **1961** MARTIN *Flora NZ* 18 *Neptune's Necklace* or *Necklace Seaweed* (*Hormosira banksii*)... Each stem & each branch resembles a string of beads.

necko, var. NIKAU.

Ned Kelly. [f. the name of *Ned Kelly* (1857–80), the Australian bush hero shot dead in 1880.] As an emblem of the superlative, in the phr. **the cheek of Ned Kelly**, very great cheek; **(as) dead as Ned Kelly**, undeniably dead; **as game as Ned Kelly** [AND 1938], very game or courageous.

1963 HILLIARD *Piece of Land* 99 'Pretty cheeky, they are,' he told the winchman. 'Got **the cheek of Ned Kelly**, some of them.' **1960** MASTERS *Back-Country Tales* 172 'Dead! **Dead as Ned Kelly**. Just shows what the wrong kind of boose [*sic*] can do to a man.' **1955** *BJ Cameron Collection* (TS July) **game as Ned Kelly** Very courageous. **1968** SLATTER *Pagan Game* 175 Mrs Archer, game as Ned Kelly, dancing about wearing nothing but three pot lids. **1977** BRUCE *Life in Hinterland* 35 They told him the position and the danger involved but he was as game as Ned Kelly.

needlefish. *Scomberesox saurus* (fam. Scomberesocidae), a small elongate long-billed saury. See also SKIPPER.

1966 DOOGUE & MORELAND *Sea Anglers' Guide* 205 The needlefish is preyed on by many large surface fishes and to escape these it skips across the water surface... *Other names*: *Scomberesox forsteri*; saury, skipper, double beak, ocean garfish, ocean piper. **1981** WILSON *Fisherman's Bible* 169 Needlefish... The seagoing version of the common Piper, or Garfish, this fellow is a common, surface-water fish that is widespread in our territory and is often found well out to sea. **1982** AYLING *Collins Guide* (1984) 171 Saury (Needlefish) *Scomberesox saurus*... It is similar in shape to the piper but on the saury both the upper and lower jaws are projected forward to form a sharp beak.

negro: see NIGGER.

negrohead, *n.*[1] [Ellipt. for *negrohead tobacco*: see OED 2, 1839.] A strong dark plug tobacco in the form of sticks or twisted string, or a stick or twist of such tobacco, commonly smoked by early traders, settlers, etc., and often used in early colonial days in trade with the Maori. Cf. NAILROD, NIGGERHEAD *n.*[1]

1834 *NZ* (Independent) (1979) 9 Aug. 31 Tobacco is the *currency* of the Island: you could no more travel without it than in Europe with '*the ready*'; nothing however but American negro-head will pass; Brazil they [*sc.* the Maori] will scarcely accept as a gift. **1835** YATE *NZ* (1970) 127 Those [weapons] made of wood..may be purchased..sometimes for a mere trifle of a fig of negro-head tobacco. **1841** HODGSKIN *Narr. Eight Months Sojourn NZ* 38 I purchased a pig..for a few negro-heads of tobacco and two gun flints. **1848** WAKEFIELD *Handbook for NZ* 180 [Prices] tobacco, negro-head, [per] lb, 6^{1}/2d. to 10d. **1857** HURSTHOUSE *NZ* II. 568 Tobacco.—The 'Lion' brand (negrohead) is getting much liked. **1889** [see NEGROHEAD *n.*[2]]. **1903** *TrNZI* XXXV. 87 Their names for the brands of tobacco..are *purupuru*, *pongi*, and *parehe*, not to mention *nikahere* (negrohead). **1971** HALL-JONES *Mr Surveyor Thomson* 21 Foetid negrohead through a 'cutty pipe'.

negrohead, *n.*[2] [f. the appearance: prob. a 'polite' form of the more common NIGGERHEAD.] NIGGERHEAD *n.*[2]

1888 BULLER *Birds NZ* II. 255 I cast my eyes for a moment below, and there, in a 'negro-head' swamp..I witnessed a very pretty picture of wild bird life. **1889** WILLIAMS & REEVES *Colonial Couplets* 3 Only think how much more graceful all the landscape will appear... *Negro-heads* shall be re-christened. I for one will take no heed, While to me there yet remaineth Negrohead, the fragrant weed.

nei, var. (erron.) of NE?, see EH?

neinei /ˈnæinæi/. Also **nene**. [Ma. /ˈneinei/: Williams 220 *Nei* (ii)..*neinei*.. *Dracophyllum latifolium*.] Any of several small trees or shrubs of *Dracophyllum* spp. (fam. Epacridaceae), distinguished by the clusters of long tapering leaves at tips of branches, esp. *D. latifolium* (NI); *D. traversii* (also **mountain neinei**) (NI & SI);

less commonly *D. longifolium.* See also DRACOPHYLLUM, GRASS-TREE 2, HEATH, INANGA *n.*², *mountain mop* (MOUNTAIN 2), PINEAPPLE 2, *snow-tree* b (SNOW *n.*¹ 3 b), SPIDERWOOD.

1838 POLACK *NZ* II. 400 There are many other woods of much service to Europeans, differing in quality, among others: the.. *Maihoi..Néné* &c. **1858** SMITH *Notes of Journey* 8 Jan. in Taylor *Early Travellers* (1959) 355 [We found] what was to us quite a new kind of tree, called *Nei Nei*. It is something like a diminutive ti. **1867** HOOKER *Handbook* 766 Neinei..*Dracophyllum latifolium.* **1879** HAAST *Geol. Canterbury & Westland* 119 There were some very large groves of *nene* (*Dracophyllum traversii*), surrounded by a great number of good sized shrubs of *Dracophyllum latifolium.* **1882** HAY *Brighter Britain* II. 197 The Neinei (*Dracophyllum latifolium*) is but a small tree. The wood is hard, and is valued for making mallets. **1890** *PWD Catalogue Timbers* (NZ & South Seas Exhib.) 12 Neinei..Dracophyllum latifolium..Wood of a reddish brown colour, prettily figured. **1926** COWAN *Travel in NZ* II. 95 We have climbed above the pines [on the West Coast]..and up here on the mountain side..is.. the semi-tropical *neinei*, half-shrub, half-palm, and whole forests of fern trees. **1936** *Hills & Valleys* 38 The Mountain Neinei (D. Traversii) bears aloft its tufts of long, wide, grass like leaves. **1937** BUICK *Moa-Hunters NZ* 85 Portions of spear, made of nene (*Dracophyllum* sp.). **1961** MARTIN *Flora NZ* 192 Reference has ever been made to the Pine-apple Tree of the western uplands of Nelson and Westland, otherwise known as the Nei-nei or less commonly as the Spider-wood. **1978** MOORE & IRWIN *Oxford Book NZ Plants* 114 *Dracophyllum traversii*. Mountain neinei is an example of the larger mop-headed species. **1981** DENNIS *Paparoas Guide* 163 The..New Zealand cedar..stands over a skeletal mountain neinei..near the bushline in Heniker Creek.

nekau, neko, varr. NIKAU.

nelly. [Spec. use of northern hemisphere *nelly* (of uncertain orig.) a large petrel.]

1. Either of the southern giant petrel *Macronectes giganteus* or northern giant petrel *Macronectes halli* (fam. Procellariidae); PETREL 2 (10). See also *black molly* (BLACK *a.*² B 2), STINKPOT 1.

1871 HUTTON *Catalogue Birds* 44 *Ossifraga gigantea*... Nelly. **1873** [see PETREL 2 (10)]. **1888** DOUGALL *Far South* 18 [We] had two nellies on board, which are reckoned valuable birds. **1904** HUTTON & DRUMMOND *Animals NZ* 251 *The Nelly. Ossifraga gigantea*... The bird is very voracious, hovering over the sealers when they are engaged cutting up a seal, and devouring the carcass the moment it is left. **1925** [see PETREL 2 (10)]. **1949** *NZ Bird Notes* III. 170 In the air, nellies are fine big petrels, and their gliding, purposeful flight is a pleasure to watch; but when a large number are collected and feeding on whale refuse, neither their habit nor their behaviour is calculated to arouse admiration. **1955** OLIVER *NZ Birds* 109 *Giant Petrel Macronectes giganteus* Called by sailors the Nelly or Stinkpot, the Giant Petrel has long been known to voyagers to the southern seas. **1966** [see PETREL 2 (10)]. **1982** GRADY *Perano Whalers* 114 Many giant petrels, larger scavenger birds, known [to the Cook Strait whalers] as Nellies or stinkers, were also found.

2. As **nelly-birding** *fig.* or *transf.,* a modern whalers' term for the taking (or 'scavenging') of a whale first chased by another crew.

1982 GRADY *Perano Whalers* 227 Quite often the Peranos would pursue a pair of whales. If the cow was harpooned first, the bull whale would hang around. The whalers, therefore, tried to get a bomb into a bull in a near vital spot. But sometimes the chaser got out of position, and one of the other chasers would fire their harpoon into it. This was called 'Nelly-birding'.

Nelson, *attrib.*

1. Occas. *joc.* **Nelsonic**. Of, from, or representing the provincial district (occas. the cathedral city) of Nelson. See also SLEEPY HOLLOW 1.

1859 THOMSON *Story NZ* II. 188 It is worthy of notice, that the colonists, soon after the formation of all the settlements, acquired distinguishing epithets; thus there was an Auckland cove, a Wellington swell, a Nelson snob, a Taranaki exquisite... These epithets, almost already forgotten, are too characteristic to be buried in oblivion. **1880** CRAWFORD *Recoll. of Travel* 262 There is a Nelsonic absence of wind [in Havelock]. **1961** *Merriam-Webster Third Int. Dict.* 1514 *Nelson* a. of or from the provincial district of Nelson, New Zealand; of the kind or style prevalent in the Nelson provincial district.

2. Special Comb. **Nelson boarfish**, BOARFISH; **Nelson huntaway** *mustering*, a stone rolled down to move sheep from a place dogs cannot easily reach (see also quot. 1878 and *Maori huntaway* (MAORI B 5 b)); **Nelson (school) system**, a system of religious instruction for State schools using a regular daily fifth hour of school time for its delivery without affecting the statutory four-hour-minimum laid down for secular instruction (see quot. 1986); **Nelson weather**, fine sunny weather.

[**1878** ELWELL *Boy Colonists* 169 In mustering times, Ernest used to set some of the huge boulders on the sides of [the] cliffs rolling, and they made quite a roaring noise... This noise startled the sheep..which always made upwards.] [**c1907–14**] A.G. MOWAT *Diary or Reminiscences* in McCaskill *Molesworth* (1969) 100 Danger could also be caused by a musterer rolling a large rock to frighten sheep along and save running a dog. These rocks, started on purpose, were known as '**Nelson huntaways**' because young men from that district used to come mustering with young, untrained dogs. When frustrated they would use any method to move a sheep along the beat. **1941** BAKER *NZ Slang* 59 *Nelson huntaway*, a stone rolled down a hillside to move stock below instead of sending a dog out. 'From the fact that in the early days the Nelson musterers were noted for having few and poor dogs.' **1949** NEWTON *High Country Days* 29 Brownie sent a boulder hurtling down the face—a 'nelson huntaway'. **1951** MCLEOD *NZ High Country* 42 On the hill, when sheep are sticking far below you, it's sometimes possible to roll a large rock down a steep face and scare them into movement with its crashing and bounding. This is called a 'Nelson huntaway', or just a 'Nelson'. **1968** TOMLINSON *Remembered Trails* 128 A lot of young fellows from Nelson used to start off mustering..[at Hillensden Station, Marlborough] and they became known as the Nelson College. If anyone said 'I'm going back to the college,' you knew where he was going... Stones being rolled down steep faces to frighten sheep were called Nelson Huntaways. **1911** *Maoriland Worker* 4 Aug. 3 It is the introduction of what is called the **Nelson school system**, having been originated by a Presbyterian minister settled in Nelson. **1930** *AJHR I-8A* 133 The facilities offered for religious instruction under the Nelson system are taken advantage of..in approximately only 10 per cent of the schools. **1930** PINFOLD *Fifty Yrs. Maoriland* 133 I used to attend, week by week, the State school of the town in which I lived, and gave Bible lessons to the children whose parents indicated their desire for them to remain. This is called the 'Nelson System' because it was started in that city. **1974** MCLAREN *Education in Small Democracy* 52 By 1960 it claimed that the Nelson system was in use in 80 per cent of the country's primary schools. [**1986** TAYLOR *NZ People at War* I. 129 Since schools taught for more than the four hours daily required by law, it had become usual, and was legal under the system started in Nelson, for ministers of religion with the approval of headmasters and school committees to take classes for half-an-hour weekly, though the children did not have to attend.] **1853** EARP *NZ* 143 In other settlements of New Zealand, it is not unusual, in extraordinarily fine weather, to hear the observation—'This is **Nelson weather**.'

Nelsonian. [f. NELSON + *-ian.*] Also **Nelsonite**. One born or resident in the city or (less frequently) the provincial district of Nelson.

1851 WAKEFIELD *Let. to Sir George Grey* 13 The Transalpine Nelsonian. **1916** *Chron. NZEF* 15 Nov. 134 Oh, you're from Sleepy Hollow... Nelsonites rise to the bait. **1934** MARKS *Memories* 35 The Nelsonians gave us all the encouragement and cheer they could. **1951** CRESSWELL *Canterbury Tales* 95 Everyone knows he was a Nelsonian and took his title from that town. **1960** MUIR *Word for Word* 114 Good old Nelsonians. Can't miss a chance to plug the sunshine, can you? **1980** MANTELL *Murder & Chips* 5 Behind him, Steven could hear subdued whisperings from a surprising number of curious Nelsonians. **1991** *Evening Post* (Wellington) 19 Nov. 6 If I were a Nelsonian I'd not give him my vote again.

nene, var. NEINEI.

nephrite. [A spec. use of *nephrite* a form of jade (OED 1794).] GREENSTONE 1.

1851 SHORTLAND *S. Dist. NZ* 38 In *Phillip's Mineralogy* this stone [*sc.* pounamu] is described under the name of Nephrite. **1867** HOCHSTETTER *NZ* 202 It owes this name to a mineral found there, to the Nephrite, or Jade of the mineralogists; by the colonists called 'greenstone', by the natives 'punamu'. **1892**, **1929** [see POUNAMU 1]. **1946** [see JADE]. **1982** in Forster *Resolution Journal* 17 Aug. 1774 (1982) IV. 608 The Natives are very fond of New-Zeeland green stones. [**1982** *Note*] nephrite.

Neptune's necklace. *Hormosira banksii* (fam. Hormosiraceae), an intertidal alga resembling a necklace from its strings of small swollen bladders. See also NECKLACE, *Venus' necklace* (VENUS 2).

1948 MARTIN *NZ Nature Study* 136 [Caption] Neptune's Necklace (*Hormosira*). **1966** *Encycl. NZ* III. 479 [Caption] *Neptune's necklace*, Hormosira banksii, *one of the common brown seaweeds.* **1978** NATUSCH *Acheron* 109 Hansard..could see [in Otago Harbour] large chitons and delicate seaweed overhung with beads of a coral-like growth—perhaps the seaweed that children call 'Neptune's necklace'. **1989** HULME & MORRISON *Homeplaces* 61 Neptune's necklace (again, just 'rimu') is tangy when you nibble it, and so are the young tips of rimuroa (bladderweed).

nest.

1. In the phr. **nest of gold**, see quot.

1890 *TrNZI* XXII. 401 It is very common in quartz-specimens to get what is called a nest of gold, which generally consists of one large speck surrounded by a number of smaller ones at various distances from it.

2. See LANGUAGE NEST.

nester.

1. A dog trained to find rabbits' nests.

1933 *Press* (Christchurch) (Acland Gloss.) 11 Nov. 15 *Nester.*—Dog for finding rabbits' breeding nests. Most rabbiters have one in their pack. **1980** Goldie

Brown collection nester: (?obs) a dog for finding rabbits' nests or breeding places.

2. A baby rabbit, still in the breeding nest.

1969 McCaskill *Molesworth* 160 Rabbiters..would receive a bonus for 1s. on each large skin and 4d. on each nester.

net fungus: see FUNGUS 2 (7).

nettle.

1. Any of various native species of *Urtica* (fam. Urticaceae) esp. *Urtica ferox*. See also ONGAONGA.

1777 Anderson *Journal* Feb. in Cook *Journals* (1967) III. 805 Amongst the known kinds of plants are common and rough Bindweed, and Nettles, which grow to the size of small trees. **c1835** Boultbee *Journal* (1986) 62 Nettles grow in abundance, and it is said that this alone is a proof of the goodness of the land. **1842** [see ONGAONGA]. **1853** Hooker *II Flora Novae-Zelandiae I Flowering Plants* 224 The New Zealand Nettles are similar in general appearance to the English, but quite different specifically. **1903** nettle shrub [see ONGAONGA]. **1924** native nettle [see RED ADMIRAL]. **1982** Sansom *In Grip of Island* 69 I know..that the fierce nettle also grows on Herekopare.

2. As **nettle-tree** [AND 1827], **tree-nettle** (occas. **bush-nettle**), a tall form of *Urtica ferox*.

1846 Taylor *Journal* (ATLMS) IV. 117 The **nettle-tree**, a singular but disagreeable shrub attains a height of about twelve feet, its long, narrow leaf is covered with large white spines very sharp and painful if touched. **1849** *Ibid.* 25 May VI. 99 We passed by a nettle tree which the old chief immediately cut down as being a very disagreeable thing for naked feet to come near. **1869** *TrNZI* I. (rev. edn.) 208 Nettle tree. *Urtica ferox*, Forst. **1900** *Canterbury Old & New* 184 The native fuchsia—an exile from South America—and the fierce bush-nettle are conspicuous amongst the undergrowth. **1903** *TrNZI* XXXV. 60 *Ongaonga*: The **tree-neetle** (*Urtica ferox*). The name *purihi* is also applied to it, and sometimes it is called *houhi*. It is the inner bark which is eaten, a thin film resembling the inner layers under the bark of the *houhi* (*Houheria populnea*). **1909** *AJHR* C-11 10 Ongaonga. Tree-nettle. End[emic] Near Ohakune. **1915** *AJHR* C-6 12 *Urtica ferox*. Ongaonga. Tree-nettle. Forest, or forming thickets. **1922** *NZJST* IV. 281 One plant of which the extinction would not be a matter for regret is the tree-nettle. **1978** [see ONGAONGA]. **1989** *NZ Gardener* June 11 Nettles are well known for this [*sc.* stinging] and the most dangerous is the native tree nettle or ongaonga.

never-never. Also occas. **never-nevers** (*pl.* perhaps on analogy of BACKBLOCKS); occas. init. cap. [AND far interior of Australia, 1833.] BACKBLOCK A 2, the 'back of beyond'.

1908 *Truth* 3 Oct. 4 A shearer comes along with a cheque for £80 or £100, gives it to the publican, gets rapidly drunk, and then drunker, and then D.T.'s and then wakes up and goes back into the never-never to rake up another cheque. **1916** Anzac *On the Anzac Trail* 41 You don't run across illiterates in the colonies —even way back in the Never Never. **1952** Thomson *Deer Hunter* 32 The other four shooters were out on the job for a few more days fly-camping, so the two of us had the first night in the never-nevers to ourselves. *Ibid.* 108 To have lived such an open life and then to be suddenly caged up in an enclosure such as this Army camp often tempted me to make a break for the never-never.

new, *a.* In special collocations.

1. Denoting the recently arrived usu. (from Britain, etc.): **New Enzedder** [formed on *New Australian*: AND 1905], a recently arrived, often non-British, immigrant; **new settler**, a recently arrived immigrant; also a farmer newly-arrived in a district.

1950 *Truth* 2 Jan. 6 [Heading] Truculent '**New Enzedders**'. **1952** *Evening Post* (Wellington) 18 June The [Prime Minister's] visit [to a Danish immigrant girl in Adelaide] originated a new phrase, 'New Enzedder,' which Mr Holland said would become the equivalent of 'New Australian'. The girl said to Mr Holland: 'You can't call us new New Zealanders; it's too clumsy. Why not New Enzedders?' 'That is excellent.' said Mr Holland. 'We will use it'. **1909** Barry *In Lee of Hokonuis* (1966) 161 In a comparatively short time the whole of the area was sold to the '**new settlers**' as they were called by those already farming north of the Mataura–Glendhu road. **1927** *Otago Daily Times* (Dunedin) 11 Jan. 8 A large contingent of new settlers reached Wellington on Sunday evening by the steamer Corinthic from England. **1948** *Southern Cross* (Wellington) 23 July 1 A further 327 new settlers, due here in the Rangitata.., include 237 men and women who have been granted either free or assisted passages. **1955** *BJ Cameron Collection* (TS July) new settler (n) A post-1945 immigrant from Britain or Europe.

2. Denoting one new to a job or situation: **new hand**, NEW CHUM A 2.

1845 Wakefield *Adventure NZ* I. 327 A new hand, pulling one of the oars, begins to look frightened..a volley of oaths from the headsman accompanies a threat to 'break every bone in his skin if he *funks* now'. **1871** *McLean Papers* (ATLTS) XXXVII. 161 Of course, Mr. T. is a new hand here and knows nothing of the particular case. I am sure no old hand could have so written.

new chum, *n.* and *attrib.* Also occas. with init. caps.

A. *n.*

1. [AND orig. (1812) a newly-arrived convict, thence an immigrant, 1828.] A newly-arrived immigrant; occas. a new arrival in a district, town, etc.

1853 Adams *Canterbury Settlement* (Griffiths Collect.) 18 [New arrivals] were..encountered by some..who take delight in..frightening 'new chums', as they term them, with all kinds of disheartening accounts of the colony. **1862** Chudleigh *Diary* 14 June (1950) 43 There are lots of new chums at the Tamorna House where we are staying. They came out in the Black Swan. *Ibid.* 114 He is a new chum only landed that day. **1873** Tinne *Wonderland of Antipodes* 7 A 'new chum', or novice in colonial life, was consulting my friend as to what amount of luggage he would advise for bush travel. **1882** Hay *Brighter Britain* I. 21 There's an Auckland proverb, that a new-chum never does any good until his nose has grown. **1907** *Truth* 13 July 3 You seem to be one of those new chums who think it clever to sneer at everything colonial, and delight in making comparisons between our town and your big English cities. **1913** Carr *Country Work* 5 The sooner a 'New Chum' loses his identity as such, the better for himself. **1938** Hyde *Nor Yrs. Condemn* 155 We don't call them green-horns out here. We call them new chums, or else Homies. **1947** Kenway *Quondam Quaker* 73 A 'new chum' [pronounced 'new ch'm'] in New Zealand is usually regarded [c.1880s] by the old hands with an amused and kindly contempt... This attitude of mind may, I think, be illustrated by a sentence from a letter I once saw, written by a native-born on his first visit to England: 'It's most extraordinary, the whole bally shop seems chock-a-block with new chums.' **1960** Masters *Back-Country Tales* 85 I smiled, but of course Jim, being a new chum, didn't realise wekas were flightless. **1982** Lynn *Lynnwood Tree* 125 The boss usually kept one up his sleeve to try out a new chum.

2. A novice; a person inexperienced at a job.

1870 *TrNZI* II. 43 The reckless gunner.., the self-complacent 'new chum', with the inevitable fire-arms..will sometimes destroy..both old and young [birds]. **1906** Alexander & Currie *NZ Verse* xvii He was a rotten new chum of a musterer. **1912** Booth *Five Years NZ* 15 According to bush custom it was usual to dub all fresh arrivals 'new chums' until they had satisfactorily passed certain ordeals in bush life. **c1924** Anthony *Me & Gus* (1977 Gus Tomlins) 3 I will admit that when I bought this place I was a new chum. **1930** Dobson *Reminiscences* 101 With capable men, the Buller was a fine river to work canoes on, but not for new chums. **1967** May *West Coast Gold Rushes* 527 New-chum: not a new-arrival on the diggings, but a fellow new to gold-digging. **1977** Fisher *Angels Wear Black* 38 They..[*sc.* kelpfish] have been known to be mistaken by new chums for the Spotted Black Groper.

3. In special collocations: **new chum (chums') gold** [AND 1873], fool's gold, esp. pyrites; **new chum's pigeon**, see quot.

1867 Cooper *Digger's Diary* 12 Nov. (1978) 12 Many new comers are misled by the abundance of mica and mundic, which is consequently called '**new chums' gold**', and it is difficult to convince them that they have not got the precious metal. **1889** Paulin *Wild West Coast* 14 The sand [in Dusky Sound]..glittered with scales of yellow mica. It is sometimes called New Chum Gold, as, seeing it for the first time, one can hardly believe it is not the precious metal itself. **c1890–1900** Edwards in *Penguin Book NZ Verse* (1985) 93 When the battered dish flowed empty, bar a tail of new-chum gold, Or it gave a ring of 'colour' that betokened wealth untold. **1952** Thomson *Deer Hunter* 73 We found traces of gold at different places, golden mica, known as new chum gold, and two types of pyrites. **1920** *Quick March* 10 May 39 The long grey moss which hangs in festoons and beards from some of the trees in the heavy bush [especially in mountain country in the North Island]. One kind of the moss..is almost white and very conspicuous in the gloom of the bush. The settlers' name for it in my part of the country is '**new-chum's pigeon**'. It is so called because of the imagined resemblance of the mossy bunches to the white breast of the wild pigeon;.. I'm hanged if it would deceive any New Zealander country-born or bush-bred.

B. *attrib.* [AND B, 1903.]

1. Newly-arrived in New Zealand; non-colonial-born.

1865 Chudleigh *Diary* 2 Feb. (1950) 165 Turned a swell [whip] handle for Dr Wareing a new chum doctor. He does not look as if he could use a whip. **1874** Kennaway *Crusts* 78 The captain [was] elated, and the new-chum passengers just as jolly as if they were already safe ashore. **1904** *NZ Illustr. Mag.* Dec. 177 We were all bursting with new-chum energy as we took our first steps in colonial life. **1960** Masters *Back-Country Tales* 85 On one of my hunting trips I took a gentlemanly sort of new chum Englishman named Jim along.

2. Inexperienced; inexpert.

1906 *Truth* 24 Mar. 3 The new-chum domestics. **1946** Miller *There Was Gold* 24 Without his aid I might have blundered along until I broke my new chum heart. **1953** Stronach *Musterer on Molesworth* 45 The most trying ordeal for a new-chum musterer is getting in the killing sheep. **1960** Masters *Back-Country Tales* 45 One yarn I heard tell of Alex, concerned a new chum packman. **1973** Fernandez *Tussock Fever* 1 He had not much patience with these new-chum shepherds.

3. In composition: **new chummy**, characteristic of a new chum; **new-chum-hood, new chumship**

NEW EDINBURGH

[AND 1843], the condition or phase of being a new chum or colonial apprentice.

1871 CLARKE in Money *Knocking About NZ* vii Another of the illusions of our trusting **new-chumhood** vanishes for ever. **1860** *Lyttelton Times* 16 Dec. in *Otago Witness* (Dunedin) (1862) 18 Jan. (Griffiths Collect.) I think the price asked depends in a great measure upon the appearance of the purchaser—those with a '**new chummy**' look paying through the nose. **1885** W.J. Swainson letter in *William Swainson* (1992) 107 The older the [cabbage tree] hat the more it was valued. Indeed I have known a new one willingly exchanged for a much older article—perhaps because it did not look so 'new chummy'. **1863** BUTLER *First Year* iv 55 I was anxious to become an old chum, as colonial dialect calls a settler—thereby proving my **new chumship** most satisfactorily.

New Edinburgh: see EDINBURGH OF THE SOUTH.

new iniquity. *Otago. Hist.* [A reverse play on OLD IDENTITY, with a suggestion of *Old Iniquity* the Devil: cf. OED *iniquity* 4 b.] **a.** Newcomers (esp. Australian miners) to Dunedin in the 1860s. See quot. 1874. Also with jocular variation **young iniquities** (see quot. 1903).

1874 BATHGATE *Col. Experiences* 25 [Old Identity] was the name applied by the people of Victoria, who flocked hither in thousands on the discovery of gold [in 1862], to those who had been in the province before that time. Those honest folks..were greatly startled by this immense and sudden influx of population. 16,000 persons landed in three months... It is alleged that one minister actually prayed that the stream of rogues and vagabonds which was flowing into the country might be stayed, but this I believe to have been a base invention of the 'new iniquity', as the new-comers were nicknamed. **1892** REEVES *Homeward Bound* 3 The canny Scotch 'old identity' was swallowed up in the 'new iniquity', as they mutually styled each other. **1903** *Otago Witness* (Dunedin) 25 Feb. 68 I was at the Old Identities' picnic yesterday and spent a fair time among the 'young iniquities' and 'old immensities' as Texas Jack's irresponsible brother calls the Old Identities. **1937** AYSON *Thomas* 33 Thomas had had a taste of 'the new iniquity' before leaving for the goldfields. **1938** *Press* (Christchurch) (McNab Slang) 2 Apr. 18 'The new iniquity' was the Otago settlers' name for the unwelcome Australian immigrants who arrived in the 60's. **1959** SINCLAIR *History NZ* 104 Dunedin became the largest town in the country, while, to the horror of the 'Old Identity', saloons, billiard rooms, gambling dens and dance halls sprang up to attract the gold of the 'New Iniquity'.

b. *transf.* A newcomer to any neighbourhood (as part of an unwanted influx).

1871 *Evening Post* (Wellington) 3 July 2 We got new doctors..lawyers..Jew pedlars..et hoc genus omne [in Wanganui], and this infusion of 'new iniquities' [to Wanganui] has fairly bedeviled the place.

New Leinster, Munster, Ulster: see entry for PROVINCE 1.

New Zealand, *n.*, *a.*, and *abbrev.* Also early **New-Zealand, Newzealand, New Zeeland, New Zeland**; with joc. pronunciation forms **New Zillun(d), Noo Zilland, NyaZilnd** (approaching /ˌnuˈzɪlən(d)/), etc., often so heard and written.

A. *n.*

1. [f. a transl. of Dutch *Nieuw Zeeland*, or of mod. Lat. *Zelandia Nova* which latter name appears on Frederick de Wit's world map of 1660 first printed in Hendrick Donker's atlas, and later in de Wit's atlas of 1671, for those parts mapped by Tasman. The originator, possibly a Dutch cartographer or an official, probably thought it a suitable congener of *New Holland,* the name given then to Australia, as *Zeeland* and *Holland* were neighbouring Dutch maritime provinces.] [Note] Tasman's general name for his rediscovery was *Staten Landt,* considering it to be part of a southern continent and therefore connected with the *Staten Landt* previously discovered to the south of Cape Horn.

The name of a country and a biogeographic region (see quot. 1962 below). See also AOTEAROA 2 a, *Aoteroa-New Zealand* (AOTEAROA 2 b), ENZED (see also C below), MAORILAND 2, NIU TIRANI (NIU TIRENI).

1768 COOK *Journals* 30 July (1955) I. cclxxxii [Secret Instructions from the Admiralty] Or fall in with the Eastern side of the Land discover'd by Tasman and now called New Zealand. **1769** MONKHOUSE 8 Oct. in Cook *Journals* (1955) I. 564 On the sixth of october [*sic*] 1769 the Endeavour Bark first made the land of New Zeeland. **1773** COOK *Journals* 26 Mar. (1961) II. 109 Intending to put into *Dusky Bay* or any other Port I could find on the Southern part of *Newzealand*. *Ibid.* 11 May II. 131 There is no Port in New Zealand I have been in. **1821** [see ZEALANDER]. **1840** *Letters Patent* issued 16 Nov. quoted from *The Ordinance of New Zealand* in Domett (1850) 4-8 in *Speeches and Documents* (1971) 54 And we do hereby declare, that from henceforth the said Islands shall be known and designated as the Colony of New Zealand. **1847** ANGAS *Savage Life* I. 293 She is left with several..children, who are dressed in the Maori costume, and know no language but that of New Zealand. **1855** [see AOTEAROA 1]. **1867** HOCHSTETTER *NZ* 33 The Dutch named it *New Zealand.* [1867 *Note*] English writers..protest strongly against this name... *Taylor* says..New Zealand ought to be re-christened. To this end he proposes names such as '*Austral Britain*', or '*Austral Albion*'. *Zealandia* was likewise proposed. **1872, 1898** [see AOTEAROA 1]. **1946** *JPS* LV. 141 Words that appeared to me to have become current in English, at any rate as written and spoken in Newzealand. **1961** BEAGLEHOLE in Cook *Journals* (1962) II. 1 Tasman did not call the country New Zealand but Staten Land, on the supposition that it was part of the coast of the southern continent and a westward extension of the Staten Land off Tierra del Fuego discovered by Schouten and le Maire in 1616. When this was proved to be an island by Brouwer in 1643 the second part of the supposition fell down; but who it was conferred the name New Zealand, within the next few years, we do not know. The reason for it may have been analogy with New Holland. **1980** MARSH *Photo-Finish* 31 That's what they reckon. Nothing like it anywhere else in N'yerzillun. **1987** *Dominion* (Wellington) 26 Sept. 8 Sir,—Thank you to R Herd for directing me as to where Noo Zilland is—couldn't hulp larfin. **1988** *Dominion* (Wellington) 1 July 10 It is no surprise that a conservative organisation such as the RSA has taken exception to the use of the phonetically pleasant 'Aotearoa' instead of the clumsy 'New Zealand' or colloquial 'Newzyullind'. **1989** *Listener* 15 July 11 The idea is to create an original, irreverent, NyaZilnd-flavoured teevee tonic.

2. Young New Zealand a. Young Maori, or Maori after the arrival of the Pakeha, as a group or class.

[*Note*] Maning is making a pun on 'Old New Zealand' the title of his book about Maori before the arrival of the main body of Pakehas.

1858 ASHWELL *Lett. & Jrnls.* (ATLTS) III. 332 Young N.Z, if I may use the term. **1863** MANING *Old NZ* vii 104 A few years ago the madness [for acquiring pakeha goods] ran upon horses and cattle; and now young New Zealand believes in nothing but money. *Ibid.* 105 Here I am, I find, again before my story. Right down to the present time talking of 'Young New Zealand', and within a hairbreadth of settling 'the Maori difficulty' without have been paid for it.

b. Young New Zealanders (non-Maori and Maori) collectively.

1877 *TrNZI* IX. 41 It seems pretty certain that drunkenness will not be so prevalent in young New Zealand as among the parent stock.

3. a. The Maori language. MAORI A 3.

1823 BUTLER *Jrnls. & Corr.* 252 We had prayers both in New Zealand and English. The Natives were very attentive and repeated the sentences in New Zealand correctly. **1843** *Letter* 1 Sept. in Macmorran *Octavius Hadfield* (1969) 181 Since I left England I have only studied New Zealand and Hebrew, and have found no kind of difficulty with these.

b. New Zealand English.

1993 *Sunday Times* (Wellington) 23 May 2 Fifth generation, they speak New Zealand with a Northumbrian accent. That's the kind of isolated lives they've led.

B. *attrib.* or *adj.* and *adv.*

[*Note*] Early use to c1850 includes various senses of MAORI B and NATIVE B (esp. 1 a), as well as that of *New Zealand* A 1 above (e.g. *New Zealand Company*); after the arrival of the main body of European settlers c1840–50, predominant use progressively includes reference to non-Maori society and culture.

1. a. *Obs.* MAORI B 1 a. See also NATIVE B 1 a.

1769 MONKHOUSE 10 Oct. in Cook *Journals* (1955) I. 570 We had not yet sufficient experience of New Zealand troops to trust them too far. **1778** FORSTER *Observations* 591 The New-Zeeland ladies never failed to put on the same kind of *rouge* mixed with grease, before they come on board to offer their uncouth favours to our sailors. **1815** KING 11 Aug. in Elder *Marsden's Lieutenants* (1934) 107 In the evening Terra told us that he made a fire to cook potatoes and to eat a New Zealand man. **1827** WILLIAMS *Early Jrnls.* 9 Apr. (1961) 51 Mr. Marsden entered with much apparent interest, upon the idea of a New Zealand settlement in Port Jackson. **1834** MARKHAM *NZ* (1963) 40 I was certainly ashamed that Europeans could degrade themselves so before their New Zealand Boys, but so they did. **1847** TAYLOR *Journal* 19 Mar. (ATLTS) V. 5 Thus whilst Xt. is the strength and support of the learned and enlightened believer of England he does not disdain the heart of a poor New Zealand child. **1853** EARP *NZ* 50 According to New Zealand notions of rank he [is] the highest in the scale. **1869** *TrNZI* I. (rev. edn.) 390 From a close examination..of their poetry, it is apparent, that the New Zealand poet had taken some pains towards rhythm. **1878** BULLER *Forty Yrs. NZ* 174 It is easy to make a serious mistake in the New Zealand tongue, or *reo maori*. **1884** MARTIN *Our Maoris* 134 Nor was he like some New Zealand and English boys, smart without being clean. His shirt and boots were spotless.

b. Pertaining to, or written or spoken in, the Maori language.

1770 COOK *Journals* 31 Mar. (1955) I. 286 *English* A Chief *New Zeland* Eareete *South-sea Islands* Earee **1817** NICHOLAS *NZ* II. 327 A vocabulary of English and New Zealand words. **1823** MARSDEN *Lett. & Jrnls.* (1932) Sept. 373 I remained in the house nearly all the day examining the New Zealand Grammar, which appears to be very imperfect. **1840** BUNBURY *Report* 28 June in *GBPP House of Commons 1841 (No.311)* 108 I..had on my table a New Zealand Testament which Bishop Broughton had been kind enough to lend me. **1853** HOOKER *II Flora Novae-Zelandiae I Flowering Plants* 257 The celebrated Ti of the South Sea Islands (whence the New Zealand name 'Ti' for *C. australis*) belongs to this genus.

2. Of or pertaining to New Zealand as a biogeographical entity, a place of human habitation for Maori and non-Maori people. Cf. MAORILAND 3 b, NATIONAL A 1 B.

1774 FORSTER *Resolution Jrnl.* 17 Aug. (1982) IV. 608 The Natives are very fond of New-Zeeland green stones. **1833** WILLIAMS *Early Jrnls.* 14 Nov. (1961) 347 The natives had prayers this evening by themselves, and while singing the hymn, the Europeans..who rank amongst the New Zealand merchants, struck up their vocal powers, and gave us the well known ballad, Old King Cole. **1848** *Governor Grey to Earl Grey* 29 Nov. in Rutherford *Sel. Documents* (1949) 33 The efficacy of the various general laws..for the whole of the New Zealand Islands will be tested by some years actual practice. **1853** EARP *NZ* 106 Swamps are disagreeable things..; but they are no impediment to the New Zealand traveller. **1860** BUTLER *Forest Creek MS* (1960) 48 We kept one [horse] on the tether—tethered to a tussock of grass by a peculiar kind of New Zealand knot. **1863** MOSER *Mahoe Leaves* 4 It is a picturesque spot..flanked by a noble pine bush, the most noble of all the New Zealand forests. **1874** *Letter* May in Kennaway *Crusts* 182 Last month C., B., and self started from a rough hut or den in the drear regions of this New Zealand Interior. **1945** *JPS* LIV. 225 The pig was introduced by Captain Cook... [1945 *Note*] Hence modern Newzealand slang a *Captain Cook* or *Captain Cooker*, for a wild pig. **1960** KEINZLY *Tangahano* 90 And there was the New Zealand woman, a trained nurse who stood at the ready for those who had need of her. **1976** WILSON *Pacific Star* 19 The energising force in New Zealand life up to now has been this myth of the pioneer, the frontier. **1992** *North & South* (Auckland) Jan. 83 Something which makes me feel very New Zealand is when I'm overseas and there's a Maori concert party performing songs about the arrival in the land of the long white cloud.

3. Mainly *Obs.* In the sense 'indigenous', and often interchangeable with MAORI B 4 or NATIVE B 2, in the names of plants and animals. The list below gives only main or frequent examples of this use: the earliest record is that of Yate in 1835 (*NZ* (1970) 44): Puriri (*Vitex littoralis*)—This tree, from its hardness and durability, has been denominated the New-Zealand Oak. **a.** In the names of plants, see: ACACIA, ARBOR VITAE, ASH, BEECH 1, BIRCH 1, BLUEBELL, BOX *n.*³, BRAMBLE, BROOM 1, CARROT 1 b, CEDAR 2 (2), CLEMATIS a, COFFEE, CONVOLVULUS, COTTONWOOD 2, CURRANT, DAISY 2 (8), DAPHNE, DOCK 1, EDELWEISS, EYEBRIGHT, FIG *n.*², FLAX 2 (3), GRAPEFRUIT, HAREBELL, HAWTHORN, HEMP, HOLLY, HONEYSUCKLE, ICE-PLANT, JASMINE, LABURNUM, LAUREL, LILAC 1, LILY 2 (11), MINT, MULBERRY 2, MUSK a, MYRTLE, OAK, OLIVE 1, ORANGE 1 b, ORCHID 4, PALM 1, PASSION-FLOWER 1, PASSIONFRUIT 1, PINCUSHION, PINE 2 (9), PINEAPPLE 1, PRIVET, SANDALWOOD 1, SCREWPINE, SPINACH, STRAWBERRY, TEAK, THORN, VIOLET, WILLOW 2, YEW. **b.** In the names of animals, see: BAT *n.*¹, *New Zealand blue* (see SOUTHERN *a.* 3), CANARY *n.*¹ 1, COD 2 (5), CROW *n.*¹ 1, DOG 1, DOTTEREL 2 (3), FALCON, FROG *n.*¹ 1, HAKE 1 b, HARRIER, MINNOW, PIPIT, RAT *n.*¹ 1, ROBIN 1, SEAL *n.*¹ 2 (1), SMELT, SOLE 2 (1), TEA 1 b, THRUSH, TURBOT, TURKEY *n.*¹ 1.

4. In special collocations: **a.** In the sense of B 1 a above. **New Zealand howl**, TANGI; **New Zealand language** *obs.*, the Maori language.

1832 WILLIAMS *Early Jrnls.* 28 Nov. (1961) 265 Having addressed himself to Tu and extolled the acts and brave deeds of these warriors, and viewed the payment (the fourteen heads of Nateawa) he expressed his approbation and turned to Titore, fell on his neck, and immediately both began a **New Zealand howl**. This lasted a few minutes. **1840** in Chambers *Samuel Ironside* (1982) 84 A little English composition, with some attention to the **New Zealand language**, employing my time. **1847** ANGAS *Savage Life* I. 306 There being more consonants used in the New Zealand language, *Hawaii* would become Hawaiki in the dialect of these latter people. **1871** WILLIAMS *Dict. NZ Lang.* (3edn.) iii A Dictionary of the New Zealand Language to which is added a selection of colloquial sentences. William Williams, D.C.L... [preface iii] The principal feature of this edition of the Maori Dictionary..is the arrangement of the words.

b. In the sense B 2 above. **New Zealand Alliance**, see ALLIANCE 1; **New Zealand Association**, see ASSOCIATION *n.*¹ a; **New Zealand bun**, see quot.; **New Zealand Company** (a) the 'First' New Zealand Company, promoted 1824 (see quots. 1936, 1966); (b) the second or Wakefieldian New Zealand (Land) Company, promoted in 1837 and constituted in 1839; **New Zealand cream**, see quot.; **New Zealand Cross**, a decoration given to local militia, Volunteers, and Armed Constabulary for meritorious acts during the New Zealand Wars (see quots. 1869, 1941); **New Zealand Day** *obs.*, February 6, the anniversary of the signing of the Treaty of Waitangi as a public holiday, now called WAITANGI DAY; **New Zealand death** (also called **national death**, see quot. 1960 below), death by drowning; **New Zealand disease**, *Kiwi disease* (KIWI 15), the national anti-nuclear stance; **New Zealand English**, (a) the variety of English written and spoken by native-born New Zealanders (and by others whose speech and idiom recognizably approaches that of the native-born) perceived as distinct in its features or usage from other varieties of English, esp. British, North American and Australian (see also KIWI 10, NEW ZEALANDISM 2, NEW ZILD A 1); (b) all those parts of the English language used or understood by New Zealanders including those shared with speakers of other forms of English; **New Zealand Expeditionary Force**, the name for the whole body of New Zealand troops sent overseas in WW1 (usu. **NZEF**); in WW2, the Second New Zealand Expeditionary Force (**2NZEF**); **New Zealand green**, New Zealand-grown marijuana, see GREEN *n.* 2; **New Zealand House** (a) (i) *hist.* the London headquarters of the New Zealand (Land) Company; (ii) the official London headquarters of the High Commissioner for New Zealand; (b) (also partly sense 1 a) a house displaying colonial or Maori architecture or design and using local materials; **New Zealand Legion** *hist.*, see quot.; **New Zealand** (occas. **Kiwi**) **mafia**, (members of) the informal network of New Zealand professional people (esp. academics and intellectuals) in London or Britain, occas. elsewhere; **New Zealand War Medal (New Zealand Medal)**, see quots. 1899, 1941 (see also *New Zealand Cross* above); **New Zealand Militia**, see quot.; **New Zealand mutton** *joc.*, pork, the common meat in pre-settlement times; **New Zealand Party**, an ephemeral right-wing political party founded in 1983 by a property dealer, (Sir) Robert Edward Jones (1939–); **New Zealand Sign (Language) (NZSL)**, the New Zealand dialect of the natural sign language of the deaf and hearing-impaired; **New Zealand tea**, see quot.

c1916 *Edmonds 'Sure to Rise' Cook. Book* (4edn.) 20 **New Zealand Buns**..flour..sugar..Edmonds' Baking Powder..1 egg..butter..make a stiff dough. Divide into buns... Bake in a quick oven. (a) **1936** BELSHAW et al. *Agric. Organiz. NZ* 3 The first organized attempt to colonize New Zealand occurred in 1826 when the first **New Zealand Company** was formed and sent an unsuccessful expedition to Hokianga. **1966** *Encycl. NZ* II. 658 It is one of the minor enigmas of New Zealand history that so little is known of the origin and plans of the first New Zealand Company... In the late thirties its land holdings at Hokianga and Kaipara were taken over by E.G. Wakefield's..New Zealand Company. **1993** EVISON *Te Wai Pounamu* 36 A British syndicate, the first 'New Zealand Company', was preparing to send settlers to New Zealand under Captain James Herd. (b) **1839** Let. in *William Swainson* 4 July (1992) 62 L/- [*sc.* pounds sterling] New Zealand Land Company's Office, 1 Adam Street, Adelphi. July 4, 1839... These are to certify that I have this day registered the Application of William Swainson Esq. for five Land Orders according to the printed Terms of Purchase... John Ward Secretary. **1840** *Somes to Russell* 22 Oct. in *GBPP House of Commons 1841 (No.311)* 22 New Zealand House, Broad-street Buildings, 22 October 1840... The gentlemen who have been associated under the name of the **New Zealand Company**, for the purpose of promoting the settlement of New Zealand. It is, therefore, with great satisfaction that the Company perceives in the recent proclamations..an opening for a satisfactory adjustment. **1842** Mary F. Swainson let. in *William Swainson* 21 Aug. (1992) 90 Each section [of 100 acres] had a town acre attached to it at the first sale the Land Company held. **1851** *Lyttelton Times* 7 June 6 Amongst the most important of the measures to be brought under your notice is that which relates to the settlement of titles to land within the territory which was formerly vested in the New Zealand Company. **1872** *The Taranaki New Zealand Company's Land Claims Act* 36 Vict. s2 Provided however that the award of such Commissioners..shall be deemed a final settlement of every claim whatever of such claimant in respect of the matters in the Preamble of this Act referred to, or in any way relating to his contract with the Plymouth Company of New Zealand or with the New Zealand Company. **1892** *NZ Official Handbook* 4 In 1838 a colonisation company, known as the New Zealand Company was formed to establish settlement on systematic principles. **1966** [see ASSOCIATION a]. **1990** *Family History at National Archives* (1991) 26 The New Zealand Land Company was formed in 1837 and the New Zealand Company was constituted in 1839. **1891** CHAMIER *Philosopher Dick* 26 There is a very good substitute for milk. If you pour a little cold water on the hot tea it has very much the same effect—takes off the sharpness..we call it '**New Zealand Cream**'. [**1869** *NZ Gazette* 127 His Excellency the Governor..doth by this present Order institute a Decorative Distinction, to be conferred on members of the Militia, Volunteers or Armed Constabulary, who may particularly distinguish themselves by their bravery in action, or devotion to their duty while on service... The decoration shall consist of a Silver Cross, with the name of the Colony and the name of the recipient engraved thereon.] **1887** *Auckland Weekly News* 28 May 22 Major Ropata..wore at his side the handsome sword presented to him by the Queen, and on his breast the **New Zealand Cross**. **1899** *NZPD* VI. 662 The Speaker announced that he had received from His Excellency the Governor a message, transmitting the New Zealand Cross of Hono[u]r Bill. **1912** *Free Lance* (Wellington) 10 Aug. 4 There were Crimean decorations there and New Zealand Crosses, as well as the more plentiful Maori War medal. **1940** COWAN *Sir Donald Maclean* 102 Mair was the only *pakeha*..in the action that won him a captaincy and the New Zealand Cross. **1941** SUTHERLAND *Numismatic Hist. NZ* 228 [Heading] New

Zealand Cross, 1869. A silver maltese cross with a six pointed star in gold upon each limb... Institution, Order of the Governor in Council, dated 10 March, 1869. *New Zealand Gazette* 1869, p. 127. *Ibid.* 229 This cross was instituted by the Colonial Government and awarded to members of the local Militia, Volunteers, and Constabulary for acts of bravery and distinction. **1984** *Dominion* (Wellington) 3 July 6 A rare New Zealand Cross, awarded for bravery during the New Zealand land wars, is the centre-piece of a major auction of coins and medals in Melbourne later this month. The cross, described as a non-military version of the Victoria Cross, is one of only 23 awarded to the militia, volunteers and armed constabulary during the wars. **1973** Hayward *Diary Kirk Years* (1981) 112 Mr K. announced at the Waitangi Day celebrations [1973] that henceforth it would be called **New Zealand Day** and become a public holiday, 'though I think that this will still often be called Waitangi Day rather than New Zealand Day.' [1981 *Note*] On 6 February 1976 the day again became officially known as Waitangi Day. **1978** Weir *NZ Ambassador's Letters from Moscow* (1988) 140 *Monday* 6 [February 1978] On New Zealand Day here, a function is customarily organised by the USSR/New Zealand Friendship Society. **1979** Belshaw *Man of Integrity* 255 On 6 February 1962, New Zealand Day, this suffering ended. **1993** *Dominion* (Wellington) 20 Jan. 2 Some Northland Maori leaders have called for Waitangi Day to be changed back to New Zealand Day, saying this would restore national pride. **1947** Beattie *Early Runholding* 24 In the early days [before bridges were built]..so many persons were drowned that drowning was often described as '**The New Zealand Death**.' **1960** *Over Whitcombe Pass* 15 For drowning was in those days [c1860s] called the 'national death', so often did glacier-fed mountain rivers claim victims. **1971** Griffiths *King Wakatip* 73 When the diggers came, the 'New Zealand death'—as drownings came to be termed—rose to epidemic proportions. **1984** Beardsley *Blackball 08* 70 Drowned in a river—the New Zealand death. **1991** *National Business Review* 27 Sept. 7 Washington's dilemma has been that on the one hand it feared rapprochement would encourage other allies to develop 'the **New Zealand disease**', and on the other that continued rebuffs will simply entrench the New Zealand position. (a) **1910** *Triad* 10 Aug. 37 **New Zealand English**. Mr. E.W. Andrews, of the Napier Boys' High School, is an admitted authority on English. His presidential address, recently delivered at the conference in Wellington of the Secondary Schools' Assistant Teachers, is..the more interesting. The subject was 'New Zealand English'. **1966** Turner *Eng. Lang. Austral. & NZ* 152 *Mullock* is less frequent and retains a specialist sense of 'rubbish from a mine'. It is not common in general New Zealand English. **1984** *Listener* 21 Jan. 30 There are entries [in *The Macquarie Dictionary*]..for *Australian English*..but none for *New Zealand English*, *New Zealandism* or *New Zild*. (b) **1979** *Heinemann NZ Dict.* [Front Cover] The first dictionary of New Zealand English and New Zealand pronunciation. **1991** *Dominion* (Wellington) 23 Aug. 1 When their projects are done, the countries will..have representative and comparable samples of written Australian and New Zealand English. **1994** *Cambridge Hist. of the Eng. Lang.* (L Bauer 'English in New Zealand') V. 401 Most of the vocabulary that is found in New Zealand English is general to all varieties of English. **1916** *Chron. NZEF* 15 Sept. 37 There are fifteen members of the **New Zealand Expeditionary Force** [as POWs] at Bilmedik. **1917** Thornton *With Anzacs in Cairo* 53 I consulted Chaplain-Major Luxford, the chief chaplain of the N.Z.E.Force. **1918** *Chron. NZEF* 10 May 153 For the benefit of troops who may be under a false impression as to the meaning of the letters 'N.Z.E.F.', commanding officers are asked to especially impress their men that it means 'New Zealand Expeditionary Force', and not 'N.Z. Employer's Federation'. **1918** Weston *Three Yrs. with New Zealanders* 11 The training at Trentham was good, where at that time all the reinforcements for all arms of the N.Z.E.F. were concentrated. **1936** Treadwell *Recolls. Amateur Soldier* 5 Had I not done so I might have started my adventure with the New Zealand Expeditionary Force as a captain. **1982** Maclean *Lifetime at School* 18 C.M. Bevan—Brown came..in 1914. He left to join the NZEF. **1992** Farrell *Skinny Louie Book* 73 On Fridays he had a drink down at the 2nd NZEF hall. **1990** *Sport* 5 97 I remember one night, all of us full of sharp white wine and **New Zealand green**, we discussed the ideas of 'loyalty' and 'discretion'. (a) **1840 New Zealand House** [see *New Zealand Company* above]. **1843** Chapman *NZ Portfolio* 97 I address the following observations to you [Somes, Governor of the NZ Company], because I am well aware of the anxious desire..to give your support within the New Zealand House, and your influence without, to whatever measures are calculated to promote the prosperity of the colony. **1849** in Cutten *Cutten Lett.* (1979) 35 I have chosen my town suburban and rural sections, see the map at New Zealand house—Town section 49 Block 16 Dunedin, Suburban 14 Block east side of Harbour. **1955** *Evening Post* (Wellington) 19 July 17 [Caption] Carlton Hotel, London, on the corner of Pall Mall and Haymarket, which is expected to be demolished early in 1957 to make room for **New Zealand House**. **1969** *Ibid.* 10 Apr. 12 Employers..were not fully aware of the service New Zealand House offered. **1974** *Dominion* (Wellington) 9 Mar. 3 New Zealand House received a steady flow of telephone calls from confused prospective migrants. **1993** *Contact* (Wellington) 11 Mar. 6 He's one of the key men British would-be migrants must speak to at NZ House in London. (b) **1840** Deans *Pioneers* (1964) 9 Feb. 4 I am likewise having a **New Zealand house** built on it—which is to be built for six blankets, and a more comfortable place I never saw. It is built of wood and large pieces of fern and is 34 feet in length by 17 feet broad, with three rooms—one for baggage, one for myself, and one for the servants. **1959** Sinclair *History NZ* 238 In 1933 the **New Zealand Legion**, a semi-fascist organization.. sprang up..to abolish party government and bring dynamic leadership to the nation. Fortunately it was a weed which, flourishing in sour ground, was soon crowded out by healthier growths when rising prices fertilized the land. **1984** Boyd *City of the Plains* 276 Sir Andrew Russell and other dissatisfied sheepfarmers in the Reform Party lent some support to the New Zealand Legion which advocated a return to free enterprise. **1986** *Listener* 26 Apr. 46 The chief editor of the Oxford English Dictionary is Wanganui's Robert Burchfield (cf under *mafia* [joc. phr. **New Zealand mafia**]) [*sic*]. **1995** *Dominion* (Wellington) 19 May 3 Two Britons who said they were fired for being British have won a discrimination case [in Britain] against a New Zealand-owned company [in Oxford]... An industrial tribunal ruled in their favour after hearing allegations there was a New Zealand 'mafia' at the firm. **1996** *Sunday Star-Times* (Auckland) 28 Jan. A3 Two English company executives, told they were up against a 'Kiwi mafia', have won a discrimination case..against their New Zealand bosses. **1873** Tinne *Wonderland of Antipodes* 32 Most of them distinguished themselves..during the war, which are but ill rewarded by the universal **New Zealand medal**, and a most scanty pay. **1890** *NZ Observer* 25 Jan. 16 None of the **N.Z. War Medals** presented to the Imperial Forces bear the date of their service on the medal. **1899** *NZPD* VI. 889 That this Committee concurs in the report of the Joint Committee on the granting of the New Zealand War Medal to such of the Colonial forces and friendly Natives in all cases where the claimants have been actually under fire, or otherwise conspicuous for distinguished service in the field; and recommends that the medal be also given to the nearest relatives of any who have died of wounds or have been killed in action. **1941** Sutherland *Numismatic Hist. NZ* 228 [Heading] The New Zealand (Maori War) Medal... The *Gazette* issued at Auckland on 23 October, 1869, p. 590, notifies the extension to the Colonial Forces of the grant for the decoration conferred 'for the War in New Zealand to all persons whether belonging to the local forces or loyal native tribes, who were actually under fire in any engagement with the enemy, or were otherwise conspicuous for distinguished service in the field'. **1935** Maxwell *Recollections* 73 During earlier Maori disturbances, besides troops from Home, there were many volunteer corps, and also some semi-regular troops which came under the general term '**New Zealand Militia**'. **1887** *Auckland Weekly News* 17 Sept. 8 My first meal was **New Zealand mutton**. It was very white..and I found out afterwards that was the name given to pork. **1897** Philips *Memories of Past* 38 I recollect in very early times, being served with what looked like very white meat; and, asking what it was, was told 'New Zealand Mutton', and it was some time before I was undeceived. **1994** *Tablet* (Dunedin) 17 July 8 For deaf and hearing impaired children English is a second language. Their native language is signing, whether it be the natural sign language of the deaf, now called **New Zealand Sign Language** (NZSL), or signs the children have developed among themselves for ease of communication. **1898** Morris *Austral-English* 462 **New Zealand tea.** Tea made of the leaves of the *manuka*.

5. With suffixed *pa. ppl.* **New Zealand born**, usu. of a non-Maori, born in New Zealand; **New Zealand-caught** *obs.*, of whale-oil, tried from whales caught off the New Zealand coast; **New Zealand fashion**, according to Maori practice (cf. *native fashion* (native B 5 a)); **New Zealand-made**.

1948 Sargeson in *Conversation in a Train* (1983) 29 Because as you all know Katherine Mansfield was New Zealand born. **1988** *Through the Looking Glass* 124 I hadn't ever, as my **New Zealand-born** parents had, called England home. **1992** *Dominion* (Wellington) 1 Sept. 1 A third..were New Zealand-born permanent residents of Australia. **1839** *Jones to Committee* 6 July in Eccles & Reed *John Jones of Otago* (1949) 25 If **New Zealand-caught** oil be treated in future as foreign-caught, I shall be obliged to break up my establishments. **1817** Kendall 25 Mar. in Elder *Marsden's Lieutenants* (1934) 136 In the course of this month several female scholars absent in order to get their lips and chin marked in the **New Zealand fashion** by an artist from Whangaroa. **1819** Marsden *Lett. & Jrnls.* (1932) 187 I laughed at him presenting his bloody nose for me to rub with mine, and pointed to the wound he had received; he smiled and said it was New Zealand fashion. **1834** Markham *NZ* (1963) 57 House cold, wet and Muddy, determined to build a Chimney New Zealand fashion. **1930** *NZJST* XI. 283 [Title] **New Zealand-made** Leather By Philip White

C. In composition (mainly in occasional use): **New Zealandiana**, memorabilia, items, or collectibles characteristic of New Zealand (see also *kiwiana* (kiwi 16 b)); **New Zealandic** *a.*, *New Zealand* B 1 above; **New Zealandish** *a.*, *New Zealand* B 1 above, *n.* New Zealand English; **New Zealandize** *v.* **a** *obs.*, to turn or translate into a Maori form, to make Maori; **b** to make (a thing, person, institution) New Zealand in character or ownership; hence **New Zealandization**, the making (of a thing, person, institution) New Zealand in character or ownership; **New Zealandness**, the state or condition or quality of being of New Zealand, or of having essential New Zealand characteristics or character; **New Zealandophile**, one (over)fond of New Zealand; **New Zealandy**, in a New Zealand fashion. See also NEW ZEALANDESE, NEW ZEALANDISM.

1988 *Through the Looking Glass* 124 I have no memory either of **New Zealandiana** in the *School Journal*. **1991** *Dominion Sunday Times* (Wellington) 3 Nov. 12 Richard Wolfe keeps a close eye on anything to do with the kiwi, especially its place as an image and icon. His latest book, the third in what shapes as a career cataloguing New Zealandiana, is 84 pages on the usage and mythology of the kiwi down the ages. **1874** *TrNZI* VI. 90 *Notice of the Skeleton of the New Zealand Right Whale* (Macleayius australiensis)... When first imported it was believed to be the **New Zealandic** whale, which I described..in Dr. Dieffenbach's 'Voyage'. **1963** CASEY *As Short a Spring* 117 Another paragraph on my unbounded praise for everything **New Zealandish**: the hotels, the railways, the roads..—all the best in the world. **1981** HENDERSON *Exiles Asbestos Cottage* 46 He is a handsome, slim man, thirty-nine, his bearing and dress (cocked slouch hat) and manner exactly suited to this setting. There is something distinctively *New Zealandish* focusing itself here. **1985** HOWE *Towards 'Taha Maori'* in *English* (NZATE) 3 Do New Zealanders whose cultural roots are strongly European (from Scotland, Ireland, England, Yugoslavia, Holland etc.) feel as 'New Zealand'ish as, say, those whose roots are strongly non-European (from the Cook Islands, Rarotonga, New Zealand Maori etc.). **1995** *Evening Post* (Wellington) 28 Oct. 8 Even within what we understand to be custom-built New Zealandish, there are words which have international recognition. **1835** YATE *NZ* (1970) 229 In short, there is scarcely any thing which we can imagine, but they have an expression for it, except it be some such words as express the Christian graces of hope, gratitude, charity, &c.; which words, and some few similar ones, always require to be **New-Zealandized**, and of course to be explained, as to the meaning that is to be attached to them; which is however, in no instance, a difficult task. **1993** *Evening Post* (Wellington) 2 Mar. 4 The process of 'New Zealandising' the fishing industry was 'clearly not' occurring. **1986** *NZPD* CCCCLXXII. 3007 The opposition has restated its objective as a '**New Zealandisation**' policy. **1988** FRAME *The Carpathians* 30 They now say *streams*. And *fields*. And the Minister of Agriculture has been talking of the *New Zealandisation* of Fisheries. **1994** *Dominion* (Wellington) 6 Aug. 22 [*Shortland Street* is] a soap, but there's a New Zealandisation in there. It reflects the things that do happen and it keeps current and makes people aware of issues. **1985** FRAME *Envoy from Mirror City* 19 I was much influenced by the West Indian writers and, feeling inadequate in my **New Zealandness** (for did I not come from a land then described as 'more English than England'?) **1988** CROSS *Unlikely Bureaucrat* 19 This diffident willingness to surrender our New Zealandness still has to be fought. **1988** *Dominion* (Wellington) 4 June 11 Tired notions of nationalism are paraded, so the building is..not just a work of art but the first building to be true to this place, to capture the 'real' New Zealandness of New Zealand. **1993** *Evening Post* (Wellington) 24 June 9 Central to all his works was the absence of Eurocentric inclinations. Sinclair was always a New Zealander. Today, the notion of 'New Zealandness' is the subject of occasional debate. When the young Sinclair started work, the idea barely sparked. **1988** *Dominion* (Wellington) 16 Mar. United States feminist writer and women's movement activist Robin Morgan was yesterday described by Women's Affairs Minister Margaret Shields as something of a '**New Zealandophile**'. **1922** MOUSLEY *Secrets of a Kuttite* 203 After a few miles of fern-edged [Turkish] brooks that tumbled along quite **New Zealandy**, we reached the plain again.

D. Abbreviations of the name **New Zealand**. See also ENZED, NEW ZILD 2.

[*Note*] Of the various abbreviations (in private correspondence, often idiosyncratic), **N.Z.** is the most frequent, then possibly **N. Zealand**, followed by **New Z.**, **N.Z'd**, **N. Zeeland**. **N.Z.**, in its two pronunciations, /ˌnju ˈzɪlənd/ (prob. the usual realization in the 19th c.) and /enˈzed/ (common in the 20th c.), became standard from about the mid-19th century.

1. As a noun, *New Zealand* A 1, the (orig. Maori-populated) biogeographical area; occas. (usu. *pl.*) New Zealander (see quot. 1916).

1773 FORSTER *Resolution Jrnl.* 25 Mar. (1982) II. 237 The Land was seen N.E. by E. ... so we probably off *West Cape*, on the South part of N. Zeeland or *Tavai poēnamoo*. **1792** VANCOUVER *Expedition* 26 Sept. in McNab *Hist. Records* (1908) I. 144 [We] entered Dusky Bay, N. Zealand, on the 2nd Nov. **1793** KING *Let.* to Nepean 19 Nov. in *Hist. Recs. NSW* (1893) II. 98 If N.Z. should be seriously thought on, would it not be advisable for some person to examine the country?.. I have sent you a box of N.Z'd curiosities. **1827** WILLIAMS *Early Jrnls.* 7 Apr. (1961) 51 The question again was entered upon, relative to the education of the children, when I stood alone for the education of the children in N.Z. **1838** CUNNINGHAM in Colenso *Papers* (ATLTS) IV. 6 N. Zeald. **1843** SELWYN *Journal* 97 (*et pass.*) *G.A. N. Zealand* [Selwyn's usual signature]. **1843** *Letter* 20 Jan. in Macmorran *Octavius Hadfield* (1969) 179 We were riding quietly along talking about the state of the church at home and in N.Z. **1850** *Richmond-Atkinson Papers* (1960) I. 71 I had our map of New Z. pinned to one of the struts. **1851** *Ibid.* I. 76 Auckland lies in a country level for N. Zealand. **1908** BARR *British Rugby Team in Maoriland* 54 *Said Leo*: 'What's this..that's broke my blessed head? It's called out here 'The Kiwi'—alluding to N.Z., It serves this small Dominion as an emblem for a crest.' **1914** RODGER *Blue Mountain Rhymes* 17 N.Z. are initials, I'd have you to know, They stand for New Zealand, We, Us, and Co., Who began to make history when Bobs fell in bad In the Transvaal, and cooeed, 'Come over, N.Z.' **1916** GRAY, Norman *MS Papers 4134* (ATLMS) 5 Feb. You have heard, I have no doubt of the 'Provincial pride' of most NZs. You know e.g. that Auckland is the only City in N.Z., that Wel[lington] is the hub of the business world etc. etc.

2. As an adjective. **a.** In early use, MAORI B 1 a.

1774 FORSTER *Resolution Jrnl.* 15 Mar. (1982) III. 470 They are short but almost shaped like the N.Z. battle Axes. **1794** N.Z'd [see 1 above]. **1827** WILLIAMS *Early Jrnls.* 11 Apr. (1961) 52 While in conversation with some of the Natives relative to the formation of a N.Z. settlement in the colony, Toi Tapu asked me why we were going away. **1840** WATKIN *Journal* 30 May in McNab *Old Whaling Days* (1913) 485 I am sorry to find that the little I have been able to pick of the N.Z. language that it differs materially from the language spoken in the North Island.

b. Pertaining to or characteristic of New Zealand as a biogeographic region.

1822 HUNT in McNab *Hist. Records* 9 July (1908) I. 515 It would be greatly against the N.Z. hemp. **1840** BEST *Journal* 9 Dec. (1966) 263 The usual characteristics of a N.Z. Valley viz. Narrow bounded by steep scrubby hills. **1853** MACKIE *Traveller under Concern* (1973) 74 The N. Zealand flax..was growing..by the road side. *Ibid.* 109 V.D.L. timber..is so much more durable than the N.Z. wood. **1933** *Na To Hoa Aroha* (1988) 23 Jan. III. 58 The Aussies have never played the game with us in regard to fruit, excluding N.Z. spuds. **1947** FAIRBURN *Letters* 14 May (1981) 159 You know, NZ painting is really more dead than alive.

New Zealander. Also (usu. idiosyncratic) **New-Zealander** (as in *NZPD* 1899), **Newzealander** (J.C. Andersen's spelling introduced as a house-style of the *Journal of Polynesian Society* during his editorship); also occas. early **New Ze(e)lander** (the *Zeeland* used by Forster was poss. influenced by Dutch or German); also *joc.* **New Zillunder**, etc.

1. *Hist.* (except in occas. anthropological use). **a.** MAORI A 1 and 2. See also ABORIGINE, *Aotearoan* (AOTEAROA 2 B), INDIAN, NATIVE A 1, ZEALANDER. [*Note*] With increasing European settlement after 1840, the term widened in application to include non-Maori immigrants (poss. the occas. use of *native New Zealander* from 1840 onwards implies a body of 'non-native New Zealanders'), and was replaced in its original reference by NATIVE or MAORI. In twentieth century mainly specialist use it occas. distinguishes indigenous New Zealand Polynesians from other Polynesians.

1769 PARKINSON in Cook *Journals* facing (1955) I. 209 [Caption] New Zealanders Fishing **1770** COOK *Journals* 31 Mar. (1955) I. 288 The same Language is Universally spoke by all the Islanders and this is a sufficient proff [*sic*] that both they and the New Zelanders have had one Origin or Source. **1773** FORSTER *Resolution Jrnl.* 28 Mar. (1982) II. 242 Our Gentlemen..on a sudden saw ten or twelve New Zeelanders on shore..were they back on board, when one canoe with a few Indians in appeared off the point. **1793** *Lieut.-Gov. King to Right Hon. Dundas* 19 Nov. in McNab *Hist. Records* (1908) I. 172 The decks were so full of New Zealanders that it became necessary to keep them off the poop. **1817** NICHOLAS *NZ* I. 29 The New Zealanders are looked upon at the colony [of New South Wales] as barbarians of the most ferocious and implacable dispositions. **1840** WATKIN *Journal* 15 June in McNab *Old Whaling Days* (1913) 489 I had Americans, Australians, English and New Zealanders in my congregation [in Otago]. **1853** in Mackie *Traveller under Concern* (1973) 72 A custom house boat came off to us manned by N. Zealanders or as they are called here Maoris (pronounced Mouries). **1874** DOMETT *Diary* 20 May (1953) 125 I asked him for his candid opinion whether the Ashantis of whose prowess so much had been made in the newspapers were equal in the field to the New Zealanders. 'One Maori was worth fifty of them!' he answered very decidedly. **1893** *TrNZI* XXV. 411 In some cases our English names of places have been adopted by the Maori... New Zealanders have long spoken of 'Peowhairangi,' Bay of Islands; 'Akarana,' Auckland; 'Niu Tirani', New Zealand. **1971** [see MAORI POTATO 1]. **1987** DAVIDSON *Prehistory of NZ* 16 These exercises..tend to distract attention from the essential point that the Polynesians, including the New Zealanders, are more like each other than like anybody else.

b. A Maori as distinct from a Chatham Islands Moriori (MORIORI 1 a).

1866 PARK *School Primer of Geogr. & Hist. Oceania* In 1830, the harmless natives [of the Chathams] were about 1000, but they have since been nearly all destroyed by barbarous aggression from the New Zealanders. **1879** HAAST *Geol. Canterbury & Westland* 425 The remnant, at present existing in the Chatham Islands..of a race which is allowed by the present New Zealander to be truly aboriginal, and before them in occupation.

c. As **white New Zealander**, PAKEHA-MAORI A 1.

1830 CRAIK *New Zealanders* 275 [The captain] as soon as he saw me [Rutherford, a pakeha-maori], exclaimed, 'Here is a white New Zealander.' I told him that I was not a New Zealander, but an Englishman.'

2. a. In senses or uses excluding Maori: a non-Maori person, often *spec.* a white European, born or permanently resident in New Zealand. See also *Enzedder* (ENZED 2), *New Zilder* (NEW ZILD).

[Note] The Europeans of c1830–50 were more likely to be referred to in writing as *Pakehas, Pakeha-Maoris, whalers, immigrants, colonists* (often from a particular 'colony': see quot. 1859), or *settlers* rather than *New Zealanders*; quot. 1848 may poss. refer to Maori.

1848 SELWYN in *NZ Part V* (Church in the Colonies XX) (1849) 81 And, as a natural consequence of the publication [of Selwyn's 'Protest'] in England, the Colonial police force, composed of English and New Zealanders, was the medium of communication to this large body of natives. **1852** SOUTHEY *Col. Sheep & Wools* 61 In their social and commercial relations the New Zealanders have made great progress... The best proof of their intellectual advancement is the fact that, at Wellington, a most respectable statistical almanack is now published. **1854** CHOLMONDELEY *Ultima Thule* 324 Now while I am convinced that society in such a colony as New Zealand must daily Americanise, I am also persuaded that the New Zealander will retain more of the Briton than any other colonist. **1859** THOMSON *Story NZ* II. 223 [Provincialists] were anxious to be Wellingtonists or Aucklanders, not New Zealanders. **1874** TROLLOPE *NZ* 632 And I would also observe to the New Zealander generally..that if he would blow his own trumpet somewhat less loudly, the music would gain in its effect upon the world at large. **1895** *TrNZI* XXVII. 240 Take..the land which we New-Zealanders still speak of under the familiar term of 'Home,' though many of us have never lived there. **1904** LANCASTER *Sons o' Men* 152 Colonial is nearly as loose a term as European. Don't you tell a Sydney chap..that you took him for a New Zealander. **1904** *Ibid.* 157 A New Zealander hasn't much spiritual grace. He's a Vandal, I think. He burns the bush, and plants *Pinus insign[i]s*; and he hasn't a decent picture-gallery. **1908** BARR *British Rugby Team in Maoriland* 141 I have also been very much impressed with the loyalty of the New Zealanders to the Sovereign, and this also applies equally to the Maori people. **1918** WESTON *Three Yrs. with New Zealanders* 246 Although the New Zealanders are the youngest branch of the family, their three score years and ten of vigorous, healthy life have stamped them with a separate Nationhood. **1926** DEVANNY *Butcher Shop* (1981) 46 You are a funny people, you New Zealanders. You treat your natives as if they were white. **1946** SARGESON *That Summer* 50 But you don't go back to Dalmatia. Oh no, he said, now I am a New Zealander. No, I said, but your children will be. **1959** SHADBOLT *New Zealanders* (1986) 31 'And you're not the English girl any more.' 'I don't suppose so.' 'Don't look so sad... Is it very terrible, being a New Zealander like me?' **1983** *Dominion* (Wellington) 15 Sept. 1 The term 'New Zealander' excludes people of non-European origin unless they abandon their own language and values, race relations conciliator Hiwi Tauroa says. He says 'a good New Zealander' implies a person who accepts that traditional English and European values are the best and most civilised. **1988** *Dominion* (Wellington) 24 Dec. 8 I am a white New Zealander, not a Pakeha,... and I am bewildered and angered by incessant demands and efforts to Maorify everything. **1990** [see *Enzedder* (ENZED 2)].

b. Any person born or resident in New Zealand or accepting New Zealand citizenship.

1866 CARTER *Life & Recolls.* I. ix These volumes may..become a source of entertainment..to some of those New Zealanders of British descent. **1888** BARLOW *Kaipara* 98 Horse-racing is one of the great national amusements of New Zealanders. **1899** GRACE *Sketch NZ War* 41 Well, I wish to remind the New Zealander of to-day, whether white or brown, that the Maori of my time was a gentleman. **1927** DONNE *Maori Past & Present* 5 Ethnogenic authorities class the 'Maori' New Zealander as of Malayan extraction... When the Malayan reached Aotearoa (New Zealand) he came to his Ultima Thule. **1930** *Na To Hoa Aroha* (1987) II. 12 Our progress resolves into two periods, the transition of Polynesian into Maori and the transition of Maori into New Zealander. **1946** ZIMMERMAN *Where People Sing* 12 The surest way to get into a real and earnest fight with a white, or *pakeha*, New Zealander, is to make a derogatory remark about one of his Maori fellow countrymen. **1946** *JPS* LV. 148 Kiwi is now a common name of the footballing Newzealander. **1961** [see AOTEAROA 2]. **1985** HOWE *Towards 'Taha Maori' in English* (NZATE) 4 New Zealander—combinations of the above? A Pakeha? A Maori? A Maori Pakeha? A Pakeha Maori? And what of all the other important racial and cultural groups in New Zealand? **1988** [see AOTEAROA 2]. **1992** *North & South* (Auckland) Jan. 82 We're all New Zealanders of course, but we happen to be Pakeha New Zealanders and Maori New Zealanders, not forgetting all the other nationalities here of course.

3. *Hist.* In the names of ships, etc. **a.** A general name for a ship bound for, or trading with, New Zealand ports.

1850 WARD *Journal* 3 Oct. (1951) 40 It seems we are rather too far to the eastward of the track of the Indiamen, and Australians or New Zealanders are not common enough to meet on the high seas.

b. An early given name for a particular ship operating off the New Zealand coast.

1814 MARSDEN Dec. in McNab *Hist. Records* (1908) I. 367 [Terria] afterwards watched them himself, and killed three European sailors. I understood that the Europeans belonged to a whaler called the 'New Zealanders'. **1820** KENDALL 27 May in Elder *Marsden's Lieutenants* (1934) 163 Mr. Marsden returned to New Zealand in the *Dromedary* a day or two before the *New Zealander* sailed from thence.

c. A given name for an early newspaper.

1848 WAKEFIELD *Handbook for NZ* 280 A New Plymouth correspondent of the *New Zealander* of the 16th of February, 1848, says [etc.]. **1853** SWAINSON *Auckland* 80 The *New Zealander* is published at Auckland twice a week, the number referred to chronicles the sayings and doings of the Auckland public for the four preceding days.

4. *transf.* An indigenous or endemic plant or animal, or one of New Zealand origin. See also NATIVE A 4.

1908 *Truth* 22 Feb. 2 As Mrs. Hedley and the 'old prad' are also out for life, the 'ring in' did not do the crowd behind the ex-New Zealander, Rawmire, much, if any, good, when that gelding won. **1910** COCKAYNE *NZ Plants & Their Story* 150 It contains more than fifty species, which, with the exception of three New-Zealanders, are all South Americans. **1930** REISCHEK *Yesterdays in Maoriland* (1933) 43 At length I succeeded in getting hold of a young New Zealander, whom I called Caesar. He was two months old, and so ugly that my friends congratulated me on having found the ugliest dog in the country. **1951** HUNT *Confessions* 136 New Zealand's trees..are her own exclusive property. They are true New Zealanders, for at least 89 per cent. of them are found in no other part of the globe. **1967** NATUSCH *Animals NZ* 262 Eighteen species of migratory shore birds which nest in the Northern Hemisphere have been recorded in New Zealand; only one, the snipe..is a true New Zealander.

5. As **the New Zealanders**, an early name for (esp.) the 1905 New Zealand representative rugby touring team, later called 'All Blacks'.

1905 *Evening Post* (Wellington) 2 Nov. 7 [Heading] The New Zealand football team... Rain fell throughout the match played by the New Zealanders against Surrey, and the final stages were played in a heavy storm.

6. In composition, **ex-New Zealander**, an expatriate; **non-New Zealander**.

1931 FAIRBURN *Letters* 4 Dec. (1981) 55 I know the very man for the job—an ex-New Zealander at present resident in England. **1989** *Pacific Way* Jan. 10 Suppose a friend says to me, 'You know that drongo who was on the chain with me...'. A non-New Zealander will probably require a translation.

New Zealandese.

1. [Poss. an error or influenced by French *néo-zélandais(e)*.] The Maori language.

c**1909** BELLINGHAUSEN *Journal* (c1820) transl. in *Murihiku* (1909) 240 I then explained to him [*sc.* the Maori] that I wanted some fish, pronouncing the word in New Zealandese (giyka [?=he ika]) fish. **1941** BAKER *NZ Slang* 58 *New Zealandese*, a term used before the native language of this country became known by the name Maori.

2. Distinctively New Zealand English or idiom.

1900 LLOYD *Newest England* 136 'Social Pests' is New Zealandese for land monopolists. **1939** MCKINLEY *Ways & By-ways* 111 'I go crook?' Oh, that's simply New Zealandese for 'Pourquoi s'en faire?' **1944** *Listener* 16 June 2 I suggest it is time people realised that English is not spoken in New Zealand. The language we speak is New Zealandese, with its own idiom and pronunciation, and this is just as distinctive as the language spoken by Americans, South Africans, Australians or Canadians. **1960** ASHTON-WARNER *Incense to Idols* 162 'What does that mean..''there's not a show''?'... 'It means "She hasn't got a chance". New Zealandese.'

New Zealandism.

1. a. A New Zealand national spirit.

1921 *Quick March* 10 Feb. 65 Certainly, the war fostered a strong show of 'New Zealandism' and the pride of the New Zealand soldier in his country was strong and determined, even if it was not so aggressive as the nationalism displayed by the 'Aussie'.

b. The characteristics or character associated with New Zealand or New Zealanders.

1961 *Education* Feb. 29 [James K. Baxter writes:] In the late forties and the fifties a number of poets seceded from the self-conscious New Zealandism of their immediate predecessors and began to write simply as people who happened to live in a given time and place... Mr Oliver's lucid account of the development of New Zealand poetry..should provide a salutary antidote to Mr Curnow's New Zealandism. **1989** *Dominion Sunday Times* (Wellington) 16 Apr. 24 All [these local TV programmes] reflect..aspects of New Zealand-ism.

2. An idiom, word, pronunciation or turn of phrase distinctively characteristic of, but not necessarily exclusive to, New Zealand usage. See also *New Zealand English* (NEW ZEALAND B 4 b (a)).

1957 *Listener* 22 Nov. 4 'Creek' and 'paddock' are New Zealandisms, because they mean something quite different in the English of England. **1964** ROSS & MOVERLEY *Pitcairnese Language* 13 Also [thanks] to..all those who kindly answered the two letters which I published in New Zealand about possible newzealandisms in Pitcairnese ('Words from Pitcairn'). **1966** TURNER *Eng. Lang. Austral. & NZ* 120 The expression *busting one's guts out* is a common New Zealandism. *Ibid.* 164 The term *New Zealandism* is used for a linguistic peculiarity of New Zealand English. **1989** *Pacific Way* Jan. 11 If I continue in this vein, suggesting that most New Zealandisms are in truth simply mistakes, my compatriots will go berko at me.

New Zealand War. In early use, usu. *sing.*; in later use, usu. *pl.* as *New Zealand wars*. With and without init. cap. W. The series of armed clashes between Maori and the Crown in the 19th century;

occas. early applied to inter-tribal Maori conflicts. See also WAR.

1. *Obs.* MUSKET WAR.
  1822 KENDALL 26 Feb. in Elder *Marsden's Lieutenants* (1934) 186 I beg leave once for all to observe that we have nothing to do with the New Zealand wars.

2. Applied to the European–Maori conflicts of the 1840s (see HEKE'S WAR), and more commonly to those between 1861–72. See also *Anglo-Maori war* (ANGLO-MAORI B 2), LAND WARS, MAORI WAR(S).
  1862 *Richmond-Atkinson Papers* 8 Jan. (1960) I. 739 My wife wrote to you [*sc.* C.W. Richmond] that..our opponents would demand a committee of the H.C. to enquire into the causes of the N.Z. War. **c1871** MASTERS *Autobiography* (ATLMS) 59 I know there are people in England who say that the New Zealand War was purely agrarian, arising out of disputed lordship and ownership of the soil. **1873** DOMETT *Diary* (1953) 28 Aug. 102 Having a little discussion about the New Zealand war, and to whose fault, that of the colonists or to the Maories, it was attributable. *Ibid.* 107 Thanking me in his letter [the Governor, Sir George Bowen] went on to urge me to 'write a novel on the Maories and the New Zealand war' saying that he had pressed the same thing on Anthony Trollope. **1899** GRACE *Sketch NZ War* 169 The New Zealand War lasted about ten years. **1922** COWAN *The New Zealand Wars* [Title] **1983** KING in Cowan *NZ Wars* (1983) I. xi There is at least one sense, however, in which Cowan can be said to be ahead of his time. He resolutely clung to the term 'New Zealand Wars'. He rejected the more popular but misleading expression 'Maori Wars', which implied that Maoris alone were responsible for the outbreaks of conflict. From the 1960s historians have explored more neutral and more accurate terms to characterise the period. Some opted for 'Land Wars', but this is not entirely satisfactory because issues were involved in addition to that of land. Others suggested 'Anglo-Maori Wars' but this too is less than adequate; the English were not the only Europeans involved and, as already noted, Maoris fought on both sides. For this latter reason 'Maori-Pakeha Wars' is also unsuitable... If they are referred to as the New Zealand Wars they cannot be confused with any others, particularly if earlier actions involving Maoris alone are designated 'tribal wars'. **1984** BARBER *Red Coat to Jungle Green* 38 But it was not until the Second New Zealand War, the so-called land war, that the Queen's Maori soldiers came into their own. **1986** BELICH *NZ Wars* 15 The New Zealand Wars of 1845–72 were a series of conflicts involving the British, Imperial and colonial, and the Maori tribes of the North island.

Newzie. [f. NEW Z(EALANDER + -IE.] A (former) familiar term for a New Zealander.
  1946 SOLJAK *NZ* 117 New Zealanders have coined or adapted many expressions to meet local requirements, as illustrated by the following. *Newzie:* New Zealander

New Zild, *n.* and *a. joc.* Also **Newzild, Noo Zild.** [f. a stereotyped 'broad', clipped pronunciation of *New Zeal(an)d.*]

A. *n.*

1. *New Zealand English* (NEW ZEALAND B 4 b (a)).
  1966 ACKER *New Zild* 7 Newzilders speak Newzild. **1972** MITCHELL *Pavlova Paradise* 181 You must understand New Zild as she is spoke. Elocution teachers sometimes say that New Zild is only lazy speech. In fact New Zild is a substitute for speech. **1984** *Listener* 21 Jan. 30 There are entries [in *The Macquarie Dictionary*]..for *Australian English*..but none for *New Zealand English, New Zealandism* or *New Zild.* **1986** OVENDEN *O.E.* 144 That's French slang for a cigarette. I learned it today. I'm going to use it in Godzone and make it part of Newzild. **1994** [see *blokeish* (BLOKE 2)].

2. New Zealand as a country or culture.
  1992 *Dominion Sunday Times* (Wellington) 23 Aug. 21 They work with familiar material, slyly inverting cliches as well as pure New Zild like white Valiants, but they look at it from a fresh angle. **1993** *Salient* (Wellington) 8 June 22 It aims to be a musical satire of corporationist attitudes ruining Seacliffe, a previously idyllic rural town in the backblocks of Noo Zild.

B. *adj.* Pertaining to or characteristic of stereotyped New Zealand-ness, or distinctive New Zealand speech.
  1980 THOMPSON *All My Lives* 60 'And what languages have you, Mr Thompson?'... 'English?' (I offered this in that apologetic interrogative tone that has since become the hallmark of New Zild speech.) **1985** *Evening Post* (Wellington) 31 Dec. 10 A recent review in the Christchurch Press reviewing a two-man show of Shadbolt and McCormick described them as, 'New Zild raconteuers' [*sic*]. **1986** *National Bus. Rev.* 10 Oct. 10 In buying Newzild the council was setting an example to other quangos and to private enterprise. **1992** *Political Review* Oct.–Nov. 34 Middle New Zild English must be delivered with surgical precision.

Hence **New Zilder,** the '(stereo)typical' New Zealander. See also ORDINARY.
  1966 ACKER *New Zild* 7 Newzilders speak Newzild. **1972** MITCHELL *Pavlova Paradise* 181 New Zilders speak slowly as if they were boring themselves into sleep.

nga bush: see BUSH A 2 b.

ngaiho, var. NGAIO.

ngaio /ˈnaiʌu/, early s. SI /ˈkaiʌu/. Also with much variety of early form as **gnai(o), kaio, kio** (SI.), **ngaiho, nio.** [Ma. /ˈŋaio/: Williams 227 *Ngaio.*] *Myoporum laetum* (fam. Myoporaceae), a coastal tree with gland-dotted leaves. See also LAUREL a.
  1849 TAYLOR *Journal* 16 June (ATLTS) VI. 113 On its being remarked that he [Manaku of Otaki] was going gray he said, yes, you don't see the kowarawara (an epiphyte) growing on the ngaio or mahoe, a tree which is of no value and never attains any size, but on the large and valuable timber trees. **1851** TORLESSE in *Lyttelton Times* 28 June 6 There is a less variety of pretty shrubs..but there are a few—the gnais..kowai, &c., that bear transplantation. **1857** PAUL *Lett. from Canterbury* 63 Here and there are paddocks..surrounded with hedges of the beautiful native laurel (gnaio), which flourishes luxuriantly here and in the valley of the Heathcote, but is too delicate to stand the frosty nights on the plains. **1861** *Richmond-Atkinson Papers* (1960) I. 693 [Tupaia's father] sat down in the shade of the ngaiho's [*sic*] which bordered the beach. **1867** THOMSON *Twelve Yrs. Canterbury* 29 Gnaio shrubs (the native laurel). **1874** WILSON *Diary* 15 May in Wierzbicka *Wilson Family* (1973) 191 I think we should plant a hedge inside [the fence] but the best one will be..the Matipo or the Ngaio which makes I believe a beautiful hedge..when it does not grow straggly. **1892** *Otago Witness* (Dunedin) 3 Nov. 5 *Myoporum laetum (Ngaio).* This is generally called kio by the colonists. **1898** MORRIS *Austral-English* 320 *Ngaio, n.* Maori name for a New Zealand tree, *Myoporum laetum*..generally corrupted into *Kaio*, in South Island. **1899** nio [see PIGEONWOOD.] **1900** *Canterbury Old & New* 184 The handsome ngaio, with its glossy leaves and pink-spotted flowers represents our garden verbenas. **1921** GUTHRIE-SMITH *Tutira* 102 In this light bush, tawa..mahoe or hinahina,..ngaio and koromiko were the most common trees and shrubs. **1964** BAXTER *Collected Poems* (1980) 306 What happened under the low green tarred ngaio branch cannot be clearly remembered. **1981** CAMPBELL *Collected Poems* 95 The dogs graze in the spring grass Under the ngaio tree.

ngamu, var. NAMU.

ngarara. Also **narara, nárrara,** and (erron.) **nancra.** [Ma./ˈŋaːrara/: Williams 229 *Ngārara..1.* Reptile, monster...*Ngārara pāpā*, brown gecko, a lizard.]

1. A mythical monster taking the form of (usu.) a lizard-like reptile.
  [**1815** KENDALL *New Zealanders' First Book* 48 Nárrara A lizard or reptile. **1820** LEE & KENDALL *NZ Gram. & Vocab.* 229 Nga rára; General name for reptiles.] **1841** BIDWILL *Rambles in NZ* (1952) 27 It appears, however, that the very existence of these lakes is a mere matter of tradition, as none of the present generation have ever ascended to their shores, through fear of the *nancras* [poss. a typographical error for *na[rra]ras*], or imaginary centipedes, or crocodiles (for it does not appear very clearly which is meant by the term), which inhabit the banks of all these inaccessible lakes, and with which even whole valleys are said to be so infested that it is impossible to get a native to visit them. **1857** *Lyttelton Times* 15 Aug. 3 The presiding deity has been offended:—his vengeance assuming the form of a Ngarara (lizard) enters the body of man, consumes his vitals, and thereby causes death. **1861** HAAST *Topographical Exploration of Nelson* 50 We started from the cave..respecting which..[the natives] tell a very interesting tale of a large ngarara, a monster in the form of an enormous lizard, which formerly lived here, and devoured all who attempted to pass. **1905** BAUCKE *White Man Treads* 38 [The Maori's] existence was burdened with the knowledge of huge reptilian monsters, ngarara on land, and taniwha in the water, who could speak, and roar..and decoy with satanic duplicity! **1916** DANSEY in Thomson *Naturalisation Animals & Plants* (1922) 179 I will remember the consternation and consternation in the native village, upon some native excitedly reporting his having seen a peculiar *ngarara* (reptile) in a pond near the lake, and describing that it had fingers and toes and swam like a human being. **1985** ORBELL *Natural World of the Maori* 163 Traditional tales tell of great monsters called ngarara which used to inhabit the land and threaten human beings. These ngarara were enormous reptiles.

2. TUATARA 1, or any of various native lizards.
  1842 GRAY *Fauna* in Dieffenbach *Travels in NZ* (1843) II. 205 I have been apprized of the existence of a large lizard, which the natives called *Tuatera*, or *Narara*, with a general name, and of which they were much afraid. **1875** *TrNZI* VII. 296 Unu ngarara or ngarara burrows were frequently met with on the plains..the ngarara was darker in colour than the ruatara. They varied in size from two to three feet in length, and ten to twenty inches in girth. **1882** HAY *Brighter Britain* II. 214 The only reptiles are pretty little ngarara, or lizards (*Mocoa* [spp.]). **1895** *TrNZI* XXVII. 674 The ridge-boards are carved to represent a number of *ngarara*, or lizards, running along the roof. **1949** BUCK *Coming of Maori* 61 The reptiles (*ngarara*) [carried on the *Mangara* canoe] were lizards (*moko-moko*) of the following species: *tuatara, teretere, kumukumu, mokaeparae,* and *moko-kakariki.*

Ngati /ˈnati/, *n.* and *prefix.* Also **Nati.** [Ma. /ˈŋaːti/: Williams 227 *Ngāi, ngāti,* tribal prefix.]

1. a. A Maori tribal prefix, 'tribe; clan', as in *Ngati Porou.*

NGAWHA

1856 SHORTLAND *Traditions & Superstitions* 225 *Ngati* is the word most commonly prefixed to the name of an ancestor to designate his descendents. It is the compound word *Nga-ati*, signifying the offspring. **1904** TREGEAR *Maori Race* 161 Names of tribes (*iwi*) were generally denoted by the prefix Ngati, meaning 'descendants of', as Ngati-Raukawa the descendants of Raukawa. Sometimes sub-tribes (*hapu*) or or small remnants of tribes used Ngati before their names. The prefix varied into Ati and Ngai as Te Ati-awa, Ngai-tahu.

b. As a prefix indicating humorously or ironically a quasi-Maori tribe or entity, **Ngati D.B.** [f. *D*(ominion *B*(reweries (now DB Breweries), and its well known beer, brand-named *DB*], for the displaced urban Maori having the hotel bar as a marae or meeting-place; **Ngati-drongo**, Maori regarded as stupid; **Ngati Naughty**, Maori regarded as mischievous or irresponsible (quot. 1995); **Ngati-one**, see quot. 1905; **Ngati-pakeha**, see quot. 1991.

1905 BAUCKE *White Man Treads* 241 Then I pushed [the Maori Councils Act] away, amazed that..the Minister who fathered it, should have forgotten that the Maori acts from compulsion..what Ngati-one proposes, Ngati-two will promptly oppose; while Ngati-three looks on and chuckles; and Ngati-pakeha pulls out his hair, and desperately wonders what next he shall do. **1979** TAYLOR *Eyes of Ruru* 15 My name is Tu the freezing worker. Ngati D.B. is my tribe. The pub is my Marae. My fist is my taiaha. **1986** HULME *Windeater* 130 'Don't you understand English, Ngati DB?' 'You're Ngati DB yourself, come to that.' **1988** McGILL *Dict. Kiwi Slang* 75 *Ngati Drongo* not our tribe! eg 'Was that your lot involved in the Maori Loans Affair?' 'Nah. That was Ngati Drongo.' **1991** *Metro* (Auckland) Apr. 24 Elizabeth tried to come across as Irihapeta. Alas, it is evident that she is just another Ngati Pakeha. **1995** *Dominion* (Wellington) 9 Sept. 19 But really what was the point of airing this tiff?.. *20/20* [TV programme] said that Lee and Riwia..had thrown their lot in with Duff to appeal for more loot [from film rights of *Once Were Warriors*]. Gee don't you love it when the Ngati Naughty tribe fights.

2. a. Also **Nati**. The Ngati Porou of the East Coast, as in 'The Ngati have placed a temporary prohibition on the use of this road'.

[*Note*] The prefix is distinctive as other major North Island tribes (e.g. Arawa, Tuhoe, Waikato) lack it or have dispensed with it.

1935 *Na To Hoa Aroha* (1988) III. 189 At Mangahanea in teeming rain the Nati rose to the occasion. **1951** KOHERE *Autobiography of a Maori* 134 I could see the spirit of the Nati hovering over our friend and guarding him. [1951 *Note*] Nati, short for Ngati-Porou, meaning the virile, devil-may-care, type of the tribe. **1987** *From a notice on the pohutukawa Te Wahao Rerekohu at Te Araroa* 29 Mar. (Ed.) 'According to Ngati tradition this tree dates from time of the ancestor Rerekohu who lived thirteen generations ago.'

b. Special Comb. **Ngati Blow**, a dismissive nickname applied, usu. by affiliates of other Maori tribal groups, to Ngati Porou; **Ngati Porou mafia**, a jocular nickname for the interconnected network of Ngati Porou people in positions of influence in the New Zealand community.

1989 McGILL *Dinkum Kiwi Dict.* 71 **Ngati Blow** nickname for Ngati Porou, probably from the sound in the Pakeha's inattentive ear; undoubtedly unacceptable. **1991** *North & South* (Auckland) Dec. 101 A tradition had been established as young Ngati Porou became teachers, academics and civil servants. They have so dominated key posts in a variety of government departments over the years that there has been jocular talk of 'the **Ngati Porou Mafia**'.

3. *transf.* A brumby, or wild horse of the central NI plateau.

1961 CRUMP *Hang On a Minute Mate* 54 Here's how we're going to catch ourselves some of those long-haired, tussock-eating ngatis... The brumbies are used to us coming and going along there now.

ngawha. [Ma. /ˈŋaːfaː/: Williams 232 *Ngāwhā*.. *1*. Boiling spring, or other volcanic activity.] A boiling spring. Cf. PUIA.

1843 SELWYN *Journal* 30 Oct. in *NZ Part II* (Church in the Colonies VII) (1845) 30 Here [at Ohinemutu] are to be seen all the varieties of Ngawha (hot-springs). **1859** *Auckland Provincial Gazette* 8 July 98 At intervals of considerable length..all these *ngawhas* begin to play together. **1867** HOCHSTETTER *NZ* 92 The Ngawhas, a term especially used for non-intermittent springs. **1870** *TrNZI* II. 171 The word Puia is especially used in the Taupo country, to designate the intermittent, geyser-like fountains... Ngawhas [is] a term specially used for non-intermittent springs, for the solfataras and sulphurous hot-springs on the Rotomahana, Rotorua, and Rotoiti. **1887** *Auckland Weekly News* 15 Jan. 15 Dr Hochstetter..predicted that this very spot, in the vicinity of which are numerous ngawhas, fumeroles and hotwater streams, would some time be the area of a great volcanic eruption. **1905** *TrNZI* XXXVII. 452 Hochstetter's map of Rotomahana, published in 1889..shows the location of most of the ngawhas, puias, fumeroles, and solfataras that surrounded Rotomahana. **1920** *Otago Witness* (Dunedin) 28 Dec. 27 [Caption] In the Ngawhas, Whakarewarewa, in the Thermal Springs District. **1978** FULLER *Maori Food & Cook.* 13 In the thermal areas of the North Island it is not long ago that one could watch people diving for carp..and cooking them in the ngawha (hot springs). **1989** TE AWEKOTUKU *Tahuri* 33 She walked over to the ngawha. A tukohu—cabbage tree kit—was hanging in its place..close to the steaming pool.

ngeri, *n.*[1] Also early **néri**. [Ma. /ˈŋeri/: Williams 233 *Ngeri* (i)..*2*. A rough kind of cloak.] A cloak; a raincape.

1838 POLACK *NZ* I. 158 Their dresses consisted of the kaitaka and karowai, made of the silky flax, and covered with dog-skin mats, or *néris* made of rushes, as protection against rain. **1840** POLACK *Manners & Customs* I. 178 A valuable garment for the stormy climate of the southward is called *néri*, and is made of undressed flax or of the *kierakiki*, a species of rush, impervious to rain. **1869** *TrNZI* I. (rev. edn.) 262 From [flax] the..shaggy bee-butt looking pake and ngeri..were alone manufactured. **1878** BULLER *Forty Yrs. NZ* 27 Covered with the Ngeri (a coarse flax mat), they looked like so many thatched bee-hives. **1882** POTTS *Out in Open* 23 Blankets, ngeries, shawls, mats of dressed flax..contributed a great variety of costume. **1963** KEENE *O te Raki* 193 *ngeri:* rough kind of cloak.

ngeri, *n.*[2] [Ma. /ˈŋeri/: Williams 233 *Ngeri* (i), n. *1*. Rhythmic chant with actions.] A Maori rhythmic chant with actions.

1882 POTTS *Out in Open* 14 Then was poured forth a wild ngeri, chanted in honour of Sir George. **1920** BOLITHO *With the Prince in NZ* 44 The..natives.. completed the tribal displays, which were followed by a great massed ngeri, in which thousands of natives joined in the famous 'Kamate Kamate.'

ngidu ngidu, var. NGIRUNGIRU.

ngirungiru. Also **ngídu ngídu**. [Ma. /ˈŋiruŋiru/: Williams 233 *Ngirungiru* [*Petroica* spp.]] South Island tomtit (TOMTIT, *Petroica macrocephala macrocephala*); also the note of the bird. See also MIROMIRO.

NGUTU-PARORE

[**1820** LEE & KENDALL *NZ Gram. & Vocab.* 230 Ngídu ngídu; A bird so called.] **1835** YATE *NZ* (1970) 56 *Ngirungiru*—This bird lays its eggs in the holes of trees—.. It is a very small bird, not larger than the tom-tit. **1873** BULLER *Birds NZ* 126 (Yellow-breasted Tit)... Its note in the early morning is like the Maori syllables *ngi-i-ru, ngiru-ngiru*, from which it derives its name, the first syllable being rather prolonged. **1904** HUTTON & DRUMMOND *Animals NZ* 70 The Yellow-breasted Tit.—*Ngiru-ngiru*. **1946** *JPS* LV. 154 Whilst miromiro was the name of the North Island bird, both of them bore the name ngirungiru, so that has been adopted for the South Island form, though the South Island Maori would probably give the 'ng' sound scurvy treatment and call the bird kirukiru, as he calls ngaio kaio. **1955** OLIVER *NZ Birds* 481 Yellow-breasted Tomtit. *Ngirungiru Petroica macrocephala macrocephala*. **1966** FALLA et al. *Birds NZ* 200 Tomtit... Miromiro (North Island), Ngirungiru (South Island), Wheedler, Butcher-bird (Taranaki). **1990** *Checklist Birds NZ* 209 *Petroica macrocephala macrocephala*... South Island Tomtit (*Ngiru-ngiru*).

ngoiro. Also from Ma. dial. **koiro**. [Ma. /ˈŋoːiro/: Williams 234 *ngōiro 1*... conger eel; Williams 128 also records *kōiro*.] *conger eel* (EEL 2 (2)).

[**1820** LEE & KENDALL *NZ Gram. & Vocab.* 230 Ngóiro, *s.* A fish so called.] **1855** TAYLOR *Te Ika A Maui* 625 The *Koiro*, conger eel..attains a length of about five feet, it is much esteemed by the natives. **1886** SHERRIN *Handbook Fishes NZ* 18 Known to the Natives as ngoi[r]o, and attains a very large size, with a length of 6ft... Congers are captured by hooks and lines, either used by the hand, or long lines with hooks at regular intervals. **1905** BAUCKE *White Man Treads* 5 One evening he marched up to our house and said: 'My mouth waters for "koiro" (conger eel); come, the tide and moon are rising, collect thy gear.' **1928** BAUCKE *Manuscript* (Bishop Museum Memoirs Vol.IX No.5 343–382) in Skinner & Baucke *Moriorios* 378 I see old Kirapu gather his *kupeng' tchitok'* (pole net)..to net *mararii*..and *koiro* (conger eel) and I go with him. **1947** POWELL *Native Animals NZ* 64 Conger Eel (*Leptocephalus verreauxii*), Ngoiro of the Maoris, is the common one of a number of marine eels. **1988** FRANCIS *Coastal Fishes* 19 Common conger eel (Ngoiro) *Conger verreauxi*.

ngutukaka. [In English use prob. a short form of KOWHAI NGUTUKAKA q.v.] KAKA-BEAK.

1883 DOMETT *Ranolf & Amohia* I. 302 Kowhai (scarlet)...*O*. Leguminosae; *G*. Clianthus; *S. C.* puniceus... In the natives' eyes, parrots' bills, so they call it '*gnutu-kaka*' [*sic*] the parrot-billed. **1946** *JPS* LV. 154 *Ngutukaka*, a tree (Clianthus puniceus), kaka-beak, parrots-bill *see* kowhai-ngutukaka.

ngutupare, var. NGUTU-PARORE.

ngutu-parore. Also **ngutupare**. [Ma. /ˈŋutu ˈparore/: cf. Williams 268 *Parori. 1.* a. Awry,.. twisted; also Williams 236 *Ngutu pare*..Wry-bill plover.] *wry-billed plover* (PLOVER 2 (8)).

[*Note*] The form *ngutu-parore* is not attested by Maori authorities.

1888 BULLER *Birds NZ* II. 9 Anarhynchus frontalis. (Wry-billed Plover.)... Ngutupare. **1955** OLIVER *NZ Birds* 268 Wrybill Plover. *Ngutu-parore Anarhynchus frontalis*. **1966** FALLA et al. *Birds NZ* 130 Wrybill..Wry-billed Plover, Crook-bill Plover, Ngutu-parore. **1970** *Annot. Checklist Birds NZ* 46 *Anarhynchus frontalis*..Wrybill (*Ngutu parore*). **1985** [see PLOVER 2 (8)].

nibbie. *Farming.* [f. Sc. dial. *nibby* a staff with a hook on the end: cf. OED *nibby*.] *mustering stick* (MUSTERING 2).
 1947 NEWTON *Wayleggo* 86 By dint of much labour, not to mention the ruining of several nibbies (mustering sticks) they finally chipped a hole in ice. **1990** MARTIN *Forgotten Worker* 63 The mustering stick, known as a 'hillstick' or 'nibbie', was usually made from manuka and had a metal ferrule.

nibble nook. *Obs.* [f. a proprietary name.] The name from c1950s for a shop associated with Kerridge-Odeon theatres selling sweets, ice-cream, soft drinks, etc.
 1987 *Metro* (Auckland) May 54 On the way home [in the 1950s] we'd sometimes go back down Anzac Avenue..then up Newmarket where..we'd stop for a crumpet at the new Nibble Nook next to Modelair on Broadway. **1988** JACKSON *Rainshadow* 83 I faced..men and women, munching sweets from the Nibblenook..; I turned back to the rising curtain.

nicau, var. NIKAU.

nick, *n.* [Poss. ad. *nekkid* a variant of *naked*; poss. an alteration of *nix* nothing: poss. f. an original NICKETTY-BOO, as a play on *naked*.] In the phr. **in the nick**, in the nude. (Also **nicketty boo** [*nekkid* + *y* + *-boo* (after *arsy-boo*, etc.)] also used in Marlborough and elsewhere c1940.)
 1940 Marlborough boys (Ed.). Go swimming in the nick. **1989** *Listener* 20 Nov. 36 She'd seemed so unaware of her nudity... The mother of his Pakeha friend, in the nick.

nick, *v.* [Poss. a variant of (or of similar obscure sense development as) *nip* (away, off, etc.) to move quickly: see OED *nip v.* 12; also NICK *v.*²] As **nick away** [AND *nick away* 1896], **nick out**, to slip away; **nick over**, to pay a hurried visit.
 1988 MCGILL *Dict. Kiwi Slang* 76 **nick away** to leave, usually surreptitiously or quickly; eg 'Look, I'm going to nick away before the speeches start. Let me know if they say anything important, will you?' **1960** CRUMP *Good Keen Man* 121 Flynn, sensing my decision to **nick out** for a bit of hunting, kept dashing out. **1988** MCGILL *Dict. Kiwi Slang* 76 *nick over* to visit, usually without warning; eg 'Marge, I'm just going to **nick over** and see Harry before din-dins, okay?'

nickel spinner. [f. *nickel*(-plated bullet) + *spinner* a fisherman's lure.] A humorous euphemism for a .303 bullet fired (illegally) at trout.
 1952 THOMSON *Deer Hunter* 101 Having small interest in different types of lures, flies and whatnots, I asked the field officer what kind of bait he caught it on, the reply being a 'nickel spinner'! Cliff told me that the 'nickel spinner' was a .303 rifle bullet. **1980** LELAND *Kiwi-Yankee Dict.* 70 *nickel spinner*: Another horror story for the devoted fisherman. A bullet (not necessarily nickel plated) fired at a trout (or any other fish). This almost always misses but it stuns the fish which then float to the surface to be gathered in.

nig: see NIGGLE.

nigau, var. NIKAU.

nigger. *Offensive.* [AND (Aborigine) 1845.] Occas. **negro** (see quot 1862). An abusive and contemptuous term for a Maori, esp. freq. at the time of the New Zealand wars of the 1860s (possibly reinforced by the usage of troops with Indian service). Also *attrib.*, and in compositional forms such as **antiniggerism**. Cf. BLACK *n.*¹ A 1 b, BROWNIE 1, DAGO 1 a, DARKIE, HORI.
 1858 *Richmond-Atkinson Papers* (1960) I. 175 [A.S. Atkinson] We heard that Bishop Selwyn..thinks there is a fair chance of collision with the 'niggers'. **1860** *Ibid.* I. 631 Will speaks of settling at Otago..and James agrees with him that migration to an entirely 'nigger' settlement would be preferable to living amongst those Scotchmen. **1861** *Taranaki Punch* II. 3 The bump of antiniggerism is most consolingly prominent. **1862** FITZGERALD *Native Policy NZ* 12 You will find in these papers complaints by chiefs that some of the settlers are in the habit of speaking of them as 'black niggers' and 'bloody Maoris'. **1862** *Richmond-Atkinson Papers* (1960) I. 807 Domett has promised to act decisively one way or another about Taranaki... If we cannot keep the negroes in order it would be most cheerful to clear out and try to get a bit reunited. **1868** [see BLACKFELLOW]. **1875** COCKBURN-HOOD *Chowbokiana* 51 The Vulgar Europeans call their tawny skinned neighbours 'Niggers', 'Savages' and other opprobrious epithets more applicable to themselves. **1880** SENIOR *Travel & Trout* 198 I met colonists who could not use objurgations too strong against the Maoris—'niggers' as, John Bull fashion, they term them. **1908** GORST *NZ Revisited* 118 From his deathbed [Potatau] sent a message to his friend Sir William Martin..: 'Be kind to the niggers.' **1911** *Truth* 7 Jan. 1 Heavens above, we filch the nigger's land and then we make an alien of him. Why the day will come when the Dago won't be at home here. **1926** DEVANNY *Butcher Shop* (1981) 119 He saw through Tutaki's eyes the unworthiness of the course he had decided on. He laughed grimly at the idea of 'a nigger' influencing him. **1938** LANCASTER *Promenade* 166 But the only girl Roddy liked was that Eriti Fleete. A nigger, thought Brian, who had already absorbed Auckland's notion of Maoris. **1946** BEAGLEHOLE *Some Modern Maoris* 299 Skin colour and the mixture of blood which is responsible for it [sc. the high visibility of Maori in a white world] are often commented on by one Maori to another. The terms 'mongrel', 'black mongrel', 'dago', or 'black nigger', for instance, are often used by Maoris either in referring to themselves or to other Maoris in the neighbourhood. **1984** *Dominion* (Wellington) 28 Mar. 7 Later a girl by the campfire said 'why don't you niggers do a haka and...[sic] off.' **1984** CAMPBELL *Island to Island* 93 In those days [c1939] racism was more blatant than it is now... At high school Stuart was known as Sam (short for Sambo). But 'nigger' was the ultimate, the unforgivable epithet. **1991** PAYNE *Staunch* 27 The biggest gang to come along since us [sc. the Mongrel Mob] has been the niggers [Black Power]. **1992** [see MAORI BUG b]. **1993** *Dominion* (Wellington) 2 Mar. 3 His assailants [who attacked him because they thought he was a Maori] told him they 'hated niggers'.

niggerhead, *n.*¹ *Obs.* Also abbrev. **N Hd.** [A proprietary name for a pipe tobacco: see Mathews, 1809.] NEGROHEAD *n.*¹
 1839 *Piraki Log* (stock list) (1911) 806 lb N Hd 6lb Cavendish 1 doz Pipes. **1871** MONEY *Knocking About NZ* 76 I had two or three pieces of 'Niggerhead' tobacco (Barrett's Twist) in my pocket. **1933** *Press* (Christchurch) (Acland Gloss.) 11 Nov. 15 *Nigger head...* (2) The name of the tobacco usually kept in station stores for the men in the eighties. **1957** PASCOE in *Mr Explorer Douglas* 70 In the middle nineties [Douglas] smoked 'niggerhead', a tobacco of two dozen thin sticks to the pound.

niggerhead, *n.*² Also occas. **nigger wig** (see quot. 1898). [f. the appearance (cf. quots. 1910, 1933): see OED 1 a '*U.S. & N.Z.*', 1859.] *Carex secta* or *Carex virgata* (fam. Cyperaceae), a swamp sedge of tussock form the raised clumps of which turn black when dried. See also MAORIHEAD, NEGROHEAD *n.*²
 1864 CHUDLEIGH *Diary* 27 Aug. (1950) 143 Trenching in the swamp and cutting nigger heads to fill up a bog on the track in the morning. **1878** [see MAORIHEAD]. **1882** POTTS *Out in Open* 76 Winding round and penetrating through the dead massy root of an old plant of nigger-head (*carex virgata*). **1898** MEREDITH *Reminisc. & Experiences* 20 The [Otago] country I had to travel was intersected in all directions with 'nigger wig' swamps..quite impassable for a horse. **1900** *Canterbury Old & New* 179 The vegetation may be observed in thickets of tea-tree..and that curious sedge known popularly as nigger-head. **1910** COCKAYNE *NZ Plants & Their Story* 109 Very characteristic [of swamp vegetation] is the niggerhead..a species of sedge which builds for itself tall and stout 'trunks' out of its dead roots and root-stocks, from the summit of which, like shock-heads of hair, the long leaves droop. **1920** *TrNZI* LII. 72 '*Pukio*' was the Maori name of 'niggerheads'. **1933** *Press* (Christchurch) (Acland Gloss.) 11 Nov. 15 *Nigger head.*—(1) Carex secta. A plant which grows up like a tussock out of the water in swamps and at the edges of lagoons. When it is burnt and goes black it is more or less the shape of a head; hence the name. **1950** *Bull. Wellington Bot. Soc. No.23* 11 At the creek edges *Carex secta* (niggerhead) occurs. **1968** SLATTER *Pagan Game* 20 The land of the magpie and the myna, the pukeko scuttling into raupo and niggerhead. **1970** MCNEISH *Mackenzie* 67 He crossed swamps, jumping from nigger-head to nigger-head. **1988** WARR *Bush-burn to Butter* 49 Flax, niggerheads, toitoi and rushes grew in abundance in all swampy areas.

2. [Not otherwise recorded.] See quot.
 1898 MORRIS *Austral-English* 321 *Nigger-head, n.* (1) Name given in New Zealand to hard black-stones found at the Blue Spur and other mining districts. They are prized for their effectiveness in aiding cement-washing. The name is applied in America to a round piece of basic igneous rock.

niggerhead, *n.*³ [See OED *niggerhead* 2, applied to various black rock nodules or boulders (1876); not otherwise recorded in NZ.] See quot.
 1898 MORRIS *Austral-English* 321 *Nigger-head, n.* (1) Name given in New Zealand to hard black-stones found at the Blue Spur and other mining districts. They are prized for their effectiveness in aiding cement-washing. The name is applied in America to a round piece of basic igneous rock.

nigger wig: see NIGGERHEAD *n.*²

niggle. WW2. Also **nig.** [f. Brit. dial. *nig* a small piece: see EDD.] A small drink.
 1946 WEBBER *Johnny Enzed in Italy* (Gloss.) *Nig*: niggle, small drink (very rare). **1950** THE SARGE *Excuse My Feet* (Gloss.) *Niggles*: (slang) a small (?) drink.

night.

1. Used *attrib.* in special Comb. **night-cart** *obs.* [in use until comparatively recently in NZ: AND 1840–1986; OED apparently the removal of filth from cess-pools], a sanitary cart for the removal of human excrement ('night soil') from private premises; **night demon** *Otago goldmining*, black petrel (PETREL 2 (1) *Majaqueus parkinsoni*); **night-hawk** *obs.* [poss. f. Brit. dial. *night-hawk* a bird which flies in the twilight: EDD *night* 19], MOREPORK 1 a; **night paddock** *farming*, a paddock in which stock are kept overnight, esp. dairy cows for the morning milking; **night parrot**, see

PARROT 2 (8); **night-pen** *farming*, a sheltered pen (often in a shearing shed) where sheep can be kept overnight before shearing; **nightwalker** *obs.*, red cod (COD 2 (6) *Pseudophycis bachus*).

1985 LANGDALE-HUNT *Last Entail Male* 65 There were no flush toilets, only the 'Old Dunny' in the backyard, both in town and country with the only difference that a vehicle called a **night cart** called in town in latter years. **1986** *Evening Post* (Wellington) 4 Sept. 9 Kainga [in North Canterbury] is the last place in New Zealand to have sewerage removed by night cart. **1993** RENÉE *Daisy & Lily* 33 I..stared at my new back yard with the decrepit old dunny in it... 'Means you won't be woken by the night cart,' said Auntie Maureen. **1895** *TrNZI* XXVII. 122 *Majaqueus parkinsoni...* (Black petrel.).. I am quite satisfied that this bird is the '**Night Demon**' of our diggers. I had a live one..from Collingwood... On windy nights the bird would become very excited, and then it would give vent to the hysterical laugh or scream from which it takes its name. **1871** MONEY *Knocking About NZ* 44 I struck up [a song]..electrifying the moreporks or '**night-hawks**' in the neighbourhood. **1883** DOMETT *Ranolf & Amohia* I. 247 Two loud harsh notes assail her ear—The *night-hawk's*! harsh but yet so *near*! **1928** STAPLEDON *Tour Austral. & NZ* 55 On an appreciable number of farms the system of the '**night paddock**' is largely adopted. This consists of always bringing the dairy cows to a particular paddock at night. The 'night paddock' will be rotated round the farm. **1956** DARE *Rouseabout Jane* 122 The night paddock was land surrounding the house and easily accessible. **1966** *Te Reo* IX. 54 The apparently Australian innovation lies..in the adoption of the refined terminology of the *home paddock* and the *night paddock*. **1983** STEWART *Springtime in Taranaki* (1991) 116 We were genuinely able to be of some use in the cowshed—helping..to bring up the herd from the night paddock..leg-roping them..attaching the machine's strange cups to their fleshy teats. **1885** *Wairarapa Daily* 12 Oct. 2 From each side of a central building..are the **night pens** and shearing floors. **1907** KOEBEL *Return of Joe* 305 [The fleeces] was all here on top of the nightpen rail. **1928** REES *Wild Wild Heart* 72 'Have you got any idea what a night-pen is?' 'Not the foggiest.' 'It's inside the shed. The sheep are kept in there ready for the morning's shearing.' **1955** BOWEN *Wool Away* 112 They [*sc.* tally pens] can be used as a night pen... Except in dire circumstances it is not good practice to fill the catching pens for use as night pens. **1986** RICHARDS *Off the Sheep's Back* 73 The woolshed was..enormous with..a huge night pen to cover over 1,500 sheep. **1773** FORSTER *Resolution Jrnl.* 19 May (1982) II. 283 [They] brought some Fish all of the *red Codkind* which the people on board the Adventure called *Nightwalkers*, because the[y] bite chiefly in Nighttime. **1777** ANDERSON *Journal* Feb. in Cook *Jrnls.* (1967) III. 808 [We caught another fish] of the same size [as the cole fish] of a reddish colour with a little beard which we call'd nightwalkers from the greatest number being caught in the night.

2. In the phr. **the night's a pup** [Wilkes 1915], it's early (yet).

1968 SLATTER *Pagan Game* 166 Sit down, Erik... The night's but a pup yet.

nightshade. Any of a large group of herbs and soft-wooded shrubs of the genus *Solanum* (fam. Solanaceae) esp. **black nightshade**, a native small-flowered nightshade *S. americanum* (formerly *S. nodiflorum* and *S. nigrum*) (see also *black tomato* (TOMATO 1), WONDERBERRY), which is often erroneously called **deadly nightshade** (properly applied to a completely different plant *Atropa belladonna*). Occas. as **New Zealand nightshade** *obs.*, POROPORO (*Solanum aviculare* or *S. laciniatum*).

1770 BANKS *Journal* (1962) II. 8 Sow thistle, garden nightshade were exactly the same as in England. [1962 *Note*] *Solanum nigrum*, which botanists have thought possibly introduced; but this mention seems conclusive that it was a native. **1777** ANDERSON *Journal* Feb. in Cook *Journals* (1967) III. 804 Amongst the known kinds of plants are..Nightshade..and Nettles. [1777 *Note*] Solanum Linnaei. **1864** MUELLER *Vegetation Chatham Is.* 32 Mr Travers alludes in his journal to a dwarf New Zealand Night-shade also found in the Chatham-group. This is unquestionably the now cosmopolitan *S. nigrum*. **1867** HOOKER *Handbook* 766 Nightshade. *Solanum nigrum*. **1892** HUDSON *Elem. Manual NZ Entomology* 82 Formerly this insect must have fed exclusively on the New Zealand nightshade (*Solanum aviculare*). **1964** *Press* (Christchurch) 19 Sept. 5 We do have a Nightshade properly called Black Nightshade, a very common weed all over the country and distributed widely in all parts of the world. It is this plant which people will call Deadly Nightshade. **1977** CONNOR *Poisonous Plants* 156 All local reports using the name deadly nightshade apply to the many forms of *Solanum nigrum*, the black nightshade. *Ibid.* 169 Although called black nightshade because of the generally black colour of the berries, there is a range of [ripe] fruit colours. **1980** TAYLOR *Weeds of Crops* 16 Black Nightshade (*Solanum nigrum*)..has many different forms which are regarded as variants of one species... [It] is common throughout New Zealand but less abundant in the southern half of the South Island.

nikau /ˈnikæu/.

1. Also with much variety of early form as **necko**, **nekau**, **neko**, **nigau**, **nikou**. [Ma. /ˈniːkau/: Williams 221 *Nīkau..1...*New Zealand palm.] Also **nikau palm**. *Rhopalostylis* (formerly *Areca*) *sapida* (fam. Arecaceae), a native palm, the edible flesh of its shoots or the heart of its leaf-base as a food; also its leaves as a construction material. See also CABBAGE-PALM 2, CABBAGE-TREE 3, *New Zealand palm* (PALM 1), PALM-TREE 2.

a. As **nikau**.

[**1820** LEE & KENDALL *NZ Gram. & Vocab.* 185 Níkau, *s.* A shrub, so called from its numerous leaves proceeding from the same stalk.] **1827** WILLIAMS *Early Jrnls.* 8 Nov. (1961) 83 One half of the long native house had been prepared for the reception of the females..it was nearly filled up with the *nikau* and made very comfortable. **1839** TAYLOR *Journal* 13 Nov. (ATLTS) II. 167 We rested at ten in a little shed constructed of palm leaves (the nigau) where the Waimate boys had passed the preceding night. **1854** LUSH *Auckland Jrnls.* 4 Feb. (1971) 150 [He] said he would soon get me some luncheon... We speedily spied a young *Nikau*, the native palm tree, and cutting off the upper end he cut the inside... It tasted like sweet turnip. **1854** GOLDER *Pigeons' Parliament* 75 The *necko* or *neko* is a large tree-like plant known elsewhere as the mountain cabbage. **1871** MONEY *Knocking About NZ* 61 We found a good quantity of bush plant called 'nikou,' the pith of which is much like hazel nut, and is very good eating when roasted or boiled. **1894** *NZ Official Year-book* 329 The nikau, or southern palm, is plentiful all through the district. **1900** *Canterbury Old & New* 184 Another semi-tropical plant, the nikau—New Zealand's only palm—extends as far south as Banks Peninsula. **1973** FINLAYSON *Brown Man's Burden* 141 Nikau: a palm, whose leaves can be used to thatch roofs or decorate dance-halls. **1984** MORTON *Whirinaki* 15 New Zealand has only one palm, the nikau, *Rhopalostylis sapida*.

b. As **nikau-palm**.

1847 ANGAS *Savage Life* I. 245 There is an undergrowth..composed of the *nikau* palm.., and the beautiful tree-fern. **1873** TINNE *Wonderland of Antipodes* 61 I could never resist slicing off the head of a 'nekau-palm'. **1905** WHITE *My NZ Garden* 51 Those who cut down large Nikau Palms..and use them for the decoration of ballrooms and for other festive occasions, are greatly to blame. **1948** FINLAYSON *Tidal Creek* (1979) 80 Jake leaves the creek and wanders among the groves of nikau-palms that line the lower slopes. **1959** SHADBOLT *The New Zealanders* (1986) 30 The drooping leaves of the nikau palms sprinkled a confetti of sunlight on the fern..above us. **1991** *Evening Post* (Wellington) 26 Nov. 22 Mr Corrigan said the decorated nikau palms outside the new library would no doubt get the 'wowsers barking'.

2. Special Comb. **nikau heart**, the edible centre of the leaf-base; **nikau hut, nikau whare**, a rough or makeshift hut made of (or thatched with) nikau leaves.

[**1938** *Auckland Weekly News* 21 Sept. 12 Hungry children went to the bush and got the heart of nikau, a good food.] **1982** BURTON *Two Hundred Yrs. NZ Food* 7 Succulent and sweet to the taste, **nikau heart** later became known as 'millionaire's salad' because the tree dies when the heart is removed. **1840** TAYLOR *Journal* 8 Jan. (ATLTS) II. 178 In the evening it came on very raining, we have encamped by a river in a **nikau hut**. **1873** TINNE *Wonderland of Antipodes* 53 Our nearest neighbours are a colony of gum-diggers, at the Kaiwaka swamp..they have built quite a little village of these 'nekau' huts. **1879** FEATON *Waikato War* 28 And where the **nikau whare** stood,.. Now sheltering stands in calm repose, The Saxon cot, encircled with the rose. **1907** LAING & BLACKWELL *Plants NZ* 84 Nikau whares are extremely pretty and picturesque, but are now rarely seen, owing to the cheapness of corrugated iron. Bushmen, however, still make them occasionally for temporary residences. **1920** MANDER *Story NZ River* (1974) 230 [The gum-digger] made a hut of sacks and mud and ti-tree, or he built a nikau whare, an art learned from the Maoris, out of the broad-leaved native palm. **1938** *Auckland Weekly News* 21 Sept. 12 He..took up his residence in a nikau whare with a clay floor. **1989** RICHARDS *Pioneer's Life* 88 This was to be my last time living in a bushman's nikau whare.

3. As a first element in adjectives formed with *pa. ppl.*: **nikau-bordered**, decorated with fans of nikau palms; **nikau-thatched**, of bushmen's or esp. Maori whares, thatched with nikau leaves.

1920 BOLITHO *With the Prince in NZ* 34 The train drew into Hamilton station, gay with bunting and nikau-bordered streets. **1935** COWAN *Hero Stories NZ* 159 Most of the people appeared to be gathered in the large nikau-thatched meeting-house.

nikou, var. NIKAU.

nineteener. *Obs.* [Of uncertain origin: perhaps from cribbage, 'a nineteener' being an impossible score to get; Partridge glosses as 'a swindler', quoting Sidney Baker's *Australian Slang* (1942), and proposes a derivation from a person who talks 'nineteen to the dozen'.] 'A bad lot'.

1887 *NZ Mail* (Wellington) 15 July 9 (NZ slang) If he is altogether bad he is 'a fair lady', 'a daylight robber', 'a heap'.., 'a lump of dirt', 'a bad egg', 'a nineteener' (a digger's expression rapidly becoming obsolete).

ninety nine. [A variation of SIXTY-NINE, perhaps influenced by (or mistakenly confused with) the name *Ninety-nine* of the woman agent in the 'Get Smart' TV comedy.] See quots. See also SIXTY-NINE.

1987 OGONOWSKA-COATES *Boards, Blades & Barebellies* 97 *Ninety-nine*. A more recent addition to shearers' slang. When a woman enters the usually all-male shed, the words 'ninety-nine' are passed down the board, presumably to give the shearers a chance to smarten up their language. **1989** *NZ Eng. Newsletter* III. 26 *ninety nine*: This means there is a woman on the board or at least within hearing distance, so watch your language. It originated from the Maxwell Smart television programme in the 1960s where the female agent was called 'ninety nine'.

ning nong. [f. Brit. dial. *ning-nang* a fool: cf. EDD and OED; AND 1957.] A fool, a silly or stupid person. Cf. NONG.

1960 Wellington 2YA Wellington (Radio talk). Words must be understandable by sub-editors and other advanced species of ning-nong while conveying that the writer has had college education. **1964** MCLEAN *Willie Away* 163 And if ning-nong sub-editors don't cut it out of copy. **1965** WATSON *Stand in Rain* 54 The boss was a bit of a ningnong and the customers were beginning to rely on Jerry instead. **1972** *Truth* 26 Sept. 25 Featherston County Council..forces are out to preserve privies and 'long drops' for the relief of Ning Nong locals. **1991** VIRTUE *Always the Islands of Memory* 7 Sister was a ning-nong about planning for the future. **1994** *Dominion* (Wellington) 2 Aug. 15 Leonard is one of Wellington's homeless people... Leonard, however, has no intention of becoming 'another ning-nong of society'.

nip, *n.*

1. [AND 1919.] In the phr. **to put the nips in (into, on)** (someone) (also **get the pinchers into**, see quot c1926), to ask for a loan (of money), to cadge from; also, to put pressure or 'the squeeze' on (someone). Cf. BITE *n.*²

1917 *Chron. NZEF* 19 Sept. 63 I put the nips into one the other night, 'n he come to light with a couple o' de[e]ner. **c1926** THE MIXER *Transport Workers' Song Book* 11 They've got the pinchers into me. Don't you think I ought to buck. When the Union won't take action. **1935** STRONG in Partridge *Slang Today* 287 I put the nips into the fellow in charge for a feed. **1963** PEARSON *Coal Flat* 190 'The woman's getting too serious,' he thought; 'she's putting the nips in; a man doesn't want to be trapped a second time.' **1989** *Listener* 7 Jan. 13 And it's anybody's guess what Japanese tourists make of such Kiwisms as 'She's apples' 'put the nips in'.

2. [f. *nippers* fingers.] In the phr. **to get the nips on to**, to obtain, get hold of.

1947 DAVIN *For Rest of Our Lives* 5 We were all pretty plastered and we got the nips on to some more beer.

nip, *v. Obs.* [AND 1919.] *trans.* to pinch, to steal; to steal or cadge from (a person).

1911 *Truth* 21 Jan. 6 'Oh an old fellow came in while you were out and nipped your "paper".' I said: 'Oh, did he?' 'Yes,' said the other fellow, 'he came in, looked over all the seats, and then put his peeper on your sheet and poled it.' **1917** *Chron. NZEF* 19 Sept. 54 When you are in Auckland the stiffs nip you, to raise the wind.

Nippon clipon. A nickname for the Japanese-made Auckland Harbour Bridge extensions.

1976 JOHNSTON *New Zealanders* 119 Four extra lanes were added [to the Auckland Harbour Bridge] outside the main arch—the 'Nippon clip-on' as it is known. **1980** LELAND *Kiwi-Yankee Dict.* 70 *Nippon-clipon*: The Auckland Harbor Bridge was once a two-lane bridge... Thanks to..Japanese engineering, it is now four lanes. The extra two were built in Japan, towed to Auckland and attached to the sides of the existing bridge. **1986** TEMPLE & APSE *NZ from the Air* 45 The centre four lanes [of the Auckland Harbour Bridge] were opened in 1959 but traffic flows trebled in less than a decade forcing the addition of four more outer lanes. These are affectionately known as 'Nippon clip-ons'.

niu. *Hist.* [Ma. /'niu/: Williams 222 *Niu. 1.* n. Small sticks used for the purposes of divination.] In contexts of the 19th century Maori Pai Marire cult, divination rods, or divination; but mainly a ceremonial pole, usu. in special Comb. **niu pole** (or occas. **niu mast**), a pole erected for the religious ceremonial purposes of the Pai Marire.

1864 *Richmond-Atkinson Papers* (1960) II. 125 In the flat open space behind the pa there was a pole (or niu) standing used in their new Pai Marire religion. It was about 10 feet high, square for 2 or 3 feet at top & bottom & rounded in the middle. *Ibid.* 155 I was curious to know where the first *niu*, or worshipping post, was set up & when he said at Kaitake during the present war I said I did not see it there. 'To you,' he said, 'it was a color (flagstaff) to us it was a niu. **1879** *Auckland Weekly News* 17 May 14 A pole of a certain height, to be called a Niu, should be erected, around which all true believers were to worship, standing in a circle; those found worthy would receive the gift of tongues. **1904** TREGEAR *Maori Race* 336 [The priest] cast the *niu* rods, or interpreted the 'jerkings' (*takiri*) of the limbs or body of a sleeping man. **1922** COWAN *NZ Wars* (1955) II. 6 This *niu* was the central symbol of worship under Te Ua's dispensation. The term was the olden Maori word for the short sticks used by the *tohunga* in his mystic arts of divination, particularly before a battle. Te Ua's *niu* was a tall pole or flag-mast, round which the faithful were to march in procession chanting their hymns. **1937** BABBAGE *Hauhauism* 29 The central object of worship [of the new religion] was the 'Niu'. The origin of this innovation was described in the following terms:—'The Angel Gabriel said: "Go back to your house and erect a niu." Horopapera enquired what a niu was. The Angel replied: "A post." Horopapera enquired for what purpose? The Angel replied: "To work for you for the acquirement of the languages of all the races upon the earth."' **1959** SINCLAIR *History NZ* 137 The services of the new Maori evangelism were held at a *niu*, a long pole, perhaps fifty feet high, with yard-arms from which hung ropes. The congregation revolved round this mast as round a maypole while the priests conducted a service of prayer. **1967** BRATHWAITE *Evil Day* 380 Niu. Mast erected for purposes of religous rites and observances in *Pai-marire* faith. **1983** *Listener* 31 Mar. 20 More significant are the Niu poles, erected in the early 1860s and well-known to canoeists who traverse the river today. The remaining two poles, at Marae-kowhai, are distinguished by their cross-arms reaching to the compass points, one of which (Rongo Niu) has carved hands on it.

Niu Tirani. Also **Niu Tireni, Niu Tirini, Nuitereni, Nui Tireni, Nu Tirani**. Ma. /'niu (or /'nu:) 'ti:rani/ (or /'ti:reni/, or /'ti:rini/): Maori transliterations of NEW ZEALAND A 1 a.

[*Note*] The early variation *Niu/Nu* may derive from contemporary English variant pronunciations /nju/ or /nu/ of *new*.

[**1833** *Ko te tahi wahi o Te Kawenata Hou... Ka oti nei te wakamaori ki te reo o Nu Tirani. Hirini...* 1833 [Title] in Williams *A Bibliography of Printed Maori* (1975) 3 **1840** *Treaty of Waitangi* in **1877** *Facsimiles Treaty Waitangi* (1976) [Preface] 3 Ka tiakina e te Kuini o Ingarani nga tangata maori katoa o Nu Tirani.] **1860** *Taranaki Punch* 19 Dec. 8 Niu Tirini is in a mist for the loss of his medicine. **1867** HOCHSTETTER *NZ* 203 However, the natives have no general name for the whole of New Zealand; they employ the European word for New Zealand, which in the Maori pronunciation becomes Nuitereni or Niutereni. **1868** TAYLOR *Past & Present NZ* 123 Potatau the First..in June 1858..entered [Rangiawhia] preceded by his flag, bearing the device of a cross and three stars, with the name of the country, 'Niu Tirini,' in the centre. **1893** *TrNZI* XXV. 402 New-Zealanders have long spoken of 'Peowhairangi,' Bay of Islands; 'Akarana,' Auckland; 'Niu Tirani,' New Zealand, &c. **1915** *Hawkes Bay Herald* 2 Dec. 6 We girls felt we could jump over the moon. Well done Nui [*sic*] Tireni! **1949** CURRIE *Centennial Treasury Otago Verse* 110 Whether in Niu Tireni or Te Reinga Now you live, or in countries over the ocean. **1988** *Listener* 13 Aug. 15 I very much object to Sir James Henare's suggestion that this country be known as Nu Tirini. That is merely the corruption of the English name to which so many Maoris object. **1993** [see AOTEAROA 2].

no., *abbrev.*: see NUMBER.

noa, *a.* [Ma. /'noa/: Williams 222 *Noa. 1.* a. Free from tapu or any other restriction... 2. Of no moment, ordinary.] Mainly in Maori contexts, unrestricted by tapu; ordinary.

[**1815** KENDALL *New Zealanders' First Book* 8 Noa Common.] **1839** in Wily & Maunsell *Robert Maunsell* (1938) 61 He replied that his grandfather Kukutai had sent word that he would not consent to his (Ngataru's) becoming *Noa* (common) while he retained those garments. **1841** BIDWILL *Rambles in NZ* (1952) 118 The natives always require an additional consideration for taking off the 'taboo', or making 'noa' any places which may be included in a purchase. **1851** SHORTLAND *S. Dist. NZ* 69 [The] ceremony of making 'noa' the 'taua', that is, of restoring the men who composed it to their ordinary condition, by severing the intimate connexion existing between them and the 'Atua' so long as they remained 'tapu'. **1903** *TrNZI* XXXV. 17 Up to the time when the planting commenced everything was *noa*, or 'common', but once the seed began to be handled.. the whole thing became *tapu*, or consecrated. **1948** HENDERSON *Taina* 29 The dining-house was *noa*, and slaves or any person could enter it. **1985** HOWE *Towards 'Taha Maori'* in *English* (NZATE) 21 Noa— the narrowest sense of this word is 'freeing from restriction' or 'cleansing', but like its complementary quality 'tapu'..it pervades *all* aspects of Maori life and custom. Generally it is associated with cooked food, water, women, the low-born, and the young, good, and ordinary life events.

nob.

1. *Whaling. Obs.* [Spec. use of Brit. slang *nob* a person of distinction: see OED *n.*²] In early whalers' or traders' parlance, a Maori chief.

1845 WAKEFIELD *Adventure NZ* I. 319 A chief was called a '*nob*'; a slave, a '*doctor*'; a woman, a '*heifer*'; a girl, a '*titter*'; and a child, a '*squeaker*'.

2. [Transf. and fig. use of the cribbage call *one for his nob* influenced by *nob* head: cf. OED *nob n.*¹] In the phr. **one for his nob**, a blow on the head.

1913 *Hutt Valley Independent* 29 Nov. 1 A local Red Fed bachelor nearly got one for his nob the other day from a mounted special constable who was passing through Upper Hutt.

3. *Two-up.* [Transf. use of Brit. slang *nob* head.] A double-header coin.

1928 DEVANNY *Dawn Beloved* 163 A double-tailer is called a 'grey'; a double-header a 'nob'.

nobbler. Also **nobler**. [f. *nobble v.* in a general sense of 'incapacitate': see OED *v.* 1 and 3; AND

1842.] A measure or 'nip' of spirits; the glass in which it is served.
   1856 in *Canterbury Rhymes* (1866) 41 When the hateful 'nobbler' shall be forgot. **1858** Higgins *Letters* (Hocken Lib. MS) (Griffiths Collect.) 27 Dec. 3 In the Colonies glasses of anything are called noblers so that if you want anything you ask for a nobler of what you want. **1861** *Dunedin* in *NZ Goldfields 1861* (1976) 1 Oct. 31 I subjoin the retail prices of a few articles sold at Tuapeka:- Brandy, 15s. per bottle, or 1s.6d. per nobbler. **1871** Money *Knocking About NZ* 13 And there behind the bar..was Reinecker..serving a 'nobbler' to a sashed and booted digger. **1881** Bathgate *Waitaruna* 220 There's nothing like a good stiff nobbler first thing in the morning for picking you up. **1913** Bathgate *Sodger Sandy's Bairn* 79 A box of 'nobbler glasses', as small thick tumblers of limited capacity were called. **1924** *Otago Witness* (Dunedin) 11 Mar. 60 Meals, beds, and horse-feeds were from half a crown to 5s each, and nobblers 1s. **1949** Davin *Roads from Home* 45 Putting the nobbler down empty. **1953** Mundy *Days That Are No More* 30 From a bottle of whiskey poured him out a good nobbler. **1969** *Landfall* 23 59 Sure enough there were two full whisky nobblers on my dresser. **1973** Wilson *NZ Jack* 91 The steward came over with our drinks, and by the time we'd paid for our nobblers Don had..disappeared again.

nobblerize, *v. Obs.* [f. prec.: AND 1847.] *intr.* To drink nobblers, or any spirits, esp. socially.
   1858 Hannah Richardsons' *Journal* Dec. in Rolleston *The Master* (1980) 45 The ladies nobblerise to an extent much to be regretted. **1876** *Southern Advertiser* 8 July 5 No more at even shall our fast young swells For drinks at yankee grab, or euchre play..Nor 'Justices' who guard the public weal, Stand 'nobblerising' at the public bars. **1905** Ferguson *Poems & Sketches* 86 On Saturday and market nights frequent the company of hard-gristed cockatoos—smoking and nobblerising, if you will.
   Hence **nobblerizing** *ppl. a. obs.*, given to drinking nobblers or tippling spirits.
   1856 Waitt *Progress of Canterbury* 2 Our delightful sojourn for a few days at Akaroa with the old nobblerizing Admiral and his quaint stories. **1858** Shaw *Gallop to the Antipodes* 58 You are accustomed to the lazy and lounging and nobblerising community too often to be found in the towns of New Zealand and in Sydney where people prefer..nobblers to occupation.

no-beg-pardons: see BEG PARDON.

nobler, var. NOBBLER.

nodder. [f. *nod*(ding thistle) + -ER.] A familiar shortened form of *nodding thistle*.
   1980 *Star* (Christchurch) 5 Jan. 7 But the result was that the nodders are a non-event here and the same applies to scotchies.

noddie. [Poss. f. Sc. or Irish dial. *noddy* a former two-wheeled box-like carriage: see OED *n.*³; SND *noddy n.* a kind of light two-wheeled cab having a door at the back, and a seat for the driver in front, 1825–1942.] A four-wheeled barrow or small wagon on which passenger luggage was formerly (to the mid-1970s) placed for carriage on the inter-island ferries.
[*Note*] A noddie, or a rake of them, was drawn by hand or by tractor on to the ferry, and again on to the terminal at disembarkation.
   1972 *Evening Post* (Wellington) 26 May 18 A slowly moving rake of waggons had caught a luggage 'noddie'..and the noddie in turn had caught the deceased..I instructed him to take off the centre rake of railway wagons first, and then pull off one passenger luggage barrow or 'noddie' by hand. A tractor was not needed or necessary... I then discovered a smashed luggage noddie on the port side of the linkspan [of the Cook Strait rail-ferry] and could see feet protruding from beneath it.

noddy. [Extended or transf. use of *noddy* a tropical tern-like bird.] *white-fronted tern* (TERN 2 (10) *Sterna striata*).
   1838 Polack *NZ* I. 307 The small *noddies*..abound in large flocks. **1966** [see TERN 2 (10)]. **1985** *Reader's Digest Book NZ Birds* 232 White-fronted Tern *Sterna striata... Tara, sea-swallow, kahawai bird, black cap, grenadier, swallowtail, noddy*.

no fear. [f. *no fear of that*: used elsewhere but recorded earliest and of freq. use in NZ: see OED *fear n.* 5 a, 1880; EDD 2 4.] Certainly not!
   1860 in Butler *First Year* (1863) iii 27 A few [colonial] expressions were not familiar to me. When we should say in England, 'Certainly not', it is here 'No fear', or 'Don't *you* believe it'. **1866** Burgess *Confessions* (1983) 93 He replied: 'Did you think I was going to let a bloody wretch like that best me? No fear, the — shall sweat there till Monday.' **1874** Baines *Edward Crewe* 75 'Why, Janson, I thought she was going to turn turtle.' 'No fear,' he replied. **1886** *TrNZI* XVIII. 55 As expletives 'My word' and 'No fear' are favourites, both drawn out as long as possible. **1895** Roberts *Diary of Jonathan Roberts* 5 'Can you produce them?' 'No fear'. **1905** *Truth* 24 June 2 It is the result of conviction or the dictates of conscience? No fear. Nothing of the kind. **1915** *Inglewood Record & Waitara Age* 8 Oct. 2 'Are you off to the war?'.. 'No fear. You don't catch me fighting for the Taranaki cockies.' **1960** Muir *Word for Word* 254 She didn't commit no bloody suicide, mate. No bloody fear. **1975** Davin *Breathing Spaces* 97 I'd like to see the bloody Hun who's going to make me start now. No fear, me old cobber General Freyberg, VC, 'd never forgive me. **1981** Hunt *Speaking a Silence* 20 And there was no hot water laid on, no fear.

nog. Also **nogging**. [Orig. *nogging-pieces* horizontal pieces nailed to the framing to strengthen it; *brick nogging* brickwork built up between a wooden framing: see OED *nogging n.* 1 and 2.] Usu. *pl. nogs, noggin(g)s*. See quot. 1986. See also DWANG.
   [**1853** Sewell *Journal* 3 Feb. (1980) I. 123 The building is what they call brick nogging.] **1957** *NZ Timber Journal* Aug. 59 *Nogging Pieces*: Stiffening pieces between studs. See 'partition'. **1957** Ibid. Aug. 68 *Nog*: (Bld) A block of wood the size of a brick, built into a wall to provide a means of nailing skirting, etc. Hence 'nogging', the filling in of the spaces between timber in walls and partitions. **1963** Bacon *In the Sticks* 7 The house was a mere shell, all its constructional details plainly visible. Rafters, studs and noggings, in all their naked glory, flaunted themselves unashamedly before my eyes. Ibid. 181 *noggings*—In building, horizontal spacers securely fastened between the uprights (studs) of a house frame. Usually covered by exterior walls and interior lining material. **1986** Salmond *Old NZ Houses* 232 *Nog (or dwang)*. a short piece of framing timber fixed tightly between *studs*, to which lining materials are fixed. **1992** *NZ English Newsletter* 6 10 (Bartlett *Regional Variation: Southland*) The buiding term *noggins* (also known by the short form *nogs*) is thought to be a North Island term, according to those in the Southland building trade I talked with. Certainly, all..interviewed preferred the term *dwangs*, without hesitation.

nogget, var. NUGGET.

nogging: see NOG.

nohi: see JACK NOHI.

nohi. [Ma. /'nohi/: Williams 223 *Nohi* (i).] *Luzuriaga parviflora* (fam. Philesiaceae), a small forest herb with a zig-zag creeping stem.
   1978 Moore & Irwin *Oxford Book NZ Plants* 186 *Luzuriaga parviflora*. Nohi is a stringy little plant that grows on the Coromandel Ranges and extends to Stewart Island, reaching sea-level in the south. **1982** Wilson *Stewart Is. Plants* 252 *Luzuriaga parviflora* Lanternberry..Nohi... Wiry-stemmed little plant, the leafy shoots arching from a creeping base... Fruit white, crisp-fleshed, filled with numerous small, hard, pale seeds.

no-hoper. [AND 1944.] A hopelessly ineffectual or incompetent person.
   1955 BJ Cameron Collection (TS July) no-hoper (n) A hopeless case, a good-for-nothing. **1968** Slatter *Pagan Game* 166 Her husband, whom she openly scorned as a no-hoper, sold paint in the hardware store. **1988** McGill *Dict. Kiwi Slang* 76 *no-hoper* totally incompetent or inadequate person socially or at sport; used in horse racing for a useless racehorse; eg 'Cripes, that horse is a no-hoper: six starts, and last in every one.' **1991** Eldred-Grigg *The Shining City* 17 How come they lived in a nice new suburb and not in grubby old Sydenham like other Feron no-hopers.

nondi /'nɒndi/. *Schoolboys. Obs.* [f. *non-de* (script: cf. Partridge 8 *nondescript*. A boy in the middle school: certain Public Schools': late C19–20.] A junior schoolboy or one of no account.
   1919 *Blue & White* 114 Being one of the Nondies, or in other words, one of the small fry, I have been asked to make a few remarks on their behalf. **1935** *St Patrick's College 1885–1935* 49 The students over whom he placed their fellows honoured him for the trust he reposed in them from the 'nondies' down. **1962** Lawlor *More Wellington Days* 149 I had marched gaily to camp hoping to become a soldier 'full of strange oaths and bearded like the pard'. Instead, they made me a 'Nondi' (i.e. nondescript) [Lawlor had been a student at St Patrick's College, Wellington.]

nong. [A shortened form of NING-NONG: AND 1944.] A fool; a silly or stupid person.
   1959 *Kaingaroa Forest News* 19 Feb in Boyd *Pumice & Pines* xiii Just listen to my song For a man's a bloody 'nong' To work among the pine trees row on row. **1973** Grant in *Listener Short Stories* (1977) 147 Mortimer looked a real nong. 'This here is Mortimer,' said Fred. 'He's a pongo, but he can't help it.' **1984** Duckworth *Disorderly Conduct* 12 'I love you, you silly nong.' 'There you are then.' **1987** *Evening Post* (Wellington) 1 Oct. 34 The poor little nong thinks deer velvet makes you sexy. **1994** *Dominion* (Wellington) 18 June 14 A fully-fledged *nong*..is a menace to himself and everyone else... He is, in short, a backward ning-nong.

nookie /'nʊki/, *a.* [Prob. from Ma. *noke* 'small': Williams 223.] Tiny, little; also as a nickname for a small boy or person.
   1917 Fussell *Lett. from Private Tikitamu* 19 [Written mainly in 'pidgin Maori.'] Nookie, nookie man. **1978** Tucker *Thoroughbreds Are My Life* 6 Len's nickname..was 'Nookie', which today bears a totally different connotation to that which it did in those early years [c1930s]. How he came by it I will never know.

no-remittance, *a. Obs.* A system of importing (esp. motorcars) from c1950s to mid 1970s,

where the importer already had sterling or other overseas funds and did not need to 'remit' funds from New Zealand.
   1972 *Sunday Times* (Wellington) 25 June 35 Exceptions are made only for no-remittance cars and leprosy.

normal school. [Spec. use of Brit. *normal school* (after French *école normale*) a school for the training of teachers: cf. OED *a.* 3, 1834.] A primary school associated with a specified College of Education and providing supervised classroom experience for teacher-trainees.
   1876 *Educ. Board Act* S 19 Every Board may..make such provision..for the establishment and maintenance of a normal or model school or schools. **1886** *AJHR E-1* 88 [The Otago Principal reports] I have the honour to submit my report of the training department of the [Otago] normal school for session [*sic*]. **1917** *Statute Law Amendment Act* S2 Any Education Board having control of a training college..may establish and maintain in connection with such training college one or more public schools as normal or practising schools. **1949** *Southern Cross* (Wellington) 18 Aug 9 [Heading] Normal School in 'Deplorably Filthy State'. **1976** JOHNSTON & MORTON *Dunedin Teachers College* 9 The Training Department of the Otago Normal School was opened on 15 February 1876... In New Zealand until early this century the term *Normal School* as we know it (to designate a Practising School) was not in general use. The term was used initially for the combined institution: the name Dunedin Training College was officially applied in 1880. Both names were used indiscriminately for many years. *Ibid.* 217 Regulations of Otago Normal School (1876) I. Candidates for training shall be arranged under the following classes:- (a) Pupil teachers who have attained their 18th year in the case of males, and their 17th year in the case of females, and who have satisfactorily completed their term of apprenticeship, or whose transference to the Normal School has been approved by the Board. **1987** *Evening Post* (Wellington) 2 Dec. 13 As a 'normal' school (associated with the teachers college next door) the school is used to test and evaluate new programmes and syllabuses. **1990** *Ibid.* 6 June 5 Normal and model schools, which are involved with teacher training, will receive an extra grant of $5.20 per pupil.

north: see *far north* (FAR *a.*), ROADLESS NORTH, UP NORTH, WINTERLESS NORTH.

North Cape. In phrases denoting the length and breadth of New Zealand, from one end of New Zealand to the other. See also *from Bluff to Cape Maria* (BLUFF 2), *from Reinga to the Bluff* (REINGA 2), *Three Kings to the Snares* (THREE KINGS 2). **a. from North Cape to Stewart Island** (and vice versa).
   1859 THOMSON *Story NZ* I. 36 The coast climate of New Zealand from Stewart's Island to the North Cape may be described as most changeable. **1919** *Quick March* 10 Sept. 19 Tennessee may stand for any place from the North Cape to Stewart Island. **1958** MULGAN *Making of New Zealander* 94 All people from the North Cape to Stewart Island are New Zealanders, but with a difference.
   b. from North Cape to the Bluff (with some variety of form).
   1870 *TrNZI* II. 132 Some of these introductions have largely displaced the original vegetation in many localities, from the North Cape to the Bluff. **1892** *NZ Official Handbook* 131 From the North Cape to the Bluff Hill, in the extreme south of the Middle Island, the climate and soil are eminently adapted for the growth of a large variety of fruits. **1906** PICARD *Ups & Downs* 8 [He] cussed Seddonland from N.C. to Bluff. **1923** MALFROY *Small Sawmills* 21 This is a..well-tried-out jack which is extensively used in logging operations from North Cape to the Bluff. **1931** CLOKE *Songs NZ* 210 When we see our far-flung Circuit, From the North Cape to the Bluff. **1953** *Listener* 6 Mar. 3 [Advt] From North Cape to the Bluff only the best is good enough! Get Plume [petrol] the best you can buy! **1960** KEINZLY *Tangahano* 90 From the Cape to the Bluff Hangis [*sic*] Maoris like their Hangis and Kiwis like their shindigs. **1982** *Evening Post* (Wellington) 2 Sept. 30 Industrial reaction to the Government's wage restraints has been primed to burst countrywide... 'From North Cape to the Bluff,' Federation of Labour President..said.

northern. In the names of plants and animals, see: KELPFISH 3, KINGFISH a, PETREL 2 (7) and 2 (10), RATA 2 (2).

Northern Island. *Hist.* Also **Northern Isle.** Usu. init. caps. An occas. early name for the NORTH ISLAND 1.
   1773 WALES *Journal* in Cook *Journals* (1961) II. 790 There were seven large Cannoes of these New-comers, and... They came from somewhere towards, if not actually from the Northern Island. **1826** *Memorial to Earl of Bathurst* 24 Apr. in McNab *Hist. Records* (1908) I. 664 There is every prospect of a rapid increase in the trade..under the..protection of the British Government, which could not be given so effectually from any station as from the Northern Island of New Zealand. **1834** MARKHAM *NZ* (1963) 29 New Zealand or the Northern Island, as there are three, is known to the Natives by the name of Eaheinomawe. **1853** EARP *NZ* 34 The Middle Island is separated from the Northern Island by Cook's Strait, and from Stewart's Island by Foveaux's Strait. **1868** TAYLOR *Past & Present NZ* 192 The New Zealand group chiefly consists of the Northern, Middle, and Stewart's Islands. **1875** *TrNZI* VII. 61 A patauruhe, or fernroot beater, made of maire..another strictly Northern Island tree. **1889** FEATON *Art Album NZ Flora* 5 This minute plant is a native of the Northern Island. **1905** THOMSON *Bush Boys* 174 Hark! It is ringing now, not the clang of harsh metal hanging in church steeple, but the mellow note of the *Tui*, the bell-bird of our Northern Isle.
   Hence **Northern Islander**, a Maori from the North Island.
   1853 ADAMS *Spring Canterbury Settlement* 76 A young Maori..was a child at the time, and beheld his father and mother slain and eaten by Northern Islanders. **1866** ANGAS *Polynesia* 166 The natives in the Middle Island had always been inferior in numbers..to the Northern Islanders, who from time to time made cruel and butcherly raids upon them.

North Island.
   1. Often *attrib.* **a.** Also occas. early **North Isle.** The northernmost of the two large islands of New Zealand. See also (in early use) NORTHERN ISLAND.
   [*Note*] The noun in general New Zealand use is collocated with the definite article. Select quots. only are given below.
   1773 FORSTER *Resolution Jrnl.* 24 June (1982) II. 307 This had happened at the North Isle. But in *Queen Charlotte's Sound*, no such thing had ever been remarked or apprehended. **1834** McDONNELL *Extracts Jrnl.* (1979) 20 Coffee, sugar, indigo, and rice, would succeed well on the North Island, as also all the tropical fruits. **1841** HODGSKIN *Narr. Eight Months Sojourn* 5 The beautiful..islands of New Zealand, *Eaheinomauwe*, or North Island..South Island..and Stewart's Island. **1867** [see MIDDLE ISLAND]. **1980** BRASCH *Indirections* 53 He had collected too a number of North Island trees and shrubs, at that time rareties in Dunedin.
   b. In the names of (esp. subspecies of) plants and animals, see: CROW *n.*[1] 2 (1), EDELWEISS, FANTAIL 2 (3), FERNBIRD 2, KAKA 2, KINGFISH a, KIWI 2 (1), KOKAKO 2 (1), OYSTER 2 (4), OYSTERCATCHER 2 (4), PIOPIO, RIFLEMAN, ROBIN 1, SADDLEBACK *n.*[1], THRUSH 2, TIT a, TOMTIT, WEKA 2 (3), WOODHEN 2 (3), WREN 2 (1).

   2. Of climate or weather, warm, mild.
   1951 LEVY *Grasslands NZ* (1970) 336 The South Island in an occasional 'North Island' season still suffers from rank, foggy feed, and in such season hogget ill-thrift is rampant.

North Islander. One (occas. specifically a Maori, see quots. 1850, 1873, 1877) born or resident in the North Island of New Zealand.
   1850 MANTELL in *Proc. Zool. Soc.* (Britain) XVIII. 211 According to native traditions, a large Rail was contemporary with the Moa... It was known to the North Islanders by the name of 'Moho'. **1869** BROOME *Crisis in NZ* 417 The creed of the North Islander will depend on his province. **1873** BULLER *Birds NZ* 191 It [*sc.* the notornis] was known to the North-Islanders by the name of 'Moho', and to the South-Islanders by that of 'Takahe'. **1877** CHUDLEIGH *Diary* 11 July (1950) 259 The New Plymouth boatmen are some of them great scamps... These North Islanders are a bad lot. **1917** *Chron. NZEF* 11 Oct. 134 In the afternoon [the men] played a match between the North Islanders and South Islanders among them. **1945** HENDERSON *Gunner Inglorious* 122 Unscathed in four campaigns, two North Islanders had been invalided home. **1964** DEMPSEY *Little World Stewart Is.* 6 Where the North Islander talks of his beach cottage, or bach, we call these little places *cribs*. **1972** *Dominion* (Wellington) 31 Oct. 1 He told me he had one broadside he wanted to deliver while he was still a North Islander. **1987** ELDRED-GRIGG *Oracles & Miracles* 208 Friendly, chatty..Australians, Americans, English, North Islanders.

North Isle, var. NORTH ISLAND.

Northland.
   1. The North Auckland peninsula. (*North Auckland* may still occas. be heard esp. from non-residents.) Often *attrib.* See also *far north* (FAR), ROADLESS NORTH, WINTERLESS NORTH.
   [**1889** WAKEFIELD *NZ after Fifty Years* 121 The far north of New Zealand, 'North of Auckland', as it is often familiarly called, even in official documents..is semi-tropical, and the people are like unto it.] **1919** RUSSELL *NZ Today* 27 This country, now officially called 'Northland'. **1922** *Northlander* 13 Mar. (VUW Fildes Clippings 641a/42) 1 [Masthead] The Northlander. The Organ of Progress and Democracy in the Northland Vol. I—No. 1. Kaitaia, Monday, March 13, 1922. For all information, Maps, Literature, Etc. pertaining to the Winterless Northland... Is romance all gone out of the Northland? **1946** REED *Farthest North* 13 I board the service car at Northland's capital. **1957** GOLDBLATT *Democracy at Ease* 11 We reach the capital of Northland, the busy, growing town of Whangarei. **1966** *Encycl. NZ* II. 693 The region is usually referred to as North Auckland, but the use of the shortened Northland is gaining a wider currency. **1970** THOMAS *Way Up North* 29 [Kauri] grows naturally within the restricted area of the northern part of the Auckland Province and almost wholly in Northland. **1982** PEAT *Detours* 70 Harbour and hospital boards had gone the 'Northland' way, and only a few organisations such as the North Auckland Rugby Union and the North Auckland Electric Power Board found comfort in the

old provincial name. **1990** *Checklist Birds NZ* 91 There has been a spectacular increase in the number of winterers [*sc.* cattle egrets], sizable flocks reappearing annually in many favoured localities from Northland to Southland.

Hence **Northlander**, a person born or resident in Northland; also the name of a newspaper (see quot. 1922 in 1 above).

1961 REED *N. Cape to Bluff* 81 As an old Northlander, I could trace its evolution. **1983** *Landfall 147* 384 Nick Messenger. Northlander by upbringing, B.A. in Philosophy..a West Coaster by adoption. **1990** *Dominion* (Wellington) 23 July 1 Southlanders have once again proved the cheeriest lot in New Zealand about the economic prospects for their own region. At the opposite end of the country, Northlanders hold the bleakest view of their local economy.

2. A suburb of Wellington.

1953 *Evening Post* (Wellington) 27 Feb. 8 Often your writers refer to Northland, the suburb, in a headline, and I have to read the text to see if they are referring to Northland up north or Northland down south here in Wellington. Couldn't we plan a key to this by referring to North Northland or Northland North (as in Palmerston North?).

North Sea rabbits. *WW1.* Herrings; see esp. quot. 1937.

1918 *Chron. NZEF* 22 Nov. 206 Slim Jim leaned back and held up by the tail one of the ever popular 'North Sea Rabbits'. **1935** MITCHELL & STRONG in Partridge *Slang Today* 286 [The] following [was] employed by those who served in the [Great] War..*North Sea rabbits*, English herrings. **1937** PARTRIDGE *Dict. Slang* 569 *North Sea Rabbits*. Herrings as food: New Zealand soldiers': 1916–18. Ex the abundance of herrings in N. Z. camps in England and of rabbits in N.Z.

North Shore. As **the North Shore**, a district on the north shore of Waitemata Harbour; without def. art., formerly a suburb, now a city, part of the greater Auckland conurbation.

1859 *Richmond-Atkinson Papers* (1960) I. 446 The Governor & Mrs Browne have been staying for some time on the North Shore. **1995** *Metro* (Auckland) Sept. 54 Within 20 years the cities which currently have some space—North Shore, Waitakere and Manukau—will be at their metropolitan boundaries. *Ibid.* 55 On the North Shore there's concern about expansion into..rural areas.

north-west, northwester: see NOR-WEST, NOR-WESTER.

nor-west, *a. Canterbury.* Also **nor'-west,** occas. **north-west.** Esp. in collocations: **nor-west day, nor-west weather,** hot and dry as during, or presaging, a NOR-WESTER.

1889 in Wilson *Land of Tui* (1894) 44 All these amusements would seem to be more than enough dissipation in 'nor'-west weather'. **1892** SWANTON *Notes on NZ* 57 There are [in Canterbury] what are called 'nor'-west days', when hardly any wind is perceptible, so named on account of the close, dry heat. **1948** [see NOR'WEST ARCH]. **1952** THOMSON *Deer Hunter* 21 Or, again, he thinks of a hot north-west day with the sun glinting off the shingle. **1952** BLAKISTON *My Yesteryears* 58 We never burned [tussock] in nor'-west weather, or when the ground was bone dry. **1971** CURNOW *Collected Poems 1933–1973* (1974) 92 The sensitive nor'west afternoon Collapsed, and the rain came.

nor'west arch. *Canterbury.* Also occas. **nor'-wester arch.** The arch-shaped line between the cover of cloud overhead and the clear sky above the western sky-line of Canterbury, often preceding and accompanying a nor-wester.

[**1866** BARKER *Station Life* (1870) 54 One morning an arch-like appearance in the clouds over the furthest ranges was pointed out to me as the sure forerunner of a violent gale from the north-west, and the prognostic was fulfilled. **1959** [see NOR-WESTER].] **1948** HAAST *Julius Von Haast* 128 On a Nor'-West day before the Nor'-Wester comes from the north-west across the mountains drained of its moisture, the clouds in the sky form a 'Nor'-Wester' arch. **1959** SLATTER *Gun in My Hand* 19 The sky is clouded but with some blue far to the west where the nor'-west arch sweeps across. **1960** MUIR *Word for Word* 85 White repeated in the high cloud [toward the Southern Alps] with a hint of nor'west arch.

nor-wester. *Canterbury.* Also **north-wester, nor'(-)wester,** occas. with init. caps.

1. The hot, dry wind of the Canterbury Plains.

1849 TORLESSE *Papers* (1958) 47 Heavy North-wester, smothered with sand. **1858** ACLAND *Notes Sheep-farming NZ* 5 This occurs in the early part of summer, when the snow is melted..by a hot wind, termed by the [Canterbury] settlers a nor'wester. **1863** BUTLER *First Year* viii 121 The nor'westers are a very remarkable feature in the climate of this settlement. They are excessively violent, sometimes shaking the very house; hot, dry, from already having poured out their moisture, and enervating like the Italian sirocco... They blow from two or three hours to as many days. **1875** *TrNZI* VII. 106 Usually a north-wester commences about 10 o'clock in the morning. **1887** HOPEFUL *Taken In* 93 As summer approaches, the cold winds change to nor'-westers. These nor'-westers are hot, trying, exhausting winds, and very strong, often accompanied with clouds and clouds of dust. **1910** GROSSMAN *Heart of Bush* 9 Mountains..smoothed into the velvet by the sunset light of a spring Nor'Wester. **1937** *King Country Chronicle* 4 Feb. 4 Unpleasant though the Canterbury nor'wester undoubtedly is, its freakish tricks sometimes have their humorous side. **1948** [see NOR'WEST ARCH]. **1959** SLATTER *Gun in My Hand* 190 And the nor'-westers in summer, the Old Man Nor'-westers, blowing through a great arch over the Alps. **1962** *Landfall Country* 162 The day had been very warm, with a nor-wester threshing at the tops of the firs and bluegums. **1981** MARSH *Black Beech & Honeydew* 56 Some weeks later we were visited by a hot nor'wester, a very trying and enervating wind in our part of New Zealand.

Hence **nor-westery** *a.,* of weather, days, etc., having the climatic qualities associated with a nor-wester.

1962 SHARPE *Country Occasions* 89 On a nor'westery night, when there is no dew, header operators still work long hours.

2. *Mustering.* In the phr. **head a nor'wester,** see HEAD *v.*² 2.

3. nor'-wester arch, see NOR'WEST ARCH.

nose, *n.*¹ Used in *pl.* as a predicate in various verbal phrases (esp. **to rub noses**) which attempt to describe the Maori salutation of HONGI 1 q.v., a pressing of noses. **a. to bump noses.**

1982 in O'Biso *First Light* (1987) 42 As we filed out of the great hall on our way to tea there was a 'receiving line' of sorts and we were expected to bump noses twice, Maori style, with each of the people in the line.

b. to join noses.

1773 BAYLY *Journal* 4 June in McNab *Hist. Records* (1914) II. 209 He joined noses with every one of us. **1793** *Lieut.-Gov. King to Right Hon. Dundas* 19 Nov. in McNab *Hist. Records* (1908) I. 172 Tookee then introduced [the chief] to me, and after the ceremony of etrouge (joining noses) he took off his ha-a-how..and put it on my shoulders. **1804** [see HONGI *n.* 1]. **1823** CRUISE *Journal* 17 Feb. (1957) 30 It is customary with these extraordinary people to go through the same ceremony upon meeting as upon taking leave of their friends. They join their noses together, and remain in this position for at least half an hour.

c. to press noses. (This is a preferred modern English use; see quot. 1984 at e (a) below.)

1838 POLACK *NZ* I. 75 Every one of them came up to press noses. **1847** ANGAS *Savage Life* I. 237 On entering one of the enclosures..these visitors commenced their salutations by pressing noses with each in succession. **1853** GRACE *Letter* 29 Dec. in *Pioneer Missionary* (1928) 35 They should shake hands and 'hongi' (press noses) in the presence of all. **1866** ANGAS *Polynesia* 150 The usual mode of salutation amongst the New Zealanders is that of pressing their noses together. **1945** *JPS* LIV. 97 There is a set pattern for the hongi—clasp hands, briefly press together the tips of the noses, make a wailing sound, press noses briefly for a second time. **1953** LINKLATER *Year of Space* (1954) 201 This old lady cannot speak English, but she has asked me to say that she would like to press noses with you. **1985** ROSIER-JONES *Cast Two Shadows* 88 'Kapai. Kei te pai.' Tui presses noses with the old lady, then Maude.

Hence **nose-press** *n.,* HONGI.

1945 *JPS* LIV. 97 Close relatives hongi for a longer period than the formal brief nose-press.

d. to put noses together.

1769 PARKINSON *Journal* (1773) 19 Nov. 106 We observed that the natives mode of salutation was by putting their noses together.

e. to rub noses. This is a freq. use which does not accurately describe the practice. (a) [Compare OED *rub* 5 d, 1822, of Eskimos (Inuit).]

1819 MARSDEN *Lett. & Jrnls.* (1932) 187 When the public confusion was a little over, Moodee Why and the hoary warrior rubbed noses as a token of reconciliation. **c1835** BOULTBEE *Journal* (1986) 71 These people saluted us by rubbing noses. **1832** EARLE *NZ* 69 We thanked him for the invitation, rubbed noses with him (their token of friendship), and parted. **1840** BEST *Journal* Aug. (1966) 233 To rub noses is a mark of great esteem. **1857** *Lyttelton Times* 2 Sept. 5 Just before Mr. MacLean went away..the contending chiefs met and rubbed noses. **1866** HUNT *Chatham Is.* 17 The usual amount of shaking hands and rubbing noses being over, a long *korero,* or talk, ensued. **1881** CAMPBELL *Poenamo* 142 Had we been Maoris of course we should there and then have also squatted down and rubbed noses. **1911** SHAND *Moriori People* 5 After the recital of this, they then saluted by rubbing noses (*hongi*), as with the Maori. **1933** *Na To Hoa Aroha* (1988) III. 66 I was introduced to him and metaphorically rubbed noses with him on behalf of the Race. **1957** FRAME *Owls Do Cry* (1967) 13 There were, say, six years of peace when Maoris and white people spent every day and night of the years smiling at each other and rubbing noses. **1965** SHADBOLT *Among Cinders* 24 They [*sc.* old Maori women] rubbed noses in the old Maori fashion instead. **1984** CORBALLIS & GARRETT *Witi Ihimaera* 23 Further changes were made before the first 'Tangi' (in *Contemporary Maori Writing*) became the definitive version (in *Pounamu, Pounamu*)... The characters 'rub' noses in the earlier version; they 'press' them in the later one.

(b) *transf.* In European use.

1941 BAKER *NZ Slang* 21 In modern colloquial speech we find that *to rub noses* is used loosely for (a) to greet (a person), (b) to kiss (someone), (c) to plunge into a private conversation with heads close together.

Hence **nose-rubbing** *vbl. n.*; **nose-greeting** *vbl. n.*, HONGI.

1843 DIEFFENBACH *Travels in NZ* I. 61 Observing his embarrassment, we withdrew to some distance, leaving him to indulge his natural feeling in hongi and tangi, or **nose-rubbing** and crying. **1869** *TrNZI* I. (rev. edn.) 355 It is evident that the nose salutations (*hongi*, nose-rubbing), [the baby] was continually receiving from its mother and relatives, must have had a great tendency that way [*sc.* to flattening its nose]. **1881** CAMPBELL *Poenamo* 140 The principal chiefs then..squatted down..to receive the visitors, who are expected to walk up to where the chiefs are sitting and commence nose-rubbing. **1906** *Truth* 17 Mar. 4 The ardent pakeha finds no satisfaction in nose-rubbing. **1905** BAUCKE *White Man Treads* 278 Our college graduate arrives; the home-coming tangi and **nose-greeting** is over.

f. to touch noses.

1769 MONKHOUSE 9 Oct. in Cook *Journals* Oct. (1955) I. 567 But tho' the man saw C. Cook give away his weapon to put himself on a footing with him..he had not courage enough to wait his arrival..., however he at last ventured forward, there was a saluting by touching noses. **1817** NICHOLAS *NZ* I. 91 Duaterra immediately recognised [the chief]..touching noses with him. **1820** MCCRAE *Journal* (1928) 12 On taking leave of these boys I touched noses with them. **c1835** BOULTBEE *Journal* (1986) 68 An old man named Ooree Pahbah came to us..who saluted us by touching noses (the New Zealand custom). **1843** DIEFFENBACH *Travels in NZ* II. 109 When they meet one another, or a European, after the first salutation, by touching noses, they do not remain standing upright, but squat down on their heels. **1981** SUTHERLAND & TAYLOR *Sunrise on Hikurangi* 47 When Bill went back to the shed Dumby touched noses with him.

nose, *n.*² [AND 1941.] In the phr. **on the nose**, of a person or thing, objectionable; unfair.

1946 WEBBER *Johnny Enzed in Italy* 9 You're on the nose, aren't you, pinching a man's letter to his popsie. **1964** HELMER *Stag Party* 48 'Aren't you going to look for what's causing the stink?'... 'It is a bit on the nose, isn't it?' **1981** *Avondale College Slang Words* (Auckland) (Goldie Brown Collect.) *a bit on the nose*: unfair; smelly. **1988** MCGILL *Dict. Kiwi Slang* 77 *nose*, phr. *a bit on the nose* protest at unfairness; eg 'Hey, no spitting, okay? Come on, that's a bit on the nose. Fair dos, eh?'

nose, *v.*

1. Occas. constr. **to nose (with)** (someone), to HONGI.

1773 FORSTER *Resolution Jrnl.* 7 Apr. (1982) II. 248 Then Capt Cook..shook hands with him, & lastly went up to him & nosed him, which is the mark of friendship among these people. **1817** NICHOLAS *NZ* II. 77 Tupee, who upon Korra-korra's coming on deck, *nosed* with him (as our sailors expressed it) in the most affectionate manner.

2. Of a cattle dog, to control (a beast) by biting its nose.

1984 RENNIE *Working Dogs* 39 Cattle dogs will also 'nose' cattle by running beside the animal and biting at its nose while it charges.

nosy, *n.* Also **nosey**. **a.** A nosey-parker; a prying person. Cf. JACK NOHI 1.

1937 MARSH *Vintage Murder* 155 He may be a bit of a nosy but he doesn't look like a murderer.

b. A pry; a good look (around).

1986 *National Radio* 'Landline' (Farming Programme) June 21 [A Central Otago farmer speaks of an advantage of holding discussion groups on other people's farms:] They're also an excuse to have a nosey round other people's farms.

note, *n.*¹ [Spec. use of *note* banknote: AND 1863; cf. also EDD 4 Scottish dial.] A one-pound note; the sum of one pound.

1866 *Lyttelton Times* Aug. 6 [Burgess, Maungatapu bushranger] made use of a cant expression that he had seen 'long tailed ones' the cant phrase for notes. **1868** *Auckland Punch* 63 He asked me to lend him a note so as to make it £2-10. **1875** WOOD AND LAPHAM *Waiting for Mail* 39 When you see me working at the rate Of fifty notes a week!.. And even at half fifty notes a-week, You ought to have made a pile. **1889** WAKEFIELD *NZ after 50 years* 191 The ordinary currency consists of one pound notes of all the six banks, which circulate indiscriminately through the colony. Hence the word 'note' is commonly used for 'pound'. For instance a man may say, 'I gave 100 notes for the cattle', meaning he gave 100 pounds for them, though he may have given a check for the money or ten pound notes. **1891** COTTLE *Frank Melton's Luck* 93 He had me for a few notes I was fool enough to lend him. **1905** *Truth* 30 Sept. 3 She wouldn't return his letters as they might be worth a few hundred notes. **1953** HAMILTON *Till Human Voices Wake Us* 178 They refused to be compelled to deliver their honey to the government and when they were fined fifty notes, they refused to pay. **1961** CRUMP *Hang On a Minute Mate* 129 I reckon we were lucky to get twenty notes for the old girl.

note, *n.*² A system of measuring (and publishing on a 'Board of Honour') weekly attainment in subjects and discipline at Marist Fathers' colleges using a scale of 0 (heinous, but short of expulsion), through 2 (bad), to 5 (excellent)

1935 *St. Patrick's College 1885–1935* 81 Two doors with lead-glass panels..were erected to make the hall more sacrosanct than discipline-notes could make it. **1956** *St Patrick's College, Silverstream 1931–56* 16 Always..'sinker' and notes for this and notes for that. **1962** LAWLOR *More Wellington Days* 144 When he [*sc.* the Rector of St Patrick's College, Wellington, c1905] said those awful words 'a bad note for discipline', it sounded like an echo of 'depart from me...'

notice. *Hist.* Usu. as **to give notice**, to give public notice of intention to drive stock across another person's run. See also *sheep notice* (SHEEP 2).

1863 CHUDLEIGH *Diary* 15 Nov. (1950) 109 It was 5 p.m. before we got [the sheep] to the stopping place... Cooper is gone on giving notices. **1864** *Ibid.* 12 Jan. 118 I had great difficulty to keep several mobs from joining with us. I then went on with notices to King and Rhodes 40 miles again. These notices are a great bother. **1939** BEATTIE *First White Boy Born Otago* 152 In the early days when there were no fences one had to give notice of intention to go through each run... Bill Smith and my brother were once taking 50 sheep up the coast..and went to cross [Hillgrove run] without notice.

notional railway. *Hist.* A former arrangement whereby, through State subsidies, freight was carried by road transport between Nelson and the railhead at Blenheim at lower ruling rail-freight charges.

1958 *NZPD* CCCXVI. 225 Yes, we will build a new railway, but I am not dealing with the railway at the moment; I am dealing with the notional railway... The Nelson railway closed on 3 December 1955. The notional railway started on, I think, 4 November 1957. **1966** TURNER *Eng. Lang. Aust. & NZ.* 157 The oddest of all railways is Nelson's *notional railway* in New Zealand which does not exist, except as a subsidy paid to road transport. **1974** MULDOON *Rise & Fall of a Young Turk* 56 The old railway from Nelson into the interior..had been closed by the Holland Government, but a 'notional' railway had been instituted giving subsidised rail freight rates to the freight carried by road between Nelson and Blenheim.

notornis. [f. the former generic name *notornis* modern Latin (R. Owen 1848) ad. Greek νότος south + ὄρνις bird.] TAKAHE. Also *transf.* (see quots. 1933, 1949).

1848 OWEN in *Proc. Zool. Soc.* 8 The *Notornis* is a large modified form of the same natural family of the *Rallae* as the *Porphyrio* and *Brachypteryx*. **1850** MANTELL in *Proc. Zool. Soc.* 209 Notice of the discovery..in the Middle Island of New Zealand, of a living specimen of the Notornis, a bird of the Rail family. **1866** ANGAS *Polynesia* 61 The *notornis*, owing to the feeble nature of its wings, is incapable of flight, but runs with great swiftness amongst the fern. **1873** BULLER *Birds NZ* 192 Although no examples of the *Notornis* have since been obtained, it does not necessarily follow that the species is absolutely extinct. **1882** *TrNZI* XIV. 239 Perceiving the trail of a large and unknown bird on the snow..they followed the footprints until they obtained a sight of the *Notornis*... It was kept alive for three days and then killed, and the body roasted and eaten by the crew, each partaking of the dainty, which was declared to be delicious. **1900** *Canterbury Old & New* 195 The *Notornis*, longest of our living birds, has not been met with in Canterbury, and is indeed on the verge of extinction. **1927** GUTHRIE-SMITH *Birds* 92 Perhaps in the last drafting, when St. Peter races off the just..I may be there hoping to get on some improved kinematograph, films of the Notornis..yet surviving in the Elysian fields. **1933** *Press* (Christchurch) (Acland Gloss.) 2 Dec. 15 I imagined the word ['skillion'] had gone completely out of use until last month (May, 1933), when I bought five tons of chaff from a man and asked him to store it for a few weeks. He looked into his woolshed and said, 'Oh yes, there's plenty of room in the skillions.' I felt as if I had met a notornis. **1949** *Southern Cross* (Wellington) 23 Aug. 2 [Heading] Is Your Car a Notornis? The name of a New Zealand bird which until recently was thought to be extinct, is used in the additional sense—to describe a car which is so old-fashioned that it has become almost extinct. **1962** FRAME *Edge of Alphabet* 74 There's a valley of the notornis, the flightless bird. **1970** *Notornis* XVII. 67 This encounter [with a Takahe] was approximately 12 km from the closed Notornis area. **1986** HENDERSON *Jim Henderson's People* 161 There's speculation on the remote chance an odd ground owl or kakapo, or even a notornis, may yet be found here.

noxious, *a.*

1. Mainly in the collocation **noxious weed** [cf. OED *noxious a.* 3 *noxious weed* a weed growing on neglected land, esp. in Australia and New Zealand [etc.], 1913], a plant, declared harmful to farmland or stock, which the land-owner is compelled by statute to eradicate from a property; hence **noxious weed inspector**, an official responsible for implementing the control of noxious weeds in rural areas (see quot. 1904).

1844 COLENSO *Excurs. Northern Is.* in Taylor *Early Travellers* (1959) 40 Various species of the genus *Rumex* are now too frequent in several districts, in common with many other noxious European weeds. **1857** *Thistle Amendment Act* in *Acts Provincial Legislature* (1873) 178 Any person who shall fail to eradicate or cut down any noxious Thistles having seed stems growing upon land in his occupation. **1861** GREY *Memorandum* 2 Nov. in Rutherford *Sel. Documents*

(1949) 112(b) For preventing the growth and spread of thistles and other noxious weeds. **1895** *TrNZI* XXVII. 407 [Title] *On the Presence of some Noxious Weeds in Nelson District.* **1900** *NZ Statutes* No.10 20 An Act [Noxious Weeds Act] to prevent the spread of Noxious Weeds and to enforce the Trimming of Hedges... 'Noxious Weeds' means plants mentioned in the First Schedule hereto. **1904** *Free Lance* (Wellington) 20 Feb. 13 One noxious weed inspector, who thought it was 'up to him' to do something for his money, recently strolled on to a farm in Taranaki..and said: 'Hi! Look 'ere..if them blackberries ain't grubbed out by tomorrow, up you goes.' **a1927** ANTHONY *Me & Gus* (1977 Gus Tomlins) 85 He cleared his throat nervously a couple of times and..passed a few remarks on noxious weeds... I wondered if by any chance my visitor was the Noxious Weed Inspector. **1950** *NZ Statutes* No.62 778 'Noxious weeds', in relation to any area means such of the plants mentioned or included in the First Schedule to this [Noxious Weeds] Act as have been declared under this to be noxious weeds in that area. **1966** *Encycl. NZ* III. 597 As used in relation to weeds in New Zealand, the term 'noxious' is a confusing one, as it has two distinct meanings. In a general, non-specific sense, it denotes any weed regarded as significant, for one reason or another, by the use of the term. It has, however, a precise legal meaning denoting weeds whose control and eradication are required under the provisions of the Noxious Weeds Act..and its amendments. These are the so called 'noxious weeds'. **1978** MOORE & IRWIN *Oxford Book NZ Plants* 138 The grey-leaved *C. leptophylla* so invaded neglected hill pastures (as about Wellington) that it, along with the golden tauhinu *C. fulvida*, was designated a 'scheduled noxious weed'.

2. As **noxious animal**, one proscribed by statute as environmentally damaging.
  1956 *NZ Statutes* No.6 29 [Noxious Animals Act] Any noxious animal may be hunted or killed or had in possession by any person in any part of New Zealand. **1960** CRUMP *Good Keen Man* 86 Until we get some real co-operation from these near-sighted cockies, the complete eradication of noxious animals in places like this'll be impossible.

nugget, *n.* Also **nogget**. [f. Brit. dial *nugget* (also *nug*) a lump or block of anything; a short thickset person or animal (Scottish), see EDD: used elsewhere but recorded earliest (and often) in NZ use.]

1. *Southern South Island*. A dumpy islet or block-like rock outcrop in the sea; also used as a place-name.
  1844 BARNICOAT *Journal* (ATLTS) 4 May 169 By night we dropped anchor off the Head, called 'The Nuggetts'. **1844** TUCKETT *Diary* 6 May in Hocken *Contributions* (1898) 216 Within the Noggets [*sic*] I was glad to observe the schooner at anchor. **1857** THOMSON *S. Dists. Otago* 12 Feb. (1959) 333 These eastern ranges continue..to the nuggets on the eastern coast, near the mouth of the river Clutha. **1892** HOCKEN & FENWICK *Holiday Trip* 2 A remarkably beautiful reflection of the breakers and island 'nuggets' off the coast. **1944** BEATTIE *Maori Place-names Otago* 85 There is a little nugget between Te Waitaua and The Neck and this is the nugget that the whaler, 'C. A. Larsen', struck. Its name is Whero (red). **1948** BEATTIE *Otago Place Names* 11 The whalers [early 19th century] called small islets formed of jutting rock 'nuggets', and hence we get the names The Nuggets and Nugget Point. **1964** DEMPSEY *Little World Stewart Is.* 30 They were along the beach near the nugget, where the great bull-kelp writhed and twisted. **1967** NATUSCH *Animals NZ* 267 [The tern] is seen in all New Zealand bays and..nests on islets and 'nuggets'—which are little more than rocks, with a tuft of bush, set in the water.

2. a. *Goldmining*. [AND 1851.] A lump (of alluvial gold).
  1852 LUSH *Auckland Jrnls.* 23 Nov. (1971) 126 One of the boys took out..a small nugget of gold. **1866** SMALL *NZ & Austral. Songster* (1970) 25 And a fifty-pound nugget, bedad, wouldn't draw me Away from this city and my Judy again. **1876** *NZ Mag.* II. 121 *nugget*..from *niggot of gold*: West Country *nig*, *nug* 'block'. **1890** *TrNZI* XXII. 400 How is gold formed into specks and nuggets? **1901** BUTLER *Erewhon Revisited* (Everyman edn. 1960) ii 207 In these [saddlebags] he packed his money, his nuggets, some tea, sugar, tobacco, salt. **1935** BLYTH *Gold Mining Year Book* 11 *Nugget*: Alluvial gold in a solid lump.

b. *Gumfields*. A chunk or lump of kauri gum.
  1900 *Weekly News* 31 Aug. [Caption] 'Nugget' of kauri gum, and digger's spear and spade. **1902** SATCHELL *Land of Lost* 41 He lifted out a nugget about 10 inches long. **1920** MANDER *Story NZ River* (1974) 229 Men..had the chance to pick up in quantities..the nuggets of amber gum which only the Kauri tree produces. **1956** SUTHERLAND *Green Kiwi* (1960) 70 Mechanical outfits for collecting the smaller nuggets..by means of washing were invented. **1963** CAMPBELL *Golden North* 41 They could make a hole through the mud, then reach down and retrieve the nugget of gum which sometimes weighed three or four pounds. **1972** REED *Gumdiggers* 24 In general..the size varied from an occasional nugget weighing a few pounds down to 'nuts'.

3. a. [AND 1852.] A thick-set, chunky animal or person. Cf. NUGGETY *a.* 2. (Quot. 1899 may be a transf. use of 1 a 'something precious': cf. AND 1 b.)
  1871 MEADE *Ride through Disturbed Dist.* in Taylor *Early Travellers* (1959) 428 [The chief] is noted for his preference for a very little steed... It was mounted on some such little 'nugget' that he..distinguished himself at Rotoiti. **1899** BELL *In Shadow of Bush* 86 And this is your little sister, I suppose? Well, she is a nice little nugget, anyhow; and here's sixpence to buy lollies for her and you. **1968** *NZ Contemp. Dict. Suppl.* (Collins) 14 *nugget..n.* small, solidly built horse.

b. As a man's nickname.
  1912 CHUDLEIGH *Diary* 29 July (1950) 458 McGregor with a 4 horse dray, Nugget Dix with a 3 horse dray. **1918** *NZ at the Front* 110 [If you] asked 'How are you Tom?' he'd invariably answer, 'I'm thirsty, Nugget; you ain't got a pint about yer, eh?' **1973** WALLACE *Generation Gap* 209 I was horrified to hear the owner [of the mailcar], 'Nugget' they called him, say to the driver..And for Gawd's sake, don't kill 'em.

4. [In transf. use as a proprietary name of a boot and shoe polish, perh. from its being orig. sold as a 'nugget' or lump of blacking.] Boot or shoe polish, orig. black (but see quot. 1960), and orig., usu. with init. cap., a specific proprietary name. Also *attrib*.
  1903 *Supplement to the N.Z. Gazette* 1 Oct. The 'Nugget' 4349 [filed] 27th August, 1903. Preserving Leather from Cracking..The Nugget Polish Company Limited..London... Preparations for cleaning and polishing leather goods. **1914** *Letter* 18 Aug. in Pugsley *Gallipoli* 52 Please post me my nugget outfit and a spare tin or two of nugget. **1925** *Evening Post* (Wellington) 5 Jan. 11 Made by the manufacturers of Nugget Boot Polish—therefore it's good. 'Nugget' is made in Black, Brown (Tan), Dark Brown, Toney Red; also White for patent and Coloured Glace Leathers. **1948** in McKay *James K. Baxter* (1990) 116 Early that morning he turned up at Baigent's place and said: 'Lawrence, you haven't any nugget, have you? I'm getting baptized today and look at my shoes.' **1960** KEINZLY *Tangahano* 152 The cocoa was like melted shoe nugget and the toast had stuck to the cloth, soldered in its own grease. **1974** BREAM *I'm Sorry Amanda* 31 I added 'Nugget and brushes' to my shopping list. **1985** MCGILL *G'day Country* 62 I knew them well, from..playing hopscotch laid out with coloured chalk, using Nugget tins filled with earth. **1986** RICHARDSON *Choices* 95 Before the party broke up, the boys got some nugget and a brush and blackened the sleeping cook's face and bald head.

Hence **nugget-black**, a deep black colour; **nugget-blacked** *a*, blackened with nugget polish..
  1936 HYDE *Passport to Hell* 84 Exception was also taken to the words 'Rummies Retreat', which appeared in enormous words of **nugget-black** upon Tent Eight [at Trentham Military Camp]. **1986** HULME *Windeater* 120 A nugget-black bug rollicked under the till. **1936** HYDE *Passport to Hell* 176 Their **nugget-blacked** faces made them look like limp and shattered Christy minstrels.

nugget, *v.*[1] [f. NUGGET *n.* 1: AND 1851.] Usu. as **nugget out**, to dig (gold) out in nugget form.
  c1862 Sept. in 1887 PYKE *Hist. Early Gold Discoveries Otago* (1962) 82 'There,' said I 'is where the gold was got'; and on breaking up the surface, the first thing I discovered was a bit of about 3dwts; and that afternoon we nuggeted out 9oz. 6dwts. 3grs. **1977** MURRAY *Costly Gold* 7 By the end of the afternoon he had 'nuggeted out nine ounces and twelve grains'.

nugget, *v.*[2] [f. NUGGET *n.* 4.] *trans.* To apply black boot or shoe polish to, to blacken with Nugget polish.
  1963 *Dominion* (Wellington) 30 Oct. 12 The incident of the egg occurred last July, but it was also stated in evidence that the same [Fire Brigade] officer had his helmet nuggeted about four years ago. **1981** JOHNSTON *Fish Factory* 167 Danny got a bit stroppy for a while when some of the jokers had tried to nugget his knackers. **1987** KNOX *After Z-Hour* 72 It was a carved wooden gun, nuggeted black and filthy to hold. **1991** WOLFE *Kiwi* 37 Even in the home of the bird it is still more usual to 'nugget' one's boots.

Hence **nuggeting** *vbl. n.*, see quot.
  1988 MCGILL *Dict. Kiwi Slang* 77 *nuggeting* unpleasant male party habit of removing victim's trousers and underpants and applying Nugget shoe polish to testicles; eg 'Let's get him pissed then give him a good nuggeting.'

nuggety, *a.* Also **nuggetty**. [f. NUGGET *n.* 1 + -Y.]

1. [AND 1852.] Of gold, in the form of lumps.
  1857 *McLean Papers* (ATLTS) IV. 83 The gold is becoming more nuggetty ranging from a pin's head to a bean. **1861** *Otago Witness* (Dunedin) 23 Mar. 10 Where the diggers are now working, the gold is almost all nuggetly, some running as large as horse beans. **1875** HOGG *Lays & Rhymes* 176 'Twas when the Rocky River rush began..and stories told Of ounces gotten in a single pan, Of nuggety, and round, and shotty gold. **1887** PYKE *Hist. Early Gold Discoveries Otago* (1962) 60 The gold is described..as being of a very 'fine description'—'not much waterworn', and 'half-pea nuggety'. **1898** *TrNZI* XXX. 500 The effect of such matters..was rather to disperse any gold it reduces than to concentrate such gold in a nuggetty form. **1940** HOWARD *Rakiura* 232 They..obtained the heaviest gold yet seen in rough nuggety pieces up to ½ dwt. in size. **1968** TOMLINSON *Remembered Trails* 125 The gold from Digger's was more nuggety and from Patriarch it was nearly black. **1981** DENNIS *Paparoas Guide* 68 The gold soon gained a reputation for being coarse and nuggety.

2. Thickset, compactly built, and sturdy. **a.** [AND 1856.] Of a person.

1938 LANCASTER *Promenade* 67 Lean Yankee boat-steerers and harpooners, nuggetty little breeds from Quebec. **1946** SARGESON *That Summer* 66 He wasn't a rangy specimen like me, no, he was nuggetty. **1971** *Listener* 19 Apr. 56 Well, out of the boo-ai comes three trampers. One was a nuggety bloke in a sou'wester. **1986** DAVIN *Salamander & the Fire* 72 He was big and tough and nuggety and he didn't look like one of those smoothies from town.

b. [AND 1893.] Of an animal.
1953 MIDDLETON in *Short Stories* (1966) 187 Belle [a sheep-dog] was..more nuggetty, but still powerful.

number, *n.* and *attrib.*

A. *n.* [See OED *number n.* 3 f *'Austral. and N.Z.'*.] Elementary arithmetic taught to children in primary school.
1922 *NZ Education Gaz. 1 Dec.* 137 Miss Caldwell has published a book entitled 'The Simplicity of Number', a copy of which, along with the apparatus, can..be obtained from her by teachers. **1963** PEARSON *Coal Flat* 63 You'd best make sure of his reading and his number and see if he's good enough for this class.

B. *attrib.* In designatory collocations with a numeral.

1. Number 2. a. See quot.
1925 BATHGATE *Random Recolls.* 17 Pale brandy or P.B. was the favourite spirit [in Dunedin, 1860s], and a sparkling moselle, which was dubbed champagne, was popular under the name of No. 2. There was even a bar on board the harbour steamer..and I have heard No. 2 called for there on the way to Port Chalmers... I was told that owing to the large sales of No. 2 the producers sent a consignment of No. 1, which was the better liquor, but no one would buy it.

b. *Prison. Obs.* Restricted diet No. 2 (now abolished).
1982 NEWBOLD *Big Huey* 251 Number Two (n) Restricted diet No. 2 (abolished).

2. Number 5 (Five). a. *Hist.* See quot.
1898 HOCKEN *Contributions* 111 It was not long before the seed of dissension appeared in the young community. The fifth number of the [*Otago*] *News*, long known as 'Number 5', indulged in a very free and unfavourable criticism of the Otago block,.. after scolding the editor, Captain Cargill withdrew his subscription... Thenceforth the paper became an enemy.

b. *Hist.* **Number Five Scheme.** The government relief scheme in the 1930s depression.
1962 GLOVER *Hot Water Sailor* 82 Waitakiri Golf Links is a monument to what was then [1930's Depression] known as the Number Five Scheme.

3. number eight (wire). Also **No(.) 8.** With and without caps. The standard Number 8 gauge (4 mm) smooth fencing wire, esp. when used inventively and practically for other than fencing purposes. **a.** In fencing applications.
1876 *Saturday Advertiser* 8 July 10 [Advt] Fencing Wire, Nos. 6, 7, 8, 9, and 10; Fencing Staples and Wire Stretchers. **1883** *Brett's Colonists' Guide* 77 Five wires at the bottom of No. 8, and two wires at the top of No. 6, will require 1 ton 7 cwt. per mile. **1894** *NZ Official Year-book* 514 A good paling fence on ordinary bushlands with double No. 8 wires at top and bottom..can be erected at about 12s. per chain. **1946** MILLER *There Was Gold* 97 No. 8 wire was to him as string is to the average man. He could tie it..and with a strainer he could tighten a wire until it literally sang when it was flicked. **1950** *NZJAg.* July LXXXI. 10 The palings are interwoven by a double No. 8 wire at the top and a double No. 8 wire at the bottom. **1962** EVANS *Waikaka Saga* 131 The variety so well known as No. 8 has become the unwritten standard for New Zealand fences. **1985** SHERWOOD *Botanist at Bay* 131 'They were buying a roll of number eight.' 'Fencing wire,' Johnson interjected. **1992** ANDERSON *Portrait Artist's Wife* 33 Squatting on his heels he coiled it and held it up. 'It's only a bit of old number eight.'

b. In non-fencing applications, *occas. fig.*
1973 WILSON *NZ Jack* 27 Then eventually we made barbs for our harpoons, by cutting a length of Number Eight wire from some farm fence. **1973** WHEELER *Hist. Sheep Stations NI* 102 A very long toasting fork made of twisted No. 8 fencing wire, last night's unwashed coffee cups. **1978** SUTHERLAND *Elver* 37 Each bale had half a kerosine tin with handle made of number eight wire. **1987** CHRISTIE *Candles & Canvas* 150 The swing bridge, made of No 8 fencing wire, made a good support for the pipelines. **1989** GIBBONS *Recollections* 43 The home-made toasting forks... were made from No. 8 wire. **1994** *Dominion* (Wellington) 8 Aug. 9 [Kiwi shoplifters] have a number-eight fencing wire inventiveness that probably makes them the best store thieves in the world. **1994** *Quote Unquote* Nov. 30 Despite this failure Richard Pearse was a genuine Kiwi original—a No 8-wire man of the first rank.

numbfish. Also with a modifier: **blind numbfish, southern numbfish.** Any of several ray-like fishes able to deliver an electric shock. See also *electric ray* and *torpedo ray* (RAY 2 (2) and (4)), SKATE *n.*¹ 2 (1).
1898, 1927 [see RAY 2 (4)]. **1930** *NZJST* XI. 98 Southern numbfish, or Whai Repo. The Southern numbfish was first described as new by Hutton in 1872. *Ibid.* 100 Blind Numbfish. This numbfish was first described by Hamilton. **1956** GRAHAM *Treasury NZ Fishes* 90 Blind Torpedo Ray or Numbfish *Typhlonarke aysoni. Ibid.* 92 This uncommon fish has several names, all of which relate to its manner of producing electric shocks, some of which are Numb-fish, Crampfish and Electric Skate. These vernacular names are given by fishermen on account of the fish benumbing or paralysing the person who unwittingly grasps one with his hands. **1967** NATUSCH *Animals NZ* 202 [The ray] *T[orpedo] aysoni*, the numbfish or cramp fish, is round, with short tail and pelvic fins, and grows up to 3 ft. **1981** WILSON *Fisherman's Bible* 198 Blind Torpedo Ray. A rare ray, *Typhlonarke aysoni*, as he is called in Latin, has the ability to emit sparks and make a needle magnetic—yet not to see. Variously named Numbfish, Crampfish and Electric Skate.

nut, *n.* [Poss. f. *nut* a small lump (or a specific grade) of household coal: cf. OED *n.*¹ 19 *pl.*, 1870.] A small piece or grade of kauri-gum. See also GUM 2 and 3, *gumnut* (GUM 3 b).
1923 *NZJST* VI. 96 One ingenious individual, knowing that white 'range nuts' were twice as valuable as black 'nuts', obtained a quantity of the latter and carefully shook them up with some white pipeclay from the hillside. **1948** REED *Gumdigger* 13 A few 'nuts' of gum. **1960** BOSWELL *Ernie* 137 Then there was the washing of the 'nuts' (gum too small to be scraped). **1963** CAMPBELL *Golden North* 48 It was not nut gum but large pieces that meant hard digging. **1966** [see CHIP *n.*¹ 2]. **1972** REED *Gumdiggers* 60 To clean 'nuts'—anything up to the size perhaps of a pullet's egg—a different method was used.

nut, *v. Two up.* [f. *nut* slang for 'head'.] As **nut 'em!,** see quot.
1937 PARTRIDGE *Dict. Slang* 575 *nut' em.* Mostly as *nutted'em!*, an exclamatory c[atch]p[hrase] when the pennies turn up two heads in 'two-up': Australian and New Zealand: C. 20. Ex *nut*, the head.

nutmeg-tree. [f. the taste of the leaf.] HOROPITO 1, PEPPER-TREE 2.
1919 in *TrNZI* (1927) LVII. 944 nutmeg tree *Drimys axillaris* Ver. (WB) [=Vernacular names, used by early settlers, supplied [to Johannes Andersen] by W. Best of Otaki, on 29th July, 1919.].

N.Z.: see also ENZED; NEW ZEALAND D.

Nzder. Abbrev. of NEW ZEALANDER; var. ENZEDDER (see ENZED 2 a).

NZEF *WW1.* and *WW2.*: see *New Zealand Expeditionary Force* (NEW ZEALAND B 4 b).

O

-o. Also **-oh**. The *-o(h)* suffix, in nouns prob. deriving from street cries (e.g. *bottle-oh!*), is not as frequent and widespread in New Zealand as the *-ie* suffix. Nor is it common (as in Australia, see AND) as a final syllable added to shortened polysyllabic nouns (*journo*) or to monosyllabic forms (Australian *Greeko*). See separate entries for ARVO, BERKO, BOTTLE-OH, COMPO, DERO, DONKO, JOURNO, METHO, *rabbit-o(h)* (RABBIT *n.* 1), SMOKO, SPELL-OH; and -IE suffix.
1984 *Listener* 14 Apr. 13 Smoko was held in the donko, where we'd adjourn after working like billyo. (The old tendency for working argot to end words in 'o' appears to have been displaced by modern tendencies to end it in 'ie' like 'bikkie' and 'prezzie'.)

oak. Usu. as **New Zealand oak**, any of various trees whose wood is thought to resemble English oak, esp. PURIRI q.v.; the wood of these trees.
c1826–27 BOULTBEE *Journal* (1986) 110 oak— ēnak [inaka]. **1835** YATE *NZ* (1970) 43 Puriri... This tree, from its hardness and durability, has been denominated the New-Zealand Oak. **1840** *NZ Jrnl.* I. 139 Among the hard woods the Puriri.., which has been called the oak of the Pacific, and the New Zealand oak, seems to bid fair to be the most useful. **1860** BENNETT *Gatherings Naturalist* 347 [The pohutukawa] is the New Zealand Oak and Fire-tree of the Europeans. **1869** [see TEAK]. **1883** *Brett's Colonists' Guide* 190 Puriri, or New Zealand Oak..is one of the most valuable trees on the North Island... It is sometimes called ironwood, and is considered equal to English oak in stiffness, strength, and durability. **1892** BROOKES *Frontier Life* 174 The puriri is called the New Zealand oak. **1907** LAING & BLACKWELL *Plants NZ* 350 *Vitex lucens* (*The Puriri*). A fine tree, from 50ft. to 60ft. in height, often called the *New Zealand Oak*, on account of the strength and durability of its timber. **1963** KEENE *O te Raki* 194 *Puriri*: New Zealand oak, a large, handsome tree with hard timber.

Oamaru stone. [f. *Oamaru* a town in North Otago near which the stone is quarried.] A white, easily worked limestone formerly much used for building.
1870 *TrNZI* II. 168 I presume this formation has been generally considered to overlie immediately the Oamaru building stone... Interposed between the 'Blue clay' and Oamaru stone, is a layer of sand. **1876** *TrNZI* VIII. 140 The most important building material that hitherto has been used in Otago. viz. the *Oamaru Stone*. The use of this material is coeval with the settlement of the district in which it occurs, but it was little known beyond until 1866, when an export trade commenced with Dunedin. **1883** HECTOR *Handbook of NZ* 64 A white, granular limestone, called the Oamaru stone, is worked in extensive quarries in the Oamaru district... A considerable quantity has been exported to Melbourne. **1923** *Auckland Capping Book* 16 There are some men sawing Oamaru stone in Princes Street [for the university building]. **1938** *NZ Observer* 28 July 8 Oamaru, with its brilliant white buildings of Oamaru stone, can be seen a long way off on a sunny day. **1951** CRESSWELL *Canterbury Tales* 81 The architect..set up on the bare plain an Elizabethan style in brick, faced with white Oamaru stone. **1982** MARSHALL *Master of Big Jingles* 68 Our farm was in two parts... The bottom place had an old Oamaru-stone house on it when my father bought it. **1990** *Dominion Sunday Times* (Wellington) 18 Nov. 13 Stonemason Kerry Dooley says Oamaru stone is good to carve and cut because it doesn't shatter.

oarfish. [See quot. 1927.] *Regalecus glesne* (fam. Regalecidae), a long silvery eel-like fish.
1872 HUTTON & HECTOR *Fishes NZ* 35 Regalecus gladius... Oar Fish. **1881** *TrNZI* XIII. 196 They are usually long, deep and very much compressed and flattened on the sides, so much so that their local appellations always embody some idea of these peculiarities—such as ribband-fish, lath or deal fish, band-fish or blade-fish, and also oar-fish. **1891** *NZJSc.* (NS) I. 154 On its arrival in Christchurch..I found the fish to be a species of *Regalecus*, or oar-fish of unusually large proportions. **1902** DRUMMOND & HUTTON *Nature in NZ* 74 The flesh of deep sea fishes, such as the ribbon fish and the oarfish, becomes a jelly when boiled, and is quite unfit to eat. **1927** SPEIGHT et al. *Nat. Hist. Canterbury* 198 The Oar-fish, 12 to 20 feet long, with a high, flame-tipped head-crest (the elongated fin rays) is probably the sea-serpent of repute. Its pelvic fins are narrow, elongated processes, hence the name Oar-fish. **1930** *NZJST* XI. 428 The capture of an oar-fish seems to be worth putting on record... It was washed ashore at Warrington, Otago..in calm weather. **1947** POWELL *Native Animals NZ* 65 Silvery Oarfish (*Regalecus argenteus*). This is a bizarre inhabitant of the ocean depths, which comes to the surface on rare occasions in New Zealand. **1982** AYLING *Collins Guide* (1984) 190 *Oarfish Regalecus glesne* (*Regalecus pacificus*)... It has been suggested that sightings of large oarfishes have been responsible for sailors' reports of sea serpents. As adult oarfish range in size from 3m, and the longest specimen recorded from New Zealand was over 5.5m, this confusion is easy to understand.

oat grass: see GRASS 2 (27).

oath. [See OED *oath* 1 c.] In exclamations of enthusiastic assent, 'certainly!' **a.** As **my colonial oath** [AND 1859]. Also *ellipt*. **my colonial**.
[**1892** KIPLING *One Lady at Wairakei* (1983) 41 With savage gestures and a hundred hurrying colonial oaths, told a tale of a riotous living.] **1897** WRIGHT *Station Ballads* 29 But, my blooming straight Colonial! there are two things in that cart..and them things is *grit and heart*. **1946** *Johnny Enzed Italy* 35 'My oath!' said the Bloke. 'My Colonial oath!' **1988** MCGILL *Dict. Kiwi Slang* 74 *my colonial oath!* a mild expletive used usually as reinforcement, with variations such as *my oath!*, *my bloody oath!*, *my bloody colonial oath!*
b. As **my oath** [AND 1869].
1906 [see BOSKER A]. **1909** *Truth* 29 May 5 When one comes to think of it, instead of saying 'Rightly, sir,' Connelly would have remarked, 'They picked it, my oath,' or words to that effect. **1918** *Quick March* 1 Nov. 17 But, my oath! They plays up 'Ell wiv our chaps. **1925** COOK *Far Flung* 12 'Perhaps you'll square up?' 'My oath!' said the debtor. **1932** SCANLAN *Pencarrow* 248 'Hot driving today?' 'My oath!' **1945** HENDERSON *Gunner Inglorious* 140 'And on top of that we'll be eligible for Social Security.' 'My oath yes.' **1951** MARSH *Opening Night* (1968) iv 43 'My oaff,' he said, 'what a daisy!' **1962** *Landfall Country* 119 'My oath I'll ring the Mayor,' Larry said. **1976** O'SULLIVAN *Miracle* 14 The man who had called for order said 'Hear, hear,' and this was taken up by several others, some of whom said 'Oath' or 'Too right' or 'That's the line to take'.
c. (a) As **(my) bloody, bloomin'**, etc. **oath** [AND 1848].
1943 JACKSON *Passage to Tobruk* 19 My bloomin' oath I am. **1947** DAVIN *For Rest of Our Lives* 352 My bloody oath they did. **1960** MUIR *Word for Word* 254 'She knew all right,' the man said. 'Bloody oath. That's why she done it.' **1986** HULME *Windeater* 79 I have never won anything. I reach across, grab his hand, shake it... 'Bloody oath, Mat what good luck!' **1990** EDWARDS *AWOL* 7 'My bloody oath I do!' I was beginning to do my block.
(b) As **'kin oath, k'noath**, euphemisms for '(my) fuckin' oath'.
1985 O'SULLIVAN *Shuriken* 58 I'll have to report this, Jacko. Jacko: K'noath. We'll both report it. **1988** MCGILL *Dict. Kiwi Slang* 66 '*kin oath* rude avowal; contraction of 'fucking oath'; eg 'That was a bastard of a stump to dig out.' ''Kin oath, mate. 'Kin oath.'

oatmeal water. A refreshment for shearers or outdoor workers, a mixture of water, sugar and oatmeal. See also BEER, BROSE, BURGOO 2.
1949 NEWTON *High Country Days* 196 Oatmeal water: A billy of water in which oatmeal and sugar is mixed is kept in the shearing shed. Plain water is inclined to have a weakening effect on anyone who is working hard. **1987** HARTLEY *Swagger on Doorstep* 188 After breakfast Dad left the house with mugs and a cream can of oatmeal water—a refreshing drink of rain water, lemon juice and a large handful of oatmeal.

octopus clamp. *Obs.* **a.** A hold in wrestling, reputedly difficult to remove once put on, the trademark of Meynell Strathmore ('Lofty') Blomfield (1908–71), a New Zealand champion wrestler in the 1930s. See quot. 1973.
1938 *Auckland Weekly News* 19 Jan. 63 Thereby hangs the tale of the 'Octopus Clamp' and the new name of Maynell Lofty Blomfield. The hold is a cross between that Boston crab of Jack Forsgren's and Chief Thunderbird's Indian deathlock. **1940** in *In Their Own Words* (1988) 89 A Sergeant Major in the forces with a longing desire to put the old octopus clamp on Hitler and Mussolini... [Lofty Blomfield:] And if I ever get the clamp on Hitler and Mussolini it will take more than a referee to take it off again. **1950** *Southern Cross* (Wellington) 22 June 11 Today, when anybody finds himself in an inextricable position, he is said to be in an 'octopus clamp'. **1962** INGRAM *Legends in their Lifetime* 18 Wellingtonians saw Alf Jenkins..untangling the wrestlers from what was reported as 'a clamp applied by an octopus'. Thus was born the octopus clamp. **1973** MCCARTHY *Listen...!* 55 Lofty [Blomfield] was just perfecting his own special hold, the Octopus Clamp or,

as Hutter used to call it, the Rangitoto special. It was applied by Blomfield scissoring his opponent's legs while on the ground, then by force of his legs bringing the opponent over on to his face, at the same time forcing the opponent's knee up over his own knee while still retaining the scissors.

b. *transf.* or *fig.* A strong grip.
   1981 *Listener* 28 Nov. 33 St Kilda: Famous for lifesavers and brass bands. Labour's plan to give Golden Kiwi grants to brass bands composed of life-savers should strengthen its octopus clamp on St Kilda.

OE /ˈʌuˈiː/. Also **O.E.** A familiar abbrev. of *overseas experience* (OVERSEAS B).
   1975 *Listener* 5 July 10 We are both suffering from what the rich call a jaded palate, others call 'Cultural Imperialism' and what my sophisticated friends call OE depression. OE, of course, is the abbreviation for overseas experience—and no New Zealander, it is claimed, is complete without it. As well as being vital to emotional and intellectual (and sexual) development, OE very nicely fills that awkward gap between high school and marriage. **1976** *Ibid.* 21 Aug. 12 I found on my brief OE that Englishmen everywhere warmed appreciably when I was able to prove I wasn't from Queensland. **1982** *Pacific Index Abbrev.* 229 OE.. Overseas Experience. **1986** OVENDEN *O.E.* 6 O.E., as every New Zealander knows, means Overseas Experience. The term refers, as in such colloquial phrases as: 'He's gone to get his O.E., eh,'; or 'Got your O.E. yet then?' to that most rare of concepts, an abstract consumer durable. **1986** *Evening Post* (Wellington) 8 Apr. 22 We are now at their OE stage—Deborah lives with her older sister Lee-Ann in Kansas, Lisa and Shirleen flat together in Sydney. **1995** *Sunday Star-Times* (Auckland) 28 May sect. D 22 This is my last column before I take off on OE.

Hence **OEing**, undertaking or gaining 'overseas experience'.
   1986 *Wellington City Magazine* Nov. 14 It seems that his hard-scrabble idea of OEing did not engage the imagination of several other Wellington expats.

off.
1. *Shearing.* See quot.
   1933 *Press* (Christchurch) (Acland Gloss.) 11 Nov. 15 *Off*... Slang. A shearer speaks of being *o[ff]* when he has finished a sheep and put him out through the port hole.

2. In the phr. **off like a robber's dog** [cf. EDD *long dog*], an expression of speedy departure.
   1959 *The Standard* (Wellington) 19 Aug. 9 When the whistle goes, some workers are 'off like a robber's dog'.

3. off the blades, off (the) shears, see BLADE *n.*[1] 2, SHEAR *n.* 1 b.

off course substitute. *Horse-racing.* See quots.
   1954 *Truth* 2 June 3 The off-course substitute is the horse favoured most in the second-leg wagering by backers using the T.A.B. The decision to employ this method of transferring the winning first-leg tickets when the punters' nominated second leg does not start was arrived at after mature consideration. **1970** *Horse Racing [etc.] in NZ* 78 If the horse nominated for the second leg [of an off-course double] is withdrawn, the TAB substitutes for that horse the favourite for the race shown by the TAB doubles bets. The horse is known as the 'off-course substitute'.

office. *Musterers. Obs.* See quot.
   1934 *Press* (Christchurch) (Acland Gloss.) 27 Jan. 15 *Office.*—A small patch of grass high up in an almost perpendicular rock wall, which offers only one way in and out for a few sheep or even a dog. The word was in general use among the genuine high country men of 40 or 50 years ago, but may (a correspondent says) not be much used now, as too many modern musterers are conveniently blind to an *o[ffice]*.

official stamp. Also *ellipt.* **official.** A current stamp overprinted 'Official' for use by Government Departments from 1907 until 1954, from which latter time special designs were used until the issue was discontinued in 1965.
   1906 *NZ Gazette* 20 Dec. 3287 The 'Official' overprinted stamps shall on no account be used for prepaying other than official correspondence or telegrams, and no officer or other person shall exchange 'Official' stamps for cash, or for stamps of the ordinary issue. **1914** *AJHR F-1* 5 To minimize illicit trafficking in 'official' stamps issued for the use of Government Departments, it was decided in November, 1913, to sell the stamps to the public on the understanding that they were not available for the prepayment of postage. **1938** *Postage Stamps of NZ* I. 461 In August, 1906, Cabinet decided that 'as from 1st January next, the existing system of franking letters, packets and telegrams sent on public service is to be abolished and that in lieu thereof such correspondence is to be paid for by means of official stamps'. **1953** LEE et al. *Penny Universal NZ* 16 On January 1, 1908, the Auckland District Officer, Department of Health, suggested that official stamps should be bound into booklets as it was not unusual for loose stamps to stick together. **1969** *NZ Bulletin (Woking)* VII. No.2 2 We had on hand..about 500 used 8d officials..all done up neatly, just as we had bought them, in bundles of 100. **1988** STRACHAN *Century of Philately* 256 As the prosecution had claimed that officials were not postage stamps but merely inter-departmental accountancy labels and could not be used by the public a licence was not required to sell them.

offside. [from team sport, esp. rugby.] In the phr. **offside with** [AND 1979], in bad odour with; esp. **to put** (oneself) **(get) offside with** (a person, etc.), to put (oneself) in bad with; **to get** (someone) **offside**, to put (someone) in bad (with another person).
   1944 COMBS *Half Lengths* 8 Harris began to put himself off-side with some of the leading citizens. **1950** SIMPSON *Chatham Exiles* 149 To be 'Off-side' with the Maori residents is to be deprived of even these unreliable services. **1969** HASCOMBE *Down & Almost Under* 32 As well as..putting us 'offside' with neighbours..[he] is now a canine luxury par excellence. **1995** ANDERSON *House Guest* 132 Once again, Murray had sidetracked the conversation, deflected the course and got him offside [*sc.* with a woman friend].

offsider.
1. [AND 1879.] A bullock-driver's assistant, orig. one attending to the 'off side' (or right-hand side facing front) of a bullock team.
   [a1914] MCCARROLL *The Days of the Kauri Bushmen* (Radio Talk 3 (1951): TS) The bullocky's offsider was the chap who helped the bullock driver, and the origin of the name 'offsider' came about this way; very often when a team is operating it is necessary for someone to run round on the off side and push or force point bullocks over quickly..for instance when going round a corner or avoiding some obstacle..also to give general help. **1934** [see 2 a below]. **1953** REED *Story of Kauri* 184 The bullock-driver usually had an assistant called an offsider. **1969** MOORE *Forest to Farm* 42 [Northland c 1920] The team was hitched to the rear of the waggon, and the Maori 'offsider', a somewhat irresponsible youth was instructed to guide the two polers.

2. a. [AND 1879.] An assistant.
   1922 TURNER *Happy Wanderer* 8 He will get you on as an offsider. **1934** *Press* (Christchurch) (Acland Gloss.) 27 Jan. 15 *Off-sider.*—Assistant. Now mostly applied to the *slushy*, or cook's mate, but the term may have originated with the old bullock drivers, who drove their teams from the near side... I have heard a bullocky speak of his dog as his *o[ff] s[ider]*. **1943** MARSH *Colour Scheme* 162 I shan't tell Simon... His present theory will lead him to behave like the recording angel's offsider. **1952** RHODES *Fly Away Peter* 122 He said it wouldn't have mattered if it had been his half-witted cowman, but Johnny Holden and that off-sider of his are two of the best musterers in the Gorge. **1969** MOORE *Forest to Farm* 88 My 'offsider' is Ralph, a young man who does not know much about bush work. **1976** SARGESON *Sunset Village* 73 Tups and his offsider were fortunate enough to be much informed by the young orderly on duty at the morgue. **1993** *Dominion* (Wellington) 16 Aug. 10 After he left the shop I heard the butcher say to his offsider, 'I don't like blokes like that in my shop'.

b. [AND 1910.] Specifically, often as **cook's offsider**, a farm, camp, or army cook's assistant; a kitchen hand. Cf. SLUSHY *n.*[1] 1.
   1917 in Miller *Camps, Tramps & Trenches* 27 Sept. (1939) 144 I missed, being cook's offsider, whose principal job is to collect wood. **1929** SMYTH *Girl From Mason Creek* 206 The Maori boy who acted as the cook's 'offsider'. **1935** STRONG in Partridge *Slang Today* 288 It's the offsider I'm talking about because he winked at me when the trump of the dump asked him if he had barbered the spuds for tomorrow's breakfast. **1944** BRUNO *Desert Daze* 49 [The cook] hearing of the unexpected arrival of a number of reinstouchments snarled to his offsiders. **1951** MCLEOD *NZ High Country* 27 One classer..[etc.] make up the shed contingent and the cook and 'offsider' complete the total. **1962** SHARPE *Country Occasions* 36 A contract shearing gang is complete, right down to the cook's offsider. **1973** FERNANDEZ *Tussock Fever* 16 The only people left working were the cook and her two off-siders, cleaning up after the meal. **1975** HARPER *Eight Daughters* 56 The [station] cook's offsider..was a gullible chap and the boys often played practical jokes on him. **1995** ANDERSON *House Guest* 60 He was promoted to mains... He was Spiro's right-hand man, his offsider.

c. In a weakened sense companion, mate, 'sidekick'.
   1938 *Auckland Weekly News* 23 Nov. 96 If you and that off-sider of yours step it out, you'll just about catch a train. **1991** ELDRED-GRIGG *Shining City* 116 Mark Hand was an offsider, someone who drifted along and agreed with us.

3. An offside bullock, any one of a team on the right-hand side facing front.
   1953 REED *Story of Kauri* 184 The cleared land would then be ploughed with one or two pairs of bullocks, and though the ploughman would not have the assistance of a driver..the offsider would not put a foot out of the furrow from end to end.

og(g): var. HOG *n.*

-oh, var. -O.

ohau. *South Island.* FIVE-FINGER 1. See also WHAUWHAU a.
   1907 [see WHAUWHAU a]. **1940** LAING & BLACKWELL *Plants NZ* 331 *Schefflera digitata*... Maori name *Patete, Ohau,* (the latter name chiefly on Banks Peninsula). The wood is soft, and was used by the Maoris in obtaining fire. **1940** STUDHOLME *Te Waimate* (1954) 246 In this bush were..Ohau, (panax or five-finger)..and other shrubs.

ohi, var. OI.

ohu /ˈʌuhu/. [Ma. /ˈohu/: Williams 238 *Ohu* (i) *1*. n. Company of volunteer workers.]

1. A group of volunteer workers; a working bee.
   1862 *Richmond-Atkinson Papers* 18 Apr. I. 755 In evg. went up to the foot of Totaraiahua to an ohu of Tutanekai who are digging potatoes there. **1921** *NZJST* IV. 88 Under the custom of *ohu* the men were assembled assisting a man to make a garden at some distance from the *whare* (houses). **1930** *Na To Hoa Aroha* (1987) II. 34 Road-making on a 50/50 basis with the local bodies, ohu or mahi-apu in relation to scrub-cutting..gave ample evidence of self-help. **1949** KOHERE *Story of a Maori Chief* 28 The work was performed by what was called an 'ohu' or working-bee. Only in this case the whole community..formed the 'ohu'. **1988** KING *Apirana Ngata* [Caption] The ohu, or working bee, which cleared and sowed the Panguru block. By 1932, groups like this were bringing Maori land into production all over the North Island.

2. *Hist.* A State-sponsored rural commune.
   1974 HAYWARD *Diary Kirk Years* (1981) 223 Arthur Faulkner, still Acting Minister of Lands, has announced that the proposed communes will be called 'ohu'—a Maori word meaning to achieve something 'by means of friendly help and work'. **1981** *Ibid.* 183 *The Listener* in 1979 published a feature on the kibbutz or ohu scheme which described it as originating from a 'chance remark by Norman Kirk'. **1988** *Dominion* (Wellington) 30 Dec. 11 [Ahu Ahu on the Wanganui River] was founded only 13 years ago, back in those heady Kirk years when the late Prime Minister gave the flower-power mob the land they yearned to return to. There they could build their communes. Ohu, he called them. This was one of eight ohu established and remains as one of only two that have seen the distance. **1991** *North & South* (Auckland) Dec. 52 This was at a time when communes and ohus were fashionable, even government-funded in some cases.

oi. Also **ohi, oii.** [Ma. /ˈoːi/: Williams 238 *Ōi*..muttonbird..grey-faced petrel. *Imitat.*] Originally any of several seabirds of the fam. Procellariidae, now only or esp. the *grey-faced petrel* (PETREL 2 (12)). See also MUTTONBIRD *n.* 1.
   1871 HUTTON *Catalogue Birds NZ* 45 Puffinus tristis... Mutton Bird. Oii. **1886** *TrNZI* XVIII. 90 Observations on Gould's Petrel..Procellaria gouldi (Ohi), *their Habits and Habitats*... After sunset, thick clouds of these Petrels swarm round the cliff, uttering the melancholy sound '*ohi! ohi!*' from which the Natives named it '*Ohi*'. **1890** *TrNZI* XXII. 292 *Procellaria gouldi*. This is the 'oii' of the Barrier Maoris. **1922, 1947** [see MUTTONBIRD]. **1955** OLIVER *NZ Birds* 131 *Sooty Shearwater. Titi. Oi. Puffinus griseus. Ibid.* 162 *Grey-faced Petrel. Oi Pterodroma macroptera gouldi.* **1966, 1985** [see PETREL 2 (12)].

oia. [Ma. /ˈoia/: Williams 238 *Oia..Caesioperca lepidoptera,* red perch.] *butterfly* (or *red*) *perch* (PERCH *n.* 2 (2) and (3)).
   1927 PHILLIPPS *Bibliogr. NZ Fishes* (1971) 33 *Caesioperca lepidoptera* (Forster). Red Perch; Oia. **1956** GRAHAM *Treasury NZ Fishes* 233 Red Perch (Oia) *Caesioperca lepidoptera*... This is a most highly coloured fish. **1966** [see PERCH *n.* 2 (3)]. **1982** [see PERCH *n.* 2 (2)].

oii, var. OI.

oil.

a. With a defining word, usu. as **dinkum oil** [AND 1915]; also **good oil** [AND 1916], **real oil,** **right oil,** the real truth, completely trustworthy information; the 'real thing'.
   1915 *Dominion* (Wellington) 22 June 6 I heard one man say, 'Saida, the dinkum oil at last; no more furpheys,' and that was the feeling all round. **1939** *Cappicade* (VUW Capping Book) 27 The Dinkum Oil [Name of a student Musical review]. **1944** FULLARTON *Troop Target* 18 Anyway there's no dinkum oil. Only latrinograms..it may be all hooey. **1952** *Here & Now* May 34 Unless I'm doing new things all the time I feel I'm going loopy... Dinkum. Dinkum oil. **1960** ROGERS *Long White Cloud* Slanting his glance down at the Scotch and soda on the tray. 'The dinkum oil, eh?' **1962** HORI *Half-gallon Jar* 21 The 'right oil' at the races cost me plenty... 'What about you driving me to the races on Saturday because I can get the good oil from a mate of mine?' I tell him that I don't need the oil since the old V8 has had the rebore. He say 'Crikey, I don't mean that sort of oil. What I mean is the dinkum oil, the straight griffen and the low-down about the horses.' **1987** NORGROVE *Shoestring Sailors* 50 Well..yeah, an' give it a bit of a wipe. If you want the real oil, George. **1991** *Dominion* (Wellington) 24 Aug. 8 [He]..is once again on the campaign trail giving us the good oil on the virtues of selfishness. **1993** *Dominion* (Wellington) 14 June 10 If you make no commitments, it's easy to pass yourself off as the only source of the dinkum oil.

b. Usu. as **the oil,** the truth; correct or significant information.
   1937 PARTRIDGE *Dict. Slang* 581 *the oil.* 4. Hence in New Zealand c[ant] (–1932), it = information. **1938** *Press* (Christchurch) (McNab Slang) 2 Apr. 18 [In local criminal slang]... 'oil' is significant information. **1944** FULLARTON *Troop Target* 18 'What's the oil, Noel?' 'Yes, spill it.' **1964** DAVIS *Watersiders* 22 'Wait on, mate give us the oil,' yelled Giant after him. **1988** MCGILL *Dict. Kiwi Slang* 78 *oil, the* the truth, the information you need, an excellent person or thing; eg 'Phil had the oil all right on Brierleys. Sold all he had the day before the bottom fell out of the market.'

oil: see BLACK OIL.

oilfish. *Ruvettus pretiosus* (fam. Gempylidae), a large midwater snake-mackerel, the very oily flesh being strongly purgative.
   1956 GRAHAM *Treasury NZ Fishes* 410 Oil Fish *Ruvettus whakari*. **1966** DOOGUE & MORELAND *Sea Anglers' Guide* 281 Oilfish... Usually [taken] on deep groper lines but occasionally seen in the trawl. **1986** PAUL *NZ Fishes* 122 Oilfish *Ruvettus pretiosus*... The flesh is edible but the copious oil it contains has a strong purgative effect.

oil rag, oily rag: see LIVE *v.* 1 b.

oioi. [Ma. /ˈoioi/: Williams 238 *Oi* (i) *oioi..3. Leptocarpus simplex,* a rush-like plant.] *Leptocarpus similis* (formerly *simplex*) (fam. Restoniaceae), a jointed wire rush of salt-marshes and some inland lakes.
   1853 HOOKER *II Flora Novae-Zelandiae I Flowering Plants* 265 Leptocarpus *simplex*. *Ibid.* 266 Nat. name, 'Oioi' (shaking). **1870** *TrNZI* II. 126 Leptocarpus simplex Oi or. **1950** *Bull. Wellington Bot. Soc. No.23* 10 An indication that..another vegetation-type existed..is found in..clumps of *Leptocarpus simplex* (oi-oi) which can be readily distinguished by the thin, rush-like, reddish-brown stems with closely appressed black sheaths, giving the plant a jointed appearance. **1978** MOORE & IRWIN *Oxford Book NZ Plants* 198 *Leptocarpus similis*, jointed rush, *oioi*. **1982** WILSON *Stewart Is. Plants* 324 *Leptocarpus similis* Jointed Wire Rush... Oioi... The Maori name oioi also means to shake or agitate; watch the beds of jointed wire rush when waves wash into them. **1995** CROWE *Which Coastal Plant?* 51 In spite of its common name, jointed wire rush is not really a rush. Oioi means 'to shake gently', which derives from the swaying of the stems as the wind blows though them.

okarari, var. HOKARARI.

okeoke. [Ma. /ˈokeoke/: Williams 239 *okeoke.. 4. Squalus lebruni* and *S. griffini, dogfish.*] DOGFISH 1. See also PIOKE.
   [**1820** LEE & KENDALL *NZ Gram. & Vocab.* 141 Oˈke óke, *s.* A certain fish.] **1927** PHILLIPPS *Bibliogr. NZ Fishes* (1971) 9 *Squalus fernandinus*... Spined Dogfish; Okeoke or Koinga. **1930** *NZJST* XI. 223 Spiny Dogfish. *Squalus fernandinus*... It is generally called oke-oke, or kapeta, by [Maori]; the term pioke is applied by some tribes to this species. **1956** GRAHAM *Treasury NZ Fishes* 80 The Maori name for Spined Dogfish is Koinga or Okeoke, and the fish is used by them as food. **1966** DOOGUE & MORELAND *Sea Anglers' Guide* 186 Northern dogfish... *Squalus blainvillii;* Griffin's dogfish, common spined dogfish, brown dogfish; pioke, okeoke (Maori).

old, *a.*

1. In various collocations, referring to the country which has been left on emigrating to New Zealand, usu. the British Isles. See also HOME *n.*[1] 1, MOTHER COUNTRY. **a.** Usu. as **(the) Old Country** *obs.* [also US; AND 1834].
   1840 POLACK *Manners & Customs* II. 216 If [the emigrant] expects to become emancipated from the thraldom of the aristocracy, he is soon relieved from his mistake by discovering that the invidious order is usurped by a clique, formerly, in the 'old country', (as it is feelingly termed) on a par with himself. **1848** 17 Dec. in *Lett. from Otago* (1978) 23 On the road was invited into the house by a Scotch lassie to take a drink of new milk, and..a gossip about the 'auld countrie'. **1853** ADAMS *Canterbury Settlement* 16 But straight before us lay our land of promise..the land where the losses and errors of the old country were to be retrieved. **1874** KENNAWAY *Crusts* 16 The crops grown were just those raised in the old country. **1882** POTTS *Out in Open* 78 Plants so greatly admired by fern-growers in the old country. **1905** *Truth* 12 Aug. 2 The Old Country..the Motherland. **1912** RUTHERFORD *Impressions NZ Pastoralist on Tour* 123 Visitors from our oversea dominions, when they come Home, invariably swear that they have in their own little State something better than anything in the same line to be seen in the Old Country. **1933** *Press* (Christchurch) (Acland Gloss.) 11 Nov. 15 *Old Country, the.*—England, not usually including Scotland; but sometimes Irishmen use the word to signify Ireland. **1934** *Na To Hoa Aroha* (1988) III. 145 A decision to send a delegation to the Old Country was arrived at. **1960** MUIR *Word for Word* 181 He knew the men still regarded him as a Homey, though it was well over thirty years since he'd left the Old Country.

b. As **(the) Old Dart** *obs.* [AND (1892) derives from a dial. pronunciation of *dirt*].
   1905 *Truth* 18 Nov. 4 Haughty squire of a shire in the Old Dart. **1916** old Dart [see MAORILAND 3 b]. **1933** PRUDENCE CADEY *Broken Pattern* 93 The old dart is the old country, home. **1947** *NZ Observer* 24 Sept. 9 Englishman, stranded in New Zealand, who wanted to see the 'Old Dart' again. **1964** DAVIS *Watersiders* 42 Strewth ducks, gerroutoftheway or you'll never reach the Old Dart without a harp and wings.

c. As **(the) Old Smoke,** London. Cf. BIG SMOKE a.
   1910 *Truth* 19 Feb. 1 The London money-lenders handed out £182,500,000 in loans to borrowers all over

the globe last year... No wonder he has booked his passage for the Old Smoke, the Mecca of all dead broke pilgrims after cheap beer.

2. a. In collocations implying colonial (or, later, military) experience or long residence in New Zealand, or that the referent is long established in a locality, see: OLD CHUM, *old dig* (DIG *n.* 2 c), OLD HAND 2, OLD IDENTITY, OLD SETTLER. **Oldest white inhabitant**, used ironically; **old stager**, someone or something of exceptional age, experience, size, etc.

1874 HOLLOWAY *Jrnl. of a Visit 1873–75* (ATLTS) 18 June 117 That much abused authority 'the oldest white inhabitant'. **1943** HISLOP *Pure Gold* 140 The big fish I caught..was very likely one of the old stagers which had come out of the many very deep mining holes on the flat.

b. In collocations implying a long-established or close relationship: see *old mate* (MATE *n.*² 3 b).

3. In special collocations: **old lady from Botany Bay** (and variants, see quot.) *hist.*, a children's game; **old maid** *Wellington*, KELPFISH 2.

1953 SUTTON-SMITH *Unorganized Games NZ Primary School Children* (VUWTS) II. 432 The Dialogue game of Caricature includes The **Old Lady from Botany bay**. In this game the children must not laugh at the old lady although she does her best to provoke them to do so. It has been known as Diggley Bones (Auckland [19]00), An Old Man from B.B. (Palmerston [19]10), An Old Lady from Poverty bay (Wellington [19]00). It is widely reported in the last twenty years. The Old Lady comes up to the children and says 'Here comes the Old Lady from Botany Bay, and what have you got to give her today. You must neither laugh nor smile but say ——'. Then the child would say something funny but try not to laugh when doing so... Nelson [19]49). **1963** *Evening Post* (Wellington) 31 Aug. 31 Sometimes the catch would include..the odd unlucky crayfish or several fat kelpfish, known locally [on Wellington's east coast] as '**old maid**'.

old chum. [A reflex of NEW CHUM: AND 1832.] OLD HAND 2.

1863 BUTLER *First Year* iv 55 I was anxious to become an old chum, as colonial dialect calls a settler—thereby proving my new chumship most satisfactorily. **1868** HOYLE *Fragments of Jrnl.* 23 My fellow passengers [were] both 'old chums'. **1930** GUTHRIE *NZ Memories* 159 In an incredibly short time,.. the 'new chum' was quite able to sit a stock-horse, no easy task even for an 'old chum'. **1968** *NZ Contemp. Dict. Suppl.* (Collins) 14 *old chum n.* used in 1870s for a person who had been in N.Z. for some time.

old hand.

1. *Hist.* [AND an experienced convict, 1826; later, an ex-convict.] An Australian former convict, an 'old lag'.

1845 MARTIN *NZ in 1842* 104 The 'old hands' (a name which emancipated convicts take to themselves). **1858** THOMSON *Reconn. Survey S. Dist. Otago* in Taylor *Early Travellers* (1959) 346 The house that we got into at the end of our long journey belonged to an 'old hand', and was as primitive as its owner. **1874** BATHGATE *Col. Experiences* 156 Many liberated convicts found their way hither during the great rush from Australia in 1862... I have in my sojourn in the colony met with a few who were admittedly 'old hands', as the phrase is. **1967** MAY *West Coast Gold Rushes* 527 'Old Hands': ex-convicts who had been transported to Australia and eventually found their way to the West Coast goldfields.

2. [AND 1839.] A person of (colonial) experience as distinct from a NEW CHUM q.v. Cf. OLD CHUM.

1842 BEST *Journal* 16 Oct. (1966) 377 New arrivals working and contented Older hands in better spirits. **1858** THOMSON *S. Dists. Otago* 314 From these stirring times of whaling, so often conned over by the 'old hand' as he smokes his pipe at the door of his hut. **1870** *TrNZI* II. 173 One day some 'old hands' (surveyors' men) were having dinner in the hut. **1881** BATHGATE *Waitaruna* 67 He can punch the bullocks almost as well as an old hand already, even to the swearing at them. **1913** CARR *Country Work* 37 Fossicking is carried on by Chinamen and old hands practically all over the province. **1933** *Press* (Christchurch) (Acland Gloss.) 21 Oct. 15 *Hand, old.*—Experienced person in Colonial matters. **1941** BAKER *NZ Slang* 44 *Old hand*, in the first place used for an ex-convict, but later for any man who had had his *colonial experience*, was more often used than *old chum*.

old identity. Also *ellipt.* IDENTITY. [Spec. use of *identity*, connoting 'uniformity' (of outlook, background, etc.); see also OLD *a.* 2.]

1. *Otago Hist.* [It is uncertain whether Cargill or Thatcher originated the phrase 'the Old Identity': poss. Thatcher, with his acute sense of the locally (and aptly) ridiculous, transformed and popularized Cargill's original.] **a.** (a) As a collective *sing.*, usu. as **the Old Identity**, or *ellipt.* **the Identity**, the mainly Scottish Presbyterian and reputedly strait-laced original settler community of Otago.

1862 THATCHER *Dunedin Songster 1* 18 [Title] *The Old Identity*. Mr Cargill in the Council made such a funny speech; He got up and he stated that it devolved on each Of all the early dwellers to preserve safe as could be Amid the Victorian influx, The Old Identity. **1862** WEKEY *Otago As It Is* 76 'Old Identity' is an entirely Otagonian idiom. It is meant to designate the early settlers of the province and their adherents. **1887** PYKE *Hist. Early Gold Discoveries Otago* 2 [The first digger immigrants] alighted on a golden country—a circumstance which some of '*the Identity*'—a phrase first brought into use by Mr Edward Cargill—still profess to regard in the light of a calamity. **1898** HOCKEN *Contributions* 201 The origin of the descriptive term 'Old Identities' has been involved in some doubt. Not only is it a convenient one, but it is now widely used throughout the Colonies to denote the oldest inhabitants, as distinguished from the newcomers, or 'new iniquities'... Mr. E. B. Cargill was seeking a seat in the Council, and addressing the electors, regretted that the old settlers were being thrown into the shade, and that to prevent this they must make a strong and united effort. This was food for Thatcher, who thereupon [in 1862] brought down the house with a witty song of eight verses, each of which terminated with the refrain of 'The Old Identity.' **1959** SINCLAIR *History NZ* 104 Dunedin became the largest town in the country, while, to the horror of the 'Old Identity', saloons, billiard rooms, gambling dens and dance halls sprang up to attract the gold of the 'New Iniquity'.

(b) In distributive use, a Scottish founding settler of Otago.

1862 THATCHER *The Great Customs Seizure* in *Dunedin Songster 3* 11 Mister Monson in the Customs Is a most efficient chap; His dad's an Old Identity—I once gave him a rap. **1874** BATHGATE *Col. Experiences* (1974) 26 The term 'old identities' took its origin from an expression in a speech made by one of the members of the Provincial Council, Mr. E.B. Cargill, who, in speaking of the new arrivals, said that the early settlers should endeavour to preserve their old identity. The strangers, who were inclined to laugh at the aboriginals as a set of old stagers, caught up the phrase, and dubbed them 'old identities'. A comic singer helped to perpetuate the name by writing a song... So that anything effete came to be styled a regular 'old identity'. **1876** *Saturday Advertiser* 8 July 5 Act ii. scene i.—A sly grog-shanty... [*Enter New Chum and Old Identity*] **1893** FROBISHER *Sketches of Gossiptown* 2 It would seem that this place had been an isolated settlement of Old Identities, long ere the Otago Goldfields had been thought of. **1903** *Otago Witness* (Dunedin) 25 Feb. 68 I was at the Old Identities' picnic yesterday and spent a fair time among the 'young iniquities' and 'old immensities' as Texas Jack's irresponsible brother calls the Old Identities. **1919** *Otago Witness* (Dunedin) 24 Feb. 5 There was a large attendance at Portobello on Saturday when the annual picnic of the Port Chalmers Old Identities' Association was held. **1924** *Otago Witness* (Dunedin) 11 Nov. 68 Get, if you can, speech with an 'old identity'.

b. The barracouta fish as a too regular Dunedin boarding-house dish.

1874 BATHGATE *Col. Experiences* (1974) 27 So much did the name ['old identity'] come to be a term of reproach among the Australian diggers that the barracouta..., a rather coarse fish, very abundant at certain seasons, and which was consequently very cheap, and a great favourite with boarding-house keepers, was christened by them 'the old identity'. **1896** MOFFATT *Adventures* (1979) 64 There seemed to be a plethora of bread and barracouta [at Dunedin], the principle [*sic*] cry being 'Here you are, a loaf and an old identity (barracouta) for a shilling.' **1925** BATHGATE *Random Recolls.* 17 The barracouta was the fish..as it was cheap was often served by the [Dunedin] boarding house-keepers [c1860s], and I remember a fish-hawker while selling it calling out: 'Here you are: two yards of old identity for a bob!' **1952** LYON *Faring South* 131 In early Dunedin large shoals of barracouta were easily caught and sold at sixpence or less for a fish... No wonder the old Dunedinite of a former generation referred to them, those wide-jawed and projecting toothed long fish, as 'Old Identities'.

2. In general or non-Otago use, occas. with some development of meaning or application, often with a descriptive term (freq. a local place-name) infixed or prefixed: a person long identified with a place, position, institution, etc.; a long-time resident, incumbent, practitioner, etc. **a.** As **old identity**.

1864 THATCHER *Songs of War* 15 This Auckland's getting civilized,—Victorians come this way, And show these Old Identities The proper time o' day. **1864** PRESHAW *Banking Under Difficulties* (1888) 124 The police—Old Nelson identities—were quite unprepared for any such emergencies. **1872** CLYDE *Te Kooti* 37 A penniless new chum was I, A wealthy carle was he; One of those ancient ones, y clept The Old Identity. **1888** D'AVIGDOR *Antipodean Notes* 171 One of the most curious expressions...is 'an old identity', used for a person long 'identified with a place'—in fact an old inhabitant, or one whose interests have long been bound up in it. This expression is unfortunately now universal even in newspapers. **1894** WILSON *Land of Tui* 256 A mixed gathering, containing some members of the class who in this country are known as 'Old Identities', but whom I heard an aged man designate, with a *lapsus linguae*, that had in it much unconscious irony: 'Old Nonentities'. **1898** HOCKEN *Contributions* 33 The whaling station in Preservation Inlet, founded in 1829, and belonging to Captain Peter Williams—an old Otago identity, better known as 'Billy Williams'. **1916** STALLWORTHY *Early N. Wairoa* 20 One of the oldest identities of the Wairoa district was Dan Lane. **1935** MAXWELL *Recollections* 16 To all but the few remaining 'old identities' it is now vain to endeavour to visualise what these pioneers had to face. **1947–48** BEATTIE *Pioneer Recolls.* (1956) 22 One by one the old identities of Gore are slipping away. **1952** *Evening*

Post (Wellington) 23 July When Wellington College farewelled Lord and Lady Freyberg yesterday, an old identity on the platform was the former first assistant master, Mr T. Brodie. **1984** EDMOND *High Country Weather* 31 But my father you know—very old identity—big holdings in those days.

b. As **identity**.
1905 *Truth* 23 Sept. 5 [Caption] Three Auckland Identities. **1926** BLACKWELL *Lost Tribute* [Dustcover blurb] Another well-known Taranaki identity is introduced. **1952** *Evening Post* (Wellington) 16 Oct. 16 [Caption] Union Identities Differ.**1934** HYDE *Journalese* 225 The son of one of the wealthiest town identities..used to drive his spanking equipage here. **1980** *Dominion* (Wellington) 11 Aug. 3 Poet Denis Glover..was as much at home talking football and boats with hard-case, down-to-earth folks as he was talking craft with the most fastidious literary identity. **1991** *Press* (Christchurch) 14 Oct. 1 Born and educated in Nelson, Mrs Urquhart made friends easily and had a wide circle of acquaintances, including many local identities.

3. Sometimes used with a sense of 'colourful (local) character', DAG 1 a.
1956 BLAIR *Life & Work at Canterbury Agric. College* 139 That identity of the House of those days, J.A. Lee, Labour member for Grey Lynn. **1964** ANDERSON *Doctor in Mountains* (1974) 75 Like all small places, Queenstown had its quota of old identities, interesting personalities, some with very odd and often amusing characteristics. **1981** HUNT *Speaking a Silence* 58 Reggie was seventy-seven,.. a well known character in the Bay. The locals would ask, 'Have you seen Reggie yet? He's a real old identity.'

4. In *attrib.* use in various senses, often transf. to animals and things.
1866 SMALL *NZ & Austral. Songster* (1970) 26 Any man but a Scot would be soon sent to pot, For Dunedin was then an 'Identity' shop. **1878** *TrNZI* X. 310 Gradually they [house flies] appeared, first in Dunedin..then..they overspread the whole province, entirely supplanting..the genuine old-identity blow-fly. **1878** *TrNZI* X. 321 I know that this statement will be questioned by many who have never believed that there were genuine old-identity wild dogs in New Zealand before Europeans brought them here. **1879** BARR *Old Identities* 317 There are in Princes-street [Dunedin] certain Old Identity places of business. **1978** MANTELL *Murder in Fancydress* 67 'One of the locals thought so, too... Probably wouldn't have moved if it hadn't been for the old identity competition.'

old man, *n.* and *attrib.*
A. *n.* WW1. One who runs a Crown and Anchor game.
1917 *NZ at the Front* 106 Murder on the old sergeant-major [*i.e.* the Crown], and the bottom line goes for the old man. **1918** *Quick March* 1 Oct. 3 Diggers' Rules of Crown and Anchor.—When the limit is laid on the spade, club, heart, diamond, and anchor, and the banker throws three crowns, he shall forthwith cry in a loud, clear voice : 'The old man smiles again,' and folding his tent like the Arabs, silently beat it. **1921** *Quick March* 10 Aug. 27 'Come on me lucky lads, you pick 'em. Hop in, digs, and have a fly with the old man. Come on, thick and heavy, for I'm here today and gone tomorrow.'

B. *attrib.* Also occas. **old-man, Old Man**.
1. [AND 1845.] Of exceptional size, toughness, intensity, duration, etc. See esp. quot. 1933. See also *old man snapper* (SNAPPER 2 (3)); cf. GRANDFATHER.
1889 KIRK *Forest Flora* 93 C.H. Gorton..of Burnt Hill..informed me that mature specimens [of entire-leaved beech] are commonly termed 'old-man birch', and are much disliked by the woodmen, as they are very difficult to split. **1897** MCKAY *Older Auriferous Drifts of Central Otago* 48 It seems to be confined to a comparatively narrow run, which is at considerable angle against the 'Maori bottom', or 'Old man reef'. **1926** HILGENDORF *Weeds* 49 Twitch..is sometimes called..blue, English, white, or old man, twitches or couch. **1933** *Press* (Christchurch) (Acland Gloss.) 11 Nov. 15 *Old man.*—Slang. Striking, big, remarkable; e.g., an *o[ld] m[an]* rock, flood, nor'-wester, cabbage tree, etc. Hence the *o[ld] m[an]* is a common name for paddocks, though some hills are probably so called from a fancied resemblance to a man's face. **1938** HYDE *Nor Yrs. Condemn* 144 You've got to be cunning as a fish; there's nothing to look for but a little bump in the mud, and that's old man flounder. **1959** SLATTER *Gun in My Hand* 190 And the nor'-westers in summer, the Old Man Nor'-Westers, blowing through a great arch over the Alps. **1969** BAXTER *Collected Poems* (1980) 241 A cord of old man manuka, I cut it in a day. **1973** FERNANDEZ *Tussock Fever* 47 The pools frequented by the old-men trout who defied the fishermen year after year.

2. Pertaining to an earlier or ancient non-white race.
1900 *TrNZI* XXXII. 314 At all events, close to Bunny Cliffs,.. there are some 'old men's workings', as the remains of what are taken to be ancient surface streaming of the prehistoric races are called.

3. In special collocations: **old man bottom** mining, see quots. (the sense, and that of *old man gravel*, may be connected with 2 above: see also BOTTOM *n.* 1); **old man flood** [AND 1916], a very high flood; **old man gravel**, see quot.
1896 *AJHR* D-4 240 What do you say is the '**Old-man bottom**'?—It is the gravel... They are river gravels, though they may often be found on the sea-coast. **1897** MCKAY *Older Auriferous Drifts Central Otago* 49 The 'old man' or 'Maori bottom' on which these claims are working, runs up at a steep inclination as it approaches the Deep Lead, having the quartz drift standing against it in nearly vertical layers. *Ibid.* 50 At the time of my visit they were working on what appears to be the bed of an ancient river; the 'old-man' bottom being cut away shows the direction of the current, and indicates that it had at one time been the bed of a large river. The width of this river-bed has not yet been determined, but on the eastern side the 'old man' bottom again crops up. **1898** *AJHR* C-9 3 The coal-bearing series is followed by heavy deposits of conglomerate and coarse gravels, locally known as 'Old-man bottom'. **1908** *NZGeol.SB (NS)* No.6 113 In Westland these ancient gravels [Moutere Gravels] form the true Old Man Bottom of the gold-miners. **1938** *N.Z. Geol. Memoir* No.4 49 It was shown that it is possible to differentiate between a lead formed of less consolidated gravels, if imbedded in more consolidated gravel, locally [in Westland] known as 'Old Man' bottom. **1896** HARPER *Pioneer Work* 134 I feel confident that any one who has seen a Westland river in an '**old man' flood** would credit the actual upheaval of any sized boulder. **1939** BEATTIE *First White Boy Born Otago* 173 This was the famous Old Man Flood [of the Shotover in 1863]; it was the biggest I ever knew. **1943** HISLOP *Pure Gold* 19 It was in 1878 that the Old man flood, as [the Otago miners] called it, happened and swept all the bridges away between Cromwell and Balclutha. **1969** MOORE *Forest to Farm* 45 But a real 'old man' flood in the autumn ultimately swept the tangle away and cleared the bed of the stream. **1981** DENNIS *Paparoas Guide* 139 Great thicknesses of these sediments were laid down..some two thousand metres of them still lie beneath the **Old Man Gravels** of the Grey River valley... More recent and perhaps better known are the Pliocene Old Man Gravels of the Grey-Inangahua Valley, a conglomerate that is part of the large sheets of aggradation gravels deposited both east and west of the..Southern Alps early in the Kaikoura Orogeny.

old man's beard.

1. [AND 1914.] Also formerly **old Maori's beard**. *Usnea capillacea* or *U. xanthophana* (fam. Parmeliaceae), a pendulous lichen growing on trees.
[**1879** HAAST *Geology Canterbury and Westland* 109 The beech forest..now had become dwarfish and covered with *Usnea barbata* (that peculiar pendant greenish white lichen).] **1844** WILLIAMS *NZ Jrnl.* (1956) 104 [When the rimu] tree becomes old these splendid leafs [*sic*] become smaller and grow in tufts..giving it the appearance of being dead, or 'covered with old Mauries beards' rather than natural leafs. *Ibid.* 117 [1956 *Note*] usually known as Old Man's Beard, a lichen (*Usnea*). **1888** D'AVIGDOR *Antipodean Notes* 152 From the branches hang bunches of that wonderful lichen, 'old man's beard'. **1893** *TrNZI* XXV. 316 Of these are some of our larger..tree-lichens, such as..*Usnea barbata,..* ('old man's beard'), several varieties. **1927** GUTHRIE-SMITH *Birds* 144 The pendent 'old man's beard' that, yards in length, swings from the tawa boughs. **1961** MARTIN *Flora NZ* 51 [Caption] Foliaceous Lichens—mainly *Sticta fossulata*, and tufts of Old Man's Beard (*Usnea*), on dead tree branches in Stewart Island forest. **1989** PARKINSON *Travelling Naturalist* 156 Higher up..[are] stunted beech, leatherwood and mountain fuchsia, their branches festooned with hanging, delicate grey lichen called Old Man's Beard.

2. [Used elsewhere but of special noxious significance in New Zealand: see OED *old man* 8, 1760.] A rampant, troublesome, introduced clematis, *Clematis vitalba* (fam. Ranunculaceae), the flowers of which are replaced in autumn with long feathery ('beard-like') seed heads.
1969 *Standard Common Names Weeds* 54 *Old man's beard* [=] *traveller's joy.* **1984** *Karori News* 8 May 8 The fast-growing introduced vine Old Man's Beard is smothering native bush in many parts of the city and surrounding hills.

old Maori's beard: see OLD MAN'S BEARD 1.

old settler. [AND *settler*, 1827.] See also SETTLER 1, *missionary settler* (SETTLER 1 b (a)).

1. A European (esp. a shore whaler, missionary trader, etc.) settled in a district before the start of the organized immigration of the 1840s.
1842 DEANS *Pioneers* (1964) 2 Apr. 10 The old settlers in New Zealand, missionaries and others, you are aware, purchased land to a great extent from the natives. **1878** HEBERLEY *Autobiography* (ATLTS) 34 I think that the old settlers ought to be entitled to our part [*sc.* Te Awaite c1839] as well as the NZd company.

2. An early settler in New Zealand, or in a particular district.
1849 TORLESSE *Papers* (1958) 117 The evil consequences of employing beach-combers, escaped convicts and sailors are becoming every day more apparent. Many excellent old settlers have been prevented from coming here, on the supposition that they [*sc.* the beach-combers, etc.] could not be ousted from the land they first squatted upon when the settlers arrived. **1853** ADAMS *Spring in Canterbury Settlement* 78 I obtained an interesting anecdote of their affectionate attachment to those who treat them kindly from an old settler at Christchurch. **1854** PAUL *Some Account Canterbury Settlement* 5 Having resided more than two years in the Canterbury Settlement [and]..considering the rapid growth of colonial life..[I] may almost call [myself] an 'old settler'. **1882** POTTS *Out in Open* 33

Old settlers can doubtless recollect the rise, progress, and decay of the willow and poplar period. **1911** *TrNZI* XLIII. 438 Old settlers will tell you that the seasons have changed of late years. **1953** *NZ Observer* 7 Jan. 19 They will all 'gang up' on you if you are not an old settler.

olearia /ʌuliˈeriə/. [f. the name of Johann Gottfried *Olearius* (1635–1711), German theologian and horticulturalist: OED 1839; 1852 (Austral.).] A mainly Australasian evergreen shrub; in New Zealand any one of over 30 native species of the *Olearia* genus (fam. Asteraceae or Compositae) having clusters of variously (creamy-)white or purplish flowers. See also AKEAKE, AKEPIRO, AKIRAHO, DAISY TREE, HEKETARA, *mountain musk* (MUSK b), TETEAWAKA, TREE DAISY.

1869 *TrNZI* I. iii. 4 Along the shore there is a profusion of shrub Veronicas and Olearias. **1886** in HILL *Richard Henry of Resolution Island* 163 There were many varieties of veronicas in full flower..olearias of all kinds. **1957** WILKINSON *Kapiti Diary* 88 We may still trace a sweet perfume to a branching Olearia with tufts of little white flowers. **1966** *Encyclop. NZ* I. 440 Amongst the Olearias are several species occurring commonly in lowland shrubland. *Ibid.* III. 712 Olearia, purple-flowered .. .. teteaweka .. *Olearia angustifolia*. **1979** WILSON *Titi Heritage* 64 The 'muttonbird trees' (Olearias) have a very limited life.

olive.

1. [Transf. use of the northern hemisphere *olive Olea europaea* (fam. Oleaceae) for NZ *Nestegis* (formerly *Olea*) spp. of the same family.] Usu. with a modifier: **mountain, native,** or **New Zealand olive.** MAIRE 1 a.

1882 *TrNZI* XIV. 375 [Title] *On the New Zealand Olives*. By T. Kirk. **1898** HUDSON *NZ Moths & Butterflies* 139 *Olea apetala* (Maire, New Zealand Olive). A shrub or small tree with broad leaves, and insignificant flowers growing on opposite sides of the flower-stalk. **1911** *TrNZI* XLIII. 200 The true New Zealand olive is the maire—*Olea*. **1917** WILLIAMS *Dict. Maori Lang.* 405 Rororo... *Olea montana*, mountain olive. **1980** LOCKLEY *House Above Sea* 95 Plump brown wallabies peering at us tamely from among the stunted pohutukawas, native olive..manuka. **1988** DAWSON *Forest Vines to Snow Tussocks* 42 Three of the four species of *Nestegis* or 'native olives' have narrow adult leaves.

2. Either of two native trees with fruits resembling olives, TAWAPOU 1 (*Planchonella costata*) or HINAU (*Elaeocarpus dentatus*).

1911 *TrNZI* XLIII. 200 Among the..plants on or near sea cliffs..may be mentioned..the tawapou..., sometimes called the New Zealand olive, from the resemblance of its fruit to that of the olive. **1924** [see TAWAPOU 1]. **1979** STARK *Maori Herbal Remedies* 17 Hinau (Olive Tree) *Elaeocarpus dentatus*.

3. *transf.* As **olive branch**, an offspring.

1912 *Truth* 17 Aug. 5 Stuart, in evidence, said that Pehipa and he were married in September, 1909, at the Thames [*sic*], and there were no olive branches.

o.m.: see *overland mail* (OVERLAND B).

ombudsman. [f. Swedish *ombud* agent: see OED.] In New Zealand, an officer of Parliament appointed to investigate complaints by individuals against central and local government agencies, including state-owned enterprises and statutory boards; to act as a review authority for the whole education and health systems; and to act as a review authority in respect of the Official Information Acts 1982 and 1987.

1962 *NZPD* CCCXXXI. 1758 It has recommended a small change in the title from Parliamentary Commissioner for Investigations Bill to Parliamentary Commissioner (Ombudsman) Bill. The reason is that the public is not talking about the parliamentary Commissioner for Investigations but about the appointment of an ombudsman. **1962** *NZ Statutes* I. No.10 107 [Parliamentary Commissioner (Ombudsman) Act] There shall be appointed, as an officer of Parliament, a Commissioner for investigations, to be called the Ombudsman. **1966** TURNER *Eng. Lang. in Aust. & NZ* 174 In July 1961 he was to be called the 'Parliamentary Commissioner for Investigation'... The office was modelled on the Scandinavian *ombudsman* and this word was used in the meantime... The plural *ombudsmen* appeared, and a man checking hotel measures was called a drinker's *ombudsman*. **1974** *NZPD* CCCXCV. 5735 The term 'ombudsman' has general acceptance and has passed into common usage. The reservations that existed 12 years ago over using an unfamiliar term are no longer supportable. *Ibid.* 5737 There will be a Chief Ombudsman who will be the prime Ombudsman. **1975** *NZ Statutes* I. No.9 98 [Ombudsman Act] It shall be a function of the Ombudsmen to investigate any decision or recommendation made, or any act done or omitted..relating to a matter of administration and affecting any person or body of persons in his or its personal capacity.

on, *a.* or *adv.* [AND 1903.] In the phr. **to be on with** (someone), to be keen on or amorously involved with, to be 'on a fuss' with (someone).

1980 LELAND *Kiwi-Yankee Dict.* 73 *on with*: 'Sally and Sam are on with each other'. They enjoy the benefits of the marriage bed without benefit of clergy. **1984** BEATON *Outside In* 103 Di:.. She's 'on with you' because of me!

on, *prep.*

1. In the phr. **on it. a.** *Goldmining.* As **to be on it**, to be *on gold* (GOLD 1).

1914 PFAFF *Diggers' Story* 66 [We were] getting excellent gold. From that time until May 1867, we were always 'on it'.

b. In the phr. **to be (get, look)** + *adj.* + **on it** [f. Brit. dial.: see OED *on* prep. 10 c (b) dial.; EDD II 1 (1)], indicating a particular, usu. distressing, condition or situation.

1946 SARGESON *That Summer* 96 He looked pretty crook on it. **1976** SARGESON *Sunset Village* 35 You don't look too good on it what's wrong?

c. As **to be on it** [AND 1908], to be 'on the booze', to be on an alcoholic binge.

1959 SLATTER *Gun in My Hand* 14 The news soon got around that we were on it. Horns peremptory at the gate, blokes coming up the drive every night, some lumping cartons of beer, some carrying jars of draught, many of them with nothing but a nose for parties. **1988** McGILL *Dict. Kiwi Slang* 79 *on it* drinking alcohol; eg 'I'm sick of footy practice. Let's get on it instead, eh?'

2. [See OED 6 b and 26 b: AND 1958.] In the phr. **on the weekend, on weekends,** at or during the weekend(s).

1989 *NZ English Newsletter Number 3* 15 The preposition used with the noun *weekend* is variable in New Zealand English, and..at, on, and in are all heard... [In an elicitation experiment] three items were presented to [103] informants [including]... (b) I wanted to play football on the weekend, but they are forecasting rain... When presented with *on*, 64 informants maintained *on*, 9 changed the preposition to *at*, 23 to *in* and 4 to *during*. *Ibid.* 16 [Reproducing a copy of an advt.] For Lunch on the Weekend. Due to the popularity of Pizza Hut Special Delivery we have extended our hours to include Weekend Lunches.

3. In the negative phr. **not to be on board**, to be mentally irresponsible, not to be 'with it'.

1973 LEE *Political Notebooks* 41 Said [Sir Thomas Wilford]: 'Sir Joseph [Ward] wasn't on board half the time he was prime minister.'..One day a deputation came to see him... It was one of Ward's mentally irresponsible days.

4. As **on and off the bridge** *obs.*, a children's game.

1982 SUTTON-SMITH *Hist. Children's Play* 231 There are games recorded in this period for which there is no record before 1900 though they may well have existed under other names... *Wellington*: Who Goes Round My Stone Wall, Beg o' My Neighbor, Bellahonie, Run a Mile, On and Off the Bridge, Here Come Two Nuns.

5. As **on side** [transf. use from rugby football], in the phr. **to keep on side (with)**, to keep in favour (with a person). Cf. OFFSIDE.

1979 ASHTON-WARNER *I Passed This Way* (1980) 312 Mr Flake has the whole of the department behind him and it's best for a young teacher to keep on side... [**1979** *Note*] *on side* a Rugby football term meaning in favour.

one. Used in various combinations and collocations where the number or value *one* is of significance: **one another** *prison*, rhyming slang for 'mother' or 'brother'; **one-o'clock** [origin uncertain: perh. from a children's rhyme said when blowing on a dandelion seed-head to demolish it], a floating head of 'thistledown'; **one out of the box**, see BOX $n.^2$ 3; **one-star artist**, see ARTIST 1; **one-stepper**, see DEBT-DODGER; **one-striper**, a chaff or wheat sack marked with one stripe (usu. blue) running vertically down the middle; **one-winged** *WW1*, of a (returned) soldier, having one arm.

1982 NEWBOLD *Big Huey* 252 **One another** (n) Mother or brother. **1982** FRAME *To the Is-land* (1984) 115 The flowers still came out in their proper time, the dandelion seeds or **one-o'clocks** never failed to float away into the sky. **1986** OWEN & PERKINS *Speaking for Ourselves* 72 The wagga rug was made out of the old **one-striper** sacks... The old one-striper was the fair-dinkum chaff sack... Later came the three-striper bag. It was a much shorter, smaller bag with a very much lighter weave, but the old heavy one-striper made a wonderful wagga. **1920** *Quick March* 10 Jan. 23 [Title] The Inconvenient 'Wingy'. A lady sitting comfortably in a tram-car, saw a **one-winged** soldier hanging to a strap, and advised him thus: 'You men should wait for a car that has seating accommodation.'

Onehunga weed /ʌuniˈhʌŋə/, –/ˈhʊŋə/. [f. *Onehunga*, a port within the greater Auckland conurbation.] *Soliva sessilis* (fam. Asteraceae), a South American lawn weed noted for its sharp-spined fruits in early summer, named for Onehunga where it first came into prominence. Also called **jo jo weed**.

1967 HILGENDORF & CALDER *Weeds* 192 [Not found in 1926 edn.] Onehunga Weed (*Soliva sessilis* and *S. valdiviana*), also called Jo Jo weed, is a small spreading weed with trailing stems and much divided leaves... The weed was introduced from Chile and is now common in waste places and grasslands chiefly in the northern half of the North Island, but also in Nelson and Marlborough. **1969** *Standard Common Names Weeds* 41 *jo-jo weed* [=] Onehunga weed [*Soliva* spp.]. **1980**

TAYLOR *Weeds of Crops* 69 Onehunga Weed (*Soliva* spp.). Several similar South American species go by this name... The common name is derived from the Auckland suburb where the weed came under early notice. Onehunga weed is common in many districts of the North Island and is spreading fast in the South Island. **1988** *Listener* 26 Nov. 13 This is the last chance this year to prevent seed setting on Onehunga weed (prickle weed).

ongaonga. [Ma. /ˈoŋaˌoŋa/: Williams 240 *Onga* (i)..*ongaonga*. *1*. n. *Urtica* [spp.], nettle.] NETTLE.
[**1820** LEE & KENDALL *NZ Gram. & Vocab.* 142 O´nga ónga. A certain shrub.] **1842** TAYLOR *Journal* 23 Nov. (ATLTS) 7 This morning I was showed a real stinging nettle which the natives assured me as it grew turned into a tree & loses its stinging quality the onga onga, which though they affirmed I confess I very much doubt. **1853** HOOKER *II Flora Novae-Zelandiae I Flowering Plants* 225 Urtica *ferox*... Nat. name, 'Onga Onga'. **1867** HOOKER *Handbook* 766 Onga-onga... *Urtica ferox*, and others. **1903** *TrNZI* XXXV. 111 The *ongaonga* (nettle shrub) has no leaves now (August). **1916** COWAN *Bush Explorers* (VUWTS) 7 That plant, from which all of us suffered for some days, was the native stinging nettle, the ongaonga, which botanists have christened urtica ferox. **1924** *Otago Witness* (Dunedin) 9 Sept. 6 Really bad onga-onga stings provoke feverish sickness. **1969** *Standard Common Names Weeds* 54 Ongaonga [=] *tree nettle*. **1978** MOORE & IRWIN *Oxford Book NZ Plants* 82 *Urtica ferox*, *ongaonga*. The tree nettle can form great thickets taller than a man. Pale stinging hairs on leaves and stems are poisonous, a real danger to horses and dogs. **1988** *Pacific Way* June 48 It is possible to proceed..but beware of the native tree nettle, ongaonga! **1989** [see NETTLE 2].

ongkus, var. ONKUS.

onion.

1. Usu. as **onion flower**, **onion weed** and **wild onion**, species of *Allium* (fam. Liliaceae), occurring as naturalized weeds in New Zealand.
1926 HILGENDORF *Weeds* 55 Wild Onion (*Allium vineale*), is also called wild garlic and crow garlic. **1963** FRAME *Reservoir* 71 The tap leaked, the earth was bogged with moss and onion flower. **1972** FRAME *Daughter Buffalo* 39 Some tombstones were broken, others were hidden by the grass and the onion flowers. **1973** MCELDOWNEY *Arguing with My Grandmother* 78 Onion weed grew all over Auckland. **1981** GEE *Meg* 15 I saw him in the flowering onion weed. **1982** WILSON *Stewart Is. Plants* 294 *Allium triquetrum* Three-cornered garlic... Onion weed... Native to: Europe and North Africa. ranges through the drier eastern mountains of the South Island from North Canterbury southwards. **1992** PARK *Fence around the Cuckoo* 127 Prolific was the growth of wild garlic, which we children [in Auckland] called onionflower.

2. As **Maori onion**, *Bulbinella* (formerly *Chrysobactron*) species (fam. Asphodelaceae), a native, summer-green, fleshy-leaved herb with swollen storage roots and an onion-like odour, commonly found in damp, grazed grasslands. See also *bog lily*, *golden lily*, *swamp lily* (LILY 2 (1), (4), and (17) a).
1884 *NZJSc.* II. 295 The Moa hunters were more favoured..in this district [Canterbury] with a supply of food..there being an abundance of 'Maori onion', fern-root, and birds, together with caves to dwell in. **1908** DON *Chinese Mission Work 1907–8* 22 Some slopes are golden with the 'Maori Onion', others bright with the 'Maori Tobacco'. **1933** *Press* (Christchurch) (Acland Gloss.) 4 Nov. 15 *Maori.—*Used as an adjective synonymous with *native*, except that it seems slightly contemptuous... M[*aori*] onion (*Chrysobactron hookeri*)..[etc.] are caricatures of their English namesakes. **1940** LAING & BLACKWELL *Plants NZ* 106 *Bulbinella Hookeri*, is found in lowland and sub-alpine pastures in both the Northern and Southern Islands of New Zealand... It is frequently—at least in the Southern part of New Zealand—known as the *Maori Onion*. **1961** MARTIN *Flora NZ* 249 Where the ground was moist but scarcely swampy the Maori Onion (*Chrysobactron hookeri*) with tall spikes of yellow flowers added a touch of colour. **1970** MOORE & EDGAR *Flora NZ* II. 22 Fls are yellow in all N.Z. [*Chrysobactron*] spp. and all emit a faint but characteristic odour when crushed. 'Maori onion' is the name most commonly used, but 'swamp lily' and 'golden star lily' have also been applied to one or more spp. **1981** HENDERSON *Exiles Asbestos Cottage* 71 Chaffey, despite his extraordinary toughness, is said to have nearly poisoned himself with brews of varying hideosity from trees, leaves, shrubs, modest growths such as Maori onion.

onion water. WW2. *Egypt*. Also **onion juice**. [Transf. f. *onion water*, a medicinal liquor prepared from onions: see OED *onion* 8.] A soldiers' name for Stella beer, an Egyptian brew, having an onion flavour, sold in Services canteens to the troops.
1944 BRUNO *Desert Daze* 22 The stella beer (you remember that—onion water, Kiwi? *Ibid.* 47 A modest glass [of] 'onion-water' beer. **1983** HENDERSON *Down from Marble Mountain* 265 We drift into various canteen-tents for the military [in Egypt], we buy eggs and tomatoes.., a limited amount of onion juice (ie Stella beer, Egyptian) usually runs out a fraction ahead of us.

onkus /ˈɒŋkəs/, *a. Obs.* Also **ongkus**. [Origin unknown: AND 'disagreeable', 1918.] Good; 'profitable'; pleasant. (The 1944 quot. is ambiguous: ?'in a happy condition' or ?'in an unhappy condition'.)
1910 *Truth* 11 June 1 But 'Critic' asks the said gentleman to submit the following sentence to any school boy or a semi-intelligent adult: 'The Opposition are whipping the cat because they've got Buckley's chance of pulling the leg of the farmer with an onkus [*sic*] freehold lurk.' **1937** PARTRIDGE *Dict. Slang* 589 *ongcuss* or -*cuss; onkiss*; mostly *oncus* or, esp., s[lang] *onkus*. (Of food) good; (of a place) passable: New Zealanders': from ca. 1914, chiefly among the soldiers. **1938** *Press* (Christchurch) (McNab Slang) 2 Apr. 18 New Zealanders have their curiously sounding slang... 'ongkus' (good). **1944** BRUNO *Desert Daze* 55 Now Auld Jock and Bluey, having successfully partnered a crown-and-anchor board in their Naafi, and having 'done up' the feloose A.W.L. in Cairo Y.M.C.A.'s, had arrived back at Maadi decidedly 'onkus'. [**1967** MILLER *Ink on My Fingers* 27 For many years he was followed into the office [of the *Otago Daily Times* (Dunedin). c1920s] by his faithful fox terrier, Onkus.]

on one's pat: see PAT *n.*[1]

on-the-drop: see DROP *n.* 1 b.

oozle, *v. Obs.*

1. Also **ouzle**. [Origin uncertain.] To wangle.
1937 PARTRIDGE *Dict. Slang* 594 *ouzle*. pronounced and gen. spelt *oozle*. To obtain illicitly or schemingly: New Zealand soldiers': 1915; ob. Perhaps ex *ooja* + *wangle*.

2. *Wellington tramping.* [?f. *ooze* 'pass slowly through' in transf. use + -*le*.] To meander; take one's time.
1938 *Tararua Tramper* Aug. 5 We were keen to see the renowned 'Whareiti' and oozled off one by one in search thereof. **1958** MASON *Tararua* Sept. 29 The critics will no doubt note that *to oozle* and *to trickle*, which denoted much slower modes of locomotion, were comparatively little used.

opah: see MOONFISH.

opalfish. Any of various small slender greyish marine fishes of fam. Percophidae having bright iridescent markings, esp. *Hemerocoetes monopterygius*.
1938 *TrRSNZ* LXVIII. 415 *Hemerocoetes acanthorhynchus*... Opal-fish. **1956** GRAHAM *Treasury NZ Fishes* 317 Both anglers and commercial fishermen of Port Chalmers knew this fish [sc. *Hemerocoetes monopterygius*] and had bestowed the common name of Opal-fish prior to my having seen one. The opalescent display of colours left no doubt in my mind as to the appropriateness of the common name... The iridescence, when just out of the sea, left no other name for it. **1967** NATUSCH *Animals NZ* 226 The opal fish and blue bonnet are two handsome and colourful species of *Hemerocoetes*. **1986** PAUL *NZ Fishes* 116 *Opalfishes* Family Percophidae. There are several New Zealand species, one of which is common in harbours and over the shelf. The opalfish, *Hemerocoetes monopterygius*, is so named from its iridescent striped and banded colouring of blue, orange, brown and yellow.

open, *a.* [Spec. use of *open* unobstructed, clear: see OED *a.* 8; also US, see Mathews; AND 1829.]

1. a. Most often collocated with **country** or **land**. Not covered with bush; having few or scattered trees; unobstructed by heavy scrub or undergrowth.
1841 *NZ Jrnl.* II. 286 There is much open or fern country. **1849** in Deans *Pioneers* 20 Jan. (1964) 147 Our opinion is, that the greatest part of the plain was covered with timber at no distant period, and that the bush land is not superior to the open land in any respect. **1864** HURSTHOUSE *NZ Handbook* 95 In the..South Island there is a large and magnificent area of 'open country'. [**1864** *Note*] I include in this term all tracts and districts which are not true or dense forest districts. **1872** *TrNZI* IV. 73 In the term 'open' I include plains and hill-sides in the low-lands covered with grass, fern, tutu..spaniards, wild Irishman and snow grasses. **1882** HAY *Brighter Britain* I. 207 We prefer bush-land to open-land for pioneer farming. **1899** BELL *In Shadow of Bush* 10 His father, who owned a large farm..in the open country, some fifty miles nearer the coast, had..started him in life on his own account here in the bush. **1935** MAXWELL *Recollections* 99 There was between the tall bush and the sea a coastal belt of flax, cabbage tree and scrub-covered land. It is described as open land to distinguish it from that covered with big heavy bush.

b. As **open winter**, one reasonably free from snow thus allowing sheep to move freely.
1949 NEWTON *High Country Days* 196 *Open winter*: In winter snow forms a boundary for stock. If the winter is mild this boundary may not be sufficient; the country is then open for sheep to get away back into dangerous areas—hence the term 'open winter'.

2. *South Island.* [AND 1830.] Of land, without obstruction to title; available for settlement. See also OPEN *v.*
1948 SCOTTER *Run Estate & Farm* 1 In April, 1853, six months after his arrival in New Zealand, he bought

820 sheep in Nelson and drove them to Canterbury in search of land and it was only after he saw that all the open country was taken up..that he..decided to cross the Waitaki River. *Ibid.* 15 Yet, until the land was fenced stock had to be herded. There was also the unsold land open for grazing. Each year, therefore, those who wished to graze stock on this open country applied for a depasturing licence.

3. As **open shed** *shearing* [spec. use of *open* available to all, unrestricted], a farm or station where shearers are not contracted before the start of shearing. Cf. SHED *n.*[1] 2.

1872 BARKER *Christmas Cake* iii Brown and Wetherby's was an 'open shed', where any shearers that came were taken on until there were hands enough. **1934** *Press* (Christchurch) (Acland Gloss.) 27 Jan. 15 *Open shed.*—S[*hed*] where the shearers are not engaged beforehand, but roll up on the advertised day and take their chance of employment. I think the custom has quite gone out of use now. **1946** [see PEN 2 b]. **1979** TEMPLE *Stations* 93 It's the last year Ben Griam's an open shed. Those picked this year can book their place for next. **1986** *National Radio* 'Landline' (Farming Programme) 11 Oct. 'Do you have open shed or contract shearing?' 'I prefer the contract gang, but you have to help your local shearers; some wives are on the table, and we're often on the board too.'

4. As **open-pointed** *ppl. a.*, of a sheep, having no wool on the points.

1955 BOWEN *Wool Away* 9 The present-day Romney, with wool to the toe and even on the 'top lip' is much different from the clear open-pointed Romney of fifty years ago.

5. Said of shearing or of fleeces in which the comb and cutter run easily or unhindered through the wool.

1955 BOWEN *Wool Away* 76 On good open shearing, when the grease is up, and the comb enters easily, give the comb a lead on the cutter of one-eighth of an inch.

open, *v.*[1]

1. Also **open up**. [Spec. use of *open* to make land available for settlement: see OED *v.* 12.] To make esp. Crown or waste land available for purchase and settlement.

1853 *Richmond-Atkinson Papers* (1960) I. 131 Some... [*sic*] who wished to stop, intend proceeding to Auckland as they are frightened of bush land, and the block containing fern, which will be next opened, is hardly likely to be in the market for 6 months to come. **1888** D'AVIGDOR *Antipodean Notes* 233 'The country is now comparatively opened up,' Sir Julius Vogel was able to boast. **1902** *Settler's Handbook NZ* (Lands Department) 11 This industry gives employment to a large number of persons, both directly..and indirectly to those who labour at bushfelling, grass-seed sowing, fencing, and otherwise opening up new country.

2. In the phr. **to open the books**, to make available an organization's records for outside scrutiny, now a mainly political catchphrase popularized by the 1984 (Lange) Labour Administration in reference to making public confidential economic, etc. advice given to the previous Administration by its advisers.

[**1984** *Evening Post* (Wellington) 11 July 60 Labour..cannot release such detail until Labour has seen the books and the IMF report has been one of the books Labour has been demanding to be opened.] **1986** *Dominion* (Wellington) 1 Nov. 5 The National Party opened its books to the writer, and made available its records and files. **1987** ROBERTS *Politicians, Public Servants & Public Enterprise* 118 The document was released as part of the pledge by the new [Labour] Government to 'open the books'. [footnoted to a reference to R.O. Douglas's Preface to *Economic Management*, The Treasury, 1984: p. 111] **1987** *National Bus. Rev.* 2 July 3 The opening of the books on Strathmore follows hard on the heels of major shareholder Omnicorp Investments taking effective control..last month. **1992** *Evening Post* (Wellington) 13 June 5 They will..stand up to any investigation as pure canards..unravaged by the now-ritual post-election opening of the books.

open, *v.*[2] [Spec. use of *open* to make a cut in to.]
1. *Goldmining.* [AND 1845.] To break open ground preparatory to mining.

1863 PYKE *Report* in *Handbook NZ Mines* (1887) 8 About the same time several gullies were opened in the Umbrella Ranges; and on the banks of the Waikaia..a permanent goldfield..was also discovered. *Ibid.* 11 Other gullies and beaches further up the river were shortly afterwards opened up.

2. *Shearing.* [AND 1882.] Usu. as **to open up**, to begin shearing, or removing the fleece from a particular area.

1904 LANCASTER *Sons o' Men* 81 A big Maori was making the [shearing] pace; opening up in a scientific fashion with a clean-run cut over the ear-root. **1914** SMITH *Sheep & Wool Industry Australasia* 37 The machine is then driven up the front of the neck several times till the neck wool is well opened up. **1955** BOWEN *Wool Away* 32 Three short sharp blows are essential here to open up the neck for clean shearing. **1981** SUTHERLAND & TAYLOR *Sunrise* 45 He leaned well over the sheep, placed the forelegs under his left arm, and opened up the right side of the belly with a few deft strokes. **1989** *NZ Eng. Newsletter* III. 26 *open up:* To shear wool from a certain area. An example is to 'open up the neck'.

open slather: see SLATHER.

Opo /ˈʌʊpʌʊ/. [f. *Opo*(noni, a coastal township in Northland.] A much-publicized dolphin frequenting Opononi in the 1950s. Cf. PELORUS JACK.

1956 *Weekly News* (Auckland) 15 Feb. 27 Opononi Jack, the man-loving mammal... 'Opo's' antics and shows of delight in human company have already made him Opononi's celebrity No. 1. **1956** *Listener* 23 Mar. 4 The untimely death of Opo George (who turned out to be Georgina) caused sadness in Opononi... Opo was touching the fringe of a world that was stranger than she could know. **1963** ALPERS *Book of Dolphins* 209 The dolphin had become generally known by the nickname 'Opo', having first been known as 'Opononi Jack'. **1972** GASKIN *Whales, Dolphins & Seals* 131 'Opo' was a partly grown female *Tursiops*..believed to be the offspring of a female shot by a local youth. **1988** DOAK *Encounters with Whales & Dolphins* 59 With some famous cases, such as Opo in New Zealand,.., the dolphins have been described as 'social outcasts' or 'bulls ostracised from the herd'. **1991** *Dominion* (Wellington) 13 Apr. 9 Opo's influence in the novel seems to make almost everyone more sensitive and perceptive.

opossum. [AND *possum* 1, 1770 transferred from North American use.]

1. a. POSSUM. (First recorded in NZ as an *attrib.* in *opossum rug*.)

1851 [see 2 below]. **1860** in CUTTEN *Cutten Lett.* (1979) 60 Contemplating me from the open doorway was my friend the bulldog, and in another corner on a bundle of clothing or something of the sort was an opossum. **1892** *Ann. Rep. Wellington Acclimatisation Soc.* Some years after [1858], one or two opossums (presumably Australian Grey Opossums) escaped from confinement in the same neighbourhood [*sc.* Riverton]. **1913** *NZ Gazette* 7 Aug. 2371 Opossums of every variety shall be deemed to be absolutely protected..under the..Animals Protection Act, 1908. **1922** THOMSON *Naturalisation Animals & Plants* 557 [Professor H. B. Kirk's] general conclusions are that opossums do very little real damage in the bush. **1937** *King Country Chronicle* 3 Dec. 4 A live opossum was belched forth from the printing machine. **1949** BAXTER *Collected Poems* (1980) 83 No opossum leaping Stir thee from thy sleeping. **1950** WODZICKI *Introduced Mammals of NZ* 19 The name 'opossum' applies strictly to the true American opossum (family of Didelphidae)... The opossum, now so well established in New Zealand, belongs to the tree-dwellers of the genus *Trichosurus*..(brush-tailed opossum). **1983** *Star* (Auckland) 28 June 4 A security officer outside Telethon headquarters at the Auckland Town Hall on Sunday was confronted with a drunken man dangling a decomposing opossum.

b. *attrib.* passing into Comb.

1931 *Tararua Tramper* Feb. 4 Opossum trappers have blazed a trail of sorts down the upper portion of the valley. **1950** WODZICKI *Introduced Mammals of NZ* 27 Little is known of the value of opossum skin exports before 1921. **1965** SHADBOLT *Among the Cinders* 13 We had opossum stew for dinner. What more did we want? **1980** *NZJAg.* Aug. CXLI. 63 The first farmer with whom I worked in setting up an opossum farm is still in business and operating successfully.

2. Special Comb. **opossum rug** [AND 1841], a rug made from cured opossum skins, popular in Victorian New Zealand.

1851 TORLESSE *Papers* (1958) 5 Jan. 190 I am on a rough trip, laying off 60 miles of roadline, and have nothing but an opossum rug with me. **1866** BARKER *Station Life* (1870) 85 The only thing to remind me that I was not in an English cottage was the opossum rug with which..the bed was covered. **1871** MONEY *Knocking About in NZ* 74 A share of his [*sc.* a digger's] damper and bacon,... a pannikin of tea, or half his blanket or opossum rug, are always at your disposal. **1892** *NZ Official Handbook* 294 [Table of Duties of Customs] Rugs, woollen, cotton, opossum, or other, £20 per cent. *ad valorem* **1917** JAMES STRACHAN *Experiences* in *Neave Land of Munros* (1980) 65 [In 1858] I had to make myself a cap out of a piece of an old opossum rug. **1968** SEDDON *The Seddons* 30 Two of us would find ourselves wrapped in the old grey opossum rug, the rug with the red cloth lining.

opossuming, *vbl. n.* [AND *v.*, 1847.] Trapping, poisoning, or otherwise killing opossums. (Used much earlier than 1970.)

1970 SANSOM *Stewart Islanders* 199 On the runs, opossuming had always been a sideline.

opportunity shop. Usu. in the shortened form **op(p) shop**, orig. a shop selling donated used goods (esp. clothing) to raise funds for charitable purposes; also occas. applied to any secondhand shop dealing mainly in clothing. Often *attrib.*

1933 *NZ Tablet* (Dunedin) 11 Jan. 23 The opportunity shop is still operating satisfactorily, and considering the time of stress, we may say the results are good. **1983** OLIVER *James K. Baxter* 108 The long unkempt beard and straggling hair, the opp-shop clothes and the bare feet were still to come. **1984** DUCKWORTH *Disorderly Conduct* 109 Punks, bikies, trainee civil servants, inner-city fringe people, clad in Opportunity Shop garments. **1989** *Landfall* 172 466 The three of them went to pubs together, handed on news of the best takeaways, op shops, likely exam questions and model answers. **1991** *More* (Auckland) Sept. 44 You don't get bargains like you do with opshop things.

Hence **opshop** *v.*, to patronize an opshop; **opshopper**, one who patronizes an opshop.
1991 *More* (Auckland) Sept. 46 My friends opshopped, too. **1991** *More* (Auckland) Sept. 45 A true opshopper doesn't sort of casually drop into a shop once a week..you're constantly working them.

op shop: see OPPORTUNITY SHOP.

O.P.S.O. /ˈɒpsʌu/. Also **OPSO**. The initials of **On Public Service Only** used on mail from Government Departments sent overseas from 1891–1906 (similar to the use of *O.H.M.S.*) or on stamps identifying such mail; hence *n. pl. Opsos*.

1913 JOLLIFFE *History NZ Stamps* 31 The Postal Department in 1892 introduced the practice of overprinting current stamps as required for its own foreign correspondence with the letters O.P.S.O. (On Public Service Only) diagonally by means of a rubber stamp... This practice was followed until the introduction of 'official' stamps in 1907. **1919** *NZ Stamp Collector* I. 17 Forged O.P.S.O.s... 'I have just been shewn some forged O.P.S.O. stamps which have been offered for sale in Christchurch.' **1938** *Postage Stamps of NZ* I. 460 On December 17, 1891, the instruction was given to officers of the General Post Office that 'all letters posted with stamps from this office will have impressed on each stamp "O.P.S.O."' **1940** *NZ Stamp Collector* XXI. 4 There is..a mint block of four of the 1d Christchurch Exhibition claret..and a representative lot of the rare O.P.S.O.'s. **1950** *Postage Stamps of NZ* II. 177 Certain items which [it was said] had been produced in 1913 by the use of the rubber stamp with inscription O.P.S.O. [were] not issued during the period 1891–1907. **1987** *NZ Specialist* II. 3 Shown below is a rather aged and worn example of the Exempt from Postage Official OPSO Parliamentary Debates Wrapper still with original unopened documents.

orange.

1. In the names of plants with orange-coloured berries, orange-yellow wood, or features resembling those of an orange tree. **a.** As **orange-leaf, orange-wood**, KARAMU 1, having orange-coloured berries, a leaf reminiscent of that of an orange-tree, and yellowish wood.

1867 HOOKER *Handbook* 766 Orange-leaf of Otago. *Coprosma lucida*, etc. **1868** Orange-leaf [see BROADLEAF 2]. **1890** *PWD Catalogue Timbers* (NZ & South Seas Exhib.) 12 Orangewood..Coprosma lucida. **1982** WILSON *Stewart Is. Plants* 108 *Coprosma lucida* Glossy Karamū... Orangewood.— Shrub or small tree. Leaves rather glossy... Flowers clustered creamy... Fruit (on female plants) bright orange in stalked clusters.

b. As **New Zealand orange blossom**, LACEBARK 1 a.

1889 FEATON *Art Album NZ Flora* 55 Hoheria populnea... The 'Houi' or 'Whau-whi'... grows abundantly in both Islands... Owing to the chaste [snow-white] appearance of its flowers, it has not inaptly been termed by some the 'New Zealand orange Blossom'.

c. As **orange-tree**, TARATA, from the odour of the crushed leaf. Cf. LEMONWOOD.

1898 MORRIS *Austral-English* 332 *Orange-Tree, n.* The *New Zealand Orange-Tree* is a name given to the *Tarata*.., from the aromatic odour of its leaves when crushed.

d. As **orange berry**, the native passionfruit (see PASSION-FLOWER 1) from its orange-coloured fruits.

1919 July 29 Vernacular names supplied to J.C. Andersen by W. Best, Otaki in *TrNZI* (1927) LVII. 944 orange berry *Tetrapathaea australis*.

2. See *poorman's orange* (POOR MAN 2).

3. Special Comb. **orange barrel** (also *ellipt.* **barrel**) *drug users*, a capsule or tablet orange in colour and barrel-like in shape; **orange roughy**, see ROUGHY 2.

1982 *Dominion* (Wellington) 16 Feb. 10 At the flat Parker had unwrapped the package which contained five plastic bags. In each was a thousand orange barrels... At this stage of your operation what experience had you had, if any, with barrels or tablets of that type?..I had made many purchases..of those particular orange barrels... 'The details were that I was to give him $6 a barrel.' **1982** *Evening Post* (Wellington) 16 Feb. 20 They drove back to Mr Hansen's flat in Mount Victoria, where Parker took out a package and unwrapped it, showing five clear plastic bags containing thousands of orange barrels (tablets). 'I estimated that in each packet there would have been at least 1000 of these barrels,' he said.

orange-wattled crow: see CROW *n.*[1] 2 (2).

orchardist. [AND (1887) notes that 'App. in more freq. use in Aust. and N.Z. than elsewhere.'] A commercial fruit-grower.

1885 *Wairarapa Daily* 6 Oct. 2 The beetles..experimented with fruit and other cultivated trees, and..they are now inclined to make extensive use of them, to the horror of the orchardist. **1894** *Ann. Rep. Dept. Agric.* II. 109 I will instance the case of an orchardist in the neighbourhood of Auckland, who this year sold over two tons of plums. **1993** *Metro* (Auckland) Feb. 102 Kiwifruit orchardists were the darlings of the banks. **1993** *Dominion* (Wellington) 19 Mar. 10 Other markets are not as particular as the US which is a major orchardist itself.

orchid. Various native species of the plant family Orchidaceae.

1. bamboo orchid. *Earina mucronata*.

1946 *Bull. Wellington Bot. Soc. No.14* 8 Here are some [vernacular names]... *Uncinia australis*, hook grass; *Earina* spp., bamboo orchid.

2. greenhood orchid. Also *ellipt.* **greenhood.** *Pterostylis montana*, TUTUKIWI.

1978 MOORE & IRWIN *Oxford Book NZ Plants* 194 *Pterostylis montana, greenhood*. On open grassy banks, even in cities like Wellington, on forest margins..the little greenhood orchids push up in winter in the north and well into summer further south. **1982** [see TUTUKIWI].

3. lady's slipper orchid. *Dendrobium cunninghamii*, an epiphytic orchid of coastal and lowland forest.

1964 DEMPSEY *Little World Stewart Is.* 16 On another rocky islet a cascade of beautiful dendrobium orchid hangs down. This is the lady's slipper orchid. The unopened buds are miniature white high-heeled slippers that a fairy might wear to a ball. **1982** WILSON *Stewart Is. Plants* 288 *Dendrobium cunninghamii* Lady's Slipper Orchid... Flower buds 'lady's slipper'—shaped, creamy.

4. New Zealand Easter orchid. *Earina autumnalis*, an autumn-flowering epiphytic orchid. See also RAUPEKA.

1982 SALE *Four Seasons* 116 Here [in the bush] we found, growing on a fallen log, the spiked fronds and the tiny deep-scented flowers of the New Zealand Easter orchid—raupeka or Earina autumnalis. **1994** *Dominion* 4 June 17 Both [*Earina*] autumnalis (the Easter orchid) and *mucronata* prefer cool conditions

and will grow well in Wellington. Both have tiny creamy white flowers.

5. sun orchid. *Thelymitra* spp., a terrestrial orchid whose flowers open in sunny weather.

1969 *Standard Common Names Weeds* 76 sun orchid *Thelymitra*. **1982** WILSON *Stewart Is. Plants* 284 *Thelymitra* Sun Orchids New Zealand has 12 species of this, mostly Australian genus... Unfortunately, except for *T. venosa*..the flowers tend to open only briefly on bright days.

ordinary bloke (or **joker**). Also with various collocations of **average, ordinary, real** with (**Kiwi**) **bloke** or (**Kiwi**) **joker**, the stereotypical New Zealand male regarded (often with disastrous consequences) as a touchstone of modesty and good commonsense. Also *joc.* **ordinary blokess**, similarly, a female (see quot. 1992). Cf. *good keen man* (GOOD *a.* 3).

1959 *Review* Nov. 16 It is a candid look at the present-day New Zealanders..the ordinary joker in [a] tartan shirt with his do-it-yourself concrete mixer... The practical, unimaginative, adaptable, prejudiced, smug, kindly, resilient, casual, slangy, independent, open-hearted she'll be right New Zealander. **1964** CAPE 'Taumarunui' in Reid *Book NZ* (1964) 223 A New Zealand Joker's Lament for his Sheila. I'm an ordinary joker getting old before my time For my heart's in Taumarunui on the Main Trunk Line. **1986** JAMES *Quiet Revolution* 84 Muldoon constructed a stereotype of the 'ordinary bloke' or 'ordinary citizen' whom he held, in his speeches, in exaggerated reverence as the fount of all wisdom and the touchstone of political legitimacy. **1988** MACRAE *Awful Childhoods* 47 In manner Dunc was yer down-to-earth Kiwi joker... Great man for his piss-ups. **1989** BIOLETTI *The Yanks Are Coming* 15 It was a land where..roll-yer-owns were the sign of the real Kiwi bloke, while 'tailormades' were a drawing-room affectation. *Ibid.* 16 Americans..tended to be more articulate than the average Kiwi joker. The silent 'Man Alone' New Zealand male, suspicious of language, talk and books, contrasted strongly with the fast-talking servicemen from bustling American cities. **1991** *Contact* (Wellington) 22 Aug. 2 [Column title] 'Keeping You in Contact' by the Ordinary Bloke. **1991** CLEVELAND *Great NZ Songbook* 5 Imitators in New Zealand..composed some [lyrics] of their own written from the viewpoint of a shearer..a bushman or even an 'ordinary Kiwi joker'. **1992** *Dominion Sunday Times* (Wellington) 9 Aug. 9 He took near-plenipotentiary power, the better to do all that he did for his ordinary blokes (and, near the end, because even he could not be entirely untouched by linguistic fashion, 'blokesses'.) **1992** *Dominion* (Wellington) 28 Aug. 8 Keep up the good work on behalf of the ordinary bloke and blokess, yours sincerely, Rt Hon Don McKinnon. **1993** *Dominion* (Wellington) 24 July 12 I don't know if I'm one of those ordinary Kiwi blokes. But I've tried to be. **1994** *North & South* Apr. 59 Crowe [a former national cricket captain] is not seen as being accessible to 'blokes', while Rutherford is seen as being a bloke himself.

ordinary claim. *Goldmining. Hist.* A claim of standard size worked by hand. See quot. 1892.

1862 WEKEY *Otago As It Is* 61 (quoting Otago Gfds Regs) Claims shall be classified thus;—1. Ordinary Claims, *i.e.*, alluvial claims worked without the aid of sluices or machines. 2. Sluice and machine claims [etc.]. **1892** PYKE *Gold-Miners' Guide* 7 *Ordinary claim* in alluvial.—An area *n.e.* 100ft. by 100ft. for each miner, and not more than 100,000 square feet in one claim. But the Warden may grant *double ground* on being satisfied that such extension is necessary for working the ground.

oreo /ˈɒrijʌu/. Also **oreo dory**. [*oreo* f. the family name *Oreo*(somatidae (+ *dory* f. the superficial resemblance of this to the *dory* family): Oreosomatidae derives from the generic name *Oreosoma* established by Cuvier (1817?, 1819) (*oreo* 'mountain' *soma(tos)* 'body'), the species being known for many years only from the juveniles which carry prominent pyramid-shaped projections, giving rise to a common name 'mountainsides' used elsewhere. Ichthyologists prefer the simplex *oreo* as the common name to prevent confusion with the *dory* family.]

1. Any of various large-eyed, now commercially important, deep water fishes of the fam. Oreosomatidae, esp. **black oreo** (*Allocyttus niger*). See also DORY.

    1978 *Catch* Aug. 5 Log books from Soviet trawlers fishing..since 1 April indicate that catches are almost entirely oreo dories. Before those recent Russian catches, oreos were virtually unknown in New Zealand waters as few trawlers had attempted to fish such deep water. **1986** PAUL *NZ Fishes* 76 Oreos (fam. Oreosomatidae) are deepwater dories with large eyes and sometimes a strongly scaled skin. New Zealand has three common species plus two rarer species.

2. With a modifier: **black, smooth**.

(1) **black oreo (oreo dory)**. *Allocyttus niger*.

    1978 *Catch* Aug. 5 Four species of oreo are known from New Zealand..although Soviet catches contain only two of these: the black oreo *Allocyttus* sp., and the smooth (or small-spined) oreo *Pseudocyttus maculatus*. **1983** *NZ Times* 20 Mar. 9 This week's fish is the black oreo dory, also known as black dory, deepwater dory, and at my local suppliers—deepsea dory. This fish is taken by deepsea trawling... Don't confuse it with the john dory. In spite of its name, the black oreo dory is not a member of the zeidae family of true dories. **1992** *Evening Post* (Wellington) 16 June 15 Black oreo dory could be worth a further $100 million or more a year.

(2) **Smooth oreo (dory)**. *Pseudocyttus maculatus*.

    1978 [see (1) above]. **1986** PAUL *NZ Fishes* 77 Smooth oreo *Pseudocyttus maculatus*... An important component of the commercial oreo dory catch, providing large thick and almost boneless fillets with a delicate flavour, suitable for all cooking methods.

organ bird. [f. the range of its song resembling organ notes.] Either of the TUI or the KOKAKO.

    1817 NICHOLAS *NZ* I. 335 There was however one bird that was distinguished from all the rest, as well by the compass and variety of its notes, as by their incomparable sweetness. This bird, which has been brought to Port Jackson, and highly prized there, is called by the colonists the organ bird, and is, I believe, peculiar to New Zealand. **1826** SHEPHERD *Journal* 9 Mar. in Howard *Rakiura* (1940) 359 This day returned to Albion cove saw..a large black and white Duck called a Paradise Duck, a black bird called the organ bird, shags, a Black Robin with a white breast. **1938** GORDON *Children of Tane* 227 The rare Kokako, or Organ-bird..is, rather than the Korimako, the true Bellbird of the New Zealand forest. **1966** FALLA et al. *Birds NZ* 236 Kokako *Callaeas cinerea*... Wattled Crow, Organ-bird, Gill-bird, Bluegill (N.I.). **1985** *Reader's Digest Book NZ Birds* 303 Kokako *Callaeas cinerea*... Blue wattled crow, blue gill, orange wattled crow, organ bird.

Original All Blacks, the Originals: see ALL BLACK 1 b.

orihou. Also **orihau**. [Ma. /ˈorihou/: Williams 241 *Orihou*... a shrub.] *Pseudopanax colensoi* (fam. Araliaceae), a shrub or small tree with 3–7 foliate leaves and sessile (or sub-sessile) leaflets.

    1939 COCKAYNE & TURNER *Trees NZ* 89 *Nothopanax Colensoi* (Araliaceae). Orihau, Mountain Ivy-tree. **1940** LAING & BLACKWELL *Plants NZ* 324 *Nothopanax Colensoi*... Maori name *Orihou*. **1982** WILSON *Stewart Is. Plants* 82 *Pseudopanax* sp. aff. colensoi Fivefinger.. Threefinger.. Orihou... Shrub or small, rounded tree. Leaves with 3–7 unstalked 'fingers' (mostly 5).

Orion: see SHACKLOCK.

oro-oro. [Ma. /ˈorooro/: Williams 242 *Oro* (iii)..Clump of trees, copse; generally followed by the name of the tree.] A tree of the MAIRE family, *Nestegis montana* (fam. Oleaceae), having shiny leaves in it adult form.

    1906 CHEESEMAN *Manual NZ Flora* 438 *O[lea] montana*... A much-branched round-headed..tree, 20–50 ft. high..*Orooro; Narrow-leaved Maire*. **1963** POOLE & ADAMS *Trees & Shrubs* 170 Orooro. Tree reaching 12 m. Leaves: juvenile up to 7–15 cm, narrow-linear; adult, shining, coriaceous. Drupes 6–8mm long, red. **1986** SALMON *Native Trees NZ* 290 Oro-oro is found from sea level to 600 m in forests from Mangonui in the north to Nelson and Marlborough in the south.

Oscar. Also **Oscar Asche**. [f. the name of *Oscar Asche* (1871–1936), an actor: AND 1917.] Rhyming slang for 'cash'.

    1946 COOZE *Ten Bob Each Way* (Foreword.) It's easy to laugh at a joke but it takes real humour to laugh at a joke [sc. a losing horse] which carried his oscar at the rear of the field. **1946** MILLER *There Was Gold* 31 [In the early thirties money] was also oscar, and the origin of that, I discovered, was a bit more obscure. Oscar Asche, the name of a famous figure in the theatre world some years ago, rhymed admirably with cash, and the abbreviation to Oscar was a matter of course. **1955** BJ *Cameron Collection* (TS July) oscar (n) Cash. Shortening of Oscar Ashe, a once famous actor, this in turn being rhyming slang for cash. **1984** OVENDEN *Ratatui* 195 ''is wife rang up an' said 'e 'ad to go. Always does what 'e's told. Even with 'is pocketmoney. She keeps 'er fingers on the Oscar Asche that one.'

Ossie: see AUSSIE.

ostrich foot. Also **large** (or **small** or **southern**) **ostrich foot**. Any of several univalve molluscs of the fam. Struthiolariidae but esp. the large (80 mm) handsome tan or brown-striped *Struthiolaria papulosa*.

    1947 POWELL *Native Animals NZ* 26 Ostrich Foot (*Struthiolaria papulosa*). A fine shell up to 3 inches in length, conspicuous for its strong white lip to the aperture and radiate pattern of reddish-brown bands. **1955** DELL *Native Shells* 21 Large Ostrich Foot... This characteristic New Zealand shell owes its scientific and its common name to the fact that the points on the aperture of the shell reminded its discoverer of the claws of a bird's feet. **1966** *Encycl. NZ* II. 718 Ostrich Foot (*Struthiolaria papulosa*)... It is representative of a family which has developed in New Zealand from Cretaceous times. **1970** PENNIKET *NZ Seashells in Colour* 28 The Ostrich Foots. An odd name for the New Zealand members of a widespread incredibly varied and most attractive super-family. **1983** GUNSON *Collins Guide to Seashore* 91 The ostrich foot shells are members of the large family that includes the famous Pacific conches.

Otagan: see OTAGO C.

Otago *often locally* /ʌuˈtagə/, *n*. and *attrib*. [ad. Ma. *Otakou*: cf. c1835 BOULTBEE *Journal* (1986) 79 Neffiteia was the daughter of Pohu, a chief and brother to Taāttoori, head man of Otargo.]

A. *n. WW1*. Usu. as **the Otagos**, until the formation of the New Zealand Division in 1916, the Otago Battalion of the Infantry Brigade; thence, either the 1st or 2nd Otago Battalions of variously organized Infantry Brigades. Occas. early in WW1, the Otago Mounted Rifles Regiment of the divisional cavalry.

    1917 *Chron. NZEF* 27 June 223 I think the Otagos had a fairly easy time. **1919** WAITE *New Zealanders at Gallipoli* 106 Others, particularly the Otagos, hung on grimly through the long night. **1966** *Encycl. NZ* III. 561 The four infantry battalions each 1,000-strong when they landed [at Anzac]..sailed [back] in one small ship—239 of the Canterburys, 130 of the Otagos, fewer than 100 of the Wellingtons, all looking like scarecrows. **1982, 1984** [see AUCKLAND 1]. **1987** KNOX *After Z-Hour* 174 [WW1] We met one of the wounded Otagos on his way back.

B. *attrib*. **a.** Pertaining to, originating in, or resident in the provincial district of Otago.

    1859 THOMSON *Story NZ* II. 188 It is worthy of notice, that the colonists, soon after the formation of all the settlements, acquired distinguishing epithets; thus there was an Auckland cove..an Otago cockney, and a Canterbury pilgrim. **1880** BATHGATE *NZ* 60 In the wild, mountainous districts goods were packed, and the Otago pack-saddle became so noted that it was used as a model by the Imperial Government in the Abyssinian War. **1959** SINCLAIR *History NZ* 104 In 1859..there occurred an incident known as the 'Otago Raid'. The wily Scots, hearing of unemployment in the capital, carried off a hundred settlers from the mild, temperate and fruitful North, to the frigid, bleak and snowy South.

b. In the special collocation **Otago block**, see BLOCK *n*.[1] 1 a.

C. In composition as a formant in various nouns denoting those born or resident in the Otago provincial district, or in adjectives denoting the Otago provincial district, its perceived characteristics, or those of its residents: **Otag(o)an; Otagoist** *n. hist.*; **Otagoite; Otagonian** obs.

    1862 WEKEY *Otago As It Is* 76 'Old Identity' is an entirely Otagonian idiom. It is meant to designate the early settlers of the province and their adherents. **1870** *TrNZI* II. 170 Still it has an interest..especially to Otagonians, to whom a hot spring of any sort is a natural wonder. **1874** MEREWETHER *By Sea & By Land* 187 An Otagoist [i.e. an Otago supporter of provincial government] complained to me. **1874** BATHGATE *Col. Experiences* 25 'Old Identities'. The phrase..is one familiar in the ears of all **Otagans** as household words. *Ibid*. 235 The chief beauty of Otagan bush scenery lies in the ferns. **1890** *Otago Witness* (Dunedin) 27 Nov. 7 As a rule Otagan soil is not sufficiently light..to be borne away upon the wings of a nor'-wester. **1909** THOMPSON *Ballads About Business* 86 The Grand Scotch Game (*From a Central Otagoans's Point of View.*) [sc. curling] **1924** *Otago Witness* (Dunedin) 4 Mar. 69 When one thinks of an Otagan, there flashes into the mind a certain phrase: 'Joseph was a just man'! **1947** BEATTIE *Early Runholding* 10 It must be remembered that the administration of the Waste Lands Board, controlling the runs, played a conspicuous part in Otagoan politics. **1991** *Dominion* (Wellington) 19 Dec. 26 Dowling obviously supported his fellow Otagoite Mains for the All Black coaching post.

other side: see SIDE I 1.

otter. For the so-called 'otter', a rumoured native animal, see WAITOREKE.

OURISIA

ourisia /ə'rɪziə/. [From the name of a plant genus *Ourisia* (fam. Scrophulariaceae), confined to the southern hemisphere and named by P. Commerson in 1789, from *Ouris* the name of an 18th century governor of the Falkland Islands.] Any of several *Ourisia* spp., montane-alpine herbs of shaded sites. See also FOXGLOVE.

1900 *Canterbury Old & New* 188,190 To this assemblage of plants also belong the New Zealand 'Edelweiss'..and the exquisite white-flowered ourisias. [1900 *Note*] *Ourisia macrocarpa* and *macrophylla*. **1908** *AJHR* C-11 40 *Ourisia caespitosa*. Creeping ourisia. Alpine meadows. **1933** *Canterbury Mountaineer* 40 There were keas everywhere..with three very wicked ones having a contest to see which could bite off the most ourisia stems. **1981** DENNIS *Paparoas Guide* 165 In the spring a number of ourisias flower on the Paparoa tops, including the mountain foxgloves *O. macrocarpa* and *O. macrophylla* (the latter of which also grows in the lowlands). **1982** WILSON *Stewart Is. Plants* 252 *Ourisia caespitosa* Creeping ourisia... Creeping forming deep green patches... Flowers white.

out, *a.* and *prep*.

A. *adj*. In collocations and phrases. **1.** In a sense 'distant from a main settlement': **out-blocker** *hist.*, one who lives on a remote settlement block; **out-district**, a region remote from town; **out-settlement** *hist.* [also N. Amer. and elsewhere; AND 1803, of a convict settlement], a settled place or district remote from a main town and its protection; a backblock farm; **out-settler** [also N. Amer. and elsewhere: AND 1802], one who lives and works in a district remote from a town and its protection. See also OUTBACK.

1913 *Triad* 10 May 35 It has been my calling these many years to travel up and down this land, in the course of which I have met college professors, college graduates, dungareed **out-blockers**, and the varied gamut between. **1858** *Richmond-Atkinson Papers* (1960) I. 408 The sale of spirits on the two gallon system. This I consider to be the chief curse of the **out districts**. **1868** *McLean Papers* (ATLTS) XXVIII. 227 [The enemy] will retaliate upon our **out-settlements**. **c1910** MACDONALD *Reminiscences* (VUWTS) 19 I will now refer to the outsettlements or back-blocks of the early New Zealand days. *Ibid.* 18 When I come to write of the outsettlements from Wellington, or as they are now called, the 'back blocks'. **1922** COWAN *NZ Wars* (1955) II. 138 Panapa, Nikora, and Te Rangitahau were to deal simultaneously with the out-settlements of *pakeha* and Maori and then join in the sack of Napier. **1843** *NZ Company Reports* XII (1844) 23 Sept. 135 Caution him against exciting the natives against the **out-settlers**. **1860** *Richmond-Atkinson Papers* 19 Feb. (1960) I. 522 Many people feel certain the Maoris will be overawed; the preparations already being made by the removal of out-settlers to the town, and the erection of strong block houses in one or two places have astonished them. **1879** FEATON *Waikato War* 7 (Griffiths Collect.) The Maories living in the vicinity of the out-settlers prepared for the coming struggle. **1922** COWAN *NZ Wars* (1955) I. 161 As the war went on and the out-settlers were driven in, and New Plymouth was reduced practically to a state of siege. **1959** SINCLAIR *History NZ* 76 Atiawa tribesmen, returning to the vicinity of New Plymouth and finding Europeans on their land, intimidated the 'out-settlers' and obstructed surveyors.

2. In a sense 'distant from or beyond the main building of a rural station or property': **out-flock**, sheep grazing on other than the home run or home paddocks; **out-hut** *obs*. [AND 1873], a shepherd's or musterer's hut at a distance from the home-station; **out-shepherd**, one who shepherds from an out-station. See also OUT-STATION.

1939 BEATTIE *First White Boy Born Otago* 52 I consider Jones had 4000 sheep when the 1848 settlers came, as in addition to the three **out-flocks** of 1000 each he had fully 1000 at the homestead. **1861** in Kennaway *Crusts* (1874) 182 No hour's shepherding and back..no stroll to the **out-hut**,—but a positive, unmistakable expedition, with extra-heavy packs. **1900** SCOTT *Colonial Turf* 165 Periodical rounds to the out-huts, taking the shepherds their rations. **1933** JONES *Autobiography Early Settler* 60 Nowadays, I believe most of the runs have out-huts built to save the trouble of shifting the tents etc. **1900** SCOTT *Colonial Turf* 166 Little wonder that..so many of the lonely **out-shepherds** in the high-country of Otago have gone dotty.

3. *Two-up*. In the collocation **out better**, OUTER *n*. 1.

1917 *Chron. NZEF* 16 May 137 'Out' betters tore their hair and swore—The 'ins' were in the sun!

4. In various phrases. **a. to be out** *obs.*, to be put out to foster in an institution.

1909 *Truth* 18 Dec. 6 They entered the bonds a few years back, and have a child now two and a-half years of age, which is 'out,' or, in other words, is being reared in some institution.

b. (to be) out on one's own, (to be) beyond reproach; **out on its own**, excellent of its kind.

1935 STRONG in Partridge *Slang Today* 287 Now don't say that about my tin plate or I'll go crook: He is out on his own and, in fact, he is shook on me. *Ibid.* 288 You'll do me, D! You are out on your own. **1961** PARTRIDGE *Dict. Slang.* (Suppl.) 1210 *out on its own—like a country shit-house*. Excellent; unique: New Zealand: since ca. 1910. An elaboration of the coll.: *out on one's*, or *its, own*.

c. to be out of one's tree, to be drunk.

1986 *Listener* 22 Nov. 46 MC: I'm drunk... Drunk. Tanked. Cut. Sloshed. Out of my tree. Shickered to beat the band.

d. out to it [cf. OED *adv.* 19 e], dead drunk; fast asleep.

1988 MCGILL *Dict. Kiwi Slang* 80 *out to it* unconscious, often from too much alcohol; eg 'Clive wanted to continue with the pub crawl, but Keith was out to it.'

B. *prep.* and *adv.* **1.** As **out the**, *ellipt.* for *out at the* [cf. OED *out prep.* 2 *Obs.* or *dial.*]; **out the monk**, see MONK.

1985 MCGILL *G'day Country* 171 Alan didn't have a bad life in Dunedin, probably because a good deal of it was out the point, at Puratanu. 'I've got a wee crib there.'

2. *Chatham Islands*. To or in mainland New Zealand, esp. as **to go out**. See also UP *adv.* 2.

1996 TV1 'Heartland' programme about the Chatham Islands. Interviewees use *go out*. One says: 'I stayed out for two months'.

outback, *adv.*, *a.*, and *n*. Often separable as in **way out back**. [Ellipt. *out* (in) the *back* (country), etc.): AND 1869.]

A. *adv*. In a rural district remote from a town or settlement.

1904 LANCASTER *Sons o' Men* 2 Seven–ninths of the Mindoorie men had been born out-back, and bred in the hill-country. **1909** THOMPSON *Ballads About Business* 43 Now I've been around some stations way out back upon the hills, **1915** *Countess of Liverpool's Gift Book* 40 Curious things take place outback. **1936** MASON *Collected Poems* (1971) 85 The lone bush digging gum and the starving bushie outback. **1971** TAYLOR *Plekhov*

OUTER

Place 26 Gray and I had been out back and, as usual, had lost track of time.

B. *adj*. Pertaining to or characteristic of areas remote from a town or settlement.

1905 BAUCKE *White Man Treads* 262 In my recent outback explorations I have met with scenes which..brought home to me..the imperative necessity..that it be a criminal offence..to practise tohungaism. **1914** in *Hist. N. Otago from 1853* (1978) 111 Their carts full of groceries scoured the country..supplying the wants of the outback settlers. **a1927** ANTHONY *Dave Baird* in *Follow the Call* (1975) 112 If you searched the outback district..I doubt if a worse built whare than that could have been found. **1958** MULGAN *Making of New Zealander* 17 But road or bridge could be life or death to an outback settler. **1965** MCLAGLAN *Stethoscope & Saddlebags* 172 Air Travel Limited had inaugurated a modest but adventurous service for those outback settlers south of Franz Josef. **1952** THOMSON *Deer Hunter* 23 What looms more important [than danger] in our lives outback is boredom, or a shortage of tobacco. **1986** WATSON *Address to a King* 59 All sorts of characters used to gather there, hunters and miners, ringers from outback stations.

C. *n*. [AND 1893.] **a.** As **the outback** (occas. **the outbacks** on analogy of **the backblocks**), sparsely settled country remote from a town or settlement.

1905 *Truth* 11 Nov. 7 'Look here,' said the bushie..said the man from the outback. **1933** *Press* (Christchurch) (Acland Gloss.) 9 Sept. 15 Two new-fangled literary expressions, *out back* and *backblocks*, are driving *back-country* out of newspaper use. **1938** HYDE *Nor Yrs. Condemn* 145 The town, to which many bushfellers and men from the outback came when they drew their pay cheques, was accustomed to small troubles. **1959** SINCLAIR *History NZ* 97 Puhoi (the name of which, corrupted, is apparently the origin of the slang term 'the Boo-ay', a synonym for 'the out-backs'). **1960** ROGERS *Long White Cloud* 13 I told you to stay in the outback till you got all those crossbreeds. **1973** WHEELER *Hist. Sheep Stations NI* 99 Today the remoteness of the outback is fading.

b. A person from the outback, a BACKBLOCKER q.v.

1905 BAUCKE *White Man Treads* 295 I asked a farthest outback his tenure : 'Well,' and he lingered on the 'well', 'mine is a perpetual lease.'

outdoor education. Also **outside education**. Outdoor leisure activities organized by schools.

1973 *NZ College of Ed. Occasional Papers* IV. No.2 5 Outdoor education—be it specialised, like canoeing, scuba-diving, climbing or skiing,... or generalised, like camping. **1986** *Policy Statement on Educ. outside Classroom* 1 The term 'outside education' has been generally used to describe the more physical activities conducted in a range of environments.

outer. *n*.

1. *Two-up*. An out-better; one 'outside the ring' who, not being the person in charge of the ring ('ringie'), places a bet on the result of the spin against the betting choice of the 'spinner' and the 'inners' ('in-betters') who support the spinner's choice. Cf. OUT *a.* 3.

1917 *Chron. NZEF* 16 May 137 'Up and do'em!' yelled the 'inners', The 'outers' said, 'No Chance!'

2. In the phr. **to be on the outer** [cf. AND *outer* 1 (1915) the non-members' area of a race-course; also (an onlooker) on the periphery of a two-up ring: 2 (1902) disadvantaged]. **a.** To be unpopular or unacceptable; to be excluded from a group.

1955 B J Cameron *Collection* (TS July) on the outer 1. Almost penniless. 2. On the way out, had it. **1988** McGill *Dict. Kiwi Slang* 80 *outer* phr. *on the outer* out of favour, or penniless; from the outer enclosure at a racecourse; eg 'After Dick was seen in the big anti-apartheid march on telly, he was on the outer at the rugby club.'

b. *Prison.* To be on the outside (of prison).
1953 Hamilton *Till Human Voices Wake Us* 147 Good God, said Neil, he was barely six shillings in the pound, used to talk all day about the colours of a motorbike he had on the outer.

3. [Poss. f. *outer* something which puts one 'out of action'.] **a.** *WW2.* A minor wound.
1944 Fullarton *Troop Target* 171 I'll have to get an 'outer'.

b. An alcoholic binge.
1913 Ferguson *Marie Levant* 8 (Griffiths Collect.) I consider that I was a temperate young man, and as such was respected by my acquaintances. On the night of the first day of May, I indulged in an 'outer'.

outside education: see OUTDOOR EDUCATION.

out-station.
1. *Hist.* [f. STATION I.] A subsidiary missionary station serving outlying areas too remote for convenient regular travel from the main mission station.
1841 Bidwill *Rambles in NZ* (1952) 62 I was joined by a native called Peter, who had been left..to superintend the building of a house..which he will use as an out-station to visit every two or three months, just as the clergymen do in England with their distant flocks. **1961** Reed *N. Cape to Bluff* 20 Te Paki was one of several outstations during Yates's reign.

2. [f. STATION III: AND 1829.] A subordinate living quarters of a large grazing property at some distance from the main establishment or 'home station'. See also *shepherd's hut*, *station*, *whare* (SHEPHERD *n.*).
1848 Torlesse *Papers* (1958) 40 Captain Thomas..& I breakfasted at Rhodes's; afterwards pulled across the harbour..to Mt. Pleasant, an out-station of Rhodes. **1859** Fuller *Five Years Residence* 157 Outstations are started for the shepherds, who watch separate flocks, to live in. **1863** Butler *First Year* x 150 As your mob increases, you can put an out-station on the other side of the run. **1870** Prentice *A Tale of NZ* (GALMS) 37 After the first lambing was over I was detailed to take my turn at out-station duty. **1881** Nesfield *Chequered Career* 32 [We were] sent to learn the art of sheep-farming at different out-stations. At these out-stations are shepherds and boundary-riders stationed. **1898** Hocken *Contributions* 168 The runholder was also allowed a pre-emptive right of purchase on his run of eighty acres for his principal station and ten acres for each out-station. **1904** *NZ Illustr. Mag.* Apr. 48 To facilitate the working of the station, there were..places where the hands resided. The Homestead,... the chief one, was at the end of the station nearest civilisation. About eight miles further back was a cottage, known as the 'Out-Station'. **1916** Gascoyne *Soldiering NZ* 8 But I usually reached an out-station or a shepherd's whare before dark, and was always welcome to a meal. **1947** Newton *Wayleggo* 154 *Out-station*: Some high country stations are so extensive that it is necessary to have a second homestead situated in some distant part of the property. Such a place is termed an 'out-station'. **1973** Fernandez *Tussock Fever* 15 Each week..Bessie packed up stores for the cooks at the two out-stations. **1988** *Through the Looking Glass* 114 The cottage which was built as an outstation residence for the original Home Station taken up by Edward Elworthy in 1856.

3. *Hist.* [Spec. use of military *out-station*: AND 1817.] An Armed Constabulary outpost.
1852 *Rules & Regs. of Constabulary Force NZ* The Superintendent, Inspector, or other Officer in charge of a Police District, or Out-station.

ouzle, var. OOZLE.

oven.
1. *Hist.* HANGI 1. Cf. EARTH OVEN, MAORI OVEN, *native oven* (NATIVE B 3 a).
1819 Marsden *Lett. & Jrnls.* (1932) 193 The cooks opened their ovens and served all their separate portions. c**1826–27** Boultbee *Journal* (1986) 111 oven—oòhmoo. **1835** Yate *NZ* (1970) 108 When the stones are heated to redness, they are taken out of the oven, and the place cleared from any remains of burning wood.

2. In the phr. **to have (a bun, scone, etc.) in the oven**, to be pregnant.
1959 Middleton *The Stone* 53 Reg would say there was another scone in the oven and how he hoped it was a boy. **1987** Eldred-Grigg *Oracles & Miracles* 198 'I don't want to wear white,' I said... 'Something in the oven?' I said. **1988** Lay *Fools on Hill* 52 Baby. Nobody said baby. Sprog, kid, up the duff, one in the oven, but not baby.

over. In various phrases.
1. *prep.* **a. over the hill**, see HILL 4.
b. over the fence, see FENCE *n.*[1] 2 c.
c. over the plimsoll [f. *plimsoll line* marking the limit of loading of a ship], drunk.
1921 Lord *Ballads of Bung 'Stunology'* (1976) 11 'Over the plimsoll', 'rocking' or that 'you're on the roll'—All these expressions clearly show you love the flowing bowl.

2. *adv. Ellipt.* for **over at**.
1964 Harvey *Any Old Dollars Mister?* 3 Then the eggs..would start to roll around and he was more worried about cracking them than falling into the gully over Chadwicks' place next door.

overland, *adv.* and *a. Hist.* [Spec. use of *overland* proceeding across land.] In early colonial times, of, pertaining to, or with reference to cross-country travel and transport, esp. in the South Island, and often with stock, as distinct from the usual (and, then, often easier) travel by sea.

A. *adv.*
1850 Torlesse *Papers* (1958) 150 Captain Mitchell and Mr Dashwood have lately arrived here overland from Nelson, after a six weeks' trip: they..appear to have found a very practicable road for driving stock. **1865** Chudleigh *Diary* 4 May (1950) 180 The cattle are being brought overland and he has come to see about selling. **1879** Haast *Geol. Canterbury & Westland* 72 Only those diggers went back overland who had not the means to take a passage in a steam or sailing vessel. **1889** Mitchell *Rhymes & Rambles* 19 I travelled overland to Christchurch on two pounds of bread and two Maori hens. **1898** Hocken *Contributions* 150 In May, 1852,... Valpy..made the journey overland from Christchurch in twelve days' hard travelling. **1914** Pfaff *Diggers' Story* 111 From there [Hyde, Otago] I walked overland to the West Coast, landed in Hokitika in the latter end of 1865.

B. Used *attrib.* in collocations: **overland mail** (also abbrev. **o.m.**), mail carried overland as distinct from sea-mail; **overland route**, a (usu. stock) route across country.
1848 Wakefield *Handbook for NZ* 291 The overland mail, between the two first of these places [Wellington and Auckland], passes through New Plymouth each way once a fortnight. **1856** *McLean Papers* (ATLTS) III. 10 No less than a dozen native letters were received by yesterday's o.m. **1861** in *Richmond-Atkinson Papers* (1960) I. 709 By the overland mail, the answer from Waikato to the Governor's proclamation came in. **1865** Chudleigh *Diary* 4 July (1950) 192 The first Overland Mail to the West Coast went through today. They had to borrow a horse from Enys to go on one stage. **1865** Mueller *My Dear Bannie* (1958) 41 The **Overland Route** [from Christchurch to Hokitika] was perfectly frightful.

overlander. *Hist.* Mainly *SI.* [AND 1841.] A man who drives stock long distances across country.
1851 Torlesse *Papers* (1958) 211 His brother too is now on his way [from Marlborough]—the first overlander with fat sheep for the Canterbury market. **1854** *Canterbury Almanac* 59 During the summer of 1852–3, several more overlanders from Nelson imported sheep and cattle into the Canterbury district. **1865** [see MATEY]. **1930** *Press* (Christchurch) in *Studholme Coldstream* (1985) 4 With the exception of Valpy, they were the first white overlanders between Christchurch and Dunedin, and they were the first to cross cattle over the Waitaki river. **1933** *Press* (Christchurch) (Acland Gloss.) 11 Nov. 15 *Overlander.*—An Australian word for a man driving sheep or cattle a long distance. It was sometimes used in Canterbury in the early days. (*Lyttelton Times*, March 27 1852.)

overseas, *adv.* and *a.*

A. *adv.* [f. *oversea a.* foreign: the Old English for *foreigner* was *ofersæwisca* 'over-sea(w)ish person'.] Abroad, esp. applied to service outside New Zealand in WW1 and WW2, and with verbs of movement or travel (esp. **to go overseas**), or referring to servicemen in WW2, **the boys overseas**.
1919 Waite *New Zealanders at Gallipoli* 17 The body of the first soldier of the New Zealand Expeditionary Force to die overseas was reverently committed to the deep. **1936** *Na To Hoa Aroha* (1988) III. 211 A race which had no count beyond mano [*i.e.* 1000]..cannot be expected to evince surprise that one of their number should take a foremost place among the millions of pakehas overseas. **1942** *NZEF Times* 2 Feb. 3 They were asked by the announcer..to remember the 'boys' overseas—the members of the New Zealand Forces. **1957** Frame *Owls Do Cry* (1967) 35 My uncle, the bank manager. My cousin, who's gone overseas. **1968** Slatter *Pagan Game* 165 He had been overseas and he had been up and down the island picking up jobs. **1985** Rosier-Jones *Cast Two Shadows* 10 'She's a bit upset today. Her brother's just gone overseas.' 'I hope he gives that Hitler what-for,' says the grandmother.

B. *adj.* or *attrib.* in special collocations in the sense 'foreign, situated beyond New Zealand': **overseas consultation**, see CONSULTATION; **overseas experience** [poss. influenced by COLONIAL EXPERIENCE], an originally humorous term for a working holiday (popularly considered as a mandatory pilgrimage) to Britain and Europe undertaken by young New Zealanders as part of their informal education (see also OE); also in a jocular composition **overseasia**, the state of feeling inadequate in face of foreign culture, etc.
1976 Johnston *New Zealanders* 144 [Tatts] was euphemistically known as..an '**overseas consultation**'. Tickets were sold fairly widely; a few tobacconists still discreetly advertise 'We post to Hobart'. **1982** *Pacific*

Index Abbrev. 229 OE..**Overseas Experience. 1986** REILLY *Deputy Head* 17 They were an attractive couple at training college, and their 'overseas experience' had made them even more so. They had come back from the years in Britain to learn the Maori language. **1994** *Dominion* (Wellington) 13 Aug. 15 Simon went [to Australia] too, later returning [to New Zealand] before leaving on his overseas experience. **1984** RHODES *Frederick Sinclaire* 1 Long before an Australian critic was talking about 'the cultural cringe', or Allen Curnow was referring to the malady of '**overseasia**' in New Zealand, Sinclaire had declined to regard himself as a spiritual exile from anywhere.

overseer. *Rural. Hist.* [Spec. use of *overseer* one who superintends: AND 1806.] The manager of a stock station; see esp. quot. 1933.
 1853 ROCHFORT *Adventures of Surveyor* 23 We..went on up the river to a station belonging to Mr. H-n, managed by his overseer. **1860** in Butler *First Year* (1863) vi 76 They will..find no great difficulty..getting an overseer's place, with from 100*l.* to 200*l.* a year, and their board and lodging. **1873** TINNE *Wonderland of Antipodes* 37 I found the overseer..'mustering' sheep. **1883** FERGUSON *Castle Gay* 167 But by-and-bye the overseer Rode out to learn the shepherds' cheer. **1912** BOOTH *Five Years NZ* 18 One of these [huts, c1859] contained the general kitchen.., the other was the residence of the squatter and his overseer. **1933** *Press* (Christchurch) (Acland Gloss.) 11 Nov. 15 *Overseer.—* Under manager. O[*verseer*]s were kept on most of the large stations in former days, and where the owner lived on the station he often managed it himself but kept an o[*verseer*]. The word is rarely used here now..but O[*verseer*]s all call themselves *managers*; but the real difference between them is that a m[*anager*] can sign cheques and an o[*verseer*] can't.
 Hence **overseership**, the position of overseer.
 1912 BOOTH *Five Years NZ* 22 The opportunity was an excellent one, and would in all probability lead to his..being offered the overseership.

overstay, *v.*

1. *WW1.* To overstay one's leave. Also *n.*, a soldier who does this.
 1976 LEE *Soldier* 6 Another New Zealander overstayed o[n] leave came to cadge a few bob as I walked down the street. *Ibid.* 12 And a swine of a military MP came in and demanded my leave pass... 'Just where you might hang around. Cocoa and biscuits for pennies. Cheap for the overstays.'.. 'Well don't let me catch you overstaying your leave.'

2. To remain in New Zealand beyond the expiry date of a visitor's or work permit.
 1981 KENNEDY *Straight from Shoulder* 9 Besides there was the advantage that these [Pacific island] people were not admitted permanently, and if things got tough, we could..round up, with dawn raids in the best totalitarian tradition, those who had overstayed and forcibly deport them.
 Hence **overstayer** [f. *overstay* + *-er*: also Brit. 1976 (OEDAS I. 150)], originally and mainly a Polynesian immigrant who remains in New Zealand beyond the expiry date of a visitor's or work permit; **overstaying** *vbl. n.*
 1976 *Evening Post* (Wellington) 1 Nov. 16 Amnesty Aroha, the national group seeking an amnesty for immigrant **overstayers**, last night appealed to the Prime Minister. **1977** *NZ Herald* (Auckland) 5 Jan. secti. i 1 While expressing sympathy for the plight of overstayers, the Maori leader said the laws of the nation had to apply to everyone, regardless of race. **1980** *Dominion* (Wellington) 3 Jan. 6 Overstayer was added to our vocabulary [in 1975], as was dawn raid as police sought illegal immigrants. **1992** *Dominion* (Wellington) 28 Jan. 3 The second time I stayed longer and I wasn't aware that I was an overstayer. **1986** *Evening Post* (Wellington) 16 Apr. 16 The plaintiff is charged with staying in New Zealand after her temporary permit had expired, the offence commonly known as **overstaying**. **1986** *Evening Post* (Wellington) 12 Aug. 6 In a report on discrimination against Pacific Island visitors, Mr Hirsh said the former National Minister of Immigration, Mr Frank Gill, in 1977 linked overstayers with 'communicable disease' and talked of an 'overstayer epidemic.' Such an equation of overstaying with disease was both revealing and irrational.

owl.

1. Usu. as **New Zealand owl**, a nocturnal bird of prey of the fam. Strigidae, usu. MOREPORK 1 a.
 1849, **1873** [see MOREPORK 1 a]. **1888** BULLER *Birds NZ* I. 13 As the night closed in upon us we heard all round the solemn notes of the New-Zealand Owl: first, a distinct *kou-kou, kou-kou*;.. and then, in alternation, the alarm note and ever familiar cry of 'more-pork'. **1893** *TrNZI* XXV. 71 *Spiloglaux novae-zealandiae*... The New Zealand Owl. **1905**, **1984** [see MOREPORK 1 a].

2. With a modifier: **laughing, little** (or **German**), **rock**.

(1) **laughing owl.** WHEKAU (*Sceloglaux albifacies*). Cf. LAUGHING JACKASS 1.
 1871 HUTTON *Catalogue Birds NZ* 2 Athene albifacies... Laughing Owl. Laughing Jackass. Wekau. **1884** *NZJSc.* II. 86 Sceloglaux albifacies (Laughing Owl). *Ibid.* 87 The uncontrollable outburst of laughter, i.e. the call peculiar to this species, is only heard when the birds are on the wing and generally on dark and drizzly nights or immediately preceeding rain. **1891** *TrNZI* XXIII. 191 The name 'laughing owl' is applied from the sound they make, which is a kind of ridiculous laugh in a descending key. **1904** HUTTON & DRUMMOND *Animals NZ* 157 *The Laughing Owl.—Whekau*... The peculiar cry which has given this Owl its name..is heard only when the birds are on the wing. **1923** *NZJST* VI. 84 The undoubted diminution in the numbers of the laughing-owl is usually ascribed to the practical extinction of the 'Maori' rat. **1947** STEVENSON *Maori & Pakeha* 56 The [bouquet] sachets were made from the skins of laughing owls (whekaus), birds that were once quite common in this locality, but now appear to be extinct. Occasionally their weird laughter could be overheard on dark..nights up to about 1900. **1957** MONCRIEFF *NZ Birds* 56 Laughing Owl... Lives in crevices of rocks, South Island in bleak tracts of country. Moves in series of hops, also walks with long strides, body erect. Strictly nocturnal. **1966** FALLA et al. *Birds NZ* 184 Laughing Owl... Whekau... According to early accounts the call from which this species received its name is heard mainly on dark nights accompanied by rain or drizzle, or before rain; it is 'a loud cry made up of a series of dismal shrieks frequently repeated'. **1973** HENDERSON in *NZ Short Stories III* (1975) 211 'Hear the morepork?' asked the boy. 'Laughing owl,' said the man. **1985** [see WHEKAU].

(2) **little** (**little grey** or **German**) **owl**. *Athene noctua* (fam. Strigidae), a small white-faced owl similar to but smaller and of lighter colour than a morepork, introduced c1906 from the northern hemisphere (orig. from Germany) and apparently confined to the South Island..
 1924 *Otago Witness* (Dunedin) 5 Feb. 1 A class of bird commonly referred to as the little grey owl was the subject of some unfavourable comment..at the meeting of the..Otago Acclimatisation Society last week. *Ibid.* 13 May 73 When I was trapping I caught a little grey German owl. **1938** *Auckland Weekly News* 30 Mar. 60 I dissected the body of a Little Owl, or German Owl. **1944** *Korero* (AEWS Background Bulletin) 23 Oct. 24 The introduction in 1906, of the European Little Owl, frequently called the 'German Owl', and its subsequent establishment, chiefly in parts of the South Island, hardly compensates us for the loss of the Laughing Owl. **1966** FALLA et al. *Birds NZ* 185 Little Owl *Athene noctua Local name*: German Owl... Between 1906 and 1910 several shipments were liberated in Otago whence other districts were stocked. **1985** FRAME *Envoy from Mirror City* 170 The trees heaved and rocked in the rising wind; moreporks and the little 'German' owls called from the macrocarpa. **1990** *Checklist Birds NZ* 186 *Athene noctua*..*Little Owl*... No recent records from Stewart Island..or the North Island (seen at Rotorua 1958).

(3) **rock owl.** *laughing owl* 2 (1) above; see quot. 1972.
 1972 *Notornis* XIX. 8 [The laughing owl] apparently hunted for its food over open ground..and roosted and nested in fissures in rocks (having an alternative name of rock owl as well as its common Maori name of whekau). **1985** [see WHEKAU].

owl parrot: see PARROT 2 (9).

owl's-foot moss. *Lycopodium volubile* (fam. Lycopodiaceae), a club moss up to several metres long which clambers up other vegetation or sprawls down banks, having leaves set on the stem in a fashion fancifully resembling an owl's foot. See also WAEWAEKOUKOU.
 1905 SATCHELL *Toll of Bush* 236 The boys on the [Northland] station were getting the big shed ready for a dance... Another young man..was engaged in looping up garlands of 'waiwaikoko' or owl's-foot moss, together with branches of Christmas tree, aflame with blood-red flowers. **1961** MARTIN *Flora NZ* 90 The first named [*Lycopodium volubile*]—the Owl's-foot or Climbing Club-moss—is found abundantly throughout New Zealand.

own your own. Also **O.Y.O.** (Applied to) a self-contained flat or unit, part of a block of flats, the freehold of which can be individually held by the occupier.
 1985 MARSHALL *Nest of Cuckoos* 164 I'll sell this house soon and move into an own-you-own... No garden to worry about. No kanukas lying across the lawn. **1987** *Evening Post* (Wellington) 7 Jan. 20 Kelburn: OYO. $79,500 ono. Architect designed 2 dbr unit in block of 2, sep amenities, parking, unit title.

ox-eye. See quot. 1915.
 1915 MCCREDIE *Patriotic Fete... Bungalow recipe Book* 37 Ox-eyes..thick slices of bread into rounds, smaller rounds..soak the rings..in milk... Break an egg in each hole..sprinkle with chopped parsley and bake. **c1936** *Bread;—The Basic Food. Facts & Recipes.* 8 Ox-eyes..slices of stale bread cut into rounds..pour over..milk..press down the centre..break an egg..in... Bake.

oxtongue.

1. *Glossophora kunthii*, (Class Phaeophyta), a brown alga with rough outgrowths on its strap-like fronds.
 1961 MARTIN *Flora NZ* 20 *Ox-tongue* (*Glossophora kunthii*). The fronds of this dichotomously branched seaweed are covered with rough outgrowths bearing the organs of reproduction, which resemble the surface of a cow's tongue.

2. *Picris echioides* (fam. Asteraceae), an introduced daisy weed with bristly stems, and leaves reminiscent of a cow's tongue.
 1969 *Standard Common Names Weeds* 55 *oxtongue*

Picris echioides. **1981** TAYLOR *Weeds of Roadsides* 109 All true leaves have raised spots, each carrying a short hooked bristle, which give Oxtongue a rough feel. **1983** ELL *Wildflowers & Weeds* 11 Another plant with a flower like a dandelion is the prickly ox tongue, so named for its leaves. These are prickly and warty.

OYO: see OWN YOUR OWN.

oyster, *n.*

1. Any of various edible bivalves of the family Ostreidae esp. the rock oyster *Saccostrea cucullata,* the Bluff oyster *Tiostrea chilensis lutaria,* and more recently the Pacific oyster *Crassostrea gigas;* rarely, members of the fam. Anomiidae. Often *attrib.* See also STEWART ISLANDER 2, TIO. Cf. *mountain oyster* (MOUNTAIN 2).

1769 *An 'Endeavour' Log* 12 Nov. in McNab *Historical Records* (1914) II. 147 Got two Longboat loads of Oysters from a small River at the Head of the [Mercury] Bay. **1826** SHEPHERD *Journal* in Howard *Rakiura* (1940) 357 Cockles Mussels & oisters are plentiful and excellent. **1849** POWER *Sketches in NZ* 78 Oysters of various kinds and of excellent quality are found on every rock; and it is a favourite amusement in some places to go out with a stock of bread and butter, a hammer and a knife, to enjoy an 'al fresco' entertainment. **1873** DOMETT *Diary* (1953) 102 'Do you know the difference between a good oyster and a bad one?'—'No!' 'Do you give it up?'—'Yes!' 'Well, a good oyster's a *Native*—and a bad one's a *Settler!*' **1896** *AJHR H-15* 3 During the year petitions were received from oyster-dealers..praying that the export of rock-oysters from the colony might be prohibited. **1909** MCNAB *Murihiku* 386 The *Argo* probably claims the honour of being the pioneer of the oyster trade. **1929** BOLITHO *The Glorious Oyster* (1960) 19 Thus I came to the pleasure of eating oysters with black velvet, sitting on a beach, with the blue ocean stretched before me. **1938** HYDE *Nor Yrs Condemn* 163 They say Stewart Islanders and the souls of oysters always go back to the old place. **1942** CURNOW *Verses by Whim-Wham* 19 There was a dispute between merchants and oystermen at Bluff, and no oyster-boats had put to sea. **1977** SARGESON *Never Enough!* 11 It was my first beach picnic..potatoes in their jackets were cooked in sea-water, oysters were eaten raw from the shell. **1989** *Listener* 25 Feb. 5 The nostalgic call of the oyster, we are told, is likened to the word 'knitting needle'.

2. With a modifier: **Bluff** (or freq. **Stewart Island,** also **flat, mud, dredge, Foveaux Strait**); **golden; Pacific (Pacific rock); rock oyster** (or freq. **Auckland rock,** also **New Zealand, northern, North Island rock oyster;** occas. **coxcomb, crested, drift, mangrove, shore oyster**).

(1) **Bluff oyster** [from *Bluff,* the mainland port of Foveaux Strait oysterboats], or freq. **Stewart Island oyster** (known in Melbourne c1910 as 'Stewarts'), formerly occas. **flat** or **mud oyster,** also **Foveaux Strait oyster,** occas. **dredge oyster** (esp. when harvested from other localities). *Tiostrea chilensis lutaria* (fam. Ostreidae), the celebrated deepwater dredge oyster, esp. that found in the Foveaux Strait beds. See also STEWART ISLANDER 2.

1887 *Auckland Weekly News* 26 Feb. 20 The Northern rock oyster was found only north of the East Cape; the Southern oyster was not found further north than Banks' Peninsula, and the mud oyster was found all over the colony. **1904** *Free Lance* (Wellington) 14 May 12 'Two shillings' worth of Stewart Island oysters please, and be sure the pearls are black.' 'Yes mum; certainly!' **1905** *AJHR H-15* 6 The quantity of Foveaux Strait oysters exported to Australia during the year..was 335,868 dozen, valued at £2,785. **1913** CARR *country Work* 25 In the straits between Bluff and Stewart Island large beds exist of the flat, or mud oyster. **1919** *AJHR H-15* 7 During the year the Department obtained eighty sacks of Foveaux Strait oysters and planted them in Cook Strait. **1919** WAITE *New Zealanders at Gallipoli* 182 The oyster question raged furiously... With an Aucklander present, it was never safe to say that Stewart Island oysters were the finest in the sea. **1929** *How to Cook NZ Fish* 80 The so-called 'mud oyster' or 'Stewart Island oyster' is dredged from between 12 and 25 fathoms in the Foveaux Straits. **1938** *Auckland Weekly News* 9 Feb. 9 After an absence from the menu for four months, the popular Foveaux Strait oysters appeared in Bluff and Invercargill for evening meals and supper. **1955** DELL *Native Shells* 38 The Stewart Island or Mud Oyster..is found throughout New Zealand. **1967** NATUSCH *Animals NZ* 79 Both rock and mud oysters are found all round New Zealand, but only the North Island rock oyster..and the Foveaux Strait mud oyster..are taken commercially. **1982** BURTON *Two Hundred Yrs. NZ Food* 70 A lesser name for the Bluff oyster is the Stewart Island oyster. **1985** *Metro* (Auckland) May 28 The dredge oyster, Bluff oyster or Foveaux Strait oyster is by far the most popular in New Zealand. **1995** *Dominion* (Wellington) 9 Dec. 17 Variously known as dredge oysters, flat oysters, mud oysters, Bluff oysters, Foveaux Strait oysters, their proper name is *Tiostrea chilensis.*

(2) **golden oyster.** *Anomia walteri* (fam. Anomidae), see quot. 1947.

1947 POWELL *Native Animals NZ* 19 Golden Oyster (*Anomia walteri*)... It has a thin wrinkled upper valve varying from white to a beautiful golden colour, but the lower valve is greenish or white with an oval hole through it, near to the hinge. **1966** *Encycl. NZ* II. 738 *Oyster, Golden* (*Anomia walteri*). This is not a true oyster... The golden valves can be fashioned into very realistic imitation Iceland poppies. **1970** PENNIKET *NZ Seashells in Colour* 90 Golden Oyster or Jingle Shell (*Anomia walteri*) 2 in... Common on northern beaches, this shell is identified by its crinkled, yellow to orange upper valve. **1988** *Short Stories from NZ* 70 The shell I have in my hand is a bivalve commonly known as a golden oyster though it is not a true oyster.

(3) **Pacific (Pacific rock) oyster.** *Crassostrea gigas* (fam. Ostreidae), introduced accidentally in the 1950s and now widespread.

1972 *AJHR H-15* 52 A second rock oyster—the Japanese or Pacific rock oyster, *Crassostrea gigas*—has been recognised... The original source of this oyster in New Zealand is unknown. **1986** PAUL *NZ Fishes* 165 *Pacific oyster Crassostrea gigas*... A native of Japanese waters, this oyster is now widely distributed through the Pacific... First noticed at Mahurangi in the Hauraki Gulf in 1970—though undoubtedly present for many years before that.

(4) **rock oyster** (or freq. in modern use **Auckland rock oyster,** also occas. **New Zealand, northern, North Island rock oyster**; occas. formerly **coxcomb** [i.e. cock's comb] **crested,** also **drift, mangrove, shore oyster**). *Saccostrea cucullata* (fam. Ostreidae), esp. associated with Auckland and northern coasts. See also *monkey oyster* (MONKEY 3).

1769 PARKINSON *Journal* (1773) 11 Nov. 105 A long-boat full of rock oysters, too, were brought aboard of us at one time. **1821** *McCrae's Evidence before Commissioner Bigge* May in McNab *Hist. Records* (1908) I. 550 There are snappers (schnapper..and..some rock oysters. **1847** ANGAS *Savage Life* I. 295 The rocks along the sea-shore, in the bays surrounding Waitemata harbour..are covered with a small species of oyster called the crested or coxcomb oyster (*Ostrea cristata*), which is very palatable. **1887** Northern rock oyster [see (1) above]. **1888** *AJHR H-19* 6 The question of the taking of the oyster which is stated to be a 'shore' and 'mangrove' oyster, and which scientific authorities and the department hold to be 'rock-oyster' still remains unsettled. **1892** *AJHR H-29* 3 On the 6th October last an Order in Council was made prohibiting the export of rock, shore, drift, or mangrove oysters. **1908** *AJHR H-15* 6 Under the Authority given by The Sea fisheries Act Amendment Act, 1907, this Department is to pick and sell the North Island rock-oysters. **1915** *AJHR H-15* 7 There are now large quantities of mangrove-oysters growing on the mangrove-trees in the north of Auckland, and as there is no market for these oysters in New Zealand it would be advisable to export them to Australia, which found a good market for them before the export of rock and mangrove oysters was prohibited. **1924** *Weekly News* (Auckland) 19 June [Caption] A fine specimen of Auckland rock oyster. **1936** HYDE *Check to your King* (1960) 185 Delicious rock oysters were sixpence a kit of three hundred. **1966** *Encycl. NZ* II. 738 *Oyster, Auckland Rock*... This is found only in the upper tidal rocky zone of the northern portion of the North Island and at the Chatham Islands. **1971** POWNALL *NZ Shells & Shell Fish* 61 Gourmets argue mightily as to the respective merits of the fat, juicy Stewart Island oyster as compared to the sweet, small rock oyster from the opposite end of the country. **1985** *Metro* (Auckland) May 28 The rock oyster is also known as the Auckland rock oyster. **1986** PAUL *NZ Fishes* 164 *Rock oyster Saccostrea glomerata*... Native to New Zealand, but very similar to the Sydney rock oyster... A delicious and popular oyster... Rock oysters are marketed fresh in the shell.

3. *fig.* and *transf.* Freezing works. Usu. *pl.* Sweetbreads. Compare *mountain oyster* (MOUNTAIN 2).

1951 17 May Feilding Freezing Works terms p.c. Colin Gordon. Sweetbreads are called *oysters* and are reputed good for sexual potency. If a person is seen pinching them there are comments of 'He's going out tonight'.

4. Special Comb. **a. oyster bird, oyster eater, oysterpicker,** OYSTERCATCHER.

1894 DUCHESS OF BUCKINGHAM *Glimpses Four Continents* 127 [At Bluff] saw some colonial robins; and also **oyster birds,** or 'red bills', with black bodies and red legs and beaks. **1862** WEKEY *Otago As It Is* 66 Among gulls, albatrosses, and other sea birds ... , the *toria,* or **oyster eater,** and the *korora,* also living on a species of shell-fish, called *pipi,* is met with on the sea shore. **1855** DRURY *Sailing Directions* 66 Birds met with in Pelorus... **Oysterpickers**—two kinds, called Toria by the natives.

b. oyster-borer (also *ellipt.* **borer**), *Lepsiella scobina* (fam. Muricidae), a small carnivorous whelk; **oyster fishery,** the business of taking and selling oysters.

1869 *AJHR D-15* 10 Care should be taken to destroy the enemy of the young brood [of oysters]; the enemies are the five-fingers, the dog whelk, the starfish, the **borer,** the stingaree, with his tail. **1929** *AJHR H-15* 19 The chief enemy of the rock-oyster [is] the whelk-like animal (*Thais scobina*) commonly known as the 'borer'. **1937** POWELL *Shellfish NZ* 21 The rock oyster is..open to attack by a voracious little shellfish less than half an inch in length, but quite capable of devouring the largest and strongest of our oysters. This little oyster borer is..*Lepsiella scobina.* **1955** DELL *Native Shells* 28 Oyster Borer... *Lepsiella scobina*... In other parts of New Zealand, it preys upon small intertidal barnacles, drilling a small hole and extracting its prey. **1968** MORTON & MILLER *NZ Sea Shore* 85 Our smallest and most abundant species is the oyster-borer, *Lepsiella* *scobina*. **1983** Gunson *Collins Guide to Seashore* 93 The oyster borer..often hunts in gangs when food is scarce. **1869** *AJHR D-15* 9 There are many men employed in connection with **oyster fisheries**, shops and hawkers. **1888** *AJHR H-19* 6 The whole question of the oyster-fisheries requires grave consideration. **1898** *AJHR H-15* 2 The beds in the Northern Oyster-fishery..were examined by the Inspector before the end of the close season. **1908** *Ibid.* 6 The most important matter in connection with oyster fisheries during the past year is the adoption of a new system of working the rock-oyster beds. **1980** *Catch '80* Dec. 12 Boat permits for the Foveaux Strait Dredge Oyster Fishery in 1980 were issued to the same 23 boats which have traditionally fished the oyster beds.

5. In the phr. **as tight as an oyster at low water**, characterizing extreme parsimony.

1928 *Free Lance* (Wellington) 25 Jan. 10 The last farmer I worked for was tighter than an oyster at low water.

oyster, *v*. Usu. as *pres. ppl.* or *vbl. n.*, also *attrib.* To gather oysters for trade or pleasure.

1875 in Howard *Rakiura* (1940) 308 Each had its cutter..lying ready for oystering which was just commencing. **1921** *Quick March* 10 Aug. 31 [Heading] *Oystering in the Straits* [Foveaux]. **1949** *AJHR H-15* 26 One vessel which was under overhaul for practically the whole of the 1947 season operated throughout 1948, bringing the number of vessels oystering up to ten. **1952** *AJHR H-15* 33 Weather conditions during 1951 were generally more favourable for oystering than was the case the previous year. **1973** *NZ Heritage* 99 2767 Brett, aware of the need to control the oystering industry, applied to the Commissioner of Crown Lands for directions for a closed season. **1989** *NZ Geographic* III. 64 'Wake up! You're going oystering!' hisses the hotelier's voice through the door.

oystercatcher. [Transf. use of *oystercatcher* (fam. Haematopodidae) for the similar southern hemisphere species.]

1. Any of three species of shorebird of the genus *Haematopus* (fam. Haematopodidae), feeding mainly on shellfish but rarely on oysters. See also *oyster bird*, *eater*, *picker* (OYSTER 4), PARSON 1.

1773 Forster *Resolution Jrnl.* 29 May (1982) II. 243 I shot two Curlews or rather *Oister catchers*, which are quite black & have very bright vermillion bills of the same structure as the English Sea Pie. **1817** Nicholas *NZ* II. 256 Towards the southward there are also..cormorants, oyster catchers, or sea-pies, penguins, and some other sorts of aquatic birds. **1838** Polack *NZ* I. 307 The small *noddies* (sterna [*sic*] solida) abound in large flocks, as also the *oyster-catchers* and *water-hens*, whose excessive tameness has nearly annihilated them. **1843** Dieffenbach *Travels in NZ* I. 59 Kingfishers, oystercatchers, tuis and cormorants enlivened the trees on its shores. **1867** Thomson *Twelve Yrs. Canterbury* 15 Several kinds of birds are indigenous to the woods and waters; among them the oyster-catcher. **1872** Domett *Ranolf & Amohia* 274 Slim oyster-catcher, avocet, And tripping beach-birds, seldom met Elsewhere. **1882** Potts *Out in Open* 131 The dottrel.., the oyster-catcher or sea-pie (*Haematopus longirostris*), both..do 'yeoman's service' as insect feeders. **1898** [see TOREA 1]. **1952** Richards *Chatham Is.* 79 Oyster Catchers are found in New Zealand, Australia and the Moluccas west of New Guinea. **1976** Soper *NZ Birds* 118 Oystercatchers are fast and powerful flyers and I have seen one chase a falcon and match it in speed. **1989** *NZ Geographic* IV. 111 Love me as I am Not just an ordinary oystercatcher But an elegant host of ancient times.

2. With a modifier: **black, Chatham Island, South Island pied, variable (North Island)**.

(1) **black oystercatcher**. *Haematopus unicolor*, the black phase of the *variable oystercatcher* (see (4) below) See also RED-BILL 3 b, TOREA 1.

1777 Forster *Voyage Round World* I. 133 Ducks, shags, black oyster-catchers, and some sorts of plovers were very numerous here [at Dusky Bay]. **1871** Hutton *Catalogue Birds NZ* 26 Haematopus unicolor... Black Oyster-catcher. Red-bill. Torea. **1872** *Appendix Proc. Otago Prov. Council* 39 The following is a list of the birds shot... *Haematopus unicolor* black oyster catcher, or red bill; *Haematopus longirostris*, pied oyster catcher. **1873** [see TOREA 1]. **1885** [see RED-BILL 3 b]. **1948** *NZ Bird Notes* III. 16 In 1928 I photographed a young black oystercatcher (*Haematopus unicolor*) in its kelp nest on the beach on the South Coast of Stewart Island. **1967** Natusch *Animals NZ* 260 There are two species [of oystercatcher], the pied (*Haematopus ostralegus finschi*..) common on South Island estuaries and shingle flats, and the black (H. unicolor..) common on Stewart Island and breeding also as far north as Cook Strait and up the East Coast of the North Island. Northern Hemisphere pied oyster-catchers are known as sea pies.

(2) **Chatham Island oystercatcher**. *Haematopus chathamensis*, a strongly territorial and rare seabird.

1966 Falla et al. *Birds NZ* 120 Chatham Island Oystercatcher *Haematopus chathamensis*... Confined to the Chatham Islands where it is widely distributed around the coast. **1976** Soper *NZ Birds* 217 Also on the shore line are Chatham Oystercatchers, a rare species, totalling perhaps no more than fifty birds. **1985** *Reader's Digest Book NZ Birds* 176 Chatham Island Oystercatcher *Haematopus chathamensis* Redbill. The Chatham Island Oystercatcher forages on rocky coasts between the high and low water marks. **1996** *Dominion* (Wellington) 15 Mar. 16 The world's rarest oyster-catcher—the Chatham Islands oystercatcher—has been built back up to a population of 100.

(3) **South Island pied oystercatcher**. *Haematopus ostralegus finschi*. See also RED-BILL 3 a, TOREA 1.

1871 Hutton *Catalogue Birds NZ* 26 Haematopus longirostris... Pied Oyster-catcher. Red-bill. Torea. **1948** *NZ Bird Notes* III. 65 On the estuary were..eight South Island pied oyster catchers (*Haematopus finschi*). **1955** Oliver *NZ Birds* 246 *South Island Oystercatcher. Torea Haematopus ostralegus finschi* It is hardly possible to say to which of the two New Zealand species of pied oystercatchers the birds recorded by the early visitors to New Zealand should be referred, but probably the 'Pied Oistercatcher' recorded by Latham in 1785 as from New Zealand belonged to this species. **1966** Falla et al. *Birds NZ* 118 South Island Pied Oystercatcher *Haematopus finschi* Other names: Redbill, Torea... The plumage of the South Island Pied Oystercatcher presents a strikingly clear-cut pattern of black and white, especially in flight. **1985** *Reader's Digest Book NZ Birds* 174 South Island Pied Oystercatcher *Haematopus ostralegus finschi*... Torea, redbill... During the winter the South Island pied oystercatcher probes with its long powerful bill in estuaries, mudflats and sandy beaches, mainly catching and prising open bivalve molluscs such as cockles and pipis. **1990** *Checklist Birds NZ* 128 *Haematopus ostralegus finschi*.. South Island Pied Oystercatcher (*Torea*)... Breeds inland in the South Island.

(4) **variable (North Island) oystercatcher**. *Haematopus unicolor*. See also RED-BILL 3 b, *torea-pango* (TOREA 1).

1885 [see RED-BILL 3 b]. **1957** Moncrieff *NZ Birds* (5edn.) 54 North Island Oystercatcher... Abundant in the North Island... Interbreeds with the Black Oystercatcher. **1964** [see RED-BILL 3 b]. **1985** *Reader's Digest Book NZ Birds* 175 Variable Oystercatcher *Haematopus unicolor Torea-pango, redbill*... In flocks of up to 150 birds the variable oystercatcher lives scattered around the New Zealand coast... It occurs in three colour types: black, pied and an intermediate colouring that is a hybrid of the other two. **1990** *NZ Geographic* VII. 43 Variable oystercatchers are also strong enough to resist the unwanted attentions of hungry gulls, and are still able to raise young on more isolated part of [Matakana] island.

P

pa /pa/, *n.*¹ Also with much variety of early form as **eppah**, **hèpa**, **heppa**, **hippa(h)**, **hipparr** (=he pa); **paa**, **pah** (freq.), **parr**. [Ma. /pa:/: Williams 243 *Pā* (ii) 4...Stockade, fortified place.]

1. *Hist.* A fortified Maori settlement; a stronghold.

1769 Cook *Journals* 15 Nov. (1955) I. 203 They have strong holds or Hippa's as they call them. *Ibid.* 4 Dec. I. 217 We pass'd round a point of land on which stood a Heppa or fortified village. **1769** Parkinson *Journal* (1773) 20 Nov. 106 Near the entrance to this river..there was a village, and a Hippa, or place of refuge, erected to defend it. **1773** Forster *Resolution Jrnl.* 18 May (1982) II. 282 Where the strong hold of the Natives is & which they call a *Hèpa*. **1817** Nicholas *NZ* I. 266 [Korra-Korra] thought it most advisable for us to accept an invitation..to visit his *hippah*, or fortified village. **1823** Cruise *Journal* (1957) 45 In the morning some of the gentlemen accompanied Krokro [sic] to his *pah* or fort. **1834** Markham *NZ* (1963) 33 Hattay or Ettay is a Tea tree [=TI]..; as Parr a Fort and Hipparr a Fort in Cooke..is put down[,] The Hip or Hit..is only the Article. **1835** Yate *NZ* (1970) 122 The Pa, or native fortification, is a place in which the natives..assemble in times of war. **1840** *Bunbury Rep.* 17 June in *GBPP House of Commons 1841 (No.311)* 112 This island..was accordingly taken possession of..and Her Majesty's colours hoisted at the paa of Hoiakaka, Cloudy Bay. **1869** Thatcher *Local Songs* 16 He'd shelled an empty pa there, To rush it then he tried. **1882** Potts *Out in Open* 16 It was struck in cases of alarm, when the people immediately flocked in to the pah. **1904** Tregear *Maori Race* 300 A Maori village of the old days was, if of importance, always a *pa* or fortress. **1951** Cresswell *Canterbury Tales* 9 This pah..was soon afterwards captured by Te Rauparaha. **1959** Sinclair *Hist. NZ* 24 The fortified hill-top village, the *pa*, was capable of offering resistance to weapons much more formidable than those of the Maori. **1990** *Evening Post* (Wellington) 29 Sept. 1 A kaumatua with the group..placed a pouwhenua..on the pa site behind a lodge as an important step toward their planned takeover of the island.

2. a. In a weakened sense, a Maori village or settlement; in modern (post c1960) English use replaced by MARAE, occas. by KAINGA.

1840 *NZ Jrnl.* I. 232 A Pah..is a fortified village, but as all the villages *are* fortified, we call them Pahs, and so do the Mauri. **1853** Adams *Canterbury Settlement* 49 On the north side of the harbour..there is a small 'paa' or village. **1863** Moser *Mahoe Leaves* 14 Two very natural questions arise from the heading of this article, the first being what is a pah? And the second why do I style it *pah?*... A pah is strictly a *fortified village*, but it has ceased to be applied to a fortified one only, and a collection of huts forming a native settlement, is generally termed a pah now a days. **1871** Money *Knocking About NZ* 30 A few Maories were in the habit of going over every year..to see their friends at a pah or village on the Grey river. **1907** Mansfield *Letters* 20 Nov. (1984) I. 30 We drove on through sheep country..past Maori 'pahs' and nothing else. **1920** *Quick March* 10 Apr. 27 For six months, while 'batching' near the pah I made a study of these..animals. **1938** Hyde *Nor Yrs. Condemn* 133 Most Maoris still slept on the floor..when they were in the guest-house of a big *pa*. **1959** Shadbolt *New Zealanders* (1986) 20 I mean it's common knowledge what happens at the pa when there's a big hui. **1960** Hilliard *Maori Girl* 9 Near this bridge [in backblock Taranaki] is the cluster of tin shacks known locally as 'the *pa*'. **1984** Edmond *High Country Weather* 28 Tom insisted on calling at the pa on the way home... Louise had several times passed the scattering of houses and sheds that clustered round the meeting house and the open space in front of it.

b. In various dismissive phrases in which *pa* connotes a non-European Maori life-style of supposedly lower quality or attainment than the European; esp. as **back to the pa**, of a Europeanized Maori, to return to Maori ways.

1938 Hyde *Nor Yrs. Condemn* 189 'Taihoa', that's what they [sc. Maori] say, and they all go back to the *pa* in the long run. **1951** Kohere *Autobiography of a Maori* 102 Boys who have been educated at Te Aute..and who have gone back to the pa, have done neither good for themselves nor good for anybody else. **1973** Finlayson *Brown Man's Burden* 141 pa:.. loosely, any Maori village. To get away from the pa, to make an effort to assimilate into pakeha society. **1974** Preston *Lady Doctor* 77 The maids were all young Maori girls straight from the pa, nearly always entirely ignorant of European ways, and some could speak only a few words of English.

3. a. Special Comb. **pa Maori**, one who has not been assimilated into European society; also *spec.* collectively **pa lot (mob)**, non-urbanized Maori.

1938 Hyde *Nor Yrs. Condemn* 1-69 I'm not just a *pa* Maori, I've been about. Once I went to Sydney and they took me on in a café. **1963** Bacon *In the Sticks* 109 Even young Tamu..sidled up to me and whispered, 'They [sc. new Maori schoolchildren] real Maori, eh, sir? Real pa Maori, eh?' **1992** Costello *Howard* 18 Even though the village was small, there was a division on what we used to call 'the pa lot' and 'our lot'. We were the 'suburban marae Maori'. We would watch 'the pa mob' making their semicircle.

b. In composition **paful** *joc.*, a great number (of Maoris).

1927 Guthrie-Smith *Birds* 29 When..the lagoon has become very full..whole pafuls of Maoris arrive.

pa /po/, *n.*² Also **paw**. [Ma. /'pa:/: Williams 244 *Pā* (vii)..Fish-hook made with *pāua* shell in lieu of bait.] *couta stick* (COUTA 2). Also *v.*

c1920 Beattie *Trad. Lifeways Southern Maori* (1994) 191 Towai wood was greatly favoured for making pa (jiggers used in catching barracouta fish). **1956** Graham *Treasury NZ Fishes* 310 A bent nail was secured to this piece of wood in the form of a hook but no bait was used. When a school of Barracouta was found the Couta stick, or paw, was brought out ready for fishing. *Ibid.* 311 Should there be any Barracouta about the..Couta sticks were then set to work to paw the water and attract Barracouta to the spot. *Ibid.* 314 The Maori also knew he could catch Barracouta without bait and he, too, used a short piece of stick and line with a baitless hook and leaned over his canoe and threshed the water to and fro, which is known as 'Kaihau manga!' When the European fisherman called his fishing outfit 'paw', the Maori used the term 'pa'. Old Maoris of Opotiki told me they used a chip of Tawhai..which is dark red, in the making of a pa (paw).

paa, var. PA *n.*¹

paakirikiri, var. PAKIRIKIRI.

paanui, var. PANUI.

paapa, var. PAPA.

Pachia, var. PAKEHA.

Pacific bench. *Sawmilling.* A moving sawbench for handling large logs (see also quot. 1952–53).

1928 *NZ Free Lance* (Wellington) 25 July 7 When the loco arrives at the mill skids, the logs are hauled off by two winches, cut to the required length by the fiddling saw, then kicked to the Pacific bench which does the 'breaking down'. **1951** *Awards, etc.* 453 [Westland Timber-Workers Award] [Rates of wages] Band sawyer Pacific bench 4 4. **1952–53** *NZ Forest Gloss.* (TS) Pacific bench. A wheeled travelling saw bench on which logs are held while it moves past a circular or band saw. It is fitted with knees which permit accurate sawing to thickness or width, and thus can be used for recutting as well as breaking down.

Pacific Islander. Also familiarly **PI**. ISLANDER 1. Contrast the earlier, Europe-orientated, *Southsea islander*.

1877 *TrNZI* IX. 65 The Pacific Islanders appear to be principally derived from two stocks. **1988** *Dominion* (Wellington) 16 Sept. 8 The Government has been urged to redefine the term Pacific Islander so more people can qualify for scholarships. Melanesian and Micronesian students are excluded from some grants... [The Pacific Island Education Foundation] says grants can only go to pupils of Samoan, Cook Island, Niuean, Tongan or Tokelauan descent. **1988** *Dominion* (Wellington) 25 Nov. 10 Shore had claimed two Pacific Islanders had abused him. **1990** *Ibid.* 2 Aug. 1 This year the university employed a Pacific Islander person to work with students. **1995** *Mana* 10 (Spring issue) 16 Today, there are signs that PIs and Maori are rediscovering that shared kinship.

Pacific oyster: see OYSTER *n.* 2 (3).

Pacific Slope.

1. The Pacific Islands, or the Pacific area or countries on the Pacific rim, esp. as refuges for criminals or the hard-pressed.

1871 Clarke in Money *Knocking About NZ* v There was a rumour that a travelling journalist, who had condescended to visit Melbourne on his way to the Grand Pacific Slope, was about to temporarily abandon the abodes of sweetness and light, and sing 'Whiskey in the jar'. **1883** *NZ Educational Monthly* 4 Aug. 7 He [sc. the 'larrikin'] is essentially colonial, English cities may have 'gamins' and the Pacific Slope can boast of 'hoodlums'. **1906** *Truth* 24 Feb. 1 There must be a powerful lot of people on the Pacific Slope who are wanted in this colony.

2. In the phr. **to do the Pacific slope**, of a 'wanted' person, to flee the country to the Pacific Islands, South America or other places on the Pacific rim.

1902 Walker *Zealandia's Guerdon* 292 Perhaps he [*sc.* a missing man] accomplished the 'Pacific Slope'. *Ibid.* 326 He [*sc.* the detective] has packed so many 'confidence men' off to penitentiary..that the others have done the 'Pacific Slope' in various directions, chiefly towards Australia. **1934** Mulgan *Spur of Morning* 42 Poor old Tom! He's never been the same since his partner did the Pacific slope. **1938** Gilkison *Early Days Dunedin* 133 In the 'seventies and 'eighties many fraudulent debtors, embezzlers and rich thieves escaped from New Zealand before arrest, by doing what came to be known as the 'Pacific Slope'. Someone discovered that the Sandwich Islands, which were then ruled by a native queen, had no extradition treaty with New Zealand and consequently rogues who were much 'wanted' by the police in this country on reaching Honolulu could laugh at writs and law proceedings. **1956** Gore *Levins* 186 Tetley had done what in those days was termed 'The Pacific Slope', and was last heard of in South America, that haven for absconders and those anxious to shelve their responsibilities.

pack, *n.*[1] [Spec. use of *pack* a bundle packed for convenient transport on the back of beast or human.]

1. In colonial New Zealand, usu. personal gear (and often food) rolled or packed, often in a waterproof sheet or in a blanket, for carrying on the back or on the shoulders during rural travel. See also swag *n.*[1] 1 a.

1849 Torlesse *Papers* (1958) 63 Left Goashore at 6 a.m. and commenced arranging our packs. **1858** Smith *Notes of a Journey* in Taylor *Early Travellers* (1959) 351 We now..shouldered, or rather 'backed' our packs, which..weighed over 40 lbs., and principally consisted of biscuits, bacon, sugar, chocolate. **1874** Kennaway *Crusts* 187 We rolled our packs roughly together, crossed the river below us on horse-back. **1883** Green *High Alps* 185 I then dragged my pack through the thorns..to ease my shoulders I took off my knapsack. **1905–06** in Grave *Beyond Southern Lakes* (1950) 64 We put off our packs and scouted round for a good spot to spend the night. When we went to pick up the swags again, we couldn't locate them anywhere.

2. a. *Orig.* tramping. [Cf. OED *pack n.*[1] e 'Chiefly *Forces* and *N.Z.*', 1916.] A rucksack or light bag, usu. stiffened with a frame, and carried on the back. See also *kidney-rotter* (kidney).

1928 *Tararua Tramper* Dec. 3 Next morning, with our packs on our backs, we climbed gradually up easy slopes. **1933** *Tararua Tramper* Feb. 2 Some twenty odd people and thirty odd packs strewn in indescribable chaos everywhere. **1940** *Tararua Tramper* Apr. 2 *Rucsacs*.—There are two main types of pack, the frame pack, which in its present form was originally introduced by Bergan of Norway, and the frameless pack. **1958** *Tararua 12* 27 England since 1895 has borrowed *rucksack* from German dialect; New Zealand has preferred *pack*. Not that *rucsac* is not used here; it is noticeable that older Club members used it in several articles in early numbers of *Tararua*, and it still appears in advertisements... *Pack* as a synonym for *rucksack* is used in Australia to some extent at any rate. **1960** Masters *Back-Country Tales* 28 It is 3,011 feet above sea level, and about a two and a-half [*sic*] hour journey with a light pack. **1971** *Listener* 22 Feb. 51 Pack carrying is still the same old personal battle between man and gravity. **1987** Sinclair *Rail* 128 The guards..only occasionally 'went crook' when the van was cluttered with sleeping bags, packs and, sometimes, roaring primuses.

b. With a prefixed adjective indicating a particular type of pack: **flat pack**, **frame pack** or **A-frame pack**, one with (an A-shaped) frame; **frameless pack**.

1958 *Tararua 12* 27 The two main varieties of packs are the *frame pack* and the *frameless pack*, sometimes called a *flat pack*. The frameless pack of course receives that name only on formal occasions, being more familiary known by that elegant term, *kidney-rotter*. **1966, 1988** frameless pack, A-frame pack [see kidney].

3. Special Comb. **pack-box**, a box in which the cook's and other gear is transported by pack-horse to a musterers' hut or camp; **pack-boy**, rouseabout cook at a musterers' camp; **pack-bridge**, a bridge safe under non-vehicular loads only; **pack-bullock** [AND 1832], one trained as a pack-animal rather than as a draught-animal; **pack dray**, a dray which carries musterers' packs and gear to an out-station; **packhorse mail**, a mail delivery carried by pack-horse.

1949 Newton *High Country Days* 39 The 'droppers' were first slung into place, swags, tents, or **pack boxes**, which were known as 'side-loads', were hung above them. **1981** Charles *Black Billy Tea* 35 When a gang goes out to muster the merinos..the men work as a team. The '**pack boy**', whose age may be seventeen or seventy, carries all the provisions and other gear..on his team of packhorses. He is the cook and odd job man. **1879** Barry *Up & Down* 203 The connection between Cromwell and the country lower down the river Clutha, was a **pack-bridge** erected over that river. Wagons with stores and goods had to unload, and everything was packed across on horses. **1853** Collinson *Remarks Military Operations* 31 The country is too difficult for **pack-bullocks**. **1862** Hodder *Memories NZ Life* 184 Two pack-bullocks loaded with moa bones. **1947** Newton *Wayleggo* 35 It was all walking country..the musterers travelling either per 'Harry Pannell' (walking) or riding on the **pack dray**. **1984** Marshall & Startup *From the Bay to the Bush* 51 To get despatches and mails to their field parties the Public Works then arranged for a weekly **packhorse mail** to run westward from Moawhango to the accommodation house at Karioi.

4. A fabric container into which wool is pressed for transport; an empty wool-bale.

1922 Perry *Sheep Farming* 121 The 'bellies' can be placed in a pack hung on the shearing-board, and when two of these are filled they can be pressed. **1950** *NZJAg.* Oct. LXXXI. 313 Today the 42in. pack is the standard size for New Zealand. **1985** Bremner *Woolscours NZ* 9 Pack see bale.

5. [Cf. OED *pack*[1] 13.] *Ellipt.* for pack-horse.

1866 Chevalier *Reminisc. of Journey* (ATLTS) 7 The pack a strong heavy old chap, the third pretty good. The fourth—a flea bitten Arabian mare.

pack, *n.*[2]

1. *Farming.* [Spec. use of *pack* a company of hunting dogs: see OED *n.*[1] 5 a.] A musterer's or rabbiter's team of dogs. See also *rabbit-pack* (rabbit *n.* 1).

1858 *Puketoi Station Diary* (Hocken TS) 2 Dec. 'Dick', Hepburn's dog nearly worried by our pack. **1889** *TrNZI* XXI. 430 I had now only one pack of dogs employed [rabbiting]... Early in the year I noticed that my rabbiter's pack of dogs were looking miserably-poor..mangy skeletons. **1913** Carr *Country Work* 27 In the North Island a pack of dogs and a gun are the rabbiter's stock-in-trade. **1933** [see *rabbit-dog* (rabbit *n.* 1)]. **1951** McLeod *NZ High Country* 46 I often hear [musterers] say they're selling up the pack and turning in the mustering. **1966** *NZ Short Stories* (1976) 126 Never saw such a great pack in all the King Country, as old Charlie's. See him coming in from the back country at mustering-time..his dogs handling each woolly as though its fleece was worth its weight in gold. **1984** *NZ Times* 28 Oct. 13 Immediately a broken down mongrel from a rabbiter's pack sneaked over the skyline.

2. [AND 1919.] In the phr. **to go to the pack**, to go to the 'dogs', to go to 'pieces'.

1937 Partridge *Dict. Slang* 598 *pack, go to the*. To go to pieces (fig.); lose a leading position... New Zealand: C. 20. **1938** *Press* (Christchurch) (McNab Slang) 2 Apr. 18 [The traveller to New Zealand] might be..told that things had 'gone to the pack.' **1948** Ballantyne *Cunninghams* (1976) 67 Some saying it was awful how a man with connections in the Old Country could go to the pack like this. **1959** Slatter *Gun in My Hand* 39 The rejection of it [*sc.* a book] knocked me back completely. I went to the pack and drifted around the country from job to job. **1988** McGill *Dict. Kiwi Slang* 51 *go to the pack* to deteriorate; eg 'Since his wife left him for his best mate, Reg has gone rapidly to the pack.'

pack, *v.*

1. [Spec. use of *pack v.* to carry or convey (in a pack): see OED *v.*[1] 9 a.] **a.** As **pack in** also *absol.*, to tramp (into the back-country, mountains, etc.) carrying provisions, etc. in a pack; to carry (provisions) into the back-country (cf. pack *n.*[1] 2).

1970 Severinsen *Hunt Far Mountain* 123 Bill had just seen off his party [of hunters],.. having sadly decided that his ageing heart wasn't up to packing in. **1981** Hunt *Speaking a Silence* 24 And they got me a job. Pretty hard yakker too, packing in stuff.

b. As **pack up**, to transport by back-pack (up to a camp, etc.).

1849 Torlesse *Papers* (1958) 63 Found that Jim had only packed up 96lbs biscuit.

2. In the phr. **to pack a sad**, to become severely depressed; to reveal a dismal or depressed state of mind; (?)to become disturbed by or to withdraw support from (a person) in a sad but angry fashion (see quot. 1994).

1980 Leland *Kiwi-Yankee Dict.* 74 *pack a sad*: to get ostentatiously depressed. **1982** O'Sullivan *Rose Ballroom* 28 As he moved to the porch and found her packing a sad *how blokes kept their distance*—*did he fancy a bit?* **1985** *Press* (Christchurch) 22 May 4 Because of a row with his girlfriend, a young man who had been drinking and was disqualified 'packed a sad' and drove. **1991** Duff *One Night Out Stealing* 172 Oh, yet again when she remained silent. Hahaha, she's packing a sad now. **1994** *Evening Post* (Wellington) 3 Dec. 3 Mr Storey told the National Party's Waikato division last night it was time the New Zealand Government 'packed a sad' with Paul Keating and his Government.

Packaha, Packeah, varr. pakeha.

packer, *n.*[1] [See OED *packer*[1] 3 a. 'Now N. Amer., Austral.'.]

1. See also packman, packie. **a.** One who transports supplies by pack-animal.

1864 *Hexameters* in Kennaway *Crusts* (1874) 124 Sawyers, and stockmen, carpenters, packers, and shinglers and loafers, Smoke as they work to assist them. **1881** Nesfield *Chequered Career* 76 A packer offered me higher wages to drive pack-horses down..towards Hokitika. **1896** Harper *Pioneer Work* 224 The packer came up from the beach with more provisions. **1960** Rogers *Long White Cloud* Good healthy work, mustering. Up in the ranges... We send a packer up each week with supplies. **1981** HENDERSON *Exiles of Asbestos Cottage* 24 A similar signal later was used by packers coming in from Takaka.

b. One who manages provisions, makes camp, and cooks for musterers.

1912 *Sheepowners' Handbook* 6 [Title] Musterers, Shepherds & Packers' Dispute..relating to musterers, shepherds and packmen. **1923** *Awards, etc.* 456 [Marlborough Musterers, Packers, and Drovers] Any musterer or packer required to do snow-raking shall be paid £1 5s. per day while engaged in such work. **1938** BURDON *High Country* 105 Like an army [the musterers] moved with their baggage train..in charge of the 'packer', who also fulfilled the duties of cook, butcher, and numerous other roles. **1952** BLAKISTON *My Yesteryears* 18 Two packers, with some of the mules..had gone ahead of us to pitch camps for the night. **1978** JARDINE *Shadows on Hill* 32 In high-country station operations the part played by the packer is of no minor importance.

2. [See OED 3 c 'Chiefly *Canad.*'.] One whose business is to transport supplies by back-pack.

1865 *Evening Post* (Wellington) 3 Aug. 2 The township..is full of life and excitement caused by the crowds of diggers, packers and storekeepers, all anxiously waiting to be off to..the Golden Grey. **1892** BROOKES *Frontier Life* 117 I have often watched packers, who would carry a load of seventy five pounds on their backs, through a rough survey line. **1928** GREY in Heinz *Bright Fine Gold* (1974) 30 Packers, that is men exceptionally strong who acted as beasts of burden for the storekeepers, were arriving every now and then with great packs on their backs.

packer, *n.*² *Obs.* One employed to squeeze as many people as possible into the gallery of a theatre.

1962 LAWLOR *More Wellington Days* 45 When the gallery was charged to a point of suffocation along would come 'the packers', two hired men who would exhort the crowd in ungentlemanly terms to move up closer.

packet of salts. [A var. of Brit. *dose of salts*, that is, Epsom, etc. salts for loosening the bowels.] In the phr. **to go through (something) like a packet of salts**, to run or cut through (opposition, etc.) quickly and easily.

1955 *BJ Cameron Collection* (TS July) go through something like a packet of salts (v) To go through something very quickly. **1968** SLATTER *Pagan Game* 155 Played a blinder against Maungaraki [rugby team]. Went through them like a packet of salts. **1986** DAVIN *Salamander & the Fire* 21 'Went through them [*sc.* the enemy] like a packet of salts for a start,' said Dawson. 'Got right up to the edge of the drome.'

packhorse: see CRAYFISH 2 (2).

Packia, var. PAKEHA.

packie. PACKER *n.*¹, esp. 1 b.

1945 *NZ Geogr.* I. 21 Next on the list is the 'packie'—half-cook, half-handyman, always good with horses or mules—who takes blankets and provisions into 'camp', as hut or tent life is called. **1951** MCLEOD *NZ High Country* 32 [Packhorses] set off in single file with the packie bringing up the rear on his hack. **1960** MASTERS *Back-Country Tales* 26 Fergie yelled to the packman to get the swags before they got wet, and he and Dave rushed down to the packie's assistance. **1973** NEWTON *Big Country SI* (1977) 87 Although they [*sc.* mules] are renowned for their dirt [*sc.* bad behaviour]..most of the old packies swear by them.

packman. Also occas. **packman-cook.** PACKER *n.*¹ 1 b.

1910 *Awards, etc.* 584 [Drovers and Shepherds Award] The minimum rate of wages to be paid to packman with dog shall be 10s. 6d. per day. **1917** *Triad* 10 Apr. 66 In the midst of them [*sc.* the musterers in the whare] the packman was filling his bread baskets. **1933** *Press* (Christchurch) (Acland Gloss.) 11 Nov. 15 *Packer, packman.*—One who loads the packhorses and leads or drives them from camp to camp. He also cooks for the musterers. **1951** MCLEOD *NZ High Country* 9 The packman, who cooks for the musterers and carries their equipment on packhorses, had to make a day's journey of 28 miles. **1961** CRUMP *Hang On a Minute Mate* 76 The packman-cook [on the sheep-station] was a muttering-to-himself old man called Joe. **1973** FERNANDEZ *Tussock Fever* 2 Weeks out mustering without a packman-cook, crowded..in the little smoky huts out-back. **1981** HENDERSON *Exiles of Asbestos Cottage* 122 The rare perspiring trackmaker and the flitting packman were Chaffey's passing neighbours.

pack-track. Mainly *Hist.* [Used elsewhere but recorded earliest in NZ.] A track made for use by pack animals.

1870 *AJHR D-40* 5 Metalled Pack-track, four feet wide, from mouth of Cockabulla Creek to Clifton, two and a half miles. **1887** *Handbook NZ Mines* 220 A pack-track is now being made to this reef. **1896** MOFFATT *Adventures* (1979) 67 [We] came back down the Buller from the Grip, the pack track being then under construction. **1922** COWAN *NZ Wars* (1955) I. 303 [In February 1864] In he succeeded in getting commissariat through to the troops..by rapidly cutting a pack-track from Raglan Harbour over the ranges to the Waipa. **1930** DOBSON *Reminiscences* 172 In the open country there were pack tracks everywhere. **1953** STRONACH *Musterer on Molesworth* 1 Molesworth is forty-four miles from Hanmer by pack-track, about seventy-five from Blenheim by road. **1975** NEWTON *Sixty Thousand on the Hoof* 4 Access to the back country was by packtrack only. **1988** *Dominion Sunday Times* (Wellington) 25 Dec. 7 There's roads all round here now, but they were just pack tracks in those days. **1995** WINTER *All Ways Up Hill* 168 There was a pack track, good enough for bullock teams with a few improvements, that ran from the block to Makuri.

paddle crab: see CRAB 2 (2).

paddock, *n.*¹ [Spec. use of *paddock* a small field or enclosure: see OED *n.*² 1; AND 1808.]

1. A piece of land of any size marked off by a fence or natural boundary; a field large or small.

1840 MATHEW *Journal* 11 Mar. in Rutherford *Founding of NZ* (1940) 76 His house is handsomely furnished, and is prettily situated with a nice Lawn and paddock green with clover. **1848** in Deans *Pioneers* (1964) 51 We have now all but finished one paddock of about 400 acres, with a ditch and bank. **1848** EARP *Handbook* 11 Good land has been laid down to English grasses, and enclosed in paddocks. **1874** TROLLOPE *NZ* 80 Vast paddocks containing perhaps 20,000 acres each. **1883** FERGUSON *Castle Gay* 251 Former swamps could now display Rich harvest paddocks dense with sheaves. **1892** *NZ Official Handbook* 121 The percentage of increase [in lambing]..is very high, particularly so in the paddocks..while on the hill or unimproved country it varies from 45 to 80 per cent. **1912** MANSFIELD *Poems* (1988) 36 I lay down in the paddock And listened to the cold song of the grass. **1924** GIBSON *Gibbie Galoot* 56 By the way, you colonials call a field a paddock, or more often a paddick. **1940** *Tales Pioneer Women* (1988) 199 Here the material had to be unloaded and jinkered across a 2000-acre paddock to Inchbonnie. **1969** HASCOMBE *Down & Almost Under* 80 Leaving the precincts of the house, we came to the paddocks—'ram', 'killing', 'holding' and 'horse', they each served a particular purpose. **1974** GRACE in *Some Other Country* (1984) 171 I started over the paddocks towards him then. **1982** *Agric. Gloss.* (MAF) 5 *Paddock*: a confined area of any size (field).

2. An outdoor area for sun-drying (and bleaching) flax fibre before further processing (cf. PADDOCK *v.*¹ 2); an outdoor area where scoured wool is dried (in Comb. only, as *paddock-hand*). Cf. BLEACHING PADDOCK, DRYING GREEN, GREEN *n.* 1.

1888 COX *Diaries 1888–1924* (ATLMS) 28 Nov. I was working in the paddock..and my hands were worse tonight, the Flax poisoned them. **1913** CARR *Country Work* 44 [The flax fibre] is carted..to the drying green, generally called the 'paddock', where it is spread out to dry and bleach. **1985** BREMNER *Woolscours NZ* 9 Paddock hand: hand who spread and turned wool on drying screen.

3. *transf.*, often *joc.* [AND 1839.] A playing field, esp. for rugby football.

1947 GASKELL *Big Game* 11 We're going to play fifteen backs and run them off the paddock. **1959** SLATTER *Gun in My Hand* 90 Tell your cobbers what they should have done on the paddock..why your team should have won. **1975** HOWITT *NZ Rugby Greats* 172 Tennis in those days meant as much to Lochore as Rugby..for he achieved more tangible results around the court than on the paddock. **1980** *Dominion* (Wellington) 29 July 1 The sort of thing described was becoming far too prevalent on rugby paddocks in New Zealand, he said. **1992** *Sunday Times* (Wellington) 22 Nov. 8 Rugby players would not like the idea of prosecution [for rough play]—the notion of 'what happens on the paddock should stay on the paddock'.

4. As **the paddock**, in specific uses. **a.** *Hist.* An area of pakihi near Hokitika on the old Canterbury–West Coast foot-route, used as a staging place by gold-diggers, etc.; also other such areas.

1865 CHUDLEIGH *Diary* 20 Apr. (1950) 176 We are getting very short of food and all reports say there is nothing to be had at the paddock... *21st*..I shall have to push on to Okitikie... Under favourable circumstances I could regain the paddock in six days. **1867** in May *West Coast Gold Rushes* (1962) 527 The *West Coast Times*, 1 July 1867, gave another meaning: 'The name 'paddock' must not be accepted in its Australian significance, as it is unfenced by the familiar post and rails, and is merely one of those patches of country free from timber, and generally very boggy, peculiar to the West Coast. The native name is 'Pakihi'.' Hence 'Natural Paddock' (or Bruce's Paddock) at Lake Brunner, and Big and Little Paddocks at the Ho Ho. **1885** *NZJSc.* II. 484 Some specimens [of native quail]..taken from 'the paddock', near Hokitika, are slightly in excess of this measurement.

b. Formerly, the railway yards at Waltham, Christchurch.

1959 SLATTER *Gun in My Hand* 22 Chalking the curved E on the empty wagons, the railwayman's shorthand like *PDK* for paddock, the wide Waltham Yards outside. **1966** TURNER *Eng. Lang. Austral. & NZ* 157 PDK in Christchurch means send to the 'paddock', the wide railway yards at Waltham.

c. As **the long meadow (paddock)**, see LONG *a.* 1 b and c.

5. *transf.* or *fig.* **a.** *transf. WW1.* No-man's-land.

1916 *Chron. NZEF* 30 Aug. 9 Would far rather hop over the parapet and gallop across the paddock than crouch in the bottom of a trench waiting for a trip west.

b. *fig.* See quot.

c1962 BAXTER *Horse* (1985) 106 Zoe felt that her labours in the paddock of culture were at last bearing fruit.

c. In the phr. **one's own paddock**, one's own neighbourhood or 'backyard'.

1988 *Karori News* 11 Oct. 1 He says he did not have the resources to get the petition circulating in Karori. 'I had hassles in my own paddock.'

6. a. In Comb. and special Comb. (a) Of or pertaining to a paddock: **paddock fence**, **paddock gate**; **paddock manure**, dung etc. collected from stock paddocks.

1852 *NZGG* 19 Nov. V. 28:169 On the south of the southern extremity of C.B. Robinson's **paddock fence**. **1920** MANSFIELD *Stories* (1984) 233 A lovely kingfisher perched on the paddock fence preening his rich beauty. **1867** PHILLIPS *Rockwood & Point Jrnl.* 1 May (Canterbury Pub. Lib. TS) 102 T.A.P. mending **paddock gates**, Bill & Co. fencing. **1988** HILL *More from Moaville* 37 At herringbone shed. 150 Jerseys..waiting patiently by paddock gate... 600 hooves pass placidly through herringbone. **1905** WHITE *My NZ Garden* 5 The ground first received a good dressing of **paddock manure**—this means free from straw.

(b) Characteristically farmed from or pastured in paddocks as distinct from hill or high-country ranges or runs; pertaining to such farming: **paddock farmer**, one whose lowland farm is divided by fencing as distinct from a high-country farmer whose farm can also be organized by terrain (cf. *forty-acre farmer* (FORTY-ACRE)), hence **paddock-farming**; **paddock lambing**, lambing managed in an enclosed paddock rather than on the open run; **paddock-mate**, another animal as company for a paddocked animal; **paddock-sheep (paddock wether)**, a sheep, one of a mob, pastured in a paddock as distinct from one pastured on a (high-country) run; **paddock-shepherd**, one who looks after paddock sheep.

1969 MCCASKILL *Molesworth* 192 How many down-country **paddock farmers** would be happy with an equal result? **1864** MARSHMAN *Canterbury 1862* 44 The writer..would..prefer **paddock farming** to a run... It is a more pleasant kind of life. **1890** *Otago Witness* (Dunedin) 27 Nov. 7 The paddock lambing was luckily pretty well finished before the wet weather set in. **1988** *Sunday News* (Auckland) 10 July 7 'In February, my sister answered an advert for a **paddock mate** for a weaning foal on a Glen Murray farm,' she said. **1883** Brett *Colonists' Guide* 214 All **paddock sheep** should be yarded before shearing. **1889** CHUDLEIGH *Diary* 15 Nov. (1950) 368 Run sheep much better. Ewe and paddock sheep not so good. Lice in wool and [dust from] ploughed ground all through Ewe mob. All the paddock sheeps wool must be scoured. **1950** *NZJAg.* Feb. LXXX. 140 The Merinos were not as successful as paddock sheep. **1953** STRONACH *Musterer on Molesworth* 25 Two lucky men were selected as **paddock shepherds** to stay behind and help at shearing time. *Ibid.* 29 The paddock shepherds were fattening up and loafing about the shed. **1975** HARPER *Eight Daughters* 42 Joe Ferris was head shepherd and Chris McCauley and Jimmy Muir paddock shepherds. **1950** *NZJAg.* Oct. LXXXI. 349 Shearing usually begins about November 20 with the rams, which are followed by the **paddock wethers**, hoggets, and hill wethers, and finally the ewes.

b. As a second element of special Comb. indicating the specific use to which the paddock is dedicated, see: ACCOMMODATION PADDOCK, BACK *a*. B 2, BLEACHING PADDOCK, COW 6, DREDGE *n.* 1, HAY-PADDOCK, HOLDING PADDOCK, HOME *n.*³, HORSE *n.*¹ 5, HOUSE 5, LAMBING *vbl. n.* 2, NIGHT 1, RAM 1, RATION 2, SACRIFICE PADDOCK, SADDLING PADDOCK, SCRUB *n.* 1 c, SHEARING B 3, SHEEP 1, SPELLING 1.

paddock, *n.*²

1. *Goldmining.* **a.** [AND 1855.] A shallow opencast excavation from which wash-dirt was systematically taken (see esp. quot. 1967).

1852 GRACE *Rep. Turanga Dist.* in *Pioneer Missionary* (1928) 20 One large paddock of 3 acres was dug in two weeks by 12 of them with the help of 3 boys. **1865** *Evening Post* (Wellington) I. No.7 2 One party, about four miles from Canvastown, has bottomed, and out of a paddock twelve by sixteen feet has taken 70 ounces. c**1875** *Colonial Songster No.5* 64 If you want some tin to spend, To paddocks rich your footsteps bend, And your time there well employ; When no one's findings fill your dish, And you may wash out what you wish. **1894** *NZ Official Year-book* 368 When the gold is found in what promises to be payable quantities the sluice-boxes are set up..and 'paddocks' of auriferous gravel excavated. **1911** *Maoriland Worker* 2 June 1 Smith and Joseph Bates were working on the Round Hill..Co.'s claim, sinking a paddock, or hole, in drifting sand. **1953** SUTHERLAND *Golden Bush* (1963) 119 My only dividend from the flood, the ample tailings-dump, made a great difference to work on the claim and returns took a turn for the better over the new few paddocks. **1967** MAY *West Coast Gold Rushes* 527 Paddock: applied to alluvial mining, this term was used in many ways. A paddock was an excavation made for procuring wash-dirt in shallow ground; an excavation in which the wash-dirt was dumped; a wooden bin in which the wash-dirt was stored. To 'paddock' a claim meant to work it systematically by means of a series of small, shallow pits.

b. In full *dredge paddock* (DREDGE *n.* 1).

1919 *Alexandra Herald* 20 Aug. 5 Water from the dam was used for keeping the paddock open [for the dredge]. **1900** KITTO *Pract. Dredgeman's Manual* 18 If you are working a bank claim it is important that you keep the hole or paddock wide... This can only be done by taking out the corners every time you move ahead, and..to do this it is necessary to keep the stern of the dredge out towards the centre of the paddock. **1935** *NZ Free Lance* (Wellington) 7 Aug. 19 The Bendigo Goldlight Dredge has recently set to work to open out a paddock. **1992** LATHAM *Golden Reefs* 420 The grass-covered dip of the paddock or pond in which the dredge was built is still discernible.

2. *Goldmining.* [AND 1858.] A place for storing excavated washdirt, or ore (see quot. 1992).

1862 *Otago Goldfields & Resources* 34 Sod walls for tents are everywhere common, and..are largely used in making dams and 'paddocks'. **1874** BATHGATE *Col. Experiences* 130 Removing auriferous dirt from the paddock to the 'long tom' or sluice-box. **1887** *Handbook NZ Mines* 18 A large paddock is excavated out of the bed-rock and into this the whole of the material is sluiced from the face. **1914** PFAFF *Diggers' Story* 114 Some friends gave me their washdirt paddock to clean up after they had finished. **1946** MILLER *There Was Gold* 76 I would have a wash-up in a very short time, and I began to speculate on the amount of gold the ever-widening paddock contained. **1992** LATHAM *Golden Reefs* 431 Paddock: Ore in bins, or stored or stacked at the surface was said to be 'in the paddock'.

3. *Gumdigging.* An area of ground systematically excavated for kauri gum.

1971 SMITHYMAN in Satchell *Land of Lost* 212 'Paddock' had also a special gumdigging meaning, for an area dug out sod by sod in a search for surface gum.

paddock, *v.*¹ *Farming.*

1. a. *trans.* [AND 1847.] To enclose, run, or provide secure pasture for, (stock) in a paddock, often temporarily or overnight.

1866 BARKER *Station Life* (1870) 86 We..reached the station..in time to see our horses paddocked safely before the train started for Christchurch. **1875** *Official Handbook NZ* 238 He can make terms with his neighbour for the right of paddocking his cattle. **1901** *TrNZI* XXXIII. 197 Messrs. Nelson Brothers, of the meat-freezing works.., kindly offered to receive and paddock any black lambs forwarded..to their works until such time as a drive of black lambs should be collected together. **1933** ACLAND *Early Canterbury Runs* 111 He paddocked the sheep one night at the Rangitata Bridge. **1953** STRONACH *Musterer on Molesworth* 21 That night we paddocked the sheep, ready for the trip to Molesworth for shearing. **1960** SCRYMGEOUR *Memories of Maoriland* 49 A draft of stud ewes paddocked handy..to make a handy mob. **1984** BOYD *City of the Plains* 83 When an account of 15/- for paddocking the borough horse had to be passed for payment, it auctioned the horse.

b. *intr.* To hold (or place) stock in a paddock.

1989 RICHARDS *Pioneer's Life* 86 I paddocked that night in a holding paddock adjoining the Taupiri saleyards.

Hence **paddocking** [AND 1871], the holding or feeding (of stock) in paddocks.

1881 *Rep. Committee on Frozen Meat Trade* 21 Dec. in Macdonald *Canterbury Frozen Meat Co.* (1957) 77 The operations can best be carried on by having the freezing works..adjacent to a line of railway..and where paddocking can be got for holding the stock until slaughtered. **1959** MASTERS *Tales of Mails* 50 On arrival, after arranging for a feed and paddocking for his horse George wandered into the hotel bar.

2. *Flaxmilling.* [Recorded in derived forms only: see PADDOCK *n.*¹ 2.] To spread scutched flax fibre in a paddock or an outdoor area for sun-drying, hence **paddocked** *ppl. a.*, of flax, so spread; **paddocker**, a flaxmill worker employed to spread and attend to flax fibre in the drying paddock; **paddocking** *vbl. n.*, the activity or occupation of so spreading flax fibre.

1928 *NZJST* X. 238 The tests were too small to discriminate much, but they show that there is no loss of strength in comparison with **paddocked** fibre. **1891** Cox *Diaries 1888–1924* (ATLMS) 3 June Jones talks of closing the mill, the weather is so bad that the paddockers cannot get any fibre in. **1913** CARR *Country Work* 44 Wages...—Stripper keeper and feeder... Shaker 30s a week... Paddocker 30s a week to 1s an hour. **1977** FURNISS *Servants of the North* 15 Now the paddockers took over, hanging the lengths of fibre over fences of plain wire or laying them out on the grass of the hillside to bleach in the sun and wind. **1938** *TrRSNZ* LXVIII. 7 He painted the house, helped in the **paddocking** of the flax, constructed a tennis court.

3. [AND 1873.] To enclose or fence (land); to divide (land) into paddocks.

1941 BAKER *NZ Slang* 40 *To paddock land*, to put up fences.

paddock, *v.*² *Goldmining.*

1. Also **paddock out.** *trans.* To excavate a PADDOCK *n.*² 1.

1862 CHUDLEIGH *Diary* 3 June (1950) 41 Went down several more feet with our pit. One of the digers [*sic*]..came to the conclusion we should have to paddock it which is to work it like a quarry, large at the top instead of driving levells [*sic*]. **1863** *AJHR* D-6 18 Many..who held river claims worked..so as to cut off a portion of its bed, which, being drained by pumping, was paddocked out and passed through the cradle. **1906** GALVIN *NZ Mining Handbook* 204 The washdirt was 'paddocked' or 'driven' out, and carried or carted to where there was water. **1962** EVANS *Waikaka Saga* 15 Then they began 'paddocking'. They marked off a strip of land and stripped off the soil down to the wash... When all this first area of wash had been put through the sluice box, they began on the second 'paddock'.

2. [AND 1871.] To store (excavated washdirt) in a PADDOCK *n.*² 2, or other area or receptacle.

   1884 REID *Rambles on Golden Coast* 66 I accosted a party of four who were paddocking a goodly looking wash. **1974** HEINZ *Bright Fine Gold* 200 *Paddock*: To work an area of a certain size: To paddock washdirt, that is hold it in a bin, until water is available for washing.

   Hence **paddocking** *vbl. n.*, working a gold-bearing area by excavating a paddock; the (process of) storing excavated washdirt. See also quots. 1953, 1983.

   1879 BRACKEN *The NZ Tourist* 24 The operations of 'paddocking' and 'sluicing'. **1916** STALLWORTHY *Early N. Wairoa* 54 On the higher and drier lands, the here-and-there-pot-holing practice gave place to continuous digging, known as paddocking. **1946** MILLER *There Was Gold* 74 But even at that [sluicing] was going to pay me much better than paddocking. **1953** *NZ Geogr.* Apr. 29 Workings [at Mount Ida, Otago, in 1871] were for the most part alluvial, the distinctive process used being 'paddocking'. [1953 *Note*] Paddocking was the systematic sluicing of large areas of flat ground from which the surface layers were first removed to reveal the 'wash-dirt' beneath. **1983** NOLAN *Gold Fossicker's Handbook* 113 *Paddocking*: working alluvial gold in a dry region by storing the paydirt in a gully or bin and washing it when water is available; also, digging or sluicing a claim one section at a time methodically.

Paddy. [f. the common familiar Irish alteration of Patrick.]

1. In various collocations: **Paddy's apple** [f. the association of the Irish with the potato], a potato; **Paddy's lantern** [f. Brit. dial. and nautical use: cf. EDD supp.], a jocular name for the moon; **Paddy McGinty's goat** [cf. Partridge 8 *up goes McGinty's goat*, the excitement starts], indicating a wide inclusiveness, 'Uncle and Tom Cobley and all'; **Paddy's pig** in the phr. **as ignorant as Paddy's pig**, very ignorant; also occas. heard **as Irish as Paddy's pig**, fully Irish.

   1922 COWAN *NZ Wars* (1955) II. 408 The rations consisted of potatoes..or, as Mr. James Carroll, sen., the facetious one of the party, observed: 'Potatoes for breakfast, spuds for dinner, and Paddy's apples for tea.' **1933** EADDY *Hull Down* 104 Work round the deck and up aloft is a hundred times easier when 'Paddy's Lantern' is hung out. **1960** KEINZLY *Tangahano* 91 From the Cape to the Bluff Hangis [sic] Maoris like their Hangis and Kiwis like their shindigs, and it's just too bad if you, I and Paddy McGinty's goat don't like either! **1974** AGNEW *Loner* 185 There's one who reminds me of Crawford from the Dunedin gaol—as ignorant as Paddy's pig.

2. As **Paddy Webb** *West Coast obs.* [f. Patrick (*Paddy*) Charles Webb (1884–1950), M.P. for Buller 1933–46], see quot.

   1990 CHURCHMAN & HURST *Railways of NZ* 196 The mixed train which arrived at Rewanui about 11.30 pm Sunday to Thursday was known as the 'Paddy Webb' or 'Bob Semple' after the miners who became Cabinet Ministers in the first Labour Government, and who first arranged this train to make it easier for the miners changing shift at midnight.

pa-degga-degga, var. PAREKAREKA.

paekirikiri, var. PAKIRIKIRI.

paepae. [Ma. /ˈpaepae/: Williams 245 *paepae*..n. Beam, bar.] The beam forming a bench at the threshold of a meeting house.

   1937 BUICK *Moa-Hunters NZ* 203 'This looks like the *paepae* of a large house,' said Mr. Teviotdale. **1986** IHIMAERA *Matriarch* 74 She nodded in the direction of the paepae where the speakers were sitting. **1989** TE AWEKOTUKU *Tahuri* 102 paepae: bench or seat for orators; ritual threshold. **1995** *Dominion* (Wellington) 2 Oct. 6 One assumes that Sir Hepi's political calculation is that nailing the Government as the source of Maori woes is a pretty safe line both on the *paepae* (orator's bench) and TV news.

pagoda plant. [f. the shape of its inflorescence.] Himalaya honeysuckle, *Leycesteria formosa*; WHISTLEWOOD.

   1943 *Bull. Wellington Bot. Soc. No.7* 2 *Leycesteria formosa* was common in parts [of Durville Island]... Large red fruits hang down surrounded by tiers of red bracts, from which the local name of Pagoda plant arises. **1946** *Ibid. No.14* 8 Here are some [vernacular names]... *Leycesteria formosa*, whistlewood, pagoda plant, (both in the Hutt Valley), Japanese spiderwort, twitch elder.

pah, var. PA *n.*¹

pahautea. [Ma. /ˈpaːhauˈtea/: Williams 247 *Pāhau* (i) *1. Beard... Pāhau-tea* [=? 'white beard' from the peeling bark], *Libocedrus bidwillii*.] *Libocedrus bidwillii* (fam. Cupressaceae), a smallish tree of high altitudes, having pinkish bark which peels off in narrow strips; also its light, red wood. Occas. confusingly termed KAIKAWAKA. See also CEDAR 2 (1) and (2).

   1867 HOOKER *Handbook* 766 Pahautea...*Libocedrus Bidwillii.* **1875** KIRK *Durability NZ Timbers* 13 Cedar—Pahautea.—(*Libocedrus bidwillii*). **1889** KIRK *Forest Flora* 159 *Libocedrus Bidwillii* is generally known as 'kaikawaka' by surveyors and bushmen, although Mr. Colenso states the the correct Native name is 'pahautea'. **1902** *Settler's Handbook NZ* 119 Cedar, or pahautea, pokaka, and hinau are not unfrequent, while most of the beeches are plentiful. **1910** COCKAYNE *NZ Plants & Their Story* 41 The pahautea (*Libocedrus Bidwillii*), a very light wood, of a red colour, out of which canoes have been made. **1961** MARTIN *Flora NZ* 171 [Kawaka] is the commoner species [of *Libocedrus*] in the North Island as the Pahautea or Mountain Cedar is in the South Island. **1978** *Manawatu Tramping Club Jubilee* 99 [We] take the track into splendid kaikawaka (pahautea) and mountain beech bush. **1986** SALMON *Native Trees NZ* 90 Pahautea wood is red, soft and straight-grained but splits easily.

pahiwah, var. PAUA.

Pahkihow, var. PAKEHA.

pahrarra, var. PARAERAE.

pahutukawa, var. POHUTUKAWA.

pai (ana): see PIE ON; see also KAPAI.

pai kare, var. PY KORRY.

Pai Marire. *Hist.* Also **Paimarire**, occas. **Pai mariri, Pai Maririe**. [Ma. /ˈpai ˈmaːrire/: *pai* 'good' + *mārire* 'quiet, gentle, appeased': Williams 250 *Paimārire*.]

1. a. The name given to a spiritual movement founded by Te Ua, of Taranaki, in 1862 (see esp. quots. 1871, 1986). See also HAUHAU *n.*¹ Contrast RINGATU.

   1864 *AJHR E-8* [unpaged title] [Title] Papers Relative to the Pai Maririe, or Hau Hau Religion... illustrating the new superstition called 'Pai Maririe', or 'Hau hau' religion. Te Ua then made me [on 28 June 1864] a long speech, singing several Waiata's [sic] and 'Pai Marire' hymns. **1868** [see HAUHAU *n.*¹ A a]. **1871** MEADE *Ride through Disturbed Dist.* in Taylor *Early Travellers* (1959) 440 We met a small party of mounted natives, who brought news that an apostle of the new *Pai Marire*, or *Te Hau*, fanaticism had arrived at Taupo... They are called *Pai Marire*, from the words which they subscribe to their signatures and use in greeting or parting from their co-religionists. The words literally mean 'good! be appeased'; but the real tendency of the belief is to unite the Kingites of all sects in one common bond of fanatical hostility to the pakehas. *Te Hau* means only the *hau* (faith). **1889** [see HAUHAU *n.*¹ A a]. **1922** COWAN *NZ Wars* (1955) II. v The description of the Pai-marire, or Hauhau religion..contains much that has not previously been recorded. **1959** SINCLAIR *Hist. NZ* 137 But there was a new and intractable fact to be taken into account in Taranaki: *Pai marire*—the Good and Peaceful Religion. In 1862 the Angel Gabriel had appeared in a vision to Te Ua, a Maori who had fought the Europeans in Taranaki. **1967** BRATHWAITE *Evil Day* 380 Pai-marire. The Taranaki form of the Hauhau faith. (There was a modified form, even more barbaric, if anything, founded by Te Kooti and rife in East Coast and Urewera Country, known as *Ringa-tu*. *Pai-marire*, which revived ritual cannibalism and other revolting practices, strangely enough means 'Good and Peaceful'.) **1986** BELICH *NZ Wars* 204 *Pai Marire*—'The Good and Peaceful', also known as 'Hauhauism'—was a syncretic religion originated by the prophet Te Ua Haumene, of the Taranaki tribe, in 1862. It had messianic and millenarian aspects, and theologically combined traditional Maori religion and the Maori versions of Christianity with Te Ua's own innovations... The original form of Pai Marire may have died out as early as 1866, with the death of its founder, but related or similar cults developed around leaders such as Hakaraia, Te Whiti O Rongomai, Titokowaru, Te Kooti, and Tawhiao himself.

b. A follower of Pai Marire.

   1865 *Evening Post* (Wellington) I. No.53 2 They are Pai Marires themselves. **1870** [see 1 a above].

c. A cry or prayerful ejaculation used by Pai Marire adherents.

   [**1864** *AJHR E-8* 4 Atua Pai Marire, rire, Atua Pai Marire, haw!.. the 'Haw' is said to be a substitute for 'Amen'.] **1912** *NZ Free Lance* (Wellington) 20 July 4 Down came the Hauhuas, a whole mob of them, armed, yelling 'Pai-mariri!' and such-like war-cries.

2. a. *attrib.*

   1864 *Richmond-Atkinson Papers* (1960) II. 125 In the flat open space behind the pa there was a pole (or niu) standing used in their new Pai Marire religion. **1868** TAYLOR *Past & Present NZ* 167 The other commanded him to go lie down and die, making pai marire signs at him. **1879** *Auckland Weekly News* 26 Apr. 12 This was..while the Pai Marire superstition was rife. **1940** COWAN *Sir Donald Maclean* 86 In..the early part of 1866, there were indications of the spread of Pai-marire propaganda in Hawke's Bay.

b. Special Comb. **Pai Marire pole,** NIU.

   1867 *Richmond-Atkinson Papers* (1960) II. 228 There is a flagstaff here [on Waimate Plains], fenced in & surmounted by the figure of a bird, probably a kawekawea as it was a great *niu* or Pai Marire pole at one time. **1892** KELLY *Journey Upper Waitara Valley* 11 There remains a huge paimariri pole, round which renegade Christians danced, and held their superstitious ceremonies.

PAINKILLER

3. As **pai marireism**, a belief in and practice of Pai Marire.

1866 P.C.B. *Two Yrs. Experience of Maoris* 700 That fierce outbreak of fanaticism known as pai marireism.

painkiller. [f. *Perry-Davis Painkiller*, a proprietary preparation, much used in early New Zealand, often on account of its alcohol content: see OED *pain*[1] 7 e, 1853.]

1. The proprietary tonic of the Perry Davis Company.

1873 BARKER *Station Amusements* 135 I always purchase myself a box of Holloway's Pills..and also a bottle of pain-killer; but last shearing they was out o' pain-killer. **1874** BATHGATE *Col. Experiences* 144 [A digger speaks.] 'Here's the only liquor I've got. Will you have a nip.'.. So we had a pannikin of hot water each with a nobbler of pain-killer in it. **1889** PRINCE *Diary of Trip* 17 They bought a good supply of provisions, not omitting..a bottle of Perry Davis' Painkiller, the latter a valuable bush medicine, for it has a healing, stimulating and satisfying effect when taken internally. **1896** HARPER *Pioneer Work* 182 For medicinal purposes, Douglas carried 'pain-killer' and pills. **1904** *NZ Illustr. Mag.* Dec. 252 The men held the beasts' heads up in turn, and the skipper poured the painkiller down their throats. **1948** FINLAYSON *Tidal Creek* (1979) 58 We got 'em and kept 'em in a painkiller bottle for a long time. **1965** HENDERSON *Open Country* 250 These old-timers used to wean themselves on 'Painkiller', a patent medicine of the time having a high alcoholic content, and possibly a little morphia. **1983** COOPER *Wag's Tales* 27 Sometimes a scent can stir unpleasant memories..and one such is Painkiller, that old-fashioned remedy for many minor ills.

2. *transf. Obs.* **bush (Maori) painkiller.** A decoction of the leaves of the HOROPITO; or (occas.) the KAWAKAWA *n.*[1] a.

1889 FEATON *Art Album NZ Flora* 13 A decoction of the leaves is known as Maori painkiller, and I have heard the tree itself so called. **1907** [see PEPPER-TREE 2]. **1923** *NZJST* VI. 151 Of the two plants which furnish 'bush-painkiller', one *Macropiper excelsum*, is a true pepper. **1924** *Otago Witness* (Dunedin) 29 Jan. 6 Two plants that furnish 'bush painkiller', the pepper tree [*sc.* kawakawa] and the pepper-wood, or horopito, both with leaves that have a hot taste, have been investigated. **1925–26** *NZJST* VIII. 107 Among bushmen a decoction of the leaves [of *Drimys axillaris*] used to be much in vogue as a medicine, under the name of 'Maori painkiller'.

painted duck: see DUCK 2 (5).

pai on, var. PIE ON.

pairairai, var. PARAERAE.

pair of bastards on a raft. Poached eggs on toast.

1985 HUNT *I'm Ninety-five* 29 And what did we call the poached eggs [c1916]? A pair of bastards on a raft.

pakadu, var. PAKARU.

pakaha. Also **pakahaa.** [Imitative of the bird's call: Ma. /paka'ha:/: Williams 250 *Pakahā*..fluttering shearwater.] *fluttering shearwater* (SHEARWATER 2 (3)). See also RAINBIRD.

1888 BULLER *Birds NZ* II. 236 Puffinus gavia. (Forster's Shearwater)... *Native name.*—Pakahaa: 'Rainbird' of the colonists. *Ibid.* 237 They fly low but swiftly, and utter a note resembling the native name by which the bird is called, but somewhat prolonged, as *paka-ha-a—paka-ha-a*. **1925–26** *NZJST* VIII. 208 Forster's Shearwater, or Pakaha (*Puffinus gavia*). **1955** [see SHEARWATER 2 (3)]. **1966** FALLA et al. *Birds of NZ* 43 On their approach to nesting grounds after dark, they are very noisy with a rapid staccato repetition of a call which can roughly be rendered by one of the Maori names for the bird 'Pakaha' with the emphasis on the last syllable. **1985, 1990** [see SHEARWATER 2 (3)].

pakapaka *Hist.*: see PAKE 1 for possible (variant) forms.

pakapoo /'pækəpu/. Also **pakapu.** [Recorded earliest in Australia: AND 1886, ad. 'Chinese *pai ko p'iao* white pigeon ticket': of historical significance in New Zealand as a once widely-known and generally popular illicit gambling game closely associated with early immigrant Chinese. See further GRANT *On a Roll* (1989) pp.157–8.] A gambling game involving the marking of a number of Chinese characters on a ticket to try and match those on a master ticket. Often *attrib.* or in Comb. as in **pakapoo den, saloon, ticket,** etc.

1892 DON *Chinese Mission Work* 2 He won £120 at a pakapu lottery. **1904** *NZ Observer* 3 Sept. 4 He got pak-a-pu struck out of the Gaming and Lotteries Bill as a lottery. **1922** *Auckland Weekly News* 22 June 20 Two bits of 'documents printed in a foreign language' were stated to be pakapoo tickets. **1934** *Fielding Star* 10 Mar. 6 The Wellington police believe that there are from 40 to 60 houses about the Chinese quarter..being used as pakapoo dens. **1936** HYDE *Passport to Hell* 10 The..bawdy-houses of Upper Queen Street..mingled happily with Chinese grocery-shops, masonic clubs, and pakapoo saloons. **1942** FINLAYSON *Brown Man's Burden* (1973) 93 A serious middle-aged man in short sleeves..sat at one table with brush and ink for the marking of pakapoo tickets. **1960** *Listener* 22 July 9 Some of the last of the old Chinese dwellings of the opium-smoking and pakapoo-playing generation are being pulled down in Haining Street in Wellington. **1980** MCGILL & TILLY *In Praise of Older Buildings* 116 You paid sixpence for a pakapoo ticket, each ticket bearing 80 Chinese characters. Ten had to be marked. You won a prize if five or more corresponded with the master ticket.

pakaru /pʌkə'ru/, *v. trans.* Also with much variety of form as (early) **pakādu, puikero, pukeru;** (later) **buckeroo, puckaroo, puckeroo, pukaroo, pukaru, pukeroo, pukkaroo.** [Ma. /'pa:karu/ (*v.*); /'pakaru/ (*adj.*): Williams 251 *Pākaru.. 1.* v. trans. Break in pieces, break through. *Pakaru. 1.* a. Shivered, broken, shattered.: in the anglicized form *puckerood* at times associated by English speakers with *buggered*.]

1. In mainly Maori contexts, variants of orig. Ma. *pakaru.* To damage; ruin; kill.

[**1820** LEE & KENDALL *Gram. & Vocab.* 187 Pakádu, *v. n.* Bursting.] **1840** BEST *Journal* 13 Dec. (1966) 267 The Mauries swore that we should all be Puckarooed as well as the gun and away they scuttled. **1844** BARNICOAT *Journal* (ATLTS) 19 Mar. 160 Gideon [a Maori guide, foreseeing a collision]..shouted out 'puikero! puikero! puikero!' (broken). A boat would have been stove..in such a passage. **1863** MORGAN *Journal* 16 Sept. (1963) 85 As they retreated from our troops into the bush..they sung out in Maori, 'Soldier, aramay; Pukaru the soldier,' accompanied by shouting and yells. **1885** HANCOCK *Short Sketch* 19 [The Maori said] 'We will *pukeru* you'. 'Very well,' I said 'Pukeru me.'

PAKE

Hence, as quasi-noun, **te pukeroo,** the ruination (of).

1931 *Aussie* (NZ Section) 15 Apr. xi If you no bring him, I make-a te *pukeroo* you!

2. Variants of an anglicized form PUCKEROO (also **buckeroo**), in mainly non-Maori contexts. *v. trans.* To ruin, freq. in passive use.

1913 *NZ Observer* 19 July 13 [Caption] The Pakeha poss in Werrington he want to 'pukeroo' te exhipition. **1941** BAKER *NZ Slang* 42 We had begun to *pukaroo* things, when we broke something, confused an issue, or ruined some plan of action. This is derived..from the Maori *pakaru*..though..many New Zealanders [have thought] that it comes from the verb b——r. **1948** FINLAYSON *Tidal Creek* (1979) 126 He never would have..used his axe [to bash in iron wedges]..which is the surest way to buckeroo an axe Uncle Ted says. **1955** *BJ Cameron Collection* (TS July) puckeroo (v) To put paid to, to spoil. Also spelt *buckeroo.* **1960** MUIR *Word for Word* 174 *I* don't know. His old man was pretty strict, of course... Probably pukarooed any romances. **1963** CASEY *As Short a Spring* 284 It used to be a real crackerjack, but I'd puckerooed it completely, *eh.* **1969** MASON *Awatea* (1978) 43 Haangi puckerooed by now, I bet. Kumaras like bullets, pigs all burnt up. *Ibid.* 99 *puckerooed*: English version of Maori *pakaru*, meaning shattered, or broken or rendered useless. **1971** *Listener* 19 Apr. 56 He had a compass..but it was puckeroo'd. Well, he decided it was a dead loss. **1991** *Dominion* (Wellington) 12 Oct. 13 The most active thing, the only thing in your body, is the mind, your brain. And if anything affects that, then you're puckerooed. You've had it.

pakaru /pʌkə'ru/, *a.* [Mainly f. Ma. *pakaru a.*] In predicative use, broken; smashed; ruined; out of order.

[*Note*] Used in both Maori and non-Maori contexts; in the latter, less frequently than *puckerood*, and perh. often perceived as a variant of a participial adjective.

1843 DIEFFENBACH *Travels in NZ* II. 377 Pakaru—breaking, bursting. **1917** *NZ At the Front* xiv (Gloss.) Pakaru.—Broken, smashed. **1937** PARTRIDGE *Dict. Slang* 601 *pakaru.* Broken, crushed, smashed: New Zealand military: G.W. Ex Maori *pakaru* (to destroy), common as N.Z. coll. in late C. 19–20. **1943** BENNETT *English in NZ* in *Amer. Speech* XVIII. 93 Pukkaroo, adjective and noun, (to make) worthless, useless—it could be used, for instance, of an engine that had broken down—is of dubious origin;.. perhaps from the Maori *pakaru*,.. or conceivably..an adaptation of 'buggered'. **1946** SOLJAK *NZ* 117 New Zealand colloquialisms which are of Maori origin include..*pakaru*: broken, ruined. **1952** LYON *Faring South* 76 Bob related how a row of Maoris would push him off the paths of Wellington's main streets, and with many insulting gestures, tell him to go to Taranaki, where they said he would be pukaru or finished. **1969** MASON *Awatea* (1978) 89 Then they come, to visit. But no hui! The hui is pakaru, pakaru.

pake. Also with much variety of early form as **boghee-boghee, bugabuga, bugge(e) bugge(e), buggy, bugy bugy** representing an anglicized pronunciation ?/bʌgi/ reduplicated. [Ma. /'pakapaka/: Williams 250 *Paka* (i)..*pakapaka..4.* A coarse rough cloak of flax.: or Ma. /'pa:ke:/: Williams 252 *Pākē*, n. A rough cape made of undressed leaves of *kiekie* or flax.]

[*Note*] Mead 1969 (*op. cit.* 2 a below 60f.) identifies the Bayly, Edgar and Forster forms with Ma. *pākē*, and this is certainly the form which came into English use in the 19th c. However, it would be reasonable to suppose, from Mead's comments on the early local provenance of *pākē* and from phonetic considerations and the persistent recording of reduplicated forms, that early

PAKEA

English-speaking observers may have been hearing a concurrent use of Ma. *pakapaka*, with possibilities of cross-identification between *pākē* and *pakapaka*.

1. Poss. forms from Ma. *pakapaka*. A coarse rough cloak of flax.

   1773 FURNEAUX *Narrative* in Cook *Journals* (1961) II. 740 Their Cloathing (both Men [and] Women) is a kind of matt or cloth made of silk grass or fine flax..and over it they have one of a coarser sort made of Grass well thrumbed with the same to keep out the wet which they call a Bugy Bugy. **1773** BAYLY *Journal* 12 Apr. in McNab *Hist. Records* (1914) II. 204 Over this [*sc.* Ahoo, a wrap-round mantle] they have a rough garment which they call a Buggy. **1777** SAMWELL *Account* 24 Feb. in Cook *Journals* (1967) III. 1002 That night they lay..covered with their Cloaks or Bugge bugge's. **1777** FORSTER *Voyage Round World* I. 214 The *boghee-boghee*, or shaggy-cloak, which hangs round their necks like a thatch of straw, was almost constantly worn by them. **1777** EDGAR *Log 'Discovery'* 25 Feb. in McNab *Hist. Records* (1914) II. 226 That Night they lay in the Steerage on the bare Deck cover'd with their Cloaks or Buggee buggees. **1783** LEDYARD *Journal* (1963) 14 They add what they call the Bugabuga or Toga.

2. Forms from Ma. *pākē*. **a.** A rough rain cape made of the undressed leaves of kiekie or flax.

   1869 *TrNZI* I. (rev. edn.) 262 From [flax] the Chief's..shaggy bee-butt looking Pake and Ngeri..were alone manufactured. **1921** GUTHRIE-SMITH *Tutira* (1926) 52 To be in sympathy with this *hapu*..readers would be well-advised..to imagine themselves bare-limbed, bare-headed, brown, the *pake* of everyday wear thrown over their shoulders. **1949** BUCK *Coming of Maori* 160 The *pake*, as we know it, is the roughest type of rain cape with an outer thatch of overlapping free ends to shed the rain. **1969** MEAD *Traditional Maori Clothing* 60 *P-class: paakee, ornamental and rain capes* [quoting the 18c. references in 1 above] *Ibid.* 61 Although the Maori word paakee seems mainly to have been associated with the Queen Charlotte Sound area, and as it is the only name recorded it is perhaps appropriate that we should use it to designate the class [of ornamental and rain capes] as a whole.

b. *transf.* /ˈpaki/. A sacking rain-cape or hood, usually made by punching in one corner of a grain sack to make a peaked hood with the tail covering shoulders and back.

   1898 MORRIS *Austral-English* 337 *Pakē*, *n*. Maori name for a coarse mat used against the rain. A sack thrown over the shoulders is called by the settlers a *Pake*. **c1930** *Whitcombe's Etym. Dict. Aust.-NZ Suppl.* 8 *pake n*. a mat or piece of sacking used as a protection from rain. **c1940–45** *parkee* was a term used in Marlborough for a sack hood, esp. as a makeshift protection when humping hundredweight sacks of coal or lime (Ed.).

Pakea, var. PAKEHA.

Pakeha /ˈpakiˌha/, /ˈpakiə/, *n*. and *a*. Also with much variety of early form as **pachia**, **packahâ**, **packeah**, **packia**, **pahkihow**, **pakea**, **pakia**, **pakiha (mouri)**, **Pakkahah**, **Parkeha**, **Parkiah**, **Parkiar**, **pekeha**, **pokeey**, **Pughia**, with *pakeha* and *Pakeha* being the accepted forms in both English and Maori orthography from c1850, a standardization prob. aided by the spelling used in the Williams *Dictionary* of 1844, and subsequent editions. Spellings indicate early anglicized pronunciations were variously /ˈpakəˌha/, /ˈpʌk-/, ?/ˈpʊkjə/. Maori orthography has seemed to prefer *Pakeha* with initial cap. as a full congener of the forms *European* and *Maori*, though some Maori scholars (e.g. Apirana Ngata) vary their English usage; and Maori examples are not always capitalized in Williams (7edn. 1971), as at 20: *Atua* 3... *Toku atua he pakeha* (*A European is the most disagreeable thing to me*). The house rules of publishers and newspapers have been variable, though the trend is towards capitalization. *Pl. Pakehas* and *Pakeha*. [Ma. /ˈpaːkeha:/ Of uncertain origin, the association with *pakepakehā*, var. *pākehakeha* 'imaginary pale-skinned beings' is the least unlikely of those suggested: Williams 252 *Pākehā*, *1. n*. A person of predominantly European descent. *2. a. Foreign...3. n. Silver eel..4. A flea*. Earlier editions define it variously: 1871 (3edn.) 105 '*Pākehā*, n. *foreigner*'; 1917 (5edn.) 293 '*Pākehā*, *1. n. Foreigner* (not necessarily light-skinned, but probably connected with *pakepakehā*)', the semantic connection being formally made by its inclusion as a sub-entry of *Pākehā* in the 1957 (6 edn.). Compare from A 1 below *tangata pora* a southern use, quots. 1826–27 (Boultbee) and 1851 (Shortland) (Williams 293 *Pora 2. Ship. 3. Stranger, wonderful person; also called tangata pora*.); and *tangata tupua* an early northern use recorded from 1801 in the *Missionaries Journale in the Royal Admiral* (ATLMS) 19 June 'Some of the natives here [*sc.* Firth of Thames northwards] have informed us that Tongatta [*sic*] Tubua or white people took with them two of Tongata Maura (New Zealanders) to their own country, and some time after they returned they say they lived well with the white people eating Bunga Bunga (bread) and Gure (flesh of all kinds).' The reference is prob. to the Maori men taken to Norfolk Island by Governor King: see further Williams 458 '*Tupua, tipua 1. n.* Goblin, demon, object of terror... *3.* Foreigner. *5.* a[djective]. Strange.' where the senses, all recorded from at least the mid-19th century, mix or fuse ideas of 'goblin, demon, foreigner; and strangeness', in a manner appropriate to first or early perceptions of European seafarers.]

[*Note*] Early written sources are unhelpful or ambiguous in respect of the origin of *Pakeha*, or of whether a Polynesian or a non-Polynesian etymon or source underlies the present word-form, and if the former, what was its essential meaning. They suggest, however, that *Pakeha* was a northern New Zealand word (see esp. quots. c1826–27 and 1851 A 1 below), a hypothesis strengthened by the evidence of J.S.C. Dumont d'Urville, who was familiar with the word from his visits to northern New Zealand in the 1820s as designating all whites in general. (See *Les Zélandais: Histoire Australienne* c1825–1826, translated as *The New Zealanders: a story of austral lands* (1992) by Carol Legge.) Pierre Lesson (who was in New Zealand in 1827) remarks in *Voyage de découvertes autour du monde et à la recherche de La Pérouse* in *La Librarie Encyclopédique de Roret* 1832 (XIX. 2:2:516) that the New Zealanders designate all Europeans 'or rather all white people' ('ou plutôt tous les blancs') by the generic term 'pakeha', and was surprised to find that it had been adopted in widely separated New Zealand localities. It may be mere chance that in English written use the senses 'white man, European' pre-date those for 'stranger' by about 20 years; white males would be the 'strangers' or 'foreigners' (from the sea) most likely to be met with in late 18th and early 19th century New Zealand. It is also well to remember that Maori, not English, was the major language of communication between the races until at least the 1860s. The first written record of the word *pakeha* occurs in Maori (see A 1 below, quot. 1814). It is found in the preamble to the Maori version of the Treaty of Waitangi (but not in the English translation) as a distinguishing congener of *tangata maori*: *ki te tangata maori ki te pakeha* 'the Maori people and the Europeans'.

A. *n.*

1. A pale-skinned non-Polynesian immigrant or foreigner as distinct from a Maori; thence, a non-Polynesian New Zealand-born New Zealander esp. if pale-skinned. In *pl*. Europeans as an ethnic category. See also ENGLISH 1 b, EUROPEAN A. **a.** Illustrations of sense and use.

   [**1814** W. Hall to CMS 15 June in Wilson *From Hongi Hika to Hone Heke* (1985) 87 They..expressed their joy by saying 'Nuee nuee rangateeda pakehaa—a very great Gentleman white man. **1815** KENDALL *New Zealanders' First Book* 22 [Sentences] Na! Iesu Christ ta Atua Nue, ta Atua Pi, ta wanhoungha Nue, ta wanhoungha Pi, ke ta notungata na, Pakkahah, ke ta na tangata maoude, ke ta tungata katoa katoa. *Ibid.* 23 Behold! Jesus Christ is the great and good Atua, the great and good friend to white and black men; to all men.] **1817** NICHOLAS *NZ* I. 181 We could easily perceive..that the *packahâ*, or white man, was the subject of some extraordinary remarks. [**1820** LEE & KENDALL *Gram. & Vocab.* 187 Pakéha, *s*. An European; a white man.] **1820** McCRAE *Journal* (1928) 23 They then remarked that that might be the way of the Pakeha (or white men) but with them the belief was that their God had fished up New Zealand. **1823** EARLE *Nine Months Residence* (1966) 146 The white taboo'd day [*sc.* Sunday], when packeahs (or white men) put on clean clothes. [c**1826–27** BOULTBEE *Journal* (1986) 109 white man—tongata bulla (Bay of Islands—tongata páhkihow).] **1834** MARKHAM *NZ* (1963) 51 One [Chief] said he liked the 'Parkiars' or Europeans and said he would protect them. *Ibid.* 66 The old people believe that the (Atua) God of the Parkiars Strangers is killing or eating the Mouries or Natives. **1839** TAYLOR *Journal* 6 Apr. (ATLTS) II. 88 Their exclamations of admiration were very frequent when they beheld the *pakeas* (so they call strangers) wash. *Ibid.* 119 They notice the pakias (the Europeans) whom they copy in everything. **1840** BEST *Journal* (1966) 239 Our First Step was to bundle all the armed Packias out of the Pah. **1842** in *Lett. from Settlers* (1843) 81 The natives have been taking too much *Whipe ha[r]o* of the *pokeeys*, that is, *whipe ha[r]o* is spirits, and *pokeeys* white men. [Orig. *havo* corrected from the text in the *NZ Journal*.] **1850** LUSH *Auckland Jrnls.* (1971) 46 Mrs Martin and Mr and Mrs Abraham were the *Parkeha's* [baptismal] sponsors: Mrs Selwyn and two natives were the sponsors for the little Maori. **1851** SHORTLAND *S. Dist. NZ* 312 Pora, a ship. 'Takata pora', a man of a ship, or whiteman, equivalent to the term 'pakeha', used commonly in the North Island. [Cf. Williams 293 *Pora 2. Ship. 3. Stranger, wonderful person; also called tangata pora*.] **1859** THOMSON *Story NZ* I. 59 This word [*sc.* Maori] rendered, by linguists 'native,' is used in contradistinction to pakeha, or stranger. **1861** *Gov. Grey to Duke of Newcastle* 8 Dec. in Rutherford *Sel. Documents* (1949) It is the desire of the Queen, and this also is the thought of Governor Grey and of the runanga of the Pakehas, that the Maoris should also do for themselves as the Europeans do. **1884** MARTIN *Our Maoris* 138 Indeed, it is a strong proof of the earnestness of his wish to become a 'Pakeha' (an Englishman), that he submitted to the restraint. **1909** *TrNZI* XLI. 139 The word *pakeha* serves them to signify all whites, whom they also call 'Iouropi' (Europeans). I did not observe that they had a special name for the English. **1929** *Na To Hoa Aroha* (1986) I. 163 With that generation also had largely passed the pakeha who was wedded to the idea of England being 'Home'. The native born New Zealand pakeha is looking nearer to his native heath for objects of study, literary effort and missionary care. **1951**

COMPTON *Through Open door* 64 Party of Pakehas (people other than Maoris). **1967** BRATHWAITE *Evil Day* 380 Pakeha Stranger. Usually Europeans are pakeha. Rarely, if ever, applied to other races. **1983** HULME *Bone People* 466 Pakeha = stranger, now used for a New Zealander of European descent. Used here as an adjective, hence the lower case. **1983** *W5* 5-18 Dec. 15 At Thorndon school my children mix with an amazing cross-section of New Zealand—Greek, Maori, Pakeha, Cambodian, Samoan, Chinese, Sri Lankan, Buddhist, Christian, atheist. **1986** *Listener* 16 Aug. 50 [A NZ Chinese woman writes] I thought for a while that the way to live in New Zealand society was just to be a yellow Pakeha. **1988** *Dominion* (Wellington) 30 Apr. 8 Recent letters opposing the use of the word 'Pakeha' claim that it means 'foreigner' or 'stranger'... Whatever the word meant when it was first bestowed, it has taken on a new and special meaning. Maoris today use it to identify non-Maori New Zealanders of European and especially of British stock, people whom they recognise as having a history of residence and commitment to this country. Maoris use it not only to distinguish Pakehas from themselves but to couple them with themselves. The word has meaning only within the New Zealand context, in relation to and partnership with 'Maori', the shared reference point being the land of Aotearoa/New Zealand.

b. Illustrations of conjectural origins.

1817 NICHOLAS *NZ* II. 338 Packahâ A white man, (the flea is also called by this name, as they assert it to have been introduced into their country by Europeans—the turnip is likewise called packahâ from its whiteness). **1843** DIEFFENBACH *Travels in NZ* II. 7 They call themselves *Maori*, which means *indigenous, aboriginal*..in opposition to *Pakea*, which means a stranger, or *Pakea mango mango*, a very black stranger, a negro. **1898** MORRIS *Austral-English* 337 *Pakeha, n.* Maori word for a white man. The word is three syllables, with even accent on all... Mr. Tregear, in his 'Maori Comparative Dictionary,' s.v. *Pakepakeha*, says: 'Mr. John White [author of 'Ancient History of the Maoris'] considers that *pakeha*, a foreigner, an European, originally meant 'fairy', and states that on the white men first landing sugar was called 'fairy-sand,' etc.'... Some express this idea by 'fairy'. Another explanation is that the word is a corruption of the coarse English word, said to have been described by Dr. Johnson (though not in his dictionary), as 'a term of endearment amongst sailors.' The first *a* in *Pakeha* had something of the *u* sound [*sc.* /ʌ/]. The sailors' word would have been introduced to New Zealand by whalers in the early part of the nineteenth century. **1904** TREGEAR *Maori Race* 523 It is said that when the Deluge swept over the earth some of those who escaped were a god-sprung little people, the fairies known as *Pake-pakeha* who dwelt in flowers and shrubs. This was the reason that the white men on coming to New Zealand were named *Pakeha*, because they were fair and were supposed to have come from fairyland. **1905** *NZ Herald* (Auckland) 7 Jan. Suppl. 1 Sir George [Grey].. addressing himself to me, said 'As long as I have been in the colony, I have never been able to discover the origin of the term pakeha. *Ibid.* I asked [an old chief] why his people gave the name pakeha to the strange human beings they had seen for the first time in their lives... He mea pakewhakewha'. I took the phrase..to signify 'A thing wafted from the ocean to the shore'. **1946** ANDERSEN in *JPS* LV. 145 *Pākehā*, foreigner, not necessarily light-skinned; probably connected with pakepakehā, or pākehakeha, imaginary beings... Very often spelt with small initial letter, but wrongly... The Maori himself was clearer on the point than the Pākehā, for in his Maori publications he would print 'Maori and Pakeha' while the Pakeha was still printing Maori and *pakeha*—a quite inconsistent proceeding.

2. In censorious or derogatory uses. **a.** Attributed to (fictional) Maori speakers or interlocutors.

1857 *Lyttelton Times* 8 Aug. 3 Their reply to him was, 'Oh, you are a pakeha, you don't know our ideas and customs.' **1938** HYDE *Nor Yrs. Condemn* 148 *Plurry pakeha*, eh? You, got the skin like the Maori, but you're not *tangata* Maori. **1944** FINLAYSON *Brown Man's Burden* (1973) 15 They didn't like the pakehas slinging off about Maori prophets. 'The pakeha haven't got one damn prophet,' they said. **1953** HAMILTON *Till Human Voices Wake Us* 2 The Pakehas. I don't know what it sounds like to ordinary ears, when the Minister of Maori Affairs talks about Maoris and Pakehas getting together, but when a Maori says Pakeha, there isn't any mistake, unless that's one of your dead senses. He says it like a man would say s—t. I mean a Maori, not a white Maori. Pakeha, Pakeha, Pakeha. He spits it out. **1965** SHADBOLT *Among Cinders* 24 This brother business could go too far; I mean he had enough real brothers without having a dozy pakeha thrown in too. **1976** WILSON *Pacific Star* 146 'Don't talk to him—damned pakeha,' he said. 'But I wasn't,' she said with a gentle smile. **1980** BERRY *First Offender* 42 The Islanders were Coconuts or Raros to the biased Maori; the Maoris were Black Bastards to the bigoted Pakeha; the militant Maori spat 'Paak-ia' as an obscenity.

b. As perceived by non-Maori, often regarded as derogatory.

[*Note*] The word *Pakeha*, unlike *Maori*, is still essentially monocultural in active use being infrequently seriously used (and rarely in spoken English) by non-Maori of themselves. Hence when it is used by Maori people in English contexts it is open to perceptions by non-Maori that it is not merely exclusionary in connotation but implicitly derogatory.

1946 SARGESON *That Summer* 34 I asked Bill [a Northland barman] if there weren't any *pakehas* and he said there were a few. I can't describe what they're like, he said, except they wouldn't wake up — It was a good crack, but there's a law against putting such things in print. **1960** *Dominion* (Wellington) 17 Oct. 10 If the Hon. Mr. Algie knew the true origin of the word 'pakeha' he would be even more anxious to see it removed from daily use... My great-great uncle was a signatory to the Treaty of Waitangi. He told my father that 'pakeha' was never used in polite language and most certainly never written. **1962** *Dominion* (Wellington) 17 Sept. 8 In taking exception to the use of the term 'pakeha,' a correspondent..suggested that not only is it derogatory but also an affront, being spelled invariably with a small 'p,' whereas its antonym carries a capital 'M.'. **1986** *Dominion* (Wellington) 11 July 11 The word 'Pakeha' is a Maori word that is being increasingly used in a derogatory way against Europeans, and should be banned from use on radio and television and in the newspapers. **1988** *Dominion* (Wellington) 24 Dec. 8 I am a white New Zealander, not a Pakeha,.. and I am bewildered and angered by incessant demands and efforts to Maorify everything.

c. In jocular use alluding to the anthropophagous reputation of the early Maori. (*Pakeha and puha* is also heard in occas. joc. use.)

1905 BRANDON '*Ukneadit*' 104 *Pakeha a la tohunga (an entree)* Pakeha Steaks, Dried Shark.. Kumaras, Pork Fat, Mutton Fish, and Karaka Berries.

3. In Maori and occas. early English use, applied to various things coloured white or associated with 'white': a (white) turnip, a leper, a flea, an eel.

1817 packahâ [see A 1 b above]. **1840** POLACK *Manners & Customs* II. 129 A leper ironically termed as a Pakeha by the natives. [**1842** GRAY *Fauna* in Dieffenbach *Travels in NZ* (1843) II. 291 137. *Pulex*. Keha, or flea. *Polack I .c.i.,p.321. Tuiau. Dieffenbach...* The natives say that fleas were introduced by the Europeans, and for that reason call them sometimes 'he pakeha nohinohi', the little stranger.] **1960** HILLIARD *Maori Girl* 218 Netta warmed to Shirley immediately, especially when she heard her refer to pakeha customers as kehas (fleas). They made numerous jokes: 'Will you be quick with the Keha's oysters, please?' 'Look out for the keha with the moustache—he bites.' **1918** *TrNZI* L. 306 *Kopakopako*. Silver-eel. The Ngai-Tahu people call this *pakeha*, a name they used long before the advent of the Europeans.

4. The English language in New Zealand.

1969 MASON *Awatea* (1978) 60 Werihe..Matt writes to me in pakeha, I talk back to him in Maori. I speak: Gilhooly writes—Brett. She knows Maori? **1973** *Reflections: Voices from Paremoremo* 16 Once I spoke Maori but teacher strapped me so hard and made me learn pakeha so hard.

5. In attrib. use in various Comb. and special Comb. **a. Pakeha Native**, a native-born non-Maori New Zealander (cf. PAKEHA-MAORI); **Pakeha-style**; **Pakeha-trained**.

1932 BRUCE *Early Days Canterbury* [Foreword] As a **Pakeha Native** of our garden city of Christchurch, I have..taken keen interest in the annals of early days. **1960** HILLIARD *Maori Girl* 20 The boys neglected it [*sc.* an eel-weir], preferring to work with lines **pakeha-style**. **1989** TE AWEKOTUKU *Tahuri* 23 But she hated..using the pakeha-style ones instead. Too small, those baths. **1959** TAYLOR *Early Travellers* 350 He was one of the few collectors of Maori lore..who got their knowledge direct from the Maori, before it..was subtly changed by the younger men with **pakeha-trained** minds.

b. As the second element in compounds: **anti-Pakeha**; **pre-Pakeha**, denoting the period of Maori society and culture before the 18th century European contact; **pseudo-Pakeha**, a Maori having adopted the superficialities of European society and culture.

1922 COWAN *NZ Wars* (1955) I. 147 The **anti-pakeha** crusade was given its first expression in a great conference of the west-coast tribes held in 1854. **1940** COWAN *Sir Donald Maclean* 110 To him..fell the task of conciliating..the anti-*pakeha* party. **1879** *TrNZI* XI. 71 The few surviving fragments of **pre-pakeha** civilization in our land have to be sought for in our museums. **1900** *TrNZI* XXXII. 397 The old-time pre-pakeha Maori and his history..are becoming year by year more interesting. **1915** *TrNZI* XLVII. 71 The staple food of the Taupo Maoris in pre-pakeha days was fern-root. **1926** DEVANNY *Butcher Shop* (1981) 32 In pre-pakeha days Tutaki's leg would have caused his fellow-tribesmen much envy. **1936** in *Na To Hoa Aroha* (1988) III. 213 Three hours were devoted to talks on Maori migrations..and the Maori in pre-Pakeha days. **1945** *JPS* LIV. 228 Among composite forms in which the adjective appears are *pre-pakeha times, Journal of the Polynesian Society*, 27 (1918), *pre-pakeha days*, V. Roberts *Kohikohinga* (1929), etc. **1983** HULME *Bone People* 324 'It hasn't got a name,' she is saying. 'It's a family piece though, and it is guaranteed pre-pakeha.' **1990** *Metro* (Auckland) Nov. 172 Our concern, however, is for those Maori who do not wish to be made into **pseudo-Pakeha**. That is not easy in a society which strives to forcibly Europeanise everyone.

c. In a jocular reformation of *pakehas*: **pake-has**, **pake-hasn't** with syllable stress on the second element /pakiˈhæs(ənt)/.

1941 BAKER *NZ Slang* 16 The colloquial uses of *pake-has* (the *has* being accented), for a wealthy white man, and *pake-hasn't*, for a penniless white, may be noted. **1945** *JPS* LIV. 228 Among composite forms in which the adjective appears are..the jocular uses *pakehas* (the 'has' being accented) and *pakehasn't*, for a rich and penniless white man respectively. (These uses may have occurred in print, but I have not seen them; only heard them.)

6. In composition, mainly as a reflex of a form orig. with *Maori-* as a first element: **Pakehadom**, European people and their world; **pakehafied**, converted to Pakeha ways; **pakehaness**, the character of being Pakeha; **pakehatanga**, Pakeha traditions, culture, etc. as distinct from those of the Maori and Maoritanga.

1988 *Listener* 5 Mar. 16 How a project..with the blessing..of all the tribes, including some but not all the tangata whenua Ngai Tahu, plus **Pakeha-dom**..could have become so unstuck..is a complex tale of human foibles. **1988** *Sunday Star* (Auckland) 23 Oct. A12 Pakehadom, as controllers of media, choose and create the so-called spokespersons for Maoridom. **1912** *NZ Free Lance* (Wellington) 10 Feb. 4 Nowadays, they [*sc.* Atiu Islanders] are all quite '**pakehafied**' as to religion. **1985** *Landfall 156* 491 If his blackness has been whitened, his Maoriness pakehafied, then his story is another tragedy. **1988** *Through the Looking Glass* 128 Even an educated 'Pakeha-fied' Maori would end by going 'back to the mat'. **1993** *Evening Post* (Wellington) 27 Apr. 6 I regarded my Maori classmate as a bit 'pakehafied'. **1969** HILLIARD *Green River* 56 But you can't bring your **pakehaness** into my home unless I say so and I won't! This is a Maori home..bringing up his children to be Maoris and not half-pie imitation pakehas. **1991** KING *Pakeha* 19 One essential ingredient of Pakeha-ness..is contact with and being affected by Maori things. **1992** *Metro* (Auckland) Jan. 114 I am Pakeha and aware of my Pakeha-ness. **1986** *Victoria Univ. Faculties of Arts & Lang. & Lit. 'Format First Year Courses'* 14 May Introduction to **Pakehatanga** (in this I include such things as classical mythologies, Bible stories, cultural institutions, etc...). **1988** *Dominion Sunday Times* (Wellington) 12 June 10 In fact, exploring our Pakehatanga can be a very rewarding experience. **1988** MCGILL *Dict. Kiwi Slang* 82 pakehatanga emerging word for cultural attitudes and origins of European and/or Pakeha New Zealanders.

B. *adj.*

1. a. Of, pertaining to, or designating a (usu. fair-skinned) non-Polynesian or European as distinct from a Maori. (Quot. 1834 follows Maori adjectival word order.)

1834 MARKHAM *NZ* (1963.5) 57 But I told her it was for a Waheinee Parkiah, European Woman. **1840** *NZ Jrnl.* I. 221 *Pachia* (English) missionary. **1850** *Emigrants' Lett. from Brit. Colonies* 96 In the minds of these poor heathens we..are classed under two denominations—the Pughia Christians and the Pughia devils. **1863** MANING *Old NZ* i 4 I do not understand the pakeha way of beginning a story in the middle. **1875** CHUDLEIGH *Diary* 15 Sept. (1950) 241 A pakeha hotel is started..amongst hot baths and boiling cauldrons. **1882** POTTS *Out in Open* 15 Ingress or egress only permitted to the pakeha party and their numerous escort of Kupapas. **1905** *Truth* 7 Oct. 5 The opening of the Maori and Pakeha Carnival some four weeks back. **1928** *Na To Hoa Aroha* (1986) I. 150 I had no notion how the pakeha [election] battle was going, being immersed in the fight against Ratanism in four electorates. **1946** BEAGLEHOLE *Some Modern Maoris* xviii Throughout this report we have used the words 'Maori' and 'pakeha' in referring to the two major cultural groups which are in contact. We have however always thought of these terms as being used as adjectives, not nouns, as adjectives followed by such words as 'New Zealander', 'man', 'woman', 'teacher', 'doctor'. **1959** SHADBOLT *New Zealanders* (1986) 16 I should have to share a tiny schoolroom..with some thirty other Maori, half-caste, and pakeha children. **1964** DEMPSEY *Little World Stewart Island* 132 Like most pakeha New Zealanders I had..pronounced the word..as *Mo-ah'-na*. **1985** *Listener* 7 Sept. 77 This is why the debate of the lowest common denominator, couched in terms such as 'social disaster', 'utu' and 'Pakeha backlash' is irresponsible to say the least.

b. In jocular or mildly derogatory use.

1964 HELMER *Stag Party* 104 I was introduced to a huge Maori... 'Got a flash new pakeha car, Crump. How you like him?' he boomed. **1969** MASON *Awatea* (1978) 67 Werihe. My son will look after you. Not pakeha hotel style, you know. **1978** HILLIARD *Glory & Dream* 127 'Sounds like another stupid pakeha idea to me,' she said. '*We* don't carry on like that.'

2. Referring or pertaining to the English language; occas. 'English-speaking'.

1920 *Quick March* 10 Jan. 13 Their remote ancestors were a light-skinned tribe called the Whanau-a-Rongi [*sic*], which in the pakeha tongue is 'Offspring of Heaven'. **1952** *Here & Now* Sept. 31 In this context, ['whare'=] combined lunch and locker room. Pakeha pronunciation, 'warrie'. **1994** *Sunday Star* (Auckland) 23 Jan. A8 Recently a RNZ interviewer discussing the new Maori-English dictionary used the term 'Pakeha word' and 'Maori word'.

3. As **Pakeha time**, rigorous 'clock time', as distinct from the more flexible 'Maori time' measured by human self-interest, convenience or need.

1980 THOMPSON *All My Lives* 115 They [*sc.* two Maori actors] turned up in the end, of course, and, just to prove me prejudiced and wrong, subscribed more rigorously than anyone to 'pakeha time'. **1983** *Listener* 24 Sept. 59 All people who live in urban industrial societies have their lives regulated by measured time. This concept of time is referred to by Maoris as 'Pakeha time' and they conform to its dictates inasmuch as they are on time for work, to catch buses or to fulfil engagements. However, because they are bicultural, Maoris function in their own time-frame as well, which they refer to as 'Maori time'.

Pakeha Maori, *n.* and *attrib.* Also **pakeha-Maori, Pakia Maori, Pakiha Mouri, pekeha mauri**, modern use preferring init. caps.; *pl.* often *Pakeha-Maoris*.

[Note] The suffixed *Maori* is an adjective, the collocation following the rules of Maori grammar, though in modern English use *Maori* is probably felt as a noun qualified by *pakeha*. The word *Pakeha-Maori* was popularized by its use in 1863 as the pseudonym of F.E. Maning, the author of *Old New Zealand*.

A. *noun.*

1. *Hist.* A white or European man living as a Maori, at first used as a respectful epithet, and later, esp. by English speakers, taking on a measure of contempt.

1832 WILLIAMS *Early Jrnls.* 16 Dec. (1961) 268 [Warekaua] pleaded hard for Missionaries to live in his neighbourhood, as they would never be *ora* [?'satisfied'] by the *Pakeha Maori*. **1837** White to Rev. Hinds in *Voyages of Adventure & Beagle* (1839) 42 *pekeha mauri* (foreign heathen) [1839 *Note*] The true meaning is 'naturalised white man'. **1838** POLACK *NZ* II. 239 A native feels much gratified at a European being conversant with the language, and terms him a native white man (*pakehá* maori). **1840** TAYLOR *Journal* (ATLTS) II. 200 *Nopera Pani Karao*..I am jealous of the speeches of the Pakia Maori be careful and don't listen to the speeches of bad white men. **1841** BIDWILL *Rambles in NZ* 21 [The missionary natives] often fancy that they know quite as much as the 'Pakiha Mouries,' (a name applied to the pork-traders etc. who have native women for wives). **1847** [see *pork trader* (PORK 3)]. **1853** *Austral. & NZ Gaz.* 19 Feb. 174 Since the foundation of the colony the natives have became acquainted with a different class of people, and the Pakeha Maori has gradually sunk in their estimation, and has now not only ceased to be appreciated, but treated with contempt. They are, however, almost extinct—and at the present time [1852] there is not more than one specimen in the whole of the Waikato district. **1865** HURSTHOUSE *England's NZ War* 37 Pakeha-Maories consist, chiefly, of old Whalers and runaway Sailors, Australian Expirees, Sawyers and Pedling Traders, who have taken Native Concubines and left civilization for the bush. **1871** MEADE *Ride through Disturbed Dist.* in Taylor *Early Travellers* (1959) 483 At Oruanui, Dr. Hooper and a pakeha-Maori named Frank..accompanied me to the pah. **1890** FIRTH *Nation Making* 228 He was a young 'Colonial', a sailor, a born engineer and a *Pakeha* Maori—that is—a European with a Maori training. **1900** *Auckland Weekly News Xmas Number* 17 I might have been a Pakeha-Maori to this day. **1921** *Quick March* 10 Sept. 11 A pakeha-Maori who was there—he was attached to the [Maori] household by domestic ties—took other methods of first aid. **1930** GUTHRIE *NZ Memories* 9 With the coming of the settler this curious existence of the 'pakeha Maori' vanished quickly; for it was no longer necessary to have a go-between for trade. **1941** SUTHERLAND *Numismatic Hist. NZ* 176 This was no doubt facilitated by the attachment to paramount chiefs of a 'Pakeha-Maori,' who acted as an interpreter-agent. **1959** SINCLAIR *Hist. NZ* 23 Judge F.E. Maning..in his younger days had been a 'Pakeha-Maori' (... a white man living with and more or less as the Maoris).

b. As a Comb. and in a weakened sense, a Pakeha, usu. one sympathizing with Maori aspirations. Cf. *bone people* (BONE 3).

1887 *Auckland Weekly News* 27 Aug. 30 It is all very well for a few pakeha Maoris to roll round such words as Waipukurau and descant upon the beauty of the Maori lingo. **1945** *JPS* LIV. 228 There is also an..adjectival use in which *pakeha maori* is employed (seemingly a 20th century development) to describe a native-born New Zealand white, or the white population in general, although they may have no contact, or only a minor contact, with the Maori race.

2. A Europeanized Maori. (The construction follows English grammar with *pakeha* used attributively.)

1937 MARSH *Vintage Murder* xxii 241 Really? You mean a real Maori—not a *pakeha-*Maori? **1943** MARSH *Colour Scheme* 37 Eru is not a satisfactory youth. He is a bad *pakeha* Maori. **1964** FRANCES *Johnny Rapana* 37 And when he walked towards the silent men, he walked not as a Maori-pakeha or pakeha-Maori, but as a Maori and a pakeha, possessed now of a rare thing that made him equal to all men. **1982** SANDYS *Love & War* 104 [Wiri] had lived too much of his life as a 'pakeha-Maori'. **1985** HOWE *Towards 'Taha Maori'* in *English* (NZATE) 4 New Zealander... A Pakeha? A Maori? A Maori Pakeha? A Pakeha Maori?

3. A combination or mixture of English and Maori language elements.

1947 STEVENSON *Maori & Pakeha* 40 Names described as 'pakeha maori' are Maori words which have been used as names by Europeans. **1982** SANSOM *In Grip of Island* 120 Taipo is a hybrid word, a mixture of pakeha-maori for a mythical fiend or demon.

4. In composition: **Pakeha-Maoridom**, the world and interests of the Pakeha-Maori; **Pakeha-Maori-ship**, the state of being a Pakeha-Maori.

1881 CAMPBELL *Poenamo* 289 We had got news from that late seat of kingly power, Herekino; it had lapsed into its primitive state of **Pakeha-Maoridom**, and Waipeha was no longer a king, but only Taniwha's white man, married to his daughter. **1931** *Taranaki The Herald* 22 May (VUW Fildes Clippings 621/38) [Heading] The Pakeha-Maori... Whites who took the blanket. Bent and Cockburn and their like, the renegade

PAKERIKERI

soldiers who 'took the blanket' represented the lowest stratum in Pakeha-Maoridom. **1866** HUNT *Chatham Is.* 21 So, leaving the insignia of my **Pakeha-Maori-ship** in the care of Bolt's wife, and borrowing a jacket and pair of trowsers, I prepared for a final start in the morning.

B. *attrib.*

1. Characteristic of, or as, a *Pakeha-Maori* A 1.
   1877 *NZPD* XXV. 316 The man who takes up the Native's case is a low-class practitioner—a pakeha-Maori lawyer—because he exposes the honourable gentleman's transactions to view. **1870** *TrNZI* II. 170 With the assistance of a Pakeha-Maori friend..we here [at Rangiriri] engaged a Maori canoe and crew. **1881** CAMPBELL *Poenamo* 305 It was said a pair of Pakeha-Maori sawyers had taken possession of the island. **1911** *Triad* 10 Apr. 23 They [*sc.* detectives] even employed a Pakeha-Maori interpreter, who lived among the tribes for months. **1956** GORE *Levins* 4 This was the principal hostelry..presided over by the rotund and jovial Dicky Barrett, Pakeha-Maori adventurer, whaler, and now publican.

2. Pertaining to a mixture of Maori and Pakeha descent, race, culture, etc.; comprising or involving both Pakeha and Maori.
   1882 *TrNZI* XIV. 127 Cleanliness and better living were not the only pleasures I found in the houses of the Pakeha Maori families. (I prefer to use the term *Pakeha*, for that includes Americans, and these might object to being termed Europeans.) **1890** *NZ Observer* 8 Nov. 7 A Pakeha-Maori agitator, He will soon be a cooked pertater. **c1920** BEATTIE *Trad. Lifeways Southern Maori* (1994) 336 Is [kapa-maori] genuine or merely pakeha–Maori lingo. **1922** COWAN *NZ Wars* (1955) I. 3 Regarding these old wars in the light of the ordeal of battle from which the civilized world has lately emerged, the *pakeha-Maori* conflicts seem chivalrous tournaments. **1927** DONNE *Maori Past & Present* 42 [Heading] *Pakeha-Maori Marriages.* There was no marriage ceremony between white and brown in old Maoridom. **1940** COWAN *Sir Donald Maclean* 81 The present town of Gisborne—then [c1860s] a *pakeha-Maori* settlement known as Turanganui.

pakerikeri, var. PAKIRIKIRI.

paketi. [Not recorded by Williams: poss. from an alteration of *pakiri(kiri)* to a form based on /ˈpakɪdi/.] SPOTTY 1 (*Notolabrus celidotus*).
   1966 DOOGUE & MORELAND *Sea Anglers' Guide* 257 Spotty... *Other names: Pseudolabrus celidotus;* butterfish, kelpie, guffy. None is widely used. Paketi, pakirikiri (Maori). **1986** HALEY *Settlement* 121 You're still talking about paketi? **1987** *Listener* 8 Aug. 61 Well out into the [Auckland] harbour was the 'paketi pond', where children could easily catch 'paketi', as we called the fish usually called 'spotties' or, by the Maori, pākirikiri. **1991** BRADSTOCK *Fishing* 17 Spotty. Other names paketi, butterfish, guffy.

paki, var. PAKIHI.

Pakia, var. PAKEHA.

pakidikidi, var. PAKIRIKIRI.

Pakiha, var. PAKEHA.

pakihi /ˈpaki/, /ˈpakəhi/. Also (following pronunciations) **paki, parke(e); parkihi.** *Pl.* often *pakihis.* [Ma. /ˈpaːkihi/: Williams 253 *Pākihi...* 3. Open grass country, barren land.]

1. *Esp. w. South Island.* A tract of open as distinct from bushed country. **a.** A tract of open fern, etc. land; a stretch of open land surrounded by bush; a large natural clearing in the bush.
   1844 in Shortland *S. Dist. NZ* (1851) 195 These plains [near Moeraki] are called 'pakihi,' a word used in the North Island to signify dried up. **1851** SHORTLAND *S. Dist. NZ* 311 Pakihi, open country, bare of trees, covered with coarse wiry grass, stunted fern, and low shrubs. It does not necessarily signify 'a plain'. The 'a' is sounded long and broad in this word. **1861** HAAST *Topogr. Explor. Nelson* 53 After travelling a mile through dense bush..we arrived at an open tract of swampy land, a *paki*, as the natives call it, covered with rushes, swamp grasses, and..with manuka and ferns. **1863** MARTIN *Diary* (Hocken MS) 7 Oct. Crossed Parke plain by 4-35 the only open country I've seen these 4 months. **1879** HAAST *Geol. Canterbury & Westland* 81 I had been assured..that I should be able to obtain new provisions at the so-called Pakihi, a large forest meadow near Lake Brunner. **1896** *NZ Alpine Jrnl.* II. No.9 148 A patch of rata bush on the flat, the rest being partly open 'pakihi'. **1907** *NZGeol.SB (NS)* No.3. 24 The Wakamarama Range [Nelson] is for the most part densely forested, though there are patches of open *pakihi* on its summit. [1907 *Note*] *Pakihi* (bare) is a Maori term applied to flat, open spaces. **1931** *Tararua Tramper* Mar. 3 An hour or two brought us to the big grass parkee. **1947** NEWTON *Wayleggo* 110 Little pakihis ran up into the bush every here and there. **1951** MCLEOD *NZ High Country* 43 Parkee is very expressive. It is used of an open space partly surrounded by the dark green birch bush... A clearing completely surrounded by bush will be called a 'blind Parkee'. **1985** MCGILL *G'day Country* 156 Their wartime job was to drain..the stunted manuka swamps Bill calls parkee (pakihis).

b. A swampy, barren terrace or flat.
   [*Note*] This sense is often hard to distinguish from a above; the reference is mainly to Westland.
   1896 *AJHR* D-4 210 These 'pakihis' are valueless for agriculture? Absolutely so. **1907** *TrNZI* XXXIX. 385 The pakihis..are open swampy plains..having an impervious substratum of cemented gravel where the rain-water accumulates and is held as in a sponge. **1929** *NZJST* XI. 231 Large areas of marshy lands on the west coast of the South Island of New Zealand are known locally as 'pakihi' lands, or the 'pakihis'. **1936** BELSHAW et al. *Agric. Organiz. NZ* 61 Much of the terrace land consists of 'pakihi'—barren treeless moorland with an undrained, sour, peaty soil, deficient in lime and phosphates, and resting on hard ferruginous gravel. **1970** *Listener* 7 Dec. 6 So what about all the pakihi? It is red-brown, depressing land whose drainage is blocked by an impervious iron pan. **1981** DENNIS *Paparoas Guide* 161 On the lowland fringes of the range..there are considerable tracts of boggy treeless land called pakihis (locally 'parkees'). **1988** DAWSON *Forest Vines to Snow Tussocks* 120 The progression from bog to bog forest has been studied in South Westland where island-like patches of bog, known locally as pakihi, are scattered in forest on the lowland gravel plain.

2. a. *attrib.* Of the nature of, characteristic of, pertaining to pakihi.
   1907 *NZGeol.SB (NS)* No.3 31 Though much of the *pakihi* country near Rockville is wet, there are almost no true swamps actually within the subdivision. **1930** *NZJST* XII. 241 The vegetation consists of the usual stunted 'pakihi' growth of fern and rushes. **1944** WOOD *Understanding NZ* 243 The Otira Tunnel through the mountains now gives [the West Coaster] a new way of escape from his rain and his parkihi, waterlogged land. **1959** MCLINTOCK *Descr. Atlas* 30 Waterlogged counterparts of these soils, the *grey podzols* or 'pakihi soils', cover ¾ million acres..in Westland. **1970** *Listener* 7 Dec. 6 The 33 million acres of sour and barren 'pakihi' soil [on the West Coast.]. **1988** DAWSON *Forest Vines to Snow Tussocks* 118 [Caption] Aerial view of

PAKURA

the transition from pakihi bog through silver pine... South Westland.

b. Special Comb. **pakihi land, pakihi terrace,** a patch of open flat or terrace land, often swampy and surrounded by bush; **pakihi rush,** see RUSH *n.*[1] 2 (5).
   1896 HARPER *Pioneer Work* 220 Extensive flats of open '**pakihi**' **land,** in the birch forest. **1912** *NZJAg.* Aug. V. 126 [Title] Experiments on the Pakihi Soils of Westland... There are in Westland large areas of sour, swampy, terrace land which supports a flora such as rushes, fern, moss, and plants one usually associates with sour, water-sodden soils... This type of country is usually known locally as pakihi land, or 'the pakihis'. **1948** *Our Own Country* 103 Westport is surrounded by worthless, sour, marshy pakihi lands rather like the Russian podsol. **1987** GEE *Prowlers* 105 But I had only a glimmering yet of my real work..the reclamation of pakihi lands. **1933** WASHBOURN *Reminisc. Early Days* 4 With the exception of the **pakihi terraces** all the country was covered with bush.

4. *transf.* and *fig.* A human bald spot.
   1949 p.c. R. Mason (Wellington). Paki [paːkiː] Heard in Christchurch for a bald spot on the head from a man who was often on the West coast in the course of his work. **1959** *Tararua 12* 46 As pakihis are frequently surrounded by bush, a bald spot on one's head may be called a pakihi, but that is slang.

pakiri, var. PAKIRIKIRI.

pakirikiri. Also with much variety of form as **paakirikiri, paikere, paekirikiri** (freq.), **pakerekere, pakídi kídi; pakiri.** [Ma. Ngapuhi dial. /ˈpaːkirikiri/: Williams 254 *Pākirikiri..2... blue cod* 3. A fish..4... spotty; a fish.]

1. SPOTTY 1 (*Notolabrus celidotus*).
   [**1820** LEE & KENDALL *NZ Gram. & Vocab.* 188 Pa kídi kídi; A fish so called. **1842** GRAY *Fauna* in Dieffenbach *Travels in NZ* (1843) II. 218 Fam. Labroideae *Labrus paecilopleura.* M. Lesson ascertained that the native name of this fish is 'Parèquiriquiri.'] **1843** WILLIAMS *NZ Jrnl.* (1956) 41 Of this variety of 78 species [of fish] I will name a part, viz... Pakerekere. **1927** PHILLIPPS *Bibliogr. NZ Fishes* (1971) 41 *Pseudolabrus celidotus*... Spotty; Paekirikiri. **1959** MIDDLETON *The Stone* 13 Around the wharf piles where barnacles and mussels clung..flitted the little pakirikiri and maomao. **1983** STEWART *Springtime in Taranaki* (1991) 104 We fished [near Mokau] for *paikere*, a pretty but tasteless kin of parrotfish. **1987** pākirikiri [see PAKETI].

2. blue cod (COD 2 (3) *Parapercias colias*).
   1855 DRURY *Sailing Directions* 67 Fish [met with in Pelorus]. Rock Cod—Pakiri of the natives, red and brown, or black, very numerous. **1872** [see COD 2 (3)]. **1957** [see COD 2 (8) a]. **1966** DOOGUE & MORELAND *Sea Anglers' Guide* 264 Blue Cod... *Parapercis colias*; coal fish; rawaru, pakirikiri. **1988** FRANCIS *Coastal Fishes NZ* 48 Blue cod (Paakirikiri, Raawaru) *Parapercis colias.*

pakkahah, var. PAKEHA.

pakura. *Obs.* in English use. [Ma. /ˈpaːkura/: Williams 256 *Pākura..1... = pūkeko.*] PUKEKO 1.
   1873 BULLER *Birds NZ* 185 (Swamp-hen)... Pukeko and Pakura. [*Note* to 1888 edn. II. 79 So called [pakura] by the Ngatipukeko tribe of Whakatane.] **1897** *TrNZI* XXIX. 166 They [Moriori] also had the pakura (*Porphyrio melanotus*). **c1920** BEATTIE *Trad. Lifeways Southern Maori* (1994) 387 The pakura or the swampturkey of settlers; pukeko in North Island. **1985** [see PUKEKO 1 a].

pakurakura. [Ma. Ngapuhi dial. /'pa:kurakura/: Williams 256 *Pākurakura..4. Verreo oxycephalus*, a fish (Ng[apuh]i).] PIGFISH 2 (1).
[**1820** LEE & KENDALL *NZ Gram. & Vocab.* 188 Pa kúra kúra; A fish so called.] **1921** *NZJST* IV. 117 *Verreo oxycephalus... Spotted Pigfish; Pakurakura.* A common food fish, Bay of Islands. Secured up to 10lb. near rocks and kelp. **1967, 1982** [see PIGFISH 2 (1)].

pakuta, var. PATAKA.

palagi /pa'laŋi/. Mainly *Auckland.* [/'pa:laŋi/: ad. colloquial Samoan *pālagi* (from *papalagi*) European.] Also *attrib.* A European.
1964 WENDT in *Listener Short Stories* (1977) 71 The palagi attendant called, 'Do you want to go up?' 'Yes,' the [Samoan] man replied in English. *Ibid.* 72 'Thank you,' said the [Samoan] man. 'She's jake,' called the palagi. **1985** MITCALFE *Hey Hey Hey* 20 As they came into the grounds, a palagi boy came rushing out to meet them. **1991** *Evening Post* (Wellington) 26 Oct. 25 The six-member band played mainly palagi music, a bit of reggae and rock and roll, and some Samoan songs.

palm. Usu. with a modifier, a native tree of the palm family (Arecaceae), usu. NIKAU or a plant resembling a palm, esp. CABBAGE-TREE 1. Cf. CABBAGE-PALM, PALM-LILY, PALM-TREE.

1. Usu. **New Zealand palm**, also **southern palm**. NIKAU 1.
1844 COLENSO *Excurs. Northern Is.* in Taylor *Early Travellers* (1959) 16 Here it was [at Tolaga Bay] that..the first New Zealand Palm (*Areca sapida*, Sol.) was cut down [by Cook's people] for the sake of its edible top. **1853** HOOKER *II Flora Novae-Zelandiae I Flowering Plants* 261 The New Zealand Palm [*Areca*] is a plant of great interest as being the most southern representative of the fine Natural Order to which it belongs. **1869** *TrNZI* I. (rev. edn.) 261 The young inner blanched leaves and heart of..the Nikau, or New Zealand Palm,.. were eaten both raw and cooked. **1872** *TrNZI* IV. 249 The southern palm (*Areca sapida*) attains its extreme height of fifty feet. **1894** southern palm [see NIKAU 1 a]. **1957** WILLIAMS *Dict. Maori Lang.* 221 *Nikau*,.. *Rhopastylis sapida* New Zealand palm.

2. Also occas. **mountain palm.** CABBAGE-TREE 1.
1926 COWAN *Travel in NZ* II. 148 There are mountain palms or *titoi* (cordyline indivisa), and *mamaku* fern-trees.

3. Stewart Island palm. *Melanoselinum decipiens* (fam. Apiaceae), a robust introduced herb with a spreading crown of pinnate leaves.
1982 WILSON *Stewart Is. Plants* 80 Parsnip Palm (*Melanoselinum decipiens*) has been grown in Halfmoon Bay gardens for so long that some people call it 'Stewart Island Palm'. In fact it is a curious member of the umbellifer family, not a palm, and is native to the Azores.

palm-lily. *Obs.* [The *Cordyline* spp. (now Asphodelaceae) were formerly assigned to fam. Liliaceae.] CABBAGE-TREE 1.
1887 *Auckland Weekly News* 5 Nov. 7 The palm-lily cordyline or dracaena Australis..or 'cabbage-tree' is peculiar also to the scene. **1888** MUELLER *Sel. Extra-tropical Plants* 112 *Cordyline Banskii*..New Zealand. This lax- and long-leaved Palm-Lily attains a height of 10 feet. **1896** *TrNZI* XXVIII. 509 The most appropriate name..'palm-lily', for which we are indebted to the learned Baron Von Mueller, is sufficiently elegant and euphonious to be generally adopted. **1908** BAUGHAN *Shingle Short* 160 *Cabbage-tree*, an ugly name for a beautiful thing: the Palm-Lily, the Maori *ti.* **1928** DEVANNY *Dawn Beloved* 25 And then there remains only the scent of the cabbage or palm-lily to be added to create 'a wilderness which is Paradise enow'. **1946** [see TI *n.*[1] 1 a]. **1969** *Standard Common Names Weeds* 56 palm lily [=] cabbage tree. **1971** WILLIAMS *Dict. Maori Lang.* (1975) 487 *Whanake...* 3. *Cordyline australis*, palm lily, so-called *cabbage-tree.* **1986** DEVANNY *Point of Departure* 6 Followed [the rata] the blooming of the cabbage tree, or palm lily, which grew mostly along the banks of streams.

palm-tree. *Obs.*

1. CABBAGE-TREE 1.
1773 FORSTER *Resolution Jrnl.* 27 Apr. (1982) II. 267 We saw here a great many *Palmtrees*, of the same kind as had been found on April Ye 24th. **1856** [see CABBAGE-TREE 1]. **1868** PYKE *Province Otago* 21 Honey-suckles twine around cottage-porches..and fragrant violets bloom beneath the shade of picturesque palm-trees. **1884** MARTIN *Our Maoris* 41 Honeysuckle..hung in masses over the verandah, and here and there a tall aloe or native palm-tree rose towering up.

2. As **New Zealand** (or **savoury**) **palm-tree**, NIKAU 1. See also PALM 1.
1835 YATE *NZ* (1970) 153 [New Zealanders' houses] are built of bulrushes and lined with the leaves of the palm-tree, neatly platted [*sic*] together. **1871** WILLIAMS *Dict. NZ Lang.* (3edn.) 83 *Miko, n. areca sapida*; New Zealand palm-tree. **1883** DOMETT *Ranolf & Amohia* II. 40 The *savoury palm-tree's* pithy heart, By Ranolf just cut down. *Ibid.* II. 336 Savoury Palm-tree (Nikau)... *O.* Palmeae; *G.* Areca; *S. A.* sapida.

pampas grass. Also **New Zealand pampas-grass.** [Spec. use of *pampas grass* South American *Cortaderia selloana* (fam. Poaceae) for New Zealand *Cortaderia* spp.] TOETOE 1 a. [*Note*] Introduced *pampas grass* is now often planted ornamentally by roadsides, etc., and by some confused with native toetoe.
1874 KENNAWAY *Crusts* 40 We struck up..towards the [Canterbury] mountains, the country being all level..with a strong growth of coarse tussocks, pampas-grass, snow-grass (similar to the pampas, but having a deep red tinge in the blade). **1883** GREEN *High Alps* 298 Bitterns..flew lazily over the stagnant pools to islets covered with flax and pampas grass... *Arundo conspicua.* **1900** BOYD *Stolen Summer* 78 On the high cliffs..clumps of pampas grass grew side by side with the regal spikes of native flax. **1911** *Piraki Log* (1911) 155 All the open ground surrounding the settlement [at Piraki]..[was] covered with tussac-grass, raupo, or tohitohi (N.Z. pampas-grass). **1920** BOLITHO *With Prince in NZ* 157 The Prince of Wales feathers were outlined in pampas grass, and the entire street was lined with greenery. **1939** BEATTIE *First White Boy Born Otago* 10 [Early station owners] dwelt in whares (huts) built in the traditional shape of an inverted V, roofed with grass, and lined inside with the reeds of the toetoe or New Zealand pampas grass. **1940** COWAN *Sir Donald Maclean* 146 And along the river bank the *kakaho*, the *toetoe* or pampas grass, once waved its plumes abundantly. **1970** MCNAUGHTON *Tat* 59 They travelled over miles of silver tussock country with..clumps of pampas grass..growing in patches of peaty swamp.

pan, *n.*[1] A gold pan; also a quantity of wash-dirt held in a pan. Cf. DISH *n.*[1]
1853 SWAINSON *Auckland* 103 'I went there [to Coromandel]..on yesterday,' says the reporter, 'prospecting, and found gold in the first pan washed.' **1863** *Diary of an Unsuccessful Digger* 22 May in *Star* 27 Aug. (1931) in Heinz *Bright Fine Gold* (1974) 95 Went out to Dome Gully and had only washed three pans of dirt. **1875** HOGG *Lays & Rhymes* 176 'Twas when the Rocky River rush began..and stories told Of ounces gotten in a single pan. **1935** BLYTH *Gold Mining Year Book* 11 *Pan*: To wash metalliferous dirt; also the dish used to wash sand, clay, etc. from gold. **1968** [see DISH *n.*[1]]. **1981** HENDERSON *Exiles of Asbestos Cottage* 113 Odd nuggets up to the size of a small fingernail bare their beauty in black sand in pan or sluicebox.

Hence **panful** *n.*, an amount of washdirt convenient to wash in a pan.
1852 *NZGG* 9 Nov. V. 26:165 (Rep. Gold Discovery in Coromandel) Your committee had a quantity of stuff taken out of this hole and washed under their inspection, and every panful produced a few specks of gold.

pan, *n.*[2] Also **pan iron.** [Poss. f. the shape, the turned up part resembling a pan.]

1. SHOE.
1961 HENDERSON *Friends In Chains* 187 Pan: Flat iron with turned up nose placed under forward end of log.

Hence **panman** *logging*, a bush workman who arranges the pan under the nose of a log to be hauled out of the bush.
1908 *Awards, etc.* 339 [Wellington Sawmills Award] [Rates of wages] Trackmen, cutters or otherwise [£] 14[s.] 0[d.] Panmen 2 17 0 Bullock-drivers 2 17 0.

2. See quot.
1986 SALMOND *Old NZ Houses* 232 *pan iron* flat iron roofing sheets with edges turned up against adjacent sheets and covered over to exclude water.

pan, *v.*

1. [Used elsewhere, with some uses recorded earliest in NZ: see OED *pan v.*[1] *trans.*, 1839.] To wash gold-bearing sand, gravel, etc. in a pan to recover the gold. Usu. as **pan off, pan out. a.** As **pan off.**
1868 *Thames Miner's Guide* 53 Color [*sic*].—A minute quantity of gold left behind in panning off. **1874** BATHGATE *Col. Experiences* 147 I panned it off carefully. **1883** *Brett's Colonists' Guide* 720 In choosing a spot in a stream from whence to *pan off* a trial, the miner seeks some part of the stream below a junction with another water-course. **1900** KITTO *Pract. Dredgeman's Manual* 46 Save all the cleanings [gained by washing the gold, etc.] until there is a dishful, which you may silverise. Work the quicksilver in in an iron dish and when all of the gold is taken up pan off the sand. **1977** MURRAY *Costly Gold* 8 If you watch a skilful..miner panning-off a dish of gravel you might say 'There's nothing much to it'.

Hence **panning (off)** *vbl. n.*, washing pay-dirt in a pan to recover the gold.
1892 WARDON *MacPherson's Gully* 13 A capital hand at panning off. **1909** *TrNZI* XLI. 72 No gold was visible in the stone, but panning-off showed a little free gold. **1946** MILLER *There Was Gold* 24 Panning off, it seemed, was a simple process. **1953** SUTHERLAND *Golden Bush* (1963) 39 At the end of the day, the panning-off of the grit collected in the matting showed the takings. **1962** EVANS *Waikaka Saga* 228 In order to have a daily supply of water for cradling and panning many miners combined to build this dam. **1970** WOOD *Gold Trails Otago* 7 During prospecting the gold was separated from the dirt by hand panning in a gold-dish.

b. As **pan out** *trans.* and *intr.* Also *transf.* and *fig.*, to sift, to separate out (information, facts).
1864 *Press* (Christchurch) 6 May in Turner *Eng. Lang. Austral. & NZ* (1966) 17 After painfully panning out, he threw the dish down with disgust, and exclaimed... 'Not even the colo[u]r!' **1882** HAY *Brighter Britain* II. 274 Here, the mining is all quartz... There is no alluvial washing to enable one to pan out one's dust.

1933 WASHBOURN *Reminisc. Early Days* 4 I have frequently [c1860s] seen large specks floating in and out of the dish when panning out there. 1980 MCGILL *Ghost Towns NZ* 147 Alistair Murray Isdale offers the evidence, and he has spent a lifetime panning out the information on the Hauraki goldfields.

panada, var. PARERA.

panako, var. PANOKONOKO.

panapana. [Ma. /ˈpanapana/: Williams 256 *Pana* (i)..*panapana*..a species of cress.] Usu. an introduced *bitter cress* (CRESS), *Cardamine* spp. (fam. Brassicaceae), esp. *C. hirsuta*.
    1853 HOOKER *II Flora Novae-Zelandiae I Flowering Plants* 13 Cardamine *hirsuta*... Nat. name, 'Panapana'. 1867 HOCHSTETTER *NZ* 157 Panapana, Hanea, Nau, (*Cardamine*) New Zeal. cress. 1870 *TrNZI* II. 124 Cardamine hirsuta Panapana 1882 HAY *Brighter Britain* II. 210 There are..the Pana-pana, or cress..and the Retireti, or sorrel..which do for salad and green vegetables. 1889 [see CRESS]. 1952 RICHARDS *Chatham Is.* 29 Cardamine..*heterophylla*... Land Cress. Pana-pana.

panel.
1. The section between the posts of, originally, a post-and-rail fence, then of any fence. Occas. *ellipt.* for SLIP-PANEL.
    1859 *Puketoi Station Diary* (Hocken TS) 10 Mar. Put up two panels of stockyard. 1882 CHUDLEIGH *Diary* 25 Oct. (1950) 313 His posts look like one line of wood... 236 panels; all the gates soaked in tar boiling hot. c1930 *Whitcombe's Etym. Dict. Aust.-NZ Suppl.* 8 *panel n.* a section between two posts in a post and rail fence; a movable fence.
2. [Poss. from fencing panel.] A wire suspension bridge, having a rough deck made of 'panels' of wood.
    1926 GREY *Angler's Eldorado* 189 'You came down easy,' he said. 'But this panel over the river will be hard.' 'Huh! What's a panel!' I asked. 'Hoka, I've begun to have suspicions about you.' He soon showed us the panel. It was no less than a rickety pole bridge, swung on wires attached to branches of trees, and spanning a dark rushing little river that must have been beautiful at some other time.

panican, var. PANNIKIN.

pan iron: see PAN *n.*² 2.

panman: PAN *n.*² 1.

Pannells: see HARRY PANNELL.

pannikin. Also **panican, pannican.** [f. Brit. dial. *pannikin* a small (usu. earthenware) drinking vessel: cf. EDD; AND 1830.]
1. a. A large metal cup serving also as an all-purpose vessel or container.
    1834 MARKHAM *NZ* (1963) 57 We went to Showracky to get some more 'Go ashores' or Iron pots, for Household purposes, tin pannikins to drink out of. 1841 BIDWILL *Rambles in NZ* 11 Tea boiled in a common tin pot, or pannikin as the sailors call it. 1858 *Richmond-Atkinson Papers* (1960) I. 430 To purchase timber for floors, tables, beds, forms, panicans, plates, soap, [etc]. 1866 CHEVALIER *Reminisc. of Journey* (ATLTS) 10 The billey (a tin pot for boiling the water) and three pannikins (tin cups). 1871 MONEY *Knocking About NZ* 6 He was considered sufficiently rewarded in having the 'honour' to drink his '*pannikin*' of tea out of the boss's deal table. 1889 PAULIN *Wild West Coast* 1 Tin mugs, or pannikins as they are called, holding about a pint at least. 1896 MOFFATT *Adventures* (1979) 61 [I] caught and roasted a woodhen, boiled some flour in my pannikin. 1904 *NZ Illustr. Mag.* Sept. 408 Pigeon and kaka stew..and..several large pannikins each of choice billy tea. 1933 *Press* (Christchurch) (Acland Gloss.) 11 Nov. 15 *Pannikin*.—Tin drinking mug, holding a pint as a rule. In the early days the explorers used them for boiling to save carrying billies... They are now usually made of enamel and called *pints* or *mugs*. 1953 STRONACH *Musterer on Molesworth* 8 We cooled our tea by placing the pannikins in [the snow]. 1960 MASTERS *Back-Country Tales* 21 The ordinary enamel pannikins generally used by men on stations were not good enough for Jeff. 1986 RICHARDS *Off the Sheep's Back* 59 A large round 'wheel' of bread..a butcher's knife and three large enamel pannikins (mugs).

b. A drinking vessel of totara bark.
    1864 *Richmond-Atkinson Papers* (1960) II. 87 [At the abandoned Maori camp was] a pannikin of native manufacture made of totara-bark.

2. Used *attrib.* in Comb. or special Comb. **pannikin-full**; **pannikin tea**, tea made in a pannikin.
    1874 CAIRD *Sheepfarming NZ* 12 A shepherd or drover would think himself hardly used indeed if he had not his **pannikinful** of tea three or four times a day. 1884 MARTIN *Our Maoris* 24 We were doubly anxious to be liberal after hearing a very good-tempered Maori man contrast the large-handed hospitality of his people to English travellers, with the 'one pannikinful' of flour,—about half a pound,—doled out to him when he visited any one in Auckland. 1892 *NZ Official Handbook* 171 On the arrival of the first wagon with flour..it was surrounded by a crowd of miners from the field, when the whole of the flour was handed out..at 2s. 6d. a pannikinful. 1897 *Otago Witness* (Dunedin) 14 Dec. 57 I remember the times when **pannikin tea** and 'brownie' with the shearers was the joy of my life.

3. *transf.* **a.** Obs. [AND 1894.] In the phr. **off one's pannikin**, off one's head, crazy.
    1906 *Truth* 24 Feb. 5 If this writer is not right off his 'pannikin'. 1906 *Truth* 26 May 2 Waterloo [a footballer], however, 'goes off his pannikin' with excitement at times. 1968 *NZ Contemp. Dict. Suppl.* (Collins) 15 *pannican..n...(Coll.)* the head; *off one's pannican*, insane, demented.

b. Special Comb. **pannikin-struck** [f. (off one's) *pannikin* + ?a var. of *panic-stricken*], panic-stricken, highly disturbed.
    1986 RICHARDS *Off the Sheep's Back* 124 [The liquor] fired their imagination... Panic and fear is contagious—it was not long before several of the gang became 'pannikin struck'. *Ibid.* 146 A bugle sounded and whistles blew. Someone yelled, 'The Japs are on us.' Our tent was 'pannikin struck'. Some of us were not even out of bed before the enemy struck [on a Home Guard exercise]. 1989 RICHARDS *Pioneer's Life* 86 All hell broke loose. Dogs, sheep and horse all became 'pannikin-struck'.

4. [AND 1951.] *Ellipt.* for PANNIKIN BOSS.

pannikin boss. Also *ellipt.* **pannikin.** [AND 1898.] A person with minor authority, an 'under-boss'; a foreman or leading-hand or other person put in charge of a work-gang.
    1911 *Maoriland Worker* 20 Apr. 15 The 'pannikin' boss usually is in evidence. This is the man who for a wretched shilling a day more than his fellow Unionists sells his body to a mercenary employer to rush, wear, and sweat others. c1926 THE MIXER *Transport Workers' Song Book* 7 I'm the man who runs the job—I'm a Pannikin, get me? *Ibid.* 13 There's not a pannikin can say That we could not do our work. *Ibid.* 69 He'll criticise each one told off As a 'pannikin devotee' [*sc.* a boss's stooge]. 1933 *Press* (Christchurch) (Acland Gloss.) 28 Oct. 17 *Pannikin boss*.—Slang. B[*oss*] who has little authority. B[*oss*] of rouseabouts, etc. 1946 ACLAND *Early Canterbury Runs* 119 The 'pannikin boss' (head general hand), used to carry it [*sc.* a bale of wool] out of the shed single-handed. 1959 SLATTER *Gun in My Hand* 226 All the half-pie pannikin bosses ordering me about because there's no-one like the working man for putting the boot into the working man. 1966 TURNER *Eng. Lang. Austral. & NZ* 146 The manager of a sheepstation was called a *pannikin boss*, a term I have heard used, along with *straw boss*, for a foreman on building jobs in New Zealand. 1983 BREMER *Port Craig* 17 A man called Bob Donoghue was the second in command or pannikin boss of the navvies as they were called, and besides being pannikin he was also the first aid man.

panokonoko. Also **panako.** [Ma. /paːˈnokonoko/, /ˈpanoko/: Williams 257 *Panoko.. pānokonoko.. papanoko* [and many other variant forms].] TORRENTFISH. See also PAPANOKO.
    1922 *NZJST* V. 96 Cheimarrichthys forsteri. *Panokonoko*, or *Papane*. Large numbers are annually secured by the Maoris of this locality [on the Wanganui River]. The panokonoko is much esteemed as a food fish. 1929 BEST *Fishing Methods* 190 The Panoko... This fish is also known as *panokonoko, parikou, papane,* and a number of other names... The *panokonoko* is a scaly fish with very small scales; it is 6in. to 8in. long, having a fairly big head, thick body and tapering quickly to the tail. 1945 panako [see TROUT 2 (6)]. 1949 BUCK *Coming of Maori* 234 Some of the smaller fish which migrated down the stream in the autumn to spawn in the river estuaries were..the smelt..and the panokonoko (*Cheimarricthys fosteri*).

panther. Also often **panther's.** Prefixed to **milk, piss, purge,** a jocular name for any strong or crude liquor, often home-brewed.
    1934 *Canterbury Mountaineer* 4 Pemmican stew and soup went down—well 'watered' with a little Roger Rum. Perhaps this 'panther's milk' was the cause of early slumber. 1968 SLATTER *Pagan Game* 149 He stood fondling a bottle of his Panther Purge. 1977 JOSEPH *Time of Achamoth* 40 Hollister took a mouthful [of wine], and found it thin and poor. 'Panther piss,' said Piotr. 'This is what they sell to the workers.'

panui. Also **paanui.** [Ma. /ˈpaːnui/: Williams 257 *Pānui..4. n.* Public notice. *Note.*—This is said, with some probability, to be a modern Maori word invented in a context of Christian instruction by the early missionaries.] A public notice.
    [1892 WILLIAMS *Dict. NZ Lang.* (4edn.) 124 *Pānui, v.t.*... 2 publish; proclaim. 3 advertise publicly.] 1910 MATTHEWS Apr. in *Northlander* (VUW Fildes Clippings 461a/50) (1922) 20 The season for fishing the *kapeta* (dogfish) was restricted to two days only in each year... It was he who issued a *panui*, or notice, of the date. 1910 *Southland Daily News* Feb. in Wilson *Titi Heritage* (1979) 155 At the Native Land Court's enquiry concerning the Titi Islands, Mr John Moffett..submitted that part one of the 'Panui' of the Native Minister for ascertaining the persons entitled to the rights conferred under section 24 of the Land Act, 1908, to the Titi Islands [etc.]. 1986 *Victoria Univ. Weekly Staff Circular* 31 Oct. No.813 [Heading] He Paanui. Regular meetings are now being held at Te Herenga Waka Marae for the kaiawhina (helpers) in preparation for the opening of the new wharenui on 6th December.

papa /ˈpʌpə/.

1. [Ma. /ˈpapa/: Williams 259 *Papa* (i). *1.* Anything broad, flat and hard; flat rock, slab, board.] A bluish calcareous marl found in the North Island; occas. applied to other formations elsewhere.

   1851 Shortland *S. Dist. NZ* 311 Papa, a hard sandstone found in thin slabs, used as a saw to cut the 'pounamu'. **1873** St John *Pakeha Rambles* in Taylor *Early Travellers* (1959) 565 We..landed on a reef composed of a peculiar and disagreeable kind of rock. Its Maori name is *papa*, its scientific appellation I know not; it is blueish in colour when dry; gets reddish under water. **1891** Wallace *Rural Econ. Austral. & NZ* 231 The term 'papa' is applied in the South Island, not to clay or heavy soil, but to a porous, brittle limestone rock. **1902** *Settler's Handbook NZ* 7 The country is generally broken, and the formation is known as papa—a calcareous blue clay, capped in many places by shelly limestone. **1907** *NZGeol.SB (NS)* No.3 59 The blue and yellow clays, often locally [at Parapara, Nelson] called 'papa', are sometimes well banded. **1921** *TrNZI* LIII. 60 The Patea claystones are of the type which throughout New Zealand is popularly called 'papa'. **1931** *Na To Hoa Aroha* (1987) II. 117 Wherever there is papa there will be a mess when the heavy rains come, as whole hill sides will slip away. **1959** Shadbolt *New Zealanders* (1986) 45 Giant ulcers of erosion scabbed with weeping crusts of clay and papa. **1990** *Dominion Sunday Times* (Wellington) 23 Sept. 22 Papa is slippery stuff. On the East Coast it causes hillslides to slide into the valleys.

2. As **papa rock**.

   c1875 Meredith *Adventuring in Maoriland* (1935) 119 In the *papa* rock on the north-east cape of the North Island there was the facsimile of a gigantic human footprint. **1892** Brookes *Frontier Life* 150 The country [in Taranaki] is principally composed of papa rock. **1905** Thomson *Bush Boys* 62 The Papa Rock, of which many of the cliffs in the bush country of New Zealand are formed is really a very hard blue clay... It lies in distinct strata, and, when the wet penetrates to one beneath, the surface of this latter becomes as slippery as glass. **1924** Anthony *Follow the Call* (1975) 111 It was a steep hill..not improved by the fact that it was of papa rock foundation. **1950** *Truth* 14 Oct. 1 Skin broken..by a piece of papa rock.

3. *attrib.* passing into Comb., esp. **papa country**.

   1893 *TrNZI* XXV. 356 The rich limestone and papa country already described. **1903** King *Bill's Philosophy* 23 Weary years of farming on a *papa*, slipping farm. **1911** *TrNZI* XLIII. 177 The steep papa cliffs of the Wanganui River above and near the junction. **1922** *Auckland Weekly News* 12 Jan. 17 It is papa country—that bluish-grey old sea mud which is found on this eastern seaboard from Napier up to Hicks Bay—a soft, unstable, crumbling formation, which water and weather easily shapes into irregular contours, which is slipping and changing all the time. **1947** Gretton in *The Spike* 17 Where trees on papa cliffs Are shedding crimson stamens on the tide. **1954** *Here & Now* Aug. 17 The blue *papa* can grow wonderful clover, and it is mostly blue *papa* country. **1960** Masters *Back-Country Tales* 131 Where a tributary creek flows into the Ohara stream,..stands a small, almost impregnable papa bluff. **1973** Wheeler *Hist. Sheep Stations NI* 11 In the East Coast papa soils, selecting a fenceline is a serious job. **1989** *NZ Geographic* III. 113 Long periods of low water flow have meant increased exposure of the 'papa shelves' of the river bed.

papaauma, var. papauma.

papa-kainga. [Ma. *papa* + *kāinga* village. /ˈpapa ˈkaːiŋa/: Williams 259 *Papa* (i)..*2*. Earth floor or site of a native house... Hence the modern expression *papa kāinga*.] The homeground of one's kinship group; a marae or village site.

   1900 *NZ Statutes* No.55 470 [Maori Lands Administration Act] 'Papakainga' means an inalienable reserve set aside for the occupation and support of any person of the Maori race as in this act provided. *Ibid.* 475 Provided that nothing in this [Maori land] Act contained shall be construed to authorise the alienation of papakaingas. **1930** *Na To Hoa Aroha* (1987) II. 29 A central Tuhoe papakainga or marae of ten acres has been fixed near the school, with a tribal title like Porourangi... [1987 *Note*] The earth floor or site of a house, but, as Ngata indicates, it has become synonymous with marae. **1985** Howe *Towards 'Taha Maori' in English* (NZATE) 21 Papakainga—'homeground' does not reveal the spiritual and emotional connotations this word implies. Papakainga is that area where one's original kinship group came from and lived. Whether or not the area has buildings on it, it has strong emotional overtones for any Maori. In this age of the urban Maori, the ability to refer to ancestral areas—the place where one's own history was made—is a matter of deep pride. Once known, one can never leave it—though one may be physically absent all one's life.

papanga, var. papango.

papango. Also **papanga** (erron.). [Ma. /ˈpaːpaŋo/: Williams 258 *Pango*. *1.* a. Black, of dark colour... *Pāpango*..New Zealand scaup, black teal.] scaup. See also *black teal* (teal *n.*[1] 2 (2)).

   1870 *TrNZI* II. 73 Fuligula novae zelandiae... Papango. **1873** [see scaup]. **1882** Hay *Brighter Britain* II. 225 The species we have identified in the Kaipara..are..the Papanga, or 'teal', or 'widgeon'..and some other varieties. **1904** [see teal *n.*[1] 2 (2)]. **1921** Guthrie-Smith *Tutira* (1926) 204 Tutira lake bore on its bosom a fleet of eight or nine hundred papango, widgeon. **1966** [see scaup]. **1985** [see teal *n.*[1] 2 (2)]. **1990** *Checklist Birds NZ* 106 Aythya novae-seelandiae..New Zealand Scaup (Papango).

papanoko. [Ma. /ˈpapanoko/: Williams 257 (see panokonoko).] torrentfish. See also panokonoko.

   1855 Taylor *Te Ika A Maui* 499 The *papanoko* is a scaleless fresh water fish, about five inches long. **1880** *TrNZI* XII. 315 *Papanoko* are small fish, from six to eight inches in length, and very deep in proportion..and weigh about the eighth of a pound. At this season of the year they are very fat, full of spawn, and are most delicious eating. **1886** Sherrin *Handbook Fishes NZ* 143 The papanoko..is called..the hidden fish of Tane..for they are never found in the streams or rivers unless during a flood, and then only during the night. **1929** *NZJST* XI. 166 [*Cheimarrichthys fosteri*] is the 'shark-bully' of Canterbury and the 'torrent-fish' of Westland but is better known by one or other of its Maori names—papanoko, papane, panokonoko, or papauma. **1936** [see shark-bully]. **1963** Woods *Freshwater Fishes* 48 Torrent Fish *Cheimarrichthys fosteri* Papanoko... The long single dorsal fin, the square-cut tail, and the pattern..distinguish the Papanoko. **1990** McDowall *NZ Freshwater Fishes* 416 The Maoris know the torrentfish as papanoko. It seems surprising that this small and rather obscure fish had much interest to the Maori as a food, but it seems to have been a fish to which considerable ceremony was attached.

papa-taniwhaniwha. [Ma. /ˈpapa taːˈnifanifa/: Williams 261 *Papa-tāniwhaniwha*..a native daisy.] Either of *Lagenifera petiolata* or *L. pumila* (fam. Asteraceae), small native daisies of grasslands. Cf. daisy 2 (8) a, parani.

   1899 [see daisy 2 (8) a]. **1906** Cheeseman *Manual NZ Flora* 272 L[agenophera] Forsteri.. Papataniwhaniwha. **1921** Guthrie-Smith *Tutira* (1926) 104 On the damp cliffs grew..Lagenophora Forsteri, the native daisy—Papataniwhaniwha..and other plants. **1940, 1952** [see daisy 2 (8) a]. **1961** Allan *Flora NZ* I. 607 Lowland to montane grassland, open places and light forest... *Papataniwhaniwha*. **1982** Wilson *Stewart Is. Plants* 200 *Lagenifera pumila Papatāniwhaniwha*... Small rosettes or tufts, often forming patches... *Lagenifera petiolata Papatāniwhaniwha*... Very small rosettes or tufts.

papauma. Also **papaauma**, **papa-umu**. [Ma. /ˈpaːpaːuma/: Williams 261 *Pāpāuma*..*1. Griselinia littoralis*, a tree. *2. Coprosma* [sp.], a shrub.]

1. broadleaf 1 (*Griselinia littoralis*).

   1889 Kirk *Forest Flora* 69 W.L. Williams informs me that in the East Cape district its [*sc. Griselinia littoralis*] native name is papauma. **1890** [see broadleaf 1]. **1906** Cheeseman *Manual NZ Flora* 239 Kapuka; Papaumu; Broad-leaf. Timber strong, close-grained and durable. **1946** *JPS* LV. 155 *pāpāuma*, a tree (*Griselinia littoralis*), broad-leaf. **1966** *Encycl. NZ* I. 252 *Broadleaf, Papauma* (*Griselinia littoralis*). This is a common hardwood tree. **1981** Dennis *Paparoas Guide* 157 The Maori *papauma* is rarely used for this tree [*Griselinia littoralis*, in Westland].

2. kanono (*Coprosma grandifolia*).

   1867 Hooker *Handbook* 767 Papaauma, Col[enso]. Coprosma grandifolia. **1869** *TrNZI* I. (rev. edn.) 261 Several species of *Coprosma*,—particularly..the papaauma (*C. grandifolia*). **1886** *TrNZI* XVIII. 211 To find specimens [of aweto at Petane] it is best to look under the papa-umu (*Coprosma grandifolia*). **1981** Brooker et al. *NZ Medicinal Plants* 86 *Coprosma australis*... Maori names: Manono, papauma.

paper.

1. In the sense 'drawn on paper', as **paper road**, **paper street**, **paper town (township)**, one existing only on paper or on a plan, not in formed actuality. [Cf. OED *paper* 12, *paper town* N. Amer.]

   c1890s Douglas in *Explorer Douglas* (1957) 15 'Weld Town', for example he noted as 'another paper town situated on the beach in Bruce Bay bight'... Gillespies [was] sketched by Douglas as 'never even a paper township, but entirely a digging one'. **1959** *Tararua* 13 49 *Paper road* and *paper town*..describe those roads and towns which have been surveyed but whose actual existence has got no further than the maps. **1993** *Dominion* (Wellington) 23 July 11 It appears that 'paper roads' (surveyed but not formed), may be used for walkways. Technically district councils still own this land. **1993** *Evening Post* (Wellington) 10 Nov. 29 Fifty-five years ago my father bought what was considered to be an impossible steep section on a 'paper' street.

2. In the sense 'resembling paper', as **paper-leaf**, rangiora, having a large leaf, white on the underside and able to register written messages; **paper mulberry**, see mulberry 1 (the inner bark can be used to make a paper-like cloth).

   1919 July 29 Vernacular names supplied to J.C. Andersen by W. Best, Otaki in *TrNZI* (1927) LVII. 945 paper leaf *Brachyglottis repanda*.

3. In the senses 'made of paper' or 'wrapped in paper'. See also poke 2. **a.** Often *pl.* [Cf. Partridge 3, 'Prison'.] A cigarette paper.

   c1940 Known to and commonly used by Ed. 'A book of Zigzag papers.' **1980** MacKenzie *While We*

Have Prisons 98 *paper* a cigarette paper. **1987** [see TISSUE *n.*].

b. As **paper lolly**, a sweet, usu. a toffee, wrapped in fancy paper.

1961 FRAME *Faces in Water* 98 The paper lollies would be showered into the middle of the day room and it would be first come first served.

4. In the sense 'newspaper', as **paper-car**, a mail-car or service-car delivering newspapers as part of its service; **paper-run** *n.* and *v.*, (to work at) a newspaper delivery round.

1960 TUWHARE 'The Old Place' in Hilliard *Maori Girl* 9 On the cream lorry or morning **paper car** no one shall come. **1888** PRESHAW *Banking* 133 There's a fortune to be made **paper-running** at the diggings. **1948** BALLANTYNE *Cunninghams* (1976) 47 Gilbert wanted..a bike for Christmas so's he could have a **paper run**. **1992** *North & South* (Auckland) Apr. 106 I had a paper run, and with the tips I got from selling papers..I'd go to the Star Cafe.

paper-collar. *Obs.* [With derog. reference to the cheap 'paper' (rather than genuine starched cloth or celluloid) collars worn by indigent clerks pretending to elegance or style.] Also **paper-collared**. Used in collocations to denote a town-based clerkly attitude to an easier, 'non-physical' life or work: **paper collar bushman**, a bush-boss who prefers supervision to 'pitching in' beside his workmen; **paper-collar life**, **paper-collared swell**.

1871 MONEY *Knocking About NZ* 29 He was not one of these **paper-collar bushmen**, who expect their men to do every thing while they look on, but always took his share of work or of tucker as one of themselves. *Ibid.* 86 I will go on to Christchurch, where I enjoyed a real spell of what diggers call a '**paper-collar life**'. **1874** BATHGATE *Col. Experiences* 86 [The population of a goldfield] includes a section of the community known as the '**paper-collared swells**' who are the government officials, medical men etc. **1881** BATHGATE *Waitaruna* 183 'The paper-collared swells' did not number ten.

para, *n.*[1] Also **he-para** (=he para). [Ma. /'para/: Williams 262 *Para* (ii)..4. A fresh-water fish, similar to *kōkopu*.] rock trout (TROUT 2 (6)).

[**1820** LEE & KENDALL *NZ Gram. & Vocab.* 189 Pára. *s.* A fish so called.] **1842** GRAY *Fauna* in Dieffenbach *Travels in NZ* (1843) II. 219 *Galaxias alepidotus*... Named by the natives of Dusky Bay 'He-para,' and by Cook's sailors 'Rock-trout.' **1872** HUTTON & HECTOR *Fishes NZ* 129 Para.—A small fish found near the sources of the Wanganui River. **1886** SHERRIN *Handbook Fishes NZ* 138 The kokopu of the stream is caught by them with bobs... It is also called rawaru and para. **1927** PHILLIPPS *Bibliography of NZ Fishes* (1971) 13 *Galaxias fasciatus*... Kokopu or Para. **1940** PHILLIPPS *Fishes NZ* 16 Para... Hawkes Bay and Waiapu-Gisborne natives call the species [*Galaxias fasciatus*..] para. Auckland, Bay of Plenty and Wellington tribes call it kokopu. **1978** [see KOKOPU 1].

para, *n.*[2] [Ma. /'pa:ra/: Williams 261 *Pāra*... frost-fish.] FROSTFISH.

1855 TAYLOR *Te Ika A Maui* 625 The *Para*..is a long narrow fish, shaped like a broad sword, from three to five feet long..; it is only obtained after a sharp frost, being then drifted on the shore. **1886** SHERRIN *Handbook Fishes NZ* 300 *Lepidopus caudatus* Frost-fish, Hiku, or Para. **1921** *NZJST* IV. 118 *Frost-fish*; *Para*... Distribution: New Zealand coasts (rarer south of Bay of Plenty). **1932** [see FROSTFISH]. **1947** POWELL *Native Animals NZ* 71 Frost-fish..Para of the Maoris, is like a long narrow ribbon of burnished silver, from 3 to 5 feet in length. **1966** DOOGUE & MORELAND *Sea Anglers' Guide* 277 Frostfish... Other names: *Lepidopus caudatus*; para, hiku, taharangi (Maori). **1981** WILSON *Fisherman's Bible* 66 The Maori name Para means 'to spring' or 'to leap' and refers to the last moments of the average specimen when it seems to leave its own element to spring to its death. *Lepidopus* means 'small scales' and *caudatus* refers to the small tail.

para, *n.*[3] Also **pura** (prob. a typographical error). [Ma. /'para/: Williams 262 *Para* (ii)..2. *Marattia salicina*, a large fern.] *Marattia salicina* (fam. Marattiaceae), a large fern of nw. New Zealand and elsewhere, having a root covered with edible scales. See also *horseshoe fern*, *king fern*, (FERN 2 (8), 2 (11) c).

1855 HOOKER *II Flora Novae-Zelandiae II Flowerless Plants* 49 *Marattia Salicina*... Nat. name, 'Para'. **1869** *TrNZI* I. (rev. edn.) 261 The following roots and plants were often eaten, *viz.*, the roots..of the large Fern, Para. **1874** BAINES *Edward Crewe* 198 Another giant fern, the pura..[with] a bulbous-looking root, like Brobdingnagian dahlias. **1882** POTTS *Out in Open* 17 Para, the rootstock or rhizome of a grand fern (*Marattia fraxina*). **1911** *TrNZI* XLIII. 205 The para..is not uncommon in gullies in the Maungataniwha Ranges. **1921** [see FERN 2 (8)]. **1930** REISCHEK *Yesterdays in Maoriland* (1933) 194 I went..into the Pirongia Range to look for para, a kind of fern which the Maoris plant in the bush. When the bulbs are ripe, they are dug up and boiled in the hangis. **1948** [see FERN 2 (11) c]. **1961**, **1981** [see FERN 2 (8)].

paracuta, var. BARRACOUTA.

paradise, *a.* In the names of birds of *Podiceps* spp., see: DUCK 2 (6), SHELDUCK; and also as below.

1856 PHILLIPS *Rockwood & Point Jrnl.* 27 Dec. (Canterbury Pub. Lib. TS) 60 Seal killed a Paradise Flapper on a Lagoon. **1867** *Richmond-Atkinson Papers* (1960) II. 237 As I write I hear the quacking, or rather cawing, of a paradise drake... The drake caws exactly like a 6d. woolly dog.

paraerae. *Hist.* Also with much variety of early form as **pāhrarra**, **pairairai**, **parala**, **parara**, **pararo**, **pereira**, **porrara**. Often felt as *pl.* [Ma. /pa:'raerae/: Williams 263 *Pāraerae*... A sandal made of leaves of flax or *tī* twisted into a pad; also 263 *Pārahi*.. *pārahirahi*, n. A sandal made of flax.] A native or Maori sandal made of the plaited leaves of flax, cabbage-tree, etc. See also *Maori sandal* (MAORI B 5 a), *native sandal* (NATIVE B 3 a).

[c**1826–27** BOULTBEE *Journal* (1986) 111 shoes—pāhrarra] c**1835** *Ibid.* 38 On the beach we saw a broken spear and a pair of old porraras, (a kind of sandal made of flax). **1844** in Shortland *S. Dist. NZ* 13 Jan. (1851) 209 This evening, Huruhuru made me a pair of sandals, such as are in common use among these natives. They are called 'paraerae', and are made either with the leaves of the flax-plant, or of the 'ti'... Mine were a pair with double soles, called 'torua'. **1847** BRUNNER *Exped. Middle Is.* 21 Oct. in Taylor *Early Travellers* (1959) 288 Now I can trudge along..with a pair of native sandals, called by the natives *pairairai*, made of the leaves of flax, or, what is more durable, the leaves of the ti. **1848** in *Lett. from Otago* 20 July (1978) 16 They [natives] wear shoes made of flax, which they call *paralas*. **1861** HAAST *Topogr. Explor. Nelson* 48 The next day,.. the coast becoming very rocky, we exchanged our boots for Maori sandals (pereiras), which allowed better foothold on the smooth boulders. **1896** HARPER *Pioneer Work* 231 To allow Bill to make himself some Maori sandals, or 'parara' out of flax. **1904** TREGEAR *Maori Race* 240 Sandals made from the leaves of the cabbage-palm..were sometimes made; they were called *parewai* in the North and *tahitahi* in the South Island... The southern name for a sandal generally was *paraerae*. **1926** COWAN *Travel in NZ* II. 85 Accidentally the [Maori] fugitives..shod with *paraerae* or sandals of flax-leaves,... crossed the dividing range. c**1930** McKILLOP *Topsail Schooner 'Lark'* (MS Tasmanian Collection, State Library of Tasmania) 78 We followed [the sealers returned c1870s from West Coast] with our eyes admiring their new hand made seal skin caps with the crest of a penguin or some other Antarctic bird sewn on front. Still wearing their flax *pararos* as it takes a long time to get used to wearing boots after a sealing trip... It is in such places that the sealer is seen at his very best; travelling at great pace over rugged sea-piled rocks.. with their feet covered with flax or grass mats tightly laced. **1939** BEATTIE *First White Boy Born Otago* 12 When their boots gave out [early Europeans] would sometimes wear Maori 'pararas' or sandals. **1940** SMITH *Early Adventures in Otago* 42 I secured a pair of native sandals or pararas.

paraha. [Ma. /'paraha/: Biggs 39 *convolvulus*.. paraha; cf. Williams 330 *Rauparaha*..*Calystegia sepium*, a creeper used as food.] CONVOLVULUS (*Calystegia sepium*).

1937 HYDE *Wednesday's Children* 75 This convolvulus was called paraha in the native tongue. In the good old days, Maritana's father and uncles used to tie their captives up in paraha vine, wrap them in paraha leaves, dig a Maori oven..line it with red-hot stones and green fern, and then roast them alive. **1938** HYDE *Godwits Fly* (1970) 70 But always..[*sic*] the sand had splayed out in fawn-coloured drifts, and the pale paraha bells had trembled their taut mauve silk, elastic to the touch, against the wind. **1946** *JPS* LV. 155 Paraha, a climbing plant (Calystegia sepium), a convolvulus. The far-famed Te Rauparaha took his name from this plant as a reminder that when the body of his father was eaten by his enemies they used the leaf (rau) of this plant as a relish.

parakeet. The variety of early spelling derives from two main forms: (a) **parakeet** with variants **parrakeet**, **perrokeet**; and (b) **parroquet** with variants **paraquet**, **paroquet**, etc. [Spec. use of *parakeet* a small bird of the parrot kind.]

1. Any of several small long-tailed mainly green parrots of the genus *Cyanorhamphus* (fam. Psittacidae, subfamily Platercinae) existing in many sub-species and colour-forms. See also KAKARIKI *n.*[1] Cf. PARROT. **a. parakeet** forms.

1773 FORSTER *Resolution Jrnl.* 2 Apr. (1982) II. 245 In the morning..I went..to the Indian Cove, & shot there..a small Perrokeet, green with a red forehead. **1869** *TrNZI* I. (rev. edn.) 104 Platycercus pacificus. Kakariki. Parrakeet. Common. **1883** DOMETT *Ranolf & Amohia* I. 154 Let but a grass-green *parrakeet* alight To pluck from some wild *coffee-bush* in sight, And nibble... The scarlet berries. **1888** BULLER *Birds NZ* I. 14 The Parrakeet chased its mate through the tree-tops with sharp cries of 'twenty-eight'. **1914** PFAFF *Diggers' Story* 11 Parrakeets were very common, and developed a keen appetite for fat. **1930** GUTHRIE *NZ Memories* 89 Kaw-kaws and parakeets made splashes of colour as the sun caught their iridescent wings. **1962** EVANS *Waikaka Saga* 129 Bush robins, parakeets, tomtits, grey warblers, riflemen, pigeons and the bush hawk are still to be seen.

PARAKI

b. parroquet forms.

1773 BAYLY *Journal* in McNab *Hist. Records* 12 Apr. (1914) II. 206 There are great numbers of large grey Parrots..and small Parroquets flying in great plenty. 1817 NICHOLAS *Voyage NZ* II. 255 We saw two or three beautiful species of the parrot and the paroquet, a small bird resembling the sparrow. 1838 POLACK *NZ* I. 297 *Parroquets*, with crimson-feathered heads and breasts, with silver gray, purple, and green bodies. 1848 WAKEFIELD *Handbook NZ* 163 *Kakariki*. There are two species of this little green parroquet..neither of them much larger than a canary bird. 1855 DRURY *Sailing Directions* 65 Birds met with in Pelorus... Paroquets—two kinds. 1860 BUTLER *First Year* (1863) iv 58 There was sufficient wood..to harbour abundance of parroquets—brilliant little glossy green fellows. 1870 *TrNZI* II. 64 The smaller Parroquet is a beautiful object, as with merry note, it darts across the forest glade, with its bright green plumage glinting in the sunshine, giving at once a foreign impress to the scene, in the mind of the English settler. 1889 BLAIR *Lays of the Old Identities* 29 'Twas in the year of fifty-six When some odd million paroquets Came practising their evil tricks. 1896 HARPER *Pioneer Work* 41 If one is hard pushed for food, the smaller birds, such as the crow, tui, paraquet and saddle-backs are all acceptable. 1912 FERGUSON *Castle Gay* 60 See here are met... The robin's chirp and lintie's trill..And parroquet's green clamouring shrill.

2. With a variety of modifiers distinguishing subspecies based (a) on colour: **crimson-top** (rare, see (7) below); **red (orange-fronted)**; **red-crowned**, etc.; **yellow (yellow-crowned, yellow-fronted, yellow-top)**; or (b) on provenance: **Antipodes, Chatham, Kermadec Island**; or (c) from the names of those associated with the discovery of the species: **Forbes'** (see (3) below), **Reischek's**. (Usually only the earliest and latest quotations for each are printed below.)

(1) **Antipodes Island (Antipodes green) parakeet**. *Cyanoramphus unicolor*, lacking prominent red or yellow markings. See also (8) below.

1892 *TrNZI* XXIV. 64 *Platycercus unicolor*. (The Antipodes Island Parakeet.) 1985 *Reader's Digest Book NZ Birds* 250 *Antipodes Island Parakeet Cyanoramphus unicolor*... Other name: *Antipodes green parakeet*.

(2) **Chatham Island red-crowned (red-fronted) parakeet**. *Cyanoramphus novaezelandiae chathamensis*.

1955 OLIVER *NZ Birds* 559 Chatham Island Red-fronted Parakeet... The Chatham Island parakeet was discovered in 1840 [when] it flocked in hundreds to the potato fields when seed potatos were planted. 1990 *Checklist Birds NZ* (1980) 178 *Cyanoramphus novaezelandiae chathamensis*... *Chatham Island Red-crowned Parakeet*.

(3) **Chatham Island (Chatham Island yellow-crowned** or **yellow-fronted) parakeet**. *Cyanoramphus auriceps forbesi*. Also, from the specific name, called **Forbes' parakeet**.

1952 RICHARDS *Chatham Is.* 77 *Cyanoramphus... Forbesi*. The Chatham Island parrakeet is very like the yellow-mind of New Zealand. 1985 *Reader's Digest Book NZ Birds* 251 *Yellow-crowned Parakeet Cyanoramphus auriceps* (1820).. *Chatham Island Yellow-crowned Parakeet C. a. forbesi* 1893. Other names: *Kakariki, Forbes' parakeet*.

(4) **Forbes' parakeet**. See (3) prec.

1976 SOPER *NZ Birds* 214 Like the Black Robin, Forbes' Parakeet is confined today to Little Mangere—only a short flight for the parakeet but too far for the robin. 1984 HOLMES *Chatham Is.* 99 Forbes Parakeet,

Cyanoramphus auriceps forbesi—was formerly widespread throughout Chathams but is now mainly found on Little Mangere.

(5) **Kermadec (Kermadec Island(s)) parakeet**. *Cyanoramphus novaezelandiae cyanurus*.

1904 HUTTON & DRUMMOND *Animals NZ* 140 The Kermadec Island Parakeet. *Cyanorhamphus cyanurus*. 1976 SOPER *NZ Birds* 208 Although the Kermadec Parakeet..has been extinct on Raoul since shortly after the cats became wild about 1860, it is still present in good numbers on the Herald Islands—even the treeless and windswept Chanters. 1985 [see (7) below].

(6) **orange-fronted parakeet**. Now considered a colour form of the *yellow-crowned parakeet*, *Cyanoramphus auriceps auriceps* ((9) below).

1888 BULLER *Birds NZ* I. 146 *Platycercus alpinus*. (Orange-fronted parrakeet). 1985 *Reader's Digest Book NZ Birds* 247 *Orange-fronted parakeet Cyanoramphus malherbi*... Since European settlement the orange-fronted parakeet has never been as common as other New Zealand parakeets... Other name: *Alpine parakeet*.

(7) **red-crowned (red-fronted) parakeet**. (Also **crimson-top parroquet** (early, rare); **red-headed parakeet, red-topped parakeet**). *Cyanoramphus novaezelandiae* with a subspecies *C. n. novaezelandiae* very rare on the mainland but still common on offshore islands. Cf. (2) above and (8) below. See also POWHAITERE.

1871 HUTTON *Catalogue Birds NZ* 19 *Platycercus novae zealandiae*... Crimson-top Paroquet. Kaka[r]iki. 1873 BULLER *Birds NZ* 59 The Red-fronted Parrakeet is very generally dispersed over the whole country—but is more plentiful in the southern portion of the North Island than in the far north. 1936 GUTHRIE-SMITH *NZ Naturalist* 100 It was a delight once again to see New Zealand forest unspoiled. Birds noted were Weka, Bellbird, Tui, [and] Red-fronted Parakeet. 1970 SANSOM *Stewart Islanders* 146 Half Moon Bay straight out to the..island of Herekopare, at one time a paradise for native birds, especially red-crowned parakeets. 1985 *Reader's Digest Book NZ Birds* 248 *Red-crowned Parakeet Cyanoramphus novaezelandiae*... There are four subspecies of the red-crowned parakeet in New Zealand: the New Zealand red-crowned parakeet *Cyanoramphus novaezelandiae novaezelandiae*, the Kermadec parakeet *C. n. chathamensis*, and Reischek's parakeet *C. n. hochstetteri*.

(8) **Reischek's (or Antipodes Island red-fronted) parakeet**. *Cyanoramphus novaezelandiae hochstetteri*.

1955 OLIVER *NZ Birds* 560 The food of the Antipodes Island Red-fronted Parrakeet consists..mainly of plant substances. 1985 *Reader's Digest Book NZ Birds* 248 *C. n. hochstetteri*... Antipodes red-crowned parakeet... Reischek's parakeet occurs on all parts of the Antipodes and Bollons Islands.

(9) **yellow-crowned (yellow-fronted, yellow-top) parakeet**. *Cyanoramphus auriceps auriceps*. Cf. (3) above.

1872 *Appendix Proc. Otago Prov. Council* 39 *Platycercus auriceps*, yellow-top paroquet. 1873 BULLER *Birds NZ* 62 *Platycercus auriceps*. (Yellow-fronted Parrakeet). 1985 *Reader's Digest Book NZ Birds* 251 *Yellow-crowned Parakeet Cyanoramphus auriceps*... Kakariki.

paraki. Also **parauki**. [Ma. /ˈparaki/: Williams 264 *Paraki*..2... smelt.] The (adult) SMELT (*Retropinna retropinna*).

1848 BRUNNER *Exped. Middle Is.* Nov. in Taylor *Early Travellers* (1959) 293 The rivers, large or small, abound in eels, *hawera, upukuroro, haparu, patiki* and *parauki*. 1851 SHORTLAND *S. Dist. NZ* 312 Paraki, a

PARAPARA

small fish like white bait, caught at the mouth of Waitaki. 1925–26 *NZJST* VIII. 291 At present Canterbury residents refer to *R. retropinna* as 'silvery',... Maoris refer to this 'silvery' as 'tikihemi,' and to the adult as 'paraki'. 1963 WOODS *Freshwater Fishes* 17 Common Smelt *Retropinna retropinna*..Paraki... River smelts were taken in large numbers as a matter of routine by the Maoris in the upper Wanganui. 1990 MCDOWALL *NZ Freshwater Fishes* 414 The Maori certainly caught and ate smelt, which seem variously to have been called porohe, paraki, inanga and other names.

parala, var. PARAERAE.

parani. [Ma. /ˈparani/: Williams 264 *Parani*..native daisy.] Any of several *Lagenifera* spp. (fam. Asteraceae), small native daisies of grasslands and scrub. Cf. PAPA-TANIWHANIWHA.

1905 *TrNZI* XXXVII. 116 *Lagenophora forsterii*. (*Parani*; Native Daisy.) 1979 STARK *Maori Herbal Remedies* 75 Parani (New Zealand Daisy) *Lagenifera pumila*. The Parani is a small native Daisy which is available in both the main islands of New Zealand. 1981 Parani [see DAISY 2 (8) a]. 1982 WILSON *Stewart Is. Plants* 200 *Lagenifera strangulata Parani*... Very small rosettes or tufts in open patches... Daisies white, but tiny.

paraoa, *n*.[1] Also **paráua, paráwa**. [Ma. /paˈraːoa/: Williams 264 *Parāoa. 1*... sperm whale.] *sperm whale* (WHALE 2 (17)).

[1820 LEE & KENDALL *NZ Grammar and Vocabulary* 190 Parāwa, *s*. A sperm whale.] 1838 para párāua [see WHALE 2 (17)]. 1904 HUTTON & DRUMMOND *Animals NZ* 47 *The Sperm Whale.—Paraoa. Physeter macrocephalus*. Black above and grey below. Length, from 55 to 60 feet. 1929 BEST *Fishing Methods* 51 The sperm whale is called *paraoa*, while *paikea* denotes some other species. 1966 PHILLIPPS *Maori Life & Custom* 31 The paraoa or sperm whale, the pakake..and the black fish..were used as food.

paraoa, *n*.[2] [Ma. transliteration of *flour*, /paˈraːoa/: Williams appendix, *Parāoa*, flour, bread; Duval III. 294 *paraua* flour, 1833.] Maori bread (MAORI B 5 a).

[c1826–27 BOULTBEE *Journal* (1986) 112 bread—pahbah [paraoa]] 1966 BAXTER *Collected Poems* (1980) 347 I saw the Maori Jesus... His breath smelt of mussels and paraoa.

Hence also **paraoa rewana** [Ma. /paˈraːoa ˈrewana/: *rewana* a transliteration of Eng. *leaven*], leavened bread.

1970 IHIMAERA in *Listener Short Stories* (1977) 86 I used to take seven pieces of porou [*sic*] rewana or Maori bread to school for lunch. 1986 IHIMAERA *Matriarch* 282 Local farmers had donated..money to purchase flour for the paraoa rewana.

parapara. [Ma. /ˈparapara/: Williams 262 *Para* (ii)..*parapara*... the bird-catching tree.] BIRDCATCHING TREE.

1853 HOOKER *II Flora Novae-Zelandiae I Flowering Plants* 209 *Pisonia Sinclairii*... Nat. name, 'Parapara'. 1867 HOOKER *Handbook* 767 Para-para, *Col[enso]. Pisonia Sinclairii*. 1889, 1898, 1907, 1924 [see BIRDCATCHING TREE]. 1946 *JPS* LV. 155 *Parapara*..bird-catching tree: its sticky leaves are liable to entrap small birds; the tree does not eat them as the sundew does entrapped insects. 1961 MARTIN *Flora NZ* 163 Parapara leaves opposite..4–15 in. long;.. fruits long thin, very viscous. 1978 MOORE & IRWIN *Oxford Book NZ Plants* 60 Parapara is a small tree of quick, rather soft growth carrying leaves up to 40cm long, of dark glossy green...

PARAQUET

Nodular ridges down the length of the 'fruit'..secrete a glutinous substance. **1988** parapara [see BIRDCATCHING TREE].

paraquet, var. PARAKEET.

parara. [Ma. /paraˈraː/: Williams 264 *Pararā* (i)..2.n. *Pachyptila vittata*.] PRION 2 (*Pachyptila vittata*).
    1914 GUTHRIE-SMITH *Mutton Birds & Other Birds* 21 The fierce Parara, very easily distinguished on account of his broad bill with laminated edges, we found to be the most forward of the petrels. **1940** HOWARD *Rakiura* 205 Parara: *Prion vittatus*, or Broad-billed Petrel. Bill very wide. **1955** OLIVER *NZ Birds* 125 Skuas killed large numbers of parara and skeletons were found on nests of the Black-backed Gull. **1964** DEMPSEY *Little World of Stewart Island* 53 I..came upon Arthur, who'd just dug out two adult parara, another species of petrel, also called the broad-billed prion. **1985**, **1990** [see PRION 2].

parara, pararo, varr. PARAERAE.

parataniwha. Also **parataniwa.** [Ma. /ˈparaˈtanifa/ /ˈparataːˈnifanifa/: Williams 265 *Parataniwha, paratāniwhaniwha*.] *Elatostema rugosum* (fam. Urticaceae), a robust native herb having succulent stems and colourful, long, serrated leaves and found alongside rocky stream banks. See also BEGONIA FERN.
    1843 TAYLOR *Journal 1842–43* (ATLTS) Aug. 51 Parataniwa a slimy succulent plant growing in the dense forest. **1853** HOOKER *II Flora Novae-Zelandiae I Flowering Plants* 227 *Elatostemma rugosum*... Hab. Northern Island. Nat. name, 'Parataniwha'. **1869** *TrNZI* I. (rev. edn.) 265 For their Kao, or prepared sweet potatoes, they used the leaves of the Parataniwha. **1906** CHEESEMAN *Manual NZ Flora* 637 [*Elatostemum rugosum*] Damp shaded ravines from North Cape..to the middle of Wellington Province... *Parataniwha* above, sparingly branched, 1–5 ft. high. **1922** *Auckland Weekly News* 27 Apr. 56 *Elatostema rugosum*, or parataniwha of the Maoris, is the name of the very distinct plant with bronzy-green foliage. **1940** LAING & BLACKWELL *Plants NZ* 143 *Elatostema rugosum* (The Wrinkled Elatostema)... Maori name, Parataniwha. **1961**, **1978** [see BEGONIA FERN].

paraua, var. PARAOA *n.*¹

parauki, var. PARAKI.

parawa, var. PARAOA *n.*¹

parawai. [Ma. /ˈparawai/: Williams 265 *Parawai. 1*...A superior kind of flax cloak.] A traditional Maori fine flax cloak. Compare KAITAKA, KOROWAI.
    1847 ANGAS *Savage Life* I. 323 The other dress, called *parawai*, is exceedingly scarce; it comes from the Southern Island, and is made of strips of dog's fur, arranged indiscriminately all over a very large mat of the finest flax. **1860** BUDDLE *Maori King Movement* 29 Teira laid at His Excellency's feet a *Parawai* (a Taranaki Mat) as a symbol that the offer was accepted. **1922** [see KAITAKA]. **1930** REISCHEK *Yesterdays in Maoriland* (1933) 69 He showed me several beautiful mats, kaitaka and parawai cloaks made of flax, with plaited border. **1969** MEAD *Traditional Maori Clothing* 50 *Kaitaka* (*parawai*) *cloaks*... Kaitaka is the eastern term used for this class, the western equivalent is parawai.

parcel, *n.*¹ *Goldmining*. [Prob. f. Brit. dial., a spec. use of *parcel* a small amount: see OED 4 b.] A quantity of gold or gold ore, esp. one prepared for sale.
    1852 *Cornell & Ridings* 13 Dec. in Swainson *Auckland* (1853) 106 The parcel offered for sale [by auction, 11 Dec. 1852] comprised about six ounces of gold dust, and about ten ounces of auriferous quartz. **1863** Capt. Anderson 26 July in Cowan *Down the Years in Maniototo* (1948) 38 Mr W. Parker produced a parcel of gold (five ounces) the proceeds of one day's work of his party of five. **1870** *TrNZI* II. 174 One parcel of calcined stuff from the 'John O'Groat', weighing only 11 tons, yielded 11oz. 4dwt. retorted gold. **1925** BATHGATE *Random Recolls.* 28 On one occasion I had bought a parcel of gold from the representative of a party of diggers. **1964** ANDERSON *Doctor in Mountains* (1974) 84 He told me in a most secretive and confidential manner that he had come down with a nice parcel of gold.

parcel, *n.*² [Poss. an alteration of *particle*.] A tea-leaf floating in a cup. (In Marlborough in the 1930s also called 'a stranger' (Ed.).)
    1963 FRAME *Reservoir* 82 She handed him his special teacup on its matching saucer... He took it, and blew the parcels from the top.

Pare, var. PARRY.

pareira, var. PARERA.

parekareka. Also early **Pa-degga-degga**. [Ma. /paːˈrekareka/: Williams 266 *Pārekareka* (ii)..spotted shag.] SHAG 2 (16).
    1842 GRAY *Fauna* in Dieffenbach *Travels in NZ* (1843) II. 201 *Graucalus punctatus*... Pa-degga-degga of the Natives of Queen Charlotte's Sound... Common in Cook's Strait. They are social birds, and build their nests..on high trees overhanging the rivers and coasts. **1955** OLIVER *NZ Birds* 229 *Spotted Shag. Parekareka Phalocrocorax punctatus punctatus*. **1988** *Pacific Way* June 98 [Names used for Air NZ fleet aircraft include:] ZK-NAP 'Parekareka' (Spotted Shag)

parengo. *East Coast.* [Ma. /ˈpareŋo/: Williams 266 *Parengo*..2... Edible seaweed..= *karengo*.] An edible seaweed, KARENGO.
    1844 COLENSO *Excurs. Northern Is.* in Taylor *Early Travellers* (1959) 7 On them [*sc.* the rocks] grew a peculiar kind of large procumbent *Algae*, which, boiled, is commonly used as an article of food by the natives of these parts; they call it Parengo. [1959 *Note*] Parengo, often now called Karengo, is a name given to seaweeds of the genus *Porphyra*. **1941** *NZEF Times* 17 May 6 I want to get it back to New Zealand before they ship the parengo. **1973** GRACE in *Listener Short Stories* (1977) 108 Parengo. You stink Parengo! Who told you to put your haunga seaweed in my drier? **1978** [see KARENGO]. **1982** BURTON *Two Hundred Yrs. NZ Food* 9 Karengo or parengo (*Porphyra columbina*) is a species of seaweed common on the East Coast of the North Island and was well known to the Maori for its nutritive qualities.

parera. Also with much variety of early form as **panada, pareira, parra, parrera.** [Ma. /ˈpaːrera/: Williams 267 *Pārera*... grey duck (*parera* [Ngapuhi and Waikato dial.]).] grey duck (DUCK 2 (4)).
    [**1817** NICHOLAS *Voyage NZ* II. 339 A duck Panada. **1820** LEE & KENDALL *NZ Gram. & Vocab.* 190 Paréra; A duck, goose, &c.] **1835** YATE *NZ* (1970) 57 *Parera*, or Wild Duck—These birds exactly resemble the English wild-duck. **1838** POLACK *NZ* I. 299 The *pareira*, or ducks, are principally found up deserted creeks, or unfrequented rivers. **1842** GRAY *Fauna* in Dieffenbach *Travels in NZ* (1843) II. 198 *Anas superciliosa*... He-Parrera of the natives of Dusky Bay and Queen Charlotte's Sound... Parera. **1855** TAYLOR *Te Ika A Maui* 407 Family, *Anatida*—Parera, turuki (*Anas superciliosa*), the duck; very similar to the wild duck of England. **1867** HOCHSTETTER *NZ* 293 The wild-duck Parera (*Spatula rhynchotis*). **1870** [see DUCK 2 (4)]. **1882** HAY *Brighter Britain* II. 225 The species we have identified in the Kaipara and Hokianga are..the grey duck, or Parera (*Anas superciliosa*)..and some other varieties. **1894** [see DUCK 2 (4)]. **1903** *NZ Illustr. Mag.* Nov. 117 It was a parra duck, a pretty little grey, timid-looking thing. **1935** *NZ Free Lance Christmas Annual* 14 Oct. 31 The native grey duck or 'parera'..is one of the Dominion's finest sporting birds. **1946** *JPS* LV. 155 *Pārera*, a water-duck (*Anas superciliosa*), grey-duck: this is also the general name for the north-west wind, but is restricted by the Pakeha to the duck. **1966** FALLA et al. *Birds of NZ* 90 Grey Duck *Anas superciliosa*... Parera... It remains a common duck in many parts of New Zealand. **1988** MIKAERE *Te Maiharoa* 75 There were putakitaki (paradise ducks), parera (grey ducks), tataa (brown ducks) and whio (blue ducks).

pari, var. PARRIE.

parish. *Hist.* [Spec. use of *parish* a district constituted for purposes of civil government: see OED *n.* 2 a.] In parts of the North Auckland, Auckland and East Coast land (survey) districts, a subdivision of a county.
    1848 WAKEFIELD *Handbook NZ* 317 ['Terms of Purchase of Land in the Settlement of Otago' agreed on by the 'Otago Association' and the Company] 11. Reservations to be made..of the Sites of Villages and Towns..in the Several Parishes and Hundreds. **1916** STALLWORTHY *Early N. Wairoa* 142 In the year 1894, a letter was received from the Lands and Survey Department, notifying that section 42, Kopuru Parish, had been gazetted an Aratapu Domain. **1952–53** *NZ Forest Gloss.* (TS) Parish Under the old land-subdivision system in the Auckland Provincial District, a subdivision of a county. Still in use in parts of the North Auckland, Auckland and Gisborne Land Districts.

park, *n.* [Spec. use of *park* a parking area for motor-vehicles: see OED *n.* 5 b.] A parking space for a single vehicle off a roadway, in a parking building, etc.
    1963 *Evening Post* (Wellington) 4 Apr. 11 Notices mean nothing to a driver in search of a handy park... There were four cars parked right under the clearly marked notice: Private property. **1980** LELAND *Kiwi-Yankee Dict.* 74 *park*: The place where one parks a car is called a park.

park, *v.* In the phr. **to park one's ears to,** to listen in (to).
    1948 BALLANTYNE *Cunninghams* (1976) 125 'Come off it. You wouldn't like your sister-in-law to park her ears to all I know about you. You and your bow-tie.'

parke(e), varr. PAKIHI.

Parkeha, var. PAKEHA.

Parker's boy: see PARKHURST BOY.

Parkhurst boy. *Hist.* Also erron. **Parker's Boy.** Usu. *pl.* [f. the name of *Parkhurst Prison*, Isle of Wight: AND 1844.] A juvenile offender sent for rehabilitation to New Zealand 1842–43 (and also to Australia) after having served part of a sentence in Parkhurst Prison.

[1847 ANGAS *Savage Life* I. 285 A number of boys, reformed juvenile offenders, from the Parkhurst prison in the Isle of Wight, have from time to time been sent out to Auckland, for the purpose of being apprenticed to such of the settlers as would take them.] **1859** THOMSON *Story NZ* II. 65 [In 1842 the Secretary of State] sent out one hundred Parkhurst boys as emigrants; and these reformed prisoners, in one year after their arrival, doubled the felony cases in the colony. **1897** PHILIPS *Memories of the Past* 11 A great deal of mischief was done..by the importation of 'Parkhurst Boys' as they were termed, who were sent out from home. **1936** BEASLEY *Pioneering Days* 18 Runaway sailors, escaped convicts from Sydney, (locally known as 'Parker's Boys' on account of the association of some of them with Parker's Gaol in Sydney) and others of a similar type provided the principal labour supply [in Auckland in the 1840s]. **1990** *Family History at National Archives* (1991) 29 *Parkhurst Boys.* In 1842 a scheme was adopted to rehabilitate boys discharged from Parkhurst Prison. They were granted pardons on condition that they went to New Zealand, and, in some cases, that they served apprenticeships. Ninety-two boys were sent out in 1842 and another 33 in 1843.

Parkiah, Parkiar, varr. PAKEHA.

parkihi, var. PAKIHI.

Parnell /paˈnɛl/. [A suburb of Auckland, once (c1920s) shabby-genteel and poor but independent, now trendy and nouveau-riche.]
1. As special Comb. **Parnell shout** *Auckland*, a 'dutch treat' where each member of a group pays his or her own share of the treat; in the phr. **to go Parnell**, to pay for one's share of a treat, etc.
1916 *Wairarapa Daily Times* 6 Sept. 4 A 'Jamie Woodser' is the exact equivalent of a 'Parnell Shout' which is the only kind of 'shout' now permitted. **c1930** Auckland p.c. Professor P.S. Ardern. *Parnell shout*, a 'dutch treat', from Parnell's 'poor but independent' outlook. **c1940** Auckland p.c. Raydia Farquhar. *To go Parnell with* someone is to pay for one's own share of an outing, treat, etc. **c1945** Auckland p.c. Ruth Mason (Wellington, 1953). A *Parnell shout* is a 'Dutch treat'.
2. Symbolic of conspicuous wealth or trendy display.
1987 *Evening Post* (Wellington) 26 Sept. 2 'I think it is important,' he said, 'that people get a perspective of me as not someone that comes from a background of pink gins, quiche and Parnell but someone who had to come up the river in a cabbage boat.

paroquet, var. PARAKEET.

parore /pəˈrori/. [Ma. /ˈparore/: Williams 268 *Parore...* mangrove fish.] *Girella tricuspidata* (fam. Kyphosidae), a northern New Zealand seafish. See also *black bream* (BREAM 2 (1)), BLACKFISH *n.*², *mangrove fish* (MANGROVE 3), ROCKFISH, SHITFISH, *black snapper* (SNAPPER *n.*¹ 2 (1)).
[**1820** LEE & KENDALL *NZ Gram. & Vocab.* 190 Paróre, *s.* A fish so called] **1849** *NZ Jrnl.* IX. 125 Black rockfish Parore. **1875** [see MANGROVE 3]. **1886** SHERRIN *Handbook Fishes NZ* 70 Parore or Mangrove Fish... A fish 18in. long, Dr. Hector says, with black bands on a dark ground; height equal to half the length; peritoneum black. Does not take bait, but frequents rocks among the mangroves at high water. **1899** *TrNZI* XXXI. 97 My specimen was the parore, a fish excessively plentiful on the water-covered mangrove-flats..it being a great nuisance to the mullet-fishermen on account of its unwittingly occupying net-space. **1921** *NZJST* IV. 116 *Girella tricuspidata... Mangrove-fish*; *Parore*. Very common in the vicinity of kelp and mangrove, North Auckland Peninsula. **1957** [see BLACKFISH *n.*²]. **1963** AUDLEY *No Boots for Mr. Moehau* 13 One day it's only parore – all black guts, only fit for dogs; another time it's kawhai, good. **1972** DOAK *Fishes* 51 With broad muscular tails and compressed bodies, parore are fast-moving reef fishes feeding extensively on seaweeds... Parore may spend considerable time in estuaries and are thus of considerable economic importance being easily netted as bait for crayfishing. **1987** [see SHITFISH].

parr, var. PA *n.*¹

parra, var. PARERA.

parrakeet, var. PARAKEET.

parrera, var. PARERA.

parrie. Also **pari.** *Pl. paris, parries.* [f. *par*(adise + -IE.] A familiar short form of *paradise duck* (DUCK 2 (6)).
1946 MILLER *There Was Gold* 136 The melancholy honk of a flock of 'Parries' flying overhead..accentuated the eeriness of the night. **1950** *Canterbury Mountaineer* 77 We were unable to eat even a morsel of our parrie stew. **1965** WALL *Long and Happy* 122 Mrs Sutherland [of Milford Sound] kept some parrie ducks. She told me [c1902–3] how she saw one of a group of tourists aiming a gun at them. She gave him a rare scolding 'trying to shoot my parries!' **1981** *NZ Times* 5 July 13 For many years, the pari has been considered just another duck. **1985** [see DUCK 2 (6)]. **1988** PICKERING *Hills* 32 In some valleys a discordant orchestra of parries follows you for hours.

parroquet, var. PARAKEET.

parroquet's beak: see PARROT'S BEAK.

parrot.
1. [Spec. use of *parrot*, any of various birds of the fam. Psittacidae for NZ species.] Any of various New Zealand parrots or parakeets. See also KAKA 1 a, KAKAPO, KEA *n.* 1 a, PARAKEET.
1770 PARKINSON *Journal* 15 Jan. (1773) 115 The woods abound with diverse kinds of birds, such as parrots, wood-pigeons, water hens. **1777** FORSTER *Voyage Round World* I. 158 The parrots were of two sorts; one small and green, and the other very large, greyish-green, with a reddish breast. **1817** [see PARAKEET b]. **1833** WILLIAMS *Early Jrnls.* 30 Mar. (1961) 302 The Parrots making a great deal of noise in the trees close to us, but we slept well till daylight. **1841** BIDWILL *Rambles in NZ* (1952) 95 I bought for two blue beads a cockatoo—or rather parrot (nestor), the most common bird in New Zealand, and good to eat. **1853** EARP *NZ* 105 We had a pudding for dinner today..composed of a green parrot and some parson-birds..; they were delicious, particularly the parrot. **1865** [see KAKA 1 a]. **1874** YONGE *Life of John Coleridge Patteson* I. 282 Small green parrots getting up actually in coveys, eight at a time and perching close to me; large red ones in numbers. **1882** HAY *Brighter Britain* II. 151 Pigeons, nestors, parrots..all these and more were eaten. **1949** BAXTER *Collected Poems* (1980) 87 The carrion parrot with red underwing Clangs on the roof by night.
2. With a modifier: **brown, bush, green, ground, mountain, Mount Cook, native (New Zealand), night, owl.**
(1) **brown parrot.** KAKA 1 a.
1871 HUTTON *Catalogue Birds NZ* 19 Nestor meridionalis... Brown Parrot. Kaka. **1882** POTTS *Out in Open* 44 We once had the gratification of witnessing a most interesting trial of powers between a sparrow-hawk and the brown parrot. **1936** GUTHRIE-SMITH *NZ Naturalist* 39 A mode used for the taking of the Brown Parrot—Kaka..was termed *taki*. **1946** *JPS* LV. 143 *Kākā*, a bird (Nestor meridionalis), brown parrot. **1982** SANSOM *In Grip of Island* 78 The kaka or brown parrot is the earliest bird to wake up in the morning.

(2) **bush parrot.** KAKA 1 a.
1870 *TrNZI* II. 64 Nestor meridionalis... Kaka. Bush Parrot. **1926** ALEXANDER & CURRIE *NZ Verse* 288 *Kaka*: bush parrot. **1986** RICHARDS *Off the Sheep's Back* 27 The kaka, or bush parrot, was killed and eaten in large numbers.

(3) **green parrot.** KEA *n.* 1 a.
1882 POTTS *Out in Open* 184 Nestor notabilis..green or mountain parrot, kea of the Maoris. **1889** KNOX *Boy Travellers* 276 Among the mountains there were flocks of the *kea*, or green parrot, living in the glens and feeding entirely on fruit and leaves.

(4) **ground-parrot. a.** KAKAPO.
1847 BRUNNER *Exped. Middle Is.* in Taylor *Early Travellers* (1959) 306 On the hills bounding the Grey river I caught four kakapos or green ground-parrots. **1851** *Lyttelton Times* 12 Apr. 7 A great addition has been made to our knowledge of the kiwi and ground parrot (kakapo) peculiar to New Zealand. **1863** BUTLER *First Year* ix 139 There is a green ground parrot too, called the kakapo, a night bird, and hardly ever found on the eastern side of the island. **1879** HAAST *Geol. Canterbury & Westland* 52 [The Maori judged] its value not by its extent but by the great number of..Kakapos (Ground parrots) which..had here enjoyed an undisturbed existence. **1885** *NZJSc.* II. 479 Ground parrot, Night parrot, Kakapo. It is still abundant in many parts of Westland; notwithstanding the persecution that constantly pursues it. **1926** [see KAKAPO a]. **1957** WILLIAMS *Dict. Maori Lang.* 91 *Kākāpō... Strigops habroptilus*, ground parrot. **1985** *Reader's Digest Book NZ Birds* 242 *Kakapo Strigops habroptilus...* Tarapo, tarepo, owl parrot, ground parrot, night parrot.
b. fig. *cockatoo farmer* (COCKATOO *n.* 1).
1877 BROOMHALL *Fragments from the Jrnl.* 41 The man who farms less than 100 acres is a ground parrot; more than 100 acres but less than 1000 acres, a gentleman.

(5) **mountain parrot.** KEA *n.* 1 a.
1873 [see KEA *n.* 1 a]. **1879** HAAST *Geology Canterbury and Westland* 117 A number of Keas (the green mountain parrot)..broke the stillness of nature with their plaintive notes. **1882** [see (3) above]. **1898** *Merriam-Webster Internat. Dict.* (Australasian Suppl.) 2028 *Par´rot..n.* [Add.] *Mountain parrot.* (*Zoöl.*) See Kea. **1917** WILLIAMS *Dict. Maori Lang.* 131 *Kea* (i), *keha*, *n. Nestor notabilis*, mountain parrot. **1938** *NZ Observer* 8 Sept. 10 Polly is a kea, or mountain parrot. **1982** BAXTER *Selected Poems* 188 Kea *mountain parrot*

(6) **Mount Cook parrot.** *Obs.* KEA *n.* 1 a.
1883 GREEN *High Alps* 171 While engaged in making our *cache*, two keas or Mt Cook parrots came wheeling round us screaming loudly. **1934** ROSS *Mixed Grill* 10 A stew of keas or Mount Cook parrots.

(7) **native (New Zealand) parrot.** KAKA 1 a.
1835 [see KAKA 1 a]. **1847** ANGAS *Savage Life* I. 274 I obtained a *kaka*, or New Zealand parrot (*nestor meridionalis*). **1917** [see KAKA 1 a]. **1936** HYDE *Passport to Hell* 31 Through the forests the outlaws and the native parrots, the red-plumed kakas, had swept in varying degrees of magnificence. **1947** [see KAKA 1 a].

(8) **night parrot.** KAKAPO.
1848 TAYLOR *Leaf from Nat. Hist.* xii kaka-po ground parrot night-parrot. **1851** WELD *Jan.* in *NZGG* 21 Feb. (1851) 31 [The Maori]..said that formerly he

had often been there to catch kakapos (green night parrots) in a black birch wood. **1859** THOMSON *Story NZ* I. 28 Night parrots are almost extinct. **1862** HAAST in *Julius Von Haast* (1948) 282 We were separated from the whole world, our only neighbour the abnormal night parrot, whose shrill cry enlivened the dismal nights. **1869** *TrNZI* I. (rev. edn.) 223 The remarkable genus Strigops, or night parrot, is strictly a New Zealand one. **1885** [see (4) a above]. **1922** COWAN *NZ Wars* (1955) II. 459 The range..had in old times been a well-known hunting-ground for the *kakapo* (night-parrot or ground-parrot). **1985** [see (4) a above].

(9) **owl parrot**. [f. the owl-like appearance of its face, and its nocturnal habits.] KAKAPO.

1873 BULLER *Birds NZ* 28 This [Kakapo] is one of the very remarkable forms peculiar to New Zealand, and has been appropriately termed an Owl Parrot... As its name *Strigops* indicates, its face bears a superficial likeness to that of an owl. **1889** *TRNZI* XXI. 211 *Strigops habroptilus* (Owl Parrot, or Kakapo). **1898** MORRIS *Austral-English* 333 Owl-parrot..a bird of New Zealand. See *Kakapo.* **1957** WILLIAMS *Dict. Maori Lang.* 391 *Tarepo... Strigops habroptilus owl parrot* or *ground parrot.* **1966** DURRELL *Two in the Bush* 108 The Kakapo's name is Owl Parrot, and this is singularly apt for even a professional ornithologist could be pardoned for mistaking it for an owl at first glance. **1985** [see (4) a above].

parrotfish. [Transf. use of *parrotfish* tropical fish of the fam. Scaridae having fused teeth resembling a parrot's beak: AND 1827.]

1. A name used in New Zealand for any of various brightly-coloured reef fish of fam. Labridae, more properly called wrasses. See also SOLDIER $n.^2$, WRASSE.

1777 ANDERSON *Journal* Feb. in Cook *Journals* (1967) III. 808 The natives now and then brought Hake, Paracutas, a small sort of Mackarel, parrot fish and leather jackets. **1817** NICHOLAS *Voyage NZ* II. 14 The canoes came alongside, bringing us..various descriptions of fish; among which were snappers, bream, parrot-fish. **1838** POLACK *NZ* I. 323 Many other fish are equally numerous, answering to our *hakes..parrot-fish.* **1844** BARNICOAT *Journal* (ATLTS) 6 May 170 A Singular fish which was new to all on Board except one man who called it a parrot fish, was hauled in this morning. It derives its name from a beak-like projection at the nose. **1886** SHERRIN *Handbook Fishes NZ* 70 Parrot Fish (*Labrichthys psittacula*)... Very little is generally known about the species called in Dunedin the parrot-fish. **1896** *TrNZI* XXVIII. 54 The mullet, latris, and parrot-fish are always after them [*sc.* mackerel]. **1922** *Auckland Weekly News* 15 June 14 Further along are parrot fish with their beak-like mouths and their round bodies. **1967** [see KELPFISH 2]. **1977** FISHER *Angels Wear Black* 37 A number of Parrotfish (they do not live in schools) were following me around and picking up the broken off crayfish legs. **1982** AYLING *Collins Guide* (1984) 251 Most members of this family [*sc.* Labridae: wrasses] have been known in New Zealand as parrotfish although in all other countries they are collectively called wrasses and the name parrotfish is applied to a completely different family.

2. With a modifier: **banded, girdled, Sandager's, scarlet**.

(1) **banded parrotfish**. *banded wrasse* (WRASSE 2 (1) *Notolabrus fucicola*). See also CHINAMAN $n.^5$, KELPFISH 2.

1911 WAITE *Rec. Canterbury Museum* I. 226 *Pseudolabrus Pittensis..* Banded Parrot Fish. **1922** *Auckland Weekly News* 9 Mar. 15 The banded parrot-fish—kelp-fish or Chinaman in the Stewart Island waters—is the most plentiful fish in the inlet after cod. **1956** GRAHAM *Treasury NZ Fishes* 277 The Banded Parrot-fish is not by any means the most beautiful of our New Zealand fish, but it is most strikingly coloured. **1966** DOOGUE & MORELAND *Sea Anglers' Guide* 259 Banded Parrotfish... Eats any marine animals, including firmly fixed shellfish which it pulls off rocks by means of its strong teeth. **1977** FISHER *Angels Wear Black* 37 The Banded Parrotfish is the most common in the shallows—it blends right in with the seaweed. **1982** [see WRASSE 2 (1)].

(2) **girdled parrotfish**. *Notolabrus cinctus*. See also *deepsea butterfish* (BUTTERFISH 3).

1911 WAITE *Rec. Canterbury Museum* I. 226 *Pseudolabrus Cinctus..* Girdled Parrot Fish. **1921** *NZJST* IV. 116 Pseudolabrus cinctus... Girdled Parrot-fish. Odd examples are exposed for sale in Wellington during the later summer and winter months. Sold as 'deep-sea butterfish'. **1956** GRAHAM *Treasury NZ Fishes* 275 Girdled Parrot-fish *Pseudolabrus cinctus*... This fish was sold on the Wellington Fish Market as 'deep sea Butterfish', inferring that it is the Greenbone. **1982** [see WRASSE 2 (2)].

(3) **Sandager's parrotfish**. [After A.F.S. Sandager (1851–1904), Asst. Lighthouse Keeper at Moko Hinau Island and elsewhere, amateur naturalist.] *Coris sandageri*. See also *Sandager's wrasse* (WRASSE 2 (5)).

1927 PHILLIPPS *Bibliogr. NZ Fishes* (1971) 41 *Coris sandageri...* Sandager's Parrot-fish. **1966** DOOGUE & MORELAND *Sea Anglers' Guide* 260 Sandager's Parrotfish... *Other names: Coris sandageri;* king parrotfish (Australia). **1972** DOAK *Fishes* 88 It seems that the Sandager's Parrotfish has a remarkable learning capacity and social organisation. Whenever we return to study one particular tribe even after weeks of absence they immediately recall us and approach for food. **1982** [see WRASSE 2 (5)].

(4) **scarlet parrotfish**. *Pseudolabrus miles*. See also PAU, PUWAIWHAKARUA, *scarlet wrasse* (WRASSE 2 (6)).

1913 *TrNZI* XLV. 231 *Pseudolabrus coccineus*... The scarlet parrot-fish was originally described from Dunedin by Hutton..as *Labrichthys roscipunctata*. **1921** THOMSON & ANDERTON *Hist. Portobello* 77 Scarlet Parrot-fish; Wrasse *Pseudolabrus miles...* It is a beautiful fish in the water, the ground colour varying from pink, red, or yellowish to a bright green, but a black blotch behind the pectoral fin is always a conspicuous mark. **1938** *TrRSNZ* LXVIII. 412 *Pseudolabrus coccineus*... Scarlet parrot-fish. **1956** GRAHAM *Treasury NZ Fishes* 271 Scarlet Parrot-fish are of a peaceful disposition... If snapped at, the Scarlet Parrot-fish will peacefully swim away. **1966** [see PAU]. **1972** DOAK *Fishes* 82 The depth range of the scarlet parrotfish seems to begin where that of the spotty and banded parrotfish tapers off. **1982** [see WRASSE 2 (6)].

parrot's beak. Also **parrotbeak**, occas. **parroquet's beak**. KAKA-BEAK 1.

1905 WHITE *My NZ Garden* 92 *Clianthus puniceus* (Parrot's Beak) is the most gaudy-looking plant possible, here in its native land. **1907** LAING & BLACKWELL *Plants of NZ* 210 *Clianthus puniceus* (*The Scarlet Clianthus*)... It is also called in the Urewera Country *Ngutu-Kakariki,* the *Parroquet's Beak.* **1943** [see KAKA-BEAK 1]. **1961** *Merriam-Webster Third Internat. Dict.* 1644 *parrot's-beak* or *parrot's-bill* or *parrotbeak, n, pl parrot's-beaks* or *parrot's-bills* or *parrotbeaks* [so called from its curved standard] : Clianthus; *esp* : Kaka Beak.

parrot's-bill. Also **parrotbill, parrots'-bill, parrot-billed kowhai**. KAKA-BEAK 1.

1835 [see KOWHAI NGUTUKAKA]. **1843** DIEFFENBACH *Travels in NZ* I. 250 The banks of the Keri-keri are also the only known habitat of the elegant Clianthus puniceus, a leguminous plant, which the natives appropriately call parrot's-bill—ko-waingutu kaka. **1848** DILLON *Letters* (1954) 1 May 67 The seeds are those of a very handsome shrub with a very large scarlet flower. The translation of the Maori name for it is parrot-billed Kowhai. It is a clianthus. **1857** HURSTHOUSE *NZ* II. 365 The perfumed manouka [*sic*], the scarlet myrtle and giant fuchsia, the red and yellow parrot's bill. **1869** [see KOWHAI NGUTUKAKA]. **1872** DOMETT *Ranolf & Amohia* 261 Deep-dyed as of trogon or lory, How with parrot-bill fringes 'tis burning, One blood-red mound of glory! **1886** *TrNZI* XVIII. 293 In New Zealand..it is said to be called 'Kowhaingutu-kaka,' or Parrot's-bill, and to grow to the size of a large tree. **1898** [see KAKA-BILL]. **1910** COCKAYNE *NZ Plants & Their Story* 160 Then there is the parrotbill (*Clianthus puniceus*), which is related to Sturt's desert-pea of central Australia. **1946** [see KOWHAI NGUTUKAKA]. **1961** [see PARROT'S BEAK].

Parry. Also **Pare**. [f. *Par*(emoremo + -Y.]

1. A familiar name for Paremoremo high security prison.

1982 NEWBOLD *Big Huey* 128 Thought I might as well give it a bash. 'Anything's a go,' they used to say in Pare. *Ibid.* 252 Parry, Pare (n) Paremoremo Prison. **1985** *Listener* 5 Oct. 19 If you are in Parry you understand those jokers who came back from the war and stayed all stuffed up... Parry is just a holding pen. **1987** *Metro Fiction* 8 Sometimes the heavies arrive..crims edgy from Pare release, quick off the draw. **1992** *Listener* 5 Dec. 7 It's more than folklore. I'm told that at least one child has been conceived in the Pare visitor's room.

2. Special Comb. **Parry blues**, the blue uniform of inmates of Paremoremo prison; **Parry syndrome**, an independent attitude in a long-term prison inmate.

1982 NEWBOLD *Big Huey* 252 **Parry Blues** (n) The uniform of inmates as above. **1991** *Listener* 4 Nov. 17 Being from Pare, I..had the audacity to question the rules [at Kaitoke prison], but the standard reply was, 'You know your problem, don't you? You have the **Pare syndrome.**'.. I assume the symptoms were an ability to think for oneself.

parsley. [Transf. use of northern hemisphere *parsley Petroselinum crispum* (fam. Apiaceae).] Any of various edible native plants of the parsley family Apiaceae, esp. *Apium prostratum.*

1. A coastal herb *Apium prostratum,* usu. as **native, prostrate, shore,** and **wild parsley**. See also *Maori celery* (CELERY 2 (1)).

1817 NICHOLAS *Voyage NZ* II. 249 The herbaceous productions indigenous to the country are, wild celery, canary grass, wild parsley. **1836** RHODES *Jrnl. Barque 'Australian'* (1954) 36 There are a few stunted trees and a little wild parsley..on the most elevated part [of Macauley Island]. **1846** HEAPHY *Exped. to Kawatiri* in Taylor *Early Travellers* (1959) 244 We..lived upon..*toretore* or sea anemonies, making the latter into what we termed a 'soup', flavoured with salt water and the wild parsley which grows among the rocks of that [west] coast. **1907** LAING & BLACKWELL *Plants NZ* 334 *Apium prostratum* (The Prostrate Parsley). Leaves bi- or tri- pinnate on a stout prostrate or decumbent stems. Flowers white, rays 4–15. Both islands: common... (Maori celery). **1981**, **1982** prostrate, shore parsley [see CELERY 2 (1)].

2. Any of various other edible plants of fam. Apiaceae, usu. as **wild parsley**. **a.** *Anisotome* or *Gingidia* spp., subalpine herbs.

1891 WALLACE *Rural Econ. Austral. & NZ* 297 *Barley Grass..*and *Wild Parsley* both superior feeding value, have also practically disappeared from the natural pastures. **1926** CROOKES *Plant Life Maoriland* 154 The family is a very large one, containing..the Ligusticums, the native parsley, and that highly aromatic plant, the native aniseed.

b. *Scandia* (formerly *Angelica*) *geniculata*, a slender climbing plant of coastal cliffs.

1896 HARPER *Pioneer Work* 33 Wild parsley (*Angelica geniculata*), [and] spinach (*Tetragonia expansa*)..are also eatable.

parsnip. [Transf. use of European parsnip *Pastinaca sativa* (fam. Apiaceae).] Usu. as **Maori parsnip**, occas. **wild parsnip**, *Anisotome* (formerly *Ligusticum*) *lyallii* (fam. Apiaceae), a robust native herb with carrot-like leaves.

1867 HOOKER *Handbook* 766 Maori Parsnip, *Hector. Ligusticum Lyallii*. **1869** *TrNZI* I. (rev. edn.) 203 Maori parsnip. *Ligusticum Lyalli*. **1946** ACLAND *Early Canterbury Runs* 15 There were some very valuable plants growing between the tussocks, such as wild parsnip, wild carrot and aniseed. They have become scarce now.

parson. *Obs.*

1. [Prob. from the black and white colouring.] OYSTERCATCHER, or poss. in quot. 1863, some other black-and-white seabird.

1773 FORSTER *Resolution Jrnl.* 24 May (1982) II. 285 We saw great flocks of Curlews or *Oyster-catchers* [at Queen Charlotte Sound], whom the people on board the Adventure called *Parsons*. We found several black & white ones amongst them, perfectly like those we have in England. **1863** BUTLER *First Year* i 12 The great feature of the southern seas is the multitude of birds... Huge albatrosses..parsons..mutton birds and many more, wheel continually about the ship's stern.

2. In full PARSON-BIRD. TUI 1.

1834 [see PARSON-BIRD]. **1840** JOHNSON *Plain Truths* 65 The whalers call [tuis] parsons from the two white feathers hanging out. **1841** HODGSKIN *Narrative of Eight Months Sojourn in NZ* 28 The most harmonious is the toi or tue, to which we gave the nickname of parson, from its being a beautiful glossy black, and having a small patch of snow-white feathers on the neck. **1853** MACKIE *Traveller under Concern* (1973) 77 In a cage I saw a bird called the parson. It takes its name from two curious white feathers on its breast.

parson-bird. [f. the tufts of white feathers on the throat being reminiscent of a 19th century Anglican parson's white throat-bands.] A formerly popular name for the TUI. See also PARSON 2.

1834 MARKHAM *NZ* (1963) 34 The Toi bird or Parson... With two bands under the Chin of white Feathers,..called Parson birds. **1847** ANGAS *Savage Life* II. 29 The graceful *tui*, or parson-bird..sported amongst the yellow blossoms of the *kowai*. **c1850** in Hall-Jones *Mr Surveyor Thomson* (1971) 55 Our parson bird being beyond reach held on his discourse with much nonchalance. Altogether this bird is a most remarkable one: clothed in feathers of deep black from head to foot, he wears a most grave and sacerdotal aspect... He bears out closer the clerical resemblance by the possession of two pure white feathers under his chin, and the parody is complete when he commences to utter his guttural yet energetic notes. Sitting on the branch of a tree as a..pulpit, he wags his paw and shakes his head, bending to one side, and then to another; as if he remarked to this one and to that one. **1866** BARKER *Station Life* (1870) 93 Then we crept softly up..to have a good look at the Tui, or Parson-bird, most respectable and clerical-looking in its glossy black suit..and white wattles of very slender feathers..curled coquettishly at each side of his throat, exactly like bands. **1881** CAMPBELL *Poenamo* 99 The full rich carol of the tui or parson-bird..fell faintly upon the ear. **1908** GORST *NZ Revisited* 120 The most striking objects were the kohai [*sic*] trees..generally full of large black parson birds. **1940** LAING & BLACKWELL *Plants NZ* 225 The tuis or parson-birds will not take the trouble to insert their brush-tongues to get at the honey. **1957** WILLIAMS *Dict. Maori Lang.* 527 *Tui… Prosthemadera novae-seelandiae, parson bird*. **1966** FALLA et al. *Birds of NZ* 221 Tui *Prosthemadera novaeseelandiae*... Parson Bird. **1981** HENDERSON *Exiles Asbestos Cottage* 182 Parson bird's benediction.

partial impact. *Hist.* An astrophysical theory, of some note and much controversy in its day, put forward by Alexander W. Bickerton (1842–1929) when Professor of Chemistry at Canterbury University College.

1879 *TrNZI* XI. 121 Partial impact appears competent to explain the occurrence of temporary double, and variable stars, nebulae of various kinds (the kind depending on the nature of the impact), comets, and finally stars or suns accompanied by bodies of smaller size. **1880** *TrNZI* XII. 191 The hypothesis I [*sc.* Bickerton] am about to describe suggests that this [*sc.* a series of collisions] is the case, but especially says further that if they do knock against each other that the blow may be a mere graze of the two outsides, or sometimes a large piece of each may be struck off, and in extremely rare cases they may meet fair; but as this latter is so extremely rare the other cases are those chiefly considered, and so the theory is called *Partial* Impact. **1910** *Triad* 11 July 49 I want to know..why your theory of partial impact is not being recognized and accepted in the scientific world. **1923** *College Rhymes* 14 He will never get weary Of answering any query On the partial impact theory; Will you, Bick? **1940** JENKINSON *New Zealanders & Science* 130 It was on 4 July 1878..that Bickerton read before the Philosophical Institute of Canterbury his paper 'On Temporary and Variable Stars' in which the main facts of the theory of partial impact were first announced. **1965** LEE *Rhetoric at Red Dawn* 110 As a youngster I remember the New Zealand press talking of Bickerton and his theory of partial impact.

partike, partikie, varr. PATIKI.

part up, *v.* [AND 1889.] To pay up.

1906 *Truth* 15 Sept. 3 When woolly whiskers of the Wayback goes into the township and is fined a quid for being drunk his boss never thinks of parting up for him. **1943** BENNETT *English in NZ* in *Amer. Speech* XVIII. 92 *to part up*, to pay up **1964** SARGESON *Collected Stories 1935–63* (Pearson gloss.) 302 part up: hand money over.

paruwhatitiri. Also early **paruwhatiri.** [f. Ma. *paru* excrement + *whatitiri* thunder. Ma. /'paru'fatitiri/: Williams 268 *Paru* (i).. 2. Excrement. *Paru whatitiri, Clathrus cibarium*, a net-like fungus. =*tūtae whatitiri.*] *basket fungus* (FUNGUS 2 (1)). See also THUNDER-DIRT.

1867 HOOKER *Handbook* 767 Paruwhatiri... *Ileodictyon cibarium*. **1869** *TrNZI* I. (rev. edn.) 261 [Also eaten were] several *Fungi* [especially]..the Paruwhatitiri (*Ileodictyon cibarium*), the Pukurau. **1881** *TrNZI* XIII. 30 Several fungi were also eaten..such as the *paruwhatitiri* (*Ileodictyon cibarium*). **1882** HAY *Brighter Britain* II. 213 Their chiefest dainty and most esteemed treasure among fungi, is the Paruwhatitiri, or 'thunder-dirt'.

pass. *Goldmining.* [Spec. use of rare Brit. *mining pass* an ore chute: see OED *n.*[1] 4.] **a.** An ore chute. See esp. quot. 1978.

1874 HOLLOWAY *Jrnl. of Visit 1873–75* (ATLMS) 17 June 116 [West Coast] A man got killed in a 'Pass'. (A Pass is a Narrow or small aperture, down which the quartz is passed from the upper to the lower tunnels). **1944** *Korero* (AEWS Background Bulletin) 24 Apr. 20 Clad in trousers and singlet, they are busy shovelling the quartz down a 'pass' to the level below. **1978** MCARA *Gold Mining Waihi* 193 As the mine workings reached greater depths the ground generally became more solid and stable and more and more shrinkage stopes were worked, until this method became the principal one in use for stopes up to about forty feet in width. The method consisted of putting in the level timbers in the usual way, with short chutes or 'passes' installed every other set to allow all the ore in the stope to be lowered evenly as it was worked. *Ibid.* 209 Including..chutes for ore-handling, or 'passes' as they were generally known.

b. Special Comb. **pass-bar**, a bar manipulated to control the passage of material through a pass.

1978 MCARA *Gold Mining Waihi* 329 *Pass-bars*: Pinch-bars, fitted with 'D' handles, used to work the passes and chutes.

passenger. [Spec. use of a colloq. sense of *passenger* one who takes a passive role: cf. OED 6.] A lazy working-dog. Cf. SUNDAY DOG.

1949 NEWTON *High Country Days* 196 *Passengers*: A musterer's name for a dog which does not do its share of the work—it is 'carried' by the rest of his team.

passion-flower, passionfruit. [Spec. use of northern hemisphere *passion-flower, passionfruit* (also *passion-vine*) *Passiflora* spp., for native and introduced spp. of fam. Passifloraceae.]

1. Also **passion vine**, and with the modifiers **native** (or **New Zealand**), *Passiflora tetrandra* (formerly *Tetrapathea tetrandra* and *T. australis*), a native high-climbing vine of lowland forest, also its attractive flowers and bright orange fruit about the size of a cherry with seeds (from which the Maori formerly expressed oil) embedded in a sparse crimson pulp. See also KOHIA, *orange berry* (ORANGE 1 d).

1846 *The Calendar of St. John's College (NZ Church Almanac)* attested in *TrNZI* (1927) LVII. 945 *Tetrapathaea australis* passion-flower. **1853** HOOKER II *Flora Novae-Zelandiae* I *Flowering Plants* 72 The New Zealand Passion-flower is a perfectly smooth climbing plant, with alternate, simple, petiolate leaves, axillary tendrils, and small axillary panicles of green flowers. **1866** ANGAS *Polynesia* 51 In the New Zealand forest the blossoms of the clematis and the passionflower enliven the sombre foliage of the larger trees. **1900** *Canterbury Old & New* 184 Climbing forest plants or 'lianes' are abundantly represented by the lawyer, the native passion-flower..and the beautiful clematis. **1911** *TrNZI* XLIII. 199 The native passion-vine (*Passiflora tetrandra*)..also occur[s]. **1925–26** *NZJST* VIII. 86 *Passiflora tetrandra*, the New Zealand passion-fruit, is a tendril climber very often found on tree-ferns. In autumn it produces beautiful bunches of round orange berries. **1940** LAING & BLACKWELL *Plants NZ* 281 *Tetrapathaea tetrandra* (The New Zealand Passion-flower)... Maori name, Kohia. **1957** WILLIAMS *Dict. Maori Lang.* 125 *Kohia, n. Tetrapathaea tetrandra* a vine, New Zealand passion-fruit. **1961** MARTIN *Flora NZ* 145 The native Passion Fruit (*Tetrapathaea australis*) is yet another scrambler on forest margins north from Banks Peninsula and Deans Bush in Christchurch. **1978** MOORE & IRWIN *Oxford Book NZ*

Plants 64 *Tetrapathaea* (*passiflora*) *tetrandra, kohia.* The native passion fruit reaches its southern limit about Banks Peninsula. **1982** BURTON *Two Hundred Yrs. NZ Food* 145 The passionfruit family includes several subtropical species, one of which, the New Zealand passionfruit or *kohia*, is native to New Zealand. However, this species has non-edible fruits. **1992** [see KOHIA].

2. banana passion-flower, banana passionfruit. *Passiflora mollissima*, a naturalized South American vine or its edible yellow ellipsoid fruits.

1955 *BJ Cameron Collection* (TS July) banana passionfruit (n) 1. A variety of passion fruit, oval in shape and yellowish in colour. 2. The vine producing this fruit. **1969** *Standard Common Names Weeds* 56 *passion flower, banana Passiflora mollissima.* **1980** ADAMS *Wild Flowers* 28 Commonly known as banana passionfruit for its long, pendulous yellow fruits, this beautiful passion flower is a vigorous climber in frost-free areas... Botanical name: *Passiflora mollissima.* **1982** WILSON *Stewart Is. Plants* 44 *Further exotic climbers in Halfmoon Bay:..* Banana Passion Vine (*Passiflora molissima*) has spectacular pink-purple flowers and pendent yellow fruit. **1986** RICHARDS *Off the Sheep's Back* 140 The dunny was still in the same place,... but was now hidden..by a prolific banana-passionfruit bearing vine.

pastoral, *a.* [Spec. use of *pastoral* relating to or occupied in the care of herds; (of land) used for pasture: see OED *a.*, and the substantial entry in AND: as in Australia, *pastoral* in NZ use is virtually free of literary connotations.]

1. Of land, used for or suitable for stock farming as distinct from arable farming or cropping.

1847 in Deans *Pioneers Canterbury* (1937) 114 In the good pastoral districts of New Zealand they [*sc.* bullocks] will be worth about one-half more. **1848** WAKEFIELD *Handbook NZ* 15 Pastoral ranges will be allotted to purchasers of freehold land in the Settlement [of Canterbury]. **1866** ANGAS *Polynesia* 120 The south-eastern portion of Marlborough consists mainly of the Wairau plains, one of the richest and first occupied pastoral districts in New Zealand. **1931** LOVELL-SMITH *Old Coaching Days* 109 We were passing through a fine pastoral country, with grassy valleys. **1940** COWAN *Sir Donald Maclean* 3 The experience he gained in work on the newly broken-in settlements was useful..when he came to take up a pastoral block in Hawke's Bay.

2. Pertaining to or engaged in stock-raising, usu. sheepfarming, as distinct from 'agricultural' farming, i.e. arable farming or cropping.

1856 FITTON *NZ* 91 The pastoral occupations of New Zealand..are described in another chapter. *Ibid.* 127 The pastoral stations north of Otago extend..until they meet the stock-owners' out-stations South of Canterbury. **1892** *NZ Official Handbook* 157 To those whose proclivities tend towards a pastoral life, occupation as stockriders, shepherds, &c., on one of the large cattle- and sheep-runs common in the colony may be obtained. **1902** *Settler's Handbook NZ* (Lands Dept.) 15 There are open grassy plains, of no great fertility, but yet suited to pastoral pursuits. **1914** PFAFF *Diggers' Story* 89 The fat stock of Westland is another adjunct to our pastoral wealth. **1938** BURDON *High Country* 150 The first two stages of the Colony's growth, pastoral and agricultural, had clashed. The time when the pastoral industry had been of supreme importance was passing by. **1951** CRESSWELL *Canterbury Tales* 29 [He] entered into partnership with..Mallock and Lance, giants in the North Canterbury pastoral world. **1971** GRIFFITHS *King Wakatip* 73 The Rees family barely had time to get settled again at their home station before the quiet pastoral barony..was invaded by a noisy..avalanche of gold-seekers. **1985** *Standards* (Standards Assoc. of NZ) Sept. 16 Fencing wire has been part of New Zealand's pastoral tradition for many years.

3. In special collocations. **a.** In the sense 'pertaining to stock-grazing': **pastoral land**, see quot. 1902; **pastoral lease** [AND 1850], a lease of an area of land restricted in use to grazing stock (see also PASTURAGE LEASE or LICENCE, DEPASTURAGE LICENCE); **pastoral licence**, a licence to use a specified piece of land for stock-grazing; **pastoral road**, a rural road giving access to remote stations; **pastoral run**, RUN *n.*¹ 2.

1902 *Settler's Handbook NZ* (Lands Dept.) 71 'Pastoral lands' are defined in the Land Act as 'lands suitable exclusively for pasturage, and not capable of being used with profit in areas of a carrying-capacity of less then five thousand sheep'. **1906** ROBERTS in *Hist. N. Otago from 1853* (1937) 7 In 1849, a law was passed that pastoral lands should be leased as runs, at a low rental,.. with an agistment charge of one penny a head per annum on every sheep,... in addition to the rent. **1993** *Sunday Times* (Wellington) 23 May 2 Most of the station..is crown **pastoral lease** land with a perpetual renewal right. **1938** BURDON *High Country* 150 The land companies and absentee owners came in for the greatest execration; but those who held **pastoral licences** of rough hill country were usually excepted. **1858** in Beattie *Early Runholding* (1947) 21 In 1858 the Otago Provincial Council voted £336 6s 8d towards a '**pastoral road**' from Waikouaiti to Manuherikia. **1898** HOCKEN *Contributions* 185 Roads of some sort—metalled horse or dray tracks, and what by a pleasant conceit were termed 'pastoral roads'—extended [by c1858] from the Waitaki to Riverton. **1871** in Evans *Waikaka Saga* (1962) 19 Miners have commenced mining on **Pastoral Run** No. 167C leased by Hugh McIntyre Esquire. **1902** *Settler's Handbook NZ* (Lands Dept.) 63 Pastoral runs are limited to areas which will carry 20,000 sheep or 4,000 cattle. **1915** MACDONALD *NZ Sheepfarming* 94 To buy a large pastoral run requires a lot of capital. **1936** BELSHAW et al. *Agric. Organiz. NZ* 32 The variation in the size of holding ranges from the very large 'Pastoral Runs' (Crown leases) which average about 15,000 acres and are frequently as large as 50,000 acres, to small market gardens and orchards. The 'Pastoral Runs' are the poorest of occupied land, and are found mainly in the South Island. **1939** BEATTIE *First White Boy Born Otago* 116 He duly repaired to Coal Creek where Johnny Jones had the third of his trio of pastoral runs.

b. In the sense 'pertaining to large runholders as a political power group': **pastoral interest, pastoral lobby.**

1862 *Otago Daily Times* (Dunedin) 9 Jan. in *Sketch of Otago* (1862) 52 [Heading] The Pastoral Interest. **1939** BEATTIE *First White Boy Born Otago* 171 Soon after the diggings got going properly the Hog Burn was made a sludge channel. The old pastoral interests had to give way before the new mining interests. **1985** MCGILL *G'day Country* 82 We were all agreed it was absurd the pastoral lobby kept getting subsidies in the face of continued failure to sell its produce.

pastoralism. The practice of large-scale stock-farming.

1938 BURDON *High Country* 150 The time when the pastoral industry had been of supreme importance was passing by; but pastoralism still lay..across the path of progress in agriculture. **1940** HOWARD *Rakiura* 313 Scott made his pioneer venture when pastoralism was in its period of maximum development in the South Island. **1990** MARTIN *Forgotten Worker* 9 Extensive pastoralism and mixed crop-livestock farming employed a large number of wage earners.

pastoralist. [AND 1880.] A person who grazes sheep or cattle, usu. on a large property. Cf. GRAZIER.

1905 *Weekly Press* (Christchurch) 25 Jan. 11 This was due to the action of several large pastoralists who, instead of shipping their wool to London.., decided to offer it locally. **1915** MACDONALD *NZ Sheepfarming* 30 The small run grazier has, like the large pastoralist, often to contend with distance from the market. **1928** *Na To Hoa Aroha* (1986) I. 152 A Cabinet strongly redolent of the farm did not satisfy the farmer, because it really represented the large pastoralists. **1949** REED *Story Canterbury* 111 The farmer and the pastoralist each had an indispensable part to play in building up a prosperous community. **1952** MEEK *Station Days* 111 ['Squatter'] has been superseded by the term 'pastoralist'. **1964** DEANS *Pioneers* 61 The purchase by the Crown of the greater part of the South Island..placed in doubt the position of all pastoralists grazing stock on native lands. **1970** MCNEISH *Mackenzie* 22 Gulls perched on top of the pole. This was a Pastoralists' Club. **1978** POPE *Mobil NZ Tour Guide South Island* (3edn.) 261 As a pastoralist he [*sc.* Dillon Bell] realised from the outset that his class would retire automatically before the advance of the agriculturalist. **1986** IHIMAERA *Matriarch* 47 Turanga, as..Mclean said in February 1851, was..'A Veritable Paradise for Pastoralists'.

pasturage lease or **licence.** The lease of, or licence to stock, an area of land restricted in use to the grazing of stock. See also DEPASTURAGE LICENCE.

1851 *Lyttelton Times* 12 Apr. 6 They one and all protest against the rental to be charged for pasturage licenses. **1857** *Richmond-Atkinson Papers* 29 Jan. (1960) I. 257 We have just advised the Governor to assent to the new land regulations of the [Otago] province under which pasturage leases will be granted for 14 years at a yearly rate of 1d. per head on the sheep depastured. **1863** *NZ Statutes* No.39 157 [Nelson Waste Lands Act 1863] No portion of the land occupied by the holder of a pasturage license whereon a homestead shall have been erected or improvements made shall be offered for sale until the offer of purchasing such land shall have been made to such license-holder. **1902** *Settler's Handbook NZ* (Lands Dept.) 72 The pasturage lease or license entitles the holder to the sole right of pasturage; gives no right to the soil, timber, or minerals; and is no bar against prospecting or mining. **1946** ACLAND *Early Canterbury Runs* 51 When Row united the two runs, a new pasturage license was issued for both.

pat: see *cow-pat* (COW 6).

pat, *n.*¹ [AND 1908.] Abbrev. of PAT MALONE, in the phr. **on one's pat**, on one's own, alone.

1918 *Chron. NZEF* 16 Jan. 13 I'll stick on me belt and gas bag, and buzz off to the village on me pat. **a1927** ANTHONY *Me & Gus* (1977 Gus Tomlins) 73 He said 'No,' a man should be able to build a round stack on his pat, and he didn't want any boy [helper]. **1938** HYDE *Nor Yrs. Condemn* 214 The fact is, I'm a stranger here, and on my pat. **1949** SARGESON *I Saw in My Dream* (1974) 216 But why not stay the night, Dave? Mr Anderson went on. Don't leave a man all on his pat. **1970** SLATTER *On the Ball* 135 Good old Johnny... Remember him getting two tries all on his pat at Castelraimodo? **1988** MCGILL *Dict. Kiwi Slang* 82 *pat*, phr. *on one's pat* single-handed or alone, short for rhyming slang 'on one's Pat Malone/alone' or on your 'own'; eg 'Since Mabel passed on, Ron's been on his pat far too much.'

Pat, *n.*² [Orig. unknown.] A Chinese.

1910 *Truth* 26 Nov. 4 Only a few weeks ago 'Truth'

pataka. Also **patáaka**. [Ma. /ˈpaːtaka/: Williams 270 *Pātaka 1*. Storehouse raised upon posts, elevated stage for storing food.] A Maori storehouse raised upon posts. See also STOREHOUSE, WHATA 1.

[**1820** LEE & KENDALL *Gram. & Vocab.* 190 Patáka, *s.* A stone so called: a store-house.] **1843** DIEFFENBACH *Travels in NZ* II. 70 A third sort of structure are the provision-houses (pataka), which are built on poles to prevent rats from entering them. **1858** SMITH *Notes of a Journey* in Taylor *Early Travellers* (1959) 365 Not far from [Te Heuheu's] house is a splendid *pataka*, or store house; and it is elevated on four red posts, in fact the whole concern is painted red. **1903** *TrNZI* XXXV. 22 Sometimes the storehouse was set up on legs 3 ft. or 4 ft. high and called a *pataka*. **1917** *Truth* 8 Sept. 8 I soon had plenty of it [*sc.*] cooked and dried and stored away in a rat-proof pataka. **1938** LANCASTER *Promenade* 227 The [Maori] women brought filled baskets of kumeras and maize and onions..to fill the patakas against the time of war. **1946** *JPS* LV. 155 *pātaka*, a food-storehouse raised on posts: the one on a single post is a whata. **1964** HELMER *Stag Party* 'What are those little things like bird houses [at Whakarewarewa Pa]?' I asked. 'Patakas... Food storehouses.' **1972** BAXTER *Collected Poems* (1980) 579 Or the wind that shakes the tree above the pataka. **1982** BURTON *Two Hundred Yrs. NZ Food* 3 Food was stored in the *pataka*, a small house standing on a high platform out of the way of dogs and rats.

patapatow, var. PATU.

patate: see PATETE.

patch, *n.*[1]

1. *Goldmining.* [AND 1857.] A discrete piece of ground rich in gold, esp. in the phr. **to strike a patch**.

1862 *Otago Goldfields & Resources* 18 This field surpassed all others in a series of rich patches. **1873** PYKE *Wild Will Enderby* (1889, 1974) I. i 9 Say, stranger! you ain't struck a patch anywhere about up there, have you? **1875** WOOD & LAPHAM *Waiting for Mail* 13 Mrs. Arkwright had been hoping that..he might strike a patch this week. **1897** MCKAY *Geol. SW Nelson* 80 Within [the block] lie the rich alluvial diggings of Lyell Creek, famous for its 'patches' and the coarse character of its gold.

Hence **patchy** *a.*, of a claim or ground, auriferous only in patches.

1862 *Otago Goldfields & Resources* 18 Many of these ventures have paid well, but the progress will naturally be slow, particularly as the ground is so very patchy. **1871** MONEY *Knocking About NZ* 69 Though the ground had proved in general very 'patchy' yet a large amount of gold had been taken out. **1906** GALVIN *NZ Mining Handbook* 17 The lodes are what the [quartz] miner terms 'very patchy'.

2. *Gumdigging.* An area similarly rich in gum.

1970 THOMAS *Way Up North* 31 The possibility of finding a 'pocket' or better still a good 'patch' added interest to the [gumdigger's] day's work.

patch, *n.*[2] [Spec. use of *patch* a piece of material sewn on a garment as a badge: see OED 1 d.] The insignia of a gang sewn to the back of a member's jacket; by synecdoche, a gang member. Often in *attrib.* use as **patch member** (see also PATCH *v.* 2); **no-patch zone**, an area where the wearing of patches is forbidden (see quot. 1995).

1975 *Dominion* (Wellington) 17 Aug. 3 I was wearing my colours—the insignia of the Epitaph Riders which is sometimes referred to as a patch... If a member of the gang lost his patch he had to try and get it back himself. **1985** MITCALFE *Hey Hey Hey* 63 'So, Winston's joined a gang has he?'.. 'Hasn't got his patches, or his jacket yet, I know that.' **1989** *Sunday Star* (Auckland) 4 June A6 The police said that the gang grew to more than 30 patches. **1989** *Dominion* (Wellington) 27 June 3 'Would it be true there were about 43 members of Black Power?'.. 'Yes, that would be true but not patch ones.' **1989** THOMSON & NEILSON *Sharing the Challenge* 261 Full acceptance into the *Epitaph Riders* gang entitled the member to wear a backpatch displaying the gang insignia. The patch is regarded as a mark of esteem and is highly prized among gang members. To become a 'patch member' of a gang, a recruit first had to become a 'prospective member', riding with the gang for a probationary period. **1991** *Dominion* (Wellington) 13 Aug. 3 A spate of serious crime in Wanganui was being committed by Maori gang prospects trying to earn their patches.., Detective Senior Sergeant Peter Scott said yesterday. **1991** PAYNE *Staunch* 12 No self-respecting gang has their president, or any patch member of real importance, answering the doorbell; the task is usually saved for a prospect or a hanger-on. **1995** *Dominion* (Wellington) 20 Jan. 13 A staunch no-patch zone in the town [of Gisborne] still holds.

patch, *v.*

1. Also **patch up**. To receive, or wear, a patch as a sign of full gang membership.

1990 *National Radio* 'Spectrum Documentary' 16 Sept. 'You had some connection with Black Power?' 'Yeah, my two uncles were patched up for Hastings.' **1991** PAYNE *Staunch* 123 I first patched up in 1972 and I've been part of one chapter ever since.

Hence **depatch** *trans.*, to expel (a member) from a gang by removing the identifying membership patch.

1986 *Dominion* (Wellington) 16 Dec. 1 'If we find the..people responsible, we will 'depatch' [expel them from the gang] [*sic*] them and ensure they give themselves up to the police,' Mr Mamfredos said. **1991** PAYNE *Staunch* 30 In the grave lies..a Mobster who died of a drug overdose on this date four years earlier, just days after he had been de-patched.

2. *ppl. a.* In the special collocation **patched member**, one who is a full member of a gang having earned and being entitled to wear a patch, as distinct from a PROSPECT q.v. See also *patch member* (PATCH *n.*[2]).

1988 *Dominion* (Wellington) 11 Nov. 8 Nikora had been associated with the Nomads gang, but was not a 'patched' member, Mr Justice Barker said. **1991** *Dominion* (Wellington) 14 Dec. 11 They win their patch by doing the bidding of a patched member.

patch-plant. A cushion- or mat-forming plant of the alpine zone, esp. *Raoulia* spp. (fam. Asteraceae) the mats of which have the appearance of moss-like patches. Cf. SCABWEED.

1867 BUCHANAN *Notes on Bot. of Mt. Egmont* Feb. in *Linnean Soc. Jrnl.* X. 58 Strong hopes were entertained by myself that many of the more minute plants of various genera known as Patch-plants..were yet to be found; but..no Patch-plant was seen on Mount Egmont. **1889** FEATON *Art Album NZ Flora* 45 Many of these class [*sic*] of plants..are known as 'Patch Plants', having only one terminal flower [at the end of] each branch. **1907** *TrNZI* XXXIX. 330 This subalpine 'patch plant' is also common on stony river-beds of the lowland region.

patchy *a.*: see PATCH *n.*[1]

pate. [Ma. /ˈpaːte/: Williams 270 *Patē* (i)..*Schefflera digitata*, a tree. = *patatē, patete.*] *Schefflera digitata* (fam. Araliaceae), a small forest tree having palmately compound leaves, and soft wood used by the Maori in making fire. See also FIG *n.*[2], *Maori ivy* (IVY 1), PATETE, SEVENFINGER.

[**1820** LEE & KENDALL *NZ Gram. & Vocab.* 190 Páte, *s.* A tree, the branches of which are used by the natives in producing fire by friction.] **1838** POLACK *NZ* II. 400 *Paté* (*Aralia polygama,*) trunk slender, and pithy, grows to twenty feet, leaves virent digitated and epinated at the edges; the wood is made use of for procuring fire by friction. **1844** WILLIAMS *NZ Jrnl.* (1956) 107 The Pate tree is by no means handsome as a tree or shrub, having nothing remarkable, only that its wood when decayed produces fire by rubbing or friction, if rubbed by a harder piece of wood. **1853** HOOKER *II Flora Novae-Zelandiae I Flowering Plants* 95 Aralia Schaefflera... Nat. names, 'Pate'..; 'Patete', Middle Island. **1869** *TrNZI* I. (rev. edn.) 236 Of our shrubs and smaller timber trees, several are of strikingly beautiful growth..(*e.g.*)...the Pate..and the truly evergreen Ngaio. **1906** CHEESEMAN *Manual NZ Flora* 233 [*Schefflera digitata, Forst.*] *Pate*; *Patete*. **1966** FALLA ET AL. *Birds of NZ* 234 On Hen Island pate..and whauwhaupaku..are an important berry source [for the saddleback]. **1988** DAWSON *Forest Vines to Snow Tussocks* 103 Other common shrubs are the..kanono..and pate..with its large palmately compound leaves.

pateke. Also **patete, puteke**. [Ma. /ˈpateke/: Williams 270 *Pāteke*.] Either of two members of the fam. Anatidae, the SHOVELLER *Anas rhynchotis variegata* (*obs.*), or the *brown duck* (*brown teal*) (DUCK 2 (3), TEAL *n.*[1] 2 (3) *Anas aucklandica chlorotis*).

1870 *TrNZI* II. 72 Anas chlorotis,... Puteke. Teal. **1871** HUTTON *Catalogue Birds NZ* 36 Anas chlorotis... Red Teal. Pateke. **1888** BULLER *Birds NZ* II. 257 Anas chlorotis. (Brown Duck)... Tarawhatu, Patete, Tete, and Tete-whero. *Ibid.* II. 269 Rhynchapsis Variegata. (New-Zealand Shoveller)... Tete, Pateke..'Spoon-bill Duck' of the colonists. **1904** HUTTON & DRUMMOND *Animals NZ* 312 The Brown Duck—*Pateke*. c**1920** BEATTIE *Trad. Lifeways Southern Maori* (1994) He thought the spoonbill was called pateke as it says 'patek', patek', at night. **1955** OLIVER *NZ Birds* 413 *Brown Duck. Pateke Anas chlorotis* The Brown Duck was first collected in New Zealand about 1840 by P. Earl who forwarded a number of specimens to the British Museum. **1966** [see DUCK 2 (3)]. **1979** *Dominion* (Wellington) July 5 Mr F N Hayes holds one of two female brown teal or pateke ducks which are being airfreighted to a new home in England... The pateke is a New Zealand species and was until the 1900s widespread. **1985** [see TEAL *n.*[1] 2 (3)].

pateketeke. Also freq. modern **puteketeke**. [Ma. /paːˈteketeke/: Williams 270 *pāteketeke*..crested grebe.] The *crested grebe* (GREBE 2 (1) *Podiceps cristatus australis*).

1888 BULLER *Birds NZ* II. 283 Podiceps cristatus. (Great Crested Grebe)... Pateketeke. **1955, 1966** Puteketeke [see GREBE 2 (1)]. **1990** *Checklist Birds NZ* 10 *Podiceps cristatus australis... Australasian Crested Grebe* (*Puteketeke*).

Paterson's curse. [AND 1904: prob. f. the name of Richard Eyre *Patterson* (1844–1918), a grazier.] A European pasture weed of *Echium* spp. (fam. Boraginaceae) introduced from Australia and locally abundant in Auckland. Contrast CURNOW'S CURSE.

1926 HILGENDORF *Weeds* 144 Paterson's Curse (*Echium plantagineum*).— This is the local name of this weed where it is commonest in New Zealand, viz., in the Thames and neighbouring districts. **1969** *Standard Common Names Weeds* 56 *Paterson's curse Echium lycopsis.* **1980** ADAMS *Wild Flowers* 32 Paterson's curse is a serious weed in Australia. It is mainly found as a garden escape in New Zealand on dry wasteland. **1981** TAYLOR *Weeds of Roadsides* 161 Paterson's Curse (*Echium plantagineum*) Biennial like viper's bugloss... Introduced from Eurasia, it is uncommon in New Zealand although locally abundant in parts of Auckland and Hawke's Bay provinces.

patete. Also formerly occas. **patate**. [Ma. /'patete/, /pata'te:/: Williams 271 *Patete* (ii)..*Schefflera digitata* ... = *patatē, patē*.] PATE.

1853 patate [see PATE]. **1882** HAY *Brighter Britain* II. 196 The Patate..is another small tree. **1906** [see PATE]. **1940** LAING & BLACKWELL *Plants NZ* 331 *Schefflera digitata* (*The Patete*)... Maori name Patete, Ohau, (the latter name chiefly on Banks Peninsula). **1946** *JPS* LV. 155 *Patete*, a tree.., a five-fingered Maori ivy (the fruit only being similar). **1951** LEVY *Grasslands NZ* (1970) 87 Such species as lancewood..five finger, patete, toru. **1961** MARTIN *Flora NZ* 159 Patete (*Schefflera digitata*) 7–9 finely serrated leaflets. **1982** WILSON *Stewart Is. Plants* 86 *Schefflera digitata*..Sevenfinger... Patete... Small tree with large, tropical looking leaves..with 5–9 stalked leaflets (often 7).

patiki. Also early **battik; partikē, partikie.** [Ma. /'pa:tiki/: Williams 271 *Pātiki*..sand flounder.]

1. FLOUNDER *n.* 1.

[**1820** LEE & KENDALL *NZ Gram. & Vocab.* 190 Pátiki, *s.* A fish so called; also a game. **c1826–27** BOULTBEE *Journal* (1986) 110 flatfish—battik.] **1834** MARKHAM *NZ* (1963) 46 Partikies or Soles, are speared with a Bayonet or a stick at night. **1848** BRUNNER *Exped. Middle Is.* in Taylor *Early Travellers* (1959) 293 The rivers, large or small, abound in eels..*patiki*, and *parauki.* **1851** SHORTLAND *S. Dist. NZ* 11 Every now and then, we had a present of 'patiki', a fish not unlike the sole in appearance, and quite equal to it in flavour. **1865** CARBERRY *Journal* (ATLMS) 24 Feb. We killed several flat-fish like place [*sic*] they are about the best kind of Fish for cooking and are called Partikē by the natives. **1872** HUTTON & HECTOR *Fishes NZ* 117 The Patiki (*Rhombosolea monopus*), is very common in shallow bays and tidal estuaries on every part of the coast. **1886** SHERRIN *Handbook Fishes NZ* 21 Lake Ellesmere, in Canterbury, is also a famous place for patiki. **1929** BEST *Fishing Methods* 191 The *patiki* of brown colour, light underneath, is found in the swifter-running, clear streams. **1938** [see FLOUNDER *n.* 1]. **1947** [see FLOUNDER *n.* 2 (9)]. **1956** GRAHAM *Treasury NZ Fishes* 191 New Zealand Sand-flounder (Patiki) *Rhombosolea plebeia*... The common Sand-flounder is known from one end of New Zealand to the other, sometimes by other names in different localities. In Auckland it is known as the Dab. **1967** [see FLOUNDER *n.* 2 (9)]. **1970** THOMAS *Way Up North* 57 But the memory will be far more enjoyable to me if I call the flounder a patiki. **1982** BURTON *Two Hundred Yrs. NZ Food* 73 Both flounder (*patiki*) and sole (*patiki rori*) have a fine, delicate flesh with little bone. **1992** EDWARDS *Mihipeka* 86 I cook the patiki with two eggs each, also mashed potatoes.

2. *transf.* /'patɪki/ A small sailing yacht. Mr Robin Elliott (Auckland) notes (p.c. 5 May 1993): Around the turn of the century a *patiki* was a fast, shallow-draft, unballasted centreboarder, having a hull of clinker or carvel construction, between 18 and 27 feet (5.486 and 8.230 m) total length, spoon-bowed, with a flat tuck-stern, and carrying a large mainsail and small jib on a stem-headed rig. The term came into common use c1898 when it was used by the Parnell (Auckland) Sailing Club for its class of small (18ft 6in. or 5.638 m) clinker-built racing yachts. Patikis as a racing class lapsed in Auckland from 1904 until 1922 when the '18 foot restricted Patiki class' was launched. From 1904 the term was elsewhere widened to include various patiki-type boats, the class and the term surviving in Napier until the sheltered inner harbour was drained following the Napier earthquake of 1931.

1898 *Star* (Auckland) 30 July 2 The Parnell Sailing Club has decided on a specific class of boat... On the suggestion of Mr. T. Ryan the proposed class has been given the appropriate name of 'Patiki', the M[ao]ri equivalent of 'flat-fish'. **1902** *Cyclopedia of NZ, Auckland* II. 456 Among the mosquito fleet most of the one-design Patiki class owe their origin to the firm [of Logan Bros], and have been large prizewinners. **1944** CARTER *Little Ships* 57 So the fame and the skill of the Logans spread through the Australian yachting world, just as it did in New Zealand and South Africa, for although it may not be readily known, several small yachts of the *Patiki* type were built and shipped to that country. **1970** SMITHYMAN in *Te Reo 16* 9 Local [Auckland] variations on yacht-design abounded, and local namings (*patiki*, *mullety*, *fourteen-footer*, *zeddy*) were coinages. **1993** ELLIOTT AND KIDD in *Boating World* Apr. XLXI. 114 [Title] Napier—Where Patiki was King.

3. Combined with Maori suffixes in the names of various flatfishes. **a. patiki-mohoao.** Also in shortened form **mohoao.** [Ma. /'pa:tiki 'mohoao/: Williams 271 *pātiki mohoao, R. retiaria*, river or black flounder.] *black flounder* (FLOUNDER *n.* 2 (1)).

1921 [see FLOUNDER *n.* 2 (1)]. **1929** BEST *Fishing Methods* 191 At Otaki the Natives call the spotted flounder *mohoao*; it is found in streams having a slow current and muddy bed. **1956** [see FLOUNDER *n.* 2 (1)]. **1966** DOOGUE & MORELAND *Sea Anglers' Guide* 215 Black Flounder...*Rhombosolea retiaria*; mud flounder, river flounder, estuary flounder; patiki-mohoao (Maori). **1982** AYLING *Collins Guide* (1984) 310 *Black Flounder* (Mud flounder, patiki-mohoao) *Rhombosolea retiaria*.

b. patiki-rori. [Ma. /'pa:tiki 'rori/: Williams 271 *Pātiki rori*..sole.] SOLE 2 (1).

1921 [see SOLE 2 (1)]. **1927, 1947** [see SOLE 1]. **1947** POWELL *Native Animals NZ* 67 Sole *Peltorhamphus novae zelandiae*. Patiki rori of the Maoris. **1956** [see SOLE 2 (1)]. **1966** DOOGUE & MORELAND *Sea Anglers' Guide* 218 Common Sole... *Peltorhamphus novaezeelandiae*; English sole, sole, New Zealand sole; patiki-rori (Maori). **1982** [see PATIKI].

c. patiki-totara. [Ma. /'pa:tiki 'to:tara/: Williams 271 *Pātiki tōtara*..yellow flounder.] *yellow (yellow-belly) flounder* (FLOUNDER *n.* 2 (11)).

1921 [see FLOUNDER *n.* 2 (11)]. **1927** PHILLIPPS *Bibliogr. NZ Fishes* (1971) 28 *Rhombosola leporina* Guenther. Yellow Flounder; Patiki-totara. **1956, 1966** [see FLOUNDER *n.* 2 (11)]. **1982** AYLING *Collins Guide* (1984) 308 *Yellow-belly Flounder* (Patiki-totara) *Rhombosolea leporina*.

patiti. [Ma. /'pa:ti:ti:/: Williams 271 *Pātītī* (i) 1..*Microlaena stipoides*, a grass...*Pātītī taranui*,

Agropyron scabrum, tussock grass.] Either of two native tussock grasses of fam. Poaceae, *Elymus rectisetus* (formerly *Agropyron* or *Tritium scabrum*), *blue-grass* (GRASS 2 (5)), or *Chionochloa antarctica*, a tall tussock grass of subantarctic peat soils (quot. 1870).

1844 in Shortland *S. Dist. NZ* 9 Jan. (1851) 195 We now advanced along the plain [towards Moeraki], which was covered with 'patiti' and..stunted fern and 'tutu'. **1851** SHORTLAND *S. Dist. NZ* 10 The hills [at Otakou] are clothed with wood, or a species of grass (*triticum scabrum*), known by the name of 'patiti'. **1870** *TrNZI* II. 177 The soil [on Campbell Island] is very wet..the surface between the tussocks (Patiti) carpeted with beautiful mosses. *Ibid.* 178 Greatest elevation [Antipodes Islands] 700 feet, the hills dotted with high tussock (pa-ti-ti).

Pat Malone /'pæt mə'lʌun/. Also occas. **Pat Maloney.** [AND 1908.] Rhyming slang for 'own', esp. in the phr. **to be on one's Pat Malone,** to be on one's own, alone. Cf. PAT *n.*¹

1937 PARTRIDGE *Dict. Slang* 609 *Pat Malone.* Alone: Australian and New Zealand rhyming s.: C. 20. Gen. *do a thing, go, on one's Pat Malone,* hence *on one's Pat* (hence *pat*). **1950** WHITWORTH *Otago Interval* 111 This strictly to my Pat Maloney. **1984** BEATON *Outside In* 79 Di: Scared you might spend the Festive Season on Your Pat Malone? **1986** OWEN & PERKINS *Speaking for Ourselves* 68 There was I, on my Pat Malone, starting off on my first experience at humping a swag.

patoo, patoo-patoo, varr. PATU.

patotara. [Ma. /'pa:'to:tara/: Williams 272 *Pātōtara*..1. *Cyathodes juniperina.* 2. *Leucopogon australe (fraseri).* 3. *Botrychium ternatum.*]

1. *Leucopogon* (formerly *Cyathodes*) *fraseri* (fam. Epacridaceae), a low-growing bronze-coloured, prickly shrub of tussock grasslands, having juicy edible orange fruits. See also GOBLIN ORANGE, HEATH 1, *penny orange* (PENNY), TOTARA *n.*²

1867 HOOKER *Handbook* 767 Patotara...*Leucopogon Fraseri.* **1907** LAING & BLACKWELL *Plants NZ* 328 *Leucopogon Fra[s]eri* (*Fra[s]er's Leucopogon*)... Maori name *Pa-totara.* **1921** GUTHRIE-SMITH *Tutira* (1926) 169 A small densely rooting heath, patotara (*Leucopogon Fra[s]eri*), during this third period began to colonise suitable localities. **1947** [see GOBLIN ORANGE]. **1951** LEVY *Grasslands NZ* (1970) 10 Poa tussock..mingimingi, tauhinu, patotara, and *Pimelea* were the more dominant plants of the poorer areas. **1961** MARTIN *Flora NZ* 277 The Patotara (*L[eucopogon] fraseri*) is a dwarf, bronze-coloured, pungent-leafed, golden-fruited epacrid..common in heaths..throughout New Zealand. **1990** CROWE *Native Edible Plants* 40 According to Peter Buck and William Colenso, patotara fruits were eaten by the Maori. They taste sweet and juicy... (They are still popular with children on the Coromandel.)

2. *Botrychium australe,* a fern.

1867 HOOKER *Handbook* 767 Patotara...*Botrichium Virginicum.* **1872** *TrNZI* IV. 252 The bracken of the British Islands is represented by a closely similar plant..and the same remark applies to the representative forms, with the exception..of the patotara. **1952** RICHARDS *Chatham Is.* 17 *Botrychium*..*australe*... Southern Moonwort. Pa Totara.

pattie, pattoe, pattoo, varr. PATU.

patu. *Hist.* Also with much variety of early form as **patoo, pattie, pattoe, pattoo,** including reduplicated forms **patapatow**, **patoo-patoo**, **patu patu**. [Ma. /ˈpatu/: Williams 272 *Patu. 1.* v. trans. Strike, beat... *8. n.* Weapon.] **a.** A stone club used as a weapon. Also as **patu-pounamu**, a highly-valued patu made of greenstone. Cf. MERE 1, WADDY 1.

1769 MONKHOUSE 9 Oct. in Cook *Journals* (1955) I. 567 A short hand weapon which was fastned by a string round the wrist, was about 18 inches long, had a rounded head and thence formed into a flat elliptic shape: this weapon, we afterwards learnt, was called *Pattoo*. **1769** BANKS *Journal* 11 Oct. (1962) I. 406 One of [the Indians] sold his *patoo patoo* as he called it, a short weapon of green talk [= talc]. **1777** Feb. in Ledyard *Journal* (1783) (1963) 18 And when the men were busy..the warriors rushed out upon them and killed them with their Patapatows, and then divided their bodies among them. **1814** MARSDEN *Lett. & Jrnls.* (1932) 91 Some of his officers stood up and regulated all their movements both by word of command and signal made by their large pattoes ornamented with feathers which they held in their hands and kept in constant motion. **1830** CRAIK *New Zealanders* 266 These [spears], or rather the shorter sort, are also sometimes called by English writers Patoos, or Patoo-patoos. **1851** [see *mere pounamu* (MERE 2)]. **1878** BULLER *Forty Yrs. NZ* 249 They used a variety of manual weapons, such as the mere, the hani, the hoeroa, the patu..etc. **1882** POTTS *Out in Open* 171 They adopted a variety of methods for their [*sc.* eels'] capture..by means of the spears of different forms, or by the patu or club. **1898** MORRIS *Austral-English* 343 *Patu, n.* Maori generic term for all hand-striking weapons. **1930** REISCHEK *Yesterdays in Maoriland* (1933) 69 He showed me..also..a patu-punamu, or greenstone axe. **1967** BRATHWAITE *Evil Day* 380 Patu Club-like weapon, made from stone, bone or greenstone (jade) and occasionally elaborately-carved hardwood. In spite of club-like appearance, it was a short-sword, and with its sharpened edge, could lift the top from a man's skull, or pierce between his ribs with comparative ease. **1986** *Listener* 8 Feb. 19 Archaeologists sifted middens 50 years ago hoping to find glamorous artefacts, such as greenstone patu—the fighting club.

b. A pestle or pounder.

[**1820** LEE & KENDALL *Gram. & Vocab.* 191 Pátu pátu; A club for the purpose of extracting the roots of trees from the ground.] **1882** POTTS *Out in Open* 82 When used, it was soaked, roasted, and repeatedly beaten with a small club (patu) on a large smooth stone.

patu-paere, var. PATUPAIAREHE.

patupaiarehe. Also **patu-paere**. [Ma. /patuˈpaiarehe/: Williams 272 *patupaiarehe, paiarehe, patuparehe, parehe..* Sprite, fairy, malign or beneficent.] A supernatural being; a fairy-like being. Cf. TUREHU.

1883 DOMETT *Ranolf & Amohia* I. 168 To be as best he might, moreover, That *Patu-paere's* pet and lover! **1889** *TrNZI* XXI. 32 In those good old times the interior was occupied, they say, by Turehu or Patupaiarehe, a race short in stature and of fair skin. **1905** BAUCKE *White Man Treads* 63 Directly [the Maori] enters the domain of witchcraft, 'tipau' (ghouls), 'patupaiarehe' (fairy demons)..he becomes a fear-haunted, helpless perverter of truth! **1912** *NZ Free Lance Christmas Annual* (Wellington) 35 She was..as pretty as one of the patu-paiarehe, the 'little' people that in Waikato belief haunted the fairy mountain Pirongia. **1921** *Quick March* 11 Apr. 47 She knew what it was to become the wife of a Patu-paiarehe. **1936** LAMBERT *Pioneering Reminisc. Old Wairoa* 58 Even to-day the Tuhoe folk speak of what they called the Tangata Whenua (the race of men that dwelt in this little region), a smaller, much more gentle, and fair-skinned people called the 'Patu-pai-arehe,' or the fairy people. **1974** HENDERSON *Open Country Muster* 213 It led to tiny waterfall, as if this were the goal of the patupaiarehe. **1986** IHIMAERA *Matriarch* 15 We are immortal you and I, just like the patupaiarehe, the dream people who live in the hills. **1992** *Evening Post* (Wellington) 17 Jan. 13 [Caption] Moss-covered grottos—home of patupaiarehe, the little people.

patu patu, **patu-pounamu**: see PATU.

pau. [Ma. /ˈpau/: Williams 273 *Pau* (iv)..*Pseudolabrus coccineus*, red parrot-fish = *pūwaiwhakarua*.] *scarlet parrotfish* (PARROTFISH 2 (4)).

1927 PHILLIPPS *Bibliogr. NZ Fishes* (1971) 40 *Pseudolabrus coccineus*... Scarlet Parrotfish, Soldier; Puwai-whakarua or Pau. **1956** GRAHAM *Treasury NZ Fishes* 269 Scarlet Parrot-fish (Puwai-whakarua or Pau) *Pseudolabrus* (*Lunolabrus*) *miles*. **1966** DOOGUE & MORELAND *Sea Anglers' Guide* 258 Scarlet Parrotfish... *Other names*: *Pseudolabrus coccineus*; soldier, red soldierfish; pau, puwaiwhakarua (Maori).

paua /ˈpawə/. Also early **hepaooa** (=he paua), **pàhiwah**; freq. **pawa**. [Ma. /ˈpaːua/: Williams 273 *Pāua..1. Haliotis* of several species.] *Pl.* often *pauas*.

1. Also occas. as **common paua**, any of several species of the edible univalve *Haliotis* (fam. Haliotidae), close relative of the European ormer and North American abalone; also its iridescent shell, a popular material for jewellery and much used as a decorative inlay in Maori carving. See also EAR-SHELL, HALIOTIS, MUTTON-FISH, *sea-ear* (SEA 1 b), *Venus's ear* (VENUS 1). Cf. PAUA-SHELL. Often *attrib.*

[**1770** PARKINSON *Journal* (1773) 127 A Vocabulary of the Language of New Zealand... Hepaooa, *Ear-shells*. **1820** LEE & KENDALL *NZ Gram. & Vocab.* 191 Páua, *s.* A shell-fish so called. **c1826–28** BOULTBEE *Journal* (1986) 110 Muttonfish—pàhiwah.] **1840** POLACK *Manners & Customs* I. 121 The eyes in these figures are inlaid with pieces of the pearl mutton-fish-shell (*paua*) each in size to a tea-cup. **1843** DIEFFENBACH *Travels in NZ* II. 378 Pawa—a shell-fish (*Haliotis*). **1866** HUNT *Chatham Is.* 32 At her feet would be laid the treasures of the deep, the finest *pawa*, or the fattest *tarakia*. **1879** *Auckland Weekly News* 4 Jan. 17 At low water the great delicacies called pawa and pipis are to be obtained in any quantity. **1904** TREGEAR *The Maori Race* 188 A hook used with the line running behind a canoe was decorated with the iridescent shell of the haliotis (*paua*). **1924** BUCKNILL *Sea Shells NZ* 19 When two or three inches in length, the Pawa is, if anything, slightly paler inside, but very iridescent; rose pink and gold are the prevailing hues, with golden green and a suggestion of sky blue, the margin exhibiting a narrow edging of opaque slate blue. **1937** POWELL *Shellfish of NZ* 28 Pauas are seldom exposed to view even at lowest spring tides. **1946** *JPS* LV. 155 *Pāua*, a shellfish (*Haliotis iris*); there are three species (H. rugusoplicata and H. virginea also) but iris is much the most common, and is the one with the red-blue-green opalescence that has made it so popular for use as ornaments, etc., within the last few years: it was exported from the beginning of settlement for the making of buttons, but a rage has set in for the wearing of paua jewellery and the use of paua..goods, ink-stands, serviette-rings, etc., and a new name has been given to it sea-opal, and its deeper tints are as beautiful as opal if not as durable. **1959** SHADBOLT *New Zealanders* (1986) 117 'Who cares if we don't find pauas?' 'Me. I like them.' **1971** POWNALL *NZ Shells & Shellfish* 71 Paua Fritters... Soup or fritters are the only way to treat paua whose early beating has been neglected. **1988** *Listener* 9 Jan. 42 Marinated paua kebabs with tarragon and bacon.

2. With a modifier: **black (blackfoot, blackfooted), queen, silver(y) (pink, southern), virgin (white-footed), yellow-footed**.

(1) black (black-foot, blackfooted) paua. *Haliotis iris*, the common paua of the New Zealand coast.

1982 *Catch '82* Mar. 15 The blackfoot paua (*Haliotis iris*) is found all round the New Zealand coast. **1983** *Catch '83* June 13 The black-footed paua, *Haliotis iris*, is probably more strongly associated with New Zealand world-wide than any other shellfish, both through the export of meat..and especially through the souvenir and jewellery items made from its shell. **1985** *Shellfisheries Newsletter 25* 15 Of the three species of paua that occur around the New Zealand coastline only the black paua, *Haliotis iris* is fished commercially. **1986** PAUL *NZ Fishes* 170 Common paua *Haliotis iris*... Alternatively, black-footed paua. (The scientific name means rainbow-tinted sea-ear.)

(2) queen paua. *Haliotis australis*, a small yellow-footed paua having a shell pale yellow-brown on the outside and a silvery internal lustre. See also *silvery paua* (3) below.

1964 DEMPSEY *Little World of Stewart Island* 41 The first cod opened had something hard in its stomach, a queen paua shell, pale and lovely as pearl. **1970** [see 2 (3) below]. **1983** *Catch '83* June 13 A second New Zealand species..is the yellow-footed or queen paua, *H[aliotis] australis*. **1985** *Shellfisheries Newsletter 25* 15 We are looking at the possibility of culturing and on-growing the queen paua, *Haliotis australis*.

(3) silver(y) (pink, southern) paua. *Haliotis australis.* See *queen paua* (2) above.

1947 POWELL *Native Animals NZ* 24 Silvery Paua (*Haliotis australis*). Hihiwa. **1966** *Encycl. NZ* II. 757 *Paua, Silvery* (*Haliotis australis*), or hihiwa... This shellfish is smaller than the paua and easily distinguished from it by its silvery internal lustre, corrugated shell, and colour. **1970** PENNIKET *NZ Seashells in Colour* 34 Silvery or Queen Paua... Iridescent silvery interior, tinged with pink. **1983** GUNSON *Collins Guide to Seashore* 84 There are three species of paua in New Zealand; the virgin paua *Haliotis virginea* (70mm); the pink, silver or southern paua *H. australis* (100mm), and the common paua *H. iris*, usually about 150mm in length.

(4) virgin (white-footed) paua. *Haliotis virginea.* See quot. 1983.

1947 POWELL *Animals NZ* 24 Virgin Paua (*Haliotis virginea*). This is from 1 to 2½ inches in diameter and is more brilliantly iridescent than [the other two] species. **1970** PENNIKET *NZ Seashells in Colour* 8 Virgin Paua (*Haliotis virginea*)... A much smaller and rarer shell. **1983** *Catch '83* June 13 The virgin paua's foot does not appear to concentrate pigments to the same extent as either H[aliotis] iris or H. australis. This accounts for H. virginea's other name, the white-footed paua. **1985** *Shellfisheries Newsletter 27* 1 The sub-antarctic Auckland Islands possess fair-sized populations of the white-footed paua, *Haliotis virginea*.

(5) yellow-footed paua. *Haliotis australis.* See *queen paua* (2) above.

1986 PAUL *NZ Fishes* 171 Yellow-footed paua *Haliotis australis* Alternatively, queen paua. Distinguished by a pale yellowish brown shell with prominent exterior ridges;.. the animal's foot bright yellow with a black rim.

3. *Special Comb.* **paua diver**, one who dives for paua for sport or profit; **paua poacher**, one who takes paua illegally; **paua steak**, a paua foot

cooked as a whole, often tenderized by beating before cooking.
1991 *Dominion* (Wellington) 21 Feb. 3 Dr Day was giving evidence against [X] unemployed, and [Y] **paua diver**, who have pleaded not guilty to kidnapping and raping the woman. **1992** *Evening Post* (Wellington) 8 Feb. 44 The **paua poachers** off Barrett Reef..take note—we saw you. **1977** *Glenfield College Maori Cookbook* 50 **Paua Steaks**... Using a rolling pin or hammer, beat the white part of the paua to a pulp. Slice into long thin strips. **1988** *Listener* 9 Jan. 48 The following dish has become my favourite summer dinner—aside from those simplest beachside tastes of barbecued paua steaks and freshly boiled crayfish. **1990** CONEY *Out of the Frying Pan* 47 Endless summer evenings were spent sitting round the old dining room table..eating the tender paua steaks my mother cooked.

paua-shell.
1. The internally iridescent shell of species of paua, used by Maori craftsmen, and later, by New Zealanders generally, for the manufacture of artefacts and jewellery, for decoration and ornament, for fish lures, for use as a utensil, or as an article of trade. See also PEARL-SHELL.
1838 POLACK *NZ* I. 92 The eyes [of the carved figures] were formed of pieces of the pearl, paua, or mutton fish-shell. **1843** DIEFFENBACH *Travels in NZ* II. 44 They are caught..with a..(canoe-shaped) piece of wood, lined on one side with a thin plate of the pawa-shell (Haliotis). **1863** MOSER *Mahoe Leaves* 7 I feign sleep so successfully, that the paua shell is passed across my face. **1875** *TrNZI* VII. 61 Amongst the other objects..exhumed..were... several large pawa shells.., in which the holes near the exterior border are filled with fibres of flax or ti leaves, thus forming a vessel for the preservation of oil and other liquids. **1898** MORRIS *Austral-English* 344 *Paua*..the Maori name for the *Mutton-fish*. Also used as the name for Maori fish-hooks, made of the *paua* shell. **1912** MANSFIELD *Stories* (1984) 111 We walked together up the garden path... One little patch was divided off by pawa shells—presumably it belonged to the child. **1920** MANSFIELD *Stories* (1984) 245 There were three daisy heads on a laurel leaf for poached eggs, and the chocolate custard which she had decided to serve in the pawa shell she had cooked in it. **1936** HYDE *Check to your King* (1960) 158 Over the *pa* the dead man looks down, and the women cut their flesh with sharp *paua* shell until blood streams. **1972** MITCHELL *Pavlova Paradise* 183 *paua shell:* Product of West German jewellery industry. **1984** BRASCH *Collected Poems* 48 I send this peacock paua shell Azured in the rich under-sea.
2. a. *attrib.*
1938 LANCASTER *Promenade* 114 On her knees by the bright thread of the stream..Tiffany prayed to the stiff little god with its blank paua-shell eyes. **1949** BUCK *Coming of the Maori* 309 In New Zealand, owing to the abundance of the *Haliotis* (*paua*), elliptical and round eyes with *paua* shell inlay were in general use. **1957** [see DUCHESSE]. **1967** ASHTON-WARNER *Greenstone* 50 Above him the painted rafters, about him the glaring paua-shell eyes of the carving on the walls. **1981** MARSH *Black Beech & Honeydew* 59 The only [presents] I can remember were an extremely fancy paua-shell napkin ring engraved with a fisherman's head.
b. Special Comb. **paua-shell ashtray**, a paua shell used or fashioned as an ash-tray.
1959 SHADBOLT *New Zealanders* (1986) 107 She stubbed out her cigarette in the polished iridescent bowl of a paua-shell ashtray and walked to the window. **1960** HILLIARD *Maori Girl* 201 An empty cigarette packet, a paua-shell ashtray, full of butts. **1991** *Evening Post* (Wellington) 3 Jan. 16 We live in a time..where Kiwi culture is turned into fashionable accessories for a lifestyle. Paua shell ashtrays are the most obvious example.

paua slug. Any of several species of the land snail *Schizoglossa* (fam. Paryphantidae) from the resemblance of its shell to that of the marine paua *Haliotis*.
1937 POWELL *Shellfish NZ* 44 *Schizoglossa*. This is the 'paua' slug of which only one living species, *novoseelandica*, is known. **1953** *NZJST* XXXVB. 60 *Schizoglossa*, the endemic 'paua-slug', has a rudimentary shell which is 'incapable of containing the animal, being reduced to the function of a shield to the heart and lungs.' **1967** NATUSCH *Animals NZ* 75 [Caption] Paua slug, *Schizoglossa*. **1976** POWELL *Shells of NZ* (5edn.) 60 Schizoglossa. This is the 'paua' slug of which there are three living and two subfossil kinds: The shell is much smaller than the animal and it is shaped rather like the marine 'paua', *Haliotis*, but without the row of holes. **1990** FOORD *NZ Descr. Animal Dict.* 302 Paua Slug. *Schizoglossa novoseelandica*. A large land snail of the central NI with the shell only a shield, 6–20mm long, shaped like a paua shell, on its back.

pav.
a. [AND 1966.] Abbrev. of PAVLOVA.
1966 TURNER *Eng. Lang. Austral. & NZ* 173 Cooking terms noticed by newcomers (other than Australians) are..*pikelets*..and *pavlova cake*, a meringue sweet, sometimes shortened to *pav*. **1973** *Truth* 9 Oct. 17 A big do, with 500 guests. Oysters, crays, chook, ham on the bone, pav, the works. **1982** BURTON *Two Hundred Yrs. NZ Food* 131 But whichever way it crossed the Tasman at first, 'pav' quickly made its way to both nations' hearts..: the mystique surrounding the expert pav maker is largely over-rated. **1988** MCGILL *Dict. Kiwi Slang* 83 *pavs and savs* pavlovas and savaloys, the once typical serving at Kiwi gatherings.
b. *fig.* See quot.
1987 *Evening Post* (Wellington) 24 Aug. 2 [Heading] Kiwis still aspire to 'pav' property. The average New Zealander still aspires to a slice of the great New Zealand property pavlova, says Roger Hallinan, the new president of the New Zealand Institute of Valuers. He says more than two decades have passed since political scientist, and now UK Labour MP, Austin Mitchell, described New Zealand as a quarter-acre, pavlova paradise.
Hence **pav** *v. joc.*, to use (an ingredient) in producing a pavlova.
1992 *Evening Post* (Wellington) 2 Jan. 6 The average rhode island red is at fever pitch all summer, churning out a never-ending stream of yolks and whites to be stuffed, quiched, pavved, pied, sandwiched.

pavlova /pæv'lʌuvə/. Also **pavlova cake**. Occas. init. cap. [f. the name of Anna *Pavlova* (1885–1931), Russian ballerina, who toured New Zealand in 1926, the shape and appearance of the original gelatine dessert also suggesting a ballerina's tutu: AND 1940.]
[*Note*] The name *pavlova* has been applied to two distinct foods: (a) first, to a moulded jelly with multicoloured layers; (b) second, as *pavlova cake*, thence elliptically *pavlova*, to a meringue cake, possibly orig. as one of a number of small cakes, later mainly as a larger filled or topped confection, at first eaten as a cake, then as a dessert or party sweet.
1. *Obs.* A moulded jelly with multicoloured layers, suggesting a tutu in shape and appearance.
1927 *Davis Dainty Dishes* (6edn.) 11 [Heading below a coloured picture of a fluted ('pleated' or 'tutued') turned-out moulded jelly mound, coloured in layers from top to bottom green, white, orange-yellow, and red, and standing on a plain dish, with no background] *Pavlova*... 1½ cups hot water 1 cup orange juice ½ cup milk 3 dessertspoons Davis gelatine 6 dessertspoons sugar Flavouring cochineal—sap green colouring... Dissolve all but a teaspoonful of Gelatine..[arrange orange or other fruits around base: serve with cream or custard]. **1937** DAVIS *Dainty Dishes* (13edn.; also 1943 edn.) 57 Pavlova. 6 Servings. Ingredients. Davis Gelatine, Hot water, Sugar, ¼ cup milk, Slices of oranges, ¾ cup orange juice, Lemon essence, Vanilla essence, Cochineal, Green colouring, Citric acid.
2. A meringue shell or cake usu. topped or filled with whipped cream and/or fruit.
[*Note*] The cake or confection was formerly called a *meringue cake* or *meringue (sandwich) sponge*, in which vinegar was included at least by 1934. Cf. 1934 *The Marigold Book of Recipes* 14 *Meringue Cake* Beat very stiff three egg whites..sugar..vinegar..vanilla..bake in slow oven till meringue is firm... Turn upside down..spread with whipped cream flavoured with passionfruit... decorate with chopped nuts and cherries.
a. As **pavlova cake** (distinguish esp. quot. 1929 which may refer to small cakes), **pavlova sponge** (a 'sandwich' variety); occas (see quot. 1971) **pavlova meringue**. Also *attrib.* or Comb. **pavlova cake tin**.
1929 MCKAY *Practical Home Cook.* 155 *Pavlova Cakes* whites of two eggs beaten.. sugar..cornflour.. coffee essence..chopped walnuts. Cook like meringues. They are delightful..a novelty. **c1933** FINLAY *Cookery* 125 Meringue Sponge Sandwich or Pavlova Cake... Whites of 3 eggs 7 or 8 ozs. Sugar Pinch of Salt 1 Teaspoon vanilla essence 1 Teaspoon vinegar. Suitable tins, 8in. diam. Sandwich tins or special Pavlova cake tin. Method.—Add salt to egg whites. Whisk them stiffly; add sugar gradually and continue beating for a few minutes. Carefully mix in vinegar and essence. Place in greased tins and cook in a slow oven for 1 to 1½ hours. [When cooked, turn out carefully. Fasten cakes together with a filling of whipped cream, add fruit, and top off.] **1936** *St. Mary's Recipe Book* 63 *Pavlova Cake*..sugar..vinegar..egg whites... Beat egg whites very stiff, add sugar..add any colouring matter required..bake slowly. **c1939** BASHAM *Aunt Daisy's Book of Recipes* 153 *Pavlova Cake*..castor sugar..whites of 3 eggs, beaten very stiff..vanilla..vinegar... Grease a piece of grease-proof paper, hold it under the cold tap for a second, shake the water off, then pile the cake upon it either in a round or square shape and bake. **1969** HASCOMBE *Down & Almost Under* 67 However, those people holding the view that the meringue-like delicacy..the Pavlova Cake, is her ultimate achievement, are guilty in their assessment of women. **1971** ARMFELT *Catching Up* 18 Never had he seen such cakes: pavlova meringues, jelly sponges, passion-fruit cream sponges. **1974** *Otago Daily Times* (Dunedin) 2 May 10 Pavlova cake has for so many years been a staple of any party.
b. *Ellipt.* as **pavlova**.
1953 *Listener* 31 Dec. 143 A delicious party sweet—a New Zealand specialty is called Pavlova. I understand the name was given to it when the famous dancer came to New Zealand with a company many years ago. **1961** *Edmonds Sure to Rise Cook. Book* 25 Pavlova. 3 Egg Whites... Beat egg whites until quite stiff, fold in sugar, add vanilla and vinegar. **1964** DICK *High Country Family* 42 By this time I had sneaked a backward glance. Feet *and* rifles were reposing on the boxes of meringues..sponges and pavlovas. **1973** MCELDOWNEY *Arguing with My Grandmother* 38 My mother dispensed tea and pavlova from the tea wagon. **1987** *Otago Daily Times* (Dunedin) 1 Jan. ('Prester John' column.) I would like to point out that both the Irish version and the Australian recipe are for a *meringue* cake (sugar and egg whites) and not for the traditional New Zealand

pavlova which has a *soft centre*, because of the inclusion of vinegar and cornflour in the N.Z. recipe. I don't think we'll ever discover who had the original idea which transformed a hard oversweet dessert into the delicious dessert of today. **1991** More (Auckland) Mar. 66 I felt there should have been cheerios and tomato sauce, meat pies, tinned spaghetti pizzas, pavlovas, lamingtons, sausage rolls, fat club sandwiches, beer and thick cups of steaming tea.

3. Used *attrib.* in special Comb. **pavlova cake-tin**, see quot. 1933 1 a above; **pavlova mouse**, a mouse-shaped pavlova meringue.

1988 *Press* (Christchurch) in *Listener* Mar. 5 The Wellington District Court heard how the pair left with 24 **pavlova mice** after a Johnsonville bakery was burgled on December 18.

4. *transf.* or *fig.* **pavlova brigade**, home cooks confined to the competitive cooking of conventional dishes; **(Quarter-acre) Pavlova Paradise**, see QUARTER-ACRE 3.

1987 SLIGO *Final Things* 29 It will help civilization..to know your wife is independent. Not of the pavlova and cream-puff brigade.

paw, var. PA n.²

pawa, var. PAUA.

pawaiwhakarua, var. PUWAIWHAKARUA.

pay, *v. Goldmining*. [Spec. use of *pay* to yield a return or profit: AND 1852.] Of a claim or a mineral deposit, to be worth working.

1862 *Otago Witness* (Dunedin) 23 Aug. 7 We tried a number of small bars that we thought would pay about an ounce a-day by working with a cradle. **1862** *Otago Goldfields & Resources* 24 With an immense number of blind gullies, all more or less auriferous, and a creek that paid and is promising to pay for a considerable distance yet..who can predict the future of the Woolshed?

Hence **paying** *ppl. a.*, of a claim, profitable to work.

1857 *Lyttelton Times* 5 Aug. 5 We are now satisfied that we have a good paying claim; my mates think that now we have not less than 48 ounces which we have got in these six days.

payable, *a.*

1. *Goldmining*. [Spec. use of *payable* capable of yielding an adequate return: see OED *a.* 3; AND 1859.] **a.** Of gold recovered, of a profitable amount; of auriferous ground, a claim, etc., profitable to work, returning more than expenses.

1861 *NZ Goldfields 1861* (1976) 34 Thus the gold which, when spread over a large area is not 'payable', is found in 'rich' quantities when circumstances have brought it to one spot. **1862** *Otago Goldfields & Resources* 2 The river and creeks that run through them are auriferous—are payable. **1871** MONEY *Knocking About in NZ* 81 We had no discovery of anything payable in the way of gold. **1879** HAAST *Geol. Canterbury and Westland* 101 They were bound for a creek..where some payable finds..had just been made by some prospecting party. **1939** *NZGeol.SB* (NS) No.39 110 The gravel beds are quite payable, but a difficulty is that bands of clay overlie the wash.

b. In the collocations: **payable gold, goldfield, prospect, washdirt**.

1866 ANGAS *Polynesia* 133 During the first fortnight there have been several rushes up to the..Southern Alps, where the diggers are finding good, **payable gold**. **1871** MONEY *Knocking About NZ* 47 The hope of being the first to discover either a prospect of payable gold, or some open country fit for farming purposes. **1914** PFAFF *Diggers' Story* 42 We..did not locate payable gold. **1862** *Otago Witness* (Dunedin) 23 Aug. 4 I am of the opinion that it is a **payable gold-field**. **1898** HOCKEN *Contributions* 198 A petition was presented to the Council asking that a substantial reward should be offered for the discovery of a payable gold-field, and so prevent a further loss of population. **1863** *AJHR* D-6 14 I consider the prospects of this [Tuapeka] Gold-field are very much above the average of what, in Victoria, would be called '**payable ground**'. **1887** PYKE *Hist. Early Gold Discoveries Otago* (1962) 60 [He] did not succeed in discovering payable ground anywhere. **1862** *Otago Witness* (Dunedin) 23 Aug. 7 About twelve or fifteen miles below the junction..we first obtained **payable prospects**. **1892** PYKE *Gold-Miners' Guide* 8 [R.124] Holders of prospecting *areas* must report the discovery of **payable wash-dirt** to the Warden within three days from the date of such discovery.

2. *transf.* Of fleeces, returning a good profit to the farmer.

1922 PERRY *Sheep Farming* 96 Wethers will thrive..and clip big payable fleeces, besides taking little attention.

pay out, *v. Obs.* To scream.

1866 *Lyttelton Times* 26 Sept. [Maungatapu murder trial] Yes, you old bu— if you pay out—that is scream.

pay-rock. *Quartzmining*. [Used elsewhere but recorded earliest in NZ: see OED *pay-* 2.] Auriferous rock which yields a return greater than the cost of working it.

1868 *Thames Miners' Guide* 13 The 'pay-rock' forms bands or streaks.

pay ten shillings in the pound: see SHILLING 1.

peacow, var. PIKAU.

peak, *v.* [Prob. a spec. use of Brit. dial. *peak* to look sickly: cf. also OED *peak v.*¹ 4.] To fail to perform; to lose performance.

1937 SCOTT *Barbara Prospers* 206 The horses had peaked on him. **1947** NEWTON *Wayleggo* 49 The sheep 'peaked', and the six-mile drive over the Birdwood Saddle took us ten hours. **1971** NEWTON *Ten Thousand Dogs* 145 I nearly peaked when the time came [to shoot my old dog] but the old chap never even knew I was there, and it was over in a split second. *Ibid.* 168 *Peak*: To knock up or jib at doing a certain job.

Hence **peaked** *ppl. a.*, become exhausted.

1949 NEWTON *High Country Days* 196 Peaked: Knocked up—become exhausted.

pea, pie, pud /pʌd/. Also **pea, pie and spud**. [An alteration of *pea, pie, and spud*.] The usual familiar name of the former main fare at pie-carts, a pie topped or surrounded with mashed potatoes and boiled peas.

1959 SLATTER *Gun in My Hand* 163 We strolled down [to the pie-cart] late at night for pea pie and spud steaming hot in the white wrapping paper through the hatch. **1962** LAWLOR *More Wellington Days* 64 It was a rare treat [c1905]..[to] order a 'pea-pie-pud'. For sixpence you would have juggled up for you from the stove a steaming plate of pie surrounded with a collar of green and white (peas and potatoes). **1963** WALLIS *Point of Origin* 201 This is called pea pie pud. It is written on the menu over there on the wall and you may order it simply by saying pea pie pud without any inflection. **1978** in Cole *It Was So Late* (1978) xii John was..treated to a fare markedly superior to the 'pea, pie, and pud' he had at the pie cart on the way back from university on week nights. **1983** HENDERSON *Down from Marble Mountain* 201 I got slender payments to buy pea pie an' pud. **1992** *North & South* (Auckland) Apr. 106 I went to a place they called the Star Cafe and they had..a guy serving sloppy old pies that they called pea, pie and pud.

pea rifle.

a. Recorded earliest in New Zealand in the obsolete sense of 'a rifle with a thick barrel and a small round bullet like a pea' (see OED *pea* 6, 1862).

1845 DEANS in *Pioneers* (1964) 43 Some people shoot them with small pea rifles; they are nearly as large and as handsome as a cushat [= wood-pigeon (Sc. dial.)] and fine eating.

b. *transf.* A common name for a .22 rifle.

1904 *NZ Observer* 23 Apr. 3 We were promised legislation to put down the pea rifle nuisance. **1913** *Ibid.* 24 May 5 The average mother is quite deceived by the term 'pea' rifle—believing, no doubt, that the weapons are used for throwing small vegetables about. **1938** *Auckland Weekly News* 20 Apr. 13 We had a row and I shot him with a pea-rifle. **1950** THE SARGE *Excuse my Feet* 9 It would be great..being a real soldier—not just a blundering Home Guard..with a pea rifle or a broomstick for a weapon. **1976** LORETZ *Moments of Life* 6 The family has been sitting eating their evening meal at the kitchen tale when a pea rifle bullet shot between them and lodged in the wall behind them. **1994** LASENBY *Dead Man's Head* 63 I'm saving for a pea-rifle when I'm old enough.

pearler, var. PURLER.

pearl-shell. *Obs.* In occas. early use for PAUA-SHELL 1.

1838 POLACK *NZ* I. 92 The eyes [of the carved figures] were formed of pieces of the pearl, paua, or mutton fish-shell. **1847** ANGAS *Savage Life* I. 263 Many of the natives..were employed in cooking the fish of the *pawa*, or pearl-shell (*haliotis*), in the ashes.

pearlside. Also **southern pearlside**. *Maurolicus muelleri* (fam. Sternoptychidae). See esp. quot. 1990.

1875 *TrNZI* VII. 250 Maurolicus australis... The Southern Pearlside. **1927** PHILLIPPS *Bibliogr. NZ Fishes* (1971) 15 *Maurolicus pennanti australis*... Southern Pearlside. **1956** GRAHAM *Treasury NZ Fishes* 400 Pearlside *Triarcus australis* (Hector) **1982** AYLING *Collins Guide* (1984) 114 *Pearlside* (Elongate hatchetfish)... Off New Zealand this species is one of the commonest fishes caught in midwater trawls. **1990** FOORD *NZ Descriptive Animal Dictionary* 305 Pearlside. *Maurolicus muelleri*. A green-blue fish with purple light-organs..common offshore from surface to deep water... Other Names: Elongate Hatchetfish,.. Southern Pearlside.

pea souper. *Obs.* A teetotaller.

1893 JACOBSON *Tales of Banks Peninsula* 246 The Chaplain said [to the Publican] 'I'll take a glass of water.' 'We don't sell that here; there's plenty in the creek, and if you ever come in again don't expect any bunting, because we don't fly it for peasoupers.'

pea walker, var. PIWAKAWAKA.

peel, *v. Shearing*. [Joc. use of *peel* to strip: AND 1912.] *trans.* See quot. 1952.

1952 MEEK *Station Days* 110 Peel: To shear the wool from a sheep. **1981** SUTHERLAND & TAYLOR *Sunrise*

45 Pine placed the sheep on its back on the board and began the long blow. 'Like peeling bananas, eh?' Pine laughed. Bill didn't know that was a traditional shearing expression. **1987** OGONOWSKA-COATES *Boards, Blades & Barebellies* 97 *Peel.* To shear the wool from a sheep.

pee-u /'pi͵u/, *Obs.* Also **pee-oo**. [f. the call.] *sooty albatross* (ALBATROSS *Phoebetria palpebrata*).
1865 HUTTON *Birds Southern Ocean* 233 Sooty Albatross—called 'Pee-u' by sealers. **1966** FALLA et al. *Birds of NZ* 35 At nesting places a distinctive call [of the sooty albatross], seldom heard at sea, consists of two clear notes which may be transcribed as 'Pee-oo'. Hence its vernacular name current among sealers and seafarers.

peewee. Also *joc.* **piss-wee**. [Found also in US and Brit. dial.: see OED 3 b, 1848.] A marble.
1933 SCANLAN *Tides of Youth* 153 Reverend Mother talks of when she used to give you marbles for being a good little boy—pee-wees and agates. **1951** FRAME *Lagoon* (1961) 116 I had pee-wees and bully taws and changers that weren't made of glass mind you. **1972** peewee, piss-wee [see GLASSIE].

peg, *n.*[1] WW1. *Obs.* [f. Sc. dial. *peg* a shilling: AND 1882.] A shilling.
1887 [see HERRING *n.*[2]]. **1917** *Chron. NZEF* 16 May 137 He dreamt he'd got his fourteen 'peg' And buttoned it 'Down South'. **1937** PARTRIDGE *Dict. Slang* 615 peg... A shilling: Scottish c[ant]: 1839, Brandon; Jennings, 1926. Also among New Zealand soldiers in G.W.

peg, *n.*[2] [f. Sc. dial. *peg* a policeman: see EDD *n.*[3]; SND *n.* 3, 1862.] A policeman.
1862 *Puketoi Station Diary* (Hocken TS) 25 Aug. Fine. Diggers passing all day [to rush at Molyneux]. Keddell & two pegs came and stayed all night.

peg, *v. Goldmining.*
1. Usu. **peg out**, occas. **peg** or **peg off**. To mark out (a mining claim) with pegs or stakes.
[**1892** PYKE *Gold-Miners' Guide* 9 Every claim and licensed holding must be marked by a post 3in. square or 3in. in diameter, standing 2ft. above the surface, erected at each corner of the claim, or as near there to as the nature of the ground will permit.] **1867** COOPER *Digger's Diary* 8 Nov. (1978) 10 Then the word is given to the intruders by their leader, to peg off the claim..and the claim is thus unjustly, though..legally seized. **1873** PYKE *Wild Will Enderby* (1889, 1974) I. iv 17 He progressed up the Gorge trying 'prospects' in many places, and at length he was satisfied to 'peg out'. **1881** NESFIELD *Chequered Career* 74 My 'gaffer' pegged out a claim for himself on which to erect our butcher's shop. **1896** MOFFATT *Adventures* (1979) 51 When we arrived at 'One Spec Gully' we found it pegged out from the Falls nearly to the Forks. **1968** SEDDON *The Seddons* 44 Could I peg out a claim of my own and in a dish swill dirt to find if there were any specks of gold in the pan? **1976** BROWN *Difficult Country* 63 Many preferred the independent life of the alluvial miner, and claims were soon pegged off at the Doughboy.

Hence **pegging**, **pegging off**, **pegging out** *vbl. n.*, see quot. 1892.
1867 COOPER *Digger's Diary* 8 Nov. (1978) 10 The whole day taken up in pegging off, an important and essential operation, as till that is done we are not safe, being liable to the unpleasant visits of any who are inclined to jump our claim. **1892** SWANTON *Notes on NZ* 149 'Pegging out' means planting pegs at the four corners of the piece of ground. **1940** HOWARD *Rakiura* 296 Claims had been staked from the coast upward. (This pegging was duly carried out..afterwards.)

2. *fig.* In the phr. **peg out one's last claim** [an elaboration of *peg out*], to die.
1876 KENNEDY *Colonial Travel* 236 'Ah,' said the captain, his conversation acquiring a local colouring, 'many a poor fellow has pegged out his last claim there.'

peggy bag. [Used elsewhere but recorded earliest in NZ: see OED *peggy n.* 7.] A kind of woman's handbag, usu. with handles (and, so OED, with outside pockets).
1910 *Truth* 9 July 7 The things stolen were easily portable... There were a number of 'peggy' bags... Gladys Wood, Bealey Avenue, said that between 9 and 10 p.m. on February 18 a trinket..two tiki curios and a peggy bag were stolen from her bedroom. **1955** BOSWELL *Dim Horizons* (1956) 146 [Mother and daughter c 1890s] made pretty necklaces from the dried seed-pods of the field flax..and, most treasured of all, little peggy-bags of velvet, lined with bright silk or satin and threaded with silk cord for handles.

peggy square. [f. the name of *Peggy* Cook (née Huse) (1926–1994), who was associated with popularizing 'blanket squares' during the 1930s Depression: see obituary in *Hutt News* (Lower Hutt) 18 Jan. 1994.] A knitted, occas. crocheted, woollen square with a side of about 15 cm, numbers of which are sewn together to make rugs, etc., often for charitable purposes; elsewhere usu. called 'blanket square'.
1932 TS Letter of 9 July from H.C. Hassall, Merchandise Manager, DIC, Wellington to Miss Peggy Huse, Lower Hutt. For a little girl of six you have become quite famous during the last week..since we know that you worked out the number of stitches and the size of the needles to use for the Wool Squares the 2YA Children knit and which have been given your name. That is why we were so glad to have your photograph in our windows with the beautiful bedcovers made from Peggy Squares that are to be given to people who are badly in need of warm blankets. **1951** 21st May Correspondence School request on radio 2YA Wellington. Peggy squares for rugs for displaced children. **1982** BREAM *Island of Fear* 82 Mrs Wetherby probably knits peggy squares for the Ladies' Guild. **1989** *The Web* (Quarterly Jrnl. NZ Spinning, Weaving and Woolcrafts) 20 Nov. 4 I thought knitters all over the world knew about peggy squares, and was not aware that it is a New Zealand term. Recently, Elizabeth Prescott of Christchurch sent me copies of several short items published in 'Reporter's Diary' of the Christchurch Press, July 1986. The story goes that a visitor to this country was puzzled about the term 'peggy squares', although she was familiar with 'blanket squares'. **1992** *Listener* 6 Jan. 6 In late October, the staff at R. Nielsen's Footwear in Blenheim..began to knit a 'blanket of concern' for the unemployed... The staff set out to knit one 15cm x 15cm (6 x 6 inch) peggy square for every unemployed person in the country. **1992** p.c. Heather Halcrow Nicholson (North Shore) 12 Mar. In 1930 a Mrs Lewis [known to 2YA Wellington's listeners as 'The Wool Woman'] visited..a farm at Haywards in the Hutt Valley... The younger daughter of the family then..4..was learning to knit and had made several little squares from scraps of wool. Her mother had joined them together to make a cover for the..dolls cradle... Mrs Lewis discussed the idea [of promoting mass knitting of squares to make blankets for the Depression needy] with Aunt Molly who conducted the children's session... If anything came of her idea Mrs Lewis had already decided that she would call the squares 'Peggy Squares' after the little girl [Peggy Huse] who had given her the idea... With Aunt Molly's help the idea caught on... Thousands of squares came in from all over New Zealand.

pekapeka. [Ma. /'pekapeka/: Williams 275 *pekapeka..1.* [Various] bats.] BAT *n.*[1]
[Note] *pekapeka* is often commonly known from its use in the name *Ruapekapeka*, conventionally transl. 'Bats' Nest', the stronghold pa of the northern chief, Hone Heke (1810?–50).
1838 POLACK *NZ* I. 304 The *pekápeká* or bat, and various small batlets, are very common in the land, but none of the vampire species. **1843** DIEFFENBACH *Travels in NZ* II. 378 Peka peka—a bat, a game so called. **1867** HOCHSTETTER *NZ* 160 New Zealand possesses only..the bat (*Pekapeka*, two species) and a small indigenous rat (*Kiore*). **1888** BULLER *Birds NZ* II. 98 We are standing on the banks of the Horowhenua Lake..a solitary Pekapeka is flitting silently overhead, chasing..the minute insect-life upon which this bat subsists. **1904** HUTTON & DRUMMOND *Animals NZ* 33 The Long-tailed Bat.—Pekapeka. *Chalinolobus morio.* c**1920** BEATTIE *Trad. Lifeways Southern Maori* (1994) 190 Another old man said that the pekapeka raised an awful smell. It had a skin like a kiore..or like a hinereta (English mouse). **1930** REISCHEK *Yesterdays in Maoriland* (1933) 77 The only original New Zealand mammal is a little bat, called pekapeka by the Maoris. **1947** POWELL *Native Animals NZ* 92 Long-tailed Bat (*Chalinolobus morio*), Pekapeka of the Maoris, shelters in caves and hollow trees. **1966** *Encycl. NZ* II. 169 Two species of bat occur in New Zealand... The Maoris called them 'pekapeka' and they were the subject of an old native proverb predicting evil. **1990** [see BAT *n.*[1]].

pekau, peko(w), varr. PIKAU.

Pekeha, var. PAKEHA.

Pelorus Jack.

1. The name of a dolphin (prob. a Risso's dolphin, *Grampus griseus*), famous in folk legend (see esp. quot. 1950) and protected by Order in Council in 1904, which escorted ships through French Pass near the entrance of Pelorus Sound between 1888 and 1912. Compare OPO.
1904 *Weekly News* 4 Feb. [Caption] Pelorus Jack, the white porpoise, which attends all the steamers crossing French Pass. **1912** *Truth* 27 July 1 Pelorus Jack hasn't been seen lately. It's too good to be true. Pelorus Jack has made more liars of men than did the old-time 'Bona-fide traveller' gag. **1914** *JPS* XXIII. 176 It was about the year 1860 that Te Matoro-hanga gave me the history of Tuhi-rangi, the fish you Pakehas call Pelorus Jack. **1917** *Chron. NZEF* 25 July 244 Quicker 'un Pelorus Jack after a chunk of rump steak..I was. **1924** LYSNAR *New Zealand* 104 In the Nelson and Picton waters of Cook Straits is to be seen a remarkable white fish, known as 'Pelorus Jack'. **1933** *Proc. of the Linnean Soc. of London* CXLVI. 2 Dr. W. Rushton Parker exhibited lantern-slides of Pelorus Jack alongside of a common dolphin. **1947** [see DOLPHIN 2 (5)]. **1950** in *In their Own Words* (1988) 91 It was this Pelorus Jack... He was a species of whale and he used to come up and blow and then he would go down and get some more fish. **1966** *Encycl. NZ* II. 761 After his protection, wide publicity made Pelorus Jack world famous; postcards based on photographs were much used, and many tourists..made the trip to Nelson specially to see him. **1985** DAWSON *NZ Whale & Dolphin Digest* 105 Risso's Dolphins are active animals... They are not especially interested in boats (although the famous Pelorus Jack was a Risso's Dolphin). **1990** BAKER *Whales & Dolphins* 103 The famous New Zealand dolphin 'Pelorus Jack', which rode the bow waves of

steamers passing across the outside of Pelorus Sound and Admiralty Bay, Marlborough, between 1888 and 1912, was a Risso's dolphin.

2. *transf.* or *fig.*, a nickname for a self-appointed escort.

1968 SLATTER *Pagan Game* 50 On Sunday mornings he always tapped on the bedroom window of Mr O'Meara to wake them up and then he walked with the whole family of them to the Catholic church, waited outside.. and walked home with them again. Mr O'Meara always called him Pelorus Jack.

pen, *n.* [Spec. use of *pen* a small enclosure for domestic animals.]

1. *Whaling.* See quot.

1838 POLACK *NZ* II. 417 These vessels are fitted with tryworks or fire-places..; the fire-place is built of bricks, so laid below as to form channels for water to preserve the floor or main deck from injury. The water is kept confined by a square, formed with a two-inch plank, around the sides, negligence in leaving this pen (as it is termed) dry, has caused many accidents.

2. *Farming.* **a.** [AND 1879.] Any one of a number of small enclosures in the sheep-holding area of a shearing shed from which a shearer draws his sheep. See also CATCHING-PEN 1, HOLDING-PEN 1.

1880s *Teviot Station shearing rules* in Martin *Forgotten Worker* (1990) 95 No Shearer shall go into a pen to catch a Sheep after 'Smoke-oh' or any interval, or 'Clear the Board' has been called. Any Shearer already in a pen may take out a Sheep. **1912** BOOTH *Five Years NZ* 27 Each man has his pen, which is cleared out and refilled as often as necessary. **1933** *Press* (Christchurch) (Acland Gloss.) 11 Nov. 15 *Pen.*—(1) A small yard; a division in the sheep-holding part of a wool shed. (2) Shearers catch out of a *p[en]*, and when they apply for work they ask for a *p[en]*. 'Will you keep me a *p[en]* for next year, boss?' is often their farewell. Two shearers usually catch out of one pen and are called *p[en]-mates*. **1987** OGONOWSKA-COATES *Boards, Blades & Barebellies* 97 *Pen.* A small fenced-in area. The sheep-holding part of a wool shed is divided into pens connected to the board by a swing door. Shearers catch their sheep out of these pens, which are usually shared, the shearers being pen-mates.

b. By synecdoche, a job shearing; the right to shear in a shed.

1933 'keep me a pen' [see 2 a above]. **1946** ACLAND *Early Canterbury Runs* 166 Clayton was an 'open shed', that is, the shearers were not engaged beforehand, but turned up and took their chance of a pen on the advertised starting day. **1964** DICK *High Country Family* 70 Lend me some suitable clothes and I'll take a pen alongside you. Must be nigh on forty years since I held a pair of shears. **1978** JARDINE *Shadows on Hill* 130 Applications for a pen (the right to shear) had closed months ago. **1986** RICHARDS *Off the Sheep's Back* 108 When Charlie told me that the award for shearing in Australia was two pounds one shilling per 100, I told him I would like to get a pen over there.

c. Special Comb. **pen-mate**, a shearer who takes sheep from the same pen as another shearer.

1897 WRIGHT *Station Ballads* 58 But I somehow fancy we'll all be pen-mates on the day when they call the Roll of the Sky. **1933** [see 2 a above]. **1952** MEEK *Station Days* 111 When two shearers share a catching-pen, they are said to be 'Penmates'. **1975** HARPER *Eight Daughters* 56 Two of the shearers in particular..who were pen mates, carried on a friendly conversation the whole day. **1986** RICHARDS *Off the Sheep's Back* 94 On the third day we were joined by the sixth shearer, who was to be my pen-mate.

3. The area on the waterfront where men gathered in search of work.

1964 MIDDLETON *Walk on Beach* 216 He taught me more about handling cargo..than anyone else I met. Every morning I used to look for him among the crowd at the pen. *Ibid.* 228 The morning found me down at the pen as usual. The..pen was full of seagulls looking for work.

pen, *v.* Usu. as **pen up**. [Spec. use of *pen v.* to confine animals: cf. OED *pen v.*¹ 3 b.]

1. *intr.* Of a sheep-dog, to work sheep into pens.

1934 LILICO *Sheep Dog Memoirs* 26 A bitch pup I sold..went direct to freezing works to pen up and developed into a first class forcer and backer.

2. *trans.* and *intr. Shearing.* To keep catching-pens full of sheep; to move (sheep) into catching pens. See also PENNER-UP.

1960 SCRYMGEOUR *Memories of Maoriland* 50 Loppies, rousies, and even young Jim, who was assisting to pen up, followed out from the side door to where the shoots from the stands gave the nearest exit. *Ibid.* 110 The Maori buck did the shearing, with machines, boys penned, and did pick-up work. **1981** CHARLES *Black Billy Tea* 72 I was the rouseabout—penning up the sheep, sweeping the shearing board and bailing [*sic*] the wool.

Hence **penning up** *vbl. n.*, the work of ensuring that catching-pens are full of sheep.

1922 PERRY *Sheep Farming* 16 The shearing board should be of good width, and be separated from the holding pens by a solid wall, so as to facilitate penning up. **1950** *NZJAg.* Oct. LXXXI. 310 One daggy sheep can stain quite a few clean sheep when penning up is in progress. **1975** HARPER *Eight Daughters* 43 Latterly he..did all the penning up in the shed and helped in any way he could. **1981** [see SHEEPO A].

pen and ink.

1. WW1. [f. a play on *peninsula*.] The Gallipoli Peninsula. See also PENINSULA 1.

1935 MITCHELL & STRONG in Partridge *Slang Today* 286 [The] following [were] employed by those who served in the [Great] War. *Pen and Ink* and *Inch and Pinch*, the Peninsula of Gallipoli. **1937** PARTRIDGE *Dict. Slang* 616 *Pen and Ink*, Gallipoli *Pen*insula: New Zealand soldiers': in 1915; occ. after.

2. [AND 1967.] Rhyming slang for 'drink'.

1963 *Truth* 21 May 19 We wander over to the bar for a pen and ink, where the talk gets round to tomato sauces. pen and ink... drink

penguin.

1. a. [In locally significant use mainly with a defining word.] A flightless seabird of the fam. Spheniscidae with webbed feet and flipper-like wings, found only in the southern hemisphere. See also HOIHO, KORORA.

1773 FORSTER *Resolution Jrnl.* 1 Apr. (1982) II. 244 We described..fish & birds & a Seal..& a small Pinguin, of about the size of a small Teal; and different of all those I have seen before. **1899** DOUGLAS in *Mr Explorer Douglas* (1957) 286 It is a wonderfull [*sic*] sight to see a penguin coming through the surf. **1964** GLOVER *Enter Without Knocking* 37 In Plimmerton, in Plimmerton, The little penguins play. **1987** SPARKS & SOPER *Penguins* 15 Although Antarctica boasts the greatest concentration of penguin numbers, New Zealand and its associated islands have no less than six species.

b. Special Comb. **penguin oil**, oil rendered from penguin carcasses (also *attrib.*); **penguin ranch**, a rookery area used continually by penguins.

1910 *NZ Free Lance* (Wellington) 11 June 4 They are the **penguin-oil** hunters on Macquarie Island, stationed there boiling down the penguins for a south New Zealand firm. **1987** SPARKS & SOPER *Penguins* 204 The most famous of all penguin-oil factories was on the Macquarie Islands. In 1891 Joseph Hatch was granted a lease by the New Zealand government to collect penguin oil. **1892** CARRICK *NZ's Lone Lands* 6 The chief sights of the place [*sc.* The Snares] are its sea-washed caves and its **penguin ranches**... The ground is closely cropped of its verdure, and to a large extent the soil has been broken up and furrowed.

2. With a modifier: **blue (little (small) blue, fairy), crested (Fiordland crested, Fiordland, yellow-crested), erect-crested (big-crested), king, rockhopper (tufted, Victoria), royal, Snares (Snares crested, Snares Island), white-flippered, yellow-eye(d) (yellow-crowned, yellow-headed)**.

(1) **blue (little blue, small blue,** occas. **fairy) penguin**. *Eudyptula minor* (fam. Spheniscidae), the smallest of the penguins and previously divided into a number of subspecies (see quot. 1985) but now (see quot. 1990) recognized as one taxon. See also KORORA, *white-flippered penguin* (8) below.

1870 *TrNZI* II. 75 Korora. Small Penguin. One of our commonest sea-fowl, and certainly a frequent burrower in its mode of nidification. **1873** BULLER *Birds NZ* 349 Eudyptyla minor. (Little Blue Penguin). **1898** [see KORORA]. **1938** *Auckland Weekly News* 27 Apr. 38 Common visitors are little blue penguins. **1955** OLIVER *NZ Birds* 84 The Northern Blue Penguin swims under the surface of the water with great speed. *Ibid.* 86 The Southern Blue Penguin burrows in the peaty ground on Mangere Island. **1967** NATUSCH *Animals NZ* 252 The little blue penguin..up to twenty inches long, nests in caves and crannies of rugged coasts; it also moves in, sometimes, under seaside houses, causing complaints about its fearful caterwauling at night. **1988** *Press* (Christchurch) 24 Aug. 21 Canterbury has its own distinctive penguin, the white-flippered penguin, which is a local variant of the Little blue or fairy penguin found only in New Zealand and Australia. **1990** *Checklist Birds NZ* 69 Eudyptula minor... Blue Penguin (Korora). *Ibid.* 70 In view of this [1988] uncertainty about the taxonomic status of these various populations, we have placed all the New Zealand birds in one taxon, *E. minor*, including the white flippered birds often classified as *E. albosignata* or *E. m. albosignata*.

(2) **crested (Fiordland crested, Fiordland**, occas. early **yellow-crested) penguin**. *Eudyptes pachyrhynchus*.

1871 HUTTON *Catalogue Birds NZ* 53 Eudyptes pachyrhynchus........ Crested Penguin. Tawaki. **1885** *TrNZI* XVII. 193 *Eudyptes pachyrhynchus*. Yellow-crested penguin. **1890** *Otago Witness* (Dunedin) 30 Jan. 15 As we left the ship..the braying noise of the crested penguins became incessant. **1917** WILLIAMS *Dict. Maori Lang.* 337 Pokotiwha, Catarrhactes pachyrhyncus, crested penguin. **1952** RICHARDS *Chatham Is.* 92 Eudyptes.. Sclateri... Big Crested Penguin. Tawaki. **1966** FALLA et al. *Birds NZ* 24 Fiordland Crested Penguin *Eudyptes pachyrhyncus*. **1976** SOPER *NZ Birds* 169 Like all penguins the Fiordland Crested has an immaculate white front and a bluish/black back but its most attractive features are the two golden/yellow crests that sweep back above the eyes and adorn the head. **1990** *Checklist Birds NZ* 73 Eudyptes pachyrhynchus... Fiordland Crested Penguin... Nests under forest or in caves.

(3) **erect-crested (big-crested) penguin**. *Eudyptes sclateri*. See also quot. 1955.

1904 HUTTON & DRUMMOND *Animals NZ* 282 The Big Crested Penguin. Catarrhactes sclateri... New Zealand only. **1955** OLIVER *NZ Birds* 76 The Erect-crested Penguin differs from all the other members of the genus Eudyptes in the parallel-sided culminicorn longitudinally ridged at the base. **1990** *Checklist Birds NZ* 74 *Eudyptes sclateri*... Erect-crested Penguin... Breeding in large numbers on the Antipodes and Bounty Islands and in small numbers on Campbell Island and on Disappointment Island (Aucklands Group).

(4) **king penguin**. *Aptenodytes patagonicus*. See quot. 1985.

1881 Douglas in *Mr Explorer Douglas* (1957) 32 I..saw an unfortunate King Penguin that had fallen in, and..I'll never forget the piteous emploring [*sic*] look of that wretched hypocritical bird. **1888** Buller *Birds NZ* II. 306 (King Penguin)... The specimen of this noble penguin..was obtained on Stewart's Island, where this bird is extremely rare. **c1920** Beattie *Trad. Lifeways Southern Maori* (1994) 165 Tokoraki is the King Penguin while the penu is a small kind with yellow eyebrows. **1938** *Auckland Weekly News* 30 Mar. 96 Two kinds of penguins—the rock-hopper, and the crested king penguin—swarmed here. **1985** *Reader's Digest Book NZ Birds* 41 *King Penguin Aptenodytes patagonicus*... A large, erect and dignified bird, with a sleek black head and bright-orange neck patches. The king penguin could only be compared with its much rarer relative the emperor penguin.

(5) **a. rockhopper** (**tufted**, formerly **Victoria**) **penguin**. *Eudyptes chrysocome filholi*. See esp. quots. 1955 (b), 1985.

1904 Hutton & Drummond *Animals NZ* 281 *The Tufted Penguin*...a band of golden feathers over each eye... This bird is sometimes called the Victoria Penguin by New Zealanders. **1938** [see (4) above]. **1990** *Checklist Birds NZ* 71 *Eudyptes chrysocome filholi..Eastern Rockhopper Penguin*... Breeds abundantly on Heard, Macquarie, Campbell, Auckland and Antipodes Islands.

b. *Ellipt.* as **rockhopper**, formerly any of various penguins, but now restricted to (5)a above (*Eudyptes chrysocome*).

1883 *TrNZI* XV. 401 *Pygoscelis taeniala*, 'Rockhopper'. A name much more suited to the 'Victorias' than to this variety. **1914** Guthrie-Smith *Mutton Birds & Other Birds* 201 *Eudyptula minor*—Blue Penguin known in Stewart Island as the Rock Hopper, a name elsewhere given to Pygoscelis papua. **c1920** Beattie *Trad. Lifeways Southern Maori* (1994) 165 One old man said that 'rock-hoppers' were called korora. **1955** Oliver *NZ Birds* 68 On land the Rockhopper progresses by hopping and, if the surface be steep, helping itself along with its bill and flippers. **1986** Fraser *Beyond the Roaring Forties* 25 The rockhopper, *Eudyptes chrysocome*, is the smallest but most common of the crested penguins.

(6) **royal penguin**. *Eudyptes chrysolophus schlegeli*, a penguin with an orange-yellow crest.

1883 *TrNZI* XV. 401 *Eudyptes schlegeli*, 'Royal Penguin'... The 'Royals' leave the island in June, and return in October. **1895** *TrNZI* XXVII. 563 The chief industry now [on Macquarie Island] is the boiling-down of the royal penguin. **1987** Sparks & Soper *Penguins* 204 At first, Hatch concentrated on the king penguins but found it was difficult to extract their oil without getting it contaminated with blood, so he turned his attention to the smaller but more plentiful royal penguins. **1990** *Checklist Birds NZ* 72 *Eudyptes chrysolophus schlegeli*... Royal Penguin... Birds evidently of this subspecies have reached Cook Strait, Hawke's Bay and Dunedin.

(7) **Snares (Snares crested) penguin**. *Eudyptes robustus*. See quot. 1966.

1948 *NZ Bird Notes* III. 70 Snares Crested Penguin. It has been said that the penguins..by forming rookeries in the bush, kill out the olearia in a few years. **1966** Falla et al. *Birds NZ* 25 Snares Crested Penguin... This species forms dense and compact nesting colonies in clearings a short distance from the sea on the Snares Island. **1990** *Checklist Birds NZ* 74 *Eudyptes robustus*..Snares Crested Penguin... Endemic, breeding on the Snares.

(8) **white-flippered penguin**. See *blue penguin* (1) above, esp. quot. 1990.

1904 Hutton & Drummond *Animals NZ* 284 *The White-flippered Penguin. Eudyptula albosignata*... Both margins of the flipper widely bordered with white. **1965** Gillham *Naturalist NZ* 89 It can claim as its own the white-flippered penguin which breeds only on Banks Peninsula.

(9) **yellow-eyed** (formerly **yellow-crowned**, **yellow-headed**) **penguin**. Also *ellipt.* **yellow-eye**. *Megadyptes antipodes*, having a pale golden forehead and crown with black shaft stripes, and a yellow iris to the eye. See also Hoiho.

1873 Buller *Birds NZ* 346 *Eudyptes antipodum*. (Yellow-crowned Penguin.) **1889** *TrNZI* XXI. 379 Here [at Stewart Island] I noticed the yellow-headed penguin..so seldom seen by collectors. **1904** Hutton & Drummond *Animals NZ* 283 *The Yellow-eyed Penguin.—Hoiho*... It is sometimes called the Grand Penguin. **1917** Williams *Dict. Maori Lang.* 66 *Hoiho, Megadyptes antipodum, yellow-eyed penguin*. **1966** Durrell *Two in the Bush* 56 Yellow-Eyes like to nest inland, in the forest or scrub. **1987** Sparks & Soper *Penguins* 70 Study of the New Zealand yellow-eyed penguins shows that in any particular breeding season there is a divorce rate of 13–18 percent among those pairs where both mates turned up. **1988** *Pacific Way* June 48 Here [at Nugget Point, South Otago] is the habitat of the world's rarest penguin: the yellow-eyed penguin. Yellow-Eyes like to nest inland. **1990** *Evening Post* (Wellington) 18 Oct. 13 Dunedin-based Mainland Products Ltd will provide a range of support for the Yellow-eyed Penguin Trust over the 1990–91 breeding season.

3. *transf.* and *fig.* [f. the colour and style of the former habits of some religious orders.] A nun.

c1940 Used at Patea Convent School (p.c. Dr. Desmond Hurley). **1948** in Pearson *Six Stories* (1991) 47 We used to call the nuns penguins. **1990** *Matriarchs* 117 Like most non-Catholics, I have always been fascinated by nuns...Gliding along the streets in their long black habits, arms folded out of sight..; the 'penguins' we called them. **1994** *Dominion* (Wellington) 15 Sept. 11 The nuns I knew were 'the penguins' who glided in pairs up the path to visit.

Peninsula.

1. *WW1*. As **the Peninsula**, the Gallipoli Peninsula. Also *attrib*. See also pen and ink 1.

1916 *Great Adventure* (1988) 131 At about 10 p.m. we drew in to what is known as Anzac Cove..the whole Peninsula from Anzac to Suvla Bay was fairly lit up. *Ibid.* 266 I am feeling as fit as a fiddle after my seven months sojourn on the Peninsula. **1918** *NZ at the Front* 15 The Peninsula vocabulary was notorious. **1937** Marsh *Vintage Murder* 238 'Dikkon.' It's the same as if you'd say 'come off it'. Used to hear it on the Peninsula. 'Aw dikkon, dig.' **1987** Knox *After Z-Hour* 145 Our platoon commander was at school with him—he was on the Peninsula too.

2. The Otago Peninsula; Banks Peninsula (Canterbury); the Coromandel Peninsula.

1890 *Otago Witness* (Dunedin) 6 Mar. 9 Ask the same prices demanded by Southern agents, or lose forever the grip they had on the [Banks] Peninsula trade. **1946** *NZ Farmers' Weekly* 21 Mar. 28 Cocksfoot is a dying industry on the [Banks] Peninsula. **1956** Fairburn *Letters* (1981) 245 As a mandarin of letters you can't very well get yourself voted a jaunt on the Peninsula, can you? **1963** Audley *No Boots for Mr. Moehau* 90 But on the third morning the [Coromandel] Peninsula was once more calm. **1971** Adcock *High Tide in the Garden* 6 [Title] A Surprise in the [Otago] Peninsula. **1979** Glover *Towards Banks Peninsula* 16 Mick, you took the Peninsula As a strong man might. *Ibid.* 18 The Peninsula still looks insular, Banks Island now Peninsula created.

penner-up. [f. pen *v*. 2: AND 1908.] *Pl.* **penners-up.** In sheep-shearing, one who keeps the shearers' pens supplied with sheep. See also sheepo B.

1897 Wright *Station Ballads* 101 And the penner-up is cursing at the back. **1933** [see sheepo A]. **1940** Studholme *Te Waimate* (1954) 130 The shearers were, of course, the autocrats of the shed, but the 'sheep-oh' (penner-up) also held an important position. In addition to filling up the catching pens, he weighed the bales and recorded them, with their descriptions, in the wool book. **1953** Stronach *Musterer on Molesworth* 31 At the back of the shed worked the 'penners-up' whose job was to keep the small catching pens full for the shearers. We always alluded to them as the 'pen-uppers'. **1967** Harper *Kettle on Fuchsia* 87 Sandy became the sole penner-up for sheep for over thirty shearers in the Orari Gorge woolshed. **1989** [see sheepo A].

penny. Special Comb. **penny bun**, see quot.; **penny Dominion** (usu. as **1d. Dominion**, also occas. in shortened form **Dominion**) [from the design: that of the *penny universal* with the words 'Dominion of' added before 'New Zealand'], a stamp of one-penny value issued in 1909 to commemorate Dominion status; **penny orange**, patotara 1, a small alpine shrub bearing juicy orange fruits; **penny tote** *obs*. [f. the former use of a penny to unlock the penny-in-the-slot cubicle], a (public) lavatory; **penny universal** (also occas. in shortened form **universal**) [an altered short form of *Universal Penny Postage*], a penny stamp first issued in 1901 to commemorate the introduction of Universal Penny Postage.

1961 Martin *Flora NZ* 36 **The Penny Bun** (*Boletus edulis*), so very abundant in pine-tree plantations, is the best known member of the fleshy mushroom-shaped polypores. **1938** *Postage Stamps of NZ* I. 238 To distinguish the stamp of 1909, it is referred to as the 1d 'Dominion Universal' (or **1d 'Dominion'**). **1958** *NZ Stamp Collector* XXXIX. 12 Brief reference was made to the major flaws in the 1d. Dominion and in the Government Life Insurance stamps. **1970** *NZ Bulletin* (Woking) XI. No.1 1 We were recently shown..a registered cover bearing the left half of a vertically bisected 1d Dominion and a 3d Edward. **1988** Gwynn *Collecting NZ Stamps* 75 On 26 September 1907, the colony became a dominion. There were immediate suggestions that the new status be celebrated by a stamp, and these bore fruit two years later when the 1d Universal was succeeded by another 1d stamp of similar design but bearing the inscription 'Dominion of New Zealand'. This stamp is always known as the '1d Dominion'. **1951** Frame *Lagoon* (1961) 12 Once she went for a holiday down South where snowberries and **penny oranges** grow on the hills. **1991** p.c. Jack Coulter, *fide* Maggy Wassilieff (Wellington). The *penny orange* is a name for *Cyathodes fraseri*, patotara. **1920** *NZ Stamp Collector* I. 111 January 1st 1901.—The birth of the '**Penny Universal**' was to be a new era in the history of the Post Office: 'The beginning of the new century will fittingly mark the event'. **1938** *Postage Stamps of NZ* I. 213 With the exception of the special booklet plate..all the plates used for the penny Universal contained 240 impressions in ten horizontal rows of 24 each. **1953** Lee *Penny Universal NZ* 1 The Penny

Universal was a true pioneer in the penny post system. It has a unique place not only in the postal history of New Zealand but in that of the world. **1970** *NZ Bulletin (Woking)* VII. No.7 1 At any philatelic level, the Penny Universal provides fun. **1988** STRACHAN *Century of Philately* 104 Chalon stamps, 1898 Pictorials, Penny Universals, King Edward VII and King George V stamps have always been popular.

penny doctor.

1. [Transf. use of Brit. dial. *doctor* or *penny doctor* for a small insect: see EDD *penny n.*¹ 3 *penny doctor* (*penniless doctor*) a small red-bodied insect. (Cumberland); SND *doctor n.* 3 (1) a black insect with red streaks [used in a boys' game, 1923] (2) A ladybird, 'supposed to cure cuts when placed on them' (1948): *doctor* is applied to the cleg or horse-fly in n. English dial.] The *butcher-boy* (BUTCHER 1 a), the larva of the tiger beetle, *Neocicindela* spp. (fam. Cicindelidae).

1929 MARTIN *NZ Nature Book I* 119 This name [*sc.* tiger beetle] is appropriately given in allusion partly to the active manner in which they search out the flies and other insects that serve as food and partly to the way their larvae—the well known penny doctors—lie in wait for their prey at the entrance to the tunnels excavated in sunny clay banks... The '*penny doctors*' during sunshine, may be noted with their heads filling the entrances to their tunnels ready to seize in an instant the unwary fly that alights or passes within reach. **1935** [see BUTCHER 1 a]. **1947** POWELL *Native Animals* 50 The larvae are the 'penny doctors' of the children, who often endeavour to fish for them by placing straws in the long straight tunnels which are made in clay or hard earth. The larvae may be seen at times with their heads just emerging from the tunnels, ready to seize any insect that unsuspectingly comes within range. **1967** NATUSCH *Animals NZ* 148 In summer [tiger beetles] are seen on sunny clay banks; holes in the ground contain the voracious larvae ('penny doctors'). **1978** HILLIARD *Glory and the Dream* 9 'See those holes in the ground?'.. 'When we was little we use [*sic*] to stick dry grass-stalks down them to catch penny-doctors.'

2. A children's game. See BUTCHER 1 b and quots. 1951, 1953, 1984 there.

penny section: see SECTION *n.*³

pennyweight. [f. a transf. use of *pennyweight* a twentieth of a troy ounce, in allusion to the small size of the bird.] SILVEREYE.

1922 *Auckland Weekly News* 10 Aug. 17 Among their familiar English names are, wax-eyes, blighties, winter migrants, pennyweights, and twinkles.

pennywort. [Spec. use of European *pennywort Hydrocotyle* spp. (fam. Apiaceae).] Usu. with a modifier, esp. as **American** (or **shining marsh) pennywort**, *Hydrocotyle heteromeria* (often also *americana*) (fam. Apiaceae), a common native weed of damp lawns (often called 'waxweed'); and **New Zealand marsh pennywort** *Hydrocotyle novae-zeelandiae*, a sprawling low herb with dull brownish-green leaves.

1869 *TrNZI* I. (rev. edn.) 203 Penny wort. Hydrocotyle elongata. **1907** *AJHR C-8* 20 [*Hydrocotyle*] *americana*..American marsh-pennywort..Coastal heath, forest. **1911** *AJHR C-13* 39 [*Hydrocotyle*] *novae-zealandiae*. New Zealand marsh-pennywort. End[emic]. Sand-hollow. Herb, small, creeping... *Hydrocotyle americana*..American marsh-pennywort.. Sand-hollow. Herb, small, creeping. Dunes of Southland occasionally. **1982** WILSON *Stewart Is. Plants* 276 Hydrocotyle americana A pennywort. American... Hydrocotyle novae-zelandiae A pennywort. New Zealand. **1984** *Standard Common Names Weeds* 78 pennywort, shining [=] waxweed.

Pensioner. *Hist.* [Spec. use of *pensioner* military pensioner.] **a.** The usual early name in Auckland and elsewhere for a FENCIBLE. Also *attrib.*

1847 *New Zealander* (Auckland) 27 Nov. in La Roche *Hist. of Howick & Pakuranga* (1991) 108 Much insubordination has shown itself amongst the Pensioners in the villages on the Tamaki. *Ibid.* Dec. Oh ye Pensioners, avoid intoxicating drinks as poison! **1852** MUNDY *Our Antipodes* II. 87 Howick is some ten miles further from the capital than the other pensioner settlement. **1887** *Brett's Auckland Almanac* 89 *Howick*, a pretty little pensioner settlement of about 220 inhabitants, lies..on the south bank of the Tamaki river.

b. *fig.* See quot.

1991 LA ROCHE *Hist. of Howick & Pakuranga* 12 A local drink measure was called [c1840s] 'a pensioner' such was their great thirst!—unique to the 'Fencible' or 'Pensioner Settlements'.

pen up: see PEN *v.*

penwiper. [See quot. 1988.] Also **penwiper plant**. *Notothlaspi rosulatum* (fam. Brassicaceae), a grey, fleshy-leaved herb of alpine screes.

1899 KIRK *Students' Flora* 38 *Notothlaspi rosulatum* (pen-wiper plant)... Erect, 3in.–10in. high, stemless or nearly so... [1899 *Note*] One of the most remarkable plants known; now becoming very rare owing to the ravages of sheep... The flowers have the fragrance of orange-blossoms. **1907** LAING & BLACKWELL *Plants NZ* 178 *Notothlaspi rosulatum*... An erect stemless herb... Shingle beds in the alpine districts of the South Island. The *Pen-wiper Plant* of the Settlers. **1924** *Otago Witness* (Dunedin) 18 Mar. 10 I was desirous of securing..the pen-wiper plant, but found no trace of it. **1969** MCCASKILL *Molesworth* 14 On the higher levels, up to 5,000 feet and over, a scattered alpine vegetation, including pen-wiper and mountain buttercups. **1978** MOORE & IRWIN *Oxford Book NZ Plants* 40 The penwiper plant..grows on South Island scree slopes... The leaves form a neat circular rosette,... in appearance much like the now forgotten penwipers made of overlapping strips of soft cloth on which Edwardian writers wiped the ink off their steel-nibbed pens. **1988** DAWSON *Forest Vines to Snow Tussocks* 191 The best known scree species is the penwiper plant which belongs to the cabbage family (Cruciferae). Its rosettes of grey, fleshy leaves closely overlap in a dome-like arrangement, which reminded early settlers of the similarly arranged and sewn together diamonds of felt on which they wiped their..pens.

pepi, var. PIPI.

pepper. Also **pepper plant**. [Transf. use of *pepper Piper nigrum* (fam. Piperaceae).] See also PEPPER-TREE, PEPPERWOOD.

1. Also **long pepper**, **native pepper**, **New Zealand pepper**. KAWAKAWA *n.*¹ (*Macropiper excelsum*).

1773 FORSTER *Resolution Journal* 25 May (1982) II. 286 My Son found a new kind of *Pepper* in flower with large cordated leaves... The flowers grow like all other Peppers in long spikes. Its tast[e] participates sometimes of the Ginger. **1777** ANDERSON *Journal* Feb. in Cook *Journals* (1967) III. 805 A species of long pepper is found in great plenty but it has little of the aromatic flavour which makes spices valuable. **1838** POLACK *NZ* I. 295 To the southward a species of *long pepper* is found, of little value; the *kauá kauá*, or *kává* (bitter), of the Friendly Islands, is also abundant. **1852** *Wellington Gazette* in Earp *Hand-Book for Intending Emigrants* (1952) 230 In the [alluvial bush land], which is wooded chiefly with *pukateas*..and thick underbrush of..*kaua kaua* (or pepper), &c. **1853** HOOKER II *Flora Novae-Zelandiae I Flowering Plants* 227 The New Zealand Pepper is a small tree, 12–20 feet high, or sometimes a rambling shrub, with a very aromatic smell; it has been used for Tea, and for the cure of toothache; it is found also in Norfolk Island, and belongs to a subgenus (Macropiper). **1867** HOOKER *Handbook* 767 Pepper, native. *Piper excelsum*. **1940** LAING & BLACKWELL *Plants NZ* 133 *Macropiper excelsum* (The Lofty Pepper). A small tree, sometimes 20 ft. in height, shining, aromatic. Leaves heart-shaped, 3in.–5in. long, pointed at the tip... Maori name *Kawakawa*.

2. HOROPITO (*Pseudowintera* (formerly *Drimys*) *colorata*).

1900 *Canterbury Old & New* 184 Even the semi-tropical true pepper [*Piper excelsum*] disputes with the false native pepper [*Drimys colorata*] the right to its name. **1925–26** *NZJST* VIII. 107 The New Zealand South Island pepper-plant, *Wintera colorata* (better known under its old name, *Drimys axillaris*), is one of our few magnolias.

pepper-pot, *v. Hist.* [Fig. from an allusion to 'sprinkling' Maori tenants over a predominantly non-Maori urban housing area: cf. the similar Austral. use in an Aboriginal context, AND 1980.] *trans.* To dot state-financed houses for Maori tenants in and throughout a predominantly non-Maori urban housing area. Often as *vbl. n.*

1967 *The Maoris of New Zealand* 80f. In urban areas, the Government favours the interspersing of Maori homes among Pakeha ones (pepper-potting). **1971** *Housing in NZ* 204 [Maori and Island Affairs Department's] houses for sale are intended to be dispersed singly or in groups of two or three throughout cities and towns, according to a practice known in the jargon of housing administrators as pepper-potting, but perhaps more accurately described as sprinkling. **1988** *Dominion Sunday Times* (Wellington) 27 June 10 Other Maori people are 'pepper potted' through the structures, diluting their voice. **1988** MCGILL *Dict. Kiwi Slang* 83 *pepperpotting* Maori Affairs past housing policy of sprinkling Maori families among Pakeha ones.

Hence, occas. as a *n.* in *attrib.* use, **pepper pot policy**, the policy of distributing Maori tenants throughout general housing areas.

1968 *Pol. Science* Sept. 70 Still, here [in Sutch's *The Quest for Security in New Zealand*]..is a discussion of..one of the Maori 'Harlems' without the 'pepper pot' policy by which the Department of Maori Affairs is trying to obviate them.

pepper-tree. See also PEPPER, PEPPERWOOD.

1. KAWAKAWA *n.*¹ (*Macropiper excelsum*). [*Note*] The name is also applied in northern New Zealand (as elsewhere) to the introduced *Schinus molle* (fam. Anacarsiaceae), a South American tree of spreading habit.

1773 FORSTER *Resolution Jrnl.* 8 June (1982) II. 296 The *pepper-Tree* is peculiar to this place: and grows..in joints & knots. **1842** pepper-tree [see KAWAKAWA *n.*¹ a]. **1855** TAYLOR *Te Ika A Maui* 181 The word is still preserved, in the *kawa kawa*, the *piper excelsum*, or pepper tree of New Zealand, and perhaps in the *casava* of America. **1868** PYKE *Province of Otago* 34 So also [elegant] is the native pepper-tree (*Kawa-kawa*). **1907**

AJHR C-8 18 *Macropiper excelsum.* Kawakawa. The tall pepper-tree. **1924** *Otago Witness* (Dunedin) 25 Mar. 6 The kawa, or native pepper-tree..is almost identical with the common kawa or kava of the South Sea Islands. **1936** *NZ Railways Mag.* June 29 The *kawakawa* or pepper tree (*piper excelsum*) is a useful medicine tree. **1988** Dawson *Forest Vines to Snow Tussocks* 103 Kawakawa is sometimes called 'native pepper tree' because of its hot tasting leaves, and it is in fact related to the true pepper plant of Indonesia... Horopito (*Pseudowintera axillaris*) with its dark green shiny leaves has also been termed 'pepper tree' for the same reason, but it is not in fact related to the kawakawa. **1992** Poole *Skinny Louie Book* 32 The Conlon's territory was marked by a peppertree hedge sneezy-dusty in the sun.

2. Also **native peppertree**, occas. **red pepper tree**. horopito (*Pseudowintera axillaris* and *P. colorata*).

1856 Tancred *Nat. Hist. Canterbury* 23 Pepper-tree, from its round black seeds being used for pepper. **1870** *TrNZI* II. 122 Pepper-tree, *Drimys axillaris*. **1883** Hector *Handbook NZ* 129 Horopito, Pepper-tree Winter's Bark. —A small slender evergreen tree, very handsome. Whole plant aromatic and stimulant. **1890** pepper tree [see horopito 1]. **1907** Laing & Blackwell *Plants NZ* 172 A decoction of the leaves is often used by bushmen as a medicine, and has earned the name of 'Maori Painkiller.'..Called by the settlers the Pepper Tree. **1915** *AJHR* C-6 12 *Drimys Colorata.* Horapito. Blotch-leaved pepper-tree. Forest. **1923** Cockayne *Cultivation NZ Plants* 62 W[intera] (Drimys) *axillaris*..is..a small tree.. with black bark... *W. colorata* (pepper-tree vh) is smaller; *Lvs.* beautifully coloured, blotched with reds and purples. *Hab.* lowland and subalpine forest. **1946** *JPS* LV. 149 *horopito*, a small tree..pepper-tree; (an aromatic evergreen in Supplement). **1950** Wodzicki *Introduced Mammals* 223 [Wapiti] nibble all other growth except beech and the pepper tree (*Wintera colorata*). **1981** *Field Guide to common NZ Trees and Shrubs* 5 Red Horopito (Red Pepper Tree) *Pseudowintera colorata* Small tree up to 3m. **1988** native pepper tree [see 1 above].

pepper weed: see cress 1 (quot. 1926).

pepperwood. See also pepper, pepper-tree.

1. horopito.

1923 *NZJST* V. 151 The horopito or pepperwood..is a member of the Magnoliaceae, being a sister plant to the South American *Drimys winteri*, source of the once important but now almost forgotten medicine Winter's bark. **1924** pepper-wood [see painkiller 2]. **1952** Thomson *Deer Hunter* 129 Going became fairly difficult..at times, a dense thicket of pepperwood shrubs. **1960** Crump *Good Keen Man* 122 Cutting through a patch of pepperwoods, we came out on the first clearing. **1984** Morton *Whirinaki* 26 Pepperwood (*Pseudowintera colorata*), one of our most archaic flowering plants.

2. kawa kawa.

1965 Gillham *Naturalist NZ* 229 The coastal scrub includes..red matipo and pepperwood. This last..has unusually large leaves, so large that it has been given varietal status as *Macropiper excelsum* var. *majus*.

peppi, peppy, varr. pipi.

perch, *n.* [AND for various fish, 1825.]

1. In New Zealand, any of several fishes of the families Kyphosidae, Labridae, Scorpaenidae and Serranidae.

1840 Best *Journal* (1966) 222 The Bay abounds with fish and..I saw the Gurnard, Mullet, a kind of Perch..and a species of Sole. **1879** *TrNZI* XI. 382 [Native or Settlers' Name] Wrasse, or Perch..[Scientific Name] *Labrichthys celidota* **1892** *TrNZI* XXIV. 211 Perch (*Labrichthys celidota*). Only one example of this fish was recorded from Puysegur Point. **1957** Williams *Dict. Maori Lang.* 215 *Muritea,* n. *Girella tricuspidata, perch*; a sea fish... *parore*. **1970** Sorensen *Nomenclature NZ Fish* 40 *Perch* (two species) *Scorpaena cardinalis, Helicolenus papillosus* (or *percoides*).

2. With a modifier: **black, butterfly, red, sea**.

(1) **black perch**. parore (*Girella tricuspidata*).
1875 *TrNZI* VII. 243 Girella percoides. Sp. nov..Black Perch. **1886** Sherrin *Handbook Fishes NZ* 13 Black Perch (*see* Perch) *Ibid.* 71 Perch (*Girella simplex*). **1966** Doogue & Moreland *Sea Anglers' Guide* 242 Parore... *Girella tricuspidata;* blackfish, black perch; black bream (Tasmania). **1981** Wilson *Fisherman's Bible* 25 Black Perch: *see Parore*.

(2) **butterfly perch**. *Caesioperca lepidoptera* (fam. Serranidae), having a large dark blotch on each side of the body. See also oia.

1957 Parrott *Sea Angler's Fishes* 73 The Red Perch... is also known as the 'Red Snapper', 'St. Peter's Fish' [usu. applied to *John Dory* from similar blotches said to be St Peter's finger-marks] or 'Butterfly Perch'. **1967** Moreland *Marine Fishes* 38 Butterfly Perch... Other names are red perch when this colour predominates. **1972** Doak *Fishes* 30 Another of the plankton-feeding perch gropers, the butterfly perch has a similar life-style to the pink maomao. **1982** Ayling *Collins Guide* (1984) 207 Butterfly Perch (Oia) *Caesioperca lepidoptera*... The butterfly perch is similar in shape and habits to the pink maomao but is deeper bodied and smaller.

(3) **red perch**. See *butterfly perch* (2) above. See also St Peter's fish.

1921 *NZJST* IV. 115 *Caesioperca lepidoptera*... Red Perch. Called 'red snapper' or 'St. Peter's fish' in Queen Charlotte and Pelorus Sounds, where it is occasionally taken in the seine net during July and August. **1938** *TrRSNZ* LXVIII. 410 *Caesioperca lepidoptera*... Red perch. **1957** Parrott *Sea Angler's Fishes* 73 The Red Perch may be distinguished from other New Zealand fishes by its unusually bright colouring and the black mark on each side of the body. **1957** Williams *Dict. Maori Lang.* 238 *Oia,.. Caesioperca lepidoptera*, red perch, a fish. **1966** Doogue & Moreland *Sea Anglers' Guide* 228 Butterfly Perch... *Caesioperca lepidoptera;* red perch; oia (Maori).

(4) **sea perch**. Any of several species of the family Scorpaenidae but usu. *Helicolenus percoides*. See also five-finger 3, flinger, highlander, Jock Stewart, Maori chief *n.*² 3, pohuiakaroa, scarpee, scroddie. Cf. *sea salmon* (salmon 1).

1773 Forster *Resolution Jrnl.* 27 Mar. (1982) II. 240 The *Sea-Perch* is a fine hard fish. **1872** Hutton & Hector *Fishes NZ* 108 Sea Perch. The Pohuiakaroa.. though not figured deserves mention... It is the proper *Sea Perch* of these waters. **1886** Sherrin *Handbook Fishes NZ* 88 Sea Perch ([*Helicolenus*] *percoides*)... It is one of the most frequent and troublesome fish, caught in a moderate depth of water round the coast, and especially in rocky harbours, being almost worthless as food. **1921** *NZJST* IV. 121 Helicolenus percoides... Sea-perch; *Pohuiakaroa*. Secured in rocky localities among blue cod. Large numbers common in Christchurch Markets during early summer months. **1938** *TrRSNZ* LXVIII. 416 *Helicolenus percoides*... Sea perch, so called John Dory (scroddie, fivefinger, soldier-fish, Jock Stuart, Highlander). **1957** Parrott *Sea Angler's Fishes* 161 There are two species of scorpion fishes (Family *Scorpaenidae*) that are of interest to New Zealand sea-anglers..the Sea Perch (*Helicolenus percoides*) and the Red Rock Cod. **1967** Natusch *Animals NZ* 231 Family Scorpaenidae includes the sea perch, *Helicolenus percoides*, better known as Jock Stuart..an ugly, spiny customer related to the dangerous stone fish and scorpion fish of tropical reefs. **1972** Doak *Fishes* 24 Nestling beneath a ledge, the sea perch is ready to dash out and swallow a blenny or crab that ventures too near. **1982** Ayling *Collins Guide* (1984) 196 Sea Perch are similar in shape and appearance to the scorpion fish but have smoother heads... It is a deep water species..more common to the south of Cook Strait. **1991** Bradstock *Fishing* 21 *Sea perch*. Other names: scarpee, Jock Stewart, highlander, flinger, pohuiakaroa, *Helicolenus percoides*.

perch, *v. Obs.* [f. Brit. dial. *perch* (also *perk*) a frame against which sawn timber is set to dry: cf. EDD *perch n.*², *perk n.* 5.] To stack sawn timber upright for seasoning.

1879 *TrNZI* XI. 460 When converted it [*sc.* timber] should be 'perched' or 'stripped' in such a way that no two planks should be in contact.

perei. [Ma. /ˈperei/: Williams 278 *Perei,* n. *Gastrodia cunninghamii* and *Orthoceras strictum,* orchids with a tuberous edible root.] *Gastrodia cunninghamii* (fam. Orchidaceae), a parasitic orchid with edible tubers.

1845 Taylor *Journal* 17 Mar. (ATLTS) III. 97 Forde one of my boys brought me some roots which when cooked were superior to the potatoe, the Perei. **1869** *TrNZI* I. (rev. edn.) 208 Perei. Gastrodia Cunninghamii. **1881** *TrNZI* XIII. 31 Another fleshy root..the *perei*..was also eaten. **1904** Tregear *Maori Race* 99 A plant resembling a long red radish (*perei*: Gastrodia cunninghamii) was valued for its root, but it was scarce, and only found in dense forests. **1929** Firth *Primitive Econ. NZ Maori* 51 The perei orchid..also furnished vegetable food. **1937** Buick *Moa-Hunters NZ* 231 When digging for the *perei*, an edible root..the diggers were warned against mentioning the name *perei,* or the root would never be found. **1978** [see maikaika 1]. **1982** [see maikaika 2].

pereira, var. paraerae.

Perendale. [f. the name of (Sir) Geoffrey Sylvester *Peren* (1892–1980), a student of sheep husbandry and a founder of Massey University.] A sheep bred in New Zealand from Cheviot and Romney genes, for both wool and meat.

1975 *NZ Patent Office Jrnl. No.1145* 17 Jan. Perendale B104798 [filed] 3 July 1973..woollen knitting yarns made wholly or predominantly of Perendale wool. Perendale Genetic Development Holdings Limited. **1977** Brooking *Massey—its early years* 91 In 1960 a society was formed in order to standardise type and promote the breed which was named the Perendale in recognition of the founder's work. **1989** *Illustr. Encycl. NZ* 930 *Perendale* sheep have been described as 'New Zealand's classic, hardy, hill country foragers', with equal emphasis on meat and wool, an easy-care breed with minimal lambing problems and easy to muster. **1991** *Dominion* (Wellington) 26 Jan. 6 While we may not live on the sheep's back as we did during the Korean War boom in the 1950s, romneys and perendales still put the caviar on a great many triangles of toast.

perf, *v.* Often as **perf out**. [Acronym of *P*(olice *E*(mployment *R*(ehabilitation *F*(und.] *intr.* To accept money-payments from the Police Employment Rehabilitation Fund for taking early retirement by claiming to be medically unfit.

1987 *Dominion Sunday Times* (Wellington) 26

Apr. 1 [Heading] 'Perfing out' for $80,000. The number of seemingly fit police quitting the force with average payouts of $80,000 under recently introduced medical discharge provisions is being criticised within police ranks. A total of 125 officers have been granted medical disengagement on the grounds they are no longer able to carry out police work... The medical option is colloquially known within the police as 'perfing out', based on the acronym of the scheme's original name—police employment rehabilitation fund. **1991** *Evening Post* (Wellington) 17 Jan. 5 There has been some controversy lately over the police employment rehabilitation fund (Perf), which allows police to leave the force early for medical reasons, with enough money to retrain and re-educate them... Police officers 'perfed out' received what they had paid in superannuation, plus the employers' contribution, and some interest.

Hence **perfed** *ppl. a.*, of a police officer, to have accepted disengagement under such conditions; **perfing** *vbl. n.* and *ppl. a.*

1995 *Evening Post* (Wellington) 11 Mar. 18 Another '**perfed**' officer..claimed police officers know what to say in medical interviews. **1990** *Evening Post* (Wellington) 13 Dec. 8 [Heading] **Perfing** Policemen... I am concerned about the journalistic ability of the individual responsible for the editorial (The Post, Dec. 6), Police '**perfing**' under scrutiny... Perf stands for Police Employment Rehabilitation Fund and not Police Early Retirement Fund as stated in the editorial. **1991** *National Business Review* 20 Sept. 5 A recent report..found psychological factors were the main reason for police officers PERFing. **1995** *Evening Post* (Wellington) 11 Mar. 17 'Perfing', as it is commonly but inaccurately known (in reference to the police employment and rehabilitation fund), is considered by some offficers a joke, a scam, and is routinely abused by officers who wish to leave the force and find the lure of leaving on medical grounds..just too tempting to pass up... 'Perfing' happens under section 28D of the Police Act which allows police to disengage on grounds of physical or psychological impairment, either compulsorily or voluntarily, and take their super contributions, those of their employer and interest in a taxfree lump sum.

perishable. [f. *perishable*(-goods train.]
1. A train carrying perishable goods overnight between Christchurch and Greymouth, formerly much used by mountaineers to get to and from the Alps.
   1948 *Canterbury Mountaineer* 266 He refused to be cheered by tales of how George..and Bill..used to scamper up the Wanganui between perishables to look for gold. **1966** TURNER *Eng. Lang. Austral. & NZ* 157 The *Perishable*, the train taking perishable goods from Christchurch to Greymouth. **1974** AGNEW *Loner* 124 [In Greymouth] I catch the perishable to Christchurch, convinced I have more chance..in the city than in a small town like Greymouth. **1987** SINCLAIR *Rail* 128 The Perishable, introduced some time during the mid-twenties, was an express goods train that ran between Christchurch and Greymouth—in both directions—on six nights of the week. As well as its usual duties, the train provided a convenient weekend service for Canterbury Mountaineering Club members travelling to Arthur's Pass.
2. A train formerly carrying fruit and vegetables from Hawke's Bay to Wellington markets.
   1974 AGNEW *Loner* 112 After calling into Te Aute..we caught the perishable to Wellington.

periwinkle, *n.*[1] A transferred use of *periwinkle* for any of various medium-sized, snail-shaped shellfish with a more or less circular shell aperture, often known as *top shells* (from their resemblance to a whipping top). See also MUD SNAIL.

1773 WALES *Journal* in Cook *Journals* (1961) II. 787 Amongst the crustaceous Tribe we found..Scollops, Whelks, Periwinkles. **1879** HAAST *Geol. Canterbury & Westland* 416 Then follows a series of shell beds, consisting of the remains of the following species, now still inhabiting the estuary..*Amphibola avellana* (Periwinkle) Hetikutiku, and..(Mussel) Kuku. **1924** BUCKNILL *Seashells of NZ* 37 *Litorina cincta*... This is a small periwinkle..found on rocks, in crevices or sheltered parts. **1947** POWELL *Native Animals NZ* 26 Periwinkle (*Melarhaphe oliveri*). A most abundant shell on high tidal rocks throughout New Zealand... This is a true periwinkle, but that name is frequently applied locally to other shellfish, some of the top-shells and the cat's-eye. **1951** KOHERE *Autobiography of a Maori* 21 Everywhere she looked even in caverns, where crayfish were usually found, the only object that met her eyes was a solitary periwinkle. **1966** *Encycl. NZ* III. 710 Periwinkle or mud snail . . takarepo, titiko, whetiko . . *Amphibola crenata*. **1968** MORTON & MILLER *NZ Sea Shore* 80 The name 'periwinkle' is sometimes used for topshells, but properly belongs to a small snail of the littoral fringe, *Melarapha oliveri*. **1983** GUNSON *Collins Guide to Seashore* 91 The common cat's eye *Turbo smaragdus* (30mm) is one of the best known univalves of the north, and is sometimes mistakenly referred to as a periwinkle. **1983** KING *Whina* 38 The sea also brought them snapper, mullet, parore and flounder; whitebait in season; and oysters, pipi and karahu (periwinkles).

periwinkle, *n.*[2] [Transf. use of *periwinkle* (*Vinca* spp.) a trailing plant with blue flowers.] Usu. as **native** or **New Zealand periwinkle**, JASMINE (*Parsonsia* spp.).

   1961 MARTIN *Flora NZ* 144 Two species of *Parsonsia*..have a..[climbing] habit though lacking in prickles. They are variously termed Kaiku, Native Periwinkle, or New Zealand Periwinkle.

perk, *n. Obs.* [From a shortening of 19th century British slang *perkins* beer, itself from the name of a brewing firm *Barclay, Perkins*, in full a cockney term for 'stout': AND 1913.] Beer. Also **perked**, drunk. (Partridge notes that *perked* is 20th century military slang.)
   1887 *NZ Mail* (Wellington) 15 July 9 (NZ slang) A drunken man is 'screwed', 'boozed'..'got his tank full', 'perked' (I should have explained that 'perk' is the theatrical slang for beer), or 'shikkar'.

perk, *v.* To get by a perk or lucky gift, or occas. by pilfering.
   1962 CRUMP *One of Us* 78 Then he..wheeled out the old push-bike he'd perked off a neighbour.

Hence **perking** *vbl. n.*, pilfering from the work-place.
   1983 *National Bus. Rev.* 22 Aug. 36 Perking is the name for fringe benefits that are taken by employees and should not be confused with the 'perk' that is an authorised addition to a salary. The word originated on the floor of the factory but the practice is not confined to that area. Those who make a habit of perking don't consider it dishonest but factory owners disagree and waste time and effort trying to stamp it out. **1985** MARSHALL *Secret Diary Telephonist* 105 R.A. told Lew and Harry the pilfering has reached an 'Unacceptable level.' 'Pilfering' is their word. In the plant it's 'perking'.

perla, perler, varr. PURLER.

perna: see MUSSEL 2 (5).

perpetual lease: see LEASE.

perrokeet, perroquet, varr. PARAKEET.

perv, *v.* [AND 1941.] *intr.* To watch (intently) with prurient interest. Also *vbl. n.* **perving**.
   1980 MACKENZIE *While We Have Prisons* 98 *perv.* (*v.*) to look at with lust **1981** *Avondale College Slang Words* (Auckland) (Goldie Brown Collect.) *give us a perv*: let's see. *to perv*: to admire sexually. **1984** BEATON *Outside In* 63 Di: You never do get used to the screws pervin' at you, do you, Ma? *Ibid.* 110 Perving: watching (as a peeping Tom does) with prurient interest. **1996** PERKINS *Not Her Real Name* 14 We call him [sc. an art teacher] Stiff O'Donnell because he gawks at the girls all the time he is so disgusting... Yuck Stiff O'Donnell is perving I better go. [sic]

peter, *n.*[1] [f. Brit. slang *peter* a (cash-)box (OED 1859), a safe, with a general sense of enclosed space for holding (people or things) safe: see OED *n.*[1] 6.]
1. A cash-register or till, often in the phr. **to tickle (the) peter**, to regularly pilfer petty cash, esp. by removing it from a till without recording the transaction.
   1937 PARTRIDGE *Dict. Slang* 883 *tickle*... To steal from, to rob, as in *tickle a peter*, to rob the till: New Zealand c[ant] (–1932). Perhaps ex *to tickle trout*. **1943** *Penguin New Writing* 17 66 He pushed me over one more double gin which he only pretended to ring up on the peter. **1946** SARGESON *That Summer* 124 I risked going to the Dally's [hash-house], and as usual at that time he was standing behind the peter. **1965** SHADBOLT *Among Cinders* 143 'We've only just discovered that our senior salesman..has helped himself to a vacation in Australia.' 'Did he tickle the peter?' Hubert asked. 'To the tune of two thousand quid.' **1971** SHIRLEY *Just a Bloody Piano Player* 50 He was accused of 'tickling the peter' when he was on door duty.

2. [AND 1895.] A witness box.
   1910 *Truth* 31 Dec. 6 'I'll mount the Peter in the morning and give evidence about it,' she said, shrilly. His Worship: What does 'mount the Peter' mean?—To come here, your Worship.

3. [AND 1890.] A prison cell.
   1945 BURTON *In Prison* 38 A cell or 'peter' at Mt. Crawford is..somewhere about nine feet long by seven wide and ten or eleven in height. **1953** HAMILTON *Till Human Voices Wake Us* 125 For a while he had charge of the pound and he was a fair soandso down there, doing over your peter for tobacco two or three times a day. **1964** DAVIS *Watersiders* 110 So that was that. I spend what's left of the night in the peter and when I come out I'm out of work. **1982** NEWBOLD *Big Huey* 77 And I'd always give my drink a little jerk outside Whippy's peter so a bit of tea would splash out on to the floor *Ibid.* 180 A tealeaf is just a cunt in my eyes, and you'd be about the lowest... You're a peter thief and you're a dog.

peter, *n.*[2] [Prob. f. *blue peter* a chemist's or other blue jar or (square-sided) bottle, a use reinforced by allusion to the name *blue peter* for the marine signal flag indicating an intention of leaving port.] Orig. a half-gallon or gallon jar or stoneware demijohn, occas. (as *blue peter*), a square-sided blue bottle used to hold draught beer; thence a half-gallon flagon of draught beer or wine. Cf. *half-g* (HALF- 3 a (b)), *blue peter* (BLUE *a.* 1), BLUEY *n.* 7. Compare RIGGER, SQUARE RIGGER 1.
   1914 as *blue peter* [see BLUE *a.* 1]. **c1930s** Canterbury: p.c. Jack Columbus (Blenheim). Originally blue peter, a chemist's blue jar of about three-quarter gallon, used to hold beer for consumption off the licenced premises. **1955** *Evening Post* (Wellington) 17

PETER SCHOOL

Jan. 8 The fact is that 15 years ago in Dunedin [c1940] we regularly had our half and one-gallon jars filled in the bar. So well established was the custom that the 'gang' I was with kept special wooden cases to carry the 'peters,' as the jars were called. *Ibid.* 19 Jan. 8 I am also a South Islander, and the statement [above] is correct concerning half and one gallon jars. Many one gallon were covered in wicker covering to protect them. Some half-gallon jars were known as 'Blue-Peters' on account of the colour. In Christchurch..twenty to 25 years ago they started selling and filling these jars. **1967** BAXTER *Collected Poems* (1980) 392 [Title] *The Jar.* I'd bought a peter of wine From the owner of a Dalmatian vineyard. **1968** SLATTER *Pagan Game* 173 Sitting up all night over a peter to listen to the 1949 series. **1972, 1982, 1988** peter [see *half-g* (HALF 3 a (b))]. **1992** *NZ English Newsletter* 6 11 (Bartlett *Regional Variation: Southland*) [Other items which may be diagnostic of Southland English are:] *peter* (a flagon, or half-gallon bottle, usually of beer).

peter school. *Obs.* [Origin unknown.] A gambling school.
   1938 *Press* (Christchurch) (McNab Slang) 2 Apr. 18 [In local criminal slang]... a 'peter school' is a gambling den. **1949** PARTRIDGE *Dict. Underworld* (1961) 507 *peter school.* A gambling den: New Zealand and Australian: 1932, Nelson Baylis (private letter; N.Z.).

petrel.
1. [In locally significant use mainly with a defining word.] Any of various tube-nosed seabirds, Order Procellariiformes, esp. species of *Pterodroma* and *Procellaria*.
   1777 FORSTER *Voyage Round the World* I. 153 Here they found an immense number of petrels of the bluish species, common over the whole southern ocean, some being on the wing, and others in the woods, in holes under ground formed between the roots of trees and in the crevices of rocks, in places not easily accessible, where they probably had their nests and young. **1853** ADAMS *Canterbury Settlement* 8 Among these may be noticed the albatross, the molimawk, the Cape pigeon, and several varieties of tern and petrel. **1914** GUTHRIE-SMITH *Mutton Birds & Other Birds* 16 We also got four kinds of Petrel in their burrows,—the Mutton Bird, Parara, Titi Wainui, and the Kuaka. **1932** STEAD *Life Histories NZ Birds* 73 Owing to the similarity in appearance of different species of Petrels, and also to the fact that the one trivial name 'Mutton-bird' was applied indiscriminately to a number of different kinds, records concerning them are most unreliable. **1978** HARPER & KINSKY *Southern Albatrosses & Petrels* 41 If..the albatrosses..and the storm petrels..are separated from the other Procellariiformes, a large and varied assemblage of birds still remains: to many people these are the 'true' petrels. **1984** *Notornis* XXXI. 97 On predator-free 'petrel islands', [warblers'] nests were low to the ground.

2. Among the many common names of petrels, mainly formed with a modifier + *petrel*, the following are most frequent, and are accepted both in 'informed' usage and in that 'popular' usage which can, and prefers to, distinguish species and varieties of petrel: **black (brown, Parkinson's), black-capped (white-naped), black-winged, Chatham (Chatham Island(s)), Cape, Cook's, diving** (also in subsp. **northern, southern, subantarctic), dove, frigate, giant (Hall's giant, northern** or **southern giant), grey (brown), grey-faced (great-winged), Kermadec, laughing, magenta, mottled (Peale's, scaled), pintado, Pycroft's, soft-plumaged, storm** (with numerous modifiers), **Westland (Westland black), white-chinned, white-headed**.

(1) **black (brown, Parkinson's) petrel**. *Procellaria parkinsoni* (fam. Procellariidae), a large yellowish-billed petrel. See also TAIKO 1, TOANUI.
   1871 HUTTON *Catalogue Birds NZ* 47 Procellaria atlantica... Black Petrel. **1873** BULLER *Birds NZ* 302 Procellaria Parkinsoni. (Black Petrel.) **1886** *TrNZI* XVIII. 87 Observations on *Procellaria parkinsoni*... Brown Petrel (Taiko). **1895** *TrNZI* XXVII. 122 Black petrel... I am quite satisfied that this bird is the 'Night Demon' of our diggers. I had a live one..from Collingwood... On windy nights the bird would become very excited, and then it would give vent to the hysterical laugh or scream from which it takes its name. **1908** *TrNZI* XL. 503 I became personally acquainted with the black petrel. **1917** WILLIAMS *Dict. Maori Lang.* 180 *Kuia* (b) n. *Majaqueus parkinsonii*, black petrel. **1949** *NZ Bird Notes* III. 185 We searched hopefully, but in vain [on Hen Island] for evidence of the black petrel. (*Procellaria parkinsoni*). **1979** FALLA et al. *New Guide to Birds of NZ* 49 Black Petrels are known to breed on the tops of Little Barrier and Great Barrier and on a few bush-clad mountain tops some distance inland in Taranaki, Nelson, Westland, Fiordland, and Stewart Island. **1985** *Reader's Digest Book NZ Birds* 90 *Black Petrel Procellaria parkinsoni... Taiko, Parkinson's petrel...* Black petrels may still be killed occasionally for food on Great Barrier Island. **1993** *Evening Post* (Wellington) 8 Nov. 21 Cook's petrel and the rare black petrel arrive in spring to breed.

(2) **black-capped (white-naped) petrel**. *Pterodroma cervicalis* (fam. Procellariidae), having a black cap and a white nape.
   1904 HUTTON & DRUMMOND *Animals NZ* 246 *The Black-capped Petrel... Ibid.* 247 It is altogether nocturnal in its habits, and rarely leaves its burrow in the daytime, and therefore it is not seen at sea. **1955** OLIVER *NZ Birds* 158 *Black-capped Petrel Pterodroma externa cervicalis*. **1979** FALLA et al. *New Guide Birds NZ* 40 Black-capped Petrel... Known mainly from the vicinity of the Kermadecs where it breeds abundantly on Macauley. **1980** *Notornis* XXVII. (Suppl.) 22 *P[terodroma] externa cervicalis... White-naped Petrel.* **1984** SOPER *Birds NZ* 42 The White-naped Petrel *Pterodroma externa cervicalis*... This is a subtropical species now breeding only at Macauley Island of the Kermadec group, having been exterminated on Raoul by cats and rats. **1990** *Checklist Birds NZ* 52 *Pterodroma cervicalis*... White-naped Petrel.

(3) **black-winged petrel**. *Pterodroma nigripennis* (fam. Procellariidae), a small grey-backed subtropical petrel.
   1904 HUTTON & DRUMMOND *Animals NZ* 246 *The Black-winged Petrel. Oestrelata nigripennis*... Under surface of the wings white, with a dark brown border. **1955** OLIVER *NZ Birds* 148 The Black-winged Petrel breeds on all the islands of the Kermadec group except French Rock. **1970** *Annot. Checklist Birds NZ* 24 *P[terodroma] hypoleuca nigripennis*... Black-winged Petrel. **1984** SOPER *Birds NZ* 38 The Black-winged Petrel's inclination for coming ashore in daylight is especially notable at the Kermadec Islands where, on the outer islands, their *weet-weet* calls, as they circle endlessly overhead, form a muted background of sound as soothing and unceasing as the murmur of surf.

(4) **Cape petrel:** see PIGEON 3 a.

(5) **Chatham (Chatham Island(s)) petrel**. The rare *Pterodroma axillaris* (fam. Procellariidae). See also RANGURU.
   1904 HUTTON & DRUMMOND *Animals NZ* 250 *The Chatham Island Petrel. Oestrelata axillaris.* **1955** OLIVER *NZ Birds* 149 *Chatham Island Petrel. Ranguru...* This species was discovered by Hawkins on South-east Island, Chatham group, in 1892. **1966** Chatham Island Petrel [see RANGURU]. **1984** HOLMES *Chatham Is.* 60 It has no land mammals and..has retained its original population of Shore Plover, Chatham Islands Petrel and insular sub-species of Antarctic Snipe. **1984** SOPER *Birds NZ* 38 The Chatham Island Petrel is a very rare endemic breeder not yet recorded away from Chatham waters and is, so far as is known, confined to a small colony on South East Island. **1990** *Checklist Birds NZ* 51 *Chatham Petrel...* Breeds now only on South East Island, Chatham Island.

(6) **Cook's petrel**. *Pterodroma cookii* (fam. Procellariidae), a grey and white small petrel. See also TITI 1.
   1873 BULLER *Birds NZ* 307 Procellaria cookii. (Cook's Petrel). **1888, 1904** [see TITI 1]. **1924** *Otago Witness* (Dunedin) 26 Feb. 6 Cook's petrel is grey and white. **1938** *Auckland Weekly News* 27 Apr. 38 At night..these birds chase each other all over the sky in courting display, the Cook's petrel uttering a rapid 'ti-ti-ti' while the larger black petrel voices a 'purring' note. **1947** *NZ Bird Notes* II. 137 Cook's petrel has many distinct calls. Perhaps the most frequently used are the quick 'whi-kek-kek' and the goat-like bleating. **1966** FALLA et al. *Birds of NZ* 52 The strong wheeling flight of Cook's Petrel presents to the eye in turn the characteristic pattern of the back and the pure white under-surface. **1989** PARKINSON *Travelling Naturalist* 25 In the evenings you can often hear the faint cries of Cook's petrels passing far overhead as they fly from their breeding burrows on Little Barrier. **1993** *Evening Post* (Wellington) 8 Nov. 21 Cook's petrel and the rare black petrel arrive in spring to breed.

(7) **diving petrel**. Any of a distinctive group of small dumpy short-winged petrels of *Pelecanoides* spp. (fam. Procellariidae) assigned to two subspecies (formerly to three—**northern** (also locally called **dipchick**), **southern** and **subantarctic**), in present 'informed' use named **common diving petrel** *Pelecanoides urinatrix urinatrix*, and **subantarctic diving petrel** *P. u. exsul*. See also KUAKA b.
   1871 HUTTON *Catalogue Birds NZ* 45 Diving Petrel. Titi. *Pelecanoides urinatrix*. **1904** HUTTON & DRUMMOND *Animals NZ* 255 *The Diving Petrel...* It is gregarious, living in small flocks all round the New Zealand coasts. There are two species. *Pelecanoides urinatrix... Pelecanoides exsul.* **1914** GUTHRIE-SMITH *Mutton Birds & Other Birds* 201 Diving Petrel—Kuaka. Kuaka is also in the North Island a name given to the Southern Godwit. **1955** OLIVER *NZ Birds* 94 *Diving Petrel. Kuaka Pelecanoides urinatrix urinatrix.* The Diving Petrel was discovered at Queen Charlotte Sound in 1773 during Cook's second voyage. *Ibid.* 95 *Chatham Island Diving Petrel Pelecanoides urinatrix chathamensis...* The Diving Petrel occurs in immense numbers along the southern coast of New Zealand. **1966** FALLA et al. *Birds NZ* 57 Northern Diving Petrel *Pelecanoides urinatrix...Local name:* Dipchick. *Ibid.* 58 Southern Diving Petrel; *Pelecanoides chathamensis...* Kuaka (at Stewart Island only). **1982** SANSOM *In Grip of Island* 91 With [the titi] were scatterings of the smaller titi-wainui, the Fairy Prions, and a sprinkling of kuaka, the Southern Diving Petrels, which ducked and rose on the outskirts. **1990** *Checklist Birds NZ* 32 *Pelecanoides urinatrix urinatrix... Common Diving Petrel (Kuaka)... Pelecanoides urinatrix exsul... Subantarctic Diving Petrel.* Breeding Auckland and Antipodes Islands.

(8) **dove petrel**. *Pachyptila desolata* (fam. Procellariidae), *Antarctic prion* (PRION 1). See also WHALEBIRD.
   [*Note*] The name is occas. also applied to *Pachyptila turtur*, fairy prion (PRION 3), see quots. 1914, 1951 below.

1873 Buller *Birds NZ* 309 Prion turtur. (Dove petrel). **1888** [see WHALEBIRD]. **1914** GUTHRIE-SMITH *Mutton Birds & Other Birds* 201 *Prion turtur*—Dove Petrel—Titi Wainui. **1938** *Auckland Weekly News* 23 Mar. 42 Dove petrels are not the only residents of the island. **1951** *NZ Bird Notes* IV. 136 Dove Petrel (*Pachyptila turtur*). Most nights in the autumn, winter and spring, 'doveys,' as we call them, are about in great numbers. They sometimes keep us awake, especially on wet nights, when they seem to offer hymns of praise for the rain. **1957** WILLIAMS *Dict. Maori Lang.* 497 *Whiroia...Pachyptila desolata, dove prion (dove petrel or whale-bird)*. **1969** HENDERSON *Open Country Calling* 166 Perhaps the most memorable sight on Stephens Island was the dove petrels.

(9) **frigate petrel**. See *white-faced storm petrel* (19) b (e) below.
1982 SALE *Four Seasons* 38 [The white-faced storm petrel] has many other names—skipjack, Dancing Dolly, frigate petrel—from the Pakeha; and takahikaremoana from the Maori.

(10) **giant petrel**. Either of two closely related very large petrels (fam. Procellariidae) with huge yellowish bills, noted for their scavenging habits; also with modifiers: **northern (Hall's) giant petrel** *Macronectes halli*, and **southern giant petrel** *Macronectes giganteus*; NELLY 1. See also *black molly* (BLACK *a*.² B 2), STINKER *n*.¹
1873 BULLER *Birds NZ* 297 *Ossifraga gigantea*. (Giant Petrel)... The Giant Petrel, or 'Nelly', as it is called by sailors, is by no means uncommon in our seas. [Cf. *op cit.* 1888 II. 227 This bird [a Giant Petrel] is habitually silent, except when fighting or when voiding its natural excrement, on which occasions it utters a grunting note.] **1891** *TrNZI* XXIII. 492 As we came out [of the Snares Islands], flocks of sea-birds flew and swam around us, and we headed up a great herd of nellies (*Ossifraga gigantea*, giant petrel or breakbones), and chased them awhile. **1925** GUTHRIE-SMITH *Bird Life* 97 We had heard of a small outlying colony of Giant petrel or Nellies on an islet in the harbour... Nellie Island it is called. **1966** FALLA et al. *Birds NZ* 35–36 Giant Petrel *Macronectes giganteus*... Nelly, Stinker, Black Molly... Mainly scavengers, Giant Petrels are amongst the best documented of ocean wanderers. **1985** *Reader's Digest Book NZ Birds* 68 *Southern Giant Petrel Macronectes giganteus... Nelly, stinker, giant fulmar...* Southern giant petrels are seen most often in New Zealand in the summer when they flock around outfalls of freezing works, and inshore fishing boats. *Ibid.* 69 *Northern Giant Petrel Macronectes halli... Nelly, stinker, Hall's giant petrel, giant fulmar*. The northern giant petrel is very similar to the southern giant petrel and, in fact, it was not until 1966 that they were recognised as two separate species.

(11) **grey** (occas. early **brown**) **petrel**. *Procellaria cinerea* (fam. Procellariidae), a large petrel (see esp. quot. 1984).
1904 HUTTON & DRUMMOND *Animals NZ* 241 *The Brown Petrel... Ibid.* 242 The cry is something like the bleating of a lamb. **1955** OLIVER *NZ Birds* 142 *Grey Petrel Procellaria cinerea*. The Grey Petrel, like many of the species of Puffinius, takes its food in the open sea by diving. **1984** SOPER *Birds NZ* 41 The Grey Petrel is a cold-water species, grey above and white below with dark grey underwings.

(12) **grey-faced (great-winged) petrel**. *Pterodroma macroptera gouldi* (fam. Procellariidae), a dark-plumaged petrel, the common muttonbird of the North Island Maori. See also MUTTONBIRD 1, OI.
1871 HUTTON *Catalogue Birds NZ* 47 *Procellaria gouldi*... Grey-faced Petrel. **1888** Grey-faced Petrel [see OI]. **1904** HUTTON & DRUMMOND *Animals NZ* 245 *The Grey-faced Petrel*... At sea this bird is solitary and wild, never coming near a vessel; and on the wing it looks like a large Swift. **1925–26** *NZJST* VIII. 17 A young *Pterodroma macroptera*, or grey-faced petrel, was found scrambling up a reclining tree-trunk. **1955** OLIVER *NZ Birds* 163 The Grey-faced Petrels breed on most of the off-lying islands of the Auckland Province. **1966** FALLA et al. *Birds of NZ* 47 Grey-faced Petrel... Oi. Great-winged Petrel... Entire plumage blackish-brown, pale grey on the forehead, face and throat. Heard only at nesting grounds, a whistling call with a guttural undertone rendered roughly by the Maori name. **1985** *Reader's Digest Book NZ Birds* 72 *Grey-faced Petrel Pterodroma macroptera gouldi... Oi, muttonbird...* Around the northern part of the North Island, the grey-faced petrel is the most common breeding petrel.

(13) **Kermadec petrel**. *Pterodroma neglecta neglecta* (fam. Procellariidae), a medium-sized variably-coloured petrel breeding in the Kermadec island group.
1955 OLIVER *NZ Birds* 156 The Kermadec Petrel may be considered as consisting of a light phase, a dark phase and innumerable intermediates. **1966** FALLA et al. *Birds of NZ* 49 Kermadec Petrel... Bills are black in all forms; feet usually parti-coloured, being dark at their extremities. **1976** SOPER *NZ Birds* 198 During the early 1900s Kermadec Petrels were reported breeding on Raoul to a density of 800 nests to the half acre and in 1899 twelve thousand chicks were salted down as muttonbirds. **1985** *Reader's Digest Book NZ Birds* 79 At the beginning of this century, more than 200[,]000 Kermadec petrels bred on Raoul Island. Many of their young were harvested as muttonbirds and in the first three weeks of April 1908, over 2000 were slaughtered.

(14) **laughing petrel**. LAUGHING JACKASS 2.
1940 laughing petrel [see LAUGHING JACKASS 2].

(15) **magenta petrel**. *Pterodroma magentae* (fam. Procellariidae) of the Chatham Islands; TAIKO 2.
1985 *Reader's Digest Book NZ Birds* 78 *Chatham Island Taiko Pterodroma magentae...* This extremely rare bird is hardly ever seen... Other names: *Magenta petrel, tchaik* of the *Moriori.* **1987** *Dominion* (Wellington) 16 Dec. 15 For several years now they've been hunting a bird that the rest of the world has been telling them was extinct, the taiko, or the magenta petrel, to give it its European name.

(16) **mottled (Peale's, scaled) petrel**. *Pterodroma inexpectata* (fam. Procellariidae), a small grey and white petrel, having a variety of common names. See also RAINBIRD, TITI 1.
1922 *Auckland Weekly News* 24 Aug. 16 I picked it up to discover it was a mottled petrel, a somewhat rare species at Puysegur Point. **1932** STEAD *Life Histories NZ Birds* 80 Mottled Petrels are such beautiful birds, that it seemed all wrong to find them destroyed [by skuas]. **1955** OLIVER *NZ Birds* 153 *Mottled petrel. Rainbird. Korure...* The Mottled Petrel was discovered in the South Pacific Ocean during Cook's second voyage... All observers have reported the usual call of the Mottled Petrel as a high pitched te-te-te rapidly and continuously repeated when the bird is in flight. **1966** FALLA et al. *Birds of NZ* 50 Mottled Petrel *Pterodroma inexpectata...* Korure, Rainbird. **1985** *Reader's Digest Book NZ Birds* 76 *Mottled Petrel Pterodroma inexpectata... Scaled petrel, Peale's petrel, rainbird, korure, titi...* At one time the mottled petrel may have bred on the mountains of the North and South Islands and on Banks Peninsula.

(17) **Pycroft's petrel**. [f. the name of Arthur Thomas *Pycroft* (1875–1971), naturalist and collector.] *Pterodroma pycrofti* (fam. Procellariidae), a small grey and white petrel.
1949 *NZ Bird Notes* III. 185 The three of us who were familiar with the calls of Cook's petrels..all agreed that the calls of Pycroft's petrel were similar but softer and rather less staccato. **1955** OLIVER *NZ Birds* 149 *Pycrofts Petrel Pterodroma pycrofti*. Andreas Reischek found this petrel on the Chicken Islands in burrows with the tuatara in December 1880 but failed to distinguish it from Cook's Petrel. [**1990** *A Flying Start* 189 When an unknown species of petrel was discovered on Hen Island, Falla expressed his gratitude by naming it in [Pycroft's] honour *Pterodroma pycrofti*.] **1992** *North & South* (Auckland) Apr. 17 Rare and endangered species which stand to benefit from the work include..Pycroft's petrel.

(18) **soft-plumaged petrel**. *Pterodroma mollis* (fam. Procellariidae), a small grey and white petrel.
1976 SOPER *NZ Birds* 227 A new species for the island [*sc.* Antipodes], only recently recorded, is the Soft-plumaged Petrel. **1985** *Reader's Digest Book NZ Birds* 82 Until recently, it was thought that soft-plumaged petrels did not breed in the Pacific Ocean. Then, in February and March 1969, they were seen and heard flying over the Antipodes Islands.

(19) **storm petrel. a.** Any of several tiny petrels of the fam. Oceanitidae which characteristically flutter over the surface of the sea with legs dangling, appearing to walk on the water (hence the names DANCING DOLLY, JESUS CHRIST BIRD, SKIPJACK *n*.² qq.v.). Cf. STORM BIRD.
1917 WILLIAMS *Dict. Maori Lang.* 391 *Reoreo..Garrodia nereis,* storm-petrel. **1932** STEAD *Life Histories NZ Birds* 72 Ranging in size as its members do, from the tiny Storm Petrels (the smallest of all web-footed birds, being not as big as a common Blackbird) to the lordly Albatross..[petrels] have been associated with myths and superstitions for ages. **1984** SOPER *Birds NZ* 46 Storm petrels are tiny seabirds of delicate and frail appearance, whose flight, erratic and flitting, has been likened to that of butterflies. In the hand they feel like thistledown.

b. With a modifier: **black-bellied, grey-backed, Kermadec (Kermadec white-faced), white-bellied, white-faced (New Zealand white-faced), Wilson's**.

(a) **black-bellied storm petrel**. *Fregetta tropica* (see quot. 1904).
1904 HUTTON & DRUMMOND *Animals NZ* 236 *The Black-bellied Storm Petrel...* This species..is at once distinguished from all the other Petrels by the broad black mark which passes down the centre of the abdomen. **1955** OLIVER *NZ Birds* 105 In a bare earth face, I found two tiny burrows about eighteen inches long, in each of which was a Black-bellied Storm Petrel sitting on an egg. **1979** FALLA et al. *New Guide Birds NZ* 55 Black-bellied Storm Petrel... General colour sooty black, brownish grey on the secondary wing-coverets. **1984** SOPER *Birds NZ* 47 In the New Zealand region, the Black-bellied Storm Petrel breeds at Antipodes Islands and Auckland Islands.

(b) **grey-backed storm petrel**. *Oceanites nereis*.
1904 HUTTON & DRUMMOND *Animals NZ* 235 *The Grey-backed Storm Petrel. Garrodia nereis*. **1955** OLIVER *NZ Birds* 100 *Grey-backed Storm Petrel...* This species was first taken off Kaikoura during Cook's first voyage to New Zealand and was described in Solander's manuscript. **1966** FALLA et al. *Birds NZ* 54 Grey-backed Storm Petrel... [B]urrows, like 'rat-holes' have been found..among sitting mollymawks on Disappointment Island. **1984** SOPER *Birds NZ* 47 The Grey-backed Storm Petrel is a bird of subantarctic waters, seldom seen away from the vicinity of its breeding islands. **1990** *Checklist Birds NZ* 58 *Oceanites nereis...* Grey-backed Storm Petrel.

(c) **Kermadec (Kermadec white-faced) storm petrel**. *Pelagodroma marina albiclunis*.

1955 OLIVER *NZ Birds* 103 *Kermadec White-faced Storm Petrel*... Cheeseman, who visited the Kermadecs in 1887, recorded the 'Storm Petrel' as common at sea all round the Kermadec Islands. **1985** *Reader's Digest Book NZ Birds* 104 The rare Kermadec storm petrel is found round the Kermadec Islands. **1990** *Checklist Birds NZ 60 Pelagodroma marina albiclunis..Kermadec Storm Petrel... Breeding* grounds unknown. About 30 records from around Kermadec Islands but only once ashore.

(d) **white-bellied storm petrel**. *Fregetta grallaria grallaria*.

1955 OLIVER *NZ Birds* 105 White-bellied Storm Petrel *Fregetta grallaria*. **1979** FALLA et al. *New Guide Birds NZ* 56 White-bellied Storm Petrel... A circum-sub-tropical species known to breed in the New Zealand region only on the vermin-free outliers of the Kermadecs. **1984** SOPER *Birds NZ* 47 The White-bellied Storm Petrel... This is a subtropical relative of the Black-bellied Storm Petrel and differs from it in having a wholly white belly and less conspicuous nostril tubes. **1990** *Checklist Birds NZ* 62 *Fregatta grallaria grallaria...* White-bellied Storm Petrel.

(e) **white-faced (New Zealand white-faced) storm petrel**. *Pelagodroma marina maoriana*. See also DANCING DOLLY, JESUS CHRIST BIRD, SKIPJACK *n.*²

1893 *TrNZI* XXV. 81 The White-faced Petrel... I have recently obtained a number of specimens from Otago, together with the skins of the birds, taken from the burrows. **1949** *NZ Bird Notes* III. 152 White-faced Storm Petrel... Some scores were seen on both crossings [to Little Barrier]. **1966** White-faced Storm Petrel [see JESUS CHRIST BIRD]. **1979** FALLA et al. *New Guide Birds NZ* 55 White-faced Storm Petrel *Pelagodroma marina...* Takahikare-moana, Skipjack, Jesus Christ Bird, shortened to 'J.C Bird'), Dancing Dolly. **1984** SOPER *Birds NZ* 48 The White-faced Storm Petrel is the common storm petrel of New Zealand inshore waters... It is the only storm petrel with a white face broken by a dark line through the eye, and a black cap. **1990** *Checklist Birds NZ* 59 *Pelagodroma marina maoriana*..New Zealand White-faced Storm Petrel (*Takahikare-moana*).

(20) **Westland (Westland black) petrel**. *Procellaria westlandica* (fam. Procellariidae), a large, pale-billed, all-black petrel. See also SHOEMAKER.

1966 FALLA et al. *Birds of NZ* 46 Westland Black Petrel... The entirely dark plumage is exactly similar to that of the Black Petrel, as are the bill and feet. **1970** *Annot. Checklist Birds NZ* 26 *Procellaria westlandica... Westland Black Petrel*. **1980** LOCKLEY *House Above Sea* 36 There were some petrels I had never seen before —..the large all-black Westland petrel whose only known resting place is a remote rainy valley in Fiordland. **1989** PARKINSON *Travelling Naturalist* 172 In the hills..nests one of the world's rarest seabirds, the Westland black petrel. This bird, once called the Westland shoemaker..survives only here.

(21) **white-chinned petrel**. *Procellaria aequinoctialis aequinoctialis* (fam. Procellariidae), a large dark petrel. See also SHOEMAKER, STINKPOT 1.

1904 HUTTON & DRUMMOND *Animals NZ* 243 *The White-chinned Petrel*... This bird breeds in holes at the Auckland Islands. By the sealers it is called Stink-pot, or Stinker. **1955** OLIVER *NZ Birds* 147 Sorensen examined a small nesting colony of the White-chinned Petrel on Campbell Island. **1966** [see SHOEMAKER]. **1984** SOPER *Birds NZ* 42 White-chinned Petrels dig enormous burrows, usually in the wettest, most saturated ground they can find, a behaviour unique among petrels. **1990** *Checklist Birds NZ* 35 *Procellaria aequinoctialis aequinoctialis*..White-chinned Petrel.

(22) **white-headed petrel**. *Pterodroma lessonii* (fam. Procellariidae), a pale-grey, dark-winged petrel.

1871 HUTTON *Catalogue Birds NZ* 46 Procellaria lessoni... White-headed Petrel. **1889** *TrNZI* XXI. 384 Among the other birds seen [on Auckland Islands] were the skua gull, the black-backed gull..and the white-headed petrel. **1904** HUTTON & DRUMMOND *Animals NZ* 246 *The White-headed Petrel...* This bird breeds in holes on the Antipodes Island... It is solitary and wild, like the Grey-faced Petrel. **1955** OLIVER *NZ Birds* 160 At the Auckland Islands, E.F. Stead found the White-headed Petrel breeding. **1985** *Reader's Digest Book NZ Birds* 73 White-headed Petrel... By day this nocturnal bird is rarely seen near its breeding places; but at night the White-headed petrel performs noisy aerial displays.

(23) **white-naped petrel**, see *black-capped petrel* (2) above.

phantom. *Goldmining*. An apparently well-defined lead of gold which proves a 'duffer'.

1862 *Otago Goldfields & Resources* 21 Waipori has no 'pile claims', and the miner, who is searching after that New Zealand 'phantom', a defined lead, would be surely disappointed here. **1868** *Auckland Punch* 76 There is a phantom in every shaft.

pheasant. *Obs*. Also **ground pheasant**. WEKA 1.

1842 BARNICOAT *Journal* (ATLTS) 6 May 53 The [Waimea] pla[i]n abounds with a kind of bird about the size and very much of the appearance of a common hen. We call them pheasants which they also resemble. **1842** HEAPHY *NZ* 47 The *Weka*.., an Apterix [Heaphy is mistaken], termed by some of the settlers the 'Ground Pheasant'.

pheasant weed: see INKWEED.

phormium. In full **Phormium tenax**. Also with init. cap. [Cf. OED modern Latin (J.R. & G. Forster *Characteres Generum Plantarum* (1776) 47), ad. Greek diminutive φορμίον, mat, basket, in reference to the use made of the fibres of the leaves.] FLAX 1.

1817 NICHOLAS *Voyage NZ* II. 249 The herbaceous productions indigenous to the country are, wild celery..the phormium tenax or flax-plant, and a species of the fern. **1821** YULE in *Edinburgh New Philos. Jrnl.* V. 345 The following results..manifest the comparative superiority of strength of the fibres of the Phormium. **1826** SHEPHERD *Journal* 18 Mar. in Howard *Rakiura* (1940) 361 A considerable quantity of Phormium ten[a]x grows here. **1830** CRAIK *New Zealanders* 179 Mr. Nicholas brought some of the seeds of the New Zealand phormium with him to England. **1841** [see FLAX I 2 (3)]. **1860** in Butler *First Year* (1863) iii 34 The distinctive marks which characterise it as not English are the occasional Ti palms..the luxuriance of the Phormium tenax. **1892** *NZ Official Handbook* 153 The preparation of Phormium for export is an industry of New Zealand which has not made vast progress. **1910** COCKAYNE *NZ Plants & Their Story* 109 The manufacture of fibre from phormium—'New Zealand hemp', as it is now called—has become one of the staple industries of the Dominion. **1930** [see AUTE]. **1950** *NZJST* XXXI. 4 The Phormium industry in New Zealand..was built largely on an export trade to cordage fibre markets overseas.

pia. Also **pia-manuka**. [Ma. /ˈpia/, /ˈpia ˈmaːnuka/: Williams 279 *Pia* (i)..*1*. Gum of trees, or any similar exudation.] *manuka manna* (MANUKA 3).

1867 HOOKER *Handbook* 767 piamanuka... Manna exudation of *Leptospermum scoparium*. **1869** *TrNZI* I. (rev. edn.) 262 [They] thought highly of a sugary manna-like exudation (of doubtful vegetable origin) called pia-manuka, and found..on the branches of the *Leptospermum scoparium*. **1882** HAY *Brighter Britain* II. 196 A sort of manna, which exudes from the [manuka] plant in all stages, is called by [the Maori] Piamanuka. **1981** [see MANUKA 3].

piarau, var. PIHAPIHARAU.

picaninny. *Obs*. Also **picaninni, piccaninny, pickaninny, pickeeninnee**. [Transf. use of West Indian *picaninny* a (black) child: AND 1 Aboriginal child, 1817.] **a**. A Maori or half-caste child.

1817 NICHOLAS *NZ* II. 171 This fellow [sc. a native servant]..met me..telling me that Mrs. King had got a *pickeeninnee* [sic], (a child,) he began to describe her groans..while..under the pains of labour. **1830** REV. LEIGH 4 Aug. in McNab *Hist. Records* (1908) I. 709 They observed they could not let me have it, for if they did all their pickaninnies (their children) would all die. **1842** *Piraki Log* 18 May (1911) 129 Richards and Mould returned yesterday with some traps, his woman, and the Picaninnies. **1854** *Richmond-Atkinson Papers* (1960) I. 159 Most of the picaninnies have been 'down with the measles' as the people here phrase it. c**1867** in Wily & Maunsell *Robert Maunsell* (1938) 187 We found three large canoes filled with natives—men, women, and picaninnies—all covered with green leaves, the mourning costume of the Maoris. **1873** TINNE *Wonderland of Antipodes* 9 Fancy these *tamariki*, picaninnies or brats of one or two years old, indulging..in the herb nicotiana. **1891** COTTLE *Frank Melton's Luck* 97 Little Maori pickaninny. **1900** *Canterbury Old & New* 116 On being hauled out [of the lilipi gruel] the [Maori] child was handed over to the women..very little stuff from the picannini was wasted. **1905** BRANDON 'Ukneadit' 104 Pickled picaninnies... Picaninnies from neighbouring tribes may be preserved for winter. **1925** MANDER *Allen Adair* (1971) 85 He loved to carry her about in a shawl on his back as the Maoris did the picaninnies. **1939** GRIEVE *Sketches from Maoriland* (1961) 43 'The kids at them school he the cheeky brat..', volunteered a lady with a piccaninny fastened to her back. **1949** SARGESON *I Saw in My Dream* (1974) 229 Johnny said yes, and did Dave know what Rangi and Eileen and the pickaninnies would do when they got to town? **1964** MORRIESON *Came a Hot Friday* (1981) 170 Pakeha visitors to the abode of Tui Porano were few and far between and news of the occupancy of the guest chamber soon circulated among the piccaninnies.

b. *transf*. Occas. applied to the young of animals.

1853 EARP *NZ* 145 [The natives] are very fond of horses... They will buy nothing but mares, having a great desire to have 'pickaninny' horses of their own.

Piccadilly. *WW1*. and *WW2*. [Poss. alluding to the reputed sartorial, etc. smartness of the London West End set.] Applied to the 'spit-and-polish' insistence and results of Imperial drill instructors, seen as an unnecessary 'Homey' or 'Pommy' display; also in the phr. **to do the Piccadilly**, to perform an ultra-smart sentry patrol. Also used *attrib*. in special Comb. **Piccadilly stunt**, a full-dress, 'spit-and-polish' Army routine march or exercise, occas. a parade.

1917 in Miller *Camps, Tramps & Trenches* 31 Mar. (1939) 49 At about 11.15 every morning we go through a piece of agony known as 'Piccadilly'. All the New

Zealanders in [? Sling] camp, three to four thousand strong, march along a certain section of the road in column of fours. On either side are about sixteen Sergeant Instructors, beautiful fellows, their superb figures almost bursting through their London tailor-made tunics. Their duty and pleasure it is to blast us up in a loud voice for any little irregularity of deportment they may notice or think they notice. **1918** *Chron. NZEF* 13 Sept. 88 Our camp..has witnessed..many strange Piccadilly stunt parades in the morning... This dink camp is some size now; and the Piccadilly, twice weekly, some stunt. *Ibid.* 25 Oct. 150 The rest was carried out in the usual way: inspections, parades, Piccadilly stunts, and recreation. **1919** *Chron. NZEF* 24 Jan. 309 Are we advertisements for New Zealand or not?.. If we are, dress us up smart..riding breeches and leggings, a tunic that fits, and a good felt hat with a Piccadilly pugaree. **1959** SLATTER *Gun in My Hand* 185 [The Pongo sentry] was in full gear with blancoed web and anklets and rifle sling and he did the full Piccadilly up and down outside the door and slapping salutes right left and centre.

piccaninny, var. PICANINNY.

pick, *v.*

1. *trans.* To guess rightly; to predict.
1909 *Truth* 29 May 5 When one comes to think of it, instead of saying 'Rightly, sir,' Connelly would have remarked, 'They picked it, my oath,' or words to that effect. **c1926** THE MIXER *Transport Workers' Song Book* 128 I'm picking we'll soon have a row. **1943** MARSH *Colour Scheme* vi. 100 There's a bit of a shelf above the cliff... I picked that was where he'd go. **1959** MASTERS *Tales of Mails* 14 The boss..exclaimed, 'why blow me down if here isn't His Excellency and party now!' Clarrie glanced up. 'Well; by crikey old chappie; how quickly you picked us,' he responded. **1985** GORDON & DEVERSON *NZ Eng.* 48 *pick* (for example, *I'm picking*—I reckon *the All Blacks will win*)

2. In the phr. **to pick the eyes out** (of land), see EYE 2.

pick, *n.* *Farming.*[AND 1960.] Also **picking**, usu. *pl.* [AND 1901]. (A snack for stock from) sparse pasture.
1985 STEWART *Gumboots & Goalposts* 65 We drove around..and had a good leisurely look at the stock while tossing a bit of hay about—just to 'provide a pick'. **1973** FERNANDEZ *Tussock Fever* 60 How about I get half a dozen [sheep] down into the pen this evening... There's enough pickings for them there.

pickaninny, var. PICANINNY.

pickapo, var. PIKOPO.

pickaroo. *Forestry.* [Orig. unknown.] A long pole with a spike at one end used to tilt a tree being felled in the direction of its proposed fall so as to keep the feller's saw-blade free-moving. Cf. PIKE-POLE.
1992 BOYD *Pumice & Pines* 148 [Caption] Carl Taylor felling a Douglas fir with a Lowther circular saw in 1953. His mate assists with a 'pickaroo'; a long pole with a spike in one end.

pickeeninnee, var. PICANINNY.

picker.
1. *Shearing.* A *picker-up* (PICK UP *v.* 1).
1913 CARR *Country Work* 14 As soon as a shearer has taken the fleece off..the picker gathers the fleece up in such a manner that she or he can on getting to the rolling table, throw it out with the breech part at the right end.

2. [AND 1913.] A fruit-picker.
1950 *NZJAg.* Nov. LXXXI. 427 Careful handling of fruit..is essential. Pickers are shown placing the picking receptacles into the cases. **1987** GEE *Prowlers* 105 The Coxes and the Galas and the Golden and Red Delicious are harvested now and the pickers are working on the Granny Smiths.

3. *Wool-scouring.* See quot.
1985 BREMNER *Woolscours NZ* 9 *Picker* hand who picked residual foreign matter out of scoured wool before packing. *Ibid.* 23 After conditioning..hours, scoured wool is put onto the wire-netting table where any residual discoloured or stained wool is removed by the pickers before the bales are packed.

pick handle. As a rough measure of (human bodily) breadth. Compare *axe-handle* (AXE 3).
1974 GIFFORD *Loosehead Len's Big Brown Book* 20 He'd have gone about 15 or 16 stone and he was about three pick handles across the shoulders. **1986** *Marist Messenger* Dec. 36 She's a big woman, the boss's wife, two pick handles across the backside and an arm that can fell a bullock.

pickings, *vbl. n.*
1. [f. *pick (out)* to distinguish from surroundings: cf. OED *pick*[1] 19 d.] Of a building, the external features painted in a colour different from the main colour.
1913 MANSFIELD in *Undiscovered Country* (1974) 301 And at last it was finished. Old Tar's house, painted white with green 'pickings', reared up ready at the top of the hill.

2. See PICK *n.*

picking up, *vbl. n.* In various senses of 'collecting', 'lifting up': **a.** *Shearing.* See PICK UP *v.* 1.

b. *Rabbiting.* The activity or process of collecting dead rabbits from a poison or trap line.
1953 STRONACH *Musterer on Molesworth* 61 'Picking up' on a frosty morning is an unpleasant job and, with a big 'kill' takes a long time. Rideable country is the best because a man carrying twenty-five rabbits had quite a good load, and a horse can take many more.

c. *Whaling.* Collecting a whale killed by a chaser.
1982 GRADY *Perano Whalers* 228 *Pick-up boat*—The boat used for picking-up whales killed by whale-chasers. The pick-up boat would then tow the whales to the whaling station for processing. Sometimes, if the mother ship was not available for pick-up work, a spare chaser or the one with the least work on hand would take on the task of picking up.

d. *Carpentry.* See quot.
1987 SCOTT *Imported Timbers* 71 *Picking up* The process by which a planing machine produces planed timber which has a hairy surface. This may be the result of blunted or wrongly angled planing knives or reverse grain or tension wood in the timber, or a combination of these. Such hairiness is very hard to eradicate.

pickle, *v.* In exclamations of surprise or disbelief: **pickle me bloody agates** [i.e. testicles], **pickle my daisies, pickle my tit!**
1964 HELMER *Stag Party* 82 I gets down to the stag. Wull, pickle me bloody agates, would you believe it? The bullet has caught the old boy clean in the family jewels. **1964** DAVIS *Watersiders* 109 'Well pickle my tit,' he says, 'if it isn't young Blue'. **1988** MCGILL *Dict. Kiwi Slang* 83 *pickle my daisies!* exclamation of doubt; eg 'Pickle my daisies if that's true.'

pick up, *v.*

1. *Shearing.* [AND 1897.] **a.** *trans.* To gather up (a newly-shorn fleece) and place it on the sorting table for skirting, classing, etc.
1862 WALKER *Journal* (ATLTS) 10 Nov. 24 My job at first was picking up fleeces. **1878** ELWELL *Boy Colonists* 46 His work was to pick up fleeces. **1889** WILLIAMS & REEVES *Colonial Couplets* 9 I'm engaged in the baling and pressing of wool, And when picking up fleeces my hands are quite full. **1922** PERRY *Sheep Farming* 83 A boy or man to five shearers is sufficient for picking up the fleeces. **1933** *Press* (Christchurch) (Acland Gloss.) 21 Oct. 15 When a shearer finishes a sheep, the *f[leece]* is left lying on the *board*... It is *picked up* by a boy (the *f[leece]-p[icker]*), who carries it to a table throws it out flat to be skirted, rolled and classed. The verb, to *f[leece]-pick*, means 'to be a fleece-picker'. To *p[ick] up* is to do the actual *job*. **1964** MIDDLETON *Walk on Beach* 167 There was nothing new to me in picking up fleeces. **1986** RICHARDS *Off the Sheep's Back* 55 I was allowed to miss school to help in the shed by picking up the bellywool.

b. *intr.* or *absol.* To gather up a shorn fleece for skirting, etc.
1926 DEVANNY *Butcher Shop* (1981) 29 But the wonder of wool..the naked feet of the brown women 'picking up' from the shining greasy floor. **1965** MACNICOL *Skippers Road* 89 'I don't need a shearer, but I need shed hands. Can you pick up?' **1981** CHARLES *Black Billy Tea* 72 Jack Frost..was 'picking up' and I was the rouseabout.

Hence **picker-up**, *pl. pickers-up* [AND 1870], a person who clears fleeces from the shearing board (see also FLEECE-OH, FLEECE-PICKER); **picking up** *vbl. n.*, see also FLEECE-PICKING.
1875 *Otago Witness* (Dunedin) 18 Sept. 18 First, clean all the points, the crutch and the belly wool, and let this be swept aside and taken away at once by the 'picker-up'. **1881** BATHGATE *Waitaruna* 172 Meanwhile the 'pickers up' were busy gathering up the fleeces..and carrying them to the sorting table, where they were stripped of the 'pieces', which were thrown aside. **1913** BATHGATE *Sodger Sandy's Bairn* 57 The pickers-up gathered the fleeces as they fell intact from the shears and bore them to the sorting table where they were quickly 'skirted' and 'classed'. **1926** DEVANNY *Butcher Shop* (1981) 65 The singing of the Maoris on the boards, interspersed with raucous yells at a careless 'Picker-up'..all conspired to dazzle her. **1940** STUDHOLME *Te Waimate* (1954) 208 At shearing time [at Benmore, 1892] about 55 men were employed in the shed: 28 to 30 shearers, 2 penners-up, 4 pickers-up. **1952** MEEK *Station Days* 111 *Picker-up.* One who picks up the fleece, and carries it to the wool-table. **1975** HARPER *Eight Daughters* 30 They both helped too with the drafting and dipping, and **picking up** in the woolshed—usually barefoot.

2. [Alluding to William Ellis's supposed founding of rugby football by 'picking up the ball and running with it'.] In the phr. **to pick up the ball (to pick the ball up) and run with it**, to take a forward-moving initiative.
1984 *2YA Wellington*: Local News Bulletin 3 Oct. 8.05 a.m., Wellington Chamber of Commerce members, criticising Economic Summit Meeting, said that now they 'should pick up the ball and run with it' if things were to get done. **1986** *Dominion* (Wellington) 27 Dec. 31 Maori Affairs secretary Tamati Reedy picked it [*sc.* the loan proposal] up and ran with it. Then it became a government negotiation.

picnic, *n.*[1] [AND 1896.] An awkward or unpleasant venture; a troublesome experience; a 'mess'.

PICNIC

c1930 *Whitcombe's Etym. Dict. Aust.-NZ Suppl.* 9 *picnic* n. sl. a troublesome job; an awkward experience; a difficult adventure. **1943** BENNETT *English in NZ in Amer. Speech* XVIII. 90 The expressions 'too true', 'too right', in which *too* has its old intensive value, are in common use; so are 'that'll be a picnic', 'what a picnic' (where *picnic* = 'trouble, bother'). **1988** MCGILL *Dict. Kiwi Slang* 83 *picnic* problem; ironic, reversal of what is usually a pleasant occasion; eg 'If you take the boat out in that weather, mate, it's your picnic.'

picnic, n.²

1. *Horse-racing.* [AND *picnic-meeting* 1896, *-races* 1911.] Usu. *attrib.*, often in Comb. **picnic meeting**, applied to a racing club, or a race-meeting held by such a club, which perhaps once a year on a public or local holiday holds a meeting in a 'picnic' or informal atmosphere.
1944 *Matamata Record* 21 Dec. 7 Picnic Race Meeting... The Morrinsville Picnic Racing Club has now issued its programmes for the Club's Annual race meeting. **1944** *Wairoa Star* 29 Dec. 1 At Tauherenikau (which incidentally is a lovely picnic course, being surrounded by beautiful native bush), the big event is the Wairarapa Cup. **1970** *Horse Racing, Trotting in NZ* 172 *Wairoa*... This is one of the North Island 'picnic' clubs and holds a 3-day meeting around the local anniversary day... It relies on the picnic atmosphere as its main attraction. **1972** PREBBLE *Horses, Courses & Men* 50 The racing enthusiasm of the locals was absorbed in picnic meetings which had a strong Maori influence. **1987** WILLIAMS *Racing for Gold* 72 [Caption] Maori picnic meeting 1890s. Note the discarded kai baskets in front of the bookmakers. **1992** *Evening Post* (Wellington) 18 May 21 I think we should be sticking to the picnic-type meetings... They are successful and it can be a pleasant day out for families.

2. See *school picnic* (SCHOOL 1).

Picton herring: see HERRING 2 (1).

picture.

1. *pl.* As **the pictures** [used elsewhere but recorded earliest, and in freq. use in New Zealand: see OED *picture* 2 i.], a usual popular term for the cinema in New Zealand. Also *sing.* as *attrib.*
1910 16 Mar. in *Evening Post* (Wellington) (1952) 1 Oct. 14 [King's Theatre Programme] West's and Royal Pictures. **1914** *Evening Post* (Wellington) 6 Jan. 2 Eight million individuals attend 'the pictures' every week. **1938** HYDE *Nor Yrs. Condemn* 13 'Tea's coming up in the lift? Going to the pictures?' 'I suppose so.' **1944** *Short Guide NZ* 37 And most New Zealanders have a fair working knowledge of American slang, having heard it from the movies (called 'the pictures' or 'the flicks'). **1967** HOLDEN *Empty Hills* 24 The picture crowds had already gone home and there was hardly anyone about. **1982** FRAME *To the Is-land* (1984) 107 Going out with boys or loitering..outside the pie cart after the pictures.

2. Special Comb. (now mainly archaic) **picture hall**, a (country) hall used as a picture house; **picture night** *obs.*, esp. in the country, the night of the week on which a picture show occurred; **picture show** [AND *obs.* 1915], a cinema programme; **picture theatre** [AND 1947], a cinema.
1938 HYDE *Nor Yrs. Condemn* 138 Nothing much happened to break the days or evenings, except young 'prentices in the **picture-hall** banging their seats and chanting: 'Siddown, siddown'. **1964** ANDERSON *Doctor in Mountains* (1974) 55 It seemed to me that the whole population of the town must be there—being Saturday it was of course '**picture night**'. **1927** *NZ Dairy Produce Exporter* 3 Sept. 43 In the backblocks, we backblockers have to lead a pretty quiet life. No **picture shows**, or even shops. **1926** *NZ Dairy Produce Exporter* 28 Aug. 42 The nearest **picture theatre** is six miles. **1955** *BJ Cameron Collection* (TS July) *picture theatre* (n) Almost always used in speech instead of cinema. **1967** HOLDEN *Empty Hills* 40 Elsie would lie awake afterwards trying to decide whether he went to the pictures hoping to see her there or whether he had merely discovered that the picture-theatre was a pleasanter place to spend his evenings than the boarding-house.

pidi-pidi, var. PIRIPIRI n.¹

pidgin-Maori. Also **pigeon-**.

1. An often reduced form of the Maori language affected by English vocabulary, pronunciation, or grammar.
[*Note*] Early reduplicated examples are KAIKAI v., *tappy-tap(py), tabby-tab(by)* for TAPU v., *crackee crackee* for KARAKIA n. 2 (see quot. 1817). See also TOKI 2, quot. 1817 ('no tokee, no tokee, no porkee, no porkee').
1874 BAINES *Edward Crewe* 115 One trouble to the learner [of Maori] is that natives will persist in talking easy 'pigeon' Maori to new 'pakehas'; perhaps that is one reason why so few Europeans 'talk Maori well', though many know enough of the language for ordinary purposes, such as buying or selling. **1936** LAMBERT *Pioneering Reminisc. Old Wairoa* 75 We had been out fishing and were expecting at any time to hear the signal, 'There she spouts!' or '*Ehi pauta*!' the pigeon-Maori version of the warning.

2. Also as **Maori pidgin**, a form of the English language affected by Maori vocabulary, pronunciation, or grammar and often used by entertainers, etc., and formerly by writers, to represent working-class Maori use of spoken English. See esp. *Maori English* (MAORI B 5).
1995 *Dominion* (Wellington) 29 Mar. 2 Speaking in pseudo Maori pidgin the Far North MP rang a Radio Pacific talkback show..to bemoan the Government fiscal envelope as a threat to his 'free ride' on the dole.

pie: see PIE ON; HALF-PIE.

pie. *Freezing works.* [f. Brit. dial. *pie* a heap (of maturing root crops or dung): see EDD 6 and 7.]

1. The collected or heaped up remnants of sheepskin (often rotted) from which the wool is to be plucked.
1913 CARR *Country Work* 19 There is only one job that the most fastidious could refuse, and that is 'picking pie'. This consists in pulling the wool off the trimmings that have been taken off by the 'wool pullers' at the beam. These trimmings are..allowed to rot until the wool comes away easily. [Pie pickers] live and eat by themselves.

2. Special Comb. **pie-heap**, the heap of pie at a freezing works; **pie-house**, a building in a freezing works where the pie is collected and worked; **pie man, pie-picker**, one employed to pick the wool out of pie, notorious for having the stink of pie clinging to the person, hence **as popular as a pie-picker at the pictures**, very unpopular; **pie-wool**, wool retrieved from pie.
1951 pie-heap [see *pie-picker* below]. **1950** *NZJAg.* Sept. LXXXI. 261 Pie Wool All the head, ear, cod, shank, and pullers' skin pieces..are taken to the **pie house**, where under normal atmospheric conditions they are allowed to sweat in heaps. **1959** SLATTER *Gun in My Hand* 67 You were on hourly rates shoving the heavy-laden trolleys of sheepskins from the painters to the pullers or working in the piehouse where it got into you and you could never go to the pictures. **1951** *Awards, etc.* 327 [NZ Freezing-Workers Award] [Rates of wages] Piece or **pie men** (piecework at per pound on weight of dry wool)..per 10 lb. [£]0 2[s.] 8³/₄[d.]. **1951** 17 May Feilding Freezing Works terms p.c. Colin Gordon. The *chopper* also *scalps* them which gets taken off as the *ear-piece*, and goes down to the *pie-house*, on to the *pie-heap* where [the piece] rots and is plucked by the **pie-pickers**. In Southland there was supposed to be a special session [of the pictures] for pie-pickers. **1950 pie wool** [see *pie-house* above]. **1953** *Shaw, Savill & Albion Coy Timetable* 16 Dec. [A passenger vessel] does not accept first slipe, 2nd slipe, pie wool class 1, pie wool class 2, Hides, Clippings. **1957** *NZ Farmer* 13 June 6 Some 7 per cent of this freezing works wool is produced from the skin... In the past these skin pieces were rotted and the wool recovered, since skin rots faster than wool. The process was unpleasant and the wool (known as 'pie' wool) often suffered fibre damage.' **1957** MACDONALD *Canterbury Frozen Meat Co.* 69 Some mention should be made of 'pie-wool'. This is the wool from pieces which are trimmed off the woolly skin, and are not 'painted' with depilatory. Pie-wool is loosened by allowing the skin to putrefy, a repulsive and laborious job, and after separation the wool is washed and dried.

Hence occas. as a v. intr. (usu. *vbl. n.*) **pieing**, rotting, decomposing (in a pie-heap).
1957 MACDONALD *Canterbury Frozen Meat Co.* 69 A great deal of research work has been done in Australia recently in the use of 'enzyme' preparations to get quick sanitary 'pieing', but unfortunately so far costs have proved too high.

pie-cart.

a. A mobile eating place, usu. set up nightly on a regular street-stand and serving meals (traditionally PEA, PIE, PUD q.v.), or (now mainly) takeaway foods.
1920 *NZ Free Lance* (Wellington) 1 Dec. (Xmas Annual) 33 There were a few points which appealed to the aesthetic tastes of the pie-cart frequenter. **1922** TURNER *Happy Wanderer* 37 We [*sc.* New Zealanders in England] drifted down to the pie-cart (coffee-stall in your speech). **1938** HYDE *Godwits Fly* (1970) 125 Two cadgers whined for the price of a meal. Timothy felt his panache come back... 'Come along to the pie-cart, boys.' **1949** DAVIN *Roads from Home* 70 Somebody having a feed at the pie-cart. **1959** SLATTER *Gun in My Hand* 163 Over the road now I see the pie-cart halted by the kerb. *Ibid.* 164 Pie-cart food always tastes the same. **1960** MUIR *Word for Word* 201 The rest of the staff..spent the hour dining or having a snack at the pie-cart. **1977** *Dominion* (Wellington) 8 Oct. 2 I hoped..to devote a separate chapter to the famous pie-cart men of the city [*sc.* Wellington]... It was a treat..to push yourself up under the surrounding canvas, right into the bright lights and warmth of stove, and order a 'pea-pie-pud' for sixpence. **1991** *North & South* (Auckland) Mar. 29 Jim Jennings..was Auckland's true hero of 'different' cuisine (from the pie-cart, boarding-house stodge).

b. *transf.* See quots.
1928 *Free Lance* (Wellington) 25 July 7 The 'bush express', which consists of one carriage known as the 'pie-cart' and a light locomotive, leaves the cookshop daily at 7.15 a.m. **1937** *NZ Railways Mag.* Jan. 35 Here [*sc.* at Port Craig] we had a ride on the sawmill train, great high unwieldy object, known locally as 'the pie-cart'.

piece. [Spec. uses of *piece* a portion or fragment.]
1. *Farming.* [AND 1891.] Usu. *pl.* Body wool trimmings and oddments removed from the shorn

PIECEY

fleece when it is skirted. Cf. BELLY 1 a, LOCK, SKIRTINGS, TRIMMINGS.

1856 FITTON *NZ* 234 New Zealand.—Scoured fleece, 1s. 8½d... average flocks, 1s. 5d... pieces and locks, 1s. 1d... unwashed, 10½d. **1881** [see *picking up* (PICK UP v. 1)]. **1894** WILSON *Land of Tui* 244 The waste pieces [*sc.* wool trimmed from fleeces by the fleece-picker] are thrown into a heap. **1901** [see BELLY-WOOL]. **1917** STRACHAN in Neave *Land of Munros* (1980) 65 We had [in 1858] an old tent pitched inside and had about half a bale of pieces as a field bed. **1922** PERRY *Sheep Farming* 121 The skirtings of the neck and shoulder can be called first pieces, and the britch ends made into second pieces. **1936** BELSHAW et al. *Agric. Organiz. NZ* 710 'Pieces' are mainly skirtings other than necks or bellies and consist of heavy-conditioned, stained or inferior wool removed from the fleece. **1940** GASKELL *All Part of the Game* (1978) 2 I take the next [bale of wool] and weigh it. 'Bellies and pieces,' they say. **1950** *NZJAg.* Oct. LXXXI. 311 Baskets or skeps on wheels are handy for holding pieces. **1964**, **1973** [see BELLY *n.* 1 a]. **1982** *Agric. Gloss.* (MAF) 57 *Pieces*: Body wool trimmings removed from the fleece when it is skirted after shearing. The longer pieces are termed first or bulky pieces while the shorter pieces are termed second pieces.

2. Also occas. **piecey**. [f. Brit. (esp. Sc.) dial. *piece* a piece of bread (and butter): see SND *piece n.* 2.] A piece of bread and butter (and jam), to be eaten as a snack.

1881 BATHGATE *Waitaruna* 87 After breakfast, taking what Renwick called a 'piece' in their pockets, Gilbert and Leslie started on foot for Waterfall Gully. **1938** HYDE *Godwits Fly* (1970) 7 Run along and brush yourself, do. Eliza, dearie, wouldn't you like a piece before you go? **1947–48** BEATTIE *Pioneer Recolls.* (1956) 39 My chief recollection of that visit is that Mrs McKellar gave me a big piece. **1963** PEARSON *Coal Flat* 120 'I want a piece,' he said. *Ibid.* 121 'You pick up your schoolbag..or there won't be any piece!' **1963** FRAME *The Reservoir* (1966) 105 We banged on the bedroom wall, 'Mum, bring us a piece!' She brought us a piece of bread and jam. **1968** BALLANTYNE *Sydney Bridge* 13 'Would anybody here fancy a piecey?' asked Mrs Kelly... I followed her to the pantry, hoped she would get out some of her great plum jam on the pieces of bread. **1975** KNIGHT *Poyntzfield* 30 I do not seem to remember breakfast that morning—we had 'pieces' in the boat [at Porirua, c1850s].

3. In various phrases. **a. a piece of piss**, something easy to accomplish, or easily attained. See also *piss-easy* (PISS *n.* 2).

1981 JOHNSTON *Fish Factory* 84 I've got it all worked out and your part is a piece of piss. **1981** *Avondale College Slang Words* (Auckland) (Goldie Brown Collect.) *a piece of piss*: easy **1991** DUFF *One Night Out Stealing* 41 Yeah, a breeze, a cinch, a piece of piss, an easy-meat bowl-over.

b. to have a piece of, to scold, to reprimand.

1958 HORNBY *Mystery in Maori land* 26 'Try some more apricots,' he suggested. 'Better than having a piece of Danny.' 'What do you mean?' Julie wrinkled her brows. 'That's a New Zealand expression for telling someone off,' explained Danny. **1982** GILDERDALE *Sea Change* 241 *have a piece of* Reprimand.

piecey: see PIECE 2.

pied. In the names of birds, 'particoloured', see: FANTAIL 2 (3), OYSTERCATCHER 2 (3), SHAG 2 (11) and 2 (13), STILT 2 (2), TIT *n.*[1] a.

pie on. *Obs.* Also **pai**, **pion**, **pye-on**. [ad. Ma. *pai* /'pai/, and prob. from the phr. *e pai ana* '(It) is

good': Williams 249 *Pai* (a) *1. a[djective]* Good, excellent... *10. v.* Be willing.: *Ana* (b) A particle denoting continuance of an action or state, used after verbs or adjectives... *1.* When 'e' precedes the adjective or verb, *ana* denotes a temporary condition, a continuing action, or an action intended to be performed immediately: P. Ranby notes—Williams's 'adjective' 1. is a 'stative'; 10. is a transitive verb which can be glossed 'to agree to, approve of'.] Very good, 'dinkum', 'ship shape'; all right, 'OK'; formerly used as an exclamation of agreement or commendation. Cf. also HALF-PIE, KAPAI.

[**1807** SAVAGE *NZ* 76 Piannah—Good. **1843** DIEFFENBACH *Travels in NZ* II. 376 Pai—good, kind, well; e pai ano—please, good.] **c1890–1910** p.c. Professor P.S. Ardern (1954, Auckland): In my youth in Auckland before the World War [*sc.* WW1] *Pie on*! was used rather like 'she's jake' is now. **1916** GRAY, Norman *MS Papers 4134* (ATLMS) 26 Aug. I still have my sanitary work, but there is practically nothing to do and it's a pye-on kop (excuse)! **1917** let. 25 July in *Boots, Belts* (1992) 18 We had a showerbath, first hot and then cold... As the cold water came down, what yells! It was pion all the same. **1918** *Stratford Evening Post* 13 July 4 What does 'pie on' mean?.. It means 'all right', volunteered a solicitor. **1948** FINLAYSON *Tidal Creek* (1979) 119 When we gets the old gig properly worked over everything should be pie-on. *Ibid.* 124 'Well,' thinks Jake, 'this is a nice sort of hitch. Just as we were getting everything pie-on as Uncle Ted calls it.' **1980** SMITHYMAN in *Te Reo* 22–23 106 The date 1941 [given as the earliest use] for *pie on* seems to me unduly late, perhaps because my father had an expression 'It's pie on the diddle', uttered with stress on *pie* and *on*. The sense was of *right on, smack on, bang on*, informal, a sense of approval. [**1983** HULME *Bone People* 301 'I didn't see you come back.' 'O, I been here,' the old [Maori] lady grins. 'Listening. E pai ana.']

pig, *n.*[1]

1. [Of special historical association for New Zealand (cf. PIG ISLANDS: AND 1854.] As **bush pig** and **wild pig**, a feral descendant of domestic pigs, *Sus scrofa* (fam. Suidae), released by Europeans since c1769, the time of Cook's first voyage, and often associated with him; also the meat of these animals (see also *bush pork* (BUSH C 2 a). See also CAPTAIN COOKER. **a.** As **bush-pig**. [See OED *pig* 11.]

1838 POLACK *NZ* I. 64 It appeared that one of the eldest..was upset in the path by a wild bush-pig, at full gallop, running against him with its utmost force. **1849** POWER *Sketches in NZ* 76 The bush-pig is occasionally hunted by both white men and Maories, but never with any other view than to obtain cheap pork. **1868** TAYLOR *Past & Present NZ* 274 Mawai compared him to a bush pig, which, when you think it is caught, suddenly slips out of your hand and escapes. **1874** BAINES *Edward Crewe* 239 Some said it was only an old bush pig. **1888** COLENSO *Fifty Years* 28 Pork was the only Butcher's meat..the flesh of wild, or Bush pigs, and very good it was. **1907** KOEBEL *Return of Joe* 20 What with mutton down to the price of bush pig..fresh hands has..hard work to find a billet. **1920** *Quick March* 10 Jan. 41 [Title] Bill's Foundling. The Story of A Bush Pig.

b. As **wild pig**.

[**1848** WAKEFIELD *Handbook for NZ* 167 The wild hog, which is caught with dogs, and afterwards domesticated and home-fed, partakes a good deal of the Chinese breed about the head, and frequently grows to a great size.] **1849** TORLESSE *Papers* (1958) 5 Jan. 46 Abundance of wild pigs. **1853** MACKIE *Traveller under*

PIG

Concern (1973) 14 Mar. 87 The supply of wild pigs scattered all over the islands are quite a boon for which the colonists are indebted to Captn Cook. **1868** LINDSAY *Contributions to NZ Botany* 49 'Spear-grass Scrub'..forms one of the favourite hunting grounds of the Wild Pig. **1874** BAINES *Edward Crewe* 228 Nominally we were supposed to be going on a pig-hunting expedition..not to return minus a back-load each of wild-pig. **1911** ANSON in *Piraki Log* (1911) 155 Wild Pigs—a legacy from Captain Cook. **1923** *Dominion* (Wellington) 11 Jan. 3 The man's point was whether hunting wild pigs was part of the farm work in that district, where wild pigs are plentiful and very destructive. **1939** BEATTIE *First White Boy Born in Otago* 99 Wild pigs were a great nuisance; the runs were overrun with them, and they started to eat the lambs. **1990** *Handbook NZ Mammals* 359 The common name 'wild pig' should be avoided, since it can apply both to feral pigs of domestic origin and to the true wild boar of Eurasia, as well as to other members of the Family Suidae.

2. In special collocations. **a.** As **pig's whisper** *obs.* [spec. use of Brit. dial. *pig's whisper* a loud whisper: see EDD *n.*[1] 58 (a)], a whisper made so as to be overheard; to whisper loudly. Also occas. as a verb.

1889 DAVIDSON *Stories NZ Life* 50 The schoolmaster and his wife. The dominie was telling his good lady, in somewhat of a 'pig's whisper', all about Thirza's history. **1912** *Hutt Valley Independent* 11 May 3 Why did Mr Ronayne 'pig's whisper' to the Hon. Mr Myers that Upper Hutt was 21 miles from Wellington?

b. pig's face (**pigs' faces**) (also **pig-face(s)**, occas. **pig's ear**). [AND *Disphyma* sp., 1830] ICE-PLANT *Disphyma* (formerly *Mesembryanthemum*) *australe*.

1905 *TrNZI* XXXVII. 67 A decoction made from the *rauriki* (*Sonchus*), and the expressed juice of the '**pig's ear**' (*Mesembryanthemum* sp.) were used locally. **1899** KIRK *Students' Flora* 184 *Mesembrianthemum australe* pig's faces. **1909** *AJHR* C-12 54 *Mesembryanthemum australe*. Horokaka Pig's face, ice-plant. Coastal cliff. Not common. South end of Mason Bay. **1910** [see ICE-PLANT]. **1940** LAING & BLACKWELL *Plants NZ* 167 *Mesembryanthemum australe*... Called by the colonists, *pigs' faces* or *ice-plant*. **1961** MARTIN *Flora NZ* 244 Bare clay banks free from other vegetation commonly have sheets of the pink-flowered Iceplant or Pig's-face. **1981** pigface [see ICE-PLANT].

c. As **pig's back**, in the phr. **home on the pig's back** [AND (1930), 1948], an extended form and use of **on the pig's back** (cf. OED *pig n.*[1] 11 h), in a happy or successful situation, having arrived at a successful conclusion.

1937 PARTRIDGE *Dict. Slang* 400 *home on the pig's back!* Very successful!; thoroughly (and easily): a c[atch] p[hrase], mostly among New Zealanders and Australians: from ca. 1910. **1943** HISLOP *Pure Gold* 34 Sir Swithen [*sic*, a horse] was not home and dried, nor was he home on the pig's back, as some would also say of an easy win. **1955** *BJ Cameron Collection* (TS July) home on the pig's back Cut and dried. **1968** SLATTER *Pagan Game* 158 Got into the reps and when they won the Shield he was home on the pig's back. Never looked back. Everything went right. **1988** MCGILL *Dict. Kiwi Slang* 57 *home on the pig's back* very successful or easy; eg 'If this horse wins, we're home on the pig's back.'

d. With various, usu. anatomical, nouns, expressing disbelief, disagreement, derision, etc.: **pig's arse** (**bum, ear**) [AND 1919]; **pig's christmas parcel** [euphemistic rhyming slang for 'pig's arsehole'].

1968 SLATTER *Pagan Game* 102 The Head's always

asking them to come along and claim watches and pens and what have you. And do they? **Pig's arse**. They're all too well off. **1977** ELDRED-GRIGG *Of Ivory Accents* 38 Never mind Davie, she said. We won't tease you. Pig's arse we won't, said Emma, and laughed. **1988** MCGILL *Dict. Kiwi Slang* 83 **pig's arse/bum/ear** derisive exclamations; eg 'In a pig's arse to that notion, mate.' **1944** BRUNO *Desert Daze* 23 And did he marry poor blind Nell? He did—**pig's christmas parcel**. *Ibid*. 50 Minefield, pig's Christmas parcel.

e. pig's breakfast, see ROUGH A 2 c.

f. pig's bucket, see PIG-BUCKET.

3. Used in various phr. with reference to cuisine: **pig and potatoes**, see *pork and potatoes* (PORK 1); **little pigs in blankets (pigs in a blanket)**, oysters wrapped in cooked bacon (elsewhere called 'angels on horseback'); occas. sausage pieces similarly cooked and served; also occas. pre-cooked sausages fried in a coating of mashed potato.

1916 *Celebrated Amuri Cook. Book* (1927) 7 *Little Pigs in Blankets*... Season the quantity of oysters required... Wrap each oyster in slice of bacon. **1917** MILLER *Econ. Tech. Cook. Book* 38 '*Little Pigs in Blanket*' Bacon..Oysters..roll an oyster in each piece. **1928** *Everybody's Cook. Book Tested Recipes* 68 *Little Pigs in Blanket*..bacon..oysters..wooden skewers.. buttered toast..hard boiled egg..parsley and pepper... Cook the little pigs long enough to crisp the bacon. Place one on each piece of toast. Serve on a hot dish garnished with egg..parsley. **c1939** BASHAM *Aunt Daisy's Book of Recipes* 40 *Little Pigs in Blanket*..oysters... bacon..roll..up.... Don't put butter or fat in pan, but see it is quite hot before the 'pigs' are put in. **1955** *New Home Cook.* 33 Pigs in a Blanket. Season two cups mashed potatoes... Fry..1 dozen small sausages... Roll each sausage in the mashed potatoes..then..in breadcrumbs, and fry a golden brown.

4. Special Comb. **pig-bridge** *obs.*, a makeshift bridge to allow Maori-owned pigs across a river; **pig-fence**, see quot.; **pig-jobber** *hist.*, one who trades in Maori pigs, also used as a derogatory name given to a Government agent in Maori land-negotiations (see also *pork trader* (PORK 3)); **pig-knife**, a long knife for sticking or killing (usu. wild) pigs; **pig-proof**, usu. of a fence, able to keep wild pigs out (cf. OED *pig n.*^{1} 13 c); **pig-rooting**, a patch of ground rooted up by wild pigs; **pig-run**, uncultivated tracts of land on which pigs run wild (see also RUN *n.*^{1}), or a track made by wild pigs; **pig-sign**, the droppings of wild pigs; **pig-sticking** [contrast OED 1], the hunting of wild pigs with dogs and a sheath-knife; **pig track**, a track beaten by a wild pig; **pigweed** [f. a name given to various herbs eaten by pigs: AND *portulaca*, 1862], any of *Polygonum* spp., *Amaranthus* spp., or *Portulaca* spp. (cf. WIREWEED 1); **pigwood**, HANGEHANGE.

1842 SELWYN *Jrnl. & Let.* 24 Dec. in *NZ Part I* (The Church in the Colonies) (1847) 91 The path crosses the river by a native **pig-bridge**, composed of two trees, with a hollow wattle of brushwood in the middle. **1982** *Agric. Gloss.* (MAF) 28 **Pig-fence**: Usually made of wire netting 1.07 m high. **1899** *Richmond-Atkinson Papers* (1960) II. 622 His [*sc.* the M.P.'s] venom not being quite exhausted he called me [*sc.* Robert Parris] a '**pig jobber**' which I never was. **1853** ADAMS *Canterbury Settlement* 71 Thick boots, duck trousers, blue sailor's shirt, serge shirt, with a belt containing a **pig-knife**, and a broad-leaved cabbage-tree hat, will form the dress. **1905** THOMSON *Bush Boys* 183 At the belt of each hung a billy, a tin pannikin, and a sheath carrying a large pig knife. **1894** ARTHUR *Kangaroo & Kauri* 98 Settlers whose produce is grown in the proximity of bush or scrubby ground have..[to make] their ground **pig-proof**. **1939** BEATTIE *First White Boy Born Otago* 99 Both kinds [of fence], when properly made, were pig-proof, which a modern wire fence might not be. **1921** GUTHRIE-SMITH *Tutira* 169 [Manuka] now began to colonize the paddock..appearing about **pig-rootings**, along sheep-tracks. **1848** CHAPMAN *Lett. & Jrnls.* (ATLTS) II. 381 Thousands of acres on all sides of you..here and there little patches are under cultivation—the rest are '**pig-runs**'. **1860** BUDDLE *Maori King Movement* 21 [The Maori] desire to have large tracts of land for pig and cattle runs, over which the herds may range without danger of trespass on the white man's cultivation. **1950** *NZJAg.* Apr. LXXX. 346 This type of utilisation..at the same time allows some rejuvenation of the pasture in the permanent pig runs. **1960** CRUMP *Good Keen Man* 57 I was thoroughly interrogated every evening as to the whereabouts of any fresh **pig-sign** I had seen that day [in the bush]. **1878** LINDSAY-BUCKNALL *A Search for Fortune* 44 We had any amount of '**pig-sticking**' all round our new quarters. **1894** ARTHUR *Kangaroo & Kauri* 97 Wild-pig hunting, or, as it is more commonly called, pig-sticking. **1834** MARKHAM *NZ* (1963) 35 If you diverge from the Beaten Track, either to the Right hand or the left You lose ground with those you are with As all Tracks seem to be **Pig tracks** in the first instance. **1938** BURDON *High Country* 90 They [put]..in charge of the station a manager known as 'Pig Track' Hudson, thus called from his unwavering faith in getting on to a pig track and following it up, to wherever it led, whenever he had the misfortune to get lost. **1937** AYSON *Thomas* 102 So up a pig track he started to the ferny face where the dogs were barking. **1870** *TrNZI* II. 126 Polygonum aviculare **Pigweed**. **1911** *Triad* 11 Dec. 36 Any gardener who wishes to grow roses must be meritorious in regard to pigweed. **1926** HILGENDORF *Weeds* 70 Red root (*Amaranthus* [*hybridus*] and *A. retroflexus*), also called red shank and pig weed, is found in gardens and waste places all over the North Island and as far south as Nelson. *Ibid*. 72 Portulaca (*Portulaca oleracea*), called also pig weed, hog weed, purslane, and ice plant, is very common on garden paths etc., in Auckland, becoming less and less common as far south as Nelson. *Ibid*. 61 pigweed (*Polygonum aviculare*). **1969** *Standard Common Names Weeds* 58 pigweed [=] redroot: rhagodia: twincress: wart cress: wild portulaca: willow weed: wireweed. **1978** MOORE & IRWIN *Oxford Book NZ Plants* 118 *Geniostoma ligustrifolium*, hangehange... The waxy-surfaced, apple-green leaves..might commend this as a desirable garden shrub were it not that the small greenish flowers,.. have an odd smell that gives rise to the name '**pigwood**' in some districts.

pig, *n.*^{2} [f. northern English and Sc. dial. *pig* an earthenware pot or jar; a stone bottle.] Orig. a stone jar or rigger for beer; later, a half-gallon glass flagon or jar.

1938 HYDE *Nor Yrs. Condemn* 45 Starkie slipped down the fire-escape, and came back with a pig of beer. Word went round the wards. 'Starkie's got a pig.'..All went well, until, as the pig passed from bed to bed, one man dropped the mighty bottle. **1988** MCGILL *Dict. Kiwi Slang* 83 *pig* flagon of beer.

pig, *n.*^{3} [?Transf. use of *pig*(-iron.] The anchor.

1952 *Diary* 20 Apr. in Sansom *In Grip of an Island* (1982) 153 In Buddie Willa's Viking:.. Into Horomamae and dropped the 'pig'.

pig-bucket. Also **pig's bucket**; occas. **pig barrel**, **pig tub**. A receptacle for organic kitchen waste such as could be fed to pigs.

1851 KENNAWAY *Biscuit & Butter* (1973) 58 *Thursday Morning, Sep. 4*... again we have biscuits..[the shipboard authorities] have opened a new bag and in consequence [we] have not the disagreeable fusty taste the old dusty scraps (which are now swimming in the pigs' bucket) used to have. **1905** *Truth* 4 Nov. 5 Putting potato chips into the pig barrel..if you don't stop putting them into the pig tub. **1926** GLEN *Uncles Three* 27 The bottom of the pig-bucket. **1954** MCDONALD *Stinson's Bush* 83 If you were for giving Uncle William coffee he'd just be pouring it into the pig's bucket, and there's be your white stuff wasted! **1964** HOSKEN *Life on Five Pound Note* 28 Mrs T. was helping me and as she cleaned up some spilt sugar and flour, said, 'What shall I do with this?' I looked at it and said, 'Oh put it in the pig bucket.' **1978** PRESTON *Woolgatherers* 41 Leaving the cookhouse, they scraped their plates into the pig bucket, then filed past three basins of hot water. **1992** ANDERSON *Portrait Artist's Wife* 40 Heads down, as busy as Bernadette [a sow] at her pig-bucket but with less result.

pig-dog. [AND 1925.] Any of various dogs of mixed breed used for hunting wild pigs. Cf. BULLY *n.*^{2}

1845 WAKEFIELD *Adventure NZ* II. 6 Pig-dogs are of rather a mongrel breed, partaking largely of the bulldog, but mixed with the cross of mastiff and greyhound which forms the New South Wales Kangaroo dog. **1856** FITTON *NZ* 266 Pig-hunting is a most ignoble and stupid sport; there are in the country plenty of so-called pig dogs. **1863** CHUDLEIGH *Diary* 15 Sept. (1950) 102 [We] started with tent blankets, knives, spears..pig dogs and a large amount of provisions. **1873** BARKER *Station Amusements* 49 We could seldom procure the loan of a good pig-dog. **1881** NESFIELD *Chequered Career* 37 We had a breed of dogs on the station called pig-dogs, a cross between a mastiff, and kangaroo dog. **1899** *TrNZI* XXXI. 145 Unfortunately, birds caught by pig-dogs are generally torn and useless. **1921** *Quick March* 10 Sept. 23 Mildred and Hongi, after an exciting day with the pig-dogs in the bush behind the homestead, were wandering down..under the scented wattles. **1935** MAXWELL *Recollections* 200 A pig dog—a bull mastiff—was almost a necessary possession in the outlying districts. **1967** GROVER *Another Man's Role* 12 The best pig dog for miles. Look at his scars. **1986** RICHARDS *Off the Sheep's Back* 30 He was a very good pig dog, but when he was with us he only hunted for kiwis.

pigeon.

1. *Hemiphaga novaeseelandiae novaeseelandiae* (fam. Columbidae), a large, beautiful, green, copper and white, native bush pigeon. See also ILLEGAL TEGEL, KERERU, KUKU *n.*^{1}, KUKUPA.

1773 FORSTER *Resolution Jrnl.* 2 Apr. (1982) II. 245 I went..to the Indian Cove, & shot there..a fine large green and brown Pigeon. **1807** SAVAGE *Some Acc. of NZ* 10 The only [bird] species I saw that struck me as new, was a pigeon, of beautiful plumage, large size, and delicious eating. **1834** [see KUKUPA]. **1840** BEST *Journal* May (1966) 222 The Pigeon or Wood Quest (Kukupa) is a very beautiful bird and capital eating. **1855** [see KUKU *n.*^{1}]. **1863** BUTLER *First Year* ix 138 The pigeon is larger than the English, and far handsomer. **c1899** DOUGLAS in *Mr Explorer Douglas* (1957) 283 A pigeon would be about the last bird one would expect to alter its coat, but I once saw one nearly pure white. **1905** [see KUKU *n.*^{1}]. **1921** GUTHRIE-SMITH *Tutira* 204 He recollects pigeons so plentiful that, on certain favourite perching-trees, their weight was sufficient to break down the smaller boughs. **1966** DURELL *Two in the Bush* 46 The plumage of this pigeon, as it waddled about like an over-dressed Dowager Duchess, made the green grass look positively drab. **1986** RICHARDS *Off the Sheep's Back* 62 Every day we applied pigeon fat to our hands to prevent cracking.

2. With a modifier: **bush, Chatham Island(s), native (New Zealand), wild, wood-**.

(1) **bush pigeon**. See 1 above.
   1850 McLean *Journal* in Cowan *Sir Donald Maclean* (1940) 52 At Tautara..the party was hospitably entertained..with abundance of taro, potatoes and bush pigeon. **1894** [see KUKUPA]. **1911** *TrNZI* XLIII. 603 The bush-pigeon..known in the north by the Maori name *kukupa*, is fast becoming scarce. **1940** Studholme *Te Waimate* (1954) 240 Bush Pigeon... Few, but increasing. **1957** Baxter *Collected Poems* (1980) 185 Your single grief enlarges now The voice of night in kumara gardens, Prayer of the bush pigeon. **1984** Wilson *S. Pacific Street* 8 A bush pigeon sometimes sat in that tree in the quiet morning sunshine.

(2) **Chatham Island(s) pigeon**. *Hemiphaga novaseelandiae chathamensis.*
   1904 Hutton & Drummond *Animals NZ* 167 The Chatham Island Pigeon. *Hemiphaga chathamensis.* **1923** *NZJST* VI. 82 *Hemiphaga chathamensis...* Chatham Islands Pigeon. I have no recent news of this species. **1955** Oliver *NZ Birds* 443 Chatham Island Pigeon. *Kuku Hemiphaga chathamensis...* From being in former times exceedingly abundant, the Chatham Island Pigeon, through the invasion of the Maoris in 1835 and of Europeans soon afterwards, became nearly extinct about 1896. **1984** Holmes *Chatham Is.* 97 Chatham Island Pigeon..is confined to the broadleafed forest remnants on the southern half of Chatham Island. **1992** *Evening Post* (Wellington) 26 Sept. 11 The species in question is the parea, or Chatham Island pigeon. The parea used to be thought of as just a larger version of the mainland New Zealand pigeon or kereru.

(3) **native** (or **New Zealand**) **pigeon**. See 1 above.
   1819 Hall 3 Aug. in Elder *Marsden's Lieutenants* (1934) 223 The New Zealand pigeons are as small as half-grown fowls. **1834** McDonnell *Extracts Jrnl.* (1979) 16 The New Zealand pigeon is as splendidly beautiful in plumage as it is exquisitely delicious to the taste. **1843** Dieffenbach *Travels in NZ* I. 27 The berries..form the favourite food of the beautiful New Zealand pigeon. **1853** Mackie *Traveller under Concern* (1973) 96 Strolling in the bush adjoining our inn, observed the native pigeon a large and beautiful bird. **1873** Buller *Birds NZ* 157 (New-Zealand Pigeon)... Kuku, Kukupa, and Kereru. **1904** [see KERERU]. **1930** Guthrie *NZ Memories* 90 The handsome native pigeon lazily flew from tree to tree. **1966** Durrell *Two in the Bush* 45 It was a New Zealand Pigeon, and it circled once round the house in fat, rather self-satisfied flight. **1985** *Reader's Digest Book NZ Birds* 238 The New Zealand pigeon is also found in some towns and cities, especially if the cities are not too densely populated.

(4) **wild pigeon**. See 1 above.
   1823 Cruise *Journal* 14 Mar. (1957) 56 We saw a few small birds of very rich plumage, and shot some wild pigeons. **1844** Williams *NZ Jrnl.* (1956) 112 The Wild Pigeon of New Zealand reigns the undisputed king of beauty amongst this feathery tribe. **1867** Barker *Station Life* (1870) 181 Overhead the trees were alive with flocks of wild pigeons, ka-kas, parroquets, and other birds. **1905** White *My NZ Garden* 73 Our Wild Pigeon is a very handsome bird with coloured plumage and white breast, two or three sizes larger than the English Wood Pigeon. **1936** Hyde *Check to your King* (1960) 120 Your wild pigeon (*kuku*)..beds itself on the fern.

(5) **wood-pigeon**. [Spec. use of Brit. *wood-pigeon*: OED 1668.] See 1 above.
   [*Note*] *wood-pigeon* is prob. more freq. in popular use than the synonyms *bush pigeon* or *wild pigeon*.
   1770 Parkinson *Journal* (1773) 15 Jan. 115 The woods abound with diverse kinds of birds, such as parrots, wood-pigeons, water hens. **1838** Polack *NZ I.* 297 *Wood-pigeons* are very numerous in the woods, from January to April; they are delicious nutriment. **1842** Heaphy *NZ* 47 The wood-pigeon is in New Zealand very large... The plumage of the bird is very beautiful, and the flesh is excellent. **1855** Taylor *Te Ika A Maui* 406 (Morris) Kereru, kukupa (kuku..), the wood-pigeon. **1874** Kennaway *Crusts* 58 In the bush were numbers of wood-pigeon, large and in good condition. **1904** Hutton & Drummond *Animals NZ* 163 The beautiful plumage of the native Wood Pigeon gives it rank among the most handsome birds belonging to this colony. **1926** Cowan *Travel in NZ* II. 64 Wood-pigeons (*kukupa*)..are found in the forests. **1936** Hyde *Check to your King* (1960) 207 The greedy wood-pigeons would plump down berries with soft, dull little thudding noises from the *Karaka* trees. **1946** Soljak *NZ* 9 Another fearless bird is the wood pigeon, one of the finest in the world for its size, beautiful plumage and strength of flight. **1980** [see ILLEGAL TEGEL].

3. In transf. uses, applied to members of other families of birds thought to resemble pigeons in form or colour. See also MUD PIGEON. **a. Cape (Snares Cape) pigeon** (or **Cape petrel**). [Used elsewhere: cf. OED *Cape*⁴, 1798.] *Daption capense* (fam. Procellariidae), a scavenging black-and-white, southern hemisphere petrel, the pintado, well known to ocean-travelling early immigrants.
   1853 Adams *Canterbury Settlement* 8 The Cape pigeon, which is a beautifully marked black and white bird about the size of a wood pigeon, will follow the vessel to the end of the voyage. **1873** Buller *Birds NZ* 299 Daption capensis. (Cape Petrel)... So familiar is the so-called 'Cape Pigeon' to all who have made a voyage to the southern seas. **1930** Reischek *Yesterdays in Maoriland* (1933) 280 Cape pigeons were here [at Campbell Island] in plenty, and great numbers of Magellan shags were fishing round about. **1959** Wilson *Bird Is. of NZ* 164 [Dr Falla] found..large numbers of cape pigeons nesting in the rocks. These supplied the first authentic eggs of the cape pigeon for the New Zealand region. **1984** Soper *Birds NZ* 34 There are 2 races: the New Zealand race (known as the Snares Cape Pigeon) breeding at Snares, Bounty, Antipodes, Auckland and Campbell Islands, and the Antarctic race breeding on Antarctica. **1990** *Checklist Birds NZ* 39 *D. capense australe*..Snares Cape Pigeon... Breeds on The Snares, Bounty, Antipodes, Auckland..and possibly Campbell Islands... Ranges in New Zealand seas.

b. *Hist.* The nickname of a group of early Waikato settlers.
   1864 Drummond in Lush *Waikato Jrnls.* (1982) 15 Later William Berg of Capetown sponsored a small group of South Africans, to be known to their fellow settlers as 'the Cape pigeons'.

4. In special Comb. with reference to introduced homing pigeons or to rock-pigeons acclimatized to urban habitats: **pigeongram** *hist.* [spec. use of *pigeongram* (f. *pigeon* + tele)*gram*): see OED 1885], mail carried by homing pigeons with reference esp. to the Great Barrier Island and Marotiri Islands pigeon posts of 1897–1908, linking those islands with mainland New Zealand; **pigeon post** *hist.* [a spec. local use of *pigeon post* a postal service delivered by means of carrier pigeons], a postal service via carrier pigeon *spec.* that established in 1897 between Great Barrier Island and mainland New Zealand; **pigeon park** (often caps.), a name given to a small central city park, a haunt of people and pigeons.
   1879 *Auckland Weekly News* 20 Sept. 18 A Thames Star **pigeongram** from Paeroa, this afternoon, states that the judgment of the native council was delivered at 3 p.m. today. **1899** *Ibid.* 15 Sept. Each bird has a distinctive number and underneath the wing has 'Original Great Barrier Pigeongram Services.' **1920** *NZ Stamp Collector I.* 33 The next 'air post' of any interest was that started in 1896, by W.W. Fricker, and known by the high sounding title of 'The Great Barrier Pigeongram Agency'. **1938** *Postage Stamps of NZ* I. 435 In 1899 a more pretentious message form was provided, with..the title 'The Original Great Barrier, Marotiri Copper Syndicate, and Port Charles Pigeongram Services' across the top. **1955** *Postage Stamps of NZ* III. 309 Because the carriage of letters is a prerogative of the Post Office, official objection was made to the inclusion in the Great Barrier Island stamps of the inscription 'Special Post' and this had to be changed to read 'Pigeongram'. **1970** *NZ Bulletin (Woking)* VII. No.9 6 Auckland Philatelic Society produced special covers in 1948 and again in 1958 to mark the Golden Jubilee of the Pigeongram stamp. **1991** *NZ Geographic* Jan.–Mar. 115 On one well-publicised occasion a bird was despatched with a pigeongram to Auckland at 8am and a reply received at 9.15 the same morning. [**1897** *NZ Herald* (Auckland) 8 May [Advt] Great Barrier Postal Pigeon Service. J.E. Parkin.] **1948** *NZ Stamp Collector* XXIX. 38 **Pigeon Posts**. The 19th November, 1948, is the Golden Jubilee of the World's first adhesive air-mail stamp—the Great Barrier Pigeongram stamp. **1968** Walker *Great Barrier Is. Pigeon Post Stamps* 9 The genesis of the Great Barrier Pigeon Post has been a matter of considerable controversy. *Ibid.* 13 The Great Barrier Island Pigeon Post developed from the tragic circumstances surrounding the wreck of the 'Wairarapa'. **1977** Franks *All the Stamps of NZ* 12 In 1899 a pigeon post service was company-operated from Great Barrier Island to Auckland and vice versa. **1947** *NZ Woman's Weekly* 23 Jan. 7 The unofficial name by which [this reserve] is known to the citizens of Wellington is '**Pigeon park**', and most fitting is the description, for..the pigeons have established for themselves a veritable sanctuary. **1979** Baxter *Collected Poems* 532 I lay down on the grass In Pigeon Park. **1986** *Metro* (Auckland) Sept. 113 Their customers are the city's [*sc.* Auckland's] homeless, who will be waiting for them in K Road's Pigeon Park, Myers Park, and down near the docks. **1991** *Dominion* (Wellington) 23 Sep. 8 Why is the city council spending half a million dollars on tarting up Pigeon Park..when tourism is suffering because visitors can't find street names clearly marked.

5. *transf.* SAILER.
   1947 Brereton *No Roll of Drums* 78 He was chopping a tree when a pigeon (a loose branch) fell on his head.

6. In the phr. **to mind one's own pigeon**, to mind one's own business.
   1941 Baker *NZ Slang* 53 *To mind one's own pigeon*, to mind one's business (an interesting extension of the English slang *someone's pigeon*, someone's business or private affair).

pigeon-berry: see PIGEONWOOD.

pigeon-maori: see PIDGIN-MAORI.

pigeonwood. Also **pigeon-berry**. *Hedycarya arborea* (fam. Monimiaceae), a small forest tree having long red berries much favoured by the native pigeon. See also KAIWHIRIA, POROKAIWHIRI.
   1899 *NZ Times* (Wellington) 28 Oct. 3 Nio, matipo..pigeon wood, etc., struggle one with another in rich profusion for an existence. **1919** Cockayne *NZ Plants & Their Story* 170 The *Monimiaceae* is represented by only 2 species—that noble tree the pukatea..and the pigeonwood. **1919** *NZJST* II. 257 In addition to the karaka and nikau..the most notable were the pigeon-berry, titoki, and broad-leaved cabbage-tree. **1923** Cockayne *Cultivation NZ Plants* 131

Hedycarya arborea (porokaiwhiri, pigeonwood..) is small, dense, fairly quick. **1939** COCKAYNE & TURNER *Trees NZ* 59 *Hedycarya arborea*... Porokaiwhiri, Pigeonwood. **1950** *NZJAg.* Oct. LXXXI. 320 *Pigeonwood. Porokaiwhiri*... Small tree 20 to 40 ft. high; trunk up to 20 in. in diameter. **1961, 1978** [see POROKAIWHIRI]. **1988** DAWSON *Forest Vines to Snow Tussocks* 102 Other species which tend to be more wide ranging are mahoe.., pigeonwood (*Hedycarya arborea*), toro.

pig-face: see PIG *n.*¹ 2 b.

pigfern: see FERN 2 (13).

pigfish. [AND 1842.]

1. Any of several unrelated fishes either those with pig-like head and elongated snout or occas. those making grunting noises when first taken out of water, esp. *Congiopodus* (formerly *Agriopus*) *leucopaecilus* (fam. Congiopodidae). See also SKIPJACK 2, SNAP JACK.
   1876 *TrNZI* VIII. 211 *Agriopus leucopoecilus*... *Pig Fish.* **1886** SHERRIN *Handbook Fishes NZ* 300 *Agriopus leucopoecilus*... Pig-fish. **1892** *TrNZI* XXIV. 207 Pig-fish—*Agriopus leucopoecilus*...called 'leatherjacket' in Dunedin, where the fish occurs in immense numbers. **1906** *TrNZI* XXXVIII. 545 *Congiopodus leucopoecilus*... The fish is popularly known as 'pigfish', on account of the grunting noise it makes when taken out of the water and has to gasp for air. **1956** GRAHAM *Treasury NZ Fishes* 350 Pigfish (Puramorua) *Congiopodus leucopaecilus*... The name Pigfish is given on account of its snout and the general appearance of the head when looked at from the front... It also has the habit of making a grunting noise when left for a while out of water. **1967** NATUSCH *Animals NZ* 231 The pigfish (*Congiopodus*..) has a protractile mouth, blotchy protective coloration, and long spines; it grunts when taken from the water.

2. With a modifier: **red** (or **spotted**), **southern**.

(1) **red** (or **spotted**) **pigfish**. *Bodianus vulpinus* (formerly *Verreo oxycephalus*) (fam. Labridae). See also PAKURAKURA.
   1922 *Auckland Weekly News* 15 June 14 The spotted pig-fish are browns and ambers and silky greens, with touches of flame on their fins, and with mouths ridiculously like a pig's mouth. **1956** GRAHAM *Treasury NZ Fishes* 408 Red Pigfish *Verreo unimaculatus*. **1967** MORELAND *Marine Fishes* 22 Red Pigfish [*Verreo oxycephalus*]... Other names are pigfish, spotted pigfish, and the Maori pakurakura. **1972** DOAK *Fishes* 94 With its royal red body, an iridescent blue-black ocellus on its bold dorsal fin and a white patch near the tail, the male red pigfish is one of the most handsome of our reef fishes. **1982** AYLING *Collins Guide* (1984) 252 *Red Pig Fish* (Pig wrasse, pakurakura) *Bodianus vulpinus* (*Bodianus oxycephalus, Verreo oxycephalus*). Ibid. 253 The long pointed snout..and forward projecting, fleshy lips suggested the name pig fish for this species.

(2) **southern pigfish**. *Congiopodus leucopaecilus* (fam. Congiopodidae). See also LEATHERJACKET 2, PURUMORUA, *silver trumpeter* (TRUMPETER 2 (2)).
   1922 *NZJST* V. 95 *Congiopodus leucopaecilus. Southern Pigfish.* An attempt to sell this species under the name of 'silver trumpeter' in Christchurch was unsuccessful. **1982** AYLING *Collins Guide* (1984) 199 *Southern Pigfish Congiopodus leucopaecilus*... The southern pigfish is a moderately deep-bodied fish that..attains a maximum size of about 35cm. **1988** FRANCIS *Coastal Fishes NZ* 24 Southern pigfish are usually seen resting on the bottom often nestled in seaweed or against rocks. **1991** BRADSTOCK *Fishing* 21 *Southern pigfish.* Other names: purumorua.

pig-hunt, *v.* Usu. as *vbl. n.* often in *attrib.* use. [Recorded elsewhere but of special significance in NZ.] *intr.* To pursue on foot and kill wild pigs for food, sport, or (more recently) for sale for export, usu. with the help of trained pig-dogs. Often as a *vbl. n.*, the sport or occupation connected with this activity.
   1837 *Piraki Log* 16 Nov. (1911) 60 The Natives and one Man started a Pig hunting the remainder employed grass cutting. **1843** DEANS in *Pioneers* (1964) 16 But what you would count the best sport of any is wild pig hunting. **1849** TORLESSE *Papers* (1958) 119 After a rainy night..we all sallied out to pig hunt..and caught 2 large boars. **1853** ADAMS *Canterbury Settlement* 72 [The settler's] principal amusement will be pig-hunting, a sport by no means realising the expectations usually formed of it by enthusiastic colonists on this side of the globe; and possessing none of the glorious excitement of an Indian boar-hunt. The animal is pursued by every variety of mongrel, and when one of them catches him by the ear, the hunter dismounts, sticks him with his long knife in a most business-like manner, and then remounts and pursues the chase. The spoils are afterwards collected, and carried home for use. **1867** BARKER *Station Life* (1870) 106 We were all returning from a great pig-hunting expedition, when I saw one of the party coming..with a small..wild pig under each arm. **1878** *TrNZI* X. 321 But pig-hunting, the New Zealand sport of sports, has long become only a tradition of the past. **1951** ACLAND *Early Canterbury Runs* 262 In 1878..one of the shepherds took a pig-hunting contract. **1983** STEWART *Springtime in Taranaki* (1991) 220 I do remember discussing it..with my ridiculous pig-hunting dog, Bill.

Hence **pig hunt** *n.*, a hunt on foot for wild pigs; **pig-hunter**, one who hunts wild pigs for pleasure or profit.
   1864 *Gold Digger's Notes* (1950) 51 I lived on salt wild pork for weeks after that **pig hunt**. **1882** HAY *Brighter Britain* II. 318 [Chapter heading] A Pig-hunt. **1904** *NZ Observer Xmas Issue* 10 Harry proposed that next afternoon I should join him in a pig-hunt. **1961** REID *Kiwi Laughs* 9 The misfortunes of that pig-hunt which is an almost indispensable episode in fiction or memoirs. **1837** *Piraki Log* 16 Nov. (1911) 60 The **Pig hunters** returned but with no luck. **1848** 20 July in *Lett. from Otago* (1978) 15 The pig-hunters wear boar-skin shoes when they go a pig-hunting. **1852** DEANS *Pioneers* (1964) 155 Four pig-hunters came here; stopped all night. c**1871** MASTERS *Autobiography* (ATLMS) 47 I had frequently seen pig hunters about in various places. **1893** FROBISHER *Sketches of Gossiptown* 48 Now's your chance for winning your spurs as a pig-hunter.

Pig Island(s).

1. [A name celebrating the long (since c1769) association of New Zealand with domestic pigs escaped into the wild: cf. PIG *n.*¹ 1.] Usu. init. caps. New Zealand. **a.** As **the Pig Islands.**
   1906 *Truth* 25 Aug. 5 Your Worship, for forty long years, and the rest, I've battled the Pig Islands doing my best. **1918** *Kia-ora Coo-ee* (1981) 15 Dec. 5 An Aussie invariably greet[s] a Maorilande[r] as 'Digger', and the men from the Pig Islands, in common with us, use the term in relation to one another, whether Infantry, Artillery, or Mounted. **1941** BAKER *NZ Slang* 43 It is traditional that Cook introduced pigs into this country. *Pig-islands* for the Dominion and *pig-islander* for an inhabitant would not have come into being but for that fact. We find these two latter terms widely used on the east coast of Australia. **1945** *JPS* LIV. 225 Modern Newzealand slang... *Pig-islands,* Newzealand, *Pig-islander,* a Newzealander. **1946** MACFARLANE *Amuri* 117 He returned to the Pig Islands.

b. As **Pig Island.**
   1917 *Chron. NZEF* 22 Aug. 15 We wish them [*sc.* Canterbury troops] a safe return and every happiness and prosperity in our dear old 'Pig Island'. **1945** HENDERSON *Gunner Inglorious* 149 Back home in old Pig Island. **1946** SIMPSON *If You'd Care to Know* 58 Arising out of all this [breeding of wild pigs], the Australians have a good-natured name for New Zealand. They call it Pig Island, and New Zealanders are Pig Islanders. This applies particularly to the North Island and its people. The citizens of the Dominion are quite happy about it, and use the term themselves. **1956** DAVIN *Sullen Bell* 167 It all helps to put good old Pig Island on the map. **1963** BAXTER *Collected Poems* (1980) 266 [Title] An Ode to the Reigning Monarch on the Occasion of Her Majesty's Visit to Pig Island *Ibid.* 627 [In *Pig Island Letters* (1966)] Baxter notes that: The term 'Pig Island' is used to refer to the South Island in New Zealand vernacular, very likely on account of the wild pigs found there; but in the title of this [sequence] [*sic,* =*Pig Island Letters*] it is used more generally, with a satirical nuance, to refer to the whole country. **1970** *Listener* 21 Dec. 8 Another guy got black-mailed into taking a sheila half-way around Pig Island. **1983** OLIVER *James K. Baxter* 43 The colloquial name for New Zealand 'Pig Island' gains an added significance [in Baxter's poems] by association with the Celtic goddess of death with a pig's face.

2. *attrib.* Usu. with init. caps.
   1912 *Free Lance* (Wellington) 27 July 4 He had been let in for it by a 'Pig Island mug'. **1917** *Chron. NZEF* 5 Sept. 28 Pig Island n.c.o.s only go for the extra couple of bob a day... The hoot is all they're chasing. **1918** *Ibid.* 10 May 154 I think I will wait and give some Pig Island girl the chance of turning me down. **1927** DEVANNY *Old Savage* 278 I'll back one pig island miner against three of the best that ever came out of England. **1948** FINLAYSON *Tidal Creek* (1979) 144 'Good for you!' the men shout. 'The good old Pig Island spirit!'

3. Occas. in address, with init. caps., PIG ISLANDER.
   1918 *Chron. NZEF* 22 Nov. 206 An Aussie on a passing motor-bike yelled to me: 'Hulloa, Pig Island. Want a pull?'

Pig Islander. Also occas. **Pig-Islander, Pigislander.** NEW ZEALANDER 2 a.
   1909 *Truth* 18 Sept. 6 The lady didn't call Arthur a blanky pig-islander, and she didn't tell him to go to a warm place. **1917** 25 Apr. in Miller *Camps, Tramps & Trenches* (1939) 65 We Pig Islanders are not nearly so hot-blooded in our manner of speaking [as Aussies]. **1919** *Quick March* 10 Oct. 33 But, Tom, do yer think —..that a whole million Pig-Islanders is a goin' to let the Chows snavel Noo Zealand? **1938** HYDE *Nor Yrs. Condemn* 164 A lot of people called the New Zealanders Pig Islanders, and the Australians the Aussies. **1946** SARGESON *That Summer* 92 He was a big matelot, though not a Pom, it was easy to tell he was a Pig Islander. **1959** SLATTER *Gun in My Hand* 223 Yes, and my guardian was a Pommie too. Always running down New Zealand. Pig Islanders. **1960** ASHTON-WARNER *Incense to Idols* 23 I'm not one of these tight little Pig-Islanders you know. I've moved about. **1981** HENDERSON *Exiles of Asbestos Cottage* 60 The old name of Pig Islanders for New Zealanders at times seems singularly apt.

pig-jump, *v.* [AND 1884.] *intr.* Of a horse, to jump as a pig does, from all four legs but without bringing them together (as in buckjump). Also as *vbl. n.* Contrast PIGROOT *v.*
   1904 LANCASTER *Sons o' Men* 145 The colt shivered..and began to buck... He pig-jumped, kicked mulewise, struck out with swift, savage forefeet. **1907** KOEBEL *Return of Joe* 11 He bucked before I was ready. Not pig-jumped—he bucked hard. **1940** STUDHOLME *Te Waimate* (1954) 257 I well remember one disastrous

PIGMY PINE

start when the pannikins rattled in the billy and Tom, the pack horse, who was a flighty brute, set to work kicking and pig-jumping. **1992** REILLY *Jim's Elvis* 103 One day he would be a dream to ride, the next he'd refuse to move, or try pig-jumping.

Hence **pig-jump** *n.*
1953 SUTHERLAND *Golden Bush* (1963) 80 Again he went up and finished by executing a couple of pig-jumps for good measure.

pigmy pine: see PINE 2 (12).

pigroot, *n.*[1] A name given to a kind of hill or to a steep track on such a hill; *spec.* as **the Pigroot**, an informal name for a hill and track in Otago (see quots. 1944, 1995).
1889 WILLIAMS & REEVES *Colonial Couplets* 3 Only think how much more graceful all the landscape will appear. No more pigroots, whalebacks, hogbacks—these names that shall not last. **1944** BEATTIE *Maori Place-names Otago* 8 No map the collector has consulted has shown Pigroot Hill or hotel, and yet it is the most prominent and most used name between Palmerston and Kyeburn. Again and again the collector has heard the remark, 'I am going into the Central by the Pigroot,' or 'I came down by the Pigroot.' So frequently is it used that one might imagine that certain people used it thinking that the word 'root' is in reality 'route,' but be that as it may, common usage is the deciding factor in place-names, and Pigroot, with its associations back into the fifties, has come to stay. The name was originally bestowed because the wild pigs rooted up the hillside looking for the roots of the taramea, or speargrass. **1995** ANDERSON *House Guest* 176 They shot through Palmerston [Otago] and headed up the Pig Root.

pigroot, *n.*[2] [AND 1917.] The act of pigrooting performed by a horse (see PIGROOT *v.*).
1921 *Quick March* 10 Feb. 36 **Pigroots**, bucks and other forms of equine misdemeanour. **1983** STEWART *Springtime in Taranaki* (1991) 118 She could still give a gentle pig-root which failed to dislodge me.

pigroot, *v.* [AND 1900.] *intr.* Of a horse, to kick upwards with the hind legs, head down and forelegs firmly planted. Contrast PIG-JUMP *v.*
1968 *NZ Contemp. Dict. Suppl.* (Collins) 15 *pigroot v.i.* used of a horse, to plant both forelegs on the ground and kick with the hind legs; whence *pigrooter*.

pigskin. [Spec. or collocative use of Brit. (also NZ from 1908) sporting slang *pigskin* a riding saddle: see OED 1 a, 1876.]
1. In various (mainly farming) phrases. **a. per pigskin, in the pigskin**, on horseback.
1888 BARLOW *Kaipara* 204 He also has an immense amount of riding to do, and is as much at home in the pigskin as some men are in their easy chairs. **1947** NEWTON *Wayleggo* 120 We travelled..just on forty [miles] per pig skin. **1975** NEWTON *Sixty Thousand on Hoof* 99 Today..it [*sc.* mustering] is all done in the 'pig-skin' (saddle) where the few feet of height gained from being mounted make all the difference to visibility.
b. to stick to the pigskin, to stay in the saddle (on a frisky horse).
1952 NEWTON p.c. Apr. 21 'Stick to the pigskin' is the converse of 'show daylight' (between one's seat and saddle). **1960** BOSWELL *Ernie* 117 Once Togo got the bit between his teeth, it was a case of 'Stick to the pigskin' and hope for the best.

2. Special Comb. **pigskin country**, country which is negotiable on horseback.

1947 NEWTON *Wayleggo* 90 The bulk of Castle Hill was pigskin country (i.e., rideable).

pig tub: see PIG-BUCKET.

pihapiharau. Also **piarau, piharau.** [Ma. /ˈpihaˈpiharau/ /ˈpiharau/: Williams 279 *Piharau, pihapiharau, pipiharau*..lamprey.] LAMPREY. Cf. PIPIHARAU.
1845 WAKEFIELD *Adventure NZ II.* 15 We procured an abundant supply of piarau, a 'lamprey', which is taken in large numbers in this river. **1846** TAYLOR *Journal* 2 June (ATLTS) IV. 33 I found my former quarters not very fragrant, having about 400 piha piharau, (lampreys) which were presented to us when we were here before. **1855** TAYLOR *Te Ika A Maui* 412 Pihapiharau (the lamprey), is almost eighteen inches long, of a silvery color... The name of the fish is derived from its many gills. **1886** SHERRIN *Handbook Fishes NZ* 306 *Geotria chilensis*..Lamprey, Piharau, or Puhikorokoro **1898** MORRIS *Austral-English* 353 *Piharau*... Maori name for *Geotria chilensis*..a New Zealand *Lamprey*. **1904** [see LAMPREY]. **1922** *NZJST* V. 97 *Lamprey*. Called 'pihar[a]u' and 'korokoro' by the Maoris. **1929–30** *TrNZI* LX. 139 *Geotria australis*... Lamprey. Maori: Korokoro, Piharau. **1983** *Listener* 28 May 19 There were mussels..and also..piharau (lamprey eel from the Waitara River). **1992** [see TUERE].

pihoihoi. Also **pihoi; piohiohi, pi ói ói.** [Ma. /piˈhoihoi/: Williams 280 *Pīhoihoi*..*1*... ground-lark.] PIPIT.
[**1820** LEE & KENDALL *NZ Gram. & Vocab.* 193 Pi ói ói; A bird so called.] **1835** [see LARK 2 (1)]. **1838** POLACK *NZ* I. 300 The *piohiohi* [*sic*] is a species of 'poor cock-robin', equally fitted to 'point a moral, and adorn a tale', as his antipodal species. **1842** GRAY *Fauna* in Dieffenbach *Travels in NZ* (1843) II. 192 Alauda Novae Seelandiae... 'Ground Lark' is given under the name of Pihoihoi, by Mr Yate; Piohiohi, by Mr Polack; Pi-o-oie, by M. Lesson. **1873** BULLER *Birds NZ* 132 (New-Zealand Pipit)... *Native names.* Pihoihoi and Whioi; 'Ground-Lark' of the colonists. **1882** pihoi [see LARK 1]. **1898, 1939** [see LARK 2 (1)]. **1955** OLIVER *NZ Birds* 460 New Zealand Pipit. Pihoihoi Anthus novaeseelandiae novaeseelandiae. **1966** [see LARK 2 (2)]. **1985** [see LARK 2 (1)].

pikapo, var. PIKOPO.

pikau /ˈpikæu/, *v.* Also with much variety of early form as **peacow, pekau, pekou, peko(w), pikaw.** [Ma. /ˈpiːkau/: Williams 280 *Pīkau. 1*...*v.* trans. Carry on the back, pick-a-back. ..*4.* n. Load for the back.]

1. *trans.* To carry (a load or swag) on the back.
[**1817** NICHOLAS *NZ* II. 337 To get upon the back Pekou] **1834** MARKHAM *NZ* (1963) 61 Jake exerted himself and got five Boys to Pekow the Traps across at 2lb [tobacco] each to Kiddy Kiddy. **1863** MANING *Old NZ* viii 129 'I tell you what we must do..we will not carry (*pikau*) the provisions, we will *hiki* them' (*Hiki* is the word in Maori which describes the act of carrying an infant in the arms.) **1882** HAY *Brighter Britain* II. 94 Both [Maori] men and women are able to pikau (hump, or carry on the back and shoulders) great weights. **1891** A TRAMP, ESQ. *Casual Ramblings* 79 'Tommy' and Rairaina *pikaued* the swag. **1892** *Auckland Weekly News* 2 Apr. 30 It will scarcely be argued that exhibitors will *pikau* the result of their labour 10 or 15 miles to a show when they have neglected one at their own doors. **1931** *Aussie* (NZ Section) 15 Apr. 11 You *pikau* te canoe, quick. **1946** *JPS* LV. 155 *Pikau*, pack carried on the back: to carry on the back: to mount on the back of another.

PIKAU

2. *trans.* To pick-a-back.
1834 MARKHAM *NZ* (1963) 72 He picked out two of the strongest of the Boys about the place to carry 'Pekow' us over the River. **1840** POLACK *Manners & Customs* I. 59 [The Maori] may with due deference to public opinion, carry (Pekau) Pickback the said foreigner. **1879** FEATON *Waikato War* 86 (Griffiths Collect.) Riria Raihi came to his assistance.., took him on her back and pikaued him to the top. **1905** BAUCKE *White Man Treads* 89 Woe betide the tender, forming backs, as they grew strong enough to waha, or pikau (carry) the baby. **1946** [see 1 above].

3. *intr.* To travel on foot with a swag.
1916 COWAN *Bush Explorers* (VUWTS) 6 Three grand days in the saddle, the last winding down the bush road that skirted the..Ohura..then 'pikau' and foot-slog for the great roadless forest.

pikau, *n.* Mainly NI. [See PIKAU *v.*: there is no etymological connection with English *pick-a-back*.] Pl. usu. *pikaus*.

1. *Obs.* A pick-a-back.
1834 MARKHAM *NZ* (1963) 42 I crossed a Stream a dozen times, mostly on a Mans back called a (Pekow is to carry..) [syntax *sic* and obscure]. **1840** POLACK *Manners & Customs* I. 59 Nay, he may with due deference to public opinion, carry (*pekau*) pickback, the said foreigner, be his dimensions long or short.

2. a. Any load (to be) carried on the back or shoulders. Also *fig.*
1836 WILSON *Missionary Life & Work in NZ* 23 Aug. (1889) III. 48 Our natives weary with their *pikaus*. **1843** DIEFFENBACH *Travels in NZ* II. 378 Pikau—a load, burden, a garment **1851** *Richmond-Atkinson Papers* (1960) I. 82 The Maoris..speedily made up all our packages..into three *pikaws* or bundles of about 35lb each which they tied up & slung over their shoulders with strips of native flax leaf. **1874** BAINES *Edward Crewe* 49 So 'there and then' [the wild pig's] inside was torn out..and, his legs tied together so as to make him a handy 'pikau'. **1882** POTTS *Out in Open* 12 Here a brief stay allowed time for..dividing the pikaus. **1915** *Canterbury Times* 3 Mar. (VUW Fildes Clippings 421:59) A tin wash-dish for testing the creek gravels, and his old black billy, made [the prospector's] 'pikau'. **1930** COWAN *The Maori* 16 But the Maori generally is manfully shouldering the *pikau* of this twentieth century and is in some quarters showing that, given the same facilities, he can even outstrip the *pakeha* in the walks of civilized life.

b. A back-load carried in a pack or as a swag; a pack for such a load, in later use esp. one made of a sugar-bag.
1847 ANGAS *Savage Life* II. 3 My fellow traveller and myself set off..accompanied by five Maori lads, who carried our baggage..in their *pikau* or knapsacks, strapped over their shoulders with the leaves of flax. **1863** MORGAN *Journal* Nov. (1963) 123 One [Maori prisoner]..had on an oilskin, a hat, and carried a small 'pikau', his wardrobe I suppose. **1887** *Auckland Weekly News* 12 Feb. 8 We carefully packed in our blankets, which, fitted with 'pikau' straps, formed our swags. **1892** BROOKES *Frontier Life* 148 Most of us were now loaded with heavy pekoes or swags on our backs. **1916** COWAN *Bush Explorers* (VUWTS) 10 A week's provisions and other fixings in your rolled-up 'Pikau' of oilskin on your back. **1922** COWAN *NZ Wars* (1955) I. 122 These Ngati-Mutunga..made up small casks of powder in flax-basket *pikaus* or back-loads. **1940** [see SWAG *n.*[1] 1 a]. **1959** MASTERS *Tales of Mails* 101 I often wonder..how I ever managed, wet and almost numb with the cold as I sometimes was, to keep the pikau of mail and parcels in place, and get through some of those dreadful gates. **1969** MOORE *Forest to Farm* 88 As we leave the hut for the day's work we each have on

our backs a 'pikau'—a sugar-bag rucksack containing tucker. **1972** REED *Gumdiggers* 50 The pikau (load for the back) was a half-sack, with a strap attached to each of the bottom corners and joined at the middle of the top—in the manner of a knapsack. **1982** HOLDEN *Wild Pig* 43 Both of [the Canterbury pighunters] carried a pikau (a daypack which fits snugly over one's shoulders and is often fashioned out of a sugar-bag) as they ranged those big [sheep] stations. **1992** BOYD *Pumice & Pines* 56 Many [Depression relief workers] carried their few possessions in a *pikau*—a sugar sack, tied with string at the top and at one of the bottom corners to form a loop which could be slung across the shoulders and chest.

3. *Northland gumfields.* A kind of knapsack (often made from a sugarbag fastened with rope at the neck and two corners) for holding kauri-gum; *gum-bag* (GUM 3 a).
1900 *Auckland Weekly News* (Suppl.) 31 Aug. 8 The outfit required [for gum-digging] is a spade, a spear, and a pikau. **1911** *Truth* 29 Apr. 5 The last time he saw deceased alive was about 9 a.m. on April 5 going..to follow his occupation of gum-digging, having his pikau, with spear, spade, and axe in his possession. **1948** REED *Gumdigger* 5 Lonehand gumdiggers..spade in hand, pikau on back. **1958** *Tararua* Sept. 27 The gumdiggers used a *pikau*, a bag with shoulder straps, a good deal smaller than the usual tramper's pack. They were sold under that name by Leroy's in Auckland in the thirties. If *pikau* had been current further south trampers might have adopted it.

4. A makeshift saddlebag, often two sacks (or a split sack) slung each side of the horse's back. See also POCKET *n.*²
1951 p.c. D. Singe: the usual name on the East Coast for two sacks side-slung and balanced on both sides of a pack-horse. **1960** MASTERS *Back-Country Tales* 39 He vaguely remembered..cutting the tail off the animal and putting it in the pekau on the saddle of his horse. **1973** FERNANDEZ *Tussock Fever* 102 David hunted up a sacking pikau to drop over his saddle in case there should be venison..to bring back. **1983** FRANCIS *Wildlife Ranger* 65 The heavy canvas pikau bags which draped over the saddle and hung down on either side to about stirrup level..were waterproof when fording rivers. **1986** RICHARDS *Off the Sheep's Back* 34 Dad led the pack horse, and a troop of us youngsters followed on our ponies (bareback), each with a pikau laden with goods. *Ibid.* 66 After removing our pikaus, saddle bags and swag, we unharnessed the horses and turned them loose. **1990** WATTS *Wild Horses & Me* 52 They would arrive about lunchtime with peacows slung over their saddles. A peacow is a chaff sack, sewn up at both ends with a slit made across the centre of one side of the sack. When slung over the saddle it formed two large pockets in which the men carried their 'glad rags' or best clothes.

pikaw, var. PIKAU.

pike. Also **pike barracuda, sea pike.** BARRACUDA.
1927 PHILLIPPS *Bibliogr. NZ Fishes* (1971) 30 *Sphyraena obtusata*... Pike. **1956** GRAHAM *Treasury NZ Fishes* 405 Pike *Sphyraena grandisquamis.* **1982** AYLING *Collins Guide (1984)* 250 Pike Barracuda (Striped sea pike) *Sphyraena obtusata*... The pike barracuda is a small relative of the large tropical barracudas, being very similar in shape. **1986** PAUL *NZ Fishes* 113 Pike barracuda. *Sphyraena obtusata.* Alternatively sea pike.

pike(d), pike-headed whale: see WHALE 2 (9).

pikelet. [f. a shortened and altered form of *bara-picklet* (ad. Welsh *bara pyglyd*: *bara* =bread), a small leavened cake made of fine flour: a Western and Midland British local name for a small round tea-cake; elsewhere, a crumpet (so OED): cf. also EDD *pikelet-stone* (Warwickshire) a circular disk of iron suspended over the fire, on which pikelets are baked; cf. also SND *dropp(ed) scone* (*scone* 1) one made by allowing the mixture to drop on to a girdle or hot plate.]

1. a. A small pancake made of a batter which includes a rising agent. Cf. GEM (see esp. quot. 1910 below).
1905 BRANDON *'Ukneadit'* 66 *Pikelets..* Flour..Soda..[Tartaric] Acid dissolved in a Cupful of Good Milk..Sugar..Milk to make a good batter. **c1910** BEATON *Universal Cook. Book* 30 *Pikelets..*same mixture as for gems..nice and hot; take sharp-pointed tablespoon of the mixture..drop off the point of the spoon onto the hot greased girdle. Brown on both sides. **1917** MILLER *Econ. Tech. Cook. Book* 264 *Pikelets or Drop Scones* Flour..Soda..Eggs..Cream of Tartar..Sugar..Milk. **1957** FRAME *Owls Do Cry* (1967) 57 She..was greasing the girdle for pikelets that would be made on the coal stove, the batter dropped in spoonfuls on the smoking girdle, and rising and bubbling and browning. **1963** BACON *In the Sticks* 18 The wife gave me a few pikelets for supper. **1982** BURTON *Two Hundred Yrs. NZ Food* 152 Early Scottish immigrants added baking powder to a recipe known in their home country as 'drop scones' and the result—pikelets—has become a New Zealand specialty.

b. With a modifier: **potato pikelet,** see quot.; **yeast pikelet,** a muffin cooked on a girdle.
1928 *Everybody's Cook. Book Tested Recipes* 40 **Potato Pikelets**..mashed potatoes..flour..baking powder..dripping..one egg with milk... Fry in boiling fat. **1917** MILLER *Econ. Tech. Cook. Book* 264 **Yeast Pikelets** *or Muffins* Flour..1 Egg..Salt..lukewarm water..Yeast..let it stand all night to rise.

2. In the phr. **as plain as a pikelet,** of a girl, very plain (influenced by the form of *plain as a pikestaff,* 'clearly seen').
1981 Feb. 25 p.c. Rev. Dr. Frank McKay. *Plain as a pikelet* is a phrase applied to a homely girl. **1989** *Listener* 18 Dec. 8 [Heading] Plain as a pikelet. It's candidate selection time again, and all over the country aspiring MPs are jockeying for position in a sort of political beauty contest.

pike-pole. *Logging.* [f. N. Amer. lumbering usage: DCan. 1830.] A pole with a spike and hook at one end used to shift floating logs. Cf. PICKAROO.
1874 BAINES *Edward Crewe* 177 The remaining seven [men]..I stationed two miles above the boom, where they had to lend a hand as occasion [*sc.* a log-jam] may require. All were armed with either a 'pike-pole,' timber-jack, or axe. **1953** REED *Story of Kauri* 225 Succeeding logs were pushed in position by pike poles.

piker. *Obs.* [Transf. use of Brit. slang or dial. *piker* a vagrant: see OED *piker n.*³ 2; AND 1887.] A wild bull.
1904 LANCASTER *Sons o' Men* 24 [They] swung the roaring tangle of pikers, steers, and fierce old scrub bulls by..whips. **1907** LANCASTER *Tracks We Tread* 52 [The wild cattle] were a mixed haul: two-year-olds, poddies and pikers.

pikiarero. [Ma. /'piki'arero/: Williams 281 *Pikiarero..2. Clematis* [spp.].] *Clematis forsteri* (formerly *hexasepala*) (fam. Ranunculaceae), a small native clematis. See also CLEMATIS.
1843 DIEFFENBACH *Travels in NZ* II. 379 Pikiarero—the ligament of the tongue, a climbing plant. **1850** [see CLEMATIS a]. **1867** HOCHSTETTER *NZ* 157 Mr. Probert has exhibited in London a liana Pikiarero (a species of *Clematis*) which is said to contain a fine silky fibre. **1889** FEATON *Art Album* (Plant Names) 178 Pikiarero [Maori name]..Clematis [Settlers' name]..Clematis hexasepala..Climber. **1946** *JPS* LV. 155 *pikiarero*, a climbing plant (Clematis hexasepala); pua-wānanga is C. indivisa. **1959** *NZ Philatelic Bull.* 3 Dec. 1 6d [postage stamp] Pikiarero (Clematis).

piki-pik(i), varr. PIKOPIKO.

pikipo, var. PIKOPO.

pikopiko. Also **piki-pik(i).** [Ma. /'pikopiko/: Williams 281 *pikopiko..2.* n. Young curved shoots of fern, etc... *pikopiko,* n. *1...* a fern.] A young curved fern frond of the hen and chicken fern (*Asplenium bulbiferum*), or of the shield fern (*Polystichum richardii*), eaten by the Maori as a delicacy.
1882 POTTS *Out in Open* 97 The tender unfolding fronds (piki-piki) are made use of by the Maoris as an article of food. **1896** HARPER *Pioneer Work* 33 I have often been glad of even a small feed of Piki-piki fern (*Asplenium bulbiferum*) [when bushed]. **1922** [see MAUKU]. **1934** HARPER *Windy Island* (Gloss.) Piki-pik—edible fern. **1978** FULLER *Maori Food & Cook.* 7 Pikopiko, the young uncurled shoots of the *Asplenium bulbiferum* fern, were also sought after, as they are today. *Ibid.* 36 Fern Shoots (Pikopiko). The *Polystichum richardii* shield-fern is found growing in the damper shady part of the bush. **1982** BURTON *Two Hundred Yrs. NZ Food* 8 Pikopiko, the young, curling buds of the hen and chicken fern (*Asplenium bulbiferum*), were collected in the spring. They taste similar to asparagus when steamed. **1988** *Evening Post* (Wellington) 13 Aug. 3 On Wednesday afternoon..Mr Stan Phillips disappeared while picking piko piko with friends.

pikopo. *Obs.* Also with much variety of early form as **Pickapo, Pikapo, pikipo, Pikypo.** *pl.* *pikopo; pikopos, pikopoes; pikipoi.* [Ma. /'pikopo/: Williams Appendix. *Pikopo* Roman Catholic: a Maori alteration of Latin *episcopus* bishop (cf. quot. 1842 below): contrast *pihopa*, an alteration of *bishop*.]

1. With init. cap. A Maori name for Bishop Pompallier, the first Catholic bishop.
1839 WILLIAMS *Early Jrnls.* 6 Oct. (1961) 446 Conversation with some who had attended 'Pikopo' (The Roman Catholic Bishop). [Bishop Pompallier arrived on 10 Jan. 1838.] **1841** BRIGHT *Handbook Emigrants* 126 M. Pompaliere; the natives call him *Pikypo,* for what reason I know not. [**1842** *Ko te Epikopo Katorika Romana, ko Hoane Papita Werahiko Pomaparie* [Title] in Williams *A Bibliography of Printed Maori* (1975) 21] **1890** COLENSO *Treaty of Waitangi* 13 'If Pikopo and his priest go in, we [*sc.* Colenso et al.], for the sake of our position among the Natives, should go in also.' [1890 *Note*] The common Maori name by which the Roman Catholic bishop and the priests were known.

2. A (Roman) Catholic.
1842 TAYLOR *Journal 1842–43* 17 Oct. (ATLTS) 4 Encamping close by the sea by a beautiful amphitheatre of powa takawa trees..Mr Williams addressed a party of Pickapos the best part of the afternoon **1843** DIEFFENBACH *Travels in NZ* I. 369 The Protestant natives regard their Roman Catholic brethren as belonging to the devils: they are called pikipo, which M. Pompalier explained as being derived from *episcopus*, which seems to me the most probable derivation. The Protestant

pikypo, var. PIKOPO.

pilchard. [Trans. use of *pilchard* a small seafish.] *Sardinops neopilchardus* (fam. Clupeidae), a predominantly blue-green and silver sea-fish, having a dark oily flesh. See also *Picton herring* (HERRING 2 (1)), MOHIMOHI, SARDINE.

1842 10 Feb. in *Lett. from New Plymouth* (1968) 3 There are plenty of mackerel here, but no nets to catch them, and there are pilchards; please to bring one good pilchard net. 1872 HUTTON & HECTOR *Fishes NZ* 63 *Clupea sagax*... Pilchard or Sardine. 1886 SHERRIN *Handbook Fishes NZ* 73 As the New Zealand pilchard is regarded as only 'a climatal variety' of the English pilchard, some details about the pilchard industry may not be out of place. 1892 *TrNZI* XXIV. 213 Pilchard, or Sardine (*Clupea sagax*)... Sprat (*Clupea sprattus*). The recorders were mostly unable to distinguish between these species. 1903 [see MOHIMOHI]. 1927 SPEIGHT et al. *Nat. Hist. Canterbury* 195 The pilchard appears to shoal in immense numbers in bays and harbours in the winter and from Queen Charlotte Sound the fishing interests supply smoked 'Picton Herring' regularly to the Wellington market. 1938 *TrRSNZ* LXVIII. 402 *Sardinia neopilcharda*... Pilchard. Mohimohi. 1956 GRAHAM *Treasury NZ Fishes* 104 The Pilchard is known from the northern end of the South Island as the Picton Herring, and off Picton large shoals of these fish have from time to time been recorded. 1967 NATUSCH *Animals NZ* 207 Schools of pilchard (*Sardinops*... related to the Norwegian sardine) enter harbours in the winter. 1982 AYLING *Collins Guide* (1984) 104 Around New Zealand pilchard schools are most abundant in the Bay of Plenty, and in Tasman Bay and the Marlborough Sounds. 1990 *Evening Post* (Wellington) 22 Aug. 50 The success of pilchards as a bait lies in the fact that they are particularly oily fish, affecting predators [*sic*] sense of smell, together with being very shiny which attracts species such as kingfish, kahawai and tuna.

pilchers. [f obs. or dial. Brit. *pilch* a triangular flannel wrapper worn over an infant's napkin: see OED *pilch n*.¹ 3; SOD *pilcher* (= *pilch*) Canad. dial. *rare* a baby's nappy; *Macquarie Dict* (1981) 1310.] A water-absorbent or waterproof covering (formerly usu. flannel, but now often plastic) for a baby's nappy.

1954 *pilchers* known to Wellington informants as (at that date) a flannel overcloth for waterproofing nappies. 1980 LELAND *Kiwi-Yankee Dict.* 77 *pilchers*: Babies [*sic*] plastic pants. 1996 *Evening Post* (Wellington) 5 Feb. 6 I am aware of tremendous advances in babywear, [*sic*] since my family has grown up. Were the pilchers used or new, woollen or brushed cotton, or some newfangled plastic variety?

missionaries however, say that it means piki-po—always bowing—(piki, bend—po, night). The Protestants, therefore, call their bishop pihopa, while the Roman Catholics have retained the title pikipo for theirs. 1844 *NZ Jrnl*. IV. 621 The natives at Taupo are nearly all *pikipoi* (*episcopoi*) as they call themselves. 1845 WAKEFIELD *Adventure NZ* I. 168 We were Pikapo. 1878 BULLER *Forty Yrs. NZ* 295 They took the name of Pikopo. This no doubt was maorified from the Latin word *episcopos*; but, unfortunately for them, it had an ominous meaning in the Maori tongue,—*creeping in the dark*. 1936 BUICK *Treaty of Waitangi* 118 In his discussions with the Maoris, Bishop Pompallier had stressed the point that he held the advantage over the Protestant missionaries in that he was a member of the Episcopacy. The best attempt on the part of the natives to render into their own language the word Episcopos, in its varied forms, was *pikopo*, hence the Bishop and his converts became known as *Pikopo*.

pile, *n*.¹ *Goldmining.* Also **piler**. [Transf. use of *pile* a heap of wealth: AND 1854.] Usu. as **pile claim**, a rich claim.

1862 LINDSAY *Place & Power Nat. Hist.* 12 'Good finds' and 'piles' have been hitherto unknown. 1862 *Otago Goldfields & Resources* 21 In the one or two holes that have been sunk gold has been obtained... Waipori has no 'pile claims'. 1888 PRESHAW *Banking Under Difficulties* 155 We found the miners doing fairly, but no 'pile' claims. *Ibid.* 157 Nearly all were on gold, but no pile claims. 1967 MAY *West Coast Gold Rushes* 244 The digger recognized four classes of payable ground: 'tucker ground'..a 'wages claim'..a 'riser' was a rich claim; and a 'piler' or 'homeward bounder' the richest of all. Probably most of the 'pilers' were beach-claims. 1974 HEINZ *Bright Fine Gold* 200 *Claims* Worthless claims or ground were called schicers or duffers. Those yielding..above £8 were known as 'pilers'. 1992 LATHAM *Golden Reefs* 120 Every quartz discovery was assumed to be the the beginning of a 'pile claim'.

pile, *n*.² [Spec. use of *pile* a long heavy beam driven into the ground as a foundation.] A block of wood or stone on which the underfloor beams of a house or other building rest; a *house-block* (HOUSE 5).

1850 TORLESSE *Papers* (1958) 183 Bill Holland carting piles and Pollard's goods on return trips. 1866 BARKER *Station Life* (1870) 49 It was preceded by two dray-loads of small rough-hewn stone piles, which are first let into the ground six or eight feet apart: the foundation joists rest on these, so as just to keep the flooring from touching the earth. 1887 CHUDLEIGH *Diary* 14 Oct. (1950) 358 Put 2 piles under the cottage. 1892 CARRICK *NZ's Lone Lands* 24 Timber, fencing, building-piles..could all be had within the place. 1987 MS *Cellany* 6 The heart of it was still decaying, the borer spreading, the piles left to rot.

pilgrim. *Hist.* [A short familiar form of CANTERBURY PILGRIM, perhaps also recalling US *Pilgrim Father*, an original (religious) settler.]

1. a. Often init. cap. Also occas. **Pilgrim Father**. CANTERBURY PILGRIM.

[1851 *The Times* (London) 5 July in Carrington *Godley* (1950) 117 A slice of England cut from top to bottom was despatched to the Antipodes last September..a deliberate, long-considered, solemn and devoted pilgrimage to a temple erected by nature for the good of all comers. At the head of the pilgrims stood an actual bishop, behind him were working clergy, working schoolmasters, working landlords, working labourers, workers every one.] 1851 *NZ Spectator and Cook's Strait Guardian* (Wellington) 7 May [unpaged 3] [see SHAGROON]. 1851 *Austral. & NZ Gaz.* 29 Nov. 483 This gale has completely startled the 'big-hearted Pilgrims'. 1853 DEANS *Pioneers* (1964) 82 I do not wish to sell any to the Pilgrims, as they are not good payers. 1859 [see SHAGROON 1]. 1865 BARKER *Station Life* (1870) 20 Fifteen years ago a few sheds received the 'Pilgrims', as the first comers are always called. I like the name; it is so pretty and suggestive. 1877 PRATT *Col. Experiences* 234 In the 'Dream of a Shagroon'..the term Pilgrim was first applied to the settlers. 1883 *Canterbury Rhymes* iv The pilgrim was not only quite another man from those who have followed him: he was also a colonist of a stamp distinct in many respects from any other class of pioneer in Australasia. 1890 *Otago Witness* (Dunedin) 25 Sept. 36 By the end of the previous year ('51) the Pilgrim Fathers..had begun stringing up the steep bridle-track. 1898 [see SHAGROON 1]. 1933 *Press* (Christchurch) (Acland Gloss.) 11 Nov. 15 *Pilgrim*.—One of the Canterbury Association's settlers. 1949 [see PRE-ADAMITE 1 a]. 1951 CRESSWELL

Canterbury Tales 26 The Pilgrims could cross the hills to the Plain over the Bridle Path.

b. A Canterbury agriculturalist as distinct from a pastoralist (contrast PROPHET 1).

1851 *Lyttelton Times* 9 Aug. 7 Gaily the pilgrim harnessed his plough, When he had built up a roof o'er his head; Singing, 'From Albion hither I come;' 'Land of mine! land of mine! grow me some bread.' Proudly the prophet flourished his crook.

2. *attrib.* or *a*. Pertaining to the Canterbury Association foundation settlers.

1853 *Canterbury Papers* II. 91 Weld shows out the true blood of an old settler. Your *pilgrim muffs* were too slow even to have stirred themselves in the matter. 1886 HART *Stray Leaves* 6 It was hardly a matter for surprise that amongst the ranks of the Pilgrim Settlers who—as the Puritan founders of new England did in the *Mayflower*—set sail for Canterbury in 1850, we should have many scions of the aristocracy. 1912 BAUGHAN *Brown Bread* 130 Narrated this Pilgrim mother. 1932 BRUCE *Early Days Canterbury* 193 Even at this early period [c1850s]..there were some four-wheeled open chaises... The pilgrim mothers and daughters..who occupied the humbler contraptions were none the less happy. 1970 MCNEISH *Mackenzie* 16 But how, he thought, as the pilgrim town loomed on the edges of the plain, do I explain it to a bullock driver?

pillion pussy. *Obs.* A girl (or occas. a youth) riding pillion with a MILKBAR COWBOY. Also **pillion pickup** (heard Wellington, 1953).

1956 *Street Society Christchurch* 15 'Have you got a motor-bike?' I asked Bill. 'Yes. A two stroke... [I] Got pinched.' 'How?' 'Riding over eighty-five down Blank Road with a pillion pussy. Came off once too.' 1993 YSKA *All Shook Up* 144 These cowboys..dressed in army greatcoats and peaked train-driver's caps..roared around on bikes..attracting girls, known as 'pillion pussies'.

pinchers: see NIP *n*. 1 (*to get the pinchers into*).

pincushion. Also **New Zealand pin-cushion**. Any of various native plants resembling a pincushion, esp. *Raoulia mammillaris* (VEGETABLE SHEEP), *Gaimardia setacea* (syn. *ciliata*) (fam. Centrolepidaceae) ('bog pincushion'), and *Colobanthus buchananii* (fam. Caryophyllaceae).

1885 *NZ Country Jrnl*. IX. 140 [*Raoulia mammillaris*] is also called the New Zealand pincushion and is often used for that purpose by the shepherds' wives. 1909 *AJHR* C-12 52 *Gaimardia setacea*. Bog-pincushion. End[emic]... Bog. 1982 WILSON *Stewart Is. Plants* 258 *Colobanthus buchananii* Pincushion... Small, compact, green, prickly cushions a few cm in diameter.

pine. [Spec. uses of *pine*, applied (in early times) to various native, and (in modern use) to introduced gymnosperm trees, and to their wood or timber.] See also KAURI, PINUS, RADIATA PINE, SCREWPINE.

[*Note*] In general, Maori-derived names have replaced the -*pine* names of 19c. immigrant English speakers, a process which has taken place more slowly in the South Island than in the North, and more slowly in respect of timber than for the trees themselves: e.g. *rimu* has for some time now replaced *red pine* as the name of the forest tree; but *red pine* could still in the 1970s, poss. later, be heard in South Island timber yards as a usual name for the timber.

1. Also **pine-tree. a.** *Obs.* KAURI. See also *New Zealand pine* 2 (9) below.

1814 KENDALL 17 June in Elder *Marsden's*

PINE

Lieutenants (1934) 63 Loads of excellent pine are to be found. **1819** MARSDEN *Lett. & Jrnls.* (1932) 210 There is here and there the root of a pine..and pieces of rosin, which have come from the pine tree, are lying on the ground in all directions. **1841** BIDWILL *Rambles in NZ* (1952) 28 The Cowrie or pine of the country..is abundant here. **1881** CAMPBELL *Poenamo* 73 Waiheki had many a stately kouri growing on it. [1881 *Note*] *Pine-tree*. **1925** MANDER *Allen Adair* (1971) 41 He was delighted with the houses in the pines and the suggestion of old and rambling gardens about them.

b. Applied to various members of the podocarp family. Often *attrib.*

1810 Leith *Report* 15 Apr. in *Hist. Recs NSW* VII. 333 The pine I consider is not of good quality, possessing very little turpentine or rosin. **1817** NICHOLAS *Voyage NZ* I. 233 Another species of the pine, but much inferior to the one I have described, and the same that Captain Cook mentions as bearing a berry with a leaf like that of the yew, presented itself in great abundance upon the banks which bordered the sides of the cove. **c1835** BOULTBEE *Journal* (1986) 103 The trees are easily cleared away, being either pine or other soft wood. **1848** WAKEFIELD *Handbook for NZ* 322 [Inland from Kaikoura the country is] dotted with groves of pine-trees. **1866** BARKER *Station Life* (1870) 78 Blazing logs of pine and black birch made every room warm and cheery. **1879** HAAST *Geol. Canterbury & Westland* 102 Towards evening we camped..near a grove of pine trees and arborescent ferns. **1898** HOCKEN *Contributions* 79 Beyond these [small trees] rise the lofty pines and other forest giants. **1935** STACK *More Maoriland Adventures* in Wily & Maunsell *Robert Maunsell* (1938) 139 The river presented a striking contrast to the dark pine trees that lined its opposite bank. **1966** [see PINUS].

2. With a modifier in names of native genera: **Barrier, black (bastard black, black rue), bog, celery (celery-leaved, celery-top, celery-topped), alpine (mountain) celery, king, mahogany, mountain, New Zealand, pink, pitch (New Zealand pitch), pygmy, red, rue, silver, sugar-loaf, swamp, Westland, white, yellow.**

(1) **Barrier pine.** [f. the name of (*Great*) *Barrier* Island in the Hauraki Gulf.] MANOAO 2, and its timber.

1878 *TrNZI* X. 384 This species [*D. kirkii*] was sufficiently plentiful on the Great Barrier Island to admit of its conversion [to timber] a few years ago, and the timber was placed in the Auckland market under the name of Barrier pine. **1889** KIRK *Forest Flora* 192 [*D. kirkii*] was occasionally converted..as 'Barrier pine'. **1985** in Satchell *Toll of Bush* (1905) 42 [1985 editorial note to *manoa*, p. 41] Correctly, manoao, a podocarp tree also known as Barrier pine. **1957** WILLIAMS *Dict. Maori Lang.* 176 *Manoao,.. 2. Dacrydium kirkii, Barrier pine.*

(2) **black pine.** *Southern New Zealand.* **a.** Also as **black rue pine**, MATAI 1, and its timber.

1851 *Lyttelton Times* 28 June 6 The timber in [the groves] is chiefly Kaikatea, (white pine), Mahi, (black pine), Remu, (red pine)..and Totara. **1861** *NZ Goldfields 1861* (1976) 23 Here [at Taieri] was the tall and graceful black pine. **1877** [see MATAI 1]. **1889** KIRK *Forest Flora* 5 The matai is commonly termed 'black-pine' by the settlers except in the Nelson District, where it is known as 'red-pine', a name applied to the rimu..in other parts of the colony. **1898** HOCKEN *Contributions* 201 'With hearts devout by the hill we climb To hear the Word by the old black pine'... The verses refer to the little bush congregation by the clay cottage at Green Island. **1915** *AJHR* C-6 11 *Podocarpus spicatus*. Matai. Black-pine. Forest. **1926** COWAN *Travel in NZ* II. 90 The way is through the tall woods, chiefly *rimu* and *kahikatea* pines, with large *rata* and *matai*

(black pine). **1939** BEATTIE *First White Boy Born Otago* 13 I liked the berries..of the black pine and of the supplejack. **1940** *Otago Daily Times* (Dunedin) 6 Feb. 6 The black pine towers above the surrounding bush. **1961** MARTIN *Flora NZ* 161 Black pine (*P. spicatus*) leaves rather smaller in adult. **1985** MCGILL *G'day Country* 156 It was once, he said, a great area for red pine, rimu, and the black pine, matai.

b. Also as **bastard black (black rue) pine.** MIRO *n.*[1] a, and its timber.

1867 HOOKER *Handbook* 767 Pine, black. *Podocarpus ferruginea*. **1869** *TrNZI* I. (rev. edn.) 169 Miro, black rue or black pine in Otago. *Ibid*. 31 The most valuable for sawn timber [in Otago] are Black Pine, or Miro.., having red, hard, durable wood. **1875** KIRK *Durability NZ Timbers* 11 Miro, also called Black Pine in Otago. **1883** HECTOR *Handbook NZ* (3edn.) 123 Miro, Bastard Black-pine of Otago, ornamental and useful tree; attains a height of 40-60 feet, trunk 2-3 feet in diameter. A useful wood, but not so durable as the matai or true black-pine wood. **1890** *PWD Catalogue Timbers* (NZ & South Seas Exhib.) 12 Miro (bastard black pine)..*Podocarpus ferruginea*..Wood hard, elastic, strong, and grain prettily figured. *Ibid*. 24 Miro (bastard black pine) slab.

c. *Early local.* RIMU *n.*[1]

1879 HAAST *Geol. Canterbury & Westland* 81 Along the rather wet track appeared, besides the Totara pine, white pines.., and black pines (*Rimu* or *Dacrydium cupressinum*), which..towered high above the other forest foliage. **1882** HAY *Brighter Britain* II. 90 The Rimu..is a beautiful species of cypress; 'Black Pine', as bushmen call it.

(3) **bog pine.** *Halocarpus* (formerly *Dacrydium*) *bidwilli*, occas. *Lagarostrobos* (formerly *Dacrydium*) *colensoi*, trees often found on low-lying or peaty land. See also *mountain pine* (8) b below, *silver pine* (15) b below, TARWOOD 2.

1889 KIRK *Forest Flora* 57 In the Te Anau district, where this species [*D. bidwillii*] is plentiful, it is termed 'bog-pine' or 'tar-wood' by the shepherds, but does not seem to have received a distinctive name elsewhere. **1896** BIGGAR *Diary* in Begg *Port Preservation* (1973) 360 As soon as you get four or five hundred feet above the sea the timber..becomes very small interspersed with birch, and bog or silver pines. **1911** *TrNZI* XLIII. 248 The track leads on to low peaty land..which has recently been covered by a young forest of bog-pine (*Dacrydium Bidwillii*). **1939** COCKAYNE & TURNER *Trees NZ* 42 *Dacrydium bidwillii* (Podocarpaceae). Bog-pine, Mountain Pine. **1961** ALLAN *Flora NZ* I. 110 Montane to subalpine scrub..also lowland... *Bog Pine.* **1988** DAWSON *Forest Vines to Snow Tussocks* 40 A group of conifers formerly included in *Dacrydium*..yellow silver pine (*Lepidothamnus intermedius*), bog pine (*Halocarpus bidwilli*), *H. biformis* and manoao (*H. kirkii*).

(4) **celery (celery-leaved, celery-top, celery-topped [AND 1832]) pine.** *Phyllocladus* spp. **a.** TANEKAHA, TOATOA 1.

1853 HOOKER *II Flora Novae-Zelandiae I Flowering Plants* 234 The 'Celery-leaved Pines' [Gen. *Phyllocladus*] are natives of New Zealand, Tasmania, and the mountains of Borneo. **1869** *TrNZI* I. (rev. ed.) 158 From 1000 feet upwards..in addition to the common kinds [of Pine], the Toa-toa or Celery Pine..becomes abundant. **1876** *TrNZI* VIII. 104 Celery pine..is covered with large well-defined leaves like the common celery plant, from which the name is derived. **1877** *TrNZI* IX. 163 *Celery-Pine—Phyllocladus trichomanoides*. The genus to which the celery pine belongs only embraces three timber trees, one each in Borneo, Tasmania, and New Zealand... The leaves are quite different from the other conifers of Otago. Instead of a mere cluster of thin foliage, the tree is covered with large well-defined

PINE

leaves like the common celery plant, from which the name is derived. **1883** HECTOR *Handbook NZ* 125 *Phyllocladus trichomanoides*... Tanekaha, Celery-leaved Pine. A slender handsome tree, 60 feet high. **1889** KIRK *Forest Flora* 9 The tanekaha is one of the remarkable 'celery-topped pines,' and was discovered by Banks and Solander during Cook's first voyage. **1889** [see TOATOA 1 b]. **1895** *TrNZI* XXVII. 408 *Phyllocladus trichomanoides*. This species of the so-called celery-leaved pine is reported..as growing in the Maitai Valley, Nelson. **1895** *NZ Reader* quoting Potts *Out in Open* (1882) 82 The silvery parsley pine. [1895 *Note*] Or celery-top pine of settlers—tanekaha, *Phyllocladus*. **1898** MORRIS *Austral-English* 84 *Celery-topped Pine*... The tree is so called from the appearance of the upper part of the branchlets, which resemble in shape the leaf of the garden celery. **1907** LAING & BLACKWELL *Plants NZ* 76 *Phyllocladus trichomanoides* (Celery-leaved Pine). **1935** *Star Sun* (Christchurch) 12 Oct. 14 Not so many know the curious philocladus [*sic*], the tanekaha, or celery pine, so odd in details of growth, so shapely in whole. **1940** [see TANEKAHA]. **1946** *JPS* LV. 146 *tanekaha*, a tree (Phyllocladus Trichomanoides), celery-leaved tree. **1961** MARTIN *Flora NZ* 171 The name Celery Pine in common usage is almost restricted to *Phyllocladus alpinus*, the others being called tanekaha and toatoa. **1981** BROOKER et al. *NZ Medicinal Plants* 32 *Phyllocladus trichomanoides*..*Celery pine*..*Tanekaha*

b. As **mountain** (earlier **alpine**) **celery pine.** *alpine toatoa* (TOATOA 1 b, *P. aspleniifolius* var. *alpinus*).

1900 *Canterbury Old & New* 188 The undergrowth consists largely of the alpine celery pine [*Phyllocladus alpinus*], an almost unique member of the order *Coniferae*, with the customary needle-like leaves replaced by flattened leaf-like branches. **1919** COCKAYNE *NZ Plants & Their Story* 97 This unexpected association [of high mountain flora] consists of..the alpine celery-pine (*Phyllocladus alpinus*)..and the white mountain-musk. **1940** [see TOATOA 1 b]. **1988** DAWSON *Forest Vines to Snow Tussocks* 120 Bog forest is low in stature, up to 15 m, and the usual dominant tree is silver pine..intermixed with small trees of the mountain celery pine (*Phyllocladus aspleniifolius* var. *alpinus*).

(5) **kauri pine**, see KAURI 1 b.

(6) **king pine.** *Obs.* KAURI.

1883 DOMETT *Ranolf & Amohia* II. 48 The *King-pine* that grandly towers:—The fuchsia-tree with its flowers... The *clematis*-garlands that cure. *Ibid*. II. 236 King-pine (Kauri).

(7) **mahogany pine.** *Obs.* [f. a (fancied) resemblance between the woods of both, reddish, durable, and able to take a high polish.] TOTARA *n.*[1] 1 a.

1857 HURSTHOUSE *NZ* I. 141 Totara..(Mahogany Pine.)..Principal inner house and furniture wood in the south. **1867** HOCHSTETTER *NZ* 159 Totara N.Z. Mahagony [*sic*] Pine Podocarpus totara. **1868** *Province Otago* 34 The stately black pines (*Matai* and *Miro*),.. and the noble mahogany pine (*Totara*), are ever prominent objects in the forest. **1898** MORRIS *Austral-English* 354 Mahogany pine *Podocarpus totara*... Maori name, *Totara*.

(8) **mountain pine. a.** *Obs.* KAURI.

1817 NICHOLAS *Voyage NZ* I. 233 The mountain-pine, called by the natives *cowrie*, which we found growing upon the sides and summits of the hills, and rising to an enormous size, was the most remarkable.

b. *Halocarpus* (formerly *Dacrydium*) *bidwillii*. See *bog pine* (3) above.

1889 KIRK *Forest Flora* 57 This charming mountain-pine [*D. bidwillii*] has until recently been confused with other species of Dacrydium. **1890** *PWD Catalogue*

Timbers (NZ & South Seas Exhib.) 13 Pine, mountain (tarwood)..Dacrydium Bidwillii..Timber hard, and used for firewood. *Ibid.* 17 Mountain pine slab. **1909** *AJHR C-12* 29 The mountain-pine (*Dacrydium Bidwillii*) will form one-half of the formation. **1939** [see (3) above]. **1940** HOWARD *Rakiura* xviii From about 900 feet upward the forest merges into a manuka scrub..and mountain pine (*Dacrydium Bidwillii*) up to..about 1,500 feet. **1957** *NZ Timber Jrnl.* Dec. 59 Mountain Pine: *Dacrydium bidwillii*..Bog pine. N.Z.

c. *Lepidothamnus* (formerly *Dacrydium*) *intermedius*. See *silver pine* (15) b below.
1889 KIRK *Forest Flora* 167 The yellow silver-pine [*Dacrydium intermedium*] or mountain-pine, as it is less frequently termed, was originally described by the writer in 1877. **1906** CHEESEMAN *Manual NZ Flora* 655 *D[acrydium] intermedium*... Mountain-pine; Yellow Silver-pine. Wood reddish-yellow, highly resinous..; largely used in Westland..for railway sleepers,... &c.

d. *Lagarostrobos* (formerly *Dacrydium*) *colensoi*. MANOAO 1. See also *silver pine* (15) a below.
1957 WILLIAMS *Dict. Maori Lang.* 176 Manoao, n. 1. *Dacrydium colensoi*, mountain pine.

(9) New Zealand pine. *Obs.* KAURI.
1834 MARKHAM *NZ* (1963) 48 The Sawn Plank is very cheap in the Colonies and lately there is some prejudice against the New Zealand Pine. **1834** [see KAURI 1 a]. **1840** MATHEW *Journal* 25 Apr. in *Founding of NZ* (1940) 126 Here I first saw the famed Koudi tree which is now so extensively used for masts and spars under the name of New Zealand pine. **1867** HOCHSTETTER *NZ* 140 The two most characteristic plants of New Zealand are the Kauri and the Harakeke or the New Zealand Pine..and the New Zealand flax plant.

(10) pink pine. [f. the colour of the wood.] *Halocarpus* (formerly *Dacrydium*) *biformis*, a small montane forest tree or subalpine shrub with needle-like juvenile foliage and scale-like adult foliage. See also TAR-WOOD 2.
1939 COCKAYNE & TURNER *Trees NZ* 43 *Dacrydium biforme*... Pink-pine. **1958** *NZ Timber Jrnl.* Jan. 46 Pink Pine: *Dacrydium biforme*... Small tree of subalpine forest of New Zealand. Often a shrub. **1961** MARTIN *Flora NZ* 176 The pink pine (*D[acrydium] biforme*) is..named [*biforme*] because..both juvenile and adult leaves are commonly developed on different parts of the same branch. **1981** DENNIS *Paparoas Guide* 163 The montane forest is mainly made up of large tracts of mountain beech usually over an understorey of pink pine. **1982** WILSON *Stewart Is. Plants* 48 *Dacrydium biforme* Pink Pine... Small tree up to 9m... (=*Halocarpus biformis*).

(11) pitch (New Zealand pitch) pine. [Transf. use of European *pitch-pine*.] TANEKAHA (also TOATOA 1) *Phyllocladus* spp.
1796 MURRY *Journal of the 'Britannia'* Jan. in McNab *Hist. Records* (1914) II. 534 He [*sc.* Capt. Cook] has not taken any notice of the Pitch Pine... The Pitch Pine is remarkable for its black bark, which when cut and rubbed with the finger smells agreeably... **1857** HURSTHOUSE *NZ* 141 Tanekáha..(say Pitch Pine)..A handsome small Pine, common in the north. In quality of timber it may be termed a superior dwarf Kauri. **1867** HOCHSTETTER *NZ* 159 Tanekaha or Tawiwai N.Z. Pitch Pine Phyllocladus trichomanoides. **1879** [see (20) a below]. **1882** POTTS *Out in Open* 186 These and numerous other shrubs or trees, such as the pitch pine and totara, furnish some of the means of life to this parrot. **1907** *TrNZI* XXXIX. 80 [The kea] feeds on..the fruit of the pitch-pine and the totara.

(12) pygmy (pigmy) pine. *Lepidothamnus* (formerly *Dacrydium*) *laxifolius*, a sprawling subalpine shrub with scale-like leaves.
1908 *AJHR C-11* 35 *[Dacrydium] laxifolium*. Pigmy pine. Shrub-steppe, bog. **1923** COCKAYNE *Cultivation NZ Plants* 47 *Dacrydium laxifolium* (pygmy pine, vh.) forms a carpet on boggy ground, or scrambles over low shrubs... *Hab.*, usually in mountains where rainfall is high. **1940** LAING & BLACKWELL *Plants NZ* 77 *Dacrydium laxifolium* (*The Loose-leaved Dacrydium*)... Pigmy pine. **1951** HUNT *Confessions* 136 It (New Zealand) has the largest tree in the world in the Kauri..and the smallest pine in the world, the Pygmy Pine.., of sub-alpine areas, the height of which is normally about twelve inches. **1961** MARTIN *Flora NZ* 176 To this genus belong the Pygmy Pine..the smallest conifer in the world. **1973** MARK & ADAMS *Alpine Plants* (1979) 22 Small trailing shrubs—the pygmy pine..creeping heath plants. **1988** DAWSON *Forest Vines to Snow Tussocks* 170 The pigmy pine (*Lepidothamnus laxifolius*), sometimes called the smallest conifer in the world, forms even lower mat-like patches in poorly drained sites.

(13) red pine. Usu. RIMU n.¹ but occas. in early writing applied (from the colour of the wood) to other genera and species. **a.** RIMU n.¹, esp. its timber.
1821 *McDonald's Evidence before Commissioner Bigge* in McNab *Hist. Records* (1908) I. 560 Q. Whereabouts do the red and white pine trees grow? A... The red pine grows on the sides of hills. Q. Is the red pine like the cowrie? A. It is the same grain, but not the same colour. **1841** *NZ Jrnl.* II. 51 The rimu is somewhat better. It is this tree which the sawyers call the red pine. **1857** [see RIMU n.¹]. **1861** *Otago Witness* (Dunedin) 19 Jan. 5 In the decoration of the [Otago Horticultural Society] show-room, the graceful young Red Pine..ranked first among our native trees. **1877** [see RIMU n.¹]. **1889** KIRK *Forest Flora* 29 The rimu, or red-pine as it is most frequently termed by the settlers, occupies a larger area of New Zealand forests than any other timber-tree. **1896** *Interim Rep. No.3 Timber Conf.* 17 July in *AJHR H-1* 24 The Committee recommends the disuse of the terms 'red-pine', 'white-pine', and 'black-pine', in favour of rimu, kahikatea and matai, in order to prevent their being confused with timbers having similar names in Europe. **1902** *Settler's Handbook NZ* 118 North Island Red-pine District. **1939** [see RIMU n.¹]. **1946** *JPS* LV. 146 *rimu*, a fine tree..., red-pine; the young tree, a fountain of weeping foliage considered one of the most beautiful trees in the world. **1966** *Encycl. NZ* III. 85 The European name for rimu, especially in the South Island, is red pine. **1978** MOORE & IRWIN *Oxford Book NZ Plants* 208 *Dacrydium cupressinum*, rimu, red pine. **1985** MCGILL *G'day Country* 149 Ruatapu has a sawmill, New Forest, has, appropriately, red pine for prefabs.

b. *Obs. Nelson–Marlborough local.* Occas. in early writing for MATAI 1, usu. called *black pine*.
1842 HEAPHY *NZ* 42 The red pines are the *Totara*, *Towa*, *Mahi*, and *Rata*, all of which are close-grained and moderately hard... They are all of a red colour, and when oiled and polished are very ornamental. **1844** TUCKETT *Diary* 19 Apr. in Hocken *Contributions* (1898) 208 I observed a fine stream of water, and the wood with abundance of timber—the red pine, or, as it is here [in Otago] called, the black..throughout the district. **1869** *TrNZI* I. (rev. edn.) 165 On drier ground [in Marlborough Sounds] he would find the Mai or Red Pine (*Podocarpus spicata*)..festooned with parasites. **1882** HAY *Brighter Britain* II. 194 The Matai, or 'Red Pine' (*Podocarpus spicata*), needs special mention. **1889** KIRK *Forest Flora* 5 The matai is commonly termed 'black-pine' by the settlers except in the Nelson District, where it is known as 'red-pine', a name applied to the rimu..in other parts of the colony. **1933** *Press* (Christchurch) (Acland Gloss.) 18 Nov. 15 *Pine, Black p[ine]*... Called *matai* in the North Island and, I am told, *red pine* in Nelson.

c. *Obs. Rare.* TOTARA n.¹
1838 POLACK *NZ* II. 391 *Totárá* (*taxus australis*) g. coniferae..is known as red pine. **1840** POLACK *Manners & Customs* I. 227 The most superior [canoes] are to be found at Wairoa, (Hawkes' Bay) the tribes at that place employ the *totara* or red pine. **1842** [see b above].

(14) rue pine, see *black pine* (2) above.

(15) silver pine. ?Mainly *Sl.* **a.** MANOAO 1 (*Lagarostrobos* (formerly *Dacrydium*) *colensoi*). Also with a modifier: **Westland silver pine, white silver pine** (the latter distinct from *yellow silver pine* b below).
1869 *TrNZI* I. (rev. edn.) 192 A large round-headed tree, also called white pine in Otago, and Silver pine in Nelson, is not uncommon near Dunedin. **1878** *TrNZI* X. 384 *D[acrydium] westlandicum*, the Westland or white silver pine, is of great durability, probably owing to the large quantity of oily and resinous matter which it contains. **1889** KIRK *Forest Flora* 165 The Westland pine is frequently termed 'silver-pine' or 'white silver-pine', but does not appear to have been specially distinguished by the Maoris. **1894** *NZ Official Yearbook* 330 Westland silver-pine, yellow silver-pine, and quintinia, although not peculiar to Westland, are more abundant there than in any other part of the colony. **1898** MORRIS *Austral-English* 355 Silver P[ine].—*Dacrydium colensoi*..i.q. [idem quod='the same as'] *Yellow Pine*. **1908** *AJHR C-14* 35 Manoao. Silver-pine, Westland silver-pine. Small tree, with dimorphic foliage. **1918** *NZJST* I. 143 *Dacrydium Colensoi*..Manoao, silver-pine. **1922** *Auckland Weekly News* 25 May 19 The silver pine logs, which were in a wonderful state of preservation..were mostly utilised for fencing posts. **1939** BEATTIE *First White Boy Born Otago* 111 On the face to the south the bush was either silver pine or silver birch and so open you could drive cattle through it. **1940** LAING & BLACKWELL *Plants NZ* 77 *Dacrydium Colensoi*, the silver-pine of Westland, produces a valuable timber, largely used for poles and railway sleepers. **1981** HENDERSON *Exiles Asbestos Cottage* 60 Silver pine for kindling, none better, and for boiling the billy fast. **1990** GEORGE *Ohakune* 204 Gangs were working the silver pine stands for posts, strainers and telephone poles or splitting kawakawa battens.

b. yellow silver pine. *Lepidothamnus* (formerly *Dacrydium*) *intermedius* (formerly *intermedium*). See also *bog pine* (3) above.
1878 *TrNZI* X. 384 *D. intermedium*, the yellow silver pine is considered still more durable [than *D. westlandicum*], and is highly valued on the West Coast of the South Island. **1889** KIRK *Forest Flora* 167 The yellow silver-pine..or mountain-pine, as it is less frequently termed, was originally described by the writer in 1877... The wood of the yellow silver-pine is of a reddish-yellow. **1890** *PWD Catalogue Timbers* (NZ & South Seas Exhib.) 13 Pine, yellowish silver..Dacrydium intermedium..Timber reddish yellow, of great durability. **1906** CHEESEMAN *Manual NZ Flora* 655 *D[acrydium] intermedium*... Mountain-pine; Yellow Silver-pine. Wood reddish-yellow, highly resinous..; largely used in Westland (together with *D. Colensoi* [Silver-pine, Manoao]) for railway sleepers. **1981** DENNIS *Paparoas Guide* 159 In less fertile places stunted rimu is regularly joined by..silver pine (*Dacrydium colensoi*), yellow silver pine (*D. intermedium*), and mountain toatoa. **1988** [see (3) above].

(16) sugar-loaf pine. *Local. Obs.* KAHIKATEA. See also *white pine* (19) below.
1889 KIRK *Forest Flora* 43 In Marlborough I was repeatedly informed that the more durable kind [of white pine] with yellowish heartwood, which is there termed 'sugar-loaf' pine, was the male plant, while that with the white heart was the female.

(17) **swamp pine.** KAHIKATEA. See also *white pine* (19) below.
   1869 *TrNZI* I. (rev. edn.) 270 The Kahikatea, or White, or Swamp, Pine..is the next commonly used timber tree..almost invariably found in wet spots and swampy situations. **1877** *Ibid.* IX. 176 [Popular Name] White Pine—[Synonyms] Kahikatea..Kaikatea

(18) **Westland pine.** MANOAO 1. See also *silver pine* (15) a above, and *yellow pine* (20) b below.
   1881 *TrNZI* XIII. 139 The Westland pine appears to merit particular attention. **1890** *PWD Catalogue Timbers* (NZ & South Seas Exhib.) 13 Pine, Westland..Timber of a yellowish tint, straight, tough, elastic. **1910** COCKAYNE *NZ Plants & Their Story* 41 The matai..is a fine wood for resisting weather, and is only excelled by the..Westland pine (*Dacrydium Colensoi*), the *D. westlandicum* of the 'Forest Flora' and the yellow-pine (*D. intermedium*). **1911** *TrNZI* XLIII. 202 the Westland pine (*Dacrydium Colensoi*), which is not uncommon along the west coast of the South Island, is found in the North Island at a few widely separated spots.

(19) **white pine.** [Prob. from the whitish colour of the wood.] **a.** *Dacrycarpus* (formerly *Podocarpus*) *dacrydioides*, KAHIKATEA 1, esp. its valuable timber.
   [*Note*] *white pine* was in fairly regular use for the tree and its timber, esp. in the South Island, until c1970.
   1821 *McDonald's Evidence before Commissioner Bigge* May in McNab *Hist. Records* (1908) I. 560 Q. Whereabouts do the red and white pine trees grow? A. The white pine grows in wet swampy places. **1823** KENT *Journal* in Begg *Port Preservation* (1973) 315 The northern pines produce a vast quantity of rosin.., the best bears a cone not unlike an acorn, the other or white pine a berry very similar in taste to the juniper. **1835** YATE *NZ* (1970) 40 It [*sc.* kahikatea] is, what has commonly been designated, the White Pine. **1838** POLACK *NZ* II. 389 Few of the Kauri pine spars were procured by these vessels, their lading..consisting of the inferior white pine, called Kahikátea. **1841** *NZ Jrnl.* II. 51 The kahikatea, or white pine, as the sawyers call it, is an inferior New Zealand timber, and if for a short time exposed to the weather, easily rots. **1855** [see KAHIKATEA 1]. **1869** *TrNZI* I. (rev. edn.) 192 White Pine, or Kahikatea... This is a straight, narrow, sometimes conical tree, growing on wet flats; wood of little value. **1889** [see KAHIKATEA 1]. **1892** WILLIAMS *Dict. NZ Lang.* 45 *Kahika* or *kahikatea*, n. *podocarpus dacrydioides*; *white pine*. **1911** *Truth* 13 May 1 Says a simple country paper:- 'The borer, which is so destructive to white pine, is not at all particular what he bores through. **1923** COCKAYNE *Cultivation NZ Plants* 39 P[*odocarpus*] *dacrydioides* (kahikatea, white-pine, vh) remains for long time as juvenile, poor for gardens; later is of cypress-like form..grows naturally in swamp-forest. **1936** [see KAHIKATEA 1]. **1964** HARVEY *Any Old Dollars Mister?* 1 There was a big pussy willow..with a green seat underneath made out of white pine. **1970** MIDDLETON in *Some Other Country* (1984) 147 [The men at the timber-yard] had taught him..how to tell rimu from matai, totara from kauri and white pine. **1982** WILSON *Stewart Is. Plants* 50 *Dacrycarpus dacrydioides* kahikatea white pine.

b. *Stewart Island. Obs. Lagarostrobos colensoi* and *Lepidothamnus intermedius*. See *silver pine* (15) a and b above.
   1885 *TrNZI* XVII. 216 *Dacrydium colensoi* and *D. intermedium* are abundant in certain localities [on Stewart Island] and yield the 'white pine' of the saw mills; the true white pine (*Podocarpus dacrydioides*) does not appear to occur on the island. **1889** KIRK *Forest Flora* 44 [Kahikatea] is abundant in Southland, but is extremely rare in Stewart Island, where *Dacrydium intermedium* is converted at sawmills, and sold as 'white-pine'.

(20) **yellow pine.** As a popular name applied indiscriminately to various trees with yellowish wood, esp. to *silver pine*. **a.** *Obs.* An early name for KAURI.
   1838 POLACK *NZ* I. 105 We did not perceive any kouri, or yellow pine-trees; but the totará or red pine, grew in vast abundance. *Ibid.* II. 387 The tree which has hitherto attracted most attention has been the Kauri or yellow pine. **1857** HURSTHOUSE *NZ* I. 140 Kauri.— Yellow Pine... The most valuable Tree in New Zealand... Produces large quantities of resinous gum, an article of export. The only cone-bearing tree in New Zealand. **1867** HOCHSTETTER *NZ* 159 Kauri N.Z. Yellow Pine *Dammara australis* **1879** *Auckland Weekly News* (Suppl.) 13 Dec. 1 The various kinds of timber that are found in New Zealand that are valuable for building and other purposes are:- kauri; yellow pine (Dammara Australis)... pitch pine (Phyllocladus [sp.]).

b. *Obs.* MANOAO 1. See also *silver pine* (15) a above, and *Westland pine* (18) above.
   1877 *TrNZI* IX. 163 Yellow Pine—*Dacrydium colensoi*... It is a small tree seldom exceeding forty feet in height, with a trunk twenty feet long and two feet six inches in diameter... The bark is like that of young red pine, but the timber is quite different. It is of a clear yellowish colour, with little sap. **1878** *TrNZI* X. 384 *D. Colensoi*, the yellow pine or tar-wood of the Otago settlers, is another species [of Dacrydium] of great durability, although of rather small dimensions. **1883**, **1889** [see MANOAO 1]. **1898** MORRIS *Austral-English* 354 Yellow P[ine].—*Dacrydium colensoi*... Maori name, *Manoao*.

c. *Lepidothamnus intermedius*. Locally called *Kirk pine*. See *yellow silver pine* (15) b above.
   1889 *Canterbury Exhib. Catalogue, NZ Midland Railway* 52 Yellow Pine (*Dacrydium Intermedium*) Height, 40 feet... The timber is of a reddish yellow. **1909** *AJHR C-12* 48 *Dacrydium intermedium*. Yellow-pine, yellow silver-pine. This is known by everyone on Stewart Island as the 'Kirk pine'. Southern forest. **1923** COCKAYNE *Cultivation NZ Plants* 28 D[*acrydium*] *biforme, D. Colensoi* (silver-pine) and *D. intermedium* (yellow-pine)—all (vh.)—are cypress-like low trees of slow growth occurring in bogs, or where climate very wet. **1940** HOWARD *Rakiura* xviii In damp and boggy situations they are displaced by the Yellow Pine..which is usually accompanied by huge cushions of moss and liverwort. **1951** LEVY *Grasslands NZ* (1970) 92 The name 'pines', which is loosely applied to our podocarps, that is white pine.., red pine.., and yellow pine (*D. intermedium*).

d. *Obs. Halocarpus* (formerly *Dacrydium*) *biformis*. See *pink pine* (10) above.
   1889 KIRK *Forest Flora* 167 *Dacrydium intermedium*... The yellow silver-pine or mountain-pine, as it is less frequently termed, was originally described by the writer [*sc.* Kirk] in 1877. **1906** CHEESEMAN *Manual NZ Flora* 653 D[*acrydium*] *biforme*... Mountain districts... Yellow-pine; Tar-wood. This is for the most part the *D. Colensoi* of the [Hooker] Flora. **1908** *AJHR C-11* 35 *Dacrydium biforme*. Yellow-pine, tarwood. End[emic]... Sub. scrub, upper forest of S. and W.

e. *Nelson. Obs.* KAHIKATEA. See also *white pine* (19) a above. Cf. *sugar-loaf pine* (16) above.
   1883 HECTOR *Handbook NZ* 124 A variety of this tree [kahikatea], known as yellow-pine, is largely sawn in Nelson, and considered to be a durable building timber.

f. *transf. joc.* [f. the colour.] Straw used as firewood.
   1976 VEITCH *Clyde on Dunstan* 17 Waggoners used wood substitutes for fuel for cooking during the journey from Central to Dunedin. 'Buffalo chips' (dried dung),

'yellow pine' (straw), or 'kaladdies' (the flower and stem of flax) were burned in a can which was hung behind the waggon.

3. Used *attrib.* in special Comb.: **pine beer**, *matai beer* (MATAI 2); **pine-flat**, a river flat forested with podocarps.
   1926 *TrNZI* LVI. 662 From the leaves of the rimu Cook brewed 'spruce beer', and the black-pine [*sc.* matai] furnishes a beverage known to bushmen as '**pine-beer**'. The tree containing beer may usually be known by a black, smutty-looking stain that extends some way up the trunk; and if a hole be bored at the base the tree may be plugged and tapped like a barrel. **1862** ROCHFORT *Jrnl. Two Expeds.* 301 Good **pine-flats** on each side of river.

4. In the common names of exotic *Pinus* species, usu. *P. radiata* (formerly *insignis*), in early use called **Californian pine**, **insignis pine**, occas. **Monterey pine**, now usu. RADIATA PINE (freq. *ellipt.* **radiata**) or PINUS. See also FIR.
   1889 *Zealandia* I. 31 The grey shingles..could be..seen..looking out from some straggling plantations of blue-gum, willow, and Californian pine. **1936** BELSHAW et al. *Agric. Organiz. NZ* 576 A notable development has occurred in the production of the exotic insignis pine (*Pinus radiata*), which increased from about 7½ to 13½ million feet between 1928 and 1932. **1939** CRESSWELL *Present Without Leave* 26 Most of all the wind when it meets with the thick belts of pine-trees..gives a music so subtle and soft the ear is charmed. **1957** *NZ Timber Jrnl.* Aug. 57 *Insignis Pine: Pinus radiata*..Monterey, California. The name radiata pine is more commonly used. **1969** *Standard Common Names Weeds* 40 insignis pine [=] *pinus radiata*. **1984** BRASCH *Collected Poems* 91 Farmer ploughing and sowing the unbroken hill, Laying out fields, setting byre and barn, Planting pine-belts, raising stone walls. **1992** SMITHYMAN *Auto/Biographies* 29 Even insignis find it tough going..on tableland of rapacious yet mainly stunted teatree.

pineapple. [Transf. use of *pineapple Ananas comosus* (fam. Bromeliaceae) applied to New Zealand fruits or shrubs.]

1. Usu. **New Zealand pineapple.** KIEKIE 1, esp. its fruit.
   1849 HURSTHOUSE *New Plymouth* 18 The Kiekie, a creeping thing, called by some the 'New Zealand Pine-apple', fruits every third year. **1857** HURSTHOUSE *NZ* I. 136 The Kie-kie (New Zealand's pine-apple)..is a vegetable impostor, like a sweet artichoke flavoured with turpentine. **1867** HOCHSTETTER *NZ* 158 Kiekie, Uriuri... The fruit..when fully ripe, is very sweet and of an agreeable flavour; this may be considered by far the finest native fruit in New Zealand. It is called the New Zealand pine-apple. **1880** in Sutton-Smith *Hist. Children's Play* (1982) 117 The *tawheras* that had been missed had dried and shrivelled, and the white of the *tiore* had decayed, but the fingers of the 'gentlemen' had swollen considerably and now provided us with New Zealand 'pineapples'. The really good ones were eight inches long and two-and-a-half inches in diameter... They were tricky eating too. You bit off all the outside hard, nobbly but not prickly covering, and then gnawed the soft, sweet flesh to the bone.

2. Applied as a modifier to *Dracophyllum* spp. esp. NEINEI q.v., a subalpine shrub distinguished by its leathery curved leaves crowded at the tips of branches, fancifully reminiscent of the tufted appearance of the pineapple plant: **pineapple forest**, a grove of NEINEI; **pineapple scrub**, **pineapple tree**.
   [**1900** *Canterbury Old & New* 188 The quaint *Dracophyllum traversii*, a much-branched tree, whose

PINEX

branches end each in a tuft of stiff foliage, reminding one of the crown of a pine-apple.] **1988** DAWSON *Forest Vines to Snow Tussocks* 165 Indeed, mountain groves of *Dracophyllum traversii* are sometimes known locally as '**pineapple forests**' [from similarity of leaves]. **1968** HALL-JONES *Early Fiordland* 44 His collection of specimens [from Dusky Sound] included..the **pineapple scrub** (*Dracophyllum menziesii*). **1973** MARK & ADAMS *Alpine Plants* 116 *Dracophyllum menziesii*..Pineapple scrub... The broad, hard, tapered leaves..are crowded near the tips of the branches, resembling the crown of a pineapple. **1982** WILSON *Stewart Is. Plants* 80 *Dracophyllum menziesii* Pineapple Scrub... Distinctive shrub... Leaves stiffly curving in tufts like pineapple tops at the branch tips. **1925** BAUGHAN *Arthur's Pass & the Otira Gorge* 45 Giant Grass-trees, *nei-neis*, or '**pine-apple trees**', as they are sometimes called. **1946** *Wellington Bot. Soc. 14* 8 There are some popular names, including those of introduced species, which seem to have hitherto escaped print and are only known locally... Here are some to start with... *Dracophyllum traversii*, candelabra tree, mountain mop, pineapple tree. **1961** [see NEINEI].

3. pineapple weed. [Cf. OED 3 b *Matricaria* sp., 1908.] The rayless chamomile *Matricaria dioscoidea* (fam. Asteraceae).

1983 ELL *Wildflowers & Weeds* 8 Pineapple Weed. This strong-growing plant has a feathery appearance and tiny yellow flowers... Another name used for this plant in New Zealand is the rayless chamomile. This is because it is a flower without white petals.

pinex /ˈpaɪnəks/. [f. a proprietary name.] A soft, pulp-based interior wallboard or insulating board.

1941 *NZ Patent Office Jrnl.* [no number given] 31 July Pinex 38709 [filed] 24th March, 1941. N.Z. Forest Products Limited..Timber, including treated timber; hard-board, soft board, and wood pulp; goods included in Class 50 manufactured from wood. **1944** *Weekly News* June 25 [cover] [Advt] Build comfort into your home with Pinex. Pinex Insulating Board. **1968** SLATTER *Pagan Game* 99 The pre-fab, stifling in February..a criss-cross of rafters and beams; pinus and pinex and unpainted corrugated iron. **1970** *Evening Post* (Wellington) 16 July 25 [Advt] Pinex insulating board and hardboard, all sizes. Evans Bay Timber, Kilbirnie. **1985** HILL *Moaville Magic* 59 The sheet of pinex that for years had leaned up against his Borough Office wall..accompanied Hedley to his new premises. **1991** KEITH *Lovely Day Tomorrow* 54 The baches all smelt..a wonderful summer smell of Pinex wall board.

ping, *n.*[1] *Drug-users*. A dose of narcotic from a syringe.

1982 NEWBOLD *Big Huey* 252 Ping (n) 1. Dose of narcotic in a syringe. **1986** *Evening Post* (Wellington) 5 Apr. 19 Peter's early-days addiction routine started with a 'ping' in the morning and a cup of coffee.

Hence **ping** *v.*, to inject a dose of a drug.

1986 17 Apr. TV1, 'Close Up' programme: Today Gretchen [an addict] has pinged, that is injected with an illegal dose. **1993** *Metro* (Auckland) Sept. 120 If it [*sc.* any drug] got him high and was injectable, he'd ping it.

Ping, *n.*[2] An oriental person.

1982 NEWBOLD *Big Huey* 252 Ping (n)..2. Oriental person. **c1985** p.c. Melissa Gough (Hutt Valley). *Ping* used for an oriental person at a family fancy-dress party in the Wairarapa on Labour Weekend 1985.

pingae, var. PINGAO.

pingao. Also early **pingae**. [Ma. /ˈpiːŋao/: Williams 281 *Pīngao*, n. 1... a plant which grows near the seashore.] *Desmoschoenus spiralis* (fam.

Cyperaceae), a hardy sand-dune plant having golden-brown foliage, used by the Maori for weaving baskets or belts. See also *sand-grass* (GRASS 2 (35) a).

1853 HOOKER *II Flora Novae-Zelandiae I Flowering Plants* 272 Desmoschoenus *spiralis*..Nat. name, 'Pingao'. **1867** HOOKER *Handbook* 767 Pingae or pingao, *Desmoschoenus spiralis*. **1874** *TrNZI* VI. 46 The pingao..and the *Spinifex hirsutus*, which may be obtained in unlimited quantities on all coast sand-hills in the colony. **1890** *Otago Witness* (Dunedin) 16 Jan. 18 The bright yellow leaves of the pingao were woven into useful purse-like girdles. **1904** TREGEAR *Maori Race* 238 Sometimes a sea-side-spreading plant named *pingao*..was used for making belts. **1911** [see GRASS 2 (35) a]. **1946** *JPS* LV. 155-6 Pingao, sea-shore plant.., tumble-weed, after the stiff-spined globular seed-heads: the leaves, drying a bright-orange much used for plaiting ornamental girdles and for tuku-tuku (lattice-work) lacing in wall-panels of whares. **1959** SLATTER *Gun in My Hand* 52 I cross over and go along the sand track, pocked with prints, between the native *pingao* and the introduced marram. **1978** MOORE & IRWIN *Oxford Book NZ Plants* 204 Pingao..provided Maori women with bright strands for their weaving. **1982** WILSON *Stewart Is. Plants* 368 *Desmoschoenus spiralis* Pingao.. Orange tufts about 30 to 70 cm tall, growing in rows along stout, woody, sand-binding rhizomes which appear like frayed ropes where the sand has blown out. **1986** HULME *Windeater* 43 There, suitable low sandhills are covered with marramgrass and pingao and sand convolvulus.

pinguin, var. PENGUIN.

pink, *n.* [From its call.] *pied stilt* (STILT 2 (2)).

1955 OLIVER *NZ Birds* 300 When disturbed, the Pied Stilt makes a snapping noise which has been compared to the yapping of a pup, or has been rendered 'pink', hence these birds have sometimes been called 'pinks'.

pink, *v.* Shearing. [AND 1897.] *trans.* To shear (a sheep) carefully and so closely that the pink skin shows, esp. in the phr. **pink 'em**. Contrast ROUGH *v.*

1897 WRIGHT *Station Ballads* 37 Dick could shear if he was willing, pink 'em if he wanted to. **1955** BOWEN *Wool Away* 156 Pink 'em. To make a very good or better than average job of a sheep. Shearers sometimes call this a 'special cut'. **1989** *NZ Eng. Newsletter* III. 26 *pink*: To make the pink skin of the sheep show by shearing closely.

pink batt, pink maomao, pink pine: see BATT, MAOMAO 2 (2), PINE 2 (10).

pinna mussel: see MUSSEL 2 (6).

pinnie. [*pin*(ball + -IE.] Usu. *pl.* An arcade pinball machine.

1994 *North & South* (Auckland) Apr. 51 Her other son..was out playing pinnies in Newlands Mall.

pinus /ˈpaɪnəs/. *Ellipt.* for *Pinus radiata* (formerly *insignis*) (fam. Pinaceae), a usual name for the tree and timber of a widespread, introduced, commercial species. Cf. PINE 4.

[**1880** GRANT & FOSTER *NZ* 15 The various kinds of pine seem the favourite trees. At Cambridge it took two men to span with their arms the trunk of a *pinus insignis* planted only 14 years ago. **1904** LANCASTER *Sons o' Men* 157 A New Zealander hasn't much spiritual grace. He's a Vandal, I think. He burns the bush, and plants

PIONEER

Pinus insign[i]s; and he hasn't a decent picture-gallery.] **1952** FAIRBURN in *Letters* 5 Oct. (1981) 209 I have..an invoice from the firm of Residential Construction Ltd... It is for pinus, plus cartage. **1954** DUFF *Shepherd's Calendar* 22 Dec. (1961) 202 In addition the boys have cut down rimu..and pinus growing on the property and built a 4-stand woolshed. **1966** TURNER *Eng. Lang. Austral. & NZ* 60 The word *pine*, with various colour adjectives, is used for so many native trees in the South Island of New Zealand that a builder who wants to refer to timber which is really pine (*Pinus radiata*) has to call it *pinus*. **1977** ELDRED-GRIGG *Of Ivory Accents* 10 And those bookshelves made from Pinus boards and concrete blocks. **1990** *Greenpeace* 20 Aug. [unpaged] A substance called DHAA..occurs naturally in pinus bark.

piohiohi, pioio, varr. PIHOIHOI.

pioke. [Ma. /ˈpioke, piːˈokeoke/: Williams 282 *Pioke, piokeoke*... Spined dogfish. = *okeoke*.] Usu. *Mustelus lenticulatus* (formerly *antarcticus*), GUMMY *n.*[3]

[**1820** LEE & KENDALL *NZ Gram. & Vocab.* 193 Pīoke; A fish so called.] **1922** *NZJST* V. 97 The pioke has been found in the Auckland market continuously throughout the year. It is popularly sold as 'silver-strips', or 'silver-spots'. Probably many of the fish are *Mustelus antarcticus*. **1936** *Handbook for NZ* (ANZAAS) 71 *Mustelus antarcticus*: Common dogfish, pioke (Auckland), rigg (Canterbury). **1958** *AJHR* H-15 73 Scientific names of Fish and Shellfish... Pioke.. *Mustelus antarcticus* (chiefly). **1966** BRAMBLEY *Sea-cockies of Manukau* 43 I lose patience with people who prattle about 'gummy' sharks when they mean pioke, or dogfish—'lemon-fish' when it reaches the shops. **1970** SORENSEN *Nomenclature NZ Fish* 44 Smoothhound... Other common names: Kini; Pioke; Lemons; Lemonfish; Dogfish; Rig; Silver Strip (fillets); Sweet William; Flake. **1986** PAUL *NZ Fishes* 30 Rig *Mustelus lenticulatus*... Other names include spotted dogfish, gummy shark, smoothhound and pioke.

pioneer. [f. US *pioneer* one who leads settlement in a new country: AND 1842.]

1. a. One of the early or foundation European settlers of a province or district.

1849 POWER *Sketches in NZ* 192 [There are] numerous other places, of which very little is known, and where pioneers are gradually finding their way, on sufferance from the Maories, or on payment of a small consideration for the use of the land. **1894** WILSON *Land of Tui* 65 As we wound about the [Rimutaka] hills the devastation and desolation became more apparent, for pioneers burn all before them. **1900** *Canterbury Old & New* 8 Anyone who considers what Canterbury is to-day and what she was fifty years ago must be filled with admiration for those early settlers we well name 'pioneers'. **1926** COWAN *Travel in NZ* II. 85 [*Pounamu*] was as great an attraction to the New Zealanders of that [pre-European] era as the nuggets..of Westland were to the white pioneers two and a half centuries later. **1933** SCANLAN *Tides of Youth* 59 Trees were the pioneer's natural enemy. **1948** FINLAYSON *Tidal Creek* (1979) 80 There's a loneliness about the bush and something that pulls taut the nerves... No wonder the pioneers burnt the bush. **1957** FRAME *Owls Do Cry* (1967) 14 Each page seemed, to the children, like something out of a museum, to be kept under a glass case, like the handwriting of a pioneer or governor. **1976** WILSON *Pacific Star* 19 The energising force in New Zealand life up to now has been this myth of the pioneer, the frontier. **1985** LANGDALE-HUNT *Last Entail Male* 128 Jim and Nance Gregory are buried in the Hunt cemetery on Pitt Island where the old Hunt pioneers are buried. **1993** *Dominion* (Wellington) 27 Mar. 20 How much

PIOPIO

longer are taxpayers to be punished for the crimes committed [against the Maori] by the pioneers?

b. In *attrib.* use, also as Comb. **pioneer settler** [AND 1852], pertaining to or characteristic of early European settlement.

1906 *TrNZI* XXXVIII. 499 By this means the bush was thoroughly explored by Natives and pioneer settlers. **1935** MAXWELL *Recollections* 19 The period from about 1840 to the 'seventies, especially of course the earlier part, can be taken as the real adventurous pioneer period, during which the main work of colonisation took place. **1936** BELSHAW et al. *Agric. Organiz. NZ* 358 The natural pastures provided the only grazing available for the stock of the pioneer settlers. **1939** BEATTIE *First White Boy Born Otago* 118 [When] Kennard went up-country early in 1860 he found things still in the pioneer state as a rule. **1940** [see BIDDY-BID *n.* 3]. **1944** BEATTIE *Maori Place-names Otago* 73 Long after the time of the 'land-grabbers' of the 'thirties and 'forties of last century, we have pioneer documents giving Maori names. **1959** SHADBOLT *New Zealanders* (1986) 18 She was a member of the third generation of a famous pioneer family. **1966** SCOTT *Days That Have Been* 154 Basil Champion is a Gallipoli veteran and his wife belongs to one of the pioneer New Zealand families. **1974** MORRIESON *Predicament* (1981) 40 An open sesame to the Pioneer Club, the best homes in town and the most exclusive circles of the racing world.

Hence **pioneer** *v.*, *trans.* and *intr.* to open up new land or a new country as a foundation or early settler, esp. as **pioneering** *vbl. n.* and *ppl. a.*

1851 *Lyttelton Times* 24 May 6 We readily admit the palm of pioneering in the colony of New Zealand to be due to the settlers in Wellington. **1940** *Tales Pioneer Women* (1988) vii We have tried..to depict every phase of women's part in pioneering. **1962** EVANS *Waikaka Saga* 87 A study..shows that there was a marked interest in these lands by Australian settlers who..settled and pioneered them. **1985** LANGDALE-HUNT *Last Entail Male* 65 Everyone in latter years seems to want to equate living conditions of today with the pioneering conditions of the nineteenth century and even of the first half of the twentieth.

2. *WW1.* A member of the New Zealand (Maori) Pioneer battalion, a complete Maori unit formed on 1 September 1917, developing from the (First) Maori Contingent and the New Zealand Pioneer Battalion, the latter a mixture of races. See also EHOA 2.

1917 *Chron. NZEF* 18 Apr. 78 Unfortunately, though we could fight like the Infantry, the Infantry could not dig like us. So the Powers that be made us Pioneers. [1917 *Note*] The Pioneer battalion was formed from the Otago Mounted Rifles and the Maori Contingent. *Ibid.* 25 July 251 A Maori Pioneer was 'lambed down' last week. **1982** SHADBOLT *Once on Chunuk Bair* (1990) 53 This is not the Maori contingent... You have no combat duty. You're a Pioneer, man. Your lot. **1989** BOYACK *Behind the Lines* ix Pioneer Member of the New Zealand Pioneer Battalion, which was made up mostly of Maori but did include some white soldiers. The term itself was commonly used to describe Maori.

piopio. Also early **biobio.** [Ma. /'piopio/: Williams 282 *Pio* (ii)..*piopio..1..* native thrush.] The name now preferred by ornithologists to THRUSH q.v. for *Turnagra capensis*, and the two subspecies *T. c. tanagra* **North Island piopio**, and *T. c. capensis* **South Island piopio**.

1841 *NZ Jrnl.* II. 86 [A bird] called Biobio. **1843** DIEFFENBACH *Travels in NZ* I. 119 The forest was enlivened by many of the common birds, and I brought home one of a new species, called pio-pio. **1859** THOMSON *Story NZ* I. 25 The *Turdidae* family has only one species in the colony; the Piopio, a bird about the size of the thrush, which is supposed to be a visitor in the North Island from the south. **1861** HAAST *Rep. Topogr. Explor. Nelson* 140 Another..belonging to the family Turdidae, is the piopio.., the thrush of the settlers. **1873**, **1886** [see THRUSH 2]. **1898** MORRIS *Austral-English* 356 *Piopio*..Maori name for a thrush of New Zealand, *Turnagra crassirostris*. **1904** [see THRUSH 2]. **1938** GORDON *Children of Tane* vi 160 The southern Piopio has been more often encountered than the northern. **1955** OLIVER *NZ Birds* 524 North Island Piopio *Turnagra tanagra* Although the North Island Piopio was at one time said to be common in the southern portion of the North Island, it was not described until 1865. *Ibid.* 525 South Island Piopio *Turnagra capensis* Formerly the Piopio was exceedingly abundant in forests throughout the South Island. **1966** [see THRUSH 1]. **1989** PARKINSON *Travelling Naturalist* 59 There have been a number of reports of piopio surviving in the bush. **1990** *Checklist Birds NZ* 228 *Turnagra capensis*... Piopio... It is feared that both subspecies are extinct.

pi-oua-ka-oua-ka, var. PIWAKAWAKA.

pipefish.

1. Any of various small slender long-snouted marine fishes of the family Syngnathiidae.

1838 POLACK *NZ* I. 323 Many other fish are equally numerous, answering to our *hakes*, *tench*,.. *pipe-fish*. **1855** TAYLOR *Te Ika A Maui* 625 The Fam. Lophobranchii contains several varieties of the pipe fish. **1888** BARLOW *Kaipara* 133 The *dog fish*, *eels*, and a small fish with a long snout called the *pipe fish*, complete the list. **1906** *TrNZI* XXXVIII. 552 *Ichthyocampus filum*... The pipe-fish; another very common fish in the harbour. **1967** NATUSCH *Animals NZ* 213 The pipefishes are like long-drawn-out seahorses, but they retain the caudal fin—a ridiculous frill—at the spindly tail end. **1986** PAUL *NZ Fishes* 135 Pipefishes. Family Syngnathiidae. Thin and elongated fishes, encased in segmented ring-like plates, and with a coiled tail. There are several New Zealand species, including the well-known seahorse.

2. With a modifier: **long-snouted (long-headed) pipefish** *Stigmatophora macropterygia*; **short-snouted pipefish** *Lissocampus filum*.

1911 WAITE *Rec. Canterbury Mus.* I. 173 *Syngnathus Norae*... Long-snouted Pipe Fish. *Ibid.* 174 *Syngnathus Blainvillianus*... Short-snouted Pipefish. **1927** PHILLIPPS *Bibliogr. NZ Fishes* (1971) 20 *Syngnathus norae*... Long-snouted Pipe-fish... *Syngnathus blainvillianus*... Short-snouted Pipe-fish. **1947** POWELL *Native Animals NZ* 65 Long Beaked Pipe Fish (*Stigmatophora longirostris*)..The Pipe-fishes are like stretched-out sea-horses but they always remain thus and the tail is not prehensile. **1956** GRAHAM *Treasury NZ Fishes* 147 These Short-snouted Pipefish are extremely poor swimmers, and after storms and gales..they lose their hold on seaweed, and, unable to find another anchorage, they are washed ashore to die. **1966** DOOGUE & MORELAND *Sea Anglers' Guide* 203 The name 'long-snouted pipefish' has been used for another pipefish with a shorter snout, but the term is much more appropriate for the present species. **1982** AYLING *Collins Guide* (1984) 193 The short-snouted pipefish is a small stick-like fish that reaches a maximum length of only 10cm. *Ibid.* 194 Long-snouted pipefish are found throughout New Zealand but are nowhere as common as the short-snouted species.

piper. GARFISH.

1871 *The Field* (London) 25 Nov. 457 I do not think that the New Zealand piper is as perfect in flavour as the Melbourne one. **1872** HUTTON & HECTOR *Fishes* 118 Angling for Gar Fish in Auckland Harbour, where it is known as the piper, is graphically described in..'The Field' [London, Nov. 25, 1871]... 'The Pipers are 'jest awfu' cannibals', and you will be often informed on Auckland wharf that 'pipers is deeth on piper'. **1887** *Auckland Weekly News* 29 Oct. 7 The waste bran..used to attract myriads of piper, or gar fish. **1898** MORRIS *Austral-English* 356 *Piper, n.* an Auckland name for the *Garfish*... The name is applied to other fishes in the Northern Hemisphere. **1927** [see GARFISH]. **1947** POWELL *Native Animals NZ* 66 Piper (*Hemirhamphus intermedius*). This is common in the harbours and estuaries of both the North and South Islands. **1956** [see GUARDFISH]. **1966** DOOGUE & MORELAND *Sea Anglers' Guide* 206 Garfish... *Reporhamphus ihi*; piper, half-beak; ihe, takeke (Maori). **1987** *Listener* 8 Aug. 61 The tip of Point Chevalier was a park known as 'the Reserve'..which led to the Piper Rocks, where boys and men..caught sprat and piper, which were excellent eating.

pipi. Also with much variety of early form as **pēpā**, **pepi**, **peppy**, **pippee**, **pippi**, **pippy**. *pl. pipi, pipis* also occas. early *pippies*. [Ma. /'pipi/: Williams 282 *Pipi*.. 1. Cockle in general; particularly applied to *Chione stutchburyi* and *Amphidesma australe*.]

1. The entry is laid out thus: **a.** Unidentified spp. indicating period and range of early usage; (occas.) **b.** the ribbed cockle *Austrovenus* (formerly *Chione*) *stutchburyi* (fam. Veneridae); (usu.) **c.** the edible, smooth-shelled bivalve *Paphies australis* (fam. Mesodesmatidae); and (occas.) **d.** in the South Island, the mussel *Mytilus edulis* (fam. Mytilidae); (occas.) **e.** TUATUA a.

a. Unidentified spp., but prob. mainly *Paphies* spp.

[**1815** KENDALL *New Zealanders' First Book* 11 Pippee. A cockle. **1820** LEE & KENDALL *NZ Gram. & Vocab.* 193 Pípi, *s.* Cockle.] **1834** MCDONNELL *Extracts Jrnl.* (1979) 15 There are abundance of lobsters, crawfish,.. and shrimps; besides clams, peppies, muscles, limpets, and cockles. **1834** MARKHAM *NZ* (1963) 45 I have many times made a grand Meal in a Kanga Mouri or Native Village on Pippies, sitting round the Coppre Mouries, each helping themselves till all was done. **1847** ANGAS *Savage Life* I. 246 As the tide was out, the [Maori] women were busily employed in gathering *pipis*, a species of cockle, from the uncovered flats. **1855** TAYLOR *Te Ika A Maui* 415 The common name..of all univalve shells, *pupu*; and of bivalves, *pipi* and *anga*, which includes both kinds. **1879** *Auckland Weekly News* 13 Dec. 8 One youthful urchin afterwards declared that for two days they had been 'living on pipis'. **1881** CAMPBELL *Poenamo* 321 [We dug] *peppies* out of the beach at low water. **1882** POTTS *Out in Open* (1976) 15 Kumaras seemed to be most appreciated, dried pipis giving the proper zest of salt. **1908** BAUGHAN *Shingle-Short* 50 They jeer'd in delight 'Aha! So art thou Caught, little *Pipi*? **1929** BEST *Fishing Methods* 63 An old folk-tale describes a quarrel that arose in remote times between the Kuku and Pipi families at Waikaru—that is, between the mussels and the cockles. **1948** BALLANTYNE *Cunninghams* (1976) 44 Two Maori women bending over and half a dozen kids putting the pippis in flax kits. **1971** POWNALL *NZ Shells & Shell Fish* 67 Apparently the Maori people were not too fussy as to names of shell-fish and hence called them all 'pipis'. The hungry hunter of today is no less careless in terminology. **1989** *A New Zealand Prayer Book* 64 Dolphins and kahawai..pipi and shrimp: give to our God your thanks and praise. **1990** STEAD *Voices* 116 pipi hot from the hangi—these were our welcome.

b. *Austrovenus* (formerly *Chione*) *stutchburyi* (fam. Veneridae). COCKLE 1 b. See also TUANGI.

1842 GRAY *Fauna* in Dieffenbach *Travels in NZ* (1843) 250 *Venus intermedia*. Called 'Pēpā' by the natives; they are extremely abundant, and are eaten as food by the natives. The name appears generic for this edible bivalve. **1878** BULLER *Forty Yrs. NZ* 27 On those shoals the women gather cockles (pipi). **1913** SUTER *Manual NZ Mollusca* 987–988 *Chione Stutchburyi... Maori.*—Huai or pipi (teste Hutton and Captain Bollons). **1924** [see COCKLE 1 b]. **1934** HYDE *Journalese* 169 Pipis, on his death-bed, he desired, pipis (a small shellfish similar to the English cockle) he must have. **1967** BRATHWAITE *Evil Day* 380 Pipi Shellfish, cockle group. *Chione Stutchburyi*, *Mesodesma australe*, etc.

c. *Paphies* (formerly *Amphidesma* or *Mesodesma*) *australis* (fam. Mesodesmatidae), now the main use. See also COCKLE 1 c.

1879 HAAST *Geol. Canterbury & Westland* 416 Then follows a series of shell beds, consisting of the remains of the following species, now still inhabiting the estuary;—*Chione stutchburyi* (Cockle); *Huai* or Pipi, *Mesodesma chemnitzii*, Pipi. **1898** MORRIS *Austral-English* 356 *Pipi, n.* Maori name of a shellfish, sometimes (erroneously) called the cockle, *Mezodesma* [sic] *novae-zelandiae*. **1924** BUCKNILL *Sea Shells NZ* 90 Mesodesma australe... One of the two Maori Pipis. **1937** POWELL *Shellfish NZ* 23 Allied to the toheroa is a heavier and more triangular species, the tuatua, *Amphidesma subtriangulatum*, and the common oval pipi of the Maoris, *Paphies australis*. **1942** ANDERSEN *Maori Place Names* 446 Europeans frequenting our sandy beaches have given the name pipi to Mesodesma australe, a smooth-shelled bivalve..generally keeping the name cockle, for the smaller, roundish, ridged bivalve more common on mud-flats. **1955** *AJMFR* VI. 348 It is convenient, and more correct use of the Maori language, to employ the name 'tuatua' for the northern *A*[*mphidesma*] *subtriangulatum*..reserving 'pipi' for *A. australe*. **1963** PEARSON *Coal Flat* 375 Now Mrs Torere brought out..some pipis, and a half-kerosene tin of cooked mutton-birds preserved in fat. **1970** PENNIKET *NZ Seashells in Colour* 102 Pipi (*Amphidesma australe*)... A harbour-dwelling member of the family, it lives just below the surface on sandy flats. **1986** PAUL *NZ Fishes* 159 The name pipi is sometimes applied to a number of New Zealand's common bivalves which are collected for food, but it properly refers to this species [*Paphies australis*], a close relative of the tuatua and toheroa. **1990** EDWARDS *AWOL* 1 I was a skinny specimen, tall with pipe-stem arms and pipi-sized biceps.

d. ?Mainly SI. *Mytilus edulis aoteanus* (fam. Mytilidae), MUSSEL 2 (1).

c1920 BEATTIE *Trad. Lifeways Southern Maori* (1994) 503 [The blue mussel] is called pipi in Canterbury and Otago although the term kuku has crept in during the past forty years until now both terms are regarded as synonymous by the younger Maoris. **1967** NATUSCH *Animals NZ* 19 Even pipi does not mean the same thing all round New Zealand (a Stewart Island Maori of the older generation would use this name for the mussel) and it would mean nothing at all outside New Zealand.

e. Occas. TUATUA (fam. Mesodesmatidae).

1981 WILSON *Fisherman's Bible* 179 Once the staple diet of coastal-dwelling Maori tribes the name pipi covers a variety of small shellfish which include tuatuas and cockles. **1986** [see TUATUA].

2. In *attrib.* use often as Comb., esp. **pipi-bed**, **pipi fritter**, **pipi-gatherer**, **pipi-shell**.

1844 WILLIAMS *NZ Jrnl.* (1956) 48 The poor and needy instead of hearing as they do from another party 'bear up for a **Pippy Bed** and sail large for no man need starve in New Zealand'. **1931** *AJHR H-15* 16 Many cockle and pipi beds in Hawke's Bay have been totally destroyed by having been lifted above the level of the tides. **1973** WILSON *NZ Jack* 72 Yeah, we were glad of a good feed of **pipi fritters**. **1984** BRASCH *Collected Poems* 58 Beneath the infinite whorls of Whiria Pa Hill **Pipi-gatherers** stray about the wet shore. **1847** ANGAS *Savage Life* I. 296 The whitened heaps of **pepi shells** that lie scattered in immense quantities about these slopes, that once formed the sites of their fortified pahs. **1865** CARBERRY *Journal* (ATLMS) Apr. One of them scooped out his eyes with a pepi (or mussel) shell and eat [*sic*] them. **1874** BAINES *Edward Crewe* 116 'There, she is a wife for you,' he said, nodding his head in the direction of a good-looking native young lady, at that moment..scraping potatoes with a pipi-shell. **1881** CAMPBELL *Poenamo* 148 He then and there appealed to Mrs. Rangi Pama, squatting at that moment on the ground scraping potatoes with a peppy-shell for her Pakeha's dinner. **1882** POTTS *Out in Open* (1976) 356 As they sit chatting away, each female is busily employed in scraping the potatoes thoroughly with pipi shells. **1937** BUICK *Moa-Hunters NZ* 121 The deposit consisted of a layer of cockle and pipi shells about 2 feet in depth.

Hence **pipi** *v. intr.*, to collect pipis for food.
1973 WILSON *NZ Jack* 68 Sailboats. Fishing and pipi-ing. What fun we'll have, eh, boys?

pipiharau. [Ma. /ˈpipihaˈrau/: Williams 282 [see *piharau*.] LAMPREY. Cf. PIHAPIHARAU.

1859 THOMSON *Story NZ* (1974) 30 The lamprey, Pipiharau, is, properly speaking, a salt-water fish which enters the river to spawn. **1870** TAYLOR *Te Ika A Maui* 498 The principal ones are the *tuna*, eel, the *pipiharau*, lamprey, the *kokopu*, and *inanga*. **1882** HAY *Brighter Britain* II. 151 In the fresh-water creeks are eels (tuna), lampreys (pipiharau), and whitebait (inanga).

pipipi. [Ma. /ˈpiːpipi/: Williams 282 *pīpipi, 3*...brown creeper.] *brown creeper* (CREEPER *n.*[1]).

1873 BULLER *Birds NZ* 105 (New-Zealand Creeper)... Pipipi and Toitoi. **1946** *JPS* LV. 156 *Pīpipi*, a gregarious bird (Finschia novaeseelandiae), tree-creeper: the flock sings a long song in time and in unison. **1955** [see CREEPER *n.*[1]]. **1966** FALLA et al. *Birds of NZ* 207 Brown Creeper *Finschia novaeseelandiae*... Pipipi. **1985** *Reader's Digest Book NZ Birds* 275 *Brown Creeper Finschia novaeseelandiae*... Pipipi.

pipit. [Extended use of Brit. *pipit*, *Anthus* sp.] *Anthus novaeseelandiae novaeseelandiae* (fam. Motacillidae), a small, brown, insect-eating, ground-nesting bird. Often with modifiers indicating local provenance, in general (**common, native, New Zealand pipit**) or in particular for sub-species (**Antipodes pipit** *A. n. steindachneri*, **Auckland Islands** or **Southern Islands pipit** *A. n. aucklandicus*, **Chatham Island pipit** *A. n. chathamensis*). See also KATAITAI, LARK 2 (1), PIHOIHOI.

[*Note*] *New Zealand pipit* is the preferred ornithological use; *ground-lark* and less often *pihoihoi* are prob. still the most freq. popular uses.

1873 BULLER *Birds NZ* 132 Anthus novae zealandiae. (New-Zealand Pipit)... Pihoihoi and Whioi; 'Ground-Lark' of the colonists. **1882** POTTS *Out in Open* 131 The native lark, or perhaps it should more properly be called the pipit (*Anthus Novae Zelandiae*), is not a dweller in woods. **1884** *NZJSc.* II. 84 [The hawk] may be seen almost daily pursuing the common Pipit..on the wing. **1898** MORRIS *Austral-English* 356 *Pipit*... another name for *Ground-Lark*. **1914** GUTHRIE-SMITH *Mutton Birds & Other Birds* 158 I have also seen [the Weka] working the ground for a Pipit's nest..the anxious owners meanwhile hanging about, their very solicitude possibly enlightening and stimulating the searcher. **1923, 1947** [see LARK 2 (1)]. **1953** GUTHRIE-SMITH *Tutira* (3edn.) 206 Of all the birds on the run, the Native Pipit or Ground Lark..has been the greatest gainer by change. **1955** OLIVER *NZ Birds* 462 *Southern Islands Pipit Anthus novaeseelandiae aucklandicus* Pipits were first collected on the Auckland Islands during the visit of the British Antarctic Expedition in 1840. **1964** BACON *Along the Road* 52 Over Joe's front paddock we trekked, flushing pipits from clumps of grass under our very feet. **1976** SOPER *NZ Birds* 132 Found from one end of New Zealand to the other, from the sea coast to the mountains, the Pipit is the lark-like bird seen on such open tracts of country... Often called the Ground Lark, the Pipit is frequently confused with the introduced Skylark. **1990** *Checklist Birds NZ* 198 *Anthus novaeseelandiae novaeseelandiae*... *New Zealand Pipit* (*Pihoihoi*)... *Anthus novaeseelandiae chathamensis*... *Chatham Island Pipit*... Chatham Islands: Common throughout. *Anthus novaeseelandiae aucklandicus*... *Auckland Islands Pipit*. Auckland Islands... *Anthus novaeseelandiae steindachneri*... *Antipodes Pipit*. Antipodes Island.

pipiwharauroa. Also **pipiwarauroa, pipiwawaroa.** [Ma. /ˈpiːpiːfaˈrauroa/: Williams 282 *Pīpīwharauroa..1...* shining cuckoo.] *shining cuckoo* (CUCKOO 2 (3)); also its call.

1835 YATE *NZ* (1970) 64 *Pipiwawaroa*—This is a bird of passage. **1844** COLENSO *Excurs. Northern Is.* in Taylor *Early Travellers* (1959) 15 By the natives of [the East Coast the shining cuckoo] is called Koekoeā; but by the northern tribes, Pipiwarauroa. **1855** *Richmond-Atkinson Papers* (1960) I. 179 I heard a pipiwharauroa today—first time this spring. **1869, 1873** [see CUCKOO 2 (3)]. **1885** [see CUCKOO 2 (1)]. **1904** [see CUCKOO 2 (3)]. **1929** DUGGAN *NZ Bird Songs* 20 I remember once in Para how I heard your mother calling, 'Pipi-wha-rau-roa' from a poplar by the river, Crying slowly the one word. **1946** [see CUCKOO 2 (1)]. **1966** FALLA et al. *Birds of NZ* 180 Shining Cuckoo... Pipiwharauroa, Whistler... A small cuckoo, much more often heard than seen. **1985** [see CUCKOO 2 (3)]. **1992** GRACE *Cousins* 104 In its branches a pipiwharauroa chick screeched for food.

pippee, pippi, pippy, varr. PIPI.

pirikahu. Also (?erron.) **piripiri-kahu.** [Ma. /ˈpirikahu/: Williams 284 *Pirikahu. 1...* = *hutiwai, piripiri.*] PIRIPIRI *n.*[1] 1 a.

1848 TAYLOR *Journal* 9 Nov. (ATLTS) V. 282 Having no tea or sugar left I used the Pirikahu a creeping burr instead. It was a pretty fair substitute. **1853** [see PIRIPIRI *n.*[1] 1 a]. **1868** [see BIDDY-BID *n.* 1 a]. **1889** FEATON *Art Album* (Plant Names) 178 Piripiri-kahu [Maori name]..Burr [Settlers' name]..Acaena sanguisorbae..Herb

piripiri, *n.*[1] Also **pidi-pidi.** Usu. found in the anglicized form BIDDY-BID q.v. and its variations. [Ma. /ˈpiripiri/: Williams 283 *Piri. 1. v. intr.* Stick, adhere, cling..*piripiri. 1*...*Acaena anserinifolia*, a creeping burr. = *hutiwai, pirikahu, piriwhetau... 3. Haloragis incana* and *H. micrantha*, plants. *4. Bulbophyllum pygmaeum.*] Any of various unrelated plants, but usu. *Acaena* spp.

1. *Acaena* spp. (fam. Rosaceae). **a.** Also **red piripiri.** *A. novae-zelandiae*, BIDDY-BID *n.* 1 a. See also HUTIWAI, PIRIKAHU.

1853 HOOKER *II Flora Novae-Zelandiae I Flowering Plants* 54 Acaena *Sanguisorbae*... Nat. names, 'Hutiwai', Middle Island, Lyall; 'Pirikahu' and 'Piri piri'. **1868** [see BIDDY-BID *n.* 1 a]. **1870** *TrNZI* II. 177 The soil [on Campbell Island] is very wet... The inevitable Piri-piri appears everywhere. **1882** CHUDLEIGH *Diary* 17 Nov. (1950) 314 Clearing piri-piri from edge of the native bush and planting tomatoes. The piri-piri is 7 ft. high round many trees. **1891** WALLACE *Rural Econ. Austral. & NZ* 301 Unlike the New Zealand bur Atwai or Pidi-pidi, [Australian burclover] cannot be easily broken up in working. **1899** KIRK *Students' Flora* 133 Red piripiri. *Ibid.* 134 This species is distinguished from *A. Sanguisorbae* by the large heads, the longer spines, and the achene narrowed at both ends. **1907** LAING & BLACKWELL *Plants NZ* 202 The common *Acaena* was called by the Maoris Piripiri, but colonists frequently corrupt the Maori name, and call the plant Bidi-bidi. **1911** *AJHR* C-13 37 *Acaena novae-zealandiae*. Red piripiri; red New Zealand burr. Subshrub, prostrate, spreading. **1926** HILGENDORF *Weeds* 99 Piri Piri... This name is commonly corrupted into bidi bid. **1946** *JPS* LV. 156 *piripiri*, a scrambling plant-pest..burr, biddy-bid (corruption of Maori name); also called hutiwai. **1951** LEVY *Grasslands NZ* (1970) 239 He [*sc.* the pioneer] did not realise the insidious spread of secondary growth..and piripiri under the close and continuous nibbling of the turf by sheep. **1969** *Standard Common Names Weeds* 59 *piripiri Acaena anserinifolia.., Acaena novaezelandiae..Acaena viridior piri piri* [=] *piripiri*.

b. mountain piripiri. *Acaena caesiiglauca*; **spineless piripiri** *A. inermis.*

1919 COCKAYNE *NZ Plants & Their Story* 149 Various unpalatable indigenous species have greatly increased on these upland pastures—*e.g...*the mountainpiripiri (*Acaena Sanguisorbae* var. *pilosa*)... the spineless piripiri (*A. inermis*). **1969** *Standard Common Names Weeds* 73 spineless piripiri *Acaena inermis*.

c. Also occas. **Australian piripiri.** Used loosely for *sheep's burr* (BURR *n.*¹ 2 a *Acaena ovina*).

1919 COCKAYNE *NZ Plants & Their Story* 154 The Australian piripiri (*Acaena ovina*)..and..the well-known garden annual *Eschscholzia californica* grow along the roadsides of Marlborough and Central Otago. **1926** HILGENDORF *Weeds* 99 Sheep's Burr (*Acaena ovina*), called also Australian burr, false bidi bid, and very loosely piri piri or bidi bid, is not uncommon in fields and waste places in certain localities of both islands, but is commoner in the north.

2. *Obs.* Gronocarpus (*Haloragis*) spp. (fam. Haloragaceae), a small creeping herb of damp sites.

1867 HOOKER *Handbook* 767 Piri-piri, *Cunn. Haloragis tenella*. **1869** *TrNZI* I. (rev. edn.) 202 Piripiri. *Haloragis depressa*.

3. *Obs. Bulbophyllum pygmaeum* (fam. Orchidaceae), a tiny native orchid that forms a spreading mat of rhizomes and pseudobulbs.

1853 HOOKER II *Flora Novae-Zelandiae* I *Flowering Plants* 241 *Bolbophyllum*[sic] *pygmaeum*... Nat. name, 'Piri-Piri'. **1869** *TrNZI* I. (rev. edn.) 208 Piri piri. Bolbophyllum pygmaeum.

4. *Pittosporum cornifolium* (fam. Pittosporaceae), a native epiphytic shrub.

1853 HOOKER II *Flora Novae-Zelandiae* I *Flowering Plants* 23 Pittosporum *cornifolium*, A. Cunn... Hab. Northern Island;.. Nat. name, 'Karo', Colenso; 'Piripiri'. **1867** HOOKER *Handbook* 767 Piri-piri, *Lindsay*. *Pittosporum cornifolium*. **1889** FEATON *Art Album NZ Flora* 36 Pittosporum cornifolium... The 'Piripiri'.— This remarkable and interesting plant is peculiar to the eastern and southern coasts of the Northern Island, where it is common; always..growing epiphytically on trunks of forest trees.

5. *Local.* ?*Obs. Marrubium vulgare* (fam. Labiatae), the introduced plant, horehound.

1926 HILGENDORF *Weeds* 151 Horehound (*Marrubium vulgare*), is actually called piri piri and bidi bid in some localities. It is common in waste places and sheep camps in both islands. It is a perennial, growing one to two feet high.

6. As **piripiri (piripiri fern)**. *Hymenophyllum sanguinolentum* (fam. Hymenophyllaceae), a filmy fern.

1978 *Bull. Wellington Bot. Soc.* No.40 48 The piripiri fern..is, I think in this case, *Hymenophyllum sanguinolentum* though *H. demissum* also seems to go by this name. **1989** BROWNSEY & SMITH-DODSWORTH *NZ Ferns* 77 *Hymenophyllum sanguinolentum*..Piripiri. *Ibid.* 78 A very drought-resistant filmy fern, frequently curling into a tight ball in dry weather.

piripiri, *n.*² [Ma. /'piripiri/: Williams 283... *piripiri...5...* rifleman, a wren.] Usu. the RIFLEMAN; occas. (perh. erron.) the *grey warbler* (WARBLER 2 (3)) (see quots. 1870, 1884).

1835 YATE *NZ* (1970) 57 Piripiri—A small bird, three inches long; with brown plumage tinged with yellow and dark purple. **1838** POLACK *NZ* I. 301 The *piripiri* is also like to our swallow. **1870** *TrNZI* II. 48 The grey warbler (Piripiri) with quivering notes fluttered near its cosy, dome-shaped nest. **1873** [see RIFLEMAN]. **1884** *NZJSc.* II. 284 *Gerygone flaviventris*... Grey Warbler, Teetotum, Piripiri. The warbler is a true pensile nest-builder. **1988** *Pacific Way* June 98 [Names used for Air NZ fleet aircraft include:] ZK-NAY 'Piripiri' (Rifleman).

piripiriwhata. [Ma. /'piripiri'fata/: Williams 284 *Piripiriwhata..Carpodetus serratus*.] PUTAPUTAWETA.

1853 HOOKER II *Flora Novae-Zelandiae* I *Flowering Plants* 78 Carpodetus *serratus*... Nat. name, 'Piri Piri Whata'. **1869** *TrNZI* I. (rev. edn.) 199 White mapau, or piripiriwhata (*Carpodetus serratus*). An ornamental shrub-tree, with mottled-green leaves, and large cymose panicles of white flowers. **1889** KIRK *Forest Flora* 77 [*Carpodetus serratus*] is frequently termed 'piripiriwhata', but Mr. Colenso considers this to be an error. **1890** [see PUTAPUTAWETA]. **1906** CHEESEMAN *Manual NZ Flora* 137 *C*[*arpodetus*] *serratus.. Piripiriwhata*; *Putaputawheta*.

pirita. [Ma. /'pirita/: Williams 284 *Pirita..1. Rhipogonum scandens..2. Loranthus* and *Elytranthe* species, semi-parasitic plants. *3. Tupeia antarctica,* mistletoe.]

1. SUPPLEJACK 1 a.

1867 HOOKER *Handbook* 767 Pirita... *Rhipogonum parviflorum*. **1869** *TrNZI* I. (rev. edn.) 264 The creepers, Aka, (*Metrosideros scandens,*) and Kareao or Pirita, (*Rhipogonum parviflorum,*) were extensively used for tying up fences. **1905** *TrNZI* XXXVII. 59 The Tuhoe people sometimes cauterised wounds by holding near the cut a burning piece of dry *pirita* or supplejack. **1906** CHEESEMAN *Manual NZ Flora* 703 *R*[*hipogonum*] *scandens*... Supplejack; *Kareao*; *Pirita...* an extract from the root has been employed in the place of sarsaparilla.

2. MISTLETOE 1.

1867 HOOKER *Handbook* 767 Piri-ta, *Col*[*enso*]. *Tupeia antarctica*. **1869** *TrNZI* I. (rev. edn.) 203 Pirita. Tupeia antarctica, Cham. and Schl. **1961** MARTIN *Flora NZ* 152 The Pirita (*Tupeia antarctica*) is the sole representative of its abundant but strictly New Zealand genus.

piss, *n.*

1. In the phr. **piss in the hand**, easy or easily achieved or done.

1980 LELAND *Kiwi-Yankee Dict.* 77 *piss in the hand*: Easy, usually applied to exams. (see *piss in, in* the hand). **1985** SHERWOOD *Botanist at Bay* 44 'How did you get in?' she asked. 'That padlock is a piss in the hand, princess, when you know how.' **1988** MCGILL *Dict. Kiwi Slang* 84 *piss in the hand* something easily achieved; eg 'That cross-harbour swim was a piss in the hand.'

2. As a quasi-adverbial intensifier: **piss-awful** 'extremely awful'; **piss-easy** 'extremely easy' or easily achieved.

1983 HULME *Bone People* 138 They still think I'm making a pissawful job of bringing him up. **1988** MCGILL *Dict. Kiwi Slang* 84 *piss awful* very unpleasant; eg 'The party was piss awful.'... *piss easy* very easy; eg 'The exam was piss easy.'

piss, *v.*

1. In various phrases (see quot.).

1988 MCGILL *Dict. Kiwi Slang* 84 *piss in someone's pocket* attempt to ingratiate; eg 'If you want to get in the team you'll just have to piss in his pocket.'... *piss in the wind* self-defeating activity; eg 'You're pissing in the wind trying to beat him on his own turf.'... *piss on regardless* continue drinking without considering consequences; eg 'Whether you stay or not, we intend to piss on regardless.'... *piss all over* easily beat the competition; eg 'We pissed all over Marist, even though they had that Junior All Black joker.'

2. As **piss down**, to rain heavily or suddenly.

1951 WILSON *Brave Company* 172 It fairly pissed down on top of me.

3. As **piss in**, to achieve or succeed with ease.

1980 LELAND *Kiwi-Yankee Dict.* 77 *piss in*: Succeed. Sam will piss in on that exam. **1988** MCGILL *Dict. Kiwi Slang* 84 *piss in* achieve with consummate ease; eg 'Reckon I'll piss in with this line-up for the 100 metres.'

pisser. [f. *piss v.* to drink liquor + -booz)*er*.] A pub; a 'boozer'.

1980 *Islands* 29 132 Caught up in an inane conversation about some barmaid with big tits. Mason kept saying she was in Palmerston and Boswell kept saying there were no pissers in Palmerston. **1988** MCGILL *Dict. Kiwi Slang* 84 *pisser* the pub; eg 'Who's coming down the pisser?'

pisshead. [Used elsewhere but recorded earliest in and freq. popular use in NZ.] A confirmed or heavy drinker; an alcoholic.

1951 WILSON *Brave Company* 22 Shut up, you pisshead. **1961** PARTRIDGE *Dict. Slang* 1223 *piss-head.* An habitually heavy drinker: New Zealand low: since ca. 1930. **1968** *Landfall* 22 50 My old man was a piss-head too. **1988** MCGILL *Dict. Kiwi Slang* 85 *pisshead* heavy drinker..eg 'You guys are nothing but a bunch of permanent pissheads.'

pisswee, var. PEEWEE.

pit. [Spec. or transf. use of *pit* a hole (in the ground).]

1. *Obs.* An outdoor privy of the 'long drop' type, consisting of a seat over a hole in the ground. Cf. LONG DROP.

1916 *Hutt Valley Independent* 15 Apr. 4 He went and hid in the pit when he found the parade was held over ten weeks ago.

2. *Marlborough. Hist.* **a.** The name for shallow excavations once thought by some to be the remains of the dwellings of a supposed preMaori people.

1917 HOWES *Marlborough Sounds* 22 [The Marlborough Sounds] contain remains of the old pit villages and cremation mounds of Moriori tribes.

b. *Special Comb.* **pit-dweller**, according to a discredited hypothesis, a member of a supposed early Polynesian people (cf. MORIORI 3) preceding and distinct from the Maori, alleged to have dug pits as a dwelling-base, on the evidence of remains of pit-like shallow excavations found in the Marlborough Sounds and occas. in other parts of New Zealand; **pit-dwelling**, the 'pit' supposedly excavated as a dwelling base.

1898 *TrNZI* XXX. 554 Mr. Rutland appeared convinced there were two distinctly marked periods in the history of New Zealand—viz., that of the **pit-dwellers** and of the modern Maoris. The evidence for the pit-dwellers had been mainly collected by Mr. Rutland himself, and the general consent of Maori scholars to the theory had not yet been expressed. **1940** MCINTOSH *Marlborough* 387 Much has been written concerning the so-called pit dwellers, who formerly inhabited the district. When Europeans commenced to settle in the Sounds the bush had practically established itself to the water's edge. The few vestiges of aboriginal cultivation were rapidly becoming clothed with a dense second growth and, except for a few localities occupied by the remnants of native tribes, had been practically obliterated. As the colonists commenced to clear the bush..vestiges of an ancient occupation were brought to light in the..square or oblong pits. These pits were of varying shapes and sizes, many bunched into steep spurs and forming a series that reached from the shores to the tops of the low hills, and all placed in secure positions on land not liable to slip. These numerous pits were widely scattered throughout the Sounds and, some being similar to those in use in the North as store pits, they were called by the settlers' 'Kumera pits' under the impression that they had been used to store those tubers for food supply. Investigation proved this idea to be erroneous; the pits were found in positions unsuitable for such storage and the presence of shell heaps amongst them proved that they had formed part of the dwellings of an ancient people. **1968** HALL-JONES *Early Fiordland* 125 At Indian Cove he came across several Maori huts and fireplaces. Because of their depth, he described the ovens as belonging to the 'pit-dwellers'. **1901** *TrNZI* XXXIII. 325 The abandoned **pit-dwellings** of the ancient Moriori inhabitants..prove beyond question that much of the bush on the shores of the Pelorus Sound was a regrowth. **1952** TAYLOR *Lore and History of the South Island Maori* 18 The Maoris of Pelorus Sound affirm that prior to their arrival the inhabitants were a small dark-skinned race, who cultivated land and lived peacefully in pit dwellings on hillsides.

3. *transf.* A sleeping bag; occas. a bed.

1980 *Listener* 22 Sept. 35 While you are lurking slothfully in your pit—bed for those not familiar with the language of the hills. **1988** PICKERING *Hills* 8 So to cope with the rituals of tramping..a slang language has developed to suit. Lots of quick short words... 'Pit' (the tramper's true friend, a sleeping bag), 'pog' (porridge).

4. See *kumara pit* (KUMARA 2).

pitau. Also **pito**. [Ma. /ˈpiːtau/: Williams 284 *Pītau* (i) *1*. Young succulent shoot of a plant, especially circinate frond of a fern.]

1. The succulent pith or young central fronds of the mamaku; less commonly, the heart of the nikau palm.

1844 WILLIAMS *NZ Jrnl.* (1956) 108 At the bottom of the leafs [*sic*, of the nikau], a fruit or white substance is found, out of which grows the leafs. This substance is called by the natives 'Pito' (pronounced peetaw [pitau]). The middle is in seperate [*sic*] layers called 'Muka' from its resemblance to the flax, eaten by the natives. **1846** TAYLOR *Journal* (ATLTS) IV. 149 [We] received several presents of Pitau the inside of the stem of the mamaku or korau the Cyathea medullaris, which forms a wholesome and palatable food. **1904** TREGEAR *Maori Race* 331 Raw heart-fronds (*pitau*) of tree-fern were offered to the god, and then the same substance cooked. **1926** CROOKES *Plant Life Maoriland* 10 Attacking a suitably sized fern, he would split open the stem and extract from it the slimy pith, the 'pitau'. This would be..baked in the 'hangi', or Maori oven.

2. Applied to the MAMAKU itself q.v.

1845 WAKEFIELD *Adventure NZ* I. 57 The pitau, or tree-ferns growing like a palm-tree, form a distinguishing ornament of the New Zealand forest. **1850** TAYLOR *Journal* 9 Jan. (ATLTS) VII. 45 At Korinito a bowl of tutu juice boiled with the pith of the Pitau fern tree was presented our party. It is a very palatable dish and soon disappeared. **1867** HOCHSTETTER *NZ* 158 Mamaku, Pitau, Korau *(Cyathea medullaris)*, an arborescent fern; the entire stem being peeled is eaten and when cooked is very good; it is a favourite dish of the natives. **1982** BURTON *Two Hundred Yrs. NZ Food* 6 Alternatively, it [*sc.* tutu juice] was boiled with the pith of the pitau fern or pieces of bull kelp seaweed (*rimurapu*).

pitch. *Goldmining. Obs.* [f. Cornish mining *pitch* a part of a mine allotted to a particular workman: see OED *n.*² 12.] See quot.

1868 *Thames Miner's Guide* 55 Pitch.—A portion of a vein prepared and set apart for working.

pitch pine: see PINE 2 (11).

pit-dweller, pit-dwelling: see PIT 2.

pitiki, var. PATIKI.

pito, var. PITAU.

pitoitoi. [Ma. /piːˈtoitoi/: Williams 285 *Pītoitoi*.] ROBIN 1.

1843 DIEFFENBACH *Travels in NZ* I. 29 The white-breasted motacilla longipes (Pitoitoi) alone was heard pursuing its search from branch to branch after small dipterous insects. **1888** BULLER *Birds NZ* I. 34 This bird is the subject of an article—the Pitoitoi or Toutouwai of the natives and the 'Robin' of the colonists. **1948** HENDERSON *Taina* 121 He showed me how to catch *pitoitoi*.

pitoko, pitoku, varr. TITOKI.

pit spider. *Mining.* [f. the resemblance to a spider-shape.] A device consisting of a spike with hooks affixed, for use in a mine. See also *tommy stick* (TOMMY *attrib.*).

1981 HUNT *Speaking a Silence* 133 And they'd go down the mine... scrape the coal down and load it into the skips by hand with great big 'banjo' shovels. Then there were the old 'pit-spiders', steel hooks you'd jab into the mine wall and hang your lamp on. **1984** [see *tommy stick* (TOMMY *attrib.*)].

pittosporum /pəˈtɒspərəm/. A generic plant name [given by Sir Joseph Banks (1788), a modern Latin adaptation of Greek πίττα pitch σπόρος seed, the seeds being imbedded in gluten] often used as a vernacular name for common plants such as KARO, MAPAU, TARATA qq.v.

1874 WILSON *Diary* 15 May in Wierzbicka *Wilson Family* (1973) 191 I think we should plant a hedge inside [the fence] but the best one will be Pittosporum or as they call it here the Matipo. **1882** POTTS *Out in Open* 186 The beautiful pittosporum with their small dark seeds packed in gluten, and the black-berried aristotelia. **1898** HOCKEN *Contributions* 79 Two or three hundred yards beyond begins an irregular fringe of native bush, broadleaf, veronica, fuchsia, pittosporum, and tangled supplejack. **1935** *Star-Sun* (Christchurch) 12 Oct. 14 The pittosporums, or matipos, take prominent place among spring flowering trees. **1968** *NZ Contemp. Dict. Suppl.* (Collins) 15 *pittosporum n.* genus of handsome evergreen shrubs with fragrant white flowers. **1986** HALEY *Settlement* 123 Walter found a convenient pittosporum leaf. **1993** ANDERSON *All the Nice Girls* 29 He saw the large amiable shape outlined against the pittosporum at the back door.

pi-tui, var. TUI.

piupiu /ˈpjupju/, *n.*¹ [Ma. /ˈpiupiu/: Williams 285 *Piu*. *1.* v. trans. Throw or swing.. *piupiu*. *1.* v. trans. Oscillate, move to and fro.... *4.* A garment consisting of a heavy fringe, about 18 in. wide, attached to a band for the waist.] In traditional Maori dress, a skirt comprising a fringe of treated dried flax-blades attached to a waist-band; a flax skirt or kilt worn now mainly on ceremonial occasions or for concert performances.

1882 POTTS *Out in Open* 23 Mats of dressed flax, robes of piu piu, korowai, or of dogskin, contributed a great variety of costume. **1905** BAUCKE *White Man Treads* 90 Who so cunning and skilful in the weaving of piu piu, korowai, fancy mats, fancy plaits..as Te Aatarangi? **1917** *NZ At the Front* xiv (Gloss.) Piupiu.—A Maori garment extending from waist to knee, from which the kilt was copied. **c1920** BEATTIE *Trad. Lifeways Southern Maori* (1994) 48 Piupiu is a waist mat... It can be made of whitau in the roll or twist known as the miro fashion, or of the prepared bark of the ribbonwood. Made thus it is practically a silent garment but it can also be made of dried flax to make a swishing, rustling sound when the owner is engaged in hakas or in twirling the poi balls. **1930** ANDERSEN in *NZ Short Stories* 30 There moved the young women in *piupiu* whose pipe-strings, dyed yellow and black, and hanging from the waist, showed well under their cloaks as they walked, and rattled softly to the movement of their limbs. **1946** *JPS* LV. 156 *piupiu*, a garment consisting of a heavy fringe, about nine inches wide or more, made of flax and craped at intervals and dyed black. The flax when drying curl[ed] up into pipes. This fringe hung down the bare thighs, and as the wearer moved the gentle click-click of the hard tubes made a sound that was likened as to the frou-frou of a silk dress. **1969** BAXTER *Collected Poems* (1980) 449 They have taken the piupiu from the body of the land. **1971** *New Zealand's Heritage* I. 74 Maori child wearing a piupiu, typical costume worn nowadays by Maori concert parties. **1986** IHIMAERA *Matriarch* 107 Maori action songs at Takitimu Hall... The swishing and crackling of the piupius.

piupiu, *n.*² [Ma. /ˈpiupiu/: Williams 285 *Piu*... *3.* n. *Blechnum capense, B. discolor*, and *Dryopteris pennigera*, ferns.] Any of several large forest ferns: *crown fern* (FERN 2 (4), *B. discolor*) or *gully fern* (FERN 2 (5), *Pneumatopteris pennigera*). See also KIOKIO (*Blechnum* spp. esp. *B. capense*).

1844 WILLIAMS *NZ Jrnl.* (1956) 110 Piupiu, species of fern grows very ornamental. **1867** HOOKER *Handbook* 767 Piu-piu... *Polypodium pennigerum*. **c1920** BEATTIE *Trad. Lifeways Southern Maori* (1994) 359 A Wairewa Maori said the piupiu fern of the South Island was called mouku in the North Island. **1950** *Bull. Wellington Bot. Soc. No.23* 21 We..traversed a level stretch of mixed forest where piupiu (*Blechnum discolor*) rustled to our strides. **1952** RICHARDS *Chatham Is.* 11 *Blechnum*..or *Lomaria*..*discol*[*or*]... Bird's Nest Fern. Piu Piu. **1969** *Standard Common Names Weeds* 59

PIWAKAWAKA

piupiu [=] *kiokio* [=*Blechnum capense*]. **1981** BROOKER et al. *NZ Medicinal Plants* 28 *Cyclosorus penniger...* Common name: *Gully fern* Maori name: *Piupiu* This common fern is found in woods throughout New Zealand. **1982** WILSON *Stewart Is. Plants* 460 *Blechnum discolor* Crown Fern..Piupiu... Crowns of numerous, stiffly upright fronds up to a metre long.

piwakawaka. Also **pea walker, pi-oua-ka-oua-ka.** [Ma. /piːˈwakawaka/: Williams 285 *Pīwakawaka..fantail..pīwaiwaka, tīrairaka*: and numerous variations of these forms.] FANTAIL 1.

1834 MARKHAM *NZ* (1963) 41 There is another small bird called a Pea Walker. **1835** YATE *NZ* (1970) 57 *Piwakawaka*, or *Tirakaraka*—This restless little bird is continually on the wing, or hopping from twig to twig. **1840** POLACK *Manners & Customs* I. 124 A small bird called *Piwákáwáká* struck up its vocal strain, which sounded as peculiarly plaintive in the deserted place. **1842** GRAY *Fauna* in Dieffenbach *Travels in NZ* (1843) II. 190 *Rhipidura flabellifera.—* ..Diggowagh Wagh of the natives of Dusky Bay... Piwáka-waká... Pi-oua-ka-oua-ka. **1855** TAYLOR *Te Ika A Maui* 403 Piwakawaka, tirakaraka, the fan-tailed fly-catcher, a pretty, restless, lively bird; very sociable, and fond of displaying its beautiful little fan-tail. **1869** *TrNZI* I. (rev. edn.) 104 Rhipidura flabellifera. Piwakawaka. Fantail. Common. **1873** BULLER *Birds NZ* 143 (Pied-Fantail)... Piwaiwaka, Tiwaiwaka, Piwakawaka, and Tiwakawaka. **1886** *TrNZI* XVIII. 102 Rhipidura—fantail (Piwakawaka). Every one admires the two species of these fly-catchers, and their graceful evolutions in catching their prey. **1895** [see FANTAIL 2 (3)]. **1910** [see FANTAIL 1]. **1946, 1966** [see FANTAIL 2 (1)]. **1979** FRAME *Living in Maniototo* 30 Fluttering black fantail, the piwakawaka. **1985** [see FANTAIL 2 (1)].

piwauwau. [Ma. /piːˈwauwau/: Williams 285 *Pīwauwau*..wren. = *mātuhituhi*.] **a.** *bush wren* (WREN 2 (1)).

1842 GRAY *Fauna* in Dieffenbach *Travels in NZ* (1843) II. 188 Piwauwau of the natives, a bird confined to the upper regions of the hills. **1843** DIEFFENBACH *Travels in NZ* II. 154 A little bird, which is peculiar to these heights [of Mt. Egmont], busied itself in our neighbourhood... It is..called piwauwau by the natives. **1873** BULLER *Birds NZ* 115 Xenicus longipes. (Bush-wren.).. Matuhituhi, Piwauwau, and Huru-pounamu.

b. Occas. RIFLEMAN, called erroneously 'wren'.

1870 *TrNZI* II. 57 Acanthisitta chloris... Pi wau wau. Wren. **1884** *NZJSc.* II. 282 *Acanthisitta chloris*... Wren, Titipounamu, Pi-wau-wau.—Often builds in a small hole in a tree.

pizzle. *Farming.* [f. Brit. dial. *pizzle* an animal's penis, apparently more frequent now in Australasian technical use than elsewhere: AND 1891.]

1. The penis of an animal, esp. of a wether sheep. Also *attrib.*

1899 *Dept. Agric. Rep.* 15 The pizzle disease exists, but to no great extent. **1951** 17 May Feilding Freezing Works terms p.c. Colin Gordon. *Pizzles* (undeveloped penises) are cut off wethers. **1955** BOWEN *Wool Away* 4 The two worst cuts of all are ewes' teats cut or cut off, and wethers' pizzles cut or cut off.

2. Special Comb. **pizzleguard,** see quot.; **pizzle stain,** see quot. 1982.

1989 *NZ Eng. Newsletter* III. 26 **pizzleguard:** An imaginary piece of equipment called for when shearing rams or wethers. Good for a joke with a green shedhand. **1982** *Agric. Gloss.* (MAF) 57 **Pizzle Stain:** Unscourable urine staining in wether and ram bellies, and ewe crutchings. **1986** RICHARDS *Off the Sheep's Back* 55 I was allowed to miss school to help in the shed by picking up the bellywool and removing the pizzle stains from the wether bellywool.

placer, *n.*[1] *Goldmining.* [Introduced from US (cf. OED *n.*[2] 1842) and common in early New Zealand mining parlance.] A shallow alluvial gold deposit, esp. in *attrib.* use in Comb. **placer-claim, placer field, placer-mine (miner, mining),** also **deep placer,** a non-surface deposit.

1869 deep placer mines [see DIGGER *n.*[1] 1]. **1869** *AJHR* D-6 6 I should say what has to be said as to the prospects of a gold-mining industry of a still more stable nature than that of placer-mining being developed on the alluvial fields. **1873** PYKE *Wild Will Enderby* (1889, 1974) III. i 75 They've struck a big old placer somewhere, you bet. They are on heavy gold too. **1889** KNOX *Boy Travellers* 215 Some of the mines are wholly alluvial, or placer, diggings, others are wholly quartz-mines, which are called reefs in New Zealand and Australia. *Ibid.* 216 The placer miners do not confine themselves to the valleys of the rivers. **1890** *TrNZI* XXII. 404 If the gold in the deep placers had come ready formed from the vein-matter in the reefs, it would be laid down in layers of unequal richness. **1903** *Ibid.* XXXV. 129 It must be remembered that gold is now chiefly obtained by quartz-mining. The placer-claim is no longer the chief source of the gold-supply. **1934** *NZJST* XV. 349 Placer deposits. The comprehensive mining term 'placer' is here used to cover the deposits of valuable minerals formed by subaerial concentration. **1950** ISDALE *Hotels of Old Thames* 1 About 1871, it.. [became] increasingly evident that the Thames was not a 'placer' field for individual effort, but a quartz reef area for working by big companies.

placer, *n.*[2] *Farming.* [f. *place* locality + -ER.]

1. A sheep which will not leave the neighbourhood ('place') of an object to which it became bonded as a lamb. Cf. HERMIT.

1921 GUTHRIE-SMITH *Tutira* 383 Rock, log, nettle-clump, bush, or tree stump may, as chance determines, become the foster-parent of the 'placer'... To begin with, it must happen that the dam of the future 'placer' shall perish within measurable distance of some such conspicuous object as one of those named; it must happen likewise that she shall perish when her lamb is..old enough to be able to support life on grass... When compelled by hunger to crop the turf, it never strays far. **1934** *Press* (Christchurch) (Acland Gloss.) 27 Jan. 15 *Placer*.—When a ewe dies, her lamb usually stays by her body. If he is old enough to survive, and does not follow other sheep away, he sometimes transfers his filial affection to some object close to where his mother died, perhaps a bush or large stone. He then becomes a *hermit* and a great nuisance to get in at mustering. In the North Island these sheep are called *p*[*lacer*]*s*. I have never heard the word used in Canterbury; but the thing undoubtedly occurs here. **1948** WALL in Woodhouse *Farm & Station Verse* (1950) 149 [Title] The 'Placer Sheep' [about a lamb, whose mother died, transferring its attachment to a block of stone, and not leaving its neighbourhood].

2. *transf.* [This sense is not elsewhere attested: Guthrie-Smith may be confusing or conflating PLACER *n.*[1] and [2].] A solitary miner.

1921 GUTHRIE-SMITH *Tutira* 383 'Placer' is a term used to denote a gold digger who remains year after year on the one spot, on the one place. **1936** GUTHRIE-SMITH *NZ Naturalist* 34 Now, however, from new sprung mushroom townships, from the bark huts of 'hermits', the tents of 'placers'—solitaries who work alone—devastation radiated.

PLAIN

plaice. *sand flounder* (FLOUNDER 2 (9)).

1841 in Ross *Voyage of Discovery* (1847) II. 117 The soles, though small, are very good, and the plaice of large size are equal in flavour to the Dutch fish. **1848** WAKEFIELD *Handbook NZ* 160 The only sorts [of fish] similar to ours are the *Conger-eel, Sole, Plaice,* and *Flounder.* **1901** *TrNZI* XXXIII. 559 The flounder, or patiki, wrongly named 'plaice'. **1956** GRAHAM *Treasury NZ Fishes* 191 In and around Nelson the Sand-flounder is known as Plaice. It is not unlike this fish in shape, but the English Plaice is of a deep brown colour with orange-red spots on the upper surface. **1970** SORENSEN *Nomenclature NZ Fish* 24 Flounder... Rhombosolea plebeia... Other common names..Square, Dab, Plaice, Diamond or Diamond-back, Tin-plate, Three Corners.

plain, *n.* [Spec. use of *plain* a tract of country the surface of which is comparatively flat.] Usu. *pl.* as **the plains,** an extensive tract of open country, often undulating, lightly treed, and generally suitable for pasture. **a.** Often, with init. cap., the Canterbury Plains.

1851 SHORTLAND *S. Dist. NZ* 210 [13 Jan. 1844] The sharp prickles of the small shrub 'tumatakuru'..is very common on the plains. **1854** *Canterbury Almanack* 104 [Advt] Gentlemen and families visiting the Plains will find every accommodation at the above Establishment. **1860** in *Canterbury Rhymes* (1866) 79 The folks on the plains Turned..uncommonly brown, In all the Nor'-westers and easterly rains. **1873** BULLER *Birds NZ* 218 Any one acquainted with our 'plains' must have observed..how certain parts (termed by the geologists 'fans') are thickly covered with stones. **1886** HART *Stray Leaves* 18 All huddled in vain are the sheep of the Plain. **1902** *Settler's Handbook NZ* (Lands Dept.) 25 The lower hills, downs, and better kinds of plain country have now been widely cultivated. **1930** ACLAND *Early Canterbury Runs* 5 Until wire fences were introduced about 1862, all sheep on the plains were kept more or less in hand. **1951** the Plain [see *bridle-path* (BRIDLE)]. **1960** SCRYMGEOUR *Memories of Maoriland* 152 Wallie..did enjoy the jaunts around the agricultural areas, situated near the environs of the city of 'The Plains'.

b. In non-Canterbury reference.

1845 TAYLOR *Journal* 17 Mar. (ATLTS) III. 97 These plains [about Taupo] or Mania agree with the prairie and pampas of America. **1859** THOMSON *Story NZ* I. 17 On the coast plains in the North Island ferns and flax plants supply the place of grasses. **1873** PYKE *Wild Will Enderby* (1889, 1974) II. iii 57 Never was he happier than..when..madly galloping over the plains, he chased the wild cattle. **1882** HAY *Brighter Britain* II. 283 The river [Thames] winds through what are called plains here, but the term is only relatively applied. The 'plains' are broken with spurs and undulations from the higher ranges that bound them, and the country is anything but one uniform level. **1939** BEATTIE *First White Boy Born Otago* 120 There were innumerable lagoons on the plains in those days [c1860s].

plain, *a.*

1. *Farming.* **a.** Of sheep-dogs, without 'eye' or the ability to work sheep by fixed gaze, usu. in collocations: **plain-eye(d), plain-working.** Cf. EYE 3.

1953 STRONACH *Musterer on Molesworth* 43 At Molesworth in those days most of our heading dogs were the 'plain-working' kind. They did not 'eye' the sheep or exercise any mesmerism, as is done by the present-day trial dog. **1959** McLEOD *Tall Tussock* 124 *Plain Working Dog*: Heading dog with no 'eye'. **1966** NEWTON *Boss's Story* 188 *Plain-eyed*: Most of our heading dogs show what is known as 'eye', i.e. when working a few sheep they 'set' them much as does a setter or pointing dog setting game. Those that do not have this trait are called plain-eyed. **1971** Lethbridge *Sunrise on Hills* 118 Glen was a plain-eyed heading dog. That is, he did not try to mesmerise the sheep by staring them in the eyes till their wills broke and they would turn and run. **1982** 'plain-eye' [see EYE 3 a].

b. As **plain-bodied**, of sheep, having a smooth skin, free from wrinkles.
   1955 Bowen *Wool Away* 130 However, with the modern trend of breeding, tending to eliminate excessive skin folds and wrinkles, there are many nice-cutting reasonably plain-bodied Merinos that shear well. *Ibid.* 132 The average Corriedale is..plain-bodied apart from an odd neck wrinkle or dew-lap.

2. In the phr. **plain as a pikelet**, see PIKELET 2.

planny. [f. PLAN(TATION + -Y.] A familiar form of PLANTATION 2.
   1957 Frame *Owls Do Cry* (1967) 28 Not many girls of my age have left school, have they Daphne? And not many been in the plannies with a boy, have they Daffy? **1982** Frame *To the Is-land* (1984) 56 The pine plantations, to be known as the 'plannies'.

plant, *v.* [f. Brit. slang *plant* to hide (stolen goods).]
1. *trans.* [AND 1793.] To hide.
   1846 *McLean Papers* (ATLTS) III. 86 If compelled to give up the guns I shall 'plant' the locks. **1864** *Gold Digger's Notes* (1950) 50 I had always carried the gold about with me; but on that day I left it planted in my stretcher. **1871** Money *Knocking About NZ* 112 Here we began to look out for signs of stores..that we should find 'planted' in the bush out of reach of rats. **1905** *Truth* 2 Sept. 1 The main crime [of the University students] was entering the girls' quarters with no other ulterior motive than to 'plant' their academic gowns. *Ibid.* 21 Oct. 1 They either mix the stolen [sheep] with their own flock, or travel at night, or 'plant' them. **c1924** Anthony *Me & Gus* (1977 Gus Tomlins) 8 I carried it [*sc.* a calf] home and tied it in the cow-yard, in the hope that if I planted myself out of sight the heifer would eventually pluck up enough resolution to pay it a visit. **1934** *Press* (Christchurch) (Acland Gloss.) 27 Jan. 15 *Plant.*—To hide (trans. and intrans.).

2. *intr.* or *reflexive.* [AND 1890.] Of an animal, to hide or be hidden.
   1865 Chudleigh *Diary* 29 Apr. (1950) 179 We all looked for him [*sc.* a horse]..but could not finde [*sic*] him. I supposed him to be planted in the bush as he is given to that. **1900** *TrNZI* XXXII. 283 The new-born lamb will follow its mother, and does not 'plant'... The kid is liable to 'plant' or bolt away for hiding when the flock is mustered.

   Hence **planting** *vbl. n.*, the action of hiding objects away.
   1888 Barlow *Kaipara* 167 It was..on a regatta day that I became acquainted with a singular colonial institution known by the name of 'planting.'..There were plants (of the class alcoholic) in all directions that day, from the humble beer to the haughty three star brandy plant.

plant, *n.* [Extended use of Brit. slang *plant* (a hiding-place of) a hoard of stolen goods: see OED *n.*¹ 7 a; AND 1812.] Something, or a hoard of things, hidden away.
   1856 Phillips *Rockwood Jrnl.* 28 Dec. (Canterbury Pub. Lib. TS) 60 The rest packed up and went on to little Peninsular [*sic*] where..they came on to an old Maori plant of some Eel baskets, Flax rope Paddles &c. **1862** Chudleigh *Diary* 19 Aug. (1950) 54 Made a plant of some 60 yds. of rope near 22 trig pole. **1873** Pyke *Wild Will Enderby* (1889, 1974) III. viii 99 Well, now, I guess the plant ain't sprung. **1888** [see PLANT *v.*]. **1920** Mander *Story NZ River* (1974) 53 He guessed that..every man about the place knew of the plant of money at the boss's cottage awaiting the arrival of the bush contractor.

plantain. [Local use of *plantain* for mainly introduced *Plantago* spp. (fam. Plantaginaceae).] Usu. with a modifier: **broadleaved (greater) plantain** *Plantago major,* **buck's horn (elkhorn) plantain** *P. coronopus,* **New Zealand plantain** for the native *P. raoulii,* **swamp (hoary) plantain** *P. australis* (formerly *P. hirtella*). See also RATSTAIL 1, SOLDIER *n.*¹ 1 a.
   1843 Dieffenbach *Travels in NZ* I. 393 From having formerly been the principal abode of the Rotu-rua natives..[Mokoia] was always well cultivated, and grasses, both native and European, plantain, chickweed, and others..vary agreeably the usually brown tint of the lower native vegetations. **1907** *AJHR* C-8 21 *Plantago raoulii.* Common New Zealand plantain. Meadow, forest. **1926** Hilgendorf *Weeds* 161 Broad-leaved Plantain (*Plantago major*), also called ratstail, birdseed, lamb's tongue, and greater plantain, is common on roadsides and trodden places throughout the country and in pastures in the King Country... Plantain (*Plantago lanceolata*) is commonly called rib grass, lamb's tongue, horse plantain, and soldiers. It is common in pastures and waste places throughout. *Ibid.* 163 Buck's Horn Plantain (*Plantago coronopus*), also called elk horn plantain, is found in sandy or gravelly places in scattered localities over both islands [usually in seaside marshes]... Hoary Plantain (*Plantago media*), is also called lamb's tongue and swamp plantain; it is found in fields and waste places, but appears nowhere very common. **1969** *Standard Common Names Weeds* 8 *buck's-horn plantain Plantago coronopus. Ibid.* 59 *plantain* [=] *broad-leaved plantain: narrow-leaved plantain: swamp plantain. Ibid.* 38 *hoary plaintain* [=] *swamp plantain. Ibid.* 76 *swamp plantain Plantago hirtella.* **1981** Taylor *Weeds of Lawns* 88 Plantains (*Plantago* spp.)... This plant, native to Eurasia, is one of the most widespread weeds in New Zealand, common in lawns, playing fields, untended ground, pasture and in arable crops sown out of pasture. *Ibid.* 29 Bucks Horn Plantain (*Plantago coronopus*) Small annual recognised by its divided leaves [like buck's horns].

plantation. [Spec. uses of *plantation* an assemblage of growing plants which have been planted.]
1. [A specific application of OED *plantation* 2 a.] *Hist.* In early New Zealand use applied to a Maori garden or area of planted food-crops, esp. of potatoes and kumara.
   [**1773** Forster *Resolution Jrnl.* 4 June (1982) II. 292 We..went there ashore, & showed them [*sc.* Natives] our Gardens & plantations [of vegetables, etc], & traded with them for some trifles.] **1815** Marsden *Lett. & Jrnls.* (1932) 105 In this place there were some very fat hogs and fine plantations of potatoes. **1832** Williams *Early Jrnls.* 8 Sept. (1961) 258 Boys at the Karaka at their plantation. **1841** Bidwill *Rambles in NZ* (1952) 58 We left this potatoe plantation, and, after about two hours' walk, emerged from the wood. **1888** Colenso *Fifty Years* 32 Not a house nor even a Maori plantation nor fishing-village. **1930** Reischek *Yesterdays in Maoriland* (1933) 169 The bridle-track led past little bush-clearings with fenced-in Maori plantations.

2. [The usu. modern sense: a specific application of OED 2 b.] A small patch of exotic trees, esp. of *Pinus radiata*, planted for timber and/or shelter often as part of a farm's economy; a woodlot. Cf. PLANNY.

   1865 Barker *Station Life* (1870) 26 Here and there clumps of tall trees rise above the shrubs, and..there is a thick plantation of red and blue gums, to shelter the garden. **1880** Chudleigh *Diary* 17 June (1950) 289 I can get trees and gardener from the station and received directions how to plant for a solid plantation. **1899** Mansfield *Stories* (1984) 7 On Sunday mornings Pat..took us for a walk in the great pine plantation. **1917** Glen *Six Little New Zealanders* (1983) 27 We raced through the tussocks again, scrambled up the bank, through the plantation, and out on to the lawn. **1959** Slatter *Gun in My Hand* 57 It was El Dorado at last among the lupins offering cones of gold to the blue sky and the black battalions of the pine plantations. **1973** Fernandez *Tussock Fever* 11 The girls skirted the plantation as far as the gate and soon entered the homestead horse paddock. **1984** Boyd *City of the Plains* 43 [He] then drained land and planted trees along roadsides and in plantations for Tanner.

plant-caterpillar. VEGETABLE CATERPILLAR.
   1892 Cooke *Vegetable Wasps and Plant Worms* 139 The New Zealanders' name for this plant-caterpillar is 'Hotete', 'Weri', and 'Anuhe'. **1930** Reischek *Yesterdays in Maoriland* (1933) 70 Under the rata roots I also found the Aweta, or plant-caterpillar, which to change into a chrysalis creeps underground, and in many cases instead of becoming a moth becomes—a mushroom!

plastic fantastic. [Alluding to the fibreglass hull.] **a.** A nickname for a New Zealand fibreglass ('plastic') entrant (esp. KZ-7) in the 1986–87 America's Cup challenges.
   1986 *Dominion* (Wellington) 9 Oct. 24 The boat..is a development of the racer New Zealand trounced in their first venture in their plastic fantastics, the world championships in February. **1989** McGill *Dinkum Kiwi Dict.* 81 *plastic fantastic* revolutionary all-plastic hull designed by Bruce Farr for the yacht KZ7, in the Kiwi challenge for the 1987 America's Cup.

b. *transf.* or *fig.* A credit card, or credit cards as a medium of exchange. See also quot. 1990.
   1987 *Dominion Sunday Times* (Wellington) 22 Feb. 1 Simply ask for credit cards in New Zealand and you will almost certainly receive. The national debt on plastic fantastic is soaring past $600 million. **1990** *Salient* (Wellington) 5 Mar. 11 Think of *Salient* as a Plastic Fantastic. Space age styling (with a partially padded interior). **1995** *Sunday Star-Times* (Auckland) 3 Dec. A17 [Business page] Swipe 'n' gripe could well be the cry as we pull out the plastic fantastic in the weeks before Christmas to pay for those parties and presents.

plate: see LADY 1 b.

play, *v. Farming.* In the phr. **to play the piano**, see quot. 1933.
   1933 *Press* (Christchurch) (Acland Gloss.) 18 Nov. 15 *Play the piano.*—To run the fingers over the sheeps' backs in order to find the softest and easiest to shear. **1941** Baker *NZ Slang* 42 *To play the piano*, to run one's fingers over the backs of sheep to find which are the easiest to shear.

playcentre. A pre-school institution designed to encourage very young children to learn and socialize through constructive play, affiliated to the New Zealand Playcentre Federation, established, organized, maintained and, in particular, supervised by parents rather than salaried teachers.
   1944 *Rep. Ministerial Conf. on Educ.* (Ministry of Education library) 13 Each playcentre is controlled by

player. [Spec. use of *player* one who plays (seriously) at a sport.]

1. Of a racehorse, a good runner, a stayer.
1946 COOZE *Ten Bob Each Way* 18 She was a player and let nothing go past.

2. Of a woman, one who, from a male point of view, 'plays around' sexually, or is reputed to; a 'good sport'.
1968 SLATTER *Pagan Game* 48 His mind began to dwell on another player at the College, a Fourth Former named Cheryl. **1988** MCGILL *Dict. Kiwi Slang* 85 *player* person, usually female, prepared to play at sex; c.1950; eg 'I reckon that one in the corner would be a player. Want to find out?'

play-lunch. [AND 1963.] A snack (apple, etc.) taken to school to eat during the morning play period or 'interval'. Also *transf.*
c1930 p.c. P.B. Trapp, Dept. of Education, Wellington (10 Oct. 1963). Playlunch was used at least from 1930. **1960** HILLIARD *Maori Girl* 13 The family shared one schoolbag and fought over who was to open it and give out the play-lunches. **1962** *Listener* 27 July 39 Children like to take the special little packets of [dried fruit] to school for their playlunch. **1986** *Listener* 4 Oct. 6 Why don't you have two chocolate biscuits for play-lunch. **1991** *North & South* (Auckland) June 33 Beatings those days [were] accepted as a normal part of a boy's day, like play-lunch and a cigarette behind the bike sheds. **1994** *Tablet* (Dunedin) 6 Mar. 1 Mr Bolger purred with satisfaction at this sign of approval..with a possible added bonus in the shape of the US Secretary of State..dropping in for playlunch on his way to Australia.

playtime. *Hist.* [Spec. use of *playtime* a time for play or recreation.] At a primary school, a break or 'interval' for play between classes, usu. mid-morning.
[*Note*] Present official usage enforces 'interval'.
1922 MANSFIELD *Stories* (1984) 501 Playtime came and Isabel was surrounded. The girls of her class nearly fought to put their arms round her. **1968** SLATTER *Pagan Game* 13 Dignity would become the keynote. Play-time would become interval. Second year Fifth would become the Remove. **1983** STEWART *Springtime in Taranaki* (1991) 91 We would proudly return ['stolen' articles] when the blessed release of playtime or lunchtime arrived. **1991** O'REGAN *Aunts and Windmills* 14 We used [in the 1920s] to have a playtime in the morning and afternoon at school. Now I hear children talk of an 'interval' or morning and afternoon 'break' in much the same way as people talk of a coffee break..as a temporary cessation of work.

playway. [Cf. OED *play n.* 17 an educational method which seems to utilize play (1914).]
[*Note*] The concept was introduced to New Zealand prob. in 1930 in the 'Red Book' of P.B. Strong, Director of Education, which promised 'a new freedom' for teachers to adapt methods to the needs of pupils, and recommended (among other texts) *The Play Way: an essay in educational method* by Henry Caldwell Cook, London, 1917.

a. In New Zealand, in mainly derog. use to categorize any educational method emphasizing the special needs of children and thus considered non-traditional; often wrongly associated with Dr. C.E. Beeby, Director of Education 1940–60. Contrast BEEBYISM.
1947 *NZ Observer* 12 Feb. 5 There was great harm in too liberal application of an educational slogan: 'Learning the playway'. **1951** *Here & Now* Jan–Feb. 16 'Bah!' you say, 'the play way'. Wait a bit, my friends. Reflect on what your children of five here learnt by the play way before they ever went to school. *Ibid.* 17 What is the 'play-way'? Is it universally practised in schools today? The term 'play-way' is well known to students of education as the name given by Caldwell Cooke to a highly successful experiment, mainly in the teaching of English, carried out by him at the Perse School, Cambridge—a fee-paying school, with a high staffing rate and a tradition of experimentation. **1958** in Holcroft *Voice in Village* 9 May (1989) 73 An occasional folly or weakness at an individual school is built up into an indictment of the system as a whole; and the 'playway', a misleading term that must be haunting its inventor, is brandished recklessly. **1964** BOOTH *Footsteps in Sea* 61 The tots who learned at school the play way. **1972** MITCHELL *Pavlova Paradise* 51 The collapse of morals, the untidiness of state house gardens..were all authoritatively attributed to 'play-way'. **1990** 24 Oct. p.c. Dr. C.E. Beeby (Wellington). P.B. Strong towards the end of the 1920's became Director of Education and set to work with his senior inspectors on a new syllabus for primary schools producing in 1930 the famous 'Red Book' which promised 'a new freedom' for teachers to adapt teaching methods, etc., to the needs of the pupils. One of the books recommended there for trainee and teacher reading was Caldwell Cook's *The Play Way*. C.E. Beeby who attained the Directorship eleven years later was blamed for a *term* he never used—he prefers the term 'activity methods' esp. in respect of infant rooms. **1992** *NZ Tablet* (Dunedin) 23 Dec. 14 We..will appreciate the benefit of the biffs we got in those 'bad old days' before they discovered the 'play-way' of educating kids.

b. *attrib.* and *transf.*
1983 *Dominion* (Wellington) 1 Sept. 8 New schemes which approach educational problems with vision and imagination are frequently dismissed by outside commentators with such phrases as 'playway stuff', 'airy fairy nonsense' and provoke cries 'to get back to basics'. **1989** NEWBOLD *Punish. & Politics* 155 In the House, conservative MPs demanded a toughening up of the country's gaols and an end to the 'play-way' method of dealing with convicts.

pleura, var. PLEURO.

pleuro. Also occas. **pleura, ploorer.** [f. contagious) *pleuro*(-pneumonia: AND 1871.] **a.** A disease of farm stock, esp. cattle.
1863 CHUDLEIGH *Diary* 13 Aug. (1950) 98 [We] docked a horse that is showing symptoms of pleura. It is a very severe inflammation of the lungs and if not attended to often kills in 24 hours. **1865** THATCHER *Otago Songster* 15 And in the cattle came, Before pleuro broke out, and spoilt That rosy little game. **1937** AYSON *Thomas* 115 The danger of tutu poisoning and the pleuro scare made constant observation of the cattle necessary. **1968** *NZ Contemp. Dict. Suppl.* (Collins) 15 *pleuro, ploorer n.* shortened forms of pleuro-pneumonia.

b. *Obs.* A beast that has pleuro-pneumonia.
1864 THATCHER *Songs of War* 13 We are by this Pleuro haunted. **1865** *Puketoi Station Diary* (Hocken TS) 5 Apr. Killed a pleuro of F's.

c. *Obs.* Beef from a beast infected by pleuro-pneumonia.
1864 THATCHER *Songs of War* 5 Butchers are talking of raising Pleuro to a shilling a pound. **1865** THATCHER *Otago Songster* 9 And they'd come to live [in Otago] on trouble, Pleuro and barracouta.

plonk. [In the general English colloquial sense '(cheap or inferior) wine' ('orig. *Austral.*', so New SOD; AND 1933), *plonk* (prob. altered from French *blanc* as in *vin blanc*) is recorded in NZ from 1943 mainly in WW2 contexts or specifically in that of 2 below.]

1. Any alcoholic liquor, 'booze'. Also *fig.*
1941 BAKER *NZ Slang* 62 Terms for strong drink [shared with Australia] as *lunatic soup, Africa speaks, plonk.* **1943** *NZEF Times* 6 Sept. 6 I hiked along to Madame Plonk's bar for some inspiration. *Ibid.* 20 Dec. 5 Scene. Two plonk artists on floor of packed truck. **1960** MUIR *Word for Word* 235 Boy, am I going to get silly with the plonk when this year's over? **1976** WILSON *Pacific Star* 134 I really liked the flavour of it, after the Australian and American plonk we'd drunk up in the Islands.

2. As **Dally plonk, Henderson plonk,** wine made by mainly Dalmatian vintners esp. in the Auckland district of Henderson, and formerly sold cheaply at the vineyards.
1950 *Landfall* 14 127 You can buy an awful lot of Dally plonk for 4 pounds. **1984** *Insight* Feb.–Mar. 81 Plonk can be defined as 'badly made wine', and fortunately in New Zealand, the ridiculed 'Henderson Plonk' is almost a thing of the past.

plonked, *a.* [AND 1972 plonked up.] Drunk.
1949 THE SARGE *Excuse my Feet* 42 George was difficult and Herbert was slightly *plonked.* **1955** *BJ Cameron Collection* (TS July) plonked (adj) Drunk. **1984** WILSON *S. Pacific Street* 51 She looked very plonked.

ploorer, var. PLEURO.

plough bird. Also **plough boy.** *black-fronted tern* (TERN 2 (2) *Sterna albostriata*).
1888 BULLER *Birds NZ* II. 72 Mr. Kirk writes that the local name of this bird [*sc.* Black-fronted Tern], in the neighbourhood of Cape Kidnappers, is the 'Plough Bird' or 'Plough Boy', given on account of the persistent manner in which it follows the farmer's plough for the purpose of picking up the grubs and worms that are exposed in this operation. **1966** FALLA et al. *Birds NZ* 157 Black-fronted Tern *Chlidonias albostriatus. Other names*: Tara, Sea Martin, Ploughboy, Inland Tern, Riverbed Tern.

plover.

1. Transf. use of the name *plover* for any of various small to medium-sized wading birds of the family Charadriidae. Cf DOTTEREL.
1777 FORSTER *Voyage Round the World* I. 133 Ducks, shags, black oyster-catchers, and some sorts of plovers were very numerous here [at Dusky Bay]. **1870** *TrNZI* II. 48 Plover chimes in, as it sidles slyly off with alternate run and halt, nor could you find its slight grassy nest till half a dozen times the ground had been stepped over.

2. With a modifier: crookbill (crookbilled), dusky, golden, red-breasted, sand, shore (New Zealand shore), spur-winged, wrybill (wrybilled).

(1) crookbill (crookbilled) plover. *Obs.* See *wrybill plover* (8) below.
   1870 *TrNZI* II. 45 The reason for the lateral curvature of the beak of the Anarynchus, or Crook-billed Plover, as yet requires explanation. 1885 *NZJSc.* II. 509 Crookbill Plover, Sand-lark. The Crookbill at breeding season is less wary than perhaps any other species of the family. 1966 FALLA et al. *Birds of NZ* 130 Wrybill... Wry-billed Plover, Crook-bill Plover, Ngutu-parore.

(2) dusky plover. *Obs.* [*dusky* f. a translation of the specific epithet *obscurus* 'dark, dusky', poss. also (but prob. coincidentally) containing an allusion to the name of the type locality, *Dusky Sound.*] *New Zealand dotteral* (DOTTEREL 2 (3) *Charadrius obscurus*).
   1844 COLENSO *Excurs. Northern Is.* in Taylor *Early Travellers* (1959) 44 The Dusky Plover (*Charadrius obscurus*) and the Southern Godwit..were in large flocks. 1882 POTTS *Out in Open* 216 Donald Potts..once found an egg of this species laid in the nest of the dusky plover. 1885 *NZJSc.* II. 506 *Charadrius obscurus*... Dusky, Red-breasted, or Mountain Plover, Big Dottrel [*sic*], Tuturiwatu, Paturiwhata, Tituriwhatu-pukunui. This excellent gamebird formerly bred on the Canterbury Plains.

(3) golden plover. Also as **eastern (Pacific) golden plover**, and with other modifiers, the migratory *Pluvialis fulva*.
   1871 HUTTON *Catalogue Birds NZ* 24 Charadrius fulvus... Golden Plover. 1949 *NZ Bird Notes* III. 127 At the Ohau I have seen the golden plover. 1955 OLIVER *NZ Birds* 255 *Eastern Golden Plover Pluvialis dominicus fulvus* In 1835 Yate recorded the takahikahi from the Bay of Islands. 1990 *Checklist Birds NZ* 138 *Pluvialis fulva..Pacific Golden Plover*... Breeds on the tundras of Siberia and western Alaska... Very few overwinter in New Zealand.

(4) red-breasted plover. *New Zealand dotterel* (DOTTEREL 2 (3) *Charadrius obscurus*).
   1870 *TrNZI* II. 68 Charadrius obscurus... Tituriwhatu-pukunui. Red-breasted Plover. 1871 [see TUTURIWHATU]. 1885 [see (2) above].

(5) sand plover. *Obs.* See *shore plover* (6) below.
   1838 POLACK *NZ* I. 306 Blue herons, auks, sand larks, sand plovers, terns. 1871 HUTTON *Catalogue Birds NZ* 25 Thinornis novae zealandiae... Sand Plover. Kukuruatu. 1885 *NZJSc.* II. 508 Masked Plover, Sand Plover, Shore Plover... This pretty plover is..seen in the southern part of this island fossicking about the sandy shores at the mouths of rivers. 1904 HUTTON & DRUMMOND *Animals NZ* 205 Kukuruatu. Thinornis novae-zealandiae... The Sand Plover was once common in sandy bays from the Great Barrier Island southward to Otago, but it is now very rare. *Ibid.* 207 The Auckland Island Sand Plover. *Thinornis rossi*. 1923 *NZJST* VI. 76 *Thinornis novaeseelandiae... Shore-plover; Sand-plover*. It is a matter for regret that no recent records of this beautiful endemic plover are forthcoming... It may still occur at the Chatham Islands.

(6) shore (New Zealand shore) plover. *Thinornis novaeseelandiae*, an endangered sedentary species formerly of sandy shores but now confined to South East Island (Chatham Islands). See also BOWING-BIRD, KUKURUATU, *sand plover* (5) above, TUTURUATU.
   1897 *TrNZI* XXIX. 191 *Thinornis novaezealandiae*... (New Zealand Shore-plover.) 1925 [see (5) above]. 1952 RICHARDS *Chatham Is.* 79 The shore plover is found on the Chathams and has no near relative left in New Zealand. 1966 FALLA et al. *Birds of NZ* 127 Shore Plover... Tuturuatu... Now apparently confined to South-east Island in the Chathams, where in 1937 the population was estimated at about 70 pairs. 1985 *Reader's Digest Book NZ Birds* 188 *New Zealand Shore Plover... Tuturuatu*... Once found on mainland New Zealand and all over the Chatham Islands, the New Zealand shore plover is now confined to South East Island in the Chathams. 1991 *Evening Post* (Wellington) 26 Nov. 3 The first of 17 eggs of the shore plover, one of the world's most endangered species, hatched at Mount Bruce national Wildlife centre last night.

(7) spur-winged plover. *Vanellus miles novaehollandiae*, a large, yellow-wattled bird of open grasslands, self-introduced from Australia.
   1957 MONCRIEFF *NZ Birds* 47 Spur-winged Plover... One of the most beautiful plovers. 1976 SOPER *NZ Birds* 131 The Spur-winged Plover is a bird of the open grasslands and farmlands and it prefers areas containing patches of swampy ground. 1985 *Reader's Digest Book NZ Birds* 178 Although it has now established itself in New Zealand's three main islands, the spur-winged plover is a sedentary bird that, once it has settled somewhere, lives within a range of three or four kilometres.

(8) wrybill (wrybilled) plover or (freq.) *ellipt.* **wrybill.** *Anarhynchus frontalis* (fam. Charadriinae), a unique plover which has its beak deflected to the right to enable it to spoon for small insects and crustaceans. See also NGUTU-PARORE, *crookbill plover* (1) above.
   1873 BULLER *Birds NZ* 216 Anarhynchus frontalis. (Wry-billed Plover). 1889 PARKER *Catalogue NZ Exhib.* 116 The curious wry-billed plover..the only bird known in which the bill is turned not up or down, but to one side—the right. 1898 MORRIS *Austral-English* 519 *Wry-billed Plover*... a very rare bird of New Zealand. 1904 HUTTON & DRUMMOND *Animals NZ* 207 The Wry-bill. 1923 *NZJST* VI. 76 *Anarhynchus frontalis*... Wry bill... The habits of the bird are apparently such as to elude any but the sharpest observation. 1936 GUTHRIE-SMITH *NZ Naturalist* 110 For we all know it may be a silent grief to respectable Wrybill to see their little ones grow up with this horrid distortion of the probiscis, to reflect that in the councils of the Great Plover family their breed has been..relegated for all time to South Canterbury. 1946 SOLJAK *NZ* 10 Other waders are the wrybill, the only bird in the world with a twisted beak. 1954 WINKS *These New Zealanders* 163 Another bird of interest is the Wry-bill Plover, the only bird in the world which has its beak to one side; a sharp curvature to the right gives the plover a chance to forage under flat stones. 1967 NATUSCH *Animals NZ* 262 The wrybilled plover..winters in the North Island and breeds along the great shingle flats of the Canterbury rivers. It has a curiously skewed beak. 1976 SOPER *NZ Birds* 114 For breeding purposes Wrybilled Plovers require a vast expanse of shingle..bare of all growth, driftwood, and debris and composed of fairly large round stones. 1985 *Reader's Digest Book NZ Birds* 189 No bird in the world has a beak like the wrybill. The last third of its long bill turns to the bird's right at an angle of 15 to 22 degrees... Other names: *Ngutu-parore*, *wrybilled plover*. 1990 *NZ Geographic* VII. 49 [Caption] Unfortunate wrybill has its toe caught in the embrace of a cockle.

Plumb. [f. a proprietary name.] A favoured brand of axe. Cf. KELLY.
   1913 CARR *Country Work* 29 For many years to come the 'whoof' of the bushman, as he sinks the 'Kelly', or the 'Plumb' (two favourite brands of American axes, the latter especially) into..rimu..will be heard.

plume grass, plume tussock: see GRASS 2 (29), TUSSOCK 3 (7).

plunge, *v. WWI. trans.* To send (men) on an unplanned, sudden or violent attack. Also occas. as a noun. Cf. STUNT.
   1915 *Great Adventure* (1988) 45 [Our Brigadier] seems to resent my asking for information and for not too readily allowing my men to be plunged ahead without reconnaissance and information. *Ibid.* 52 I had heard that a 'plunge' attack by 100 men of the Mounted Rifles had been ordered by Headquarters for a couple of days ago. A mad fatal thing. It was to be a dash across open ground commanded by machine guns..to the Turkish trenches and then back.

Plunket. [f. the name of Lady *Plunket*, wife of Lord Plunket, Governor of NZ, 1904–10.]

1. a. Usu. init. cap. The popular name of the Royal New Zealand Plunket Society Inc., formerly the Royal Society for the Protection of Women and Children, founded 1907 by Sir Truby King (1858–1938); also used with reference to the methods and system of baby care advocated by the Society. Also *absol.* as **Plunket**, or **the Plunket**. Cf. KARITANE.
   1909 [see *Plunket nurse* 3 below]. 1913 [see c below]. 1939 MULGAN *First with Sun* 119 I have been wondering whether this country has much to show in the way of original words, especially those taken from names. There is 'Plunket' applied to Sir Truby King's famous method of raising babies. 1941 BAKER *NZ Slang* 58 For the past twenty years [the Plunket Society] has been known as *the Plunket*. 1957 FRAME *Owls Do Cry* (1967) 41 It was Mrs Peterson from the Plunket. 1967 HOLDEN *Empty Hills* 197 Plunket says it's all right, and aren't they somebody? 1979 ROCHE *Foreigner* 196 'What are you going to do when the baby comes?' 'I don't know'. 'Have you been to the Plunket?' 'What's the Plunket?' 1987 *NZ Woman's Weekly* 4 May 13 Looking to the future, Plunket plans to become more involved in child health research, especially into cot deaths. 1992 *Metro* (Auckland) Jan. 18 Plunket is so underfunded it's *designed* to encourage massive non-use and dropouts.

b. A Plunket clinic or establishment.
   1990 *Sunday Mag.* 1 Apr. 43 Last year the Health Department ran a cot death campaign in Plunkets and hospitals. 1991 *Dominion* (Wellington) 10 Dec. 7 I've washed till I'm blue And I've walked to Plunket 'Cos I've got someone new.

c. In *attrib.* use or as an *adjective* (rarely in predicative use). Pertaining to, or following the regime of, the Plunket Society.
   1913 *NZ Observer* 13 Sept. 5 'Plunket Saturday' for the kiddies naturally reminds one of the Plunket kiddies and their pa and ma. 1926 *NZ Dairy Produce Exporter* 18 Dec. 38 Mother does everything including helping in the shed and 'Plunket' feeding babies as well as calves. *Ibid.* 45 Last Saturday the Town Hall was the scene of the Plunket Party. 1937 HYDE *A Home in This World* (1984) 73 I..left with many admonitions to her not to forget..[the baby's] lime juice; above all to keep him goodly and Plunket. 1930 *Evening Post* (Wellington) 4 Dec. 5 Reviewing the published reports of the Plunket Conference, we would like to add our tribute to the excellent work accomplished. 1939 GRIEVE *Sketches from Maoriland* (1961) 55 The nearest I got the Maori mothers to 'Plunket feeding' was in administering the babies' food out of a bottle instead of with a spoon. *Ibid.* 56 The pride of the first Plunket mother when she discovered that her baby, properly fed, slept all night. 1946 BEAGLEHOLE *Some Modern Maoris* 295 Round here none of us mothers are Plunket. If you're Plunket

you have to measure everything and we just like the rough way for feeding our children. **1960** [see KARITANE 1]. **1992** *Metro* (Auckland) Jan. 121 [The baby] age 15 months, is Plunket-made.

2. Used in trade-names, occas. slightly altered in form as in **Plunkette**, a brand-name for a toilet soap.

c1920s Union Oil, Soap and Candle Co. [Notice to shareholders.] As you are specially interested in the welfare of the Company, we trust you will include the undermentioned articles in your regular household requirements:- 'Taniwha' soap. 'Taniwha' sandsoap 'Plunkette' toilet soap 'Tiki' toilet soap. **1925** *NZ Patent Office Jrnl.* [no number given] 26 Mar. Plunkette 'P.W.' 20734 [filed] 6th November, 1923. Union Oil, Soap, And Candle Co., Ltd..Toilet soap. **1927** *NZ Patent Office Jrnl.* [no number given] 1 Dec. Plunket 24120 [filed] 9th July, 1926. Ross and Glendining, Limited..Blankets included in Class 34.

3. Special Comb. **Plunket baby**, a baby reared according to the Plunket system; **Plunket Ball**, formerly a fund-raising social occasion held often with great formality in major centres, and also often as (for example) a children's 'fancy dress ball' in minor centres; **Plunket book**, a 'Baby Record' in which details of the weight, etc., and physical progress of a baby are recorded by the Plunket nurse; **Plunket centre**, a clinic wherein mothers can receive help with advice about babycare; **Plunket nurse**, a registered nurse with further training in the Plunket Society's baby-care methods who advises mothers on care of their babies (cf. *Karitane nurse* (KARITANE 2, esp. quot. 1992)); **Plunket rooms**, public baby clinics run by the Plunket Society; **Plunket Society**, the Royal New Zealand Plunket Society Inc.; **Plunket system** (also *transf.*), one requiring baby feeding at regular hours, etc.

1934 HYDE *Journalese* 168 They are **Plunket babies**, and their absurdly plump little brown cheeks nestle on snowy starched white pillows. **1944** WOOD *Understanding NZ* 130 Nearly three-quarters of the children born in New Zealand become 'Plunket Babies'. **1966** TURNER *Eng. Lang. Austral. & NZ* 173 A New Zealander is likely to begin life as a *Plunket baby*. **1984** BOYD *City of the Plains* 217 A very successful fundraising..was held..with Plunket babies present 'to show the good results of the work'. **1960** HILLIARD *Maori Girl* 52 Netta's coming out was not at Government House or at the **Plunket Ball**, but at the Matiti tennis club. **1954** SQUIRE *Family Daze* 68 **Plunket Book** memories of hot and cold baths..kept getting in the way of my driving. **1954** [*Cover Page of the Society's* 'Baby Record'] The Royal N.Z. Society for the Health of Women and Children Incorp. 'Plunket Society'... *Baby Record*... Plunket Nurse's Advice to Mothers. Instructions written in this book—are for Your baby only. **1983** OLIVER *James K. Baxter* 14 There are very few traces of James's early life. He arrived before he was due..; his Plunket book traces the growth of a healthy infant. **1994** *Contact* (Wellington) 8 Sept. 2 The official Plunket book was not introduced until 1922, but any record that proves the person was a Plunket baby is enough to claim the title [of oldest Plunket baby]. **1922** *Auckland Weekly News* 20 July 58 The Society would gladly welcome an effort among the larger county districts to establish **Plunket centres** with nurses of their own. **1909** *Ann. Rep. Soc. for Promotion of Health of Women & Children* I. 9 The doctor was pleased to have the assistance of the **Plunket nurse**, and at once consented to the children being fed on humanised milk. **1911** *Truth* 7 Oct. 5 Mrs Williams said that the child..continued all night until..a plunket nurse came and ordered a change of food. **1924** *Otago Witness* (Dunedin) 1 Apr. 61 Plunket nurses..are taught there specially how to look after the mothers and babies in the districts where they travel. **1938** HYDE *Nor Yrs. Condemn* 114 Have you taken her [*sc.* a child] to a Plunket nurse or a doctor? She'd soon get over it. **1942** SMITH *Medical Advice from Backblock Hospital* (1943) 25 Some Plunket nurses are specially active [in circumcision]. They appear to collect foreskins with the same enthusiasm as the Red Indians did scalps. **1951** HUNT *Confessions* 23 My mother..was always ready to smooth over their cares, act as 'Plunket' nurse to their babies. **1963** BAXTER *Collected Poems* (1980) 291 The Plunket nurse ran in To scissor off my valued foreskin. **1988** *Univ. Entr. Board Bursaries English Exam.* 6 There was the Plunket Nurse, of course, when the baby was little. **1992** *Metro* (Auckland) Jan. 18 I have yet to see a Plunket nurse driving a Rolls-Royce with $300,000 yuppie plates. **1944** WOOD *Understanding NZ* 48 The town will have..**Plunket rooms** (baby clinics). **1946** SOLJAK *NZ* 86 Every town, however small, has within close distance its community clinic or 'Plunket room' where pre-natal and infant care is taught. **1974** MULDOON *Rise & Fall of a Young Turk* 81 For the next nine years [I] always appeared at the Glen Innes Plunket Rooms on the first Saturday morning of the month to be available to constituents. **1976** BROWN *Difficult Country* 190 The Anglican Hall was available as a 'Plunket Room'. **1988** FRAME *The Carpathians* 83 We didn't want the Plunket Rooms here, with nurses coming to tell us what to do with our babies. **1917** *NZ Free Lance* (Wellington) 2 Mar. 14 The **Plunket Society** has outlived the time when people laughed at it. **1922** *Auckland Weekly News* 20 July 58 [Heading] The Plunket Society. **1930** *Evening Post* (Wellington) 4 Dec. 5 While in the Dominion the nurses of the Plunket Society are trained in one method, as the only sound method, of feeding the unfortunate infant who is denied his birthright (breast-feeding). **1960** *NZ Dairy Exporter* 11 Jan. 59 The Plunket Society..is an integral part of New Zealand life, and this new 'Plunket News' will have a great appeal to young parents. **1970** *Evening Post* (Wellington) 16 July 12 A sherry party was held..by the Hutt Valley branches of the Plunket Society..to launch the new official Plunket handbook. **1925** *Evening Post* (Wellington) 6 June 13 Instead of studying the trade and commerce of New Zealand, I spent the morning reading the wonderful account of the **Plunket system**. **1938** *Auckland Weekly News* 18 May 82 Replacements [*sc.* calves] here are well reared—quite on a Plunket system.

Plunket Shield: see SHIELD 2.

plurry, *adv.* and *a.* [A representation of *bloody* pronounced with Maori consonant substitution: AND 1900.] Occas. used as a euphemism for *bloody*. Formerly in jocular use to suggest the attempts at English speech of a simple and uncultivated, usu. rural, Maori stereotype. Compare *py korry* (KORRY a).

1917 *NZ At the Front* xiv Plurry.—The great Australian adjective as expressed in the more mellifluous language of the Maori. Ibid. 161 He t'e plurry Porangi, I t'ink. **1938** HYDE *Nor Yrs. Condemn* 148 *Plurry pakeha*, eh? You got the skin like the Maori, but you're not *tangata* Maori. **1941** BAKER *NZ Slang* 71 As appears to be suggested by raconteurs and cartoonists, the Maori finds *plurry* (bloody) and *py korry* necessary ingredients of normal conversation. **1959** SLATTER *Gun in My Hand* 206 He could speak beautiful English but often he put on the plurry Maori eh just to have a crack at us. **1960** MUIR *Word for Word* 109 Anyway, it's no bloody good for a title. No one would know how to pronounce it [*sc.* a Maori name]. Let's get right away from this plurry native stuff. **1973** WALLACE *Generation Gap* 224 The roughest timber will be left lying across the plurry line. **1986** [see POTAE].

plush. *Goldmining.* Plush, or similar long-napped cloth, used as a surface on gold tables, etc., to trap fine gold particles washed over it.

a1882 in MOFFATT *Adventures* (1979) 70 [A poem of Walter D. Moffatt, died 3 Jan. 1882] Yet still they dig and delve, be the weather foul or fair, And talk of plush and tables, and a thousand pounds a share. **1905** *Otago Daily Times* (Dunedin) 25 Feb. in Evans *Waikaka Saga* (1962) 42 Cheyne then got a board and one of the plushes from the manager's office, laid the plush on the board, and fixed the board from the gold box to the streaming down pipe. Cheyne then took a quantity of sand out of the box, put it on the board, and turned the water on, and washed the sand back into the gold box. The gold remained on the plush. **1977** *Sunday Times* (Wellington) 27 Nov. 17 He shovels the black sand into the gold box, washes it through... The gold falls on to the plush ('I just use an ordinary towel') which is then shaken into a baby's bath.

plutie, *a.* Also **pluty**. [f. *plut*(ocrat + -IE: cf. *plute* a wealthy man, AND 1894 (NZ 1907).] Moneyed, well-to-do, wealthy, 'upper-class' in accent or appearance.

1952 Wellington p.c. Ruth Mason. *Plutie type*, 'one who has money'. **1988** MCGILL *Dict. Kiwi Slang* 85 *pluty* wealthy, but worse, perceived as assuming airs and graces above the level of the egalitarian Kiwi herd; refers also to suburbs that fancy themselves, such as Fendalton in Christchurch, Khandallah or Karori ('We are the Park Lane of New Zealand' overheard comment in London of a woman from Karori) in Wellington, Remuera in Auckland; comes from 'plutocracy', the land barons of the South Island last century. **1989** *Pacific Way* Jan. 10 Well, it seems that he's shacked up with some pluty Remmers sheila and she's about to drop her bundle. **1995** WILLIAMS *Bishops* 65 Everyone used that phrase [taken from a BBC cricket commentator] to death, speaking in a pluty English accent, then collapsing with laughter.

pn: see POSTAL NOTE.

poa: see GRASS 2 (30).

poached egg. *dog daisy* (DAISY 2 (3)), the 'oxeye daisy' so called.

1926 HILGENDORF *Weeds* 176 Oxeye Daisy (*Chrysanthemum leucanthemum*), also called dog daisy, moon daisy and poached eggs, is common in pastures on somewhat heavy and damp land throughout the islands.

poaka, *n.*[1] Also early **porka, puerko, puorka**. [Ma. /ˈpoaka/: a Maori alteration of English *pork*, or *porker* 'a young hog fattened for pork' (Williams Appendix and p.301), re-introduced into English contexts.] A pig, esp. one Maori-owned or wild; pork. Some instances are difficult to separate from those of PORKER q.v.

[**1820** LEE & KENDALL *Gram. & Vocab.* 194 Pórka, *s.* Pork.] **1830** CRAIK *New Zealanders* 185 As the New Zealanders call a dog pero, so they call a pig *porka*, evidently another European term. **1838** POLACK *NZ* I. 311 The *puorka* (so pronounced for pork or pig) is especially well acclimated to the country. **1839** WALTON *Twelve Months' Residence* 26 The puerko, (so the natives name the pig or hog,) has proved himself to be a highly beneficial importation to the country. **1843** DIEFFENBACH *Travels in NZ* II. 49 Pigs have only of late been generally introduced into many parts of the country... The native name is poaka; and although

POAKA

English men think this word to be their own 'pork', with a native termination (porka), I am doubtful whether the New Zealanders had not some knowledge of this animal previous to its introduction by us. **1851** *Richmond-Atkinson Papers* (1960) I. 103 Ancient grey headed cannibals who..discriminate the saltness of the 'pakeha' from the sweetness of the maori & the superiority of both to 'poaka' pork. **1889** *TrNZI* XXI. 448 The Maori word *poaka*, for pig, was probably given them by the Tahitian interpreter, Tupaea, who was with Captain Cook when he gave the New-Zealanders their first pigs. Had the Englishmen given a word they would probably have said 'pig,' not 'porker,' and the Maoris would have called the animals *piki*. **1910** *NZ Free Lance* (Wellington) 4 June 12 It happened..all on account of the family 'poaka'. **1930** Reischek *Yesterdays in Maoriland* (1933) 156 She was immensely delighted about my coming, and immediately prepared a meal of 'porka' and kumera. **1949** Buck *Coming of Maori* 64 The pig, though present in Polynesia, is not mentioned in Maori traditions. After its introduction by Europeans, it was named *poaka* after the English name pork or porker which resembles the old Polynesian name of *puaka* but must not be confounded with it. **1969** Mason *Awatea* (1978) 18 Ana... Oh, boy. Here we go. Gee, they fine poakas. **1986** Ihimaera *Matriarch* 282 The wild pig—the poaka from the hills

poaka, *n.*² [Ma. /ˈpoaka/: Williams 286 *Poaka... 1...* pied stilt and..black stilt.] *pied stilt* (STILT 2 (2)).

1870 *TrNZI* II. 70 Poaka. Pied Stilt... The monotonous call of pink, pink, has, in some places, fixed on it the trivial name of Pink. **1885, 1904** [see STILT 2 (2)]. **1947** Powell *Native Animals NZ* 80 White-headed or Pied Stilt..Poaka... is widely distributed in both the North and South Islands of New Zealand. **1966** [see BARKER]. **1989** Parkinson *Travelling Naturalist* 136 The opening up of the country..better suited..the pied stilt, or poaka. **1990** *Checklist Birds NZ* 130 *Himantopus himantopus leucocephalus..Pied Stilt (Poaka)...* Throughout New Zealand; partly migratory.

poanamo, var. POUNAMU.

pocket, *n.*¹

1. *Goldmining.* [Used elsewhere but freq. in NZ use esp. with reference to alluvial gold: see OED *pocket* 7, 1850.] A crevice or cavity in rock (holding gold).

1858 Thomson *Reconn. Survey S. Dist. Otago* in Taylor *Early Travellers* (1959) 336 We washed the sands of the river and examined the 'pockets' of the rocks for gold. **1867** Hochstetter *NZ* 97 Their irregular upturned edges [afford] the most convenient and abundant 'pockets' for the storage and detention of the alluvial gold washed from the higher grounds. **1874** Pyke *George Washington Pratt* 51 Gold lay in a series of rich 'pockets' (as the crevices were termed). **1889** Knox *Boy Travellers* 216 Deposits, or 'pockets', are occasionally discovered in the sand under the loose stones. **1914** Pfaff *Diggers' Story* 115 I bought and sold flour..got a 3-1/2 oz. nugget from the bottom of a hole that had been left, made a rise of £300 out of a pocket of gold like horse beans.

2. *Gumdigging.* An isolated patch or collection (of kauri gum).

1873 Tinne *Wonderland of Antipodes* 54 If a man hits on a good 'pocket' of gum, he may make five or six pounds a week. **1970** Thomas *Way Up North* 31 The possibility of finding a 'pocket' or better still a good 'patch' added interest to the [gumdigger's] day's work.

pocket, *n.*² A pack for carrying wool often slung as one of a pair from each side of a pack-horse. Cf. PIKAU *n.* 4.

1907 Koebel *Return of Joe* 239 A train of pack horse, heavily laden with the weighty 'pockets' of wool, toil weekly past. **1921** Guthrie-Smith *Tutira* (1926) 116 [Caption] *Packing wool pockets.* **1940** Studholme *Te Waimate* (1954) 183 For the first part of the journey over the hills it [*sc.* the wool] was carried by pack horses—sixty-two of them—each taking about 150 lb. in what were called 'pockets'—long shaped packs slung one on each side of the saddle. **1952** Newton *High Country Journey* 78 The wool is baled out at the shed..and the 'pockets', which weigh from 70 to 90 lb. each, are packed out to the homestead by horses. **1981** Anderson *Both Sides of River* 50 The wool clip of twenty-one bales was packed out in 'pockets'. These were small bales which held about thirty-one kilograms of wool.

poddly. SPOTTY 1.

1872 Hutton & Hector *Fishes of NZ* 108 [The Pohuiakaroa] is the proper *Sea Perch* of these waters, that name having been by mistake applied in the Catalogue to a small Wrasse..[*Labrichthys celidota*]), which is generally called the Spotty or Poddly.

poddy. Also **poddie.** [Spec. use of Brit. dial *poddy* corpulent: AND 1872.] **a.** A hand-fed calf (also as **poddy-calf**), or lamb.

1906 *Truth* 13 Oct. 7 One day he got a telegram from his dear, forgiving old dad to come home and eat of the fatted poddie calf. **1922** Perry *Sheep Farming* 94 Any undue disturbance of the [Merino] ewes at this time will result in much mis-mothering of lambs, many of which will subsequently die or survive as 'poddies' and 'weeds'. **1968** *NZ Contemp. Dict. Suppl.* (Collins) 15 *poddy, poddy-calf n.* hand-fed calf.

b. Any young calf.

1907 Lancaster *Tracks We Tread* 52 [The wild cattle] were a mixed haul: two-year-olds, poddies and pikers.

poe, var. POI.

poe. *Obs.* Also **poe-bird** (and with much variety of form **poey-, pohe-, poi-, poy-** representing probable anglicized pronunciations /ˈpʌui/, /poi/). [f. Polynesian *poe* (/poe/) pearl, used in reference to the tuft of white feathers at the tui's throat.] A name for TUI q.v. used by Cook's company and some other early visitors.

[**1840** in Wilkes *US Exploring Exped.* (1852) I. 317 [The tui's] note [is] rather louder than that of the bird called by the Samoans 'poe'.] **1773** Wales *Journal* in Cook *Journals* (1961) II. 786 Another..was by the Gentlemen in the Endeavour's Voyage, called the poy-Bird... Under its Throat hang two little tufts of curled, snow-white feathers called its *poy*, which is an Otahitean word for Ear-rings. **1773** Forster *Resolution Jrnl.* 11 Apr. (1982) II. 253 The great noise caused by the Cascade is now & then conquered..by the graver pipe of wattle birds, Pohebirds..& Mocking-birds. **1773** Bayly *Journal* 12 Apr. in McNab *Hist. Records* (1914) II. 206 There are great plenty of a kind of birds much resembling our black birds... These are called Poey-birds. They are thought to be the finest eating for delicacy & richness. **1791** Menzies *Journal* 21 Nov. in McNab *Hist. Records* (1914) II. 492 I..shot about a dozen & half of the Poe birds. **1817** Nicholas *Voyage NZ* II. 254 The poe, with its pendents tufts of white feathers. **1830** Craik *New Zealanders* 187 Another..is called by the English the poe, or poi bird, from a little tuft of white curled feathers which it has under its throat, and which seemed to them to resemble certain white flowers worn as ornaments by the people of Otaheite, and known there by a similar name. **1842** Gray *Fauna* in Dieffenbach *Travels in NZ* (1843) II. 187 Poe, or Toi of the natives of Queen Charlotte's Sound... Toni... Tui. **1884** *NZJSc.* II. 276 Parson-bird, Poe-bird, Tui, Koko. Often builds under the shelter of *Rubus* twines, which many of us have learnt to fear or respect as bush-lawyer. **1898** Morris *Austral-English* 363 *Poë, n.* same as *Tui..*and *Parson-bird...* The name, which was not the Maori name, did not endure.

poeanamy, poenammoo, poenamu, varr. POUNAMU.

po-e-tere, var. POWHAITERE.

poey-, var. POE-.

pog. *Tramping.* An alteration of *porr*(idge.) Porridge.

1945–46 p.c. D. Close (May 1951): used by Auckland Tramping Club members. *Pog* a name for porridge. **1988** Pickering *Hills* 8 So to cope with the rituals of tramping, its pains and camaraderie, a slang language has developed to suit. Lots of quick short words... 'pog' (porridge), 'bastard grass' and 'lawyer'. **1990** *Dominion Sunday Times* (Wellington) 4 Mar. 19 Down a steep hill to Long Beach, a winding road, the Pioneer Pog 'N' Scroggin Bush Band can cope, they know the rules.

poha. [Ma. /ˈpo:ha:/: Williams 286 *Pōha... 1.*] A receptacle made of kelp or totara bark to hold preserved muttonbirds. See also *bull-kelp bag* (BULL-KELP 2), *kelp bag* (KELP 2), *rimu bag* (RIMU *n.*² 1 b).

1844 in Shortland *S. Dist. NZ* 18 Jan. (1851) 224 The cargo with which they had been freighted, consisting chiefly of 'poha-titi' or casks of preserved mutton birds. Many of these were from five to six feet high, and ornamented with feathers... The 'poha,' which I have called a cask—as it performs the office of one—is constructed by the natives in an ingenious manner, worthy of description. A kelp bag—the air bladder of a fucus—is easily found of the size required, made by nature. In this the young 'titi' are packed, after being cooked, and the oil which has escaped in the cooking is poured on them. Over the exterior of the bag is then laid the bark of the 'totara' tree. **1847** Brunner *Exped. Middle Is.* in Taylor *Early Travellers* (1959) 285 There is great taste shown by the natives in the *poha*, or bag of preserved wekas; and I believe it is always made for a present, for which they expect a return. **1851** Shortland *S. Dist. NZ* 312 Poha, a sort of cask shaped like a sugar loaf, constructed from the air bladder of a species of sea-weed, strengthened outside by layers of the bark of the 'totara', and kept firmly together by means of stakes tied with flax. **c1920** Beattie *Trad. Lifeways Southern Maori* (1994) 177 The poha was blown up by means of a pupuhi-rimu, a hollow tube which was inserted into the orifice. **1952** *Diary* 20 Apr. in Sansom *In Grip of an Island* (1982) 153 Out on line by door bull-kelp bags blown up and drying. Under the table finished pohas stacked. Birds in kelp bags with totara bark wrapping, looking fine in their new flax baskets.

pohe, var. POE.

pohowera. Also early **ha-poho-wera** (=?he poho-wera). [Ma. /ˈpohowera/: Williams 287 *Pohowera..*banded dotterel.] DOTTEREL 2 (1). Cf. TUTURIWHATU.

1842 Gray *Fauna* in Dieffenbach *Travels in NZ* (1843) II. 195 *Charadrius obscurus...* Ha-poho-wera

POHUA

of the natives of Dusky Bay. **1871** [see DOTTEREL 1]. **1888** [see TUTURIWHATU]. **1904** [see DOTTEREL 2 (1)]. **1952** RICHARDS *Chatham Is.* 80 Below white with a band of black on the chest and another of chestnut on the upper abdomen. Banded Dotterel. Pohowera. **1966**, **1985** [see DOTTEREL 2 (1)].

pohua, var. POHUE.

pohue. The spelling **pohuehue** has equal standing. Also early **pohua**. [Ma. /ˈpo:hue/ /po:ˈhuehue/: Williams 287 *Pōhue..,pōhuehue*..A name given to several trailing or climbing plants.] Any of various native and introduced climbing plants. **a.** *Calystegia* spp., esp. *C. sepium*. CONVOLVULUS; also BINDWEED 1 a.
 1843 TAYLOR *Journal 1842–43* (ATLTS) Aug. 50 [Word list] Pohua the convolvulus. **1853** HOOKER *II Flora Novae-Zelandiae I Flowering Plants* 183 Calystegia *sepium*... Nat. name, 'Panake and Pohue'... This beautiful plant, the English 'Bind-weed', is as common in the Southern Hemisphere as it is in the Northern. **1867** HOOKER *Handbook* 767 Pohue, *Col[enso]. Convolvulus sepium*. **1882** POTTS *Out in Open* 17 Amongst the edibles was a preparation of the roots of the pohua (*Convolvulus sepium*), the favourite food of the pheasant. **1906** CHEESEMAN *Manual NZ Flora* 476 [*Calystegia sepium*..] *Pohue*..Bindweed... Widely dispersed in most temperate countries and everywhere highly variable. **1926** HILGENDORF *Weeds* 137 Greater Convolvulus (*Calystegia sepium*) has the same popular names as the last species, [i.e. convolvulus] and in addition, beautiful white devil, and its native name of pohue. **1946** *JPS* LV. 156 *pōhue*, a vine (Calystegia Soldanella), sand-bine: C. sepium is paraha. **1966** [see CONVOLVULUS].

b. *Muehlenbeckia* spp. (fam. Polygonaceae), a stout forest or coastal climbing plant. See also MUEHLENBECKIA, *wirebush, wire vine* (WIRE 1).
 1867 HOOKER *Handbook* 767 Pohuehue, *Col[enso]*. *Polygonum complexum*. **1952** RICHARDS *Chatham Is.* 51 *Muehlenbeckia..australis*... Maori Vine. Po-hue-hue (creeper). **1969** *Standard Common Names Weeds* 60 *pohuehue* [=] *large-leaved muehlenbeckia*: *wire vine*. Ibid. 70 *small-leaved pohuehue* [=] *wire vine*. **1976** *Hist. & Nat. Hist. Boulder Bank* 21 On the inner side..of the bank there are prostrate shrubs of pohuehue [*Muehlenbeckia complexa*], [and] some bachelor's button. **1989** PARKINSON *Travelling Naturalist* 73 This coast gets the full blast of Wellington's famous winds, resulting in..ground-hugging plants..as pohue, mikimiki and tauhinu. **1995** CROWE *Which Coastal Plant?* 13 *Pōhuehue* Wire Vine *Muehlenbeckia complexa*... The drought-resistant wire vine gets established on sand dunes once the dunes are sufficiently stabilised by other plants.

pohuiakaroa. [Ma. /ˈpohuiakaroa/: Williams 287 *Pohuiakaroa..Helicolenus percoides*.] *sea perch* (PERCH *n.* 2 (4) *Helicolenus percoides*).
 1872 HUTTON & HECTOR *Fishes of NZ* 108 The Pohuiakaroa..deserves mention... It is the proper *Sea Perch* of these waters. **1886** SHERRIN *Handbook Fishes NZ* 88 Sea Perch (*Sebastes percoides*)... 'The pohuiakaroa'. **1898** MORRIS *Austral-English* 384 *Red Gurnet-Perch*.. name given in Victoria to the fish *Sebastes percoides*..family *Scorpaenidae*. It is also called..in New Zealand, *Pohui[a]karoa*. **1921** *NZJST* IV. 121 Helicolenus percoides... *Sea-perch*; *Pohuiakaroa*. Secured in rocky localities among blue cod. **1956** GRAHAM *Treasury NZ Fishes* 344 Seaperch (Pohuiakaroa). **1988** FRANCIS *Coastal Fishes NZ* 23 Sea Perch (Pohuiakaroa) *Helicolenus percoides*. **1991** BRADSTOCK *Fishing* 21 *Sea perch*. Other names: scarpee, Jock Stewart, highlander, flinger, pohuiakaroa, *Helicolenus percoides*.

pohute, pohuterkaura, pohutokaua, pohutukaua, varr. POHUTUKAWA.

pohutukawa. Also with much variety of early form as **pahutukawa, pohuterkaura, pohutokaua, pohutukaua, pootacow, potikákawa, pou te cowa, póutu kaua, powa takawa.** [Ma. /ˈpo:hutukawa/: Williams 288 *Pōhutukawa, pohutukawa*.. *1. Metrosideros excelsa*.]

1. Also *ellipt.* **pohute** (see quot. 1963), *Metrosideros excelsa* (formerly *M. tomentosa*) (fam. Myrtaceae), a NI coastal native evergreen tree with bright red blossom appearing near the end of December. See also CHRISTMAS TREE 1, *fire-tree* (FIRE 3).
 [**1820** LEE & KENDALL *NZ Gram. & Vocab.* 195 Póutu kaua, *s.* A tree so called.] **1833** WILLIAMS *Early Jrnls.* 24 Feb. (1961) 285 After breakfast assembled..under the shadow of the wide spreading *Pohutukaua*, and held service. **1834** McDONNELL *Extracts Jrnl.* (1979) 34 The *Courie Croeka* and *Pou te Cowa*, I think, are the finest trees in the Island..and the [latter] for the splendour of its flower, which grows in such thick clusters and is of so rich a color, that looking at it from a short distance, one would imagine a sumptuous scarlet pall had been thrown over the top of the tree. **1838** POLACK *NZ* II. 392 The *Pohutokaua or Potikákawa*..is of the same genus as the preceding [Rata]. **1840** *NZ Jrnl.* I. 139 The Pohuterkaura is a heavy and exceedingly dark wood, capable of receiving a very fine polish, and strongly resembling rosewood. **1842** TAYLOR *Journal 1842–43* (ATLTS) 17 Oct. 4 Encamping close by the sea by a beautiful amphitheatre of powa takawa trees. **1844** COLENSO *Excurs. Northern Is.* in Taylor *Early Travellers* (1959) 7 The Pohutukawa..here forms a thick and evergreen rampart between the sea beach and the main land. **1855** GREY *Polynesian Mythol.* 142 As they drew near to land, they saw..some pohutukawa trees of the sea-coast, covered with beautiful red flowers. **1882** POTTS *Out in Open* 32 Kauri..pohutukawa, kowhai, rata, and a host of other timber, possessing qualities of known value for building or general purposes. **1908** BAUGHAN *Shingle-Short* 54 *Kauri* and *Totara, Rimu*, and *Matai* and *Maire*..and bright-as-blood *Pohutukawa, Manuka*. **1911** *Truth* 10 June 6 Edith and Harry Hodges..have been married 13 years, and there was a time when..the crimson blossom of the pohutukawa symbolised the affection that subsisted between them. **1920** MANSFIELD *Stories* (1984) 194 All the poor little pahutukawas [*sic*] on the esplanade are bent to the ground. **1943** MARSH *Colour Scheme* 71 'You'd been to Pohutukawa Bay?'.. 'My God, why shouldn't I go to see the pootacows?' **1959** SINCLAIR *Hist. NZ* 22 There it climbed down the roots of an ancient *pohutukawa*, a tree which in the summer is covered with fine, blood-red flowers. **1990** *Landfall* 174 207 among the dream polaroids jacaranda diamante simulacra of before and after the visceral rub of pohutukawa in bloom [*sic*]

2. With a modifier: **inland, Kermadec (Kermadec Island)**.

(1) **inland pohutukawa.** *Metrosideros excelsa* (formerly *tomentosa*) and *M. robusta*.
 1870 *TrNZI* II. 93 *M. tomentosa*... In woods near the sea it attains its greatest height, and is of comparatively close and erect growth; known to bushmen as 'Inland Pohutukawa'. **1872** Ibid. IV. 269 In some localities [the non-epiphytic rata, *M. robusta*] are frequent enough to attract the special attention of the bushman, who calls this form the 'inland pohutukawa', a designation he also bestows upon symmetrical specimens of true pohutukawa sometimes found in the forest.

(2) **Kermadec (Kermadec Island) pohutukawa.** *Metrosideros kermadecensis*, a small tree widely cultivated in New Zealand, native to Raoul and Kermadec Is., similar to the mainland pohutukawa, but with smaller leaves and a tendency to flower throughout the year.
 1965 GILLHAM *Naturalist NZ* 173 From then on I took only flowers..the massed crimson of the Kermadec Island pohutukawa which, unlike the true New Zealand 'Christmas tree' flowers from August to November. **1986** *NZ Herald* (Auckland) 7 Nov. 6 One said that there was nothing unusual in a pohutukawa blooming at any time of the year if it was a Kermadec pohutukawa.

3. In *attrib.* use as special Comb. **pohutukawa honey**, honey obtained predominantly from the nectar of pohutukawa flowers in bloom over the Christmas period.
 1991 *NZ Geographic* Jan.–Mar. 113 Pohutukawa honey from Barrier was so sought after, claims Les, that it found its way to King George V's table.

poi. Also early **poe**. [Ma. /ˈpoi/: Williams 288 *Poi. 1*...Ball, lump...*2*. a light ball with a short string attached to it: PPN. **po(e,i)* 'rounded, ma[d]e into a ball' Walsh & Biggs 88.]

1. a. Also **poi-ball**. A light ball on a long or a short string (**long poi, short poi**), swung and twirled to a rhythmic beat in Maori songs and dances.
 1817 NICHOLAS *NZ* I. 318 They made Mr. Marsden a present of a ball called a *poe*, with which the ladies amuse themselves by throwing it repeatedly backward and forward; it is..made of their cloth or canvas, stuffed with the down of the bull-rush, having a long string appended to it. [**1820** LEE & KENDALL *Gram. & Vocab.* 194 Pói, *s.* A round ball with which children play.] **1835** YATE *NZ* (1970) 113 Climbing, swimming, wrestling, flying kites, and tossing the *poi*, a ball about the size of a good cricket-ball, are most of the games of native origin. **1843** DIEFFENBACH *Travels in NZ* II. 57 Another game is with one ball (poi) suspended from a string. **1927** DONNE *Maori Past & Present* 130 The *Poi* is for girls or women; they stand in line, the performers holding in each hand a string of twisted, dressed flax about nine inches in length, to which is attached a ball of the size of a tennis ball made of dry leaves of the bullrush plant (*raupo*) and termed '*poi*'. **1935** GUTHRIE *Little Country* (1937) 147 The poi women began their dance to slow chanting..the tiny pois danced against arms and shoulders and breasts. **1949** BUCK *Coming of Maori* (1950) II. ix 243 The women's *poi* dance..used an accessory in the form of the *poi* ball... The *poi* balls in common use in modern times are made of dry bullrush leaves (*raupo*), about the size of an orange but slightly elongated, and with a short string... The movements with the long *poi* were slower than with the modern short *poi*. The string of the *poi* was held in the right while various movements were made over the shoulder, to the sides, the thighs, the knees, the head, the *poi* balls being kept twirling in perfect time to the songs sung by the leaders. **1960** HILLIARD *Maori Girl* 201 Whirling poi was easy, but flipping it so that it slapped first on the top of the wrist, then underneath, was the hard part. **1973** FINLAYSON *Brown Man's Burden* 141 poi: a ball of flax swinging on a flax thong, swung in unison by girl performers.

b. An informal game. See also quots. 1817, 1820, 1835 in 1 above.
 1883 DOMETT *Ranolf & Amohia* I. 156 Amid her damsels, scarlet-crowned With *kowhai*-flowers, a lively ring Playing at '*poi*' sent flying round The ornamented ball o'erwound.

c. Any of various poi dances or songs (see 2 b below) performed using a poi-ball on a long string (**long poi**), a short string (**short poi**), two poi-balls each on its own string (**double poi**), or performed seated in a row, as in a canoe (**canoe poi**).

1900 *Canterbury Old & New* 155 Among other dances was the *poi*, danced by Maori maidens, who..manipulated a couple of balls,... one in each hand. **1936** HYDE *Passport to Hell* 141 The Maori girls sing them, weaving lithe arms and bodies in the canoe *pois*, the graceful dance of the womenfolk. **1960** HILLIARD *Maori Girl* 32 Mum taught them the short, long and double poi. [**1960** *Note*] *poi*—dance performed to music with a light ball attached to a string. **1969** MASON *Awatea* (1978) 24 Miri. Oh yes! I'm going to do the long poi! **1986** *Dominion* (Wellington) 16 July 13 After a stirring poi performed by Putiki Maori Club, Prince Edward said he was delighted to be back in New Zealand.

2. a. In *attrib.* use.

1905 BAUCKE *White Man Treads* 89 Now, also, are sedulously practised, haka and poi swinging; but these do not irk; oh, dear, no! **1915** WILLIAMS *New Zealander's Diary* (c1922) 12 Mar. 30 [The Maoris] sang grandly, especially a very fine poi song. **1943** FINLAYSON *Brown Man's Burden* (1973) 88 The rhythm of their dancing and the beauty of their poi girls. **1958** ASHTON-WARNER *Spinster* 47 The Maori love-songs..and the poi tunes and melodies they use in canoes.

b. Special Comb. **poi-ball**, see 1 a above; **poi dance**, any of various dances or songs accompanied by the rhythmic manipulation of poi; **poi dancer**, one who performs poi dances.

1869 *TrNZI* I. (rev. edn.) 367 The old men often amused themselves with..encouraging the younger ones..in playing with the **poi-ball**. **1920** BOLITHO *With the Prince in NZ* 42 The wahines (women)..held their poi balls ready for a word of command. **1936** 28 Mar. in *Na To Hoa Aroha* (1988) III. 212 The arts and crafts section comprised tukutuku..taniko work and making poi balls. **1905** BAUCKE *White Man Treads* 91 Be sure that when a **poi dance** is suggested, and while the maidens are displaying their most captivating attitudes, one of them..glides outside [to a tryst]. **1920** BOLITHO *With the Prince in NZ* 38 The warriors withdrew, and their place was taken by a hundred poi girls, who performed a canoe poi dance in front of the meeting house. **1939** GRIEVE *Sketches from Maoriland* (1961) 18 He contorted his pseudo-tattooed features and performed frenzied *hakas*, or lent his voice to the haunting rhythm of the *poi*-dances. **1946** *JPS* LV. 156 *poi*, a light ball made from raupo blades, with a short string attached to it which is swung and twisted rhythmically, in the manner of Indian clubs, to the accompaniment of a song; the so-called poi-dance, which is less a dance than a whirling of the balls and a swaying of the body in time with the song. **1950** *Landfall 16* 310 Doing poi dances on the stage in front of lots of people! **1913** *Auckland Univ. College Students Carnival Programme* 27 Interpreters (1st, 2nd and 3rd grade), Poets Laureate, **Poi Dancers**, Guides, &c.

poi, var. POE.

point, *n.*¹ Usu. *pl.* [AND 1871.] The hock of a sheep; the wool on (or from) the hocks forming the main extremities of the fleece.

1875 *Otago Witness* (Dunedin) 18 Sept. 18 First, clean all the points, the crutch and the belly wool, and let this be swept aside. **1922** PERRY *Sheep Farming* 44 The wool should be lustrous, soft to the touch, free from kemp, with a blocky tip, and well spread on the back, belly, and points. **1938** BURDON *High Country* 84 The sheep they shore..carried less wool on the points than they do now, so that fewer short blows were required to take off the trimmings. **1948** ACLAND *Early Canterbury Runs* (1951) 379 *Fribby*..the yolky locks round the points taken off by the..roller from a decently skirted fleece. **1955** BOWEN *Wool Away* 132 The Corriedale..grows more wool than hair on the hocks... These points or socks do not have a tendency to lift or rise off the skin.

point, *n.*² *Obs.* [AND 1889.] One hundredth of an inch of rainfall as measured in a standard receptacle.

1908 in *Atea, Nireaha, Putara 1887–1987* (1987) 32 1908 27 January: Only seventeen points of rain have fallen for the month. **1923** 26 Mar. in Henderson *Exiles Asbestos Cottage* (1981) 135 So began the rainfall record from Asbestos Cottage, from 26 March 1923 (52 points), recording daily at 9 am unfailingly for twenty-eight and a half years. **1964** DEANS *Pioneers* 171 Four months had over six inches of rain, February being highest with 12.34 points, which produced a major flood... An extraordinary rainfall was experienced on January 21st, 1936, when 75 points of rain fell in 15 minutes.

point, *v.*¹ *Obs.* [f. the phr. *to score points* to gain an advantage: AND 1853.] *intr.* To impose upon dishonestly or dishonourably, to take an unfair advantage of a person.

1910 *Truth* 29 Oct. 2 A certain section of bookmakers make a practice of 'pointing' during the progress of a race by roaring out a short price about a horse they say is in front is another prad altogether, and in luring the public to invest on it they are doing nothing short of obtaining money under false pretences. **1934** *Press* (Christchurch) (Acland Gloss.) 27 Jan. 15 *Point*.—Loaf on (your mates); let them do the hardest of the work. **1941** BAKER *NZ Slang* 62 *To point*, to impose upon.

Hence **pointer**, a sharper or trickster.

1935 STRONG in Partridge *Slang Today* 288 I believe he is a bit of a pointer because he asked me what billet I was coming to and I wouldn't be surprised if he came along any minute. **1943** HISLOP *Pure Gold* 22 I suppose at that time [c 1860s goldrush] I would be more interested in grabbing my 'dumps' out of the ring at school, when some quick eye had noticed that a young pointer had tried to get away with placing a stinkie or a chalkie into play with the rest of his marbles.

point, *v.*² [Spec. use of *point the finger at* to accuse.] In the phr. **to point the finger**, to testify for the Crown.

1982 NEWBOLD *Big Huey* 252 Point the finger. Testify for the Crown.

pointer: see POINT *v.*¹; SHARK 2 (4) and 2 (20).

pointer, *n.*¹ [Transf. use of *pointers, pl.* the two bright stars in the Great Bear: AND 1864.] Usu. init. cap. Either of the two stars *Alpha* or *Beta Centauri*, a line drawn through both of which indicates the head of the Southern Cross constellation.

1897 *TrNZI* XXIX. 146 Here in our southern skies we have..Crux Australis..and Centaurus, with the two neighbouring first-class stars in the legs of the Centaur, commonly called the 'Pointers'... The constellation Crux Australis, or the Southern Cross..forming with the two 'Pointers' such a glorious sight on a starlight night, has ever been an object of universal attraction. **1926** GREY *Angler's Eldorado* 38 When I looked out of my tent window I could see the Southern Cross and the Pointers that pointed to it. **1936** in Lee *Politician* (1987) 71 The Southern Cross and the Pointers are clear in the sky.

pointer, *n.*² *Hist.* Usu. *pl.* [AND 1872.] Either of the 'point bullocks', the pair of bullocks next ahead of the polers in a bullock team.

[**c1914**] MCCARROLL *Days of Kauri Bushmen* (1951) (Radio Talk 3: TS) Usually the third pair of bullocks from the back were called the 'point' bullocks or pointers... strongest in the team..to pull hard in chain when rounding corners. **c1930** *Whitcombe's Etym. Dict. Aust.-NZ Suppl.* 9 *pointers n. pl.* in a bullock team, the pair ahead of the pole pair.

poison, *v.* [Spec. use of *poison* to kill with poison.] *intr.* or *absol.* To kill rabbits (or possums) with poisoned baits.

1897 WRIGHT *Station Ballads* 38 I went poisoning out at the back.

Hence **poisoning** *vbl. n.*, the killing of rabbits with poisoned baits.

1905 ACTON-ADAMS 6 May in McCaskill *Molesworth* (1969) 92 He has failed to do the Rainbow poisoning, he has failed to keep the boundary fences up.

poison, *n.*

1. *Rabbiting.* Special Comb. **poison line**, a line of poisoned baits laid out to kill rabbits.

1946 MILLER *There Was Gold* 129 Rabbiters guard their rights with a jealous eye, and indeed a man moving over a block with a gun can upset all the work on a poison line.

2. *transf.* A term in marble-playing.

1966 TURNER *Eng. Lang. Austral. & NZ* 159 Marble games, with terminology far too extensive to go into, included *follies*, the simplest, or *holes*, in which one had to roll a marble into the last of a series of holes, called *poison*, before attacking an opponent's taw.

poisoner. *Rural.*

1. A person employed to poison rabbits.

1899 AYTON *Diary* 15 Oct. (1982) 9 5 poisoners called made them Tea for lunch told them about Skins. **1933** *Press* (Christchurch) (Acland Gloss.) 18 Nov. 15 *Poisoner*.—(1) Man employed to poison rabbits... (2) Slang name for a cook.

2. *transf.* [AND 1905.] A nickname for a camp (esp. shearers') cook.

1933 [see 1 above]. **1953** REED *Story of Kauri* 122 The cook was rather an old man, quite a 'poisoner'. *Ibid.* 137 Inferior cooks were known by such uncomplimentary names as 'The Snake', 'Death Adder' and 'Poisoner'.

3. *fig.* See quot.

1934 *Press* (Christchurch) (Acland Gloss.) 27 Jan. 15 *Poisoner* (3).—Mischief maker among the men.

pokaka. Also **bokaka, bokako, pokako**. [Ma. /ˈpoːkaːkaː/: Williams 289 *Pōkākā*... 5. *Elaeocarpus* [spp.].] *Elaeocarpus hookerianus* (fam. Elaeocarpaceae), a small forest tree with distinctly different juvenile and adult forms; less commonly, *E. dentatus*, HINAU.

1844 MONRO *Notes of a Journey* in Hocken *Contributions* (1898) 249 The native name of it is pokaka, and with the bark of it a black dye is made, which is equal to the dye of the hinau. **1844** BARNICOAT *Journal* (ATLTS) 1 June 178 [In Otago] I sketched a tree called Pokaka from the bark of which the natives procure a beautiful black d[y]e like that of *hinow*. **1851** *Lyttelton Times* 28 June 6 The timber in [the groves] is chiefly Kaikatea, (white pine)..Pokaka, Kowai, and Totara. **1867** HOOKER *Handbook* 764 Bokako.— *Elaeocarpus Hookerianus*. *Ibid.* 767 Pokaka.— *Elaeocarpus dentatus* and *Hookerianus*. **1869** *TrNZI* I.

POKAKO

(rev. edn.) 195 Pokako (*Elaeocarpus Hookerianus*). A large round-headed tree, near Dunedin; common also on the west coast. **1878** McINDOE *Sketch Otago* 29 Timbers most in demand are..red pine..bokaka (Eleocarpus dentatus). **1889** FEATON *Art Album NZ Flora* 65 Eloeocarpus hookerianus... The 'Pokako'.— This species is indigenous to the hilly portions of the Northern, and common in the Middle Island... Its native name is 'Pokako', or 'Mahi-mahi', but it is very commonly called 'Hinau' by the settlers. **1890** *PWD Catalogue Timbers* (NZ & South Seas Exhib.) 13 Pokaka..Elaeocarpus Hookerianus..Timber white and tough. **1922** [see HINAHINA]. **1940** LAING & BLACKWELL *Plants NZ* 261 *Elaeocarpus Hookerianus* (*The Pokaka*). A smaller species, called Pokaka by the Maoris. The flowers do not open out so widely as those of the Hinau. **1953** DEWAR *Chaslands* 82 At the season when bokakas dropped their berries the wild pigs made a migration from tree to tree. **1982** WILSON *Stewart Is. Plants* 72 *Elaeocarpus hookerianus* Pōkākā... Tree with very pale, corky bark.

pokako, var. POKAKA, PUKEKO.

poke.

1. *Obs.* [A survival of obs. or arch. Brit. *poke* pocket: see OED *n.*¹ 1 c.] A pocket.
1866 BURGESS *Confessions* (1983) 117 Kelly observed after he had passed, 'Did you take notice what a poke he had?'—meaning thereby the bulk of his pocket.

2. a. Mainly *SI.* [f. Brit. dial. *poke* a bag: see OED *n.*¹ 1 a.] A bag or twisted paper spill (for sweets).
c1920 p.c. 1951 Les Souness: heard in Southland and Dunedin. A twisted paper spill for lollies with top folded over. **1934** LEE *Children of Poor* (1949) 131 'Hullo, Milly.' 'Hullo.' 'Have a lollie?' he had a poke of sweets. Milly had one. **1970** SANSOM *Stewart Islanders* 153 We were not encouraged to buy lollies [on Stewart Island c1901] if we had a penny, although it was tempting when other children seemed to have pokes of lollies so often. (A 'poke' was a cone-shaped twist of newspaper.) **1982** HARWOOD *Heritage Trail* 58 A penny could [in early 20C.] buy a full 'paper poke'— that popular lolly bag made of a triangle of paper. **1983** MANTELL *Murder to Burn* 13 Even when a poke of amphetamines was found hidden behind the switchboard, he blandly claimed it must have been there when he took over the bach. **1988** SOMERSET *Sunshine & Shadow* 7 Inside [the general store c1900] were treasures of all kinds..chocolate buttons in poke bags, and..the wonderful penny classics we loved.

b. The contents of a poke.
1980 NEAVE *Land of Munros* 51 Our Annual Meetings were held in the hall... Then there was supper. There was always a number of children who were usually given a 'Poke'—a sandwich, a bun, a piece of cake, and an apple, and a mug of tea.

Hence **pokeful** [cf. EDD, Scot. and northern Eng. dial.].
1934 LEE *Children of Poor* 67 I would sneak pokefuls of brown sugar.

poke borak, borax: see BORAK, BORAX.

poked, *ppl. a.* [Prob. a euphemism for 'fucked': cf. *poke v. trans.* to have sexual intercourse with.] Exhausted.
1978 O'SULLIVAN *The Boy, The Bridge, The River* 115 He had told the boys he'd be out at the lake by nine, it was no good getting up on the skis if you felt poked.

Pokeey, var. PAKEHA.

pokeka. *Hist.* Also early SI **bogek**. [Ma. /ˈpoːkeka/: Williams 289 *Pōkeka* (i)..A rough cape of undressed flax leaves, sometimes made of the inferior *Phormium cookianum*.] A coarse rain cape formerly used by the Maori.
1868 LINDSAY *Contribs. NZ Bot.* 78 The principal sorts of cloak or mantle at present made by the Maoris from their native flax are..The 'Korowai'..The 'Kaitaka'..and..The 'Pokeka,' or rain cloak. **1939** BEATTIE *First White Boy Born Otago* 12 In those old days [the 1840s; Maori weavers] were very skilful at making 'bogek' (pokeka in standard, or northern, Maori—it means raincloaks). They seemed to pleat the flax in layers, and all round they left little tails in rows hanging over each layer. **1940** *Tales Pioneer Women* (1988) 252 The high class women..stayed at home and made mats..pokeka, rain mats from dried flax.

pokekha, pokeko, varr. PUKEKO.

pokokatea, erron. var. POPOKOTEA.

polach, var. POLLOCK.

polar, erron. var. POLER.

pole /pʌul/, *v.*

1. Also **poll**. *trans.* and *intr.* To steal (something).
1908 *Truth* 12 Sept. 1 T'other day in a Lambton Quay pub, he, with some friends, was drinking, and the pimp thought he saw the barman 'poleing', and reported him to the boss, who subsequently sacked the bartender, who informs 'Truth' that he did not thieve. **1910** *Ibid.* 12 Mar. 7 What does 'polled' mean? That's a new word to me?.. It means 'shook' them; stole them, you know. **1938** *Press* (Christchurch) (McNab Slang) 2 Apr. 18 [In local criminal slang] 'to clout,' 'to pole,' 'to fend off' are to steal. **1964** LEE *Shiner Slattery* 140 Did you ever hear of a man called Arthur Beaumont who poled three hundred thousand pounds?

Hence **poled** *ppl. a.*, stolen.
1937 PARTRIDGE *Dict. Slang* 645 *poled. ppl. adj.* Stolen: New Zealanders': C. 20. **1941** BAKER *NZ Slang* 53 [Underworld slang includes] *poled* for stolen.

2. As **pole on** [AND 1906], to impose on, sponge on; to take an advantage of (someone).
1910 *Truth* 14 May 5 Many times during its career 'Truth' has had to use the scalpel on the hidebound quacks who wax fat and wealthy by poling on the credulity of the people.

Hence **poler**, one who imposes or sponges on another.
1968 *NZ Contemporary Dict.* 16 *Poler n.* any one who sponges on his mates.

pole, *n.* [Spec. uses of *pole* denoting a wooden construction material.] Special Comb. **pole chimney**, a chimney built of green poles cut from the bush; **pole house**, a house supported on poles built out over a slope.
1960 CRUMP *Good Keen Man* 16 Next day I built a pole chimney round the fireplace and lined it with flat stones from beside the river. **1992** MAHY *Underrunners* 16 It was what was called a pole-house, built on a platform which hung out over the slope on great poles, driven deep into the rocks and stones of the peninsula.

pole bullock: see POLER 1.

poler.

1. Also erron. **polar**. [AND 1860.] Usu. *pl.* Often as **pole bullock**, one of a pair of draught bullocks working beside the pole of a dray or wagon.
1860 in Butler *First Year* (1863) vii 105 In the small river Ashburton..we had a little misunderstanding with the bullocks; the leaders..slewed sharply round, and tied themselves into an inextricable knot with the polars. **1863** CHUDLEIGH *Diary* 16 Dec. (1950) 114 He [sc. a new chum] was getting on the dray to ride just behind the off polar and of course got cicked. **1878** ELWELL *Boy Colonists* 234 The polers..are always the quietest. **1891** CHAMIER *Philosopher Dick* 9 He could [with a whip]..tickle the ear of the leader, or flip a fly from off the rump of a poler. **1900** *TrNZI* XXXII. 280 I had 3 generations of white bulls, all of whom learned this trick..when I used them in the bullock team as 'polers'. **1916** THORNTON *Wowser* 22 That blanked poler, Strawberry. **1933** *Press* (Christchurch) (Acland Gloss.) 18 Nov. 15 Polers, pole-bullocks.—The two bullocks which work on the *p[ole]* of a dray or waggon. **1938** BURDON *High Country* 47 The poler's yoke had a ring in the middle, fixed by means of two pins to the end of the pole. **1961** HENDERSON *Friends In Chains* (1961) 188 Polers: Last pair in bush team of bullocks two abreast. **1991** MACKAY *Working the Kauri* 38 Squat, powerful bullocks—the 'polers'—were at the back of the team to take most strain.

2. A coach-horse working next to the coach behind the leaders or other horses in the team.
1863 *Otago Colonist* 25 July in Lovell-Smith *Old Coaching Days* (1931) 35 On Monday last, at 6 o'clock, Cobb's coach..left Dunedin for Dunstan all right, but..one of the fore wheels collapsed... Upon [the driver's] arrival at the Union Hotel with his polers, he was rushed with enquiries. **1914** in *Hist. N. Otago from 1853* (1978) 169 The leaders reached the shore, and the polers had just got their footing when the coach turned over. **1968** SEDDON *The Seddons* 12 Each team comprised five horses—three leaders and two polers.

poley /ˈpʌuli/, *a.* and *n.* Also **poly**. [f. Brit. dial. *poley, polley* hornless, 'polled'.]

A. *adj.* Of a cattle-beast, having no horns, 'polled'.
1844 PARNELL *Farm Diary & Notebook* (ATLMS) Bought a poly cow. **1846** PHARAZYN *Journal* (ATLMS) 36 Yearling Poley heifer. **1848** WAKEFIELD *Handbook for NZ* 169 Some poley Devons, and a few long-horned Devon and Hereford working bullocks have also been received. **1869** *Auckland Punch* 140 Poley bullock. **1946** ACLAND *Early Canterbury Runs* 192 A new chum had a theory that if you turned your back on a beast..and looked at him through your legs he wouldn't charge, and how a noted poley bullock completely exploded his theory.

B. *n.* [AND 1843.] A hornless beast.
c1875 *Colonial Songster No.1* 100 I say, Mum, will you be so kind as to 'low me to damn that 'ere Poley. **1879** *Auckland Weekly News* 3 May 16 He swore that the beast killed by the prisoner belonged to him, and that it was a poley, about seven years old. **1884** COLENSO *In Memoriam* 65 By-the-bye the red poley was killed just after calving. **1900** HASELDEN *Winter's Night* 1 The cow had nothing wrong with her at all, but was a poley, and..many cattle were polies. **1940** STUDHOLME *Te Waimate* (1954) 135 In the nineties we tried breeding polled shorthorns from freaks which occurred at intervals amongst the horned beasts, but soon gave it up, for the poleys seemed to be deficient in the body.

poli, var. POLLIE.

policeman. *Obs.* A log or length of wood laid alongside a water-table to prevent over-running by wagon wheels.
1961 HENDERSON *Friends In Chains* 188 Policeman: Stout sapling fitted on roadside to safeguard watertable.

poll, var. POLE *v.*

pollie. Also **poli**. [f. *poli*(tician: cf. OED, orig. U.S.; AND 1967.] A politico, a politician.
  1989 *National Bus. Rev.* 18 Aug. W17 A local pollie was invited to launch the venture..but when he looked up 'politician' in the handsome tome..he had to be persuaded not to stalk off the platform. **1992** *Cuisine* (Auckland) June–July 101 The Polis' restaurant, Bellamy's, is further away than before and many MPs now eschew the place.

pollock. Also **polach**. [Cf. OED *pollock*.] Prob. a mis-identification by Polack of the Atlantic *pollock* or coal-fish with the New Zealand *blue cod* (COD 2 (3) *Parapercis colias*) then known as COAL-FISH q.v.
  1838 POLACK *NZ* I. 323 Many other fish are equally numerous, answering to our *hakes, tench, bream, snapper, haddock, elephant-fish, pollock*. **1840** POLACK *Manners & Customs* I. 202 Among the piscivorous tribes, are those well known in Europe under the appellations of snapper, tench, haddocks, pollock, salmon. **1842** GRAY *Fauna* in Dieffenbach *Travels in NZ* (1843) II. 222 Polack mentions 'cod-fish', bearing the native name of 'Wapuka,' but we do not know the fish he alludes to. The 'polach' he speaks of are, perhaps, the young of the *Percis colias*, the adult of which are known to the settlers as the 'cole-fish'.

Polly. Also **Poly**. [f. *Poly*(nesian.] A Polynesian. Also as an *adjective*.
  1989 *National Radio* Aug. [An Auckland school teacher speaks:] They can join our Poly Club. **1990** *Motoring Today* July 37 New Zealand's most popular thermal complex is probably Rotorua's *Polynesian Pools*..The Poly Pools, as they are affectionately known.

poly, var. POLEY, POLLY.

Pom. [Australian evidence records *pom, pommy* and *pomegranate* from the same date (AND 1912) suggesting that *pom* in Australian use was orig. an abbreviation of *pomegranate*, and only subsequently of *pommy*. NZ evidence confirms that the NZ use is a shortened form of POMMIE q.v.]

1. a. POMMIE A a.
  1946 SARGESON *That Summer* 92 He was a big matelot, though not a Pom, it was easy to tell he was a Pig Islander. **1972** MITCHELL *Pavlova Paradise* 183 *Pom*: Suspected Englishman. The confirmed case is referred to in the clinical term of Pongo. **1974** *Dominion* (Wellington) 9 Mar. 3 To talk of slogans like 'Punch a Pom a Day' is absurd. **1977** HALL *Glide Time* 48 Hugh. I'm not a Pom..I'm Welsh. Jim. Same bloody difference as far as I'm concerned. **1985** O'SULLIVAN *Shuriken* 23 Tiny: A Pom? Jacko: Yeah. A homey.

b. As **whingeing (wingeing) Pom** [AND 1962], a name for the stereotype of a complaining British immigrant dissatisfied with life in New Zealand.
  1985 SHERWOOD *Botanist at Bay* 18 A wingeing pom is a person from the United Kingdom who never ceases to complain in a loud whine about aspects of this country's arrangements which displease him. **1988** McGILL *Dict. Kiwi Slang* 122 *whingeing Pom* any British immigrant complaining about life here; a stereotype of the British immigrant.

2. a. Special Comb. **Pomland** *joc.*, Britain.
  1974 GIFFORD *Loosehead Len's Big Brown Book* 62 Home: The good lady wife's domain; may also be used to refer to Pomland. **1996** *Sunday Star-Times* (Auckland) 17 Mar. A2 I must confess to sometimes being puzzled by politicians in Pomland.

b. In composition **Pomerania** [a word-play on *Pom* with *pom*(eranian (dog), and a jocular use of the regional suffix -*ania*], Britain; hence **Pomeranian.**
  1963 GLOVER *Bedside Book* 147 I was trying to explain that this fellow came from England. 'You know—Angleterre, Pomerania, Kipperland.' **1988** McGILL *Dict. Kiwi Slang* 86 *Pomeranian* a Pom, fancifully extended by association with mythical Middle European country.

pomegranate. *Obs.* [The use, not directly recorded in writing from within NZ, is a word-play associating *pomegranate* (perh. /ˈpɒmiˌɡrænət/) with the rhyming series JIMMYGRANT (*immigrant*), *Pommy Grant* (Austral. /ˈpɒmiˌɡrænt/) or *pummy grant* (the last two recorded in Australia but not in NZ; thence to *ellipt*. or familiar forms POM, POMMIE: AND 1912.] A (British) immigrant to New Zealand.
  1916 [see POMMIE A a]. **1950** *Evening Post* (Wellington) 18 Nov. 8 There is no obscurity about the origin of 'Pommy'. The origin is the obvious one—'Emigrant'. The emigrants themselves corrupted this to 'Pomegranate'. From 1914 to 1925 I frequently heard and used 'pomegranate' to describe a new arrival. Over recent years this has become abbreviated to 'Pommy'. [**1964** *Dominion* (Wellington) 3 Sept. 4 Every now and then some one puts forward a new theory on why Englishmen are occasionally referred to in these southern latitudes as 'Pommies'. The following note from Mr. G.T.M., of the coastal motor vessel Squall, at Wellington, may clear things up: 'I first visited Aussie in 1911—Western Australia, Victoria, New South Wales, and Queensland. Immigrants were variously termed-Immygrant', 'Jimmy grants', and up among the bananalanders, quite often 'Pommy grants' (pomegranates). Very soon this became 'Pommy'; and this, I think, would be the true derivation.']

Pomgolia. [A word-play on POM + Mon)*golia*.] Britain. Cf. PONGOLIA.
  1976 GIFFORD *Loosehead Len's Bumper Thump Book* 14 Now it was true that the spudbashers [*sc.* the Irish rugby union team] had about as successful a season in Pomgolia as a bomb disposal man with hay fever. **1988** 5 Mar. TV1 Third Cricket Test England v. NZ [Crowd sign held up read:] Greetings to Outer Pomgolia.

Pommie, *n.* and *a.* Also **Pommy**. [f. *pome*(granate (see POMEGRANATE) an immigrant from Britain + -IE: AND 1912: erron. derivations include: *Prisoners of Mother England; Permit of Migration Ireland or England; Pommes* potatoes, eaten by British troops in WW1; *Pompey*, naval slang for Portsmouth.] Usu. init. cap.
  [*Note*] Homie, homey, most often a non-derogatory use, was the common New Zealand colloquial term for 'Briton' up to WW2. *Pommie*, often derogatory, was orig. an Australianism, and so regarded until it came into more frequent use in New Zealand during and after WW2.

A. *n.*

a. A British (esp. English) immigrant; thence, a resident of Britain. See also HOMEY, POMEGRANATE, PONGO A b.
  1916 ASH in *Anzac Book* (1916) 31 'Never met him, matey, but he is all right, you bet. A Pommy can't go wrong out there if he isn't too lazy to work.'..'Oh, well, yer see, mate, we don't call the like of 'im "Pommies" because we dislike 'em, but just as a matter of description.' [1916 *Note*] Pommy—short for pomegranate, and used as a nickname for immigrants. **c1926** THE MIXER *Transport Workers' Song Book* 69 He'll corner a bloke often that's 'shickered', Who looks like a 'pommie' or a 'yob'. **1929** DEVANNY *Riven* 158 Why don't you dump Janet and Laura and get a couple of Pommies? They'll do it [*sc.* housework] for much less money and work longer hours. **1938** SCANLAN *Guest of Life* 141 '[New Zealanders] like the English, provided they are the right type; the educated young man gets on well. They don't like the "Pommie" as they call him, God knows why, and no one can tell you where the name came from, but it's more common in Australia than in New Zealand'. 'What is a Pommie?' 'Blest if I know; it's hard to define, but usually the short, shrunken industrial worker, the man with the broad accent, from Yorkshire or Lancashire.' **1945** HENDERSON *Gunner Inglorious* 143 And even the poor old Pommies will find things tough in bashed-about over-crowded England. **1950** *Here & Now* Nov. 8 The average 'Pommie' can be forgiven if he is apt to harp on those things he has left 12,000 miles behind him. **1950** [see POMEGRANATE, PONGO]. **1959** DAVIN *No Remittance* 104 Being a pommy or a homey as they called it I was just as much a freak for the rest as I was for the Irish. **1965** MALLABY in Sinclair *Nash* (1976) 318 New Zealanders..never quite knew where they had Mr. Nash. Was he one of them or was he still, if you scratched below the surface, just another Pommy? Certainly he never exchanged his Worcestershire accent for the very individual New Zealand version of our language. **1986** OWEN & PERKINS *Speaking for Ourselves* 78 [The immigrants] were 'Homeys'—the word 'Pommy' wasn't in use then [during the early 1930s], and we called them 'Homeys'.

b. Special Comb. **pommie-bashing** *vbl. n.*, subjecting Britons to harsh, often unfair, criticism.
  1987 *National Bus. Rev.* 10 July 49 Apart from pommie-bashing, the commentators in the world cup matches spent an extraordinary amount of time telling viewers what they could easily see.

B. *adj.*

1. Usu. derog., British, esp. English; occas. as a soubriquet (see quot. 1968).
  1933 PRUDENCE CADEY *Broken Pattern* 130 'You should have heard the English accent.' 'Pommy gab, eh?' commented his mate. **1944** FULLARTON *Troop Target* 18 A Pommie ambulance. **1949** SARGESON *I Saw in My Dream* (1974) 110 Look at Wally's ma—get over her Pommy ways. **1968** *Dominion* (Wellington) 8 May 4 They met a boy they knew, Ricky Hatch, who was joined by another boy, 'Pommie' Paul. **1972** SARGESON *Man of England Now* 26 Well, Pommy pay in the army was just a joke to a New Zealander. **1975** DAVIN *Breathing Spaces* 124 We never really talked the same language anyhow. 'I don't know,' he said and his accent seemed to have gone a bit pommier than usual, or what he thought was pommy, only that was another thing that meeting a lot of pommies had made some of us wise to. **1987** GEE *Prowlers* 124 He made some comment about the trees—how ours were better than the pommie ones.

2. In special collocations: **Pommy accent**, the speech of British people, esp. those from the Midlands, or those with a pronounced Southern British educated accent; **Pommy bastard**, a term of (occas. friendly) abuse; **Pommie-land**, Britain.
  1952 *Landfall* 23 213 Think of the uncalled-for occasions on which a fictional 'Oxford accent' is introduced to be made fun of, or cowboy-film American, or phoney Lancashire which makes do for the '**pommie accent**'. **1959** SLATTER *Gun in My Hand* 30 The BBC announcers with their Pommie accents crackled by the static. **1986** DAVIN *Salamander & the Fire* 72 Anyway, she'd been to some posh school in England and been presented at Court and she spoke with rather a pommy accent. **1940** in Taylor *NZ People at War* (1986) I. 233 [Aitken, a railway ganger says] I hope the **Pommy —**

get beaten'. **1959** SLATTER *Gun in My Hand* 218 'You were tight then all right... That's the time you called me a Pommie bastard.' **c1962** BAXTER *Horse* (1985) 35 'You may think I'm a bit of a drongo,' said Ivan surprisingly. 'Letting that big Pommy bastard horn in on me and Mollie.' **1963** CASEY *As Short a Spring* 22 A fellow that's come all the way from **Pommieland** to have a quick look at Kiwi-Country..at least ought to have an overcoat to put on himself. **1990** *Listener* 27 Aug. 114 These hedgehogs in Pommie-Land find a half full bottle of champagne lying on the lawn after a garden party. They all get drunk, grab one of the sheilas, and start sticking champagne corks on her prickles.

Pommy, var. POMMIE.

Pommy-ism. [f. POMMY + *-ism.*] The assumption of an air of superiority in respect of British customs, etc. compared with those of New Zealand. Also **anti-Pommyism**.
  1920 *Quick March* 11 Oct. 13 Has anybody heard of 'Pommy-ism' and, if so, what is it. **c1925** AIREY *NZ a Nation* 2 Nationality..does not lie in 'anti-pommyism' prejudice against British immigrants, because they say 'choom' when they mean cobber.

ponamu, var. POUNAMU.

pond. [Spec. use of *pond* a small artificial lake.] An artificial hollow filled with water for fire-protection or stock-management purposes in forests or on farms.
  1991 *Press* (Christchurch) 14 Oct. 1 An extensive search of bush and ponds in the Golden Downs Forest..failed to uncover [the] body. Police diving teams returned to Wellington last night after scouring ponds in the area and parts of the Buller River.

Poneke: see PORT NICK.

ponga /ˈpɒŋə/, /ˈpʌŋə/. The large variety of form represents two main English pronunciations of **ponga**: (1) with initial unvoiced /p/ as /ˈpʌŋə/, /ˈpɒŋə/ (occas. early /-ŋɡə/) represented by **ponga** (early **pongo**, occas. **ponja**; and Ngai Tahu **poka**), **punga** (the common, almost standard, misspelling); and (2) (mainly South Island) with initial voiced /b/ as /ˈbʌŋə/, /ˈbʌŋɡə/ (or /bʌŋ(ɡ)i/) represented by **bunga, bunger, bungi(e), bungy**. [Ma. /ˈpoŋa/: Williams 291 *Ponga* 1. n. *Cyathea dealbata*, a tree fern.] Plural often *pongas, pungas*, etc.

1. Also **ponga fern, ponga tree-fern.** *Cyathea dealbata* (fam. Cyatheaceae), a tall (3 to 10 m) New Zealand silver tree-fern, having fronds green or yellow-green above and silver-white beneath; also its trunk and fronds used as a construction material or for decoration. See also *silver tree-fern* (FERN 2 (20) b (c)). **a.** As **ponga**.
  1773 FORSTER *Resolution Jrnl*. 23 Nov. (1982) III. 426 I got a Man who went & fetched me a Fern-tree with root and all, he called it *Mā[m]āgu*, & as I pointed to a large ferntree near me, with leaves whose underside is white, he shewed me the difference & called the latter *Pònga*. This Tree is full of tender pulp. and I believe this Fern is nearly related to the *Sago*-tree, which is likewise a Fern. **1838** POLACK *NZ* II. 399 The *Pongo*... The fronds are five feet long, virent, circumference of trunk one and a half foot, covered with chaffy scales. **1844** WILLIAMS *NZ Jrnl.* (1956) 109 The Ponga fern is perhaps the male tree, as it grows frequently near the Korau and is like it in leaf, with the exception of growing taller and the stalk bare. **1855** TAYLOR *Te Ika A Maui* 115 Some of the trees were so alarmed that they held down their heads, and have never been able to hold them up since; amongst these were the ponga (a fern-tree) and the kareao. **1864** MUELLER *Vegetation of Chatham Is*. 65 *Cyathea cunninghami*...Common in the woods of the Chatham-Islands, where it is called by the natives 'Ponja'. **1875** [see FERN 2 (20) b (c)]. **1882** POTTS *Out in Open* 10 The..shades of evening gradually conceal the spreading fronds of the..silvered ponga. **1905** BAUCKE *White Man Treads* 266 He had bought a complete smithy outfit, built himself a workshop of ponga, and fitted it up in every detail like mine! **1921** [see FERN 2 (18) (a)]. **1946** *JPS* LV. 149 *Ponga*, a tree-fern (Cyathea dealbata), silver tree-fern; very often corrupted to bunger. **1964** JEFFEREY *Mairangi* 13 The ferns by the camellias are tree-ferns. Do you know what the Maori name is? Ponga! They're natives, of course. **1987** *Listener* 8 Aug. 61 There were..many small trees and shrubs on our section, including ponga, which Dad called 'king ferns'.

b. As **punga**, or occas. reduplicated **punga-punga**.
  1874 BAINES *Edward Crewe* 198 Then there were the magnificent tree-ferns, one kind growing some forty feet high, called punga by the natives. **1886** *TrNZI* XVIII. 86 [The nest was] lined with hairy substance off the fronds of the *punga*. **1892** [see c below]. **1911** MORELAND *Through South Westland* 75 We..entered a narrow path where high grasses brushed against our knees as we rode past, and every few yards streams ran across it in inverted culverts of punga logs. **1920** BOLITHO *With Prince in NZ* 157 The neighbouring forest had been raided to make Hokitika beautiful. Towering punga ferns were linked together with festoons of lycopodium. **1930** REISCHEK *Yesterdays in Maoriland* (1933) 193 The first night in this bush I camped under a punga-punga (fern-tree). **1946** ZIMMERMAN *Where People Sing* 4 And there was a vague and somewhat disturbing unfamiliarity about the trees, the fantastic, prehistoric looking *punga* tree fern, for instance. **1959** SHADBOLT *New Zealanders* (1986) 92 He wheeled his cycle off the road..and hid it behind a ragged cluster of pungas. **1972** BAXTER *Collected Poems* (1980) 539 Hilltop behind hilltop, A mile of green pungas Bow their heads to the slanting spears of rain. **1986** OWEN & PERKINS *Speaking for Ourselves* 156 They would first rig up a platform..and on top of it they put trunks of punga fern, because they gave grip to the feet.

c. As **bunga, bungee, bunger, bungi(e), bungy**, or occas. reduplicated **bunga-bunga**.
  1892 HOCKEN & FENWICK *Holiday Trip* 15 We made our way..over the well made track of punga-pungas (or in the vernacular of the camp 'bungies'.) **1898** MORRIS *Austral-English* 65 *Bunga* or *Bungy*... a New Zealand settlers' corruption of the Maori word *punga*. **1900** BOYD *Stolen Summer* 89 A wealth of *bunga-bungas* (tree-ferns) clothed the declivity, and spread their huge fronds like a procession of giants' umbrellas beneath. **1914** PFAFF *Diggers' Story* 70 Building a hotel of 'bungies'. **1920** *Quick March* 10 Jan. 41 The construction..was that of most bush bunks; the main supports consisting of a section of 'bungi' laid on the ground at each end. **c1920** BEATTIE *Trad. Lifeways Southern Maori* (1994) 122 The familiar poka (known as ponga further north and called the bungee by white bushmen) was no good from a food standpoint. **1921** DOBBIE *NZ Ferns* 100 The 'bunga' of the bushman, used for all manner of purposes—fences, verandah posts, even for making roads. **1926** *TrNZI* LVI. 670 In some instances the Maori name has been adopted but corrupted:.. 'bunger' (now fortunately seldom heard) for 'ponga'. **1934** *Press* (Christchurch) (Acland Gloss.) 13 Jan. 13 *Bungy*.—I understand from both West Coasters and North Islanders that this term is used throughout New Zealand (but so far as I know not in Canterbury). **1953** DEWAR *Chaslands* 11 The principal building material used [on the Southland bush farms c1900] was fern-tree, known locally as bungie. **1967** MAY *West Coast Gold Rushes* (1962) 147 The ramshackle shanty-town of calico tents and 'bungy' stores on the Hokitika sandspit had a temporary air about it. **1970** McNAUGHTON *Tat* 86 Bluey made a kennel for him of bungy ferns and manuka scrub.

2. With a modifier: **black, silver**.

(1) **black ponga.** MAMAKU.
  1922 *Auckland Weekly News* 15 June 60 No other members of the vegetable kingdom can produce a more telling effect than those noble specimens of Cyathea medullaris, the black punga or tree fern. **1951** LEVY *Grasslands NZ* (1970) 88 *Table 1. Ecological Classification*... Black punga. **1965** [see MAMAKU]. **1969** *Standard Common Names Weeds* 5 *black punga* [=] *mamaku*.

(2) **silver ponga.** *ponga* 1 above. See also *silver king, silver tree-fern* (FERN 2 (18) a and (20) b (c)).
  1951 LEVY *Grasslands NZ* (1970) 88 *Table 1. Ecological Classification*... Silver punga. **1969** *Standard Common Names Weeds* 70 *silver punga* [=] *ponga*.

3. In *attrib.* use. **a.** Of, made of, associated with pongas, including use in local place-names.
  1868 *Thames Miner's Guide* 83 Brickmakers', near Punga Flat. Five men's ground, taken up in March 1868. **1870** *TrNZI* II. 90 The Ponga Flat..owes its name to the large grove of Black Tree-ferns with which it was formerly covered. **1892** BROOKES *Frontier Life* 139 The Survey Department graded a zigzag track up the side to the top, fixing in punga steps, so that horses could climb up. **1922** *Auckland Weekly News* 14 Dec. 17 Shall I see the Ponga Fairy and the cross old Bush Lawyer. **1938** HYDE *Nor Yrs. Condemn* 173 A tree-fern, punga stump hollowed..hit him under the chin, and he sprawled in the mud. **1952** *Landfall* 23 Sept. 209 We raid the bush for punga fronds and lycopodium to decorate dance-halls, we knock down pigeons with stones and forestall protest with a sneer.

b. In special Comb. denoting *ponga* as a construction material: **ponga fence**, a fence constructed from ponga stems; **ponga house, hut, shack, whare**, a 'log' house or hut constructed from ponga stems, esp. as a Maori or pioneer bush dwelling.
  1968 *Listener* 11 Apr. 10 He built himself a ten-foot high **punga fence** and was snug. **1911** MORELAND *Through South Westland* 42 We drove to the little old accommodation-house at the edge of the bush—a **punga house**, i.e. built of fern logs on end, filled with moss and grass. **1963** PEARSON *Coal Flat* 420 A **bungy hut** is a hut made of the trunks of tree-ferns. *Ibid.* 123 He would dream that he was a lone woodsman living in a bungy hut deep in the bush. **1930** *Na To Hoa Aroha* (1987) II. 26 There is the danger of a pakeha supervisor with his pakeha standard imposing on a people just out of raupo and **ponga shacks** a type of dwelling far above their requirements. **1886** *Hawera Star* 18 Jan. in Arnold *New Zealand's Burning* (1994) 144 Punga whare burnt on leasehold land., also dairy, cowshed, clothing and furniture. **1905** BAUCKE *White Man Treads* 123 We came to his [*sc.* Maori's] homestead—a ponga whare with a bark roof, stained with smoke. **1994** ARNOLD *New Zealand's Burning* 152 The [bush settler's] first home was commonly a ponga whare, followed shortly by a split timber one.

pongo, var. PONGA.

Pongo, *n.* and *a. Derog.* [Transf. use of Brit. nautical slang *pongo* a soldier or marine: see OED 2 a; AND 1944.]

A. *n.*

a. *WW2* (North Africa). A British soldier. Occas. derog. for a 'base-wallah', any soldier not usually in the firing line (see quot. 1944).
  1939-45 *Expressions & Sayings 2NZEF (TS N.A. WAII DA 420/1)* Pongo—English soldier. **1942** *NZEF Times* 7 Sept. 5 A big bronzed Pongo came in. **1944** FULLARTON *Troop Target* 127 The [supply] vehicles were obviously driven by 'base-wallahs'—'pongoes' is the expression. *Ibid.* 151 Hear about the Pongo up in the blue for the first time. *Ibid.* 159 It is characteristic of Kiwis that they will approach a 'Pommie' and say, 'You know, you Pongoes are a hopeless lot.' **1945** HENDERSON *Gunner Inglorious* 148 The successful applicant [for the job of batman], an elderly quiet-spoken Pongo was a dinkum butler. **1963** GLOVER *Bedside Book* 77 Don't like these shells falling round, but its worse for the Pongos. **1978** HENDERSON *Soldier Country* 112 Some of the nearby Pongos cried: 'E-e-e-e! What a Fred Karno's Army!' **1984** OVENDEN *Ratatui* 197 He felt rattled and puzzled,.. like some poor bloody pongo pinned down under an artillery barrage.

b. *Post WW2.* A Britisher; POMMIE A.
  1949 *Here and Now* Oct. 11 He long ago began featuring himself as 'New Zealander born and bred', a sop to the vague..feeling against Pommies, Pongoes, Homies. **1950** *Evening Post* (Wellington) 21 Nov. 8 The New Zealand term was 'Homie' until superseded by the Australian adjective. And even now Pommie is being superseded by the term 'Pongo'. The term certainly was derisive in origin, and as to whether it is still derisive depends entirely upon the individual addressed as such. **1959** SLATTER *Gun in My Hand* 219 'A real Pommie eh? Imagine that.' 'Yes, we're all Pommies here.' 'A real bloody Pongo.' 'This Pongo business annoys me. You haven't even got it right. Pongo's the naval word for soldiers or marines. Out here they use it as just another form of Pommie.' 'Oh well, it's all the same to me.'..'They're all right really. The Pommies, I mean. The Homeys, the Chooms, the Pongos.' **1962** *Evening Post* (Wellington) 23 Feb. 8 [Correspondent writing on the word *pommie* signs himself] Drongatus Pongorum. **1973** GRANT in *Listener Short Stories* (1977) 147 Mortimer looked a real nong. 'This here is Mortimer,' said Fred. 'He's a pongo, but he can't help it.' **1984** *Listener* 21 Jan. 30 Others I had no idea were pure New Zild (*jacksy*, *pongo*). **1995** *Dominion*(Wellington) 21 Nov. 25 [Death notice] *Morris, John (John Der Pom) (Pongo)...* You may be gone John (Der Pom), but you will always be remembered.

B. *adj.* Usu. *derog.* British; POMMIE B.
  1944 *NZEF Times* 18 Dec. 4 Those guys in D company might not understand if we talked to them with a Pongo accent. **1947** DAVIN *For Rest of Our Lives* 165 Like that pongo cobber of yours, the homo. **1949** THE SARGE *Excuse my Feet* 130 'You can call me "chum", lad,' he added, breaking into a broad Pongo dialect. **1959** SLATTER *Gun in My Hand* 93 We strolled up the main *strada* in the evening..and the Pongo red-cap stopped us to demand where our hats were. Bloody cheek said Mick, as if we're in their damned Pongo army. **c1962** BAXTER *Horse* (1985) 35 'You may think I'm a bit of a drongo,' said Ivan surprisingly. 'Letting that big Pommy bastard horn in on me and Mollie... If I turfed that Pongo bastard out of the house she'd go with him.' **1993** *Dominion* (Wellington) 5 Mar. 20 He..could come from a Welsh coalmining village, with his white Pongo body and mole-adorned face.

Pongolia. *Joc.* [f. PONG(O + Mong)*olia*.] Britain. Cf. POMGOLIA.
  1985 *Contact* (Wellington) 7 June 5 During his month-long mission to Pongolia, Trev made a bird of talking to shopkeepers on their experience of the British version of GST. **1987** GEE *Prowlers* 69 When Phil bought the property he found the name changed to something English... 'Some bloody name from Pongolia.' He had it off the gate in no time. **1993** *Dominion* (Wellington) 20 Sept. 6 I have a niece..who gets on the blower..and rings up all her old mates in outer Pongolia or wherever.

  Hence **Pongolian** *n.*, a person born or resident in Britain. As an adjective, British.
  1967 *Comment* 32 Sept. 12 And indeed even the barbarian Pongolians to whom he normally sells the bulk of his produce have said that they will soon wish to buy their foodstuffs elsewhere. **1987** GEE *Prowlers* 70 His English stallion Thundercloud (no prejudice against Pongolian horses) earns him four thousand dollars every time he serves a mare.

ponja, var. PONGA.

pony. *Obs.* [Transf. use of Brit. slang *pony* £25: an uncommon early use in NZ, hence the uncertainty of denomination.] ? A pound, or occas. poss. a £5, note.
  1911 *Truth* 11 Feb. 7 Rumo[u]r has it that before leaving Wellington this youthful nobleman 'tapped' a Minister of the Crown for a pony, and soon after his arrival in the northern city he suddenly became short of the 'needful'. **1916** CHURCH *Tonks* 148 Done for a pony... Make it a fiver.

poofter /'pʊftə/, *n.*[1] Also occas. **pouffey; pooftah, poufter, pufter**. [Prob. from *poof* 'a puff', in a transf. use of *puff* 'an overblown promotion'.]

1. A blowhard, one full of 'wind' or 'hot-air', a skite; a socially or intellectually pretentious person. See also POOFIE.
  1916 *Hutt Valley Independent* 15 Apr. 4 He's a puny poofter. **1952** *Here & Now* Jan. 19 The butcher's assistant was as likely to have a star bird dog..as the richest pooftah—indeed, he was likely to have a better-trained and more efficient beast. **1972** MITCHELL *Pavlova Paradise* 183 *poufter:* Air mattress assembler or M.P. **1974** MORRIESON *Predicament* (1981) 223 He carried no brief for a poufter like Vernon Branwell who he knew had swindled the General's Widow. **1974** SIMPSON *Sugarbag Years* 52 We went and looked at five places which met all these requirements [for a cheap family house] and ended up in Remuera Road among the high-life pouffeys, paying heaven knows what tiny rent by today's standards. **1979** ASHTON-WARNER *I Passed This Way* (1980) 318 We hear [the official] is only the director general [of Education], Dr Benjamin Gully, on the prowl by proxy and that he's a bit of a pufter. 'What's a pufter?' I say. One says, 'It's someone called the director of visual and audio aids when a debutante could do the job.' **1983** *Dominion* (Wellington) 25 Nov. 1 In a tense exchange over the Government's refusal to extend the normal hours of broadcasting of Parliament for last night's late sitting, Mr Lange shouted at the Leader of the House, Mr Thomson: 'The minister is a poofter.' **1983** FRANCIS *Wildlife Ranger* 147 While vicegeral ADCs were a very decent type when they were New Zealand bred, those originating in the United Kingdom were often 'poofters', or so I found. **1990** CHAVASSE *Integrity* 40 'I don't like my boss,' he said. 'He's a stuck-up poofter, and he makes mistakes.'

2. [Prob. related to schoolboys' use of *poof*, *poofter* for a fart.] As a nickname.
  1943 HISLOP *Pure Gold* 79 Nicky, Curley, Fatty, Skish..[were schoolchildren's nicknames in Dunedin in the 1880s]... Poofter and Irish were two of the girls,

but I will leave them at that, as I must keep off the grass with my evergreen memories.

poofter /'pʊftə/, *n.*[2] Also **poufter**. [f. *poof* homosexual: AND 1903, and now (borrowed from the Australian) the main NZ use.] A male homosexual.
  1965 SHADBOLT *Among Cinders* 80 All this bull I been hearing about you. About you not getting up. And sitting here sulking. Is it true, you little poufter? **1980** LELAND *Kiwi-Yankee Dict.* 80 *pouf, poufter: (A) queer.*

pook /pʊk/. Also **puke**. Familiar abbrev. of PUKEKO 1.
  1957 *pook* p.c. R. Mason, heard /pʊk/ at Wildlife course from K. Miers. **1966** FALLA ET AL. *Birds of NZ* 108 Pukeko *Porphyrio melanotus* Other names: Swamp-hen, Pukaki, Pook. **1982** SALE *Four Seasons* 148 One or two pukeko are shot for every gun during the [duck-]shooting season. I recall a friend returning one early May morning with a disgusted report: 'Only a pook'. **1985** puke [see PUKEKO 1 a]. **1994** LASENBY *Dead Man's Head* 110 'Pooks!' said Polly... Among some rushes a couple of pukekos strode gawkily,

pool house. *Obs.* A State-owned house, part of a pool or allocation of such reserved for State servants on transfer.
  [**1947** *PSA Jrnl* July 244 After four months' operation, the Housing Bureau located in the office of the Public Service Commission, reports that the housing needs of..public servants on transfer..have been satisfied... Active steps need to be taken to avoid..loss from the 'pool' [caused by public servants giving up tenancies to non-public-servants]. **1950** *Ibid.*Sept. 47 The Minister claims that State servants who are allocated houses from the pool are receiving special treatment.] **1954** *PSA Jrnl.* Dec. 9 Mr Tuohy suggested certain lines of approach..to increase quickly the number of pool houses available not only in the main centres. **1963** *PSA Jrnl.* Nov. 4 [Heading] Pool House Rentals. The Combined State Service organisations are currently discussing with the Government the question of pool house rental increases. **1993***Evening Post*(Wellington) 15 Sept. 25 With a change of [Government] job came a State pool house in Chaffey Crescent, Titahi Bay.

poonamoo, var. POUNAMU.

poo-ree-dee, var. PURIRI.

Poor Knights lily: see LILY 2 (12).

poor man. Also **poorman's**, occas. **poor men's**. Used in collocations suggesting that the object referred to is in some way easier to attain (see 1), or inferior to or cheaper than a standard article (see 2, 3, 4).

1. *Goldfields.* **poor man's** (occas. **poor men's**) **diggings, poor man's goldfield** [AND 1855], a diggings or goldfield returning relatively easily-got 'wages' to a miner of limited means or equipment.
  1862 *Otago Goldfields & Resources* 19 I fully believe it will, as a 'poor man's' diggings, prove second to none. **1865** *Evening Post* (Wellington) I. No.85 3 They all described [the claims] as a 'good poor man's diggings'; meaning thereby that anybody could be sure of earning a living from them, but few would realise large sums. **1874** BAINES *Edward Crewe* 265 The latter place..having rich alluvial, or poor men's diggings, was a very bank with an ever-ready balance in favour of the clever and the muscular. **1967** MAY *West Coast Gold Rushes* 240 The term 'poor man's

diggings' was used by contemporaries to describe the West Coast goldfields. This term referred not to their richness or otherwise but to the fact that gold could be readily obtained by any 'poor man' with limited means. 'Gold is the great friend of the masses', ran a line in the chorus of a diggers' song. **1976** BROWN *Difficult Country* 34 A 'poor man's goldfield' they called the whole Buller area, not because of a shortage of gold but because a man with a minimum of equipment could at least make wages.

2. poorman's (poorman, poor man's) orange. Often init. cap. Occas. ellipt. poorman. A small grapefruit used for marmalade, now usu. the New Zealand grapefruit (GRAPEFRUIT).

1884 ALDERTON *Treat & Handbk. Orange Culture in Auckland* 66 The Poor Man's Orange is only good for preserving. **1887** *Auckland Weekly News* 20 Aug. 30 These are all of this variety known as 'The Poor Man's Orange.' They grow to a large size, are hardy, coarse in texture, harsh in flavour, and possessed of a degree of bitterness which many do not like. **1899** *Annual Rep. Dept. Agric.* VII. 245 Both sweet and 'poor man' oranges also succeed remarkably well along this coast. **1929** *Jrnl. NZ Inst. Horticulture* I. 65 The Poorman Orange is really a Pomelo. **1937** *NZJST* XVIII. 409 This development [*sc*. the popularity of grapefruit] has a particular interest for New Zealand in that a type of grapefruit has been evolved from citrus introduced by Sir George Grey and named by him the Poorman orange. New Zealand grapefuit..is a selected strain known generally as Morrison's Seedless, after the late Mr. H. Morrison, of Warkworth, who sought to improve the original Poorman orange, which was at one time considered suitable only for the manufacture of marmalade. **1938** *NZJST* XX. 56A At Kerikeri..infection occurred roughly in the following order: Ponderosa lemon..grapefruit (Marsh's Seedless)..New Zealand grapefruit or Poorman Orange (Pommelo X Sour Orange). **1938** *Auckland Weekly News* 27 Apr. 79 There is the famous strain of poorman called 'Morrison's Seedless'. **1946** MULGAN *Pastoral NZ* 81 Kerikeri [with] its groves of sweet orange, grapefruit..and what is known as the Poorman Orange, which is much in demand for marmalade making. **1956** WILSON *Sweet White Wine* 30 We had three lemon trees and a poorman's orange and two nectarines. **1966** TURNER *Eng. Lang. Austral. & NZ* 116 *Poor man's orange* (New Zealand grapefruit: a once standard term now abandoned for advertising reasons). **1978** *Otago Daily Times* (Dunedin) 1 July 7 (Griffiths Collect.) [Heading] N.Z. Grapefruit Wrongly Named. New Zealand grapefruit are not, in fact grapefruit at all. They are a type of orangelo, and probably more accurately described by the nickname 'poor man's orange'. **1986** *New Outlook* XXI. 48 'What's that you brought for us?' 'Poorman's oranges.'..I hate grapefruit.

3. As **poor man's weather glass** *obs*. [f. obsolete Brit. dial.: see OED *poor man* 5, 1847], the introduced weed scarlet pimpernel *Anagallis arvensis* (fam. Primulaceae), from its habit of closing its flowers before rain.

1926 HILGENDORF *Weeds* 132 Scarlet Pimpernel (*Anagallis arvensis*), sometimes called poor man's weather glass, is found in cultivated fields and waste places throughout the islands.

4. In cookery in a sense of 'mock, imitation': **poorman's goose**, a liver savoury, poss. an imitation *pâté de foie gras*; **poor man's whitebait**, strips of shredded skate wing.

c1940s *Tui's Commonsense Cookery* 57 Liver Savoury (**Poorman's Goose**)... 1 lb. liver. 1 lb. potatoes. 4 oz. onion. 1 teaspoon salt. teaspoon pepper. pint water. Little powdered sage. **1986** BROWN *Weaver's Apprentice* 43 Rachel stripped the last of the skin from the steamed skate's wing... When fried with beaten, seasoned eggs, it was almost identical in taste and appearance to whitebait. Skittleback: **poor man's whitebait**, but as good as the real thing.

poor pretences. [A spelling re-formed from a pronunciation /ˌpoəprə'tensəz/ of *Poa pratensis*.] A name for brome-grass (*Bromus mollis*), an unfavoured pasture plant. Compare GALLANT SOLDIER.

1921 GUTHRIE-SMITH *Tutira* (1926) 284 'Poor Pretences' was then [in the early 1880s] the name by which this brome-grass [sprung up after grass-fires] was known on the east coast... As regards the sound, 'poor pretences' can, I think, only be a corruption of *Poa pratensis*; the Latin name of the one plant done into English has been fitted to another. The reader will recollect how this grass—more widely known as goose-grass—was sown wholesale over the trough of the run.

pootacow, var. POHUTUKAWA.

poozle /'puzəl/, *v*. [A fanciful word: origin unknown.] To scavenge for collectibles, usu. as *ppl. a.* or *vbl. n.*

c1974 p.c. P.B. Orsman. Used in Wellington and Christchurch by bottle collectors, etc. 'Their bottle collection came from *poozling* under old houses.' **1980** LELAND *Kiwi-Yankee Dict.* 79 *poozling:* Going through abandoned houses scheduled for demolition and removing the (usually antique) fittings that strike your fancy. Until recently this was a socially acceptable practice (although not strictly legal), however, as demolition contractors catch on to the value of these fittings legal and moral pressure is exerted to discourage the practice. **1986** *Listener* 15 Nov. 69 Peter was fighting to save old houses once he felt so strong he was shouting about the old people who had lived in Grafton so long for instance himself he had built his own room out of poozled pieces of glass. **1988** McGILL *Dict. Kiwi Slang* 87 *poozling* scavenging in abandoned buildings before the demolisher gets there, old bottles favoured, but anything of antique significance or value.

Hence occas. as a *n*. **poozle**, a collectible, antique, etc. salvaged from old buildings or their sites.

1971 SHADBOLT *Bullshit & Jellybeans* 57 Leo would spend his sober periods worrying about Jill's poozles—a variety of antiques with great sentimental and artistic value.

pop: see GO *v*. 4 a (go (send) off pop).

popokotea. Also **popokatea** (an error well-established in the 'scientific' and general literature), rarely **pokokatea**. [Ma. /'po:pokotea/: Williams 292 *Pōpokotea*..whitehead; a bird. Sometimes misspelled *pōpokatea*.] Either of two *Mohoua* spp., WHITEHEAD or YELLOWHEAD, but prob. applied more to the North Island *whitehead* than to the South Island *yellowhead*. See also POPOTEA. Cf. UPOKOTEA.

1842 GRAY *Fauna* in Dieffenbach *Travels in NZ* (1843) II. 189 *Mohoua ochrocephala*... Mohoua houa of the natives of Tasman Bay... Popokatea, natives of Cook's Straits. **1859** THOMSON *Story NZ* I. 25 The *Certhidae*, or Creeper family of birds, possesses five species, none of which are very remarkable save the Pokokatea [*sic*], a social bird not unlike the English finch in its habits. **1862** *Richmond-Atkinson Papers* (1960) I. 782 He was telling me..[*sic*] how old Potatau (Te Wherowhero) had likened himself to a ruru mobbed by a flock of popokoteas, the latter representing the Waikato worrying him to be King. **1873** BULLER *Birds NZ* 101 *Orthonyx albicilla*. (The White-head.)..Native names. Popotea..Popokotea, and Upokotea. **1882** POTTS *Out in Open* 199 [It] coolly pursues its occupation without..the watchful distrust of the popokatea, that defends his home with almost the courage of the falcon or tern. **1904** *TrNZI* XXXVI. 119 Sir Walter Buller says..that the Blue Crow..leaves the care of the chick to the Popokatea, or Canary. **1947** REED *Dict. Suppl.* 175 *popokatea*: whitehead, forest bird. **1966** FALLA et al. *Birds NZ* 209 Whitehead *Mohoua albicilla* Maori name: Popokatea. **1985** *Reader's Digest Book NZ Birds* 276 Whitehead *Mohoua albicilla*... Popokatea. **1990** *Checklist Birds NZ* 204 *Mohoua albicilla*..Whitehead (*Popokatea*)... North Island only.

poporo: see POROPORO.

poporo-kaiwhiri: see POROKAIWHIRIA.

popotea. [Ma. /'popotea/: Williams 292 *Popotea*..whitehead.] POPOKOTEA.

1873 [see POPOKOTEA]. **1882** HAY *Brighter Britain* II. 224 The Popo or Popotea..is a little brown bird with a white head, which sings like a chaffinch, and principally lives about rata trees. We see them not infrequently. **1946** [see UPOKOTEA].

popper. [f. the sound made.] A pneumatic tunnelling drill.

1911 *Maoriland Worker* 15 Sept. 6 He considered that 'poppers' (a small boring machine) should be abolished altogether as they caused dust [in the coal mines]. **1938** HYDE *Nor Yrs. Condemn* 151 The air shimmered and beat with sound. The poppers, eating with their thin blue tongues into rock. **1978** McARA *Gold Mining Waihi* 185 It was not until considerably later that the 'swing type' stoper with its pneumatic-feed-leg for drilling uppers, and known as the 'popper', came into use. In it the drill was rotated in the hole by swinging the machine handle backwards and forwards. At first the miners did not like it, as they considered it 'shook up' the roof too much, causing falls of ground, but it was light and easily transportable and was fast in good ground. It remained in use in the stopes for many years, until the much later introduction of the rotary stoper. At one stage the popper was given the rather undeserved name of the 'widow-maker'. **1986** RICHARDS *Off the Sheep's Back* 85 For the first time in my life I saw, and heard, pneumatic drills at work. They were referred to as 'poppers'.

pop-pop boat. [f. the sound made when under steam.] A child's small toy boat moved by the emission of a steam jet from a candle-fired 'boiler'. (Known to Ed. by this name from before WW2.)

1951 FRAME *Lagoon* (1961) 9 People whizzing round the harbour in motor-boats like the pop-pop boats we used to whizz round in the bath on Christmas morning.

poppy.

1. Special Comb. **poppy show** [f. Brit. dial. *poppy-show*, also *puppy-show*, a (children's) peep-show, puppet show: EDD *poppy n*.² Sc. 1798; so OED *poppy-show* 'dial. and Sc.', also 1887 Cheshire 'A pin to see a poppy-show.'] Apparently used elsewhere but recorded only in Partridge 1937– and Macquarie 1981, a term used mainly by schoolchildren to describe the sudden, usu. accidental (white or coloured) show or glimpse of a girl's petticoat and underpants (see also quot. 1982). Cf. SNOW *v*. 1.

c1950s p.c. Dr. Kathryn Walls (Wellington, 1989) has known *poppy-show* since the 1950s for a show of underclothes. **1968** SLATTER *Pagan Game* 51 The poppy shows with the Robertson tart in the pine plantation behind the hospital. **1982** SUTTON-SMITH *Hist. Children's Play* 223 Pin dips were known also as 'poppy shows' (perhaps it was the similar flash of color that gave the same name—'the poppy show'—to the exciting experience of seeing a girl's dress blown upward by the wind; pins were not charged for flowers of this sort).

2. As **tall poppy** [f. Austral. use: AND 1902], a conspicuously successful person, usu. one exciting envy.

1992 *Dominion Sunday Times* (Wellington) 23 Aug. 11 There's no such thing as a tall poppy playing rugby.

Hence *v.*, to cut (an apparently successful person) down to size.

1991 *Evening Post* (Wellington) 21 Sep. 2 The Maori partners in the controversial Quality Inn buyout are being 'tall poppied' by other New Zealanders.

popular, *a.* In various phrases indicating unpopularity: **as popular as a pie-picker**, SEE PIE 2; **as popular as shit (at a nightmen's picnic)**.

1935 FAIRBURN *Letters* 11 Sept. (1981) 97 I'm going to be as popular as shit at a nightmen's picnic if it ever gets into print intact.

porae. Also erron. **porahi**. [Ma. /ˈpoːraeː/: Williams 293 *Pōrae... 3. Cheilodactylus douglasi.*] *Nemadactylus* (formerly *Cheilodactylus*) *douglasi* (fam. Cheilodactylidae), a large, tarakihi-like, greenish-grey sea-fish of North Island waters.

[**1820** LEE & KENDALL *NZ Gram. & Vocab.* 195 Poráe, *s*. A fish so called.] **1875** *TrNZI* VII. 244 Cheilodactylus douglasi... Native name—Porae. **1882** HAY *Brighter Britain* II. 231 We prefer the substantial schnapper, the goodly whapuka or kanae, or the luscious porahi. **1918** *NZJST* I. 6 Its nearest allies amongst New Zealand fish are *Cheilodactylus macropterus* (the tarakihi) and *C. douglasi* (the porae). **1921** *NZJST* IV. 115 *Porae*. Secured up to 40 fathoms among tarakihi. Uncommon at Russell, but more plentiful in Hauraki Gulf. **1966** DOOGUE & MORELAND *Sea Anglers' Guide* 249 Porae..morwong (Australia)... These are feeders which are normally found on tarakihi grounds and which will take almost any type of bait. **1972** DOAK *Fishes* 70 From the edge of the tide to depths of 180 feet and beyond, porae fossick for crabs, marine worms, brittle stars and molluscs. **1981** WILSON *Fisherman's Bible* 181 Porae. A big, green, delicious inhabitant of our warmer waters found in a variety of habitats from surf-beaches to rocky depths.

porahi, var. PORAE.

porangi, *a*. [Ma. /ˈpoːraŋi/: Williams 293 *Pōrangi. 1...Hurried... 2.* Headstrong, wrongheaded... *3.* Having the mind fully occupied, distracted. *4.* Beside oneself, out of one's mind, mad.]

1. In various senses of foolish; distracted; crazy or eccentric; occas. 'in a hurry' (see quot. 1847).

[**1820** LEE & KENDALL *Gram. & Vocab.* 195 Pórangi, *a.* Hasty.] **1847** *McLean Papers* (ATLTS) V. 13 The bearer is porangi to get off and makes me almost raruraru by his impatience. **1863** MOSER *Mahoe Leaves* 38 The majority..did not appear to pay much attention, [one observing]..that the koroheka (old man) was 'porangi' (foolish). **1867** GRACE *Journal* 18 Dec. in *Pioneer Missionary* (1928) 167 At first I thought he was a Hauhau; but, when I came up to some other Maoris, they told me that he was porangi (mad). **1872** DOMETT *Ranolf & Amohia* 435 'Twas nothing—he was not to mind her—she Was foolish—was '*porangi*' and would be Better directly—and her tears she dried. **1883** *TrNZI* XV. 423 A man who told such marvellous stories that he was deemed to be porangi or insane. **1891** *Richmond-Atkinson Papers* (1960) II. 583 All the witnesses on one side declare the testatrix was 'porangi' (mad). The other side say she was a 'tohunga' and a prophet and had gifts of healing. **1917** *NZ At the Front* 161 He t'e plurry Porangi, I t'ink. **1933** EADDY *Hull Down* 34 Te Maori, he can't get to sreep. Bruddy well porangi. **1941** BAKER *NZ Slang* 42 We slipped into the easy way of calling a person *porangi* instead of crazy or stupid. **1960** HILLIARD *Maori Girl* 49 He's porangi, that fellow, sick in the head. **1970** IHIMAERA in *Listener Short Stories* (1977) 91 Some people called my nanny crazy, porangi. **1983** *Dominion* (Wellington) 12 Nov. 6 The class was in fits. The teacher marched him off to the headmaster where Patu did his porangi act again. **1992** *North & South* (Auckland) Jan. 110 We had words you didn't find in the dictionary but which we all used: 'porangi', 'whare', 'taihoa'.

2. Occas. as a noun, madness; madman. Also as a nickname.

1845 WAKEFIELD *Adventure NZ* I. 137 The combatants took..especial pains to tell us that it was no fault of ours, but the porangi or 'foolishness' of the Maori. **1858** *Richmond-Atkinson Papers* (1960) I. 410 During the debate..I frequently heard him called by leading men as Hori te Waru, Wiremu Tamihana etc., etc., 'a porangi'. **1912** *NZ Free Lance* (Wellington) 18 May 4 Harry McIntosh..some time known to Wellingtonians as 'Porangi' has left Australia.

porarra, var. PARAERAE.

porbeagle: see SHARK 2 (14).

porcupine-fish. Occas. *ellipt.* **porcupine** (see quot. 1960). *Allomycterus jaculiferus* (fam. Diodontidae), a large self-inflating sea-fish with prominent, permanently erect spines on the body and head. See also KOPUTOTARA.

1872 HUTTON & HECTOR *Fishes NZ* 73 Chilomycterus jaculiferus... Porcupine Fish. **1886** [see KOPUTOTARA]. **1892** WILLIAMS *Dict. NZ Lang.* 71 *Koputotara*, n. *chilomycterus jaculiferus*; *porcupine fish*. **1913** *TrNZI* XLV. 234 The porcupine-fish is occasionally met with in Otago Harbour. **1927** SPEIGHT et al. *Nat. Hist. Canterbury* 202 The porcupine fish..has the tubercles specialised into long spines. **1938** *TrRSNZ* LXVIII. 418 *Allomycterus jaculiferus*... Porcupine-fish. **1947** POWELL *Native Animals NZ* 72 Porcupine-fish (*Allomycterus jaculiferus*). This belongs to a group of poisonous tropical fishes, most of which have the power of greatly inflating the body as a means of defence. **1956** GRAHAM *Treasury NZ Fishes* 381 Porcupine-fish (Koputotara). *Ibid.* 382 The Porcupine-fish belongs to the family of poisonous tropical fish. **1960** BAXTER *Collected Poems* (1980) 218 Barracouta, Sergeants of the under-deep? Porcupines like sleepy mayors With poison in their spikes? **1967** NATUSCH *Animals NZ* 234 The porcupine fish..has small fins, but is inflatable like the globe fish, and also has three-pointed spines embedded in its skin. Dried-up castaways are common after storms on the south coast of Wellington. **1982** AYLING *Collins Guide* (1984) 318 *Porcupine fish* (Koputo tara)... An inflated porcupine fish, looking like a large prickly ball, is not a very appetizing meal for any predator.

porcupine grass. *Obs.* SPANIARD 1.

1849 ALLOM *Letter* in Earp *Handbook* (1852) 28 [The porcupine grass] when young, is devoured by sheep with avidity, and the root is a favorite and agreeable food both with natives and stockmen. But when the grass is fully grown..the stems..closely resemble the quills of the porcupine and are pretty nearly as formidable to the legs of the stockmen. Porcupine grass is abundant in the Wairarapa. **1853** EARP *NZ* 119 There is a great variety of native grasses [in the Wairarapa].. mixed with other kinds of vegetation, such as the coarse grasses, fern, *tohi-tohi*, porcupine grass, flax, *tutu*, *manuka*, and others.

porcupine shrub. Also **porcupine scrub**. *Melicytus* (formerly *Hymenanthera*) *alpinus* (fam. Violaceae), a native shrub of subalpine habitats having spiny branchlets and a divaricating growth form.

1969 *Standard Common Names Weeds* 60 *porcupine shrub Hymenanthera alpina*. **1976** *Hist. & Nat. Hist. Boulder Bank* 21 Along the outer slope we find..tauhinu..and porcupine shrub (*Hymenanthera*). **1982** WILSON *Stewart Is. Plants* 62 *Hymenanthera alpina* Porcupine Shrub... Rigid shrub with short, stout, whitish or grey branchlets. **1984** *Hanmer Forest Park* 36 The screes support a number of specialised plant species which include porcupine scrub (*Hymenanthera alpina*), penwiper..and New Zealand harebell.

porina /pəˈrainə/, /pəˈrinə/. [f. *porina* mod. Latin (F. Walker *List of Specimens Lepidopterous Insects in Brit. Mus.* (1856) VII 1572), the former generic name: see OED.] *Wiseana* (formerly *Porina*) spp. (fam. Hepialidae), a native moth (**porina moth**); also its subterranean caterpillar (**porina caterpillar**), a night-feeder on grass foliage, hence a major pasture pest. Also *attrib.* See also *grass caterpillar* (GRASS 6), GRASS GRUB 2.

1929 MARTIN *NZ Nature Book* I 153 The Porinas, Swifts, or Bull Moths... The subterranean larvae thus attacked [by fungi] have long been known as Vegetable Caterpillars. **1940** *NZJAg.* Apr. LX. 245 The Porina moth makes its first appearance in early October... It is the caterpillar..which causes the damage during the winter. **1951** LEVY *Grasslands of NZ* (1970) 348 It is a fascinating concept to envisage the control of weeds and insects—grass grub, porina. **1969** *NZ News* 9 Apr. VII. 1 Grass grub and porina caterpillar, numbered among the most devastating of New Zealand pasture pests. **1973** WILLIAMS *Nat. Hist. NZ* II. 198 The practice of closing paddocks for hay and seed crops frequently appears to have accentuated the porina problem. **1975** *NZ Nature Heritage* LVI. 1564 Porina caterpillars, unlike grass-grubs, denude the pasture but do not eat the roots. **1989** LESSITER *Butterflies & Moths* 23 There are several species of swift moths, often called Porina. Their caterpillars live in underground tunnels during the day, and come to the surface at night to feed... Porina caterpillars, usually those living in forested areas, are sometimes destroyed by the 'vegetable caterpillar' fungus.

pork.

1. In the phr. **pork and potatoes** (occas. **pork and puha**), a common food offered to travelling Pakehas in the 19th century, and thus perceived as a favourite Maori food, and used almost as a catchphrase, with occas. jocular modern variants heard in spoken use as *pork and Pakeha*, having a light allusion to the anthropophagous reputation of the early Maori. See also PUHA.

1839 TAYLOR *Journal* 20 Mar. (ATLTS) II. 75 Very light winds almost becalmed..our fare [on the schooner] very ordinary tea pork and potatoes for breakfast, dinner and supper. **1840** MATHEW *Journal* 26 Feb. in *Founding of NZ* (1940) 63 After taking some dinner—the usual New Zealand fare, pork and potatoes—we left on our return in Fairburn's boat. **1881** CAMPBELL

Poenamo 306 Had he not brought his own it could only have been the hospitality of pork and potatoes that we could have offered, for as yet we were destitute of any more civilized supplies. **1955** BOSWELL *Dim Horizons* 41 What do we eat [in the Northland bush in the late 19 century]? Is it the usual pigeons and potatoes? Is it the pickled pork and puha? Is it even the dumplings with golden syrup? **1964** FRANCES *Johnny Rapana* 167 When this big bloke, the young chap's stepfather, got up in court, you could almost *taste* the puha and pork. **1986** OWEN & PERKINS *Speaking for Ourselves* 109 There would be kiwi and pigeon, wild duck and trout, pork and puha, potatoes and kumara—a great feast, with plum pudding to follow. **1990** *Dominion* (Wellington) 12 July 3 Maori Battalion veteran..shows some of the pork and puha battalion members are serving up in their Maori kai stall at the touring expo New Zealand 1990. **1992** *Listener* 8 June 38 Whether it's an Irish stew, a delicious French *pot-au-feu*, or an old-fashioned Kiwi pork and puha, a boil-up will satisfy winter appetites.

2. WW1. As **pork and cheese**, rhyming slang for 'Portuguese'.

1917 26 May in Miller *Camps, Tramps & Trenches* (1939) 85 The Portuguese or 'Pork and Cheese' camp [at Sling]. **1937** PARTRIDGE *Dict. Slang* 650 *Pork and Beans* Portuguese. Milit. from 1916. The New Zealanders called them *Pork and Cheese*.

3. *Hist.* Special Comb. **pork trader**, a Pakeha or Pakeha-Maori who traded in Maori-grown pork. See also *pig-jobber* (PIG *n*[1] 4).

1841 [see PAKEHA-MAORI 1]. **1847** ANGAS *Savage Life* II. 43 We met a large canoe coming down the stream, having in it two Europeans, accompanied by about a dozen Maories. They were pork-traders, a class of men in New Zealand corresponding somewhat to the overlanders of Australia. These individuals go up the rivers into the interior, and procure pigs from the natives in exchange for powder, tobacco, and blankets. The pigs thus obtained they bring down to the coast, where they sell them for a good price, either to the people at the European settlements, or to the captains of whalers and trading vessels. The native terms these men 'Pakeha Maories', or 'white men of no consequence'.

porka, var. POAKA *n.*[1]

porker. [Spec. use of *porker* a young hog fattened for pork: early instances are difficult to separate from those of POAKA *n.*[1] q.v.] A Maori-bred pig for slaughter; occas. a wild pig hunted for pork.

1840 BEST *Journal* 13 Dec. (1966) 267 During the day we killed many pigs and at length so satiated were our party [of Mauries] that they cruelly murdered the wretched porkers only taking their hearts and livers. **1849** POWER *Sketches in NZ* 68 If a Maori porker objects to go into a canoe, he is not forthwith kicked and punched..but he is coaxed, and patted. **1891** ALPERS *Three in a Coach* 22 Three little porkers. **1909** VOGEL *Tragedy of Flirtation* 42 The Maori Porker. **1929** SMYTH *Girl from Mason Creek* 169 The dogs were holding a 'porker' somewhere. **1933** EADDY *Hull Down* 48 How far to go for the wild porker? [Question addressed to a Maori in Northland.] **1951** HUNT *Confessions* 34 'Captain Cookers', with sharp snouts and formidable tusks, waged constant war with a group of dogs.. that rushed towards..food thrown out on to the open spaces [of the pa]. Running from place to place, the half-grown porkers led a precarious life.

porokaiwhiri. Also as Ma. variants **poporo-kaiwhiri, porokaiwhiria, porokaiwiria**. [Ma. /'porokaifiri(a)/ (/'po:porokaifiri/): Williams 295 *Porokaiwhiri, porokaiwhiria, pōporokaiwhiri,*

poroporokaiwhiria..a tree.] PIGEONWOOD (*Hedycarya arborea*).

1867 HOOKER *Handbook* 767 Porokaiwhiri, Col[enso]. Hedycarya dentata. **1882** POTTS *Out in Open* 16 The Hauhau call to prayers is sounded by the beating of the pahu, a sounding piece of wood..it is made (when procurable) of the wood of the Poro Kaiwhiria.., an aromatic tree. **1888** BULLER *Birds NZ* I. 12 The spot fixed upon was..sheltered all round by close-growing porokaiwhiri, torotoro, and other shrubby trees. **1889** KIRK *Forest Flora* 217 The porokaiwhiri forms a tall shrub or small tree, sometimes from 40ft. to 50ft... It does not appear to have received any distinctive appellation from the woodman or settler. **1906** CHEESEMAN *Manual NZ Flora* 600 A small tree 20–40 ft. high..*Porokaiwhiri*. **1923**, **1939** [see PIGEONWOOD]. **1940** LAING & BLACKWELL *Plants NZ* 181 *Hedycarya arborea* (*The Pigeon Wood*)... Maori name *Porokaiwhiria* or *Poporo-kaiwhiri*. **1950** [see PIGEONWOOD]. **1961** ALLAN *Flora NZ* I. 138 Lowland to montane forest..*Porokaiwhiri, Pigeonwood.* **1978** MOORE & IRWIN *Oxford Book NZ Plants* 36 *Hedycarya arborea, pigeonwood, porokaiwhiri.* A medium-sized tree, rather common in mixed forests except in eastern districts south of Banks Peninsula.

poroporo. Also with much variety of early form as **bura bura, poraporo, pura-pura, puru-puru**; occas. as a Ma. variant **poporo** /'po:poro/ (see quots. 1882, 1906); see other variants at BULL-A-BULL. [Ma. /'poroporo/: Williams 294 *pōporo, poroporo..Solanum nigrum, S. aviculare.*] BULL-A-BULL (*Solanum aviculare* and *S. laciniatum*), and the orange-yellow berries edible when ripe. Also *attrib*. See also *Maori gooseberry* (MAORI B 4 b), NIGHTSHADE, *potato berry, plant* (POTATO 1).

1840 WAKEFIELD *Diary* (ATLMS) 7 Oct. Bura bura..beads of berries. **1843** DIEFFENBACH *Travels in NZ* II. 380 Poraporo [*sic*]—berry, fruit. **1847** ANGAS *Savage Life* II. 88 I had to cut down a large and spreading *pura-pura* bush, that almost concealed the verandah. **1853** HOOKER *II Flora Novae-Zelandiae I Flowering Plants* 182 Solanum *aviculare*... Nat. name, 'Poroporo' in the northern, and 'Kohoho' in the southern parts of the Islands. **1857** HURSTHOUSE *NZ* I. 136 The poroporo, the nicest or least nasty of the wild fruits, is a sodden strawberry flavoured with apple-peel. **1869** *TrNZI* in Brooker et al. *NZ Medicinal Plants* (1981) 15 As a cataplasm for ulcers they used the leaves of the kohoho or poroporo. **1883** DOMETT *Ranolf & Amohia* II. 109 Potato-apples of the *poro-poro* tall Rich-mellowing from their crude lip-burning green. **1898** REEVES *Long White Cloud* 403 Not to call the poro-poro shrub 'bull a bull' would be considered affectation. **1906** CHEESEMAN *Manual NZ Flora* 482 *Poporo; Poroporo; Kohoho.* Also common in many parts of Australia... The fruit is edible, and was made into jam by the early colonists. **1926** HILGENDORF *Weeds* 152 Poro poro (*Solanum aviculare*), also called bullibull (a corruption of the Maori name), and potato berry. **1943** *NZ Farmers' Weekly* 11 Mar. 40 How many readers know the native shrub, with its dainty blue flower, nasty-smelling foliage and bright orange berries—purupuru by name but commonly called bullabull? **1946** [see BULL-A-BULL]. **1952** LYON *Faring South* 130 Native fruits were few; the purapura, tawha and karaka are the only ones that occur to me. **1965** [see *potato bush* (POTATO 1)]. **1981** [see BULL-A-BULL].

porphyrio. [f. Latin *porphyrio* (ad. Greek) purple water-hen.] A vernacular use of *Porphyrio* the generic name of the PUKEKO (*Porphyrio porphyrio melanotus*).

1843 DIEFFENBACH *Travels in NZ* I. 362 Ducks,

teals, the red-billed porphyrio or pukeko..are found here. **1875** DOMETT *Randolf & Amohia* 213 The crimson-billed porphyrio, that jerking struts Among the cool thick rushes.

porpoise. Any member of the fam. Delphinidae having spade-shaped teeth and no beak.

[*Note*] There are no true porpoises in New Zealand waters: the term, often as **common**, or **New Zealand porpoise**, is usu. applied in default to various species of DOLPHIN q.v.

1892 WILLIAMS *Dictionary of the NZ Language* 34 *hopuhopu..porpoise.* **1917** WILLIAMS *Dictionary of the Maori Language* 549 *Upokohue,...Globicephalus melas, blackfish,* and *Cephalorhynchus hectori, porpoise.* **1918** *NZJST* I. 137 *Porpoises* and *dolphins* are most valuable for their skins and oil. **1922** *Ibid.* V. 140 The dusky dolphin..is perhaps as plentiful round the coast of New Zealand as the common porpoise [*Cephalorhynchus hectori*]. It can be distinguished from it by the falcate dorsal fin and the more pointed snout. **1966** DOOGUE & MORELAND *Sea Anglers' Guide* 305 Hector's Dolphin... Confined to New Zealand.. *Cephalorhynchus hectori*; native dolphin, New Zealand porpoise.

porridge pot. A small mud volcano; a natural pool of boiling mud. See also *mud-pool, mud volcano* (MUD 2).

1886 KERSHAW *Col. Facts* 250 'Pretty hot business in Auckland some years ago,' said Mac,.. look[ing] down on the twenty extinct porridge pots. **1887** WADDINGTON *Notes of a Tour* 31 Near [Rotorua], after a little climb, a small plateau was gained where the 'porridge pot' was continually on the boil, the mud is relished by the natives, but its appearance was not tempting to us. **1888** WILLIS *Geysers & Gazers* 12 Porridge pots.

port: see PORTSAMMY.

portable soup. *Hist.* Also **portable broth**. [Of historical significance in early NZ: OED 1758; AND 1843.] A base of dried meat, etc. for reconstitution into soup by adding water.

1769 COOK *Journals* 28 Oct. (1955) I. 185 I have caused it [*sc.* sellery] to be boild with Portable Soup and Oatmeal every morning for the Peoples breakfast..because I look upon it to be very wholesome and a great Antiscorbutick. **1777** FORSTER *Voyage Round World* I. 105 The prophylactics..which were regularly served to the crew, namely portable broth, and sour krout, had a wonderful effect of keeping them free from sea-scurvy. **1862** in Butler *First Year* (1863) iv 40 Should means be found of converting the meat into portable soup, the carcase of a sheep might..be considerably higher than 10*s*.

Port Craig cocktail. [f. *Port Craig* (named after a locally drowned millhand, John *Craig*), a remote locality on the western shoreline of Te Waewae Bay, on the Foveaux Strait coast of Wallace County, South Island, once a thriving sawmilling settlement and port.] See quots.

1967 MILLER *Ink on My Fingers* 176 They decided to try as a reviver a 'Port Craig cocktail', made as follows: Take a cup—or a round tobacco tin—and drop in one egg. Add one tablespoonful of Worcester sauce and one eggcup of methylated spirit. Mix well, hold nose, swallow rapidly. **1976** MCCLENAGHAN *Travelling Man* 47 'I got on to Port Craig cocktails once'... He explained, 'You get a cup, drop in an egg, add a spoonful of Worcester sauce, an egg cup of methylated spirits, hold your nose and swallow rapidly.'

porthole. *Farming.* [AND 1882.] The opening in the woolshed through which a newly-shorn sheep leaves the shearing-board and enters the counting-out pen. **1913** CARR *Country Work* 14 As soon as a shearer has taken the fleece off and let the sheep go through the port-hole to the counting-out pen, the picker gathers the fleece up. **1922** [see COUNT 2 b]. **1933** *Press* (Christchurch) (Acland Gloss.) 30 Sept. 15 Each shearer has his own [counting-out pen] and passes his [shorn] sheep through a *port hole* into it, so that his tally may be counted. **1949** NEWTON *High Country Days* 50 [The shearer] sent the sheep bundling out the porthole. **1960** MILLS *Sheep-O* 59 As fast as shorn sheep went through the porthole into the counting-out pens, woolly ones were coming up the ramp into the catching pens. **1973** FERNANDEZ *Tussock Fever* 3 He pushed his completed, naked sheep through his legs and out the porthole. **1989** RICHARDS *Pioneer's Life* 51 Although the shed had twelve portholes only six had been adapted for machines.

Port Nick. *Hist.* Also **Portnic**. A sailors' and early settlers' shortening of *Port Nicholson*, the early name [after Captain John *Nicholson* (d. 1863), harbourmaster at Sydney] for Wellington and its harbour; also adapted by Maori speakers as *Pōneke*, adopted into English as *Poneke* /ˈpɒnɪki/, /pəˈniki/ (see quot. 1917), and also used in modern Wellington reference.
1840 WAKEFIELD *Diary* (ATLMS) (1839) 14 Mar. Started from Port Nick for Porirua. **1841** WEEKES *Journal* (ATLMS) 12 Port Nicholson, or as it is here universally called, Portnic. **1887** *Auckland Weekly News 13 Aug.* 7 The incident adds another of the wrongs of Port Nick. **1890** *Otago Witness* (Dunedin) 28 Aug. 36 We determined to return to our first love, 'Port Nick'—as it was usually called. **1910** *NZ Free Lance* (Wellington) 5 Feb. 4 He is perfectly amazed at the number of sceptics who now live on the shores of Port Nick. **1917** BROWN *Lay of Bantry Bay* 5 Cockies scratching the Wairau Plain Offer a frequent freight: Hay and chaff for Poneke main. **1968** *NZ Contemp. Dict. Suppl.* (Collins) 16 *Port Nick n.* whaling sl. for Port Nicholson, Wellington. **1992** *Dominion* (Wellington) 8 Aug. 10 Along with earth tremors, Port Nick's waters rose and fell for at least eight hours.

portsammy. *Obs.* Also *ellipt.* **port**. [f. *port*(manteau + *sammy*.] A suitcase, gladstone bag, etc. (often one already packed for a trip).
1905 *Truth* 7 Oct. 7 Pack your 'ports' and hurry up. **1943** HISLOP *Pure Gold* 107 One evening, on answering a knock on the homestead front door, he was met by a traveller with 'port sammy' all set for the usual kind invitation to come along inside. **1969** NEWTON *Big Country NI* 215 As green as grass, he arrived [at the sheep station] riding a horse bareback and carrying a flash Queen Street port sammy. **1980** LAWRY *Good Luck & Lavender* 63 A classy gentleman's travelling chest... It had strong metal clasps and a lock, and a leather handle was attached to each end... Ed nonchalently [*sic*] referred to this piece of elegant luggage as his 'port sammy'.

portulaca. [Local use of *Portulaca* for *Portulaca* and other genera.] **a.** Also **wild portulaca**. Introduced *Portulaca* spp.; also occas. applied to *Calandrinia* spp. See also HORGAN'S WEED, *pigweed* (PIG *n.*[1] 4).
1926 HILGENDORF *Weeds* 72 Portulaca (*Portulaca oleracea*), called also pig weed, hog weed, purslane, and ice plant, is very common on garden paths etc., in Auckland, becoming less and less common as far south as Nelson. **1951** LEVY *Grasslands of NZ* (1970) 4 Many introduced weeds typical of subtropical climates are present, the more common ones being wild portulaca, inkweed, redroot, thorn apple, and apple of Sodom. **1969** *Standard Common Names Weeds* 60 *portulaca, wild Portulaca oleracea*. **1980** TAYLOR *Weeds of Crops* 114 Wild Portulaca (*Portulaca oleracea*)... This Asiatic weed of arable crops is common in many warmer countries. In New Zealand wild portulaca occurs in gardens and cropping land.
b. *Calandrinia* sp. CURNOW'S CURSE.
1967 [see CURNOW'S CURSE]. **1969** *Standard Common Names Weeds* 60 portulaca [=] calandrinia: wild *portulaca*.

posi, var. POSSIE.

position of responsibility. *Education.* Often abbrev. **P.R.** A designated position, ranking between teacher and deputy principal, involving responsibility for areas of a school programme.
1965 *Teachers' Legal & Service Handbook* 456 Positions of Responsibility..in any secondary school shall be determined according to a scheme approved by the Minister. **1968** SLATTER *Pagan Game* 92 It would be a splendid stepping stone to a position of responsibility at any of the numerous schools in and about Wellington.

possie /ˈpɒsi/, /ˈpɒzi/. [f. *pos*(ition + -IE.] Also **posi, posse(y), possy, pozzy**.
1. *WW1* and *WW2*. [AND 1915.] A place of shelter, poss. orig. a firing position.
1916 *Chron. NZEF* 30 Aug. 9 He shot one after the other of the enemy as they sprang out of their underground H.E.-proof 'possies'. **1917** 2 Feb. in Miller *Camps, Tramps & Trenches* (1939) 11 We repaired to our 'possie' on the dispensary roof. **1917** LANGFORD, E.H. *MS Papers 2242* (ATLMS) 19 July A terrible long way up to posse and q 'L' [*sic* =hell] of a place to arrive in. **1920** *Quick March* 10 Feb. 27 'How many more miles have we got to go to get to this 'possie' of yours?' asked the exasperated voice of a Digger. **1924** *Aussie (NZ Section)* 15 May I Look out, Bill [Massey], Jerry's over and we're in a crook possie here! **1937** PARTRIDGE *Dict. Slang* 652 *possy*; occ. *possie, pozzy*. A *position*; esp. a dug-out, or other shelter: military, mainly Australian and New Zealand: from 1915. **1944** FULLARTON *Troop Target* 11 Those M.G. Blokes have camouflaged their 'possies' well.
2. a. A personal place or space; a secluded place.
c1926 THE MIXER *Transport Workers' Song Book* 70 You'll hear him in his bar-room 'possie'. **1943** BURDON *Outlaw's Progress* 25 Swell little pozzy this. **1944** *NZ New Writing* III. 8 Don't y'think it's a lovely little possey? I only just found it. **1948** BALLANTYNE *Cunninghams* (1976) 114 The autumn was mild for Gladston; the veranda, sunny and swept by cool breezes, was really a bonzer possy. **1963** PEARSON *Coal Flat* 31 He had taken girls outside the [dance] hall before..for a cuddle..and sometimes more, if the night was fine, in a pozzy he knew of under the blackberries. **1972** FRAME *Daughter Buffalo* 38 We found it to be divided into small plots like the private places or 'possies' which my friends and I claimed for ourselves when in the midst of games we suddenly decided we wanted to be alone and inaccessible. **1986** CARR *Diary Pig Hunter* 6 Not having the right sort of dog and the 'posi' to hunt in..combined to keep me from ever catching a pig. **1990** *North & South* (Auckland) May 94 By now passengers have already separated themselves into possies on the ship.
b. A position, situation, place or predicament.
1937 MARSH *Vintage Murder* 238 Messing about on the scene of the crime... She's going to find herself in a very, very uncomfortable little pozzy. **1971** GRANT & GABBARA *Land Uprooted High* 44 They [*sc.* the Canterbury pioneers] had, in New Zealand idiom, 'a good pozzy'. **1992** *Marlborough Express* (Blenheim) 31 Jan. 5 'It [*sc.* a high-country farm] was a beauty possie up the Puhi..' Sam says wistfully.
c. A position or job.
1953 *Landfall* 28 251 She'd not Be loony enough to leave a good Pozzy, a husband and a house to rot.

possum. Also **'possum.** [An aphetic form of OPOSSUM.]
1. a. [AND 1770.] The presently preferred scientific and official name for *Trichosurus vulpecula* (fam. Phalangeridae), a brush-tailed, tree-living, mainly nocturnal, vegetarian marsupial introduced from Australia. Recorded earliest in *attrib.* use. See also OPOSSUM.
1851 as *possum skin* [see 2 below]. **1880** SENIOR *Travel and Trout* 260 [We] fed and stroked the Tasmanian 'possum [in Acclimatisation Society grounds at Christchurch]. **1912** *NZ Free Lance* (Wellington) 3 Feb. 14 'Possums have been a tarnation nuisance ever since they were introduced into New Zealand. **1921** *Quick March* 11 July 17 Gran'pa has been very excited lately about 'possums. **1938** HYDE *Nor Yrs Condemn* 147 No hou-hou, no 'possum, no wild pig, pretty soon we starve. **1965** *Tuatara* XIII. 30 A glance through the scientific papers published on *Trichosurus* in the last ten years shows that most zoologists (and all Australian zoologists) have used 'possum'. **1985** BENTLEY & FRASER *Grand Limerick Tour* [No.] 56 It's Fair Day at Mangatainoka, What's the guts for your average joker? Pitching possums is big, There's calf roping, greased pig, And a yahoo, with untold strip poker. **1990** *Handbook NZ Mammals* 68 Brushtail possum *Trichosurus vulpecula*... In New Zealand, its common name has traditionally been 'opossum'.., especially in the fur trade... The standard common name for *T. vulpecula* adopted by the Australian Mammal Society is common brushtail possum..or, as here, simply possum.
b. *attrib.*
1971 CRUMP *Bastards I Have Met* 99 A possum-man is like a possum dog. They're a special kind of people. **1985** HILL *Moaville Magic* 33 Once a year, they [*sc.* the Moaville saleyards] become the venue for the Central North Island All-Comers Possum-Skinning Championships. **1986** *Listener* 26 Apr. 16 Try buying two-inch possum-proof wire-netting in Whakatane or Opotiki between October and December, and you will be out of luck. **1991** *Dominion Sunday Times* (Wellington) 31 Mar. 21 The [Hokitika Wildfoods] festival is famous for its possum pate, but this year the delicacy was almost dropped from the menu. The furry pests are carriers of tuberculosis.

2. Special Comb. **possum block**, see BLOCK *n.*[2] 6 a; **possumburgers**, a joc. fanciful formation on *hamburger*, suggesting possum meat as the filling; **possum line**, a line of traps or poison baits for taking possum, usu. for their skins; **possum rug** (occas. *ellipt.* **'possum**) [AND 1840], a rug made out of possum skins (see also WOGGA); **possum skin** [AND 1854], a possum pelt cured for sale; **possum token**, the ears and a strip from the back to be redeemed for cash under a former State eradication programme; **possum-trapper**, one who traps or poisons possums for a living.
1991 *Examiner* 27 June 8 [Heading] Nothing But Blood, Sweat, Toil And **Possumburgers**. **1986** *Woman's Weekly* 14 July 12 We've always lived on the road up to now... We do a bit of gold now and again. And Robin runs a good **'possum line**. **1853** in *Canterbury Rhymes* (1866) 18 This mutton chop—and this damper queer—A stretcher—a **'possum rug**—So wretched all that the traveller here But seldom shows his mug. **1873** ST JOHN *Pakeha Rambles* in Taylor *Early Travellers* (1959) 528 I took a pull at the flask,

wrapped myself up in my 'possum [sic] with the saddle for a pillow..and lit my pipe. **1896** Moffatt *Adventures* (1979) 61 I..took the kindly offer of a 'possum rug and turned in [Nelson c.1860]. **1913** Carr *Country Work* 6 Sheets are not fashionable, while three sacks sewn together make what is termed a 'New Zealand Possum Rug' or 'Wogga'. **1991** Eldred-Grigg 15 A worn possum rug on the floor. **1851** *Lyttelton Times* 3 May 1 [Advt] 2 **Possum skins**. **1873** Tinne *Wonderland of Antipodes* 67 The fur of the rat was..rather like a baby 'possum skin from Tasmania. **1988** *Dominion* (Wellington) 23 July 8 Bent into s-shapes..it becomes hooks upon which one may hang..new possum skins, and the keys for the trail bike. **1993** *Dominion* (Wellington) 26 May 5 [Caption] Mr Falloon wearing a possum-skin hat with a golden totara. **1961** Crump *Hang On a Minute Mate* 145 Well, a man could sell deerskins and **possum tokens**. **1960** Crump *Good Keen Man* 114 Harry found four traps that a **possum-trapper** had left hanging in a hollow rata.

possuming, *vbl. n.* The trapping, poisoning or shooting of possums, usu. for their skins.
1980 Glen *Bush in Our Yard* 67 'Have you caught any possums yet?' asked Rex Findlay... Eventually everyone at work began to greet me with the same question, 'How goes the possuming?' **1987** 6 Sept. TV1 Country Calendar (West Coast) I like fishing, shooting, possuming and all that. **1995** Crump *Bushwoman* 27 There must be a knack to this possuming.

possy, var. possie.

postal fiscal. *Hist*. A fiscal stamp originally used to collect State revenue other than postal, but authorized for postal use.
1903 *Sterling Monthly* II. The great bulk of the postal fiscals of the early issues are stamps which were placed on deeds or receipts and never cancelled, and which collectors, taking advantage of the legal permission of 1882, have passed through the post. **1938** *NZ Stamp Collector* XIX. 55 the latest edition of Gibbon's catalogue..shows that increases in value have been made in all sections with the exception of the postal fiscals and the postage dues. **1943** *NZ Stamp Collector* XXIV. 12 New Zealand Postal Fiscals... Philatelists are not yet in agreement as to the status of the early fiscals as postage stamps. **1970** *NZ Stamp Collector* L. 119 The only true 'postal fiscal' in New Zealand is the same design in blue, which, in 1882, prior to the abolition of the distinction between fiscal and postage stamps, was specially authorized for postal use owing to a shortage of 1d stamps. **1988** Strachan *Century of Philately* 108 There was clearly a need for full information on at least some issues of Fiscal Stamps, if only to make understanding of the Postal Fiscals much easier.

postal note. *Hist*. Also occas. abbrev. **PN**. [Elsewhere called a *postal order*: AND 1885.] A type of money order for limited amounts, in various fixed denominations, formerly bought and cashable at any post office.
1890 *NZ Observer* 10 May 4 Postal notes and money orders are just equivalent to bank notes and cheques. **1901** *NZJE* 1 Mar. III. 1 Remittances.— Money can be forwarded by post-office order or postal note. **1917** Lawson *Historic Trentham* 40 More letters, parcels, postal notes, and telegrams pass through that [Trentham] office than there does in a town like..Gisborne, for instance. **1937** *NZ Railways Mag.* Jan. 5 A postal note for 17/- must accompany each initial entry. **1944** Scott *Life with Barbara* 20 Elizabeth rushed to my aid with her tea coupon for the month and a postal note for seven and sixpence. **1950** McKenzie in *Hyacinths and Biscuits* (1985) 73 I suppose you'll accept a postal note... It's as good as money. *Ibid*. 74 'Don't you keep tins?' she asked when my milkman, plus my p/n's, had finally departed. **1960** Startup *Travelling Mails* 3 The rural residents are also able through their rural contractor to obtain postal notes, money-orders, postage stamps and to register correspondence. **1981** Peterson *Glasshouses* 7 Many years earlier [c1890s] Mother had sent Don to the Post Office for a 2/6 postal note. Unfortunately she forgot to give him the poundage. 'That's another penny, Sonny,' said the Postmaster cheerfully. With eyes flashing fire the small boy held up the PN.

post-and-rail.
1. [Used elsewhere but of special significance for early rural New Zealand.] **a**. [AND 1802.] Each of the component posts and rails of a *post-and-rail fence* (see c (b) below).
1835 Yate *NZ* (1970) 44 No plant in New Zealand furnishes such excellent materials [as Puriri] for..posts and rails for fences. **1849** Deans in *Pioneers* (1964) 150 We believe that this sort of fence [sc. ditch and bank] would not cost more at first than one of post and rail, even where timber abounded. **1859** *Puketoi Station Diary* (Hocken TS) 25 Mar. Hood left with dray for Kyeburn to bring Stockyard posts and rails. **1871** Money *Knocking About NZ* 145 I joined an old troopmate who had been post-and-rail splitting for some Maories at Rangitaiki. **1965** Henderson *Open Country* 53 The next type of fence was of posts and rails for a stockyard.

b. *Sing*. *Ellipt*. for *post-and-rail fence*.
1844 Dillon *Letters* 10 Apr. (1954) 39 My outer fences are post and rails..and the inner ones of what is called in England staple and board. **1861** *Butler to Tripp* 13 Oct. in Maling *Samuel Butler* (1960) 56 I want a man..to do all sort[s] of station work—a little fencing sod work and post and rails. **1883** *Brett's Colonists' Guide* 18 These [dog-leg fences] will, in later years, give place to the post-and-rail, or wire, thorn, hakea, or other live fences. **1895** *Fencing Act* in *Settler's Handbook NZ* (1902) 160 (1.) Post and rail, at least 3 ft. 9 in. high, of substantial material, firmly [ere]cted, with not less than four rails. **1982** *Agric. Gloss.* (MAF) 28 *Post and rail*: Made from wooden posts joined by rails.

c. [AND 1820.] (a) In *attrib*. use.
1849 Allom *Letter* in Earp *Handbook* (1852) 118 The only farm buildings requisite are, a strong post-and-rail stock-yard for the purposes of milking and occasionally mustering the stock. **1857** [see catching-pen 1].

(b) In the special collocation **post-and-rail fence (fencing)**, a strong fence of usu. three to four wooden rails slotted through holes in, or morticed to, upright wooden posts.
1853 Rochfort *Adventures of Surveyor* 25 The run is bounded on one side by the Turakina river, on the other three by a good post-and-rail fence. **1865** Chudleigh *Diary* 4 July (1950) 192 Chas and I put up post and rail fencing. **1875** Kirk *Durability NZ Timbers* 6 Totara post and rail fences are expected to last from ten to thirteen years. **1888** Barlow *Kaipara* 92 When outside the post and rail fence..I breathed once more. **1922** Cowan *NZ Wars* (1955) I. 380 He bade the *tupara* men hold their fire until the soldiers were close up to the post-and-rail fence. **1940** Studholme *Te Waimate* (1954) 103 The first fences were made of split totara posts and rails... Post and rail fences took a very long time to erect. **1950** *NZJAg*. July LXXXI. 9 *Post-and-rail Fence*. Posts and rails form a strong and durable fence. **1984** Locke *The Kauri & the Willow* 62 I thought your house was all shut in with the post-and-rail fence.

2. *transf*. or *fig*. *Obs*. As **posts and rails tea** [AND 1843] (also *ellipt*. **post-and-rails**), a coarse tea leaving stalks, etc. (the 'posts and rails') floating in the billy.
1914 Pfaff *Diggers' Story* 43 I forgot tea, 4s... but the quality; we used to call it Posts and Rails [on the diggings c1860s]. **1940** Studholme *Te Waimate* (1954) 91 It has to be remembered that..bread cost only 6d. or 7d. a 4lb. loaf, and tea (post and rails) could be bought for 1/- per lb. **1968** *NZ Contemp. Dict. Suppl.* (Collins) 16 *post-and-rails (tea)* n. strong, coarse, inferior tea made in a billy..with pieces of stalk or leaves floating in it. **1982** Burton *Two Hundred Yrs. NZ Food* 16 The tea was 'of the commonest kind'. The brand was Young Green Hyson, but the settlers nicknamed the foul brew 'post and rails'. This was a reference to the twigs which floated about on the surface, large enough to form the posts and rails of a wooden fence. **1991** La Roche *Hist. of Howick & Pakuranga* 105 Tea [c1840s] was 'young Green Hyson' but this astringent brew was called by the settlers 'post-and-rails'.

post and stake. Applied to a kind of fence. See quot.
1940 Studholme *Te Waimate* (1954) 105 A little later..sod fences were reduced to about 2 ft. 6 in. in height... Then post and stake fences came in; posts nine feet apart, with stakes in between, the posts being bored to let the wire through.

poster. *Rugby football*. A shot at goal which hits one of the upright goal-posts.
1885 *Wairarapa Daily* 6 July 2 The referee, however, gave it as a poster. **1963** *Dominion* (Wellington) 17 June 6 [He] went to 99 points for the season, then kicked a 'poster' with the conversion. **1987** 13 June TV1 Rugby Commentator. It all stemmed from a poster by Grant Fox the Auckland fullback.

post-primary. [Used elsewhere but recorded earliest in NZ: see OED.] Of education or schools, following a 'primary' stage, secondary; of a pupil (usu. of the age of 13 years or over) receiving such (secondary) education. (The term prob. became official in the Education (Post-Primary Teachers) Regulations 1945/24.)
1919 *AJHR* E-6 15 Suffice to say the main aim we have had in view is the bringing of the post-primary work into closer touch with the vocational needs of the pupils. **1929** *NZ Educ. Gaz.* 1 Mar. 36 The teaching of French pronunciation in our post-primary schools. **1963** *Evening Post* (Wellington) 18 July 23 At present being built are 25 schools—17 primary, seven intermediate and one postprimary.

post splitter. A bushman who fashions posts, battens, etc. by splitting tree trunks.
1952–53 *NZ Forest Gloss.* (TS) Post Splitter. A bushman engaged on splitting posts, sleepers or battens out of found timber, usually on a contract basis.

Hence **post-splitting**.
1920 *Quick March* 10 Apr. 31 While we were waiting for the billy to boil..taking the mid-day spell after a strenuous morning of post-splitting.

pot, *n.*[1] *Rugby football*. [f. *pot*(-shot a random shot at a target (see quot. 1902).] (An attempt at) a drop-kicked field-goal.
1888 in *Otago Univ. Review* in *College Rhymes* (1923) 21 Cresswell attempted a pot, but somehow or other he missed it. **1900** *NZ Illustr. Mag.* III. 237 As in England, drop-kicking is conspicuous by its absence, unless when resorting to a 'pot'. [**1902** Ellison *Art of Rugby Football* 30 [A full-back's] duties are almost purely defensive, except when in a position to take a

pot shot at goal.] **1908** BARR *British Rugby Team in Maoriland* 33 In an even game with no tries on; he's certain to frighten the enemy with a 'pot' which..will skim the paint off the uprights. **1928** *NZ Free Lance* (Wellington) 6 June 37 [Caption] Take a pot. **1947** MCCARTHY *Broadcasting with the Kiwis* 34 Leinster scored from a lovely 'pot' by the blond stand-off half Carry. **1959** SLATTER *Gun in My Hand* 74 Dave kicked his usual pot for them. **1968** SLATTER *Pagan Game* 217 The Ruamahanga forwards bullock into the ruck and Keith Maxwell, given the ball, takes a snap pot at goal. **1975** HOWITT *NZ Rugby Greats* 20 With time almost up and Wanganui ahead 12–11, Brown tried for a 'pot'. **1986** KNIGHT *Shield Fever* 262 He had the happy sight of seeing his pot soar between the uprights for three of the game's most important points.

pot, *n.*² In the phr. **to put (one's) pot on. a.** [Poss. a shortening of, for example, *to put one's pot on (to boil, on the fire)* to put the heat on (a person); AND 1864.] To inform on, to tell on; to 'put (one's) weights up'.

1905 *Truth* 11 Nov. 5 'Tongue-murdering' appears to be a new term applied to slandering a man, or 'putting his pot on' with intent to do him harm. **1908** *Ibid.* 13 June 6 Walsh was abusing Mrs. Kerr, the landlady, when she said she would 'put his pot on' with the police. The term is familiar. **1913** REES *Merry Marauders* 206 You ought to put the Liquor Party's pot on. **1928** SMYTH *Jean of Tussock Country* 59 Dalton has put your pot on [i.e., told the boss]. **1945** BURTON *In Prison* 103 I played one of my [prison] pals for the life of a girl 'who had done him wrong' or, even in more classical language, had 'put his pot on with the police'. **1951** MARSH *Opening Night* (1968) ix 160 If you put me pot on with the management for what I done leaving 'er to lay—all right... Finish! **1962** *Landfall Country* 114 I been there about the same time as you, Tom, and I haven't had a rise yet. Wonder if Myers put my pot on. **1974** *Sunday Times* (Wellington) 4 Aug. 3 'If Mrs Moore and her child are living in the gully no one would put her pot on. They would just accept it and say nothing about it,' she said. **1985** MITCALFE *Hey Hey Hey* 121 The cheek of them! I didn't 'put their pot on'.

b. To give the game away to another person's disadvantage; to ruin things (for a person).

1906 *Truth* 8 Sept. 5 The first [indecent post-]card was enough to put his pot on. **1915** *Hutt Valley Independent* 17 Apr. 3 Squarehead and Co. had a try to rope in Tom Wilford to put our pot on. Tom W. smelt a rat and wasn't to be had that way. **1943** HISLOP *Pure Gold* 91 It also shows how a smart Alec, by saying too much, can put his own pot on if he is not careful. [He lost a sale.]

Hence **pot** *v. trans.*, to inform on; **potting** *vbl. n.* acting as an informer, tale-telling.

1968 SLATTER *Pagan Game* 164 He's a moral to get potted. **1983** *National Business Review* 26 Sept. 28 [There is] a kiwi aversion to sneaking, grassing, potting or squealing. **1990** KIDMAN *True Stars* 60 Have you been potting Larissa to the cops?

pot, *v. Rugby union.* [See POT *n.*¹] To score a drop-kicked field-goal; often as a *ppl. a.* in the collocation **potted goal**, a field goal; also **potter** *n.*, **potting** *vbl. n.*

1884 BAKER *Daughter of King* 178 An old boy 'Chum'—son of a chief..had joined the group..to inform the young man, with whom he had..struggled many times on football grounds for the mastery of the ball, or the potting of a goal, that he was now a missionary amongst his people. **1887** *Auckland Weekly News* 1 Oct. 12 The Canterbury match was very interesting... The visitors sticking closely to the 'potting' tactics as a means to score. **1890** *Otago Witness* (Dunedin) 8 May 28 This advantage was shortly followed up by Laurenson potting a goal for Kaikorai. **1902** ELLISON *Art of Rugby Football* 32 A centre three–quarter should possess..the additional qualifications of being a clever potter or try getter. **1905** *Evening Post* (Wellington) 2 Nov. 7 The only bright spot in the match for them was the potted goal by the full-back, Lillicrap, a fine performance. **1906** DIXON *Triumphant Tour of the NZ Footballers* 99 Sloan elected to 'pot' instead of passing. **1908** BARR *British Rugby Team in Maoriland* 44 He kicked superbly..while his potted goal was a fine effort. **1924** *NZ Free Lance* (Wellington) 28 May 36 He..wound up..with a slashing potted goal. **1959** *Listener* 24 July 6 Five potted goals—that was when a pot was worth five points. **1968** SLATTER *Pagan Game* 206 I have seen a boy pot a goal and not know he was doing it. **1986** KNIGHT *Shield Fever* 262 John Boe potted one of the six goals he landed in the shield era.

potae /ˈpʌutai/. Also **potai, poti**. [Ma. /ˈpoːtae/: Williams 296 *Pōtae. 1*... Covering for the head, cap, hat.] A hat, a head covering.

[**1770** PARKINSON *Journal* (1773) 127 A Vocabulary of the Language of New Zealand... Potai, *A feather ornament on their head.* **1815** KENDALL *New Zealanders' First Book* 12 Poti. Hat. **1820** LEE & KENDALL *Gram. & Vocab.* 195 Potai; A hat, cap, pot-lid; any round covering. **c1826–27** BOULTBEE *Journal* (1986) 111 hat—pòtai.] **1840** POLACK *Manners & Customs* I. 180 Coverings for the head (*potai*) are rarely made use of. **1881** CAMPBELL *Poenamo* 71 How pretty she'll look in her new *potai*. Te-na. [1881 *Note*] *Potai*, cap or hat. **1900** *Auckland Weekly News Xmas Number* 12 A dumb and touching expression of the chief's woe is his *potae* lying beside the dead boy, where he has flung it down in a paroxysm of grief and despair. **1912** *NZ Free Lance* (Wellington) 29 June 4 How pretty she'll look in the new potae. **1916** *Chron. NZEF* 29 Sept. 55 So—Put on your potae in the latest style, and smile, boys, smile. **1923** *Aussie (NZ Section)* 14 Apr. X I ket Winnie Hawkena's poti (hat) from the keyser. **1946** REED *Farthest North* 72 My hat blew off,.. I ran to retrieve my potai. **1961** MACKAY *Puborama* 53 When that potai was returned to its bewildered owner, it took him some time to adjust the extra load. **1962** *Australasian Universal Dict.* 3 Again, the New Zealander has drawn less upon Maori words than the Australian has called upon the Aborigine. However 'puku' (stomach) and 'potae' (hat) are freely used in New Zealand. **1976** FINLAYSON *Other Lovers* 96 I'll lend you an old pair of jeans and a shady potae. You'll need a shady hat out there. **1986** LATHAM *WAAC Story* 3 And we made our own hats. Believe me, there were some beauts! One Maori girl's remark summed it up in a lot of cases—'Call that plurry thing a potae (hat)? Looks more like a mimi pot!'

potai, var. POTAE.

potato.

1. Usu. in various Comb. in transf. uses, applied to other *Solanum* spp., esp. the POROPORO: **potato apple**, **potato berry** (also for *Gaultheria* sp.), **potato bush**, **potato plant**. See also MAORI POTATO.

1883, 1926 potato-apple, potato berry [see POROPORO]. **1970** SANSOM *Stewart Islanders* 141 We would hang on..while we gathered the 'potato berries' which grew on its sunny faces... It is a heath, *Gaultheria*, and its flowers too are delicately scented. **1965** GILLHAM *Naturalist in NZ* 51 Only four..species [of *Solanum*] were natives and one of these, the **potato bush** or poroporo, was probably not one of the original inhabitants of the islet [off Stewart Island]. **1898** HUDSON *NZ Moths & Butterflies* 139 *Solanum aviculare* (Poroporo, or **Potato Plant**). A shrub, with very dark green, pointed leaves, purple underneath, and bright purple flowers resembling those of the potato.

2. In the phr. **to have one's potato cooked**, to be done for, to be finished, to 'have one's goose cooked'; also as **the potato is cooked** (when attributed to, or after, Te Whiti-o-Rongomai (d. 1907), Maori leader and prophet), the 'die is cast', 'it is done'.

1897 WRIGHT *Station Ballads* 13 Your potato's cooked with Mary. **1935** MAXWELL *Recollections* 84 Owing to Te Whiti's peculiar mentality..it turned out otherwise, he making the somewhat oracular announcement, 'The Potato is not yet cooked.' **1974** SLATTER *Great Days at Lancaster Park* 84 [Referring to the refusal of the British Secretary of State to allow Maori volunteers for the Boer War.] One [advertisement, December 1900] in the [Christchurch] *Press* boldly declared: 'The War and the Maori... Alas the potato is cooked; the Maoris have been stopped by Chamberlain. Ka Kino, too bad.'

pot-head. A translation of a Maori insulting phrase *upoko kohua* (='head' a sacred part of the body + 'pot') implying that the head of the person referred to is fit only for cooking.

1905 BAUCKE *White Man Treads* 149 And who may this *upoko kohua* (pot head) be? **1947** FINLAYSON *Brown Man's Burden* (1973) 76 Just a silly pothead, a doormat for those damn tourists! **1973** *Ibid.* 141 Pothead: translation of a Maori insult more serious than it sounds in English.

pothole. Also **potch hole**. [AND a shallow excavation (goldmining),1890.]

1. *Gumfields.* [?Spec. or transf. use of *pothole* a hole from which the clay has been taken (for pottery): cf. OED 2.] A hole remaining after an excavation to obtain kauri-gum.

1911 *TrNZI* XLIII. 203 The few plants I saw were growing on the edges of 'potholes'—*i.e.*, small pits from which gum has been dug—a rather unusual situation. **1915** *Ibid.* XLVII. 77 It is growing..on the margins of 'potholes' from which gum has been dug on the moorlands. **1916** STALLWORTHY *Early N. Wairoa* 53 The [gum-land] ground was left in great pot-holes, which..made the land dangerous to get over.

2. [Cf. OED 3. *N. Amer.*, 1902.] A water-filled or boggy hole in a swamp.

1867 THOMSON *Rambles of a Philosopher* 35 Its blind swamps—its intersecting boggy creeks, and its interspersed *potch* holes. **1936** HYDE *Passport to Hell* 59 Apart from the fishy reek of it, [the mud] clung in great soggy dollops to the shovels, and underfoot the ground gave into pot-holes where the men sank knee-deep.

poti, var. POTAE.

poua. Also **pouwa, puoa.** A mythological, or alleged, huge bird of the Chatham Islands. See quots. Cf. Ma. *pouakai* a name for *Haast's eagle*.

1875 *TrNZI* VII. 117 [This is the article by Cockburn-Hood referred to in 1989 below, Anderson *Prodigious Birds.*] It appears that the Morioris have traditions about a great bird, called by them Puoa... The Morioris have a song about it, and repeat the first syllable as a chorus, Pu, pu—Pu, pu—Pu, o-a, in a manner which recalls the hollow drumming noise made by the emu. The word is probably a contraction for pu-pu-moa. **1890** *Otago Witness* (Dunedin) 18 Sept. 31 The poua-kai and the hokioi are probably different names for the same gigantic bird of prey, contemporary with the Moa. **1893** *Fortnightly Review* May in *TrNZI* (1897) XXIX. 163 I knew from various sources that the Morioris had a tradition of a great bird they called the poūwa. **1897** *TrNZI* XXIX. 162 In this paper I will endeavour to prove that the large, mythological, and extinct bird the poua, traditionally spoken of by the remaining survivors of the Moriori people who inhabit the Chatham Islands, was not allied to the moa..but was a species of swan, and belonged to the family *Anatidae*. **1989** ANDERSON *Prodigious Birds* 91 Post-European re-working of different legends about big birds..seems..evident in the names *poua* and *pouakai*. These were alleged by Tare Te Maiharoa, an influential South Island chief about the turn of the 20th century, to be the true, ancient names for moas. *Ibid*. 92 It was later argued by Forbes, however that *pouwa* was the Moriori term for the extinct Chathams swan, while Tregear suggested *poua* and *poouakai* were related (White 1897). Duff (1977:289) accepted this later speculation in attributing *pouakai* to the extinct mainland swan *Cygnus (Chenopis) sumnerensis*... [**1989** *Note*] *Poua* was also a common term for grandfather, yet another source of potential bird-man confusion.

poudi, var. POURI.

pouffey, poufter, varr. POOFTER.

poukatea, var. PUKATEA.

pounamu. Also with much variety of early form as **poanamo**, **poeanámy**, **poenammoo**, **poenamu**, **ponamu**, **poonamoo**.
1. [Ma. /ˈpounamu/: Williams 298 *Pounamu*. *1*...Greenstone, jade.] GREENSTONE 1.
1770 PARKINSON *Journal* (1773) 8 Feb. 119 On his ears hung a bunch of teeth, and an ear-ring of Poonamoo, or green stone. **1778** FORSTER *Observations* 6 Among the fossil productions of this country, we must likewise reckon a green stone, which sometimes is opaque, and sometimes quite transparent... We asked for its native place, and they called it *Poēnamoo*, from whence the abovementioned part of the country obtained the denomination of Tavai Poēnamoo. [**1820** LEE & KENDALL *NZ Gram. & Vocab*. 195 Póu námu; A green stone so called.] **1835** YATE *NZ* (1970) 151 'Manatungos'..are mostly made of the ponamu, the green stone found only in the Southern Island. **1840** POLACK *Manners & Customs* I. 194 The green talc, *poeanámy* and pieces of red jasper chipped off adroitly, resembling in shape our common gun-flints. **1846** HEAPHY *Exped. to Kawatiri* in Taylor *Early Travellers* (1959) 241 In [the Arahura's] bed, after freshets, is found the *poenamu*, in shingles or slabs. **1851** SHORTLAND *S. Dist. NZ* 4 Te Pehi..[was] killed treacherously by some of Tamaiharanui's tribe, among whom he had trusted himself, in order to barter muskets for Pounamu stone. **1867** [see NEPHRITE]. **1892** *TrNZI* XXIV. 481 It is called *pounamu* or *poenamu* by the Maoris, and 'jade', 'jadeite', or 'nephrite', by various writers, while old books refer to the 'green talc' of the Maoris. **1929** FIRTH *Primitive Econ. NZ Maori* 388 Among the Maori, considerations of aesthetic interest helped quite materially..to decide the relative worth of objects made of the *pounamu*, the nephrite so much prized for pendants, *mere*, and adzes. **1941** SUTHERLAND *Numismatic Hist. NZ* 8 The best *pounamu* pendants were worn by the chiefs. **1962** JOSEPH *Pound of Saffron* 113 'The jade, the pounamu... It's a beautiful stone. **1983** HULME *Bone People* 14 There is a gap between two tiers of bookshelves. Her chest of pounamu rests inbetween [*sic*] them.
2. *Obs*. With init. cap. An occas. early elliptical form of TE WAIPOUNAMU q.v., the South Island or possibly a place on its west coast.
1778 [see 1 a above]. **1793** *Capt. Raven to Lieut.-Gov. King* 19 Nov. in McNab *Hist. Records* (1908) I. 179 They [natives] took to the woods, and we never saw them again [at Dusky Bay], nor did Mr. Leith see any inhabitants during his residence at Poenammoo. **1834** McDONNELL *Extracts Jrnl*. (1979) 20 Coffee, sugar, indigo, and rice, would succeed well on the North Island, as also all the tropical fruits. New Zealand, more particularly Poenammoo, is yet but little known.

pound, *n*.[1] [Transf. or fig. uses of *pound*, a former unit of NZ currency.] In various phr.: **to be (or pay) (only) [x] shillings (bob) in the pound**, see SHILLING 1; **to be not (quite) the full pound**, to be mentally deficient, see QUID 1; **a pound to a pinch of shit**, an expression of certainty.
1982 SHADBOLT *Once on Chunuk Bair* (1990) 73 A pound to a pinch of shit he's scared he'll never live to be a real sinner.

pound, *n*.[2] *Prison*. [An extended use of *pound* an enclosure for detaining stray stock.] A detention unit; a punishment block or area in a prison. Cf. DIGGER *n*.[2]
1953 HAMILTON *Till Human Voices Wake Us* 72 It's a pretty rare specimen who won't do anything for a man in the pound. *Ibid*. 83 The exercise yard of the pound is the place where they used to hang and flog. **1971** SHADBOLT *Bullshit & Jellybeans* 15 The day before the following weekend I was locked up in the pound. A pound is for locking up animals. If only we'd been animals the RSPCA and all the animal lovers would have caused a public outcry—but we were only humans so no one cared. **1980** MACKENZIE *While We Have Prisons* 14 The punishment block, known as the 'pound' or the 'dummy', was a prison within the [Mt Eden] prison. In the basement, through a steel grille and a wooden door, it was a dimly lit and silent annexe leading at its far end to the tiny execution yard. **1982** NEWBOLD *Big Huey* 25 You're in *jail* now, son! Another peep from you and you'll be down the fookin pound. *Ibid*. 252 Pound (n) Detention unit. **1993** *Dominion* (Wellington) 30 June 3 His alleged assailant was put in the 'pound', a jail within the jail.

poupou. [Ma. /ˈpoupou/: Williams 297 *poupou..2*.] Any one of the upright slabs forming the solid framework of the walls of a whare.
1921 GUTHRIE-SMITH *Tutira* (1926) 95 It was his [*sc*. Te Rangi-nukai's] body which was to be buried beneath the *poupous*—uprights supporting the framework of the *whare*. **1937** *King Country Chronicle* 9 Jan. 4 Carvers..at Ohinemutu are at present on the last of the heavy pou pou slabs for the Wairoa..meeting house. **1946** *JPS* LV. 157 *poupou*, upright deeply-carved slabs forming the solid framework of a whare: between every pair of poupou is the panel of tukutuku work. **1955** PHILLIPPS *Maori Carving Illustrated* 40 Rafters are supported below by upright slabs, poupou, which are often carved.

pouri, *a*. Also early **póudi**. [Ma. /ˈpoːuri/: Williams 299 *Pōuri..2*. Sorrowful, sad, distressed.] Sad, sorrowful; distressed. Occas. used as a noun.
[**1820** LEE & KENDALL *Gram. & Vocab*. 195 Póudi, *a*. Dark, dull, heavy, sorrowful.] **1832** WILLIAMS *Early Jrnls*. 7 Sept. (1961) 258 Very *pouri* from the idleness of the boys. **1849** TAYLOR *Journal* 19 May (ATLTS) VI. 92 My boys are all pouri, because they think we have taken the wrong [path]. **1867** GRACE *Journal* 23 Dec. in *Pioneer Missionary* (1928) 169 They appeared quite satisfied that I had done all in my power for them; still, they were very pouri (sad). **1911** *Triad* 11 Dec. 23 When it was rumoured that Morland was missing, she [Roro] was *pouri*—wouldn't eat, and cried all the time. **1938** WILY & MAUNSELL *Robert Maunsell* 88 Mihi, the east wind comes. My husband is very full of *pouri*.

pouriedie, var. PURIRI.

poutama. [Ma. /ˈpoutama/: Williams 299 *Poutama..1*.] A stepped pattern of tukutuku ornament on the walls of a Maori meeting house, and in weaving.
1931 *Na To Hoa Aroha* (1987) 8 Mar. II. 120 The Rangiatea Church is being renovated, I hear, and the School of Art has been asked to reconstruct the arapaki work. It is I believe all poutama, and kakaho work, the real thing. **1986** IHIMAERA *Matriarch* 1 The hill was a gigantic crescent of eleven terraces, like the poutama pattern, the wondrous Stairway to Heaven.

pou te cowa, poutu kaua, varr. POHUTUKAWA.

pouwa, var. POUA.

poverty plant. Also **poverty weed**. [So called from its ability to grow in the poorest soil.] KUMARAHOU 1.
1869 MAY *May's Guide to NZ Farming* 29 This plant of the fuchsia species which has an oval-shaped leaf of light-green color, and bears clusters of yellow flowers..is always a sign of sterility [of soil] and is known by many settlers as the 'poverty plant'. **1934** MORRISON *Poems* 2 Kumerahau is Poverty Plant... Shy plant that waves its yellow crest Where even bracken scorns to grow. **1969** HARVEY & GODLEY *Bot. Paintings* 48 Kumarahou Rhamnaceae... Another local name, 'poverty weed', probably arose because the plant is common in poor clayey soil. **1981** BROOKER et al. *NZ Medicinal Plants* 84 Common names: *Poverty weed, gumdigger's soap* Maori names: *Kumarahou, papapa*

powaitere, var. POWHAITERE.

powa takawa, var. POHUTUKAWA.

powha, var. POHA.

powhaitere. Also early or poss. adapted from Ma. dial. forms, **po-é-tere**, **powaitere**, **powhytarnee**. [Ma. /poːˈfaitere/: Williams 299 *Pōwhaitere*..parrakeet.] *red-crowned parakeet* (PARAKEET 2 (7)).
1817 NICHOLAS *Voyage NZ* II. 339 A parrot Powhytarnee. **1835** YATE *NZ* (1970) 54 *Powaitere* A Parrot, or Paroquet.—Of these birds there are several kinds; all of them small. **1842** GRAY *Fauna* in Dieffenbach *Travels in NZ* (1843) II. 193 *Platycercus Novae Seelandiae*... Kakariki... Powaitere... Po-é-tere. **1873** BULLER *Birds NZ* 58 Red-fronted Parrakeet... Kakariki, Kakawariki, Powhaitere, Porere, and Torete.

powhiri. [Ma. /ˈpoːfiri/: Williams 300 *Pōwhiri, pōhiri..2*. Beckon anyone to come on, welcome.] A ceremonial welcome to a marae.
1899 *NZ Illus. Magazine* Oct. 38 [Caption] A Maori 'powhiri' of welcome. **1925** *Patea & Waverley Press* 26 Jan. 2 A few weeks ago, numbers of Taranaki Natives went to Ratana to accord the 'Saviour' of the Maoris a fitting 'powhiri' (welcome) in true Maori fashion by the waving of leaves and the branches of trees before the advancing party. **1932** ELDER in Marsden *Lett. & Jrnls* (1932) 179 When they came within a few paces they stopped and performed the war dance, distorting their features in the most frightful manner and making at the same time the most horrid yells. [**1932** *Note*] Strictly speaking this was not a war-dance but a *powhiri*, or dance in reception of visitors. **1986**

Evening Post (Wellington) 14 Aug. 6 Tomorrow there will be a powhiri (welcome) at the Town Hall... Anyone can attend the powhiri. Guests are asked to be seated by 6pm. **1996** *Sunday Star-Times* (Auckland) 21 Jan. C2 Pakeha 'trot out' indigenous Maori culture—a waiata (song) or haka—in lieu of other recognisable Kiwi symbols. Dr Montgomery calls it 'rent-a-powhiri'.

powhiwhi. [Ma. /ˈpoːfifi/: Williams 300 *pōwhiwhi..1*. Several climbing plants.] Either of two native climbing plants, *Calystegia tuguriorum* or *Ipomoea cairica* (formerly *palmata*) (fam. Convolvulaceae), CONVOLVULUS.

1952 RICHARDS *Chatham Is.* 51 *Calystegia.. tuguriorum*... Small Bindweed. Po-whi-whi (creeper). **1966** [see CONVOLVULUS]. **1982** SALE *Four Seasons* 47 It was at this time last year I first saw the powhiwhi—a pale purple trumpet flower... It was a New Zealand native convolvulus.

powhytarnee, var. POWHAITERE.

poy, var. POE.

pozzy, var. POSSIE.

prad. *Obs.* [Spec. use of obsolete Brit. (and Austral.) slang *prad* a horse: AND 1812.] A racehorse.

1897 SCOTT *How I Stole 10,000 Sheep* 6 If there were no races on we would beg or 'borrow' out of a paddock a couple of 'prads' and have a race meeting on our own account. **1905** *Truth* Aug. 19 The towel-horse is the safest prad. **1908** *Ibid.* 22 Feb. 2 As Mrs. Hedley and the 'old prad' are also out for life, the 'ring in' did not do the crowd behind the ex-New Zealander, Rawmire, much, if any, good, when that gelding won. **1946** COOZE *Ten Bob Each Way* 9 He put what he had on his favourite prad. **1962** HORI *Half-gallon Jar* 22 I tell my pakeha friend that I will put ten bob each way on this prad.

pre-Adamite. *Hist.* [Fig. use of *pre-Adamite* one who existed before Adam; pre-human.] An early nickname for those settled in Canterbury before the arrival of the first Canterbury Association 'pilgrim' immigrants. Often *attrib*. Contrast SHAGROON.

1930 ACLAND *Early Canterbury Runs* 3 The old 'Pre-Adamites'..were those who had bought land from the New Zealand Company and settled here before the Canterbury settlers arrived. **1949** REED *Story Canterbury* 55 To the Hays and Sinclairs and other 'pre-Adamites'— as those few who had arrived before the 'Pilgrims' came jocularly to be called—these ships represented shops, schools, churches. *Ibid.* 183 He had further aroused the hostility of the leaders of the settlement by his decisions on certain complicated 'pre-Adamite' Banks Peninsula land claims. **1951** in Ward *Journal* (1951) 132 The Canterbury Association settlers were 'Pilgrims', while those established in Canterbury before their arrival were 'pre-Adamites'. **1972** in Stack *Through Canterbury* (1906) 18 This was no doubt Charles Hunter Brown, the pre-Adamite Canterbury settler.

pre-empt: see PRE-EMPTIVE RIGHT.

pre-emptive right. Also abbrev. **P.R.** (see quot. 1878), and *ellipt*. **pre-empt, pre-emptive**. [Spec. use of *pre-emptive, pre-emption* (with reference to) the prerogative of the Crown to monopolize purchase.] An occupant's right of preferential purchase at a low or nominal price of stated areas of public land on the condition of the occupant's improving it; concretely, the land so acquired.

1856 WAITT *Progress of Canterbury* 13 The largest run-holder has only a pre-emptive right. **1863** BUTLER *First Year* viii 115 Every [Canterbury] run-holder has a preemptive right over 250 acres round his homestead, and 50 acres round any other buildings he may have upon his run. **1863** *Richmond-Atkinson Papers* (1960) II. 37 As to the preemptive right, please send me the best description you can of what we should apply for. We have a right to '80 acres at one of the stations and 10 acres at each of the other stations erected upon the run'... It seems, however, that there must be a station of some sort at the place where preemptive is applied for; but it would be easy to have a hut put up at any place where we wanted to take our land. **1873** WILSON *Diary* 2 Feb. in Wierzbicka *Wilson Family* (1973) 164 The settler was allowed a pre-emptive right for every 50,000 acres or so which he could choose where he liked. In this way the owner of this station got about 4,000 acres pre-emptive right on this run at £1 per acre. **1878** MCCAW in Crawford *Station Yrs.* (1981) 122 You have bought a good bit of the run now... The P.R. up the White Rock river is very stoney. **1898** HOCKEN *Contributions* 168 The runholder was also allowed a pre-emptive right of purchase on his run of eighty acres for his principal station and ten acres for each out-station. **c1930** *Whitcombe's Etym. Dict. Aust.-NZ Suppl.* 9 *pre-empt n.* abbrev. for pre-emptive right. **1946** ACLAND *Early Canterbury Runs* 37 The farmers did not begin buying [the run land] until 1874, but when they did they bought it quickly. In eighteen months nearly all the run except the pre-emptives had gone. **1962** EVANS *Waikaka Saga* 117 The pre-emptive right was the right of a lessee to freehold one square mile of land. This became the station headquarters. **1981** CRAWFORD *Station Yrs.* 126 Another four acres were to be planted on the 'Pre-emptive' (which by then was freehold). **1981** PINNEY *Early N. Otago Runs* 70 There was a house and woolshed on a pre-emptive right.

pre-fleet: see FLEET *n*.¹ 2.

Premier. *Hist.* [Spec. use of *Premier* head of government.] In the 19th century formally, and since c1900 informally and less frequently, the title of the first or chief minister of the Government party in the New Zealand parliament, now formally PRIME MINISTER q.v.; see esp. quots. 1966, 1982.

1854–55 *NZPD* I. 11 Fitzgerald, Mr. J.E., Town of Lyttelton (Premier). **1877** *NZPD* XXV. 46 There is no accusation brought against the Premier. **1880** CHUDLEIGH *Diary* 10 July (1950) 289 Wellington. Interviewed the premier Sir John Hall... Dined at Bellamys. **1892** *NZ Official Handbook* iii The preparation of this Handbook was undertaken by direction of the Hon. John Balance, Premier of the Colony. **1905** BAUCKE *White Man Treads* 227 They practise the mission which the Premier in jaunty abandon has mapped out for them. **1911** *Maoriland Worker* 26 May 6 'Bob' Semple—dubbed 'the Demon of Dissension' by those who want the mob tame flunkeys—said at Waihi that New Zealand's Premier was being gushed over by the 'snobs'. **1934** [see SEDDON 4]. **1943** MARSH *Colour Scheme* 133 On the back [of the meeting-house] were hung coloured prints of three kings of England, two photographs of former premiers, and an enlargement of Rua as an M.P. **1948** LIPSON *Politics of Equality* 98 The head of the ministry [from 1856] and leader in Parliament was at first known as the colonial secretary. In the early sixties..the highest position was designated by the title and office of premier. *Ibid.* 293 Savage and Fraser, the two Labor premiers, began life under the severe economic handicap of poverty. **1966** *Encycl. NZ* II. 868 In the constitutional debates of 1854 during the first session of the New Zealand Parliament, the term 'Prime Minister' was frequently used in a somewhat casual fashion. This explains in part why it was some years before the term 'Premier' came into general usage. William Fox..who took office in July 1861, was described in the *Gazette* as Attorney-General 'with first seat in the Ministry'. In November 1864 Weld..was gazetted as holding 'a seat in the Executive Council and the office of Premier'. Stafford..his successor, in October 1865 was termed 'First Minister'. In June 1869, when Fox again headed a Ministry, he was described officially as 'Premier and member of the Executive Council.' Thereafter the term 'Premier' was regularly used. Nevertheless, in the Schedule of the Civil List Act of 1873, provision was made for the salary of the Leader of the Government 'being the Prime Minister'. The first Premier to use the title 'Prime Minister' officially was Richard John Seddon... It was used in the *New Zealand Year Book* of 1900 and the Imperial Conference of 1903 confirmed the practice.

Hence **premiership**, *n*. (tenure of) the office of Premier.

1937 BABBAGE *Hauhauism* 62 The second phase of the campaign was inaugurated by the accession of Mr. Stafford to the premiership on October 17th [1865]. **1948** LIPSON *Politics of Equality* 98 During the twenty-five ministries from 1856 to 1890, the premiership was filled by thirteen different persons. *Ibid.* 295 Once he attains the premiership, a man is not easily dislodged. **1980** McIntyre (ed.) in Sewell *Journal* I. 104 Sewell's premiership—the first under full responsible government—lasted less than three weeks.

press, *n. Woolhandling.* [AND 1848.]

1. *wool-press* (WOOL 3). Cf. MONKEY 1 a.

1862 *Puketoi Station Diary* (Hocken TS) 2 Jan. Kennards dray came with press, sorted woolshed. **1865** BARKER *Station Life* (1870) 33 There was a constant emptying of these bins into trucks to be carried off to the press, where we followed to see the bales packed. **1904** LANCASTER *Sons o' Men* 78 The bare-armed..gang that swarmed over the presses worked bars and cranks to a tune of their own. **1936** SARGESON *Conversation With Uncle* 24 After we'd pulled the bellies off the fleeces we had to roll them up and put them in the press. **1959** MIDDLETON *The Stone* 49 When we had washed the dung and oil and sweat from the shearing board..we..sat on a bale near the press. **1973** [see PRESSER a]. **1985** BREMNER *Woolscours NZ* 9 Press machine for pressing wool into bales.

2. Special Comb. **pressman**, *wool presser* (WOOL 3); **press-room**, the room in a woolshed where wool is pressed.

1878 CHUDLEIGH *Diary* 16 Nov. (1950) 274 My **press men** are two fools. Abner pressed more wool in 40 minutes than they did from 2 to 6. **1882** *Ibid.* 15 Dec. 316 One press-man gave in, W. Baucke. None of the family have any last in them. **1985** LANGDALE-HUNT *Last Entail Male* 104 It came time for shearing and again I was able to get the services of Rangi and his wife in the capacity of pressman and housekeeper. **1874** CAIRD *Sheepfarming NZ* 23 Behind the bins again is the **press-room** where the wool is pressed into bales either by a screw-press or by a lever-press.

press, *v. Woolhandling.* [Spec. use of *press* to compress: AND 1840.] *trans.* and *intr.* To compress (wool) into bales; to operate a wool-press.

1862 CHUDLEIGH *Diary* 24 Nov. (1950) 67 You put from 90 to 120 fleeces in a bail which way [*sic*] from 300 to 350 lbs. It is hard to press the wool into so small a compass. **c1875** MEREDITH *Adventuring in Maoriland* (1935) 41 We have just started shearing, and I am kept

PRESSER

pretty busy mustering sheep, wool-rolling, pressing, and dipping. **1882** Chudleigh *Diary* 28 Nov. (1950) 315 Pressed the first bale of this seasons wool with the Williams press. **1894** Wilson *Land of Tui* 242 At the main entrance of the shearing-shed..stands a wool-press, and behind this are the bins into which the fleeces..are placed preparatory to being pressed. **1922** Perry *Sheep Farming* 121 The 'bellies' can be placed in a pack hung on the shearing-board, and when two of these are filled they can be pressed. **1945** *NZ Geogr.* I. 39 'Press' and 'sweep' are technical terms for necessary operations in the woolshed at shearing time. The former refers to pressing the fleeces into tight-packed bales..to facilitate the transport of an otherwise bulky commodity. **1986** Richards *Off the Sheep's Back* 113 While one press was being filled and pressed, the already pressed bale would have the cap clipped (not sewn).

Hence **pressing** *vbl. n.*, **wool pressing** (wool 3), the compressing and baling of wool in a wool-press. (Quot. 1879 is grammatically ambiguous.)

1879 Kiernan *Diary* 31 Jan. in Guthrie-Smith *Tutira* (1921) 125 Finished pressing and weighing all wool in the shed. **1889** Williams & Reeves *Colonial Couplets* 9 ['A New Chum's Letter Home'] I'm engaged in the baling and pressing of wool. **1894** Wilson *Land of Tui* 244 The next operation is that of pressing. Into a large iron receptacle, with movable sides, an empty sack is placed, when the iron box is raised by means of machinery to the level of the bins. **1913** [see monkey 1 a]. **1922** [see presser a]. **1936** Belshaw et al. *Agric. Organiz. NZ* 708 Competent pressing can contribute to the final appearance of the clip. **1982** *Agric. Gloss.* (MAF) 58 *Pressing*: Compressing loose wool into bales in either a shearing shed or woolstore.

presser. *Woolhandling.* [press n. + -er: AND 1872.] **a.** *wool presser* (wool 3), one who operates a wool-press. Cf. press v.

1881 Chudleigh *Diary* 16 Nov. (1950) 303 The pressers are not up to the mark. **1897** *Otago Witness* (Dunedin) 2 Dec. 58 The pressers had put in a bale. **1912** *Gisborne & East Coast Shearers' Award* in *Sheepowners' Handbook* (1912) 32 17(a) Pressers and wool-rollers, when engaged by the week, £1 10s. per week. **1922** Perry *Sheep Farming* 123 In pressing, fleeces should be handed singly to the presser who is trampling the wool, and who, placing one fleece in each corner of the pack, tramples it well down, and so on until both boxes are filled. **1940** Studholme *Te Waimate* (1954) 127 At Waimate there were about 50 men and boys employed for the shearing—22 shearers..3 pressers, 1 waggoner. **1951** McLeod *NZ High Country* 27 One classer..two pressers, one penner up, make up the shed contingent. **1964** Middleton *Walk on Beach* 167 I had often given a hand in the smaller woolsheds at shearing time..helping the presser. **1973** Fernandez *Tussock Fever* 5 The pressers made the most of the break to catch up. They tramped down the fleeces in the two compartments of the press. **1988** *More* (Auckland) Mar. 30 At smoko the presser's assistant said to the eye roller: 'Well, at least I didn't have to help her.'

b. presser-sheep-o. A woolshed worker who combines the work of a *presser* and sheep-o q.v.

1957 *NZJAg.* Oct. XCV. 334 An example of the staff required..one presser-sheepo.

press noses: see nose *n.*[1] c.

pricker. [AND (1945) associates the phr. with *pricker* a device studded with sharp points attached to the side of the snaffle to correct a horse with a one-sided mouth (1871); prob. the association is with *prickly* 'tetchy-tempered' and the form of *get one's back up* and/or *get the needle*, to become annoyed.] In the general sense of 'temper', 'sulks', variously in the phr. **to get one's pricker up**, **to get the pricker**, **to give** (somebody) **the pricker**, to become, get, make (somebody) angry, annoyed, nettled; **to get the pricker with**, to become annoyed with.

1947 Davin *For Rest of Our Lives* 296 Even if they're only up against Italians, front-line troops get the pricker if you sneer. *Ibid.* 311 They were all beginning to get the pricker a bit. No wonder. On the go since Syria. **1951** p.c. W. Cameron (Wellington) *To get one's pricker up* is to get one's temper up; *get the pricker* is to get annoyed or fed up. **1959** Slatter *Gun in My Hand* 91 Got the pricker with me. Slingin off at me he was. You're up the boo-ay he told me. **1963** *Home Life* Jan–Feb. 2 I'm feeling as cheerful as a Fijian in a freezing chamber... What is really giving me the pricker is the fact that I have got the plurry toothache. **1964** Frances *Johnny Rapana* 94 'Miro's got the pricker,' Ben said, flopping his lips in a grin. 'He cleared off by himself.' **1975** Davin *Breathing Spaces* 107 Boxer got to his feet, his fist bunched. 'Now, now, Boxer, don't start getting the pricker.' **1984** Wilson *S. Pacific Street* 69 'You deserve everything you get.' 'Now don't get the pricker, Len.' She smiled and patted my hand. **1985** O'Sullivan *Shuriken* 35 That joker's been giving me the pricker for weeks.

priest, *n.*[1] *Hist.* [Spec. use of *priest* one trained to perform certain rituals.] tohunga 1.

1804 [see tohunga 1]. **1814** Marsden *Lett. & Jrnls.* (1932) 69 He [*sc.* Duaterra, a chief] endeavoured to persuade them that he would return in four moons... Their priest told him that his head wife was sure to die before his return. **1833** Williams *Early Jrnls.* 14 Mar. (1961) 294 The party assembled naked,.. the Priest an old greybearded man..stood up in front with outstretched arms..and repeated over his *karakia*, or prayer, to Tu, the God of War. **1857** [see tohunga 1]. **1864** Campbell *Martin Tobin* I. 64 When he had eaten, she told him the war party had gone across the river, meaning the Pelorus, and that the women and priests only were left. **1872**, **1904**, **1983** [see tohunga 1].

Hence **priestess**, a Maori wise-woman.

1814 Marsden *Lett. & Jrnls.* (1932) 86 An old woman, whom I took to be a priestess.

priest, *n.*[2] [Of unknown origin.] A fish-stunning club. Cf. waddy.

1989 Haley *Transfer Station* 2 First [fish] were hard to find and then if you did hook one it came in with open sores..and you either tapped it with a priest or threw it back

priests' weed. [See quot.] The thornapple, *Datura stramonium* (fam. Solanaceae), as a medicinal plant.

1921 Guthrie-Smith *Tutira* (1926) 270 Thornapple (*Datura stramonium*), or, as it is still called in Hawke's Bay, 'Priests' Weed', has on two occasions appeared at Tutira. As a plant likely to be of use in pulmonary affection, it was distributed in early days throughout the *pas* of Hawke's Bay by the Rev. Father Regnier of the Meanee Mission Station.

prime, *a.* Applied to stock bred for slaughter, replacing fat *a.* as a trade term; esp. as **prime stock**, meat animals ready for slaughter.

1943 *NZJST* XXIII. 323A Even when properly treated..these lambs, now checked in growth, needed a much greater quantity of rape and supplementary feed and a longer 'fattening' period to raise them to the 'prime' state. **1974** *NZ Agric.* 185 Frozen prime beef is increasingly shipped as special 'primal' cuts, wrapped in polythene and packed in cartons. **1982** *Agric. Gloss.* (MAF) 35 *Prime stock*: Animals ready for slaughter. The term 'prime' is now preferred to 'fat'.

PRIMER

Prime Minister. [Spec. use of *Prime Minister* head of government.] The formal title of the first or chief minister of the Government party in the New Zealand Parliament. See also premier.

[*Note*] The term *Prime Minister* replaced *Premier* in official documents c1900 (see quot. 1900[2]), though it was in sporadic use before this date.

1856 Sewell *Journal* 20 Apr. (1980) II. 227 Here we are once more..only now trying Responsible Government in earnest... And I am Prime Minister. **1877** *NZPD* XXV. 316 If I became a member of the Cabinet, or if accident made me Prime Minister—I doubt very much whether I should be equal to such an onerous position. **1900** *Ibid.* CXII. 333 This opportunity now given will prove the sincerity of those who..have said to me, 'As Prime Minister of this country, you are underpaid.' **1900** *NZ Statutes* No.8 16 [Ministers' Salaries and Allowances Amendment Act] There shall be payable..the annual sum of eight thousand pounds for..the annual salaries of Ministers, as follows:- The Prime Minister..£1,600. **1900** *NZ Official Yearbook* 27 [Inset pasted on to p. 27 amending the previous formula of 'Executive Council..Rt. Hon. R.J. Seddon, P.C., LL.D., Premier'.] The Executive Council now consists of..Right Honourable Richard John Seddon, P.C., Prime Minister. **1901** *Whitaker's Almanac* 520 New Zealand... Prime Minister, Colonial Treasurer etc., Rt. Hon. Richd. J. Seddon. **1966** [see premier]. **1971** *Speeches & Documents* 467 Responsible government was inaugurated in 1856 when Henry Sewell, as head of the Ministry, assumed the office of Colonial Secretary, and became the first 'Premier'... [This usage] did not become standard for some years, and styles such as 'First Minister', occasionally 'Prime Minister' were used. The term 'Prime Minister' was adopted by Seddon towards the close of the century and appeared in the official Year Book in 1900.

primer /ˈprɪmə/. [Prob. f. *primer* an elementary reading book.]

[*Note*] *primer* is now replaced in official use by *junior* (class, school, etc.), *juniors n*.

a. One of the classes covering the first years of instruction in a primary school; also *pl.* as **the primers**, the junior school of a primary school. Often *attrib.*

1928 *Syllabus of Instruction Primary Schools* (Ministry of Education library) 55 In all schools teachers of Primer classes will use 'Physical Exercises and Games for Infants'. **1942** *NZ Educ. Gaz.* 2 Feb. XXI. 19 To keep Primer 4 employed I generally left a note on each child's desk. **1948** Ballantyne *Cunninghams* (1976) 62 Then they got a couple of primer kids under the stage and scared them with spooky noises. **1948** in Pearson *Six Stories* (1991) 40 When I was in the primers I was pretty pleased with myself. **1957** Frame *Owls do Cry* (1967) 103 He is in primer three at school, and anxious for the holidays to finish. **1963** Hilliard *Piece of Land* 191 It seemed no time since he'd been in the primers. **1970** Johnson *Life's Vagaries* 16 At three o'clock some of the children, generally from the Primers and Standard 1, would be racing to the foot of the hill. **1978** *Education* VI. 19 There was also the primer swing to work up, to leap from and catch a branch. **1987** Eldred-Grigg *Oracles & Miracles* 72 Things got worse when we left the primers.

b. A member of a primer class. (The plural does not take the def. article.)

1928 *Syllabus of Instruction Primary Schools* (Ministry of Education library) 55 Where there are three teachers: Primers do infant work; Squad I, Tables 1–36; [etc.]. **1947** Gaskell *All Part of the Game* (1978) 88 And there was Micky, her smallest primer, a little wizened creature with sad eyes like a monkey. **1980** Mantell *Murder & Chips* 71 Primers get out at two-thirty in case you didn't know. **1990** *Dominion*

(Wellington) 25 Sept. 12 [Heading] Maori course for primers.

Prince Alberts. *Hist.* [Ironic use of the name of *Prince Albert* (1819–61), Prince Consort of Queen Victoria: AND 1893; *Royal Alberts*, 1900.] *Pl.* Strips of cloth or foot rags worn (esp. by swaggers) round the feet to take the place of socks. See also DUKE OF YORKS.
1917 STRACHAN in Neave *Land of Munros* (1980) 65 I was to get a liberal screw..for four months [at Otematata Station], beginning the 8th of March [1858], with..two cotton shirts..no underclothing, no socks, but pieces of blanket rolled round your feet (we called them Prince Alberts). **1944** LEE *Shining With Shiner* 71 Just wrap around [your feet] as much Prince Albert [that is ladies' stockings] as you need, and cut the stockings off and throw the rest away. **1952** LYON *Faring South* 180 [The early bushman's] socks were often replaced by a long strip of calico bound from the toe upwards to a few inches above the boot top. These strips of calico were usually termed Prince Alberts. **1974** AGNEW *Loner* 71 The cocky's wife spotted my Prince Alberts, a piece of blanket cut into eighteen-inch squares which I wound over my feet... Prince Alberts were more serviceable than ordinary socks, were warmer, longer-wearing and would take up the slack in my boots, preventing blisters.

Prince of Wales feather(s). Usu. with init. caps. and various placements of apostrophe. Also occas. **Prince of Wales fern**. The ornamental fern *Leptopteris* (formerly *Todea*) *superba* (fam. Osmundaceae). See also *crape fern*, *king fern* (FERN 2 (3) and (11) a), HERUHERU.
1873 TINNE *Wonderland of Antipodes* 36 The dense undergrowth of the Prince of Wales' Feathers. **1882** [see FERN 2 (11) a]. **1890** FIELD *Ferns NZ* 149 'Prince of Wales' Feather', 'Chenille Fern', and 'Crape Fern'. This is confined to New Zealand and southward to the Auckland Islands. **1909** *AJHR* C-12 48 Heruheru, punui. Double crape-fern, Prince of Wales's feather. Forest, especially southern forest. Local, but very abundant and of large size where it occurs. **1911** MORELAND *Through South Westland* 58 A little further on grow huge clumps of Prince-of-Wales' Feather, its tips bent exactly like an ostrich plume. **1920** BOLITHO *With the Prince in NZ* 157 The Prince of Wales feathers were outlined in pampas grass, and the entire street was lined with greenery. **1930** GUTHRIE *NZ Memories* 171 There were carpets of delicate kidney ferns..Prince of Wales's feathers, umbrella and many other varieties. **1961** MARTIN *Flora NZ* 116 The double crepe fern..also known as the Prince of Wales Feathers. **1988** DAWSON *Forest Vines to Snow Tussocks* 127 Larger ferns on the forest floor include the well-known crepe fern or Prince of Wales Feathers (*Leptopteris superba*) and *Blechnum discolor*.

prion. [Spec. use of *prion*, *Pachyptila* spp. of small saw-billed petrels: in locally significant use mainly with a defining word.] Any of several similar small petrels of the genus *Pachyptila* (fam. Procellariidae), usu. with a modifier: **Antarctic** (or **dove**), **broad-billed**, **fairy**, **fulmar** (**Bounty Island, cliff, thick-billed**).

1. Antarctic (or **dove**) **prion**. *Pachyptila desolata banksi*, a prominently-billed blue-grey petrel. See also *dove petrel* (PETREL 2 (8)).
1873 [see PETREL 2 (8)]. **1955** OLIVER *NZ Birds* 120 Antarctic Prion. Dove Prion *Pachyptila desolata*. The Antarctic Prion was taken at Kerguelen or Desolation Island in 1768 during Cook's first voyage. *Ibid.* 121 At the Auckland Islands in certain localities the whole of the peat along the coast line is riddled by the burrows of the Dove Prion. **1957** WILLIAMS *Dict. Maori Lang.* 442 Totorore... *Pachyptila desolata* Antarctic prion (*dove prion*). **1985** *Reader's Digest Book NZ Birds* 86 Antarctic prion *Pachyptila desolata desolata*... Dove Prion... Between May and September, winter storms regularly cast young Antarctic prions ashore on the New Zealand mainland. **1990** *Checklist Birds NZ* 45 *Pachyptila desolata desolata..Antarctic (Kerguelen) Prion.*

2. broad-billed prion. *Pachyptila vittata*, having its bill at the widest part as broad as the bird's head. See also *blue-billy* (BLUE *a.* 2 b), PARARA, WHALEBIRD.
1948 *NZ Bird Notes* III. 28 This morning a bird which I believe to be a broad-billed prion (*Pachyptila vittata*) appeared in the dredge pond beside the Austral New Zealand Mining Co.'s dredge... The shift men fed it biscuits. **1955** OLIVER *NZ Birds* 125 The Broad-billed Prion breeds on islands that lie on the borderline between the subantarctic and subtropical zones of ocean water temperature. **1966** [see *blue-billy* (BLUE *a.* 2 b)]. **1985** *Reader's Digest Book NZ Birds* 85 Broad-billed Prion *Pachyptila vittata vittata*... Whalebird, scooper, blue-billy, parara... In the shape and function of its remarkable bill, the broad-billed prion is unique among petrels. Its bill, as wide as its head, is fringed with small comb-like growths called lamellae. **1990** *Checklist Birds NZ* 46 *Pachyptila vittata..Broad-billed Prion* (*Parara*).

3. fairy prion. *Pachyptila turtur*, a small short-billed blue-grey petrel. See also TITI-WAINUI, WHALEBIRD; occas. *dove petrel* (PETREL 2 (8)).
1947 POWELL *Native Animals NZ* 79 Fairy Prion (*Pachyptila turtur*), Titi Wainui..is the small dove grey petrel which skims the surface of the sea in its energetic quest for food. **1955** OLIVER *NZ Birds* 119 On the Brothers..the Fairy Prion..breeds in burrows under low-growing taupata. **1967** NATUSCH *Animals NZ* 257 There are six species of prions (*Pachyptila*) of which the likeliest to be seen is the dainty fairy prion or titi-wainui (*P. turtur*). **1985** *Reader's Digest Book NZ Birds* 87 Fairy Prion *Pachyptila turtur*...Titi-wainui... Fairy prions patrol the seas in large, loose flocks... Fairy prions are one of New Zealand's most abundant petrels. **1990** *Checklist Birds NZ* 42 *Pachyptila turtur..Fairy Prion* (*Titi Wainui*).

4. fulmar (Bounty Island, cliff, thick-billed) prion. *Pachyptila crassirostris*, a rare blue-grey petrel with subspecies *P. c. crassirostris* (**fulmar prion**) and *P. c. pyramidalis* (**Chatham fulmar prion**).
1955 OLIVER *NZ Birds* 115 The Bounty Island Prion was first collected by Reischek in 1888. **1966** FALLA et al. *Birds of NZ* 41 Fulmar Prion *Pachyptila crassirostris*. **1985** *Reader's Digest Book NZ Birds* 88 Fulmar Prion *Pachyptila crassirostris*... Cliff prion, thick-billed prion... The fulmar prion nests on lava outcrops or on steep cliffs overlooking the sea, either in the shelter of small rock crevices or in tunnels under the surface. **1990** *Checklist Birds NZ* 43 *Pachyptila crassirostris crassirostris*... *Fulmar prion. Ibid.* 44 *Pachyptila crassirostris pyramidalis..Chatham Fulmar Prion.*

private bag. Often abbrev. **P.B.** esp. as a form of mail address. Indicating in modern use (compare earlier use in quot. 1960[2] below) either of two forms of mail service given by New Zealand Post: an urban service requested and paid for by (usu.) large mail customers whose mail is enclosed in a bag and collected from and delivered to a specified address; and a rural service (the 'rural bag' of quot. 1992 below commonly identified by the public as 'private bag') provided to make mail handling easier and more secure to and from those customers in remote areas who are normally not on a rural mail delivery route. Also *attrib*. Cf. RURAL DELIVERY.
1960 STARTUP *Travelling Mails* 1 Others [*sc.* settlers] had organised a privately financed private-mail bag service from the nearest post office. One such rural private bag service had been established as early as 1858 in the Wairarapa, from Masterton to Brancepeth station 18 miles distant, this station even had its own mailbag wax sealer. Mails for outlying stations and farms are delivered today by private-bags, usually handled by rural mail contractors. **1960** *Post Office Guide* 65 [Town Districts] Private bags. The charge for a private bag, which must be conveyed by the user or his agent to and from the post office, is £3 a year... Rural Districts... If a resident in a rural district desires to have correspondence delivered at his house in a private bag conveyed by the postman, and to enclose correspondence for posting in a private bag to be handed to the postman, an inclusive annual fee of £3 is charged... A rural private bag may be used for all postal packets. **1984** MARSHALL & STARTUP *From the Bay to the Bush* 51 Today the district is served, for mail, partly by rural mail delivery and partly by a private bag service from Hastings. **1992** *NZ Post Guide* (internal manual) Issue 7 Aug. Sheet 20 7.22 A rural bag is not the same as a private bag. The purpose of mail being carried in a bag for some rural customers is to make handling easier. A rural bag is an operational method of providing rural delivery, chosen by New Zealand Post and is not a customer choice... Private bags are a separate service that customers may choose to have.

private hotel. [Spec. use of *private hotel*, in Britain, usu. a hotel which receives guests only by private arrangement.] A hotel (or boarding-house) not having a licence to sell alcoholic liquor. Cf. ACCOMMODATION HOUSE.
1907 *NZ Free Lance* (Wellington) 8 June 14 [Advt] Day's Bay House, Day's Bay. The Most Delightful Seaside Private Hotel in New Zealand. **1922** *Auckland Weekly News* 5 Jan. 3 Reserve your Accommodation at Stonehurst Residential Hotel. The ideal private hotel, renowned for its good management, excellent table, numerous lounge rooms, elegant furnishings, and an acre of beautiful grounds and tennis court. **1936** *NZ Railways Mag.* Apr. 44 [Advt] A High-class Private Hotel at a Reasonable Tariff. **1943** MARSH *Colour Scheme* 110 Delightful surroundings. Homelike residential private hotel. **1962** CRUMP *One of Us* 45 Sam booked Ponto into a private hotel. **1992** *Evening Post* (Wellington) 11 Nov. 28 Her earlier search for a boarding house when first in Wellington saw her approaching a little private hotel in Ghuznee St.

private school. A school outside the State system, though receiving a measure of State financial and other support; now often termed 'independent school'. Contrast PUBLIC SCHOOL.
1890 *Otago Witness* (Dunedin) 8 May 24 He had supported the Private School Bill, which applied principally to the Catholics. **1892** [see COLLEGE a]. **1944** MURDOCH *High Schools NZ* 61 The Inspectors were obviously overworked inspecting a number of private and district high schools as well as all the State high schools. **1966** *Encycl. NZ.* I. 557 One of the most interesting features of the history of education in New Zealand has been the part played by the registered private schools. **1976** JOHNSTON *New Zealanders* 126 Outside the State system there are 115 private secondary schools... The question of State aid to private schools has occasioned much debate in recent years... 'Old-boy networks', typical of the British 'public' schools, are also products of New Zealand's 'private' schools, though they are by no means as influential. **1986** *Illustr. Encycl. NZ* 983 The main educational issue of

the 1960 General Election was state aid for private schools. **1991** *Dominion* (Wellington) 24 Sept. 6 A controversial survey that found many people thought private schools did a better job than state schools. **1993** [see PUBLIC SCHOOL].

privet. [Transf. use of *privet Ligustrum* spp. (fam. Oleaceae) for a privet-like species of fam. Loganiaceae.] Usu. as **Maori (native, New Zealand) privet,** HANGEHANGE (*Geniostoma rupestre*).
1841 Diary in *William Swainson* 1 July (1992) 85 Papa finished the hedge of native Privet. **1907** *AJHR C-8* 20 Hangehange. New Zealand privet. Forest (not common). **1929** [see COPROSMA]. **1940** LAING & BLACKWELL *Plants NZ* 357 *Geniostoma*... A shrub with shining, pale-green leaves... Maori privet. **1956** [see HANGEHANGE]. **1981** BROOKER et al. *NZ Medicinal Plants* 63 *Geniostoma ligustrifolium*... Maori privet... Hangehange, papa.

pro, *n.*

1. a. [f. *pro*(bationer.] A probationer nurse.
1938 HYDE *Godwits Fly* (1970) 167 Presently a senior probationer comes back, a Scotch-looking little nurse in blue. Pros. wear pink, senior pros. pale blue, Sisters indigo, Matron white with red and silver nursing medals.

b. [f. *pro*(bation (officer).] A probation officer of the former probation Service (now Community Corrections) of the Department of Justice.
1982 MCCAULEY *Other Halves* 64 'He thought you was from Welfare, or a pro or something.' 'Pro?' Did they solicit door to door? He grinned. 'Probation Officer.'

2. [f. PRO(FICIENCY.] *Hist.* PROFICIENCY 1.
1986 O'REGAN *A Changing Order* 42 By the time I got to Standard Five, the black cloud of the Proficiency exam was casting its shadow over my young life. You could not leave primary school until you had passed your Pro. You could not get a job without your Pro.

pro, *v.* [f. PRO(HIBITION ORDER.] *trans.* To put a prohibition order upon, or to take a prohibition order out against (an alcoholic or heavy drinker).
1949 DAVIN *Roads from Home* 12 Nellie, you should have him pro'd. The magistrate'd give you the order all right and not a publican..would dare serve him a drop. **1959** [see PROHIBITION ORDER]. **1968** SLATTER *Pagan Game* 163 Been hitting it along too hard. His wife is going to pro him.

probationary assistant. Also **probationer**. Formerly, a teacher during the first year of teaching after training (usu. at a Teachers College or College of Education) but before certification (see also 1888 quot.). Previously also called *Student Assistant*.
1888 BARLOW *Kaipara* 202 Teachers at elementary schools are supposed to pass examinations, and receive certificates..but in small up-country districts, teachers are often placed in charge who are not certificated, but are what are termed probationers. **1920** MANDER *Story NZ River* (1974) 210 Betty, who now taught in the Kaiwaka school, and Mabel, who was a probationer in the school at the head of the bay, were not yet home. **1921** *NZ Educ. Gaz.* 1 Dec. 21 1 Central classes for the instruction of pupil-teachers, probationers, and uncertificated teachers in science and in drawing and hand-work may..be established by an Education Board. **1963** BACON *In the Sticks* 182 *Probationary Assistant*- New Zealand student teachers normally do two years' training in one of the country's Teachers' Colleges. During this time, they work about five separate monthly practice periods in selected schools. Their third year of training is as Probationary Assistant in a larger school. If this probationary year's service is satisfactory, trainees receive their Teacher's Certificate. **1963** PEARSON *Coal Flat* 8 You were here [*sc.* at this school] before, as probationer, weren't you?

probationer: see PROBATIONARY ASSISTANT.

probie. [f. *pro*(bation + –IE.] A probation officer of the former Probation Service (now Community Corrections) of the Department of Justice.
1993 *Dominion* (Wellington) 2 Aug. 1 I expected a decent sentence. My lawyer reckoned I'd get one to two years and my probie (probation officer) said it'd be 18 months.

procesh. [An alteration of *process*(ion.] A university students' (annual) procession through town with humorous satirical floats, hi-jinks, etc.
1959 SLATTER *Gun in My Hand* 226 The Procesh Day lorry decorated with fernery like our tanks on a triumphal procession through liberated San Giorgio. **1962** JOSEPH *Pound of Saffron* 176 There had been a procesh party in someone's flat, with a lot of beer. **1977** BROOKING *Massey—its early years* 118 The first Massey 'Procesh' was held in 1935 and was greeted with enthusiasm..as establishing a tradition that was a feature of the older New Zealand Universities. **1986** *Campus News* 3 June 2 The Procesh, held on Friday, was judged by the Police Chief.

Also as **procesh** *v. intr.*, to form, execute, or take part in a public procession.
1888 MCHUTCHESON *New Zealander Abroad* 127 And thereafter 'procesh' around with beating drums and flying banners.

proddyhopper. *Obs.* An abusive term for a Protestant formerly used mainly by Catholic schoolchildren.
1960 KEINZLY *Tangahano* 165 'It was the proddyhopper, Sister—' 'What is a *proddyhopper*, Augustine?' 'A protestant kid.' **1973, 1992** [see CATTLE-DOG 2].

proficiency. *Obs.*

1. *Ellipt.* for *Proficiency Examination*. A former public examination, abolished in 1935, a pass in which, duly certificated by a Proficiency Certificate, entitled a student to enter upon secondary schooling.
1916 *Dannevirke Evening News* 28 Nov. 4 The proficiency examination was held by the Department's inspectors on November 17th. **1919** *Evening Post* (Wellington) 15 July 6 Proficiency and competency certificates he considered an unwanted evil, and other means infinitely more efficient could be found to judge the capacity and work of the child. **1924** *Otago Witness* (Dunedin) 12 Feb. 71 I obtained my proficiency last year, and I think I will be going on to the High School this year. **1938** HYDE *Godwits Fly* (1970) 37 It was quite a good school, and Mr Duncan said that Carly, though a nervous little idiot, was safe to get her Proficiency. **1970** THOMAS *Way Up North* 70 At the age of twelve and a half years [c1904] I had passed the final school examination for my 'certificate of proficiency'. **1980** THOMPSON *All My Lives* 11 They had left school early, he at 14, she at 13, both having obtained their proficiency. **1982** FRAME *To the Is-land* (1984) 84 She was in her Proficiency Year at school, and all the talk at home was of whether she'd get her proficiency.

2. As **Proficiency Certificate, Proficiency exam (Examination).**
1926 *NZ Observer* 3 Nov. 7 If a boy secures his **proficiency certificate** it by no means follows that he is therefore prepared mentally to receive the education..provided by a secondary school. **1983** MARSHALL *Memoirs* I completed my primary education, at the age of thirteen and gained, by examination, the Proficiency Certificate which in those days marked the high point, and usually the end, of formal education for most children. **1916** *Dannevirke Evening News* 28 Nov. 4 The **proficiency examination** was held by the Department's inspectors on November 17th. **1948** FINLAYSON *Tidal Creek* (1979) 20 You know you've got to get strong and pass your proficiency exam and get your scholarship. **1987** CHRISTIE *Candles & Canvas* 139 I was still only fifteen and had left school with the gaining of the Proficiency Examination which entitled me to enter high school. **1987** *Listener* 8 Aug. 64 In my last year at primary school, 1935, the Proficiency exam, which was the qualification for going to secondary school, was abolished.

prohibition order. Also in shortened form **pro. order**. An order made by a court forbidding a person's purchase of intoxicating liquor. See also PRO *v.*
1905 *Truth* 12 Aug. 7 The issue of a prohibition order, granted on the application of a runner of one of those cheap boarding-houses. **1904** LANCASTER *Sons o' Men* 105 Seepose Joe's havin' a wet... There's a pro. order out agin' him. **1959** DAVIN *No Remittance* 198 'Sorry, I'm not allowed to serve you.' 'Why not, I say?' 'Well,' he looked at my friends and tried to say it quietly but they heard all right, 'your wife's had you pro'd.' Imagine it, a prohibition order taken out against me. And they say it's a man's world, when a woman can stop her husband buying a drink. Not just buying one either, she can even stop him from getting his friends to buy him one.

pro. order: see PROHIBITION ORDER.

prop, *v. Prison slang.* [Prob. f. *prop* to stop suddenly.] To hold a sit-down (or other protest) strike. Also as a *n.*, an institutional protest strike.
1982 NEWBOLD *Big Huey* 89 Because we were late starting practice we all decided to prop for ten minutes extra. *Ibid.* 252 Prop (v) Sit-down strike. **1985** *NZ Times* 12 May 5 After Alofoe's suicide, A Block inmates began 'a prop'. One man started a hunger strike and others planned to join him... The original unpublished plan involved a mass 'prop' by all Paremoremo inmates.

property. [Spec. use of *property* a landed estate: see OED *n.* 2 b: AND 1825.] A rural holding used for agricultural or pastoral purposes.
1891 WALLACE *Rural Econ. Austral. & NZ* 320 On the property..ten men have to be kept 'rabbiting' all the year round. **1899** BELL *In Shadow of Bush* 10 Frank Ashwin, to whom the property belonged, was a New Zealander born, the son of one of the early settlers. His father..had..started him in life on his own account here in the bush, by purchasing this property of about five hundred acres. **1924** *Otago Witness* (Dunedin) 4 Nov. 54 A great deal of the property was still heavily bushed, and the bush would have to be felled and burnt off before the station could be put down in grass, and used for sheep and cattle. **1947** BEATTIE *Early Runholding* 115 It is usually understood that in the early days, the word 'station' denoted the owner's house and its immediate buildings, while 'run' meant the whole property. **1992** *Evening Post* (Wellington) 7 Sept. 12 They [*sc.* a Russian family] live and work on Kalinin Farm, a property with 8000 inhabitants.

prophet.

1. *Canterbury Hist.* [Transf. use of *prophet* one who foretells the future.] A nickname for the Australian sheepmen in the early Canterbury settlement, supporters of a pastoralist or sheepfarming regime as distinct from the 'agriculturalists' (mainly newly-arrived English 'pilgrim' settlers); see esp. quot. 1866. Cf. PILGRIM 1 b, SHAGROON a.

1851 *Lyttelton Times* 9 Aug. 7 Gaily the pilgrim harnessed his plough, When he had built up a roof o'er his head; Singing, 'From Albion hither I come;' 'Land of mine! land of mine! grow me some bread.' Proudly the prophet flourished his crook, When he had landed his sheep from the west; Singing, 'From Philipland hither I come;' 'Silly men! silly men! wool pays the best.' **1859** [see SHAGROON a]. **1866** *Canterbury Rhymes* 101 During the first year of the Settlement, Canterbury was invaded by a body of Sheep-farmers from Port Philip (Victoria), who were regarded by the Settlers partly with admiration as successful colonists, and partly with horror as disbelievers in the art of colonization and the 'Canterbury System'... One of the visitors, who seem to have delighted in the *soubriquet* of 'Shagroon', ventured to prophesy, in a letter which found its way into print, that the 'Canterbury Pilgrims' would soon be ruined... The 'pilgrims' sought no harsher revenge than to nick-name their Port Philip visitors 'prophets', and to take example from their experience in pastoral pursuits. **1933** *Press* (Christchurch) (Acland Gloss.) 18 Nov. 15 *Prophet.—* Nick-name of the Australian squatters who came down to Canterbury in 1851. They were called P[rophet]s because they prophesied ruin for the farming pilgrims. **1966** *Encycl. NZ* III. 231 Not only did Australian sheep arrive, but during the 1850–60 period many Australian squatters (disgruntled by the fickle rainfall) also sold or abandoned their properties and migrated to New Zealand... They became known as the 'Prophets' because they forecast failure for the small-area arable farm plans of the established settlements.

2. [f. *prophet* a divinely-inspired spokesman; a teacher or spiritual leader.] A leader or spokesperson for a Maori spiritual movement, *spec.* for Pai-marire; a person with reputed gifts of far-sight; a TOHUNGA q.v. Also occas. **prophetess**, a female prophet.

1885 *Wairarapa Daily* 25 Mar. 2 Mr. Hakuere M.H.R., has visited the Maori prophetess, and reports that everything is quiet. **1888** PAYTON *Round About NZ* 293 Here lives the great Te Whiti, the Maori prophet and fanatic. **1891** [see TOHUNGA 1]. **1922** COWAN *NZ Wars* (1955) II. 7 Kimble Bent, the *pakeha-Maori*, related to me that when Te Ua was in Otapawa *pa*..a *ruru* flew from the forest at dusk and perched on the ridge-pole of the house in front of which the prophet was sitting. *Ibid.* II. 72 Kereopa te Rau..and Patara Raukatauri were the two prophets despatched by Te Ua early in 1865 to convert the tribes of the East Coast to the Pai-Marire faith. **1950** *Southern Cross* (Wellington) 6 May 8 [Caption] The famous temple of Rua, the Ringatu prophet. **1973** PEARSON note to Finlayson *Brown Man's Burden* (1973) 134 'The Ratana preacher'. He is a clergyman of the Ratana Church, founded in the 1920s by Tahupotiki Wiremu Ratana, a faith healer and prophet.

proppy, *a.* [f. *prop* a sudden stop + -Y.]

1. [AND 1866.] Of a horse, restive or given to sudden stops and starts when ridden.

1937 AYSON *Thomas* 96 The horse was so 'proppy' that Thomas decided he was past using as a stock horse, so he had to leave him to his fate.

2. [AND 1904.] *transf.* Shaky.

1910 *Truth* 8 Jan. 1 But it is not only Bob's memory that would appear to be weak. He would seem to be pretty proppy on his pins, judging by their appearance on Monday at the stadium, and the paltry support they provided to the poor old bloke.

propstick. *Obs.* Usu. *pl.* Wooden supports to take the weight of dray-shafts during a rest.

1872 in Mitchell *Rhymes & Rambles* (1889) 25 It was in 1872, while carting wheat into Timaru from Cave Valley way, I composed the following piece,.. Hold hard, Jock, put the prop-sticks down, And let the cattle spell. O for a gill of Campbellton, Or a pint of Tennant's ale. **1961** HENDERSON *Friends In Chains* 188 Propsticks: To hold up shafts of dray or stretcher while horses feed.

prospect, *n.*[1] *Goldmining.* [Used elsewhere but of significance in NZ and recorded early in sense 1 below: see Mathews *n.*, 1850; OED *n.* 4 c, 1879.]

1. A trial sample of washdirt or ore containing gold; the gold recovered from such a sample.

1853 SWAINSON *Auckland* 94 Early in November..the prospect began to be of a more promising character: one party being reported to have washed out two or three ounces of gold. **1861** in *NZ Goldfields* (1976) 16 This morning a man..showed me a prospect which he had obtained from several dishes of washing-stuff, in a claim on the Waitahuna. It consisted of about half-a-dozen specks of gold. **1871** MONEY *Knocking About NZ* 99 No less than fifteen shafts did we sink..but found a prospect of nothing sufficient to encourage us in working it. **1887** PYKE *Hist. Early Gold Discoveries Otago* (1962) 61 'Fair prospects' at the Lindis; 'nice prospects of fine gold' in the Mareburn, and so on throughout. **1914** PFAFF *Diggers' Story* 43 We pushed on into maiden country, i.e. the Right Hand Branch, and got very good prospects. **1946** MILLER *There Was Gold* 69 I had sunk my first prospect hole at the lower end of a shallow depression..and had struck the deepest part of the lead. **1967** MAY *West Coast Gold Rushes* 528 Prospect: (*noun*) the yield of gold won from a dish of wash-dirt, or from the bottom of a shaft, or from roughly reduced quartz.

2. [See OED *n.* 4 b.] A test-search of a place, or of material, to discover its prospective yield of gold.

1861 *Otago Witness* (Dunedin) 10 Aug. 5 We are indebted for the following graphic description of the result of a 'prospect' to a gentleman who has been a successful digger on the Tuapeka. **1864** *Nelson Mail* in 1952 *Marlborough Express* (Blenheim) 16 Apr. 6 The result of their several prospects was 3.5 dwt of gold. **1873** PYKE *Wild Will Enderby* (1889, 1974) I. iv 17 Borrowing a pan (*Anglice*: tin-dish) from some neighbourly miners, he progressed up the Gorge trying 'prospects' in many places.

prospect, *n.*[2] Orig. in full **prospective member**; also occas. **prospector**. A junior or probationary gang member.

1986 *More* (Auckland) May 26 Out-of-towners and new-comers in the gang—'prospectors' still earning their patch—tend to be an unknown quantity. **1988** *Dominion* (Wellington) 21 Oct. 1 Among gangs junior members or 'prospects' often admit ownership of drugs as a gang initiation, Mr Keefe said. **1989** [see PATCH *n.*[3]]. **1991** PAYNE *Staunch* 74 Everyone's sitting around, the bro's, the prospects even the gash... 'You scared, bro?' sneers a prospect. 'Got no balls, cuz?' says another. *Ibid.* 91 Other than prospects—who were young heavies out to prove how staunch they are—there was no problem [in prison].

Hence as a verbal form **prospecting** *vbl. n.*, the approaching or recruitment of prospective gang members.

1991 PAYNE *Staunch* 75 He went into corrective training and I have my suspicions the prospecting started there.

prospect, *v. Goldmining.*

1. [Orig. US but of historical interest in early NZ: see Mathews *v. intr.* 1841, *trans.* 1851.] *intr.* and *trans.* To explore or search (an area) for gold. Mainly significant as a *ppl. a.* or *vbl. n.*

1852 *NZGG* 10 Dec. V. 30/183 (Heaphy's Rep.) Kapanga River Diggings, Coromandel harbour, 4th November, 1852. The annexed tabular report of the work at this Gold-field since my arrival. Wherever I and the Messrs. Ring have 'prospected' on the Kapanga..we have found gold. **1853** *NZGG* 12 Jan. VI. 1/3 Many of these had been much employed in 'prospecting'. **1862** ARCHIBALD *Lett.* in *AJHR* D-7 (1863) 2. We prospected the bars and the banks.

2. As a *ppl. a.* in special collocations [OED *prospecting* 2 a, 1848; Mathews 1850], **prospecting claim,** a claim registered for the purpose of prospecting only; **prospecting dish** [OED 2 b, 1944], DISH *n.*[1]; **prospecting licence,** one granted to prospect a defined area (see quot. 1896 for *sluice-claim* (SLUICE 2)); **prospecting party** [OED 2 b, Mathews 1848], a group joined in a search for gold; **prospecting track,** a pathway made in un-tracked country to facilitate prospecting.

1892 PYKE *Gold-Miners' Guide* 7 Claims are classified as follows:—Alluvial deposits, and river-or creek-beds; Quartz lodes, reefs, and leaders; Sea-beach claims; **Prospecting claims. 1852** *NZGG* 10 Dec. V. 30:183 Kapanga River Diggings, Coromandel harbour, 4th November, 1852. We have found gold, and that the greatest number of flakes in the **prospecting dish**, appeared upon washing some earth yesterday at a bar about half a mile lower down the stream. **1935** COWAN *Hero Stories NZ* 273 Sutherland and Mackay, with guns, slash-hooks, and prospecting-dish..were clambering the rocky side of Lake Ada. **1943** HISLOP *Pure Gold* 20 A day with a prospecting dish is real good fun. **1853** SWAINSON *Auckland* 87 Several '**prospecting**' **parties** now started in various directions, all eager for the search [for gold]. **1907** *TrNZI* XXXIX. 396 A **prospecting-track** has been cut along the range for some twenty odd miles.

prospector: see PROSPECT *n.*[2]

prospector. [Used elsewhere but of historical significance, and recorded early, in NZ: see Mathews 1846; OED 1857.] One who searches an area or district for (signs of) gold. Also as **prospectors' claim, Prospectors' Right**, see quots. 1974, 1976.

1853 SEWELL *Journal* 10 Feb. (1980) I. 135 We found much excitement from the report of gold diggings on the plains. A party of prospectors had gone up the country. **1882** POTTS *Out in Open* 105 Within were all necessary appliances for the dreary life and calling of the lonesome prospector. **1896** HARPER *Pioneer Work in the Alps* 158 It is sad to see these old-time prospectors disappearing. **1918** *NZJST* I. 12 The coarse nature of the alluvial gold..and the fact that many of the 'specks' had fragments of gold attached, early induced prospectors to seek for lodes. **1974** HEINZ *Bright Fine Gold* 110 Two 'extra men's ground' was allowed by the Commissioner [at Thames, 1867], as a reward for the finding of the claim; thus, in diggers' parlance it was known as the 'prospectors' claim'. **1976** NOLAN

protected, *a. Obs.* [Spec. use of *protected* kept safe from injury or interference.] Applied to a mining claim, one that could legally be left unoccupied at certain times.

1873 PYKE *Wild Will Enderby* (1889, 1974) III. i 74 The Regulations provided for this contingency [of not working beach claims during summer floods]; and the miners, having duly registered their claims as 'protected', scattered themselves over the country.

Hist. Gold Trails Nelson & Marlborough 12 The Miner's Right, used on the goldfields from the earliest days until replaced by the Prospectors' Right in 1971.

Protector of Aborigines. *Hist.* Also popularly **Protector of the Aborigines**, *ellipt.* **Protector**. [The choice of official term was prob. earlier made in respect of Austral. aborigines: cf. AND 1835.] An official (post) established in 1840 to look after Maori interests *vis-a-vis* European, and abolished in 1846; also a deputy or assistant **Sub-Protector of Aborigines.** Cf. *Native protector* (NATIVE B 3 b).

1839 *Instructions from Secretary of State to Hobson* 14 Aug. in *Speeches & Documents* (1971) 13 All such [land-purchase] contracts should be made by yourself, through the intervention of an Officer expressly appointed to watch over the interests of the Aborigines as their Protector. *Ibid.* 16 Amongst the Officers thus to be created, the most evidently indispensable are those of a Judge, a Public Prosecutor, a Protector of Aborigines. **1843** DIEFFENBACH *Travels in NZ* I. 398 One [former slave]..went with us chiefly for the purpose of applying to the *Protector of the Aborigines* appointed by the Government, to obtain back some of the land which formerly belonged to his relatives. **1848** DILLON *Letters* 6 Aug. (1954) 74 I am now a kind of 'protector of aborigines' tho [*sic*] that name is abolished. **1848** WAKEFIELD *Handbook NZ* 75 Like his predecessor,.. [Fitzroy] merged the duties of Governor in those of Sub-Protector of Aborigines. **1902** IRVINE & ALPERS *Progress of NZ* 133 The appointment by Hobson of a catechist, George Clarke, as Protector of the Aborigines, was ill advised. **1938** WILY & MAUNSELL *Robert Maunsell* 58 On Sunday, July 4, 1840, His Excellency Lieutenant-Governor Hobson, accompanied by Mr. George Clarke, Protector of the Aborigines..paid a visit to Maraetai. **1966** *Encycl. NZ* I. 354 The position of Protector of Aborigines was created on the instructions of the British Government, and its purpose was to protect the Maoris from injustice, cruelty, and wrong, to establish and maintain friendly relations with them, to encourage the development of their capacities, to preserve their health and general well-being, to educate their youth, and to diffuse the blessings of Christianity. **1982** MORTON *Whale's Wake* 220 Edmund Halswell, a one-time Protector of Aborigines, argued that missionary egalitarianism..upset the Maori social structure.

province. [Spec. uses of *province* an administrative division of a country.]

1. *Hist.* Until 1876, a statutory administrative unit of regional government. Cf. *provincial district* (PROVINCIAL *a*. 2). **a.** One of the political-administrative units, New Ulster (the North Island), New Munster (the South Island), New Leinster (Stewart Island), set up in 1846 under the Constitution proposed by Orders in Council under the British Acts 9 and 10 Vict. cap. 103.

1846 *An Act to make further provision for the government of the New Zealand Islands* 9 and 10 Vict. c. 103 (28 Aug. 1846) in Rutherford *Sel. Documents* (1949) No. 20 III... it shall be lawful for Her Majesty..to divide the said Islands of *New Zealand* into two or more separate Provinces. **1848** WAKEFIELD *Handbook NZ* 86 On 28th January, 1848, [Grey] appointed and swore in some of the officers of the Southern Province, which is called 'New Munster'; and on the 10th of March proclaimed as the boundary between that and 'New Ulster', or the Northern Province, the parallel of latitude running..about 39° 46´ S. **1958** MCLINTOCK *Crown Colony Government in New Zealand* 214 Earl Grey decided in mid-1846 to confer on the colony a most complex constitution which, inter alia, provided for the creation of two provinces, New Ulster and New Munster, whose boundary line was to run due east across the North Island from the mouth of the Patea River.

b. Until their abolition in 1876, any one of a number (varying from time to time) of self-governing regional administrative units developed from the original provinces (and settlements) and distinct from a central General Assembly, having an elective Provincial Council, and an elective Superintendent as an executive head.

1849 *Earl Grey to Governor Grey* 22 Dec. in Rutherford *Sel. Documents* (1949) 35b The separation from New Munster of the other two projected provinces, of which Otago and New Canterbury are to form the nuclei respectively, must, for the present, be postponed, until the settlement of the latter is somewhat more advanced and the general convenience can be consulted with more certainty as to its limits. **1851** *Gov. Grey to Earl Grey* 30 Aug. in Rutherford *Sel. Documents* (1949) 64 At Auckland, Wellington, and Nelson, which would be the capitals of three separate provinces, Governments have already been constituted. **1851** *Lyttelton Times* 23 Aug. 3 Public meeting at Christchurch. Erection of Canterbury into a separate province. **1856** FITTON *NZ* 21 The novelty of the New Zealand constitution consists in a number of gubernatoria[l] departments, for the most part independent of all the acts of the general government... For this purpose, the Colony is divided into six Provinces [*sc.* Auckland, New Plymouth (later Taranaki), Wellington, Nelson, Canterbury, Otago]. **1866** BARKER *Station Life* (1870) 75 F— asked me if I would like to ride across the hills, and pay my first visit to some..old friends..who were among the earliest arrivals in the province. **1868** *Marlborough Express* (Blenheim) 25 July 3 The Provincialists consider themselves that they gained a triumph..by limiting the Bridges and Ferries Bill to districts outside Provinces. **1875** KIRK *Durability NZ Timbers* 12 Tanekaha [is]..more abundant in the Province of Auckland. **1894** *NZ Official Year-book* 70 As a result [of the distance of settlements from each other] the colony was formerly divided into nine provinces, each having its capital town. Of these, the principal are the Cities of Auckland, Wellington, Christchurch, and Dunedin. **1902** [see COUNTY 1]. **1959** SINCLAIR *Hist. NZ* 89 Of the six Provinces set up under the 1852 constitution, five were Wakefield settlements.

c. *Pl.* As **the Provinces**, provincial governments collectively as distinct from central government.

1857 *Richmond-Atkinson Papers* 15 May (1960) I. 265 Every six pence which is borrowed by the Provinces must be paid by the Colony at large. **1939** CRESSWELL *Present Without Leave* 9 These [Centralists] now had control of the central government, and when the Provinces hampered their aims they swept them away.

2. a. After 1876, a provincial district based on the boundaries of former Provinces (Auckland, Taranaki, Hawke's Bay, Wellington, Nelson, Marlborough, Westland, Canterbury, Otago, Southland) existing as a focal point for local identity or as a geographical basis for boundaries of local government administrative units or of various other regional sporting, etc. organizations.

1882 POTTS *Out in Open* 85 It is said to be found in Canterbury, but as yet we have not been so fortunate as to meet with it in this province. **1926** *NZ Observer* 9 June 6 Hawke's Bay had lost the shield and that after getting Cookie and half the All Blacks to go and live in the capital of the province of the wool kings. **1966** TURNER *Eng. Lang. Austral. & NZ* 52 [Provinces] were abolished in 1876 but the names remain. A province is now a region without administrative significance. **1970** THOMAS *Way Up North* 29 [Kauri] grows naturally within the restricted area of the northern part of the Auckland Province and almost wholly in Northland. **1972** SUTTON-SMITH *Folkgames Children* 177 In most of the provinces the game was known as Knucklebones.

b. *Spec.* in rugby union (and some other sports), a union or administrative body defined by its local catchment area and forming part of a national competitive network. (The use is at times extended to areas never within the former provincial network (e.g. Waikato, King Country Rugby Unions, etc.).

1905 THOMSON *Bush Boys* 80 Both were fine athletes and great footballers, the young minister as centre three-quarter and Malcolm as wing, proving 'crack' representatives not only of their college but also of their province. **1934** MULGAN *Spur of Morning* 24 That Bryan. A regular top-notcher. Be playing for the province in a couple of years.

provincial, *a.* Occas. init. cap.

1. Of or belonging to the provinces (or a province) in various senses of PROVINCE before and after 1876. **a.** *Hist.* In senses deriving from PROVINCE 1 a.

1848 WAKEFIELD *Handbook NZ* 84 Each Municipal Council was to elect members to the Representative Chamber of a Provincial Assembly in one of two Provinces, into which the islands were to be divided. **1857** *Richmond-Atkinson Papers* 16 June (1960) I. 276 The Provincial System is giving evident signs of infirmity. **1862** LINDSAY *Place & Power Nat. Hist.* 7 It would give them pleasure..making collections for a Provincial museum..and by affording every information in correspondence with a Provincial naturalist, were there such an officer. **1874** TROLLOPE *NZ* 59 The Provincial Assembly will be a real Parliament with a 'Bellamy'. **1894** WILSON *Land of Tui* 44 There were also..dances and a ball given in the [Canterbury] Provincial Chamber. **1938** BURDON *High Country* 166 Today a man from Invercargill may get into a train or service car and, within twenty-four hours, propose to and be accepted by a girl in Blenheim... Surely it is not to be wondered at that provincial distinctions have disappeared. **1948** LIPSON *Politics of Equality* 45 Up to 1876 political sentiment was regionalized...Provincial loyalties were paramount; people considered themselves Aucklanders or Wellingtonians rather than New Zealanders... Provincial politics were close at hand. **1969** BASSETT *Sir Harry Atkinson* 31 Provincial Superintendent: In the provincial system, the Superintendent was usually the man who led the majority group in the provincial assembly.

b. In modern use, applied to local sporting and other organizations, groups, events or contests (PROVINCE 2).

1910 *Evening Post* (Wellington) 8 Jan. 9 [Heading] Plunket Shield. Given by the 16th Governor, Lord Plunket, to Canterbury for the best record in provincial cricket in 1906–07. **1993** *Dominion* (Wellington) 13 Aug. 12 With..sprig-stomping..players..representing the game at provincial, national and international level, is it not time it was renamed thugby?

2. Special Comb. **Provincial Council** *hist.* (also as **Council**, and early **Provincial Legislative**

Council), the elective administrative council controlling a PROVINCE 1 b; **provincial district**, an official or semi-official name applied to a former province after abolition; **provincial government** hist. (also attrib.), applied before abolition to the elected government of a province with its elected executive head, the Superintendent.

1848 Grey 16 Nov. in Rutherford Sel. Documents (1949) 34 The large powers which will thus be vested in the Local Legislatures, will enable the **Provincial Legislative Council** of New Munster..to devise and frame all those measures. 1849 Gov. Grey to Earl Grey 30 Nov. in Rutherford Sel. Documents (1949) 39 And I think it should be further provided that if any new Province or Provinces were established, the **Provincial Council** of any such Province should in the usual manner be nominated by the Crown, until its European inhabitants amounted to such a number..when it would be replaced by a representative Legislative Council. 1850 GREY in GBPP NZ (Irish Univ. Series) VII. 1420 56 I propose to avail myself of the powers vested in me by the Act 11 & 12 Vict. c.5 which empowers me, with the advice of my Legislative Council, to constitute Provincial Councils. 1851 Gov. Grey to Earl Grey 30 Aug. in Rutherford Sel. Documents (1949) 44 I would..allow the electors of every province to elect the Superintendent or officer administering the Government of that province, to hold office for the same period of time as the members of the Provincial Councils are elected to serve. 1853 Richmond-Atkinson Papers (1960) I. 136 He is made clerk of the Council (our Parliament that is) and is proposed as Attorney for the Province by the Superintendent and Council. 1858 ACLAND Notes Sheepfarming NZ 11 The provincial council (i.e. the parliament) of the province of Canterbury have passed some very stringent laws on [scab]. 1860 BUDDLE Maori King Movement 16 Between the provincial Councils and the General Assembly the wants of the Natives in these respects have..been wholly neglected. 1873 NZPD XIV. 98 That honourable member was one of the great 'Truly Rural' party which was to bring about an entire revolution in [the] political system by sweeping away the Provincial Councils altogether. c1875 MEREDITH Adventuring in Maoriland (1935) 58 I have joined the Ice Creams [sic] assemblies, which have dances fairly often in the old provincial council room. 1898 HOCKEN Contributions 154 The first session of the [Otago] Provincial Council extended from the 30th of December, 1853, to the 25th of April following. 1946 ACLAND Early Canterbury Runs 34 Ross became the first clerk of the Canterbury Provincial Council. 1959 SINCLAIR Hist. NZ 87 The 1852 constitution was extremely democratic... The six Provincial Councils, the House of Representatives, and the Superintendents of the Provinces were all elective, though the members of the Legislative Council (the Upper House) were nominated for life by the Governor. 1883 Brett's Colonists' Guide 761 The Waste Lands of the Colony are administered in each **Provincial District** by a Board of Commissioners appointed by the Governor. 1894 NZ Official Yearbook 67 The following table gives the population in each provincial district estimated for the 31st December, 1893. 1851 WAKEFIELD Let. to Sir George Grey 35 The public buildings erected by the **Provincial Government** are, a small lock-up, called a jail. 1866 ANGAS Polynesia 122 Christchurch possesses a provincial government building and council-chamber..a hospital, a lunatic asylum, and other public buildings. 1876 Richmond-Atkinson Papers (1960) II. 427 The Otago Provincial Govt. backed by the Dunedin mob naturally do not like losing control of the provincial purse strings. 1939 NZ Centennial News 29 May 11 Two seals purporting to be the official seals of the Canterbury Provincial Government have been found.

Provincial, n. Hist. Also **co-provincial**. Provincialist (PROVINCIALISM 1).

1855 STAFFORD Papers (ATLTS) II. 13 You Provincials have all the legislation. 1867 Richmond-Atkinson Papers (1960) II. 244 Your brother has no enviable task at Dunedin... Will your old co-provincials go? 1939 CRESSWELL Present Without Leave 9 When the Provinces hampered their aims they [sc. the Centralists] swept them away... For these Provincials had aims other than acquisition.

Provincialism. Hist.

1. In 19th century New Zealand, the political system of regional government by elected Provincial Councils as distinct from central government; the political ideology which would advocate or support such a system. Contrast CENTRALISM.

1854 Richmond-Atkinson Papers (1960) I. 150 I [sc. C.W. Richmond] see you are a very prominent figure in the G.A. I expect to see the intense provincialism of you Aucklanders a good deal softened down. 1856 [see CENTRALISM]. 1858 Lyttelton Times 11 Sept. in Speeches and Documents (1971) 105 'Centralism', properly so called, is repugnant to all the political instincts of Englishmen. 'Provincialism' is as repugnant. Their educated sympathisers who are called or erroneously call themselves Centralists are truer friends of local self-government than many of the defenders of 'Provincialism'. 1868 Marlborough Express (Blenheim) 4 Jan. 6 On the question of Provincialism v. Centralism, he expresses our own views. 1870 Evening Post (Wellington) 28 Feb. 2 Under the wretched system of Provincialism, educational measures in our own Province ha[ve] been shamefully neglected. 1879 Auckland Weekly News 4 Jan. 10 There is still some heat left in the smouldering ashes of Provincialism. 1893 FROBISHER Sketches of Gossiptown 37 Let us now, for argument's sake, suppose Provincialism to be the best form of internal Government for New Zealand. 1953 Pol. Science Sept. 3 [Title] A Study in Provincialism versus Centralism Politics and the East Coast War 1865–69. 1966 [see CENTRALISM]. 1979 in CUTTEN Cutten Lett. 20 Macandrew's avowed Provincialism was seen by Cutten as constituting a difference too deep to bridge.

Hence **Provincialist** n. and attrib., one favouring Provincialism or the keeping of power in the hands of provincial governments; **Provincialist party**, the political faction advocating government by Provincial Councils.

1856 Richmond-Atkinson Papers (1960) I. 216 Hall of Canterbury, a clever young man and rather a strong provincialist. Ibid. I. 306 All these women are of course fanatical Provincialists. 1858 Lyttelton Times 11 Sept. (Editorial) in Speeches and Documents (1971) 105 After all, the names 'Centralist' and 'Provincialist' do not in most cases give a truer impression than party nick-names generally convey... Some who find themselves classed under the name of Provincialists have the most profound contempt for the assumption and local tyranny that have distinguished one or two of our little centralisms. 1859 THOMSON Story NZ II. 223 Two parties were now [mid 1850s] developed in the colony; one was called Centralists, the other Provincialists... The latter..insisted that the Imperial Parliament had established two independent governments in New Zealand, each for its own sphere, the provinces having exclusive jurisdiction in all provincial matters, and only under the control of the General Assembly on matters of general concern. 1868 Provincialists [see PROVINCE 1 b]. 1876 Richmond-Atkinson Papers (1960) II. 413 Of course, that the abolition of the provinces is a fait accompli is hardly denied now by even the hottest Provincialist, but how can Auckland and Otago work together harmoniously now the provincialist war cry cannot be used to rally them? 1953 Pol. Science Sept. 10 The strongly provincialist..Hawkes Bay Herald.. investigated..his preparations. 1959 SINCLAIR Hist. NZ 106 There were in the House of Representatives in the fifties, less clearly thereafter, two loose groups which were called the 'Centralist' and the 'Provincialist' parties. 1966 Encycl. NZ I. 358 A strong provincialist, Clifford did all possible to assist Wellington. 1987 [see CENTRALISM].

2. With a combining prefix (init. caps various): **ultraprovincical, ultra-provincialism, ultra-provincialist**, used mainly by the Richmonds and H.A. Atkinson to categorize extremist political views supporting a system of Provincial government.

1856 SEWELL Journal 20 Apr. (1980) II. 228 Featherston, Fox, and FitzHerbert together, want to establish ultra Provincialism, at Wellington as Headquarters. 1857 Richmond-Atkinson Papers (1960) I. 269 I am perfectly ready for a struggle with the Ultra Provincialists. Ibid. I. 355 I believe no man in this Province..has done more to let down ultra-provincialism & to strengthen the hands of the General Government. Ibid. I. 383 I will not reply to your insinuations about our being 'ultraprovincial'. 1868 DILKE Greater Britain I. 343 The Southern people now aim at 'Ultra-Provincicalism', declaring for a system under which the provinces would virtually be independent colonies. 1869 Richmond-Atkinson Papers (1960) II. 289 The blind Southerns and Ultra-provincials will support [Fox] through all. 1877 Ibid. II. 440 The localisation of the land fund..was the inevitable result of the Ultra-Provincialism which he [sc. Sir George Grey] did his best to introduce.

Provisional Matriculation. Now usu. called **provisional admission**, admission to a university for persons over 21 years of age without the need to pass an entrance examination.

[1921–22 Calendar University NZ 53 Soldiers that have been placed at a disadvantage by their service as members of the New Zealand Forces may be exempted provisionally from the examination for Matriculation.] 1924 Calendar University NZ 19 Applications for Provisional Matriculation shall be made to the chairman of the Professorial Board. 1936 Calendar University NZ 23 Provisional Matriculation will be accepted for the courses in Arts, Science. 1948 Calendar University NZ 15 Any candidate not under twenty-one (21) years of age may be granted provisional admission to a course for a degree or diploma. 1990 Calendar VUW 60 Every person who, prior to 1972, was granted provisional admission to the University..shall be deemed to have matriculated on the first day of March.

ptui, var. TUI.

puarangi. [Ma. /ˈpuaraŋi/: not recorded by Williams.] Hibiscus trionum (fam. Malvaceae), an attractive herb of coastal habitats, once considered native, now thought to have been introduced from Africa.

1959 NZ Philatelic Bull. 3 Dec. 1 4d Puarangi (Hibiscus). 1964 Postage Stamps NZ IV. 186 Hibiscus trionum, the botanical name of the plant known to the Maoris as puarangi, is the smaller of the two New Zealand hibiscus. 1981 BROOKER et al. NZ Medicinal Plants 64 Hibiscus trionum... Starry hibiscus... Puarangi. Mr A.H. Watt obtained the Maori name from older people at Te Kao, when the New Zealand Post Office wished to use an illustration of Hibiscus on a postage stamp.

puawananga. Also **puawhananga**. [Ma. /pua'wa:naŋa/: Williams 303 *Puawānanga.. Clematis paniculata.*] A native clematis *Clematis paniculata* (formerly *C. indivisa*) (fam. Ranunculaceae), a robust forest climber with large white flowers. See also CLEMATIS a.

1853 HOOKER *II Flora Novae-Zelandiae I Flowering Plants* 6 Clematis *indivisa*... 'Puawhananga'... It is the most common species. **1869** *TrNZI* I. (rev. edn.) 353 The elegant climbing *Puawananga (Clematis, sp.).* **1889** FEATON *Art Album NZ Flora* 2 Clematis indivisa... The Entire-leaved Clematis... The 'Puawananga'. **1910** [see CLEMATIS a]. **1926** CROOKES *Plant Life Maoriland* 27 The loveliest of our native flowers, Clematis indivisa... Puawananga, indeed, is one of our few New Zealand plants that has large and conspicuous flowers. **1930** ANDERSEN in *NZ Short Stories* 31 Many had twined the moony-white clematis in their hair—the *pua wananga*, child of two bright stars. **1946** *JPS* LV. 157 *Puawanānga*, a climbing plant..., a child of the stars Rehua (Antares) and Ruanga (Rigel). **1965** SHADBOLT *Among Cinders* 33 '*Pua wananga*,' Sam said. 'That's the old Maori name for those flowers [*sc.* of bush-clematis]. It was supposed to be sacred. **1983** *Evening Post* (Wellington) Weekender 23 Sept. 4 You can see it, clematis paniculata, Child of the Stars, puawhananga, sprawling over the trees in the bush now with its mass of white starry flowers.

pub. Used *attrib.* in special Comb. **pub pet**, a two-litre plastic beer flagon or its contents; **pub-stiff** *obs.* [prob. f. *stiff* a penniless man: see OED], a hotel worker or rouseabout guarding the door of a hotel after-hours, letting in approved customers and looking out for the police.

1988 *Pacific Way* July 50 Depending on regional expressions, [draught-beer containers] are variously known as a 'jar', 'peter', 'half-gee' (half-gallon) or the more modern '**pub pet**' two-litre plastic bottle. **1946** SARGESON *That Summer* 63 The **pub-stiff** that was on the door told us to go upstairs. **1964** PEARSON *Gloss.* to Sargeson *Collected Stories 1935–63* (1964) 302 pub-stiff: hotel worker.

pubbery. [f. *pub* + *-ery* a suffix designating place or establishment: AND 1910.] A public house.

1910 *Truth* 28 May 7 Williamson's procedure is a daring one; he simply walks into a store or pubbery, buys goods, and hands over a cheque which gives him a handful of ready money to move on to the next town and do likewise. **1934** MARKS *Memories* 182 A motherly old lady running a 'pubbery' in the Lyell Gorge. **1960** SCRYMGEOUR *Memories of Maoriland* 157 Nearby was a 'pubbery' (certainly not a hotel, for anybody would wonder why the Licensed Victuallers Association ever granted a licence for meals or liquor to be dispensed), and was typically designated 'The Trap'. Truly, this pubbery was just short of shanty.

publican-fish. [See quot. 1981.] GLOBEFISH.

1956 GRAHAM *Treasury NZ Fishes* 378 Globe-fish *Contusus richei*... It has several other popular names such as Balloon-fish and Mouse-fish... The most humorous name is that of Publican-fish. **1981** WILSON *Fisherman's Bible* 182 Publican-fish Another name for the Globe-fish, given apparently because of its round, bloated resemblance to early New Zealand publicans.

public school. [AND 1813.] In New Zealand, a primary or secondary school established and financed by the State. See also *State School* (STATE). Contrast PRIVATE SCHOOL.

[*Note*] Before 1876, *public school* was occas. used in a wider sense of any school (even one under the aegis of a private foundation) admitting the children of members of the general public (see quot. 1853).

1853 EARP *NZ* 66 Public Schools..St. John's College..Roman Catholic Day School. **1876** *NZ Statutes* No.42 134 [Educ. Boards Act, 1876] 'Public School' shall mean any school established and maintained under the provision of this Act. **1892** [see COLLEGE a]. **1902** [see CADET CORPS]. **1921** *NZGG* 20 Jan. VI. 137 The Inspectors of the Department, [shall] proceed annually to grade in accordance with the regulations herein contained the certificated teachers employed in the public schools. **1932** SCANLAN *Pencarrow* 256 The term 'public school' has a different connotation in New Zealand. It implies the Borough or County school; the school provided by the State. **1955** *BJ Cameron Collection* (TS July) public school (n) A State school. **1993** *Dominion* (Wellington) 12 June 2 If private schools were so much better, why did 96 per cent of New Zealanders still choose public schools?

public servant. [AND a *civil servant*, 1812.] An employee of certain State authorities, formerly, post-1912, usu. of the Public Services (now State Services) Commission. Now usu. called *State servant*. Cf. PUBLIC SERVICE.

[*Note*] The term *civil servant*, except for a period in the 19th century, has not been commonly used in New Zealand.

[**1890** *Otago Witness* (Dunedin) 7 Aug. 23 The civil servant is popularly supposed to be composed of dignity and a tall collar, tempered by red tape and a retiring allowance.] **1890** *NZ Observer* 8 Feb. 4 [Heading] Public Servants and Gambling. **1914** *PSA Jrnl.* 15 Apr. 29 That Public Servants in remote places be allowed extra leave to enable them to reach the railway. *Ibid.* 15 Sept. 3 The Public Servant is at the mercy of the market. **1948** LIPSON *Politics of Equality* 425 From fear and dislike the public servants called him [*sc.* Seddon] their executioner. **1955** *AJHR H-14* (43rd Report of the Public Service Commission) 5 Is it an honour to be a pubic [*sic*, corrected to 'public' in a later version] servant? **1962** SCOTT *NZ Constitution* 140 Public servants owe a duty of loyalty to their minister and to the government generally. **1977** HALL *Glide Time* 98 Christ, they [*sc.* State Services Commission] spend weeks checking to see if you're fit to be a public servant.

public service. Often with init. caps.

1. [AND 1793.] The personnel of State departments responsible for administering Government policy and enterprise in their respective areas of interest; *spec.* those State departments whose staff presently or formerly have come under the provisions of the State Services Act (formerly the Public Service Act 1912) and have the State Services Commission (formerly Public Service Commission(er)) as their employing authority.

[*Note*] In Britain and North America *Civil Service* is the usual term.

1890 *Evening Post* in *PSA Jrnl.* Apr. 20 [Meeting of July 31, 1890] If any gentlemen were present who did not belong to the Public Service, he trusted they would have the good taste to withdraw. **1896** *NZPD* XCII. 85 While we have..a Liberal Government..we have got Conservative administration in the public service... 70 or 80 per cent of the public service of the colony are undoubtedly conservative. **1907** *NZ Statutes* No.63 286 An Act to Provide a Superannuation Fund for the Public Service. *Ibid.* No.63 287 'Public Service' includes the High Commissioner's Office, the Legislative Branch, and every Department of the Government Service except the Government Railways Department, so much of the Police Department as is included in the Police Provident Fund Act, 1899, and so much of the Education Department as is included in the Teachers' Superannuation Act. **1912** *AJHR H-34* 1 I..do hereby..appoint you to be a Commission to inquire..as to the following matters in the case of each unclassified Department of the Public Service. [Earlier Commissions of Enquiry (1866, 1880) had used 'Civil Service'.] **1921** BRYCE *Modern Democracies* (1929) II. 307 In few countries, if in any, is the proportion of members of the public service to the whole nation so large as in New Zealand. **1948** LIPSON *Politics of Equality* 436 The personnel of about forty-five departments, forming in New Zealand parlance the 'Public Service', have been controlled first by the public service commissioner (1912–46) and since 1946 by a three-membered commission... The plural term 'public services' covers all employees of the central government. **1951** *PSA Jrnl.* Jan. 4 As a newcomer to the Public Service I have just worked my first overtime. **1962** SCOTT *NZ Constitution* 137 There are three separate career services: the public service (using that term in a narrow sense to mean the departmental staffs that are under the control of the Public Service Commission), the Railways service, and the Post and Telegraph service. **1977** HALL *Glide Time* 94 In those days, as now, we were known as the Public Service. **1988** RENNIE *Super Man* 151 The large Public Service desk with his folder on it brought back the memory of the day he had received a dressing down.

2. Special Comb. In full **Public Service Entrance Examination**, but mainly in shortened forms **Public Service Entrance**, **Public Service** *obs.*, a competitive public examination formerly held among second or third-year secondary pupils as a recruitment device for the Public Service.

1924 *Otago Witness* (Dunedin) 28 Oct. 73 I am at present busy swatting for Public Service Entrance and Matriculation examinations. **1964** MIDDLETON *Walk on Beach* 165 I agreed to sit for the Public Service exam.

Public Trust (Office).

1. A State organization handling all matters of trusteeship, wills, etc. Also *attrib.*

1870 *NZPD* IX. 109 The Government..had made a provision which merely left it open to the trust office to make such investments, if desirable, and if an agreement could be made with the colonial government by the public trust office. **1872** *NZ Statutes* No.26 124 [Public Trust Office Act] There shall be an office called the Public Trust Office, administered by an officer called the Public Trustee, who shall be appointed by the Governor. **1894** *NZ Official Year-book* 270 The Public Trust Office was constituted by 'The Public Trust Office Act, 1872'. **1936** BELSHAW et al. *Agric. Organiz. NZ* 35 The remaining financial requirements for land purchase and establishment of farms being obtained mainly from private individuals, the State Advances Office and the Public Trust.

Hence **Public Trustee**, the national (or district) head of a Public Trust office.

1870 *NZPD* IX. 17 The Bill would authorize public trust property to be placed in charge of a public trustee. Private persons, as well as charitable bodies, might also vest property in the trustee, subject to the approval of a board, consisting of the Colonial Treasurer, the Government Annuities Commissioner, the Auditor-General and the Public Trustee. **1894** *NZ Official Year-book* 269 The Public Trustee is also authorised by 'The Lunacy Act, 1882,' to undertake the administration of the estates of lunatics. **1905** BAUCKE *White Man Treads* 237 He can entrust [his estate] to the enervating mediation of that passé invention, the Public Trustee, whose very mention dries up the blood in their veins. **1964** HINDE *Mozley & Whiteley's Law Dict.* 308 The

Public Trustee is a corporation sole with perpetual succession and a seal of office. See s.5 of the Public Trust Act 1957. **1978** *Who's Who in NZ* 179 McGhie, John Gordon..dist. Public Trustee Napier '46–49.

2. *transf. Car-salesmen.* Rhyming slang for 'rust'.
1986 *NZ Herald* (Auckland) 22 Jan. 1 Car dealers have a collection of jargon they use on the yard, so if you are thinking of taking up selling cars as a career, there are a few terms you should know... Nowadays most cars have 'fires,' or heaters, but not all of them have 'public trust,' or rust.

puckaroo, puckeroo, varr. PAKARU.

puddle, *v. Goldmining.* [Spec. use of *puddle* to work clay, etc. with water to form a liquid; used elsewhere but mainly in Australia (AND 1852) and NZ.] *trans.* To work (clayey washdirt) with water in a special apparatus to separate the gold or gold-bearing material from the mullock.
c1875? *NZ Songster No.5* 64 When no one's looking fill your dish [with another person's washdirt], And you may wash out what you wish, Puddling mullock's knocked into a 'mish,' Hard work will but annoy. **1887** PYKE *Hist. Early Gold Discoveries Otago* 111 There was nothing to 'puddle'—anything like the stiff-clays of Bendigo being non-existent.

Hence **puddler**, a machine, or person, that puddles washdirt; **puddling** *vbl. n.*, washing clayey washdirt to obtain gold; **puddling machine** [AND 1855], an apparatus used to wash gold from mullock.
1935 BLYTH *Gold Mining Year Book* 11 **Puddlers**: Circular machines used for washing paydirt. **1943** HISLOP *Pure Gold* 20 A day with a prospecting dish is real good fun, and will often give the novice **puddler** visions of gold that will put to shame the goose that laid the golden eggs. **1967** MAY *West Coast Gold Rushes* 528 **Puddling**: separating gold from clay. **1862** WEKEY *Otago As It Is* 61 Claims shall be classified thus;—1. Ordinary Claims, *i.e.*, alluvial claims worked without the aid of sluices or machines. 2. Sluice and machine claims, *i.e.*, alluvial claims worked with the aid of sluices or **puddling machines**. **1862** *Otago Goldfields & Resources* 18 The puddling machine interest is stronger here than in other parts of the Province, but the results..offer no very cheering assurance of its adaptability to these gold fields. **1871** MONEY *Knocking About NZ* 17 For three days I 'did duty' on a puddling machine until the 'gaffer', finding me not equal to the others, who were all old hands, gave me the sack.

pudidi, var. PURIRI.

puffer: see PUFFERFISH.

pufferfish. Also *ellipt.* **puffer.** [Spec. use of northern hemisphere *puffer(fish)* for round-bodied, self-inflating fishes of fam. Tetraodontidae.] GLOBEFISH.
1966 DOOGUE & MORELAND *Sea Anglers' Guide* 296 Globefish... *Spheroides richei*; puffer, common toado, sand toado. **1967** [see TOADO]. **1974** *NZ Nature Heritage* XXI. 569 Small inflatable pufferfish occur in some localities. **1982** AYLING *Collins Guide* (1984) 316 Globefish (Pufferfish, prickly toadfish) *Contusus richei*. The globefish is a round bodied puffer with a blunt rounded snout. *Ibid.* 317 Green Pufferfish *Sphoeroides hamiltoni*... The green pufferfish is a small fish with..a distinctive colour pattern. **1986** [see TOADO]. **1989** PAULIN *NZ Fish* 244 Family Tetraodontidae, puffers. *Ibid.* 245 Puffers are circumglobal in tropical and temperate seas in depths of 0–1000 m.

pug. *Mining.* [Transf. use of *pug* clay used as a building material: AND 1896.] A clay or clay-like material, often auriferous, associated with reefs. Also *attrib.*
1907 *NZGeol.SB (NS)* No.4 102 An undetermined kaolinic product—the 'pug' of the miners—is fairly abundant in the reefs. **1912** *Ibid.* No.15 127 The more steeply dipping contacts between these andesites and the older land-surface..are usually marked by a heavy band of slickensided pug. **1918** *Ibid.* No.19 45 There was merely a narrow vein of pug, showing no scheelite, but a little gold. **1922** *NZJST* V. 174 This silica settled in pockets, forming the siliceous 'pug' common in the workings of the New Zealand quick-silver mines.

Hence **puggy** *a.* [AND 1932], characteristic of pug; including pug in its composition.
1907 *NZGeol.SB (NS)* No.3 98 The conglomerates and graywackes of the Haupiri Series here encountered contain ramifying stringers of quartz and puggy material. **1911** *Ibid.* No.12 58 Here a very soft puggy seam was found on the west side of the drive. **1912** *Ibid.* No.15 85 The foot-wall country almost throughout is shattered and frequently puggy. *Ibid.* 88 The vein-material consists of soft puggy mineralized andesite.

Pughia, var. PAKEHA.

puha /ˈpuwa/, /ˈpuha/. The spelling **puwha** has equal standing (it is given precedence in the Ma. usage of Williams), though **puha** is preferred in modern English language contexts. Also occas. early **poowha, púa.** [Ma. /ˈpuːfaː/, /ˈpuːhaː/: Williams 318 *Pūwhā, Pūhā. 1*...sow-thistle; or any vegetable used as greens.]

1. a. A sowthistle of the genus *Sonchus* (fam. Asteraceae) used as a vegetable. See also *bush thistle* (BUSH B 4), *Maori cabbage* (CABBAGE 2), RAURIKI, *sow-thistle* (THISTLE *n.* 2 (5)). Cf. *pork and puha* (PORK 1).
[**1815** KENDALL *New Zealanders' First Book* 12 Poowha. A sow thistle. **1820** LEE & KENDALL *NZ Gram. & Vocab.* 196 Púa, *s.* A sow-thistle.] **1848** [see RAURIKI]. **1868** TAYLOR *Past & Present NZ* 88 When I reproved a chief for not compelling his children to attend school, his excuse was, that as soon as they arose in the morning, they went and gathered little bundles of *Puwha*, sow thistles or sticks, which they carried to the town and sold, either for a few pence or a little food. **1873** BULLER *Birds NZ* 159 It [*sc.* the pigeon] also feeds on the tender shoots of the puwha, a kind of sow-thistle. **1881** *TrNZI* XIII. 27 The next is the *puwha*, or common sow-thistle (*Sonchus oleraceus*, var., or two varieties, exclusive of the later introduced British one). **1905** BAUCKE *White Man Treads* 177 And all was ready for the contents of the haangi—pork, puha, and potatoes. **c1920** BEATTIE *Trad. Lifeways Southern Maori* 119 *The Sowthistle* played a not unimportant part in providing vegetable food for the ancient Maori. It grew plentifully in the bush (and hence is often called bush thistle by settlers) and the aged people at Temuka enumerated at least three kinds, viz. the rauriki, a very fine soft variety; the ordinary puha; and the puha-taratara, a coarse kind of recent appearance in that district. Further south the people appeared to have just the one name, puha (often pronounced buha in the extreme south). **1946** ZIMMERMAN *Where People Sing* 66 Almost always there was *puha*, a green, leafy weed that grows in profusion over the whole countryside. **1952** [see RAURIKI]. **1963** BAXTER *Collected Poems* (1980) 279 Sea-eggs, puha, pork, and kumara: The Maori owned the land. I have a camera. **1976** HILLIARD *Send Somebody Nice* 18 We passed..three Maori women..stooping to cut puha from a manuka burn-off. 'A readymade Van Gogh,.. Or rather The Puha Gatherers.' **1985** *Listener* 7 Sept. 12 Then, I'd roll out my threadbare Whaariki..spread an old newspaper on the floor and on it place a steaming pot of puha.

b. *Spec. Sonchus asper*, the prickly sowthistle, not always distinguished from a above. See also RAURIKI.
1894 *TrNZI* XXVI. 264 The Rev. W. Colenso..considers this var. [*Sonchus oleraceus* L. *asper*..leaves clasping, sharply toothed] to be the puwha of the Maoris, who formerly used it for food, but abandoned it for the introduced European plant, which is less bitter. **1906** [see THISTLE *n.* 2 (5) a]. **1926** [see THISTLE *n.* 2 (5) b]. **1951** PARK *Witch's Thorn* 152 Mrs Hush..preferred to cook the wild sow-thistle that was called puha in those parts, a prickly dark green weed. **1965** [see RAURIKI]. **1982** BURTON *Two Hundred Yrs. NZ Food* 7 The smooth-leaved puha rauriki (*Sonchus oleraceus*) is the most favoured for eating, though the slight bitterness of the prickly-leaved *S. asper* (puha tiotio) is not unpleasant.

Hence *joc.* in composition **puhaologist**, a student of puha.
1988 *Sunday Star* (Auckland) 30 Oct. B2 One suspects if a new strain of puha appeared in Inner Mongolia tomorrow we'd have an instant gang of puhaologists zapping off with due ceremony..to the land of Ghengis Khan.

2. *transf.* As **electric puha**, marijuana, usu. locally grown. In *transf.* use, the name of a Maori pop group.
1989 MCGILL *Dinkum Kiwi Dict.* 28 *electric puha* marijuana. **1990** *Evening Post* (Wellington) 30 Nov. 9 [Heading] The electric puha story. New Zealand Green. The Story of Marijuana in New Zealand. **1995** *Dominion* 3 Mar. 16 A showcase for Maori music – *Electric Puha* —is on at Wellington's Taki Rua theatre tomorrow night.

puhaiwhakarua, var. PUWAIWHAKARUA.

puharakeke. [Ma. /puːˈharakeke/: Williams 304 *Pūharakeke..* yellow salt-water eel.] *Gymnothorax prasinus* (fam. Muraenidae), a moray eel having a yellow, gold or orange body, also called *yellow moray* (MORAY) q.v.
1918 *TrNZI* L. 302 *Tuna puharakeke* the large yellowish brown-skinned eel with which most of us are more or less familiar, is also taken in the *hinaki*... The natives use lamprey as bait as the puharakeke is very greedy for this food. **1927** PHILLIPPS *Bibliogr. NZ Fishes* (1971) 18 *Gymnothorax prasinus*... Yellow Eel; Puharakeke. **1929** BEST *Fishing Methods* 83 *Puharakeke*... A large eel, yellowish-brown, large head, small eyes with black pupils surrounded by yellow ring, projecting lower jaw; grows to a great size. **1967** MORELAND *Marine Fishes* 30 Yellow Eel... Other names are moray, muraena, and the Maori puharakeke. **1982** AYLING *Collins Guide* (1984) 91 *Yellow Moray* (Puharakeke) *Gymnothorax prasinus*... This species is the most abundant and the most widespread of the morays found in New Zealand.

puharitaiko, var. PUHERETAIKO.

puheretaiko. Also **puharitaiko, puheritaiko**. [Ma. /ˈpuːhereˈtaiko/ /ˈpuːhareˈtaiko/: Williams 304 *Pūharetāiko* [Ngai Tahu]... *Pūheretāiko* = *pūwharetāiko*.; Williams 318 *1. Senecio rotundifolius*.] *Brachyglottis rotundifolia* (formerly also *Senecio reinoldii* or *rotundifolius*) (fam. Asteraceae), a small tree or shrub of southern New Zealand, having leathery leaves with white or buff tomentum on the underside. See also MUTTONBIRD SCRUB, MUTTONWOOD.

1867 Hooker *Handbook* 767 Puheritaiko, *Lyall. Senecio* [sp.]. **1869** *TrNZI* I. (rev. edn.) 198 Puheritaiko [*Senecio* spp.]..are very ornamental shrub-trees, having large leathery leaves, covered on the back with white wool. **1885** *Ibid.* XVII. 216 The traveller who visits Stewart Island in December or January will have his attention arrested by..the deep green leaves of the puheretaiko. **1910** [see MUTTONBIRD SCRUB]. **1926** Cowan *Travel in NZ* II. 169 One of these [curious plants of Stewart Island] is the *puharitaiko* (*Senecio rotundifolius*) with large glossy-green leathery leaves, on which messages can be written in ink. These leaves could be stamped and sent through the post-office a few years ago, but the practice is now interdicted. **1936** Guthrie-Smith *NZ Naturalist* 149 They creep over the thinly scattered flat, fresh fallen *Puheretaiko* leaves [on the Snares I.] **1982** Wilson *Stewart Is. Plants* 102 *Senecio reinoldii* Muttonbird Scrub.. *Pūheretāiko*... Muttonwood... Shrub or small tree.

puhia, var. PUIA.

puhoi, var. BOOHAI.

puia. Also early **puhia**. [Ma. /ˈpuia/: Williams 305 *Puia* (i)..2. Hot spring.] A boiling spring. Cf. NGAWHA.
1843 Dieffenbach *Travels in NZ* I. 327 About three miles from this place I saw masses of white vapours rising in jets, and the natives told us that they were caused by the hot-springs (puhia). **1853** Taylor *Journal* 6 Feb. (ATLTS) VIII. 74 We caught a pig..which is to be cooked in the puia. **1864** Hochstetter & Peterman *Geol. NZ* 35 The geysers..of Iceland..have..strong rivals in the *puias* and *ngawhas* of New Zealand. **1878** Buller *Forty Yrs. NZ* 11 Hochstetter divides the steam jets into three kinds: 1. *Puias*, which are geysers, continuously or intermittently active. 2. *Ngawas*, which are inactive *Puias*—emitting steam, but not throwing up columns of water. **1905** *TrNZI* XXXVII. 459 Strange to say, several large masses of waterworn gravel cemented by puia-deposit into a compact rock are to be seen a short distance below the bridge at Taupo. **1911** *Triad* 11 Dec. 22 Tell you what, Jim. We'll get up in the cool of the dawn, and have a dip in O'Rorke's *puia*. **1920** *Quick March* 10 Sept. 47 The rheumaticky greybeard was bending over his own little mud steam-hole, a boxed-in 'puia' covered with a sack in which his pot of potatoes was boiling. **1930** Reischek *Yesterdays in Maoriland* (1933) 298 During the time I was in New Zealand practically none but Maoris enjoyed the salutary effects of the puias.

puikero, var. PAKARU.

puk /pŭk/: see PUKU.

puka. [Ma. /ˈpuka/: Williams 306 *puka 1. Meryta sinclairii... 2. Griselinia lucida*, a shrub.] Either of two native trees with large glossy leaves.

1. Occas. **pukanui** (see quot. 1988). *Meryta sinclairii* (fam. Araliaceae), a small tree found on the northern Three Kings, and Hen and Chickens islands, and distinguished by its large, oblong leaves crowded at the tips of branches.
1867 Hooker *Handbook* 767 Puka... *Polygonum australe* and *Meryta Sinclairii*. **1870** *TrNZI* II. 100 [Title] An account of the *Puka* (*Meryta Sinclairii*...) By T. Kirk. **1889** Kirk *Forest Flora* 245 *Meryta sinclairii*... The Puka... This noble species is one of the rarest plants in the world. **1898** Merriam-Webster *Internat. Dict.* (Australasian Suppl.) 2029 Puka..n. [Maori.] *1. (Bot.)* A New Zealand tree (*Meryta Sinclairii*). **1910** Cockayne *NZ Plants & Their Story* 83 Very interesting, too, must be the Three Kings where Mr. T.F. Cheeseman found abundance of that magnificent tree, supposed to be almost extinct, the puka (*Meryta Sinclairii*). **1922** *Quick March* 11 Sept. 15 Another notable thing about these off-shore islands the Chickens..is the fact that they are the original habitat of that gigantic broadleaf the puka. **1936** Guthrie-Smith *NZ Naturalist* 154 The huge leafed *Puka*... was the most conspicuous small tree of [the Hen and Chicken group] island. **1981** Brooker et al. *NZ Medicinal Plants* 37 *Meryta sinclairii*... Puka... This handsome tree grows on small islands off the coast... It has been planted widely as an ornamental. **1988** Dawson *Forest Vines to Snow Tussocks* 110 Pukanui *(Meryta sinclairii)*: a small tree with very large simple leaves which is also found on the Hen and Chicken Islands off the Northland east coast.

2. *Griselinia lucida*. BROADLEAF 2.
1886 Kirk in *Settler's Handbook NZ* (1902) 122 [Native name] Puka..[Settlers' name] Broadleaf..[Family] Corneae. **1889** Kirk *Forest Flora* 69 This handsome tree [*Griselinia littoralis*] is known as the puka in many districts, but, in Mr. Colenso's opinion, the name is applied erroneously. **1906** Cheeseman *Manual NZ Flora* 239 [*Griselinia lucida.*] *Puka.* **1940** [see BROADLEAF 2]. **1966** *Encycl. NZ* I. 252 The other native species [of *Griselinia*] is a handsome large-leaved tree, *G. lucida* or puka, which occurs throughout lowland forest.

pukahau, var. PUKAHU.

pukahu /ˈbukæu/. Also **bookau** (a freq. form), **pukahau, pukau.** [Ma. /ˈpukahu/: Williams 306 *Pukahu*..*3*. Any matted fibrous formation.] Any matted fibrous formation, esp. the mound formed under a kauri tree.
1897 *TrNZI* XXIX. 494 Wherever the kauri-trees grow..the ground is covered with a thick layer of humus (*pukahau*), composed of vegetable fibre intermingled with fallen leaves, particles of gum, and scales from the resinous bark, the latter helping to form a solid bank, sometimes several feet in height, round the base of the trees. **1899** *Ibid.* XXXI. 479 The floor of the kauri bush is covered with a thick coating of vegetable humus (*pukahu*). **1951** Levy *Grasslands of NZ* (1970) 94 In high humidity forests,.. pukahu—undecomposed dead forest litter—may accumulate on the forest floor, feet in depth. **1952–53** *NZ Forest Gloss.* (TS) *Pukau*... The mound at the base of mature kauri trees. syn. Cone. **1953** Reed *Story of Kauri* 208 The platform enabled a man to go from side to side, in order to pour *pukahu* down the face of the dam as a preventive of leaks in the planking. This pukahu (bookau to the bushman) was the matted, fibrous material which gathered at the foot of large Kauris. *Ibid.* 272 I have known these bookau fires to stay alight through fairly heavy falls of rain. **1975** *Evening Post* (Wellington) 20 Aug. 32 Stumps can vary in height up to 3.2 metres above ground level... When the stumps are covered by a pukahu—a mound of shed bark and other forest litter—it is necessary to dig down to find the stump height. **1991** La Roche *Hist. of Howick & Pakuranga* 205 Once the dam was being filled, the cracks were plugged with 'bookau'.

Hence **pukahu** *v. trans.*, to stop leaks in a dam with pukahu.
1953 Reed *Story of Kauri* 219 Some of the men were sent to *pukahu* it [the dam].

pukake, pukaki, pukako, varr. PUKEKO.

pukanui: see PUKA a.

pukapuka. [Ma. /ˈpukapuka/: Williams 306. *pukapuka*..*1. Brachyglottis repanda*.]

1. RANGIORA.
1838 Polack *NZ* II. 400 There are many other woods of much service to Europeans, differing in quality, among others:.. *Pukapuka*. **1852** Lush *Auckland Jrnls.* 9 June (1971) 117 I..succeeded in getting a number of Pohutukawas, Pukapukas, and several handsome evergreens. **1869** *TrNZI* I. (rev. edn.) 236 Of our shrubs and smaller timber trees, several are of strikingly beautiful growth..(*e.g.*)..the Pukapuka. **1885** *Ibid.* XVII. 419 The few clumps of trees consist of pohutukawa, mapou..pukapuka. **1900** *Auckland Weekly News* (Xmas Number) 6 The puka-puka with its hoary leaves. **1922** *Ibid.* 14 Dec. 17 He carried piles of pukapuka leaves. **1981** Brooker et al. *NZ Medicinal Plants* 40 *Brachyglottis repanda*... Maori names: *Rangiora, pukapuka, wharangi*.

2. *Obs.* in non-Maori use. Also **booka-booka**. [Ma. /ˈpukapuka/: Williams 306 *pukapuka. 3.* Book. (Probably partly from similarity of sound, partly with the underlying idea of a flat surface.) (mod.) *4.* Paper. (mod.) *5.* Letter. (mod.); Duval III. 351, 1833.] Something written; a book; a cheque.
1838 Polack *NZ* I. 180 It was agreed that a canoe..should be lent to us, for the amount of a blanket and some tobacco, for which I instantly wrote a check (pukápuká), on the spot. **1840** *NZ Jrnl.* I. 14 You will take care to mention in every *booka-booka*, or contract for land, that a proportion of the territory ceded, equal to one-tenth of the whole, will be reserved by the Company, and held in trust by them for the future benefit of the chief families of the tribe. **1843** Dieffenbach *Travels in NZ* I. 141 He [*sc.* an old tohunga recently converted] almost invariably kept his puka puka (hymn and prayer books) upside down when he pretended to sing his psalms or read the service. **1868** Taylor *Past & Present NZ* 16 *Pukapuka*—the word applied either to paper or books—at first sight appears to be derived from our English word *book*; it is not so, but from the large white leaf of the Pukapuka Rangiora (*Brachyglottis repanda*), to which the natives likened paper when they first saw it. They said, 'He rau pukapuka tenei!' 'Oh! this is a leaf of the Pukapuka.'

pukapuka, var. PUNGAPUNGA.

pukaroo, pukaru, varr. PAKARU.

pukatea. Also with much variety of early form as **buccatea, buckatee(r), buckyteer, bukatea, bukitea** (all prob. representing /ˈbʊkə-/). [Ma. /ˈpukatea/: Williams 307 *Pukatea, puketea*... *1. Laurelia novaezealandiae;... 2. Gnaphalium luteo-album;* a small plant.]

1. *Laurelia novae-zelandiae* (fam. Monimiaceae), a large native tree of swampy areas, distinguished by its deeply buttressed trunk, and valued for its timber, esp. as used for boat building. See also LAUREL a.
1841 *NZ Jrnl.* II. 51 The pukatea is easily known by its roots forming a pedestal for the tree above ground. *Ibid.* II. 213 The box containing the above is made of various woods. The white and red pine, the buccatea, and the plank inside is totara. **1842** Heaphy *NZ* 44 The *Bukitea* is also used for building; it is of a darker colour, and rather a softer nature than [kahikatea]. **1854** Golder *Pigeon's Parliament* 5 But still bear up thou! [pine] And bend not!—If thou shouldest, I vow You'll render mine a grevious [*sic*] lot! And crush to ruins my poor cot! Aye, more than when the buckateer Such havock made me t'other year! **1889** Kirk *Forest Flora* 129 The pukatea is one of the loftiest trees in New Zealand. **1910** Cockayne *NZ Plants & Their Story* 41 The pukatea (*Laurelia novae-zelandiae*), with pale-brown,

soft but strong and tough wood, which has been used for boat-building and furniture. **1936** *NZ Railways Mag.* June 29 The bark of the forest tree *pukatea* (*Laurelia*) has a reputation as a backblocks remedy for toothache and neuralgia. **1940** Laing & Blackwell *Plants NZ* 180 One of the loftiest of New Zealand forest trees, sometimes reaching the height of 150 ft... Maori name *Pukatea*, often misnamed *Bukatea*. **1957** *Dominion* (Wellington) 12 Aug. 10 Bushmen usually called a pukatea, buckyteer; a kowhai, goey; and a kaponga, bunger. **1988** Dawson *Forest Vines to Snow Tussocks* 31 In New Zealand pukatea (*Laurelia novae-zelandiae*) often has well-defined plank buttresses.

2. Usu. as **pukatea weed**, *Gnaphalium luteo-album*, a cudweed.

1883 *Brett's Colonists' Guide* 483 Puke-tea Weed.—This weed is boiled (roots and all), and applied, hot, as a poultice to cuts. **1952** Richards *Chatham Is.* 45 *Gnaphalium..luteo album*... Common Cudweed. Puke-atea (white lump).

pukateine /'pʊkətin/. [f. *pukate*(a + *-ine*.] A plant alkaloid contained in pukatea bark. Cf. pukatea 1, quot. 1936.

1977 Connor *Poisonous Plants NZ* 128 Bernauer (1967) isolated seven new alkaloids..in this species... Pukateine is the best known of them. **1981** Brooker et al. *NZ Medicinal Plants* 11 In 1910 he [*sc*. Aston] isolated pukateine, the poisonous principle of pukatea bark.

pukau, var. pukahu.

puke, pukeka, varr. pook, pukeko.

pukeko /ˌpuːˈkekʌu/, /ˌpjuːˈkekʌu/, /ˌpjuːˈkækʌu/; /ˌbʌuˈkækə/ [etc.]. With much variety of form deriving from non-Maori perceptions of Maori /p/ as [p] or [b], and /uː/ /e/ and /o/ as a variety of vowels. Variants fall broadly into two regional types: /p/ forms in mainly NI spoken and general New Zealand written use: **pokako, pokekha, pokeko, pukake, pukaki, pukako, pukeka**; /b/ (mainly SI) forms in older or more informal use: **bokak(k)a, bokak(k)er, bukaka**; and with (usu. informal) shortening: **bok(i)e, bowie; pook, puke** /puk/. Pl. is often *pukekos*, with a freq. older Canterbury and Otago plural form *pukaki* (perh. influenced by the Latin *pl.* in *-i*, but occas. also used as a singular form). [Ma. /ˈpuːkeko/: Williams 307 *Pūkeko*. 1...Swamp hen... = *pākura*.]

[*Note*] Though a Maori alternative name *tangata tawhito* (Williams 409) suggests 'old, ancient, original, primeval', the bird may be self-introduced from eastern Australia.

1. *Porphyrio porphyrio melanotus* (fam. Rallidae), a common red-billed, black-and-purple, hen-sized, tail-flicking rail. See also *bald coot, bald pate* (bald), pakura, pook, porphyrio, red-bill 1, sultana bird, *swamp-hen* (swamp 2 b), swampie, *swamp-turkey* (turkey n.¹ 1), water-hen b. **a. pukeko** forms.

[**1820** Lee & Kendall *NZ Gram. & Vocab.* 196 Pu kéko; A flute made of the bird *Kéko*. Name of a person.] **1835** Yate *NZ* (1970) 62 *Pukeko*—A species of water-hen, the size of a well-grown capon. **1840** *NZ Jrnl.* I. 288 I amused myself by pursuing some pukekas over the swamps and potato grounds at the back of the pah. **1841** Best *Journal* 15 May (1966) 311 I also saw a fine Bittern a small white Gull a wader like a Godwit and shot a Pukako. **1850** Godley *Letters* 4 June (1951) 170 Teal, ducks, and pukakos innumerable. **1868** Pyke *Province Otago* 31 Swamp-hens (*Pukeko*) are plentiful. **1874** Evans *Over the Hills and Far Away* 2 Pokekhas..swamp hens. **1884** Martin *Our Maoris* 114 The place was populous with large black birds, called by the Maoris pu-ke-ko. **1886** *TrNZI* XVIII. 99 Porphyrio melanotus... Swamp-hen (*Pokako*). **1891** Wallace *Rural Econ. Austral. & NZ* 52 The Swamp-hen or Pukeko..of New Zealand is in the habit of pulling up the affected grass..to get at the grub. **1911** Foston *Bellbirds' Lair* 47 In the swamp 'pukake' abound. **1928** Baucke *Manuscript* (Bishop Museum Memoirs Vol.IX No.5 343–382) in Skinner & Baucke *Moriioris* 362 Rail and pukeka were caught by snares set in their sphagnum moss runs. **1934** Hyde *Journalese* 109 But here, a little stream meandered under cream-plumed shimmer of huge toi-toi bushes, crimson-billed pukekos with thoughtful expressions waded downstream. **1946** *JPS* LV. 157 *pūkeko*, a swamp-bird.., the swamp-hen; makes a comical pet, but inquisitive and destructive in the garden. Pukaki, name in the south, not recognized by Williams. **1957** Frame *Owls Do Cry* (1967) 59 Pukekos took long strides through the swamp, flicking their white envelopes of tail. **1966** Pook [see pook]. **1976** Soper *NZ Birds* 104 Who, for example, having once read the late Charles Douglas's classic description of the Pukeko's mincing stepping gait as being like that of a man in too tight boots can ever see it again in any other way? One sees immediately the hobbling, head-jerking action so characteristic of the Pukeko's walk. **1985** *Reader's Digest Book NZ Birds* 171 *Pukeko Porphyrio porphyrio melanotus*... Swamp hen, pakura, puke, pukaki... Essentially a bird of the lowland swamps, the pukeko has expanded its range with the development of agriculture... So while farmers and market gardeners argue that pukekos are pests, conservationists are worried by declining populations.

b. bokaka forms (mainly SI).

1898 Morris *Austral-English* 449 Called..by New Zealand colonists *Sultana-bird, Pukáki*, or *bokáka*. **c1899** Douglas in *Mr Explorer Douglas* (1957) 234 Besides being a jack of all trades, this bird has a variety of names, no two people being agreed as to which is correct. The Maories call it the bu-ka-ka—is this spelling correct? **1913** *Auckland Univ. College Student Carnival Programme* 27 Pukeko. A bokakker out of season. **c1940–50** A variety of speech-forms known to the editor from Marlborough: *bokakka, boke, bokie, bowie*: also used as a nickname for thin, long-legged men or boys. **1975** Anderson *Milford Road* 99 'No—it's more like a big bo-kakka' the local [Southland] slang for pukeko. **1983** Henderson *Down from Marble Mountain* 100 The raupo..where the glossy blue..bo-kaker peered out, winced, and bolted back into cover.

c. pukaki forms (mainly SI).

1874 Bathgate *Col. Experiences* 85 The pukaki or swamp-turkey. **1889** Williams & Reeves *Colonial Couplets* 26 And the swamp hen on the rail Pertly tilts her scanty tail. [**1889** *Note*] 'swamp-hen'—The 'pukaki', it wants jugging. **1890** Grossman *Angela* 47 I may shoot pukakis. **1900** *Auckland Weekly News* (Suppl.) 13 Apr. 7 The pakeha boat..gliding across raupo-fringed lakes, where the wild duck and pukaki..muster in countless mobs. **1911** Moreland *Through South Westland* 27 A fairly straight road ran between dykes and tall marsh-grass, where the red-legged pukakis rose and flapped away, their blue-black plumage shining in the sun. **1933** Acland *Early Canterbury Runs* 175 There were thousands and thousands of pukaki in the [Waimate] swamp. **1947** Stevenson *Maori & Pakeha* 78 Notornis... resembled the pukaki, but was a much heavier bird. **1954** Macfarlane *Te Raka* 58 Pukaki, the swamp hen, treats man rather as a joke and helps himself to whatever he wants. **1981** Hooper *Goat Paddock* 17 A bird or two rustled somewhere, a pukaki screeched across the stream, but otherwise it was very still.

2. In recipes as **stewed pukaki, pukeko stew, pukeko soup**.

1908 Col. *Everyday Cookery* 99 *Stewed Pukaki*. Hang for some time, then..stew or jug like wild duck or hare. **1936** *Recipe Book* (St. Mary's) 33 *Stewed Pukaki*..cut into pieces..lay in stewpan..bacon..pukaki..onion..thyme..salt and pepper..water....Cook..slowly. **1953** *Whitcombe's Cook. Book* [no page] Stewed pukaki. **1982** Burton *Two Hundred Yrs. NZ Food* 22 [Quoting an anonymous early poem.] And can you really make, man, Proper **pukeko soup**? **1977** *Glenfield College Maori Cookbook* 28 **Pukeko Stew**. Skin the bird. When cutting off the legs, make sure the sinews are removed.

3. a. In elaborations forming evasive or dismissive replies to children or importunate questioners. (Often associated with boohai, see also boohai 3.)

1959 Slatter *Gun in My Hand* 230 Ronnie doesn't live here any more he's up the creek shooting pukekos with a long-handled shovel.

b. *fig*. (Young) feller-me-lad.

1914 Grace *Tale Timber Town* 12 A half-fledged young *pukeko* like you, presumes to cut me out!

pukeroo, pukeru, pukkaroo, varr. pakaru.

puku /'pʊku/. Also early **buk**. [Ma. /ˈpuku/: Williams 308. *Puku* (i)... 2. Abdomen, stomach.]

1. Occas. in a shortened form **puk** /pʊk/, the stomach, belly; tummy. See also pukunui.

[**1820** Lee & Kendall *Gram. & Vocab.* 197 Púku, s. The stomach. **c1826–27** Boultbee *Journal* (1986) 113 belly—buk]. **1917** *Chron. NZEF* 30 May 151 My 'puku' feel werry bad. **1918** Weston *Three Yrs. with New Zealanders* 70 The Medical Officer..injected the serum in what the Maories call my *puku*. **1931** *Aussie* (NZ Section) 15 May X Te punch in the *puku* wind him. **1948** Henderson *Taina* 176 'I'm all right now,' I said, although my *puku* was feeling very sore. **1960** Rogers *Long White Cloud* 17 That 'good name' business seemed to hit the old man in the *puku*. **1970** Mason in *Solo* (1981) 15 'Aw, tonight a course... Look at that puk! Big fat slob!' [**1981** *Note*] Puk: contraction of *puku*, a Maori word meaning belly; much used by both races. **1971** Baxter *Collected Poems* (1980) 516 Nikki goes down to have a wash..with her little bulging puku. **1987** Cox *Dirty Work* 59 Nah, just slapped on some shades, stuck out the puku, stood really big in the doorway with a bad attitude. **1995** *Quote Unquote* Nov. 20 He is agitating the waistband of his pyjamas... I can see his tummy looking all pokey-outey. 'Put away your puku and brush your teeth.'

2. In the phr. **a pain in the puku**, a stomach-ache; occas. applied to a person who is a nuisance or 'pain'.

1941 Baker *NZ Slang* 42 A stomach-ache became..a pain in the puku. **1988** McGill *Dict. Kiwi Slang* 81 *pain in the puku* a bellyache or irritating person; Maori 'puku', stomach; eg 'That Pom's a pain in the puku.'

pukunui.

1. /ˈpʊkuˈnuwi/. [f. puku + Ma. *nui* 'big'.] A protuberant belly; also used as a nickname. See also puku 1.

1848 Power *Sketches in NZ* (1849) 159 [Maori nicknames for the pakehas in Power's party] A stalwart officer of the grenadiers, for instance, is generally known as Puku-nui, or Big-belly. **1943** Bennett *English in NZ* in *Amer. Speech* XVIII. 93 *puku*, stomach, and *pukunui*, big stomach (used jocularly). **1985** Bentley & Fraser *Grand Limerick Tour* [No.] 16 A novel librarian at Tui Found a way to avoid 'puku nui' Was rotating male members From July to December On a system according to Dewey.

2. [Ma. /'pukunui/: Williams 309 *Pukunui. 1.* a. Greedy...2... dotterel: see quot. 1835.] DOTTEREL 2 (3) (*Charadrius obscurus*).

1835 YATE *NZ* (1970) 68 *Pukunui*—A bird so called from the largeness and rotundity of its breast, about the size of the crow, and remarkable for the deep red with which the feathers are tinged upon the back and under the wings. **1842** GRAY *Fauna* in Dieffenbach *Travels in NZ* (1843) II. 195 *Charadrius obscurus...* Ha-poko-wera of the natives of Dusky Bay... Tuturiwatu... To this order may also be referred two other birds spoken of by Mr. Yate under the names of Pukunui, Pututo. **1985** *Reader's Digest Book NZ Birds* 183 New Zealand Dotterel *Charadrius obscurus... Tuturiwhatu, pukunui, paturiwhata,* red-breasted dotterel.

pukurau. [Ma. /'pukurau/: Williams 309 *Pukurau*: Williams defines only as *Clathrus cibarium*, the basket fungus.] A large puff-ball of the genus *Calvatia* (formerly *Lycoperdon*), (fam. Lycoperdaceae) edible in its young form.

1867 HOOKER *Handbook* 767 Pukurau, Col[enso]. *Lycoperdon Fontainesii*. **1869** *TrNZI* I. (rev. edn.) 261 [Also eaten were] several *Fungi* [especially]..the paruwhatitiri (*Ileodictyon cibarium*), the Pukurau (*Lycoperdon Fontainesii*). **1882** HAY *Brighter Britain* II. 212 The Maori also ate the Pukurau..and possibly other species of puff-balls besides. **1981** BROOKER et al. *NZ Medicinal Plants* 23 *Calvatia caelata*... Common name: *Puffball* Maori name: *Pukurau*. In Hooker's 'Handbook..', the name 'pukurau' or 'pukuvau' is applied to *Lycoperdon fontanesei*..which is now known as *Calvatia caelata*.

pull, *v.*

1. *trans.* Of a sheep-dog, to bring (sheep) directly towards its handler; to use a dog to do this. Also *intr.* (see quots. 1934, 1949, 1970).

c1875 MEREDITH *Adventuring in Maoriland* (1935) 47 He covered more ground than was necessary, by running wide, but eventually 'pulled' the mob on the slope of a hill, and sat down wagging his tail... I might have to pull every mob of sheep on the run. **1934** LILICO *Sheep Dog Memoirs* 4 Once you have a strong-eyed dog trained to pull he does so with care and control of sheep. **1938** BURDON *High Country* 107 The silent dog is used to 'pull' or bring sheep back to the shepherd. **1949** HARTLEY *Shepherd's Dogs* 3 The system I have devised..gives the trainer greater command where there is a likelihood of the dog 'setting' sheep and failing to lift or pull. *Ibid.* 26 As the young dog begins to pull sheep the trainer should go forward and work matters so that the sheep will be brought along a fence line. **1953** STRONACH *Musterer on Molesworth* 44 It is said by some that on rough country he [*sc.* the eye dog] spends too much time eyeing the sheep and not enough 'pulling' them. **1970** MCLEOD *Glorious Morning* 141 Once he had headed them he 'pulled' relentlessly, following hard on the heels of the mesmerised animals. **1978** JARDINE *Shadows on Hill* 7 Steve had told him to pull a small mob down to the flat 'to see what your heading dog is like'; she pulled too hard and nearly put them over a bluff.

Hence **pulling** *vbl. n.,* see quot.

1947 NEWTON *Wayleggo* 154 *Pulling:*... The act of a heading dog bringing sheep back to his master is termed pulling.

2. In deer-hunting, of a hunting dog, to draw (the deer) towards the hunter. Also as **deer-puller,** a hunting dog which does this; **pull** *n.,* the process or result of 'pulling' deer.

1951 *Here & Now* Dec. 15 These crosses [*sc.* greyhound-collie/terrier, etc], sometimes euphemistically called lurchers, are excellent deer-pullers... Only with great luck and fitness..can the hunter be in on the pull with the knife. On the whole it is better not to have dogs so fast as to be able to pull deer unless you are going in for that line exclusively.

3. *transf.* In the phr. **to pull** (one), to trick (successfully), to 'pull a fast one'.

1984 BEATON *Outside In* 20 Kate: Reckon she'll get away with it. Sandy: No way. Kate: You never know. Lav's a softie. Ginny might pull one. *Ibid.* 47 Ma:.. they don't mean no harm. Always pullin' a few..to stir, you know.

pull, *n.* [See PULL *v.* 1.]

1. The action of a sheep-dog bringing sheep directly to its handler.

1970 MCNAUGHTON *Tat* 122 It was a perfect head and pull. Tat got them into the twelve o'clock hold in the ring. **1970** MCLEOD *Glorious Morning* 253 *Heading dog:* One which casts wide to reach the 'head' of sheep, and brings them back. Their work divides into the 'head' and the 'pull'. **1982** *Agric. Gloss.* (MAF) 25 *Pull:* Action of dog bringing sheep directly to its handler.

2. *Dog-trialling.* As **long pull.** See quots.

1970 MCNAUGHTON *Tat* 88 When Bluey finally got him [*sc.* a sheep-dog under training] started on what is known as the 'long pull', on flat ground..he would naturally take a wide run out..to head his sheep. **1971** NEWTON *Ten Thousand Dogs* 11 There are five standard classes [in dog trialling], each incorporating three events. The standard classes are as follows: Class I (the Long Pull); Class II (the Drive and Yard); Class IIA (a South Island event); Class III (the Zig-zag or Slew) and Class IV (The Straight Hunt.)

puller. [f. *pull* to pluck + -ER.] *wool puller* (WOOL 3), a person or machine that removes wool from a sheepskin or carcase.

1908 *Awards, etc.* 211 [Meat-workers award] [Rates of wages] Fellmongery hands, pullers, painters, fleshers, pelt-classers, curing-dolly, steam-drier, dollymen, scudders, skin-washers, wool scourers and trimmers, 8s. per day. **c1927** SMITH *Sheep & Wool Industry* 186 The men employed [by fellmongers] pulling the wool off the skins are called 'pullers'. **1951** *Awards, etc.* 327 [NZ Freezing-Workers Award] [Rates of wages] Pullers, South Island—per dozen skins [£]0 1[s.] 2½[d.] All skins shall be counted and placed as conveniently as practicable near each puller who shall be required to pull and sort the wool. **1959** SLATTER *Gun in My Hand* 67 You were on hourly rates shoving the heavy-laden trolleys of sheepskins from the painters [*sc.* those who paint woolled sheepskins with a depilatory] to the pullers.

pulpie. [f. *pulp* (and-paper-worker + -IE.] A pulp-and-paper worker.

1986 *Evening Post* (Wellington) 5 Sept. 3 Pulp and paper workers have been locked out by management..Mr Knox reported to 464 'pulpies' at the meeting on his efforts to end the row. **1986** *Sunday News* (Auckland) 21 Sept. 3 Claims that her husband received a..loan from the Pulp and Paper Federation have prompted the wife of controversial pulpies secretary John Murphy to go public.

pum: see PUMICE.

pumice. Also *ellipt.* **pum** (see quot. 1919, sense b below). Used *attrib.* of the abundant pumice originating on the central volcanic plateau of the North Island. **a.** Comb. **pumice-drying, -dust, -topped, track, -whitened.**

1983 *Whakarewarewa Forest Park* 30 The props were sold to the Waihi Goldmining Company and to a local **pumice-drying** company. **1872** *Weekly News* (Auckland) 7 Dec. 20 Patches of snow covered with **pumice dust**. **1965** OLLIVIER *Petticoat Farm* 1 Harry stood at the roadside and watched the white pumice dust rising between the bracken at each side of the road. **1891** WALLACE *Rural Econ. Austral. & NZ* 229 **Pumice-topped** land..covers unfortunately about thirty per cent. of the area of the North Island. **1943** MARSH *Colour Scheme* 233 And drive it he did..bouncing slightly as he negotiated the inequalities of the **pumice track**. **1883** DOMETT *Ranolf & Amohia* I. 247 She staggers, falls—upon the **pumice-whitened** shore.

b. Special Comb. **pumice country, pumice flat, pumice-land(s), pumice soil,** an area of land, or its soil, comprising or containing broken-down pumice; **pumice-stone** rounded pieces, or blocks, of pumice used for sanding, skin cleaning, etc.; or, in larger trimmed blocks, for construction work; **pumice sweep** an area outside an entrance covered with pumice material.

1892 *NZ Official Handbook* 8 A large area adjacent to the lake [Taupo] is at present worthless **pumice-country**. **1912** *Otago Witness* (Dunedin) 17 July 15 Thanks to Dr. Reakes..a tremendous stretch of pumice country has been freed from its bad reputation [for bush sickness]. **1950** *NZJAg*. Feb. LXXX. 115 In its natural state the open pumice country..looks barren and unattractive... The pumice land of the central plateau area of the North Island consists of soils derived from volcanic-ash showers. **1959** *NZ Dairy Exporter* Sept. 63 Perhaps pumice country farmers could follow the practice adopted by those South Taranaki farmers who have no summer problem. **1946** SARGESON *That Summer* 173 Here the valley began to close in and there were no **pumice flats**. **1892** *Auckland Weekly News* 23 Apr. 31 My experience..may be of some use in suggesting one or two plants which are worthy of extended trial..on..the **pumice land** of Waikato and Taupo. **1912** *NZJAg*. July V. 24 [Heading] Pumice Lands. Pumice country varies in quality in just the same degree as do the more fertile lands on the Canterbury Plain. **1919** *Quick March* 10 June 45 In a leading article recently a daily paper referred to the gum lands and the 'pum' lands (pumice) selected by the Government for returned soldiers. **1922** *Auckland Weekly News* 20 July 55 The term 'King Country Pumice Lands' is largely a misnomer in that the area which can actually be described by the words is much smaller than the title as generally used gives credit for. **1955** *BJ Cameron Collection* (TS July) pumice lands (n) A large area in the centre of the North I. with a pumicy soil. **1986** EVANS *Change Agent* 19 He was..able to prolong the toughness by taking on a new block in the sparse pumice land of New Zealand's North Island. **1912** *NZJAg*. Jan. IV. 374 **Pumice soils** are classified as coarse sands, but the word 'sand' conveys rather a wrong impression. **1950** *Ibid.* Jan. LXXX. 17 In the north and north-west, where annual rainfall is over 50 in., the soils are classified as yellow-brown pumice soils. They are light fluffy pumice soils formed on volcanic ash. **1773** FORSTER *Resolution Jrnl.* 8 June (1982) II. 296 Among the loose Shingles on the beach two pieces of **Pumice-stone** were found. [1982 *Note*] Rounded pumice pebbles commonly cast on New Zealand beaches were mainly produced by the prehistoric Taupo eruption (circa 1800 years ago). **1853** ROCHFORT *Adventures of Surveyor* 26 A small depth of soil brings you to pumice-stone, much used for building chimneys to wooden houses. **1943** MARSH *Colour Scheme* 24 She walked round the house, crossed the **pumice sweep**, and set off along a path that skirted the warm lake.

punamu, var. POUNAMU.

punch, *v.*[1]

1. *trans.* **a.** [AND 1859.] To work or drive (cattle, esp. bullocks as a team).
[*Note*] The term used of dairy cows is SPANK q.v.
1881 BATHGATE *Waitaruna* 67 He can punch the bullocks almost as well as an old hand already, even to the swearing at them. **1888** D'AVIGDOR *Antipodean Notes* 170 A *bullock puncher* is a man engaged to drive bullocks to market or port. The expression is painfully true, as these men, who receive but very poor wages, are recruited from the worst class, ill-treat the poor animals by *punching* their sides with pointed stick. **1889** SKEY *Pirate Chief* 178 Puncher of the stolid beast, Punch him not from morning feast;.. Goad him not until he reel,.. Fling that cruel whip from thee.

b. [AND 1967.] To drive (sheep) vigorously.
1933 *Press* (Christchurch) (Acland Gloss.) 18 Nov. 15 *Punch*.—To drive [sheep] forcibly up hill or when they are tired. **1953** SUTHERLAND *Golden Bush* (1963) 154 They were punching the last mob down to the shearing shed..when two merino wethers broke and set off back. **1975** HARPER *Eight Daughters* 90 When I hear the old men talk I have to grin, And often wonder how they got the dam sheep in. When punching sheep down through the snow.

Hence **punching** *vbl. n.*, the vigorous driving (of stock).
1970 MCNAUGHTON *Tat* 99 It was a slow process, getting those sheep down. The hillside was benchy and rough. But once they were started on the downward journey..all that remained was hard punching to keep them together.

2. *trans.* [Cf. EDD *punch v.*[3] to work very hard.] To lug; to carry or move with effort or difficulty.
1891 DOUGLAS in *Mr Explorer Douglas* (1957) 124 Punching up remainder of Swag, what a weary heart braking [*sic*] thing it is, staging swags going over the same ground twice or thrice... 11 Feby Punched a Camp to above the Forks. **1896** HARPER *Pioneer Work* 249 Taken the risk—rather than going down the river and 'punching' up more stores over that rough ground.

3. *Wood-chopping.* To make the final, direct, vigorous blow or blows to sever the block or log in a chopping contest.
1983 *TV1 Axemen's carnival.* He's punched through the block.

punch, *v.*[2] [f. *punch* to hit with the fist.]

1. *Freezing works. trans.* To remove (the pelt from sheep briskets) by working it with fists and hands.
1959 SLATTER *Gun in My Hand* 67 Lambs hooked on to the chain and progressing slowly along while the row of men..slash and tear..with knives while others punch briskets or pull the skins from the swinging carcases.

Hence **puncher**, one who strips the pelt from a sheep.
1949 STRONACH in Woodhouse *Farm & Station Verse* (1950) 188 The legger slits as a surgeon does, And the puncher strips the pelt.

2. In the phr. **to punch** (someone) **over**, to give (someone) a beating with the fists. Cf. DO OVER.
1984 *Press* (Christchurch) 7 Dec. 4 I have been raging all day. I punched him over because he tried to punch me over, and put me in my place... Detective Rex Barnett said that Gilbert admitted that he had 'punched over' a man in the toilets 'because he was trying to buy something I do not like'.

punched. [Transf. or fig. emphatic use of carpentry terms.] In the phr. **not to know whether one is punched, bored or countersunk**, to be not 'with it'; not to know whether one is coming or going.
1968 SLATTER *Pagan Game* 162 Doesn't know if he's punched, bored, or countersunk—A tiger for punishment.

puncher. *bullock-puncher* (BULLOCK *n.* 2 a); occas., a drover.
1889 SKEY *Pirate Chief* 178 Puncher of the stolid beast, Punch him not from morning feast. **1900** SCOTT *Colonial Turf* 76 Using the whip with all the skill of a professional 'puncher'.

punga, var. PONGA.

pungapunga. Also (SI) **pukapuka**. [Ma. /ˈpuŋapuŋa/: Williams 311 *pungapunga,..3.* Pollen of raupō..or a cake made of the same.] Raupo pollen, and a kind of bread or cake made from it.
1801 Bunga Bunga (bread) [see TANGATA MAORI]. **1867** HOOKER *Handbook* 767 Pungapunga, *Geolog. Surv.* Pollen of *Typha angustifolia*. **1869** *TrNZI* I. (rev. edn.) 262 The pollen also of the flowers of the large bulrush..was..collected..by the Southern tribes, and made into large gingerbread like cakes, called Pungapunga. **1881** *TrNZI* XIII. 28 Another highly curious article of vegetable food was the *pungapunga*, the yellow pollen of the *raupo* flowers—the common bulrush, or cat's reed mace (*Typha angustifolia*)... To use it as food it is mixed up with water into cakes and baked. It is sweetish and light, and reminds one strongly of London gingerbread. **1890** *Otago Witness* (Dunedin) 9 Jan. 17 Here we have a cake of Maori bread, called punga punga. **1898** MORRIS *Austral-English* 372 *Punga-punga, n.* Maori name for the pollen of the *raupo.* **c1920** BEATTIE *Trad. Lifeways Southern Maori* (1994) 299 In old days the people made a bread called punga from raupo dust. **1982** BURTON *Two Hundred Yrs. NZ Food* 5 The inner parts and roots of the raupo (*Typha orientalis*) provided a meagre amount of food, but the seed heads were prized for their bright yellow pollen which was made into loaves known as *pungapunga*.

punk. [Spec. use of *punk* a touchwood: see OED *n.*[3] 1 a; AND 1798.] Rotten wood or dry fungus used as tinder, occas. also known by its Maori name *putawa* (see quot. 1947).
1853 MACKIE *Traveller under Concern* (1973) 125 We had no lucifer matches but my friend had some fungus called 'punk' which is very inflammable and shooting this from a pistol it ignited. **1924** *JPS* XXXIII. 155 The Maori..carried live fire. To do so he procured..dry material of slow combustion... A kind of punk that grows on trees, [was] used for this purpose. **1947** BEATTIE *Early Runholding* 155 [W.H.S. Roberts writes] we also carried 'touch-paper'..as well as a fungus that grew on the black birch called punk, or by the Maoris putawa. **1966** PHILLIPPS *Maori Life & Custom* 61 Light has been recorded of the bracket fungus [*Polyporus*] and its importance in the generation of fire... Dr G.B. Cone has spoken to an old Pakeha bushman who has used it in the Thames district where it was known as 'punk' to the early settlers, who learned of its use from the Maoris. Punk burns very slowly and persistently. It can be put out only when smothered... Punk has now been recognised as the dried flesh of the *Polyporus* [fungus]..which may be found in many parts of the North Island. **1972** SUTTON-SMITH *Folkgames Children* 156 'Punk' [a fungus] taken from the trees was at hand everywhere in the bush, and was used for a [home-made cricket] ball. Large pieces of punk two or three pounds in weight would cut out three balls... [Carterton, Wairarapa, 1880] **1978** FULLER *Maori Food & Cook.* 15 A dried bracket fungus—*Polyporus* [sp.], called punk by the European settlers and bushmen, was collected and prized for its slow-burning properties.

punui. [Ma. /ˈpuːnui/: Williams 310 *Pūnui..2., 3.* [*Stilbocarpa* spp.] [=] *pūniu. 4. Cyathea cunninghamii*, a fern. *5. Dicksonia fibrosa*, a tree-fern.]

1. Any of various *Stilbocarpa* spp. (fam. Araliaceae), large-leaved mega-herbs of Stewart Island and subantarctic islands. Cf. MACQUARIE CABBAGE 1.
1885 *TrNZI* XVII. 293 For the sake of conciseness..the native name *punui* will be restricted to the Stewart Island plant; the generic name *Stilbocarpa* to that from the Auckland Islands. **1891** *NZJSc.* (NS) I. 163 The most striking herbaceous plant is..the punui..the large orbicular leaves of which are sometimes two feet in diameter. **1907** LAING & BLACKWELL *Plants NZ* 317 *Stilbocarpa polaris* (*The Polar Stilbocarpa*)... Auckland, Antipodes, Macquarie, and Campbell Islands... Maori name *Punui*. **1922** *Auckland Weekly News* 12 Oct. 17 The punui of the Auckland Islands, with leaves sometimes 12 in. broad, and purple-eyed flowers, and its near relation on Stewart Island, are important members of this family. **1950** WODZICKI *Introduced Mammals NZ* 155 Goats have also been placed..on small mutton bird islands in order to destroy punui. **1964** DEMPSEY *Little World of Stewart Island* 50 A deft shake..and the [muttonbird] bodies were..neatly packed into casks lined with the large leaves of the punui, a plant which grew near the hut. **1978** MOORE & IRWIN *Oxford Book NZ Plants* 96 *Stilbocarpa lyallii*, the punui of Stewart Island, has less hairy leaves and reddish-purple flowers. **1982** WILSON *Stewart Is. Plants* 126 *Pūnui...* Robust herb forming large clumps up to 1 m or more tall.

2. Either of the tree ferns WHEKI-PONGA (*Dicksonia fibrosa*), or *gully tree-fern* (FERN 2 (5), *Cyathea cunninghamii*.
1855 HOOKER *II Flora Novae-Zelandiae II Flowerless Plants* 7 *Cyathea Cunninghamii...* Nat. name, 'Punui', *Col.* **1867** HOOKER *Handbook* 767 Punui, *Col[enso]. Cyathea Cunninghamii.* **1961** MARTIN *Flora NZ* 109 The second species [of *Dicksonia*] known as the Punui or Wheki-ponga (*D. fibrosa*).

puoa, var. POUA.

pup. [AND 1915.] In the phr. **the night's (still) a pup**, it's early yet.
1957 *Numbers Seven* 8 'Is it really so late? Amazing how time... The night's only a pup. Goodnight; goodnight. You don't mind, dear? Just the tiniest peck?' **1976** MCCLENAGHAN *Travelling Man* 75 The night's a pup yet.

pupu /ˈpupu/, /ˈbubu/. Also freq. (esp. SI) **bubu**; early **e-poo-poo** (=he pupu). [Ma. /ˈpuːpuː/: Williams 300 *Pū* (i)..*pūpū..3.* General name for volute univalve molluscs of the *winkle* type.] Usu. CAT'S EYE 1; occas. a periwinkle (see quot. c1920).
[**1804** *Collins Eng. Colony in NSW* 561 E-poo-poo, *Shells.* **1820** LEE & KENDALL *NZ Gram. & Vocab.* 197 Púpu, *s.* A periwinkle.] **1855** TAYLOR *Te Ika A Maui* 415 The common name..of all univalve shells, *pupu*; and of bivalves, *pipi* and *anga*, which includes both kinds. **1905** BAUCKE *White Man Treads* 2 White seashore sandhills, representing the accumulated deaths of ages of pipi, pupu, kuku, and other molluscs. **c1920** bubu [see CAT'S EYE]. **1939** BEATTIE *First White Boy Born Otago* 22 They ate many kinds of shellfish such as bubu

and pipi. **1947** *AJHR H-15* 29 Bay of Islands: 394,000 borers and 1,200 pupu destroyed. **1970** Sansom *Stewart Islanders* 134 They had no gun but they cooked limpets and bu-bus (the catseye shell)..to keep them going. **1982** Sansom *In Grip of Island* 144 Green..fitted on a suitable shell, usually a whelk or a cat's eye shell, the lunella ('Bu-bu' to us) for a hand-grip [on the walking stick]. **1989** *Listener* 20 Nov. 35 She would've admired his every kina, even his pupu.

pupuharakeke. [Ma. /ˈpuːpuːˈharakeke/: Williams 300 *Pūpū-harakeke*.] *flax snail* (FLAX 5 c).

1937 Powell *Shellfish NZ* 38 Unfortunately, both the Pupurangi and the Pupuharakeke are fast declining, due to the ravages of pigs, which consume great numbers of these snails. **1947** [see *flax snail* (FLAX 5 c)]. **1955** Dell *Native Shells* 58 Flax Snail... *Pupu-harakeke*, size 3 inches, Whangarei to Kaitaia. **1966** [see *flax snail* (FLAX 5 c)]. **1976** Powell *Shells NZ* 522 Being coastal in distribution, the Pupuharakeke has now almost disappeared from the mainland. **1989** Parkinson *Travelling Naturalist* 31 Another rarity of the far north is the pupuharakeke, the flax snail.

pupurangi. [Ma. /ˈpuːpuːˈraŋi/: Williams 300 *Pūpū-rangi*..a land mollusc.] Any of various large (9–10cm), carnivorous, often brilliantly-coloured, land snails of the genus *Paryphanta* (fam. Paryphantidae). See also *bush snail* (BUSH C 4), *kauri grub* (KAURI 5), KAURI SNAIL.

1898 *TrNZI* XXX. 535 On asking a Maori of North Auckland if the great [pu]purangi, our largest land-shell (*Paryphanta busbyi*), was edible, the answer was a decided negative. **1937** Powell *Shellfish NZ* 41 In such situations the Pupurangi hunts its staple food, which consists of earthworms and slugs. **1947** Powell *Native Animals NZ* 32 The pupurangi is coincident in range with the kauri tree, but there is no relationship between the two—in fact the snail shuns the immediate vicinity of the ground for the ground there is usually too dry for the existence of worms, upon which the pupurangi feeds. **1950** *NZJAg.* Sept. LXXXI. 285 The shell exhibits ranged from the humble pupurangi or kauri snail (which numbers nearly 50 varieties in New Zealand alone and lays large white shelled eggs in a leafy nest on the floor of the forest and, like the much publicised early bird prefers a worm diet) to the proud argonaut. **1966** [see KAURI SNAIL]. **1976** Powell *Shells NZ* (5edn.) 53 The best known member of this group [of land snails] is the Pupurangi, or kauri snail. **1990** *NZ Geographic* VII. 96 In Northland..the kauri snail (termed pupurangi or whistling snail by the Maori) is still common in places.

pura, var. PARA *n.*³

puramorua, var. PURUMORUA.

purapura: see POROPORO, BULL-A-BULL.

purge. [Joc. use of *purge* an aperient medicine: AND *Obs.* 1891.] Alcoholic liquor.

1905 *Truth* 11 Nov. 5 Piously Pulverise Purge-Purveying Publicans. **1909** *Ibid.* 4 Sept. 6 There were in the house at the time three other men under the influence of purge. **1959** Slatter *Gun in My Hand* 43 Come on now, force that purge down ya gullet and have a man's drink with me. **1968** Slatter *Pagan Game* 150 Great drop of purge this... Down the hatch. *Ibid.* 173 Green Band, Red Band, Gold Top, Double Brown, Nut Brown..all the colours of purge. **1974** Gifford *Loosehead Len's Big Brown Book* 60 *Beer*: The pause that refreshes, see also under 'Slops, Turps, Frosty Fluid, The Old Amber Liquid, Suds, Purge, etc, etc.'

puriri. Also with much variety of early form as **booreedy, boridé, periri, pouriedee, pudídi, pyriri** (prob. a typographical error). [Ma. /ˈpuːriri/: Williams 314 *Pūriri*.] *Vitex lucens* (fam. Verbenaceae), a large spreading tree of the North Island, having glossy leaves and pinkish-red flowers; its dark, heavy wood. See also IRONWOOD b, OAK, TEAK.

[**1820** Lee & Kendall *NZ Gram. & Vocab.* 196 Pudídi, *s.* A shrub so called.] **1834** Markham *NZ* (1963) 33 *Pouriedee* is a fine hard wood like Lignum Vitae, grows into immense trees, but you can not get planks out of it as the Worms..make places like Nail holes. **1834** McDonnell *Extracts Jrnl.* (1979) 19 The boridé, is a fine-limbed, large, and spreading tree; very crooked, close-grained, stringy, and tough; much resembling teak; of a darker colour, harder, and of an oily nature. **1841** Wade *Journey in Nthn Is.* 40 The Puriri has been improperly called the New Zealand Oak. **1844** Williams *NZ Journal* (1956) 108 This peculiar..insect travels up..both rata and periri trees. **1853** Lush *Auckland Jrnls.* 10 May (1971) 136 I took with me two stout puriri planks. **1863** Maning *Old NZ* xiv 213 He would sit whole days on a fallen puriri near the house. **1879** *Auckland Weekly News* 13 Sept. 8 This lathe was at work turning puriri rollers for straining fencing wire. **1883** Hector *Handbook NZ* 128 Puriri. A large tree, 50–60 feet high; trunk 20 feet in girth. Wood hard, dark olive-brown, much used; said to be indestructible under all conditions. **1892** [see OAK]. **1904** *NZ Illustr. Mag.* Dec. 178 Booreedy Jack was a specimen of the old-time bushman.. kauri-cutting..and mill-work, etc. He acquired the soubriquet of 'Booreedy' (settlers' name for puriri). **1907** *Wairoa Bell & Northern Advertiser* 13 Sept. [unpaged] Puriri posts, house blocks and firewood. **1938** Hyde *Nor Yrs. Condemn* 149 Many trees were old and in decay, and the little rosy apples of the *pyriri* [sic] tree smothered the moss. **1960** Hilliard *Maori Girl* 10 Wiwi, blackberry, clusters of puriri..no patch of grass visible sufficient to graze a solitary cow. **1992** *NZ Geographic* 13 Jan.–Mar. 106 Puriri groves are still used as a burial place.

puriri moth: see MOTH 8.

purler. Also **pearler, perler**. [Spec. use of *purler* a knock-down blow (see OED 1), f. Brit. dial. *purl* go head over heels (recorded in NZ in 1856 and 1863).]

1. Often in the phr. **to come (go) a purler**, (to have) a heavy or spectacular fall; a cropper. Also *transf.* and *fig.*

[**1856** Abraham *Walk with Bishop NZ* in Taylor *Early Travellers* (1959) 96 The Bishop [Selwyn] fell in over head and ears at once. The only remarks he made was one of anxiety for his..pedometer; the other..was, that he now understood the full meaning of the poet's language about '*purling* brooks'.] **1906** *Truth* 19 May 2 The grassing of Mana [football team]..raised a hurricane of plaudits from the..barrackers. Mana went a 'perler' that time. **1934** *Canterbury Mountaineer* 37 H... when in mid-stream tripped, landing feat—a 'purler'. **1939** Combs *Harrowed Toad* 86-87 On the first two essays [at jumping] he came absolute 'pearlers'. **1951** 14 M 10 Wellington H.S. 16 Pearler [M2] **1963** *Truth* 17 Sept. 48 The police seemed to have come a purler in trying to invoke the aid of doctors in tracing pregnant women.

2. Also formerly **purter** (perh. influenced by Brit. dial. (see EDD) *peart* lively, in good spirits; smart). [AND 1935.] Something fine or exceptional. Often adjectival (*What a purler bike!*), and occas. adverbial (*He went through the whole thing purler*).

1941 Baker *NZ Slang* 51 In constant use by our youngsters..swinjer, pearler, stunner..rumptydooler, purter. **1955** *BJ Cameron Collection* (TS July) purler (adj) Wonderful. Possibly derived from 'superlative'. **1967** Macnicol *Echoes Skippers Canyon* 128 'He's a pearler,' he declared, picking him up and extolling his fine features. **1976** Wilson *Pacific Star* 152 'Isn't she a little pearler, Dick?' Tom said 'She's a beauty, all right,' I said. **1980** Mantell *Murder Or Three* 45 Never thought he'd ever get around to having any then they produce a purler like that. She's a real little darling. **1985** Jones *Gilmore's Dairy* 57 'How did Fog go?' 'A pearler. Kicked three penalties and dropped a goal. He was terrific.' **1994** *Dominion Infotech Weekly* (Wellington) 5 Sept. 1 [Heading] Hi-tech system [of computerized knitting patterns] a pearler for knitters.

puroa grass, var. PURUA GRASS.

purourou. [Ma. /puːˈrourou/: Williams 314 *pūrourou*.] SADDLEBACK.

1835 [see TIEKE]. **1838** Polack *NZ* I. 301 The *purourou* agrees with our lark; but with a plumage of glossy black. **1842, 1873** [see TIEKE]. **1988** *Pacific Way* June 98 [Names used for Air NZ fleet aircraft include:] ZK-NAW 'Purourou' (Saddleback).

purple death. Mainly *WW2*. Cheap red (Italian) wine. Compare *rooster's blood* (ROOSTER 5).

1939–45 *Expressions & Sayings 2NZEF* (TS N.A. WAII DA 420/1) Purple death—Vino Rosso. **1944** *NZEF Times* 18 Sept. 5 Any soil with the taste of this purple death couldn't even support a poisonous cactus. *Ibid.* 2 Oct. 10 A few gallons of Purple Death..would just about do the trick. *Ibid.* 1945 22 Jan. 4 He should be able to hold his liquor... Even Purple Death, Crocodile's Tears and Camel's Bile. **1959** Slatter *Gun in My Hand* 92 And we drank the purple death because there were more rivers to cross and more men to be maimed. **1965** Gee *Special Flower* 37 When she came in she was carrying a half-gallon jar of wine. 'Purple death,' she grinned at her father. **1970** Slatter *On the Ball* 153 Of course there were other diversions in the Division. Looting casas and drinking plonk and Purple death has some supporters. **1987** *Sunday News* (Auckland) 4 Jan. 3 The Purple Death has scored a few hits over the festive season. It's a wine with a difference, recommended as 'rough-as-guts' drinking... Word of the Purple Death has been spread by mouth but has even reached as far south as the Antarctic... At around $10 a bottle, few liquor outlets sell it as well as the Sapich brothers out Henderson way, in West Auckland. **1991** *Evening Post* (Wellington) 9 Jan. 17 A glass of red plonk reminds him of the 'purple death' he and his mates went on 'rekkies' for between battles [in the Italian campaign].

purple-top. *Verbena bonariensis* (fam. Verbenaceae), an introduced South American verbena, having a mauve or purplish corolla.

1969 *Standard Common Names Weeds* 62 purple-top *Verbena bonariensis*. **1975** *Tane* 21 8 *Verbena bonariensis* purple-top. **1981** Taylor *Weeds of Roadsides* 117 Purple-top (*Verbena bonariensis*)... Stiff upright square stems with prominent corners... Small purple flowers in prominent clusters on top of plant... native to Argentina, is common in..the North Island and northern part of the South Island. **1983** Ell *Wildflowers & Weeds* 19 Purple-top, *Purple Verbena*. The purple verbena grows around a metre and a half before it produces the heads which give it the nick-name purple top. **1988** Webb et al. *Flora NZ* IV. 1277 Purple-top is presumably an escape from cultivation although it is rarely grown now. Occasional plants in different parts of both main islands correspond to *conglomerata* Briq. rather than *bonariensis* but others seem intermediate.

purter: see PURLER 2.

purua grass. Also **puroa grass.** [Not recorded in Williams: prob. f. *Purua* the name of a settlement approx. 20 km nw. of Whangarei; but poss. (as P. Ranby suggests) either *puroa* f. Ma. *pū* a bunch or tuft + *roa* tall; or f. *pūrua* abundant.] *Bolboschoenus* (formerly *Scirpus*) *fluviatilis*, *B. medianus* and *B. caldwellii* (fam. Cyperaceae), a group of robust, summer-green, native swamp sedges (not true grasses) with broad leaves and woody tubers.
1927 *TrNZI* LVII. 948 purua grass *Scirpus maritimus* Ver. [= Vernacular names supplied to [J.C. Andersen] by B.C. Aston.] **1969** *Standard Common Names Weeds* 62 purua grass *Scirpus maritimus*. **1984** *Standard Common Names Weeds* 85 Purua grass *Scirpus caldwellii, S. fluviatilis, S. medianus*. **1987** HARTLEY *Swagger on Doorstep* 170 The ground cover [on the Hauraki Plains section] included heavy and light manuka, flax, puroa grass and raupo, with mangroves in some places.

purumorua. Also **puramorua.** [Ma. /puruˈmorua/: Williams 315 *Purumorua*..pig fish.] PIGFISH 2 (2) (*Congiopodus leucopaecilus*).
1921 *NZJST* IV. 121 *Pigfish; Puramorua*. Large numbers commonly sold throughout the year in Christchurch under the name of 'silver trumpeter'. **1956** [see PIGFISH 1]. **1967** MORELAND *Marine Fishes* 24 Pigfish... The Maori name puramorua is not now heard. **1988** FRANCIS *Coastal Fishes NZ* 24 Southern pigfish (Purumorua) *Congiopodus leucopaecilus*.

push. *Obs.* [Spec. use of *push* a 'press' of people, a crowd: see OED *n.*¹ 8 and 9; AND (1812), 1884.] A (street) gang; a crowd or clique of larrikins or youths.
1891 A TRAMP, ESQ. *Casual Ramblings* 94 The sporting 'push'. **1896** BRACKEN *Tom Bracken's Annual* 38 In spite of my being in with a clever 'push'. *Ibid.* 40 When he did see that the cad was going to chuck the push, he tried to get up. **1912** *Truth* 3 Feb. 7 There used to be much more of the push element around Christchurch than there is now, and it frequently occurred that pushes [ie. youths belonging to these groups] like the 'Tigers', the 'Diehards', the 'Scalpers', and the 'Skull-Draggers', faced the music before the beak. **1913** *Hutt Valley Independent* 25 Sept. 4 Don't pledge your votes to anyone till you've heard McCurdy's address to the people, not to the push. **1946** HARPER *Mems. of Mountains & Men* 53 Mention of..1890 reminds me of another side of Christchurch in those days—namely the gangs, or 'pushes' as they were called—of larrikins. They wore bell-bottomed trousers, fancy shoes and well-oiled forelocks. These young ruffians frequently assaulted any lone pedestrian who happened to come their way.
Hence **pushism**, the distinctive doctrine held by or distinguishing members of a push; **pushite**, a member of a 'push'.
1909 *Truth* 2 Oct. 6 In other places the pushite is not thoroughly respected until he has been before the 'beak'; it is his baptism in the principles of pushism, and the glory of going to 'quod' is like unto no other form of fame.

put, *v.*

1. In various phrases: **to put the acid on**, see ACID; **to put the boot in**, see BOOT *n.* 2; **to put (one) in crook with**, see CROOK *a.* B 5; **to put the hard word on**, see HARD WORD; **to put the nips in**, see NIP *n.* 1; **to put (one) off the board**, see BOARD *n.*¹ 1 d; **to put (one's) pot on**, see POT *n.*²; **to put a ring round**, see RING *n.*²; **to put up a smoke**, see SMOKE *n.*¹ 1.

2. In the phr. **to put one around**, to trick, to 'put one across' (someone).
1986 RICHARDS *Off the Sheep's Back* 93 I did not intend to be caught with 'roughies' left in my pen when the pressure was on. A shearer will always try to put one 'around' his mate when he has a full pen of sheep to pick from.

3. As **put down** *v. farming*, of wool, to press, to bale.
1940 STUDHOLME *Te Waimate* (1954) 92 Kane and his mates worked from 4a.m. to 9p.m. and put down seventy-three bales—about fifty..was considered a good day's work with one of these mankilling presses.

4. As **put through. a.** To complete an operation on a group or number; to handle, do work with. (a) [AND 1908.] To shear (sheep).
1878 CHUDLEIGH *Diary* 8 Mar. (1950) 267 Put about 5000 sheep through the yards of which nearly 3000 must have been ewes.
(b) To complete a milking (of a dairy herd).
1924 ANTHONY *Follow the Call* (1975) 9 Being but an indifferent milker it used to take me quite three hours..to put my herd through.
(c) To move or draft (stock) through stockyards.
1937 AYSON *Thomas* 86 They got a good muster of cattle, took them to the yards, put them through, kept those that were to be tamed in the paddock, and let the rest out in a mob, each to find its way to its own beat.
(d) To complete a kill (of stock) on a freezing works chain.
1968 SLATTER *Pagan Game* 166 On the chain at Whakatu when they put through 13,000 lambs a day.
b. To complete proceedings for bankruptcy against (someone).
1986 *Sunday News* (Auckland) 20 July 18 [X, an actor,] has been adjudged bankrupt over an alleged $8000 maintenance bill. The actor..was 'put through' on July 2 on an application by [an] Auckland lawyer.

5. As **put up** *v. a. Obs. Criminals.* To hold up and rob. Cf. STICK UP *v.*¹ 2.
1866 BURGESS *Confessions* (1983) 76 While we were at the township [in Otago, c1862 March], one of our acquaintances came to me and told me there was a man in a disreputable shanty, that had plenty of money and would I come and put him up? Now the Wetherstone diggings were very quiet, so that I objected to men being put up and let go to alarm the place—for I anticipated robbing this banker sooner or later, and that would do me. **1866** *Narr. Maungatapu Murders* 17 Sullivan [the bushranger] said, 'Here's a young fellow and a woman carrying a swag; I'll put them up.' *Ibid.* 18 'I'll put them [the victims] up and you give me your gun while you tie them.'
b. In the phr. **to put up a blue**, see BLUE *n.*² 1.

putakitaki, var. PUTANGITANGI.

putangitangi. Also early **pooa dugghie dugghie**; occas. **putangi**; SI **putakitaki**. [Ma. /puːˈtaŋitaŋi/: Williams *Pūtangitangi* (i.).] *paradise duck* (DUCK 2 (6)).
1842 GRAY *Fauna* in Dieffenbach *Travels in NZ* (1843) II. 198 *Casarca variegata*... Pooa dugghie dugghie of the natives of Dusky Bay... Putangi tangi of the natives of Cook's Strait; Paradise Duck of the settlers. **1851**, **1873** Putakitaki [see DUCK 2 (6)]. **1882** HAY *Brighter Britain* II. 225 The species we have identified in the Kaipara and Hokianga are—the Putangi, or 'paradise-duck'..; the grey duck. **1890** *Otago Witness* (Dunedin) 20 Nov. 41 The native name [of the paradise duck] is Putangi-tangi, which means the waterfowl that makes a great funeral crying—and this she does to perfection with her loud clarionet vocal. **1904** TREGEAR *Maori Race* 105 The paradise duck (*putangi-tangi*: *Casarca variegata*) a bird of beautiful plumage..was considered a prize. **1926** [see DUCK 2 (6)]. **1946** *JPS* LV. 157 *Pūtangitangi*..a goose but called the paradise-duck; always found in pairs. **1966** FALLA et al. *Birds NZ* 87 Paradise Duck... Putangitangi, Rangitata Goose. **1988** MIKAERE *Te Maiharoa* 75 There were putakitaki..and whio (blue ducks). **1990** *Checklist Birds NZ* 100 *Tadorna variegata*..Paradise Sheldrake (*Putangitangi*).

putaputaweta. [Ma. /putapuˈtaːweːtaː/: Williams 317 *Putawētā, putaputāwētā*.. *Carpodetus serratus*..Cf. 316 *Puta* (i)..*putaputa*, a. Full of holes, pitted: (see also quot. 1907).] *Carpodetus serratus* (fam. Escalloniaceae), a small tree with a marbled leaf. See also HAWTHORN, MAPAU 2 (3) b, MARBLE-LEAF, PIRIPIRIWHATA, *snow-tree* a (SNOW *n.*¹ 3).
1886 KIRK in *Settler's Handbook NZ* (1902) 122 [Native name] Putaputa-weta..[Family] Saxifrageae. **1889** FEATON *Art Album NZ Flora* 133 The '*Puta-puta-weta*'.—This graceful looking shrub, or sometimes small tree, is found in both the Northern and Middle Islands. **1889** KIRK *Forest Flora* 77 I am indebted to..W.L. Williams for the correct Native name, 'putaputaweta'. **1890** *PWD Catalogue Timbers* (NZ & South Seas Exhib.) 13 Putaputa-weta (piripiriwhata).. Timber white and open of grain. **1907** LAING & BLACKWELL *Plants NZ* 188 The native name *Puta-puta-weta* signifies full of weta holes. In the North Island trees of this species are rarely cut down unperforated by longitudinal insect galleries. Another name by which it is known is *Puna-weta*. In the Urewera country it is called *Kai-weta* (i.e., weta food). **1910** COCKAYNE *NZ Plants & Their Story* 37 The putaputaweta (*Carpodetus serratus*) is a rival of the English may. **1961**, **1978**, **1981** [see MARBLE-LEAF].

putawa: see PUNK.

puteke, puteketeke, varr. PATEKE, PATEKETEKE.

put in, *n. Rugby football.* The act or process of introducing a football into a set scrum.
1910 *Truth* 23 Apr. 3 Presumably, the side was penalised by the referee for the ball being put unfairly in the scrum. The question of what constitutes a fair 'put in' produces a wide divergence of views among the whistling brigade. **1971** *Evening Star 7 O'clock* 18 Sept. 1 (Griffiths Collect.) Norton profited from his misfortune to grasp Canterbury's only strike against the put in, which led to the home side's first try.

putoto. [Ma. /ˈpuːtoto/: Williams 317 *Pūtoto* (iii)..*Porzana tabuensis plumbea*, spotless crake (swamp rail.)] *spotless crake* (CRAKE b).
[**1820** LEE & KENDALL *NZ Gram. & Vocab.* 198 *Putóto, s.* A bird so called; a partridge.] **1835** YATE *NZ* (1970) 67 *Putoto*—A small black bird, about the size of the thrush, found in the swamps of New Zealand. **1873** BULLER *Birds NZ* 181 *Ortygometra tabuensis*. (Swamp-crake)... Pueto and Putoto. **1882** HAY *Brighter Britain* II. 225 The Putoto (*Ortygometra Tabuensis*) is a crake, often confounded by settlers with the patatai. It is a smaller bird altogether, having partridge tints on the back, and a grey breast. It chiefly inhabits raupo swamps. **1904** HUTTON & DRUMMOND *Animals NZ* 182 *The Swamp Rail.—Putoto. Porzana tabuensis*. **1966** [see RAIL 2 (10)]. **1985** *Reader's Digest Book NZ Birds* 167 Spotless Crake *Porzana tabuensis plumbea*... Putoto, puweto.

putty. [Poss. f. an extended or transf. use of *putty* 'a patching substance' and the phr. *up to putty* giving a sense 'ready, or in a state to be patched up'; but cf. AND (1916) which derives f. a poss. fig. use of *putty* a powder in contradistinction to *snuff* in the phr. *up to snuff* 'up to scratch'.] In the phr. **up to putty**, in a bad way; in a mess. (The phr. is also known to Ed. from Marlborough c1940.)

1918 *Chron. NZEF* 19 July 274 The much perturbed Digger would immediately seek out the M.O..pitching a yarn about feeling feverish and generally 'up to putty'.

puwaiwhakarua. Also **pu(h)aiwhakarua, puuwaiwhakarua.** [Ma. /ˈpuːwaifakarua/: Williams 318 *Pūwaiwhakarua..Pseudolabrus coccineus*, red parrot-fish: according to Williams, when caught it is considered a sign that the northwest wind will blow; cf. *whakarua* a north-east sea breeze.] *scarlet parrotfish* (PARROTFISH 2 (4)).

c1920 BEATTIE *Trad. Lifeways Southern Maori* 313 The puaihakarua at Otago Heads and Moeraki is a sort of perch and is called Soldier Fish. **1927** [see PAU]. **1945** BEATTIE *Maori Place-names Canterbury* 62 The..list of fish to be caught along the Canterbury coast has some notable omissions... Omitted are the tarakihi..the puhaiwhakarua (red-jacket), koiro. **1956** GRAHAM *Treasury NZ Fishes* 269 Scarlet Parrot-fish (Puwaiwhakarua or Pau). **1966** [see PAU]. **1988** FRANCIS *Coastal Fishes NZ* 44 Scarlet wrasse (Puuwai whakarua) *Pseudolabrus miles.*

puweto. [Ma. /ˈpuːweto//ˈpuːeto//puːˈwetoweto/ /puːˈetoeto/: Williams 318 *Pūweto, pūeto, pūwetoweto, pūetoeto, Porzana tabuensis,* swamp rail... = *pūtoto*.] *spotless crake* (CRAKE b). See also *swamp rail* (RAIL 2 (10)). Cf. PUTOTO.

1955 OLIVER *NZ Birds* 357 *Spotless Crake. Puweto Porzana tabuensis plumbea...* The Spotless Crake is presumably the putoto of Yate, 1835. **1966** [see RAIL 2 (10)]. **1970** *Notornis* XXVII. (Suppl.) 15 *Porzana tabuensis plumbea...* (*Puweto*). **1985** [see PUTOTO].

puwha, var. PUHA.

puwhananga, var. PUAWANANGA.

pygmy pine: see PINE 2 (12).

py korry: see KORRY.

pyriri, var. PURIRI.

Q

quack. [Joc. use of *quack* (medical) charlatan: see OED *n.*¹ 1 b; AND 1919.] Often as **the quack**, a familiar though somewhat contemptuous name for any qualified medical practitioner.

1917 *Chron. NZEF* 17 Oct. 108 The scathing criticism of the 'quacks' and 'heads' kept the house in a continual uproar. **c1926** THE MIXER *Transport Workers' Song Book* 43 [They] ask me if I want a 'sub.' For to take me to the 'quack'. **1939** BROWN *Farmer's Wife* 49 Been to the Quack again, Anne? **1946** SARGESON *That Summer* 132 I was remembering what the young hospital quack had said. **1964** MORRIESON *Came a Hot Friday* (1981) 208 My wrist's broken... You'll have to get me to a quack, boy. I can't stand this.

quail.

1. [Transf. use of *quail*, any of several small plump game-birds of the family Phasianidae, for the native *Coturnix* sp.] Also **New Zealand** (occas. **Maori, native**) **quail**. *Coturnix novaezelandiae novaezelandiae* (fam. Phasianidae), once abundant, but extinct since about 1870. See also KOREKE.

1769 MONKHOUSE 21 Oct. in Cook *Journals* (1955) I. 583 Saw two or three quails [in Teegadu Bay]. **1823** CRUISE *Journal* 29 Aug. (1957) 149 We went on shore, and shot some red-bill and quail. The latter are smaller than those seen in England, & rather darker in their plumage. **1843** DIEFFENBACH *Travels in NZ* I. 417 [Dogs] are perhaps the cause that the New Zealand quail..is so scarce in the northern island. **1859** THOMSON *Story NZ* I. 26 The Quail..was once numerous over the whole country, now it is chiefly met with on the Middle Island. **1861** *NZ Goldfields 1861* (1976) 38 In fact the only wild birds..were one or two quails, about the same number of New Zealand larks. **1873** BULLER *Birds NZ* 163 On one occasion about the year 1848,... he went out to his own [Nelson] estate..for a day's Quail-shooting; and in the course of a few hours the party bagged 29½ brace. **1885** *NZJSc.* II. 484 It seems a strange statement..that probably no youngster has ever found a nest of native quail. **1893** *TrNZI* XXV. 106 Of the remaining birds, perhaps the most interesting is the now extinct New Zealand quail. **1900** *Canterbury Old & New* 196 True game birds are represented by the native quail, once abundant on the Canterbury Plains. **1922** [see KOREKE]. **1939** BEATTIE *First White Boy Born Otago* 121 I never saw the native quail. **1946** *JPS* LV. 152 *koreke*, a bird (*Coturnix novae zealandiae*), Maori quail, now extinct, its place being taken by the imported California and Tasmania quail, now very plentiful. **1966** *Encycl. NZ* III. 7 The New Zealand quail was once common in parts of the North and South Islands... By the mid-nineteenth century the koreke, as it was known to the Maori, was already uncommon in the North Island, though..it was still abundant in parts of Nelson and Otago. **1985** *Reader's Digest Book NZ Birds* 308 The extinction of the New Zealand quail is as deplorable as it is unexplained. **1990** *Checklist NZ Birds* 115 *Coturnix novaezelandiae novaezelandiae*.. New Zealand Quail (Koreke)... Extinct since about 1870.

2. Californian quail. Also as an informal short form **callie** (see quot. 1985). *Callipepla* (formerly *Lophortyx*) *californica brunnescens* (fam. Phasianidae), a small grey-blue game-bird introduced from N. America 1860–70.

[*Note*] New Zealand usage prefers *Californian quail* to the orig. *California quail* (see OED 1831).

1868 PYKE *Province of Otago* 31 Various kinds have been introduced... Especially may be named..Californian quail, and Victorian quail. **1870** *TrNZI* II. 49 The Pheasant, the Partridge, and Californian Quail, are amongst the best of the game birds..established amongst us. **1907** *Ibid.* XXXIX. 249 The two species of quail introduced, the swamp-quail (*Syno[i]cus australis*) and the Californian quail..have been hardly more successful than the pheasants. **1927** SPEIGHT et al. *Nat. Hist. Canterbury* 225 Californian Quail, though not so numerous as they were twenty years ago, are still plentiful. **1947** FAIRBURN *Letters* (1981) 160 [Sargeson] is no more distinctively 'New Zealand' than I am..or wedgie shoes—or Californian quail. **1985** *Reader's Digest Book NZ Birds* 159 California Quail *Lophortyx californica brunnescens*.. Californian quail, callie.

3. brown (occas. **Australian, Australian brown, swamp** [AND 1849], **Tasmania**) **quail**. [AND 1843.] *Synoicus ypsilophorus* (fam. Phasianidae), a small brown quail introduced from Australia and Tasmania 1860–70 and still widespread in the North Island.

1887 *Auckland Weekly News* 9 Apr. 17 It appears that pheasants, Californian quail and Australian quail may be taken..from the 1st May, 1887, to the 31st July in the same year. **1907** swamp quail [see 2 above]. **1922** *Auckland Weekly News* 4 May 15 The Australian quail has transverse arrowhead bars of brownish black on its undersurface, while on the undersurface of the New Zealand quail the marks are horse-shoe shaped, with pale centres. **1946** Tasmania quail [see 1 above]. **1966** FALLA et al. *Birds NZ* 100 Australian Brown Quail (*Synoicus australis*)... North Island. Two races were introduced. **1990** *Checklist Birds NZ* 116 *Synoicus ypsilophorus*..Brown Quail... Introduced to New Zealand and widely liberated in the 1860s and 1870s.

quail-hawk. *Obs.* FALCON.

1870 *TrNZI* II. 48 We might perhaps have seen the Quail-hawk, rapidly ascending with spiral flight, till it appeared like a dark speck against the cloudless sky, its shrill jarring scream distinctly heard the while. **1882** POTTS *Out in Open* 71 A female quail-hawk was observed with a tui, trussed in her talons; we tried to make her drop the tui without success. **1904** HUTTON & DRUMMOND *Animals NZ* 149 The Quail-hawk—Karewa-rewa... The Quail-hawk, a true Falcon, with a distinctly toothed bill, stands at the head of the diurnal birds of prey. **1929** DUGGAN *NZ Bird Songs* 32 And worse than men, the quail-hawk, The bird that keeps no law.

quarter. *Hist.* A quarterly stipend paid to a Native Assessor.

1877 GRACE *Journal* Aug. in *Pioneer Missionary* (1928) 266 They then went furiously to the 4th point— that we were all hirelings and worked for money like the Assessors. One fellow said, 'Don't you get your quarter?' I replied, 'Certainly! I do not live by stealing.' 'Quarter' has, of late years, become a proverbial term; the Government Native Assessors, being paid once a quarter, talk commonly of getting their quarters. The Kingites despise these Maoris who have been bribed over, and hate and deride the 'quarter' as conclusive of all that is bad. Hanauru, the King's great priest, who was present, pointed out how he could go about anywhere, all the year round, and wanted no quarter.

quarter-acre. Also ¼**-acre.** [f. the name of a common size (1012.5 m²) of a NZ urban residential building section.]

1. a. *Ellipt.* for *quarter-acre section* (2 below).

1841 WEEKES *Journal* 25 Apr. in Rutherford & Skinner *Establish. New Plymouth* (1940) 49 I have put in several seeds in my 'garden' or quarter-acre. **1845** *Arrangements Establish. of Settlement* Sept. in Hocken *Contributions* (1898) 280 On payment of his purchase-money, each purchaser to receive, for each sum of £120 10s. so paid, three separate Land-Orders, namely, for the Town quarter-acre, the ten acres of Suburban Land, and the fifty acres of Rural Land, respectively. **1898** HOCKEN *Contributions* 99 Mr. David Garrick..was the first private individual to select in Dunedin, and..he chose what is now probably the most valuable site— that quarter acre upon which now stands the Bank of New Zealand. **1972** MITCHELL *Quarter-acre Pavlova Paradise* 102 As in everything else, they [*sc.* New Zealanders] conform to a norm: a quarter-acre, one-car, three-children, two-orgasm family. **1988** *Through the Looking Glass* 130 Never once do I remember hearing [in Tauranga in the 1930s] about the confiscation of Maori land although the name 'the Quarter Acres' for an area of town sections allotted to Pakeha after the Battles of Gate Pa and Te Ranga (1864) was commonly used.

b. *fig.* or *transf.* A quarter-acre section as a symbol of the family home.

1910 FANNING *Players & Slayers* 80 Thus has the mighty Bernard Fanning, some-time representative of New Zealand, fallen into the quarter-acre of domesticity. **1971** SHADBOLT *Bullshit and Jellybeans* 89 [Kiwis] all became little capitalists... 'She'll be jaker on my quarter acre' became the basis of New Zealand life. **1980** MCGILL & TILLY *In Praise of Older Buildings* 50 So much for the cult of the quarter acre.

2. As **quarter-acre section**, a standard size of urban section from the time of early European settlement.

[**1843** *NZ Jrnl.* 5 Aug. in *Speeches and Documents* (1971) 24 For £120 a property consisting of 50 acres of rural land, 10 acres of suburban land, and a town lot of ¼ acre, can be had [in Otago]. **1883** HECTOR *Handbook NZ* 104 Town sections are usually one quarter acre each, having a frontage of 66 feet to a street, and running back 165 feet.] **1848** *Plan of Colonization of Canterbury* in Wakefield *Handbook NZ* 19 The remainder of the block to be divided into quarter-acre sections, as Town Land. **1849** *Lett. from Otago* 13 Sept. (1978) 37 He is obliged to go and take a quarter-acre section from the church trustees or company, for which he has to pay the exorbitant rent of 4*l.* a year.

1886 Hart *Stray Leaves* 14 My father bought at auction, for £46 [in 1851], the quarter-acre section upon which our tent was erected. **1899** Bell *In Shadow of Bush* 21 The 'town' itself remained a solid block of standing bush, and the absentee owners of its acre or quarter-acre sections were only reminded of their possessions by the persistent recurrence of the notices to pay rates. **c1919** Ford in *NZ Yesterdays* (1984) 82 A New Zealand statesman has said upon more than one occasion that the ideal for New Zealand is a detached house with a quarter-acre section for every working-man. **1922** *Evening Post* (Wellington) 2 Oct. 1 [Advt] £150 Deposit—5-rd. Bungalow..¼-acre section. **1934** Mulgan *Spur of Morning* 261 The political outlook of these men could not be the same as that of the town-dweller on his quarter-acre section. **1959** Stone *Verdict on NZ* 9 Over 2,000,000 people know what it is to be a New Zealander. For some it means..a house on a quarter-acre section. **1961** Crump *Hang On a Minute Mate* 126 They..swung their lines..to catch the snapper, kahawai..and tarakihi that..boiled in the surf in shoals the size of quarter-acre sections. **1977** Hall *Glide Time* 64 Jack's as good as his master, the quarter acre section. **1989** *Press* (Christchurch) 14 Feb. 2 Friday evening shopping was as once as Kiwi as six o'clock closing, the pavlova and the quarter-acre section.

3. Special Comb. **quarter-acre act**, see quot. 1982; **quarter-acre pavlova paradise** (and variants), a phrase, coined by Austin Mitchell, as a satirical name for middle-class New Zealand.

1982 Sutton-Smith *Hist. Children's Play* 43 In some rural areas it was the custom to allow the teacher to keep a cow and a horse, which further extended the normal playground space (e.g., 1875, in Tahataki). It was only in the towns, and at a much later date in rural areas, that the effects of the '**quarter-acre act**' were felt. [1982 Note] The quarter-acre was the space to be given over to the playground in public schools. **1972** Mitchell *The Half-gallon* **Quarter-acre Pavlova Paradise** [Title] **1987** [see pav. b]. **1990** *Sunday Mag.* 17 June 7 A man's home is his castle... Growing numbers are choosing to leave the quarter-acre pavlova paradise for life in a caravan. **1990** *NZ Gardener* May 28 [Heading] Quarter acre paradise.

quarter-back. *Farming.* Also formerly **comeback** [AND 1891] (see quots. 1891, 1933). A sheep bred from a Merino ram on a cross-bred ewe. See also QUARTER-BRED.

1891 Wallace *Rural Econ. Austral. & NZ* 360 When a pure Merino ram is put to a cross ewe the produce is termed a 'come-back' or 'quarter-back'. **1933** *Press* (Christchurch) (Acland Gloss.) 30 Sept. 15 *Comeback.*—A sheep three quarters merino and one quarter long wool. The word is often used; but in New Zealand I think these sheep are oftener called quarterbreds or quarter-backs. **1940** Studholme *Te Waimate* (1954) 111 When the sheep became too coarse, it was tried to bring them back by using Merino rams on the cross-bred ewes, the progeny being known as quarter backs.

quarter-bred. QUARTER-BACK.

1891 Wallace *Rural Econ. Austral. and NZ* 259 In 1890, the better portion of the greasy quarter-bred wool fetched 1s. 2½d. **1892** *NZ Official Handbook* 122 The average clips for the various breeds of sheep are approximately as follow: Merino, from 4lb. to 7lb.; quarter-breds, about 6½lb.; half-breds, 7½lb.; three-quarter breds, 8½lb. **1933** [see QUARTER-BACK]. **1936** Belshaw et al. *Agric. Organiz.* 416 The progeny of merino rams mated with half-bred ewes, or of half-bred rams mated with merino ewes are commonly termed 'quarter-bred,' but the wool produced falls within the 'half-bred' range.

quarter-caste. A person of mixed race having one quarter Maori and three-quarters non-Maori ancestry.

1913 *NZ Observer* 20 Sept. 16 A quarter-caste man, who is not affected [*sc.* with smallpox] was prohibited from using the train. **1938** *NZ Observer* 10 Feb. 6 They got a quartercast [*sic*] who was working with him. **1948** Ballantyne *Cunninghams* (1976) 13 He guessed that being up the duff to a young quarter-caste who was out of town was no joke even if she *had* been a fast number. **1952** Finlayson *Schooner came to Atia* 51 The crew with the exception of the quartercaste mate were all Maori. **1979** *Church Times* 9 Mar. 4 Bishop Reeves is a 'quarter-caste' Maori and a graduate of St. Peter's College, Oxford.

quarter-loaf. Also *ellipt.* **quarter.** [The 1843 quot. is poss. a transf. use of the Scottish name *quarter-laif* a quartern loaf, that is a four-pound loaf, or alternatively one made from a quarter pound of flour: see SND.] In esp. SI districts, a half of a 'split' loaf made from a nominal minimum 1½lb (680 g) of dough, and itself considered equivalent to a 'half-loaf', that is half a former nominal 4lb. square or raised 'tin' loaf.

1843 in Deans *Pioneers Canterbury* (1937) 51 [From Kilmarnock] The quarter-loaf for instance, which was 9d. last year, is now as low as 6d.] **1966** Turner *Eng. Lang. Austral. & NZ* 178 What is called a *quarter* (loaf of bread) in the South Island is *half* a loaf in the North Island. **1972** [see BARRACOUTA 3]. **1980** Leland *Kiwi-Yankee Dict.* 83 *quarter white*: Southland term for half a 700 gramme loaf of bread. I know it doesn't make any sense! **1989** McGill *Dinkum Kiwi Dict.* 84 *quarter-loaf* South Island version of a half-loaf.

quartz. Used *attrib.* in special Comb. **quartz-reefer**, a miner or mining company that operates by quartz-reefing; **quartz-reefing**, the mining of auriferous quartz-reefs using heavy machinery.

1869 *AJHR* D-6 26 Everything which will render the miners on the alluvial gold fields..disposed to take up their permanent abode in New Zealand, will have an equally..satisfactory influence on the **quartz-reefers** of the North. **1869** *AJHR* D-6 26 There is a pressure about **quartz-reefing** which does not appertain to alluvial digging. **1879** Barry *Up & Down* 228 The newspapers continually reiterate that 'quartz-reefing' is only in its infancy. **1887** *Handbook NZ Mines* 15 Quartz-reefing is a slow and tedious process. **1894** *NZ Official Year-book* 369 The most important work in mining for precious metals is quartz-reefing; here the system differs little from underground mining in general..the ore..when brought to the surface, is committed to 'batteries' or crushing-mills, where the stone is stamped or ground into powder. **1953** *NZ Geogr.* Apr. 29 The Dunstan field had expanded..[to] where [a] variety of natural conditions provided for dredging on the Clutha, tunnelling and sluicing on the Cromwell Flats, and quartz reefing in the Carrick Range.

queen. Often with init. cap.

1. With init. cap. applied to a Maori hierarchy, esp. later to the Maori Queen q.v.

1819 Marsden *Lett. & Jrnls.* (1932) 175 She told me..that her aunt's name was Heena (Hine-mati-oro) and a great queen. **1853** Rochfort *Adventures of Surveyor* 42 Next morning..I borrowed the queen's horse as far as Hapuka's, a distance of fifteen miles. [1853 Note] Queen of the Maories, and sister of the celebrated chief Hapuka.

2. In the names of animals, see: PAUA 2 (2), SCALLOP; see also *queen bird* 4 a below.

3. In various phrases: **a. not to call the Queen one's aunt**, see CALL *v.* 3.

b. *Goldmining.* **sinking for the Queen**, sinking a duffer shaft from which the Crown would profit from the fees charged.

1967 May *West Coast Gold Rushes* 526 At Ross in 1866 putting down a duffer shaft was termed 'sinking for the Queen'.

c. Queen Anne in front, Mary Anne at the back, said of a building architecturally presentable only in its frontal facade.

c1920 p.c. R. Mason (Auckland). In the 1920s 'Queen Anne in front, Mary Anne at the back' was applied to the Auckland Museum. **1981** Mason *Solo* 174 Queen Anne at the front; Mary Anne at the back.

4. a. Special Comb. **queen bird**, see quot.; **Queen City**, a nickname for Auckland.

1918 *TrNZI* L. 145 On the 14th June, 1916, I had an interview with Mrs. Sidney Ladbrook..who had just then returned from a birding expedition to Evening Island... Mrs. Ladbrook informed me also that [a pure white muttonbird] is called a 'jimmy bird' if it has white or pink eyes, but if the eyes are black it is known as a '**queen bird**' and the portent is less serious. **1890** *NZ Observer* 1 Feb. 7 Auckland! **Queen City** of the Austral Seas. **1917** *NZ Free Lance* (Wellington) 20 July 16 Nor does our cheerful friend from the Queen City of the North pretend to be a prophet or a seer. **1924** *Auckland Capping Book* 13 Uphold, uphold, we entreat you, the hoary traditions of your Queen City. **1939** *Tomorrow* 15 Mar. 319 Auckland is a beautiful city, the Queen City, fair and lovely. **1947** *NZ Observer* 16 Apr. 5 The local inhabitants seem much gloomier than in the Queen City. **1955** *BJ Cameron Collection* (TS July) Queen city (n) Auckland.

b. In the special collocation **Queen's chain** [f. *chain* a unit of measurement (66 feet, 20.13 m), the collocation poss. an adaptation of an orally attested (p.c. Gilbert Natusch, Wellington) *Crown chain*], a public right-of-way or public access strip of orig. one chain, now 20 m, often less, reserved along the margins of coasts, rivers and lakesides.

[Note] The expression (as distinct from the practice) is often popularly thought to be of 19th c. 'Victorian' origin. There is no evidence to support this supposition.

1977 *The Landscape* Dec. 14 (Graham E. Anderson) [Heading] The Queen's Chain (Not a limp wrist ornament). *Ibid.* 15 In many places in New Zealand the Queen's Chain, as the coastal reserve became known because of its nominal width, has been the foundation of coastal land subdivision, but in others it has not... The fault lies not in the laws but in ourselves that we have crowded the coast, and the Queen's Chain concept is as appropriate right now to the new idealism of environmental management as it was to the nineteenth century problems of land grabbing, coastal shipping by sail, river communication, and lack of roads. **1992** Milne *Handbook of Environmental Law* 132 Esplanade reserves, often referred to as part of the *Queen's chain*, are reserved areas along the banks of some rivers and lakes and along the seashore. *Ibid.* 133 Marginal strips are strips of land very like esplanade reserves except that their origins are in the disposal of crown land rather than subdivision of private land. Like esplanade reserves they are often referred to as the *Queen's chain.* **1993** *Dominion* (Wellington) 28 Mar. 8 The public campaign in respect of the Queen's chain and esplanade reserves..is questionable. **1993** *Sunday Times* (Wellington) 14 Mar. 6 Largely unfettered and unhindered access around and along margins of the sea and waterways—commonly thought of by the public as 'the Queen's Chain'—is dear to the hearts of most New Zealanders. **1993** *Dominion* (Wellington) 15 July 2 Many New

Zealanders will know that the Queen's chain, the 10-metre strip around coasts, rivers, streams and lakes, is land reserved from sale or lease.

Queenite. *Hist.* [f. QUEEN + *-ite* on the pattern of KINGITE q.v.] A North Island Maori loyal to the English Queen (Victoria) as distinct from a Kingite, a follower of the Maori king. See also FRIENDLY B, KUPAPA 1.

1861 *Otago Witness* (Dunedin) 6 Apr. 6 Karapama Te Kapukai (kingite) stood up and upbraided the kingites for turning away from them... Napai Tarratoa (queenite) stood up and said, 'I have nothing to ask you; you have been questioned but will not answer. You have chosen a king, I have chosen a church, a queen, and a governor. You have chosen one; I have three.' **1871** MEADE *Ride through Disturbed Dist.* in Taylor *Early Travellers* (1959) 427 Amongst the whole of the 'Queenites' (in contradistinction to the 'Kingite' followers of the so-styled Maori King), Poihipi is probably the most influential chief. **1879** SIMMONS *Old England & NZ* 19 The Maories of the South Island—the Queenites—are..friendly towards the English-speaking people. **1922** COWAN *NZ Wars* (1955) II. 90 A party of the enemy had built another *pa*, hemming in the Queenites on the north. **1940** COWAN *Sir Donald Maclean* 79 Mr. Maclean quickly sent a supply of rifles..which enabled the Queenite section of the Ngati-Porou to take the field well equipped for their campaign. **1976** *Tall & Short Stories* (2edn.) 32 Every Kingite, and just about every neutral, and, on the quiet, many Queenites were on his [*sc.* Te Kooti's] side. **1986** BELICH *NZ Wars* 211 The *kupapa*, Maoris fighting on the British side, were variously known as 'loyalists', 'Queenites', and 'the friendly natives'.

Queensland tomato: see TREE TOMATO.

Queen Street. [the name of a central business street in Auckland city.]

1. Symbolic or emblematic of urban opulence or (business) sophistication as distinct from rural plainness or simplicity.

1905 BAUCKE *White Man Treads* 293 Today he taketh an unblenched heart his axe, and his billy; he humpeth his bluey and setteth his face to the wilderness... Put him in Queen Street today as he stands, and watch. The constable layeth a steady eye on him. **1985** SHERWOOD *Botanist at Bay* 45 'But princess,' he drawled, 'us sex-starved bushwhackers buried out here in the sticks have to make do with what we can get.' 'Queen Street bushwhackers from a commune in Auckland, more likely.'

2. Special Comb. **Queen Street Cocky**, **Queen Street farmer**, a city businessman owning a farm as an investment (cf. FEATHERSTON STREET FARMER); **Queen Street yank**, a New Zealander aping North American ways or accent (cf. CUBA STREET YANK).

1981 KENNEDY *Straight from Shoulder* 144 Of the thirty million acres of [British] farmland which changes hands there each year, more than a third is sold to non-farmers. That is already beginning to happen here; the '**Queen street cocky**' is now part of the New Zealand scene. **1959** SLATTER *Gun in My Hand* 229 And the **Queen Street farmers** leant on the bonnets of their dusty cars and chatted or looked in the windows of parked cars... You see them in every country town in tweed sports coats and turned-down hats and shoes mucky from going around the sheep in the morning. Good old Queen Street farmers. They carry us on their broad backs. **1966** TURNER *Eng. Lang. Austral. & NZ* 49 It is permissible to call a member [of Parliament] a 'Queen Street farmer' (from the main street in Auckland) and to ask him to 'stick to the truth occasionally'. **1985** SHERWOOD *Botanist at Bay* 26 A 'Queen Street farmer' was a city slicker who owned land or stock for tax-fiddle reasons. **1990** *Dominion* (Wellington) 11 Aug. 3 Budget changes have removed the tax advantages for 'Queen Street farmers' in the ownership of such farms as Taumata. **1993** *Dominion* (Wellington) 3 Mar. 10 Sometimes the expression 'Have a nice day' is a sincere wish... But in New Zealand it sounds forced and odd, like the accent of a **Queen Street Yank**. **1993** YSKA *All Shook Up* 185 Some bodgies [c1955 in Auckland]..were so infatuated with American culture that they assumed Bronx accents... Somewhat pityingly, Hastie and his friends called them 'Queen Street Yanks'.

quickfire raffle: see QUICK RAFFLE.

quick raffle. Also **quickfire raffle**. A money-raising raffle (often for frozen meat, poultry, etc.) where the winning ticket is drawn immediately after the limited number of tickets is sold. Often called a *rapid raffle*.

1941 *NZEF Times* 4 Aug. 3 The holding of what have come to be known in New Zealand as 'quick raffles' has been banned by the police. **1981** JOHNSTON *Fish Factory* 74 Get them tourists..with their bulging wallets... Quick raffles in the boozer here. Chooks raised and fattened by the maestro of the poultry business. **1985** MCGILL *G'day Country* 63 Matata School was advertising its bring-and-buy with quickfire raffles, 'come one, come all'.

quid.

1. *transf.* [f. *quid* a colloquial word for a pound (note) and its component 20 shillings; AND 1944.] In the phr. **(to be) not the full quid**, **to be short of the full quid**, **to be [x] shillings in the quid** (occas. **pound**), to be mentally or intellectually deficient. See also SHILLING 1.

1941 *Troopship Tattoo* (H.M.Transport 32, Troopship pub.) 4 'That cove looks about seven and six in the quid to me,' remarks a lance-jack. **1947** NEWTON *Wayleggo* 140 Honey snorted that I was mad—only about 'two bob in the quid'. **1960** HILLIARD *Maori Girl* 213 Not that she was simple in the sense that she was short of the full quid. **1982** OLIVER *Poor Richard* 24 Or they say he isn't quite the full pound though useful enough in the front row. **1987** VIRTUE *Redemption of Elsdon Bird* (1988) 50 I heard Mum saying that I'm not the full quid. **1993** O'SULLIVAN *Let the River Stand* 55 'Gone in the swede,' Alex said. 'I beg your pardon?' 'It's what they say at school. Means not the full quid.' **1996** *Dominion* (Wellington) 2 Mar. 23 She's not a bit like the dim-witted..barmaid [in *Coronation Street*]... The actress who plays Raquel..looks entirely the full quid.

2. In the phr. **to make a quid**, to make or earn money.

1977 *Sunday Times* (Wellington) 27 Nov. 17 'Get this,' he insists. 'To make a quid I've got to swim my cattle out.'

3. In the phr. **the whole quid**, genuine, real.

1980 MANTELL *Murder Or Three* 41 'Yes, Kylie. Y'know, woman's angle. Does she think it's the whole quid or a put on?' 'She says real.'

quiet. [Used elsewhere but recorded earliest in NZ.] In the phr. **on the quiet**, on the sly, secretly.

1862 *Otago Goldfields & Resources* 35 Unless men can work [the gold] on 'the quiet', they are not likely to make 'piles' so rapidly as Messrs. Hartley and Riley. **1871** *Evening Post* (Wellington) 27 July 2 Obtain contracts 'on the quiet'. **1887** PYKE *Hist. Early Gold Discoveries Otago* 108 There must be diggers working on the quiet somewhere on the run.

quietly, *adv.* [AND 1938.] As **just quietly**, in confidence, 'between you and me'.

1938 *Press* (Christchurch) (McNab Slang) 2 Apr. 18 [Slang of the N.Z.E.F.]..a good phrase and one that came back to New Zealand to be used for some years after the [1914–18] War was 'just quietly.' **1941** BAKER *NZ Slang* 50 Terms originated in the first Great War [include]..*just quietly*, between you and me! **1963** PEARSON *Coal Flat* 43 I'm a full Maori and proud, too... Old Mum she meant I'm still a savage, that's what she meant. Just quietly, eh? **1964** HELMER *Stag Party* 80 Crump said... 'I could scoff a real binder, just quietly.' **1988** MCGILL *Dict. Kiwi Slang* 64 *just quietly* confidential aside, WW1; eg 'Just quietly, this is the best steak I've ever had.'

quintinia. Also **common** (or **Westland**) **quintinia**. [A genus of southern hemisphere trees and shrubs of the family Escalloniaceae, named by the Swiss botanist A.P. de Candolle in 1830 for J. de la *Quintinie* (1626–88), a French writer on plant breeding.] TAWHEOWHEO (*Quintinia serrata*).

1894 *NZ Official Year-book* 330 Westland silver-pine, Yellow silver-pine, and quintinia, although not peculiar to Westland, are more abundant there than in any other part of the colony. **1907** LAING & BLACKWELL *Plants NZ* 186 *Quintinia serrata* (The Serrated Quintinia). **1939** COCKAYNE & TURNER *Trees NZ* 120 *Quintinia acutifolia*..Westland Quintinia. *Ibid.* 121 *Quintinia serrata*..Tawherowhero, Common Quintinia. **1951** in PEARSON *Six Stories* (1991) 63 Round his head was a mad red garland of horopito and quintinia leaves. **1981** DENNIS *Paparoas Guide* 157–158 Most prominent among the broadleaf species here [in Westland] are toro..Westland quintinia (*Q. acutifolia*)..and pate.

quota. In general, the total allowable commercial catch, namely that quantity of any particular fish which can be caught in any specified area within the New Zealand Economic Zone during a particular season under rights assigned by the State; the quota assigned to a person or organization can be sold or transferred, such quota being termed *transferable quota*.

[*Note*] The Fisheries Act does not define 'quota', but speaks of 'Quota Management Areas' and 'Quota Management System'.

1986 *NZ Statutes* II. No.34 526 [Fisheries Amendment Act] Any fishery management plan and..any quota management system..may..(a) Designate areas, within the fishery management area where, and the period when, fishing for certain species of fish shall be prohibited or restricted, or permitted only by specified types of vessels or by specified methods, or subject to such other conditions as may be specified. **1992** SMITHYMAN *Auto/Biographies* 43 that's the whole fishing fleet these days since the Ministry went to work on quotas. **1992** *Evening Post* (Wellington) 29 Oct. 16 Two fishing companies..involved in quota fraud investigations are appealing the decision..to refuse name suppression. **1995** *Dominion* (Wellington) 22 Sept. 6 [Heading] Kidd takes a tough line to slash fish quota... The total allowable commercial catch has been cut by almost 40 per cent.

R

rabbit, *n.*

1. Special Comb. mainly alluding to the professional killing, extermination, or containment of rabbits: **rabbit** (or **rabbiting**) **block**, BLOCK *n.*[1] 6 a; **Rabbit Board** [AND 1898], a local authority charged with the control of rabbits in its area; **rabbit camp**, see *rabbiters' camp* (RABBITER 2); **rabbit-cart** *obs.*, the vehicle travelling around rabbiters' camps collecting carcasses or skins for sale; **rabbit club** *obs.*, a private rabbit-shooters' club whose members have exclusive rights of rabbit-hunting over a specified area; **rabbit-dog**, any of various dogs trained to specific tasks in the hunting of rabbits; **rabbit factory**, a factory processing rabbit carcasses for food; **rabbit fence** [AND 1896], a *rabbit-proof fence* (RABBIT-PROOF 2); **rabbit-fencing**, (lengths of) such fences collectively; **rabbit-hole** *transf. WW1* (Gallipoli), a place of refuge dug out of the ground; **rabbit inspector** [AND 1896], an official appointed to enforce (usu.) local rabbit control measures; **rabbit-netting** [AND 1925], netting of a small enough gauge as to prevent a rabbit slipping through it; hence **rabbit-net** *v. trans.*, to make (a fence or boundary) rabbit-proof with netting sunk into the ground (cf. RABBIT-PROOF); **rabbit-o(h)** [OED Austral., 1911], an itinerant seller of rabbit carcasses; **rabbit pack**, a team of *rabbit-dogs* (see also PACK *n.*[2] 1); **rabbit plough**, a special plough for making a furrow in which to lay baits for rabbits; **rabbit-sick** *a.*, of land, infertile or unproductive through overgrazing by rabbits (cf. SICK 2); **rabbit-skinner** *transf.*, a nickname for a slow shearer.

  1943 *NZ Farmers' Weekly* 25 Mar. 34 Our local **Rabbit Board** has not employed a rabbiter for the last six months. **1955** *BJ Cameron Collection* (TS July) Rabbit Board (n) A local authority having rating powers, whose function it is to control and if possible exterminate rabbits in a particular area. **1964** DICK *High Country Family* 109 Even before the advent of Rabbit Boards there were always only just enough rabbits for the odd pie and the succulent braised pot-roast. **1971** ARMFELT *Catching Up* 67 Kane Potts..helped Terence on the Rabbit Board. **1984** *Knapdale Run* 195 About the 1950s, a new concept of rabbit control was emerging. This was 'Rabbit Board' control. Within a defined area, the farmers, as rate-payers, elected the members of the Board whose task was to destroy the rabbits within that area. But by no means did the Otama Rabbit Board have a gentle and smooth passage to life. **1921** *Quick March* 10 Feb. 45 We were struggling home with a big night's catch [of rabbits]—struggling down to the road-line, along which the **rabbit-cart** would travel next day. **1882** POTTS *Out in Open* 117 But what member of a **rabbit club** or possessor of a shooting license would willingly permit the appearance of a hawk near the sacred limits of the reserve? **1912** *NZJAg.* Dec. V. 605 This later gang should be provided with a few quiet-working **rabbit-dogs** to 'hole' any rabbits that may be in the grass or scrub. **1933** *Press* (Christchurch) (Acland Gloss.) 18 Nov. 15 *Rabbit dogs*.—Those spoken of such include greyhounds, lurchers, spaniels, and nondescript terriers; sometimes, retrievers. They are called the *r[abbit] pack* and in the 'nineties some station *r[abbit] p[ack]s* had as many as 30 dogs in them. If one of them retrieved he was called a *carrier* and sometimes rabbiters point out a dog as a great *nester* (smeller out of *r[abbit]* nests). **1946** ACLAND *Early Canterbury Runs* 168 During the late 'eighties and onwards most stations kept large rabbit packs... The 1903 diary [of Clayton station] remarks 'feeding 19 rabbit dogs'. **1980** NEAVE *Land of Munros* 40 [Caption] Taking a load of rabbit carcases to the Kurow **Rabbit Factory** established by Thompson and Finlayson in 1891. **1901** ACTON-ADAMS *Letter* 7 Feb. in McCaskill *Molesworth* (1969) 85 By an agreement.. dated 25 July 1899 they agreed that 'the said W. Acton-Adams might depasture cattle..northward..of the **rabbit fence** which runs along the Clarence and over Maling's Pass.' **1902** *Settler's Handbook NZ* 216 [Rabbit Nuisance Act] [Heading] *Rabbit-proof Fencing. Rabbit Fences.*—In respect of rabbit fencing, the different legal rabbit-proof fences are [etc.]. **1938** BURDON *High Country* 163 Though rabbit fences are still used by individuals, no attempt has since been made to protect a whole province, as in 1887. **1987** [see *rabbit inspector* below]. **1889** *TrNZI* XXI. 431 I placed as little reliance on the ferret as I did upon poisoning or **rabbit-fencing**. **1894** in WILSON *Land of Tui* 202 There are fifty miles of rabbit-fencing on this property which will, doubtless, in time prove beneficial. **1936** HYDE *Passport to Hell* 119 The men crept away into their dug-outs and bled to death. Their mates..found them stiffened up in the **rabbit-holes**. *Ibid.* 122 If you start thinking..your being stowed away in a rabbit-hole where the next whirling, twisting fire-cracker coming down..may be your own packet. **1889** *TrNZI* XXI. 429 A reference to Mr. Bayley's (the Chief **Rabbit Inspector** of the colony) annual report for 1888 will show that the Government and every Rabbit Inspector are willingly allowing the use of traps. **1893** ACTON-ADAMS *Letter* 1 Jan. in McCaskill *Molesworth* (1969) 78 I find it impossible to comply with the requirements of the present Rabbit Inspector. **1906** rabbit inspector [see RABBIT *v.*[1] 2]. **1950** *NZJAg.* Dec. LXXXI. 517 The rabbit inspector at Ashburton was sufficiently alarmed by the discovery of a colony of rabbits in the Upper Rangitata to recommend the building of a rabbit-proof fence from the upper reaches of the river to the sea. **1987** CHRISTIE *Candles & Canvas* 121 The local county council employed a full-time rabbit inspector to visit farmers and ensure that active steps were taken to eradicate the pest and to enforce the erection of rabbit fences on the perimeter of those farms bordering the wasteland. **1981** PINNEY *Early N. Otago Runs* 68 The old mustering and boundary huts were of stone and the fences were **rabbit-netted**. **1984** *Knapdale Run* 195 Farmers within the proposed area who had no rabbit problem naturally objected to paying another rate as did farmers who had cleared their farms of the pest, some even having their boundaries 'rabbit-netted'. **1905** *Weekly Press* (Christchurch) 25 Jan. 2 [Advt] Timber and Coal Merchants..In stock—Galvanised Iron..Sheep and **Rabbit Netting**. **1959** LAWLOR *Old Wellington Days* 30 Stronger notes of colour were to be found in the occasional street musicians..butcher boys..'**rabbit-oh's**', 'milk-oh's'. **1987** ELDRED-GRIGG *Oracles & Miracles* 40 The milko would rattle past with his cart of a morning... Then there was the rabbit-o [c1930], who sometimes talked Mum into buying a couple of his little skinned carcases. **1933, 1946 rabbit pack** [see *rabbit dog* above]. **1985** HAWKE & SCOTT *Early Farm machinery in NZ* 27 **Rabbit ploughs** seemed to come in several different shapes, although probably the most common was the light walking plough used for making a shallow furrow in which to lay bait... Another..had a tank which would be used for carrying oats or cut carrots along the furrow. **1969** MCCASKILL *Molesworth* 121 The best country..was 'covered by rabbits in countless numbers'. Even the small paddocks adjoining the homestead were in a disgraceful condition and the greater part of the land was rapidly becoming hopelessly **rabbit-sick**. **1904** LANCASTER *Sons o' Men* 81 **Rabbit-skinner** felt..[the shed boss's] power long after the lean man had gone, and he chipped at his sheep painstakingly.

2. In the phr. **as eccentric as a rabbit on skates**, very eccentric.

  1941 MARSH *Surfeit of Lampreys* (1951) xii 180 But of course she may be as eccentric as a rabbit on skates and not come within the meaning of the act.

3. *fig.* or *transf.* A novice Rastafarian gang member. Cf. PROSPECT *n.*[2]

  1988 *Dominion* (Wellington) 25 Mar. 1 The court was told that Kennedy was a 'rabbit' or junior associate, of the Rastafarians and acted on the instructions of two senior members.

rabbit, *v.*[1] [Spec. use of *rabbit v.* to hunt or catch rabbits: used elsewhere but of special significance in NZ.]

1. *intr.* To hunt rabbits; to do the work of a professional rabbiter.

  1875 RIVES *Jottings on the Spot* (Canterbury Pub. Lib.TS) 11 Feb. 1 I went out rabbitting with the Trolove boys but never got a shot. **1882** *TrNZI* XIV. 239 A man who was engaged 'rabbiting' on the run, had camped on the Maruroa Flat, not far from the homestead. **1891** WALLACE *Rural Econ. Austral. & NZ* 320 On the property..ten men have to be kept 'rabbiting' all the year round. **1926** DEVANNY *Butcher Shop* (1981) 60 The rabbiters' whare was a two-roomed shanty occupied by two old cronies who were rabbitting for Messenger. **1933** *Press* (Christchurch) (Acland Gloss.) 18 Nov. 15 *Rabbit*.—To kill *r[abbit]s*, to be employed as a *rabbiter*.

2. *trans.* To free (an area) from rabbits.

  c1930 *Whitcombe's Etym. Dict. Aust.-NZ Suppl.* 9 *rabbit v.t.* to render an area free from rabbits. **1969** MCCASKILL *Molesworth* 128 Leighton said: '..To attempt to rabbit Molesworth [a sheep station] with unemployed would involve the presence of an ambulance.'

Hence **rabbiting** *vbl. n.* [OED 1841], the occupation or practices of a professional rabbiter. Also *attrib.*

  1887 *Auckland Weekly News* 4 June 8 There he spotted the prodigal, 'keeping body and soul together'..by 'rabbiting', that is by destroying rabbits

RABBIT 651 **RACE**

as vermin. **1906** Acton-Adams *Letters* in McCaskill *Molesworth* (1969) 93 *Rainbow Rabbiting*. You weakly gave in to the Inspector against my instructions... The rabbit Inspector fairly bluffed you. **1956** Cresswell *Early NZ Families* 167 After the final clean-up on Marchburn there was no rabbiting done there for thirty years. **1966** Barry *In Lee of Hokonuis* 65 He had a great many rabbiting dogs of all breeds.

rabbit, v.² *Rugby football.*

1. *trans. Obs.* [Prob. a transf. use of Australian National (Rules) Football *rabbit*: to duck down in the path of an opposing player, so causing the player to trip or fall; AND 1885.] To duck down in the path of an opposing player bringing him to the ground; also ?to scurry hither and thither with the ball.

c**1870s** Meredith *Adventuring in Maoriland* (1935) 59 He [a six foot seven inch player] was chasing the smallest member of the [football] club, who was running with the ball; when close up to his quarry, the little fellow 'rabbited' him. The giant went sprawling and the little fellow jumped up and continued his run amid roars of laughter from the spectators. **1930** *Northern Advocate* 4 July 7 After 'rabbiting' for a while, Abbott all but scored as a result of such a movement.

2. To attempt to claim a rugby try by touching down over the goal-line with a 'second movement' a ball already touched down in the field of play. Apparently mainly recorded as a *vbl. n.* (Quot. 1877 poss. belongs with 1 above.)

1877 in Swan *Hist. NZ Rugby Football* (1948) I. 70 Members of the [Auckland] City Clubs held a meeting to modify the Laws of the Game... This meeting, on June 19, decided that:- 'Slinging, **Rabbiting** and Butting be added to Rule 57.' **1944** Gaskell *All Part of the Game* (1978) 33 Offside a mile. Rabbiting. You handled it on the ground. **1973** *Dominion* (Wellington) 6 Sept. 16 The big Jeremy Janion decided to go on his own, only to be picked up in a tackle of the covering Dougan. Janion then wriggled his way over the line but rightly was penalised for rabbiting. **1988** McGill *Dict. Kiwi Slang* 91 *rabbiting* illegal carrying of grounded rugby ball over try line.

Hence **rabbiter** n., a rugby player who practises rabbiting.

1910 Fanning *Players & Slayers* 24 The backs..may be classified as setters, retrievers,.. and rabbits (to be distinguished from the '**rabbiter**', who may be quite a useful quadruped if overlooked by the referee).

rabbit, v.³ To rifle surreptitiously (esp. potatoes by digging out potato tubers, leaving the tops still growing). Also *ppl. a.* **rabbiting**, thieving. Cf. BANDICOOT V.

1952 *Rabbiting* used in Wellington of potato plants which have had the tubers stolen but the tops left intact (Ed.). **1978** Glover *Men of God* 10 On the way out at the gate Joe [an ex-convict] hesitated then said to himself, No, it wouldn't be fair to rabbit the old codger's letterbox. **1995** Winter *All Ways Up Hill* 207 As Sid turned around to look, his mate grabbed two handfuls of hot sausages out of the pan... [Sid's] giant form loomed large in the firelight..'Any more uv you rabbiting little bastards want sausages? Come on!' he challenged.

rabbiter. [Spec. use of *rabbiter* one who hunts rabbits: see OED n. 1872.]

1. A professional killer of wild rabbits; one who is paid to attempt to clear farmland of rabbits.

1882 *TrNZI* XIV. 240 On the following day the station manager..visited the camp. The rabbiter had just struck his tent. **1892** Swanton *Notes on NZ* 133 The men so employed [*sc.* destroying rabbits] are called 'rabbiters'. **1909** Thompson *Ballads About Business* 54 And rabbiters experienced knew, Or thought it safest to eschew All labour under 'Skinflint' Kenn. **1933** *Press* (Christchurch) (Acland Gloss.) 18 Nov. 15 *Rabbit*.—To kill r[abbit]s, to be employed as a *rabbiter*... He may be a permanent or a temporary hand, or may *take a block* for the skins. He may use dog, gun, and spade, poison, or traps. **1941** Curnow *Island and Time* 2 The cowman home from the shed went drinking with the rabbiter home from the hill. **1971** Henderson *Our Open Country* 242 That truck quaffed petrol like a beerdrinking rabbiter hitting town after six months in the back of the Dunstan. **1987** Ogonowska-Coates *Boards, Blades & Barebellies* 97 *Rabbiter*. Hand employed on the station to kill rabbits, usually with poison or traps.

2. In special collocations: **rabbiters' breakfast**, see quot.; **rabbiters'** (or **rabbit**) **camp**, the field headquarters of a rabbiting gang; **rabbiters' hut**, a hut on a farm or other property used by rabbiters.

1975 Anderson *Men of Milford Road* 68 Next morning we were up too early for a meal at the cookhouse, so Mae said, 'It'll have to be a **rabbiters' breakfast** for us today—a trip to the toilet and a cigarette.' **1897** Wright *Station Ballads* 44 **Rabbit camp**. **1973** Fernandez *Tussock Fever* 15 Each week..Bessie packed up stores for the cooks at the two out-stations, for the **rabbiters' camp** and for the station cook-house. **1951** Duff *Shepherd's Calendar* (1961) 24 It has always interested me in the back country to study the printed and pictorial matter in shepherds' and **rabbiters' huts**.

rabbit-proof, a. [Recorded elsewhere, but of local significance in the South Island.]

1. Secure against rabbits.

1886 *AJHR H-9* 2 Rabbit-proof fencing has been found to afford a certain amount of protection. **1902** *Settler's Handbook NZ* 163 *Swing Gates*.—Swing gates or rabbit-proof gates can be put up across roads and bridges with the consent of the local authority. **1912** *The Sheepowners' Handbook* 57 *Second Quality Rabbit-Proof Wire Netting*. **1938** *NZJST* XX. 229A [Caption] Rabbit-proof enclosure, same species within and without. **1981** Pinney *Early N. Otago Runs* 29 Rabbit-proof netting was mentioned in Middleton's [c1880s] reports only when an enclosure of one acre was planned to lure rabbits on to a crop.

2. Special Comb. **rabbit-proof fence** [AND 1883]; **rabbit-proof fencing**, a fence or fencing secure against rabbits. See also *rabbit fence* or *fencing* (RABBIT n. 1).

1884 *AJHR I-5* 127 We have no **rabbit-proof fences**, not to any extent. **1895** *Fencing Act* in *Settler's Handbook NZ* (1902) 161 (2.) *Sufficient Rabbit-proof Fence*. **1902** *Settler's Handbook NZ* 71 Valuation for improvements at the end of a lease is not to exceed three times the annual rent... Rabbit-proof fences are extra. *Ibid*. 217 It enables rabbit-proof fencing districts to be set up by the Governor (as small as 1,000 acres in area, with as few ratepayers as three) on petition of a majority of the ratepayers. **1922** Perry *Sheep Farming* 15 No hard and fast rules can be laid down as to the class of fence to erect, as so much depends on the purpose..*e.g.*, whether boundary, rabbit proof, etc. **1973** Fernandez *Tussock Fever* 39 'We'll put the mob through the rabbit-proof fence,' Rusty instructed. **1980** Neave *Land of Munros* 122 As some protection, a great rabbit proof fence was erected which ran for 80 miles from the Waitaki River..to the Tekapo River. **1886** *AJHR H-9* 2 **Rabbit-proof fencing** has been found to afford a certain amount of protection. **1890** *AJHR H-9* 2 Phosphorized grain, shooting..erecting rabbit-proof fencing. **1889** *TrNZI* XXI. 429 With regard to rabbit-proof fencing, I always thought it a weak thing, and I would have nothing to do with it. **1912** *NZJAg.* Dec. V. 602 [Heading] Rabbit-proof Fencing Necessary... The first and most important step is the erection of rabbit-proof netting fences on the boundaries. **1948** Cowan *Down the Years in the Maniototo* 150 In order to cope..with the rabbit pest there must be..a great extension of rabbit-proof fencing.

race, n.¹ [Spec. use of *race* a channel: cf. OED n.¹ 8 c and f.]

1. *Goldmining.* [f. *race* an artificial channel for water.] In New Zealand use (first recorded 1860), associated with goldfields, with main significant uses HEAD-RACE, TAIL-RACE qq.v., and the special Comb. (mostly obsolete) **race holder**, the owner of a goldfields water-race and water rights; **raceman**, a local body worker attending to the 'races' or channels at roadsides which carry away surface water; or, one attending to water-races carrying water to goldmines or farms; also as **race** v., to move water by means of a race.

1911 Bremner in *Mt. Ida Goldfields* (1988) 15 One could not blame the **race holders**... The supply was far too small for the demand for water at any time. **1946** Miller *There Was Gold* 13 There is the..runholder and more important station owner; there is the cow cocky, the gold miner..the Public Works **raceman**. *Ibid*. 108 At the end of the summer the water is turned out of the race, and the winter tries its best to see that the racemen earn their money the following spring. **1962** Evans *Waikaka Saga* 228 The dam filled by night and gave a steady supply by day, the water being raced down the flat as far as the cemetery.

2. *Farming.* **a.** [AND 1862.] A narrow passage along which stock walk in single file for drafting, branding, etc.; or in which they can be held for drenching, and other farm operations; also the passage by which dairy cows enter or leave the bails or milking shed.

1862 Chudleigh *Diary* 4 Oct. (1950) 61 Made an attempt to brand but the race was too wide..we had to drag three cows out by the horns. **1865** Barker *Station Life* (1870) 34 The newly-shorn ones..being turned out after they have passed through a narrow passage, called a 'race', where each sheep is branded. **1872** Routledge *Every Boys Annual* LIII. 2 Each lamb was driven through the narrow passage..called a hurdle race. **1881** Bathgate *Waitaruna* 69 The sheep were driven through a narrow race from one yard to another. **1902** *Brett's Colonists' Guide* 315 Drafting... To effect this they have to go through the yards, passing through a narrow race, at the end of which there is a swing gate. **1924** [see DRAFT V. 1 a]. **1956** Dare *Rouseabout Jane* 167 I drove the sheep..down the race—a narrow lane boarded up on either side, just wide enough for one sheep to go down at a time, and with a set of three narrow gates at the bottom. **1963** Duggan *Collected Stories* (1981) 199 Dried off all four tits and let the cow out into the race where..she squittered off wild in the eyes. **1978** Sutherland *Elver* 36 While the MacLellans were having their snack the cows were coming down the race. **1989** Richards *Pioneer's Life* 50 A strong bail was made at the end of the race to secure his head. **1992** *Dominion* (Wellington) 28 Mar. 10 If there's no trace of a race, a place will hide its face in disgrace.

b. Also **raceway**. A fenced roadway through a farm.

1974 *NZ Agric.* 86 The paddocks all open on to the central roadway (the 'race') which leads to the farm dairy. **1982** Yerex *Farming Deer* 103 The provision of central farm raceways enables deer to be moved from paddock to yards quickly. **1982** *Agric. Gloss.* (MAF) 7 *Race*: A fenced roadway through a farm.

c. Special Comb. **race-bail** *dairy-farming*, a stall to hold cows in a race-shed (see SHED 4 b) during milking; **race-gate**, a swinging gate in a farm race used for drafting animals.

1912 *NZJAg.* Jan. IV. 536 Could you kindly inform me through the *Journal* the measurements of **race-bails** to hold five cows each side... A *race* milking-shed to hold five cows on either side should measure 43 ft. in length, and a total width of 10 ft. 9 in. (inside measurement). **1973** WALLACE *Generation Gap* 251 The man on the gates would be the boss..swinging the **race-gate** from side to side as the sheep were pushed forward by the shepherd.

Hence **race** (or **race off**) *v. trans.*, to separate or draft (stock) by means of a race. Also *fig.*

1927 GUTHRIE-SMITH *Birds* 92 Perhaps in the last great drafting, when St. Peter races off the just—whom I take to be those who protect their native birds. **1947** BRERETON *No Roll of Drums* 172 Gavin was of the opinion that he could race the lot out of the flock without previous marking.

race, *n.*² *West Coast coalmining.* [f. Brit. dial. *race* a row or series: see OED *n.*¹ 9 b.] **a.** A series of rail-tracks in a mine.

1901 *NZ Illustr. Mag.* IV. 614 The driver takes the trucks through the mine races, and deposits them in lay-bys, places similar to..railway sidings. Here the trucks are received by the hangers-on, boys who attach the trucks to an endless rope.

b. A 'rake' of coal trucks.

1963 PEARSON *Coal Flat* 421 race (of boxes): A local expression for a rake (of trucks). **1981** *Listener* 2 May 43 The wheeled vehicles that transport the coal (trucks, tubs, or skips elsewhere) are in the Strongman called *boxes*, and when they are linked together in a string they become a *race of boxes*. This *race* is the same word you hear in a railwayman's *rake of waggons*, *rake* being the northern-dialect form. *Race* was usually the southern form, used by miners in Cornwall.

race-caller. [See CALL *v.*] One who gives a running commentary on a horse-race. See also *caller* (CALL *v.*).

1984 *Listener* 16 June 21 Tonks was a race-caller for 33 years, based in Auckland. He got his start as an on-course commentator, but nowadays many race-callers begin with horse trials. **1992** *Evening Post* (Wellington) 11 Dec. 31 Simon says New Zealand has some of the best race callers in the world.

Hence **race-calling** *ppl. a.* and *vbl. n.*

1984 *Listener* 16 June 20 Bright's race-calling accent shares the flat Manawatu vowels of his predecessor Peter Kelly. *Ibid.* 21 Haub's talent for race-calling emerged when a commentator broke down at Dargaville. 'I was there calling to my mates where our horses were and they said 'Why don't you have a go?' **1990** *Evening Post* (Wellington) 11 Dec. 31 He also says race-calling was a pretty 'cruisy' sort of life-style.

racehorse. [Spec. use of *racehorse* symbolic of anything lean and racy: AND 1953.] A thinly-rolled roll-your-own cigarette. Cf. GREYHOUND.

c1940 a common use in Marlborough for a thin hand-made cigarette (Ed.). **1953** *Evening Post* (Wellington) 29 Aug. 8 Judged on 'roll-your-own' standards..the average per head [consumption of tobacco in New Zealand] might reach as high as 3000 cigarettes depending on whether the smoker concerned rolled 'racehorses' or 'steamrollers'.

race relations. As **Race Relations Conciliator**, a statutory official appointed to arbitrate on complaints of racial slur or deprivation. (Also *Race Relations Office*, the base or institution from which the conciliator works.)

[*Note*] The term *race relations* is first recorded in NZ use in 1934 (OED 1911, US).

1971 *NZ Statutes* IV. No.150 2250 [Race Relations Act 1971] There shall be appointed a Conciliator to be called the Race Relations Conciliator. **1974** *Dominion* (Wellington) 14 Mar. 3 The Attorney-General..has decided not to refer the recent spate of 'pom baiting' to the Race Relations Conciliator. **1983** *NZ Statutes* II. No.56 694 [Human Rights Commission Amendment Act 183] The powers and functions of the Race Relations Conciliator under the Race Relations Act 1971 shall be vested in the Commission, but shall be exercised by the Race Relations Conciliator and his Deputy and officers and employees. **1986** *Dominion* (Wellington) 14 May 14 Surely our new race relations conciliator has misread his instructions? Or has he? Is he merely a Coloured Race Protector?

racing, *ppl. a.* In special collocations **racing axe**, **racing saw**, an axe or saw prepared for, and used in, chopping or sawing contests.

1984 *Dominion* (Wellington) 31 Aug. 13 Eddie is a saw doctor with a difference. He has become a craftsman of racing axes and saws, and for both of these he has created a growing demand in New Zealand and overseas. **1992** *Evening Post* (Wellington) 3 Jan. 2 [Caption] Eddie Fawcett with a Tuatahi axe. 'We're the only commercial racing axe makers left in the world that we know of.'.. Along with axes and racing saws Mr Fawcett also makes throwing tomahawks for the US market.

raddle, *n.* [Transf. use of *raddle* red ochre.] In obsolete *attrib.* use, mainly referring to the (allegedly often unfair) employer's practice of using coloured chalk or raddle to mark badly shorn sheep for which the shearer is not paid.

1912 *Maoriland Worker* 29 Mar. 12 Raddle in those days [1880's] was in great demand, and when the boss of the board was in a bad humor [*sic*] or perchance did not like the color of the shearer's hair he used the raddle on the sheep shorn by the shearer and the raddle sheep were counted out and the shearer not paid for them. **1960** MILLS *Sheep-O* 122 This [South Island] shed is often said..to have been paid for with 'raddle money', a term that many of our younger shearers have never even heard. In those days..a shearer had to shear cleanly, or have many of his sheep heavily marked in the count-out pens and excluded from his tally. Inevitably the boss stood to benefit from such a one-sided bargain, hence the term, raddle money.

raddle, *v. trans.* [Spec. use of *raddle* to mark with raddle: AND 1879.] **a.** *Obs.* To mark an unsatisfactorily shorn sheep.

1910 *Maoriland Worker* 15 Oct. 4 'Well, boss' says he, 'I shear for myself in the morning, and for my girl in the afternoon, and he wouldn't be much of a man who could raddle a sheep on a girl, would he, boss?' **1946** ACLAND *Early Canterbury Runs* 167 In 1886 there is mention [in the Clayton station diary] of 'raddling' (and not paying for) badly shorn sheep. I think by the 'nineties the shearers had managed to get this custom abolished. **1987** OGONOWSKA-COATES *Boards, Blades & Barebellies* 97 *Raddle*. To declare a sheep badly shorn and therefore not included in the shearer's tally. This practice was outlawed in the 1890s.

Hence **raddled** *ppl. a.*, see quots.; **raddling** *vbl. n.* and *ppl. a.*, (pertaining to) the marking of a badly-shorn sheep with raddle.

1989 *NZ Eng. Newsletter* III. 26 **raddled:** This word means 'robbed' in the sense of being deprived of one's proper payment. It is an extension of 'raddling', carried out by unscrupulous farmers before the Shearers' Union looked after shearers' interests. Any sheep considered unsatisfactorily shorn was marked with red or blue raddle and such a sheep would not be counted in the shearer's tally... This must not be confused with marking a sheep for other purposes, such as identification of certain sheep for easy selection later. **1911** *Maoriland Worker* 8 Dec. 14 This is like going back to the good old **raddling** days. **1934** *Press* (Christchurch) (Acland Gloss.) 27 Jan. 15 *Raddling*.— An old-time shed practice, whereby the shed boss put a raddle-mark on any sheep in the counting-out pen not shorn to his satisfaction, and the shearer was not paid for it. Old hands often spoke of this practice. I think the great shearers' strike at the beginning of the 'nineties ended it. **1990** MARTIN *Forgotten Worker* 94 Most runholders tried to maintain quality through so-called 'raddling' clauses, under which bad shearers were penalised and lost a certain proportion of their earnings. Raddled sheep were those which had been marked with coloured chalk by the shed boss as badly shorn and not to be paid for.

b. To mark a shearing cut; to mark (a sheep) as an aid to drafting.

1988 *More* (Auckland) Mar. 31 The new rousie [was] instructed to raddle (mark with colour for the farmer's attention) the cut pizzle on the underside of a ram. **1989** RICHARDS *Pioneer's Life* 26 If the forthcoming sale was the Ewe Fair all the ewes..would be mustered and sorted in the 'crush pen', then 'raddled' (chalk marked) ready for drafting.

radi, var. RARI *n.*¹

radiata pine. Often *ellipt.* **radiata**. [f. *radiata* the specific name of *Pinus radiata* given by D. Don (1837), in *Trans. Linn. Soc.* XVII. 442.] *Pinus radiata*, the member of the exotic pine family most commonly cultivated to provide timber and wood products in New Zealand. See also FIR 2, PINE 4, PINUS.

1953 *NZ Jrnl. Forestry* V. 374 The development of major industries, dependent wholly or substantially on radiata pine as a basic raw material, is well advanced. **1957** [see PINE 4]. **1973** SIMPSON *Kauri to Radiata* 310 By 1959 radiata would have achieved prominence in sawn output over that of our indigenous timbers. **1988** HILL *More from Moaville* 22 The rows of two-tiered spectator benches within the corrugated-iron enclosures are composed of radiata from Ballantyne's Sawmills. **1991** *National Business Review* 21 May 3 [Heading] Radiata lure for Thai delegation.

radicky, var. RAURIKI.

radish. Usu. as **wild radish**, *Raphanus raphanistrum* (fam. Brassicaceae), a naturalized European weed of coastal sites and waste land distinguished by its hairy leaves and constricted seed pods.

1838 POLACK *NZ* I. 291 The *turnip* is found in a wild state over the entire country, as also wild *radishes*, *garlick*, *celery*, *cress*, &c. **1926** HILGENDORF *Weeds* 96 Wild Radish (*Raphanus sativus*) is found in many scattered localities. It is much like the garden plant, with the same shaped leaves, purplish flowers, and jointed pods. **1969** *Standard Common Names Weeds* 86 *wild radish Raphanus raphanistrum*. **1981** TAYLOR *Weeds of Roadsides* 171 Wild Radish (*Raphanus raphanistrum* and *R. maritimus*)... This European plant..is now common in several districts.

Rafferty, *a.* [f. a Brit. dialectal alteration of *refractory*, felt as an Irish surname (hence init. cap.): AND 1918; see also EDD.] Usu. as **Rafferty('s) rules**, having no apparent rules, or sense of order or method. Also occas. heard as an *adj.* [AND 1948], rough; raffish: e.g. a rafferty old car; rafferty friends.

1917 *Chron. NZEF* 17 Oct. 114 It was Muldoon's picnic, and the rules were Rafferty's. **1918** *Great Adventure* (1988) 17 Mar. 237 And you should have seen what a mess we made of it. Rafferty Rules was the order of the day and our company..were all over the place. **1936** LAMBERT *Pioneering Reminisc. Old Wairoa* 189 The day was hot..and the rules were those of the well-known 'Mr. Rafferty'. **1953** *Truth* 4 Mar. 3 'Rafferty's Rules,' said Miss M.B. Howard M.P. as soon as..the Board had finished discussing the housing plight of two of its registrars. **1963** PEARSON *Coal Flat* 53 The bus seemed to have no regular stops, the driver knew where anyone wanted to get off and stopped there; 'Rafferty rules,' she thought. **1972** MITCHELL *Pavlova Paradise* 183 *Rafferty's rules*: Standing Orders of the House of Representatives. Named after William Ewart Rafferty, the second Speaker who, because of his high voice, was also referred to as Mr Squeaker. **1986** OVENDEN *O.E.* 236 Out here it's always been Rafferty's Rules. Make 'em up as you go along.

rag, *n.* [Used as a figure for something flimsy, easily torn, or of low value.]

1. *Obs.* A one pound note.

1899 *Bulletin* (Sydney) 14 Jan. (Red Page) [Letter from *Loafer*, Tauranga.] Following are other local money-names:—1 pound note—*flimsy*, *rag* or *carpet*. **1977** *NZ Numismatic Jrnl.* Oct. 16 The pound note of pre-decimal days was var[i]ously known as a *quid*, *nicker*, *smacker*, *flimsy*, *rag*, and *carpet*. The latter term was apparently peculiar to New Zealand and Australia.

2. A low card (the 2, 3, or 4) in some card-games, esp. 'five-hundred'.

c1940 Marlborough (Ed.), e.g. 'I got two diamonds from kitty—the left bower and a rag'.

rage, *n. Adolescents.* [OEDAS *Austral.* and *N.Z. colloq.*] An exciting and noisy party or event.

1980 *Listener* 6 Dec. 56 The notice-board told me [*sc.* Professor I.A. Gordon] that the last rage of the year would take place that night and later in the evening the sound of the rage filled the campus. **1991** PAYNE *Staunch* 36 Harry was expected at a rage in the Mob clubhouse. **1993** *Evening Post* (Wellington) 29 Jan. 3 Problems which include 'legless' 13 and 14-year-old girls being driven home from 'rages' (dances) by police.

Hence **ragey** *a.*, of a party or event, noisy and exciting.

1993 *Evening Post* (Wellington) 4 Aug. 12 It was a warm and affectionate portrait of a community, from the old men laying wreaths..to the ragey party at the Mussel Inn.

rage, *v.* [OEDAS *Austral.* and *N.Z. colloq.* to revel, to 'party': Aust. 1979.][Cf. *Macquarie Dict. New Words* (1990), *rage* 1981; *rager* 1984.] To behave in a noisy, excited or abandoned way in the course of a party or as part of a group; to dance in an abandoned manner; to be high on drugs.

1984 *Press* (Christchurch) 7 Dec. 4 Gilbert said that he had plenty of money as he played pool, toss the coin and won quinellas at the races. He refused to 'point the finger' at where Mr Maddox got the dope. 'This has spoilt a good day. I have been raging all day. I punched him over because he tried to punch me over, and put me in my place.' **1986** *More* (Auckland) May 22 Tonight is club night..when Butch's group of dauntingly attired females..show how staunch they are in the chapter by showing up to rage. **1991** *Dominion* (Wellington) 8 Apr. 1 While student union, university and civic leaders looked for reasons for the rampage, students continued to rage at several parties in the city yesterday. **1991** PAYNE *Staunch* 12 There's a party going on. Huckory-looking biker girls wander back and forth, swigging beer from the bottle and raging to the music.

Hence **rager** *n.* [OEDAS *Austral.* and *N.Z. colloq.*: Aust. 1972.], one who is given to raging.

1986 *Woman's Weekly* 30 June 76 [A 15-year-old writes] Finally, I don't turn up my nose at flash new clothes that my relations give me. As I said before, I'm not into some gears, so I just give them to Mum, who's my size too. (My mum's a bit of a rager.)

rahui. Also early **rahue**, **raoui**. [Ma. /'raːhui/: Williams 321 *Rāhui* (i). *1.* n. A mark to warn people trespassing; used in the case of *tapu*, or for temporary protection of fruit, birds, or fish, etc.] Mainly used in Maori contexts, orig. a mark or warning to trespassers; now often a formal or ritualized warning-off from an activity or area.

1832 WILLIAMS *Early Jrnls.* 13 Dec. (1961) 267 Tohitapu expressed a wish to *Rahue* the spot, which was granted. The act of *Rahue* is the fixing of a piece of carved wood, about 5 feet high, smeared over with red ochre, in some conspicuous spot to signify that no one must trespass, or that it is *Tapu*ed [*sic*]. **1838** POLACK *NZ I.* 71 On the north bank were placed, among the bushes, three *raouis*, or carved monuments, painted with red earth. These had been erected here to prevent native travellers or strangers from grubbing in the sand for a favourite large cockle. **1896** *TrNZI* XXVIII. 54 *Rahui*.—In the case Airini Donnelly *v.* Broughton..*Hawkes Bay Herald*... 26th March, 1892, the witness Noa Huke says, 'The whole of this block from Te Whanga to Puketitiri..was affected... They went and put up rahuis all over it. At Puketitiri, Piko (a man) was the *rahui*.' **1910** *Ibid.* XLII. 477 The fruit of the *tutu* is sometimes preserved for the owners by means of a *rahui*, which warned persons. **1954** *Landfall* 32 275 Here is the sea's hand on the yielded shore, Here is the benediction and the prayer. No rahui to stay the steadied step. **1983** HULME *Bone People* 393 It will take most of the day to go round his rahui. **1989** PARKINSON *Travelling Naturalist* 143 In many cases it seems that the rahui of the Maori was often more a desperate attempt to preserve food sources than a true conservation measure. **1994** *Dominion* (Wellington) 4 Nov. 13 The source of the conflict is a rahui, or reserve, imposed by the Whakarara Maori Committee on scallop beds about 200 metres off the Matauri Bay mainland to give the beds time to recover.

rail. [Spec. use of *rail* a bird of family Rallidae.]

1. Any of various, mainly swamp-living, birds of the family Rallidae, esp. the *banded rail* 2 (2) below. See also COOT, CRAKE, MOHO-PERERU, PUKEKO 1, TAKAHE, WEKA.

1773 FORSTER *Resolution Jrnl.* 17 Apr. (1982) II. 257 These Water-hens [*sc.* wekas] or rather *Rails* have so short wings. **1817** NICHOLAS *NZ II.* 256 Towards the southward there are also water hens of a large species, rails in vast numbers..and some other sorts of aquatic birds. **1830** CRAIK *New Zealanders* 187 Among them are many sorts of wild ducks..rails, parrots, and parroquets. **1840** DIEFFENBACH *Acc. Chatham Islands Jrnl. Royal Geogr. Society* XI. 195–215 in Holmes *Chatham Islands* (1984) 95 A new kind of rail was formerly very common. **1873** [see WEKA 1]. **1882** HAY *Brighter Britain* II. 151 Pigeons, nestors, parrots, rail..all these and more were eaten. **1904** TREGEAR *Maori Race* 105 The rail (*mohoperu* and *moeriki*: Rallus sp.) and many other land-birds were cooked or potted down. **1922** *NZJST* IV. 278 I recall, however, a pretty little rail (*Hypotaenidia philippensis*) which was taken in the bush at Littlebourne. **1953** GUTHRIE-SMITH *Tutira* (3edn.) 214 Injurious as the cat may be to the Rail, its presence is still more baneful to the rat. **1970** MCNEISH *Mackenzie* 11 A rail sounded to his left. 'Swamp country,' he muttered. **1984** SOPER *Birds NZ* 81 Rails are mostly secretive and skulking with laterally compressed bodies for slipping through dense vegetation. **1990** FOORD *NZ Descr. Animal Dict.* 329 Rails. Ground-living birds with short legs and no web on the toes; poor flyers with short, rounded wings.

2. With a modifier: **Auckland Island(s), banded (New Zealand banded), Chatham Island (Hutton's, little Chatham Islands), Dieffenbach's, landrail, Macquarie Island (Macquarie Island banded), Mangere, marsh, striped, swamp (sooty)**.

(1) **Auckland Island(s) rail.** *Rallus pectoralis muelleri*, a small brown rail of the subantarctic Auckland Islands.

1904 HUTTON & DRUMMOND *Animals NZ* 171 The Auckland Islands Rail. *Hypotaenidia muelleri*. **1923** *NZJST* VI. 76 *Rallus muelleri* Roths. Auckland Island Rail. Buller wrote in 1905, 'presumably extinct'. **1966** FALLA et al. *Birds NZ* 102 The Auckland Island Rail which is known only from two specimens, may be identical with or derived from a small Australian rail. **1976** SOPER *NZ Birds* 237 The Auckland Island Rail, not seen since 1890, was rediscovered on Adams Island by the Wildlife Service in 1966. **1985** *Reader's Digest Book NZ Birds* 166 Auckland Island Rail. *Rallus pectoralis muelleri*... The only live Auckland Island rail obtained for study was captured on Auckland Island in 1966 foraging in a garbage dump.

(2) **banded (New Zealand banded) rail.** *Rallus philippensis assimilis*, a large brown rail, streaked black above and barred black and white below. See also *landrail* and *striped rail* ((5) and (9) below), MOHO-PERERU.

1888 BULLER *Birds NZ* II. 95 Rallus philippensis. (Banded Rail.)... Patatai... Moho-pereru, and Puohotata; 'Land-Rail' of the colonists. **1892** WILLIAMS *Dict. NZ Lang.* 277 *Pepe... banded* or *land rail*. **1904** HUTTON & DRUMMOND *Animals NZ* 170 The Pectoral Rail.— *Mohopereru*... These birds live among tangled masses of grass, sedges and rushes, which border swamps and lagoons. **1925** GUTHRIE-SMITH *Bird Life* 87 Like the Pukeko, the Banded Rail leaves his bath with a series of leaps and bounds. **1949** *NZ Bird Notes* III. 121 Banded Rail... Possibly a common bird locally [at Tauranga], appearing to favour the salt-marshes. **1955** OLIVER *NZ Birds* 352 Banded Rail. Moho-pereru... In 1839 Heaphy found the Banded Rail plentiful around Wellington. **1967** NATUSCH *Animals NZ* 268 New Zealand banded rail, is the only species of this genus left in the country. It frequents swampy places throughout, and is not easily seen. **1985** *Reader's Digest Book NZ Birds* 165 Banded Rail *Rallus philippensis...* Moho-pereru... If alarmed in the open, the banded rail is unwilling to take to the air. **1990** *NZ Geographic* VII. 40 Banded rails, which are related to weka and pukeko, are secretive birds, and most active in early morning or late afternoon when they feed at the fringes of mangrove mudflats and in beds of rushes.

(3) **Chatham Island (Hutton's, little Chatham Islands) rail.** The now extinct *Rallus modestus* of the Chatham Islands. See also *Mangere rail* (7) below.

1893 PROF. PARKER *Catalogue of NZ Exhibition*

(Morris) 116 Hutton's rail, the third of the endemic rails..is confined to the Chatham Islands. **1923** Little Chatham Islands Rail [see (7) below]. **1955** OLIVER *NZ Birds* 356 Through the work of collectors..aided by cats..the Chatham Island Rail was exterminated about twenty-five years after it was discovered. **1990** *Checklist Birds NZ* 119 *Rallus modestus..Chatham Island rail...* Extinct since about 1900.

(4) **Dieffenbach's rail**. The extinct *Rallus philippensis dieffenbachii* of the Chatham Islands, a subspecies of the *banded rail* ((2) above). See also MOERIKI.
1873 BULLER *Birds NZ* 179 Rallus dieffenbachii. (Dieffenbach's Rail.)... Moeriki. *Ibid.* 180 This beautiful Rail was brought from the Chatham Islands by Dr. Dieffenbach in 1842. **1904** HUTTON & DRUMMOND *Animals NZ* 172 *Dieffenbach's Rail. Nesolimnas dieffenbachii...* (Extinct). **1955** OLIVER *NZ Birds* 354 *Dieffenbachs Rail. Moeriki...* Although at one time common in the Chatham Islands, only one specimen of Dieffenbachs Rail has been obtained. **1966** FALLA et al. *Birds NZ* 105 Dieffenbach's Rail.., once abundant in the Chatham Islands, was similar to the Banded Rail in so many respects that that it may be regarded as a strong sub-species of *philippensis.* **1990** *Checklist Birds NZ* 119 *Rallus philippensis dieffenbachii..Dieffenbach's Rail* Extinct. Known from one skin collected on Chatham Island in 1840.

(5) **landrail**. See *banded rail* (2) above.
1869 *TrNZI* I. (rev. edn.) 228 Our representative of the restricted genus Rallus (*R. assimilis*) resembles closely an Australian species, but is distinguishable by the pectoral band and rufous colouring of the head and neck being less prominent. This is the 'Land Rail' of the colonists. **1888** BULLER *Birds NZ* II. 95 Banded Rail... 'Land-Rail' of the colonists. **1892** WILLIAMS *Dict. NZ Lang.* 277 *Pepe..banded* or *land rail.* **1966** FALLA et al. *Birds NZ* 104 Banded Rail *Rallus philippensis...* Landrail, Striped Rail.

(6) **Macquarie Island (Macquarie Island banded) rail**. The extinct *Rallus philippensis macquariensis* of the subantarctic Macquarie Island, a subspecies of the *banded rail* ((2) above).
1904 HUTTON & DRUMMOND *Animals NZ* 171 *The Macquarie Island Rail. Hypotaenidia macquariensis.* **1955** OLIVER *NZ Birds* 353 *Macquarie Island Banded Rail...* Elder, Cormack and Company, during the time they were engaged in sealing at Macquarie Island, brought back alive to New Zealand, in March, 1879, a specimen of the Banded rail that was then common at the south end of the island. **1976** SOPER *NZ Birds* 229 Two of Macquaries' birds have become extinct since discovery by man: the Macquarie Island Rail and the Macquarie Island..Parakeet. **1990** *Checklist Birds NZ* 119 *Rallus philippensis macquariensis...* Macquarie Island Banded Rail... Extinct since about 1880.

(7) **Mangere** (also erron. **Mangare**) **rail**. [Named from Mangere Island in the Chathams group.] See *Chatham Island rail* (3) above.
1904 HUTTON & DRUMMOND *Animals NZ* 172 *The Mangare Rail. Cabalus modestus.* **1923** *NZJST* VI. 76 *Cabalus modestus...* Little Chatham Islands Rail; Mangare rail. Buller (1905) considered this almost certainly extinct. **1950** ed. note to **1905** CHUDLEIGH *Diary* 27 June (1950) 428 Saw a bird I never saw before. Nearly black... It looked like a platypus flying with penguins flippers only short and round, not long like a penguins. [1950 *Note*] Mangere (Chatham I.) rail.

(8) **marsh rail**. *marsh crake* (CRAKE a *Porzana pusilla affinis*).
1888 BULLER *Birds NZ* II. 103 (Marsh-rail)... *Native name.*—Koitareke. **1904** HUTTON & DRUMMOND *Animals NZ* 181 *The Marsh Rail.—Koitareki...* These solitary little birds live in flax swamps and hide themselves with much dexterity. **1917** WILLIAMS *Dict. Maori Lang.* 175 *Kotoreke..Porzana affinis*, marsh-rail. = *kareke*. **1928** *NZJST* IX. 188 Marsh-rail... A shy little bird which frequents swampy situations, being very seldom seen.

(9) **striped rail**. *Obs.* See *banded rail* (2) above.
1871 HUTTON *Catalogue Birds NZ* 32 Rallus Pectoralis... Striped Rail. Mohopereru. **1886** *TrNZI* XVIII. 127 *Rallus philippensis...* Striped Rail. **1904** *NZ Illustr. Mag.* Oct. 39 A medium-sized footprint..shows where a striped rail has been fossicking for tit-bits. **1966** FALLA et al. *Birds NZ* 104 Banded Rail... Landrail, Striped Rail, Mohopereru, Mioweka.

(10) **swamp** (or **sooty**) **rail**. See *spotless crake* (CRAKE b *Porzana tabuensis plumbea*). See also PUWETO.
1888 BULLER *Birds NZ* II. 101 Ortygometra tabuensis. (Swamp-rail)... Pueto and Putoto. **1904** HUTTON & DRUMMOND *Animals NZ* 182 *The Swamp Rail.—Putoto...* The Swamp Rail also frequents swampy places, especially raupo swamps. **1917** WILLIAMS *Dict. Maori Lang.* 187 *Kuweto..Porzana tabuensis*, swamp-rail; a bird. = *puweto.* **1927** GUTHRIE-SMITH *Birds* 77 In the wet, undrained lands round about the lake are to be found..the Swamp Rail and the Marsh Rail. **1952** RICHARDS *Chatham Is.* 79 *P[orzana] tabuensis..*Swamp Rail. Putoto. **1966** FALLA et al. *Birds NZ* 105 Spotless Crake... Sooty Rail, Putoto, Puweto.

rain, v. In the phr. **rain Duke Georges, rain like a drunken dog**, to rain heavily.
1938 SCANLAN *Guest of Life* 339 She says it's raining Duke Georges in Wellington. **1950** SCANLAN *Confidence Corner* 14 It's going to rain Duke Georges if you ask me. **1988** MCGILL *Dict. Kiwi Slang* 91 *raining like a drunken dog* raining heavily; variant on 'raining cats and dogs'.

rainbird. [AND 1827.] Any of several birds thought to augur rain, including the *grey warbler* (WARBLER 2 (3)), *mottled petrel* (PETREL 2 (16)), PAKAHA (or *fluttering shearwater*, SHEARWATER 2 (3)), and *shining cuckoo* (CUCKOO 2 (3)). See also HAKOAKOA 1, LAUGHING JACKASS.
1871 HUTTON *Catalogue Birds NZ* 45 Puffinus gavius... Rain-bird or Wet-bird. **1888** [see PAKAHA]. **1892** KELLY *Journey Upper Waitara Valley* 7 In the early morning the notes of solitary tuis are heard, and later on the cheerful warble of the rerorero (the rain bird). **1904** *TrNZI* XXXVI. 134 Like the Cuckoos in other parts of the world, [shining cuckoos] appear before rainy weather or coincident with it, and have thus come to be known in many widely different localities as 'Rain-birds' and 'Storm-birds'. **1904** HUTTON & DRUMMOND *Animals NZ* 249 *The Rain Bird. Oestrelata inexpectata* [mottled petrel]... It is known as the Rain Bird in many places, as it is often heard at night calling as it flies to the sea; and in New Zealand rain often falls in the night. **c1920** BEATTIE *Trad. Lifeways Southern Maori* (1994) 167 The Rainbird, a kind of petrel with a very harsh screech before rain, was called karae. **1937** MOORE *Reminiscences* (ATLTS) Letter 3. Riroriro or Rainbird, the only true song bird in New Zealand. **1948** MONCRIEFF *NZ Birds* 42 Rainbird (or mottled petrel)... Flight rapid and erratic... Like other Petrels calls at night before rain, hence name. Horrible scream. **1955** [see PETREL 2 (16)]. **1968** *Listener* 15 Mar. 6 *Screech!* went the rainbird, not really meaning it. **1985** [see PETREL 2 (16)]. **1986** HULME *Windeater* 119 I hear them singing in the hills, *kui kui kui, whiti whiti ora.* Rainbirds. I used to think, O hell, rain coming.

rainbow.
Used *attrib.* in special Comb. **rainbow cake**, a plain cake with multicoloured layers and (often) coloured icing; **rainbow-fish**, *Suezichthys arquatus* (fam. Labridae), a small highly-coloured, slender wrasse having several colour phases.
1901 *NZ Ilustr. Mag.* IV. 855 **Rainbow cake**. **1926** *NZ Observer* 6 Mar. 22 Rainbow Cake... Divide the mixture into three parts... As ordinary tins are not big enough, as the cake rises very high, cut the bottoms off three petrol tins, leaving them with sides about 3 ins. high. **1948** FINLAY *Dunedin City Gas Dept. Cookery Book* 120 Rainbow Cake... Divide mixture into 3 parts. Flavour 1st with teaspoon grated lemon rind. Flavour 2nd with teaspoon orange rind, and colour pink with cochineal... Add to the 3rd 1 dessertspoon cocoa... Fasten together with lemon honey, and ice all over with chocolate icing. **1968** BASHAM *Aunt Daisy Cookbook* 99 Rainbow Cake... Divide into three lots. Make one pink; leave one plain; and add 1 dessertspoon cocoa or allspice to the next. Cook in three tins and stick together with jam. **1972** DOAK *Fishes* 94 A male **rainbow fish**..approached a female, spread his median fins slightly, and undulated horizontally alongside the female. **1982** AYLING *Collins Guide* (1984) 260 *Rainbow-Fish Suezichthys* sp. 2 (*Halichoeres* sp.)... The rainbow fish is closely related to the crimson cleaner but is even more colourful... All the colours of the rainbow are incorporated into the colour pattern of this species but these bright colours do not show up fully unless the fish is taken out of the water. **1988** FRANCIS *Coastal Fishes* 44 Rainbowfish *Suezichthys arquatus...* Rainbowfish appear to form stable male-female pairs which are home-ranging.

rajah. An erection, a tumescent penis.
c1941 *rajah* for erection freq. used at St Patrick's College (Silverstream) (Ed.). **1988** MCGILL *Dict. Kiwi Slang* 91 *rajah* tumescent penis; eg 'Boy, the moment she came into the room I could feel this gi-normous rajah coming on.'

rakau. Also **rakkoo**. [Ma. /'ra:kau/: Williams 321 *Rākau. 1.* Tree... *2.* Wood, timber... *3.* Stick, spar, mast.] Wood; spar, 'flagstaff'.
[**c1826–27** BOULTBEE *Journal* (1986) 111 wood— ràkkoo.] **1858** *Richmond-Atkinson Papers* 10 May (1960) I. 396 The fighting ought to be stopped at once by our Govt. (not by Potatau), who as our natives working here tell me is but a 'rakau' (flagstaff). **1863** MANING *Old NZ* 225 Kawiti, who is himself a *tohunga*, throws a *rakau* for his own path. **1943** BENNETT *English in NZ* in *Amer. Speech* XVIII. 93 *rakau,* wood; *wahine,* woman; [etc]

ram.

1. [f. *ram* a male sheep.] Special Comb. **ram-paddock** [AND 1882], a farm paddock reserved for rams.
1857 PAUL *Lett. from Canterbury* 90 [Make] a horse-paddock, ram-paddock,..oats or wheat-paddock, and a good, permanent washing-place. **1868** *Puketoi Station Diary* (Hocken TS) 20 Aug. George & Bill began rampaddock [*sic*] fence. **1900** *TrNZI* XXXII. 282 Rams, when the season is off..if fences allow, will come to the gate of the ram-paddock as to their proper home. **1921** GUTHRIE-SMITH *Tutira* (1926) 384 Then again, at the very suggestion, say, of..utilisation of the ram paddock for an aviary, not one of his friends..but would go back on him. **1953** SCOTT *Breakfast at Six* 17 This is the ram paddock... I don't go in for fat lambs right through. Like to breed my own ewe-hoggets.

2. *Canterbury Hist.* In transf. use (not otherwise recorded), homosexuality.
1980 ELDRED-GRIGG *Southern Gentry* 52 On the wool stations women were hard to find, so that

RAMARAMA

consolations were homosexuality (known in [19th cent.] Canterbury as 'ram') and grog.

3. *Obs.* A greeting among males.

  1952 *Landfall* 23 208 Among young people greetings like 'Hophead', 'Ram', 'Burglar', 'Sheik', 'Stopout', are accepted as flattery: 'burglar' I heard only in the army.

ramarama. Also **ramiram**, **rum-a-rum**, **rummy-rum**. [Ma. /ˈramarama/: Williams 322 *ramarama*..2... *Myrtus bullata*.] *Lophomyrtus* (formerly *Myrtus*) *bullata* (fam. Myrtaceae), a native shrub or small tree of coastal and lowland forest, distinguished by its bubbly-surfaced leaves. Often *attrib*. See also *New Zealand myrtle* (MYRTLE, esp. b).

  [**1820** LEE & KENDALL *NZ Gram. & Vocab.* 199 *Ráma ráma*; A shrub so called.] **1848** TAYLOR *Leaf from Nat. Hist.* 93 Nat. Ord. Myrtaceae. *Ramarama, Rohutu, New Zealand Myrtle.* **1851** *Richmond-Atkinson Papers* 15 Jan. (1960) I. 97 The ramiram for ramming in the posts in fencing [in Taranaki]. **1853** HOOKER *II Flora Novae-Zelandiae I Flowering Plants* 71 *Myrtus bullata*... Nat. name, 'Rama-Rama'... An erect shrub or small tree, 10–15 feet. **1882** HAY *Brighter Britain* II. 196 The Rama-rama..has a good hard wood, but is small. **1890** *PWD Catalogue Timbers* (NZ & South Seas Exhib.) 13 Ramarama...Timber reddish brown, hard, tough, and often prettily figured. **1910** [see MYRTLE b]. **1927** GUTHRIE-SMITH *Birds* 2 The limestone range east of the lake [Tutira] at one time grew..a considerable area of..kowhai, fuchsia, rama rama. **1949** SARGESON *I Saw in My Dream* (1974) 273 rummy-rum: (ramarama) a native running plant..'a bundle is springy..: some call it micky-mick'. [Sargeson appears to be confusing *ramarama* with *miki-miki* and both with a climber or creeper.] **1966** [see MYRTLE b]. **1970** JOHNSON *Life's Vagaries* 16 During the warm months there was a long season for koninis..then..the ramarama berries (Myrtaceae) were ripe. **1981** BROOKER et al. *NZ Medicinal Plants* 72 Common name: *Native myrtle* Maori name: *Ramarama*... It was known as *Myrtus bullata*.

ramshorn shell. Also **ram's-horn shell**. The internal shell of a small deepwater squid, *Spirula spirula* (fam. Spirulidae).

  1924 BUCKNILL *Sea Shells NZ* 116 The Ram's Horn shell. These exceedingly fragile white shells are occasionally thrown up on the beach in great numbers, but the animal itself is extremely rare. **1937** POWELL *Shellfish NZ* 50 Most visitors to our West Coast will recognise the ram's-horn shell, *Spirula spirula*, a small, flat, open, spiral white shell about an inch in length. **1947** POWELL *Native Animals NZ* 32 Rams Horn Shell (*Spirula spirula*). This is the white openly coiled shell about an inch long, which washes ashore in great numbers on our West Coast beaches. **1968** MORTON & MILLER *NZ Sea Shore* 472 Coming in with the flotsam we shall find the small rams-horn shells of the squid *Spirula*, washed ashore in their thousands. **1970** SANSOM *Stewart Islanders* 186 Ramshorn shells, the spirula, the internal shells of a small squid and coiled like a watchspring but papery-looking, lie..among the 'violets' [*sc*. sea-snails].

ranchslider. A glassed sliding door opening onto an outside space or patio.

  1980 MANTELL *Murder Or Three* 169 Smart looked once at Danny, remote on his humpty by the ranchsliders then he pulled a rocker closer to his wife's wing chair. **1989** *Property Press* 23 Mar. in *Listener* 22 Apr. (1989) 5 Tidy 3-bedroom brick home, private section. Ranchsliders open from lounge, double garage plus games room. **1990** O'SULLIVAN *Snow in Spain* 38 Several other friends moved through the open ranch-slider doors, between the wide handsome living-room and the patio.

Ranfurly Shield: see SHIELD 1 a.

rangatera, var. RANGATIRA.

rangatira, *n.* and *a.* Also with much variety of early form as **etan-ga-teda** (=he rangatira), **rangatera**, **rangitira** (a freq. modern error), **rangiterer**, early **rungateeda**. [Ma. /ˈraŋatira/: Williams 323 *Rangatira. 1*...Chief, male or female... *2*. Master or mistress... *3*. Person of good breeding.] A chief or noble person; commonly used by English speakers for people of recognized importance or mana.

A. *n.*

1. In Maori contexts. **a.** A high-born Maori; one of superior rank.

  [**1804** *Collins Eng. Colony in NSW* 344 Etan-ga-teda Epodi, a subordinate chief or gentleman.] **1817** NICHOLAS *Voyage NZ* I. 227 He assisted us..but reflecting at intervals on the rank he held among his countrymen, which was that of a *rungateeda*, or gentleman, he would several times shake his head, and cry out against this indignity. **1823** CRUISE *Journal* 26 Apr. (1957) 87 Saying, 'that if it were the child of a *rungateeda*, or gentleman, it should be laid in tabbooed ground.' **1830** CRAIK *New Zealanders* 204 Rungateeddas, or, as it has been more recently written, Rangatiras, which appears to answer nearly to the English term gentry. **1840** *NZ Jrnl.* I. 80 I have said the captains of companies should consist *for the most part*, of native chiefs, and my reason for having some British officers among the captains and lieutenants is, to establish a perfect equality between the English gentleman and the New Zealand *rangatira*. **1863** MANING *Old NZ* viii 120 The fighting men and petty chiefs, and everyone indeed who could by any means claim the title of *rangatira*—which in the sense now used it means gentlemen—were..possessed of this mysterious quality. **1893** *Otago Witness* (Dunedin) 21 Dec. 11 Te Kooti is at Puketapu with many Rangatiras. **1905** BAUCKE *White Man Treads* 216 She was a rangatira's daughter when Te Rauparaha took her with others prisoner to Kapiti. **1929** DUGGAN *NZ Bird Songs* 13 They say that in the old days stately rangatiras Slit his [*sc*. tui's] tongue, and made him speak instead of sing. **1943** MARSH *Colour Scheme* 37 'I am a *rangitira*. My father attended an ancient school of learning...,' said Rua. **1964** FRANCES *Johnny Rapana* 2 He was a rangatira and, above a chief, he was a tohunga pouwhiro, high priest and teacher.

b. Used to or of a pakeha, a leading citizen.

  1863 MANING *Old NZ* i 6 The chief also, having made some enquiries..—such as, whether I was a *rangatira*..gave me a most sincere welcome. **1881** CAMPBELL *Poenamo* 141 The two Pakehas who had come to live with them were Rangatiras. **1938** *Labour pamphlet for Northern Maori* in Gustafson *Cradle to Grave* (1986) [facing 232] Today it is our Rangatira Savage who is fishing up this Maoriland of ours from the gloom and slime of depression.

2. In non-Maori contexts, a person of importance in the community.

  1840 MATHEW *Journal* 14 Mar. in *Founding of NZ* (1940) 80 I first visited a native Pah..and I made myself known to them as a Rangatira or chief in the service of Her Majesty. **1842** RETTER in Manson *I Take up My Pen* (1971) 27 There is not many days but some of our rangiterers are walked to jail for debt. I hope I shall soon be a rangiterer but not go to jail. **1918** *Featherston Camp Weekly* 19 Oct. 17 The 'officer' was a mere man wearing the coat of the rangatira. **1941** BAKER *NZ Slang*

RANGATIRATANGA

59 *rangatira*, a leading citizen, a magistrate (taken directly from the Maori), in very early use. **1964** DAVIS *Watersiders* 36 The big rangatira standing by him's the meat inspector.

B. *adj.*

1. High-born; of superior rank.

  1845 WAKEFIELD *Adventure NZ* I. 173 I took care to tell them that the rangatira, or 'chief' missionaries, would come out with the settlers. **1847** ANGAS *Savage Life* II. 85 The grace and gentle bashfulness of this *rangatira* damsel were in strong contrast with the coarse and rude appearance of the half-clad slaves. **1887** *Auckland Weekly News* 12 Mar. 22 There are many of these rangatira landlords, who have leased large blocks of first-class land at a good figure. **1935** MAXWELL *Recollections* 120 Many writers have..failed to..recognise the great difference between the chieftain, or rangatira, class, and the ordinary, let alone the slave class. **1935** *Na To Hoa Aroha* (1988) III. 200 Te Puea says that the family are convinced that Rugby is the rangatira code, and the one on which the elect of all the tribes can meet in friendly contest. **1984** *Te Maori* 155 Some aptitude for carving was expected of all men of rangatira status.

2. Comb. **rangatira girl**, a high-born Maori woman or girl; **rangatira pakeha**, a European of importance; **rangatira wahine**, a high-born Maori woman.

  1958 MILLER *Early Victorian NZ* 141 The native women often welcome the squatters with bouquets of flowers and became very attached to their young men. The high-born **Rangitira** [*sic*] **girls** were sometimes richly beautiful. *Ibid.* 166 Always quick to imitate new fashions, the young Maoris would turn out for their own flat and hurdle races attired in true jockey style..while the attractive Rangatira girls also took to the saddle, equipped with gauntlets and silver whip, habit, hat and plume. **1863** MANING *Old NZ* 236 *Rangatira*—A chief, a gentleman, a warrior. **Rangatira pakeha**—A foreigner who is a gentleman (not a *tutua*, or nobody,...), a *rich* foreigner. **1881** CAMPBELL *Poenamo* 140 The excitement consequent upon our arrival, which extended through the whole tribe, was not simply because two Pakehas had arrived, but because they were two Rangatera Pakehas who had come to live amongst them. The ordinary Pakehas the natives had hitherto come in contact with had been for the most part runaway sailors. **1939** GRIEVE *Sketches from Maoriland* (1961) 46 And here was the *rangatira Pakeha* a whole day before his time. *Aue Aue.* **1948** HENDERSON *Taina* 134 I replied that I wanted to stay with..my father, who was a *rangatira pakeha*, just as my mother was a *rangatira* Maori. **1930** DOBSON *Reminiscences* 68 This good *whata* belonged to Purua, a **rangatira wahine**, who lived here with her servants.

rangatiratanga. Often with init. cap. [Ma. /ˈraŋatirataŋa/: Williams 323 *rangatiratanga*, n. Evidence of breeding and greatness.: f. *rangatira* + *-tanga* one of a number of suffixes forming abstract nouns from common nouns.] The state or quality of being (a) rangatira, or noble; chieftainship. Also as **tino rangatiratanga**, see quot. 1994.

  [**1837** *He Wakaputanga o te Rangatiratanga o Nu Tirene* [Title] in Williams *A Bibliography of Printed Maori* (1975) 7 **1840** *Treaty of Waitangi* in *Facsimiles of the Declaration of Independence and the Treaty of Waitangi* (1877) [unpaged 4] Ko te Kuini o Ingarani ka wakarite ka wakaae ki nga Rangatira, ki nga Hapu, ki nga tangata katoa o Nu Tirani, te tino Rangatiratanga o o ratou wenua o ratou kainga me o ratou taonga katoa.] **1858** GRACE *Letter* 24 Mar. in *Pioneer Missionary* (1928) 76 Sir George Grey when on his visit to Taupo saw the said [damaged] Pataka and told Te Heuheu (no doubt in a jocose way) that it was a sign of his 'Rangatiratanga'. **1946** *JPS* LV. 157 *rangatira*, a chief, male or female: *rangatiratanga*, evidence of breeding and greatness. **1989** *Principles for Crown Action on the Treaty of Waitangi* 7 The Principle of Self-Management. The Rangatiratanga Principle. The iwi have the right to organise as iwi, and, under the law, to control their resources as their own. *Ibid.* 11 The New Zealand Maori Council has explained the concept of Rangatiratanga as meaning more than 'possession': 'it means the wise administration of all the assets possessed by a group for that group's benefit: in a word, trusteeship' (*Te Wahanga Tuatahi*, 1983, p 5). In the Crown's view, the First and Second Articles of the Treaty are both strong statements which necessarily qualify one another. *Kawanatanga* is subject to a promise to protect *Rangatiratanga*. *Rangatiratanga* is subject to an acknowledgment of *Kawanatanga*. **1994** *Landfall* 188 313 This would lead to a conclusion that Ngai Tahu *rangatiratanga* over these lands was secure. **1994** *Evening Post* (Wellington) 21 May 11 The [Conservation Authority] document..aims to initiate a public debate on the degree of power given to iwi—possibly developing a new mechanism recognising the balance between tino rangatiratanga (rights of autonomous self-regulation) and kawanatanga (Government powers and systems).

range, *n.* Usu. *pl.* [Spec. use of *range* a line of mountains: see OED 2 c; AND 1805.]

1. a. Often as **the ranges**, mountainous or high country not necessarily forming a single divide.
1843 *Jrnl. Roy. Geogr. Soc.* XIII. 184 The pass through which he [*sc.* Mr Cotterell] gained the Wairoo from the Wairoa does not appear really to cross the principal mountain range. **1855** *Austral. & NZ Gaz.* 27 Jan. 88 The land between the Inch Clutha and these ranges..is laid off in sections extending 16 miles from the coast. **1864** CHUDLEIGH *Diary* 4 Oct. (1950) 146 The others went down the sides of the ranges, clearing the sheep off as they went. **1864** *Gold Digger's Notes* (1950) 50 We carried home the boar..—a long tramp over the ranges. **1874** KENNAWAY *Crusts* 135 While C., who had been on the ranges all day, was refitting himself..we killed it [*sc.* a sheep] by starlight. **1882** HAY *Brighter Britain* II. 11 The logs are easily collected.., as they can be sent down the sides of ranges by means of screw-jacks, rollers and slides. **1894** *Richmond-Atkinson Papers* 22 Mar. (1960) II. 597 He has had a rough time of it surveying a block on the ranges up the Wai-o-hine in the Wairarapa. **1938** HYDE *Nor Yrs. Condemn* 126 It was a good life on the hydro. Men dragged home quarters of deer from the ranges to fill the cook-pots. **1952** *Here & Now* Mar. 27 Willie and his old man were panning for uranium in the ranges at the time. **1960** MASTERS *Back-Country Tales* 57 Deer were then starting to, and have now become, something of a problem in our range country. **1987** VIRTUE *Redemption of Elsdon Bird* (1988) 34 The hills were called the Ranges. The Ranges spread along the skyline all the way to Wellington.

b. As **dividing range**, a range forming a divide between two watersheds.
1848 WAKEFIELD *Handbook NZ* 88 East of the dividing range lies an extensive plain, or series of plains. **1863** PYKE *Report* in *Handbook NZ Mines* (1887) 8 Contiguous to [Moa] creek there is a large extent of auriferous country, bordering on the Nokomai, and extending over the dividing-range through the valley of the Nevis to the Kawarau River. **1872** *TrNZI* IV. 10 [These sounds] reach far into the wild solitudes of the lofty mountains which form the *cordillera*, or 'dividing range', of the Middle Island. **1949** REED *Story of Canterbury* 246 After cutting a track for forty miles over the great dividing range down to the Taramakau River, they struck across to Lake Brunner, where they pitched their camp.

c. As **main range** [OED *main a.* 11 'Austral. and N.Z.', 1888], the principal ridge of a chain of mountains. See also *Main Divide* (DIVIDE b).
1950 *NZJAg.* Jan. LXXX. 19 The barren and unproductive land consists of bare mountain tops, and native bush areas on the slopes of the main ranges. **1952** PASCOE *Land Uplifted High* 25 An unusual exercise..was to cross over the tops of the main range in the dark. **1971** *Listener* 19 Apr. 56 A *main range* is the major backbone of any individual group of mountains.

2. In the phr. **over the range(s)**, across the mountains or hills; occas. on the other side of a tract of mountainous country.
1848 TORLESSE *Papers* (1958) 16 Dec. 40 Accompanied by Rhodes..walked over the ranges to the bay..called Terape [near the future Christchurch]. **1872** BUTLER *Erewhon or Over the Range* [Title] **1922** COWAN *NZ Wars* (1955) I. 303 [In February 1864] he succeeded in getting commissariat through to the troops..by rapidly cutting a pack-track from Raglan Harbour over the ranges to the Waipa. **1930** PINFOLD *Fifty Yrs. Maoriland* 65 Many times has the pioneer worker gone on foot from Coromandel over the 'range' to Mercury Bay. **1986** RICHARDS *Off the Sheep's Back* 6 During the early days..the only access to Waihi was by bridle track over the range.

3. Special Comb. **range gum**, kauri gum found in the soil, see GUM *n.* 2.

range, *v.* As **range up**, of a racehorse, runner etc., to come up within range, or level with, another.
1929 *Evening Post* (Wellington) 16 Sept. 6 Laughing Prince went up to Admiral Drake, and Vertigern also ranged up. **1939** *Taranaki Herald* (New Plymouth) 31 Aug. 24 Ranging up on the outside, Autosweep won going away from Eupatrid. **1959** *Landfall* 50 135 At the turn it was the same except that..Royal Return had ranged up on the outside of Conformist. **1991** *Radio NZ Sporting Annual* 31 Peter Johnson on Flying Luskin ranged alongside ensuring Horlicks went back behind those ahead.

Ranger, *n.*[1] *Hist.* Usu. init. cap. [Spec. use of *ranger* one of a body of armed militia employed in ranging over country: see OED 3 *pl.* 'Chiefly U.S.'.] In the New Zealand Wars, a short form of FOREST RANGER *n.*[1], a volunteer citizen militiaman; as *pl.* the body of troops formed from such volunteers. Cf. BUSHRANGER *n.*[1] 2.
1879 FEATON *Waikato War* 72 Captain Jackson's Forest Rangers... The Rangers had the most perilous duty to perform. If the troops advanced, the Rangers scoured the country in front. **1879** GUDGEON *Reminisc. War in NZ* 17 The rangers and the militia were also present. **1922** COWAN *NZ Wars* (1955) I. 266 The Rangers' arms were..in Von Tempsky's company, a bowie knife with a blade 10 inches or 12 inches long... 'We find them long enough to reach our enemies with,' so the Rangers could have said of their bush-knives. **1935** COWAN *Hero Stories NZ* 234 The patient Colonel probably did not venture to inform his wife that the Rangers preferred their bush-ranging costume, and would not wear trousers if they had them—on active service at any rate.

ranger, *n.*[2] *Obs.* [AND 1817.] Short form of BUSHRANGER *n.*[2] 1.
1878 ELWELL *Boy Colonists* 221 When we saw the troopers coming..we thought they were the rangers.

ranger, *n.*[3] [Spec. use of *ranger* forest officer, gamekeeper, warden of a park: see OED *n.*[1] 2.]

1. a. *Hist.* Earlier **Crown (Lands) ranger**. A State official or field officer supervising Crown land in the public domain.
1841 *Hobson Despatch* 4 Aug. in *GBPP House of Commons 1843 (No.134)* 3 Superintendent of the Government Domain — [£]136 17 6 Ranger, at 4*s.* 6*d* per diem. **1899** *AJHR* C-1 22 The work done by the Crown Lands Rangers, whose manifold duties comprise inspecting settlement holdings, reporting on transfers, applications for leases of Crown lands, reserves..&c., resuming possession of forfeited holdings, inspecting pastoral runs, and watching over the preservation of bush lands, &c., can only be very imperfectly indicated in any tabular statements. **1902** *Settler's Handbook NZ* 180 *Crown rangers*.—These officers are appointed by the Governor. Under the Commissioners they watch over the provisions of the Land Act, laying informations against offenders, examining and reporting as to the fulfilment of the various conditions under the various leases; they are, in fact, the eyes of the Land Board, and they have the right of entry upon all properties and of answer from the occupiers to reasonable questions. **1908** STEWART *My Simple Life* 48 [1880 Kati Kati] The Crown Lands Ranger called again, expressed himself much pleased with our improvements. **1913** *AJHR* C-12 10 You are the Crown Lands Ranger for Otago?—Yes. **1948** SCOTTER *Run Estate & Farm* 57 He was one of three Otago Crown land rangers whose chief duty was the inspection of the estates to see that lessees and purchasers of Crown lands adhered to the conditions of lease or sale. **1985** HUNT *I'm Ninety-five* 249 He was a ranger for the Departments of Lands and Survey, Forestry and Internal Affairs for thirty-four years. **1994** ARNOLD *New Zealand's Burning* 153 The Crown Land Ranger often became a friend and mentor of the settlers [in 1880s Taranaki].

b. In full **National Park ranger**. A State official supervising National Parks.
1935 ODELL *Handbook Arthur's Pass National Park* 18 There are a number of Honorary Rangers, whose function is to safeguard the scenery and report any breaches of the by-laws and regulations governing the Park. **1938** HYDE *Nor Yrs. Condemn* 153 'You want to be careful of the ranger, young fellow. He nurses these trees like a mother [to an English new chum wanting to cut firewood]. **1966** *Weekly News* 3 Aug. 7 Fiordland's chief ranger..emphasises that the authority's huts are 'spartan'. **1973** in FINLAYSON *Brown Man's Burden* 136 [1973 *Note*] The rangers are men employed by the government to take care of national parks and reserves and see the laws that pertain to them are observed.

2. Also occas. **county ranger**. [Local use of (mainly) US *ranger*: see OED *ranger*[1] 2 b.] A local official appointed to impound wandering stock or domestic animals (esp. dogs).
1880 *Tuapeka Times* 15 Dec. in Marks *Hammer & Tap* (1977) 307 On 15 December 1880, the *Tuapeka Times* reported Matheson's death from heart failure. 'The appointment of Ranger seemed to bring with it too much excitement for his naturally excitable temperament and he gave way to drink. **1885** *NZ Statutes* No.30 77 [NZ State Trusts Act] Any ranger.. may drive any cattle or other animal..to the nearest public pound. **1925** WEBB *Miss Peters' Special* 47 One of them was the county ranger, and in pursuance of his business of impounding straying stock he rode upon an aged bay horse. *Ibid.* 51 The ranger's got the cow.

3. An honorary or paid official of an Acclimatisation Society appointed to regulate the taking of protected fish or game.
1902 *Settler's Handbook NZ* 140 [Animals Protection Act] *Administration*.—The law is worked by the acclimatisation societies, who usually recommend the appointment of the rangers. The latter

RANGIORA

are appointed by the Governor, and have the same power as constables of seizing game, guns, nets, &c. **1925** MANDER *Allen Adair* (1971) 54 He saw a man coming towards him... He too had a gun and a dog. 'Had any luck?' asked Allen as they came together. 'Only a brace [of pheasants]. You're not the ranger, are you?' 'Lord no,' smiled Allen... 'Good. I haven't got a licence.' **1938** HYDE *Godwits Fly* (1970) 89 Boy Scouts caught the trout and..stuffed them into their shirts so that the Ranger would not see. **1943** HISLOP *Pure Gold* 23 To add further to my unpleasant surprise [in spearing a trout]..the ranger was on top of the bank getting an eyeful of fun at my expense. **1961** MACKAY *Puborama* 83 'Well..'tis the way them poachers have been at it [*sc.* trout-poaching] again..' 'Isn't there a ranger about?' 'Ranger?.. he's too busy puttin' out little fish without worryin' about big 'uns.' **1964** DAVIS *Watersiders* 112 The duckshooting season was open, but Blue had neglected to purchase a licence. This made it somewhat embarrassing for him when he bumped into a ranger along the track. **1982** BREAM *Island of Fear* 56 The ranger lives at Shingle Bay too, and old Ernie was constantly in trouble with him. You know it's illegal to take the rock oysters?

4. Also **forest ranger**. The occupational title given to a forest manager in the former New Zealand Forest Service.

1902 *Settler's Handbook NZ* 115 In 1876 a Forest Department was created, forest legislation passed, and many timber reserves were made. Within these the department was supreme. It was under a Chief Conservator of Forests..and a staff of conservators and rangers. **1908** *AJHR C-1* 22 In this district the services of Rangers and Surveyors were requisitioned. **1958** *NZ Timber Jrnl.* May 56 *Ranger*: A forest officer responsible for the organised work of the forest. **1992** BOYD *Pumice & Pines* 131 Amongst the wives of foresters and rangers I made many firm friends.

Hence **rangership**, the official position or status of a ranger under various authorities; **ranging** *ppl. a.*

1905 BAUCKE *White Man Treads* 303 But there can be no finality to a system of inspector, valuer, and rangerships; where coercion is juxtaposed to base compliance. **1983** FRANCIS *Wildlife Ranger* 6 Without the past years of stock farming, horse riding..I could not have coped with the varied ranging duties, which were the first step towards my becoming New Zealand's first Wildlife Oficer.

rangiora. [Ma. /'raŋiora/: Williams 324 *Rangiora..1. Brachyglottis repanda.*] *Brachyglottis repanda* (fam. Asteraceae), a shrub or small tree having fragrant flowers and leaves with white hairy undersides. See also *paper-leaf* (PAPER 2), PUKAPUKA 1.

1867 HOOKER *Handbook* 767 Rangiora, *Col[enso]. Brachyglottis repanda.* **1906** CHEESEMAN *Manual NZ Flora* 367 B[*rachyglottis*] *rangiora*... Rangiora. **1921** GUTHRIE-SMITH *Tutira* (1926) 51 Later, appeared slender matapo [*sic*]..and rangiora. **1934** *Tararua Tramper* Dec. 3 The Tauherenikau..look[s] very beautiful with the sweet-scented rangiora and heketara in bloom. **1940** LAING & BLACKWELL *Plants NZ* 472 Plants of this genus [*Brachyglottis*] are well-known to the Maoris, under the name *Rangiora*. The leaves were much used by them for application to wounds and old sores. **1959** MASTERS *Tales of Mails* 68 On one occasion the buggy horses were tethered to some rangiora bushes... They had a good old feed of leaves from the bushes, which, of course caused them to become intoxicated. **1966** *Encycl. NZ* II. 785 Gums and resins for..[chewing gums] were obtained from kauri..rangiora..and wharangi. **1988** DAWSON *Forest Vines to Snow Tussocks* 103 The familiar large-leaved rangiora (*Brachyglottis repanda*). **1992** FARRELL *Skinny Louie Book* 273 She takes a rangiora leaf and wipes Tia's watery eyes.

Rangitata goose. [Ma. /raŋi'ta:ta:/: f. *Rangitata* the name of a river and district in Canterbury favoured by the bird.] A local name for the *paradise duck* (DUCK 2 (6)).

1966 FALLA et al. *Birds NZ* 87 Paradise Duck *Tadorna variegata...* Putangitangi, Rangitata Goose.

rangitira, var. RANGATIRA.

Rangitoto yank. Also **Rangitoto yankee.** [Ma. /'raŋitoto/: f. *Rangitoto*, the name of an island in Auckland's Waitemata harbour.] A non-Auckland nickname for Aucklanders perceived as brash loudmouths.

1984 p.c. David More (Waihi). The Rangitoto Yanks.—S. Island name for Aucklanders, c1960–70 **1985** MCGILL *G'day Country* 49 'Do you know what they call us in Wellington?' Dad asked on the way. 'What?' 'Rangitoto Yankees.' I had never heard it, but I figured it was a small price..to pay for what Dad reckons is Paradise. **1987** *Metro* (Auckland) May 66 The rest of New Zealand has always hated Auckland and Aucklanders, seeing us variously as parasites and 'Rangitoto Yanks'. **1992** *Ibid.* Oct. 56 Not for me a bout of fisticuffs when provoked by the natives of Canterbury bleating, 'Our power keeps you Rangitoto yanks afloat'.

ranguru. [Poss. a Chatham Island Maori name; or an altered shortened form of Ma. /pa:'ŋuruŋuru/: Williams 258 *pāngurunguru*... A dark-coloured species of petrel.] *Chatham petrel* (PETREL 2 (5)).

1955 OLIVER *NZ Birds* 149 *Chatham Island Petrel. Ranguru Pterodroma axillaris* This species was discovered by Hawkins on South-east Island, Chatham group, in 1892, and was described by Salvin the following year. Only a few specimens have since been obtained. **1966** FALLA et al. *Birds NZ* 52 Chatham Island Petrel *Pterodroma axillaris* Maori name: Ranguru. **1970** *Annot. Checklist Birds NZ* (1980) 24 [*Pterodroma axillaris*] (Salvin, 1893) *Chatham Island Petrel* (*Ranguru*). **1985** *Reader's Digest Book NZ Birds* 81 Chatham Island Petrel *Pterodroma axillaris* Other name: *Ranguru*... Fewer than 20 specimens of this rare petrel have been banded.

raòoroo, var. RAWARU.

raoriki, var. RAURIKI.

raoui, var. RAHUI.

rapeoo, rapo(o), rapou, rappoo, rapu, varr. RAUPO.

rapt, *a.* [A narrowed use of *rapt* enthralled, enraptured (with a person or thing): AND 1963.] Very pleased.

1985 JONES *Gilmore's Dairy* 206 Aw, I hoped so. Terry'll be rapt. **1990** *Dominion* (Wellington) 26 Jan. 14 Anderson..was rapt to have won his opening bout..on a unanimous points decision. **1991** *Ibid.* 8 Aug. 1 The New Zealand-born chief executive of Avaiki Air..said yesterday Ms Evans was on her first day at work. 'She was rapt out of her brain with her new job.'

rapu, var. RAUPO.

rare as hen's teeth: see HEN 3 a.

RAT

rari, *n.*[1] Also early **rádi, rarii.** [Ma. /ra'ri:/: Williams 327 *Rarī* (ii)..butterfish.] BUTTERFISH 1. Cf. MARARI.

[**1820** LEE & KENDALL *NZ Gram. & Vocab.* 198 *Rádi, s.* A fish so called.] **1908** HAMILTON *Fishing & Sea-Foods* 64 With the following results:..a few snapper and kahawai; hundreds of red cod and rarii. **1967** MORELAND *Marine Fishes* 28 The term greenbone is widely used in southern waters... The Maori names marari, and rari are seldom used. **1981** WILSON *Fisherman's Bible* 33 Kelp-fish and Kelpie are names sometimes used [for the butterfish] as are the Maori names 'marari' and 'rari'.

rari, *n.*[2] ?*Obs.* [Not recorded in Williams but prob. related to Williams 56 *Hokarari.. Genypterus blacodes,* the ling.] LING.

1855 TAYLOR *Te Ika A Maui* 628 The *Rari*, a fish often found eight feet long, the body is large and tapers suddenly into a narrow tail, which is surrounded by a fin above and below, as that of the eel. **1886** SHERRIN *Handbook Fishes NZ* 304 *Genypterus blacodes*... Ling, or Rari.

rarii, var. RARI *n.*[1]

rarikis, var. RAURIKI.

Raro /'rarʌu/.

1. A shortened form of *Rarotongan*, occas. applied to any Pacific Islander; also in occas. use for the island of *Rarotonga*.

1918 *Kia-ora Coo-ee* (1981) 15 Aug. II. 14 In the Rarotongans, we have representatives of a race naturally endowed with song, and nothing pleases a New Zealand audience more than to secure items, wonderful in the harmonious blending of the part singing and most moving in vivid expression, from their doughty fellow soldiers and fellow-countrymen, the 'Raros'. **1978** DRYDEN *Out of the Red* 48 The story was typical of what I was to hear that week on Rarotonga... A day later I was to put the question to Mrs King as we filmed young Lisa riding round Raro on her bike. **1980** BERRY *First Offender* 42 The Islanders were Coconuts or Raros to the biased Maori. **1988** *Metro* (Auckland) Aug. 111 It began with the question, many months ago. 'Sir, will you organise a trip for us to Raro?' **1995** *Ibid.* June 26 Robert Budwig..flew in from Rarotonga..where he'd been busy drawing the coconut trees. *Moi* imagines there's little else to draw up in Raro.

2. A proprietary name for a former brand of (esp.) orange juice; also now for the powdered components of a fruit drink.

1992 FARRELL *Skinny Louie Book* 74 Could she have some Raro instead? **1995** COCHRANE *Tin Nimbus* 51 'Save me? From what?' 'From George bloody Thingme and his crypts. From Raro and meths on Sundays.'

rarzoo, var. RAZOO.

rat, *n.*

1. Also as **bush** (or **Maori, native, New Zealand, wild**) **rat**, the Polynesian rat *Rattus exulans* (fam. Muridae) introduced by the Maori; KIORE a.

1769 COOK *Journals* 29 Oct. (1955) I. 186 We saw no four footed Animals either tame or wild or signs of any except Dogs and Ratts and these were very scarce especialy [*sic*] the latter. **1821** *Evidence of Ensign McCrae before Commissioner Bigge* in McNab *Historical Records* (1908) I. 543 Q. Are there any quadrupeds in New Zealand, wild or tame? A. This [dog] and a species of small wild rat are the only quadrupeds. **1834** MARKHAM *NZ* (1963) 53 The Native

Rat was more like a field Mouse and was considered a Luxury in old times, but the Rat from Norway or England came and is called Rah Parkieah or Stranger rat. **1843** [see KIORE 1 b]. **1851** *Pap. Proc. Roy. Soc. Van Diemen's Land* I. 301 I have procured two specimens of the ancient, and all but quite extinct, New Zealand Rat. **1861** HAAST *Topographical Exploration of Nelson* 135 The native rat (Mus rattus) is the only known indigenous land quadruped; but..I was unable to find any. **1865** HURSTHOUSE *England's NZ War* 40 The Pakeha-Rat ate up the Maori-Rat. **1871** *TrNZI* III. 3 Relative to the New Zealand rat: I never possessed but one, and it hung up till it rotted away. **1885** *Wairarapa Daily* 17 July 2 The whole lot were, in probability, native rats, though they are supposed to have become extinct in the Wairarapa upwards of twenty years ago. **1891** *TrNZI* XXIII. 196 The tradition at that time among the Canterbury settlers was that the Maori rat was of a red colour. **1895** *Ibid.* XXVII. 258 [Title] *Arboreal Nests of Bush-rat* (Mus maorium). **1911** [see KIORE 1 a]. **1920** *TrNZI* LII. 56 My Maori friends were careful to explain that the Maori rat was an altogether different creature from the filthy-eating European rat. **1934** *Feilding Star* 10 Apr. 7 It was plain from earlier records that the native rat existed in hordes in the early days of the Maori in New Zealand. **1971** OGILVIE *Moonshine Country* 131 Other pioneers in the Opihi district [of Canterbury] refer to the abundance of native pigeons..and Maori rats—which were small, grey, fluffy, vegetarian and evidently succulent. **1986** DANIEL & BAKER *Collins Guide* 66 Polynesian Rat *Rattus exulans*... Kiore (Maori), Maori rat, native rat.

2. [AND 1855.] As **bush rat**, either of the European ship rats *Rattus rattus* and *R. norvegicus* (fam. Muridae) found in or associated with the bush.

1871 MONEY *Knocking About in NZ* 31 I smoked my evening pipe..by the light of a good bush-fire, that danced and flickered on the trees and scrub around me, and showed the only living animals that formed my society—grey bush rats. **1889** *TrNZI* XXI. 207 The bush-rats (Mus rattus)..depend for food..on the ripe berries falling from the trees. **1904** *NZ Illustrated Magazine* Nov. 109 [Caption] The Bush Rat is a noted Egg Stealer. **1914** PFAFF *Diggers' Story* 148 Two days after our arrival [at Hokitika in 1865] there was a flood..and bush rats were swimming in hundreds, to the fearsome delight of the youngsters. **1942** ANDERSEN *Maori Place Names* 285 The bush-rats are experts in extracting the kernels from the nuts [of the tawa]. **1950** WILSON *My First 80 Years* 107 All the bush rats I have seen in the King Country..were the ordinary grey vermin. **1967** ELLIOTT & ADSHEAD *Cowshed to Dog Collar* 16 Then came a plague of bush rats, huge brutes that were eaten by the moreporks. **1983** *Whakarewarewa Forest Park* 57 Black rats (also known as ship rats, roof rats, bush rats) differ from brown rats..in that they have longer, non-furry ears and tail and are smaller.

3. Special Comb. **rat-hunting**, hunting the kiore.

1872 *TrNZI* IV. 400 The Rev. Mr. Stack stated..that the maoris took great care to protect the plains from fire on account of..being their rat-hunting grounds.

4. In various phrases mainly connoting emotional excess or mental instability. **a.** In the phr. **give one rats** [AND 1894], to give one a scolding, to become angry with one.

1906 *Truth* 3 Nov. 5 The daughter, Mrs Atholwood, who has been only a few weeks over from Sydney said that she called on her dear father and gave him rats for not providing her mother with money, even for trams to the hospital three times a week.

b. In the phr. **to get (have) a rat** (occas. **in one's garret**) [AND 1898], to be or become eccentric, cracked; to have an obsession; (occas.) to become angry (cf. RATTY *a.* 'angry', RAT-HOUSE, a psychiatric hospital).

1904 LANCASTER *Sons o' Men* 135 Harry's whistle soared out of the darkness... 'He's got a pertickler rat to-night,' murmured Cressit... 'But though Harry's cuttin' th' soul out 'n hisself wi' that tune 't won't do him much comfort.' **1910** *Truth* 16 Apr. 1 His Worship: 'Was the accused sober?' Witness: 'Well, he looked muzzy.' His Worship: 'What do you mean by that?' Witness: 'He looked either drunk or a shingle short.' His Worship: 'A what?' Witness: 'A screw loose.' His Worship: 'I don't understand you.' Witness: 'He seemed to have a rat in his garret.' His Worship: 'Oh, speak English!' Witness: 'Off his dot—balmy [*sic*]—dilly.' Sergeant: 'He says the man was mad, your Worship.' Witness: 'No, I didn't. I said he was either drunk or ratty.' **1921** *Quick March* 11 July 15 The clever chap who wrote the epistle would have no hesitation in speaking to this effect: 'Dicken! I done me block right enough! I come home and the old finger hit the roof. Tike it from me, he's gotter rat.' **c1926** THE MIXER *Transport Workers' Song Book* 12 'Lend us a quid!' 'Lend you a what! Blime, have you got a rat?'

c. In the phr. **in the rats** [AND 1937], hallucinating through liquor, in the 'dingbats'.

1921 LORD *Ballads of Bung 'Stunology'* (1976) We say a man is... A 'ribald reveller', 'on the rag', or mayhap 'in the rats'.

d. In the phr. **like a rat up a drainpipe** [AND 1962], very quickly.

c1962 BAXTER *Horse* (1985) 15 'He's not a blacksmith's arsehole,' said a voice from the door... 'He's an old brown-hatter. Watch out, Tim. He'll be up you like a rat up a drainpipe.'

rat, *v.*

1. [AND 1898.] *trans.* and *intr.* To ransack or loot; to rob (someone); to steal property.

1906 *Truth* 4 Aug. 7 That night as the old man slept the reprobate son crept into his bedroom, 'ratted' the old man's pockets, and lit out for another glorious orgie. **1917** *Chron. NZEF* 27 Sept. 105 The chief pastime of the month has been 'ratting', otherwise known as salvaging. **1918** INGLIS in Boyack *Behind the Lines* (1989) 107 The same Maoris would show the gentle Hun points..when it comes to 'ratting a joint' which is the diggers expression for looting a house. **1937** LEE *Civilian into Soldier* (1937) 157 He saw a New Zealander stoop to rat a Hun who had lost his backside. *Ibid.* 194 There must be a lot of dead Huns to rat. **1962** HORI *Half-gallon Jar* 27 And old bluebeard had the plenty trouble to stop [them] ratting the cupboard for the small drop of plonk which he kept for the toothache. **1971** TAYLOR *Plekhov Place* 109 I made an instant soup with a pint of milk and ratted through Vic's medicine box until I found a sedative. **1986** DAVIN *Salamander & the Fire* 11 The shot echoed. He was dead... 'Did you rat him?' 'I forgot.' 'You're crazy. He might have had a Leica.'

Hence **rat** *n.*, ?a swindle.

1873 *Richmond-Atkinson Papers* 6 Apr. (1960) II. 347 We are now in the thick of the cross examinatn. by Sheehan of the chiefest of the apostles—Tizzey the Tanner (Ko Tanera)... We have not found anything that can be called a rat; nor even got the scent very strong.

2. As **rat on** [see OED 2 c 'rat on a contract', 1938], to abandon (lit. or *fig.*), to go back on.

1912 *Hutt Valley Independent* 14 Dec. 1 Rather than rat on his principles as some members did.

rata. Also with some variety of early form as **arata**, **e ratta**, (?=he rata), **lāhtah**, **rattah**, **ráttár**. [Ma. /'ra:ta:/: Williams 327 *Rātā*..1. *Metrosideros robusta*.]

I. As **rata**, a tree. **1.** *Metrosideros robusta* (fam. Myrtaceae), a tall tree (often called *northern rata*, see 2 (2) below), having attractive red flowers and a close-grained heavy timber; (*rarely*) the related *M. umbellata*, now usu. *southern rata* (see 2 (3) below); the wood of these trees. Also *attrib.* See also IRONWOOD a, MYRTLE c. Contrast *rata-vine* II below.

1771 PARKINSON *Journal* (1773) 40 E ratta, or e pooratta... This tree, or shrub, grows upon the Tooarao, or Lower Hills... The flowers are full of beautiful scarlet stamina. [**c1826–27** BOULTBEE *Journal* (1988) 110 Ironwood—lāhtah.] **1834** MCDONNELL *Extracts Jrnl.* (1979) 20 The ráttár is a beautiful, lofty, spreading tree; very hard, stringy, and tough; close-grained, and in appearance not unlike the live oak. **1835** YATE *NZ* (1970) 50 Rata... This is a fine and useful tree, producing a heavy, close-grained, durable red wood. **1851** *Lyttelton Times* 12 Apr. 8 Her timbers are of Picked Rata, and the said vessel is planked with the best Mai. **1867** BARKER *Station Life* (1870) 118 [We] were running right into what appeared to be a grove of rata-trees growing at the water's edge... When the bowsprit touched the rata-branches..H— made a signal to lower the mast. **1871** MONEY *Knocking About NZ* 54 The brilliant vermilion of rata blossoms relieving the varied green and yellow of the forest trees high above us. **1896** HARPER *Pioneer Work* 35 There is also the rata tree, the prince of firewoods. **1908** BAUGHAN *Shingle-Short* 54 Red-as-blood *Rata*, and bright-as-blood *Pohutukawa*. **1926** COWAN *Travel in NZ* II. 95 Up here on the [West Coast] mountain side the vegetation is the flowering *rata*. **1949** SARGESON *I Saw in My Dream* (1974) 119 Mr Anderson and Dave sat with their backs against the twisted barrel of a fallen rata. **1967** MCLATCHIE *Tang of Bush* 34 Rata, or 'Ironwood', so called because of its hardness, made a splash of crimson in summertime.

2. With a modifier: **mountain, northern, southern.**

(1) **mountain rata**. *Metrosideros umbellata* (formerly *M. lucida*), a tall tree with a habitat extending from sea level to approx. 1000 m. See also IRONWOOD, and *southern rata* (3) below.

1889 *TrNZI* XXI. 382 The lower portions [of the Auckland Islands] are usually covered with bush, which consists mostly of mountain rata (*Metrosideros lucida*), which grows to a height of 30ft. **1909** *AJHR* C-12 57 *Metrosideros lucida*. Rata. Ironwood, southern rata, mountain-rata. Forest, sub-alpine scrub. Principally in a belt near the shore, and in the upper forest and sub-alpine scrub. **a1927** ANTHONY *Gus Tomlins* (1977) 152 They said the timber we were amongst was all mountain rata, and very difficult to split.

(2) **northern rata**. *Metrosideros robusta*, as 1 above.

1875 KIRK *Durability NZ Timbers* 3 The Northern rata (*Metrosideros robusta*), when growing in moist places, produces timber of inferior quality. **1889** [see (3) below]. **1902** *Settler's Handbook NZ* 118 Amongst the most conspicuous trees of this area there are two worthy of special mention, the northern rata and the black-maire. **1910** COCKAYNE *NZ Plants & Their Story* 37 The northern rata..frequently behave[s] in this most ungrateful manner. **1926** CROOKES *Plant Life Maoriland* 68 The northern rata has the apt name of Metrosideros robusta, which means literally 'the strong iron heart'. **1940** LAING & BLACKWELL *Plants NZ* 297 Northern Rata is also found on the west coast of the South Island as far south at least as Karamea. **1972** *Islands 1* 5 Metrosideros robusta, the northern rata... becomes a tall, massive tree 60 to 100 feet high. **1981** DENNIS *Paparoas Guide* 157 Tall northern rata..and kahikatea..are scattered emergents. **1992** SMITHYMAN *Auto/Biographies* 50 Soon he discovered factually the most part of the kauri forest is taraire but also..northern rata.

(3) **southern rata**. *Metrosideros umbellata*, as 2 (1) above, of mainly southern, esp. West Coast, habitats.

1889 KIRK *Forest Flora* 99 Although the two plants [*sc. Metrosideros robusta* and *M. lucida*] are easily distinguished..it may be advisable to term this species the southern rata, and *M. robusta* the northern rata. 1894 *NZ Official Year-book* 330 The southern rata, which extends to Stewart Island, is especially plentiful in the Tautuku Forest. 1905 WHITE *My NZ Garden* 88 *Metrosideros lucida* revels in the cold of the South. 1935 ODELL *Handbook Arthur's Pass National Park* 100 Southern rata forest..is found in the headwaters of all the Westland streams. 1940 LAING & BLACKWELL *Plants NZ* 294 *Metrosideros umbellata* (*The Southern Rata*)... It grows in masses on the slopes of the Southern Alps, and in a good rata year, adds much to the beauty of the scenery. 1980 ADAMS *NZ Native Trees I* 49 The leaves of southern rata are dark green and shiny with long tapering tips.

II. As **rata-vine** or **rata**, a climbing vine to be distinguished from the tree-forms of I above. **3. a.** As **rata-vine**, a climbing vine of the genus *Metrosideros* (fam. Myrtaceae), esp. *M. fulgens* with distinctive scarlet stamens, and *M. perforata* with white stamens. See also AKA, TOROTORO.

c1875 MEREDITH *Adventuring in Maoriland* (1935) 84 Between the tops of the inside posts and the..outside posts [of the pa fortifications] is a platform of spars, strongly laced to both by rata vine. 1892 KIPLING *One Lady at Wairakei* (1983) 36 Now he will become a rata-vine. 1905 THOMSON *Bush Boys* 27 A *rata* vine caught his foot and down he went in a headlong plunge. 1911 *TrNZI* XLIII. 198 Other lianes are various forms of rata-vines. 1926 [see AKA]. 1940 LAING & BLACKWELL *Plants NZ* 292 *Metrosideros scandens* (*The Rata Vine*)... A shrub, or lofty climber... North Island, Marlborough, Nelson, and Westland; common on forest trees... Maori name, *Aka Akatawhiwhi, Pua-tawhiwhi*. English name *Rata-vine. Ibid.* 296 *Metrosideros albiflora* (The White-flowered Rata Vine). A climbing shrub. 1975 *Tane 21* 8 Myrtaceae *M[etrosideros] fulgens* rata vine 1986 RICHARDS *Off the Sheep's Back* 28 If thirsty..a very palatable drink could be obtained by cutting a length of rata vine.

b. As **rata**.

1882 HAY *Brighter Britain* II. 187 The twisting, squirming rata. 1884 MARTIN *Our Maoris* 30 I saw, for the first time, a grand, old pine dying in the vigorous, cruel embrace of the Rata.

4. white (white climbing, white-flowered, white-flowering) rata. Usu. a climbing plant of white-flowered species of the genus *Metrosideros*, esp. *M. albiflora* of the North Island. See also AKATEA.

1888 HETLEY *Native Flowers NZ* The lovely white Rata (*Metrosideros albiflora*)..hanging down a bank and climbing the branches of the trees in masses of white feathery balls. 1889 FEATON *Art Album NZ Flora* 160 The 'White-flowering rata'. This handsome climber is indigenous to..the Bay of Islands and the East Cape, but is not abundant. 1901 *TrNZI* XXXIII. 387 The flowers of the white rata..are probably the most productive in insect life. 1908 *AJHR* C-14 40 [*Metrosideros albiflora*]. White climbing rata. Forest. Woody root climber. 1926 CROOKES *Plant Life Maoriland* 45 One very common white rata is Metrosideros [perforata], which is prevalent in both islands... Another white rata very similar to the above is Metrosideros hypericifolia [now *M. diffusa*], which differs chiefly in the position of its flowers. The largest of the white ratas is Meterosideros albiflora. 1951 *Bull. Wellington Bot. Soc. No. 25* 24 Several bushes of white rata, *Metrosideros perforata*, were flowering on the face of the [Kapiti Is.] cliffs. 1981 BROOKER et al. *NZ Medicinal Plants* 73 *Metrosideros albiflora*... Common name: *White-flowered rata*. Maori name: *Akatea* 1982 WILSON *Stewart Is. Plants* 44 *Metrosideros* [=*ironwood*] *diffusa* White Climbing Rātā..Akatea... Leafy creeper becoming a high-climbing vine... Flowers white, often flushed pink.

5. Special Comb. **rata grub** (or **rata tree caterpillar**), VEGETABLE CATERPILLAR.

1960 BOSWELL *Ernie* 101 I recall [the botanist-Inspector's] chuckle when we showed him..the huge white caterpillar known throughout bushland [in North Auckland] as the 'rata grub', so-called because it was always found at the foot of a rata and was supposed to be the origin of the tree itself. It is a curious creature—a great caterpillar with a strange tree-like fungoid growth, growing to a height of several inches, from its body. I think everybody believed in the legend of the rata-tree caterpillar.

ratahuihui. [Ma. /ˈraːtaːhuihui/: Williams 327 *Rātāhuihui*..sun-fish.] Any of various extremely large oceanic sunfishes of the family Molidae (esp. *Mola mola*) found in northern New Zealand waters, having abruptly truncated, vertically-compressed bodies.

[*Note*] The word *sunfish* has been recorded from the New Zealand coast from 1770 (Parkinson's *Journal*).

1927 PHILLIPPS *Bibliogr. NZ Fishes* (1971) 57 *Mola mola* Linnaeus. Sunfish; Ratahuihui. 1956 GRAHAM *Treasury NZ Fishes* 383 Sunfish (Ratahuihui) *Mola ramsayi* (Giglioli)... The sunfish is surely one of the oddest looking of all known fishes. 1982 AYLING *Collins Guide* (1984) 319 Ocean Sunfish (Ratahuihui)... The ocean sunfish cannot be confused with any other fish. Its body is a huge flat disc up to 1.5m across. 1987 POWELL *Native Animals NZ* 65 Ocean Sunfish (Ratahuihui) *Mola mola*. A giant..for it grows up to 4m high with a length of 2.9m and a weight of over 2,000 kg.

Ratana, *a.* and *n.* [Ma. /ˈraːtana/: f. the name of Tahupotiki Wiremu *Ratana* (1870–1939) a faith healer and prophet, the founder of the Ratana Church and its associated religio-political movement.]

A. *attrib.* or *adj.* Of or concerning the Maori religious movement founded by T.W. Ratana in 1918.

1921 *Quick March* 10 Feb. 15 The 'Ratana' railway station lies between Marton and Wanganui. 1925 *Patea & Waverley Press* 26 Jan. 2 A good deal of prominence has been given to what has become known as the Ratana Movement in New Zealand, and this has again become more pronounced since the return of Ratana and his party from their visit to England and Europe. 1935 *Na To Hoa Aroha* (1988) III. 198 Then there is one of the Ormond [*sc.* Omana] boys of Mahia out as the Ratana candidate. 1938 HYDE *Nor Yrs. Condemn* 180 It was at the soft-drinks shop that he met Dickie Kotara, a..scraggy young Ratana Maori, who wore a plug hat and an unspeakable ex-pink shirt. 1968 *Evening Post* (Wellington) 26 Jan. 7 Some busloads of Ratana adherents left for home late today. 1992 *Dominion Sunday Times* (Wellington) 30 Aug. 3 The Ratana Church is seen by many Maori, especially the younger ones, to be an expression of organised Christianity that has not been imported by missionaries; it is not colonial.

B. *n.*

1. *Ellipt.* for **Ratana Church**, or a member of the Church.

1955 *BJ Cameron Collection* (TS July) Ratana (n) A Maori Christian sect with a considerable following. 1992 *Dominion Sunday Times* (Wellington) 30 Aug. 3 [He] believes Ratana has become a form of Maori expression that has replaced politics as the race breaks its traditional ties with the Labour Party. 1992 *Capital Times* (Wellington) 7–14 Oct. 11 People say are you a Ratana? Are you a born again Christian?

2. In composition: **Ratanaism**, the ideology and practice of Ratana and his followers, esp. as a political movement; **Ratanaite**, a political follower of Ratana.

1928 *Na To Hoa Aroha* (1986) I. 150 I had no notion how the pakeha battle was going, being immersed in the fight against **Ratanaism** in four electorates. 1930 *Na To Hoa Aroha* (1987) II. 30 The Mohaka people had got into a very bad position owing to a set back during the slumps succeeding the war, the purchase of substantial interests by the Crown, and Ratanaism. The last factor was the finish of them. 1925 *Patea & Waverley Press* 26 Jan. 2 Many **Ratanaites** were present at the customary meeting held at Waitara on a recent Sunday by the Te Whitiites. 1930 *Na To Hoa Aroha* (1987) II. 28 There has been a set back here owing to the influence of Pepene Eketone and other Ratanaites. 1935 LEE *Letter* 3 Dec. in Sinclair *Nash* (1976) 118 As we sit down Tirikatene and his co Ratana-ite call a Moari [*sic*] greeting. Old Joe hands out a few kind words to the Moari [*sic*]. Old fellow deeply stirred.

rata-vine: see RATA II.

ratbag. [AND 1890.] In early use as **ratter** (see quot. 1917), a disagreeable, worthless or contemptible person; something insignificant or beneath notice. Often *attrib.*

[*Note*] The term **old ratbag** can be used in an ameliorated sense.

1917 INGLIS in Boyack *Behind the Lines* (1989) 130 I'm sadly afraid the average chap is by no means a plaster saint or even coming up the straight to that goal, but I'm sure that often the difference between his turning out a decent sort of ratter rests with the girl. 1952 *Here & Now* Jan. 16 Rat-traps in her hair, old ratbag, can I shoutcha down. 1959 SLATTER *Gun in My Hand* 206 An easy-going boy kicked to death by ratbags. 1960 HILLIARD *Maori Girl* 193 That's Sir Walter Peach. He's an old ratbag, really, I suppose what I've heard about him, but he's not a bad stick. 1963 CASEY *As Short a Spring* 161 'What do you think you're going to do with the old ratbag [*sc.* a horse] now that you've caught him?' 1970 *Listener* 12 Oct. 13 A bit late to find that out, you snobbish ratbag wowser. 1987 *Metro* (Auckland) May 61 The editor of the *Taupo Times* wrote back to tell me that I was a fool to want to..follow a ratbag career like journalism.

rat double. [So called because it dealt in small entry fees and small prizes.] A horse-racing double picked from a chart showing first-leg horses across and second-leg down, often formerly sixpence (5c) or a shilling (10c) a choice for a prize of five or ten shillings (50c or $1.00). (According to informants it was popular in secondary schools in the 1930s to 1950s.)

1942 *NZEF Times* 13 July 2 Charged with running a 'rat' double on the Manawatu races, a Wellington bookmaker said the double meant 70/- to the winner. 1954 *Evening Post* (Wellington) 27 Sept. 17 Detective-Sergeant F.A. Gordon..found Riley running a doubles chart—familiarly known as a 'rat double'. 1987 WILLIAMS *Racing for Gold* 173 It was real heart-stopping stuff, especially for those dealing with the bookmakers and rat-double investors.

rat-factory: see RAT-HOUSE.

rat-house. Also later **rat-factory.** [AND 1900.] A psychiatric hospital. Cf. RAT *n*.4 b.

1907 *Truth* 8 June 8 It was cruel in various ways, the cruellest being that Dr. Reid proposed to have Shields shut up in the 'rat-house'. **1913** REES *Merry Marauders* 25 It was a rat-house—an asylum. **1949** SARGESON *I Saw In My Dream* 117 They work it so he's taken away up to the rat-house. **1961** CRUMP *Hang On a Minute Mate* 68 They tried to get Tonker certified crackers..but the people at the rat-factory must been a bit cagey about taking him on. **1988** McGILL *Dict. Kiwi Slang* 92 *rat factory* psychiatric hospital; eg 'Poor Julie's been sent off to the rat factory again.'

ration. *Hist.*

1. *pl.* /ˈræʃənz/ or occas. /ˈreɪʃənz/. [Transf. use of *rations* a daily allowance of some articles of food given to military personnel: see OED 3 a; AND 1843.] An allowance of food over and above cash wages as part of the conditions of employment of early station and farm hands and other outdoor workers; often expressed as '[cash amount] *and rations*', and often equivalent in sense to 'board and lodging'. See esp. quot. 1933.

[**1842** *Piraki Log* 18 May (1911) 129 I can prove that the men have had their rations of meal up to breakfast-time this day.] **1848** in *Lett. from Otago* 17 Dec. (1978) 21 One farmer told, that he was going to offer 60*l*. and rations (sixty pounds!) for a ploughman. **1852** SHAW *Tramp to Diggings* 302 Many of the working men obtain thirty to forty pounds, with board and lodging besides, or rations as they term them in that part of the world. **1866** *Puketoi Station Diary* 24 Dec. in Beattie *Early Runholding* (1947) 115 On December 24, 1866, the diarist remarks: 'Sent rations to Stotburn hut.' I understand 'rations' was the common term, although I did not see its use elsewhere in the diary, the word 'stores' being used quite a few times. On May 20, 1867, we note that 'J. Gavin drove to Drysdale's with provisions'—the solitary use of this word. **1878** ELWELL *Boy Colonists* 157 Contrary to the custom of most run-holders in New Zealand at that time, Walker had introduced the Tasmanian and Australian plan of rations, or 'rashuns', as the men called them. **1883** PASH *Report on NZ* 6 The rations [for farm labourers] differ somewhat with locality... [There is] more food [than at Home] under hut and rations system. **1898** HOCKEN *Contributions* 186 Labourers got 7*s*. to 8*s*. a day;..farm servants, £40 to £50 with rations. **1912** *The Sheepowners' Handbook* 25 The rate for shearing by hand shall be not less than £1 per hundred, with rations. **1933** *Press* (Christchurch) (Acland Gloss.) 18 Nov. 15 *Rations*.—Pronounced to rhyme with 'nations', not with 'passions' as in the army. The *r[ation]* system went out of general use in Canterbury in the 'seventies. The old scale was 16lb meat, 10lb flour, 2lb sugar, ¼lb tea a man a week; or sometimes 12lb meat, 12lb flour, 2lb sugar, and ¼lb tea. **1964** ANDERSON *Doctor in Mountains* (1974) 84 They were very generous and if anyone visited their camp they would cook their best rations for their visitors.

2. Special Comb. **ration-paddock**, a small, handy farm paddock where sheep to be killed for food are kept.

c**1875** MEREDITH *Adventuring in Maoriland* (1935) 41 I sometimes have to do the slaughtering. There is no 'ration paddock'. I go out on the run, bring in the first mob of sheep I come across, and select one that is not too fat.

ratstail.

1. [f. the resemblance of the seed head to a rat's tail.] *broadleaved plantain* (PLANTAIN).

1926 HILGENDORF *Weeds* 161 Broad-leaved Plantain (*Plantago major*), also called ratstail.

2. *Children*. [f. the appearance.] Also called **French knitting**. See quot. c1936.

c**1930s** p.c. George Turner. *Ratstail* was the term used by Wairarapa children. c**1936** *Rats-tail* was the usual name at Havelock School, Marlborough, for what has been called 'French knitting' done by manipulating wool over four nails set in a cotton-reel to make a round length of knitted 'tail' which emerges from the 'tunnel' of the cotton-reel, and which, when of a sufficient length, can be used to make various useful articles such as tea-cosies. (Ed.) **1960** *Ratstail* used by children at Karori (Main) School, Wellington. (Ed.)

rattah, var. RATA.

rattail. [Spec. use of *rat-tail* (a member of a) family of fish with tapering, rat-like tails: see OED 4.] Any of numerous species of deepwater fishes of the family Macrouridae having a large head and short body tapering to a pointed tail. See also GRENADIER *n*.², JAVELINFISH.

1927 SPEIGHT et al. *Nat. Hist. Canterbury* 200 The Rat-tails, which have the tail tapering off to a point, belong to the same order, and two of them (*Coelorhynchus* [now *Coelorinchus*] *australis* and *C. aspercephalus*) have the mouth placed below the sharp snout in a very shark-like manner. **1938** *TrRSNZ* LXVIII. 404 *Coelorhynchus australis*... Javelin-fish (rat-tail). **1967** NATUSCH *Animals NZ* 213 [The order Anacanthini, true codfish] includes rat-tails (big, rare, spiny fish with spear-shaped heads). **1988** *Evening Post* (Wellington) 22 July 14 The fish, known as the 'rattail' or *Coelorhynchus*, were caught off the coast of..Taranaki... The rattail also known as the grenadier is closely related to the codfish family, feeding on the bottom of the ocean.

rattar, var. RATA.

ratter: see RATBAG.

rattle, *v.* In the phr. **(to) rattle one's dags** [f. the noise often made by the (dried) dags of hurrying, un-crutched sheep: AND 1980], usu. *imp.*, hurry up, get moving! Hence quasi-*ppl. a.* **dag-rattling** in transf. use, inducing panic or thoughtless movement (see quot. 1995).

[**1874** KENNAWAY *Crusts* 135 Just then..in the indistinct light we could just make out our old friend C..bringing in a small mob of rattling sheep.] **1968** SLATTER *Pagan Game* 161 I'm not overstruck on that new cop.—Told me to rattle my dags out of there. **1970** DAVIN *Not Here Not Now* 328 'I'll be with you in two shakes of a lamb's tail.'..'You'd better rattle your dags, then.' **1982** SANDYS *Love & War* 271 Come on, come on. Rattle your dags. **1987** *Listener* 8 Aug. 49 [Cartoon caption] Was ist das 'rattle your dags'? **1995** *Dominion*(Wellington) 29 Nov. 2 Dr Smith [Minister of Education], still playing semantic football over what his last dag-rattling speech about school funding really meant, offered the Labour Party the services of a reading recovery programme.

ratty, *a*. [f. *rat* + -Y.]

1. [Used also in Brit. slang: see OED 2 b, 1909.] Angry, irritable. Cf. *have a rat* (RAT *n*. 4 b).

1904 LANCASTER *Sons o' Men* 190 It's prime millin' wheat booked [to be loaded on to railway wagons but held up] ter Cotton, an' he's goin' fair ratty over it. He's wantin' the money, yer know. **1906** PICARD *Ups & Downs* 28 Slush was ratty, and plucked them first, and slaughtered them after. **1926** DEVANNY *Butcher Shop* (1981) 62 She began ter get ratty. **1941** BAKER *NZ Slang* 62 A person is..*ratty* when he is stupid or angry. **1995** ANDERSON *House Guest* 190 I liked her voice too..and there was a kind of swing you know, a sort of snap to it. Not ratty. I don't mean that.

2. [AND 1895.] Eccentric, dotty; deranged.

1904 LANCASTER *Sons o' Men* 20 Muggins was calling him 'ratty'. **1906** *Truth* 1 Dec. 8 He is as ratty as they make them in regard to all forms of gambling, and the result is that he is never likely to be able to command anything more than he has at the present moment—a bare billet. **1910** *Ibid*. 16 Apr. 1 Sergeant: 'He says the man was mad, your Worship.' Witness: 'No, I didn't. I said he was either drunk or ratty.' **1988** McGILL *Dict. Kiwi Slang* 92 *ratty* silly, stupid or slightly eccentric; eg 'The guy's ratty.'

rauhuia. [Ma. /ˈrauhuia/: Williams 329 *Rauhuia*..*Linum monogynum*.] FLAX 6.

1853 HOOKER *II Flora Novae-Zelandiae I Flowering Plants* 28 *Linum monogynum*... Nat. name, 'Rauhuia', *Colenso*; 'Kaho', *Cunn*.; 'Nao', *D'Urville*. **1867** HOOKER *Handbook* 767 Rauhuia, *Col[enso]. Linum monogynum*. **1889** FEATON *Art Album NZ Flora* 68 *Linum monogynum*... The 'Rauhuia' or 'Kaho'.—This interesting little plant is common, especially on rocky coasts, throughout both Islands. **1907** LAING & BLACKWELL *Plants NZ* 218 (*The True New Zealand Flax*)..Native name *Rauhuia*. This is the true New Zealand flax; the plant which is usually so called being a lily. **1946** *JPS* LV. 157 *rauhuia*, a plant (Linum monogynum), a good rock-plant with its long soft-leafed branchlets white-tipped like huia-feathers (whence the name). **1952** [see FLAX 6]. **1969** *Standard Common Names Weeds* 63 *rauhuia Linum monogynum*. **1981** TAYLOR *Weeds of Roadsides* 117 Rauhuia (*Linum monogynum*) Spindly native..common in some regions especially on rocky or broken ground.

raukawa. [Ma. /ˈraukawa/: Williams 329 *Raukawa*..*1*. An aromatic plant used as a scent; *Nothopanax edgerleyi*...2. The scent from the same.] *Pseudopanax* (formerly *Panax* or *Nothopanax*) *edgerleyi* (fam. Araliaceae), a forest tree, the aromatic leaves of which were used as a scent by the Maori.

1867 HOOKER *Handbook* 767 Raukawa, *Col[enso]. Panax Edgerleyi*. **1869** *TrNZI* I. (rev. edn.) 266 The aromatic leaves of the raukawa, a very scarce small tree, sparsely growing in the high dense forests..were also sought for [scent]. **1889** KIRK *Forest Flora* 73 The raukawa is a small but handsome evergreen tree, rarely exceeding 40ft. in height, with glossy foliage which emits an agreeable odour. **1890** *PWD Catalogue Timbers* (NZ & South Seas Exhib.) 14 Raukawa..Timber white with silver grain; of little value. **1907** LAING & BLACKWELL *Plants NZ* 305 (*Edgerley's Nothopanax*)... Maori name *Raukawa*. The leaves are aromatic, and were used by the Maoris in the making of perfumed oils. **1946** *JPS* LV. 157 *raukawa*, a fragrant shrub (Panax Edgerleyi); a tribe named after it, Ngati-raukawa, and Cook Strait, Raukawa, after the tribe. **1978** MOORE & IRWIN *Oxford Book NZ Plants* 98 *Raukawa*. A small tree of hill forests from Auckland to Stewart Island. **1988** DAWSON *Forest Vines to Snow Tussocks* 37 Raukawa..has palmately compound juvenile leaves with up to five deeply lobed leaflets.

raupatu. [Ma. /ˈraupatu/: Williams 330 *Raupatu*. *1.* v. t. Conquer, overcome..2. n. Conquest. 3. quarrel, fight.] In modern use associated with the confiscation of Maori land during and after the New Zealand Wars of the 19th century, often as **raupatu (land) claim**, a claim (made to the

Waitangi Tribunal) for compensation for land so confiscated. See also CONFISCATION.
   1928 *Na To Hoa Aroha* (1986) I. 90 The Raupatu Commission has recommended your Taranaki people a fund of £5000 per annum, Waikato £3000, Whakatohea £300, and N'Kahunganu, Wairoa £300. **1986** SORRENSON in *Na To Hoa Aroha* I. 33 But the most notable of the grievances was the raupatu—the confiscation of Maori land during the New Zealand wars of the 1860s in Taranaki, Waikato, Bay of Plenty, and the East Coast. **1995** raupatu land claim [see BENEFICIARY 2].

raupeka. [Ma. /ˈraupeka/: Williams 330 *Raupeka* (ii)..*Earina* [sp.].] New Zealand Easter orchid (ORCHID 4 *Earina autumnalis*).
   1926 CROOKES *Plant Life Maoriland* 18 For the Raupeka (Earina suaveolens) may justly claim to be one of the most exquisite of our New Zealand blooms. **1946** *JPS* LV. 157 *raupeka*, a fragrant orchid (Earina autumnalis), flowering in autumn as name suggests. **1952** RICHARDS *Chatham Is.* 22 E[*arina*] *autumnalis*..Brides' Bouquet. Rau Peka (branch plant). **1982** [see ORCHID 4].

raupo /ˈræupʌu/, /ˈrapʌu/, *n.*
1. Also with much variety of early form as **rapa, rapeoo, rapo, rapoo, rapou, rappoo, rapu, raupu, repo, roupo.** [Ma. /rauˈpoː/: Williams 330 *Raupō..bulrush.*] **a.** *Typha orientalis* (formerly *angustifolia*) (fam. Typhaceae), a tall native summer-green plant of swampy places distinguished by its large flowering spike, the stems being used by the Maori as a construction or decoration material, the pollen as a kind of flour (see PUNGAPUNGA), and the down from the ripe seed-head for mattresses, etc. and as a poultice (see HUNE); less commonly applied to other tall robust swamp plants. Often *attrib.* See also BULRUSH, COOPERS' FLAG, FLAG 1.
   [**1815** KENDALL *New Zealanders' First Book* 13 Roupo. Flaggy grass. **1820** LEE & KENDALL *NZ Gram. & Vocab.* 201 Raupó, *s.* A species of reed of a soft and spungy nature.] **1827** EARLE *NZ* (1966) 106 Another party were collecting rushes (which grow plentifully in the neighbourhood, called Ra-poo). **1827** WILLIAMS *Early Jrnls.* 17 Dec. (1961) 91 The circumstance of the burning of Capn. Duke's house has made us somewhat thoughtful relative to *raupo* buildings. **1834** MARKHAM *NZ* (1963) 37 Rappoo is a Flag or Marsh Reed, used in England by Coopers to put between Staves of Casks. **1840** MATHEW *Journal* 26 Feb. in *Founding of NZ* (1940) 63 Fairburn's house is built by the natives of what they call 'rapou', that is, long reeds matted thickly together and tied. **1843** DIEFFENBACH *Travels in NZ* I. 426 Under the name of repo, or raupo, it is a most useful building-material to the natives. **1864** VON TEMPSKY *Memoranda* (ATLTS) 181 The troops had hutted themselves for the winter in huts built of a sapling framework, walls of 'raupu' (a species of rush in New Zealand swamps) and roofs of long grass. **1882** POTTS *Out in Open* 19 The buildings have very much of the ancient style of warri about them... most of them are built of raupo, tied closely in bundles. **1898** [see COOPERS' FLAG]. **1903** *TrNZI* XXXV. 22 The roof was..covered with raupo. **1939** BEATTIE *First White Boy Born Otago* 29 What we used to call flags then [in the 1840s], but now known as bulrushes or by the Maoris called rapo (or raupo), were used by the coopers then. They were inserted between the joints and kept the oil casks as tight as a drum. **1942** *NZEF Times* 25 May 9 in Cleveland *The Iron Hand* (1979) 23 I hear the lifting sea-borne breeze Trill on the lute-edged toi-toi spear, And passing up the valley to the falls Curtseys the rapa reeds along the creek. **1946** *JPS* LV. 146 *raupo*, a waterside plant (Typha angustifolia), bulrush; much used for thatch: often mispronounced rapoo. **1954** *The NZ Farmer* 30 Dec. 3 At one time the gully slopes were covered with toitoi, rapu and scrub. **1966** *Encycl. NZ* III. 54 Next to the harakeke, raupo was probably the plant most used by the Maoris. **1984** WILSON *S. Pacific Street* 7 In my spare time I went continually down to our muddy creek among thick blackberry bushes, dark soft raupo and high teatree.
   b. The 'down' of ripe raupo seed heads; HUNE.
   1851 *Lyttelton Times* 28 June 2 Raupo! Raupo!! Raupo!!! The Undersigned is prepared to supply the Inhabitants of the town with this invaluable article. It can be warranted free from maggots, &c. &c.
2. *Ellipt.* for *raupo hut* or *cottage* (3 a below).
   1840 MATHEW *Journal* 20 Mar. in *Founding of NZ* (1940) 96 Among them are some native huts of neat and curious construction, which they call Rapas, and some enclosures for cultivation or that have been cultivated. **1851** LUSH *Auckland Jrnls.* 25 Apr. (1971) 75 Reached Lusk's *raupo* about 9. **1991** [see *raupo house* 3 a below].
3. Special Comb. **a. raupo church, raupo cottage, raupo house, raupo hut, raupo whare** *hist.*, one thatched with (or with walls of) raupo stems and leaf-blades.
   1940 MATTHEWS *Matthews of Kaitaia* 58 A **raupo church**, 25 x 18 feet, was built. **1850** LUSH *Auckland Jrnls.* 26 Oct. (1971) 30 Reached Mr. Lusk's **raupo cottage** about ½ past 12. **1866** LUSH *Waikato Jrnls.* (1982) 72 An empty *Raupo* cottage which a Captain had lately vacated, and this he had immediately fitted up with bedding... Cooper escorted me to my *Raupo* hut—where I had a glorious night's rest. **1831** WILLIAMS *Early Jrnls.* 29 Mar. (1961) 174 Gave instruction for the erection of a small **raupo house** for any of us who might be up there. **1851** *Richmond-Atkinson Papers* (1960) I. 81 They have a large raupo house, very roomy and very draughty. **1883** *Brett's Colonists' Guide* 20 The raupo slab or log house has disappeared, giving place to the comfortable-looking weatherboard house. **1940** MATTHEWS *Matthews of Kaitaia* 42 Before leaving Kaitaia sites were chosen and staked out for three raupo houses—Mr. Baker's 30 x 18, and Matthews's and Puckey's 30 x 14. **1991** LA ROCHE *Hist. of Howick & Pakuranga* 256 There were 150 raupo houses in Howick in December 1848, and only 50 wooden cottages... A 'raupo house' in the official records could include sod cottages with a raupo roof. They called them a 'raupo'. **1823** WILLIAMS *Journal* 15 Sept. in *Tales Pioneer Women* (1940) 14 Within an enclosure of paling stood our **raupo hut**, which had, except in shape, the appearance of a beehive. **1840** MATHEW *Journal* 12 Apr. in *Founding of NZ* (1940) 109 It contains a number of Rapoo houses or huts, and one of the neatest looking is a church where native missionaries perform the services. **1870** *TrNZI* II. 173 The excess of my care of both bottles caused me to place them on a shelf in the raupo hut. **1931** COAD *Such Is Life* 29 Lord of his own lands, king of his own castle; at least, owner of his own raupo hut. **1942** BUTLER *Early Days, Taranaki* 17 By 1850 there were 'homesteads' in place of the rude raupo or slab huts. **1840** CAMPBELL *Present State NZ* 17 A great number of '**rapeoo forras**' [whares]. **1864** NICHOLL *Journal* 29 Apr. (ATLMS) 209 The worst was that we could not see the Maoris as they were in the pits covered over with rapoo whares through the roofs of which they put their rifles. **1881** CAMPBELL *Poenamo* 147 So we propounded this plan to Pama—that we should get the natives to build us a small *raupo whare*, which they could run up easily in a week. **1907** MANSFIELD *Urewera Notebook* (1978) 49 Raupo whare in distance—Picture. At the City [*sc.* Murupara village] gates we pull up and walk into the 'city'. **1913** *NZ Observer* 2 Aug. 17 Then you build a tin hut or a wattle and daub humpy or a raupo whare and call it an hotel. **1941** SUTHERLAND *Numismatic Hist. NZ* 38 Writing of a visit to the Bay of Islands in 1837, and of his stay with a Christian Maori in a two-roomed *raupo whare*, a medical man named Shaw stated: 'The inner room is a sleeping apartment.' **1966** SCOTT *Days That Have Been* 128 They [*sc.* pioneer bush settlers] had lived first in raupo whares..pit-sawing the timber with which later they built their little homes.
   b. Special Comb. **raupo swamp**, a swamp whose dominant plant is raupo.
   1844 TUCKETT *Diary* 6 Apr. in Hocken *Contributions* (1898) 204 The predominance of a russet tint far and near lowered my expectations [of good farm land], indicating too truly the extent of Raupo swamp (a bulrush) already struck by the frost. **1857** *Lyttelton Times* 5 Apr. 5 The new road has been nearly completed, with the exception of the part over the Raupo swamp. **1860** DONALDSON *Bush Lays & Rhymes* 5 Entangled in a foul morass, A raupo swamp, one name we know. **1886** HART *Stray Leaves* 13 At the back..was a large raupo swamp, which was a rare resort for wild ducks and pukaki. **1897** *TrNZI* XXIX. 342 Passing through an almost continuous raupo swamp..we at last arrived at Awanui Township itself. **1925** MANDER *Allen Adair* (1971) 53 Allen liked even the raupo swamps smellful of patches of stagnant water. **1938** *Auckland Weekly News* 8 June 7 A Maori boatman..waits to ferry the party through a raupo swamp.

raupo, *v. intr.* To line or build (a hut, etc.) with raupo. Also as *vbl. n.*
   1840 Mar. in Wilkes *US Exploring Exped.* (1852) I. 300 The manner of making the roof is to tie the materials on the horizontal strips or poles..; the *rappooing* is then cut square off at the upper horizontal beam or plate-piece. **1881** CAMPBELL *Poenamo* 276 Had they shown the same assiduity in *raupo*-ing the walls of the house as they did in smoking their pipes we should have had no cause to grumble.

raupu, var. RAUPO.

raurekau. Also occas. **heraurekau** (=he raurekau), **raureka, raurikau.** [Ma. /rauˈre:kau/: Williams 330 *Raurākau, raurēkau...Coprosma.*] KANONO (*Coprosma grandifolia*).
   1843 *NZ Jrnl.* IV. 216 We made a meal of some *tuées* roasted in the leaf of a tree called *heraurekau*. **1892** KELLY *Journey Upper Waitara Valley* 3 [The eels] are then covered with the broad leaves of the raurikau (or bullock's kai as it was known by the early settlers). **1904** TREGEAR *Maori Race* 45 The officiating priest stuck a twig of the shrub (*raurekau*) in the middle of the stream. **1950** WODZICKI *Introduced Mammals NZ* 164 Miss Mason identified the leaves of the following plants [from Egmont National Park]:.. raurekau (*Coprosma grandifolia*)..and broadleaf. **1970** MASON in *Solo* (1981) 27 An old rock garden, writhing with weeds. A jungle of raureka and gorse. **1975** *Tane 21* 8 C[*oprosma*] *australis* raurekau. **1982** *Field Guide Common NZ Trees & Shrubs* 26 Raurekau *Coprosma australis*.

raurau. Also **rou-rou.** [Ma. /ˈraurau/: Williams 328 *Rau* (i)..*1.* Leaf. *raurau..1.* Foliage... *2.* Thatch.] An often foul-tasting inferior or substitute tobacco. Cf. TORORI.
   1909 OWEN *Philip Loveluck* 82 He considered [tobacco] a luxury for a man who was often reduced to *rou-rou* on a back country block... 'I'm not sure a pipeful of niggerhead ain't as good'... [1909 *Note*] Locally grown tobacco of vile flavour.

raurikau, var. RAUREKAU.

rauriki /'ræurəˌki/, /ˈrarəˌki/, /ˈrærəˌki/, /ˈrædəˌki/. Also **radicky**, **raoriki**. [Ma. /ˈrauriki/: Williams 331 *Rauriki..Sonchus oleraceus*, sow-thistle.] PUHA 1 a and b.

1848 TAYLOR *Leaf from Nat. Hist.* 94 Korau, Poronea, Puwa, Rauriki, Aotea, Puroa, *sow-thistle..*is generally used as a vegetable by the natives. **1900** *Canterbury Old & New* 21 The native wild cabbage and 'rauriki' (sow thistle) were used as vegetables until gardens had been made. **c1920** [see PUHA 1]. **1926** [see THISTLE *n.* 2 (5) a]. **1940** *Tales Pioneer Women* (1988) 207 For vegetables [in early Banks Peninsula] there was plenty of pora, the Maori turnip, and puwha (rauriki) or sowthistle. **1952** LYON *Faring South* 198 The younger pigs did little harm, except to graze on the raoriki, which the Maori boils and as 'puha' uses as cabbage. **1958** radicky [see THISTLE *n.* 2 (5) a]. **1962** *Evening Post* (Wellington) 22 Nov. 72 The sow thistle, better known as 'rauriki' in the Wellington district, which, marketed [in East Coast and Rotorua districts] as 'puha' finds a ready sale. **1965** GILLHAM *Naturalist in NZ* 51 Around them grew..the yellow sow thistle, which although probably not native to New Zealand, has been known to the Maoris for a long time..under the name of puha or rauriki. **1982** [see PUHA 1 b].

Raurimu Spiral: see SPIRAL.

rautini. *Chatham Islands.* [Ma. /ˈrautini/: Williams 331 *Rautini..Senecio huntii.*] *Brachyglottis* (formerly *Senecio*) *huntii* (fam. Asteraceae), a small native tree of the Chatham Islands distinguished by its heads of yellow flowers and lemon-scented leaves.

1910 COCKAYNE *NZ Plants & Their Story* 122 In the neighbourhood of these [Chatham Island] bogs the margin of the forest often consists entirely of the rautini (*Senecio Huntii*), a magnificent tree-groundsel, which produces immense bunches of yellow flower-heads. **1918** *NZJST* I. 144 *Senecio Huntii..Rautini.* **1952** RICHARDS *Chatham Is.* 69 *Senecio..Huntii...* This tree-groundsel has a stout erect trunk... Rautini. **1984** HOLMES *Chatham Is.* 93 *Senecio Huntii* (Rautini)—this endemic tree grows in the natural forest [at the south of Chatham and Pitt Islands].

rawa rawa, var. REWAREWA.

rawaru. Also early **raòoroo**. [Ma. /ˈra:waru/: Williams 332 *Rāwaru..Parapercis colias.*] blue cod (COD 2 (3)).

[**c1826–27** BOULTBEE *Journal* (1986) 113 cod fish—raòoroo] **1903** *TrNZI* XXXV. 319 Hundreds of..what I believe are young rock-cod, or kokopu or rawaru. **1921** *NZJST* IV. 123 Blue Cod; *Rawaru.* A highly esteemed food fish; secured in water up to 100 fathoms. **1938** [see COD 2 (3)]. **1947** POWELL *Native Animals NZ* 69 Blue Cod (*Parapercis colias*) Rawaru of the Maoris, is our most esteemed food fish. **1957** [see COD 2 (8) a]. **1966** DOOGUE & MORELAND *Sea Anglers' Guide* 264 Blue Cod... *Parapercis colias;* coal fish; rawaru, pakirikiri, patutuki (Maori). **1982** AYLING *Collins Guide* (1984) 267 *Blue Cod* (Blue weever, rawaru) *Parapercis colias.*

rawiri. [An adaptation or variant of Ma. *rauwiri, rauiri,* /ˈrauwiri/, /ˈrauiri/: Williams 331 *Rauwiri, rauiri* (i)..4...a tree.] KANUKA.

1843 DIEFFENBACH *Travels in NZ* II. 382 Rawiri—a shrub (*leptospermum ericoides*). **1853** HOOKER *II Flora Novae-Zelandiae I Flowering Plants* 70 Leptospermum *ericoides...* Nat. name, 'Rawiri', Northern Island,... *D'Urville.* **1867** HOCHSTETTER *NZ* 132 Only Manuka and Rawiri bushes (species of *Leptospermum*)..are intermixed with *Pteris.* **1872** *TrNZI* IV. 249 The rawiri..or tea-tree, with spray-like branches laden with myriads of white flowers. **1889** KIRK *Forest Flora* 124 Mr. Colenso informs me that 'rawiri', as it [*sc. L. ericoides*] is sometimes called in the North Island, is erroneous, and that the proper name is manuka-rauriki.

raw prawn. [f. Austral. slang: see AND 1942.] In the phr. **to come the raw prawn** (**with, over** a person), to attempt to deceive; esp. as a negative phr. **don't come** (etc.).

1965 SHADBOLT *Among Cinders* 202 'Break it down, Pop,' said the farmer. 'Don't you come the raw prawn with me.' **1980** LELAND *Kiwi-Yankee Dict.* 34 *raw prawn with, don't come the* Don't try to feed me that line. **1982** NEWBOLD *Big Huey* 82 The lads..started discussing plans..if the [prison] administration tried to come the raw prawn over Christmas parcels.

ray.

1. Any of various fishes of the Order Rajiformes with a flattened kite-like body and usu. a whip-like tail. See also STINGAREE, WHAI, WHAI-REPO.

2. Significant New Zealand uses are mainly those with a modifier: **eagle** (**whip, whiptail**), **electric** (**New Zealand electric**), **stingray, torpedo**.

(1) **eagle** (**whip, whiptail**) **ray**. *Myliobatis tenuicaudatus* (fam. Myliobatidae).

1872 HUTTON & HECTOR *Fishes NZ* 121 There goes an Eagle Ray.., and there another and another, more flying than swimming. **1886** SHERRIN *Handbook Fishes NZ* 128 Whip Ray (*Myliobatis Aquila*)... It swims pretty rapidly, with a kind of sailing motion, and little action of the pectoral fins, and when taken vibrates its tail violently; the first care of the fisherman, therefore, is to cut off the caudal spine, which..is a very formidable implement. **1927** PHILLIPPS *Bibliogr. NZ Fishes* (1971) 11 *Aetobatis tenuicaudatus...* Eagle-ray. **1930** *NZJST* XI. 107 *Aetobatis tenuicaudatus...* Stingaree; Eagle-ray; Manumanu. **1967** MORELAND *Marine Fishes* 14 Eagleray [*Myliobatis tenuicaudatus*]..Whiptail, stingray and cowfish are among other names in use. **1981** WILSON *Fisherman's Bible* 198 Eagle-ray A graceful, swimmer capable of high speeds this ray has powerful teeth which it uses to crush oysters.

(2) **electric** (**New Zealand electric**) **ray**. Any of several rays with almost circular body shape able to deliver an electric shock esp. *Torpedo fairchildii* (fam. Torpedinidae) and the blind electric ray or numbfish *Typhlonarke aysoni* (fam. Narkidae); NUMBFISH. See also WHAI-REPO.

1872 HUTTON & HECTOR *Fishes NZ* 121 The New Zealand Electric Ray (*Torpedo Fairchildii*)..is an interesting addition to our Fauna, named after the collector, Capt. Fairchild, of the Colonial Government gun-boat 'Luna'. **1927** [see WHAI-REPO]. **1930** *NZJST* XI. 98 *Narcobatus fairchildi...* Southern Numbfish, or Whai Repo. *Ibid.* 99 The species is also called 'torpedo' or 'electric ray'. Hutton states that the Natives (presumably of Napier) call it whai-ngenge. **1947** [see WHAI-REPO]. **1986** PAUL *NZ Fishes* 35 In a separate family (Torpedinidae) [from skates] there is the torpedo or electric ray *Torpedo fairchildi,* similar to an Australian species and to others elsewhere... In a second family (Narkidae) there are two species of the blind electric ray *Typhlonarke.*

(3) **stingray**. Either of two species of barb-tailed rays of the genus *Dasyatis* (fam. Dasyatidae), often distinguished by the defining words **short-tail(ed)** and **long-tailed**. (Some early quots. may refer to the *eagle ray* (see (1) above).) See also STINGAREE, WHAI, WHAI-REPO.

1769 COOK *Journals* 5 Dec. (1955) I. 219 We got only fish..and these of Various sorts, such as..sting-rays, Breams, Mullet, Mackerel. **1817** NICHOLAS *NZ* I. 269 On these stages were placed a quantity of the dog-fish and sting-ray, which were drying there as a supply against the winter. **1838** POLACK *NZ* I. 323 Many other fish are equally numerous, answering to our *hakes, tench..sting-ray* and *dog-fish.* **1873** TINNE *Wonderland of Antipodes* 95 We went out 'stingareeing', or spearing sting-rays. **1929** BEST *Fishing Methods* 48 The *whai,* or sting-ray, was speared, and the spike on its tail (hoto and tara whai) was used as a point for fighting-spears. **1938** *NZ Observer* 8 Dec. 8 I have bathed from practically every well-known beach in New Zealand, and I know the fear in which the vicious stingray is held. **1946** [see WHAI]. **1956** [see WHAI-REPO]. **1982** AYLING *Collins Guide* (1984) 79 Short-tailed Stingray *Dasyatis brevicaudatus.* Both the species of stingray found in New Zealand waters are bulky animals that grow to a large size. *Ibid.* 80 Long-tailed Stingray *Dasyatis thetidis...* The tail of the long-tailed ray is thin, rounded and whip-like and covered in small prickles as well as bearing one or more large barbs.

(4) **torpedo ray**. Also *ellipt.* **torpedo**. An alternative name for the *electric ray* (*Torpedo fairchildi*), and occas. for the blind electric rays *Typhlonarke* spp. (NUMBFISH). See also (2) above.

1872 HUTTON & HECTOR *Fishes NZ* 83 Torpedo fairchildi. sp. nov. Torpedo... The natives call it Whaingenge. **1898** MORRIS *Austral-English* 475 *Torpedo, n.* a fish, well known elsewhere, and also called elsewhere, the *Numb-fish* and *Cramp-fish.* **1927** SPEIGHT et al. *Nat. Hist. Canterbury* 193 The Torpedo Ray (*Typhlonarke aysoni*) or blind numb-fish is a small brown, soft-bodied fish which lurks on the bottom in moderately shallow water. **1930** [see (2) above]. **1936** *Handbook for NZ* (ANZAAS) 71 *Narcobatus* (*Torpedo*) *fairchildi* and *Typhlonarke aysoni*: Electric or torpedo rays. **1956** [see NUMBFISH]. **1967** MORELAND *Marine Fishes* 14 Electric Ray [*Torpedo fairchildi*]... Other names are torpedo and sometimes numbfish. **1981** [see NUMBFISH]. **1986** PAUL *NZ Fishes* 35 In a separate family (Torpedinidae) there is the torpedo or electric ray *Torpedo fairchildi,* similar to an Australian species and to others elsewhere.

razoo /raˈzu/. Occas. **rarzoo, razzoo.** [Origin unknown: the connection of Ma. *raho* 'testicle' with (*brass*) *razoo* is most unlikely: AND 1919, then 1932.] **a.** Also **brass razoo** (on the form of *brass farthing*). A small or worthless (imaginary) coin, usu. in neg. constructions.

1937 PARTRIDGE *Dict. Slang* 690 *razoo.* A small coin; *razoos,* (human) testicles: New Zealanders': C. 20. App. a corruption of the Maori *rahu.* **1941** BAKER *NZ Slang* 52 *Razoo..*is in currency for a small coin. The term also has wide use in Australia and..is heard mainly in the negative phrases *I haven't a razoo* or *I haven't a brass razoo* for 'I have no money at all'. **1948** MUNDY *There's Gold* 93 I haven't got a rarzoo. **1951** PARK *Witch's Thorn* 177 No work, no custom. Nobody's got a razoo left anywhere, especially to buy fish with. **1956** SUTHERLAND *Green Kiwi* (1960) 197 When I was up before him that last time last year he never found [*sc.* fined] me any fiver—never found me a dam' razzoo. **1964** ASHTON-WARNER *Bell Call* 142 And I've got nothing in my pocket... I haven't got two razoos to rub together. **1966** *Evening Post* (Wellington) 1 Feb. 21 'The United States Air Force didn't give us a brass razoo for financing the trip,' Sir Edmund [Hillary] added. **1977** HALL *Glide Time* 55 Hugh. Don't you get anything? Jim. Not a brass razoo. **1986** *Evening Post* (Wellington) 6 Jan. 14 [Advt] No Deposit. Not a cent. Not a sausage. Not a brass razoo. **1995** *Sunday Star-Times* (Auckland) 21 May sect. C 2 Not only did it aggravate other worthy sports and cultural strivers who are seldom within scrounging distance of a state razoo. [*sic*]

RAZOR-BACK

b. *fig.* or *transf.* A jot, a tittle.

1976 Sargeson *Sunset Village* 53 And she didn't give a razoo whether they knew already or they didn't. **1981** Hunt *Speaking a Silence* 127 It benefits the petrol people, the shops and the butcher... But the rank and file..I don't think it affects us one razoo.

razor-back. [f. its silhouette of razor-like sharpness: see OED 4, 1874; AND 1831.] A steep-sided sharp-backed ridge or spur; also the given name of such a local ridge or hill. Also *attrib.*

1851 Cooper *Journal of an Expedition* 110 Gullies ran down from each side of a razor-back ridge. **1867** Thomson *Rambles of a Philosopher* 1 The sharp, razor-back ridges that extend between Waikouaiti River and the Snowy Mountain. **1874** Baines *Edward Crewe* 247 At length..from a high 'razor-back', I had a magnificent view of the Waikato. **1885** *TrNZI* XVII. 353 At 7,500 feet we reached the top of the range, which is a mere razor-back, being only a few feet wide, and composed of loose angular and slab-like rocks. **1902-3** *NZ Illustr. Mag.* VII. 91 We entered on a long narrow ridge, like the roof of a church... It is what the New Zealand people call a razor-back. **1922** Cowan *NZ Wars* (1955) I. 250 The troops in December, 1861, marched along the Maori track over the range called the Razorback. **1933** *Press* (Christchurch) (Acland Gloss.) 18 Nov. 15 *Razor back*.—Sharp ridged spur or hill. A very common local name. **1954** *Here & Now* Aug. 17 If he were only young again, by God he'd be with us too, but looking ruefully at the razorbacks saying 'but I should need bagbooks in the arse of my pants to get me up there!' **1976** Wilson *Pacific Star* 141 We carried Alf down..along the snow covered, razorback ridge from the ski hut.

razor mussel: see mussel 2 (8).

razzoo, var. razoo.

R.D.: see rural delivery.

read, *v.* [AND 1950.] In the phr. **you wouldn't read about it**!, an exclamation expressing a range of feeling from chagrin to tolerant surprise; 'you wouldn't believe it!'.

1955 *BJ Cameron Collection* (TS July) read: you wouldn't read about it! It's fantastic! **1962** Hori *Half-gallon Jar* 15 Well, fair dinkum, you wouldn't read about it. This entree fish is about the size of a packet of razor blades. **1988** McGill *Dict. Kiwi Slang* 128 *you wouldn't read about it!* something that amazes.

reading recovery. A process which identifies children with reading difficulties at six years of age and provides specialized one-to-one assistance from a teacher trained in remedial ('Reading Recovery') procedures. Also *attrib.*

1979 *AJHR E-1* 10 Support for Professor Marie Clay of Auckland University to introduce a 'reading recovery' programme aimed at helping 6-year olds with incipient reading problems. **1983** *AJHR E-1* 9 Reading recovery is a preventative programme, of which the key features are early identification of children at risk followed by intensive teaching. **1988** *Evening Post* (Wellington) 26 Oct. 3 Aimed at six year olds, Reading recovery is an early intervention programme which provides a second chance for children who cannot read or write after a year in school. **1993** *City Voice* (Wellington) 9 Sept. 8 [Heading] Reading recovery. Adults with reading difficulties are being treated in an adult way at last.

ready, *v.* [f. racing slang *ready up* to prevent a horse from winning: see OED.] As **readied** *ppl. a.*, of police evidence, manufactured, falsely contrived.

1910 *Truth* 6 Aug. 7 Two men (strangers to each other) recently came out of the Police Court after listening to evidence in a case. Said one: 'It looks like a "readied" case'; to which the other replied: 'Yes.' They said no more and went their several ways; but the joke of the matter lies in the fact that it came out later that the first man intended to libel the police, while the second sought to libel the defence.

Hence **ready** *n.*, an illegal or questionable arrangement.

1975 Anderson *Men of Milford Road* 120 I remembered that old saying 'If you're not one up you're one down.' I am sure, however, that the auditor sensed that this was a bit of a 'ready'.

ready-made. In full, **ready-made cigarette**, a factory-made cigarette, a 'tailor-made'.

1940 *Dominion* (Wellington) 9 Dec. 10 [Advt] I want a tobacco with a character. I've been used to 'ready made' cigarettes. **1952** *Here & Now* Jan. 32 No matter if you've bought nothing but ready-mades before you get busted.

rebel, *n.* and *a. Hist.* [Spec. use of *rebel* one who resists, or rises in arms against, the established governing power.] A European-oriented term for a Maori who fought (or defended principles and land) against the Crown, esp. during the New Zealand Wars. Cf. hostile *a.* and *n.*, Kingite.

1846 in Deans *Pioneers of Canterbury* (1937) 108 The number of these rebels [in the Hutt] is quite insignificant, from all accounts not exceeding 300 or 400... The natives chiefly engaged in rebellion are of the tribe Ngatitoa. **1860** Grace 23 Oct. in *Pioneer Missionary* (1928) 94 Had the Treaty of Waitangi been fully and faithfully carried out, the war would not have occurred; instead, it has been ignored until now that it is useful to make rebels of the Natives. **c1875** [see savage a]. **1876** *Saturday Advertiser* (Dunedin) 22 July 3 *Orakau* [a poem] The swarthy rebels answered with a fierce defiant shout, 'Ka whawhai tonu! Akè! Akè! Akè!' **1966** *Encycl. NZ* II. 483 In confiscating the land, little heed was paid to the degree of 'guilt' of the 'rebels'. **1987** *NZJH* XXI. No.1 17 I used to hear how [Te Kooti] was a rebel and all that, and I didn't think I was connected with him.

receiving yard. [AND 1848.] The enclosure or special yard in a stockyard into which mustered stock are first driven for further drafting.

1922 Perry *Sheep Farming* 16 [The sheep yards] should consist of receiving yards at each end, forcing pen, and drafting race. **1933** *Press* (Christchurch) (Acland Gloss.) 18 Nov. 15 *Receiving yard*.—A very large yard which sheep come into first when brought into the *sheep yards*. **1950** *NZJAg.* July LXXX. 7 In general large drafting yards embody the following subsections or divisions... *The receiving yards*, into which the sheep enter, which usually have a large capacity. **1955** [see forwarding yard].

red, *a.*

1. a. In the names of plants, see: beech 2 (7), birch 3 (9), horopito 2, kowhai 2 (1), manuka 2 (2), mapau 2 (2), matipo 2 (2), mistletoe 2 (1), pine 2 (13), tea-tree 3 (1), tussock 3 (9). **b.** In the names of fish, see: cod 2 (6) and 2 (7), crayfish 2 (4), gurnard 2 (2), herring 2 (2), moki 2 (4), mullet 2 (2), perch *n.* 2 (3), snapper *n.*¹ 2 (4), soldier *n.*² See also *red jacket* 2 below.

RED ADMIRAL

2. In special collocations and phrases: **red back** *obs.* [f. the crimson colour], a 50-pound note (not recorded of the 50-dollar note); **red boy** (often init. cap.) [f. the picture of a boy against a red background], the penny value of the 1931 Health Stamp; **red collar** *farming*, in the phr. **to put a red collar on**, to cut the throat of; **red jacket** *scarlet parrotfish* (parrotfish 2 (4)); **red light** *shearing* [AND 1915], a warning of the approach of a woman (see sixty-nine); **red tribe** *obs.*, the 'tribe' of imperial British 'redcoated' or red-uniformed troops of the early-mid nineteenth century; **red white and blue**, a betting game played with darts thrown into a board or revolving wheel with stripes of the three colours, betting money being placed on a chosen colour (known to Ed. as a showground gambling game in Marlborough from c1936).

1966 *Sunday Times* (Wellington) 31 July 5 [Heading] '**Red Back**' Poison. Mr. Percival cashed a cheque six months ago and asked for a £50 note as part payment. He tried unsuccessfully to cash the '**red back**' in Auckland hotels, and hoped for better luck in Wellington. **1947** *NZ Observer* 29 Jan. 8 Roughly 75,000 of the '**red boy**' and 112,000 of the 'blue boy' were sold. **1974** *NZ Bulletin* (Woking) XI. No.6 4 The cover bearing the Red Boy also carries a 1d Field Marshal to make up the recently-increased postage rate. **1988** Gwynn *Collecting NZ Stamps* 93 The 1d '**red boy**' was sold in considerably smaller quantities than the 2d 'blue boy', and is the rarer of the two stamps in used condition. **1951** McLeod *NZ High Country* 42 I've heard a head shepherd say to a man 'go down to the shed and put the **red collar** on those two dog tuckers in the yard.' He meant the man to cut the throats of the sheep and skin them for the dogs. **1945** Beattie *Maori Place-names Canterbury* 62 The above list of fish to be caught along the Canterbury coast has some notable omissions... Omitted are the tarakihi..the puhaiwhakarua (**red-jacket**), koiro (conger eel). **1970** Porter *Nor'west Arch* 29 I [Grace Porter] used to wonder why the boys called out '**Red Light**' as I approached the shed..and later found it was their signal to stop all flowery language. **1906** Buick *New Zealand's First War* 118 in Barber *Red Coat to Jungle Green* (1984) 15 A number of the **red tribe** who had not joined in the attack on our pa came at our people with a rush. **1939** Belton *Outside the Law* 204 [Sideshowman speaks] Can a man play **Red, White and Blue** tomorrow?

red admiral. [Transf. use of European *red admiral Vanessa atalanta*.] Either of *Bassaris gonerilla gonerilla* or *B. g. ida* (fam. Nymphalidae), large, dark, native butterflies, having red patches on the upperside of the wings.

1902 Drummond & Hutton *Nature in NZ* 58 One of the best known..is the red admiral, named after the European species, which it resembles. **1907** Lancaster *Tracks We Tread* 80 On the spears of sunlight between the cabbage-trees the Red Admiral flickered like an elusive thought. **1910** *School Jrnl. Part III* May 96 The red-admiral butterflies are sometimes tempted out on brilliant days. **1924** *Otago Witness* (Dunedin) 28 Oct. 6 New Zealand's Red Admiral butterfly, characterised mostly by dark red, black and brown colours, usually deposits its eggs on a leaf of the common native nettle. **1966** Gaskin *Butterflies and Common Moths* 87 The Red Admiral Butterfly. This very common garden-haunting species with its black background belted with red on both wings is too well known to merit a detailed description here. **1971** Miller *Common Insects* 3 Red Admiral..; it was known by the pre-European Maori as *kahukura*, a word also applied to the rainbow and to the god that took care of travellers. **1989** Lessiter *Butterflies*

red-bill. [In spec. local use as the name of any of various (usu. water or shore) birds with red bills: AND 1799.]

1. *Obs.* PUKEKO 1.
  1824 CRUISE *Journal* 29 Aug. (1957) 149 At eleven, it becoming moderate, we went on shore, and shot some red-bill and quail. **1849** STRANGE *Journal* 10 Mar. in *Canterbury Papers* (1851) 79 The red-bill, *porophyrio melanotus* or *pukeko* of the natives. **1854** MALONE *Three Yrs. Cruise* 13 We shot [at Whangarei] a capital eating bird which we called a red-bill. **1968** *NZ Contemp. Dict. Suppl.* (Collins) 16 *redbill* n. gregarious bird, the swamp-hen.

2. Any of various unidentified red-billed water or shore birds, prob. mainly the shore-birds of 3 below.
  1826 SHEPHERD *Journal* in Howard *Rakiura* (1940) 357 He shot several ducks Red bills in a wood hen and killed a hare seal. **c1835** BOULTBEE *Journal* (1986) 64 To add to our misery, our potatoes were consumed, and..we could not shoot any Red-Bills, altho' they were on the beach in immense quantities. **1863** BUTLER *First Year* ix 133 There are also paradise ducks, hawks, terns, red-bills, and sand-pipers.

3. a. *pied oystercatcher* (OYSTERCATCHER 2 (3) *Haematopus ostralegus finschi*).
  1861 HAAST *Rep. Topogr. Explor. Nelson* 50 We continued our route along this beach..endeavouring in the meantime to shoot some toreas (redbills), in order to add a little to our small stock of provisions. **1870** *TrNZI* II. 47 A pair of Harriers..floating high above..alarmed the pyebald Redbill. **1882** POTTS *Out in Open* 199 Its habit..frequently is to pipe thrice, in a way that at once recalls the red-bill (*Haematopus*). **1945** BEATTIE *Maori Place-names Canterbury* 18 An island further up the river is known as Torea (redbill) because these birds nest there. **1966** FALLA et al. *Birds NZ* 118 Oystercatchers are sturdily built waders.. with red..legs and strong orange-red bills... In some districts they are commonly called redbills. **1985** [see OYSTERCATCHER 2 (3)].

b. Also **black red-bill.** OYSTERCATCHER 2 (1) and (4) (*Haematopus unicolor*).
  1869 *TrNZI* I. (rev. edn.) 105 Haematopus unicolor. Torea. Red-bill. East Coast. **1871** [see OYSTERCATCHER 2 (1)]. **1885** *NZJSc.* II. 511 Black Oyster-catcher, Black Red-bill, Torea.—Breeds out on 'the plains' in riverbeds. **1894** DUCHESS OF BUCKINGHAM *Glimpses of Four Continents* 127 [At Bluff] saw some..oyster birds, or 'red-bills', with black bodies and red legs and beaks. **1904** HUTTON & DRUMMOND *Animals NZ* 199 The Red Bill.—Torea... Ibid. 200 The Red-bill is rarer than the Oyster-Catcher. It is found chiefly in the sounds and inlets of the west coast of the South Island. **1919** *TrNZI* LI. 224 Along the coast, wherever masses of rock are to be found in conjunction with sandy shores, the redbill is not uncommon. **1964** DEMPSEY *Little World Stewart Is.* 95 The oystercatchers, or red-bills as we call them sometimes, on our beaches are black. **1985** [see OYSTERCATCHER 2 (4)].

red-billed gull: see GULL 2 (3).

red-crowned parakeet: see PARAKEET 2 (7).

Redfed /ˈredˌfed/. Also **Red Fed**(.). [Poss. ellipt. for *Red Federal* or *Red Federationist*; or directly f. *red* left-wing + (the name of the) NZ *Fed*eration of Labour (established 1909) popularly known as 'the Red Federation'; Hickey's surmise that the term *Red Fed* was coined by the *Evening Post* is not supported by the evidence, though *Red Federation* is recorded in that paper from early 1912.]

1. a. *Hist.* Orig. (c1911–35) a member of the 'Red' Federation of Labour, or one supporting its social and industrial ideals and policies; RED FEDERAL. Occas. used for the Federation itself (see quots. 1912, 1968).
  [**1912** *Evening Post* (Wellington) 7 Mar. 6 The blame for the bluster of syndicalism lies with the Red Federation of Labour.] **1912** *NZ Free Lance* (Wellington) 22 June 1 [Caption] A slap in the face for the 'Red Feds'. *Ibid.* 26 It is Town Talk... That a nickname has been found for Bob Semple's Federation of Labour. It's the 'Red Fed.'.. That the Red-Fed's game is about up in New Zealand. That Waihi strike has just about put their pot on the fire. **1912** *Evening Post* (Wellington) 3 Oct. 8 Presently a score or so of school boys wearing red, white, and blue ribbons, commenced to follow the 'Red Feds', giving the latter a taste of their own medicine by hooting the red flag and cheering the Union Jack. **1917** *NZ At the Front* 90 'Of course, they call me a bit of a Socialist.' 'I heard you were a Red Fed,' interjected my companion. **1925** HICKEY *'Red' Fed. Memoirs* 48 I issued a circular, stating that the Federation would stand behind the tramwaymen in any action that they might take... The leaflet (which happened to be printed on red paper, this giving the idea to the 'Evening Post' [in early 1912] that was responsible for the coining of the term 'Red Federation', which was afterwards abbreviated to 'Red Fed'.) caused a wave of militancy to sweep through the tramway service. **1931** COAD *Such Is Life* 24 'They [*sc.* NZ customs officials] are on the look-out for Bolshevists, Red-Feds and I.W.W's,' replied the New Zealander, looking at him suspiciously. **1959** SINCLAIR *Hist. NZ* 199 In contrast to the United Labour Party, the 'Red Feds' eschewed political action. **1968** BOLLINGER *Against the Wind* 100 As things turned out, the U.F.O.L. never became much broader than the old 'Red Fed'. **1988** *Dominion* (Wellington) 20 May 8 In 1912 the federation pledged support for the disgruntled tramwaymen in Wellington, and the Evening Post made its contribution to history by declaring: 'A victory for the Reds in the present quarrel would be a public disaster, possibly on a national scale. The Reds are out to fight...'. The tramwaymen struck and won, and henceforth that first Federation of Labour became known as the Red Federation and its leaders as Red Feds.

b. *Derog.* A person perceived to be a left-wing 'agitator', militant unionist, or other assertive person ('troublemaker') of the left.
  1920 *NZ Free Lance* (Wellington) 1 Dec. (Xmas Annual) 45 The aviator pinned the tribute to the breast of the Right Honourable R. Fedd. 'He died for a principle!' **1947** DAVIN *For Rest of Our Lives* 102 Who cares if he is a red-fed? I've gone a bit bolshy myself after some of the balls ups I've seen out here. **1959** *Star* (Christchurch) 9 Mar. 2 I have always prided myself on my British descent and our fair play and am not a Red-fed, but I admire the natives for kicking over the traces and striking on this account. **1965** HILLIARD *Power of Joy* 213 To the well-off it seemed that all who worked for wages [in the 1930s] were dolies or red-feds, whatever that was. **1970** DAVIN *Not Here Not Now* 280 He sounded a bit of a red-fed, though. No time for Baldwin or any of that lot over in England. **1992** FARRELL *Skinny Louie Book* 58 Nancy-boy..was of the opinion that the country's salvation had lain with Campbell Begg and not some ex-Red Fed.

2. *attrib.* Left-wing, 'socialist'.
  1917 *NZ Free Lance* (Wellington) 30 Mar. 6 Mr Webb's interference in municipal elections is on behalf of the 'Labour'—otherwise the Red Fed.—ticket. **1920** *Ibid.* (Wellington) 6 Jan. 8 When the Red Fed candidates came before the electors last December, they included quite a number of the 'radish' fraternity. **1956** DAVIN *Sullen Bell* 59 'Isn't that the red-fed lawyer?' Hugh laughed..at the combination of respect for a headline name and honour of political notoriety so characteristic of the New Zealander. **1963** *Letter* in McKay *Baxter* (1990) 195 It is not 'Marxist' or 'Red-fed'—it is a certain kind of love. **1978** SUTHERLAND *Elver* 44 When it comes to the pinch you can trust the New Zealander. We don't go for these red-fed ideas here.

Hence **red-fedism**, an ideological attitude of holding and expressing militant left-wing opinions.
  1917 *Wanganui Herald* 18 Apr. 23 [Heading] Red Fedism. Akin to Prussianism. **1920** *NZ Free Lance* (Wellington) 1 Sept. 6 Red Fedism hasn't a hope in rural New Zealand. **1959** *Listener* 26 June 4 Those dark days [of the 1930s] when many a university lecturer and many a student were being hauled across the coals for radicalism, Communism, red-Fed-ism, and all sorts of other nonsense.

Red Federal; **Red Federationist.** *Hist.* A member of the 'red' Federation of Labour. See also REDFED 1a.
  1912 *Evening Post* (Wellington) 16 Sept. 6 There is a diversity that doth hedge a 'strike' is practically the doctrine of some of the Red Federationists. **1914** *Evening Post* (Wellington) 17 Jan. 9 Messrs. Semple, Hickey, Fraser and other leading Red Federals. **1919** FANNING *Politics and the Public* 78 While it is well known..that 'The One Big Union' is the objective of the Red Federals in New Zealand, it is not so well known that [it] seems to be the objective of the Labour Party.

Hence **Red Federalism** *hist.*, the left-wing policies and beliefs of the 'red' Federation of Labour.
  1914 *Evening Post* (Wellington) 17 Jan. 9 The creed of Red Federalism.

redshank. In the phrases: **to run like a red shank** [f. nw. Brit. dial.: see OED *redshank* 2, 1804], to run off quickly; **to be off (out) like red shanks** [see OED 1903], to move quickly away.
  1910 *Truth* 19 Nov. 1 Dr. Findlay..**ran like a red shank** until he got the ear of a reporter, and to him he confided his utter astonishment at such a charge being made by a retired magistrate against his administration. **1891** CHAMIER *Philosopher Dick* 466 Without another thought or look behind us **we were off like red shanks**. **1903** *NZ Illustr. Mag.* VIII. 93 They would be off into the bush like redshanks. **1918** LAWSON *Historic Trentham* 26 Whoop! goes the engine-whistle. We're out like redshanks after her.

red-tailed tropic bird: see TROPIC BIRD.

reed sparrow, **reed warbler.** FERNBIRD.
  1914 GUTHRIE-SMITH *Mutton Birds & Other Birds* 202 *Sphenaeacus punctatus*—Fern Bird—Reed Sparrow. **1940** STUDHOLME *Te Waimate* (1954) 235 [The following diagrams may give some idea of the varying flights of birds:] *Fantail*... Reed warbler.

reef, *n.* Goldmining.

1. [Transf. use of *reef* a narrow ridge or chain of rocks: AND 1854.] A lode or vein of auriferous quartz; also, a quartz-mine.
  1862 *Otago Witness* (Dunedin) 23 Aug. 6 On the hill sides there are numbers of large quartz reefs. **1874** KENNAWAY *Crusts* 230 These fields—or *reefs*, as they

are called—are at present worked by many thousands of diggers. **1889** KNOX *Boy Travellers* 215 Some of the mines are wholly alluvial, or placer, diggings, others are wholly quartz-mines, which are called reefs in New Zealand and Australia. **1918** *NZGeol.SB (NS)* No.19 37 The greater part of the auriferous belt is locally termed 'reef formation', and consists of much crushed and contorted mica-schist. **1978** MCARA *Gold Mining Waihi* 330 *Reefs*: The quartz veins which were contained in the country rocks at Waihi. They were more correctly described as fissure veins; the term 'reefs' is considered to be more appropriately applied to them than the term 'lodes' formerly used.

Hence **reefy** *a.*, of gold, originating in a (quartz) reef.

1910 *NZGeol.SB (NS)* No.11 37 The gold won from Glasseye Creek [Mt. Radiant] was for the most part of a coarse 'reefy' nature, the particles generally varying in weight from 0.5 (half) gr. to 5 dwt.

2. Special Comb. **reef bottom**, bedrock; **reef country**, the area in which a reef of auriferous ore originates; **reef gold**, gold obtained from crushing auriferous ore; **reef-track**, see quot.

1908 *NZGeol.SB (NS)* No.5 37 The basement rock is known to alluvial miners as 'reef bottom'. The '**reef bottom**' may be slate and sandstone, as in Victoria; mica-schist, as in Otago; or granite, as in some parts of New South Wales and Queensland. *Ibid.* 42 Towards the dip it passes off the schist or 'reef' bottom on to the lignite series. **1959** MILLAR *Westland's Golden' Sixties* 158 The **reef country**..apart from being much more difficult to work, was hidden in the wooded hills. **1976** BROWN *Difficult Country* 107 Similarly in the Lyell, Antonio Zala had discovered a reef in 1869... Naturally, this led to a renewed search for gold.., and an endeavour to trace the gold back to 'reef country'. **1890** *TrNZI* XXII. 402 That alluvial gold is of a higher quality than **reef-gold** from the same neighbourhood. **1898** *Ibid.* XXX. 499 There is a great difference in the standard of fineness bewteen alluvial and reef gold. **1948** *NZGeol.SB (NS)* No.42 18 When they contain only small veinlets of quartz or merely bands of faulty pug, vein-fissures are referred to as '**reef-track**' by the miners. *Ibid.* 38 A crosscut put out eastward for 800ft, from which three reef-tracks were explored. **1992** LATHAM *Golden Reefs* 432 When the quartz feathers out, the space between the fissure-walls is generally occupied by crushed rock known as 'reef formation' or [on the Reefton field] 'reef track'. This 'track' often leads to another quartz body, the whole constituting what is usually defined as a 'lode'.

reef *v. intr.* Goldmining.

1. [AND 1859.] To mine auriferous quartz (usu. as a *vbl. n.* or *ppl. a.*, 2 and 3 below).

1879 BARRY *Up & Down* 164 We must sell out the business and go reefing. **c1930** *Whitcombe's Etym. Dict. Aust.-NZ Suppl.* 9 *reef. n.* a vein of gold-bearing quartz; *v. trans.* to work at a reef.

2. As a *vbl. n.*, **reefing.** [AND 1859.] The mining of auriferous reefs as distinct from alluvial mining. Cf. *quartz-reefing* (QUARTZ).

1862 *Otago Witness* (Dunedin) 23 Aug. 5 Any expectations of great gold finding until the dry summer weather [i]s decidedly premature, and even then 'quartz reefing' will, I am convinced, be the main source of a gold export. **1874** *AJHR* H-9 7 Quite recently attention has been turned to reefing, and a party is at present prospecting specially for reefs. **1906** GALVIN *NZ Mining Handbook* 5 Reefing is being carried out at a number of places. **1914** PFAFF *Diggers' Story* 88 As to reefing, the efforts to prospect have been largely sporadic. **1952** HEINZ *Prospecting for Gold* 21 Reefing is made more difficult by the bush cover over most of the hill country and no doubt many rich reefs have thus been passed over. **1992** LATHAM *Golden Reefs* 104 Reefing was not then the main aim of the prospector so Shiel had not troubled himself with the quartz pieces.

3. As a *ppl. a.*, **reefing,** connoting the existence of workable quartz-reefs, usu. in the collocations **reefing-country**, -**district**, -**field**, -**locality**.

1867 reefing country [see REEFER]. **1885** *Wairarapa Daily* 26 Sept. 2 Dunn..is satisfied that the country..is both an alluvial field and good reefing country. **1890** *Mines Report* 157 in *NZGeol.SB (NS)* No.42 (1948) 39 Stone is found in detached blocks along the line of reefing country for 600ft. to 700ft. and runs in narrow scams rich in gold. **1874** HOLLOWAY *Journal of a Visit* 24 June (ATLTS) 121 The rising **reefing district** of Lyell. **1887** *Handbook NZ Mines* 362 The oldest reefing-district in New Zealand [is]..Coromandel. **1907** *NZGeol.SB (NS)* No.4 16 The Try Fluke vein or branches of this vein carrying payable values, were soon traced... It was therefore considered that here at least, a permanent **reefing-field** existed. **1874** *AJHR* H-9 16 It is remarkably strange that this place, so well thought of by practical miners as a likely **reefing locality** should receive so little attention at their hands.

reefer. *Goldmining.* [f. REEF *v.* + -er: AND 1859.] A quartz-miner, as distinct from an alluvial miner; **public-house reefer** (see quot 1992), an 'armchair' quartz-miner having little field experience.

1867 *Trip to Thames Goldfields* (1978) 29 As a reefing country, I am convinced that the small portion of land now open is wonderfully rich. Let the reefers once obtain machinery, and depend upon it the yield will be enormous. **1869** THATCHER *Local Songs* 24 A digger comes up here [to Grahamstown], say from the West Coast... Discovers a reef, and his fortune is made... He rides in a carriage, race-horses he buys, And the people who fawn on this reefer the most, Would have turned up their nose at him on the West Coast. **1892** in McGill *Ghost Towns NZ* (1980) 46 Joseph Berry wrote in the *Cromwell Argus*: Gone is the old 'forty-niner', Gone, like the days that are past, Gone is the sturdy old reefer, Gone to his haven at last! **1992** LATHAM *Golden Reefs* 103 The encouraging results of the..assay performed in September 1870..had been dismissed by some 'public-house reefers' as the product of picked stone.

reef heron: see HERON 2 (1).

refreshment room. *Hist.* Formerly, the official name for a New Zealand Railways cafeteria.

1957 FRAME *Owls Do Cry* (1967) 34 You could never get anything in the refreshment rooms except a bun stuffed with a dirtyfoam of cream, or a stale sandwich, or a pie. **1959** SHADBOLT *New Zealanders* (1986) 42 There were three stale-looking refreshment room sandwiches inside. **1966** TURNER *Eng. Lang. Austral. & NZ* 157 The New Zealand *refreshment rooms* on railway stations are notable. **1976** WILSON *Pacific Star* 150 I walked across [the Palmerston North platform] and went into the refreshment rooms. **1985** *Listener* 28 Sept. 19 You'd have a problem finding a cup of tea at the Taumarunui railway station—the refreshment rooms were closed down in 1975... So you pop off to Refreshments for a cupper tea and pie In Taumarunui, Taumarunui, on the main trunk line. **1990** EDWARDS *AWOL* 61 We went into the crowded refreshment room where there seemed to be an endless queuing up at the counter for the mountains of pies and sandwiches.

regatta shirt. *Obs.* [Used elsewhere but recorded earliest in NZ: f. *regatta* a cotton fabric: see OED 3, 1861.] An informal lightweight striped shirt, in early colonial times often used in trade with the Maori.

1840 in Chambers *Samuel Ironside* (1982) 78 At last he suggested we might make a peace offering..a regatta shirt or two, some figs of tobacco, etc. **1842** *Piraki Log* 14 July (1911) 139 Give to Richards Whaheen 10 regatta shirts..and 5 pairs of lambs-wool hose to get daubed. **1847** ANGAS *Savage Life* II. 161 The payment which I made each of them [*sc.* Maori guides] consisted of a couple of large blankets, a regatta shirt, and a pair of trousers. **1854** *Canterbury Almanack* 93 [Table of Duties of Customs] Slops, Trousers, Moleskin and Tweed..shirts..Regatta and cotton striped. **1866** HUNT *Chatham Is.* 12 Upon that day I had donned a fancy regatta shirt of a most florid pattern.

rehab. *Hist.* Also with init. cap. [f. *rehab*(ilitation or *Rehab*(ilitation Department: AND 1945.]

1. Usu. with reference to the *Rehabilitation Department* set up to help servicemen returned from WW2; often as an *attrib.* or in Comb. denoting its activities (*rehab. loan*, etc.). Compare Brit. *repat*. **a.** Often as **the Rehab.**, the Rehabilitation Department; any or all of the services provided by the Department.

c1945 SIXES & SEVENS (Troopship pub.) 16 Now, chaps, what about a spot of Rehab.? **1953** SCOTT *Breakfast at Six* 12 'This block's a Soldiers' Settlement. You know the sort of thing. Under Rehab.' I didn't know till he explained. Rehab meant the Rehabilitation of Returned Soldiers, a Government department. It advanced money to buy farms. **1959** *Upper Hutt Leader* 25 Mar. 5 'I had a bursary,' said the Grim Dig. 'Reading, writing and rehab.—every soldier's right.' **1969** HILLIARD *Green River* 39 He'd had to bum around for a few years before approaching the rehab [for a loan].

b. *Ellipt.* for *rehab. bursary*, *rehab. loan* or *rehab. payment* (see 2 below).

1959 SLATTER *Gun in My Hand* 28 I was living in Christchurch at different times, at varsity on Rehab for a while. **1960** KEINZLY *Tangahano* 50 There's a dozen jobs waiting to walk into. I can even apply for my rehab and crash out on my own. **1966** TURNER *Eng. Lang. Austral. & NZ* 172 Rehab..was a common word in the years following the Second World War for 'rehabilitation', referring to loans, bursaries and other help given to returned soldiers.

c. In *attrib.* use.

1945 *People's Voice* 5 Dec. 3 [Heading] Value of Maori Rehab. Officers. **1963** PEARSON *Coal Flat* 26 When he came out of the army he got a Rehabilitation grant to finish his B.A. The clerk at the Rehab. office advised him to do this. **1969** HILLIARD *Green River* 22 He'd never really thought of himself as a soldier or an ex-soldier even though he'd had two years of it before..eventually going farming on rehab money. **1976** WILSON *Pacific Star* 156 Well, the Rehab people were sympathetic to my request. **1988** *Univ. Entr. Board Bursaries Exam. Eng.* 6 We lived out in the wop-wops then—on a rehab place, miles from town up a metal road.

2. Special Comb. **Rehab. bursary**, a bursary given to returned servicemen for tertiary study; **Rehab. farm**, one balloted for by returned servicemen and usu. purchased with a rehab. loan; **rehab. farmer** (also *attrib.*); **Rehab. loan**, a loan at a special low rate of interest often with generous suspensory provisions; **Rehab. officer**, a Public Servant responsible for managing rehabilitation services.

1959 SLATTER *Gun in My Hand* 37 The others made good use of their **Rehab Bursary**, made up for the years in the services or behind the wire in the stalag, but I was a washout. **1968** SLATTER *Pagan Game* 16 While on a Rehab Bursary he gained his Masters Degree. **1993** SINCLAIR *Halfway Round the Harbour* 111 On a 'rehab bursary', this was the first time that I had been a full-time university student. **1935** in *Alfredton* (1987) 315 Dave McGovern took over until after W.W.I. when..a returned serviceman was settled on it as a **Rehab. farm**. **1953** *Landfall* 28 263 Then when we saw his name in the paper for winning the Rehab. farm ballot he wrote and said he was coming up. **1974** SIMPSON *Sugarbag Years* 48 I sent the local secretary of the RSA ten pounds towards expenses in getting the man made secure on his farm, which was a rehab. farm. **1983** *Dominion* (Wellington) 24 July 6 They were breaking in their 526 hectare rehab farm..nearly 70km east of Masterton, **1991** *North & South* (Auckland) Nov. 40 Uncle Pat came back from the war [*sc.* 1945] and got a rehab farm. **1978** HENDERSON *Soldier Country* 141 Mac, a canny **rehab. farmer**, took his truck into Invercargill. **1983** *Listener* 4 June 11 Most rehab farmers did make some sort of a fist of it... I fully agree..about the rehab farmers' wives. **1959** SLATTER *Gun in My Hand* 117 My own house and paying it off on the **Rehab. Loan** at three percent. **1966** TURNER *Eng. Lang. Austral. & NZ* 172 A house may be bought with a *rehab* loan or a State Advances loan. **1973** MCELDOWNEY *Arguing with My Grandmother* 20 The interstices had been filled up after the war with rehab-loan bungalows. **1992** *North & South* (Auckland) Jan. 61 With the help of a rehab loan, I belatedly sat for and obtained my engineering qualifications. **c1945** SIXES & SEVENS (Troopship pub.) 5 A **Rehab. officer** outlined the scheme; he offered opportunities for learning carpentering,... and a host of other trades. **1953** SCOTT *Breakfast at Six* 53 It was the Rehab officer in charge of this settlement and others.

Reinga /ræɪˈɪŋə/.
1. Also early **Terry-inga** (=Te Reinga). [Ma. /ˈreːiŋa/: Williams 334 *rēinga*..*1*. Leap, rush...*2*. Place of leaping; so of the place whence spirits of the departed took their final leap; abode of departed spirits: Cape Reinga is situated (as is the North Cape) on the northern tip of the NI.] Often as **the Reinga** (formed after Ma. **Te Reinga**), the place in the far north of New Zealand from which the spirits of Maori dead were believed to enter the otherworld.
1804 *Collins Eng. Colony in NSW* 345 In his chart Too-gee has marked an imaginary road which goes the lengthways of Ea-hei-no-mawe, viz. from Cook's Strait to the North Cape, which Too-gee calls Terry-inga. While the soul is received by the good Ea-tooa, an evil spirit is also in readiness to carry the impure part of the corpse to the above road, along which it is carried to Terry-inga, whence it is precipitated into the sea. **1822** KING 2 Aug. in Elder *Marsden's Lieutenants* (1934) 254 I am told the spirit hovers about the body and place of the deceased until the third day, when the priest prays and directs the spirit to the *reinga*, a place at the North Cape where the natives say the spirits go to and descend. **1833** WILLIAMS *Early Jrnls.* 23 June (1961) 320 They had much to say about Te Uarahi having died and after taking a survey of the Reinga returned to deliver his account. **1840** POLACK *Manners & Customs* I. 58 The chiefs are accounted of divine origin by their followers, whose spirits after death are supposed to reign in an abode of the gods called *Te Reinga*, whose entrance is situated at the gloomy caverns beneath the sea-worn cliffs of the North Cape, (*Muri wenua*). **1862** MANING *War in the North* 22 One of the ancestors of Haurake..hearing, even in the R[ei]nga, (the Maori hades) of the warlike renown of one of his sons, became jealous of his fame. **1878** BULLER *Forty Yrs. NZ* 201 The abode of spirits, they ascribed to a place called *Te Reinga*, at the north cape. **1904** TREGEAR *Maori Race* 169 The spirits of dogs were supposed, like those of men, to pass to the World of Shadows (*Te Reinga*) but they travelled by a different path than that taken by the souls of human beings. **1935** COWAN *Hero Stories NZ* 115 Her warrior brother Hitiri..was not long in following her to the Reinga. **1949** CURRIE *Centennial Treasury Otago Verse* 110 Whether in Niu Tireni or Te Reinga Now you live, or in countries over the ocean. **1982** HULME *Silences Between* 38 Love of dolphins, love of whales show me the way to Te Reinga

2. In the phr. **from Reinga (Cape Reinga, the Reinga) to the Bluff** (occas. **Stewart Island**), varr. of *North Cape to the Bluff* (see NORTH CAPE).
1882 HAY *Brighter Britain* II. 204 It [*sc.* flax] is plentiful everywhere..hill and dale, from the Reinga to the Bluff. [**1940** DUGGAN *NZ Poems* 52 Holding us in from the tip of Reinga To where the Bluff folds down a heavy paw.] **1979** GEBBIE & MCGREGOR *Incredible 8-Ounce Dream* 11 But it never ceases to amaze me that those who spend so long hanging on handles in public bars from Cape Reinga to Bluff should know so little about how they can be exploited in these places. **1981** CHARLES *Black Billy Tea* 94 You can steal a car and drive it From Reinga to the Bluff. **1986** BROWN *Weaver's Apprentice* 150 The name Crocker Quarries would be known from Cape Reinga to Stewart Island.

Reischek's parakeet: see PARAKEET 2 (8).

reiva reiva, var. REWAREWA.

relief. *Hist.* Often init. cap. [Spec. use of *relief* aid given to persons in a state of want: see OED *relief n.*² 3 a.]
1. Applied in the Depression of the 1930s to the Government 'scheme 13' whereby the unemployed were paid a small amount by the State in return for work on public amenities, and also to the similar 'scheme 15' for subsidized farm labour. Usu. in the phr. **on relief**, or as *attrib.* passing into Comb.
1936 HYDE *Passport to Hell* 15 They..work three days a week shovelling bits of coast in the relief gangs, for whom award wages are a bright and sweet dream from a dead generation. They cadge vegetables and coal at relief depots and welfare departments. **1937** *Tomorrow* 6 Jan. 154 Jackson could not get regular work and in the end he went on 'relief'. **1946** SARGESON *That Summer* 55 He was pretty red, too, though he said he hadn't been until he'd had experience of being on relief. **1959** DAVIN *No Remittance* 190 The Depression was knocking at the door..half the people on Relief. **1964** PEARSON *Glossary* to Sargeson *Collected Stories 1935-63* (1964) 302 relief: a Government work scheme for unemployed during the depression. Relief work was often part-time and often work of little perceivable immediate value—clearing drains, grubbing gorse, draining swamps, making roads, planting trees, etc. **1970** MIDDLETON in *Some Other Country* (1984) 153 Then the Slump came. The builder went broke and for months I was on relief. **1986** TAYLOR *NZ People at War* I. 72 Men still on relief had little urge to fight for the country that had given them so little.

2. Special Comb. **relief camp**, a camp, usu. of tents, housing workers on a relief work project; **relief work (works)**, usu. work provided by the Government scheme for occupying and paying the unemployed (but see also quots. 1888, 1921); **relief worker** (occas. **reliefer**, see quot. 1934), one employed on relief works; **relief worker's jam**, golden syrup as a cheap spread.
1932 *Weekly News* (Auckland) 1 June With the object of providing satisfactory useful work for unemployed men in return for sustenance and a small wage the Government has established **relief camps** in many parts of New Zealand. **1959** SINCLAIR *Hist. NZ* 250 The unemployed were put to work draining swamps, making roads—or golf courses—planting trees, and were paid a miserable sum partly raised by special taxation. In many of the rural 'relief camps' conditions were extremely primitive. **1965** SHADBOLT *Among Cinders* 140 You remember what it was like in the depression? All the single men being shipped off to relief camps? **1987** *Metro* (Auckland) May 143 But of all the schemes to help the unemployed help themselves, the one that aroused most hostility was that of the relief camps. **1991** VIRTUE *Always the Islands of Memory* 95 Tom was in a relief camp, somewhere south of Hamilton, digging ditches and felling trees for the Government. **1888** BRADSHAW *NZ of To-day 1884-7* 175 The New Zealand Government is pestered by applicants who desire more '**relief works**' to be undertaken at public expense. **1921** *Quick March* 10 Sept. 36 A number of local bodies also provided a limited amount of 'relief work' [for unemployed]. **1938** HYDE *Nor Yrs. Condemn* 275 Men on relief works were being turned off, unless they had wives and families. **1946** SARGESON *That Summer* 152 As a single man, I'd only get about a day and a-half's relief work a week, and drew fourteen shillings. **1959** SINCLAIR *Hist. NZ* 250 The ragged army of men 'on the dole'—as they called the payments for 'relief work'; architects, teachers, carpenters, chipping weeds on the footpaths. **1987** ELDRED-GRIGG *Oracles & Miracles* 23 Then he was on a scheme they had going [c.1930], what they called relief work. **1964** NORRIS *Settlers in Depression* 210 A scheme for creating some work for the unemployed was developed at Te Kauwhata... The men on relief work cleared the ground of scrub and 810 acres were then ploughed by contract. **1934** *Fielding Star* 27 Feb. 5 The case of the **reliefer** today was particularly hard when sickness came his way. **1975** SARGESON *More Than Enough* 42 But the first of these people with a purpose was a fellow **relief worker**, and I will call him X. **1981** STEWART *Hot & Copper Sky* 63 Groups of 'relief' workers lived under canvas, a sad army separated from wives and families in pursuit of the only work available to them, moving on as the road moved. **1984** LOCKE *The Kauri & the Willow* 175 She regularly walked two miles to a shop which sold '**relief workers' jam**' (golden syrup) a halfpenny cheaper.

relieving teacher. Also occas. **relief teacher**, **reliever**. A teacher temporarily replacing a teacher who is absent. Cf. Brit. *supply teacher*.
1916 *NZ Educational Institute Rep. of Thirty-Third Annual Meeting* 19 Review 31—That relieving teachers be paid travelling expenses. **1922** *NZ Gaz.* 13 Apr. No.29 Regulations relating to Secondary Schools. S49..a relieving teacher employed for two months or more during any calender year. **1966** TURNER *Eng. Lang. Austral. & NZ* 158 Later he may become a *relieving teacher* (corresponding with the English teacher on supply). **1976** *Secondary School Boards Assoc. to Dept. of Educ.* 20 Oct. in *STA archives* [Heading] Administrative Aspects of the Employment of Relief Teachers. **1987** *Evening Post* (Wellington) 17 Dec. 9 In the 1062 schools which replied to the survey, there were 2873 times during the year when regular teachers were absent and there were no relieving teachers to take over the classes. The relievers were appointed..before the required certification... The employment of relief teachers [was confirmed].

religo /rəˈlɪdʒʌu/. WW2. [f. *relig*(ious + -o.] One who conscientiously objects to war on religious grounds. Cf. HOON 1.
1953 HAMILTON *Till Human Voices Wake Us* 164 There was a sort of line drawn in the [detention] camps

between the Hoons and the religoes... The religoes were divided again into God knows how many sects and amongst the hoons were absolute pacifists, pacifists, Communists, Anarchists, humanists, and plain dodgers. *Ibid.* 215 The third group [in conscientious objectors' detention camps], the religoes, could hardly be called a group at all. It was a mixed bag of Methodists, Presbyterians, Brethren, Church of England and some Catholics.

rellie. [f. *rel*(ation or *rel*(ative + -IE.] A relation or relative.
　1988 *North & South* (Auckland) Sept. 41 Where else are they so big on hypocorisms?.. They're those dinky little words we make up, like these: kiddies (children), cardies (cardigans)..rellies (relations). **1989** *Evening Post* (Wellington) 10 Jan. 6 Those strangely infantile condensations—'prezzies' and 'rellies' (for presents and relatives) were bandied about on the radio quite a bit recently. **1991** *Metro* (Auckland) July 51 If we go away for a holiday we don't stay in flash pubs, we stay with rellies.

rema, var. RIMU *n.*[1]

remit. [f. *remit v.* to send: cf. OED *v.* III 8, *n.* 3 b.] A recommendation sent by a branch or by an affiliated organization to the main body of the organization (often to an annual conference) for consideration, and possible adoption and action.
　1902 *NZJE* 1 Feb. III. 247 Mr. Johnson moved the Taranaki remit, That the desirableness be urged upon the Minister of having a uniform set of text books in use in the schools throughout the colony. **1912** [see EXPERT]. **1916** *Maoriland Worker* 12 July 4 Messrs. Hutchison and Harper moved that the Order Paper Committee put on a remit dealing with Conscription. Carried. **1921** *Quick March* 10 Feb. 40 The following are some of the remits proposed for discussion at the Empire Conference by the N.Z.R.S.A. **1958** *Listener* 5 Sept. 8 We might see that New Zealand would put a remit up to the International Board and it would be turned down. **1966** TURNER *Eng. Lang. Austral. & NZ* 174 The noun *remit*..means a directive from a branch to a central organization for consideration. **1972** MITCHELL *Pavlova Paradise* 183 *remit:* Resolution.

remittance. *Hist.* [Used elsewhere, but of significance to New Zealand's colonial past.]
　1. A payment made from a 'home' country source to ensure the exile of a (usu.) undesirable relative or friend who has been removed to New Zealand.
　1853 MACKIE *Traveller under Concern* (1973) 26 Apr. 102 [The Wakatu inn] is frequented by young men of some education with a little money, and whilst their money lasts they give themselves up to riot and excess. They are probably such as their friends in England are glad to send to a distance and as if to confirm their ruin supply them with a small income. As soon as this is squandered they go to the Wairau as shepherds... Here they remain in obscurity till their remittance brings them again to the Wakatu. **1861** HARPER *Lett. from NZ* (1914) 61 We have fewer of those failures at home who are sent out to the Colonies, in the faint hope that a man who is a ne'er-do-well in England will succeed elsewhere, and in too many cases sent out with the promise of small remittances, to be out of sight and out of mind. **1881** BATHGATE *Waitaruna* 145 'Oh! bother my uncle, though he did send me a small remittance the other day,' was Arthur's rejoinder. **1899** BELL *In Shadow of Bush* 126 What the devil brought you here? Did I not tell you to keep to yourself and not cross my way, except when you come to my office for your remittance. **1910** *Truth* 2 July 6 They [*sc.* station cadets] get a remittance which keeps them in clothes, l[e]ggings and riding breeches, and an occasional trip to town... They are practically banished from the old country to save the family from being disgraced, and this place is being made a dumping ground for these wastrels. **1938** LANCASTER *Promenade* 135 No good record attached to this young sprig of the nobility who (said rumour) had been cashiered from the Hussars..the relatives promising that he would receive a handsome remittance so long as he stayed [in the colonies].

　2. Special Comb. **remittance day**, the day a remittance man's remittance is paid; **remittance man**, a (usu.) upper-class immigrant in some way found undesirable by his home family and for that reason supported 'in exile' by remittances from Britain; often a folk or stock character in New Zealand popular literature.
　1944 LEE *Shining with the Shiner* 76 Fill it up [with whisky] it's **remittance day**. **1965** MCLAGLAN *Stethoscope & Saddlebags* 185 Each remittance day they used to get very drunk indeed, often got the D.T.s and had to be taken into the Auckland Hospital for treatment. **1888** BRADSHAW *NZ To-day* 171 He ultimately settled down into the position of a '**remittance man**'—living, that is, upon a pittance sent out from home and doled out in weekly instalments by a solicitor. **1892** KIPLING *One Lady at Wairakei* (1983) 35 Two of her loves were just sheep-men, but the third was a remittance-man, if you know what that is, and he had been a gentleman in England. **1911** *Truth* 8 Apr. 7 For many years New Zealand has been the dumping ground for social derelicts 'who left their country for their country's good'... They are called remittance men, and when their little div. arrives from 'Ome they are millionaires for an hour. **1925** BATHGATE *Random Recolls.* 36 One not infrequently came across remittance men, generally on the goldfields, at some public house, employed as groom and general rouseabout, or perhaps cook. **1943** MARSH *Colour Scheme* 45 They [*sc.* English-born upper-class misfits] used to be called remittance men, and in this extraordinary country received a good deal of entirely misguided sympathy from native-born fools. **1965** MCLAGLAN *Stethoscope & Saddlebags* 89 In those days New Zealand, including especially the gumfields, was the haunt of remittance men, black sheep from good families whose relatives had shipped them off to the colonies and sent them an allowance as long as they stayed there. **1978** TAYLOR *Twilight Hour* 12 Our parents told us that Daddy was a remittance man. **1991** *NZ Geographic* Apr.–June 37 The fields were populated by rebels, drifters, remittance men, unemployed mechanics and clerks—underdogs of every description.

remo, remu, varr. RIMU *n.*[1]

rengarenga. [Ma. /ˈreŋareŋa/: Williams 336 *rengarenga*..5... *Arthropodium cirratum.*] *Arthropodium cirratum* (fam. Asphodelaceae), a herb having drooping leaves and branching flower-stems, found in open rocky situations northwards from the Marlborough Sounds. See also *Mabel Island lily, New Zealand lily, renga lily, rock lily* (see LILY 2 (7), (11), (13), (14)), MAIKAKA.
　[**1820** LEE & KENDALL *NZ Gram. & Vocab.* 202 *Rénga rénga*; A plant so called.] **1835** YATE *NZ* (1970) 89 The root of the Rengarenga..scraped and applied..to bring forwards any abscesses or tumours, where matter is forming. **1848** [see LILY 2 (11)]. **1853** HOOKER *II Flora Novae-Zelandiae I Flowering Plants* 254 Arthropodium *cirratum*... Nat. name, 'Renga Renga', in Northern Districts, and 'Maikai Ka', in Southern. **1879** *Auckland Weekly News* 3 May 17 This is..a good year; the *rengarenga* (lily of the valley) is in bloom. **1881**, **1904** [see LILY 2 (11)]. **1924** *NZJST* VII. 187 On the rocky knoll near the middle of the [Karewa] islet the rengarenga, or rock-lily.., grows in profusion. **1946** *JPS* LV. 157 *Rengarenga*, a lily (Arthropodium cirratum), likes open rocky situations. **1969** [see LILY 2 (7)]. **1973** [see LILY 2 (12)]. **1981** BROOKER et al. *NZ Medicinal Plants* 63 Arthropodium *cirratum*... Common name: *Rock lily* Maori names: *Rengarenga, maikaika, maika ka*

rental, *a.* [Spec. use of *rental* something rented.] Formerly, a public library book (usu. popular fiction) for which the borrower paid a fee to borrow. Also *attrib.*
　1962 MCELDOWNEY *NZ Library Association* 75 The Fiction Committee of the Association in 1942 compiled a list..with the division into free and rental collections in mind. **1966** TURNER *Eng. Lang. Austral. & NZ* 159 Another of New Zealand's contributions to library science, the *rental collection* or *pay collection*, reflects the other side of the New Zealand character. Rental collections in free Public Libraries provide 'popular' books not justifiably bought with public money, and sometimes also duplicate books in heavy demand. **1968** *NZ Libraries* 31(4) Aug. 131 How would life without rentals be carried on? **1981** *Ibid.* 43(6) June 98 A recent review..has shown that desk income from rentals is not keeping pace with spending on the collection.

reo: see TE REO.

rep. [Spec. use of *rep*, a shortened form of *rep*(resentative (footballer, etc.).]
　1. a. A member of a provincial (occas. national) representative sports team, very often a rugby union footballer. Also as **the reps**, a provincial representative sports team.
　1896 EYTON *Rugby Football* 10 Joe..has annually played and led the Tauranga reps. against the Auckland teams. **1900** *Auckland Weekly News* (Suppl.) 6 July 9 There is little doubt but that Mr. Arneil will succeed in getting together a fifteen that, even if not quite up to last year's touring 'reps.', will nevertheless be equal to making a good fight of it with the best the sister provinces can put in the field against them. **1917** INGRAM *Anzac Diary* (1987) 16 Sept. 44 The afternoon was spent in watching the 1st. and 2nd. Batalion [*sic*] football reps. in action against each other. **1928** *Na To Hoa Aroha* (1986) I. 139 The Maori Reps under George Nepia defeated N.S. Wales by 9 to 8 on Athletic Park last Saturday. **1943** HISLOP *Pure Gold* 36 Everybody knew him as a rep. in the Otago [rugby] team. **1968** SLATTER *Pagan Game* 158 Got into a good team in the city, got into the reps and when they won the Shield he was home on the pig's back. Never looked back. Everything went right for him. **1985** STEWART *Gumboots & Goalposts* 13 And that's what the reps need too, a few good country forwards who know how to 'get stuck in'.

　b. *attrib.* usu. in reference to a team sport, very often rugby union, at provincial level.
　1905 *Truth* 12 Aug. 2 Junior rep. match. **1908** BARR *Brit. Rugby Team in Maoriland* 39 Colin Gilroy, rep. footballer and Rhodes scholar. **1916** THORNTON *Wowser* 270 Didn't you play wing-threequarters in such and such a 'rep' match? **1956** SUTHERLAND *Green Kiwi* (1960) 140 Family..plays rep. tennis and hockey and handles a horse better than most men. **1968** SLATTER *Pagan Game* 174 The rep games when the log of wood has gone. **1974** GIFFORD *Loosehead Len's Big Brown Book* 9 Where I go once I'm in the park depends on whether it's a club day or a rep match. **1985** STEWART *Gumboots & Goalposts* 13 The rep selector is here today.

2. *Hist.* [AND 1899.] A Shearers' (Union) representative.

1933 *Press* (Christchurch) (Acland Gloss.) 18 Nov. 15 *Rep.*—Sometimes *shed r[ep]*. Under the arbitration award it is laid down that 'the shearers shall elect a representative', who deals with the employer whenever any dispute or question arises. If the *r[ep]* is a sensible man of good will, shearing goes through with hardly a hitch. **1949** NEWTON *High Country Days* 197 In a shearing gang a man is elected as a representative in the event of any disputes. He is known as the 'rep'. **1955** BOWEN *Wool Away* 156 Rep. Shearers' voted representative who speaks for all the shearers in the gang in regard to complaints, decisions, etc. **1987** OGONOWSKA-COATES *Boards, Blades & Barebellies* 97 *Rep.* In the terms of the 1894 Industrial Conciliation and Arbitration Act, shearers were to elect a representative to negotiate any disputes or grievances directly with their employer.

repat /ri'pæt/. *WW1*. The Repatriation Department, a State department formerly responsible for helping returned servicemen from WW1 settle back into civilian life. Compare REHAB.

1925 SCANLON *Much in Little* 10 That 'coot' who just got out is one of the Repat 'heads'. [**1984** BOYD *City of the Plains* 208 The Repatriation Department was wound up in 1922.]

reperepe. Also early **eraperape** (=he raperape), ?erron. **rerepe**. [Ma. /'reperepe/: Williams 336 *reperepe..2...* elephant fish.] ELEPHANT FISH.

1770 PARKINSON *Journal* (1773) 127 Eraperape, *A fish called Chimaera*. **1921** *NZJST* IV. 123 Callorhynchus milii... *Elephant-fish; Reperepe*. In Christchurch large numbers are sold under the name of 'silver trumpeter'. **1938** [see ELEPHANT FISH]. **1956** GRAHAM *Treasury NZ Fishes* 84 Elephant-fish (Reperepe) *Callorhynchus milii*. **1967** MORELAND *Marine Fishes* 12 Elephantfish... Other names are elephant and reperepe. **1982** BURTON *Two Hundred Yrs. NZ Food* 73 This bizarre, silvery fish, known to the Maori as *rerepe*..occurs mainly along the east coast of the South Island.

repo, var. RAUPO.

reputation. Usu. in non-personal application, **to hang by** (or **on**) **its reputation**, to hang by 'a thread', to be in a 'touch and go' position or situation.

1949 *hanging by its reputation* used at Kaitaia, of physical objects p.c. R. Mason. **1949** (Wellington) A man describes a nearly-amputated finger as 'hanging by its reputation'. (Ed.) **1972** July Radio Talk. The JBL industrial group, which had gone into receivership, described as 'hanging on its reputation for more than a year before the crash'.

reremai. [Ma. /'reremai/: Williams 338 *Reremai*..basking shark.] *basking shark* (SHARK 2 (1)).

[**1820** LEE & KENDALL *NZ Gram. & Vocab.* 202 Rére mai; A fish so called.] **1927** PHILLIPPS *Bibliogr. NZ Fishes* (1971) 8 *Cetorhinus maximus*... Basking-shark; Reremai. **1947** POWELL *Native Animals NZ* 62 Basking Shark..Reremai of the Maoris, is our largest shark. **1963** KEENE *O te Raki* 194 *Reremai*: basking shark, New Zealand's largest shark, has blunt teeth about ¼ in. in length; harmless; eats crustaceans. **1967** NATUSCH *Animals NZ* 198 Family Cetorhinidae contains the enormous basking shark or reremai (*Cetorhinus*).

rerepe, var. REPEREPE.

rerepe, rerepi, varr. LILIPI.

reserve. [Spec. use of *reserve*, land, or a place, set apart: see OED 5 b; cf. also U.S., Mathews 6 any piece of land set aside for a special purpose, 1807.]

1. [AND 1815.] A piece of land set aside for public or special use, often with a modifier denoting the nature or purpose of the reservation as *bush*, *education*, *native*, *roads*, *scenic*, etc. Often **The Reserve** as a local place-name indicating a bush reserve, recreation area, etc.

1848 WAKEFIELD *Handbook NZ* 94 A town-site [for Wellington] was laid out, consisting of 1100 sections of one acre each, besides reserves for public purposes. **1879** KIERNAN *Diary* 1 Mar. in Guthrie-Smith *Tutira* (1921) 128 Kite and Jim went mustering the reserve for stragglers. **1882** POTTS *Out in Open* 30 The subject of national domains, parks, or reserves, is a matter of such general interest, that probably no long time will elapse before the question will thoroughly engage the attention of the public. **1898** HOCKEN *Contributions* 100 An instruction to Mr. Kettle when commencing his surveys was to lay off certain portions of land for public use, not open for sale, and termed 'reserves'. **1911** KOEBEL *Maoriland Bush* 97 A patch or two of 'reserve' bush. **a1927** ANTHONY *Me & Gus* (1977 Gus Tomlins) 81 How a man can fancy that a job of sawdust boy..can help him to locate cattle in Mount Egmont Reserve beats me. **1936** BELSHAW et al. *Agric. Organiz. NZ* 603 In New Zealand a large area of land in different parts has been permanently reserved as 'scenic reserves' and 'National Parks'. **1957** FRAME *Owls Do Cry* (1967) To decide if the reserves where grew native trees and shrubs should be offered for sale as housing sections. **1960** MASTERS *Back-Country Tales* 149 'One of the wonders of the world.' Such was the manner in which the scenic reserve known as Ball's clearing at Puketitiri, was referred to by the writer of an article in an overseas magazine years ago. **1987** *Listener* 8 Aug. 61 The tip of Point Chevalier was a park known as 'the Reserve', ringed with pine trees and macrocarpa.

Hence **reserved** *ppl. a.*, of land or forest, retained for public use.

1861 *Otago Witness* (Dunedin) 6 Apr. 7 The reserved bush is within two minutes' walk of the house.

2. Special Comb. **Maori** (or earlier **native**) **reserve,** land reserved by statute for Maori purposes and intentions; esp. in early colonial times, in respect of sales of Maori land, areas required to be set aside for exclusive Maori ownership and use.

1846 *Wakefield to Gladstone* 20 Jan. in Rutherford *Sel. Documents* (1949) 15(A) It strikes me that a portion of the funds derived from Native Reserves might be very suitably set apart for the payment of outside Protectors and the promotion of Christian Missions. **1847** William Swainson let. in *William Swainson* 25 Oct. (1992) 134 The natives of Epuni are now going on their two Reserves at the Taita. **1853** ROCHFORT *Adventures Surveyor in NZ* 31 All the land of any use is purchased by the government, except a sufficient quantity to support the aborigines, which is called a native reserve. **1853** ADAMS *Canterbury Settlement* 49 On the north side of the [Lyttelton] harbour..is situated the Maori Reserve, a beautiful..valley which was retained by the natives. **1872** *Appendix Proc. Otago Prov. Council* 39 The peninsula..is a Maori Reserve, but is unoccupied except by..an old whaler. **1879** *Auckland Weekly News* 23 Aug. 8 Suppose..that 10,000 acres of this 100,000 is to be a 'native reserve,' this reserve should be made inalienable. **1888** D'AVIGDOR *Antipodean Notes* 105 There are now 'Native Reserves' in both islands, the increasing revenues from which are administered by a minister for the benefit of the various tribes interested, who are yet tacitly acknowledged by everybody to be as unable to look after their own property as children or lunatics. **1914** PFAFF *Diggers' Story* 1 Mackay, after fixing up some Native Reserves at the Buller, agreed to shepherd them [*sc.* a party wishing to return to 'civilisation'] to Massacre bay. **1943** MARSH *Colour Scheme* 36 Down in the native reserve a collection of small brown boys milled about. **1944** BEATTIE *Maori Place-names Otago* 51 A statement in print that 'Wairakinui is a Maori Reserve at the Waiau' greatly intrigued an old friend of mine, as he said Wairakinui was the name of a remote ancestor of his. **1952** TAYLOR *Lore and History of the South Island Maori* 16 At present [*sc.* early 1950s] the Native Reserves of Nelson are numerous, but small; the total area being 58,565 acres take. **1972** *Coastal Development. Policy Issues & Planning Techniques* 49 In counties, owners of coastal lakes and riverside land who subdivide it into sections smaller than 10 acres are normally required to dedicate a strip of land above the foredune for access and use by the public. The minimum width of this strip of so-called '**esplanade reserve**' is generally 66 feet (one chain) measured from mean high water mark.

Reserve Bank. In full **Reserve Bank of New Zealand.** [AND 1959.] The central bank holding deposits of reserves of other banks, and having certain statutory obligations in the regulation of money supply.

1933 *NZ Statutes* No.11 53 There shall be established in New Zealand in accordance with this Act [Reserve Bank of NZ Act] a bank to be called the Reserve Bank of New Zealand. *Ibid.* 56 It shall be the primary duty of the Reserve Bank to exercise control..over monetary circulation and credit in New Zealand, to the end that the economic welfare of the Dominion may be promoted and maintained. **1936** *NZ Statutes* No.1 7 [Reserve Bank of NZ Amendment Act] It shall be the general function of the Reserve Bank..to give effect as far as may be to the monetary policy of the Government, as communicated to it from time to time by the Minister of Finance... The bank shall regulate and control credit and currency in New Zealand, the transfer of moneys to or from New Zealand, and the disposal of moneys that are derived from the sale of any New Zealand products and for the time being are held overseas. **1952** *NZPD* CCXCVIII. 1223 The great temptation to any Government is..to use Reserve Bank credit. **1959** SINCLAIR *Hist. NZ* 254 In the same year [1933] the Government set up the Reserve Bank of New Zealand so that it could secure cheaper credit for the state..so and, more important, so that it could determine general monetary policy. **1968** GLEN *Holy Joe's People* 13 She was a woman of considerable importance..who..was reputed..to have more money than the Reserve Bank. **1994** *Dominion* (Wellington) 29 June 15 The Reserve Bank's hints at interest rate rises to control New Zealand inflation exacerbated worries.

resin. *Obs.* Also **rosin**. An early name for KAURI GUM.

[**1769** COOK *Journals* 16 Nov. (1955) I. 204 [The first reference to kauri gum which Cook mistakes for an exudation from coastal mangroves.] In speaking of Mercury Bay I had forgot to mention that the Mangrove trees found there produce a resinous substance very much like rosin, something of this kind I am told is found in both the East and West Indies. We found it first in small lumps upon the Sea beach.] **1814** MARSDEN in Elder *Marsden's Lieutenants* (1934) 55 Pork, if it is to be obtained, and salt fish, rosin, or any other natural productions. **1819** MARSDEN *Letters and Journals* (1932) 22 Oct. 210 There is here and there the root of a pine which has been burnt into the surface of the ground,

retireti. *Obs.* [Ma. /ˈretireti/: not recorded in Williams or Biggs: poss. a Maori adaptation of *lettuce*.] Sorrel, *Oxalis* spp.

1867 HOCHSTETTER *NZ* 157 Retireti, Tutaekahu (*Oxalis*), is a wholesome vegetable when boiled. **1882** HAY *Brighter Britain* II. 210 There are the native spinach or Renga-renga..the Pana-pana, or cress..and the Reti-reti, or sorrel (*Oxalis magellanica*), which do for salad and green vegetables.

retread /ˈriːˌtred/. [Transf. use of *retread* a used tyre which has been re-capped for further use: AND 1941.] A superannuated or retired person returned into the work force.

1968 *NZ Contemp. Dict. Suppl.* (Collins) 16 *retread n.* soldier who re-enlists; superannuated public servant who re-enters the Service as a casual officer. **1974** BREAM *I'm Sorry Amanda* 28 Mr Willis had taught for forty years, and then retired. He had now returned to the school..to help relieve the teacher shortage. He was a very nice person, as were all our retreads.

return. A second helping (esp. at a public eating-place).

c1945 Table menu in a Wellington eating-place 'No returns'. **1950** *Post Office English Course* (TS) 14 New Zealand has developed many phrases that depend on local interpretation: e.g. 'The Limited', 'the six o'clock rush'..'return (at meals)'. All these are immediately understandable to New Zealanders, but not always to others.

returned, *a.* [AND 1902; OED 2 b.] The usual term applied in New Zealand (as elsewhere) to a serviceman discharged from the forces and returned home after a war. Usu. in collocations, earlier (WW1) **returned soldier** (later as **returned serviceman**), occas. **returned man** or **ex-serviceman**. See also **RSA**.

1917 *Truth* 5 May 2 Truth saw one official at the Returned Soldiers' Club... The next time the Returned Soldiers' Association gives a dinner, those responsible..will make it clear that the soldiers themselves are giving the dinner. **1918** *Quick March* 1 Oct. 3 On 30th April, 1916, about thirty returned soldiers assembled in Wellington for the purpose of forming a Returned Soldiers' Association. **1920** BOLITHO *With the Prince in NZ* 21 It was an impressive gathering of returned soldiers. **1936** HYDE *Passport to Hell* 17 Yet, potentially at least, the returned soldier's desperate desire to fit in again..is one of the most valuable things remaining in our world. **1948** *Our Own Country* 53 Today the supervisor is a man of Maori blood, a returned soldier of the last war. **1963** BACON *In the Sticks* 62 The Government partly developed the land, then put returned soldier farmers on it. **1970** LEE *Mussolini's Million* 101 Paddy Murphy had been District President of the Returned Soldiers Association since 1918. **1992** *Metro* (Auckland) Feb. 7 Often 'returned' men like Muldoon, went to him for financial advice.

rewai, var. RIWAI.

rewarewa. Also with much variety of early form as **ráwa ráwa, reivá reivá, river river, riwariwa, ruva-ruva**. [Ma. /ˈrewarewa/: Williams 339 *rewarewa. 1.*] *Knightia excelsa* (fam. Proteaceae), a tall forest tree of the North Island and Marlborough Sounds, having long, toothed leaves and bearing racemes of tomentose red-brown flowers followed by woody pods; also its timber, valued for cabinet and decorative work. (Occas. mistakenly applied to KOHEKOHE *Dysoxylum spectabile*.) See also BUCKET-OF-WATER-WOOD b, HONEYSUCKLE.

1817 NICHOLAS *NZ* II. 245 The trees which the natives chiefly make subservient to their purposes, are..the henow..the *river river*, the grain of whose wood is similar to that of the beech. [**1820** LEE & KENDALL *NZ Gram. & Vocab.* 201 Ráwa ráwa; A tree so called.] **1834** McDONNELL *Extracts Jrnl.* (1979) 19 A great variety of hard-wood grows at New Zealand, admirably adapted for the timbering of any sized ships; among them is the boridé..reivá reivá..and many others. **1835** YATE *NZ* (1970) 264 Give him this Rewarewa-box, for his wife to put her needles and thread in. **1842** HEAPHY *NZ* 43 The Ruva-ruva or honeysuckle, is mostly used for timbers and other parts requiring great strength. **1864** *Richmond-Atkinson Papers* 25 Mar. (1960) II. 100 The flagstaff was a rewarewa—the cap (or truck) of it I brought away. **1874** BAINES *Edward Crewe* 144 On either side much of the land was covered with a growth of..rewa-rewa, towai..and other smaller kinds of timber. **1879** riwariwa [see RIBBONWOOD]. **1883** HECTOR *Handbook NZ* 129 Rewarewa... A lofty slender tree, 100 feet high. Wood handsome, mottled red and brown. **1898** MORRIS *Austral-English* 386 *Rewa-rewa* pronounced *raywa*, Maori name for the New Zealand tree *Knightia excelsa*.., *N.O. Proteaceae*, the Honey-suckle of the New Zealand settlers. **1907** LAING & BLACKWELL *Plants NZ* 146 *Knightia excelsa* (*The Honey-suckle*)... Maori name, *Rewa-rewa*. It is sometimes called the *Bucket-of-water-tree*, because it is so slow of combustion. **1910** COCKAYNE *NZ Plants & Their Story* 41 The New Zealand honeysuckle (..rewarewa) is one of the handsomest woods in the world. **1926** CROOKES *Plant Life in Maoriland* 31 Few people seeing our modestly attired rewa rewa (or native honey-suckle as it is sometimes called) with its sprays of dark brown or red-brown flowers, would dream of associating it with the flamboyant bottle brushes..of our gardens and parks. **1989** THOMSON & NIELSON *Sharing the Challenge* 128 [Caption] Police baton fashioned from native Rewa Rewa (Honeysuckle) for the Foot Specials during the 1913 strike.

rhubarb.

1. *Flaxmilling*. The red stalk-base of a blade of New Zealand flax.

1913 CARR *Country Work* 43 The cutter, armed with a sickle, stoops down and cuts the plant as near the base as he can get without taking in too much of the white growth, commonly called 'rhubarb'. **1952** p.c. R. Mason (Wellington). *Rhubarb* is used for the reddish coloured base of the flax leaf used by Foxton flax-mill workers. Probably much older than when I heard it, 1943, and could be much more widespread.

2. In the phr. **up (someone) for the rhubarb season,** see UP YOU; cf. BOOHAI 3 (quot. 1930).

ribaldo /riˈbældʌu/. [Origin unknown.] *Mora moro* (formerly *pacifica*) (fam. Moridae), a large-eyed, deepwater cod, a good food fish.

1956 GRAHAM *Treasury NZ Fishes* 404 Ribaldo *Mora pacifica*. **1960** PARROTT *Queer & Rare Fishes* 86 Ribaldo. *Mora pacifica*... The Ribaldo is included in this book because..this fish may sometimes be taken by commercial fishermen. **1986** PAUL *NZ Fishes* 58 *Ribaldo Mora moro*... Alternatively, googley-eyed cod... Greyish pink above, flecked with brown, paling to white below... A regular by-catch in offshore trawl and longline fisheries... Often marketed as deepsea cod. **1993** PAUL & MORELAND *Handbook Marine Fishes* 69 *Ribaldo* (*Mora moro*). A moderate-sized cod of deep waters... Also present off southern Australia, and quite widely distributed from Northern Africa through European waters... Alternative names include googly-eyed cod and deepsea cod. It is sold commercially under the latter name... Flesh is white and flaking but moderately firm.

ribbandfish: see RIBBONFISH.

ribbonfish. Also **ribbandfish.** [Spec. use of *ribbon-fish* a flat, elongate species.] Formerly applied somewhat indiscriminately to several species of large, elongated 'ribbonlike', usu. silvery, fishes of three related families: Lophotidae (crestfishes), Trachipteridae (ribbonfishes, dealfishes), and Regalecidae (oarfishes).

1855 TAYLOR *Te Ika A Maui* 625 A large fish, most probably a..ribbon fish, thrown up on the Nelson coast..was described..as having a small head..and a body fifteen feet long tapering to the tail. **1881** ribband-fish [see BANDFISH]. **1886** SHERRIN *Handbook Fishes NZ* 303 *Regalecus argenteus* Ribbon-fish, or Mataura. **1902** DRUMMOND & HUTTON *Nature in NZ* 74 The flesh of deep sea fishes, such as the ribbon fish and the oarfish, becomes a jelly when boiled, and is quite unfit to eat. **1912** *Otago Witness* (Dunedin) 18 Sept. 45 [Caption] A ribbon-fish, 12 feet in length, the most perfect specimen yet found in New Zealand. **1927** PHILLIPPS *Bibliogr. NZ Fishes* (1971) 26 *Trachipterus trachypterus*... Ribbon-fish... *Agrostichthys parkeri*... Benham's Ribbon-fish. **1956** GRAHAM *Treasury NZ Fishes* 185 Ribbon-fish *Trachipterus arawatae*... This comparatively rare fish is strictly a deep sea fish and few Ribbon-fish are seen alive. *Ibid.* 186 It is stated that Ribbon-fish twenty feet in length have been seen and these have given rise to a number of stories of sea serpents. **1960** PARROTT *Queer & Rare Fishes* 97 Ribbonfish *Agrostichthys parkeri*... The New Zealand Ribbonfish is characterized by its elongated body, the length of which is between 30 to 40 times its greatest height. **1982** AYLING *Collins Guide* (1984) 189 *Ribbonfish* (Dealfish) *Trachipterus trachypterus*... Ribbonfish are silver in colour with a few irregular dark spots, and have pink fins. **1986** PAUL *NZ Fishes* 69 *Ribbonfish. Agrostichthys parkeri.* New Zealand and South Atlantic.

ribbon-tree. *Obs.* LACEBARK 1 b, RIBBONWOOD 2 (1) (*Plagianthus* spp.).

1866 *Treasury Bot.* 981 Ribbon-tree, *Plagianthus betulinus*. **1889** FEATON *Art Album NZ Flora* 53 Plagianthus betulinus..is abundant in forests in most districts..reaching as far south as Otago, where it is generally known as the 'Ribbon Tree', on account of the tough, fibrous, inner bark which it possesses.

ribbonwood. [f. the ribbon or lace-like character of its layered inner bark: see quot. 1907.]

1. Any of several trees of the family Malvaceae having fibrous, layered, lace-like inner bark, usu. of the genera *Hoheria* and *Plagianthus*, incl. *P. regius* (formerly *betulinus*) of the North Island, South Island, and off-shore islands. See also LACEBARK 1.

1867 HOOKER *Handbook* 767 Ribbon-wood of Otago. *Hoheria populnea.* **1869** *TrNZI* I. (rev. edn.) 192 In some cases, such as the ribbon-woods, plants of different genera are included in the one group. **1879** *Auckland Weekly News* 4 Oct. 7 The pillars and styles of this are of rimu, the panels of ribbonwood, and the mouldings of riwariwa. **1882** POTTS *Out in Open* 186 The small leaved kohai and the soft bright foliaged ribbon-wood contrast well with the dusky hue of the dark-leaved fagus. **1894** WILSON *Land of Tui* 285 Overhanging the tossing creek [at Lennox Falls, Otago] bend Ribbon-wood trees, with masses of soft, white blossom. **1907** LAING & BLACKWELL *Plants NZ* 252 The varied names given by the Maoris in different districts to this plant [*Hoheria* spp.], are all said to spring from the same root. *Whau* signifies *wrapped about, netted,—like lace*, and the tree is so called from the character of its inner bark. The settlers name it lace-bark, ribbon-wood, or thousand-jacket. **1922** *Auckland Weekly News* 20 Apr. 15 Ribbon-wood 'jacket' packed over swellings and lumps, made useful substitutes for dressings of abscesses and tumours. **1938** *Tararua Tramper* Feb. 15 Ranunculus gave way to..native broom, alpine scrub to ribbonwood. **1949** [see HOUI]. **1952** THOMSON *Deer Hunter* 99 Most of these valleys were covered with stunted scrub and large patches of ribbonwood trees. **1981** [see CANVAS 2]. **1988** DAWSON *Forest Vines to Snow Tussocks* 154 The species..are not confined to such sites, but some are most frequent there, including ribbonwood (*Plagianthus regius*), and species of lacebark (*Hoheria*).

2. With a modifier: **lowland, mountain, saltmarsh (marsh, shore)**.

(1) **lowland ribbonwood**. *Plagianthus regius*, LACEBARK 1 b. See also MANATU.

1915 *AJHR* C-6 13 [*Plagianthus*] *betulinus*. Manatu. Lowland ribbonwood. Forest. **1940** LAING & BLACKWELL *Plants NZ* 270 *Plagianthus betulinus* (*The Lowland Ribbonwood*). **1961** MARTIN *Flora NZ* 166 Lowland ribbonwood (*Plagianthus betulinus*). **1982** WILSON *Stewart Is. Plants* 92 *Plagianthus regius* Lowland Ribbonwood..Mānatu... Small deciduous tree.

(2) **mountain ribbonwood**. Either of the two small deciduous trees *Hoheria* (formerly *Gaya*) *lyallii* or *H. glabrata* of lowland to subalpine SI forest.

1906 THOMSON *Intro. Classbook Bot.* 146 *Plagianthus* (Ribbon-wood) 3 sp., *Gaya* (Mountain Ribbon-wood) 1 sp., *Hoheria*, 1 sp...occur in New Zealand. **1910** COCKAYNE *NZ Plants and Their Story* 170 The following plants are..not difficult to procure:—Trees... *Gaya Lyalli*, *G. ribifolia* (mountain-ribbonwood). **1933** *Canterbury Mountaineer* 43 The higher terraces [on the approaches of the Canterbury Alps]..were bright green with colonies of mountain-ribbonwood. **1965** *NZ Weekly News* (Britain) 28 July 39 In this village..we found a nursery garden and there I saw a flowering tree of our New Zealand mountain ribbonwood. **1971** *New Zealand's Heritage* I. 114 [Caption] The mountain ribbonwood, *Hoheria lyallii*, was discovered at Dusky Sound by Forster on Cook's second voyage. **1988** DAWSON *Forest Vines to Snow Tussocks* 165 *Hoheria glabrata* or mountain ribbonwood colonises young, deep, moist, well-drained and often stony soils such as those provided by slips, talus slopes and alluvial fans.

(3) **saltmarsh (maritime, marsh, shore) ribbonwood**. *Plagianthus divaricatus*, a coastal and estuarine shrub of the NI, SI, and offshore islands, usu. having flexible interlaced branchlets. See also *wire-netting bush* (WIRE *n.* 1).

1909 *AJHR* C-12 56 *Plagianthus divaricatus*. Salt-marsh ribbonwood. Salt meadow. Not common [on Stewart Island]. **1940** LAING & BLACKWELL *Plants NZ* 270 The Salt-marsh Ribbonwood..grows only by the seaside, where it forms dense bushes. **1975** *Tane 21* 8 Malvaceae *Plagianthus divaricatus* marsh ribbonwood. **1980** LOCKLEY *House Above Sea* 199 Less comfortable for lying upon is the tougher, more twiggy, shore ribbonwood..which likes its feet in salt water at times. **1982** WILSON *Stewart Is. Plants* 56 Saltmarsh Ribbonwood..in shrubland bordering tidal estuaries. **1995** CROWE *Which Coastal Plant?* 56 Saltmarsh ribbonwood grows not far above the high-tide mark... Here, it forms mats or low-growing clumps of tangled dark-brown stems, which can create such an impenetrable barrier that it has been graphically nicknamed 'wire-netting bush' (not to be confused with *Corokia cotoneaster*)... Also sometimes known as maritime ribbonwood, shore ribbonwood or marsh ribbonwood.

ricker. Also occas. **rika** (from a misapprehension that the word has a Maori origin), **rikka, rikker**. [Spec. use of orig. nautical *ricker* (see OED) a spar or pole made out of a young tree.]

1. A long slender tree trunk or a pole cut therefrom.

1834 *Log 'Lucy Ann'* 26 Apr. in McNab *Old Whaling Days* (1913) 102 [Cargo from NZ] 10 logs of timber, 890 rickers, 165 handspikes, 13 casks of black whale oil. **1838** POLACK *NZ* II. 93 I was employed collecting a quantity of spars, for ships' masts..and rickers or trunks of trees, of narrow diameter but great length. **1871** *TrNZI* III. 88 The noose [was] made of a slender strip of flax leaf attached to the end of a ricker or rod. **1882** POTTS *Out in Open* 172 Rods and lines were always kept in readiness, hooked and weighted, stuck in the rickers of the thatched roof. **1902** *Brett's Colonists' Guide* 94 On many farms in this colony 'rickers' [for fence-making] can be got for the cutting. **1912** BOOTH *Five Years NZ* 24 The roof [of the station buildings, Canterbury c1859] were of round pine framing covered with rickers (young pine plants) and thatched with snow grass. **1928** BAUCKE *Manuscript* (Bishop Museum Memoirs Vol. IX No.5 343–382) in Skinner & Baucke *Morioris* 363 Having provided.. ricker saplings and other materials of wood, he [*sc.* the Moriori] gathered dry flower stalks of *Phormium*. **1952** THOMSON *Deer Hunter* 48 There was not enough room to erect ricker (small round rails or saplings) bunks for four men.

2. A kauri sapling; a kauri-tree in the pole stage.

1930 *Northern Advocate* 29 July 6 The fifty-feet kauri rika goal posts excited much admiration. **1949** *NZ Geogr.* 57 A vigorous second growth interspersed with young kauri rickers soon appeared. **1953** REED *Story of Kauri* 61 The sapling [of kauri] is known as a 'ricker', sometimes incorrectly spelt 'rika'. **1966** *Encycl. NZ* II. 679 *Rikka*, the bushman's word for a young kauri, long supposed to be a Maori word, turns out to be an English dialect word for a pole, apparently introduced by workers from England in the kauri timber trade as long ago as the 1790s. **1978** MOORE & IRWIN *Oxford Book NZ Plants* 212 The spire-like young [kauri] tree is called a 'ricker'. **1986** OWEN & PERKINS *Speaking for Ourselves* 150 Then it would be necessary to use the smaller kauris, the young trees known as rikkers. Ibid. 162 They used kauri rikkers as cranes.

ride, *v.*

1. As **ride boundary**, see BOUNDARY 2 b.

2. *trans.* Usu. as **ride in**, to drove or muster (stock) on horseback.

1852 GODLEY *Address* Dec. in Fitton *NZ* (1856) 354 I have seen here clergymen ploughing,... officers of the army..riding in stock, and no one thought the worse of them, but the contrary. **1856** ROBERTS *Diary* 18 Dec. in Beattie *Early Runholding* (1947) 43 At Macfarlane's the men saddled fresh horses and rode in some cattle which we had a great bother to yard. **1867** THOMSON *Rambles With Philosopher* 147 [Old Yarmouth sailor speaks] I know you are the 'cove' to ride in a bullock. **1912** BOOTH *Five Years NZ* 30 I learned to ride stock, shoe horses, shear sheep.

3. As **ride work** [used elsewhere but recorded earliest in NZ: see OED *ride v.*¹ 1 k], to exercise a racehorse.

1950 *Landfall 13* 19 Gordon, did you know I ride work now in the mornings? **1959** GEE in *NZ Short Stories* (1966, 1976 repr.) 271 He'd ridden work on the horse and knew her well.

ridgepole. [Spec. use of *ridgepole* the horizontal timber at the ridge of a roof.]

1. a. As **ridgepole rafter** [from its resemblance to the ridge-pole and end rafters of a Maori meeting-house], a local name for the stick-insect, fam. Phasmidae.

1888 BARLOW *Kaipara* 186 Another curious insect found here is the 'Mantis', commonly called, on account of its shape, 'the ridge-pole rafter'.

b. Symbolizing the main characteristics of family love.

1986 IHIMAERA *Matriarch* 107 The whanau was my home. The love and affection they held for each other were the ridgepoles of my heart.

2. *Tramping*. [f. the *ridgepole* of a tent or hut.] In the phr. **throwing the ridgepole**, a game or contest among trampers, resembling tossing the caber.

1930 *Tararua Tramper* Dec. 4 *Throwing the Ridgepole*—1, Tom Smith; 2, Dave Thomas; 3, Bert Smith.

ridie. *Show people.* [f. (*sideshow*) ride + –IE.] One who controls the assembly and running of a sideshow machine offering rides to customers.

1996 *Dominion* (Wellington) 4 Mar. 27 The 'ridies and jointies' who travel round setting up rides and sideshows were less than enthusiastic when first approached about the [TV] show.

riding. *Hist.* [Local use of *riding* a territorial administrative division of Yorkshire and also occas. elsewhere, ultimately ad. Old Norse *þriðjungr* a third part.] A territorial sub-division, often for electoral purposes, of a county. See quot. 1902.

1888 *NZ Statutes* No.11 37 [Counties Amendment Act, 1888 s2] The Pahiatua County is hereby constituted, and shall comprise all that portion of the Wairarapa North County which is included within the boundaries of the Pahiatua Riding of the last-named county. **1888** BARLOW *Kaipara* 95 The main road through the county is supposed to be constructed by the County Council, which is composed of representatives from the several ridings or districts forming the county, each riding electing a councillor every three years. **1902** *Settler's Handbook NZ* 142 When the nine provinces were abolished in 1876 the colony was divided for local government purposes into counties, regard being had to boundaries of existing road districts, and the counties were subdivided into ridings, each riding being empowered to elect a certain number of members of the Council of the county. The ridings comprise one or more of the above three districts. They have no governing body—they are simply the electoral divisions of the county, and their maximum number is nine. **1918** *Hawera & Normanby Star* 9 July 5 He noted that £400 had been allocated to the Waverley riding. **1930** *Northern Advocate* 7 July 2 He considered his road the worst in the riding. **1970** THOMAS *Way Up North* 75 The term 'riding' as part of a county would have little meaning today.

rifleman. [Poss. f. the similarity of its plumage to an early military uniform.] *Pl.* **riflemen**. *Acanthisitta chloris* (fam. Acanthisittidae), a tiny, short-tailed, greenish (male) or brownish (female and juvenile) bird, in two subspecies **North Island rifleman**, *Acanthisitta chloris granti*, and **South Island rifleman**, *A. c. chloris*. Occas. erron. applied to a wren (see quot. 1871). See also PIRIPIRI *n.*², THUMB BIRD, TITIPOUNAMU (and variants), WREN 2 (1).

1871 HUTTON *Catalogue Birds NZ* 7 Xenicus stokesii... Grey Wren. Stripe-faced Wren. Rifleman. A broad white streak from each nostril over each eye to the back of the head. 1873 BULLER *Birds NZ* 113 Titipounamu..Kikirimutu, Pihipihi, Piripiri, Tokepiripiri, and Moutuutu. *Ibid.* 114 The Rifleman is the smallest of our New-Zealand birds. 1898 [see TITIPOUNAMU]. 1900 *Canterbury Old & New* 195 Amongst the creepers there are the bush-wren, the rock-wren, the rifleman and the yellow-headed native canary. 1914 GUTHRIE-SMITH *Mutton Birds & Other Birds* 123 Although but a very little bird the Rifleman adds much to the life of the woods with his faint 'zee', 'zee', 'zee', his endlessly repeated wink and twinkle of wing. 1930 *Evening Post* (Wellington) 6 Dec. 17 The rifleman wren..was seen on several occasions diligently searching among the nooks and crannies of some large tree trunk. 1953 SUTHERLAND *Golden Bush* (1963) 108 The robins, riflemen and tomtits tamed very soon. 1965 GILLHAM *Naturalist in NZ* 233 There were bellbirds, tuis..and..two tiny riflemen or New Zealand wrens. 1985 *Reader's Digest Book NZ Birds* 264 *North Island Rifleman*: Larger tracts of native bush in the North Island but not north of the Coromandel Pennisula... *South Island Rifleman*: Widespread throughout forests of the South, Stewart and Codfish Islands. 1990 *Checklist Birds NZ* 192 *Acanthisitta chloris granti..North Island Rifleman (Titipounamu)... Acanthisitta chloris chloris... South Island Rifleman (Titipounamu)*.

rig, *n.*[1] Also **rigg**. [Transf. use of Brit. dial. *rig* a shallow-water shark: see OED *n.*[1]] GUMMY *n.*[3] (*Mustelus lenticulatus*).
1936 *Handbook for NZ* (ANZAAS) 71 *Mustelus antarcticus*: Common dogfish, pioke (Auckland), rigg (Canterbury). 1977 *Dominion* (Wellington) 8 Nov. 1 'But many wholesalers have told us they are moving away from marketing school shark,' Mr Gradwell said. 'They prefer rig, elephant fish or spotty shark.' 1979 *Catch* Sept. 22 A rig by any other name... Dogfish, gummy shark, spotty, kini, lemonfish, pioke, rig..the smooth-hound dogfish (*Mustelus antarcticus*) probably has more common names than any other New Zealand fish. 1983 *Dominion* (Wellington) 2 Apr. 5 It seems mystery surrounds the fish commonly served..in our fish and chip shops—the rig, or spotted dog fish. 1986 BROWN *Weaver's Apprentice* 91 Not too many flat fish..a good proportion of cod and elephants with a few rig sharks..thrown in for good measure. 1991 *Dominion* (Wellington) 12 Aug. 9 During the 1989-90 fishing year, rig landed from boats..was misdeclared as ghost shark, a non-quota species.

rig, *n.*[2] *Otago-Southland*. [f. Sc. dial. *rig*, orig. the 'ridge' between furrows; a measure of land: see OED *rig n.*[1] 3 a and b.] A measure of ploughland.
1949 SHAW & FARRANT *Taieri Plain* 218 At that time [c1860] the land was ploughed in 'rigs' five and a half yards in width, and each man when sowing or harvesting kept to his allotted strip.

rigg, var. RIG *n.*[1]

rigger. [Ellipt. for SQUARE RIGGER; ultimate etymology unknown.] Orig. a quart-sized square-gin bottle esp. one used for holding draught beer (see SQUARE RIGGER); thence a quart bottle of beer; thence any glass (occas. early, stoneware) flagon or half-gallon jar, usu. for beer, but also for other liquids such as draught vinegar. Cf. PETER *n.*[2]
1911 *Truth* 16 Dec. 5 This drew a crowd round, and he tried to humo[u]r her by first getting her home, and then getting a jar and two riggers of beer from the hotel. 1943 BENNETT *English in NZ* in *Amer. Speech* XVIII. 89 A quart bottle of beer is a *rigger*, and a pint bottle a *marine*; doubtless neither of these terms is peculiar to New Zealand, but they are rarely, if ever, heard in England. 1946 SARGESON *That Summer* 132 He was hanging on to an armful of riggers... They'd brought a lot of riggers and I was worried, because I thought beer wouldn't do Terry any good. 1955 *Truth* 14 Dec. 4 Any bloke who's had to carry a half-dozen riggers..all the way to New Lynn could simply laugh at forced marches. 1957 SHEEHAN ('Kerbstone') in *Truth* June in *Acid Test* (1981) 72 We were just getting back to normal again when he produced an old-time rigger which, he said, contained wampo. 1983 19 Feb. p.c. C.R. Francis (Christchurch). I notice that the word 'rigger' [in 1979 *Heinemann NZ Dict.* 936] does not include the sense which used to be common, of a 1 litre JDKZ gin bottle filled at the pub with draft beer. I distinctly remember the notice at 'His Lordships' a very scruffy tavern in St Asaph St. Christchurch 'No jars or riggers filled after 5-45 pm.' This was deciphered by an elderly habitue for the innocent student. The word is apparently a contraction of the term 'square rigger' used to describe a JDKZ bottle. 1991 *North & South* (Auckland) June 32 The Club Hotel—where little old ladies with woollen caps, sandshoes and string bags in which to carry their riggers of beer would gossip together... A rigger, or square gin bottle, would be filled with beer for a few pence.

right, *a.* and *adv.*

1. As **too right** [in freq. use in NZ: recorded earliest in Austral.: AND 1919; see OED *right a.* 14 c, *too adv.* 5 g 'orig. Austral.'], used as an exclamation or assertion expressing emphatic agreement; 'yes, indeed'.
c1930 *Whitcombe's Etym. Dict. Aust.-NZ Suppl.* 12 *adv.—too right a.* sl. satisfactory; very good. 1934 SCANLAN *Winds of Heaven* 'Too right I could.' 'You're not allowed to say too right.' 1943 BENNETT *English in NZ* in *Amer. Speech* XVIII. 90 The expressions 'too true', 'too right', in which *too* has its old intensive value, are in common use. 1954 WINKS *These New Zealanders* (1956) 54 'Too right' especially common in North Auckland, and 'goody-oh' are two fascinating phrases [for Americans]. 1962 JOSEPH *Pound of Saffron* 152 'I'm terribly sorry, Stan.' 'She's right, Mr Keogh,' said the boy with a grin. 'We'll do it this time, eh?' 'Too right we will.' 1976 HULME in *Some Other Country* (1984) 182 'Bloody oath, Mat what good luck!'.. 'Shout you eh?' 'Too right you can. Double whisky.' 1985 SHERWOOD *Botanist at Bay* 49 'He can be tiresome, I imagine.' 'Too right he can, and I'm exhausted.'

2. In the phr. **She'll be** (or **She's**) **right**, expressing confidence in a happy outcome, reassurance, agreement, etc.; also often, an overconfident or couldn't-care-less attitude of 'who's to care!' **a.** As **She'll be right** [AND 1947].
1947 DAVIN *For Rest of Our Lives* 19 'But I think the way I said should work.' 'She'll be right.' 1958 *Political Science* Sept. 90 [Advt of the National Safety Association featuring a cartoon character *Sheel B. Wright*] You see my secret is to lull managers and workers into believing that 'she'll be right'. 1965 SHADBOLT *Among Cinders* 43 Don't worry, son. She'll be right. 1972 MITCHELL *Pavlova Paradise* 183 '*She'll be right*': An expression of faith in divine providence. 1985 *Standards* (Standards Assoc. of NZ pub.) Dec. 17 [Heading] *Do it right* and *She'll be right mate*. If you have a lingering attitude to house painting that whispers 'slap it on, she'll be right'—then you must definitely order a copy of the new painting Standard which will be available in the New Year. 1991 *Listener* 10 June 8 Remember the expression 'She'll be right, Mate'? That sort of upbeat attitude has long ago disappeared in New Zealand.

b. In *attrib.* use with lower case initial *s*.
1959 SLATTER *Gun in My Hand* 148 Poor country lads the Hun radio called them... The easy-going jokers who jacked things up with the she'll-be-right spirit. 1964 BOOTH *Footsteps in Sea* 101 Hans..the Dutch migrant..was making money and losing friends in this 'she'll be right' country by working too hard. 1973 WHEELER *Hist. Sheep Stations NI* 93 Perhaps this remark, made quite spontaneously, combines the often criticised 'she'll be right' attitude with a more serious one. 1984 OVENDEN *Ratatui* 12 The more homely, bluff, she'll-be-right democratism that fitted better with acceptable standards in New Zealand. 1991 *Dominion* (Wellington) 10 Apr. 1 A big problem confronting New Zealand was the habit of short term thinking..and an underlying feeling that something would turn up: the she'll be right philosophy.

c. As **She's right** [AND 1958].
1950 *Listener* 3 Mar. 12 'She's right!' Miss Cooper said, with a good Pig Islander's inflexion. 1963 *Dominion* (Wellington) 30 Jan. 8 As a Grim Dig I feel that it is my duty to point out..'she's right'. 'She's right' or 'She'll-Be-Right' originated in the Army and was only used when the person using the saying was satisfied that he had done his particular job to the best of his ability and took pride in it. If, on the other hand, he had done the job to the best of his ability but he was not satisfied with the job, he used the phrase 'She's not too good' or 'She's pretty poor'. Never was the phrase 'She's right' used in the sense that politicians and various other people not in the know use it to refer to a job badly done or done with a 'couldn't-care-less' attitude. 1974 AGNEW *Loner* 63 'The boss said I should see you.' 'She's right, boy. Keep your shirt on.'

right whale: see WHALE 2 (14).

rika, rikka, rikker, varr. RICKER.

rim-rap, var. RIMURAPA.

rimu /'rimu/, /'rimju/, *n.*[1] Also with much variety of early form as **demo, dímu dímu, rema, remo, remu**. [Ma. /'rimu/: Williams 340 *Rimu..1*.] *Dacrydium cupressinum* (fam. Podocarpaceae), a valued coniferous timber tree common throughout the wetter lowland areas of New Zealand, distinguished by its scale-like drooping foliage, flaking bark and great height; also its timber, now much prized for furniture manufacture, and formerly of great commercial importance as a common building timber. See also *red pine* (PINE 2 (13) a), SPRUCE 1.
[1820 LEE & KENDALL *NZ Gram. & Vocab.* 165 Ko dímu dímu; A certain tree.] 1820 MCCRAE *Journal* (1928) 20 Here we found the trees..of that kind called by the natives Demo and Totara. The former resembles the pine and the latter has a leaf like the yew tree. 1835 YATE *NZ* (1970) 40 Rimu... This elegant tree comes to its greatest perfection in shaded woods, and in moist rich soil. 1841 HODGSKIN *Narr. Eight Months Sojourn NZ* 27 Rema, a beautiful, high, and majestic tree, growing upwards of 80 feet in length. 1844 TUCKETT *Diary* 16 Aug. in Hocken *Contributions* (1898) 223 The prevailing species of tree are remo, totara, and tall manuka. 1857 HARPER *Lett. from NZ* 4 Nov. (1914) 45 At work in the forest, sawing up Rimu, *i.e.* Red Pine, a finely grained timber which literally seemed to bleed under the saw, as its red sap flowed out. 1877 *TrNZI* IX. 163 Rimu, the native name of this tree, is now tolerably well known in Otago. So if professional men and timber merchants would only encourage its use, it would soon supersede the vague conventional term of 'red pine'. 1890 *PWD Catalogue Timbers* (NZ & South Seas Exhib.) 14 Rimu (red-pine)..Dacrydium

cupressinum... A strong, handsome, reddish coloured timber, grain beautifully marked and figured. **1939** BEATTIE *First White Boy Born Otago* 13 Rimu is the red pine, and for the miro I never heard an English name. **1941** MYERS *Valiant Love* 10 Today, they saw only the dense, rimu-wooded hills. **1966** [see PINE 2 (13) a]. **1982** PEAT *Detours* 196 'What are you milling mainly?' 'Rimu. It's almost all red pine. But we're [*sc.* West Coast sawmillers] rationed.'

rimu(rimu), *n.*² Also early **dímu, limmoo**. [Ma. /ˈrimu/ /ˈrimurimu/: Williams 340 *Rimu.. rimurimu...* Seaweed.]

1. a. BULL KELP 1. Cf. RIMURAPA.

[**1820** LEE & KENDALL *NZ Gram. & Vocab.* 150 Dímu, *s.* Sea weeds. **c1826–27** BOULTBEE *Journal* (1986) 113 kelp -limmoo.] **1848** TAYLOR *Leaf from Nat. Hist.* 33 Rimu, *a sea weed.* edible. **1867** HOCHSTETTER *NZ* 139 When [tutu-berry juice is] boiled with Rimu, a seaweed, [it] forms a jelly which is very palatable. **c1920** BEATTIE *Trad. Lifeways Southern Maori* (1994) 125 The kelp (rimu) was out to various uses in the South. Boiled with tutu wine it formed the edible rehia.

b. Special Comb. **rimu bag**, a receptacle made out of split kelp used by Maori to hold birds preserved in their fat. See also *bull-kelp bag* (BULL KELP 2), POHA.

1847 BRUNNER *Exped. Middle Is.* in Taylor *Early Travellers* (1959) 284 The natives here preserve the birds..in a *rimu* or seaweed bag... They..place the cooked birds in the *rimu* bag, and pour over them the extracted fat, and tie tightly the mouth of the bag. **1850** ACHERON *Journal* May in Howard *Rakiura* (1940) 390 Thus prepared the [weka] meat is put into a rimu bag filled up with the fat extracted in cooking.

2. Also **rimu-rimu, sea rimu**. *Caulerpa brownii* (fam. Caulerpaceae), a green seaweed which forms dense patches with upright shoots resembling twigs of the rimu tree.

c1920 BEATTIE *Trad. Lifeways Southern Maori* (1994) 499 The masses of very fine and tangled seaweeds found along seashores were called rimurimu. **1961** MARTIN *Flora NZ* 8 Rock pools..are the favourite haunt of several species of *Caulerpa*, much the most widely distributed and commonest member being the Rimu-rimu..thought confined to areas South of Castle Point. **1962** FRAME *Edge of Alphabet* 110 Featherweed, she said, in a chanting tone.—Feathery-weed, pop-kelp, sea-rimu, tree-daisy. **1978** MOORE & IRWIN *Oxford Book NZ Plants* 8 *Caulerpa brownii*. Sea rimu grows in dense patches at or below low tide level on open rocky coasts. **1982** WILSON *Stewart Is. Plants* 318 Sea Rimu... Green patches, often dense, the creeping stems giving rise to numerous more or less upright shoots resembling the foliage of rimu.

rimurapa. Also early **dímu rápa**, occas. **rimrap'** (indicating unvoicing of final vowels). [Ma. /ˈrimurapa/: Williams 341 *Rimurapa*..bull kelp.] BULL KELP 1. Cf. RIMU *n.*² 1 a.

[**1820** LEE & KENDALL *NZ Gram. & Vocab.* 150 Dímu, *s.* Sea weeds. Dímu rápa; Name of a place.] **1848** TAYLOR *Leaf from Nat. Hist.* 33 Rimurapa, *a sea weed,* edible; largest kind. **1869** *TrNZI* I. (rev. edn.) 262 A few also of the sea-weeds were eaten; such as, the karengo..the rehia, the rimurapa..and some others. **1881** *Ibid.* XIII. 29 [Karengo] together with two other species of sea-algae, *rehia* and *rimurapa*..was mixed with the sweet juice of the *tutu*. **1908** BAUGHAN *Shingle-Short* 190 Thick grew the *Rimurapa*, fringing the shore, Thick grew the long-shore kelp... [1908 *Note*] *Rimu-rapa*. A seaweed. **1928** BAUCKE *Manuscript* (Bishop Museum Memoirs Vol.IX No.5 343–382) in Skinner & Baucke *Morioris* 363 The accepted tale that he [*sc.* the Moriori] caulked the seams of his crate-like affair [*sc.* a reed boat]..with 'rim-rap', bull-kelp, and used inflated bladders of this material..is, to put it mildly, tosh! **1982** [see BULL KELP 1]. **1985** *Dominion* (Wellington) 22 Feb. 9 The great bull kelp—rimurapa— with writhing slimy arms up to 10 metres or more long, clothes the coasts of many parts of New Zealand.

ring, *v.*¹ [f. *ring* to form a circle or encirclement.]

1. [Spec. use of *ring* to deprive (a tree) of a ring of bark: AND 1846.] **a.** *trans.* RING-BARK *v.* 1.

1875 *TrNZI* VII. 186 During these two months, July and August, let them 'ring' the trees, that is cut out a ring of bark and sap 3 or 4 inches wide round all the trees they intend to cut down or 'fall' during the next 12 months. **c1930** *Whitcombe's Etym. Dict. Aust.-NZ Suppl.* 10 *ring v. trans.* to kill a tree by cutting the bark round the trunk.

b. As a *vbl. n.* **ringing**, a method of deep-scarfing round the circumference of a (kauri) tree-trunk.

1953 REED *Story of Kauri* 157 Deeper scarves were cut out of all leaning trees to prevent them from splitting up. After sawing to a certain depth..each man alternately cut round his side of the tree almost to the front scarf. The adoption of this plan, known as 'ringing', caused the wood to break clean when falling.

2. *Farming.* [AND 1868.] Usu. *intr.* Of stock in a mob, to make a circling movement round a stationary group (see esp. quot. 1934). Also *vbl. n.*

c1875 MEREDITH *Adventuring in Maoriland* (1935) 66 It was risky swimming them over the rivers. If the cattle fail to make for the opposite bank the leaders may turn back and start 'ringing' in midstream, the cattle in the middle of the ring being forced under water and drowned. **1928** *Weekly News* 12 Jan. [Caption] A view..of the Riversdale yards, White Rock, showing drafting in progress and the beasts 'milling' or 'ringing' on left. **1934** *Press* (Christchurch) (Acland Gloss.) 27 Jan. 15 Merino sheep on the flat, especially when coming to a gate, are apt to circle. The centre of the mob may stand still or move slowly forward; but the outside sheep gallop round and round them. This is called *ringing*. It is annoying to see the sheep racing past the gate instead of going through it. **1963** NORRIS *Armed Settlers* 198 To drive stock to Auckland it was necessary to cross the river twice... The danger of swimming the stock across was that they might 'ring', that is swim round and round in the centre of the water till exhausted and then drown.

3. *Farming. intr.* Of an inadequately trained sheep-dog, to turn in a complete circle around the sheep and come back to the handler, that is, to fail to stop after its out-run. Also as a *vbl. n.*

1982 *Agric. Gloss.* (MAF) 25 *Ringing Sheep*: Fault in a dog where it goes in a complete circle around the sheep and comes back to the handler. It fails to stop after its out-run, halfway around the sheep, and directly opposite the handler.

ring, *v.*² [Cf. Partridge 8 *ring it on* outwit.] In the phr. **to ring it on** (to a person), **to ring** (something) **on** (to a person), to pass (something fraudulent, exaggerated, untruthful) on (to a person). Cf. RING IN *v.*²

1912 *Truth* 6 Jan. 7 This sort of excuses make his Worship tired. 'The same old cold,' he remarked. 'It is no use ringing that kind of stuff on to me.' *Ibid.* 16 Mar. 6 After giving the [counterfeit] coin to the cabby he repented, and wanted to get it back, but Watson said, 'Never mind, it's all right; he'll ring it on to someone else.'

ring, *v.*³ [A back-formation from RINGER *n.*¹: AND 1894.] *trans.* To outshear (other shearers) by gaining the highest aggregate tally of sheep shorn; usu. in the phr. **to ring the board**, or **to ring the shed**, to have the highest tally of shorn sheep.

1941 BAKER *NZ Slang* 38 The terms *to ring a shed* and *to be a ringer*, i.e. to be the fastest and most expert shearer in a shed, have been used for so many generations that they are quite orthodox in the antipodes. **1951** ACLAND *Early Canterbury Runs* 372 Sleeveless singlet... Named after the famous Jack Howe who rang many of the South Island sheds in the 1890s. **1955** BOWEN *Wool Away* 6 [Young shearers should] take notice of the man who shears in a quiet, business-like way, and..[by] the end of the day rings them [*sc.* his mates] by quite a few sheep. **1960** MILLS *Sheep-O* 21 Many a tense drama was enacted as individuals vied..for the honour of 'ringing the shed'. For a shearer to be able to say that he 'rang the board' at so-and-so station the previous year was as good a testimonial as he could wish for. **1978** JARDINE *Shadows on Hill* 131 The man who has shorn the most sheep from any particular shed is said to have 'rung' it, as is the man with the highest tally for a particular day. **1989** *NZ Eng. Newsletter* III. 27 *ring:* To outdo all other shearers by 'ringing the board' or 'ringing the shed'.

ring, *n.*¹

1. a. [f. *ring* a circle: AND 1896.] The site or operational area of a two-up game.

1935 STRONG in Partridge *Slang Today* 287 Anyhow, to give you the fair dinkum guts I put across a beauty when I found the double-headed penny in the ring, and that's how I won 200 francs.

b. Special Comb. **ring-keeper** [AND 1911] (occas. **keeper**), **ring-master** [AND 1896], the person who 'keeps the ring', that is, controls a two-up school (see also RINGIE *n.*¹).

1917 *Chron. NZEF* 16 May 137 The poor 'tail' betters heaved a sigh..But Bill consoled them with a 'quid' (The keepers got ten more). **1928** DEVANNY *Dawn Beloved* 162 One man takes the kip and places two pennies on it... He hands [his bet] to the **ring-keeper**. **1935** STRONG in Partridge *Slang Today* 287 I'll admit I was stiff when I lost that fifty francs, but my cobber produced another ten; and when the ring-keeper said 'Up and do 'em,' I collected 200 francs. **1937** LEE *Civilian into Soldier* 99 'Come on, come on, come on!' the ring-keeper would yell as he gave the new chance to spin to the biggest better. **1912** *Truth* 20 Jan. 7 Once upon a time the free and easy [two-up] 'school' with the '**ring-master**', and his 'All set—a fair go' broke upon the stilly night.

2. Usu. as **rings**, a marble game, see RINGIE *n.*²

ring, *n.*² [f. *ring* to circle an important calendar date (cf. **1987** *Dominion* (Wellington) 4 Apr. 8 If I kept a diary, today would have a red ring round it. Not because it's anyone's birthday.), or poss. from throwing a ring around a desired object at *hoop-la*.] In the phr. **to put a** (occas. **the**) **ring around that**, expressing certainty, strong agreement, approval, etc.; 'that's for certain'.

1959 SLATTER *Gun in My Hand* 228 If it had been me she'd have kids all right. You can put a ring around that one. **1960** KEINZLY *Tangahano* 131 There's still a couple of hundred that haven't told me yet—but they will tonight. You can put a ring around it! **1978** O'SULLIVAN *The Boy, The Bridge, The River* 130 'It had better be good weather then,' Latty said. 'You can put a ring round that,' Len said. **1980** BALLANTYNE *Penfriend* 13 'Made recently by a truck, I'd say.' 'Yes, I reckon you can put the ring around that.'..'I beg your pardon.'.. '"Put the ring around that"? Meaning?' 'Only that I

Ringatu, *n.* and *attrib.* Also **ringa-tu.** [Ma. /riŋaˈtuː/: *ringa* hands + *tū* raised up, in prayer fashion.] (Of or concerning) the Maori religious movement founded by Te Kooti Rikirangi in 1867; a member of the Ringatu religion or church.

1905 *TrNZI* XXXVII. 87 When she returned here [from treatment in a Pakeha hospital] I heard an old woman ask her, 'In what state are you now?' (*i.e.,* 'Have you deserted our *ringa tu* religion, are you *noa*?') **1921** *Quick March* 10 Feb. 15 The combined [Ratana] service was most impressive..other sects were all represented—even the modern Maori 'Ringa-Tu' was represented. **1922** Cowan *NZ Wars* (1955) II. 25 As we [recited the incantation '*Hapa, hapa, hapa! Hau, hau, hau! Pai-marire, rire—hau!*']..we held our right hands uplifted, palms frontward, on a level with our heads—the sign of the *ringa-tu*. This, we believed, would ward off the enemy's bullets. **1934** Hyde *Journalese* 227 Te Kooti, terrible leader of the Hau-Haus, was worshipped as a god by one small section of the Maori people—the Ringatus, whose name literally means 'lifted hands', signifying the phosphorescent palm with which the wily Te Kooti used to impress his followers. **1948** *Our Own Country* 55 Many of the Maoris are followers of the Ringatu religion started by Te Kooti, the prophet, last century. **1959** Sinclair *Hist. NZ* 142 In 1868 he [*sc.* Te Kooti] escaped [imprisonment] and founded a new religion, *Ringatu*, which was a genuine Maori variant of Christianity, though retaining some elements of the *Hau hau* cult. **1963** Henderson *Ratana* (1972) 6 The Ringatu church has earned respect. It was fully constituted at Ruatoki in 1938. **1979** Binney et al. *Mihaia* 25 His [*sc.* Eria Raukura's] right hand is raised in the act of homage to god, the gesture of the Ringatu worshippers from which they took their name: 'Ringa-tu', the upraised hand. **1986** Belich *NZ Wars* 218 [Te Kooti's] power arose from his religion, *Ringatu*, the Upraised Hand. *Ringatu* is a syncretic millenarian belief similar in some respects to *Pai Marire*. Te Kooti originated the religion in 1867 at the Chathams.

Hence **Ringatuism**, the doctrines and beliefs of Ringatu.

1930 *Na To Hoa Aroha* (1987) II. 80 Some tribes have the marae instinct and a psychology that influences the collection of food supplies. Such is Waikato. And you will find the same condition where cults like Ringatuism prevail.

ring-bark, *v.* [f. RING *v.*¹: AND 1866.]

1. To kill a tree by cutting away a ring of bark from around the trunk. Cf. RING *v.*¹ 1 a.

1905 Baucke *White Man Treads* 13 And so, instead of felling these forest giants, he simply..ring-barked the trees, and when they were dead..burnt out a farm from the stubborn wilderness of forest around him. **1928** Baucke *Manuscript* (Bishops Museum Memoirs Vol. X No. 5 pp. 343–382) in Skinner & Baucke *Morioris* 366 Firewood was procured [by the Moriori] by ring-barking trees and waiting until some gale overthrew the tree at the ring-bark rot. **1955** *BJ Cameron Collection* (TS July) ringbark (v) To cut a strip of bark right around a tree so that the tree is killed.

2. *fig.* or *transf.* [AND 1899.] In mainly jocular use, see quots.

1905 *Truth* 24 June 1 Or, if [the unruly hair] were too stiff and strong, to ring-bark and use a cross-cut saw [on it]. **1987** Norgrove *Shoestring Sailors* 138 'Of course skinboys pick it up quicker than those who have been ringbarked.' 'Ringbarked?' 'Circumcised.'

Hence **ringbarked** *ppl. a.*, having had forest cleared by ringbarking; *fig.* of a person, debilitated (as a tree by ringbarking); **ringbarking** *vbl.n. fig.*, an attempt to destroy a policy, course of action, etc. (or the person promoting it) by injuring an essential part.

1906 *Truth* 17 Mar. 4 Barren, ring-barked hills. **1983** Henderson *Down from Marble Mountain* 129 A great old bushwhacker..and shearer in his day but now a bit **ringbarked** himself with a depressed and hagridden mustache but twinkling eyes. **1995** *Sunday Star-Times* (Auckland) 26 Feb. sect. C1 Mike Moore was among ministers who witnessed the new Prime Minister face up to a currency crisis ringbarking by his predecessor Sir Robert Muldoon.

ringbolt /ˈrɪŋˌbɒlt/, *n.*

1. [Poss. a play on *ring bolt* an eye-bolt with a ring through its eye to which ropes, etc. can be attached: with a fanciful play on *bolting* escaping, running away, and poss. orig. with sexual allusion to *bolt* penis, and/or to *ring* vagina or anus as a *quid pro quo* for right of passage.] A clandestine passage by sea hidden by members of the crew often in their quarters; hence, one who travels by this means, a stowaway. Occas. *attrib.*

1965 Watson *Stand in Rain* 16 They would go possum-trapping..or maybe even..do a ringbolt on a ship somewhere. **1982** Newbold *Big Huey* 192 Because Mata was a seaman he knew he'd have no trouble getting a ringbolt or a stowaway back to the Islands. **1987** Norgrove *Shoestring Sailors* 48 Maybe she's scared he'll do a ringbolt and take off. **1989** *Dominion* (Wellington) 11 Jan. 3 Officially Hinckesman was a stowaway, but the Auckland Star said he had done a 'ringbolt', paying a crew member to hide him during the voyage. **1991** *Metro* (Auckland) July 94 She went to Australia as a 'ring bolt', a stowaway, on the *Monowai*. **1995** *Metro* (Auckland) Dec. 164 Many more people talk about *Man Alone* than have read it... It could make quite a movie, especially the Ringbolt ending [when the hero is smuggled out of the country on a ship].

2. As **ringbolt-kicker**, a nickname for a seaman.

1991 *Dominion* (Wellington) 9 Nov. 13 They ordered me out of my cosy radio shack and sent me to the irascible company of ring-bolt kickers (seamen) on the upper deck.

ringbolt, *v.* [f. *n.*] *intr.* To stow away or travel clandestinely by sea with a crew member's connivance. Often as a *vbl. n.*

1981 *Listener* 14 Nov. 45 For seamen, well-hidden ring-bolting was a way of getting between islands without paying. **1988** *Sunday Star* (Auckland) 10 July A10 He vanished..possibly using a technique known as 'ring bolting', catching an illegal passage on a crew member.

ring crutch, *v. Farming.* To crutch or shear a circular area around a sheep's anus (see CRUTCH *v.*¹). Also used as a noun.

1950 Coop *Shearing Ewes before Lambing* 28 With August shearing it is customary and generally advisable to 'ring-crutch' or 'bullseye' the ewes before putting the rams out at tupping. **1986** Richards *Off the Sheep's Back* 98 As we completed shearing each mob of ewes, we would follow on by ring crutching their lambs. *Ibid.* 148 As tupping season was approaching I also gave them a light ringcrutch (a honeymoon shear) before turning them out into a larger paddock

ringer, *n.*¹ [Spec. use of Brit. dial. *ringer* anything superlatively good: see EDD *n.*² Yorks.]

1. *Shearing.* Also occas. **ringie** (see quot. 1965). [AND 1871.] The shearer with the highest aggregate tally in a gang, or a shearing-shed; the fastest shearer in a shearing gang. Cf. DON, *gun-shearer* (GUN *n.*¹ 1).

c1875 Meredith *Adventuring in Maoriland* (1935) 143 Two of them [*sc.* shearers] were running one another for the title of 'ringer' (the one who shore the most sheep in one day). *Ibid.* 144 The two ringer contestants then called to [the boss]. **1876** [see DON]. **1889** *Bulletin* (Sydney) 8 Sept. in Bailey & Roth *Shanties* (1967) 121 And when each shearing season came... She'd take the 'snips' and put to shame The 'ringer' of the crowd. **1894** Wilson *Land of Tui* 242 Some [shearers] are so proficient at their craft that they can shear as many as a hundred and sixty sheep in a day, the best and quickest of whom is called the 'ringer'. **1911** *Maoriland Worker* 7 July 14 'Ringer'..persists for the fastest hand in a shed; with about an equal probability of derivation from the man, horse, or ship that runs 'rings' round an antagonist, or from the ringer of the bell that has marked success in many games or contests besides that of the sportive 'shooting gallery'. **1933** *Press* (Christchurch) (Acland Gloss.) 18 Nov. 15 *Ringer.*—The fastest shearer in the woolshed. He is said to *ring the shed*. **1955** Bowen *Wool Away* 156 Ringer. The fastest shearer on the board. He usually shears on the first stand next to the wool table. Any rival shearer must shear a bigger tally for three consecutive days before he can take the ringer's stand. **1986** Richards *Off the Sheep's Back* 115 I was up with the 'guns' with a top tally of 163 and had my eye on the 'ringer' status, the highest and most coveted accolade in any large shed. **1990** Martin *Forgotten Worker* 48 Bob Tutaki..was a gun shearer... He first joined the union in 1906 when he was the ringer of the sixteen-stand Moawhango shed outside Taihape.

2. [AND 1848.] One outstandingly superior or expert in any activity.

c1926 The Mixer *Transport Workers' Song Book* 24 I don't stand up to look for work, I come down to make a start; For I'm classed among the 'ringers', and from others stand apart. **1927** Donne *Maori Past & Present* 248 Bill Blake was a mighty hunter of gigantic fishes, 'ringer' of the crew. **1941** Baker *NZ Slang* 39 The term *ringer* is now applied to a person who is particularly competent at any manual labour. **1981** *Evening Post* (Wellington) 24 Jan. 7 The best men on the killing board [ca1914], called the Ringers were Ellis and Pettit.

ringer, *n.*² [f. *ring* a circle drawn in games of marbles + *-er*.] A marble which, when fired in a ring game, lodges in the track of the ring.

1953 Sutton-Smith *Unorganized Games NZ Primary School Children* (VUWTS) II. 770 It is important to distinguish..the innumerable merely descriptive marble terms which have no effect on the course of the action—terms such as Ringer, In, Smug, Dead Stick. **1972** Sutton-Smith *Folkgames Children* 176 [Waitara, Taranaki, 1899: reference, to the game of Little Ring] A 'ringer' was a taw which, when fired at the commencement of the game, lodged in the track of the ring itself; that, and knocking a marble out when he 'fired' were the perfect shots.

ringer: see RING IN *v.*² 1.

ringey, var. RINGIE *n.*²

ringeye. Mainly *SI.* SILVEREYE.

1888 Buller *Birds NZ* I. 81 The natives distinguish the bird as Tau-hou (which means stranger), or Kanohi-mowhiti (which may be interpreted as spectacle-eye or ring-eye)... By the settlers it has been variously designated as Ring-eye, Wax-eye, White-eye, or Silver-eye, in allusion to the beautiful circlet of satiny-white feathers which surrounds the eyes. **1890** *Otago Witness* (Dunedin) 11 Dec. 41 The beautiful little ringeye..builds in scrub along the banks of watercourses. **c1920** BEATTIE *Trad. Lifeways Southern Maori* (1994) 345 The ringeye (also known as whiteeye, silvereye, waxeye and blightbird) was called (at Akaroa) pihipihi. **1946** [see BLIGHT-BIRD]. **1951** FRAME in *Some Other Country* (1984) 101 But she was big and warm and knew about cats and little ring-eyes. **1967** NATUSCH *Animals NZ* 282 Family Zosteropidae (silvereyes). *Zosterops lateralis*..called ring-eye in the south. **1975** DAVIN *Breathing Spaces* 11 The very first time they tried it they caught a blackbird and two ring-eyes.

ring fence, *n.* [Of special significance in early colonial NZ, obsolescent in British use: see OED *ring-fence,* 1769.] A fence completely enclosing a property or an area; a boundary fence. Also in *transf.* use (see *v.*, quot. 1994).

1891 A TRAMP *Casual Ramblings* 54 A ring fence had been placed round the property at the snow-line. **1902** *Settler's Handbook of NZ* (Lands Department) 77 (1.) The lessee shall, within two years from the date of his lease, have the land fenced with a ring-fence; and such fence shall be a sufficient fence within the meaning of 'The Fencing Act, 1895'. **1962** EVANS *Waikaka Saga* 283 When he got his first sheep the only fences were known as 'ring' fences. There was one ring fence round the whole farm.

ring fence, *v. trans.* [See *n.*] To completely enclose (a property or an area) with a ring fence. Also *transf.* [cf. OED *v.*], to secure or reserve (esp. public money) for a particular purpose (see quots. 1994).

1894 *NZ Official Year-book* 486 The clearing of forest-lands, ring-fencing and grassing them, will cost about £3..per acre. **1925** WEBB *Miss Peters' Special* 98 We had got it [*sc.* the section] ring-fenced, because..the drawers of the adjoining sections had done their share towards that. **1930** *Na To Hoa Aroha* (1987) II. 26 280 acres in grass and turnips, ring fenced. **1948** SCOTTER *Run Estate & Farm* 15 The first job of the purchaser [of a run], that of ring fencing his whole property could not be done quickly or cheaply. **1951** LEVY *Grasslands NZ* (1970) 245 As soon as possible after sowing, the burn was ring-fenced and later subdivided. **1970** THOMAS *Way Up North* 93 He decided to take up the other section 'as forty pounds was sufficient at slump prices to buy wire for ring-fencing'... He then ring-fenced the new land, ramming as many as fifty posts into position in one day. **1986** RICHARDS *Off the Sheep's Back* 164 The property was ring-fenced and divided into nine paddocks. **1994** *Evening Post* (Wellington) 20 Sept. 20 A suggestion that money from donors is building Wellington City Missioner..a house has been refuted by [the City Mission Director]... 'We ring-fence any donations for the purpose they are intended,' he said. **1994** *National Radio* 'Morning Report' 19 Dec. [The Medical Director of the National Heart Foundation speaks:] 'The Public Health Commission had a ring-fence budget [for preventive health measures]... Money needs to be ring-fenced.'

Hence **ring fenced** *ppl. a.* [OED 1898], surrounded by a ring fence.

1943 HISLOP *Pure Gold* 73 There are plenty of [hares] in that ring-fenced paddock, and as they can't get out of there you should have a lot of fun.

ring fern: see FERN 2 (15).

ringie: see RINGER *n.*[1] 1.

ringie, *n.*[1] *Two up.* [f. *ring*(-keeper + -IE: AND 1941.] *ring-keeper* (RING *n.*[1] 1 b).

1917 *Chron. NZEF* 16 May 137 And swift the 'ringie' shouts with might, 'Then, two pounds heads, I'll take!' **1938** *Press* (Christchurch) (McNab Slang) 2 Apr. 18 A 'boxer' is a gratuity to the 'ringie' at two-up.

ringie, *n.*[2] Also **ringey**, **rings**. A children's marble game played in or about a ring marked on the ground. Cf. RINGER *n.*[2]

[**a1946**] *Alfredton* (1987) 75 Colin Houlbrooke recalled [from the period 1927–46] the two main areas for battle with marbles as being the sealed area for 'rings' and the dirt area behind the shed for 'holes'. **1951** FRAME *Lagoon* (1961) 116 I played ringie and holie. I played funs and keeps. **1984** KEITH & MAIN *NZ Yesterdays* 288 [Caption] Marbles became 'in' or 'out' capriciously but someone always knew the rules of the various games—'holey', 'liney' and, seen here, 'ringey'—which could be played for 'funs' or 'keeps'. **1995** *Independent* 8 Dec. 20 Liney was the game the big [Dunedin] boys played when they were intent on quickly taking all the marbles from the little kids. I preferred holey and ringey.

ring in, *v.*[1] [f. RING *n.* 1 a + *in.*] To enter into a two-up game; also in the phr. **to ring in a grey** [AND 1898], to use an illegal double-headed coin in a two-up game.

1912 *Truth* 20 Jan. 7 Too often, he falls a ready victim to the crook and speiler [*sic*] who is adept in the art of 'ringing in a grey'; i.e., using a double-headed penny, and resorting to other devious, and dirty dodges. **1913** REES *Merry Marauders* 71 The fly-manager rings in at a 'two-up' school.

ring in, *v.*[2]

1. *Horse-racing.* [Spec. use of *ring in* to substitute fraudulently: see OED *v.*[2] 13 b; AND 1898.] To fraudulently substitute one horse for another or to change the name of a horse entered in a race.

1924 REES *Heather of South* 90 He was not 'ringing in' the horse. **1962** GLOVER *Hot Water Sailor* (1981) 59 When somebody or other rings in a racehorse even in those days, takes it to Australia with painted fetlocks.

Hence **ring in** *n.* [AND 1918], (also **ringer** [see OED *ringer*[2] 2. 'U.S. slang', 1890]), a fraudulent substitution, esp. a horse fraudulently substituted for another in a race (see also RINGTAIL), also in a weakened sense, any substitute; **ringing-in** *vbl. n.*, and *attrib.*

1900 SCOTT *Colonial Turf* 222 He fumed at being beaten..winding up his vituperation by saying that [the racehorse] was a **ringer** from Australia. **1908** *Truth* 22 Feb. 2 As Mrs. Hedley and the 'old prad' are also out for life, the '**ring in**' did not do the crowd behind the ex-New Zealander, Rawmire, much, if any, good, when that gelding won. **1957** *Racing in Rangitikei* 7 Credit is due to those lovers of the 'Sport of Kings'..who did their best to put a stop to 'ring-ins' and 'Rafferty Rules'. **1992** SMITHYMAN *Auto/Biographies* 20 Sweet Mystery of Life at last, that's what the tenor sang who was a ring in spruced up with three stripes and a crown. **1924** *Auckland Weekly News* 14 Feb. 24 The hearing of the charge in connection with the alleged '**ringing-in**' trotting case was proceeded with in the Police Court, Dunedin.

2. rung-in *ppl. a.*, substituted unexpectedly or at short notice.

1910 FANNING *Players & Slayers* 45 They are..disgusted at seeing a 'rung-in' man in the place which they had been fitting themselves to fill in many a hard battle.

ring loaf: see *tank loaf* (TANK *n.*[1] 3).

ringtail. *Horse-racing.* [AND 1908.] See *ring in n.* (*v.*[2] 1).

1934 *Truth* 28 Feb. 2 Has the '**ringtail**' entirely been eliminated from trotting in New Zealand?.. The majority of cries of 'ringer' that are heard after a hitherto unknown, or poorly performed horse wins a heat in impressive style..are simply the result of 'pipe-dreams'. **1955** *Truth* 20 July 25 This time it is..an allegation that there has been a 'ringtail' racing. A 'ringtail' is a colloquialism employed to describe a horse which is raced under the name of another, usually with the desire to deceive and defraud.

rip, *v.*

1. [Spec. use of *rip* to slash.] In the phr. **to get ripped**, of a dog, to be slashed by a wild boar's tusks.

1849 TORLESSE *Papers* (1958) 17 Nov. 113 Caught a fine young boar and Jock got ripped by a large boar.

2. As **to rip into** [AND *rip it into*, 1940], to attack (a person with blows or words) or (a task) vigorously; to 'tear a strip off' a person; to 'tear into' a job of work.

1958 *Listener* 16 May 21 There was — with a walking stick, his leg in plaster. And he was ropeable! He came down and ripped into them. **1988** McGILL *Dict. Kiwi Slang* 93 *rip into* attack with fists or words, often in positive fashion, such as aiming to move a pile of rubble; eg 'Let's rip into this digging of the swimming pool, should only take us a few hours.'

ripple, *n.*[1] *Obs.* [Used elsewhere but recorded earliest in NZ: see OED *ripple* 1 b, 1869.] A rip (short for *tide rip*), a disturbed state of the sea caused by strong or contrary currents.

1823 KENT *Mermaid* log 29 May in Howard *Rakiura* (1940) 342 Commences with strong Gales and thick misty weather; a strong ripple, and a heavy cross-sea running, the vessle [*sic*] shipping a quantity of water. **c1835** BOULTBEE *Journal* (1986) 105 After leaving Lord's Harbour, you come to a critical boat passage between 2 reefs: here are two tides meeting at the flood, which causes a dangerous ripple, this instantly subsides at the ebb when the waters recede from each other.

ripple, *n.*[2] *Goldmining.* Also as **ripple-board**, **ripple-plate**. [Not exclusively NZ, but freq. in goldmining usage: see OED *ripple*[4] = *riffle* 5. 1879; *ripple-box* 1853, U.S.] See quot. 1967.

1862 WEKEY *Otago As It Is* 65 They had the advantage..of going from one bar of the river to another..which, probably for ages, served as *ripples on a grand scale*, to catch and accumulate the gold-dust brought down by the river. **1903** *TrNZI* XXXV. 403 Mr. William Beetham..in Nelson, mentioned the trouble..occasioned at the periodical 'clean-up' by the presence of..lead which collected in the ripples with the gold. **1939** BEATTIE *First White Boy Born Otago* 172 There was a minor rush to Coal Creek..and I think a little gold was got in the ripples. **1940** *Tales Pioneer Women* (1988) 291 The water and debris then ran down a sluice channel into boxes fitted with coconut matting and 'ripple plates'; these caught and retained the gold which was collected at the regular 'wash-up'. **1959** MILLAR *Westland's Golden Sixties* 9 Presently, the white men poked gently with their fingers among the fine sand which had been caught on small flanges nailed across a plank which extended from the open, lower end of the box. From these little ledges, ripples the men called them, one began to pick out pieces of yellow metal. **1967** MAY *West Coast Gold Rushes* 528 Riffle or ripple: both terms were used for the grooves cut across the bottom of a sluice-box or for the much

rip, shit, and (or) bust. [Poss. orig. from a folk story: the reference is to desperate straining at stool for relief: see also near congeners in Brit. dial. and slang: EDD *rip n.*¹ 11 (1) *a rip and tear*, a noisy person who makes a great show of himself; Partridge *be shit or bust* do a thing and damn the consequences.] Said of a person or action (occas. in *attrib.* use), having no consideration of the consequences nor of the quality of the result; often as an exclamation or asseveration indicating a vigorous (or over-vigorous) approach to a job, problem, etc. Variously euphemized as *rip, tip or bust, rip, split or bust*, with the latter suggesting a wood-splitting origin.

c1940 *rip, shit, or bust* in freq. use in Marlborough for a violent, thoughtless approach to a job or problem. (Ed.) **1956** SUTHERLAND *Green Kiwi* (1960) 120 If anything breaks grab our standby truck and keep hauling. It's rip, tip or bust at this game [hauling road metal] and no please or thank you. **1981** CHARLES *Black Billy Tea* 49 We'll get that old Buster [*sc.* a wild boar]! Rip, split or bust! **1983** *National Bus. Rev.* 11 Nov. 57 It didn't ever seem to occur to him that a leisurely, measured approach might work better than rip shit and bust. **1986** *Metro* (Auckland) Sept. 48 He'd already picked a name—it would be Loosehead Len and he'd be a right-wing, rip shit and bust Kiwi bloke, opinionated about everything. **1995** *Listener* 1 Apr. 42 [They] have gone a long way towards changing public perceptions of shearers as ripshitorbust hard-drinking riffraff.

riripi, var. LILIPI.

riro, var. RIRORIRO.

riroriro. Also occas. **riro.** [Ma. /ˈriroriro/: Williams 343 *riroriro..*grey warbler.] *grey warbler* (WARBLER 2 (3)).

1835 YATE *NZ* (1970) 58 *Riroriro*—A very small brown bird, with white feathers under the wings and tail. **1860** *Richmond-Atkinson Papers* 20 Oct. (1960) I. 645 Found a fantail nest (young ones) & a riroriro's with two young ones & an egg. **1873** [see WARBLER 2 (3)]. **1889** *Cassell's Picturesque Australasia* IV. 163 A little wren managed to squeeze itself through, and it flew off to Kurangai-tuku, and cried, 'Kurangai-tuku, the man is riro, riro!'—that is, gone, gone, gone. And to this day the bird is known as the riro-riro. **1905** THOMSON *Bush Boys* 174 The silver-bellied warbler, the Riroriro, with unpretentious plumage of quiet grey[,] trills with bursting throat, from a thick clump of bush. **1934** HYDE *Journalese* 109 A dart of wings meant riro-riro, the Maori's little bird of laughter, adventuring in the sunlit spaces. **1946** *JPS* LV. 157 *Riroriro*, a bird..grey-warbler; favourite foster-parent for young bronze-wing cuckoo. **1955** OLIVER *NZ Birds* 477 When the Riroriro begins to sing is the time to begin planting and the proverb 'Where were you when the Riroriro began to sing?' is applied to a lazy man who has neglected his work. **1984** BRASCH *Collected Poems* 46 The riro's note Crosses the ripening day. **1990** *Checklist Birds NZ* 206 *Gerygone igata..Grey Warbler (Riroriro)*.

rise. *Goldmining.* [f. US: AND 1876.] In the phr. **to make a rise**, to make a good profit or gain over 'wages'.

1896 HARPER *Pioneer Work* 30 True, there are still many working the alluvial ground [on the West Coast], but those making more than 'tucker' are few, and it is many years since 'a rise' of importance has been made by anyone. **1899** BELL *In Shadow of Bush* 30 I have been knocking round the Colonies..pretty hard up generally—but not always. I made a rise in Queensland once, at the Towers, but it all went soon. **1914** PFAFF *Diggers' Story* 115 I bought and sold flour..got a 3½ oz. nugget from the bottom of a hole that had been left, made a rise of £300 out of a pocket of gold like horse beans. **1976** VEITCH *Clyde on Dunstan* 30 By mid-June [1864] disappointed miners were returning from Picton to try once again to 'make a rise' from the banks of the Clutha where it was possible to realise at least a couple of pennyweights a day using only the humble cradle.

Hence **riser** *n.*, a profitable claim.

1928 *Grey River Argus* in Heinz *Bright Fine Gold* (1974) 29 The rush [to Welshman's in 1867] was not remarkable for the richness of the ground though a few 'risers' were found.

rising. [OED *vbl. n.* 15 Brit. *dial.* yeast; leaven.] Leaven; material added to make a cooked article rise.

c1940 Known from Marlborough as a common term for baking powder, baking soda, and the like. (Ed.)

river.

1. Mainly *Auckland province. Hist.* Occas. **saltwater river.** An arm of the sea, or a tidal inlet, into which a freshwater river or creek often runs; a harbour. Cf. CREEK 1.

[*Note*] In Auckland province the narrow or partially enclosed harbours or arms, mainly on the west coast, are often called rivers and were so named on old maps: e.g. Whangape River, Herekino River, Hokianga River, Waiuku River: see also the title of Jane Mander's novel (1920) *The Story of a New Zealand River* which refers to the Kaipara harbour as well as to the Wairoa river running into it.

1769 *An 'Endeavour' Log* 12 Nov. in McNab *Historical Records* (1914) II. 147 Got two Longboat loads of Oysters from a small River at the Head of the [Mercury] Bay. **1823** KING in Elder *Marsden's Lieutenants* (1934) 255 May 3rd.—The Rev. J. Butler came and informed us of the wreck of the American schooner *Cossack* at Shokeehanga River. **1832** Steine in *Courier* 14 Sept. in McNab *Old Whaling Days* (1913) 20 Captain Steine discovered another large river near the entrance of the river William The Fourth, which he named Queen Adelaide River. *Ibid.* 21 [1913 *Note*] The term river was, at that time, applied to what we would now designate a sound, [William IV River] was Tory Channel. **1840** POLACK *Manners & Customs* I. 169 The salt-water rivers are joined at their entrances by fresh-water creeks, many of which pursue routes inland, through perhaps eighty miles of country. **1867** HOCHSTETTER *NZ* 143 In the vicinity of the Hokianga river of the West Coast. **1884** *Maoriland* 162 The town, [of Auckland] as seen from a vessel sailing up the river, presents a very picturesque appearance. **1896** *TrNZI* XXVIII. 141 The usual name for the inlet [on Dunedin harbour] appears to have been 'The River'. **1939** BEATTIE *First White Boy Born Otago* 38 European families had by this time either returned to Sydney or shifted over to 'Otago' (the district around the Otago Harbour, or Otago River as the whalers called it). **1974** PRESTON *Lady Doctor* 79 We had a call to a farm well up the river [*sc.* Hokianga harbour], at the head of one of the tidal creeks. **1983** KING *Whina* 37 Most of Whina's earliest memories are of 'the river', as they always called the [Hokianga] harbour.

2. Special Comb. **a. river-beach** [see OED *n.*¹ 5], the sloping sand and shingle areas at a river's edge; **river-bed**, the bed of the river including the flood plain (cf. BED 1); as **Riverbed Mould** *obs. joc.*, a common nickname of a local brand of cigarette tobacco *Riverhead Gold*; **River Board**, a statutory elective local authority responsible for river control; **river crow**, SHAG 2 (18); **river flat**, a FLAT (*n.*¹ 2 a) adjoining a river; **river flounder**, see FLOUNDER *n.* 2 (1); **river-horse**, a horse naturally (or trained to be) efficient in river crossing.

1863 PYKE *Report* in *Handbook NZ Mines* (1887) 10 The fortunate prospector was Mr. Thomas Arthur, who..obtained 200oz. of gold in eight days, by washing the sands of the **river-beach**. **1879** *TrNZI* XI. 388 We find..along the **river-beds** [in Westland] swarms of Maori hens. **1915** *Ibid.* XLVII. 334 A number of introduced plants..have made their appearance on the shingle-fan and in the river-beds. **1916** *Ibid.* XLVIII. 175 Popularly included in the term 'river-bed' is the more stable ground, formerly the flood-plain, on either side of the bed proper, and this we likewise include in our treatment of river-bed. **1955** *BJ Cameron Collection* (TS July) riverbed (n) The flood plain of a river. **1945** *NZ Dairy Exporter* 1 Dec. 41 Matches, ashtray, packet of **Riverbed Mould** handy? **1884** *NZ Statutes* No.49 227 [River Boards Act] In every river district there shall be a **River Board**. *Ibid.* 235 All rivers, streams, and water courses within any river district constituted under this Act shall..be to all intents and purposes within and subject to the jurisdiction of the Board. **1938** *Auckland Weekly News* 16 Mar. 18 All work will close down on the Hawke's Bay River Board's diversion and flood control scheme. **1959** MCLINTOCK *Descr. Atlas* 76 A considerable superstructure of other bodies has gradually come into being—river boards, catchment boards, milk boards, rabbit boards, and the like. **1888** BULLER *Birds NZ* II. 171 Not the least interesting feature to me [by the Huka Falls] was this, that a dozen or more of these little [white-throated] Shags (or '**River Crows**' as they are sometimes called) kept passing and repassing through the misty spray. **1879** *TrNZI* XI. 442 The whole valley of the Wangapeka consists of a narrow gorge, with here and there a small **river-flat**. **1917** *TrNZI* XLIX. 4 This 'river-bed' is bounded on either side by a broad expanse of flat land, chiefly tussock-covered, termed colloquially 'river-flat', but in this paper 'terrace'. **1925** MANDER *Allen Adair* (1971) 15 It was in his first month, as he passed a river flat one day, that he saw a young man begin the cutting of a sledge track. **1959** MCCLYMONT *Exploration of NZ* 80 Every creek and river-flat was prospected. **1960** SCRYMGEOUR *Memories Maoriland* 157 'Te Rapa' was not of an investment purpose, gorse in golden bloom spread its noxious mantle across some beautiful river flats. **1860** in Butler *First Year* (1863) iii 32 He is a good **river-horse**, and very strong.

b. *Goldmining.* **river claim** [AND 1859], **river diggings**, a goldmining claim or diggings that extends into a watercourse; **river-workings**, *wet diggings* (WET *a.* 3).

1862 WEKEY *Otago As It Is* 61 Claims shall be classified thus... Creek or **river claims**, *i.e.*, alluvial claims in the bed of creeks or rivers. **1863** *Otago Witness* (Dunedin) 18 July 7 Dunstan, 13th June... At the Kawarau..all the river claims are submerged, the paddocks and tunnels in the banks are mostly fallen in. **1864** *AJHR* C-4 7 [Regulations under Goldfields Act (1862) Otago.] River claims shall means claims in the beds of rivers. **1857 river diggings** [see *dry diggings* (DRY *a.* 1 b)]. **1864** HOCHSTETTER & PETERMAN *Geol. NZ* 88 There are, therefore, two principal descriptions of diggings; either 'river diggings', in the beds of streams, or 'dry diggings', in the conglomerate and gravel accumulated on the slopes of the mountains. **1863** PYKE *Report* in *Handbook NZ Mines* (1887) 8 Before the close of the year 1862, 70,000oz. were transmitted by escort from the Dunstan Goldfield; but this was not all derived from the **river-workings**.

river river, var. REWAREWA.

riwai. Also occas. **rewai**, **rewi**, **riwi**. [Ma. /'ri:wai/: Williams 344 *Rīwai..Potato*; a general name; Duval (III. 390) records *riwai* from 1842 and, without evidence of origin or discussion, treats it as a loanword.] MAORI POTATO 1. Cf. TAEWA.

1851 SHORTLAND *S. Dist. NZ* 309 Mahetau, a potato. Syn. riwai; besides which a variety of other words are used to denote their different kinds. 1867 HOCHSTETTER *NZ* 298 The 'men' of one party were represented by small potatoes cut in two, called Riwai. 1916 *Chron. NZEF* 30 Oct. 107 These same two Australians on the previous weekend had turned up and peeled all our rewis (otherwise 'spuds'). 1917 *NZ At the Front* 163 Maori, all t'at pomme-de-terre, t'at riwai, t'at spud, for you. 1924 *Kai Tiaki* XVII. 34 One kit contained riwi of different varieties. 1930 REISCHEK *Yesterdays in Maoriland* (1933) 148 First of all, quantities of provisions were brought to the place, kumara, taro, hire, and rewai, birds preserved in oil. 1948 HENDERSON *Taina* 167 'We're not going to eat dirt like this,' said Jance. 'Who peeled the *riwai* today?' 1966 FINLAYSON *Brown Man's Burden* (1973) 120 There on the river flats were our crops of corn and kumara and riwai that we kids had to hoe. 1972 BAXTER *Collected Poems* (1980) 537 To others my love is a plaited kono Full or empty, With chunks of riwai, Meat that stuck to the stones. 1985 *Listener* 7 Sept. 12 Then, I'd roll out my threadbare Whaariki..spread an old newspaper on the floor and on it place a steaming pot of puha, kamo-kamo, riwai, brisket-on-the-bone.

riwariwa, var. REWAREWA.

roa. *South Island.* Also **roa-roa**, **rua**. [Ma. /'roa/: Williams 344 *Roa* (ii), *roaroa..large grey kiwi*;.. ([Ngai]Tah[u].)] The *great spotted kiwi* (KIWI 2 (2)). (Occas. the *brown kiwi* (KIWI 2 (1)), more correctly the ROWI).

1862 HAAST in Haast *Julius Von Haast* (1948) 226 It was the same call as that of the Roa, but much louder and deeper. 1869 *TrNZI* I. (rev. edn.) 226 *Apteryx maxima* is described [from Nelson] as 'a Kiwi, about the size of a turkey...' The natives distinguish it as the Roaroa. 1882 W.J. Wheeler let. from Dusky Sound (March) in Begg *Port Preservation* (1973) 275 I have some very good Roa skins on hand..the Price list..is posibally [*sic*] the tourist price..Roa skins and skeletons 20s. 1885 *NZJSc.* II. 506 *Apteryx haastii*..Roa-Roa.— Nothing is known of the breeding habits of this fine species. 1896 HARPER *Pioneer Work* 68 While camping on the shore of this lake [Maporika], I heard the cry of the rua, or large brown kiwi, now nearly extinct and very valuable. 1904 [see KIWI 2 (2)]. 1906 *TrNZI* XXXVIII. 338 Another remarkable flightless bird..is the member of the *Apteryx* family commonly called by naturalists the '*roa*'. The Maoris say that the proper name of this bird is the '*tokoweka*'. 1923, 1947 [see KIWI 2 (2)]. 1955 OLIVER *NZ Birds* 53 *Large Grey Kiwi. Roa...* Though many stories regarding a large Kiwi called by the Maori Roaroa, were current prior to 1871, it was not until that year that two specimens were received from Westland at the Canterbury museum. 1964 DEMPSEY *Little World Stewart Is.* 74 At nights, the others..heard the distant call of a kiwi, 'roa' the big Stewart Island kiwi is called, but we saw no trace of the bird. 1984 SOPER *Birds NZ* 14 The Great Spotted Kiwi or Roa... *Apteryx haasti*. 1990 [see KIWI 2 (2)]. 1993 *Dominion* (Wellington) 23 Apr. 3 Till now scientists had recognised three species—the great spotted kiwi or roa in the northwest of the South Island, the little spotted kiwi on Kapiti.., and the brown kiwi, scattered from Northland to Stewart Island.

road.

1. In the phr. **on the road. a.** [AND 1901.] Used allusively with reference to droving.

1874 KENNAWAY *Crusts* 48 [It] recalls one of our evening camps 'on the road'.

b. Used allusively with reference to swagging in the phr. **to be on the road**, **to walk the long road**, to go on the swag (in search of work).

1900 SCOTT *Colonial Turf* 162 The pair were 'on the road'. In other words, they were carrying their swags. 1986 *Islands* 37 Aug. 42 In middle and later years of Depression walked the 'long road' picking up odd jobs rather than rest on penurious safety of Public Works Relief Camps.

2. *Kauri logging. Hist.* **a.** As **rolling road**, a cleared logway, often with a base of logs laid lengthwise to the line of the road, along which logs are rolled (using timber-jacks) from the bush to a collection point.

[1867 HOCHSTETTER *NZ* 147 A broad clearing leads from the interior of the forest..and forms a kind of road along which the logs are rolled down to the head of a regular tramway.] 1889 KIRK *Forest Flora* 149 [Caption] Kauri Logs on a Rolling Road. *Ibid.* 150 When growing at any considerable distance from a creek or river it is necessary to form rolling-roads; these are broad tracks from 30ft. to 60ft. wide. 1889 in Reed *Story of Kauri* (1953) 172 An article in the *Building World*, 1889, had this to say: 'Logging the Kauri in New Zealand is a rather exciting occupation—that is by the "rolling road" method of extraction.' 1894 *NZ Official Year-book* 331 After the [kauri] trunks are cut into lengths a 'rolling-road' is formed to the nearest creek. All the scrub is closely cut down for a width of from twenty-five to thirty feet..to obtain an approximately even surface, inclined towards the creek. The logs are forced along this road by timber-jacks, which the bushmen use with remarkable skill, and are impelled with a rapidity which is simply astonishing to persons unused to the process. If the creek contains plenty of water the logs float to the nearest booms without further trouble. 1953 REED *Story of Kauri* 171 Rolling roads were formed by laying three rickers or other small trees lengthwise to the line of road, and logs were placed crosswise on this road. There might be thirty or forty or more in a fleet [of logs]. Three men with timber jacks usually operated this job.

b. As **(skidded) road**, a logway with a base of greased logs laid across the line of road over which logs are dragged to a collection point.

1906 LAING & BLACKWELL *Plants NZ* 64 If far from water, the carriage [of kauri logs] is more difficult. A skidded road, six to eight feet wide, is formed of greased logs. Thus a sort of rough wooden tramway is made. The logs are hoisted onto this road by means of 'jacks', or dragged by a team of bullocks. 1951 p.c. R. Gilberd (Okaihau). *Road* an old name for *logway* among kauri bushmen.

3. In the phr. **to be sent (to go) down the road**, to be sacked. See also TRACK *n.* 2.

1951 p.c. Miss J. Hall (Otago). *To be sent down the road...* Expressions heard used in Central Otago and Fiord Country, by people engaged in gold-mining or bush work. In the beginning, I should imagine, it was a literal description of what happened to the man— since there was only one road leading out of the community... It is now used in isolated communities to describe someone being dismissed, even if he can get another job that keeps him in the community. 1959 SLATTER *Gun in My Hand* 91 You'll go down the road if ya don't wake ya ideas up, I said. 1984 BEARDSLEY *Blackball 08* 85 By God, he'd keep a close eye on Master Hickey and at the first opportunity..he'd be sent down the road so fast he'd wonder what hit him. 1986 *Metro* (Auckland) July 82 But it didn't compensate for the..slack period when workers went down the road.

4. Special Comb. **Road(s) Board** [used elsewhere but recorded early in NZ and earliest in Australia (AND 1856): see OED *road n.*[1] 10 a], an elected local authority with responsibility for roads and roading and bridges; **Road Code**, a set of rules issued officially for guidance of road-users; **road-hopper**, a hitch-hiker; **road-keeper** *obs.*, a bushrangers' lookout; **road-line**, the surveyed line of a road often cut through bush or scrub (see also LINE *n.*[1] 1 a); **road trusteeship** *hist.*, a local initiative for the provision and upkeep of district roads.

1864 CHUDLEIGH *Diary* 14 May (1950) 132 Acland came home in the evening having had to attend a **Road Board** at Shanks when, like other road boards they squashed all their own actions of the last four months. 1887 *Auckland Weekly News* 23 July 15 When a member of the Road Board is voted to the chair, does he remain chairman for a year, or for three years? 1897 A TRAMP, ESQ. *Casual Ramblings* 11 Another remedy that might be tried with advantage is the abolition of the County Councils and Road Boards. 1992 LATHAM *Golden Reefs* 234 The commonly called 'Roads Boards' were, in theory, permitted to use a portion of the money raised in each district. 1986 RICHARDS *Off the Sheep's Back* 80 **Road code**, drivers' licences and warrants of fitness were unheard of in those days. 1993 *Dominion* (Wellington) 16 June 8 [Advt] Psst want your driver's licence?.. Each Driver's Licence Test Kit includes..Road Code; Oral Test Questions. 1933 GRAEME-HOLDER *Restless Youth* 99 Did you ever see such a lot of **road-hoppers**? 1866 *Narr. Maungatapu Murders* 11 He was '**road-keeper**' in the gang; that is, he preceded the others, and while they were engaged with their victims, stood ready to give warning of danger to his companions. 1898 HOCKEN *Contributions* 160 Was there a little bridge to build, a small cutting to make, or a portion of an impassable **road-line** to be improved, there were many to contribute labour. 1898 *TrNZI* XXX. 399 The burnt area on each side of the road-line. 1899 BELL *In Shadow of Bush* 8 A large clearing opened out on the right, and a little way back from the road-line stood a slab hut—or wharé, as it is generally called in New Zealand. 1921 *Quick March* 10 Feb. 45 We were struggling home with a big night's catch [of rabbits]— struggling down to the road-line, along which the rabbit-cart would travel next day. 1861 *Otago Witness* (Dunedin) 6 Apr. 5 There are plenty of opportunites for a young gentleman to take part in the public business of the district in which he resides; there are the **road trusteeships**, the school committees, &c. &c.

roadie.

1. [f. *road*)man + -IE.] A roadman, one employed in the upkeep of roads and verges (see also LINESMAN); also, one employed by a road-building or tar-sealing contractor.

1983 HULME *Bone People* 241 I've known roadies who knew theirs was a high place in the scheme of things. 1986 *Sunday News* (Auckland) 15 June 25 [Heading] Roadies riled. Speed freaks are putting road builders in potentially life-threatening positions.

2. A road-service operator or driver.

1985 *National Bus. Rev.* 10 June 8 Despite all the ranting..it would appear that even NZ Railways concede that costs by road are cheaper than by rail... It is certainly satisfying to have a 'roadies' view endorsed by the corporation.

roadless north. A name for the North Auckland peninsula arising from an early lack of or difficulty with road access for wheeled vehicles, with a consequent dependence on coastal shipping. Cf. WINTERLESS NORTH.

1906 *Weekly News* 3 May [Caption] The oft-reiterated appellation of the 'roadless North' is thoroughly deserved as far as the Hokianga district is concerned. **1925** MANDER *Allen Adair* (1971) 6 But the north was not respectable. It was the land of lost men. It was peopled with nomads and wasters. And it was 'the roadless north', the 'barbaric north', where the Maoris still might war upon you in the night. It had no railway beyond Helensville. **1946** REED *Farthest North* 34 A post bearing the legend 'Waihopo Landing' seemed to indicate that in comparatively recent times, when the term 'roadless north' expressed the literal truth, the little settlement was saved by boat. **1953** REED *Story of Kauri* 235 The mill was closed in winter, for the reason that may be apparent only to those who remember the 'roadless north' in the later decades of the nineteenth century. **1961** REED *N. Cape to Bluff* 30 The building was erected when this part of the country [Pukenui] could literally be described as 'the roadless north'. **1970** THOMAS *Way Up North* 72 Nevertheless the 'Roadless North', to use the term in general use at that time [c1904], was still well named.

roads and bridges. *Hist.* Used allusively as an attributive in early New Zealand with reference to the assiduous promotion of local roading and bridging in their electorates by members of the House of Representatives.

1858 *Roads & Bridges Ordinance* in *Ordinances of Taranaki* (1867) 93 [Title]. **c1850s** W.B.D. MANTELL in Hocken *Contributions* (1898) 126 Roads and bridges, and schools and churches Were among the original terms of purchase, Churches and schools and roads and bridges Were promised as our most esteemed privileges, But bridges and schools and churches and roads Are sought for in vain near settlers' abodes. **1883** *NZPD* XLIV. 15 It was the numerous and very large votes to favoured districts which gave them [*sc*. the Whitaker-Atkinson ministry] their support... The estimates were loaded with votes for roads and bridges. **1958** MULGAN *Making of New Zealander* 17 Often settlers went right out into the wilds and had to wait long for reasonably good communications. This partly explains the importance of the 'roads and bridges member' in the New Zealand Parliament, a term that has well-nigh disappeared. One might laugh at him and deplore his preoccupation with local matters, but road or bridge could be life or death to an outback settler. The central Government was the main source of bounty, so grants were continually asked for. **1966** *Encycl. NZ* I. 365 Among a rather mediocre team Coates stood out for initiative and vigour. By his sustained use and encouragement of experts, by his disregard for the time-honoured 'roads and bridges' system, Coates broke new ground [c1920–26]. **1991** LA ROCHE *Hist. of Howick & Pakuranga* 213 The Hundred of Howick [in Auckland] also included..1055 acres of 'Waste Land'... Wardens were elected to control the grazing rights. These Wardens were the first recognisable local administrators. They used the revenue from 'depasturing' leases..to provide a common fund for the provision of roads, bridges, and other essential community needs.

roarer. In the phr. **to go a roarer**, of a creek, to be in violent flood. Cf. ROARING MEG.

1960 MASTERS *Back-Country Tales* 59 Next morning the creek in front of the hut was going a roarer, making it useless my attempting getting the horses over.

Roaring Meg. Also erron. **Roaring Mag.** [f. *roaring* noisy, boisterous: the name has been given to various noisy things, e.g. a famous Londonderry cannon, a top, a flow or exudation of water: see OED *Roaring Meg*; see also ROARER.]
a. A common name from gold-digging and coaching days for a swift, rapid-rising creek or small river, *spec.* a tributary of the Kawarau River in Central Otago. Cf. GENTLE ANNIE 2.

1874 PYKE *George Washington Pratt* 3 The mountain torrent..was the stream named by surveyors as the 'Kirtleburn', but which is best known by the fantastic appellation conferred on it by the miners— 'Roaring Meg'. There are three creeks in succession on this line of road—tributaries of the Kawarau River. The first is very small, and in a dry season merely drips from the rocks, and is called 'Crying Jenny'. The second, which tumbles down from the mountains impetuously and with great noise, is 'Roaring Meg'. The third, being a sluggish stream, has received, by popular assent, the designation of 'Gentle Annie'. **1875** HOLLOWAY *Journal of Visit 1873–75* (ATLMS) 21 Mar. Drove over Annie's Creek. And on till we came to within half a mile of Roaring Mag... We crossed a Beautiful Mountain Torrent call'd Roaring Mag, and not inaptly. **1891** DOUGLAS in *Mr Explorer Douglas* (1957) 149 T'was [*sic*] sweet upon a Summers eve To wander with my Nannie To hop accross [*sic*] the Roaring Meg And climb up gentle Annie. **1943** HISLOP *Pure Gold* 20 There are now several bonnie burns coming down the mountain sides to the river, the largest of which are the famous Roaring Meg and Gentle Annie. *Ibid*. 53 This heavy stream, which breaks so suddenly on a stranger from its very rough surroundings, got its name (according to early-day tradition) from the fact that Meg, one of the two girls on their way to a dancing saloon at Arrow, created such a fuss at crossing this turbulent water that vibrations of her voice loosened rocks on the mountain side to add still further to the roaring of the stream and of Meg herself. There are different versions concerning the naming of this stream, and maybe some of this one is my own... A few miles further on the next stream to be crossed is the Gentle Annie, called after Meg's pal, who no doubt was a much quieter type of tourist than Meg herself. **1959** *Tararua* 13 49 *Roaring Meg*, usually a creek and..rough and tumble, is apt to be in the neighbourhood of *Gentle Annie*... *Roaring Meg* may come from the name of the famous gun of Londonderry.

b. As **Roaring Meg Creek**, a West Coast place-name.

1981 DENNIS *Paparoas Guide* 64 This side-track crosses two old water races, Wessels' [*sic*], and Roaring Meg (the latter diverting water by a 30 metre tunnel from nearby Roaring Meg Creek).

c. The Pukeatua stream in the north central North Island.

1992 *Evening Post* (Wellington) 6 Oct. 3 They are prepared to borrow $1.3 million to harness the Pukeatua Stream, also known as Roaring Meg.

roa-roa, var. ROA.

Robert, Roberto: see COLONIAL ROBERT.

robin. [Transf. use of the northern hemisphere name *robin Erithacus* species.] Any of several small birds of the genus *Petroica*, subgenus *Miro* (fam. Eopsaltriidae).

1. Also occas. as **bush, New Zealand**, or (*obs.*) **wood, robin**, (usu.) *Petroica australis*, a tame, inquisitive small bird of the New Zealand bush, having three subspecies often individually identified by modifiers indicating provenance: **North Island** (*P. australis longipes*), **South Island** (*P. a. australis*), **Stewart Island** (*P. a. rakiura*). See also PITOITOI, TOUTOUWAI, *whitethroat* (WHITE *a.* 1).

1773 FORSTER *Resolution Jrnl.* 3 May (1982) II. 269 We hitherto had taken [the bird] for a variety of the small yellow legged Thrush, commonly called *Robin* by our Ship's-crew. **1777** ANDERSON *Journal* Feb. in Cook *Jrnls.* (1967) III. 806 One [bird] in figure and tameness exactly resembles our Robin. **1845** DEANS *Pioneers* (1964) 44 The robin here has not a red breast, he is black and has a white breast; every country has the robin, although of many different colours. **1853** LUSH *Auckland Jrnl.* 9 June (1971) 140 We have a bird called the Robin but though like his British cousin in shape and habits his breast is black. **1866** BARKER *Station Life* (1870) 93 The New Zealand Robin was announced, and I could only see a fat little ball of a bird, with a yellowish-white breast. **1871** HUTTON *Catalogue Birds NZ* 12 *Petroica albifrons*... Wood Robin... *Petroica longipes*... Wood Robin. Totowai. **1873** BULLER *Birds NZ* 119 Miro longipes. (North-Island Robin.) *Ibid.* 120 This bird is..the 'Toutouwai' of the natives and the 'Robin' of the colonists. *Ibid.* 122 Miro albifrons. (South-Island Robin.) **1881** BATHGATE *Waitaruna* 150 [They saw only] a wretched bush-robin, which Arthur insisted on shooting..which was so close that it was actually blown to pieces. **1889** *TrNZI* XXI. 215 *Miro albifrons* (South Island Robin). The wood-robin is an almost constant attendant..in the bush or about the tents. **c1899** DOUGLAS in *Mr Explorer Douglas* (1957) 271 My attention was attracted by a couple of Robins who were playfully hoping [*sic*] about, jumping on my head or standing on my breast, innocently looking in my face with that ernest [*sic*] gaze so peculiar to them. **1914** GUTHRIE-SMITH *Mutton Birds & Other Birds* 39 I had never before seen the South Island Robin sitting. **1921** *Quick March* 10 Oct. 25 Has any reader seen a South Island robin lately? **1938** *Auckland Weekly News* 27 Apr. 38 On the lower slopes we found that rare bird, the North Island robin. **1938** LANCASTER *Promenade* 96 Tiffany, wooing bush robins..with a bellbird ringing its chime for her, came at length to lie in dusty hay in the dray bottom. **1955** OLIVER *NZ Birds* 488 The South Island Robin quickly retreated before the advance of civilization and it was feared that it might become extinct. *Ibid.* 489 No doubt well known to the early sealers and settlers, the Stewart Island Robin first appeared in an ornithological paper in 1872. **1960** MASTERS *Back-Country Tales* 286 On our arrival back at Hollyford late that afternoon we found our former camp friends, the bush robins waiting to greet us. **1964** BACON *Along the Road* 53 Then, from nowhere, there was a robin on a rotted stump, his navy and white jacket gleaming, his large eyes button-bright. **1976** SOPER *NZ Birds* 389 The New Zealand Robin is a plump, grey and white, rather long-legged bird with pert stance and beady eyes that immediately arrives to investigate anything you may be doing in its territory. **1981** *Dominion* (Wellington) 13 Feb. 11 A flutter up ahead and a North Island robin hops nervously from branch to branch hoping for the ground to be disturbed and some insects uncovered. **1988** *Listener* 12 Nov. 17 The feathers of the bush-robin plumping BA pillows.

2. *Petroica traversi*, a robin of the Chatham Islands, recovered from near extinction, now rare and confined to (esp.) Mangere Island in the Chatham group. **a.** As **black** (occas. **black wood**) **robin**, the present preferred common name. Also *fig.*

1884 *NZJSc.* II. 288 Black Robin.—Information concerning the breeding habits of this Chatham Island robin is as yet wanting. **1893** *TrNZI* XXV. 57 The Black Robin. I have received several more specimens of this bird from the Snares. **1952** Black Wood Robin [see MIRO *n.*²]. **1976** SOPER *NZ Birds* 213 Little Mangere..lies just off Mangere Island. At its top is a small area of bush in which the last few Black Robins, no more than twenty, survive. **1990** *Dominion* (Wellington) 23 Nov. 12 The nine-year black robin programme..had been one of the most spectacularly successful endangered species stories in the world.

b. As **Chatham Island (Chatham Islands, Chatham Island black) robin**.
1873 BULLER *Birds NZ* 123 Chatham-Island Robin... This species was discovered by Mr. Henry Travers during an exploratory visit to the Chatham Islands in [1871]. **1891** *TrNZI* XXIII. 37 I exhibit..a pair of so-called Chatham Island Robin, obtained at the Snares. **1923** *NZJST* VI. 88 Chatham Islands Robin. Buller (1895) stated, on the authority of Hawkins, that this bird was extinct. **1966** FALLA et al. *Birds NZ* 204 The remaining population of the Chatham Island Robin (estimated at 20–35 pairs in 1937) lives in a small area of coastal forest and the ledges of scrubby vegetation on the surrounding cliffs on Little Mangere Island. **1984** HOLMES *Chatham Is.* 96 Chatham Island Black Robin, *Petroica traversi*—Little Mangere Island is the native home of this little member of the flycatcher family. **1995** ANDERSON *House Guest* 254 Old Blue, the last breeding female Chatham Island robin, had saved her race from extinction.

Rob's mob. Also occas. **Robsmob**. The name given to the loose coalition of political supporters (inside and outside Parliament) of the late Hon. Robert D. Muldoon and his (interventionist) policies. Cf. MOB *n.* 3.
1985 *Listener* 5 Oct. 39 About half the callers confessed they were not part of 'Rob's Mob'. **1986** JAMES *Quiet Revolution* 91 On his way to victory in 1975, Muldoon had recruited 'Robsmob'—'ordinary citizens' from outside National's normal ranks. **1991** *Listener* 23 July 34 Call them Rob's mob if you like; older, considerably greyer, but no less loyal to the man who led not wisely but too well. **1992** *Dominion* (Wellington) 26 Jan. 6 'Rob's mob' was a figment of a warped imagination. This mythical horde of rabid adherents could have held a meeting in a Taranaki long drop.

rock. In *attrib.* use.
1. In the names of plants and animals found on, around, or in the vicinity of, rock or rocks, see: COD 2 (7) and (8), DAISY 2 (6), LILY 2 (14), LOBSTER 2 a, OWL 2 (3), OYSTER *n.* 2 (3) and (4), TROUT 2 (6), WREN 2 (4). See also ROCKFISH.
2. Special Comb. **Rock College**, prison, or (in WW2) a field punishment centre; **rock melon** [recorded earliest in Austral.: AND 1841], in New Zealand a general name for any of several musk melons, in US often called *cantaloupe*.
1942 HARCOURT *Parson in Prison* 164 I found that some of the alumni of '**Rock College**'—as the inmates call H.M. Prison, Mt. Eden. **1946** WEBBER *Johnny Enzed in Middle East* (Glossary) Field Punishment Centre, Budgie Cage, Rock College. **1988** MCGILL *Dict. Kiwi Slang* 93 *rock college* prison. **1871** LUSH *Thames Jrnl.* 16 Mar. (1975) 105 Blanche bought 8 fine rock melons for 4/0. **1882** HAY *Brighter Britain* I. 223 We grow large quantities of melons—water-melons, musk-melons, **rock-melons**, Spanish melons, pie-melons, and so on. **1893** CRICHTON *Australasian Fruit Culturalist* II. 129 The Rock, or Sweet, melon is known as *Cucumis melo*. **1949** Brett's *Gardening Guide* 87 Melons, Rock and Musk. It does not pay to sow melon seeds too early. **1983** SCARROW & GOODING *Scarrow's Guide to Gardening in NZ* (1984) 112 Try growing rock melons; these have a delicious perfumed flesh quite different from water melons. **1991** MCDONNELL *Grow Your Own Fruit & Vegetables* 86 The Rock Melons can be hollowed out and used as a receptacle for fruit salad.

rocker. Goldmining. [AND 1851.] CRADLE *n.* 1.
1868 *Thames Miners' Guide* 20 'The rocker' for concentrating tailings. **1906** GALVIN *NZ Mining Handbook* 8 When sufficient water was not available, the use of a tom (or rocker) had to be resorted to.

rockfish. [Spec. use of *rockfish* a fish frequenting rocks.] Any of various unrelated marine fish frequenting rocky shores, esp. *Taumakoides* (formerly *Acanthoclinus*) spp. (fam. Acanthoclinidae), and occas. formerly *Girella* sp. See also HIWIHIWI, PARORE, TAUMAKA.
1770 PARKINSON *Journal* (1773) 15 Jan. 114 All the coves of this bay teem with fish of various kinds, such as cuttle-fish, large breams..scorpenas or rock-fish. **1849** black rockfish [see PARORE]. **1850** ACHERON *Journal* May in Howard *Rakiura* (1940) 391 There has been a great catch of fish..and some red rock fish. **1870** *TrNZI* II. 325 The Hapuka, Baracouta..and a few varieties of Rock fish, are the sea fish chiefly obtained. **1886** [see HIWIHIWI]. **1938** *TrRSNZ* LXVIII. 415 *Acanthoclinus quadridactylus*... Rockfish. Taumaka. **1947** POWELL *Native Animals NZ* 72 Rockfish.., Taumaka of the Maoris, is the small brownish-olive fish, about 7 inches in length, which is found lurking under boulders at low tide. **1956** GRAHAM *Treasury NZ Fishes* 322 Those who do know this fish call it Rockfish, but I prefer the Maori name, Taumaka. **1967** NATUSCH *Animals NZ* 229 The rockfish..a long, straight fish with the tips of the dorsal fin running parallel to the back, and to the line of the anal and belly fin-tips, is common as a small fish of rock pools, where it hides under stones and seaweed; bigger ones occur in deeper water. **1973** MILLER & BATT *Reef & Beach Life* 72 One of the largest and commonest [of the shore fishes] is the rockfish..which is not the least bit easy to catch even when the rocks are high and dry. It is strong and slippery and remains very active out of water. **1986** PAUL *NZ Fishes* 135 The rockfish..is dark green with a pale head and stripe, and lives under stones or in crevices in rock pools.

rock-hop, *v.* Usu. as *vbl. n.*
1. *trans.* To negotiate (a stream or river-bed) by stepping from boulder to boulder; also, Cf. *boulder-hop* (BOULDER 2).
1982 HOLDEN *Wild Pig* 75 Sneaking along, he rock-hopped a small stream. *Ibid.* 128 When I reached the creek I rock-hopped my way down it. **1952** THOMSON *Deer Hunter* XII [Caption] Rock-hopping to keep dry feet dry. The creek bed is typical of Canterbury high-country streams. With experience one rivals the mountain goat.
Hence **rock-hopper**, one who negotiates river-beds, etc. by stepping from boulder to boulder; also the familiar name of a penguin (see PENGUIN 2 (5)).
1978 JARDINE *Shadows on Hill* 115 In rock-hoppers' slippers By Pannells made We'll tramp the peak Bluff, chutes and glade.
2. *intr.* To fish from coastal rocks. Hence **rock-hopper**, one who fishes from coastal rocks.
1981 WILSON *Fisherman's Bible* 183 Rock-hopping. One of the most exciting, dangerous and rewarding types of fishing is undoubtedly rock-fishing. The rock-hopper gets added spice in his fishing by his sometimes death-defying attempts to get to the best possie.

Rockwood lily: see LILY 2 (15).

Rogernomics. [f. *Roger* (Douglas + eco)*nomics*, a variation of US *Reaganomics* a portmanteau of (President) *Reagan* + eco)*nomics*: first used as a heading to an inset placed within an article by a journalist, Gordon Campbell (see 1985 quot.).] Also facetiously **Roger Nomic**. A label applied to the financial and monetary policies of (Sir) Roger Douglas (1937–), Minister of Finance in the 1984 Labour Government, involving a non-interventionist, free-market approach to economic management.
1985 *Listener* 23 Feb. 8 [Heading] Rogernomics in Finland. *Ibid.* 15 June 35 We hear a lot these days about the so-called 'Rogernomics' a name derived from the so-called 'Reaganomics', which in turn is shorthand for 'supply-side economics'. **1987** ROBERTS *Politicians, Public Servants & Public Enterprise* 146 The coinage 'Rogernomics', originally intended to draw attention to the idiosyncracies of an untried experimenter, is passing into the political language as a description of a wide ranging programme of organisational and economic reform. **1992** *Metro* (Auckland) June 76 It is basic to the Rogernomics creed that political action be decisive and as far as possible irreversible. **1992** *Dominion* (Wellington) 16 July 12 I found myself thrown once more against the aforementioned forces of cultural darkness, a truly awful coalition led by Mammon and the dreaded Roger Nomic supported by Low Common Denominator, Market Madman and Treasury Philistine. **1993** *Listener* 3 Apr. 16 Take 'Rogernomics', for instance. The term was born on February 23, 1985, as a headline on a *Listener* interview with Roger Douglas. The following week it was picked up by Bernard Lagan in the *Dominion* and went on from there to enter the language as a term for mad dog monetarism, Kiwi style.

Hence **Rogernome** [a play on *Rogernom*(ics with g)*nome* (of Zurich)], a supporter of Rogernomics esp. an adviser recommending strict fiscal policies as a national benefit; **Rogernomic** *a.*; **Rogernomicize** *v. trans.*, to apply the policies of Rogernomics (to a country, a problem, etc.).
1991 *Sunday Star* (Auckland) 1 Dec. B8 I believe Sir Robert [Muldoon] had the right recipe for New Zealand and it is you **Rogernomes** who have ruined it. **1993** *Independent* 8 Oct. 10 The Rogernomes are set to abolish import licensing..and lower the playing field. **1992** *Dominion Sunday Times* (Wellington) 16 Aug. 11 Simon Upton was in vogue for a thoughtful speech on what a **post-Rogernomic** conservative should be. **1986** *National Bus. Rev.* 7 Nov. 11 Whatever did happen to that old comfortable world; has it all been **Rogernomicised** out of existence? Happily no. What we used to call social justice and now term wimpishness still lives.

rohe, var. ROI.

rohito, var. ROHUTU.

rohutu. [Ma. /'ro:hutu/: Williams 345 *Rōhutu*, *rōutu.. 1. Myrtus* [spp.].] Either of two native forest shrubs of fam. Myrtaceae. **a.** Also early **rohito**. *Lophomyrtus* (formerly *Myrtus*) *obcordata*, a small shrub with heart-shaped leaves and dark red berries.
1838 POLACK *NZ* II. 395 A very similar wood [to the Kahikatoa] exists to the southward, called *Rohito*, of which carved boxes, for holding small trinkets and feathers, are made by the people. **1848** [see RAMARAMA]. **1889** KIRK *Forest Flora* 221 *Myrtus pedunculata*... The Rohutu... This species bears the same native name as *Myrtus obcordata*. **1894** COLENSO *Excurs. Northern Is.* in Taylor *Early Travellers* (1959) 29 I also found a species of *Myrtus*, a small slender tree bearing orange-coloured juicy berries... [The natives] call the tree rohutu. **c1920** BEATTIE *Trad. Lifeways Southern Maori* (1994) 68 The rohutu was a good wood to make

[Maori] tops from. **1961** MARTIN *Flora NZ* 230 The Rohutu (*M[yrtus] obcordata*) is more widespread [than Ramarama, *M. bullata*]. **1981** BROOKER et al. *NZ Medicinal Plants* 72 *Lophomyrtus obcordata*... Maori name: *Rohutu*... This shrub, and the closely allied *Neomyrtus pedunculata*..are found throughout New Zealand. Both are known as 'rohutu', and it is possible that both were used for medicine.

b. *Neomyrtus* (formerly *Myrtus*) *pedunculata*, a small shrub with obovate leaves, bearing its flowers and berries on long stalks ('peduncles'). See also MYRTLE b.

1867 HOOKER *Handbook* 767 Rohutu... *Myrtus pedunculata*. **1869** *TrNZI* I. (rev. edn.) 261 The fruit of the tutu-papa..of two of the New Zealand myrtles, the ramarama (*Myrtus bullata*), and the rohutu (*M. pedunculata*). **1889** [see a above]. **1907** LAING & BLACKWELL *Plants NZ* 288 *Myrtus pedunculata* (*The Pedunculate Myrtle*)... Maori name *Rohutu*. **1961** ALLAN *Flora NZ* I. 331 *N[eomyrtus] pedunculata*... Coastal to lower montane forest and shrubland... *Rohutu*. **1971** *VUWTC '71* 55 A jungle of pepperwood..rohutu.., or the crown fern..does not represent regeneration..but marks areas of extreme modification. **1982** WILSON *Stewart Is. Plants* 61 *Neomyrtus pedunculata* Rōhutu... Shrub or small tree up to 6 m.

roi. Also early **rohe**. [Ma. /ˈroi/: Williams 345 *Roi* (i)..fern root.] FERN-ROOT a.

[**1820** LEE & KENDALL *NZ Gram. & Vocab.* 203 Rói, *s*. Fern-root:] **1838** POLACK *NZ* I. 397 The principal sustenance, anterior to the time of Cook, was the *roi*, or fern-root, answering the same purpose that bread does with us. **1842** BEST *Journal* 8 Apr. (1966) 343 We were regaled with Rohe (Fern root). **1867** HOOKER *Handbook* 768 Roi, *Col[enso]. Pteris aquilina* (root of). **1882** POTTS *Out in Open* 18 Roi—The rhizome or root of the bracken (*Pteris aquilina var. esculenta*). **1906** CHEESEMAN *Manual NZ Flora* 971 Common fern; Bracken; Rau-aruhe; Rahurahu; of the root, *Aruhe, Roi*. **1915** *TrNZI* XLVII. 79 Certain places became noted for '*roi*', the edible rhizome.

rolie. *Drug users*. A shortened altered form of *Rohypnol*; see quot.

1989 *Dominion* (Wellington) 30 Apr. 3 Dr John Dobson, a drug clinic consultant.., says flunitrazepan, marketed as Rohypnol, is supposed to be a sleeping tablet. But it has become a favourite with pill popping addicts, and 'rolies' as they are known, sell on the street for up to $7 each... 'It's the drug that druggies use.'

roll, *v*. [Spec. use of *roll* to form into a (cylindrical) roll.]

1. *Farming*. Also **roll up**. [AND 1874.] *trans*. To roll up (a newly-shorn fleece) after skirting, etc. Occas. *intr*. or *absol*.

1863 CHUDLEIGH *Diary* 30 Jan. (1950) 75 Commenced shearing at five a.m. I was picking up and rowling [*sic*] the fleeces. **1881** BATHGATE *Waitaruna* 173 The best of the fleece was quickly classified, rolled together, and deposited in a kind of bin. **1901** *TrNZI* XXXIII. 196 The latter is always skirted and classed, whereas the black fleece was rolled up just as taken from the sheep's back. **1903** *Bill Reardon's Roadman's Diary* 22 Oct. in *Alfredton* (1987) 163 Rolling wool for three shearers at Saunders. **1929** *NZJST* X. 326 It is hardly necessary to state that fleeces from March-shorn sheep were not able to be rolled. **1943** HISLOP *Pure Gold* 18 [Helping press wool] was only one of the many ways I was glad to put in a week-end, if it was not skirting and rolling for some good friend. **1982** WOODHOUSE *Blue Cliffs* 89 It is difficult to imagine how these two men could skirt, roll, class and carry away the 1600 or so fleeces shorn in a day.

Hence **rolling** *vbl. n.*, see quot. **1922** (see also *wool rolling* (WOOL 3)); **rolling-table**, the table or stand in a woolshed on which newly-shorn fleeces are rolled (cf. *wool-table* (WOOL 3)).

1922 PERRY *Sheep Farming* 122 *Rolling*.—When the wool is opened at the sale it is in the best interests of the seller if the best and most attractive part of the fleece, viz., the shoulder, is exposed to view. *Ibid*. 123 There are many ways of rolling, but two common ways are as follows:- (1) First throw in the neck so that it will rest on the shoulder and then turn in the two sides to the middle of the back. Commencing at the tail, roll the fleece towards the neck. **1936** BELSHAW et al. *Agric. Organiz. NZ* 708 [Heading] *Rolling*. There are several methods of rolling a fleece. **1986** RICHARDS *Off the Sheep's Back* 113 The wool tables for rolling and skirting were in the centre of the woolboard. **1883** *Brett's Colonists' Guide* 215 There are many so-called wool-classers whose experience is limited to a few years at the **rolling table**. **1913** CARR *Country Work* 14 As soon as a shearer has taken the fleece off..the picker gathers the fleece up in such a manner that she or he can on getting to the rolling table, throw it out with the breech part at the right end. **1924** *Otago Witness* (Dunedin) 23 Sept. 54 The picker-up..collected the shorn fleece, carried it to the rolling table, where the wool roller, after pulling off and tossing the skirts to one side, rolled it and passed it in his turn to the wool classer.

2. [Used elsewhere but recorded earliest in NZ: see OED *roll v.*¹ 8 *U.S.*, 1932.] Usu. in the phr. **to roll (one's) own** (cigarettes), **to roll** (oneself) **one**, to roll a cigarette from tobacco and a cigarette paper. Cf. ROLL-YOUR-OWN.

1922 *Quick March* 10 Mar. 4 The 1921-Model of flapper..can 'roll her own' whether it be cigarettes or hosiery! **1935** *NZ Free Lance* (Wellington) 11 Sept. 19 Some time ago for instance, rolling one's own cigarettes became a fashion that spread through the country like wildfire. **1937** COWIE *NZ from Within* 13 At least half the cigarette smokers [of Christchurch] 'rolled-their-own'. **1949** SARGESON *I Saw in My Dream* 111 While he rolled himself one he looked across the flat. **1950** CHERRILL *NZ Sheep Farm* 40 I mostly roll my own cigarettes down home. **1987** GEE *Prowlers* 165 She rolled her own, fine-cut Greys from a Desert Gold tin.

roll, *n*. [Spec. use of *roll* a quantity of material rolled up in cylindrical form: see OED *n.*¹ 6.] Ellipt. for ROLL-YOUR-OWN.

1935 *Canterbury Mountaineer* 36 Patient work in the boulders and bush was punctuated with the cry for a cigarette. 'Have a roll.' **1955** BJ *Cameron Collection* (TS July) roll. have a roll. Have some of this [roll-your-own] tobacco to roll yourself a cigarette. **1965** *Weekly News* (Auckland) 29 Dec. 35 He wouldn't give his own mother a roll. *Ibid*. 35 If we play it right they'll give us a roll.

Hence **roll-up** *adolescents*, an illicit smoke.

1984 16–17 F E3 Pakuranga Coll. 33 Roll up [M4 F4]

roller. Also occas. **roller-up**. [f. ROLL *v*. 1: AND 1899; OED 1890.] *wool roller* (WOOL 3).

1892 SWANTON *Notes on NZ* 96 There is the wool-classer with his assistant rollers who number five or six. **1900** *TrNZI* XXXII. 367 They brought their own cook, fleece-pickers, and rollers-up, and also their children and dogs. **1901** *Ibid*. XXXIII. 196 White wool divides, when skirted by the roller at the wool-table, thus: Belly pieces [etc.]. **1904** CHUDLEIGH *Diary* 5 Nov. (1950) 425 I am to keep and pay a cook..1 roller who expects to roll 1000 fleeces a day. **1933** *Press* (Christchurch) (Acland Gloss.) 30 Dec. 13 Wool-classer.—Besides classing the wool, he is responsible (at least in my own sheds) for the work of the shed hands—pressers, rollers, and fleece-pickers. **1940** STUDHOLME *Te Waimate* (1954) 208 At shearing time [at Benmore, 1892] about 55 men were employed in the shed: 28 to 30 shearers..6 rollers. **1951** MCLEOD *NZ High Country* 27 One classer, two rollers..make up the shed contingent. **1982** WOODHOUSE *Blue Cliffs* 89 Fred Stuthridge came as a wool-classer in 1904 and was paid £1 for each 1000 fleeces with 25/- a week extra for wool-rolling. He was helped by one roller at 25/- a week.

rollie. [f. ROLL(-YOUR-OWN + -IE.] ROLL-YOUR-OWN.

1984 COX *Waiting for Einstein* 62 Peter was smoking again—it would have been rollies back then, with longer hair and that faded jacket. **1991** *Metro* (Auckland) Nov. 117 'Rowdy buggers,' says John, spitting a thread of baccy off his tongue. That's the problem with rollies—no filter to keep it in.

rolling dock, road, table: see DOCK 1, ROAD 2 a, ROLL *v*. 1.

roll up. *Obs*. [AND 1861.] A general public meeting or assembly (often of goldminers) on a matter of public interest.

1890 *Lyttelton Times* 11 Jan. The escort robbery and 'Roll up' are taken from events well within his recollection when he was a youth on the West Coast. **1895** *Hawke's Bay Herald* 10 June [3] There is a 'roll up' of the diggers to hunt [the bushrangers] down and the mounted troops appear upon the scene to aid in capturing the outlaw[s]. **1895** *Evening Star* (Dunedin) 27 June [Advt] Act 5- The Deathbed Confession—The Western Gully—The Roll Up—Lynch Law—The Burning House—A Fugitive—Life for Life. **c1930** *Whitcombe's Etym. Dict. Aust.-NZ Suppl*. 10 *roll up. n.* sl. a meeting.

Hence *v*. [AND 1861], to attend or turn up for (a meeting).

1941 BAKER *NZ Slang* 62 *To roll up at a meeting*, [etc.] these are phrases which came almost as easily to the New Zealand tongue as to the Australian. **1968** *NZ Contemp. Dict. Suppl*. (Collins) 17 *roll-up v*. arrive.

roll-your-own /ˌrʌuljəˈrʌun/. Also **roll-yer-own, rollyown**. [Also US: cf. Random House, 1975-80.] A hand-rolled cigarette. Often *attrib*. See also ROLL *n*., ROLLIE.

1937 *King Country Chronicle* 22 Oct. 5 I suppose it is a bit of a blow—coming back to New Zealand and down to roll-your-owns and beer. **1938** *National Tobacco Company* Advertisement featured 'Rollyown'. **1945** *NZ Geogr*. Apr. I. 23 The background of all this [bunkhouse life] is tobacco. There are but few pipes, and 'tailor-made' cigarettes are only a luxury. 'Roll your own' is on most lips. **1950** *Dominion* (Wellington) 14 July 11 [Advt] Everywhere you go—Roll-your-own-smokers say..Silver Fern for preference. **1959** SLATTER *Gun in My Hand* 21 He hid behind the truck for a few quick puffs at his roll-your-own. **1978** TAYLOR *Twilight Hour* 30 That evening I handed round my box of cigars, but everyone seemed to prefer their roll-your-own cigarettes. **1989** BIOLETTI *The Yanks Are Coming* 15 It was a land where..roll-yer-owns were the sign of the real Kiwi bloke, while 'tailormades' were a drawing-room affectation.

Hence in verbal use, **to roll one's own**, to make one's own cigarettes; **roll-your-owner**, one who makes or prefers hand-rolled cigarettes.

1939 *Dominion* (Wellington) 15 Sept. 13 [Advt] Prize Crop. For Every Man who Rolls his Own. **1986** *National Radio* (9.00 p.m. News) 31 July 9.00pm news Roll-your-owners and pipe-smokers will pay an extra

Rongopai. Also **Rongo Pai.** [Ma. /roŋo'pai/: see quot. 1946.] The gospel; Christianity.
1928 BAUCKE *White Man Treads* 133 The old *tohunga Maori*, schooled in the ancient religion, were the first to accept Pai-marire; they were astute enough to recognize that by adopting it they would secure the ancient ascendancy of their class over the people which the Rongopai had impaired but not destroyed. 1935 COWAN *Hero Stories NZ* 53 He was a middle-aged man when the missionary impulse set him seeking a field beyond his tribal district, in the cause of the new religion, the Rongo Pai, and the reconciliation of old enemies. 1946 *JPS* LV. 157 *rongopai*, Gospel (rongo, to hear or something heard; pai, good, good news).

roniu. [Ma. /'roniu/: Williams 346 *Roniu.. Brachycome radicata.*] *Brachyscome* (also formerly *Brachycome*) *radicata* (fam. Asteraceae), a small tufted daisy of grasslands and herbfields.
1853 HOOKER *II Flora Novae-Zelandiae I Flowering Plants* 127 *Brachycome radicata*, the only New Zealand species, is a small herb with stout woody roots of many thick fibres, no stem... Nat. name, 'Roniu'. 1867 HOOKER *Handbook* 768 Roniu, *Col[enso].Brachycome odorata.* 1868 *TrNZI* I. (rev. edn.) 266 The daisy like flowers of the roniu..and the flowering tops of the sweet-scented grass *karetu*..were worn around the neck. 1982 WILSON *Stewart Is. Plants* 196 *Roniu*... Tufted herb, often forming small patches... Flower heads rather inconspicuous daisies.

rookery. *Sealing. Obs.* [Recorded earliest on the NZ coast: see OED 2 b, 1832.] A seal colony.
1831 BISCOE *Journal* 19 Nov. in McNab *Old Whaling Days* (1913) 418 They had only seen a few seal, it was thought these were only stragglers from some Rookery near at hand. 1845 MCLEAN *Journal* (ATLTS) I. 42 A boat goes out on search of a 'rookery' as [sealers] term the collected seals on any spot. 1851 SHORTLAND *S. Dist. NZ* 144 This rugged part of the coast was formerly thickly inhabited by seals; and several spots, once their favourite resorts, called rookeries by the sealers, were pointed out by some of the crew.

rooster. [f. transf. or fig. uses of *rooster* a male domestic fowl: see OED *n*. 'Chiefly *U.S.* and *dial.'*.]
1. *Rooster* is the common New Zealand use for the male domestic fowl; *cock* is, in its common local use, 'penis', or *ellipt.* for *poppycock* 'nonsense'.
2. A fellow, chap, bloke, JOKER *n.*¹ 1. (In the 1911 quot. prob. more directly *fig.*, poss. for 'noisy cocks of the walk'.)
[1911 *Maoriland Worker* 7 July 9 'Blatant megaphones' and 'roosters' who have been 'got at' are the terms used to describe 'highly-paid' officials of the Labour Federation.] 1944 [see SPRUIKER 2]. 1952 PASCOE *Land Uplifted High* (1961) 162 'Rooster' is another variant of 'joker' [in high country slang]. 1960 CRUMP *Good Keen Man* 43 The note invited me to see if I could make head or tail of this rooster. As far as Jim had been able to make out, his name was 'Bloodywell Clarry'. 1963 MORRIESON *Scarecrow* 22 Something weird about that rooster... Another of ole McDermott's scrub-cutters..going off on a spree. 1987 *Dominion Sunday Times* (Wellington) 20 Sept. 17 Gold is easy enough to find on the West Coast. Those in the know can..pan out a few flecks of the precious metal. Any rooster can go out and do that. 1992 ANDERSON *Portrait Artist's Wife* 46 We were all there, the whole lot of us and this rooster from Walters Carriers arrives for the wethers.
3. A male who will not get up and dance, but prefers to 'roost' in one place all evening (a once common sight in New Zealand dance halls).
1946 SMITH *Poetical Works* 273 The mayor [of Greymouth] in a happy mood Told a funny tale or two. When you want to grip the roosters That's the best thing you can do. [1946 *Note*] 'Roosters'—those on the high seats near the door [of a dance or social hall].
4. *Canterbury. Hist.* See quot.
1980 ELDRED-GRIGG *Southern Gentry* 121 In Canterbury [in the 1880s], men looking for harvest jobs perched along fences in country townships, and were called 'roosters'.
5. *WW2* (Italy). As **rooster's blood** [f. the colour], cheap red wine. Compare PURPLE DEATH.
1944 *NZEF Times* 23 Dec. 18 Rooster's Blood. 1952 NEWTON *High Country Journey* 40 I had drunk 'Zibib' and 'Rooster's Blood' with their brother George in the Middle East and this seemed introduction enough. 1956 DAVIN *Sullen Bell* 66 'And I remember how you bust up that pommy officers' club in Bari.'.. 'But that was after drinking Roosters' Blood.'

root, *v.* [Poss. from a fancied brutal similarity of the movements of a pig's snout in foraging and an Australasian male's penis and loins during intercourse: AND 1958.] *trans.* and *intr.* To have sexual intercourse (with).
1941 *root* first heard by Ed. at St Patrick's College, Silverstream. **c1950** Cf. the common jocular catch-phrase: A Kiwi is a swine who eats roots and leaves. 1971 ARMFELT *Catching Up* 37 'He's just about rooting her on the way round.' Graham did not know what Ted meant by 'rooting'. 1974 HILLIARD *Maori Woman* 91 'Yes, I had to make a full confession.' Maisie smirked. 'And you told the priest about Richard rooting you?' 1980 LELAND *Kiwi-Yankee Dict.* 86 *root:* (A) Root most often means Copulate.
Hence **rooted** *a.* [AND 1944], exhausted (compare *fucked*, *stuffed*), or as an exclamation of contemptuous dismissal, **get rooted!** [AND 1961]; **rooting** *vbl. n.*, (a bout, or result, of) sexual intercourse.
1988 MCGILL *Dict. Kiwi Slang* 49 **get rooted!** vigorous objection; eg 'Me play Aussie rules? Ahh. Get rooted!' *Ibid.* 94 **rooted** exhausted, not necessarily from sexual activity; eg 'That second half really took it out of me. I'm rooted!' 1988 LAY *Fools on Hill* 181 'You're looking a bit rooted, old chap.' 'Yeah, had a late night last night.' 1976 SARGESON *Sunset Village* 83 Anyhow full house, rape on the screen, or it could have been mutual, just plain **rooting**. 1987 *Chosen Place* 22 'Rooting around the drawers' caused consternation and a few raised eyebrows in the early days. *Ibid.* 104 Rooting. colloquial term for fornication. 1988 JACKSON *Rainshadow* 97 I am inducted into the mysteries of 'rooting'. 1990 DUFF *Once Were Warriors* 15 Made her feel like..bringing the youth back to her bed and giving him, you know, a real good rooting.

root, *n.*
1. [See *v.*: AND 1959.] An act or instance of sexual intercourse.
c1960 *Truth* newspaper billboard p.c. Don Bryant (Wellington), former editor. 'En route in boot' [referring to serial intercourse carried on in the boot of a car circling a shopping centre]. 1977 HALL *Glide Time* 77 Hugh. Well, didn't you ask him whether he was having naughties, or roots or knee-tremblers, or all the other.
2. [AND 1961.] A female (seldom a male) regarded as a sexual object.
1984 17 M E101 Pakuranga Coll. 28 Root. 1984 16 M E93 Pakuranga Coll. 28 Root bag(s) [M5]

ropable, var. ROPEABLE.

rope, *v. Farming.* **a.** As **rope up**, to secure (an animal, usu. a cow) with a rope. Cf. LEG-ROPE *v.* 1 and 2 a.
1854 CHAPMAN *Diary* (ATLTS) 4 Alfred roped up and milked Lilly.
b. [AND (also US) 1827.] *trans.* To catch or secure (stock) with a rope (cf. *roping stick* below).
1862 CHUDLEIGH *Diary* 17 Nov. (1950) 66 MacCluchey came..and branded etc. a lot of young horses. It is very hard work ropeing [*sic*] them. 1878 ELWELL *Boy Colonists* 189 Harold with a long pole, had been 'roping'—that is, throwing the slip-knot over the heads of the cattle that required to be branded... Harold had successfully roped an animal.
Hence **roping stick** [AND 1846], a pole with a noose at one end used for securing a farm animal, usu. a cattle-beast.
1878 ELWELL *Boy Colonists* 190 Ernest..had to get behind the animal, and by dint of prodding with the roping stick..force it to run up towards the corner.

rope, *n.*
1. *Logging. Spec.* use of *rope* for the wire rope used to haul logs out of the bush.
c1950 p.c. R Gilberd (Okaihau). A log can be hauled forward on 'the rope', backwards on the 'tail-rope' and the direction of pull can be varied by the use of a snatch block temporarily attached to a tree on one side or other of the log-way.
2. *Special Comb.* **ropeboy** *coalmining,* a junior workman who assists in attaching trucks to the hauling rope; **ropeman** *logging,* a bush workman who attaches saw-logs to the hauling rope (see also ROPEY); **rope road,** see quot.
1952 *Landfall* 23 206 An Italian has trucked in a West Coast mine for twenty years; he is still alone..**ropeboys** just starting can feel cocky pride in shouting: 'Good day, you — rotten Skypoo bastard!' 1908 *Awards, etc.* 339 [Wellington Sawmills Award] [Rates of wages] Engine-drivers for loco. or traction [£]3 3 0 **Ropeman** who splices his own ropes 3 0 0. 1951 *Awards, etc.* 520 [Marlborough Timber-Workers Award] [Rates of wages] Other crosscutter and scarfer 4[s.] 2¼[d.] Breaker-out, snigger, ropeman (hauling rope), to apply to only one man in each hauling team 4 4½. 1961 HENDERSON *Friends in Chains* 70 [I] had taken one of the first of Westland's mechanical log-haulers out to Bourkes Creek mill..Alf acting as ropeman. 1984 BEARDSLEY *Blackball 08* 245 **rope road** (the) ropeway for hauling coal trucks to surface.

ropeable, *a.* Also **ropable.** [AND 1874.] Violently angry, needing restraint, 'fit to be tied'.
1913 *NZ Observer* 13 Sept. 16 When he come round he was ropable. 1947 DAVIN *For Rest of Our Lives* 315 Well, I must get back to the G1. He's absolutely ropable about the tanks. 1958 [see RIP *v.* 2]. 1966 *People's Voice* 2 Nov. 3 The young bloke had completed [a security questionnaire]—but the father was ropable. 1976 WILSON *Pacific Star* 131 Oh, Dick. What a ropeable young idiot I've been. 1988 *Sunday News* (Auckland) 17 Apr. 15 Hastings cowboy Brian Denton is ropeable. He is angered that the word cowboys is being used as a label for wild, reckless behaviour.

rope up: see ROPE *v.* a.

ropey. *Logging.* Also **ropy.** [f. ROPE *n.* 1 + -Y.] A *ropeman* (ROPE *n.* 2).

1951 p.c. R. Gilberd (Okaihau). The breaker-out is assisted by a 'ropey' whose duty is chiefly to carry the snatch-block. **1953** REED *Story of Kauri* 195 Immediately a log was drawn to the whim, the pole was released from the niche, whereupon the 'ropey' pulled back the rope and hitched on another log. **1981** MARRIOTT *Life in Gorge* 21 A steam log hauler he would put up with, as long as the ropies would hook on to the tree he had felled and get it out of the way. **1990** GEORGE *Ohakune* 95 Among the other employees there was..the 'ropey' whose job it was to fasten a heavy steel rope to the log.

roping stick: see ROPE *v*. b.

rori. [Ma. /'rori/: Williams 347 *Rori... 4.* n..sea-slug.] *Scutus antipodes* (formerly *breviculus*) (fam. Fissurellidae), a univalve shellfish (see quot. 1987).
1870 TAYLOR *Te Ika A Maui* (2edn.) 631 The..*Rori*, is a large black slug, with a shield-like shell on its back, it is abundant on the coast of Taranaki, where it is eaten the same as the Pawa. **1881** *TrNZI* XIII. 71 There is a proverbial comparison for a woman's lips when well tattooed; such are said to resemble a *rori*..; the plump black smooth and glossy mantle of this shellfish. **1922** ANDERSEN *Maori Life in Ao-Tea* 28 How..gnawing hunger makes the soul-less frame to stagger, when at dim eventide the reeling form oft seeks to eat the refuse rori, cooked and left by Pare-korau! **1954** BEATTIE *Our Southernmost Maoris* 60 Rori—a black shellfish in a small white shell. **1987** POWELL *Native Animals* 22 *Shield Shell (Rori) Scutus antipodes*. An internal shell just sufficient to protect the vital organs of the animal, which is a large black slug very like a Paua animal minus its shell. **1989** HULME & MORRISON *Homeplaces* 8 When I lift the lid, the rori is undulating beautifully round and round in the steaming water, singing to itself.

rort. [Origin obscure; poss. related to Brit. slang *rorty a*. (OED 1864) splendid; rowdy; coarse; of dubious propriety.] An act or bout of sexual intercourse; a woman regarded as a sexual object. Cf. ROOT *n*.
[*Note*] The Austral. sense 'an act of sharp practice' (AND 1926), and those of the verb 'to engage in sharp practice' (AND 1919) and 'to rig (a ballot, etc.)' (AND 1980) have recently come into NZ understanding and use.
1976 HILLIARD *Send Somebody Nice* 127 Ian thought of Valerie Kemp. By God, what a rort!

Hence *v. trans.*, to fuck.
c1949 Football Song: *My Old Man's a Fullback*. My old man's a blacksmith, a blacksmith [etc.]... All day he wroughts iron, wroughts iron, [etc.] At night he comes home and rorts me.

rorter. *Obs*. [f. Brit. slang *rorty* fine, splendid.] Occas. heard as **rorter-snorter.** Something superior or excellent of its kind.
1941 BAKER *NZ Slang* 51 In constant use by our youngsters..rorter, rumpty, rumptydooler. **1955** *BJ Cameron Collection* (TS July) rorter (n) A beaut.

rosebud. Also **rosie.** A kind of marble.
1938 HYDE *Godwits Fly* (1970) 30 The boys knelt at the side of the big rings, and very deliberately cannoned one another's rosies and glimmers out of the way. **1962** LAWLOR *More Wellington Days* 128 Cat's-eyes were a variety [of marble]..and I think they came in early in my marble-playing time [c1905]. With me they were always officers in British regiments, the agates were Boers, and rosebuds and glassies were women.

rosella. *Shearing*. [AND 1849.] A sheep which has cast or lost most of its wool.
c1900–10 GOLDSTONE *'The Man From Kaiveroo'* in Woodhouse *Farm & Station Verse* (1950) 49 We'd a bunch of Aussie shearers, and they come from New South Wales, They entertained the 'rouseys' with a lot of fairy tales Of how they shore the jumbucks and rosellas from the hills. **1933** *Press* (Christchurch) (Acland Gloss.) 18 Nov. 17 *Rosella*.—A sheep that has cast most of his wool before shearing, so is very easy to shear. *R[osella]* is a shearers' word, probably brought from Australia. **1940** STUDHOLME *Te Waimate* (1954) 130 When the pen had been re-filled, [the old hand would] quickly catch and shear all the 'rosellas', or easily shorn sheep. **1960** MASTERS *Back-Country Tales* 257 In it [*sc*. the catching-pen] I noticed right near the front, one rosella (sheep bare of wool except for a few tufts around the neck), and several others that appeared to be bare-bellies. **1989** *NZ Eng. Newsletter* III. 27 *rosella*: A sheep with wool falling out of it.

rosie: see ROSEBUD.

rotary cowshed: SHED *n*.[1] 4 b.

rotate: see *wouldn't it rotate you* (WOULDN'T 3 d).

rotten, *a*. In special collocations: **rotten corn**, KANGA; **rotten eggs** [AND 1957], *egg cap* (EGG 3); **rotten fish plant**, *fish-guts plant* (FISH 3).
c1875 MEREDITH *Adventuring in Maoriland* (1935) 146 I sampled a new Maori dish on this trip—*kanga kopirau* (**rotten corn**). It has a bouquet just about as potent as the dead whale I mentioned in my last. **1966** TURNER *Eng. Lang. Austral. & NZ* 159 In small schools without proper playing fields, games were spontaneous and enjoyable, and holes could be dug freely in the school grounds for **Rotten Eggs**, in which a tennis ball is rolled into the nest [or hole] of one of the players and all run while the boy with the ball has to *brand* another player (i.e. hit him with the ball). **1969** *Standard Common Names Weeds* 65 **rotten fish plant** [=] *fish-guts plant*.

rough, *a*.

1. In special collocations in senses 'inferior'; coarse; tough; 'difficult': **rough country** *mustering*, see quots.; **rough-guts**, a roughly-behaved or uncouth ill-bred person (cf. *rough-as-guts* 2 d below); **rough sheep**, ROUGHIE 2 b and quot. 1947; **rough stock**, inferior stock; **rough stuff**, in the phr. **to cut the rough (stuff)**, see CUT *v*.[2] 2; **rough tree-fern**, see FERN 2 (20) b (b).
1888 SHIRRES *Diary* in Neave *Land of Munros* (1980) 54 This is, in fact, a region which is appropriately spoken of, as '**rough country**'—a region where a horse will plunge without hesitation into a rushing stream. **1947** NEWTON *Wayleggo* 56 I might here explain that to a musterer, the term rough country does not imply hard shingle country, but rock-bound bluffy country. **1949** *Landfall* 9 50 How dare that little **rough-guts** make fun of Firpo. **1947** NEWTON *Wayleggo* 154 **Rough Sheep**: Domesticated sheep which have escaped musterers and gone semi-wild. Distinct from the real wild sheep of Canterbury, and unlike them do not shed their wool. Consequently they become overburdened with wool, which at times reaches such length that it drags on the ground. **1966** NEWTON *Boss's Story* 154 These sheep were real wild sheep—not the ordinary domestic sheep gone wild. The latter, long-tailers and wool[l]ies which have escaped muster and gone semi-wild, are known as 'rough sheep'. **1933** CRAY *National Welfare* 32 The 'window dressing' has covered a good deal of '**rough stock**' of doubtful value.

2. In various phrases using **rough** *as* in comparisons indicating extreme crudeness or roughness of make-up, behaviour etc.; roughly made or done; rough and ready; very untidy; most uncouth. (Phrases heard but not found in writing include **rough as boots**, **rough as houses**.) **a.** (a) **rough as bags** [AND 1919], **rough as a bag**, very rough, untidy, uncouth, etc.
1918 let. 4 Jan. in *Boots, Belts* (1992) 58 He was an Australian and seemed to be proud of it. Although he was as rough as a bag, he had the look of a man. **1933** *Press* (Christchurch) (Acland Gloss.) 9 Sept. 15 Idiomatic use of *as* to introduce a simile... Two may possibly be Canterbury expressions: At least, I never heard them outside the province: (1) As rough as a bag. (2) As rough as a pig's breakfast. **1938** HYDE *Godwits Fly* (1970) 144 I haven't seen a dance in months, outside of the local hops, and they're rough as bags. **1941** BAKER *NZ Slang* 53 *rough as a bag* (the Australians also have *rough as bags*), and *rough as a pig's breakfast*. **a1950** WHITWORTH *Otago Interval* 50 The kids were rough as bags and the food wasn't very choice. **1966** TURNER *Eng. Lang. Austral. & NZ* 115 There is simile: 'as mad as a snake'..'rough as bags' (which I know better in the variant 'rough as sacks'). **1974** MASON *Hand on Rail* (TS 1987) 30 Maori Girl:.. I took him on after my girl friend Tui got fed up with him. But he could be rough, rough as bags. Beat me up once, and that was the finish.

(b) **rough as a soojee bag** *obs*. [prob. f. *soojee* (ad. Hindi *sūjī*) a flour from Indian wheat: see OED: hence, its container].
1939 BEATTIE *First White Boy Born Otago* 97 [Sugar] came in mats, the big ones weighing 180 lbs, and was often called 'mat sugar'. This mat was native made..and was pretty well square. Outside this mat, and covering it, was a coarse bag called a soojee (or suji?) bag. A familiar saying of the early days was, 'As rough as a soojee bag', and this saying was applied to both people and things. Up to 1863 I never saw sugar except in mats.

(c) **rough as a bag of files**.
1918 *Kia-ora Coo-ee* (1981) 15 Sept. III. 2 But as the engine was still rough as a bag of files, the pilot..headed for home.

b. rough as sacks.
1943 BENNETT *English in NZ* in *Amer. Speech* XVIII. 91 The Australian 'rough as bags' has became 'rough as sacks'. **1966** [see a (a) above].

c. rough as a pig's (occas. **dog's**) **breakfast.**
1933, **1941** rough as a pig's breakfast [see a (a) above].

d. rough as guts [OED 14 d, 1966 'Chiefly Austral. and N.Z.']. Also *attrib*. Cf. *rough-guts* 1 above.
1918 *Chron. NZEF* 5 July 253 Our Sergeant sez we are as 'rough as gutz'. **1982** HOLDEN *Wild Pig* 10 A pretty typical pighunter's firearm: rough as guts but still capable of delivering the goods. **1987** *Sunday News* (Auckland) 4 Jan. 3 The Purple Death has scored a few hits over the festive season. It's a wine with a difference, recommended as 'rough-as-guts' drinking. **1989** RICHARDS *Pioneer's Life* 44 I knew..that they had already judged me. I would be like my clothes and swag, as rough as guts and soon be down the track.

rough, *v. Shearing*. [AND 1878.] *trans*. To shear (sheep) roughly and badly, esp. as **rough 'em (out)**.
1897 WRIGHT *Station Ballads* 37 But he wouldn't shear [sheep]..in to rough them through. **1955** BOWEN *Wool Away* 156 Rough 'em. The opposite to 'pink 'em', and meaning rough shearing and a bad job of the sheep. **1960** MILLS *Sheep-O* 129 To keep level [with the

roughage. [Cf. OED *roughage* 1 'dial., U.S. and N.Z.' 1883.] Rough growth or scrub; tough grass or the less nutritious or palatable parts of pasture or crops.

1940 STUDHOLME *Te Waimate* (1954) 96 The first work of the settlers was to burn off the roughage on large areas of country. **1950** *NZJAg.* Feb. LXXX. 122 On much of the country a fairly high proportion of cattle to sheep is carried, the cattle being used to clean up roughage left by the sheep. **1951** LEVY *Grasslands NZ* (1970) 362 *Roughage*—Pasture growth grown to maturity and remaining *in situ* for winter and summer grazing.

roughie. See also ROUGHY.

1. An unqualified or poor tradesman; one who makes a rough job of what has to be done.

1910 *Truth* 16 July 2 It is wonderful the difference a fashionable jockey makes to a horse's price. With a 'roughie' on they go out at 20 to 1, but when a crack jockey is up they are often 6 to 4 propositions. **1915** WILLIAMS *New Zealander's Diary* (c1922) 27 Feb. 20 A *type*..leading characteristics anarchical tendency. Pride in being a 'roughie'. **1975** *Dominion* (Wellington) 10 Mar. 2 Mr Quigley expressed concern that there were some 'roughies'—unqualified carpenters—engaged in building.

2. Also **roughy. a.** A poorly-performing racehorse or one considered an outsider.

1908 *Truth* 7 Mar. 2 It was of very little avail to them when the 'roughie' won easily. **1910** *Truth* 11 June 2 The jockey became unseated during the race and..let the 'roughie'..win comfortably. **1989** *Sunday Star* (Auckland) 31 Dec. B12 Backing a roughie gives as good a chance of a return as following the money—favourites have a poor record in the cup. **1995** *Dominion* (Wellington) 27 Jan. 21 [Heading] Trainer put faith in roughie Rastes. Rastes didn't fool everyone when he won the 1987 Wellington Cup at odds of 55–1.

b. A sheep difficult to shear because of a double-fleece, or matted wool, etc. See also *rough sheep* (ROUGH *a*. 1).

1947 NEWTON *Wayleggo* 115 The hiding place of..those odd little lots of dodging old 'roughies'. **1973** NEWTON *Big Country SI* (1977) 86 When he took over [the station], the only domestic sheep were 'roughies'—long tailers and doubles that had multiplied from those which had escaped the wind-up muster four years before. **1986** RICHARDS *Off the Sheep's Back* 93 I did not intend to be caught with 'roughies' left in my pen when the pressure was on.

c. A disobedient or poorly-trained sheep-dog.

1949 HARTLEY *Shepherd's Dogs* 45 Of course these methods [of correcting faults in sheep-dogs] would not do for very young beginners but for the..'roughy' there is nothing better.

d. A wild-mannered cattle-beast.

1985 *NZ Times* 12 May 8 I hasten to explain, the stock agent bought on our behalf, a further dozen 18-month steers. 'They're roughies,' he advised by phone on the day of the purchase and I admit we waited with just a little trepidation for them to arrive.

Rough-on-Rats. [AND *Rough-on-Rats,* 1885.] A former well-known brand of rat-poison comprising arsenic, magnesia and a little charcoal, often associated with suicide by poisoning. Occas. *transf.*

1885 *Wairarapa Daily* 6 Jan. 2 [Advt] Don't die in the House. 'Rough on Rats' cleans out rats, mice, beetles, roaches, bed-bugs, ants..moles, jack-rabbits, gophers, 7½d. **1888** DUNCAN *Wakatipians* 53 [The dog] became..'rough on rats'. **1890** *Otago Witness* (Dunedin) 17 July 18 The jury returned a verdict 'That the deceased took a dose of "rough on rats" while in a state of temporary insanity caused by reading sensational literature'. **1917** *Wairarapa Daily Times* 13 Oct. 4 The deceased..took the greater portion of a box of 'Rough on Rats' and immediately became seriously ill. **1946** ACLAND *Early Canterbury Runs* 103 He went to shoot at a neighbouring station [in the 1880s] and the host invited the party to have a nip before they started out, but gave them 'Rough-on-Rats' by mistake for whisky. Six of them were badly poisoned. **1962** LAWLOR *More Wellington Days* 79 [c1905 children's 'Willie' rhymes.] Willie, and two other brats, Licked up all the Rough-on-Rats. Father said, when Mother cried, 'Never mind, they'll die outside.'

Rough Rider. *Hist.* [Spec. or transf. use of *rough rider* a horse-breaker (OED 1 and 2 a: recorded in NZ from 1856), 2 b an irregular cavalryman, 1884.] Used mainly in *pl*. A member of any of the New Zealand contingents to the Boer War.

1900 *Auckland Weekly News* (Suppl.) 16 Feb. 5 [Caption] Auckland Rough Riders for Fourth Contingent; The First Parade at Potter's Paddock. **1904** BAUGHAN *Life in NZ* in *Empire Review* (1902) 176 [A farmer,] his hat a 'rough-rider' felt [i.e., a slouch hat]. **1906** MOORE *With the Fourth NZ Rough Riders* 10 It may not be amiss to explain how the name 'Rough Riders' came to be applied to the contingents. The Premier..expressed a strong opinion that we should not accept the title of 'Bushmen' which had been adopted in Australia [because of possible confusion with the Bushmen of South Africa]... As they were not regularly trained troops, and were to be good riders ready for rough work, he thought they should be called 'Rough Riders', and expressed the hope that they would be particularly rough on the enemy. Accordingly the name was adopted, and under it the Third and Fourth Contingents have been raised. **1949** BROWN *Short History of Belfast, Canterbury* 12 The departure of a few lads to the Boer War at the turn of the century—Rough Riders they were called. **1951** CRESSWELL *Canterbury Tales* 86 When however, the Boer War began and Canterbury started recruiting her special contingent of Rough Riders, prices for many commodities, and especially for oats on which the Rough Riders' horses were to be fed..began to rise. **1982** HARWOOD *Heritage Trail* 64 At the start of the Boer War he enlisted in the 5th Contingent of 'Rough Riders'. The name 'Rough Riders' was given to the New Zealand troops by the Premier, the Right Hon. Richard John Seddon.

rough-up. [Spec. use of *rough-up* a boxing contest: AND 1891.] An aggressive encounter; a fight, a free-for-all. Also *attrib.*

1910 *Truth* 10 Sept. 2 There is a rough-up jockey in America named Duggan, who is not particular as to whether he causes a jockey to be knocked over the rails, under the rails, or any other old place. **1916** CHURCH *Tonks* 91 I enjoyed that rough-up. **1917** Aug. in Miller *Camps, Tramps & Trenches* (1939) 121 Hurt my knee a little in a wrestling match on my bunk during one of the usual roughups.

roughy. [AND 1864.] Any of several deep-bodied rough-skinned fish of the family Trachichthyidae.

1. As common (pink-finned) roughy (*Paratrachichthys trailli*)(see also SANDPAPER FISH), **long (slender, violet) roughy** (*Optivus* (or *Hoplostethus*) *elongatus*), **silver roughy** or SAWBELLY (*Hoplostethus mediterraneus*).

1927 PHILLIPPS *Bibliogr. NZ Fishes* (1971) 24 *Paratrachichthys trailli*... Roughy... *Hoplostethus elongatus*... Long Roughy. **1928–29** *TrNZI* LIX. 375 *Hoplostethus elongatus*... Long Roughy. **1939, 1956** [see SANDPAPER FISH]. **1967** NATUSCH *Animals NZ* 215 Related [to golden snapper, *Trachichthodes*] is the roughy of Otago and Stewart Island (*Paratrachichthys trailli*). **1972** DOAK *Fishes* 23 Slender roughy *Hoplostethus elongatus*... The slender roughy is one species [of roughies] that comes well within the range of skindivers. **1979** *Catch* Feb. 12 Common Roughy *Paratrachichthys trailli*. Pink-finned roughy, sandpaper fish... Slender Roughy *Optivus elongatus*. Long roughy, violet roughy... Saw Belly *Hoplostethus mediterraneus* Silver roughy. **1982** AYLING *Collins Guide* (1984) 174 *Common Roughy* (Sandpaper fish) *Paratrachichthys trailli*... This species of roughy has small rough scales and because of this feature it is sometimes known as the sandpaper fish... Common roughys are found throughout New Zealand, although they are rarely seen north of Cook Strait. *Ibid.* 175 *Slender Roughy*. *Optivus elongatus* (*Hoplostethus elongatus*)... The slender roughy is a small fish..and is more elongate than the other members of this family. *Ibid.* 176 *Silver Roughy*. *Hoplostethus mediterraneus*... The silver roughy is a moderately sized deep water species... This species is silver in colour with a rosy-pink tinge on the back and black-edged pink fins. **1986** PAUL *NZ Fishes* 71 *Slender roughy. Optivus elongatus*. Also called long or violet roughy. Well described by its names but more quickly distinguished by the vent near the anal fin. **1989** PAULIN *NZ Fish* 152 *Hoplostethus mediterraneus* silver roughy, sawbelly.

2. As orange roughy (also occas. *ellipt.* **roughy**). **a.** *Hoplostethus atlanticus* (fam. Trach-ichthyidae), a popular, orange-coloured, fine-fleshed mid-water fish of great commercial importance.

1979 *Catch* Feb. 12 Orange Roughy *Hoplostethus atlanticus*... Deep body, massive head with conspicuous bony ridges and cavities... No NZ catch, a probable foreign by-catch on some deep grounds. **1981** *NZ Times* 17 Nov. 22 Trawling at 1000 metres in the rough waters off the Chatham Rise three years ago the Wesermunde began hauling in loads of a strange orange fish... It had beautifully white, desirable flesh, thick fillets with no small bones, it cooked well..and it was sizeable (cheap to process)... Now known as orange roughy. **1983** *National Bus. Rev.* 1 Aug. 33 Orange roughy: kiwifruit of the sea, the fish which is a blueprint for the export market, with its firm-textured, white, odourless fillets... The Japanese research ship, Shinkai Maru in 1975 made the first significant catches of orange roughy on the northern Chatham Rise. **1986** PAUL *NZ Fishes* 70 *Orange roughy. Hoplostethus atlanticus*... Widespread in deep water of most temperate oceans, from the North Atlantic to South Africa and Australasia. **1991** *Evening Post* (Wellington) 21 Oct. 15 The orange roughy fish roe is the product of three years' work by a small family fishery in Cuba Street.

b. *transf.* As the name of an orange-coloured machine, or one which is in a 'rough' condition; as a nickname for a person with flaming orange hair.

1991 *Dominion* (Wellington) 20 Feb. 10 The 'Orange Roughy' Iroquois helicopter returns to New Zealand next week after..supporting New Zealand..scientific programmes in Antarctica. The helicopter, named for its vivid orange colour, took passengers and cargo to remote field scientific parties. **1991** *Metro* (Auckland) Aug. 111 We had to get rid of the orange roughy. The old Austin needed work on its engine, in addition to the extensive panel damage. **1992** *Dominion* (Wellington) 23 Oct. 22 With her agent-orange hair and colourful costumes she [*sc.* Belinda Todd] blazes a trail on TV3's late-night show...We grew up with pleasant news presenters..and then along came the Orange Roughy.

roundabout. *Hist.* A simple all-enveloping long garment once provided (esp. by early missionaries) as respectable European clothing for Maori women.
  1856 LUSH *Auckland Jrnls.* 17 Jan. (1971) 176 In two minutes the whole lot [of the bathing Maori schoolgirls] stood quietly looking at us, clothed from top to toe in their long full roundabouts. *Ibid.* 177 In came a file of five young Maori women, the head scholars in their blue striped roundabouts. **1861** PAUL *NZ as It Was & Is* 17 [The Maori women's] usual dress is..a shapeless sack of printed calico, called a 'roundabout', tied round the neck but loose at the waist. **1874** BAINES *Edward Crewe* 118 I also gave [the Maori girl] eight yards of Navy blue print (which every one knows is enough for a 'roundabout'). **1890** PHILIPS *Reminisc. Early Days* 7 The hostess [at Waiwera 1850] did not dress for dinner..her usual attire being a Maori roundabout. **1922** COWAN *NZ Wars* (1955) I. 8 Ngapuhi girls..well plumped-out of figure, swing up and down the roadway flaunting the print gowns and the brightly-coloured 'roundabouts'..bought with the dollars of the sailormen. **1940** COWAN *Sir Donald Maclean* 33 The payment..consisted of..100 figs of tobacco, four greenstone pendants,... two 'roundabouts' (loose brightly coloured blouses for the ladies), and one axe.

roundie. *Prison.* Also **roundy.** [f. the cylindrical shape of a factory-made cigarette compared with that of a roll-your-own.] A factory-made cigarette.
  1948 Used in the NZ Navy p.c. Les Cleveland (1968). **1982** NEWBOLD *Big Huey* 253 Roundie (n) Factory-made cigarette. **1984** *Roundie*: prison slang for a tailor-made cigarette; p.c. Ray Hancox (Marlborough): also *round*. **1991** roundy [see BOOB 1].

round the world for ninepence. Methylated spirits (as a drink), referring to its ability to take the addict into dream trips.
  1984 *NZ Times* 10 June 10 Round the World for Ninepence, Jessie's Dream, Fix Bayonets, devotees called methylated spirits, recommending orange juice as a dilutant. Diluted or neat, it can, and does, cause blindness. **1988** McGILL *Dict. Kiwi Slang* 94 *round the world for threepence/fourpence/ninepence* drinking methylated spirits.

roupo, var. RAUPO.

rourou, var. RAURAU.

rousabout, var. ROUSEABOUT.

rouse /ræus/, /ræuz/, /ræust/, *v.* Also **rouse (at, on, onto)** [AND 1896]; **roust (rowst) on** [AND 1904]. [f. Sc. dial. *roust* roar, bellow: see EDD *roust v.*²] *intr.* To become very angry, to make a fuss; *quasi-trans.* (usu. with **on**) to scold, berate; to turn on (a person).
  1904 *NZ Observer* 13 Feb. 2 He 'rousted', as the saying goes, on the man who sacked him. **1906** *Truth* 27 Jan. 8 She told her..husband she'd 'rowst' on him. Her idea of 'rowsting', as she called it, was to send for a peeler. **1906** *Truth* 20 Oct. 1 About time the Manawatu Railway Company started running Sunday trains. The religion relating rummies will rouse a bit, but that's only a detail. **1911** *Truth* 15 Apr. 1 For in the Australasian vernacular the person who 'rousts' or 'rouses' goes temporarily mad and yells, and is an irresponsible person while he is 'rousting' or 'rousing', and the condition so nearly approaches the mild insanity of the wowser in his neurotic outbursts of oratory that Churchill must be congratulated upon stumbling upon a great truth. **1940** SARGESON *Man and His Wife* 27 Then Mrs Bowman roused on to me for putting too much sugar in her tea. **1964** PEARSON *Glossary* to Sargeson *Collected Stories 1935–63* (1964) 303 roused him up hill and down dale: dressed him down thoroughly; *roused on to me*, scolded me. **1966** NEWTON *Boss's Story* 104 His aversion to children nearly got Madge down... He was always inclined to rouse onto our kiddies.

rouseabout. Also occas. **rousabout.** [Spec use of Brit. dial. *rouseabout* a rough, bustling person: see OED 2; EDD.] Cf. ROUSIE, ROUSTABOUT.
1. *Farming.* [AND 1881.] **a.** A general hand in a shearing-shed.
  1861 HARPER *Lett. from NZ* 20 July (1914) 54 Shearing..is in full swing, so there are a number of extra men, besides the shepherds of the station, shearers, fleece-pickers, wool sorters, and 'rouse-abouts'. **1888** DUNCAN *Wakatipians* 57 They stayed with us for a week or so, until the main body of shearers and rouseabouts arrived. **1902** LANCASTER in *Happy Endings* (1987) 106 And the mantle of the rouseabout, and one who must obey fell on Crandeck's shoulders and chafed him. **1913** CARR *Country Work* 14 The boss Maori undertakes to supply all the rouseabouts (as shed hands are termed). **1933** *Press* (Christchurch) (Acland Gloss.) 18 Nov. 15 *Rouseabout*.—(1) General station hand, employed at fencing, bush-work, etc. (2) Shed hand as opposed to a shearer. **1953** STRONACH *Musterer on Molesworth* 31 It was a common expression among the 'flash' shearers of years ago, when wanting tar for a cut sheep, to say, 'Tar, boy, and step back. I hate the smell of a rouseabout.' **1964** MIDDLETON *Walk on Beach* 165 I..answered an advertisement for a rouse-about in the Walford Bugle. **1973** FERNANDEZ *Tussock Fever* 54 The rouseabout was a half-witted teenager... The men called him Harpic—clean around the bend. **1981** CHARLES *Black Billy Tea* 28 At the very bottom [of the shearing shed scale] are the rouseabouts—the boys and old men who sweep the floors, fill the individual shearers' 'catching' pens.

b. A general farm-hand, usu. employed on unskilled or menial work.
  1887 INGLIS *Our NZ Cousins* 163 The whare with its idle group of Crimean-shirted..stockmen..bullock-punchers, horse-breakers, fencers and general rouseabouts..came back to us. **1895** GRACE *Maoriland Stories* 132 This new man was made 'rouse-about' at a fixed though modest salary. **1909** [see FOSSICKER 1]. **1913** BEATTIE *Trade Hunting* 10 I was cook, housemaid, cowboy—for I had a cow and 'lashings of milk'— rouseabout, ploughman. **1921** *Quick March* 10 Feb. 36 In the succeeding two years the..boundary-rider, stockman, boiling-down works labourer, shearer, rouseabout..examined a mining boom. **1945** *NZ Geogr.* Apr. 39 A 'rouseabout' is a 'handy man' who does the menial odd-jobs around the homestead; 'hired man' is probably the American equivalent. **1950** CHERRIL *NZ Sheep Farm* 73 'You..you *rouseabout.*' [she said to the Maori stationhand.] 'You calling *me* a rouseabout?' he shouted, with blazing eyes.

2. [AND 1906.] A general handyman, or odd-job worker, employed usually on menial work. Also *fig.*
  1904 *NZ Observer* 25 June 7 Hotel-keepers complain that they are unable to get the aristocrats of labour to work for them when they advertise 'Wanted, a rouseabout.' **1925** BATHGATE *Random Recolls.* 36 One not infrequently came across remittance men, generally on the goldfields, at some public house, employed as groom and general rouseabout, or perhaps cook. **1934** MULGAN *Spur of Morning* 211 I'm going to put you in the Ministry... You won't have any departments, but you'll be general rouseabout; and I'll give you the first vacancy. **1961** MACKAY *Puborama* 28 In some manner or other Tim, the [pub] rouseabout, displeased Mrs Ted. **1971** BAXTER *Collected Poems* (1980) 531 Not a single house in Wellington Empty and usable for the boobhead and the rouseabout. **1987** HARTLEY *Swagger on Doorstep* 114 Bushwhackers, sugar-bag men, tramps, swaggers, rouseabouts—all these expressions became familiar as I grew older.

3. *attrib.* Of work or workers, of the nature or quality associated with rouseabouts.
  1925 BATHGATE *Random Recolls.* 33 The waiter was a rouseabout sort of fellow, wearing a flannel shirt without coat or waistcoat. **1934** LILICO *Sheep Dog Memoirs* 27 [The dogs] would head, lead, hunt away, force and back, though, of course, they were best at rouseabout work.

Hence **rouse about** *v. intr.* [AND 1897], to do general labouring work; **rouseabouting** *vbl. n.*, working as a rouseabout, esp. in a shearing-shed.
  1983 *Dominion* (Wellington) 27 Sept. 11 Her involvement with netball was encouraged by her mother. 'I used to go along to practices and if Mum needed someone to **rouse about** on the court she'd yell out to me.' **1988** *More* (Auckland) Mar. 29 [Caption] Above: **Rouseabouting** can be an international job. Here Margaret Way (in red) and friend Robin are pictured atop a wool pile in an English woolshed.

rousey, var. ROUSIE.

rousie /ræusi/, /ræuzi/.
1. Also **rousey, rousy.** [f. ROUSE(ABOUT *n.* + -IE: AND *rousie*, 1906.] ROUSEABOUT 1.
  c**1900–10** GOLDSTONE in Woodhouse *Farm & Station Verse* (1950) 49 They entertained the 'rouseys' with a lot of fairy tales. **1952** MEEK *Station Days* 11 And the rouseys in their shirt-sleeves passed the pannikins around. **1955** BOWEN *Wool Away* 157 Rousie. This is the poor old rouseabout who has a great variety of jobs. **1964** MIDDLETON *Walk on Beach* 166 Don't tell me you're one of the rousies, Sonny? **1978** JARDINE *Shadows on Hill* 132 Then he slips off his coat and hands it to a rousy and nods to the classer. **1984** BEATON *Outside In* 106 Ginny: Nah. Only time I stopped was when I worked the sheds... I was a fucken good rousy. **1988** *More* (Auckland) Mar. 33 A rousie, or wool winder as they're called in England, would at least pay for half a return ticket from New Zealand in the two-month season there.

Hence **rousie** *v. intr.*, to work as a woolshed hand.
  1981 *Dominion* (Wellington) 23 Apr. 6 [Caption] A change from school work: Christine McIntyre, a fifth former at Wanganui Girls College and daughter of Apiti farmer Rusty McIntyre, rousies during the [shearing] competition.

2. Special Comb. *joc.* **rousie's chewing gum,** sheep-dags.
  1989 *NZ Eng. Newsletter* III. 27 *rousie's chewing gum*: Dags.

roust: see ROUSE *v.*

roustabout. [Orig. US.]
1. Occas. in short familiar form **roustie.** ROUSEABOUT 1 and 2.

roustie: see ROUSTABOUT 1.

rousy, var. ROUSIE.

rowdy hat. *Obs.* A slouch hat made of felt.
  1863 BUTLER *First Year* iii 29 Hither come more of the shaggy clear-complexioned men with the rowdy hats; looked at them with awe and befitting respect. **1948** HAAST *Julius Von Haast* 44 It was practically all over when [c1860s] the opposing witnesses..[found] their old friend in the 'rowdy' hat now attired in the wig and gown of the cross-examining counsel. **1959** SINCLAIR *Hist. NZ* 101 The working settler commonly dressed in a blue woollen shirt or blouse, moleskin or cord trousers, boots, and the slouch felt hats known as 'rowdy' (that is, backwoodsmen's) hats. Butler called them 'exceedingly rowdy hats'.
  Hence **rowdy-hatted**, wearing a rowdy-hat.
  1863 BUTLER *First Year* iii 28 The healthy clear-complexioned men shaggy-bearded, rowdy-hatted, and independent, pictures of rude health and strength.

rowi. [Ma. /ˈrowi/: Williams 349 *Rowi*..*Apteryx australis*, South Island kiwi;... = *tokoeka*.] brown kiwi (KIWI 2 (1) *Apteryx australis*).
  1885 *NZJSc.* II. 505 *Apteryx australis*... Rowi, Big Kiwi. **1904** HUTTON & DRUMMOND *Animals NZ* 328 The Southern Kiwi.—*Rowi*... which was the first species made known to science, is called Rowi by the Maoris, and Big Kiwi by the miners. **1955** OLIVER *NZ Birds* 51 *South Island Kiwi. Tokoeka. Rowi*... The call of the female is somewhat like 'ro-ar ro-ar' with both syllables accented. **1985** *Reader's Digest Book NZ Birds* 39 Brown Kiwi *Apteryx australis*... Rowi, totoeka.

rowst, var. ROUSE *v*.

royal. *Obs.*
1. Also **boss's royal**. A derogatory name for a watersider favoured by the employer in competition for jobs under the auction block system of allocating work; a boss's stooge.
  1888 CHUDLEIGH *Diary* 25 June (1950) 362 Only the roustabouts count among all hands. Not the ploughmen. **1906** ELKINGTON *Adrift in NZ* 145 When a man first goes on a station and is not an old hand he is engaged as a 'roustabout', which means he is given jobs which do not require much experience and in which he works under other men. **1925** MANDER *Allen Adair* (1971) 4 I didn't send you to Oxford to become a roustabout. **1934** LEE *Children of the Poor* (1949) 26 Rabbiters..ploughmen, roustabouts, leaving their jobs..were frequently headed off by the hotels. **1949** BIERNACKI *Poems, Verses & Rhymes* 6 One of the roustabouts [on the station] kicked him. **1963** FRAME *The Reservoir* 162 Alan found it hard to decide..finding a job as a wharfie, farm roustabout, shearing hand. **1969** HENDERSON *Open Country Calling* 258 The rousties flew up and down the board while the table hands tore at the neck and skirtings the moment the fleece was thrown. **1983** *Dominion* (Wellington) 20 Dec. 5 The work of roustabouts was covered by the New Zealand Oil Exploration Award and their membership should be that of the New Zealand Labourers Union. **1990** EDWARDS *AWOL* 3 Daisy was a roustabout. She did most of the chores of preparing meals and keeping the place clean.

2. Special Comb. **roustabout steward** (also heard as **patrol steward**) *shipping*, one on a shift with no fixed work location who can be called to wherever needed.
  1989 11 Sept. Public address system of interisland ferry 'Arahura'. Would the roustabout steward please call at the shop. (Ed.)

1938 *NZ Observer* 24 Nov. 7 Invariably the 'royals' receive preference. These watersiders are well known to the stevedores. **c1963** p.c. J. Winchester (Wellington). *boss's royal* is a waterfront term for a boss's stooge or pet.

2. A rejected name for the unit of decimal currency.
  1974 MULDOON *Rise & Fall of a Young Turk* 76 We [on the Decimal Currency Board] had had trouble with the name of the major unit... Other names [than dollar] flooded in: zealer, crown, royal, zeal, tui, fern, doubloon.

royal albatross, spoonbill: see ALBATROSS, SPOONBILL 2.

royaller. An outstanding event or coup.
  1963 *Truth* 21 May 19 On the first Saturday I was out, I decided to make it a royaller. To make it a royaller..to have a really good time. **1987** WILLIAMS *Racing for Gold* 174 Joe Devcich almost brought off a 'royaller' in the last when Peranui ran third.

RSA /ˌaresˈæɪ/. Also **R.S.A.** [Acronym of the (*New Zealand*) *Returned Services*' (formerly *Soldiers*') *Association*.]
1. a. An association founded at a meeting held in April 1916 and incorporated as the *New Zealand Returned Soldiers' Association* on 31 January 1917, having as its members service personnel most of whom have served (orig. overseas) on active duty. Often *attrib*. See also RETURNED *a*.
  1918 *Kia-ora Coo-ee* (1981) 15 Apr. 8 The Dunedin R.S.A. at once urged the Government to award the [Gallipoli Star] to all who served on Gallipoli. **1920** *Otago Witness* (Dunedin) 7 Dec. 23 There was an impression abroad that the R.S.A. was opposed to the scheme. **1936** HYDE *Passport to Hell* 16 In New Zealand..many of the best..are too shabby..to attend R.S.A. ceremonials. **1953** HAMILTON *Till Human Voices Wake Us* 197 Venomous statements that were made about C.O.s on the part of the so-called responsible members of R.S.A. executives. **1988** *Dominion* (Wellington) 1 July 10 It is no surprise that a conservative organisation such as the RSA has taken exception to the use of the phonetically pleasant 'Aotearoa'. **1993** *Metro* (Auckland) Feb. 113 I parked..where the RSA used to gather on Anzac Day, their lapels ablaze with paper poppies.
b. An R.S.A. club, its building or headquarters.
  1982 MARSHALL *Master Big Jingles* 73 Mr Meechin was preparing to march back to the R.S.A... Mr Meechin didn't stay long at the R.S.A. and I drove him home. **1988** *More* (Auckland) Mar. 29 He'll be the bloke with the hat in the parking lot behind the RSA with the others at 6.30 tomorrow morning. **1992** *Metro* (Auckland) Feb. 8 And now the RSAs are emptying.
2. Special Comb. **RSA badge**, the identifying badge of the Association worn on the right lapel.
  1948 in Pearson *Six Stories* (1991) 4 He fingered his RSA badge. **1953** HAMILTON *Till Human Voices Wake Us* 197 I'm not asking you to spit in the eye of every individual you see..merging from an insurance office wearing an R.S.A. badge. **1977** HALL *Glide-Time* 10 Boss. Short, fussy, worried..Wears RSA badge and very conservative. **1980** BENNETT *Canterbury Tale* 106 So I put up an R.S.A. badge but soon took it down. **1990** *Evening Post* (Wellington) 30 Apr. 6 I once toyed with the idea of crossing the Tasman to live. I looked at Pop's RSA badge and thought 'Nay not so!'.
3. *fig*. A censorious conservative authority.
  1984 *Listener* 22 Dec. 8 Who is writing this poem? who is reading it? academics the RSA of language.

rua, var. ROA.

rua, *n*.[1]
1. Also early **dúa**. [Ma. /ˈrua/: Williams 349 *Rua* (ii)..1. Pit, hole... 2. Store for provisions.] A storage pit for root vegetables, *spec*. kumara and potatoes. See also *kumara pit* (KUMARA 2).
  [**1820** LEE & KENDALL *NZ Gram. & Vocab.* 151 Dúa, *s*. A house, vessel, &c. to contain stores.] **1831** WILLIAMS *Early Jrnls.* 11 June (1961) 181 In the afternoon shifted our quarters on account of the rain to a *Rua* where we were very comfortable by the aid of a good fire. **1863** MANING *Old NZ* xi 171 The *kumera* were dug..then all hands set to work..to..carry off the crop to the storehouse or *rua*. **1898** MORRIS *Austral-English* 396 *Rua*. Maori word (used in North Island) for a pit, cave or hole. A place for storing roots, such as potatoes, etc. Formerly some of these *rua* had carved entrances. **1903** *TrNZI* XXXV. 21 The object was very simply attained in the dry porous soil by the *rua*. This was a circular pit sunk in the ground 5 ft. or 6 ft. deep and about the same in diameter, narrowing in at the top and closed by a trap-door made of a wooden slab. **1930** *Na To Hoa Aroha* (1987) II. 64 In the 'ngahuru' he would turn up with a horse to haul the 'kumara' to the rua. **1952** LYON *Faring South* 158 Their chief quest was a pot hole which might be described as much like a Maori *rua* or potato pit. **1970** JENKIN *NZ Mysteries* 56 At the south end of the beach he found several *rua* (kumara pits) half washed away by the sea. **1982** BURTON *Two Hundred Yrs. NZ Food* 3 Apart from kumara, which usually had to be kept in the *rua* or storage pit, the pataka was used to store all the food.
2. In contexts of the New Zealand Wars, a Maori rifle-pit; also an anti-artillery bunker.
  1922 COWAN *NZ Wars* (1955) I. 52 These subterranean chambers [for protection from shell attack, etc.] (*ruas*, or pits, the Maoris called them) were usually 6 feet deep. **1986** BELICH *NZ Wars* 52 Kawiti had independently invented the anti-artillery bunker. These pits, or *rua* as they were called by the Maoris, were underground compartments roofed with beams of timber.

rua, *n*.[2] [f. Ma. *rua* /ˈrua/ the number 'two' (Williams 349): experimental potato varieties were orig. distinguished by assigning numbers from the Maori numbering system.] A main-crop domestic potato variety.
  1960 *AJHR* H-34 37 'Rua' is a selection from the cross Katahdin by Harford... Rua may be a safer variety to grow where there is a risk of soils being wet in the autumn. **1980** BRANDENBURG *Outdoor Vegetable Growing* 111 Rua. This is a maincrop variety still gaining ground in Canterbury... Rua produces a large, coarse-leafed plant keeping up top growth well into the autumn. **1985** BENTLEY & FRASER *A Grand Limerick Tour* [No.] 5 A chap growing spuds near Opua Sent a ton to a lady, to woo'er, Of ancient King Edwards, But what got her bedwards Were newer, and fewer, and Rua. **1994** *Dominion* (Wellington) 24 June 13 You wanna try ruas. They'll grow for anyone—almost.

ruatara. *Obs.* Also **dueterra**. [Ma. /ˈruatara/: Williams 350 *Ruatara*... = *tuatara*.] TUATARA 1.
  1833 WILLIAMS *Early Jrnls.* (1961) 26 Mar. 301 We pulled to Karewa, a small island 8 miles from Tauranga... Upon the island are *Ruataras*, a species of the lizard about a foot in length, which are regarded by the natives as *Atua*. **1834** MARKHAM *NZ* (1963) 30 The only Animal a native of the Island is a Lizard (Dueterra). **1840** POLACK *Manners and Customs* I. 264 Should the patient recover, the doctor takes credit to himself that he has ejected his godship, and will not hesitate to assert that he discovered the rascal leaving the mouth, nostrils, or ears, of the sick man in the shape of a lizard, (*ruatára*) or some such animal. **1875** *TrNZI* VII. 296

Unu ngarara or ngarara burrows were frequently met with on the plains..the ngarara was darker in colour than the ruatara.

rub: see RUB-A-DUB 1.

rub-a-dub.

1. Also in a shortened form **rub.** [AND 1941.] Rhyming slang for 'pub'. Cf. RUBBITY-DUB.
 1906 *Truth* 23 June 3 The genial Sandy Serves out the shandy And keeps up the 'rep' of the 'rub'. **c1926** The Mixer *Transport Workers' Song Book* 81 I gazed upon the motley crowd Within this 'rub-a-dub'. **1965** WEBBER *Try Again Friday* 107 There will be streets, shops, houses, parking meters, schools, hospitals, TABs,.. bowser stations,... pubs, clubs, and rubadub-dubs. **1981** *Auckland Savings Bank* (Queen Street) (Goldie Brown Collect.) *Rub-a-dub*: hotel, pub.

2. An elaboration of *rub*, a massage.
 1979 WILLIAMS *Skin Deep* 18 What's the matter with you bums, anyway? My rub-down not classy enough for you anymore?.. What about you, Les? You'd be in for a bit of the ah..[*sic*] other, the high-class rubadub, wouldn't you?

rubberty dub, rubbidy(-dub), varr. RUBBITY(-DUB).

rubbish, *v.* [See OED *rubbish n.* 1, 1953 'Orig. and chiefly *Austral.* and *N.Z.*'] *trans.* To criticize (someone, something) severely.
 1968 *Comment* 33 June 2 The paper..was recently rubbished in the Catholic *Tablet*. **1988** McGILL *Dict. Kiwi Slang* 94 *rubbish* to dismiss, criticise harshly or tease; eg 'I wouldn't rubbish him just yet, he could still come good.' **1993** *Sunday Star* (Auckland) 1 Aug. A2 Whenever he brought up the micro chip we would just rubbish him. As a result I think he lost his trust in us.

rubbity /ˈrʌbəti/. Also **rubby, rubberdy, rubbidy.** [AND 1898.] Abbrev. of RUBBITY-DUB.
 1963 *Truth* 21 May 19 I hop off at the rubbidy, borrow a couple of Plymouth Sounds and get on the pig's ear. rubbidy (dub)... pub. **1978** HILLIARD *Glory & Dream* 166 'Anybody seen Charlie?' 'In the rubbity this arfto. He's probably flakers.' **1988** McGILL *Dict. Kiwi Slang* 94 *rubbidy* pub, rhyming slang 'rub-a-dub/pub'; aka *rubbity, rubbidy-dub, rubberdy* and *rubby.*

rubbity-dub /ˌrʌbətiˈdʌb/. Also with much variety of form as **rub(b)erty dub, rubbidy dub, rubblededub, rub-de-dub.** [AND 1898.] Rhyming slang for 'pub'.
 1950 *Truth* 23 May 15 I thought you might like to take me and the publisher over to the rubbity-dub for a sarsaparilla snifter. **1959** SLATTER *Gun in My Hand* 165 'Give us a bloody beer.'... 'Turn it up, Tom. This isn't the rubbleededub. This is the pie-cart.' **1962** HORI *Half-gallon Jar* 85 So on a Saturday I went down to the local rubberty dub to have a few with the boys. **1982** NEWBOLD *Big Huey* 253 Rub-de-dub (n) Pub. **1988** rubbidy dub [see RUBBITY].

rubblededub, var. RUBBITY-DUB.

rubble, *v. Obs. intr.* To scour gumland soils for small pieces of kauri-gum. Also as *vbl. n.*
 1926 *NZ Observer* 20 Feb. 2 An expert has estimated that the industry [*sc.* gum-digging] will keep 3000 men employed for the next hundred years if rubbling is resorted to to gather in the chips, dust and small nuts.

rub-de-dub, var. RUBBITY-DUB.

rube, *n.* and *attrib. Obs.* Also **ruby.** Abbrev. of RUBYDAZZLER.
 1941 BAKER *NZ Slang* 51 In constant use by our youngsters..rubydazzler..rube, grouce [etc.]. **1953** 14 M A16 Thames DHS 8 Ruby. **1988** [see RUBYDAZZLER].

rub noses: see NOSE *n.*¹ e.

ruby: see RUBYFISH.

rubydazzler. [An alteration of orig. Brit. dial. *bobby-dazzler.*] Anything excellent or superior of its kind. Also used *attrib*. See also RUBE.
 1941 BAKER *NZ Slang* 51 In constant use by our youngsters..bobbydazzler, rubydazzler. **1955** BJ *Cameron Collection* (TS July) rubydazzler (n) Something marvellous, superlative. (Mainly children's slang.) **1963** CASEY *As Short a Spring* 275 The old man took a ruby-dazzler on the nose and went reeling back. **1988** McGill *Dict. Kiwi Slang* 94 *rubydazzler* excellent person or thing, a rube for short; variant of Brit. 'bobbydazzler'; eg 'All those scones, for how many of you ratbags! That Noeline's a rubydazzler, and I hope you appreciate it.'

rubyfish. Also *ellipt.* **ruby.** [From its red coloration.] *Plagiogeneion rubiginosus* (fam. Emmelichthyidae, the 'bonnetmouths' having extensible bonnet-like jaws), a dark pink or red fish with small yellow spots along the scale rows, and having a strongly forked tail.
 1982 AYLING *Collins Guide* (1984) 223 *Ruby Fish Plagiogeneion rubiginosus* size 25–35cm... The rubyfish is a moderately elongate midwater fish... Body colour of this species is a uniform dark red, with a small yellow spot on each scale sometimes giving the fish an orange tinge, and red–pink fins. **1994** *Evening Post* (Wellington) 21 June 17 One of these [little known food fish] is the ruby fish... A handsome fish, rather like a red snapper in appearance, the ruby varies in size from 25 to 35cm. As its name implies, it is red in colour... The only reason we see so little of the ruby..is that fishermen consider them too difficult to sell.

rudderfish. *Centrolophus niger* (fam. Centrolophidae), a moderately large (80–100 cm) deepwater fish.
 1956 GRAHAM *Treasury NZ Fishes* 405 Rudderfish *Centrolophus maoricus* Ogilby. **1982** AYLING *Collins Guide* (1984) 302 The rudderfish is an elongate species with a rounded snout. **1986** PAUL *NZ Fishes* 139 *Rudderfish. Centrolophus niger* Widespread in temperate seas..., in some areas known as blackfish... Regularly taken, though in small numbers, by offshore trawlers working in 300–700m.

rue: see PINE 2 (2).

rum-a-rum, rummy-rum, varr. RAMARAMA.

rumble. [See OED *n.* 2 b 'Chiefly *U.S.*'.] A (gang) fight.
 1958 in *In Their Own Words* (1988) 81 A bodgie is a type to carry a knife..and go round in gangs and get into fights and rumbles. **1976** *Evening Post* (Wellington) 29 June 14 Words and sayings sent in by 'Tuesdate' readers—things their parents said when they were at school: *rumble* fight. **1984** 16–17 F E4 Pakuranga Coll. 30B Rumble [fight] [F7 M9]. **1993** YSKA *All Shook Up* 145 On successive weekends late in 1955, major fights [between Army conscripts and bodgies], known as 'rumbles', became a regular occurrence.
 Hence **rumble** *v. trans.* and *intr.*, esp. of gangs, to fight (another gang); to raid, to attack. Also *transf.*, to be given a 'hard time'. to be 'done over'.
 1979 20 Aug. TV1 *Dateline Monday*. Rumbling another gang is called 'spooking'. **1979** *Press* (Christchurch) 21 Aug. 19 We were not formed to be rumbling (fighting) all the time. **1982** NEWBOLD *Big Huey* 213 If they touch you, we'll rumble them. **1994** *Contact* (Wellington) 14 July 3 He'd [*sc.* author, Karl Stead] been 'rumbled vigorously' by Kim Hill [a radio host and interviewer], put through the mill by a previous interviewer and was ready to pack his bags for Christchurch and more interviews.

rumpty.

1. Also occas. **rumty,** and elaborated as **rumptydooler.** [Poss. from an alteration of Brit. dial. *rumty-tummer*: see EDD *Rumty-tummer* Oxf. a surprisingly large potato; a fine large fruit, etc. EDD Sup. *Warw*: 'This is a rumty-tummer, this is', would be used of unusually large vegetables or fruits, or by schoolboys of a favourite top, taw, or cobbler etc.; poss. related to obs. Brit. slang *rumtitum* fine.] Anything fine or superior of its class. Also *attrib*.
 1941 BAKER *NZ Slang* 51 In constant use by our youngsters..rorter, rumpty, rumptydooler. **1945** *NZEF Times* 29 Jan. 2 What a rumpty. *Ibid.* 5 Feb. 45 It's a rumpty. **1959** SLATTER *Gun in My Hand* 200 I've seen some rumpty parties in kitchens. Real humdingers. **1988** McGILL *Dict. Kiwi Slang* 94 *rumty* excellent person or thing.

2. In *attrib.* use. **a.** Used of something unlovely, in a bad state of repair; disreputable.
 1950 p.c. Ken Griffiths (Auckland). *Rumpty*. Used in derogatory senses 'rank' or 'unlovely'; occas. 'violent'. **1958** p.c. Breward (Whakatane) 25 Jan. The other day I came across an expression at work which was a new one to me—'rumpty'. It was used by two different people. One used it of a car which was almost in the last stages of disrepair. The other used it of the sawmill in its early stages when it was badly designed and rather 'Heath Robinsonish'. **1985** *National Radio* (Correspondence School) 4 Nov. [A story in NZ speech includes:] Baching in a rumpty old shack. **1995** *Dominion* (Wellington) 20 Sept. 36 Turner [NZ cricket coach] was not unduly concerned about the size of the [NZ] defeat. 'It was a pretty rumpty wicket, we didn't take good advantage of it and they did.'

b. [Poss. an alteration of *rumpus* uproar.] A fuss, an uproar.
 1974 MORRIESON *Predicament* (1981) 21 [Written by schoolboy on flyleaf of his North and Hillard's Latin Grammar] Stay for me, I shall not fail To meet you in that hollow vale, But what a rumpty there will be If thou shouldst bring this book with thee!

rumptydooler, rumty: see RUMPTY 1.

run, *n.*¹ [AND *run*², 'Prob. Br. dial. in origin, superseding *walk* both in the sense of an enclosure for poultry, etc. [cf. *fowl-run*] and a tract of land used for pasture.' 1804; see OED *n.*¹ 2 b and 22; 11 a and 12, a stretch of pasture, the right of pasturing. Acland's summary of the possible senses is helpful (1933 *Press* (Christchurch) (Acland Gloss.) 18 Nov. 15): 'Run... (1) The country held under a particular lease or pastoral license... (2) Group of r[un]s held by one owner, or in one station. The whole area is spoken of as a r[un]... (3) Leasehold as opposed to freehold. (Sheep returns, 1878) (4) Open as opposed to fenced country. 'Out on the r[un]'; i.e., not in any of the paddocks... [e.g. *run sheep*] (6) As equivalent to *station*: e.g. 'He has sold his *r[un]*'; 'One of the best *r[un]s* in Canterbury.' In this sense *r[un]* did not always include the sheep, as the word *s[tation]* does. This usage is now uncommon and *r[un]* in these contexts would probably mean *small grazing r[un]*... (7) A block of country, a division of a *r[un]*. E.g. *ewe r[un] upper r[un]*. This sense was always rare, but is still in use on some *s[tation]s*.']

1. [AND 1820.] *Obs.* Pasturage.
   1831 Chapman *Jrnl. & Lett.* (ATLTS) I. 50 Thirty acres of average available land may be found with many miles of run for the cattle.

2. [AND 1804.] A tract of open grazing land held orig. under pastoral lease or licence from the Crown or provincial authority. Compare Brit. *sheepwalk*, North Amer. *range*. Also *attrib*. See also *cattle run* (CATTLE 2), *dairy-run* (DAIRY 4), *pastoral run* (PASTORAL 3), *sheep run* (SHEEP 2).
   1834 [see *cattle run* (CATTLE 2]. **1848** Wakefield *Handbook NZ* 169 The custom has been, like that of New South Wales, to let the cattle..rove at large over a tract of country, generally called a run. **1851** Weld *Hints to Intending Sheep-farmers* 6 The first care of the intending sheep-farmer will naturally be to select a 'run' or sheep-walk. **1859** Fuller *Five Years' Residence* 147 The dwelling-house is generally termed the 'Station'; while the land, the pasture of which is rented from the Government, is termed the 'Run'. **1863** *Richmond-Atkinson Papers* 3 July (1960) II. 54 When two or three adjoining runs are in one man's holding he must have as many flocks and establishments as runs to fulfil the exact letter of the regulations, which require stock to be on every run during the whole term of the license. **c1875** Meredith *Adventuring in Maoriland* (1935) 41 I go out on the run, bring in the first mob of sheep I come across, and select one that is not too fat. **1898** Hocken *Contributions* 139 Under the original terms, land purchasers were entitled upon payment of an annual license fee of 10s. 6d. to depasture or *run* sheep and cattle upon such waste lands within the block as remained unappropriated... Though Captain Cargill was then gazetted Commissioner of Crown Lands for the Otago block only, he received no definite instructions upon the subject of granting the runs. **1934** Mulgan *Spur of Morning* 261 Mark felt a real sympathy for some of the men and women out back in the high country—where runs ran right up to the glaciers. **1948** Scotter *Run Estate & Farm* 65 The run was then taken up by Mrs. Margaret Preston..of Longlands Station. **1974** *NZ Agric.* 57 The stock on these high-country farms may graze in altitudes as high as about 1500 to 1800 metres, though most of the 'runs' utilise areas up to about 900 m only. **1981** Anderson *Both Sides of River* 8 The areas shown as 'high country' runs or stations vary in size from 2,000 to 40,000 hectares and are used for grazing sheep... There were no fences on these early high country runs.

3. [AND 2, 1810.] STATION *n.* 3 a.
   1858 Acland *Notes Sheepfarming NZ* 7 It will be as well to mention the way in which a sheep-farmer settles himself on his sheep-walk, or 'run', as it is called. **1865** Chudleigh *Diary* 21 June (1950) 191 [Friends] have been abusing me for not coming to stay with them ever since they started the [Castle Hill] run. **1892** Swanton *Notes on NZ* 93 We now leave the smaller class of sheep farm and come to the large 'runs' or 'stations', as they are called. **1902** *Settler's Handbook NZ* 30 155,500 acres of similar land, the temporary licenses of which expired in 1901; and 22,918 acres of pastoral land passed in at the last run-sale. **1947** Beattie *Early Runholding* 26 Next day the two run-seekers [in Otago Central in 1859] met her husband coming with the cattle. *Ibid.* 115 It is usually understood that in the early days, the word 'station' denoted the owner's house and its immediate buildings, while 'run' meant the whole property. **1965** McLaglan *Stethoscope & Saddlebags* 184 A distant connection of mine had a run in a lonely place touching the upper reaches of the Wanganui River. **1982** *Agric. Gloss.* (MAF) 5 *Run*: an extensive grazing property usually in South Island tussock country.

4. a. Special Comb. alluding to stock pastured on open country and likely to be wild as distinct from those pastured in an enclosed paddock, as **run bull**, **run cattle**, **run cow**, **run sheep**; also in the phr. **to kick like a run cow**, to kick violently as one not trained to the bail or legrope (see quot. 1963[2]).
   1889 Chudleigh *Diary* 15 Nov. (1950) 368 I think sheep and wool will be up to last year; run sheep much better. Ewe and paddock sheep not so good. **1920** Powdrell *Dairy Farming* 42 Practical farmers sometimes put two calves on to one duffer cow, or to a run cow for five or six weeks. **1933** *Press* (Christchurch) (Acland Gloss.) 18 Nov. 15 *R[un]* sheep, *r[un]* cattle, as opposed to paddock sheep or milking cows and hand-reared calves. **1950** *NZJAg.* Sept. LXXXI. 215 With fertility declining pastures are becoming more difficult to control for sheep, and because of this, run cattle numbers are being increased. **1963** *Weekly News* (Auckland) 10 July 38 Run cattle..can be moved on a mob basis from one paddock to another. **1963** *Ibid.* 30 Oct. [farming page] If the share struck anything these [swing ploughs] had a kick like a run cow. It is said that a good man could land on his feet six yards in front of the horses. **1968** *NZ Farmer* 21 July 24 The greater number of unwanted tail-enders will tend to affect the price of the breeders' actual 'bread-and-butter' bulls, the general crossing bulls, the bulls which we call in New Zealand run bulls. **1986** Richards *Off the Sheep's Back* 149 It is also necessary to have a certain number of run-cattle on a sheep farm. They eat out any rank and tufty grass.

b. Special Comb. **run country**, open grazing-land; **run licence**, a licence to graze stock on a tract of Crown land (cf. DEPASTURAGE LICENCE); **run-owner**, RUNHOLDER.
   1950 *NZJAg.* Oct. LXXXI. 349 A wool-blind sheep is seriously hampered on **run country** in its search for feed and consequently does not thrive. **1970** Thomas *Way Up North* 63 He proceeded to raise cattle on a large area of leasehold run country, mostly north of Hukatere. **1857** Hursthouse *NZ* II. 512 Pastoral lands are the wild grazing lands..leased..for a term of years under a deed termed a '**run licence**', to the emigrant who, embarking on pastoral pursuits, becomes what is indifferently termed a run-holder, sheep-farmer, flock-master, or Squatter. **1888** D'Avigdor *Antipodean Notes* 72 The **run-owners** are clamouring for more ships, though they grumble at the average price of 4½d. a pound, which is all their mutton realizes in London. **1947** Beattie *Early Runholding* 11 I found thirteen [terms for 'runholders'], viz., 'flock owners', 'flock masters', 'pastoralists', 'run holders', 'run owners', 'sheep owners', [etc.].

run, *n.*[2]

1. Shearing. **a.** [AND 1904.] A period of uninterrupted shearing between breaks. Also a period of work during the working day at a freezing works.
   1909 Meek in Woodhouse *Farm & Station Verse* (1950) 52 The record shearing run of nineteen-nothing nine. **1933** *Press* (Christchurch) (Acland Gloss.) 18 Nov. 15 *Run*... (3) Stretch of work [shearing]. Shearers work for an hour before breakfast, two stretches in the morning and three in the afternoon. The stretches are divided by meal-times and *smokos*. **1955** Bowen *Wool Away* 7 No one knows better than I how a bad run can tend to get a man down—a run of sticky sheep, or gear not cutting the best. *Ibid.* 157 Run. The shearing time worked between official stops, smokos, or meals. **1966** *Encycl. NZ* III. 229 Actual shearing time is probably nine hours, with 'spells' (breaks) between six typical 'runs' totalling three hours. **1973** Fernandez *Tussock Fever* 64 Andrew was troubled about the [shearing] gang's knocking off... He had enough sheep in for another run. **1989** *NZ Eng. Newsletter* III. 27 *run*: (1) This word has several uses but the most common refers to a stretch of work. The official shearing time of two hours is called a 'run'. The day is divided into four of these. 7.30am-9.30am, smoke-o; 10.00am–12 noon, dinner; 1.00pm-3.00pm smoke-o; 3.30pm–5.30pm, tea.

b. A circuit of shearing sheds that a shearer or gang might contract (or intend) to work at during a season.
   1911 *Maoriland Worker* 26 May 11 When a man [*sc.* a shearer] made arrangements to go to a 'run' of two or three sheds he only deposited 20s, which carried him through the run. **c1927** Smith *Sheep & Wool Industry* 72 As an inducement for the men to work for them [shearing contractors] arrange a 'run of sheds' to follow one another. **1962** Sharpe *Country Occasions* 36 Each group of Maoris developed its own 'run', or succession of woolsheds in which the group did shearing as of right. **1989** *NZ Eng. Newsletter* III. 27 The contract circuit. A shearing contractor will arrange a 'run' of sheds for his gang each season.

c. In the phr. **to lose** (one's) **run**, to be sacked from the shearing board or from a shearing gang.
   1955 Bowen *Wool Away* 46 No learner has ever been put off the board because he has shorn sheep well, but many have lost their run through..rough shearing.

2. [OED *spec.*, of horses only.] A working dog's performance.
   1947 Newton *Wayleggo* 154 *Run*: Also a dog's performance during a particular job is referred to as his 'run', i.e., he puts up a good run or otherwise.

run, *n.*[3] As **to get the run** [AND 1889], to be dismissed from one's employment.
   1941 Baker *NZ Slang* 53 To *give a person his running shoes*..an extension of the phrase to *get the run*, to be dismissed or fired.

run, *v.*[1] [AND *run v.*[1] 'used elsewhere but recorded earliest in Aust. and apparently chiefly Austral.' 1795; see OED *v.* 43 c.]

1. *trans.* To (de)pasture or graze (livestock) on a run; of a stockowner, to graze (livestock); of land or pasture, to carry (livestock).
   1848 Pharazyn *Journal* (ATLMS) 169 Asked 80 acres and back hill..to run sheep and cattle upon. **1885** W.J. Swainson let. in *William Swainson* (1992) 107 A settler of the name of Duke made an arrangement with the natives to run cattle at Otaraia. **1898** [see RUN *n.*[1] 1]. **1933** *Press* (Christchurch) (Acland Gloss.) 18 Nov. 15 *Run*... To keep or carry. 'He *runs* merinos'; 'The station *runs* 10,000 sheep'.

2. *intr.* Of livestock, to graze at large, to range over open pasture.
   1848 Wakefield *Handbook NZ* 149 We have about 1400 [sheep] running in the Upper Motueka Valley. *Ibid.* 310 On the site of Dunedin..a Mr. Anderson had, in April 1847, 300 sheep and 50 head of cattle running. **1854** *Richmond-Atkinson Papers* 8 Aug. (1960) I. 154 We have 36 head of cattle running this winter on the back bush land. **1857** *Lyttelton Times* 1 July 1 All persons are hereby cautioned against disturbing the Horses now running in the neighbourhood of Rangiora, or driving any of them without permission of J.H.

Ward, Rangiora. **1865** in *Hist. N. Otago from 1853* (1978) 177 Mr. Holmes' sheep are running on native grass and the above increase has been obtained at one lambing.

run, *v.*² *Mustering.* [Transf. use of *run* to pursue, to trail: see OED *v*. 34 b.]

1. Usu. *trans.* To work (a dog); to send (a dog) out (for sheep).
   1933 *Press* (Christchurch) (Acland Gloss.) 18 Nov. 15 *Run.*—(1) To send [a dog]. (2) Work [of a young dog]. 'That dog is just beginning to r[un].' **1953** STRONACH *Musterer on Molesworth* 24 Never run a dog unless you must; never run a dog behind you. *Ibid.* 34 It was wise to start them from a distance, because if started suddenly they were likely to scatter, and that meant running a dog. **1973** WALLACE *Generation Gap* 211 You, Dickie, to the shepherd, run a dog around that black lamb.

2. As **run out**, also as *vbl. n.*, of a dog, to move quickly away from the shepherd to head sheep. Also as *n.* **run-out**, see quot.
   1971 NEWTON *Ten Thousand Dogs* 67 He [a sheep-dog] wasn't particularly good at running out and he was a bit slack at hand—he was too kind and sheep had no fear of him whatever. *Ibid.* 169 *Run-out:* The act of running out to head sheep. *Outrun*—the manner in which the dog runs out.

3. In the phr. **run on the blind**, see BLIND B a.

run, *v.*³ In phrases using various senses of *run v.*:
a. to run for (one's) **colours**, see COLOUR *n.*²; **to run like a bushfire (hairy goat, redshank)**, see BUSH-FIRE 3 a, HAIRY GOAT a, REDSHANK a; **to run the cutter**, see CUTTER *n.*¹; **to run on terms**, see TERMS *n.*¹

b. to run the ship *obs.*, see quot.; **to run up the calico** *obs.*, to pitch a tent.
   1912 *Truth* 3 Aug. 4 It has been the custom for a good number of years for the Shipping Companies to select an experienced man from the ranks of the Union to act as Foreman, or what is known in waterside parlance as 'running the ship'. **1934** *Press* (Christchurch) (Acland Gloss.) 27 Jan. 15 *Run up the calico.*—Pitch the tent.

runa. [Ma. /'runa/: Williams 352 *Runa..1. Rumex flexuosus*, dock.] DOCK 1, the native dock.
   1867 HOOKER *Handbook* 768 Runa, Lindsay. *Rumex* sp. **1922** COWAN *NZ Wars* (1955) II. 26 Boiled flax-root water poured on the wounds, and also dock-root (*runa*), well scraped and boiled, were our favourite remedies for gunshot and bayonet wounds. **1982** [see DOCK 1].

runanga.

1. [Ma. /'ru:naŋa/: Williams 352 *Rūnā..6. v. intr.* Assemble... *rūnanga. 1*...Assembly, council.] **a.** In Maori society, an assembly or council.
   1843 DIEFFENBACH *Travels in NZ* II. 384 Runanga—assembly, council. **1858** *Richmond-Atkinson Papers* 21 June (1960) I. 411 This arrangement was proposed by Potatau's *runanga*. **1863** MOSER *Mahoe Leaves* 28 A few years back we used to hear a meeting of the tribes simply termed a 'korero', a 'talk', or a 'ko-miti', a 'committee', and it is only lately that our ears have been regaled with the high sounding term, 'runanga'. **1908** GORST *NZ Revisited* 210 The supreme authority, legislative and judicial resided in the village Runanga. **1922** COWAN *NZ Wars* (1955) I. 184 This *runanga* consisted of Rewi Maniapoto (the *tumuaki*, or head of the council), his..cousins..and several other chiefs. **1937** *NZ Railways Mag.* Nov. 18 Te waka..paddled three miles up the river..where the Kingite *runanga*, a Council of the districts chiefs, was sitting. **1946** *JPS* LV. 157 *runanga*, assembly; council; so, whare-runanga, meeting-house. **1959** SINCLAIR *Hist. NZ* 132 Grey and the New Premier, William Fox, set about introducing in Maori districts a system of 'indirect rule' such as the Stafford ministry had advocated in 1858. Maori *runanga* (assemblies) in the various districts were to recommend to the Governor the laws they required. He could introduce them by Order-in-Council without seeking parliamentary assent. **1986** IHIMAERA *Matriarch* 68 Here [in Turanga, c1851], particularly, the native council, the runanga, was in control of Pakeha trading, and *it* set the price of products, not the Pakeha. **1992** *Metro* (Auckland) Dec. 148 In the absence of authentic tribal structures such as runanga, trust boards have, in recent years, expanded their functions to include lobbying Parliament.

b. Transf. to European assemblies or councils.
   1861 Gov. Grey to Duke of Newcastle 8 Dec. in Rutherford *Select Documents* (1949) 115 It is the desire of the Queen, and this also is the thought of Governor Grey and of the runanga of the Pakehas, that the Maoris should also do for themselves as the Europeans do. **1863** *Richmond-Atkinson Papers* 8 Mar. (1960) II. 29 Candid comments may be made on any species of public entertainment, in which class huis..and runangas and koreros with the Governor, probably, are included.

2. A house or place of assembly, MEETING HOUSE, *whare runanga* (WHARE 2). **a.** As **runanga**.
   1868 HARPER *Lett. from NZ* 5 Feb. (1914) 126 After service they provide dinner for me in their 'Runanga' or Social Hall, a low long wooden room. **1876** KENNEDY *Colonial Travel* 252 The building was formerly a Runanga, or meeting-house of the Hau-Hau rebels. **1930** REISCHEK *Yesterdays in Maoriland* (1933) 149 The baskets were bound together..and piled up..on the free places before the meeting-house (*runanga*). **1968** SEDDON *The Seddons* 63 And then to write sitting down on the floor of a Maori runanga and without table, chair or other convenience to record word by word a series of rapidly delivered translated speeches.

b. As **runanga house**.
   1879 *Auckland Weekly News* 1 Feb. 15 At Okahu, a *runanga* house has been erected. **1899** GRACE *Sketch NZ War* 2 They assisted him to re-robe, and led him to their runanga-house, treating him with every consideration. **1905** *Truth* 19 Aug. IX. V. 5 [SI use] The tangi..lasted for several days..the remains laid [*sic*] in state in the runanga house at Tairooa [*sic*] Pah. **1931** *Na To Hoa Aroha* (1987) II. 152 But the marae and runanga house discussions between hosts and distinguished visitors must have resulted in a fair amount of interpolation. **1983** *Land of Mist* 30 Matuahu—Te Kooti's most important pa where he had his runanga council (house) but which was found abandoned.

run crayfish: see CRAYFISH 2 (3).

rungateeda, var. RANGATIRA.

runholder. [AND 1863.] The owner (occas. manager and, in early use, 'lessee') of a stock-run or station. (For various (near) synonyms see quot. 1947 below.) See also *run-owner* (RUN *n.*¹ 4 b), *station-holder* (STATION 5). Cf. *sheep king* (SHEEP 2), SQUATTER 3.
   1857 HURSTHOUSE *NZ* II. 512 Pastoral lands are the wild grazing lands..leased..for a term of years under a deed termed a 'run licence', to the emigrant who, embarking on pastoral pursuits, becomes what is indifferently termed a run-holder, sheep-farmer, flock-master, or Squatter. **1865** *Evening Post* (Wellington) I. No.26 2 The runholders, squatters, sheepfarmers, or whatever else they may be called. **1875** *Official Handbook NZ* 128 The tenants of the waste lands, or 'runholders' were allowed a right of pre-emption. **1898** HOCKEN *Contributions* 150 I 'cooeed' for a long time, and when I had given up all hope Mr. Clapcott, the runholder, kindly came across for me. **1902** *Settler's Handbook NZ* 73 Boundary disputes between adjoining runholders are settled by arbitration under the direction of the Land Board. **1922** PERRY *Sheep Farming* 92 For these reasons it usually pays a runholder best in the long run to breed up his own flock. **1933** *Press* (Christchurch) (Acland Gloss.) 25 Nov. 15 *Run holder.* — Squatter, station owner, or (recent) owner of a small grazing run. This or *stock owner* was the proper designation of a squatter in the early days. **1947** BEATTIE *Early Runholding* 11 So aghast was I [at the wrong use of synonyms for 'runholder'] that I spent weeks collecting every old term for 'runholders' I could, and I found thirteen, viz., 'flock owners', 'flock-masters', 'pastoralists', 'run holders', 'run owners', 'sheep owners', 'sheep holders', 'sheep masters', 'squatters', 'station holders', 'station owners', 'stock holders', and 'stock owners'... Of the thirteen terms found in old documents, the word 'runholder' was the most used. **1951** MARSH *Opening Night* iii 55 He was the son and grandson of a high-country run-holder—sheep-farmer—in the South Island. **1960** OLIVER *Story NZ* 107 Sheep brought the runholders and later the station-owners. The runholders owned only the sheep which they pastured on great stretches of leased land. **1970** McNAUGHTON *Tat* 89 Jim, the runholder, persuaded Bluey to stay on and give a hand to lamb the paddock ewes.

Hence **runholding** *vbl. n.* and *attrib.* [AND 1872 only], (pertaining to) the occupation of runholder.
   1939 BEATTIE *First White Boy Born Otago* 92 Hopkinson was a Swede who left his mark on Otago runholding annals. *Ibid.* 117 In the fifties he early became aware of the efforts of the runholding class to open up the backblocks. **1947** BEATTIE *Early Runholding in Otago* 10 [Title] **1965** McLAGLAN *Stethoscope & Saddlebags* 130 In a well-to-do run-holding area were a popular doctor pair.

run in, *v.* [Transf. use of *run* to chase, to hunt: cf. OED 42 a; AND 1885.] *trans.* To drive (stock) to a place where they may be handled, as sheep to yards, dairy cows to the milking shed.
   1889 *Colonia: the Colonial College Mag.* 23 He has to 'run in' the cows by himself which takes a long time for sometimes they are feeding some little way from the homestead. **1986** RICHARDS *Off the Sheep's Back* 130 Unfortunately in the afternoon we got ahead of the musterers, so the manager had to run in a mob of undagged cotty sheep that were being held until the cut out.

runner, *n.*¹ [?Spec. use of *runner* a rope rove through a single block.] Usu. *pl.*, the small intestines of an animal killed for meat.
   1912 *Truth* 19 Oct. 1 It came out in a sausage skin case... It was explained that the matter removed from the 'runners' or plain guts from the abattoir created the atmospheric unpleasantness. **1957** MACDONALD *Canterbury Frozen Meat Co.* 69 From certain intestines sausage casings are prepared, and in 1887 Henry Berry & Co. contracted to purchase..clean 'runners'. *Ibid.* 72 An important by-product is sausage casings, which are made from several parts of the gut, the main source being the very long small intestine of the sheep. This, in the untreated state, is called a 'runner'.

runner, *n.*² [Spec. use of *runner* errand-bearer: see OED *n.* 3 a and c.] A person who delivers newspapers.

1946 SIMPSON *If You'd Care to Know* 134 Into these tubes the 'runner' pops the morning or evening newspaper.

running shoes. *fig.* [From a phr. popularized by the Hon. Robert Semple (1873–1955), Minister of Public Works in the first Labour Government.] In the phr. **to give** (one his) **running shoes**, to dismiss a person.

1936 GILMOUR Cartoon in *Truth* in Grant *The Unauthorised Version* (1980) 136 The Hon. R. Semple has told the country that members of Government boards who obstruct the Government will..be given 'running shoes'. **1941** BAKER *NZ Slang* 53 To *give a person his running shoes*, to dismiss a person from office (also a political use), which is an extension of the phrase to *get the run*. **1943** BENNETT *English in NZ* in *Amer. Speech* XVIII. 92 'To give a man his running shoes' [was] coined by a New Zealand Minister of the Crown [Hon. R. Semple] as a vivid substitute for the English 'sack' or the American 'fire'. **1955** *BJ Cameron Collection* (TS July) *running shoes, give someone his running shoes* (v) To dismiss from an office or job. **1963** PEARSON *Coal Flat* 111 Like Bob Semple used to say about hit-and-run drivers—give them their running shoes. **1988** MCGILL *Dict. Kiwi Slang* 50 *give somebody their running shoes* dismiss from political office.

run-off, *n. Farming.*

1. Often in the phr. **to take a run-off**, a group of sheep drafted from a main mob. Also occas. as a verb.

1933 *Press* (Christchurch) (Acland Gloss.) 25 Nov. 15 *Run-off.*—(1) Sheep counted out from a mob without being drafted: e.g., 'I cannot buy the whole line. I will take a *r[un-]o[ff]* of 300.' Usually 'fair *r[un-]o[ff]*'... (3) to separate: e.g., 'I will *r[un] o[ff]* the strangers when we draft the mob.'

2. As **run-off (block, paddock)**, an area which is not part of a developed farm but which is used for intermittent grazing or feeding of stock. See also quot. 1982.

1933 *Press* (Christchurch) (Acland Gloss.) 25 Nov. 15 *Run-off*... Paddock used with turnips or green feed on which the sheep may camp and get what extra feed they can. **1950** *NZJAg.* Apr. LXXX. 366 Utilisation of the heavier pockets [of coastal land] and sand dunes is complementary, the latter being used mainly as a winter run-off. *Ibid.* 389 During early winter they [*sc.* ewes] are rationed turnips, fed good hay, and driven off their turnip break on to a large run-off paddock daily. **1973** WALLACE *Generation Gap* 254 I suppose we could make do with the netting we used for a run-off on the turnips. **1982** *Agric. Gloss.* (MAF) 5 *Run off*: an area of land, perhaps separated from the main area where young stock or dry (non-lactating) animals are run. **1994** *Dominion* (Wellington) 20 May 12 The five properties sold at auction were bought as runoff blocks for dairy or beef.

run out: see RUN *v.*² 2.

run out, *v. Shearing.* Of the shears or shearing comb, to move through the fleece to the end of the shearing stroke. Also **running out** *vbl. n.*

1955 BOWEN *Wool Away* 26 This way the comb enters nicely on the off leg and it takes little time to run out. **1989** *NZ Eng. Newsletter* III. 27 *running out*: Allowing the shears to run beyond the intended length of the blow into the unshorn fleece wool. This is bad shearing and results in costly second cuts.

rural, *a. Hist.* [Spec. use of *rural* characteristic of the country as distinct from the town.] Applied as a defining word in early European settlement (or in emigration prospectuses) to distinguish the non-urban allotments in (esp. Wakefield) systems of land purchase, often in combinations as **rural land, rural section** as distinct from **town land, town section**, etc.

1848 WAKEFIELD *Handbook NZ* 317 ['Terms of Purchase of Land in the Settlement of Otago' agreed on by the 'Otago Association' and the Company] 16 In exchange for each sum of 120*l*. 10*s*... each Purchaser to receive..three separate Land-Orders, namely, for the Town quarter-acre, the ten acres of Suburban Land, and the fifty acres of Rural Land, respectively. These lands to be severally selected according to priority of choice, to be determined by Ballot. *Ibid.* 284 Two hundred and fifty Town-sections [at New Plymouth], with their orders of choice..each with a Rural section of 50 acres attached. **1943** *St Michael's Anglican Church A Century of Christian Witness* 6 The rural sections, to be allotted further out in the country, were not surveyed at this time and were therefore unavailable.

Rural Bank. Formerly, a familiar short form of *Rural Banking and Finance Corporation*, a State-sponsored lending institution for financing the primary sector or primary producers, which, after privatization, was eventually (c1993) absorbed into the corporate structure of the National Bank of New Zealand Ltd.

1985 *Listener* 6 Apr. 72 Today's Rural Bank is responsible for realising much of New Zealand's export potential, from the sea as well as the land. **1986** *Illustr. Encycl. NZ* 1080 Rural Banking & Finance Corporation, known commonly as the Rural Bank, was a government-funded bank charged with providing loans to individuals or organisations engaged in any sort of farming or farm support industry, or the fishing industry. **1991** *Dominion* (Wellington) 18 Oct. 14 A $2 billion guarantee by the Government for Rural Bank borrowing was not recorded by the Treasury in the Government accounts as the result of an 'administrative oversight', according to the Audit Office.

rural delivery. Also **rural mail delivery**, and in shortened form (used mainly as an address indicator on envelopes) **R.D.** A mail and general delivery service to rural areas. Often *attrib.* Cf PRIVATE BAG.

1918 *Quick March* 1 Oct. 19 [Heading] Outback Settlers... Mr. Guthrie has replied that at the opening of the war a system of rural mail delivery services was in process of being introduced. **1949** *Here & Now* Oct. 17 We can still number by thousands the homes (not all of them R.D.) where meals are cooked on the wood range. **1955** *BJ Cameron Collection* (TS July) RD (n) Rural delivery. A system of mail delivery in country areas. **1955** *Postage Stamps of NZ* III. 149 The Postmaster-General's Report for 1916 stated:- 'On the 1st November, 1916, a travelling post office was established on the Masterton-Waingawa-Matahiwi rural-delivery route.' **1960** STARTUP *Travelling Mails* 6 A rural delivery service had been commenced in 1913 from Masterton to Rangitumau, 9 miles to the north, on the closure of the post office in that locality. **1964** MORRIESON *Came a Hot Friday* (1981) 4 He had caught the rural delivery car on its return journey. **1964** MIDDLETON *Walk on Beach* 15 Every afternoon it was Zelda's job to collect the paper and the mail from the rural delivery box. **1985** HILL *Moaville Magic* 63 There were no simple wooden boxes with a red metal flag on a hinge that the Rural Delivery driver could raise to show when the cream cheque called. **1987** *MS Cellany* 25 The first run, RD9 is over for the day. RD8, seventy-nine miles begins after breakfast.

rura rura, var. RURU.

ruru. Also with much variety of early form as **dúdu, heroòroo** (=he ruru), **looloo, rura rura, ruru ruru**. [Ma. /'ruru/ /'rurururu/: Williams 352 *Ruru* (i) *rurururu*..morepork, = *ruru-peho, koukou*.] MOREPORK 1 a. See also OWL 1.

[**1815** KENDALL *New Zealanders' First Book* 16 Looloo An owl. **1842** GRAY *Fauna* in Dieffenbach *Travels in NZ* (1843) II. 186 *Athene Novae Seelandiae*... Heroòroo of the natives of Queen Charlotte's Sound... Eou Hou of the natives of Tasman Bay... Kou Kou... Kao Koa... Ruru ruru. **1847** *NZ Jrnl.* VII. 219 The Rura Rura, a small owl, kept up its incessant and monotonous cry of 'More Porke, More Porke'. **1859** THOMSON *Story NZ* I. 23 Many of the native names of the birds are derived from their cries: thus the pigeon is Kukupa, the brown parrot Kaka, and the owl Ru-ru or Kou-Kou. **1861** HAAST *Rep. Topogr. Explor. Nelson* 139 Some [birds] are seldom seen..as for instance the ruru..the 'more pork' of the settlers. **1873** [see MOREPORK 1 a]. **1894** WILSON *Land of Tui* 94 No voice came to mar the utter stillness, until..the Ruru shuddered past, croaking his eerie cry: 'Moepok! Moepok!' which sounded like an uneasy wraith. **1922** COWAN *NZ Wars* (1955) I. 25 Owl called to owl, and the regularly repeated cries grew nearer until they formed a semi-cordon of melancholy notes about the flagstaff hill... It was a fatal cordon, for the *rurus* were the pickets of Heke's war-party. **1946** *JPS* LV. 157 Ruru, koukou, an owl.., morepork: the name, which is echoic, should really be kroukrou; but as the Maori disliked the sound of paired consonants, the two forms resulted according to the sound more prominent to the ear of the name-giver—koukou, or ruru: ruru much the more common. **1978** *Manawatu Tramping Club Jubilee* 87 We watched Kaka fly overhead and later listened to the Ruru answering each other. **1989** *Listener* 2 Sept. 7 A ruru dropped out of the trees to land on the telephone wire—a dark shape with only the stars behind.

rush, *n.*¹ [Extended use of *rush* fam. Juncaceae.]

1. Specifically, native and naturalized species of *Juncus* (fam. Juncaceae), or, generally, any member of the rush family Juncaceae, or a plant bearing some resemblance to a rush. See also WIWI *n.*¹ 1 a.

1867 HOOKER *Handbook* 768 Rush. *Juncus*. **1909** *AJHR* C-11 11 [*Juncus*] *effusus*. Wiwi. Rush. Cos[mopolitan]. Swampy forest openings. Pokaka, &c. [*Juncus*] *bufonius*. Wiwi. Rush... Common in swamp. **1910** COCKAYNE *NZ Plants & Their Story* 162 The rush family (*Juncaceae*) is an extensive one, consisting of the alpine or subantarctic *Rostkovia*, the true rushes (*Juncus*), and the wood-rushes (*Luzula*). **1926** HILGENDORF *Weeds* 54 Rushes (*Juncus polyanthemos* [spp.]) often called by their Maori name of Wiwi, are well known in all damp pastures. **1969** *Standard Common Names Weeds* 65 rush [=] *bog-rush: cladium: leptocarpus: spike-rush: wire-rush*.

2. With a modifier: **alpine, bog, common, jointed, pakihi, red, spike, wire, wood**.

(1) **alpine rush.** *Juncus novae-zelandiae*, a small tufted and rhizomatous plant bearing shining black capsules and found in damp sites.

1908 *AJHR* C-11 36 [*Juncus*] *novae-zealandiae*. Wiwi. Alpine rush. End[emic]. Bog. **1961** MARTIN *Flora NZ* 141 The Alpine Rush..occurs abundantly in alpine swamps from Taranaki southwards.

(2) **bog rush.** *Schoenus pauciflorus* (fam. Cyperaceae), a tussock-forming sedge of subalpine sites.

1868 *TrNZI* I. (rev. edn.) 209 Bog Rush. Schoenus pauciflorus. **1969** *Standard Common Names Weeds* 7 *bog-rush. Schoenus pauciflorus*.

(3) **common rush**. *Juncus gregiflorus* or *J. usitatus* (formerly *J. polyanthemos*), a tall, clumped native rush.
 1870 *TrNZI* II. 126 Juncus communis. Common rush. **1908** *AJHR C-11* 36 *Juncus effusus*. Wiwi. Common rush... Wet ground. **1915** *AJHR C-6* 12 *[Juncus] effusus*... Common rush. Tussock pasture.

(4) **jointed rush**. *Leptocarpus similis* (OIOI); or the naturalized *Juncus articulatus* (formerly *lampocarpus*).
 1909 *AJHR C-12* 52 *[Juncus] lampocarpus*. Jointed rush N. temp. region. Wet ground, lowland. **1956** *Standard Common Names Weeds* 41 *jointed rush. Juncus articulatus*. **1961** MARTIN *Flora NZ* 140 The third of these bastard-rushes is that known as the Jointed Rush, which forms such extensive stands on salt-marsh and saline flats all round the coast.

(5) **pakihi rush**. *Baumea* (formerly *Cladium*) *teretifola* (fam. Cyperaceae), a tufted rhizomatous sedge of West Coast bogs and pakihi.
 1929 *NZJST* XI. 236 Pakihi rush *Cladium teretifolium*. **1969** *Standard Common Names Weeds* 55 *pakihi rush. Cladium teretifolium*.

(6) **red rush**. *Leptocarpus similis* (OIOI); or *Schoenus pauciflorus*.
 1909 *AJHR C-12* 52 *Leptocarpus simplex*. Oioi Red rush. Swamp Both in brackish and fresh water, very common; follows course of old strait from head of Paterson Inlet to Mason Bay. **1969** *Standard Common Names Weeds* 63 *red rush* [=] *bog-rush*.

(7) **spike-rush**. *Eleocharis sphacelata* (fam. Cyperaceae), a tall leafless swamp sedge.
 1869 *TrNZI* I. (rev. edn.) 210 Spike Rush. Eleocharis gracilis. **1969** *Standard Common Names Weeds* 73 *spike-rush, tall. Eleocharis sphacelata*.

(8) **wire rush**. *Empodisma* (syn. *Calorophus*) *minus* (formerly *Hypolaena laterifolia*) (fam. Restionaceae), a peat-forming plant.
 1961 MARTIN *Flora NZ* 139 Next the Wire-rush (*Hypolaena*) claims attention. This rush-like plant is strictly a bog plant, with slender, wiry, much-branched stems. **1969** *Standard Common Names Weeds* 88 *Wire-rush. Hypolaena laterifolia*. **1973** MARK & ADAMS *Alpine Plants* (1979) 22 Several species are virtually confined to peat-bogs—the wire rush (*Calorophus minor*) and the tangle fern.

(9) **wood rush**. *Luzula* species (fam. Juncaceae).
 1907 *AJHR C-8* 18 *Luzula campestris*. Wood-rush. End[emic]. Coastal rocks. **1969** *Standard Common Names Weeds* 88 *wood rush. Luzula*.

rush, *n.²* Hist. [Used elsewhere and recorded earliest in Austral. (AND 1841), but of historical and social significance in early NZ: cf. OED *n.²* 4 a; EDD *n.²* 3 a great assembly of people; a crowd.]

1. a. A sudden migration or 'rushing off' of people to a new goldfield; often with a modifier indicating locality (see quot. 1873); also in transf. use, of things connected with new goldfields (see quot. 1869). See also *gold-rush* (GOLD 3).
 1853 SWAINSON *Auckland* 104 In order to check an immediate and indiscriminate rush to the spot,... the Government now issued provisional regulations. **1862** in *Canterbury Rhymes* (1866) 92 I've circulated rumours... Of people finding nuggets by the score, To cause a rush. **1869** *Mount Ida Chron*. in Bromby *Eye Witness Hist.* (1985) 52 Kyeburn, April 14... Permit me..to call attention..to the rush of grog shanties which has taken place in our locality. **1873** PYKE *Wild Will Enderby* (1889, 1974) I. ii 8 It was the time of the great Dunstan 'Rush', and a host of miners were hurrying from all parts of New Zealand. **1898** HOCKEN *Contributions* 198 Some old Australian diggers.. discovered the precious metal in sufficient quantity to create a fever of expectation and a 'rush'. **1968** SEDDON *The Seddons* 38 The exciting days when fresh finds of gold were reported and wild rushes took place were over.

b. Similarly, a 'rush' to a new gumfield.
 1955 BOSWELL *Dim Horizons* 58 Then new gumfields were opened farther north..and a diggers' rush gave my brothers intermittent employment.

c. Similarly, a 'rush' to a sealing ground.
 1907 MCNAB *Murihiku* 118 [Heading] Macquarie Island Rush, 1810 to 1812.

2. A place where gold has been recently found and to which diggers and others 'rush'; often with a modifier, esp. as **new rush**.
 1863 WALKER *Jrnl. & Lett.* (ATLTS) 12-13 Jan. He [sc. the miner] was very civil, told us that two of his mates had followed a man to see if they could find a new rush. **1866** FARJEON *Grif* 39 When the diggings first broke out, he was a Cheap Jack, as they call them, trading at all the new rushes. **1914** PFAFF *Diggers' Story* 8 We were on the Five Mile, and then went on to Hunt's rush. I was there when Hunt got away from a big crowd. **1939** BEATTIE *First White Boy Born Otago* 81 Their father lived at Caversham, and at the time of Gabriel's rush he built an hotel at Caversham. **1967** MAY *West Coast Gold Rushes* 526 Duffer: applied to a rush, a shaft, or a claim generally. A failure. Synonyms were 'shicer', 'stringer' or, in the case of a false rush, 'store-keepers' rush'. **1968** SEDDON *The Seddons* 37 Undefeated, on they came to the West Coast rush.

rush, *v.¹* Goldmining. Hist. [AND 1852 'Used elsewhere but recorded earliest in Aust.'; cf. OED *v.²* 5 d.]

1. a. *trans*. To occupy or over-run (a locality) by an influx of gold-diggers.
 1862 *Otago Goldfields & Resources* 26 The Highbury has been rushed, condemned, almost deserted, and yet survives. **1887** PYKE *Hist. Early Gold Discoveries Otago* (1962) 74 Our object was to work only the richest spots, as we did not know how soon we might be discovered and 'rushed'. *Ibid.* 85 The fact that we were liable to be 'rushed' at any time, and our claims limited to 24 feet square did not affect Fox's or West's parties. **1896** HARPER *Pioneer Work* 30 Westland..was rushed by gold-diggers in the early sixties.

Hence **over-rushed** *ppl. a.*, of a new goldfield, having received more prospective miners than it can support; **rushing** *ppl. a.* and *vbl. n.*, taking part in a rush.
 1869 *Grey River Argus* 11 Mar. 3 These diggers will be greatly disappointed, as there are no grounds sufficient to justify such a rush. Camp Mountain creek is **over-rushed**, and many of the new arrivals will go on to the West Coast. **1863** HEYWOOD *Vacation Tour Antipodes* 162 Our old friends, Cobb and Co., had followed their '**rushing**' friends from Victoria. **1967** MAY *West Coast Gold Rushes* 280 The goldfields press complained of 'headstrong and indiscriminate **rushing**' in 1865, a complaint still being echoed in 1867.

b. *trans*. and *intr*. to join a rush (to a new goldfield).
 1863 HEYWOOD *Vacation Tour Antipodes* 161 We brought from Sydney several men *rushing* to the Otago diggings. **1903** *NZ Illustr. Mag.* Nov. 108 Joe Potter, humping his bluey across the scrub-covered Waitui flats, when he and Steel rushed Flannigan's Find, little thought he would ever see an important town in that place.

2. As **rush ho!**, a (verse) exclamation.
 1914 PFAFF *Diggers' Story* 26 Thatcher sang [c1860s]:—The cry is now 'Rush Ho!' and away the diggers go, To the norrard now they make their way.

rush, *v.²*

1. *intr*. Of cattle, to stampede.
 1863 CHUDLEIGH *Diary* 2 Oct. (1950) 105 [We] went to get some more cattle for Mellish out of Rowleys mob... We brought some home and vainly endeavoured to yard them but as all took to rushing we let them go.

Hence **rush** *n.*, a stampede; **rusher** [AND 1892], a stampeding animal; **rushing** *ppl. a.*, stampeding.
 c1930 *Whitcombe's Etym. Dict. Aust.-NZ Suppl.* 10 *rush n*. a stampede of cattle, etc. **1882** HAY *Brighter Britain* I. 158 Only occasionally we find it necessary to slaughter some unmanageable **rusher**, a cow, or bullock. **1910** CHUDLEIGH *Diary* 1 Nov. (1950) 452 [Rev. J.G. Engst] would face man or the devil bible in hand but he would take a stick to a **rushing** cow.

2. *trans*. To hurry (stock) along.
 1938 STUDHOLME in Woodhouse *Farm & Station Verse* (1950) 67 Down the slopes we rushed them [sc. cattle] hell for leather, Towards the open country and the yard.

rush ho!: see RUSH *v.¹* 2.

rush the kip: see KIP 2.

rust bucket. [AND 1965 'Transf. use of (orig. U.S.) *rustbucket* an old and rusty ship'.] A rust-infested vehicle.
 1981 *Avondale College Slang Words* (Auckland) (Goldie Brown Collect.) *rust bucket*: old car. **1986** *Marist Messenger* Dec. 34 We had a good look at the ute which had its passenger door open... It was an old rust bucket. I wouldn't have driven it anywhere on these roads. **1993** *Evening Post* (Wellington) 12 Mar. 8 Last night's main..item was a gripping piece of journalism concerning the rust-bucket oil tankers and bulk carriers that ply the world's shipping lanes.

rusticated. [Transf. use of *rusticate* to mark masonry by sunken joints or roughened surface: see OED *rusticate v*. 4, *rusticated* 3 a.] See quot. 1986.
 1883 *Brett's Colonists' Guide* 728 Rusticated weatherboards for front 350 @ 17/-. **1935** *NZ Institute of Architects Jrnl.* Apr. 20 The rusticated weatherboard made its appearance [in the 1870s]—the invention of it being attributed to Toxwood [sic for Toxward], who was an architect trained in Denmark. **1986** SALMOND *Old NZ Houses* 114 Another kind of weatherboard which became popular in the 1880s was the 'rusticated' board, where the top edge was planed down to fit behind a rebate in the edge of the next board. The completed wall showed pronounced grooves which resembled channel-jointed stonework, and in more elaborate houses timber *quoins* at corners assisted the illusion. The introduction of the rusticated board has been attributed to the Wellington architect Julius Toxward in the 1860s.

rusty gold. Gold coated with a thin layer of iron oxide, thus hindering or preventing amalgamation with mercury.
 1890 *Otago Witness* (Dunedin) 6 Mar. 21 Mr. Gordon referred to the existence in this colony of 'rusty' gold, which was coated with oxide of iron and refused to amalgamate easily. **1967** MAY *West Coast Gold Rushes* 238 The mercury plates were seldom perfect: the finest gold was lost by flotation while with cemented gold a thin coating of iron oxide ('rusty gold') often prevented amalgamation.

ruva-ruva, var. REWAREWA.

S

Sa. An informal shortening of *Samoan*, a person of Samoan ancestry. See also SAMI.
    1992 *Sport* 8 Mar. 121 Dixon the Niuean said the same so did Stephen the Sa and Dennis the other Maori.

sacrifice paddock. A paddock heavily stocked and completely grazed (that is, 'sacrificed') in order to save feed in other paddocks.
    1958 *Star-Sun* (Christchurch) 14 Oct. 13 The farming technique known as the 'sacrifice' paddock, in which one paddock on a farm is heavily stocked during the winter to save pastures elsewhere on the farm for use by cattle after calving was criticised by the Society for the Prevention of Cruelty to Animals in the Palmerston North Magistrates' Court today... In Dalefield's case it had been the stock rather than the paddock which had been 'sacrificed'.

sad: see PACK *v.* 2.

saddle.
1. a. As **colonial saddle**, see COLONIAL A 5.
b. In the phr. **to talk to one's saddle**, of a solitary musterer, to talk to oneself.
    1946 MACFARLANE *Amuri* 97 Men became so strange and quiet in the back, so much alone, begin 'talking to their saddle' as the old saying is.
2. Special Comb. **saddle-track**, *bridle-track* (BRIDLE 3).
    1982 MARSHALL *Master Big Jingles* 35 Letty has for days now been..sneaking off... The Golightlys happened to see her today on the saddle track, and brought her home.

saddleback. [f. the saddle-like markings on its back (see quot. 1899).] *Philesturnus* (formerly *Creadion*) *carunculatus* (fam. Callaeatidae), a now rare glossy-black bird of the size of a starling, distinguished by a bright chestnut saddle-marking and orange-red wattles and found in two localized subspecies **North Island saddleback** (*P. c. rufusater*) and **South Island saddleback** (*P. c. carunculatus*). See also BROWNIE 5, JACKBIRD, PUROUROU, TIEKE, WATTLE BIRD.
    c1835 BOULTBEE *Journal* (1986) 104 The Saddle back is a brown bird with a bright red spot on its back like a saddle. **1869** *TrNZI* I. (rev. edn.) 217 The 'saddle-back' (*Creadion carunculatus*) of the North is represented in the South Island by *C. cinereus* a closely allied species. **1882** POTTS *Out in Open* 64 It is the sharp, quick call of the saddle-back. **1899** DOUGLAS in *Mr Explorer Douglas* (1957) 268 The saddle back is in shape something like a tui... Accross [sic] the back is a marking in shape and colour like a new riding saddle, giving the bird a strange appearance and it[s] equally strange name. **1914** PFAFF *Diggers' Story* 11 Every flock was accompanied by two or three Saddlebacks, a bird now wholly extinct [in Westland]. **1923** *NZJST* VI. 97 The disappearance of the saddleback occurred so early in the history of the colony that it is very difficult to explain in terms of any known introduced factors. **1955** OLIVER *NZ Birds* 513 The North Island Saddleback is doubtless the 'starling' that Crozet mentions during his stay at the Bay of Islands in 1772. *Ibid.* 514 The South Island Saddleback was collected by Forster at Queen Charlotte Sound during Cook's second voyage. **1966** *Weekly News* (Auckland) 1 June 17 A pair of saddlebacks point like hunting dogs... They snap from one rigid position to another, head down, tail erect, wattles a blood crimson, the fragmented sunlight burnishing the chestnut saddle on their backs. **1990** *Dominion* (Wellington) 7 July 10 Once common in the North Island, saddlebacks were easy prey for rats and ferrets and by the 1970's they survived only on the Hen Islands.

saddle with *v.* [f. *saddle n.* a long, concave ridge connecting two hills, the whole being saddle-shaped, a frequent feature of the New Zealand landscape: cf. OED *n.* 4.] Of a geographical feature, to join by or across a saddle.
    1877 *TrNZI* IX. 579 Showing that the southern branch of the Cook River saddles with the Karangarua, at a point to the Mount westward of Sefton. **1950** *Tararua* 90 This shows the Blue some miles east of the Okuru, though in fact one saddles with the other. **1957** HARDIE *In Highest Nepal* 57 The pass at its head actually saddled with what appeared to be a tributary of the Hongu to the west.

sailer. *Forestry.* Also occas **sailor**. [Transf. use of *sailer* something which sails (through the air).] A falling tree-branch, esp. from a tree being felled. Cf. PIGEON 5, WIDOW-MAKER.
    1952–53 *NZ Forest Service Gloss.* (TS) *Sailer*. A falling branch. syn. Widowmaker. **1958** *Press* (Christchurch) 3 Oct. 5 Quarter of an hour later, the sailer..came down, striking Scott across the forehead and scalp. **1961** CRUMP *Hang On a Minute Mate* 42 He learned that..broken-off branches—sailors—can fly fifty yards when a tree comes down, and bowl a man stone stinking dead if he's not careful. **1983** *National Radio* 'Spectrum Documentary' 12 Nov. [G.W. Johnson's working life, 1940–46:] A sailer—a danger well-known to bushmen. When a tree was felled a branch might break off and stay high up in another tree—stay up for years—one day..you can have 30 to 40 feet of branch coming down to earth.

sailor, var. SAILER.

sale: *n.* see SELL OUT.

sale day. *Rural.* Also **saleday**, occas. with init. caps. [See OED *sale n.* 3 a.] In country towns, the day on which the farm-livestock sale is held.
    1881 HURNDALL in Warr *Bush-burn to Butter* (1988) 52 September 2: first cattle sale day. **1904** *NZ Illustr. Mag.* Dec. 251 Sale day, Christmas week, and not a beast to be got for love or money. **1949** SCANLAN *Rusty Road* 10 Thursday was Sale Day, when the farmers came in to buy and sell sheep or calves, heifers and pigs, and the farmer's wife to trade her butter and eggs at the grocer's for stores, and to buy towels and sheets and shoes. Market day, they would call it in England, but there was no market in these small New Zealand towns. **1956** MIDDLETON in *NZ Listener Short Stories Volume 2* (1978) 40 Tell him I'll be wanting another pup and I'll look him up next saleday. **1967** HENDERSON *Return to Open Country* 172 I came to appreciate the farmers' saleday when I was running a small country town bakery and tearooms. **1970** MCNAUGHTON *Tat* 104 Next morning was sale day, and Stewart went to the saleyards with his hack and his dogs. **1982** KEENE *Myrtle & Sophia* 45 Sale Day was always exciting in Kaitaia—especially in those early times when wild frightened cattle from the most northerly stations.. were driven down the main road to the saleyards. **1991** *North & South* (Auckland) June 31 Some [relatives] appeared twice a week, some only on Sale Day at the stockyards.

saleyard.
1. [AND 1839 *pl.*] Usu. *pl.*, often as a collective. A set of conveniently situated pens from which a district's farm livestock is sold. See also YARD *n.* 1.
[*Note*] Saleyards were once to be found in most small towns and townships serving rural areas.
    1863 WALKER *Jrnl. & Lett.* (ATLTS) 30 June There was a free dinner to all comers in the [Otago] Provincial sale yards. **1870** *TrNZI* II. 219 The means for draining the swamp near the Remuera saleyards..have been provided. **1887** *Auckland Weekly News* 12 Feb. 8 Attached to his hotel there is half an acre of sale yards, at which periodical sales of stock take place. **1908** *Truth* 8 Feb. 1 Instead of going to the Addington saleyards..Topham quietly went down to Sumner. **1923** ANTHONY *Gus Tomlins* (1977) 6 I think now that the reason I got a cheap heifer that morning was because he had made up his mind that he could never get her as far as the saleyards. **1949** SCANLAN *Dusty Road* 10 The cows and sheep and horses and other farm stock were gathered into pens at the saleyard, and sold by auction. **1975** *NZJAg.* Sept. CXXXI. 61 Normally stud stock are sold either from yards on the farm itself, or by auction at recognized centrally situated saleyards. **1990** *Dominion Sunday Times* (Wellington) 30 Sept. 11 Mr Garnett recalls a long chase after a large Captain Cooker that had escaped from the city saleyards.
2. Special Comb. **saleyard rig**, a countryman's best clothes, stereotypically (and ironically) tweed coat and trousers, and hat with the brim turned down.
    1948 FINLAYSON *Tidal Creek* (1979) 100 In saleyard rigs or blazers or holiday frocks, Maori and pakeha..jostle around the booths.

sally-up, *n.* [Poss. f. Brit. dial. *sally* a dash, a sortie: see OED *sally n.*[1] and *v.*[2]; see also EDD *sallet n.* and *v.* a blow; to give a severe thrashing.] A stir-up; a scolding. Also used as a verb **to sally up**, to berate, to scold.
    1973 WALLACE *Generation Gap* 304 Mrs..Maclean rang me up and gave me a sally-up a few weeks ago... What did she sally you up about? **a1974** SYDER & HODGETTS *Austral. & NZ Eng.* (TS) 944 *A sally-up*. Brisk urging to hurry. 'I'll go back and give those stragglers a sally-up and try to hurry them along.'

salmon. Obs.

1. [Transf. use of *salmon* fam. Salmonidae for *Arripis trutta* fam. Arripidae.] Usu. with a modifier indicating either a New Zealand provenance as in **Maori (native, New Zealand) salmon**, or a saltwater habitat as in **sea salmon**. KAHAWAI 1.

1777 ANDERSON *Journal* Feb. in Cook *Journals* (1967) III. 808 Sometimes we got a sort of small Salmon, Gurnards, Skate and Nurses. **1838** POLACK *NZ* I. 322 Some deep banks lie off the east coast, on which the *kanai*, or mullet, *wapuka*, or cod-fish, and the *káháwai*, or colourless salmon, abound. **1842** HEAPHY *NZ* 48 The *Kawai*, or New Zealand Salmon, is esteemed by many as equal to the European species in excellence; it is of the same size, and much resembles it in appearance and taste. **1872** HUTTON & HECTOR *Fishes NZ* 105 Kahawai. This fish..is frequently termed the native Salmon, from its elegant form and lively habits. **1880** SENIOR *Travel & Trout* 202 At Tauranga I saw the first kahawai, or New Zealand salmon. *Ibid.* 291 I found the kahawai, or native salmon, a favourite object of sport. **1946** *JPS* LV. 149 *kahawai*, a sea-fish..sometimes called Maori salmon: vulg. ka(ha)wai, the 'h' suppressed. **1957** PARROTT *Sea Angler's Fishes* 169 Kahawai..Native Salmon; Sea Trout. **1966** DOOGUE & MORELAND *Sea Anglers' Guide* 236 Kahawai... Sea salmon, salmon, Australian salmon (Australia). **1986** PAUL *NZ Fishes* 92 Known principally by its Maori name, kahawai, in New Zealand and only occasionally (and erroneously, despite its scientific name) as sea trout or salmon.

2. As **salmon trout** [transf. use of Brit. *salmon-trout, Salmo trutta*], KAHAWAI 1.

1817 NICHOLAS *NZ* I. 88 In the [canoe's] cargo was also a very fine fish resembling the salmon trout, besides many others equally excellent. **1877** *TrNZI* IX. 488 Kahawai, Salmon... On the 24th..another Salmon Trout, 10½ lbs. weight, was caught in the Lower Harbour. **1978** NATUSCH *Acheron* 157 The 'salmon trout' as Chaseland called kahawai [c1851], showed no interest in English trout flies.

salt grass: see GRASS 2 (34).

salt lick: see LICK *n.*²

saltmarsh ribbonwood: see RIBBONWOOD 2 (3).

salubriate: see SALUBRIOUS.

salubrious, *a. Tramping.* [Spec. use of *salubrious* favourable or conducive to health: see esp. quot. 1958.] Pleasantly healthful, applied to pleasant, esp. sunny, weather and places.

[*Note*] The term was prob. coined by J.D. Pascoe when in Canterbury, and brought to Wellington to be adopted (with derivatives) by members of the Tararua Tramping Club, thence by other trampers.

1933 *Canterbury Mountaineer* 7 [J.D. Pascoe writes.] On the Whitehorn, it looked rather salubrious higher up. **1938** *Tararua Tramper* Aug. 5 Our Hutt Valley comrades are to be congratulated on the erection of this 'salubrious'..bivvy. **1941** *Canterbury Mountaineer* 73 It was not until 2.30 a.m. that we woke up the 'salubrious' sleepers in the hut. **1958** *Tararua* 28 To offset these rather gloomy expressions [about weather] there are those that derive from *salubrious*. They are J.D. Pascoe terms and were brought by him from Canterbury to Wellington. They obviously arose from the habit of describing sunny, pleasant weather or places as 'salubrious'. First is the *salubrium*, a rest or sunbake in salubrious conditions. This first appeared in *The Tramper* in 1937. About 1939 people were *salubriating*, or taking a *salube* in the sun. The previous year Te Matawai was described as a 'salube hut'. By 1943 trampers were sunbathing and *salubing*. So far as Tararuas are concerned, *salube* as a noun and a verb is the word that has survived. **1966** TURNER *Eng. Lang. Austral. & NZ* 161 *Salubrious*..became a common word for good weather and developed many derivatives, e.g. *salubing* 'sunbathing', *salubriating* 'taking a salube', and *salubrium* 'rest in the sun'.

Hence, by back-formation, **salubriate** *v. intr.*, to rest or relax in the sun; **salubrium** (occas. as **salube**) *n.* [*salub-* + a transf. use of Latin *-(r)ium* as in *atrium*], in early use, a pleasantly sunny place to rest or camp; later, a rest in the sun.

1934 *Canterbury Mountaineer* 31 Hearty approval was registered regarding Gran Clark's camp site, a truly alpine salubrium... We sunbathed, slept and tasted lotus for many hours. **1937** *Canterbury Mountaineer* 16 We ate and sunbathed, generally having a typical Pascoe 'high alpine salubrium'. **1937** *Tararua Tramper* Jan. 4 Salubrium over, we descended by the main Haast Ridge. *Ibid.* Oct. 3 [We] had 'brunch'; a salubrium on the menu, being two tins of pineapple which had frozen solid overnight. **1939** *Ibid.* Jan. 4 On top of the ridge, it'd be perfect for a salubrium (sorry, sun-bake). *Ibid.* Jan. 5 The sun shone forth and so we were able to salubriate in true pasconian [*sc.* John Pascoe] style. *Ibid.* Oct. 5 Sunday proved calm and sunny, a day even worthy of a Pascoe salube.

Sami /'sæmi/, *n.* A shortened, poss. derog., form of *Samoan*, a person from Samoa or of Samoan ancestry.

1982 NEWBOLD *Big Huey* (Gloss.) 253 Sami (n) Samoan.

sammie. [f. a pronunciation *sam*(wich + -IE: Ayto-Simpson, 1978.] A sandwich.

1995 *City Voice* (Wellington) 27 July 8 When I'm making school lunches or sammies to take to work, one of the ways to make them more interesting is to use different breads.

sammy: see SAMSON.

sammy. A shortened form of PORTSAMMY.

1910 *Truth* 8 Jan. 1 It was a venerable looking hansom, and the proprietor had just put a fare's 'sammy' on the top of the cab, when the elderly vehicle got tired and collapsed just where the shafts join the body.

Samoan. In special collocations.

1. Samoan cricket, a variant of English cricket orig. played in Samoa at village level and introduced into New Zealand by the Samoan community (see quot. 1987), spreading thence to other Pacific Island communities. Also called **kilikiti, kirikiti** [ad. *cricket*].

1987 *NZJH* Apr. 148 [Arthur Tyndall] was impressed by..the great abundance of amusements, Samoan cricket, singing, dancing and the King's Birthday sports at Apia. **1987** *Metro* (Auckland) May 110 Kilikiti: Samoan cricket bears about as much resemblance to the..territory of Lords as the sound of the word does to English... The bat—fashioned in triangular shape from the springy fau tree, decorated in gaudy splashes of colour and bound with coconut fibre—has nothing to do with the sissy wider blade of the willow. It's an out-and-out war club of such bold length... The ball, spun by hand from liquid rubber tapped from a living tree and compressed to rock-hard consistency, bounds down the pitch with a dangerously unpredictable velocity... [T]eams are of indefinite size—15 a side is considered a minimum for serious competitions... When the batting team reaches 35 runs, to keep the action alive, the teams swop over. **1991** *Evening Post* (Wellington) 28 Dec. 1 [Caption] Scorekeepers Elisapeta Fruean..and Elisapeta Paiaaua enjoyed the excitement of a game of Samoan cricket yesterday. **1996** *Evening Post* (Wellington) 6 Feb. 1 Waitangi Day celebrations turned a little sour for a group of Samoans and Tokelauans..involved in a dispute at Fraser Park... Police were called to the dispute between two large groups at a kirikiti tournament.

2. Samoan Force, the New Zealand military force occupying Samoa in 1914 (through to 1918).

1971 MCKEON *Fruitful Yrs.* 46 [c1914] In retrospect, the occupation of Samoa was in the nature of a picnic, but one must never lose sight of the fact that the Samoan Force was ready, bright and early.

samson. Also **sammy**. [Poss. f. a proprietary name.] A flatbed trolley for moving heavy objects, often balanced on a fulcrum of centrally-placed wheels. See also JIGGER 2 d.

c1950 Levin's Woolstores. Wellington (Ed.). *Samson* was the name given to a platform trolley balanced on central wheels, and used for moving bales of wool. **c1950** p.c. Ralph Wheeler (Wellington). A *sammy* is a cradle with a series of bearers or rollers underneath to move heavy weights and objects; also called a dolly. **1963** Sept. (Ed.) The name *samson* used by men shifting a grand piano at Victoria University, Sept. 1963, and applied to a small trolley about two feet long with a pair of centre-wheels, which was slid under the piano to take the weight. The men said the term had for years been commonly applied to all such balancing trolleys, and came originally from a brand-name *Samson* of a particular kind of trolley.

sand. In the names of plants and animals, see: CRAB 2 (2), DAPHNE, FLOUNDER *n.* 2 (9), LARK 2 (2), PLOVER 2 (5). See also SANDFISH, SANDFLY, SANDPIPER.

Sandager's parrotfish: see PARROTFISH 2 (3).

sandal: see *Maori sandal* (MAORI B 5 a), *native sandal* (NATIVE B 3 a), PARAERAE.

sandalwood.

1. Also **Maori (native, New Zealand) sandalwood**. MAIRE 1 b (*Mida salicifolia*).

1886 KIRK in *Settler's Handbook NZ* (1902) 122 [Native name] Maire..[Settlers' name] Sandalwood.. [Family] Jasmineae. **1889** KIRK *Forest Flora* 138 The wood of the New Zealand sandal-wood [*sc.* maire] is of a rich deep-brown hue, with darker streaks and markings, and an agreeable odour. **1896** *TrNZI* XXVIII. 497 The process would be closely analogous to that exhibited by the native sandalwood (*Fusanus cunninghamii*). **1906** [see MAIRE 1 b]. **1939** COCKAYNE & TURNER *Trees NZ* 79 *Mida myrtifolia*—syn. *Fusanus Cunninghamii* (Santalaceae). Maire, Sandalwood. **1940** LAING & BLACKWELL *Plants NZ* 153 (*Maori Sandalwood*). A small tree, with variable leaves. **1967** *Bull. Wellington Bot. Soc. No.34* 31 One shrub.. somewhat a rarity south of the Ohau River..is the sandalwood (Mida salicifolia).

2. bastard sandalwood. *Chatham Islands.* AKEAKE 1 (*Olearia traversii*).

1864 MUELLER *Vegetation of Chatham Is.* 19 *Eurybia Traversii* (Sect. cardiostigma)... A very beautiful not viscid tree..called inappropriately by the colonists Bastard Sandalwood-tree and passing under the native name 'Ake-Ake'. **1867** HOOKER *Handbook NZ Flora* 732 It [*sc. O. traversii*] forms the principal wood, and is called 'Ake-Ake' and 'Bastard Sandalwood-tree'. **1889** KIRK *Forest Flora* 47 Mr. H. Travers states that

SANDBAG DUFF

it [*sc.* akeake, *Olearia traversii*] is called 'bastard sandalwood-tree' by the settlers on Pitt Island. **1890** *PWD Catalogue Timbers* (NZ & South Seas Exhib.) 9 Akeake (bastard sandalwood)... Timber compact and heavy, valued in cabinet making and ornamental work; a native of the Chatham Islands

sandbag duff. *WW1.* An army pudding made from ground biscuit.
   1935 STRONG in Partridge *Slang Today* 287 I suppose he has been making it too hot lately and they have kept him in the line.—He will get plenty of sandbag duff up there. **1938** *Press* (Christchurch) (McNab Slang) 2 Apr. 18 [Slang of the N.Z.E.F.] 'Shell shock bread' and 'sandbag duff' were not much liked.

sand cracker: see THROWDOWN.

sandfish. *Gonorynchus gonorynchus* (fam. Gonorynchidae). See quot. 1982. See also *sand eel* (EEL 2 (6)).
   [*Note*] p.c. L.J. Paul, July 1994: The spelling of the scientific name given here seems to be the orig. Linnaean (1766, 12edn.) form, though other forms appear to have been in majority use since c1780.
   1927 PHILLIPPS *Bibliogr. NZ Fishes* (1971) 13 *Gonorhynchus gonorynchus* [*sic*] (Linnaeus). Sandfish. **1938** [see EEL 2 (6)]. **1940** PHILLIPPS *Fishes NZ* 13 Sand-fish *Gonorhynchus forsteri* (Ogilby)... The sandfish, also called sand-eel has a long eel-like body and large fins. **1956** GRAHAM *Treasury NZ Fishes* 399 Sandfish *Gonorhynchus forsteri* Ogilby. **1967** NATUSCH *Animals NZ* 207 The sand fish..is an eely-looking, sharp-snouted burrower in the sand. **1982** [see EEL 2 (6)]. **1986** PAUL *NZ Fishes* 55 *Sand fish*... None of its common names—sand fish, sand eel, beaked salmon— is particularly appropriate.

sandfly. [Extended use of Brit. *sandfly* of fam. Simuliidae, Psychodidae, and Ceratopogonidae.] *Austrosimulium* spp. (fam. Simuliidae), a common small black native fly. See also NAMU.
   1773 FORSTER *Resolution Jrnl.* 3 Apr. (1982) II. 246 We had been plagued all the time of our stay [at Dusky Bay] by a very minute black *Tipula alis incumbentibus* [1992 ed. note: ?'a fly of the *Tipula* genus with wings which attacks (?settles on) one': here wrongly assigned to the *Tipula* (cranefly) genus (HWO)], which the people called a *Sandfly*: its Sting is very painfull & causes..a most intolerable itching. **1791** BELL *Jrnl. Voyage H.M.S. 'Chatham'* (ATLMS) 51 Nor in short did we see any living thing on shore except the Birds— a small Sand fly—but this annoy'd us more than perhaps fifty animals wou'd. **1835** YATE *NZ* (1970) 72 A small sand-fly, not larger than a flea, but very noxious—its bite is sharp, and leaves an unpleasant itching for many hours. **1848** TAYLOR *Leaf from Nat. Hist.* xii The only noxious insects are the *namu*, a small black sand-fly, the *waeroa* or mosquito, and the small black spider. **1853** MACKIE *Traveller under Concern* 14 Feb. (1973) 79 Mosquitos and sand flies (a small black fly) I find very troublesome, they inflame my hands very much. **1888** PRESHAW *Banking Under Difficulties* 104 Sandflies (a little black fly which bites hard and raises a lump like a mosquito) being here in thousands. **1911** MORELAND *Through South Westland* 163 The fly in the ointment was the abominable sand-fly, which proved a veritable nuisance. **1929** MARTIN *NZ Nature Book I* 134 The first to claim attention are two of our..pernicious *Sandflies* (*Simulium caecutiens* and *S. australense*). **1946** [see NAMU]. **1969** KNOX *Nat. Hist. Canterbury* 485 In the family Simuliidae (sandflies) five of the seven species of *Austrosimulium* described from New Zealand occur in Canterbury. **1973** *NZ Entomologist* V. 336 In New Zealand, Simuliidae are called 'sandflies', a usage that has persisted since the voyages of exploration of Captain Cook between 1769 and 1775 (Dumbleton 1973). Throughout the remainder of the English-speaking world, Simuliidae are generally referred to as 'black flies', a name apparently of North American origin. **1986** ANDREWS *Southern Ark* 162 At long last that villain of so many previous expeditions, the sandfly—or more correctly the New Zealand Blackfly—was collected and later described and named.

sandhill fescue: see GRASS 2 (17) e.

sandpaper fish. ROUGHY 1.
   1939 *TrRSNZ* LXIX. 231 *Paratrachichthys trailli*... The Roughy or Sand-paper Fish..is not uncommon in trawler catches in New Zealand and southern Australia. **1956** GRAHAM *Treasury NZ Fishes* 177 The fish derives the common name of Roughy or Sandpaper-fish from its skin, which is as rough as the coarsest grade of sandpaper. **1966** DOOGUE & MORELAND *Sea Anglers' Guide* 213 Roughy... Other names: *Paratrachichthys trailli*; sandpaper fish (Australia). **1982** [see ROUGHY 1].

sandpaper suit. *Obs.* A school cadet uniform.
   1941 St Patrick's College, Silverstream. (Ed.) *Sandpaper suit*, a freq. term for the cadet uniform. **1983** *Evening Post* (Wellington) 29 July 12 Whatever happened to those 'sandpaper suits?'—the khaki shorts and battledress tunics worn by thousands of boys during the heyday of the school cadets. Most of the uniforms were manufactured during the Second World War and proved so durable that they were recycled... 'They were issued to a cadet, returned at the end of the year, drycleaned and given to another cadet,' said Major Don Stewart. He understood the uniforms went out of use some time in the 1960s. **1989** McGILL *Kiwi Baby Boomers* 53 In summer..secondary school lads were dressed in sandpaper suits and given a taste of..standing on parade. **1995** SLATTER *One More River* 48 On 3 September 1939..my khaki uniform was hanging..in the back bedroom, not the uniform of a real soldier but the 'sandpaper suit' of a secondary school cadet.

sandpiper. Transf. use of Brit. *sandpiper* a limicoline bird, not a plover nor a stilt, for any of several small migratory shore-birds, esp. members of the sub-family Calidrinae (fam. Scolopacidae).
   1841 BEST *Journal* 8 Mar. (1966) 280 Our guns procured us a plentiful supply of Sand pipers which were just then in excellent order. **1863** BUTLER *First Year* ix 134 The sand-piper is very like the lark in plumage. **1888** BARLOW *Kaipara* 138 We only secured there..a couple of New Zealand sandpipers. **1904** HUTTON & DRUMMOND *Animals NZ* 215 *The Red-necked Sandpiper. Limonites ruficollis*... *The Sandpiper. Heteropygia acuminata*. **1939** BEATTIE *First White Boy Born Otago* 120 There were sandpipers and waders along the Molyneux. **1984** SOPER *Birds NZ* 95 Sandpipers are small or medium-sized with straight tapered bills. Stints are tiny sandpipers. All arrive in New Zealand in September and depart in March.

sandwich.
1. In the phr. **to be a (one) sandwich short of a picnic**, to be intellectually deficient.
   1988 McGILL *Dict. Kiwi Slang* 96 *sandwich short of a picnic, a* a brick short of a load. **1990** *Contact* (Wellington) 15 June 7 You may think John Banks is one sandwich short of a picnic, but he has/is a good speechwriter.

2. Special Comb. **sandwich loaf** [used elsewhere, but recorded earliest in NZ: see OED *sandwich n.²* 3], an oblong loaf baked in an enclosed mould square in section, used esp. for making sandwiches.
   1934 *Bread Baking in NZ* [Caption] Large Flat or Sandwich Loaf. **1982** FRAME *To the Is-land* (1984) 58 I ran home for lunch each day, stopping only at Mrs Feather's corner store to collect the freshly baked sandwich loaf.

sandy-back. *Shearing.* Also **sandy cobbler.** A sheep with sand or other gritty matter in its wool. See also COBBLER $n.^1$ 1.
   1955 BOWEN *Wool Away* 157 Sandy Back. A sheep with sand, grit or dirt in the back wool. **1960** MASTERS *Back-Country Tales* 257 On strolling along and glancing casually into Syke's catching pen, I noticed that he had eight tough looking, old sandy-backs in it. **1972** McLEOD *Mountain World* (Gloss.) 310 *Sandy-backs*: Sheep which have rubbed sand and stones into the wool by scratching under banks. **1982** *Agric. Gloss.* (MAF) 58 *Sandyback*: Sheep with sand, grit, or dirt in the back wool. **1989** *NZ Eng. Newsletter* III. 23 It was a simple transfer to use the term 'cobbler' or 'sandy cobbler' to describe a rough hard sheep at any time.
   Hence **sandy-backed** *ppl. a.*, applied to a sheep with gritty matter in its fleece.
   1953 STRONACH *Musterer on Molesworth* 29 The wethers were sandy-backed and hard shearing—things sounded busy at the station! **1960** MASTERS *Back-Country Tales* 256 Frank Nurse and the musterers..kept the tough old sandy-backed wethers well out of sight and gave the five of us..some nice little hoggets to start on.

sandy cobbler: see SANDY-BACK.

sandy hooker. *South Island mustering.* [Perh. f. a poss. nickname *Sandy Hook* for Farewell Spit, a long, 24-km sickle-shaped sand-spit, a feature of n.w. Nelson.] A Nelson musterer.
   1941 BAKER *NZ Slang* 59 In the slang of Canterbury and Marlborough shepherds, *sandy hooker* is used for a Nelson musterer. **1953** STRONACH *Musterer on Molesworth* 11 The general plan of our muster was this: down each spur went one man... One of the Nelson chaps—the 'Sandy Hookers', as they were called— took the first spur. *Ibid.* 32 Good. I'll show these Sandy Hookers some speed. **1968** TOMLINSON *Remembered Trails* 128 Nelson men in Marlborough and North Canterbury used to be called Sandy Hookers. **1988** McGILL *Dict. Kiwi Slang* 96 *Sandy Hookers* people from Nelson; after Farewell Spit.

sante /sænti/. [Perh. f. a proprietary name: ad. French *santé* health.] **a.** As **sante bar**, a small bar of dark chocolate.
   c**1938** Marlborough (Ed.) Used of a popular small bar of chocolate costing a penny, manufactured by the confectionery and biscuit firm, Griffins & Sons. **1948** BALLANTYNE *Cunninghams* (1976) 30 He bought a penny sante bar. **1974** PRESTON *Lady Doctor* 11 The cost of these outings [c1920]..and also the..one santé bar of chocolate apiece..was..half-a-crown per term. **1983** HENDERSON *Down from Marble Mountain* 98 An ideal place..to eat..a precious Sante bar of chocolate.

b. As **sante biscuits**, a sweet biscuit made from chopped up sante bars in a biscuit mix.
   1966 *Edmonds Cookery Book* 34 [Also 1978 edn. 47] Santé Biscuits... Butter..Flour..Sugar..Sweetened Condensed Milk..Baking Powder..*Dark* Chocolate... Cream butter, sugar and condensed milk... Add dry ingredients and chopped chocolate. Roll into small balls... Flatten with a fork. Bake.

sao cracker. [A proprietary name registered by Griffin's Foods, an acronym of *Salvation Army*

Ordinance.] A plain, unsweetened, square cracker biscuit having usu. less fat in its recipe than, for example, a 'cream cracker'. See quot. 1994.

c1939 Sao cracker known to the editor as a popular name used in Marlborough for a square cracker-type biscuit. **1989** McGill *Kiwi Baby Boomers* 73 We used to have Sao biscuits whistling contests. You'd eat the biscuits, which were very dry, then try to whistle. **1994** p.c. Mr Peter Chaney of Griffin's Foods. The formulation for *sao cracker* was brought to New Zealand by an English chemist in the 1930s. It was originally called *Salvation Army Ordinance* being for a biscuit made very cheaply as a food for poor people. It is a proprietary name registered in New Zealand by Griffin's Foods, and by Arnott's in Australia (where it is the largest selling cracker biscuit but formulated nearer the New Zealand 'cream cracker').

sardine. [Spec. use of *sardine* a small fish of the herring family.] Any of several small marine fish, esp. PILCHARD (*Sardinops neopilchardus*).

1849 *NZ Jrnl.* IX. 125 English Name Sprat or sardine. Native Name Aua. **1872** [see PILCHARD]. **1892** *TrNZI* XXIV. 204 *Catlin's River*—Mullet (sea), flounders, sole, sardines. **1918** *NZJST* I. 136 The sardine (*Sardinia neopilchardus*) is found in all the coastal waters. **1924** *NZJST* VII. 191 During the month of July, 1924, Wellington harbour was visited by an enormous shoal of pilchards, or sardines. **1945** *Korero* (AEWS Background Bulletin) 15 Jan. 18 Before the war a few hours in Queen Charlotte Sound would keep the fishermen in sardines for a month. **1950** *Fisheries General Regs.* (1956 reprint, 16) [2] 'Sardine' means the fish of which the scientific name is *Sardinia neopilcharda*, also known as the Picton herring. **1986** Paul *NZ Fishes* 40 *Pilchard. Sardinops neopilchardus...* Sometimes called the sardine.

sark. [Poss. a transf. use of Sc. dial. *sark* a woman's undergarment: SND 3.] A sanitary napkin.

1989 Te Awekotuku *Tahuri* 68 'What are these for?'..'Sark... You know..for us women when we have the rags on.' Ibid. 103 sarks: sanitary napkins

sarsaparilla. [Transf. use of *sarsaparilla*, esp. *Sarsaparilla smilax* (fam. Smilacaceae) and the preparations made from it.] Usu. as **bush (native, New Zealand) sarsaparilla**, (a medicinal concoction or tonic made from the root of the) SUPPLEJACK 1 a.

[**1906** Cheeseman *Manual NZ Flora* 703 *R[hipogonum] scandens...Supplejack...* an extract from the root has been employed in the place of sarsaparilla.] **1867** Hooker *Handbook* 768 Sarsaparilla, native. *Rhipogonum scandens*. **1883** Brett's *Colonists' Guide* 481 The roots [of supplejack]..are beaten into a pulp, and steeped in a little water; the decoction..is taken in cases of severe rheumatism... (It has been called the bush sarsaparilla). Females drink the decoction to procure abortion. **1889** Neil *Family Herb Doctor* (1980) 41 The supple jack is our New Zealand Sarsaparilla, not unlike it in outward appearance. **1907** Laing & Blackwell *Plants NZ* 93 The roots of the Rhipogonum are used by bushmen as a medicine, and the plant is sometimes called 'Bush Sarsaparilla'. **1948** Irvine-Smith *Streets of My City* 33 In times of accident and sickness the native flora supplied a whole pharmacopoeia..soothing drinks from the houhere and bush sarsaparilla from the supplejack.

sarvo. Also **s'arvo.** Ellipt. for *this arvo*, this afternoon.

1968 *NZ Contemp. Dict. Suppl.* (Collins) 17 *sarvo, this arvo..* corruption of *this afternoon.* **1976** *Evening Post* (Wellington) 29 June 14 *S'arvo..* words and sayings sent in by 'Tuesdate' readers—things their parents said when they were at school.

satchel-snatching. Also **satchel-snatch.** The reference is to a cause-célèbre of the 1940s, when a satchel containing a potentially politically damaging letter was stolen ('snatched') from the car of Cecil W. Holmes, a left-wing public servant, by a colleague who wished to ingratiate himself with the authorities.

1949 *Here & Now* Oct. 26 The 'Satchel-Snatching Section' of the Prime Minister's department is a label likely to stick. **1976** Sinclair *Nash* 277 The famous 'satchel snatch' was one of the few occasions when Nash—then acting Prime Minister and acting Minister in charge of Police—had a central role in such an illiberal act.

sausage-sizzle. The open-air cooking of sausages either at campfires or on barbecues often as part of a demonstration or promotion of a product, or as a fund-raising occasion.

1971 Ogilvie *Moonshine Country* 135 These excursions [*sc.* evening eel-hunts] can be both exciting and pleasurable especially if followed by a riverside camp-fire and sausage-sizzle. **1986** *Listener* 5 July 79 There are quickfire raffles, cups of tea in the tea tent and a sausage sizzle outside. **1991** *Dominion* (Wellington) 22 Nov. 13 Peter Leitch, aka The Mad Butcher, will star at a sausage sizzle tomorrow morning to mark the official opening of the Kingsway Carpet Centre. **1996** *Sunday Star-Times* 7 Jan. A1 We'll be putting together ACT's [*sc.* a right-wing political party] 'sausage' with some other people's 'sizzle'. I'd be surprised if the party's name changes [on any amalgamation with another political party].

sausie /'sɒsi/. Also **sossie.** [f. *saus*(age + -IE.] A familiar name for a sausage.

1994 *City Voice* (Wellington) 15 Dec. 25 Whack another sausie on the Barbie, mate! Ibid. 27 The usual nutritious selection of..candy-floss and glistening sossies.

savage, *n.* and *a. Obs.*

A. *n.* Used freq. during the nineteenth century, and occas. in the twentieth, not necessarily pejoratively, of a Maori. Cf. CANNIBAL.

1804 Collins *Eng. Colony in NSW* 350 These two worthy savages (if the term may be allowed) will, I am confident, ever retain the most grateful remembrance of the kindness they received on Norfolk Island. **c1835** Boultbee *Journal* (1986) 76 I had now become tired of spending my time to no purpose, and amongst wild savages, where I felt myself like one cast away. **1840** Watkin *Journal* 5 June in McNab *Old Whaling Days* (1913) 486 The inhabitants of this Island [*sc.* southern South Island] in common with some savages are very superstitious. **c1875** *Otago Guardian* in Tonkin *Dunedin Gaol* (1980) 16 Altogether some 76 rebel savages were transferred to Dunedin gaol, among them being the chief Tauraū. **1901** Chudleigh *Diary* 9 Sept. (1950) 407 Himeona is building a whare... He is a most elated old savage now. **1939** Grieve *Sketches from Maoriland* (1961) 85 [With the introduction of a school bus service] my Infant Room was inundated with a weird assortment of little savages straight out of the bush. **1940** Cowan *Sir Donald Maclean* 42 Te Rangihaeata rose, a tall gaunt savage in appearance, clothed in a dogskin mat. **1963** Pearson *Coal Flat* 43 I'm a full Maori and proud, too... Old Mum she meant I'm still a savage, that's what she meant. Just quietly, eh? *Haka* and *tangi*.

Hence **savagery** *n.*, a perceived pre-European condition of the Maori.

1959 Sinclair *Hist. NZ* 112 As with most similar [*sc.* to the Kingite] movements, there was a dark and primitive strain in Maori nationalism. Some Maoris longed to drive the settlers into the sea so that they could return to ancient savagery.

B. *adj.* Pertaining to the Maori perceived as a primitive, but often noble, non-European.

1831 Williams *Early Jrnls.* 30 Oct. (1961) 199 Many new things have they heard today, surprising in their savage ears. May the Lord bless and sanctify the same to them. **1856** Shortland *Traditions & Superstitions* 212 These works, and many others requiring great and continued labour, have been often cause of wonder to foreigners, who were surprised to find a savage people able to accomplish them. **1858** *Memo. by Responsible Advisers on Native Affairs* in Rutherford *Sel. Documents* (1949) 104a.5 The [native] race, it is said, is irredeemably savage. **1859** [see CIVILIZE v.]. **1862** *Otago Witness* (Dunedin) 23 Aug. 2 Statesmen could learn very readily the peculiar characteristics of the Maori, and when he contemplated these characteristics he knew of no savage race which could make such progress in a life-time. **1924** Lysnar *NZ* 65 Few savage races were greater adepts in the art of canoe-building than the Maoris. **1933** Scanlan *Tides of Youth* 107 Erena's [*sc.* a beautiful half-caste Maori] mother, even into middle-age, retained that native aristocratic bearing which marked out the rulers of this savage race.

Hence **half-savage**, of New Zealand, only partly under European cultural and social influence.

1930 Reischek *Yesterdays in Maoriland* (1933) 7 Perhaps, also, he will help to remind them how good, how strenuous life was 'in the good old days,' when their Dominion was still half-savage, still unsettled after the toughest of colonial wars.

sawbelly. silver roughy (ROUGHY 1).

1979 [see ROUGHY 1]. **1986** Paul *NZ Fishes* 71 *Silver roughy. Hoplostethus mediterraneus*. Sometimes called sawbelly, from a row of enlarged scales along the belly midline.

saw-doctor. *Sawmilling.* [f. Brit. dial. or provincial use: see EDD *saw* 1 (North. Ireland).] A sawmill employee who maintains and repairs saws.

1901 *Awards, etc.* 8 [North Auckland Timber-Workers Award] Men in charge of main goose-saws, 7s... saw-doctor, £3 per week. **1920** *Quick March* 10 Nov. 11 'What reminds you,' interrupted the saw-doctor. **1923** *Awards, etc.* 111 [Westland Timber Yards and Sawmill Employees] [Rates of wages] Engine-driver, second class [£]3 15[s.] 0[d.] Saw-doctor 5 5 0 Wagon-drivers 4 5 0. **1938** *Auckland Weekly News* 23 Nov. 96 I'm a dinkum saw-doctor, too, though I sez it meself. **1944** *Korero* (AEWS Background Bulletin) 8 May 28 An interesting section of any mill is the 'saw-doctor's' shop. **1983** Bremer *Port Craig* 23 One..very important part of the mill was the saw doctor's workshop. **1988** Hill *More from Moaville* 61 Loft was a saw-doctor as well. Any sort of saw—anything he could get his teeth into—rip saws, cross-cut saws, circular saws, chain saws.

Also as a *vbl. n.* **saw-doctoring,** the work of keeping mill saws in good condition.

1951 *Awards, etc.* 453 [Westland Timber-Workers Award] [Rates of wages] Leading yardman 4[s.] 4[d.] Sawdoctoring and sharpening 4 7 [per hour].

sawyer. *Bushmen.* [f. the scraping or sawing sound it makes.] tree weta (WETA 2 (5)).

1885 *Wairarapa Daily* 23 Dec. 2 The so-called mosquito was a 'Weita' or 'Ti-tree Sawyer' which is found at times in this district and is very common in Auckland and other provinces. It is called a scorpion by some settlers, and is considered to be poisonous. 1898 MORRIS *Austral-English* 404 *Sawyer, n.* (1) Name applied by bushmen in New Zealand to the insect *Weta*. c1930 *Whitcombe's Etym. Dict. Aust.-NZ Supplement* 10 *sawyer n.* a large New Zealand grass-hopper. 1941 BAKER *NZ Slang* 46 *Sawyer*, a bush nickname for the repulsive grasshopper called *weta* by the Maoris. 1951 p.c. R.Gilberd (Okaihau). The old bushmen..called a 'weta' a 'sawyer' [but] none of us younger chaps. You know the noise it makes at night—krrar-krrar... That's where it got the name.

sax. *Obs.* [f. a (?joc.) shortening of (stage) Scottish dial. *sax*(pence.] A sixpenny piece. Cf. ZACK.

1943 BENNETT *English in NZ* in *Amer. Speech* XVIII. 91 In New Zealand slang a penny is a *brown*, a threepenny piece a *thray*..a sixpence a *sax*, presumably from Scottish *saxpence*.

scab. *Hist.* [An ancient name for a once common sheep disease of special significance in early pastoral NZ: first recorded from c1386 in Chaucer's *Canterbury Tales* (see OED *scab* 2).]

1. A contagious disease of sheep formerly rife esp. in the South Island (see esp. quot. 1967).

1848 DEANS *Pioneers* (1964) 49 The scab broke out among our sheep in the beginning of autumn, but we gave them a thorough dressing, and I think they are now quite clean. 1851 *Lyttelton Times* 14 June 6 The scab in sheep is the pest of all the settlements of Australia and New Zealand. 1883 *Brett's Colonists' Guide* 174 *Scab*.—It spreads among sheep, not so much by direct contact as by means of the rubbing places, and is caused and propagated by minute insects called *acari*. 1890 *Otago Witness* (Dunedin) 8 May 36 The station owners were..Mr. Anderson (called the 'father of the scab'). 1902 *Settler's Handbook NZ* (Lands Dept.) 98 Scab is now eradicated. 1967 RICKARD *Strangers in Wilderness* 102 Scab, the worst menace, was an ailment of sheep caused by a tiny mite which burrowed beneath the skin and lived on the tissues there, setting up an intolerable irritation in the process... The disease was highly contagious:.. Scab was noticed in Australia in the 1830s and was brought from there to New Zealand where its first reported appearance was in Nelson in 1845. It had spread to the Wairarapa by 1846; to Riccarton, where the Deans brothers discovered it among some of their sheep, by 1848; and to Banks Peninsula by 1850... Scab was not finally eliminated from New Zealand until 1892 when D'Urville Island, where it had lingered longest, was pronounced clean. 1992 *Dominion* (Wellington) 21 Mar. 14 The scab boiler sheds produced a hell-brew based on tobacco leaves, into which sheep were slung to rid them of the dreaded mange mite.

Hence **scab** *v. trans.*, to infect (sheep) with scab; **scabbed** *ppl.a.*, SCABBY *a.* 1.

1969 MCCASKILL *Molesworth* 72 Fuhrmann..would have in turn to sue Acton-Adams, whose Tarndale sheep had [c1884] 'scabbed' the Molesworth flock. 1849 PHARAZYN *Journal* (ATLMS) 269 Pronounced Ewe to be **scabbed**. 1938 BURDON *High Country* 79 It is notorious that, whereas the whole of the province of Nelson is scabbed, Canterbury is clean.

2. a. Special Comb. **scab-hunter**, a hunter once paid to find and kill scabby sheep; **scab-inspector**, an official formerly charged with the duty of inspecting flocks and farms for scab.

1968 TOMLINSON *Remembered Trails* 56 It was on Mt Patriarch [Marlborough]..that the last scabby sheep was killed by the '**scab hunters**'. Ibid. 119 The first man to own land at the head of Lake Rotoiti was Hans Fanselow, a German who is believed to have been a sheep **scab inspector** during the scab years. 1863 CHUDLEIGH *Diary* 3 Nov. (1950) 108 Arthur had to go to Lyttelton to get a clean certificate from the scab inspector. 1939 BEATTIE *First White Boy Born Otago* 153 Logie, the Scab Inspector [c1860 Central Otago], had only one eye, but it was a very good one.

b. As **scab-infected** *a.*, SCABBY *a.* 1.

1938 BURDON *High Country* 85 Quite apart from the long, expensive business of dipping scab-infected sheep, the lack of wire fences entailed constant vigilance. 1976 VANCE *Bush, Bullocks & Boulders* 36 If sheep were driven through scab-infected country, there was a danger of the sheep contracting the disease.

scabby, *a.*

1. [f. SCAB + -Y.] Of a sheep, infected with scab; of a property or run, having scab among its sheep.

1851 *Lyttelton Times* 19 July 1 Wanted to purchase, 500 scabby sheep, to depasture at Rhodes Bay. 1865 BARKER *Station Life* (1870) 35 This fine station is in technical parlance, 'scabby', and although of course great precautions are taken, still some 10,000 sheep had an ominous large S on them. c1875 MEREDITH *Adventuring in Maoriland* (1935) 145 A little further up the [East] coast the Maoris have a flock of very 'scabby' sheep, which roam over a large area of land. 1885 ACTON-ADAMS in McCaskill *Molesworth* (1969) 57 I hear that Molesworth may lose its certificate through having scabby sheep from Kekerangu. 1939 BEATTIE *First White Boy Born Otago* 153 I never have to do with scabby sheep, and mine is a hearsay knowledge. 1946 ACLAND *Early Canterbury Runs* 122 On one occasion [a1880] Mr Reed..was taking a mob of sheep out to one of the paddocks when he met two 'commercials' (swaggers). One of them said to him 'Good day, mate, is old Scabby at home?' (He went by the name of 'Scabby'.) 1968 [see SCAB 2 a].

2. scabby mouth. [See OED *scabby* 1 a, 1938.] A viral disease of sheep characterized by ulceration around the mouth.

1950 *NZJAg.* Aug. LXXXI. 100 On farms where scabby mouth occurs each new crop of lambs should be vaccinated, and this is most conveniently done at marking. 1961 *Merriam-Webster Third International* 2022 *scabby mouth n, Austral & NewZeal*: Sore mouth.

scabweed. Also **native scabweed.** [Cf. OED *scabwort.*] Any of several mat-forming daisy species of the genus *Raoulia* (fam. Asteraceae), pioneering plants of coastal gravels, river sands and alpine places. Cf. PATCH-PLANT.

1922 *NZJST* IV. 281 Now in many parts even the hardy tussock..has disappeared, leaving the earth bare, or perhaps occupied by the native scabweed (*Raoulia lutescens*). 1936 BELSHAW et al. *Agric. Organiz. NZ* 365 This [Central Otago] country in its natural state carries a very poor type of vegetation..where scabweed..may form the dominant cover. 1944 *Bull. Wellington Bot. Soc. No.9* 3 The scabweed [of Central Otago]..really appears to be painted on the earth. 1955 BAXTER *Fire & Anvil* 78 It survives many droughts... Like the scabweed in Central Otago. 1969 MCCASKILL *Molesworth* 154 The oldest part of the infested ground is distinguished by the rabbit's unmistakable trade mark—the great circular, silvery or green, dense, low cushions of the scabweed. 1978 *Manawatu Tramping Club Jubilee* 89 Scabweeds cover the rocks [in the Waimakariri country]... The downy seeds of the scabweeds fill the hollows like swansdown. 1988 DAWSON *Forest Vines to Snow Tussocks* 150 The tussocks were largely replaced by grey patches of *Raoulia australis*, unflatteringly termed 'scabweed'.

scale, *n.* Goldmining. [AND *Obs.* 1851.] A flake of gold; also as **scale gold**, alluvial gold found as flakes.

1852 *NZGG* 9 Nov. V. 26:165 (Gold Discovery in Coromandel) A panful was taken from about two feet below the surface and washed, it produced a number of scales of gold. 1857 *Lyttelton Times* 5 Sept. 4 We yesterday saw a small specimen of scale Gold said to be found by a sawyer named Jones. c1861 STACK in Reed *Annals Early Dunedin* (1973) 15 The gold is what is called 'scale', in little flat pieces, varying in size from a pin's head to a threepenny bit. 1879 HAAST *Geol. Canterbury & Westland* 84 They [sc. the colours] were generally thin, small scales, often only slightly rolled, and could not, therefore have been brought any distance.

Hence **scaly** *a.*, of gold, characteristically flaky.

1861 [see SHOTTY *a.*]. 1862 LINDSAY *Place & Power Nat. Hist. in Coloniz.* 12 The gold here is very fine, scaley or granular, generally in mere specks. 1879 HAAST *Geol. Canterbury & Westland* 85 The wash gold is fine, scaly, and very much rolled. 1887 PYKE *Hist. Early Gold Discoveries Otago* (1962) 12 The late Mr. John Hyde Harris showed me a small quantity of fine scaly gold, which he informed me was obtained in 1853. 1890 *Otago Witness* (Dunedin) 6 Mar. 18 Some coarse scaly gold is from Quartz Reef Point, Clutha River.

scale, *v.*

1. [f. Brit. dial. *scale* to depart (hurriedly): see EDD *v.* 31.] *intr.* To rush, go fast.

1917 24 Feb. in Miller *Camps, Tramps & Trenches* (1939) 29 We had to scale for the 10.16 to town.

Hence **scale** *n.*, a hurried departure often to avoid debts or responsibilities, esp. as **do a scale**.

c1926 [see SCALER a].

2. a. [AND 1904.] To swindle or cheat (a person); to steal (a thing).

1937 PARTRIDGE *Dict. Slang* 730 scale... To steal (a thing), rob (a person): New Zealanders': C. 20. 1941 BAKER *NZ Slang* 62 When we are taken down financially we are *scaled*.

Hence **scaling** *vbl. n.*, swindling, esp. in a context of a bookmaker cheating or welshing on bets.

1912 *Truth* 22 June 4 The origin of the term 'scaling' is not definitely known, but it conjures up the spectacle of Isaac Moses flying with full bag before the wrath of infuriated punters, who backed the winner in the last race. It is also known as 'balancing'.

b. To cheat on the payment of a fare by deliberately over-riding the end of a fare-section during urban train or bus (and formerly, tram) travel.

1951 p.c. F.M. O'Brien (Wellington). Used by Wellington tramwaymen. *Scale*: to over-ride the distance paid for as a fare. *scaler*: one who over-rides the fare paid. 1968 *NZ Contemp. Dict. Suppl.* (Collins) 17 *scale, scale a ride v.t.* and *i.* ride on a tram, bus or other vehicle without paying whence, *scaler.* 1988 MCGILL *Dict. Kiwi Slang* 96 *scale* disappear quickly or furtively, to steal or rob; originally from scaling a ride on trams or trains, or taking a free ride.

scaler. [f. SCALE *v.*] **a.** [AND 1915.] A cheat, *spec.* one who bilks a prostitute.

1907 *Truth* 12 Jan. 5 Indeed, one girl in that same district did succumb to that same storekeeper only to find, after the Chinaman had sated his lust on her, that he was a 'scaler' who laughed at her for a soft fool and who refused to give her sixpence, let alone a tenner. **c1926** The Mixer *Transport Workers' Song Book* 5 *The Scaler*: He hates to pay his Union fees And holds out to the last... He's not the man to say 'goodbye' Before he hits the trail He waits until his dues are due The bloke who does a scale.

b. A bookmaker who decamps without paying out.
1908 *Truth* 8 Feb. 2 It was a win for the racing clubs in general to know that there was a 'scaler' amongst the bookmakers at Pahiatua, as it will have the effect of driving money into the machine where the punters know they will get paid.

c. Among criminals, one who decamps with his mates' share of the loot.
1932 in Partridge *Dict. Underworld* (1961) 596 A burglar, or other criminal, that decamps with a confederate's share of the loot: New Zealand since ca. 1920 and, after ca. 1935, Australia: 1932, Nelson Baylis (private letter). **1941** Baker *NZ Slang* 52 Underworld slang [includes]..a *scaler*, a criminal who absconds with his partner's share of the booty.

d. One who cheats on a fare on a bus or tram. See scale *v.* 2 b.

scallop /ˈskæləp/, /ˈskɒləp/. Any of various species of usu. edible bivalves of the family Pectinidae that do not attach themselves but swim rapidly by opening and closing their fluted shell valves, esp. the commercially harvested **queen scallop** *Pecten novaezelandiae*, the smaller cold water scallop *Chlamys delicatula* now occas. also marketed as queen scallop, and the **fan scallop** or **fan shell** *Chlamys zelandiae*. Also *attrib*.
1773 Wales *Journal* in Cook *Journals* (1961) II. 787 Amongst the crustaceous Tribes we found Crawfish..Scollops [sic], Whelks, Periwinkles. **1924** Bucknill *Sea Shells NZ* 92 *Pecten zelandiae*... The most brilliantly coloured of all the scallops, this beautiful little species, commonly known as the Fan Shell, is from half an inch to an inch and a-half in height. **1947** Davin *For Rest of Our Lives* 8 The smoke of the cigarette he had just stubbed stinking up from the scollop [sic] ashtray. **1947** Powell *Native Animals* 20 Queen Scallop... This is the large scallop with one valve convex and the other one flat... Fan Scallop (*Chlamys zelandiae*). A small scaly ribbed shell of two equally convex valves. It is brilliantly coloured. **1966** *Encycl. NZ* III. 177 Queen scallops are our most delicately flavoured shellfish. The Maori name is tipa. **1970** Penniket *NZ Sea Shells in Colour* 76 Queen Scallop (*Pecten novaezelandiae*), 3in. This large handsome shell..is a favourite culinary delicacy and is fished commercially at Nelson. **1981** *Catch '81* Sept. 9 A considerable amount of interest has been shown recently in the possibility of scallop farming in New Zealand. **1990** *Dominion Sunday Times* (Wellington) 26 Aug. 1 Poachers cross Cook Strait in high-speed boats to pluck scallops from the Nelson area for sale to Wellington restaurants.

scalping, *vbl.n. Gang members*. [Transf. or fig. use from *scalp v.* to take the scalp (of an enemy) as a trophy.] See quot.
1996 *Sunday Star-Times* 3 Feb. A2 Detective Constable Brett Watene, the Tokoroa police iwi liaison officer, said beating and taking the patch of a rival gang member is known as scalping—and regarded as a declaration of war.

scaly: see scale *n.*

scamperdown: see whale 2 (15).

Scandy, *n.* and *a.* [f. *Scand*(inavian + -y.]
A. *n.* A Scandinavian.
1887 *Auckland Weekly News* 23 July 21 I am told the 'Scandies' lived on the rabbit. **1912** Baughan *Brown Bread* 126 A whole tribe of little 'Scandies'. **1951** Lochore *From Europe to NZ* 16 If any continental Europeans have ever been popular in this country it is the 'Scandies'. **1968** Slatter *Pagan Game* 161 Erik, the scandalous Scandy from the Skagerrak. **1987** Gee *Prowlers* 41 The place is full of Yanks and Scandies with flags sewn on their back packs.

B. *adj.* Scandinavian.
1902 *NZ Illustr. Mag.* V. 489 He got on his horse..and went a mile down the metal to spend the night with some Scandy friends. **1912** Baughan *Brown Bread* 121 The Scandinavian settler, to whom [the house] belonged, industrious and 'fore-handed' as Scandy settlers are wont to be, had already finished his milking.

Hence **Scandywagon** *obs.*, former local Pahiatua district term for a wagon home-made by Scandinavian settlers (see quot.).
1995 Winter *All Ways Up Hill* 162 [The Scandinavian settlers] were a thrifty and ingenious people who bought nothing they could make... They made butter churns, and most notable of all, 'Scandywaggons'. These were strange contraptions with wheels shaped out of rata vine, or slices off a round log, pegged across the grain to prevent splitting, with fencing-wire tyres. They saved a lot of heavy carrying by replacing manpower with horse or bullock.

scarce as frog's feathers: see frog *n.*[1] 4.

Scarecrow Ministry. *Hist.* Also **scarecrow Cabinet.** The nickname of a makeshift Ministry holding power from c1887–91.
1888 *NZPD* LX. 511 He [sc. Atkinson] formed what they are pleased to call 'a scarecrow Cabinet', and of this they have been prating ever since. **1891** *NZPD* LXXIII. 491 He put a Ministry on those benches which was called in a Conservative newspaper 'a scarecrow Ministry'. **1963** Chapman & Sinclair *Studies of a Small Democracy* 102 [Heading] The Significance of 'The Scarecrow Ministry', 1887-91. *Ibid.* 118 In the end Atkinson formed what the free traders called 'a scarecrow Cabinet', leaving out most of his old friends. **1971** *NZ's Nature Heritage* IV. 1312 The Cabinet he [sc. Harry Atkinson] patched together was so makeshift that it was called 'the Scarecrow Ministry' but it remained in office because there was no alternative. **1985** *Dominion* (Wellington) 2 Mar. 9 With amazing resilience Harry Atkinson was back in the premier's seat in 1887 to lead what was disparagingly dubbed The Scarecrow Ministry. **1990** *DNZB* I. 9 [Atkinson's] leadership [c1887–91] of the so-called 'Scarecrow' ministry was insecure and led to defeat.

scarf, *v.* [Prob. a var. of Brit. dial. *carf n.* a cut ('carve'), recorded in 19th c. Australia in the sense 'scarf' (see AND), influenced by *scarf v.* to cut a scarf-joint in timber: see OED *v.*[2], *n.*[5], *v.*[3]]
[Note] The noun *scarf* is in general forestry (1861 US) and whaling (1851 US) use: see OED *n.*[5]

1. *Whaling.* [Used elsewhere but recorded earliest from the NZ coast.] *trans.* To make a 'scarf' or horizontal incision in (the blubber of a whale).
1836 *Piraki Log* 23 May (1911) 36 Sent three boats out to tow but could do no good in consequence of their being too much wind—scarfed her.

2. *Logging.* **a.** *trans.* [AND 1909.] To make a 'scarf' or incision (in a standing tree) to determine the direction of fall. See also dip *v.* 1.
1899 Bell *In Shadow of Bush* 83 [The big rimu] fell, driving before it in its line of fall a dozen or so of the smaller trees, which had been 'scarfed' or cut partly through in readiness. **1904** Lancaster *Sons o' Men* 165 [He] scarfed the timber for the saw [which was to make the back-cut]. **1947** 'belly scarf', 'back scarf' [see drive *n.*[1] 2]. **1983** Lambert *Illustr. Hist. of Taranaki* 83 [Caption] Here, two axemen chopping from jiggers, have begun to scarf a large tawa. **1986** Owen & Perkins *Speaking for Ourselves* 62 As regards felling ability, take scarfing; when you scarf a tree you scarf it in the direction it is going to fall, and the bottom cut, the underswing of the cut, is level.

b. *absol.* To cut a scarf in a standing tree.
1972 Newton *Wake of Axe* 155 [Axemen] usually worked in gangs of four, and a gang would sometimes scarf for a full week before they let the 'king' tree go... A certain defined area would be 'scarfed' i.e. each tree in that area would have a scarf cut in it to the point where it was about to fall.

Hence **scarfer**, the member of a logging team expert in scarfing trees; **scarfing** *vbl. n.* [AND 1938].
1943 Bennett *English in NZ* in *Amer. Speech* XVIII. 85 Other [timber-trade] terms..*scarfer.* **1951** *Awards, etc.* 520 [Marlborough Timber-Workers Award] [Rates of wages] Other crosscutter and scarfer 4[s.] 2[1/4][d.] Breaker-out, snigger, ropeman (hauling rope), to apply to only one man in each hauling team 4 4[1/2]. **1961** Crump *Hang On a Minute Mate* 42 [During the next few weeks] Jack learned about scarfing, backing, limbing, deeing, sniping, jigger-boards, platforms, toms, strops, drives, triggers, and saw and axe sharpening. **1986** Richards *Off the Sheep's Back* 15 The three brothers spent the first few weeks clearing, learning the art of chopping, scarfing, driving and working a face. **1987** TV1 Country Calendar 6 Sept. Finding out where to put in the first cut. That's called scarfing up the tree.

scarfie. An Otago (university) student, from the custom of wearing long scarves in university colours.
1990 *Listener* 20 Aug. 112 [Heading] Otago's scarfies. **1991** TV2 *More Issues* 7 Nov. 'The University, thank you.' 'Au-wee. You a scarfie, too?' **1993** *Sunday Times* (Wellington) 8 Aug. 20 Such pearls are contained in Speight's..sought-after poster..reputedly adorning many a scarfie (Southern lingo for student) flat.

scarlet. In the names of plants and animals, see: kowhai 2 (1), mistletoe 2 (1), parrotfish 2 (4).

scarpee. Also **common scarpee.** [Alteration of Brit. dial. *scarpen* a form of *scorpion* (also used for *scorpionfish*) influenced by the generic name *Scorpaena.*] *sea perch* (perch *n.* 2 (4)). See also scorpionfish.
1932 *NZJST* XIII. 233 [*Scorpaena cruenta*] is the common scarpee of Cook Strait and the cobbler of Napier. Wellington Maoris call it ngutoro or puraruraru. **1957** [see cobbler *n.*[2]]. **1966** Doogue & Moreland *Sea Anglers' Guide* 267 Sea Perch... *Helicolenus papillosus*; Jock Stewart, scarpee, highlander. *Ibid.* 288 Red Scorpionfish... *Other names*: *Scorpaena cardinalis*; red rock cod, scarpee. **1970** [see scorpionfish]. **1986** Paul *NZ Fishes* 78 Scarpee. *Helicolenus percoides*... Known from New Zealand and southern Australia. These fishes, known variously as scarpees, sea perches..etc. were once thought to comprise a single species. **1991** Bradstock *Fishing* 21 Sea perch. Other names: scarpee, Jock Stewart, highlander, flinger, pohuiakaroa, *Helicolenus percoides.*

scat, *ppl. a.* [Poss. f. Brit. dial. *go scat* to become bankrupt: see OED *scat adv.*; see also EDD.] 'Cleaned out' or 'skinned' (of marbles).

1953 SUTTON-SMITH *Unorganized Games NZ Primary School Children* (VUWTS) II. 770 It is important to distinguish these 'Action-Terms' of marbles from the innumerable merely descriptive marble terms which have no effect on the course of the action—terms such as..Skun, Skinned, Sported off, Scat, Cannons, Dubs. **1972** SUTTON-SMITH *Folkgames Children* 178 [Waitara, Taranaki, 1899: in reference to a game of Little Ring.] When a boy lost all his marbles at play he was 'scat'.

scaup /skop/. Often **New Zealand scaup**. [Spec. use of northern hemisphere *scaup*.] *Aythya novaeseelandiae* (fam. Anatidae), a small compact diving duck. See also *black teal* (TEAL *n.*[1] 2 (2)), PAPANGO, WIDGEON.

1873 BULLER *Birds NZ* 259 (New-Zealand Scaup)... Papango, Tetepango, Matapouri, Titiporangi, and Raipo; 'Black Teal' and 'Widgeon' of the colonists. **1889** PARKER *Catalogue NZ Exhib.* (Morris) 117 Among the most interesting..are the Paradise Duck..and the Scaup or Black Teal. **1897** *TrNZI* XXIX. 201 *Fuligula novae-zealandiae* (New Zealand Scaup). **1927** GUTHRIE-SMITH *Birds* 39 The little Scaup..were tiny brown creatures with disproportionate feet, enormous for their bodies' size, and reminding one of children wearing their father's fishing brogues. **1955** OLIVER *NZ Birds* 417 The New Zealand Scaup, or Black Teal as it is generally called, was discovered at Dusky Sound during Cook's second voyage. Forster, who accompanied Cook, recorded that it was gregarious and found at the mouths of rivers in bays little exposed to the wind. He left a drawing from which Latham described his 'New Zealand Duck', a title adopted by Gmelin when founding the specific name. **1966** FALLA et al. *Birds NZ* 94 New Zealand Scaup (Black Teal) *Aythya novaeseelandiae*. *Maori name*: Papango. **1976** SOPER *NZ Birds* 86 The New Zealand Scaup, or Black Teal, is the alert, perky, chubby little duck now seen on most freshwater lakes and lagoons, especially inland. **1989** PARKINSON *Travelling Naturalist* 43 Scaup, the diving duck, occurs in scattered groups along the margins of most lakes.

scenic reserve: see RESERVE 1.

schedule. *Freezing works.* The regularly published list of prices offered by meat companies for various weights and grades of meat. Usu. *attrib.* or Comb. **schedule price**.

1936 BELSHAW et al. *Agric. Organiz. NZ* 629 In 'schedule' buying the purchaser gets the complete carcass, including all skin and offal, for 'per lb.' price based on the weight of the dressed carcass. **1974** *NZ Agric.* 187 The schedule rate itself varies throughout the year, depending on the supply and on the overseas demand for beef. *Ibid.* 188 Farmers are paid schedule rates on the killing weights. **1982** *Agric. Gloss.* (MAF) 35 *Schedule*: The price offered by Meat Companies for various weights and grades of meat.

schicer, var. SHICER.

schleinter, schlenter, varr. SLINTER.

schnapper, var. SNAPPER.

schnein, /ʃnain/, *a. Obs.* [Origin unknown: not found elsewhere.] Of imitation material or base metal; paste.

1866 *Narr. Maungatapu Murders* 34 The purse contained a ring..[which was] 'Schnein'—a cant word for base metal. **1914** GRACE *Tale Timber Town* 153 If [the diamond] is schnein, the bargain's off.

school.

1. See PRIVATE SCHOOL, PUBLIC SCHOOL, SIDE SCHOOL, *State school* (STATE).

2. Used *attrib.* in special Comb. **school bag** [used elsewhere but recorded earliest in NZ: see OED 16 a, 1895], originally prob. a satchel, but applied to many and various bags used by pupils to carry to and from school books, lunches, etc; **school camp**, a study period spent in a rural or bush outdoor camp, also the group of huts, tents and amenity buildings forming such a camp; **school committee** *hist.*, formerly, a group of parents and householders elected to manage State primary and intermediate schools (see also *school trustee* below); **school dental clinic**, the building (or room) usu. in a primary school grounds set aside for the treatment of first teeth by a dental nurse under the school dental programme introduced in 1921 (cf. MURDER HOUSE); **school dental nurse**, usu. shortened to **dental nurse**, a nurse trained by the State to provide dental care for the first teeth of primary schoolchildren; **school dental service** (occas. init. caps.), a service established soon after WW1 to provide dental care for the first teeth of primary schoolchildren; **school dentist**, see *school dental nurse* above; **schoolhouse**, used elsewhere, but in New Zealand always for the residence of a country schoolteacher; **School Journal**, often abbrev. as **the Journal**, a periodical containing a range of graded reading material, published by the State and distributed free to all primary schools; **school-kit**, a *Maori kit* (KIT *n.*[1] 2) used as a school-bag or satchel; **school picnic**, a usu. annual outing for pupils, teachers, and parents to some local picnic spot; **school trustee**, any of the several members of a Board of Trustees set up in 1991 under statute to administer the staffing and maintenance of New Zealand schools.

1877 *NZPD* XXV. 206 [Vincent Pyke MHR] I have seen barefooted children trudge fully four and five miles to school with nothing but a little food in their **school bags**. **1927** *NZ Dairy Produce Exporter* 26 May 46 Each was wearing a very bulgy school bag (they didn't mean to put the lunches in his schoolbag and went outside. **1960** HILLIARD *Maori Girl* 13 Netta began school. The family shared one schoolbag and fought over who was to open it and give out the play-lunches. **1989** *Dominion Sunday Times* (Wellington) 16 Apr. 1 Back problems [are] caused by carrying heavy, book laden school bags. **1957** *Education* VI. No.3 28 During last summer groups of children, sometimes a class from a city school, sometimes a group of senior classes from several country schools, lived for a week to ten days at a **school camp**. **1974** *Educ. Amendment Act* s21 Having regard to the intellectual, social, physical and cultural aspects of education that can be given to advantage by the provision of school camps. **1855** *Act to Promote Establish. Common Schools in Province of Wellington* s.1. Ratepayers..shall be elected to be the **school committee**..for the management of any school. **1867** *Native Schools Act* 56 The committee elected as aforesaid shall be called the District School Committee of such district. **1877** *NZ Statutes NZ* [Gold Fields Act] No.21 122 For every school district constituted under this Act there shall be a School Committee consisting of seven householders within the school district, to be elected as hereinafter provided. **1889** CHUDLEIGH *Diary* 3 Sept. (1950) 367 The Island school committee have larger powers given them and their duties defined.

1897 *Otago Daily Times* (Dunedin) 11 Sept. 4 The annual meeting of the Dunedin and Suburban Schools Committees' Conference showed that this body continued to exercise vigilance over educational matters. **1902** CHUDLEIGH *Diary* 18 Jan. (1950) 410 Held a School Committee meeting, recommended the removal of Mr Williams from the Chathams as a teacher. **1929** BUTCHERS *Young NZ* 316 Such rate should be collected [in 1849] by means of school committees..appointed by the ratepayers. **1947** GASKELL *Big Game* 87 And to crown it all the damned School Committee had to pick on this Saturday for their school picnic. **1957** *Mangamaire School 1897–1957* [15] The grounds were being transformed from a paddock into a nice level playing area, by an energetic school committee and local labour. **1961** *Carterton District School Centennial Celebration* 3 The school committee..agreed that a school rate of one pound per household would be levied in order that the school need not close its doors. **1989** *Illustr. Encycl. NZ* 347 Under the Education Act, every grammar or high school under the charge of a school committee or education board was deemed to be a district high school. **1952** *Here & Now* Dec. 30 In numbers of Auckland schools children from Standard 2 upwards will no longer receive dental care at the **School Dental Clinics**. **1961** *Carterton District School Centennial Celebration* 13 The School Committee..were also busily engaged [in 1928] in watching the progress of the 'Schools Dental Clinic' proposals. **1980** LELAND *Kiwi-Yankee Dict.* 68 *school dental clinic*: At most large schools, and for each collection of small ones, there is a small prefabricated building set slightly apart in which you can find one or more School Dental Nurses who do all of the preventive, and most of the corrective dental work (free) for the children in their schools. The children..consider a visit to the school dental clinic an unpleasant necessity. **1952** *School Dental Service Gaz.* Nov. XII. No.6 1 Six nurses from Ceylon to train as **School Dental Nurses**. **1954** *Truth* 5 May 11 [Heading] **School Dental Service** Pioneers Get Raw Deal. **1966** *Encycl. NZ* II. 522 The School Dental Service in New Zealand is unique in that it has successfully accomplished its task in a manner never before attempted. **1989** *Illustr. Encycl. NZ* 298 Dental Health care in New Zealand is provided by a school dental service and by private practitioners. **1953** SUTTON-SMITH *Unorganized Games NZ Primary School Children* (VUWTS) I. 382 There is a tendency to refer to the game-dentist (and to the real **school dentist**) in an exaggerated manner. 'Here's for the butcher shop'. **1889** CHUDLEIGH *Diary* 12 Dec. (1950) 369 Settled the fence question about the **school house** and garden. **1911** MORELAND *Through South Westland* 128 The first stage was but six miles, to a little school-house where a Christmas service was to be held. **1939** GRIEVE *Sketches from Maoriland* (1961) 60 He would whinny apologetically, making off..in the direction of the school-house. **1957** *Mangamaire School 1897–1957* [10] Crossing the railway line we turned right and came in sight of the unlovely neglected schoolhouse. **1988** SOMERSET *Sunshine & Shadow* 38 Our square two-storied school-house..faced north into the school grounds. **1907** *AJHR* E-1E 6 I might mention..the **School Journal**, because it will give an opportunity of explaining the place it should occupy in the school system. **1908** *AJHR* E-1 xxii It was decided in 1906 that the Department should publish a *School Journal* for free distribution to schools... The first number was issued in May, 1907. **1935** GUTHRIE *Little Country* v. 102 The word [*sc.* Australasia] was expurgated from school journals. **1938** HYDE *Godwits Fly* (1970) 32 Sometimes the school journal called New Zealand 'Maoriland' or 'Ao-te-aroa'. There, again, you hardly ever saw a Maori, and if you did, it was in town. **1948** BALLANTYNE *Cunninghams* (1976) 154 Bary put his finger on the school journal, whispered out the side of his mouth. **1952** FRASER *Ungrateful People* 40 School children were to be charged a penny for *The School Journal*. **1973** DAKIN *Education in New Zealand* 127 [The School Publications Branch's] *School Journal*, enriched by nearly seventy years of experience, has become an educational vehicle of great utility. Each year a special issue of the *Journal* is designed for use by backward readers. **1991** O'REGAN *Aunts & Windmills* 74 There were very few New Zealand poets in our lives in those days. Those there were spoke to us mainly through the pages of the *School Journal* and gave us a yearning for songs of our own land. **1922** MANSFIELD *Journal* (1954) 304 Her hat was like a child's with its wreath of daisies, and she carried a bag like a child's **school-kit**, stuffed very full and covered with a cloth. **1885** *Wairarapa Daily* 22 Jan. 2 The Featherston **School picnic** has been postponed. **1890** *Otago Witness* (Dunedin) 23 Jan. 41 The annual school picnic at Dunrobin took place on the 3rd inst. **1924** *Ibid.* 12 Feb. 71 I went to the Presbyterian Sunday School picnic. **1947** [see *school committee* above]. **1968** SEDDON *The Seddons* 24 However, we had happy days too. There was the annual school picnic. **1980** NEAVE *Land of Munros* 48 Our school picnics were held at Otekaieke Station [c1900]... The Duntroon School also joined us, and we looked forward to the refreshments and soft drinks provided, lolly scrambles etc., and small silver coins for winning races and competitions. **1987** *Alfredton* 75 Bryce Napier is among the many pupils who remember the school picnics. These family outings were held during this era [1927–46] at the domain. **1991** *Dominion* (Wellington) 19 Dec. 8 When the **School Trustees** Bill was originally introduced into Parliament in 1989, some submissions expressed concern about the prospect of student representation. *Loc. cit.* The School Trustees Association represents the views of 96 per cent of the country's boards to the Government.

School C: see SCHOOL CERTIFICATE.

school cadet; school cadet corps: see CADET *n.* 4; CADET CORPS.

School Certificate. Also in the familiar short forms **School C., School Cert.** [Spec. use of *School Certificate*: see OED *school* 19.]

1. a. In New Zealand, a qualification gained usu. at the end of the fifth form year usu. by examination, and since 1969 by passes in one or more separate subjects.
 1932 *NZ Educ. Gaz.* XI. No.5 77 The prescription for the new School Certificate Examination will be available..in the next issue. **1934** [see MATRICULATION]. **1946** *NZ Educ. Gaz.* XXV. No.6 166 Candidates..have secured only a partial pass in the School Certificate Examination. **1959** SHADBOLT *New Zealanders* 90 He began at the bank after he passed his school certificate. **1969** *AJHR E-1* 19 Approval was given to a School Certificate examination based on passes in separate subjects to replace the group-pass examination. **1990** *Evening Post* (Wellington) 12 June 3 Further changes to School Certificate could be in store if the Government accepts the recommendations of a group looking at educational assessment.

b. As **School C., School Cert.**
 1950 *Blue & White* 85 History for School C. **1968** SLATTER *Pagan Game* 204 A second year fifth former..should be swotting maths for School Cert. **1971** SHADBOLT *Bullshit & Jellybeans* 30 You know these days Shadbolt School Cert doesn't mean very much. **1983** *Landfall 147* 276 I wouldn't know. All I got was School C. from Hokitika High School. **1984** MARSHALL *Day Hemingway Died* 30 'I had two tries at School Cert,' he said. **1992** *Dominion Sunday Times* (Wellington) 13 Apr. 9 The Otago front row wouldn't get School Cert between them.

2. *transf.* The qualification used as a scale of success.
 1986 *Listener* 5 July 32 I'll also say that some of its [TV drama] characters are already in imminent danger of caffeine poisoning, that its fight scenes have been C2 on the School Cert scale.

school shark: see SHARK 2 (15).

schooner. [A local use of *schooner* a tall beer-glass: orig. US, see OED *n.*²; AND 1892.] A very large or long beer glass, esp. associated with the South Island West Coast.
 [*Note*] Of various reputed capacities, of which 20 fluid ounces (an imperial pint or 568 ml) seems a standard.
 1933 EADDY *Hull Down* 163 Long schooners of steamed beer, and various small mugs of 'Tom and Jerry'. **1937** *Truth* 20 Oct. 22 'Schooners' are still dispensed in some of the Coast hotels which knew the glory of the gold rush days, but they are more or less in the form of oversize tumblers. **1945** *NZEF Times* 26 Feb. 7 [The young men] were usually very thirsty and drank from long glasses, or 'schooners'. **1947** NEWTON *Wayleggo* 41 We stopped that night in Hokitika.., and with a few West Coast 'schooners' (extra long glasses) of beer under our belts, wet clothes..were forgotten. **1962** CRUMP *One of Us* 168 He had already got into his stride and drank a schooner each of Scrubby's and Sam's eight-ounce beers [in the West Coast pub]. **1974** AVERY *The Ken Avery Songbook* [Title 'Tea at Te Kuiti'] I'm going to.. Drink a handle or a schooner as I tack my Takapuna. **1983** HULME *Bone People* 27 She pours a schooner full [of stout], and settles back on the sheepskins. *Ibid.* 28 A twelve-ounce schooner should stop you, my lad.

scissor-snip. [From similarities of its wing-case movement and sound to that of scissors.] A nickname of the katydid, *Caedicia simplex* (fam. Tettigoniidae).
 1925 *NZJST* VII. 372 *Caedicia simplex* (Walker), popularly known as the katydid, or scissor-snip, is a green leaf-like insect which is very abundant in certain localities throughout the summer. **1948** MARTIN *NZ Nature Study* 204 Katydid or Scissor-snip. From Marlborough and Nelson northwards, this green nocturnal insect is well known. It feeds on leaves and flowers, emitting at short intervals a short staccato 'zip' by moving the left wing-case over the right wing-case.

scone, *n.* [Poss. a survival of an altered form of *sconce* the head (see OED *n.*²) influenced by the fancied resemblance of the head to a *scone* (*loaf*), and by the similiar expressions *do one's bun, do one's loaf.*] In the phr. **to do one's scone**, to become angry or excited; to lose self-control. See also BLOCK *n.*³ 2, BUN *n.*¹
 1939-45 [see BUN *n.*¹]. **1942** *NZEF Times* 19 Oct. 5 'Don't do your plurry scone, Dig!'.. 'Who's sconing? **1949** THE SARGE *Excuse my Feet* 49 Immediately pandemonium broke loose and scones were done in all directions. *Ibid.* 134 Don't do your scone... Don't do your block. **1959** SLATTER *Gun in My Hand* 98 I must say something or I'll do my scone properly. **1975** DAVIN *Breathing Spaces* 97 'She's jake, boys, don't panic,' Ted said. 'Don't do your scones.' **1983** *Dominion* (Wellington) 12 Nov. 6 Well the teacher did his scone and Patu did his porangi act.

Hence **scone** *v. intr.*, to become excited or angry, to lose control; **scone-doer**, one given to losing self-control; **scone-doing** *vbl. n.*, a show of anger; loss of emotional control.
 1942 sconing [see quot. above]. **1944** *NZEF Times* 20 Nov. 5 He decided it was no good sconing over a lost jersey. **1942** *NZEF Times* 20 Apr. 43 (Gloss.) **Scone-doer**—a person subject to sudden fits of excitement or irritation. **1944** Sergeant's Mess Racing Club, Bari, 'Rules' in Latham *WAAC Story* (1986) 174 2nd Race: Hophead Hurdles Scone Doer by Demon Dan out of Good Temper Nightmare by Grim Dig out of Odd Noggin. **1944** COOZE *Kiwis in the Pacific* 8 The camp at Pahautanui was much as all military camps. Tedsons training, fatigues and '**scone doing**' from 6 am to 4 pm.

scone, *v.* [f. Brit. dial. *scon, scun* to hit with the flat of the hand: see EDD.] *trans.* To strike or hit; now often interpreted as to 'hit about the head'.
 1951 *16+ M* 26 Marlborough C. 30A Scone [M2] **1957** CROSS *God Boy* 30 Joe was worried in case he had really sconed the girl. **1988** MCGILL *Dict. Kiwi Slang* 97 *scone* head, or hit somebody on the head, usually its top.

Hence **to get sconed**, to get struck; to get hit (by an object, fist, etc.).
 1953 Jan. p.c. R. Mason quoting Geoff Milne, guide: 'He'll get sconed one of these days if he doesn't look out'—of a careless or overventurous climber. **1963** BALLANTYNE *The Last Pioneer* 15 The damned jalopy tipped over. I got sconed, that's all.

scone-hot, *a.* [Prob. an elaboration of *hot* (*stuff*) applied to praiseworthy or excellent things or people.] Excellent.
 1975 ANDERSON *Men of Milford Road* 56 Dan asked him how the convenience was going. 'Scone-hot', was his description, and Dan..asked if I could view the installation. **1988** MCGILL *Dict. Kiwi Slang* 97 *scone hot* very good; perhaps euphemism for 'shit hot', though hot scones are very good indeed; eg 'That new batsman is scone hot!'

scoop. A standard measure of chips in takeaway food shops.
 1986 *Listener* 21 June 35 Once the convention [of ordering takeways] is established, it is just a matter of stating one's preference for two meat patties and a scoop, over a frankfurter. **1992** FARRELL *Skinny Louie Book* 145 In Soutano's..there would be the usual queue for fish, a pineapple ring and two scoops.

scoot. [Poss. a survival and alteration of *on the scoop* on the 'booze' (see OED *scoop n.*² 3); or a transf. use of *scoot* to hurry off suddenly: AND 1916.] In the phr. **on the scoot**, on the drink, on the spree.
 1959 SLATTER *Gun in My Hand* 219 I must have been boozed up all right... You know what it's like when a man's on the scoot. **1988** MCGILL *Dict. Kiwi Slang* 79 *on the scoot* drinking spree; eg 'I'm surprised he's still upright, let alone at work. I hear he's been on the scoot every night this week.'

scoria. [Found elsewhere but of frequent widespread use in NZ, esp. in Auckland.] **a.** Clinker-like porous dark rock, the result of lava fragments cooling quickly, used esp. as a roading or building material.
 1839 TAYLOR *Journal* 24 Mar. (ATLTS) II. 76 [Tauranga]..a lofty volcanic isolated hill in front of this table land is formed of alluvial deposits of sand and scoriae containing..veins of steatite. **1846** *Narr. Exped. into Interior NZ* in *Colburn's United Service Jrnl.* Aug. 580 I much doubt the correctness of the appellation given to it by the European settlers, of Scoria... This stone is to be found almost everywhere in New Zealand, in pieces ranging from 4 inches to 18 inches and

sometimes longer. It is very hard and durable, and excellent for making roads. **1857** ASKEW *Voyage Austral. & NZ* 329 The presbyterians have also a place of worship, built of scoria. **1869** THATCHER *Local Songs* 13 There's nothing that cuts into 'em, so very fast no doubt, As when we go marching on the scoria. **1881** CAMPBELL *Poenamo* 274 The structure was to be scoria and 'dab'. **1904** *NZ Observer* 16 Jan. 4 A few boulders of scoria were deftly touched up with gold leaf and dropped into the waggons of road metal. **1951** HUNT *Confessions* 141 Jagged masses of scoria cover the whole surface of the island, and, as the scoria is extremely porous, no water or streams exist. **1978** SINCLAIR & HARREX *Looking Back* 36 Maori stone masons helped build the Auckland barracks and the stone wall surrounding it—'a strong scoria wall some twelve feet high'... (The stone was not the porous reddish-brown stone called 'scoria' today, but a solid blue basalt.) **1988** GEE *Prowlers* 36 We followed him up a path spread with scoria... Volcanic slag, all the way [to Nelson] from Auckland.

b. *attrib.*

1859 THOMSON *Story NZ* II. 60 The military force in the colony erected at Auckland a loop-holed barrack, the first scoria-building in the colony. **1887** *Auckland Weekly News* 15 Oct. 7 Who can forget the scoria footpaths, and the discomfort of walking on them? **1922** *Auckland Weekly News* 9 Mar. 14 By the time that little hill with the red scoria quarry on one side of it has come into sight, we are running through the fields of Wiri.

scorpion. [Transf. use of *scorpion*, an arachnid having a poisonous sting, by settlers most of whom would have had no direct experience of scorpions: see also OED 1 f.] WETA.

[**1857** HURSTHOUSE *NZ* I. 123 The weta, a suspicious-looking, scorpion-like creature, apparently replete with 'high concocted venom', but perfectly harmless. **1863** BUTLER *First Year* ix 141 It is called 'weta', and is of tawny scorpion-like colour.] **1885** *Wairarapa Daily* 23 Dec. 2 The so-called mosquito was a 'Weita' or 'Ti-tree Sawyer'... It is called a scorpion by some settlers, and is considered to be poisonous. **1942** ANDERSEN *Maori Place Names* 452 The female [weta has] a stout ovipositor which has been stigmatised as a sting and earned for the insect the undeserved names, scorpion, and herself and her mate wood-devil and taipo.

scorpionfish. [Spec. use of *scorpionfish* for a fish of the fam. Scorpaenidae, esp. one having (venomous) spines, the element *scorpion* being prob. partly an alteration of the generic *Scorpaena*.] In New Zealand, also **red scorpionfish**. Applied mainly to any of several spiny, large-bodied, red fishes of fam. Scorpaenidae of rocky coasts. See also COBBLER n.², COD 2 (7), *grandfather hapuku, hapuku's grandfather* (HAPUKU 3), JOCK STEWART, *sea perch*, PERCH *n.* 2 (4)), SCARPEE.

1932 *NZJST* XIII. 232 *Scorpion-fish or cobbler. Scorpaena cruenta.* **1965** *Evening Post* (Wellington) 20 Aug. 29 The scorpion fish, variously known as red rock cod, grandfather hapuku, Jock McKenzie or scarpee is not good to eat. **1967** MORELAND *Marine Fishes* 26 Red Scorpionfish [*Scorpaena cardinalis*]... A variety of names is in use including cobbler and grandfather hapuku. **1970** SORENSEN *Nomenclature NZ Fish* 40 *Perch* (two species) (a) Scientific name: (i) *Scorpaena cardinalis* (ii) *Helicolenus papillosus* (or *percoides*)... (c) Other common names: (i) Rock Perch; Jock Stewarts (ii) Sea Perch; Scorpion Fish; Scarpees. **1982** AYLING *Collins Guide* (1984) 195 *Scorpion Fish. Scorpaena cardinalis* (Grandfather hapuku, red rock cod, pahuiakaroa). *Ibid.* 196 They are basically red in colour... They should be handled with care as the toxic head and fin spines can cause extremely painful stab wounds.

scorpion fly. *Obs.* [From a fancied resemblance to a (winged) scorpion: see SCORPION.] A cicada (fam. Cicadidae).

1777 ANDERSON *Journal* Feb. in Cook *Journals* (1967) III. 808 Insects are very rare, of which we only saw..vast numbers of Scorpion flies which as we mention'd before fill the woods with their chirping. **1830** CRAIK *New Zealanders* 186 There are not many..insects..only a few dragon-flies, butterflies, grasshoppers, spiders, and black-ants, vast numbers of scorpion-flies, and a sand-fly. **1835** YATE *NZ* (1970) 72 The principal [insects] are, the locust and the grasshopper,... the dragon-fly and scorpion-fly.

Scotch, *a.* In special collocations: **Scotch chest** [poss. a variant of *Scotch press*, orig. a portable box for holding linen, etc. (p.c. John F. Johnson, Christchurch, June 1994), often in colonial or emigrant times comprising a set of two or three such 'presses' or chests for holding personal belongings, each with handles, and able to be packed one on top of the other for convenient and compact stowage; *Scotch* may connote 'space- or money-saving economy, compactness', or the Comb. *Scotch press* may have had a dialect application to a (compact) freestanding 'cupboard' or 'holdall': cf. *SND press n.* 2 'A large cupboard, gen. one built into a recess in the wall but also applied to freestanding cupboards of all kinds... Gen. Sc. and Eng. dial. In Scot. in wider application than in Eng. where it gen. refers only to cupboards for books, occas. for clothes.'], in modern use, see quot. 1993; **Scotch thistle**, see THISTLE *n.* 2 (4); **Scotch whist**, a card game played in Otago in the 1860s.

1982 SANSOM *In Grip of Island* 104 The **scotch chest**, bedroom tallboy of those years, [c1888] had a drawer especially for the bell-topper. **1993** *Evening Post TV Weekly* (Wellington) 21 June 13 [Advt.] Scotch Chest (100 [cm] h x 80w x 42d) $225 [Chest pictured with 3 wide (80 cm) drawers, and a top set divided into 3 sections of equal width comprising a central deep drawer flanked on each side by a set of two shallow drawers]. **1939** BEATTIE *First White Boy Born Otago* 125 I could play cards, however. Catch the Ten was then called **Scotch whist**. People did not want games then, but news.

Scotchie: see SCOTCHMAN 2.

Scotchman.

1. [Poss. transf. f. *scotchman* 'scotch thistle' to another spiny plant.] A small species of *Aciphylla* (fam. Apiaceae), a grassland herb with sharp-tipped leaves, esp. *A. monroi.* Cf. SPANIARD.

1895 ROBERTS *Southland in 1856* 39 Speargrass of the smaller kind, known as 'Scotchmen', abounded, and although not so strong and sharp-pointed as the 'Spaniard', would not have made a comfortable seat. **1896** *The Australasian* Aug. XXVIII. 407 One could not but be forced to find the name Scotchman applied to a smaller kind of Spaniard. **1968** *NZ Contemp. Dict. Suppl.* (Collins) 17 *Scotchman n.* N.Z. grass, with sharp points, called also *Spaniard*.

2. Also **scotchie, Scotsman**. *Scotch thistle* (THISTLE 2 (4)).

1907 KOEBEL *Return of Joe* 301 We took them to the paddocks where the 'Scotchmen' lay closest. **1921** GUTHRIE-SMITH *Tutira* (1926) 173 There was the customary waning recrudescence of the 'Scotsman' (*Cnicus lanceolatus*), a plant which, whatever its name might seem to infer, does not thrive..on hungry soils. **1980** *Star* (Christchurch) 5 Jan. 7 But the result was that the nodders [*sc.* nodding thistles] are a non-event here and same applies to scotchies.

3. Scotchman's (Scotsman's), used with nouns to connote something obtained for nothing or for lower than standard cost: **Scotchman's feed** *WW2 prisoners-of-war*, food or drink cadged from another; **Scotsman's grandstand** (also **Scotsmen's stand**), a stand erected on private property overlooking a sportsground and hired to those wishing to watch an important event usu. for less than the official price of admission; occas. a vantage point used as a free grandstand; **Scotchman's half-crown** *obs.*, the two-shilling piece, worth sixpence less than the half-crown; **Scotchman's shout**, a 'Dutch' treat where each of the treated pays a share.

c**1945** *Sixes & Sevens* (Troopship pub.) 4 By this time the inner-man is calling loudly..so down you go to the brewing-up place for a '**Scotchman's feed**.' That means going round sniffing the brew of the odd hoarder who has saved something from his Red Cross parcel. **1973** *Dominion* (Wellington) 2 Sept. 17 The dismantling of the last big '**Scotsman's grand-stand**' beside Eden Park on Saturday in accordance with a Court order. But many people still watched the rugby test from the stand in Mrs Monica O'Sullivan's back garden. **1979** ZAVOS *After the Final Whistle* 103 The crowd was in good humour, and even people in the luxurious Scotsmen's grandstands that circled the ground were relaxed and good-humoured. **1986** KNIGHT *Shield Fever* 49 For this match [*sc.* Otago v. Southland] 35,000 people crammed into Carisbrook with plenty more standing in the 'Scotsmen's Stand' on the high hills overlooking the ground. **1993** *Sunday Times* (Wellington) 11 July 41 The Scotsman's grandstand will still be there..and there will be the ultimate Scotsman's grandstand, a stationary train overlooking the ground. **1970** SANSOM *Stewart Islanders* 125 The bottles [in which coins were saved] were labelled 'Pennies', 'Church Mice' (that was the threepence), 'Bobs' (the shillings) and '**Scotsman's Half-Crown**' (the florin). **1942** HOLLAND & LILIENTHAL *Meet the Anzacs* 14 **Scotchman's shout**: Dutch treat.

Scotsman, var. SCOTCHMAN.

Scotty. A kind of marble, poss. with tartan-like coloration.

1972 SUTTON-SMITH *Folkgames Children* 174 Then there were the terms referring to particular kinds of marbles: for example, agates, aggies..American alleys..Scotties, Scottish alleys, smokies.

scour. [AND 1896.] In full **wool-scour**. A place or plant in which dirt, natural grease, etc. are removed from wool.

[*Note*] Verbal and participial uses of *scour* with reference to cloth and fibre date from the 15th century.

c**1907–14** MOWAT *Diary* in McCaskill *Molesworth* (1969) 103 The dry wool was pressed at the scour and the bales taken to the woolshed. **1913** CARR *Country Work* 18 A number of stations..run a scour... From five to seven men are generally employed..at the wash, and the balance on the drying green. **1925** ACLAND *Early Canterbury Runs* 123 The Creek Station..was leased to T.P. Bartrum from 1870 onwards, and he established a wool scour there. **1969** MCCASKILL *Molesworth* 103 The bulk of the clip..went to the scour on the bank of the Awatere River... Water was drawn from the river to run the four circular tubs. **1975** NEWTON *Sixty Thousand on*

SCOW

the Hoof 13 Gerard established his own wool scour at Mesopotamia and one old waggoner, Charlie Dunstan, recalls that in the 1911–12 season he carted 640 bales from the shed to the scour. **1985** BREMNER *Woolscours NZ* 16 Scours were part of the Otago goldrush boom of the 1860s.

scow. *Hist.*

1. [OED evidence suggests that the term is restricted to US, Scotland, Ireland in the main sense of a large, flat-bottomed lighter or punt; see also EDD.] **a.** In New Zealand, (usu.) a sailing scow, any of various shallow-draft, flat-bottomed, centreboard craft formerly engaged in coastal transport and trade, esp. in the North Auckland and Cook Strait areas. (See K. Smithyman 'The Auckland Scow' *Te Reo* 16 pp.9ff. (1970).)

1879 *Auckland Weekly News* 20 Dec. 17 A seafaring man..who was employed in the Makarau scow, was..on board the Nightingale. **1887** *Ibid.* 2 July 30 We refer to the scows. These vessels are copied from those in use on American lakes, and were first introduced for harbour work here, but being found so suitable for carrying large logs that their shape has rapidly improved, so much that some of them are now fit to go to any part of the world, and are large enough to carry cargoes of up to 50,000 and 60,000 feet of timber. **1897** A TRAMP, ESQ. *Casual Ramblings* 108 Scows can get up the Whangapoua Harbour to within two or three miles of the mine. **1904** LANCASTER *Sons o' Men* 159 Up the first grade that climbed into the bush the jigger rocked like a scow in a tideway. **1913** *NZ Observer* 17 May 17 Chips from the tree he [*sc.* W.E. Gladstone] cut down were sent in scow loads all over the Empire. **1925** MANDER *Allen Adair* (1971) 15 Then a scow unloaded windows and doors, and corrugated iron for the roof. **1933** EADDY *Hull Down* 145 'What are your Auckland scows like?' 'The larger scows have two centreboards, and sometimes a smaller one, called a fin, fore-part of the mast. They have long sticks [masts] in them too and carry an enormous amount of sail.' **1946** SARGESON *That Summer* 33 They say he's got a job on a scow. **1960** HAWKINS *Out of Auckland* 147 The first long coastal voyage undertaken by a scow (schooner barge) was that of the *Makarau* which was built by George Darroch at Makarau, on the west coast of the North Auckland peninsula, in 1879. **1975** ASHBY *Phantom Fleet* 8 The *Vindex* and *Vesper* weren't true scows as we define them, for though flat-bottomed, they were round-bilged timbered vessels with shallow keels and fore-and-aft planked, whereas the true scow was hard-chined, with no keel, and the bottom planking ran athwartships from the stern log right through to the turn of the bow. **1983** MANTELL *Murder to Burn* 84 Elsewhere [in Wellington Harbour]..the inter-island scow made its weekly trip to Petone wharf. **1991** *NZ Geographic* Jan.–Mar. 104 The homeload of building materials, shipped across on the scow *Te Aroha*, was off-loaded by hand.

b. With various modifiers as **Auckland, cattle, deck, log, New Zealand, New Zealand sailing, sand, stock scow** (see also quot. 1933 a above).

1913 *NZ Observer* 20 Sept. 4 He [*sc.* Truby King] was particularly angry with boots that were not as broad in the toe as a sand scow. **1963** AUDLEY *No Boots for Mr. Moehau* 178 The sand scow will start grabbing up the clean white stuff right away in a fathom or less. **1986** OWEN & PERKINS *Speaking for Ourselves* 139 In a deck scow you can go below and she's all open, and you can see the water tumbling in, and you can set to work and somehow block it up. *Ibid.* 139 On the log scows they [*sc.* the crew] had to be about as good as a bushman, because they had to know how to jack timber and how to load timber and how to stow timber. *Ibid.* 135 They [*sc.* the owners and skippers and builders] slowly evolved the New Zealand scow—the Auckland scow—which proved the only really adequate method of water transport for our type of work. *Ibid.* 139 On the stock and cattle scows, the skipper and the crew had to be as good as a good back-country farmer; they had to know how to handle cattle.

2. Special Comb. **scowman**, one owning, sailing or working on a scow; **scowmaster**, the master of a scow; **scow skid**, a marine skidway for beaching scows for survey, maintenance, etc.

1986 OWEN & PERKINS *Speaking for Ourselves* 140 So you had to be a very versatile animal to be a good **scowman**—you had to practically be about six tradesmen in one. **1913** *NZ Observer* 8 Mar. 7 **Scowmasters** want Fisher to blow up the dangerous D'Urville Rock. *Ibid.* 19 July 16 Auckland has.. innumerable places where a **scow skid** could be placed without offence.

3. *Canterbury.* A former type of flat-bottomed, usu. square-bilge centreboard yacht, up to 30 feet (9.15 m) in length, having minimal freeboard, and sailed for sport on the Heathcote River and Christchurch Estuary from c1900 to the late 1920s.

1948 CARTER *Little Ships* 143 I..sailed with [Aub. Round] on several occasions on the scow Te Arai, which, in spite of poor sails, had no difficulty in showing the rest of the fleet the way home. **1964** MANDER *Give a Man a Boat* 35 First, the motor launch that was to lay the marks [for the 1945 Cornwell Cup contest held on the Christchurch Estuary] broke down..and the sailing scow..skippered by the late Aub Round..had to do the job. **1991** HARRISON *Ebb & Flow* 41 Most of the fleet were [c1900–14] thirty footers [*sic*] known then as 'skimming dishes'. Some, such as the scows, were copied from the Great Lakes designs. They were 30ft. long with a beam of 8ft., square ended and low wooded... They were flat bottomed with a slight rocker in their keels.

scrag, *n.*¹ [f. Brit. dial. *scrag* in depreciatory use for inferior or useless residue, etc.]

1. *Whaling.* The residue of whale blubber after the oil has been tried out.

1845 WAKEFIELD *Adventure NZ* I. 145 Into [the try-works] the blubber is put..and the oil is boiled out. The residue is called scrag, and serves to feed the fire. **1864** CAMPBELL *Martin Tobin* I. 193 When the [whale] oil is extracted a stringy dry portion remains called scrag, this burns like wood. **1940** McINTOSH *Marlborough* 43 Into these [boilers] the blubber cut into lumps two feet square..was thrown and boiled until the oil was extracted. The residue, called scrag, then served to feed the fires.

2. An inferior whale deficient in blubber.
[*Note*] The 1839 quot. is poss. *ellipt.* for *scrag-whale*: see OED *scrag-whale* (*scrag,* n.¹ 5), a finner whale of the sub-family Agaphelinae, esp. *A. gibbosus*, common in the North Atlantic.

1839 *Piraki Log* 16 Apr. (1911) 83 Saw a scrag: pursued her, but did not succeed. **1913** McNAB *Old Whaling Days* 230 The cow whales produced the most oil, and they had been the scarcest, their places being filled by young bulls and 'scrags'.

scrag, *n.*² [Prob. f. *scrag* a rough tackle: see OED *v.* 1 b and *n.*³] A boys' chasing and catching game.

1978 SUTHERLAND *Elver* 61 'Do you play shinty or football?' 'Yeah. Football. And we play scrag in the winter and tippeny runs in the summer.' **1982** SUTTON-SMITH *Hist. Children's Play* 231 There are games recorded in this period for which there is no record

SCRAPE

before 1900 though they may well have existed under other names... *Wellington*:.. Isaac and Rebecca, Scrag, Diabolo.

scrag, *v.* [f. Brit. dial. *scrag* stump of a tree: see OED *n.*² 1.] *intr.* To work already cut-over bush in the hope of getting some useful logs.

1948 MUNDY *There's Gold* 44 The bush had been previously cut through, and we were as it is generally called, scragging, and we had a good many [logs] condemned.

Hence **scragging area**, see quot.
1953 *NZ Forest Service Gloss.* (Commercial Div.) (TS) *Scragging (area)*: An area available for splitting operations which has been worked over previously.

scran. [f. Brit. (and military or nautical) dial.: see OED 2 a 'of obscure origin'.] Food.

c**1875**? *NZ Songster No.3* 22 ['John Chinaman's Marriage'] She then repudiated rice, And swore such scran would not suffice. **1906** PICARD *Ups & Downs* 23 I put some more scran on his menu and smoodged to him quite a lot. **1919** *Quick March* 10 Oct. 33 'Roll up for yer scran!' said Tom, as he..limped to the fence for the nosebags. **1926** DEVANNY *Butcher Shop* (1981) 33 [Shepherds speak to cook] Hurry up with the scran. A chap's belly is like a concertina. **1947** BEATTIE *Early Runholding* 12 A common expression among a number of men approaching a meal-time was 'Get your scran'. **1959** SLATTER *Gun in My Hand* 218 Sausages and eggs. That's what a man needs. Decent scran like that. **1975** DAVIN *Breathing Spaces* 95 When we were at camp in Kaisariani..we used to cook up our scran..and have a few drinks together. **1984** 16 M E90 Pakuranga Coll. 22B Scran [name for food].

scrape, *v.* [Spec. use of *scrape* to free from excrescent matter.] *trans.*

1. *Gumdigging.* To remove dirt and impurities from the surface (of kauri-gum) by scraping.

1873 TINNE *Wonderland of Antipodes* 54 They generally work in parties..taking it in turn to remain at home to..scrape the gum clean. **1882** HAY *Brighter Britain* II. 27 When enough [gum] has been collected and scraped it is carried down to the nearest bush-store. **1904** *NZ Illustr. Mag.* Mar. 429 One might have scraped gum and cooked 'doughboys' among less interesting surroundings than those of the diggers' camp. **1963** CAMPBELL *Golden North* 61 At weekends the children went into the gumfields and collected sugar bags full of the smaller nuts that the diggers considered too small to scrape and clean. **1991** *NZ Geographic* Apr.–June 37 On depressing wet days there was always..the onerous job of scraping gum ready for sale at the local store.

Hence **scraped** *ppl. a.*, of kauri-gum, cleaned of surface impurities; **scraping** *vbl. n.*, the action or occupation of so cleaning gum; **scrapings**, the surface refuse scraped from gum.

1874 BAINES *Edward Crewe* 158 At the time of which I write, well **scraped** kauri gum could readily be sold in Auckland for £20 per ton. **1888** BARLOW *Kaipara* 151 The more successful his day's digging, the more **scraping** lies before him in the evening, and it is considered a good ten hours' work to scrape a hundredweight of gum. **1904** *NZ Illustr. Mag.* Mar. 431 Ye might try Jim Jackson's tent over there, Missus... He's doin' a bit of scraping to-day. **1916** STALLWORTHY *Early N. Wairoa* 54 At one time the dust, and **scrapings**, of the gum were not saleable... Since then there has always been a price of some sort for all dust and scrapings.

2. To dress (flax), Maori-fashion, using a shell to remove the green matter from the fibre.

SCRAPERS

1823 KENT *Log 'Mermaid'* 1 June in Howard *Rakiura* (1940) 345 Inside were many bed places built of wicker work..upon which lay their shells &c. for dressing and scraping flax. **1884** MARTIN *Our Maoris* 71 It was a busy time of year, when all were scraping flax. **1933** BURN in *Centennial Treasury of Otago Verse* (1949) 36 Never a swamp or hillside lacks Store of tall, sabre-bladed flax; Cut, scraped, hardened, twined. **1939** BEATTIE *First White Boy Born Otago* 12 The whites would copy the native way of scraping flax for various purposes [c1840].

scrapers, *n. pl.* [A survival of an *obs.* Anglo-Irish dial. use: see OED *scraper* 9, 1792–1842.] In the phr. **to take to one's scrapers**, to take to one's heels, to decamp.
1961 CRUMP *Hang On a Minute Mate* 63 Tonker took to his scrapers and hid in a hedge.

scratcher. [f. *scratcher* something which scratches: cf. Partridge 8, a bed (Glasgow, 1934, also, later, Services slang).] A (makeshift) bed or bunk; a sleeping bag.
1959 SLATTER *Gun in My Hand* 92 Mick efficiently putting me to bed in my blankets on the hard stone floor.—Come on stick your feet down there. Get into the scratcher. **1960** CRUMP *Good Keen Man* 33 We lit a fire and discussed how we were going to get our sleeping-bags. Jack said someone should..distract Allan's attention while the others..grabbed our scratchers. **1964** HELMER *Stag Party* 56 'After all, getting out of this old scratcher takes a lot of effort.' He hopped back to his bunk. **1992** *Dominion* (Wellington) 27 Nov. 10 Prebble worries that people might leap into the scratcher solely to stave off prosecution.

scratchie. [cf. *Macquarie Dict. New Words* (1990) *scratchie*, 1987.] An 'instant' lottery ticket, from which, to discover a possible prize, one must 'scratch' or scrape off a covering material. See also INSTANT KIWI q.v., occas. heard called 'scratch Kiwi'.
1990 *Dominion* (Wellington) 19 Sept. 3 He had spent the whole of his benefit on 'scratchies' like Instant Kiwi, the first week they were available. **1991** *Ibid.* 24 July 8 The scratchies are helping 'squash the squelch mentality', that the Conservation Department says too many New Zealanders have toward insects.

scratching, **scratch muster(ing)**: see *straggle muster(ing)* (MUSTER *n.* 2), MUSTERING *vbl. n.*

screamer. Also **screecher.** [f. its harsh cry.] *long-tailed cuckoo* (CUCKOO 2 (2)).
1946 *JPS* LV. 152 *koekoeā, kōhoperoa* a migratory bird (Urodynamis taitensis), long-tailed cuckoo, screamer. **1985** Screecher [see CUCKOO 2 (2)].

screecher: see SCREAMER.

screwpine. Also **native** (or **New Zealand**) **screwpine.** [Spec. use of *screw-pine* for plants of the fam. Pandanaceae having aerial roots, narrow leaves arranged in spiral tufts, and fruits resembling a pineapple.] KIEKIE.
1907 *AJHR* C-8 17 *Freycinetia banskii*. Kiekie. Native screw-pine. Forest. **1908** *AJHR* C-14 35 *Freycinetia Banskii*. Kiekie New Zealand screw-pine. Forest. Root-climbing, woody liane. **1910** COCKAYNE *NZ Plants & Their Story* 46 High up some of the stems climb the New Zealand screw pine, the kiekie. **1979** WEBSTER *Rua* 80 Known to the Maori as kie kie this plant has narrow, sword-shaped leaves which droop curiously at the ends and are arranged in compact spirals (hence the English name of Screwpine). **1982** *NZ Gardener* Dec. 23 In the last few years interesting finds have included *Freycinetia banksii*, the kiekie, or New Zealand screwpine, which has edible fruit.

screw press. *Obs.* A woolpress worked by a screw mechanism.
1865 BARKER *Station Life* (1870) 33 The fleeces are tumbled in, and a heavy screw-press forces them down till the bale..is as full as it can hold. **1938** BURDON *High Country* 85 The shorn wool was packed into five foot six inch bales by means of a wooden spade, with which the wool was pressed down into the corners; screw presses were not used until towards the end of the sixties. **1952** BLAKISTON *My Yesteryears* 21 [The large tally] meant hard work for all hands, especially the three men on the old screw press [c1869].

scroddie. Also occas. **scrodie**. [Poss. f. US *scrod* a young fish, esp. cod or haddock: cf. OED *scrod*.] *sea perch* (PERCH *n.* 2 (4)).
1938 *TrRSNZ* LXVIII. 416 *Helicolenus percoides*... Sea perch, so called John Dory (scroddie, fivefinger, soldier-fish). **1956** GRAHAM *Treasury NZ Fishes* 344 The name Scroddie, commonly used at the northern end of the South Island, is derived from the word Scrod which means a young Dogfish. It appears from my researches that when the early colonists first saw a small Seaperch they at once named it Scrod and later the 'ie' was tacked on to make Scroddie. **1966** scrodie [see FIVE-FINGER 3].

scrodie, var. SCRODDIE.

scrog, **scrogen**, varr. SCROGGIN.

scroggin. *Tramping.* Also **scrogen**, and occas. abbrev. **scrog** (see quot. 1971). [Origin uncertain: poss. f. *scr*(an + h)*og* (*in*).] A mixture of dried fruit, nuts, chocolate, etc., eaten by trampers as a high energy snack. Also *attrib*.
1940 *Tararua Tramper* Mar. 7 We had our breakfast of 'scroggin'. **1948** MOIR *Guide Book* (2edn.) 88 The best quality of raisins, dates, nuts, etc., should be selected to make up a 'scroggin' mixture to nibble when stopping for a spell. **1950** *Canterbury Mountaineer* 45 The 'Scroggin Bag' was produced with heavy demands on chocolate etc. **1958** *Tararua* Sept. 26 If any word originating in the mountain clubs deserves to be incorporated in the language it is perhaps *scroggin*. That mixture of raisins, sultanas, chocolate, nuts, boiled lollies, a mixture of bits and pieces of whatever one fancies, was evolved to fill the need for a sustaining, palatable, easily-carried food, one as readily available for a bite snatched in a cold, wet, momentary halt as for a welcome spell in the warmth and sun. The word seems to come from Otago but its derivation is not clear. **1971** ARMFELT *Catching Up* 137 'I brought some scrog, and a thermos of hot coffee.' He..handed him the mixture of raisins, nuts and squares of dark chocolate. **1971** *Listener* 19 Apr. 56 It was hard yakka, nothing but a plate of burgoo and a handful of scroggin since sparrow-chirp. **1980** *NZ Woman's Weekly* 7 Jan. 83 Scrogen 1 cup peanuts ¾ cup dried apricots 1 135 gram block energy chocolate ½ cup mixed dried fruit ¼ cup sunflower seeds ½ cup coconut 2 tablespoons powdered glucose. Roast the peanuts at 180 degrees C for 10–15 minutes, or until lightly golden. Cool. Chop the apricots and chocolate coarsely. In a strong plastic bag, put the peanuts, apricots, chocolate, mixed fruit, sunflower seeds, coconut and glucose. Shake to combine. Secure cool. Use as a high energy snack food. **1991** *Dominion* (Wellington) 9 Mar. 10 'Scroggin? What the hell's scroggin?' Scroggin, I can tell you, is the tramper's friend—an energy-sustaining mixture of peanuts, chocolate and raisins.

scrub, *n*. [Used elsewhere but mainly in NZ and Austral.: see OED *n.*[1] 2.]

1. a. In *collective* use. [AND 1805.] An association of generally low-growing or stunted vegetation, often thick or impenetrable. See also UNDERSCRUB *n*.
1839 COLENSO *Journal* (ATLTS) I. 28 Natives knew not the road obliged to muku thro' swamps, reeds, rushes, burnt scrub. **1841** *NZ Jrnl.* II. 285 Every part is covered with vegetation, fern, scrub, copse and forest. **1852** SMITH *The Settler's New Home* 19 There is abundance of fern, scrub, brushwood, and timber. **1869** *TrNZI* I. (rev. edn.) 186 This scrub, as it is termed, is often found impenetrable, both from the closeness of the growth and the presence of spinous plants. **1879** HAAST *Geol. Canterbury & Westland* 11 The growth of the scrub was in many places so dense, that it was necessary to walk literally on top of it. **1888** BARLOW *Kaipara* 108 Small Tea-tree..grows in large and dense patches called scrub. **1896** HARPER *Pioneer Work* 32 In New Zealand the forest is always spoken of as 'bush' as opposed to lower growth of vegetation, which is called 'scrub'. **1912** FERGUSON *Castle Gay* 56 Ere yet the ruthless Pakeha Appeared with desolating axe..where chance some pah, Was hidden there, 'mid scrub and flax. **1951** LEVY *Grasslands NZ* (1970) (Gloss.) 362 *Scrub*—Short growing, hardy trees or shrubs, often densely packed to form a thicket. **1981** HENDERSON *Exiles Asbestos Cottage* 18 The little blue ornament remained very dear to her..among the scrub, manuka, and the ancient remembering cries from the stalking brown woodhens. **1991** *Historic Places* June 31 By the time Brickell arrived at Driving Creek, the land was covered in scrub and gorse.

b. In *distributive* use. (a) A patch of scrub; a thicket, a copse.
1840 TAYLOR *Journal* (ATLTS) II. 230 A kahikaitea scrub [along which] we forced our way with difficulty. **1853** ADAMS *Canterbury Settlement* 59 Immediately on the other side of the river is a considerable tract of land, known as the Manuca Scrub... The 'Scrub' which extends about two miles, consisted of a number of [Manuca] shrubs. **1868** LINDSAY *Contribs. NZ Bot.* 49 Hence a 'Spear-grass Scrub' on the hill ranges is frequently most formidable..to men and horses. **1874** KENNAWAY *Crusts* 57 We pitched..our blankets in the shelter of a small *scrub* or copse. **1925** *NZJST* VIII. 16 In the pohutukawa scrubs the bell-bird greets the visitor with animated song. **1947** REED *Dict. Suppl.* 175 *scrub*: patches of small bush.

(b) A scrub plant or shrub as a constituent of scrub or a scrub; also, cut scrub or brushwood (see quot. 1860).
1851 SHORTLAND *S. Dist. NZ* 195 My other natives..had lingered behind unable to resist a 'tutu' scrub black with fruit. **1860** *Puketoi Station Diary* in Beattie *Early Runholding* (1947) 93 Drays went and brought in two loads of scrub. **1861** HAAST *Topogr. Explor. Nelson* 37 Towards evening..we lit a fire with the roots and short stems of a few Alpine scrubs. **1906** ROBERTS in *Hist. N. Otago from 1853* (1978) 4 Tumatakuru, a small thorny scrub..which Europeans nick-named 'Wild Irishman'.

c. Special Comb. **scrub bar**, an attachment to a mowing machine enabling it to deal with light scrub; **scrub bull** [AND 1881], a wild bull bred or living in the scrub (also *transf.*); **scrub bush** (a) see b (b) above; (b) a bush or shrub which forms part of a scrub association; **scrub cattle**, wild or range cattle living in scrub or on scrub country; **scrub fence**, a fence made of cut scrub,

a brush fence; **scrub fire**, a fire burning through scrub; **scrub flax** (i.e. a stunted flax often forming a scrub-like mass), see FLAX 2 (4); **scrub horse** [AND 1897], a horse bred to work in scrub; **scrub hut**, a hut built of cut scrub; **scrub knife** [AND 1882], a large knife with a hooked blade for use in cutting (through) scrub; **scrubland** [AND 1833], land (once) covered by, or fit only to grow, scrub; also **scrublands**, scrubland viewed extensively or collectively; **scrub line**, the upper limit of altitude for the growth of scrub; **scrub paddock** [AND 1955], an uncleared paddock, or one let go back to scrub; **scrub pen**, a stock pen formed and fenced with cut scrub, a brush pen; **scrub-thorn**, MATAGOURI; **scrubyard**, a stockyard formed and fenced with cut scrub.
1950 *NZJAg.* Feb. LXXX. 116 The scrub covering on pumice land should be cleared and burnt before cultivation. Hand cutting or mowing with a **scrub bar** have now been replaced..by rolling the standard scrub with a heavy flanged roller which crushes and breaks the scrub. *Ibid.* 127 Many farmers are faced with the problem of clearing gorse and scrub..and though the mower fitted with a scrub bar will deal very effectively up to the thickness of a man's thumb, a method that can be used with even heavier scrub [etc.]. **1993** *Evening Post* (Wellington) 7 Jan. 6 A device called a scrub bar is identified as Good for Gorse. In between waiting for the gorse scrubber to arrive..we idle away the time. **1904** LANCASTER *Sons o' Men* 19 It was the savage low warning of a **scrub bull** somewhere back in the manuka-blocked night. **1920** POWDRELL *Dairy Farming* 99 Don't buy scrub bulls unless you anticipate scrub results. **1936** BELSHAW et al. *Agric. Organiz. NZ* 345 The 'scrub' bull (a cross-bred bull of poor milking strain) is now the exception. **1950** WOODHOUSE *Farm & Station Verse* [p. i in unpaged introduction] The bull, whether scrub or stud, is unhonoured and unsung. **1977** *Listener* 15 Jan. 34 The 'scrub bull', eccentric conservationist station owner who has parted company with the local 'establishment'. **1978** JARDINE *Shadows on Hill* 88 It was a major operation rounding them up out of the rough, scrub-covered gullies. Older scrub bulls and any others completely intractable were destroyed, younger bulls..were marked. **1847** WHITE *Journal* (ATLTS) 64 Set the **scrub bush** on fire at Ohauiti. **1897** WRIGHT *Old Station Days* 11 Cobwebs..jewelled the **scrub-bushes** o'er. **1958** *Tararua 13* 45 One curious term is *scrub bush.* So far as I can make out it is applicable to the individual plants which go to make up tall scrub... A tall plant of teatree may be called a *scrub bush.* **1949** BAXTER *Collected Poems* (1980) 86 Though the wild **scrub cattle** Acclimatized, may learn Shreds of her purpose. **1955** *BJ Cameron Collection* (TS July) scrub-cattle (n) Cattle that have run wild and deteriorated in condition. **1871** MONEY *Knocking About NZ* 147 I obtained a contract for the erection of a **scrub fence**. **1983** *Whakarewarewa Forest Park* 22 Several Europeans who visited Rotorua in the late 1830s and 1940s [*sic*] reported on the uncontrolled bush and **scrub fires** they saw. **1893** FERGUSON *Bush Life* 301 The scrub confused and handicapped [the thoroughbred] whilst Selim was a **scrub-horse**. **1982** STUART *Satyrs of Southland* 14 It was rumoured at that time [*sc.* c1880s] that the still was located to the eastward of South West Cape, in a little **scrub hut**. **1900** *NZ Illustr. Mag.* III. 150 I never carried a..gun [while pig-hunting], only a **scrub knife** and a small butcher's knife. **1855** TAYLOR *Te Ika a Maui* 264 The sum per acre that the..emigrant must give for **scrub land** in Canterbury. **1884** CUMMING *NZ in Blooming December* 123 It is far from the scrub-land. **1915** MACDONALD *NZ Sheepfarming* 106 The fallen bush lands and some of the scrub lands have been surface sown in English grasses. **1926** *NZJST* VIII. 205 The total number of species recorded is twenty-four, of which ten are common to the forest and scrublands. **1943** WALL & CRANWELL *Botany of Auckland* 22 Go to the hill-top drive above Waikumete cemetery; there..typical scrubland can be seen. **1959** MCLINTOCK *Descr. Atlas* 24 There were many islands of forests within the scrub lands and many pockets of scrub land within the forest. **1966** *Encycl. NZ* I. 52 Most New Zealand endemic ants are forest or scrub-land inhabitants. **1974** CHINNOCK *Ferns & Fern Allies* 24 'Bracken'... Very common along the margins of forest, forest clearings, along the edges of roads, scrublands and mountain regions. **1980** GIBBS *NZ Butterflies* 184 The latter species prefers the margins of streams in light bush or scrubland where the vegetation is lush. **1892** DOUGLAS in *Mr Explorer Douglas* (1957) 176 Up at point B the **Scrub line** is close on ? [*sic*] 5000 feet, nearly the limit of vegetation. **1912** *TrNZI* XLIV. 23 Above the scrub line, pigs had eaten freely of *Pleurophyllum Hookeri.* **1946** *Tararua Story* 31 In September of the same year, Wilson..crossed Richard's Knob to the Butcher blaze and the scrub-line on Pukematauai. **1959** *Tararua 13* 45 *Scrubline* for the upper limit of the scrub seems to be confined to New Zealand as does the corresponding *grassline.* **1929** *Love & Chiffon* 144 Through the **scrub paddock**. **1847** PHARAZYN *Journal* (ATLMS) 147 Draft out the Ewes and bring them to the **scrub pen**. **1874** KENNAWAY *Crusts* 185 A thin fire of a little **scrub-thorn** is induced to show itself in the chilly air. **1968** TOMLINSON *Remembered Trails* 58 Most of the sheep went on, except about fifty wild and double-fleece sheep that were put in a **scrubyard**.

2. With a modifier: **black, yellow**.

(1) **black scrub**. See quot. 1952.
1892 DOUGLAS in *Mr Explorer Douglas* (1957) 175 Similar country [in Westland] extends on the other side of the river..but it is much drier and covered to a great extent with Black Scrub, which is easily fallen and burnt off. **1908** *NZGeol.SB* (NS) No.6 9 Mingimingi, or black scrub (*Coprosma propinqua*). **1952** p.c. Ruth Mason (Wellington). *black scrub*: a name given to smallish divaricating shrubs with dark stems and, often, small dark-green leaves: e.g. *Plagianthus betulinus, Coprosma propinqua, Hymenanthera* spp., *Aristotelia* spp. etc. These shrubs are sometimes clothed with a black fungus. **1995** CRUMP *Bushwoman* 41 A black scrub bush grew by the grave, perfect for nailing up a [possum] trap.

(2) **yellow scrub**. TAUHINU 1.
1926 HILGENDORF *Weeds* 212 *Tauhinu*..also called yellow scrub; grows as a woody shrub, 3 to 4 ft. high with yellow leaves and white flowers.

3. a. In *attrib.* use in the senses pertaining to, characteristic of, or comprising scrub; of plants, found in or forming a thicket; of animals, living or ranging in scrub.
1882 POTTS *Out in Open* 198 A large island in that river more or less covered with scrub-brush, dotted with ti-trees. **1918** *TrNZI* L. 154 The present plant-covering might be called a 'scrub' association. **1935** ODELL *Handbook Arthur's Pass National Park* 95 Two scrub associations are found on the old river terraces, one, the bane of the bare legged travellers, open scrubland. **1940** STUDHOLME *Te Waimate* (1954) 247 Many of the bush and scrub gullies extended from the Waihao River to the top of the range. **1950** *NZJAg.* Feb. LXXX. 116 Because of the [fire] danger..scrub burning on pumice areas is now controlled strictly. **1953** LINKLATER *Year of Space* (1954) 203 Big trees abound, and lianas and scrub-growth fill the intervals between them.

b. Comb. scrub-belt, country [AND 1847], **track**.
1980 HOLDEN *Stag* 14 They were just on the point of whirling around and racing pell-mell to the nearby **scrub-belt** when the strange object suddenly moved. **1951** LEVY *Grasslands NZ* (1970) 265 Most of the **scrub country** of the harder parts of coastal Otago could be vastly improved. **1988** WARR *Bush-burn to Butter* 43 Scrub country was brought into cultivation and pasture much more easily. **1986** *Islands 37* 39 Apart from me, swag on shoulder, it was empty, but he'd know it promised more than the **scrub track** down to the hidden bach.

4. With *pa. ppl.* forming adjectives: **scrub-clad; -covered; -clothed; -filled; -hidden; infested**.
1960 MASTERS *Back-Country Tales* 222 That amazing gift makes it possible for a horse to find its way..along dangerous bush and **scrub clad** mountain tracks, over which it may have been only once. **1964** HINTZ *Trout at Taupo* 36 It is scrub-clad, with some lovely remnants of native bush. **1916** ANZAC *On the Anzac Trail* 117 Back of the crescent strand [at Anzac] rose the..**scrub-clothed** slope, its breast seamed and gashed by *dongas*. **1881** NESFIELD *Chequered Career* 54 The Hen and Chickens..are simply **scrub-covered** islets. **1905** SATCHELL *Toll of Bush* 5 Low scrub-covered hills walled it in; beyond rose great bush-clad ranges. **1911** *Triad* 11 Dec. 24 [They] rode at a walk, along the undulating track through the broken scrub-covered country. **1922** COWAN *NZ Wars* (1955) I. 309 They had not been long there before a sudden volley was fired from a scrub-covered bank of the river. **1935** MAXWELL *Recollections* 99 There was between the tall bush and the sea a coastal belt of flax, cabbage tree and scrub-covered land. **1960** MASTERS *Back-Country Tales* 120 The heavy scrub covered country in which Doug had been injured, was very rugged. **1986** IHIMAERA *Matriarch* 107 This place of old wooden shacks and scrub-covered foothills. **1959** MIDDLETON *The Stone* 56 Around and beneath us **scrub-filled** gulleys fell away to green flats. **1951** PARK *Witch's Thorn* 87 He knew a secret, **scrub-hidden** place under the bridge where a fellow could hide and have a bonzer view of Mrs Hush's place. **1960** MASTERS *Back-Country Tales* 52 It now stands a deserted habitation, in a **scrub infested** area of abandoned country, that 30 odd years ago, carried..1,000 sheep.

5. In transf. use in the phr. **in the scrub**, in the remote countryside, 'in the sticks'.
1991 *Evening Post* (Wellington) 24 May 4 My daughter as a group leader has spent a fair bit of time in the scrub, and did her job well.

scrub, *v.* [AND 1860.] *trans.* and *intr.* To clear scrub from country, or undergrowth from forested areas. See also UNDERSCRUB *v.*
1921 FOSTON *At the Front* 69 Others could divert streams or creeks, scrub or fell bush, use a wheelbarrow. **1973** *Islands 4* 116 One of us would go ahead scrubbing. Slashing the undergrowth. The others cut the trees. **1983** *NZ Times* 8 May 4 This old chap's job for many years was scrubbing the packtrack... 'I never failed to picture him down on his knees, soap and hot water, scrubbing.' The old chap, the scrubber, lived in an ancient hut, a mere shell of wood, a door at one end, a chimney at the other. **1989** RICHARDS *Pioneer's Life* 89 I instructed him on how to sharpen..his slasher, and how to 'scrub' or cut the small undergrowth.

Hence **scrubber**, SCRUB-CUTTER.
1889 SKEY *Pirate Chief* 178 Scrubber, stay thy arm so strong, Stay thy slasher keen and long; Let the scrub yet graceful wave... And the scrubber let the scrub wave on. **1983** [see verb above].

scrubbed, *ppl. a.* [AND 1899.] Scrub-covered.
1870 WHITWORTH *Martin's Bay Settlement* 13 The [bush] land was densely scrubbed with undergrowth. **1878** HARRIS *Southern Guide Hot Lake Dist.* 50 The banks on either hand are high and densely scrubbed with fern.

scrubber.

1. [AND 1874.] An ill-favoured, ill-bred, or ill-thrifty animal (esp. a horse) or person.
1876 KENNEDY *Colonial Travel* 249 Then we four adventurers in Indian file..mounted on the shaggiest of small 'scrubbers'. **1878** MCINDOE *Sketch of Otago* 62 With regard to horse hire..the legitimate charge is 7/6 per day for the use of a Maori 'scrubber'. **1883** BRADSHAW *NZ As It Is* 63 We do not for a moment assert that 'scrubbers' are to be found. **1912** WILSON *Reminisc. Early Settlement Dunedin* 216 They should have good stock instead of scrubbers. **1948** FINLAYSON *Tidal Creek* (1979) 96 You remember Nancy? You wouldn't even try to milk her like the silly little scrubber you used to be. *Ibid.* 138 'That cattlelick man,' says Uncle Ted. 'The dirty scrubber! I'll give him a kick to blazes.' **1968** *NZ Contemp. Dict. Suppl.* (Collins) 17 *scrubber n.* wild bullock or cow, poor quality animal.

2. An animal bred or living in the scrub. See also *scrub bull* (SCRUB *n.* 1 c).
1897 WRIGHT in Alexander & Currie *NZ Verse* (1906) 70 New fences climb the warm brown spurs to guard the scrubber ewes, Because the run is broken up for hungry cockatoos. **1904** LANCASTER *Sons o' Men* 21 He considered the chance of picking these scrubbers out of the gullies. **c1930** *Whitcombe's Etym. Dict. Aust.-NZ Suppl.* 10 scrubber n. a bullock that has escaped into the scrub and become wild.

scrubbing, *vbl. n.* **underscrubbing** (UNDERSCRUB *v.* 1). Compare SCRUB-CUTTING *vbl. n.*
1955 WILSON *Land of My Children* 5 A thoughtless owner who delayed in passing the scrubbing [*sc.* as done well enough to allow felling of trees]. **1986** RICHARDS *Off the Sheep's Back* 58 The first operation when starting a bush job is to do the scrubbing (cutting the small undergrowth, supplejack, kiekie and vines) with a slasher.

scrubby, *a.* Of land, covered with scrub; of vegetative cover, consisting of scrub; of a shrub or plant, stunted in form.
1840 BEST *Journal* 9 Dec. (1966) 263 The valley was nothing remarkable not differing from the usual characteristics of a N.Z. Valley viz. Narrow bounded by steep scrubby hills and watered by a fine stream. **1844** STEPHENS *Journal* (ATLTS) 257 Travelling today..partly through wood and partly through scrubby brushwood and fern. **1857** HURSTHOUSE *NZ* II. 330 Grass land, consists of coarse grasses, intermixed with scrubby fern, flax..and ti tree. **1860** in Butler *First Year* (1863) iii 28 The little townlet..the scattered wooden boxes of houses, with ragged roods of scrubby ground between them. **1873** *TrNZI* V. 416 Ranges found covered with rich sub-alpine, scrubby vegetation. **1883** GREEN *High Alps* 80 They [*sc.* moas] may not have frequented the plains so much as the scrubby valleys. **1902** *Settler's Handbook NZ* (Lands Dept.) 2 The forests contain a mixture of trees of all kinds, from the giant kauri to scrubby tea-tree or manuka. **1919** WAITE *New Zealanders at Gallipoli* 323 Snipers' Nest.—A scrubby hill about 1000 yards from the sea. **1948** FINLAYSON *Tidal Creek* (1979) 54 The Crummer's place at Tidal Creek is..stuck on a scrubby kind of no-man's-land behind old Aspey's section. **1959** SHADBOLT *New Zealanders* (1986) 10 I grew to awareness rejecting as alien our scrubby backblocks farm. **1977** MARKS *Hammer & Tap* 510 He found 'some very good sheep country' but also a great deal of 'scrubby' land. **1982** *Listener* 31 Mar. 19 Here, on a scrubby river terrace..is the pa where Tihu's grandfather..lived. **1986** RICHARDS *Off the Sheep's Back* 64 The farm was poor and only partially improved, the majority being in its original state of scrubby tea tree and tawhine.

scrub-cutter.

1. A tool or machine for cutting scrub.
1886 STOUT *Notes on Progress NZ* 28 The following are manufactured in the colony—viz., ploughs, chaff-cutters,..disc-harrows,..horse-powers,..scrub-cutters.

2. [AND 1845.] One employed to cut scrub to clear land.
1910 *Truth* 27 Aug. 7 In the Arcade they met one William Walker, who was introduced..as the man who wanted scrub-cutters. **1927** GUTHRIE-SMITH *Birds* 52 During the past season another Grey Duck's nest was got, found accidentally by one of a party of scrub-cutters. **1936** WEST *Sheep Kings* 87 Timber-men and scrub-cutters and post-splitters. **1965** SHADBOLT *Among Cinders* 139 Hubert studied his slick suit, then the parked Jaguar, in disbelief. His face said he'd never seen anyone less like a scrub-cutter in all his life. **1974** AGNEW *Loner* 104 Thirty yards away a dozen scrub-cutters, brandishing slashers, were charging down on us. **1995** WINTER *All Ways Up Hill* 201 When he got the offer of a job in a scrub-cutter's camp he took it at once.

scrub-cutting, *vbl. n.* Also in quasi-participial use (see quots. 1943, 1960, 1974). [AND 1891.] The work of cutting down and clearing scrub. Also *attrib.*
1905 *Weekly Press* (Christchurch) 25 Jan. 68 [The] manager of Te Awaite station, knew Collinson as a contractor for scrub cutting. **1910** *Truth* 9 Apr. 6 He had to take some scrub-cutting contracts at 3s 6d an acre, and his Worship surmised that it depended upon how thick the scrub was. **1919** HOLLAND *Armageddon or Calvary* 177 A raid..was made on this scrub-cutting camp. **1927** GUTHRIE-SMITH *Birds* 3 The great pumiceous region..has not yet—though scrub-cutting and ploughing are in progress—been seriously affected. **1930** *Na To Hoa Aroha* (1987) II. 31 Scrub-cutting and the clearing of black-berry are seen all along the road. **1943** *Pattie Perano Diary* 13 Apr. in Grady *Perano Whalers* (1982) 85 Dad and Olsen scrub cutting again. **1960** MASTERS *Back-Country Tales* 142 On February 26, 1904, a man named Ross who was scrubcutting with Collinson.., heard a shot followed by a groan. **1974** HILLIARD *Maori Woman* 53 He'd had eight months as a knife-hand in a bacon factory, a month scrub-cutting. **1985** HUNT *I'm Ninety-five* 36 I..wrote a whole poem about that scrub cutting.

scrubie /ˈskrubi/, *a. Obs.* [f. a Brit. dial. var. of *scurvy*, often found also as *scrubby*: see OED *scruby*; EDD *scrooby*.] In the quot. prob. used generally as a pejorative: 'scrubby', 'dirty', difficult or unpleasant (to shear).
1955 *Star-Sun* (Christchurch) 19 May 4 There was hardly a fleece free from sand in the whole clip, and it is no wonder that the old-time shearers used to complain about the 'scrubie' sheep because they were really tough shearing.

scrum, *n.*[1] *Obs.* [AND 1891.] Rhyming slang for 'thrum', a threepenny-bit. Cf. THRUM.
1905 *Truth* 16 Sept. 5 Couples who did not possess the necessary 'brown' or 'scrum' would recline on the grass [instead of paying for seats]. *Ibid.* 4 Nov. 3 They would find more people ready to chuck a scrum in the [church] plate.

scrum, *n.*[2] [Transf. use of *scrum* a rugby union scrummage.] In *transf.* or *fig.* uses. A competitive struggle. Also as a *v. intr.*, to struggle competitively for a goal.
1938 LAWLOR *House of Templemore* 98 Young calves 'scrumming' to dip their heads in the long troughs of milk. **1987** ROBERTS *Politicians, Public Servants & Public Enterprise* 104 One famous Permanent Head in discussing his life as an administrator said that he could not 'abide the annual scrum for resources'.

scull: see SKULL.

scunge /skʌndʒ/. [f. *scungy a.*]

1. [Cf. *Macquarie Dict. New Words* (1990) 1988.] A nasty or morally-objectionable person.
1966 *Salient* (Wellington) 29 July 11 Now! about the scunge who is flogging my Fanta bottles from the Caf. **1967** *Comment 31* June 14 He obviously thought I must be a bit of a scunge asking political questions when it was my job to report on how well the war was going.

2. a. Bodily and other filth or muck, 'gunge'.
1972 *2ZB Wellington Commercial* 18 Sept. 11.08 am Relda Familton (speaking from a down-town sauna bath): 'And feel all that muck, and sweat, and scunge rolling off you in the sauna.' **1985** *Listener* 2 Feb. 58 It [*sc.* an old movie film] was so dirty and disgusting that we had to clean it all and put it through the machines to take all the scunge off. **1988** *Short Stories NZ* 73 The cracks and corners were full of scunge, like dirty fingernails.

b. *Special Comb.* **scunge-bucket**, a term of abuse.
1986 *Listener* 26 Apr. 45 He says he will never vote Labour because they are the party of 'union bosses, carpet-baggers, scunge-buckets, window-dressers and vegetarians'.

scungy /ˈskʌndʒi/, *a.* Also **scungie**, **skungy**. [Prob. a new formation, e.g. from *sc*(um or *sc*(urf + g)*unge*, g)*ungey*, rather than a survival or revival in NZ and Austral. of a transferred use of Sc., Irish and Shetland Island *scunge n.* a sly or vicious fellow; *v.* to slink about, fawn: see EDD *v.* and *n.* 1, 4, 5; also OED.] Of people, things, ideas, filthy, greasy, smelly; nasty; morally obliquitous; sordid.

[*Note*] The word appeared suddenly in the early 1960s first among students. (*Scungy a.* was first heard by Ed. in 1962 from an Auckland University person.) OED derives from Sc. dial. (origin unknown) and quotes mod. Brit. use. See also the following from Australian surfie slang (the earliest Austral. recorded use): 1964 *Quadrant 30* June–July (Vol.VIII. No.2) 18 If someone's got a car..a few of us might take one of these scungy birds and promote her [i.e., arrange serial gang intercourse with her]... *Scungy*: a rough-headed Bird. See also 1980 POHL *Beyond the Blue Event Horizon* (Gollancz) 110 A male and a female, standing side by side. They had faces and arms and legs, and the female had breasts. Both had skungy beards and long hair pulled into bands. Cf. Bloomsbury *Neologisms* (1966) *skungy* unpleasant.

1964 *Salient* (Wellington) 16 Apr. 1 *Pitch-hacking* has been in the news lately. The story goes that some scungy anonymous louts tore up the sacred turf for the first cricket test in a savage outburst of meaningless destruction. **1966** *Critic* (Otago University) 8 July 6 But I'm much more concerned about My own old skungy body. **1971** BAXTER *Collected Poems* (1980) 532 She [*sc.* a reporter] took a photograph of the scungiest bedroom... And stuck it in her rag, with a long rave on hygiene. **1974** AGNEW *Loner* 166 They were the dirtiest, scungiest, most scurrilous, no-good mutts a man could ever hope never to set eyes on. **1987** GEE *Prowlers* 33 In my opinion you were a scungy lot, with few exceptions. **1991** *Evening Post* (Wellington) 16 Oct. 48 Drop that ya scungy mongrel.

scunner. Also occas. **skunner**. [f. Sc. dial.] A (strong) dislike.

1939 BEATTIE *First White Boy Born Otago* 188 The sale was at Invercargill, but I did not go down as I had got what the Scot calls a 'scunner' at the district. **1943** MARSH *Colour Scheme* 80 Young Simon's so disgusted he's taken a scunner on anything that looks like smart business. **1978** COWLEY *Growing Season* 126 Oh, Mary, you know I've got a skunner against a collar and tie, anyway. Could you not have brought something comfortable? **1992** PARK *Fence around the Cuckoo* 13 Disliking..[Te Kuiti] on earlier..visits, she now took a scunner to the town that lasted till her dying day.

scurvy-grass. Also **(Captain) Cook's scurvy-grass, scurvy weed**. Any of a wide variety of plants, esp. of the family Brassicaceae, believed or known to be a remedy for scurvy. **a.** As **((Captain) Cook's) scurvy-grass**, any of several native and naturalized herbs or subshrubs of *Lepidium* spp. (fam. Brassicaceae) with small crucifer flowers and pouch-shaped pods, esp. the native *Lepidium oleraceum* used by Captain Cook as a fresh vegetable, once common but now confined mainly to some offshore islands. See also *Captain Cook's cress* (CRESS).

1769 COOK *Journals* 27 Oct. (1955) I. 184 The other place I landed at was at the north point of the Bay where I got as much Sellery and Scurvy grass as loaded the Boat. **1773** COOK *Journals* 19 May (1961) II. 165 Knowing that sellery and Scurvey grass and other vegetables were to be found in this Sound and that when boiled with Wheat or Pease and Portable Soup makes a very nourishing and wholesome Diet which is extreemly beneficial both in cureing and preventing the Scurvey, I went my self at day light in the Morn in search of some. **1891** *TrNZI* XXIII. 412 Here and there patches of Captain Cook's scurvy-grass (*Lepidium oleraceum*) were growing vigorously on the highly-manured ground. **1906** CHEESEMAN *Manual NZ Flora* 39 [*Lepidium oleraceum*] Best known as 'Cook's scurvy-grass'. The whole plant has a heavy disagreeable smell and hot biting taste. **1910** COCKAYNE *NZ Plants & Their Story* 161 *Lepidium* is the most important New Zealand [crucifer] genus, and *L. oleraceum*, Cook's scurvy-grass, the most celebrated plant. **1926** HILGENDORF *Weeds* 95 Narrow-leaved Cress (*Lepidium ruderale*) is also called swine cress, wart cress, way-side cress, wild cress, pepper cress, pepper weed, and scurvy grass. It is common on waste lands, especially near the sea. **1927** *TrNZI* LVII. 919 Cook's scurvy-grass *Lepidium oleraceum* var. *acutidentatum*. **1952** RICHARDS *Chatham Is.* 30 *Lepidium..oleraceum*... The famous Cook's scurvy grass is 10–24 in. high... Found on rocky shores here and in New Zealand... Nau, Eketara. **1968** JOHNSON *Turn of Tide* 74 On making New Zealand, Cook was pleased to find wild celery growing in profusion as well as 'scurvy grass' of the cress family. **1971** *New Zealand's Heritage* I. 113 Cook's famous scurvy grass, *Lepidium oleraceum*, belongs to the cabbage family. Nowadays it is hard to come by, for it has been largely eaten out by sheep. **1984** *Press* (Christchurch) 11 Dec. 25 A rare herb known as Cook's scurvy grass, thought to have vanished from the South Island, has been found in the Moeraki area near Oamaru. **1995** CRUMP *Bushwoman* 148 Captain Cook's scurvy grass even started growing again. It's extremely rare and doesn't look like a grass, with its celery-like leaves. It grows on cliff faces by the sea in the rich droppings of the nesting seabirds.

b. As **scurvy weed**.

1889 FEATON *Art Album NZ Flora* 178 Nau [Maori name]..Scurvy weed [Settlers' name]..*Lepidium oleraceum*..Herb.

sea.

1. Used *attrib.* or as special Comb. in the names of plants and animals. **a.** See BASS, BINDWEED 1 b, BREAM 1 a, 1 c, MULLET 2 (1), PERCH *n.* 2 (4), RIMU *n.*² 2, SALMON 1, TROUT 2 (7).

b. sea-bear *obs.* [spec. use of *sea-bear* for local seal species: cf. OED *sea-bear* 2], the New Zealand fur seal (*Arctocephalus forsteri*), SEAL *n.*¹ 2 (1); occas. the female *sea-lion* (*Phocarctos hookeri*); **sea-devil** *obs., sea leopard*; **sea-ear** *obs.* [spec. use of *sea-ear*, *Haliotis* spp. for local species: see OED 1], PAUA; **sea-elephant**, ELEPHANT SEAL; **sea-elephant oil**, oil obtained from the blubber of sea-elephants; **sea-hawk**, see HAWK 2 (4); **sea-holly** [spec. use of the name *sea-holly* for local species], *Eryngium vesiculosum* (fam. Apiaceae), a tufted coastal herb with rigid toothed leaves or submerged linear leaves; **sea leopard**, see *leopard seal* (SEAL *n.*¹ 2 (3)); **sea lettuce**, *Ulva* spp. (fam. Chlorophyceae), a green seaweed of shallow and estuarine waters, esp. the widespread *U. lactuca*; **sea-lion**, usu. **New Zealand sea-lion**, or occas. **Auckland Islands** or **Hooker's sea-lion**, *Phocarctos hookeri* (fam. Otariidae), a lively, totally-protected hair seal of very restricted distribution, breeding mainly on the Auckland Islands; **sea-opal**, a commercial name for polished iridescent PAUA-SHELL (q.v.) used in ornaments and costume jewellery; **sea potato**, KAEO; **sea swallow**, in New Zealand usu. the *white-fronted tern* (TERN 2 (10)), from a similarity of its forked tail and pointed wings to those of a swallow; **sea tulip**, the long-stalked tulip-like sea-squirt *Pyura* (formerly *Boltenia*) *pachydermatina* (Sub-Class Ascidacea) (see also KAEO).

1775 COOK *Journals* 31 Jan. (1961) II. 605 Here [in Staten Land] were also the same sort of Seals which we found in New Zealand generally known by the name of **Sea Bears**, at least so we called them. **1817** NICHOLAS *NZ* II. 318 The ursine-seal or sea-bear, and the sea-lion, are found in congregated herds to the southward. **1838** POLACK *NZ* I. 317 The *sea-bear* (phoca ursina) was formerly the largest seal; but these animals are so well known, that they require no further description. **1861** HAAST *Topographical Exploration of Nelson* 134 Mr. John Rochfort..killed a sea-bear (Ursina marina), seven feet long. **1866** [see *sea-lion* below]. **1893** *TrNZI* XXV. 256 Fur-seals, or Sea-bears, which have an under-fur as well as a clothing of long hair, both of which are cast and renewed each summer, so that the skin of the animal when taken at the proper season is of value as a 'pelt' or furrier's material. **1909** CHILTON *Subantarctic Islands NZ* II. 544 The female [sea-lion], or sea-bear, is smaller and sleeker, and grey in colour. **c1920** BEATTIE *Trad. Lifeways Southern Maori* (1994) 156 Rapoka is the sea-leopard, also known as the **sea-devil**. It is not so fearsome as its name and one veteran remarked, 'An old woman could kill the rapoka it is so easily dealt with.' **1770** COOK *Journals* 31 Mar. (1955) I. 284 An od design'd figure of a man with..large white eys made of the Shells of **sea ears**. **1848** WAKEFIELD *Handbook NZ* 160 The natives fish for (kawai) with a hook lined with pieces of the parti-coloured shell of the..sea-ear. **1892** WILLIAMS *Dict. NZ Lang.* 74 *Kororiwha..haliotis virginica*; a small species of *sea-ear*. **1904** TREGEAR *The Maori Race* 241 The mat-pins..were often made from..the iridescent shell of the *paua* (the sea-ear: *Haliotis iris*). **1924** BUCKNILL *Sea Shells NZ* 19 This species is mostly known by its Maori name—Pawa,—but it is also called the Sea Ear. **1942** ANDERSEN *Maori Place Names* 14 Paua (sea-ear, or mutton-fish-Haliotis). **1957** WILLIAMS *Dict. Maori Lang.* 273 *Paua..Haliotis* of several species, *sea-ear, mutton-fish*. **1977** *Auckland at Full Stretch* 29 We dived for a few paua—abalone, ormer, or sea-ear. **1893** *TrNZI* XXV. 256 **Sea-elephants**. These are massive, unwieldy, and gigantic animals, which have a very restricted distribution, being confined to the islands in the extreme south. **1909** CHILTON *Subantarctic Islands NZ* II. 549 The sea-elephant has occurred at Campbell Island. **1938** *Auckland Weekly News* 6 Apr. 96 Besides the fur seals,.. sea leopards and sea elephants thronged the reefs and cliffs, rocks and beaches on the Solanders. **1945** *NZEF Times* 22 Jan. 7 Billy, a sea elephant, who recently adopted the Hutt River as his regular habitat, is dead. **1947** POWELL *Native Animals NZ* 91 Sea elephants were formerly killed in numbers for their blubber, but not for their fur. **1951** SORENSEN *Wild Life in the Subantarctic* 6 'Something awful' might also be well used to describe the smell of the sea elephants. **1969** KNOX *Natural History of Canterbury* 521 A female sea-elephant gave birth to a pup on a beach close to Kaikoura in the spring of 1967. **1986** GRADY *Sealers and Whalers* 53 The name 'sea elephant' comes from the inflatable, trunk-like proboscis which is very conspicuous in bulls. Early sealers simply called them 'elephants'. **1889** *Otago Daily Times* (Dunedin) 19 Jan. 4 [Advt] **Sea Elephant Oil**, refined by ourselves, is the best of lubricants, and the most suitable for Harvesters and all other Agricultural Machinery. Sample Free. **1890** *Otago Witness* (Dunedin) 13 Feb. 15 The Resident Magistrate..was called on to adjudicate on two cases..that occurred during the last voyage of the Janet Ramsay in search of sea elephant oil... No attempt was made to get elephant oil. **1907** MCNAB *Murihiku* 176 A vessel called the Caroline..engaged in the Macquarie Island trade..is first noted as returning with sea elephant oil on 11th July, 1823. **1940** LAING & BLACKWELL *Plants NZ* 334 *Eryngium vesiculosum* (The **Sea-holly**). **1969** *Standard Common Names Weeds* 68 sea holly Eryngium. **1958** *Whitcombe's Modern Jun. Dict.* (8edn.) 358 **Sea lettuce**. A name used in New Zealand for a soft green maritime plant growing in vast quantities in the estuaries of New Zealand rivers. **1964** DEMPSEY *Little World Stewart Is.* 25 Every shallow pool is a garden of seaweed, with long ruffles of sea lettuce, carrageen and Neptune's necklace. **1979** NATUSCH *Wild Fare for Wilderness Foragers* 26 Sea lettuce (*Ulva lactuca*) spreads glistening sheets and frilly ribbons of glossy green among the rocks and pools. **1984** DUCKWORTH *Disorderly Conduct* 112 The moon spotlights the flat water... A pile of sea lettuce slithers under one foot. **1773** FORSTER *Resolution Jrnl.* 28 Nov. (1982) III. 430 Saw few Petrels & several Seals or perhaps rather Sea-Cows, or **Sea-Lions**. **1817** [see *sea-bear* above]. **1826** SHEPHERD *Journal* in Howard *Rakiura* (1940) 357 The Male [hair seal] generally called the Sea Lion grows much larger and of a darker colour than the female. **1838** POLACK *NZ* I. 316 The amphibious *sea-lion and lioness* (phoca leonina) have been often met with on the coasts by the sealers who have been residents on the southern island and islets to the south-west of the Island of Victoria. **1866** ANGAS *Polynesia* 56 The sea-lion is found on the west coast of the Middle Island of New Zealand; where also the fur-seal of commerce (probably the sea-bear) was formerly hunted in great numbers. **1893** *TrNZI* XXV. 256 Hair-seals, or Sea-lions, which are covered with long coarse hair and have no under-fur, and are therefore only commercially valuable for the production of oil, and formerly as food and clothing. *Ibid.* XXV. 257 This group, the sea-lions..is represented in the south by *Protoarctus hookeri*, which is supposed to be a different species frequenting the islands in the longitude of New Zealand and southward, and is best known at the present time as the Auckland Islands sea-lion. **1909** CHILTON *Subantarctic Islands NZ* II. 544 The male, or sea-lion, is a large bulky animal of dark-brown colour, and the old bulls

SEAGULL

have a thick mass of long hair, disposed mane-like over the neck and shoulders. **1945** [see WIG *n.*¹]. **1951** SORENSEN *Wild Life in the Subantarctic* 18 In the breeding season, the long sandy beach is covered from end to end with harems, each bull sea lion having about twelve females, or sea bears as they are called. **1966** *Encycl. NZ* III. 203 Sea lions are generally larger and heavier than fur seals; large males measure up to 10 ft and have a characteristic 'mane'; mature females range from 5 to 7 ft in length. **1983** KING *Seals of the World* 33 Hooker's Sea Lion, New Zealand Sea Lion *Phocarctos hookeri*... Hooker's Sea Lion is an animal of very restricted distribution. **1990** *Handbook NZ Mammals* 256 *New Zealand sea lion. Phocarctos hookeri*... Also called Hooker's sea lion, hair seal. *Ibid.* 261 In pre-European times, the New Zealand sea lion ranged up the east coast of the North Island and was exploited by the Maori for food. From the discovery of the Auckland Is. in 1806 to the end of the main sealing period in the 1830s, large numbers of sea lions were killed by sealers and whalers for hides, oil and food. **1942** ANDERSEN *Maori Place Names* 15 Haliotis iris, the largest and commonest species [of paua], the one so popular under the name of **sea-opal**. **1946** *JPS* LV. 155 A rage has set in for the wearing of paua jewellery..and a new name has been given to it—sea-opal, and its deeper tints are as beautiful as opal if not as durable. **1967** NATUSCH *Animals NZ* 187 Kaeo and **Sea Potatoes** subclass Ascidiacea. **1871** HUTTON *Catalogue Birds NZ* 42 Sterna frontalis... **Sea Swallow**. Tara. **1873** BULLER *Birds NZ* 282 The term 'Sea-swallow', as applied to this Tern, is a very appropriate one; for on watching the evolutions of a flock..one is forcibly reminded of a flight of Swallows coursing in the air. **1886** *TrNZI* XVIII. 99 Sterna—Sea swallows (*Tara*). Five species in New Zealand. **1936** GUTHRIE-SMITH *NZ Naturalist* 118 The Sea Swallow..still survives in vast numbers..on the North Island coast-line. **1947** [see KAHAWAI BIRD]. **1952** RICHARDS *Chatham Is.* 82 *Sterna..frontalis*... Sea Swallow, Tom Noddy. Tara. **1966** [see TERN 2 (10)]. **1982** SALE *Four Seasons* 105 Each evening the young sea swallows gather with their elders on the shore... They derive one of their popular names from the forked tail, pointed wings and agile flight which make them so like the welcome swallows of the land. **1947** POWELL *Native Animals NZ* 58 **Sea Tulip**... A tunicate with a long stalk attachment known as Kaeo by the Maoris of the Chatham Islands. **1952** RICHARDS *Chatham Is.* 95 *Boltenia..pachydermatima*... Sea Tulip. Kaeo. **1968** MORTON & MILLER *NZ Sea Shore* 357 Attention will first be caught by the forests of long-stalked sea tulips..girdling the reefs within the fringes of bladder kelp. **1972** *JPS* LXXXI. 354 Shellfish were a staple food [in the Chathams] especially *paua, pipi,* and *kaeo* (sea tulips). **1983** GUNSON *Collins Guide to Seashore* 37 The most spectacular tunicate is the sea tulip..known to the Maori as the Kaeo, the edible inner body apparently having a rather piquant, briny taste... The diver may come across dense fields of them in shallow water, all waving gently together in the current like a vast garden of tulips.

2. Special Comb. **sea cockie** [transf. use of *cockie* small farmer], a fisherman; **seaweed pencil** *obs.*, a crude 'instrument' formerly used for procuring illegal non-medical abortion.

1966 BRAMBLEY *Sea-cockies of Manukau* [Title] **1907** *Truth* 28 Sept. 4 She did not know what a '**seaweed pencil**' was, nor what a 'tent' was. She had informed no girl that she had used a crochet needle for a certain purpose, and she had, as a matter of fact, never used the needle.

seagull, *n.* See also GULL *n.*¹ In various *fig.* and *transf.* uses.

1. *Watersiders.* Occas. also **gull**. [f. one who, like a seagull, sits around on the wharf waiting for a livelihood to turn up: AND 1965.] A casual (non-union) wharf-labourer.

[**c1926** THE MIXER *Transport Workers' Song Book* 44 As they sit upon the stringer While the stop-work meeting's on. What a study! Let us paint it As the seagulls fly about While the stringer birds are anxious For the meeting to come out.] **1938** *NZ Observer* 24 Nov. 7 If the port is exceptionally busy, 'gulls' may be needed to work an entire ship... This practice of transferring unionists from a ship which has been completed to a 'seagull' ship is the fly in the ointment. **1939** *Auckland Capping Carnival Book* 24 Lest a wharfie should suffer a strain; Seagulls unsavory National knavery. **1945** MUNDY *Body-snatcher & Seagull* (unpaged) A Seagull may be classed as a permanent casual worker who puts in a good deal of his time sitting down upon the stringers on the wharf for the purpose of being able to say that he is a watersider and thereby gain a fictitious status as being one of the best paid workers in the country. **1959** SLATTER *Gun in My Hand* 225 Ended up as a seagull on the Wellington wharves loading up the Home boats. **1963** CASEY *As Short a Spring* 275 His father had been a sea-gull—a casual wharfie who had earned enough in three days of the week to keep him in the pub the other four. **1975** HENDERSON *Log of a Superfluous Son* 33 The wharfies sat on forms at the tables... 'She called us seagulls,' said Alec Morrow. **1984** MARSHALL *Day Hemingway Died* 38 The union men were the aristocracy of the shift; anyone else was a seagull, no matter how regular. **1991** *National Business Review* 13 Sept. 6 Dickson represents the bad old days..when 'seagulls' lined up in the mornings in the hope their brawn would be needed to load or unload a ship. **1995** *Independent* (Auckland) 24 Mar. 7 Auckland stevedoring companies are limited by collective employment contracts to the amount of casual labour they can hire and the type of work carried out by 'seagulls', as they're known.

2. *Rugby union.* A loose forward who positions himself around scrums, line-outs, rucks, etc. as though scavenging for pickings on the outskirts of tight play.

1975 HOWITT *NZ Rugby Greats* 37 Probably because he was a loose forward himself and appreciated the need for a 'seagull', he chose me for the North Island team four years in a row, from 1953 to 1956.

seagull, *v.*

1. *Watersiders. intr.* To work as a casual waterside labourer. Often as a *vbl. n.*

1938 *NZ Observer* 24 Nov. 7 There are those who have adopted 'seagulling' as a livelihood. **1947** *NZ Observer* 25 Jan. 9 We agree that 'seagulling' is not too strenuous an occupation. **1964** MIDDLETON *Walk on Beach* 217 Some of the men seagulled on the wharf. **1978** GARNIER et al. *The Hunter and the Hill* 34 During the evenings, when he wasn't working night shift on the ferry, Kirk 'seagulled' on the Auckland waterfront for one shilling an appearance. **1980** HALL *Prisoners of Mother England* 29 I got my non-union card—seagulling it's called. **1991** *National Business Review* 13 Sept. 6 To Dickson the union represents the more recent bad old days when seagulling was replaced with effective control of the industry by union officials.

2. *Rugby union.* To play as a SEAGULL *n.* 2. Also as a *vbl. n.* and *ppl. a.* (Occas. also heard as *swanning.*) See quot. 1951.

1951 June p.c. J. Clancy (Wellington). A person who gets offside through waiting for opportunities, e.g. at the side of the scrum, is said to be 'seagulling'. Probably from the opportunistic habits of 'seagull' labourers on wharves, waiting for something to turn up. **1953** *NZ Observer* 23 Sept. 23 Jones..will have to curb a 'seagulling' tendency. **1975** HOWITT *NZ Rugby Greats* 36 It didn't stop young Clark, seagulling flanker

SEAL

exceptional, from making an instant hit with the selectors.

seal, *n.*¹

1. [In locally significant use mainly with a defining word.] Any of various large fish-eating marine mammals of the family Phocidae having sleek, furry bodies of special commercial significance in late 18th and early 19th century New Zealand. See also CLAPMATCH, ELEPHANT SEAL, WIG *n.*

1773 FORSTER *Resolution Journal* 1 Apr. (1982) II. 244 We described..fish & birds & a Seal, which was but small. **1793** in McNab *Historical Records NZ* (1908) I. 182 Captain Raven sailed from Port Jackson in October last for Dusky Bay, in New Zealand..to kill seals. **1821** in McNab *Historical Records NZ* (1908) I. 559 The best season for taking seals for the China market is when the pups are six months old. **1966** *Encycl. NZ* III. 203 Three species of seals breed at present in the New Zealand region..: two are eared seals, and the third is the largest of the true or Phocid seals, the sea elephant.

2. With a modifier: **fur (New Zealand fur), hair, leopard**.

(1) **fur (New Zealand fur) seal**. *Arctocephalus forsteri* (fam. Otariidae), a common coastal seal breeding in the South Island esp. around the Fiordland coast and as far south as Macquarie Island. See also KEKENO, *sea-bear* (SEA 1 b).

1806 BANKS in McNab *Historical Records NZ* (1908) I. 273 A certain portion of the seals of the southern hemisphere, called fur seals, have under the shaggy hair with which they are cover'd a coat of wool almost as fine as that of the beaver, and much more valuable than that of the rabbit. **1826** SHEPHERD *Journal* in Howard *Rakiura* (1940) 357 The Furr seals are here [Stewart Island] also but not so plentiful as the [hair seal]. **c1835** BOULTBEE *Journal* (1986) 105 [Hair seals] grow to larger size than the fur seal, which generally live on the barren rocks on the seaside. **1866** [see *sea-lion* (SEA 1 b)]. **1893** [see *sea-bear* (SEA 1 b)]. **1904** [see KEKENO]. **1922** *Auckland Weekly News* 19 Oct. 19 Provided certain rituals were observed at kills, and no blood was spilt, nor carcase flensed nor left upon the camping rocks, the fur-seal took no heed of man. **1966** *Encycl. NZ* III. 203 The New Zealand fur seal is peculiar to this country, although very similar to a closely related form inhabiting southern Australia and Tasmania. **1989** [see KEKENO]. **1990** *Handbook NZ Mammals* 255 Fur seals were killed by the Maori for food and clothing, and the teeth were used to make composite fishhooks... James Cook's crew killed fur seals in Dusky Sound in 1773, using the flesh for food, the skins to repair rigging and the fat for lamp fuel.

(2) **hair seal**. [So called from the mane of coarse hair on the adult male.] *Phocarctos hookeri* (fam. Otariidae), *New Zealand* (or *Hooker's*) *sea-lion* (SEA 1 b).

1826 SHEPHERD *Journal* in Howard *Rakiura* (1940) 357 Seals of the Hair kind are numerous here [on Stewart Island]... The Hare seal is a singular looking animal of the brownish colour. **c1826–27** BOULTBEE *Journal* (1986) 112 hair seal pàhkàk. **1830** MORRELL in McNab *Old Whaling Days* (1913) 82 Although the Auckland Isles once abounded with numerous herds of fur and hair-seal, the..seamen..have made such clean work of it as scarcely to leave a breed; at all events there was not one to be found on the 4th of January, 1830. **1893** [see *sea-lion* (SEA 1 b)]. **1938** *Auckland Weekly News* 30 Mar. 96 The coarse scrub and grasses..were the sheltering places of hair seals and sea-lions. **1950** BEATTIE *Far Famed Fiordland* 24 The seal called pakake by the Maori is the hair seal. **1986** FRASER *Beyond the Roaring Forties* 79 Hooker's sea lion pups at Sandy Bay on Enderby Islands. A hair seal, this

SEAL

species was slaughtered for its oil. **1990** *Handbook NZ Mammals* 256 *New Zealand sea lion Phocarctos hookeri...* Also called Hooker's sea lion, hair seal.

(3) **leopard seal**. Also **sea leopard**. *Hydrurga leptonyx* (fam. Phocidae), a long, spotted seal, fast in the water and of solitary habit.
    1874 *TrNZI* VI. 87 *Stenorhynchus leptonyx*. The sea Leopard. **1893** *Ibid.* XXV. 256 Sea-leopards..are large spotted seals covered with coarse hair. **1904** HUTTON & DRUMMOND *Animals NZ* 40 The natural home of the Sea Leopard is in the ice-pack and the islands near it; but it sometimes wanders north to New Zealand, Tasmania and New South Wales. **1917** WILLIAMS *Dict. Maori Lang.* 340 *Popoinangore.. Hydrurga leptonyx, sea-leopard*. **1930** REISCHEK *Yesterdays in Maoriland* (1933) 271 We also saw a sea-leopard fishing among the kelp. **1986** FRASER *Beyond the Roaring Forties* 30 The leopard seal..is the only other true or earless seal found round New Zealand's subantarctic islands. **1990** *Handbook NZ Mammals* 271 The leopard seal is built for speed.

3. As **seals' ballast**, see quot. for an engaging theory.
    1872 *TrNZI* IV. 416 Anyone who had ever been about old whaling and sealing stations must have seen collections of round smooth stones of various sizes but mostly about the size of cannon-balls, lying on the beach... You will..be told that they are 'seal's ballast'..that the seal is a migratory animal, and that when it is about to take a long journey it will trim itself to exactly the proper weight for long and easy locomotion through the water. It picks up one of these stones and swallows it and goes into the water to try the effect. If it finds it requires more ballast it comes ashore again and repeats the dose. If it has too much weight... it vomits one or two of the stones out on the beach. Hence the stones are always termed 'seals' ballast'.

seal, *n.*² TARSEAL *n.* 1.
    1967 HENDERSON *Return to Open Country* 213 He put a home-lettered notice on the edge of the sacred seal announcing Hot Pies and Ice Cream, but the cars..roared past without stopping. **1985** SHERWOOD *Botanist at Bay* 23 At a warning notice 'Seal Ends' the tarmac stopped and gave way to loose chippings the size of potatoes.

seal, *v.* [spec. use of *seal* to make a surface impervious.] *trans.* TAR-SEAL *v.* 1.
    1969 HENDERSON *Open Country Calling* 276 It was too big an expense to seal the whole road. **1976** MCALLISTER *Old Taranaki & its Mountain* 66 Years were to pass before other counties attempted to overtake the Eltham lead and seal their roads. **1987** *Metro* (Auckland) May 52 A lot of suburban streets..were only sealed down their centres.
    Hence **sealed** *ppl. a.* [AND 1938], TAR-SEALED; **sealing** *n.*, TAR-SEALING.
    1966 *Weekly News* (Auckland) 5 Dec. 47 It was good to be back on a **sealed** highway. **1980** MANTELL *Murder Or Three* 13 The walkway had been placed in one of the latter areas [of bush]. Wide enough—four feet—and sealed. **1945** *NZ Dairy Exporter* 1 Sept. 91 'I wonder if I could get through all that sealing?'.. 'But—what do you want to go through the ceiling for?' **1969** HENDERSON *Open Country Calling* 276 We might be getting to the point where sealing is cheaper than maintenance. **1977** HOLCROFT *The Line of the Road* 168 After reconstruction came sealing; and this was what everyone was looking for... W.L. Carter pushed on with its programme for sealing with renewed vigour.

seasoning. [An extended use of *seasoning* salt, spices, etc. added to food as a relish.] A culinary stuffing comprising usu. a mixture of breadcrumbs, onion, herbs, etc. Also **seasoned**, filled or stuffed with such a mixture.

705

1955 *Journal of Agriculture Cookery Book* 149 Seasoning... Make breadcrumbs from pieces of stale white or brown bread with the crusts removed. **1961** MESSENGER *Dine with Elizabeth* 118 Roast Duck. Stuff with sage and onion seasoning and roast about one and a half hours in a moderately hot oven. **1976** MCDERMOTT *Lost & Found NZ* 20 'Seasoned' chickens means they are stuffed.

second cut. *Shearing.*

1. A second blow of the shears made to remove wool which has not been cut close enough to the sheep's skin with the first blow. See also *doublecut* (DOUBLE B), *two-cut* (TWO).
    1890 PEACHE *Journal* in Gray *Quiet with Hills* (1970) 82 But the machine does far better work and neither cuts the sheep nor the fleece (i.e. second cut, or cutting the fleece, or staple of the wool). **1899** *Hawera & Normanby Star* 9 Sep. 2 It is impossible to make a good 'second cut' to the wool as with the shears, therefore the clip is longer and more valuable. **1950** *NZJAg.* Oct. LXXXI. 311 An efficient shearer will not make many 'second cuts', but the presence of them among the fleeces in a bale will antagonise the wool buyer. **1965** *Listener* 26 Feb. 15 *Second cut:* (1) a blow made to remove wool which has not been cut close enough to the skin. **1973** FERNANDEZ *Tussock Fever* 13 He was past his best [as a shearer] and could only maintain his number by some very rough work, making second cuts to clean up the job. **1989** *NZ Eng. Newsletter* III. 27 *second cut:* This results when the shears are allowed to move off the sheep's skin and so into the fleece.

2. [AND 1882.] The short pieces of wool which result when a shearer takes two cuts of the shears when the first is too far above the sheep's skin and above the base of the staple; also in *attrib.* use as **second-cut wool**.
    1897 WRIGHT *Station Ballads* 34 Mighty lot of wool you've lost! Second cuts? Well, that ain't my fault, you've his wrinkled hide [to thank]. **1915** MACDONALD *NZ Sheepfarming* 69 The wool table..is made of battens about 1½in. wide..to permit the locks or second cuts to fall through. **1936** BELSHAW et al. *Agric. Organiz. NZ* 710 'Locks' consist mainly of short pieces of wool such as second cuts, sweepings and short wool. **1955** BOWEN *Wool Away* 3 The loss to our annual wool clip by second cuts is very large. **1960** MILLS *Sheep-O* 100 In money value the absence of second-cut wool certainly adds up. **1977** *Dominion* (Wellington) 24 Feb. 11 *Second cut* (1) A blow made to remove wool that has been left too long in shearing. (2) Short wool that was cut in a 'second cut'. **1982** *Agric. Gloss.* (MAF) 58 *Second cut*: Wool which is cut twice during shearing when the first cut is above the base of the staple. These short pieces of wool are of little value.

second five-eighth: see FIVE EIGHTH 2 b.

second shear. Also **second shearing**.

1. As **second shear**, usu. *attrib.* **a.** Of wool, from the second shearing of a sheep in any one season.
    1957 *NZJAg.* Oct. XCV. 331 Second shear is a fairly loose term used to describe wool from sheep shorn more than once in a season. **1958** *Ibid.* Oct. XCVII. 305 At Invercargill this season buyers refused to bid on certain lines of heavily branded second-shear wool. **1973** WHEELER *Hist. Sheep Stations NI* 58 Wool is cleaner if removed twice a year... And second-shear wool is in good demand for carpets. **1988** *More* (Auckland) Mar. 30 And skirt the dirty bits off the sides as they're shearing—it's only second shear wool, you see.

b. Of a sheep, shorn more than once in a season.

SECTION

    1963 WALLIS *Point of Origin* 181 Neil..supervised the last of the second-shear ewes through the yard gate. **1986** RICHARDS *Off the Sheep's Back* 169 Conditions are changed—second shear sheep are shorn—but fundamentally the shearers are much the same.

2. As **second shearing**, the second of two shearings of a sheep in any one season. See also quot. 1974.
    1974 *NZ Agric.* 68 The practice of shearing sheep twice a year or three times in 2 years is popular, especially in the North Island. This is known as 'second shearing' and tends to extend these 'out of season' offerings. **1988** *More* (Auckland) Mar. 32 I made enough money to put some in the bank and fly home to the King Country for second shear.

section, *n.*¹ [Spec. use of *section* one of the parts into which something is divided, for a surveyed parcel of land which is a subdivision of a larger area.]

1. *pre-1840*. [Orig. US, one square mile of undeveloped land (see OED *section n.* 2 e (b) and (d)); also Austral. (AND 1830, superseded by *block*).] An area of a square-mile (640 acres or 259 ha) of undeveloped land purchased from the Maori. (Later superseded by BLOCK *n.*¹ 1.)
    1839 *Weller's evidence to Legislative Council Committee* (Sydney) 8 July in McNab *Old Whaling Days* (1913) 279 Attached to one of my whaling stations is about thirty-six square miles or sections, which my brother, who is residing in New Zealand, purchased from a Chief.

2. *Hist.* In early settlement, a subdivision of blocks of undeveloped land (cf. BLOCK *n.*¹ 1) purchased from the Maori by the Crown or by land companies for allotment, sale or lease for settlement, and of sizes varying according to locality, whether urban or rural, etc.: often with a modifier: **country (rural), town section**. See also *town acre* (TOWN 2), the preferred use in some settlements.
    1839 *Terms of Sale NZ Land Company* in *GBPP* (1852) xxxv. 570 1 June 18 in *Speeches & Documents* (1971) 19 These doubly-selected lands will be divided into 1100 sections, each section comprising one town-acre, and 100 country-acres. *Ibid.* 20 The choice of sections, of which the priority has been so determined by lot in England, will take place in the settlement, as soon after the arrival of the first body of colonists as the requisite surveys and plans shall have been completed. **1842** Mary F. Swainson let. in *William Swainson* 21 Aug. (1992) 90 I will now explain to you about the quantity of the land: each section is one hundred acres, and Papa rents three... Each section had a town acre attached to it at the first sale the Land Company held. **1842** DEANS *Pioneers* (1964) 10 To prove to you how little the Nelson settlement is in vogue here, I may mention that out of 200 sections reserved for sale in the colony, only six or eight were sold. **1842** HEAPHY *NZ* 81 A section in the Hutt Valley..lately sold for 900 *l.* On this section the village of Richmond is to be laid out. **1842** in *Lett. from New Plymouth* 7 Feb. (1968) 1 We have bought a section of land in the town... The country section we have got together... We have paid..for the town section £25. **1843** SWAINSON in Manson *I Take Up My Pen* (1971) 25 The allotments were made to consist of 100 acres each, and these are what we call 'sections'. **1848** WAKEFIELD *Handbook NZ* 94 A town-site [for Wellington] was laid out, consisting of 1100 sections of one acre each, besides reserves for public purposes, and there were also laid out 1100 rural sections of one hundred acres each. **1857** *Lyttelton Times* 1 July 1 For Sale The Lease of Two 50–acre Sections. To Let Several Town Sections in Lyttelton. **1862** LINDSAY

Place & Power Nat. Hist. in Coloniz. 6 I did not come to New Zealand to study science, but to drive bullocks and grub up flax, and buy sections and found a clan. **1930** GUTHRIE *NZ Memories* 118 Sections were allotted upon which..they first built wattle and daub huts. **1943** *St Michael's Anglican Church A Century of Christian Witness* 5 Under the plan for Nelson settlement, allotments of 150 acres of rural land, one accommodation (suburban) section of 50 acres and one town acre were sold to purchasers for £300.

3. From the time of later settlement to the present.
a. An often extensive parcel of rural land, a part of a block surveyed and subdivided for farming settlement or timber-felling. See also *bush section* (BUSH C 3 a).

1864 MUTER *Travels* II. 260 'Cockatoos'..'spotted' his run all over with fifty and hundred acre sections, and worried him for trespass. **1898** HOCKEN *Contributions* 78 For fifty-acre sections, the price [for clearing] ranged from 8*d.* to 1*s.* 9*d.* per acre. **1899** BELL *In Shadow of Bush* 84 I mean to have a buck at some of those sections in the Whakatangi Block that'll be thrown open shortly. **1913** *NZ Observer* 15 Mar. 8 Four hundred acres of the 'Glen Innis' Estate at Tamaki West, divided into sections from one to 28 acres, are to be sold on Friday. **c1924** ANTHONY *Me & Gus* (1977 Gus Tomlins) 20 His idea was that he and I should get the firewood rights on a thousand-acre section, up under the mountain reserve. **1937** BUICK *Moa-Hunters NZ* 136 The summer of 1895 was a particularly dry one, and..the settler who owned the section adjoining..was prospecting for a better supply of water. **1946** REED *Farthest North* 14 The father..had come down to the wharf to meet his boys, who were trudging after him to the recently purchased little gumland Government section three miles up in the hills. **1957** *Mangamaire School 1897–1957* [6] It has been said that this land was to be divided into 100-acre sections, making good dairy farms. **1968** TOMLINSON *Remembered Trails* 28 The bush in the locality [of Tophouse], known as Big Bush Settlement, was cut into sections in 1906 and we had quite a few neighbours. **1976** BROWN *Difficult Country* 47 The land at the junction of the Matakitaki and Buller which was not heavily bushed was lined and later surveyed in sections. **1988** HILL *More from Moaville* 28 30-odd wethers, all pattering..along the tarseal on their way from Wally's paddock six sections down the road to Wally's other paddock eight sections up the road.

b. Also **building section**. An urban building lot, now usually applied to a small parcel of urban land for residential use, often formerly of an area of a quarter of an acre (0.101 ha or 1012.5 m²). See also *quarter-acre section* (QUARTER-ACRE 2). [*Note*] It is often difficult to distinguish the sense here from that of 2, esp. in respect of a *town section*.

[**1841** *Sinclair & others, Wellington to Sir George Gipps* 10 Feb. in *GBPP 1842 (No.569)* 131 By the Government advertisement for the sale of town lands at Auckland, it was stated that sections..would be exposed to sale by auction.] **1849** TORLESSE *Papers* (1958) 100 Packed up my boxes and prepared bush outfit. Took section up Dublin St. **1865** *Richmond-Atkinson Papers* (1960) II. 147 Invercargill is a very dull place... The sections are divided in the back streets by rough fences inside of which stand the usual wretched little boxes which do duty in N.Z. for houses. **1879** SIMMONS *Old England & NZ* 94 They have..bought a 'section' of land—some an eighth, some a quarter, and others half an acre or more—and have then had their cottages erected upon their several sections. **1899** BELL *In Shadow of Bush* 3 Some indeed of these townships never reach any further stage..which..the unfortunate individuals who were induced to buy sections there, may have looked forward to. **1923** *Dominion* (Wellington) 3 Jan. 3 A horse dropped dead last Thursday morning..in Dunedin, and it[s] carcass, partially concealed by a light cover, has since lain on a vacant section there. **1934** LEE *Children of Poor* (1949) 47 The [railway] line had always beckoned, but the admonitions of the elders were prohibitory. 'Stay in the section.' **1943** BENNETT *English in NZ* in *Amer. Speech* XVIII. 87 A plot of land suitable for a building site is in New Zealand a *section*, in Australia a *block*. **1979** *SANZ Gloss. Bldg. Terminol.* 98 *Section*—Small parcel of land intended for residential use. **1991** *Independent Herald* (Wellington) 3 Oct. 21 Work Wanted... Section clearing, tree felling & removal. Free quotes.

4. Special Comb. **section** (or **corner**) **peg**, a land boundary marker.

1901 *TrNZI* XXXIII. 492 In these colonies especially the proportion of land occupiers and owners is so large that most of us are directly or indirectly interested in 'section pegs', 'trigs', and such-like, while at Home the expression of this interest is practically limited to the impersonal 'beating the bounds of the parish'. **1975** KNIGHT *Poyntzfield* 37 Father pointed it out the first time we passed it [*sc.* a white pine] saying that this was the end of our Section, and the pine tree was the 'corner peg'.

section, *n.*² *Education.* Esp. in the phr. **on section**, a course of practical 'hands-on' teaching under the supervision of a permanent classroom teacher undertaken by student teachers as part of their teacher-training, now officially termed 'teaching experience'.

c1930 p.c. Patrick Macaskill, Wellington Teachers College (1960). To be *on section* was equivalent to the English term to be *on TP* (or Teaching Practice). **1943** BENNETT *English in NZ* in *Amer. Speech* XVIII. 87 A probationary student teacher describes himself as 'on section' when he is paying a periodic visit to the school to which he is assigned. **1966** TURNER *Eng. Lang. Austral. & NZ* 158 A New Zealand [trainee] teacher..*goes on section*, that is, he visits classes to observe and take lessons. **1987** *Metro* (Auckland) May 58 We [teacher trainees] went on section and I fell silently in love with 23-year-old associate teachers. **1993** SINCLAIR *Halfway Round the Harbour* 57 After six weeks at [training] college each section spent about six weeks in the schools working as pupil-teachers in the classrooms. This was called being 'on section'. **1996** *Evening Post* (Wellington) 5 June 36 Read is on section at Levin's Waiopehu College as part of her Teacher's Training College requirements.

section, *n.*³
1. A fare-stage on municipal transport (in some jurisdictions the term *zone* is used). Also *attrib.* as **one-section**, **two-section**, etc., indicating the length or duration of a public transport ride.

1904 [see 2 a following]. **1907** *NZ Free Lance* (Wellington) 29 June 12 The careful Scot is surprised that he has to pay another section when the conductor says so. **1926** *NZ Observer* 13 Mar. 20 Otherwise the tram conductor would never have charged him sixpence for a one-section ride on the trams. **1936** *Tramway Journal* Aug. 1 A short distance rider purchasing one of the new one-section tickets and paying 1 d. [= penny] for an average section one mile in length is being called upon to bear an undue proportion of the increase. **1942** GILBERT *Free to Laugh* 18 Quite alone, buying a two-section ticket, getting off somewhere past Kilbirnie. **1952** Glover in *In Their Own Words* (1988) 120 A chap would wait hours before it dawned on him that the tram had broken down two sections before. **1973** STEWART *End of the Penny Section* 62 Threepence had been the fare on horse-cars irrespective of the distance travelled; now, as promised, it was one penny a section on the new-fangled electric contraptions. **1976** HILLIARD *Send Somebody Nice* 34 It costs twice as much today for a five-section ride as it did only a few short years ago. **1984** KEITH & MAIN *NZ Yesterdays* 244 The canny city fathers insisted that the company provide a public transport service on the one-mile section from the corner of Hardy and Trafalgar Streets to the port [of Nelson]. **1992** *Evening Post* (Wellington) 24 Apr. 7 What's there is the Cook Islands equivalent of the whacking with the damp one-section Big Red bus ticket.

2. As **penny section**. **a.** *Obs.* The first, or main central, transport section through a city or town centre charged at a special 'round' rate of orig. a penny (1 cent), 'the end of the penny section' marking the beginning of suburban travel.

1904 *NZ Observer* 6 Feb. 23 [Advt] It's only a hop, skip and a Jump! From the end of the Penny Section to H.W. Bateman's. **1908** *Back Then—Volume Two* (Oral History Birkenhead) 26f. [Photocopy of an invoice] Upper Symond Street, End of 1d. Section, Auckland, June 11th 1908. Bought of Smith & Brown. **1910** *Truth* 14 May 7 The disturbance continued until the 'penny section' was completed, and there the conductor called a policeman. **1917** *Wanganui Herald* 10 Sept. 7 If they want to get at these penny section people, why on earth don't they stop using penny tickets after 10 at night.

b. Usu. in transf. use in the phr. **end of the penny section**, the end of easy or cheap progress or action; 'the end of the golden weather'.

1951 MARSH *Opening Night* (1968) i 17 'Personally escorted tour abaht to commence.'.. She followed him to the stage and round the back of the set... 'End of the penny section,' he said. **1973** STEWART *End of the Penny Section* [Title] **1977** McLEAN *Winter of Discontent* 151 End of the Penny Section? Lions 34, Auckland 15.

section 218. Also *ellipt.* **218**. A demand for payment of a company debt under section 218 of the Companies Act, 1955.

[**1955** *NZ Statutes* No.63 I. 747 [Companies Act, 1955 Section] 218. A Company shall be deemed to be unable to pay its debts—(a) If a creditor to whom the company is indebted in a sum exceeding fifty pounds..has served on the company..a demand under his hand requiring the company to pay the sum so due, and the company has for three weeks thereafter neglected to pay the sum..; or (c) if it is proved to the satisfaction of the court that the Company is unable to pay its debts.] **1985** *NZ Times* 1 Dec. 1 A satellite television firm involving prominent National Party members is under threat of a winding-up petition. Two 218s have been taken out against [it]. A 218 demands that an outstanding debt be paid within 21 days or else the court will be petitioned to wind up the business of the company. **1985** *Metro* (Auckland) Dec. 167 My major supplier..took me to court on a 218. (Section 218 of the Companies Act under which creditors can apply for a winding up.) **1990** *Dominion* (Wellington) 23 July 27 A section 218 claim for $48,000..was incorrectly served.

sectionist. *Obs.* An immigrant who had paid a land company in Britain for a section or sections of land in New Zealand (or the right to ballot for such).

1841 DEANS *Pioneers Canterbury* (1937) 32 The secondary sectionists are to choose their land at Wanganui. **1843** WOOD *Twelve Months in Wellington* 26 Colonel Wakefield, at the last selection of land in November, promised that the New Zealand Company would return to the sectionists any amount of property (*under* 10 *l.*) they might give to the natives as payment for the land. **1868** TAYLOR *Past & Present NZ* 275 The holders of the company's land orders were called, in

Seddon. In various mainly obsolete forms alluding to Richard John *Seddon* (1845–1906), Premier and Prime Minister (1893–1906), his politics or policies. See also *since Dick Seddon died* (SINCE).

1. As **Seddonism**, the style and policies of the administration of Richard John Seddon, associated with an autocratic control of parliament, liberal social policies, and an imperialistic vision of external relations.

1898 *Ensign* (Gore) 14 May in Bromby *Eye Witness Hist.* (1985) 74 Electors will recognise, however, that consistency can scarcely be expected of one who is prepared to swallow the whole creed of Seddonism with its falsities, its injustices, and its masses of corruption without so much as a wince. **1899** *Auckland Weekly News* (Suppl.) 15 Sept. 8 A further 'Slap at Seddonism', and 'New Zealand's Socialistic Policy', is given today by the Financial News. **1904** *NZ Observer* 20 Aug. 24 'Twas ever thus, even in the 'good old days' that preceded Seddonsim. **1907** DRUMMOND *Life & Work of Richard John Seddon* 311 The whole modern movement in favour of annexation had been described as another phase of 'Seddonism'. **1968** SEDDON *The Seddons* 114 This blaze of 'Seddonism' was criticised as an ambitious move 'to extend the realms of his kingship'.

2. As **Seddonite**, a supporter of, or believer in, the policies and governing style of Richard John Seddon.

1968 SEDDON *The Seddons* 174 There was a scuffle outside the kitchen door and then a man, a non-Seddonite, banged open the door and fled, an irate Seddonite armed with a waddy chasing him.

3. As **Seddonland** [f. King Dick *Seddon* + MAORI)LAND], New Zealand, under the premiership of Seddon.

1906 *Truth* 28 Apr. 6 In wider Seddonland. **1906** PICARD *Ups & Downs* 8 [He] cussed Seddonland from N.C. to Bluff.

4. As **Seddonian** *a.*, pertaining to the personal or political style of Richard John Seddon.

1899 *Taranaki Herald* (New Plymouth) 7 Sept. 3 In speaking of the evil effect of party government worked on the Seddonian principle, Mr. Monkhouse got in a thrust at the sitting member. **1934** *Feilding Star* 3 Apr. 4 There is a Seddonian and Massey touch of masterfulness in the reply by Premier Forbes to a statement current in Wellington.

seed.

1. [Transf. use of *seed* a small particle.] Usu. *pl.* A grade of kauri-gum comprising seed-sized particles.

1936 *NZJST* XVII. 371 The terms dust, seeds, chips, nubs, &c., are the names given to certain of the lower kauri gum grades according to the relative sizes of the pieces. **1956** [see *rescraped gum* (GUM *n.* 2)]. **1966** *Encycl. NZ* II. 207 An increasing demand for poorer grades of gum [after 1900], used in making linoleum, made it profitable to search for smaller gum: 'nuts', 'chips', 'seeds', and 'dust'.

2. Special Comb. **seed gold**, particles of gold 'sown' by a miner in auriferous material in the hopeful fancy that it will attract further gold; **seed merchant**, a wholesale firm which buys, or produces, seed in bulk and processes it for sale.

1898 *TrNZI* XXX. 498 Nor was this wild theory [*sc.* that nuggets grow in drift] of the digger and the miner merely a speculative one, for they believed in it to such an extent that they acted up to it by purposely leaving gold—a little '**seed-gold**', as they termed it—in their tailings to draw the precious metal to itself for a profitable rewashing thereof. **1944** SCANLAN *March Moon* 157 I introduced Owen at the bank, at the stock agent's and at two **seed merchants**.

select, *v.* [Spec. use of *select* to choose in preference to another or others: AND 1826.] *trans.* and *absol.* During early settlement, to select or be allotted, often after a ballot (sections of land already purchased); later, to select, often after a ballot (sections of crown rural land) for farm settlement.

1841 Sinclair to Russell 19 July in *GBPP 1842 (No.569)* 134 From the extreme value of allotments with water frontages for commercial people, the [Auckland] waterside was subdivided into very small allotments..but two of the best of these..have been selected by Government officers. **1848** WAKEFIELD *Handbook NZ* 317 ['Terms of Purchase of Land in the Settlement of Otago' agreed on by the 'Otago Association' and the Company.] In exchange for each sum of 120*l.* 10*s.*.each Purchaser to receive..three separate Land-Orders, namely, for the Town quarter-acre, the ten acres of Suburban Land, and the fifty acres of Rural Land, respectively. These lands to be severally selected according to priority of choice, to be determined by Ballot. **1849** DEANS *Pioneers* (1964) 63 [To William Fox, Principal Agent of New Zealand Company.] [The run] we now occupy will most probably be speedily selected for sections [on arrival of the settlers]. **1851** TORLESSE *Papers* (1958) 195 He was to have selected the town sections for me during my absence in the country..I purpose selecting in Christchurch for the following reasons. **1894** *NZ Official Year-book* 202 Where the choice of selection is by ballot, the poor settler has the same chance as the rich one... The limit that a selector may hold is fixed as to encourage the class of small farmers, and up to that limit the amount he selects is left entirely to himself. **1898** HOCKEN *Contributions* 99 The 21st of April [1848] was fixed for the formal selection of their own town sections by the land purchasers... Mr.David Garrick..was the first private individual to select in Dunedin. **1902** *Settler's Handbook NZ* 4 It is quite possible within this district to select land early in the winter, fell and burn off by the ensuing summer, sow in grass in the autumn, and put on stock within twelve months from selection. **1959** SINCLAIR *Hist. NZ* 156 Where leaseholders were not permitted to 'select' land, or where conditions of residence were enforced, 'dummyism' was rife—that is, a leaseholder would pay some 'swaggie' to act as the ostensible selector and fufil the requirements for him.

selection.

a. [AND 1826.] The operation or act of selecting Crown land for occupation or settlement.

[*Note*] The concrete sense 'land so acquired' freq. in Austral. since 1830 (see AND) is usu. replaced by *section* in NZ.

1843 *Lett. from Settlers* (1843) 67 By the end of April..about 2,500 acres of suburban land will be ready for selection. **1851** TORLESSE *Papers* (1958) 201 Went to the [Land] Office and plotted the sections that I had laid off, and present at selections of 2nd Series of the first body. **1854** *Richmond-Atkinson Papers* (1960) I. 145 A great opportunity for investment will be opened in a few months when the Hua Block and the Waiwakaiho Block will be proclaimed as open for selection. **1873** [see SELECTOR]. **1883** *Brett's Colonists' Guide* 16 On looking for land open for selection..the intending settler will find the greater proportion described as bush. **1892** *NZ Official Handbook* 284 On the fulfilment of conditions [of homesteading], which are five years' residence, the erection of a house, and the cultivation of one-third of the selection if open land, and one-fifth if bush-land, the Crown grant is issued. **1902** [see SELECT *v.*]. **1937** AYSON *Thomas* 74 Out came the maps and he learnt that the land was still open for selection. **1959** SINCLAIR *Hist. NZ* 155 The system of 'free selection' enabled a would-be 'cockatoo' to choose land in localities 'thrown open' to selectors..and to buy the freehold. **1973** NEWTON *Big Country SI* (1977) 27 The Lands Department took over the running of the Molesworth and Tarndale country but the Rainbow..was offered for selection. **1982** WOODHOUSE *Blue Cliffs* 59 On 6 January 1891 the runs were offered by the Crown 'for sale or selection'.

b. [AND 1878.] A mining claim.

1931 COAD *Such Is Life* 55 And there are others [*sc.* nuggets] like it, about here on this selection. Thank God we bought this hut. It's the site of a rich seam.

selector. *Hist.* [AND *free selector*, 1864.] One who takes part in a ballot for sections of Crown land for farm settlement.

1873 WILSON *Diary* 2 Feb. in Wierzbicka *Wilson Family* (1973) 164 The land up here is far too hilly for anything but grazing purposes and unless they allow the selector the right of running over so much ground besides his selection as they do in New South Wales it will be a long time before it is taken up. **1885** *Wairarapa Daily* 19 Jan. 2 The first year the selector will have to pay 10 per cent of his purchase money. **1892** MURPHY in *Settler's Handbook NZ* (1902) 102 The very nature of the industry renders it peculiarly suited to small selectors. **1892** *NZ Official Handbook* 280 During 1891–92 there were 1,953 selectors of Crown land in the colony, who took up holdings of the following sizes. **1902** *Settler's Handbook NZ* 63 It is with these land offices the selector has to transact all business. **1934** MULGAN *Spur of Morning* 261 In this high country he met some of the original selectors—men who had pushed out into the unknown in bullock drays. **1948** SCOTTER *Run Estate & Farm* 58 Of the original selectors [of Elderslie No. 1]..only four remained in 1919. **1955** WILSON *Land of My Children* 25 In company with most of the other selectors, Frank had willy-nilly to leave the firing in Blow's hands. **1987** HARTLEY *Swagger on Doorstep* 170 When the first sections were balloted in 1910 the department had cautioned 'that rough sleeping provisions will be made for intended selectors who must..provide their own blankets'.

Self Help. [See quots. 1949, 1966.] Formerly the name of a chain of cut-price grocery stores. Usu. as **the Self Help**, a Self-Help store.

1938 *NZ Observer* 7 Apr. 7 Another far-sighted business-man is Benjamin Sutherland, of Wellington, the 'self-help king'. **1949** *Dominion* (Wellington) 3 Jan. 8 He [*sc.* Ben Sutherland (1873–1949)] began a small shop near the old Lambton Station under the name of Self Help and introduced new ideas of retail grocery selling. **1952** *Landfall 24* 330 There is Ben Sutherland, the civil servant, 'a man without initiative' according to his staff record card in the Railways Department. Yet he lived to found the Self-Help 'co-ops' to do battle against price rings, and to revolutionize the grocery trade. **1966** *Encycl. NZ* III. 331 Sutherland's Self Help Cooperative Ltd..was founded in Wellington on 27 October 1922... A year later there were seven Self Help Stores in Wellington... In October 1932, to mark the tenth anniversary of Self Help, he inaugurated a liberal staff benefit fund. **1974** SIMPSON *Sugarbag Years* 55 There was a great deal of shame [during the Depression] in the minds of working men..who had to go with an order from the Charitable Aid Board for groceries up to the local Self Help. **1987** *Metro* (Auckland) May 52 Down further on the Great South Road [in the 1950s] were the Auckland Savings Bank..and the Self Help.

self-reliance. *Hist.* Also as **self-reliance (self-reliant) policy**, the policy of New Zealand governments of the 1860s of not relying on British military (and other) aid to solve internal problems.

1869 Hawthorne *Dark Chapter NZ Hist.* 7 On the 12th October [1865] Mr. Weld resigned. He was the author of what is termed the 'Self-Reliance Policy', which might have issued differently to what it has hitherto done if a regiment or two had been left in the colony for a year or two, and the mother country had granted the pecuniary assistance to which New Zealand was fairly entitled. 1925 Bathgate *Random Recolls.* 18 The feeling of irritation [with Britain in late 1860s] soon passed away, and the success of the self-reliant policy became recognised. 1948 Lipson *Politics of Equality* 54 Weld became the next premier [in 1864] with a policy of war and self-reliance. As New Zealand intended to fight without British troops or generals, the ministry took over from the governor the control of defense and native affairs. 1959 Sinclair *Hist. NZ* 140 The first fruit of colonial 'self reliance' was the confiscation of nearly three million acres of Maori land. 1966 *Encycl. NZ* I. 462 In 1864 the Weld..Ministry proposed its 'self reliant' policy, the substance of which was that New Zealand should dispense with the Imperial troops for which they were paying an annual capitation of £40. Reliance would instead be placed on local forces and on Maori auxiliaries.

sell, *v.*

1. In the phr. **to sell a canary**, see canary *n.*[2]

2. As **selling a horse**, a bar-game to determine who in a group is to pay for drinks.

1928 *Auckland Univ. College Students' Association Souvenir Programme* 16 Another form of gambling..is that known as 'selling a horse'. *Ibid.* 17 A member of the party thinks of, or writes down a number and another member starts counting, beginning at any number below ten, and the party takes it in turn to count, much as in the Army a platoon is numbered off. The member saying the number thought of or written down collects the pool. 1938 Hyde *Nor Yrs. Condemn* 85 'That doesn't buy our drinks,' said Sam. Another man said: 'We'll sell a horse, and find out who pays.' They were selling the horse, when a big black car slid up against the kerb. 1939 Belton *Outside the Law* 139 The procedure is sometimes referred to as 'selling a horse'. Each person pools so much money and a number is written down and hidden from view. The person who writes a number down requests one of the others to start counting, commencing at any number desired, provided that it is lower than the winning number. The counting is then carried on in rotation and stops when the written number is reached. The winner then takes the pool and pays for whatever has been purchased.

sell out. To vomit (esp. after excess liquor). (Also freq. heard as **to make a sale**.)

c1941 St Patrick's College, Silverstream. To sell out used for 'to vomit'. (Ed.) 1941 Baker *NZ Slang* 53 *To make a sale*, to vomit. 1952 *VUC First Yr. Eng. Class* 6 May I would include among New Zealand English words: *to sell out*: to be ill. 1960 Hilliard *Maori Girl* 187 'Why don't you have some kai?' 'The very sight of it makes me want to sell out.' 1984 12 Aug. TV1 4-time Gold medal kayak winner in Olympics said: 'I sold out in the tent a few times afterwards.'

send, *v.* In various phr.: **send her (it) down Hughie**, see hughie; **send off the blue**, see blue *n.*[2] 2 b; **to send (be sent) down the road**, see road 3.

separated, separator butter: see butter 2.

septic tank. Rhyming slang for 'bank' or 'Yank' (cf. AND *Yank*, 1976).

1982 Newbold *Big Huey* (Gloss.) 253 Septic tank (n) Bank. 1988 Macrae *Awful Childhoods* 88 I take it the blondie mate's a septic tank? What a strong accent!

serang, var. sherang.

sergeant-major. [f. the Crown on a military tunic sleeve, denoting the rank of Sergeant-Major.] A name for the Crown in the game of Crown-and-Anchor.

1917 *NZ at the Front* 106 Murder on the old sergeant-major, and the bottom line goes for the old man [*sc.* the owner of the board]. 1921 *Quick March* 10 Aug. 27 'Murder on the old sergeant-major.'.. 'The last spin, digs, so plank it down thick and heavy now; you pick 'em and I'll pay 'em.'

serpent stone. *Obs.* [Transf. use of *serpent(ine) stone*: f. the dull-green colour of serpentine rock: cf. OED *serpentine n.*[3]] greenstone.

1777 Anderson *Journal* 25 Feb. in Cook *Journals* (1967) III. 809 Neither is there any mineral worth notice but a green jasper or serpent stone of which the natives make their tools and ornaments. 1840 [see jade].

serpentine superphosphate. Also **serpentine super.** [See OED *serpentine n.* 4.] A mixture of superphosphate with crushed serpentine or serpentinite, used as a fertilizer.

1941 *NZJAg.* Sept. LXIII. 179 The name serpentine superphosphate will be used in future in place of 'silico superphosphate', as it is a more accurate description of the material. It is made by mixing three parts of hot, newly-made superphosphate with one part of ground serpentine and allowing the mixture to 'mature' in heaps for several days. 1960 *NZ Dairy Exporter* 10 Feb. 8 The seed was mixed with its own weight of serpentine super. 1965 Williams *Econ. Geol. NZ* 143 Serpentinite is quarried in considerable quantity in New Zealand for the manufacture of 'serpentine superphosphate'. 1966 *Encycl. NZ* I. 651 The use of serpentine-reverted superphosphate is peculiar to New Zealand. Serpentine superphosphate has three advantages. 1978 *Ann. Rep. NZ Fertiliser Manufacturers' Assn* 21 The serpentine superphosphate contained approximately double the amount of magnesium soluble in 2% citric acid than the dolomite superphosphates.

service. *Obs.* or *Hist.*

1. Used *attrib.* in respect of public transport providing (or allowing) a regular service between stated points of departure and arrival: **service bus**, **service car** (occas. early **service motor-car**) [poss. f. *mail-service car* one contracted to regular delivery of post-bags], formerly, a long-distance passenger car or bus, orig. with bench-type seats extending across the body of the car, and entered by side doors; now usu. called (*motor-*)*coach* or *bus* (see also *mail car* (mail); **service-car driver** (or **service driver**); **service lorry**, a lorry with some passenger capacity running a regular delivery service.

1937 *Taranaki Daily News* 26 Feb. 6 At 9 am, three cars had been removed from where they had stranded..but the **service bus** has remained with the water swirling deep above..the wheels. 1938 Hyde *Nor Yrs. Condemn* 139 On both sides of the service 'bus gorse streamed in a mass of flower. 1952 Thomson *Deer Hunter* 97 Here [at Lake Wanaka] we parted company and travelled by service bus for the remainder of our journey. 1917 Ingram *Anzac Diary* (1987) 9 Left Whakatane by **service motor-car** in company with a few other fellow recruits for Rotorua. 1924 Rees *April's Sowing* 19 I'd have gone up in the **service car**. 1938 Burdon *High Country* 166 Today a man from Invercargill may get into a train or service car and, within twenty-four hours, propose to and be accepted by a girl in Blenheim. 1943 Bennett *English in NZ* in *Amer. Speech* XVIII. 87 Often the only transport is by large limousines, which are always known as *service-cars*. 1956 Dare *Rouseabout Jane* 5 I should explain that a service car is well named, and is used for everything. This one was a type of lorry, with seats at the back, and it collected children for school, took in the mail, collected the cream cans, brought out parcels or luggage, and was used as a bus by any would-be travellers. 1963 Casey *As Short a Spring* 111 The service car only runs into town and back twice a week and then only from the store. 1974 Hilliard *Maori Woman* 177 At a coastal town on the Taranaki Bight she left the train..and boarded the service-car for the last few miles home. 1988 *Short Stories NZ* 35 Nevertheless..they were still out the front waiting when the service-car pulled up to drop the mail bag off. 1990 Henderson *Home Country* 9 The legendary Tinny Solly, driver..of Newman's red service car to Takaka, was reaching for the last cigarette in his yellow Three Castles packet. 1939 *Silhouettes of Past* 150 So entered the **service car driver**—late from a pioneering point of view, but still equally important. 1946 Miller *There Was Gold* 26 People of all kinds—farmers, racemen,.. mail carriers, service car drivers. 1926 *NZ Observer* 20 Feb. 4 The party set forth..having as a pilot one of those resourceful **service drivers** of the North. 1989 Richards *Pioneer's Life* 47 A slow..train from Frankton allowed me to get to Ngaruawahia in time to catch Gibbs' **service lorry** to Te Akau.

2. As **service road**, an access road; a (temporary) road made specially for transporting supplies and enabling other work to progress.

c1880s an anonymous tourist in Masters *Tales of the Mails* (1959) 46 Leaving Moawhango, we went by the Tikirere, where we came upon the service road being formed by the Government, for the purpose of getting supplies through to the Main Trunk Railway. 1921 Foston *At the Front* 66 Unmetalled portions of the 'service' road.

sesqui. A shortened form of *sesquicentennial*, *spec.* (often with init. cap.) a Wellington celebration in 1990 of 150 years of European settlement, an occasion which went notoriously awry, thus giving to the word a connotation of disastrous incompetence. Compare centennial.

1989 *Dominion* (Wellington) 15 Nov. 15 A lot of people get a glazed look in the eye when you talk to them about 1990 and say, 'Oh yes, sesqui' and we say it's slightly different. 1990 *Evening Post* (Wellington) 17 Mar. 56 *sesqui* (ses'kwe), *n.* An event doomed to failure, an abandoned place, a secret or unmentionable occurrence. *v. t.* To inflict severe personal or corporate damage, to induce trauma through the provision of an unwanted service. *dry as a sesqui*: unprofitable. *to be away with the sesquis*: to be forced to complete only one-third of a task. *to get a good sesquiing*: (*colloq.*) to be duped, to lose heavily in a gambling situation, to become or take on the appearance or nature of a gittus. 1990 *Dominion Sunday Times* (Wellington) 16 Sept. 14 [Heading] Mainlanders miss sesqui symphony. 1991 *Evening Post* (Wellington) 2 Oct. 8 The ghost of Sesqui will continue to haunt the Wellington Show Association for years to come as it services a $1.99 million debt left in the wake of the flopped 1990

SESSION

carnival. **1991** *Listener* 4 Nov. 12 Sorry. Post-Sesqui grief clouded my memory. **1995** *Evening Post* (Wellington) 7 Mar. 9 [Heading] The Sesqui survivors... The tale of..Display Promotions is a good story to tell —especially as its near disaster was born out of Sesqui, a real disaster.

Hence **Sesqui-type**, indicative of expensive failure on a grand scale.
1992 *Evening Post* (Wellington) 2 Feb. 4 The Post..has leaned over backwards to give a fair view of this Sesqui-type fiasco.

session. [AND a drinking session, 1949.] A period of time occupied with one activity, esp. drinking and gambling; a spell or bout of drinking, usu. in company. Occas. a difficult interview or one involving criticism or reprimand: 'I had a session with the Head this morning over irregular attendance'.
1944 *NZEF Times* 8 May 7 Football and Shafto's and Ensa shows, Plonk sessions under the stars. **1949** COLE *It was So Late* (1978) 48 'Don't shoot the barman, he's half shot already.'.. 'Bit of a session, eh?' **1950** *Landfall* 14 125 Late two-up sessions. **1981** JOHNSTON *Fish Factory* 32 Moody bugger when he's had a session on the top shelf. **1986** DAVIN *Salamander & the Fire* 75 I didn't see much of him, except for an occasional night when I could get back to have a session with the boys. **1992** ANDERSON *Portrait Artist's Wife* 81 They seldom spoke about their experiences except for an occasional story of..a heavy session with a booze artist named Arnold in Noumea.

set, *n.* [Spec. use of *set* dead set: see OED *n.*¹ 7; AND 1866.] In the phr. **to have a set on (against)** (someone), **to have** (someone) **set**, to have a prejudice against, to have a down on (someone).
1910 *Truth* 2 Apr. 6 There's two girls go to the Kaiapoi. They've got to go clean and tidy, or the other girls will have a set on them. **1943** BENNETT *English in NZ* in *Amer. Speech* XVIII. 90 'To have a set on or against someone' represents a conflation of the old-established 'to have a down on' and the Australian 'to have (a person) set'. **1948** BALLANTYNE *Cunninghams* (1963) 155 He had a bit of a set on Frank and Sydney and was always pinching their cheeks and telling them they were young roughnecks.

set, *v.*

1. In various phr. **a. to set** (something) **in a crack**, to settle (a matter) quickly.
1935 MITCHELL & STRONG in Partridge *Slang Today* 286 [The] following [was] employed by those who served in the [Great] War..*set in a crack*, to settle (a matter) quickly. **1937** PARTRIDGE *Dict. Slang* 746 *set* (something) *in a crack*. To settle (a matter) quickly; e.g. *set a bet in a crack*, to wager smartly at two-up; *be set in a crack*, (of persons) to be comfortably placed (lit. or fig.), to be very pleased with circumstances: New Zealanders': from the 1890's. Perhaps ex. the idea of doing a thing as sharply as the crack of a whip.

b. to set (something) **alight**, to get (something) started. Also as **set it alight!**, get a move on, hurry up!
1945 WEBBER *Johnny Enzed in Middle East* 31 Pious injunctions [to the gharry driver] to 'yella', 'igri', 'hoop it along' and 'set it alight'. **1971** NEWTON *Ten Thousand Dogs* 169 *Set alight*: A slang term referring to the act of starting a dog on its run.

2. *Farming*. **to set stock**, to allow stock to graze continuously over most of a farm; often as a *ppl. a.* **set-stocked**, of a farm, grazed over the whole area; or *vbl. n.* **set-stocking**, see quot. 1959.

1952 *Here & Now* Dec. 50 They are usually old family farms, mortgage-free, and what is called 'set-stocked', i.e., not intensively grazed paddock by paddock. **1959** *NZ Farmer* 2 Apr. 15 Set stocking is the opposite method [to mob stocking or rotational grazing], used quite commonly on hill country, where the flock is spread out over the whole farm, or most of it, the individual paddocks grazed continuously. **1982** *Agric. Gloss.* (MAF) 7 *Set stock*: To leave herd or flock to graze uninterrupted in one paddock for a long period or in several paddocks with gates.

set in, *v. Obs.* [Cf. Brit. dial. *set* to occupy land.]
1. *Whaling*. Of whales, to move into bays for calving.
1831 BELL *Let.* Nov. McNab *Old Whaling Days* Nov. (1913) 3 The black whales visit the bays and coasts of New Zealand for calving, and begin to set in about the beginning of April and remain till about the beginning of September.

2. *Goldmining*. [Prob. Brit. dial. *set* to occupy a piece of land for mining purposes (see EDD), poss. infl. by *set in* to set to work (OED 14 d *dial.*).] To get settled into, or occupy, a claim.
1853 ROCHFORT *Adventures of Surveyor* 64 Our first hole, where we 'set in', produced more than a pound of gold. **1866** *Evening Post* (Wellington) 4 Jan. 2 A party of four men..who, 'setting in' promiscuously on the beach..divided 198 pounds after a week's work. **1873** PYKE *Wild Will Enderby* (1889, 1974) I. iii 15 Here they halted, and proceeded first to encamp, then to explore the diggings and make necessary enquiries for a likely place 'to set in'. **1892** WARDON *Macpherson's Gully* 14 They duly pegged off and 'set in' on a piece of ground where nobody supposed they would get the colour... They shifted their pegs and again 'set in'. **1974** HEINZ *Bright Fine Gold* 200 *To set into work*: Preparation of the claim is completed, and all is ready for the recovery of gold.

settlement. [Spec. use of *settlement*: see OED 6, 14, 15.]

1. *Hist.* **a.** Applied before 1840 to any of various non-Maori local or sporadic communities of whalers, traders, or missionaries established in New Zealand; also the places these communities occupied, or the land so occupied.
1777 FORSTER *Voyage Round World* I. 179 Our caulkers and riggers[']..occupations gave life to the scene..whilst the anvil on the hill resounded... Already the polite arts began to flourish in this new settlement [at Dusky Bay]..and the romantic prospects of this shaggy country, lived on the canvas in the glowing tints of nature, who was amazed to see herself so closely copied. **1814** KENDALL 16 Apr. in Elder *Marsden's Lieutenants* (1934) 53 Should the [Church Missionary] Society..succeed in the formation of a settlement at New Zealand, one settler must not have to depend upon another, in my opinion, in anything of a temporal nature. **1832** WILLIAMS *Early Jrnls.* 10 Dec. (1961) 267 About 10 at night Tohitapu very vociferous on account of one [of] his *Wahitapu* (sacred spots) having been invaded by some of the lads belong[ing] to the Settlement. **1839** BALLENY *Journal 'Eliza Scott'* 1 Jan. in McNab *Old Whaling Days* (1913) 477 Got the Whale boat from the Settlement [sc. John Jones's whaling station] and gave them the Jolly boat. **1848** WAKEFIELD *Handbook NZ* 309 Near the mouth of the [Otago] harbour,.. there is a Settlement of 50 to 100 white people. **1932** Elder in Marsden *Lett. & Jrnls.* (1932) 412 In drawing up these drastic regulations, it is plain, Marsden practically confessed, that 'the settlement system', which depended upon the missionaries growing enough to support themselves, had failed. **1945** HALL-JONES *Hist. Southland* 36 A

SETTLEMENT

settler is one who establishes himself with the intention of permanent residence—a settlement is a party of such men, congregated together. The establishments of Leith at Dusky and many other sealing gangs elsewhere were but temporary or seasonal settlements.

b. Often as **Maori settlement**, **native settlement**, applied to an established Maori community. See also *native settlement* (NATIVE B 3 a), KAINGA a, PA *n.*¹, VILLAGE 1.
1820 MARSDEN *Lett. & Jrnls.* (1932) 323 One was Mowenna's daughter, whose husband had been killed and eaten at Terranakka in an engagement with the people of that settlement. **1823** [see MUTTONBIRD]. **1843** DIEFFENBACH *Travels in NZ* I. 399 We passed a native settlement, Reka-reka. **1920** *Quick March* 10 Jan. 13 The lonely little settlement of the Maori sheep-farming hapu was more than two thousand feet above the sea. **1940** *Tales Pioneer Women* (1988) 35 There were few white people in the neighbourhood [of Raglan], although a great many Maoris lived in their whares in the settlement and surrounding country. **1943** MARSH *Colour Scheme* 24 [Huia] lived with her family at a native settlement on the other side of the hill. *Ibid.* 155 The Colonel..astonished them all by offering to go to the Maori settlement.

c. As **pre-settlement**, in *attrib.* use, describing the period before the main body of European settlers arrived in the 1840s.
1940 HOWARD *Rakiura* 355 The Journal [of Shepherd, c1826]..is undoubtedly the most valuable document bearing on pre-settlement days in southern New Zealand.

2. a. *Hist.* Any of the non-Maori immigrant communities established in New Zealand in the 1840s and subsequently enlarged; often *spec.* (with init. caps and a local modifier) for any one of those established under the aegis of land companies, as Canterbury, Otago, Nelson Settlement. See also COLONY 1.
1839 [see SECTION *n*¹ 2]. **1840** WAKEFIELD *Letter* 8 Jan. in Fawcett *Sir William Molesworth* (1901) 173 But I am satisfied..that the more and greater settlements there are in New Zealand..the better for the Wellingtonians. **1849** TORLESSE *Papers* (1958) 104 There are three main points in which he errs to the probable great disadvantage of the Canterbury Settlement. **1851** *Gov. Grey to Earl Grey* 30 Aug. in Rutherford *Sel. Documents* (1949) 44.11 The group of colonies comprised in the New Zealand islands are composed at present of what might be termed nine principal European settlements besides smaller dependencies of these. **1853** ADAMS *Canterbury Settlement* 16 A loud and hearty cheer..spoke our arrival in the Canterbury Settlement. **c1861** WRIGHT in Jones *Samuel Butler* (1919) I. 106 [On Captain Simeon's leaving still owing house-rent] He was leaving the Settlement, half broken-hearted, For his friends to his going would hardly consent. **1900** HALL in *Canterbury Old & New* 120 When in 1852 I landed in Canterbury, there were but few sheep in the province, or settlement as it was then called. **1943** *St Michael's Anglican Church A Century of Christian Witness* 6 Full of expectancy, they pushed out on to the suburban sections as soon as possible after arrival in the settlement.

b. As **military settlement** *hist.*, a settled locality occupied by *military settlers* (SETTLER 1 b (c)).
1964 NORRIS *Settlers in Depression* 1 These military settlements were formed with the object of stopping the Maoris, who had retreated to what is now called the King Country.

3. a. A settled area (usu. smaller than a township and often having no cluster of residences in its vicinity) defined about, or with respect to, some central point of non-residential reference (e.g. a store, a rural hall).

1882 Hay *Brighter Britain* II. 27 It [*sc.* gum] is carried down to the nearest bush-store or settlement, where it is at once sold. **1885** *NZJSc.* II. 506 Since farms and settlements have occupied the waste lands of the plains, for the most part it [*sc.* the dusky plover] has retired to the mountains of the back country. **1904** *NZ Illustr. Mag.* Dec. 180 His 'slap-jacks' were the envy of all the housekeepers in the settlement. **1934** Mulgan *Spur of Morning* 268 He and his party were staying the night in a settlement, and a social had been arranged in their honour in the hall. **1946** Sargeson *That Summer* 192 But just before I was clear of the settlement I had to pass the little building that was known as the police station. **1958** *Tararua Tramper* Nov. 8 For the past eight months, my wife..and I have been living in Toa Toa, a backblocks settlement. **a1964** Texidor in *In Fifteen Minutes* (1987) 193 But when they went down to the settlement to shop Lili sat in the car. **1982** Sansom *In Grip of Island* 15 We left early to carry the billies of milk..to the settlement to the homes of children. **1990** Edwards *AWOL* 2 She was working at a dairy factory hostel in the little settlement of Manawaru.

b. A temporary-permanent camp or cluster of huts for workers on a project, often with a cookhouse and recreation hall as centre.

1967 Grover *Another Man's Role* 19 It was originally a timber milling settlement.

4. a. Often as **land settlement**, the act or process of settling potential farmers onto land (often compulsorily purchased by the Crown) developed for farming.

1894 *NZPD* LXXXIII. 638 Now I will come to the [Land for Settlements] Act itself... It first provides for getting land for settlement by purchase voluntarily from people who are prepared to sell it... We should meet the demands of all classes of settlers who come to the colony, and the demands of those who are now here... We can make these settlements prosperous. **1963** Bacon *In the Sticks* 87 They've [*sc.* the Lands and Survey Department] got this land settlement business down to a fine art.

b. As **soldier (soldiers') settlement** [AND 1919], a scheme under which soldiers returned from WW1 were allocated grants of land for farm development. Cf. *soldier-settler* (SETTLER 4).

1922 *Auckland Weekly News* 19 Jan. 29 I visited the Wharikaka and Paramatta soldiers' settlements where about 20 returned men have recently acquired small holdings. **1945** *Korero* (AEWS Background Bulletin) 18 June 3 Nine miles from Ngaruawahia is the Paerangi Soldiers' Settlement. **1975** Newton *Sixty Thousand on the Hoof* 169 After the Second World War 1,600 acres of the Waimahaka country was offered to the Crown for soldier settlement.

settler. [Spec. use of *settler* one who settles in a new country: see OED 2.]

1. *Hist.* Any of those settling in New Zealand before the 1840s. **a.** Also as **first settler**, a Maori.

1879 Thomson *Story NZ* I. 75 According to tradition, the first settlers in New Zealand were not tattooed on their faces. **1949** Buck *Coming of Maori* 19 From the presence of the word moa in even a few Maori references, it seemed evident that the first settlers, having no introduced moa, applied the spare name to a local bird.

b. A member of any of several non-Maori immigrant groups often having specialized communal interests (in evangelization, trade, etc.). (a) Also as **missionary settler**, a European resident who is part of a Christian mission to the Maori (often with reference to the policy that missionaries should settle or live among their potential converts).

1814 Marsden *Lett. & Jrnls.* (1932) 91 The next day (24th) we landed the horses and cattle, and fixed upon a place for the present residence of the settlers. **1816** Kendall in Elder *Marsden's Lieutenants* (1934) 132 He had asserted before that if Governor Macquarie would not give him free pardon he would by his influence with the natives drive every missionary settler back to Port Jackson. **1819** *Agreement among Settlers* 30 Mar. in Marsden *Lett. & Jrnls.* (1932) 234 Bay of Islands, March 30th, 1819. We the undersigned missionary settlers in the service of the Honourable Church Missionary Society, actuated by a desire to promote the general comfort and prosperity of this settlement, do hereby promise and agree... And provided any individual settler should procure from the natives at his own private expense..any of the above-mentioned articles. **1821** Kendall in Elder *Marsden's Lieutenants* (1934) 174 I am certain you are aware of the extreme difficulty of withstanding their incessant importunities, having yourself witnessed them at the doors of the missionary settlers.

(b) One who has settled in New Zealand with a view to trading as a sealer, whaler, flax-trader, etc.

1826 Shepherd *Journal* 8 Mar. in Howard *Rakiura* (1940) 359 I went from the ship with the Settlers to Albion Cove about 3 miles distant to the place fixed upon yesterday to cut down timber trees. **1831** Biscoe *Journal* 8 Nov. in McNab *Old Whaling Days* (1913) 416 Although there are several Missionaries..they refuse to educate the children of the White Settlers, their excuse being that they were sent out to instruct the Heathen only. **1945** Hall-Jones *Hist. Southland* 36 James Caddell, the pakeha chief, must be considered the first settler in Southland, if not from his capture in 1810, then from his voluntary return by the *Mermaid* in 1823... A settler is one who establishes himself with the intention of permanent residence.

(c) As **military settler** *hist.*, one recruited as a reserve soldier to combat Maori recalcitrants, and given land in a 'disturbed' North Island district on the understanding that immediate recall to active duty would take place if necessary; also applied to Fencibles (see quot. 1846). See also 4 below.

1846 Earl Grey to Governor Grey in *Hist. Howick & Pakuranga* 24 Nov. (1991) 57 In each of the proposed villages for these military settlers [*sc.* the Royal NZ Fencibles] there must therefore be erected two or three log-houses. **1863** *Colonial Defence Office* 31 Dec. in Norris *Armed Settlers* (1963) 21 I am directed to authorize you to proceed to New South Wales for the purpose of enrolling a company of Military Settlers for service in the Northern Island of New Zealand, under the conditions dated 5th August 1863, published in the New Zealand Gazette of the 12th September. **1867** Smith *Taranaki Jrnl.* 26 Feb. in Cowan *NZ Wars* (1955) II. 534 [British troops] are every bit as good [as bushmen] as the Military Settlers who formed part of the column which took Opotiki. **1879** Gudgeon *Reminisc. of War* 27 The military settlers had been enrolled only a few weeks. **1922** Cowan *NZ Wars* (1955) I. 177 He became captain in 1863, and served in the Military Settlers, and later in the Armed Constabulary as Sub-Inspector. **1936** Lambert *Pioneering Reminisc. Old Wairoa* 142 The other redoubts were garrisoned by the Hawkes Bay Military Settlers, and those from Taranaki. **1963** Norris *Armed Settlers* 16 It was hoped to tempt some of the goldminers in the South Island and Australia to enlist as military settlers. **1986** Belich *NZ Wars* 126 The colonial forces fell into three categories: two small permanent corps, the Colonial Defence Force (cavalry) and the Forest Rangers; the Waikato Militia or 'Military Settlers'; and the Auckland Militia and Volunteers.

(d) *Early Canterbury*. As **old settler**, one who was resident in Canterbury (or occas., in settlements other than Canterbury) before the arrival of the main body of organized settlers ('Pilgrims') in December 1850. See also SHAGROON.

1849 Torlesse *Papers* (1958) 117 Many excellent old settlers have been prevented from coming here. *Ibid.* 144 Most of the [intending] settlers..would do wisely in the opinion of all old settlers here to immediately purchase stock. **1853** *Canterbury Papers* II. 91 Weld shows out the true blood of an old settler. Your *pilgrim muffs* were too slow even to have stirred themselves in the matter

2. a. An immigrant brought out to New Zealand usu. from Europe and usu. as part of the 'Wakefield' or other organized system of permanent settlement or colonization; or as part of a scheme of organized immigration leading to permanent settlement or residence in New Zealand. Also occas. in early use, **first settler**. Cf. COLONIST a.

[**1839** *Instructions Secretary of State to Hobson* 14 Aug. 209/4 25 1–81 in *Speeches & Documents* (1971) 13 Having by these methods obviated the dangers of the acquisition of large tracts of Country by mere Landjobbers, it will be your duty to obtain, by fair and equal contracts with the Natives, the Cession to the Crown of such Waste Lands as may be progressively required for the occupation of Settlers resorting to New Zealand.] **1843** Chapman *NZ Portfolio* iv No body of colonists ever had larger claims upon the sympathies of their fellow countrymen at home than the first settlers under the Company. **1857** *Lyttelton Times* 1 July 2 The large majority of [these sales of Waste Lands] have been made to persons of the working classes and to bona fide settlers and cultivators of the soil. **1863** Moser *Mahoe Leaves* 10 [You] have anathematised the settlers of these Islands as the source of much mischief in the minds of the New Zealanders. **1886** Hart *Stray Leaves* 10 An old 'Shagroon', as those who were here [in Canterbury] when the settlers arrived were called, had given us the salutary advice to cut a ditch around our hut. **1898** Hocken *Contributions* 115 Another point of political contact with which the [Otago] settlers made early acquaintance was that connecting them with the general government of the country. **1930** Guthrie *NZ Memories* 9 But with the coming of the settler this curious existence of the 'pakeha Maori' vanished quickly. **1943** *St Michael's Anglican Church A Century of Christian Witness* 5 In Edward Gibbon Wakefield's ideal of 'planting a vertical slice of English society beneath the Southern Cross' religion held a foremost place and the Company's hand-picked settlers, many of them of exceptional calibre and attainment, clung fast to their English traditions. **1953** *NZ Herald* (Auckland) 12 Oct. 8 The Dutch plane brought 64 immigrants, who received a great reception from hundreds of Dutch settlers. **1971** Curnow *Collected Poems 1933–1973* (1974) 92 But you can't attribute to either Awareness of what great gloom Stands in a land of settlers With never a soul at home. **1993** *Evening Post* (Wellington) 26 July 2 I am writing..concerning the fate of four settlers' cottages in Newtown. These cottages..are part of a collection of settler [*sic*] cottages near the zoo.

b. In later use, esp. from the 1870s, as a development of the preceding sense, one who intends to settle, or has settled or taken up land in a rural area as a resident, esp. as a farmer; one who has lived long in a district (see quot. 1868 'old settler').

[*Note*] Often in *pl.* interchangeable with *colonists*, as a collective for non-Maori people who have roots in the country or are permanent residents in a locality, as

distinct from itinerants, gold-diggers, etc. (see as typical quots. 1894, 1924 below).
1843 SELWYN in *NZ Part II* (Church in the Colonies VII) 17 Aug. (1845) 11 [We] came to the house of a respectable English settler..who lent us his whale-boat. **1845** W.J. Swainson letter in *William Swainson* 2 Apr. (1992) 111 Amongst a few settlers who have just arrived at Wairarapa is an old school fellow. **1853** EARP *NZ* 116 The settlers there [in Wairarapa] state that the past winter has resembled the month of May in England. **1861** *Otago Witness* (Dunedin)19 Jan. 10 Culling & Thompson beg respectfully to inform the inhabitants of Dunedin, Country Settlers, and others, that they have commenced business. **1868** *Marlborough Express* (Blenheim) 11 Jan. 3 On Saturday..Mr. Joseph Blaymires, an old settler, and well-known resident in the province, left his home in Picton. **1894** *NZ Official Year-book* 340 A Commission appointed last year..gives the number of persons on the gumfields in May, 1893, as under: British, 4,303; settlers, 416; Maoris, 1244; Austrians, 519; other foreigners, 415: total, 6,897. **1907** LAING & BLACKWELL *Plants NZ* 288 By the settlers, the tree is often known as the Christmas Tree, because it flowers about the end of the year. **1924** *NZJST* VII. 186 The third..is..the parapara, or 'bird-catcher' of the settlers. **1936** BELSHAW et al. *Agric. Organiz. NZ* 581 Fires, originating generally from settlers' clearing-off operations, or the operations..have in the past done considerable destruction. **1944** *Hauraki Plains Gazette* 22 Dec. 5 The engineer was instructed to deal with the..eradication of ragwort on the property of a settler in the district. **1964** BACON *Along the Road* 69 I judge [calves] at quite a few places..where new farms are being opened up, and it does my heart good to see the way the settlers, even in their first year or so, start encouraging their bairns to put a calf in the show. **1973** MCELDOWNEY *Arguing with My Grandmother* 61 My father's A40 crawled around precipitous gullies [on the road to Wainuiomata], each of which to the locals bore the name of a settler who had gone over the side in a trap or dray.

3. *transf.* Locally applied to a mullet.
1897 *AJHR* H-17 7 The fishermen in Kaipara distinguish between 'school fish' and 'settlers'... The 'settlers' are those mullet of moderate size which stay in the harbour and run up the rivers.

4. *Hist.* **soldier-settler. a.** Occas. **settler-soldier.** *military settler* 1 b (c) above.
1922 COWAN *NZ Wars* (1955) I. 1 There was..a wide difference in..forest fighting-ability between the Imperial troops..and the soldier settlers who scoured the bush after Titokowaru and Te Kooti. *Ibid.* I. 211 Yet there were not only settler-soldiers but many of the veterans of the 65th which could have been formed into an excellent forest-ranging corps, competent to follow the Maori into the roughest country. **1991** LA ROCHE *Hist. of Howick & Pakuranga* 256 The Fencible, soldier-settlers of Howick were housed, 'in long weatherboard sheds'. **1992** PARK *Fence around the Cuckoo* 48 In 1863 [at Ngaruawahia] there was only a small white hamlet clustered about a military post. John Park became what was called a soldier settler.

b. A returned soldier of WWI settled on farmland under a State farm-settlement scheme.
1922 *Marlborough Express* 2 Mar. 'I am very much afraid I shall not be able to pay rates this year,' wrote a soldier-settler to the Wairau Road Board. **1924** *Otago Witness* (Dunedin) 5 Feb. 13 All local auctioneering firms..had agreed to reduce the accounts of all soldier settlers whom the Government intends assisting. **1938** HYDE *Nor Yrs. Condemn* 117 In the end the banks and the stock and station agents got them; the soldier settlers started in to work. **1984** BOYD *City of the Plains* 208 Mounting indebtedness and falling export prices produced much hardship among soldier settlers.

sevenfinger. [f. the fingerlike shape of the palmate leaf.] PATE. Cf. FIVE-FINGER 1.
1965 GILLHAM *Naturalist in NZ* 27 Shrubs such as five-finger and seven-finger..were cut back and gave way to other species. **1981** BROOKER et al. *NZ Medicinal Plants* 39 *Schefflera digitata* Common name: *Seven finger* Maori name: *Patete*. **1982** [see PATETE].

seven-ounce. *Obs.* Also heard as *ellipt.* **seven**, or as **seven ouncer**. [AND 1962.] A seven-ounce (200 ml) beer glass, or its contents.
1954 in Bailey & Roth *Shanties* (1967) 152 Left their nips and their seven-ounces. **1992** *Dominion* (Wellington) 11 Dec. 10 Most at home..with a seven-ounce at an aftermatch, the scribe couldn't resist an invitation to drinks..with the former [rugby] World Cup captain. **1993** *Listener* 9 Jan. 30 A seven ouncer whistled overhead and thudded into the wall.

seven-wire fence. A standard farm boundary fence.
1883 CHUDLEIGH *Diary* 21 Apr. (1950) 321 A 7-wire fence works out at £50.5.0. per mile. **1904** *Ibid.* 9 July 422 Trying to strain sheep netting outside a 7 wire fence. We are not well versed in wire netting. **1965** HENDERSON *Open Country* 54 About this time the seven-wire fence became almost the universal standard.

sexo.
1. Also **sex-oh**. *Prison slang*. A sexual offender; a person convicted of a sex-crime.
1945 BURTON *In Prison* 146 The thieves..were quite emphatic that there was nothing else to be done [except imprisonment] with the 'sexos' and murderers. The 'sexos' thought that while they were a special and rather superior class needing quite different treatment, common thieves deserved what was coming to them. **1949** *Landfall* 3 136 The sexo shows me gin-rummy. The boys stop kidding me about my Limey accent and call me Kiwi. **1962** *Landfall Country* 204 'He's a sexo sure enough,' he whispered..and quickly the news went from cell to cell that Tiny's case was not a nice one; that it involved a girl, a *little* girl. **1963** MORRIESON *Scarecrow* 113 'Maybe it's only me,' said Prudence. 'Maybe he's only laying for me. Maybe he's a sex-oh.'

2. An 'oversexed' person; a person whose main interest is in sexuality or sexual accomplishments. Also *attrib*.
1951 a joke in a Victoria University College Extravaganza. 'Dial 60 60 60' [i.e. /ˈseks,ʌu/] **1953** *Here & Now* Nov.–Dec. 43 Well, Lofty would say after a pause in the talk, time for the sexo hour. **1959** SLATTER *Gun in My Hand* 179 Sefto you old sexo! How the hell are you? *Ibid.* 230 Amy won't open the window because you're too sexo she says. **1976** SARGESON *Sunset Village* 49 There was a young hound just the other day, and another of the cold-ice breed, a sexo who had talked back, quoted somebody..who had laid it down, twice a week—to keep a man healthy. **1988** McGILL *Dict. Kiwi Slang* 98 *sexo* used to suggest another male is well-sexed, randy, ready to go sexually, often affectionately or as a greeting.

Shacklock. [A proprietary name from Henry Ely *Shacklock* (1839–1902), a Dunedin ironfounder and manufacturer of (coal) ranges: see DNZB II. 453f.] A well-known New Zealand brand of wood or coal range, esp. the *Orion* models (named from Shacklock's interest in astronomy) first built in 1873.
c**1920** BEATTIE *Trad. Lifeways Southern Maori* (1994) 294 The Maori matron or cook looks to her Orion or Champion or other range. **1924** *Otago Witness* (Dunedin) 16 Dec. 73 He could have the little Shacklock roaring in a few minutes. **1959** SLATTER *Gun in My Hand* 184 You could kid those Pongos up a gum tree. Told them I had a big cattle ranch back in Enzed. Told them me mother had the Shacklock Range and they took it all in. [**1982** BURTON *Two Hundred Yrs. NZ Food* 23 In 1873, however, an enterprising English settler by the name of Henry Shacklock produced the prototype of a new coal range, which he later called the Orion. Here at last was an oven designed for New Zealand conditions.] **1991** KEITH *Lovely Day Tomorrow* 36 A common joke of New Zealand soldiers abroad was to impress gullible foreigners with a description of the sheep station they owned on the Shacklock Range. **1992** ANDERSON *Portrait Artist's Wife* 71 'What is there to sort out?' Sarah asked the [telephone] mouthpiece, her eyes on her mother's watchful face above the Shacklock. [**1993** BERTRAM *Capes of China* 20 The [kitchen, c1924] had two Orion coal ranges.]

shade. [Alluding to the taking of atmospheric temperature 'in the shade' on the Fahrenheit scale.] In the phr. **sixty (seventy, ninety**, etc.) **in the shade**, said derogatively of an old or aging person, esp. a woman.
1928 p.c. R. Mason used in the 1920s. 'She was fifty in the shade, if she was a day.' **1950** WHITWORTH *Otago Interval* 137 Sixty-three in the shade and what a phiz.

shady, *a.* [Spec. use of *shady* shaded from sunlight.] Used of a hillside, a face, land, etc., usu. of a southern aspect, which in winter loses sun early or gets no sun at all. Cf. FACE 1 b.
1909 THOMPSON *Ballads About Business* 46 Sendin' all the sheep a-pantin' to the shady-sided slopes Of the tussock-covered foothills. **1951** LEVY *Grasslands NZ* (1970) 245 Wherever possible, sunny country was fenced off from shady country to facilitate control of stocking.

shafter. [Transf. use of *shafter* a shaft-horse: AND 1843.] A shaft bullock, one trained to work between shafts of a two-shafted vehicle.
1905 CHUDLEIGH *Diary* 20 Nov. (1950) 430 My ploughman upset his dray... The leaders got away leaving the shafter on his back. **1937** AYSON *Thomas* 97 They bought a good-looking pair of harness bullocks, one a shafter, the other a leader. **1969** HAMILTON *Wild Irishman* 105 The two leaders plunged in from the bank and disappeared under the water. Fortunately the good old shafter stood firm.

shag.

1. Also occas. **New Zealand shag**. Applied to any of various medium to large fish-eating and surface-diving sea-birds of the family Phalacrocoracidae having long, flexible necks, elsewhere usu. known as cormorants. See also CORMORANT, KARUHIRUHI, KAWAU, KAWAUPAKA. Also *attrib*.
[*Note*] Many of the species, now assigned elsewhere, were orig. placed in the genus *Phalacrocorax*.
1770 COOK *Journals* 31 Mar. (1955) I. 276 Those known in Europe are Ducks, Shags, Gannets & gulls all of which were eat [*sic*] by us and found exceeding good. **1773** FORSTER *Resolution Jrnl.* 27 Mar. (1982) II. 285 We met with several Shags, especially with a new Species, less than the common *New Zeeland shag*. **1838** *Piraki Log* 15 Jan. (1911) 65 A Boat and crew out fishing and Shag shooting. **1848** WAKEFIELD *Handbook NZ* 164 There are six or seven varieties of the Cormorant or *Shag*..called *kauwau* by the natives. **1885** *Wairarapa Daily* 18 Mar. 2 We are informed that a large shag took up it's abode on the cross of the spire of St. Patrick's Church... 'Sure enough, what else is it but the spirit of

St. Patrick himself, resting on the top of his own church!' **c1899** DOUGLAS in *Mr Explorer Douglas* (1957) 244 It is heartrending to come suddenly on thirty or forty shags suning [*sic*] themselves on a river bank, and if startled they will throw up enough of white bait to supply a ministerial dinner. **1932** STEAD *Life Histories NZ Birds* 1 The crude method adopted of putting a price on the birds has resulted in all species of Shags being persecuted. **1955** OLIVER *NZ Birds* 201 Sixteen species and subspecies of shags are found in the New Zealand region. **1966** *Encycl. NZ* III. 226 Shags are long-necked aquatic birds with hooked beaks, long, stiff, wedge-shaped tails, and webbed feet. **1984** SOPER *Birds NZ* 53 In New Zealand all cormorants are known as shags, the terms are interchangeable.

2. With a modifier: **Auckland Island, black, blue, Bounty Island, bronze (pink-footed), Campbell Island, Chatham Island, frilled, king (carunculated, Marlborough, New Zealand king), little (or little pied), little black, Macquarie Island, pied, Pitt Island** (formerly **Chatham Island(s)**, occas. **double-crested), rough-faced, spotted (crested), Stewart Island, white-throated**.

(1) **Auckland Island shag**. *Leucocarbo colensoi*, a glossy black and white, pink-footed shag.

1888 BULLER *Birds NZ* II. 161 Phalacrocorax colensoi. (Auckland-Island Shag.) **1910** COCKAYNE *NZ Plants & Their Story* 117 The Auckland Island shag [is] conspicuous with its glistening black back, spotless white breast, and flesh-coloured feet. **1955** OLIVER *NZ Birds* 216 *Auckland Island Shag*... Although this shag is abundant at the Auckland Islands it was not collected by the English, American or French expeditions that called there about 1840. **1976** SOPER *NZ Birds* 235 Auckland Island has its own shag..yet another of the complex assemblage of 'blue-eyed', flesh-footed, white-fronted shags present at all the islands except the Antipodes and Snares. **1985** *Reader's Digest Book NZ Birds* 123 The Auckland Island shag breeds in alcoves, on ledges or along the tops of very steep cliffs.

(2) **black shag**. A large black shag of the New Zealand subspecies *novaehollandiae* of the widespread species, *Phalacrocorax carbo*. See also KAWAU.

1773 FORSTER *Resolution Jrnl.* 13 May (1982) II. 276 Abounding with New Zeeland black Shags. **1844** WILLIAMS *NZ Jrnl.* (1956) 115 The Kauau or common diver, the Raruhiruhi, the first name is generally used [for] the Black Shagg or diver. **1870** *TrNZI* II. 48 On the rifted top of a huge lifeless tree, the great Black Shag, perched motionless. **1882** POTTS *Out in Open* 211 The cormorant, or great black shag, *Phalacrocorax carbo*..Kawau-tua-whenua of the Maoris. **1904** HUTTON & DRUMMOND *Animals NZ* 295 The Cormorant, or Black Shag, is found not only on the sea-coast, but also on rivers and lakes, far away from the sea. **1932** STEAD *Life Histories NZ Birds* 10 Owing to their constant persecution by the sailors in New Zealand are generally shy and wary. **1966** *Encycl. NZ* III. 226 Only in special circumstances is one single species—the black shag—likely to vie with man as a predator of trout. **1984** SOPER *Birds NZ* 53 The black shag is overall black with an oily-green sheen.

(3) **blue shag**. *Stictocarbo punctatus steadi*, the Stewart Island subspecies of the *spotted shag* (16) below. See also BRAVO DUCK.

1872 *Appendix Proc. Otago Prov. Council* 39 The following is a list of the birds shot..another species of shag, locally called the 'blue shag'..pretty highly esteemed by the sailors as an article of food. **1925–26** *NZJST* VIII. 326 Spotted Shag (*Stictocarbo punctatus*)... This is the 'blue shag' of the inhabitants [of Stewart Island]. **1948** *NZ Bird Notes* III. 79 On the west side of the middle entrance [to Port Pegasus] was a colony of blue shags (Stictocarbo punctatus steadi) nesting in well sheltered clefts on a cliff. **1966** FALLA et al. *Birds NZ* 73 Probably best treated as a subspecies of the Spotted Shag, the Blue Shag is nevertheless distinguishable by being slightly dark in tone of plumage. **1981** DENNIS *Paparoas Guide* 180 These cormorants were almost certainly the *blue shags*, which have rare northern breeding colonies..at Twelve Mile Bluff.

(4) **Bounty Island shag**. *Leucocarbo ranfurlyi*, a rare, cliff-breeding shag of Bounty Island.

1904 HUTTON & DRUMMOND *Animals NZ* 302 *The Bounty Island Shag. Phalacrocorax ranfurlyi*. **1909** CHILTON *Subantarctic Islands NZ* II. 583 Bounty Island shag... This is the latest addition to the avifauna of the New Zealand region. **1955** OLIVER *NZ Birds* 218 The Bounty Island Shag is apparently a sedentary species, remaining near the islands all the year round. **1984** SOPER *Birds NZ* 56 The Bounty Island Shag..resembles the Stewart Island Shag in size and general plumage. **1990** *Checklist Birds NZ* 84 *Leucocarbo ranfurlyi... Bounty Island Shag*... Breeds on Bounty Islands and (?) Antipodes Islands.

(5) **bronze (pink-footed) shag**. *Leucocarbo chalconotus*, the dark phase of the *Stewart Island Shag* (see (17) below).

1914 GUTHRIE-SMITH *Mutton Birds & Other Birds* 202 Pink-footed Shag and Stewart Island Shag, may, I think, prove to be one and the same breed. **1923** *NZJST* VI. 75 Bronze Shag; Pink-footed Shag. Guthrie-Smith (1914) records this with the other Stewart Island species, with which he thinks it probably conspecific. **1967** NATUSCH *Animals NZ* 260 The bronze and Stewart Island shags..which interbreed, are confined to the Foveaux Strait area. **1984** SOPER *Birds NZ* 56 The dark phase [of the Stewart Island Shag] known as the Bronze Shag, is uniformly greenish-black all over, with a bronze sheen. **1990** *Checklist Birds NZ* 83 *Leucocarbo chalconotus... Stewart Island Shag, Bronze Shag*... A dimorphic species, of which the dark phase is commonly called the Bronze Shag.

(6) **Campbell Island shag**. *Leucocarbo campbelli*, a black-necked shag of Campbell Island.

1888 BULLER *Birds NZ* II. 167 Phalacrocorax nycthemerus. (Campbell-Island Shag.) **1904** HUTTON & DRUMMOND *Animals NZ* 300 *The Campbell Island Shag. Phalacrocorax campbelli*. **1923** *NZJST* VI. 75 *Hypoleucus campbelli*... Campbell Island Shag. **1955** OLIVER *NZ Birds* 214 The Campbell Island Shag, readily recognised by its black neck, was first collected..in 1874. **1985** *Reader's Digest Book NZ Birds* 122 Campbell Island Shags hunt in large flocks. **1990** *Checklist Birds NZ* 84 *Leucocarbo campbelli... Campbell Island Shag*... Breeds on Campbell Island.

(7) **Chatham Island shag**. *Leucocarbo onslowi*, a colourful shag, of metallic sheen, and having a blue eye-ring and orange face and throat.

1899 *TrNZI* XXXI. 28 I have now before me two specimens of the Chatham Island Shag. **1904** HUTTON & DRUMMOND *Animals NZ* 300 *The Chatham Island Shag. Phalacrocorax featherstoni*. **1955** OLIVER *NZ Birds* 225 The Chatham Island Shag was discovered by H.H. Travers..in 1871. **1985** *Reader's Digest Book NZ Birds* 121 The Chatham Island shag builds its nest of ice plant, grass and other plants on level and sloping rocks not far above the high tide line and the spray zone. **1990** *Checklist Birds NZ* 83 *Leucocarbo onslowi..Chatham Island Shag*.

(8) **frilled shag**. *Obs*. See *little shag* (11) below.

1871 HUTTON *Catalogue Birds NZ* 50 Graculus melanoleucus... Frilled Shag. **1886** *TrNZI* XVIII. 100 *P. melanoleucus* (Frilled Shag)..and *P. punctatus* (Spotted Shag)..which I have often found in the inland bays, rivers, and lakes. **1896** *Ibid*. XXVIII. 367 The frilled shag is, owing to its cautious habits, called the 'duckscarer' by the sportsmen living in the [Kenepuru] sound. **1904** HUTTON & DRUMMOND *Animals NZ* 297 *The Frilled Shag. Phalacrocorax melanoleucus*... In New Zealand this bird is rare, but is occasionally found in both Islands. **1914** GUTHRIE-SMITH *Mutton Birds & Other Birds* 170 The Frilled Shag possesses no frill visible to the field naturalist.

(9) **king (carunculated, Marlborough, New Zealand king) shag**. *Leucocarbo carunculatus*, a large rare white-throated shag of Cook Strait. See also *rough-faced shag* (15) below.

1949 *NZ Bird Notes* III. 182 Inhabiting a restricted area at the northern end of the South Island, the king, Marlborough, or carunculated shag..is the rarest species of shag in New Zealand. **1955** OLIVER *NZ Birds* 223 Rough-faced Shag. King Shag... An example of this magnificent species was collected by Forster in Queen Charlotte Sound during Cook's second voyage. **1966** DURRELL *Two in the Bush* 69 The White Rocks [in Cook Strait] are one of the only two nesting places for the King Shag in the world. **1976** SOPER *NZ Birds* 162 With its black head, brilliant cobalt eye and carunculated bill, the King Shag, New Zealand's rarest shag and one of the world's rare birds, has indeed been aptly named. **1984** SOPER *Birds NZ* 55 The King Shag breeds in compact colonies on the rock platforms..building substantial nests of seaweed and debris. **1990** *Checklist Birds NZ* 83 *Leucocarbo carunculatus... New Zealand King Shag*... Breeds on islands on the south side of Cook Strait.

(10) **little black shag**. *Phalacrocorax sulcirostris*, a small entirely-black shag, having a long, thin bill. See also LOUSY HEAD.

1904 HUTTON & DRUMMOND *Animals NZ* 296 In New Zealand a single colony of Little Black Shags is known at the Bay of Islands. **1949** *NZ Bird Notes* III. 170 At Matata Lagoon, Bay of Plenty, my wife and I watched at very close range a party of seven little black shags. **1966** FALLA et al. *Birds NZ* 67 Little Black Shag... This is the most sombrely plumaged of all the New Zealand shags. **1984** SOPER *Birds NZ* 55 Little Black Shags breed in colonies, sometimes with other black-footed shags, usually in trees overhanging water. **1990** *NZ Geographic* VII. 52 [Caption] Flock of little black shags loafs on the mudflats at Uretara Estuary.

(11) **little** (occas. **little pied**) **shag**. *Phalacrocorax melanoleucos brevirostris*, a small long-tailed shag with variable black and white plumage. See also *dusk scarer* (DUCK 3 a), *frilled shag* (8) above, KAWAUPAKA, *white-throated shag* (18) below.

1955 OLIVER *NZ Birds* 204 The Little Pied Shag is mainly an Australian species which was first described by Vieillot in 1817 from New South Wales specimens. **1966** FALLA et al. *Birds NZ* 67 Little Shag *Phalacrocorax melanoleucos brevirostris*. Maori name: Kawaupaka. The name White-throated Shag is also in general use for the most abundant phase of a rather variable species. **1984** SOPER *Birds NZ* 55 The Little Shag is a small and distinctive, though variable, shag with a short, yellow bill and a long tail. **1990** *Checklist Birds NZ* 82 *Phalacrocorax melanoleucos brevirostris... Little Shag* (*Kawaupaka*).., A dimorphic subspecies with some intermediate variants; the relative scarcity of the latter suggests that the white-breasted phase may be maintained by occasional immigration from Australia.

(12) **Macquarie Island shag**. *Leucocarbo atriceps* (formerly *albiventer*) *purpurascens*, a glossy blue-black and white shag having large conspicuous yellow caruncles at the base of its bill.

1904 HUTTON & DRUMMOND *Animals NZ* 303 The

Macquarie Island Shag. Phalacrocorax traversi. **1955** OLIVER *NZ Birds* 228 The Macquarie Island Shag was first collected by Bellingshausen, commander of the Russian Antarctic Expedition, in 1820. **1984** SOPER *Birds NZ* 57 The Macquarie Island Shag is confined to Macquarie Island and the outlying stacks, such as the Bishop and Clerk Rocks.

(13) **pied shag**. *Phalacrocorax varius varius*, a large black and white shag. See also KARUHIRUHI.

1871 HUTTON *Catalogue Birds NZ* 51 Graculus varius... Pied Shag. **1873** *TrNZI* V. 151 I observed the nests of the common pied shag. **1882** POTTS *Out in Open* 210 The Pied Shag..another handsome sea-bird. **1904** HUTTON & DRUMMOND *Animals NZ* 296 The Pied Shag is the common coast Shag of the North Island, but is not so common in the south. **1932** STEAD *Life Histories NZ Birds* 14 The Pied Shag is an exceedingly handsome bird. **1949** *NZ Bird Notes* III. 182 In the large pied shag only the top of the head is black, the sides of the face and neck being white, as well as the underparts. **1955** OLIVER *NZ Birds* 209 The Pied Shag breeds in trees along the shore and breaks away leaves and twigs so as to get an unobstructed view. **1976** SOPER *NZ Birds* 160 The Pied Shag is the common large black and white shag of New Zealand waters. **1984** SOPER *Birds NZ* 54 The Pied Shag is a large and quite approachable, elegant bird.

(14) **Pitt Island** (formerly **Chatham Island(s)**, occas. **double-crested**) **shag**. *Stictocarbo featherstoni*, a sedentary shag of the Chatham Islands.

1873 BULLER *Birds NZ* 338 Phalacrocorax featherstoni. (Chatham-Island Shag.) **1904** HUTTON & DRUMMOND *Animals NZ* 301 *The Pitt Island Shag. Phalacrocorax onslowi.* **1923** *NZJST* VI. 75 *Stictocarbo featherstoni...* Chatham Islands Shag. **1955** OLIVER *NZ Birds* 233 *Pitt Island Shag. Stictocarbo featherstoni.* Equally as beautiful as the spotted shags, this representative of them in the Chatham Group was discovered by H.H. Travers during his visit in 1871. **1966** FALLA et al. *Birds NZ* 73 Pitt Island Shag... Double-crested Shag. **1976** SOPER *NZ Birds* 217 On the cliffs are Pitt Island Shags—the Chatham representative of the Spotted Shag. **1985** *Reader's Digest Book NZ Birds* 126 *Pitt Island Shag. Stictocarbo featherstoni... Double-crested shag...* Like its close relative the spotted shag, the Pitt Island shag builds a nest of ice plant, grass and other plants in the alcoves of steep cliffs.

(15) **rough-faced shag**. [f. a paraphrase of the Latin *carunculatus*.] See *king shag* (9) above.

1873 BULLER *Birds NZ* 332 Phalacrocorax carunculatus. (Rough-faced Shag.) **1904** HUTTON & DRUMMOND *Animals NZ* 303 *The Rough-faced Shag. Phalacrocorax carunculatus.* **1923** *NZJST* VI. 75 *Hypoleucus carunculatus...* Rough-faced Shag. **1955** [see *king shag* (9) above]. **1985** *Reader's Digest Book NZ Birds* 118 *King Shag. Leucocarbo carunculatus... Carunculated shag, Marlborough Sounds shag, rough-faced shag, Cook Strait cormorant.*

(16) **spotted** (or **crested**) **shag**. *Stictocarbo punctatus punctatus*, having grey wing feathers tipped with black to give a spotted appearance. See also FLIP-FLAP, PAREKAREKA. See also *blue shag* (3) above.

1855 DRURY *Sailing Directions* 66 The Phalacrocorax Punctatus, or Cristatus (Spotted Shag) is said to be common in Pelorus. **1873** *TrNZI* V. 201 The spotted shag, or flip-flap, well known to our shore folk, is stated by ornithologists to be peculiar to New Zealand; its active movements enliven many a bluff headland or rocky inlet of our island coast line. **1892** Ibid. XXIV. 84 *Phalacrocorax punctatus...* (The Spotted Shag.) **1904** HUTTON & DRUMMOND *Animals NZ* 298 *The Spotted Shag. Phalacrocorax punctatus...* This is the common coast Shag of Canterbury and Westland. **1923** *NZJST* VI. 75 *Stictocarbo punctatus* Spotted Shag. This is a common species in several portions of both Islands. **1938** *Auckland Weekly News* 30 Mar. 96 The crested shag, or cormorant, was another beautiful bird found there! **1948** *NZ Bird Notes* III. 26 Spotted Shag... This was the commonest bird observed round [Banks] Peninsula. **1955** OLIVER *NZ Birds* 231 The voice of the Spotted Shag is quite different from that of all other New Zealand shags. It might be described as a high pitched whistle. **1967** NATUSCH *Animals NZ* 260 The spotted shag..is a smallish coastal shag nesting in eastern cliff colonies of Otago and Canterbury. **1976** SOPER *NZ Birds* 164 When in full plumage the Spotted Shag is a bird of striking and exotic appearance. **1984** SOPER *Birds NZ* 58 The Spotted Shag is one of 3 closely related, totally marine shags with spotted plumage and orange-yellow feet, confined to the New Zealand region.

(17) **Stewart Island shag**. *Leucocarbo chalconotus*, a pink-footed shag. See also *bronze shag* (5) above.

1904 HUTTON & DRUMMOND *Animals NZ* 301 *The Stewart Island Shag. Phalacrocorax stewarti.* **1914** GUTHRIE-SMITH *Mutton Birds & Other Birds* 175 On the larger and more elevated northern portion [of the rock], there is established..a rookery of the Stewart Island Shag. **1948** *NZ Bird Notes* III. 80 If, as is indeed probable, the whalers and sealers used any considerable number of shags for food, it is much more likely that they used the common Stewart Island shag..which could be quite easily obtained and in much greater numbers than the blue shag. **1955** OLIVER *NZ Birds* 221 The Stewart Island Shag was collected on several occasions in Otago prior to 1888. **1964** DEMPSEY *Little World Stewart Is.* 52 The lonely Kane-te-toe..is the rookery of the Stewart Island shag. **1985** *Reader's Digest Book NZ Birds* 119 The Stewart Island shag has two colour forms and typically nests and roosts on the bare rocks of headlands and small islands. **1990** [see *bronze shag* (5) above].

(18) **white-throated shag**. See *little shag* (11) above. See also KAWAUPAKA, *river crow* (RIVER 2 a).

1871 HUTTON *Catalogue Birds NZ* 51 Graculus brevirostris... White-throated Shag. **1873** [see KAWAUPAKA]. **1904** HUTTON & DRUMMOND *Animals NZ* 298 The White-throated Shag is not a coast bird, but is found chiefly near the ends of long winding sounds and inlets, or else on the rivers. **1914** GUTHRIE-SMITH *Mutton Birds & Other Birds* 164 The Pied Shag, the Frilled Shag, and the White-throated Shag breed in the same communities, and by day perch together in the same roosting quarters. **1925–26** *NZJST* VIII. 208 White-throated Shag (*Microcarbo melanoleucos*). **1949** *NZ Bird Notes* III. 156 One of the most interesting discoveries of the expedition was a shaggery of the white-throated shag. **1955** OLIVER *NZ Birds* 203 The food of the White-throated Shags consists in large part of fresh-water fishes and crustacea. **1966** FALLA et al. *Birds NZ* 67 Little Shag *Maori name*: Kawaupaka. The name White-throated Shag is also in general use for the most abundant phase of a rather variable species. **1985** *Reader's Digest Book NZ Birds* 117 *Little Pied Cormorant... Kawaupaka, white-throated shag, frilled shag, little river shag, little cormorant, little shag.*

3. In comparisons denoting misery in the phr. **as miserable as a shag on a rock**, or loneliness, **like a shag on a rock**.

1834 MARKHAM *NZ* (1963) 53 A Thunder Storm came on. It Blew and rained, I was all afloat and as miserable as Shag on a Rock. **1988** McGILL *Dict. Kiwi Slang* 98 *shag* in phr. *like a shag on a rock* alone, abandoned, forlorn.

4. Special Comb. **shag-tree**, a shag's roosting tree. Cf. SHAGGERY.

1953 SUTHERLAND *Golden Bush* (1963) 72 He knew the range between the corner of the steading enclosure and the shag-tree to a foot.

shagaroon, var. SHAGROON.

shaggery. [f. SHAG + -*ery*.] A breeding-place of shags; a shag 'rookery'.

1878 *TrNZI* X. 207 In the Lake district there are 'shaggeries' of considerable magnitude. **1882** HAY *Brighter Britain* II. 222 The Kawau..is one of the commonest birds... They build in trees, in large 'shaggeries'. **1888** BULLER *Birds NZ* II. 151 I visited one of these 'shaggeries' on the Rurima rocks, off Whakatane,.. the young birds being then fledged and preparing to take their flight. **1920** *TrNZI* LII. 69 By the Mataura River, in the South Wyndham Bush, there used to be a shaggery, and he had seen a Maori bring away about two or three hundred young shags caught just before they were ready to fly. **1957** *15th Ann. Rep. Soil Conservation & Rivers Central Council* 55 Shaggery Road.

shagroon /ʃəˈgrun/. *Hist.* Also early **shagaroon** (freq.), **shagrun, shaproon** (?misprint), occas. with init. cap. [Poss. f. Gaelic *seachrán* 'wandering', transliterated *shaughraun* /ʃɒxˈrɒn/ (so Morris and OED): the only evidence for Wall's *shabroon*, Earp's (1850) *Shaproon*, is prob. a misprint of *p* for an orig. *g*.] **a.** Often used derogatorily for an early non-Canterbury Association settler in Canterbury, often one who had settled there before the main influx of 'pilgrim' settlers, and often or esp. an immigrant from Australia. Cf. PRE-ADAMITE, PROPHET 1.

1849 TORLESSE *Papers* 14 Aug. (1958) 93 I went to show Jollie a bush near the roadline where he should put up his house, and set 3 shagaroons to work upon it... [Aug. 15] Jollie and I surveying the roadline. Reached the waterfall nearly, near Shagaroon Bush, with Diamond, Moses, and Fitch. **1850** *Notes from a Jrnl.* 8 Mar. in Earp *Handbook Intending Emigrants* (1852) 176 We visited the warri or hut of a Shaproon, *i.e.*, one of the retired whalers who have married Maori wives, and live a half-savage life in the bush with the natives. **1850** TORLESSE *Papers* (1958) 149 The *Shagaroon* launched (1st vessel out of Port Victoria)... [1958 *Note*] Presumably so named because it was repaired [in Canterbury]..by two Hobart Town carpenters. **1851** *NZ Spectator and Cook's Strait Guardian* (Wellington) 7 May [unpaged 3] [Title] *Dream of a Shagroon.* As I lay upon my bed..methought I saw a long train of Pilgrims proceeding from a far country of the West towards an unknown land... I saw men of another aspect arrive at the pilgrim-land. [Etc., ironising an outburst in the *Lyttelton Times* deploring the mixed composition of the Canterbury settlement of 'stragglers from other settlements, of whale-fishers and stock-drivers' a far cry from 'the body of English gentlemen' intended.] **1851** *Lyttelton Times* 1 Nov. 6 We need only to point to the numbers of careless, free-and-easy, undisciplined shagroons, which infest every colonial port town; men who live from hand to mouth, whose employment is generally precarious, and whose earnings have an evident tendency towards the pocket of the publican, or of the tobacco merchant. **1851** *Austral. & NZ Gaz.* 29 Nov. 483 The Eudora and Raven have arrived with a good stock of Shagaroons who will soon infuse a new vitality into the drooping pilgrims. It's true the Shagaroons don't know what to think at the great change between the arid plains of Australia, and the moist green sward of New Zealand. **1852** *Lee to Elliot* in *Nelson Examiner* May 29 in McIntosh *Marlborough* (1940) 126 I think that many of the Canterbury pilgrims and many also of the Nelson

Shagroons may be expected to exchange visits next year. **1853** Sewell *Journal* 31 May (1980) I. 297 Rhodes is a shrewd fellow—one of the old Shagroon race. [He had come to Canterbury via Australia, not as a Canterbury Pilgrim.] **1859** Thomson *Story NZ* II. 187 An old Australian squatter, who visited the Canterbury settlement in 1851, divided the inhabitants into pilgrims, shagruns, and prophets; the first were the original colonists, the second were people from other parts of New Zealand, and the last were settlers from Australia. **1866** [see prophet a]. **1886** [see settler 2 a]. **1898** Morris *Austral-English* 410 When the province of Canterbury, in New Zealand, was first settled, the men who came from England were called *Pilgrims*, all others *Shagroons*, probably a modification of the Irish word *Shaughraun*. **1900** *Canterbury Old & New* II. 109 I therefore dressed myself in the garb of an up-country 'Shagroon' [in pursuit of McKenzie c1855-56] and searched the vessel. **1948** Arnold Wall *Let.* 25 Nov. in Reed *Story Canterbury* (1949) 110 My belief is that the word was not originally 'Shagroon' but 'Shabroon', 'shabberoon', 'shabbaroon' (all spellings occur) which is on record from the 18th century onwards, meaning 'a mean, shabby fellow'... I conjecture that the 'shabroon' of the English Pilgrims was by some pronounced with the 'b' and by others with the 'g', nobody ever having seen the word written or printed. **1959** Sinclair *Hist. NZ* 92 Even the Canterbury Association, almost as soon as its settlement was founded, had to let in the 'shagroons', as the Australian stock-men were called. **1975** Acland *Early Canterbury Runs* (4edn.) 94 Stoddart was a 'shagroon' who came from Australia with sheep in 1851. **1980** Eldred-Grigg *Southern Gentry* 76 The typical South Island landowner..was an upper-middle class Englishman... Australians were rare—the tales of Australian 'shagroons' must be exploded forever.

b. *attrib.*
1851 Ward *Journal* 20 Feb. (1951) 132 Started with Henry and a 'shagroon' cattle-driver. **1854** *Canterbury Papers* II. 137 [Sewell] has had enough of 'shagroon' letters.

shagrun, var. shagroon.

shake: see milkshake *n.*

shake, *v.*
1. In the phr. **to shake one's shirt,** to get a move on, to 'shake a leg'.
1959 Slatter *Gun in My Hand* 91 You'll haveta shake ya shirt and get down to some hard yakker. **1988** McGill *Dict. Kiwi Slang* 98 *shake your shirt* get stuck in.

2. In the phr. **to be shook on,** see shook *ppl. a.*

shake, *n.* [Spec. use of *shake* irregular vibratory movement: see OED *n.* 3 b, 'Now *U.S.* and *N.Z.*'.] (The shock of) an earthquake.
1845 Wakefield *Adventure NZ* II. xv 308 The most severe earthquake occurred that I had yet felt... The natives acknowledged that they had never experienced so bad a *ru*, or 'shake'. **1866** Carter *Life & Recollections* II. 11 These *shakes* I afterwards noticed, occurred at intervals. **1880** Leathes *An Actor Abroad* 179 My first experience of a 'Shake'. **1929** Milton *Love & Chiffon* 219 In good old New Zealand, you realise these shakes are mere nothings. **1934** Scanlan *Winds of Heaven* 264 You remember that little shake we had this morning: well, Napier had it badly. **1940** *Tales of Pioneer Women* (1988) 100 The shakes continued and we were taken up to sleep for several nights at the large strongly-built Military Hospital. **1953** Guthrie-Smith *Tutira* (3edn.) 45 My daughter estimated that approximately fifteen or twenty seconds elapsed before the shake felt at Tutira was experienced in Napier. **1963** McRae *By the Braes of Balquether* 61 Then in the early morning of the 1st September came the big shake. **1972** Anderson *Let. from James* 143 The shake [in Christchurch, 1888]..was described as the most severe since the arrival of the pilgrims. **1990** *Listener* 26 Nov. 38 You couldn't go inside for a gold clock..because every time you went inside a shake came.

Hence **shaky** *a.*, prone to earthquakes.
1906 Elkington *Adrift in NZ* 202 Wellington..is a shaky place.

shaker. *Flaxmilling.* See quot.
1913 Carr *Country Work* 44 The fibre as it leaves the stripper is caught by the 'fly boy', who collects enough to make into a hank, which he places convenient for the 'shaker'. The latter, with a motion like cracking a whip, gets rid of as much rubbish as possible.

shandygaff. [A transf. use of *shandygaff* a mixture of beer and (usu.) gingerbeer.]
1. In *attrib.* use. [AND a compromise, 1897.] Wishy-washy, compromising.
1911 *Maoriland Worker* 16 June 2 How long are the workers going to stand this treatment at the hands of this shandy-gaff Government, wherein the honest ale of democracy is drowned by the washy lemonade of alleged Liberalism?

2. *Farming.* A mixture, of kinds of stock or of breeds of dog, the result of which is in some way inferior to the components taken singly.
1933 *Press* (Christchurch) (Acland Gloss.) 25 Nov. 15 *Shandygaff.*—Various sorts of sheep mixed together in a yard. Wet and dry sheep together. Hence the verb use: to put wet sheep with dry ones in the woolshed in order to deceive the shearers. (Since 1918 in Southland, but probably it is in use here.) **1971** Newton *Ten Thousand Dogs* 169 *Shandy-gaff*: A dog bred from the crossing of heading dogs and huntaways.

shang. A shortened form of shanghai.
1904 *NZ Illustr. Mag.* Nov. 111 I did not flatter myself that he [*sc.* a cat] did this out of pure love..for me, but rather for the pickings which my prowess with the shang afforded him. **1926** Peacocke *His Kid Brother* 45 Dal's beloved 'shang'. **1938** *Auckland Weekly News* 1 June 62 He threw the shang into Jennie's hand, and fled.

shangeye, var. shanghai.

shanghai. Occas. also **shangeye.** [Ad. Sc. dial. *shangy* a stick split at one end for clipping on a dog's tail (prob. either to keep it down, or to enable messages to be attached): ad. Gaelic *seangan* 'a cleft, stick', influenced by the form and poss. pronunciation of the place-name *Shanghai*: see OED *shangy*; EDD *shangan* 'a stick cleft at one end for putting on a dog's tail'; AND 1863.] A catapult. See also shang.
1884 *NZ Statutes* No.24 64 [Police Offences Act, 1884] Rolls any cask, beats any carpet, flies any kite, uses any bows and arrows, or catapult, or shanghai, or plays at any game to the annoyance of any person in any public place. **1897** Wilmot *Journal* in Reed *Farthest West* (1950) 138 Andy knocked over a nice crow with his shanghai. **1901** *TrNZI* XXXIII. 216 Two small boys saw him [*sc.* a morepork] at the same time. I caught a whisper of 'Watch him while I get my shanghai.' **1919** *Ibid.* LI. 222 They were so tame that a boy with a 'shanghai' could soon make a fair bag. **1923** *NZJST* VI. 86 This species..still occurs far back in the great timbered areas, but is much more timid than in the old 'shanghai' days. **1934** Lee *Children of Poor* (1949) 145 We..broke windows with the careless use of the shanghai. **1949** Davin *Roads from Home* 135 He had helped them..to cut prongs out of peeled willow forks for their shangeyes. **1961** Crump *Hang On a Minute Mate* 152 I asked the girlfriend if she wanted to come down to the tip with me the next day, shooting rats with shanghais. **1970** Davin *Not Here Not Now* 133 My big brother..he hit the Stott's drake with his shangeye and killed him. **1982** Sutton-Smith *Hist. Children's Play* 99 Shanghais have been the all-time most popular improvised weapon of New Zealand boys. Occasionally they were known as catapults.

Hence **shanghai** *v. trans.*, to hit or kill (birds, etc.) with a shanghai shot. Also as a *vbl. n.*
1974 Bream *I'm Sorry Amanda* 82 [It] fosters in those selfish adolescents the streak of cruelty which urges them in the weekends, when no teachers are available as prey, to shanghai thrushes. **1985** Hunt *I'm Ninety-five* 261 No, my father didn't mind us shanghaiing thrushes and that, but he always said don't touch the natives. **1995** *Independent* 8 Dec. 20 There was [among Dunedin boys' games] also hopscotch.. shanghaiing, peeing up the dunny wall..and marbling.

Shanghai ballast. [f. *Shanghai*, a Chinese city.] Boiled rice, poss. occas. sago.
c**1910** p.c. Mr. C.R. Carr, Mowai Red Cross Home (1950): *shanghai ballast* for rice, also freq. in WW1. **1939–45** *Expressions & Sayings 2NZEF* (TS N.A. WAII DA 420/1) Shanghai ballast—Rice. **1946** *Tararua Tramper* Apr. 7 A vote whether to have Christmas dinner at midnight or a cup of cocoa and a plate of rice in half an hour, brought a hundred per cent for Shanghai ballast. **1953** Stronach *Musterer on Molesworth* 52 Rice was our mainstay. 'Shanghai Ballast' we called it, and we got dead sick of it. **1956** Sutherland *Green Kiwi* (1960) 67 Hare..had eaten a few thick slices of this [meat], together with boiled potatoes..some sago or 'shanghai-ballast'.

shanty. [See OED *n.*[1]: prob. an altered form of Canadian French *chantier* a woodcutters' hut; 'Chiefly *U.S.* and *Canada*', 1820.]
1. A rough shack or hut, often in the bush.
1840 in Wilkes *US Exploring Exped.* (1852) I. 296 Kororarika is still the principal settlement, and contains about twenty houses..and many shanties, besides tents. **1851** Torlesse *Papers* (1958) 191 Built a shanty at the creek. **1860** *Voices from Auckland* 67 A 'bushman' would run up a 'settler's first home' at a tithe of the expense..his trained and ready hand runs up his hut—'shanty', or whatever you like to call it. **1871** Money *Knocking About NZ* 17 I was much amused by a trio who arrived in the township and put up opposite my 'shanty'. **1882** Hay *Brighter Britain* I. 116 In its Canadian and original sense, the term [*sc.* shanty] means a log-house... Such log-huts are not common in this country, though they may be see here and there... A shanty here, is a name applied to almost any kind of nondescript erection, which would not come under the designation of wharè, or be honoured by the ambitious title of house. Rough edifices of planking are the common form. **1920** Mander *Story NZ River* (1974) 59 Later on, Bruce and many other men built shanties and houses for themselves. **1947** [see hut]. **1953** Reed *Story of Kauri* 130 A sheltered site having been selected near to running water, an advance party would be sent to clear the necessary space and build a 'shanty' which, in the earlier days, served inclusively as dormitory, dining hall and cookhouse. **1970** Severinsen *Hunt Far Mountain* 97 The night was spent at the Forks Hut, a rough, dark, musterers' shanty. **1986** Owen & Perkins *Speaking for Ourselves* 50 And do you know where we lived? At Te Karaka, where I was born, in a little shanty near the beach.

2. *Obs.* [AND *shanty* 1863.] A small, rough, wayside public-house or low-grade accommodation-house, usu., though unlicensed, selling alcoholic liquor; a grog-shop or sly-grog shop. See also BUSH SHANTY 1, *grog-shanty* (GROG *n.* 1).

1848 in Power *Sketches in NZ* (1849) 168 We had heard that a 'pakeha' had built a shanty on the opposite side of the river for the purpose of entertaining travellers, and ferrying them across. **1856** HARPER *Lett. from NZ* 25 Dec. (1914) 10 There happened to be at the foot of the hill a little wooden shanty where refreshments were on sale. **1862** *Otago Goldfields & Resources* 28 Every four or five miles on the road an accommodation house is met. These..are not mere 'shanties', and the traveller, with ordinary precautions, is always safe. **1871** MONEY *Knocking About NZ* 83 I walked back..to a small wayside shanty... The landlord was a digger. **1881** BATHGATE *Waitaruna* 270 Rather more than an hour's ride brought them to a roadside public-house or shanty where they hoped to breakfast. **1892** KIPLING *One Lady at Wairakei* (1983) 34 He loved a woman at a sheep station—one of the women who serve up the 'colonial goose' to the tourist when he stops at the wooden shanties..a red-faced raddled woman who talks about 'ke-ows', and 'bye-bies'. **1931** LOVELL-SMITH *Old Coaching Days* 33 [Drunken Woman's Creek] took its name from a shanty nearby..where lived an old woman, who sold whisky 'on the sly'. **1940** in Reid *Book NZ* (1964) 284 How the devil can a man keep sober In those shanties by the way? **1964** LEE *Shiner Slattery* 9 Don't blame the Colonial Government, If your children lack for bread—But blame the wayside shanty For the reckless life you've led. **1975** HARPER *Eight Daughters* 20 Pubs provided liquor and accommodation..; shanties provided just liquor. **1985** *Listener* 12 Jan. 26 Virtually every settlement in the young colony originally clustered around its taverns—even if they were only tattered calico shanties.

3. Special Comb. **shanty-keeper** *hist.* [AND 1862] (**shanty owner**), the landlord of a shanty; one who keeps a sly-grog shop.

1869 *Grey River Argus* 9 Jan. 3 What desolation... Deserted buildings and uncalicoed huts..hard-hearted storekeepers and melancholy shanty-keepers, broken newspaper men and unemployed shoemakers. **1875** WOOD & LAPHAM *Waiting for Mail* 45 Mrs Smith was the shanty-keeper's wife. **1881** BATHGATE *Waitaruna* 299 Do you mean to say that [he] has become the landlord of a low bush public-house?.. I little thought he would ever come down so far in the social scale as to become a shanty-keeper. **a1900** DOUGLAS in *Mr Explorer Douglas* (1957) 14 The Shanty Keeper is a cross between the store & the pub, he calls himself a storekeeper, but a few tins of sardines, and a side of bacon is about all he possesses in that line. He depends upon whiskey and cardplaying, and sometimes calls his place an Accomodation [*sic*] house or restaurant. **1905** *Truth* 4 Nov. 8 The police seldom run these jokers in, but they did so a few days back when a worthless shanty-keeper..was caged on two charges. **1992** LATHAM *Golden Reefs* 108 Hotel and shanty owners were the only winners.

shaproon, var. SHAGROON.

sharemilker. A person who works another's dairy farm for a share of the profits, often owning a herd of cows (see esp. quot. 1943).

1919 *Hawera & Normanby Star* 8 Aug. 4 The facts..were that..a sharemilker was drinking at the hotel on the day in question. **1920** POWDRELL *Dairy Farming* 9 The share-milker's remuneration consists of $^1/_3$ of all milk moneys, [two-fifths] of calves sold, and $^1/_2$ of the profits from the pigs sold. **1934** *Truth* 21 Feb. 11 [Heading] Sharemilker's grave offense [*sic*]. **1943** *NZJST* XXIV. 231A A feature of dairy-farming in New Zealand has been the development of share-milking, akin to the old French system of métayage or the sharefarming common with annual crops such as cotton in the United states of America. Under this system the owner usually provides the land, plant, and herd, while the share-milker provides labour and receives in return one-third to one-half of the gross returns. In other cases the sharemilker also provides the dairy herd and receives two-thirds of the gross receipts. **1963** BACON *In the Sticks* 183 Many farmers who today have their own farms in New Zealand started off as 39 per cent share milkers, saved enough to buy their own herds..then saved again to purchase land themselves (or on which they put sharemilkers!). **1972** SARGESON *Man of England Now* 27 There was the share-milking system, a kind of partnership almost, with a written agreement that farmers and share-milkers signed. **1988** HILL *More from Moaville* 50 We'll put you between Madge O'Sullivan the Yodelling Sharemilker, and the Moaville Glee Club. **1990** *Pacific Way* June 38 A still worked for a farmer for 18 months before becoming a share-milker.

sharemilking, *vbl. n.* and *attrib.* The business or occupation of a sharemilker.

1920 POWDRELL *Dairy Farming* 9 Share-milking is an annual contract in which the landowner provides the land, buildings, stock, and machinery, and the tenant all labour. **1934** SCANLAN *Winds of Heaven* 174 He..found the family he employed on a share-milking basis to be hard working if not too competent. **1943** [see SHAREMILKER]. **1960** *NZ Dairy Exporter* 10 Mar. 58 A 50/50 share-milking agreement can often limit the expansion of profit from the farming enterprise. **1974** *NZ Agric.* 88 A sharemilking agreement allows men with little capital to share in a dairy farm's production and profits. **1991** *Metro* (Auckland) July 47 There are..three ways to get into farming: 'share-milking, fornication or nepotism'.

Hence, by back formation from *n.* or *vbl. n.*, **sharemilk** *v. trans.* or *intr.*, to follow the occupation of, or to milk cows as, a sharemilker; *ppl. a.* **sharemilked**, of a farm, to be run on a share-milking basis.

1937 GORDON & BENNETT *Gentlemen of the Jury* 67 Two months later the mother is 'out in the sheds' helping to **share-milk** a hundred cows. **1963** HILLIARD *Piece of Land* 82 And he'd share-milked for three years. **1982** MOURIE & PALENSKI *Graham Mourie Captain* 160 Financially, I was in a precarious position, wanting to buy the farm on which I was share-milking. **1989** STIRLING *On Four Legs or Two* 36 My old Dad.. thirty-nine percent sharemilked for a cocky up there. **1960** *NZ Dairy Exporter* 10 Mar. 59 Another frequent cause of lowered productivity on **share-milked** farms is the kind of clause that states that no more than 10 per cent of calves may be reared.

shark.

1. [Spec. use of *shark* any of many cartilaginous fishes of the Order Selachiformes, of local significance as an important source of food for early Maori, and later for all New Zealanders as a mainstay of fish and chips: in locally significant use mainly with a defining word.] Often *attrib.* Cf. DOGFISH, MANGO.

[*Note*] Generic and specific names in early quotations may differ from those now accepted.

1838 [see MANGO 1]. **1840** POLACK *Manners & Customs* I. 202 Among the larger tribes that sport in shoals in the vicinity of the shore, are..shark, *mango* (squalus). **1851**, **1882** [see MANGO 1]. **1982** AYLING *Collins Guide* (1984) 41 There are 225–250 species of sharks of which 39 have been recorded from New Zealand to date.

2. Usu. with a modifier: **basking, black (brown, seal), blue (great blue, blue pointer, blue whaler), blue pointer, bramble, bronze (New Zealand) whaler, carpet (cat, ground, swell), ghost (dark ghost), gummy, hammerhead(ed), mackerel, mako, Plunket('s), porbeagle, school (sand), sevengill(ed), smooth-hound, thresher, tiger, white (great white).**

(1) **basking shark.** *Cetorhinus maximus* (fam. Cetorhinidae), see quot. 1924. See also REREMAI.

1886 SHERRIN *Handbook Fishes NZ* 115 *Selachus maximus*..Basking shark. **1891** *TrNZI* XXIII. 126 Notice of the Occurrence of the Basking Shark..in New Zealand. **1924** *NZJST* VI. 266 The basking-shark..is among the largest of living fishes... The name has been applied because of its peculiar habit of lying motionless in the sunshine on the surface. **1936** *Handbook for NZ* (ANZAAS) 71 *Cetorhinus maximus*: Basking shark. **1947** [see REREMAI]. **1966** *Encycl. NZ* III. 227 Shark, Basking..or reremai of the Maoris, is our largest shark, but is quite harmless, for its teeth are blunt and only $^1/_4$ in. in length. **1986** PAUL *NZ Fishes* 27 Basking shark... Occurs sporadically around New Zealand with most sightings in the Cook Strait to Kaikoura and the Dunedin to Foveaux Strait regions.

(2) **black (brown, seal) shark.** *Dalatias licha* (fam. Dalatiidae), see quot. 1986.

1898 MORRIS *Austral-English* 412 Black Shark.- *Carcharodon melanopterus*... Brown S[hark]— *Scymnus lichia* [*sic*]. **1913** *TrNZI* XLV. 235 *Dalatias licha*... The brown shark has been taken in Otago Harbour. **1946** PHILLIPPS *Sharks NZ* I. No.2 19 *Dalatias phillippsi*... Black Shark. **1958** PARROTT *Big Game Fishes* 110 The skin of the black shark is fairly smooth, the denticles being very fine. **1986** PAUL *NZ Fishes* 33 Seal shark... Often just called black shark, being the darkest species most regularly seen by New Zealand fishermen until recently..but seal shark (referring to the short snout) is more apt.

(3) **blue shark (great blue**; also **blue pointer, blue whaler). a.** Some early writers confusingly use **blue shark** as a common name for the *bronze whaler* (*Carcharinas brachyurus*) (6) below.

1872 HUTTON & HECTOR *Fishes NZ* 75 Carchari[n]as brachyurus... Blue Shark. **1886** SHERRIN *Handbook Fishes NZ* 116 Blue Shark... Grows to a length of 12ft.

b. *Prionace glauca* (and early variations) (fam. Carcharinidae), see quot. 1966.

1917 WILLIAMS *Dict. Maori Lang.* 207 *Mango pounamu*, (*blue shark*). **1929** BEST *Fishing Methods* 49 *Mango-taha-pounamu* (blue shark)... *Ngerongero* (blue shark)... *Mata wha* (blue shark)..*Tuatini* (blue shark). **1935** *NZJST* XVI. 238 Blue shark from Lyall Bay. **1946** PHILLIPPS *Sharks NZ* I. No.2 11 The Blue Shark is known in New Zealand from two small specimens found in Wellington. **1966** DOOGUE & MORELAND *Sea Anglers' Guide* 178 Great Blue Shark... Living and freshly caught specimens are indigo blue on the back, shading to bright blue on the sides and to snow white below... *Other names: Prionace glauca;* blue shark, blue whaler shark, blue pointer; mango-pounamu (Maori). **1986** PAUL *NZ Fishes* 26 *Blue shark. Prionace glauca.* Alternatively blue pointer, blue whaler. Widespread in all tropical to cool temperate oceans.

(4) **blue pointer.** Either of two species, *Prionace glauca* (see (3) b above) or *Isurus oxyrinchus*, MAKO *n.*[1] b.

(5) **bramble shark.** *Echinorhinus brucus* (fam. Echinorhinidae), called 'bramble' from its rough skin.

1929 *NZJST* XI. 221 Bramble-shark... I can detect no difference between [a Cook Strait specimen] and the true bramble-shark of the Mediterranean. **1946** PHILLIPPS *Sharks NZ* I. No.2 19 *Echinorhinus maccoyii* Whitley. Bramble Shark. **1958** PARROTT *Big Game Fishes* 111 The skin of the Bramble Shark is very rough. **1982** AYLING *Collins Guide* (1984) 72 The bramble shark is a heavy bodied species that grows to a length of about 3m... The most obvious feature..are the enlarged thorn-like dermal denticles.

(6) **bronze (New Zealand) whaler**, also occas. **bronzie, whaler**. *Carcharinus brachyurus* (fam. Carcharinidae). See esp. quot. 1986.

1927 SPEIGHT et al. *Natural Hist. Canterbury* 192 Neither [the tope] nor the ten foot whaler (*Carcharinus brachyurus*) seem to be dangerous. **1946** PHILLIPPS *Sharks NZ* I. No.2 11 New Zealand Whaler... In North Auckland [it] is regarded as a rather shy fish and not dangerous to man. **1958** PARROTT *Big Game Fishes* 90 The food of the N.Z. Whaler Shark consists of mainly fish and crustacea. **1966** *Encycl. NZ* III. 709 Bronze whale . . toiki . . *Carcharhinus brachyurus*. **1984** bronzies [see KINGIE]. **1986** PAUL *NZ Fishes* 26 Bronze whaler... Sometimes called New Zealand whaler, although species is now known to be world wide...Greyish-brown to bronze above, white below... Average size about 2 m... Dangerous when captured. **1990** *Evening Post* (Wellington) 26 Sept. 46 At Whatipa..a well-known big bronze whaler shark haunt, land based gamefishermen use big cut baits on long wire traces suspended from a balloon for the sharks.

(7) **carpet (cat, ground, swell) shark**. [*carpet* from its mottled skin pattern: see also quots. 1956, 1986.] *Cephaloscyllium isabella* (fam. Scyliorhinidae), see quot. 1986.

1913 *TrNZI* XLV. 235 The carpet-shark..is common in the harbour and along the coast. **1927** SPEIGHT et al. *Nat. Hist. Canterbury* 192 The rather flat headed, broadly mottled Carpet Shark or Cat Shark..does not seem to grow much more than three feet in length. **1938** *Auckland Weekly News* 5 Oct. 60 One such 'egg-purse' of a carpet shark..contained a lively sharklet swimming round inside with yolk-sac attached. **1946** PHILLIPPS *Sharks NZ* I. No.2 7 The carpet shark is common around Kapiti. When brought up in the trawl an involuntary barking noise is heard as its air bladder explodes. **1956** GRAHAM *Treasury NZ Fishes* 67 The Carpet Shark is well-known to all sport and commercial fishermen, who call it Ground Shark..as it's usually found on the ground or floor of the ocean. **1966** DOOGUE & MORELAND *Sea Anglers' Guide* 188 Swell Shark... carpet shark; draughtsboard shark (Australia); pekapeka (Maori). **1979** *Catch* May 16 Carpet Shark. Cephaloscyllium isabella. Cat Shark, Swell Shark. Family Scyliorhinidae (cat sharks). **1986** PAUL *NZ Fishes* 28 *Carpet shark*... Alternative names include swell shark (from its ability to inflate with water or air) and catshark (its eyes are like a cat's). The latter is more appropriate than carpet shark as a common name; the true tropical to subtropical carpet sharks are unrelated.

(8) **ghost (dark ghost) shark**. [Named poss. f. the pale ghostlike appearance or luminescence of some of the non-NZ species (esp. Australian, from c1914, also called there 'spookfish'), the name now being restricted mainly to Australasian species.] *Hydrolagus novaezelandiae* (fam. Chimaeridae).

1947 POWELL *Native Animals NZ* 60 Ghost Shark... This is related to the Elephant-fish, but is not common. It lacks the trunk-like appendage and has a long tapering tail. **1956** GRAHAM *Treasury NZ Fishes* 398 Ghost Shark *Phasmichthys novaezelandiae*... (Syn. *Chimaera monstrosa australis*). **1967** NATUSCH *Animals NZ* 202 The ghost shark..differs from the [elephant fish] in having a blunt snout with no proboscis. **1978** *Catch* May 13 Dark Ghost Shark *Hydrolagus novaezelandiae*. Chimaera, ratfish, N.Z. ghost shark. Family Chimaeridae (Chimaeras). **1986** PAUL *NZ Fishes* 39 *Dark ghost shark*... The commonest New Zealand member of this family (Chimaeridae), although only occasionally seen by coastal fisherman. **1991** *Dominion* (Wellington) 12 Aug. 9 During the 1989–90 fishing year, rig landed from boats..was misdeclared as ghost shark, a non-quota species.

(9) **gummy shark**. GUMMY *n*.³ (*Mustelus lenticulatus*). See also SMOOTH-HOUND.

1947 POWELL *Native Animals NZ* 61 Gummy Shark or Dogfish (*Emissola antartica*), Manga of the Maoris, grows up to 3 ½ feet in length... It is easily recognized by its small blunt teeth, arranged like a pavement which render it inoffensive to man. **1957** WILLIAMS *Dict. Maori Lang.* 170 Makō = mangō, n. *Mustelus antarcticus*, gummy shark. **1966** BRAMBLEY *Sea-Cockies of Manukau* 43 I lose patience with people who prattle about 'gummy' sharks when they mean pioke, or dogfish—'lemon-fish' when it reaches the shops. Instead of teeth, the doggy has cross-hatched boney ridges. **1979** [see GUMMY *n*.³]. **1982** BURTON *Two Hundred Yrs. NZ Food* 79 Of the many sharks found in New Zealand waters, the gummy and school sharks are the most commonly eaten. Both are relatively small in size, and are marketed as lemon fish or flake. **1986** PAUL *NZ Fishes* 30 *Rig. Mustelus lenticulatus*... Other names include spotted dogfish, gummy shark, smoothhound and pioke. Often listed as *M. antarcticus*... Fished commercially, in fact one of the most valuable coastal species.

(10) **hammerhead (hammerheaded) shark** (often *ellipt*. **hammerhead**). *Sphyrna zygaena* (fam. Sphyrnidae), a shark with a head that resembles a double-headed hammer. See also *mango-pare* (MANGO 2 (1)).

1838 POLACK *NZ* I. 162 They almost rolled their eyes out of their sockets, distending their mouths, like hammer-headed sharks, from ear to ear. **1844** COLENSO *Excurs. Northern Is.* in Taylor *Early Travellers* (1959) 50 A species of the Hammer-headed Shark..is sometimes met with on these shores. **1855** TAYLOR *Te Ika A Maui* 412 *Mango pare* (*squalus zygaena*) hammer-headed shark. **1892** WILLIAMS *Dict. NZ Lang.* 87 *Mango pare*. Hammer-headed shark; *Zygoena malleus*. **1926** GREY *Angler's Eldorado* 88 I lost two fish, one a hammer-head that first bit my bait in two, and then came back for the second portion. **1947** POWELL *Native Animals NZ* 60 Hammerhead Shark..Mangopare of the Maoris, is well named, for the lateral extensions of the skull are shaped just like a double-headed hammer. **1958** PARROTT *Big Game Fishes* 98 The Hammerhead is reported to be not uncommon off the coasts of the North Island. **1986** PAUL *NZ Fishes* 27 *Hammerhead shark. Sphyrna zygaena*. A widely distributed species in this family (Sphyrnidae), occurring in warm temperate seas, mainly in coastal waters.

(11) **mackerel shark**. See *porbeagle shark* (14) below.

1956 [see (14) below]. **1966** DOOGUE & MORELAND *Sea Anglers' Guide* 183 Porbeagle Shark... *Other names: Lamna nasus;* mackerel shark. **1981** WILSON *Fisherman's Bible* 163 Mackerel Shark. Another name for the Porbeagle Shark, given because of its great liking for devouring the fish. Sometimes also used for Mako shark. **1982** [see MAKO *n*.¹ 1 b].

(12) **mako shark**, see MAKO *n*.¹ b.

(13) **Plunket (Plunket's, Plunkets) shark**. [f. Lord *Plunket* (1864–1920), Governor of New Zealand 1904–10.] *Centrocymnus plunketi* (fam. Squalidae).

[**1910** *TrNZI* XLII. 386 *Centrocymnus plunketi*... With His Excellency's kind permission, I [*sc*. E.R. Waite] have dedicated this new species to Lord Plunket, Governor of the Dominion, recognising his interest in the Canterbury museum, and gratefully remembering His Excellency's kindness when..I accompanied him on his cruise to the southern islands of New Zealand in 1907.] **1929** *NZJST* XI. 225 The Plunket shark..is a deep-sea species which may be taken off Kaikoura. **1946** PHILLIPPS *Sharks NZ* I. No.2 17 Plunket shark. This shark named by Waite after Lord Plunket, is a deep-sea species. **1958** PARROTT *Big Game Fishes* 117 Plunket's Shark is a deep water dogfish..first described and named by Waite in 1910. **1982** AYLING *Collins Guide* (1984) 66 Plunkets shark is the largest of a group of three similar deep water spiny dogfishes.

(14) **porbeagle shark**. *Lamna nasus* (fam. Lamnidae), a widespread shark related to the mako (see esp. quot. 1956). See also *mackerel shark* (11) above.

1875 *TrNZI* VII. 237 On the Occurrence of *Lamna cornubica*, Porbeagle Shark.., the Mako of the Maoris, in New Zealand. **1886** SHERRIN *Handbook Fishes NZ* 115 No creature is more voracious; three large hakes have been found in the stomach of a porbeagle. **1913** *TrNZI* XLV. 235 *Lamna nasus* Bonnaterre... The porbeagle-shark. **1927** SPEIGHT et al. *Nat. Hist. Canterbury* 192 The Porbeagle..has long sharp teeth, each with a small cusp at the base on either side. **1935** *NZJST* XVI. 241 New Zealand porbeagle shark, *Lamna whitleyi*. **1946** PHILLIPPS *Sharks NZ* I. No.2 8 New Zealand Porbeagle Shark... The Porbeagle lives in very deep water up to 200 fathoms in Cook Strait and off the Kaikouras. **1956** GRAHAM *Treasury NZ Fishes* 78 The porbeagle..is often called the Mackerel Shark on account of its habit of devouring so many Mackerel. It is sometimes erroneously called Mako Shark, but when the two species are seen the difference is most apparent. **1966** DOOGUE & MORELAND *Sea Anglers' Guide* 183 Porbeagle Shark... A fast swimmer but not as swift as the related mako. **1986** PAUL *NZ Fishes* 25 *Porbeagle shark. Lamna nasus*. A widespread oceanic and pelagic shark of cool to temperate waters.

(15) **school (or sand) shark**. *Galeorhinus galeus* (fam. Triakidae), a small shark (to 180 cm) brownish-grey above and white below, having firm textured flesh sold as white fillets, flake, or lemonfish. See also *big boy* (BIG *a*.), KAPETA, LEMONFISH, TOPE.

1886 SHERRIN *Handbook Fishes NZ* 116 Tope... It is the 'school-shark' of the Sydney fishermen. **1924** [see TOPE]. **1936** *Handbook for NZ* (ANZAAS) 71 Southern tope or school shark; perhaps the most common of the sharks proper. **1947, 1956** [see TOPE]. **1963** *Commercial Fishing* Apr. 8 A record netload of fish—300 three-foot school sharks—filled a medium-sized commercial boat..near Russell. **1977** *Dominion* (Wellington) 8 Nov. 1 'But many wholesalers have told us they are moving away from marketing school shark,' Mr Gradwell said. **1982** BURTON *Two Hundred Yrs. NZ Food* 79 Of the many sharks found in New Zealand waters, the gummy and school sharks are the most commonly eaten.

(16) **sevengill (sevengilled) shark**. Also *ellipt*. **seven-gill, seven-giller**. *Notorynchus cepedianus* (fam. Hexanchidae), a large shark with seven gills instead of the usual five; also the deeper water species *Heptranchias perlo*. See also TUATINI.

1924 *NZJST* VI. 259 The 7-gilled shark is a viviparous species of the open ocean, and is rarely taken. **1935** *NZJST* XVI. 236 Seven-gilled Shark... As its name implies, the seven-gilled shark is distinguished from all other species of shark in New Zealand waters by the fact that it has seven gill-slits. **1947** POWELL *Native Animals NZ* 61 Seven-gilled Shark..Tuatini of the Maoris,.. [has] seven gill slits instead of the usual five. **1966** BRAMBLEY *Sea-cockies of Manukau* 44 Among the various species [of shark] we have landed, the seven-gilled..and the white-pointer have one similarity... The seven-gillers we catch all the year. **1986** Paul *NZ Fishes* 24 Sevengill shark *Notorynchus cepedianus*... A related but more slender and grey species, the sharpsnouted sevengill *Heptranchias perlo*, is sometimes taken by trawl in deep water.

(17) **smooth-hound shark (dogfish)**, see SMOOTH-HOUND.

(18) **thresher shark**. Also *ellipt*. **thresher**. *Alopias vulpinus* (fam. Alopiidae), see esp. quot. 1947. See also *mango-ripi* (MANGO 2 (2)).

1872 Hutton & Hector *Fishes NZ* 78 Alopecias vulpes... Thresher. **1886** Sherrin *Handbook Fishes NZ* 115 Thresher... Its most remarkable peculiarity is the great elongation of the upper lobe of the tail-fin, which is nearly equal in length to the whole body. **1921** Thomson & Anderton *Hist. Portobello* 68 Thresher... This shark is occasionally met with on the coast of Otago. **1947** Powell *Native Animals NZ* 61 Thresher Shark..Mango ripi of the Maoris, is very easily recognised by the extremely large upper fluke of the tail. **1956** Graham *Treasury NZ Fishes* 75 Thresher Shark (Mango-ripi)... When a Whale's back appears above the water, the Threshers have been said to spring several feet into the air, descending with great violence upon the object of their onslaught and inflicting upon it the most severe slaps with their long tails. **1966** *Encycl. NZ* III. 228 *Shark, Thresher*..or *mango ripi*... The thresher is not uncommon in Northland waters. **1982** Sansom *In Grip of Island* 78 Wonderful days those were..to see a single thresher shark whacking the water with a tail as long as its body. **1991** *Listener* 25 Mar. 33 Two days later Keith Wilson caught the first thresher shark, 166 kg. Collins reckons you get threshers occasionally as far south as Kaikoura.

(19) **tiger shark**. Also *ellipt*. **tiger**. [Named from the young having dark stripes.] *Galeocerdo cuvieri* (fam. Carcharhidae), a large shark visiting New Zealand summer waters. Also occas. erron. for *mako* and *porbeagle* shark.

1847 Angas *Savage Life* I. 295 An annual fishery for the tiger-shark is carried on by the natives in Hauraki Gulf, at a certain season of the year. **1866** Angas *Polynesia* 157 The tooth of the tiger-shark, drilled, and the end covered with red wax, is also an esteemed ornament as an ear-drop. **1872** [see MAKO *n.*¹ 1 a]. **1886** Sherrin *Handbook Fishes NZ* 117 Tiger Shark (*Lamna glauca*). **1917** Williams *Dict. Maori Lang.* 275 *Ngutukao*,.. *tiger-shark.* **1929** Best *Fishing Methods* 49 Toiki (tiger-shark); Ngutukao (tiger-shark). **1936** *Handbook for NZ* (ANZAAS) 71 *Galeocerda articus*: Tiger shark, shovel nose. **1946** Phillipps *Sharks NZ* I. No.2 12 Tiger Shark... Lately [this shark] has come into prominence as a sporting fish. **1966** Doogue & Moreland *Sea Anglers' Guide* 179 Tiger Shark... Proverbially one of the most voracious of sharks, the tiger will eat any kind of animal... Other names: *Galeocerdo cuvieri*; leopard shark, toiki (Maori). **1982** Ayling *Collins Guide* (1984) 58 The tiger must surely rank with the great white as one of the largest and most dangerous of sharks.

(20) **white (great white) shark**; also with a variety of names **great white, man-eater, white death, white pointer**. *Carcharodon carcharias* (fam. Lamnidae).

1872 Hutton & Hector *Fishes NZ* 78 Carcharodon rondeletii... White Shark. **1886** Sherrin *Handbook Fishes NZ* 119 White Shark... Greatest length, 36ft. **1891** *TrNZI* XXIII. 126 I felt confident that it was an unusually large specimen of the White Shark..., which visits our coasts every summer. **1913** *Ibid.* XLV. 235 The great white shark..is an occasional visitant. **1924** *NZJST* VI. 269 On account of the pure white colouring of its under-surface, this species is usually referred to as 'white pointer' or 'white shark'. **1927** Speight et al.

Nat. Hist. Canterbury 192 The Great White Shark..has large triangular teeth with serrated edges. **1947** Powell *Native Animals NZ* 60 White Shark..Mango tuatini of the Maoris, is a large, heavy-bodied shark. **1958** Parrott *Big Game Fishes* 102 The White Pointer or Man-eater may be at once recognised by the large serrated triangular teeth..which are placed in five or six rows in the jaws. **1966** *Encycl. NZ* III. 228 *Shark, White*..or *mango tuatuini*..is a large, heavy-bodied shark. **1982** Ayling *Collins Guide* (1984) 52 *Great White Shark*... (White death, white pointer, man-eater). No animal has been responsible for more unreasoning fear and horror than the great white shark.

3. In the phr. **shark and ('n') taties**, a jocular nickname for fish and chips.

1986 *Metro* (Auckland) Aug. 194 This delicacy of the English-speaking world is referred to in other circles as 'shark and taties', 'Maori roast', or 'greasies'. **1988** McGill *Dict. Kiwi Slang* 99 *shark 'n' taties* fish and chips.

shark *v*.: see SHARKING *vbl. n*.

shark-bully. *Canterbury*. TORRENTFISH.

1910 *TrNZI* XLII. 389 I was told that [in the Ashley and Hurunui river areas, torrentfish] were known as 'shark bullies', in allusion to the inferior position of the mouth, coupled with some resemblance to the gobies, commonly called 'bullies'. **1936** *Handbook for NZ* (ANZAAS) 73 *Cheimarrichthys forsteri*: [European Name] Torrent-fish or shark-bully [Maori Name] Papanoko.

sharking, *vbl. n*. A shortened form of LAND-SHARKING. Occas. as **shark** *v. intr.*, to 'landshark'.

1839 *Col. Gaz.* 2 Oct. 627 Shark away, gentlemen, he must say. **1936** Buick *Treaty of Waitangi* 33 The speculators swarmed over to the Bay of Islands, and in..1837 the land fever in all its phases of 'sharking', 'jobbing' and legitimate purchase..raged throughout the country. **1940** Waite *Port Molyneux* 15 This land fever [after 1840] has been described as 'sharking' or 'grabbing', and 'bona fide speculation'.

she, *personal pron*.

1. [See *OED she* 2 e, 'esp. in *Austral.* and *N.Z.*': AND 1863.] Applied to things (both material and immaterial) to which the female gender is not conventionally attributed, often replacing the impersonal pronoun *it*.

1874 Baines *Edward Crewe* 180 Suppose a piece of timber..is on the carriage... 'Kreash,' says the saw, and in twelve seconds she is out at the other end. **1881** Bathgate *Waitaruna* 75 'I shall not care to venture on that rapid river in a tub like that [*sc.* a Maori canoe],' said Gilbert... 'Oh! She will be getting more colonised py and py [*sic*], and not caring so much', was Dougal's patronising remark. **1894** Wilson *Land of Tui* 206 Along the [Kaituna] road we met various pedestrians, who asked our driver the rather obscure question: 'How is she?' They meant of course, the [Wairau] river... 'Oh she's a bit thick,' was his laconic reply. **1902** Lancaster in *Happy Endings* (1987) 101 She's a young country, I grant you, but she's got the biggest future of all Australasia. **1919** *Quick March* 10 July 21 We'll just catch her [*sc.* a sunset] by the time we get to the beach. **1924** Anthony *Follow the Call* (1975) 18 You haven't got your skeith set properly. Give her more land, and just notice the different work she makes. **1937** Marsh *Vintage Murder* 49 We tried her out till we was sick and tired of her and she [*sc.* a gadget] worked corker every time. She worked good-oh, didn't she. **1943** *NZEF Times* 26 Apr. 3 She's a whopper when she rolls... 'She' was the New Zealand Division. **1963** Kinross *Please to Remember* 18 Then

they turned round and surveyed the edifice and said, Yes, by cripes, she's a fine building. **1987** *Listener* 29 Aug. 46 The Ned said, 'I reckon she's safe.' So we all ran across the open gap.

2. For the use of **she'll be** and **she's** with complements to introduce common idiomatic phrases expressing confidence or reassurance in an outcome, etc., see APPLES, JAKE, RIGHT 2, SWEET 2; other less frequent complements from the questionnaire put to adolescents are exemplified below (question 12 asked for synonyms of 'It doesn't matter'). Cf. 1973 *Islands* 6 344 'Thank you, that'll be all right,' he says, using that strange future tense which is one of the ways New Zealanders have of avoiding direct affirmations ('Looks pretty good', 'Reckon it'll do'..instead of 'It's good, fine, in order').

1951 14 M 14 St Bede's, Chch 12 She's fine. **1953** 14 M A14 Thames DHS 12 She's o.k., ok, oke [M4] **1953** 15–17 M A29 Thames DHS 12 She's set [M3] **1984** 17 M E107 Pakuranga Coll. 12 She's cool [M1F2] **1984** 16 M E82 Pakuranga Coll. 12 She'll be joe **1984** 16 M E75 Pakuranga Coll. 12 She's keen

sheaf-tossing. [AND *sheaf-tossing* 1961; *-tosser* 1947.] The rural sport of pitch-forking a 'sheaf' (usu. now a bag of straw) over a bar able to be raised to test and eliminate competitors. (Known to Ed. from c1938 as once a regular event at Easter sports gatherings in Marlborough.)

1962 Evans *Waikaka Saga* 164 He also won the sheaf-tossing at Browns in 1935.

shear, *v. trans*. To own (sheep); of a farm, to carry (sheep).

1928 *NZ Free Lance* (Wellington) 14 Mar. 7 The H.B. Williams station shears nearly 40,000 sheep. **1933** *Press* (Christchurch) (Acland Gloss.) 25 Nov. 15 *Shear*.—To own [sheep]. E.g., 'How many sheep have you?' 'I generally s[hear] about 8000.' **1947** Newton *Wayleggo* 37 Lake Coleridge station itself..shore 22,000 sheep. **1987** Ogonowska-Coates *Boards, Blades & Barebellies* 97 *Shear*... Also used to count the number of sheep owned—e.g., 'I shear about six thousand.'

shear, *n*.

1. *pl. a. Obs.* As a shearers' cry for a break from work.

1873 Barker *Station Amusements* 268 'Spell, oh!' or else 'Shears!'.. [1873 *Note*] The shearers' demand for a few minutes rest.

b. In the phr. **off the shears** or **off-shears** [AND 1896], of a sheep, newly shorn. See also *off the blades* (BLADE *n.*¹ 2).

1888 Bradshaw *NZ Today* 110 The hogget in 1882 could be readily sold 'off the shears' at twelve shillings. **1929** *NZJST* X. 326 The twice-shorn sheep came off the shears in October in a very much better condition than the once-shorn. **1930** Acland *Early Canterbury Runs* viii 216 He drove them over Porter's Pass off the shears. **1951** McLeod *NZ High Country* 26 The machines shear too near the skin and when the almost naked sheep go out into the high tops 'off the shears', the first cold storm..sends them cowering under every ledge of rock. **1960** *NZ Dairy Exporter* 11 Jan. 20 Sheep may be dipped straight 'off-shears'. **1982** *Agric. Gloss.* (MAF) 51 *Off-shears*: Newly-shorn sheep. A sale term.

2. *sing*. A shearing of a single sheep, or of all the sheep in a shed or on a farm. See also HONEYMOON SHEAR.

1984 Marshall *Day Hemingway Died* 143 'When will you do your main shear?' said Sully. **1986** *Marist*

SHEARER

Messenger Dec. 33 'You're wrong,' I said. 'It's going to be a scorcher of a day and we're set to do a record shear.'

shearer. [Spec. use of *shearer* one who removes the fleece from an animal: AND 1826.]

1. An itinerant worker, often a member of a shearing gang, hired or contracted seasonally to shear sheep.

1847 in Wakefield *Handbook NZ* (1848) 250 Some good shearers are much wanted. **1858** ACLAND *Notes Sheepfarming NZ* 11 The shearers get through their work with a rapidity unknown in England. **1863** BUTLER *First Year* x 158 The shearers will want to begin with daylight. **1894** *NZ Official Year-book* 252 'The Electoral Law Amendment Act, 1893' extends the provisions relating to voting by commercial travellers..to shearers, the word 'shearer' being held to mean a person who is *bona fide* employed by an owner of sheep for shearing purposes during the season of the year. **1911** MORELAND *Through South Westland* 130 The place was full of shearers and tourists. **1933** *Press* (Christchurch) (Acland Gloss.) 25 Nov. 15 *Shearer.*- One who shears (and while so employed does nothing else). S[hearer]s, who always work in company. **1986** RICHARDS *Off the Sheep's Back* 94 All his shed hands, shearers and his wool classer had been with him before. **1989** *NZ Eng. Newsletter* III. 27 *shearer:* Like other shed employees, the shearer has many names, for example, 'greasy', 'gouger', 'stooper', 'bladesman', 'woolhawk', 'brute' and 'tiger'.

2. In special collocations: **Shearer's Award**, the agreement setting out the wages and conditions pertaining to shearers; **shearers' bun**, a sweet bun made orig. for shearers' smoko; **shearers' camp**, temporary quarters for a shearing gang; **shearers' dance**, see *woolshed dance* (WOOLSHED 2); **shearers' hut** (occas. **house**, see quot. 1888 at *shearers' whare*), also *shearers' quarters*, the accommodation on stations and larger farms for seasonal shearing gangs; **shearers' joy**, beer; **shearers' whare**, see *shearers' hut* above.

1982 WOODHOUSE *Blue Cliffs* 88 The **Shearer's Award** of 1905 contained a clause stating that the employer would find free grazing for one horse for each shearer. **1955** *New Home Cook. Book* 93 **Shearers' Buns**. Eight ozs. butter, 1 lb. flour, 1/2 lb. sugar, 3 eggs, 1 teaspoon baking soda and 1 of cream of tartar, fruit if desired. **1968** JOHNSON *Turn of Tide* 72 A frugal lunch: hard-boiled eggs, home-made bread and butter, garden lettuce and shearer's buns. **1911** MORELAND *Through South Westland* 135 The **shearers' camp**, a long row of white tents, seemed to have been newly pitched, the flaps up for coolness sake. **1864** CAVERHILL in Deans *Pioneers Port Cooper Plains* (1964) 103 Improvements on sheep station, consisting of dwelling house,..men's hut... Woolshed and yards, drafting yards and **shearers' hut**. **1866** *Puketoi Station Diary* (Hocken TS) 12 Oct. Wilson & James carting clay into shearers hut. [Dec. 17] Remainder of Shearers went... James cleaning Shearers hut. **1888** *Diary Christian Shirres re* June in Neave *The Land Munros* (1980) 53 There is the woolshed, stable, the shepherd and shearers' huts, and the house itself. **1890** *Otago Witness* (Dunedin) 21 Aug. 34 Were a Royal Commission appointed to examine..the general sanitary conditions of shearers' huts, I imagine their report would be quite as startling..as some of the sensational disclosures *re* London lodgement houses. **1953** GUTHRIE-SMITH *Tutira* (3edn.) 152 Later, when a newer and larger kitchen was made, our original domicile was again moved, and became part of the shearers' hut. **1968** SLATTER *Pagan Game* 99 As a room used mainly for Geography there were maps on the rear wall,... so many cuttings from newspapers that George Webster had called it a shearers' hut. **1968** *NZ Contemp. Dict. Suppl.* (Collins) 17 **shearer's joy**...

n. (*Coll.*) beer. **1964** ANDERSON *Doctor in Mountains* (1974) 90 So I travelled out to the woolshed and **shearers' quarters**, where the station-owner met me. **1984** BRASCH *Collected Poems* 57 In woolshed and shearers' quarters, on city wharves, Learning the arts and facts of living. **1992** ANDERSON *Portrait Artist's Wife* 33 A narrow..bridge led to the shearers' quarters and the rust-red woolshed. **1888** CHUDLEIGH *Diary* 13 July (1950) 362 My shearers house, cookhouse and all was burned to the ground... *20th.* Mr Deighton held an inquest on the burning of the Taupekas **shearers whare**. **1910** FANNING *Players & Slayers* 81 It got me some tea in bunk in a shearers' whare at the Grassmere station. **1915** CHUDLEIGH *Diary* 24 Jan. (1950) 464 Miller and I inspected the new woolshed and shearers whare. **1930** GUTHRIE *NZ Memories* 154 A queer assortment..would live together in the shearers' whare for weeks.

shearing, *vbl. n.* and *attrib.* Also early **sheep-shearing**. [Spec. use of *shearing* the process of cutting the fleece off an animal: used elsewhere but of special historical and economic significance in NZ.]

A. *vbl. n.*

1. a. [AND 1834.] The period or time within which a property's sheep are shorn.

1834 WILLIAMS *Early Jrnls.* 4 Nov. (1961) 400 My boys commenced sheep shearing. **1848** WAKEFIELD *Handbook NZ* 123 The facilities for washing the wool at sheep-shearing are very great... The shearing..usually commences about the middle of December. **1853** ADAMS *Canterbury Settlement* 73 Sheep-shearing is of course the most busy as well as the most expensive season of the year. **1865** CHUDLEIGH *Diary* 20 Sept. (1950) 201 He said he should be glad for me to go down [to Chathams] after the shearing but he cannot afforde [*sic*] it now. **1874** BATHGATE *Col. Experiences* 207 When this great business of the year is over, the squatter often allows himself a holiday, and 'after shearing' makes a run to Wellington. **1881** BATHGATE *Waitaruna* 180 Even Mr Ramshorn, though he had gone through quite a few 'shearings', was thoroughly glad when it was over. **1913** CARR *Country Work* 17 I spent Christmas..two shearings ago in a shed. **1950** COOP *Shearing Ewes before Lambing* 20 There should be no check of mismothering at the December shearing. **1975** NEWTON *Sixty Thousand on the Hoof* 10 The big 10-stand shearing shed..has weathered sixty shearings. **1982** WOODHOUSE *Blue Cliffs* 43 The main shearing was earlier that season.

b. As **pre-lamb shearing**, the shearing of ewes preparatory to lambing.

1982 WOODHOUSE *Blue Cliffs* 227 Since the introduction of pre-lamb shearing, which takes place in August, the shearing hours have been from 7.30 a.m. to 5.30 p.m.

2. The occupation or activity of a shearer; the shearing process.

1853 ADAMS *Canterbury Settlement* 73 The English farmers would be astonished at the roughness and rapidity of the shearing. **1856** FITTON *NZ* 220 The shearing of the sheep is generally done by contract. **1874** KENNAWAY *Crusts* 175 He has, perhaps, been hindered..in his shearing by drawbacks which he could not better with all his labour. **1902** *Settler's Handbook NZ* (Lands Dept.) 11 This industry gives employment..both directly and to those engaged in breeding, shearing, freezing, and shipping. **1980** ELDRED-GRIGG *Southern Gentry* 29 The first shearing on the Ledard estate was done on a drawing room carpet, with a maid servant acting as a shearing hand.

B. *attrib.*

1. [AND 1829.] Pertaining to the occupation, process, or practice of shearing.

SHEARING

1902 *Hawkes Bay Herald* in Gore *Levins* (1956) 131 Today will witness a sheep-shearing competition for which there are 36 entries. The shearing competition will be unique. **1975** NEWTON *Sixty Thousand on the Hoof* 164 Shearing gear and shearers' clothing are his main lines.

2. Comb. **shearing season** [AND 1833], **time** [AND 1842].

1849 ALLOM *Letter* in Earp *Handbook* (1852) 125 The **shearing season** commences [in Wairarapa] in December. **1882** HAY *Brighter Britain* I. 198 Except at shearing and lambing seasons, our Lincolns and Leicesters give us but little trouble. **1892** *NZ Official Handbook* 157 On a sheep-run the lambing and shearing seasons tax every power of the station-hands. **1912** BOOTH *Five Years NZ* 26 The breeding season is spring and the shearing season summer, which corresponds to our winter in England. **1959** SLATTER *Gun in My Hand* 205 Sonny's dead for ages. Flashing his roll after the shearing season... Some pakehas..into him with the boot. **1964** DICK *High Country Family* 25 In the 1915–16 shearing season the whole clip was sold privately for 10d per pound. **1987** *Listener* 29 Aug. 47 On the floor..there was a sort of shakedown—you know, the kind of lair you associate with rouseabouts in the shearing season. **1851** *Lyttelton Times* 12 July 1 The Undersigned desires to rent..sufficient pasturage for 2,000 Sheep after landing, till after lambing and **shearing time**. **1863** BUTLER *First Year* x 150 You will be able to turn the tables on them [*sc.* sheep] at shearing-time. **1888** CHUDLEIGH *Diary* 12 Nov. (1950) 365 Everything as is usual at shearing time gone mad. **1892** *NZ Official Handbook* 157 A large number of men move about the country as shearing time approaches. **1907** *TrNZI* XXXIX. 292 At shearing-time the sheep are confined to small paddocks. **1938** BURDON *High Country* 86 Even in these days..[of] devices to save the human frame from exhaustion, shearing time is still considered a fairly busy one. **1959** MIDDLETON *The Stone* 52 At shearing time when we were all around the long table..she would break in. **1964** MIDDLETON *Walk on Beach* 167 I had often given a hand in the smaller woolsheds at shearing time. **1982** WOODHOUSE *Blue Cliffs* 124 It was shearing time and there was no other man available.

3. Special Comb. **shearing-board** [AND 1882], BOARD *n.*[1] 1 a; **shearing contractor** [AND 1936], one who employs a gang of shearers and contracts with an owner to shear sheep; **shearing floor** [AND 1850], see quots; **shearing gang (contract shearing gang)**, an organized group of workers employed or contracted by a farmer to shear sheep, and, often, to sort and bale the wool clip; **shearing machine** [AND 1852], a powered mechanism for shearing sheep; **shearing muster**, see MUSTER *n.* 2; **shearing paddock**, see quot. 1933; **shearing-shed** [AND 1829], WOOLSHED 1; **shearing stand**, see quot. 1882 (see also STAND *n.*[2] 1); **shearing tally**, TALLY 1 a.

c**1875** MEREDITH *Adventuring in Maoriland* (1935) 41 Pater showed me how to class wool. This is about the least strenuous job on a **shearing-board**, and suits me down to the ground. **1888** DUNCAN *Wakatipians* 57 Eight shearers—all Maoris—occupied the shearing board [in 1862–63]. **1922** PERRY *Sheep Farming* 16 The shearing board should be of good width, and be separated from the holding pens by a solid wall, so as to facilitate penning up. **1947** NEWTON *Wayleggo* 92 [The gun shearer] achieved his fame on the shearing board by sheer courage. **1959** MIDDLETON *The Stone* 49 When we had washed the dung and oil and sweat from the shearing board..we..sat on a bale near the press. **1964** ANDERSON *Doctor in Mountains* (1974) 32 They also swept up the bellies and pieces, and so kept the shearing board clean and tidy. **1981** HENDERSON *Exiles*

SHEAR-LEGS 719 **SHED**

Asbestos Cottage 15 He knocked up excellent tallies on neighbouring shearingboards. **1912** *Sheepowners' Handbook* 50 [Advt] **Shearing Contractors.** We are prepared to make shearing contracts in any part of New Zealand. **c1875** MEREDITH *Adventuring in Maoriland* (1935) 41 They [Maori shearers] sleep on the **shearing-floor**, with a blanket or two over them and a flax mat..for a mattress. **1885** *Wairarapa Daily* 12 Oct. 2 From each side of a central building..are the night pens and shearing floors. **1936** BELSHAW et al. *Agric. Organiz. NZ* 706 Large sheep stations usually have their sheep shorn by organized **shearing gangs** who travel the districts shearing at each station in an arranged rotation. **1962** SHARPE *Country Occasions* 36 A contract shearing gang is complete, right down to the cook's offsider. **1975** NEWTON *Sixty Thousand on the Hoof* 164 His shearing gangs—anything up to 50 shearers—have included such notable men as Snow Quinn. **1986** *Marist Messenger* Dec. 37 At lunch break the shearing gang came over to the house to see the woolshed baby. **1887** *Auckland Weekly News* 2 Aug. 20 What about that **sheep-shearing machine** you spoke of just now? Is there such a machine? **1890** PEACHE *Journal* in Gray *Quiet with Hills* (1970) 82 In town last week I saw a new shearing machine for shearing the wool off sheep... I think the stroke of the cutter might be lengthened. **1892** *NZ Official Handbook* 121 Shearing-machines are gradually coming into use, and will doubtless become general when better understood. **1905** *Weekly Press* (Christchurch) 25 Jan. 13 [Advt] 'Wolseley' sheep-shearing machines... Pioneers of machine shearing. **1915** MACDONALD *NZ Sheepfarming* xv [Advt] Cooper's Little Wonder Shearing Machine... The Shearing Attachments comprise..two *Latest Model Cooper Handpieces*. **1934** SCANLAN *Winds of Heaven* 80 Kelly had recently installed new shearing machines, and Martin was eager to see them. **1963** WALLIS *Point of Origin* 18 Somewhere outside..there were salesmen talking to farmers,... discussing dips and shearing machines. **1982** WOODHOUSE *Blue Cliffs* 190 He would be available if he got into difficulties with the old Hornsby oil engine that supplied power for the shearing machines. **1933** *Press* (Christchurch) (Acland Gloss.) 25 Nov. 15 **Shearing paddock.**—Handy paddock to hold sheep during shearing. **1851** WELD *Hints to Intending Sheep-farmers* 9 The wool and **shearing sheds**..are of less immediate importance. **1870** PRENTICE *A Tale of NZ* (GALMS) 30 Erecting a shearing or wool shed. **1894** WILSON *Land of Tui* 242 At the main entrance of the shearing-shed, which is a long building with pens down the centre, and an outlet at each end, stands a wool-press. **1908** *NZ Consolidated Statutes* V. No.177 254 [NZ Shearers' & Agric. Labourers' Accommodation Act, 1908] 'Shearing-shed' means any building used for the purpose of shearing sheep, or for any operation connected with shearing, and includes all buildings and premises connected therewith or adjacent thereto wherein shearers sleep or take their meals. **1922** PERRY *Sheep Farming* 16 *Shearing Shed.*—The erection of a shearing shed is quite an expensive matter. **1933** *Press* (Christchurch) (Acland Gloss.) 25 Nov. 15 *Shearing shed.*- Woolshed. A word favoured by land agents in their advertisements... W[ool]s[hed] has always been the usual word. **1968** JOHNSON *Turn of Tide* 68 Hilda..quite enjoyed the novel spell of work in the shearing shed. **1988** *More* (Auckland) Mar. 28 I've worked in shearing sheds—from ramshackle one-standers to sparkling new eight-standers. **1982** *Agric. Gloss.* (MAF) 53 *Catching pen*: Pen adjacent to a **shearing stand** in which a shearer catches sheep for shearing. **1953** GUTHRIE-SMITH *Tutira* (3edn.) 154 We took delivery 'off the books'—that is, we accepted the flock on the previous **shearing** and lambing **tally**. **1975** NEWTON *Sixty Thousand on the Hoof* 42 [He] would be paid a bonus only if the shearing tally exceeded 17,000.

shear-legs. Also **sheerlegs**. [Recorded earliest in NZ, associated with whaling stations and as a synonym of *shears* (see OED *n.*¹ 4, 1661) recorded in NZ from 1795: OED records *shear-legs* from 1860, the three quots. suggesting mainly dial. or mining use.] A scaffold made of three raised poles sloping towards an apex from which a tackle for raising heavy weights may be hung.

1839 *Piraki Log* 2 Oct. (1911) 99 Fore part, people employ'd getting a spar out of the Creek for a windlass, and one for the sheer legs. At 11 A.M. took the Sheers down, and brought two legs ashore to put the cross-piece on. **1926** COWAN *Travel in NZ* II. 23 Near by the foot of the old whalers' shear-legs is the place..where Tama..landed [from his canoe]. **1939** BEATTIE *First White Boy Born Otago* 53 The sheerlegs [of the shore whaling station] were still standing. **1958** *NZ Timber Journal* Aug. 68 *Shear Legs*: a hoisting and loading device of two poles, tied at the top and spread at the base which can be tilted and used to raise loads with a pulley. **1965** *Listener* 15 Oct. 9 Mum and me, we rigged a sheerlegs in the garden with four-by-twos and took him [*sc.* the bull] to bits.

shearwater.

1. Also occas. early **sheerwater**. [Transf. use of northern hemisphere *shearwater*.] Any of the many southern sea-birds of the genus *Puffinus* (fam. Procellariidae), usu. nesting in underground burrows, the young of some of which are eaten as muttonbirds. Cf. MUTTONBIRD *n*. 1 and 2 (6) below.

[**1769** PARKINSON *Journal* (1773) 27 Aug. 81 27 August 1769 [on the way to NZ] We saw several albatrosses, pintados, and shear-waters. Latitude 33° 35´.] **1773** FORSTER *Resolution Jrnl.* 11 Feb. (1982) II. 225 We saw immense flocks of blackbanded Petrels, common & black Shearwaters. **1844** MONRO *Notes of Journey* in Hocken *Contributions* (1898) 254 This [*sc.* muttonbird] I take to be the bird which is sometimes called the sheerwater [*sic*], or the sooty petrel. **1871** HUTTON *Catalogue Birds NZ* 45 Puffinus gavius... Rain-bird or Wet-bird. Shearwater. **1904** HUTTON & DRUMMOND *Animals NZ* 238 *The Shearwater.—Hakoakoa. Puffinus gavia*. **1984** SOPER *Birds NZ* 41 Shearwaters are medium-sized, long-winged petrels with long slender bills, strongly hooked at the tip.

2. With a modifier: **Buller's, flesh-footed, fluttering** (or **Forster's**), **Hutton's, little** (or **allied**), **sooty**.

(1) **Buller's shearwater**. [f. the name of Sir Walter *Buller* (1838–1906), ornithologist.] *Puffinus bulleri*, a long-tailed, distinctively-plumaged shearwater.

1955 OLIVER *NZ Birds* 136 *Bullers Shearwater...* Until recently this species was considered to be one of the rarest of sea birds. The first specimen recorded was found by Sir Walter Buller on the beach at Waikanae in 1884. **1966** FALLA et al. *Birds NZ* 42 Buller's Shearwater... In summer conspicuously abundant in the Hauraki Gulf and Bay of Plenty. **1985** *Reader's Digest Book NZ Birds* 93 The Buller's Shearwater usually vigorously reclaims the nesting burrow it has used the year before. **1990** *Checklist Birds NZ* 25 *Buller's Shearwater...* Breeds on 7 of the 12 Poor Knights Islands (c. 2.5 million birds).

(2) **flesh-footed shearwater**. [f. the specific name (Modern Latin) *carnei-pes* = 'flesh-coloured foot'.] *Puffinus carneipes*, a dark-brown shearwater with pale-pink feet.

1924 *NZJST* VII. 183 By far the most plentiful amongst the bird community at Karewa is the flesh-footed shearwater..or taonui of the Maoris. **1955** OLIVER *NZ Birds* 139 *Flesh-footed Shearwater. Taonui...* The Flesh-footed shearwater was first obtained off the Three Kings Islands during Cook's first voyage. **1966** FALLA et al. *Birds NZ* 41 Flesh-footed Shearwater... An all brown shearwater distinguishable on sight by its *pale beak*, darker only at the tip, and the pale *flesh-coloured feet*. **1985** *Reader's Digest Book NZ Birds* 95 Around dusk and dawn flesh-footed shearwaters hunt small squid, crustaceans and little fish.

(3) **fluttering** (or **Forster's**) **shearwater**. [f. the name of Johann Reinhold *Forster* (1729–1798), German naturalist and traveller.] *Puffinus gavia*, a small, inshore shearwater of rapid, whirring flight. See also HAKOAKOA 1, PAKAHA, RAINBIRD.

1873 BULLER *Birds NZ* 318 Puffinus gavia. (Forster's Shearwater). **1925–6** [see PAKAHA]. **1955** OLIVER *NZ Birds* 128 *Fluttering Shearwater. Pakaha...* The Fluttering Shearwater was first collected by J.R. Forster, one of the naturalists of Cook's second voyage, in 1773 in Queen Charlotte Sound, and the publication by Lichtenstein in 1844 of Forster's description was the first introduction of the bird to science, hence it is sometimes called Forster's Shearwater. **1966** FALLA et al. *Birds NZ* 43 Fluttering shearwaters spend much time resting on the surface of the sea and in flight they skim the water with a rapid wing-action. **1985** *Reader's Digest Book NZ Birds* 100 *Fluttering shearwater...* Pakaha, Forster's shearwater. The Fluttering shearwater flies with rapid, stiff wing-beats, interspersed with very short glides, usually close to the water's surface. **1990** *Checklist Birds NZ* 28 *Puffinus gavia..Fluttering Shearwater* (*Pakaha*)... Breeds only in New Zealand on Three Kings (major colony) [and on many offshore islands from Three Kings to Cook Strait].

(4) **Hutton's shearwater**. [f. the name of F.W. *Hutton* (1836–1905), scientist and New Zealand academic.] *Puffinus huttoni*, a South Island shearwater. See also TITI 1.

1966 FALLA et al. *Birds NZ* 44 A few scattered dusky underwing-coverts..together with the fact that the plumage is of a uniformly darker brown, give Hutton's Shearwater the general appearance of a darker bird altogether [than the Fluttering Shearwater]. **1985** *Reader's Digest Book NZ Birds* 99 *Hutton's Shearwater...* Titi, pokaha, muttonbird... Hutton's Shearwater breeds only on the South Island. **1990** *Checklist Birds NZ* 29 *Puffinus huttoni..Hutton's Shearwater...* Breeds only in New Zealand on the Seaward Kaikoura Mountains.

(5) **little** (or **allied**) **shearwater**. *Puffinus assimilis* in several local subspecies **Kermadec little shearwater** *P. a. kermadecensis*, **North Island little** *P. a. haurakiensis*, and **subantarctic little** *P. a. elegans*.

1966 FALLA et al. *Birds NZ* 44 Allied (little) shearwater *Puffinus assimilis*. **1985** *Reader's Digest Book NZ Birds* 101 *Little Shearwater...* Other Names: *Allied shearwater, whistler*. **1990** *Checklist Birds NZ* 30 *Puffinus assimilis kermadecensis... Kermadec Little Shearwater...* [*P. a.*] *haurakiensis* North Island Little Shearwater. Ibid. 31 [*P. a.*] *elegans...* Subantarctic Little Shearwater.

(6) **sooty shearwater**. *Puffinus griseus*, MUTTONBIRD *n*. 1. Cf. also TITI 1.

1938 *Auckland Weekly News* 23 Mar. 42 Behind the lighthouse are burrows occupied by female sooty shearwaters. **1955** OLIVER *NZ Birds* 131 *Sooty Shearwater. Titi. Oi...* The Sooty Shearwater, or, as it is generally called in New Zealand, the Mutton Bird, was first met with during Cook's first voyage off the coast of Chile. **1966** FALLA et al. *Birds NZ* 42 Sooty Shearwater..is one of the best known of the shearwaters. **1982** [see MUTTONBIRD *n*. 1].

shed, *n*.¹ [Spec. use of *shed* a (slight) structure built for shelter.]

1. *Obs*. Applied by early missionaries and travellers to a makeshift Maori-built shelter constructed for special occasions; occas. applied to other makeshift bush shelters. (Brunner's 1848 use may be influenced by or allude to 'shedding' water.)

1820 MARSDEN *Lett. & Jrnls.* Aug. (1932) 283 A shed had also been prepared and covered with clean fern for us to sit on. *Ibid.* 284 After the common introductions and salutations we all sat down under a shed. **1832** WILLIAMS *Early Jrnls.* 4 Jan. (1961) 212 They [*sc.* the Maori] cut a few sticks..tie them together with the flax plant, and thus form the frame of their shed, and cover it with *toetoe*, a kind of long grass. **1848** BRUNNER *Exped. Middle Island* 12 Apr. in Taylor *Early Travellers* (1959) 313 There being no material for erecting a shelter, we had to hoist our blankets for a shed, but found a year's bushing had made a sad alteration in their waterproof qualities.

2. *Shearing.* [Abbrev. of WOOLSHED, or *shearing-shed* (SHEARING B 3): AND 1853.] **a.** WOOLSHED 1.

1863 CHUDLEIGH *Diary* 6 Feb. (1950) 76 Shearing was stop[p]ed..the sheep being wet through the shed. **c1875** MEREDITH *Adventuring in Maoriland* (1935) 144 As I was finishing the counting-out, the boss came towards the shed..and invited me to come for a swim. **1881** BATHGATE *Waitaruna* 171 He had seen sheep shorn at home, but he had never beheld such a scene as the shed at Waitaruna. The shed, a large building of corrugated iron, was surrounded outside by innumerable pens, most of them crowded with sheep packed as close as they could stand. **1897** WRIGHT *Station Ballads* 101 They're a ripping lot of shearers in the shed. **1911** *Maoriland Worker* 26 May 11 When a man [*sc.* shearer] made arrangements to go to a 'run' of two or three sheds he only deposited 20s. **1933** *Press* (Christchurch) (Acland Gloss.) 25 Nov. 15 *Shed.*—(1) Woolshed. Hence to *s[hed]* sheep; i.e., put them in the *w[ool]s[hed]*. **1955** BOWEN *Wool Away* 2 Good weather, good shed, good sheep, good boss, and a good gang create an atmosphere of work and action. **1973** WHEELER *Hist. Sheep Stations NI* 70 Huiarua's big fourteen-stand shed..holds 3,000 woolly sheep, and has a shearing board seventy feet long. **1982** WOODHOUSE *Blue Cliffs* 279 Shed: Woolshed. The term shearing shed seems to be coming into use. On dairy farms shed refers to the milking shed.

Hence **shedful** *n.*, all the sheep enclosed in a woolshed or needed to keep shearers fully employed.

1867 *Puketoi Station Diary* (Hocken TS) 25 Nov. Shearing in afternoon... [Nov. 26] Shore the Shedful in the morning. **1959** MIDDLETON *The Stone* 42 Hullo Charlie. Got a shedful for the morning?

b. The body of shearers and shed hands comprising the total complement employed in a particular woolshed. A **union shed** is one in which the shearers are members of an industrial union.

1878 *Otago Witness* (Dunedin) 28 Sept. 3 In some sheds the managers insist on the cuts made in shearing being tarred. **1889** CHUDLEIGH *Diary* 4 Nov. (1950) 368 Commenced shearing. Meikana and Piripi Nehu as press men stuck me up. I..sacked them... I..put on my two station boys as fleece boys. The shed did not stop one minute. **1910** *Truth* 23 July 6 Laracy pointed out that..the resolutions were carried at the sheds after a vain attempt to get the wool kings to meet them [*sc.* shearers] in conference. **c1920s** verse in Harper *Eight Daughters* (1975) 78 We've mustered in the Southern Alps And shorn in a Union shed. **1953** SUTHERLAND *Golden Bush* (1963) 154 The shed boomed with the topic.

c. The number of sheep to be shorn on a particular property or farm.

1897 WRIGHT *Station Ballads* 34 And that something might get broken long before that shed was shore. **1905** COX *Diaries 1888–1925* (ATLMS) 25 Nov. Another days shearing. The shed was cut out about 5 p.m. and no more dry sheep. **1986** RICHARDS *Off the Sheep's Back* 123 Until the shed was cut out, I shore a little over 300 each day.

d. In various phr. **to apply for** or **get a shed**, to (apply to) obtain a job shearing; **to be over the shed**, to be the boss over the shed; **to work the sheds**, to work in a shearing gang on a shearing circuit.

1910 *Awards, etc.* 113 When a shearer applies for a shed, and his application is granted, he shall forward his union ticket (if a unionist) to the employer. **1911** *Maoriland Worker* 20 Mar. 15 They got another shed at better wages and better conditions. **1924** REES *Heather of South* 139 Gillespie, who was 'over the shed', had conducted the party around. **1984** BEATON *Outside In* 106 Ginny: Nah. Only time I stopped was when I worked the sheds..I was a fucken good rousy. Even sheared a sheep once.

e. Special Comb. **shed boss** [AND 1887], the overseer in charge of shearing and shearing-shed; **shed hand** [AND 1898], an unskilled worker in a shearing gang or woolshed; **shed-manager** [AND 1879], *shed boss*; **shed rep.**, the shearer's union shed representative; **shed shearing**, shearing as part of a shed or shearing-gang; **shed shepherd**, one employed to control the sheep coming into and leaving the shearing-shed yards; **shed stain**, see quot.; **shed time**, see quot.

1892 SWANTON *Notes on NZ* 97 Then there is the '**shed boss**' who looks after everything, sees the sheep are shorn properly, takes the tally, looks after pressing etc. **1904** LANCASTER *Sons o' Men* 81 A shed-boss must know all that breathes under the roof. **1940** STUDHOLME *Te Waimate* (1954) 127 In the early days the manager acted as shed boss. Later, when the agricultural work increased, a special shed boss was engaged. **c1885** ACTON-ADAMS in McCaskill *Molesworth* (1969) 87 I have instructed my new manager..to cooperate with you as to working the two stations with one staff of musterers, shearers and **shed hands**, whereby we can save a lot of money. **1905** BAUCKE *White Man Treads* 229 The shed-hands and shearers were mostly Maoris. **1913** CARR *Country Work* 14 The boss Maori undertakes to supply all the rouseabouts (as shed hands are termed) i.e., fleece pickers, wool rollers and 'Sheep oh!'. **1933** *Press* (Christchurch) (Acland Gloss.) 21 Oct. 15 *Hand...* Everyone employed on a station is a *s[hed] h[and]* except the manager and cadets, and perhaps the cook. **1943** HISLOP *Pure Gold* 35 To use the expression of a wayback shed hand, it is real dinkum. **1953** SUTHERLAND *Golden Bush* (1963) 154 After the day's work was over Tazzy took a walk to the top of the hill..and half a dozen shed hands went with him. **1962** SHARPE *Country Occasions* 39 In the North Island there are, in a properly organised contract gang, six rouseabouts, as shedhands are called, and two pressers. **1986** RICHARDS *Off the Sheep's Back* 94 All his shed hands, shearers and his wool classer had been with him before. **1990** MARTIN *Forgotten Worker* 85 Shedhand work was..very demanding, despite being looked down on by the shearers. **1906** *Awards, etc.* 625 When shearing wet ewes the **shed-manager** may alter the smokes and extend the hours..to complete the cut-out. **1911** *Maoriland Worker* 8 Dec. 14 The union owes a very great deal of appreciation to the **shed reps.** in this district. **1986** RICHARDS *Off the Sheep's Back* 115 The shed rep called for a vote, and shearing was suspended for the day. **1965** *Listener* 26 Feb. 15 In **shed shearing** the position of 'Ringer' is sought after and competition among shearers has always been keen. **1933** *Press* (Christchurch) (Acland Gloss.) 2 Dec. 15 *Shepherd.*—(1) Man employed to work sheep. Except a *lambing s[hepherd]*, or *shed s[hepherd]*, who are specially employed for a certain time, a *s[hepherd]* is a permanent hand. **1988** *More* (Auckland) Mar. 31 Other types of fleece..are..**shed stain** which is good body wool spoilt when one sheep empties bowels on another while penned up closely. **1982** WOODHOUSE *Blue Cliffs* 224 **Shed time** is what is shown on the shed clock, irrespective of what may be shown on anybody's watch.

3. *Freezing works.* **a.** A freezing works, or its main building; any of the various buildings in which killing is done.

1951 May 17 Feilding Freezing Works terms p.c. Colin Gordon. The freezing works generally called *the works*. The building is called *the shed* (W.H. Mabbett comments (1952): 'especially among older hands who pride themselves in keeping up the traditional terms'). **1983** *National Bus. Rev.* 3 Oct. 16 But Waitaki [freezing works] has nine sheds and a quantity of mutilation can be absorbed into its total operation. **1984** *Dominion* (Wellington) 20 Sept. 3 The National executive [of the Meat Workers' Union] would hold a shed meeting soon to tell members what happened at the Christchurch meeting.

b. The body of freezing-workers at a particular works.

1963 HILLIARD *Piece of Land* 104 During the big trouble in 1951 he had been a freezing workers' delegate, and when it was all over he decided to quit the shed and get steady work closer to the middle of town. **1986** *Metro* (Auckland) July 82 And it certainly isn't the big money people have come to associate with freezing works. With the Auckland sheds solidly behind the strike, there was none of the media pandemonium occurring further south.

4. *Dairy-farming.* **a.** Occas. (prob. on the form of *bails*) collective *pl* as **the sheds**, ellipt. for COWSHED or MILKING SHED; also, the number of cows being milked at a particular time.

1924 ANTHONY *Follow the Call* (1975) 55 As we stripped out our last shed of cows that evening Clive surprised me. **1937** GORDON & BENNETT *Gentlemen of the Jury* 67 Two months later the mother is 'out in the sheds' helping to share-milk a hundred cows. **1978** SUTHERLAND *Elver* 36 To John—because his nose was new to the shed, it smelled overpowering—mud, cowdung, stale milk. **1986** *National Radio Rural Programme* 14 June [A dairy farmer says:] My wife has been out of the shed for three years now and is not looking forward to going back.

b. With defining words indicating the names and types of modern cowsheds (the quots. below consolidate instances of the full forms **cowshed**, **milking shed** and the elliptical form **shed**): **angle-park, chute, herringbone, internal race; race milking-shed**, one arranged in the form of a double race (see RACE *n.*¹ 2), with the cows milked in two lines of bails facing each other; **rotary (rotary herringbone, rotary turnstyle), tandem, walk-through**, see esp. the various 1982 quots. below.

1982 *Agric. Gloss.* (MAF) 39 *Cowshed... Angle-park*: Cows stand on raised step at an angle to the milker, cups put on from the side. Cows leave each bail through the front. *Ibid.* 39 *Cowshed... Chute*: Where cows are held in a straight line for milking at the side. They all enter and leave the shed together (now obsolete). **1959** *NZ Dairy Exporter* Sept. 66 I was called in here to give advice on **Herringbone Sheds**. **1960** MCMEEKAN *Grass to Milk* 150 The herringbone is a New Zealand development of the tandem type... In this type of shed the cows are angle-parked in two rows separated by the milkers 'well' which is 30 inches below the cow platforms... The cows are milked in batches, those on each side being milked alternately. **1972** *Sunday Times* (Wellington) 23 July 9 Now he looks as much at home coaxing reluctant cows through a herringbone milking shed as he must have been in a Dutch lecture theatre. **1982** *Agric. Gloss.* (MAF) 39 **Herringbone cowshed**. Cows are milked in two rows standing at an angle to the milker who is in a pit at udder level. Cup put on from the side. All the cows enter and leave together. **1991** *Dominion* (Wellington) 26 Jan. 6 'A building is a string of events belonging together,' wrote one authority. That's certainly true of your average herringbone after a morning's friesians have passed through. **1982** *Agric. Gloss.* (MAF) 39 **Cowshed... Internal race**: Similar to walkthrough except that cows leave shed by an internal race. **1912** *NZJAg.* Jan. IV. 536 Could you kindly inform me..[of] the measurements of race-bails to hold five cows each side... A **race milking shed** to hold five cows on either side should measure 43 ft. in length, and a total width of 10 ft. 9 in. (inside measurement). **1972** *NZ Dairy Exporter* Feb. 2 A lot has been written about the various types of **rotary shed**. Most of these articles have been concerned with the characteristics of the shed in comparison with the herringbone shed. **1982** *Agric. Gloss.* (MAF) 39 *Cowshed... Rotary herringbone*: Similar to rotary turnstyle except that the milker is in the centre and the cows face outwards. *Ibid.* 39 *Cowshed... Rotary turnstyle*: Cows are milked on a rotating platform with the milker on the outside and the cows facing the centre. The cows step on to the platform and reverse off. Cups are put on from behind. **1961** McMeekan *Grass to Milk* 148 There are three commonly used types of milking shed in New Zealand— the walk-through, the **tandem** and the herringbone. *Ibid.* 149 The tandem shed consists of a set of bails within which the cows stand in line, head to tail..on a platform 30 inches above the milker's level. **1982** *Agric. Gloss.* (MAF) 39 *Cowshed... Tandem*: Cows stand in a straight line for milking at the side. They can enter and leave each unit individually. **1920** Powdrell *Dairy Farming* 22 There are many types of cow-shed, for example the Race, the Double bail, the Single back-out, and the **Walk-through** type of shed. **1936** Belshaw et al. *Agric. Organiz. NZ* 456 In modern sheds the walk-through type of bail has completely superseded the old back-out type. **1950** *NZJAg.* Apr. LXXX. 374 The walk-through [milking-shed] with doors at the rear of the shed in the conventional manner. **1974** *NZ Agric.* 81 Farm dairies are of various types. Most of them used to be of the 'walk-through' type, where cows stand side by side and are milked by pipeline milking machines. **1982** *Agric. Gloss.* (MAF) 39 *Cowshed...Walkthrough*: Cows stand on floor level or raised step and are milked from the side. Cows leave each bail through the front. **1991** *More Earlier Days on the Coast* 18 The first cow-shed was a walk-through type, and each cow had to be leg-roped.

5. *Waterfront.* A wharf storage shed.

1911 *Maoriland Worker* 25 Aug. 5 When you [*sc.* the watersider] show grey under your skull cap you find you are not selling so freely as formerly... The young emigrant..take[s] your place in the hold and shed.

shed, *n.*² [f. *shed v.* to separate sheep from a group.] The act or result of drafting off or separating a group of sheep from a mob, or of dividing a mob. See also SHED *v.*²

1981 [see SHED *v.*² 1]. **1982** *Agric. Gloss.* (MAF) 7 *Shed*:.. the act of drafting off animals from a group— shedding.

shed, *v.*¹ *Farming.* Also **shed up**. [Spec. use of *shed* to place in a shed: see OED *v.*²] *trans.* To shut (woolly sheep) in a woolshed or under other cover before shearing to prevent them getting wet from rain or dew.

1950 *NZJAg.* Oct. LXXXI. 310 Sheep brought in for shearing should be spelled before shedding up, otherwise the pens in the shed get very dirty. **1981** *Listener* 27 June 86 When you shed-up sheep you put them under cover to prevent their fleeces from getting wet before shearing. **1981** Charles *Black Billy Tea* 28 You will be shedding up the sheep with the boss on your tail!

shed, *v.*² *Farming.* [f. *shed* to separate: see OED *v.*¹ 'Now only *dial.*, chiefly in farming uses'.]

1. Also **shed off (out)**. *trans.* To draft, split off, or cut out (one or more farm animals, usu. sheep) from a group or mob.

1933 *Press* (Christchurch) (Acland Gloss.) 25 Nov. 15 *Shed*... To separate two lots of sheep in the open... I think the word is Scotch. **1934** Lilico *Sheep Dog Memoirs* 5 These dogs got to know the [scabby] sheep..so there was no difficulty in shedding them out. **1951** *NZJAg.* Aug. LXXXIII. 13 Lambs are 'shedded out' as necessary. **1956** *NZ Farmer* 23 Aug. 4 This system is coming to be known commonly as the 'shedding' system—from the fact that the lambing flock is shifted from paddock to paddock daily and those ewes which have lambed since the previous shift 'shedded' off from the mob as it leaves the paddock. **1960** *Proc. of 10th Lincoln College Farmers' Conference* 75 Ewes are then used to being shifted when shedding off the lambs. **1981** *Listener* 21 Mar. 49 The New Zealand farmer..*sheds out* his ewes (separating off those that have lambed, for better pasture). His better dogs can *shed* sheep (separating them into groups) and what the dog has managed to achieve is also called the *shed*.

2. *vbl. n.* **shedding (out)**, the separating of groups of sheep. Also *attrib.*

1934 Lilico *Sheep Dog Memoirs* 5 [The dog] was no use in forcing, but at shedding and control of a small lot, he was perfect. **1957** *Weekly News* (Auckland) 7 Aug. 34 Shedding system..by which every ewe that lambs is immediately left behind, with others in like case, as the flock makes its daily trek on to the next paddock. **1981** *Listener* 21 Mar. 49 *Shedding out* comes from a quite different *shed*, this time an old verb which meant to divide or to split up, which in its turn produced a noun—*shed* meaning a division or split-up.

sheelah, sheeler, varr. SHEILA.

sheep.

1. Used *attrib.* in Comb. **sheep country** [AND 1822], **-dag, -docking, land** [AND 1832], **master, musterer, netting** [AND 1837], **-owner** [AND 1839], **paddock, -proof** [AND 1872], **shearing,** see SHEARING *vbl. n.*, **track, washer, work** [AND 1931].

1834 *NZ Independent* (1979) 9 Aug. 33 [Hokianga] would be splendid **sheep country**; if English grasses could be got to grow upon it. **1860** in Butler *First Year* (1863) vi 73 There can be, I imagine, no doubt that this is excellent sheep country; still, I should like to see it in winter. **1874** Kennaway *Crusts* 35 We started upon an expedition to get back into the interior, with a view of discovering..available sheep-country. **1882** William *Shirres Copybook* in Neave *Land of Munros* (1980) 55 It is one of the best blocks of sheep country in New Zealand, and I intend bidding for a portion of it. **1907** Mansfield *Urewera Notebook* (1978) 39 The manuka and sheep country—very steep and bare. **1922** *NZJST* IV. 282 When he..first travelled over the Lammerlaw in search of sheep-country they found a good deal of scrub. **1937** Ayson *Pioneering Otago* 94 It was very much infested with wild dogs and wild pigs,..but it was very good sheep country. **1975** Newton *Sixty Thousand on the Hoof* 44 A balance of mineral content seldom found elsewhere makes it a naturally good sheep country. **1979** *Islands* 27 504 The frost melted stealthily away on the thistle-heads, the bits of **sheep-dag**. **1991** *Dominion* (Wellington) 7 Dec. 12 At **sheep-docking** time: 'Let not thy right hand lose her cunning. Psalm 31, verse 14.' **1965** Shadbolt *Among Cinders* 2 Inland there is more **sheepland**, more rough country, and then mountains. **1947** Beattie *Early Runholding* 11 I spent weeks collecting every old term for 'runholders' I could, and I found thirteen, viz., 'flock owners', 'flock masters'..'**sheep masters**'..and 'stock owners'. **1885** *NZJSc.* II. 481 By all these names is this troublesome bird [*sc.* kea] known by the highland shepherds and **sheep musterers** in alpine districts. **1904** Chudleigh *Diary* 9 July (1950) 422 Trying to strain **sheep netting** outside a 7 wire fence. We are not well versed in wire netting. **1977** Bruce *Life in Hinterland* 86 In 1935 I decided to build a holding paddock on the top of Blo'ard... To get the sheep netting and iron standards packed up by horses was a mighty big undertaking. **1855** *Letter* Mar. in Fitton *NZ* (1856) 183 A **sheep-owner** need not reside on his run, but live in a more civilised district, and visit his flock at times. **1865** *Southern Cross* 14 Dec. in Stevens *John Grigg* (1952) 17 Many other purchases were made on behalf of sheep owners in other Provinces. **1874** Kennaway *Crusts* 157 Nevertheless, to run them [*sc.* wild pigs] down was, to the sheep-owner of the day..still one more imperative necessity. **1912** *Sheepowners' Handbook* 3 [Heading] The New Zealand Sheepowners' and Farmers' Federation **1982** Bream *Island of Fear* 75 If he [*sc.* a dog] got himself shot for being in a **sheep paddock**, it served him right. **1863** *Accommodation House Regs.* (Canterbury) in Gillespie *South Canterbury* (1958) 471 To provide..a good and sufficient moveable **sheep-proof** yard. **1864** [see BOUNDARY 1]. **1938** Burdon *High Country* 80 On the runs that had neither natural boundary nor sheep-proof fence..there was a fine..for every sheep found unherded by a shepherd within half a mile of the boundary. **1966** Barry *In Lee of Hokonuis* 46 The fences on the whole were sheep proof. **1982** Woodhouse *Blue Cliffs* 49 Although repairs continued to be made to boundary fences, it was next to impossible to keep them sheep-proof. **1864** Muter *Travels* II. 212 On reaching the crest we turned to our left over some rough **sheep-tracks**. **1867** Barker *Station Life* (1870) 128 The ascent was very steep, and there were no sheep-tracks to guide us. **1947–48** Beattie *Pioneer Recolls.* (1956) 18 There were no bridges and no proper roads but there were sheep tracks through the tussocks. **1982** Woodhouse *Blue Cliffs* 214 As we rode up the steep sheep track..he confessed that he had been composing a verse himself. **1990** *Dominion* (Wellington) 28 Apr. 6 Back in the days when New Zealand was linked by a series of glorified sheep tracks. **1878** Elwell *Boy Colonists* 42 December has now arrived. The Waikoura house and washpools were quite finished..: and the sheep-washing commenced. With the exception of Mr. J. the **sheep-washers** were all ordinary working men. **1892** *NZ Official Handbook* 162 Pastoral labour... Stockkeepers, with board, per annum... Hutkeepers, with board, per annum... Station-labourers: With board, per week... Sheep-washers: With board, per day. **1982** Woodhouse *Blue Cliffs* 53 Charles Hendry's younger brother..came to Blue Cliffs when required for mustering and other **sheep work**.

2. Special Comb. **sheep baron,** see *sheep king* below; **sheep-camp,** a place where sheep prefer to assemble, or to rest at night (cf. CAMP *n.* 2 a); **sheep-cocky** [AND 1897], a small-scale sheep-farmer; **sheep dip,** the bath or artificial pool in which sheep are washed in an insecticide solution (see OED *sheep* 8); **sheep-dipping** *ppl. a.*, *vbl.n.*

[used elsewhere but recorded earliest in NZ], (pertaining to) the washing of sheep in an insecticidal bath; **sheep-feed** [AND 1903], vegetation suitable for sheep (rather than cattle) to graze; **sheep inspector** *hist.*, an official who formerly inspected flocks for scab or other diseases; **sheep killer**, KEA *n.* 1 a; **sheep king** [AND 1899], a sheep farmer on a large scale; **sheepman**, one experienced or expert in the management of sheep; **sheep notice** *obs.*, a notice to a run-holder of an intention to drive sheep across his run (see also NOTICE); **sheep nut**, a proprietary supplementary sheep food; **sheep plant**, see quot. (not otherwise recorded); **sheep return**, an annual stock census form filled in by a farmer, and also the official publication of the consolidated results of such forms; **sheep run** [AND 1823], RUN *n.*[1] 2; **sheep-sick** *a.* [AND 1895], of pastures, exhausted or deteriorated from continual overstocking with sheep, hence **sheep-sickness**; **sheep station** [AND 1825], a station or large farm on which sheep are raised for meat and wool (see STATION 3 a); **sheep-wash** *fig. obs.* [AND 1891], inferior liquor; **sheep-wash tobacco** *obs.* [AND 1860], an inferior tobacco used in solution to combat scab (see quot. 1851); **sheep-yard** [AND 1809] (usu. *pl.* but often *sing.* in early use), YARD *n.*

1991 *Dominion Sunday Times* (Wellington) 24 Feb. 15 The property was once a huge station owned by South Island **sheep baron** Robert Campbell. **1908** *TrNZI* XL. 517 It will survive..on well-manured **sheep-camps**. **1921** GUTHRIE-SMITH *Tutira* (1926) 154 The sheep camps were each season ploughed and reploughed by innumerable wild pig. **1926** HILGENDORF *Weeds* 151 *Horehound*..is common in waste places and sheep camps in both islands. **1933** *Press* (Christchurch) (Acland Gloss.) 25 Nov. 15 *Sheep-camp*.—A place where sheep camp at night. It is usually marked by hore-hound. **1944** MARSH *Died in the Wool* 12 They were the wool-growers, the runholders, the **sheep-cockies**, the back-countrymen. **1949** SARGESON *I Saw in My Dream* (1974) 198 I never can teach my wife that a sheep-cocky's dogs aren't pets. **1980** LELAND *Kiwi-Yankee Dict.* 27 A cocky is a New Zealand farmer... There are also men who you could describe as sheep cockies. **1879** *Auckland Weekly News* 19 July 14 It was unanimously resolved: 'That the **sheep-dip** works about to be erected at Remuera are in an unsuitable place.' **1882** WILLIAMS *Diary* 9 July in Stevens *John Grigg* (1952) 64 We saw also the sheep dip, the washing pond &c., the manager's house &c. **1939** BEATTIE *First White Boy Born Otago* 91 As he could not take the sheep off the run a sheep-dip had to be constructed. **1851** *Lyttelton Times* 2 Aug. 2 A. Bayfield, Chemist and Druggist, Canterbury St., Lyttelton, begs to call the attention of the Farmers and Flockmasters of the settlement to his valuable **Sheep Dipping Composition**, for effectually destroying the Tick Lice, and all other insects injurious to the flock, preventing the attacks of the Scab, and cleansing and purifying the skin. **1855** *Nelson Examiner* 22 Nov. 2 The plan..of growing tobacco for sheep-dipping, reduces the expense of this treatment. **1953** GUTHRIE-SMITH *Tutira* (3edn.) 138 The master and main difficulty was lack of **sheep-feed**. **1982** WOODHOUSE *Blue Cliffs* 213 *Celmisia spectablis* var. *magnifica*, though interesting to the botanist, is worthless as sheep feed. **c1858** in Beattie *Early Runholding* (1947) 139 Wm. Pinkerton, the **sheep inspector** for the Southern District, wrote a long report headed 'Popotunoa, November 2, 1858'. [**1864** *The Sheep Ordinance* Session xxii No.13 s.24 in *Canterbury Ordinances 1857-67* 71 The owner of such sheep..shall cause such rams to be kept separate from such ewes until they shall be certified by the Inspector of Sheep to be entirely free from scab. **1879** *Auckland Weekly News* 19 Apr. 15 As yet, no Inspector of Sheep had been appointed for the Raglan County.] **1882** *TrNZI* XIV. 271 Sheep Inspector Simpson..reports as follows. **1949** CRAWFORD *Sheep & Sheepmen Canterbury* 54 The kea, or **sheep killer** (Nestor notabilis) [in the Wanaka district]. **1861** *Gabriel's Gully* in Manson *Take up My Pen* (1971) 87 Our **sheep kings** have now put an extra 2d a lb. on beef and mutton. **1953** *NZ Observer* 18 Feb. 7 That was the beginning of the fabulous career which made Edward Joshua Riddiford known throughout New Zealand as 'King' Riddiford—the king of the 19th Century sheep-kings. **1946** ACLAND *Early Canterbury Runs* 121 In 1875..D. Oliver, the head shepherd, became manager. He was a very good **sheepman** from Australia and in those days one of the best judges of merino sheep in Canterbury. **1963** WALLIS *Point of Origin* 11 He'd had plenty of experience and he was a first-class sheep man. **1973** FERNANDEZ *Tussock Fever* 34 He felt that they [*sc.* shepherds] looked down upon him for not being a sheep man. **1984** HOLDEN *Razorback* 11 Now..Bob's sheep would start to give birth, a highly critical time for any sheepman. **1864** *Puketoi Station Diary* (Hocken TS) 6 May Smith Tokie..sent **Sheep notice**. **1986** *Dominion* (Wellington) 4 Oct. 1 Esmerelda is the boss of the paddock and no questions are asked when the goat barges past the other animals to get to the **sheep nuts**. **1961** *Merriam-Webster Third International* 2091 **sheep plant** *n*: any of several New Zealand plants of the genus *Raoulia*..with white woolly tufted foliage that when viewed from a distance suggests the form of a sheep—called also Vegetable Sheep. **1950** *NZJAg.* May LXXX. 421 The Hawkes Bay **sheep returns**, as on May 1, 1872, gave the number of sheep on Rissington as 28,500. **1834 sheep run** [see *cattle run* (CATTLE 2)]. **1848** WAKEFIELD *Handbook NZ* 124 From the various description of the land included in the sheep runs, it is difficult to state..the average number of sheep per *acre*. **1856** FITTON *NZ* 215 The intending stock-owner can hardly do better..while seeking for a profitable investment of his capital in either a sheep run, a cattle station, or in..dairy-farming. **1872** in Meredith *Adventuring in Maoriland* (1935) 27 I have been given charge of one of the sheep-runs [of the Wairarapa station]. My duties are to look after the boundaries. **1882** POTTS *Out in Open* 168 For years there was offered a standing reward of one pound for an eel captured in the streams on this sheep run. **1892** *NZ Official Handbook* 157 On a sheep-run the lambing and shearing seasons tax every power of the station-hands. **1958** PASCOE *Great Days in NZ Mountaineering* 68 They spent a night at a homestead at Lake Heron with a sheeprun manager who took their gear on a pack-horse the following morning. **1984** HOLCROFT *Way of Writer* 148 Aunt Rose came down from Pinaki, the Hamilton sheeprun beyond Scargill. **1899** WILLIAMS *Page from Hist.* 9 [The land] is now what is called **sheep-sick**. **1909** OWEN *Philip Loveluck* 50 [His paddocks] are sheep-sick from boundary to boundary. **1937** *King Country Chronicle* 24 June 5 Struggles..against 'sheep sick' country..were described in New Plymouth on Monday. **1968** *NZ Contemp. Dict. Suppl.* (Collins) 17 *sheep-sick adj.* of pastures, exhausted for carrying sheep. **1931** *NZJST* XII. 1 [Heading] The relation of geology to **sheep sickness** in Mairoa district. **1844** in Shortland *S. Dist. NZ* (1851) 191 Hughes's partner and another man accompanied us as far as Orere, where they had a **sheep station**. **1853** ADAMS *Canterbury Settlement* 71 The simple and primitive mode of living at a sheep-station affords scanty materials for the pen. **1867** BARKER *Station Life* (1870) 107 There is no place..where you can live so cheaply..as on a New Zealand sheep station, when once you get a start. **1907** *TrNZI* XXXIX. 75 Various sheep-stations have suffered loss from the attacks of the [kea] bird. **1928** BAUCKE *White Man Treads* 240 When, in 1874, America sent parties to observe..the transit of Venus.., one such party set its station on the Chatham Islands, not many miles from our sheep-station home. **1944** *Short Guide NZ* (Gloss. Slang) 39 *Sheep station*—big sheep farm, ranch. **1953** GUTHRIE-SMITH *Tutira* (3edn.) 149 It was upon the 4th of September 1882 that the new owners of Tutira took delivery of their sheep station. **1963** WALLIS *Point of Origin* 181 On a sheep station in the hill country behind Awatere, Neil..supervised the last of the second-shear ewes through the yard gate. **1986** EVANS *Change Agent* 24 Brought here as a future mistress of the homestead and a kind of queen of this close-knit sheep station community. **1941** BAKER *NZ Slang* 62 [Australasian] terms for strong drink are *lunatic soup*, *Africa speaks*, *plonk*,... **sheep wash**. [**1851** *Lyttelton Times* 21 June 6 His Excellency laid on the table a memorial which had been presented to him, praying that tobacco for sheep washing might be taken out of bond free duty, or subject only to a light imposition... Mr. Cantley strongly urged the exemption of tobacco used for sheep washing from duty, as important to the interests of the sheep owners, and their efforts to eradicate the scab from the colony.] **1861** *Otago Witness* (Dunedin) 30 Mar. 4 On Sale by the Undersigned, in quantities to s[u]it settlers—**Sheep-wash Tobacco** Leaf, in bales. **1868** *Marlborough Express* (Blenheim) 29 Feb. 1 Sheep Station & Farming Goods—Sheepwash Tobacco, 10 tons **1855** PHILLIPS *Rockwood Jrnl.* 3 July (Canterbury Pub. Lib. TS) 1 H.P. John Harry & Jem making **Sheep-yard**. **1857** PAUL *Lett. from Canterbury* 88 The next point will be to make a sheep-yard. I should say make it of short stiff hurdles with a post and rail catching pen. **1863** CHUDLEIGH *Diary* 5 Oct. (1950) 105 Cleared by 12. Mr Acland and I went up the run to look at the new sheep-yard. **1922** PERRY *Sheep Farming* 16 Sheep Yards.—The erection of drafting yards is one of the first improvements to be attended to by the young sheep farmer. **1933** *Press* (Christchurch) (Acland Gloss.) 2 Dec. 15 *Sheep yards.*—Y[ards] for *drafting sheep*..or putting them into a wool-shed. **1982** WOODHOUSE *Blue Cliffs* 68 We could go up on to the balcony and watch them [*sc.* the sheep] pass on their way to the sheep-yards.

3. a. In special collocations: **sheep's back**, in the phr. **live off the sheep's back** [AND 1932], indicating or alluding to prosperity from wool growing; **sheep's burr**, see BURR *n.*[1] 2 a.

1963 WALLIS *Point of Origin* 24 And I think it's time this country stopped being so complacent about living off the sheep's back.

b. In the phr. **sheep on terms**, see TERMS *n.*[1]; **sheep shit on the brain**, see quot.

1989 *NZ Eng. Newsletter* III. 28 *sheep shit on the brain:* A fairly common expression to describe one obsessed with shearing, sheep and anything to do with the sheds.

sheepo, *int.* and *n.* Shearing. Also **sheep-oh**.

A. *int.* [AND 1900.] A shearer's cry for the catching pen to be refilled with sheep.

1878 *Otago Witness* (Dunedin) 28 Sept. 3 Very little conversation goes on among the men... Only the cry of..'sheep oh', when a man has taken the last sheep out of his pen and wants more. **1913** CARR *Country Work* 17 Another job suitable for a new hand is 'Sheep O!' The work consists of filling up the 'catching pens' when empty. The shearer who takes the last sheep..calls out 'Sheep O!' when the boy..immediately fills up the back pen. **1933** *Press* (Christchurch) (Acland Gloss.) 25 Nov. 15 *Sheep-oh!*—When a shearer empties his pen he calls 'S[heep]o[h!]' and the *penner-up* refills it. **1949** NEWTON *High Country Days* 52 The cry of 'Sheepo!'..would rouse the 'penner-up'. **1955** BOWEN

Wool Away (Gloss.: Shearing Terms) 157 Sheepo. The man who fills the catching pens and works sheep in the shed. Shearers give the call of 'sheepo' when they have caught the last sheep in the catching pen, and to signify that the pen is empty. **1968** *Straight Furrow* 21 Feb. 20 Sheep-o: The call, timid from beginners, imperious from guns for the rousie (rouse-about) to fill the catching pen. **1981** Sutherland & Taylor *Sunrise* 48 As his job also included helping with the penning-up, Bill was soon running in response to the cry of 'Sheep-oh!' **1989** *NZ Eng. Newsletter* III. 28 *sheep-oh:* The call of the shearer when he wants the penner-up to refill his catching pen. This call cannot be made while there are more than two sheep left in the pen.

B. *n.* [AND 1900.] A person who fills the catching pens. See also PENNER-UP.
1913 [see A above]. **1925** Rees *Lake of Enchantment* 111 The [shearing-] gang [included]..some boys to act as 'sheepo's'—that is to keep the pens in the shed filled up from the yards outside. **1926** Devanny *Butcher Shop* (1981) 65 The noise of the dogs and the shouting of the 'sheepos'..all conspired to dazzle her. **1933** [see A above]. **1940** [see PENNER-UP]. **1955** [see A above]. **1979** Temple *Stations* 93 If you can stomach the food, I need ten shearers, one sheep-oh, two fleece pickers, a classer, two rollers and two pressers. **1982** *Agric. Gloss.* (MAF) 59 *Sheepo:* Person who works sheep in a shearing shed and fills the catching pens.

sheerlegs, var. SHEAR-LEGS.

sheerwater, var. SHEARWATER.

sheila /'ʃilə/. Also **sheelah**, **sheeler**, **shieler**. [Prob. from a generic use of the orig. Irish personal name *Sheila* (Gaelic *Síle*, poss. an adaptation of *Celia*): AND 1832; also from 1839 Brit. slang.] A girl or girl-friend; a woman.
1902 in Lawlor *More Wellington Days* (1962) 42 June 27 Tom says I am a sheeler for playing Poor Jenny. **1918** *Chron. NZEF* 5 July 252 I goes..and stays at Ngaire with my shieler's people. **1921** *Auckland Univ. College Carnival Souvenir* 19 [Cast of Carnival play includes] Watersiders, Factory Girls, Cabinet Ministers,.. Tabbies from Takapuna, Sheelahs from the Salvation Army. **1938** Lawlor *House of Templemore* 42 'What does 'sheila' mean..?' 'Sheila is Irish for girl.' **1948** *Landfall* 6 110 Say, there was a sheila down my section today; boy, I bet a joker could make her on a cup of coffee. **1959** Middleton *The Stone* 35 Aw he goes out after sheilas in the park with those jokers from Central. **1963** Mason *Pohutukawa Tree* (1978) 13 Roy: Because, as Maori sheilas go, you're pretty hot stuff. **1973** Sargeson *Once Is Enough* 109 He was taking out his 'sheila' (a girl whom he eventually married). **1988** Rennie *Super Man* 116 One of the officer cadets..wanted me to ring his sheila to say he wouldn't be home for a naughty. **1990** *Listener* 27 Aug. 114 They all [*sc.* hedgehogs] get drunk, grab one of the sheilas, and start sticking champagne corks on her prickles.

shelduck. Also **sheldrake**, usu. with a modifier **paradise**, occas. **New Zealand**; occas. erron. **shellduck**. *Tadorna variegata* (fam. Anatidae), the 'informed' but occasional name for *paradise duck* (DUCK 2 (6)).
1873 Buller *Birds NZ* 241 *Casarca variegata*. (New Zealand Sheldrake.).. Putangitangi; Putakitaki in the South Island; 'Paradise Duck' of the colonists. **1983** *Land of Mist* 68 The river areas..host many waterfowl including the Paradise shelduck. **1987** *Dominion* (Wellington) 4 Apr. 8 Increased bag limits have been announced for..Paradise Shellduck and Canadian Geese. **1992** Smithyman *Auto/Biographies*

47 where his milkers used to browse another herd flocks; Paradise shelduck.

shelf, *n.* Criminals. Also **shelfer**. [Prob. in allusion to the phr. *to put on the shelf* to put out of the way: AND 1916.] A police informer. Cf. *topper* (TOP v.).
1932 in Partridge *Dict. Underworld* (1961) 616 *Shelfer*. One who, upon a companion or an associate, informs to the police: New Zealand since ca. 1925; and by 1935 at latest, Australian: 1932 Nelson Baylis (private letter). **1941** Baker *NZ Slang* 53 Underworld slang [includes]..*shelfer*, a police informer (*fizgig* is the Australian term). **1955** *BJ Cameron Collection* (TS July) shelfer (n) A police informer. **1989** Newbold *Punish. & Politics* 75 So along with the other privileges, life was made easier for the inmates Haywood favoured. Not all of them were 'shelves'... A 'shelf' is an informant.

shelf, *v.* Criminals. Also **shelve**. [f. *shelf n.*: AND 1936.] *trans.* To inform upon (someone).
1910 *Truth* 16 Apr. 5 Asked where he got it, he said he would sooner go to gaol than 'shelve' anybody. **1982** Newbold *Big Huey* (Gloss.) 253 Shelf (n) and (v) Police informant, inform upon.

shelfer: see SHELF *n.*

shelling, *ppl. a.* Drug-users. Applied to the process of taking out of their capsules or foil-containers the drugs or pills to be used in manufacturing 'home-bake' drugs.
1986 *Evening Post* (Wellington) 5 Apr. 19 It takes about two hours to complete a bake excluding 'shelling time'. (Taking pills out of packets.)

shellshock.

1. As **shell-shock bread** (*WWI*), bread damaged or rendered less palatable during transport to the front.
1937 Partridge *Dict. Slang* 754 *shell-shock bread.* Bread arriving, impaired, to those in the front line: New Zealand soldiers': 1916–18. **1938** *Press* (Christchurch) (McNab Slang) 2 Apr. 18 [Slang of the N.Z.E.F.] Food gave an idiom or two: 'shell shock bread' and 'sandbag duff' were not much liked.

2. A potent mixed alcoholic drink.
1955 *BJ Cameron Collection* (TS July) shellshock (n) 1. Port wine and stout. 2. Any mixed and highly potent drink.

shelter. *Obs.* A special building housing tuberculosis patients, so constructed as to be partly open to the air.
1946 Sargeson *That Summer* 116 They're going to put me down in a shelter. **1964** Pearson *Glossary* to Sargeson *Collected Stories 1935–63* (1964) 303 shelter: hut or single-room annexe for a tuberculosis patient.

shelter-shed. [Spec. use of *shelter-shed* a structure affording protection from inclement weather: AND 1911.] A name for the partially enclosed building or 'shed' in a school playground in which children 'shelter' on wet days.
1908 *Dominion* (Wellington) 22 Sept. 4 On a wet day..should we send the children outside to the shelter-sheds or allow them to use the class-rooms? **1921** *Educ. Dept. Bldg. Standards for Primary Schools* 14 Shelter sheds should be simple in design and construction. **1951** *Educ. Dept. Bldg. Code for Public Primary Schools* 13 Where, however, children are transported to school before it opens, a shelter shed of appropriate

size is approved. **1963** Aitken *Gallipoli to the Somme* 66 A Yorkshire guide showed us to our billets, my section being quartered in..a French school, with holes in the roof of the shelter-sheds and craters in the playground. **1987** *Alfredton* 71 By 1936..the education board gave permission..to remove one of the latter's [*sc.* Saunders Road School's] shelter-sheds to Alfredton. **1990** Patrick *From Bush to Jubilee* 54 At different periods classes had to be held in the corridor, in the shelter shed, and in similar places.

shelve, var. SHELF.

shepherd, *n.* In special collocations: **shepherd's basket fungus**, see FUNGUS 2 (8); **shepherd's grummet** [fig. use of *grummet* or *grommet* a rubber ring or eyelet], a sheep's behind as a sexual object; **shepherd's hut**, **station**, **whare**, OUT-STATION 2; **shepherd's needle**, see quot. 1926.
1958 Fairburn *Poetry Harbinger* 21 ('Deep South') A bottomless lake, a loud wind-break, storms raging round the summit, a tailored cassock woven of tussock, a wiggle of **shepherd's grummit**. **1853** Mackie *Traveller under Concern* (1973) 86 A few miles further brought us to a **shepherd's hut**; we found the shepherd..unwell. **1863** *Over Whitcombe Pass* (1960) 20 We..went 25 miles further, to an old shepherd's hut. **1873** Pyke *Wild Will Enderby* (1889, 1974) III. v. 90 They halted at a shepherd's hut..windowless, with walls of mud, standing beneath the shadow of a gloamy terrace. **1881** Nesfield *Chequered Career* 35 It is a very great change..suddenly to find himself in a shepherd's hut with an uneducated companion. **1933** Scanlan *Tides of Youth* 120 In his lonely shepherd's hut, a jar of whiskey and the Odyssey were his companions. **1947** Beattie *Early Runholding* 12 Provisions became 'rations'..when served out to the men at the 'shepherds' huts' (or out-stations). **1951** Duff *Shepherd's Calendar* (1961) 24 It has always interested me in the back country to study the printed and pictorial matter in shepherds' and rabbiters' huts. **1980** Bennett *Canterbury Tale* 10 But there was another house across the creek, a sort of shepherd's hut. **1926** Hilgendorf *Weeds* 132 **Shepherd's Needle** (*Scandix Pecten-Veneris*), is found in both islands on waste ground, but is not common [1967 edn.: very rare]. It is an annual 6 to 8 inches high, much branched, somewhat hairy leaves like a carrot['s]. **1969** *Standard Common Names Weeds* 69 *shepherd's needle. Scandix pecten-veneris* L. **1861** *Otago Witness* (Dunedin) 29 June 5 The runholders in the district..show every disposition to be obliging, opening their **shepherds' stations** as accommodation houses, with very reasonable charges. **1868** *Marlborough Express* (Blenheim) 8 Feb. 4 Mr. Ivanhoe Augarde despatched a letter to some lady..by the hand of Dutch Charlie, who is said to have taken it to the **shepherd's whare**, where it was opened, and its contents discussed and animadverted on.

shepherd, *v.* [Transf. use of *shepherd* to tend or guard.]

1. *trans. Obs.* **a.** [AND 1852.] To carry out (a token occupation of a claim) to satisfy the goldfields regulations (see quots. 1864, 1967); to guard (a claim) against 'claim-jumpers' (see quot. 1887); occas., to watch for a claim-holder's absence in order to occupy the claim (see quot. 1867). Also as *vbl. n.*
1864 *AJHR C-4* 8 *Shepherding forbidden.* No person shall be deemed to possess a valid title to any claim unless the same shall be fairly worked during the entire period of occupancy. **1867** Cooper *Digger's Diary* 28 Nov. (1978) 17 The prowling, dastardly enemy..plants

himself at the claim, and there..he patiently waits during the absence of his future victim. This, in the language of the diggers, is called 'shepherding a claim'. At the end of twenty-four hours he seizes it, and..appropriates..the hard-earned property. **1887** PYKE *Hist. Early Gold Discoveries Otago* (1962) 118 They were all working miners, and one of them always 'shepherded' the claim, whilst the others wrought for wages elsewhere. **1892** WARDON *MacPherson's Gully* 13 The majority of claims were simply being shepherded, their occupiers waiting till some of their more enterprising neighbours had bottomed in order to decide by the result whether to sink or shift their pegs. **1908** *TrNZI* XL. 169 Every one aspiring to a share must have done something to demonstrate the fact that he is an owner... He must, in fact, 'shepherd his claim', or his claim will be jumped. **c1930** *Whitcombe's Etym. Dict. Aust.-NZ Suppl.* 10 *shepherd*..-v. trans. to do only sufficient work on a mining claim to retain legal hold of it. **1967** MAY *West Coast Gold Rushes* 528 Shepherding: holding possession of a claim without working on it, or by doing the minimum amount of work necessary to satisfy the regulations and the warden. Shepherding was common on a new rush. Old timers often pegged out a claim and waited to see what success their more anxious neighbours had—especially where deep shafts or log tunnels were necessary to reach the lead.

b. [Prec. use transferred to land holding.] To hold (a Crown lease) with minimal occupation of (or work on) the land by the leaseholder.

1869 *McLean Papers* (ATLTS) XXXI. 189 There are at this moment, many large tracts of land, leased, which are lying, for all purposes of reproductiveness, utterly valueless; in fact, to use an old Victorian expression, being 'shepherded', the lessees of which, are Micawber-like, 'waiting for something to turn up' in their neighbourhood, before they turn to with a will and work the ground

2. *trans.* [See OED v. 4: AND 1853.] To follow or shadow (someone) surreptitiously or slyly to discover the whereabouts of a payable claim.

1863 BARRINGTON *Diary* 27 Dec. in Taylor *Early Travellers* (1959) 394 There is great talk of a man called M'Guirk, alias the 'Maori Hen', getting gold somewhere out towards the West Coast... He has been shepherded by a dozen men on several occasions, but always managed to give them the slip. **1873** PYKE *Wild Will Enderby* (1889, 1974) III. ii 77 But they're on gold anyhow... And there's a whole mob of fellows shepherding them [to discover their claim].

sherang /ʃəˈræŋ/. Also **serang**. [Transf. use of Anglo-Indian *serang* a native boatswain or captain of a Lascar crew: see OED; AND 1911.] Now usu. as **head sherang**, a, or the, boss; a person in authority.

1917 in Miller *Camps, Tramps & Trenches* (1939) 49 The Camp Commandant and half a dozen of the sherangs dressed in their best. **1917** *The Digger* (Troopship pub.) 4 The 'head serang' was in the store. **1953** HAMILTON *Till Human Voices Wake Us* 98 For the first three weeks [in prison] I was almost exclusively concerned with the head serang. **1968** SLATTER *Pagan Game* 172 Tank Tarrant the head sherang. Tank Tarrant the greatest thing since sliced bread.

shi-ack /ˈʃai(j)æk/, var. CHIACK.

shicer /ˈʃaisə/. *Obs.* Also **shiser**. [Transf. use of Brit. slang *shicer* a worthless person: see OED; AND 1853.] A worthless or unproductive claim, mine, or gold-rush.

1862 THATCHER *Canterbury Songster* 13 Vy you tell me dere vos gold now! 'Te's von shicer. **1865** *AJHR* C-4A 12 The..extensive [race]..is that cut across some minor tributaries..to the terrace ground of Shicer Gully. **1887** HOPEFUL *Taken In* 135 Supposing a man is digging, but without success, and he therefore abandons his hole, it is called a 'shicer'—that is, the *ground* was called a 'shicer' or duffer. **1914** PFAFF *Diggers' Story* 113 'Kangaroo Jim'..caused a rush to Lake Brunner, which turned out a 'shicer'. **1967** MAY *West Coast Gold Rushes* 526 Duffer: applied to a rush, a shaft, or a claim generally. A failure. Synonyms were 'shicer', 'stringer' or, in the case of a false rush, 'store-keepers' rush'. **1974** HEINZ *Bright Fine Gold* 200 Worthless claims or ground were called shicers or duffers. **1992** LATHAM *Golden Reefs* 52 The diggers' derogatory term, 'a shiser', was levelled at the Inangahua.

shicker /ˈʃɪkə/, *a.* and *n.* Also with much variety of form as **schick(k)er, shikkar, shikker, shikkur**. [ad. Yiddish *shikker* drunk, poss. reinforced by earlier Brit. dial. or slang SHICKERY q.v.]

A. *adj.* [AND 1898.] Drunk.

1887 *NZ Mail* (Wellington) 15 July 9 (NZ Slang) A drunken man is 'screwed', 'boozed', has a 'skinful', is 'full right up to the knocker', 'squiffy', 'got his tank full', 'perked'..or 'shikkar'. The latter is a popular, because comparatively new, word; and I shall never forget hearing a horsey-looking individual, en route for the Hutt races a year or two ago, say that he had seen 'Arry Rickards' schlintering shikkar' (shamming drunk) at the Theatre the night before. **1905** *Truth* 10 Oct. 5 What penalty will fall on the head of a man who gets schickker. **1921** LORD *Ballads of Bung 'Stunology'* (1976) 11 'Not sober', is another mode and 'sozzled' and 'schicker' as well. **1953** HAMILTON *Till Human Voices Wake Us* 24 The first smoke I had, I was reeling round the hut as if I'd been half-shikker. **1961** CRUMP *Hang On a Minute Mate* 119 'Why didn't they give him a bunk for the night if he was so shikker?' I asked him. **1963** BACON *In the Sticks* 75 I didn't mind when he tried to get the parson shicker, because..you expect good clean fun at a wedding. **1970** *Listener* 12 Oct. 12 After midnight, Jerry got so shicker that he was quarrelling with everyone. **1992** *Evening Post* (Wellington) 17 Oct. 8 No copper on the beat stood over a bloke because he was a bit shicker at 6.30. Being a bit shicker was quite different from being slightly P-word.

B. *n.*

1. a. [AND 1901.] Alcoholic liquor; booze, esp. in the phr. **on the shicker**; occas. drunkenness (see quot. 1906), a drink (see quot. 1910), a drinking bout (see quot. 1917).

1906 *Truth* 4 Aug. 1 A man..who got run in for shicker. **1907** *Ibid.* 16 Mar. 8 Her bad books are to good books what 'Bulletin' bards are to Byron and Shelley—sham, shicker and skite. **1910** *Ibid.* 30 Apr. 1 I wuz in the bar havin' a shikkur. **1911** *Ibid.* 28 Jan. 6 The disgrace attending the circumstance of a highly-respectable citizen being 'shot in' for shikkur was felt by other leading respectable members of Dannevirke community. **1913** CARR *Country Work* 17 Others..could..were it not for the 'shicer' (as drink is called out here) cook for a..passenger boat. **1917** let. in *Boots, Belts* (1992) 47 He..went to the pub and had a glorious shicker. **1943** BENNETT *English in NZ in Amer. Speech* XVIII. 89 *Shicker*..has produced *shickered* and on the *shicker*. **1956** SUTHERLAND *Green Kiwi* (1960) 149 He had known most of the famous bushmen of those days..and also the many instances of their riotous inclinations when 'on the shicker'. **1984** WILSON *S. Pacific Street* 48 It's very naughty of you, Joff. It's a real pain..when you get on the shicker like this.

b. In composition: **shickerhood**, alcoholism; **shikarologist** *joc.*, an expert in, or expert practitioner of, drink or drunkenness; **shicker-up**, a drinking bout.

1920 *Quick March* 10 July 41 He was now at the penultimate State of **shickerhood**. **1914** *The Maunganui Mirror* (Troopship Paper) in *Quick March* 11 Apr. (1921) 27 Marvellous results from using our special ointment, made from the recipe of the famous Maori **Shikarologist**. **1921** FOSTON *At the Front* 57 The men..returned to get another cheque for the next '**shicker-up**'.

2. a. [AND 1906.] A drunk or drunkard.

1906 *Truth* 17 Nov. 5 Magistrate Bishop here wanted to know what an 'old shicker' meant, and he was politely informed..that it was a slang term for a drunken man. **1913** *NZ Observer* 13 Sept. 16 Met a schicker last night. **1947** DAVIN *For Rest of Our Lives* 177 Joy's a shicker..as my old man used to say. **1975** DAVIN *Closing Times* 160 'I thought it was the goy who was supposed to be the shicker,' I said. 'Isn't that your proverb?' 'Where did you learn it?' I told him. A 'shicker' was a drunk in the New Zealand slang of my boyhood and American Jewish friends in Balliol before the war had told me the saying. He was delighted that I knew at least two words of Yiddish. **1984** BEARDSLEY *Blackball 08* 59 'Fine words from a couple of shickers,' said Elizabeth. **1992** *Evening Post* (Wellington) 17 Oct. 8 From time to time the magistrate's Court hosted an absolutely shicker or two from the 6 o'clock swill of the day before.

b. As **shicker express**, a train or tram leaving a terminal shortly after 6.00 p.m. in the days of six o'clock closing of public bars.

c1954 *shicker* (or *drunks'*) *express*: the 6.15 pm train from Wellington to Upper Hutt. (Ed.) **1966** TURNER *Eng. Lang. Austral. & NZ* 131 This gives in New Zealand the terms *vertical drinking*..the *six o'clock swill* and, at least among students in Wellington about 1940, the *shicker express*, the first tram after six o'clock. **1988** MCGILL *Dict. Kiwi Slang* 100 *Shicker Express, The* the first tram running after 6 pm in the days of 6 o'clock pub closing.

shickered /ˈʃɪkəd/, *ppl. a.* Also **shikkared, shikkered, shikkured**. Drunk, boozed.

1905 *Truth* 2 Sept. 1 It isn't always plain when coves who drink are screwed, Though nine or ten would make them 'shickered' in the lingo of the rude. **1910** *Ibid.* 27 Aug. 1 Constable: 'The man with the complainant was also shikkured.' **1916** ANZAC *On Anzac Trail* 27 The boys had fixed to give us a boncer welcome, but..in the words of our informant 'they..got skikkared, and the show bust up'. **1921** FOSTON *At the Front* 121 Some of them were frequently intoxicated, or 'shickered', as it was termed on the works. **1933** PRUDENCE CADEY *Broken Pattern* 130 When he's shickered he drives full out the whole time. **1943** MARSH *Colour Scheme* 10 Bert was half-shickered... He's on the booze again. **1967** MCLATCHIE *Tang of Bush* 97 See that I get on the train, Davy: I'm shickered. **1963** MORRIESON *Scarecrow* 142 To live in that place you'd want to be blind-shickered all the time. **1986** *Listener* 22 Nov. 46 I'm drunk... Drunk. Tanked. Cut. Sloshed. Out of my tree. Shickered to beat the band. **1987** SLIGO *Final Things* 103 They put Big Tom, shickered as a goat, under the showers. **1991** *Metro* (Auckland) Aug. 111 If the old man's always half-shickered and the only thing you're likely to get from him is a smack in the mouth, then the gang is quite an attractive proposition.

Hence by back-formation **shicker** *v. intr.*, to drink alcoholic liquor to excess; to become drunk.

1917 *Hutt Valley Independent* 28 July 4 Though some people do shicker and hand some of their money over to the old woman there are others who obtain a similar reputation owing to ignorant gossip.

shickery /ˈʃɪkəri/, *a. Obs. Rare.* [Poss. f. Brit. slang *shickery* ricketty (see OED); or f. northern

Brit. dial. *shiggry* (*shig* a variant of *jig*) shaky: see EDD.] Shaky; ricketty.
1862 THATCHER *Dunedin Songster 1* 7 The Grand Stand really made me laugh, Up there I did'nt [*sic*] go For fear the shickery planks might break, And pitch me whop below. **1906** *Truth* 1 Dec. 1 Magistrate McArthur..roundly rated an individual named Allbright for having put the police to the trouble of arresting his own companion for the alleged paltry theft of a foul pipe and a bit of tobacco. Why didn't the magistrate rate the police also, who acted on Allbright's shickery charge?

Shield. With or without init. cap. An abbrev. of the names of various sports trophies in the form of shields, esp. (for interprovincial rugby union football) *Ranfurly Shield* [from the name of the donor, the fifth Earl of *Ranfurly*, Governor of NZ 1897–1904, patron of the NZ Rugby Football Union; presented 13 Sept. 1902]; and (for interprovincial cricket) formerly the *Plunket Shield* [from the name of the donor, Lord *Plunket*, Governor of NZ 1904–10; presented in 1907].

1. a. In full **Ranfurly Shield**. See also LOG OF WOOD.
1904 *NZ Observer* 17 Sept. 10 If Taranaki can lift the Shield, it will mean matches next season that we will otherwise not get. **1913** Ibid. 17 May 10 Wellington will meet our reps. in Auckland in a special Ranfurly Shield match. **1926** *Ibid.* 9 June 6 Hawke's Bay had lost the shield and that after getting Cookie and half the All Blacks to go and live in the capital of the province of the wool kings. **1935** *NZ Free Lance* (Wellington) 5 June 51 The same season, Auckland regained the shield. **1958** MCCARTHY *Rugby in My Time* 59 They have one ambition and one only—to hold the Shield, she's a money-spinner. **1968** SLATTER *Pagan Game* 158 When they won the Shield he was home on the pig's back. **1973** WILSON *NZ Jack* 82 We..won the Ranfurly Shield from Auckland. But Auckland's team might have been weakened..the Saturday we took that Log of Wood off them. 'You think Waikato will keep the Shield the whole of this season?' Don asked. **1987** *Dominion* (Wellington) 26 Sept. 2 But this Saturday will be the first time he has ever called a Ranfurly Shield challenge.

b. Used *attrib.* in Comb. **Shield (shield) game, match, team**.
1957 FRAME *Owls Do Cry* (1967) 66 The Saturday night Sports Special..where the racing news was printed, and the results of football and **shield games**. **1959** SLATTER *Gun in My Hand* 45 Gotta see me boy play footie this morning and then we're off to the Shield game. I reckon Canterbury'll run all over them. **1986** KNIGHT *Shield Fever* 124 In these two shield games the Taranaki pack laid the foundation and the backline supplied the finish. **1987** *Evening Post* (Wellington) 26 Sept. 3 **Shield match** live on tv. **1963** GLOVER *Bedside Book* 110 Though we have no players in the **Shield team** as yet, I appear to have belittled Rugby.

c. Special Comb. **shield fever**, the excitement surrounding the build-up to a Ranfurly Shield game; **shield holder**, the provincial union for the time being the winner of a Ranfurly Shield challenge.
1953 *NZ Observer* 9 Sept. 4 Mr. Willis, contemplating..the evidence of '**Shield fever**' in Wellington, delivered himself of this ponderous and humourless observation. **1987** *Evening Post* (Wellington) 15 Sept. 36 Shield fever heightened this time. **1992** *Ibid.* 11 Aug. 21 This time it's only a mild dose, but 1973 saw a severe outbreak in Marlborough of Shield Fever. **1938** *Auckland Weekly News* 7 Sept. 67 Hawkes Bay was confident that it could 'stay' the **Shield holders**.

2. *Hist.* (Usu.) in full **Plunket Shield**. A former interprovincial cricket trophy (see esp. quot. 1982). Also *attrib.*
1910 *Evening Post* (Wellington) 8 Jan. 9 [Heading] Plunket Shield. Given by the 16th Governor, Lord Plunket, to Canterbury for the best record in provincial cricket in 1906-07. **1925** *Ibid.* 3 Jan. 17 Plunket Shield—Auckland's Poor Showing-Canterbury Bowlers in Form. **1930** *Ibid.* 6 Dec. 11 Invariably the Otago cricket selectors experience difficulty in getting players who are chosen to travel North for the Plunket Shield at Christmas. **1934** *Truth* 28 Feb. 5 Canterbury saved their revenge on Wellington for their defeat in the Shield match by properly stoushing the touring team by eight wickets. **1938** *Auckland Weekly News* 5 Jan. 61 He has a century to his credit in Shield cricket. **1957** FRAME *Owls Do Cry* (1967) 13 The same way people stand outside theatres and cricket grounds waiting for the films or the shield match to begin. **1970** *Evening Post* (Wellington) 17 Jan. 9 Otago wickets fell cheaply this morning and the new Plunket Shield-holders were 196 for nine in their second innings against Canterbury. **1982** *NZ Almanac* 384 Plunket Shield... It was competed for on a challenge basis [from 1906–7] until 1921. It was replaced by the Shell Series in the 1975–76 season. *Ibid.* 385 The Plunket Shield, formerly the symbol of provincial supremacy, is now at stake in the intermittent interisland match. On December 19, 1981, the North Island beat the South Island by eight runs in Alexandra.

shield fern: see FERN 2 (17).

shieler, var. SHEILA.

shift, *v.*
1. *intr.* As **shift along**, to move speedily; to travel at a fast pace.
1900 SCOTT *Colonial Turf* 231 And trot! He'd just shift along. **1943** *NZ New Writing* I. 9 I didn't lose any time shifting along.

2. [Spec. use of *shift*: see OED *v*. 20.] *intr.* To move house. Also *trans.*, and as a *vbl. n.*
1927 PEACOCKE *When I was Seven* 175 We 'moved'—the children next door called it a 'shifting', but we were instructed that while it was permissible to say 'moving', only the vulgar said 'shifting'. **1957** p.c. W.J. Jimpson (Tolaga Bay) 1 Dec. [Words heard in N.Z. but not in Britain] 'Shift'; the equivalent is 'move' or, in the words of the professional carrier, 'to remove.' We [British] never shift from one house to another, though a student may 'shift his quarters'. **1992** *North & South* (Auckland) Jan. 87 I learned to wear jandals and say truck (not lorry), chips (not crisps), shift (not move house).

shikkar, shikker, shikkur; shikkared, shikkered, shikkured, varr. SHICKER; SHICKERED.

shilling. [Fig. or transf. uses of *shilling*, a former unit of NZ currency equivalent in value to 12 *pence* or one-twentieth of a *pound*.]

1. In various phrases indicating or alluding to degrees of intellectual handicap or dull-wittedness expressed as 'x pence in the shilling', 'x shillings in the pound'. See also QUID 1. [Prob. f. Brit. dial.: see EDD *shilling: ninepence to the shilling* to be half-witted.] **a. not to be the full shilling, to be a halfpenny short of a shilling, to be sixpence in the shilling**, to be half-witted or simple-minded.
1913 HOWE *Travel Lett.* 112 [Mr. A. said] 'I don't believe he is the full shilling' meaning, 'I don't believe he has good sense'. **1939** EADDY *Neath Swaying Spars* 117 The old captain..must have been what some people term 'a hapenny short of a shilling'.

b. to be (pay) x shillings (bob) in the pound [f. the language of totalisator betting on horse-races], or *ellipt.* **x shillings** (see quot. 1968), **to be x bob short** (*sc.* of a twenty-bob pound: see quot. 1996), to express a degree of intellectual or mental simplicity, handicap or eccentricity on the part of the addressee based on a rough scale from say 1/6 (of low intelligence or severe handicap) to 19 shillings.
1939 NIALL ALEXANDER in Partridge *Dict. Slang Addenda* (1949) 1166 *shillings in the pound.* E.g. *eighteen* or, say, *twelve and six*, to indicate slight mental dullness or mild insanity; 'He's only twelve and six in the pound': New Zealand: since ca. 1925. Niall Alexander, Oct. 22, 1939. **1947** DAVIN *For Rest Our Lives* 118 He wasn't a bad bloke even if he was only fifteen bob in the pound. **1953** HAMILTON *Till Human Voices Wake Us* 147 Good God, said Neil, he was barely six shillings in the pound, used to talk all day about the colours of a motor-bike he had on the outer. **1962** HORI *Half-gallon Jar* 37 I come to the idea that this pakeha is only about eighteen bob in the pound, so I give him the brush off on the excuse that I must go home. **1968** SLATTER *Pagan Game* 153 Every small town has its characters... Joey who was only eighteen shillings,.. the local pervert, the local anarchist. **1981** HUNT *Speaking a Silence* 95 He used to tell the story of one old bloke who wasn't quite twenty bob in the pound, a sort of village idiot. **1993** SINCLAIR *Halfway Round the Harbour* 85 I told off one man..and said that he was only 2/6 in the pound, meaning less than a half-wit. **1996** *Dominion* (Wellington) 24 Feb. 2 Mrs. B.. was shocked at her sister's condition. 'She was two bob short—gross looking,' she said.... Her sister displayed no personality and only opened her mouth when she was told.

2. *Obs.* As **shilling-a-month-man** [AND 1898], an immigrant (usu. of low character) who had worked the passage to New Zealand at the nominal pay of a shilling a month and the passage.
1890 MOORE *NZ for Emigrant* 204 A few rapscallions exported by their friends or who had come as 'shilling-a-month-men' from London, New York, or San Francisco.

3. *Obs.* As **shilling in (and winner shouts)**, a bar-room gambling game to determine who is to pay for drinks in which each participant contributes a shilling and the winner shouts. Cf. *bob in* (BOB *n.*[1] 1).
1880 *Evening Post* (Wellington) 7 Jan. 17 A man had paid his shilling in a game of 'shilling in and winner shout'. **1911** MACAIRE *The Disease & Remedy* 21 That throwing for drinks and gambling ('shilling in-winner pays for drinks') shall be stopped.

4. [f. the shape and size.] A rounded notch in the edge of an axe-blade. Cf. GAP *v.*
1952 LYON *Faring South* 182 To use such [a well-ground] axe on rimu stone veins, as they were termed, on maire, or on certain hard timbers, meant many hours' grinding, and to 'knock a shilling' out of the face of an axe brought one to the soft core.

shimmy. [See OED 'dial. and U.S.', a familiar alteration of *chemise*; see also EDD.] A child's singlet. Cf SINGLET 1.
c1930s Children's rhyme (Ed.). The boy stood on the burning deck In nothing but his shimmy. The flames rolled up and up and up, And burnt his little jimmy. **c1984** p.c. Bill Griffiths (Pakuranga College) July Also I note in the *Macquarie Dictionary* that *shimmy* is given as a diminutive of *chemise*, but in NZ it means a child's singlet. **1988** SMITH *Southlanders at*

Heart 34 Then, as over his head, shirt and 'shimmy' were shed... [1988 *Note*] One-time slang term for 'singlet'.

shingle, *n.*[1] [Fig. use of *shingle* a thin wooden house-tile.]

1. In various phr. alluding to mental retardation. Cf. *have a tile loose.* **a.** In the phr. **to be (have) a shingle short,** to be intellectually 'missing', 'not all there'.

1862 THATCHER *Canterbury Songster* 2 And here you have a *Thatcher* If you're a shingle short! 1868 LYTTELTON *Two Lectures* (Canterbury) 34 Mr. Acland used an odd colonial phrase for a half-witted person: 'shingle-short'. Wooden shingles being used..for house-roofs, it means, weak in the head. 1899 GRACE *Sketch NZ War* 22 I smiled, and ranked him [*sc.* an eccentric major] a shingle short. 1910 *Truth* 16 Apr. 1 His Worship: 'Was the accused sober?'.. Witness: 'He looked either drunk or a shingle short.' His Worship: 'A what?' Witness: 'A screw loose.' His Worship: 'I don't understand you.' Witness: 'He seemed to have a rat in his garret.' His Worship: 'Oh, speak English!' Witness: 'Off his dot—balmy [*sic*]—dilly.' Sergeant: 'He says the man was mad, your Worship.' Witness: 'No, I didn't. I said he was either drunk or ratty.' a1927 ANTHONY *Gus Tomlins* (1977) 106 He was a shingle short, in some ways, and farmed on original lines. 1933 *Press* (Christchurch) (Acland Gloss.) 2 Dec. 15 *Shingle short.*—Silly fellow; foolish. 1957 FRAME *Owls Do Cry* (1967) 21 Francie Withers has a brother who's a shingle short. *Ibid.* 62 Toby Withers, the shingle-short with the dirty fingernails. 1963 CAMPBELL *Golden North* 84 He was a few shingles short in the head but he was harmless. 1970 DAVIN *Not Here Not Now* 8 Her mouth was always open: the lower lip very thick and always wet. She wasn't bad really, but a shingle short somewhere.

b. In the phr. **a shingle loose (off)**, intellectually deficient.

1865 *Punch in Canterbury* 24 We think there are more shingles loose than he speaks of. *Ibid.* 73 Screws loose in the head are rivetted. Shingles off are fixed.

2. In the phr. **to take a shingle off**, to become angry or offended; to 'hit the roof', 'blow one's top'.

1881 BATHGATE *Waitaruna* 132 Gilbert, thinking it best to be civil, thanked the [digger], but declined his offer [of a shout]. 'You must not take a shingle off,' said the landlord addressing him, 'that won't do.'

shingle, *n.*[2] [Extended use of *shingle* small roundish stones, loose water-worn pebbles such as are found on the seashore: see OED *n.*[2] 1 (1598)]

1. In New Zealand *shingle*, in freq. and common general use, is applied to any loose gravel (not necessarily rounded or water-worn, or connected with beaches or river-beds) such as is found on hill or mountain slopes, in the shingle-piles of crushing-plants, or on metalled roads.

[1777 FORSTER *Voyage Round World* I. 204 The latter [*sc.* argillaceous slate] is commonly found in great quantity, and broken pieces, on the sea beaches, and is what our seamen call shingle, by which name it is distinguished in the account of captain Cook's former voyage. 1851 *Lyttelton Times* 21 June 6 The water flows in several streams through a wide bed of shingle.] 1863 GOLDIE in Beattie *Pioneers Explore Otago* (1947) 141 Titaroi [a hill], whose singularly looking shingle upon its top brings it the appellation of 'Whitehead'. 1879 HAAST *Geol. Canterbury & Westland* 174 In examining these angular fragments (usually called shingle in New Zealand, whence the expression 'shingle slips' for these huge taluses of debris covering the mountain sides), we find that they have a polyhedrical shape, their planes being sharply defined, and cutting, as seen in the conglomerates, clean through even the hardest pebbles of which the latter are composed. 1926 *NZ Dairy Produce Exporter* 28 Aug. 29 William, after you have carted a load or two of shingle, set to work and hoe those mangels. 1933 *Press* (Christchurch) (Acland Gloss.) 2 Dec. 15 *Shingle.*—Loose, rather sharp shale or similar rock. Hence *S[hingle] tops*, *shingly basins*, *s[hingl]y facings*, etc. 1959 *Tararua* 13 46 The word *shingle* is given an unusual meaning in New Zealand. In standard usage it refers only to the small roundish water-worn stones of the seashore or rivers. In NZ it is also used of moderately-sized, angular stones, such as in fact are found in shingle slides or are the result of crushing boulders for road metal. 1991 *Dominion* (Wellington) 2 Nov. 10 Progress along Moaville's rural thoroughfares has been a mixture of pounding over potholes, sloshing across sloughs and skidding through shingle.

Hence **shingle** *v. trans.*, to surface a road with road metal; **shingled** *ppl. a.*, of a road, surfaced with road-metal.

1976 VANCE *Bush, Bullocks & Boulders* 200 Through the slump years, Charles Totty went out contracting for the County Council **shingling** the roads with horse and dray for 6/- a yard. 1862 CHUDLEIGH *Diary* 17 Mar. (1950) 58 George and I packed the medium and started tandem for Ch.Ch..breaking the splinter bar coming out and a few such trifles until I got on to the **shingled** road near Ch.Ch. where I stuck.

2. a. Comb. in the sense 'composed of shingle': **shingle-face, flat, slope, terrace**.

1915 *TrNZI* XLVII. 59 Messrs Crosby Smith and Cuthbert again collected it on the **shingle-faces** of Mount Burns, Fiord County. 1883 GREEN *High Alps* (1976) 145 Then came a **shingle flat**, across which we ran to restore circulation to our extremities. 1918 *Chron. NZEF* 2 Aug. 14 With William and James, as with all other residents of Shingle Flat, to think is to act. 1937 *NZ Alpine Jrnl.* VII. 57 It was a mixture of boulder-scrambling and 'bush-hiking' interspersed with a few shingle-flats. 1882 *TrNZI* XIV. 313 *Haastia sinclairii*..[is] not uncommon on **shingle slopes**. 1898 *Ibid.* XXX. 416 And on the edge of the ridge above the shingle slopes were patches of *Euphrasia cuneata*. 1921 *Ibid.* LIII. 96 And it is so upon the steep shingle-slopes of the dry eastern mountains of the neighbourhood. 1862 *Otago Witness* (Dunedin) 23 Aug. 6 The [Clutha Valley] soil consists of rich alluvial flats and **shingle terraces**.

b. Special Comb. **shingle-bank**, in *transf.* or *fig.* use, a stony piece of land; **shingle-bed** [recorded earliest in NZ: see OED *n.*[2] 3], a bed of shingle left by a river; **shingle(d) country**, see quot.; **shingle crusher** (also *ellipt.* **crusher**), a plant for crushing (usu. river) shingle and boulders into various sizes of chips, sand, etc. for building or road-making purposes; **shingle fan**, FAN 1; **shingle heap**, see *shingle-fan* or *slip*; **shingle plant,** any of various native plants adapted to growing on screes and shingle slips; **shingle slide** [OED has NZ quots. only], see *shingle-slip*; **shingle-slip** [OED '*N.Z.*'], the action or result of small stony debris breaking free and slipping down the face of a hillside (see also SLIP *n.*[1]).

1904 *NZ Illustr. Mag.* X. 193 I'm not half sweet enough to invest money in the old man's **shingle-bank** of a farm. 1861 BOWEN *Poems* 76 Ghastly white beneath, Lay stretched the rough, drear, **shingle-bed**. 1879 HAAST *Geol. Canterbury & Westland* 150 These shingle-beds form a plateau—a continuation of the Canterbury plains—the line being easily traced through the Waimakiriri gorge. 1922 *Auckland Weekly News* 23 Feb. 57 Then it was..out of the bush into the water: here it was simply shingle bed and rapids. 1976 VANCE *Bush, Bullocks & Boulders* 75 The bullocks refused to go on the shingle bed. 1991 *Dominion Sunday Times* (Wellington) 3 Nov. 24 [The piano] had to be off-loaded and stand covered by a tarpaulin on a shingle bed for weeks before resuming its journey. 1966 NEWTON *Boss's Story* 189 **shingle country:** Typical South Island high country is characterised by bare shingle tops and face—the latter often 'running' shingle. Accordingly the high country is commonly referred to as shingled country. 1983 STEWART *Springtime in Taranaki* (1991) 197 The shingle bank where the gaunt old **crusher** stood. 1991 *Evening Post* (Wellington) 23 Dec. 2 [Heading] **Shingle crusher** site to be park. The massive crushing plant on the Hutt River bank..is being demolished and piles of boulders and shingle removed... The operators of the concrete block plant just south of the old shingle crusher have a lease which has 18 years to run. 1879 HAAST *Geol. Canterbury & Westland* 131 For two miles more we kept along the eastern side of the valley, travelling mostly on the slopes of huge **shingle-fans**. 1915 *TrNZI* XLVII. 334 A number of introduced plants..have made their appearance on the shingle-fan and in the river-beds. 1864 HOOKER *Handbook NZ Flora* 142 **Shingle heaps** on the alps. 1908 *TrNZI* XL. 281 This [*Veronica spathulata*] is a true **shingle-plant**. 1912 *Ibid.* XLIV. 209 Only specially adapted shingle-plants, such as *Muehlenbeckia*, could, therefore hope to survive in such a station. 1914 *Ibid.* XLVI. 42 The extensive shingle-slips of the Ruahine tops are worthy of a more searching examination, but a hasty one revealed a South Island shingle-plant hitherto unrecorded from the North Island in *Epilobium pycnostachyum*. 1927 WALL *Alpine & Sub-Alpine Flora* in *Nat. Hist. Canterbury* 151 'Shingle plants', e.g. form a perfectly distinctive group and hardly one of them is ever found in any other locality than a true 'scree' or 'shingle-slip'. 1948 HAAST *Julius Von Haast* 181 The names of the friends are associated in the 'Shingle Plant', *Haastia Sinclairi*. 1959 *Tararua* 46 *Shingle plant* for the type of plant which grows on shingle or shingle slides may be noted in passing. 1873 *TrNZI* V. 286 Habitat, **shingle slides**. 1896 *NZ Alpine Jrnl.* IX. 189 Once off the rock we were able to enjoy the pleasure of a shingle slide, a few minutes of which soon saw us at the base of the hill. 1934 *Press* (Christchurch) (Acland Gloss.) 27 Jan. 15 *Shingle slide.*—Shingle slip, loose shale on a facing. 1952 THOMSON *Deer Hunter* 15 Where bush and tussock had grown before, bare and barren shingle slides began to fan out. 1981 CHARLES *Black Billy Tea* 91 I was sitting on a shingle slide in the bush beneath the snow. 1864 HOOKER *Handbook NZ Flora* 11 **Shingle slips**, Wairau Gorge, alt. 4500 ft. 1879 HAAST *Geol. Canterbury & Westland* 36 The shingle-slips..are also not without an interesting vegetation. 1885 *TrNZI* XVII. 352 At times we were scrambling through the thick bush or over steep shingle slips. 1900 *Canterbury Old & New* 190 One of the most characteristic features of our Canterbury Alps is afforded by the numerous 'shingle-slips' formed by the weathering of the rocks, and often covering almost entire hill-sides. 1910 COCKAYNE *NZ Plants & Their Story* 97 As the traveller wearily ascends these 'shingle-slips', as they are called, the stones constantly slip beneath his tread. 1927 *TrNZI* LVII. 82 There are a few moderate sized shingle-slips on the slopes of Middle Peel. 1928 COCKAYNE *Vegetation of NZ* 289 Shingle-slip, in its unstable typical form, is confined to those mountains of South Island with a tussock-grassland climate. 1944 *Modern Jun. Dict.* (Whitcombe & Tombs 7edn.) 365 Shingle-slide or *-slip*... a term used in New Zealand for (steep) mountain-sides covered with loose, sliding stones, in England called 'screes'. 1958 PASCOE *Great Days in NZ Mountaineering* 42 Scrambling through thick bush or over steep shingle slips..was laborious. **1966** shingle country [see 2 b above]. **1971** *Listener* 19 Apr. 56 The creek beside the shingle slip just below the confluence.

shingly, *a.* [Spec. use of *shingly* f. SHINGLE *n.*²] Consisting of, mixed with, or covered with shingle or scree.

1857 *Richmond-Atkinson Papers* (1960) I. 318 Their beds are often a mile wide or more banded by shingly cliffs. **1863** GOLDIE in Beattie *Pioneers Explore Otago* (1947) 141 The Takatimos, whose shingly sides and high backed rugged peaks plainly show the effect of Time's destroying influence. **1873** BARKER *Station Amusements* 55 Grass would not grow there except in summer, and its gray, shingly sides were an eye-sore. **1939** BROWN *Farmer's Wife* 42 Often has he discussed subsoil, sandy, clayey or shingly. **1949** WOODHOUSE in Currie *Centennial Treasury Otago Verse* 87 The shingly rivers seaward swirling.

shining cuckoo: see CUCKOO 2 (3).

shin plaster. Also **shin plaister**, **skin plaster**. [Orig. US *shin-plaster* a piece of privately issued low denomination paper money: see OED *shin* 5.] Applied to small-denomination tokens or paper issued by private traders; occas. applied to official or quasi-official issues often considered of low real value.

c1871 MASTERS *Autobiography* (ATLMS) 26 Many tradesmen [in the early 1840s] had to make their own money on strips of paper called by the settlers 'shin plaisters'. Governor Grey [*sic*] established a bank issue and issued one pound promisery [*sic*] notes, to get change for one of these, you would get a hat full of shin plaisters. **1890** *Otago Witness* (Dunedin) 20 Feb. 17 A feature of this exhibit is a number of debentures or 'shin plasters' as they were irreverently termed, which were put into circulation during the term of governorship of Captain Fitzroy... The Government debentures were for 5s., but the private ones were for sums ranging down as low as 3d. **c1910** MACDONALD *Reminiscences* (VUWTS) 109 The retail business in the town was carried on [c1840s] mostly by means of little bits of printed paper, issued by shopkeepers, for from one penny to two or three shillings. This currency went by the general name of 'shin plaster'. *Ibid*. 117 When eggs fell [c1840s] from six silver shillings per dozen to one shilling of 'shin plasters', the Hutt, Porirua Road and Karori settlers looked anxious. **1941** SUTHERLAND *Numismatic Hist. NZ* 158 *Shinplasters.*—The fact that private traders found it necessary themselves, to issue paper notes in denominations below five shillings suggests that at the outset..the Fitzroy notes were not issued for values below five shillings. The private paper notes were issued for small change, redeemable mostly in 'Five Shillings, in Government debentures.' Both the debentures and the private notes were issued on poor paper, and soon became known as 'Government Rags' and 'Shinplasters' respectively. The term 'Shinplaster' for paper money appears to have come to New Zealand from America, via New South Wales. **1972** HARGREAVES *Beads to Banknotes* 40 The [Governor Fitzroy's (1844)] Debentures, popularly known as 'government rags', were given various nicknames such as 'assignats', 'shinplasters', and 'flash notes'... 'Shinplasters'—sometimes written 'skinplasters'—had its origin in North America, and again referred to depreciated paper money. *Ibid*. 78 The Southland Treasury had no legal liability for the payment of the notes if issued as they had never been sanctioned by law, and would circulate merely as the personal promissory note of whoever signed them. It is no wonder, then, that the *Otago Daily Times* (Dunedin) called them 'Southland Shinplasters'.

ship-girl. A young woman or (often part-time) prostitute, who seeks a good or profitable time with seafarers. **a.** In early North Island use.

1827 WILLIAMS *Early Jrnls.* 22 Apr. (1961) 53 I afterwards visited three settlements towards Waitangi. The first a few Natives from inland; the second a company of Ship girls. **1908** *TrNZI* XL. 159 One of the heaviest prices paid for the guns—and, in its far-reaching effects, one of the principal causes of the decay of the Maoris—was the institution known as that of the 'ship-girls'. **1922** COWAN *NZ Wars* (1955) I. 7 From the dawn of civilized enterprise on our coasts we hear of Kororareka and its fleets of whalers at anchor, its Maori 'ship-girls', its gun-play between quarrelsome Maori *hapus*, and its all-pervading flavour of licence and lawlessness. **1993** *Defence Quarterly* No.1 12 Clusters of canoes and boats [at Kororareka c1845]..that were quickly launched to carry out the shipgirls to meet each whaler as it arrived.

b. In modern use. Also **ship-moll**, **shippie**. See also BOATGIRL.

1968 *Crime in NZ* 247 Most of the 'ship girls' in New Zealand are not prostitutes. They are more often girls who find it difficult to establish ordinary boy-girl relationships—the lonely girls, the plain girls. **1973** *Salient* (Wellington) 19 Sept. 10 Two of my shippie mates who were both butch actually 'cracked it' so seldom they were more sexually moral than most varsity students. *Ibid*. 11 The other main regulars of the bistro are the ship molls and the hillybins (lesbians). **1982** *Truth* 19 Jan. 7 Napier is the best place for new ship girls to get used to the ropes. **1987** *Dominion* (Wellington) 21 July 13 Probably the least prestigious members of Wellington's prostitution community are the 'ship girls', who work on the boats or the wharves. **1989** 12 Apr. TV1 drama *Shark in the Park*. There was a shippie working the coastline riddled with clap. Ship-molls make me sick. **1993** *Dominion* (Wellington) 23 Jan. 6 She was said to have caught a ride on a ship leaving port that night... Speculation Judy was a 'ship girl' was also denied.

ship-moll, shippie: see SHIP-GIRL b.

shirker. WW1. [Spec. use of *shirker* one who evades responsibility: AND 1918.] A young man not volunteering for military service in WW1.

1915 *Hutt Valley Independent* 16 Oct. 4 A 'shirker wedding'.

shirt: *shake one's shirt*, see SHAKE *v*. 1.

shiser, var. SHICER.

shit, *n*. In various phrases: **a. not to be able to tell (or not to know) shit from clay**, to be very stupid or ignorant.

1944 FULLARTON *Troop Target* 121 I can't tell excreta from clay where strategy is concerned. **1984** *Islands* 33 3 Poor young android Americans from the new-clear warship *Truxton* who wouldn't know shit from clay if it was hurled in their faces. **1993** O'SULLIVAN *Let the River Stand* 11 Does he see a great deal, people would often wonder, or doesn't he know shit from clay?

b. to push shit uphill, to work hard at an (apparently) worthless enterprise, argument, etc.

1985 BINNEY *Long Lives the King* 26 'I reckoned Andy was pushing shit uphill,' said Burnsie, 'setting up that sort of a show; but I got to hand it to him... It must be worth a buck or two for him now.' **1991** *Sunday Star* (Auckland) 22 Dec. C11 Insipid Sports Segment. TVNZ's..America's Cup..clips from Jane Dent... Not her fault. The lady is pushing the proverbial uphill.

shit, *v*. In various phrases: **a. rip, shit, and (or) bust**, see RIP, SHIT AND (OR) BUST.

b. he'd (she'd) shit anywhere, said of a person who can fit into any company.

1952 *Landfall* 23 208 Think of the animal comeback in the remark, common among New Zealand troops, usually said with a touch of flattery: 'He's a nice chap, he'd shit anywhere.'

shit, *int*. As **shit-a-brick!**, a rhythmic elaboration of 'shit!' expressing surprise.

1965 SHADBOLT *Among Cinders* 83 'A queer thing...' 'Shit a brick,' he said. **1974** MORRIESON *Predicament* (1981) 160 The buzzing ceased. 'Shitabrick,' said the Spook. The winking man held up his hand. 'Don't panic.' **1988** MCGILL *Dict. Kiwi Slang* 101 *shit a brick* exclamation of annoyance and/or surprise.

shit-fish. [See quot.] A local Auckland term for PARORE.

1987 *Listener* 8 Aug. 61 Sometimes men, using bread for bait, caught parore [off Point Chevalier], which we called black snapper or 'shit-fish', because they were reputed to eat at sewer outlets.

shitty. [AND 1982.] A fit of bad temper, esp. in the phr. **to throw (crack) a shitty**, to put on a display of bad temper.

1971 SHADBOLT *Bullshit & Jellybeans* 34 Jo went off on an oasis crawl and when he came back she [*sc*. his chick] was up the duff. Well, old Jo throws a bit of a shitty but Mary tells him about this invisible guy God who'd done it. **1980** *Islands* 29 137 Now he was drinking and Miller heard him say, 'My old man'd throw a shitty if he was here.' **1988** MCGILL *Dict. Kiwi Slang* 101 *shitty* bad mood, phrs. *crack a shitty, pack a shitty, throw a shitty*; eg 'I bet you he throws a shitty now we're starting to win.'

shivery dick. *Obs.* A schoolchildren's exclamation.

1953 SUTTON-SMITH *Unorganized Games NZ Primary School Children* (VUWTS) II. 677 Some of the [slang] expressions listed by children..are 'Up the shoot..shivery dick, shiver me timbers'. **1972** SUTTON-SMITH *Folkgames Children* 138 [c1920–50] there are vigorous *Slanging Contests* in which the contestants try to outdo each other by using phrases like the following: 'You're up the shoot.'.. 'Shivery dick'.

shivoo /ʃɪˈvuː/. [ad. French *chez vous* 'at your place', variously anglicized, hence an 'at home', a party: see OED *shiveau*; EDD *sheevo* Yorkshire and Cornwall; AND 1844.] A social gathering or celebration; a meeting.

1900 *Otago Witness* (Dunedin) 18 Jan. 57 Reveille was called a little bit later after this shivoo, which one and all had voted a fitting end to a great night! **1906** *Truth* 18 Aug. 5 Amid mighty applause, from deadheads particularly, the mutual admiration shivooed ended. **1913** *NZ Observer* 28 June 7 Canadian Commissioner Beddoe, who was one of the few bachelors at the shivoo, said it was a 'survival of the fittest'. **1914** PFAFF *Digger's Story* 34 Dick stepped forward, much to the consternation of the organisers of the 'shivoo' [*sc*. a political meeting]. **1946** BRUNO *Maleesh George* 28 He had a bit of a head himself from a shivoo in the Officers' Mess. **1955** *BJ Cameron Collection* (TS July) shivoo (n) A celebration, drinking-bout. **1968** *NZ Contemp. Dict. Suppl*. (Collins) 18 *shivoo..n*. (*Sl*.) party celebration, entertainment.

shleinter, shlinter /ˈʃlɪntə/, varr. SLINTER.

shoddy-dropper. *Obs.* [f. *shoddy* woollen yarn + *dropper* one who delivers goods: AND 1950.] A seller of cheap goods, orig. serge cloth.
   1932 BAYLIS in Partridge *Dict. Underworld* (1961) 620 A seller of cheap serge: New Zealand: 1932, Nelson Baylis (private letter). **1941** BAKER *NZ Slang* 52 Underworld slang [includes]..*shoddy dropper*, a seller of cheap serge.
   Hence **shoddy-dropping** *vbl. n.*, see quot. 1953.
   1953 *NZ Observer* 16 Dec. 5 'Shoddy dropping' consist of talking men into buying cheap watches by pretending they are costly ones which have come into the country illegally. **1953** *Ibid.* 23 Sept. 7 'Shoddy dropping' and 'dudding' are lawful occupations at present.

shoe. *Forestry.* [Spec. use of *shoe* for a shoe-like fitting: see OED *n*. 5.] A metal sheet (or equivalent device) placed under the nose of a log to facilitate ground-hauling. See also DISH *n.*², PAN *n.*² 1, *snigging-pan*, *shoe* (SNIGGING 2).
   1904 LANCASTER *Sons o' Men* 165 He heaved up the shoe—which is a much over-grown road-scoop tilted at the nose..and wrenched at the wire-rope that had its beginnings on the engine-drum. **1952–53** *NZ Forest Service Gloss.* (TS) Shoe. Snigging pan. **1982** SANSOM *In Grip of Island* 32 Behind one heap of fireplace stones is a whale's skull, once used as a 'shoe' to bring out logs.
   Hence **shoeman**, see quot. 1985.
   1904 LANCASTER *Sons o' Men* 158 Lavel was a shoeman, and Cornell was driver of the little eight–horse power engine that hauled the shoe. **1924** *Otago Witness* (Dunedin) 22 Jan. 72 A man called a shoeman follows the logs up till they get to the mill. **1983** BREMER *Port Craig* 5 The man accompanying the logs to the hauler was known as a shoeman and he generally had a whistle boy who stopped the hauler by means of a whistle when the log reached one of the snatch blocks. **1985** May p.c. Ivan Bannister (Canvastown). In logging to the mill skids the man who puts the shoe over the nose of the log to save sniping is the shoeman.

shoemaker. [Poss. from its tapping or clattering call reminiscent of a cobbler cobbling: see OED 2 b, applied to the Antarctic skua.] A name applied to various species of petrel, usually the white-chinned shoemaker; also as **Westland shoemaker**, the closely related Westland black petrel (see PETREL 2 (20), (21).
   1955 OLIVER *NZ Birds* 145 *Westland Shoemaker. Procellaria aequinoctialis westlandica. Ibid.* 146 *White-chinned Petrel. Shoemaker. Procellaria aequinoctialis aequinoctialis.* **1966** FALLA et al. *Birds NZ* 47 White-chinned Petrel... A clacking sound is made from within the burrow and is said to be uttered also by birds sitting at the mouth of the burrow. Hence the old sealers' name 'shoemaker'. **1970** JENKIN *NZ Mysteries* 157 The identity of this bird [*sc.* hakuwai] is still in doubt. Most of the petrels have been suggested at some stage, including the bird the whalers called the Shoemaker because of the tapping noise it made. **1985** *Reader's Digest Book NZ Birds* 92 An alternative name for the white-chinned petrel is the shoemaker. This refers to the chattering call which may sound like a cobbler stitching a shoe. **1989** PARKINSON *Travelling Naturalist* 172 This bird [*sc.* the Westland black petrel], once called the Westland shoemaker because of its distinctive call, survives only here.

shonky, *a.* [Prob. from *shonk* (abbrev. of *shonicker*) an offensive name for a Jew: AND 1970.] Dishonest, shady (esp. in business dealings); shaky, unsafe (of physical things).
   1987 *Sunday Star* (Auckland) 10 May M2 Australian authorities have cracked down on fringe market operators on their side of the Tasman. As a result a number of these shonky operators have set up shop in deregulated New Zealand. **1991** *Evening Post* (Wellington) 17 Oct. 19 The economic future of New Zealand is being prejudiced by shonky economic advice with ridiculous and unacceptable margins of error. **1992** *Ibid.* 22 June 4 This is not to say public anxiety about shonky political goings on has no validity. **1992** *North & South* (Auckland) Nov. 99 Even back in '72, its foundations were so shonky that the floor was like a roller coaster.

shook, *ppl. a.* [f. an archaic or dial. *pa. ppl.* of *shake v.* to quiver with emotion: see OED *shake v.* 11, and *shook*; AND *shake v.*, 1868.] **a.** In the phr. **(to be) shook on** (a person or thing), (to be) greatly taken with, (to be) keen on, (to be) enamoured of.
   1875 WOOD & LAPHAM *Waiting for Mail* 80 That cousin of her's [*sic*] is awfully shook on her. **1908** *Truth* 28 Nov. 1 You may be dead shook on the girl, but that doesn't give you license to gently bite her ear as you go spinning round..in a merry waltz. **1915** *Triad* 10 July 415 Alan's a bit shook on Miss Lestrange, isn't he, mother? **1926** DEVANNY *Butcher Shop* (1981) 51 The state of mind described by girls she knew as being 'shook' on a man. **1937** MARSH *Vintage Murder* 9 What they used to call 'shook on the pros'... He hangs around Carolyn [the star actress]. **1955** *BJ Cameron Collection* (TS July) shook on Fond of, in love with.
   b. In negative constructions, poss. the most freq. modern use, esp. as **not too shook (on)**, not (too) keen on.
   a**1927** ANTHONY *Me & Gus* (1977 Gus Tomlins) 73 I can't say I was shook on Gus's style. **1933** PRUDENCE CADEY *Broken Pattern* 95 If you find you're not too shook on it up there..just come and look us up. **1936** SARGESON *Conversation with Uncle* 26 He wasn't shook on women anyhow. **1960** MUIR *Word for Word* 109 I told you I'm not shook on those Maori words. **1965** SHADBOLT *Among Cinders* 209 'Still not keen on it, are you?' 'On what?' 'The bush. Still not too bloody shook on it, are you? I can tell.' **1988** McGILL *Dict. Kiwi Slang* 101 *shook on* very keen on person or thing; eg 'I can't say I'm much shook on a guy who marches in as if he owns the place.'

shoot *n.*: see CHUTE.

shoot through, *v.*
   1. [AND 1947.] To leave quickly; to disappear; to escape.
   1956 *Evening Post* (Wellington) 11 Aug. 15 'The bloke who really started the blue isn't here—he shot through,' said Purda [a 22-year-old Hungarian workman]. **1962** *Ibid.* 31 Oct. 19 Auckland Prison escaper..claimed..he 'shot through' because he was not being fairly treated. **1968** BAXTER *Collected Plays* (1982) 123 Well—he puts me in the family way—and then he shoots through. I've not seen hide nor hair of him since. **1987** *Metro* (Auckland) May 62 Men shed their responsibilities by shooting through to places unknown. **1991** *Listener* 10 June 40 When he got there it turned out that James had decided, rather than confront the might of Don McKinnon, to shoot through to the Middle East.
   2. In the phr. **to shoot through on** (someone), to desert (a person), to leave in the lurch. Cf. *blow through* (BLOW *v.*⁴ 2).
   1961 CRUMP *Hang On a Minute Mate* 11 He'd probably never miss the Old Girl if he shot through on her. *Ibid.* 190 What'd y' do, Sam? Shoot through on 'im? **1963** DUCKWORTH *Barbarous Tongue* 158 'Why are you home, anyway? I thought you had a job up north?' He shrugged. 'Did have. Bob's shot through on me.' 'What?' He was using expressions picked up from Bob and I wasn't sure of their meaning. **1965** WATSON *Stand in Rain* 57 That's what I come [*sic*] all the way up here for, to get me old mate Tommy, he wouldn't shoot through on a man.
   Hence *ppl. a.* **shooting-through**, with reference to (the need for) a sudden departure.
   1993 *Evening Post* (Wellington) 28 May 9 Many women had nest eggs, with some describing them as 'my shooting-through money'.

shoot in, *v.* To throw (someone) into gaol, esp. in the passive phr. **to be shot in**.
   1910 *Truth* 14 May 7 More care should be taken by the police in shooting in people for making themselves offensive in a public place. **1911** [see SHICKER B 1 a]. **1947** NEWTON *Wayleggo* 38 How we saw that day out without getting 'shot in' is a mystery to me yet. **1949** NEWTON *High Country Days* 14 [He] had nearly got 'shot in' for getting into a drunken argument with a fishmonger.

shooting-stick. *Obs.* In early whalers' or traders' parlance, a gun.
   1845 WAKEFIELD *Adventure NZ* I. 319 Every article of trade with the natives has its slang term,—in order that they may converse with each other respecting a purchase without initiating the natives into their calculations. Thus pigs and potatoes were respectively represented by '*grunters*' and '*spuds*', guns..by '*shooting-sticks*'.

shooting-timber. [Poss. an alteration of a dial. pronunciation /ˈʃʊtɪŋ/ of *shutting*, that is, timber which 'shuts' in on the saw-blade: see EDD.] See quot.
   1953 REED *Story of Kauri* 162 After the saw had bitten well into the heart-wood..it might encounter what was known as 'shooting-timber'. This was a peculiar condition which caused the interior wood to close in on the saw, impede its movement, and, in a bad case, bring it to a complete standstill.

shop butter: see BUTTER 2.

shore.
   1. *Hist.* Used *attrib.* in special Comb. denoting whaling (occas. sealing) carried out from a shore-based as distinct from a ship-based station: **shore fishery**, **shore-fishing**, a whale fishery, or whaling, operated from a shore base; **shore-party**, a whaling party which operates from a shore-station; **shore sealing**, see quot.; **shore station**, the coastal headquarters of a local shore-whaling operation; **shore-whale** *attrib.*, see *shore-whaling*; **shore whaleman, shore-whaler**, one who engages in shore-whaling; **shore-whaling**, whaling carried out entirely from a shore-based whaling station taking whales close to the coast, as distinct from deep-sea or coastal whaling carried out from a whaler (cf. *bay whaling* (BAY 2)); **shore-whaling station**, see *shore-station*.
   1848 WAKEFIELD *Handbook NZ* 193 [Table] **Shore fisheries** depending on the port... Name of Station..Tons of Black Oil. **1842** HEAPHY *NZ* 123 The great number of whale-ships..proves the Chathams to be a fit locality for **shore-fishing**. **1831** BELL *Let.* Nov. in McNab *Old Whaling Days* (1913) 3 The black whale fishery..was abandoned until last year, when it was renewed by one vessel and two **shore parties** from Sydney, and one vessel from Hobart Town. *Ibid.* 9 If the fishing is to be

short-finned eel: see EEL 2 (7).

shortie. *Crayfishing.* [f. *short* + -IE.] An undersized crayfish with a tail less than 150 mm in length.

1983 2YA Wellington 3 Dec. Rural Programme on Crayfishing in the Fiordland Sounds used the term *shortie* and defined it as an undersized crayfish. **1984** *NZ Times* 2 Sept. 9 Des did what he reckons almost every crayfisherman does; he bought home a feed of 'shorties' (illegal-sized crayfish) for his mates. It was to be a treat, Southland hospitality... A fisheries inspector was on the wharf at Riverton when Des returned. The inspector seized the sacks of 'shorties'.

shot, *n. Goldmining.* [Prob. a dial. var. of *shoot* a considerable mass of ore in a vein: see OED *shoot n.*[1]] A considerable mass of auriferous material occurring at intervals in a quartz lode.

1892 *NZ Official Handbook* 184 The gold [in lodes] is found in shots, which seldom exceed 400ft. in length; the barren part will come in and cut off the gold, though the structural appearance of the quartz may remain almost the same; still by driving along the lode for some distance, another shot of gold is likely to be found. **1898** 'H' *Grain of Gold* 13 He told of rich 'shots' which had to be abandoned because the water came in and flooded the miners out.

shot, *ppl. a.* Also **half-shot.** [See OED *ppl. a.* 'Chiefly *U.S., Austral.* and *N.Z.*'; AND 1913.] Drunk, tipsy; also in the phr. **shot full of holes,** drunk.

1941 BAKER *NZ Slang* 50 *shot full of holes*, drunk (an elaboration of *shot*). **1943** MARSH *Colour Scheme* x 187 The chap was half-shot... He smelt of booze. **1957** *Nelson Evening Mail* 18 May 7 He asked the man: 'Are you shot?' The man said: 'Yes'... It was ascertained that he had fallen down while intoxicated.

shottie, *n.* [f. *shot*(gun + -IE.] A shotgun.

1980 BATTYE & EAKIN *Shadow of Valley* 42 He set his trap and sat down to wait behind a tree—with his shottie in his hand. *Ibid.* 72 shottie *shot-gun*.

shotty, *a. Goldmining.* [Spec. use of *shotty* resembling shot or pellets of lead: AND 1860.] Esp. as **shotty gold,** alluvial gold found in a pellet form resembling gun-shot.

1861 *NZ Goldfields 1861* (1976) 29 The general character of the gold being scaly and fine, the reverse of shotty. **1875** HOGG *Lays & Rhymes* 176 'Twas when the Rocky River rush began..and stories told Of ounces gotten in a single pan, Of nuggety, and round, and shotty gold. **1887** *Handbook NZ Mines* 130 The gold was heavy and shotty. **1890** *Otago Witness* (Dunedin) 6 Mar. 18 From Torrie Bros.' claim..there is a sample of coarse shotty gold. **1906** GALVIN *NZ Mining Handbook* 134 Gold is from fine to shotty. **1924** *Grey River Argus* 9 Feb. 7 It is shotty, not flaky gold, that is the Diggers Delight. **1937** AYSON *Thomas* 29 The result was that in a few afternoons he had filled a tin matchbox with coarse, shotty gold. **1953** SUTHERLAND *Golden Bush* (1963) 119 There was nothing very big but it was chunky and rough, 'shotty' as the diggings called it. **1967** MAY *West Coast Gold Rushes* 161 The gold was shotty and coarse compared with the fine, flaky deposits of Waimea and Kaniere. **1970** WOOD *Gold Trails Otago* 81 Crevicing can be a fascinating occupation, for one never knows when one might find a virgin crevice with its quota of shotty gold and even a small nugget. **1984** BEARDSLEY *Blackball 08* (Gloss.) 245 shotty gold[:] hard, round pieces of gold.

shouse. Also **shoush.** [Syncopated form of *sh*(ith)*ouse*: AND 1941.] A toilet.

1968 SLATTER *Pagan Game* 71 He had heard a shoush rumour that they were going down to Trasimeno to get all regimental for the transfer to the Pacific. **1988** McGILL *Dict. Kiwi Slang* 102 *shouse* something very bad; contraction of 'shithouse'; eg 'It's total shouse out there, why not wait until it eases, eh?'

shout, *v.* [Transf. use of *shout* to call (for drinks).]

1. [AND 1854.] *trans.* **a.** As **shout** (a drink), to stand (a drink).

1855 *Nelson Examiner* 14 Nov. 2 The supposed digger..'shouted' champagne *ad. lib.* **1868** DILKE *Greater Britain* I. 339 At every halt one or other of the passengers is expected to 'shout', or 'stand', as it would be called at home, 'drinks all round'. 'What'll yer shout?' is the only question. **1967** HARPER *Kettle on the Fuchsia* 49 I've known good men..go down to..Christchurch, and knock down £200 in a week, shouting grog on all sides to anyone that..can be induced to drink. **1981** HUNT *Speaking A Silence* 42 They were always trying to kid me to shout drinks.

b. As **shout** (a drink) **for** (someone), to buy (a drink or round of drinks) for (a person or group).

1856 HARPER *Lett. from NZ* 25 Dec. (1914) 10 To say nothing of the fact that the first person in New Zealand to 'shout' for me, which here means to ask you into a house of call and stand treat, should be the great Bishop! **1863** *Lyttelton Times* 31 Dec. 4 We have seen boys encouraged by their elders to think it manly to 'shout' and to drink at bars. **1874** BATHGATE *Col. Experiences* 90 [Diggers] 'shout for all hands' (ie., treat everyone in the house to drink). **1888** D'AVIGDOR *Antipodean Notes* 48 The chap would hang about till some digger would *shout* to all comers. [1888 Note] Shout: Colonial for offering drinks. **c1895** DOUGLAS in *Mr Explorer Douglas* (1957) 16 The few cityzens [*sic*] [of Okarito] spend their time shouting for each other. **1904** *NZ Observer* 4 June 17 An Otahuhu farmer..was betrayed the other day into..'shouting' for a company of some fourteen persons. **1935** STRONG in Partridge *Slang Today* 287 I bet our guns will lay it down thick and heavy, and if I get out of the smack-up with a whole skin I will shout for all hands. **1953** STRONACH *Musterer on Molesworth* 69 Then—the old, old custom—he took us over to the hotel and shouted for us. **c1962** BAXTER *Horse* (1985) 83 Gandhi..insisted on shouting seven dog's-noses for Horse in the bar of the Shamrock. **1971** TAYLOR *Plekhov Place* 132 Had three double brandies and shouted a round for all the others which set me back considerably more than I had bargained for.

c. As **shout** (someone), to treat (someone) to (a drink), to stand (someone a drink).

1877 BROOMHALL *Fragments from the Jrnl.* 41 When at the Bay of Islands a native asked me to 'shout' him, I thought him mad. He saw my difficulty and vociferated, 'a pint of beer! a pint of beer!' My guide explained that to 'shout' a man is 'to stand treat'. **1934** *Truth* 16 May 15 Claridge shouted him another whisky. **1946** SOLJAK *NZ* 115 Following are examples of colloquialisms common to New Zealand and Australian English, with their English or American equivalent... *shout*: treat; e.g. *I'll shout you to a drink*. **1947** GASKELL *Big Game* 23 In I goes and he shouts me a couple.

2. *intr.* To stand treat.

1862 HODDER *Memories NZ Life* 123 Among this class [of Wairau shepherds], going to these [public houses] and 'shouting' (which is another word for spending their evenings in drunken, disgraceful revelry, which lasts for a week or a fortnight at a time) is considered the acme of pleasure. **1869** *Grey River Argus* 23 Jan. 2 If the girls went to bed at twelve o'clock when [bar-room] dancing was over, they would be 'growled' at by Mrs Crawford if there were men about the bar 'shouting'. **1875** WOOD & LAPHAM *Waiting for Mail* 79 'Will you shout if she comes?' 'Yes, I'll shout.' **1881** BATHGATE *Waitaruna* 220 The doctor got the credit..of never refusing a drink and seldom 'shouting'. **1943** BENNETT *English in NZ* in *Amer. Speech* XVIII. 89 *to shout* is, specifically, to 'stand a drink'..but it now also means to treat another person, no matter what the place or occasion. **1960** HILLIARD *Maori Girl* 233 As Arthur pushed to the door the Samoan girl thrust her face into his and demanded, 'Aincha gonna shout?'

3. [AND 1896.] *trans.* To stand treat (for other than liquor), to make a present of (something) to (a person).
 1904 *NZ Observer* 11 June 4 His wife 'shouted' the trip. **1944** *Short Guide NZ* (Gloss. Slang) 39 *Shout*—buy something for someone (often a drink). **1965** MCLAGLAN *Stethoscope & Saddlebags* 184 She shouted the two elder teenage boys a trip to Wellington. **1968** GRUNDY *Who'd Marry a Doctor?* 50 At Christmas, George had shouted me a call home to my family.

shout, *n.* [f. SHOUT *v.*: used elsewhere, but recorded earliest in Austral., then NZ.]

1. [AND 1854.] A free drink, or round of drinks, purchased for or given to a person or group; a 'treat'.
 1869 THATCHER *Local Songs* 33 Eicke's constitution, we hear, Was so delicate... That on the journey he'd be queer, Unless sustained by bottled beer... So of grog they took a good supply When they went to Ohinemuri. Their life was one continual shout, They stayed up there and idled about. **1887** HOPEFUL *Taken In* 135 When one friend meets another very often the greeting will be, 'Are you going to stand "shout"?' in other words, 'Are you going to stand drink or "treat"?' If this is agreed to they will adjourn to the nearest inn, or hotels as these poor little match-boxes are called. **1906** *Truth* 12 May 1 Half-a-dozen luggers, Waiting for a shout. **1909** THOMPSON *Ballads About Business* 27 A poundt a shout vos a common ding. **1924** *Otago Witness* (Dunedin) 11 Mar. 60 Before banks had been established, the diggers frequently paid for shouts..by doling out gold dust with a teaspoon from a chamois leather bag.

2. [AND 1882.] **a.** A turn in paying for (a round of) usu. alcoholic drinks.
 1880 LAPHAM *We Four* 25 There were two of three more shouts. **1904** *NZ Observer* 11 June 16 Last week's story about the canny Otahuhu farmer who managed a seven-shilling 'shout' with a five-shilling bottle of whisky is capped by another. **1917** *Truth* 1 Dec. 2 He would swear he saw two shouts. **1960** KEINZLY *Tangahano* 72 If you like to bring your wife and a glass they'll let you through the door. Also, you don't have to knock with your elbow—it's his shout. **1969** MASON *Awatea* (1978) 56 Gilhooly... My shout! Always shout yer, New Year's Eve.

b. As **house shout,** the turn of the 'house' or publican to by a free drink or round of drinks for a customer or school.
 1939 *Taranaki Herald* (New Plymouth) 19 Aug. 3 Employees of the Addington railway workshops are in accord with the..waterside workers in their attitude towards..the elimination of the house 'shout' by the publicans. **1948** *Evening Post* (Wellington) 6 Feb. 12 The 'house shout', which in the majority of hotels follows the fourth drink, has again been abolished.

Hence **shouted** *ppl. a.*, of a drink, paid for by other than the drinker.
 1946 MANDERSON *Beer Slops* 6 Sometimes..the barman having sipped a 'shouted' drink, will tip the remainder into the bucket.

3. *transf.* (A turn in paying for) a treat or present other than liquor.
 1934 *Truth* 16 May 15 He returned the shout, paying only for some ginger ale. **1957** FRAME *Owls Do Cry* (1967) 38 A sixpenny shout from her [*sc.* an older sister's] pay for blackballs or acid drops or aniseed balls. **1987** VIRTUE *Redemption of Elsdon Bird* (1988) 1 When Dad left for work Elsdon's mum made him some cocoa for a shout.

shouter. [AND 1862.] One who shouts, or stands treat.
 1863 [see SHOUTING *vbl. n.*]. **1913** *NZ Observer* 1 Nov. 9 Later you shall see him condescending to some hospitable 'shouter' in a select bar. **1927** DEVANNY *Old Savage* 170 They were lavish 'shouters', more spendthrift than the New Zealanders in this direction.

shouting, *vbl. n.* [AND 1850.]

1. Treating to (a round of) liquor.
 1863 *Lyttelton Times* 31 Dec. 4 Perhaps some of our readers do not know the extent to which the practice of 'shouting' or of inviting to drink at the shouter's expense is carried even here. **1868** *Evening Post* (Wellington) 16 Jan. [Leader] A meeting has been held in..Otago for the purpose of forming a 'Non-Shouting Society',... all present pledged themselves to abstain from treating their neighbours, friends and acquaintances, to liquor of every sort. **1874** BATHGATE *Col. Experiences* 99 One of the greatest social evils in the gold-fields is the system of 'shouting'. **1888** D'AVIGDOR *Antipodean Notes* 222 Either he takes to 'nips' and degenerates into a mere loafer, scrambling..for odd shillings which he spends in 'shouting' (standing drinks to his friends). **1917** *Truth* 1 Dec. 2 Police witnesses were convinced that 'shouting' had taken place. **1924** *Otago Witness* (Dunedin) 11 Mar. 60 Shouting was universal. **1939** *Taranaki Herald* (New Plymouth) 22 Aug. 5 'Shouting' has not passed into the discard in Stratford bars but it is not done as often as it was before the beer tax.

2. See ANTI-SHOUTING LAW.

shoveler, var. SHOVELLER.

shoveller. Also **shoveler**, the presently preferred ornithological standard spelling. [Transf. use of *shoveller* the name of the northern hemisphere shovel-billed duck, *Anas clypeata*: see OED *shoveller*[2] 2.] Also as **New Zealand shoveller,** *Anas rhynchotis variegata* (fam. Anatidae), a duck with a shovel-like beak. See also KURUWHENGI, SPOONBILL 1.
 1870 *TrNZI* II. 48 Amongst them [*sc.* the visitors], the Black Widgeon and variegated Shoveller were rarely to be seen. **1873** [see KURUWHENGI]. **1886** *TrNZI* XVIII. 127 Shoveller, or Spoonbill. This beautiful species is not at all uncommon about the district [*sc.* Petane, Hawke's Bay]. **1897** *Ibid.* XXIX. 202 *Rhynchaspis variegata*... (New Zealand Shoveller). **1904** HUTTON & DRUMMOND *Animals NZ* 314 The Shoveller.—Kuruwhengi... The Shoveller, or Spoonbill Duck, is common in both Islands, and frequents the muddy shores of lakes and streams. **1917** WILLIAMS *Dict. Maori Lang.* 186 *Kuruwhengi*... *Spatula rhynchotis*, shoveller; a bird. **1939** BEATTIE *First White Boy Born Otago* 121 I never saw the rare shoveller duck except as a wee lad. My father called them shovel-bills. **1947–48** BEATTIE *Pioneer Recolls.* (1956) 49 A handsome member of the duck family was the spoonbill or shoveller. **1955** OLIVER *NZ Birds* 415 Shoveller. *Tete. Kuruwhengi*... The Shoveller was first discovered in Australia. **1966** [see SPOONBILL 1]. **1967** [see TEAL *n.*[1] 2 (5)]. **1985** *Reader's Digest Book NZ Birds* 148 *New Zealand Shoveler*... *Kuru whengi, spoonbill, spoonie*. **1990** *Checklist Birds NZ* 104 *Anas rhynchotis variegata*... New Zealand Shoveler (*Kuruwhengi*).

show, *n.* [See OED 3 c 'Now only *U.S., Austral.* and *N.Z.*': AND 1876.] A chance (to make good), a 'look-in', esp. in the phr. **to give** (one) **a show.**
 1866 HARPER *Lett. from NZ* 6 Oct. (1914) 102 'I want to introduce myself,' I said [to the diggers]. 'I'm going to have a service tomorrow..I hope you will come.' There was a general response: 'We'll be there and give you a show,' a bit of diggers' slang, which I found meant—'Here's your chance, can you use it.' **1888** *Evening Post* (Wellington) 15 Mar. 3 His selected bowlers would have a 'show'. **1891** CHAMIER *Philosopher Dick* 154 When these fellows started shingle-splitting, he asked them as a favour to give me a show. **1905** THOMSON *Bush Boys* 51 His fear..lest this [food] should entirely disappear before he got a 'show' at it. *Ibid.* 63 Give him a show [to tell his yarn]. **1913** BATHGATE *Sodger Sandy's Bairn* 58 'Give the man a show, boss,' said Cranstown who occupied the next place on the board. **1950** *Landfall 16* 296 I wish I could take you on but there isn't a show. **1963** MORRIESON *Scarecrow* 115 I felt pretty mean to Les Wilson, sicking her [*sc.* an upset sister] on to another guy in this way, but whadda hell? Les never had a show anyway.

show, *v.*

1. In the phr. **to show** (one) **a point (dirty point),** to swindle, trick.
 1907 *Truth* 19 Jan. 2 When the bettor went round to collect, every mother's son of a book showed him a dirty point declaring that he had backed Splendid Point for the first race he was entered for and not for the first start. **1941** BAKER *NZ Slang* 53 Underworld slang [includes]..*to show a point to someone*, swindle a person

2. In the phr. **to show a trick,** to outwit, to fool, to deceive.
 1982 NEWBOLD *Big Huey* (Gloss.) 253 Show a trick (v) Outwit, fool, deceive.

show day. [f. *show* a display of objects: see OED *n.*[1] 12.] The day on which a local, usu. Agricultural and Pastoral, show is held; *spec.* in Christchurch, a holiday in November, the day of the Agricultural and Pastoral Show and corresponding to the Anniversary day in other provinces.
 1912 *Otago Witness* (Dunedin) 25 Dec. 71 What a lot of friends you meet on Show Day. **1980** LELAND *Kiwi-Yankee Dict.* 7 *A & P Show*: The Agricultural and Pastoral Show. Local equivalent of a State fair. The major event in every region and nearly all businesses..etc. close down for 'Show Day'. **1981** CHARLES *Black Billy Tea* 34 I've been down to the show and got on the booze And I'm heading back home with the show-day blues!

shower. Also **tea-shower.** A light fabric protective cover placed over food, cups, etc. on a tea-table or tray. See also THROWOVER.
 1943 BENNETT *English in NZ* in *Amer. Speech* XVIII. 86 A *shower* is not now what it once was—a party for the bride-to-be—but a light decorated covering spread over cups and saucers set out on a tray or table. **1944** SCANLAN *March Moon* 5 He stood about awkwardly while Julia plugged in the electric kettle, and whipped the muslin shower off the tea-table, which was already set. **1957** FRAME *Owls Do Cry* (1967) 20 Mothers..with their parcels from the handwork sale, table-runners and tea-showers in lazy-daisy and chain and shadow stitch. **1967** SARGESON *Hangover* 108 All was out of sight beneath a large and snowy fabric..—the kind of gossamer thing he could remember his mother had coveted many years ago in a shop window and described as a shower.

shrap: see SHRAPNEL.

shrapnel.

1. Also abbrev. **shrap**. A copper coin; usu. as a collective *sing.*, copper coins, or any small change.

c1915 p.c. C.R. Carr: used during WW1. 'Coppers' are heavy and rattle like copper shrapnel fragments, and were considered not much more valuable, and quite often coppers were referred to as 'shrapnel' or 'the iron'. **1974** Morrieson *Predicament* (1981) 238 'Anything in his pockets?' 'Nothing. Some matches... And about two bob in shrapnel.' **1983** *Sunday News* (Auckland) 23 Oct. 7 He used to pinch 'shraps' from his mum's purse or dad's wallet. **1989** *Dominion* (Wellington) 8 Aug. 3 'Shrapnel' won Lotto for chef... The young woman bought her Lotto ticket..with a collection of 20-cent coins because she had no banknotes at the time. **1990** *Sunday Star* (Auckland) 29 Apr. A2 The Reserve Bank expects to collect between $3 million..worth of 1c and 2c pieces... But canny punters looking for an inflation-proof investment should hold on to their shrapnel.

2. WW1. French currency notes of low denomination.

1935 Mitchell & Strong in Partridge *Slang Today* 286 [The] following [was] employed by those who served in the [Great] War.. *shrapnel*, the French currency notes of small denomination were generally very worn and holey, like a man sieved with shrapnel-pellets **1938** *Press* (Christchurch) (McNab Slang) 2 Apr. 18 [Used by soldiers overseas during the Great War] 'Shrapnel' was the name given to tattered French paper currency.

shrewd head. SHREWDIE 1.

1935 Strong in Partridge *Slang Today* 287 He is a shrewd head, but I think he would give a man a fair go although he is a base-walloper. **1962** Webber *Look No Hands* 26 I know all about roosters like you who already have cars you got cheap because you are shrewdheads.

shrewdie. [*shrewd* + -IE.] Also **shrewdy**.

1. [Used elsewhere but recorded earliest in Austral. and NZ: AND 1904.] A shrewd or cunning person. See also SHREWD HEAD.

1916 *Triad* 10 Jan. 43 To rush blindly into the high gear would be fatal. They are 'shrewdies', some of those people outside the windows. A man must keep his head. **1917** in Miller *Camps, Tramps & Trenches* (1939) 11 The shrewdies had used up all the hot water. **1922** *Quick March* 10 Mar. 11 There was among them he whom they called Shrewdy. **1939** in Lauridsen *Linton 1889–1989* (1988) 194 One of the local lads came to light with the following limerick: 'Certain young fellow, Mick Moody. Thought that he was a shrewdy. Bred hens with short legs Thought he'd get more eggs, But all they would do was go broody. **1948** Ballantyne *Cunninghams* (1976) 16 People reckoned Fred was a shrewdie because he did some bookmaking outside his warehouse business. **1956** Davin *Sullen Bell* 161 There'd been none of the shrewdies who dug themselves into good hospital jobs. **1964** Booth *Footsteps in Sea* 16 Charlie Mills, who prided himself on being a shrewdie, had slipped farther south than the rest of the fleet. **1974** Morrieson *Predicament* (1981) 16 Fancy an old shrewdie like him getting taken for a ride like that.

2. [AND 1960.] A shrewd or crafty trick, ploy or move.

1961 Crump *Hang On a Minute Mate* 27 Everything was as good as he said it was, but I knew he was pulling a shrewdie in there somewhere. **1970** Slatter *On the Ball* 138 Fred Allen comes racing out with the ball for the drop-out, puts in a little shrewdy and sprints away upfield in a sensational run. **1972** *Otago Daily Times* (Dunedin) 15 Sept. 4 This time, they and their publishers decided to work a shrewdie. They took full advantage of the 30 days allowed under the Copyright Act before sending the three copies north.

shunter. *Railways.*

1. A person engaged in shunting operations. Also *attrib.*

1928 *NZ Free Lance* (Wellington) 17 Mar. 17 Just recently, a shunter lost his life there [*sc.* in the Middleton yards]. **1984** *Listener* 11 Aug. 16 Richard Prebble had helped produce a package whereby Picton shunters would work 'as directed' by the corporation.

2. A wagon waiting on a shunting line to be put on a train.

1987 Virtue *Redemption of Elsdon Bird* (1988) 99 He..stared..at some bulls in a shunter on the other side of the hedge.

3. A railway engine designed to shunt rolling-stock.

1990 Churchman & Hurst *Railways of NZ* 106 [Caption] A NZR built DSC twin bogie diesel shunter locomotive from the mid 1960s on the Newstead bridge on the Cambridge Branch on a local shunt. *Ibid.* 216 The club [*sc.* the Bush Tramway Club] owns seven diesel shunters, and a Goodman built battery-electric locomotive.

shy mollymawk: see MOLLYMAWK 2 (8).

shypoo /ʃaiˈpuː/, *n.* and *a.* Also erron. **skypoo**. [Orig. unknown: AND 'inferior liquor', 1897.]

A. *n.*

1. Cheap or inferior liquor; also as **shypoo shanty**, an inferior hotel or booze-den.

1908 *Truth* 8 Feb. 5 As it is, this den, ostensibly a club, in reality a shypoo shanty, is such that its charter should be revoked. **1988** McGill *Dict. Kiwi Slang* 102 *shypoo* inferior booze, as once sold in a sly grog shop known as a 'shypoo shanty', from Cantonese 'sai po', little shop.

2. *transf.* Jocularly applied to people considered inferior, here *spec.* Italian soldiers.

1943 *NZEF Times* 25 Oct. 11 They were at war at the time with the Skypoos, a race which showed far more talent at cutting hair, teaching dancing and selling fish than it did at soldiering.

B. *adj.* Inferior; also as a term of abuse.

1952 *Landfall* 23 206 An Italian has trucked in a West Coast mine for twenty years; he is still alone..the fear of his broken English and the contempt for his pleading eyes have been handed down from his first workmates, so that ropeboys just starting can feel cocky pride in shouting: 'Good day, you — rotten Skypoo bastard!' **1955** BJ Cameron Collection (TS July) shypoo (adj) Inferior, low-grade, shoddy.

Siberia.

1. Applied to various, usu. cold, windy, remote places (esp. on a farm), or to places otherwise climatically uncomfortable (see 1982 quot.).

1980 Chapman in Neave *Land of Munros* (1980) 72 Two of my Uncles..had the property they called 'Siberia', but the Munro family called 'Sunny Peaks'... [My father] never attempted to winter sheep on what my Uncles..called 'Siberia'. **1982** Newbold *Big Huey* 162 We were working in an arid burnt-off part of the [Hautu prison] farm the inmates called Siberia where there is no shade and where the summer sun beats down relentlessly, as if upon a desert. **1985** McGill *G'day Country* 150 That's called Little Siberia over there. When the frost is on, it never leaves all winter.

2. *Obs.* A part of the former railway line across the Rimutaka range.

1959 Slatter *Gun in My Hand* 19 The exasperated huffing of the Fell engines hauling the slow creaking train up through Price's and Siberia and Summit with the pungent smoke seeping under the doors. **1981** *Listener* 24 Jan. 57 A five-engine train climbs through the area [over the Rimutakas] locally known as Siberia because of the strong winds. **1990** Churchman & Hurst *Railways of NZ* 158 On 13 September 1880 a strong wind gust on the long Siberia Curve blew the two leading coaches and a brake van of a mixed train off the tracks.

3. A name for (part of) the old General Assembly Library wing of Parliament Buildings and later for pre-fabricated buildings at some distance from the Chamber, and usu. housing Opposition members.

1973 Lee *Political Notebooks* 20 They would move to a side door of parliament [buildings] on a warm night and stand one at each side of the door. The messengers used to call the door Siberia because it was cold and lonely in winter. **1980** *Dominion* (Wellington) 15 Dec. I. 7 Some of the papers were recovered by security guards in 'Siberia'—an alleyway directly below Mrs Tirikatene-Sullivan's third floor office windows. **1984** Davies *Bread & Roses* 137 I often tottered along the creaky corridor from the Siberia wing [of Parliament Buildings] about 1 a.m. to meet my taxi. **1989** *Dominion Sunday Times* (Wellington) 4 June 2 Siberia, the name given to freezing prefabs on the outer fringes of Parliament buildings, houses lowly Government back-bench MPs.

sick, *a.*

1. Of land, reduced to infertility or poor yields by overstocking or overgrazing: see BUSH-SICK b, *rabbit-sick* (RABBIT *n.* 1), *sheep-sick*, (SHEEP 2), *stock-sick* (STOCK 2 b).

2. *Goldmining.* Of mercury, having lost its amalgamating properties. Also as a *v.* **sicken**, and *n.* **sickening**, see quot. 1992.

1967 May *West Coast Gold Rushes* 238 The mercury plates were seldom perfect: the finest gold was lost by flotation while with cemented gold a thin coating of iron oxide ('rusty gold') often prevented amalgamation. The mercury itself became 'sick' or 'floured'. *Ibid.* 527 Floured Mercury: mercury that has lost its amalgamating properties because of impurities in the ore or the wash. The mercury is then 'sick'. **1992** Latham *Golden Reefs* 120 Metallurgically, the antimony was to become a major problem, for it had the property of 'sickening' the plates. *Ibid.* 433 *Sickening:* A scum which formed on the surface of mercury and retarded amalgamating... In the Reefton district antimony sulphide (stibnite) was often responsible for 'sickening of the plates'.

sickie. [f. *sick*(-leave + -IE: AND 1953.] (A period of) sick-leave, esp. in the phr. **to throw a sickie**, to take a period of sick-leave often without a good medical reason.

1975 Wedde in *Some Other Country* (1984) 174 Because he [*sc.* a postman] was so wet the walking no longer kept him warm. Sickie time tomorrow. **1976** Fisher *Divers of Arakam* 27 [His boat] looked so fancy..that it would have been taken as unmistakeably belonging to a senior public servant 'throwing a sickie'. **1978** Ballantyne *Talkback Man* 142 The odd day off sick is pretty well vital if one is to remain sane. 'A sickie for sanity's sake' should be the motto on every office and workshop wall. **1987** Moore *Hard Labour* 13 I thought of getting out of it by throwing a 'sickie', but went in the end. **1992** *Metro* (Auckland) June 132 It's much better to take extra rest days than have them as 'sickies'.

sicko. [f. *sick* + -O.] A person thought to be mentally sick.

1984 16 F E41 Pakuranga Coll. 1 Sicko [F1 M1] 1984 14 F E125 Wgton Girls C. 1 Sicko. **1988** *Dominion Sunday Times* (Wellington) 17 Jan. 1 The man said the police should concentrate their efforts on the 'sickoes' in Napier if they wanted to catch Teresa Cormack's killer. **1995** *Dominion* (Wellington) 14 Feb. 3 [Heading] Police hunt 'sicko'. A police hunt for an 'extremely sick individual' who trashed a Whangarei woman's home and pinned her goldfish to the wall with butcher's knives continued last night.

side.

I. [Ellipt. for *side of the world* or *ocean*.] **1.** In the phr. **the other side. a.** *Hist*. The other side of the world: from a northern hemisphere point of view, New Zealand; from a New Zealand point of view, the northern hemisphere.

1874 KENNAWAY *Crusts* 8 [Heading] *Landing on the Other Side* [*sc.* in New Zealand]. **1874** BAINES *Edward Crewe* 21 The natives seemed intuitively to know that I was a new 'pakeha' by that ship from 'the other side'.

b. Often with prepositions **from, on, over**, and occas. as **on that side**, the other side of the Tasman Sea; Australia.

1884 COX *Recollections* 125 Christchurch Magistrates' [Court] I ax your pardon, zur, but were you ever at the Yan Yean works over the other side. **1889** SKEY *Pirate Chief* 129 On 'the other side', Sam, you'd have swung on a tree, To warn other liars about. [1889 *Note*] New Zealanders signify by this expression, Australia. **1912** *Triad* 10 Aug. 52 The English spoken in New Zealand is very far ahead of the English spoken in Australia. The Australian accent is everywhere on that side, and everywhere appalling and disfiguring. **1897** WRIGHT *Station Ballads* 53 Every boat that crosses from the sunny 'other side' Is bringing waves of shearers. **1906** *Truth* 7 Apr. 5 He made the mistake [of]..describing himself as an Australian! Some..have peculiar ideas about our neighbours 'on the other side'. **1912** BOOTH *Five Years NZ* 39 [In the accommodation house was] the villainous-looking 'lag' from 't'otherside'. **1933** *Press* (Christchurch)(Acland Gloss.) 11 Nov. 15 *Other side, the*.—Australia. I suppose it is a contraction of 'the o[ther] s[ide]' of the water'. The expression is still in common use. The word *o[ther] sider* has never been in use here. **1941** BAKER *NZ Slang* 43 *The other side* has for long been current in this country for the Commonwealth, i.e. the other side of the Tasman. **1951** MCLEOD *NZ High Country* 16 Lean Australian blademen from 'the other side' across the Tasman [and] tough old Merino shearers. **1966** TURNER *Eng. Lang. Aust. and NZ* 147 A professional New Zealand shearer is likely to spend some time working 'over the other side' as shearers call Australia.

Hence **othersider, tothersider** [AND c1872, used in W.A. of easterners], an Australian.

1900 *Canterbury Old & New* 33 In those early years the whaling vessels often brought doubtful characters from Australia, most of them ticket-of-leave men or ex-convicts, commonly called 'T'othersiders', or 'Van Demonians', etc. **1905** *Truth* 9 Sept. 1 T'Othersiders are still calling Maoriland legislation 'experimental'. **1933** [see above].

c. *Stewart Island*. 'Mainland' New Zealand, on the 'other side' of Foveaux Strait.

1964 DEMPSEY *Little World Stewart Is.* 6 If we are told that someone has gone over to the Other Side..we understand he has gone to Invercargill or to Bluff. *Ibid*. 92 It was sad to have to disillusion these nice people and confess that we rarely saw an oyster, unless we crossed over to the Other Side and saw them in the fish shops of Invercargill.

II. [Transf. use of a rugby football term.] **2.** In the phr. **to put** (one) **on side** (for), to put (one) in a satisfactory position or situation.

1960 MASTERS *Back-Country Tales* 223 Over bowled the rabbit. That, boiled with a bit of rice as a sort of stew, put me on side for food for the time being.

sidecars. *Adolescents.* [Poss. f. motorcycle sidecar racing, where the passenger leans out to stabilize cornering.] A game of 'dares' involving a passenger leaning out a car window while the driver tries to drive as close as possible to a car parked on his left, without injuring the passenger.

1983 *Dominion* (Wellington) 21 Dec. 6 A misunderstanding over what the game 'sidecars' meant led to one youth leaning most of his body out of a car's passenger window while the car's driver tried to drive as close as possible to a parked car, the Wellington Coroners Court heard yesterday... 'When the deceased had asked me if I had done sidecars I thought he meant side-swiping cars,' Beattie said.

sideling /ˈsaɪdlɪŋ/. Also **sidling**. [f. (mainly) Brit. (esp. Sc.) dial. *sideling* a slope, esp. one along the side of which a track or road runs: see OED *n.* 2, Sc. 1808, Austral. 1852.]

1. a. A steep hillside slope. Also *attrib.* See also SIDING. Cf. FACE 1 a.

1864 BARRINGTON *Diary* 30 Apr. in Taylor *Early Travellers* (1959) 409 Continued on our course up the river—a very bushy sideling of a steep mountain gorge, with the white foam of the river some hundreds of feet below us. **1878** ELWELL *Boy Colonists* 197 He gave up the attempt of climbing the ridge, and made away back along the sidling. **1889** ROSS *Lakes Central Otago* 43 At every 'spell ho!' the outlook from our sideling bush was lovely. **1892** WARDON *McPherson's Gully* 11 The giant pine tree went crashing down the precipitous sidling into the bottom of the gully. **1900** *Auckland Weekly News* (Suppl.) 26 Jan. 2 The sideling was so steep that in some places the clearers must have had to cling on with one hand while they cut with the other. **1925** BATHGATE *Random Recolls.* 25 When we reached the hills we passed along many a sloping piece of ground, called a sidling, with the coach tilted at an angle that seemed to invite an upset. **1934** *Press* (Christchurch) (Acland Gloss.) 20 Jan. 15 *Face* and *sidling*.—S[idling] is generally used in connection with mustering and connotes the idea of steepness or roughness, and is never used when discussing the aspect. You do not say 'a dark s[idling],' though you often hear 'dark side'; but *f[ace]* can be used in either sense. **1953** SUTHERLAND *Golden Bush* (1963) 167 Directly ahead lay several miles of snow-grass sidling falling from a long ridge flanking its southern side. **1966** NEWTON *Boss's Story* 189 *Sidling*: The face of a hill, i.e. hillside. A man sidles round the face of a hill. **1989** *NZ Gardener* May 27 The biggest block covers two hundred acres of steep sidlings which was cleared out of kanuka and gorse only a few years ago.

b. SIDLE *n.*

1864 CHUDLEIGH *Diary* 10 Oct. (1950) 148 [We] made a sideling under the top to cross a valley and then go down on a lower ridge.

c. A *sideling track* (2 below).

1939 BEATTIE *First White Boy Born Otago* 134 It was only a small cutting at first, but later a long sidling was made on the same ridge and was also called Sailors' Cutting.

2. Used *attrib*. in Comb. **sideling route, track**, one made across a sideling; **sideling run** *mustering*, see quot.

1958 *Tararua* Sept. 29 From 1936 to 1938 in *The Tramper* there are a number of references to 'sidling tracks' and '**sidling routes**'. **1971** NEWTON *Ten Thousand Dogs* 169 **Sidling run**: A run directly round through the face of a hill, as distinct from running either uphill or down.

side-row. *Rugby union*. One of the two players attached to the side of the scrum; earlier often called 'breakaway'.

1939 FLETCHER *School Football* 95 In forming down, the two side-row men must have their backs quite straight. **1947** *Sports Post* (Wellington) 10 May 12 Brown, a side-row man, played an inspired game. *Ibid*. 24 May 12 Australian scrum halves can look forward to an interesting time under the attention of the players who will grace New Zealand's side row. **1960** CROSS *Backward Sex* 75 Then, right on full-time, their side-row man was a mile offside in a ruck.

side-scarf. *Kauri logging.* A cut put into the bole of a large-diameter tree at right-angles to the front-scarf to reduce the diameter and thus enable greater lengthwise movement for a crosscut saw.

1951 MCCARROLL, H.S. *The Days of the Kauri Bushmen* Radio Talk 2 (TS) Deep side-scarfs on a tree too large for a cross cut—at right angles to the felling scarf. **1969** MOORE *Forest to Farm* 89 I decide to put in a 'side-scarf' to give a better 'run' for the saw, even though this is a 9-foot one.

side school. [f. Sc. dial.: SND *Hist.* a subsidiary school, gen. one in an outlying part of the parish; cf. also OED *side*[1] 'Sc. dial.' 27.] A school subsidiary to a main primary school.

1885 *Wairarapa Daily* 26 Jan. 2 If Masterton does not take the £500 for the additions to the present school, it will not get the money for a side school. **1993** *Sunday Times* (Wellington) 21 Mar. 13 Possibilities already talked about by schools include..developing 'side schools', where a school has extra classrooms on the suite of another school, or building a new school.

sideways. *Prison*. A euphemism and partial rhyming slang for 'suicide'.

1964 DAVIS *Watersiders* 106 Last time I saw a fish stupid enough to commit sideways on that anchor cable of yours was a good three years ago. **1982** NEWBOLD *Big Huey* (Gloss.) 253 Sideways (n) Suicide. **1984** BEATON *Outside In* 81 Di: If this keeps up for much longer Ma, I'll end up committing sideways.

Sidey time. *Hist.* Also **Sidey's Time**. [f. the name of Sir Thomas *Sidey* (1863–1933) who introduced a 'Summertime' or daylight saving time bill in 1909 to be finally passed in 1927.] Summer 'daylight-saving' time involving the advancing of clocks by one hour from standard usu. from approx. October to March.

1927 *NZ Tablet* (Dunedin) 30 Nov. 58 [Heading] Sidey's Time. A teacher tells me that the children have a new chorus..and it runs like this: 'Oh give us back our hour in bed!' **1928** *Greymouth Evening Star* 12 Mar. 5 The population of New Zealand had got to extend the palm to Mr. Sidey and shout 'Sidey time for ever'. **1938** *NZ Observer* 29 Sept. 9 His [*sc.* Thomas Sidey's] name will always be fondly revered by the sports-loving public of New Zealand as the 'inventor' of 'Sidey-time'. **1966** TURNER *Eng. Lang. Austral. & NZ* 176 Terms now historical are Red Fed..and *Sidey Time* 'summer time' from the name of the politician who urged its adoption. **1984** *National Radio* 15 Mar. [Correspondent writes to Sharon Crosbie on the subject of daylight saving:] When I was a young girl it was called Sidey time.

siding. [See OED 5 c; AND 1852.] SIDELING 1 a.
1891 CHAMIER *Philosopher Dick* 360 He told him to mind the siding by the shoot [when driving his dray]. **1904** LANCASTER *Sons o' Men* 28 [He] must have gone over the siding. **1922** TURNER *Happy Wanderer* 7 Only eighteen months ago I was whacking some bush on a siding. **1975** *NZJAg.* Sept. CXXXI. 27 The animal which grazes mostly on non-treated areas—such as gullies or sidings -..will not be fully protected.

sidle, *v.* [Spec. use of *sidle* to move sideways or obliquely, influenced by SIDELING *n.* 1 a.] *intr.* Usu. with prep. **across, along, around, up,** to negotiate or traverse a steep slope by making one's way across it at an angle; occas. *trans.* (see quot. 1953).
1896 *NZ Alpine Jrnl.* IX. 189 We sidled along the base of a mass of rugged peaks known as the Hawk's nest. **1926** HILGENDORF in Blair *Life & Work at Canterbury Agric. College* (1956) 83 There was heavy snow as we sidled along above Bealey gully. **1934** *Press* (Christchurch) (Acland Gloss.) 27 Jan. 15 *Sidle.*— To work one's way round, up, or down a facing by an easy grade. Usually *s[idle] out, s[idle] round*, etc. **1949** NEWTON *High Country Days* 30 Sidling to a handy shoulder, he scanned the basin ahead. **1953** STRONACH *Musterer on Molesworth* 23 Most of the Clarence block is 'sidled'. That is to say, the spurs are so big that it is necessary to have several men sidling on the 'face' or side of each spur. **1958** *Tararua* Sept. 29 To *sidle*, to go around the side or across the face of a hill, is a characteristic New Zealand expression, strange to the Englishman or Australian... *Sidle* is well known among high-country musterers. As it is a word most likely to be used in open hilly or mountainous country, one may guess that musterers and up-country people gave it currency, whence it was adopted by mountain club people. **1971** *Listener* 19 Apr. 56 They got up the lower scree, sidled across the first face into a couloir, but they were getting bombed so they cramponed up to just below. **1981** [see *mustering stick* (MUSTERING 2)].

sidle, *n.* [See verb.] An act of sidling. Also *attrib.* in Comb. **sidle track**, a track which runs at an angle across a slope.
1960 Pascoe in *Over Whitcombe Pass* (1960) 33 When the Whitcombe River is in flood there are many such whirlpools which the usual route avoids by a high steep sidle in the thick bush. **1958** *Tararua* Sept. 29 In 1940 comes 'on a long sidle', and from then on the noun is as common as the verb. *Ibid.* 70 From Mitre Flats a good sidle track avoids the Waingawa gorge, leading out to the easy flats of the Wairarapa plains.

sidling, var. SIDELING.

signs of the Zodiac. *Hist.* See quot. Cf. TWELVE APOSTLES.
1933 *Press* (Christchurch) (Acland Gloss.) 30 Dec. 13 *Zodiac, signs of.-* When the Christchurch Club was started by 12 squatters as a place to live when in town, there were never more than two of the 12 visible at the same time, so they were nicknamed the *s[igns] of the Zodiac*.

silence. As **two minutes silence** [an ironic transf. use of the term for the brief commemorative silence demanded on solemn occasions], a (local) newspaper.
1978 HENDERSON *Soldier Country* 198 Off she went to the pictures, while the grand old gunner with the local 'two minutes silence' (newspaper) and the fat cat dozed happily before the cozy kitchen stove.

silent army: see SILENT DIVISION.

Silent Division. *WW1*. Also **silent army** (see quot. 1946). The New Zealand Division in WW1 reputedly not given to singing on the march.
c1917–18 DIAL *Sights.* (250 NFA) The Silent Division. **1921** STEWART *NZ Div.* 616 With a highly developed esprit de corps, the troops generally impressed the outsider as stern dour and grim. On the march the cheerful and spontaneous gaiety of the English regiments was conspicuous by its absence. The undemonstrative reception of battalions returning after notable achievements suggested to an English observer the not inapt name of 'The Silent Division'. **1921** *Quick March* 10 Mar. 15 On the march the New Zealanders never sang: the Australians scarcely stopped singing. But the men of 'The Silent Division' had at times a wistful sense of loss. **1936** TREADWELL *Recolls. Amateur Soldier* 21 In France the New Zealand troops were always known as the Silent Division because of their disinclination to sing on the march. **1946** SOLJAK *NZ* 85 Even in his lighter moods the New Zealander reflects the dour outlook of his Scottish forbears [*sic*], a characteristic which in 1914–18 won for Dominion forces the name of 'the silent army'. **1984** PUGSLEY *Gallipoli* 23 'Silent' is the word invariably used with New Zealanders—in France the New Zealand Division was called 'The Silent Division'. Not for them the singing to and fro from the trenches.

silent policeman. A raised concrete mound or other construction in the centre of a road to control traffic flow and speed. In Britain termed *sleeping policeman*.
1965 SARGESON *Memoirs of a Peon* 88 A silent policeman had been prized from its street moorings. **1971** WATT *Centenary Invercargill* 70 In June, 1925, the council had erected..a 'silent policeman' at the intersection of Dee and Esk Streets. On August 13, 1936, the council decided it should be replaced by a dome and centre line. The inspector said the 'silent policeman' had been the means of training motorists to keep to the left of the centre line.

silk grass. *Obs.* [Extended use of *silk-grass*, any of various American or West Indian grasses: see OED.] An archaic term for finely scutched or dressed flax.
1773 *Furneaux's Narr.* in Cook *Journals* (1961) II. 740 Their Cloathing (both Men [and] Women) is a kind of matt or cloth made of silk grass or fine flax, curiously wove and tied about the shoulder. **1777** LEDYARD *Journal* Feb. (1963) 14 The Toga is their ne plus ultra in this sort of manufactory... The materials of the manufacture are the grass before-mentioned, which is a kind of silk-grass, said to be indigenous to the country, and the hair of their dogs blended together.

silly, *a.* and *n.*
A. *adj.* In comparisons suggesting 'very silly'.
a. (as) silly as a chook (or **hen**). See also WET HEN a.
1947 NEWTON *Wayleggo* 93 One decent nip [of whisky] had me as silly as a hen. **1982** NEWBOLD *Big Huey* 110 Pretty soon we were all as silly as chooks, and having increasing difficulty acting normally.

b. (as) silly (crazy, screwy) as a two-bob watch [AND 1954] (or **a Woolworth's watch**), very silly; as undependable as a cheap watch.
1955 BJ Cameron Collection (TS July) silly as a two-bob watch Very silly. **1956** SUTHERLAND *Green Kiwi* (1960) 125 It would surely be a long time before anyone..would remark: 'There goes young Sutherland—silly as a two-bob watch.' **1974** MASON *Hand on Rail* (TS 1987) 30 Footballer 1: Ah, what can you do? He's screwy as a two-bob watch. **1976** HILLIARD *Send Somebody Nice* 136 That Val Kemp. She's a real bloody tease that one. What a crow! Silly as a Woolworth's watch. **1978** COWLEY *Growing Season* 74 'You're mad!' he said. 'You know that? You're as crazy as a two-bob watch. I don't know how Evan puts up with you.' **1980** LELAND *Kiwi-Yankee Dict.* 10 *silly as a two bob watch*: Any timepiece that sells for 20c could be expected to keep somewhat irregular time, if any at all. Usually used to describe people, e.g. 'Jack is as silly as a two bob watch', implies eccentricity approaching the Harebrained.

B. *n.* A schoolboys' euphemism for an erection.
1974 MORRIESON *Predicament* (1981) 83 And did I see some sights!.. I used to get a silly on..I reckon if I'd fallen down I'd've pole vaulted into the lake.

silver. In the names of plants and animals, see: BEECH 2 (9), BIRCH 3 (10), DORY 2 (2), EEL 2 (8), FERN 2 (18), 2 (20) b (c), KINGFISH b, PINE 2 (15), ROUGHY 1, TRUMPETER *n.*[1] 2 (2), TUSSOCK 3 (10), WAREHOU 2 (3). See also SILVER BEET, SILVERBELLY, SILVEREYE, SILVERFISH, SILVER PENNY, SILVERSIDE, SILVER-SPOT, SILVER STRIP, SILVERWEED.

silver beet /ˌsɪlvəˈbiːt/. The New Zealand name for a leafy cultivar of beet *Beta vulgaris* (fam. Chenopodiaceae) used as a vegetable, and distinguished by its large green leaves on white stems; called elsewhere *Swiss chard, spinach beet*.
1902 *Brett's Colonists' Guide* 487 Beet... Varieties.—The principal varieties are—Henderson's, Pine-apple, Silver or Sea-kale, Blood Red. **1913** *NZJAg.* Jan. VI. 595 In commerce there are eight varieties of Swiss chard, or silver-beet. **1944** SCOTT *Life With Barbara* 63 I saw Barbara rush into the garden and..pick an armful of silver beet. **1966** TURNER *Eng. Lang. Austral. & NZ* 172 Among cultivated plants, *silver beet, tree tomato* and *Chinese gooseberry* seem to be commoner in New Zealand than in other English-speaking countries. **1982** BURTON *Two Hundred Yrs. NZ Food* 122 Silverbeet, or Swiss chard as it is known by other peoples, is significantly more popular in New Zealand than in Britain or elsewhere. **1991** ELDRED-GRIGG *Shining City* 15 We'd follow an asphalt path past..a clump of silverbeet run to seed.

silverbelly. Also **silver-bellied (silverbelly) eel**. A native freshwater eel of *Anguilla* spp. See also EEL 2 (8).
1945 BEATTIE *Maori Place-names Canterbury* 34 I..saw him put a hinaki in the river, and next morning it was full of silver bellies. **1961** HENDERSON *Friends In Chains* 67 The eels were so plentiful..that we often hauled the line up with two fat silver-bellies clinging to one bob. **1965** McLAGLAN *Stethoscope & Saddlebags* 112 So he went and caught a little, silver-bellied eel, Doctor, just the kind she liked. **1978** FULLER *Maori Food & Cook.* 69 Silver-bellies and small eels. **1983** HULME *Bone People* 366 Then one night I added [to the soup stock] two silverbelly eels. **1984** WILSON S. *Pacific Street* 7 She said they tasted muddy, though they were beautiful silver-bellies. **1990** McDOWALL *NZ Freshwater Fishes* 55 Other common names [for the long-finned eel] include..sometimes silverbelly, which is a migrant longfin or one from a clean flowing, stony-bedded stream. *Ibid.* 61 Anguilla australis..Shortfinned Eel... It is very often referred to as 'silverbelly', although this name also applies to the longfin at times.

silvereye. [AND 1862.] *Zosterops lateralis lateralis* (fam. Zosteropidae), a familiar small green and grey bird of esp. urban gardens distinguished by a white eye-ring; self-introduced from Australia in the early to mid 19th century. See also (dates of first record given) BLIGHT-BIRD (1870), BUTTON-EYE (1946), *fish-eye* (FISH 3) (1888), GLASS-EYE (c1920), JEWEL BIRD (1905), PENNYWEIGHT (1922), RINGEYE (1888), TAUHOU (1870), TWINKIE (1922), WAXEYE (1871), *white-eye* (WHITE *a.* 1) (1869), *winter migrant* (WINTER) (1888).

 1873 BULLER *Birds NZ* 80 (The Silver-eye)...*Native names.* Tau-hou, Kanohi-mowhiti, Karu-patene, Karuhiriwha, Poporohe, and Iringatau. **1888** [see RINGEYE]. **1897** *TrNZI* XXIX. 285 We found the 'bill of fare' for that day to have been a silver-eye. **1905** WHITE *My NZ Garden* 71 The little 'Silver Eye'..has a silvery circle round its eyes, composed of tiny white feathers which are sweetly becoming. **c1920** BEATTIE *Trad. Lifeways Southern Maori* (1994) 345 The ringeye (also known as whiteeye, silvereye, waxeye and blightbird) was called (at Akaroa) pihipihi. **1930** *Evening Post* (Wellington) 6 Dec. 17 A few white-eyes or silver-eyes were noted flitting about the foliage of the forest trees. **1940** STUDHOLME *Te Waimate* (1954) 201 The silver-eyes their fragile nests did make. **1976** SOPER *NZ Birds* 74 Silvereyes are sociable birds and in autumn and winter large flocks move into our gardens, calling to one another with their plaintive 'zee-zee' notes as they feed on the rose bushes, ornamental shrubs, household scraps and so on. **1985** *Reader's Digest Book NZ Birds* 288 Silvereyes were noticed in New Zealand as early as 1832, but they did not arrive in large numbers until 1856. **1992** PARK *Fence around the Cuckoo* 226 'But she hasn't the sense of a silvereye!' This metaphor touched me when I was older.

silver fern: see FERN 2 (18), (20) b (c).

silverfish. [Spec. use of *silverfish* silver-coloured fish: see OED 1.] Any of various silver-sided fishes esp. *Retropinna retropinna* (SMELT) and *Seriolella punctata* (WAREHOU 2 (3)). See also SILVERY *n.*

 1870 *TrNZI* II. 86 There are only three fish in the River Avon..that may be the adult form of the Whitebait; these are the Bull-head, the Silver-fish, and the Smelt. **1879** *Ibid.* XI. 275 This fish is called Silverfish by Mr Powell, but Smelt (*Retropinna richardsoni*) by Dr Hector. **1921** *NZJST* IV. 120 *Seriolella punctata... Silver-fish.* Occasionally seen in Dunedin markets, but not now so common as several years ago. **1921** *TrNZI* LIII. 473 Common Name of Fish... Silver-fish... Scientific Name... *Callorhynchus antarcticus.* **1938** *TrRSNZ* LXVIII. 408 *Seriolella punctata...* Silver-fish. **1940** PHILLIPPS *Fishes NZ* 45 According to Thomson and Anderton the silverside [*Argentina elongata*] is common along the Otago Coast being called silver fish or snodgall by the local fishermen. **1956** GRAHAM *Treasury NZ Fishes* 217 Silver-fish *Seriolella maculata...* The silver-fish was not common during 1930-33. **1967** NATUSCH *Animals NZ* 217 Sub-order Stromateoidae. This group includes..the warehou..and the silverfish..; the latter two are species of *Seriolella*.

silver king: see *tree-fern* (FERN 2 (18), (20) b (c)); also PONGA 2 (2).

silver penny. A shell-fish shell. See quot.

 1970 SANSOM *Stewart Islanders* 185 One of our favourites [on Stewart Island] was the silver penny or *Myadora* [shell]. The flat valve was the 'silver penny' but the concave valve was lovely too, and much rarer. Both were lined with a pearly lustre, the 'silver pennies' sometimes in hundreds high up on the beach..gleaming in the sun.

silverside /'sɪlvəˌsaɪd/. *Argentina elongata* (fam. Argentinidae), an elongate yellowish silver-banded fish; less commonly, any of various fishes of the family Scopelosauridae (see quot. 1982). See also SNODGALL.

 1911 WAITE *Rec. Canterbury Museum* I. 161 *Argentina Elongata...* Silverside. **1913** *TrNZI* XLV. 234 The silverside..is common along the east coast. **1921** THOMSON & ANDERTON *Hist. Portobello* 70 Silverside *Argentina elongata...* It is sometimes called the 'silverfish' or 'snodgall' by the local fishermen, and is taken in seine nets. **1938** [see SNODGALL]. **1940** PHILLIPPS *Fishes NZ* 45 The silverside is yellowish or silvery with very pale brown semi-cross bands, at least in the young, and a polished silvery band along the middle of the sides. **1956** GRAHAM *Treasury NZ Fishes* 121 Although Silverside is the correct name, almost all fishermen continue to call this fish Snodgall... The name Silverside is derived from its glistening, silvery body, though in medium sized fish the colour is yellowish. **1978** *Catch* Mar. 15 Catches of silverside by the *Kaiyo Maru* showed a high potential for the fish as a quality food eaten raw. It commands high prices in Japan. **1986** PAUL *NZ Fishes* 54 *Silverside. Argentina elongata*..small quantities of silverside are caught by offshore trawlers.

silver-spot. A former trade name for a fillet of (*spiny*) *dogfish.* Cf. DOGFISH, GUMMY *n.*[3]

 1921 *NZJST* IV. 123 *Squalus Fernandinus* (Molina). *Spiny Dogfish; Pioke.* Large numbers are smoked and readily sold in the Auckland markets under the name of 'silver-spots'. Distribution: New Zealand coasts. **1922** [see PIOKE].

silver strip. A trade name for a (smoked) fillet of (usu.) dogfish or elephant fish.

 1922 [see PIOKE]. **1946** PHILLIPPS *Sharks NZ* I. No.2 16 *Squalus griffini...* This species has good edible qualities and is one of the dogfish cut up and sold as silver strips in Auckland. **1970** SORENSEN *Nomenclature NZ Fish* 22 *Elephant Fish..Callorhynchus millii...* Other common names: Silver trumpeter, Silver strip (smoked), Elephants. **1970** [see PIOKE].

silverweed /'sɪlvəˌwid/.

1. *Potentilla anserinoides* (fam. Rosaceae), a native herb of damp sites, having compound leaves, brownish green above, silvery below.

 1899 KIRK *Students' Flora NZ* (And) North and South Islands: Auckland Isthmus to Southland; ascends to 3,000 ft. Chatham Islands. *Silverweed.* Dec., Jan. Also in the arctic regions, and in most temperate countries in both hemispheres var. *anserinoides* endemic in New Zealand. **1909** *AJHR* C-12 55 *Potentilla anserina*..var. *anserinoides.* Silverweed. Bog. Rare. **1926** HILGENDORF *Weeds* 101 Silver Weed..is found in damp pastures in both islands. It is a perennial about 6 inches high, with creeping and rooting stems. **1952** RICHARDS *Chatham Is.* 31 The root-stock, used as a food by the Maoris, can be either roasted or boiled and tastes like parsnip... Silverweed. Kowhai-kura (yellow-red). **1978** MOORE & IRWIN *Oxford Book NZ Plants* 30 The name silverweed refers to the pale shining underside of the soft brownish leaves. **1982** WILSON *Stewart Is. Plants* 178 *Potentilla anserinoides* Silverweed... Herb creeping by slender runners... Leaves dark brown-green above, silvery white with appressed fine hairs beneath.

2. Occas. *Pseudognaphalium* (formerly *Gnaphalium*) *luteo-album* (fam. Asteraceae), a native cudweed covered in soft woolly silver white hairs. See also CUDWEED.

 1926 HILGENDORF *Weeds* 171 Cudweed (*Gnaphalium luteo-album*).—This or an allied species is sometimes called silver weed. It is found all over the world including New Zealand, in all soils and climates.

silvery, *a. Obs.* Possessing silver coin, *holding* (HOLD *v.*[2] 2).

 1906 *Truth* 15 Sept. 3 If they are 'silvery' they will walk out again; if 'stiff' they will work a week or two to get a few shillings to take them on the road again.

silvery, *n.* Mainly *Canterbury and Westland.* SMELT (*Retropinna retropinna*).

 1916 ANDERSON *Jubilee Hist. South Canterbury* 28 Silveries and smelts were caught and highly esteemed by the Maoris, and whitebait by both the Maoris and Europeans. **1925–26** *NZJST* VIII. 291 Canterbury residents refer to *R[etropinna] retropinna* as 'silvery', on account of the silver line running along the side of the half-grown fish. **1930** [see SMELT]. **1937** BUICK *Moa-Hunters NZ* 174 Then there came [up the Waitaki] what from its bright appearance was known as the 'silvery' (*Argentina retropinna*), and, from its odour when young, as the 'cucumber' smelt. **1940** PHILLIPPS *Fishes NZ* 54 Certain races of fish [*sc.* NZ smelt] have a broad silvery band running along the side; hence the term 'silvery'. **1967** NATUSCH *Animals NZ* 208 New Zealand smelts [*Retropinnidae*] are true smelts, but here they are often called by the pretty name of silveries. **1978** MCDOWALL *NZ Freshwater Fishes* 40 Common names for the species include Silvery, Cucumber-fish or just Cucumber, or Estuarine Smelt. **1981** WILSON *Fisherman's Bible* 288 Silvery. The bane of professional whitebaiters. This small silver fellow is usually removed by hand from the catch when he appears not so much because he doesn't taste good but because he looks like a 'foreigner'. The Silvery is the young of the smelt. **1990** [see CUCUMBER FISH 1].

since. Introducing various phr. indicating a time in the distant past, alluding to the infrequency of the happening under discussion or review; 'in donkey's years': **since Adam was a cowboy** [poss. a variant of the English expression *when Adam was an oakum boy in Chatham Dockyard*; *cowboy* 'a boy who looks after cows' (cf. COWBOY)]; **since Dick Seddon died, since Dick Seddon was a boy** (Richard J. Seddon, Prime Minister, d. 1907: cf. SEDDON.); **since God called the chickens home; since the Lord had the measles.**

 1968 SLATTER *Pagan Game* 102 I've been slogging me guts out in this school **since Adam was a cowboy** and it takes me all my time to figure some of them out. **1993** *Evening Post* (Wellington) 8 Feb. 4 Both these clubs have raced on this [Anniversary] day since Adam was a cowboy. **1952** p.c. Bruce Mason (Wellington) 7 June **since Dick Seddon died** used since c1943 (Wellington). **1953** *Listener* 23 Jan. 8 That afternoon [in 1918 the] *Times* came out in a leading article which started like this: 'The most important thing that has happened in Westport *since Dick Seddon died* is...' *since Dick Seddon died*, for a long time, in donkeys' years. **1979** *Otago Daily Times* (Dunedin) 28 Mar. 21 A curious word called 'perquisite', which hasn't been used in New Zealand English **since Dick Seddon was a boy.** **c1945** p.c. R. Mason (Wellington). **Since God called the chickens home; since the Lord had measles** were once in frequent use.

singer. The cicada (fam. Cicadidae).

 1891 *TrNZI* XXIII. 49 The *Cicadae.* These creatures are generally called 'singers' and are familiar to nearly every New Zealand child. **1920** *Ibid.* LII. 431 The family Cicadae, often popularly known as 'locusts' or 'singers'.

singlestick. An alternative name for the game LAZY STICK q.v.

 1865 THATCHER *Otago Songster* 6 They threw the

singlet.

1. [AND 1882.] A woven or knitted undergarment, usu. sleeveless or short-sleeved, reaching from shoulders to somewhat below the hips; also worn as an outer garment; (British) *vest*. Cf. SHIMMY.

1890 *NZ Observer* 22 Mar. 10 The writer remembers well an experience he hopes never again to undergo, being burnt out..and having to start..again with no more wealth nor capital than a pair of ragged cotton pants and a worse singlet. **1905** *NZ Herald* (Auckland) 4 Feb. Suppl. 1 Who causes the ship to be filled..but he of the unshaven face..who in singlet and dungaree pants..hews and grubs, plants trees and clothes the hills with green grass. **1913** *NZ Observer* 31 May 16 The Dunedin Corporation neglects to enquire whether he wears silk or cotton singlets. **1922** *Auckland Weekly News* 9 Feb. 44 [Advt] Men's Colonial Singlets [9s 6d]. **1938** FINLAYSON *Brown Man's Burden* (1973) 30 The old man was in just a singlet and baggy old trousers. **1947** *NZ Observer* 15 Jan. 8 The Maori in the singlet had the same look about him. **1953** *Ibid.* 21 Jan. 19 You can't tell me that a baby swan is called a singlet. **1960** MASTERS *Back-Country Tales* 129 His apparel consisted of a singlet and a pair of trousers cut off at the knees. **1985** Hughes in *Hyacinths and Biscuits* 136 As was common those days he wore bowyangs and a pink woollen singlet with short sleeves. **1991** *North & South* (Auckland) June 33 If I was to continue my journey to freedom right then it would be in my singlet and socks.

2. With a modifier: **black**, **bush**, **bushman's**, a black or dark sleeveless singlet as part of the traditional clothing of a New Zealand outdoors workman, esp. of a bush worker or shearer. See also JACKIE HOWE. **a.** As **black singlet**.

1973 *Islands* 6 360 His visual sense records the black singlets, the stretched cords and arms of the shearing blades. **1987** *Country Calendar* 123 Wearing the traditional black singlet and sacking moccasins, he first mops up the dags. **1990** *Art New Zealand* LVII. 58 Kiwi as any black singlet or twenty-five-yard penalty. **1992** *Listener* 29 June 57 The *Black Singlet Legacy*, a history of the Maori in the freezing works, gets a repeat broadcast this week.

b. As **bush singlet**.

c1910 p.c. W.H.B. Orsman (Marlborough) (1972). As long as I can remember, and certainly before the First World War, black woollen singlets were always called, and sold in the store as, 'bush singlets'. **1965** *NZ Weekly News* 28 July 19 [Advt] Bush Singlets. New, navy blue, all-wool athletic-type singlets. Ideal for outdoor winter workers. **1971** LETHBRIDGE *Sunrise on Hills* 40 Standing there in his black bush singlet and leather apron, turning the handle of the forge. **1981** HENDERSON *Exiles Asbestos Cottage* 200 Bits of drapery too, the black bush singlets, work trousers and shirts, singlets. **1991** *New Zealandia* 3 Mar. 3 At my golf club there is a large notice (abbreviated): 'T-shirts, bush singlets, beach shorts, jeans, jandals, sneakers are not acceptable.'

Hence **bush-singleted**.

1978 HENDERSON *Soldier Country* 135 He cannot be visualised as an uneloquent slang-spattered nasal bush-singleted clumping Kiwi—few of us are.

c. As **bushman's singlet**.

1964 BACON *Along the Road* 47 He laughed heartily, his great stomach wobbling under his black bushman's singlet. **1969** MOORE *Forest to Farm* 49 Their [*sc.* Maori bushmen's, 1920s] usual garb was a sleeveless knitted bushman's singlet, and denim or palmer-nap pants. **1974** HENDERSON *Open Country Muster* 187 We wear saddletweed trousers and the sleeveless woollen dark navy-coloured 'bushmen's singlet'. **1981** CHARLES *Black Billy Tea* 83 In his ragged bushman's singlet And no backside in his breeks, He's the roughest-looking cocky That ever left the sticks. **1986** RICHARDS *Off the Sheep's Back* 61 A bushman's singlet is a black, heavy woollen sleeveless garment that keeps the body warm even when it is soaking wet.

sink, *v.*[1] *Goldmining.* [Spec. use of *sink* to excavate (a well, shaft, etc.) by digging downwards: see OED *v.* 18; AND 1851.] **a.** *intr.* To dig down in search of gold.

1852 *NZGG* 9 Nov. V. 26:165 (Rep. Gold Discovery in Coromandel) They reached a bend of the Creek, where they found Ring's party at work, sinking into the bed of it. **1857** *Lyttelton Times* 4 July 5 Attempts have been made to sink on the hills near Agpoo's and Lightband's Gullies. **1861** *Otago Witness* (Dunedin) 29 June 5 We tried a number of places along the bed of the creek, sinking in each from two to four feet. **1871** MONEY *Knocking About NZ* 28 I am myself of opinion that the bed-rock on the eastern side of the dividing range is at so much greater depth..as to render it unlikely that it would ever pay for the labour of sinking for a prospect. **1918** *NZJST* I. 11 Near Deep Creek..miners in search of alluvial gold have sunk through 80 ft. of gravel in the stream bed before reaching solid rock.

b. *trans.* [AND 1852.] To dig (a hole or shaft) in search of gold, or, occas., of kauri-gum.

1861 *NZ Goldfields 1861* (1976) 28 The ground sank through consisted only of the upper soil, a bed of clay, and a little coarse gravel, below which was the washing-stuff—a layer of rotten slate, interspersed with quartz rubble, and other *débris*. **1863** WALKER *Jrnl. & Lett.* (ATLTS) 11 Jan. Found ourselves in the evening on a high gulley where somebody had sunk a hole but found nothing. **1909** THOMPSON *Ballads About Business* 66 Comes a miner treasure seeking,... Sinks a hole with pick and shovel. **1970** THOMAS *Way Up North* 30 To see a fit and experienced gumdigger sinking a hole large enough to allow freedom of action, deep enough to get the gum,.. was to see something special as a test of competence, fitness and endurance.

Hence **sinker**, a miner who has excavated a hole in search of gold; **sinking** *vbl. n.* [AND 1851], a hole dug in search of gold.

1862 *Otago Witness* (Dunedin) 23 Aug. 5 The 'Driving Creek' claims are nearly worked out, and the **sinkers** are discouraged by the late floods and heavy rain. **1861** *NZ Goldfields 1861* (1976) 13 His opinion is that a party can make an ounce a man, as the **sinking** is very shallow, and the working dry. **1874** BATHGATE *Col. Experiences* 107 We were working a first rate claim, with about a hundred feet sinking. **1895** GRACE *Maoriland Stories* 51 I expect we'll see 'sinkings' if we look for them. **1967** MAY *West Coast Gold Rushes* 219 The sinking was shallow, the ground dry, and the gold coarser than usual for beach-gold.

sink, *v.*[2] [Spec. use of *sink* to cause (a thing) to descend: used elsewhere but recorded earliest in NZ: see OED *v.* 17 e; AND 1911.] To drink down or consume (liquor).

1906 PICARD *Ups & Downs* 6 He's got a slog on, and could about sink a long beer. **1948** *Landfall* 6 111 Duggan must look at the clock, sink his beer. **1971** SHADBOLT *Bullshit & Jellybeans* 85 A real shithot bloke. Jesus, can he sink the piss. **1982** O'SULLIVAN *Rose Ballroom* 28 [Skull'd] sunk piss with a bishop. **1992** FARRELL *Skinny Louie Book* 65 The new chap..preferred a quiet smoke..to sinking a few convivial beers in the farm kitchen.

sinker. [f. *sinker* something that will not float.]

1. a. *Logging. Obs.* A log which will not float (and so cannot be 'driven' in water).

1889 KIRK *Forest Flora* 42 Many logs have the same specific gravity as water, and will only float when fully immersed; others will not float at all at all, and are termed 'sinkers' by the bushmen. **1907** LAING & BLACKWELL *Plants NZ* 72 Some of these [kahikatea] logs, however, will not float at all, and are known to the bushmen as 'sinkers'. **1953** REED *Story of Kauri* 96 The 'gummy' kauri, as its name implies, was weighted with an overload of resin, and a log—known as a 'sinker'—cut from such a tree could be very troublesome. **1958** *NZ Timber Jrnl.* Sept. 87 *Sinker*: A log or other timber too heavy to remain afloat in water.

b. *Whaling.* See quot.

1982 GRADY *Perano Whalers* 228 (Gloss.) *Sinker*— A whale that sinks before it can be inflated and made buoyant with the air-spear and pump.

2. *fig.* [Cf. OED *n.*[1] 5 d *slang* (orig. *U.S.*). A doughy cake, esp. a doughnut; a dumpling. Now *rare.* 1870.] A heavy (often unattractive) steamed (suet) pudding, with or without raisins, associated with institutional or camp cookery. Cf. CLAGGER.

1905 BRANDON *Ukneadit* 105 Dough boys, 'sinkers', or 'water boys' are prepared in exactly the same manner as damper, except that the dough need not be so stiff. **1956** *St Patrick's College, Silverstream 1931–56* 16 Always..'sinker' and notes for this and notes for that. **1981** *St Patrick's College, Silverstream 1931–80* 11 The most notorious dish was 'sinker', the steamed pudding which provoked the no food strike in my time [c1943]. **1982** MACKENZIE *WAAF Book* 67 It [*sc.* custard] was eaten every day [in the RNZAF in WW2]—custard with dried apricots,.. custard with 'sinker' (steamed pudding). **1996** *Dominion* (Wellington) 24 May 12 Try them [*sc.* carrots]..with celery, stored onions and horseradish dumplings, which we used to call '10-minute sinkers'.

sinking lid. A name given to the policy of reducing public service staff numbers (in the interests of cutting costs) by not replacing deceased or departing workers.

1984 OVENDEN *Ratatui* 19 Her absence was believed to be another part of expenditure restraint..Flukie referred to her as 'the visible evidence of the sinking lid'. **1995** ANDERSON *House Guest* 70 She told him..how the sinking lid was making things virtually impossible.

sink the boot in(to): see BOOT *n.* 2.

sit up like jacky: see JACKY *n.*[2]

six. Used in various combinations and collocations where the number (of) **six** is of significance: **six and eight**, rhyming slang for 'mate'; **six-day-bike-rider**, a Seventh-day Adventist; **sixer** [prob. from being worth 6 lesser marbles in exchanges], a kind of marble; **six-figure man** WW2 [f. the Army personal number: lower in early recruits, higher in later], a late enlistment in the 2NZEF (cf. *four-figure man* (FOUR)); **six-finger**, a species variant of FIVE-FINGER 1; **six-tooth**, a sheep just before it reaches full maturity (eight-tooth).

1966 *NZ Short Stories* (1976) 51 Your mums [*sic*] old school-mate Jancy Andrews called in to see me the other week she was down on holiday just the same old **six and eight** but very deaf and failed a lot. **1943** JACKSON *Passage to Tobruk* 11 Mrs. Mudge, apart from being a Seventh-day Adventist (a **six-day-bike-rider**, in the language of MacNeil). **1900** in Lawlor *Old*

Wellington Days (1959) 36 October 2... Marbles are in. Lost a **sixer** and two stinkers. **1972** SUTTON-SMITH *Folkgames Children* 174 When I first went to school, bottlies were good currency, being classed as two-ers, but usually sodawaters and black bottlies counted as the equivalent of six-ers [?for exchange purposes] (Petone, Wellington, 1913). **1944** FULLARTON *Troop Target* 214 Raw rookies arriving from New Zealand (**six-figure men**! 800,000!). **1951** in Pearson *Six Stories* (1991) 63 For somewhere across a tangle of supplejack and kiekie vines in a creek-bed soft with **six-finger**, Red was prowling. **1963** PEARSON *Coal Flat* 47 She was afraid..as if she had entered a quiet gully in the bush where there were only mossy rotten logs and supplejack and soft fronds of six-finger. **1855** *Nelson Examiner* 7 Feb. 2 The sheep were two, four, and **six-tooth** ewes. **1860** *Puketoi Station Diary* (Hocken TS) 14 Mar. Ewe lambs 32 two tooth ewes 402 four & six tooth 638 full mouthed 1322 broken mouthed 11, wedders 290 total 2695. **1987** [see FULL-MOUTHED].

six-o'clock. *Hist.* Used *attrib.* in Comb. and special Comb. with reference to the period when public bars were required to close at 6.00 p.m. **a.** As **six-o'clock closing**, the statutory closing at 6.00 p.m. of all hotel bars open to the public, introduced as a war measure in 1917, made permanent in 1918, and lifted 9 October 1967 (see also 1919 quot.). Also *attrib.*

1916 [see ANTI-SHOUTING LAW]. **1917** *Truth* 6 Oct. 1 The Government did believe that six o'clock closing was of greater moment than the War Pensions. **1919** FANNING *Politics and the Public* 68 On 1st August, 1917, a report of the National Efficiency Board [recommended to Parliament]..the restriction of the hours for the sale of liquor to from 9 a.m. to 6 p.m. The Liquor Restriction Bill went into committee on 21st September, 1917, and with provision for 8 o'clock closing. Without debate, and by a majority of 41 to 28, the hour was struck out, with a view to fixing another hour, and the Prime Minister then proposed 6 o'clock. This amendment was passed after very little discussion... Six o'clock closing came into force on 1st December, 1917. **1925** *NZ Dairy Produce Exporter* 26 Sept. 61 An amusing relationship between six o'clock closing and the number of cars in New Zealand was drawn by the Hon. W.P. Reeves in his address to the shareholders of the National Bank of New Zealand. **1936** HYDE *Passport to Hell* 76 Six o'clock closing, that most devastating custom of the New Zealander's country, emptied the soldiers out of the bar. **1948** FINLAYSON *Tidal Creek* (1979) 74 'Don't y'*know* about six o'clock closing,' says the [hotel] porter, blinking with amazement. **1959** BOLLINGER *Grog's Own Country* 54 Six o'clock closing came about in the first place as the result of a high-pitch campaign by prohibitionists to have Prohibition imposed as an emergency measure during the First World War. **1967** *NZ Jrnl. of Hist.* Apr. 31 1917..was the year of 6 o'clock closing! **1979** GEBBIE & MCGREGOR *Incredible 8-Ounce Dream* 46 During six o'clock-closing days supplies of after-hours beer and spirits would always be charged in round figures. **1984** FRAME *Angel at My Table* 23 The people were poorer..and sometimes, perhaps, there were a few more drunks outside the pub at six-o'clock closing. **1992** *North & South* (Auckland) Jan. 94 The six o'clock closing culture wasn't violent.

b. As **six o'clock rush**, *six o'clock swill* (d below).

1950 *NZ Post Office Eng. Course* (TS) 14 New Zealand has developed many phrases that depend on local interpretation: e.g. 'The Limited', 'the six o'clock rush', 'off the bitumen'... All these are immediately understandable to New Zealanders, but not always to others.

c. As **six o'clock scrum**, *six-o'clock swill* (d below).

1955 *BJ Cameron Collection* (TS July) six o'clock scrum (n) The packed mass of men in bars just before closing time.

d. As **six o'clock swill** [AND *swill* 1955], the rapid consumption of (mainly) beer between office closing and bar-closing, and esp. from just before the final serving-time of 6.00 p.m. to 6.15 p.m., when bars were cleared. See also SWILL.

1959 BOLLINGER *Grog's Own Country* 2 Junior Chambers of Commerce claim that two-thirds of opinion in their areas want to 'get rid of the six o'clock swill'. **1963** *Dominion* (Wellington) 13 Aug. 4 Like the great majority of New Zealanders who finish work at 5 or 5.30 p.m. I like two or three beers and a chat to my friends before I go home for dinner... They call it the 'six o'clock swill', but we enjoy it. **1976** JOHNSTON *New Zealanders* 147 Most notorious was the 'six o'clock swill', the mass consumption of beer by workers in the hour after work, followed by a semi-drunken journey home. **1986** HOLCROFT *Sea of Words* 9 We were then..in the heyday of the six o'clock swill, an institution so notorious that visiting Americans..were taken to selected hotels to see for themselves an operation otherwise unbelievable. **1993** *Independent Herald* (Johnsonville) 20 Jan. 1 They have become booze barns run by a private company which is still in the six o'clock swill mode.

Hence **six o'clock swiller** [cf. AND *swiller*, 1964], one who took part in heavy public-bar drinking between 5.00 p.m. and 6.15 p.m.

1965 GILLHAM *Naturalist in NZ* 87 Nor was there a 6.10 p.m. bus, though I was directed to stop to catch it, staggering under my heavy luggage like one of the many '6 o'clock swillers'.

sixty in the shade: see SHADE.

sixty-nine. *Shearing.* [Origin unknown.] In New Zealand, a shearers' code cry, warning that women or visitors are approaching the shearing shed. See also *ducks on the pond* (DUCK 3 b), NINETY NINE, *red light* (RED *a*. 2).

1955 BOWEN *Wool Away* 157 'Sixty-nine.' The call made to let the shearers and hands know that ladies and visitors are entering the shed, and to give them a chance to put on their best job and be on their best behaviour. Visitors, of course, take this call of 'sixty-nine' to be just a sheep number. **1965** *Listener* 26 Feb. 15 *Sixty-nine*: The shearers' code warning that ladies or visitors are approaching and bad language is out of order—it is intended to sound like some kind of tally. **1982** *Agric. Gloss.* (MAF) 59 *Sixty-nine*: Call made to let shearers and shedhands know that ladies and visitors are entering a shearing shed.

skate, *n.*[1]

1. As a large flat cartilaginous 'fish of the genus *Raia*' (so OED *n.*[1] 1) of the fam. Rajidae, *skate* has been recorded from New Zealand coastal waters since 1777 (ANDERSON *Journal* Feb. in Cook *Journals* (1967) III. 808 Sometimes we got a sort of small Salmon, Gurnards, Skate and Nurses.), but in distinctive local use only in the common names of two species (**rough** and **smooth skate**), and in the application of the name to members of families Arhynchobatidae and Narkidae.

2. With a modifier: **electric, long-tailed, rough, smooth**.

(1) **electric skate**. *Typhlonarke aysoni* (fam. Narkidae), a species able to produce electric shocks. See also NUMBFISH.

1956, 1981 [see NUMBFISH]. **1984** *Marlborough Express* (Blenheim) 22 Aug. 6 There are also ling and school shark..electric skates and others with saw toothed snouts.

(2) **long-tailed skate**. *Arhynchobatis asperrimus* (fam. Arhynchobatidae). See esp. quot. 1982.

1927 PHILLIPPS *Bibliogr. NZ Fishes* (1971) 10 *Arhynchobatis asperrimus*... Long-tailed Skate. **1929** *NZJST* XI. 104 The long-tailed skate is known so far by one example only. **1982** AYLING *Collins Guide* (1984) 78 *Long-tailed Skate*. *Arhynchobatis asperrimus*. The long-tailed skate is similar in shape to the deepsea skate but has only one small dorsal fin and a small yet distinct caudal fin at the tip of the tail.

(3) **a. rough skate**. *Raja nasuta* (fam. Rajidae). See esp. quot. 1982. See also WHAI.

1966 [see WHAI]. **1974** *TrRSNZ* IV. 345 The common 'rough' skate, usually referred to as *R. australis*..is shown to be *R. nasuta*. **1982** AYLING *Collins Guide* (1984) 75 *Rough Skate. Raja nasuta*... The rough skate is named for the many small prickles on the upper surface of the disc that give the skin a distinctive rough texture.

b. smooth skate. *Raja innominata* (fam. Rajidae).

1974 *TrRSNZ* IV. 345 The 'smooth' skate usually referred to as *R. nasuta*, has not in fact been named, and is now described as *R. innominata* n. sp. **1982** AYLING *Collins Guide* (1984) 76 As the name suggests the skin is smooth... The smooth skate is common throughout New Zealand waters but is usually found in deeper water than the rough skate. It..is also unpopular as an eating fish. **1986** PAUL *NZ Fishes* 35 *Smooth skate*... Larger, smoother, and greyer than the rough skate; less common... An occasional but spectacular catch for an angler.

skate, *n.*[2]

1. [f. *skate v.* to slide: see OED *v.* 1 b.] In the phr. **to go for a skate**, to slip or slide; also *transf.*, to fail; to be brought up before Court.

1955 *BJ Cameron Collection* (TS July) skate go for a skate (v) To slip or slide. **1962** CRUMP *One Of Us* 105 You'd have gone for a skate if they'd caught you out. **1974** HILLIARD *Maori Woman* 99 I don't want the cops here, yous guys'll go for a skate, for sure.

2. [f. *skate v.* to depart speedily: see OED *v.* 1 d.] In the phr. **to do a skate**, to depart quickly; to decamp.

1988 MCGILL *Dict. Kiwi Slang* 103 skate phr. *do a skate* to disappear hurriedly; aka *skate off*; eg 'Potts figured there was trouble brewing and did a skate.'

skee. [AND 1962.] A shortened form of *whisky*.

1959 SLATTER *Gun in My Hand* 145 In this country a bulged pocket would not mean a gun. More likely a flask of skee or mother's ruin.

skelp. *Otago-Southland*. [f. Sc. dial. *skelp* a long strip or an indefinite area of land: cf. SND *n.*[2] 3.] An area, a piece (of land).

1992 ANDERSON *Portrait of the Artist's Wife* 132 Humphrey Potter's father..had farmed a skelp of the original Lookout Point land [in Central Otago].

skep: see SKIP.

skerrick /ˈskɛrɪk/, /ˈskærɪk/. [f. Brit. dial. *skerrick* a small amount, the least particle: see OED and EDD; AND 1854.] A scrap, the least amount. [*Note*] The word is of much earlier use in New Zealand than its first recorded date.

1960 Mills *Sheep-O* 100 During the slump after World War I, a farmer told his shepherds..that he wanted every skerrick of wool brought in off the run. **1973** Newton *Big Country SI* (1977) 88 The stores..were stored in the Dump..and a freak flood took shed and all, and every skerrick was lost. **1983** Mantell *Murder to Burn* 122 'Oscar, you saw the composite of the fair man we're looking for. Anything like Nolan?' Oscar laughed heartily. 'Not a skerrick. Gerry's got a Kirk Douglas chin.' **1987** *Dominion* (Wellington) 9 Jan. 2 A 'Skerrick of information' led to the uncovering of the $600 million Maori loan affair, National MP Winston Peters said yesterday. **1993** *Ibid.* 16 Feb. 2 There is not a skerrick of substance in the Prebble allegation.

skid. [Spec. use of *skid* one of several beams on which something rests, or along which something is moved.]

1. *Sawmilling.* Also **log-skids**. Usu. *pl.* as **the skids**, a slipway, often in the form of a ramp or platform, for storing and handling logs or timber at a sawmill or a bush site.

1834 Whiteley *Journal* (ATLTS) 56 Attempted to get up a large log, but the rope broke and down it went and broke the skids. **1879** *Auckland Weekly News* (Suppl.) 13 Dec. 1 There is, also, a powerful hauling apparatus, capable of drawing nine logs up on the skids at a time. **1889** Kirk *Forest Flora* [facing] 145 [Caption] Kauri Logs on the Skids. **1920** Mander *Story NZ River* (1974) 198 They watched the progress of the log from the booms up the skids to the side of the breakdown platform. **1923** Malfroy *Small Sawmills* 17 The logging-delivery tram, mill log-skids, engine, breakdown bench. **1939** *NZ Centennial News* 29 May 8 He supplied them with rice, which, when boiled, made an excellent substitute for skid grease. **1951** *Awards, etc.* 529 All mills, excluding log-skids, shall be suitably roofed. **1958** *NZ Timber Jrnl.* Sept. 87 Skids: Platforms for holding logs or sawn timber. The verb 'to skid' implies the removal of logs from the forest. **1961** [see SNIG *v.* 1]. **1982** Newbold *Big Huey* 209 Every few days we'd drive around in the tractor, load the logs on to a cradle-trailer, and haul them out to the skid. **1992** *Dominion* (Wellington) 9 Jan. 15 The hauler driver then dragged the trees out to a cleared landing area called the skids, where they were set free of the strops by workers called skiddies (what else).

Hence occas. **skid** *v. trans.*, to remove (logs) from the bush (to the skids). See quot. 1958 above.

2. *Freezing works.* ?Inferior pieces that go down a chute ('the skids') to be processed.

1976 Morrieson *Pallet on Floor* 93 He strode briskly, a quarter-filled sack of skids and gambols [=gambrel 'hock'] over his shoulder, along the siding.

skidded road. [A var. of *skid road*, OED *skid n.* 5.] A logging roadway made from (peeled) saplings laid on the surface of the ground (see quot. 1953).

1907 Laing & Blackwell *Plants NZ* 63 A skidded road, six to eight feet wide, is formed of greased logs. **1953** Reed *Story of Kauri* 180 For the preparation of the skidded road the ground would first be made as level as possible... The next proceeding was to procure good solid saplings, ten to twelve inches diameter, from nine to twelve in length, and lay them across the road, from seven to nine feet apart, and partly sunk in the ground to enable the bullocks to pass over them. It was..these cross pieces or skids, that gave the road its name. **1969** Moore *Forest to Farm* 40 Forming..the 'skidded roads' that were so often used in getting the timber out. These were roads..10–12 feet in width and of easy grade, on which the skids 8–9 inches in diameter and 10 feet long, were transversely spaced about five feet apart. These were carefully levelled. **1986** Owen & Perkins *Speaking for Ourselves* 160 The bushmen would build a special road for them [*sc.* logging catamarans]—a corduroy road, or 'skidded' road, as we used to call it.

skiddy. *Sawmilling.* [f. SKID or SKID(MAN + -Y.] SKIDMAN.

1916 Thornton *Wowser* 45 Good, the skiddy, and his wife. **1951** *Awards, etc.* 454 [Westland Timber-Workers Award] [Rates of wages] Second bushman 4[s.] 1¼[d.] Skiddy 4 0¾ Dogger-on and tracker 4 1¾ **1954** *NZ Geogr.* Apr. 98 The story is told at all levels—from that of the millionaire sawmilling combines down..to the parts played by the cooks, the crosscutters, the climbers and the 'skiddies'. **1992** [see SKID 1].

skidman. [f. SKID 1 + *man.*] *Sawmilling.* A workman who receives logs at the bush or sawmill skids, cuts them into appropriate lengths, and loads them on to the skids. See also SKIDDY.

1908 *Awards, etc.* 337 [Wellington Sawmills Award] [Rates of wages] Sawdust-men [£]2 11[s.] 0[d.] Slabmen 2 14 0 Skidmen or carriers from travelling or breast benches per week 2 17 0.

skilion, skillen, varr. SKILLION, SKILLING.

skilling. Also occas. **skillen-room**. [Spec. use of *skilling* a shed or outhouse: see EDD *skeeling*, OED *skilling*; AND 1799.] A lean-to or a built-on room. See also SKILLION, the usual NZ form.

1834 Markham *NZ* (1963) 63 I..was told there was a skilling for me, which I readily accepted. **1852** *Col. Church Chron.* VI. 294 As in the case with bush houses, two skillen-rooms would be added behind. **1986** [see SKILLION b].

skillion. Also **skilion**.

1. a. [A variation of *skilling*: AND 1808.] SKILLING.

1866 Chevalier *Reminisc. of Journey* (ATLTS) 23 A skillion kitchen with a big fire. **1947–48** Beattie *Pioneer Recolls.* (1956) 21 Mr Busbridge drew me a plan of the place, and its five compartments. One of these, a long room known as the 'Skillion' had rows of bunks along each wall. **1991** La Roche *Hist. of Howick & Pakuranga* 243 [Caption] Interior of Johnsons [colonial cottage, late 1840s]—note the old skillion line in the whitewashed kitchen.

b. As **skillion roof**, see quot.

1986 Salmond *Old NZ Houses* 233 Skillion (roof). a single-pitch roof or 'lean-to' attached to a building to enclose extra rooms; also known as a *skilling*.

2. *pl. Obs.* A section built on, often in lean-to fashion, to each side of a woolshed for the purpose of holding sheep under cover.

1863 Butler *First Year* x 158 The wool-shed..has a large central space, and an aisle-like partition on each side. These last will be for holding the sheep at night... In a wool-shed, the aisles would be called skilions (whence the name is derived, I know not, nor whether it has two 'l's' in it or one). All the sheep go into the skilions. The shearers shear in the centre..[and] pull the sheep out of the skilions as they want them. **1865** Barker *Station Life* (1870) 34 A constant succession of woolly sheep being brought up to fill the 'skillions' (from whence the shearers take them as they want them). **1933** *Press* (Christchurch) (Acland Gloss.) 2 Dec. 15 Skillion... In old Australian and New Zealand books (up to about 1880) it is common and means the sheep holding part of a woolshed. I can remember an old hand mentioning the word in the 'nineties. I have tried it on several elderly shepherds since the war and none of them understood it. I imagined the word had gone completely out of use until last month (May 1933), when I bought five tons of chaff from a man and asked him to store it for a few weeks. He looked into his woolshed and said, 'Oh yes, there's plenty of room in the skillions.' I felt as if I had met a notornis. **1979** Temple *Stations* 99 He saw the clearest satisfaction in the sunlight falling through the skillion door over the heaving backs of the sheep and on to the board, slick with wool grease.

skim-dick. [f. Brit. dial. *skim-dick* thin, watered or skimmed milk: see EDD 1 (3) (b).] Skim-milk or milk which has had the cream removed in a separator.

1917 *Horowhenua Chronicle* 4 Jan. 3 [Heading] 'Skim-Dick' Scrap... The defendant..backed his cart into the whey tank before his turn. **1948** Finlayson *Tidal Creek* (1979) 32 Uncle Ted gives Blackie, the youngest, whole milk, but the older ones which are already able to graze he feeds on skim-dick. **1981** Hunt *Speaking a Silence* 16 You'd just put on some skim dick—that's what we called the separated milk they gave us—half the time it tasted sour. **1981** Sutherland & Taylor *Sunrise* 25 Alison skimmed the cream from one of the full setting pans..and poured off the skim dick into a full-sized kerosene tin.

skimmer. [f. *skim*(ming) *dish* + *-er*, an adaptation of a British yachtsmen's term *skim(ming) dish* to describe fast, shallow-draft Rater yachts, and also once used in NZ to describe the 'patiki' type yacht as in the 1911 quots.: prob. fig. from a fancied resemblance to the rounded, shallow-scooped skimming-dish used to hand-skim cream off milk.] A fast, beamy, centreboard yacht, usu. 14 to 18 feet (4.27 to 5.5 m) long, with a flat ('transom') bow, but sometimes with a rounded ('spoon') bow.

[*Note*] The 'skimmer' designer could gain an advantage by replicating the underwater sections of a much longer hull, and also chop off a section of the bow (or stern) to enable the hull to measure in a smaller class.

1911 *NZ Yachtsman* 1 Apr. It was a pity that the skimmer, *Maroondah*, did not work close in shore all the way round from Station Bay Point. *Ibid.* 21 Nov. A very good start was made at 3.15 p.m. when the 5 skimmers held well together till the turn up the Heathcote. **1946** *Lee Rail* (Official organ of Richmond Yacht Club) 21 Feb. The way George McKeown is just 'mooching' about with his new 18ft. skimmer, it looks like he's waiting for something. **1950** in Carter *A Yachtsman's Memories of Long Ago* (1976, repr. from *Sea Spray* Mar. 1950) 115 He drew it out, chopped off the bow, giving her a transom in place of a pointed stem. The public called her a skimmer; Jack called her a frying-pan, 'complete with handle'. **1957** *Sea Spray* June 34 Stan Pascoe's skimmer Quiz, again won the 18ft...Auckland Championship. [**1991** Harrison *Ebb & Flow* 41 Most of the [Christchurch Yacht Club] fleet were [in the early 20th c.] thirty footers [*sic*] known then as 'skimming dishes'.]

skin.

1. [AND 1955.] In the phr. **(one's) skin is cracking**, of a person, 'dry' with a craving for alcoholic liquor.

1934 *Press* (Christchurch) (Acland Gloss.) 27 Jan. 15 Skin cracking.—Anxious to get away to town for a burst. **1975** Anderson *Men of Milford Road* 170 He took his money with him and as 'his skin was cracking a bit', to use the expression of the time, he called in at a few 'boozers' on the way.

SKINK

2. [f. *skin* a flayed animal pelt.] **a.** Special Comb. with main reference to deer-culling. **skin-fly**, a fly or fly-tent arranged to shelter deer-skins from the weather; **skin-money**, payment received for deer-skins; **skin shelter**, see *skin-fly*; **skin-shooting**, shooting deer professionally for their skins.
   1952 THOMSON *Deer Hunter* 177 We used the canvas canoe to bring ashore a few odds and ends, and a **skin fly** which we pitched to store dry wood for firing, as well as to use for a cooking galley. 1960 CRUMP *Good Keen Man* 24 It took me three trips to get [my deer skins] down to the hut where I proudly arranged them under the skin-fly. *Ibid.* 31 The only thing that didn't increase with time was my roll of **skin-money**. 1952 THOMSON *Deer Hunter* 34 When sun-dried, or dried in the **skin shelters**, the hides were branded ready for marketing. 1947 NEWTON *Wayleggo* 137 **Skin-shooting** is really a job for one man.

b. Special Comb. **skin hole**, the chute-opening for the disposal of pelts at a freezing-works.
   1989 PERRIAM *Where it all Began* 164 Ron Summers, a pelter, fell down the skin hole one day.

c. *transf.* Usu. *pl.*, cigarette papers.
   1982 NEWBOLD *Big Huey* (Gloss.) 253 Skins (n) Cigarette papers.

3. [f. *skin* the covering of the body of a live animal.] Special Comb. **skin boy**, an uncircumcized male; **skin scratch** *shearing*, see quot.
   1987 NORGROVE *Shoestring Sailors* 138 'Of course **skinboys** pick it up quicker than those who have been ringbarked.' 'Ringbarked?' 'Circumcised.' 1955 BOWEN *Wool Away* 4 There is a big difference between what is termed a **skin scratch** and a cut. Shearing sticky sheep is practically impossible without skin scratches (a small mark on the outer skin that does not bleed and is not apparent the next day).

skink. A spec. use of *skink* for any of various shiny-scaled small-eyed lizards of the family Scincidae, most of the New Zealand species of which give birth to live young; also with many modifiers forming mainly 'book names' to distinguish species, including **common skink** (*Leiolopisma nigriplantare*), **copper skink** (*Cyclodina aenea*), **egg-laying skink** (*L. suteri*), **Smith's skink** (*L. smithi*) and **speckled skink** (*L. infrapunctatum*). See also MOKOMOKO.
   [*Note*] Skinks would in general be referred to in New Zealand popular speech merely as 'lizards'; see also note at GECKO *n.*[1]
   1937 BUICK *Moa-Hunters of NZ* 162 [The Waitaki-mouth site's] principal inhabitants are skinks, or large green rock-lizards, and rabbits. 1947 POWELL *Native Animals* 74 Our true lizards are referred to as either skinks or geckos—the former have small heads, are smooth and scaly all over and live on the ground—the latter have broad heads, a soft skin, with scales found only on the head and belly and are to be found mostly amongst the foliage of trees and shrubs. 1966 SHARELL *The Tuatara, Lizards & Frogs of NZ* 51 The Common lizard or skink (*Leiolopisma zelandica*...) Occurs in great varieties of colour and patterns in..brown, and is found all over New Zealand. 1967 NATUSCH *Animals NZ* 246 Skinks..are mostly active by day, retiring to shelter at night; but a few are nocturnal. 1979 *Forest & Bird* 214 35 The skinks, though the most recently established endemic reptiles in New Zealand, constitute the greatest number of species. 1986 *Illustr. Encycl. NZ* 1 134 Skinks are the commonest form of lizard found in New Zealand with about 22 species. 1986 GILL *Collins Handguide to Frogs & Reptiles* 56 Egg-laying Skink *Leiolopisma suteri*... The only native lizard that lays eggs. *Ibid.* 60 Speckled Skink *Leiolopisma infrapunctatum*... Widespread but localised... Open scrubby areas and tussock country. *Ibid.* 64 Smith's Skink *Leiolopisma smithi*... The common beach skink of northern New Zealand. *Ibid.* 72 Common Skink *Leiolopisma nigriplantare*... The most widespread New Zealand skink and the common garden skink of the South Island and many parts of the southern North Island. *Ibid.* 84 Copper Skink *Cyclodina aenea*... New Zealand's smallest native lizard. The commonest garden skink in Auckland and the more wooded suburbs of Wellington.

skinnamalink. [f. Sc. dial.: see OED *skinny a.* 6 'Chiefly *Sc.*'.] A weedy child; occas. used in friendly address to a child.
   1933 BAUME *Half Caste* 44 'Pooh, nigger!' This from a skinnamalink of thirteen with two plaits of mousey coloured hair. c1935 Taranaki p.c. Dr. D.E. Hurley. 'Young skinnamalink' was a common form of address to a child.

skinner, *n. Obs.* [Transf. use of Brit. slang *skinner* one who 'fleeces' or strips another of money or property: see OED 4 b.]
1. *Canterbury.* See quot.
   1892 SWANTON *Notes on NZ* 75 At one time in Canterbury there were people who took up land for about four or five years at a time and simply grew nothing but wheat. Of course this ruined the land for some time to come. When they had finished one patch they took up another and repeated the operation. From this they obtained the title of 'skinners'.

2. [AND 1891.] A horse that wins at very long odds.
   1905 *Truth* 26 Aug. 2 All this [*sc.* a big win of £800] in addition to having a 'skinner' on his own double book. 1906 *Ibid.* 24 Feb. 1 Jack and Jill went on the kill To pick a long-priced winner, But Jack came down— He dropped a crown, And Ikey had a 'skinner'. 1918 *Kia-ora Coo-ee* (1981) 15 Aug. II. 5 Perhaps he was on his way to try his luck with us, knowing what good sports we are. He was lucky right enough, receiving a 'skinner' first pop. 1960 SCRYMGEOUR *Memories Maoriland* 105 'Stewie,' he [*sc.* the bookmaker] exclaimed..'you gave me almost a skinner [when you looked like losing].'

skinner, *quasi-adjective.* [Formed on *skinned* penniless.] As **a skinner** used predicatively (esp. **to be a skinner**), (to be) penniless, broke, 'skint'; empty, finished; having no (liquor, food, etc.) left.
   1946 SARGESON *That Summer* 69 I didn't have the price of a tram fare because Ted had left me a skinner. 1951 LAWSON *Gold in Their Hearts* 130 'Ain't they gettin' gold there now?' 'Not much—she's a bit of a skinner, I reckon.' 1964 MORRIESON *Came a Hot Friday* (1981) 149 'He's broke,' said Don. 'He ees a skinner for dinner,' agreed Esmerelda. 1970 DUGGAN *O'Leary's Orchard* 96 Sure you're a skinner? Not a drop in the place, I mean? 1988 MCGILL *Dict. Kiwi Slang* 103 *skinner* broke or empty; in latter case you might say 'the beer's a skinner'.

skinnier than a gumdigger's dog: see GUMDIGGER *n.*[1] 2.

skinnies, *n. pl. Obs.* As **the skinnies**, BUSH SICKNESS a.
   1928 *NZ Free Lance* (Wellington) 22 June 7 New Zealand 'bush sickness' or 'the skinnies' as it is graphically labelled by the farmers of this country. 1929–30 *TrNZI* LX. 47 As a descriptive title 'the skinnies' is much more appropriate and quite descriptive... The animal appears like nothing so much as a walking skeleton.

skinplaster: see SHINPLASTER.

skip. Also **skep.** OED *n.*[2] covers a wide range of applications for *skip* or *skep* as a basket, container, bin, box on wheels, etc., most of which are, or have been, recorded in New Zealand use, esp. in mining uses, but also in those of railways or woolstore. *Spec.* used in some localities for a large removable rubbish-container (often called a BIN (q.v. *n.* 3)). Hence (Invercargill) **skip-truck**, a truck with a special hoist for lifting and transporting skips.
   1904 *Awards, etc.* 9 [Hikurangi Coal-Miners Agreement] The skips are estimated at 12cwt. 1950 *NZJAg.* Oct. LXXXI. 311 Baskets or skeps on wheels are handy for holding [wool] pieces and can be wheeled to the press from the table. 1972 *Marlborough Express* (Blenheim) 12 Oct. 1 The crane on the site was used to lower a skip, containing the stretcher, to the ambulance waiting below. 1982 *Listener* 4 Dec. 21 All this passes Otago and Southland by. They don't have bins at all. Perpetuating the linguistic independence which began when whey decided to call baches 'cribs', the goodly citizens of Dunedin and Invercargill refer to bins as 'skips'. 1982 *Agric. Gloss.* (MAF) 59 *skep*: Pronounced skip. Trolley for carrying loose wool in a woolstore or mill. Also called a dobbin. 1985 Nov. 21 p.c. Nicholas Ransom. *Skip-truck*..is the name in Invercargill for the special vehicle used to move a *skip*. 1986 *National Bus. Rev.* 1 Aug. 56 The New Zealand listing follows the signing of franchising agreements by Miniskips New Zealand to establish operations here based on the rapid acceptance in Australia of its waste disposal concept using small, on-call collection vehicles and minibins, known in Australia as 'skips'.

skipjack. [f. the habit of appearing to 'skip' across the surface of the sea.]
1. a. Either of TREVALLY (*Pseudocaranx dentex*) (*obs.*) or mainly now as elsewhere (see DSAE) **skip jack tuna** (*Katsuwonis pelamis*, fam. Scombridae, see also TUNA *n.*[2]) which is found in New Zealand northern waters from about December to May.
   [1769 MONKHOUSE 3 Oct. in Cook *Journals* (1955) I. 166 Saw some fish like skip Jacks and a small sort that appear'd very transparent.] 1791 BELL *Jrnl. Voyage H.M.S. 'Chatham'* (Vancouver exped.) (ATLMS) 51 Fish..was in very great plenty..the best are the Cole Fish & Skip-Jack. 1872 HUTTON & HECTOR *Fishes NZ* 111 [Trevally] is the Skipjack of the sealers, [and] used to be a staple article of food with the natives. 1898 MORRIS *Austral-English* 419 Skipjack used also to be given by the whalers to..*Trevally*. 1956 GRAHAM *Treasury NZ Fishes* 238 The early sealers called [trevally] Skipjack. It was a staple diet of the Maoris who assembled on fine calm days and drove the fish into weirs formed of branches. 1966 DOOGUE & MORELAND *Sea Anglers' Guide* 268 Striped Bonito... *Other names*: Katsuwonis pelamis; striped tunny or tuna, skipjack, bonito, and sometimes, skipper. 1978 *Catch* Aug. suppl. 8 Many large surface schools of skipjack were encountered in New Zealand waters during the 1977–78 season. 1986 PAUL *NZ Fishes* 128 Skipjack tuna *Katsuwonus pelamis*. Skipjack are world wide in distribution in tropical and sub tropical waters.

b. Occas. and locally a fish-trade name for PIGFISH. See quot. at SNAP JACK.

2. *white-faced storm petrel* (PETREL 2 (19) b (e)).
   1966 FALLA et al. *Birds NZ* 55 White-faced Storm

Petrel...*Takahikare-moana, Skipjack,* Jesus Christ Bird (shortened to 'J.C. Bird'). **1985** [see DANCING DOLLY].

skipper. [See quot. 1982.] NEEDLEFISH.
1872 HUTTON & HECTOR *Fishes NZ* 118 Gar Fish. This name is applied..to the Skipper (*Scombresox Forsteri*). **1886** SHERRIN *Handbook Fishes NZ* 305 *Scombresox Forsteri...* Skipper. **1921** *NZJST* IV. 120 *Skipper.* A highly esteemed edible fish, known as 'deep-sea piper' at Bay of Islands. **1966** [see NEEDLEFISH]. **1982** AYLING *Collins Guide* (1984) 172 Sauries are often called skippers in reference to their habit of leaping clear of the water and skipping along on their tails for short distances.

skirt, *n. Shearing.* [f. Brit. dial. *skirt*: see EDD *n.* 8.] Often *pl.*, the edges of a fleece; occas. SKIRTING 1.
1851 WELD *Hints to Intending Sheep-farmers* 8 The Merino has the more valuable wool, being finer, and particularly superior in the 'skirts', which are remarkably deficient in crossed sheep. **1884** CHUDLEIGH *Diary* 31 Dec. (1950) 331 Shearing and drying sheeps skirts till Dec. 31 when the Omahe anchored at Taupeka. **1955** BOWEN *Wool Away* 92 In skirting a fleece use two hands—holding the edge of the fleece in one hand, take off the skirt with the other.

skirt, *v. Shearing.* [f. Brit. dial.: see EDD *n.* 8 and *skirting* 5; OED 5 b; AND 1833.] *trans.* To trim or remove (the skirtings) from a fleece.
1883 *Brett's Colonists' Guide* 172 Fleeces should be carefully skirted, and all daggings and faulty parts removed. **1901** *TrNZI* XXXIII. 196 The latter is always skirted and classed, whereas the black fleece was rolled up just as taken from the sheep's back. **1913** CARR *Country Work* 15 When the fleece is thrown on the table by the fleece-picker, the wool rollers..skirt—i.e., take off the dirty wool—the neck (in some sheds) and legs. **1922** *Auckland Weekly News* 7 Dec. 21 Other lots were discounted through careless classing and not being skirted. **1936** BELSHAW et al. *Agric. Organiz. NZ* 710 'Necks', which are generally removed when skirting, are baled separately in the case of large clips. **1955** [see SKIRT *n.*]. **1988** *More* (Auckland) Mar. 30 [They] skirt the dirty bits off the sides as they're shearing.

Hence **skirted** (also **unskirted**) *ppl. a.*, of a fleece, having the skirtings removed; **skirter** [AND 1883], a shed hand who skirts fleeces.
c1927 SMITH *Sheep & Wool Industry* 80 Badly skirted wool will often bring a penny a pound less. **1936** BELSHAW et al. *Agric. Organiz. NZ* 707 It may be taken for granted that a buyer faced with a mass of unskirted wool will, on the average, shade the price as a sort of insurance against the risk he runs in buying it. **1981** SUTHERLAND & TAYLOR *Sunrise* 43 The shearers brought their own cook and fleecos and **skirters**.

skirting, *vbl. n. Shearing.* [f. SKIRT *v.*]

1. *pl.* [AND 1881.] The inferior parts trimmed off a fleece.
1883 *Brett's Colonists' Guide* 216 There is a portion of the fleece near the breech which is very coarse and hairy, and should be removed and packed with the pieces and skirtings. **1904** LANCASTER *Sons o' Men* 81 'Clear out these skirtings again,' he said; and Walt passed on to the presses. **1920** MACDONALD *Austral. & NZ Sheepfarming* 144 The big stations..may even divide up the skirtings or pieces from the fleece into different classes. **1936** BELSHAW et al. *Agric. Organiz. NZ* 710 'Bellies' form the bulk of the skirtings and are seldom classed except for type or condition. **1955** BOWEN *Wool Away* 92 If skirtings are pulled off without one hand holding good wool, a lot of this good wool tears out of the fleece and goes in with the skirtings. **1973** FERNANDEZ *Tussock Fever* 166 Grade 2, pieces—that's skirtings—hogget wool. **1985** BREMNER *Woolscours NZ* (Gloss. Old Wool Terms) 10 *Skirtings* wool removed form edges of fleece, below average quality of bulk of fleece, of inferior commercial value—short stapled pieces, sweated locks, stained wool etc.

2. *sing.* The action or process of trimming a fleece.
1922 PERRY *Sheep Farming* 121 In cases where a farmer has only a few sheep..good skirting, neat rolling, and careful pressing..is about all that can be done. *Ibid.* 122 *Skirting.*—Proper skirting is most essential. While it is unnecessary to rob the fleece of good wool, all fribby and inferior pieces must be removed. **1936** BELSHAW et al. *Agric. Organiz. NZ* 707 *Skirting* The removal of stained, dingy, heavy-conditioned and seedy wool improves the evenness of the fleece both in regard to condition and yield. **1950** *NZJAg.* Oct. LXXXI. 312 Skirting should always be done at shearing time. **1982** *Agric. Gloss.* (MAF) 59 *Skirting*: Removing oddments from a fleece after shearing.

3. Special Comb. **skirting-board**, **skirting table** [AND 1890], the table in the woolshed on which fleeces are spread and skirtings removed.
1885 VINCENT *Forty-Thousand Miles* 218 We saw the **skirting-board** on which the fleece is laid out. **c1927** SMITH *Sheep & Wool Industry* 84 Two wool-rollers should be at each **skirting table**. **1959** MIDDLETON *The Stone* 49 When..I had spread the fleece on Charlie's skirting table, the shearers began to sharpen their combs and cutters for the next shed. **1974** *NZ Agric.* 66 The shorn fleeces are picked up from the board floor and thrown out on to a slatted 'skirting' table, where they are trimmed of all inferior pieces.

skite, *v. intr.* [See *n.*]

1. a. [AND 1857.] To boast, to show off. Cf. BLATHERSKITE.
c1875 THATCHER in *NZ Songster No.3* 69 He'll drink and commence then to skite. **1906** in Hull *College Songs* (1907) 25 If you really want to skite The remainder of the night, Would you speechify in ordinary prose, please? **1918** *Chron. NZEF* 5 July 252 He used to skite like that at times. **1926** PEACOCKE *His Kid Brother* 83 Don't skite, kid. **1938** *Auckland Weekly News* 23 Nov. 96 Don't ever let me hear yer skitin' about sawing timber. **1940** SARGESON *Man & His Wife* (1944) 79 I suppose he went back to his ship and skited about the time he'd had. **1952** *Public Service Official Circular* No.17 Sept. 4 [A slogan for a Safety Campaign] 'Don't Skite'. **1965** HENDERSON *Open Country* 101 I don't like talking too much about narrow escapes—people reckon you're skiting. **1978** GRACE *Mutuwhenua* xiv. 102 Everyone laughing, hugging Nanny who was skiting about her hat.

b. *Farming.* See quot. 1933.
1933 *Press* (Christchurch) (Acland Gloss.) 2 Dec. 15 *Skite.*—(Of a dog) to caper about in front of sheep; to race about.

2. As **to skite up** (someone, something), to puff, to exaggerate the good qualities of.
1950 *Landfall* 13 20 I'm a damn sight better rider than he is. It's only that they skite him up.

3. In the phr. **nothing to skite about**, used depreciatingly of something inferior; 'nothing to write home about'.
a1974 SYDER & HODGETTS *Austral. & NZ English* (TS) 782 *Nothing to skite about.* Of no great significance; or, conduct better left unmentioned. 'You might've hoodwinked the boss, but it's nothing to skite about.'

Hence **skiting** *vbl. n.* and *ppl. a.*, boasting. Also used as a nickname or appellation.
1897 *Otago Witness* (Dunedin) 11 Nov. 60 There are others..like Skiting Harry. **1906** *Truth* 20 Jan. 5 The sickening skiting of the boodling blowhards of our doltish dilly-dailies. **1915** POCOCK in Pugsley *Gallipoli* (1984) 12 The Australian, and more especially the town bred man, is a skiting bumptious fool who thinks nobody knows anything but himself. **1934** SCANLAN *Winds of Heaven* 86 Such bad form—skiting. **1984** 16 F E15 Pakuranga Coll. 17 Skiting [F2 M1]

skite, *n.* [f. Brit. (esp. northern) dial. *skite* 'Opprobrious epithet for an unpleasant or conceited person' (see EDD *n.*[1] 3); see also EDD *blather n.* 1 (7) *blather(um) skite* nonsense.]

1. [AND 1860.] Boasting; blather; ostentation. Also occas. in special Comb. **skite tape**, a curriculum vitae (see quot. 1996).
1905 *Truth* 25 Nov. 3 We abhor cheap 'skite'. **1907** *Truth* 16 Mar. 8 Her bad books are to good books what 'Bulletin' bards are to Byron and Shelley—sham, shicker and skite. **1913** *Auckland Univ. College Student Carnival Programme* 39 [Cartoon 'A guaranteed flight' with notice pinned to fence reading:] Monster aviation carnival to day Blizzard Sloane will fly the hero of Two Thousand Skites. **1928** *NZ Free Lance* (Wellington) 16 May 6 Noisy riding is a form of 'skite'. **1934** MARKS *Memories* 178 I noted the bored look that usually comes over one's listeners when 'blow' is indulged in, more especially if they know it is pure 'skite', and not in accordance with fact. **1972** NEWTON *Sheep Thief* 149 I thought I had a good district run but you've taken the skite out of me. **1996** *North & South* (Auckland) Jan. 85 As soon as I don't get work, I'll probably take a skite tape to Australia.

2. [AND 1897.] A boaster; a 'show-off'; a conceited person. See also BLATHERSKITE, SKITER.
1928 *NZ Free Lance* (Wellington) 25 Apr. 33 [Caption] Went to school with yer friend Maurice Brownlie did yer? I'll learn yer—yer big skite. **1943** BENNETT English in NZ in *Amer. Speech* XVIII. 89 A boaster is a *skite*, and there is a verb of the same form. **1983** MANTELL *Murder to Burn* 156 Like to have a look around. Nice outfit. One of our local skites and we can give you permission. **1995** ANDERSON *House Guest* 171 'Because it's better,' said the skite.

skiter. *Obs.* [AND 1898.] SKITE *n.* 2.
1887 *NZ Mail* (Wellington) 15 July 9 (NZ Slang), If he talks too much he is 'a skiter', 'a wind bag'..'a gasser'. **1890** *NZ Observer* 12 Apr. 11 Hanlan, the prince of 'skiters', is again seeking notoriety through the columns of the Press. **1905** *Truth* 12 Aug. 7 With Samson's Weapon Alf Paralyses Pug Champions and Wins the Skiters' Stakes Against All Comers... 'Airy Alf Woods..is a well-known champion skiter. He has now talked himself into the limelight. **1906** *Truth* 17 Feb. 1 Hell and fury think you skiters, Where are Britannia's boasted fighters? **1912** *NZ Free Lance* (Wellington) 23 Nov. 14 The local 'skiter' was giving his views.

skitey, *a.* Boastful.
1948 BALLANTYNE *Cunninghams* (1976) 144 She didn't look at Gilbert, and he felt she wasn't looking at him on purpose and that made him seem skitey. **1961** PARTRIDGE *Dict. Slang Suppl.* 1276 *skitey*. Boastful: New Zealand: since ca. 1925.

skitters, *n. pl.* [f. Brit. dial. (northern *sk-* = southern *sh-*): see OED *n.*[1] 1 'Chiefly *Sc.* and *dial.*'.] An attack of diarrhoea or loose bowels in animals or people.
1944 FULLARTON *Troop Target* 65 Phillipson's been evacuated with the skitters. **1959** SLATTER *Gun in My Hand* 59 Men with skitters running desperately for the

SKIVVY

latrines and slowing to a dejected walk. **1978** Cowley *Growing Season* 71 'Notice any difference in the way [the cows] shit. It's all runny, no firm plops...' 'They get permanent skitters.'

skivvy. [f. an orig. N. Amer. *skivvy* undershirt, thence N. Amer. & Austral. 'pullover': see OED (& NewSOD) *n*² 2 (Austral. 1967).] A high-necked pullover of thin or lightweight material.

1971 *Evening Post* (Wellington) 5 May 21 [Advt] Skivvies by Canterbury. A host of colours. **1979** *Ibid.* 3 Apr. 34 [Advt] Girls smart striped skivvies. Long sleeved in popular carnival stripes. **1988** *Ibid.* 4 Apr. 12 [Advt] Boys and Girls Trew and Skivvie Specials. Girls and Boys fleecy skivvies. **1994** *Dominion* (Wellington) 21 Nov. 8 After 14 years of marriage I can safely say my husband has the sexual charisma of a Val Doonican skivvy.

skol: see SKULL *v*.

skua. [Transf. use of northern hemisphere *skua*.] *Catharacta skua lonnbergi* (fam. Stercorariidae), the **southern skua**, a predatory, gull-like bird of the southern hemisphere; occas. also any of various other similar small migrant visitors, esp. the Arctic skua. See also HAKOAKOA 2, *sea hawk* (HAWK 2 (4)).

1873 BULLER *Birds NZ* 267 Stercorarius antarcticus. (Southern Skua.) **1909** *Subantarctic Islands NZ* II. 557 It seems probable that the skuas actually enter the [petrel] holes and drag the birds out. **1914** GUTHRIE-SMITH *Mutton Birds & Other Birds* 40 Sea Hen, Skua, and Sea Hawk are other [Stewart] island names for this great gull. **1932** STEAD *Life Histories NZ Birds* 62 I am prepared to admit that a Skua flying straight at one's head..is somewhat unnerving. **1955** OLIVER *NZ Birds* 319 The Southern Skua, or, as it is more commonly called in New Zealand, the Sea Hawk, was taken off the east coast of the South Island in 1770 during Cook's first voyage. **1957** WILLIAMS *Dict. Maori Lang.* 32 Hakoakoa, (ii) = hakuakua.., southern skua. **1967** NATUSCH *Animals NZ* 265 The southern skua breeds in the subantarctic island and northwards to the Snares, Stewart Island and the Chathams. **1976** SOPER *NZ Birds* 177 The Southern Skua, our resident breeding skua, is seen more as a predator of petrels and other birds, and as a scavenger, than as an aerial pirate. **1985** *Reader's Digest Book NZ Birds* 218 Southern Great Skua... Hakoakoa, southern skua... A powerful and belligerent bird, the southern great skua—like all skuas—defends its eggs and young ferociously.

skull, *n.*¹ [Transf. use of *skull* head.] A 'head' or headed coin in the game of two-up.

1976 HILLIARD *Send Somebody Nice* 75 'Two notes for skulls! I'm betting skulls. Anyone?' 'Ten here to say we see their butts this time.' *Ibid.* 76 'He's headed them! Skulls it is!'

skull, *n.*² Also **scull**. [An alteration of *skol* a toast in drinking, ad. Danish (etc.) skaol: see OED *skoal*.]

1. A bar-game involving the loser drinking off a glass of liquor.

1979 *Dominion* (Wellington) 12 Dec. 1 The game involved trying to throw a match into the other person's drink. If this happened, the loser had to drink a full glass of whisky. They called the game 'skull'.

2. Orig. a drinking contest among tertiary students involving the rapid drinking of containers of liquor against a time limit; hence, any rapid 'tossing back' of liquor.

1986 *Campus News* (Auckland) 3 June 2 The Drinking Horn, held later that afternoon, was compered by Ross Blanch, OUSA President-elect. The 8 oz Individual Sculls were again won by Philip McDonald, of the Southlanders' Society. *Ibid.* 3 June 14 Some [student association] presidents manage better than others at jug sculls! With suitable decorum and dignity, one nameless Auckland Prez managed to scull a jug in the public bar... He was pressed into sculling another Jug—which he did, maintaining his dignity, and most importantly of all, his liquor, all the while. *Jug sculls*, a simple matter of either *being able to* or *not being able to* were won by a Canterbury drinker.

skull, *v. Orig. tertiary students*. Also **scull, skol**. [See *n.*: AND *skol*, 1976.] *trans.* To quaff (a container of liquor) rapidly or in a single draft, esp. in a drinking contest; also occas. to drink up (liquor). Cf. SLOG *v*.²

1980 *Listener* 6 Dec. 56 [I.A. Gordon]... confessing [my] ignorance of the origin of the verb 'to skull' (to drink quickly). **1985** JONES *Gilmore's Dairy* 55 Later he stopped by the dairy to scull a milkshake. **1986** *Sunday Star* (Auckland) 21 Sept. A3 After a 'fair amount of booze' [schoolboy] James was dared to 'skol' half a bottle of whisky. **1988** *Salient* (Wellington) 18 Apr. 15 You're still there, with your cup of coffee... It's cold by now, so you scull the rest. **1989** *Listener* 20 May 12 A tough job when you're sculling beer with the lads after work. **1990** *Evening Post* (Wellington) 31 July 10 A 20-year-old woman, after 'sculling' spirits at Chips nightclub, climbed to the seventh floor of the Hotel St. George. **1993** *Dominion* (Wellington) 16 Oct. 12 The days of sculling back pints..driving home and bashing up your partner are over.

Hence **skulling** *vbl. n.* and *attrib.*, fast drinking of draughts of (usu.) beer.

1986 *Listener* 20 Dec. 13 An integral part of the hoon-ethos itself, is the drinking game... The drinking game perhaps found its purest expression in the version entitled Next. Down a drink as fast as possible (commonly known as 'sculling'), turn to the bloke on your left and say 'Next', whereupon he does the same. **1991** *Dominion* (Wellington) 6 Dec. 24 She [sc. Philippa Baker] won this year's world sculling champs in Austria, and those Austrians drink pretty fast.

skull-draggers. *Obs.* [Cf. AND *skull-drag* to haul (someone or something) along by force, 1872.] The name of a Christchurch gang.

1912 *Truth* 3 Feb. 7 There used to be much more of the push element around Christchurch than there is now, and it frequently occurred that pushes [*i.e.* youths belonging to these groups] like the 'Tigers', the 'Diehards', the 'Scalpers', and the 'Skull-Draggers', faced the music before the beak.

skunge, skungy, varr. SCUNGE, SCUNGY.

skunner, var. SCUNNER.

skyblue. *Obs.* [Transf. use of Brit. slang *sky-blue* watered milk (which has a bluish tint): see OED 2.] A name or nickname for a milkman.

1864 THATCHER *Songs of War* 5 Milkmen give their customers warning, They're leaving their usual walks, And off to the Wakamarina [goldfield] Old Skyblue is walking his chalks [i.e. departing, with a play on adding chalk to watered milk to obviate the blue tinge].

skypoo: var. SHYPOO.

slab, *n.*¹ and *attrib*. [Spec. use of *slab* a flat, broad, thick piece of wood: see OED *n.*¹ 2 b.]

SLAB

A. *n.*

1. *Hist.* Also **split slab**. [AND 1829.] A rough plank split or hewn from a log for use as a building material.

1840 in Chambers *Samuel Ironside* (1982) 101 The only place of shelter my dear wife and I could obtain, on being landed [at Cloudy Bay]..was an old disused kauta [native cooking place], built of rough slabs of timber, roofed in the same material. **1856** PHILLIPS *Rockwood Jrnl.* (Canterbury Pub. Lib. TS) 1 May 37 John & Seal cutting firewood Jem & Georgie splitting slabs for pig-stye. **1866** MURRAY *Descr. Prov. Southland* 28 He will make his house..of slabs split in the bush from Totara. **1879** FEATON *Waikato War* 52 To strengthen their defences two detachments..were detailed to cut slabs in the bush. **1883** *Brett's Colonists' Guide* 16 The slabs should be of kauri, rimu, totara, or kahikatea, split about 2 inches thick, 10 to 12 inches wide, and about 7 feet long. **1905** BAUCKE *White Man Treads* 259 It is a low whare of split slabs, adzed over, and sunk into the earth as closely as the inequalities of adze-joining will permit. **1916** in Winter *King Country* (1938) 13 Our new home of two rooms with timber hewn out of trees and split into lengths called 'slabs' and put up in the rough state. **1935** GUTHRIE *Little Country* (1937) 352 How you worked at felling that tree and splitting it into slabs. **1958** MILLER *Early Victorian NZ* 140 Sometimes the whare is built of large 'Slabs'; sometimes of toi-toi.., sometimes of wattled clay; and sometimes of brushwood. **1995** WINTER *All Ways Up Hill* 168 Jabe camped in a big hollow rata tree while he split slabs and built a two roomed whare.

2. A sawn mill slab, an outside cut of sapwood, often with bark still adhering, trimmed by the saw from a log, and in New Zealand considered mainly as waste timber or firewood, but once used on occasion for rough or makeshift building. [*Note*] This sense, of high frequency in NZ use, is international and recorded from 1573 (see OED *n.*¹ 2 a).

c1846 WEEKES *My Island* in Rutherford & Skinner *Establish. New Plymouth* (1940) 118 Edwards knew a saw-mill down the harbour and was sent off..to tow up some slabs which he said would make an excellent chimney. **1851** *Richmond-Atkinson Papers* (1960) I. 94 The partitions which are very rough (made of slabs, the outside board in sawing up a tree, bark on one side) do not reach up to the roof. **1964** BACON *Along the Road* 31 The mill area was no longer a raw muddy clearing... The houses with their slab fences were probably bleached more silver. **1983** BREMER *Port Craig* 9 We lowered the truck down as far as the slab heap.

3. [Wilkes 1991.] A (usu.) 24-can pack of beer in its carton. Cf. BRICK 3.

1994 *Listener* 22 Oct. 38 If they felt you had played well, you found a couple of slabs of Fosters in your dressing room.

B. *attrib.* in the sense 'split slab'.

1. Constructed from split slabs.

1871 MONEY *Knocking About NZ* 23 They were in an out-house, where, upon a slab table, Miss Dampier was peeling potatoes for dinner. **1905** BAUCKE *White Man Treads* 296 The house measures 10 ft. by 20 ft.; the walls and roof are of split palings, bush-carpentered... A slab chimney, if put there for ornament, is a mistake. **1925** MANDER *Allen Adair* (1971) 15 The slab door of the camp was unbarred by a man who expected some suppliant for shelter. **1959** MASTERS *Tales of Mails* 92 Donald, assisted by Horace Wall, built himself a slab woolshed. **1976** VANCE *Bush, Bullocks & Boulders* 22 He [sc. A. McDonald] lived in a slab and cob cottage.

2. Comb. **slab-built** *ppl. a.* [AND 1854], **slab fence, house** [AND 1839], **hovel, hut** [AND 1836], **slab-splitting** *ppl. a.*, **whare**.

SLAB

1857 HARPER *Lett. from NZ* 1 Sept. (1914) 45 A **slab-built** hut. **1940** *Tales Pioneer Women* (1988) 211 Next day she walked back home, elated that the little two-roomed, slab-built cottage set in the thick manuka bush was just a little more their own. **1950** *NZJAg.* July LXXXI. 10 The **slab fence** is seldom put up now because it is extravagant of timber... The whole fence is composed of posts, or rather slabs, say 3in. x 8in., which are set in the ground like posts with 3in. or 4in. spaces between them. Sometimes a wire or capping rail is run along the top. **1851** *Richmond-Atkinson Papers* (1960) I. 96 What with the various discomforts of shipboard, bush travelling, New Zealand hotels & **slab houses** I find it most uphill work to write. **1860** *Voices from Auckland* 54 'A split-slab house' in the Bush. **1878** GRACE *Journal* Feb. in *Pioneer Missionary* (1928) 289 A rough slab house, in which we were able to have a fire, was placed at our disposal. **1883** *Brett's Colonists' Guide* 16 If a slab house is preferred..some experience in bush work will be required, not only to select the right trees, but to split them. **1916** in Winter *King Country* (1938) 14 The 'slab-house', with a few additions, still exists. **1987** WILSON *Past Today* 62 The party crossed over to visit Hori Patene whose house Crawford described as 'a wretched **slab hovel**'. **1848** let. in Swainson *William Swainson* 24 Feb. (1992) 135 We are cooking in the open air..until we can knock up a **slab hut**. **1860** BUTLER *Forest Creek MS* (1960) 43 A person would understand the almost oppressive feeling of newness about everything were he to enter into a colonial slab hut and see an old carved oak chest in a corner. **1871** MONEY *Knocking About NZ* 24 [The run manager's residence] consisted at this time of only one small slab hut, with four bunks and a chimney. **1883** FERGUSON *Castle Gay* 187 When Harry's song came to a pause The old slab hut rang with applause. **1894** *Richmond-Atkinson Papers* (1960) II. 597 I have a smudgy sketch made in 1859... A wretched little slab hut in the foreground and burnt bush. **1903** *NZ Illustr. Mag.* Nov. 108 He had seen weatherboard shanties and slab huts replace gumdiggers' tents and Maori whares. **1940** STUDHOLME in Woodhouse *Blue Cliffs* (1982) 10 Poingdestre lived in a slab hut near where the Waimate creek runs into the Waihao estuary. **1988** HILL *More from Moaville* 31 Jack had roughed it in tents or slab huts. **1922** COWAN *NZ Wars* (1955) I. 452 On returning to the bush one day after lunch, members of the **slab-splitting** party, who had a bull-dog with them, surprised some Maori scouts, who fired at the dog. **1871** MONEY *Knocking About NZ* 33 The old **slab-wharry**. **1899** BELL *In Shadow of Bush* 2 The slab wharé will have given place to the weatherboard cottage. **1946** SARGESON *That Summer* 53 It was only a slab whare they lived in with two rooms. **1962** EVANS *Waikaka Saga* 221 Board houses replaced slab whares. **1976** McALLISTER *Old Taranaki & its Mountain* 52 Pioneers lived in tents, punga or slab whares.

slab, *n.*[2] [Prob. transf. f. SLAB *n.*[1] A 1 as resembling a thin, rough timber slab: cf. OEDAS *Angling* (orig. N.Z.), 1952 Aust., 1986 Brit.] A trout in poor condition, or suffering from a disease. Hence **slabby, slab-sided** *a.*, of a trout, in poor condition.

1921 *NZJST* III. 272 No less than 140 [small molluscs] were counted in the stomach of a 'slab' taken at Rotorua... A considerable number of the trout examined were definitely 'slabs'. The slabby condition appeared to be due not only to the usual poor health of the fish for some months after spawning..but more definitely..both semi-starvation and indigestion. **1964** HINTZ *Trout at Taupo* 171 If you land your fish you are well rewarded. The kelts and slabs seem to have little chance of competing with vigorous, well-conditioned trout during a green beetle rise. **1975** ANDERSON *Men of Milford Road* 197 It was a rainbow and it was a 'slab'. I don't know what was wrong with it but its body was just bones and not very much longer than its big head. **1982** AYLING *Collins Guide* (1984) 229 The fish that stay in estuaries for some time lose condition and become thin and slab-sided indicating that this diet is not ideal for them. **1993** *Sunday Star* (Auckland) 14 Feb. A12 They'd caught 32 [trout]. Most to be returned. 'Slabs' they explained. Out-of-condition fish that would taste horrible.

slab, *v.* [f. SLAB *n.*[1] A 1]

1. *Mining.* [AND 1854.] *trans.* To support (the sides of a shaft) with slabs.

1873 BARKER *Station Amusements* 3 Whenever any wood was wanted for building a stockyard, or slabbing a well..we were obliged to take out a Government license to cut wood. **1967** MAY *West Coast Gold Rushes* 280 Drives, too scantily lathed, collapsed; shafts, too hastily slabbed, caved-in.

Hence **slabbed** *ppl. a. mining* [AND 1859], of a shaft, drive, etc., reinforced with slabs.

1967 MAY *West Coast Gold Rushes* 188 The deep whim-shafts, carefully slabbed for 120 feet from top to bottom, with their closely-lathed horizontal drives, were engineering feats.

2. *transf.* As **slab over**, to trim 'the rough edges off' (something), to smooth over.

1880 CRAWFORD *Recoll. of Travel* 232 The country is either a mountain or a morass; it wants slabbing over, sir.

3. As **slab up**, of a tree, to split during felling. Also *ppl. a.* **slabbed**, split.

1947 BRERETON *No Roll of Drums* 156 It commonly happened that a tree slabbed up from the back after a few blows and splitting far up, the slabbed tree fell just where the man was standing and unless he jumped clear he would be under it.

slabbing, *vbl. n.*

1. The operation of reinforcing (mine shafts, etc.) with slabs; any reinforcing composed of slabs.

1862 WEKEY *Otago As It Is* 60 [Trees are] available for fuel as well as for slabbing and other purposes. **1865** *Evening Post* (Wellington) I. No.245 2 The slabbing in a mine. **1967** MAY *West Coast Gold Rushes* 528 Slabbing: close timbering between 'sets of timber' in a shaft.

2. *Sawmilling.* See quot.

1958 *NZ Timber Jrnl.* Sept. 87 Slabbing: (Mill.) the operation of squaring a log on the saw.

slabby. [f. SLAB *n.*[1] 2 or SLAB(MAN + -Y.] A sawmill hand who handles the slabs. See also SLABMAN.

1907 LANCASTER *Tracks We Tread* 87 The bench sawyers felt it; and the trolley-men..down to the least and clumsiest slabby that lumped in the mill. **1916** THORNTON *Wowser* 180 Barrabas was a slabby..working in the timber-yard. **1923** *Awards, etc.* 112 [Westland Timber Yards and Sawmill Employees] [Rates of wages] Slabby [£]0 13[s.] 0[d.] Fiddler, steam crosscut 0 11 0. **1924** *Otago Witness* (Dunedin) 22 Jan. 72 The man who cuts the wood for the engine is called a 'slabby'. **1938** *NZ Observer* 20 Oct. 7 His first job in this country was that of a 'slabby' in a sawmill near Hokitika. **1955** BOSWELL *Dim Horizons* 19 Why the mill hands, from the tally clerk down to the 'slabby', should be on the top of the social ladder, while the bushmen [etc.]. **1967** GROVER *Another Man's Role* 34 He was a slabby, loading slabs of useless wood onto a trolley and carting them away. **1970** SANSOM *Stewart Islanders* 142 A slabby was a mill hand who sorted the timber on the wharf before loading it on to the cutters and..steamers.

slabman. [f. SLAB *n.*[1] 2 + *man.*] *Sawmilling.* SLABBY.

1908 *Awards, etc.* 337 [Wellington Sawmills Award] [Rates of wages] Sawdust-men [£]2 11[s.] 0[d.] Slabmen 2 14 0 Skidmen or carriers from travelling or breast benches per week 2 17 0.

slack, *a.* In mainly adolescents' use, unattractive; reprehensible.

1981 *Auckland Secondary Teachers College* (Goldie Brown Collect.) *slack*: weak, poor, unattractive *she's a slack sheila.* **1984** 16–17 F E4 Pakuranga Coll. 3 Slack [F6M3] **1986** MACRAE in *New Outlook 21* 47 If he moves in I'm moving *out*. I mean it. I'd rather be a street kid than live with that slack bastard. *Ibid.* 49 Once a week you see them stagger up to the Post Office and the Indian superette. It must be slack to be sick all the time.

slag. *Obs.* [f. (*basic*) *slag*, the slag from the basic or Bessemer steel-making process, finely ground as a fertilizer.] **a.** As **slagged**, of pasture, treated with basic slag.

1936 BELSHAW et al. *Agric. Organiz. NZ* 389 The relative merits of superphosphate and basic slag for pasture top-dressing are much discussed in certain districts... Many experienced farmers are firmly of the opinion that slagged pastures have better milk production and fattening capacities than ones treated with superphosphate.

b. Special Comb. **slag boat**, a cargo boat transporting basic slag.

1987 *Listener* 8 Aug. 66 My mother hated him being a wharfie, especially when he worked on a slag boat and came home as black as a coalminer.

slap-jack. [Orig. US.] FLAP-JACK *n.*[1]

1871 MONEY *Knocking About NZ* 113 We had finished the fifth or sixth frying-pan of bacon and slapjacks. **1873** BARKER *Station Amusements* 269 I only had a shoulder [of mutton]..that night, half-a-dozen slap-jacks, and a trifle of mussrooms [*sic*]. **1904** *NZ Illustr. Mag.* Dec. 180 He was a light and dexterous hand with the frying-pan, and his 'slap-jacks' were the envy of all the housekeepers in the settlement. **1983** p.c. Dr Chris Corne (Auckland) 11 Nov. A Maori woman from Matakana Island was showing me how to make 'Maori bread' the other day, and she referred to it as *slapjack*.

slapsie-maxie. Rhyming slang for 'taxi'.

1963 *NZ Truth* 21 May 19 I was caster for Gene Tunney [=money], so I took a slapsie maxie to the course.

slash, *v.* [See OED *v.* 1 b 'Chiefly N. Amer.'.] *trans.* To cut down (scrub, etc.) with a slasher or like tool.

1849 HURSTHOUSE *Acct. Settlement New Plymouth* 93 The cane-like fern stalks should be cut at once..and the 'Tutu' slashed down with a bill-hook. **1958** PASCOE *Great Days in NZ Mountaineering* 132 Mountaineers were amazed to see that a bushman with a heavy swag could slash a track just about as fast as they could walk.

slasher. [f. SLASH *v.* + -ER, poss. infl. by Brit. provincial *slasher*, or by *slash-hook*: see OED 2 b 'a bill-hook'.] The common name in New Zealand for a heavy-bladed cutting tool, with a straight or curved blade (the curvature described as 'quarter-moon' or 'half-moon') fastened to (usu.) a long handle, and used for cutting down ('slashing') scrub, undergrowth, etc. See also SLASH-HOOK, and distinguish from *bill-hook*, the usual term in early settlement for a common tool having usu. a short handle and a curved or hooked blade.

1871 Money *Knocking About NZ* 129 Though it should be..thick tangled and heavy bush and undergrowth, the party with their bill-hooks and fern slashers must cut their way. **1882** Hay *Brighter Britain* I. 186 A bill-hook, or slasher, supplements the axe, for the purpose of clearing all the undergrowth. **1900** *NZ Illustr. Mag.* III. 265 We had..4 slashers, 2 billies, a cooking 'clobber'. **1913** Carr *Country Work* 30 The work [of underscrubbing] is done with a long-handled tool called a slasher. **1922** *Auckland Weekly News* 5 Oct. 9 [Advt] Handled half-moon slashers... Price 9s 11d. **1936** Guthrie-Smith *NZ Naturalist* 40 Ferns, tree fern, smaller trees and shrubs were cleared by billhook and slasher. **1945** Harper *Camping & Bushcraft in NZ* 20 A bill-hook, or short-handled slasher is essential in bush country. **1952** Lyon *Faring South* 179 The slashers used [for scrubcutting in early Rangitikei settlement] were a style of long-handled bill hook. **1967** Henderson *Return to Open Country* 70 The slasher is like a butcher's chopper with a three-foot handle. **1974** Simpson *Sugarbag Years* 86 There we stood while the foreman presented each of us with a slasher. **1989** Richards *Pioneer's Life* 89 I instructed him on how to sharpen..his slasher, and how to 'scrub' or cut the small undergrowth. **1992** Mahy *Underrunners* 102 I'll have to sharpen the old family slasher.

slash-hook. [Used elsewhere but recorded earliest in NZ: poss. f. slash v. + bill)*hook*.] slasher.

1883 *Brett's Colonists' Guide* 17 The best tools for bush-falling are an American axe, about five pounds weight, and a light slash-hook with a keen edge. **1891** Wallace *Rural Econ. Austral. & NZ* 231 These [sc. undergrowth plants] require to be carefully cut by slash-hooks. **1905** Baucke *White Man Treads* 304 He is a slogger who fondles his axe and slash-hook with the affectionate ease of familiarity. **1922** *Auckland Weekly News* 5 Oct. 9 [Advt] Handled slash hooks... Price 8s 9d. **1935** Cowan *Hero Stories NZ* 273 Sutherland and Mackay, with guns, slash-hooks, and prospecting-dish..were clambering the rocky side of Lake Ada. **1951** Levy *Grasslands NZ* (1970) 74 The slash-hook, the fire stick, and grazing animals..are all important in the maintenance of this essential balance. **1974** Simpson *Sugarbag Years* 152 'Job here waiting bring boots and packs' or 'Bring boots and slash hooks'. **1992** Park *Fence Around the Cuckoo* 26 Mera and I often went to auctions in the hope of picking up..a slash hook, a grindstone.

slater. [Sc. and northern Brit. dial.: from its slate-coloured shell: see OED, EDD.] Any of various terrestrial Crustacea of the Order Isopoda, commonly the imported European species found around houses, esp. *Porcellio scaber* (fam. Porcellionidae), but also any of numerous native species of various families commonly found in bush litter; the wood-louse.

1882 Hay *Brighter Britain* I. 151 [The kauri bug] is flat, black, hard and shiny, and resembles a cross between a black-beetle and the woodlouse or slater. **1909** Thomson *NZ Naturalist's Calendar* 58 The woodlouse,—or slater as it is often called,—is not an animal of high intelligence, but it seems to have enough to know that it is sometimes a wiser plan to stand still than to run away. **1917** Williams *Dict. Maori Lang.* 302 Papapa..4. Armadillium [sic] *vulgare*, wood-louse, slater. **1920** *Yates Garden Guide* (14edn.) 138 Woodlice or Slaters. These are long, oval, flattish, slate-colo[u]red insects, with many legs and a hard shelly back; they thrive in damp places under decayed wood, leaves or old timber. **1933** *NZJAg.* May XLVI. 320 A good deal of damage has been done among tobacco and tomato seedlings by earwigs and slaters. **1951** Frame *The Lagoon* (1961) 44 A slater with hills and valleys on his back fell to the floor and moved slowly along..to a little secret place by the wall. **1961** *TrRSNZ* I. 260 Around houses and under rotting wood, the introduced species *Porcellio scaber* (the common woodlouse or 'slater') and *Armadillidium vulgare*; in leafmould or native bush—any of the numerous native species. **1979** Hulme *in Islands* 25 238 The one with a slater in it. There was a slater in the pot. **1989** Virtue *Upon the Evil Season* 20 We might hear the cicadas in the bush and the slaters on the earth praising His name! **1992** *NZ Gardener* Apr. 7 Here, in Cromwell, we are this year overrun with earwigs, slaters etc.

slather /'slæðə/. [f. Brit. dial. and US *slather* a large amount: see OED and Webster 1961.] As **open slather** [AND 1919], indicating a situation where there is no hindrance to action; a free-for-all.

1959 Slatter *Gun in My Hand* 180 It's worth a go. Come round, she said, it'll be open slather. **1964** Ashton-Warner *Bell Call* 77 Aren't you supposed to have anything at all if her kids can't have it? Or are you supposed to give them open slather, baby and all? **1988** McGill *Dict. Kiwi Slang* 79 *open slather* unconstrained and often riotous gathering available to allcomers; possibly from Irish 'slighe', access; eg 'It's open slather, I hear, at the golf clubrooms this Saturday. Coming?'.

slather up v. [f. Brit. slang *slather* to thrash.] To scold, to 'slate'. Also occas. (perh. originally) as a noun, a violent brawl or 'beating up' (see quot. 1916).

1916 Anzac *On Anzac Trail* 100 Before we got shut of it the battle [sc. a street-fight] had developed into a first-class slather-up. **c1926** The Mixer *Transport Workers' Song Book* 23 Then he slathers up the 'trammies' As the conductor goes through. **1952** Meek *Station Days* 21 To hear him slather up the crowd as slackers, sticks, and sap—You would think Joe was the only one who worked.

slaughterboard. *Freezing works.* Also **slaughtering-board.** board *n*.[1] 2.

1951 *Awards, etc.* 334 [NZ Freezing-Workers Award] The slaughtering-boards shall be kept clear at all times and the slaughterhouse shall be properly ventilated. **1982** *Dominion* (Wellington) 16 Feb. 1 Staff would have nothing to do with the..meatworkers' union, two officials of which were on the slaughterboard. **1987** *Ibid.* 7 Jan. 3 Miss Robin..spent the last two Christmas holidays working on the slaughterboard at Whakatu [freezing works].

sledge, *n*. [Transf. use of *sledge* a conveyance on runners for transport over snow: see OED *n*.[2]] A low farm-conveyance on runners or skids, occas. with a pair of back wheels, originally horse- or bullock-drawn. See also *bullock-sledge* (bullock *n*. 2 a); koneki 1.

1873 Barker *Station Amusements* 3 These stacks..had to be brought down to the flat in rude little sledges, drawn by a bullock. **1890** *Otago Witness* (Dunedin) 6 Mar. 9 The seed has to be packed on horses..to tracks, where a sledge will take it to the main road. **1892** Williams *Dict. NZ Lang.* 68 Koneke,.. sledge. **1903** [see sledge v. 1]. **1913** Carr *Country Work* 11 The jobs to look for [in haymaking] are..loading the drays or sledges when ready. **1934** *Truth* 6 June 15 [Heading] Not Human Blood Stains on Bayly's Sledge Boards. **1952–53** [see konaki 1]. **1961** Henderson *Friends In Chains* 188 Sledge: Dragged by power on ground, mostly used by farmers. **1975** Davies *Outback* 7 Closer at hand, the flat gave way..to hills..crisscrossed with walking and sledge tracks. **1976** McAllister *Old Taranaki & its Mountain* 68 He built a sledge with ironshod runners for the rough track, but it also had a boat-like body for other sections of the route, which crossed many swamps so boggy and wet that a floating vehicle was drawn over the surface of the water and mud so much more easily. **1981** [see konaki 1].

Hence **sledger**, one who operates a sledge.

1915 *Canterbury Times* 3 Mar. (VUW Fildes Clippings 421:59) There were piles of firewood..ready for the sledgers, who would haul them on their konekes down a short cut on the mountain side.

sledge, v.

1. *trans.* To transport by sledge.

1903 *Bill Reardon's roadman's diary* 10 June in *Alfredton* (1987) 163 Medill was sledging wood on Saunders Road with 8 bullocks, sledge 10ft x 6ft.

2. *transf.* As **sledge out**, to hand out (liberally); to produce.

1903 [see sledge *n*.]. **1904** Lancaster *Sons o' Men* 127 They're goin' ter sing up to the house Crismus night, an' Lane'll sledge 'em out beer an' terbaccer.

3. As **sledge into**, to skid into, to slide into.

1984 *Listener* 21 July 37 'He can't stop if he wants to,' said bush-shirt. 'Not with that load on. He'll sledge right into you.'

sleep v.: see Mrs Green, star hotel.

sleeping-mat: see mat 2.

sleepout. [AND 1927.] Sleeping accommodation provided by an out-building, bach, etc., separate from a main house.

1972 *Press* (Christchurch) 7 Nov. 2 On the way out she went into the sleepout where her other sons, John and Robert, normally slept. She went to the sleepout to see what he had been doing there. **1975** *Dominion* (Wellington) 3 Nov. 2 [X], 17, of Lincoln, was found dead by police in a sleepout near a house on the Main South Road. **1988** *Sunday Star* (Auckland) 12 June A1 A mentally retarded woman was killed in a sleepout behind her family's Mt Maunganui home on Friday. **1991** *Contact* (Wellington) 28 Nov. 7 [Advt] A Profile Sleep-out. Do you need an extra room but the extension costs are prohibitive?

Sleepy Hollow. [f. the name in Washington Irving's story *The Legend of Sleepy Hollow* (1820).]

1. A nickname for Nelson town and city.

1857 *Nelson Examiner* 2 May 2 Nelson appears to have become a second 'sleepy hollow', and unless we rouse ourselves speedily, we shall be known, like the inhabitants of 'Tarry Town', as 'sleepy-hollow boys' throughout the neighbouring country. **1877** *Country Jrnl.* I. 251 The 'Sleepy Hollow' boys [sc. the Nelson football team] rode rough shod over boisterous Wellington. **1887** *Auckland Weekly News* 24 Sept. 28 Our visit ended at Nelson—generally spoken of as 'Sleepy Hollow'. **1891** in Wilson *Land of Tui* (1894) 218 In summer, when the heat is semi-tropical, I am told that Nelson fully merits its soporific title of 'Sleepy Hollow'. **1910** Fanning *Players & Slayers* 87 In his time B. Fanning was in some fierce battles, and the roughest of them was at Nelson, misnamed 'Sleepy Hollow'. **1937** *NZ Railways Mag.* Oct. 23 In spite of the fact that Nelson is called 'Sleepy Hollow' it seems to me always that it is Marlborough that is the quiet province. **1956** Sutherland *Green Kiwi* (1960) 172 While we were driving along..Nelson harbour..Glennie remarked: 'They call this place "Sleepy Hollow", you know. I've heard it said that you'll sleep a couple of hours longer here than you will anywhere else—it's something to do with the air, they say.'

2. Any quiet provincial place.

1985 McGill *G'day Country* 77 Through the [Rimutaka] tunnel are the country's most regular run of sleepy hollows, from Featherston through Greytown and Carterton.

Sleepy Joe. [The flowers close up ('sleep') in the late afternoon.] The eschscholtzia; see *four-o'clock* (FOUR).

1945 *NZ Dairy Exporter* 1 Dec. 90 It was the gay eschscholtzia, the 'four o'clocks' or 'Sleepy Joes' (as we called them as children), that furnished me with my pen name.

sleets, *n. pl.* A term in a game of marbles. See quot. 1953.

1949 *Hilltop* I. 2 19 'Huh, sleets again,' said Sid but Ginger only flicked his marble even further from the hole. **1953** Sutton-Smith *Unorganized Games NZ Primary School Children* (VUWTS) II. 770 Consider..the use of the borderline action terms Sleets (Caversham) and Do's (Nth. East Valley [Dunedin]).. meant to overcome a difficulty which sometimes arises in the marble game of Holey. The first player to reach the hole may discover that although he is now entitled to fire at his opponent, the opponent's marble is too far away for him to hit it. He may then attempt to force the opponent to bring his marble nearer to the hole by the use of the action-term 'Sleets'.

sleever. *Obs.*

1. [AND 1901.] In full LONG SLEEVER q.v. A tall beer-glass or the drink it contains.

1936 Hyde *Passport to Hell* 89 [Mabel] knew everything from the zoo to the places where the police weren't so quick off the mark if the landlord passed a few sleevers over the counter after six o'clock. **1941** Baker *NZ Slang* 57 *Sleever*, a drinking straw (the Australian expression *long sleever* for a long drink should be noted).

2. A drinking straw. See quot. 1941 above.

slender roughy: see ROUGHY 1.

slenter, var. SLINTER.

slew, *v.* Also **slue.** [Spec. or transf. uses of *slew trans.* to turn round: see OED.]

1. *Obs. trans.* **a.** To overcome or 'work round' (an obstacle).

1863 Butler *First Year* v 67 This [waterfall] 'stuck us up', as they say here concerning any difficulty. We managed, however, to 'slew' it, as they, no less elegantly, say concerning the surmounting of an obstacle.

b. To outwit; to baffle (someone).

1873 Pyke *Wild Will Enderby* (1889, 1974) I. xi 41 Of their reputation, the miners spoke with bated breath... The general impression seemed to be, that Jack Ketch had been 'slued' (*anglice*—robbed of his dues) by the trio. **c1875?** *NZ Songster No.3* 89 In London the peelers down areas will go, To make love to the cook and the victuals, But here there're no areas down which to intrude, So of course the New Zealand bobbies are slewed. **1889** Mitchell *Rhymes & Rambles* 25 Or levant from Oamaru Without bidding them adieu And the merchants we will slew—let them catch us if they can.

2. *trans.* and *intr.* Of a heading dog, to turn (a mob of sheep).

1933 *Press* (Christchurch) (Acland Gloss.) 25 Nov. 15 Some men have a special *slewing d[og]*; but a well-trained, *h[ea]d[in]g* dog or *h[un]t[a]w[a]y* will usually slew. *Ibid*. 30 Dec. 13 *Turn*—when a dog heads or slews sheep, shepherds speak of his having done a good (etc.) *t[urn]*. **1949** Crawford *Sheep & Sheepmen Canterbury* 40 If you 'slewed' a mob of strong merino wethers. **1966** Newton *Boss's Story* 190 *Slew*: To slew sheep is to turn them in a different direction to that in which they are going. If sheep are sidling round a face and they have to be turned downhill a dog is run out and above them to 'slew' them down. **1971** Newton *Ten Thousand Dogs* 15 A mob of those wethers, slewed out of a high basin, would disappear down a spur in a cloud of dust.

Hence **slewing** *vbl. n.* and *ppl. a.*; also **slew** *n.*, an act or result of turning a mob of sheep.

1933 slewing [see above]. **1949** Hartley *Shepherd's Dogs* 76 In slewing, good clean work, with ample clearance between the dog and sheep is looked for. **1971** Newton *Ten Thousand Dogs* 169 Slewing is done mainly with huntaways and in one of the huntaways events at our trials..the sheep are hunted on a zig-zag course. This is often called a **slew**.

slimy, *n.*

1. HAGFISH.

1938 *TrRSNZ* LXVIII. 399 *Hepatretus cirrhatus*... Hagfish (slime-eel, hag, slimy, borer). *Tuere*.

2. A slimy mackerel; MACKEREL 2 (1).

1991 *North Shore Times Advertiser* (Auckland) 11 May 13 Slimy mackerel, better known as 'slimies', are one of the best baits you could use... The popular name comes from their extremely slippery and slimy skin... Their irregular blotchy or bright wavy greenish markings mak[e] them highly visible to predators.

sling, *v.*

1. In various phrases in the senses of *sling* 'to suspend' or 'to throw'. **a. to sling the billy** [AND *billy* 1879], to put the billy on to boil; to prepare a drink of tea.

1873 Pyke *Wild Will Enderby* (1889, 1974) III. v 88 They lighted a fire, and 'slung the billy',—(*Anglicé*: a tin vessel used for preparing tea)—the indispensable concomitant of all repasts, and the chief luxury of dwellers in bush land. *Ibid*. III. x 105 The billy was slung for tea. **1900** Scott *Colonial Turf* 168 I'll sling the billy and get you a drink of tea

b. to sling off (at) [AND 1900], to throw off (at), to jeer (at), to mock.

1911 Kiwi *On the Swag* 6 They had now altered their time, instead of 'slinging off' at the scraggy moke. **1936** Sargeson *Conversation with Uncle* 18 They used to sling off at me. **1944** *NZNW-3* (Texidor) 41 He was always slinging off at everything. **1959** Slatter *Gun in My Hand* 91 Got the pricker with me. Slingin off at me he was. **1960** Hilliard *Maori Girl* 221 The *pakehas* think you're slinging off about them for saying something rude. **1987** Virtue *Redemption of Elsdon Bird* (1988) 38 They look like a bunch of bodgies to me. They'll only start slinging off.

c. to sling the lead [Partridge 8, a 20C. Glasgow variant of *swing the lead* (cf. OED *lead* 6 b, *swing the lead* 1917)], to malinger.

1916 *Chron. NZEF* 30 Aug. 10 It has been rumoured that they prefer to 'Sling the lead at Sling' [Camp].

d. In the phr. **to sling the dirt (at)**, to slander (a person).

1938 Hyde *Nor Yrs. Condemn* 170 You wouldn't be slinging the dirt.

2. *trans.* [AND c1907.] To bribe.

1982 Newbold *Big Huey* (Gloss.) 253 Sling v. Pay off, bribe.

Hence **sling** *n.* [AND 1948], a payment or bonus for good work done.

1982 *Truth* 11 Aug. 2 How's this for confidence? An owner of a horse racing at Pukekohe on Saturday told a jockey what his 'sling' would be for winning.

slink. Also **slinkie, slinky.** [f. Brit. dial. *slink* (the skin or flesh of) a premature calf or other animal: see OED *n.* 1 and 2.] The skin of an unborn (or newly born) lamb, fawn, or calf; a lamb, fawn, or calf providing such a skin. **a.** As **slink.**

1952 Thomson *Deer Hunter* 116 The tails were salted as was the 'slink' (unborn calf) carcass, while the sinews and antlers in velvet were sun-dried. **1971** *Otago Daily Times* (Dunedin) 22 July 3 (Griffiths Collect.) [Heading] N.Z. 'Slink' In High Demand. A coat made from New Zealand 'slink' is expected to be shown in the Paris autumn-winter fashion shows, which open here next week. For the uninitiated, 'slink' is made from the skins of stillborn lambs. **1973** Hayward *Diary Kirk Years* (1981) 182 We also called in at a venison-processing plant. In one cool store hung rows of slinks—the bodies of unborn fawns. **1980** *Dominion* (Wellington) 19 Sept. 8 The slink skin industry in New Zealand had grown in 10 years to a million dollar export business... It is an industry born out of the statistical fact that even in ideal climatic conditions 10 per cent of all lambs born each season die at birth. **1982** *Agric. Gloss.* (MAF) 22 *Slink*: Calf or fawn in utero valued for skin markings. *Ibid*. 51 *Slink*: Dead lamb (i.e., born or died soon after birth) which is processed for its skin.

b. As **slinkie, slinky.**

1965 Macnicol *Skippers Road* 47 I tanned slinky (unborn deer) hides and nanny-goat skins to make mats. **1967** Macnicol *Echoes Skippers Canyon* 39 Archie was keen to secure pelts of the unborn fawn. These 'slinkies' tan beautifully and make lovely mats.

slinkie, slinky: see SLINK.

slinter, *n.* and *a.* Also **schlenter, schleinter, shlinter, slenter.** [ad. Dutch or Afrikaans *slenter* knavery; a trick, perh. adopted from S. African English: see OED *schlenter*; AND *slanter*.]

A. *n.* [AND 1864 (Thatcher), 1919.] An underhand trick, 'a fast one', a sham, esp. **to work** (occas. **pull**) **a slinter**.

1864 Thatcher *Invercargill Minstrel* 15 'Twas a 'shlinter' for the tenant one morning departed Without paying his rent in the Lowther Arcade. **1887** *NZ Mail* (Wellington) 15 July 9 (NZ Slang) 'Schlinter' is shamming. **1906** *Truth* 14 July 3 The controlling officials [of boxing] don't care a dump what the professional stoushers' views may be on the subject; their plain duty will be to protect the public from a recurrence of the 'schleinters' which took place in this city in past years. **1913** *NZ Observer* 5 July 18 Pure spoof we all are swopping..'Schlenters' ready-made. **1916** Gray, Norman *MS Papers 4134* (ATLTS) 26 Nov. As you know many men..are drafted to Stationary and Base Hospitals..and many of them work all manner of 'slinters' to stay there for the duration. **1938** *Auckland Weekly News* 23 Nov. 96 There is a slinter somewhere—but where? **1945** *NZ Geogr.* Apr. I. 24 Shearers are still better organized and most sheds have somebody articulate to voice their worries if any slinters are feared. *Ibid*. 39 Finally [among unusual words] there is 'slinter', which alone presented the editor [*sc*. Professor K. Cumberland] with any difficulty. To 'work a slinter' apparently is—to utilize alien idiom—to 'pull a fast one'. **1950** *Southern Cross* (Wellington) 22 June 11 Most people know that a slinter is a conspiracy..a take-down. **1959** Slatter *Gun in My Hand* 166 He worked

SLIP 744 **SLOT**

a slinter at the end. Ref shoulda penalised him for deliberate infringement of the rules. **1964** MORRIESON *Came a Hot Friday* (1981) 41 Cyril and I have worked out a slinter or two to work at the game. **1974** MORRIESON *Predicament* (1981) 74 So it's the dirtiest, lowest down crime..but what about the slinter they pulled on Granny? Did they show any mercy? **1983** *Metro* (Auckland) July 81 Origin only to be guessed at. A false call or call where the driver can't locate the person who ordered the cab. Can be used as a noun—'It's a slinter'; adjectivally—'The slintered car will get the next job'; or as a verb—'I've been slintered'. **1984** BEARDSLEY *Blackball 08* 215 Somebody tried to work a bloody slinter on the union. **1995** *Dominion* (Wellington) 4 Nov. 16 I [*sc.* Frank Haden, 'Words' columnist] told a colleague the best way of grasping the essence of *scam* was to think of it as a *slinter*. He looked disbelieving, and accused me of making the word up. *Slinter* is a perfectly acceptable word, or it was when I was growing up in Christchurch. I've tried it on a relative who till recently lived in Christchurch, and he assured me he knew exactly what it meant: a trick, particularly a cunning confidence trick.

B. *adj. Obs.* Dishonest, crooked.
 1889 WILLIAMS & REEVES *Colonial Couplets* 51 Broke! Broke! Broke! At the will of the C.J.C. For the slenter [1904 edn. *schlenter*] race with the favourite *dead* Will never come back to me. **1900** SCOTT *Colonial Turf* 35 [These perjuring race-course rogues] can draw deductions so beautifully, piecing together imaginary 'schlenter goes', and 'put up jobs' with the cleverness of a whole courtful of..lawyers. **1906** *Truth* 28 July 3 The [Boxing] Association is making a 'dead set' against the professional talent which has come into such prominence in Wellington of late, and the stoushers' chance of fixing up 'shleinter goes' is 'Buckley's'.

slip, *n.*[1] [Abbrev. of *land-slip*: see OED *slip n.*[3] 12 b, 1838: not exclusively NZ, but the common word in freq. use.] A land-slip or *shingle-slip* (SHINGLE *n.*[2] 3 b), the slipping of a mass of earth, etc. from a higher level; the mass thus fallen.
 1853 *NZGG* 12 Jan. VI. 1:2 The slip has filled with a mass of decayed vegetation, gravel..the former hollow of a small rivulet. **1882** *TrNZI* XIV. 85 These hills are scarred by..small isolated slips. **1896** HARPER *Pioneer Work* 136 It was on a very steep hillside..falling stones and slips had to be feared in wet weather. **1905** THOMSON *Bush Boys* 59 'You don't mean that big slip about a fortnight ago?'.. 'Why it was enough to bury a town.' **1935** ODELL *Handbook Arthur's Pass National Park* 62 The earthquake in 1929 marred this beauty by causing slips. **1949** SARGESON *I Saw in My Dream* (1974) 117 But they'd come to a place where a big slip had come down and blocked the track. **1951** LEVY *Grasslands NZ* (1970) 273 Slips generally occur in periods of heavy rainfall when soil water adds to the weight and mobility of the surface soil upsetting slope equilibrium. **1987** KNOX *After Z-Hour* 66 'It would have to be *Wahine*-storm weather for them not to clear the slip off in the morning,' Hannah said.

slip, *n.*[2] [f. Cornish dial.: see OED *n.*[2] 3 a.] A young store pig.
 1950 *NZJAg.* Dec. LXXXI. 559 The usual practice is to buy the pigs as slips.

slip-bar: see SLIP-RAIL.

slipe, *n.*[1] *Obs.* [f. Sc. and northern Brit. dial. *slipe* sledge: see OED *n.*[1] 1.] A sledge. Also as a *v. trans.*, to transport by sledge.
 1851 in Ward *Journal* 15 Mar. (1951) 149 [The bullock] drew the slipe from the first as quietly as a lamb. *Ibid.* 170 We attempted to slipe our load across the mud.

slipe, *n.*[2] and *attrib.* [See OED *slipe n.*[4], 1856; and *v.*[2] dial.]

1. In New Zealand, a wool-industry term for wool plucked from dead sheep, or (chemically loosened) from pelts, usu. *attrib.* in collocations **slipe wool,** occas. **sliped wool**.
 1909 *TrNZI* XLI. 42 Sliped wool is the wool obtained from skins which have been washed in water to remove adhering sand and dirt together with a certain amount of the fat. **1918** *NZJST* I. 165 The chemical action of this solution loosens the wool from the skin, and it is easily plucked off by hand. The wool (called 'slipe') is then dried and packed in bales for shipment. **1982** *Agric. Gloss.* (MAF) 59 *Slipe wool*: Wool recovered from pelts in abattoir. *Ibid.* 62 *Slipe*: Wool recovered by a wool puller, chemically loosened with a sodium sulphide and hydrated lime mixture.

2. As **Slipemaster** [f. a proprietary name], a machine used to recover wool from pelt trimmings in a fellmongery.
 1957 *NZ Farmer* 13 June 6 This machine, known as the Slipemaster, is now in operation in the majority of New Zealand freezing works, and New Zealand-made machines have been sold to Australia and England. **1976** MORRIESON *Pallet on Floor* 94 He had expected to find Entwistle standing at the bend of one of the slipe masters, the machines which had replaced the outcast but fabulously paid gang of men whose job had been to save the precious strands of wool after maggots had devoured the adhering meat. **1982** *Agric. Gloss.* (MAF) 62 *Slipemaster*: Machine used to recover wool from pelt trimmings in a fellmongery.

slip-panel. *Obs.* [AND 1844.] A panel of a post-and-rail fence the rails of which can be slipped out and removed. Cf. PANEL 1.
 1853 DEANS *Pioneers Canterbury* (1937) 263 I was thinking of making another slip panel at the gate..but as it is twenty horses could not yard them. **1867** *Richmond-Atkinson Papers* (1960) II. 236 His master took the slip-panel down and the dog then rounded the sheep in and yarded them. **1879** KIERNAN *Diary* 5 Feb. in Guthrie-Smith *Tutira* (1921) 125 Went up the fence as far as the slip panel and found the fence burnt. **1881** PYKE *White Hood & Blue Cap* 121 'Get off here, Marion,' said Nellie, herself dismounting at the Melrose slip-panel. **1891** CHAMIER *Philosopher Dick* 11 One of the bullocks charged furiously against the rails [of the stockyard], bursting out a slip-panel.

slipper shell. Any of various univalve shells of the family Calyptraeidae bearing a fancied resemblance to a slipper.
 1870 TAYLOR *Te Ika A Maui* 631 The slipper shell, very common both in New Zealand and Australia, some attain a considerable size, one is round and covered with a thick epidermis. **1947** POWELL *Native Animals NZ* 26 White slipper shell... A limpet-shaped shell, up to 1½ inches long, with a curious internal shelf.

slip-rail. Also **slip-bar** (see quot. 1892). [AND 1827.] A rail of a post-and-rail fence which can (with others) be removed to provide an opening. See also SLIP-PANEL.
 1860 *Voices from Auckland* 62 The manufacture of rough farm gates..[would] assist to do away with those abominations—slip rails. **1873** BARKER *Station Amusements* 68 [He] bounded over the slip-rail of the paddock before Karl could get it down. We were too primitive for gates in those parts. **1892** HINEMOA *Travels of a NZ Feather* 7 I forgot to put the slip-bars up. **1910** GROSSMAN *Heart of Bush* 42 He leant on the slip-rails and forgot even to smoke. **1948** SCANLAN *Rusty Road* (1949) 81 For an hour Ambrose smoked his pipe as he leant over the slip-rail behind the cow-bails. **1968** *Bull. Wellington Bot. Soc. No.35* 24 Slip rails fencing off a portion of the track show where horses used to be held in the old days. **1986** RICHARDS *Off the Sheep's Back* 103 Most of the gateways were either 'Taranakis' or slip-rails.

slittie. WW2. [f. *slit*(-trench + -IE.] A slit-trench.
 1944 FULLARTON *Troop Target* 18 He'd built the deepest slittie in the Balkans. **1959** SLATTER *Gun in My Hand* 113 That was where you really got to know a man. Sitting in a slittie in the front line. **1978** HENDERSON *Soldier Country* 144 Maybe if I hold a leg out of the slittie during the raid, I will be returning on the truck.

slog, *v.* [Spec. uses of *slog v.* to work hard.]

1. In the phr. **to slog one's guts out,** to work very hard, to slave or toil.
 1949 DAVIN *Roads from Home* 58 I've slogged my guts out all these years. **1968** SLATTER *Pagan Game* 102 I've been slogging me guts out in this school since Adam was a cowboy.

2. As **slog down,** to drink quickly (with effort, or) in large gulps. Cf. SKULL *v.*
 1950 WHITWORTH *Otago Interval* 9 A noisy bar and he-men slogging down long beers.

 Hence **slogger** *n.,* a pub.
 1971 ARMFELT *Catching Up* 9 Safer not to go to the slogger before half-past five, because if they did, they might get through too much between then and closing-time at six.

slop.

1. a. As *pl.* **slops** or **slop beer,** the overflow from the bar-room filling of glasses, returned to the barrel for resale. See also WAMPO.
 1946 MANDERSON *Beer Slops* 6 [The pressure for profits] also causes the revolting practice of tipping the slops back into the barrel. *Ibid.* 11 He still wants those companies who have..sold hundreds of thousands of gallons of slop beer..to be still retained in their privileged position. **1946** *AJHR H-38* 113 The word 'dregs' refers to the drippings from the taps in a bar and to the overflow from the glasses as they are filled. These dregs are sometimes called 'swill'..or 'slops'. **1947** *People's Voice* 26 Mar. 4 [Heading] Are Beer Slops being Used?... On occasion it [*sc.* the beer] has been so bad that suspicion of slop beer being used..is again aroused. **1959** BOLLINGER *Grog's Own Country* 98 This concerned the filthy practice..engaged in by certain licensees of pouring the slops (or dregs) left in the customer's glasses into a special container and emptying this..back into the bulk supply for resale the next day.

b. *attrib.* Pertaining to slop beer or its sale.
 1946 MANDERSON *Beer Slops* 5 He had worked in a number of slop hotels in Auckland. **1946** MANDERSON *Beer Slops* 14 I have an idea this slop practice is being worked in Wellington and Christchurch also. **1959** BOLLINGER *Grog's Own Country* 111 The positive.. recommendations to prohibit slops-selling were overlooked completely.

2. A familiar name for any beer.
 1887 *NZ Mail* (Wellington) 15 July 9 (NZ Slang) It's only in the country..that a man going into a public house calls for a pint of 'colonial wallop', 'tearer' or 'slop', 'slush'..all and any of which elegant terms are used instead of 'colonial beer'. **1976** GIFFORD *Loosehead Len's Bumper Thump Book* 31 There's a lot more to downing slops than sendin' a kid to the bar with his quids in his mitt.

slot. *Prison.* [AND 1947.] A prison cell.
 1973 JUSTIN *Prisoner* 23 'Yeah! Here's my slot. Twenty-two. Come on in.'.. So, a slot was a cell. **1980**

BERRY *First Offender* 14 Prison terminology. Boob for prison; slot for cell. **1982** NEWBOLD *Big Huey* 26 Ha! you reckon this [prison wing] looks bad..wait'll you see the slots! *Ibid*. 107 I was allocated a slot of my own. It was a nice little cell. **1991** STEWART *Broken Arse* 16 Tama is in his slot.

sloucher. [f. *slouch* hat + *-er*.] A slouch-hat.
1903 KING *Bill's Philosophy* 28 That is, if we wear slouchers, and boots a bit square-toed—It ain't for bluey-humpers to travel on his road.

slousher. [Prob. an alteration of *sloucher* a lazy person: see EDD (Lanc.): cf. also *be no slouch at*.] In the phr. **to be no slousher at**, to be competent or vigorous at.
1904 LANCASTER *Sons o' Men* 247 'He's no slousher at this [*sc.* bush-falling],' murmured Bassett.

sloven /ˈslʌvən/. *Logging*. [Cf. OED *sloven* 6 *Forestry*, 1946: poss. a transf. use of (?Cornish) mining *slovan* the cropping out of a lode or strata.] The splintered or uneven part projecting between the front and back scarf (or saw-cut) on the stump, or on the butt-end of the trunk, of a felled tree. (Occas. heard used of the projecting convex part of a 'split' loaf which has been broken apart.)
1946 SARGESON *That Summer* 175 The stumps still had the sloven sticking up. **1952–53** *NZ Forest Service Gloss.* (TS) *sloven* The end of a log cut off to give an even face. **1961** HENDERSON *Friends In Chains* 69 When we reached the bushmen, we found them busy on their knees, cross-cutting the sloven, or rough outer edges, off a fallen silver pine. **1973** SARGESON *Once Is Enough* 69 The severed end of the tree faced us; and its concentric rings, marred by the jagged area of broken timber (the sloven as my uncle afterwards named it), made it look like a sort of improvised target for distant shooting.

sludge channel. *Goldmining*. [Transf. use of *sludge* finely crushed ore + *channel*.] A constructed channel, or a stream, into which drain the tail-races carrying non-auriferous tailings away from alluvial claims.
1896 *AJHR* I-4 2 Petitioners pray that the Main Totara River..and the Four-mile River may be proclaimed sludge-channels. **1900** *NZ Mines Record* 16 Feb. 273 They wanted to induce the government to declare the Waikaka Stream a sludge channel. **1911** BREMNER in *Mt.Ida Goldfields* (1988) 16 This [solution] was to tack on a sludge channel to the head race. **1939** BEATTIE *First White Boy Born Otago* 171 Soon after the diggings got going properly the Hog Burn was made a sludge channel. **1956** *Weekly News* (Auckland) 28 Jan. 45 He ceased his talk of his mates, of the rival claims that used No. 1 and No. 3 sludge channels. **1968** SEDDON *The Seddons* 24 Then like the rumbling of distant thunder came the noise of horses and vehicles rushing to No. 3 sludge channel. **1987** WILSON *Past Today* 89 The building of sludge channels, the main canals into which the numerous tail races draining the claims fed, occupied the alluvial miners for many years in the seventies and eighties. *Ibid*. 90 Similarly, for the sludge channel proprietor. He charged miners to deposit tailings and waste water into his channel at the rate of sixpence a 'head'.

slue, var. SLEW.

slug. [Transf. or fig. use of *slug* a slow-moving land-snail.] A cake or sweetmeat resembling a slug in shape.
1934 *Marigold Book Recipes* 27 *Slugs*..butter..sugar creamed..one egg..flour..B.P... cocoanut essence, vanilla..little roll, dip in cocoanut..[bake]... Put together with butter icing. *Ibid*. 28 *N.Z. Slugs*..butter,..sugar..egg..flour..B.P... cocoanut, roll small pieces the shape of slugs, press a date in the side, dip in cocoanut; bake. **1936** *Merry Meal Maker Cook. Book* 26 *Slugs*..butter..sugar..flour..egg..cocoanut..cream of tartar..soda..Roll small, oblong pieces in cocoanut... Bake..join together with icing.

sluice /slus/. *Goldmining*. [Used elsewhere but of local mining significance: see OED *n*. 5 (1851 US).]

1. An artificial channel comprising a sloping trough or series of troughs fitted with riffled (transversely grooved or cleated) sluice-boards to trap the heavier gold particles deposited when auriferous material is washed through the apparatus.
1861 *Let. from Tuapeka* in Hochstetter *NZ* (1867) 110 I would also advise parties of six to..provide themselves with a California pump, sluice, picks, shovels. **1871** MONEY *Knocking About NZ* 16 Meanwhile, our Oxonian 'chips' had prepared three boxes or sluices, open at both ends, each 12 feet in length, 2 in width, and 1 in depth. **1935** BLYTH *Gold Mining Year Book* (Gloss.) 11 *Sluice*: A long trough along which the wash-dirt is forced by a stream of water leaving behind the metallic particles which are caught by the riffles.

Hence **sluice** *v. transf*. in the phr. **to get sluiced out**, to get washed out.
1873 PYKE *Wild Will Enderby* (1889, 1974) I. viii 31 See here, our claim is a mighty small part of them beaches, and if we get sluiced out of one, we can darned soon get another.

2. Special Comb. **sluice board**, a grooved or riffled board (or occas. one lined with coarse matting) forming the bottom of (or part of the length of) a sluice-box, and designed to trap gold particles; **sluice-box** [OED 1857], one of the long wooden troughs which comprise a gold-washing sluice (cf. RIPPLE *n*.²); **sluice-claim (sluicing-claim)**, an alluvial claim worked by means of sluicing and sluices; **sluice-fork** [OED 1856] (**sluicing-fork**), a long-pronged fork used to remove small boulders from sluice-boxes; **sluice-head**, see HEAD *n*.³ 1 a.
1914 PFAFF *Diggers' Story* 84 We made rough coffins from old **sluice boards**, and buried them in one grave. **1861** *NZ Goldfields 1861* (1976) 12 Could they get long toms or **sluice-boxes** they say, perhaps a decent yield might be obtained. **1873** PYKE *Wild Will Enderby* (1889, 1974) I. v 20 And with the word he..kicked the enemy's offending sluice-box into the river, and five pounds' worth of deal boards went careering down the stream. **1889** KNOX *Boy Travellers* 216 Some of this gold is obtained by washing the sands in sluice-boxes, just as in operations among the mountains. **1892** *NZ Official Handbook* 185 The beds of all the gulches are merely Nature's sluice-boxes, and the rough uneven surfaces of the rocks in their beds are ripples for saving the gold. **1906** GALVIN *NZ Mining Handbook* 276 in Evans *Waikaka Saga* (1962) 44 The advent of the sluice-box dredge may be looked upon as a blessing in this [Waikaka] locality. **1926** COWAN *Travel in NZ* II. ix The men of wash-dish and pick and sluice-box had their rugged prototypes in the pioneers of 'Forty-nine'. **1962** EVANS *Waikaka Saga* 15 When all this first area of wash had been put through the sluice box, they began on the second 'paddock'. **1970** WOOD *Gold Trails Otago* 7 In the sluicebox, water from a stream, pipe, or bucket was played over the dirt while it was stirred, so that the gravel was carried away. Most of the black sand and gold..sank into the matting. **1981** HENDERSON *Exiles Asbestos Cottage* 113 Luring, encouraging, enticing, odd nuggets up to the size of a small fingernail bare their beauty in black sand in pan or sluicebox. **1862** WEKEY *Otago As It Is* 61 Claims shall be classified thus... **Sluice** and machine **claims**, *i.e.*, alluvial claims worked with the aid of sluices or puddling machines. **1896** Biggar *Diary* in Begg *Port Preservation* (1973) 357 At Gulche's Head Mr John McKinna..has a sluicing claim and has taken up some three hundred acres of ground on a prospecting license. **1942** GILBERT *Free to Laugh* 87 My grandfather..worked on a sluicing-claim. **1959** MILLAR *Westland's Golden 'Sixties* 146 In spite of heavy costs in the preparation of..flumes, most of the sluicing claims were 'turning out first rate', as a report..had it. **1966** BARRY *In Lee of Hokonuis* 291 However, with the opening of a new sluicing claim, a representative meeting of farmers, miners, and Mines Department was held in Mataura. **1988** BREMNER *Mt. Ida Goldfields* 38 [Caption] Chinese miners working a sluicing claim at the Upper Kyeburn diggings. **1873** PYKE *Wild Will Enderby* (1889, 1974) I. v 20 Then Barney and his mates set up a wild shout, and rushed at the Co. with uplifted shovels and **sluicing forks**. **1874** BATHGATE *Col. Experiences* 92 The smaller [stones] are sometimes taken out [of the tail-race] with a long handled long pronged sluice-fork. **1909** THOMPSON *Ballads about Business* 70 In the seeming open sewer that extends beyond the claim, Slinging stones out with his sluice-fork. **1937** AYSON *Thomas* 26 'What is that continuous roar?' he asked... 'It's just the noise of the cradles and the sluice forks and the other sounds of a huge mining camp,' he was told. **1985** BREMNER *Woolscours NZ* 19 A hot soak preceded the cold-water wash, and in the Medieval manner a strong arm wielded the six-foot potstick or the sluice fork stirring and lifting sodden wool.

sluicer. [AND 1855.] An alluvial miner who uses a sluice or sluicing to recover gold.
1904 *NZ Illustr. Mag.* X. 182 We saw some sluicers at work further on. The branchman had a big nozzle on a stand, and was directing a powerful jet of water..against the face of gravel. **1909** THOMPSON *Ballads About Business* 71 You'll find these hardy sluicers doing as they're doing now. **1967** MAY *West Coast Gold Rushes* 198 The energetic army of Waimea sluicers washed the terraces through the boxes and into the gully-beds. **1976** VEITCH *Clyde on Dunstan* 48 Below Clyde, on each side of the river, scores of sluicers worked at Mutton Town Point, Sandy Point, Coal Point and Poverty Point.

sluicing, *vbl. n.* and *ppl. a. Goldmining*.

1. [Used elsewhere but recorded earliest in NZ: see OED *sluicing* b.] Recovering gold by washing out alluvials with high-pressure water and passing them through a sluice.
1857 *Lyttelton Times* 4 July 5 There is every reason to believe that many other gullies that have not paid for tomming, will yield well to sluicing parties, especially for a ground sluice. **1862** *Otago Goldfields & Resources* 20 All the wash-dirt is auriferous..but this sluicing party calculate that half a pennyweight to the load will pay them a pound sterling per day. **1873** WILSON *Diary* 30 Jan. in Wierzbicka *Wilson Family* (1973) 158 At last we see the gold in the bottom of the sluicing box and they tell us after about a month's work they have only got three ounces..—not wages, as they express it. **1935** BLYTH *Gold Mining Year Book* (Gloss.) 11 *Sluicing*: Washing alluvials with water under pressure. The wash dirt eventually passing through a sluice box, or over gold saving tables. **1962** EVANS *Waikaka Saga* 11 The term 'sluicing' in this book refers to the use of the sluice box, rather than the nozzle.

SLUMGULLION

2. Spec. collocations **sluicing-claim, sluicing-fork**, see *sluice-claim, sluice-fork* (SLUICE 2).

slumgullion. *Whaling.* [f. US *slum gullion* the offal of fish, etc. mixed with blood and blubber oil: see OED 2 a, 1893 only.] See quot.
 1982 GRADY *Perano Whalers* 228 (Gloss.) *Slumgullion*—Offal from the blubber of a whale.

slushie, var. SLUSHY *n.*²

slush lamp. *Obs.* Also **slush-light** (see quots. 1883, 1917, 1981). [f. *slush*, a sailor's word for refuse fat or grease + *lamp*: used elsewhere but recorded earliest, and freq. used, in early rural NZ: see OED *n.*¹ 6.] A lamp improvised from a wick (or piece of cloth, etc.) set in a shallow container of fat. See also *bush lamp* (BUSH C 3 d), SLUSHY *n.*²
 1862 CHUDLEIGH *Diary* 27 May (1950) 40 [In the hut]..turned into our blankets and read by the light of some slush lamps which is a pot full of fat with a bit of lighted rag in the middle. **1872** in Meredith *Adventuring in Maoriland* (1935) 30 But I mustn't forget the 'slush-lamp'. This consists of an old pannikin about three parts filled with clay, and the other part with tallow, in the middle of which is a small piece of rag of some sort (cotton, of course) sticking out of the fat about a quarter of an inch. The rag is lit with a match or a stick from the fire; the wick is fed by the surrounding fat, and the surrounding darkness is made visible. **1883** FERGUSON *Castle Gay* 193 Now by their [*sc.* shepherds'] languishing slush light... They rose and... Abruptly tumbled into bed. **1908** BAUGHAN *Shingle-Short* 75 Oh! a letter.—Then, 'twas 'Get the slush-lamp, quick!' ('Twas a hollow'd raw potato, stuff'd with stocking round a stick, An' stuck, swamp'd with porpoise-oil, in a pannikin—Smelt, Uncle used to say, worse than home-made sin). **1912** BOOTH *Five Years NZ* 31 The only light [in a shepherd's hut c1860s] is that..from what is called a slush lamp, made by keeping an old bowl or pannikin replenished by refuse fat or dripping in which is inserted a thick cotton wick. **1917** BROWN *Lay of Bantry Bay* 57 In Shannon, Buckley, Kereru..The Sports are piling up their glue, And conning weights by slush-light blue. **1924** *Otago Witness* (Dunedin) 9 Dec. 44 There were to be seen [in old Maori middens]..slush lamps (made of pumice)..and fishhooks of bone. **1947** BEATTIE *Early Runholding* 112 Presumably before this..the hut had been lit with that abomination of pioneer life—a slush-lamp. **1967** MAY *West Coast Gold Rushes* 188 When it was dark the light of the slush-lamps shone like so many glow-worms among the pines. **1971** WATT *Centenary Invercargill* 5 There were few..sewing machines and often womenfolk..sat late into the night sewing by the indifferent light of a candle or slush lamp. **1981** HUNT *Speaking a Silence* 30 We'd get a little tin and put a wick in it, then fill it up with fat. Slush lights we called them.

slushy, *n.*¹ [Transf. use of *slushy* a ship's cook: see OED.]
 1. An assistant to a cook, esp. on a stock station or for a shearing gang. Cf. *cook's offsider* (OFFSIDER 2 b).
 1911 *Maoriland Worker* 20 Oct. 1 [Caption] Get out, and take that 'prying slushy' with you. I want a new cook. **c1930** *Whitcombe's Etym. Dict. Aust.-NZ Suppl.* 10 *slusher, slushy n.* the cook, esp. for shearers. **1940** STUDHOLME *Te Waimate* (1954) 127 At Waimate there were about 50 men and boys employed for the shearing..[including] 1 cook, 1 cook's mate, generally known as the offsider or 'slushy'. **1968** *NZ Contemp. Dict. Suppl.* (Collins) 18 *slushy n.* cook's assistant on a station. **1982** WOODHOUSE *Blue Cliffs* 88 The station cook, with a slushy to help him, would cook for all hands. **1990** MARTIN *Forgotten Worker* 79 The whole army of [shearing] labour was fed by a cook and cook's mate (known as the 'offsider' or 'slushy').
 2. *transf.* Compulsory menial work tidying up the school grounds.
 1980 BRASCH *Indirections* 75 [c 1923] I escaped in this way the Saturday afternoon 'slushy' or forced labour in the [Waitaki Boys' High] school grounds for which the Man used now and then to round up boys.

slushy, *n.*² Also **slushie.** [f. SLUSH (LAMP + -Y: AND 1928.] SLUSH LAMP.
 1984 Kerse ed. *Knapdale Run* 130 [Donald Millar of Knapdale, Southland reminisces] Kerosene lamps were the only means of lighting and were a big improvement on the early 'slushies' which gave more smoke and bad smell than light.

sly grog. [Spec. use of *sly* secretive + *grog*.]
 1. [AND 1825.] Alcoholic liquor sold illicitly, usu. from unlicensed premises. Often *attrib.*
 1842 [see *sly-grog shop* 2 below]. **1904** *NZ Observer* 2 Jan. 7 There is a surprising demand for patent medicines..in the [dry] King Country. Nobody ever calls them 'sly grog', however. **1910** *Evening Post* (Wellington) 4 Jan. 6 The occupier of the premises, alleged to be Mary Jane Barrie, is to be charged with keeping sly-grog. **1921** *Quick March* 10 May 37 Mr A.B. Sievwright..appeared for the defendant in a sly-grog case..at Wellington recently. **1947–48** BEATTIE *Pioneer Recolls.* (1956) 31 McKenzie had a license but she was selling sly grog and later the police had to prosecute her. **1953** SCOTT *Breakfast at Six* 26 Great trade in sly grog—you do know that this is one of those districts where the fools won't allow a licence. **a1964** TEXIDOR in *In Fifteen Minutes* (1987) 200 They said if it would be sly grog or a cat shop. **1986** DAVIN *Salamander & the Fire* 164 Mum cried like hell but I took her for a few drinks and everyone in the sly-grog joints after closing time in the pubs said she ought to be proud of me.
 Hence **sly-grog** *v. intr.*, to sell liquor illicitly.
 1984 WILSON S. *Pacific Street* 9 Some kids reckoned he had a secret whisky still hidden in the bush, where he made hokonui to slygrog to the local people.
 2. Special Comb. **sly-grog seller** [AND 1826], an unlicensed vendor of alcoholic liquor; **sly-grog selling** [AND 1827]; **sly-grog shanty** [AND 1882], **sly-grog shop (sly grog-shop)** [AND 1826], an unlicensed public house.
 1897 *AJHR* H-16 3 Sly-grog selling has existed..in parts of the district where there are no public-houses... Sly-grog sellers are strongly shielded by those who purchase liquor from them. **1900** *Egmont Star* (Hawera) 29 Dec. 18 It was useless to fine these 'sly grogsellers' £5, £10, or £20. **1904** *NZ Free Lance* (Wellington) 30 Apr. 10 Some of these Ashburton sly-grog sellers are humorists. **1861** *NZ Goldfields 1861* (1976) 19 Hotels are not numerous, owing to a restrictive law, but **sly grog-selling** exists everywhere. **1885** *Wairarapa Daily* 2 Mar. 2 The Constable..had been sent in for the special purpose of discovering whether sly grog selling was going on. **1900** *Evening Post* (Wellington) 28 Dec. 6 The Council [under the Maori Councils Act] may also make by-laws providing for the health and cleanliness of Maori settlements, for the suppression of common nuisance, for the prevention of drunkeness and sly-grog selling. **1913** HOWE *Travel Lett.* 73 Sly grog-selling..is what we would call bootlegging. **1954** MILLER *Beyond the Blue Mountains* 104 The police were empowered to raid anyone they suspected of sly-grog selling. **1975** ACLAND *Early Canterbury Runs* (4edn.) ix 328 Green, though more intent on sly-grog selling..made some success of the station. **1866** FARJEON *Grif* 167 It was past nine o'clock in the evening when Richard, who had been drinking at some of the **sly-grog shanties**, came to the tent. **1876** *Saturday Advertiser* (Dunedin) 8 July 5 Act II. Scene I.—A Sly grog-shanty... Enter New Chum and Old Identity. **1904** *NZ Observer* 9 Apr. 7 Two individuals who have been running a sly-grog shanty..claim to have cleared £400 each. **1910** *Truth* 25 June 4 Since prohibition was carried in the [Waihi] district, it has been nothing else but police raids on sly-grog shanties. **1939** BEATTIE *First White Boy Born Otago* 161 Another who kept a sly-grog shanty was a woman known as the Bullpup. **1943** HISLOP *Pure Gold* 118 Heaps of stonework of the old sly-grog shanties can still be seen all along the [Dunstan] road. **1980** MCGILL *Ghost Towns NZ* 63 And you could probably treble the licensed numbers if you included the sly-grog shanties. **1842** *NZ Gaz.* II. 113 Encourage the opening of **sly grog-shops**. **1862** CHUDLEIGH *Diary* 5 June (1950) 41 We had meals in a sly-grog shop. **1876** *Saturday Advertiser* (Dunedin) 8 July 5 And o'er the town, sly grog shops shall be found, And crime and wretchedness still more abound. **1887** HOPEFUL *Taken In* 147 Some of the small fruit-shops are really sly grog-shops. **1912** *NZ Free Lance Christmas Annual* (Wellington) 35 It was in the days when..sly-grog shops and policemen were alike unknown from the Puniu River to Taumaranui. **1959** SHADBOLT *New Zealanders* (1986) 113 Down a narrow path,.. around a sagging ruin that had once been a sly-grog shop and brothel.

sly-grogger. [AND 1897.] A seller of sly-grog, either in a 'dry' area, or after legal hours esp. during the period of six o'clock closing.
 1916 THORNTON *Wowser* 196 Sly-grogger. **1936** LAMBERT *Pioneering Reminisc. Old Wairoa* 104 There were two anchorages..and both were the business places of two sly-groggers. **1988** SMITH *Southlanders at Heart* 24 Those were the days of prohibition... When you cut your own 'sly-grogger' if you met him on the trams. **1993** YSKA *All Shook Up* 182 At 9.30 [p.m. in 1935], he headed out to a sly grogger for more beer, rounded up more girls, and returned to the party.

sly-groggery. [AND 1907.] An establishment from which sly-grog is sold.
 1899 *Hawera & Normanby Star* 18 Nov. 2 There were sly-groggeries, but the young men were not found therein. **1911** *Truth* 28 Oct. 4 It is possible to get as much liquor as one wants in Masterton, and while much of it..is of good quality, much more (surreptitiously dispensed at sly-groggeries..at enhanced prices) is atrocious and harmful liquor. **1972** *Truth* 18 July 41 So that's what you're up to? Running a slygroggery and using this fragile, delicious, 17-year-old bit of feminine fluff as a decoy.

sly-grogging, *vbl. n.* [AND 1952.] The illegal dealing in alcoholic liquor.
 1943 BENNETT *English in NZ* in *Amer. Speech* XVIII. 89 *Sly-grog* was originally an Australian term for illicit liquor; the verbal noun, *sly-grogging*, for the traffic in this liquor, is worth recording. **1959** SINCLAIR *Hist. NZ* 320 (Colonial Gloss.) sly-grogging: selling alcoholic liquor illegally. **1973** SARGESON *Once Is Enough* 81 When I first visited the farm he had told me stories about King Country drinking, that was to say, 'sly-grogging' and 'dropping'.

smack. *WW1.* [Spec. use of *smack* a sharp blow.] A wound, an injury. Also as a verb *trans.* See also SMACK-UP 1.
 1917 *Great Adventure* (1988) 172 I think because there is so little chance of getting a 'smack' that there is a corresponding small chance of getting back to my Rhoda. **1918** *Quick March* 1 Oct. 13 Life was so simple

SMACK-UP

when I was with the old Hard-Doers in Gallipoli and Armentieres. You carried on until you got a smack. **1918** let. 7 Sept. in *Boots, Belts* (1992) 120 I was in No. 2 Stationary in Abbeville after I was smacked..while we were digging in... A Sixth Co corporal bandaged me up.

smack-up.

1. *WW1*. A fight or battle.
1918 *Chron. NZEF* 30 Aug. 56 Our boys are just itching to have a 'smack-up'. **1935** STRONG in Partridge *Slang Today* 287 I believe we are in for a big smack-up... I bet our guns will lay it down thick and heavy, and if I get out of the smack-up with a whole skin I will shout for all hands. **1937** PARTRIDGE *Dict. Slang* 786 *smack-up*. A fight: New Zealanders': from ca. 1906. 2. Hence, a battle: id.: in G.W.

Hence **to be smacked up**, to be wounded or injured.
1937 PARTRIDGE *Dict. Slang* 786 *smacked up, be*. To come off worst in a fight of any kind: New Zealanders': C. 20. 2. Hence, in G.W., to be wounded: id. Also *be smacked*. **1938** *Press* (Christchurch) (McNab Slang) 2 Apr. 18 [Slang of the N.Z.E.F.] 'To be smacked up,' 'to take one's hook,' 'to be where the whips are cracking' are clear.

2. *Secondary schools*. Corporal punishment with the cane, usu. in the phr. **to get (give) a smack-up.**
1941 St Patrick's College, Silverstream (Ed.) **1951** 14–15 M 33 Wellington H.S. 23 Smack up. **1951** 16–18 F 23 Marlborough C. 23 Smack-up. **1953** 14–17 M A2 Thames DHS 23 Smack up [M3]

small beans: see BEAN.

small-goods.

1. [AND 1905.] Edible meat by-products, and (esp. sausage-like) foods manufactured from them, often sold pre-cooked.
1879 BARRY *Up & Down* 181 I had also tradesmen at work making up 'small goods' which I sold to the retail butchers. **1908** *Awards, etc.* 968 [Meat-workers award] [Rates of wages] Gut-house hands 8[s.] 0[d.] Trimmers, butchers' assistants, small-goods packers, and chilling-room hands 7 0 Hide-room hands 7 6. **1909** *Souvenir Programme Jubilee Band Contest* (Marlborough) 30 [Advt] The Most Up-to-date Butchery in Marlborough... We stock only the Best of Meat and make only the best of Small Goods, which comprise—*German Sausage..White & Black Pudding.. Brawn. Pork Sausages.* **1934** *NZJST* XV. 248 One of the outstanding changes in the New Zealand frozen-meat industry..is the development of a valuable export trade in certain edible by-products (livers, kidneys, hearts, and sweetbreads)... Even when low prices prevail for animal products, the market for these 'small-goods' is usually a profitable one. **1959** SLATTER *Gun in My Hand* 67 More men rip out the guts and throw the heart and liver on to the small-goods table. **1974** [see CHOPPER *n.*[1]].

2. As **small-goods man. a.** In transf. joc. use, one with a liking for small-goods.
1910 FANNING *Players & Slayers* 20 [Saturday night football-pub dialogue] Hook: 'I lifted a piece of Paddy Murphy's neck last week...' Boot: 'Oh, I'm more a vegetarian in the things I go for.' Hook: '...What are you getting at? Do you take me for a cannibal or a small-goods man?'

b. *Shearing*. Jocular for a rough shearer who slices the skin, flesh, etc. from sheep.
1952 MEEK *Station Days* 111 small-goods man: A rough shearer who cuts his sheep.

smart-fart. A person thought to be too clever for his or her own good; one too quick at repartee; a know-all.
c1938 Marlborough boys' reply to a smart Alec: 'Smart-fart, who blew you?'. **1971** CRUMP *Bastards I Have Met* 26 How's *that* for a Clever Bastard (*Bastardus Smartfartus*). **1980** *Islands* 29 131 A smart young fart of twenty or twenty-one.

smart weed. [Poss. from a stinging or pungent taste.] A species of *Polygonum*.
1926 HILGENDORF *Weeds* 59 Redshank (*Polygonum persicaria*) is also called persicaria, spotted persicaria, knot weed, smart weed, willow weed, and lady's thumb. **1969** *Standard Common Names Weeds* 71 *smartweed* [=] *pale willow weed*: *water pepper*: *willow weed*.

smell of an oily rag: see LIVE *v*. 1 b.

smelt. [Transf. use of *smelt* a small European fish.] A very small, often silvery, coastal and freshwater fish esp. of the fam. Retropinnidae, usu. *Retropinna retropinna*. Often with a locality modifier: **Canterbury smelt**, **Chatham Islands smelt**, **estuarine smelt**, **New Zealand smelt**, **Rotorua smelt**, **Southland smelt**. See also CUCUMBER FISH 1, PARAKI, SILVERFISH, SILVERY *n*., *second-class whitebait* (WHITEBAIT 2 a).
1848 WAKEFIELD *Handbook NZ* 161 Smelts are abundant on some parts of the coast; both they and the fish called *herring*..readily take a fly in the estuaries of rivers, which they enter with the tide. **1857** HURSTHOUSE *NZ* I. 122 These, with the smelt, lamprey, whitebait..are all the fish. **1860** in *Canterbury Rhymes* July (1866) 85 My friend... You like hapuku drying; Kapai the smelt, the duck, the eel, And shark when putrifying. **1872** HUTTON & HECTOR *Fishes NZ* 126 In my paper I distinguished two species of Smelt... The larger variety..following the flood-tide in numerous shoals..the Maoris catching them as the tide fell by closing weirs made of flax net across the small creeks. **1894** *NZ Official Year-book* 431 Several varieties of smelt (*Retropinna*) called by the Natives 'inanga'..are widely distributed. **1901** *TrNZI* XXXIII. 243 The only true representative of the *Salmonidae* is the beautiful little *Retropinna*, or smelt, two varieties of which are found in our rivers and lakes. **1922** *NZJST* V. 94 The larval smelt, which has a strong cucumber-like smell, is rarely sold as 'whitebait'. **1930** *NZ Fishing & Shooting Gaz.* 1 Feb. 10 The large size inanga, smelt or silvery make a delicious table fish (with a cucumber smell and flavour)... Early settlers often netted quantities and preserved them in bottles with weak vinegar and cloves. **1940** PHILLIPPS *Fishes NZ* 53 New Zealand Smelt... The smelt is the cucumber fish of some localities and the silvery of others. *Ibid.* 54 It is to be regretted that in Canterbury the term smelt is still used to apply to the minnow, *Galaxias attenuatus*. **1956** GRAHAM *Treasury NZ Fishes* 399 Canterbury Smelt *Retropinna* spp. nov. (unnamed)... Chatham Islands smelt *Retropinna chathamensis*... Southland Smelt *Retropinna osmeroides*... Rotorua Smelt *Retropinna lacustris*. **1986** PAUL *NZ Fishes* 49 *Common smelt*... Also called silvery, estuarine smelt, or cucumber.

smiddy. *Otago-Southland*. [f. Sc. and northern Brit. dial.] A smithy.
1937 AYSON *Thomas* 50 I just had a keek into Rab Macgregor's smiddy before I left hame and watched them awee, and soon saw there was naethin' in 't. **1939** BEATTIE *First White Boy Born Otago* 69 On the beach down Rattray Street, north side, was Davie Macdonald's smiddy or blacksmith's shop. **1967** MCLATCHIE *Tang of Bush* 101 'I never heard such rot,' exclaimed Andy Richardson. 'Do you mean to say that when my smiddy

SMOKE

fire is stoked up the heat going out the chimney is not wasted?' **1982** SANSOM *In Grip of Island* 37 All the ironwork was done in his own smiddy.

smoke, *n*.[1]

1. [AND 1770; also US.] A column of smoke serving as a signal or the sign of an encampment, esp. in the phr. **to make** (or **put up**) **a smoke**.
1874 KENNAWAY *Crusts* 60 We arranged a signal, often used up country, agreeing that if either party found the sheep, they should *make a smoke* to telegraph the fact to the other. **a1916** SMITH *Reminiscences of a Pioneer Surveyor from 1840 to 1916* (Auckland Inst. & Museum MS) in Hunt *Twenty-five Years Experience* (1866, new edn. 1990) 101 [In 1868] [a]ccording to prior arrangement with Hunt we had been making 'smokes' at Cape Fournier but after a week, getting no answering signal, we made arrangements with the natives..to let us have a boat. **1933** *Press* (Christchurch) (Acland Gloss.) 18 Nov. 15 *Put up a Smoke*.—To light a snowgrass bush, etc., as a signal when mustering. **1952** Dec. Davie Gunn (Hollyford Valley) advising tyro trampers (Ed.) 'Make a smoke for the steamer at Greenstone [on Lake Wakatipu].'

2. [AND 1908.] In the phr. **in smoke**, in hiding.
1937 PARTRIDGE *Dict. Slang* 422 *in smoke*. In hiding: New Zealand c[ant] (–1932). Thereby shrouded. **1938** *Press* (Christchurch) (McNab Slang) 2 Apr. 18 [In local criminal slang] 'in smoke' is in hiding. **1966** *NZ Contemp. Dict. Suppl.* (Whitcombe's) 625 *v. int. smoke* to decamp escape: (phrase) in smoke, usually of criminals in hiding.

3. In the phr. **like smoke in a wheelbarrow**, an expression of disbelief.
1953 SUTTON-SMITH *Unorganized Games NZ Primary School Children* (VUWTS) II. 677 Some of the [slang] expressions listed by children in two schools are: 'Up the shoot..like smoke in a wheelbarrow' (Kaitaia).

4. [AND 1892.] Abbrev. of BIG SMOKE b.
1980 MACKENZIE *While We Have Prisons* 98 *smoke* city. **1988** SMITH *Southlanders at Heart* 134 For a bloke from the 'smoke' who has never a bean, An' no knowledge of farming, it's almost obscene.

5. Special Comb. **smoke concert** [AND 1891], an informal male gathering for light entertainment, smoking and drinking (see also SMOKER[1], SMOKO *n*.[2]); **smoke fly**, see quot.; **smoke hole**, a fumarole (see OED 1899); **smoke-pole**, a cigarette; **smoke social** *obs*. [AND 1901], *smoke concert*.
1887 *Auckland Weekly News* 1 Jan. 7 They had a **smoke concert** with a Salvation Army accompaniment. **1898** *NZ Times* (Wellington) 2 Nov. 2 A smoke concert to celebrate the opening of the Port Nicholson Cycling Club's rooms in Willis Street was held last night. **1904** *NZ Observer* 2 July 5 Frank Seccombe..was entertained at a smoke concert by the staff and employees of the Great Northern Brewery on Monday evening. **1921** *Quick March* 11 July 44 [Heading] A 'Smoko'. The entertainment committee..has in hand..arranging a smoke concert for the Diggers of this city. **1934** MULGAN *Spur of Morning* 344 One of the boys told a story he had heard of a smoke concert with which the victorious Rugby club had ended the season. **1948** FINLAYSON *Tidal Creek* (1979) 148 No smoke concert is a proper success without Uncle Ted. **1977** BROOKING *Massey—its early years* 106 'Smoke concerts', a kind of stag party and forerunner of the Massey 'bash', and dances were held frequently. **1933** WASHBOURN *Reminiscences of Early Days* 12 There were then [c1857 near the bush] millions of small flies which were known as '**smoke flies**'... Most flies..do not like smoke, but these seemed to delight in it and over a camp fire they would form a

SMOKE

high column in the smoke. They did not bite or interfere in any way. **1865** CHUDLEIGH *Diary* 25 July (1950) 195 There are lovely clumps of bush in the rocky portion of the [Rakaia] gorge. There is a **smoake hole** [*sic*] a curious cleft from whence comes a sulphurous steam at times vis[i]ble from a long way though very slight when I visited the hole some time since. **1970** *Listener* 21 Sept. 14 A long time since he'd fired the old **smoke-pole**, anyway. **1911** *Maoriland Worker* 7 July 12 A **smoke social** was tendered Comrade Semple on Saturday, June 24, by the Waihi Miners' Union Committee and Executive, and a few personal friends. **1912** *Ibid.* 26 Jan. 12 At the conclusion of the conference between the waterside workers' representatives and the shipping companies, a smoke social was tendered visiting delegates.

smoke, *n.*² In occas. use for SMOKO *n.*¹ b.
1875 *Otago Witness* (Dunedin) 18 Sept. 18 Shearing to commence each working day at sunrise, and end half an hour before sunset... Morning smoke half an hour... Afternoon smoke for twenty minutes. **1906** *Awards, etc.* 625 When shearing wet ewes the shed-manager may alter the smokes and extend the hours..to complete the cut-out.

smoke, *v.*
1. *trans.* to hide.
1910 *Truth* 16 Apr. 5 Warren said he had the chain and 'smoked' it. After that James and Ted pawned the watch.
2. *intr.* Also as **smoke off.** [AND 1893.] To depart hastily and unobtrusively.
1910 *Truth* 24 Sept. 7 Lawyer Hindmarsh protested that the warrant was a high-handed proceeding, while Mr Dix, on the other hand, declared that he had ample evidence to show that Sarah intended 'smoking off.' **c1930** *Whitcombe's Etym. Dict. Aust.-NZ Suppl.* 11 *smoke v..i. sl.* to escape; to run away. **1966** *NZ Contemp. Dict. Suppl.* 625 *v. int. smoke* to decamp, escape. **a1974** SYDER & HODGETTS *Austral. & NZ English* (TS) 966 *To smoke off.* To depart unobtrusively. 'I don't see him—he was here a few minutes ago. He must have smoked off somewhere.'

smoke-o(h), var. SMOKO *n.*¹ and *n.*²

smoker, *n.*¹ Obs. [f. US: see OED *smoker* 4 c, 1899.] *smoke-concert* (SMOKE *n.*¹ 5).
1904 *NZ Observer* 3 Sept. 10 The Ponsonby Lacrosse Club wound up the season with an enjoyable 'smoker' on Friday night. **1910** FANNING *Players and Slayers* 72 The subtle know well how to convert her [the football follower's] enthusiasm into tea and cakes for the 'smokers' or the mixed 'socials'. **1916** ANZAC *On the Anzac Trail* 9 Concerts and 'smokers' on week nights.

smoker, *n.*² [Poss. f. a proprietary name.] Occas. (?erron.) **smokos** (see quot. 1984). Usu. *pl.* Tiny, cylindrical pink sweets with a musky taste or odour, perh. orig. meant to take the smell of smoking from the breath.
c1938 *smokers* known to Ed. as popular small pink pill–like lollies supposed to sweeten the breath. **1950** GASKELL *All Part of the Game* (1978) 141 'I had a cigarette the other day after school,' I said... 'We ate all sorts of things to take the smell away.'.. 'Chewing gum's best,' said Cliff. 'Or Smokers.' *Ibid.* 190 [1978 *note*] Tiny, hard, pink, musky scented sweets. **1984** TRAIL *Child of Arrow* 56 So off we went together and what a big bag of chocolate fish, cinnamon bars, Turkish delight, Bulgarian rock, little pink smokos and other lovely sweets I got for my shilling. **1985** *Women's Work* 67 The toothpaste on her breath reminds me of the pink smokers we buy in cellophane packets.

smoker, *n.*³ *Shearing. Obs.* A former shearing-machine handpiece.
1960 MILLS *Sheep-O* 19 The handpieces of these earlier machines, resembling somewhat those of modern barbers, caused much dissatisfaction. Through overheating and blistering the shearer's hand they were labelled 'Hot Boxes', 'Smokers' and similar uncomplimentary terms. *Ibid.* facing 144 [Caption] The 'smoker', an 1886 Bergen narrow-gear handpiece.

smokey, var. SMOKY.

smoko, *n.*¹ Also **smoke-ho**, **smoke-o(h)**. [f. *smoke* an act of smoking tobacco + -O; poss. orig. a call to cease work for a smoke: AND 1865.]
1. a. A break from work for refreshments. See also *tea-oh* (TEA 2 c). (a) **smoke-o(h)** forms.
1864 *Hexameters* in Kennaway *Crusts* (1874) 124 Sawyers, and stockmen, carpenters, packers, and shinglers and loafers, Smoke as they work to assist them, and then knock off for a '*smoke oh*!' **1881** BATHGATE *Waitaruna* 173 During the morning, when there was a cessation of [shearing] work for a few minutes for 'smoke oh', a large bucket filled with tea and a number of pannikins were brought up to the shed. **1904** *NZ Observer* 3 Dec. 17 The operatives demanded a 'smoke-oh' break in the morning. **1908** *Awards, etc.* 245 [Canterbury Slaughtermen Agreement] Work to commence at 7 a.m. on five days in the week and cease at 5 p.m., with ten minutes 'smoke-ho' in the morning and ten minutes 'smoke-ho' in the afternoon. **1919** WAITE *New Zealanders at Gallipoli* 42 Wherever the troops went in the desert, at smoke-oh, up would come the boys with the 'oringies'. **1938** HYDE *Nor Yrs. Condemn* 171 'They've got to give us time for our smoke-oh,' said a heavily-bearded man. 'We get wet as tykes, and they grudge us knock-off time for our smoke-oh.' **1943** BENNETT *English in NZ* in *Amer. Speech* XVIII. 86 When [a] morning break is taken alfresco or in factories it is known as a *smoke-oh.* **1952** *Here & Now* Sept. 31 [Title] Smoke-o. The siren blows: time to breathe, tea In the grim whare. **1969** MOORE *Forest to Farm* 88 As we leave the hut for the day's work we each have on our backs a 'pikau'—a sugar-bag rucksack containing tucker for our lunch and 'smoke-o's'.

(b) **smoko** forms.
1900 *Auckland Weekly News* (Suppl.) 26 Jan. 2 I stayed and talked with them through a short 'smoko'. **1948** BALLANTYNE *Cunninghams* (1976) 13 Jokers at work breaking the day into periods. From early morning to morning smoko, to lunch, to afternoon smoko, then to knockoff. **1955** BOWEN *Wool Away* 12 Whether it be contract gang shearing or individual shearing, 'smokos' and meals must be on time for the shearer. **1962** SHARPE *Country Occasions* 73 So about 9 a.m. our dipping party knocks off for smoko. Coffee break, they call it in America, morning tea, in New Zealand family circles. To the outdoor worker it is always smoko. **1983** *Dominion* (Wellington) 18 Aug. 13 The boys work from nine to five, with an hour for lunch and two 10 minute tea breaks—or 'smokos'. **1991** *Dominion Sunday Times* (Wellington) 10 Nov. 24 Smoko came and there was no let-up in the banter.

b. *Obs.* A break from work for a smoke. See also SMOKE *n.*²
1906 *Truth* 22 Sept. 6 The men work eight hours a day, and only twice in that time are they allowed to smoke. There are two 'smokos', one in the morning, and the other later in the day, and the watch is put on them for seven minutes, during which time they have to draw like the devil and have a supply of matches before the start. **1913** *AJHR* C-12 23 The men are allowed to smoke, and are given 'smoke-ohs' in the morning and afternoon. **1921** *Quick March* 10 Feb. 35

SMOKO

[He] had to wean himself from the impulse to sit on kegs of blasting powder to indulge in 'smoke-oh'. **1946** REED *Farthest North* 34 [The occupant] may have been on holiday; he may have been out of sight amongst the scrub, at work or enjoying a quiet 'smoko'.

c. The refreshments supplied during a break from work.
1921 *Quick March* 11 July 17 Well, this morning we were topping off a stack; the young man was left on top when morning 'smoke-oh' arrived... The girls poured out the tea. **1994** *Listener* 15 Jan. 28 He made the smoko [for the bridge-building gang], carried the tools, got in the way.

2. The cry or call of 'smoke-oh' as a signal to stop work for refreshment.
c1880 *Teviot Station Shearing Rules* in Martin *Forgotten Worker* (1990) 95 No Shearer shall go into a pen to catch a Sheep after 'Smoke-oh', or any interval, or 'Clear the Board' has been called. **1881** BATHGATE *Waitaruna* 151 This is no go, and we must give it best!.. I think it's time to cry 'Smoke oh'. **1938** HYDE *Godwits Fly* (1970) 129 When the Boss called, 'Smoke-oh', the men scrambled down like baboons.

3. a. *attrib.*
1959 SLATTER *Gun in My Hand* 37 I saw the England of working with a tamper..sweating under the interested eyes of city men with rolled umbrellas and Big Ben for a smoko whistle. **1973** FERNANDEZ *Tussock Fever* 33 Back at the homestead, smoko hour came around again. **1981** HENDERSON *Exiles Asbestos Cottage* 14 'These were 240-lb bags,' Chaffey would stress, leaning against the bar or squatting with smoko-oh pannikin of tea. **1984** *Listener* 11 Aug. 15 [Caption] Around the smoko table at Picton; sometimes there is a break of only nine hours between shifts.

b. Special Comb. **smoko room**, **smoko-shed**, a room or building at a work-site in which workers take their smokos; **smoko-time**, *smoko* 1 a above.
1988 JACKSON *Rainshadow* 90 In the lean-to that served as a storeroom and **smoko-room**, my grandfather poked among rusty saws. **1993** *Evening Post* (Wellington) 24 Feb. 5 The explosion is thought to have been caused when vapours..collected on the [service] station roof and dropped into the smoko room below. **1971** SHADBOLT *Bullshit & Jellybeans* 45 At smoko we all just stopped drilling and started climbing down the jumbo, walking to the **smoko sheds**. **1985** *Evening Post* (Wellington) 28 May 2 Their refusal to ferry electricians in mini-vans to and from smoko sheds unless they get a time-and-a-half 'raindrops' payment has led to their suspension. **1991** *Dominion* (Wellington) 10 Aug. 11 [Speaking about where workers smoked cannabis during breaks] On the site... In the smoko sheds, in the company vans. **1964** DAVIS *Watersiders* 94 Whiskey Bill went away at **smoko-time** and came back with the full story. **1972** NEWTON *Sheep Thief* 27 By 'smoko' time..the three drivers had arrived in from the bail.

smoko, *n.*² Also freq. **smoke-oh**. [f. *smoke*(-concert + -O; AND 1918.] *smoke-concert* (SMOKE *n.*¹ 5).
1918 *Chron. NZEF* 13 Mar. 61 The A team mopped them at a Smoko in the evening—good sports, these flyers, diggers. **1921** *Quick March* 10 Mar. 39 Instead [of a wedding reception] there was a free-and-easy 'smoke-oh' in the lounge room of the Bon Ton Hotel. *Ibid.* 11 July 44 [Heading] *A 'Smoko'*. The entertainment committee..has in hand..arranging a smoke concert for the Diggers of this city. **1938** HYDE *Nor Yrs. Condemn* 76 It was after Captain Hyne's farewell smoke-oh that Starkie took the one step too far. **1959** SLATTER *Gun in My Hand* 99 Rata singing *Manu Rere* in the hut and the Maori returned man shouting at the drunks who wouldn't quieten for his song at the smoko. **1981** KENNEDY

Straight from Shoulder 23 There was a time when no end-of-year function of a local body..or football club 'smoko' was complete without a toast to 'the press'.

smokos: see SMOKER *n.*²

smoky. Also **smokey**.
1. [Alluding to dark skin colour.] An offensive word for a Maori.
   1984 Landfall 150 177 Men from the Canterbury Plains snigger in the bar at night when the *smokeys* are asked to leave but those dark locals hear only what they want.
2. [f. the appearance of the marble.] An opaque brown and grey marble. Also occas. heard called 'oyster' (Ed.).
   1949 DE MAUNY *Huntsman in his Career* 136 Once he gave him a bag of marbles, good ones, too, 'smokies', not the useless little clay things. **1972** SUTTON-SMITH *Folkgames Children* 174 Then there were the terms referring to particular kinds of marbles: for example..smokies, stinkies, stonies.

smoodge, smoodger, varr. SMOOGE, SMOOGER.

smooge /smudʒ/, /smutʃ/, *v.* Also **smoodge**, occas. **smouge**. [f. Brit. dial. *smudge* to kiss: see EDD *v.*¹, *n.*¹; also *smouch*, see OED *smooch v.*³]
1. [AND 1898.] Often as **smooge to**, to flatter; to behave in an ingratiating manner; to curry favour.
   1905 *Truth* 9 Sept. 4 Dick [Seddon] smooged to [the Employers' delegation] a bit, and tried to comfort them in their distress. **1917** *Truth* 29 Sept. 6 On Monday night, Mac Callum Mor was bent on 'smooging' to the Prime Minister.
2. *intr.* Esp. of children or (often amorous) of lovers, to show affection. Occas. formerly **smooge to** (someone).
   1904 *NZ Observer* 24 Sept. 22 Q.S. and A.S. looked quite at home smooging on the bridge. **1906** PICARD *Ups & Downs* 26 No thanks to this party who had been smooging to a clina up the line instead of slinging the roaring lion his hash. **1969** *Landfall* 89 27 We'd better go in now or he'll think we're smooging with each other out here.
   Hence **smooging** (also occas. **smoozing**) *vbl. n.* [AND 1904] and *attrib.*, flattery; a show of affection.
   1904 *NZ Observer* 9 July 22 They evidently preferred sitting out in the 'smooging' room to dancing. **1913** *NZ Bull.* 8 Feb. 11 There is too much smoodging about the [Hastings Borough] council, and the staff do nothing. **1926** DEVANNY *Butcher Shop* (1981) 54 She had seen their loving intimacy, their 'smoozing' even after twenty years of married life. **1953** *Landfall* 7 20 He would be putting his arms around her. 'Smooging won't get you out of it,' she said. **1960** MUIR *Word for Word* 80 He tucked her into bed himself tonight... 'Bring anything for me, Father? Dad-dee?' 'Cut out the smooging, you transparent horror.' **1963** PEARSON *Coal Flat* 304 You do your smooging somewhere else. **1984** BEARDSLEY *Blackball 08* 75 Goodness, it was hot—too hot for smoodging.

smooge, *n.* Also **smoodge**. [f. SMOOGE *v.*: AND 1909.] Smooth and devious talk; flattery.
   1913 *Hutt Valley Independent* 22 Nov. 1. [Heading] Smoodge versus Straight Talk.

smooger. Also **smoodger**.
1. *Obs.* [AND 1897.] A flatterer.
   1906 *Truth* 18 Aug. 1 There are few politicians who aren't smoodgers. **1915** *Hutt Valley Independent* 25 Dec. 4 [Samuel Marsden.] A smoodger of Maories and a flogger of British men and women.
2. One who shows (often amorous) affection.
   1904 *NZ Observer* 20 Aug. 21 Miss H. and Miss B. looked nice dancing with the little smoodgers. **1920** *NZ Free Lance* (Wellington) 43 Then I gets the blinkin' smoogers As they come home from the Bay. **1946** SARGESON *That Summer* 67 Ted just rolled over and curled himself round Mavis. Don't make out you're a smoodger, she said. **1951** 14 M 14 St Bede's, Chch 4 Smooger. **1964** PEARSON *Glossary* to Sargeson *Collected Stories 1935–63* (1964) 303 smoodger: one who gains his end by fondling.

smooth-hound. In full **smooth-hound dogfish** (or **shark**). Any of various small sharks in the fam. Triakidae, in New Zealand esp. GUMMY *n.*³ (*Mustelus lenticulatus*).
   1773 FORSTER *Resolution Jrnl.* 2 May (1982) II. 269 They caught a *smooth Hound* (*Squalus Mustelus*) about 5 feet long. **1886** SHERRIN *Handbook Fishes NZ* 91 *M. antarcticus*, known as the smooth hound, is the only shark that is properly edible, living, as it does on shell-fish and crabs. **1892** *TrNZI* XXIV. 203 *Portland Island.*—Tarakihi, moki..smooth-hound, soldier fish. **1913** *Ibid.* XLV. 235 The smooth hound is the smallest of the New Zealand sharks. **1927** [see GUMMY *n.*³]. **1958** PARROTT *Big Game Fishes* 95 The Spotted Smooth-hound may be easily recognised by the grey body with conspicuous white spots along the upper parts of the back. **1966** DOOGUE & MORELAND *Sea Anglers' Guide* 181 Spotted Gummy Shark... smooth hound, spotted dogfish, gummy; mango (Maori). **1982** AYLING *Collins Guide* (1984) 56 The boneless and tasty flesh of the spotted smooth-hound is sold under the trade-name of lemon fish and is often used in the fish and chip trade. **1986** [see SHARK 2 (9)].

smoozing, var. *smooging* (SMOOGE *v.*).

smother, *v.* Farming. [Spec. use of *smother* to suffocate by the prevention of breathing: see OED *v.* 1 b.] *trans.*, occas. *intr.* Of sheep, to suffocate (others) by crushing or falling (on them), esp. when driven or frightened; to cause (sheep) to die in this way. Often in passive use, and also as a *vbl.n.* (see quot. 1947).
   1848 *Pharazyn Journal* (ATLTS) 15 Jan. 152 Teddy and W. to lambs to drive them to pen, smothered 10 in a blind gully, one brought home eatable, broke window. **1862** CHUDLEIGH *Diary* 2 May (1950) 36 In a minute half the mob were in. We pushed our horses in and prevented the others from going in. If they had 3 out of 4 would have been smothered. **1872** BARKER *Christmas Cake* 290 I had to bring 'em [*sc.* the mob of sheep] down uncommon easy, for it was a nasty place, and I didn't want half of 'em to be smothered in the creek. **1889** COX in Woodhouse *Blue Cliffs* (1982) 50 When coming in from the hill country with the wethers, I had the misfortune to smother some sheep. **1933** *Press* (Christchurch) (Acland Gloss.) 2 Dec. 15 *Smother.*—Run sheep especially merinos, are very easy to s[mother] on broken hill ground. An injudicious turn with a dog in an abrupt gully may stop the lead and cause some sheep to be knocked over. Other sheep make a rush and are brought down too, so that in a second or two there is struggling heap; and before the shepherd can pull them off one another the bottom ones are *smothered*. **1938** BURDON *High Country* 108 Of all breeds the Merino is the easiest to smother, for he moves freer, faster, and more recklessly than any other. **1947** NEWTON *Wayleggo* 118 While at Mt. White I experienced..the worst case of 'smothering' on the hill that I have known. **1987** OGONOWSKA-COATES *Boards. Blades & Barebellies* 97 Smother. If the pens in a woolshed are filled too tight sheep may smother during the night.

smother, *n.*¹ *Farming.* [f. *v.*] The death of sheep by suffocation in a mob, caused by mob-crushing, stampede, etc.
   1930 ACLAND *Early Canterbury Runs* 128 They once had a bad smother there. **1938** [see HAND *n.*² 2 a]. **1949** CRAWFORD *Sheep and Sheepmen* 42 Mt Peel [station] was unlucky with smothers. **1952** BLAKISTON *My Yesteryears* 20 If such a mob runs into a steep-sided gully, they are likely to pile up at the bottom until those behind are running across a bridge of bodies, and, in hundreds, are suffocated. Shepherds dread a 'smother'. **1962** CRUMP *One of Us* 88 I've been off water for years, ever since we had a smother up the back and the creek ran dry before it came down in a stinking flood. **1975** NEWTON *Sixty Thousand on the Hoof* 88 Sam Welsh also recalled an occasion when they had a bad smother when coming off the Mt Dalgety country with 10,000-odd wethers. **1982** WOODHOUSE *Blue Cliffs* 50 During the shearing muster of 1889 there was a disastrous smother.

smother, *n.*² *Horseracing. Obs.* The preventing of a horse from winning by allowing it to be hedged in or blocked by other horses.
   1910 *Truth* 26 Feb. 2 The rider of Nukuhan was in sore straits in the Scurry at Taranaki, as his instructions were to give the chestnut a good smother. Across the bottom bend he was on the outer, but then he came in to the rails, and despite the boy's efforts, he finished second.

smouge, var. SMOOGE *v.*

snag, *n.*¹ [Fig. use of *snag* an obstacle.]
1. [AND 1905.] An adversary to be reckoned with.
   1912 *Auckland Univ. College Capping Book* 43 He never gave his teacher 'cheek' and he never 'played the wag'. In time a scholarship he got; For indeed he was a 'snag'. **1939** BEATTIE *First White Boy Born Otago* 172 This man, to use a colonial term, was a 'snag' to anyone who tried to take a 'rise' out of him.
2. Something (or someone) disagreeable.
   1947 NEWTON *Wayleggo* 83 A snag of a beat fell to my lot one day.

snag, *n.*² Also **snaggle**. [Ayto & Simpson 1992 'Prob. from Brit. dial. *snag* a morsel'; poss. from Lanc. dial. *snackles* little delicacies of food (see EDD); AND 1941.] A sausage.
   1963 *Dominion* (Wellington) 22 Aug. 8 'Snags', 'bangers', sausages..call them what you will. **1968** *NZ Contemp. Dict. Suppl.* (Collins) 18 *snags, snaggles n.* (*Sl.*) sausages. **1988** McGILL *Dict. Kiwi Slang* 105 *snag* sausage.—*a few snags short at the barbie* not quite right in the head.

snag, *v. Obs.* A 1930s 'Depression' use, to search for bargains: often as **snagger**, one who thus searches; and as **snagging** *vbl. n.*, searching for bargains.
   1992 PARK *Fence around the Cuckoo* 115 *Snagging* was the depression word for bargain-hunting. But in this specific case one did not snag for economy, but in order to live. *Ibid.* 118 Other snaggers' attributes appeared in due course in my own stories, as did the unforgettable odour of people wearing aged garments from secondhand shops.

snaggle: see SNAG *n.*²

snail: see BUSH C 4, FLAX 5 c, KAURI SNAIL, MUD SNAIL.

snake.

1. See *mad as a snake* (MAD *a.* d).

2. A traffic policeman.
   1971 Shadbolt *Bullshit & Jellybeans* 36 It was a snake and his leg was pinned under his bike... We..got his bike off him. That was the last time that snake gave a Queen Street bikie a ticket. **1984** 16–17 F E3 Pakuranga Coll. 24C Snake ['traffic cop' F3M2]

3. In various (often fanciful) special Comb. **snakebite**, see quot.; **snakejuice** [AND 1890], potent, often inferior, liquor; **snake-proof**, of trousers, with narrow or tapering legs; also earlier heard (c1940) used of 'plus-fours'.
   1993 *Sunday Times* (Wellington) 28 Feb. 40 Punctures are common, usually caused by 'snakebite'—hitting a rock with such force the tube is pinched against the wheel rim. **1905** *Truth* 26 Aug. 1 Every bottle of **snakejuice**. **1906** Picard *Ups & Downs* 9 She [*sc.* a barmaid] simply made the hops flow... I was passing the snake juice on to the Merican. **1946** Webber *Johnny Enzed in Italy* 35 They don't sell Snake Juice there. It's a four star house. **1968** *NZ Contemp. Dict. Suppl.* (Collins) 18 *snakejuice n.* strong drink. **1953** Cody *21 Battalion* 17 The ill-matched uniforms, especially the narrow '**snake-proof**' trousers, were thankfully discarded in favour of the easy fitting..comfortable battle dress.

snaky, *a.* [AND 1894.] Usu. in the phr. **to go (get) snaky**, to become angry, to turn nasty.
   1943 Bennett *English in NZ* in *Amer. Speech* XVIII. 90 The verbs *to go snaky*, *to go maggoty*..have the same implications [as *to go crook*]... (some though not all..may heard be in Australia; cf. Australian *snake-headed*, annoyed). **1950** *Listener* 3 Mar. 8 'Turning the job in?' said Bill 'No, Bill. Just a day in town.' 'Big chap going snaky?' **1964** Harvey *Any Old Dollars Mister?* 108 Well, this warden got awfully snaky and said some terrible things about people having no respect for others' feelings. **1974** Mason *Hand on Rail* (TS 1987) 38 June:.. Then we had to get dug in again to that bloody pigsty in town..and he got all snaky again. **1981** Charles *Black Billy Tea* 39 The men get short and snaky And they have their little tiffs. **1984** [see SNITCH].

Snap Jack. An occas. and local trade-name for PIGFISH.
   1956 Graham *Treasury NZ Fishes* 351 Many years ago [pigfish] were sold to the public in large numbers but only for a short period when others were exceptionally scarce. The fish were skinned so that they looked quite different from the fish in its natural state. They were then railed to a country town and sold readily under the name of Snap Jacks or Skip Jacks.

snapped, *ppl. a.* Prison. In the phr. **to get snapped**, to get caught (out) by authority; to get picked up (by police).
   1984 Beaton *Outside In* 22 Kate: [Ginny] Dunnit to the new chick. Sandy: Should've seen her face! Ma: Ginny get snapped? Kate: Sure did. *Ibid.* 54 Helen: Don't you get snapped by the screws? Kate: Yeah. It's me hair that really fucken pissed 'em off, but. *Ibid.* 110 *Snapped*: caught.

snapper, *n.*[1] Also occas. **schnapper**, a spelling orig. generated in imitation of the form in German. [Spec. use of *snapper* a widespread name for a fish.]

1. Usu. *Chrysophrys auratus* (fam. Sparidae), a pinkish-white fish highly valued as food. See also BREAM 1 a and b, TAMURE.
   1807 Savage *Some Acc. of NZ* 11 The snapper and bream are uncommonly fine. **1817** Nicholas *NZ* I. 88 They brought with them some fish, which Europeans call snappers. **1834** Markham *NZ* (1963) 46 Mullet is very plentiful and Snappers, and half a dozen different kinds of fish. **1840** Mathew *Journal* 20 Apr. in *Founding of NZ* (1940) 121 Very fine fish they are [off Whangarei]—schnappers, gurnet and what is called salmon in these seas. **1851** Lush *Auckland Jrnls.* 21 Nov. (1971) 93 Buying 6 snapper (a large fish about the size of a well-grown salmon) for 6 pence. **1872** Hutton & Hector *Fishes NZ* 106 There are few fishes better known in the northern parts of the Colony than the Snapper. **1882** [see TAMURE]. **1904** *NZ Observer* 5 Mar. 7 His sorrow at the struggles of the dying schnapper was pitiful to behold. **1918** *NZJST* I. 136 The class of fish supplied to this market before the war contained nothing so good as our groper (hapuku) or snapper. **1929** [see TAMURE]. **1938** Hyde *Nor Yrs. Condemn* 60 They fed on great slabs of schnapper fried in deep oil, crumbling slabs of bread into their mouths. **1956** *Dominion* (Wellington) 5 Mar. 8 Bellamy's menu has qualified as the most snobbish of all State papers. Whenever the well-known New Zealand fish called snapper is an item of Parliamentary diet it is invariabl[y] spelled 'schnapper'. **1966** [see TAMURE]. **1986** Paul *NZ Fishes* 96 A sea bream (family Sparidae), not closely related to the true snappers of tropical and subtropical seas... Small snapper are often called bream or brim, and the brightly coloured, medium-sized fish caught during the spring spawning season are often called school snapper. **1990** *Evening Post* (Wellington) 21 Nov. 59 There can be no denying that in the past two seasons more monster snapper have been caught than in any other period in the past decade.

2. With a modifier: **black, golden, old man, red, school**.

(1) **black snapper**. [f. the colour.] PARORE (*Girella tricuspidata*).
   1986 Paul *NZ Fishes* 101 *Parore. Girella tricuspidata*. Known variously as blackfish, black snapper, black bream, and mangrove fish. **1987** [see SHIT-FISH]. **1991** Bradstock *Fishing* 21 *Parore*. Other names: black snapper.

(2) **golden snapper**. *Centroberyx affinis* (fam. Berycidae). See also KOAREA, *red snapper* (4) below.
   1921 *NZJST* IV. 121 *Golden Snapper; Koarea*. A highly esteemed food fish, of very beautiful colours when first taken from the water. **1938** *TrRSNZ* LXVIII. 406 *Trachichthodes affinis*... Golden snapper. **1956** Graham *Treasury NZ Fishes* 175 Golden Snapper (Koarea) *Centroberyx affinis*... As an edible fish the Golden Snapper in my opinion ranks high in favour. **1966** Doogue & Moreland *Sea Anglers' Guide* 211 Red Snapper... The red snapper belongs to a very different group of fishes to our common snapper... Other names..golden snapper; nannygai (Australia); koarea (Maori). **1972** Doak *Fishes* 21 Swimming slowly in midwater, seldom near the surface and never resting on the bottom, the golden snapper hide their brilliant shotsilk bodies by day in the gloom of caves or in deeper water. **1982** Ayling *Collins Guide* (1984) 177 In spite of its name the golden snapper is not related to the true snapper and is in fact more similar to the roughys... Schools of golden snapper..are..regularly caught in bottom trawls and sold as red fish.

(3) **old man snapper**. See quot. 1956.
   1946 Sargeson *That Summer* 43 Those nibbles might be old men snapper. **1956** Graham *Treasury NZ Fishes* 245 Many large Snapper are caught with a peculiar hump on the head which is caused by a thickening of the frontal bone. When a fisherman lands such a fish he immediately states: 'I've caught an old man Snapper' under the erroneous impression it is an old male fish. I have often dissected these 'old man' Snappers and found there was as many female as male fish with this conspicuous bony knob. The name 'old man Snapper' comes from the likeness to the face of an old man with bulbous red nose, a short clipped moustache and tight upper lip. **1981** Wilson *Fisherman's Bible* 227 'Old man snapper' are those fish which develop a hump on top of the head as they become older; often the fleshy upper lip also increases in size.

(4) **red snapper**. Any of several fishes esp. *butterfly perch* (PERCH *n.* 2 (2) *Caesioperca lepidoptera*), and *golden snapper* (see (2) above).
   1872 Hutton & Hector *Fishes NZ* 106 Red Snapper. (*Scorpis Hectori*). This is described as a new species by Captain Hutton, and is not unfrequently caught in the sands on the west coast of Otago. **1886** Sherrin *Handbook Fishes of NZ* 83 The red schnapper belongs to the same family as the hapuku and kahawai, the Percidae. *Ibid.* 84 It is generally called the red schnapper by seamen who are acquainted with the fish of the coast, the colour being a uniform bright red. **1892** *NZ Official Handbook* 167 The following is a list of the fishes which are chiefly met with in the market: hapuku, kahawai, red-snapper. **1921** *NZJST* IV. 115 *Caesioperca lepidoptera*... Red Perch. Called 'red snapper' or 'St. Peter's fish' in Queen Charlotte and Pelorus Sounds, where it is occasionally taken in the seine net. **1957** [see PERCH *n.* 2 (2)]. **1967** Moreland *Marine Fishes* 36 Red Snapper... Also known as golden snapper, and koarea. **1979** *Catch* Feb. 12 Red Snapper..Family Berycidae (golden snappers). **1982** Ayling *Collins Guide* (1984) 177 *Golden Snapper*..(Nannygai, red snapper, koarea).

(5) **school snapper**. A young adult snapper swimming in a shoal of (usu.) evenly-sized fish. Cf. BREAM 1 a.
   1922 *NZJST* V. 92 In December and January this species is often seen on the surface associated with school snapper, among which it appears to spawn. **1972** Doak *Fishes* 40 Many young snapper from 15cm upwards swim in silvery schools and are called 'bream' or 'school snapper' by the fishermen, each school of uniform size and age. **1986** [see 1 above].

snapper, *n.*[2] *Obs.* [Orig. unknown.] A sixpence.
   1868 Dilke *Greater Britain* I. 332 [The Hokitika newsboy] put [a newspaper] into my hand. 'How much?' I asked. 'A snapper.' 'A snapper?' 'Ay—a tizzy.' Understanding this more familiar term, I gave him a shilling. [Dilke is either mistaken or generous. (Ed.)] **1972** Hargreaves *Beads to Banknotes* 151 Sixpence [:] tanner, sprat, tizzy, bender, snapper.

snapperback. *Northland logging.* [Orig. uncertain.] A tree whose shape or form makes it lean or sit back (?'snap' back) on to the stump during felling.
   1952 p.c. Roy Gilberd (Okaihau) 9 Nov. You run across a tree sometimes, ought to open up when you cut it, but instead it pinches even though it's lying right across a ridge. *Snapperbacks* we used to call them... If you can't get your saw out buy another one. **1953** Reed *Story of Kauri* 96 Instead of the perfectly erect, cylindrical trunk, the snapper-back has an oval, tapering and curved butt, which no doubt suggested the name.

Snares (Islands). An island group south of Stewart island in the far south of New Zealand, used as a modifier in the names of birds, see: PENGUIN 2 (7), *cape pigeon* (PIGEON 3 a), SNIPE *n.* 2, TIT *n.*[1] b.

snarler. [Poss. a play on the fancy that stray dogs are used in the manufacture; poss. also because sausages can seem to spit (or 'snarl') when fried.] A sausage. See also SNAG *n.*[2]

1939–45 *Expressions & Sayings 2NZEF (TS N.A. WAII DA 420/1)* Snarler—Sausage. **1941** *2NZEF* p.c. Len Climo (Marlborough). Sausages are always reputed to be made out of cats, dogs, or any unfortunate animal that comes along; so much so that extra bad ones could be expected to sit up and *snarl*. **1944** *Korero* (AEWS Background Bulletin) 17 July 24 Interesting..is 'snarlers' for the inevitable Army sausages. 'Growlers' is another form, 'barkers' still another. **1955** *BJ Cameron Collection* (TS July) snarler (n) A sausage. **1963** MORRIESON *Scarecrow* 121 Are there any more snarlers in the pan? **1984** *Listener* 16 June 20 Rita the cook offers crumbed 'snarlers' and Irish stew to all her regulars. **1988** *Univ. Entr. Board Bursaries Eng. Exam.* 6 But she usually gave me a good feed—savs or snarlers, and sometimes a whole chip of strawberries. **1991** *Consumer* 297 Sept. 5 A very hot pan..can break down the sausage mixture..leaving you with a small, tough and dry snarler.

sniffer. [f. *sniff* + *-er*.] A device which when held a short distance from the face of a subject detects alcohol on the breath.
  1993 *Evening Post* (Wellington) 21 Mar. 3 The sniffers, called Alcotech AR1005, were being imported from Australia.

snig, *v.* Mainly *logging*. [f. Brit. dial. *snig*: see EDD. *v.*¹ 5; OED *v.*²]
1. [AND 1897.] *trans.* To drag (a log or logs) with a rope or chain.
  1866 TRIPP *Day Book* June in Harper *Kettle on Fuchsia* (1967) 69 Blair. Snigging firewood out of bush. **1933** *Press* (Christchurch) (Acland Gloss.) 2 Dec. 15 *Snig*.—To drag along the ground by horse or bullocks, especially to drag logs or other timber. The stout chain which goes round the log has a ring at one end, and a hook to which the horses' chains are attached. It is called a *snigging chain*. **1937** *Morrinsville Star* 1 Oct. 4 He brought [the bullocks] from Hoe-o-Tainui, where they had been used for snigging logs from the bush. **1955** WILSON *Land of My Children* 28 The mill hands took chains, hooked them ingeniously round the bundles of timber, hitched a horse to each pile and proceeded to 'snig' it to its destination. **1961** CRUMP *Hang On a Minute Mate* 37 You just get the log ready and hook her on to the winch-rope when the tractor comes to snig her out to the skids. Skids? That's the ramp where they load the logs on to the trucks. **1986** RICHARDS *Off the Sheep's Back* 24 Fortunately, there was a timber mill operating nearby. By borrowing horses, they were able to snig the timber home through the bush track.
2. [AND 1976.] *trans.* To catch and hold (something) by a rope; to drag (something).
  1949 SARGESON *I Saw in My Dream* (1974) 96 He could go..and start snigging posts up to where the fence had got buried. **1965** HENDERSON *Open Country* 101 He was going to snig it [*sc.* a crocodile]. **1966** NEWTON *Boss's Story* 99 Anyway five days later he landed back snigging a pretty civilised colt... There was a fair sort of banging going on..and..I saw one of the chaps snigging a dog away by its tail.

snig, *n.* [See *v.*] Used *attrib*. in Comb. and special Comb. alluding to the 'snigging' or hauling of logs: **snig-chain**, *snigging-chain* (SNIGGING 2), **horse, -mare, snig-pan**, see SHOE, **track** [AND 1979].
  1953 SUTHERLAND *Golden Bush* (1963) 155 He got the blacksmith to make him a really big hook and attach it to a length of **snig-chain**. **1972** NEWTON *Wake of Axe* 119 **Snig horses**, mainly draughts, sometimes got away, and were left behind when a mill closed down. **1981** MARSH *Black Beech & Honeydew* 102 It was followed by a man and a one-eyed horse. This was Jock the snigger and his **snig-mare**. **1961** HENDERSON *Friends In Chains* 69 Hammering in the dogs with angry vigour, I adjusted the **snigpan** under the nose of the log, and..manoeuvred the horses into position. **1952–53** *NZ Forest Service Gloss.* (TS) **Snig Track** A path constructed for snigging.

snigger. A forest workman in charge of hauling logs from the bush.
  1909 *Greymouth Evening Star* 20 Apr. 3 [Advt] Wanted—Good SNIGGER, must be able to slice. **1923** MALFROY *Small Sawmills* 27 The *snigger* has charge of the rope, dogs, and blocks, and must see that his hauling tracks are cut in the best direction. **1951** *Awards, etc.* 520 [Marlborough Timber-Workers Award] [Rates of wages] Other crosscutter and scarfer 4[s.] 2¹/₄[d.] Breaker-out, snigger, ropeman (hauling rope), to apply to only one man in each hauling team 4 4¹/₂. **1981** MARSH *Black Beech & Honeydew* 102 Here..were a winch, a loco-driven circular saw and, close to the ground a steel cable that ran..into the forest. As we watched it, it quivered. From a hidden and remote distance a human voice gave a..cry. 'That's the snigger,' Sandy said.

snigging, *vbl. n.*
1. See quot. 1923.
  1923 MALFROY *Small Sawmills* 39 Snigging... The pulling of a log endwise along the ground by wire-rope haul, bullock-team, or other power. In America called 'skidding'. **1944** *Korero* (AEWS Background Bulletin) 8 May 25 This [hauling] is done by a low or high lead and is called 'snigging'. **1986** OWEN & PERKINS *Speaking for Ourselves* 160 It was astonishing the tremendous loads they could pull out of the bush along the ground—'snigging', that was called.
2. Used *attrib*. in special Comb. (see also SNIG *n.*) **snigging chain**, the special chain used to fasten a log to the hauling team or hauling device; **snigging-pan** (see also SNIG *n.*), **snigging-shoe**, SHOE; **snigging-track** [AND 1910], an often corduroyed bush track prepared for log haulage.
  1933 *snigging chain* [see SNIG *v.* 1]. **1966** TURNER *Eng. Lang. Austral. & NZ* 153 To *snig*, to shift a log with a *snigging chain*, is still sometimes heard on farms. **1984** LOCKE *The Kauri & the Willow* 88 After about five years the stumps had rotted enough to be pulled out, using horses and snigging chains. **1948** JEWELL *Accounting in Timber Industry* 128f. (Gloss.) *Snigging-pan*: A metal sheet held under the nose of the log to facilitate haulage operations. **1952–53** *NZ Forest Service Gloss.* (TS) *Snigging Pan*. A metal sheet held under the nose of a log to facilitate ground movement. syn. Dish, Shoe. **1923** MALFROY *Small Sawmills* 13 A good snigger..will use his **snigging-shoe**..to lift the log out of bad places. **1923** MALFROY *Small Sawmills* 13 **Snigging-tracks**... Good straight tracks make hauling easy. A few pieces of corduroy placed across the track are a great help. **1961** CRUMP *Hang On a Minute Mate* 44 They dug their axes into a handy stump and trudged off down the snigging-track.

snipe, *n.* [Spec. use of *snipe* a northern hemisphere, migratory bird of *Gallinago* genus to which the NZ bird was occas. assigned in early reference.]
1. Also **native snipe**. *Coenocorypha aucklandica* (fam. Scolopacidae), a secretive, dumpy, richly-plumaged russet, black and brown bird. Occas. applied to various other wading birds, esp. to the godwit.
  1777 ANDERSON *Journal* Feb. in Cook *Journals* (1967) III. 807 No other sort of game was seen except a single snipe which was shot and differs but little from that of Europe. **1823** CRUISE *Journal* 30 Aug. (1957) 150 At noon we went on the island to shoot, and killed some red bill and a snipe; the only one that any of us had seen in this country: in its plumage it resembled those found in England, but the bird itself was much smaller. **1833** WILLIAMS *Early Jrnls.* 28 Mar. (1961) 302 We have had fresh baked bread, puddings..ducks, snipe and pigeons. **1840** MATHEW *Journal* 29 Apr. in *Founding of NZ* (1940) 132 We saw myriads of snipes [in North Auckland] in the shoal water and shot a dozen of these graceful birds. **1871** HUTTON *Catalogue Birds NZ* 31 Gallinago pusilla... Native snipe. **1905** [see KUAKA a]. **1928** BAUCKE *Manuscript* (Bishop Museum Memoirs Vol.IX No.5 343–382) in Skinner & Baucke *Moriori s* 358 [Maori] kuaka [Moriori] kūk snipe. **1955** OLIVER *NZ Birds* 275 About 1870 two snipes were seen on Little Barrier Island by Captain Bennett of the schooner *Mary Ann.* **1966** FALLA et al. *Birds NZ* 116 Godwits are sometimes referred to as 'snipe' or 'curlew'. Both these names are quite incorrect. **1985** *Reader's Digest Book NZ Birds* 202 Snipe..found on some of New Zealand's outer islands are named for their resemblance to the migratory *Gallinago* species of the northern hemisphere. **1987** SCOTT *Seven Lives on Salt River* 90 At that age he began standing in for his father..shooting snipe (godwits) on the dunes.

2. With modifiers indicating provenance: **Antipodes Island snipe**, *Coenocorypha aucklandica meinertzhagenae*; **Auckland Island snipe**, *Coenocorypha aucklandica aucklandica*; **Chatham Island snipe**, *Coenocorypha pusilla*; **Snares (Snares Island) snipe**, *Coenocorypha aucklandica huegeli*; **Stewart Island snipe**, the extinct *Coenocorypha aucklandica iredalei*, **subantarctic snipe**, *Coenocorypha aucklandica*.
  1873 BULLER *Birds NZ* 196 Gallinago aucklandica. (Auckland-Island Snipe.) **1888** BULLER *Birds NZ* II. 33 Gallinago pusilla.. (Chatham-Island Snipe.) **1891** *NZJSc.* (NS) I. 161 Several interesting land birds inhabit [Snares] island, the more noticeable being the Auckland Island Snipe. **1904** HUTTON & DRUMMOND *Animals NZ* 218 The Auckland Island Snipe are tame and by no means numerous. They fly badly, and only for a short distance. *Ibid.* 219 *The Chatham Island Snipe. Gallinago pusilla... The Snares Snipe. Gallinago huegeli.* **1917** WILLIAMS *Dict. Maori Lang.* 543 *Tutukiwi.. Snares Island snipe.* **1923** *NZJST* VI. 76 *Coenocorypha aucklandica...* Semi-woodcock; Subantarctic Snipe. **1948** *NZ Bird Notes* III. 73 Snares Snipe. The snipe..is the least in evidence of the three land birds, but that is quite likely chiefly on account of its somewhat skulking habit, and because it is largely nocturnal. **1955** OLIVER *NZ Birds* 274 The Chatham Island Snipe is characterised by its smaller size and undersurface without blotches. *Ibid.* 275 *Stewart Island Snipe. Coenocorypha aucklandica iredalei. Ibid.* 276 *Snares Island Snipe. Coenocorypha aucklandica huegeli. Ibid.* 277 An account of the Snares Island Snipe has been published by E.F. Stead... *Auckland Island Snipe. Coenocorypha aucklandica aucklandica. Ibid.* 278 *Antipodes Island Snipe. Coenocorypha aucklandica meinertzhagenae.* The Antipodes Island Snipe was first collected by Fairchild in 1887. **1967** GODLEY in Fraser *Beyond Roaring Forties* (1986) 198 Unmolested by cats..[on Adams island] the Auckland Island snipe is here in abundance. **1986** FRASER *Beyond Roaring Forties* 75 Just as much at risk are..the Snares fernbird..and the Snares snipe. **1987** *Notornis* XXXIV. 112 All the available evidence indicates that the hakawai of the southern mutton bird islands was an aerial display of the Stewart Island Snipe. **1988** MERTON in Morris & Smith *Wild South* 126 We've experimented with the Chathams Island snipe. They need a large and constant supply of insects day and night.

snipe, *v. Logging.* [Brit. and US dial. *snipe* to cut off: see EDD *v.* 10; OED *v.* 3.] *trans.* To trim or round (the end of the log) for ease of handling. See esp. quots. 1950, 1951.

1902 *NZ Illustr. Mag.* V. 375 If the weather is favourable, the log is 'sniped' or rounded at one end, an iron grip driven into it, and to this the team is fastened. **1950** p.c. R. Gilberd (Okaihau). A 'ropey' will learn to 'snipe'..which is a highly-skilled operation. Butt-end of clean-trimmed log is trimmed of angles. Vees are cut at points opposite each other at the butt-end (usually) and are connected by a chopped Dee which runs around in a semi-circle from one to the other. In the Dee is laid a 'strop', a short length of cable with an eye in each end. The eyes are connected with each other and to a short chain by a shackle; and the chain is attached to 'the [hauling] rope' with a hitch. **1951** H.S. McCarroll *The Days of the Kauri Bushmen* (Radio Talk 2: TS) After the logs were cut, each was sniped. To snipe a log, the end is chipped all the way round so that it can be handled without catching humps in the ground, stumps and so on; in fact you might say that a log when it is sniped looks rather like the blunt end of a whale. **1953** Reed *Story of Kauri* 180 To prevent the log from 'biting' into uneven ground, and enable it to slip over minor obstacles, it was 'sniped'—that is, somewhat rounded or tapered at the front. **1969** Moore *Forest to Farm* 42 The front end of the log was carefully 'sniped', that is, its sharp edge was rounded to allow it to skid like a sledge-runner. **1986** Owen & Perkins *Speaking for Ourselves* 159 First of all they tapered one end, rounding the log so that it would be able to slide over impediments in its path... Now these men were called 'snipers', and having sniped the log, they then made two cuts, one on each side of the log opposite each other, right into the rounded part—the sniped end. That was for the purpose of holding a heavy chain which attached the log to the yoked bullocks. **1995** *NZ Geographic* Jan.–Mar. 16 The breaker-out..jacked it clear, so that he could snipe the end and drive the sidedogs to take the hook of the single hauling chain.

Hence **sniper** [OED 1905], a bush-worker who snipes logs; **sniping** *vbl. n.*, see quot. 1948.

1958 *NZ Timber Jrnl.* Sept. 87 **Sniper**: One who snipes logs before they are skidded. **1986** [see quot. above]. **1948** Jewell *Accounting in Timber Industry* 128–130 *Sniping*: Rounding the end of a log for easier transport (haulage). **1961** Crump *Hang On a Minute Mate* 42 During the next few weeks Jack learned about scarfing, baching, limbing, deeing, sniping, jigger-boards, platforms, tome, strops, drives, triggers, and saw and axe sharpening.

snitch. [Origin obscure: see OED *n.* 4.] Esp. in the phr. **to get (have) a snitch on**, to have a down on, to have a grudge against. See also snitcher *n.*²

1943 Bennett *English in NZ* in *Amer. Speech* XVIII. 90 A person complaining of another's ill-will might also say, 'He's got a proper snitch on me'—obviously a variant of 'to snitch upon' (to inform against). **1948** *Landfall* 6 June 109 These jokers didn't understand the snitch Myers had on you. **1959** Slatter *Gun in My Hand* 91 Got a snitch on me and put me in crook with the boss. **1966** *NZ Short Stories* (1976) 128 He wasn't a man to get a snitch on his neighbours because of a bit of bad luck. **1984** Edmond *High Country Weather* 74 Mr Brooker kept on making snaky remarks about him. He's got a snitch on our boy.

snitcher, *n.*¹ [Origin obscure.] In mainly children's use, anyone or anything excellent, fine or attractive. Often *attrib.*

1938 *Press* (Christchurch) (McNab Slang) 2 Apr. 18 New Zealanders have their curiously sounding slang. 'Prejaganint', 'snitcher' or 'snozzler' (a good specimen). **1941** Baker *NZ Slang* 51 Of children's terms..we may note *snitcher*, *snitch*, [etc.]..descriptive of something superlative or excellent, both as nouns and adjectives. **1942** Cottrell *Lost Cave of Pukerangi* 15 [A child speaks.] Look at the snitcher nikau palms. **1955** BJ Cameron Collection (TS July) snitcher (adj) Marvellous. **1970** McNaughton *Tat* 55 So far they were delighted with her [*sc.* a sheep-dog]. She was easy to command, knew her drill...She was a 'snitcher'. **1988** McGill *Dict. Kiwi Slang* 105 *snitcher* attractive person or thing.

snitcher, *n.*² A dislike, esp. in the phr. **to take a snitcher to** (someone), to take a dislike to; **to get a snitcher on**, to take offence (at); to have a grudge (against), to get a down (on). See also snitch.

1953 *Here & Now* Apr. 35 Sirs: Your 'Housewife' has apparently taken a 'snitcher' on us schoolteachers. **1964** Davis *Watersiders* 49 Most times he lets us get away with it. But if he gets a snitcher on..all we'll collect is the thick edge of tongue. **1976** Sargeson *Sunset Village* 29 It was Brixton's habit, this talking to himself, a long monologue which reproduced the slang of forty years ago. Sometimes..he might..tell about some bloke he had a snitcher on. **1984** Beardsley *Blackball 08* 38 But listen, Paddy, don't call my wife 'missus'. She'll take a snitcher to you straight away if you do. *Ibid.* 111 The missus had got a real snitcher on the place. **1993** O'Sullivan *Let the River Stand* 42 She was blowed if she'd go along with her husband.., getting a proper snitcher like that from someone else's report.

snitchy, *a.* [f. Brit. dial.: see EDD *snitch adj.* cross.] Ill-tempered; disdainful. Cf. snitcher *n.*²

1979 Heinemann *NZ Dict.* 1037 *Snitchy adjective* (*informal*) bad-tempered. **1985** Rosier-Jones *Cast Two Shadows* 89 'Emma's playing with her knuckle-bones,' says Tina in a snitchy voice.

snivelling snufflebuster: see snufflebuster 2.

snob, *n.*¹ In a derogatory sense of one who sets great store on rank or wealth, in Comb. or in composition: **snob-nobs** *pl.* [poss. recalling Austral. terms *snobs* the aristocracy, *nobs* the wealthy merchants], the (self-appointed) rural aristocracy; **snobocracy** *hist.* [used elsewhere but recorded earliest in NZ: see OED], the class of snobs as one wielding social or political power; **snobshop,** a (select) private school.

1906 *Truth* 22 Sept. 6 They are fair sticklers for tone in the country districts, and the country newspaper panders to the little **snob-nobs** with all the might of its scissors and paste pot. **1853** *Richmond-Atkinson Papers* 17 July (1960) I. 129 His impartiality..is not satisfactory to the '**snobocracy**', as Jas calls the genteel of this place [*sc.* New Plymouth]. **1913** *NZ Observer* 8 Mar. 5 He has had to come up hard against a 'snobocracy' whenever he has had to attend several functions in his capacity of Mayor. **1948** Lipson *Politics of Equality* 292 New Zealand's educational system is on the whole more democratic than that of Britain, but it still preserves some relics of privilege (for example, the survival of certain expensive private schools, known as '**snob-shops**').

snob, *n.*² *Shearing.* [f. a play on *snob* a Brit. term for a *cobbler* or shoemaker: AND 1915.] cobbler *n.*¹ 1.

1955 Bowen *Wool Away* (Gloss.: Shearing Terms) 157 Snob. The last sheep in the pen. **1982** *Agric. Gloss.* (MAF) 59 *Snob*: Last sheep in the catching pen. **1989** *NZ Eng. Newsletter* III. 28 *snob:* Sometimes used instead of 'cobbler' to describe a sheep which is left to last in the catching pen because it is difficult to shear.

snodgall. [Poss. a variation of *snot-gall*: see Century Dict. and OED.] silverside.

1921 Thomson & Anderton *Hist. Portobello* 70 Silverside *Argentina elongata*... It is sometimes called the 'silverfish' or 'snodgall' by the local fishermen. **1938** *TrRSNZ* LXVIII. 402 *Argentina elongata* Hutton. Silverside (snodgall). **1940** Phillipps *Fishes NZ* 45 The silverside [Argentina elongata] is common along the Otago Coast being called silver fish or snodgall by the local fishermen. **1956** [see silverside].

snook. [Abbrev. of snooker¹ child.] A child. See also snork.

1946 Sargeson *That Summer* 180 To run the house, with the snooks are growing up fast, his missus could have always done with considerably more money. **1964** Pearson *Glossary* to Sargeson *Collected Stories 1935–63* (1964) 303 snooks: children.

snooker, *n.*¹ [Poss. f. military *snooker* a new cadet; or an alteration of *snook(um)s* a trivial endearment for a child: see OED.] A child, a boy. See also snook.

[Note] The 1962 quot. contains a play on *snoek*, *snook* a barracouta fish.

1908 *Truth* 8 Feb. 2 In response to my enquiry for suitable light-weight boys for apprentices, I have received several applications... One 'snooker' was offered a billet in one of our leading local stables. **c1962** Baxter *Horse* (1985) 15 Gandhi grasped Charlie from behind..and strained to lift him from the floor..'An eight-pound snooker, I'd say. Or else a barracouda.' **1968** Baxter *Collected Plays* (1982) 109 She wasn't a wife, Rosie—we lived together, that is. We had a couple of snookers.

snooker, *n.*² *Prison.* [Prob. f. *snooker* to stymie: AND 1967.] A hiding place; also quasi-*attrib.* as **heavy snooker**, well hidden, secret. Also as a verb, to hide.

1982 Newbold *Big Huey* 85 Every smoko time..[they] would pull their bombs out of snooker and brew up a cup of tea or cocoa. *Ibid.* 148 He had a secret compartment in his slot where he hid all his goods,.. and a couple of screws swooped on [his] place and sprung his snooker. *Ibid.* 249 Heavy Snooker (adj) Well hidden, secret. *Ibid.* 254 Snooker (n) and (v) Hide, hiding place. From the term in billiards.

snooze. [Orig. unknown.] See quot.

1953 Dewar *Chaslands* 90 Fishing was to be taken seriously [in Southland c1900]. The lads spent the evening hours 'snoozing' hooks; that is, fastening to them short lengths of flax-fibre string, lighter than the line; the idea being that if a hook becomes fast on anything in the sea the fisherman will lose the hook and not the line.

snore, *v.* [Apparently a survival of a Brit. (OED *v.* 1 c 'Chiefly *Sc.*') dial. *snore* to move or cut *through* the water with a roaring sound; to sail or travel quickly.] To cut through (a wave).

1985 Langdale-Hunt *Last Entail Male* 89 The weight of this tow-line seemed to place a fair weight on the bow of the towed launch and although the sea was moderately rough, the launch seemed to just snore through each sea without rising very much.

snore off. [AND *n.* 1952, *v.* 1925.] A (short) sleep; a nap.

1950 *Landfall* 14 127 I notice Little Spike's legs

SNORER

sticking out from an empty tallow cask where he is having a snore-off. **1963** PEARSON *Coal Flat* 77 Saying 'Yes, that's not a bad idea. Have to think it over,' saving it up to be looked into after a snore-off.

Hence *v. intr.* **snore off**, to have a (short) sleep.

1962 HORI *Half-gallon Jar* 54 Others snore off, some go to Bellamy's for the light refreshment or the quiet pot.

snorer. Obs. WW2. [Cf. Partridge 8, *snorer* 2. Bed: Army: 20C.] As **the snorer**, a bed; 'the sack'.

1945 *NZEF Times* 21 May 5 We trust you will deny any allegations that our disappearance is due to the fact that we are (a) out the monk (b) [AWL] (c) in the boob, and (d) on the snorer.

snork. [f. Brit. dial. *snork* a young pig: see OED *n.* 2; AND 1941.] A baby. See also SNOOK.

1941 BAKER *NZ Slang* 57 Other twentieth century New Zealand expressions..include..*snork*, a baby. **1956** DAVIN *Sullen Bell* 136 What I wasn't expecting was to find her living with the same bloke again and well on the way to having another snork. **1963** PEARSON *Coal Flat* 303 What'll they think if you have a snork that's got no father? **1970** DAVIN *Not Here Not Now* 108 Have to give up being on the bum once there's a snork or two to be looked after.

snorter.

1. [An elaboration of Brit. slang *snorter* anything exceptionally remarkable.] As **ring-tail snorter**, an exceptional person.

1908 *Truth* 2 May 1 When it comes to hot stuff this man North is out on his own, he's a hummer, a ring-tail snorter.

2. [Transf. use of Brit. slang *snorter* one who snorts in scorn: see OED *snorter* 1.] A peevish, cross-grained person.

c1926 THE MIXER *Transport Workers' Song Book* 127 If the pannikin's a 'snorter' with a look that's woebegone?

snot-eel: see SNOTTIE.

snottie. Also **snot-eel**. [f. the exudation of mucus.] HAGFISH.

1986 28 Oct. TV2 University Challenge: the host, Peter Sinclair, explains: In New Zealand they are called blind eels or snotties... Hagfish is the answer I had to have. **1991** BRADSTOCK *Fishing* 23 *Hagfish*. Other names: tuere, blind eel, snot-eel, snottie... Some very rude names are also used.

snotty-gob. [In allusion to the profuse exudation of sap when the plant is cut: cf. AND *snottygobble*; also Brit. dial. *snotty-gobble* var. of *snottergob* the fruit of the yew-tree.] Any of several plants exuding profuse sap esp. PATETE (*Schefflera digitata*) and FIVE-FINGER 1.

1927 *TRNZI* LVII. 957 snotty gob *Schefflera digitata* Ver. (Otago) [Vernacular names heard by [J.C. Andersen] among settlers, sawyers, etc.] **1940** LAING & BLACKWELL *Plants NZ* 324 [*Nothopanax arboreum*] is known by a variety of names, e.g. Five-fingered Jack (Canterbury), Snotty-gob (Taranaki), New Zealand Fig (Otago).

snout. [Fig. use of *snout* the nose: AND 1919.] In the phr. **to have (get) a snout on** (a person or thing), to bear a grudge against, to have a 'down' on.

1905 *Truth* 12 Aug. 1 The Grey candidate has a snout on the law courts. 'I got fourteen days,' he said. *Ibid.* 19 Aug. 3 Prisoners [in the Terrace Gaol] frequently complain that if the chief gaoler gets a snout on them they go into the dig-out on the slightest provocation.

Hence **snout** *v.* [see also EDD *snout v.*²; AND 1913], in the phr. **to get (someone) snouted**, to bear a grudge against (someone), to have it in for (someone).

c1926 THE MIXER *Transport Workers' Song Book* 30 Seems to me [the boss] has got me 'snouted' What it's for, hell only knows.

snow, *n.*¹

1. In the names of plants, usually synonymous with '(sub-)alpine', see: TOTARA *n.*¹ 2 (1), TUSSOCK 3 (11). See also SNOWBERRY, *snow-tree* 3 below.

2. [f. its short staple giving an appearance of snowflakes.] Second-cut wool.

1965 *Listener* 26 Feb. 15 *Snow*: Second cut wool. When a shearer is racing, if the quality of his shearing is not up to standard, wool flies about like snow.

3. Special Comb. **snowbirding** *vbl. n.*, stealing women's underwear or night-wear from clothes-lines (generally known as *snow-dropping*); **snow comb** shearing [f. *snow* + COMB *n.*], see quot. 1954; **snow fence** (also **snowline fence**) *n.*, a fence below the snowline to keep sheep safe from heavy winter snow; **snow-fence** *v.*, to erect snow-fencing on an area; **snowgrass**, **snow-patch grass**, see GRASS 2 (36), (37); **snowline** [spec. use of *snowline* the lower limit of perpetual snow: see OED 1835], the lower limit of winter snow, esp. in the phr. **above the snowline**, referring to the land snow-bound in winter but open to grazing in summer; **snowman** *freezing works obs.*, see quot.; **snow-pole** *Central Otago*, a pole placed upright to mark out a road or track (liable to be) covered with snow; **snow river** [see OED *n.*¹ 8 a, 1844], a snow-fed river; **snow-tree** (a) [f. the profuse white blossom], PUTAPUTAWETA; (b) [f. the sub-alpine location], NEINEI.

1980 MANTELL *Murder Or Three* 34 They kick up a stink if washing's left out overnight... There's been a few cases of **snowbirding** in that area lately. And if the girls lost washing from the lines, the hostel could be culpable. *Ibid.* 84 Peacock grimaced. 'So what have you got? A repressed old man who's done a bit of snowbirding?' **1954** *Press* (Christchurch) 17 July 5 **Snow comb**—a special type of comb used in shearing machines which leaves more wool on the sheep than an ordinary comb, meant for use in the high country where sheep are exposed to the cold. **1958** *NZ Farmer* 2 July 21 He thought the snow comb had had too much publicity, said..[the] chief shearing instructor for the New Zealand Wool Board. **1960** MILLS *Sheep-O* 62 Two devices are employed to reduce the risk of loss of stock through exposure after shearing. One is the 'snow comb', a thick comb on the handpiece that ensures that sufficient wool is left on the sheep to keep it from freezing. **1964** DICK *High Country Family* 144 'Blades or machines?' I asked. 'Oh, we use the snow-comb—know it?' 'Yes, yes I do.' **1933** *Press* (Christchurch) (Acland Gloss.) 2 Dec. 15 *Snow fence*.— A fence to keep sheep down on the winter country. **1962** SHARPE *Country Occasions* 158 Instead of putting boundaries along the tops of snow-swept ranges, modern high-country owners try to establish a 'snow-fence' which runs along the side of a range perhaps 3,000 feet above sea-level. Below this, sheep will be reasonably safe through the winter. **1968** TOMLINSON *Remembered Trails* 126 He went to fill his billy in the last little creek that runs into the Motueka River before the snow fence.

1981 ANDERSON *Both Sides of River* 8 A greater number of stations have snowline fences on their winter blocks. **1952** NEWTON *High Country Journey* 30 At one time boundary-keeping after the autumn muster was a major job, but over the years, a big proportion of the block has been **snow fenced**. **1898** MORRIS *Austral-English* 425 *Snow-line, n.* In pastoralists' language of New Zealand, 'above the snow-line' is land covered by snow in winter, but free in summer. **1902** *Settler's Handbook NZ* (Lands Dept.) 92 The merino occupies and thrives on the wild lands of the colony, from the snow-line to the border of the plains. **1933** *Press* (Christchurch) (Acland Gloss.) 2 Dec. 15 *Snow line.*—Roughly the line above which snow lies all the winter and therefore the country above the *s[now] l[ine]* is only useful for sheep from October (or even after shearing) until May. **1981** ANDERSON *Both Sides of River* 8 In winter the high tops remain permanently snowbound down to a line of about 900 metres; hence the word 'snowline'. **1981** CHARLES *Black Billy Tea* 35 There's no place I'd rather be, Than the top beat With a snow-line boundary. **1957** MACDONALD *Canterbury Frozen Meat Co.* 66 All freezing was done for the first ten years [from c1882] by the cold air machines... The carcases were hung in the chambers, and the cold air was blown through kauri ducts or trunks at a temperature of minus 40° Fahrenheit. The carcases, being relatively warmer than the air, always lost moisture to it; this formed snow which blocked the trunks, cutting down the air circulation and giving the '**snow-men**', who had to crawl through the trunks, a bad time in clearing them. **1862** *Otago Witness* (Dunedin) 19 July 7 The miners..appreciate the care and thoughtfulness of the Government in erecting **snow poles** between the Teviot township and Tomahawk Gully. **1875** WOOD & LAPHAM *Waiting for Mail* 36 They got snowed up at Potter's, and tried to make their way out by the snow poles over there. **1887** PYKE *Hist. Early Gold Discoveries Otago* (1962) 106 The first snow poles were put up on the track from Tuapeka to 'the Portuguese'..below Miller's Flat; these were only Manuka poles. **1898** HOCKEN *Contributions* 172 It was sought to make the track over Flagstaff, or the Snowy Mountains as they were then called, safer by erecting snow poles sunk into mounds, and of these there were seventeen to the mile. **1970** MCLEOD *Glorious Morning* 219 Coming down Starvation Gully, where the striped 'snow-poles' marked the winding road for winter travellers. **1988** PICKERING *Hills* 26 Routes became, as the maps put it, 'poled', which meant that metal standards were studded along the tops, These can also be called snow-poles or sometimes waratahs. **1862** CHUDLEIGH *Diary* 4 May (1950) 36 It [*sc.* Waitaki] is a **snow river** looks milky before it rises. **1865** MUELLER *My Dear Bannie* (1958) 26 Sept. 46 All these rivers here are snow rivers, fed by melting snow on the mountains and are consequently ice cold. **1871** *TrNZI* III. 86 The Rangitata, one of the great *snow rivers*, as they are termed. This stream..is periodically swollen by the melting of the snow..from the north-west. **1881** BATEMAN *Colonist* 26 Very many [in Canterbury] are known as 'snow' rivers, owing to the icy coldness of the water. **1959** *Press* (Christchurch) 7 Aug. 12 We travelled far and wide, on foot for many weary miles, by car, by buggy, and by bicycle; penetrated to the headwaters of the great snow rivers and the shores of the great lakes. **1888** HETLEY *Native Flowers of NZ* 3 Small **Snow-Trees** (*Carpodetus serratus*)—so called from the quantities of little white flowers making it appear that there had been a fall of snow. **1908** *NZ Geol. SB* (NS) No.6 9 The most noticeable of these are various Olearias, usually with moss-covered trunks..[and] **snow-tree** or neinei.

snow, *n.*² Also **snowy**. Used in address often to a youngster (not necessarily a blonde); also occas used ironically (and possibly offensively) to a Polynesian.

SNOW 754 **SNOW-RAKE**

c1935 In Taranaki use: p.c. D. Hurley. **1951** 14 M 14 St Bede's, Chch 11 Snow. **1951** 14 M 14 St Bede's, Chch 11 Snow(y) [M2] **1984** CAMPBELL *Island to Island* (1984) 93 In those days [c1939] racism was more blatant than it is now... I had become accustomed to being addressed as 'snow', 'darky', and even 'Hori', often by adults who would have been surprised had they known they were giving offence.

snow, *v.*

1. In the phr. **It's snowing down below (down south)**, a cry to girls whose petticoat is showing in what is generally called a POPPY-SHOW q.v.

c1935 Taranaki schools, p.c. D. Hurley: 'It's snowing down south.' **c1940** Mangapai School (Whangarei) Northland, p.c. Jean Watson: 'It's snowing down below.'

2. As **snow ink**, to snow heavily.

1936 *Hills & Valleys* II. 44 Not caring if it 'snowed ink' we crawled into our wet sleeping bags.

snowball (waltz). A waltz (or occas. another popular dance) which begins with a single dancing pair each of whom when the music pauses chooses a new partner from spectators, and so on through pauses and starts until all able dancers present are on the dance floor. Often elsewhere called a 'chain waltz', it is a social device to encourage participation. Known to informants from the 1920s, 1930s and 1980s, though apparently rarely found in writing.

1995 *Listener* 15 Apr. 88 Take your partners, please, for *The Snowball Waltz*, a play by Renee that, according to producer Steve Danby, evokes the trestle tables, beetroot and red lemonade of dancehalls gone by.

snowberry. [Transf. f. Brit. *snowberry* (OED 'A name given to various plants..bearing white berries') and applied to any of several unrelated NZ plants, often sub-alpine in habitat, and often with a 'berry' colour of white through pink to red.]

1. See also GAULTHERIA. **a.** Also locally **nardoo berry**. *Gaultheria antipoda* or *G. depressa* (fam. Ericaceae) native shrubs of mainly sub-alpine habitats, having bell-like flowers and seed capsules surrounded by a fleshy edible calyx. See also HEATH 3, *weka-berry* (WEKA 5).

1856 WAITT *Progress of Canterbury* 10 My great delight was to gather the New Zealand snowberry. This little pure white berry..the fruit pure as the snow, the leaf and plant like a Scotch blac[k]berry. **1864** BARRINGTON *Diary* 17 May in Taylor *Early Travellers* (1959) 413 I was so weak that I thought I must give in, but I ate plenty of the little snow-berries which grow under the snow. **1888** HETLEY *Native Flowers NZ* I. 3 At the edge of the lake there were bushes with lovely berries of different colours, and such large white snow berries (*Gaultheria antipoda*). **1891** *NZJSc.* (NS) I. 200 Besides grubs, they feed on the berries of various alpine shrubs..such as the snow berry. **1909** *AJHR C-12* 59 *[Gaultheria] perplexa*. Narrow-leaved snowberry. Heath. Fairly common in its station. **c1920** BEATTIE *Trad. Lifeways Southern Maori* (1994) 118 Tapuka is the Murihiku name of the familiar snowberry, so sought after by back-country musterers, by kea parrots and by weka. *Ibid.* 356 The tapuku [*sic*] was the snowberry, the white berry growing so close to the ground. **1918** *NZGeol.SB* (NS) No.19 3 The kaka used to visit the grass country..when the berry of the *Gaultheria rupestris* (snowberry, or so-called 'nardoo berry' of Waipori) was ripe. **1939** BEATTIE *First White Boy Born Otago* 13 The snowberries were fine. We called the red hill kind [c1840] 'mulberries', but I do not know why. **1947** [see WEKA 5 b]. **1978** MOORE & IRWIN *Oxford Book NZ Plants* 110 *Gaultheria depressa* variety *Novae-zealandiae*... White succulent edible 'fruits'..are called 'snow-berries', but red and pink ones are almost equally common. **1982** WILSON *Stewart Is. Plants* 64 Bush Snowberry... Tāwiniwini... False beech... Shrub up to 1–2 m tall... Fruit berry-like, red or reddish pink, formed by swollen calyx around thin capsule.

b. As **Tarawera** (or **Taupo**) **snowberry** [f. the names of Mount *Tarawera* and Lake *Taupo* in the central NI], *Gaultheria oppositifolia*.

1961 MARTIN *Flora NZ* 235 *Gaultheria oppositifolia* Niniwa or Tarawera Snowberry. *Ibid.* 226 Outstanding..is the Taupo Snowberry (*Gaultheria oppositifolia*), with its..pure 'lily of the valley' flowers. The shrub is abundant in the southern half of the Auckland Province.

2. [f. the white colour.] *Luzuriaga* (also *Enargea*) *parviflora* (fam. Philesiaceae), a small creeping forest-floor plant bearing white berries.

1908 *AJHR C-11* 36 *Luzuriaga parviflora*. Puwatawata. Snowberry. Forest. **1909** *AJHR C-12* 52 Nohi, puwatawata. Snowberry, forest snowberry. Forest. Very abundant. Not found north of the Thames mountains. **1961** MARTIN *Flora NZ* 245 Lilies are represented by two perching *Astelias* and..by the Forest Snowberry (*Enargea parviflora*). **1964** DEMPSEY *Little World Stewart Is.* 14 Eileen Willa..occasionally brought in..mosses and arranged amongst them..the fragile white bells and the translucent white berries of what in Stewart Island we call the snowberry. It is a lily, she told me.

3. *Pernettya* spp. (fam. Ericaceae), a genus of sprawling shrubs bearing dry berries.

1973 MARK & ADAMS *Alpine Plants* (1979) 110 *Pernettya macrostigma*... Snowberry.

4. *Cyathodes* or *Leucopogon* spp. (fam. Epacridaceae). MINGIMINGI a.

1966 *Encycl. NZ* III. 712 Snowberry... mingimingi, tumingi . . *Cyathodes* spp.

snow cave, *n. Mountaineering.* Also *ellipt.* **cave**. [Used elsewhere but recorded earliest in NZ: see OED *snow n.*[1] 8 a.] A cave hollowed out of snow and used for shelter.

1941 *Canterbury Mountaineer* 83 The use of snow caves in providing adequate shelter..may yet be included in the plans of New Zealand climbers. **1948** *NZ Alpine Jrnl.* XII. 248 A party established in a snow cave can literally laugh at the weather. **1952** *Ibid.* XIV. 274 I went down..to borrow a new ice-axe and the others improved the cave. **1955** *Ibid.* XVI.190 Perhaps the most important of a number of changes in the first post-war decade in this country is the development and use of snow caves. **1990** *Evening Post* (Wellington) 16 Aug. 1 Mr Iwama..was last seen on Saturday digging a snow cave to escape the storm... Mr Iwama said his first snowcave was close to the crater lake.

snow-cave, *v. Mountaineering.* [f. SNOW CAVE *n.*] To use a snow cave as a base for further mountaineering.

1948 *Canterbury Mountaineer* 258 In reality of course they were the tracks of another club party who had been 'snow caving' near Katie's col.

Hence **snow-caver** *n.*, one who excavates or uses a snow cave; **snow-caving** *vbl. n.*

1949 *NZ Alpine Jrnl.* XIII. 93 We advise future **snow-cavers** to have the top of the entrance tunnel no higher than the floor of the living space. **1948** *NZ Alpine Jrnl.* XII. 248 The two great advantages of 'snow-caving' are absolute security and adequate comfort. **1955** *Ibid.* XVI. 190 [Heading] Ten years of snow caving in New Zealand. **1968** *Ibid.* XXII. 384 [Heading] Snow Caving in the La Perouse.

snowed in, *ppl. a. Shearing.* See quot. 1955. Cf. WOOLLING-UP.

1955 BOWEN *Wool Away* 157 Snowed in. Describing the state of affairs when the shearers are ahead of the wool table, so that wool is lying around the floor waiting to go on the wool table. With a good run shearers can sometimes snow the pressers in. Shearers will be seen at their best when they get ahead of the rest of the shed. They enjoy this snowing in, and usually they make the wool flow faster than ever. **1965** *Listener* 26 Feb. 15 Snowed in: The condition of the sorting table or the shearing board when shearers are working too fast for the shed hands to keep up. **1989** *NZ Eng. Newsletter* III. 28 *snowed in:* When the shearers get ahead of the men on the wool table and fleeces lie around.

snowgloo. *Mountaineering.* [f. SNOW (CAVE + i)*gloo.*] A fanciful name for a kind of snow cave.

1952 *NZ Alpine Jrnl.* 14 (39) June 363 A.J. Heine's building of a 'snowgloo' (a cross between a snow cave and an igloo). **1958** *Tararua* 12 66 We soon had a comfortable 'snowgloo'. Inflating my li-lo, I snuggled into my bag.

snow-rake, *v. High-country farming. intr.* To rescue (snow-bound sheep) from deep snow.

1907 *TrNZI* XXXIX. 75 When 'snow-raking'— that is, taking sheep from high country—keas would gather round. **1933** *Press* (Christchurch) (Acland Gloss.) 2 Dec. 15 *Snow rake*.—To rescue sheep from snow and bring them to a safer place. Hence *s[now] raker*. **1946** MILLER *There Was Gold* 136 When the snow came unexpectedly before all the sheep were off the high country, the men had to go snow raking, looking for breathing holes in the tops of deep drifts which provided the only clue to the presence below of buried sheep and shovelling them out. **1952** BLAKISTON *My Yesteryears* 32 On many places, it is customary to offer a whisky to men who have spent a day snow raking. **1965** HENDERSON *Open Country Harvest* (1970) 187 'They'll soon be snowraking out back.' I said. 'What do you mean—snowraking?' Jock asked.

Hence **snow-raker** *n.*, one who snow-rakes; **snow-raking** *vbl. n.*, the action or process of rescuing snow-bound sheep from deep snow.

1933 *s[now]raker* [see above]. **1962** SHARPE *Country Occasions* 177 Trudging away from their main track, the snow-rakers packed the snow with their feet into a sort of trail along which sheep could travel. **1992** *North & South* Oct. 17 Little two-seater Robinsons, which some of the cockies have, were ferrying snow rakers up to the tops. **1908** *Awards, etc.* 1126 Any shepherd having less than a yearly engagement, or musterer employed in **snow-raking**, shall be paid at the rate of 10s. per day. **1911** *Mowat's Diary* July in McCaskill *Molesworth* (1969) 104 The whole countryside was covered [with snow] to a depth of 18 inches. Snow raking was out of the question as there was no clear ground to which the sheep could be shifted. **1912** *Canterbury Musterers' & Packers' Award* in *The Sheepowners' Handbook* (1912) 41 Any musterer required to do any snow-raking shall be paid not less than 15s. per day while engaged in such work. **1923** *Awards, etc.* 456 [Marlborough Musterers, Packers, and Drovers] Any musterer or packer required to do snow-raking shall be paid £1 5s. per day while engaged in such work. **1938** BURDON *High Country* 157 The process of extracting sheep [from snow] is known as 'snow-raking'. **1947** BEATTIE *Early Runholding* 64 Most of the runholders have had gangs rescuing the sheep..(commonly called 'snow-raking'). **1966** NEWTON *Boss's Story* 189 *Snow-raking*: When sheep get held up in heavy snow they often have to be 'raked' out onto clear windswept country or down to lower levels. A man has to tramp a track through the snow along which the sheep can follow. This job—snow-raking—is tough, killing work. **1982** WHEELER *Hist. Sheep Stations NZ* 32 [The winter blocks'] condition allows continuous and concentrated grazing. Concentration means quick, economical snowraking.

snow-rake, *n. Joc.* [f. prec.] A name for an imaginary result of a fool's errand.
1938 BURDON *High Country* 157 The process of extracting sheep [from snow] is known as 'snow-raking', and this term gives the old hands an opportunity of playing off an evergreen joke on the new chum. He is advised to get a snow-rake made for himself.

snowy, *a. Obs.* In names for high-altitude features, as **Snowy Hills (Mountains, Ranges)**; esp. in Canterbury and Otago, old names for the Southern Alps and other ranges.
1861 *Otago Witness* (Dunedin) 23 Mar. 5 The terror of a journey over the Snowy Mountains is fast passing away. **1863** BUTLER *First Year in Canterbury* (1923) 83 On the right, at a considerable distance, rises the long range of mountains which the inhabitants of Christ Church suppose to be the backbone of the island, and which they call the Snowy Range. **1898** HOCKEN *Contributions* 172 It was sought to make the track over Flagstaff, or the Snowy Mountains as they were then called, safer. **1933** *Press* (Christchurch) (Acland Gloss.) 2 Dec. 15 *Snowy Range* or *Snowy Hills*.—The old names for that part of the Southern Alps and foothills which is visible from the plains... The original applications for the runs on the upper plains, in describing the locality, all end with the words 'and back to the Snowy Hills'.

snowy: see SNOW *n.*²

snuffle. *Obs.* [Prob. f. Brit. slang *snuffler* one who speaks cantingly: see OED.] Paltry cant, humbug.
1905 *Truth* 26 Aug. 4 Snuffle, humbug and hypocrisy like a veil.

snufflebuster. *Hist.* [f. SNUFFLE + *buster* fellow, chap: AND 1890.]
1. A sanctimonious puritanical person; a 'wowser' or spoilsport. (The term was a favourite of the early issues of *Truth* weekly.)
1905 *Truth* 23 Sept. 8 Prurient Parsonical Parasites... A Trinity of Tarnished Tray-trappers..smug snuffle-busters. **1906** *Ibid.* 1 June 4 Sanctimonious snuffle-busters. *Ibid.* 14 July 1 The object of the Nelson snufflebusters is to stir up strife. **1906** *Ibid.* 4 Aug. 1 When a cove wanting lodgings advertises himself as a staunch teetotaller, or a Christian young man, it's a sign for the other people in the house he goes to to double lock their belongings. Such snufflebusters ar[e]n't to be trusted worth a crimson anvil. **1915** *Hutt Valley Independent* 28 Aug. 4 Our editor does not believe that the snufflebusters will be able to keep him out of Heaven.
2. As **snivelling snufflebuster**, an elaboration of 1 above popularized by (and its origin often wrongly attributed to) the Minister of Works in the early Labour administrations, the Hon. Robert Semple (1873–1955), notorious for his use of pungent epithets.
1941 BAKER *NZ Slang* 53 A well-known New Zealand politician [Hon. R. Semple]..introduced this country to the term *snivelling snufflebuster*. **1952** *Evening Post* (Wellington) 7 Feb. 10 I am still so ignorant that I don't even know what a 'snivelling snufflebuster' is, except that in Mr Semple's opinion I myself am one. **1959** SINCLAIR *Hist. NZ* 262 Bob Semple, the irrepressible Minister of Public Works,..added a number of colourful expressions to the language—'snivelling snufflebusters', for instance, as a term of abuse. **1984** BEARDSLEY *Blackball 08* 241 The snivelling bloody snufflebusters, fooled by that cheap little opportunity.
3. In quasi-verbal use **snufflebustering** or **snuffle-busting** *vbl. n.* and *attrib.* [AND 1895], sanctimoniously puritanical canting.
1905 *Truth* 4 Nov. 8 Highly respectable citizens, often snuffle-busting religionists who yell loudest in church. **1906** *Truth* 17 Mar. 1 The snufflebustering ass [of a street preacher]. *Ibid.* 18 Aug. 1 The latest 'evil' that this snufflebusting clique of chad band has unearthed is the indecent postcard. **1908** *Truth* 5 Dec. 8 Snufflebusting shicers..white-eyed wowsers.

snuff-stick. [Prob. a survival of Brit. slang: see OED *snuff n.* 4, 1879 only.] A cigarette.
1978 HILLIARD *Glory & Dream* 76 Not with a snuff-stick hanging out of their gates.

soak. *Obs.* An enclosed place in or beside a stream used for sheep-washing. Also as a *vbl. n.* **soaking**, the cleansing of sheep in a soak.
1938 BURDON *High Country* 83 Washing consisted of two separate operations, the first of which was called 'soaking'. The soak was a sort of bath..let into the ground beside a creek... It was filled and kept full by water flowing in through a two-inch pipe and a supply of boiling water was kept handy... Soap and sometimes ammonia were added to it. After the sheep were let out of the soak they were driven..[to] the creek..tipped in..and washed clean by men standing in the water. **1949** CRAWFORD *Sheep & Sheepmen Canterbury* 42 The sheep were driven into 'the soak', a sort of bath about twenty feet long by ten feet wide let into the ground beside a creek. It was filled and kept full of lukewarm water to which soap and sometimes ammonia were added.

soap, *n.*
1. See *bar of soap* (BAR *n.*³ 2); *gumdigger's soap* (GUMDIGGER *n.*¹ 3).
2. Special Comb. **soapbox artist**, see ARTIST 2 b; **soap shaker**, a perforated or mesh soap-container on a handle, holding a piece of soap which is swished in water to make suds (for washing dishes, etc.).
1964 HARVEY *Any Old Dollars Mister?* 10 I was drying the dishes while Elizabeth..washed up..she started bouncing the soap shaker up and down in the water until the sink was full of bubbles.

soap, *v.*
1. [Used elsewhere but recorded earliest in NZ: see OED *v.* 2.] To flatter (someone).
1849 TORLESSE *Papers* (1958) 72 Tarawata was annoyed at my shooting the horse without his knowledge, but I soaped him down. **1910** *Auckland Herald* 10 Mar. 6 [Heading] Soaping Wairoa. Lord Kitchener at 'Whaka'.
2. In the phr. **to soap (the geyser)**. **a.** To add soap flakes to a geyser to encourage it to spout or spout more spectacularly. Also as *vbl. n.*
1904 *NZ Observer* 5 Mar. 16 Quality, not quantity, rules the soaping of the Whakarewarewa geyser. It was soaped for a German princelet..but two thousand carnival trippers..implored the Department..and there wasn't enough soap forthcoming to wash a dewdrop. *Ibid.* 1 Oct. 17 Upon what principle is the big geyser at Whakarewarewa 'soaped?' **1910** *NZ Free Lance* (Wellington) 26 Nov. 12 It would be more appropriate if the laundry whistle was blown when Wairoa geyser was soaped. **1935** POSPISIL *Wanderings on the Islands of Wonders* 243 We soaped the Dragon's Mouth which 'spat unusually high', as the Maori suspiciously remarked. **1993** *Evening Post* (Wellington) 5 Apr. 14 Alex performs the ritual of 'soaping the geyser'. He explains..that by pouring a kilo of special soap into the geyser it reduces the surface temperature allowing the geyser to erupt.
b. *transf. obs.* To get started, to get going.
1946 SIMPSON *If You'd Care to Know* 100 An expression in common use Down Under is soap the geyser... It is confined almost exclusively to New Zealand... In the Thermal Regions..there is a particular geyser that could be made to perform by throwing soap into it, and it was frequently soaped so that it would put up a display for the delight of important visitors. So today, when a New Zealander says, 'Come on, let's soap the geyser,' he means 'Come on, let's get going', or 'Let's start'.

soapie. [f. *soap* (opera + -IE).] A soap opera.
1990 DUFF *Once Were Warriors* 9 Or she'd be watching the TV. An afternoon soapie. **1993** *Evening Post* (Wellington) 21 June 20 [Heading] Visit your favourite soapies in Britain.

Social Credit. In New Zealand, *Social Credit* has been applied to various people or organizations advocating policies based on Social Credit theory (see OED *Social Credit* 1 and 2); *spec.* in New Zealand politics, the **Social Credit Party**, or the **Social Credit (Political) League**.
1959 SINCLAIR *Hist. NZ* 281 Thereafter the only serious challenge to his [*sc.* Holland's] authority came from a Social Credit party which, in the election of 1954, won 11 per cent of the votes, though no seats, and threatened to become a rival conservative party. **1966** *NZ Encycl.* II. 812 In May 1953, the New Zealand Social Credit Political League was formed. **1968** *Landfall* 88 365 The men armed with Social Credit conversation for the interval. **1975** *Landfall* 113 64 However unpalatable it may be to Social Crediteers [*sic*], a vote for the Social Credit Political League is a wasted vote in its immediate effect upon the fortunes of the two major parties.

sock. *Shearing.* Usu. *pl.* The wool between a sheep's knee and foot.
1955 BOWEN *Wool Away* 45 If the front socks are required to be taken off (this rests with the sheepowner), it is best to do it before starting the first blow on the belly, taking off the two inside front leg socks with two flicks of the handpiece. **1968** *Straight Furrow* 21 Feb. 20 Socks: The wool between the knee and the foot. In some sheds and competitions the instruction 'leave the socks on' means not to shear this wool, which usually contains hair.

sod. Used *attrib.* in Comb. 'made, formed, built, or consisting of sods' and, though often used elsewhere, of special significance in early colonial New Zealand: **sod cottage** (see also SODDIE), **fence, house, hut** [AND 'recorded earliest in Australia', 1827], **oven, whare**. Also **Sod Town**, a nickname for a settlement comprising mainly sod buildings.
1949 SHAW & FARRANT *Taieri Plain* 140 John Jefferis imported timber and added twelve rooms around and above his **sod cottage** and opened it as a licensed

house. **1952** STEVENS *John Grigg* 26 The first house [on Longbeach run] was a sod cottage built at the head of a gully close to the sea. **1991** LA ROCHE *Hist. of Howick & Pakuranga* 256 A sod cottage was cheap, quickly erected with no building experience required and using materials readily available... Sods were cut about 8 inches by 10 inches (a size easily cut and lifted with a spade); and laid horizontally like bricks. **1870** in Evans *Waikaka Saga* (1962) 14 On March 30, 1870, Shepherd also applied for a claim 'situated near Aynsleys **sod fence**, right hand side'. **1875** WOOD & LAPHAM *Waiting for Mail* 84 Frank was waiting beside the sod-fence. **1937** AYSON *Thomas* 132 Towards the close of 1869 Doull decided to fence in two paddocks with sod fences. **1947–48** BEATTIE *Pioneer Recolls.* (1956) 4 Next day they got on their own property and soon began to build sod fences along the lines marked by survey pegs. These fences were six sods high with a cap making their height between four and five feet, and they served excellently until the rabbits ruined them three or four years later. **1944** *Feilding Express* 29 June 4 The difference between a **sod house** and a cob house is that the former is made of sods cut square and laid like bricks to form a wall, while a cob house is built of clay cemented with tussock. **1867** BARKER *Station Life* (1870) 110 The next step [after buying land] is to build a **sod hut** with two rooms..thatching it with Tohi, or swamp grass. **1913** BEATTIE *Trade Hunting* 15 A lively family of rats could soon make a ruin of a sod hut; this limited the popularity of this style of architecture. **1939** BEATTIE *First White Boy Born Otago* 112 The station was just a sod hut, built against a steep bank, and the chimney was merely a wide hole cut up through the bank. **1988** MIKAERE *Te Maiharoa* 73 Whare parupuru (sod huts) were erected, gardens were planted with potatoes..and the whole settlement was neatly enclosed with takitaki (sod walls) and manuka fences. **1937** AYSON *Thomas* 27 It was fried in a **sod oven** heated with dry manuka which Thomas would bring in in dray loads from nearby. **1944** *Feilding Express* 29 June 4 The settlement was known as Arowhenua, but..it became known as **Sod Town**. **1886** HART *Stray Leaves* 9 The most popular [architecture] was what is known as the V hut... Sod **wharés**, of all kinds and designs, were also to be seen here and there. **1904** LANCASTER *Sons o' Men* 37 There were five men in the sod wharè that was rather close quarters for one. **1947–48** BEATTIE *Pioneer Recolls.* (1956) 29 The hut they built was a 'sod whare'.

soddie. *Hist.* Also **soddy**. [Orig. western N. Amer.: see OED *soddy n.* 2.] A sod cottage or hut.
  1940 *Tales of Pioneer Women* (1988) 283 Soon the sturdy young farmer..had built a comfortable enough 'soddie' from stout sods and heavy manuka branches. **1949** SHAW & FARRANT *Taieri Plain* 15 In 1852, Burns was welcomed by John Gow and his wife Catherine to their first home on 'Invermay', a 'soddie' with a long, long view of swamps. **1966** *Encycl. NZ* I. 490 Their father [Edward Dobson] meanwhile [c1854] had built a small cottage in Christchurch and a 'soddy' at Sumner.

SOE: an acronym of *State-owned enterprise*, see STATE.

solar, var. SOLLAR.

soldier, *n.*¹ [In various mainly transf. uses of *soldier* a serviceman.]

1. a. Mainly *pl.* Also **soldier-grass**. The stem and head of (usu.) the plantain *Plantago* spp. (fam. Plantaginaceae) so called from its use in a children's game (see b below). See also PLANTAIN.
  1926 HILGENDORF *Weeds* 161 Plantain (*Plantago lanceolata*) is commonly called rib grass..and soldiers... From the [leaf] rosette rises the slender flower stalk a foot or more in length, with a crowded mass of tiny brown or black flowers at its tip. These heads are used by children for playing 'soldiers'. **1938** HYDE *Godwits Fly* (1970) 146 He would have enjoyed swishing their heads off, as he used to cut off the dark heads of soldier-grass when he was a child. **1969** *Standard Common Names Weeds* 72 soldiers [=] *narrow-leaved plantain*.

b. *pl.* A game like conkers or 'conquerors', played with plantain stalks where a player has to try and strike off the head of the opponent's stalk, and, in turn, allow the opponent to try to do likewise to the striker's stalk.
  [*Note*] Also a common British children's game: EDD *soldier* 12 attests the senses a and b above in Sc. and English dial.; cf. J.G. Wood *The Boy's Modern Playmate* (London) 1891 p.151 'In the spring and summer conqueror is often played by means of the plantain-stalk, each player trying to cut off the head of the other's plantain with his own.'
  c1900 Marlborough children p.c. W.H.B.Orsman; also **c1938** (Ed.). Both *soldier*, and *soldiers* were used for the game. **1920** MANSFIELD *Letters* 17 Mar. (1993) III. 248 We shall lie in the grass..and play soldiers..& we'll blow some o'clocks. **1926** [see a above].

2. [Poss. a transf. use of *soldier* vertical timber pieces used to hold formwork in position: see OED *n*. 7 c.] An iron rod arranged so as to prevent backward movement of a wagon.
  1961 HENDERSON *Friends In Chains* 83 As a safeguard, we had fitted to the pole astern [on the horse-wagon], a 'soldier', which was an iron rod with a sharp parrot beak at the end, dragging on the ground... The backward pressure caused the soldier to pierce the surface and so hold the wagon.

3. In special collocations: **soldier's button**, *Cotula australis* (fam. Asteraceae), an Australasian daisy of disturbed sites, having a small button-like head of pale yellow flowers; also applied to BACHELOR'S BUTTON 1 (*Cotula coronopifolia*); **soldier (soldiers') settlement**, see SETTLEMENT 4 b; **soldier settler**, see *military settler* (SETTLER 1 b(c)) and *soldier-settler* (SETTLER 4 b); **soldiers' fruit cake** *WW1*, a rich cake made as a treat for soldiers on service overseas.
  1926 HILGENDORF *Weeds* 179 Bachelor's Button (*Cotula coronopifolia*), also called **soldier's button**, is found in shallow ponds in scattered localities. **1950** *Bull. Wellington Bot. Soc. No.23* 13 Growing in mud or shallow pools are..the introduced..water purslane and *Cotula coronopifolia* (soldier's button). **1969** *Standard Common Names Weeds* 72 *soldier's button. Cotula australis*. **1985** PARHAM & HEALY *Common Weeds NZ* 114 Soldier's button *Cotula australis*... Ann[ual] with weak, spreading stems to 20 cm. **1915** MCCREDIE *Patriotic Fete..Bungalow Recipe Book* 9 **Soldiers' Fruit Cake**...Flour..butter..sugar, [fruit, etc.]... Make an icing... When set replace the cake..pack so that it cannot shake about, put on the lid and solder it all round.

soldier, *n.*² Also **red soldier**, freq. **soldierfish**. [f. the red body-colour, resembling the uniform of the former 'redcoat' soldier.] Any of several red-bodied marine fish, esp. *Pseudolabrus miles* (fam. Labridae), *Helicolenus* spp. and *Scorpaena* spp. (fam. Scorpaenidae). See also PARROTFISH.
  1842 GRAY *Fauna* in Dieffenbach *Travels in NZ* (1843) II. 218 Fam. Labroideae *Julis miles*... Named the 'Soldier' by the seamen who accompanied Cook on his second voyage. **1870** WHITWORTH *Martin's Bay Settlement* 13 Trumpeter, soldier fish. **1892** *TrNZI* XXIV. 215 From Portland Island a fish called 'soldier-fish' is recorded, fourteen specimens having been taken in the months of May, June, August, and October. **1917** WILLIAMS *Dict. Maori Lang.* 369 Puwaiwhakarua, n. *Red soldier*; a fish: when caught considered a sign that a north-west wind will blow. **1921** *NZJST* IV. 116 Pseudolabrus miles... *Scarlet Parrot-fish*. Known as 'soldier' at French Pass. **1922** *Auckland Weekly News* 28 Dec. 64 Among the fish..are sea perch or soldiers as the fishermen call them, on account of their red colour and defensive spines. **1927** SPEIGHT et al. *Nat. Hist. Canterbury* 201 The Soldier-fish (*Scorpaena cruenta*) and the variegated horror with the droll name of Hapuka's Grandfather..are members of the same order. **1938** [see FIVE-FINGER 3]. **1956** GRAHAM *Treasury NZ Fishes* 269 Scarlet Parrot-fish... [Otago commercial line fishermen] also said that never at any time had they known the 'Soldier Fish', as they call it, to be abundant. **1966** DOOGUE & MORELAND *Sea Anglers' Guide* 258 Scarlet Parrotfish... *Pseudolabrus coccineus;* soldier, red soldierfish; pau, puwaiwhakarua. **1981** WILSON *Fisherman's Bible* 208 Soldierfish: The Red, or Scarlet, Parrotfish by any other name.

soldierfish: see SOLDIER *n.*²

soldier-grass: see SOLDIER *n.*¹ 1 a.

sole. [Transf. use of *sole* or *lemon sole* for New Zealand flatfish resembling the European species.]

1. Any of several species of fam. Pleuronectidae (right-eyed flounders). See also PATIKI 1, 3 b.
  1770 [see DAB *n.*¹]. **1773** FORSTER *Resolution Jrnl.* 8 Apr. (1982) II. 250 We described all this and drew a new Sole. **1821** MCCRAE *Evidence before Commissioner Bigge* May in McNab *Hist. Records* (1908) I. 550 Many of the fish are very good. There are..bream, soles. **1834** MARKHAM *NZ* (1963) 46 Partikies or Soles, are speared with a Bayonet or a stick at night the flood tide coming in. **1844** TUCKETT *Diary* 13 May in Hocken *Contributions* (1898) 220 Like Otago it is a fine place for spearing soles or patike (the best of fish). **1868** PYKE *Province Otago* 32 Many..varieties of sea-fish are caught round the coast, such as barracouta, groper. **1876** [see TURBOT]. **1901** *TrNZI* XXXIII. 574 In other parts king-fish in abundance..soles, and flounders were found. **1927** PHILLIPPS *Bibliogr. NZ Fishes* (1971) 29 *Peltorhamphus novae-zeelandiae* [sic]... Sole; Patiki Rori. **1947** POWELL *Native Animals NZ* 67 Sole (*Peltorhampus novaezelandiae*), Patiki rori of the Maoris, is distinguished from the flounders by its oval shape.

2. With a modifier: **New Zealand (common, English), lemon (New Zealand lemon).**

(1) New Zealand (common, English) sole. *Peltorhamphus novaezeelandiae* (fam. Pleuronectidae), a right-eyed flatfish with a rounded snout. See quot. 1982. See also *patiki-rori* (PATIKI 3 b).
  c1846 WEEKES *My Island* in Rutherford & Skinner *Establish. New Plymouth* (1940) 119 Then a woman came up with a string of New Zealand soles (*Patiki*). **1872** HUTTON & HECTOR *Fishes NZ* 117 The New Zealand Sole (*Peltorhampus*) is an inferior table fish to the [Patiki; *Rhombosolea monopus*], and not equal to the English Sole in flavour. **1886** SHERRIN *Handbook Fishes NZ* 25 Of the abundance of the New Zealand sole, we cannot speak with any certainty. **1913** *TrNZI* XLV. 233 The so-called 'English' or New Zealand sole is very abundant along the east coast. **1921** *NZJST* IV. 122 Common Sole; Patikirori... Distribution: New Zealand coasts (not common, North Auckland Peninsula). **1936** *Handbook for NZ* (ANZAAS) 72 *Peltorhamphus novae zealandiae*: Sole; 'English sole.' **1956** GRAHAM *Treasury NZ Fishes* 206 New Zealand Common Sole (Patiki Rori). **1967** MORELAND *Marine*

Fishes 32 Common Sole... Frequently called sole, English sole, New Zealand sole, this fish is not strictly speaking a sole. **1978** *Catch* Dec. 17 New Zealand Sole..English sole, common sole. Family Pleuronectidae (righteye flounders). **1982** *Evening Post* (Wellington) 8 Dec. 37 Our most important commercial flatfish is the New Zealand or common sole, a rather elongated fish with a distinctive, rounded snout. Although there are minor differences in eyes and shape, this is our closest relative to the famous Dover sole.

(2) lemon (New Zealand lemon) sole. *Pelotretis flavilatus* (fam. Pleuronectidae) or (*obs*.) *Colistium* (formerly *Ammotretis*) spp. See also BRILL.

1876 *TrNZI* VIII. 215 *Ammotretis rostratus*... A fish not uncommon in the Dunedin market, where it goes by the name of 'Lemon Sole'. **1886** SHERRIN *Handbook Fishes NZ* 304 *Ammotretis rostratus* Gunther Lemon Sole. **1898** MORRIS *Austral-English* 267 Lemon Sole... In New Zealand it is another name for the New Zealand *Turbot*. **1906** *TrNZI* XXXVIII. 543 *The Lemon Sole* (*Ammotretis rostratus*). This fish is popularly known as the lemon sole, to distinguish it from *Peltorhamphus novae-zealandiae*..which the local fishermen call the English sole. The names are somewhat unfortunate, seeing that they are applied to totally different species in Britain. **1921** *NZJST* IV. 122 Ammotretis guntheri Hutton. *Brill*. Received in Wellington from Timaru and sold as 'lemon sole'... Pelotretis flavilatus... *Lemon Sole*. Sold as 'brill' in Wellington. **1947** POWELL *Native Animals NZ* 67 A related species is known as the Lemon-sole. **1956** GRAHAM *Treasury NZ Fishes* 210 The Lemon Sole, like the Common Sole, Flounder, Brill and Turbot is a bottom-dwelling fish with both eyes on the upper surface of the body, known as the right side. **1966** DOOGUE & MORELAND *Sea Anglers' Guide* 219 Lemon Sole... Other names:.. New Zealand lemon sole... Considered more choice than the common sole. **1986** PAUL *NZ Fishes* 140 Lemon sole... Known only from New Zealand, but named from a similar European species... A relatively minor commercial species.

sole charge, *attrib*.

1. Applied to a country school having one teacher only for all classes, or a teaching position in such a school. See also quot. 1963.

1944 WILSON *Moonshine* 21 It's [*sc.* the school's] a sole charge. **1957** *Education* No.2 10 Of the many sole-charge positions I had enthusiastically applied for, this one was the most remote. **1963** BACON *In the Sticks* 184 *Sole Charge*—The affectionate term applied to a country school having one teacher only. Maximum number of pupils for such a school is usually thirty-five; after the roll reaches this number, an assistant is appointed, making the school 'a two teacher job'.

2. Special Comb. **sole-charge school,** a small rural school with only one teacher; **sole-charge teacher,** SOLE TEACHER.

1942 *NZ Educ. Gaz.* No.2 14 The attempt to conduct the **sole-charge school**, with its several classes, without help must inevitably result in loss or failure. **1958** *Education* No.1 9 I first met with the pre-occupation of country children in their home affairs many years ago..in a small sole-charge high country school. **1973** McELDOWNEY *Arguing with My Grandmother* 38 They were both school teachers, at sole-charge country schools in Taranaki. **1988** WARR *Bush-burn to Butter* 116 The task of milking..and then facing a walk..to the nearest sole-charge school resulted in large numbers of country children..being too tired to learn at school. **1990** *Evening Post* (Wellington) 13 July 4 Te Wharau is a sole-charge school 40 kilometres south-east of Masterton. **1941** CURNOW *Island & Time* 12 I am the sums the **sole-charge teachers** teach. **1959** McCORMICK *Inland Eye* 25 I became a sole-charge country teacher.

sole teacher. A teacher in a sole-charge school, responsible for teaching primary classes at all levels. Also *attrib*. See also *sole-charge teacher* (SOLE CHARGE 2).

1888 *AJHR E-1* viii Table K—Number of Teachers, December 1887 [Heading] Principal—Head of School —Head of Department—Sole Teachers—Assistant teachers—Pupil Teachers [Sub-heading] [Similarly-headed tables in 1890, 1900 volumes]. **1959** SHADBOLT *New Zealanders* (1986) 21 In her last year at the little.. primary school, she often helped the sole teacher with his infant classes. **1963** BACON *In the Sticks* 1 She passed the *Education Gazette* across to me... I read aloud, 'Patunui Valley School, Sole Teacher required. Thirteen pupils, sixty miles from Estuarine.' **1981** PETERSON *Glasshouses* 16 She was sole teacher at the little country school of Riversdale. **1993** *North & South* (Auckland) Oct. 32 Mrs Adams, our sole teacher at this 18-pupil school, had to take classes from primer one to standard six.

sollar. Also **solar.** [f. Cornish mining use: see OED *sollar* 3 a, 1778–1896.] A platform to provide a smooth surface on a mine floor.

1978 McARA *Gold Mining Waihi* 187 The first job to be done, on arrival at the face to commence drilling, was to lay the solars,.. three rows of two-inch thick boards, five feet long, over the full width of the floor of the drive to provide a smooth surface from which to shovel the broken rock.

solo, *a.* and *n.*

A. *adj.* [Spec. uses of *solo* acting alone or without help.]

1. In special Comb. **solo butcher, solo slaughterman,** *freezing works obs.*, formerly one who killed or butchered animals as an individual contractor, not part of a chain system; **solo butchering, solo killing,** the work or business of a solo butcher.

1951 *Awards, etc.* 323 [NZ Freezing-Workers Award] In the case of solo killing, from the time the last man cuts out on the board. *Ibid.* 334 The employer shall provide sufficient labour to ensure that all daggy sheep and lambs shall be dagged in the case of solo slaughtermen before being penned, and for chain slaughtermen before reaching the leggers. **1982** *Dominion* (Wellington) 12 Mar. 9 At least eight of the present employees at Waitaki NZR Stoke, were **solo butchers** at the time the chain system was introduced in 1956. Stoke is not unique among New Zealand meat processing plants in still employing staff who were solo butchers... **Solo butchering** was hard work. There was a lot of bending and lifting required. Lifting [a] 140lb sheep carcase on to a hook at chin height required considerable effort. Tally was 90 per day, that's what the company expected from its solo butchers. There were no make ups for lost hooks, a butcher was paid for what he killed. **1986** *Metro* (Auckland) July 76 Before then [1932], the lamb and mutton kill was handled by solo butchers who were skilled tradesmen. Your old-time solo butcher could slaughter and dress an animal in a matter of minutes.

2. Used in Comb. in respect of single parents or parenting, of a person raising a child or children alone: **solo father (mother, mum, parent);** hence **solo parenthood.**

1987 *Dominion* (Wellington) 7 Apr. 6 After preliminary hearing..[X], 26, **solo father** was committed for trial. **1991** *Metro* (Auckland) Aug. 60 These days he's a solo father on the DPB. **1977** *NZ Herald* (Auckland) 8 Jan. sect. ii 7 So far, the research has shown that few **solo mothers** are out to skin the welfare state by claiming a domestic purposes benefit and living on boyfriends. **1986** O'REGAN *A Changing Order* 9 As a country we seem to have great need for a scapegoat... At the beginning of the 1970s it was the solo mother who was 'living off the taxpayer'. **1978** BALLANTYNE *Talkback Man* 126 'Evelyn's a **solo mum**,' Janet said. **1988** *North & South* (Auckland) Feb. 34 Just once I would like to read an article with a positive approach to 'solo mums'. **1991** DUFF *One Night Out Stealing* 112 Oh, muss be a Tuesday, the solo mum (sluts)'re out in force with their benefit money; meant to be for the..kids, but they come in here with their toyboys attached, spend the day and evening boozing. **1972** *Social Security in NZ* 242 Those **solo-parent** families in or near poverty not only experience the deprivations of being poor, but have other problems due to the lack of a partner. **1974** MULDOON *Rise and Fall of a Young Turk* 6 Although a solo parent, she [*sc.* Mrs Browne] always had one or more lame ducks under her wing. **1989** *Broadsheet* June 14 Being feminist has helped me cope with **solo parenthood**.

B. *n.* A solo parent, esp. a solo mother.

1986 O'REGAN *A Changing Order* 6 In that first year, we came to know 'the solos'. In our street there were twenty-nine houses, and fourteen of them were occupied by solo mothers and their young children... Here were fourteen women whose marriages had broken up and they were known to all and sundry as 'solos'. They themselves hated the title.

so long. [Used elsewhere, but early and often in New Zealand: see OED *long adv.* 1 c comparing German *so lange*, 1865.] Goodbye, au revoir, HOORAY 1.

1866 *Narr. Maungatapu Murders* 17 Kelly said, 'Well, I wish you good day.' I said, 'So long.' **1869** *Auckland Punch* 154 [Wharf loafer] 'Ta ta, old 'um' 'So long' is his rejoinder. **1874** BATHGATE *Col. Experiences* 97 There are many words and phrases current peculiar to the mining population. Of these, one of the most inexplicable is the diggers' goodbye, as in place of using that good old Saxon word at parting, they always say 'so-long'. **1892** WARDON *MacPherson's Gully* 31 You shut up..I know my way about. So-long. **1925** MANDER *Allen Adair* (1971) 88 'You'll never get on.' 'All right. Then I won't. So long.' **1936** ALLEN *Poor Scholar* 163 Well, so long. That's New Zealand for au revoir, isn't it? **1952** DUFF *Shepherd's Calendar* (1961) 96 'Well, so long,' one said, heading for the Square. 'Ta-ta,' the other answered, and turned back into the College.

sonk, *v. trans.* In adolescents' use, to hit (someone) with the fist, to sock.

1953 13–15 M A1 Thames DHS 30 Sonk [M10] **1951** 16+ M 26 Marlborough C. 30A Sonk

soojee bag: see *rough as a soojee bag* (ROUGH A 2 a (b)).

sook /sŏk/, *n.* and *a.* Also **sookie, sook(e)y.** [f. Brit. dial. *sook* a var. of *suck*, used as a pet name for calves (*sucky-calf*) or as a call to cows and calves (see EDD and ADD): see also EDD *suck n.* 19 a 'duffer', a stupid fellow: cf. OEDAS *sook* (1850), *sookie* (1838) a name or call for cattle, Sc. (usu. for a calf) and US (usu. for a cow).]

A. *n.*

1. [AND 1941.] A timid, soft-natured, or cowardly person, a sissy; esp. of a child, a cry-baby.

c1920 p.c. R. Mason. *sookie* used by her mother in the sense of cry-baby. **1933** SCANLAN *Tides of Youth* 155 And I say Pat was a dismal failure because he didn't arrive in his brass buttons, and he looked a big sookie and wouldn't say a word. **1948** in Pearson *Six Stories* (1991) 48 'Making a damn big ninny of me!' my father said... 'Making a big sook of me, complaining to Carlyle.' **1968** *NZ Contemp. Dict. Suppl.* (Collins) 18 *sook n. (Sl.)* timid, cowardly, young person; *adj.* sooky. **1970** BALL *People Makers* 47 Sooks come in both sexes. **1981** STEWART *Hot & Copper Sky* 300 Oh, I remember you when you were a kid. Always a snivelling little sook. **1985** ROSIER-JONES *Cast Two Shadows* 67 'Sookey.'.. 'Don't be a sook,' she says. 'It was a fair fight, have my hanky and let's be friends.' **1992** POOLE *Skinny Louie Book* 24 Peg and Jack and Kath had decided that their cousin was a sook, a townie and a sook.

2. A (pet name for a) calf, often used as a call for cows and calves. Occas. **sooky-calf**.
c**1938** 'sook, sook' or 'sookie, sookie' commonly used in Marlborough as a call to calves. (Ed.) **1963** FRAME *Reservoir* 71 'Calfie, calfie,' she whispered again. 'Sook, sook. Never mind, calfie, I'll get someone to help you.' **1975** HENDERSON *Log of Superfluous Son* 33 A calf sucked Senney's fingers. 'Sook, sook,' he said. *Ibid.* 64 He kept side on to their [*sc.* milking cows'] hind-legs and spoke to them softly, 'OK sookies. OK. Gaw-ood sooks.' **1992** ANDERSON *Portrait Artist's Wife* 33 'Sookies, sookies,' he gasped. 'You lot should be in the paddock with the sucking calves.'

B. *adj.* [AND 1901.] Timid, soft-natured; sissy.
1964 *Weekly News* (Auckland) 18 Mar. 58 The boys say they feel sooky wearing caps. **1970** *Listener* 12 Oct. 13 Their attitude of tolerant resignation toward the sooky Maoris who are always getting into trouble. **1991** *Evening Post* (Wellington) 24 Dec. 4 I don't give a damn for the sook brigade who hate rugby, and boxing. **1995** *Sunday Star-Times* (Auckland) 23 Apr. sect. D 3 He's the most sooky dog in the world but he looks really tough.

sookie, sook(e)y: see SOOK.

sool, *v.* [Transf. use of Brit. dial. *sowl* of a dog, to seize (a pig) by the ears: see OED *v.*³]

1. [AND 1849.] *trans.* Often as a command (esp. **sool 'em**), to set a dog on to (a person or animal). Occas. used absolutely.
1906 MALCOM *Rudolph* 15 Pointing to the old lady, he said 'Sool 'em, Nero.' **1906** *Truth* 14 July 1 'One of the backbone,' as they [*sc.* farmers] love to call themselves was charged at the Rangiora Court for sooling dogs onto an insurance agent. c**1930** *Whitcombe's Etym. Dict. Aust.-NZ Suppl.* 11 *sool* v. trans. sl. to incite a dog; to worry, tease, torment. **1942** BUTLER *Early Days, Taranaki* 48 The owner, Mr. Samuel Joll..would act in the capacity of shaft 'horse' [*sc.* in a cart], two goats coming next, then two dogs, and a dog as leader... When an extra pull was required 'Pig, pig, pig!' or 'Sool 'em up, boys,' was shouted, with the desired effect. **1953** SUTHERLAND *Golden Bush* (1963) 122 The New Zealand Standards Institute doesn't mention the word 'sool' in its code of by-laws... 'It is to be forbidden,' says the Institute, 'in any public place, to set on, urge, encourage, aid or assist any dog to rush at, attack or worry any person or animal.' This would seem to include baiting, egging, sooling and/or sic-ing, though not specifically mentioned. **1960** CRUMP *Good Keen Man* 23 I ran over and sooled the dog after the trotting sow, yelling and barking to show him what to do.

2. a. *trans.* Of a dog, to chase or attack (stock, quarry, etc.).
1939 COMBS *Harrowed Toad* 86 [This dog] will 'sool' anything. **1990** *Evening Post* (Wellington) 8 Aug. 48 [Footrot Flats] Hey, there's a lamb and ewe caught in the blackberries. Hop in sool it out!

b. *intr.* or *absol.* Of a person, to set a dog on to quarry; to give a command 'sool'. Also of a dog, to give chase to quarry, etc.
1960 CRUMP *Good Keen Man* 24 Even the presence of another young dog would have been better encouragement than a man lumbering about..noisily skitching and sooling.

3. *transf.* [AND 1889.] *trans.* Of people, to urge or egg (on), to scold. Also as **sool off**, to drive away, **sool into**, to attack.
1911 *Maoriland Worker* 2 July 9 Or it may be that the other boys will be brought here from other countries to be 'sooled' at you [unionists]. **1919** *Quick March* 10 Oct. 33 They up an' at him... 'He [*sc.* Fritz] wants to snavel our land,' they sez, 'sool 'im and snavel his land.' **1928** *NZ Free Lance* (Wellington) 12 Sept. 4 It seems a fitting occasion to ask the [acclimatization] societies to 'sool' their gun men on to the pests now in the country. **1934** MARKS *Memories* 60 Gee whiz! How Bill did sool him! **1968** SLATTER *Pagan Game* 175 The crowd swaying on the terraces..the crowd sooling the teams on for blood. **1975** THOMPSON *Lyalldale Waltz* 60 One of the shepherds..sooled into the boy. **1985** RENÉE *Wednesday to Come* 29 Iris... Who sooled off the strikebreakers and made them leave our house alone? **1993** *Dominion* (Wellington) 6 Feb. 5 We avoid..the mindless..system of sooling whole classes at external exams.

sooner.

1. *Farming.* [AND an idler, 1892; *soonerdog*, 1936.] An idle dog. See also *Sunday dog* (SUNDAY).
1934 *Press* (Christchurch) (Acland Gloss.) 27 Jan. 15 *Sooner.*—Slack, useless dog. So called because he would s[ooner] lie in the shade than work. I have also heard *Sunday-dog* used as an equivalent, because one day's work a week is enough for him. **1951** MCLEOD *NZ High Country* 43 Another word for a lazy dog is a 'sooner' which is intended to convey that he would sooner you ran than he did. **1966** TURNER *Eng. Lang. Austral. & NZ* 146 There is the *Sunday dog* who declines to work in a difficulty, the *woolclasser* who bites at the sheep, and the *sooner* who would sooner rest than work.

2. A jibbing horse.
1939 in PARTRIDGE *Dict. Slang Addenda* (1949) 1178 *sooner*... 'A jibbing horse (one that would sooner go backward than forward),' Niall Alexander, letter of Oct. 22, 1939: New Zealand: since ca. 1920.

sooty, *a.*

1. In the names of birds, see: ALBATROSS, RAIL 2 (10), SHEARWATER 2 (6).

2. As a noun, an offensive name for a Maori.
1989 *Metro* (Auckland) Mar. 91 There aren't many Maoris around Dargaville, but when Jenny says, 'We call them sooties here,' I understand why. One mayor of Dargaville was a spokesman for the Friends of South Africa.

sore-shin. [f. a name proposed by researchers J.C. Nevill, R.M. Biren and E.E. Chamberlain.] A virus disease of lupins involving a brown discoloration of the stalk.
1934 *NZJAg.* Sept. XLIX. 139 During the past three years a disease, for which the name 'sore-shin' is suggested, has been prevalent in blue-lupin crops in various parts of New Zealand. **1951** *NZJAg.* June LXXXII. 492 Though relatively free from disease, lupins sometimes become infected with a virus disease called 'sore shin'.

sore toe. [AND 1939.] In the phr. **(all) done up like a sore toe**, overdressed; 'dressed to kill'.
1943 BENNETT *English in NZ* in *Amer. Speech* XVIII. 91 'All done up like a sore toe' describes someone dressed over-elaborately; many New Zealand children go barefoot much of the time, and it is with this circumstance in mind that we must interpret the simile.

sort, *v.* Shearing. In *absol.* use, to sort wool.
1906 CHUDLEIGH *Diary* 7 Dec. (1950) 438 J. Dix offered to take the responsibility of the shearing at Taupeka. He would bring 4 good shearers and a cook and roll and sort himself.

Hence **sorter**, *wool-sorter* (WOOL 3); **sorting table**, *wool-table* (WOOL 3).
1878 *Country Jrnl.* (1877) II. 400 When shearing commences, a **sorter** or classer's table, be it ever so simple should be erected. **1985** BREMNER *Woolscours NZ* (Gloss. Old Wool Terms) 10 *Sorter* hand who separates different qualities of wool from each fleece grouping together shoulder wool, britch, stained wool and skirtings etc. before scouring. **1881** BATHGATE *Waitaruna* 172 Meanwhile the 'pickers up' were busy gathering up the fleeces as they fell from the bereft sheep and carrying them to the **sorting table**.

souple-jack, var. SUPPLEJACK.

sour thistle, var. *sowthistle* (THISTLE *n.* 2 (5)).

south, *n.*

1. As **the South**, the (far) southern parts of New Zealand, *spec.* Otago-Southland. Cf. DOWN SOUTH.
1937 AYSON *Thomas* 115 The danger of tutu poisoning and the pleuro scare made constant observation of the cattle necessary, but all went well in this corner of the south. **1946** SARGESON *That Summer* 36 At any rate I had Maoris on the brain. You see I was brought up in the South and never saw many Maoris.

2. In the phr. **to dip south**, to put one's hand in one's pocket for money; **It's snowing down south**, see SNOW *v.* 1.
1937 PARTRIDGE *Dict. Slang* 803 *south, dip*. To put one's hand in one's pocket for money, esp. if it is running low: New Zealanders': C. 20. **1938** *Press* (Christchurch) (McNab Slang) 2 Apr. 18 'To dip South' is to spend much needed money. **1941** BAKER *NZ Slang* 50 Terms originated in the first Great War [include]..*to dip south*, to put one's hand into one's pocket.

south, *v. trans.* To pocket or hide (something).
c**1930** p.c. W.H. Oliver, Wellington (1960). To conceal, e.g. 'My school report was a bad one, and of course I southed it instead of showing it to the old man.' **1976** MORRIESON *Pallet on Floor* 48 Sue southed my share that's what. I got twenty quid owing to me.

souther. [Used elsewhere but recorded earliest in NZ: see OED.] A southerly wind or gale; SOUTHERLY 3.
1851 *Austral. & NZ Gaz.* 29 Nov. 483 During the night a 'stiff souther' put her again on shore. **1927** GUTHRIE-SMITH *Birds* 26 If, when a change is evidently coming up from the south, no mist rests on its rounded top, the change will pass off as a 'dry souther', a skiff of big cold drops blown up in fierce raw gusts.

southerly, *n.* and *attrib.*

1. a. [AND 1896.] A cold wind from the south, esp. a *southerly buster* (3 below).
c**1872** in Meredith *Adventuring in Maoriland* (1935) 35 It must be a beastly nuisance when a southerly

suddenly crops up in the middle of operations. **1933** SCANLAN *Tides of Youth* 83 And when Genevieve wrote in the midst of one of Wellington's howling southerlies that it was a 'cow of a day', Kelly remembered with affection that lanky frame. **1948** SCANLAN *Rusty Road* (1949) 126 A wild, wet spring with bitter, driving rain, a real Southerly. **1955** *Evening Post* (Wellington) 21 Oct. 13 On 13 of the days there being cold southerlies, three of them accompanied by hail. **1966** TURNER *Eng. Lang. Austral. & NZ* 163 There are several local names for winds..[including] the *southerly buster*, a name used in both Australia and New Zealand, probably more often in the shortened form a *southerly*. **1975** *Evening Post* (Wellington) 16 June 1 [Heading] 'Old man southerly' plays havoc with travel services.

b. Used *attrib.* in Comb. **southerly gale (storm)**.
1836 *Log 'Mary Mitchell'* 23 June in McNab *Old Whaling Days* (1913) 447 Latter [sic] strong Southerly gales and Rugd went out with 4 boats. **1848** SELWYN in *NZ Part V* (Church in the Colonies XX) 30 Aug. (1849) 78 *May* 10 *and* 11.—The southerly gale continuing..we remained at anchor, and looked around the Cove for traces of Captain Cook. **1986** REILLY *Deputy Head* 25 We have had a week of southerly storms, a full week of that fierce steady cold wind, and rain.

2. As **southerly burster** *obs.*, also occas. **southern burster**, and occas. with init. caps. [AND 1850], *southerly buster* 3 below.
1851 *Austral. & NZ Gaz.* 29 Nov. 483 The order of the day has been for some time past, rain, rainbows, and southerly bursters. **1856** TANCRED *Nat. Hist. Canterbury* 26 The suddenness of these [south-west] storms is expressed by the colonial name of 'Southerly Bursters'. **1863** BUTLER *First Year* viii 123 The southerly 'burster', as it is called, gradually creeps up, and at last drives the other [*sc.* north-west wind] off the field. **1883** GREEN *High Alps* 291 Large ships..now have to anchor in the open [Timaru] bay and..'cut and run' when a 'southern burster' breaks over the coast. **1933** *Press* (Christchurch) (Acland Gloss.) 2 Dec. 15 *Southerly burster* or *buster* or *Three-day sou'-wester*.—A strong wind with rain, snow or sleet from a southerly direction.

3. As **southerly buster** (also occas. **southern buster**, **sou'-west buster** (see quot. 1892), **sutherly buster**) [*buster* prob. a Brit. dial. form of *burster*: AND 1850], a violent, usu. cold, often rapidly-developing southerly storm. See also BURST *n.*², BURSTER, BUTT-ENDER, SOUTHER, *southerly buster* (2 above).
1853 *Austral. & NZ Gaz.* 12 Mar. 250 The fact is the houses..are by no means proof against the winds, so when a 'Southerly Buster' comes, you cannot keep a candle alight. **1866** BARKER *Station Life* (1870) 49 The one drawback..is the north-west wind... However, I am assured that I have not yet seen either a 'howling nor'-wester', nor its exact antithesis, 'a sutherly buster' [*sic*]. **1877** PRATT *Col. Experiences* 223 A boisterous sou'wester, known as a 'southerly buster', with a deluge of rain, caused a rude awakening of the poor 'pilgrims' encamped on the hillside. **1885** MONTGOMERY *Songs of the Singing Shepherd* 30 We're in for a 'Southerly Buster'. **1892** SWANTON *Notes on NZ* 57 At times [in Canterbury, sou-west winds] come in what is called a 'sou'-west buster', that is to say, they come suddenly with force and pass over quickly—perhaps in half an hour. **1905** *Truth* 18 Nov. 2 The southerly buster..raised quite a sea in [Cook Strait]. **1916** MANSFIELD *Aloe* (1982) 35 She had come forth squealing out of a reluctant mother in the teeth of a 'Southerly Buster'. **c1937** MOORE *Reminiscences of Thomas R. Moore of Waimarama* (ATLMS) A Southern Buster came up. **1952** RHODES *Fly Away Peter* 4 Looks like a proper southerly buster... Won't let up for a couple of days anyhow. **1966** *Encycl. NZ* II. 680 A south-west storm [in Canterbury] is a *southerly buster*. **1983** MANTELL *Murder to Burn* 78 You ought to see the beach after a southerly buster.

southern, *a.*

1. In the names of plants and animals, see: BEECH 2 (10), BOARFISH, COD 2 (1) and 2 (8) d, CRAB 2 (1) and (3), DOGFISH 1, HAKE 2 (4), KELPFISH 1, MACKEREL 2 (1), NUMBFISH, OSTRICH FOOT, PALM 1, PEARLSIDE, PIGFISH 2 (2), RATA I 2 (3), SKUA, TUNA *n.*², WHALE 2 (14), WHITING 2.

2. southern burster (buster): see SOUTHERLY 2, 3.

3. southern blue. Also **New Zealand blue.** *Zizina otis oxleyi* (fam. Lycaenidae), a little blue butterfly of lowland sites of the South Island and common in Central Otago. See also *little blue butterfly* (BUTTERFLY A 1).
1980 GIBBS *NZ Butterflies* 173 *Zizina otis oxleyi..southern blue.* Fresh specimens of this clearly marked little blue butterfly are readily distinguished from *labradus* [the 'common blue'] by the brown pattern on the underside of the hindwing... This little grey-blue butterfly flies actively across stony ground in hot sunshine. **1992** FARRELL *Skinny Louie Book* 79 They're a nuisance, Vera thinks, but what a shame it is when beauty is trapped remembering the Southern Blues which fluttered about..at Lake Hayes. **1995** ANDERSON *House Guest* 201 In the [Central Otago] summer there would be butterflies—small New Zealand blues teasing wild flowers of the same colour. Possibly a Small Black Mountain. A Tussock.

Southern Cross.

1. [AND 1842.] The constellation *Crux Australis*, four stars of which form a cross, and are so represented on the New Zealand flag. See also CROSS.
1847 TAYLOR *Journal* 31 Dec. (ATLTS) V. 168 I referred then to their constellation of Tamarereti's canoe the anchor of which is the Southern Cross I told them that when it stood on end that it was midnight so the Cross is taken for their guide: may they ever look to Him who hung on it. **1853** POWER *Recollections* xxxi See! where the Southern Cross is hung on high, That mystic symbol glitters in the sky; And beckons men across the pathless sea Lighted by that resplendent galaxy. **1863** BUTLER *First Year* 13 The southern cross is a very great delusion. It isn't a cross. It is a kite, a kite upside down..with only three respectable stars and one very poor and very much out of place. **1879** OLLIVANT *Hine Moa* 20 The Southern Cross..is the much boasted Constellation in the Southern Hemisphere... The word cross always seemed to me singularly inappropriate..the shape is rather that of a lozenge or jujube. **1888** *Diary Christian Shirres* in Neave *Land of Munros* (1980) 55 The Southern Cross, to be sure, is a fraud, in as much as it is scarcely brighter than..its neighbours. **1897, 1926, 1936** [see POINTER *n.*¹]. **1952** FINLAYSON *Schooner to Atia* 29 Where the surrounding trees were lowest he could just catch a glimpse of the Southern Cross... The stars that formed the Cross weren't so very much bigger and brighter than the bright ones about it, were they?

2. *transf.* New Zealand, esp. in the phr. **under (beneath) the Southern Cross**. Also *attrib.*
1898 MORRIS *Austral-English* 427 The Southern Cross is of course visible in places farther north than Australia, but it has come to be regarded as the astronomical emblem of Australasia; e.g. the phrase 'beneath the Southern Cross' is common for 'in Australia or New Zealand'. **1900** CRICHTON *Songs and Ballads* 20 A Southern Cross volunteer. **1915** HAMILTON *Diary* 25 Apr. in Waite *New Zealanders at Gallipoli* (1919) x They are not charging up into this Sari Bair Ridge for money, or by compulsion. There they are—all the way from the Southern Cross—earning Victoria Crosses, every one of them. **1916** *Evening Post* (Wellington) 11 Apr. 9 [Advt] 'ANZAC' Commemoration Jewellery Brooches and Pendants... What better ornament could be worn in honour of our men from under the Southern Cross. **1930** PINFOLD *Fifty Yrs. Maoriland* 81 The National Anthem, heard in Maoriland, causes men to rise to their feet, doff their hats, and unite in doing homage to that refrain which means so much to every Britisher under the Southern Cross. **1960** SCRYMGEOUR *Memories Maoriland* 40 The love of patriotism that ever burned..just as continuous in the breasts of those citizens of the outpost of the Empire, washed by the surge of the Pacific Ocean in the land of the Southern Cross.

southerner.

1. One from the (often, southern) South Island.
1925 MANDER *Allen Adair* (1971) 6 The north was..the land of lost men. It was peopled with nomads and wasters... The Southerner curled his lip at it. **1955** *Truth* 21 Dec. 4 Trust a southerner to find a good possie. **1973** *Islands* 6 357 The Maoriness of the North Island is what is best about it—to this Southerner, at least. **1988** MIKAERE *Te Maiharoa* 79 Anti-missionary feeling was common to most North Island prophets after the wars, and it is likely that southerners held similar views.

2. The name of an express train on the South Island Main Trunk line.
1972 LEITCH *Railways of NZ* 201 The 'Southerner' has reintroduced 'on train' meals, a feature lacking on the NZR since 1917. **1975** *Islands* 11 35 I was booked on the Southerner but they told me you'd pick me up. There's a slip on the line... I have to be on the ferry from Lyttelton.

southern hemisphere. As a phr. **in the southern hemisphere**, collocated with a preceding superlative adjective, is used (occas. ironically) in comparisons possibly to exaggerate or localize the size, importance, etc. of the New Zealand object referred to.
[**1841** BIDWILL *Rambles in NZ* (1952) 115 The Salmon of the English, or Carwai (Carwhy), is a most excellent fish, the best I have tasted in the Southern Hemisphere.] **1875** *TrNZI* VII. 175 A system of education which shall enable the next generation to make New Zealand the most prosperous nation in the Southern Hemisphere. **1884** *Maoriland* 179 His fine collection of manuscripts, blackletter copies, and rare editions, the finest in the southern hemisphere, has been presented by Sir George [Grey] to the Auckland Public Library. **1894** WILSON *Land of Tui* 32 The Government offices of the Capital are the largest wooden buildings in the Southern Hemisphere. **1905** *Truth* 2 Sept. 8 There is not a more demoralised police force than that of New Zealand in the Southern Hemisphere. **1928** *Auckland Univ. College Capping Book* 13 One of the largest circulations in the Southern Hemisphere. **1935** GUTHRIE *Little Country* (1937) 2 It [*sc.* Paradise Bay] has, however, neither the Finest Harbour in the World, the Finest Harbour in the Southern Hemisphere, nor even the Finest Harbour in New Zealand. **1947** FAIRBURN *Letters* 6 July (1981) 166 I found myself at the tail-end of the procession, rubbing shoulders with probably the best architect in the Southern Hemisphere. **1965** STEAD in *Some Other Country* (1984) 144 Up in the museum under glass that's supposed to be protected by the most efficient burglar alarm system in the Southern Hemisphere. **1990** *Landfall* 174 147 The Governor-General..declared that the terminal was worthy of Christchurch, which, he observed, 'must be one of the most beautiful cities in the Southern Hemisphere.'

Southern Island. *Hist.*

1. Also occas. early **Southern Isle, Southward Island.** SOUTH ISLAND 1.

1773 FORSTER *Resolution Jrnl.* 8 June (1982) II. 294 At noon the Southernmost point of the Southern Isle of New Zeeland at Cape *Campbell* bore WSW 15 leagues distant. **1777** COOK *Journals* 25 Feb. (1967) III. 73 This Water is called by them Tovy poenammoo that is the Water of green talc, and the land about it *Poenammo*, which is all of the Southern island of New Zealand they know by that name. **1830** CRAIK *New Zealanders* 184 [They] make certain of their weapons, and carving tools, of a green talc, or jasper stone, which is found only in the southern island. **1835** YATE *NZ* (1970) 144 A piece of the green talc found in Te-wai-ponamu, or the Southward Island. **1841** *Hobson Despatch* 13 Dec. in *GBPP House of Commons 1842 (No.569)* 184 Mr. Mathew also remarks on the Southern Island, which he visited with me. **1861** HARPER *Lett. from NZ* 20 July (1914) 51 In this Southern Island of New Zealand there is more sunshine than at home.

2. *Obs. Rare.* Stewart Island.

1851 *Lyttelton Times* 11 Jan. 7 [Bishop Selwyn] had written to Lord Lyttelton, to propose that the new diocese of the Bishop of Lyttelton should extend over all the Middle and Southern Islands.

Southern Isle: see SOUTHERN ISLAND 1.

Southern Lights. [Used elsewhere but of noteworthy significance in the sight of early European explorers and settlers: AND 1775.] The Aurora Australis.

1773 FORSTER *Resolution Journal* 20 Feb. (1982) II. 228 In the night the *Southern Lights* were seen after 12 O'clock... The Lat. observed 58° 42′ South. **1841** WEEKES *Journal* 2 Mar. in Rutherford & Skinner *Establish. New Plymouth* (1940) 35 The 'Southern Lights' (Aurora Australis) were being played beautifully this evening. **1862** WALKER *Jrnl. & Lett.* (ATLTS) 17 Oct. We were then just opposite Akaroa Bay... Last night we saw a light which we thought to be the Southern light, but which turned out to be a bush fire.

South Island.

1. Often *attrib.* **a.** Also occas. early **South Isle**. Collocated with the def. art., the southernmost of the two large islands of New Zealand. See also MAINLAND 2, and in early use MIDDLE ISLAND (esp. quots. 1840, 1867 noted below), SOUTHERN ISLAND or ISLE, TE WAIPOUNAMU.

1773 FORSTER *Resolution Jrnl.* 8 June (1982) II. 294 We saw Cape *Terawittee*, & on the South Isle Cape *Campbell*... In the morning..we were abreast of Cape *Palliser*, and saw on the South-Isle some very high mountains, quite covered with Snow. **1793** *Raven to Lieut.-Gov. King* 19 Nov. in McNab *Hist. Records* (1908) I. 177 All the information respecting my people whom I left for ten months on the south island of New Zealand I here subjoin. **1803** *Bass to Gov. King* 30 Jan. in McNab *Murihiku* (1909) 128 I have every proof..that fish may be caught in abundance near the South part of the South Island of New Zealand. **1839** TAYLOR *Journal* 28 Apr. (ATLTS) II. 120 Their Tikis or green jade ornaments..are only made in the South Island where the stone is found. **1867** [see MIDDLE ISLAND]. **1868** LINDSAY *Contribs. NZ Bot.* 7 I follow the eminent geographer, Keith Johnston, in what is both the best and most recently published map of New Zealand, (1864,) in designating the more southern of the two great islands of New Zealand..the *South* Island,—a designation which is being adopted by the Governor and General Assembly of the Colony. Until recently..the island in question was generally known as the *Middle* Island... What was then called the South Island is the 'Rakiura' of the natives. **1873** BULLER *Birds NZ* 155 This species is the South-Island representative of *Glaucopis wilsoni*. **1892** *NZ Official Handbook* 1 The Colony of New Zealand consists of three main islands... These three islands..namely, North island..South Island..and Stewart Island. **1924** [see MIDDLE ISLAND]. **c1945** *Sixes & Sevens* (Troopship pub.) 24 To make North Island beer Taste a little less of the sewer, We ought to send those blokes A good South Island brewer. **1958** GILLESPIE *S. Canterbury* (1971) 45 Officially, on Lands and Survey Department maps, the South Island was known as the Middle Island until 1907. That year the Minister of Lands issued instructions that the names of the three principal islands of New Zealand should be North, South and Stewart Islands. **1973** WILSON *NZ Jack* 83 We used to be amused by his South Island turns of speech..and by his smooth, well-rounded accent compared with our nasal Waikato twang. **1986** RICHARDS *Off the Sheep's Back* 35 Out of earshot he was known as Old Clem, or the South Island blatherskite.

b. *attrib.* in the names of (esp. sub-species of) plants and animals, see: CROW 2 (2), EDELWEISS, FANTAIL 2 (1), FERNBIRD 2, KAKA 2, KINGFISH b, KIWI 2 (1), KOKAKO 2 (2), OYSTERCATCHER 2 (3), PIOPIO, RIFLEMAN, ROBIN 1, SADDLEBACK *n.*¹, THRUSH 2, TIT a, TOMTIT, WEKA 2 (4), WOODHEN 2 (3), WREN 2 (1).

2. *Obs.* STEWART ISLAND.

1868 [see 1 a above].

South Islander.

a. One (occas. specifically a Maori, see quot. 1873) born or resident in the South Island of New Zealand. See also MAINLANDER 2.

1873 BULLER *Birds NZ* 191 It [*sc.* the notornis] was known to the North-Islanders by the name of 'Moho', and to the South-Islanders by that of 'Takahe'. **1917** [see NORTH ISLANDER]. **1920** BOLITHO *With the Prince in NZ* 143 There is a definite impression that South Islanders are different from the Northerners in New Zealand. **1938** *Tararua Tramper* Nov. 5 It was music..to hear the exclamations of amazement..from South Islanders with us at the beauty around us. **1944** *Listener* 11 Aug. 14 She is not even so much a New Zealander as a South Islander. 'Give me the good old South,' she says. **1963** OLIVER *Story NZ* 99 South Islanders went their own way while the North was occupied with war. **1984** MARSHALL *Day Hemingway Died* 77 His other options were to do some heavy drinking in Wellington with fellow South Islanders.

b. *transf.* A South Island animal (here the *bush canary* (CANARY *n.*¹ 1)).

1953 SUTHERLAND *Golden Bush* (1963) 108 These little South Islanders with bright canary-coloured heads, yellow-brown upper parts and palest-brown flanks, trilled with the loveliness of their yellow, caged cousins.

Southland. In *attrib.* use as special Comb. with a sense 'of or pertaining to the provincial district of Southland': **Southland beech**, see BEECH 2 (11); **Southland burr** (occas. **accent,** and *joc.* **Southlandic dialect**), the Scottish-Irish pronunciation of word final and infra-syllabic /r/ heard in Southland and south Otago; **Southland shinplaster** *hist.*, SHIN PLASTER; **Southland slipper**, GUMBOOT 1 a.

1966 TURNER *Eng. Lang. Austral. & NZ* 105 /r/ is pronounced as in RP, but its more frequent occurrence in Otago and Southland in New Zealand may be noted. It marks what is sometimes called the ***Southland burr***, in which /r/ is pronounced in words such as *dark* or *word* where it is lost in RP. **1968** GLEN *Holy Joe's People* 19 There was some visiting American professor [who]..complained that the Southland accent was the 'worrrst' he'd ever 'hearrrd' in the 'worrrld'. **1994** *The NZ Dict.* xvi Many Southland and South Otago speakers..have 'rhotic' accents where *r* is sounded in every position. The resulting pronunciation is sometimes described as the 'Southland burr'. **1996** *Dominion* (Wellington) 21 Aug. 2 Mr English [M.P.] had to bray in full-volume Southlandic dialect to be heard [by fellow M.P.s] throwing his wobbly. **1977** *NZ Numismatic Jrnl.* Oct. 16 It was perhaps natural that the *Otago Daily Times* (Dunedin) when it broke the story in May 1864 of the proposed issuance by the Province of Southland of its doubtful Treasury Notes, that the paper should label them with the nickname ***Southland Shinplasters***. **1980** LELAND *Kiwi-Yankee Dict.* 96 ***Southland slippers***: Much of..*Southland* is farmland and when it rains venturing outside your farmhouse is a muddy business. So you keep a pair of rubber boots on the porch and slip them on and off as you leave and enter the house. **1988** *Dominion* (Wellington) 24 Sept. 8 In the deepest recesses of the mainland, they're [*sc.* gumboots] supposedly called Southland Slippers.

Southlander. One born or resident in the provincial district of Southland.

1908 BARR *Brit. Rugby Team in Maoriland* 44 The doughty Southlanders could not sustain such a pace throughout. **1941** DUFF *NZ Now* 71 The people are never 'Southlanders' (except once a year at football) as the people of the West Coast are 'West Coasters'. **1951** *NZ Geogr.* Apr. 6 But the conception of Southland as a more or less distinctive unit [from Otago] has always persisted for Southlanders as well as for most other New Zealanders. **1975** ANDERSON *Men of Milford Road* 194 There was Enid..and our two Southlander sons. **1982** PEAT *Detours* 223 Southlanders, I knew, had developed a suppleness of tongue which enabled them to pronounce cerrrtain worrrds in a distinctive way—distinctive to the ear of anyone living north of about the Clutha. **1991** *Dominion* (Wellington) 12 July 1 I believe the place should be run by a Southlander and one who has never been part of the company before.

south seaman. *Hist.* A Pacific whaleman.

1838 POLACK *NZ* II. 407 A more destructive and wholesale species of enemy is found in a species of Grampus, called by the South seamen the 'Killer', which is said to be (man excepted) its [the Razorback whale's] greatest scourge. **1959** SINCLAIR *Hist. NZ* 38 While the Anglican mission was struggling to find its feet, traders and 'southseamen' slowly established a friendly intercourse with the Maoris.

South Sea whaler. *Hist.* A ship whaling in the south Pacific Ocean.

1814 MARSDEN 15 Mar. in Elder *Marsden's Lieutenants* (1934) 46 The establishment of the Mission there will tend to the security of the South Sea whalers, who put into the island for refreshments. **1825** HALL 5 Mar. in Elder *Marsden's Lieutenants* (1934) 238 On this day also, Captain Edwards of the *Mercury* brig, a South Sea whaler belonging to Mr. Jones of London, went into the harbour of Whangaroa for refreshment.

South Suffolk. A New Zealand breed of sheep, a cross between the Southdown and the Suffolk.

1989 *Illustr. Encycl. NZ* 1151 *South Suffolk* sheep were bred in New Zealand during the 1930s by a Canterbury Southdown breeder, George Gould, who was responding to overseas demand for leaner meat. *Ibid.* 1152 The South Suffolk, registered as a breed in 1958, is gaining ground as a terminal crossing sire for meat production throughout the country... The..wool..is used for fine apparel and hand-knitting yarns. **1990** *Focus* 9 South Suffolk. A cross, achieved in New Zealand of Southdown and Suffolk breeds. **1991** *NZ Post Brochure* NZ Sheep Stamp Issue. South Suffolk. New Zealand bred Southdown/Suffolk cross.

Southward Island: see SOUTHERN ISLAND 1.

souvenir, *v.* [Recorded earliest in Austral.: AND 1918.] To steal.
   1938 *RSA Review* June 6 One of the highlights of the luncheon was the fact that the liquid refreshments were provided by Tooheys, the well known Sydney brewers. A small label on the bottle indicated this fact, and these were quickly souvenired by the diggers.

sou'wester. *Canterbury.*

1. Also **sou-wester**, **sow-wester**. [Spec. use of *sou'wester* a wind from the south-west.] A cold, wet blustery wind of (esp.) Canterbury. See also SOUTHERLY 3.
   1853 ADAMS *Canterbury Settlement* 18 [The emigrants] had been greeted on their arrival (as indeed, singularly enough had almost every emigrant ship) with a '*sow-wester*'—a wind which in this island is invariably accompanied with rainy, miserable weather. **1866** BARKER *Station Life* (1870) 76 There is a tremendous sou'-wester coming up; we had better push on for shelter, or you'll be drowned. **1889** WILLIAMS & REEVES *Colonial Couplets* 1 The cold Sou'-wester knows me; it has often soaked me. **1890** *Otago Witness* (Dunedin) 23 Jan. 25 The sou'-wester may be the glory of New Zealand, but it is well, as Lord Onslow remarked on another subject, to take our glory in small glasses. **1900** *Canterbury Old & New* 125 The old-fashioned sou'wester [of the 1850s] was a very different thing from its present degenerate namesake; it generally brought torrents of rain, and lasted three days. **1966** TURNER *Eng. Lang. Austral. & NZ* 163 There are several local names for winds..[including] the *three-day sou'wester* in New Zealand, a form of the *southerly buster*.

2. Special Comb. **Sou-wester Sunday** *Canterbury*, emblematic of a miserable day, weather-wise.
   1853 *Canterbury Papers* II. 27 I am sitting by the fire with Hamilton on a Sou-Wester Sunday in Port.

sowthistle: see THISTLE *n.* 2 (5).

sow-wester, var. SOU'WESTER.

spacies. Poss. collective *sing.*, poss. *pl.* [f. *space* (invaders + -IE: recorded 1986 in *Macquarie Dict. New Words* (1990).] In mainly adolescent use, a familiar term for 'Space Invaders' or any of various similar video-parlour games.
   1984 16–17 F E17 Pakuranga Coll. 21 Spacies [M4F1] **1985** *Dominion* (Wellington) 26 Feb. 6 My main entertainment [at Opunake] with my friends is Friday nights. We all gather at the fish shop where lots of kids play spacies. **1987** *More* (Auckland) Apr. 43 [The undeserving poor] give their kids money for spacies and don't go to the Plunket nurse. **1992** *Dominion* (Wellington) 5 Dec. 14 If parents and elders had said this to their children they would not have ended up sniffing glue, playing 'spacies', and having no self-esteem.

spade. In the phr. **on the spade**, working as a gumdigger.
   1970 THOMAS *Way Up North* 39 He carted sacked..gum from the fields to the wharf or to the landing places on the harbour front and creeks. But every possible minute was still spent 'on the spade'.

spadger. Also **spadge**. [f. Brit. dial. *spadger* sparrow: see OED.] A sparrow. (Occas. heard as **spadgie** (Ed.).) Cf. SPUG.
   1969 HENDERSON *Open Country Calling* 142 Sparrows were always called 'spugs' or 'spadges'. **1985** *Reader's Digest Book NZ Birds* 299 House Sparrow *Passer domesticus domesticus*... Other names: *Spadger*, *English sparrow*.

span-'em /'spænəm/. Also **spanning**. [f. Brit. dial. *spanners* (also *spannims*): see OED *spanners*.] A marble game in which one tries to hit an opponent's taw with one's own, or to come within a (hand-)span of it.
   1972 SUTTON-SMITH *Folkgames Children* 175 In the nineteenth century the ring game seems to have been the most popular marble game... There were..on a less important scale..Span-'Em, and Backits. **1981** SUTTON-SMITH *Hist. Children's Play* 269 Here are some [marble] terms from Taranaki around 1880–90: firsts, lay-up, stakes..sips, spanning, placing.

spang-weazling /'spæŋ,wizlɪŋ/. [f. *spanwhengle*, *spangwhengle* w. Yorkshire dial. (see EDD), itself f. Sc. and northern Brit. dial. *spang* n. a leap, *v.* to cause to leap, to throw violently, used in Comb. in the names of children's games involving the torturing of small or young animals (frogs, toads, young of birds) by causing them to leap up in the air from boards, etc.: hence, (EDD) *spang-toad*, *spangie-hewit* (see OED *spang* n.^{2} v.^{2}, and EDD).] See quot. 1953.
   1953 SUTTON-SMITH *Unorganized Games NZ Primary School Children* (VUWTS) I. 406 Perhaps the most intriguing game of this nature [*sc.* tormenting insects or animals] is 'Spang Weazling'. This game was played at Denniston in 1930–35. A crawley was placed on the end of a stick the middle section of which lay balanced over a stone. Before the crawley could crawl off the stick a stone had to be thrown onto the other end of the stick so as to catapult the crawley off the stick and over the cliff. **1965** 2 Aug. WNTV1 'Any Questions' (P. Smithell, Dunedin) Some years ago there was a game among boys called 'spangweaselling'—taking kingfishers' nests with the young birds in them and knocking them to bits in the air. **1972** SUTTON-SMITH *Folkgames Children* 161 *Spang-Weazling* (K-9) was a rather odd hitting game and appeared in only one locality, namely, Denniston, a mining village on the West Coast. [1920]

Spaniard. Also **wild Spaniard**. [Prob. f. an alteration or shortening of a northern hemisphere name such as US *Spanish bayonet* for similar plants having sharply-pointed leaf blades resembling weapons; cf. *Spanish bayonet*, *Spanish dagger* (SPANISH).]
[*Note*] *Spaniard* seems to refer mainly to a clump of speargrass, having a *pl.* form of *Spaniards*; in later quotations 'Spaniard' is used collectively for the species as a whole, or for a mass of spear-grass clumps, sometimes as 'Wild Spaniard' (perh. on the analogy of *Wild Irishman*).

1. Usu. init. cap., *pl.* often *Spaniards*. Occas. **spaniard grass**. *Aciphylla* spp. (fam. Apiaceae), esp. *A. colensoi* and *A. squarrosa*, a large tussock-like herb of alpine grasslands with spine-tipped leaves. See also BAYONET GRASS, KURIKURI, PORCUPINE GRASS, *Spanish bayonet*, *Spanish dagger* (SPANISH), SPEARGRASS 1, TARAMEA.
   1852 *Austral. & NZ Gaz.* 2 Oct. 393 The country through which I have passed has been most savage— one mass of Spaniards and spear-grass. **1858** THOMSON *Reconn. Survey S. Dist. Otago* in Taylor *Early Travellers* (1959) 334 A new plant appeared here, allied to the cactus, and colonially termed a '*Spaniard*'. It has stout blades with sharp points. **1860** wild Spaniard [see SPEARGRASS 1]. **1873** BULLER *Birds NZ* 255 It was placed..on the side of one of the low downs..sheltered by..a plant of Spaniard grass (*Aciphylla*). **1895** [see SPEARGRASS 1]. **1906** CHEESEMAN *Manual NZ Flora* 209 [*Aciphylla Colensoi*] *Taramea; Spaniard*... By far the finest species of the genus. **1926** [see *Spanish dagger* (SPANISH)]. **1933** *Press* (Christchurch) (Acland Gloss.) 9 Dec. 17 *Spaniard* or *speargrass*.—Various species of Aciphylla... In the 'eighties and 'nineties at Mount Peel they used to call the broader leaved sort *Spaniards* and the narrower *Speargrass;* but most people use both names indiscriminately. **1946** *Tararua Tramper* Nov. 5 We think there must be some good in the much-cursed Spaniard. **1951** LEVY *Grasslands NZ* (1970) 35 Shrubs common in the tussock zone: matagouri..the grasslike spiky-leaved Spaniard. **1971** *New Zealand's Heritage* I. 114 [Caption] The spaniards or speargrasses, belong to a genus, *Aciphylla*, found only, in New Zealand, the Chathams and Australia. **1988** DAWSON *Forest Vines to Snow Tussocks* 174 Notable among the large alpine herbs are the spaniards or speargrasses belonging to the genus Aciphylla. **1996** *Independent* (Auckland) 15 Mar. 19 The Spaniard is one of nature's bluntest, most brutal hypodermic needles.

2. With a modifier: **bloody, giant, golden, wild**.

(1) **bloody Spaniard**. [Poss. also a (partial) play on the colloq. intensifier *bloody*.] *Aciphylla* spp.
   1868 LINDSAY *Contribs. NZ Bot.* 49 The larger species [of *Aciphylla*] are familiar to the settlers as 'Spear-grass', or 'Bayonette-grass', 'Wild' or 'Bloody-Spaniard', in allusion to their very rigid, strong, poniard-like, sharp-pointed leaves. Ibid. 50 [*A. Colensoi*: alpine plant] Familiar to the shepherds of Canterbury as 'Bloody Spaniard'.

(2) **giant Spaniard**. *Aciphylla scott-thomsonii*.
   1969 *Standard Common Names Weeds* 29 giant Spaniard. *Aciphylla scott-thomsonii*.

(3) **golden Spaniard**. *Aciphylla aurea*.
   1973 MARK & ADAMS *Alpine Plants* (1979) 22 The golden spaniard (*Aciphylla aurea*) is another of these unpalatable aggressive herbs. **1988** DAWSON *Forest Vines to Snow Tussocks* 150 The golden spaniard (*A. aurea*) also often descends into short tussock grassland from higher altitudes.

(4) **wild spaniard**. [*wild* perh. on the analogy of WILD IRISHMAN.] *Spaniard* 1 above.
   1856 TANCRED *Nat. Hist. Canterbury* in *Edinburgh New Philos. Jrnl.* (NS) 7 In some places a curious thorny plant, by the settlers called Wild Irishman.. abounds; whilst in others more moist, the Wild Spaniard (*Aciphylla squarrosa*), a sort of spear-grass, raises its formidable chevaux-de-frise. **1867** HOCHSTETTER *New Zealand* 133 On account of their slender blades terminating in sharp spines the colonists have named them 'spear grass', 'wild Irishman', and 'wild Spaniard'. **1907** LAING & BLACKWELL *Plants NZ* 321 *Aciphylla squarrosa* (The Spaniard)... Maori name *Kuri-Kuri*; Colonists' name, *Spaniard* or *Wild Spaniard*. **1981** DENNIS *Paparoas Guide* 165 One of the most striking of alpine plants is the spikey [*sic*] spaniard, of which the fiercest in this range is the wild spaniard.. (speargrass).

3. false Spaniard. *Celmisia lyallii* (fam. Asteraceae), a mountain daisy of the South Island with clumps of pointed leaves.
   1973 MARK & ADAMS *Alpine Plants* (1979) 142 *Celmisia lyallii*..False Spaniard... A distinctive tufted herb with narrow..rigid very leathery, sharp-pointed leaves. **1978** WILSON *Wild Plants Mt. Cook National Park* 139 *Celmisia lyallii*..False Spaniard.

Spaniard grass: see SPANIARD 1.

Spanish, *a.* Usu. init. cap. in special collocations: **Spanish bayonet** [transf. use of N. Amer. *Spanish bayonet* a species of *Yucca*, a liliaceous plant, with a crown of long, narrow spear-like leaves: see OED *bayonet* 5; cf. also Mathews], SPANIARD 1 (cf. BAYONET GRASS); **Spanish cream**, a gelatine-based cold sweet made with milk and eggs, and served as a dessert; **Spanish dagger**, SPANIARD 1; **Spanish gallows** [prob. f. *Spanish*(-windlass + GALLOWS], a gallows with a hoist comprising a form of Spanish windlass; **Spanish prisoner** *obs.*, a confidence trick, in which a letter is written to the victim intimating that the writer is prisoner in gaol and has a sum of money hidden, which he can get if he has ready cash to bribe warders and get out; then asking the victim for money to do this, promising to return it with a bonus.

1955 CAMPBELL *By Reef & Range* 10 Red Boar had travelled..high up among the snowgrass, lichen and **spanish bayonet**. **1912** *Dominion* (Wellington) 25 Mar. 11 **Spanish Cream**... The top of the pudding should be clear amber and the custard below, forming two distinct layers. **1916** *Celebrated Amuri Cook. Book* 42 *Spanish Cream.* Soak 1 oz. of gelatine [etc.]. **c1924–30** *Nelson Cook. Book* 122 Spanish Cream... 1 oz gelatine, 3 eggs, 1 pint milk, 3 teaspoons sugar, vanilla or lemon. **1938** *Auckland Weekly News* 23 Feb. 24 About Christmas I tried..a recipe called 'Three Minute Spanish Cream'. **1945** *NZEF Times* 17 Dec. 6 About 100 members of the nursing staff of the Waikato Hospital became ill following a meal which included spanish cream made with duck eggs in aluminium saucepans. **1966** *Edmonds Cook. Book* 44 Spanish Cream... Stir over a *low* heat until the gelatine is dissolved, then add sugar and lightly-beaten egg yolks. **1970** *Listener* 12 Apr. 47 As a change to a simpler and less ceremonial pudding let me give you Granny's Spanish cream. **1986** *Listener* 15 Nov. 93 Spanish cream is supposed to separate into two layers, or at least that's the view of no less than Aunt Daisy. **1992** ANDERSON *Portrait Artist's Wife* 42 And some Spanish cream, which she had read somewhere was an excellent culture medium for the summer-sickness bug if left unrefrigerated. **1926** HILGENDORF *Weeds* 129 Family Umbelliferae. The family of carrots, parsnips, etc., as well as of the striking native known as **Spanish dagger** or Spaniard. **1965** GILLHAM *Naturalist in NZ* 72 Hares..raced among the spinous 'Spanish daggers' or 'spear grass'. *Ibid.* 190 The genus *Aciphylla*, whose popular names are 'Spanish daggers' and 'Spear grass'. **1865** CHUDLEIGH *Diary* 7 July (1950) 192 After much labour we finished the gallows. It took five of us all the afternoon to hoist the cross bit. They are called **Spanish gallows**... (10th July) Killed a bullock on the new gallows... One man can pull or rather winde up a bullock of a thousand pounds. **1939** BELTON *Outside the Law* 142 The [confidence trick] probably best known..is the '**Spanish Prisoner**'.

spank, *v.* [Transf. use of *spank* slap.] *trans.* To milk (cows). See also COW-SPANKING *a.* Cf. PUNCH *v.*[1]

1897 SCOTT *How I Stole 10,000 Sheep* 8 We got on pretty well and spanked, that is milked, his cows for him night and morning. **1942** HARCOURT *Parson in Prison* 279 'Spanking' cows, splitting posts. **1949** SMITH *N to Z* 106 The dairy farmer..has to spank cows before breakfast and he has to spank them again before his tea. **1971** *NZ Dairy Exporter* Sept. 131 'Going to spank cows?' was usually the incredulous comment.

spanning: see SPAN-EM.

spar. *Hist.* [f. *spar*, used elsewhere but significant in early NZ as an article of (esp. kauri) trade, prob. in a mixed use of the nautical (masts, yards, etc.) and the general (a pole or piece of timber of some length): see OED *n.*[1] 2 a and 4 a.] **1.** Used *attrib.* in special Comb. **spar-dealer**, one who trades in spars; **spar station**, a trading-post for the purchase of spars.

1840 POLACK *Manners & Customs* I. 170 To perform this, the **spar-dealer** must follow the advice of Shakspeare [*sic*] to 'take at the tide the flood that leads to' the sale of his labour. **1961** ROGERS (ed.) in Williams *Early Jrnls.* 216 [1961 *Note*] Captain Ranulph Dacre brought him and fifteen men in the *Belina* to establish a **spar station** at Mahurangi in 1832.

2. As a verb *trans.*, to fell (a tree) across a creek to serve as a bridge.

1896 HARPER *Pioneer Work* 182 The half-axes were necessary in case we had to cut a tree down to 'spar' the river or a bad creek; the bill-hooks were for blazing a track. *Ibid.* 215 A small axe in case it was necessary to cut a tree for 'sparring' a creek.

spare, *v.* Used to introduce various quasi-pious, exclamatory phrases: **spare me days**! [AND 1915]; **spare the crows**, see CROW *n.*[1] 4.

1910 *Truth* 26 Mar. 8 Spare me days! Where have you lived all your life? You must have been reared in a cave. **c1926** THE MIXER *Transport Workers' Song Book* 30 [As a refrain to the poem 'On the Stringer'.] Spare me days and stone the crows. **1962** HORI *Half-gallon Jar* 1 Spare me days, this is a great game for garage proprietors and panelbeaters, or anybody else with plenty of money. **1984** Dec. Toyota advertisement on TV with Barry Crump and Lloyd Scott, with Crump saying 'Aw, spare me days, mate, there's no need for all that.'

spark. In the phr. **to get a spark up**, to become merry or excited (esp. with liquor).

1939 BELTON *Outside the Law* 50 Today young men who intend going to a dance drink until closing time..just to get a spark up, they say. **1949** COLE *It Was So late* (1978) 53 Can't get a spark up on beer tonight.

Hence **spark up** [cf. *spark* to kindle, excite: see OED *v.*[1] 2 d].

1946 SARGESON *That Summer* 89 I hadn't sparked up much [with beer].

sparkie. [f. *spark* + -IE: cf. Brit. *sparks*; *Chambers Dict.* (1993 edn.) 'esp. Aust., *sparkie*'.] An electrician.

1982 *Truth* 4 Aug. 11 Sparkie drove drunk... Police gave this evidence about..[an] apprentice electrician. **1984** *Listener* 14 July 11 The Sparkie Show... As a registered electrician..I speak for many confused and frustrated people who feel our story must be told. **1987** *Sunday News* (Auckland) 2 Aug. 2 Pakuranga, Auckland, sparkie named Gary offered to repair the powerline damage at one of his mate's homes.

sparklie. [f. *sparkle* + -IE.] A marble with sparkling material in the glass.

1959 LAWLOR *Old Wellington Days* 37 The marbles [c1900] ranged from the clay ('stinker') variety to the more elaborate coloured 'glassies', the agates and the larger varieties. Some of them were beautifully made— the 'milkies' and 'sparklies'.

sparrow.

1. In various combinations alluding to (the crack of) dawn, often as a euphemism for **sparrow-fart** [orig. Brit. dial., see EDD sparrow-fart(s); now slang (see Ayto & Simpson)], which recalls fancifully the dawn-chorus of sparrows and other birds: **sparrow-chirp**, **sparrow-hiccough**, **sparrow-spit**.

1939–45 *Expressions & Sayings 2NZEF* (TS N.A. WAII DA 420/1) Sparrow fart—First light. **1940** STUDHOLME *Te Waimate* (1954) 86 He had been up since blanky 'delight' or '**sparrow-chirp**'. **1958** PASCOE *Great Days in NZ Mountaineering.* 101 They went to sleep hoping to rise at sparrow chirp. **1971** *Listener* 19 Apr. 56 It was hard yakka, nothing but a plate of burgoo and a handful of scroggin since sparrow-chirp. **c1945** *Sixes & Sevens* 7 'My oath,' I said. 'Many a Jap binjie is going to get a hoodickey stuck in it before **sparrow-hiccough**.' **1969** MASON *Awatea* (1978) 67 They got to leave at **sparrow-spit**, right, Dr Brett?

2. See *fern-sparrow* (FERN 3 d), *swamp-bird*, *swamp-sparrow* (SWAMP 2 b).

3. *transf.* [Partridge 8, *Austral.*] One who, like a sparrow, gains free admission to a performance, event, etc. **a.** In the phr. **to get in on a sparrows' ticket**.

1917 *Truth* 13 Oct. 5 The Brothers Fuller entered the hall..one paying his cash at the door and the others getting in on 'sparrows' tickets'.

b. One who uses a *Scotsman's grandstand* to gain a free view of sporting events.

1956 *Star Sun* (Christchurch) 19 Apr. 24 The Auckland Rugby Union is worrying over the problem of Eden Park's 'sparrows'—people who watch games from private 'stands' erected in back yards of homes behind the terrace fence.

sparrowhawk. [AND 1878.] FALCON.

1835 YATE *NZ* (1970) 60 *Kauaua*—A sparrow-hawk, nothing differing from the sparrow-hawks of England. **1844** WILLIAMS *NZ Jrnl.* (1956) 113 The Kaiaia is the Sparrow-Hawk quite as troublesome and more important than the Common Hawk. **1859** THOMSON *Story NZ* I. 23 Of the *Falcon* family, there are two species in New Zealand; one, called Kahu, is about the size of a pigeon, and the other, named Karewarewa, is a sparrow-hawk. **1870** *TrNZI* II. 51 In New Zealand..the head of the family [Raptores] must be fairly assigned to this bird, which is commonly known by the name of the Quail or Sparrow-hawk. **1882** *Encycl. Brit.* XIV. 54 No Kestrel is found in New Zealand, but an approach to the form is made by the very peculiar..'Sparrow-Hawk', 'Quail-Hawk', and 'Bush-Hawk' of the colonists. **1924** *Otago Witness* (Dunedin) 30 Sept. 67 The sparrow-hawk as he hovers, a mere speck in the blue. **1945** *NZEF Times* 13 Aug. 7 A sparrow hawk, a true falcon, which was taken from the hills behind Queenstown, has been reared and trained successfully by..an Otago University student. **1955** CAMPBELL *By Reef & Range* 41 So you unfeathered animals..call me 'Sparrowhawk'. 'Tis easy to call names, but I am a falcon, fierce, proud and free. **1978** JARDINE *Shadows on Hill* 80 The kea shares the mastery..with another..rejoicing in the name of *Falco novae-seelandiae*, commonly called the sparrowhawk in the south, bush-hawk elsewhere. **1981** HENDERSON *Exiles of Asbestos Cottage* 122 Weird old Jimmy Gilfillan..spent all his time shooting every sparrowhawk (New Zealand falcon) he could find, declaring: 'They fly down and pick your eyes out.'

sparrow-hawking, *vbl. n.* Of a trial sheep-dog, running off its sheep.

1949 HARTLEY *Shepherd's Dogs* 72 Sparrow-hawking or running off the sheep is a serious fault. The over-anxious, highly-strung dog will show his state of excitement by rushing pell-mell at the movement of the sheep.

spat stick. Also **spat-catching stick**. A stick on which oyster or mussel spawn are collected.

1969 *AJHR H-15* 39 Following earlier experiments 100,000 spat catching sticks were set out at Mahurangi. **1972** *AJHR H-15* 52 The original source of [the Pacific rock] oyster in New Zealand is unknown but as it had settled on spat sticks on the Marine Department farms at Mahurangi, it has now been distributed..to most farming areas in the north. **1985** *Shellfisheries Newsletter 31* 10 Spat sticks should not be set out to catch below the 'cut-off' line.

spear.

1. *Hist.* Applied (often erroneously) to various Maori (and Moriori) weapons, esp. to the TAIAHA.

1777 FORSTER *Voyage Round World* I. 137 Behind him..two women, each of them having a long spear..held a long speech. **1791** *Jrnl. 'Chatham'* 29 Nov. in McNab *Hist. Records* (1914) II. 506 Both their [*sc.* Moriori] Spears and Clubs were subject to great variety. Some of the Spears were very long and pointed only at one end, without much neatness. **1807** SAVAGE *Some Acc. of NZ* 66 The spear..is nearly thirty feet long: it is made of hard wood, and is sometimes pointed at each extremity, but not universally. **1826** SHEPHERD *Journal* 24 Mar. in Howard *Rakiura* (1940) 364 Tommy said it was next to impossible to attack a New Zealander with a sword..as they have a method of pushing such weapons aside..and generally kill the person with a Maree or axe or spear before he has time to make a second thrust. **c1835** BOULTBEE *Journal* (1986) 82 Most of these men had their stone marees (axes) slung to their wrists, and their spears placed in order. **1841** Mary Swainson let. in *William Swainson* 5 Nov. (1992) 87 The spears are handsomely carved and red feathers arranged intended to represent a head with the tongue held out, as they dance in their war dance. **1853** ROCHFORT *Adventures of Surveyor* 39 I had a native spear with me for a walking stick, which I carried as a soldier does a fixed bayonet. **1904** TREGEAR *Maori Race* 308 The principal weapon of the Maori warrior was the spear (*tao*). A short spear of from four to six feet in length was the almost invariable appurtenance of a chief. **1913** CHUDLEIGH *Diary* 20 July (1950) 463 The wood of this tree [*sc.* ake rautangi]..is hard and tough and took a keen edge and was cultivated by the Maori for spears and battle axes.

2. a. *gum-spear* (GUM 3 b).

1873 [see *gum-spear* (GUM 3 b)]. **1882** HAY *Brighter Britain* II. 26 For work, each man struggles about all day by himself, with his spear and spade and such. He tries every likely looking place with his spear, which is simply an iron rod, sharp at one end, and with a wooden handle at the other. **1901** *NZ Illustr. Mag.* III. 208 The spear is a long, slender piece of steel, four-sided and tapering to a point. When set in a handle it is easily driven into the soft ground, and the grating of the point will tell when it has touched gum. **1925** MANDER *Allen Adair* (1971) 53 Unexpectedly he met a man with a spade and a spear. **1951** HUNT *Confessions* 40 Armed with a long spear of rod iron, we 'diggers' tested these hillocks for gum. **1970** THOMAS *Way Up North* 30 When the spear met with obstruction an experienced digger knew at once..whether he had located gum.

b. spearing *vbl. n.*, a method or process of locating fossil kauri-gum by means of a gum-spear.

1916 STALLWORTHY *Early N. Wairoa* 53 In the swamps, the method of securing the gum was by spearing or hooking or, in shallow ground, by groping.

spearfish. [Used elsewhere but recorded earliest from NZ waters: OED 1882.] Any of various fishes with an elongated bill such as the swordfish. Cf. KOKIRI *n.*[1]

1817 [see KOKIRI *n.*[1]]. **1927** PHILLIPPS *Bibliogr. NZ Fishes* (1971) 46 *Xiphias gladius*... Spear-fish, Broadbill; Paea. **1936** *Handbook for NZ* (ANZAAS) 72 *Makaira mitsukurii*: Striped marlin, swordfish, or spear-fish... *Makaira mazara*: Black marlin, swordfish, or spear-fish. **1940** PHILLIPPS *Fishes NZ* 75 Spear-fish or Broad-bill *Xiphias estara* Phillipps. The first record of this sword-fish in our waters was made by Dr..Hector. This was in 1874. **1958** PARROTT *Big Game Fishes* 52 The Marlins or spear fishes are closely related to the Broadbill Swordfish but may be at once distinguished by their shorter 'sword'.

speargrass.

1. Also occas. **spear-plant**. SPANIARD 1 (*Aciphylla* spp.). Cf. BAYONET GRASS.

1846 *Brunner Exped. Middle Is.* 24 Dec. in Taylor *Early Travellers* (1959) 262 In the Rouiti [Rotoiti] Valley is found a species of spear-plant, called by the natives *taramea*, which is much valued by them. **1851** WELD *Letter* Jan. in *NZGG* 21 Feb. (1851) 33 The ascent was not difficult, spear grass was the only impediment. **1860** BUTLER *Forest Creek MS* (1960) 41 I will now return to wild Spaniard—Irishman was a nuisance, but Spaniard is simply detestable—he is sometimes called spear grass. **1874** KENNAWAY *Crusts* 40 We struck up..towards the [Canterbury] mountains, the country being all level..with a strong growth of coarse tussocks, pampas-grass..and spaniard or spear-grass. **1882** *TrNZI* XIV. 346 In 1862, the valley of the Matukituki River was, on account of the prevalence of spear-grass (chiefly *Aciphylla Colensoi*) impassable except by frequently crossing the river. **1896** *Ibid.* XXVIII. 19 The gradual replacement of the spaniard (*Aciphylla colensoi*..) by self-sown pasturage-plants is most remarkable... The common spear-grass (*A. squarrosa*..) is often displaced in the same way. **1909** *AJHR C-12* 58 *Aciphylla Traillii*. Stewart Island spear-grass. Subalpine meadow. Probably confined to Stewart Island. **1933** [see SPANIARD 1]. **1952** THOMSON *Deer Hunter* 116 The slow, painful descent to the creek bed had me cursing everything from speargrass to broken rocks. **1971** [see SPANIARD 1]. **1981** [see SPANIARD 2 (4)].

2. *Obs.* [OED records *speargrass* applied to various English and Australian meadow-grasses, and other plants: cf. AND 1840, esp. *Stipa* spp.]
a. Any of various unrelated native plants with sharp needle-like or spear-like foliage, esp. TOETOE and KIEKIE.

1838 POLACK *NZ* I. 320 The most disgusting insects in nature exist among the spear-grass, called toi toi, of the swamps and plains. *Ibid.* I. 392 As a preservative against rain, many large garments are worn..made of the *kiakia*, spear-grass, which is impervious to the element.

b. *Stipa* spp. (fam. Poaceae), an introduced grass with stiff needle-like leaves. See also *needle grass* (GRASS 2 (26)).

1926 HILGENDORF *Weeds* 27 Speargrass [1967 edn. has Needle grass, *S. variabilis*] (*Stipa setacea*)- A perennial introduced from Australia and recently spreading greatly in the Marlborough Sounds, on Banks Peninsula, and elsewhere. **1969** *Standard Common Names Weeds* 33 grass, spear [=] blue Spaniard: Chilean needle grass: needle grass: ripgut brome: Spaniard.

spear-plant: see SPEARGRASS 1.

speccie /'spesi/. Abbrev. of *specification*, a detailed description of projected building-work.

1988 MACRAE *Awful Childhoods* 59 'Where does it say this in the speccies, Chris? Show me the speccies' The specifications mentioned only the foundations, framing timber, gib board and windows.

special, *a.* In special collocations: **special claim** *hist.*, goldmining claims to which special conditions were attached; **special constable**, see SPECIAL *n.*; **special cut** *shearing*, see *pink 'em* (PINK *v.*).

1892 PYKE *Gold-Miners' Guide* 7 [s.32] Claims are classified as follows:—Alluvial deposits, and river- or creek-beds; Quartz lodes, reefs, and leaders; Sea-beach claims; Prospecting claims; and comprise ordinary claims..special claims and dredging claims.

special. *n. Hist.* [Ellipt. for *special constable*.]

1. A special constable in the New Zealand wars.

1863 MORGAN *Journal* 9 Sept. (1963) 77 [The beasts] were taken away for a better purpose, vis. [*sic*], to feed the 'specials' at the Mauku stockade. [*Ibid.* 80 The rebels appear to have made their way..to Pukekohe... The force there consists of volunteers and special constables.]

2. a. Any of those (esp. rural recruits) sworn in to control urban strikers esp. in the 1913 labour disputes. See also *Massey's cossacks* (MASSEY 2).

1908 *Auckland Weekly News* 13 Nov. 21 This scheme required less than half the force of mounted 'specials'. *Ibid.* 25 There has been such a rush of farmers to act as 'specials' that the authorities have had to refuse applications for the present. **1913** *NZ Observer* 6 Dec. 5 An unaccompanied special, on foot, was suddenly aware of a man darting out from behind a bridge and hissing 'Scab' at him. **1936** HYDE *Passport to Hell* 51 1913 brought Prime Minister Bill Massey's cockits [*sic* ?=cockies] riding into town—strike-breakers armed with pick-handles... If one of the 'cocky' specials fell among strangers..he might be wary of the boots that would as soon kick in a strike-breaker's head as not. **1953** *Here & Now* Feb. 14 There are those who remember him [*sc.* Tregear] during the 1913 strike standing with blazing eyes in Cuba Street and shaking his fists at the mounted 'specials' shouting: 'Go home! Go home, you—scabs!' **1989** THOMSON & NIELSON *Sharing the Challenge* 128 [Caption] Police baton fashioned from native Rewa Rewa (Honeysuckle) for the Foot Specials during the 1913 strike. **1995** *Sunday Star-Times* (Auckland) 22 Oct. C7 [Police Commissioner] Cullen, concerned about police loyalty [during waterside and miners' strikes, Oct. 1913], enrolled volunteer 'special' constables, mainly young farmers and territorial soldiers. The mounted 'specials', derisively dubbed 'Massey's Cossacks', soon clashed violently with strikers on Wellington streets.

b. A special constable enrolled to help control the street protests by the unemployed in the Depression of the 1930s. See also *Glaxo baby* (GLAXO b).

1932 *NZ Herald* (Auckland) 15 Apr. in Fraser *Ungrateful People* (1952) 48 [Forty-five people were charged as a result of the riots, including one special constable.] 'He was acting as a special,' said the police in evidence, 'and had a rifle on his shoulder and a baton in his hand.' **1935** LAWLOR *Confessions of a Journalist* 20 I found myself mixed up with a violent mob intent on doing harm to the 'specials'. **1959** SINCLAIR *Hist. NZ* 250 It is hard now to recall New Zealand in 1932... A rioter running up a back street, screaming hysterically, 'The "Specials" are coming!' *Ibid.* 251 'Special police' were enrolled... The Government passed repressive legislation annulling the traditional safeguards of personal liberty. **1976** MCCLENAGHAN *Travelling Man* 152 I got mixed up in a stoush up the street with the police, and the specials.

specimen. *Goldmining.* [Specific concrete use of *specimen* some thing, or a part of it, taken as typical.]

SPECK

1. [AND 1869.] In full *specimen gold* or *specimen stone* (see 2 below). Also *attrib*.

1859 *Auckland Provincial Gazette* 8 July 90 These 'specimens', as they are called by the diggers, show no—or very little—sign of being water-worn. **1861** 2 Oct. in Pyke *Hist. Early Gold Discoveries in Otago* (1887) 12 Under the impression that the prompt communication of the discovery of auriferous quartz in this neighbourhood will be of importance to the Otago settlement, we beg to enclose you specimens which we have found in various localities in order that you may give all the publicity which you may think proper to the fact that gold exists in the Southern Island. **1868** *Thames Miner's Guide* 82 Struck gold in quantity; beautiful specimens. **1887** CHUDLEIGH *Diary* (1950) 25 July 356 I had a fire under a sheet of corrugated iron and dried my 5 small bags of specimens. **1907** *NZGeol.SB (NS)* No.3 103 Considering the 'specimen' nature, which seems to characterize the auriferous veins of the [Parapara, Nelson] district [etc.]. **1917** *Thames Goldfield Jubilee Booklet* in Williams *Racing for Gold* (1987) 49 I soon saw by the old reef that we were going to have a haul of specimens. **1983** NOLAN *Gold Fossicker's Handbook* 113 *Specimen*: colloquially, a piece of quartz with a good showing of gold. Also used by fossickers to describe an alluvial gold sample.

2. As **specimen gold**, gold visible in a matrix; **specimen stone**, quartz showing observable gold.

1887 *Handbook of Mines* 151 Evidence is shown that [reefs] exist by the presence of what is known as '**specimen gold**' in nearly every gully and range in which coarse gold has been found. **1896** Biggar *Diary* in Begg *Port Preservation* (1973) 354 Some good patches of gold was got on Sealers—at one time chiefly specimen gold. **1906** *NZGeol.SB (NS)* No.2 32 In the creek workings near its source the gold is rough, shotty or hackly, sometimes crystallized, and often enclosed in a quartz matrix, forming what is known to miners as 'specimen gold'. **1903** *NZ Illustrated Magazine* Nov. 106 Steel must have struck it rich! Why this is a **specimen stone**! **1907** *NZ Geol. SB (NS)* No.4 98 The field has been noted for its ore-shoots of the bonanza type, the rich vein-material designated in local mining terminology 'specimen stone', and valued at 'ounces to the pound'. **1931** *NZJST* XII. 155 Thames is famous for its rich bonanzas of 'specimen stone', containing up to 6 oz. of electrum per pound weight.

speck. Goldmining.

1. [AND 1852.] A small fragment of gold.

1853 EARP *NZ* 255 Out of about six pans washed, four gave gold specks and grains. **1861** HAAST *Topogr. Explor. Nelson* 18 I gave orders again to wash for gold, and every dishful of dirt yielded some specks. **1862** LINDSAY *Place & Power Nat. Hist. in Coloniz.* 12 The gold here is very fine, scaley or granular, generally in mere specks. **1890** *TrNZI* XXII. 400 How is gold formed into specks and nuggets?

Hence **speck** *v*. [AND 1888] *intr.*, to search for (surface) gold. Also as *vbl. n*.

1941 BAKER *NZ Slang* 28 The finding of gold brought *diggers,.. specking, nuggeting,* [etc.].

2. Prob. an abbrev. of SPECIMEN.

1918 *NZJST* I. 12 The coarse nature of the alluvial gold..and the fact that many of the 'specks' had fragments of gold attached, early induced prospectors to seek for lodes.

speckled whelk: see WHELK 2 (2).

speculate, *v. Rugby Football. intr.* To kick the ball on the chance of the result being in some way helpful to the kicker's team. Also as a *ppl. a.*

1908 BARR *British Rugby Team in Maoriland* 32 It was Rugby gospel in those days..that a player who speculated at a rolling ball instead of getting down to stop the rush was forever doomed. **1922** *Auckland Weekly News* 24 Aug. 54 Knox speculated, and the ball went out at half-way. **1947** *Sports Post* (Wellington) 13 May 15 A shrewd speculating effort by Freeman..put Auckland in a handy position.

Hence **speculator** *n*., such a kick. Also *attrib*.

1904 *NZ Observer* 4 June 10 The Newton backs..took on a great risk by the number of 'speculators' they indulged in. **1912** *Dominion* (Wellington) 17 June 6 Evenson had stopped one hot St. James rush by a 'speculator' to touch. **1922** *Auckland Weekly News* 24 Aug. 54 A loose Auckland rush..threatened the Otago defence, but Dickinson misjudged a speculator. **1947** *Sports Post* (Wellington) 26 Apr. 15 Shortly after Robinson gained ground with a solo speculator attack. *Ibid.* 31 May 15 When Hutt attempted to clear with a long speculator Kenny picked up the ball and coolly kicked a field goal. **1985** *Collins Compact Dict.* 465 *speculator..*2. *Rugby* random forward kick.

speedwell. [Transf. use of northern hemisphere *speedwell, Veronica* spp. (fam. Scrophulariaceae) for the NZ species of *Hebe* and *Parahebe* (fam. Scrophulariaceae), formerly treated as *Veronica*.] KOROMIKO (*Hebe* species).

1773 FORSTER *Resolution Jrnl.* 9 Apr. (1982) II. 251 It is remarkable, that though we had seen scarce ten plants in all in flower, among them were three new *Speedwells*; all of them Shrubby, although there are but few Shrubby ones upon the whole known. **1838** POLACK *NZ* I. 295 *Speedwell, sow,* and *melon thistles* (coetus). **1853** TAYLOR *Journal* 30 Jan. (ATLTS) VIII. 70 The chief plants I noticed [on Ruapehu] were..a pretty speedwell, an epacris. **1910** COCKAYNE *NZ Plants & Their Story* 57 These scrubs are the headquarters of the shrubby speedwells (*Veronica*). **1951** HUNT *Confessions* 136 It has..speedwells or veronicas which in England are modest little blue flowers..but which here in New Zealand are not only an enormous family of numerous species with a range of colours varying from white to dark purple, but, in the form of shrubs and trees (known as Hebes), reach a height of forty feet.

speel, *v. Obs.* Also **spiel.** [Var. of Brit. dial. or slang *speel* to go fast, to make off: see OED *speel* *v.*²; AND 1892.] To move at speed; to make off.

1885 *Wairarapa Daily* 21 Sept. 2 At last full inquiry revealed that horrid young [man] from the marriage had 'speeled'. By the train that morning he had vamoosed quite clean. **1904** WILLIAMS *New Chum's Let. Home* 88 They had a holy horror of backing A racehorse that doesn't spiel.

Hence **speeler** [see OED *speeler n.*³, *Austral.* 1893], a fast (race-)horse. Contrast SPIELER.

1887 *Auckland Weekly News* 20 Aug. 20 No tramp ever owned such a speeler.

speeler, speeling, speiling, varr. SPIELER; SPIELING.

spell, *n.*¹ [f. Brit. dial.: see OED *n.*³ 3 b; AND 1831.] A period of rest from work; a holiday. Often in the phr. **to give a spell**, to relieve (from work, etc.); **to take a spell**, to have a rest.

1853 ROCHFORT *Adventures of Surveyor* 62 The diggers on coming down to town for a 'spell'. **1862** CHUDLEIGH *Diary* 18 Dec. (1950) 70 Every now and then he gave us a spell for about 2 min., no more. **1874** BAINES *Edward Crewe* 104 The beauty of paddling is that any one of the crew can 'take a spell' without throwing the rest much out. **1888** D'AVIGDOR *Antipodean Notes* 164 He and his young wife are now in England for a 'spell' (holiday), after three years of hard..work. **1906** *Truth* 14 July 2 Savoury ran last at Moorefield last Saturday week. He is sore and will require a spell. **1916** COWAN *Bush Explorers* (VUWTS) 10 Grateful were the spells for rest and smoke. **1920** *Quick March* 10 Apr. 31 While we were waiting for the billy to boil..taking the mid-day spell after a strenuous morning of post-splitting. **1943** BENNETT *English in NZ* in *Amer. Speech* XVIII. 91 A *spell* in New Zealand means a period of rest, rather than of work, and 'to have a spell' is to take a rest. **1952** THOMSON *Deer Hunter* 33 We had very few spells in the three-hour trip and were about all-in by the time we reached the fly-camp. **1962** JOSEPH *Pound of Saffron* 34 What about a flick or something next Friday? We'll both need a spell by then. **1970** DAVIN *Not Here Not Now* 273 Every time there was a shunt the gang had to have a spell while they waited for the line to clear again.

spell, *n.*² [Spec. use of *spell* a turn of work: see OED *n.*³ 2 a.]

1. One of the periods into which a game of rugby football is divided; a 'half'.

1888 in *College Rhymes* (1923) 22 [Quoting *Otago Univ. Review*] Nothing was scored in the spell. **1900** *NZ Illustr. Mag.* III. 237 Usually in the second spell..play is getting more exciting. **1934** MULGAN *Spur of Morning* 23 The school won a hard game by six to nil, a try in each spell.

2. *Obs. Nautical.* The amount of water made by a leaking boat which is equivalent to one 'spell' on the pump. (A survival of OED *n.*³ 2 a, quot. a1625 'When they pump a hundred strokes,.. they call it a spell.')

1836 *Piraki Log* 29 Feb. (1911) 29 Making but little water. [Mar. 1]... Carpenter caulking on the larboard side, Ship making about One Spell in 3 hours.

spell, *v*. [f. SPELL *n.*¹]

1. *intr.* **a.** [AND 1841.] To rest.

1869 *Auckland Punch* 172 Leave off and spell a bit. **1881** NESFIELD *Chequered Career* 60 We had the tide against us.., so we stopped at a 'shanty' on the north shore, and 'spelled' for a couple of hours. **1909** THOMPSON *Ballads About Business* 63 He'd scaled the heights of Nevis..Tramped and coached it through Kawarau Gorge and spelled at Arrowtown. **1930** *NZ Short Stories* 19 When we 'spelled', grey-breasted robins fluttered about us cheekily. **1960** SCRYMGEOUR *Memories Maoriland* 181 One command was to bring back the horse 'Brownie' spelling at Ben Coldham's property, and to ride him home, and spell the mount ridden out on this tour.

b. *Waterfront. Obs.* To work for a period then rest for a period. (Often formerly called the *spelling system*, and prob. taken over from Scottish labour practices: see OED *spelling vbl. n.*⁴ 1 for a similar practice.)

1951 *Evening Post* (Wellington) 5 Dec. 10 The board had never countenanced the unlawful practice of waterside workers employed by it 'spelling' hour and hour about.

2. *trans.* **a.** [AND 1846.] To rest (a person or animal) to allow to recuperate.

1864 CHUDLEIGH *Diary* 6 May (1950) 131 I spelled the horses for an hour and returned to Mt. Peel picking up my tent..on the way. **1893** FERGUSON *Bush Life* 246 Whenever [the bullocks] look fagged I spell them. **1906** *Truth* 11 Aug. 6 Killarney..is suffering from a swollen joint and is being spelled. **1950** *Listener* 3 Mar. 8 'You can put Mac on with Monty,' I told Dawson, 'and young Jimmy can spell Arthur.' **1950** *NZJAg.* Oct. LXXXI. 310 Sheep brought in for shearing should be spelled before shedding up. **1960** [see 1 a above].

b. To rest (land by removing stock or letting it lie fallow).

1934 *Press* (Christchurch) (Acland Gloss.) 27 Jan. 15 *Spell, to.*- To take the stock off (a paddock, etc.). **1940** STUDHOLME *Te Waimate* (1954) 113 The hill lambs were weaned on to a block of country which had been spelled since shearing time. **1951** LEVY *Grasslands NZ* (1970) 261 Ridge fencing is essential to control stock and to spell country.

Hence **spelled** *ppl. a.*, of a paddock or pasture, rested from stock grazing.
1951 LEVY *Grasslands of NZ* (1970) 261 Long-spelled feed is equally disastrous to wet and young stock.

spell-ho, var. SPELL-OH.

spelling, *vbl. n.* [f. *spell v.*]
1. The resting of animals from work, or of land by withdrawing it from grazing; also in *attrib.* use, and as special Comb. **spelling paddock**, a paddock in which horses are put to rest (see quot. 1930).
1916 *TrNZI* XLVIII. 164 The increased production of feed over certain areas would enable periodical spelling of much of the land. **1930** DAVIDSON *Sketch of His Life* 69 The station horses are seldom shod, and when one becomes footsore..it is turned into a spelling paddock to recover. **1949** *Rep. Royal Comm. Sheep-farming Industry in NZ* 26 The extension of essential hill country practices such as..top-dressing, spelling, scrub-cutting and cattle-stocking. **1951** LEVY *Grasslands NZ* (1970) 261 The spelling of country demands keen judgment and is dependent on the season, and slowness or rapidity of growth. **1953** SUTHERLAND *Golden Bush* (1963) 121 After the short horizons of the clearing this panorama was always welcome and the spot became a regular 'spelling' place on the way in or out. **1989** *NZ Herald (Auckland)* (Racing Suppl.) in *Listener* (1989) 10 June 5 Normandy Farm... Offers a complete agistment service, hard feeding, breaking in, extensive teasing programme brood mares, weaklings, racehorse spelling.

2. A former system of working waterfront gangs comprising a period on work and a period off work. Cf. SPELL *v.* 1 a.
1949 *Southern Cross* (Wellington) 11 Aug. 2 '"Spelling" is resorted to even in this chamber at times,' said..Mr. McLagan in the House of Representatives. **1952** *Evening Post* (Wellington) 2 Sept. 8 Spelling has ceased, reasonable rest or 'smoko' periods should be arranged by agreement between employers and employees.

spell-oh. Also **spell-ho.** [f. SPELL + -O: OED 1837; AND 1862.] **1.** A call to stop work for a brief rest.
1873 BARKER *Station Amusements* 268 'Spell, oh!' or else 'Shears!'.. [1873 *Note*] The shearers' demand for a few minutes rest. **1916** COWAN *Bush Explorers* (VUWTS) 24 'Some day,' said Wirihana, as he called spell-oh for our toiling party. **1918** *Chron. NZEF* 22 Nov. 204 An hour's solid going and..'Spell-ho' was called. **1938** HYDE *Godwits Fly* (1970) 130 Spell-oh, Boss. We're going to drown our troubles. **c1955** *She'll be Right* record sleeve notes. Spell-oh! could be another national anthem... This song's about the kind of spell you get (if you're lucky) when you're working in a hay-paddock. **1981** CHARLES *Black Billy Tea* 91 Smoko! Spell ho! Billy on the boil! Light a fag and take a drag, And rest your bones from toil.

2. A short break for a rest, taken usu. when called for.
1889 ROSS *Lakes Central Otago* 43 At every 'spell ho!' the outlook from our sideling bush was lovely. **1895** in Alpers *Jubilee Book Canterbury Rhymes* (1900) 122 Then a long spell-oh, and a lunch in the fern. **1959** *Listener* 18 Dec. 8 He dropped his pack and sleeping-bag, and unslung his rifle. 'Spell-oh.'

Hence *v. intr.*, to take a rest from an arduous task.
1905 BAUCKE *White Man Treads* 305 Look at mother and dad; pulled the old waggon uphill together, now they can spell-ho.

sperm(aceti) whale: see WHALE 2 (17).

spider.
1. See AVONDALE SPIDER, KATIPO.
2. [AND 1850.] An alcoholic drink usu. consisting of brandy and lemonade.
1869 *Westport Times* 27 Mar. 2 The hotel-keepers..of Westport..reduced the price of the indispensable 'nobbler' to the small charge of one sixpence!.. Moreover, the reduction was made not alone for that day, but for all time; 'stout, spiders, and hot grog excepted'.
3. See *crayfish-spider* (CRAYFISH 3 b); PIT SPIDER.
4. *spider crab*: see CRAB 2 (3).

spiderwood. NEINEI (*Dracophyllum* spp.).
1908 *AJHR* C-14 41 Neinei. Spiderwood. Forest. Small tree finally branching candelabra-like and with coriaceous, recurved, leaves in terminal rosettes. **1910** COCKAYNE *NZ Plants & Their Story* 43 Certain shrubs or small trees [grow in kauri forests], especially..the spiderwood. **1926** CROOKES *Plant Life in Maoriland* 105 The most striking-looking of the heaths are undoubtedly the spiderwoods (members of the Dracophyllum family). **1939** COCKAYNE & TURNER *Trees NZ* 134 *Dracophyllum latifolium*. Neinei. Spiderwood. **1951** LEVY *Grasslands NZ* (1970) 88 [Table 1] Spiderwoods. **1961** [see NEINEI]. **1978** *Manawatu Tramping Club Jubilee* 86 Then we passed through a belt of that graceful shrub Nei-nei (Spiderwood). **1982** SALE *Four Seasons* 33 We find [toropapa] in a kauri grove,... beneath the tufted neinei, or spiderwood, amid the smooth kauri grass.

spiel /spil/ *v.*, var. SPEEL; see also SPIELING.

spieler /ˈspilə/. Also **speeler**. [Orig. US: see OED *spieler* 1, 1859 'now chiefly *Austral.*'; AND 1879.] A gambler, esp. a dishonest one; a swindler or professional confidence-man.
1880 *Evening Post* (Wellington) 15 Apr. 2 Other implements of gambling. Among them a false die or, in the 'speelers' slang, a messenger. **1887** *Auckland Weekly News* 5 Mar. 17 Twenty-six speelers went to a Maori race meeting at Otaki a day or two ago, but the brown brother refused to let them play. **1892** *Star* (Auckland) in Bailey & Roth *Shanties* (1967) 82 Give me, give me God's own the country (from a spieler's point of view), Where the scripper and the sharper conjugate the verb 'to do'. **1900** SCOTT *Colonial Turf* 96 You belong to a gang of..robbers of widows,— spielers is the term—who play 'two up' with pennies. **1905** *Truth* 19 Aug. 1 A cheerful bounder... The spieler whose only game is unsophisticated shop-girls. **c1924** ANTHONY *Me & Gus* (1977 Gus Tomlins) 19 He ended his [derogatory] remarks by alluding to me as a cross-eyed spieler, and said he could see by my looks that I just lived by sucking the life-blood out of honest farmers. **1951** *Here & Now* Apr. 9 Bookmakers, money-lenders, parasites, newspaper proprietors, spielers, chisellers, drones, drongoes and spivs. **1972** PREBBLE *Horses, Courses & Men* 46 The pious and venerable recall it [*sc.* Omokoroa racing] as a spieler's picnic, and two-up and other games of chance were in vogue. **1993** *North & South* (Auckland) Feb. 106 A goldfield wouldn't be a goldfield without cheats, rogues..spielers..prostitutes and bums.

Hence **spielerdom**, the world or sub-culture of spielers.
1910 *Truth* 5 Feb. 2 What with 'guns' and 'tugs'..and all the crafty offshoots of spielerdom that..batten upon them, honest people are beginning to wonder if..honesty and labor are not at a decided discount.

spieling /ˈspilɪŋ/, *vbl. n. Obs.* Also **speeling, speiling**. [f. *spiel v. intr.* orig. US to patter, to talk glibly: see OED *v.* 3, 1894; *spieling* AND 1879.] Card-sharping; following the occupation of a (usu. dishonest) gambler or gambling trickster. Also *attrib.*
1869 *Auckland Punch* 153 My dingy acquaintance chuckles mockingly as he replies 'Not so bad for you, old un, though your [*sic*] young at the profession yet. I twigged you on your speeling lay this afternoon whilst I was gattering my clay.' [1869 *Note*] 'card sharping'. **1887** *Auckland Weekly News* 5 Feb. 9 Zahl identified a young man.., a speeler, as one of the men, and he was arrested but no money found on him. However, there was found a complete set of 'speeling' articles. **1896** BRACKEN *Tom Bracken's Annual* 38 The Bobbies nabbed some of [my friends] for speeling.

Hence occas. as *v. intr. (transf.)*, to talk continually and volubly.
1891 WILLIAMS & REEVES *In Double Harness* 1 [The mosquitos] announce that they are spieling, By the way they ring their war-cry in your ear.

spiker. [f. *spike* a stiff sharp-pointed object + -ER: cf. US *spike-buck*.] Also **spikey**. A yearling male red deer carrying a single spike rather than a tyned antler on either side of the head.
1924 FORBES *NZ Deer Heads* xvi The same day..we saw the first bull—a spiker. **1949** NEWTON *High Country Days* 197 Spiker: A yearling stag. As yearlings, stags grow only a spike, up to eighteen inches and two feet, on either side of the head. As they age, tynes, or prongs develop. **1952** ORBELL *Comfort and Common Sense in the Bush* 52 If it is a stag with a harem take a careful look round his area for odd hinds or spikeys which may not be with the main herd. **1960** MASTERS *Back-Country Tales* 42 After several days poking about not too far from their camp in the Kawekas that pair managed to drop a spiker stag. **1971** *Listener* 19 Apr. 56 They cooeed out, and when he skinned the spiker they found a possie in a bit of a trog and boiled-up. **1984** HOLDEN *Razorback* 22 He was a handsome yearling [red deer] with two long white-tipped spikes jutting above his head... The spiker's mother, a trim, well-built three-year-old, was nearby. **1991** LENTLE & SAXTON *Red Deer* 187 *spiker* 2 year old male carrying upright straight antlers.

spikey: see SPIKER.

spiky: see DOGFISH.

spin, *n.*
1. *Two up.* **a.** [AND 1919.] The act of tossing coins in the air in the game of two up.
1917 *NZ at the Front* 106 The last spin, boys, the last throw. **1921** *Quick March* 10 Aug. 27 The last spin, digs, so plank it down thick and heavy now; you pick 'em and I'll pay 'em. **1936** HYDE *Passport to Hell* 137 They had their first close-up view of a beautiful British general when three thousand of them were playing 'two-up' outside the Lemnos wells. 'What about a spin, Alec?' yelled one hardy trooper.

b. As **spin-up**, a game of two up.
1917 *Chron. NZEF* 5 Sept. 28 The O.C. sent him

along..one afternoon to stop the boys having a bit of a spin up, and he hopped into the ring and did a trot for 700 francs.

2. a. [AND 1917.] With a modifier, a run of luck, a chance, a 'go', esp. in the collocations **a bad (crook, rough, tough) spin**, a period of adversity; **a fair (good) spin**, (a period of) honest or equitable, or favourable, treatment.
1916 ANZAC *On the Anzac Trail* 150 We had a crook spin... We followed the infantry to the attack at dusk. 1919 *Quick March* Mar. 43 The 'Red Caps' got a rough spin at a recent general meeting. 1933 PRUDENCE CADEY *Broken Pattern* 95 He's had a bit of a rough spin lately... He's queertempered, but he'll give you a fair spin. 1939 *Letter* 10 May in Bruce *Life in Hinterland* (1977) 150 I was pleased to hear that you are keeping fit and able to attend business. Farmers generally are not having too good a spin. 1946 SARGESON *That Summer* 188 So he'd missed his ship, and for a time he'd had a tough spin living from hand to mouth. 1962 CRUMP *One of Us* 105 We'd had a bit of a rough spin in a two-up game the night before and done our next week's wages in. 1964 HORI *Fill It Up Again* 54 He tells me that he is getting a bad spin... All the horses he [b]acks either fall down or dead heat for eighth.

b. In the phr. **to give it** (or something) **a spin**, to give it a chance or 'go'; to try it out.
1918 *Kia-ora Coo-ee* (1981) 15 Sept. III. 17 If an attempt was to be made to outwit the Bedouins; or if Ike found that he had only a dollar left a week before pay-day, he would always resign himself to his old maxim and 'give it a spin'... 'What is this?' asked Ike, turning to the patriarch. 'This,' was the reply, 'is Death. Are you coming?' 'I'll give it a spin,' said Ike... And the orderly sitting by his side gently drew the blanket over his cold, white face.

spin, *v.*

1. *Two up.* [AND 1913.] *trans.* To toss (two coins) up in the air so that they spin end over end. Also **spin out** (see quot. 1928).
1917 *Chron. NZEF* 16 May 137 And very soon he got the 'kip' And spun for two good 'bob'. 1928 DEVANNY *Dawn Beloved* 162 If [the pennies] come down tails up they are said to be spun out... What if the coins spin one head one tail?

2. [Poss. transf. from two-up use: see SPIN *n.* 1.] As **spin (money) up**, to spend (money) recklessly.
1963 *Home Life* June 2 You did not have your last week's pay pinched from your locker but..you spun it up at the night trots.

spinach. [AND 1770.] Occas. as **native (wild) spinach**, often as **New Zealand spinach**, either of *Tetragonia tetragonioides* (formerly *expansa*) or *T. trigyna* (fam. Aizoaceae), coastal sprawling plants with edible fleshy leaves (see esp. quot. 1978). See also KOKIHI.
1830 CRAIK *New Zealanders* 183 Among the useful plants for which we are indebted to New Zealand, we must not forget their summer spinach..which was discovered in Cook's First Voyage by Sir Joseph Banks, and was 'boiled and eaten as greens' by the crew. 1841 Diary in *William Swainson* 28 May (1992) 85 Transplanted some New Zealand spinach as an experiment also. 1843 DIEFFENBACH *Travels in NZ* I. 429 Amongst the *Ficoideae* there exists..the Tetragonia expansa, or New Zealand spinach, which, however, in the northern island is very rare. 1882 HAY *Brighter Britain* II. 210 There are the native spinach.., the Pana-pana, or cress..which do for salad and green vegetables. 1888 BULLER *Birds NZ* II. 76 In some localities the nests..were placed in the thick masses of wild spinach. 1896 HARPER *Pioneer Work* 33 Wild parsley..[and] spinach..are also eatable. 1906 CHEESEMAN *Manual NZ Flora* 192 T[etragonia] expansa..Kokihi... This has long been cultivated in Europe as an edible plant under the name of 'New Zealand spinach'. 1940 LAING & BLACKWELL *Plants NZ* 167 *New Zealand Spinach*. Kermadecs to Stewart Island on the seashore. 1978 MOORE & IRWIN *Oxford Book NZ Plants* 44 Leaves of either species can be cooked as a vegetable, but those of T[etragonia] tetragonioides are preferred and selected strains are grown in many parts of the world under the name 'New Zealand spinach'. 1982 WILSON *Stewart Is. Plants* 146 Native Spinach..Kōkihi... Rather succulent sprawling herb... Stems often red-stained. 1991 *NZ Gardener* Aug. 29 New Zealand spinach, *Tetragonia trigyna*, a succulent plant native to the Chatham Islands, was boiled and eaten by whalers for a month to rid them of scurvy.

spineback: see DOGFISH.

spine-bashing, *vbl. n.* Also **spino**. [AND *v.* 1941.] Lying in bed or bunk (flat on one's back). Cf. MAORI PT.
1944 BRUNO *Desert Daze* 61 'Two hundred — yards away!' snarled the ex-prowlers [sentries], rolling up in their blankets for a 'spino'. c1944 p.c. L. Cleveland *Spine-bashing* used by soldiers in WW2. 1968 *NZ Contemp. Dict. Suppl.* (Collins) 18 *spine-bashing n.* (*Army sl.*) having a rest, loafing, whence *spine-basher*.

spinner.

1. [Spec. use of *spinner* something which moves rapidly: see OED *spinner* 8.] A fast racehorse.
1891 WILLIAMS & REEVES *In Double Harness* 3 Or suppose you're on a 'spinner', He can never prove a winner... When he should have been a 'moral' [cert].

2. *Two up.* [AND 1911.] The player who tosses or 'spins' the coins. Also in the phr. **come in spinner**, the ringie's cry for the game to begin.
1917 *Chron. NZEF* 16 May 137 The spinner's eyes began to gleam..The big brown paw that held the 'bat' Was trembling like a leaf. 1951 LAWSON *Gold in Their Hearts* 90 Percy Gray was the spinner... Well, everything was going well till Percy spun two coins very high—trying to 'float' them. 1956 WILSON *Sweet White Wine* 137 It was like a bazaar [on the troopship]. In the centre was a boxing ring and the two-up spinners were operating inside it. 1976 HILLIARD *Send Somebody Nice* 75 In the centre stood the spinner with his kip and two pennies. 1994 Come in Spinner [see KING *n.*² 1].

spinning Jenny: see JENNY 1.

spino /ˈspaɪnʌu/: see SPINE-BASHING.

spin the bottle. A method of establishing a choice or priority (e.g. among a group) by spinning a bottle placed horizontally on a flat surface, the choice being that pointed to by the mouth of the bottle when it comes to rest.
1951 16+ M 32 St Bede's, Chch 20 Spin the bottle. 1984 14 F E134 Wgton Girls C. 21 Spin the bottle [F2] 1991 *Listener* 18 Feb. 17 Although things may go no further than a..session of spin-the-bottle kissing, they may also pair off for some heavy 'scamming' (known in their parents' day as a 'pash-up') or even 'bonking'.

spiral. Also **Raurimu Spiral**. Usu. as **the Spiral**, an unusual spiral track configuration showing considerable engineering skill on the North Island main trunk railway line at Raurimu in National Park (see esp. quot. 1972).
1926 *NZ Observer* 18 Aug. 6 The Raurimu Spiral was one of the most wonderful engineering feats in the world. 1936 *NZ Railways Mag.* Sept. 35 It has been said the Raurimu Spiral would never have been constructed if aeroplanes had existed when the reconnaissance surveys were made. 1972 LEITCH *Railways of NZ* 62 Holmes' perseverance was rewarded when he finally came up with the track location known as the Raurimu Sprial. With three horseshoe curves, two tunnels and a complete circle, Holmes made the line descend 434 ft in 4 miles. *Ibid.* 217 The passenger unused to the Spiral soon loses all sense of direction. 1981 PIERRE *North Island Main Trunk* 46 The boxing of the compass by the spiral was early adopted into King Country folk-lore. It tells of the consternation of an early driver who..found that he had merely caught up with his own guard's van. 1992 SMITHYMAN *Auto/Biographies* 12 Father and I are running away to find what makes the world go round, like Raurimu Spiral?

spirtle, var. SPURTLE.

spit.

1. See *big spit* (BIG *a.*), *dead spit* (DEAD *a.*²).

2. As **long spit**, a urination. Contrast *big spit* (BIG *a.*).
1967 in *NZ Short Stories III* (1975) 155 The uncle looked around for the Gents. 'Where are you off to now?' 'For a long spit.' 'Well don't stand there all day looking at it.'

spleenwort. [Extended use of northern hemisphere *spleenwort*, *Asplenium* spp. for NZ *Asplenium* ferns (fam. Aspleniaceae).] A native fern of *Asplenium* spp. with spore tissue distributed along the veins of fronds. Also with a modifier: **pendent (hanging) spleenwort** (*A. flaccidum*), **shining spleenwort** (*A. oblongifolium*).
1777 ANDERSON Feb. in Cook *Journals* (1967) III. 805 There is also Polypody, Spleenwort and about twenty different sorts of ferns. 1908 *AJHR* C-14 33 [*Asplenium*] *flaccidum*. Pendent spleenwort... [*Asplenium lucidum*]. Shining spleenwort. In lower forest. 1975 *Tane* 21 8 Aspleniaceae A[splenium] lucidum *shining spleenwort*. 1979 WEBSTER *Rua* 81 The tree ferns are in turn often covered in other smaller ferns, particularly the hanging spleenwort (*Asplenium flaccidum*) whose graceful, drooping foliage belies the ugliness of its name. 1982 WILSON *Stewart Is. Plants* 436 *Asplenium* Spleenworts... Both the botanical and the common names refer to the old belief that these ferns were useful medicinally against complaints of the spleen.

splitter. [Spec. use of *splitter* one who splits (wood): AND 1826.] Formerly, one whose occupation was that of splitting posts, slabs, shingles, etc. from logs.
1847 ANGAS *Savage Life* II. 161 The first Europeans we saw [at Papakura] were two splitters, working for Captain Smale. 1857 PAUL *Lett. from Canterbury* 88 The [sheep-station] party to consist of owner..a couple of men for contract work (splitters and fencers if you have a tolerable bush). 1869 *Grey River Argus* 9 Jan. 2 The deceased and Hector Morrison were employed..at the head of the Lake [Wakatip], as splitters. 1875 *TrNZI* VII. 183 It is the utter recklessness displayed by saw-mill proprietors, bush contractors, and splitters which is destroying our forests. 1891 CHAMIER *Philosopher Dick* 148 It was decided to take a stroll into the bush [and] pay a call to a party of splitters. 1968 *NZ Contemp. Dict. Suppl.* (Collins) 18 *splitter n.* timber cutter, one who splits logs for posts and and rails.

Hence **splitting** *vbl. n.*, the splitting of logs into posts, slabs, etc.

c1875 MEREDITH *Adventuring in Maoriland* (1935) 61 After a spell of 'quill-driving' it takes one a week or so to get into one's stride of splitting, fencing.

spoil, spoiler: see SPOT *v.*[1]

spoon, *n.*[1] [Spec. use of *spoon* a spoon-shaped object.]

1. A blasting tool.
1852 *NZGG* V. 31:193 (Annual Contracts, Col. Secretary's Office) [Heading] Tools For Road Parties... Blasting Tools Crowbars..per lb... Spoons and Needles..per lb.

2. a. *Obs.* The 'bucket' or receptacle of a spoon dredge (see quot. 1899 b below).
1977 MURRAY *Costly Gold* 54 The 'spoon' from one of the early types of dredge.

b. Special Comb. **spoon-dredge**, hence **spoon-dredging**, see quot. 1899.
1899 *Gold Dredging in Otago* 47 The spoon-dredge consisted of a large hide affixed to an iron rim with a sharp shovel-faced cutting-edge, and holding about a barrowful: this was affixed to the end of a long, strong, but light pole, about twenty feet in length. This was worked from a barge by means of a hand winch and tackle. *Ibid.* 48 The old system of spoon-dredging died out (such a thing as a spoon-dredge being hard to find at the present time). 1906 GALVIN *NZ Mining Handbook* 34 Spoon dredges were used in this and other countries for many years.

spoon, *n.*[2] [Poss. a survival of Brit. slang *spoon* a simpleton (OED *spoon n.* 7), or transf. f. WOODEN SPOON q.v.] A fool; a simpleton; an innocent.
1982 NEWBOLD *Big Huey* 147 I realised I was talking to a real spoon so I decided to have some humour with him. 1984 BEATON *Outside In* 31 Ginny:.. But she hates Cowface most, 'cos the cunt makes her look like a fucken spoon in front of us. *Ibid.* 84 Sandy: A dumb fucken spoon. Only a dumb fucken spoon'd do a thing like that. Ma: Bloody fools! 1984 16 F E29 Pakuranga Coll. 1 Spoon [a silly person] [M5F5] 1993 *North & South* (Auckland) Feb. 91 Some of you guys have got to be spoons or dicks to get where you want to be.

spoonbill. [Transf. use of *spoonbill* for ducks having long, spatulate or spoon-shaped bills.]

1. In full **spoonbill duck**; also familiar **spoonie** (see quot. 1966). SHOVELLER (*Anas rhynchotis variegata*).
1870 *TrNZI* II. 48 Those less common birds, the great White Crane, the Avocet, and Spoonbill Duck were seen at rarer intervals. 1886 *Ibid.* XVIII. 127 Shoveller, or Spoonbill. This beautiful species is not at all uncommon about the district [*sc.* Petane, Hawke's Bay]. c1899 DOUGLAS in *Mr Explorer Douglas* (1957) 239 The Spoonbill... The bill is soft and wider at the end than the base, somewhat resembling a spoon, hence their name. 1904 [see SHOVELLER]. 1917 WILLIAMS *Dict. Maori Lang.* 479 tete... Spatula [sp.], spoonbill duck. 1930 *Evening Post* (Wellington) 6 Dec. 17 The grey duck and the shoveller or spoonbill duck enjoy a happy existence in this refuge. 1947–48 [see SHOVELLER]. 1966 FALLA et al. *Birds NZ* 92 New Zealand Shoveler... Other names: Kuruwhengi, Spoonbill, Spoonie. 1985 Spoonie [see SHOVELLER]. 1995 ANDERSON *House Guest* 23 Robin thought about..the estuary and his chances of seeing the spoonbills before they left.

2. Usu. **royal spoonbill**. *Platalea regia* (fam. Threskiornithidae), a large, white duck self-introduced from Australia. See also KOTUKU-NGUTUPAPA.

1917 WILLIAMS *Dict. Maori Lang.* 175 Kotuku-ngutupapa, Platalea melanorhyncha, royal spoonbill. 1952 *Notornis* IV. 173 Late last year..Dr. Falla reported having seen a pair of royal spoonbills in breeding plumage at the white heronry at Okarito. 1966 *Ibid.* XIII. 105 On the inside of [Farewell Spit]..2 Royal Spoonbills roosted over high tide. 1987 *MS Cellany* 72 Could it be another kotuku? No, no. This bird flew with outstretched neck—a royal spoonbill. 1990 *Checklist Birds NZ* 95 *Platalea regia* Gould Royal Spoonbill (*Kotuku-ngutupapa*)... Australia except southwest... After a century of vagrant records, it has successfully colonised New Zealand... Sometimes treated as a subspecies of the widespread *leucorodia*.

spoonie: see SPOONBILL 1.

sport. [See OED *n.*[1] 8 e 'Chiefly *Austral.*'; AND 1923.] A familiar form of male address.
1944 *Listener* 28 Jan. 20 Talking to each other, the Kiwis [of the 2NZEF] use the terms 'Soldier' or 'Dig' mostly... Occasionally, but not very often, you hear the word 'Sport'. 1944 *NZEF Times* 24 July 4 I take your word for that unreservedly, sport. 1946 WEBBER *Johnny Enzed in Italy* 32 Hullo sport, I said. 1959 SLATTER *Gun in My Hand* 50 Ya looking for somebody, sport? 1960 MUIR *Word for Word* 74 'Not much left to the imagination, is there?' 'Depends on your mind, sport.' 1963 MORRIESON *Scarecrow* 146 'So yuh ain't raised the wind, eh, sport?' said Flash Freddy. 1989 MORRISON *Auckland City & Sea* 5 'Sport' when used as 'Hi-ya Sport!' or 'G'day Sport' is exclusively a term of socially approved male endearment.

spot, *v.*[1] *Hist.* Also occas. **spoil** (see quot. 1856). [See OED *v.* 4 d.] *trans.*

1. To select and freehold (the best spots or parts of an area of Crown land or leasehold run) with a view to future alienation. See also *pick the eyes out* (EYE 2). Cf. GRIDIRON *v.*
1856 CURR *Waste Lands Wellington* 30 The practice of which I speak is called in New Zealand '*spotting*' or '*spoiling*' country. 1868 LYTTELTON *Two Lectures* (Canterbury) 31 [The early squatters] used to *spot*, as it was called, these improvements [*sc.* homesteads, or other buildings] in different parts of the run. 1885 *Wairarapa Daily* 26 Jan. 2 The block itself could hardly have been selected by anyone having a knowledge of the ground. It certainly must have been 'spotted' out especially. 1895 CHAMIER *South Sea Siren* 165 I took 'the eyes out of it', as we say—spotted all the best patches, secured all the waterholes. 1938 BURDON *High Country* 123 Much buying was done in self-defence; for if men did not 'spot' their own runs, speculators would do it for them. 1948 LIPSON *Politics of Equality* 59 If he wished to gain control over a large area without purchasing all of it, he could pick out or 'spot' the best sections, buying only these and leaving the inferior portions which were valueless without adjacent good land. 1981 CRAWFORD *Station Years* 47 McLean brought to light some of the pitfalls of spot freeholding when he wrote in September 1870 [etc.].

Hence **spotter** (also occas. **spoiler**) *n.*; **spotting** *vbl. n.* and *attrib.* (see esp. quot. 1916).
1856 CURR *Waste Lands Wellington* 30 The '**spotters**' and 'spoilers' of the public lands. 1916 [see *spotting* below]. 1981 CRAWFORD *Station Years* 50 Later in 1873 William Rolleston..drew attention..to some abuses of land laws in Canterbury, citing the favourite ruse of the spotter: buying up land at the entrance to a valley to prevent a road being made into it. 1856 CURR *Waste Lands Wellington* 36 '**Spotting**' powers. 1870 McLEAN in Crawford *Station Years* (1981) 47 The promiscuous 'spotting' of this run with small blocks of freehold..may have in a measure attained the primary object of excluding extensive purchase. 1898 MORRIS *Austral-English* 431 Spotting, *n.* New Zealand equivalent for the Australian 'picking the eyes out', and 'peacocking'. Under *Free-selection*..the squatter spotted his run, purchasing choice spots. 1902 REEVES *State Experiments* I. 234 In Australia this process of buying up spots was called 'peacocking'; in New Zealand it was nicknamed 'spotting', or—sometimes—'gridironing', from the oblong shape of the alternate sections bought. 1916 ANDERSEN *Jubilee Hist. S. Canterbury* 332 The pastoral holder would purchase 'key' sections, such as the openings of valleys leading into basins of country... This scattering of small sections over large districts was known as 'spotting'; the eyes were picked out of the country as it were, spoiling it for future disposal, except of course to the spotter, who purchased at his leisure. 1938 BURDON *High Country* 123 The other and yet more harmful method was to buy isolated sections all over a run to prevent or hinder large purchases by anyone else; to pick out the fertile and leave the barren; to take the grain and leave the husk. This was called 'spotting'. 1948 SCOTTER *Run Estate & Farm* 13 These practices called gridironing and spotting can be defended: there is no need to do so here. If spotting is practiced—the purchase of selected areas with water and shelter for the control this gave over the surrounding country—a study of the Crown grant index maps and of the dates of the original titles supplies no evidence of it. 1959 SINCLAIR *Hist. NZ* 156 'Spotting' was the purchase of strategic points, such as the mouth of a gorge, river-banks and other watering-places, so as to exclude rivals from large areas of adjacent land. 1960 OLIVER *Story NZ* 108 'Grid-ironing' and 'spotting', as these selective practices were called, were certainly used by many runholders to tie up large areas, though probably not to the extent alleged by horrified land tenure radicals in later years.

2. *transf.* To select (a gold claim).
1878 McINDOE *Sketch Otago* 15 The goldseeker is at liberty to prospect and 'spot' any claim he may fancy as a payable one.

spot, *v.*[2] [f. SPOT *n.*[1]] *trans.* and *intr.* To treat (oneself) to a drink of liquor. Also as a *vbl. n.* **spotting,** occasional drinking.
1926 DEVANNY *Lenore Divine* 58 He knew that most girls, quite 'nice girls', 'spotted' themselves nowadays, and he had never before met a girl who shuddered at the mere smell of spirits or beer. 1930 *Northern Advocate* 11 July 7 [Heading] The 'Spotting' Habit. Young people of 16 and over..thought it bright and clever to appear 'three sheets in the wind' at country dances and made a practice of running out after every dance to motor cars to 'have a spot'. 1947 GASKELL *All Part of the Game* (1978) 84 It was a pity Taumarunui was dry. She could do with a few spots herself to take away the taste of these last two weeks. *Ibid.* 189 [1978 *note*] 'spots'. Any alcoholic drinks, but usually spirits. The verbal forms 'to spot' and 'spotting' were common. 1950 CHERRILL *NZ Sheep Farm* 73 Pa wouldn't have got into the way of spotting the way he has. 1987 HARTLEY *Swagger on Doorstep* 180 Mother believed dancing was worldly if not sinful, and she was frightened that we might start 'spotting'. Mother's twin fears were carnal sin and having a 'spot'.

spot, *n.*[1] [Spec. use of *spot* a small quantity, in Brit. use usu. with *of*: see OED *n.*[1] 7 d; AND 1922.] A drink of alcoholic liquor.
1917 *Great Adventure* (1988) 180 The rumour [of whiskey available] had..a foundation of fact so we gave them a 'spot' each. 1925 HICKEY *'Red' Fed. Memoirs* 31 [A] goodly number were non-drinkers, and those who did take a 'spot' confined their imbibing to 'bobs in'. 1930 DEVANNY *Bushman Burke* 200 The

'spot' she craved, or failing that a cup of tea, was nowhere about. **1946** SARGESON *That Summer* 59 We got a couple of them to come outside for a spot, but they went crook when we spilt beer. **1956** DARE *Rouseabout Jane* 133 Apparently it was the 'done thing' at the end of every dance to invite your partner to have a 'spot' in the car. **1967** MACNICOL *Echoes Skippers Canyon* 90 'Couple of spots, please.' suggested Archie. 'No whisky,' said Mr Leather Apron. **1976** MORRIESON *Pallet on Floor* 118 'Got a bottle of sherry here,' she said. 'Come in and have a spot, Joe.' **1987** [see SPOT *v.*²]. **1995** ANDERSON *House Guest* 44 George had always asked the neighbours in for a 'spot' at Christmas.

spot, *n.*²

1. [AND 1945.] One hundred dollars, formerly one hundred pounds; a currency note of either of those denominations.
  1963 *Truth* 21 May 19 The ice hockey gives me one, so I front at the nanny goat and see that it's paying a spot... a spot..£100.00. **1982** NEWBOLD *Big Huey* (Gloss.) 254 Spot (n) One hundred dollars. **1995** *Dominion* (Wellington) 11 Sept. 8 This was an old bookmaker, who still owed me [*sc.* David Lange M.P.] what he would call two spots. That..was my fee for defending him. If you paid your lawyer $200 today your entire defence would have to advance in four minutes.

2. *Shearing.* See quot.
  1989 *NZ Eng. Newsletter* III. 28 *spot:* This generally means a hundred and is used to refer to both a shearing tally and the amount on a pay cheque. 'He shore his first two spot yesterday' or 'I need to draw four spot'.

spotless crake: see CRAKE b.

spotlight, *v.* [See OED *v.*² 'Chiefly *U.S.*'; Webster 1934.] *intr.* To hunt game or kill wild animals (occas. to spear flounders) at night by spotlight.
  c1938 *Marlborough spotlight:* used of shooting rabbits by spotlights on automobiles, and also of fishing for flounders with spear by spotlight, usu. called torching. **1973** FERNANDEZ *Tussock Fever* 47 They even drove around the home paddocks at night spotlighting and cut a fence where they found a gate locked against them. **1983** *Press* (Christchurch) 18 Jan. 7 Counsel..submitted..that both men profoundly regretted the offence, which had been..while they were spotlighting for rabbits.
  Hence **spotlighter** *n.*, see quot. 1952; **spotlighting** *vbl. n.* and *ppl.a.*, the practice of using a spotlight to search out then kill wild animals (and occas. fish) at night.
  1952 *Straight Furrow* Oct. 7 The West Coast has coined a new term for hunters who move abroad at night shooting deer that roam down to the main highways. The name given to these hunters are 'spotlighters'. **1991** *Dominion* (Wellington) 18 Sept. 9 They set up camp about 10pm and as they walked into a clearing a spotlight shone on them. The group thought the spotlighters had seen and heard them. **1968** GLEN *Holy Joe's People* 49 He took me out in the dark as we were going on what he called a '**spotlightin**' trip' [after deer]. **1981** HOOPER *Goat Paddock* 20 About half-past twelve Max decided to take a turn along the main road, although spot-lighting from the road was illegal, but at that hour we'd be unlucky to be caught. **1995** CRUMP *Bushwoman* 93 [The possums] were keeping him awake on the nights when he wasn't out spotlighting.

spotted, *a.* In the names of animals 'marked with spots or blotches', see: DOGFISH 1, GROPER 2 (1), GURNARD 2 (4), KIWI 2 (2), PIGFISH 2 (1), SHAG 2 (16), STARGAZER 2 (5), WAREHOU 2 (3).

spotted tommy. Also *ellipt.* **tommy.** [f. *spotted* 'including dried fruit' + Brit. dial. *tommy* (a loaf of) bread, provisions (see OED *n.* 2); thus, dial. *spotted Tommy* a currant or raisin loaf or steamed pudding: see EDD *spotted* (9).] A raisin or currant loaf; a steamed raisin or currant pudding. See also BROWNIE 2 a, SPOTTY 3.
  [*Note*] The synonyms *spotted boy, spotted dick, spotted dog* have also been used in New Zealand as elsewhere.
  1913 BATHGATE *Sodger Sandy's Bairn* 148 A piece of home-made bread with currants in it, commonly called 'spotted Tommy'... It will make the 'tommy' taste of tobacco. **1918** *Chron. NZEF* 30 Aug. 61 I crept out at daylight with only a chunk of ham and 'spotted Tommy' in my pocket. **1934** HARPER *Windy Island* 221 [Shearers' rations in the 1890s included] once a week, usually on Wednesdays, bread made with currants, which the men called 'tommy'. **1941** BAKER *NZ Slang* 57 *tommy*, a country term for bread baked with currants and sugar.

spotty. Also **spottie.** [f. *spotty a.* having spots, spotted.]

1. Usu. *Notolabrus* (formerly *Pseudolabrus*, earlier *Labrichthys*) *celidotus* (fam. Labridae), a medium-sized (10–20 cm average) reef-fish of variable colour but essentially brownish-olive to yellowish with yellow fins, common in shallow water and providing a favourite children's catch; also occas. any of various other small spotted marine fishes. See also BUTTERFISH 2, GUFFY, KELPFISH 2, KELPIE *n.*¹ 3, PAKETI, PAKIRIKIRI 1.
  1878 [see BUTTERFISH 2]. **1879** *TrNZI* XI. 384 There are two kinds of spotties, big and little. The Wrasse and Parrotfish are mostly caught outside among the kelp, and with the Spotty are indiscriminately named Kelpfish by the fishermen. **1892** *Ibid.* XXIV. 211 Wrasse, or Spotty (*Labrichthys bothryocosmus*). Number of fish recorded—36. Localities—Mokohinou, the Brothers, Bligh Sound, Milford Sound. **1901** *Ibid.* XXXIII. 219 They were 'spotties', those voracious little sea-fish so well known round the wharves and harbours of our coast. **1921** *NZJST* IV. 117 Pseudolabrus celidotus... *Spotty*. Common in all shallow water in rocky localities. Large examples are sold as 'butterfish' in Dunedin. **1943** HISLOP *Pure Gold* 28 Noon saw us back [from the Pleasant River mouth]..with..a great catch which also included a few spotties. **1956** GRAHAM *Treasury NZ Fishes* 275 The name Spotty is derived from the presence of spots on each side of the fish. **1967** [see KELPFISH 2]. **1972** DOAK *Fishes* 85 Sooner or later a busy, little spotty, sculls past me near the bottom. His jerky swimming style reminds me of a butterfly. **1981** *Marlborough Sounds* 79 Frozen squid and fresh spottie meat make good baits. **1982** AYLING *Collins Guide* (1984) 255 Spotties are usually restricted to water less than 30m deep... Fishing for spotties is usually restricted to small children who often catch females when dangling their sprat lines off wharves.

2. *Deerfarming.* See quot. 1982, from fawns having a spotted hide.
  1959 SLATTER *Gun in My Hand* 169 I could get right back into the bush and live in deer cullers' huts... I know a lovely little valley where I've shot some spikers and some nice spotties when the fawns are about. **1982** *Agric. Gloss.* (MAF) 22 *Spottie*: Young deer (usually fallow) up to 3 months of age.

3. A familiar form of SPOTTED TOMMY.
  1981 SUTHERLAND & TAYLOR *Sunrise* 44 Mr Knox as he came down [to the mustering camp] for a pannikin of tea and a helping of spottie.

4. As **spotties**, a name for measles.
  1953 14 M A6 Thames DHS 31 Spotties [M3]

spout.

1. In the obsolete phr. **up the spout**, a marble game.
  1840 POLACK *Manners & Customs* I. 92 Several old gentlemen 'bearded like a pard', were distanced at full length playing with round pebbles, the primitive schoolboy game, known to vulgar ken as 'up the spout'. *Ibid.* II. 170 Playing at marbles 'up the spout' and at 'buttons in the hole'.

2. *Shearing.* In the phr. **to go up the spout**, see quot.
  1989 *NZ Eng. Newsletter* III. 24 *going up the neck:* This expression refers to the blows on a sheep from the brisket towards the head. 'Opening up the neck' or 'going up the spout' mean the same thing.

spouter. [Cf. OED *n.* 1 c, 1840, 1901.] A whaling ship.
  1981 MANSON *Widow of Thorndon Quay* 2 Port Underwood itself, puncturing the northern end of Cloudy Bay, was a hub of activity in 1842, with sometimes large numbers of whaling ships—or 'spouters'—of many nations lying at anchor for the season.

spout wind. *Obs.* A Nelson name for a local wind.
  1856 SEWELL *Journal* 20 Apr. (1980) II. 227 [We] met in Blind Bay an unexpected enemy in the shape of a wind called a Spout wind, blowing right in our teeth. **1862** HODDER *Memories NZ Life* 46 [The Waimea] is visited by a strong local wind, which blows with considerable violence, especially during the summer months. It is called the 'spout wind', and is attributable to the peculiar configuration of the mountain ranges. **1864** HOCHSTETTER & PETERMAN *Geol. NZ* 81 The 'spout wind', blowing with considerable violence during the summer from the south, is a local wind of Blind Bay, due to the same physical configuration of the country. **1873** WILSON *Diary* 14 Feb. in Wierzbicka *Wilson Family* (1973) 177 There was a pretty strong wind blowing, what they call a 'spout wind' from the fact of its coming down the valley on the town. **1875** COCKBURN-HOOD *Chowbokiana* 77 Nelson, though it has its 'spout wind' possesses generally a happy freedom from destructive gales.

sprag, *n.* [Brit. dial.: poss. related to *sprig*: see EDD *sprag n.*¹ a large nail, and *v.*¹ 4.]

1. A spike (of metal) such as a strand protruding from a wire rope, the sharp end of a single wire, or a piece of jagged metal, that can snag or spike one's flesh, clothing, etc. Also as a *verb*, to injure (a limb), or catch, on a sprag.
  1957 *NZ Forest Service* (T.S. Accident Rep.) (Nelson) 23 Nov. 'While hauling on a winch-rope [*sc.* a wire rope], I spragged my fore-finger through the glove I was wearing.' *Comment* [by the authority]. 'The wire spragg [*sic*] became embedded in [X's] finger.'

2. Special Comb. **sprag-hand**, a septic condition (mainly of wire-rope handlers) caused by spragging on wire-ropes.
  1985 *Ship n Shore* (Official Jrnl. NZ Stevedores etc. Union) May 7 For all these long years I've been lumbered With Gear-Store related complaints. From 'spragg-hand' through handling bum wires, To throwing-up, wobblies and faints.

sprat. [Transf. use of the northern hemisphere name *sprat* for any of several small New Zealand fish.] Usu. either of two similar small marine fish of the genus *Sprattus* (fam. Clupeidae), *S.*

SPREAD

antipodum or *S. muelleri*, having dark oily flesh (see also KUPAE); or the *yellow-eyed mullet* (MULLET 2 (3)), known as HERRING q.v.

1849 *NZ Jrnl.* IX. 125 English Name... Sprat or Sardine... Native Name... Aua. **1872** HUTTON & HECTOR *Fishes NZ* 133 Clupea sprattus, *var.* antipodum. New Zealand Sprat. **1886** [see KUPAE]. **1902** DRUMMOND & HUTTON *Nature in NZ* The sprats, which come into shallow water in the winter. **1913** *TrNZI* XLV. 234 *Amblygaster antipodus*... The sprat, which is very common on the east coast..is frequently mistaken for the [*Clupea neopilchardus*] species. **1927** SPEIGHT et al. *Nat. Hist. Canterbury* 195 The Southern Pilchard..and the New Zealand Sprat (*Clupea antipodum*) are known from Canterbury. **1939** BEATTIE *First White Boy Born Otago* 22 I recollect the Maoris going after sprats at Matannic... They dried the sprats on mats and ate them dried. **1957** PARROTT *Sea Angler's Fishes* 28 The New Zealand Sprat is referred to in older publications, under several names, e.g. *Clupea sprattus*, *Clupea antipodum*, *Amblygaster antipodus* and *Harengula antipodum*. **1967** [see MULLET 2 (3)]. **1970** SORENSEN *Nomenclature NZ Fish* 40 Pilchard... Other common names: Sardine; Sprat; Anchovy; Herring. **1981** WILSON *Fisherman's Bible* 164 The Yellow-Eye has a much narrower head than the Grey [mullet] and is the ubiquitous, but misnamed 'sprat' or 'herring' of our wharves.

spread, *v.*

1. In the phr. **to spread one's blanket**, to bed down.

1891 CHAMIER *Philosopher Dick* 415 The men..asked permission to 'spread their blankets' in the wool-shed.

2. Hence **spreader** *obs.*, in early whalers' or traders' parlance, a blanket.

1845 WAKEFIELD *Adventure NZ* I. 319 Every article of trade with the natives has its slang term,—in order that they may converse with each other respecting a purchase without initiating the natives into their calculations. Thus pigs and potatoes were respectively represented by '*grunters*' and '*spuds*', guns, powder, blankets, pipes, and tobacco, by '*shooting-sticks*', '*dust*', '*spreaders*', '*steamers*', and '*weed*'.

sprig.

1. [See OED *sprig n*[1] 2 'chiefly N.Z.'.] One of a group of studs on the sole of a (usu. rugby football) boot.

1949 DAVIN *Roads from Home* 1 ii 27 John hammered the last tack into a sprig of his football boots. **1952** ORBELL *Comfort & Commonsense in the Bush* 29 To overcome this difficulty..the writer buys a pair of football boots, the sprigs are removed and a thin extra sole is fitted the full length of the boot. **1967** HENDERSON *Return to Open Country* 70 The boots are very heavy, with sprigs all over the soles, and the heels have three sharps spikes to prevent slipping. **1969** bush sprigs [see *ferntights* (FERN 3 d)]. **1979** *Listener* 18 Aug. 13 It's all right... You don't feel the sprigs when you're fit! **1981** *Listener* 2 May The *sprig* (though it has acquired new meaning on the football field), was originally a short headless nail. **1986** CONEY *Playing Mantis* 112 The English malthoid..almost trips me, dragging at my [cricket-boot] sprigs.

Hence **sprigging** *vbl. n.*, an injurious raking (with sprigs) in a ruck of a grounded rugby union opponent.

1977 MCLEAN *Winter of Discontent* 119 He [*sc.* Wyllie] was shattered by..the knowledge that if he had been spared a serious sprigging of the calf muscle of one leg he almost certainly would have led Canterbury to their 20th victory.

2. Special Comb. **sprig-mark**, the result of a 'sprigging' at rugby football; also *transf.*, a sign of being visibly discomforted in an altercation; **sprig-stomping**, the deliberate stamping on a recumbent rugby (union) opponent with sprigged boots.

1972 *Guardian* 11 Nov. 21 You look at Sid [Going] when we're changing, he's got sprig (stud) marks all over him. **1987** GEE *Prowlers* 179 A Cassidy or Brady who challenged her on some union matter would end up with sprig marks on his face. **1990** SHELFORD & GRAY *Buck The Wayne Shelford Story* 107 The more sprig marks he [*sc.* Shelford] has over him, the happier he seems to be. **1993** *Dominion* (Wellington) 13 Aug. 12 With head-butting, sprig-stomping and now eye-gouging players..representing the game at provincial, national and international level, is it not time it was renamed thugby?

spruce. *Hist.* [Transf. use of northern hemisphere *spruce (fir) Pinus* or *Abies* spp.]

1. Also **spruce (New Zealand spruce) fir**. RIMU *n.*[1]

1773 COOK *Journals* 1 Apr. (1961) II. 134 The most considerable [timber] here [in Dusky Sound]..is the spruce tree as we call'd it from the similarity of its leaves to the America black spruce, but the wood is more ponderous and of a redish [*sic*] colour. **1791** MENZIES *Journal* 4 Nov. in McNab *Hist. Records* (1914) II. 484 We found large trees [at Dusky Bay] of what has been called New Zealand Spruce. **1793** *Raven to Lieut. Gov. King* 19 Nov. in McNab *Hist. Records* (1908) I. 178 She [*sc.* a ship built in Dusky Bay] is planked, decked, and ceiled with the spruce fir, which in the opinion of the carpenter is very little inferior to English oak. **1817** NICHOLAS *NZ* II. 247 Of the other trees noticed by Capt. Cook..is one resembling the American spruce fir, and from the leaves of which a very wholesome liquor was brewed. This was called the New Zealand spruce fir, from its similarity to the former tree.

2. spruce beer. [Transf. use of *spruce beer*, a fermented beverage made from the leaves and branchlet tips of the northern hemisphere spruce fir: see OED, 1744.] A name given to an antiscorbutic drink made from the tips of rimu branches by Cook and other early sailors.

1773 *Bayly's Journal* 12 Apr. in McNab *Historical Records* (1914) II. 206 The largest [trees] are the spruce tree (from the tops of the branches of which we made Spruce Beer which was very good). **1777** FORSTER *Voyage Round the World* I. 143 But the constant supply of fresh fish..together with the spruce-beer and the myrtle-tea, contributed to keep us healthy..even in this damp climate. **1791** BELL *Journal of Voyage in H.M.S. 'Chatham'* Nov. (ATLTS) 45 The Cooper was sent on shore [at Dusky Bay] to sett [*sic*] up the Casks—and a Party was sent Brewing Spruce Beer. **1839** TAYLOR *Journal* 14 Nov. (TSATB) II. 171 I feel assured a pleasant beverage like spruce beer might be manufactured from its [*sc.* kauri's] sap.

sprug: see SPUG.

spruik /spruːk/, *v. Obs.* [Of unknown origin; AND 1902.] To speak out in an exaggerated fashion; to make such a speech, esp. one advertising goods or entertainment to the public.

1907 *Truth* 6 Apr. 6 When did you see me working last? queried Diggs—Spruiking for Tanner's Ark, last week. (Smiles). **1913** *Hutt Valley Independent* 6 Sept. 2 One wonders where Chairman Webb raised all the flapdoodle he spruiked about the youthful town clerk's qualifications. **1968** *NZ Contemp. Dict. Suppl.* (Collins) 18 *spruik v.i.* (*Sl.*) make a speech, whence *spruiker*, one who talks the public into entering a booth at showgrounds or buying cheap goods.

SPUD

spruiker /ˈspruːkə/. [f. SPRUIK *v.*]

1. *Obs.* [AND 1902.] A showy talker; a 'spouter'.

1906 *Truth* 24 Feb. 5 Off to Wales the All-Blacks sped, When the Cymric spruiker started. **1917** *Truth* 13 Oct. 1 Some spruikers who start out by telling the people that they have nothing to say, take [a] long time to say it. **1926** *NZ Observer* 13 Mar. 3 And then there are..a few other similar shows the 'spruikers' of which have entertaining ways. **1962** WEBBER *Look No Hands* 83 'Very interesting [talk]!' said the Bloke. 'I always said you were the spruiker of your unit.' **1972** PREBBLE *Horses, Courses & Men* 124 The incessant call of the 'sprukers' [*sic*] and the bookmakers above the hubbub of the punters' voices, gave an air of excitement and urgency.

2. *WW2.* A fellow; JOKER *n.*[1] 1.

1944 *NZEF Times* 4 Dec. 5 'I got the NZEF Times today, he said' said the Bloke, 'and I see you two spruikers have had it.'.. 'I see you missed it this week and you're out the monk, says this rooster,' said the Bloke.

spud.

1. [Transf. or fig. use of *spud* a digging implement for 'something dug up': used elsewhere but recorded earliest in NZ: see OED *n.* 5.] An informal word for a potato.

1845 WAKEFIELD *Adventure NZ* I. 319 Every article of trade with the natives has its slang term,—in order that they may converse with each other respecting a purchase without initiating the natives into their calculations. Thus pigs and potatoes were respectively represented by '*grunters*' and '*spuds*'. **1852** *Household Words* 13 Mar. IV. 585-88 in La Roche *Hist. of Howick & Pakuranga* (1991) 102 Potatoes (colonially speaking, 'spuds') are bought at from a shilling..the hundred weight. **1858** *Puketoi Station Diary* 1 Dec. in Beattie *Early Runholding* (1947) 75 Planted spuds. **1867** PHILLIPS *Rockwood Jrnl.* 22 Apr. (Canterbury Pub. Lib. TS) 110 Digging spuds. **1871** MONEY *Knocking About NZ* 68 [We] put on a pot of spuds; [and then] made a good duff. **1928** *NZ Free Lance* (Wellington) 29 Feb. 34 The late Rt. Hon. Mr. Massey..used to proudly boast..that not even frosts..and politicians could prevent the Pukekohe 'spud' and strong onion from coming into the market. **1946** SOLJAK *NZ* 116 The following New Zealand expressions derive from British dialects. *spud:* potato. **1972** in *21 Years of Rugby News* (1991) 30 Points Not Spuds. Bob Burrell didn't play against the Lions last winter because he'd been hit in the eye by a potato.

Hence **spudding** *ppl. a.*, potato-digging or potato-collecting.

1860 *Taranaki Punch* V. 3 [Long nails] would entirely supersede the use of [forks] on the next spudding expedition [to feed the troops].

2. *transf. Obs.* As **Mokikinui spud** [f. *Mokikinui* a former goldfield, now a township and river north of Westport on the w. coast of the SI], see quot.

1884 REID *Rambles on Golden Coast* 72 They will show..specimens of alluvial gold, heavy, water-worn flattened nuggets, 'Mokikinui Spuds' they fondly call them, which miners dig out sometimes even with their sheath knives.

3. An adolescents' term of abuse or contempt.

1990 *Dominion Sunday Times* (Wellington) 22 Apr. 4 If you're called [by adolescents] a..spud..you've been insulted... Spud—spat off the tongue and accompanied by a sneer—can, in some schools, also be used as a verb or adjective, though its meaning becomes increasingly vague.

4. Special Comb. **spud-barber** [OED *n.* 8, 1935], a cook's helper who peels potatoes; **spud**

SPUG | 770 | **SQUAT**

Monday, a special day in Nelson, the first Monday in August, often dedicated to the early planting of potatoes.
1928 *NZ Free Lance* (Wellington) 21 Mar. 17 Its arrangements [*sc.* the hospital's] provide for the mechanical peeling of potatoes, only the eyes being left for the attention of the '**spud-barber**'. **1927** *NZ Tablet* (Dunedin) 14 Sept. 58 A Nelsonian became quite excited..and informed us all Nelson would be holding a holiday that day. She said they called it '**Spud Monday**' in the garden province because it was the first day of spring and the new potatoes were to be planted that week. **1937** *NZ Railways Mag.* Oct. 23 Its first of spring [*sc.* in Nelson] is called by the practical, if unlovely, name of 'Spud Monday'. **1978** *PSA Jrnl.* Oct. 14 [An endearing feature of Nelson is the holiday called 'Spud Monday'.] It started when the young settlement depended on visiting boats for many supplies... The ship was delayed... When supplies came, the half-starving community declared a holiday and a feast of potatoes. This day which coincided with England's August Bank Holiday was thereafter held as 'Spud Monday'.

5. In the phr. **spuds and mutton** (or *vice versa*), the stereotype of poor station or farm fare.
1952 BLAKISTON *My Yesteryears* 46 On the old days at some stations, when a swagger arrived, he reported himself to the owner or the manager and received a ticket which he had to present to the station cook. He then either received 'spuds and mutton' or sat down at the table with the station hands. **1975** NEWTON *Sixty Thousand on the Hoof* 103 With the usual mid-day meal simply cold mutton and spuds, these shearers one day decided that something better was called for.

spug. Also **sprug**. [f. Sc. and n. Brit. dial. *sprug*, *spug*: see EDD; cf. AND *spag*.] A sparrow. See also SPADGER.
c1920s p.c. J. Winchester (Wellington) *spug* for 'sparrow' often used by boys. **1935** p.c. A. Campbell (Dunedin) *spug* used in Dunedin by schoolboys as a name for a sparrow. **1964** LEE *Shiner Slattery* 49 I'll have you know it's a sparrow, a common spug. **1969** HENDERSON *Open Country Calling* 142 Sparrows were always called 'spugs' or 'spadges'. **1977** HOLCROFT *Line of the Road* 111 It may be assumed also that boys hunted the dread sparrows and may have called them 'spugs'—as boys did elsewhere in the country. **1984** TRAIL *Child of Arrow* 95 One Saturday morning we discovered a tree with a whole colony of sparrows'—or sprugs, as we called them—nests in the upper branches.

spur: see COCKSPUR.

spurdog: see DOGFISH.

spurge. [Spec. use of *spurge*, *Euphorbia* spp.] Usu. with a modifier **Maori (New Zealand) spurge**. Any of several naturalized or native 'milkweeds' of *Euphorbia* spp. (fam. Euphorbiaceae), herbs or shrubs with poisonous milky sap and a cup-shaped structure surrounding the flowers; also **sun spurge** *Euphorbia glauca*, a native coastal herb with pale blue-green leaves and dark red flowers. See also WAIU-ATUA.
1869 *TrNZI* I. (rev. edn.) 208 Sun spurge. Euphorbia glauca. **1911** *AJHR* C-13 37 *Euphorbia glauca*. Waiuatua New Zealand spurge. Sand-grass dune. Herb, tall, sand-binder. **1940** LAING & BLACKWELL *Plants NZ* 236 (*The Glaucous Euphorbia*). A shining, glaucous herb... Both islands: sea-beaches. Not uncommon. Fl. Oct. Feb...(Maori spurge). **1952** RICHARDS *Chatham Is.* 33 This seagreen sturdy plant 1–3 ft. high is full of burning milky juice... New Zealand Spurge. Waiu-atua

(milk spirit). **1981** BROOKER et al. *NZ Medicinal Plants* 53 Euphorbia glauca Common name: *Maori spurge* Maori names: *Waiuokahukura, waiuatua*.

spurtle /ˈspɜrtəl/. *Otago-Southland*. Also **spirtle**. [f. Sc. and n. Brit. dial. *spurtle* a stick for stirring porridge.] A wooden porridge-stirrer.
1986 OWEN & PERKINS *Speaking for Ourselves* 35 He'd arrived at one time and found the Lower Pyke hut in a mess, and he grabbed a spirtle and waved it in the air and beat it up and down and said, 'The buggers and the bastards!' **1987** *Listener* 20 June 93 I wonder how many New Zealanders of Celtic origin still do the proper thing and call oatmeal 'them' and not 'it', stir it with a stick, or spurtle, and not a spoon.

squah, var. SQUAW.

square, *a*. In special collocations: **Square Dinks**, see DINK *n*. 1 b; **square dinkum**, **Square Dinkums** see DINKUM A 1 a, B 3, C 1 d; **square-face** *obs*. [f. the shape of the square-faced bottle in which gin was sold: AND 1903], see *square gin*; also a square-faced bottle orig. holding gin, see SQUARE RIGGER 1; **square gin** [AND 1871], Geneva gin sold in a square-faced bottle.
1906 *Red Funnel* II. 201 The '**square-face**' had loosened his tongue. **1918** *Quick March* 1 Nov. 23 They have their 'square-face' and their sherry. **1934** *Press* (Christchurch) (Acland Gloss.) 27 Jan. 15 *Square face.*—Square gin. **1940** STUDHOLME *Te Waimate* (1954) 173 [Gin] at that time [in the 1880s] cost only four shillings a bottle for 'Square Face'. **1910** *Truth* 4 June 7 It is not quite certain, at least in the police court, what one should call the bottles... A good old-fashioned name is a '**square-face**,' but in the court the other day 'square rigger' was the term used..while Counsel went so far as to call it a 'square-rigged bottle.'.. A J.D.K.Z. bottle will always hold the regulation sixpence worth no matter what it's called. **1912** *Truth* 13 Apr. 7 The stranger said he had brought two square-faces of beer home. **1918** *Quick March* 2 Sept. 15 The prohibitionists are circulating petitions for a poll to abolish kegs, casks, demijohns, square-faces, pewters, and all other appurtenances of 'joy-juice'. **1970** SANSOM *Stewart Islanders* 45 He stepped off, but with no confidence, in another direction; we scrabbled around and there it was, an old 'black-jack' or 'square-face' which had held gin in the early days. **1870** *TrNZI* II. 173 Before disturbing the water, I filled two **square gin** bottles. **1873** PYKE *Wild Will Enderby* (1889, 1974) III. i. 76 The only news I could discover was that..there weren't no square gin in the market. [*Ibid.* I iv 17 So scarce was [timber at the Dunstan] that an empty gin-case—a J.D.K.Z., anchor-branded gin-case—was considered rather a good bargain at £2.] **1882** HAY *Brighter Britain* I. 99 He also sells, at seven shillings a bottle, the most atrocious rum, brandy, or 'square' gin. **1906** BULLEN *Cruise 'Cachalot'* 309 The natives evinced the greatest eagerness to get drunk [at Russell], swallowing down the horrible 'square gin' as if it were water. **1991** *North & South* (Auckland) June 32 A rigger, or square gin bottle, would be filled with beer for a few pence.

square, *n*. [Spec. use of *square n*.]
1. *Hist*. A sub-division of a South Island Survey District.
1952–53 *NZ Forest Service Gloss.* (TS) *Square*. Under the old land-subdivision system for Nelson, Marlborough and North Canterbury, a subdivision of a Provincial District.

2. [f. the angular shape.] *sand flounder* (FLOUNDER *n*. 2 (9)).
1960 [see DIAMOND]. **1970** [see PLAICE].

square, *v*. *Prison*. As **square off** [AND 1943], to settle a difference, to apologize.
1968 *NZ Contemp. Dict. Suppl.* (Collins) 18 *square (off)* v.i. apologise, produce a glib explanation for a lapse. **1982** NEWBOLD *Big Huey* 157 When he [*sc.* an unpopular screw] tried to square off and asked us if we'd like to knock off early one day, we told him we'd rather work. *Ibid.* 254 Square off (v) Apologise, make amends, attempt to justify oneself.

square rigger. Also **square-rigged bottle**. [Orig. a square quart bottle for gin, with a suggestion of a word-play on *square-rigger*, a square-rigged ship: see RIGGER.]
1. a. A 'square' gin bottle holding approx. a quart; also its contents (often beer). See also RIGGER, *square-face* (SQUARE *a*.). Also *attrib*.
1909 *Truth* 3 July 5 Square-riggers of beer and small flasks of brandy were the favorite [p]otions the ladies lovingly lapped. **1910** [see *square-face* (SQUARE *a*.)]. **1914** [see *blue peter* (BLUE 1)]. **1931** CLOKE *Songs NZ* 130 Rise, ye bushmen and gumdiggers, From the Wairoa's slimy ooze, Where you've sunk with your square-riggers, With your brain on fire with booze! **1941** *NZEF Times* 4 Aug. 4 What we really need is a few more square riggers. **1962** LAWLOR *More Wellington Days* 21 A 'square rigger' (a full-sized empty gin bottle) would be filled for 8d. **1981** HUNT *Speaking a Silence* 126 Old Gus eventually trotted out with his square rigger to take on his way. (Those riggers were the old, square gin bottles, too. They held easy a quart of grog.)

b. *transf.* A half-gallon flagon of beer.
1988 MCGILL *Dict. Kiwi Slang* 106 squarerigger half-gallon jar of beer, named after gin bottles recycled for beer pre-WW2; *Squarerigger Gully* a working class inner suburb of Wellington so called because of men coming home from the pub up Aro Street with their squareriggers of beer.

2. *Obs*. A quart-sized square-faced bottle as a common container for bulk ink for school inkwells.
1968 SLATTER *Pagan Game* 98 A square rigger of ink almost empty.

squaretail. *Tetragonurus cuvieri* (fam. Tetragonuridae), a rare elongate (20–40 cm) fish having a squarish tail peduncle.
1920 *NZJST* III. 223 In October, 1918, Mr. R. Strahl sent to the Canterbury Museum a fish..identified as a specimen of the squaretail, *Tetragonurus cuvieri* Risso, the first recorded from New Zealand. **1956** GRAHAM *Treasury NZ Fishes* 405 Squaretail *Tetragonurus cuvieri wilkinsoni*. **1967** NATUSCH *Animals NZ* 217 Sub-order Stromateoidae. This group includes rare fish like the square-tail, *Tetragonurus cuvieri*..twice found off Kaikoura. **1982** AYLING *Collins Guide* (1984) 306 Squaretail... There is a pair of distinct lateral keels on each side of the base of the deeply forked tail giving the caudal peduncle a squarish cross-section that is presumably responsible for the common name of this fish.

squashed fly biscuit. Fruit-square biscuits, comprising two crackers joined by a dried-fruit filling. See also FLY-CEMETERY.
1982 DRUMMOND in Lush *Waikato Jrnls.* 21 I also brought two penny worth of fly kooks for Martin. [1982 *Note*] Cookies, known to generations of children as 'squashed fly biscuits'.

squat /skwɒt/, *v*. *Hist*. [Orig. US *squat* to settle on unoccupied land without legal title: see OED *v*. 9.] Occas. **squat on**.

SQUATOCRACY

1. *intr.* **a.** To occupy rural Maori or Crown land without (or with doubtful) legal title.
   1840 WAKEFIELD *Diary* (ATLMS) (1839) 11 June Mr Shortland says anyone may squat anywhere, until the proposed commission from Sydney shall have decided on titles to land. **1844** MONRO *Notes of a Journey* in Hocken *Contributions* (1898) 233 We anchored in the first place in a small bay..where a Mr. Greenwood has lately squatted, and has a considerable number of cattle and sheep. **1854** GOLDER *Pigeons' Parliament* 68 Some spot, Found here and there where cotters squat With self-permission. **1857** *Richmond-Atkinson Papers* (1960) I. 278 A European squats down on Maori land and the Government grant him a license [*sic*]. The natives object to it and protest against it but in vain. **1966** SCOTT *Days That Have Been* 120 [A Lands & Survey Dept officer advises a farmer:] 'We'll settle the price [for a departmental farm, c1930] later... You can take my word for it. Just squat there with your stock and good luck to you.' **1984** MARSHALL & STARTUP *From the Bay to the Bush* 49 The Murimotu plains south of the central volcanoes were 'squatted on' by venturous sheep farmers in the late 1860s as they moved ever further westward from Hawkes Bay.

b. Occas. of a Maori, to occupy Pakeha land against the occupier's wishes.
   1942 [see SQUATTER 1 c].

2. In early settlement, to occupy temporarily a (projected) town site while awaiting more permanent accommodation.
   1840 *NZ Jrnl.* I. 220 The Oriental passengers chose to squat on [the river's] banks. **1850** TORLESSE *Papers* (1958) 183 Some of the labouring emigrants sent out to me to have pointed out the site of the market place for them to squat upon. **1930** GUTHRIE *NZ Memories* 37 Here most of the emigrants from the first three ships had squatted, but there were no barracks or shelter of any kind.

Hence **squat** *n.*, by back-formation, an area of land on which to squat.
   1887 *Auckland Weekly News* 23 July 21 Maruiceville is a 'special settlement' of Scandinavian squatters—a 50-acre section is about the average squat.

squatocracy, var. SQUATTOCRACY.

squattage /ˈskwɒtədʒ/. *Obs.* [AND 1846.] An area of grazing land taken up by a squatter.
   1875 COCKBURN-HOOD *Chowbokiana* 82 [Men] took up large squattages. **1910** *Truth* 17 Sept. 5 There was the case of bootmaker Skinner, who exchanged his city property for a run on the Wanganui river, found his squattage a sort of glorified graveyard.

squattah /ˈskwɒtɑ/. A spelling jocularly alluding to the aristocratic pretensions at times associated with the squatter class.
   1892 *Star* 15 June (Auckland) in Bailey & Roth *Shanties* (1967) 82 On we go to Canterbury, where the squattah, lordly, grand, Holds the fertile plains. **1905** *Truth* 19 Aug. 1 The big Hawkes Bay squattah, Sir William Russell, who has just returned to Maoriland.

squattaucracy, var. SQUATTOCRACY.

squatter. [Orig. US *squatter* a settler with no legal title to the land occupied: see OED *n.*¹ 1 a.]
1. *Obs.* [AND 1828.] **a.** One who occupies without (or with doubtful) legal title, Maori land, or such land as has been alienated to the Crown or to a land company.
   1840 *Bunbury's Rep.* in *GBPP House of Commons 1841 (No.311)* 111 By converting the cupidity of land jobbers and squatters into a source of remuneration and profit, the necessity for..a large and expensive force would..soon be diminished. **1840** *Evidence John Ward Rep. Sel. Committee NZ* 74 in Miller *Early Victorian NZ* 3 Aug. (1958) 21 His [*sc.* Wakefield's]..task was..then to acquire as much land as possible in order, it was stated, to 'keep off land-sharks and squatters'. **1844** TUCKETT *Diary* 18 Apr. in Hocken *Contributions* (1898) 213 There are nearly twenty other Europeans residing here [at Molyneux], most of whom have enclosures of cultivated land... If any claim has been advanced by any of these squatters, none has been approved by the Land Commissioners; yet they will consider themselves aggrieved if ejected from their dwellings without compensation. **1851** *Lyttelton Times* 12 Apr. 6 These large tracts of land if not let for pasturage, would either remain wholly useless or would be surreptitiously occupied by squatters in all directions, defying laws, and enjoying privileges to the detriment of the original land purchasers..viz., pasturage without extra payment. **1853** EARP *NZ* 238 If he do not choose to purchase or lease land, he may become a *squatter*; that is, he may set himself down beyond the boundaries of the settlement altogether... In the case of squatting, it is advisable to pay a small..tribute to the resident natives. **1958** MILLER *Early Victorian NZ* 137 Two weeks later the squatters, Bidwell, Weld and Clifford, edged warily round the coastal rocks..into the Wairarapa.

b. One who, having arranged land purchase from a land company, is, on arrival in New Zealand, temporarily occupying land belonging to others while awaiting the completion of that purchase.
   1841 PETRE *Settlements NZ Co.* 12 Squatters, waiting for our land. **1845** WAKEFIELD *Adventure NZ* I. 204 During this time, I either wandered about among the squatters, or chatted with the natives at Pitoni Pa.

c. Occas. applied to a Maori occupying land claimed by a Pakeha settler usu. in a dispute over title.
   1942 BUTLER *Early Days Taranaki* 18 Natives squatting on his land, threatening him, and robbing him, were partly responsible for William Billing losing his land near the Church Mission property at Ngamotu; this is the first instance of a settler having to give way, but in this Billing's wife was struck by the squatters.

2. [AND 1837.] One occupying a tract of Maori or Crown land to graze livestock, having title (or putative title) by lease. **a.** Of unalienated Maori land, by arrangement or lease from the Maori owners.
   1847 H.S. CHAPMAN *Let. to His Father* 24 Nov. (ATLTS) in Miller *Early Victorian NZ* (1958) 147 The Wairarapa settlers are uneasy about their tenure... At present they are the lessees of the Ngatikahunu [*sic*]... The sort of contract which the squatters make with the natives is void by the Common Law, for the 'Queen' is the only source of title. At Common Law therefore the lease is a mere nullity. **1848** WAKEFIELD *Handbook NZ* 235 [Mr Clifford] has formed a sheep-station, as a squatter, in the neighbourhood of Cape Campbell.

b. Of Crown land, by registered lease or licence.
   1851 GODLEY *Selection from the Writings* 4 June 205 Supposing a run to carry a sheep every two acres, and supposing that a squatter intending to stock a run of 20,000 acres fully in five years put 2000 sheep upon it the first year, which is the ordinary calculation. **1857** HURSTHOUSE *NZ* II. 397 Under some of the regulations..the sheep-farmer, or 'Squatter', as he is generally called, leases of the Government 15,000 to 30,000 acres of some of the wild grassy districts of the country. **1864** *Naturalization Act 28 Vict. Schedule* 4 26 May John Evans Brown, U. States of America, Squatter, Merivale Near Christchurch, Prov. of Canterbury, 1 Feb. 1864. **1877** BROOMHALL *Fragments from the Jrnl.* 41 The term squatter is well known but it is not polite to use it; and the squatter now-a-days is a settler. **1912** BOOTH *Five Years NZ* 18 It consisted of two huts... One of these contained the general kitchen.., the other was the residence of the squatter and his overseer. **1959** MCLINTOCK *Descr. Atlas* 38 From the stagnation they faced in the early 1840s, the Wakefield settlements were rescued by the energy of the young 'squatters'. **1968** DALZIEL *Vogel* 32 squatters: Men who occupy land either without any title or on easy terms from the Government.

3. [AND 1841.] A pastoralist or farmer distinguished by class-status and/or size of holding without reference to the title by which the land is held. **a.** A wealthy pastoralist as a member of a social and political elite. See also SQUATTOCRACY.
   1852 in *Canterbury Rhymes* (1866) 16 Oh! Squatters, beware of the Powers of the Air, When you come with your cattle or sheep. **1866** BARKER *Station Life* (1870) 47 The 'squatters' (as owners of sheep-stations are called) have returned to their stations to vegetate, or work, as their tastes and circumstances may dictate. **1871** MONEY *Knocking About NZ* 2 Half of the entire cuddy berths were occupied by a wealthy Canterbury squatter. **1883** MULHALL *England's New Sheep-farm* 10 The [table] above..explains..the importance that the squatters..have attained in a few years, some of them possessing fortunes equal to those of Brazilian coffee-planters. **1913** *NZ Observer* 5 July 4 To the person who has not broad lands, it is very wrong to be a squatter. **1934** MULGAN *Spur of Morning* 262 And he saw from a new angle that these big sheep people—whether they owned their land or leased it, as many back-country squatters did, from the State— were a distinct class which..was establishing its own traditions. **1943** *NZEF Times* 11 Oct. 2 [Caption] Ex-Hawke's Bay Squatters in Cairo. **1959** SLATTER *Gun in My Hand* 129 Squatters' sons never get married, they plight their troth. **1963** BAXTER *Collected Poems* (1980) 266 In a land where a wharfie's daughter can Marry some day a squatter's son. **1987** SCOTT *Seven Lives on Salt River* 85 Sir William..had escaped active service in the Anglo-Maori wars by selling his commission to become a Hawkes Bay squatter. **1991** ELDRED-GRIGG *Shining City* 15 She's been spending like a squatter since Frank Morgan kicked the bucket.

b. A pastoralist on a large-scale as distinct from a small-holding agriculturist or 'cockatoo'.
   1858 in *Canterbury Rhymes* (1866) 61 'Song of the Squatters'. He [*sc.* Robert Heaton Rhodes] the prince of all the squatters, Largest holder of runholders. **1873** TINNE *Wonderland of Antipodes* 37 On Titiowharu [=Titiokura]..I found the overseer..'mustering' sheep, which is the next important process to 'shearing' in the squatter's annual programme. **1879** SIMMONS *Old England & NZ* 63 Many farmers with small or medium sized holdings,—or 'cockatoos', as they are not too classically styled, to distinguish them from the 'squatters', who hold larger tracts of land for sheep runs and general purposes. **1886** *TrNZI* XVIII. 131 They are of great service to the squatters and farmers in consuming the larvae of *Odontria*. **1898** HOCKEN *Contributions* 197 Major Richardson was opposed to the gradually increasing encroachment of the squatters, and desired to see..the acquisition of land by all for agricultural purposes. **1899** BELL *In Shadow of Bush* 7 But de'il tak' the hour I agreed to gang amang the cockatoos wi' ye, Bill; an' I could wish mysel' back amang the squatters again. **1919** *Speeches & Documents* (1971) 301 quoting *Maoriland Worker* 3 Dec. A working farmer of New Zealand, like his fellow in Australia is beginning to realise that his interests and those of the squatter are not identical. **1944** *Short Guide NZ* 39 *Squatter*—farmer, generally sheep farmer on a big scale. **1974** AGNEW *Loner* 69 For a while he would

SQUATTERDOM

accept the..hospitality of the sheep station owners, or squatters as they were affectionately known, and put the bite on others. **1986** OWEN & PERKINS *Speaking for Ourselves* 68 Good weather and good grass, and all that sort of thing, made for a generous squatter.

4. a. Comb. **squatter interests**, **party**, **system**; see also SQUATTING 3 b.
1977 MARKS *Hammer & Tap* 510 The [Otago] Provincial Council was dominated by squatter interests. **1912** *Hutt Valley Independent* 31 Aug. 1 [Leading article] The Squatter Party: i.e., the conservative opponents of Liberalism. **1859** THOMSON *Story NZ* II. 198 Cheap land was injurious to the squatter system; as all who leased were uncomfortable until they bought them.

b. Special Comb. **Squatterland** *obs.*, an ironic early name for Hawke's Bay province where it was believed a number of large pastoralists had monopolized ownership of the land.
1912 *Hutt Valley Independent* 7 Sept. 1 Here in Upper Hutt the bulk of the land is also held by a dozen holders who, as was the case in Squatterland, steadfastly put up a fight for stagnation and oppose all progressive movements.

c. In composition **squatterine**, a jocularly contemptuous name for a squatter's wife.
1913 *NZ Observer* 8 Feb. 4 It was a fine back-scratching celebration of the triumph of Reform which Squatter Hugh Campbell gave to the squatters, squatterines and appendages down in Hastings recently.

5. In special collocations **squatter's gap**, **squatters' meeting**, see quots.
1914 *History of North Otago* (1978) 99 Old Bob had bushy whiskers but usually had his chin shaved, this particular type of whisker being known [c1880s] as '**Squatter's gap**'. Old Bob considered that the 'Squatter's gap' gave him a distinguished appearance. **1980** ELDRED-GRIGG *Southern Gentry* 96 A typical meet took place at Sowburn in November every year. It was known as the '**squatters' meeting**' because of its gentry patrons.

squatterdom /'skwɒtədəm/. [AND 1855.] A collective term for the group or class of wealthy, large-scale pastoralists.
1877 *Tapanui Courier* 11 Apr. in Marks *Hammer & Tap* (1977) 11 No doubt land and sheep lords have good grounds of complaint against being mixed up with the higgledy-piggledy cockatooing and digging settlers... It must be humiliating to Squatterdom to have to come down to such a plebeian community as Tuapeka to administer their affairs. **1887** *Auckland Weekly News* 13 Aug. 8 I entrain at Woodville and emerge upon the plains of Squatterdom. **1897** A TRAMP, ESQ. *Casual Ramblings in Gumland and Squatterdom* [Title] **1906** *TrNZI* XXXVIII. 341 Finally, there is the kea,.. the outlawed of squatterdom. **1934** MULGAN *Spur of Morning* 249 But Killigrew wondered what this enemy of squatterdom was doing in the company of John Feldon's daughter.

squatting, *vbl. n.*
1. [AND 1836.] The occupation for pastoral purposes, and without proper title, of Maori or Crown land.
1844 *NZ Gaz.* 24 Apr. in Gore *Levins* (1956) 13 Mr. Bidwill has started with sheep and cattle and Messrs. Clifford and Vavasour are about to send sheep and cattle there immediately. Squatting is evidently the order of the day. **1846** *On British Colonisation of NZ* (vi) That irregular occupation of native land [before extinction of title, or true sale], commonly designated as 'squatting', which it is understood is now becoming the practice of European emigrants to New Zealand. **1853** [see SQUATTER 1 a].

2. Pastoral farming on a large scale on leasehold land.
1857 HURSTHOUSE *NZ* II. 400 He will obtain a fair idea of the *first profits* of Squatting begun on a *small* scale and on a moderate scale. **1946** ACLAND *Early Canterbury Runs* 11 The whole spirit of the [Canterbury] Association was against cheap land and the squatting system—squatting means renting large areas cheaply and running stock on the native pasture.

3. In *attrib.* use. **a.** As a quasi *ppl. a.*, pertaining to the occupation of land for (large-scale) pastoral farming.
1843 DIEFFENBACH *Travels in NZ* I. 187 A *squatting* population, therefore, living apart from each other, but connected by a safe water communication, are the best pioneers for a colonization of that part of Cook's Straits. **1873** WILSON *Diary* 6 Feb. in Wierzbicka *Wilson Family* (1973) 170 The people we meet at our hotel [in Dunedin] seem entirely of the squatting class with a few regular town residents. The squatters are decidedly the nicest and most gentlemanly class. **c1875** MEREDITH *Adventuring in Maoriland* (1935) 163 While the maize and pigs are grazing, I am filling my time with anything that will earn money, as I am very serious about this squatting project, which looks all right.

b. Special Comb. (see also SQUATTER 4 a) **squatting interest** [AND 1842], squatters (see SQUATTER 2) collectively, esp. as a political force; **squatting licence** [AND 1839], a licence to occupy Crown leasehold land on payment of an annual fee; **squatting system**, a system of pastoral farming depending on cheap leasehold land and capital enough to stock it.
1853 SEWELL *Journal* (1980) I. 188 He is jealous of Clifford and the Squatters,—is addicted to Landscrip, Town Acres and Rural Sections, and therefore I can see evidently has a leaning in favor [*sic*] of cheap land... I suspect he gives the matter up, contenting himself with sinking his **squatting interest** in the equally lucrative pursuit of land and scrip jobbing. **1877** PURNELL *The NZ Confederation* 9 The squatting interest. **1843** DEANS *Pioneers* (1964) 9 Feb. 31 [To Colonial Secretary] That your Memorialists have been informed that altho' your Excellency has not the power to grant **Squatting Licences**, over Territory not acquired from the Natives, yet that your Excellency is convinced that it will be for the ultimate advantage of these Islands that Squatting should be permitted. **1851** *Lyttelton Times* 18 Jan. 1 Notice is hereby given, that all parties to whom squatting Licenses have been granted, *pro tem.*, from the Land Office of the Canterbury Association, will be expected to remove from, and give up possession of the land they occupy. **1857** HURSTHOUSE *NZ* II. 397 [The squatter] rudely breeds, feeds, clips, and fattens his flock, under what is popularly termed the '**Squatting system**'.

squattocracy /ˌskwɒ'tɒkrəsi/. Also **squatocracy**, **squattaucracy**. [AND 1843.]
1. The party of wealthy sheepfarmers as a political or social force; often derogatorily applied to wealthy sheepfarmers collectively; also, concretely, a squatter's family estate (see quot. 1913).
1864 *Saturday Rev.* IV. 13 The Otago Squatocracy. **1874** BATHGATE *Col. Experiences* 205 The class of run-holders..comprises for the most part men of refinement and education, and they are nicknamed by the [anti-squatter] Liberal Party the 'Squatocracy', from the word squatter which is also a name frequently applied to them. **1887** *Auckland Weekly News* 13 Aug. 8 Mr. Smith is the 'black devil' of Hawke's Bay squatocracy. **1890** *Otago Witness* (Dunedin) 21 Aug. 34 I refer of course to the 'huts' provided by the squatocracy (to

SQUEAKER

coin a word) for the lodgement of..wage-earners in their employ. **1905** *Truth* 12 Aug. 1 The municipal muddlers in that centre of snobbery and squatocracy [i.e. Napier]. **1913** *NZ Observer Christmas Annual* 20 You look as prosperous as the heir-apparent of a Hawkes Bay squatocracy. **1938** HYDE *Godwits Fly* (1970) 146 In the evening of the next day they were camped at Anakawa with the Murchisons, a family of the ex-squatocracy. **1942** MARSH & BURDON *NZ* 9 [The runholders] are the squattaucracy of New Zealand. **1948** LIPSON *Politics of Equality* 68 Hall himself [c1880] represented the Selwyn electorate in the Canterbury plains, a citadel of the 'squattocracy'. **1952** *Evening Post* (Wellington) 4 Sept. 9 'I don't want any recrudescence of landowning squatocracy in New Zealand,' said Mr Hanan, supporting provisions to prevent aggregation. **1960** SCRYMGEOUR *Memories Maoriland* 109 Pillars of 'Squattocracy' from..the former generations still stand today [in Hawke's Bay]. **1970** McNEISH *Mackenzie* 31 Talking to a grazier about the land question, he had used the phrase 'White Squattocracy'. He had said it casually and included himself in his usual derogatory way. **1988** *North & South* (Auckland) Oct. 64 They are serious squatocracy. Waiting for the young couple was the Williams family's Matahiia Station, covering 3500 acres outside Ruatoria. **1995** *City Voice* (Wellington) 19 Oct. 19 Glover Park..was named for its benefactor. Not a stout Tory or scion of the squatocracy, but, would you believe, a Trade Unionist.

2. *transf.* Any powerful elite.
1986 *Dominion* (Wellington) 18 Mar. 3 'How do you pin down the tremendous vigour in which he kicked the education squatocracy?' Mr O'Regan said.

Hence **squattocrat** /'skwɒtəˌkræt/ *n.* [AND 1910]; **squattocratic** *a.* [AND 1843].
1854 SEWELL *Journal* 23 Sept. (1980) II. 87 He seeks to extinguish the political influence of the **Squattocrats** by aggrandizing the power of the Towns. **1887** *Auckland Weekly News* 23 July 21 A property tax don't hurt the great squatocrat of Mauriceville—not much. **1893** FROBISHER *Sketches of Gossiptown* 62 This country must flourish when a squatocrat Can..Make use of the Council to answer himself. **1897** A TRAMP, ESQ. *Casual Ramblings* 59 He does not waste his ink discussing the difference between the Autocratic Government of King Seddon and a **Squatocratic** Government by King Russell. **1913** *NZ Observer* 19 July 17 In Napier there is a gaol reserve which is in a place frequented by the people, since it runs down to the Marine Parade of the squatocratic little city. **1955** *NZ Geogr.* Oct. XI. 102 Bush burn techniques had not been perfected; but younger men, unable to break into the 'squatocratic' holdings of the Middle Island, were moving north.

squaw /skwɔ/. *Obs.* Also **squah**. [Spec. use of N. Amer. *squaw* Indian wife or spouse: AND (of an Aborig. woman), 1837.] A Maori woman or wife; WAHINE *n.*[1] 1. Cf. INDIAN.
1836 *Log 'Mary Mitchell'* 21 May in McNab *Old Whaling Days* (1913) 443 3 boats out one returned from the Sounds [Te Awaiti] with 2 men and 5 squaws a necessary evil. **1865** CHUDLEIGH *Diary* 5 May (1950) 181 One old Maori kept the accounts and the old squaws kept the money. **1913** McNAB *Old Whaling Days* 195 Some times the [American whale] boats, on returning from the [Queen Charlotte] Sound, were found to contain more women (called squahs by the Americans) than men.

squeaker. *Obs.* [A survival of Brit. slang: see OED 1 c; Grose *Dict. Vulgar Tongue* (1811) *Squeaker* 'a bastard or any other child'.] In early whalers' or traders' parlance, a child.

1845 Wakefield *Adventure NZ* I. 319 A chief was called a 'nob';.. a woman, a '*heifer*'; a girl, a '*titter*'; and a child, a '*squeaker*'.

squeeze, *v*. *Obs. criminal slang*. To strangle.
1866 *Narr. Maungatapu Murders* 35 [Burgess] said 'I and Kelly took a man away and we squeezed him.' **1914** Grace *Tale Timber Town* 141 All four of them should ha' been 'squeezed'.

squib. *Obs*. [Spec. use of *squib* an insignificant person: AND 1908.] A racehorse lacking endurance.
1909 *Truth* 27 Feb. 2 Mug is a humorous sort, and seen after the race in question, he remarked, 'She has cost me about 60 googs, but I'll take my oath the squib will not cost me 6l.'

squid.
1. Any of several species of ten-armed pelagic cephalopod molluscs, the flesh of which is often now sold as calamari; of significance for New Zealand English mainly with modifiers in the names of the commonest species.
2. With a modifier: **arrow**, **broad**, **giant**.
(1) **arrow squid**. *Nototodarus* spp., esp. *N. sloani* (fam. Ommastrephidae).
1947 Powell *Native Animals NZ* 32 Arrow Squid (*Nototodarus sloanii*). This has an arrow-shaped body, four to eight inches in length. **1982** Burton *Two Hundred Yrs. NZ Food* 68 The two main species of squid found in New Zealand waters are the arrow squid and the broad squid, which is distinguished by the broad fins which extend along both sides of the hood. The broad squid is more tender and delicately flavoured, but the arrow squid is more commonly landed. **1986** Paul *NZ Fishes* 156 *Arrow squid*... Usually listed as *Nototodarus sloani*, the slender, arrow-shaped squid commonly caught in New Zealand's coastal waters are now known to comprise at least two species of *Nototodarus* (family Ommastrephidae) closely related to several Australian and Pacific species.
(2) **broad squid**. *Sepioteuthis bilineata* (fam. Sepiadariidae).
1947 Powell *Native Animals NZ* 31 Broad Squid (*Sepioteuthis bilineata*). A deep-water, soft-bodied mollusc with eight rather short sucker-bearing arms and two long arms. **1966** *Encycl. NZ* III. 710 Squid, broad . . ngu . . *Sepioteuthis bilineata*. **1982** [see (1) above]. **1986** Paul *NZ Fishes* 157 *Broad squid*. *Sepioteuthis bilineata* Family Sepiadariidae (broad squids). A coastal species, moderately common around much of the North Island... Sold as calamari or (wrongly) female squid, it is as good eating as arrow squid.
(3) **giant squid**. *Architeuthis longimanus* (fam. Architeuthidae).
1937 Powell *Shellfish NZ* 50 Even in New Zealand we have had instances of the occurrence of these monsters of the sea, for in 1881 and 1888..three species of giant squids were cast ashore at Lyall Bay... One of these, *Architeuthis longimanus*, was fifty-seven feet in total length. **1948** *NZ Herald* (Auckland) 30 Jan. 8 What is thought to be a giant squid, the largest ever seen in New Zealand waters, was washed up on..the Otago Peninsula early this week. **1982** *Catch* Aug. 11 The giant squid was caught while the *Kiso Maru* was trawling in 400m of water in the Mernao Bank area. Weighing an estimated 200 kg, the squid's total length was 8.85m, with a girth of 1.45m. The body length (without the tentacles) was 1.45m.
3. Used *attrib*. in special Comb. **squid ring**, **squid tube**, the body of a squid with contents, beak, and tentacles removed, cut either into rings or sold whole as a 'tube'.

1989 *Edmonds Microwave Cook. Book* 96 Curried squid rings. Cut squid tubes into thin rings... Add rings and toss constantly until sizzling stops. **1989** *Listener* 27 May 81 Clean the squid tubes and cut into thin rings. Place in a bowl with the sliced kiwifruit for 10 minutes, removing the kiwifruit before cooking.

squiz. Also **squizz**. [f. Brit. dial. (poss. f. *squi*(nt + qu)*iz*): see EDD *v*. (Devon) *squiz* to look, examine critically: AND 1913.] A look, glance; an inspection.
1917 Nuttall, G.W. *MS Papers 2192* (ATLTS) 21 Apr. There is a very old church here and..I had a squizz through it. *Ibid*. 16 Aug. Norm and I had a ride down to Hampton Court and a good squizz round. **1922** Mansfield *Stories* (1984) 489 'I say, Laura,' said Laurie very fast, 'you might just give a squiz at my coat before this afternoon. See if it wants pressing.' **1948** Finlayson *Tidal Creek* (1979) 70 Presently he goes below, has a good squiz at the engines, and turns in to sleep. **1951** Park *Witch's Thorn* 189 Little Maori children darted out in all directions to have a good squiz [at the passing nuns]. **1965** Shadbolt *Among Cinders* 74 Neighbours woken by the noise too must have had a great old squiz between their curtains that morning. **1974** Morrieson *Predicament* (1981) 194 'Let's have a squizz at what's wrapped in this rug.' That was one 'squizz' neither of them were ever to forget! **1982** Shadbolt *Once on Chunuk Bair* (1990) 30 Aren't you going to have a squiz? It's what we're here for. **1988** *Salient* (Wellington) 5 Sept. 8 Take a quick squizz at next week's issue when it arrives.
Hence *v*. *intr*., to look, glance.
1917 Brown *Lay of Bantry Bay* 45 So I 'squizzed' them [*sc*. racehorses] behind us A 'stipe' in the straight standing handy I spies. **1948** Ballantyne *Cunninghams* (1963) 73 They walked down the passage and squizzed in the dining-room. **1948** Finlayson *Tidal Creek* (1979) 45 I sees him sort of squizzing around for a dark corner.

stab fence. *Obs*. [f. *stab* a stake.] A fence made of upright stakes ('stabs').
1874 J.G. Wilson *Diary* 23 Apr. in Wierzbicka *Wilson Family* (1973) 180 I..assisted Linton putting up a stab fence,.. Did a good deal of it this afternoon, Peggy assisting us occasionally. She carried two stabs at once and then said, 'That's as many as I can get Daddie.' **1899** Bell *In Shadow of Bush* 234 Yelled O'Byrne, who was trying to prevent the stab fence that enclosed the garden from catching fire.

stack. A hay or straw stack. In *attrib*. use as special Comb. **stack-bottom**, the rotted hay at the bottom of a stack, often used as garden manure; **stackman** (also **stackie**), one of those building a hay or straw stack.
1978 Hilliard *Glory & Dream* 112 If they came off the farm they always brought something with them... Even a load of **stack-bottom** once for his garden. **1911** *Maoriland Worker* 20 Apr. 15 It seems to me that the **stackman** on a threshing mill has a particularly hard time of it—most work and least pay... Under the old rules one stackman has to go on one of the four drays and the cocky sends the other three men. **1976** Anderson *Water Joey* 75 It was reputed that Bill Clark hired men in bulk—ten **stackies**, so many straw-wallopers, etc.

stackie: see *stackman* (STACK).

stag. *Farming*.
1. [Brit. dial. *stag* a farm animal castrated when mature: see OED *n*.¹ 3; AND 1848 (bullock), 1919 (sheep).] An imperfectly or late castrated sheep or (occas.) bullock.

1928 *NZ Free Lance* (Wellington) 22 Feb. 34 A 'stag' is a ram that has been castrated before it was to be killed and boned for the market. **1933** *Press* (Christchurch) (Acland Gloss.) 9 Dec. 17 *Stag*.— Imperfectly or late castrated male sheep or steer. Hence *staggy*. **1947** *Puketoi Station Diary* in Beattie *Early Runholding* 85 In connection with stock the following terms were used [between 1858 and 1869]:—'Let the sheep draw down to the Taieri'; 'stags', 'crawlers', 'stragglers'. **1951** *Awards, etc*. 324 [NZ Freezing-Workers Award] [Rates of wages] Rams and genuine stags Double rates. **1966** Newton *Boss's Story* 191 Sheep that have been desexed after reaching maturity are known as 'stags'.
Hence **staggy** *a*. [see OED *a*. 1 a '*N.Z. and N. Amer*.', 1933], of an animal or its meat, having the characteristics or appearance of a mature male.
1933 [see preceding section]. **1950** *NZJAg*. Sept. LXXXI. 201 Complaints about the proportion of 'staggy' New Zealand wether lamb carcasses have been received recently from the United Kingdom.
2. *transf*. Something regarded as useless (as for example a castrated ram).
1906 *Red Funnel* II. 207 He commented profanely on the valley as being a 'fraud', a 'stag', and absolutely worthless as a mining field.

stage. Formerly, the seniority of a 'unit' in a preliminary baccalaureate or other undergraduate course of study, progressing from stage I (first year) to stage III (third year or later).
1923 *College Rhymes* 48 Where Percy is not, nor stage 3 exists. **1927** *Minutes of the Council of the Univ. of NZ* 21 Feb. 14 That the examiners for Stage II be normally the two professors who are not examining Stage I. **1941** *Salient* (Wellington) 30 July 1 The Stage I course will now be much more suitable for students taking English for only one year... A choice is allowed at Stage III of either a predominantly literary or linguistic course. **1955** *Ibid*. 24 Mar. 2 We understand that Professor Beaglehole is lecturing in Psychology to Stage I students. **1979** Parton *University of NZ* 80 The degree involving nine 'units' with two taken to stage III, did not meet all needs.

stagger-juice. *Obs*. [AND 1896.] Cheap and potent, occas. illicit, liquor. See also *snakejuice* (SNAKE 3).
1905 *Truth* 10 Oct. 5 Dry Ashburton... The stagger-juice record-book... Whiskey, or beer or other kinds of stagger-juice. **1940** Hastings in *Digger's Diary* (1941) 12 The Doc found that the youngster [*sc*. soldier] had been filling himself with 'stagger juice'.

staggerweed. [AND 1903.] *Stachys arvensis* (fam. Lamiaceae), an introduced weed inducing 'stagger' or shivering in sheep.
1926 Hilgendorf *Weeds* 149 Staggerweed.., also called by its English name[s] of wound wort and hedge nettle, is found abundantly in cultivated fields in the North Island and is one of the worst garden weeds in Wellington. **1969** *Standard Common Names Weeds* 74 *staggerweed. Stachys arvensis*. **1980** Taylor *Weeds of Crops* 95 Staggerweed..native to Europe, Asia and North America, is widespread in New Zealand and most abundant in the Nelson and Wellington provinces.

stagknife. Also occas. **stab-knife**, **stick-knife**. A boy's game, also commonly called KNIFEY q.v., and occas. early *momley-peg*.
1939 Grieve *Sketches from Maoriland* (1961) 87 [Playground] Crazes came and went [in the 1930s]. One week it would be 'stag-knife', another week

'knuckle bones'. **1972** SUTTON-SMITH *Folkgames Children* 171 *Stagknife* (K-31), a universal game of nineteenth-century childhood, was important because it was played with the most treasured play object of all boys, the pocket knife. Although known in nearly all parts of New Zealand by the name of Stagknife, the game was also known as Bites, Jackknife, Stabknife, Knifey, Momley Peg, and Throwing the Knife... There were generally two players..who each sought to deflect the point of the pocket knife from certain parts of the body by a flick of the hand in such a way that the blade would stick firmly into the ground... Every movement had to be done three times. Typical movements were: (1) Place the open pocket knife (loose) [name of movement] [*sic*] on the closed knuckles of the right hand, point the knife towards the thumb, then with a quick upward flick of the hand to the left, deflect the point of the knife into the ground. **1984** KEITH & MAIN *NZ Yesterdays* 288 But 'stagknife' or 'stick-knife' was mainly played by the boys; it provided some thrilling moments when the skilled player would somersault a sharp pocket knife twice or three times off his forehead, nose or chin into the ground.

stairdancer. [Used elsewhere but recorded earliest in NZ: see OED 5 b.] A sneak thief who specializes in stealing from multi-storey buildings.
1953 HAMILTON *Till Human Voices Wake Us* 128 Occasionally you'd see a smartly dressed guy and he nearly always turned out to be a con-man or a stair dancer. A stair dancer is a chap who raids hotel bedrooms and you want to look your best for that. **1979** *Dominion* (Wellington) 27 Nov. 9 Stairdancer..roams offices stealing bags and valuables left on desks. If spotted he makes an extremely agile exit by way of the staircase. **1982** *Dominion* (Wellington) 10 Dec. 7 Mr Chambers said the victim was 'a grubby professional thief, known well around Auckland as the "stair dancer" who entered city buildings and stole personal property of employees.' **1995** *Hutt News* (Lower Hutt) 7 Nov. 15 [Heading] Stairdancing on rise. 'Stairdancers'—thieves who nip into business premises and steal personal belongings and office equipment—are on the increase in Lower Hutt.

Hence **stairdancing** *vbl. n.*, the occupation of a stairdancer.
1975 *Otago Daily Times* (Dunedin) 24 July 12 Office workers in Dunedin have not been plagued by 'stair dancers'... 'Stair-dancing', an old term used to describe thefts from hotel rooms, is now applied by criminals to the practice of thieving in high-rise office blocks. **1985** *Press* (Christchurch) 25 Jan. 13 A woman who stole..jewellery from a staff bedroom at Christ's College..was sent to prison for three months... [She] was told by the Judge that it was 'a classic offence of stair-dancing.' **1995** [see quot. above].

stake. A marble put down to be fired at.
1972 SUTTON-SMITH *Folkgames Children* 174 There were terms for marbles such as..'dubs', 'dates', 'stakes'..referring to the marbles put down to be fired at. **1982** SUTTON-SMITH *Hist. Children's Play* 269 Here are some [marble] terms from Taranaki around 1880–90: firsts, lay-up, stakes..dubs.

stake fence. See quot. 1939.
1882 HAY *Brighter Britain* I. 190 A stake-fence ought to be proof against both pigs and cattle. **1939** BEATTIE *First White Boy Born in Otago* 99 A stake fence was made by putting in posts and a top rail and driving stakes into the ground 4 inches apart and lashing with karewao vine.

stand, *n.*[1] [Spec. use of *stand* a standing growth or crop: see OED *n.* 29, (of trees, 1905).] A group of millable trees.
1874 BAINES *Edward Crewe* 152 Good 'stands' of kauri..still untouched by the Yankee axe of the bushman. **1936** *Hills & Valleys 2* 14 Splendid stands of rimu and matai bush.

stand, *n.*[2]
1. *Shearing.* [AND 1888.] **a.** The position occupied by a shearer on the shearing board; esp. in the phr. **to get a stand**, to be taken on as a shearer.
1905 BAUCKE *White Man Treads* 230 Others have to walk from their stand to cadge a sharpening from stones, a pen or so down the board. **1922** TURNER *Happy Wanderer* 143 Four hundred men might answer the roll-call where only a hundred could 'get a stand'— that is, a chance to shear. **1952** MEEK *Station Days* 111 Stand: When a shearer is engaged to shear, he is said to have booked a 'stand'. **1966** NEWTON *Boss's Story* 189 Each shearer has his allotted space on the shearing board and this is his stand. A shed for six shearers has six stands. **1973** NEWTON *Big Country* (1977) 61 He first went to the Muller [station] in the old blade days..got a stand again the next season and shore there for..years.

b. With a prefixed number, indicating the capacity of a shearing shed (or board) according to the number of stands. Also in composition as **one-stander**, etc.
1973 WHEELER *Hist. Sheep Stations NI* 35 The second one forms part of..the present eight-stand woolshed shown in my drawing. *Ibid.* 70 Huiarua's big fourteen-stand shed..holds 3,000 woolly sheep. **1988** *More* (Auckland) Mar. 28 I've worked in shearing sheds—from ramshackle one-standers to sparkling new eight-standers.

2. *West Coast.* A registered 'whitebait stand', a riverside construction from which whitebait is netted by the standholder.
1989 *Dominion Sunday Times* (Wellington) 15 Oct. 13 Like most stand holders Betty Eggeling has a 'linger' where she can linger longer in wet weather. **1990** McDOWALL *NZ Freshwater Fishes* 436 [Caption] Whitebaiting in South Westland is carried out from rickety stands built out into the river from the banks. **1994** *Evening Post* (Wellington) 6 Sept. 2 The West Coast Regional Council has been asked to consider banning whitebait stands from the Hokitika and Haast rivers and to reduce the maximum length of 30m stands by 10m... In addition to the 70 standholders on the Hokitika River and 36 on the Haast..there were also waiting lists for stands.

Hence **standholder**, the registered holder of a whitebait stand. See quot. 1994 above.

standard. [Spec. use of *standard* an upright support.] **a.** A wood or steel stake supporting a wire fence. See also WARATAH.
1865 *Timaru Herald* Jan. in Woodhouse *Blue Cliffs* (1982) 8 Tenders for a fence 5 or 6 miles long on the Otaio River... Iron standards, 6 wires, 15 strainers to the mile. **1868** BARKER *Station Life* (1870) 232 We had left them both securely tied to the only available post, through which unfortunately five wires ran, as it was one of the 'standards' of a fence which extended for miles. **1873** WILSON *Diary* 9 Feb. in Wierzbicka *Wilson Family* (1973) 173 As a rule the fencing consists of iron standards and five wires. **1895** *Fencing Act* in *Settler's Handbook NZ* (1902) 161 Posts of durable wood or iron, well and substantially erected, the posts or standards not more than 9 ft. apart. **1909** THOMPSON *Ballads About Business* 47 While yer study architecture in a wire and standard fence. **1913** CARR *Country Work* 19 In the North Island the bulk [of fences] is constructed with wooden posts and battens. In the South..flat iron standards with from five to seven wires run through them are used. **1931** LOVELL-SMITH *Old Coaching Days* 124 Ned was stopped by some irate fencers, who declared..that during the night he had flattened out some chains of iron standards. **1950** *NZJAg.* July LXXXI. 10 Fences of standards and droppers [are useful] where suitable timber is unobtainable... Steel posts or standards [are]..quick to erect, since they are driven into the ground. **1969** HENDERSON *Open Country Calling* 196 Most of the iron standards were flattened to the ground. **1978** PRESTON *Woolgatherers* 28 The standards and wire [of fences in 1860] were iron not steel; those driven into the ground a hundred years ago are still strong; whereas the modern steel standards flake off very quickly. **1988** [see WARATAH].

b. Special Comb. **standard-lifter**, see quot.
1982 *Agric. Gloss.* (MAF) 29 *Standard-lifter*: A lever for removing standards.

standing.
1. A firm footing (at the base of a tree) for a tree-feller.
1951 McCARROLL *The Days of the Kauri Bushmen* (Radio Talk 2: TS) Another difficulty..was to get a good 'standing' alongside the tree, that is a level foot hold for each sawyer, and on the same level..more often than not a stage had to be built on which the crosscutters could get a good 'standing'.

2. As **standing chop**, see CHOP *n.*[2]

stargazer. [Spec. use of *stargazer* a fish of fam. Uranoscopidae.]
1. Any of various fishes of the families Leptoscopidae and Uranoscopidae, having eyes set on top of the head, and directed upwards. See also BULLDOG, FLATHEAD 1, MONKFISH, TOEBITER.
1773 FORSTER *Resolution Jrnl.* 21 Apr. (1982) II. 263 We found they had hauled in the Sein in the Indian Cove & got some Mullets..& one new *Stargazer* (*Uranoscopus*), which we described & drew. **1921** *NZJST* IV. 123 *Star-gazer*. I have recorded this species in Napier and Wellington markets, but it is generally considered rare. **1947** POWELL *Native Animals NZ* 73 Stargazer (*Leptoscopus macropygus*). An ugly fish with a broad depressed body and the mouth inclined upwards. **1956** GRAHAM *Treasury NZ Fishes* 280 The Stargazer, like the Catfish and Flatfish, lives in sandy or muddy situations inside and outside of harbours throughout New Zealand. **1968** MORTON & MILLER *NZ Sea Shore* 550 An equally important fish of estuarine flats is the carnivorous stargazer *Uranoscopus*, with its huge head and wide crescentic mouth, lying in soft mud in wait for unwary prey. **1985** *Evening Post* (Wellington) 18 May 56 The range [in a Wellington sea-food delicatessen includes]... Stargazer which sells at about $8 a kilo.

2. With a modifier: **brown, estuary (estuarine), giant, sand, spotted**.

(1) **brown stargazer.** *Gnathagnus innotabilis* (fam. Uranoscopidae).
1982 AYLING *Collins Guide* (1984) 272 *Brown Stargazer*... In New Zealand this species is not common but is regularly trawled in northern waters. **1986** PAUL *NZ Fishes* 119 *Brown stargazer. Gnathagnus innotabilis.* Also occurs in south-east Australia where it is also known as bulldog stargazer. Dark brown above, paler on the sides and below.

(2) **estuary (estuarine) stargazer.** *Leptoscopus macropygus* (fam. Leptoscopidae). See also *mud-grubber*, *mud-gurnard* (MUD 2).
1979 *Catch* May 17 Stargazer *Leptoscopus macropygus*. Estuary stargazer... Common in river estuaries and adjacent coasts to 60m. **1982** AYLING

Collins Guide (1984) 273 *Estuarine Stargazer. Leptoscopus macropygus...* Many years ago this species, which makes excellent eating, was caught commercially in considerable quantities off the west coast of the South Island, but it has since lost favour as a food fish. **1986** PAUL *NZ Fishes* 119 Alternatively called estuary stargazer, and mud, river, or flathead gurnard.

(3) **giant stargazer**. *Kathetostoma giganteum* (fam. Uranoscopidae). MONKFISH. See also BULLDOG.
1979 *Catch* May 17 Monkfish *Kathetostoma giganteum*. Giant Stargazer. **1982** AYLING *Collins Guide* (1984) 271 *Giant Stargazer* (Monkfish)... The giant stargazer is a large fat-bodied fish with a huge blunt head. **1986** [see MONKFISH]. **1988** FRANCIS *Coastal Fishes* 48 Giant Stargazers probably spawn during autumn.

(4) **sand stargazer**. *Crapatulus novaezelandiae* (fam. Leptoscopidae).
1979 *Catch* May 17 Sand Stargazer *Crapatulus novaezelandiae*. Family Leptoscopidae (sand stargazers). **1982** AYLING *Collins Guide* (1984) 273 *Sand Stargazer...* This species is found throughout New Zealand..often being found in the surf zone or being left stranded on mudflats at low tide. **1986** PAUL *NZ Fishes* 119 The sand stargazer..is speckled grey-brown above, white below, and generally found in the sand along the surf zone.

(5) **spotted stargazer**. *Genyagnus monopterygius* (fam. Uranoscopidae). See also CATFISH, HARDHEAD, occas. MONKFISH.
1960 DOOGUE & MORELAND *Sea Anglers' Guide* 246 Spotted Stargazer... Buries itself by a sideways wriggling movement, leaving only the eyes and upturned mouth exposed... *Other names:*... catfish, monk, dogfish; kourepoua (Maori). **1979** *Catch* May 17 Spotted Stargazer... Catfish, dogfish... Not taken commercially. **1986** PAUL *NZ Fishes* 119 *Spotted stargazer. Genyagnus monopterygius.* Apparently restricted to New Zealand. Listed alternative common names include catfish and dogfish, both inappropriate.

star hotel. Also **starlight hotel, starlight boarding house**. [A play on *star* in the celestial sense, poss. also as an ironic reference to *star* as an indicator of hotel quality.] The open air, the outdoors, esp. in the phr. **to sleep** (occas. **doss**) **in the star hotel**, to sleep under the open sky. Cf. MRS GREEN.
1937 PARTRIDGE *Dict. Slang* 825 *Star Hotel, sleep in the.* To sleep in the open: New Zealand tramps' c[ant] (–1932). **1938** *Press* (Christchurch) (McNab Slang) 2 Apr. 18 [The slang terms] 'to blow up to', 'to sleep in the Star Hotel' need no explanation. **1941** BAKER *NZ Slang* 41 In later years we have records of the phrases *to sleep with Mrs. Green* and *to doss in the star hotel*, used by tramps to describe sleeping in the open. **1964** LEE *Shiner Slattery* 12 I was the youngest member of the Starlight Boarding House Fraternity [of swaggers]. **1974** SIMPSON *Sugarbag Years* 20 There was an empty section across from our house where the word must have spread among swaggers that it was a good place to kip... and they used to make a fire and sleep in the 'Starlight Hotel' as everybody used to call it at that time [c1930s]. **1985** *Metro* (Auckland) June 63 'I've stayed..all around the city... A lot of times at the Starlight Hotel. Been there quite a few times,' he continues. The Starlight Hotel is 'under the stars'.

start. *Bullock-driving*. [Prob. f. *start* (f. Old English *steort* a tail) the handle (of a vessel, etc.): see OED *n.*¹ 2; EDD 5 the lever or beam to which a horse is yoked in a threshing machine.] See quots.
1856 ROBERTS *Diary* 19 Sept. in Beattie *Early Runholding* (1947) 42 In the centre [of the bullock's yoke was] a bolt with a ring called 'the start' passed through the yoke, to which the chain was fastened from the sledge. **1951** H.S. MCCARROLL *The Days of the Kauri Bushmen* (Radio Talk 3: TS) Through the centre of the yoke, midway between the two bullocks, there was a ring bolt with a double link on the under side. This was called the start, and the bullocks were coupled together by a chain with a hook on each end and approximately 9 foot long (that was the coupling chain). It was hooked into the back link of the start on one pair and the front link of the start of the pair immediately behind them, and so on with the next pair.

starter. [Transf. use of *starter* one who starts in a race.] In the phr. **to be a starter (for)**, to (be willing to) take part in, to be ready for.
1944 FULLARTON *Troop Target* 99 I'm not a starter [in that love-match]. **1956** *Upper Hutt Leader* 26 Sept. 5 *Be a Starter* in the Trentham Kindergarten Building Stakes Double on Saturday. **1966** TURNER *Eng. Lang. Austral. & NZ* 160 From racing such current expressions as 'I'll be a starter' meaning 'I'll take part or join in'..are derived. **1983** *Dominion* (Wellington) 7 Apr. 7 He says he's a bit of a starter for getting in his cab and waiting till the car owner cools down.

starvation country. Country which will not support stock well.
1885 'K' *Visit to Lake Rotoraira* 7 My friend S— says 'Yess, that's all right, but it's starvation country for sheep.' **1963** CAMPBELL *Golden North* 6 Five miles away to the west lay the Coast [near Kaipara], a starvation country covered with tea tree.

State. As the first element in the names of various State commercial or social enterprises, etc.: **State Advances**, *ellipt.* and familiar for **State Advances Corporation, State Advances Office**, and used *attrib.* (e.g. State Advances mortgage), a former State lending organization, making 'advances' on land and buildings to home-owners and settlers; **State aid** [AND 1856], in full **State aid to schools**, (the concept of) State financial support for non-State, sectarian or private schools; **State farm** *obs.*, a farm owned by the State as an investment, as a source of employment, and later as an experimental farm or research station (quot. 1942 is used ironically and fancifully); **State Forest**, a tract of Crown land statutorily declared a forest and usu. put under a working plan administered formerly by the NZ Forest Service; **State highway**, a designated main road, a significant part of a national or inter-regional network, for whose development and maintenance a State rather than a local government administration is responsible; **state house**, a house built and owned by the State for renting to lower income tenants (also *attrib*); **state housing; State-owned Enterprise**, often as an acronym **SOE**, a name for a corporatized State department or ministry; **State (purchase and) control**, a former option in the triennial liquor licensing poll withdrawn in 1987 (cf. CONTINUANCE); **State school** [AND 1878], a public primary, intermediate, or secondary school funded mainly by the State, and formerly under rigorous central control in staffing and other matters (see also PUBLIC SCHOOL); hence **State schoolboy**, one attending a State school and formerly on occasion regarded as socially underprivileged; **state tenant**, one renting a State house.

1926 *NZ Dairy Produce Exporter* 31 Jan. 25 Why is it..that if a man lives in town and goes to the **State Advances** Office he can get 95 per cent of his valuation [as a loan], whereas if he lives in the country, he can only get 75 per cent. **1936** BELSHAW et al. *Agric. Organiz. NZ* 35 The remaining financial requirements for land purchase and establishment of farms being obtained mainly from private individuals, the State Advances Office and the Public Trust. **1938** *Dominion* (Wellington) 12 Oct. 26 [Advt] During the time the Nationalists were in power, only 125 State Advances Loans were made for 1934 and 1935. **1938** HYDE *Godwits Fly* (1970) 76 After the war, when it was decided that their father's gratuity, helped out by the State Advance mortgage (another little Government treat for the returned soldiers), should buy the Hannays a house of their own. **1969** MASON *Awatea* (1978) Appendix II 105 Fill out their tax forms, ring State Advances. **1879** *Auckland Weekly News* 23 Aug. 19 If **State Aid** is to be given to one denomination, every other denomination would have a right to it. **1890** *NZ Observer* 1 Nov. 1 'State aid to private schools' is a cry so inherently just and reasonable that I am astonished as to the manner in which the electors are gulled. **1918** *Wanganui Herald* 15 July 7 A keen and interesting debate on the subject of State aid in denominational schools took place in the Dunedin Presbytery last week. **1954** *Truth* 8 Dec. 25 The controversy which has arisen lately over State aid for Catholic schools is being looked upon with growing concern by all Catholic people. **1986** *Illustr. Encycl. NZ* 983 The main educational issue of the 1960 General Election was state aid for private schools. **1894** *AJHR H-6* 2 **State Farms**. The..Minister of Lands has successfully initiated a system of paying parties of working-men to fell bush on Crown lands, giving to these men the option of choice of lands so felled and cleared. *Ibid.* 3 A State Farm proper of about 1,000 acres has been commenced at Levin... Fifty-two men, eight women, and twenty-five children are on the ground, the men doing the preparatory work, cutting roads through the forest, felling bush for burning, planting orchards, &c., getting laid out... The State Farm is directed by an able agriculturalist as Manager, who is appointed by the Government... There is every probability that the State farm will become a paying investment on the capital expended, as well as an outlet for a description of labour—viz., that of elderly men—which cannot find occupation elsewhere in times of pressure, but which has deserved well of the colony by previous long and hard service. **1907** *AJHR C-15* 1 That there be laid before this House a return showing..receipts and expenditure of the Levin State Farm taken over by the Department of Agriculture. **1933** *AJHR H-29* 7 This leaves only the Ruakura Farm existing as a State farm in the true sense [i.e., owned by, and for the (research) purposes of, the State], and the time has arrived when consideration should be given to utilizing a portion of this for settlement purposes. **1942** [see *State house* below]. **1885** *NZ Statutes* No.30 76 [NZ State Forests Act] Every **State forest** shall be surveyed and the boundaries thereof duly marked upon the ground. **1889** KIRK *Forest Flora* 32 In Southland the timber-supply is obtained almost entirely from State forests; in Wellington, from private forests. **1899** *AJHR C-1* vi The total amount of land set aside as reserves for State forests, plantations, scenic purposes, &c..was 1,175,622 acres. **1924** *Otago Witness* (Dunedin) 22 Jan. 6 It is estimated that that 100,000,000 ft. of timber is contained in the Waipoua State forest. **1966** *Encycl. NZ* I. 722 State forests, the setting aside of which had been provided for under the first Forests Act in 1874, were now defined in a special section of the new Act. **1986** *Illustr. Encycl. NZ* (1989) 1302 Waipoua State Forest covers 15,000 hectares in Hobson County, Northland, about 50 kilometres north-west of Dargaville. **1936** *NZPD* CCXLV. 144 As a first step, some four thousand miles

STATE OF BOB

of main highway, comprising the main traffic routes only, will be placed under the sole control of the Main Highways Board and administered as State highways. **1936** *NZ Statutes* No.39 401 [Main Highways Act, 1936] The Board may from time to time..classify any main highway or portion of a main highway as a **State highway**. **1947** *NZPD* CCLXXIX. 814 In November, 1936, approximately four thousand miles of what were main highways were declared main State highways, and the Government took full responsibility for those highways. **1966** *Encyclop. NZ* III. 97 The classification of State highways into categories I, II, or III restricts vehicle loadings to those which the road can reasonably carry without serious damage. **1973** COLERIDGE *Our Motoring Heritage* 144 In 1936 the nomenclature 'State Highway' was introduced. **1942** *NZEF Times* 21 Dec. 2 A **State house**, a State farm, a State high chair and State education for the occupants thereof. **1950** JOSEPH *Imaginary Islands* 25 Live in a state house, raise forcibly-educated children Receive family benefits, and standard wages. **1964** *Listener* 11 Dec. 5 It was a state house with shrubs and flowers in a street full of state houses with flowers and shrubs. **1978** SINCLAIR & HARREX *Looking Back* 121 State houses made their contribution to the appearance of New Zealand towns from the mid-1930s. **1986** *Listener* 20 Dec. 8 'State houses'—the words have a Kiwi magic... A nation grew up on the notion of *Savage, Semple* and *Lee*—immortalised in a famous photograph—carrying furniture into the first state house in 1937. **1989** *Listener* 29 July [Victory Square, Nelson] Pushing our pram up the long hill to Orsman Crescent and our temporary State house. **1990** *Landfall 173* 4 State houses blinked weteyed for us along avenues. **1995** *Sunday Star-Times* (Auckland) 5 Mar. sect. C1 A 1930s sturdy brick home in the state house suburb of Pine Hill was home to Fraser. **1946** *People's Voice* 17 July 3 **State housing** workers..are divided into several gangs. **1949** *Weekly News* 20 July [Caption] The extensive State housing programmes for the Hutt Valley are making good progress. **1962** MITCHELL *Waitaki Votes* 9 The workers in the state and lower valuation housing areas..tend to support the Labour Party. **1985** *Women's Work* 197 One obscure family in a State Housing area in New Zealand. **1987** *Metro* (Auckland) May 52 The notorious slum of Freemans Bay was levelled and its people were relocated in new state housing suburbs like Wesley in Mt Roskill. **1990** McKAY *Baxter* 138 That year Epuni [School] had three hundred and eighty-five pupils, most of whom came from a state housing area. **1986** *State-Owned Enterprises Act* s1 Short title and commencement—(1) This Act may be cited as the **State-Owned Enterprises** Act 1986. **1987** *Listener* 27 June 56 Complementing the reorientation of the private sector is the corporatisation of the Government's trading departments into state-owned enterprises. **1987** *National Bus. Rev.* 23 Jan. 1 Collinge told *NBR* he was also worried that too much was being decided..on the structure of the enterprises (SOEs). **1990** *Contact* (Wellington) 31 Aug. 6 All the SOE bosses gathered for a posh lunch at the Beehive to receive their 1990 medals. **1991** *Evening Post* (Wellington) 21 Nov. 4 When our railways service was converted to an SOE by the Labour Government, it was apparent privatisation was the eventual goal. **1935** *NZ Free Lance* (Wellington) 20 Nov. 58 [Advt] Why you should vote **State Control**. **1854** *Educ. Comm. Rep. A & P Wellington Session 2, 1854–55* (Council Paper 59–69) Whether it shall be given by the State, or public cost, and in the **State Schools**. **1882** ANDERSON *Chatham Islands* 24 Had he the advantages that every State school now gives..he would have made..good use of them. **1911** *Maoriland Worker* 4 Aug. 3 Many persons think that the only objection to the introduction of Bible teaching into our State schools is the fact that our community is so divided in religious opinion. **1930** PINFOLD *Fifty Yrs. Maoriland* 133 I used to attend, week by week, the

State school of the town in which I lived. **1943** MARSH *Colour Scheme* 14 Simon [*sc.* an English boy]..had attended the Harpoon State schools and, influenced..by his schoolfellows' suspicion of 'pommy' settlers, had become truculently colonial..and defiantly uncouth. **1955** [see PUBLIC SCHOOL]. **1965** McLAGLAN *Stethoscope & Saddlebags* 180 A State school was improvised for the children. **1976** JOHNSTON *New Zealanders* 126 If [private schools] meet the requirements of the..inspectors, they receive free textbooks on the same basis as State schools. **1986** *Illustr. Encycl. NZ* 347 The [1877 Education] Act gave New Zealand secular education in its public (or State) schools. **1991** *Dominion* (Wellington) 24 Sept. 6 A controversial survey that found many people thought private schools did a better job than state schools asked which provided an ideal education. **1896** HODGSON *Poems* 1 The Lay of the **State Schoolboy**. My age is ten, plus two, plus three, My height is 4[foot]10 fix, My rank is plain for all to see—I have passed Standard Six! **1982** *Collins Concise Eng. Dict.* 1135 *state house n. N.Z.* a house built by the government and rented to a *state tenant*. Brit. equivalent: *council house*.

state of bob: see BOB *n.*³

State servant: see PUBLIC SERVANT.

station. [Spec. New Zealand uses of *station* in the various senses indicated in OED *station n.* 11 a (military post), 13 a and d.] See also *trig station* (TRIG 2).

1. In various elliptical, often historical uses. **a.** [See OED 13 d.] In full MISSION STATION q.v.
  1819 MARSDEN *Lett. & Jrnls.* (1932) 200 This was a very solitary station..a day's journey from any native village or farm—our only companions being men in a state of nature, some of them having never..visited the missionary settlement. **1835** in Wily & Maunsell *Robert Maunsell* (1938) 34 We shall remain here a week or two before we proceed to our station (Mangapouri). **1853** ROCHFORT *Adventures of Surveyor* 43 The Roman Catholic Mission has a handsome station here. **1979** BINNEY et al. *Mihaia* 15 The inland Anglican Station which had been founded at Te Whaiti in 1847, had been abandoned with the onset of the Anglo-Maori wars.

b. In full, 'trading station'.
  1840 MATHEW *Journal* 17 Feb. in *Founding of NZ* (1940) 51 Accordingly..we proceeded to McDonnell's Station (before mentioned), where they [*sc.* the Chiefs] had congregated.

2. [Spec. uses of *station* a place where men are stationed and apparatus set up for a particular purpose: see OED 13 a.] Usu. with a defining word: **breeding (nesting) station**, of birds, areas where species return to nest and breed; **eel-station**, a prepared place or stand from which to catch eels; **forest (forestry) station** (often *ellipt.* esp. in Comb.), the headquarters of a State Forest comprising administrative and ancillary buildings and staff residences; **surveyor's station**, a tent or rough shed as a field headquarters for surveying; **timber station** *obs.*, a trading-post for timber. See also *milk-treatment station* (MILK), *whaling station* (WHALING).
  1882 POTTS *Out in Open* 42 We have known of **breeding stations** at Cass's Peak. *Ibid.* 45 The **nesting stations** we have notes of are on the Paringa river. **1847** BRUNNER *Exped. Middle Is.* 11 May in Taylor *Early Travellers* (1959) 270 Natives worse instead of better, but we managed to accomplish about a quarter of a mile to a fresh **eel-station**. **1992** SMITHYMAN *Auto/Biographies* 54 The sawyer..took off..to the **Forestry station** beyond Waipiro Swamp. **1850** GODLEY

STATION

Letters Nov. (1951) 147 Harewood forest where there is a **surveyor's station** (shed). **1843** SELWYN *Journal* (ATLTS) 22 Capt. Lewington's **Timber Station**.

3. [Spec. use of *station* as 2 above (OED 13 a), poss. influenced by *station* a military post (OED 11 a).] **a.** [AND 1820.] A large grazing property with its buildings and stock usu. having a main centre of occupation and control. Cf. RUN *n.*¹ 1 and 2. See also *cattle station* (CATTLE 2), *dairy station* (DAIRY 4), *sheep station* (SHEEP 2), *stock station* (STOCK 2 a).

  1839 JONES in Eccles & Reed *John Jones of Otago* 6 July (1949) 25 The stations generally occupied are purchased from the Native Chiefs, and are mostly from five to ten miles square from the beach. **1843** DEANS *Pioneers Canterbury* (1937) 58 Some of the men were taking cattle to a station along the beach. **1845** DEANS *Pioneers* 28 Sept. (1964) 45 There will be no stations so far inland here as there are in Australia... Here at the inland stations they can grow the greater part of their own supplies. **1853** ADAMS *Canterbury Settlement* 69 The station..was a large sheep farm, extending over twelve square miles of pasture land. **1866** BARKER *Station Life* (1870) 73 Our friend..owns a large station... At the back of his run the hills rise to a great height. **1882** HAY *Brighter Britain* I. 178 Our station—or, as you may choose to term it, our estate, selection, place, farm, location, homestead, or run—may be reckoned a choice bit of land. **1913** MANSFIELD *Stories* (1984) 134 The young English 'johnny' who'd been on the station learning farming—disappeared. **1924** *Otago Witness* (Dunedin) 4 Nov. 54 The bush would have to be felled and burnt off before the station could be put down in grass, and used for sheep and cattle. **1939** BEATTIE *First White Boy Born Otago* 153 In those days [c1860s] every station packed its wool and shipped it to London for sale. **1958** MULGAN *Making of New Zealander* 100 It is noteworthy that the word 'station' is commonly used for big sheep-farms in the South Island, especially in the hill country. It is less common in the North Island. 'Station' has a proprietorial and almost regal air. **1963** WALLIS *Point of Origin* 10 The station Dad manages is owned by a bloke named Dent. Thirty thousand acres, most of it high country. **1976** JOHNSTON *New Zealanders* On these stations, the sheep, often in flocks of 10,000 or more, range freely over the hillsides. **1981** CHARLES *Black Billy Tea* 48 Now on farm and on station there are tales told galore. **1993** *Dominion* (Wellington) 30 Apr. 11 Koraenui Station [Rangitikei]: 1168 ha... The station has a wintering over capacity of 10,000 stock units.

b. The homestead usu. with the headquarters buildings and amenities of a large grazing property; in early times often merely a hut or shelter for the owner or overseer. See also HOMESTEAD *n.*¹ and ². Cf. HEAD-STATION 1, *home station* (HOME *n.*³).

  1849 *Handbook to Suburban & Rural Dists. Otago* 6 Sheep or cattle owners, who, establishing their temporary homesteads or stations, near or in the bush, might run their flocks and herds amongst the hills. **1858** *Richmond-Atkinson Papers* (1960) I. 439 This [lack of timber] will somewhat increase the cost of establishing a station [on the run]. **1859** FULLER *Five Years Residence* 147 The dwelling-house is generally termed the 'Station'; while the land..is termed the 'Run'. The site of the station requires vicinity to wood and water, and the term is often applied collectively to represent the whole occupation. **1860** in Butler *First Year* (1863) iv 52 Of course everyone at stations like the one we visited [i.e. Rolleston's hut] washes his own clothes, and of course they do not use sheets. **1863** *Richmond-Atkinson Papers* (1960) II. 37 We have a [pre-emptive] right to '80 acres at one of the stations and 10 acres at each of the other stations erected upon the run'... [*sic*]

It seems, however, that there must be a station of some sort at the place where preemptive is applied for: but it would be easy to have a hut put up. **1870** [see HOMESTEAD *n.*[1] 1]. **1871** MONEY *Knocking About NZ* 6 A few words may suffice to give the reader a general idea of a station. There was the usual manager's house, with a loft for the accommodation of the hands who preferred it to the woolshed... There was the stockyard,.. besides a hut or two for the shepherds about the run. There were the various out-houses, pigstyes, &c. **1889** WAKEFIELD *NZ after Fifty Yrs.* 152 'The Station' is the manor-house of a large extent of country. **1898** HOCKEN *Contributions* 168 The runholder was also allowed a pre-emptive right of purchase on his run of eighty acres for his principal station and ten acres for each out-station. **1912** BOOTH *Five Years NZ* 18 The station, or homestead, stood [c1859] on a plateau some fifty feet above the plain; it consisted of two huts, mud-walled and thatched with snow grass. **1921** GUTHRIE-SMITH *Tutira* (1926) 150 The other buildings of the primitive homestead were an ark, 6 feet by 9 feet, a *whata* or store-house on piles, empty now in the station's dire extremity. **1939** BEATTIE *First White Boy Born Otago* 110 The Waimea run belonged to..McKellar and the station consisted of two sod huts, one for the two bosses and the other for the men. **1947** BEATTIE *Early Runholding* 25 Near Te Anau a fire [in the early days]..spared the sheep, but burnt the camp that was the station. **1951** McLEOD *NZ High Country* 10 A typical station consists of a house... Besides the house there will be men's quarters scattered about.., a cookhouse with dining room and accommodation for shearers... Stables, killing house, and cart shed make up the remaining buildings and altogether the place looks quite a little village.

c. *Obs.* OUT-STATION 2.

1864 CHUDLEIGH *Diary* 1 Feb. (1950) 120 Left Harman's station about 5, breakfasted at the upper station, crossed the Rakaia. **1879** VOGEL *Land & Farming NZ* 59 A married man with a family on a station (or what you would call an out-farm) has a cottage and lodgings.

4. *attrib.* Pertaining to or belonging to a stock station.

1853 in *Canterbury Rhymes* (1866) 19 A little drinking would ease my mind,.. The grog must stop, for every drop, Would hinder station work. **1857** *Lyttelton Times* 1 July 1 For Sale 4 Useful farm or station carts. **1861** *Butler to Tripp* 13 Oct. in Maling *Samuel Butler* (1960) 56 I want a man for about two months to do all sort [*sic*] of station work—a little fencing sod work and post and rails. **1866** BARKER *Station Life* (1870) 45 F— says that probably it was a very old 'station-screw'. *Ibid.* 137 They could not be carried on horseback, and just then the station-dray was particularly employed. **1889** CHUDLEIGH *Diary* 4 Nov. (1950) 368 I..put on my two station boys as fleece boys. The shed did not stop one minute. **1897** WRIGHT *Station Ballads* 122 I sigh for the good old days in the station whare again. **1939** CRESSWELL *Present Without Leave* 260 We were all taken to our work in the morning in the station-lorry, and I had often to keep this vehicle..waiting on account of an excellent regularity of the bowels. **1973** WHEELER *Hist. Sheep Stations NI* 68 [Caption] The station store with part of the shearers' accommodation on the right. **1982** WOODHOUSE *Blue Cliffs* 68 Sometimes the girls from the house and the station men would have dances in the laundry.

5. Special Comb. **station agent**, see *stock and station agent* (STOCK 3 b); **station blanket**, see quot.; **station book**, see *station diary*; **station-bred** *a.*, bred in the station, not bought in; **station brownie**, BROWNIE *n.*[2] 1 as typical station fare; **station butter** *joc.*, dripping; **station clerk**, the person responsible for keeping station records, etc.; **station cook** [AND 1878], a cook employed to prepare meals for station employees; **station diary**, a daily record of facts and events relevant to station life and work; **station hack**, a horse for general station use; **station hand** [AND 1872], one employed on a stock station usu. for general work; **station-holder** [AND 1869], the owner of a stock-station (see also RUNHOLDER); **station homestead**, the main residence on a stock station; **station horse** [AND 1900], a horse trained for stock-station work, see also *station hack*; **station-house**, see *station homestead*; **station life** [AND 1880], the manner of living and working on a stock station; **station manager** [AND 1878], see quot. 1933; **station mutton**, sheep killed for consumption on the station; **station-owner** [AND 1873], the owner of a sheep or cattle station (see quot. 1947 below); **station rug**, see *station blanket*.

1933 *Press* (Christchurch) (Acland Gloss.) 9 Dec. 17 ***Station blanket*** or ***rug***.—Slang. Split sack or woolbale, used to sleep under. **1948** SCOTTER *Run Estate & Farm* 36 Although no **station book** from any of the estates has been found, J. Cowie Nichols has complete records of the flock on his run. **1933** *Press* (Christchurch) (Acland Gloss.) 9 Dec. 17 ***S[tation]-bred***, not a bought sheep. **1964** ANDERSON *Doctor in Mountains* (1974) 33 Now, I decided, was the time to have a horse of my own and from the twenty-five pounds I had brought with me from England I bought for eight pounds one of the station-bred hacks. **1975** HARPER *Eight Daughters* 56 He was a good baker too and baked the wellknown '**station brownie**' (currant loaf) which we had with our early cup of tea. **1888** DUNCAN *Wakatipians* 49 We [shepherds] had to content ourselves with the humble fare peculiar to the new settler, viz. mutton, tea and bread..with an occasional treat in the way of some dripping which we spread on our bread and, under the name of '**station butter**', pretended to enjoy. **1981** PINNEY *Early N. Otago Runs* 24 The [Benmore] **station clerk**, was given the job of cleaning out the drain from the boilers. **1886** *Severed Hand* 56 I am a station cook residing at Masterton. I know the prisoner Howard. **1982** WOODHOUSE *Blue Cliffs* 88 The **station cook**, with a slushy to help him, would cook for all hands. **1881** BATHGATE *Waitaruna* 68 Mr. Ramshorn inducted Gilbert into the mysteries of the **station diary**... It seemed to savour something of ship life to have to note down day by day the state of the weather, and how the hands were employed, and such-like details of the routine of their occupations. **1907** CHUDLEIGH *Diary* 18 Feb. (1950) 439 I burnt diaries, station diaries and letters. **1904** LANCASTER *Sons o' Men* 7 In the two-hundred-acre..paddock fed the refuse of the **station hacks**. **1912** BOOTH *Five Years NZ* 18 Behind these were a woolshed..and a fenced in paddock in which a few station hacks were kept for daily use. **1930** DAVIDSON *Sketch of His life* 66 The best lot of station hacks..I ever met with was the mob purchased with The Levels estate in New Zealand in 1864. **1964** ANDERSON *Doctor in Mountains* (1974) 33 I taught him to be well-mannered and above all to be easily caught, a tremendous asset in a station hack. **1992** *Evening Post* (Wellington) 20 May 23 Forbes believes a better comparison would be with the tough station hacks found on farms in the Gisborne area. **1860** in Butler *First Year* (1863) vi 75 The **station-hands** cannot look down upon him, as they do upon the other [non-paying] cadet. **1870** PRENTICE *A Tale of NZ* (GALMS) 30 There were two station hands or general workmen. **1881** NESFIELD *Chequered Career* 35 I am not..certain that the close companionship of station-hands is so desirable. **1891** in Woodhouse *Blue Cliffs* (1982) 53 J. Duff, station hand, 25/- a week. **1912** BOOTH *Five Years NZ* 73 The station hands comprised a shepherd, bullock driver, hut-keeper. **1947** NEWTON *Wayleggo* 106 To sit there like Jacky in front of a mob of grinning, barracking station hands..made me feel a perfect fool. **1964** ANDERSON *Doctor in Mountains* (1974) 30 I was called 'the new chum' by the station hands. **1973** FERNANDEZ *Tussock Fever* 139 As a rule [the shepherds] resented this type of work—station hand work—and were not obliged to cooperate. **1865** *Punch in Canterbury* 15 Apr. 3 Diggers, **Station-holders**, and Farmers supplied with the best colonial made boots and shoes cheap for cash. **1889** REISCHEK *Wonderful Dog* 35 It would be impossible for station-holders to work without the assistance of these valuable dogs. **1892** SWANTON *Notes on NZ* 117 The wild boar is a great nuisance to the station holders and farmers in the hills and back country. **1937** MARSH *Vintage Murder* 38 [He] was a station-holder twenty miles out in the country. **1947** BEATTIE *Early Runholding* 11 I spent weeks collecting every old term for 'runholders' I could, and I found..'station holders', 'station owners', 'stock holders', and 'stock owners'. **1971** GRIFFITHS *King Wakatip* 83 He is carrier,.. gold buyer, slaughterman, land agent, station-holder,.. etc. etc. **1937** BUICK *Moa-Hunters NZ* 155 The site of Gray's Hills quarry is..close to the **station homestead**. **1867** BARKER *Station Life* (1870) 197 We used to have a quiet old **station-horse** saddled, fasten the luncheon-basket to the pommel..and start off miles away to the back of the run. **1881** NESFIELD *Chequered Career* 38 Although, there were plenty of station horses,.. I invested in a couple for my own private use. **1933** *Press* (Christchurch) (Acland Gloss.) 9 Dec. 17 *Station*... (4) Adjective as in *s[tation] horse*, belonging to the owner, not to one of the men, whose horses are *private*. **1874** KENNAWAY *Crusts* 211 We raced over the last five miles at a dead gallop, dismounting on the lee-side of the **station-house**. **1888** McKAY *Earthquakes in Amuri & Marlborough* 4 The station-house was so far wrecked. **1888** CHUDLEIGH *Diary* 9 Apr. (1950) 361 James Seymour commenced as a shepherd... He and I cleared the station house out top and bottom. **1933** [see MEN'S HUT]. **1865** BARKER *Station Life* (1870) 23 F— says that this beautiful place will give me a very erroneous impression of **station life**. **1892** *NZ Official Handbook* 157 To those who love the saddle and take interest in the care of animals station-life offers innumerable attractions. **1882** *TrNZI* XIV. 240 On the following day the **station manager**..visited the camp. **1933** *Press* (Christchurch) (Acland Gloss.) 4 Nov. 15 *Manager*.—One who directs the work of a farm or station, buys and sells the stock for it, engages and sacks the men, and signs cheques. *Ibid.* 16 Dec. 21 *Station manager*.—See *Manager*. **1959** MIDDLETON *The Stone* 42 Charlie Lawlor, the station manager, showed me my stretcher in the [shearer's] whare. **1982** WOODHOUSE *Blue Cliffs* 92 My share of the annual income was derived from the sale of fat from the sheep killed for **station mutton**. **1867** BARKER *Station Life* (1870) 123 I was much amused at the names bestowed on them, according to the tastes..of the **station-owners** whose runs happen to include them. **1874** KENNAWAY *Crusts* 110 One morning we rode down to a neighbouring station about twelve miles off..and knocked at the station-owner's door. **1926** DEVANNY *Butcher Shop* (1981) 28 Barry's mother had been governess to a neighbouring station-owner's children. **1937** BUICK *Moa-Hunters NZ* 155 The station-owner..was absent in Australia..but a shepherd showed us where the quarry was. **1947** [see *station holder* above]. **1960** OLIVER *Story NZ* 107 Sheep brought the runholders and later the station-owners. The runholders owned only the sheep which they pastured on great stretches of leased land. **1973** [see *summer country* (SUMMER)].

staunch, *a.* In gang use, completely dependable (and loyal) in a fight or tough spot.

1990 KIDMAN *True Stars* 83 'That guy's a maniac.'.. 'Don't worry, Gary's staunch.' **1991** *Listener* 28 Oct.

57 Being staunch usually meant throwing batteries through the window, or hitting a guard. I became a different kind of staunch, writing letters to the superintendent and so on. **1991** *Dominion* (Wellington) 14 Dec. 11 Police raids and fights with rival gangs breeds intense in-group loyalty from which the title of the book [*Staunch*] is derived... These initiation tests prove that a prospect is staunch, which is the primary value of the gang. **1991** PAYNE *Staunch* 23 It's better to have a small crew that's staunch, that's tight, that you can trust. **1992** *Evening Post* (Wellington) 13 Mar. 2 It's staunch being educated. **1992** MAHY *Underrunners* 113 'But you're not in a gang,' Tris said. 'Who are you being staunch to?'

Hence **staunchness** *n.*, the quality of loyalty or dependability in a gang member.

1991 PAYNE *Staunch* 22 The number one rule in the Mongrel Mob is no narking..to the extent where 18 Mobsters were prepared to go to jail over the Wairoa killing rather than inform on one member. Does that say something about the staunchness of the Mob? **1991** DUFF *One Night Out Stealing* 18 Dangerboy..bulled his way through the crowd to stand with Corky..showing his staunchness.

stay. *Fencing.* [Spec. use of *stay* support: see OED *n.*²] **a.** A support for a strainer or angle post.

1982 *Agric. Gloss.* (MAF) 29 *Stays*: Support for strainer or angle post. **1987** *Listener* 9 May 51 'Stays', which hold the strainers in position, number the same way.

b. Special Comb. **stay block**, **stay foot**, a piece of timber placed in the ground to support the stay at a strainer, angle or corner post.

1982 *Agric. Gloss.* (MAF) 27 *Breast plate:* Piece of timber placed in the ground that supports the stay at a strainer, angle, or corner post. Sometimes called stay foot. *Ibid.* 29 *Stay block:* (See breastplate).

steam. [Prob. f. *steamed* drunk: AND 1941.] Methylated spirits as a drink, alone or mixed with cheap (usu. fortified) wine. See also JESSIE'S DREAM.

1941 BAKER *NZ Slang* 62 [Australasian] terms for strong drink as *lunatic soup*, *Africa speaks*, *plonk*, *steam*, *red Ned*. **1965** BAXTER *Collected Poems* (1980) 239 I'd give my ballocks now For a bucket of steam. *Ibid.* 240 But I'd give old Rose the go-by For a bottle of steam tonight. **1988** *Dominion Sunday Times* (Wellington) 14 Feb. 19 Meths is blue or white lady, and steam is a mixture of meths and sherry... I [*sc.* Archie, an alcoholic vagrant] bought this bottle of steam (meths) from the Hindu shop round the corner. **1991** *Ibid.* 8 Dec. 9 Earlier in the morning he had had his first drink of 'steam', the street name for methylated spirits cut with water.

steamed. Also **steamed up.** [Spec. use of *steamed* (*up*) excited: used elsewhere but recorded earliest in NZ: see OED 2 b.] Drunk.

1921 LORD *Ballads of Bung* 'Stunology' (1976) 11 To say you're 'soused', 'steamed', 'stunned', or that 'you're on the swank', Is only a reflection, on the glorious way you drank. **1950** *Landfall* 14 June 126 Little Spike is six foot two and has a reputation for being a hard case when he is steamed up.

steamroller. [Fig. use of *steam-roller* alluding to its size and weight.] A thick roll-your-own cigarette. Contrast RACEHORSE.

1953 *Evening Post* (Wellington) 29 Aug. 8 Depending on whether the smoker concerned rolled 'racehorses' or 'steamrollers'.

steelie. [f. *steel* + -IE.] A ball-bearing used as a marble.

1984 KEITH & MAIN *NZ Yesterdays* 288 Marbles were the currency of childhood and there were an astonishing number of names for them. The march of technology added ball bearings—ballies or steelies— which were unbeatable when it came to smashing an opponent's miserable glassie. **1992** PARK *Fence Around the Cuckoo* 62 I..inherited her [*sc.* an old truck's] discarded ball bearings, the prized 'steelies' of the marbles afficionados. **1993** [see DAKE].

steep, *a.* In the phr. **(as) steep as (the side of) a hen's face**, very steep.

1947 NEWTON *Wayleggo* 59 To use an amusing phrase of that inimitable [Canterbury] Bush language, it was country that was 'without a word of a lie as steep as a hen's face'. **1971** LETHBRIDGE *Sunrise on Hills* 167 The lower end of this spur..was very steep, and even the sheep had to walk 'zigzag' to climb up it! As they would say in Southland: 'It was as steep as a hen's face!'

Steinie /ˈstaini/. [f. a proprietary name *Stein*(lager a brand of beer + -IE.] A (pint bottle, occas. a can, of) Steinlager beer.

1983 *Rip It Up* (Auckland) Jan. 26 Roll out the Steinies, and with a crate under my arm, I went off to get drunk at the Army 'All. **1984** COX *Waiting for Einstein* 16 A six pack of Steinies was tucked under one solid arm. **1991** *Evening Post 'TV Week'* (Wellington) 1 July 2 Chuck the gumboots in the porch and slump on to the sofa with a six-pack of Steinies and a big piece of pavlova to catch the Skellerup Young Farmer of the Year Contest.

step, *v.* In the phr. **to step** (someone) **out**, to ask someone to 'step outside' for a fight, to invite or challenge to fight; to ask to 'step outside'. Also as a noun **step-out**, a challenge to fight.

1980 SMITHYMAN in *Te Reo* 22–23 108 The Coromandel pub style, 'More of that and *I'll step you*' 'I shall ask you to step outside and settle things there'. **1982** NEWBOLD *Big Huey* 117 Brian was furious and wanted to go and step them all out, but we were hopelessly outnumbered. *Ibid.* 254 Step out (n) and (v) Challenge to a fight. **1989** NEWBOLD *Punish. & Politics* 79 We had a couple of incidents where a guy would, say, step me out, you know, say he was going to knock me over. **1991** PAYNE *Staunch* 14 I have felt more threatened at dances where amateur drunks, adolescent gigolos and butcher's apprentices want to 'step you out' for daring to look at their grotty girlfriends than I ever did inside a gang clubhouse. *Ibid.* 105 He took it upon himself to go out there..and step out the Headhunters in the pub.

Stephen(s) Island frog, wren: see FROG *n.*¹ 2 (2); WREN 2 (5).

Stewart Island. Also early **Stewart's Island**: compare also the definition of MIDDLE ISLAND. In the names of plants and animals, see: KIWI 2 (1), OYSTER *n.* 2 (1), PALM 3, SHAG 2 (17), SNIPE *n.* 2, WEKA 2 (5), WOODHEN 2 (5), WREN 2 (1).

Stewart Islander.
1. One born or resident on Stewart Island.
1938 HYDE *Nor Yrs. Condemn* 163 They say that Stewart Islanders and the souls of oysters always go back to the old place. **1962** WEBBER *Look No Hands* 35 'Why don't they pick on someone their own size?' writes an indignant Stewart Islander. **1982** SANSOM *In Grip of Island* 146 I wasn't English, I'm not a North Islander either. I'm a deep-dyed Stewart Islander. Macrae's Point and Thule are my home.

2. *transf. Obs.* The *Stewart Island oyster* (OYSTER *n.* 2 (1)).

1898 MORRIS *Austral-English* 436 *Stewart Islander*..name given to the oyster, *Ostrea chiloensis*..; so called because it is specially abundant on Stewart Island off the south coast of New Zealand. The Stewart Island forms are mud oysters.

stick, *v.* In the phr. **to get stuck in(to). a.** As **to get stuck into** [see OED *v.*¹ 23 e; AND 1941] *quasi-trans.*, to attack (work, a meal) vigorously; to attack (a person, an enemy) physically or with words.

1945 *NZ Geogr.* I. 24 Today any man who can shear, press, sweep or help get stuck into the work at the shed. **1961** *Dominion* (Wellington) 18 Apr. 5 There would be 14,000 sections from Cook Strait to Newlands 'once we can get stuck into the major subdivision..,' the mayor, Mr Kitts, said. **1962** *Listener* 19 Apr. 5 *Murphy:*... One weekend we got stuck into a patch [of pigs] down Retaruke. **1969** MASON *Awatea* (1978) 45 *Tahi*... How 'bout you tell Werry we get stuck into the haangi! **1970** DAVIN *Not Here Not Now* 115 They got stuck into the home-brew then. **1974** MITCALFE in *Listener Short Stories* (1977) 125 Kevin was a hell of a burden to me..because I'd been getting stuck into him one way and another, being a year older. **1984** BEATON *Outside In* 86 Sandy:... Although, last year was grouse when the Virgin Mary got stuck into Joseph for tryin' to get it on with one of them Wise Kings.

b. As **to get stuck in** *quasi-intr.*, to enter vigorously into a fight, argument or contest; to eat or drink up (with enthusiasm); to pitch in. Often used as an invitation or friendly command to start eating or drinking, etc.

1947 DAVIN *For Rest of Our Lives* 253 And for Christ's sake, remember, till the time we get to the wadi and get stuck in, absolute silence. **1959** SLATTER *Gun in My Hand* 51 Gets into his old mocker and gets stuck in. Just one of the boys. c**1962** BAXTER *Horse* (1985) 29 He poured a beer and drank it. 'Go on. Get stuck in. You'll need it. Don't worry about us.' **1963** *Dominion* (Wellington) 17 Sept. 2 We went and got about 11 chaps..and went back [to continue the fight]. As soon as we got in the house we got stuck in—[the fight] only took about three minutes. **1974** AGNEW *Loner* 64 I pointed to the pile of dirty dishes... [The cook's] offsider..threw me a towel. 'Get stuck in, young fellow. There's plenty of them.' **1985** STEWART *Gumboots & Goalposts* 12 They [*sc.* parents] don't ask for too much sophisticated play, but they do expect their boys to 'get stuck in'. **1992** MAHY *Underrunners* 45 'Get stuck in mate and you can move the world,' said Selsey Firebone.

sticker, *n.*¹ A notice of a traffic offence (usu. gummed on to an offending vehicle or 'stuck' under a windscreen wiper); BLUEY *n.*¹ 4 b.

1951 *Evening Post* (Wellington) 31 Oct. 12 [Mr Hannah S.M.:] Every [motorist] is annoyed when he gets a sticker.

sticker, *n.*² *Sawmilling.* FILLET.

1948 JEWELL *Accounting in Timber Industry* 128 *Fillets:* Sometimes called a 'sticker' or 'strip'. **1952–53** [see FILLET].

stick game. Any of various Maori (rhythmic) games of skill played with sticks.

1963 HILLIARD *Piece of Land* 34 'How's it going, Cyril?' 'Like a Maori stick game!' **1979** HARSANT *They Called Me Te Maari* 53 Following the big feast there were haka, songs, poi dances and stick games, until it was time for the evening meal. **1989** RYAN *Revised Dict. Mod. Māori* 61 *titorea* stick-game. **1993** SINCLAIR *Halfway Round the Harbour* 62 I also went to the Maori Club, where a lecturer..taught us stick games.

sticking-pen. *Freezing works.* The pen in which cattle are stunned and killed (orig. by 'sticking' with a knife).
1959 SLATTER *Gun in My Hand* 12 The sticking-pen far below me down the tunnelled slope from the top of the ramp. From there comes the pained lowing of goaded cattle and the sharp crack of the lethal hammer wielded by the nonchalant bloke leaning over from his platform above the trapped beast.

stick-knife: see STAG-KNIFE.

stickleback: see WHALE 2 (9).

sticks, *n. pl.* [Transf. uses of *sticks* slender branches or rods.]

1. Either of two shrubs *Corallospartium crassicaule* (fam. Papilionaceae) or *Helichrysum depressum* (fam. Compositae), having a stick-like rather than a leafy appearance. Cf BROOM 2.
1899 KIRK *Students' Flora NZ* 107 *Corallospartium crassicaule*... sticks of the shepherds. Coral broom... The robust yellow stems, cream-coloured fasciculed flowers, and villous pods distinguish this from all other N.Z. plants. **1925** WALL *Flora Mt. Cook* 55 Helichrysum depressum, 'Sticks'.., Moraine, Riverbed, Shingle. **1961** ALLAN *Flora NZ* I. 371 *1. C. crassicaule*... Montane and subalpine grassland..east of divide... *Coral broom, sticks.*

2. [AND the posts of an Australian National Football goal, 1876.] The uprights or 'posts' of a rugby union goal.
1970 SLATTER *On the Ball* 139 Bob Scott comes up for a shot at goal..and..away she goes..fair and square between the sticks and we're jumping in the air again.

stick up, *v.*[1] [Used elsewhere, but in some senses recorded earliest in NZ, and in others, of historical significance.]

1. a. [AND 1879.] To bring (a person, thing, activity, etc.) to a standstill; to hold up or halt; to hamper or frustrate. (Often constr. in the passive **to be (get) stuck up**.)
1860 BUTLER *Forest Creek MS* (1960) 37 If you get stuck up by any creeks you'll very likely see cattle marks..but there is nothing that ought to stick you up at all if you keep out of the big swamp at the bottom of the valley. **c1872** WHITWORTH *Spangles & Sawdust* 26 When we told him..we'd been stuck up by the water, he.. said..'Ah, stuck up, were you?' **1884** REID *Rambles on Golden Coast* 73 Push on or you will be stuck up. Not by bushrangers,.. but by time and tide which wait for no man. At the first opportunity he 'stuck up the mail'..merely to secure a passage to town. **1889** CHUDLEIGH *Diary* 4 Nov. (1950) 368 Commenced shearing. Meikana and Piripi Nehu as press men stuck me up. I gave them five minutes and sacked them. **1894** WILSON *Land of Tui* 88 Far more often have the rivers to be forded, as is the case with the Otira..where..it is so wild that the coaches are sometimes 'stuck up' for days. **1913** BEATTIE *Trade Hunting* (12) The back blocks of Southland are not inaccessible places. Until you are stuck up by the great West Coast mountains..you can get round. **1930** DAVIDSON *Sketch of His life* 75 The only drawback to these trips was the likelihood of being stuck up now and then by flooded rivers. **1949** DAVIN *Roads from Home* 161 You might want to coax Pompey [*sc.* a ferret] out if he sticks you up. **1959** MASTERS *Tales of Mails* 25 When they got stuck up in trying to get over the saddle..they naturally made back to get him to help them over with his horses.

b. In various *spec.* uses: (a) [AND 1884], to bail up (pigs); (b) *whaling* in the phr. **stuck up with porpoises,** of a whale, to be slowed by playful porpoises.
c1875 MEREDITH *Adventuring in Maoriland* (1935) 64 It sometimes takes up to half an hour to scramble through the rough gullies to where the dogs have the pig stuck up... A bailed-up pig makes periodical rushes at the baiting dogs. *Ibid.* 97 In the morning our dogs stuck up a mob of pigs on a small, clear-topped rise. **1982** GRADY *Perano Whalers* (Gloss.) *Stuck-up with porpoises*—Porpoises that have slowed a swimming whale down by playing with it. This assisted the whalers.

2. [See OED *v.*[1] 35 k 'Orig. *Austral.*': AND 1843.] To hold up (a person or vehicle) and rob on the highway; to rob (a bank).
1862 WEKEY *Otago As It Is* 51 The consequence [of many leaving ill-equipped] was, that some of those who carried up provisions with them were 'stuck up' on the road, and the principles of communism were practically realised on the way to the Dunstan El Dorado. **1866** BURGESS *Confessions* (1983) 107 Had he attempted to stick him up Mr Fox would have shot him dead. **1881** NESFIELD *Chequered Career* 79 Burgess..insisted on 'sticking' the old fellow up.

Hence **sticking up** *vbl. n.*, a hold-up involving robbery with violence.
1865 CHUDLEIGH *Diary* 26 Mar. (1950) 170 At some time I must have about £1000 on my person and as sticking up and robbing is quite the thing, I shall carry a loaded revolver. **1874** BATHGATE *Col. Experiences* 219 'Sticking up' as [highway robbery] is called in the colonies. **1899** BELL *In Shadow of Bush* 156 'Dastardly attempt at sticking-up!'.. He was stopped and accosted by a man..[who] presenting a pistol at the rider, demanded his money or his life. **1925** BATHGATE *Random Recolls.* 27 There was only one case of the sticking-up of a banker in Otago, when Skinner..had been robbed when returning from a gold-buying expedition to the Nevis.

3. In *absol.* use. To stop (dead); to be hindered from proceeding.
1865 CHUDLEIGH *Diary* 4 Nov. (1950) 203 The river was very high.., having got over that you had to walk some way and then get into a bullock dray and cross a branch.., the bullocks sticking up in the middle each time. **1884** TUCKER *Let. from Abroad* 83 We passed only two vehicles on the road—one being an old coach 'stuck up' two years ago and left. **1891** CHAMIER *Philosopher Dick* 247 One cursed lot [of sheep] stuck up in the middle of the stream.

4. To accost (a person usu. for a favour), to hit (someone) up (for a favour). See also BAIL *v.* I 2 c.
1886 CLAYDON *Handbook NZ* 10 I was 'stuck up'—to use a favourite colonial expression—by a newly arrived immigrant from England. **c1890** BODELL *Soldier's View Empire* (1982) 211 One day he passed my store and I stuck him up and asked for my money. **1909** THOMPSON *Ballads About Business* 11 He..stuck me oop in street..und borrowed the rhino to file. **1934** HARPER *Windy Island* 236 Suppose we stick him up tomorrow [*sc.* about a job]. **1951** Heard by editor in Wellington: He stuck us up for a donation.

stick up, *v.*[2] [Used elsewhere, but apparently infrequently: see OED *v.*[1] 35 j, 1865, 1874 quots. only.] Orig. to charge liquor on a hotel score, to 'chalk up', to 'put on the slate'; hence, to charge any goods to one's credit account.
c1875? in *NZ Songster No. 3* 69 He'll drink and commence then to skite; And replies when he's asked for the shilling, 'Stick it up, you know me, it's all right.' **1897** WRIGHT *Station Ballads* 19 [He was] sticking up his tucker at the store. **1906** ELKINGTON *Adrift in NZ* 244 We then 'stick up' provisions in the store. **1949** Havelock store (Ed.). *stick up* a common term with *book up* for charging groceries to one's account: 'Stick it up on Dad's account.'

stick up, *v.*[3] As **to stick up to** (someone) [f. Brit. dial.: see OED *stick v.*[1] 35 c, 1850–99], to make love to, to make up to.
1906 *Truth* 24 Nov. 8 He was married. But he was also sticking up to a barmaid at a Gill-street hotel, and wanted to take a trip with her to Sydney.

stick up, *v.*[4] To build or erect hastily (and roughly), to run up.
1911 *Truth* 6 May 4 Having noticed in the papers that you want a few sheds stuck up, pulled down, or some other old thing, I thought as I've nothing else to fall back on just now I'd take it on.

sticky, *a.*

1. Of sheep, awkward or slow to move or respond to handling.
1955 BOWEN *Wool Away* 7 No one knows better than I how a bad run can tend to get a man down—a run of sticky sheep, or gear not cutting the best. **1971** NEWTON *Ten Thousand Dogs* 169 *Sticky sheep:* Sheep which are stiff and sluggish to move and work.

2. As **sticky weed,** FLYCATCHER 2 (*Silene gallica*).
1926 [FLYCATCHER 2].

3. [f. STICKY *n.*] Having the characteristics of a sweet dessert wine.
1995 *Dominion* (Wellington) 12 Aug. 19 As for the sticky chardonnay, for anyone who can afford to pay $28 or $29 and likes a rich dessert wine, this is it.

sticky, *n.* [An ellipt. use of *sticky a.* glutinous, as of a syrup: prob. orig. Austral. (1992): in Brit. use *sticky* can have the sense 'liqueur'.] Usu. as **stickies,** a somewhat pejorative name for sweet dessert wines as a class.
1993 *Cuisine* 38 (Auckland) Apr.–May 77 Pressed to reveal his favourite wines, Taylor admits to a passion for 'stickies' and fortifieds. **1995** *Metro* (Auckland) Jan. 44 Sensible too is the wine list—eight champagnes-methode champenoises, 12 whites, 10 reds, and five of what have recently become known, childishly in my opinion, as 'stickies'. **1995** *Evening Post* (Wellington) 12 oct. 20 Te Whare Ra is also bringing a 1995 chardonnay 'sticky', a sweet wine made from botrytis-affected grapes. **1996** *Dominion* (Wellington) 20 Apr. 19 There were several restaurants which failed to get it right with the same light, sweet muscat, treating it as if it were a rather robust sticky.

stickybeak, *n.* [f. *sticky* + *beak* nose: AND 1920.]

1. Also occas. **sticky beaker**. An inquisitive person; a nosy-parker; the nose of a nosy-parker. Also *attrib.*, inquisitive.
1937 *Truth* 10 Nov. 9 [Heading] 'Granity is full of Stickybeaks.' Declares Wife. **1945** BURTON *In Prison* 19 [He] shuffles off with an audible..exhortation to a young policeman to keep his distance and not be a stickybeak. **1948** BALLANTYNE *Cunninghams* (1976) 28 He wasn't like those other stickybeak kids, he reckoned. **1955** BJ *Cameron Collection* (TS July) sticky beak (n) A person who sticks his (or her) nose into other people's business. **1986** *Islands* 37 45 Because every grown-up was at church..we didn't have to worry

about nosey-parkers or sticky-beaks. **1992** *Dominion* (Wellington) 4 Aug. 7 Most people would be surprised to find out just how many sticky beakers there are out there. **1992** *Evening Post* (Wellington) 17 Nov. 4 My reaction to his command that I accompany him..was a closed fist on his sticky beak.

2. A prying examination.

1992 *Metro* (Auckland) June 24 Guests were invited to have a good old sticky beak around. **1996** *Evening Post* (Wellington) 27 Jan. 11 Up to 20,000 people a year visited Government House..invited, or just for an officially sanctioned sticky-beak.

stickybeak *v.* [AND 1933.] *intr.* To pry. Usu. as a *ppl. a.* **sticky-beaked**, nosy; or as a *vbl. n.* (also *attrib.*) **stickybeaking**, prying.

1931 *NZ Dairy Exporter and Home Jrnl.* 30 May 45 [She] said she hated the matron, as she was a long-nosed, sticky-beaked, old devil. **1948** BALLANTYNE *Cunninghams* (1976) 78 She was one of those sticky-beaked tarts who know all the gossip going. **1934** *Truth* 10 Jan. 8 Pigs give officialdom full scope for its prying and sticky-beaking proclivities. **1968** *NZ Contemp. Dict. Suppl.* (Collins) 18 *sticky-beak..v.i.* pry, be inquisitive. **1991** *Dominion* (Wellington) 3 Jan. 8 Visitors need permits from the Central Land Council and these are rarely granted for mere stickybeaking.

stiff, *a.*

1. *Obs.* Horseracing. [See OED *stiff n.* 3. b, *U.S.*] Of a horse, certain not to win.

1891 WILLIAMS & REEVES *In Double Harness* 3 A horse that isn't 'trying' or is 'stiff' or isn't 'going for the stuff'. **1905** *Truth* 26 Aug. 7 Put your money on the Lord instead of planking it on stiff horses.

2. *Obs.* [AND 1898.] Penniless. Also as a noun, a penniless person.

1906 *Truth* 15 Sept. 3 If they are 'silvery' they will walk out again; if 'stiff' they will work a week or two to get a few shillings to take them on the road again. **1917** *Chron. NZEF* 19 Sept. 54 In Wellington the wind nips you... But when you are in Auckland the stiffs nip you, to raise the wind. **1935** STRONG in Partridge *Slang Today* 287 I'll admit I was stiff when I lost that fifty francs, but my cobber produced another ten; and when the ring-keeper said 'Up and do 'em', I collected another 200 francs.

3. a. Unlucky, esp. in the collocation **stiff luck** [AND 1919], alluding to a tough or hard or unfortunate time. Occas. as a noun, an unlucky person (see quot. 1918).

1917 *NZ at the Front* 107 Instead, they stood aside and murmured among themselves: 'Stiff luck!' **1918** *Chron. NZEF* 7 June 205 Remarks are heard on the 'tinny' luck or otherwise of the [poker-]players, while the 'stiffs' bemoan their luck. **1946** SARGESON *That Summer* 58 But a young joker got up..and said he wished I hadn't done that... Stiff luck, I said. *Ibid.* 73 But Terry said he was stiff because the one he would have picked [from the doubles chart] had been taken. **1958** *Listener* 27 June 6 Then came the third Test... Maybe they were a bit stiff to lose that. **1968** SLATTER *Pagan Game* 159 Whadya take in the double? Grenadier... That was a bit stiff only getting the first leg in. **1988** MCGILL *Dict. Kiwi Slang* 107 *stiff* unlucky, often expressed sarcastically in such phrases as *stiff luck, stiff cheese, stiff cheddar;* eg 'I've just eaten the last sausage roll. Stiff cheese, old boy'.

b. stiff kumara, a var. of *stiff luck*.

1965 HILLIARD *Power of Joy* 208 A roar from the back: 'He never got down here!' 'That's just stiff kumara,' Baldy said.

stiff, *n. Obs.* Anything delivered illicitly or under duress, esp. to a prison inmate.

1907 *Truth* 2 Feb. 5 Any friend of an inmate caught passing in a 'stiff', i.e. a letter, or tobacco or anything else is liable to a heavy fine or imprisonment. **1911** *Truth* 25 Mar. 1 So eager was the 'snout' to get rid of the blue paper [*sc.* summons] that he had to rush up and deliver the 'stiff' just at the moment the fares were taking their seats.

stiffen the crows: see CROW *n.*¹ 4.

stiffie. [*stiff* + -IE.] An erection.

1995 *Listener* 15 Apr. 63 PC O'Connor sneers at him for 'running around with a permanent stiffie'. Nowhere is it written that you need bad language and sexual reference to make good police drama.

stilt. [Spec. use of *stilt, Himantopus* spp.]

1. Either of two slim wading birds of *Himantopus* spp. (fam. Recurvirostridae) having very long slender legs. See also POAKA *n.*², TOREA 2.

1855 DRURY *Sailing Directions* 66 Stilts—two kinds, called Toria by natives. **1882** POTTS *Out in Open* 226 Soon after, [came] the yelping cry of the stilt (himantopus) apparently from a great height. **1917** WILLIAMS *Dict. Maori Lang.* 332 *Poaka... stilt,* and..*pied stilt;* shore birds. **1932** STEAD *Life Histories NZ Birds* 97 Despite the fact that Stilts are of proportions that are somewhat unusual among birds, their movements at all times are exceedingly graceful. **1939** BEATTIE *First White Boy Born Otago* 120 I saw stilts, the black-fellows..wading about.

2. With a modifier: **black, pied, white-headed**.

(1) **black stilt.** *Himantopus novaezelandiae,* a rare sooty-black stilt of the South Island. See also KAKI, *torea-pango* (TOREA 1).

1870 *TrNZI* II. 70 We have been told that there is not a Black Stilt, that the Black Stilt..is..but the pied species in an immature state of plumage... With the utmost deference to [Mr. Buller and Dr. Finsch]..we cannot consent to give up such an old acquaintance as the Black Stilt. **1873** BULLER *Birds NZ* 205 Himantopus novae zealandiae. (Black Stilt)...*Native name.*—Kaki. **1904** HUTTON & DRUMMOND *Animals NZ* 211 *The Black Stilt.*—*Kaki. Himantopus melas.* The Black Stilt breeds early in the season. **1917** WILLIAMS *Dict. Maori Lang.* 513 *Torea pango,* (Ar[awa])..*black stilt.* **1923** *NZJST* VI. 76 Black Stilt. It is extraordinary that I have very little recent information concerning this species. **1932** STEAD *Life Histories NZ Birds* 103 The two questions naturally arise: What was the Black Stilt, and, Why has it almost, if not completely, disappeared? **1955** OLIVER *NZ Birds* 306 Potts describes the Black Stilt as breeding on sandy river beds. **1966** FALLA et al. *Birds NZ* 148 Sometimes, perhaps as a result of crossing with the Pied Stilt, almost, but not entirely, black stilts are seen. **1976** SOPER *NZ Birds* 127 The generally accepted theory is that the Black Stilt is the original New Zealand Stilt. **1990** *Sunday Mag.* 22 July 25 Black Stilt: One of the rarest waders in the world, only 60 birds now survive.

(2) **pied stilt.** *Himantopus himantopus leucocephalus,* a common white-headed wading-bird. See also BARKER, PINK *n.,* POAKA *n.*², TOREA 2; *white-headed stilt* (3) below.

1870 [see POAKA *n.*²]. **1885** *NZJSc.* II. 558 Pied Stilt, Poaka.—Makes a slight nest of grass, often by the edge of lagoons or meres, in swamps. **1904** HUTTON & DRUMMOND *Animals NZ* 211 *The Pied Stilt.—Poaka...* The Pied Stilt usually commences to breed in October. **1917** WILLIAMS *Dict. Maori Lang.* 332 *Poaka... pied stilt;* shore birds. **1932** STEAD *Life Histories NZ Birds* 97 Among the plover which breed in New Zealand, the Pied Stilt is second in numbers only to the Banded Dotterel. **1947** [see (3) below]. **1976** SOPER *NZ Birds* 124 Pied Stilts are the common black and white, long spindle-legged waders that frequent lagoons, river beds and marshy places throughout the country. **1980** LOCKLEY *House Above Sea* 181 Pied stilt flocks are more straggling, moving about restlessly. **1992** LASENBY *The Conjuror* 13 He pointed to the swamp-hens, ducks and pied stilts by the stream.

(3) **white-headed stilt.** See *pied stilt* (2) above.

1873 BULLER *Birds NZ* 203 Himantopus leucocephalus. (White-headed Stilt)...*Native name.*—Tutumata; Torea (of Arawa tribe). **1889** *TrNZI* XXI. 220 *Himantopus leucocephala* (White-headed Stilt). **1917** WILLIAMS *Dict. Maori Lang.* 539 *Tuturi-pourewa... Himantopus leucocephalus,* white-headed stilt. **1947** POWELL *Native Animals NZ* 80 White-headed or Pied Stilt..Poaka..is widely distributed in both the North and South Islands of New Zealand. **1966** [see BARKER]. **1985** *Reader's Digest Book NZ Birds* 212 *Pied Stilt... Poaka,* white-headed stilt... Over the last 100 years, as forests have been turned to farmland, the pied stilt has greatly increased its range in New Zealand.

stingamaree, var. STINGAREE.

stingaree /ˌstɪŋɡəˈriː/. Also rarely **stingamaree, stingeree, stingy ray.** [Altered form of *sting ray* (or *stingy ray*): see OED, *U.S.* 1838; AND 1830.] *sting ray* (RAY 2 (3)). See also *eagle-ray* (RAY 2 (1)).

1843 WILLIAMS *NZ Jrnl.* (1956) 41 Of this variety of 78 [fish] species I will name a part, viz...Wai, Stingeree. **1848** TAYLOR *Leaf from Nat. Hist.* 14 Pākaurua..'stingy ray'. *Ibid.* 15 Roha, stingaree. **1855** TAYLOR *Te Ika A Maui* 627 The stingy ray, so called from its having a barbed spear beneath the tail, with which it inflicts very severe wounds, often proving fatal. **1872** HUTTON & HECTOR *Fishes NZ* 121 To this family of fishes also belongs the formidable Stingaree, or Wairepo of the Maoris. **1880** SENIOR *Travel & Trout* 300 Stingamaree, as it is vulgarly called. **1892** *TrNZI* XXIV. 215 Stingaree... Only one specimen recorded, from Ponui Passage, in July. **1917** *NZ Free Lance Christmas Annual* (Wellington) 51 There were toimunga, pipi, tuna, stingaree, and shark. **1927** *Otago Daily Times* (Dunedin) 3 Jan. 16 A mild sensation was caused amongst the bathers at Takapuna beach the other day by the capture of a stingray, or 'stingaree' as it is colloquially called. **1947** POWELL *Native Animals NZ* 63 Stingaree or Sting Ray... Our largest species..found in Southern Australia, Tasmania and New Zealand, more commonly in the North Island. **1956** GRAHAM *Treasury NZ Fishes* 100 The name Stingaree is a corruption of Sting Ray. **1962** *Sea Spray* Feb. 73 In the last 15 years two girls have been killed by stingarees. **1982** SUTTON-SMITH *Hist. Children's Play* 122 We dragged it in triumph to the township and there learned that it was a 'stingaree'. And 'stingarees' they remained for some years.

Hence **stingareeing,** see quot.

1873 TINNE *Wonderland of Antipodes* 95 We went out 'stingareeing', or spearing sting-rays.

sting ray: see RAY 2 (3).

stingy ray, var. STINGAREE.

stink, *a.* Adolescents. Used (mainly predicatively) to describe a person, thing, situation, etc. which is considered nauseously bad, unwelcome, rotten or unwholesome of its kind.

1993 *Listener* 9 Oct. 56 I needed the money for varsity so I sold some [books], but I ended up feeling stink. **1995** *Ibid.* 14 Jan. 21 Old houses are good, he

stinker, *n.*[1] Used elsewhere as a name commonly given by seamen, but well-attested from the New Zealand coast, for various ill-smelling petrels esp. (see OED *n.* 5) the *giant petrel* (PETREL 2 (10)). See also STINKPOT 1.
1893 *TrNZI* XXV. 80 M[ajaqueus] aequinoctialis... (The 'Stinker' of the whalers). The name is given on the authority of the whalers on the schooner 'Emma Jane'. **1966** [see PETREL 2 (10)]. **1982** [see NELLY]. **1986** FRASER *Beyond Roaring Forties* 21 The many petrels, fulmars, prions, and shearwaters range from the southern giant petrel, *Macronectes giganteus*, sometimes called the 'Stinker'..to the tiny fluttering prions.

stinker, *n.*[2] A clay marble of low repute.
1900 in Lawlor *Old Wellington Days* 2 Oct. (1959) 36 October 2... Marbles are in. Lost a sixer and two stinkers. **1951** FRAME *Lagoon* (1961) 116 I won nearly every game because the kids were so dazzled by the look of my stinkers... They came for miles to play marbles with me. **1959** [see GLASSIE]. **1992** PARK *Fence Around the Cuckoo* 62 One steelie to twenty-four ordinary clay stinkers was what I charged.

stinkie. Also **stinky.** [f. *stink*(er + -IE.] STINKER *n.*[2]; also occas. any unfavoured marble.
1943 [see DUMP *n.* 2]. [a**1946**] reminiscence in *Alfredton* (1987) 75 Colin Houlbrooke's glossary of marbles [of period 1927–46] lists... Stinkies—these were marbles made from clay, they did not work very well. **1955** *BJ Cameron Collection* (TS July) stinky (n) A small baked-clay marble. **1963** ADSETT *Magpie Sings* 124 Sixpence was a hell of a lot of money when you come to think of it. Worth about twenty marbles, more if they were only stinkies. **1972** *Bottle News* Dec. [unpaged] Many collectors will be familiar with the small stone marbles that one often picks up when digging for old bottles. The plain white marbles are called 'stinkies', but the more beautiful ones are called 'Agates'. **1992** GRACE *Cousins* 181 Hundreds of games [had been] played with bottlies, teapots, chinas, steelies, stinkies and stones. **1995** *Independent* 8 Dec. 20 Stinkies were clay marbles which often broke when hit hard.

stinking bug. *Obs. black beetle* (BEETLE 1).
1867 COOPER *Digger's Diary* (1978) Nov. 6 The annoyances [on Thames Goldfield] are, armies of mosquitoes..frequent visitations of the stinking or whare bug..and a deficiency..of all vegetable food.

stinko: see STINKWOOD.

stinkpot.
1. [Spec. uses of *stinkpot* a sailors' name for various species of petrel: see OED *n.* 3.] Esp. the *giant petrel*, and *white-chinned petrel* (PETREL 2 (10) and (21)). See also NELLY 1, STINKER *n.*[1]
1880 *Observer* (Auckland) 9 Oct. (Supplement) Another bird that we lived upon was what we called 'molly-hawk', but which we afterwards found out to be 'stinkpots', a carrion bird. **1888** BULLER *Birds NZ* II. 226 When the albatros[s]es have..disappeared one by one, the Giant Petrel (or 'Stink-pot', as the sailors sometimes call it) has remained. **1909** CHILTON *Subantarctic Islands NZ* II. 564 *Majaqueus aequinoctialis*... (Stink-pot; Cape hen; white-chinned petrel.) **1925** GUTHRIE-SMITH *Bird Life* 97 In all probability the Petrels—locally known as Stinkpots, and, I fear, without rhyme or reason treated as such—

had been harried and driven away from their tiny territory in wanton mischief. **1951** SORENSEN *Wild Life in Subantarctic* 21 The giant petrel..is more usually known as the 'nelly' and to sailors as the 'stinkpot', the latter appellation being bestowed because of its very strong musty odour and its habit of ejecting an evil-smelling oil if approached too closely.

2. A children's term of abuse, esp. for a piss-pants.
1963 FRAME *Reservoir* 47 Someone began to call my sister Stink-pot.

stinkwood. Also occas. **stinko.** [AND any of several trees or shrubs, 1827.] *Coprosma foetidissima* (fam. Rubiaceae), a native shrub or small tree unpleasantly odorous when its twigs or leaves are crushed or broken. See also HUPIRO.
1840 TAYLOR *Journal* (ATLTS) II. ii 302 2 Beautiful new pines a Juniper a Laurestina a stinkwood but the prevailing tree was a beech. **1889** *TrNZI* XXI. 382 There is also [on Auckland Islands]..the stink-wood (*Coprosma foetidissima*)—so called from its bad smell when cut. **1892** HOCKEN & FENWICK *Holiday Trip Catlins* 6 A delicate shrub, with pale-green foliage..is in common parlance [in Southland] the stinkwood (C. foetidissima). **1918** [see HUPIRO]. **1929** *Tararua Tramper* Oct. 2 The common stinkwood..now in bloom, is a good example of this [bisexual] arrangement. **1936** GUTHRIE-SMITH *NZ Naturalist* 232 On the moors [of Antipodes Islands] the red drupes of another crawling Stinkwood (*Coprosma repens*) is also devoured. **1947–48** BEATTIE *Pioneer Recolls.* (1956) 25 The knowing lads would select a stinkwood stick and would cut the bark just where his hand would grasp and soon his hand would smell awful. **1949** *Tararua Tramper* Aug. 6 Also noted were horopito, water fern and stinko (..*Coprosma foetidissima* to the botanist). **1952** RICHARDS *Chatham Is.* 61 [*Coprosma foetidissima*] does not smell while fresh, but Maoris do not use any of the karamus as firewood as heat makes the odour worse than ever... Stinkwood. Karamu, Hupiro. **1963** PEARSON *Coal Flat* 421 Stinkwood: A small shrub, a species of *Coprosma*, with an unpleasant smell when broken. **1988** DAWSON *Forest Vines to Snow Tussocks* 104 The coprosma is sometimes known as 'stinkwood' because the crushed leaves smell like rotten cabbage.

stinky, var. STINKIE.

stipe. [Prob. a transf. use of Brit. slang *stipe* stipendiary (magistrate), one paid a stipend: see OED *stipe n.* 2; AND 1902.] A stipendiary steward paid to enforce the rules of racing.
1917 *NZ Free Lance* (Wellington) 23 Feb. 25 It might not be generally known that the 'stipes' woke up at a recent Trentham meeting and asked a question of a Maori owner, whose horse had run nowhere at a meeting a week prior to the Wellington fixture and practically walked in at the latter. **1934** [see STRIKE *v.* 1]. **1953** *Truth* 1 Apr. 17 [Heading] Wealthy Wool Man Cites Trotting 'Stipe'. **1982** *Dominion* (Wellington) 17 Feb. 20 Ginger Tankard..is..an assistant stipendiary steward and once he gains elevation to the ranks of a fully-fledged stipe he will have to relinquish his duties.

stipendiary steward. *Horse-racing.* Also *ellipt.* **stipendiary.** A racing steward paid a stipend for services rendered. See also STIPE.
1913 *NZ Observer* 29 Mar. 16 The appointment of stipendiary stewards has caused a number of ancient and valuable stewards, who are not stipendiary, to grit their teeth in rage... Quite naturally the stipendiaries must justify their existence by 'butting in'. **1922** *Auckland Weekly News* 9 Mar. 49 The advisory position of the New Zealand stipendiary steward would break

any ordinary man's heart. **1938** *Auckland Weekly News* 19 Jan. 68 Even stipendiary stewards are not immune [from accidents]. **1977** KNIGHT *Greville* 83 The stipendiary steward of the time..remembers seeing the race from a different slant.

stir, *v.* [Prob. orig. f. a euphemistic shortening of *shit-stirring* or *stir shit.*]
1. [AND 1969.] **a.** *trans.* To make or stir up (trouble, etc.) for its own sake.
1972 *Truth* 19 Sept. 6 There's an empty pew across the chamber, and for once that doesn't mean that Rob's [sc. Hon. R. Muldoon] stirring something in someone else's electorate.

b. *intr.* or *absol.*
1974 *Evening Post* (Wellington) 27 Mar. 17 'I was trained to stir by Mr Clarke,' he alleged. **1984** BEATON *Outside In* 47 Ma:.. Don't mind some of the girls in here, they don't mean no harm. Always pullin' a few..to stir, you know.

2. *trans.* To provoke (someone) to anger or angry action.
1979 *Truth* 18 Sept. 12 Inside the tavern, some locals had been stirring them. About 30 people, including a dozen bikies, came to a sudden confrontation.

3. As *stir shit,* to make trouble.
1981 *Avondale College Slang Words* (Auckland) (Goldie Brown Collect.) Feb. *to stir shit*: to make trouble.

stir, *n.*
1. A bout of troublemaking.
1974 *Evening Post* (Wellington) 27 Mar. 17 The witness alleged a 'stir' was begun against Mr Willetts. Speeches and songs, some written by Mr Clarke and Mr Black, were taped and broadcast across citizens' band by himself, Mr Clarke, Mr Black, and others... Phone calls were also made. **1984** BEATON *Outside In* 21 Sandy: This is one helluva stir. *Ibid.* 40 Ma:.. Quick smart. Move it! The screws are gettin' jumpy! We don't want no more stirs.

2. A party, celebration; a 'rage'.
1980 *Islands* 29 131 Bit of a stir tonight in my unit, end of conference party sort of thing. **1983** *Listener* 9 July 13 'What is this place?' someone whispered. 'I'm not sure but when I was a law student we used to hire it out for stirs. The floor used to be awash with beer.' **1984** 17 F E54 Pakuranga Coll. 34 (Good) stir! [F2 M4] **1984** BEATON *Outside In* 35 Di: Pity you missed out on the fun, Ma... Sandy: Best stir we had in ages.

stirabout. *Hist.* [A transf. local use of Brit. provincial *stirabout* an oatmeal porridge: see OED 'Orig. Anglo-Irish'.] A thin gruel or hasty pudding made of flour (occas. oatmeal or rotten corn), sugar, and boiling water much liked by Maoris during early European contact. Cf. LILIPI.
1827 WILLIAMS *Early Jrnls* 30 July (1961) 63 His sick wife had a mess of stirabout and a piece of salt beef, according to her particular request. [1961 *Note*] A mixture of flour and water sweetened with sugar, of which the Maoris were very fond. The Maori name was *kororirori*. **1829** *Ibid.* 14 Apr. 152 Gave out some flour for stir-about and concluded peace [with the Maori]. **1839** TAYLOR *Journal* 13 Nov. II. 168 I gave [the natives] some flour with which they manufactured *stir about* and soon finished it using fingers for spoons. **1842** in Selwyn *Reminiscences* (1961) 23 This [promise] gave huge satisfaction as did a great supply of stirabout, simply ordinary Paste with sugar, which I brought forward. **1851** *Canterbury Papers* II. 310 Our barrel of meal gives us stirabout and oaten bread daily. **1863** MOSER *Mahoe Leaves* 22 In that state it [rotten corn] is

boiled in water, and made into 'stir-a-bout', and I have been told it has a strong taste of old Stilton cheese. **1899** GRACE *Sketch NZ War* 23 Begorra, sir, there is no stirabout and milk in this country at all, at all. **1912** *NZ Free Lance* (Wellington) 13 Apr. 5 One day the native cooks opened the bag of lime, thinking it was flour, and proceeded to mix it with water and sugar, in order to provide 'stirabout' or 'lillipee', dear to the palate of the Maori. **1947** BRERETON *No Roll of Drums* 69 Irishisms were in daily use, one was pronounced 'wan', clothes 'cloes', an apron was a 'praskeen', an idiot was an 'omadhaun', to be naughty was to be 'bold'..and porridge 'stirabout'. **1982** BURTON *Two Hundred Yrs. NZ Food* 17 'Twenty pots of stirabout' [Marianne Williams journal] (Stirabout, otherwise known as lillipee, consisted simply of flour and sugar mixed together with a little boiled water.)

stirrer. [Prob. orig. a shortened or euphemistic form of *shit-stirrer*: AND 'chiefly Aust.', 1966.] One who stirs up trouble for its own sake; often *spec.* a political or social agitator or crusader.
[*Note*] Poss. popularized from use by (and of) the publicly aggressive late Sir Robert Muldoon (cf. MULDOON).
[**1927** *NZ Tablet* (Dunedin) 9 Nov. 58 Maybe you have never heard of stick-stirrers. They are of the ancient order of trouble brewers but they brew silently.] **1972** *Dominion* (Wellington) 25 Oct. 4 He was not afraid of authority but he was not a stirrer. His provocations were incidental to caring for the losers who came to him, for shelter or for guidance. **1976** SINCLAIR *Nash* 292 Nordmeyer..had been numbered in the ranks of the dissidents as an ambitious young 'stirrer'. **1981** KENNEDY *Straight from Shoulder* 24 Was the barman right when he said that outside 'stirrers' were to blame? **1983** SINCLAIR *Hist. Univ. of Auckland* 151 By 1939 the leading academic agnostic, stirrer, and radical, and soon 'establishment figure', 'Tommy' Hunter of Victoria, was knighted. **1983** HULME *Bone People* 395 Going flat on his face in the slime, I couldn't give a damn for him, the two-faced stirrer, going to the police behind everyone's back. **1992** *Dominion* (Wellington) 6 May 3 The Maori parents..had to suffer..many accusations..calling them degrading terms like stirrers and radicals.

stirring, *vbl. n.* [See STIR *v.*] Troublemaking; agitating or crusading for a cause. Also *attrib.*
1973 MCCARTHY *Listen..!* 49 Our friend S.P. was in one of his 'stirring' moods, and immediately started on me for playing such a cissy game. **1980** MANTELL *Murder & Chips* 48 Keep all this under your cap... Time enough when we've got something concrete to go on. Then we can start stirring. And I mean stirring. **1985** MITCALFE *Hey Hey Hey* 108 'And, if it's jus' the paper "stirring", what then?'... 'Now you jus' a "stirrer" too,' said Vaine.

stitchbird. [f. one of its calls: see quots. 1873, 1948.] *Notiomystis cincta*, a bush-bird of the honey-eating family Meliphagidae, now surviving only on a few offshore islands. See also HIHI.
1871 HUTTON *Catalogue Birds NZ* 5 Stitch Bird. Ihi. **1873** BULLER *Birds NZ* 98 (Stitch-bird)... Ihi,..Hihi, Tihe, Kotihe, Kotihewera, male and female are sometimes distinguished as Hihi-paka and Hihi-matakiore or Tihe-kiore. *Ibid.* 99 At..times [the male stitch-bird] produces a sharp clicking sound like the striking of two quartz stones together: the fanciful resemblance to the word 'stitch', whence the popular name of the bird is derived. **1884** *NZJSc.* II. 276 Stitch-bird, Ihi.—This shy and now rare honey-eater is seldom met with. **1896** *Otago Witness* (Dunedin) 23 Jan. 14 For a period of 10 months prior to the protective proclamation two men were living on [Little Barrier] island doing nothing all the time but collecting stitchbirds, which they procured with dust shot, and skinned to the order of an Auckland dealer. **1904** HUTTON & DRUMMOND *Animals NZ* 104 The Stitch-birds have become quite extinct on the mainland. If they live at all, they can be seen only on Little Barrier Island. **1917** WILLIAMS *Dict. Maori Lang.* 147 *Kohihi... stitch-bird.* = *hihi*. **1923** *NZJST* VI. 94 Stitch-bird. The disappearance of this beautiful species from the mainland at a date so early in the history of colonization remains inexplicable. **1948** *NZ Forest Inhabiting Birds* The call has been rendered by some writers as 'stt' or 'sttich', and it is from a resemblance of this sound to the word 'stitch' that the bird derives its common name. **1955** OLIVER *NZ Birds* 511 The note from which the Stitchbird derives its name is the cry 'tee-tee-tee' which it always repeats as it comes round to investigate any intruder into its domain. **1970** *Annot. Checklist Birds NZ* 69 Stitchbird (Hihi)..believed extinct on mainland since about 1885. **1984** SOPER *Birds NZ* 148 Stitchbirds are active, restless and quick moving... Their call note is an explosive *tzit* or *stitch* from which the name presumably is derived. **1990** *Listener* 16 July 14 This is New Zealand the way it used to be..where a self-respecting stitch bird or kiwi can still look for food on the ground without feeling the fangs of some alien predator on its endangered throat.

stock. [Spec. use of *stock* livestock (see OED *n.*[1] 63 a) in combinations, most of which have been used elsewhere but are of New Zealand significance.]

1. Used *attrib.* in Comb. **stock doctor, fence, manager, pen** [AND 1808], **-raising, terracing, track, truck, work** [AND 1943].
1937 AYSON *Thomas* 162 Thomas had a reputation as a **stock doctor**, but this was enhanced by his first aid treatment of a man who was injured by a fall from a horse. **1930** REISCHEK *Yesterdays in Maoriland* (1933) 260 The wildest beasts, once caught and driven into the stockyard, are quickly dispatched. One such animal would have broken through the high **stock fence** had I not put a bullet through him. **1964** ANDERSON *Doctor in Mountains* (1974) 27 On Wednesday 28 August 1907 we reached Wellington. We were met..by Mr Arthur Jackman, the **stock manager** through whose agency I had secured the cadet job. **1847** RONALDSON *Journal* 19 Apr. in Taylor *Journal* (ATLTS) V. 312 On going up to the **Stock pen** at the top of the hill we found his eldest daughter with a horrible gash in her forehead. **1902** *Settler's Handbook NZ* iii The fourth gives various information about cultivation and **stock-raising**, with reference particularly to meat-freezing and dairy-farming. **1914** PFAFF *Diggers' Story* 89 Stock-raising and dairying have certainly come to stay in Westland. **1951** LEVY *Grasslands NZ* (1970) 254 On steep hillsides stock will tend to track and contour the land, and the ultimate surface formation of well-stocked country will be a series of broad or narrow terraces with steep slopes between them upon which stock seldom tread. With a view to soil conservation, this **stock terracing** could probably be encouraged by running contour furrows along the hillsides. **1902** *Settler's Handbook NZ* (Lands Dept.) 52 Tracks have also been constructed giving easy access to the Franz Josef and Fox glaciers, and in the future, as population increases, doubtless tourist and **stock tracks** will be constructed. **1986** HOLCROFT *Sea of Words* 182 Yes, he told us,.. we would see occasional **stock-trucks**. **1988** HILL *More from Moaville* 23 Home players on the Moaville Tennis Courts have also learned the wisdom of offering to take the saleyards end. From here, they can serve against a background of dust..raised by stock trucks taking off. **1960** SCRYMGEOUR *Memories Maoriland* 108 Life now throbbed with interest, mustering, plenty of **stockwork**, quite a few useful hacks.

2. a. Special Comb. **stock agent**, a specialist dealer in livestock; **stock-boy**, a lad employed to help with the care of livestock; **stock bridge**, a bridge reserved mainly for travelling stock; **stock camp**, CAMP *n.* 2 a; **stock-camping** *vbl. n.*, of stock, assembling or resting in a preferred place; **stock carrying capacity**, CARRYING-CAPACITY; **stock-cattle** *obs.*, *spec.* store-cattle imported from Australia into early New Zealand; **stock dam**, an artificial pond on a farm providing water for stock; **stock driver** [AND 1836], DROVER; **stock driving** *vbl. n.* [AND 1849], the occupation of 'droving', the moving of farm stock over long distances; **stock farmer** *obs.*, one who farms livestock rather than crops; **stock-farming**, pastoral farming; **stockholder** [AND 1804], a person who owns (usu. large herds of) livestock (see also *stockowner* below, RUNHOLDER); **stock-holding** *ppl. a.* [AND 1844]; **stock-horse (-mare, -pony)** [AND 1838], a horse trained to work with stock; **stock inspector**, one employed to inspect livestock and enforce compliance with regulations concerning livestock; **stock-master**, one owning or controlling livestock; **stockowner** [AND 1804], one who owns livestock and usu. (but not necessarily) the land the stock runs on; **stock-rider** *obs.* [AND 1844], one who is employed to drive (occas. to tend) livestock, esp. cattle, from horseback; **stock-riding** *vbl. n.* [AND 1869]; **stock route** [AND 1884], earlier, a designated route allowable and convenient for the passage of driven livestock; later, a route along which livestock are driven through a town and on which they are given right of way over vehicles; **stock station** [AND 1824], a station or large farm where beef cattle or sheep are raised (cf. STATION 3 a); **stock unit** (also called 'ewe-equivalent'), the hypothetical annual feed requirement of a ewe rearing a lamb, used as the basis of comparison for different classes and species of livestock.

1933 *Press* (Christchurch) (Acland Gloss.) 9 Sept. 15 Dealers and **stock-agents** use various terms..to make failing mouthed sheep sound younger. **1985** *NZ Times* 12 May 8 I hasten to explain, the stock agent bought on our behalf, a further dozen 18-month steers. **1988** *Univ. Entr. Board Bursaries Eng. Exam.* 6 The stock agent would arrive to do the drafting every so often. **1989** *A NZ Prayerbook* 64 All sweepers and diplomats, writers and artists, grocers, carpenters, students and stock-agents,... give to our God your thanks and praise. **1939** BEATTIE *First White Boy Born Otago* 53 He had a mare named Folly; a **stock-boy** had her out one day near Goodwood and I begged a ride. **1982** WHEELER *Hist. Sheep Stations NZ* 10 [Caption] **Stock bridge** on the Von [river]. **1950** *NZJAg.* Aug. LXXXI. 141 Variegated thistle established on a **stock camp** site under a tree. **1951** LEVY *Grasslands NZ* (1970) 31 One direct outcome..of this increased carrying capacity was to overcrowd the stock camps on the knolls and ridges. *Ibid.* 32 Almost all hill country is subject to damage by intensification of **stock camping** on the hilltops. **1866** MURRAY *Descr. Prov. Southland* 9 The **stock-carrying capacity** of the natural herbage is of course variable. **1840** WARD *Information Relative NZ* 15 Load with **stock-cattle** for New Zealand. **1842** *Jrnl. Josiah Flight* 3 Mar. in Rutherford & Skinner *Establish. New Plymouth* (1940) 200 Captain King, R.N., was also a passenger to Sydney for the purpose of purchasing stock-cattle and sheep for the New Plymouth settlement. **1984** MARSHALL *Day Hemingway Died* 17 I saw the **stock dams** I had swum in, shot ducks on: I passed the windbreaks. **1989** MARSHALL *Divided*

World 60 The stock dam is large enough to keep the water clean. **1851** *Lyttelton Times* 19 Apr. 5 The Government might have founded a colony composed of stragglers from other settlements, of whale fishers and **stock drivers**. **1862** Chudleigh *Diary* 7 Mar. (1950) 27 I rode a young horse that was partly broken and then sent up here to Draper to ride on the run to make it quiet for he is the best stock driver in the Colony. **1883** *Canterbury Rhymes* 104 Oh, well for the stockdriver's cob, For the creek where he quenches his thirst! **1947** Beattie *Early Runholding* 12 In my boyhood [1880–90s] we called a man driving sheep a drover, and a man driving cattle a stock-driver or stock-rider or stockman. **1867** Phillips *Rockwood Jrnl.* 29 Sept. (Canterbury Pub. Lib. TS) 126 T.A.P. & I.I. **stock driving**. **1891** Chamier *Philosopher Dick* 48 Some go stock-driving. **1935** Odell *Handbook Arthur's Pass National Park* 49 The adventure of the gold rush, the lively days of stock driving, and the romance of the stage coaches, have each its chapter in this history. **1849** Allom *Letter* in Earp *Handbook* (1852) 118 The favourableness of the climate..is the greatest charm of the **stock-farmer**'s life in New Zealand. **1877** *TrNZI* IX. 99 To the stock farmer or the agricultural settler the opinions..will appear hypercritical. **1851** Weld *Hints to Intending Sheep-farmers* 2 I have also found this to be the opinion..of men..possessing an extensive experience of the business of **stock-farming**. **1845** Deans *Pioneers Port Cooper Plains* (1964) 28 Sept. 45 Whether there is a settlement formed here or not, I have no doubt that this district will be occupied..by parties who are desirous of depasturing sheep and cattle..so that the first **stockholders** will have the best chance. **1851** *Lyttelton Times* 2 Aug. 6 A stockholder who will put 1000 ewes on a station can obtain a run of 20,000 acres. **1861** *McLean Papers* (ATLTS) XIX. 170 It has been in the occupation of two Stock holders. **1947** Beattie *Early Runholding* 11 So aghast was I [at the wrong use of synonyms for 'runholder'] that I spent weeks collecting every old term for 'runholders' I could, and I found thirteen, viz... 'run owners', 'sheep owners', 'sheep holders', 'sheep masters', 'squatters', 'station holders', 'station owners', 'stock holders', and 'stock owners'. **1960** Oliver *Story NZ* 109 Grey, in 1853, had provided for stockholders' licences, by which the sheepowner paid the Crown a rental based upon the size of his flocks, and not the amount of land he occupied. **1855** *Otago Witness* (Dunedin) 14 Apr. 2 The election had terminated in favour of the **stock-holding** interest. **1846** Weekes in Rutherford & Skinner *Establish. New Plymouth* (1940) 124 'Peter' was an excellent **stock-horse**, would follow cattle like a dog, being always ready to check any rebellious indications. **1862** Chudleigh *Diary* 25 Aug. (1950) 55 Every stock-horse knows he must win the race or be tossed so they *do go it*. **1874** Kennaway *Crusts* 206 If he pulled up hard and '*slewed*' sharp around on his heels, the stock-horse would come up standing. **a1906** Stack *Through Canterbury* (1972) 10 Our Maori friend was mounted on a strong, wiry Australian stock-horse. **1933** *Press* (Christchurch) (Acland Gloss.) 16 Dec. 21 *Stock horse.*—Horse used to cattle work, cutting out, etc. **1940** Studholme *Te Waimate* (1954) 139 The stock-horses were all standing tied up to the rails outside the yards. **1961** Crump *Hang On a Minute Mate* 73 One of my musterers..asked me to keep my eye open for a good stock-horse. **1909** Thompson *Ballads About Business* 30 Und tole der **shtock inspector**. **1930** Acland *Early Canterbury Runs* 47 He then became Stock Inspector in the North Island, but quarrelled with his superiors. **1878** Elwell *Boy Colonists* 102 Ernest was despatched to help, on a very good **stock-mare**. **1851** Weld *Hints to Intending Sheep-farmers* 6 Every **stock-master** will take pride in his little herd of horses. **1938** Hyde *Nor Yrs. Condemn* 122 Old Hone and Hori made rotten stock-masters. They sat in the sun, smoking and dreaming..and letting their thin Jersey cows bellow..unmilked. **1851** Wakefield *Let. to Sir George Grey* 31 The **stockowner**, though brought up as a gentleman, if long in the 'bush' learns first to be proud of the 'bush' manners. **1869** *TrNZI* I. (rev. edn.) 184 The losses sustained by the stockowners and farmers..if realised, would have eradicated [tutu]. **1882** *Ibid.* XIV. 271 Most stock-owners wean their lambs on their best feed. **1902** *Settler's Handbook NZ* (Lands Dept.) 215 On petition of stock-owners (*i.e.*, owners or managers of more than 500 sheep or 100 head of cattle) [etc.]. **1933** *Press* (Christchurch) (Acland Gloss.) 16 Dec. 21 *Stock owner.*—The early squatters always described themselves either as *s[tock]o[wner]* or *runholder*. **1947** [see *stock holder* above]. **1904** *NZ Illustr. Mag.* June 197 Howard's struck the summit this time, entered one of his **stock-ponies**, with the stockman up! **c1875** Meredith *Adventuring in Maoriland* (1935) 78 On that occasion [*sc.* a fancy-dress ball] he [*sc.* J.M. Larnach] appeared as a **stockrider**, dressed in scarlet jumper, corduroy pants, and top-boots. He had a twenty-foot stock whip. **1892** *NZ Official Handbook* 157 To those whose proclivities tend towards a pastoral life, occupation as stockriders, shepherds, &c., on one of the large cattle- and sheep-runs common in the colony may be obtained. **1912** Booth *Five Years NZ* 24 The horse was never safe for a lady..and he was soon after disposed of to a stock-rider. **1947** Beattie *Early Runholding* 12 In my boyhood we called a man driving sheep a drover, and a man driving cattle a stock-driver or stock-rider or stockman. **c1891** Cottle *Frank Melton's Luck* 52 He had not quite mastered the mysteries of **stock-riding** yet. **1912** Booth *Five Years NZ* 46 [Caption] Cattle ranching and stockriding. **1937** Ayson *Thomas* 86 This was his first experience of stock-riding, but many hundreds of miles was he to ride after cattle in succeeding years. **1931** *Tararua Tramper* Feb. 2 It was formerly used by Putara farmers..as a **stock route**. **1958** *Tararua* Sept. 76 We learned that the high-level track shown on the map is the regular stock route and it would have cut our time by half. **1977** Marks *Hammer & Tap* 510 Watson Shennan had pioneered an inland stock route in the late 1850s. **1986** Brown *Weaver's Apprentice* 166 The boy at the centre of it all..had been seen on the old stock route to the plains. **1994** Lasenby *Dead Man's Head* 68 The road down Seddon Street was too rough because it was the stock route through Waharua. **1843** Chapman *NZ Portfolio* 38 [Mr. Crawford] who proved the sincerity of his opinion by establishing a **stock-station** on the peninsula formed by Evans Bay. **1866** Angas *Polynesia* 111 This [Wairarapa] is one of the finest pastoral districts in New Zealand, now exhibiting..the homesteads and stock-stations of numbers of thriving settlers, rich in sheep and cattle. **1936** Belshaw et al. *Agric. Organiz. NZ* 412 Statistically the **stock unit** position of the Auckland land district is very similar to North Auckland. **1951** Levy *Grasslands NZ* (1970) 263 [Caption] In 1966, aircraft applied 1,000,000 tons of fertiliser to the hills, and if this practice were continued over the same country every year some 30,000,000 additional sheep stock units would be run on the hills. **1992** *Marlborough Express* (Blenheim) 31 Jan. 5 Puhi Peaks carries 5000 stock units on country classified as low hills to alpine.

b. Forming adjectives **stock-proof**, of a fence, impervious to livestock; of a pig-dog, not given to worrying livestock; **stock-sick**, of land, unthrifty through over-stocking (cf. sick *a.* 1).

1915 *NZJAg.* Feb. X. 190 If the long shoots of this plant [*sc. Eleagnus*] are interlaced while the hedge is growing it makes a close and excellent **stock-proof** fence. **1940** [see *boundary-fence* (boundary 3)]. **1982** Holden *Wild Pig* 157 [The pigdog Tip] was absolutely stock-proof. **1986** Carr *Diary Pig Hunter* 21 The boundary fence on Tony Schluter's property was in pretty good shape, stock proof for 99.9 per cent of the way around the 800 odd acres. **1939** Vaile *Pioneering the Pumice* 17 When I add that the land [in the central North Island] was reputed to be '**stock sick**'. **1955** *BJ Cameron Collection* (TS July) stock-sick (adj) Land on which stock have been grazed too long, so that it has become impregnated with disease.

3. Used *attrib.* in the phr. **stock and station**. **a.** [AND 1872.] Of a firm ('agency'), its employees, or its business of dealing in livestock, land, farm products, farm supplies or financing primary industry.

[**1922** *Evening Post* (Wellington) 10 Jan. in Newman ed. *Read All About It* (1969) 13 Representatives of New Zealand stock, station, and agency firms met in Wellington yesterday and discussed the proposed meat pool.] **1934** Mulgan *Spur of Morning* 52 When he left school..he was put into the office of a large stock and station firm to learn the business side of sheep farming. **1952** *Landfall 23* 224 Again, I want to make it clear that I am not siding with the philistines of city newspapers, stock and station agencies, and Parliament House. **1959** Slatter *Gun in My Hand* 96 'What work are you in?' 'Oh, I'm up north. Buyer for a stock and station firm in the Waikato.' **1968** Slatter *Pagan Game* 50 He was assured of a position with a stock and station firm, but he had ambitions of being a..sports commentator.

b. As **stock and station agent** [AND 1884], also occas. in shortened form **station agent** or **stock agent** (see also 2 a above), a stock and station agency, or an employee of such an agency.

1875 Rives *Jottings on the Spot* (Canterbury Pub. Lib. TS) 9 Mar. 11 I then called on Wilkin the great [Canterbury] station agent and after lunch he gave me some particulars of runs for sale. **1921** Guthrie-Smith *Tutira* (1926) 27 Riding through some such bit of country with a stock and station agent, he remarked [...]. **1938** Hyde *Nor Yrs. Condemn* 287 The Banks won't advance you money on your stock or equipment, but the stock and station agents, they're pawnbrokers, see? **1944** Scanlan *March Moon* 157 I introduced Owen at the bank, at the stock agent's and at two seed merchants. **1946** Mulgan *Pastoral NZ* 33 When such a [wealthy sheepfarmer] found himself severely rationed in petrol by his bank or stock and station agent. **1974** Maughan *Good & Faithful Servants* 7 He had been able to improve..his holdings when the other 'gentry' were..signing their names to stock and station agents' orders [*i.e.* quasi-cheques on the account of an agency]. **1986** Davin *Salamander & the Fire* 71 Herbie was working for the stock and station agents who were our clients. **1992** Poole *Skinny Louie Book* 56 Tess had a nice job typing for Dilworths Station Agents.

stockade. *Hist.* [Transf. use of *stockade* a military fortification: cf. AND 1832, a place of confinement for convicts working in outlying districts; OED 2 c, a prison, esp. a military one.] An Auckland prison.

1869 Thatcher *Local Songs* 4 'Come along now,' says Plummer, 'and let us away, 'No longer in Chokee will we be confined, 'And long ere the warders turn out for their breakfast 'We'll have left the Stockade and Mount Eden behind. 'Softly, softly, let us away.' *Ibid.* 7 The Stockade bell will ring with joy... To welcome home their darling boy;.. The warders will make merry at night. **1882** Hay *Brighter Britain* I. 23 A man..on a subsequent conviction, might be sent to the Stockade (prison) without the option of a fine.

Stockholm tar. Often *ellipt.* **Stockholm**, and early as **Stockholm coal tar**. [Used elsewhere but recorded earliest in NZ and of significance esp. in its farming uses: see OED.] A kind of tar made from fine resins and in New Zealand used in ship-building, waterproofing and preserving timber, formerly for anointing cuts made in sheep's skin during shearing, and for other farm uses. See also TAR 1 a.

1848 WAKEFIELD *Handbook NZ* 180 tar, coal..Stockholm, 2*l.* 1882 CHUDLEIGH *Diary* 25 Oct. (1950) 313 All the gates soaked in tar boiling hot ½ stockholm ½ coal. 1981 CHARLES *Black Billy Tea* 7 Black billy tea, boy, Black as Stockholm tar.

stockie.

1. [f. *stock* (bowler + -IE.] In cricket, a stock bowler.

1974 *Evening Post* (Wellington) 11 Apr. 20 'Just who is going to take over from our stockies or from Howarth?' he queried.

2. [f. *stock*(car + -IE.] A stock-car owner or driver.

1981 *Dominion* (Wellington) 21 Feb. 16 Stockies promise fireworks. Stockcars will take pride of place at Te Marua Speedway tonight.

stock-keeper.

1. a. [AND *Obs.* 1795.] A person employed to tend livestock, a shepherd; STOCKMAN 1.

1834 MARKHAM *NZ* (1963) 41 He being known as the Kangaroo having Trowsers of Skin with the Fur on them like a Stock keeper at Van diemans land. 1840 *Bunbury's Rep.* 28 June in *GBPP House of Commons 1841 (No.311)* The only respectable [European] persons [on Kapiti] was [*sic*] a stock-keeper, in charge of some sheep and horned cattle, and the captain of a whaling vessel. 1856 FITTON *NZ* 292 Shepherds and stock-keepers [*sic*] wages are high in New Zealand; about £40 a year with house room and rations. 1878 BULLER *Forty Yrs. NZ* 451 Stock-keepers..£35..per annum. Shearers..15*s.* to 25*s.* per hundred. 1892 *NZ Official Handbook* 162 Pastoral labour... Stockkeepers, with board, per annum... Hutkeepers, with board, per annum.

b. In the collocation **stock-keeper's hut**, OUT-STATION 2.

1840 BEST *Journal* Sept. (1966) 244 [He] begged me to get him a bit of bread from a stock keeper's hut hard by [at Owhiro Bay, Wellington].

2. *stockowner* (STOCK 2 a).

1844 TUCKETT *Diary* 14 Apr. in Hocken *Contributions* (1898) 207 [Banks' Peninsula] a locality adapted for..ornamental grounds for future proprietors, who may hereafter acquire property as stock-keepers on the more available and valuable land of the main.

stock-keeping, *vbl. n. Obs.* [AND 1828.] The owning or tending of livestock.

1843 CHAPMAN *NZ Portfolio* 38 [Mr. Crawford] pronounced the neighbourhood..to be admirably adapted to the business of breeding and stock-keeping. 1848 *Lett. from Otago* 5 May (1978) 14 Stock-keeping pays well, and much better than agriculture. 1850 GODLEY *Letters* 7 May (1951) 53 Going up the country to a station, to spend a little time in stock-keeping.

stockman.

1. [AND 1803.] A man employed to work with or tend livestock, esp. cattle; in later use, a stockowner (see quot. 1995).

1840 *Bunbury's Rep.* 28 June in *GBPP House of Commons 1841 (No.311)* 106 A Captain Lethart, of Sydney..has established a cattle run, with about thirty head of horned cattle, and had two stockmen in charge of them. 1854 GOLDER *Pigeons' Parliament* 96 Here and there a stockman's cottage stands. 1863 CHUDLEIGH *Diary* 16 Dec. (1950) 113 I went to the stockman's hut but he was out so I wrote a full description of missing cattle and brands and stuck in the door. 1874 KENNAWAY *Crusts* 206 In tackling these cattle out on the runs, the stockmen had their work cut out, and the horses too. 1882 POTTS *Out in Open* 44 At breeding time, these birds [*sc.* falcons] have often chased cattle dogs to the shelter of the stockman's horse. 1912 FERGUSON *Castle Gay* 49 The stockman, in knee-boots and sash; The bushman—all were in their kind Proved men of mark and force of mind. 1921 *Quick March* 10 Feb. 36 In the succeeding two years the ex-coke-shoveller, boundary-rider, stockman..examined a mining boom. 1933 *Press* (Christchurch) (Acland Gloss.) 16 Dec. 21 *Stockman.*—Man employed to look after cattle, as a shepherd is employed to look after sheep. The *stock and station agents* call their yard-men *s[tock] men* also. 1947 BEATTIE *Early Runholding* 12 In my boyhood we called a man driving sheep a drover, and a man driving cattle a stock-driver or stock-rider or stockman. 1995 *Dominion* (Wellington) 25 Aug. 21 [Farming suppl.] Processors get the blame for stockmen's heavy losses.

Hence **stockmanship**, the ability to farm, handle or judge livestock.

1958 *NZJAg.* Dec. XCVII. 553 Good Stockmanship Pays: Avoid Carcase Bruising. 1959 *NZ Farmer* 11 June 5 Such a competition..would serve to emphasise the importance of achieving higher fertility in our flocks by the practice of good stockmanship. 1982 YEREX *Farming Deer* 104 The first requisite in the handling of deer is a high degree of patience, and a high standard of stockmanship. 1986 EVANS *Change Agent* 25 He had met his wife..while he was working his way around the world learning about stockmanship.

2. A yardman at a saleyards, freezing works, or abattoir.

1933 [see 1 above]. 1991 *Evening Post* (Wellington) 27 Sept. 3 [Caption] Abattoir stockman Kevin Odlum, working sheep for the abattoir's last kill.

stockwhip. [AND 1839.]

1. A long leather whip with a short, heavy handle, used in controlling cattle (see esp. quot. 1933). Cf. also BELLY 2, CRACKER *n.*[1] 1, FALL *n.* 3, TAIL *n.*[2] 3.

1848 WAKEFIELD *Handbook NZ* 169 If you cannot avoid the attack by a swift movement of your steed, your only chance is to crack the stock-whip... The wooden handle is about fourteen inches long; the thong, of plaited hide, between twelve or fourteen feet in length. 1858 THOMSON *Reconn. Survey S. Dist. Otago* in Taylor *Early Travellers* (1959) 327 [The cattle station] gave me..an opportunity of viewing..the wielding and cracking of the huge stock-whip. 1867 BARKER *Station Life* (1870) 177 At last I gave up the stock-whip, with its unmanageable three yards of lash. 1874 KENNAWAY *Crusts* 176 He puts up his glass,.. clears his stockwhip lash, and wakes up his horse with a careful but suggestive spur. 1913 MANSFIELD *Stories* (1984) 132 It was half full of old and young men in big coats and top boots with stock whips in their hands. 1933 *Press* (Christchurch) (Acland Gloss.) 16 Dec. 21 *Stock whip.*- Whip for cattle. It had a handle about 18 inches long and a raw hide lash of 12 to 18 feet. Potts of Hakatere was supposed to be able to use a 20-foot whip. In Australia they used much shorter ones... The lash is increased in thickness for several feet. The thick part was called the *belly*, the tapering part from there to the end was the *tail*. The *fall* was a single strip of hide to which was attached the cracker, made of skinned flax... With quieter cattle and more civilised management, *s[tock]w[hip]s* have gone out of use in Canterbury. The degenerate whips used now are more like hunting crops.

Hence **stockwhip** *v. trans.*, to use a stockwhip on an animal or person.

1853 ROCHFORT *Adventures of Surveyor* 42 He readily granted my request, saying..that, if the natives had not lent her to me at the last pah, he would have gone over and stockwhipped them. 1863 CHUDLEIGH *Diary* 21 Feb. (1950) 78 An old cow stuck me up about a mile from the stockyard... Millett and I worked our whips well on her. When she rushed one, the other stock-whipped her.

2. Special Comb. **stockwhip eels**, eels elongated and marked in such a way as to resemble a stockwhip.

1949 *TrRSNZ* LXXVII. 230 It is stated by fishermen at Taumuhu that in some years large extremely attenuated L[ong] F[inned] eels, with corrugations in the skin on the ventral surface, are taken at Ellesmere, and that migrants sometimes include a proportion of these so-called 'stockwhip' eels.

stockyard. [AND 1794.] Often collective *pl.* A fenced yard, usu. divided into pens and races to facilitate the drafting, handling, or holding of livestock, usu. cattle, for various purposes. Often *attrib.* See also YARD *n.* 1.

1841 *NZ Jrnl.* II. 151 Messrs. Wade..invite their friends and the public to partake of a Cold Collation, which they will provide for the occasion, at Mr Watts' Stock-yards, Evans Bay. c1846 WEEKES *My Island* in Rutherford & Skinner *Establish. New Plymouth* (1940) 124 The turkeys had become..so independent that instead of roosting at night on the stockyard rails they would absent themselves for days together. 1849 ALLOM *Letter* in Earp *Handbook* (1852) 123 I will conclude this part of the subject with a few words about stockyards. They are generally made of stout posts and rails; the corner posts ought to be much stronger than the rest, as they often have to bear the weight of a heavy bullock in branding and other operations. The yard is generally divided into three portions—viz., a large yard for the whole herd, a drafting yard, and a milking yard. 1860 DONALDSON *Bush Lays & Rhymes* 14 Now to the stockyard crowds the mob, 'twill soon be milking-time. 1871 MONEY *Knocking About NZ* 7 There was the stockyard, a square enclosure with high posts and rails, into which the cattle, horses, &c., were driven when required for milking or other purposes. 1882 POTTS *Out in Open* 155 This particular place, from its immediate contiguity to the stockyard, bullock sheds. 1933 *Press* (Christchurch) (Acland Gloss.) 16 Dec. 21 *Stockyard.*—Yard usually containing several divisions, and a *crush*..for drafting, branding, catching, etc., horses and cattle. They were built of post and rail perhaps 8 feet high and very strong. 1986 OWEN & PERKINS *Speaking for Ourselves* 30 The next stage [*sc.* of the cattle drive] would be right on to Big Bay..where there was a hut and stockyards. *Ibid.* 170 The old stockyard fences were planks, set about four or five to a fence.

Hence **stock-yard** *v. trans.*, to put or drive (farm animals) into a stockyard; to yard (farm animals); also *transf.*, to herd (people) together for a purpose (as animals in a stockyard).

1871 *Evening Post* (Wellington) 30 Nov. 2 The Chinese were 'stock-yarded' [for inspection of Miners' Rights] at the big beach. 1874 KENNAWAY *Crusts* 110 One morning we rode down to a neighbouring station about twelve miles off, stock-yarded our horses, and knocked at the station-owner's door.

stoker. WW1. [f. a play on one who 'stoked up' the home-fires, alluding to the WW1 song 'Keep the Home-fires Burning'.] An ironical name for one who did not enlist for overseas service.

1918 *Quick March* 25 May 9 And one night in the Town Hall I heard the Stokers say: 'Hoch! Hoch! mein Gott, What a very wild lot Are the Anzacs of today!' [1918 *Note*] It might be mentioned that 'the Stokers' are the ones who 'Keep the Home Fires Burning'. *Ibid.* 32 There are two great primary classes [of Diggers] a) Aucklanders b) others. They may be further subdivided

STONE

into: 1) Nat Goulds 2) Dinks 3) Stokers 4) Main Body Men.

stone, *n.*

1. *Mining.* **a.** [See OED *n.* 7 c; AND c1860.] Vein stone or quartz in which precious metal can occur.

1868 *Thames Miner's Guide* 83 Beautiful specimens; 132ozs. obtained from 100lbs. of stone... Reef 8ft. thick, gold perceptible in the stone. **1874** *AJHR* H-9 4 Within the present year a prospecting party opened a second reef in this locality, and the prospects were sufficient to warrant capitalists in erecting a small crushing plant to test the stone. **1887** GORDON in *NZGeol.SB (NS)* (1924) No.26 6 When the stone is rich in silver not more than 20% of the bullion is saved, the whole of the silver being carried away with the water. **1908** *NZGeol.SB (NS)* No.6 145 An adit level driven on the lode for a distance of 229 ft, showed..payable stone for 200 ft. **1940** HOWARD *Rakiura* 234 Though quartz reefs and leaders were seen in several places, there were no indications of payable gold in the stone. **1965** WILLIAMS *Econ. Geol. NZ* 20 *Stone*, a miner's term for payable quartz.

b. In the phr. **to bring the stone to grass**, see quot.

1875 *Official Handbook NZ* 102 The veins of quartz run into the mountain-side or dip downwards; hundreds of feet have often to be gone over in what is called 'bringing the stone to grass', that is, to daylight.

2. See OAMARU STONE.

3. MOA STONE.

1862 CHUDLEIGH *Diary* 19 Dec. (1950) 70 We went to the Coal Hill and got some specimens. I found 4 remains of the Moa and got my pocket full of the [gizzard] stones and I have three fine bones from Butler.

stone, *a.*

1. a. As a modifier defining a pre-European Maori implement or weapon made of stone as **stone adze (axe, hatchet, toki)**.

1773 FORSTER *Resolution Jrnl.* (1982) II. 243 We observed some trees fresh cut,.. they had smooth & large cuts, which proves their Stone-hatchets to be good & very sharp. **1864** *Richmond-Atkinson Papers* (1960) II. 89 Lt. Ferguson (R.E.) called for '8 good axemen', then supplied them the regulation axe—shaped like a flint axe or old Maori stone toki. **1874** BAINES *Edward Crewe* 84 A one-handed adze..after the same plan as their old-fashioned stone adzes. **c1920** BEATTIE *Trad. Lifeways Southern Maori* (1994) 184 An old man pointed out a totara tree which had had one side barked by stone axes 'donkey years ago'.

b. In the names of animals, see: CRAB 2 (1).

2. Used as a quasi-adjectival intensifier. **a.** As **stone certainty**, an undeniable or 'dead' certainty.

1953 HAMILTON *Till Human Voices Wake Us* 126 He didn't dare put Bluey on report for that, though it's a stone certainty nothing would have been done about it. **1953** *Here & Now* Nov.–Dec. 42 It's a stone certainty he wouldn't give the police any help because Obie didn't like the police.

b. As **stone ginger**, an undeniable or 'dead' certainty. [Prob. f. the name (poss. after 'stone ginger (beer)' for that made or sold in a stoneware container) of a successful racehorse, a bay colt by Lord Rosslyn from Komuri, listed in the NZ Turf Register for 1917–18, raced in Otago in 1910 winning a number of races, and in 1917 in a spectacular dead-heat in an Otago steeplechase. Cf. **1988** COSTELLO & FINNEGAN *Tapestry of Turf* 160 In the Otago Steeples of 1917, only two of the 10 starters completed the course... They deadheated for first... Stone Ginger (H. Lorigan) and Palladio (W. Griffiths).]

1910 *Truth* 12 Nov. 2 When I got to the straight I left the rails, and after this it was 'stone ginger'. **1935** MITCHELL & STRONG in Partridge *Slang Today* 286 [The] following [was] employed by those who served in the [Great] War..*stone ginger*, certain, a certainty. **1938** *Press* (Christchurch) (McNab Slang) 2 Apr. 18 'Stone ginger,' a certainty, was the name of an apparently unbeatable..racehorse in 1910. **1943** BENNETT *English in NZ* in *Amer. Speech* XVIII. 90 Horse-racing, another popular pastime..provides... 'That's a stone-ginger' (a dead certainty) [which] conceals the name of a famous and unbeatable horse, Stone Ginger. **1985** STEWART *Gumboots and Goalposts* 88 'That's it!' he declared. 'That's the finish, J.J. To hell with her. That's the absolute stone ginger.'

c. As **stone end** [AND 1946], the very end, the 'dead' end.

1970 DAVIN *Not Here Not Now* 202 This was the finish, the stone-end of it.

stone-eye. BLUENOSE.

1986 PAUL *NZ Fishes* 138 *Bluenose. Hyperoglyphe antarctica*... Alternative New Zealand names include stoneye [*sic*], bonita, bream, Griffin's silverfish... Widely distributed in temperate waters of the Southern Hemisphere.

stone fence. *Hist.* [OED *stone*[1] 20 a; AND 1853.] Brandy and ginger-beer.

1859 THOMSON *Story NZ* II. 61 [Auckland 1842:] Two Australian customs had already taken root in the colony; one a beverage composed of brandy and ginger-beer, which was denominated a stone fence; the other a halloo used by settlers in shouting to people at a distance. **1959** SINCLAIR *Hist. NZ* 102 The colonists were very partial to a mixture of brandy and ginger beer, which was known as a 'stone fence'.

stone the crows: see CROW *n.*[1] 4.

stonewall, *n.* [Fig. use of *stone wall* a barrier, an obstruction: AND 1875.] An act of parliamentary obstructionism or filibustering.

1890 *NZ Observer* 6 Dec. 6 On one occasion when a 'stonewall' was in progress, he [*sc.* Sydney Taiwhanga] achieved the feat of speaking for nine hours at a stretch. **1919** FANNING *Politics and the Public* 40 Much could be written upon..the literature with which members were wont in the past to beguile the weary hours of a 'stonewall'. **1934** MULGAN *Spur of Morning* 154 Mark was introduced to the method of barbarism known as the 'stonewall'. The Opposition staged one of these, partly to block a piece of obnoxious legislation, and partly to show the country its power. The House sat continuously from Tuesday afternoon until Thursday evening. **1948** LIPSON *Politics of Equality* 32 In response to such a threat [in 1889, to curtail urban voting] the representatives of the four cities united to maintain a long and stubborn 'stonewall'. *Ibid.* 129 So in the stonewall fight over the Representation Bill of 1889 members divided..as town versus country. **1968** SEDDON *The Seddons* 213 This feeling and the sense that deserting friends had robbed them of the privilege of sitting on the Treasury Benches, infused into the debate a determined organised opposition best described by a term not allowable in the House itself—a 'stone-wall'.

stonewall, *v.*

1. *Obs.* [f. *n.*: AND 1880.] *trans.* To obstruct (Parliamentary business) by long speeches or by manipulation of procedures; to filibuster.

c1875 [see *vbl. n.* below]. **1917** *Free Lance* (Wellington) 10 Aug. 7 Mr Wilford, chief oppositionist, stone-walled his own ideas by telling us what the Budget means. **1950** *NZPD* CCLXXXIX. 660 Is the honourable member 'stone-walling' the Bill?

Hence **stonewaller** *n.* [AND 1904], one obstructing or delaying Parliamentary business; **stonewalling** *vbl. n.* and *attrib.*

1968 SEDDON *The Seddons* 214 For instance, a **stone-waller** would begin logically his set remarks itemised one, two, and so on, say to twelve. c1875 MEREDITH *Adventuring in Maoriland* (1935) 75 There have been some very lively passages between the Government and the Opposition..mostly arising out of a **stonewalling** fight by the Opposition which resulted in an all-night sitting. Naturally I have to be in attendance..so I wished the stonewalling in Hong Kong or some warmer place... Quite a few amusing incidents occurred during the stonewalling tactics. **1948** LIPSON *Politics of Equality* 332 At most the opposition can merely conduct delaying actions. But..opportunities for stone-walling and obstruction are now far less generous than of old. **1992** *Evening Post* (Wellington) 5 Aug. 6 The pointless stonewalling of Opposition politicians..must be banished from the chamber.

2. *transf. Shearing.* As a *vbl. n.*, see quot.

1955 BOWEN *Wool Away* 103 If it [the plant] is driven too fast the cutter goes so fast across the comb that it is like a solid block of metal. It does not cut as well as at a slightly slower pace and produces the effect known to shearers as 'stonewalling'.

stonker, *v.* [f. Brit. dial. *stonk* a stake or play in a game of marbles + *-er*: AND 1918.]

1. *trans.* To put (something) out of action; to kill (someone).

1945 SEDDON *Whims of a WAAF* 4 Since benzine restrictions have stonkered my car. **1959** SLATTER *Gun in My Hand* 201 Then he went and stepped on a bloody mine. Stonkered the poor bastard properly. **1981** HENDERSON *Exiles Asbestos Cottage* 200 Tinny was utterly incapable of sssaying 'Sssseven and ssssixpence', the only thing which ever stonkered him in his brave and long life.

2. Usu. as a *ppl. a.* in predicative use [AND 1918]. **a.** Beaten; ruined; at a complete loss.

1940 *Evening Post* (Wellington) 21 Aug. 8 Air Marshal Goering (to date): Veni, vidi, I was stonkered. **1949** FENWICK *Rhyme or Reason* ('I've Had It') [unpaged] He's quite a stranger in the roost Who says he's 'stonkered', 'sunk' or 'goosed' For he must say, 'I've had it'. **1955** *Truth* 6 July 14 Quipped one Wellingtonian as he left the ground in disgust..'I came. I never saw. I was stonkered.' **1962** CRUMP *One of Us* 67 She..let them into a kitchen so clean..that Sam was stonkered for something to lean on. **1983** HENDERSON *Down from Marble Mountain* 274 I'm really stonkered. What can I tell 'em, writing home, Jack?

b. Drunk.

1940 SARGESON *Man & Wife* (1944) 76 Once they were a bit stonkered the boys would want to have a bo-peep at the bird. **1943** BENNETT *English in NZ* in *Amer. Speech* XVIII. 89 A thoroughly drunk man is *stonkered, floored, stunned*. **1960** MUIR *Word for Word* 253 'But how did the accident take place?' 'Dunno. They found her the next morning. She was well stonkered.' **1984** WILSON *S. Pacific Street* 47 He was fonged a lot of the time. He gave me the impression that he was completely stonkered.

c. Extremely tired, exhausted.

1964 BOOTH *Footsteps in Sea* 33 Oh well, better get some shut-eye, I guess. You must be stonkered. **1975** ANDERSON *Men of Milford Road* 158 'I'm stonkered,' he said. 'Pigs or no pigs I'm going to have a cup of tea.'

stony

1981 ANDERSON *Both Sides of River* 146 Went to Ashburton, signed books from 7.30p.m. until 9... Wonderful day for the book. I'm stonkered.

stony. Also **stoney.** [f. Brit. dial.: see OED *stoney.*] A marble made of stone or stone-like material.

1932, 1933, 1972 stoney [see GLASSIE]. **1982** SUTTON-SMITH *Hist. Children's Play* 139 We played marbles [at Grovetown School c1870–85], Ring, and Eye-drop with taws, glassies, stonies, and agots.

stoomer, var. STUMER.

stop-a-bit creeper. BUSH LAWYER *n.*[1] Cf. WAIT-A-BIT 1.

1876 KENNEDY *Colonial Travel* 162 The path..wound about through ferns and creepers. Prickly bushes called 'lawyers', or 'stop-a-bit creepers', seemed in league to tear the clothes off our backs.

stopbank. [See OED '*Austral.* and *N.Z.*'.] An embankment or levee raised along the banks of waterways to prevent flooding of surrounding land.

1899 *NZ Times* (Wellington) 22 Dec. 6 Mr. Fulton thought that the material for the stopbanks should be of clay and soil above a certain height. **1924** *Otago Witness* (Dunedin) 8 Apr. 26 The stop-bank on the western side of the river diverted the flood waters on to the eastern side. **1944** *Ellesmere Guardian* 22 Dec. 3 He favoured the erection of stopbanks, until a scheme for the whole river could be commenced. **1951** WILSON *Brave Company* 196 The clean lines of the river and stopbank. **1966** TURNER *Eng. Lang. Austral. & NZ* 171 Stock and the farmer change the appearance of the countryside: the surveyor's *trig station*, the engineer's *stopbanks* along the rivers on the plain..change the scenery. **1977** *NZ Herald* (Auckland) 5 Jan. 1 The Auckland Harbour Board controls to the tidal boundary..a vast acreage that has built up outside the stopbanks. **1993** *North & South* (Auckland) Feb. 123 Wine of the Month. Babich Stopbank Chardonnay 1991... Grown in the Stopbank Vineyard in Hawke's Bay.

stopper: see STOPPING DOG.

stopping dog. *Farming. Obs.* Also **stopper.** A specialist heading dog which holds the sheep once it has headed them.

1933 *Press* (Christchurch) (Acland Gloss.) 16 Dec. 21 *Stopping dog.*—Sometimes used for *heading d[og]*... Obsolete? **1947** NEWTON *Wayleggo* 13 A breed, now almost extinct, that is peculiar to the high country, is the 'stopping dog', which may be described as a 'specialist' heading dog. *Ibid.* [Gloss.] Stopping dog: A heading dog which, once it has headed sheep, will just lie and hold the mob until its master arrives... In the early days when high country sheep were much wilder and longer heads occasioned stopping dogs—real specialists at straight-out heading—were common. **1959** MCLEOD *Tall Tussock* 71 I had a little [heading] bitch called Jean... Best little stopper ever I had. **1971** NEWTON *Ten Thousand Dogs* 165 The 'stopping' dog, for instance, is now a thing of the past.

stop-work, *a.* Esp. as **stop-work meeting**, a meeting of employees which takes place during working hours requiring work to stop so that they may attend. Also as a noun.

c1926 THE MIXER *Transport Workers' Song Book* 25 With their silly bluff and twaddle, And their stop-work meetings, too, By which I'm not allowed to work 'Till their business is through. **1957** *Landfall* 11 Apr. 278 It was a good day for a stop-work. **1977** *Listener* 15 Jan. 6 A great many immigrants, probably the majority, were never involved in any kind of trade unionism in Britain and would not have recognised a 'stop-work' meeting if they had actually fallen over one!

store.

1. [See OED *n.* 12, 'Chiefly *N. Amer.* and elsewhere outside the U.K.'.] **a.** A shop, often large, mainly rural, supplying grocery items and a wide range of other merchandise for all home, farm and work needs. Often called a GENERAL STORE q.v., and preceded by other modifiers designating main or specialist lines of goods sold ('grocery store', 'hardware store', etc.), or location ('country store').

[*Note*] *Store* is the common name for such an establishment from earliest settlement, a usage poss. reinforced in those early times by its occurrence in the names of special commissaries such as 'ship's store', 'company store', 'station store', and from Australian convict use, 'public store'.

1840 CAMPBELL *Present State NZ* 23 They are rather low grog-shops than stores. **1841** Mary Swainson let. in *William Swainson* 5 Nov. (1992) 88 Col. Wakefield's protege was married soon after her arrival to a Mr. Stafford, a cabin passenger who now keeps a store. **1845** WAKEFIELD *Adventure NZ* II. 4 I soon found myself as it were forced into keeping what would be called a 'store' in America, or a 'shop' in England. **1850** GODLEY *Letters* 23 Apr. (1951) 28 The evening we spent on shore at Lyttelton, and shopping, or as they call it here, I grieve to say, Yankee fashion, going to the *store*. **1875** *Official Handbook NZ* 234 Many additional [houses] have been built, including several shops and stores of a superior description. **1881** NESFIELD *Chequered Career* 31 These 'stores' do a very large trade with the Maoris, and allow them to run very heavily into their debt for saddles, guns, groceries. **1894** ARTHUR *Kangaroo & Kauri* 89 Nearly every house there is a 'store', or shop, as we would say in England. **1912** MANSFIELD *Stories* (1984) 110 'Oh, yes,' you says, 'I know a fine store..owned by a friend of mine who'll give yer a bottle of whisky before 'e shakes hands with yer.' **1933** SCANLAN *Tides of Youth* 120 The girl's father kept a little country store. **1954** 2ZB Wellington Aunt Daisy 4 June You can get Windex at the grocer's or at the store. **1966** TURNER *Eng. Lang. Austral. & NZ* 143 A township is unlikely to have specialist shops; everything is bought at the *store*. The word recalls American use... In Australia and New Zealand the word remained especially a country word. **1982** HARWOOD *Heritage Trail* 58 Shifted to Lauder and opened a general store... The early store stocked everything from a match to a tin bath. **1992** CONDON *Hurleyville* 80 Farmers would come to the store after going to the factory and collect groceries, mail and the morning paper.

b. A commissary on a stock station holding supplies for issue or sale to employees.

1878 CHUDLEIGH *Diary* 6 June (1950) 269 The magnitude of the farm [*sc.* Longbeach station] may be shown by..a large general store to supply the station hands.

c. Special Comb. **storeman**, STOREKEEPER 1; also a storekeeper's assistant.

1871 MONEY *Knocking About NZ* 102 Turning into the nearest store, I called for a nobbler, and asked the storeman, while he bittered the decoction, what he would give a man for bringing the various articles he required. **1920** MANSFIELD *Stories* (1984) 224 And she longed to say: 'Stand on your heads, children, and wait for the storeman.' **1986** OWEN & PERKINS *Speaking for Ourselves* 64 The fair dinkum bushman was a bloke that..well, the storeman knew him, because the storeman was a helluva important man in a workingman's life at that time.

2. [Spec. use of *store* a building where (bulk) goods are stored.] *wool store* (WOOL 3).

1936 BELSHAW et al. *Agric. Organiz. NZ* 710 With small slips they are either mixed with the pieces or sent to store to be binned. **1978** ANGUS *Donald Reid Centenn. Hist. 1878–1978* 27 (Griffiths Collect.) Only in 1893 did Donald Reid..advertise that they had a man in the store to class farmers' clips.

storehouse. In early Maori contexts usu. PATAKA or WHATA 1.

1823 CRUISE *Journal* 28 Feb. (1957) 34 The storehouse is always the longest and the best building in the village. **1858, 1903, 1946, 1964** [see PATAKA].

storekeeper. [Orig. US: AND 1828.]

1. A shopkeeper; one who keeps a general (esp. rural) store. Cf. *general storekeeper* (GENERAL STORE).

1840 CAMPBELL *Present State NZ* 22 Traders and storekeepers at the Bay. **1846** FITZROY *Remarks on NZ* 17 Every storekeeper and farmer was interested in the presence of troops. **1857** PAUL *Lett. from Canterbury* 66 Their [*sc.* French settlers'] English neighbours 'buy and sell, and get gain', the farmers and storekeepers and publicans of the district. **1863** WALKER *Jrnl. & Lett.* (ATLTS) 20 Jan. Managed to..boil the billy and beg a 2lb loaf of a store-keeper. **1879** HAAST *Geol. Canterbury & Westland* 71 A storekeeper, who also sold spirits..was doing a good business. **1889** KIRK *Forest Flora* 155 Sometimes a storekeeper will lease a block of kauri-gum land. **1898** *AJHR* H-12 10 The greatest hardship is felt by the diggers should the storekeeper also be the holder of a publican's license. **1908** STEWART *Simple Life* 51 Then another enterprising local [Kati Kati] store-keeper called with groceries. **1914** PFAFF *Diggers' Story* 23 Ashore, merchants and storekeepers were all working at high pressure receiving or delivering as fast as goods could be landed [at Hokitika]. **1922** MANSFIELD *Stories* (1984) 501 And the consequence was all the children of the neighbourhood, the judge's little girls, the doctor's daughters, the store-keeper's children, the milkman's, were forced to mix together. **1946** REED *Farthest North* 76 Hard workers,.. some [Dalmatians] became storekeepers and gum buyers. **1981** JOHNSTON *Fish Factory* 47 'You apologise to Ma-Mac or I'll do you!' The storekeeper stuck his neck out: 'Get stuffed!' **1995** WINTER *All Ways Up Hill* 198 The settlers['] real friend was the country storekeeper.

2. As **storekeepers' rush** [AND 1869], a false rush, of profit only to storekeepers. Compare *duffer's rush* (DUFFER 2).

1967 MAY *West Coast Gold Rushes* 526 Synonyms [for 'duffer rush'] were 'shicer', 'stringer' or, in the case of a false rush, 'store-keepers' rush'.

storekeeping, *vbl. n.*, keeping shop, following the occupation of a general storekeeper. Occas. *attrib.* (quot. 1875), or *v. intr.* (quot. 1914).

1875 COCKBURN-HOOD *Chowbokiana* 9 The money-mongering and storekeeping class have it all their own way. **1914** PFAFF *Diggers' Story* 63 While storekeeping here I used to supply the original prospectors with stores and other necessaries. **1924** *Otago Witness* (Dunedin) 17 June 73 The old lady..confided that they—she and her old man—had retired after fourteen years of up country storekeeping. **1933** SCANLAN *Tides of Youth* 121 But the weakness in his father, combined with the Kite family's reverence for storekeeping, failed to give him the necessary support. **1981** HENDERSON *Exiles Asbestos Cottage* 196 'The storekeeping kept us on our toes,' she added, 'and we enjoyed it though we weren't professional storekeepers.'

storm bird. *Obs.* Any of several birds (esp. petrels) said to indicate coming rain. See also RAINBIRD, *storm petrel* (PETREL 2 (19)).
  1838 POLACK *NZ* I. 307 *Storm-birds* (procellaria pelagica), and the *penguin*..also exist. **c1899** DOUGLAS in *Mr Explorer Douglas* (1957) 269 The diggers used to call..[the yellowhead] the storm bird, as they made their appearance in flocks just before rain. **1904** [see RAINBIRD].

storm petrel: see PETREL 2 (19).

story. As **the story. a.** Correct information, the 'score'.
  1951 Veterans' Session 2ZB Wellington radio You can get all the story [about a reunion] by ringing up.
  b. The correct, proper, or sensible thing to do; esp. in the phr. **that's the story**, 'that's right', 'very good' often said as an encouragement.
  1944 FULLARTON *Troop Target* 45 'I take it we're heading south?' 'That's the story,' admitted Rangi. *Ibid.* 89 Lie low and sleep is the story. **1992** GRACE *Cousins* 52 Jerry..called, 'That's the story, Ada. That's the story, Morning Glory,' as he'd swooped the trolley under the stack of paper she'd counted.

stouch, var. STOUSH.

stoush /staʊʃ/, /staʊtʃ/, *n.* Also **stouch**. [Poss. f. Brit. dial. *stashie, stushie* uproar, quarrel: see EDD.]
1. a. [AND 1900.] In the phr. **to deal out (the) stoush**, to act violently towards (a person, group, etc.); to beat or thrash; to criticize harshly.
  1905 *Truth* 2 Sept. 3 The Horowhenua [Rugby] Union has dealt out the 'stoush' [*sc.* reprimands] all round. **1906** *Truth* 11 Aug. 4 The latter was a boarder..and on two occasions did he interfere when Mercer was dealing out stoush to his wife. **1913** REES *Merry Marauders* 24 I was just about to deal out stoush to the last fellow that guyed me.
  b. (A bout or instance of) physical violence (esp. on the rugby field); a violent altercation or argument.
  1912 *Free Lance* (Wellington) 13 Apr. 24 Rugby is not a game of 'stouch'... They cannot be surprised if allegations of 'stoush' [*sic*] are made against the game. **1913** *NZ Observer* 9 Aug. 3 The proceedings in the House..are what members politely call 'stoush'. **1919** *Hawkes Bay Herald* 8 Aug. 7 We used our hits to win the Cup. We met opponents' boasts With boots and stoush. **1945** *NZ Dairy Exporter* 1 May 85 What's wrong? A stoush? Who's in it? **1956** SUTHERLAND *Green Kiwi* (1960) 202 Come on, some of you jokers—there's more than a dozen sheilas in there without partners. There's all day tomorrow for stoush. **1965** GEE *Special Flower* 39 I've seen you play dozens of times. Saw you at Rugby Park two years ago when you nearly had that stoush with Peter Jones. **1970** HOLCROFT *Graceless Islanders* 32 Journalists who travelled with the Lions have written about us predictably... We have been..advised in sounding periods to stamp out 'stoush'. **1986** OWEN & PERKINS *Speaking for Ourselves* 78 I remember one time I was asked if I wanted to be in a decent stoush... I think..that we availed ourselves of a pick handle..each. **1992** *Evening Post* (Wellington) 6 July 6 Everyone knew the worst stoush in history was looming [*sc.* in 1939] but no-one was game to throw the first punch. **1993** *Dominion* (Wellington) 25 Jan. 8 The danger is that..[talkback hosts] begin to see themselves..more as public performers—and what is more entertaining than a good old stoush.

2. *WW1* and *WW2*. **a.** A battle; (military) fighting.
  1918 *Chron. NZEF* 13 Sept. 82 Of late the N.Z.s have been doing a bit of 'stouch' in the neighbourhood of Bapaume. **1941** BAKER *NZ Slang* 62 *Stoush*, a fight. **1944** FULLARTON *Troop Target* 192 There's a great tank stoush a bit to the nor'west. **1945** *NZEF Times* 24 Dec. 3 [Caption] You won't be forgetting Faenza in a hurry—Or the Stouch across the Senio, Santano and Sillaro. **1947** DAVIN *For Rest of Our Lives* 13 They said up at Company that there'd been a stoush all day in front of the Aliakhmon.
  b. Shellfire, bullets, shrapnel.
  1935 STRONG in Partridge *Slang Today* 287 I believe we are in for a big smack-up. There will be plenty of stoush and somebody is bound to get cleaned up. **1947** DAVIN *Gorse Blooms Pale* 181 A good chap, especially in the field when stoush was flying. **1959** SLATTER *Gun in My Hand* 148 Poor country lads the Hun radio called them, poor country lads who gave the German professionals plenty of stoush.

3. Special Comb. **stoush artist** [AND 1932], a basher; a rough fighter.
  1918 *Chron. NZEF* 8 Nov. 185 The 'stoush artist' of the 'squared circle' [*sc.* 'the bullring', a military training-ground at base] lams his cooker for the good of his soul. **1956** SUTHERLAND *Green Kiwi* (1960) 200 Men who preferred to pick their bouts as they went along—the men who had reputations as fighters or merely as 'stoush artists' to uphold.

stoush, *v. trans.* [AND 1893.] To punch, to strike; to overcome (an opponent).
  1906 *Truth* 18 Aug. 1 None but the brave deserve the fare, remarked the cabman, as he stoushed the would-be bilker. **1916** THORNTON *Wowser* 48 Here comes the wowser as stoushed Bill yesterday. **1926** *NZ Observer* 8 Sept. 2 Py gorry, I go up Queen Street and stoush the first black man I see. **1934** *Truth* 28 Feb. 5 Canterbury saved their revenge on Wellington for their defeat in the Shield match by properly stoushing the touring team by eight wickets. **1947** DAVIN *For Rest of Our Lives* 75 Old Sam O'Connell had to stoush a couple to stop them fighting. **1960** BOSWELL *Ernie* 36 'I'm only sorry I can't take you on..' he said,.. 'but I'm not going to stoush a maimed bloke.'

Hence **stoushed** *ppl. a.*, beaten; stumped; **stoushing** *vbl. n.*, violent argument; a wordy or physical attack; fighting.
  a1927 ANTHONY *Gus Tomlins* (1977) 134 He was utterly **stoushed**. More like a pricked bladder than anything else, and I had to take charge and get him home to his cows. **1953** 17 M A38 Thames DHS 13 Stoushed [stumped, stuck]. **1993** *Dominion* (Wellington) 5 Apr. 2 The election is still..six months away, but already political **stoushing** is reaching full campaign pitch.

stousher. [AND 1909.] A fighter, a boxer.
  1898 BROWN *Lay of Bantry Bay* (1917) 27 The cry was up for 'stoushers'—and they [*sc.* the football team] one and all obeyed. **1906** *Truth* 14 July 3 The controlling officials don't care a dump what the professional stoushers' views may be on the subject... The [Boxing] Association is making a 'dead set' against the professional talent.

St Peter's fish. Applied, as elsewhere, to fish with dark blotches on the flanks, supposedly St Peter's finger-marks, usu. to John Dory; but also in New Zealand, to *butterfly perch* (PERCH *n.* 2 (2)) of the family Serranidae.
  1921 *NZJST* IV. 115 Caesioperca lepidoptera (Forster). *Red Perch.* Called 'red snapper' or 'St. Peter's fish' in Queen Charlotte and Pelorus Sounds. **1957** [see PERCH *n.* 2 (2)].

straggle, *n. Farming.* [f. *straggle* to stray: see OED *v.*[1] 1.] Usu. in special Comb. **straggle muster** (see MUSTER *n.* 2), also *ellipt.* **straggle**; **straggle tally**, a tally of sheep missed in the main muster.
  1953 STRONACH *Musterer on Molesworth* 37 The straggle was uneventful, and I found it much easier than the shearing muster. **1947** NEWTON *Wayleggo* 37 That season the straggle tally (sheep missed) was under 400. **1966** NEWTON *Boss's Story* 121 Straggle tallies..are made up of sheep lost through mishandling by dogs or men and of sheep not seen.

straggle, *v. Farming. trans.* To make a straggle-muster (of a block of country). See also *straggle muster v.* (MUSTER *n.* 2).
  1934 [see MUSTER *n.* 1.] **1949** NEWTON *High Country Days* 197 Straggle: To muster country a second time to get any stragglers, i.e., sheep missed the first time. 'Strangers' (sheep that have strayed from another property) are also often called stragglers. **1953** STRONACH *Musterer on Molesworth* 31 To 'straggle' a block of country means, of course, to muster in the stragglers—sheep that were missed during the main muster.

Hence **straggling** *vbl. n.*, see quot.
  1966 NEWTON *Boss's Story* 81 The boys also did a bit of straggling and collected quite a useful tally of woollies. *Ibid.* 189 *Straggling*: Mustering country a second time to get any sheep that have been missed, i.e. straggle-mustering.

straggler. *Farming.* [Spec. use of *straggler* an animal which strays from its habitat or companions: see OED 4.]
1. a. [AND 1897.] A sheep missed in a main muster.
  1860 DUPPA in Crawford *Sheep & Sheepmen Canterbury* (1949) 46 Complete dipping flock..deliver stragglers. **1866** TRIPP *Day Book* June in Harper *Kettle on Fuchsia* (1967) 69 Sutherland. Mustering the boundary for straggler ram lambs. **1873** WILSON *Diary* 2 Feb. in Wierzbicka *Wilson Family* (1973) 164 To show how different the mustering is in this country, out of 70,000 sheep Campbell..was over 15,000 short at shearing and has to muster several different times before he can get all the stragglers in. **1883** PARTINGTON *Random Rot* 306 The shearers..had been employed upon the stragglers, that is, the sheep missed in the general muster, and afterwards got together. **1933** *Press* (Christchurch) (Acland Gloss.) 16 Dec. 31 *Straggler.*—(1) Sheep that has been left on the country at a muster... It is usual to go over the country again to pick them up... (2) A sheep of your own which goes on to a neighbour's run. **1949** *NZJST* XXX. 292 Re-infestation from 'stragglers' or unmustered sheep cannot take place. **1964** DICK *High Country Family* 70 We're shearing the double-fleece stragglers. **1989** *NZ Eng. Newsletter* III. 28 *straggler*: A sheep which is missed in the muster for shearing.
  b. [AND 1846.] A stray farm animal.
  1933 [see *straggle muster* (MUSTER *n.* 2)]. **1991** *Dominion Sunday Times* (Wellington) 20 Oct. 21 Hooas don't dip. Now you'll understand what a Katene straggler can do to my clip.

2. Special Comb. **straggler shearing** [AND 1898], see quot.
  1952 MEEK *Station Days* 111 Stragglers Sheep that have been missed in the general muster, and brought in later for the 'straggler shearing'.

straight, *n.* [Transf. use of *straight* the straight portion of a race-course approaching the finish line.] In the phr. **come up the straight**, to approach a goal.

straight, *a.*[1] [Transf. use of *straight* of spirits, neat, undiluted: see OED 9.] Of beer, not mixed with lemonade. Also as a noun.

1917 INGLIS in Boyack *Behind the Lines* (1989) 130 I'm sadly afraid the average chap is by no means a plaster saint or even coming up the straight to that goal, but I'm sure that often the difference between his turning out a decent sort of ratter rests with the girl. **1938** FINLAYSON *Brown Man's Burden* (1973) 23 'A handle of beer,' he was saying..to the barman... 'Straight!' **1947** *Miscellany* (Caxton Press) IX. 30 'Four straights and a dash?' she said, gathering up the empty handles skilfully in her fingers. **1960** WILSON in *NZ Short Stories* (1966, 1976 repr.) 88 'Three straights and a dash?' she [*sc.* the barmaid] said to the Maoris.

straight, *a.*[2] Phrasally used in various senses: **a. to be straight wire** *obs.*, to be correct, true; authentic; **straight dinkum**, see DINKUM *quasi-adv.* 2 b.

1904 LANCASTER *Sons o' Men* 235 Walt, yer are a smeller, straight wire. **1910** *Truth* 11 June 1 The sound of the words may not suit 'Civis', but 'Critic' bets everybody else would understand the remark and would furthermore state that it was 'straight wire' or 'dinkum'. **1911** *Triad* 11 Sept. 45 'Is it a true bill?' 'It's perfectly straight wire.'

b. straight off the turnips, see TURNIP 2.

strain, *n. Fencing.* [AND 1930.] The length of wire between two strainer posts; see also quot. 1973.

1866 PHILLIPS *Rockwood Jrnl.* 6 Oct. (Canterbury Pub. Lib. TS) 83 All hands at wire fence—finished two strains. **1973** WHEELER *Hist. Sheep Stations NI* 11 [The fencer] explained to my wife that a coil, or *strain* of wire is ten to twelve chains in length.

strain, *v. Fencing.* Also **strain up**. [OED *strain v.* 10 c.] *trans.* To stretch and tighten fence wire. Also as a *vbl. n.*

1902 LANCASTER in *Happy Endings* (1987) 110 Crandeck learnt much regarding the grubbing of turnips, and the straining of wire-fencing. **1904** CHUDLEIGH *Diary* 9 July (1950) 422 Trying to strain sheep netting outside a 7 wire fence. We are not well versed in wire netting. **1959** MIDDLETON *The Stone* 51 When all the posts were in and we had strained-up the wires, we started battening. **1961** CRUMP *Hang On a Minute Mate* 126 Then for three weeks they dug post- and strainer-holes, ran out wires, footed posts, blocked and stayed the angles, strained up, tied off, tacked up and hung battens. **1982** [see STRAINER 1b].

strainer.

1. Also **strainer-post**. STRAINING-POST. **a.** As **strainer**.

1865 *Timaru Herald* in Woodhouse *Blue Cliffs* (1982) 8 Tenders for a fence 5 or 6 miles long on the Otaio River... Iron standards, 6 wires, 15 strainers to the mile. **1876** PEACHE *Journal* in Gray *Quiet with Hills* (1970) 50 It is to be a five-wire fence, alternate post and stake..strainers to be eight chains apart. **1880** CHUDLEIGH *Diary* 16 June (1950) 289 Smith undertakes to cart my posts..for 5d. a post, strainers to count as 3 posts. **1909** THOMPSON *Ballads About Business* 19 I dinks to meinself ve are like a vire fence,.. Mit der bank eider gifin der shtrainer a dwist. **1933** JONES *Autobiogr. Early Settler* 77 I know a wire fence which was erected with iron strainers seventy years ago. **1950** *NZJAg.* Apr. LXXX. 347 Reinforced concrete strainers and intermediate posts are preferable to wood. **1961** CRUMP *Hang On a Minute Mate* 126 Then for three weeks they dug post- and strainer-holes. **1988** *Dominion* (Wellington) 23 July 8 The typical new..farm fence is a glittering grid of gleaming and galvanised No 8 wire, with battens and strainers ranked like troops at a passing-out parade.

b. As **strainer-post**.

1921 GUTHRIE-SMITH *Tutira* 148 To ordinary eyes [the mail-box] might have seemed, as indeed it was, a kerosene case nailed to the top of a strainer-post. **1959** *NZ Dairy Exporter* 10 July 59 On long strains, attach one strainer [*sc.* a wire-strainer] to the wire between strainer posts. **1982** *Agric. Gloss.* (MAF) 29 *Strainer-posts:* Main support posts at either end of the fence to which the wires are strained. **1991** *Dominion* (Wellington) 9 Feb. 9 They [*sc.* fencers in the Golden Pliers fencing contest] each had to build 50 metres of nine-wire fencing complete with two strainer posts.

2. [Ellipt. for *wire-strainer*; see OED f, 1883.] A tool (or device fixed to the wire of a fence) used to tighten the wire in a fence.

1866 PHILLIPS *Rockwood Jrnl.* 4 Oct. (Canterbury Pub. Lib. TS) 83 T.A.P. to Bullers for strainer W.P.P. & Jack fencing. **1909** THOMPSON *Ballads about Business* 20 Giving the strainer [of wire fence] a twist. **1946** MILLER *There Was Gold* 97 No. 8 wire was to him as string is to the average man. He could tie it.., and with a strainer he could tighten a wire until it literally sang when it was flicked. **1959** *NZ Dairy Exporter* July 59 [Advt] The only method of keeping the short strains tight is to use a Hayes Paramount Strainer on each wire. **1982** *Agric. Gloss.* (MAF) 30 *Strainer:* Tool used to tighten the wires in a fence. **1992** *North & South* (Auckland) June 65 This meant working with a strainer, an implement I was still learning to use.

straining-post. [f. Brit. dial. or provincial use: see OED *straining* 4, 1882 Worcester.] A large fence-post (usu. approx. 2.5 m long), stayed to take the strain of the wire. See also STRAINER 1.

1866 in Crawford *Station Years* (1981) 27 Sheep-proof fence. Iron Standards and five-wire fence. Wooden straining posts. **c1875** MEREDITH *Adventuring in Maoriland* (1935) 68 The first thing to do is to put in the 'straining-posts'. **1883** *Brett's Colonists' Guide* 77 Straining posts, every 10 chains, should be at least 9 feet long. **1892** CHUDLEIGH *Diary* 17 Feb. (1950) 379 A large amount of fencing material has been landed without the straining posts. **1904** *NZ Illustr. Mag.* July 277 It was with a feeling of relief that I at length viewed the stout straining posts. **1920** MANDER *Story NZ River* (1974) 53 She stood as void of volition as a straining post. **1959** DAVIN *No Remittance* 157 So I went out to mend a straining post I'd accidentally hit one day with a sledge. **1975** DAVIN *Breathing Spaces* 58 Tight wire and sound totara straining posts and you're jake for ten years. **1981** *Freshwater Catch* Winter XI. 19 They made the line fast to a straining post of a wire fence.

stranger. *Farming.* [AND 1845.] A sheep, wandering or straying from a neighbouring flock.

1852 CLOUGH *Journal* 11 Feb. in Deans *Pioneers Canterbury* (1937) 290 Branded 57 calves..counted all the other cattle; 201 of them strangers. **1875** RIVES *Jottings on the Spot* (Canterbury Pub. Lib. TS) 26 Feb. 7 After dinner we draughted out strangers and woolly ones. **1933** *Press* (Christchurch) (Acland Gloss.) 16 Dec. 21 *Stranger.*—A sheep of a neighbour's on your run. **1949** NEWTON *High Country Days* 52 The 'strangers', the sheep which had strayed from adjoining properties, would be raddled from head to rump. **1964** ANDERSON *Doctor in Mountains* (1974) 32 A young Maori helped in the sheep-yards drafting out the strangers, as it is taboo to shear sheep belonging to another station. **1972** NEWTON *Sheep Thief* 137 There was nothing unusual in..having a few 'strangers' (neighbours' sheep) on the place.

strap, *v. Obs.* [Transf. use of Brit. dial. *strap* to give credit: see OED *v.*[1] 6.] *trans.* To obtain (goods) on credit.

1906 *Truth* 31 Mar. 6 If you ask a pal for money When you cannot 'strap a beer'.

Strathmore weed. [f. *Strathmore* a locality in Taranaki.] *Pimelea prostrata* (fam. Thymelaeaceae), a prostrate or sprawling native shrub sometimes poisonous to stock. Also **Strathmore poisoning**, the poisonous effects on stock of eating the weed. See also DAPHNE.

1900 *Leaflets for Farmers* (NZ Dept. Agric.) No.55 2 I am forwarding a specimen of Strathmore weed. I interviewed Mr. Hewer, coach-proprietor, Strathmore and Stratford, *re* the matter. He informs me that the weed is very injurious to strange horses... This Strathmore weed proved to be two species of native plants, *Pimelea lyalli* and *P. prostrata*. **1908** *Dominion* (Wellington) 21 Sept. 5 The first case of Strathmore weed poisoning known in the Wairarapa occurred some days ago... He noticed..little clumps of a weed very much like the garden daphne growing in the paddock where the horses had been feeding... The weed..is native, and known by the names of Mataikairanga and Strathmore. The name Strathmore was given after the name of the locality near Hawera, where the first reported case of animal sickness..was made known some eight years ago... The first symptoms of Strathmore poisoning are loss of appetite, and then dullness, followed by tremors, staggering, distressed breathing, and convulsions, which in the severe cases are followed by death. **1926** HILGENDORF *Weeds* 236 Strathmore weed (*Pimelea lyallii*), a native (poisonous), from Taranaki. **1934** *NZJAg.* Sept. XLIX. 152 There are several species of *Pimelea* in New Zealand... It is known as Strathmore weed, from the name of the Taranaki town where the poisoning of horses was first recorded. **1951** LEVY *Grasslands NZ* (1970) 305 Strathmore weed, a low-growing shrubby plant found on poor, friable soils, if eaten when stock are forced on it in a holding paddock, may cause staggers and death. **1977** CONNOR *Poisonous Plants NZ* 173 Strathmore weed formerly poisoned more horses than any other animals... Today poisoning by this native plant is more common in cattle... Sheep do not seem seriously affected by Strathmore weed. **1981** CROWE *Field Guide Native Edible Plants NZ* 49 Strathmore weed is found in dry open places at all altitudes throughout New Zealand. **1995** [see DAPHNE].

stratum title. Also **strata title(s)**. [AND *strata-title* strata plan, 1961.] A legal title to a layer (or layers) of air-space above a defined surface level. See esp. quot. 1978. Cf. *unit title* UNIT *n.*[2] 1 b.
[Note] The Land Transfer Act 1952 does not include the words 'strata title'.

1959 *NZ Law Journal* XXXV. 299 There are two possible methods of handling the 'own your own flat' principle where resort to the simple 'terrace' system is not possible: (a) the stratum or air-space title method, which can give individual Land Transfer titles to each flat occupied but which is not in use because of: (i) difficulty re creation of easements; (ii) probable reluctance of mortgagees to finance individual flats. **1965** *Otago Law Review* I. 16 Strata Titles. The strata title concept is an interesting one... In New Zealand there has never been any objection to the issue of a strata title whether for strata above or below the surface. **1978** HINDE, MCMORLAND & SIM *Land Law* I. 296 Land may be divided either vertically or horizontally and certificates of title under the Land Transfer Act 1952 may be issued either for different strata of the subsoil beneath the surface of the land or for different layers of the airspace above the surface. Such certificates of title are called strata titles. **1986** HINDE & HINDE *NZ*

Law Dictionary 151 Strata titles. Subject to the various statutory and other restrictions affecting his title, the owner of an estate in fee simple is presumed to own everything 'up to the sky and down to the centre of the earth'... When, however, a stratum title is wanted for a portion of air space intended for a flat or an office, conveyancing problems arise in relation to the definition of rights over common parts of the building such as stairways, lifts, etc. and in relation to easements for services such as water, drainage and electricity. **1986** *Dominion* (Wellington) 25 July 10 Mr Gallagher said Mr Kirk had told him he had no assets or bank accounts in the United States. Two cars he owned there had been sold..and his condominium—similar to a strata title unit—had been leased.

strawberry. *Obs.* As **New Zealand strawberry**, SNOWBERRY 1 a (*Gaultheria depressa*).
 1858 THOMSON *Reconn. Survey S. Dist. Otago* in Taylor *Early Travellers* (1959) 335 Half-way up the mountains some pretty flowers were gathered... A ground berry, called the New Zealand strawberry by the colonists, formed an agreeable but rather insipid repast to our parched lips.

strawberry basket: see STRAWBERRY BOX.

strawberry box. Also **strawberry basket** (see quot. 1971). A small box of wood-chip or cardboard, like those (now usu. plastic) designed for strawberries and other berry fruit, formerly given to cabin passengers to be seasick into, esp. on the inter-island passenger steamers.
[*Note*] Never in this use called a *chip*, *punnet*, or *pottle*, the standard words for these containers when used for berry fruit, or recently for other (unregurgitated) food items.
 1936 HYDE *Passport to Hell* 93 Not far out of New Zealand waters the ship struck heavy weather..life just one strawberry-box after another. **1943** *NZEF Times* 20 Dec. 7 Can you envisage anything more pathetic than a surreptitious 'strawberry box' in the unsteady hands of a pale-green voyager? **1959** SLATTER *Gun in My Hand* 16 It is a small cabin with compact fittings... a folding chair, drawer compartments—one labelled cuspidor, the old strawberry box of ferry legend—a wash basin..and the mirror I must soon face. **1978** TUCKER *Thoroughbreds Are My Life* 8 If you can capture a mental picture of 22 cricketers making regular use of 'strawberry boxes' [on the Lyttelton ferry *Rangatira*, c1930s]..you will have some idea of the trauma which existed. **1982** MACKENZIE *WAAF Book* 30 The boat [*Tamahine* c1941] always seemed to head for that notorious stretch of water known as 'the rip'... A nurse in white would move about among the green passengers with much-needed strawberry boxes. **1992** ANDERSON *Portrait Artist's Wife* 69 The journey involved..a night on the inter-island ferry coping with Sybil's seasickness which startled even the stewardesses. 'Poor little sparrow,' they said, dumping yet another strawberry box.

strawberry fungus: see FUNGUS 2 (9).

straw insect: see ANIMATED STRAW.

straw walloper. Also in shortened form **walloper**. The member of a thrashing-mill team who clears or stacks the straw. Cf. WALLOP *v.*
 1943 *Farmers Weekly* 28 Jan. 5 The bagmen sure were busy while the straw walloper was nearly buried. **1956** BLAIR *Life & Work at Canterbury Agric. College* 51 A spark ignited the stubble, the fire leapt into the straw stack, and the straw wallopers leapt off the other end. **1976** ANDERSON *Water Joey* 75 It was reputed that Bill Clark hired men in bulk—ten stackies, so many straw-wallopers, etc. **1985** STUDHOLME *Coldstream* 127 If the farmer wanted the straw kept, a man was put on, known as 'the walloper'. He stood at the bottom of the chute and forked the straw sideways into a heap. **1990** MARTIN *Forgotten Worker* 131 [Caption] On the right is the straw elevator with two hands, the 'straw wallopers', who build the straw stack.

strength. [AND 1908; cf. OED 2 e 'orig. and chiefly *Austral.* and *N.Z.*'] The meaning, the significance, the gist, esp. in the phr. **to get the strength of**. See also STRONG *n.*
 1906 *Truth* 26 Aug. 5 Wants a friend to get the strength of things. **1937** MARSH *Vintage Murder* 95 I wonder what's the strength of this Firm of theirs..? Any idea Sir? **1943** MARSH *Colour Scheme* v 93 I don't get the strength of it myself. He wouldn't say much. **1965** SARGESON *Memoirs of Peon* 164 One would commonly hear it said among the boys that they couldn't get the strength of Spots [*sc.* a master].

stretch, *n.* In the phr. **do a stretch**, to shoplift.
 1985 *Metro* (Auckland) June 64 [Maori adolescent speaks] Sometimes you go to the wholesalers [liquor outlet]..do a stretch (shoplift) and drink in the streets.

stretch, *v.* [Transf. use of *stretch* to eke out (food): see OED *v.* 21 c.] To adulterate or dilute spirits.
 1871 *Evening Post* (Wellington) 30 Oct. 2 Inspector Atchison said that the prisoner got his living by 'stretching'—that is, adulterating—spirits.

stretcher. Also **camp stretcher** (see quots. 1956, 1983). [Transf. use of *stretcher* a camp bed, esp. in military or hospital use: see OED *n.* 9 a; AND 1834.] **a.** A collapsible bed-base, or one with folding legs, now often used as a temporary or spare bed.
 1853 in *Canterbury Rhymes* (1883) 12 This mutton chop—and this damper queer—A stretcher—a 'possum rug—And so wretched all that the traveller here But seldom shows his mug. **1861** HARPER *Lett. from NZ* 20 July (1914) 55 Would I mind sleeping in the outhouse, where I could have a stretcher? **1874** BATHGATE *Col. Experiences* 139 My host was a 'hatter' and he always kept a spare stretcher for any chance passer-by. **1917** *Great Adventure* (1988) 178 The batman 'procured' a wire netting stretcher (last night I had to sleep on the floor). **1938** LANCASTER *Promenade* 234 'I know' said Tiffany, dropping down at Sally's knees as she sat on the narrow iron stretcher. **1943** BENNETT *English in NZ* in *Amer. Speech* XVIII. 86 A common article of furniture is a *stretcher*—a folding camp bed or cot, often used to provide temporary sleeping accommodation in a house; in England the word is practically obsolete in this meaning. **1956** MIDDLETON in *Listener Short Stories* (1978) 37 And long after I got on to my camp stretcher in the corner, Mr Larsen and Uncle stayed up playing cribbage. **1974** MORRIESON *Predicament* (1981) 210 Getting yanked outa the stretcher like this when a man's trying to grab a little shut-eye is a cruel blow. **1983** KIDMAN *Paddy's Puzzle* 115 Billy brings the camp stretcher in, dangling it under one big arm as if it is a box of matches... But it turns out that Billy has forgotten how to put it up and gets the struts jammed the wrong way round. **1990** LANGFORD *Newlands* 199 I'd been sleeping on a camp stretcher beside her. I climbed into our bed, listening to the remainder of her breath.

b. Also as **stretcher-bed (stretcher-bedstead)**.
 1881 PYKE *White Hood & Blue Cap* 12 It was a small hut..and scant of furniture—two rough 'stretcher' bedsteads..a small rude table. **1942** FINLAYSON *Brown Man's Burden* (1973) 100 Inside he saw a Chinese man lying on a stretcher-bed near a small cooking-stove.

strike, *v.* [Var. of (often joc.) mild oaths *strike me* (*pink*, etc.): see OED *strike v.* 46 c; AND 1916.] **a.** Used as a mild oath in various phrases: **strike me dead, strike me handsome, strike me (bloody) hooray, strike me lucky**.
 1906 PICARD *Ups & Downs* 10 Stri [*sic*] me dead, yer'll all as slow as a wet week. **1906** *Truth* 1 Dec. 1 'Strike me lucky', is the popular catchphrase among Auckland trammen [*sic*] just now. **1917** *Chron. NZEF* 17 Oct. 114 Oh, God stiffen the — crows. Strike me dead, and pink and blue and blind and pretty. **1934** *Truth* 21 Mar. 2 Strike me hurray... I thought that was a new look-out perch for the stipes. **1962** *Landfall Country* 148 'Strike me dead,' the railwayman said. 'No need to bite me head off, mate.' **1968** SLATTER *Pagan Game* 161 So I'm in Shit Street—God strike me bloody hooray. **1988** McGILL *Dict. Kiwi Slang* 109 *strike me handsome!* well, fancy that! Variant of strike me pink/lucky.

b. Also as **strike!**, expressing (esp.) surprise.
 1943 JACKSON *Passage to Tobruk* 15 Strike! must have slept soundly. **1960** CRUMP *Good Keen Man* 116 Strike, he went crook! Who the hell was responsible? Had we been blasting fish?

string, *v.*[1] Also **string along, string away**. [Brit. dial. *string* to move in a long line: see EDD.] *intr.* Of farm animals, to move in a long straggling line. Also *transf.* to humans.
 1862 CHUDLEIGH *Diary* 4 Oct. (1950) 61 We let them [*sc.* cattle] string along a trac[k] and so counted them and took their old brands. **1890** *Otago Witness* (Dunedin) 25 Sept. 36 By the end of the previous year ('51) the Pilgrim Fathers..had begun stringing up the steep bridle-track. **1900** *TrNZI* XXXII. 282 The animals [*sc.* sheep]..are stringing along in long lines... It is a difficult matter to stop those following when the danger is observed, for even two or three men may not at first be able to 'break the string' and direct those following into a safer course. **1921** GUTHRIE-SMITH *Tutira* (1926) 182 By them [*sc.* arbitrary barriers such as fences] sheep are forced to climb when they would prefer to wind, or in shepherd's phrase, to string to their camps on comfortable grades. **1934** *Press* (Christchurch) (Acland Gloss.) 27 Jan. 15 *String.*—When sheep are mustered, they do not move forward in a body, but in a series of Indian files, so that the lead arrives at the end of the beat hours before the musterers, with the tail sheep. This is called *stringing out*, or *stringing away*. This habit is most noticeable in merinos; but all sheep do it if they are neither feeding nor hurried. **1949** NEWTON *High Country Days* 39 The pack team was stringing round the track to the next camp site. Each horse had his correct position in the string. **1966** NEWTON *Boss's Story* 190 *String:* It is the habit of sheep on the hill to travel in single file, i.e. to string.

 Hence **stringing** *vbl. n.*
 1960 SCRYMGEOUR *Memories Maoriland* 11 When dusk fell, Mrs. Parker still defied the stringing of the sheep across [the river].

string, *v.*[2] [Spec. use of US *string* to fool, deceive: see OED *v.* 15; AND 1888.] Usu. as **string on**, to deceive, to string along.
 1881 BATHGATE *Waitaruna* 142 She is barmaid in one of the hotels..but she is popularly known..as 'Goodall's stringer'... I'm sure I saw through the meaning of the phrase at once, although I had never heard it before either... It means that she makes herself agreeable to those who frequent the house, and so she 'strings them on,' and induces them to spend their money there. *Ibid.* 184 I think he is spooney on the

'stringer'. **1892** CARRICK *Romance Wakatipu* 20 [The girls'] real duty was to dance with the diggers, and, in goldfields parlance, string them on to drink.

Hence **stringer** *obs.*, a girl who works in a bar encouraging ('stringing on') customers to drink.
1881 [see prec.]. **1913** BATHGATE *Sodger Sandy's Bairn* 93 A mate o' mine got badly struck on a young girl a publican had brought up as a stringer.

string, *n.* [f. STRING *v.*[1]: AND 1931.] A single-file column of animals, esp. sheep.
1900, 1949 [see STRING *v.*[1]].

stringer, *n.*[1] *Wool store.* [Prob. a transf. use of *stringer* a tie-beam, or tie wire: see OED 5.] A piece of wire bent at right angles at each end and used to hold a bale of wool in one row to a bale in the next, to stabilize a vertical stack.
1940 GASKELL *All Part of the Game* (1978) 4 So the gang is there with me and Joe, and Bill is up top hauling them [*sc.* bales] up and putting in stringers. **1950** *Stringer* as a term and artefact was used in Levin and Co.'s Woolstore, Wellington (Ed.).

stringer, *n.*[2] *Logging.* DRAW *n.*
1944 GILBERD in *NZ New Writing* III. 55 We would have given you the muscles of a Dinny Hoe, ears that diagnose the slightest creak of the tight-strained stringers. **1950** [see DRAW *n.*].

stringer, *n.*[3] *Freezing works.* See quot.
1951 May 17 Feilding Freezing Works terms p.c. Colin Gordon. The carcasses are washed and wiped by a *wiper*, then a *stringer*, generally a boy, puts strings on the front legs and necks.

strip, *n. Sawmilling.* FILLET.
1948 JEWELL *Accounting in Timber Industry* 128 *Fillets;* Sometimes called a 'sticker' or 'strip'. Is a strip of timber or board 1"x 1" or 2"x 1" placed between layers of boards in a pile and at right angles to the boards. **1952–53** [see FILLET].

strip, *v. Obs.* [Cf. OED *strip v.*[1] 10 *obs.* To take plunder or spoil.] The English word chosen (poss. revived) by early writers to express the verbal sense of Maori MURU *n.* q.v.
1827 WILLIAMS *Early Jrnls.* 29 Jan. (1961) 41 In the afternoon we were told that a large party were on their way to this place, for the purpose of stripping us... Tikoki had stripped an Englishman on the opposite side yesterday..out in some revenge for some property of his. **1827** *Church Missionary Register* in Marsden *Letters & Journals* (1932) 434 They replied, 'Your chief has fled, and all your people have left the place, and you will be stripped of all your property before noon; therefore, instantly be gone.' **1828** WILLIAMS *Early Jrnls.* 12 Feb. (1961) 103 The news soon spread and it was given out that our natives would have a small piece of land stripped.

Hence **stripping party,** MURU *n.*. 2.
1835 YATE *NZ* (1970) 155 Should he [*sc.* the owner of a store-platform] be visited by a stripping party, the trouble they must be at..is almost a sufficient guarantee for their not attempting it. **1967** DRUMMOND *At Home in NZ* 47 [The Halls c1816] were visited by a 'stripping' party who collected most of their bedding and many of their clothes.

striped. In the names of animals, see: BONITO, MULLET 2 (1), RAIL 2 (9).

stripper. *Flaxmilling.*
1. Also **stripping machine.** [Spec. use of *stripper* a machine for stripping: see OED 2 a.] A machine for stripping the green matter from a flax blade.
1877 BROOMHALL *Fragments from the Jrnl.* 32 The [flax] leaf..is fed into a machine called a 'stripper'. **1890** *Otago Witness* (Dunedin) 13 Feb. 9 It is this stripper which makes that peculiar wild beast-like, snarling noise. **1891** WALLACE *Rural Econ. Austral. & NZ* 251 A boy receives the [flax] fibre from the stripping machine and 'leases' it over his knee in small bundles or bunches like hanks of yarn about as thick as a man's wrist. **1913** [see FEEDER c]. **1928** *Free Lance* (Wellington) 6 June 7 After the removal of dead leaves and foreign matter, the plant is passed through the stripper for the removal of the green matter composing the major part of the vegetation. **1951** [see GLORY HOLE]. **1977** FURNISS *Servants of the North* 15 He picked up the [flax] leaves one at a time and guided them into the mouth of the stripper, an ingenious arrangement of sharp gears which stripped the green material from the fibre in the leaf. **1987** HUNT *Foxton 1888–1988* 111 In 1867 an Auckland engineer invented a machine which extracted fibre from the flax plant by beating the leaves between two metallic surfaces—a revolving metal drum (equipped with beaters) and a fixed metal bar... This machine (which became known as a 'stripper') heralded the beginning of large-scale production of flax fibre.

2. Comb. stripper-keeper, a flaxmill employee who controls the stripping machine; **stripper-waste,** the non-fibrous tissue removed from a flax-blade by the stripping process (see also VEGETATION).
1891 Cox *Diaries 1888–1924* (ATLMS) 26 May Con Dwyer started at his old job today, that is stripper keeper and benchman. **1908** *Truth* 4 Apr. 1 At Seifert's [flax] mill at Shannon three stripper-keepers, Unionists, were kept on at Unionist rate of wages. **1913** CARR *Country Work* 44 Wages...—Stripper keeper and feeder... Shaker 30s a week. **1921** *NZJST* IV. 36 It was foolish to think of turning **stripper-waste** into paper, and this fact must have been known to those who made paper from flax as far back as 1830.

stroke: see GOVERNMENT STROKE.

stroke. [Spec. use of *stroke* an achievement: see OED *n.*[1] 15.] In the phr. (**to think one is doing) a (great) stroke,** something (one) is very proud of, a considerable achievement.
1890 DOUGLAS in *Mr Explorer Douglas* (1957) 113 We think we are doing a great stroke sending away thousands of Tons [*sic*] of Coal from Greymouth. **1946** SARGESON *That Summer* 132 I thought I'd done a great stroke.

strong, *n.* See also STRENGTH. **a.** In the phr. **to get the strong of** [AND 1923], to comprehend.
1917 *Chron. NZEF* 19 Sept. 63 We sees a new stunt goin' on..'n we just 'alts for a second to get the strong of it. **1953** HAMILTON *Till Human Voices Wake Us* 150 I've got most of them [*sc.* religions] into my head, he said, but I don't get the strong of that Christ joker.

b. [AND 1915.] The truth, the significance.
1978 BALLANTYNE *Talkback Man* 193 'Why was Bernie kicked out..?' 'I dare say he was pissed and confused.' 'That would be the strong of it,' said Sid.

strong-eyed, *a.* Of a sheep-dog, having the ability to control sheep with the eyes. Occas. *ellipt.* as a noun, **strong-eye,** a dog with this ability. Cf. EYE 3.
1949 HARTLEY *Shepherds' Dogs* 3 The system..in the case of excessively strong-eyed dogs..gives the trainer greater command where there is likelihood of the dog 'setting' sheep and failing to lift or pull. *Ibid.* 5 If the pup is from a 'strong-eye' strain he will begin to stalk the rubber and the trainer can begin to employ the whistle..intended to bring him on to sheep. **1952** MIDDLETON in *Arena 31* 2 Shepherding the stragglers would be Charlie's strong-eyes, Beau and Belle. **1975** NEWTON *Sixty Thousand on the Hoof* 202 Southland dog trialist Mr Don Rogers gave exhibitions of handling and working sheep with a team of five highly-trained 'strong-eyed' sheepdogs. **1980** LELAND *Kiwi-Yankee Dict.* 97 *strong-eyed bitch, strong-eyed dog:* working dogs..that exercise remarkable control over flocks of sheep..seemingly just by crouching down and staring at them.

stub fence. *Obs.* See quot.
1965 *NZ Geogr.* Oct. 147 The stub fence needed little skill for its erection, and was considered strong enough to prevent all types of stock from encroaching on land so fenced. It consisted of two large and relatively straight tree trunks lying parallel to one another, with six-foot branches placed upright between them and packed closely together.

stuck in(to), stuck up: see STICK, STICK UP *v.*

Stud Ass /ˌstʌd ˈæs/. Also **Stud. Ass., studass.** An abbreviation of (University) Students' Association. Occas. applied to a student union building.
1929 *Spike* (Victoria Univ.) 55 Like the rest of the Stud. Ass. **1959** SLATTER *Gun in My Hand* 36 Before the war the wind-whipped gowns of hurrying students, the friendly talk in the quad afterwards, tea at Stud. Ass., the laughter and explosions and grease paint of Capping Week. **1986** *Campus News* (Auckland) 3 June 14 Imagine a campus president caught smoking illicit substances in the Canterbury studass offices.

stuff, *n.*[1] *Goldmining.* Also **washing stuff.** [f. *stuff* material containing ore: see OED *n.*[1] 4 d, 1851.] Alluvial auriferous material taken from a claim; *washdirt* (WASH *n.*[2] 2).
1852 *Rep. Sub-Committee on Recent Gold Discovery in Coromandel Dist.* 23 Oct. in Earp *NZ* (1853) 258 One or two pans of the stuff was taken out of this hole..and washed, but did not produce anything. **1866** SMALL *NZ & Austral. Songster* (1970) 21 Paddy Noolan went out to wash up his little heap; But on coming to his claim—By my conscience, what a shame!—Some thieves had stole his washing stuff while he was fast asleep.

stuff, *n.*[2] [f. *stuff n.* and *v.* fuck: see OED *n.*[1] 11.] In the phr. **not to give a stuff,** not to care a whit.
1969 MASON *Solo* television script (1981) 207 Man:.. I don't give a stuff if it was or not. That spoke to me. Opened up my life, things I'd forgotten. **1978** *PSA Jrnl.* Nov. 10 Thursday was quite a shock for me to become aware that the brass couldn't give a stuff, that they wanted us to keep coping in our conditions and cover up everything and just get on with our job. **1984** *Listener* 29 Sept. 10 A young woman speaking..to the Social Credit conference told delegates that many New Zealanders 'don't give a stuff'. Everyone knows..that this word is a substitute in many expressions for the four-letter also word commonly heard. **1993** O'SULLIVAN *Let the River Stand* 40 'Not lousy even so much as just shagged,' Dick said, 'because no one's given a stuff about them for years.'

stuff, *v.* [As a synonym or euphemism for *fuck.*]
1. *trans.* To defeat soundly, to overcome or best. Also as a *pa. ppl. a.* **stuffed,** exhausted; beaten; ruined; useless.

1959 SLATTER *Gun in My Hand* 166 Wait till we clean up Otago on Wednesday [at rugby union]. We'll stuff 'em. **c1966** BAXTER in Oliver *James K. Baxter* (1983) 103 He had his chosen weapons against academics—the sword of obscenity. 'The only way to stuff them is to speak bawdy on all occasions.' **1988** MCGILL *Dict. Kiwi Slang* 109 *stuff* to defeat severely, often in sport. **1994** *Dominion* (Wellington) 11 July 6 Maori people should expect nothing from New Zealand's 'stuffed' welfare systems..Sir Tipene O'Regan said yesterday.

2. In phrases with various prepositions or adverbial complements, in various senses replacing *fuck v.* Cf. ROOT *v.* **a. to stuff** (something) **up**, to ruin.

1984 16–17 F E9 Pakuranga Coll. 19 Stuff (it) up [F8M2] **1984** 14 F E131 Wgton Girls C. 19 Stuff it up [F4]

b. to stuff about (or **around**), to waste time, to mess around.

1984 16 M E69 Pakuranga Coll. 14 Stuff about [M3] **1984** 15–17 M E82 Pakuranga Coll. 14 Stuff (a)round [M8F8] **1984** 14 F E126 Wgton Girls C. 14 Stuff around [F2]

c. to stuff off, usu. *imp.*, go away!

1984 16 F E13 Pakuranga Coll. 35B Stuff-off. **1988** MCGILL *Dict. Kiwi Slang* 109 *stuff off!* a strong request to leave; eg 'Look, mate, nobody asked you to this party. Now why don't you stuff off before we have to call the police?'

stumer /ˈstuːmə/, *n.* Also **stoomer, stummer**, and occas. *ellipt.* **stoom**. [Spec. use of Brit. slang *stumer* something worthless, a 'dud': see OED 2.] A horse, 'fixed', or otherwise, certain not to be placed; esp. in the phr. **to run a stumer** (occas. **to run stoom**), of a racehorse, to run a dishonest, losing race. Also transferred to other kinds of competitor and race.

1900 SCOTT *Colonial Turf* 191 Aren't they piling their stuff on the stumer. **1907** *Truth* 13 July 2 At this time of the year Sunday steeds are saddled up as 'stoomers' with a view of being let loose in some more important event later on. **1908** *Truth* 11 July 2 It is their flow of language that catches the mug, just as the guesser 'mags' his pigeon into backing a stummer. **1912** *Free Lance* (Wellington) 12 Oct. 14 'D'yer' think I'm running a bloomin' stoomer?' gasped Billy as he stumbled through the fence [*sc.* chased by a bull]. **1917** BROWN *Lay of Bantry Bay* 57 'She is a mare that can't run stoom!'—(I heard this in the train.)... 'I'm weighing out my weekly lead For stooms I backed last May!' **1935** *Star-Sun* (Christchurch) 6 Nov. 19 [Heading] Is the Labour Party running a stumer... [He] said the word 'stumer' meant something containing dishonesty. **1946** SOLJAK *NZ* 116 The following New Zealand expressions derive from British dialects. *stumer*: failure; *to run a stumer*: to lose a race. **1954** *Star-Sun* (Christchurch) 14 Apr. 15 Drastic action on swimmers who 'swim a stumer'—competitors who do not try in a heat, so that they will not be rehandicapped for the final.

stumer /ˈstuːmə/, *v.* Usu. as **stumered**, earlier **stumed**, *ppl. a.*, of a racehorse, to be dishonestly 'fixed'; of a person, exhausted, 'stumped'; 'broke'.

1908 *Truth* 18 Apr. 2 Larst Wellington meetin', we wus orl stoomed right out, bar 16 ogg. **1943** BENNETT *English in NZ* in *Amer. Speech* XVIII. 92 A horse that runs crooked is said to be *stumered*, apparently derived from Glasgow sporting slang. **1988** MCGILL *Dict. Kiwi Slang* 109 *stummered* bankrupt or exhausted; from English use of 'stumer', a dud cheque; *come a stumer* a fall, usually financial; *in a stumer* in a mess, usually financial; eg 'I'm stumered, mate, you're on your own the rest of this match.'

stumping-jack. A large jack (occas. of a form similar to some kinds of timber-jack) for removing stumps.

1932 SCANLAN *Pencarrow* 289 Sometimes they used a stumping-jack [for removing stumps]. **1985** HAWKE & SCOTT *Early Farm Machinery in NZ* 129 Stumping jacks were also used for lifting and turning logs.

stun the crows: see CROW *n.*[1] 4.

stunned, *ppl. a.*

1. [Cf. OED 2 '*Austral.* and *N.Z.*' drunk, 1919.] Drunk.

1921 LORD *Ballads of Bung* 'Stunology' (1976) 11 To say you're 'soused', 'steamed', 'stunned', or that 'you're on the swank', Is only a reflection, on the glorious way you drank. **1933** PRUDENCE CADEY *Broken Pattern* 129 I am afraid I got a bit 'stunned'... I had one over the odd. **1943** BENNETT *English in NZ* in *Amer. Speech* XVIII. 89 A thoroughly drunk man is *stonkered, floored, stunned,* or..*shickered.* **1964** PEARSON *Glossary* to Sargeson *Collected Stories 1935–63* (1964) 303 stunned: drunk. **1988** MCGILL *Dict. Kiwi Slang* 109 *stunned* drunk; eg 'Can't you see he's stunned? He's been boozing since the pubs opened.'

Also, by back-formation **stun-up** *n.*, a bout of drinking, a 'booze-up'.

1953 REED *Story of Kauri* 122 On one occasion he was having a periodical 'stun-up' at one of the three Mercury Bay hotels.

2. As **stunned mullet**, a type of complete amazement or stupefaction, see MULLET 3.

stunt. WW1, WW2. [OED 1915.] A raid, attack, etc. Cf. PLUNGE *v.*

1917 *NZ at the Front* 172 In a 'stunt' few men showed up like him. He could get more out of his men then any other N.C.O. *Ibid.* xiv Stunt.—A fight, ranging from a raid to a big battle. **1917** *Great Adventure* (1988) 183 At last after all these months..of waiting the orders have come for our 'stunt' and..we are to take the road en route for the real 'business'. **1942** *NZEF Times* 27 July 5 [Caption] I picked all along we were going on a desert stunt.

Hence in verbal use **stunting** *ppl. a.*, engaged on a 'stunt' or patrol.

1918 *Chron. NZEF* 8 Nov. 175 I believe the 'stunting' company is at last '·midst where the shells are thickest'.

subaltern's butter. *Obs.* Avocado flesh. See quot.

1926 *Otago Daily Times* (Dunedin) 24 Mar. 4 It is considered that there are great possibilities in the New Zealand market for Avocado pears, more widely known in the South Seas as 'subaltern's butter'... The name 'subaltern's butter' was derived from the fact that in the old days when there were many military posts in the South Seas and supplies of fresh food, including dairy butter, were often short, the subaltern on duty in the officers' mess of any camp frequently arranged for quantities of Avocado pears to be sent to the cookhouse, and the prepared fruit was served in place of butter.

Subantarctic. Usu. init. caps. Applied to the southern islands between Stewart Island and Antarctica under New Zealand control (see esp. quot. 1909), also known earlier as the 'Sealing Islands', 'Southern Islands', or 'Outlying Islands'.

1909 CHILTON *Subantarctic Islands of NZ* I. xiv To the south and south-east of New Zealand lie a number of islands, or groups of islands, which are in these volumes called the 'Subantarctic Islands of New Zealand'... The islands included in this group are the Snares, the Auckland Island Group, Campbell Island, Antipodes Islands, Bounty Islands, and Macquarie Island. **1923** *Rec. Canterbury Mus.* II. 3 117 These notes are based on observations made during a brief visit to the Sub-Antarctic Islands during March of this year. **1955** EDEN *Islands of Despair* 203 The war-time occupation of the Sub-Antarctic Islands demonstrated their potential value to the world's meteorological service. **1965** *Proc. NZ Ecol. Soc.* XII. 37 The Subantarctic islands of the south of New Zealand lie in a narrow belt of latitudes (48°S.–55°S.). **1988** DAWSON *Forest Vines to Snow Tussocks* 203 A group comprising Macquarie, the Aucklands, Campbell and Antipodes lies south of New Zealand and is conveniently termed the subantarctic islands. **1991** HIGHAM *New Zealand's Subantarctic Islands* 18 After the earlier wrecks, castaway huts were erected on all the New Zealand subantarctic islands.

subber: see SUBBIE.

subbie. Also **subber**. [f. *sub*(-contractor + -IE (or -er); AND *subbie*, 1978; OEDAS 'orig. and chiefly *Austral.*'] A sub-contractor.

1953 REED *Story of Kauri* 146 In the case of a large enterprise the contractor would commonly sublet portions of the work..to secondary contractors, known as 'subbers'. **1987** HUNT *Foxton 1888–1988* 139 Building constructors always have their 'subbies', the electricians, plumbers and painters-paperhangers. **1989** 16 May TV1 Advt for Carter-Holt Building Supplies. [Carpenter speaks] What a day!.. First the subbies don't turn up. **1991** *Examiner* (Auckland) 28 Feb. 2 Between April and December 12 they paid the contractor $270,000 but, unbeknown to them, he 'forgot' to pay at least one of his subbies.

Sub-protector of Aborigines: see PROTECTOR OF ABORIGINES.

sucker, *n.*[1] Also **suckerfish**. [Spec. use of (an ellipt. form of) *suckerfish* a fish with a suctorial disk by which it adheres to objects: see also OED *sucker n.* 11.] CLING FISH (*Diplocrepis puniceus*). [*Note*] Also applied in New Zealand, as elsewhere, to the widely distributed remora, *Remora remora* (fam. Echeneididae): see OED *sucker n.* 11.

1872 HUTTON & HECTOR *Fishes NZ* 40 *Diplocrepis puniceus*... Sucker. **1898** MORRIS *Austral-English* 443 *Sucker*..name given in New Zealand to the fish *Diplocrepis puniceus*... This is a family of small, marine, littoral fishes provided with a ventral disc, or adhesive apparatus. **1906** *TrNZI* XXXVIII. 551 *Diplocrepis puniceus*... The sucker, common in rock-pools. **1938** *TrRSNZ* LXVIII. 417 *Diplocrepis puniceus*... Sucker-fish (sucker). **1956** GRAHAM *Treasury NZ Fishes* 366 The Sucker Fish will swim only very short distances of from three to about fourteen inches, attaching themselves to a rock again with remarkable rapidity. **1968** MORTON & MILLER *NZ Sea Shore* 345 By its pectoral disc the small suckerfish *Diplocrepis* clings to the painted rock by turns quiescent and swiftly mobile.

sucker, *n.*[2] The buttocks.

1947 DAVIN *For Rest of Our Lives* 51 When he went in we sat round on our suckers scoffing the beer and playing two-up. **1947** DAVIN *Gorse Blooms Pale* 199 After we'd had our swim in the afternoon we used to come back and sit on our suckers waiting for mess.

suckerfish: see SUCKER n.¹

sudden decline (disease). Also init. caps. A disease affecting or killing cabbage trees in the North Island from c1987. (Other scientific opinion has downplayed bacterial spread suggesting ozone depletion and increase in ultra-violet radiation as part of a complex of climatic and other changes stressing cabbage trees.)
   1991 *Evening Post* (Wellington) 6 Dec. 3 Trees around Wellington were believed to have died of Sudden Decline disease, Dr Ross Beever of the DSIR's Auckland plant protection unit said... Using the test, scientists had discovered the DNA of a bacterial organism named MLO (mycoplasma-like organism) in trees affected with Sudden Decline... Sudden Decline, evident since 1987, was thought to have arrived in New Zealand in the early 1980s and to be spread by lacy-winged Australian vine-hoppers. **1993** *Dominion* (Wellington) 25 June 4 The death of many of the North Island's cabbage trees is probably caused by a specialised bacteria... The condition called sudden decline affects more than half the cabbage trees in some parts.

sugar and blanket. *Hist.* Also **sugar and flour**. Descriptive of (alleged) systematic attempts to appease the Maori, or to induce the sale of Maori lands, by bribery with food and clothing. Usu. collocated with **policy**, occas. with other terms, and occas. as a joc. defining phr. **sugary and flowry**. See also FLOUR AND SUGAR, TRACT AND TREACLE.
   1863 MOSER *Mahoe Leaves* 69 The system of 'hoatu noatu' or 'free gift', has another name which sounds a trifle grating in the ears of the colonists; it is known as the 'sugar and blanket' system. **1863** *NZ Advertiser* (Wellington) 18 Aug. 3 The sugar and blanket policy could not last much longer. **1864** GORST *Maori King* 41 It was therefore thought most economical and prudent not to attempt to govern at all, to abstain strictly from interference in purely native affairs, and merely to purchase, by presents and pensions, the goodwill of the principal native chiefs. This has gone by the name of the 'Sugar and Flour' policy, because to distribute large quantities of sugar and flour was the keystone of the system. **1868** *Auckland Punch* 31 Mr. Maori, don't fight us and we will be sugary and flowry. **1878** WELLS *History of Taranaki* 137 At first Sir George [Grey] tried his old method of diplomacy with the natives, known as the 'sugar and blanket policy'. **1879** FEATON *Waikato War* 5 The sugar and flour policy which the government had adopted seemed to do no good, being looked upon as a sign of weakness on the part of the Pakeha. **1902** IRVINE & ALPERS *Progress of NZ* 204 The 'sugar and flour' policy begun by..[Grey] became, in other hands, merely a cheap way of getting rid of our responsibilities in relation to the Maoris and in the end it helped to demoralise them. **c1910** MACDONALD *Reminiscences* (VUWTS) 63 The way in which [McLean] managed the 'Ground Bait' policy and the 'Sugar and Blanket' policy, by which he bought many..areas of land and kept the peace all the time, won for him the applause..of Maoris and Colonists.

sugarbag. *Hist.* [Spec. use of *sugar bag* a bag for containing bulk sugar: AND 1850.] **1.** Also occas. **sugar-sack**. Formerly a bag of fine sacking, often containing a standard 70 pounds (31.75 kg) of bulk sugar, and used for many purposes as a container, as a source of household and general coarse cloth, and as a knapsack.
   1864 *Richmond-Atkinson Papers* (1960) II. 115 One man Watene who played the leading part of 'hitere' or 'taki', had for his whole dress a sugar bag (or matting) round his middle. **1919** *Quick March* 10 July 21 In front there was a candle-box..with a sugar-bag over it. **1928** *NZ Free Lance* (Wellington) 11 July 7 He dropped his swag, a sugar-bag tied with a strap. **1934** LEE *Children of Poor* (1949) 145 We would throw down pieces from the full trucks and fill our sugar bags and clear out. **1959** SLATTER *Gun in My Hand* 227 A book about the working man biking to work..with his sugar-bag tied with a rope around his shoulder. **1967** HENDERSON *Return to Open Country* 57 This was the depth of the Depression: 1934... It was the year of the sugarbag. Every week you'd see the father of a needy family trudging to the centre with his empty sugarbag for his handout. **1974** SIMPSON *Sugarbag Years* 132 He went into a shop and bought an overcoat because always up until then he used to wear a sugar bag. **1987** GEE *Prowlers* 24 She sat in a wicker chair and took some typewritten sheets from her sugar sack. **1991** VIRTUE *Always the Islands of Memory* 66 Some weeks Sister begged food from the hospital, bringing it home in a sugar-bag.

2. *attrib.*
   1927 *NZ Dairy Produce Exporter* 40 Mother..always breakfasted in a drab working dress and a sugar sack apron. **1936** LAMBERT *Pioneering Reminisc. Old Wairoa* 190 The classic event was generally the Sugar bag Handicap. **1953** SUTTON-SMITH *Unorganized Games NZ Primary School Children* (VUWTS) II. 606 The seats [of the boys' fort at Waitara, c1880–90] had..a sugar-bag pillow holding the soft to[u]sled heads of..the raupo. **1974** SIMPSON *Sugarbag Years* 90 On the Friday of the stand-down week myself and hundreds of others paraded outside the boardroom of the Canterbury Hospital Board in Christchurch. This was known as the 'sugarbag parade'. **1987** HARTLEY *Swagger on Doorstep* 114 Bush-whackers, sugar-bag men, tramps, swaggers, rousabouts—all these expressions became familiar as I grew older, but I had always thought of these wanderers as tramps and swaggers only. *Ibid.* 141 She removed her sugar-bag pinny..and put it..in a cane basket. **1992** PARK *Fence around the Cuckoo* 115 Sugarbag days they were, for nearly every man carried one.

3. Special Comb. **sugar bag carpenter** [AND 1978], an itinerant carpenter; **sugar-bag years**, a phrase coined by Tony Simpson in 1974 to symbolize the poverty and self-sufficiency of the 1930s Depression.
   1982 LYNN *Lynnwood Tree* 125 The following was the method of sorting out a tradesman from a **sugar bag carpenter** [in the 1930s]. **1974** [Title] Simpson *The Sugarbag Years*. **1984** SIMPSON *Sugarbag Years* (2edn.) 8 It has been my extraordinary good fortune..for this book to have created a cliché ('the sugarbag years' is now a way of referring to the depression of the thirties) and to have taken on a life of its own. **1984** BEARDSLEY *Blackball 08* 239 It was..exciting as the Depression cut deeper..the sugarbag and sandshoe years. **1993** *Dominion* (Wellington) 8 Mar. 93 She couldn't have picked two more different generations: the children of the sugarbag years and the children of the boom. **1993** *NZ Tablet* (Dunedin) 31 Mar. 12 Understanding I needed plenty of: oldest boy in a family of eight on a raupo-ridden dairy farm in the sugarbag years.

sugar boat. *WW1*. In the phr. **to capture the sugar boat**, said about the appearance of rations, esp. in the front line.
   1935 STRONG in Partridge *Slang Today* 287 Anyhow, he said they had captured a sugar boat, so I put a few handfuls in my kick. **1938** *Press* (Christchurch) (McNab Slang) 2 Apr. 18 [Slang of the N.Z.E.F.] Food gave an idiom or two:.. a good ration was the capture of 'a sugar boat'.

sugar-loaf pine: see PINE 2 (16).

sugar-sack: see SUGARBAG.

suicide-fish. FROSTFISH, from its reputed habit of casting itself upon the beach on frosty nights.
   1981 WILSON *Fisherman's Bible* 67 The name 'Suicide-fish' comes from the [Frost]fish's apparent sea-shore 'suicide'. No reason has been confirmed for its strange, invariably fatal, behaviour.

suicide squad. *Hist.* The nickname of the group of appointees to the Legislative Council dedicated to its abolition in 1950.
   [**1950** *NZPD* CCLXXXIX. 715 Now we have the supreme confidence of the Prime Minister that those appointees are so bound that they will 'commit suicide' on orders without even thinking.] **1966** *Encycl. NZ* I. 848 National won the [1949] election and, a few days before Parliament met, announced 26 new appointments to the Council. The new councillors were quickly nicknamed the 'suicide squad' by the Opposition. They all voted for the Abolition Bill which was introduced shortly after Parliament met. **1972** JACKSON *NZ Legislative Council* 196 The members of the 'suicide squad' as it was commonly called, were neither young nor overwhelmingly composed of farmers. **1986** *Illustr. Encycl. NZ* (1989) 675 After gaining power, the National government packed the council with members intent on voting it out of existence. These members were called the 'suicide squad'. **1992** *Dominion* (Wellington) 28 Sept. 8 The final adjournment occurred on December 1, 1950, and Legislative Councillors, including the 'suicide squad', filed out of the chamber for the last time to ensure passage of the Abolition Bill.

sukey, sukie, varr. SOOKIE.

sulky /ˈsʊlki/. [Transf. use of *sulky* a light two-wheeled carriage or chaise with seating for one person: see OED 1; AND 1902.]

1. A light horse-drawn vehicle used as a conveyance (often formerly applied to a drovers' jogger); now used mainly (as in US) as the name of the vehicle in harness racing (see quot. 1978). Cf. JOGGER.
   1894 WILSON *Land of Tui* 106 B. drove in a 'sulky' with one of his assistants, as he had often to make a *détour* to inspect the line. **1911** *Triad* 11 Dec. 21 The men had come in to O'Rorke's for Christmas... They had arrived in low-hung, dust-covered 'sulkies'. **1951** PARK *Witch's Thorn* 160 There was a tremendous commotion..when the Hush family arrived, one car and three sulkies full. **1975** HARPER *Eight Daughters* 36 If there wasn't a large load to collect, George took the sulky, which had no back, was light, well-sprung and fast. **1978** MCKENZIE *Roydon Heritage* 25 This was largely due to his hind hoof hitting the sulky stirrups on the turning track. **1986** DEVANNY *Point of Departure* 19 Each family, besides horses, owned a sulky [c1900].

2. *Otago-Southland*. In *transf.* use, applied to an older type of baby's folding push-chair, usu. with a cane body in which the child faced the pusher.
   1952 Notice in a Queenstown shop window stated: 'Sulkies for hire—2/6 a day'. (The North Island reader (Ed.) was much confused, thinking the reference was to the trotting racing-vehicle.) **1966** TURNER *Eng. Lang. Austral. & NZ* 180 A Christchurch trotting man goes to buy a *sulky* advertised in Dunedin at a surprisingly reasonable price but finds it has nothing to do with horses but is what he calls a *pushchair* or the Miami store a *stroller*. **1980** LELAND *Kiwi-Yankee Dict.* 98 *sulky*: No horses hitched to this one. Its [*sic*] a baby buggy

made of woven cane. **1992** *NZ English Newsletter* 6 10 *Sulky*. This term is virtually obsolete now. According to..older interviewees, it refers to an old style of pushchair in which the child faces the person who is pushing... The term does not seems to have been used for the modern replacements.

sulphur-bottom: see WHALE 2 (19).

sultana bird. *Obs.* Also **sultan-hen**. [Spec. use of *sultana bird* for *Porphyrio* spp. (*sultana* feminine of *sultan*, alluding to its rich 'oriental' colouring): see OED 6.] PUKEKO 1.

1867 HOCHSTETTER *NZ* 293 The Sultan-hen of brilliant plumage..or the Pukeko of the natives. **1872** DOMETT *Ranolf & Amohia* 233 Black sultana-birds, Blue-breasted as deep ocean. **1883** DOMETT *Ranolf & Amohia* I. 306 Sultana-birds (*Pukeko*)... The 'Poule Sultane' of the French, Pollo Sultano, *It.* Porphyrio Melanotus, *ib.* The New Zealand species has crimson bill; red legs; rich deep blue breast; rest of plumage velvet-black. **1898** [see PUKEKO 1 b]. **1968** *NZ Contemp. Dict. Suppl.* (Collins) 19 *sultana bird n.* the swamp hen.

summer. Used *attrib.* in special Comb. applied to areas unworkable or impassable in winter: **summer country** *high country farming*, an area that is suitable for summer pasture only (contrast *winter country* (WINTER)); **summer (summer's) diggings**, a diggings able to be worked only in summer; **summer field**, see quot.; **summer road**, one negotiable with ease only in summer.

1876 PEACHE *Journal* in Gray *Quiet with Hills* (1970) 42 I rode up the Orari run..to put a mob of sheep back on to the Blue Mountain, which is the farthest of their **summer country**. **1898** MORRIS *Austral-English* 444 *Summer Country, n.* In New Zealand (South Island), country which can be used in summer only; mountain land in Otago and Canterbury, above a certain level. **1916** *TrNZI* XLVIII. 156 The former [sub-alpine associations] are largely used for grazing purposes during the summer; hence the term 'summer country'. **1922** PERRY *Sheep Farming* 88 The higher country, and that having a southerly aspect, which is likely to hold snow to some depth in the winter months, is termed 'summer country', for it is unsafe for sheep in the winter, and is used only for summer grazing. **1947** NEWTON *Wayleggo* 14 A large proportion of the country—the shady and hindermost areas—is suitable for summer grazing only... Such country is known as 'summer country'. **1962** SHARPE *Country Occasions* 123 Sheep which act like that stay out on the summer country until they are either found in a 'straggler muster' or buried by snow. **1973** WHEELER *Hist. Sheep Stations NI* 92 In the South Island the terms 'summer' and 'winter' country have a very real meaning for the station owner. **1862** *Otago Goldfields & Resources* 26 It will hardly ever be other than a **summer's diggings**. **1873** PYKE *Wild Will Enderby* (1889, 1974) III. i 74 THE miners, having duly registered their claims as 'protected', scattered themselves over the country... Nokomai and the Nevis..became favourite summer diggings. **1908** *TrNZI* XL. 170 Gum-digging may be roughly divided into two classes—viz., that on the 'Winter-fields', or the high tea-tree ranges where the ground is too hard to work in dry weather, and that on the '**summer-fields**', or low swampy situations, where digging would be impossible during the wet season. **1888** PAYTON *Round about NZ* 47 Many of these bush roads are what are called '**summer roads**', consisting entirely of mud without any metal. *Ibid.* 84 The road is what is known as a '*summer road*' that is it consists almost altogether of mud, and in the winter is very rough.

sun. In the phr. **to think the sun shines out of (one's) arse**, to consider (oneself) far better than (one's) company or competition.

1983 HULME *Bone People* 116 O him, he'll be okay at the Tainuis. Marama and Wherahiko think the sun shines outa his arse excuse me. He's the white haired boy round there, literally. **1984** 16–17 F E37 Pakuranga Coll. 17 He thinks the sun shines out of his arse [M3] [describing a boaster].

Sunday. In special Comb. as an epithet in mainly farming use applied to a person or animal shirking work or the difficult parts of it: **Sunday dog**, a lazy working dog (cf. PASSENGER, SOONER 1, SUNDOWNER 2); **Sunday shearer**, a lazy or choosy shearer.

1934 *Press* (Christchurch) (Acland Gloss.) 27 Jan. 15 *Sooner*.—Slack, useless dog. So called because he would s[ooner] lie in the shade than work. I have also heard *Sunday-dog* used as an equivalent, because one day's work a week is enough for him. **1947** NEWTON *Wayleggo* 109 Jock was what is known among hill men as a Sunday dog—normally a damning description. *Ibid.* 155 *Sunday Dog*: One which will refuse to work if the going is hard, or the heat severe. **1966** [see SOONER 1]. **1988** MCGILL *Dict. Kiwi Slang* 109 *Sunday dog* lazy sheep or cattle dog. **1960** MILLS *Sheep-O* 104 The Bowens are no '**Sunday**' shearers. Rams..bare-pointed sheep,.. these hold no terrors for these class shearers.

sundown, *v.* [Back-formation f. SUNDOWNER: AND 1882.] *intr.* To take up the occupation or way of life of a sundowner. Usu. as a *vbl. n.*

1888 D'AVIGDOR *Antipodean Notes* 154 It [*sc.* urban unemployment] has, therefore, several advantages over 'sundowning'. The professional unemployed need not tramp ten, twelve, or twenty miles a day, and he always has congenial company. **1891** DOUGLAS in *Mr Explorer Douglas* (1957) 153 I have plenty of Tucker here certainly, but I havn't [*sic*] a cent in my pocket—I am literally without a pocket—and would have to Sundown my way amongst strangers. **1907** KOEBEL *Return of Joe* 18 No more sundowning for me;.. I hate it, boss, I hate it. **1951** HAY *Swagger Jack* 19 So let us walk with Jack's sundowning stride Towards a certain station that he sees.

sundowner.

1. [AND 1868.] An itinerant or swagger with a habit of arriving at a place at the end of the working day (i.e. at 'sundown') ostensibly seeking work. See also TUSSOCKER.

1873 PYKE *Wild Will Enderby* (1889, 1974) III. x 105 Now, a 'sundowner' or 'tussocker' for the terms are synonymous—is a pastoral loafer; one who loiters about till dusk, and then makes for the nearest station or hut, to beg for shelter and food. **1883** BRADSHAW *NZ As It Is* 26 The [peripatetic labourers] in the colony are known by the name of 'Swaggers' or 'Sundowners'... Sundowners, because they never approach a habitable place before sundown lest they should be requested to take a further stroll. **1890** *Otago Witness* (Dunedin) 20 Mar. 15 Possibly before next harvest we shall hear a cry raised by the squatter..that those who are about do not want work; that they are 'sundowners'. **c1899** DOUGLAS in *Mr Explorer Douglas* (1957) 278 Another time, a white cockatoo travelled down the Coast, visiting every hut on the beaches like an experienced sundowner. **1902** SATCHELL *Land of Lost* (1971) 20 Roller's storekeeper..liking the appearance of the young fellow, took him into the house instead of consigning him to the shed reserved for sundowners. **1912** MANSFIELD *Stories* (1984) 113 Sweet life! The only people who come through now are Maoris and sundowners. **1933** *Press* (Christchurch) (Acland Gloss.) 16 Dec. 21 *Sundowner* is either literary, or a ladies' word. I have often seen it written but do not remember hearing it spoken. **1940** LAING & BLACKWELL *Plants NZ* 4 The stock-rider, the shepherd, the swagger, and even the sundowner know every aspect of it [*sc.* the tussock country]. **1951** DUFF *Shepherd's Calendar* (1961) 39 Once when I was a real sundowner [Duff's pen-name was 'Sundowner'], carrying my swag from station to station and taking care not to arrive too soon, I came with another gentleman of the road to Earnscleugh homestead in Central Otago. **1960** ROGERS *Long White Cloud* 41 The old sundowner game, eh? Learned all the tricks. Show up at dinner time so they can't turn you down. **1987** *Listener* 29 Aug. 47 On the floor..there was a sort of shakedown—you know, the kind of lair you associate with rouseabouts in the shearing season, or tramps and swaggers and sundowners in bad times.

2. *transf.* A lazy dog or person. Cf. *Sunday dog* (SUNDAY).

1953 STRONACH *Musterer on Molesworth* 2 My dogs I tied to the iron fence outside the hotel. They were..; Maud, a bob-tailed bitch, one of the borrowed ones and already under suspicion as a 'sundowner'. **1967** MACNICOL *Skippers Canyon* 129 The playful pup grew to a large..dog. He proved too easy-going and too much of a 'sundowner' for hill work. **1982** *Agric. Gloss.* (MAF) 25 *Sundowner*: Dog that leaves its work, especially when hot and noisy. A lazy dog.

sunnies. *pl.* [f. *sun*(glasses + -IE.] Sunglasses.

1995 *City Voice* (Wellington) 13 July [facing] 11 [Wellington City Council Extra] Now you don't have to take off your sunnies in the tunnel.

Super /'suːpə/, *n.*[1] [Spec. use of *super* abbrev. of *superintendent*.]

1. *Hist.* SUPERINTENDENT.

1864 THATCHER *Songs of War* 12 The Super issued quite a rabid Proclamation. **1874** WILLMER *Courts of Archery* (Christchurch) 4 One lame Finch 'scaped to Govern'd 'House'; And there to dwell in *Super* bliss.

2. *Hist.* [AND 1849.] A superintendent of a sheep station; a manager or overseer of a rural property.

1853 in *Canterbury Rhymes* (1866) 17 It's oh, to be a Super Along with some western swell, Where a man has never a stiver to save, But sometimes gets a spell. **1883** FERGUSON *Castle Gay* 193 The ewes in camp all safe and fast And all the lambs composed at last. When shortly after on the ground The Super came and glanced around. [1883 *Note*] Bush term for overseer. Abbreviation of Superintendent.

3. A superintendent of a prison.

1973 JUSTIN *Prisoner* 60 Go and see the super tonight. It's his interview night.

super /'suːpə/, *n.*[2] [AND 1925.] Abbrev. of *superphosphate* (see quot.1974). Also heard as *aerial super*, superphosphate distributed by aerial topdressing.

1922 *NZJ Ag.* Nov. XXV. 315 Putting on a dressing of lime in the autumn, followed by super in the spring, is good practice. **1939** HILGENDORF *Pasture Plants* 68 Top dressing with super, or with lime and super, every year, is essential. **1949** SARGESON *I Saw in My Dream* (1974) 135 They say if you're a dairy farmer, a bit of super is about the one thing you can never borrow off any of your neighbours. **1951** *Awards, etc.* 237 [Chemical-Manure and Acid Workers Award] [Rates of wages] Men working on super bank 4[s.] 2¼[d.] Men operating bulldozer on basic 4 4¾. **1969** HENDERSON *Open Country Calling* 60 It was great sitting in the truck just riding round while the super flew out behind. **1974** *NZ Agric.* 165 The main type of phosphatic fertiliser produced is superphosphate (or 'super'). It is made by treating phosphate rock (imported mainly from Nauru Island) with sulphuric acid (made from imported sulphur). **1982** MARSHALL *Master Big Jingles* 76 If the ground was grazed naturally, and just a little super added from time to time, then worm action would increase the height of the soil.

super /ˈsupə/, *n.*³ Occas. early **superan**, and (*joc.*) **super-duper**. [Abbrev. of *superannuation*, a pension scheme or fund: OEDAS 'Austral. and N.Z.', Aust. 1973.] *spec.* the 'Government Superannuation Fund' (often heard as *Government super*), a work-related contributory retirement scheme for State employees now closed to new members (see quots. 1932, 1985); also the so-called 'universal super', a former non-contributory superannuation benefit available from 1938–77 to New Zealanders over the age of 65; and NATIONAL SUPERANNUATION (see also the note to that entry).
    1932 *Dunedin Souvenir Sketches* (Griffiths Collect.) So long as Coates and all that clan Will leave untaxed my Superan. **1969** MASON *Awatea* (1978) 61 Werihe: I am an old man, and need little. I have my super-duper every week; tell Gilhooly; she draws it out. **1985** MCGILL *G'day Country* 31 I retire in three years. It'll be tough if I don't get the Super. I've got Railways Super, but it makes you wonder why you're in the service if they don't give you the ordinary Super. **1988** MACRAE *Awful Childhoods* 36 Chris's grandmother.. comfortably supplemented her universal super..with palmistry readings. **1991** *North & South* (Auckland) June 45 This financial year the super bill will be just over $5.1 billion.

superannuitant. Also *joc.* **superant**. A person receiving superannuation, *spec.* before 1938 mainly a (retired State servant) pensioner of the Government Superannuation Fund; from 1938–77, with the introduction in 1938 of a scheme promised by the Labour Party in the 1935 election under the slogan 'Superannuation for All', the recipient of a *superannuation benefit*, a non-contributory 'universal' benefit (usu. called 'universal super(annuation)' distinguished from a more valuable 'age benefit' (quot. 1938 refers); from 1977, a recipient of NATIONAL SUPERANNUATION q.v. Cf. SUPER *n.*³
    [*Note*] The New Zealand use does not have the apparently pejorative overtones of the sense and (single quot.) in OED (1830): 'The word *superannuitant* seems especially favoured in New Zealand; other countries usually speak of *superannuant*', p.c. D.G. Simmers, Unit Manager, Department of Social Welfare 22 June 1993.
    1938 *Auckland Weekly News* 2 Mar. 20 There appears to be every reason to accept..that the Government is aiming at £3 a week as the basis of the minimum benefit for superannuitants. **1990** *North & South* (Auckland) May 96 Sprinkled among the beautiful backpackers are some dinkum Mark I Zephyr youths and the odd fresh-air superannuitant. **1992** *Dominion* (Wellington) 12 Feb. 10 The meeting has been organised by the superannuitants' federation. **1991** *National Business Review* 27 Sept. 54 [TV3] was rewarded with another gem of a leak last week..about what the *NZ Herald* called the claw in the government's clawback scheme for superants.

superheater. *Southland*. A hotwater cylinder.
    1964 DEMPSEY *Little World Stewart Is.* 2 In one of his letters Eric had written, 'The house has a very good superheater.' Superheater? I had wondered... The word cropped up again on the day of our arrival. 'What *is* a superheater?' My husband, surprised, asked, 'What do you call them in the North Island?' and threw open the door of the cupboard which housed the hot water cistern. **1968** GLEN *Holy Joe's People* 71 I got round to asking him if he could shove it [*sc.* a shotgun] in his superheater cupboard. **1971** WATT *Centenary Invercargill* 50 A Christchurch firm, which made a well-known superheater, was baffled by the short life the heaters normally had in Invercargill [from the corrosive property of the water]. **1992** *NZ English Newsletter* 6 11 (Bartlett *Regional Variation: Southland*) [Other items which may be diagnostic of Southland English are:] *superheater* (hot water cylinder).

Superintendent. *Hist*. The chief elected officer of a Province. See also SUPER *n.*¹ 1.
    1851 *Gov. Grey to Earl Grey* 30 Aug. in *Rutherford Sel. Documents* (1949) 44.61 The terms of the New Zealand Charter of 1846 compelled me, in the Provincial Councils Ordinance, to apply the term 'Lieutenant-Governor' to the officer administering the government of each province. Had a discretion been left to myself, I should have designated such an officer by the term 'Superintendent'; and I would still recommend the adoption of this designation for the officer administering the government of a province. **1853** *Richmond-Atkinson Papers* (1960) I. 136 [William] is made clerk of the Council (our Parliament that is) and is proposed Attorney for the province by the Superintendent and Council. **1940** COWAN *Sir Donald Maclean* 91 He had been Superintendent of the province of Hawke's Bay for several years. **1952** WILSON *Julien Ware* 36 Tales were told of how, as Superintendent of his province, he bullied his councils into passing legislation that he alone favoured. **1968** DALZIEL *Vogel* 32 Superintendent: Person who ran the Province, similar to the mayor of today but with wider powers. **1971** GRANT *Land Uprooted High* 44 Fitzgerald later became Superintendent of the province and revenged himself on his old rival by erecting a hideous statue of Godley in the Square. **1983** LAMBERT *Illustr. Hist. of Taranaki* 34 Taranaki's first election for a Superintendent was held in 1853.
    Hence **Superintendency**, the office of provincial Superintendent.
    1866 *Canterbury Rhymes* 102 The Candidates for the Superintendency were Mr. J.E. Fitzgerald, [etc.].

supertom. [A proprietary name.] A tall, grafted, heavy-cropping variety of tomato plant.
    1966 *NZ Patent Office Jrnl. No.1040* 4 Apr. Supertom B79309 [filed] 26 August 1965..tomato plants. Alan Ward Naish. **1984** MARSHALL *Day Hemingway Died* 21 Left to himself he would potter about grafting berry canes and nipping out the set fruit on his super toms. **1990** *Star Garden Book* 147 Varieties are: Under glass—Beefsteak..Euro x Extase plus your Super Toms. **1993** *Evening Post* (Wellington) 7 Oct. 19 Grafted plants, sometimes called by their trade name Supertoms, consist of an ordinary tomato variety grafted on to a type..that has a very vigorous root system.

supper.
1. *Obs.* in NZ use. The evening meal; TEA 3 a (a).
    1856 HEPBURN *Lett. from Otago* 28 June in *Journal* (1934) 161 The supper consisted of roast beef, boiled mutton, steak and kaka pies, fowls, tongues, plum puddings, custards, jellies, etc., port and sherry wines, brandy, Scotch Whisky in abundance. **c1875** *Otago Guardian* in Tonkin *Dunedin Gaol* (1980) 35 Then back to gaol [after 5 p.m.]... and not dismissed until the men have had their tea, or, as it is termed 'supper'. **1881** PYKE & TALBOT *White Hood & Blue Cap* 12 [Jim was] busily engaged in cooking the savoury chops which formed the basis of their frugal supper. **1921** MANSFIELD in *Undiscovered Country* (1974) 12 Then she called me to supper and we sat down. I suppose we ate some cold meat and salad... Then she got up, changed the plates, and went to the larder for the pudding.

2. a. A late-night snack; food or other refreshment taken during an interval in a ball or dance.
    1892 COX *Diaries 1888–1925* (ATLMS) 19 Feb. Jones came back last night about 9 p.m. and had supper, a great nuisance. **1919** *Alexandra Herald* 30 Apr. 5 A..supper was served in the small hall at the back. **1924** *Otago Witness* (Dunedin) 8 Apr. 31 As usual the ladies supplied a plentiful supper which was handed round during the interval. **1943** *Timaru Herald* 10 July 1 [Advt] Lucky Spot, Monte carlo, Good Orchestra. Good Supper. **1950** *Dominion* (Wellington) 15 July 10 The Vice Regal party was piped into the hall by the Police Pipe Band, which also played during supper. **1964** BACON *Along the Road* 152 The trestle tables had been put up along one side of the hall, with the supper set out on sheets and table cloths whisked from linen cupboards from all over the district. **1963** MORRIESON *Scarecrow* 51 I'll put on a quick supper for us all... Nothing like the old cuppa..to brighten us up. **1980** LELAND *Kiwi-Yankee Dict.* 98 *supper*: A snack before retiring, never refers to the main evening meal. An evening party at home in New Zealand will almost always include a fairly substantial meal, called supper, served 11:30–12:midnight. **1992** PARK *Fence Around the Cuckoo* 46 It cost a shilling to get into a dance hall, and that entitled a boy and his partner to supper, which was provided by the older ladies, who each 'brought a plate'.

b. Special Comb. **supper dance**, **supper waltz**, the dance after which women are escorted to supper by their partners; **supper room**, the room (often in a local community hall) used for serving supper at dances.
    1924 ANTHONY *Follow the Call* (1975) 40 I finally got her to promise me the **supper dance**... When the supper dance was announced I dashed in just in time to see her taking the arm of someone else. **1948** BALLANTYNE *Cunninghams* (1976) 62 Phil Chalmers..told him he'd hang on till the supper dance, then grab the best-looking tart on the floor and [take her] to supper. **1991** LA ROCHE *Hist. of Howick & Pakuranga* 202 The hall was originally smaller with an outside walk to the **Supper Room** where a copper boiled hot water. **1964** BACON *Along the Road* 45 Ladies and gentlemen!.. We'll make this one the **Supper Waltz**. Take your partners for the Supper Waltz! **1976** FINLAYSON *Other Lovers* 59 And then, just before the supper waltz, I saw Tom. **1987** DUDER *Alex* 44 'It's the supper dance next. Where're your shoes?'.. 'OK, OK. Let's d-d-dance. It's the supper waltz.' **1991** KEITH *Lovely Day Tomorrow* 71 The supper waltz would announce a brief respite from the music.

supple. *Ellipt.* for SUPPLEJACK.
    1849 *Emigrants' Lett.* (1850) 102 (New Plymouth) One of these [parasitical climbers] the supple, is indeed magnificent. **1913** MCNAB *Old Whaling Days* 83 The insides [of the huts] were strongly constructed and fastened with supple vines.

supplejack /ˈsupəlˌdʒæk/, /ˈsʌpəlˌdʒæk/. Also **souple jack**, **suple-jack**, **supple Jack**. [Spec. use of *supplejack* a name for various tropical and sub-tropical climbing plants, also Brit. dial.: see OED; EDD; AND 1788.] See also *black vine* (BLACK *a.*² B 2), KAREAO, PIRITA 1, SARSAPARILLA.
    [*Note*] The pronunciation [supəl] is prob. of Sc. or northern Brit. dial. origin.

1. a. *Ripogonum* (occas. *Rhipogonum*) *scandens*

(fam. Smilacaceae), a high climbing woody liane of lowland forest.

1770 PARKINSON *Journal* (1773) 15 Jan. 115 The country..is entirely covered with wood, and full of a sort of supple-jack, that it is difficult to pass through it. [**1773** BAYLY *Journal* 12 Apr. in McNab *Hist. Records* (1914) II. 206 In many places there is great quantities of a sort of vines somewhat like supplejacks in the West Indies.] **1791** BELL *Jrnl. Voyage H.M.S. 'Chatham'* (Vancouver exped.) (ATLMS) Nov. 49 The underwood which grows amazingly thick and compos'd chiefly of the Supple Jack..prevents any pleasure you might propose in walking on shore. **1817** NICHOLAS *NZ* I. 232 The supple-jack, a species of cane, was very common... This plant is very elastic, as may be inferred from its name. **1834** MARKHAM *NZ* (1963) 62 Koraddie or Flax, Vines, Rattan and number of other Creepers crossing the Path and Tripping one up. [**1834** marginal *note*] Souple Jacks. **1840** *NZ Jrnl.* I. 287 The path was much obstructed by karewau or suple-jack. **1862** AYLMER *Distant Homes* 76 Tom was very fond of bringing home branches of the supple Jack-creeper. **1882** HAY *Brighter Britain* II. 201 The Kareao.., well-known to the settlers under the detested name of 'supple-jack'. **1901** *Bulletin Reciter* (Satchell 'Ballad of Stuttering Jim') 97 For the bush was..sharp as a tiger's claw, With the supple-jack vines, and the saws and the spines of toi and tartara-moa. **1907** MANSFIELD *Urewera Notebook* (1978) 51 The fanciful shapes of the supple jacks. **1938** LANCASTER *Promenade* 96 Tiffany, wooing bush robins..swinging in supple-jack loops with a bellbird ringing its chime for her. **1966** *Encycl. NZ* III. 712 Supplejack . . kakareao, kareao, pirita . . *Rhipogonum scandens*. **1990** *Listener* 16 July 15 Tendrils of supplejack are alternately valuable handholds and infuriating impediments to one's progress.

b. The stem of the supplejack as construction material for fences, eel or crayfish pots, as a cane or walking-stick, or as an instrument of corporal punishment.

1844 *Piraki Log* 7 Feb. (1911) 148 Men in the Bush cutting supple-jacks to fence the shed. **1879** *Auckland Weekly News* 26 Apr. 10 The Maori law-giver laconically called for a stout supplejack, with which he administered a castigation severe enough to instil into her..a more exalted sense of wifely duty. **1911** MORELAND *Through South Westland* 82 That snakey rope is a lily—the 'supple-jack' of the settlers. **c1930** *Whitcombe's Etym. Dict. Aust.-NZ Suppl.* 11 *supple-jack n.* various woody climbers with tough, pliant stems; a walking-stick made from such a plant. **1982** SANSOM *In Grip of Island* 14 My fish basket cradle was oval and sturdy and made of supplejacks.

2. *Obs.* Occas. (poss. erron.) BUSH LAWYER *n.*[1] (*Rubus* spp.).

1867 HOOKER *Handbook* 768 Supple-jack. *Rubus australis*, *Parsonsia*, *Lygodium*, etc. **1868** LINDSAY *Contribs. NZ Bot.* 54 In this condition *Rubus australis*..forms one of the most..troublesome 'Lawyers', or 'Supple-Jacks', of the forest. **c1890** BODELL *Soldier's View Empire* (1982) 176 The Bush Lawyer or Supple Jack was very thick amongst the trees.

3. Special Comb. **supplejack district**, by synecdoche, a 'bush' district or backblocks.

1920 *NZ Free Lance* (Wellington) 2 June 34 At a Burns 'nicht' somewhere in the supplejack district of the North Island, a fierce argument over the correct pronunciation of 'Auchtermuchty' was solved by someone playing it on the bagpipes.

supplier. A member (or shareholder) of a cooperative dairy company supplying milk or cream to its factory; hence **supply** *v. trans.* to supply (a dairy company) with milk or cream.

1890 *Otago Witness* (Dunedin) 12 June 20 The remaining five suppliers will not..send their milk to the factory in a beastly condition. **1922** *Auckland Weekly News* 11 May 55 Suppliers were under the impression that first-grade was an inferior grade to superfine. **1934** *Truth* 3 May 10 [The] Manager of the Taupiri Dairy Factory stated that Bayly had been a supplier to his factory for the present season. **1941** ALLEY & HALL *Farmer in NZ* 106 Just under 65,000 suppliers keep these [dairy] factories going, and as a high proportion of these will be engaged only in dairying, it is plain that more individuals are engaged in this than in any other branch of farming. *Ibid.* 107 An interesting feature of the dairy industry is that practically all the factories are co-operatively owned by their suppliers. **1993** O'SULLIVAN *Let the River Stand* 39 He provided figures and dates because his own father supplied the dairy company, so of course he knew.

sure dinkum!: see DINKUM C 1 a.

surf, *n.* Used *attrib.* in special Comb. **surf-boat** [spec. use of *surf-boat* a boat specially constructed for passing through surf: see OED *surf n.* 3], an open, usu. double-ended, boat designed to carry cargo between ship and beach in heavy surf; **surf-crab**, see CRAB 2 (2); **surf-hurdling**, the transporting of (goods, etc.) between ship and shore by means of surf-boats (see also SURF *v.*); **surf-lifesaver** [AND 1963], a member of a surf life-saving club; **surf life-saving** [AND 1942], the action of saving a swimmer from drowning; the organized safe-guarding of swimmers on surf beaches.

1848 WAKEFIELD *Handbook NZ* 276 They have also provided **surf-boats**, now manned by experienced boatmen in the employ of the Government [at New Plymouth]. **1857** *Lyttelton Times* 15 Aug. 5 I had a large surf-boat towing astern. **1899** GRACE *Sketch NZ War* 22 We arrived off New Plymouth early in the morning, and landed in surf-boats. **1914** in *Hist. N. Otago from 1853* (1978) 38 *The Surf Boat Service*. Possibly a description of the method of working the surf boat may interest my readers. **1930** DOBSON *Reminiscences* 153 On several occasions small sailing vessels came in and lay on the beach, but it was found too dangerous, so several large surf-boats were provided. **1952** RICHARDS *Chatham Is.* 129 Passengers for the steamer [at Waitangi] were carried through the surf to a surf boat and then rowed out to the ship in the bay. **1973** WHEELER *Hist. Sheep Stations NI* 10 The dumped wool was taken by bullock wagon into the surf, transferred to surfboats, and rowed out to the..steamer lying offshore. **1986** OWEN & PERKINS *Speaking for Ourselves* 134 We had a big surfboat, about eighteen feet long, and generally about two, or sometimes three, of us would crew it. **1941** BAKER *NZ Slang* 57 **Surf-hurdling** seems to be a New Zealand term, though there is reason to suspect it is used extensively in the Pacific. It describes the practice of landing goods from a ship to shore in an open boat on an exposed coastline. The taking of goods, especially wool, from shore to ship in an open boat is also termed *surf-hurdling*. **1946** SOLJAK *NZ* 118 New Zealanders have coined or adapted many expressions to meet local requirements, as illustrated by the following:.. *surf hurdling:* landing goods from ship to shore, or vice versa, in an open boat. **1956** *Weekly News* (Auckland) 15 Feb. 42 Never, since the establishment of the association, has a single person been drowned in an area patrolled by **surf life-savers**! **1991** *Evening Post* (Wellington) 4 Dec. 14 Hunched over a heater poorly performing in the face of last night's southerly the *Tuesday Documentary* on surf lifesavers heightened my distress at the current weather. **1912** *NZ Free Lance* (Wellington) 11 May 20 [Caption] The Lyall Bay **Surf Life-Saving** Club has a Day Out.

1938 *NZ Observer* 27 Jan. 9 The average member of a surf life-saving club goes to a considerable amount of trouble and self-sacrifice every week-end. **1940** *Otago Daily Times* (Dunedin) 5 Feb. 11 The..Competition for senior four-men alarm surf life-saving teams and the Stevenson Cup Competitions..were held at Brighton on Saturday. **1966** *Encycl. NZ* III. 328 New Zealand is a world leader in surf lifesaving, a service sport which has been followed in this country for more than 50 years. It grew spontaneously on the country's surf beaches some five years after the birth of the parent movement in New South Wales. **1986** *Illustr. Encycl. NZ* (1989) 1181 Surf lifesaving began in New Zealand in 1910 when both the New Brighton club in Christchurch and the Lyall Bay club in Wellington were started. **1991** *Dominion* (Wellington) 9 Jan. 10 Surf lifesaving receives no taxpayers' money.

surf, *v. Obs. trans.* To transport (goods, etc.) by surf-boat between a ship and shore. Also as a *vbl. n.*

1959 MASTERS *Tales of Mails* 134 Owing to lack of harbours, mail, supplies and produce had to be what was termed, surfed. On arrival, the coastal boat would anchor in the most convenient position offshore. A connecting link between shore and ship would then be made by bullock or horse wagons going out as far into the surf as possible, and being met by surf boats from the ship. Surfing was a tricky job. *Ibid.* 138 We then headed for Wangaehu, where, in his young days, as a bullock driver for Mr. Saint-Hill Alex had taken part in the surfing of wool.

surface. *Goldmining.* Used *attrib.* in special Comb. in the sense 'near the surface of the ground': **surface diggings**, diggings which comprise mainly surface deposits; **surface stuff** [AND 1855], wash-dirt obtained by working the surface of the ground.

1867 HOCHSTETTER *NZ* 112 Since the '**surface diggings**' of the Australian gold-fields are being more and more exhausted, the individual digger no longer finds his expectations realized as formerly. **1887** CHUDLEIGH *Diary* 21 July (1950) 356 I commenced making shafts to test for gold. The water stoped [*sic*] me but I shall try the **surface stuff**.

surfaceman. [Prob. transf. use of *surfaceman* one who repairs railway tracks: see OED.] A workman who keeps road surfaces in repair, and verges and gutters clear. See also ROADIE 1. Cf. LINESMAN.

1877 *Tapanui Courier* in Marks *Hammer & Tap* (1977) 371 Within a few miles of Lawrence, I noticed two surfacemen just emerging from their homes—about half-past nine—apparently traversing the locality in search of something to do, while the condition of the roads was such that they need not have gone ten yards... A little further on two other surfacers were at work..pretending to rake gravel into the wheel-ruts on a new-made piece of road. **1927** GUTHRIE-SMITH *Birds* 15 The only bipeds who upon their feet utilize the King's Highway are surfacemen and swaggers,.. the surfacemen preoccupied with the more material problems of metal and mud. **1940** STUDHOLME *Te Waimate* (1954) 141 As we were putting 120 head [of cattle] across the Waitaki Bridge..they set off at top speed..nearly killing two surfacemen, who had foolishly come on to the bridge at the far end.

surfacer.

1. *Goldmining.* BEACHCOMBER 3.

1879, **1930** [see BEACHER 2]. **1967** MAY *West Coast Gold Rushes* 528 Surfacer: on the West Coast, applied to a digger working a sea-beach claim.

2. See SURFACEMAN (quot. 1877).

surfacing, *vbl. n. West Coast.* Gold-bearing black sea-beach sand; BLACK SAND *n.*

c1890s in Harper *Memories of Mountains and Men* (1946) 113 An old 'hatter' living just above the beach, and looking out for patches of beach gold, or 'surfacing' which was thrown up, or uncovered in stormy weather by the surf. **1896** [see BEACHCOMBING *vbl. n.*].

surface sow. [See OED *surface* 6 c, 'chiefly N.Z.'.] *trans.* To broadcast (seed) on the surface of the ground without tilling in. Found mainly as a *vbl. n.* and *ppl. a.* **surface-sowing, surface-sown.**

1921 GUTHRIE-SMITH *Tutira* 163 The land is surface-sown with grass and clover seed. **1882** HAY *Brighter Britain* I. 197 In spite of..the rough ground, and the mere surface-sowing, our grass will carry four sheep per acre. **1915** MACDONALD *NZ Sheepfarming* 106 The fallen bush lands and some of the scrub lands have been surface sown in English grasses. **1950** *NZJAg.* Feb. LXXX. 121 The more fertile surface-sown hill country. **1950** *Ibid.* Apr. LXXX. 309 The uncertain establishment of plants from the surface sowing of clover seeds.

surimi /sə'rimi/. [ad. Japanese.] An artificial fish-substitute made from the flesh of real fish.

1986 *Catch* Nov. 9 The big item of interest..is the experimental fishery being conducted to determine the viability of processing New Zealand hoki into *surimi*. What is surimi? Simply put, it is a mechanically deboned, washed and stabilised fish protein paste. **1987** *Catch* Dec. 19 Jack mackerel surimi... Some companies are looking at NZ jack mackerel..as a potential source of surimi. **1991** *Dominion* (Wellington) 2 Dec. 3 A crab salad made from surimi should either be described as a surimi salad or crab-flavoured surimi salad.

swag, *n.*[1] [Transf. use of *swag* thief's plunder or booty: see OED *swag n.* 9.]

1. a. [AND 1841.] A blanket-wrapped roll or bundle of possessions and useful articles, which, when carried by a traveller on foot, was usu. held by straps to the back or shoulders, or laid round the neck like a horse-collar (see *horse-shoe swag* (HORSE *n.*[1] 5) and quot. c1864 below), or carried in bandolier fashion across one shoulder; a load carried in or as a swag. See also BLUEY *n.*[1] 1 a, PACK *n.*[1] 1, PIKAU *n.* 2 b.

1853 ROCHFORT *Adventures of Surveyor* 49 Disregarding the state of the roads we strapped on our 'swags' (colonial word for pack). **1855** *Sidebottom's Let.* 6 Mar. in Gillespie *S. Canterbury* (1958) 459 Seventeen and I collared our swags and tracked on. **1860** BUTLER *Forest Creek MS* (1960) 46 My swag generally is as follows—A mackintosh sheet, two blankets, one rough peajacket, saddle bags and a tether rope wound round my horses [*sic*] neck—then I consider myself equipped for any emergency. **c1864** TEMPSKY *Memoranda* (ATLTS) 51 And as the sudden morning broke, we shouldered our swags. [1864 *Note*] Colonial term for a roll of blankets & clothing etc. carried either horse-collar fashion or in a roll by straps over the shoulder. **1872** BUTLER *Erewhon* (Dent, Everyman edn. 1932) iv 32 When I tied the two ends [of the seven-foot blanket roll] together, and put the whole round my neck and over one shoulder. This is the easiest way of carrying a heavy swag, for one can rest one's self by shifting the burden from one shoulder to the other. **1888** D'AVIGDOR *Antipodean Notes* 165 Nowadays 'swags' are made of stout waterproof material and are sold, with straps sewn ready, like a very long and narrow 'hold-all'. **1906** PICARD *Ups & Downs* 7 You may look down on a man who gives his swag, drum, knot, or parcel of bags a shove round the land. **1933** *Press* (Christchurch) (Acland Gloss.) 16 Dec. 21 *Swag*.—A man's blankets, rolled up and strapped. The *s[wag]* may contain spare clothes, or indeed anything else, rolled up inside the blankets, and musterers usually roll an oilskin sheet outside them. **1940** COWAN *Sir Donald Maclean* 4 Maclean..must have walked some thousands of miles..carrying his swag as the Maoris carried their *pikau*. **1958** PASCOE *Great Days in NZ Mountaineering* 132 Mountaineers were amazed to see that a bushman with a heavy swag could slash a track just about as fast as they could walk. **1963** BAXTER *Collected Poems* (1980) 284 Mother, I come alone. No books, no bread Are left in my swag. **1987** OGONOWSKA-COATES *Boards, Blades & Barebellies* 98 *Swag*. Spare clothes, tobacco and any other essential possessions rolled up inside one's blankets, which are then strapped, making them convenient to carry.

b. A knapsack; later a tramper's rucksack or pack. See also *swag-bag* 4 a below.

1862 HODDER *Memories NZ Life* 137 Our knapsacks, or swags, as they are more generally called,.. were fastened to our back with a pair of slings called 'coveys' which are made by the natives of dressed flax. **1896** HARPER *Pioneer Work* 18 While climbing the last rocks and pulling our loads up after us, one of the straps broke, and the 'swag' made a rapid descent for some 700 ft. into a *bergschrund*. **1945** *NZ Geogr.* 39 'Swag'.. was used originally..to refer to tramps... In the sheep and alpine country of the South Island, the shade of meaning is changed to include the *rucsac* of those who climb, tramp, ski or shoot for pleasure and of those who deal with sheep for a living. **1958** *Tararua* Sept. 31 *Swag*. This is surprisingly little used by trampers, though it has been standard Australian and New Zealand use for many years. **1961** REED *N. Cape to Bluff* 17 I left my home at Mornington, Dunedin..and carried my swag and a small leather case down to the railway station.

c. *spec.* Mustering. A bedroll.

1951 MCLEOD *NZ High Country* 31 The pack team..for six musterers is quite an outfit. Seven swags (the men's bedding rolls) tent and fly. **1966** NEWTON *Boss's Story* 190 *Swag*: Bedroll. Before the advent of cars it was the practice of musterers to carry their total belongings in their swag or bedroll.

2. *transf.* (Occas. *joc.*) Luggage; a load carried by a person.

1891 COTTLE *Frank Melton's Luck* 3 We at once made ourselves useful by assisting the ladies with their paraphernalia or swags as Miss Julia playfully designated them. **1911** *Kai Tiaki* Apr. 57 We each took a very small swag, consisting chiefly of 'evening dress'. **1952** *Here & Now* June 26 O honour the sad rhetorical Artist... Who will honourably uncover What the lover packs in his swag. **1954** *Tararua Tramper* Apr. 4 [Heading] The Big Swag... The party..unloaded a discouraging mass of timber, iron, wire-netting, malthoid, nails and sundry hardware.

3. In various (mainly verbal) phrases. **a. (to be** or **go) on the swag.** (a) To live or travel in the style of a swagger.

1909 COX *Diaries 1888–1925* (ATLMS) 4 June I saw Davy Gunn in Carterton about 4.30 p.m. on the swag. **1911** KIWI, *pseud.*[Title] *On the swag. Sketches of station life in Hawke's Bay...* [Napier..1911.] **1941** BAKER *NZ Slang* 41 Such expressions as *to swag it* and *to go on the swag* need no elaboration. **1960** MASTERS *Back-Country Tales* 299 The 'Boarslayer' was one of those hardy old characters of the South Island mountain country, who, in those bygone times, drifted round from place to place on the swag in search of employment. **1988** MCGILL *Dict. Kiwi Slang* 51 *go on the swag* become a tramp; eg 'During the Great Depression, many men had no choice but to go on the swag.' **1990** *Evening Post* (Wellington) 8 Aug. 25 He became a general farmhand wandering from farm to farm... 'I was on the swag for many years. Truck drivers used to call me king of the road.'

(b) (To be) on foot.

1945 MUNDY *Body-snatcher & Seagull* [no paging] The Body-snatcher arrived [for work on the wharves] in numbers, not on the swag but mostly in high-powered cars.

b. to shoulder one's swag, to take to the road.

1865 CHUDLEIGH *Diary* 24 July (1950) 194 Here I shouldered my swag and walked along the froazen [*sic*] shores of the lake at a good pace. **1914** PFAFF *Diggers' Story* 114 Next day I shouldered my swag and made for the Dunstan. **1972** *NZ Heritage* LX. 1656 He [*sc.* the Highland Chief] shouldered his swag, walked over 40 miles through the night to the Otematata station for the shearing call.

c. to carry (one's) swag. (a) To be reduced to living, or occas. to live, in the style of a swagger or itinerant in search of work.

1899 BELL *In Shadow of Bush* 125 The working-man used to be able to take care of himself... I carried my swag at first, and was often enough glad to get a job at anything. **1911** *Maoriland Worker* 7 July 14 The 'drummer', starting from the man who carried a drum, became the man who carried a swag and (then or there after) the loaded man (as a commercial traveller loaded with samples). To 'carry the load' is another synonym; and the essential point throughout the symbolry was evidently the load. **1933** *Press* (Christchurch) (Acland Gloss.) 16 Dec. 21 *To carry your swag* means to lose all your money [not *to be a swagger*]. When Alan McLean built his luxurious house..his brother John, hearing of all his magnificence, grew jealous and said, 'I should not be surprised but we shall hear of poor Alan carrying his swag before it's all done with.' **1941** BAKER *NZ Slang* 41 The phrase to *carry one's swag* is used to describe a condition of penury. **1962** HOGAN *Billy-Can Ballads* 3 When things got really tough I carried my swag.

(b) To travel on foot.

1934 LEE *Children of Poor* (1949) 26 Rabbiters, harvesters, shearers, ploughmen, roustabouts, leaving their jobs, carrying their swags, and with eyes turned towards homes in Dunedin, were frequently headed off by the hotels.

d. to pack one's swag, to (prepare to) leave.

1960 ROGERS *Long White Cloud* 31 I'm warning you, Harry. Any more and you pack your swag. Now get those horses back. **1970** MCNAUGHTON *Tat* 101 It was really because of Valerie that Stewart decided to pack his swag and drift on.

e. to hoist one's swag, to start out on foot.

1967 MCLATCHIE *Tang of Bush* 98 Before dark I decided to return to camp [c1900], so I hoisted my swag and set down hill.

4. Special Comb. **a. swag bag,** a bag designed to be carried as a swag; **swag-carrier,** a porter; **swag-carrying** *vbl. n.*, the manual transport of a load on the back or shoulders; **swag-pass,** a mountain pass negotiable for one carrying a swag; **swag-strap** [AND 1902], (either of) the straps fastened to a swag to enable it to be carried; also in the phr. **look (out) for one's swag-straps,** to be thinking of changing one's job; **swag-track,** a walking-track as distinct from a pack-track suitable for pack animals.

c1904 GRAVE *Beyond Southern Lakes* (1950) 48 The kit of each consisted of a specially constructed **swag bag**, oiled sleeping bag [etc.]. **1949** NEWTON *High Country Days* 37 Dogs were loosened, and their chains dropped into each man's swag bag. **1950** in

SWAG 797 SWAGGER

Grave *Beyond Southern Lakes* (1950) 34 Grave and I [*sc.* (Sir) Thomas Hunter] made our own swag bags [in 1905], as big as an outsize in pillowslips, with broad carrying straps... For this trip Crusoe had bought a large, elaborate and very expensive rucksack. **1940** COWAN *Sir Donald Maclean* 25 Maclean and his missionary companion, with their Maori **swag-carriers**, continued on past Tauhara mountain northward on their way to Rotorua. **1889** PRINCE *Diary of Trip* 20 With a launch..there would be no tent-pitching, no **swag-carrying**. **1933** *NZ Alpine Jrnl.* V. 235 McKenzie col will be a difficult **swag-pass**. **1924** *Otago Witness* (Dunedin) 17 June 4 The balance pole..was abandoned in favour of the kawa [*sic*], which corresponds to the bushman's **swag straps** and to the soldier's knapsack. **1930** DOBSON *Reminiscences* 157 And as we were always carrying a swag of some sort, the ends over the shoulders eased the cutting of the swag straps. **1934** *Press* (Christchurch) (Acland Gloss.) 20 Jan. 15 *Looking out for his swag straps.*—Thinking of leaving his billet. **1941** BAKER *NZ Slang* 41 We may recall the country use of the phrase *to look for one's swagstraps*, to consider leaving one's job in search of another. **1956** SUTHERLAND *Green Kiwi* (1960) 210 They greased their swag-straps, packed their 'blueys' and took the road again. **1966** PHILLIPPS *Maori Life & Custom* 172 In some localities a kawe, or swag strap, made from the bark of the lacebark tree..encircled the baby's body so that it could not fall to the ground [from its mother's back]. **1898** in Newport *Footprints* 15 Nov. (1962) 242 Last summer we constructed ten miles of **swag-track** down the Karamea towards the Crow [a tributary of the Karamea], this track diverging from the main pack-track in the vicinity of the Falls.

b. In composition forming adjectives and adverbs: **swagful, swag-laden, swagless** [AND 1902].

1956 SUTHERLAND *Green Kiwi* (1960) 116 So I went back to Roundelay again,... carrying a **swagful** of tucker on my back. **1861** *NZ Goldfields 1861* (1976) 15 There are still [prospecting] parties **swag-laden** going through the streets to make a start. **1862** *Otago Witness* (Dunedin) 30 Aug. 5 The bright, brisk, invigorating weather we enjoyed yesterday seemed to add wonderfully to the spirits of those who plodded in strings, swag-laden, out of the city. **1885** BURTON *Maori at Home* [Notes to photographs] We horsemen found ourselves **swagless**. **1889** [see SWAGMAN b].

swag, *n.*[2] [See OED *n.* 11 'now chiefly *Austral.* and *N.Z.*'.] Usu. as **a swag of**, a great amount (of), a large number (of).

1943 MARSH *Colour Scheme* 105 There's a postcard from Uncle James... And a whole swag [of mail] for the boarders. **1949** SARGESON *I Saw in My Dream* 75 I suppose you blokes get told a lot of yarns about a crook missis and a swag of kids. **1953** SUTHERLAND *Golden Bush* (1963) 123 'There's a swag of mail up at the office for you,' he said, 'letters and a couple of cables.' **1968** SLATTER *Pagan Game* 176 A swag of jokers in the bar, fourteen in the school. **1981** HUNT *Speaking a Silence* 16 There was a swag of people in Bedstead Gully those days; couldn't tell you how many. **1992** *Dominion* (Wellington) 14 Sept. (IT suppl.) 2 This year it [*sc.* Auckland Area Health Board] is buying another swag of machines (about 1500).

swag, *v.*

1. *trans.* To carry (a load) on the back or shoulders as, or in, a swag.

1861 HAAST *Rep. Topogr. Explor. Nelson* 16 We..started, on the 11th February, swagging part of the provisions, etc., down the Buller. **1877** *TrNZI* IX. 578 Having had to swag our things from this point. **1880** CRAWFORD *Recoll. of Travel* 259 He had swagged his calico tent over the hill. **1890** *Otago Witness* (Dunedin) 9 Jan. 10 The pigs were 'swagged' into Dunedin. **1914** GRACE *Tale Timbertown* 116 You'll get the tucker..and you'll help to swag it. **1946** *Tararua Story* 18 The club..prefabricated, swagged up and built late in 1922 in the Hector Saddle a tiny emergency hut. **1953** *Freedom* 8 Apr. 5 All food and equipment must be swagged out to the base in amounts for several weeks at a time, and skins and tokens swagged in again to where a packhorse can pick them up.

2. *intr.* [AND 1859.] **a.** To travel on foot carrying a swag or pack. (Often followed by a prepositional phr. (esp. with **up** or **down**) indicating the direction or goal of the travel.)

1864 CHUDLEIGH *Diary* 17 Nov. (1950) 153 I started Birmingham with the sheep whilst Thompson and I swagged up. **1914** PFAFF *Diggers' Story* 45 I accepted his offer and next morning started to swag through the Grey River. **1920** *Quick March* 10 Apr. 13 Then swag and footslog for the roadless forest..our provisions.. divided into equal sized 'pikaus' among us. **1939** PASCOE *Unclimbed NZ* 42 We left the hut in auspicious weather to swag up the Mingha riverbed. **1945** *NZ Geogr.* I. 45 He had crossed Browning's Pass to Westland and swagged down the Coast. **1958** *Tararua Sept.* 75 It was with some trepidation that Peter Beveridge, Dave Heraud and I swagged up the Hodder River for ten days' winter climbing. **1986** OWEN & PERKINS *Speaking for Ourselves* 68 Different things brought people together to swag.

b. Also **swag it**. (a) To travel as, or follow the life of, a swagger.

1877 BROOMHALL *Fragments from the Jrnl.* 41 'A swagger' is simply a man who carries his travelling luggage on his back... Bill Tiestook boasts 'he's swagged it these four year.' **1889** DAVIDSON *Stories NZ Life* 2 Kelly [*sc.* a detective] had..on more than one occasion swagged it for..miles after his prey as an orthodox sundowner. **1891** A TRAMP, ESQ. *Casual Ramblings* 108 A wondrous change all this since the days we 'swagged it' trudging on..up the Molyneux. **1941** BAKER *NZ Slang* 41 Such expressions as *to swag it* and *to go on the swag* need no elaboration. **1964** LEE *Shiner Slattery* 15 He never swagged on Sunday if he was close enough to walk to the nearest front seat in Church. **1976** VANCE *Bush, Bullocks & Boulders* 107 Some years later, Peter McCormack was swagging it on the road near Rakaia when he was struck by a motor car. **1986** OWEN & PERKINS *Speaking for Ourselves* 68 I came up north [from Southland] and swagged with a character that was well known on the track.

(b) To travel on foot carrying a swag.

1890 *Otago Witness* (Dunedin) 6 Mar. 35 Next day swagged it to Manipori station. **1896** *NZ Alpine Jrnl.* II. 9/41 After a little food, [we] were once more swagging it back. **1903** *Otago Daily Times* (Dunedin) 4 Apr. (VUW Fildes Clippings 621:46) They then had to boat the provisions to the head of Edwardson Sound, and then swag it up the creek. **1914** PFAFF *Diggers' Story* 141 The weather was very wet at the time [*sc.* 1867], and swagging it was not easy when the luck was out. **1933** *Press* (Christchurch) (Acland Gloss.) 16 Dec. 21 There is no verb meaning to be a s[wagger]. To *swag it* would apply just as well to a musterer carrying his swag out to camp, or even to a tourist. **1947–48** BEATTIE *Pioneer Recolls.* (1956) 4 When they swagged it west from Clinton father and son plodded on past their own place. **1967** MAY *West Coast Gold Rushes* 108 Nelson became the point of departure for a steady stream of diggers who had swagged it over the Mount Maungatapu range..or had sailed round from Havelock.

3. *trans.* To load with a swag (hence also **unswag**, to remove a swag from). Usu. as a *ppl. a.* **swagged** [AND 1881] (also **be-swagged**) *ppl. a.*, loaded (up) with a swag.

1860 BUTLER *Forest Creek MS* (1960) 51 Feed, water, and firewood, on having found a spot possessing these requisites..first unswag the horse. **1864** *Otago Witness* (Dunedin) 16 Apr. 16 Heavily swagged diggers and heavily swagged horses, whose heavy swags consist of all the household gods [*sic*] of a mining party. **1889** SKEY *Pirate Chief* 126 As I've said he would start at break of day, To throw us all clear off the scent; So long ere the time we were swagged and away, That nice little game to prevent. **1916** COWAN *Bush Explorers* (VUWTS) 18 Wirihana..glances round to see that all hands are be-swagged and ready, then quick march. **1935** COWAN *Hero Stories NZ* 175 That column of four hundred men..short-kilted like Highlanders, heavily beswagged, had toiled up from the Ruatoki Plain.

swagger. [AND 1855.]

1. a. An itinerant carrying a swag, esp. one in search of work; a tramp. See also *gentleman of the road* (GENTLEMEN 1), JINGLING JOHNNY, SUNDOWNER, SWAGGERMAN, SWAGGIE, SWAGMAN. [*Note*] *Swagger* is the preferred New Zealand use; *swaggie* and *swagman*, the Australian.

[**1866** *Puketoi Station Diary* (Hocken TS) 15 Sept. Five tramps at Men's hut.] **1867** PHILLIPS *Rockwood Jrnl.* 4 Aug. (Canterbury Pub. Lib. TS) 111 Fine morning but heavy snow from S.W. towards evening— an exhausted swagger arrived at midday. **1873** BARKER *Station Amusements* 180 Swaggers..are merely travelling workmen, and would pay for their lodging if it was the custom to do so. **1889** WILLIAMS & REEVES *Colonial Couplets* 27 A widewake without a band, Extremely battered at the top Sheltered a face the hue of sand, And tangled hair, a greasy crop. A belt his corduroys embraced, Whence hung a keen, worn knife for dagger; With strips of flax his boots he laced, The disappointed swagger. **1894** WILSON *Land of Tui* 249 So far as I could discriminate, swaggers (those who, snail-like, carry their worldly possessions on their backs) are men occasionally willing to do a day's work for a night's lodging and a couple of meals. **1910** FANNING *Players & Slayers* 81 I was tramping with a mate..to Westland, and it was our whim to be slouch-hatted, and 'blueyed', 'billied', unshaven, and otherwise orthodox swaggers. **1923** *Dominion* (Wellington) 15 Jan. 17 A Wanganui Resident..commented upon the absence of swaggers on Taranaki roads and regarded it as a sign of the prosperity of the district. **1933** [see SWAGGIE]. **1953** BAXTER *Collected Poems* (1980) 133 'Damn this dry shingle country,' Old Jack the swagger cried. **1963** ADSETT *Magpie Sings* 11 He remembered in one awful moment all the terrible things swaggers did. The way they chased people and chopped them up. **1978** HAYES *Toss Of Coin* 111 Swaggers were on the roads again [in the 1930's Depression], some genuinely in search of work, others looking for just a bed and a meal. **1987** HARTLEY *Swagger on Doorstep* 114 The first immigrant labourers from Britain became the nucleus of the swagger movement. It was in the early 1860s.

Hence **swagger** *v. intr.*, to travel as a swagger.

1873 BARKER *Station Amusements* 180 I am told that even now [swaggers] are fast becoming things of the past; for one could not 'swagger' by railroad.

b. *transf. joc.* A tramper carrying a pack.

1940 GILKISON *Peaks, Packs & Mountain Tracks* 108 The swagger has been compared with the curious fellow whose hobby was to hit his head with a hammer 'because it was so nice when he stopped'. In the opinion of many, the only good part of a day's swagging is the period of 'spell-oh'.

2. In special collocations: **swagger's fund**, a fund to aid itinerants in need; **swaggers' hut** *obs.*, a hut or building on rural properties to shelter itinerants; **Swagger's Rest**, a nickname for a specific *swaggers' hut*.

1952 *Evening Post* (Wellington) 7 June 11 In

Masterton a '**swagger's fund**' is still being administered under the jurisdiction of the Salvation Army from the Grey bequest. From that fund those genuinely in need are given money for a meal and a bed for the night. Apparently there are many town swaggers, judging from the fact that 65 meals have been provided for out of that fund since January, 1952. **1964** LEE *Shiner Slattery* 18 At each of the great sheep stations, or wheat stations, during the great wheat-growing bonanza period, there was a **swaggers' hut**. There the out of work could receive shelter and a meal. **1977** BRUCE *Life in Hinterland* 32 All the big [South Island] stations had a swaggers' hut for there were many men on the road [?c1920s]... They had a fireplace in the Whare especially built for these 'rolling stones'. **1986** OWEN & PERKINS *Speaking for Ourselves* 74 [Caption] This swaggers' hut was for many years a landmark at Weedons near Christchurch. **1990** MARTIN *Forgotten Worker* 34 Nearly every station had a swagger's hut where men were not supposed to arrive until sundown. **1952** *Evening Post* (Wellington) 7 June 11 [Russian Barney] paid another of his regular visits to the '**Swagger's Rest**', built at Snowdon, Mauriceville, by the late Mr. Robert Cameron for the 'gentlemen of the road'.

swaggerman. SWAGGER 1 a.

1959 MASTERS *Tales of Mails* 53 But now by Mac's and Ngamatea, The swagger men no more appear. **1972** ANDERSON *Let. from James* 141 He trusted the swaggerman, and for the next two days shared his lunch..with him.

swaggie. Also **swaggy**. [f. SWAG(GER + -IE: AND 1891.] SWAGGER 1 a.

1900 SCOTT *Colonial Turf* 163 The practised eye of the professional swaggy. **1906** *Truth* 20 Jan. 1 In America the day of the swaggie is said to be nearly done. **1913** *NZ Observer* 14 June 17 A small child observed a 'swaggy' approaching and ran in terror to his mother, telling her there was 'a funny thing just like Father coming up the track.' **1933** *Press* (Christchurch) (Acland Gloss.) 16 Dec. 21 *Swagger*.- One who carries his swag from place to place, looking for work. Sometimes called (in writing) *swagman*. The slang equivalents are *swaggy* and *commercial*. **1941** BAKER *NZ Slang* 40 *Swagman* and *swaggie*, two terms..not heard often in this country. **1951** HAY *Swagger Jack* 27 For Andy Wilson, mentioned heretofore, Is hounding now the swaggies from his door. **1961** MACKAY *Puborama* 71 The 'swaggie' of old has disappeared from the rural countryside and has to be, and so has the bar 'character'. **1984** *Knapdale Run* 152 The 'swaggie' knew which farms to call at, where..'Missus' would give him meals. **1990** LANGFORD *Newlands* 27 Swaggies came to our door, standing humbly before Mum's stern gaze.

swagging, *vbl. n.* and *ppl. a.*

1. *vbl. n.* **a.** [AND 1898.] The carrying of a swag; back-packing.

c1864 TEMPSKY *Memoranda* (ATLTS) 86 Every man and officer to carry his own swag... Majors were not excluded from the universal infliction of 'swagging'. **1883** GREEN *High Alps NZ* 180 Kauffmann gave a significant glance now and then, as he contemplated the packs, but neither he nor Boss ever grumbled, though they knew full well that the heaviest share of the 'swagging' must fall to their lot. **1898** *TrNZI* XXX. 415 The packhorses were unloaded on the banks of the Mokoiwi, where the swagging began. **1900** SCOTT *Colonial Turf* 163 Jimmy was a champion growler; long swagging had soured his mind. **1916** COWAN *Bush Explorers* (VUWTS) 16 We are off..for another day of marching and swagging. **1930** DOBSON *Reminiscences* 155 When travelling with light camps and swagging, only light utensils could be carried. **1958** PASCOE *Great Days in NZ Mountaineering* 42 Swagging was slower work than walking along with pack-horses.

b. Living the life of a swagger.

1897 *Otago Witness* (Dunedin) 11 Nov. 50 He had steadily sunk through the various stages of gentleman at large, digger.., rouseabout, to the bedrock of continual swagging.

2. *ppl. a.* Mountaineering. Back-packing (as distinct from climbing or tramping without a swag).

1883 GREEN *High Alps NZ* 268 Hard swagging work. **1892** KELLY *Journey Upper Waitara Valley* 3 The ridge..is enough to test the swagging power of a new hand. **1940** GILKISON *Peaks, Packs & Mountain Tracks* 110 A climbing day without a swag. The perfect [climbing] expedition is that in which both swagging days, and climbing days are featured. **1946** *Tararua Tramper* Apr. 7 A ration of emergency chocolate, then on and up—only 1100 feet, but at the end of a swagging day not so good.

swaggy, var. SWAGGIE.

swagman. Also early **swagsman**. SWAGGER 1 a.

a. As **swagsman** *obs.* [AND 1869].

1869 *Otago Daily Times* (Dunedin) (editorial) 27 Dec. in Stewart *Patterns on the Plain* (1975) 17 (Griffiths Collect.) As examples of bad spelling, bad grammar and execrably bad taste, the letter..could hardly be surpassed by a swagsman. **1874** BATHGATE *Col. Experiences* 212 One source of annoyance to the squatters is the 'swagsmen', as they are called, or men who travel about the country, professedly in search of work, but who do not, in reality, want it. **1881** BATHGATE *Waitaruna* 107 I really believe it is some swagsman or digger. **1894** *NZ Official Year-book* 365 As shearing-time approaches, a constant stream of 'swagsmen' seeking employment flows through the sheep-farming districts. **1897** *AJHR* H-16 7 A swag was found containing such articles as are usually carried by swagsmen.

b. As **swagman** [AND 1899].

1876 KENNEDY *Colonial Travel* 194 A foul-mouthed swagman returned from the bar. **1889** SKEY *Pirate Chief* 178 Swagman, stuff thy weighty swag In the cleft of yonder crag;.. Haste thee, swagless—loiter not, Lest Buchanan goes to pot; And the swagman got his straps undone. **1891** WALLACE *Rural Econ. Austral. & NZ* 104 Swagmen, who come round to ask for employment, get 8s. to 12s. a week. **1933, 1941** [see SWAGGIE]. **1978** HAYES *Toss Of Coin* 111 Although Normanvale was far from the main road swagmen found their way there. **1986** OWEN & PERKINS *Speaking for Ourselves* 68 Now these blokes like Riverina Dick, the established swagmen, they didn't seek company—the fair dinkum swagman, he liked to be on his own.

swagsman: see SWAGMAN a.

swallow: see *sea-swallow* (SEA 1 b).

swamp.

1. Used elsewhere, but in freq. use since earliest settlement as the term preferred in New Zealand to *bog, fen, marsh, moss*. See also *flax swamp* (FLAX 5 b), *raupo swamp* (RAUPO *n.* 3 b).

1814 KENDALL in Elder *Marsden's Lieutenants* (1934) 61 After some little conversation we proceeded on our way over some swamps and exceeding high hills. **1882** POTTS *Out in Open* 49 Beating carefully and slowly over swamps or lagoons, where raupo and sedge plants shelter the defenceless water-fowl. **1899** *Otago Witness* (Dunedin) 12 Oct. 60 And swamps—aye, swamps have charms, Though they may have alarms. **1920** MANSFIELD *Stories* (1984) 232 And plain to be heard..was the sound of the creek..spilling into a swamp of yellow water flowers and cresses. **1966** TURNER *Eng. Lang. Austral. & NZ* 57 The word *marsh* was sometimes used by explorers [in Australia]..but *swamp* was a much commoner term and *marsh* is hardly current in Australia and New Zealand now. **1987** *Listener* 8 Aug. 61 The land sloped down to 'the swamp', a wet tidal area with a drain to take the surface water to the sea.

Hence **swamp** *v.* [OED *v.* 1 *N. Amer.* ?*obs.*], in the phr. **to get swamped**, to become caught or entangled in a swamp.

1850 TORLESSE *Papers* (1958) 159 Boy's mare got swamped, but easily extracted.

2. a. Used *attrib.* in special Comb. **swamp country, swamp land,** an area of swampy land usu. distinguished by growths of flax and raupo; **swamp fever** *obs.* [transf. use of *swamp fever* a malarial fever], a complaint associated with South Island West Coast swamps; **swamp gum,** kauri-gum obtained from swamps; **swamp-hopping** *vbl. n.,* crossing swamp by leaping from tussock to tussock; **swamp horse,** a horse proficient in crossing swamps; **swamp kauri,** a kauri log, long fallen and buried, retrieved from a swamp; **swamp paddock,** a paddock being in parts low-lying, or adjoining a swamp; **swamp plough,** a plough with a large mould-board, for use on heavy soils; **swamp scrub,** low growth associated with swampy or water-logged land.

1937 AYSON *Thomas* 44 Minor adventures in rounding up wild cattle in **swamp country** running up from the lake..also befell Thomas. **1869** WAITE *West Coast Goldfields* 22 I caught what is called **swamp fever**. **1914** PFAFF *Diggers' Story* 146 I worked..three miles from the Grey South, where many miners were taken from, to the Grey hospital, ill with swamp fever... The feeling was total helplessness. **1930** *NZJST* XI. 303 The [kauri-gum] samples analysed were..(d) resin obtained from peat-bogs (**swamp gum**). **1988** [see *swamp kauri* below]. **1849** TORLESSE *Papers* (1958) 110 **Swamp-hopping** etc. My dogs Jock and Flora killed a wild dog. **1890** CHUDLEIGH *Diary* 12 Dec. (1950) 373 [I] had about 6000 sheep trying to get away over a belt of swamp... I and my 2 dogs and perfect little **swamp horse** were nearly done up when..we got the better of the sheep. **1988** p.c. Kendrick Smithyman (Auckland). An associated thing for *swamp gum* and **swamp kauri** is an 'oil'. **1994** *The Capital Letter No.768* 10 May 1 quoting *Ancient Trees of New Zealand Ltd v Attorney-General* (McGechan J, HC CP 483(93) 29 April 1994). The judgment explains that 'swamp kauri' is the name given to buried remnants of the NZ kauri..which, on average, may be 8–10 metres long (including trimmed rootball, with 6–8 metres of trunk) and perhaps 11 cubic metres..a third or less of original trunk volume. It is apparently amongst the world's most ancient surviving timber, and ATNZ has since 1992 been exporting to Japan where such antiquity is prized. **1851** *Lyttelton Times* 14 June 6 There are four distinct sections..most easily brought under cultivation. The *open grass land*, that in which *fern and tutu* easily grow, the *flax bottoms*, and the *reclaimable* **swamp land**. **1870** *TrNZI* II. 322 I apply the words 'swamp land' in the local sense of the term, to tracts usually found near the coast, covered with Phormium tenax and other plants requiring a considerable depth of vegetable soil and much moisture, and by no means in the sense in which the same words would be used in England. **1959** MCLINTOCK *Descr. Atlas* 24 Swamp lands... Only the most extensive bogs and swamps are shown on the maps. **1937** AYSON *Thomas* 137 Their larder was also enlarged by the eggs of cranes, shags and gulls which nested in thousands on trees overhanging the river below the **swamp paddock**. **1909** CHUDLEIGH *Diary* 23 Nov. (1950) 449 Mabel and I walked to the drains made by my monster **swamp plough** and scoop. **1930** ACLAND *Early Canterbury Runs* 42 They..spent a lot of money in cutting the scrub, crushing it down with rollers, and ploughing it in with swamp ploughs. **1973** *Massey-Ferguson Rev.* (NZ) Mar.–Apr. 5 He..leaves it for two years before getting to work with a 19-inch swamp plough. **1985** HAWKE & SCOTT *Early Farm Machinery in NZ* 15 Swamp plough[s] were very heavy and would require a large team to operate, as they were made for use in swampy ground. **1870** WHITWORTH *Martin's Bay Settlement* 28 Timbered with mangrove and other **swamp scrub**.

b. In the names of plants and animals, see: CRAKE b, *umbrella fern* (FERN 2 (21)), FLAX 2 (5), GRASS 2 (38), HAWK 2 (6), LAWYER 1, LILY 2 (17), *maire*, see MAIRE TAWAKE, MATIPO 2 (3), PINE 2 (17), RAIL 2 (10). See also below **swamp-bird** *obs.*, FERNBIRD 1 (see also *swamp-sparrow*); **swamp-hen** [AND 1833], PUKEKO 1 (see also SWAMPIE); **swamp-sparrow** *obs.*, FERNBIRD 1, *swamp-turkey* (TURKEY $n.^1$ 1).

1886 *TrNZI* XVIII. 102 Sphenaecus.—**Swamp-bird**, two species (*Kotata*). **1904** TREGEAR *Maori Race* 329 Some little swamp-birds (*matata*) were caught and and torn to pieces. **1855** PHILLIPS *Rockwood Jrnl.* (Canterbury Pub. Lib. TS) 7 Aug. John Harry went to old whare swamp..& killed some Kakas and a **swamp hen**. **1867** BARKER *Station Life* (1870) 168 I can never forget how beautiful some swamp-hens, with their dark blue plumage..looked. **1870** *TrNZI* II. 71 Pukeko. Swamp-hen. This beautiful rail delights in swamps. **1873** BULLER *Birds NZ* 1855 The Swamp-hen is widely distributed over Tasmania, New Zealand, and the Chatham Islands. **1882** POTTS *Out in Open* 47 The red-legged swamp-hen, in its indigo suit. **c1899** DOUGLAS in *Mr Explorer Douglas* (1957) 234 [The pukeko] has a variety of names... Swamp hen it is generally called in Westland. **1904** HUTTON & DRUMMOND *Animals NZ* 182 The Swamp Hen is generally known by its Maori name, '*Pukeko*'. **1924** *Otago Witness* (Dunedin) 1 Apr. 71 The swamp hen, or pukaki, has been noticed by some of your writers. **1938** HYDE *Nor Yrs. Condemn* 116 Dainty streams stepping up like little fillies from the marshes where Maori swamp-hen stalked. **1946** SOLJAK *NZ* 9 Another incorrigible but interesting marauder is the blue-feathered pukeko or swamp hen. **1967** MIDDLETON in *NZ Short Stories III* (1975) 69 From their grazing grounds..swamp-hens sent up their piercing earth-bound shrieks. **1977** *Glenfield College Maori Cookbook* 28 Pukeko or Swamp Hen (Porphyrio melanotus). **1985** FRAME *Envoy from Mirror City* 161 The country road to Takapuna where cows, horses, swamphens had once stared at the solitary walker. **1992** LASENBY *The Conjuror* 13 He pointed to the swamp-hens, ducks and pied stilts by the stream. **1888** BULLER *Birds NZ* I. 60 These beds of rushes..are then a favourite resort for the '**Swamp-Sparrow**', as this bird [*sc.* fernbird] is sometimes called. **1898** MORRIS *Austral-English* 450 *Swamp-Sparrow*..a nickname in New Zealand for the *Fernbird*.

swampie. [f. *swamp*(-*hen* + -IE.] PUKEKO 1.
1947–48 BEATTIE *Pioneer Recolls.* (1956) 5 'Swampies' (swamp hens) and paradise and grey ducks were abundant in the waterlogged valley, while the native lark seemed ubiquitous.

swan. A scam.
1981 STEWART *Hot & Copper Sky* 153 'That's the biggest slinter in the army.' 'The biggest which -?' 'Slinter. Fiddle. Swan. Look, don't you know?' **1986** *Sunday News* (Auckland) 27 July 1 Sunday News today roasts Television New Zealand for its involvement in a major swan at the same time the public is being softened up for a big licence fee hike.

swandri, swan-dry, swanee, varr. SWANNDRI.

swank. *Obs.* Also **swankey.** [Brit. dial. *swanky* small or poor beer or liquor: see OED $n.^2$] Liquor, booze.
1905 *Truth* 12 Aug. 1 The Terrace gaol may be a drunks' club, but the swankey is not of a headachey character. **1906** *Ibid.* 17 Nov. 5 Then he started on the wine, meeting a couple of shipmates, and also the accused Donnelly for whom he shouted swankey. **1910** *Ibid.* 1 Jan. 1 He had already had an excess of 'swankey'.
Hence **swank** *v. intr.*, to take to drink, to booze; **swankify** *v. intr.*, to tipple; also as *vbl. n.*
1907 *Truth* 26 Oct. 6 [Heading] Women who swank... When a woman takes to drink it's blazes. **1907** *Ibid.* 21 Sept. 5 Girls used to go along to the kitchen and swankify, and she had seen men in Miss Taylor's room... Quite a number of the 'tarts' that had been fired out for swankifying were run through, and Mrs. G. electrified the Court by saying that it was the rule that if any bar belle got overloaded, out they went.

swankey, swankify: see SWANK.

swanndri /ˈswɒnˌdraɪ/. Often **swandri**; also in altered form **swan(n)ee, swanni, swannie, swanny.** [A form (often altered) of a proprietary name or trademark *Swanndri*, an idiosyncratic spelling of *swan* + *dry* (=weatherproof) used in company with the image of a swan.] Also **swanndri jacket, shirt.** Orig. a knee-length single-coloured woollen outer garment, often with hood, for outdoor wear, a kind of bush shirt; now, also, a shorter, plaid, woollen outer garment, zipped up the front and in a variety of colours. Cf. *bush shirt* (BUSH C 3 d), JUMPER, LAMMIE. **a. swanndri** forms.
1914 *NZ Patent Office Jrnl.* [no number given] 29 Jan. Swanndri 11715 [filed] 23rd December, 1913. William Henry Broome..Ready-made clothing. [Trademark includes a representation of a swan.] **1919** *Dannevirke Evening News* 2 Apr. 4 [Advt] Sole agents for Swandri coats—best winter value in the trade. **1959** *Tararua Tramper* July 4 The body was clothed in a cotton shirt, swandri jacket, waterproof parka,.. balaclava, boots and socks. **1979** WILLIAMS *Skin Deep* 145 But it bursts open..revealing two burly, wild-looking bush workers... 'Hey lady, you got a customer,' giggles the one in the red and black check swandri. **1983** *Dominion* (Wellington) 1 Nov. 6 The hood of your Swandri should be up—but you'd better check it with Vincent. **1986** 6 May TV1 Country Calender (farming) Programme. On the swanndri bush shirt. The brand-name *Swanndri* with two 'n's' is a mistake left uncorrected over 40 years..[by] John McKendrick who in the 1940s built up the Swanndri trademark from a factory in Waitara, Taranaki. **1990** swandrys [see *bush shirt* (BUSH C 3 d)].

b. swannee forms.
1965 WATSON *Stand in Rain* 25 In the big mirrors..we saw two men and a girl, all dirty and wearing our swannees, with untidy hair. **1971** *VUWTC '71* 49 Hey Colonel, you reckon..two grunds, two woollen shirts, long trou, bush singlet, two jerseys, long johns, balaclava, over trou, swanee, puttees and parka will be enough [for a tramping trip]. **1971** *Listener* 19 Apr. 56 Well, out of the boo-ai comes three trampers... One was a rangy bloke in..a swannie. **1985** *NZ Herald* (Auckland) 4 June 2 Mr Johnstone [a Kaikohe fisherman] was wearing knee-length gumboots and a *bush-jacket*. 'I kicked my gumboots off and had to get down under the water to pull my *swanny* over my head,' he said last night. **1992** ANDERSON *Portrait Artist's Wife* 307 A man in a red Swanni lifted a hand and ran away.

swannee, swanni(e), swanny, varr. SWANNDRI.

sweat, *v. Obs.*
1. *Obs.* As **sweat out**, to drink or finish (a quantity of liquor) off. Also as **sweating-house**, see quot.
1890 PHILIPS *Reminisc. Early Days* 8 On the beach [at Waiwera in 1850], 'rural felicity' was obtainable at a building termed a 'sweating house' where after purchasing one or two gallons of rum you could go and 'sweat it out'.
2. In the phr. **to sweat a cheque** [AND 1882], to squander one's money on liquor.
1888 D'AVIGDOR *Antipodean Notes* 169 *Colonialisms*:.. To 'sweat a cheque' is an ugly but powerful gold-diggers' expression. When the men come into the nearest town from their washings with the gold-dust, they sell it at the bank, and receive a cheque in exchange. Some of them give the cheque to a publican, and tell him to supply them with drink and all else as long as it lasts... The digger is generally hopelessly tipsy in a couple of hours, and does not recover his senses until he is informed by the publican that he has 'sweated his cheque'.

sweat. Special Comb. **sweat locks** *n. pl. farming*, see quot.; **sweat-rag** [spec. use of *sweat-rag* a cloth used to wipe off sweat: see EDD *sweat-cloth* a handkerchief], a pocket handkerchief.
1982 *Agric. Gloss.* (MAF) 60 *Sweat locks*: Short, heavy condition staples from the upper inside of the legs. **1936** LEE *Hunted* 36 You must lift your soaked sweat-rag out of the water and thoroughly wet the whole patch.

sweating pen. *Obs.* [AND 1882.] Orig. a holding pen in a woolshed where sheep sweating after a muster were confined while drying out.
1922 PERRY *Sheep Farming* 17 There are two catching pens, and two sweating pens, and a back race 5ft. wide. **c1927** SMITH *Sheep & Wool Industry* 73 After drafting, the sheep to be shorn are run up a ramp into the sweating pens of the shed.

swee /swiː/. *Otago Scots.* Also **swie, swey, sweigh**. [A Sc. dial variant of *sway*: see EDD *sway* $v.^2$] See quots.
1952 p.c. Rutherford 6 July (Inch Clutha). The spelling of a word swee, or swie, and meaning the iron stand or standard fixed in pioneer chimneys to hold cooking pots..used in those days in this Scotch community [*sc.* Inch Clutha]. **1967** DRUMMOND *At Home in NZ* 87 A heavy iron bracket with an arm that projected from the side of the fireplace was called a swey (or sweigh). An arrangement of hooks allowed it to support cooking vessels at various levels, including the iron girdle on which scones and oatcakes were baked.

sweep, $n.^1$ [See OED $n.$ 28 A plate, frame, or the like for sweeping off or sweeping up grain, soil, etc., 1825 sole quot.] Orig. a horse-drawn device for picking up hay or silage from the paddock and delivering it to the stack, silage pit, or clamp; later a similar device attached to a lorry or tractor.
1912 *NZJAg.* Mar. IV. 168 Where the sweeps are not available, the windrows should be made in pairs. **1928** *NZ Free Lance* (Wellington) 4 Jan. 31 [Caption]

One of the big sweeps which takes the hay to the stack. **1939** *NZ Farmer* 23 May 7 [Caption] A useful item of farm equipment—modern tractor, complete with hay sweep. **1940** CONNELL & HADFIELD *Agriculture* 377 [Caption] The modern Wheeled-Sweep, eminently suited for ensilage, for which it is here being used. **1979** *Otago Daily Times* (Dunedin) 28 Mar. 21 Neither ted nor tedder are recognised and the sweep has vanished into the mists of haymaking history. **1985** HAWKE & SCOTT *Early Farm Machinery* 89 According to an article in the 'New Zealand Farmer' in 1888 a sweep or reversible horse-rake could gather as much as a quarter of a ton [of] hay at a load and take it to the stack... These sweeps were rather like a gate with hinged wings and teeth protruding on both sides, about ten feet long... Other gate sweeps which had no teeth worked in the same way, the driver standing on the bottom rail or perhaps lying on the top of the load.

Hence *v. trans.*, to collect and carry usu. grass or hay with a sweep.
1939 *NZJAg.* Feb. LVIII. 163 The implement can be requisitioned for sweeping material other than hay. **1972** *NZ Dairy Exporter* Feb. 49 Sweeping bales into a barn may well be a good idea on country where a barn can serve a large area of pasture.

sweep, *n.*[2] [Of unknown origin: AND 1840.] *Scorpis lineolatus* (formerly *aequipinnis*) (fam. Kyphosidae), an edible bluish-grey reef-fish often confused with the larger and brighter *Scorpis violaceus*, blue maomao (MAOMAO 2 (1)). See also HUI *n.*[2]
1922 *NZJST* V. 93 Scorpis violaceus. *Maomao*. Mr. Griffin, of the Auckland Museum, informs us that both this species and the sweep (*Scorpis aequipinnis*) are sold as 'maomao' in Auckland. **1957** PARROTT *Sea Angler's Fishes* 108 The Sweep is common throughout the waters of the Auckland Provincial district and is also found around the southern coasts of Australia. **1972** DOAK *Fishes* 49 One puzzle of blue maomao biology is the variant form often called the 'sweep' and regarded by some as a separate species. **1982** AYLING *Collins Guide* (1984) 231 The sweep is very similar to the blue maomao... The New Zealand sweep has always been assumed to be the same as the Australian species but it has recently become apparent that they are probably different species. **1991** BRADSTOCK *Fishing* 19 A sweep is blue-grey and never has any yellow fins [as has maomao]. It is also called hui and *Scorpis lineolatus*.

sweeper.

1. *Shearing.* Also **sweepo.** [AND 1910.] BROOMIE.
1913 CARR *Country Work* 14 On large boards a sweeper is employed who brooms away loose locks and dirt. **1933** *Press* (Christchurch) (Acland Gloss.) 16 Dec. 21 Sweeper.—In some sheds special boys are employed to sweep the board of locks, etc., though as a rule this work is done by the *fleece-pickers*... These boys are officially known as s[weeper]s, but more usually called by their nickname, *broomies*. 'The sweeper that swept the board.'—Banjo Patterson. **1966** *NZ Contemp. Dict. Suppl.* (Whitcombe's) 626 *sweeper n.* woolshed worker, called also *broomie*. **1982** *Agric. Gloss.* (MAF) 60 *Sweepo*: sweeps the shearing board clean during shearing. Also called broomie.

Hence by back-formation, **sweep** *n.*, a broom used to clear the shearing board of oddments of wool.
1988 *More* (Auckland) Mar. 31 I was still trying to come to grips with the seven-day weeks, nine-hour days and driving my sweep without crashing into the shearers. *Ibid.* 32 A rousie's best friend is her broom, or sweep. A true 'professional' never works without her own special sweeping mechanism, usually aluminium or wooden handled with a heavy plastic head which swivels.

2. *Freezing works.* A boy who sweeps out the shed.
1951 May 17 Feilding Freezing Works terms p.c. Colin Gordon. *Sweepers*: boys cleaning up the place with brooms—unofficial job to roll cigarettes for the chainies who give them fantastic promises if they roll plenty.

sweepo: see SWEEPER 1.

sweet, *a.*

1. [AND 1898.] Good, fine; of a job, easy.
1935 STRONG in Partridge *Slang Today* 287 It's time I struck a sweet job. In London, for preference. **1982** NEWBOLD *Big Huey* (Gloss.) 254 Sweet (adj) OK, good, fine **1989** RICHARDS *Pioneer's Life* 35 He said it would now cut 'sweet as a lolly'.

2. In the phr. **she'll be (she's) sweet**, expressing confidence in a successful or happy outcome, or reassurance, agreement, etc.
1945 *Korero* (AEWS Background Bulletin) 26 Mar. 29 We're sweet. After all this time, Jim. Put it there, boy. **1951** 14 M 14 St Bede's, Chch 12 She'll be sweet [M3] **a1974** SYDER & HODGETTS *Austral. & NZ English* (TS) 953 *she'll be sweet*: In social situations— our arrangements are all in order; in working routine— we have done what is necessary. 'Everything's pretty well arranged for. The wooden floor's arrived and is in place already. Brian and Mac'll be here any minute now to help put up the tent. You and I can get away now. She'll be sweet. See you tomorrow.' **1964** MORRIESON *Came a Hot Friday* (1981) 193 'She's sweet,' said Don.

3. Special Comb. **sweet potato** [spec. use of *sweet-potato*], KUMARA 1 a.
1769 COOK *Journals* 22 Oct. (1955) I. 183 We purchased of the natives about 10 or 15 pounds of sweet Potatous [sic], they have pretty large Plantations of these. [1769 Note] Sweet potatoes, like those of Carolina. **1777** FORSTER *Voyage Round World* I. 230 [Teiratu] seemed to know [potatoes] very well, evidently because a certain root, the Virginian or sweet potatoe (*convolvulus batatas*), is planted in some parts of the Northern Island, from whence he came. **1814** [see KUMARA 1 a]. **1820** MCCRAE *Journal* (1928) 14 A Crop of Sweet Potatoes (a root held in much esteem by the natives and forming part of the food of their Chiefs). **1835** YATE *NZ* (1970) 85 At the time of planting the *kumera*.. or sweet potato, all who are engaged in the work..are under precisely the same restrictions. **1840** *Hobson to Normanby* 20 Feb. in *GBPP House of Commons 1841 (No.311)* 13 The natives will not hesitate to shoot..cattle that trespass, especially on their beds of Kumera (sweet potatoe), which are considered sacred. **1851** [see KUMARA 1 a]. **1869** *TrNZI* I. (rev. edn.) 250 These were..the kumara, or sweet potato.., the taro..and the hue. **1884**, **1891** [see KUMARA 1 a]. **1943** MARSH *Colour Scheme* 36 The smell of steaming sweet potatoes was mingled with the fumes of sulphur. **1988** BROOKER, CAMBIE & COOPER *Economic Native Plants NZ* 3 Captain Jean de Surville and members of his crew recorded some of the useful plants..in 1769–1770... They noticed 'young potato crops', presumably sweet potatoes.

swelling, *ppl. a. Mining.* [Poss. a var. and transf. use of Brit. dial. *swelly* a local thickening of coal: see OED, EDD *swelly n.*] Of ground, soft and unstable enough to move into spaces left by tunnels.
1912 *NZGeol.SB (NS)* No.15 18 The vein-bearing rock [of Waihi-Tairua] is usually hard enough to stand unsupported in crosscuts, except in local areas of shattered or 'swelling' country. **1978** MCARA *Gold Mining Waihi* 334 Swelling ground: Clayey ground which squeezed slowly as pressure built up on it. To prevent breakage of the sets, the ground about them had to be removed from time to time. Laths or slabs between timber-sets in swelling ground were spaced well apart to allow the country to squeeze through without breaking the legs or caps. Swelling ground was common in the Caving Block.

swept, *a.*[1] [Transf. use of *ppl.* swept cleaned out (as with a broom).] Cleaned out of money; penniless; broke.
1935 MITCHELL & STRONG in Partridge *Slang Today* 286 [The] following [was] employed by those who served in the [Great] War..*swept*, cleaned out of money. *Ibid.* 287 When I done all my sugar and never even had the makings, he went very hostile because I never told him I was swept. **1955** *BJ Cameron Collection* (TS July) swept (adj) Had it, washed up. **1962** CRUMP *One of Us* 169 'You'll have to give me some more money,' he said to Sam. 'I'm swept again.' **1972** *Truth* 11 July 43 She was clean swept too, so it wasn't any use trying to take up a collection from her.

swept, *a.*[2] As **swept up** [transf. use of *swept-up* applied to a once fashionable hairstyle brushed up to the top of the head], fashionable, superior, 'high-class'.
1985 SHERWOOD *Botanist at Bay* 150 They met in the lounge of what proved to be a superior hotel near Parliament Building. 'Very swept up,' he apologised. **1992** *North & South* (Auckland) Jan. 87 I learned to wear jandals and say truck (not lorry), chips (not crisps)..smoko (not tea-break), swept up (not smart).

swi: see SWY-UP.

swiftie. Also **swifty.** [AND 1945.] An instance of sharp practice, a trick or deception, esp. in the phr. **to pull a swiftie.** Cf. SHREWDIE.
1985 MARSHALL *Secret Diary Telephonist* 61 Harry pulled a swiftie on us. **1986** *Salient* (Wellington) 11 Aug. 14 Could [they] explain how someone can 'pull a swifty' and make it blatant without defeating the purpose? I thought pulling a swifty was like pulling out of NZSAC without telling anyone.

swill. [Spec. use of *swill n.* pig slops, or *v.* to drink greedily: AND 1945.] Formerly applied to the rushed drinking of beer between 5.00 and 6.15 p.m. during the time of six-o'clock closing of public bars, and more usually termed *six o'clock swill* (SIX O'CLOCK d). Also *attrib.* See also *five to six rush* (FIVE).
1959 BOLLINGER *Grog's Own Country* 5 The snack bar, open about the middle of the day, has long been closed before the thirsty swill crowd arrives. **1966** DURRELL *Two in the Bush* 16 I was introduced too early to what is known as 'the five o'clock swill'... The five o'clock swill is the direct result of New Zealand's imbecilic licensing laws..[office workers] have to leave their place of employment, and make a desperate attempt to drink as much beer as they can in the shortest possible time. **1976** JOHNSTON *New Zealanders* 147 During the 'swill', drinking was fast, and on an empty stomach.

swimmers' itch: see BATHERS' ITCH.

swimming crab: see CRAB 2 (2).

swimming togs: see TOGS.

swing, *v.* In various phrases:

1. [AND 1898.] **to swing the billy** [AND 1928], see *boil the billy* (BILLY *n.*¹ 2 a).

2. *Shearing.* **to swing the gate** [prob. alluding to the gate of the counting-out pen, or poss. to the porthole being kept swinging], see quot. 1933. Cf. SWING GATE.

1933 *Press* (Christchurch) (Acland Gloss.) 16 Dec. 21 *Swing the gate.*—To be the fastest shearer in the shed. **1941** [see DRAG *v.* 1].

3. to swing one (it) across, to trick, to put one across.

1943 MARSH *Colour Scheme* iv 64 You saw Questing swing it across me. **1964** PEARSON *Glossary* to Sargeson *Collected Stories 1935–63* (1964) 303 swing one across: trick, take advantage of.

swing-bridge. Also **swing footbridge**; occas. early **swinging bridge**. A suspension bridge, esp. a footbridge.

[*Note*] Contrast the Brit. and US use *swing bridge* for a bridge, (part of) the deck of which swings out of the way of the water traffic.

1847 ANGAS *Savage Life* II. 106 We crossed a boisterous river [near Taupo] on a native bridge of teatree boughs, swung by flax from the opposite trees. The river..just above the swinging bridge, descended in a grand cataract. *Ibid.* II. 137 This mountain torrent was crossed by means of a swinging bridge. **1910** COX *Diaries 1888–1925* (ATLMS) 11 July I had a walk..to the swing bridges to the island and back by Para road. **1942** GASKELL *All Part of the Game* (1978) 6 They tell him go over the swing-bridge and leave his horse behind for today. **1951** HUNT *Confessions* 61 Across a creek running into the Otaki Lagoon the residents had erected a swing foot-bridge at considerable pains and expense. **1966** *NZ Short Stories* (1976) 91 He hopped across by the swing-bridge and proceeded to stride along the road. **1973** WALLACE *Generation Gap* 188 The local school teacher was found asleep on Fulton's swing bridge, swaying gently above the steep drop into the river. **1982** GEE *Halfmen of O* (1984) 15 He went between the concrete blocks and steel wires anchoring the swing-bridge.

swing gate. *Farming.* [Spec. use of *swing-gate* a gate constructed to swing to and fro: AND 1865.] A gate able to swing in either of two ways in a drafting race. See also *double gate* (DOUBLE *a.* and *adv.*), *drafting gate* (DRAFTING *vbl. n.* 2).

1878 ELWELL *Boy Colonists* 214 They made a 'lead' in the stockyard for drafting the cattle. This was something like a 'race' for drafting sheep, with a swing gate. **1902** *Brett's Colonists' Guide* 315 Drafting... To effect this they have to go through the yards, passing through a narrow race, at the end of which there is a swing gate. **1938** BURDON *High Country* 85 Instead of being driven through a race and separated by a swing gate, sheep had to be hand drafted. **1968** *NZ Contemp. Dict. Suppl.* (Collins) 19 *swing-gate n.* patent gate for drafting sheep.

swish, *n. Prison.* [An echoic transferral from the sound of a cane used in corporal punishment.] Abuse, heckling, harassment.

1982 NEWBOLD *Big Huey* 131 Because I was doing something which the staff didn't like I started getting a bit of swish from them. **1982** *NZ Times* 12 Sept. 8 'Kes' as everyone called him [at Waikune Prison] is a nice guy with a keen sense of humour. He took a lot of swish (heckling) and threw it back.

swish, *v. Drug users.* To distribute, esp. in the phr. **to swish (on) luckies,** to distribute LSD or DMA (a hallucogenic designer drug).

1982 *Dominion* (Wellington) 16 Feb. 10 Mark probably told you I have been swishing some luckies for him... 'Swishing' meant to distribute or to sell. 'Luckies' meant lysergide or DMA. **1982** *Evening Post* (Wellington) 16 Feb. 20 On a subsequent visit to Williams' farm, Mr Hansen told him he had been swishing on luckies—distributing LSD or DMA.

swishback. Also **switchback (switch-backed).** A men's former hairstyle in which the hair is brushed straight back from the brow.

1964 MORRIESON *Came a Hot Friday* (1981) 114 The heavy switchback of fair hair, in addition to being dirty, had been known to fall sideways and uncover a balding spot. **1973** *Dominion* (Wellington) 25 Dec. 38 The star, who was a household name in the 'fifties when his lurex jacket swishback hairstyle and rock and roll numbers were all the rage. **1974** MORRIESON *Predicament* (1981) 151 His mop of switch-backed hair felt as hot as a compost heap. **1996** *Dominion* (Wellington) 11 May 18 While working at the Supreme Court, she met Don... He was pretty radical. Had a swishback hair style and rode a motor bike.

switchback, switch-backed, varr. SWISHBACK.

switched up. *Obs.* To be set up or fixed (for money), to be 'holding'.

1911 KIWI *On the Swag* 4 I only want to get square with my merchants. I'll pay you back £150 when I am 'switched up'.

swi(-up). Also **swy.** [ad. German *zwei* two + TWO) UP: AND 1913.] TWO UP. Also in special Comb. **swy-up king,** a two-up expert; **swy-up ring,** the ring in which two up is played.

1917 *Chron. NZEF* 16 May 137 His gambling blood was hot! The 'Swi-up ring' it was his goal, He meant to break the lot! *Ibid.* 5 Sept. 28 'Talk about swi-up,' remarked No. 11... Said Martin of the Dinks, 'Why, he was the greatest "swi-up" king in the "Inverteds".' **1932** in **1949** PARTRIDGE *Dict. Underworld* (1961) 708 swi. (The game of) two-up: New Zealand and Australian: since ca. 1910: 1932, Nelson Bayliss (private letter). **1955** BJ Cameron Collection (TS July) swy (n) swy-up (n) Two-up, a gambling game very common in Australia and often played in NZ. **1976** HILLIARD *Send Somebody Nice* 75 [Title] Swy school. In the warm summer evenings the men gathered behind the bath-house after tea to play two-up.

sword. *Shearing.* In the phr. **bright and shiny swords,** blade shears. See also BLADE *n.*¹ 1 a.

1934 *Press* (Christchurch) (Acland Gloss.) 13 Jan. 13 *Bright and Shiny Swords.*—Another term for blade shears. My correspondent tells me he has only heard this used in New Zealand by Australian shearers. **1989** [see HAND SHEARS].

sword-grass. A name applied to New Zealand plants with sword-shaped leaves. **a.** TOETOE.

1872 DOMETT *Ranolf & Amohia* 172 The great plumes far and wide of the sword-grass aspire. **1898** MORRIS *Austral-English* 452 *Sword-Grass.* In New Zealand, *Arundo conspicua*..It is not the same as the English plant of that name, and is often called *Cutting Grass.* **1949** BAXTER *Collected Poems* (1980) 80 Where the salt creek broadens to a brown lagoon Fringed with matted swordgrass and sea wreck..he lives alone.

b. SPEARGRASS 1.

1883 GREEN *High Alps* 120 Now the whole surface is covered with a sparse vegetation. interspersed with clumps of Spaniards or sword grass. **1892** ROSS *Aorangi* 37 Sword-grass (Aciphylla Colensoi).

swordie. [*sword*(fish + -IE.] The swordfish *Xiphias gladius* (fam. Xiphiidae).

1974 *Sunday Herald* (Melbourne) 24 Mar. 21 If Ron Scott, chairman of the Commonwealth Games Organising Committee, is as good a fisherman as he was, and is, chairman of the Games, heaven help the swordies, the makos and the yellow-tails. **1987** *Chosen Place* 19 No-one had actually seen whether it was a swordfish or a shark. You see if it's a swordie you must give him plenty of free line.

swy-up: see SWI(-UP)

T

TAB /ˌtiæi'bi/. Also **T.A.B.** [Acronym formed from the initial letters of *Totalisator Agency Board*, the name of the State-appointed agency which provides and controls off-course betting: AND 1961.] **a.** The Totalisator Agency Board as a betting agency.

[**1949** *NZ Statutes* No.32 496 [Gaming Amendment Act] There shall be a board to be known as the Totalizator Agency Board.] **1952** *Evening Post* (Wellington) 18 Apr. 14 The collators..were on duty at the Eva Street headquarters of the T.A.B. **1963** FRAME *Reservoir* 168 Poetry was not yet as popular as the T.A.B. and there was no legitimate reason why it should be. **1973** FINLAYSON *Brown Man's Burden* 141 T.A.B.: Totalisator Agency Board; betting shop.

b. A particular local agency betting-shop.

1955 FAIRBURN *Letters* 30 Nov. (1981) 236 You will find Social Security going at full blast—long queues for the T.A.B. (off-course totalisator). **1964** BOOTH *Footsteps in Sea* 64 'Stop off at the TAB., will you, Jim.' The converted shop which now carried the big sign 'Totalisator Agency Board', the open sesame for off-course betting. **1971** ARMFELT *Catching Up* 31 The T.A.B.'s the betting shop for the races—the Totalisator Agency Board.

c. *attrib.*

1954 JOURNET *Take My Tip* 71 The T.A.B. shop is the easiest thing in the world to use. **1970** *Evening Post* (Wellington) (Race Guide) 17 July The TAB concession double at the combined Woodville-Pahiatua meeting on Wednesday will be on the Woodville and Pahiatua Handicaps. **1975** *Ibid.* 16 Jan. 11 Dufy..should improve on his recent racing to win the..first leg of the TAB double at the Greymouth meeting tomorrow.

tab-a-tab, tabboo, tabby-tab(by), varr. TAPU.

table. [Spec. transf. uses of *table* a piece of furniture with a flat top.]

1. *Goldmining.* Also **gold saving table**. An apparatus for saving gold from treated crushed auriferous quartz.

1868, 1876 [see BLANKET 2]. a**1896** MOFFATT *Adventures* (1979) 70 [Quoting a poem by Walter D. Moffatt, d. 3 Jan. 1882] Yet still they dig and delve, be the weather foul or fair, And talk of plush and tables, and a thousand pounds a share. **1935** BLYTH *Gold Mining Year Book* 11 *Gold Saving Table*: A sloping surface covered with goldsaving cloth over which are placed slats to break up the wash and catch the heavier particles. **1952** HEINZ *Prospecting for Gold* 35 Under the chute board, which carries the water and sand to the head of the table, is the long inclined board called the 'table', and on this plush is fitted for its entire length.

2. *Shearing.* **a.** [AND 1905.] *wool table* (WOOL 3).

1904 LANCASTER *Sons o' Men* 78 The classers were silent at the tables. **1973** FERNANDEZ *Tussock Fever* 3 Erina had gathered up Mutu's last fleece and thrown it expertly on the table before the classer.

b. Special Comb. **table hand** [AND 1928], **tableman** [AND 1905], one who assists at the wool-table skirting and rolling fleeces.

1897 *Otago Witness* (Dunedin) 2 Dec. 58 The **table hands** sat in their aprons, ready to start. **1955** BOWEN *Wool Away* 92 A common fault is for a wool-table to be too high, which makes harder work for the table hands and the 'fleeco'. **1885** *Ida Balley Station Letterbook* 26 Oct. in Martin *Forgotten Worker* 27 I think *yearly* wages will have to come down, before any great reduction can justly be made in wages of **tablemen** & knockabouts at shearing.

taboo, tabu, varr. TAPU.

taboo'd, tabooed, tabu'd, varr. TAPUED.

tacopa, var. TAIEPA.

taepo, var. TAIPO.

taewa. *Hist.* Also **taiwha, tawai,** (usu.) **tiver(s)**. [Ma. /'taewa/: Williams 357 *Taewa, taewha, taiawa, taiwa, taiwha...* 1. Foreigner... 3. Potato... [Williams's] Note.—In view of the meanings and varieties in spelling above, it is not improbable that the word represents the name of one Stivers, who is said to have visited the Bay of Islands before Cook.: Duval (III. 404) records *taewa* 'potato' as a loanword from 1844, without discussion.] Usu. *pl.* Potato(es). Cf. RIWAI.

[**1819** MARSDEN *Lett. & Jrnls.* 20 Oct. (1932) 208 [The old chief] told us he had seen three generations and was in the middle of life when the first ship came to New Zealand. The captain's name was Stivers. [1932 *Note*] Staivers. Hence another name for the potato, *taewa*, since he apparently supplied some seed. **1820** LEE & KENDALL *NZ Gram. & Vocab.* 107 [Waiata] E táta te winubga te tai ki a *Taiwa...* [translated] The rolling billows extend nearly as far as *Stivers** [?= 'the tempestuous north']... [1820 note] *A man who is said to have visited the Bay of Islands before Captain Cook.] **1841** *NZ Jrnl.* II. 92 [The chief] expresses grief that his 'tivers', potatoes, are all gone. **1842** *Lett. from Settlers* (1843) 46 [The natives] boiled some tea and *tivers* (potatoes). **1843** STEPHENS *Lett. & Jrnls.* (ATLTS) 113 [A Maori says] *iti-iti* bit of ground to grow the tawai (potatoes) and the leeks. c**1920** *South Island Maori Lists* 'Wahi Mahika Kai' in Beattie *Maori Place-names Canterbury* (1945) 65 Taewa—the ordinary potato introduced by early voyagers. **1935** MAXWELL *Recollections* 163 He buy the corn,.. the kumikumi, the taiwha, he buy him very cheap.

tafiri, var. TAWHIRI.

taha. [Ma. /ta'ha/: Williams 357 *Tahā*..Calabash with a narrow mouth.] A bottle gourd as a container; CALABASH.

1871 GRACE *Journal* 28 Oct. in *Pioneer Missionary* (1928) 237 The poor woman wished to do me still more honour. She took some preserved meat out of a 'taha' (Native gourd). **1882** POTTS *Out in Open* 16 Women are bringing water in calabashes (taha). **1908** BAUGHAN *Shingle-Short* 195 Of old, long ago, I had life—I have lived! And a *taha* fill'd, is it not full? A web woven, is there no rest? [1908 *Note*] Taha: A calabash. **1921** GUTHRIE-SMITH *Tutira* (1926) 93 Waitara readily handed over to them *taha*—calabashes—filled with birds preserved in their own fat. **1948** HENDERSON *Taina* 112 [The chiefs] had their share brought to them in calabashes called *taha*.

tahae, *v.* Also **tahai**. [Ma. /'ta:hae/: Williams 357 *Tāhae*. *1.* v. trans. Steal.] *trans.* To steal.

1881 CAMPBELL *Poenamo* 121 Cook..interfered and asked Te Hira why he was *tahai*-ing the *goahore*. He meant '*taking* away the pot', but in his imperfect knowledge of the language he used the word *stealing*. **1978** HILLIARD *Glory & Dream* 113 So on the way home we stopped the truck and tahaed some of his [*sc.* a mean farmer's] turnips.

taha maori, *n.* and *attrib.* [Ma. /'taha 'ma:ori/: Williams 357 *Taha...* 4. Part, portion. (mod.).] A Maori perspective or way of doing things; the 'Maori side' of affairs. Also, concretely, a subject or part of a school curriculum. (P. Ranby notes that it seems to have replaced *Maoritanga* in informed circles since c1980.)

1984 *Evening Post* (Wellington) 21 Aug. 3 A taha Maori element was included in today's opening of the Post-Primary Teachers' Association conference in Wellington. The 'Maori dimension' came in the form of a special Maori welcome for the Prime Minister, Mr Lange. **1986** REILLY *Deputy Head* 74 Anything short of revolving one's entire curriculum around 'taha Maori' will be seen as not enough. **1986** *Dominion* (Wellington) 31 July 10 There is no taha Greek, taha Indian, taha Vietnamese, taha what-have-you being taught to our children, but taha Maori, yes! **1989** HOGG *Angel Gear* 16 'No time for taha Maori around here,' he says, reflecting the mood of the locals rather than his own. The school is only 6 percent Maori.

taha pakeha. [Formed on TAHA MAORI.] The Pakeha perspective.

1983 KING *Whina* 14 Her dealings with the Education Department..had given her the reputation of being somebody who understood taha Pakeha, the Pakeha system. *Ibid.* 32 None of these responsibilities, which largely dealt with taha Pakeha or the European aspects of life, eroded Heremia's identity as a Maori. **1985** HOWE *Towards 'Taha Maori'* in *English* (NZATE) 4 It would be just as valid to talk of a 'taha Pakeha'. If we combine the definitions of Pakeha and taha above, for example, we might well refer to the way Pakehas view the world, *and* how they act upon the world.

tahepa, var. TAIEPA.

taia, var. TAIAHA.

taiaha /'tai‸ha/, /'taiə‸ha/. Formerly occas. **taia**. [Ma. /'taiaha/: Williams 362 *Taiaha...* A weapon of hard wood, about 5 ft. long, having one end (the *arero*) carved in the shape of a tongue with a face on each side and adorned with a fillet of hair or feathers, the other end being a flat, smooth blade (*rau*) about 3 in. wide.] A long wooden weapon (see Williams's description above), used

TAIAPA

for striking and jabbing; a Maori 'quarterstaff', occas. wrongly regarded as a spear.

1842 BEST *Journal* 15 Apr. (1966) 349 Mukuro, a principal chief of the place who with a Taia in his hand..occupied a prominent position. **1856** SHORTLAND *Traditions & Superstitions* 244 The *taiaha*, a kind of two-handed sword made of the hardest wood of the country. **1863** *Richmond-Atkinson Papers* (1960) II. 61 The first of them was an old man with a handsome taiaha, he..was immediately shot. **1871** MEADE *Ride through Disturbed Dist.* in Taylor *Early Travellers* (1959) 499 With Mair's advice he selected a handsome *taiaha* (a sort of spear, or sword-shaped club, of dark red wood, carved and polished, with the plume of white dog's hair and small scarlet feathers, and more as a mark of the bearer's rank as chief than as a weapon). **1890** COLENSO *Treaty of Waitangi* 10 Here and there a *hani* (or *taiaha*, a chief's staff of rank, &c.) was seen erected. **1917** *NZ At the Front* 1 The *Taiaha*, as a few New Zealanders may know, is an old-time fighting weapon of the Maori. **1935** COWAN *Hero Stories NZ* 58 The *taiaha*, the most shapely and effective wooden weapon of the Maori, is a kind of two-handed sword, with the added advantage that both ends can be used, the tongue-shaped point as well as the broad blade. **1946** *JPS* LV. 149 *taiaha*, weapon of hard brown wood, up to six feet long or more, with tongue-like point and slightly-broadening blade for thrust and stroke, the tongue proceeding as if from a carved mouth, with paua eyes inserted for realism: used somewhat in the manner of a quarter-staff:.. a weapon prized as highly by the owner or collector as the mere, and much used by chiefs in oratory as well as in war. **1979** TAYLOR *Eyes of Ruru* 13 I am the taiaha left among people who dance and twirl poi in gaudy halls of plastic maoridom.

taiapa, var. TAIEPA.

taiepa /ˈtaiəpə/, /ˈtaiˌɑp/. *Obs. in English use.* Also in early use ?**tacopa, taiápa, ta(i)hepa, tie-up, tíeupha.** [Ma. /ˈtaiepa/: Williams 363 *Taiepa, taiapa, tāepa. 1....* Fence, wall.: cf. Ma. *epa* an end-post of a house; by folk etymology, *taiepa* becomes *tie-up*.] Also as **taiepa** or **tie-up fence**, a fence, often built of at-hand, bush materials e.g. saplings interlaced with vines. See also *Maori fence* (MAORI 5 b). **a.** As **taiepa** or variants.

[**1820** LEE & KENDALL *NZ Gram. & Vocab.* 205 Taihepá; A fence. (or, Tahepa.)] **1828** WILLIAMS *Early Jrnls.* 21 June (1961) 135 Several natives on the beach from Waikari who had brought *Tacopa* for fencing. [MS apparently *tacopa*: Ed. *Note* suggests *taiepa*, or perhaps the sailing cutter *Taeopa*.] **1838** POLACK *NZ* I. 223 A taiápa, or fence, surrounded each plot of ground to prevent the dogs and pigs from following the natural bent of their inclinations. **1846** WEEKES *Journal* in Rutherford & Skinner *Establish. New Plymouth* (1940) 120 A spot was selected in front of the house and with native assistance a 'Tíeupha' fence was soon completed. This is made of stout sticks six feet high stuck in the ground perpendicularly and tied round in two or three places with rods and a tough creeper (clematis) more durable than any cord. **1863** MANING *Old NZ* iv 69 A long line of similar articles..which had graced the *taiepa* fence the night before, had disappeared. **c1875** MEREDITH *Adventuring in Maoriland* (1935) 161 I am getting on very well with the clearing; and vary the monotony by putting up a *taiepa* (fence) around my pig yard. **1948** HENDERSON *Taina* 177 Yes; he fell down by the *taiepa* of the *pa*, and then I ran home.

b. As **tie-up**.

1820 BUTLER *Jrnls. & Corr.* (1977) 72 Buying tie-up wood for fencing, and setting boundaries in order to its being put up. **1834** MARKHAM *NZ* (1963) 34 [Torotoro creeper] is soaked first, or used quite fresh, for what is called (a tie up) a fence to keep Goats out of a Garden or to answer as a railing. **1861** MORGAN *Journal* 14 July (1963) 30 Thursday and yesterday making a tie up fence. **1871** MONEY *Knocking About NZ* 139 A poor fellow..was hit out in the open in front of us, and I had to pass over the 'tie-up' [the fence around the Maori village of Pangarahu], and give a hand to carry him in. **1881** NESFIELD *Chequered Career* 43 Twenty or thirty whares with their usual 'tie-up' fences around them formed the outside Pah. **1935** MAXWELL *Recollections* 162 The one has a potato patch..inside a Maori tie-up (a very close secure fence made of long poles let down between a series of pairs of stakes which were securely tied together between each layer of poles). **1975** KNIGHT *Poyntzfield* 42 The bush..made one fence, the stream another and the Maoris made a 'tie-up' fence on the other sides [at Rangitikei, c1850].

Taieri Pet /ˈtaiəri ˈpet/. [f. *Taieri* + transf. use of *pet* fit of pique.] A spectacular local Otago cloud formation heralding an approaching storm and associated with the Taieri district.

1949 THOMPSON *East of Rock & Pillar* 4 The district is subject to high winds from the north-west quarter... Their approach is usually heralded by the appearance over the valley of a long cloud known locally as the 'Taieri Pet'. **1988** HEARN *Nenthorn: Gold & the Gullible* 15 Sod huts began to replace tents, and residents learnt to watch for the 'Taieri Pet', an ominous swirling cloud above the Rock and Pillar, a sign of approaching storm and a warning to tie down roofs and tents.

taihepa, var. TAIEPA.

taiho, var. TAIHOA.

taihoa /ˈtaiˌhʌuə/, /ˈtaiˌho/, /ˌtaiˈhʌuə/; /ˈtaiˌʃʌu(ə)/, *int.* or *adv.* and *n.* Also **taiho, taisho(a), tisho.** [Ma. /ˈtaihoa/: Williams 363 *Taihoa,* ad[verb] By and by: /ˈtaiʃʌu(ə)/ reflects a (northern) Ma. dial. pron. of /h/ perceived as a kind of [ʃ] or [hj].]

A. *interj.* or *adv.*

1. Wait on!, wait-a-bit!, hold on!; by-and-by, presently: often used by English speakers to indicate a Maori stereotype to whom the urgency of clock time has little meaning. **a.** In Maori contexts.

c1826-27 BOULTBEE *Journal* (1986) 112 soon—taishoa. **1842** WADE *Journey in Nthn Is.* 66 'Taihoa'. This word has been translated, By and by; but in truth it has all the latitude of directly,—presently,—by and by,—a long time hence,—and nobody knows when. **1851** *Richmond-Atkinson Papers* (1960) I. 90 Glad we were to pay off our Maori lad & and be done with their provoking 'taiho!' 'waiho! [=rest]' (*presently wait*). **1908** GORST *NZ Revisited* 214 The plaintiff was put off with the everlasting Maori answer—'taihoa' (by and by). **1938** FINLAYSON *Brown Man's Burden* (1973) 25 Under the old gum-tree..Peta said, 'Taihoa, wait a bit. It's not midnight yet.' **1941** SUTHERLAND *Numismatic Hist. NZ* 4 Usually when in 'funds' he [the Maori] distributes largess with a lordly air, *Taihoa* (let tomorrow look after itself) being his traditional policy.

b. Used by English speakers or in non-Maori contexts (often pronounced /ˈtaiʃʌu/) mainly as an interjection, wait-a-bit! hold on!

1889 WILLIAMS in Woodhouse *Farm & Station Verse* (1950) 16 When a forward young woman approached very near, And she dropped a remark that she meant me to hear, It was 'Tisho!' its meaning is, 'Steady! Go slow!' **1898** MORRIS *Austral-English* 453 Taihoa, Maori phrase, meaning 'Wait a bit.' Much used in some circles in New Zealand. **1905** THOMSON *Bush Boys* 170 'Taisho, Mac. I'll be there in a minute.' [**1905** *Note*] The bush-boy corruption of the Maori 'Taihoa', 'Wait a bit'. **1911** *Maoriland Worker* 2 June 1 The curse of the New Zealand trade union movement is the time-server. The man who takes a paid position in a Union and sleeps on it, lives on it, loafs on it. Taihoa. **1921** *Quick March* 10 Dec. 11 Ah, well, Dad—you never know—taihoa, old man! **1935** COWAN *Hero Stories NZ* 143 Still, the young settlers said, '*Taihoa*! We'll wait and see,' and went on with their usual duties. **1940** *Tararua Tramper* Apr. 6 There was no hurry; taihoa—tomorrow would do to go on, or the day after tomorrow. **1965** SHADBOLT *Among Cinders* 205 Stay around here, with me, you might see some you like better sooner or later. Taihoa. Take your time. **1986** *Nat. Bus. Rev.* 19 Sept. 34 A lot of eager gentlemen burst into my room and said: 'We want the logs..now.' I said: 'Taihoa, gentlemen, we haven't finished growing them yet.'

B. *n.*

1. Procrastination, delay.

1910 GRACE *Hone Tiki Dialogues* 4 There is too much taihoa about you Maoris. **1912** RUTHERFORD *Impressions NZ Pastoralist on Tour* 162 We talk of 'taihoa' in connection with our Native Department. The real home of unadulterated 'taihoa' is Italy. **1974** BARTLETT *The Emigrants* 41 A raupo cottage..could be quite comfortable if the Maori builders were allowed to take their time with plenty of Taihoa—'What's the hurry, O pakeha!'

2. *transf.* or *fig.* As a joc. translation of **wait-a-while**, applied to *Cassytha paniculata* (fam. Lauraceae), a Northland creeping plant parasitic on (or associated with) manuka; also (see quot. 1940) applied to BUSH LAWYER *n.*[1] (*Rubus* spp.).

1940 MATTHEWS *Matthews of Kaitaia* 17 There was no path..and the thorny vines of the 'bush lawyer' or, as Pene called it, *Taihoa* (Wait-a-bit) made travelling difficult. **1946** REED *Farthest North* 28 Closer inspection disclosed a curious creeper, common hereabouts [in Northland], its favourite habitat a clump of scrub, amongst which it contrives to involve itself in an inextricable tangle... This creeper bears the appropriate name of Taihoa (wait-a-while). **1948** REED *Gumdigger* 53 The stringy tendrils of the aptly named *taihoa*, or 'wait-awhile' native creeper, tough enough to trap and hold a horse.

3. a. In *attrib.* use. Given to or generating procrastination or delay.

1881 CAMPBELL *Poenamo* 269 I am persuaded that if all the swearing of my after-life was put against it in an opposite column the *taihoa* one would carry the day. **1904** *NZ Observer* 31 Dec. 4 He has as yet given no indication of a disposition to drop into the old 'taihoa' ways. **1913** *Ibid.* 6 Sept. 2 Because of Mr Parr's energy and intolerance of the 'Taihoa' Department [*sc.* Health Department], we are told the unpleasant truth that the Orakei native community is infected. **1936** LAMBERT *Pioneering Reminisc. Old Wairoa* 137 Animated by an enthusiasm that completely controverts the Pakeha's conception of a Maori as a *taihoa* worker, eight Maori carvers..have a notable work in hand.

b. Special Comb. **taihoa policy**, a policy of 'wait-and-see', of proceeding slowly, with Maori or Polynesian matters.

1912 *NZ Free Lance* (Wellington) 13 Jan. 4 Dr Pomare..is wisely adopting the 'taihoa' policy as far as a pronouncement of his intentions goes. **1921** FOSTON *At the Front* 188 Taking twelve years instead of five..was described as a Taihoa policy. **1931** *Na To Hoa Aroha* (1987) II. 148 The slump finds most of the good undeveloped lands still in Maori ownership a justification of the taihoa policy; also finds the Maori youth impatient of the old excuses for not working

TAIHOA 804 **TAIL**

these lands. **1940** COWAN *Sir Donald Maclean* 125 It was just as well that Sir Donald Maclean was of a calmer temperament; had he lived in a later day his methods would probably have been described as a 'Taihoa policy'. **1986** SORRENSON in *Na To Hoa Aroha* I. 62 Carroll, as Native Minister, was often accused of a taihoa (by and by) policy.

Hence **taihoaism** *n.*, procrastination.
1881 CAMPBELL *Poenamo* 88 Waipeha was equal to any amount of taihoaism, and Tongata Maori loved him accordingly. **1912** *Dominion* (Wellington) 23 Jan. 4 The King Country..is languishing under the fell disease, 'taihoaism', and its associate Maori landlordism. **1946** *JPS* LV. 157 *taihoaism*, procrastination.

taihoa, *v.* [See prec.] *intr.* To delay; to proceed gently or carefully (with).
1881 CAMPBELL *Poenamo* 284 We must be up and doing and not *taihoa*-ing and letting the fern grow under our feet. **1938** WILY & MAUNSELL *Robert Maunsell* 129 He succeeded in persuading the natives to keep quiet for the moment—in fact to *taihoa*. **1971** *Listener* 19 Apr. 56 Pete had a dekko up a chimney. But there was a lay-back..so they tai-hoa'd while they tucked into some brunch. **1985** BENTLEY & FRASER *Grand Limerick Tour* [No.] 41 Ecology freaks at Tryphena Say 'Taihoa' on mussels and kina. **1996** *Independent* (Auckland) 30 Aug. 29 So, with a name change in the wind, the IAFP [a financial planning association] decided to taihoa on the certificates.

taiko. Occas. (Chatham Island) **tchaik'**. [Ma. /'taːiko/: Williams 363 *Tāiko... 1...*black petrel.]
1. Any of various mainly dark petrels and shearwaters, esp. now (since its re-discovery in 1978) the *Chatham Island taiko* (see 2 below), but also the *black petrel* (*Procellaria parkinsoni*) PETREL 2 (1) and *sooty shearwater* (*Puffinus griseus*) SHEARWATER 2 (6).
1879 *TrNZI* XI. 103 In that great battle, the two birds, the *tiitii*..and the *taiko*, were made prisoners by the river-birds. **1886** *Ibid.* XVIII. 89 The Natives are very careful, when taking the young *taikos*, not to disturb the burrows. **1911** SHAND *Moriori People* 6 The young of many sea birds..were used as food [on the Chathams], such as..*Hakoakoa* (mutton bird), *Tāiko* (a smaller-sized mutton bird of slatey blue colour). **1928** BAUCKE *Manuscript* (Bishop Museum Memoirs Vol.IX No.5 343–382) in Skinner & Baucke *Morioris* 358 taiko tchaik' pied shear water. **1980** LOCKLEY *House Above Sea* 188 'Taiko' is the name for any large muttonbird, once abundant on all mountain ranges from the Waitakeres to the Rimutakas of the North Island. In the 'good old days', each Maori village had its own taiko colony, which was visited in the autumn to collect the fat 'titi' (young birds).

2. Often as **Chatham Island taiko**, the rare *magenta petrel* (PETREL 2 (15)) *Pterodroma magentae* (fam. Procellariidae), thought extinct but rediscovered in 1978.
1970 *Annot. Checklist Birds NZ* 23 *Pterodroma magentae*..*Chatham Island Taiko*. **1984** HOLMES *Chatham Is.* 97 Chatham Island Taiko *Pterodroma magentae* (Magenta Petrel)—remains one of the rarest birds in the world. **1985**, **1987** tchaik [see PETREL 2 (15)]. **1990** *Sunday Mag.* 22 July 25 Chatham Island Taiko... The rarest petrel in the world with less than 80 birds left alive.

tail, *n.*[1] [f. *tail* the hinder end of anything, the part opposite the head: see OED *n.*[1] 4.]
1. *Sawmilling*. **a.** The end of a saw-bench (often extendable on a moveable trolley) which deals with the sawn timber as it emerges from the saw. Cf. TAILER-OUT.
1874 BAINES *Edward Crewe* 180 After taking off a 'face' cut, setting the gauger rollers, and placing the flitch in position, the man at the head starts the machinery. 'Kreash,' says the saw..and in twelve seconds she is out at the other end. The man at the 'tail' at that instant reverses the motion of the table, which gigs back.

b. Special Comb. **tail-box** *goldmining*, a *sluice-box* (SLUICE 2); **tail-chain**, a heavy chain bound round the trailing end (the 'tail') of logs, as a brake, when hauling on steep slopes; **tail-drag** *v.*, to haul a log by the 'tail' or trailing end first.
1875 *Evening Post* (Wellington) 23 Mar. 2 [Dunedin] persons convicted of larceny from '**tail-boxes**' and alluvial claims. **1953** REED *Story of Kauri* 180 The bullock team was attached to the log..by a pair of grips on either side of a long chain with a ring in the centre to take what was called the '**tail chain**'. **1937** AYSON *Thomas* 99 From a little bush nearby they cut all the posts, wall plates, rafters and joists required for the hut, and by night had them **tail-dragged** on the ground.

2. [Transf. use of *tail* the rear end of a marching column: see OED *n.*[1] 4 c; AND 1849.] The end or last part of a mob of sheep.
1933 *Press* (Christchurch) (Acland Gloss.) 23 Dec. 15 The t[ail] of a mob is the last part of it; hence the weakest and worst sheep. **1987** OGONOWSKA-COATES *Boards, Blades & Barebellies* 98 Tail. The last part of a mob; often the worst sheep to shear.

3. Usu. *pl.* WW1. *transf.* See quot.
1937 PARTRIDGE *Dict. Slang* 861 Tails... Batmen completing a party of horsemen of high rank: New Zealand soldiers'; in the G.W. Opp. *the heads*, those in authority: ex the game of two-up.

tail, *n.*[2] [Spec. use of *tail* something resembling a tail of an animal: see OED *n.*[1] 2.]
1. *Goldmining*. [AND 1937.] A string or ring of sediment and (or) gold left around the bottom edge of a pan after washing auriferous material.
1898 'H' *Grain of Gold* 12 By a peculiar motion of the wrist, Old Grit separated the lighter iron-sand from a smaller quantity of heavier copper pyrites, and draws the last into a long string into the bottom of the dish, called 'the tail'. **c1890–1900** EDWARDS in *Penguin Book NZ Verse* (1985) 93 When the battered dish flowed empty, bar a tail of new-chum gold, Or it gave a ring of 'colour' that betokened wealth untold. **1912** *NZGeol.SB* (NS) No.15 139 A 'tail' of very finely divided gold (electrum) could be obtained by dish washing. **1952** HEINZ *Prospecting for Gold* 18 The quantity of small pebbles and sand in moss is surprising, and at times a good 'tail' of gold is obtained. *Ibid.* 22 An experienced miner can..judge approximately the amount of gold to the ton of quartz by the tail of gold left around the bottom of the pan **1970** WOOD *Gold Trails Otago* 80 If the quantity [of gold-bearing concentrates in the gold-pan] is down to a few spoonfuls, try swirling it around *very gently*..using only about half a cupful of water in the pan—this will form a 'tail' around the edge of the bottom with the light sand going ahead, the black sand..following, and behind that the gold flakes forming the point of the tail.

2. a. The upper, pointed end of a flax-blade producing inferior fibre.
1928 *NZJST* X. 236 On exposure to the atmosphere a golden tint is produced by the formation of the brown chlorophyllan from chlorophyll, which tones with the brown colour of the tails and portions of unstripped leaf. *Ibid.* 238 One drawback that is very apparent with chemical bleaching is the fact that while the clear fibre is given a good white colour, the green tails and unstripped portions are left unchanged and show up very unfavourably.

b. Special Comb. **tail-cutting**, the lopping of the tail of a flax blade in processing for fibre.
1928 *NZJST* X. 238 Better stripping and tail-cutting is essential to get rid of these faults if high-class fibre is to be obtained.

3. [AND 1859.] The tapering slenderer part of the thong of a stockwhip between the belly and the lash. See also STOCKWHIP.
1933 *Press* (Christchurch) (Acland Gloss.) 16 Dec. 21 *Stock whip*... The lash is increased in thickness for several feet. The thick part was called the *belly*, the tapering part from there to the end was the *tail*. **1940** [see BELLY 2].

tail, *n.*[3] [Spec. use of *tail* the tail of an animal: see OED *n.*[1] 1.] Formerly, the tail (usu. of a deer) as a token on which a bounty was paid, or as proof of an animal killed.
1969 MASON *Television Script* in *Solo* (1981) 210 Young Man: Deerstalker. Live in Hoky... Up on the tops, all on my own. Fit as a flea, no beer, no gut, no birds, come down, cash my tails, live it up. **1971** *Listener* 19 Apr. 56 Just as he reached the burn he spotted a spiker... He really wanted..a decent head—he wasn't interested in tails.

tail, *v.*[1] Also **tail shepherd**. [f. TAIL *n.*[1] 2: AND 1843.] *trans.* To shepherd (livestock) from the rear of a mob to keep them together.
1852 HOMEBUSH *Journal* in Deans *Pioneers* (1964) 154 I have had to tail the cattle on foot this five weeks as I have had no saddle. **1860** *St. Leonard's Jrnl.* 10 Nov. J.S. and Billy tail shepherding. **1863** CHUDLEIGH *Diary* 24 May (1950) 88 *24th.* Fine. We tailed the cattle all day and Swan took delivery of them in the evening. **1871** MONEY *Knocking About NZ* 133 The horses, after being 'tailed', or shepherded, all day by one of us [soldiers] 'told off' for that purpose, were tied in rows..for the night. **1904** LANCASTER *Sons o' Men* 279 In the marshy gully..a boy was tailing some cattle for the milking. **1933** *Press* (Christchurch) (Acland Gloss.) 23 Dec. 15 Tail... (2) To keep sheep or cattle together in a mob allowing them to move ahead slowly as they feed. **1941** BAKER *NZ Slang* 31 To tail, to follow or watch. **1958** *Whitcombe's Mod. Jun. Dict.* (8edn.) 403 *tail...* To move a mob of sheep or cattle along by following behind them.

Hence **tailing** *vbl. n.* [AND 1848], the shepherding from behind of a mob of livestock.
1878 ELWELL *Boy Colonists* 47 This watching of sheep and keeping them together was called 'tailing'. **1937** AYSON *Pioneering Otago* 40 As there were wild dogs about I had to follow the lambs about all day... That is what they call in Australia 'tailing', as the dingoes were very bad in the early days.

tail, *v.*[2] [f. TAIL *n.*[2] 3 .] *trans.* To put a tail on (a stockwhip).
1862 CHUDLEIGH *Diary* 20 Sept. (1950) 59 I got my old whip from McDonald. He has tailed it very nicely indeed and it is now a very valuable whip. *Ibid.* 62 I left my 14 ft. whip with a Mr Pitt to be tailed with..hide.

tail, *v.*[3] [Of stock, recorded earliest in NZ: cf. OED *v.*[1] 3, 1886.] To dock or remove the tail from (a lamb, occas. a cow). Also as a *vbl. n.*
1863 BUTLER *First Year* x 153 You must tail your lambs, in which case every lamb has to be caught, and you will cut its tail off, and ear-mark it with your own ear-mark. **1940** STUDHOLME *Te Waimate* (1954) 114 One year during the eighties we tailed 28,000 lambs from 32,000 ewes. The tailing of so many lambs was a

long business, and sometimes it lasted for three or four weeks. **1958** [see TAIL *v.*¹]. **1966** NEWTON *Boss's Story* 190 *Tail:* To tail a block means to muster it, and tail and mark the lambs. **1986** OWEN & PERKINS *Speaking for Ourselves* 179 When he was tailing [*sc.* the sheep], the girls were sent away, and I wanted to see what tailing was.

tailer. *Obs.* The lower sawyer on a two-man pit saw.
   1941 *Lower Hutt Past & Present* 53 The top man pulls the [pit] saw up and guides it along a chalk line while it is being pulled down by the 'tailer' below.

tailer-out.
   1. [AND 1895.] Also **tailman**. A sawmill worker on the tail of a breast-bench who feeds out the sawn timber (see esp. quot. 1923). Cf. TAIL *n.*¹ 1 a, TAIL OUT.
   1907 LANCASTER *Tracks We Tread* 87 The bench sawyers felt it, and the trolley-men; and each tailer-out and engine driver. **1923** MALFROY *Small Sawmills* 39 Tailer-out.. The man who controls the flitches and boards at the back end of a saw-bench. He works in conjunction with the sawyer as the timber passes through the saws. **1930** SMYTH *Wooden Rails* 32 She came upon the sawyer and his mate, the tailer-out. **1950** *Landfall 14* 125 The planer..spits out faced boards for the tailer-out to stack by the goose-saw. **1951** *Awards, etc.* 518 [Marlborough Timber-Workers Award] [Rates of wages] Twin-saw table equipment—Headman twin breakdown 4[s.] 3[d.] Tailman twin breakdown 4 0¹/₄. **1971** in Cleveland *Great NZ Songbook* (1991) 54 From the bushmen to the breaker-out, From the breaker-out to the bench; From the benchie to the tailer-out, From the tailer-out to the yard. **1981** CHARLES *Black Billy Tea* 69 One of our neighbours had a small sawmill, and I often gave him a hand—in fact I became quite an efficient 'tailer-out'.
   2. Special Comb. **tailer-out tram**, a part of a breast-bench behind the saw which moves on tram-tracks to accommodate varying lengths of timber.
   1923 MALFROY *Small Sawmills* 23 The sawyer and tailer-out trams must be solidly..laid, absolutely parallel with the saw.

tailing, *vbl. n. Farming.* [f. TAIL *v.*³]
   1. [AND 1916.] The docking or removing of a lamb's tail.
   1851 WELD *Hints to Intending Sheep-farmers* 10 About a week after the lambing is finished, the operations of castration, tailing, and ear-marking are performed. **1922** PERRY *Sheep Farming* 80 The operation of tailing is generally performed with a knife, and care must be taken to have as uniform a dock as possible. **1940** [see TAIL *v.*³]. **1982** WOODHOUSE *Blue Cliffs* 190 We completed the tailing of the hill lambs about midday.
   2. Special Comb. **tailing-band**, a band of rubber placed around a lamb's tail to stop blood circulation so that the tail eventually drops off; **tailing-muster**, a muster to bring lambs in for tailing; **tailing-yard**, a yard specially arranged to facilitate tailing of lambs.
   1984 MARSHALL *Day Hemingway Died* 141 There was nothing in it [*sc.* the farm utility] except a ten-pound tin of honey, and some **tailing-bands** scattered on the floor. **1951** MCLEOD *NZ High Country* 24 No time is wasted in a **tailing muster**. If a ewe with a young lamb drags behind, leave her; she'll come in at shearing, and the little lamb is better out of the crush of the yard. **1949** NEWTON *High Country Days* 197 On most sheep stations **tailing yards** are only temporary affairs. They are erected for the day only, and when the job is finished are pulled up, and used on the next block to be tailed. **1968** TOMLINSON *Remembered Trails* 41 We always got on well. Next day we mustered down to the tailing yards.

tailings, *n. pl. Goldmining.* [Spec. use of *tailings* (inferior) residue: see OED *vbl. n.*¹ 2 b, 1864; see also EDD *tail n.*⁴, *tailings* the refuse of tin ore. Cornwall.] The waste material removed during the processing of auriferous alluvial material or ores.
   1862 HODDER *Memories NZ Life* 166 A group of women were round the pool washing the 'tailings' in tin dishes. **1868** [see BERDAN]. **1874** *TrNZI* VI. 329 The goldminer in his sluicing operations, spreads out..drift, alluvial sludge, or tailings in strata all over the plain. **1887** PYKE *Hist. Early Gold Discoveries Otago* (1962) 140 A company formed to work these 'tailings', as they are technically termed, has been in operation some time, with payable results. **1896** *AJHR I-4A* 6 The tailings from stamper-batteries are as fine as sand. **1911** BREMNER in *Mt. Ida Goldfields* (1988) 16 They would take in all tailings from the tail races emptying into the gully. **1935** BLYTH *Gold Mining Year Book* 11 *Tailings*: Useless material discarded after most of the metal has been extracted by the treatment plants. **1953** SUTHERLAND *Golden Bush* (1963) 119 My only dividend from the flood, the ample tailings-dump, made a great difference to work on the claim and returns took a turn for the better over the new few paddocks. **1967** MCLATCHIE *Tang of Bush* 116 Ethel became very excited, and exclaimed, 'The Tailings!' We were pushing through heavy gravel at the time... The language of gold mining was unknown to me, and Ethel had to explain that tailings were the heaps of gravel left after the soil had been sluiced away.

tailman: see TAILER-OUT 1.

tail out, *v.* [Prob. a back-formation from TAILER-OUT: AND 1919.] To guide sawn timber on the saw-bench as it emerges from the saw.
   1906 COX *Diaries 1888–1925* (ATLMS) 27 Aug. I was in the Mill... I was tailing out 1¹/₂ inch timber. **1988** JACKSON *Rainshadow* 90 [He] shouted greetings to men in black singlets.., tailing out. He was answered by the..drone of the breaking-down saw as it bit into a pine log.
   Hence **tailing-out** *vbl. n.*, taking sawn timber from the saw.
   1987 *Province New Nelson Writing* 61 It was then cut into fire sized blocks, pulled away from the saw and thrown in the big heap. This was called 'tailing out'.

tail-race. *Goldmining.* [AND 1856.] The water-channel by which non-auriferous refuse from (usu. alluvial) mining is carried away. Cf. SLUDGE CHANNEL. Contrast HEAD-RACE.
   1863 *AJHR D-6* 14 Where the water is heavy, and there are no means of cutting a tail-race, water-wheels have been erected, with Californian pumps attached. **1874** BATHGATE *Col. Experiences* 92 When the water reaches auriferous ground, the earth is gradually washed away through a narrow channel, or tail-race, in mining phraseology, prepared for the purpose, and paved with stones. **1880** LAPHAM *We Four* 30 I was down in the tail-race, and Jim was working just under the face. **1909** THOMPSON *Ballads About Business* 70 While the dirt pipes keep a-drumming, You can hear the tail-race humming. **1935** BLYTH *Gold Mining Year Book* 11 *Tail Race*: The aqueduct in which tailings are carried away. **1988** BREMNER *Mt. Ida Goldfields* 11 But given water, the miners could soon wash thousands of tonnes of rock and gravel down the tail races and sludge channels.

tail shepherd: see TAIL *v.*¹

tainui. [Ma. /ˈtainui/: so called as it is traditionally reputed to have grown from the skids of the Tainui, one of the Maori founding canoes: Williams 364 *Tainui..Pomaderris apetala.*]
   1. *Pomaderris apetala* (fam. Rhamnaceae), a North Island shrub, scarce in the wild, and related to KUMARAHOU 1.
   1889 KIRK *Forest Flora* 11 The tainui of the Maoris is a comparatively recent addition to our flora, having been discovered..near the south head of the Mokau River in December, 1878... As..the genus Pomaderris is absolutely restricted to Australia and New Zealand, the legend [of its being brought from Hawaiki]..appears to be without foundation. **1890** *PWD Gen. Catalogue* (NZ & South Seas Exhib.) 16 Lithograph of tainui foliage. **1906** CHEESEMAN *Manual NZ Flora* 100 [*Pomaderris apetala, Lab.*] *Tainui...* A common Australian plant. The Maoris assert that it sprang from the rollers or skids that were brought in the canoe 'Tainui' when they first colonised New Zealand. **1924** LYSNAR *NZ* 69 There is a plant the Maoris call 'Tainui'. It is interesting because of its association with a tradition that a specimen in the North Island sprang from a green timber used in the building of the 'Tainui', a canoe which brought some of the Maori immigrants to New Zealand between five and six hundred years ago. **1950** WODZICKI *Introduced Mammals NZ* 162 Kirk (1896) says that the tainui..has been completely destroyed at Kawhia by goats. **1978** MOORE & IRWIN *Oxford Book NZ Plants* 88 *Pomaderris apetala*, tainui. An erect, rather narrow shrub growing to 5m tall... Known as a wild plant only in a few North Island sites.
   2. As **golden tainui**. *Pomaderris kumeraho*. KUMARAHOU 1, a popular ornamental shrub.
   1943 MATTHEWS *NZ Garden Dict.* 79 *Golden Tainui*—see *Pomaderris elliptica*. **1981** [see KUMARAHOU]. **1986** OVENDEN *O.E.* 28 But it's spring, and the parks are full of kowhai, and rangiora, and golden tainui.

taipa, var. TAIEPA.

taipo /ˈtaiˌpɑu/. Also **taepo, tipu, typo(o)**. [Ma. /ˈtaiˈpoː/: Williams appendix *taipō* goblin, typhoid; Williams 364 notes 'This word is used by Maoris believing it English, and by Europeans believing it Maori, it being apparently neither. Colenso suggests *tae-po*, but this is not used by the Maori.': TREGEAR *Maori-Polynesian Comparative Dict.* (1891) 440 *Taepo* 'a goblin; a spectre': cf. *tae* 'arrive'; *po* 'night'.]
   [*Note*] The origin is unknown. The earliest uses are from the far south. *Taipo* is not recorded in Williams 3edn. 1871 or 4edn. 1892, nor in the English-Maori section of the 1871 edn. at *goblin*, etc. It is first noticed in the 5edn. of 1917. *Taipo* may possibly be derived from English speakers' mishearing of *tipua, tupua* 'goblin, demon'. It is unlikely to be a Maori mishearing of an 18th–early 19th century pronunciation of *typhoid* (*fever*) as this has been recorded only from 1845 in both international and early NZ English. The adjective *typhoid* used of an infectious fever, though recorded from 1800, was apparently confined to the medical literature until the 1840s. *Typhus* applied to a fever is recorded from the 18th century, but is not found in early NZ reference, and is on present evidence an unlikely source. A possible relationship with German *teufel* 'devil' has also been suggested (p.c. Bill Pearson, Auckland).

I. In Maori contexts. **1.** An evil spirit (bringing disease and death); a devil; a night goblin. (But see also quot. 1848, Taylor.)

c1826–27 BOULTBEE *Journal* (1986) 113 devil—tāipo. **c1835** *Ibid*.95 Why? no one shall hurt you, they have no reason to do so, as the boy died a natural death. The evil spirit (or Taipo killed him). **1840** WATKIN *Journal* 5 June in McNab *Old Whaling Days* (1913) 486 The inhabitants of this [South] Island in common with some savages are very superstitious..and all sickness is ascribed to supernatural or perhaps infernal agency, Taipo being the supposed author of the disease whatever it may be. Taipo is a foreign word, its native place and etymology I cannot trace, but as it appears to mean the Devil and is of universal use I shall not disturb it. **1846** HEAPHY *Exped. S.W. Nelson* 11 Feb. in Taylor *Early Travellers* (1959) 195 [The Maori] commenced chanting his Wesleyan missionary service, mixing..special incantations to the *taipo* of the lake and river for propitious weather and easy fords. **1848** TAYLOR *Leaf from Natural Hist.* 43 *Taipo*, female dreamer; prophetess; an evil spirit. **1851** REES in *GBPP NZ* (Irish Univ. Press Series) IX. 1779 33 The old superstition of 'Atua' and 'Taipo' (exacting spirits of disease) pass away whenever Christian doctrines are received. **c1875** MEREDITH *Adventuring in Maoriland* (1935) 72 Occasionally they travel at night in a party; but they always sing *waiatas* [*sic*] (native dirges) to keep the *taipo* (devil) away. **1883** COLENSO *Three Lit. Papers* 5 Taepo means to come or visit by night,—a night visitant,—a spectral thing seen in dreams,—a fancied or feared thing, or hobgoblin, of the night or darkness; and this the settlers have construed to mean the Devil!—and of course their own orthodox one. **1895** ROBERTS *Southland in 1856* 72 They believed it was the principal rendez-vous of the fallen angel (Taipo) himself. **1906** ELKINGTON *Adrift in NZ* 46 The uneducated ones still have a superstition that the Tipu (devil) lurks there [*sc.* in the bush] and prowls about at night ready to pounce on the unwary Maori. **c1920** BEATTIE *Trad. Lifeways Southern Maori* (1994) 306 Whareatua [= house of (a) spirit] is a big round white mushroom... It was a 'taipo house' and they would not eat it. *Ibid*. 408 In conversation..the word 'taipo' came up. It is a handy word to express the works of spirits or powers of evil —although it is not much used by the younger generation, who seem to prefer the Pakeha term 'Jimmy' to express the ideas of ghosts, spirits, or supernatural manifestations... The narrator said the word was certainly taipo (and not taepo) and that it was not correct Maori. When the early whalers were learning Maori they said taipo was an easy term for anything they thought was connected with the devil or with spirits. **1937** AYSON *Thomas* 53 That evening the boys held the floor, telling all sorts of Maori stories about Taipo. **1946** *JPS* LV .150 *taipo*, supernatural being; goblin. used by the Maori believing it to be Pakeha, and by the Pakeha believing it to be Maori; often spelt taepo, which also is not a Maori word: so taipo is a word coined by no one knows whom. **1973** MCCARTHY *Listen..!* 36 Now the Taipo is something older Maoris never discussed. It was a mythical spirit, which, when it made its presence known, was a fore-runner of death. **1983** HULME *Bone People* 467 Taipo = demon, night goblin (a word of dubious origin).

2. *transf.* or *fig.* Applied (often in mixed Maori-European use) to various frightening people or things: a bogeyman, a local monstrous creature or apparition; a railway train; a surveyor's theodolite (see quot. 1898).

1853 TAYLOR *Journal* 3 Dec. (ATLTS) XIII. 134 I was told that an insane man living there had told them that the influenza was caused by the anger of the spirits of the dead... We were soon saluted by the Taepo (madman) himself..addressing us in an English accent in complete gibberish. **1855** TAYLOR *Te Ika a Maui* 49 There is the *Taringa-here*, a being with a face like a cat; and likewise another, called a *Taipo*, who comes in the night, sits on the tops of houses, and converses with the inmates, but if a woman presumes to open her mouth, it immediately disappears. **1885** *Wairarapa Daily* 28 Oct. 2 An old Maori chief..approached Mr. Crawford [an engineer] with great reverence, saying 'You taipo-master?'—meaning thereby to ascertain whether Mr. Crawford could work and control the machinery. **1898** MORRIS *Austral-English* 454 *Taipo* or *taepo* is also a slang term for a surveyor's theodolite among the Maoris, as it is the 'land-stealing devil'. **1916** COWAN *Bush Explorers* (VUWTS) 2 Now the white man was coming and presently his iron rail and his steam 'taepo' would lay the trail that was to conquer..the mana of the Maori. **1924** *Aussie* (NZ Section) 15 July XII 1 no 'fraid of te taipo... No doubt many builders possess taipos of this sort. **1965** WEBBER *Try Again Friday* 81 Rushing out of the bushes [in the night], Archie gave such a convincing imitation of an angry taipo that the [young Maori] poachers hurriedly decamped. **1973** WALLACE *Generation Gap* 75 Yes, he [*sc.* a man who had lost his hands] was 'taipo' to the Maoris, who were afraid of a man who could live without part of his arms. *Ibid*. 211 My Missus..she not eat taipo meat [from a black lamb]. Black skin, she taipo. **1982** SANSOM *In Grip of Island* 119 Smugglers and poachers were good solid flesh but taipo was an intangible. 'Look out! Taipo will get you' frightened me off dark or forbidden places when I was a child. Taipo is a hybrid word, a mixture of pakeha-maori for a mythical fiend or demon.

II. In non-Maori contexts, occas. **typo** (/ˈtaɪpʌu/).

[*Note*] The English sense derives mainly from the primary Maori sense 'evil spirit', 'devil' figuratively used, or transferred to 'a fearsome or injurious person or thing' (e.g. a weta); thence in various weakened uses, as a nickname or name mainly for animals, occas. for adult humans and, in familiar address, to (usually naughty) children.

3. In topographical applications, esp. in place-names. **a.** A name for a (dangerous) West Coast or other river.

1871 MONEY *Knocking About NZ* 49 We afterwards learnt that the Maories had named this river [flowing into the Teremakau, Westland] 'Typoo', which means the devil, and there certainly was a spice of devilry about its raging waters that suggested bad spirits in a perpetual state of frenzied agony. **1879** HAAST *Geol. Canterbury & Westland* 116 Though the Taipo was still high, we were enabled to ascend along its banks. **1921** GUTHRIE-SMITH *Tutira* (1926) 91 This crossing [of the Papakiri] has always been known in my time as the 'Taipo'—goblin-crossing, a name probably given because of a totara block which used to lie there hewn roughly to the similitude of a man's head. **1933** *Canterbury Mountaineer* 85 She [*sc.* the Taipo river] would roar and whistle and play every tune on the bagpipes, shifting boulders would vibrate the hillsides; terrific, weird, madmen..the one evil one—Taipo. **1948** HAAST *Julius Von Haast* 437 [On the Midland Railway to West Coast]..numerous bridges were erected, the most remarkable of which was the bridge over the legendary Taipo [a branch of the Taramakau], in which many a tall fellow found his doom.

b. An Otago place-name.

1939 BEATTIE *First White Boy Born Otago* 152 One of the shepherds..lived in a hut at Taipo [Central Otago].

c. A sharp-pointed, steep hill; a range of such hills.

1943 *TrRSNZ* LXXII. 347 The Brocken Range is composed of a group of these 'taipos', so-called by the Maoris, who held them in superstitious dread as the dwellings of evil spirits. **1953** p.c. Ruth Mason who instances Map N162 *Moore's Taipo* 412558; N162 *Taipo* minor. Taipo is the name given to a sharply pointed steep hill in the eastern Wairarapa district.

4. a. Mainly in a weakened sense, a name given to an animal, esp. a dog.

1896 Private letter in Morris *Austral-English* (1898) 455 *Taipo*, for instance, of course one knows its meaning, though it has been adopted chiefly as a name as common as 'Dash' or 'Nero' for New Zealand dogs; all the same the writers upon Maori superstitions seem to have no knowledge of it... I think myself it is South Island Maori, often differing a little in spelling and use. **1898** MORRIS *Austral-English* 454 *Taipo*..a New Zealand word for devil, often applied by settlers to a vicious horse, or as a name for a dog. **1948** FINLAYSON *Tidal Creek* (1979) 28 'Now for the old girls,' he says, and Taipo yaps with joy. Uncle Ted heads for the cow paddock. **1985** GREEN in *Hyacinths and Biscuits* 147 Uncle named him [*sc.* a black kitten] 'Taipo', which means black devil. **1985** MCGILL *G'day Country* 122 'Don't mind Taipo,' she said as she ushered me in. I froze... 'What the devil is it?' She chuckled. 'A Beardie.' 'Does it bite?'

b. In various weakened senses of '(little) devil' addressed in exasperation or humorous endearment to a child; or applied as a nickname to a Maori.

1930 DEVANNY *Bushman Burke* 300 [West Coast reference] Oh Mary, don't—don't be a taipo. **1939** BEATTIE *First White Boy Born Otago* 20 We did not get very far with our Maori, but I used to go to Maori services [1850s–60s] with Taipo (Joe Benson) and picked up quite a lot of it.

5. Mainly *West Coast*. The large-headed *tree weta Hemideina crassidens* (WETA 2 (5)). Cf. *bush devil* and *Maori devil* (BUSH C 4 and MAORI B 4 b), *wood-devil* (WOOD *n.*¹ 2 a).

[*Note*] The distribution of *H. crassidens* includes Wellington and the SI West Coast: it makes scraping sounds esp. at night (cf. SAWYER) of no comfort to new chums in the bush, or to the Maori who also found it in some ways frightening.

c1899 DOUGLAS in *Mr Explorer Douglas* (1959) 81 [The Open Bay Island] 'Typos' [are] swarming all over and appear to burrow in the stalks of the gei gei. **1912** *Otago Witness* (Dunedin) 2 Oct. 77 They are such big, dreadful-looking things; some call them taipos but the real name is weta. **1928** DEVANNY *Dawn Beloved* 47 The very apogee of excitement would be reached when a 'typo' was discovered. Especially if it happened to be a big fat male. **1932** *NZJST* XIII. 46 These remarkable insects [*sc.* large-headed wetas] (the taipo, or weta, of the Maori) are generally said to feed only on vegetation. **1946** SARGESON *That Summer* 176 But the wetas came out at night and he laughed. The Maoris [in the central NI] call them taipos. **1948** in Pearson *Six Stories* (1991) 48 The kids at school [on the West Coast] looked at me with fear and fascination as we looked at a taipo when we found one in a rotten log. **1957** [see *bush devil* (BUSH C 4)]. **1957** HARPER in *Mr Explorer Douglas* (1959) xii Charlie always admitted that he hated, almost to the point of fear, two things: taipos (wetas) which he spells 'typos', and those dark brown bush creeks. **1966** *Encyclopedia NZ* III. 636 The..[present fam. Stenopelmatidae] includes the tree or ground wetas and the 'taipos' of the West Coast of the South Island, the name of which to the Maori means 'the devil who comes by night'. **1971** SHARELL *NZ Insects* 139 The name taepo was also sometimes applied to the weta. **1984** WALKER *Common Insects 2* 49 Wetas (sometimes called taepo) hide under bark or in old insect holes during the day and come out at night to browse on vegetation. **1988** DEVANNY *Point of Departure* 7 Most sought after [in nw. Nelson c1900], in palm or rotting log, was the typo... Up to four inches long..this insect is of terrifying appearance.

6. *Obs.* A game often called *bagatelle*. See quot. 1955.

TAIROA   807   **TAKE**

1955 *BJ Cameron Collection* (TS July) taipo (n) 1. A Maori devil. 2. A game in which successive players try to so tap a number of balls with a stick that they will roll into the highest scoring compartments on a wooden board. **1956** p.c. W.J. Orsman (Marlborough). *Taipo*. A popular New Zealand name for the game of *Bagatelle*.

7. As **manga manga taipo** (/ˈmʌŋə/) [Ma. /ˈmaŋu/, /ˈmaŋumaŋu/: Williams 178 *Mangu, māmangu, mangumangu*, a. Black], used occas. as a children's rhythmic cry or as an insult to a Maori. Cf. *mango-mango, mungee-mungee tarpot*, an abusive nickname.

[**1847** ANGAS *Savage Life* I. 281 The young New Zealanders..were greatly amused at the dark colour of [the aboriginal's] skin, and laughed at him for being so ugly; calling him '*Mango, Mango*' or 'black fellow'.] **1941** BAKER *NZ Slang* 56 We..use the doggerel Maori *mungimungitaipo!* as a ferocious expression. **1951** PARK *Witch's Thorn* 127 Shaking showers of white quince blossom down upon herself, she yelled, '*Maunga manga taipo!*' at Mauri in an unreasoning, provocative impudence, but he did not mind being called a black devil and cuffed good-naturedly at her head with a big brown paw. **1954** *Numbers 1* July 4 The happiest days of our lives. Young white gods yelling *mangumangu taipo!* without knowing what it meant, only that it was something to be yelled at the Maori kids in the swamps on Sunday afternoon. *Mangumangu taipo*, nigger-man devils! And it didn't much matter that you yourself weren't a Maori. **1964** HOWE *Stamper Battery* 85 Wockie knew the Maori for good-day and what we pakehas thought was Maori for big black devil. They were tena koe and mangi mangi taipo, but when he went to call out in a friendly way to these [Maori] strangers he forgot which meant which. **1988** *Through the Looking Glass* 126 My brothers' slang and 'funny' sayings delighted me... I remember..many that..were corruptions of Maori words. I spell them here as they sounded to me then:.. *munga munga typo*.

tairoa, var. TOHEROA.

tairoa trousers. [Prob. f. a misspelling of *Tairua* the name of a town on the eastern coast of Coromandel Peninsula, formerly a goldmining site; there seems no obvious connection with Taiaroa Head on the Otago Peninsula.] See quot.

1986 OWEN & PERKINS *Speaking for Ourselves* 155 In those days [early 1900s] the [kauri bushmen's] customary dress was the old Blucher boots..and tairoa trousers, which were made of a kind of heavy white duck; these were tied with bowyangs below the knees.

taisho(a), varr. TAIHOA.

taiwha: see TAEWA.

taiwhenu, var. TAUHINU.

takahe /ˈtakəhi/. Also (from a Ma. variant) **takahea**. [Ma. /takaˈhe:/: Williams 367 *Takahē* (ii) *takahea..Notornis..= moho*.] *Porphyrio* (formerly *Notornis*) *mantelli* (fam. Rallidae), a large blue-green flightless rail with red bill and feet, thought to have been extinct but rediscovered in 1948. Often *attrib*. See also MOHO, NOTORNIS.

1851 MANTELL *Petrifactions* II. 128 No one had seen such a bird, but all agreed that it was the traditional Moho or Takahé which they believed was utterly extinct. **1873** BULLER *Birds NZ* 191 It was known to the North-Islanders by the name of 'Moho', and to the South-Islanders by that of 'Takahé'. **1886** *TrNZI* XVIII. 78 I was informed..that the skeleton of a Takahe had been found..near lake Te Anau. **1890** *Otago Witness* (Dunedin) 6 Mar. 35 A nearly complete skeleton of the famous takahe was found a few years ago..not far from [Lake Te Anau]. **1906** *TrNZI* XXXVIII. 337 My first note refers to the *Notornis mantelli*, the *rara avis* called by the Maoris the '*takahea*'. The name of this bird is spelled '*takahe*' in Buller's 'Birds'. **1926** COWAN *Travel in NZ* II. 122 These men..made..expeditions up into the lakes region, hunting for the..rare and elusive *takahea*, the blue-plumaged notornis which is now believed to be extinct. **1949** *Emu* XLVIII. 321 [Stoats'] droppings were found in one or two empty Takahe nests... Takahe country and unmistakable traces of the birds can now be recognised easily. **1952** *Notornis* IV. 207 Deer feed on species of *Danthonia* that the takahe have been shown to depend upon in large part for food and nesting cover. **1988** MORRIS & SMITH *Wild South* 80 Takahe make a variety of calls—a hennish cluck when feeding, the occasional frightened screech, a rhythmical *kau-kau* when recalling their chicks, and a percussive note of alarm which the Maori described picturesquely as sounding like the knocking together of pieces of greenstone underwater. **1990** *Sunday Mag.* 22 July 25 After dwindling to a low of 120 the takahe population is now 230. **1990** *Listener* 6 Aug. 114 Possibly Alice met a takahe.

takahea, var. TAKAHE.

takapu. Also occas., from a Ma. variant, **takupu**. [Ma. /ˈta:kapu/: Williams 369 *Tākapu*..gannet.] GANNET 1.

[**1820** LEE & KENDALL *NZ Gram. & Vocab.* 206 Tákapu, *s*. A bird so called.] **1844** COLENSO *Excurs. Northern Is.* in Taylor *Early Travellers* (1959) 54 Several fine Gannets attracted our attention... [The natives] call it Takupu. **1869** *TrNZI* I. (rev. edn.) 105 Takapu. Breeds on Mahuke Island. **1871** HUTTON *Catalogue Birds NZ* 49 Gannet. Takapu. *Sula capensis.* **1888** BULLER *Birds NZ* II. 177 Dysporus serrator. (Australian Gannet)... Takapu, Takupu, and Toroa-haoika. **1898** MORRIS *Austral-English* 455 *Takapu*.. Maori name for the bird *Dysporus serrator*..a *Gannet*. **1908** BAUGHAN *Shingle-Short* 186 As the plunge of the *Takapu*, straight is his speeding:—Frost-fish, we make for the shore! [**1908** *Note*] Takapu (tah-kah-poo): The gannet. **1947, 1985, 1990** [see GANNET 1].

Takapuna. [A city with marine associations within the greater Auckland conurbation.]

1. In the names of recipes: **Takapuna oyster soup** (from local rock oysters); **Takapuna surprise**, a steak stuffed with oysters.

1913 *Australasian Cook. Book* 213 *Takapuna Oyster Soup*..milk..onion..pepper..fry..flour... Allow the whole to boil... Put in the oysters and simmer... *Takapuna Surprise* top-side steak... Prepare a forcemeat..oysters [etc.] cayenne pepper..breadcrumbs..fill the steak with the mixture... Sew up..slices of bacon over the top, and bake. **1988** McGILL *Dict. Kiwi Slang* 111 *Takapuna surprise* steak stuffed with oysters.

2. An alternative name for a Z-class racing boat, designed in 1921 by Mr R.B. Brown of Northcote, having a length of approx. 3.8 m, a beam of 1.5 m, square chine vee-bottom principle, and the whole of the sailing area carried on a gunter mainsail on a short mast forward, with no bowsprit or headsail.

1921 *Star* (Auckland) 15 Oct. 18 The class letters are... Z, Takapuna one-design class. *Ibid*. 26 Nov. 18 The latest class, the Takapuna 12 ft 6 in. flatties, are very handy little craft, and ideal for racing or knocking about the sheltered bays and beaches of Takapuna. **1944** CARTER *Little Ships* (1948) 127 Next to the X class is the Z class, or what are often referred to as the Cornwell Cup boats. They owe their existence to a small band of Takapuna yachtsmen who planned the first boats [with the idea of] low first cost, ease of construction, and an ever-watchful eye on speed and performance under Auckland harbour weather conditions. The yachts were originally designed for the Takapuna Boating Club but owing to their popularity from the outset the type was quickly adopted by many other yacht clubs... From small beginnings the Takapuna one-design class rapidly expanded. **1964** MANDER & O'NEILL *Give a Man a Boat* 35 To be in a fleet of Takapunas and come about the weather mark..and fly away before the breeze..was a roundabout which made up for the swing. The [new] class letters are: A, Viking 1 to 22; B, Thistle 1 to 16..Z, Takapuna one design class. **1974** AVERY *The Ken Avery Songbook* [Title 'Tea at Te Kuiti'] I'm going to..Drink a handle or a schooner as I tack my Takapuna. **1978** TITCHENER *Little Ships of NZ* 64 A good example..was the design of the famous but ill-fated Z-class, which became known as the Takapuna class throughout New Zealand. **1989** DAVIS *Kohimarama* 113 The Z class, or 'Zeddie' as it was affectionately known, was another class which was designed as a low cost sailing boat to get the boys into something safer than tin canoes or derelict dinghies. *Ibid*. 114 The Takapuna Boating Club..was the sponsoring club and the yachts were often referred to as the 'Takapuna Class'.

take, v.[1] In various phr. or phrasal uses.

1. to take a pull, to pull oneself together; to desist in (one's) course of action.

1911 *Truth* 7 Jan. 4 On again, then through Napier... When I took a pull I was by this time heartily sick of the game, and made up my mind to give it best, and came into Hastings. **1946** HAUGHEY *Railway Reminisc.* 21 Look here—, it's about time you took a pull. Just shake yourself up a bit quick. **1968** *NZ Contemp. Dict. Suppl.* (Collins) 19 *take a pull* (Sl. phr.) to reform (oneself).

2. to take the burnt chops, see BURNT *ppl. a.* 1.

3. to take (one) **down** (for a sum of money), to cost.

1944 COOZE *Kiwis in Pacific* 20 A doughy concoction labelled cake 'took us down' for seven and six. **1952** p.c. H.S. Gajadhar (Wellington). My holiday took me down for twenty pounds.

4. to take out [see OED 87 m '*Austral. and N.Z.*', 1943], to win.

1977 *NZ Herald* (Auckland) 8 Jan. 1 The Games we play..can't..end, till Someone takes them out.

5. to take to. a. [OED 74 h '*N.Z. slang*'.] To attack (esp. with the fists).

1911 KIWI *On the Swag* 9 Take to him, Bill. **1960** HILLIARD *Maori Girl* 159 When we got home he really took to me. That was when I lost a lot of my teeth.

b. As **to take to the bush**, see BUSH A 3 a (a).

take, *n*. Muttonbirding. The right to take (or to a 'take' or catch of) muttonbirds from southern muttonbird islands. Also as a v.

1911 *Gazette* Aug. in Wilson *Titi Heritage* (1979) 41 But this presumption has been rebutted by the admission that he had no 'take', therefore he has no right to this island. **1912** *Regs. under Land Act* in Wilson *Titi Heritage* (1979) 171 'Take', and all references thereto, include taking, catching, killing, or pursuing, by any means or device. **1979** WILSON *Titi Heritage* 25 The wise old chiefs set the season for the 'take' for that certain time of the year which became known to the pakeha as half of March, all of April and May, allowing no trespassing on the island at any other time of the year. *Ibid*. 27 Especially when the pakeha took a Maori wife; he could then share her journey to her island, and help her to 'take' enough birds for their family needs. *Ibid*. 55 Ever since the beginning, to 'take' meant journeying to the islands and living there for the season and using hands or any device to catch the birds..to 'take' also includes an 'attempt to take'. *Ibid.* 66 In the season 1921 the Colac Bay and Riverton Maoris caught 24,000 birds, in 1922 the 'take' was 14,000. **1995** *Evening Post* (Wellington) 15 July 15 Previously it was unthinkable not to go and harvest titi for your family. If you were not able to go yourself, you were able to appoint someone in your place to bring your 'take' home.

takeke. [Ma. /'takeke/: Williams 371 *Takeke*.] GARFISH.
1843 WILLIAMS *NZ Jrnl.* (1956) 41 The whole of the long range of the New Zealand Coast is abundantly supplied with beautiful fish..viz... takeke, Guardfish. **1844** COLENSO *Excurs. Northern Is.* in Taylor *Early Travellers* (1959) 55 Here [near Bay of Islands, the natives] call them [*sc.* garfish] Ta[k]eke; but among the southern tribes, Ihe. **1849** *NZ Jrnl.* IX. 125 Guard fish Takeke. **1879** *Auckland Weekly News* 4 June 16 There were several kinds of shellfish including *kutai*..; of fish, *tamure* (snapper), *takeke* (guardfish). **1921** *NZJST* IV. 120 *Garfish*, or *Piper*; *Takeke*. Occurs in abundance around all the northern coasts. **1956** GRAHAM *Treasury NZ Fishes* 157 Garfish or Piper (Takeke) *Reporhamphus ihi*. **1967** MORELAND *Marine Fishes* 16 Garfish... Also called piper, halfbeak, ihi, and takeke.

take up, *v.* [AND 1831 'Used elsewhere esp. in the *U.S.* but of local significance.'; see OED *v.* 93 d (b); DAE *v.* 10 a.]
1. Of pastoral or farm land or a run and, esp. in early use, of Crown leasehold, to occupy.
1860 BUTLER *First Year* (1863) v 66 My companion and myself have found a small piece of country, which we have just taken up. *Ibid.* viii 114 Taking up the Run... I had waited to see how the land was allotted before I took it up. **1873** WILSON *Diary* 10 Jan. in Wierzbicka *Wilson Family* (1973) 164 The land up here 110 miles from the sea coast (Oamaru) was taken up in 1858, and all the habitable parts of New Zealand have now been taken up. **1898** HOCKEN *Contributions* 168 Thus fresh country was continually taken up and active explorers went further and further afield. **1908** *TrNZI* XL. 518 This had been forest..long before the run had been 'taken up' or stocked. **1924** ANTHONY *Follow the Call* (1975) 111 I took the section up in the first place through ignorance. **1933** *Press* (Christchurch) (Acland Gloss.) 23 Dec. 15 Take up.—The original occupier of country in the early days was said to have 'taken it up'. 'Who took up this station?' meant 'Who was the first occupier?' Nowadays, people tell you that Mr Jones has just 'taken up' 1000 acres of Brown's run. The old sense of the word was understood everywhere on stations up to about 1900. **1981** ANDERSON *Both Sides of River* 8 When these stations were first taken up the access was poor. **1991** LA ROCHE *Hist. of Howick & Pakuranga* 213 The Hundred of Howick [in Auckland] also included..1055 acres of 'Waste Land'. This misleading description applied to land purchased from Maori tribes, that was surveyed, and offered at auction, but not taken up by prospective settlers.

2. Of potential mining land, to register and occupy a claim (on).
1863 WALKER *Jrnl. & Lett.* (ATLTS) 10 Jan. Prospected about 10 miles up river, every place worth having seems to have been taken up... [Jan. 12–13] We went up the gully to see if there was room to put in anywhere, but found it was all taken up, so we went up to the top of the hill. **1868** *Thames Miner's Guide* 83 Brickmakers', near Punga Flat. Five men's ground, taken up in March.

takiwai, var. TANGIWAI.

tak(k)i, varr. TANGI.

takupu, var. TAKAPU.

talamea, var. TARAMEA.

talc. *Obs.* Also **green talc**, **talk**. [Transf. use of *talc* a translucent green mineral.] GREENSTONE 1.
1769 MONKHOUSE 18 Oct. in Cook *Journals* (1955) I. 581 This man had a human tooth hanging at his ear—and a piece of green talk about two and half inches long, and an inch and half broad, flat, and carved into the figure of a most uncooth [*sic*] animal of fancy. **1804** COLLINS *Eng. Colony in NSW* 344 They..carry on a traffic for flax and green talc-stone, of which they make axes and ornaments. **1823** CRUISE *Journal* (1957) 183 They also wear, fastened round the neck by a cord, and hanging on the breast, a piece of green talc, carved to represent what cannot be deemed human. **1830** CRAIK *New Zealanders* 184 [They] make certain of their weapons, and carving tools, of a green talc, or jasper stone, which is found only in the southern island. **1840** [see JADE]. **1892** [see POUNAMU 1].

talk /'tælk/, var. TALC.

talk, *v.*
1. *intr.* Of a tree being felled, to make sounds warning that it is about to fall.
1904 *NZ Illustr. Mag.* Dec. 178 'Don't you hear her talkin'?' as a gentle ticking would indicate the act of partition had commenced. Then the wedges were 'backed up', and a few solid blows from the heavy mauls would complete the operation. **1951** p.c. R. Gilberd (Okaihau). *Talking*. That means that a tree is about to fall and the weight of the top is breaking the fibres of wood. They crackle and squeak and groan—'talking'.

2. In the phr. **to talk** (oneself) **around** (something), to talk (oneself) out of (a difficult situation).
1979 *Evening Post* (Wellington) 3 Apr. 5 Here is a man who took advantage of a school situation to flog off a narcotic. Talk yourself around that one.

3. In the phr. **to talk the leg off an iron pot**, to talk excessively. (The *leg* is poss. the handle; or perh. the *iron pot* is one with legs, like a CAMP OVEN.)
1910 p.c. W.H.B. Orsman (Marlborough). *Talk the leg off an iron pot*, used before WW1. **1988** MCGILL *Dict. Kiwi Slang* 112 *talk the leg off an iron pot* you talk too much.

4. talk bullock, see BULLOCK *n.* 1.

tallamaer, var. TARAMEA.

tallo, var. TARO.

tall poppy: see POPPY 2.

tally. [Spec. usc of *tally* a count, a number or the record of a count: AND 1870.]
1. *Shearing.* **a.** The number of sheep shorn by an individual shearer during a run or other specified period, in a day, or over the whole period of a shearing. See also *shearing tally* (SHEARING 3). Also in general farming use for counting large mobs of sheep, the call for 100 sheep counted (see quot. 1933).
1881 BATHGATE *Waitaruna* 73 There was a rivalry among them [*sc.* shearers] as to who would have the biggest tally. **1897** WRIGHT *Station Ballads* in Woodhouse *Farm & Station Verse* (1950) 33 And it ain't no use to tell us of tallies that he shore, There'll be records broke this year, you take my word. **1903** BAUGHAN *Reuben* 85 I've scored my last tally, I've done my last dip... there's no crutching aboard of a ship. **1913** BATHGATE *Sodger Sandy's Bairn* 71 Any good tallies, boys. **1933** *Press* (Christchurch) (Acland Gloss.) 23 Dec. 15 *Tally*.—(1) A hundred sheep. When large mobs are counted the man counting calls out 'T[ally]!' every time he gets to 100, and then starts again. Another man answers 'T[ally]!' and cuts a notch in a stick. When the whole mob is counted the number of notches gives the hundreds and the odd number completes the total, which is also (2) called the *t[ally]*. (3) The total number of sheep shorn by each shearer in a day. **1959** MIDDLETON *The Stone* 43 For a few days George..put up some high tallies, but..he dropped back to 200. **1973** FERNANDEZ *Tussock Fever* 3 The pumice in the wool played up with the gear, blunted the cutter and combs, ruined a man's tally.

b. The record, or recording, of sheep shorn by an individual shearer.
c**1875** MEREDITH *Adventuring in Maoriland* (1935) 144 As I was finishing the counting-out, the boss came towards the shed..and invited me to come for a swim. I said I would join him as soon as I had all the tallies. **1875** *Otago Witness* (Dunedin) 18 Sept. 18 The wool must be taken off at first blow. Every breach of this rule will subject the shearer to a fine or deduction of a score of sheep from his tally. **1986** RICHARDS *Off the Sheep's Back* 68 Bob Hadfield was asked to make up the tallies. When these were completed and each shearer's account had been made up, John produced his chequebook.

Hence **tally out** *v.*, to count out sheep after shearing.
1955 BOWEN *Wool Away* 97 When 'runs' are finished the tally clerk should be ready to tally sheep out, for when the run is finished, a shearer likes to know how he has been going.

c. In the phr. **to cut (get) a tally**, to shear (and get paid for) a number of sheep.
1897 WRIGHT *Station Ballads* 38 'Close your shears and leave the shed.' Dick stopped swearing, took to sneering—'You don't mean it now!' he said. 'I came here to get a tally, not to knuckle down to you.' **1986** RICHARDS *Off the Sheep's Back* 75 I had plenty of time to stroll down the board to watch Fred's movements and still cut my tally.

2. In occupations other than shearing. **a.** A specified number (often 100) of animals dealt with in some way (deer killed, rabbits trapped) in (usu.) a specified period.
1900 WRIGHT in *Centennial Treasury Otago Verse* (1949) 58 And the fork tines flash as the sheaves are turned on the frame of the one-horse dray; The long trap-line; The tallies are big on the rock-strewn spur. **1951** May 17 Feilding Freezing Works terms p.c. Colin Gordon. *Tally*: You *cut tally* if you get 100 per man. **1953** SUTHERLAND *Golden Bush* (1963) 69 Some of the high tallies taken in the early days of the so-called 'culling' operations..show that the shooters learned the wisdom of concentrating their fire on the leader hinds. **1961** CRUMP *Good Keen Man* 21 Stan said that a dog that chases deer on your block can cost you half your tally. *Ibid.* 25 I had a tally of 185 deer.

b. An amount of work done in a given time.
1944 LEE *Shining with the Shiner* 136 They would work with a will for an hour or two at the outside [at gorse-cutting]. And their tally was good.

3. Special Comb. **tally board**, see quot. 1933; **tally book**, the book in which the record of shearers' individual tallies are entered (see also quot. 1989); **tally clerk**, the employee who counts a shearer's tally and enters it into the tally book,

TAMARIKI

or one who checks off cargo during waterside or railways goods handling, or one who takes a count of animals in a freezing works; **tally pen**, *counting-out pen* (COUNT OUT *v*. 2).

1933 *Press* (Christchurch) (Acland Gloss.) 23 Dec. 15 Hence t*[ally]* book, in which the man who counts out, writes them down... The t*[allie]s* for the day before are written up each morning on a **tally board** kept in the shed. 1955 BOWEN *Wool Away* 97 A very good practice is to have the tally board hanging up on the wall where all the shearers on that particular board can see it, allowing them at any time of the day to know how their tally is progressing. c1875 MEREDITH *Adventuring in Maoriland* (1935) 144 I said nothing, put my **tally-book** in my pocket, and followed the boss... I told him I had docked a few sheep [from the tallies] for bad shearing and cutting. 1973 FERNANDEZ *Tussock Fever* 13 The shearers..gathered around for a look at the tally book. 1978 JARDINE *Shadows on Hill* 129 Tally and wool books, all were ready. 1989 *NZ Eng. Newsletter* III. 28 *tally book:* The official record of what every man has shorn in each run of the day. It is made after the run by checking each shearer's counting out pen before clearing for the next session. Each shearer's tally for the day is then transferred to the tally book. In earlier times a 'tally board' was used with the previous day's tallies chalked up. No matter whether the book or the board is used, the tallies must be displayed in the shed. 1928 *NZ Free Lance* (Wellington) 25 Jan. 10 There are twice as many **tally-clerks** as there are tons of [wharf] cargo to tally. 1955 BOWEN *Wool Away* 97 When 'runs' are finished the tally clerk should be ready to tally sheep out, for when the run is finished, a shearer likes to know how he has been going. 1989 STIRLING *On Four Legs and Two* 84 Pete soon got a job as a tally clerk in the local freezing works. 1955 BOWEN *Wool Away* 97 **Tally pens** should be large enough, where possible to hold one run of sheep. 1973 FERNANDEZ *Tussock Fever* 13 In his tally pen..[the roughly-shorn sheep] looked a speckled mess, their injuries daubed with tar to keep the flies off.

4. In the phr. **to play tally** *obs.* [prob. from the daily *tally* or roll taken by the teacher for each class to mark attendance], to play 'wag' from school.

1982 SUTTON-SMITH *Hist. Children's Play* 41 Playing the wag was very common. We made for the bush, but it was difficult to time one's arrival at home correctly (1875; Dunedin) We called it 'playing tally.' (1875; Wakefield)

tamariki. Also early **tameheeke, e-ta-ma-ree-keé** (=e-tamariki), **tamārique**. *Pl.* occas. superogatory *tamarikis*. [Ma. /ˈtamariki/: Williams 376 *Tamariki..1. Child*, opposed to adult... *2. Pl.* for *tamaiti. Children*.] Mainly in Maori use of English, a child as distinguished from an adult; often the *pl.* of *tamaiti*.

[1804 COLLINS *Eng. Colony in NSW* 562 E-Ta-ma-ree-keé, *A young man*.] 1814 MARSDEN 9 Mar. in Elder *Marsden's Lieutenants* (1934) 58 I told you when you were at Parramatta I would send you a gentleman to teach your tameheekes..to read. [c1826–27 BOULTBEE *Journal* (1986) 109 boy—tamārique] 1847 ANGAS *Savage Life* II. 102 The *tamarikis* (children) set to work endeavouring to delineate each other. 1860 *Richmond-Atkinson Papers* I. 562 Having quoted Rehoboam's case on the danger of making tamarikis counsellors, I left. 1873 TINNE *Wonderland of Antipodes* 9 Fancy these *tamariki*, piccaninnies or brats of one or two years old, indulging..in the herb nicotiana. 1890 *Otago Witness* (Dunedin) 28 Aug. 36 The chief..claimed us part and parcel of his tribe, and said we were his 'tamariki' (children) and bosom friends. 1913 *Auckland Univ. College Student Carnival Programme* 27 Warriors, Wahines, Kuri, Poaka, Tamariki, Kumeras.. Guides, &c. on application to the Registrar. 1939 GRIEVE *Sketches from Maoriland* (1961) 110 I think the *tamariki* burn him. 1980 in *Sport 11* (1993) 140 Can you hear me down there Baxter?.. Nga tamariki have grown up & left you old man alone in that hole.

tamarillo /ˌtæməˈrɪlʌu/. [A specially contrived trade-name: see quot. 1985.] *Cyphomandra betacea* (fam. Solanaceae), a small Andean tree cultivated in warmer parts of New Zealand for its edible dark red (occas. yellow) ovoid fruit; also its fruit. Formerly TREE TOMATO q.v.

[1989 BRUCHER *Useful Plants of Neotropical Origin & Their Wild Relatives* 274 *Cyphomandra betacea* (Cav.) Sendt Tree tomato, tamarillo tomatillo, tomate d'arbre, Baumtomate. More than a dozen (some authors maintain 40) taxa of the genus Cyphomandra exist in South America. None of them has been recognized undisputedly as the ancestral form.] 1965 *NZ Patent Office application No.79697* 18 Oct. *Tamarillo.* Filed for 'fresh fruits and vegetables and sub-tropical fruits', subsequently abandoned. 1967 *Orchardist NZ* Feb. 23 On February 1, 1967, the name tamarillo officially replaced tree tomato. 1972 MITCHELL *Pavlova Paradise* 124 So the N.Z.B.C. was treated like the tamarillo (nee tree tomato). 1982 BURTON *Two Hundred Yrs. NZ Food* 141 An uncultivated native of the Andes region of Peru, the tamarillo is also found wild in India, Sri Lanka and parts of South East Asia. It was from the hilly regions of northern India that New Zealand's first seeds came, introduced by the Auckland nursery of D. Hay and Sons in 1891. At first only the yellow and purple varieties were grown and it was not until the end of World War I that the now almost universal red variety was bred at Mangere, Auckland. 1985 G.W. TURNER in *Verbatim II.* 11 Two well-known New Zealand exports, neither of them native, are tree-tomatoes and Chinese gooseberries, but neither is called that by the exporters. The tomatoes are a South American fruit, a rich source of vitamin C and long popular in New Zealand. About twenty years ago, the name *tamarillo* was deliberately contrived, much as a brand name is. On the basis of *tomato*, a diminutive *-ill-* was added; then *tomatillo* was altered, in honor of a legendary Maori tribal hero, Tama-te-kapua, to *tamatillo*; and then a change to *tamarillo* was considered more euphonious. And so a new word was born. 1990 *Listener* 6 Aug. 93 I myself have the face of a tamarillo which through some accident of Nature has acquired the furred skin of a kiwifruit.

tamore, var. TAMURE.

tamure. Mainly *NI*. Also occas. **tamore, tamuri**. [Ma. /ˈtaːmure/: Williams 377 *Tāmure..snapper*.] SNAPPER *n*.[1] 1 (*Chrysophrys auratus*).

[1820 LEE & KENDALL *NZ Gram. & Vocab.* 206 Tamure *s*. Bream fish.] 1843 DIEFFENBACH *Travels in NZ* II. 385 Tamuri—the snapper fish. 1845 WAKEFIELD *Adventure NZ* I. 93 There are many other sorts of fish, including the *tamore*, or snapper..of which the natives catch large quantities. 1850 LUSH *Auckland Jrnls.* 19 Nov. (1971) 38 Bought for the little girls' dinner two fishes, larger than English mackerel..one called Tamure—the other—Araara. 1874 BAINES *Edward Crewe* 163 But big Tamuri or Schnapper, by which name it is 'best known' to Europeans, is not very good eating. 1882 HAY *Brighter Britain* II. 151 In the bays and tidal rivers are..the tamure or schnapper, the whapuka..and many others. 1929 BEST *Fishing Methods* 48 The flesh of *tamure* (snapper)..was treated..to form an appreciated article of food, called *Kaniwha*. 1946 *JPS* LV. 150 *Tamure*, a sea-fish.., a brightly-coloured vigorous fish, a favourite in the market: often called snapper. 1952 LYON *Faring South* 131 The class of fish [available] varied with the locality—in the north the tamure or snapper, and the patiki..were the most common. 1966 *Encycl. NZ* III. 268 *Snapper*..or tamure of the Maoris, is our most popular food fish. 1982 BURTON *Two Hundred Yrs. NZ Food* 79 Snapper, or *tamure* in Maori, is our most popular food fish.

tanakaha, var. TANEKAHA.

tandem cowshed: SHED *n*.[1] 4 b.

taneewha, var. TANIWHA.

tanekaha /ˈtʌnəka/. Also **tanakaha, tani ráhá, tarnicar**. [Ma. /ˈtaːnekaha/: Williams 377 *Tānekaha. 1.*] *Phyllocladus trichomanoides* (fam. Podocarpaceae), a tall coniferous tree of lowland forest having flattened stems ('phylloclades') that act as leaves and bark rich in tannin. See also *celery pine* (PINE 2 (4) a), *pitch pine* (PINE 2 (11)), TOATOA 1 a.

1828 WILLIAMS *Early Jrnls.* 23 July (1961) 139 Mr Fairburn tried the *Tanakaha* to split for shingles. 1834 WILLIAMS *Early Jrnls.* 28 Jan. (1961) 359 Went with the Sawyers up to Waikino; felled one *Kauri* and one *Tanakaha*. 1834 MCDONNELL *Extracts Jrnl.* (1979) 19 A great variety of hard-wood grows at New Zealand..among them is the..toá toá, tani ráhá,.. and many others. 1834 MARKHAM *NZ* (1963) 33 Tarnicar resembles Coudie in size but is more perishable wood and more yellow. 1835 YATE *NZ* (1970) 38 Tanekaha... This regular, beautiful, and highly-ornamental tree, is found on hilly lands, or in dry shaded woods. 1849 MCKILLOP *Reminiscences* 162 The tanekaha tree yields a black or brown dye. 1853 HOOKER *II Flora Novae-Zelandiae I Flowering Plants* 235 *Phyllocladus trichomanoides*... Nat. names, 'Tanekaha' north of the Thames, and 'Toa Toa' south of that river. 1868 TAYLOR *Past & Present NZ* 205 The Tanekaha, a pine much prized for masts of small vessels, is almost, if not entirely, peculiar to the [Auckland] province. 1883 *Auckland Weekly News* 15 Dec. 21 The price of tanekaha bark in Auckland is usually about forty dollars per ton. 1890 *PWD Catalogue Timbers* (NZ & South Seas Exhib.) 14 Tanekaha..Timber white, heavy, tough, strong, and straight grained. 1910 COCKAYNE *NZ Plants & Their Story* 46,47 Amongst the trees not spreading much beyond latitude 42 degrees are..the tanekaha. 1940 LAING & BLACKWELL *Plants NZ* 79 *Phyllocladus trichomanoides* (The Celery Pine). The native name of this tree—*Tanekaha*—is said to signify *virile*, or *strong in growth*. 1988 DAWSON *Forest Vines to Snow Tussocks* 253 Tanekaha is absent from the southern North Island.

tanewa, var. TANIWHA.

tangata maori. Also early **tongat(t)a maori (maura)**; occas. with init. caps. [Ma. /ˈtaŋata ˈmaːori/, *tangata*, Williams 379 'man, human being' + *Māori* Williams 179 *(i) 1.* a. 'Very frequently used to distinguish objects from others having special characteristics; thus..*tangata māori*, man, human being, as opposed to a supernatural being;.. later, man of the Polynesian race, not a foreigner, the distinction not being confined to colour'.]

[*Note*] **tangata maori** (the phr. follows Ma. grammar in having the adj. post-positioned) encapsulates the earliest use of the form *maori* applied to the Polynesian *tangata whenua* (see also the discussion at MAORI 1 and 2). *tangata* 'human being' is recorded from 1770 (as *taata*, a Polynesian form) in Cook *Journals* I. 286, and from 1778 as *Tāngātā* in Forster *Observations* 284. Cf. *tangata pora* 'ship-person; stranger' used in the southern

TANGATA WHENUA

South Island, *tangata ma* 'white person' (see quot. 1834 below), *tangata pakeha* (see quot. 1867 below), *tangata tupua* 'white person, foreigner' (see quot. 1801 below), and *tangata Maoriori* 'Moriori' (see MORIORI 1 a).

The Maori as a race or people distinct from the Pakeha and other non–Maori; a Maori person; MAORI 1 and 2 a (a).

1801 *Miss. Jrnl. 'Royal Admiiral'* (ATLMS) 19 June Some of the natives here [*sc*. Firth of Thames northwards] have informed us that Tongatta [*sic*.] Tubua or white people took with them two of Tongata Maura (New Zealanders) to their own country, and some time after they returned they say they lived well with the white people eating Bunga Bunga (bread) and Gure (flesh of all kinds). [The reference is prob. to the Maori men taken to Norfolk Island by Governor King.] [**1815** KENDALL *New Zealanders' First Book* 22 [Sentences] Na! Iesu Christ ta Atua Nue, ta Atua Pi, ta wanhoungha Nue, ta wanhoungha Pi, ke ta notungata na, Pakkahah, ke ta na tangata maoude, ke ta tungata katoa katoa. *Ibid.* 23 Behold! Jesus Christ is the great and good Atua, the great and good friend to white and black men; to all men. **1820** LEE & KENDALL *NZ Gram. & Vocab.* 176 Máodi, *a*. Indigenous, native; as, 'E tángata máodi; A native man:' 'Wai máodi; Native water:' 'Kai máodi; Native victuals.' Also a proper name. **c1826–27** BOULTBEE *Journal* (1986) 109 New Zealander tongata máuree] **1834** MARKHAM *NZ* (1963) 30 Crow made all hands of the Natives (or Tangata Mouries) give us some of their Dances. *Ibid.* 71 Mr Hamlyn is so good a Linguist that..the people got up..to look at him closer as the[y] said he was a 'Tangata Mar', or white Man but that he had the Tongue of a 'Tangata Mouri', native. ['native' is a marginal note] **1836** MARSHALL *Narr. Two Visits* 108 A considerable number of natives including about thirty of the Tangata Mauri, or heads of tribes. **1840** POLACK *Manners & Customs* II. 123 The national nomenclature is that of na tangnata [*sic*] maori or native people..the word maori representing the term of native or indigenous. **1843** DIEFFENBACH *Travels in NZ* II. 7 They call themselves *Maori*, which means *indigenous, aboriginal*; or *Tangata Maori*, indigenous men; in opposition to *Pakea*, which means a stranger, or *Pakea mango mango*, a very black stranger, a negro. **1867** HOCHSTETTER *NZ* 202 Tangata maori is the native in contradistinction to Tangata pakeha, the stranger. **1881** CAMPBELL *Poenamo* 70 One of Cook's peculiarities was to run down the Maoris... Waipeha, on the other hand, always stood up manfully for Tongata Maori. **1909** *JPS* III. 34 The pas, villages, and houses of the people are not visible, not actually to be seen by mortal (Tangata Maori) eyes. **1938** HYDE *Nor Yrs. Condemn* 148 *Plurry pakeha*, eh? You got the skin like the Maori, but you're not *tangata* Maori.

tangata whenua. [Ma. /'taŋata 'fenua/: Williams 494 *Tangata whenua*, people belonging to any particular place, natives.]

1. *Obs*. A 'pre-Fleet' people once, according to a discarded theory, supposed to have settled New Zealand before the Maori, and often wrongly assigned the name of 'Moriori'. (See quot. 1877; and also quot. 1950 for an illustration of the confusion in the use of the name *Moriori*.)

1877 *TrNZI* IX. 19 The people in the canoes Rangimata, Rangihoana, and Orepuke assumed the name Mori-ori, but were termed by the first inhabitants *Tangata tare* or strangers, whilst the aboriginals called themselves *Tangata whenua*, or people of the soil. **1898** *Ibid.* XXX. 32 The editors have pointed out that I laid too much stress on the Melanesian affinities of the Moriois... [Mr. R.E.M. Campbell in *JPS* III. 53] makes the following remarks: 'How much of the blood of the present native inhabitants..is derived from the people who lived here before the arrival of the historical canoes, and how much from the conquering canoemen? At present almost every Maori..quite den[ies] any "tangata whenua" admixture.' **1904** TREGEAR *Maori Race* 446 When the Mataatua canoe drew near the shore, the voyagers saw on the cliffs above them a fort belonging to the original inhabitants of the country (*tangata whenua*). **1921** *JPS* XXX. 19 The *tangata-whenua*, or original inhabitants of New Zealand, a people that clearly had much Melanesian blood in them though otherwise a Polynesian people and speaking that language. **1937** BUICK *Moa-Hunters NZ* 228 Portion of the first migrants would..land in the North Island; but in the passage of years their identity has been lost, and they are represented to us in the mass as the *tangata whenua*, the mild-mannered people who were in possession when the more truculent migrants of 1350 arrived. **1949** BUCK *Coming of Maori* 332 The first settlers of New Zealand, who earned the name of *tangata whenua* (people of the land) by priority of occupation, consisted primarily of the three groups formed by the crews of three canoes. **1950** SIMPSON *Chatham Exiles* 24 Who were the first inhabitants of New Zealand—the *tangata whenua*, or original people, as the newly-arrived [Maori] colonists called them? **1961** *Distance Looks Our Way* 19 According to the traditions, when Toi arrived the country was well inhabited... These people are the *tangata whenua* of the traditions and they were divided into a number of groups... By an unfortunate and unjustified identification these people have become known in New Zealand by the name 'Moriori'. **1978** JARDINE *Shadows on Hill* 148 The *tangata whenua*, or Moriori as they came to be known, were apparently a gentle and simple folk.

2. Occas. *ellipt.* (see quot. 1966). A local people, the local residents of a particular place. Occas. *attrib*.

1905 BAUCKE *White Man Treads* 54 For the 'tangata whenua' (resident) took precedence on his own soil. **1928** *NZ Free Lance Christmas Annual* (Wellington) 1 Dec. 6 At large Maori gatherings when..there are visitors from other tribes whom the 'tangata whenua', the sons of the soil, delight to honour, songs are chanted..that date back centuries. **1930** *Na To Hoa Aroha* (1987) II. 51 After..the usual pupuri by the tangata whenua the casket was borne to the vault. **1946** ZIMMERMAN *Where People Sing* 37 And here again the club gave expression to a fundamental idea of Maori life, that of the obligation of hospitality of the *tangata whenua*, the man of the country, to whoever might chance to be his guest. **1966** *NZ Short Stories* (1976) 93 What was this country to him now, with its spirits of old tangata haunting the tree-tops. **1974** *Listener* 20 July 13 The body was lying in state on the stage at the end of the hall and the tangata whenua were seated. **1986** *Evening Post* (Wellington) 21 June 21 Paul Temm feels essentially unchanged by his experience on the tribunal, sitting at marae around the country..hongi-ing with both tangata whenua and manuhiri (visitors), chatting over tea and kai. **1990** *Greenpeace* Aug. 21 Ultimately the tangata whenua of the areas where the mills are sited may at least be considered.

3. a. (a) The Polynesian canoe-people as the original settlers of New Zealand as distinct from various later arrivals (cf. MAORI A 2 a (a)); (b) the Moriori as the original settlers of the Chatham Islands.

1963 HENDERSON *Ratana* (1972) 2 Peace and prosperity marked the time when there was cooperation between the newcomer and the *tangata whenua*. **1988** *Human Rights Comm. Focus* Mar. 1 Statement on the Status of Maori people as Tangata Whenua of Aotearoa New Zealand. **1988** *Evening Post* (Wellington) 10 Sept. 27 Quoting journalist Tom Scott, he [*sc*. Dun Mihaka] calls her [*sc*. Atareta Poananga, a Maori activist and Foreign Affairs employee] The Last Tangata Whenua in Paris! **1990** *Dominion* (Wellington) 18 Aug. 7 This book will help the Moriori people in their drive to be recognised as a tangata whenua people and to reinstate their culture.

b. In weakened use, occas. ironic or jocular, a Maori or the Maori; in transferred use, an Australian aborigine.

1987 *Listener* 12 Dec. 11 The paradox that still besets Australia is that it has learnt to live and prosper with its many racial migrant communities while remaining brutally ignorant..about its tangata whenua. **1988** MACRAE *Awful Childhoods* 89 That Lillian bird better watch which of the tangata whenua she mouths off like that in front of. **1992** *Sunday Times* (Wellington) 20 Dec. 3 If some councillor made a racist statement I don't think we would put them on a committee that dealt with the tangata whenua.

tangeao. Also **tánge ó**, **tangiao**, **tangio**. [Ma. /'taŋeo//'taŋeao/: Williams 379 *Tangeo, tangeao. 1... Litsea calicaris.*] MANGEAO.

[**1820** LEE & KENDALL *NZ Gram. & Vocab.* 207 Tánge ó; A tree used for fire-wood.] **1838** POLACK *NZ* II. 400 There are many other woods of much service to Europeans, differing in quality, among others: the *Warangai..Tangio..Akkas* of various kinds. **1869** [see MANGEAO]. **1889** KIRK *Forest Flora* 15 The mangeao or tangeao, as it is termed indifferently by the Maoris, was discovered..during Cook's first voyage. **1890** *PWD Gen. Catalogue* (NZ & South Seas Exhib.) 17 Lithograph of tangiao foliage. **1906** CHEESEMAN *Manual NZ Flora* 603 A perfectly glabrous closely branched leafy tree 30–40 ft. high... North Island:.. to Rotorua and East Cape... *Mangeao*; *Tangeao*.

tanghee tanghee, var. TANGI.

tangi /'tæŋi/, /'tʌŋi/. *n*. Also **tak(k)i** (SI), **tanghee tanghee**, **tangie**. *Pl*. often *tangis*. [Ma. /'taŋi/: Williams 379 *Tangi v*. 2. Weep, utter a plaintive cry, sing a dirge, as a sign of grief or of affection... 4. Salute, weep over... 6. v. trans. Mourn... 7. Cry for... 8. n. Sound... 9. Lamentation, mourning, dirge.]

I. In Maori contexts. **1. a.** A lament(ation); a dirge, occas. (see quot. 1860) a song of lamentation; a weeping.

[**1817** NICHOLAS *NZ* II. 91 This had caused, he said, *nuee nuee tanghee tanghee* (a good deal of crying) among them.] **1835** WILLIAMS *Early Jrnls.* 19 Feb. (1961) 413 An old lady put forth her miserable strains in a *tangi*. **1840** BEST *Journal* Aug. (1966) 233 At daylight we were awakened by the howlings of some Mauries..who were making the 'Tangie'... The high note of the 'Tangie' is like a dog Baying at the moon..there is the Tangie for the dead or sick—the 'Tangie' of welcome or after a long absence and the 'Tangie' at separation. **1857** HARPER *Lett. from NZ* 4 Nov. (1914) 43 His wife had lately died, and a number of Maori women..were holding a 'Tangi', or lamentation, to bewail her death. **1860** BUDDLE *Maori King Movement* 56 Here he recited a native tangi, see p. 17, of Sir George Grey's collection. ['Tera in tai o Ngamotu'] **1863** MANING *Old NZ* i 3 At least one Pakeha Maori shall raise the *tangi*; and with flint and shell as of old shall the women lament you. **1871** MONEY *Knocking About NZ* 57 This was the first occasion upon which I had ever heard the 'tangi', or melancholy wailing, which is performed by the women of the tribe on the departure or return, as well as on the death, of one of its members. **1888** PAYTON *Round About NZ* viii It is always the custom in New Zealand,

TANGI

especially in the North Island, to use Maori words frequently in referring to the natives and their doings; a colonist would no more dream of calling a Maori *whare* 'a house', or a *tangi* 'a ceremony of weeping' than he would of saluting Tawhias [*sic*] as King of New Zealand. **1898** Morris *Austral-English* 457 *Tangi, n.* (pronounced *Tang-y*) Maori word for a lamentation, a cry, or dirge. **1908** Baughan *Shingle-Short* 44 *Tangi* (*Tang-ee*): The Maori *wake*. Literally, 'a crying.' **c1920** Beattie *Trad. Lifeways Southern Maori* (1994) 91 Most New Zealanders are familiar with the 'tangi' of the Maori. In Murihiku the lamentation for the dead was called taki or takihaka. **1963** Pearson *Coal Flat* 43 I'm a full Maori and proud, too... Old Mum she meant I'm still a savage, that's what she meant. Just quietly, eh? *Haka* and *tangi*. **1978** Natusch *Acheron* 143 The coffin [was]..rowed across to a Maori burial ground [at Stewart Island]..then the women sat by the stream and began the low chanting..of the Southern taki. **1984** *NZ Times* 29 Jan. 1 As the march began, Eva Rickard [said]..'I had a big tangi (cry), didn't I?'

b. Funeral rites; the funeral ceremony. See also tangihanga.

1849 Power *Sketches in NZ* 28 *Aug.* 21*st* [1846].— All day long there had been a considerable howl over the dead and wounded, and tomorrow the bodies will be carried to Waikanahi to have a tangi there. **1882** Potts *Out in Open* 27 Of course it was not an unusual sight to witness the sorrowful tangi. **1904** *NZ Observer* 13 Aug. 3 The drunken debauchery at Maori tangis is much to be deplored. **1912** *Truth* 20 Apr. 4 Gone are the days when the Maori was summoned..to attend a tangi to the departed. **1938** Finlayson *Brown Man's Burden* (1973) 3 The time was opportune for another feast-day... There had not been a marriage..for months now; and among the long-lived little community, neither had the occasion for a tangi arisen. **1958** Ashton-Warner *Spinster* 152 I'll wash my grief away as the Maoris do after a tangi. [**1958** *Note*] Maori funeral. **1969** Baxter *Collected Poems* (1980) 448 Matiu Jackson fell from the face of the dam... They buried him without a tangi. **1973** Finlayson *Brown Man's Burden* 142 tangi: a wake, a ceremonial of mourning and farewell before burial. For an important person it may last two or three days. **1986** [see tangihanga].

2. A crying or weeping as a ceremony of welcome, or meeting.

1840 [see 1 a above]. **1849** Power *Sketches in NZ* 32 Muskets were laid aside, hands shaken, noses rubbed, news talked over; and, while the feast was preparing, a considerable majority sat down to indulge in a 'tangi', as an expression of their pleasure at meeting. **1858** Smith *Notes of a Journey* in Taylor *Early Travellers* (1959) 360 We..were enlivened by a good hour's *tangi* between our guide and the woman..in fact she had been in a state of *semi-tangi* ever since we arrived. **1864** Gorst *Maori King* 322 All the old women turned out to 'tangi' over him, according to the Maori fashion of saluting an old friend. [**1864** *Note*] The old native women always show affection by a sort of whimper, which is often prolonged for hours. This is called a 'tangi'. **1905** Baucke *White Man Treads* 278 Our college graduate arrives; the home-coming tangi and nose-greeting is over.

II. In non-Maori contexts. **3. a.** A wake, associated with (often undisciplined) eating and drinking. (See also quot. 1888 1 a above.)

[*Note*] By non-Maori speakers of English *tangi* is often perceived as the feast associated with the ceremony; in English, the noun in various senses is the main use.

1893 Alpers *College Rhymes* 36 There have been merry Irish wakes, and tangis running beer. **1936** Lambert *Pioneering Reminisc. Old Wairoa* 186 Now, there are races, shows,.. football.., dances, cinemas, *tangis*, *huis* and boxing. **1938** Hyde *Nor Yrs. Condemn* 121 [Masses of grub and long orations] were inevitable at their *tangis* and *huis*. The *tangi* was a funeral, the *hui* a feast; but there wasn't much difference.

b. A liquor party.

1904 *NZ Observer* 27 Aug. 7 Man-o'-war officers and men..held a 'tangi' on board last Saturday night over the ashes of the British team. **1917** 5 Sept. in Miller *Camps, Tracks & Trenches* (1939) 131 A barrel of beer arrived at the cookhouse after tea time, so the section settled down to a large tangi. I missed most of the tangi. **1926** Devanny *Butcher Shop* (1981) 61 They'll be having a tangi [after the wedding] in the evening, I understand. **1949** Partridge *Dict. Slang Addenda* 1194 *tangi*. n. and v... 'Now very commonly adopted here [in New Zealand] by the upper classes, especially as an equivalent of the outmoded 'beano'. E.g., Harold and I were on the tangi (or were tangi-ing) last night; or there is a big tangi on to-night,' Niall Alexander, letter of Oct. 22, 1939. **1952** Newton *High Country Journey* 132 I spent Christmas at the Bealey [hotel] for five consecutive years, and they were 'tangis' that are worth remembering. **1960** Rogers *Long White Cloud* 13 Hal's teeth flashed... 'Hislops are holding a *tangi* tonight. Tiare invited all of us... I'm taking Concertina Charlie over with me. Special invitation to bushwhackers.' **1972** Davin *Brides of Price* 170 They'd had a terrific tangi [*sc.* a student party], he said.

4. *transf.* and *fig.* A mourning ceremony; a loud crying out or wailing; a noisy disputation.

1874 Potts *On Recent Changes in Fauna* 9 These birds [*sc.* gulls]..when they meet together, after a few deep-toned barks or growls hold a regular 'tangi', and utter most dismal wails and yells. **1879** *Auckland Weekly News* 1 Feb. 21 During the whole night the poor wretch kept up a horrible 'tangi'. **1919** Mansfield *Letters* 22 Nov. (1993) III. 109 [Father] has been in bed..with a severe chill... We have had a rare tangi over this climate. **1930** Guthrie *NZ Memories* 88 Their two boys upon hearing of the projected departure had set up such a howling *tangi* (shedding tears into all his possessions, so Toby declared) that to silence them the Twins promised they should also go. **1959** Davin *No Remittance* 170 And if she was angry enough she'd go in and give him a tongue-lashing... Now it had never struck me that I might get involved in one of these tangis.

5. a. In the phr. **to hold a tangi**, to have a party or meeting, esp. a discussion or analysis after an event.

1941 Baker *NZ Slang* 56 When we refer to *holding a tangi* about a setback or problem we are putting another Maori term into colloquial use. **1946** Soljak *NZ* 116 New Zealand colloquialisms which are of Maori origin include:.. *hold a tangi:* to hold a feast, party or meeting *hold a tangi over*, a post-mortem meeting or discussion.

b. Special Comb. **tangi grant**, a state grant made to cover costs associated with a tangi.

1994 *Dominion* (Wellington) 24 Nov. 13 The [Social Welfare] department's refusal of Mr Paki's request for a $1000 tangi grant [for exhuming and re-burying his mother among her tribe] is under review.

tangi, *v.* [See *n.*]

1. *intr.* To weep over, to mourn (as part of a Maori funeral ceremony). Also occas. *trans.*

[**1815** Kendall *New Zealanders' First Book* 13 Tánge tangi [*sic*] To weep. **c1826–27** Boultbee *Journal* (1986) 112 cry—takki.] **1847** Angas *Savage Life* II. 47 She [a Maori woman] begged..that she might be permitted to *tangi* over it [a sketch].., saying, 'it was her brother and she must *tangi* till the tears came.' **1863** Maning *Old NZ* iv 74 He was..consoled by hundreds of friends who came..to condole and *tangi* with him. **1874** Norris *Amongst Maoris* 113 During the time that the

TANGIHANGA

women tangied, the men stood silent. **1924** *Otago Witness* (Dunedin) 22 July 71 A chief died in Te Karaka once, and they tangied for over a year on end. **1979** Webster *Rua* 24 Pemia went first, pulling the black shawl over her head and adjusting it before she began to cry out, tangi-ing towards the corpse for a few minutes and then getting closer, and crying out again. **1983** Hulme *Bone People* 375 I have seen dead people, but I have never seen someone die. What do you do: Hold their hand and let them get on with it? Pray? Tangi? **1990** *Te Karanga* Nov. 3 Shamed by his captivity, Te Rauparaha sat alone on the Otaki beach and tangi'd for two hours, looking out to sea.

2. *trans.* and *quasi-trans.* As **to tangi over** (a person, event, etc.), to weep over, to mourn; to greet with a tangi.

1844 Williams *Journal* 17 Oct. in Drummond *Married & Gone to NZ* (1960) 39 I..decided to send Joseph to Turanga. I could not think how I had consented and tangied over his preparations. **1885** 'K' *A Visit to Lake Rotoaira* 4 Here we stop for a few minutes to enable our native companion to be tangi'd over. **1937** Hyde *Wednesday's Children* 81 Whenever a notable Maori dies, the tribe turn out and *tangi* him, sometimes for days, feasting on dried shark, dried eel, roast pig, mussels and *kumaras*. **1972** *Marlborough Express* (Blenheim) 25 Sept. 6 The great-nephew of the chieftainess..followed Mrs Rongo into the tomb to tangi over the remains.

Hence **tangi-er**, a participant at, or performer of, a tangi; **tangi-ing** *vbl. n.*, the performing of a tangi.

c1875 Meredith *Adventuring in Maoriland* (1935) 111 A master of ceremonies was appointed whose principal duty was to see that the '**tangi-ers**' kept up to concert pitch. **1866** Hunt *Chatham Is.* 17 Here we stopped, and the canoes were drawn up in front of the *pa*, amidst much ***tangi-ing***, and shouts of '*Haeremai, haeremai, haeremai!*' **1879** Featon *Waikato War* 15 The night..was spent in speechifying, tangeying, going through the war dance. **1881** Campbell *Poenamo* 179 After each new arrival had performed the proper amount of tangi-ing wailing at the semi-circle they retired to feast, and to gossip.

tangiao, var. tangeao.

tangie, var. tangi.

tangihanga. Also **tangihana**. [Ma. /ˈtaŋihaŋa/ tangi + *-hanga*: Williams does not usu. record forms with nominalizing suffixes such as *-hanga*.] A Maori funeral and the ceremonies connected with it; the occasion of weeping, esp. at a funeral. Cf. tangi 1.

1846 Taylor *Journal* 2 July (ATLTS) IV. 70 The natives were busy preparing food for the expected Tangihana... [July 3] About ten the fleet of canoes containing the *tangihana* or crying party appeared in sight. **1856** Fitton *NZ* 106 A great meeting of natives at Te Wairoa on the occasion of a grand 'tangihana' for Apatri, an old chief drowned last year. **1916** *Wairarapa Daily Times* 2 Mar. 5 A large tangihana will be held at Papawai..in memory of the Hon. Mr. Wi Pere, M.L.C. **1948** Henderson *Taina* 181 All those taking part in the *tangihana* who were psychic or receptive hoped to catch this gift from the departing spirit. **1983** Hulme *Bone People* 238 She never went to the tangihanga. I used to go round feeling like some kind of leper for having a father so bad..that his own mother wouldn't go to his burying. **1986** *PSA Jrnl.* 18 June 6 [Heading] Tangihanga leave. The CSU [i.e. *Combined State Unions*] is to lodge a claim for the recognition of tangihanga leave. The claim is based on the belief that tangihanga is a grieving process, and that as a

tangio, var. TANGEAO.

tangiwai /'tæŋiwai/. Also **takiwai**, **tuggewai** (SI). [Ma. /'taŋiwai/: Williams 379 *Tangiwai..*A transparent variety of greenstone.] Bowenite, a hard translucent variety of serpentine, often regarded as a less useful form of greenstone. See also GREENSTONE.

1844 MONRO *Notes of a Journey* in Hocken *Contributions* (1898) 261 There are two kinds of greenstone, that which is commonly seen, and which is named the ponamoo, and another sort more glassy and transparent named tuggewai... The tuggewai is much softer, of a more transparent green, and divides easily into plates. **1868** PYKE *Province Otago* 39 Serpentine occurs in two forms—as common Serpentine.., and as noble Serpentine (*Tangiwai*) in thin veins associated with Jade. **1892** *TrNZI* XXIV. 481 With the exception of the *tangi-wai*, the various kinds of greenstone are all found in a restricted locality on the west coast of the South Island. **1911** *Encycl. Brit.* XV. 123 The green jade-like stone known in New Zealand as *tangiwai* is bowenite, a translucent serpentine with enclosures of magnesite. **1929** FIRTH *Primitive Econ. NZ Maori* 389 *Tangiwai* ('tear drop'), *bowenite*, a softer stone [than pounamu] of a clear pale green, with the appearance of drops of water in the texture, was less esteemed, though more beautiful in the European eyes. **1966** PHILLIPPS *Maori Life & Custom* 98 A material similar in appearance to greenstone, but known to the geologists as bowenite and to the Maori as tangiwai, is widely used in the same manner as greenstone. Some pieces are quite translucent while others show the characteristic yellow-brown colouration. **1978** NATUSCH *Acheron* 159 Greenstone was picked up at Anita bay—takiwai, not the esteemed pounamu. **1989** PARKINSON *Travelling Naturalist* 156 Piopiotahi in Milford Sound is the source of a soft, translucent stone known as tangiwai, which was prized, like greenstone, by the Maori.

tangle. [Cf. AND *tangle n. Obs.*, abbrev of US *tanglefoot* strong liquor.] In the phr. **to be on the tangle**, to be on the booze.

1966 NEWTON *Boss's Story* 118 Just at this time he'd got hold of some grog and was on the tangle.

tangle-fern: see FERN 2 (19).

taniko. [Ma. /'ta:niko/: Williams 377 *Tāniko..*Ornamental border of a mat.] An ornamental border or band, esp. of a cloak or mat. As an English word mainly in *attrib.* use, esp. in Comb. **taniko band** (see quots. 1969, 1982), **belt**, **border**, **work**.

1904 TREGEAR *Maori Race* 228 If men ever wove they confined their attention to the weaving of the ornamental borders (*taniko*) of mats. **1927** *NZ Tablet* (Dunedin) 21 Sept. 39 The girls try to keep up some of the Maori arts, such as weaving and doing Taniko. **1929** BUCK *Coming of Maori* 28 The *taniko* in the embroidered borders of cloaks, is from the point of technique the latest development in Maori weaving. **1933** in *Na To Hoa Aroha* (1988) III. 103 The garment was a parawai or kaitaka cloak with a taniko border. **1946** BEAGLEHOLE *Some Modern Maoris* 108 Some of the women..are skilled at taniko plaiting, but such work is hardly common enough to be called a folk art. **1969** BAXTER *Collected Poems* (1980) 449 And You are born again in a broken whare And Your Mother wears on her head the taniko band? **1992** GRACE *Cousins* 140 I've got an ordinary belt at the moment but have started making my taniko belt.

tani raha, var. TANEKAHA.

taniwha. Also early **taneewha**, **tanewa**, **tániwa**. [Ma. /'tanifa/: Williams 377 *Taniwha..1.* A fabulous monster living in rivers or lakes or the sea and also able to move through earth and air.] **a.** A legendary monster, usu. perceived as dwelling in water.

[**1820** LEE & KENDALL *NZ Gram. & Vocab.* 207 Tániwa, *s*. A sea monster so called.] **1822** KING in Elder *Marsden's Lieutenants* (1934) 255 The taneewha whom the natives say upsets their canoes and drowns them. **1832** WILLIAMS *Early Jrnls.* 28 Jan. (1961) 223 A son of old Tarea who had died long ago, and turned into a *Tanewa*, God of the Sea, had appeared to him. **1842** WADE *Journey in Nthn Is.* 34 One of our boatmen quickly repeated that the place was tapued for the tanewa (a water demon). 'And I wonder,' was his irreverent addition, 'what this same tanewa may be! An old pot leg, perhaps!' **1856** SHORTLAND *Traditions & Superstitions* 75 The creature spoken of in the traditions of the New Zealanders is..also sometimes called *Taniwha*, a word of indefinite signification, equivalent to the English monster. **1863** MANING *Old NZ* ii 32 Take care, the pakeha is *taniwha*! **c1875** MEREDITH *Adventuring in Maoriland* (1935) 42 The Maoris were frightened to go to this particular waterhole, because they alleged that a *taniwha* (a fabulous reptile) lived in it. **1881** NESFIELD *Chequered Career* 109 Whether the Taniwha was offended I do not know. **1896** *TrNZI* XXVIII. 88 Ten years ago a *taniwha* was captured in a lagoon near Hamilton..and exhibited in a butcher's shop, and it proved to be a *Stenorhynchus*. **1904** TREGEAR *Maori Race* 428 The Maoris had belief in the existence of huge monsters (*taniwha*) generally of saurian character and mostly water-dwellers. **1938** HYDE *Nor Yrs. Condemn* 136 There's a little old woman *taniwha*, who comes up behind the souls of the dead. **1946** BAXTER *Collected Poems* (1980) 45 We raced boats..Or swam..Growing cold in amber water, riding the logs Upstream, and waiting for the taniwha. **1966** SHARELL *The Tuatara, Lizards & Frogs of NZ* 59 There are many tales of giant, man-eating monsters, Taniwha, which are said to be covered with scales or with black hair and down. They lived in or near lakes and rivers or in caves. **1985** ORBELL *Natural World of the Maori* 126 Taniwha are dragons, creatures with great powers that can travel through the earth and the water.

b. *transf.* or *fig.* See quots.

1928 *NZ Free Lance* (Wellington) 26 Dec. 42 Such 'taniwhas' as this [*sc.* a 34lb eel] account for many of the fry liberated in the stream they inhabit. **1986** CARR *Diary Pig Hunter* 35 Going back a few years, I recall my first ever pig hunt. My brother-in-law had condescended to take a rather timid townie to tackle the taniwha. In my mind at least, the furtive inhabitants of the bush resembled monsters. **1986** *Listener* 1 Feb. 16 Off to Whangarei by car. Seems they've got this taniwha on their side. **1990** *Dominion* (Wellington) 28 Apr. 6 The tarseal vanished, and the road twitched like a taniwha.

taniwa, var. TANIWHA.

tank, *n.*[1] [Spec. uses of *tank* a (usu.) metal receptacle.]

1. An artificial receptacle often of galvanized iron or concrete, for storing water, significantly used mainly in special Comb. **tank stand**, a stand or support for such a receptacle; **tank water**, (usu.) rainwater collected in a tank, often as distinct from artesian water.

1902 *Brett's Colonists' Guide* 1146 **Tank Stands.**—Build tank stands with 6in. x 4in. uprights. **1960** HILLIARD *Maori Girl* 15 Washing in cold water with the basin on a box beside the tank-stand. **1986** MCCAULEY *Then Again* 116 And a handyperson is wanted to do tankstand repairs. **1994** LASENBY *Dead Man's Head* 38 Mr Tamihana chopped open the second tank... He jumped the gap to their other tank-stand. **1962** 13 July in Holcroft *Voice in Village* (1989) 24 It is one of the reasons why people who love good surroundings are prepared to rely on **tank water** and to live 20 miles out of town.

2. *transf.* [Cf. Brit. slang *tanked* drunk, *to tank up*, to drink heavily.] In the phr. **on the tank**, on the booze, on a spree.

1905 *Truth* 24 June 4 From morn to noon I scorned the world and drank... Miss LLoyd inquired, 'Pray are you on the roll?' 'No,' answered I, as best I could, 'the tank.' **1984** Apr. Heard at the Wellington Teachers' Club bar (Ed.). He's not here; he's out on the tank somewhere else.

Hence **tank-up** *n.*, a drinking session, a booze-up.

1959 SLATTER *Gun in My Hand* 181 Anyway, let's get crackin on our own tank-up. Over to the bar at the high port. I'm dry as a wooden god.

3. As **tank loaf**, a loaf baked in an enclosed cylindrical mould having corrugations at right angles to its length; often called, as elsewhere, a *concertina loaf*, occas. formerly **ring loaf** (see quot. 1935 below).

1934 *Bread Making NZ* [Caption 128f.] Tank Loaf. **1935** *Star Sun* (Christchurch) 7 Dec. 14 [Advt] Sunland's Many Varieties. Brought to you each day by the Sunland Bread Man... Long Tin..Concertina or Ring Loaf..Vienna..Barr[a]couta. **1993** *Foodtown Supermarket Advertising Catalogue* (Wellington) 26 July [7] Kahawai Tank. Serves 6. 1 Foodtown Wholemeal Tank Loaf. 1 cup milk. 400 g smoked fish, flaked [etc.].

tank, *n.*[2] [Spec. use of *tank* a constructed receptacle: AND 1950.]

1. A safe, esp. in the phr. **to blow a tank**, to blow open a safe with explosives.

1937 PARTRIDGE *Dict. Slang* 67 *blow a tank*. To dynamite a safe: post-G.W. New Zealand c[ant]. **1938** *Press* (Christchurch) (McNab Slang) 2 Apr. 18 [In local criminal slang] 'to blow a tank' is to break open a safe. **1941** BAKER *NZ Slang* 52 We have also acquired some underworld slang of our own: *blow a tank*, to break open a safe with explosive. **1953** *Truth* 1 Apr. 10 Currently being circulated in Auckland is the tale of the craftsman who, with 'jelly'..went off..to 'blow a tank'. **1963** *Truth* 21 May 19 Now, I'd been in the cooler for a tank job and my presence is not wanted on racetracks. a tank... a safe. **1963** *Dominion* (Wellington) 4 July 5 [A prison escaper speaks: 'I intended to] knock off a couple of tanks and shoot through.' **1980** MACKENZIE *While We Have Prisons* (Lag's Lexicon) 99 *tank* a safe.

2. Special Comb. **tank-artist** (see also ARTIST), **tankblower**, **tankman** [AND 1967], a professional safe-blower.

1967 SARGESON *Hangover* (1984) 87 Actually by profession he's a **tank-artist**... That's what they used to call a cracksman. **1953** HAMILTON *Till Human Voices Wake Us* 73 I'd back some of the **tankblowers** to get a smoke through a two foot wall. They're the best, the tankblowers, and the more boob they've done the better usually. **1978** *Dominion* (Wellington) 17 July 4 The old-style criminal activity such as 'breakmen' and '**tankmen**' blowing safes and so on is starting to go.

tankie. *WW2.* [f. *tank* + -IE.] A member of a military tank crew.

1944 FULLARTON *Troop Target* 30 Most of [the tanks] conked out so the tankies used them as pill-boxes. 1959 SLATTER *Gun in My Hand* 192 Chaps at work in grey jerseys or khaki drill shorts or wearing tankie berets. 1975 DAVIN *Breathing Spaces* 111 'Where else? The show's a wash-out. You tankies have let him run all over you.' The sergeant flushed. 1991 *Sunday Star* (Auckland) 3 Nov. A5 The men say they'll recall how they and their fellow 'tankies' fought their way through Italy.

tannergram. *Obs.* [f. *tanner* sixpence + *tele)-gram.*] (Cf. mod. *gorillagram, stripogram*). A sixpenny twelve-word telegram. Cf. DELAYED TELEGRAM.

1896 *Oamaru Mail* 13 June (Morris) Tannergrams is the somewhat apt designation which the new sixpenny telegrams have been christened in commercial vernacular. 1898 MORRIS *Austral-English* 457 *Tannergram, n.* very recent New Zealand slang. On 1st of June, 1896, the New Zealand Government reduced the price of telegrams to sixpence (slang, a 'tanner') for twelve words. 1941 BAKER *NZ Slang* 46 *Tannergram*, recall[s] the days when a twelve-word telegram might be sent for 6d.

taonga. Also **taoka** (SI), occas. **tonga.** [Ma. /'taoŋa/: Williams 381 *Taonga*..Property, anything highly prized.] As a *collective*, goods, valuables; treasure; as a *distributive*, in recent use, a treasured artifact (including such 'intellectual property' as language) or person.

[1820 LEE & KENDALL *NZ Gram. & Vocab.* 207 Táonga, *s.* Property procured by the spear, &c. 1843 DIEFFENBACH *Travels in NZ* II. 384 Taonga—treasure, property, goods.] 1863 MANING *Old NZ* i 6 The chief also, having made some enquiries..such as..if I had plenty of *taonga* (goods) on board..gave me a most sincere welcome. 1879 *TrNZI* XI. 3370 Old Hapuku..presented him with a great *taonga*... It is the skin of a very peculiar Huia. 1888 BULLER *Birds NZ* II. 127 The beautiful snow-white plumes from the back of this bird [kotuku] have always been greatly prized by the Maoris..and their ancient poetry abounds in references to this valued *taonga*. 1905 BAUCKE *White Man Treads* 113 [The Maori] understood that by signing [the Treaty of Waitangi] he incorporated himself into a community whose stores of taonga (goods), of guns, blankets, axes, rum, and others were illimitable. 1916 STALLWORTHY *Early N. Wairoa* 27 [The spars cut by Maori spar-contractors c1850] were paid for in tonga (that is, in goods). The tonga consisted of axes, tobacco, pipes, clothing, blankets, etc. 1927 DONNE *Maori Past & Present* 192 [The hei tiki] is..the most highly prized of all the *taonga* (treasure) of the present-day Maori. 1941 MYERS *Valiant Love* 21 She was to be married tomorrow..and the [Maori] children were laden with gifts. Each brought a little *taonga*; and into her apron, there fell the oddest assortment of things! 1986 *Evening Post* (Wellington) 21 June 27 Wellington Maori..say that the Treaty of Waitangi requires the State to uphold the greatest taonga (treasure) of all, the Maori language. 1989 HULME & MORRISON *Homeplaces* 119 Taoka, however precious to us, become forlorn junk, leftovers, on our deaths. 1991 *North & South* (Auckland) Dec. 2 With his [sc. Billy T. James's] death, Maoris lost a great taonga. All other New Zealanders lost one of our most loved cultural treasures. 1993 *Dominion* (Wellington) 14 May 12 Mr Fox lost everything, including..personal taonga associated with the house.

tao reka reka, var. TAUREKA.

Tapanui flu /'tæpəˌnuwi 'flu/. [f. *Tapanui* a town in Otago associated with an early outbreak.] A common name for a group of symptoms also called ME (Myalgic Encephalomyelitis) Syndrome or Post-viral Fatigue Syndrome (PVFS); and elsewhere *Egyptian flu, yuppie flu.*

1984 *Evening Post* (Wellington) 31 Mar. 4 About 1000 people in Otago have a virus illness with effects like having a recurring flu... The professor bases his comment on a survey of 70 sufferers from what was originally called Tapanui flu. 1984 *Listener* 19 May 21 That's Tapanui flu, Otago mystery disease, Royal Free disease, post-influenzal depression, myalgic encephalomyelitis, M.E... More than 60 symptoms have been noticed in the M.E. syndrome. They affect all parts of the body, from the head to the toes, and all body systems, including the brain. Myriad symptoms, masquerading as those of totally dissimilar conditions. No wonder both doctors and patients are confused. 1984 *Dominion* (Wellington) 19 Nov. 4 Sufferers of 'Tapanui flu' could be reacting to proliferation of man-made chemicals and drugs during the past 30 years, a seminar in Dunedin heard on Saturday. 1991 *Dominion* (Wellington) 25 May 6 Tapanui was the first town in New Zealand to identify an outbreak of ME in the late 1970s. The illness, dubbed Tapanui flu, tends to affect high achievers and has symptoms ranging from chronic tiredness to severe pain.

tap-a-tap, tappoo, tappy-tap(py), varr. TAPU.

tapu /'tʌpu/, /'tapu/, *a.* and *n.* Also with much variety of early form reflecting perceptions of Maori /p/ as English [b], the devoicing of /u/ final, with the occasional prefixing in early use of the Ma. article *he* as *(h)e-*, and a 'pidgin' reduplication in verbal forms: e.g. **etapoo, etaboo, tab(b)oo, tabu; tabba-tab, tabby-tabby, tap-a-tap, tappoo, tappy-tap(py),** etc. [Ma. /'tapu/: Williams 385 *Tapu. 1.* a. Under religious or superstitious restriction... *3.* Sacred (mod.). *4.* n. Ceremonial restriction, quality or condition of being subject to such a restriction... *taputapu,* n. *1.* Charm, incantation.]

[*Note*] The PPN form is *tapu* (Walsh & Biggs 109), appearing in most Polynesian languages as *tapu*. Cook first recorded the *taboo* form from Tongan (see OED). Modern New Zealand English uses *taboo* in the general English sense 'forbidden' by custom, morality, etc.; but usu. restricts *tapu* to reference to things Maori. In early recorded usage it is often difficult to separate the Maori-derived forms from those derived from another Polynesian language.

A. *adj.*

1. In Maori contexts in senses noted by Williams above. **a. taboo** forms.

1793 LIEUT.-GOV. KING *Journal* Nov. in McNab *Hist. Records* (1914) II. 548 At Tookes desire the poop was 'Etaboo', *i.e.*, all access to it forbidden by any other than the Old Chief. 1815 KENDALL Mar. in Elder *Marsden's Lieutenants* (1934) 77 *Atua* had then, as it was conceived, entered into him. Hence he was taboo himself, or a sacred person. 1817 NICHOLAS *NZ* I. 189 The word *taboo*, in the language of these people, means *sacred*. c1835 BOULTBEE *Journal* (1986) 78 I took occasion to remark that his illness proceeded from the vengeance of the Attooa (God) who was angry with him for stealing my book, which I told him was taboo (sacred or forbidden). 1898 REEVES *Long White Cloud* 56 Tapu (vulgarly Anglicized as taboo). 1911 *Truth* 29 Apr. 5 The Maoris told Sergeant Moore, if he once put the body in the shed it would be 'tabu', and never again would they use the shed.

b. tapu forms.

[1815 KENDALL *New Zealanders' First Book* 13 Táppoo Táppoo or Taboo táboo Sacred. 1820 LEE & KENDALL *NZ Gram. & Vocab.* 208 Tápu, *a.* Sacred; inviolable.] 1822 KING 15 Aug. in Elder *Marsden's Lieutenants* (1934) 255 They ascribe [the attack of the taniwha] to their taking some old thatch from a house which was *tapu* or sacred into their canoe to sit upon. 1842 BREMNER in *Lett. from Settlers* (1843) 74 All [women] are tattooed that are tap-a-tap or married. 1851 SHORTLAND *S. Dist. NZ* 49 The soil stained by the blood of their relations was 'tapu' or sacred. 1863 MANING *Old NZ* viii 137 This was an awkward state of things, but..I voted myself *tapu*, and kept clear of my friends till night. 1884 MARTIN *Our Maoris* 31 This little wood had been 'tapu' (sacred) in old days. 1905 BAUCKE *White Man Treads* (1928) 40 Everything connected with burial rites was tapu. All who handled the dead became tapu. 1938 HYDE *Nor Yrs. Condemn* 165 That's a *tapu* tree. The Maoris used it for drying the heads of the dead. 1946 *JPS* LV. 158 *tapu*, under religious or superstitious restriction; forbidden (verboten); sacred in a specialized meaning. 1951 HUNT *Confessions* 38 On the day appointed hundreds of Maoris..assembled at the tapu plot. 1985 HOWE 'Towards 'Taha Maori' in *English* (NZATE) 22 Tapu— this word is often translated as 'sacred' but like the concept 'noa', it means much more than this. The world was/is divided into things which are 'tapu' and things which are/were 'noa'.

2. In non-Maori contexts, found mainly in the orig. Maori sense of 'restricted', but occas. also in that of the general English *taboo* 'forbidden'.

1905 *Truth* 7 Oct. 4 There was a pretty hubbub in a toney Wellington hash-house last week..because there are not enough men to go round and the bachelors..are 'tapu' to the cousins, sisters, aunts of the proprietress. 1910 *Maoriland Worker* 15 Dec. 8 If you agree to publish letters on tabooed subjects, I suggest you should exercise a vigorous censorship... You must make it a condition that any letter admitted to your 'Tapu' column either has been refused by a paper..or..would be refused. 1927 GUTHRIE-SMITH *Birds* 109 [The pukekos] were..made to understand that the garden was tapu. 1938 HYDE *Godwits Fly* (1970) 126 Being in love was a sort of tapu state, full of constraints and superstitions, not quite real. 1990 CHAVASSE *Integrity* 14 Well, we talked about everything except our bush walk; that was tapu. [1990 *Note*] Sacred, impermissible.

B. *n.*

1. In Maori contexts in the senses noted in Williams, A above. **a. tapu** forms.

1793 *Lieut.-Gov. King to Dundas* 19 Nov. in McNab *Hist. Records* (1908) I. 172 Soon after seven other canoes..came on board, when the decks were so full of New Zealanders that it became necessary to keep them off the poop, which was effected by the ceremony of etapoo [i.e. forbidding all but the chief to come within the prescribed area]. 1835 YATE *NZ* (1970) 84 From their method of baptizing, we proceed to notice the 'tapus' of this people, with which every thing they do is more or less connected. This system of consecration— for this is the most frequent meaning of the term 'tapu'—has prevailed through all the islands of the South Seas; but no where to a greater extent than in New Zealand. 1845 WAKEFIELD *Adventure NZ* I. 25 We found no natives, the cove being under tapu, on account of its being a burial place of a daughter of Te Pehi. 1851 WILSON *NZ* 24 But chiefly thou, mysterious Tapū, From thy strange rites a hopeful sign we draw. 1863 MANING *Old NZ* viii 119 The original object of the ordinary *tapu* seems to have been the preservation of property. 1872 DOMETT *Ranolf & Amohia* 89 His sole 'tapu' a far securer guard Than lock and key of craftiest notch and ward. 1900 *Canterbury Old & New* 148 The institution of tapu was common to all Polynesians, and embraced quite a code of laws. **1926** COWAN *Travel in NZ* II. 8 Among the olden Maoris Nga-whatu were isles of *tapu* and dread. **1969** MASON *Awatea* (1978) 48 Jameson:.. Don't care how many tapus I break. **1971** *Listener* 29 Mar. 11 In old New Zealand there were two main causes of sickness and disease. One was the violation of tapu or a tapu place. **1990** *Dominion* (Wellington) 10 May 15 [Heading] Miners to rethink vote on tapu site. New Zealand Steel ironsands miners will meet today to reassess a decision to return to work despite a Maori tapu on the site near Glenbrook.

b. taboo forms.

1815 KENDALL 21 July in Elder *Marsden's Lieutenants* (1934) 86 He was tabooed, and attended by two priests and some other friends, who, notwithstanding his taboo, let me see him. **1819** MARSDEN *Lett. & Jrnls.* (1932) 212 On account of the taboo and for want of proper nourishment it was not possible for him [*sc.* Duaterra] to live. **1823** CRUISE *Journal* 21 Apr. (1957) 83 Even in the predatory excursions of the New Zealanders..the superstition of the tabboo has saved the koomeras from violation. **1834** MARKHAM *NZ* (1963) 46 But for Europeans who do not know the customs of Tabboo's [*sic*] it is rather dangerous. **1841** BIDWILL *Rambles in NZ* (1952) 118 The natives always require an additional consideration for taking off the 'taboo', or making 'noa' any places which may be included in a purchase. **1872** DOMETT *Ranolf & Amohia* 100 Avenge each minor breach of this taboo. **1889** KNOX *Boy Travellers* 232 [Mount Tarawera] is the burial-place of the Arawa tribe of Maoris and the dwelling-place of one of their tutelary gods, and for these double reasons it is held in rigid tabu.

2. In non-Maori contexts. Restriction.

1882 POTTS *Out in Open* 35 It is offered as a suggestion that considerable areas of land might be set aside and held under tapu as to dog and gun.

3. In special Comb. **tapu-lifting, tapu-removal**, applied *attrib.* to ceremonies or rituals for the removal of tapu.

1988 MIKAERE *Te Maiharoa* 41 Tapu-lifting ceremonies were also carried out to remove restrictions which had been imposed for specific purposes. *Ibid.* 43 Perhaps because St Paul had said that the old covenant was fulfilled in Christ, the tapu-removal ceremony was to be performed once only. **1995** *Dominion* (Wellington) 29 Mar. 3 A tapu-lifting service and a special ceremony were held at the campus [after a student fell to her death].

tapu, *v.* [See *a.* and *n.*]

[*Note*] The simple adjective was felt in Maori to be verbally aligned and was used as a verbal complement in copula-type constructions equivalent in form to an English passive use of *to be* (*become*) *tapued*, hence the frequency of this construction. The transitive verb was formed in Maori by prefixing the causative *whaka-*, hence *whakatapu*, to *tapu* (a person or thing): pidginized reduplications were early adopted by English speakers when using *tapu* in reference to things Maori: hence the early anglicizations *tabbatab, tabby tabby*.

1. To impose, or be subject to, a religious or ceremonial restriction; to render sacred. **a. tapu** forms.

1832 WILLIAMS *Early Jrnls.* 18 Jan. (1961) 220 The canoe was *Tapu*'d, having conveyed the body of..the principal chief. **1835** YATE *NZ* (1970) 85 A man who has touched a very young child, or has approached a corpse, or has rendered the last sad offices of friendship for a friend, is strictly tapued for several days. **1838** POLACK *NZ* I. 141 The whole of the prepared flax was tápued, and of course safe from depredation. **1851** *Lyttelton Times* 17 May 6 A principal chief, who it seems was *tapued*, or rendered sacred for the time, was knocked down and beaten by one of the Maori police. **1851** LUSH *Auckland Jrnls.* 16 Dec. (1971) 94 I saw..a native burial place which the Tryces had been obliged to fence in..so great is the natives' dread lest a spot they have *tapued* should be desecrated by man or beast. **1859** THOMSON *Story NZ* I. 153 At certain seasons places where shell-fish abounded were tapued.

b. taboo forms.

1815 MARSDEN *Lett. & Jrnls.* (1932) 100 Shunghee told me they were all tabooed and were prohibited from taking anything but water. **1820** McCRAE *Journal* (1928) 15 It was called Whari Taboo which means 'a sacred house' and in which it was usual to deposit whatever was tabooed. **1823** CRUISE *Journal* (1957) 207 He pulls a thread out of his mat, which he ties round it [*sc.* the desired article], remarking..that he has 'tabbooed' it. **1834** MARKHAM *NZ* (1963) 31 And every Log of Timber burned and then Tabbooed or Tappooed (rendered Sacred). **1841** HODGSKIN *Narr. Eight Months Sojourn NZ* 11 When land is purchased of the chiefs, it is tabooed to the buyer, the taboo being a religious ceremony performed by the chiefs. **1936** BEASLEY *Pioneering Days* 27 The chief 'tapued' (or to use the white man's pronunciation of the word 'tabooed') [the article].

c. Reduplicated forms, **tabbatab, tabie tabie,** etc.

1830 REV. LEIGH in McNab *Hist. Records* 4 Aug. (1908) I. 709 After they had done this [the native priest] assured them [the natives] he would come and *tabbatab* (consecrate) the temple, and put into it the *Atua* (with some potato), after which the *Atua* (their god) would be fed with the same. **1841** *NZ Jrnl.* II. 94 With the same ship that brought your letter, I have 'tabie tabied', that is, made sacred eighteen firkins, which will carry me on.

2. *trans.* To forbid, restrict, usu. with a Maori reference.

1856 CURR *Waste Lands of Wellington* 5 No wonder the subject is tabooed (or tapued) here [in Wellington]. **1863** MANING *Old NZ* viii 122 They were, in fact, as irreverent pakehas used to say, 'tabooed an inch thick', and as for the head chief, he was perfectly unapproachable. **1874** JOHNSTONE *Maoria* (preface) Perhaps the principal reason which has 'tapued' Maoria to the writer of fiction is the difficulty of depicting a Maori heroine.

tapued, *ppl. a.* Also **tabooed, taboo'd, tabu'd**; **untápued.** Mainly in *attrib.* use, put under ceremonial or ritual restriction; made sacred.

1801 *Miss. Jrnl. 'Royal Admiral'* (ATLMS) 25 Apr. Saw several tabu'd places, or sacred houses where the dead were deposited. **1815** KENDALL Mar. in Elder *Marsden's Lieutenants* (1934) 78 Whenever we come near a piece of tabooed ground and ask the reason why it is tabooed, if a person has been buried in it we always receive for an answer '*atua* lies there.' **1827** WILLIAMS *Early Jrnls.* 29 Jan. (1961) 41 Tikoki had stripped an Englishman..yesterday..out of revenge for some property of his, which had been stolen out of a *tapu*ed house. **1832** EARLE *NZ* 146 The white taboo'd day [*sc.* Sunday], when the packeahs (or white men) put on clean clothes and leave off work. **1838** POLACK *NZ* I. 159 I was nevertheless informed, it would be lawful to place a little tobacco in the canoe that was untápued. **1851** SHORTLAND *S. Dist. NZ* 63 About two hours after she retired to a house, in which had been hung up a tapued gun: this she loaded, and..discharged it. **1863** MANING *Old NZ* viii 134 In some cases he would be fed by another person, who..would manage to do it without touching the *tapu*'d individual. **1881** CAMPBELL *Poenamo* 171 On this fence were hung almost the whole of the deceased's personal effects..all destined to hang there forever, tabooed to the memory of the departed. **1930** GUTHRIE *NZ Memories* 80 Some of the settlers had unwittingly caused trouble by cutting down 'tapued' trees to build boats.

tapuing, *vbl. n.* Also **tabooing.** The imposition of tapu.

c1835 BOULTBEE *Journal* (1986) 88 This strange custom of tabooing I do not understand, further than it is a law strictly observed. **1846** MARJORIBANKS *Travels in NZ* 89 The power of 'tapuing' seems to be vested in the principal chief alone, and may be considered the most important bulwark of his authority. **1879** *Auckland Weekly News* 16 Aug. 14 The process of 'tabooing' the lands had caused the natives to meet and talk together. **1881** CAMPBELL *Poenamo* 293 When any article was fancied, the intending purchaser took a thumb from the fringe of his or her mat, and fastened it on to the chosen article. If the selector happened to be wearing a blanket or shirt or mat without a fringe, or wearing *nothing at all*, as was sometimes the case, from which any *tapu*-ing mark could be detached, then a neighbouring flax bush, or piece of flax from a potato kit, supplied the wherewithal to affix the *tapu*.

tar.

1. *Shearing. Obs.* **a.** Stockholm tar in its former use for disinfecting cuts made during shearing, branding, etc.: see quots. 1933; and 1 b 1989. Also the cry, **tar!**, a request from a shearer that tar be brought to treat a cut sheep. See also STOCKHOLM TAR.

1878 *Otago Witness* (Dunedin) 28 Sept. 3 Very little conversation goes on among the men in the two hours' work before breakfast. Only the cry of..'tar', when a sheep is cut. **1933** *Press* (Christchurch) (Acland Gloss.) 23 Dec. 15 *Tar*.—In the old days t[ar] was always put on sheep cut by the shears. Nowadays some carbolic dip, kerosene, or Condy's is used; but it is always called t[ar]. **1949** NEWTON *High Country Days* 197 Tar: In earlier days a pot of Stockholm tar was kept in shearing sheds. If sheep were cut during shearing, the cut was dabbed with tar. Today this has been mainly replaced by other antiseptics, but these are still referred to as 'tar'. If a shearer cuts a sheep he calls: 'Tar.' **1960** SCRYMGEOUR *Memories Maoriland* 49 [The shearing] went on but with..a rougher cut than was usual... The loppies galloping down the board, to the ever increasing cry of 'Tar'. **1974** ANDERSON *Mary-Lou* 57 'Tar' one yelled (when a sheep is cut a shearer calls for tar or sulphur to dab on the cut). **1981** PINNEY *Early N. Otago Runs* 229 A tarboy would disinfect cuts made by the shearers. He came at the cry of 'Tar'. For a bad cut the cry would be: 'Tar, and a bag for the guts'.

Hence **tar** *v. trans.*, to apply tar to wounds made by shearers or to sheep so wounded; **tarred** *ppl. a.*, of sheep so wounded (or wounds made by shearers), treated with tar.

1878 *Otago Witness* (Dunedin) 28 Sept. 3 In some sheds the managers insist on the cuts made in shearing being tarred, to prevent them being fly-blown; others use kerosene. **1906** *Awards, etc.* 625 [Otago Shearers Award] In case a shearer turns out a sheep badly cut or insufficiently tarred he shall at once sew and tar such wounds in his pen..but no shearer shall be required to tar his sheep in other cases.

b. Special Comb. **tar-boy** *hist.*, a shedhand who applied Stockholm tar to shearing cuts in response to a shearer's call; **tar-brand** *v. obs., trans.* **tar-mark** [OED *tar-mark v.* 4 b, 1825 and 1918], to identify ownership (of sheep, occas. of cattle) by branding the fleece (or hide) with tar; **tarstick,** a stick often with a cloth head attached used to dab tar on shearing cuts. See also TAR-POT 1.

1926 DEVANNY *Butcher Shop* (1981) 69 The shearer

TARA

yelled 'Tar!' The **tar-boy** rushed up and smeared hot tar upon the wound. **1933** *Press* (Christchurch) (Acland Gloss.) 23 Dec. 15 When he cuts a sheep, the shearer calls out '*T[ar]*, boy, *t[ar]* on the leg', and a fleecepicker or broomie dabs the disinfectant on with a *t[ar] stick* and puts it back in the *t[ar] pot*... I do not think a tarboy was ever employed specially in New Zealand sheds. **1968** *Straight Furrow* 21 Feb. 20 Tar-boy: The first-aid hand who in earlier days administered Stockholm tar to the wounds on badly shorn sheep. **1982** *Agric. Gloss.* (MAF) 60 *Tar-boy*: Person who walks the board where sheep are prone to fly strike and puts a smear of tar on the shearing cuts made in response to the shearers' call 'tar'. Tar is now replaced by modern antiseptics and fly repellants. **1989** *NZ Eng. Newsletter* III. 28 At one time in the big sheds when any shearer called 'tar' there was a tarboy to dab the cut, but now this is usually done by the nearest shedhand. **1878** ELWELL *Boy Colonists* 205 It took a good month to muster and **tar-brand** all the sheep. **1847** PHARAZYN *Journal* (ATLMS) 81 **Tar marked** B's and M's sheep. **1918** *Chron. NZEF* 30 Aug. 61 They had all been out together..with their cattle to Tutira, tar-marking and branding them. **1933 tarstick** [see above].

2. A shortened form of TARSEAL *n.* 1, tar-macadam as a roadway surface.

c**1939** A Havelock (Marlborough) rhyme about a child who persisted in riding his tricycle on the newly-sealed main road: Robin rode on the Havelock road, A motorist came from afar; Jim Lovell took his shovel and broom And scraped him off the tar. **1952** RHODES *Fly Away Peter* 99 'Follow the tar-sealed road as far as Darfield,' Mike Foster's instructions read... Off the tar now and on to shingle—and into clouds of dust.

3. *Offensive.* Special Comb. **tar-baby**, an offensive name for a Maori; **tar-brush**, esp. in the phr. **(to have) a touch of the tar-brush**, (to have or show) Maori (or any 'coloured') ancestry.

1959 SHADBOLT *New Zealanders* (1986) 140 Those **tar-babies** and that fellow in the sweater—if you ask me. **1935** GUTHRIE *Little Country* 390 Their progeny, whose brown skins betrayed a touch of the **tar-brush**. **1946** SARGESON *That Summer* 161 He was so dark in colouring that people said he had a touch of the tar-brush, but..he probably got his dark skin from Welsh blood. **1952** TAYLOR *Lore and History of the South Island Maori* 11 The Moriorís who went from the South Island to the Chatham Islands over 1000 years ago were actually more Polynesian than the Maori, so we must look further back than the days of Toi in New Zealand to pick up the Melynesian [*sic*] tar brush. **1970** DAVIN *Not Here, Not Now* 340 If he hadn't been an Irishman you'd think he had a touch of the tar-brush himself. **1985** O'SULLIVAN *Shuriken* 27 Suspect there might be a touch of the tarbrush there—just a smidgin, mind. **1994** LASENBY *Dead Man's Head* 15 Her mother had more than a touch of the tar brush, and the girl will end up going back to the mat, I'll be bound.

tara. [Ma. /ˈtara/, /taˈraːnui/, /taˈraːpuŋa/: Williams 386 *Tara* (iii)... *Sterna striata*, tern, and other species... *Tara iti S. nereis*...*tarā nui, Hydroprogne caspia;*..*tarā punga*..the red-billed gull: these names are frequently written as single words.]

1. As **tara**. Any of the various species of the genus *Sterna* (fam. Laridae), esp. *black-fronted tern* (TERN 2 (2)).

1838 POLACK *NZ* I. 112 Puhi..arranged the hair of the gentlemen, placing..the various feathers of the uia and tara, sea-fowl, that assisted the decoration. **1869** *TrNZI* I. (rev. edn.) 105 Sterna frontalis. Tara. Abundant. **1886** [see *sea-swallow* (SEA 1 b)]. **1898** MORRIS *Austral-English* 458 *Tara*... Maori name for the birds *Sterna caspia*..and *S. frontalis*..the Sea-Swallow, or *Tern*. **1904** [see TERN 2 (2)]. **1946** *JPS* LV. 158 *Tara*, a seabird (Sterna striata), white-fronted tern: several other birds are known as tara with suffix, as S. nereis, fairy tern, tara-iti; Hydroprogne caspia, Caspian tern, tara-nui; Larus novae hollandiae, red-billed gull, and L. bulleri, black-billed gull, tara-punga; but these are not so definitely used in general as to be adopted. **1952** RICHARDS *Chatham Is.* 82 Kahawai Bird. Sea Swallow, Tom Noddy. Tara. **1966** [see TERN 2 (5)]. **1986** HULME *Windeater* 10 Hey funny! think of all the taras in there! Tara tara tara!

2. As **tara-iti** [Ma. *iti* 'small'], any small tern but esp. the *fairy tern*, *Sterna nereis* (fam. Laridae), TERN 2 (4).

1873 BULLER *Birds NZ* 285 Sterna nereis. (Little White Tern.).. Tara-iti. **1946** [see 1 above]. **1955** [see TERN 2 (4)]. **1985** *Reader's Digest Book NZ Birds* 230 *Fairy Tern. Sterna nereis*... *Tara-iti.*

3. As **taranui** [Ma. *nui* 'large'], TERN 2 (3) (*Sterna caspia*).

1873 BULLER *Birds NZ* 279 Sterna caspia. (Caspian Tern.).. Tara-nui. **1904** HUTTON & DRUMMOND *Animals NZ* 223 The Caspian Tern.—Tara-nui. Hydroprogne caspia. **1947** POWELL *Native Animals NZ* 80 Caspian Tern.., Tara-nui..is a larger and more solidly built bird than the white fronted Terns. **1955**, [see TERN 2 (3)]. **1984** *Dominion* (Wellington) 3 Apr. 6 There are birds all round. Scolding taranui, and dotterels tiptoeing nimbly away over the wet grass of the air-strip. **1990** [see TERN 2 (3)].

4. As **tarapunga** *red-billed gull* (GULL 2 (3)).

1870 *TrNZI* II. 76 Larus scopulinus... Tara-punga. Little Gull. **1882** POTTS *Out in Open* 219 The little gull (*Larus Novae Hollandiae*), tara-punga..does the farmer 'yeoman's service' in clearing off caterpillars. **1947**, **1985** [see GULL 2 (3)].

taragehe, var. TARAKIHI.

tarahina. *Chatham Islands.* Also **tarahine**. [Not recorded by Williams: cf. Ma. *tara* spike, thorn; *hina* pale grey.] *Dracophyllum arboreum* (fam. Epacridaceae), a small tree of the Chatham Islands with long grass-like leaves clustered at the tips of branches.

1905 CHUDLEIGH *Diary* 20 Aug. (1950) 428 Huia was bare-footed and could not go on the hard bare points of Tarahine so she got on my back and I carried her with ease. **1984** HOLMES *Chatham Is.* 92 The most prolific trees were formerly *Dracophyllum arboreum* (Tarahina), broad-leaved Olearia and Corokias which grew in large areas.

taraide, var. TARAIRE.

taraire. Also with much variety of early form as **taraide, tarairi, tareeray, torairi, triddy**. [Ma. /taˈraire/: Williams 387 *Taraire*.] *Beilschmiedia tarairi* (fam. Lauraceae), a tall native forest tree of the northern North Island, distinguished by its large obovate leaves and purple fruits (see quot. 1902); also its wood. See also LAUREL b.

[**1820** LEE & KENDALL *NZ Gram. & Vocab.* 208 Táraide, *s*. A tree so called.] **1834** McDONNELL *Extracts Jrnl.* (1979) 19 A great variety of hard-wood grows at New Zealand, admirably adapted for the timbering of any sized ships; among them is the boridé, ráttár, táraidé..and many others. **1835** YATE *NZ* (1970) 42 Torairi (*Laurus macrophylla*)—This tree grows to..fifty to seventy feet... Its berries are black, exactly resembling the damson in size and appearance. **1843** ASHWORTH *Jrnl. Edward Ashworth* (ATLMS) mid-Dec. I picked up a fruit much resembling a plum, of which the rind only was soft & sweet tasted the inner part being wholly a stone, it is called tareeray. **1844** WILLIAMS *NZ Jrnl.* (1956) 105 The Taraire is a very common tree sometimes used for fencing. **1868** TAYLOR *Past & Present NZ* 205 Also the Tarairi, an ornamental but not valuable tree, only fit for firewood and charcoal. **1882** HAY *Brighter Britain* II. 196 The Taraire..is a huge and handsome tree. **1891** *NZ Country Journal* 201 His hearty salutation in its faultiness proved to be about on a par with 'rummy rum', 'triddy', and 'toot'. **1902** STEPHENS *Bulletin Reciter* (Satchell 'Ballad of Stuttering Jim') 97 And their water was most of it slime from the swamp, and the flesh of the taraire plum. **1910** COCKAYNE *NZ Plants & Their Story* 43 A kauri forest by no means consists of that tree alone, for the taraire..very handsome, with its rather large leaves..is often dominant. **1946** *JPS* LV. 146 *taraire*, a tree..no common name, and even the science name has here adopted the Maori name as the specific one. **1988** DAWSON *Forest Vines to Snow Tussocks* 100 North of 36° on the Northland Peninsula, taraire.., with its broad mesophyll leaves, dominates the canopy. **1992** SMITHYMAN *Auto/Biographies* 50 Soon he discovered factually the most part of the kauri forest is taraire but also..northern rata.

tara-iti: see TARA 2.

tarakia, var. TARAKIHI.

tarakihi /ˈterəˌki/, /ˌterəˈki/. Also **taragehe, tarakia, tára kíi, tarekihi, terakihi**; now commonly misspelt **teraki(hi)**; local Kaikoura abbrev. **tiki** (see quot. 1970). [Ma. /ˈtarakihi/: Williams 388 *Tarakihi*.]

1. *Nemadactylus macropterus* (fam. Cheilodactylidae), a commercially-important, silvery sea-fish banded behind the head with black, and valued for food and sport.

[**1820** LEE & KENDALL *NZ Gram. & Vocab.* 208 Tára kíi; A fish so called.] **1843** BEST *Journal* 24 Jan. (1966) 397 The Canoes..ran away..to the banks most frequented by the Taragehe. **1844** COLENSO *Excurs. Northern Is.* in Taylor *Early Travellers* (1959) 6 They preferred the flesh of the Tarakihi (a fish which migrates towards these coasts in great shoals in the summer). **1855** TAYLOR *Te Ika A Maui* 415 *Tarekihi*, a beautifully flat silvery fish, with a black spot on the back. **1866** HUNT *Chatham Is.* 32 At her feet would be laid the treasures of the deep, the finest *pawa*, or the fattest *tarakia*. **1872** HUTTON & HECTOR *Fishes NZ* 107 Tarakihi... This is a very common fish in the market. **1902** DRUMMOND & HUTTON *Nature in NZ* 71 The warehou, tarakihi, and gurnet are common in the north. **1918** *NZJST* I. 271 In the winter, spring and early summer months an abundance of tarakihi is constantly seen exposed for sale. **1927** SPEIGHT et al. *Nat. Hist. Canterbury* 199 The Terakihi..is said to be the commonest New Zealand food fish. c**1939** BASHAM *Aunt Daisy's Book of Recipes* 16 Curried Smoked Terakihi..cover with milk. Simmer until tender. Melt..butter with..currie powder, and cook... Add..flour..tomato soup powder... Serve with loose rice. **1956** GRAHAM *Treasury NZ Fishes* 252 Tarakihi are an all-round fish for consumption; they may be used for boiling, frying, baking and are an excellent food when smoked. **1970** SORENSEN *Nomenclature NZ Fish* 47 Tarakihi... Other common names: Tiki (Kaikoura). **1980** BAXTER *Collected Poems* 219 There's twenty other good men, Campbell, Have sold their crays and terakihi.

2. king tarakihi. [Poss. f. Three *Kings* Islands, the locality from which many of the fish are taken, influenced by the KING prefix suggesting superior size.] *Nemadactylus* sp. nova, a fish resembling a large tarakihi taken in northern waters often in the vicinity of Three Kings Islands.

1982 AYLING *Collins Guide* (1984) 242 In far northern waters, on rock pinnacles rising from deepwater on the continental slope, fishermen often catch fish they call king tarakihi that are large old tarakihi that may be over 60cm long and weigh..6kg. **1994** *Dominion* (Wellington) 6 [Caption] King–size specimen: The Museum of New Zealand's fish collection manager, Andrew Stewart, shows off a specimen of New Zealand's newest sea species, the king tarakihi... The fish sent in..had not all been caught off the Three Kings [Islands], the area that gives the fish its name.

tara kii, var. TARAKIHI.

taramea. Also **talamea, tallamaer.** [Ma. /'taramea/: Williams 388 *Taramea... Aciphylla squarrosa* and other species, spear-grass. The plant provided an exudation which was used as a scent, spoken of as *taramea* or *hinu taramea*.] SPANIARD 1; also its resinous gum once used as a scent by the Maori.

[**c1826–27** BOULTBEE *Journal* (1986) 109 gum—tallamàer] **1849** TORLESSE *Papers* (1958) 74 Thick growth of kalo and talamea near the bush which was..a black birch forest with an occasional red pine. **1851** SHORTLAND *S. Dist. NZ* 313 Taramea, a small stemless plant, having fleshy triangular leaves, terminating in a sharp point, all growing in a tuft from the level of the ground. From them the natives procure a scent. **1896** *TrNZI* XXVIII. 7 Several of the smaller species have become comparatively rare from the repeated burnings of the taramea. **c1920** BEATTIE *Trad. Lifeways Southern Maori* (1994) 63 Taramea was the commonest perfume prepared in Murihiku... This juice or gum [from the taramea plant] was mixed with woodhen oil (hinuweka) and was used to dress the hair and to rub on the body. **1946** *JPS* LV. 158 taramea, a plant..speargrass..a hill and mountain plant from whose spiny blades the Maori by heat and torsion extracted a valued scent. **1966** MEAD *Richard Taylor* 69 Crossing first a grassy plain filled with..taramea..and a pretty cream-coloured star flower. **1978** HAYES *Toss of Coin* 23 A land [at Hakataramea] of rolling downs with mile upon mile of golden tussock and yellow-green sharp thickets of speargrass or 'taramea'. **1988** MIKAERE *Te Maiharoa* 78 There was the little thing..playing about quite happily amongst the matagouri and the taramea.

taramoa, var. TATARAMOA.

Taranaki /tærə'næki:/, *n.* and *a.* [f. *Taranaki* (Ma. /'taranaki/) a provincial district in the east central NI well-known for its dairying, its name deriving from that of a distinctive local mountain (for a time called 'Egmont').]

A. *n.*

1. *Hist.* A Taranaki Maori.

1863 *Richmond-Atkinson Papers* (1960) II. 35 His 400 soldiers were *not* fired upon by the 100 or 150 hostile Taranakis. **1865** LEVY 25 Mar. in Williams *East Coast Hist. Records* (1932) 92 [The natives] again formed into double line,... the forty Taranaki's [*sic*] who had arrived with Patara continually running round them shouting.

2. In *ellipt.* use. **a.** TARANAKI GATE.

1948 FINLAYSON *Tidal Creek* 205 'What do you make of him?' says Uncle Ted when he's satisfied that the taranaki is up. **1986** RICHARDS *Off the Sheep's Back* 103 Most of the gateways were either 'Taranakis' or slip-rails.

b. As a euphemistic shortening of *Taranaki bullshit* (B 2 below).

1974 AVERY *The Ken Avery Songbook* [Title 'Tea at Te Kuiti'] Although it sounds like Taranaki, When I'm shooting at Wairakei I can always hit a geothermal boar. [1974 Note] NZ's polite version of the Germaine Greer 8 letter word [*sc.* bullshit].]

3. *Obs.* The name of a children's game.

1982 SUTTON-SMITH *Hist. Children's Play* 52 Occasionally unusual types of hiding games were played, for example All In or Taranaki. In this game there were two teams and a home base. One team, the 'outs', went and hid, while the home team, looked for the 'outs'. As soon as an 'in' player saw an 'out', he cried, 'All in for Tommy Jones' (the 'out' player who had been spotted). At that cry all the 'in' players raced for home, and all the 'out' players emerged from their hiding places and attempted to tag them. If all the 'in' players could get home without being tagged, then the person seen (Tommy Jones), was considered captured, and he had to come and sit in the home base.

B. *adj.*

1. Characteristic of or pertaining to the provincial district of Taranaki, or occas. to Taranaki Maori (see quots. 1860, 1986).

1859 THOMSON *Story NZ* II. 188 It is worthy of notice, that the colonists, soon after the formation of all the settlements, acquired distinguishing epithets; thus there was an Auckland cove, a Wellington swell, a Nelson snob, a Taranaki exquisite... These epithets, almost already forgotten, are too characteristic to be buried in oblivion. **1860** BUDDLE *Maori King Movement* 29 The Governor accepted the offer..and Teira laid at His Excellency's feet a *Parawai* (a Taranaki Mat) as a symbol that the offer was accepted. **1908** GORST *NZ Revisited* 46 A small quantity of what is known as 'Taranaki Steel' is made [from Taranaki ironsand], used chiefly for surgical instruments. **1916** COWAN *Bush Explorers* (VUWTS) 13 This Taranaki-bred pioneer has packed into his fifty years many a touch-and-go adventure. **1986** *Evening Post* (Wellington) 31 Oct. 6 The entrance to Government House, Wellington, will soon have a Taranaki flavour—carved pillars and woven mats made in the Te Atiawa (Taranaki) style. **1987** *Dominion* (Wellington) 28 Dec. 2 Mr Alley bought a Taranaki farm... He walked off the land in November 1926.

2. In special collocations often with jocular, ironic or depreciatory allusion to Taranaki's dairy-farming, its history of development from bush small-holdings and its impoverished state during the 1920s and 1930s, giving rise to a reputation for a provincial outlook and rough-and-ready, makeshift constructions or notions: **Taranaki bedside lamp,** see quot.; **Taranaki boasting, Taranaki bullshit,** excessive boasting (Taranaki province is famous for its dairy herds, hence the frequency of their droppings); **Taranaki cow,** a nondescript beast; **Taranaki drive,** a timber drive made to get a single hung tree (rather than the usual many) free of entanglement (cf. DRIVE *n.*² 2); **Taranaki lily,** see *renga lily* (LILY 2 (13)); **Taranaki salute,** see quot.; **Taranaki sunshine,** rain or drizzle; **Taranaki topdressing,** cow manure; **Taranaki violin,** a set of cowbells used as a crude musical instrument. See also TARANAKI GATE, TARANAKI WOOL.

1988 *Pacific Way* 41 [In an article *Feats of Clay,* the caption to a picture of a clay model of a rough woodblock with a crude 'gantry' bolted to it from which is hanging a light bulb, and entitled] *Taranaki Bedside Lamp* by Peter Lange. A humorous approach to the manipulation of clay. **1949** THE SARGE *Excuse My Feet* 8 **Taranaki boasting. 1941** St Patrick's College, Silverstream (Ed.); and also other secondary boarding schools (e.g. Nelson College, p.c. J.H. Brownlee). **Taranaki bullshit,** applied to skiting or boasting. **1968** SLATTER *Pagan Game* 69 At Maadi he had trained hard..had read all the good news about Hitler getting the shits, no Taranaki bullshit. **1941** BAKER *NZ Slang* 59 **Taranaki cow,** a nondescript beast of poor type. **1987** TV1 Country Calendar 6 Sept. West Coast bushmen call this a **Taranaki drive**—driving this tree onto that other one which is hung up there. I don't know where the word comes from. **1989** McGILL *Dinkum Kiwi Dict.* 99 *Taranaki drive* a technique used in bush felling whereby one tree is felled on to another, in order to lay a group of trees down. **1967** p.c. Les Cleveland -WW2 and later. **Taranaki salute**: a smart turn with an extra stamp to shake the cow shit off the heels. **1991** TV1 Network News 4 Jan. p.m. **Taranaki sunshine** came down with a vengeance in March. **1995** National Radio 'Country Saturday' rural programme. 3 Feb. We'll leave you with some taranaki sunshine. **1939** ALEXANDER in Partridge *Dict. Slang Addenda* 1195 *Taranaki top-dressing.* Cattle dung: New Zealand (mostly the South Island): C. 20. Niall Alexander, letter of Oct. 22, 1939... Taranaki Province is famous for its dairy cattle. 'Among the sheep-farming communities, Taranaki is usually referred to as a land of cows and cow cockies up to their knees in mud and cow dung' (N. Alexander, [1939]). **1941** BAKER *NZ Slang* 59 *Taranaki top dressing,* a facetious euphemism for cattle-dung. **1966** TURNER *Eng. Lang. Austral. & NZ* 31 [Baker] reports that in New Zealand cowdung is referred to as *Taranaki top dressing..*the cowyards of Taranaki [are] a stock joke for New Zealand humorists. **1953** *Evening Post* (Wellington) 13 July 6 A good-sized crowd saw items ranging from the usual tap-dancing..to a performance on the '**Taranaki Violin**', a set of cowbells manipulated by Mat Salmon.

Taranakian /,tærə'nækijən/. [f. *Taranaki* + *-an.*] Occas. **Taranakite** (see quot. 1874). A person born or resident in the provincial district of Taranaki.

1841 *Establishment of New Plymouth* (1940) 66 The last attack, and the most fatal one to the Taranakians, was made about seven years since. **1842** 16 Sept. in *Lett. from New Plymouth* (1968) 52 There were many miles of flax growing..more particularly about the Sugar-Loaves, which had once been in a state of cultivation by the [Maori] Taranakians. **1874** *Taranaki Herald* (New Plymouth) 28 Jan. in Swan *Hist. NZ Rugby Football* (1948) I. 23 The game was won by the 'Taranakites' getting three 'touch-downs', which counts a game. **1905** *Truth* 12 Aug. 1 The best thing that Taranakians can do.

Taranaki gate. With and without init. cap. **a.** [See comment at TARANAKI B 2.] A simple and rough (farm) gate usu. wire (often barbed) and batten but also of other materials, held shut by wire loops.

1937 SCOTT *Barbara Prospers* 27 She had the 'Taranaki' gate open in a twinkling. **1948** FINLAYSON *Tidal Creek* (1979) 142 'Mind you get the taranaki gate properly up,' Uncle Ted shouts after the reporter. **1952** NEWTON *High Country Journey* 15 In the saddle the track cut back through a 'Taranaki' gate, on to the Glen Lyon country again. **1964** BACON *Along the Road* 113 Those [gates] between the..paddocks were supreme examples of Taranaki gates, crazy contraptions of barbed wire and battens that wound and tangled themselves like devilish clocksprings. **1973** FERNANDEZ *Tussock Fever* 36 He dismounted to struggle with the flimsy barbed wire and manuka device. 'What the hell!.. A bloody Taranaki gate on a great place like this!' **1987** CHRISTIE *Candles & Canvas* 87 Christoffer looked at what he supposed was a gate. It was made of barbed wire and battens strung between two strainer posts to which it was tied with No 8 fencing wire. Being the first Taranaki gate he had encountered, he studied the primitive contraption with a puzzled frown, then realised it was simplicity itself. 'Just lift off this wire loop.' The gate sprang from his fingers, coiled into the air and collapsed in a tangled heap. **1991** *Metro* (Auckland) Sept. 159 These 22 yarns are wildly improbable, very funny and as New Zealand as a Taranaki gate.

b. *transf.* Any similarly makeshift mechanical or other arrangement.

1992 *Dominion* (Wellington) 5 Oct. 3 [Heading] Kiwis save yacht with Taranaki gate repairs... Yamaha was an unusual sight as it sailed into Gamagori, with the 18 metre boat looking more like a giant Optimist dinghy. 'You could say it's a bit of a Taranaki gate arrangement, but it worked very well,' Field said.

taranakite /ˌtærəˈnækaɪt/. [f. *Taranak*(i + the mineral formant *-ite*: OED 1866.] A hydrated basic phosphate of potassium (partly replaced by ammonium) and aluminium, found as a soft, whitish or gray clay-like substance composed of minute rhombohedral crystals.

1866 HECTOR & SKEY in *Rep. & Awards of Jurors NZ Exhib., 1865* 423 Taranakite, a new Phosphatic mineral..presented by H. Richmond... This singular mineral was mistaken for Wavellite. [**1883** *TrNZI* XV. 385 This mineral, which is double hydrous phosphate of alumina and potash, part of the alumina being replaced by ferrous oxide, was first discovered by H. Richmond, Esq., at the Sugar Loaves, Taranaki, where it occurs as thin seams which occupy fissures in trachytic rocks.] **1993** *DNZB* II. 467 Skey discovered and analysed the naturally occurring ferro-nickel alloy awaruite, from Westland, and a hydrated aluminium phosphate from New Plymouth, which he named taranakite.

Taranaki War(s). The land war or series of conflicts between Maori and Pakeha fought in the Taranaki province and region during the early 1860s. See quot. 1922. See also NEW ZEALAND WAR.

1860 BUDDLE *Maori King Movement* 6 Thus commenced the Native War at Taranaki, which has continued from that day [c1854] to this... [He] appears to have been one of the speakers who attended the meeting of chiefs at Wellington in April last—a meeting convened..for the purpose of hearing the views of the native chiefs in reference to the Taranaki War. **1866** *Canterbury Rhymes* 97 Ornamental scars Of blue, with red ones added in The Taranaki wars. **1879** *Auckland Weekly News Suppl.* 30 Aug. 1 That was just after the Taranaki war, and the colony was soon to enter upon the Waikato war. **1912** BOOTH *Five Years NZ* [introduction] In 1860 commenced the disastrous Taranaki war, which lasted some years. **1922** COWAN *NZ Wars* (1955) I. xvii The principal campaigns and expeditions dealt with in the History are as follows... (4) The first Taranaki War, 1860–61. (5) The second Taranaki War, 1863. **1935** *Star Sun* (Christchurch) 7 Dec. The Taranaki War was caused by some surveyors pegging out. **1966** *Encycl. NZ* II. 655 Land troubles, however, beset the Taranaki settlement almost from its beginning, the climax being reached in 1860 when the Taranaki War..broke out.

Taranaki wool. *Hist.* [A joc. allusion to the one-time commercial importance to small-farm dairying of fungus, as a cash-crop bringing a touch of pastoral affluence to an otherwise bare living.] *Jew's ear fungus* (FUNGUS 1 a, 2 (5)), once collected and dried for sale to Chinese merchants.

1899 *Taranaki Herald* (New Plymouth) 23 Mar. 3 The district has been invaded by a party of Parihaka Maoris..in pursuit of that commercially mysterious product known as fungus, and once hailed in derision 'Taranaki wool'. **1935** MAXWELL *Recollections* 165 For quite a long time it was known outside as 'The Land of Fungus', with good cause, for great quantities of fungus were collected there. It was spoken of as taranaki wool. **1947** KENNEDY *A Few Early Recollections* (ATLMS) 29 Small settlers [in the 1880s]..gathered fungus (Taranaki wool) from off dead Tawa and white wood trees. **1958** *NZJAg.* Apr. XCVI. 377 It is difficult to realise what fungus—commonly known as 'Taranaki wool'—meant to the pioneer dairyman in that province [in the 1880s]. **1966** *Encycl. NZ* I. 341 Between 1872 and 1882 more than 1,700 tons of this 'Taranaki wool' were exported from New Zealand... The sale of fungus saved many Taranaki dairy farmers, for they sold their butter to the local store in exchange for goods, and fungus was their only source of ready cash. **1978** [see FUNGUS 2 (5)]. **1987** PARKER *Not to Yield* 128 Chew Chong discovered [in the 1880s] that this fungus was considered a great delicacy by his countrymen. He paid 2d or 3d a pound for it. We called it 'Taranaki wool'.

taranga. [Ma. /ˈtaːraŋa/: Williams 388 *Tāranga*... 2. *Pimelea longifolia...* = *kōkōmākaka*.] *Pimelea longifolia* (fam. Thymelaeaceae), a native shrub having reddish-brown bark and flowerheads of fragrant whitish flowers; DAPHNE.

1906 CHEESEMAN *Manual NZ Flora* 609 *P[imelea] longifolia...* A small erect much-branched shrub 2–5 ft. high... *Taranga.* **1940** LAING & BLACKWELL *Plants NZ* 283 *Pimelea longifolia* (The Long-leaved Pimelea)... Maori name *Taranga*; an attractive plant, worth cultivation. **1961** [see DAPHNE].

taranui: see TARA 3.

tarapo. Also **tarepo**. [Ma. /taraˈpoː/ /tareˈpoː/: Williams 388 *Tarapō*... 1... ground parrot. *Ibid.* 391 *Tarepō*.] KAKAPO.

1839 TAYLOR *Journal* 26 Apr. (ATLTS) II. 117 There is a bird which abounds on the mount Ikorangi—The Tarapo—..which is the size of a turkey it is red has a beak like a parrot and is much prized as an article of food. **1886** *TrNZI* XVIII. 113 A large bird is mentioned..as having been killed by a settler's dogs; which bird, if I remember rightly, was supposed by the writer to be a Tarepo. **1985** *Reader's Digest Book NZ Birds* 242 *Kakapo... Tarapo, tarepo, owl parrot, ground parrot, night parrot.*

tarapunga: see TARA 4.

Tararua /ˌtærəˈruwə/. [f. the name of the *Tararua Range*, esp. as applied by the Tararua Tramping Club.] Special Comb. **Tararua biscuit**, see quot. 1988; **Tararua dishmop** *obs.*, *Raoulia tenuicaulis*, a creeping mat plant, one of the scabweeds; **Tararua stretcher**, a stretcher improvised from saplings, etc.

1982 BURTON *Two Hundred Yrs. NZ Food* 152 **Tararua Biscuits.** A New Zealand mountaineers' staple, one of these biscuits lies buried in the Himalayas, on the summit or Yerupaja Norte. **1983** *Listener* 4 June 55 Among the authentic local baking-terms the one I find most evocative is the Tararua biscuit. It comes in high-fibre high-calorie slabs... Two generations of Wellington dentists must have made a tidy income from its inroads. **1988** PICKERING *Hills* 71 A classic lunch food is the Tararua biscuit. This is any sort of home-baked biscuit baked out of a mixture of rolled oats, flour, golden syrup and other ingredients, and formed into a hard flat biscuit that acts as a base for butter and spreads. The principle of Tararua biscuits is that they serve as a replacement for bread on long trips. **1958** *Tararua* Sept. 30 It is unnecessary to write at length in general of New Zealand plant names, but mention may be made of the **Tararua dishmop** and the *mountain mop.* Apparently the first is given to *Raoulia tenuicaulis*, one of the scabweeds, by Heretaunga Tramping Club. No doubt plenty of Tararuas have used it with sand or ashes to clean out a billy, little thinking that their actions might inspire a new plant name, given to it by Canterbury mountaineers apparently, from the tufts of leaves at the ends of the branches. **1988** McGILL *Dict. Kiwi Slang* 112 Tararua dishmop *Raouli[a] tenuicaulis* plant, used by trampers to clean out pots and billies. **1949** *Tararua Tramper* Sept. 9 A spell was taken while the **'Tararua stretcher'** was prepared and the patient transferred from the improvised stretcher.

tarata. [Ma. /ˈtarata/: Williams 389 *Tarata*... a tree, the gum of which was used for scenting.]

1. *Pittosporum eugenioides* (fam. Pittosporaceae), a small tree with a whitish bark, having aromatic leaves and gum. See also LEMONWOOD, *white mapau* (MAPAU 2 (3) a), MAPLE, *orange-tree* (ORANGE 1 c), *turpentine tree* (TURPENTINE 1).

1855 *Richmond-Atkinson Papers* (1960) I. 183 Remember too that we are now on the road, all our lovely geranium and tarata fences are gone. **1869, 1889** [see MAPAU 2 (3) a]. **1890** *PWD Catalogue Timbers* (NZ & South Seas Exhib.) 15 Turpentine (tarata)..Timber white and elastic. **1907** LAING & BLACKWELL *Plants NZ* 194 *Pittosporum eugenioides* (The Lemonwood)... Maori name *Tarata.* (Name from *Eugenia*, a genus of myrtles.) **1946** *JPS* LV. 146 *Tarata*, a tree..lemonwood; gum used by the Maori for scenting oil. **1951** LEVY *Grasslands NZ* (1970) 87 Such species as lancewood, karamu, toro..mahoe, tarata, karo. **1987** EVANS *New Zealand in Flower* 58 Tarata has long been grown as an ornamental in New Zealand and Britain for its handsome evergreen foliage, fragrant flowers and rapid growth and hardiness.

2. *Obs.* Occas. KARO (*Pittosporum crassifolium*).

1853 HOOKER *II Flora Novae-Zelandiae I Flowering Plants* 23 Pittosporum *crassifolium...* Nat. name, 'Tarata'. **1867** HOCHSTETTER *NZ* 410 But Tarata is also the name of a tree, *Pittosporum crassifolium.* **1874** *TrNZI* VI. 48 *Pittosporum crassifolium*, sea-side tarata, or kihihi.—A fine shrub or small tree, sometimes attaining the height of twenty-five feet; common on sandy or rocky coasts, from the North Cape to Poverty Bay; produces seed freely; a most valuable plant.

Tarawera snowberry: see SNOWBERRY 1 b.

tar-brush: see TAR 3.

tarekihi, var. TARAKIHI.

tarepo, var. TARAPO.

tarnicar, var. TANEKAHA.

taro. Also early **tāllo, tarra(w), tarro**. [Ma. /ˈtaro/: Williams 391 *Taro* (i)... 1... a plant cultivated for food; OED 1769.] *Colocasia esculenta* (fam. Araceae), a robust perennial with large cordate-shaped leaves and a starchy tuber which is edible when cooked, introduced and cultivated by the early Maori, now naturalized in warm, damp places.

[*Note*] The *taro* now commonly sold by New Zealand greengrocers is imported from the Pacific Islands.

1769 MONKHOUSE 9 Oct. in Cook *Journals* (1955) I. 567 At dinner our prisoners..eat largely of bread: asked if it was Târo, a Species of Arum, the root of which we now learnt constituted a part of the food of these people. **1778** FORSTER *Observations* 284 A Comparative Table of the Various Languages in the Isles of the South-Sea... [English] *Arum esculentum* or *eddoes*... [New-Zealand] *Tāllo*. **1817** NICHOLAS *NZ* I. 351 In the plantations adjoining this village, I observed a plant very common in our West India settlements, where it is called *tacca*, and named by the natives of this island *tarro*. **1820** MARSDEN *Lett. & Jrnls.* Aug. (1932) 283 They..had prepared an immense quantity of common and sweet potatoes and some tarra, a root which they are very fond of, about the size of a small turnip. **1834** MARKHAM *NZ* (1963) 42 Indian Corn, potatoes and Cumeras or Sweet potatoes, Tarraw a kind of Yam. The Tarras comes I believe from the South sea Islands. **1844** COLENSO *Excurs. Northern Is.* in Taylor *Early Travellers* (1959) 6 Leaving Te Kawakawa..I passed by several of the Taro..plantations of those natives. **1872** DOMETT *Ranolf & Amohia* 374 May a bed, That late in such luxurious neatness spread, Of melon, maize and taro—now a wreck. **1881** CAMPBELL *Poenamo* 117 We all had a turn at the soup-making..some put *tarro*, a vegetable which is like a lump of flour, and if left long over the fire boils away by slow degrees and thickens the soup. **1905** BAUCKE *White Man Treads* 12 The staple cultivated foods of the ancient Maori, which could be preserved and stored until the next seasons crop came in, were: Kumara, taro, and hue. **1951** HUNT *Confessions* 24 Potatoes, kumeras, taros, and water melons were the chief crops. **1982** BURTON *Two Hundred Yrs. NZ Food* 4 Taro grows wild in a few places in the north, having escaped from old Maori gardens, and is not difficult to grow.

tarpaulin muster. [Transf. use of *tarpaulin muster* a seamen's collection of money, esp. to buy liquor: contributions were orig. thrown into a tarpaulin.] A collection or pooling of funds for a common purpose.

1905 BAUCKE *White Man Treads* 243 I am too poor, let us make a tarpaulin muster and call in a surveyor, that this distraction be ended. **1919** WAITE *New Zealanders at Gallipoli* 263 The crews had a 'tarpaulin muster', the result of which was a present for every man in the division of half a pound of tobacco, at a time when it was specially acceptable. **1937** *King Country Chronicle* 10 Dec. 4 The Waitomo County Council had a 'tarpaulin muster' for a staff presentation. **1955** *BJ Cameron Collection* (TS July) tarpaulin muster (n) A hand around of the hat. **1963** *People's Voice* 18 Sept. 5 If the good old fashion of a 'tarpaulin muster' among friends constitutes charity, well, what next? **1986** RICHARDS *Off the Sheep's Back* 47 Rather than cancel the trip..the females of the party decided to take up a 'tarpaulin muster' and by shedding the odd garment..they soon had Pud warm and dry and dressed in a new set of finery.

tar-pot.

1. *Shearing. Obs.* Formerly a pot of Stockholm tar (see TAR 1) for applying to shearing cuts.

c1927 SMITH *Sheep & Wool Industry* 73 Prior to the commencement of shearing the board is fitted with 'tar-pots', so called because in the early days tar was used to put on the cuts accidentally made by the shearers. **1933** [see TAR 1 a]. **1949** STRONACH in Woodhouse *Farm & Station Verse* (1950) 185 Get ready with tar-pot and brooms for the job, While the shearers stroll over to size up the mob. **1978** JARDINE *Shadows on Hill* 129 Tar in the tar pots..tally and wool books, all were ready. **1989** RICHARDS *Pioneer's Life* 45 Each stand had a tar pot nailed to the wall. The pot contained a layer of wool saturated in tar and a small flat piece of wood used for applying the tar to the cuts.

2. *Offensive.* A Maori. Also in the phr. **to hit the tarpot**, to be courting a Maori woman.

1949 SARGESON *I Saw in My Dream* (1974) 112 Wally said that if he was Mr Anderson he'd never let the tarpots inside the [shearing] shed with their lousy sheep. *Ibid.* 203 Jerry? he said, answering Mrs Brennan. Jerry's a local tarpot. Oh, a maori! Anna said. I love maoris. **1960** HILLIARD *Maori Girl* 258 I didn't know you were hitting the tar-pot these days. Arthur stood up, fists bunched. **1963** ADSETT *Magpie Sings* 88 Isabel did not say how, when at school, she had taken a leading part in the teasing of Maori kids by chanting 'Tar pot! Tar pot! Who fell in the tar pot!' **1964** MORRIESON *Came a Hot Friday* (1981) 130 He sniffed contemptuously. 'Tarpot bitch' he said as he went down the stairs. **1976** MORRIESON *Pallet on Floor* 49 'As if the crafty bitch would have it in her bag,' Miriam scoffed. 'All these tarpots are too cunning to turn their back on themselves. And half-castes are the worst of the lot.' **1992** [see MAORI BUG b].

tarra(w), tarro, varr. TARO.

tar-seal, *v.* [f. *tar n.* + *seal v.* to make impervious.] *trans.* To make (the surface of a road, path, area, etc.) impervious to water by applying tar-macadam.

1935 GUTHRIE *Little Country* (1937) 140 Councillor Whortle was hoping that the Mayor would support a motion..for tar-sealing the street in which he lived. **1983** LAMBERT *Illustr. Hist. of Taranaki* 106 The Waimate West County achieved a New Zealand first in roading, by tar-sealing roads in their area in 1914. **1984** BOYD *City of the Plains* 84 When more money became available, a start was made by forming and metalling Heretaunga Street and levelling and tar-sealing a footpath past the town hall.

Hence **tarsealer**, one employed tar-sealing roads.

1983 *Dominion* (Wellington) 6 May 10 [Heading] Tarsealer Hot on Speeding Drivers. Tarsealing gang foreman..had some harsh words for inconsiderate motorists.

tarseal, *n.* [See *v.*]

1. Tar-macadam; often as **the tarseal**, a road surfaced with tar-macadam. See also BITUMEN 1, SEAL *n.*², TAR 2.

1937 in Curnow *Collected Poems* (1974) 31 and a rubbery squeal tells the tarseal that a man goes home. **1959** SHADBOLT *New Zealanders* (1986) 88 Tar-seal gave way to a road of clay and pumice. **1963** BACON *In the Sticks* 172 As we came nearer to Estuarine, the roads improved, and once we were on the tarseal, my spirits rose. **1972** BAXTER *Collected Poems* (1980) 589 I want to go up the river road..Past Atene where the tarseal ends. **1974** SARGESON in *Islands* 7 92 On the suburban side of the Belt all to the eye was uniform and conforming, the latest tar-seal serving the affluent middle-class and their housing. **1988** HILL *More from Moaville* 28 30-odd wethers, all pattering..along the tarseal on their way from Wally's paddock. **1990** *Dominion* (Wellington) 28 Apr. 6 The tarseal vanished, and the road twitched like a taniwha.

2. *Special Comb.* **tarseal road**, a road surfaced with tar-macadam.

1987 KNOX *After Z-Hour* 110 There's a long, pot-holed tarseal road between the towns. **1990** *NZ Science Monthly* Aug. 4 An Auckland company is using microwave technology to repair tarseal roads.

tar-sealed, *ppl. a.* Surfaced with tar-macadam; often in the collocations **tar-sealed highway, road**, one so surfaced.

1914 in *Hist. N. Otago from 1853* (1978) 167 Those who have come into the world since that period have no idea of what was called a road in those days, especially those who ride leisurely over miles..of tar-sealed roads in a car, such as we have in our time. **1928** STAPLEDON *Tour Austral. & NZ* 12 The milk..is transported..by a well organized motor-lorry service, the point being that practically every mile of road so traversed is 'tar-sealed'. **1943** HISLOP *Pure Gold* 106 All the main thoroughfares there [in Central Otago] can compare very favourably with the up-to-date tar-sealed highways of today. **1957** FRAME *Owls Do Cry* (1967) 39 What better place to walk than a road, tarsealed with a white line running down the middle. **1962** GLOVER *Hot Water Sailor* (1981) 28 New Plymouth prided itself..at this time on having tar-sealed roads..practically the first in the Dominion. **1975** ANDERSON *Men of Milford Road* 163 There were however odd places where the road was tarsealed for a couple of hundred yards or so. **1984** MANTELL *Murder in Vain* 6 The white and blue mosaic-tiled frontage, together with the glowing flower boxes fencing the tar-sealed area to the right of the building added a touch of grace. **1988** HILL *More from Moaville* 25 The Moaville Co-Op Dairy Factory Milk tankers, which spend more of their time down metalled farm driveways than they do on the tarsealed roads.

tar-sealing, *vbl. n.* The surfacing of a road, path, area, etc. with tar-macadam; tar-macadam as such a surface. Also *attrib.*

1917 *Wanganui Herald* 9 Oct. 8 Shingle for tar-sealing has been started out for the road fronting Powdrell's property. **1918** *Hawera & Normanby Star* 9 July 5 As the question of tar-sealing versus tar-grouting is being considered, it seems from the result of the tar-sealing that a first-class coat will not be obtained until the third tarring... I have therefore to recommend tar-grouted metal as against sealing the surface... It would be nice to have the whole of the main road tarred, but this was going to take a lot of money. **1957** *Hurleyville School 65th Anniversary 1892–1957* 15 Who among the pupils of the time will ever forget the tar-sealing of the road. **1959** MIDDLETON *The Stone* 29 You chose a piece of footpath where there was no tar-sealing and looked for little round holes in the earth. **1959** SLATTER *Gun in My Hand* 37 I saw the England of working with a tamper..and wheeling barrows of chips for the tar-sealing gang I was on. **1964** *Evening Post* (Wellington) 10 Mar. 9 'Tarsealing originated in Taranaki,' said Mr Daniell... Traffic threw much of the metal off the roads and one day a New Plymouth councillor suggested that they 'seal the metal on the roads' with tar, and so 'tarsealing' was born. *Ibid.* 12 Mar. 14 Mr Daniells [*sic*] is 100 per cent wrong on the origin of the word 'tar-sealing' [*sic*]... The first length of tar sealing [*sic*] was done in Eltham at the insistence of the late C.A. Wilkinson, and it lasted for many, many years. **1968** HALL-JONES *Early Fiordland* 180 With the tarsealing of the road from Invercargill, Te Anau township surged ahead.

tart.

1. Occas. in children's use **jam-tart**. [AND 1892.] With a neutral connotation, a woman or girl; a girl-friend.

1905 *Truth* 19 Aug. 7 As he cavorted around the [ball-]room in a rather undignified manner, a number of the tarts turned their broad backs in his direction..and snubbed him vigorously. **1918** *Quick March* 1 Nov. 23 He'd only ninepence, and would like to treat His Sunday tart to sparkling 'fizz' and oysters. **a1927** ANTHONY *Me & Gus* (1977 Gus Tomlins) 82 Gus was busy flying all over Taranaki on his motor-bike, taking some red-headed tart to football matches and such like. **1930** *National Educ.* May 197 I heard one young fellow ask another to 'give him a knockdown to that tart in the green skirt'. I gathered he was asking for an introduction to a young lady. **1938** HYDE *Godwits Fly*

(1970) 129 Christ. Well, young or old, my old woman or the next, it's all the same in the finish. A tart's a tart. **1943** BENNETT *English in NZ* in *Amer. Speech* XVIII. 85 The slang word for girl is *tart*, used, for instance, by schoolboys; it has only lately begun to assume the derogatory sense it now has elsewhere. **1964** MORRIESON *Came a Hot Friday* (1981) 128 Every hump in town getting a skinful and us poor mugs..looking for some tart that's got herself lost. **1984** CAMPBELL *Island to Island* 89 Classrooms were smelly places in the thirties, especially on wet mornings when small boys and girls ('tarts' or 'jam tarts', we used to call them)..began to steam in their damp clothes.

2. With a belittling, dismissive or contemptuous connotation, esp. as **old tart**, an old woman, an 'old biddy'.

1905 *Truth* 26 Aug. 7 She was an old tart with a high-bridged smelling apparatus. **1948** BALLANTYNE *Cunninghams* (1976) 28 He felt crook again, remembered the old tart hitting him with a broom, the kids watching. **1949** SARGESON *I Saw in My Dream* (1974) 117 No, I don't know, but there's a yarn his father was a whaler that stayed out here and got in tow with some maori tart. **1961** CRUMP *Hang On a Minute Mate* 190 Y'see, we got a job working for an old tart who had a bit of a sheep- and cattle-run in the Hawke's Bay. **1974** MASON *Hand on Rail* (TS 1987) 20 Rangi: When I choose, Dad, I'll choose a *girl*, not a wahine! Hate that word! Makes me see fat slobbery old tarts waddling along the beach.

Hence **tart** *v. intr.*, to make up to or 'chase' girls.

1948 BALLANTYNE *Cunninghams* (1976) 32 'Where you been all this time?' his mother asked. 'Down the library,' he said. 'I bet he's been tarting,' Joy said.

tarwinie, var. TAUHINU.

tar-wood. *Obs*. A name for any of several small, resinous coniferous trees.

1. MANOAO 1.

1877 *TrNZI* IX. 390 This species is the yellow pine or tar-wood of the Otago settlers. **1889** KIRK *Forest Flora* 189 The manoao... The present species is termed 'yellow-pine' and 'tar-wood' by the Otago bushmen. **1898** MORRIS *Austral-English* 460 *Tar-wood, n.* name given by the Otago bushmen to the tree, *Da[c]rydium colensoi*.

2. Either of two subalpine shrubs *bog pine* (*Halocarpus bidwillii* PINE 2 (3)), or *pink pine* (*H. biformis* PINE 2 (10)).

1889 KIRK *Forest Flora* 57 In the Te Anau district, where this species [*sc. H. bidwillii*] is plentiful, it is termed 'bog-pine' or 'tar-wood' by the shepherds, but does not seem to have received a distinctive name elsewhere. **1890** [see PINE 2 (8) b]. **1906** CHEESEMAN *Manual NZ Flora* 653 Mountain districts... Yellow-pine; Tar-wood. **1908** AJHR C-11 35 *Dacrydium biforme*. Yellow-pine, tarwood. Sub. scrub, upper forest of S. and W.

tassel. *Shearing*. Usu. *pl*. The greasy locks of wool left on legs or brisket.

1955 BOWEN *Wool Away* 40 For the tassels right under the front leg, especially for young shearers, the fingers of the left hand stretch the skin bringing the tassels around so they are easier to cut off. *Ibid*. 157 Tassel. Greasy locks of wool left under the legs and brisket. **1965** *Listener* 26 Feb. 15 *Tassels*: Greasy locks of wool left on the legs or brisket.

Tassie, var. TASSY.

Tassy, *n*. and *a*. Also **Tassie**.

1. [f. *Tas*(mania + -IE: AND 1892.] Tasmania, or Tasmanian.

1905 *Truth* 2 Sept. 1 The Salvarmy in Tassy. **1914** PFAFF *Diggers' Story* 112 I remained in Tassy about four years, came back to Auckland,.. and then went back to Tassy. **1986** OWEN & PERKINS *Speaking for Ourselves* 63 A Tassie bushman once said to me, 'I don't like that new bloke the Old Man started.'.. The Tassie was dead serious.

2. As **the Tassy**. [f. *Tas*(man sea + -IE], the Tasman Sea.

1980 BALLANTYNE *Penfriend* 69 Saw him [a trans-Tasman yachtsman] a few days before he took on the Tassy.

tasty. Of cheddar cheese, relatively mature, as distinct from 'mild'. Also heard as **extra tasty**, quite mature.

1952 *Here & Now* Dec. 5 Cheese is bung. By long tradition this has been our tradition. Bung comes in two varieties—mild or tasty. Or soap and putty. **1993** *Salient* (Wellington) 9 Aug. 8 Place a slice of tasty cheddar cheese..on the dough.

tat, var. TATT.

tat-ta /'tæta/. In the phr. **to give** (one) **the tat-tas**, to make a dismissive gesture (towards a person); to give one 'the fingers'.

1968 SLATTER *Pagan Game* 161 He gives me the tat-tas so I hoed into him.

tataramoa. Also as a Ma. variant **taramoa**. [Ma. /ta:tara:'moa/: Williams 388 *Taramoa, tātarāmoa*... [*Rubus* spp.].] BUSH LAWYER *n.*[1]

1839 TAYLOR *Journal* 13 Apr. (ATLTS) II. 100 I also noticed a curious kind of rasp the *Tataramoa* which has a singular looking leaf. [1839 *Note*] This is the only thorn in New Zealand. **1843** DIEFFENBACH *Travels in NZ* I. 143 The primeval forest was often almost impenetrable, on account of..the thorns, tataramoa (rubus), of which several species are to be found. **1853** HOOKER *II Flora Novae-Zelandiae I Flowering Plants* 53 Rubus *australis*... Nat. name, 'Tataramoa'. **1866** ANGAS *Polynesia* 47 After passing through a dense forest, annoyed by the 'tataramoa', or New Zealand bramble..we descended a hill covered with exuberant vegetation. **1873** BULLER *Birds NZ* 154 I have sometimes found its crop provided with the ripe pulpy seed of the tataramoa (*Rubus australis*). **1887** *Auckland Weekly News* 17 Dec. 8 I ventured into the bramble, or tataramoa (tatter you more, rather). **1902** *Bulletin Reciter* (Satchell 'Ballad of Stuttering Jim') 97 For the bush was..sharp as a tiger's claw, With the supple-jack vines, and the saws and the spines of toi and tartara-moa. **1946** *JPS* LV. 158 *Tatarāmoa, tarāmoa*, a scrambling bramble (Rubus australis) bush-lawyer, wait-a-bit, both names inspired by the recurved prickles. **1963** KEENE *O Te Raki* 194 *tataramoa* or *taramoa*: climbing bramble of the bush known as 'bush lawyer'. **1982** Tātarāmoa [see BUSH LAWYER *n.*[1]].

tatare, tatatarra, varr. TOTARA.

tats, *n. pl*. [Fig. use of *tats* a set of dice: AND 1919.] *Pl*. A set of false teeth.

1906 *Truth* 28 July 1 Swift as a flash, she swished a stinging left hook on to his chin and—presto—his whole set of upper front 'tats' fell into his long beer!

tatt. *Prison slang*. Also **tat**. [f. *tatt*(oo.] A tattoo, esp. one amateurly applied (in prison, borstal, etc.). Also as a verb.

1981 HARRISON *Quiet Earth* 153 'You know what a boob tat is?'.. 'A tattoo done in jail. Or borstal. Or D.C..Detention Centre. Or remand home.' **1982** NEWBOLD *Big Huey* 255 Tatt (n) and (v) Tattoo. **1984** BEATON *Outside In* 101 Di: I can see it now. Ginny in a pretty pink dress... Tatts hidden under long sleeves. *Ibid*. 110 *tatt* tattoo, especially one applied in prison. **1989** HALEY *Transfer Station* 46 Her white arms were covered in scrawled tats. **1991** DUFF *One Night Out Stealing* 8 He thrust out a tat-covered arm and exposed forearm.

Tattersalls. Also **Tattersalls sweep**. [OED 1 c, 1895.] TATTS 1.

1904 COX *Diaries 1888–1925* (ATLMS) 12 Dec. Mrs Dumbleton won a prize in Tattersalls sweep and sent the whiskey for us. I worked all day and was in the Mill a good part of the time, I did some more tailing out and found the 12in x 1-1/2in very hard work. **1951** HUNT *Confessions* 67 She told me..that she didn't think she would invest in any of my 'tickets', as her brother had frequently taken tickets in 'Tattersall's' and had never got anything for his money. **1987** *Listener* 29 Aug. 46 I could see they wanted someone outside themselves to believe in rainbows and trout and pots of gold and that Southland would win the Ranfurly Shield..and Dad would win on his ticket to Tattersalls and take us all home to Galway.

tattoo. Also early **tatto, tattou, tattow, tatu**. [From Polynesian dialects (see OED), f. a root cognate with Ma. *tā*: Williams 354 *tā* 6. *v. cut. 7. tattoo*.] Applied (orig. by Cook) to the Maori moko (see MOKO *n.*[1] 1 a) in both verbal (esp. as *vbl. n*. **tattooing**) and nominal forms.

1769 COOK *Journals* 27 Nov. (1955) I. 213 Few of these people were tattow'd or mark'd in the face like those we have seen farther to the south, but several had their Backsides tattou'd much in the same manner as the Inhabitants of the Islands within the Tropics. **1778** FORSTER *Observations* 271 The custom of tattowing the faces in spirals and Various scrolls, which prevails in New-Zeeland. **1807** [see MOKO *n.*[1] 1 a]. **1815** KENDALL 23 July in Elder *Marsden's Lieutenants* (1934) 87 The face had been oiled in order to make the marks of the tattooing clear. **1819** MARSDEN *Lett. & Jrnls*. (1932) 172 The operation is too painful to bear the whole tattooing at one time. They appear to be several years before they are perfectly tattooed. **1832** *Deed* in McNab *Old Whaling Days* (1913) 90 In Witness whereof I have this day set my hand and Seal in my Tatto likeness Opposite. **1845** WAKEFIELD *Adventure NZ* II. 109 A very famous artist in tatu came with the party. **1851** [see MOKO *n.*[1] 1 a]. **1903** *TrNZI* XXXV. 240 They fell to pieces on being touched, as did most of the bone articles..excepting the uhis or tattooing adzes. **1940** [see MOKO *n.*[1] 1 b].

tattou, tattow, varr. TATTOO.

Tatts.

1. Usu. init. cap. [Abbrev. of 'Tattersall's Sweeps', the name of a lottery established in 1881 by George Adams (1839–1904), licensee of Tattersall's Hotel, Sydney: AND 1896.] **a.** Tattersall's sweep or lottery, esp. in the phr. **a ticket in Tatts**. See also CONSULTATION, HOBART.

1911 *Evening Post* (Wellington) 12 July 3 It did not require a tram ticket or an obsolete 31,456 in a Tatt's sweep to win admission. **1912** *NZ Free Lance* (Wellington) 9 June 1 [Caption] Thou shalt not, on the pain of death, buy a ticket in 'Tatts'. **1918** *Quick March* 1 July 10 Every member..will have the option of keeping a 'pub.' or running a 'Tatts' agency. **1922** *Ibid*. 10 Jan. 17 I was a tobacconist..with a side-line in 'Tatt's'. **1924** *Star* (Christchurch) 24 Dec. 6 At

Ashburton they arrested a man for drunkenness, and finding three tickets in 'Tatts' in his pocket, charged him with purchasing the tickets, and he was fined 20/-. **1938** HYDE *Nor Yrs. Condemn* 339 We struck a ticket in Tatt's, and we won't be needing it [*sc.* money]. **1943** HISLOP *Pure Gold* 54 [After a lucky escape] on arrival at Queenstown the few locals..came round advising me to take a ticket in 'Tatts'. **1951** FRAME *Lagoon* (1961) 52 He's going on and on to a prize in Tatts and a new home, flat-roofed with blinds down in the front room. **1960** HILLIARD *Maori Girl* 238 Was there any show of his busting out of it? None that he could see—unless he struck Tatts or a good double at the races. **1976** JOHNSTON *New Zealanders* 144 For a long time, purchase of tickets in overseas lotteries, particularly the Australian one called *Tatts*, was frequently indulged. **1988** JACKSON *Rainshadow* 105 When he failed..to win Tatts or the Art Union, he took it as a personal slight.

b. Comb. **Tatts** (occas. erron. **Tatt's**) **ticket**.
1938 *Tararua Tramper* May 4 Bike to Raumati, following wind both days, Tatts' ticket indicated. **1947** SMITH *N to Z* 17 Between [Australia and NZ] there is one of the roughest seas in the world but that has never stopped us importing Cabinet Ministers and Tatt's tickets. **1965** SARGESON *Memoirs of Peon* 197 Perhaps his share in some winning Tatts ticket. **1986** RICHARDS *Off the Sheep's Back* 25 Before leaving Raglan my mother had purchased a Tatt's lottery ticket.

2. *Christchurch*. Abbrev. of *Tattersall's Hotel*.
1959 SLATTER *Gun in My Hand* 26 See you in Tatts after the war the blokes used to say and I'll shout you a beer.

tatu, var. TATTOO.

taua. *Hist.* Also early **tear, tower**. [Ma. /ˈtaua/: Williams 397 *Taua* (i) Hostile expedition, army.] A Maori war-party; a hostile expedition. Cf. FIGHT.
1817 KENDALL 20 Feb. in Elder *Marsden's Lieutenants* (1934) 135 The tear departed from hence on the 25th. The whole consisted of about thirty canoes and eight hundred men. **1829** WILLIAMS *Early Jrnls.* 21 Apr. (1961) 153 At 9 o'clock Tohitapu with the *Taua* came round the point. **1834** MARKHAM *NZ* (1963) 53 Some Chiefs were going to get payment for the Coco again..or they would bring a Tower 'for[c]ible seizure'... [**1834** *Note*] Tower a foray for an Insult or Injury. E.M. **1845** SELWYN *Letter* in *NZ Part IV* (1847) 7 At Whanganui I found a 'taua' or fighting party of 170 natives headed by Te Heu Heu. **1863** MANING *Old NZ* iii 47 Altogether this *taua* is better armed and equipped than ordinary. **1883** DOMETT *Ranolf & Amohia* I. 140 Give up our wars—war-dances—*tauas*—taboo, Whence all our wealth, and power, and fame accrue. **1908** BAUGHAN *Shingle-Short* 54 The host of your *taua*, address'd as to fight! [**1908** *Note*] Taua (tahá-wah): A warrior band. **1921** GUTHRIE-SMITH *Tutira* (1926) 69 To rehabilitate the *mana* of Popoia two *tauas* or war-parties were sent forth from Mohaka. **1936** LAMBERT *Pioneering Reminisc. Old Wairoa* 149 A strong *taua* (war-party) was being organized. **1955** CAMPBELL *By Reef & Range* 15 Then he called in as ally the wily Waikato chief..with a taua of two hundred warriors. **1961** in Williams *Early Jrnls.* 20 And war parties immediately assembled for revenge. Henry Williams..went with the *taua*, and by his intervention peace was made.

taua taua, var. TAWATAWA.

tauhau, var. TAUHOU.

tauhinu /ˌtaˈwini/. Also with much variety of form as **taiwhenu, tarwinie, tauhinau, tauhine, tau ínu, tauwhinu, tawhina(u), tawhine, tawhini**. [Ma. /ˈtauhinu/: Williams 398 *Tauhinu*, n. *Pomaderris phylicaefolia*... *Tauhinu-korokio..Cassinia leptophylla*.]

1. *Cassinia leptophylla* (fam. Asteraceae), a native shrub-daisy of highly variable form, at one time treated as 5 separate species, common in shrubland and reverting grassland where it can be a troublesome weed; the tough many-branched bush is characterized by having young stems and the lower surface of leaves covered in dense soft white hairs sometimes overlain with yellowish glandular hairs, hence the other common names COTTONWOOD, *yellow scrub* (SCRUB *n*. 2 (2)).

[**1820** LEE & KENDALL *NZ Gram. & Vocab.* 210 Tau ínu; A shrub so called.] **1874** WILSON *Ena* 286 Tauhinau... A heath-like shrub, with numerous white flowers, sweet scented. **1874** *TrNZI* VI. 248 Most persons..visiting the Miramar Peninsula..will have noticed the increase..of an indigenous shrub commonly known by its native name as the Taiwhenu, or sea mat-cord, but known to botanists as *Cassinia leptophylla*. **1880** CRAWFORD *Recoll. of Travel* 263 [In the Marlborough Sounds] after..trees have been felled, fire will go through the forest and a scanty pasture be produced..until the shrub called *tauwhinu* take possession and smother the pasture. **1901** *TrNZI* XXXIII. 327 In the portion of Marlborough north of the Wairau River care is necessary to prevent the land..being overrun with brambles..manuka, tawhinau. **1902** LANCASTER in *Happy Endings* (1987) 110 She..helped him stalk..a stray wild pig through the manuka and tawhina scrub. **1927** DEVANNY *Old Savage* 47 Behind her, tough shrubs, tarwinie and gorse, mantled the terrace. **1940** STUDHOLME *Te Waimate* (1954) 247 There were dense thickets of manuka and other scrub, including tawhini. **1947** *Listener* 26 Dec. 12 [The Nelson farmer] called it tawhine, not tauhinu, and I've never heard a farmer call it anything else. **1958** *Tararua* Sept. 76 The river forced us to do much sidling through the tauhinau and matagouri and across a limestone face. **1967** HILGENDORF & CALDER *Weeds* 225 Tauhinu (*Cassinia leptophylla, C. vauvilliersii* and also *Senecio cassinioides*). **1973** MCCARTHY *Listen..!* 35 There were only four of us..to cut 100 acres of scrub, tauhine and ti-tree (manuka). **1975** DAVIES *Outback* 59 Well, we'd better get a bite to eat now, and then pull some tawhini. **1985** HUNT *I'm Ninety-five* 36 Gather round you chaps and I'll tell you a yarn When we pulled tawhina, down on Harris's farm.

2. Less freq. applied to *Pomaderris phylicifolia* (fam. Rhamnaceae), a small highly branched shrub of heath-like appearance found in open scrub and regenerating forest.
1867 HOOKER *Handbook* 768 Tauhinu... *Pomaderris ericifolia*. **1889** FEATON *Art Album NZ Flora* 91 *Pomaderris phylicifolia*... The 'Tauhinu'.- This small heath-like shrub is peculiar to the Northern Island, and grows abundantly in certain localities on dry fern hills. **1907** LAING & BLACKWELL *Plants NZ* 238 *Pomaderris phylicaefolia* (The Phylica-leaved Pomaderris). A strongly scented, heath-like shrub, which grows profusely amongst the small tea-tree, upon gum-lands... Maori name *Tauhinu*. **1910** COCKAYNE *NZ Plants & Their Story* 52 Smaller shrubs are *Pomaderris elliptica* (kumarahou), *P. phylicaefolia* (tauhinu). **1946** *JPS* LV. 158 *Tauhinu*, a troublesome scrub (Pomaderris Phylicaefolia). **1975** *Tane* 21 8 Rhamnaceae *Pomaderris phylicifolia* var. *ericifolia* tauhinu.

3. With a modifier: **Australian, golden**.

(1) **Australian tauhinu**. *Cassinia aculeata*, a small Australian tree with linear leaves, naturalized in northern New Zealand.
1969 *Standard Common Names Weeds* 3 *Australian tauhinu. Cassinia arctuata*.

(2) **golden tauhinu**. *Cassinia fulvida*. See also BOXWOOD.
1951 LEVY *Grasslands NZ* (1970) Appendix II 355 Golden tauhinu—*Cassinia fulvida*. **1969** *Standard Common Names Weeds* 29 Golden tauhinu. *Cassinia fulvida*. **1978** MOORE & IRWIN *Oxford Book NZ Plants* 138 The grey-leaved *C. leptophylla* so invaded neglected hill pastures (as about Wellington) that it, along with the golden tauhinu *C. fulvida*, was designated a 'scheduled noxious weed'.

tauhou. Also early **tauhau.** [f. Maori *tauhou* stranger: Ma. /ˈtauhou/: Williams 398 *Tauhōu, tauhou..2... Stranger... 3... blight-bird. (mod.)*] SILVEREYE, to the Maori a 'stranger' self-introduced from Australia in the early-mid 19th century.
1870 *TrNZI* II. 61 *Zosterops lateralis*... Tauhou. Blight-bird. **1882** HAY *Brighter Britain* II. 226 The Tauhau [*sic*]..is a beautiful little green bird, much like a wren. **1908** *TrNZI* XL. 489 Our little white-eye, or tauhou, 'the stranger', who came from Australia in 1856..is now as rare as he was common. **1922** *Auckland Weekly News* 9 Feb. 15 We named it blight-bird because of its useful habit of eating the woolly aphis on apple trees. The Maoris named it tau-hou, which means stranger. **1937** *NZ Railways Mag.* July 25 We have a flock of lively tauhou, the white-eye or silver-eye, pegging away at the scraps in tins hung on a tree for them. **1946** *JPS* LV. 159 *tauhou*, a wandering bird... Tauhou means stranger and this name was given by the Maori when the bird appeared, in 1856, in the central part of Newzealand. **1970** *Annot. Checklist Birds NZ* 69 *Z[osterops] lateralis lateralis*... Silvereye (*Tauhou*). **1989** PARKINSON *Travelling Naturalist* 72 The Maori, acknowledging it as a new arrival, called it tauhou, meaning 'stranger'.

tauinu, var. TAUHINU.

taumaka. [Ma. /ˈtaumaka/: Williams 399 *Taumaka... Acanthoclinus quadridactylus*, a fish. ([Ngai] Tahu.)] ROCKFISH (*Taumakoides* spp).
1927 PHILLIPPS *Bibliogr. NZ Fishes* (1971) 49 *Acanthoclinus quadridactylus* Taumaka. **1947, 1956** [see ROCKFISH]. **1966** DOOGUE & MORELAND *Sea Anglers' Guide* 283 Rockfish... A voracious predator at night... rock cod, butterfish; taumaka. **1987** POWELL *Native Animals NZ* 64 Rockfish (Taumaka)... A small brownish-olive fish, 150–200 mm long... It is an ugly fish.

taupata /ˈtæupətə/. [Ma. /ˈtaupata/: Williams 401 *Taupata... Coprosma repens*.] *Coprosma repens* (fam. Rubiaceae), a native coastal and near-coastal shrub or small tree, having glossy leaves, widely planted as an ornamental. See also ANGIANGI, COPROSMA, *yellow-wood* (YELLOW 2).
1867 HOOKER *Handbook* 768 Taupata, Col[enso]. *Coprosma retusa*. **1868** TAYLOR *Past & Present NZ* 225 The Taupata, which having a fine bright leaf is a very ornamental tree. **1889** KIRK *Forest Flora* 109 *Coprosma Baueriana* is a handsome evergreen shrub or small tree exclusively restricted to maritime situations... I have heard it termed 'taupata' by Maoris living at Rotorua and in the Wellington District. **1907** [see LOOKING-GLASS PLANT]. **1924** *NZJST* VII. 185 The plant which is dominant and chiefly gives character to these island shrubberies is *Coprosma Baueri*, commonly known as the taupata. **1946** *JPS* LV. 159 *Taupata*, a tree..with dark green leaves shining as if varnished; much used for hedges, cutting well till in the course of years it grows too woody. **1965** GILLHAM *Naturalist in NZ* 267 There was the shiny-leaved taupata, which I heard referred to as mirror plant. **1988** JACKSON

TAUPO SNOWBERRY

Rainshadow 98 An arthritic taupata hedge sheltered it from the sea.

Taupo snowberry: see SNOWBERRY 1 b.

Tauranga /ˈtaʊrʌŋə/, /ˌtaʊˈrɒŋə/. [f. the name *Tauranga*, a port in the Bay of Plenty.]

1. *Obs.* A small, 2.135 m (7-foot), centreboard sailing boat built for competitive sailing, usu. now known as 'P-class' (from the initial of the Ponsonby Cruising Club which established the class in Auckland in 1943).

1925 *Star* (Auckland) 24 Apr. 18 A correspondent asks where he can obtain plans of the Tauranga 7′6″ class of sailing boat. The originator of the class was Mr. H.A. Highet, now of Tauranga, but formerly of Whangarei and originally from Wellington... The class now numbers 15 or 16 on Tauranga Harbour. c1938 Marlborough (Ed.). *Tauranga.* The name of a seven-foot sailing boat with a mainsail but no jib. 1944 CARTER *Little Ships* 132 What is often referred to as the 'Baby Class' of New Zealand, the 7-foot [2.135 m] Tauranga boats, also owe their existence to the efforts of a Wellington yachtsman, Mr. M.H.A. Highet, who was the originator of the class. These tiny yachts, which are built on the chine principle, have a beam of 3.6 feet [1.098 m], and carry a single sail of the gunter type. 1955 *BJ Cameron Collection* (TS July) Tauranga (n) A type of yacht. 1978 TITCHENER *Little Ships of NZ* 73 The P-class is also known as the Tauranga class, because Mr Highet moved from Wellington soon after designing the yacht. The first yachts from this design sailed on the Tauranga Harbour. 1989 *NZ Herald* (Auckland) 6 Feb. sect. i 1 Mr Highet designed his prototype of the P-class yacht about 70 years ago. It had its first outing at Onerahi Bay, Whangarei, on New Year's Day, 1920... In 1924 the boat was officially recognised in the Tauranga seven-foot one-design class.

2. Special Comb. **Tauranga disease (sheep-disease), Tauranga sickness** *obs.*, BUSH SICKNESS a.

1892 *TrNZI* XXIV. 626 Take for instance the 'Tauranga sheep-disease', as it is called: professors of different colleges are sent for, to investigate it. 1899 *Annual Rep. Dept Agric. VII.* 87 [Heading] 'Tauranga' or 'Bush Disease'. This peculiar wasting disease, which is confined to the tract of land lying in the vicinity of Tauranga, and extending from there to Rotorua and Lichfield, was made the subject of an investigation..three years ago... It appears that both sheep and cattle will do well and put on condition for the first few months after being placed on this diseased country, but as time goes on a gradual wasting sets in, which ends in death if they are not removed to another district. 1916 *Auckland Weekly News* 1 June 57 The controversy which has raged..over what is called 'Bush Sickness' in the Mamaku district, and 'Tauranga disease' in the Bay of Plenty, has undoubtedly done much to retard settlement. 1927–28 *TrNZI* LVIII. 537 The study of the deficiency disease for many years known as 'bush sickness', 'bush disease', 'Tauranga disease', or 'the skinnies', and now definitely and officially known as 'iron starvation' was commenced by the writer in 1910. 1961 *Merriam-Webster Third Internat. Dict.* 2344 tauranga n -s [Maori] *NewZeal* : Bush sickness.

taurekareka. The spelling **taureka** has equal standing. Also with much variety of early form as **táo réka réka, taurikarike, towrikka, towra caracca**. [Ma. /tauˈrekareka/: Williams 402 *Taureka, taurekareka..* 1. Captive taken in war, slave.] A slave.

[1820 LEE & KENDALL *NZ Gram. & Vocab.* 207 Táo réka réka, *s.* A slave.] 1823 CRUISE *Journal* (1957) 198 They expressed their astonishment that we could so far forget ourselves as to sit down and eat with a towra caracca, or prisoner of war; and this degrading appellation was universally applied to the American gentleman as long as he remained amongst us. c1835 BOULTBEE *Journal* (1986) 79 Price..told the natives, Capt. K. was a towrikka, or cookie, and that he was of no note etc. 1843 DIEFFENBACH *Travels in NZ* II. 113 The rest of the men are either rangatira, free men, or tau-reka-reka, slaves... The slaves, tau-reka-reka, are the prisoners of war, male or female, and such of their children as are born in slavery. 1879 *Auckland Weekly News* 5 July 15 He answered, 'I am a Ngapuhi chief, and a *rangatira*;' 'but I found out,' says Mrs. Moran bitterly, 'on getting to the Bay that he was only a *taurekareka*.' 1900 *Auckland Weekly News Xmas Number* 17 They all jabbered and cut capers when they knew the taurikarike pakeha had mated up with the daughter of such a rangitira. 1901 GRACE *Tales of Dying Race* 88 You are a low-bred set of men, *taurekareka*, all of you. 1937 MARSH *Vintage Murder* 232 I should have forgotten that an *ariki* does not lay hands on a *taurekareka*. 1948 HENDERSON *Taina* 26 The *tohunga* made it..*tapu*, so that the *kukis, taurekarekas, tutuas*, and other varieties of slaves..would be afraid to meddle. 1986 HULME *Windeater* 115 You lost your good temper and yelled at me all kinds of rude names and swearing, taureka and sloven, 'pokokohua and bitch.

tau-reka-reka, taurikarike, varr. TAUREKA.

tauwhinu, var. TAUHINU.

tavai poe-namoo, var. TE WAIPOUNAMU.

tavern. In modern (post-1962) New Zealand use, a place licensed for the sale and consumption of alcoholic liquor but not obliged to provide sleeping accommodation for the travelling public.

1962 *Sale of Liquor Act* s75(4) On determining whether the issue of any hotel or tavern premises licence is necessary or desirable, it shall be the object of the Commission, as far as practicable, to secure the provision of reasonable and adequate accommodation, to secure the provision of reasonable and adequate facilities so that those who wish to do so may drink in reasonable comfort. 1989 *Press* (Christchurch) 13 May 14 He accompanied Tauriki..to two taverns... They consumed beer and talked.

tawa /ˈtawə/, /ˈtæu(w)ə/.

1. Also occas. early **tawha, towa, tower**. [Ma. /ˈtawa/: Williams 405 *Tawa*..a tree; also the fruit.] *Beilschmiedia tawa* (fam. Lauraceae), a common timber tree of lowland forest in the North Island and Marlborough Sounds, having willow-like leaves and large purple fruits; also its timber and fruit (see *tawa-berry* 2 below). See also LAUREL b.

[1820 LEE & KENDALL *NZ Gram. & Vocab.* 209 Taua, *s.*.a tree so called.] 1835 YATE *NZ* (1970) 42 Tawa..is a frequenter of damp and deeply-shaded woods, with leaf and branches similar to those of the Mairi-tree. 1838 POLACK *NZ* II. 396 Towá, (*laurus Australis*) is a useful timber for boarding the interior of houses. 1841 BIDWILL *Rambles in NZ* (1952) 35 The trees were chiefly the Towa, a tree strongly resembling the beech in leaf and general appearance, and bearing a fruit about the size and colour of a damson. 1849 ALLOM *Letter* in Earp *Handbook* (1852) 129 The fruit of the *tawa* resembles a prune damson. 1865 HAYNES *Ramble in NZ Bush* 18 Tower trees (so called from their towering above all the other trees of the bush). 1882 POTTS *Out in Open* 18 Tawha—the prepared berries of a very common forest tree in many parts of the North Island. 1890 *PWD Catalogue Timbers* (NZ & South Seas Exhib.) 14 Tawa..The wood is white, straight grained, and easily split. 1946 *JPS* LV. 146 *Tawa*, a tree..; from its straight-grained and light wood the Maori made his long bird-spears. 1966 *Encycl. NZ* III. 350 Tawa occurs in lowland to lower montane forest from almost the North Cape to the Seaward Kaikoura Range in the South Island.

2. Special Comb. **tawa-berry**, the edible fruit of the tawa consisting of purple flesh or rind covering a large kernel.

1842 HEAPHY *NZ* 43 The *Towa* and the Kraka berries also yield an useful oil. 1843 SELWYN in *NZ Part II* (Church in the Colonies VII) (1845) 31 Among these..pools..the natives are sitting up to their breasts in hot water, shelling Tawa berries. 1858 SMITH *Notes of Journey* in Taylor *Early Travellers* (1959) 374 Scattered about [at Rotomahana]..are..large square slabs of white stone, laid..over hot springs, and..used..for drying tawa berries. 1982 BURTON *Two Hundred Yrs. NZ Food* 6 Tawa..berries have a non-poisonous kernel. If eaten raw, however, the kernels have a distinctive, turpentine-like flavour which is unpleasant to most palates.

tawaapou, var. TAWAPOU.

tawai. The spelling **tawhai** has equal standing. [Ma. /ˈtawai/ /ˈtafai/: Williams 406 *Tawai, tawhai*... General names for *Nothofagus menziesii* and other beech-tree species and their hybrids.]

1. A general name for various species of *Nothofagus*, the native beech. See also BEECH, BIRCH. **a.** As **tawai**.

1841 *NZ Jrnl.* II. 51 The forest is again formed by one sort of trees, the tawai, or black birch as it is called. 1853 HOOKER *II Flora Novae-Zelandiae I Flowering Plants* 229 *Fagus fusca*... Hab. Mountains of the Northern Island... Common in the Middle Island... Nat. name, 'Tawai'. 1861 HAAST *Rep. Topogr. Explor. Nelson* 11 I had noticed..that the vegetation began to change; totara, kahi-katea..were intermixed with the tawai (black birch). 1873 *Catalogue of the Vienna Exhibition* in Morris *Austral-English* (1898) 462 Tawai. Large and durable timber, used for [railway] sleepers.

b. As **tawhai**.

1867 HOOKER *Handbook* 768 Tawhai, Col[enso]. *Fagus Menziesii* and *Solandri*. 1898 MORRIS *Austral-English* 462 *Tawhai, or Tawai..*Maori name for several species of New Zealand Beech-trees. 1918 *NZJST* I. 144 [*Fagus*] *fusca*... Tawhai, black-birch. 1927 *TrNZI* LVII. 906 The Maori seemed to class together [the beeches] as tawhai adding, perhaps, in our own manner, a descriptive modifying word or words, as tawhairaunui for the large-leaved beech.

2. With differentiating Ma. suffix, **tawhairaunui** (occas. **tawai-raunui**) *Nothofagus fusca*, red beech (BEECH 2 (7)); and **tawai-rauriki** *Nothofagus solandri* var. solandri, black beech (BEECH 2(1)).

1867 HOOKER *Handbook* 768 Tawhai-rau-nui... *Fagus fusca*... Tawairauriki, *Geolog. Surv. Fagus Solandri*. 1869 *TrNZI* I. (rev. edn.) 272 The tawhai, and tawhairaunui, or black and red birches, (*Fagus Solandri* and *F. Fusca*,) often form large..trees. 1882 HAY *Brighter Britain* II. 190 The Tawairaunui (*Fagus fusca*) is a species of the former, known as 'black birch'. *Ibid.* 197 The Tawai-rauriki (*Fagus Solandri*) is the 'White Birch' of the settlers. 1886 KIRK in *Settler's Handbook NZ* (1902) 121 [Native name] Tawhai-raunui..[Settlers' name] Tooth-leaved birch..[Family] Cupuliferae. 1902 *Settler's Handbook NZ* 262 244,000 acres, mainly in the back country, are covered with bush, chiefly tawhai, tawhai rauriki, and tawhai raunui. 1946 *JPS* LV. 146

TAWAI

Tawai (as tawhai), a tree (Nothofagus spp.), beech; wrongly called birch; Tawai-raunui and tawai rauriki recognized as species by Maori and Pakeha alike: there are also hybrids. Also called tawhai. **1995** *Evening Post* (Wellington) 10 Aug. 23 The appearance of some juvenile divaricating plants, such as the Red Beech (Nothofagus fusca or tawhairaunui), differs from the adult. When young the leaves are only 1–2cm long, sharp-toothed and roundish. They are reddened by direct light on interlacing branchlets.

tawai, occas. erron. var. TOWAI b (b); var. TAEWA.

tawairaunui, tawai-rauriki: see TAWAI 2.

tawapou. Also **tawaapou.** [Ma. /taʼwa:pou/: Williams 406 *Tawāpou*.]

1. *Planchonella* (formerly *Sideroxylon*) *costata* (fam. Sapotaceae), a tall coastal tree of northern New Zealand having a milky exudation from its petioles and cut branchlets. See also OLIVE 2.

1844 COLENSO *Excurs. Northern Is.* in Taylor *Early Travellers* (1959) 51 I discovered a clump of small trees, bearing a handsome fruit of the size of a large walnut... The natives call it, Tawaapou. **1867** HOOKER *Handbook* 768 Tawaapou, *Col[enso]. Sapota costata*. **1889** KIRK *Forest Flora* 277 The tawaapou, or pou as it is termed by the Maoris of the Great Barrier Island, is a handsome evergreen tree. **1890** *PWD Catalogue Timbers* (NZ & South Seas Exhib.) 14 Tawaapou.. Timber heavy, tough and close grained. **1906** CHEESEMAN *Manual NZ Flora* 436 *S[ideroxylon] costatum*... A handsome closely branched tree 20–40 ft. high... North Island:.. *Tawapou*. **1911** [see OLIVE 2]. **1924** *Otago Witness* (Dunedin) 16 Dec. 6 When the berries of the tawa-a-pou, or New Zealand olive, are ripe, a few young wood-pigeons make a fairly long visit to the place. **1961** MARTIN *Flora NZ* 162 Tawapou..milky juice... fruit large-red berry. **1988** DAWSON *Forest Vines to Snow Tussocks* 110 On the mainland as well as on islands, and extending to East Cape and beyond, are the small trees parapara..and tawapou.

2. Less commonly applied to the milk-trees *Streblus* (formerly *Paratrophis*) *banksii* (TUREPO), and *S. heterophyllus*. See MILK-TREE.

1869 *TrNZI* I. (rev. edn.) 190 Milk tree, or tawaapou... The milk tree of the settlers, from the bark exuding a vegetable milk when wounded.

tawara, var. TAWHARA.

tawari. Also occas. **tawiri.** [Ma. /ʼta:wari/: Williams 406 *Tāwari* (i)..*Ixerba brexioides*.] Usu. *Ixerba brexioides* (fam. Escalloniaceae), a tree of the northern North Island having showy white flowers. See also KUMARAHOU 2, WHAWHAKOU.

1867 HOOKER *Handbook* 768 Tawari, *Col[enso]. Ixerba brexioides*. **1889** FEATON *Art Album NZ Flora* 132 The 'Tawari'. This elegant tree, is confined to the Northern Island. **1890** *PWD Gen. Catalogue* (NZ & South Seas Exhib.) 22 Lithograph of tawari foliage. **1910** COCKAYNE *NZ Plants & Their Story* 37 The tawiri..of the Auckland upland forest is so showy that the Maoris had a special name, 'whakou', for its blooms. **1940** LAING & BLACKWELL *Plants NZ* 193 *Ixerba brexioides*. A beautiful tree, sometimes 70 ft. in height... Maori name *Tawari*. **1961** MARTIN *Flora NZ* 165 Tawari..flowers very showy, white. **1978** MOORE & IRWIN *Oxford Book NZ Plants* 78 Tawari is a northern tree found in some upland forests of the Auckland and Gisborne districts. **1981** LOCKE *Student at Gates* 73 I shan't forget the first time I saw the tawari..in flower.

tawatawa. Also early **taua taua.** [Ma. /ʼtawatawa/: Williams 405 *tawatawa 1...* mackerel.] blue mackerel (MACKEREL 2 (1)).

[**1820** LEE & KENDALL *NZ Gram. & Vocab.* 210 Taua taua; A fish so called.] **1849** *NZ Jrnl.* IX. 125 English name: Herring. Native name: tawatawa. **1855** TAYLOR *Te Ika A Maui* 413 *Tawatawa*..about the same size as the kahawai, or mackerel, which it closely resembles in color and general form. **1872** [see MACKEREL 1]. **1886** SHERRIN *Handbook Fishes NZ* 61 Mackerel... In the north of Auckland the Natives make great preparations for fishing tawatawa at the time of the new moon during summer, and capture immense numbers. **1890** *Otago Witness* (Dunedin) 30 Jan. 18 Another of our food fishes..is the true mackerel (Scomber australasicus)... The Maoris call the fish tawatawa. **1921** *NZJST* IV. 118 Scomber australasicus...*Southern Mackerel; Tawatawa*. **1949** BUCK *Coming of Maori* 212 When the catch of *tawatawa* fish was hauled in, Kahukura assisted the fishermen in stringing the fish on strips of flax. **1966** [see MACKEREL 2 (1)]. **1987** POWELL *Native Animals NZ* 63 Blue Mackerel (Tawatawa)..a surface fish usually found in schools,.. not uncommon from Cook Strait north-wards.

tawera, var. TAWHARA.

tawha, var. TAWA.

tawhai, tawhairaunui: see TAWAI 2.

tawhara. Also **tawara, tawera, tawhera.** [Ma. /ʼta:fara/: Williams 408 *Tāwhara* (i)...3... Flower bracts of *Freycinetia banksii* (*kiekie*).] The edible flower bracts of the kiekie (see KIEKIE 1); occas. by synecdoche, the plant itself.

1834 MARKHAM *NZ* (1963) 61 Then up again into an almost impervious Forest where you could not see the Light of day in consequence of a kind of Lily a sort of Parasitical Plant that has so much root hanging down all keeping the Sun out. [Blank space left for drawing with Markham's caption 'Tawara Astilia Angustifolia'.] **1838** POLACK *NZ* I. 110 On the branches of the rátá..flourished the wild indigenous parasitical plant called tawárá. **1842** HEAPHY *Residence in NZ* 45 The pulpy part for the middle of the stem of the *Tawara* or *Astilia* is an excellent substitute in pastry for the apple. **1847** ANGAS *Savage Life* I. 319 The food is served in baskets made of..the long narrow leaves of the *tawara* (*Freycinetia Banksii*), plaited so as to resemble coarse matting. **1857** HURSTHOUSE *NZ* I. 115 Vine and mulberry show fruit; tawara ripe. **1869** *TrNZI* I. (rev. edn.) 261 Also the fruit (ureure) and sugary bract-like spadices (tawhara) of the climbing plant (kiekie). **1874** *Ibid.* VI. 56 The tawera, or New Zealand screw pine, *Freycinetia banksii*. **1882** HAY *Brighter Britain* II. 193 The Tawhara or Kie-kie (*Freycinetia Banksii*) appears to be sometimes a parasite, sometimes a shrub, and sometimes a small tree. **1905** BAUCKE *White Man Treads* 16 Aye, and kie kie also, with its..sweetmeats..the first at, and before Christmas, when the plant distills its nectar juices, and collects them in that bunch of tender succulence of fleshly leaflets the Maori called tawhara. **1929** FIRTH *Primitive Economics of the Maori* 51 The fleshy bracts of the root-climbing *tawhara*..also furnished vegetable food. **1934** HYDE *Journalese* 171 You can eat the tawhara in the woods around. This is the fleshy cream flower of a great green palm—sweet as honey and water-melon in one. **1955** BOSWELL *Dim Horizons* 150 There was in spring the delicious tawhara, the fleshy edible flower of the kiekie vine. **1982** SUTTON-SMITH *History of Children's Play* 116 The soft stamens of one of these are cream-coloured and covered with creamy-yellow pollen. This we called [in Taranaki c1880s] the 'lady' or sometimes what the Maoris called it, *tawhera*.

TAWHIRI

tawheowheo. [Ma. /ta:ʼfeofeo/: Williams 408 *tāwheowheo... Quintinia serrata*.] *Quintinia serrata* (fam. Escalloniaceae), a small forest tree. See also *New Zealand lilac* (LILAC 1), QUINTINIA.

1906 CHEESEMAN *Manual NZ Flora* 135 *Q[uintinia] serrata... Tawheowheo*. **1940** LAING & BLACKWELL *Plants NZ* 193 *Quintinia serrata* (The Serrated Quintinia)... Sometimes called *New Zealand lilac*. Maori name *Tawheowheo*. North Island only: Auckland, Hawke's Bay, and Taranaki. **1978** MOORE & IRWIN *Oxford Book NZ Plants* 78 *Quintinia serrata, tawheowheo. Quintinia* is another small genus shared with New Guinea.

tawhera, var. TAWHARA.

tawhere, var. TAWHERO.

tawhero. Also early **tawhere.** [Ma. /ʼtafero/: Williams 408 *Tawhero... Weinmannia racemosa*.] A native forest tree of the genus *Weinmannia* (fam. Cunoniaceae).

1. *Weinmannia racemosa*, KAMAHI 1.

1853 HOOKER *II Flora Novae-Zelandiae I Flowering Plants* 80 *Weinmannia racemosa*... Nat. names, 'Tawai', *Cunn*.; 'Tawhere', Southern Island, *Lyall*. **1869** *TrNZI* I. (rev. edn.) 274 The towai, and tawhero, (*Weinmannia sylvicola*, and *W. racemosa*), are small trees. **1875** KIRK *Durability NZ Timbers* 19 Tawhero.—(*Weinmannia racemosa*)... Often called black birch, and substituted for that timber, to which it is greatly inferior in strength and durability. **1888** BULLER *Birds NZ* I. 12 The spot fixed upon was..under the shadow of a three-stemmed tawhero (*Weinmannia racemosa*). **1889** KIRK *Forest Flora* 133 [*Weinmannia racemosa*] is termed 'tawhero' by the East Cape Natives—the name commonly applied to..*W. silvicola*. **1890** *PWD Gen. Catalogue* (NZ & South Seas Exhib.) 25 Lithograph of tawhero foliage.

2. Occas. also **tawherowhero.** *Weinmannia silvicola*, TOWAI 1.

1867 HOOKER *Handbook* 768 Tawhero, *Col[enso]. Weinmannia sylvicola*. **1889** FEATON *Art Album NZ Flora* 136 This tree [sc. *W. silvicola*] is sometimes called Tawhero, or Kamai, and is not unusually confounded with *W. racemosa*, the Tawhero or Kamai proper. **1906** CHEESEMAN *Manual NZ Flora* 139 [*Weinmannia silvicola*] North Island:.. *Tawhero*. **1910** COCKAYNE *NZ Plants & Their Story* 46 Confined to the north are..the tawhero (*Weinmannia sylvicola*), the toatoa..and some other trees and shrubs. **1940** LAING & BLACKWELL *Plants NZ* 197 *Weinmannia sylvicola* (The Tawhero). Maori names *Tawhero, Kamahi*. **1951** LEVY *Grasslands NZ* (1970) 3 Certain poor clay soils, popularly known as gum-lands, were dominated by the kauri and its associate the tawhero.

tawhina(u), tawhine, tawhini, varr. TAUHINU.

tawhiri. Also **tafiri, tawiri.** [Ma. /ʼta:firi/: Williams 408–409 *Tāwhiri.1.* v. trans. Beckon, wave to... 5... *Pittosporum tenuifolium*. So called from its being waved as a demonstration of welcome.] Any of several small native trees of the genus *Pittosporum* (fam. Pittosporaceae), esp. *P. tenuifolium* (KOHUHU), *P. eugenioides* (TARATA 1), and *P. cornifolium*.

1860 BENNETT *Gatherings of Naturalist* 416 The Tafiri, the lemon-tree of the settlers. **1872** DOMETT *Ranolf & Amohia* I. 108 This cheerful cot... Its floor, for fragrant orange-scent With faint *tawhíri*-leaves besprent. **1883** tawiri [see MAPAU 2 (3) b]. **1884** BRACKEN *Lays of the Maori* 21 The early breeze that..stole The rich Tawhiri's sweet perfume. **1892** [see MAPAU 2 (3) b]. **1907** LAING & BLACKWELL *Plants NZ* 322 The gum of the taramea [was mixed by the Maori with]..the fragrant resin of the tawhiri (*Pittosporum tenuifolium*). **1946** *JPS* LV. 146 *Tawhiri*, a tree (Pittosporum tenuifolium); so called because small branches were broken off to wave welcome while calling out haeremai to approaching visitors: tawhiri means to beckon.

tawiri, var. TAWARI, TAWHIRI.

tawse /toz/. *Otago-Southland. Obs.* [f. Sc. dial.] A school strap.
1935 TURNBULL *Happy Voyage* 240 'Had a tawse hung up; that talked if I wanted discipline.' 'I'll neither tawse nor talk,' said Angus. **1937** AYSON *Thomas* 16 The Teacher deemed it wise next day to try the effect of his tawse upon the palms that had tied the flaxen knots. **1982** GILDERDALE *Sea Change* 242 *tawse* Strap for punishing children. E. Turnbull's *Happy Voyage* (1935) page 240 and in many books thereafter.

taxing, *vbl. n.* A euphemism for the extortion of money or property (often from prospects or other members who have fallen out of favour with the gang) or for enforced contributions to gang funds.
1996 *Dominion* (Wellington) 15 May 3 Extortion or 'taxing' by the Nomads gang had recently become more of a problem in Wairarapa...'Taxing' was often associated with threats of violence of other retribution if the victim went to the police.

tchaik, var. TAIKO.

tchakat mai-hor-r: see MORIORI 1 a.

te, var. TI *n.*[1]

tea. [Transf. uses of *tea*, the plant *Camellia sinensis* (fam. Theaceae) and the beverage produced from infusing its leaves.]
1. a. *Obs.* As **New Zealand tea**, a shortened form of TEA-TREE 1 a.
1773 FORSTER *Resolution Jrnl.* 24 Apr. (1982) II. 266 A brewery provided a salutary & palatable potion from the decoction of spruce & New-Zeeland Tea mixed with the Essence of malt & Melasses for our Ships-Company.
b. *Hist.* In special Comb. with a defining suffix **tea-broom, tea-plant, tea-shrub**, obsolete variants of TEA-TREE 1 a.
1872 DOMETT *Ranolf & Amohia* 505 Mánuka... The settlers often call it '**tea-broom**'. **1898** MORRIS *Austral-English* 463 *Tea-broom, n.* a New Zealand name for the *Tea-tree*. **1773** COOK *Journals* (1961) II. 114 Began to make Beer from a Tree of a Rosinish quality intermixt with the **Tea Plant**. **1791** BELL *Jrnl. Voyage H.M.S. 'Chatham'* (Vancouver exped.) (ATLMS) Nov. 50 The Tea plant we found in plenty and mix'd it with the Spruce in Brewing. **1838** POLACK *NZ* I. 293 There are many shrubs with myrtle-leaves. The tea-plant, *kaikátoa*, covers the plains. **1982** BURTON *Two Hundred Yrs. NZ Food* 18 Captain Cook, who had dubbed it [manuka] 'teaplant', wrote 'The leaves were used by many of us as tea, which has a very agreeable bitter taste and flavour when they are recent.' **1773** COOK *Journals* 11 May (1961) II. 137 We first made a strong decoction of the leaves of small branches of the Spruce tree & **Tea shrub**.
2. a. As a workingman's beverage, see *black-billy tea* (BILLY *n.*[1] 4 and 6), *bush tea* (BUSH C 3 d), *posts and rails tea* (POST-AND-RAIL 2).
b. Special Comb. **tea-billy** [AND 1889], see BILLY *n.*[1] 4.

c. tea-oh *int.* (occas. *n.*). (A call for) SMOKO *n.*[1] 1 a.
c1944 *Whitcombe's Mod. Jun. Dict.* 407 *Tea-oh* In Australia and New Zealand, an interval for tea during working hours. **1966** *Encycl. NZ* II. 679 The back country runs have quite a vocabulary of their own... Amongst these are..terms like *cow paddock*..and *tea-oh*.

3. [Transf. use of *tea* a (light) meal orig. at which tea was drunk: see OED *tea* 4 a; AND 1863.] **a.** (a) Formerly most freq. in rural use, the main evening meal, always substantial, often cooked. Contrast SUPPER 2 a.
1853 in Cutten *Cutten Lett.* (1979) 46 We go to bed at 10 or 11 get up at 8 dine at 2, take tea at 5 or 6 and so survive. **c1875** [see SUPPER 1]. **1883** [see DINNER a]. **1890** [see b below]. **1921** MANSFIELD in *Undiscovered Country* (1974) 10 Here I sit... And everybody else has cut away home hours ago and tea's over and it's getting on for time to light the lamp. **1924** [see MARKET]. **1936** HYDE *Passport to Hell* 84 In camp the tea bugle sounded at five; the mess orderlies went up for tea, meat, and vegetables. **c1942** *Notes on the People of NZ (3rd Marine Div., Intelligence)* in Bioletti *The Yanks Are Coming* (1989) 54 And now we come to the all-important subject of 'teas'... It may be a whole meal!... If you are invited to 'tea' perhaps the safest thing to do is to ask your host to name the hour. **1943** MARSH *Colour Scheme* 100 He went into Harpoon and had tea at the pub. You call it 'dinnah'. **1959** DAVIN *No Remittance* 95 Anyway that evening when the evening meal, tea as I was learning to call it, was finished. **1967** GROVER *Another Man's Role* 6 One night when she'd cooked tea and he hadn't turned up, she'd put it out and told us to go ahead and eat. **1970** IHIMAERA in *Listener Short Stories* (1977) 86 Dinnertime was best though, except we called it tea. **1983** FRANCIS *Wildlife Ranger* 2 The [station] midday meal was more often a cut lunch eaten on the job. The main meal, 'tea', was basically mutton, potatoes, onions,.. and, for afters, stewed dried fruit, plum duff or rice and prunes. **1990** VIRTUE *In the Country of Salvation* 10 In the end they stayed the night, after an enormous seven o'clock tea of roast lamb, fresh garden vegetables and Hokey Pokey ice-cream.
(b) Special Comb. **teatime**, the time for the taking of the evening meal, usu. between 5 and 7 p.m.
1887 *Auckland Weekly News* 12 Feb. 8 He was outvoted, and compelled to quit Cambridge about an hour before tea-time. **1890** [see b below]. **1917** in Miller *Camps, Tracks & Trenches* 5 Sept. (1939) 131 A barrel of beer arrived at the cookhouse after tea time, so the section settled down to a large evening. I missed most of the tangi. **1959** MIDDLETON *The Stone* 65 It was nearly teatime when I remembered his letter. He sat down to read it while I fried bacon and eggs for our meal. **1964** HARVEY *Any Old Dollars Mister?* 118 I cheered up around tea-time because I hadn't seen any funeral coming down the hill.
b. As **afternoon tea**, a mid-afternoon occasion (usu. between 2 and 3.30 p.m.) which could in the past range in formality from a regular afternoon work-break (SMOKO) or an informal refreshment break, to an often highly ceremonious social gathering of (mainly) women. Cf. *early morning tea* (EARLY 2).
[*Note*] The passing reference in the OED to *afternoon tea* (4 only quots.) seems to confine it in the 18th century (see *afternoon* 3 a *attrib.*, 1748, 1754) to actual tea-house tea-drinking; and in the 19th century (*loc. cit.* and *tea* 4 a, 1879, 1882) to high (five-o'clock) tea.
1890 *Otago Witness* (Dunedin) 4 Sept. 36 After dinner, another lounge and gossip, afternoon tea, another drive to the baths, bathing, home again, tea time. After

tea, walking or riding. **1905** BRANDON *'Ukneadit'* 69 *Gem scones*..Split open and butter for afternoon tea. **1905** *NZ Herald* (Auckland) 27 Feb. 6 The party proceeded to the bowling green, where they were hospitably entertained at afternoon tea. **1924** ANTHONY *Follow the Call* (1975) 55 After an inspection of our hard-case looking crockery..the ladies refused my tentative offer of afternoon tea. **1939** [see FLY CEMETERY]. **1943** BENNETT *English in NZ* in *Amer. Speech* XVIII. 86 Visitors reading notices in New Zealand papers, might be puzzled by phrases like 'Rooms with tray' and 'Ladies bring basket'; in both cases the container stands for the thing contained—breakfast and afternoon tea delicacies respectively. **1980** WOOLLASTON *Sage Tea* 10 They grew like a pretty throwover, all embroidered, that you put over the food [c1915] to keep flies off when afternoon tea is waiting for visitors. **1992** *Dominion* (Wellington) 12 Jan. 6 Do New Zealand ladies still entertain their friends to afternoon tea?.. Just after the war my mother was renowned for her afternoon teas... Afternoon tea was the done thing, the social highlight, the acid test of a good cook... My mother's guests would be invited for about two o'clock in the afternoon... Tea would be served shortly after three o'clock... The real point of the afternoon, apart from the gossip and the cup of tea, was the food. It was not only the lavishness of the display but the degree to which it complied with the strict rules which made or marred a hostess's reputation.

c. As **morning tea** [AND 1916], a mid-morning break for tea, coffee, etc. Cf. *early morning* (cup of) *tea* (EARLY 2), SMOKO *n.*[1] 1.
1927 *NZ Dairy Produce Exporter* 24 Mar. 41 Return and run the morning tea..up to the men. **1943** BENNETT *English in NZ* in *Amer. Speech* XVIII. 86 *Morning tea* is an institution characteristic of New Zealand, where housewives and workers habitually make tea in the middle of the morning (in England the phrase usually denotes tea in bed). **1953** LINKLATER *Year of Space* (1954) 194 I had my first experience..of an entertainment common throughout New Zealand. They call it *morning tea*, and serve it about ten o'clock; but it may be a formidable meal. **1962** SHARPE *Country Occasions* 73 So about 9 a.m. our dipping party knocks off for smoko. Coffee break, they call it in America, morning tea, in New Zealand family circles. **1987** *Chosen Place* 23 I'd better put on some tights (tut-tut—pantihose) and buy some morning tea (which we'll eat, not drink) and pay for it.

teak. *Obs.* Also **native teak, New Zealand teak**. [Extended or transf. use of *teak*, applied, usu. with defining words, to trees which produce a strong or durable timber: see OED 2.] Any of several native trees (but usu. PURIRI q.v.) yielding teak-like wood.
1848 TAYLOR *Leaf from Nat. Hist.* 21 *Puriri*, a tree; *the New Zealand teak*; the most durable of all the timber trees in this country. **1866** ANGAS *Polynesia* 33 The New Zealand teak (*Vitex littoralis*) grows near the sea, and produces a fine durable wood, which takes a fine polish, and is of great use in ship-building. **1868** PYKE *Province Otago* 34 Rata (native teak or 'ironwood' of the colonists). **1869** *TrNZI* I. (rev. edn.) 272 The puriri, or New Zealand oak, or teak..is a large tree of irregular growth. **1875** KIRK *Durability NZ Timbers* 15 [Puriri] has been appropriately styled the New Zealand teak: it is..closely related to the Asiatic teak, and affords a timber of great density and durability. **1882** HAY *Brighter Britain* II. 190 The Puriri..is sometimes called 'teak', or 'ironwood'... The timber is hard, heavy, very durable, very hard to work, and of a greenish colour. **1898** MORRIS *Austral-English* 463 The original Teak is an East Indian timber-tree... In New Zealand, it is *Vitex littoralis*..*Puriri*.

teal, *n.*¹

1. [Transf. use of European *teal, Anas crecca.*] Any of several small compact ducks (fam. Anatidae) thought to resemble the European teal. See also WIDGEON.

[*Note*] In popular speech *duck* would prob. be preferred to *teal* as the generally used name for the bird.

1842 HEAPHY *NZ* 47 The Paradise and common duck, teal, widgeon, water-hen, and diver are all found in great numbers on the rivers. **1853** [see DUCK 1]. **1863** BUTLER *First Year* ix 137 Our teal is, if not the same as the English teal, so like it, that the difference is not noticeable. **1870** *TrNZI* II. 47 The light-eyed Teal slunk silently from view. **1882** [see PAPANGO]. **1945** BEATTIE *Maori Place-names Canterbury* 14 At this season great numbers of paradise and grey ducks and teal were taken. **1952** WILKINSON *Kapiti Bird Sanctuary* 98 When [the fishermen] had pulled the net ashore..they discovered one of the little teal, tangled up in the net.

2. With a modifier: **Auckland Island, black, brown (red), Campbell Island, grey, little**.

(1) **Auckland Island teal**. *Anas aucklandica aucklandica*. See also DUCK 2 (1).

1955 BAILEY *Birds NZ* 55 The Auckland Island..and the Campbell Island Teal..are local forms. **1972** *Notornis* XIX. 390 A surprising range of birds..is listed, including a number of rarely-visited species, such as the Auckland Island Teal. **1986** FRASER *Beyond the Roaring Forties* 75 The Auckland Island teal, or flightless duck, is one of the world's rarest woodfowl. **1990** *Checklist Birds NZ* 104 *Anas aucklandica aucklandica..Auckland Island Teal (Flightless Duck)*.

(2) **black teal**. SCAUP (*Aythya novaeseelandiae*). See also PAPANGO.

1871 HUTTON *Catalogue Birds NZ* 38 *Fuligula novae zealandiae*... Black Teal. Papango. **1873** [see SCAUP]. **1886** *TrNZI* XVIII. 113 Papango, Scaup, Black Teal. Both Islands. Flight very feeble. **1897** *TrNZI* XXIX. 201 On the Papaitonga Lake, a 'Black Teal' brought out a brood of five young ones about the middle of December. **1904** HUTTON & DRUMMOND *Animals NZ* 316 The Black Teal. Papango. *Ibid.* 317 This species, in colour, is very like the Scaup Duck of Europe, but, unlike that species, it does not frequent the sea-shore, but lives among rushy streams in small flocks. **1917** WILLIAMS *Dict. Maori Lang.* 300 *Papango, Fuligula novae-zealandiae*, widgeon, black teal. **1945** BEATTIE *Maori Place-names Canterbury* 64 Kukupako—the black teal once common, now uncommon. **1955** [see SCAUP]. **1967** NATUSCH *Animals NZ* 271 Fairly common on North and South Island lakes is the little black scaup..more familiarly known as the black teal. **1985** *Reader's Digest Book NZ Birds* 150 *Scaup. Aythya novaeseelandiae*... Other names: *New Zealand scaup, black teal, papango*.

(3) **brown (red) teal**, occas. **teal duck**. *brown duck* (DUCK 2 (3)).

1826 SHEPHERD *Journal* 9 Mar. in Howard *Rakiura* (1940) 359 This day returned to Albion cove saw..a Parot of brownish colour and a large white bird as large as a turky and a small sort of brown teal duck. **1854** in Studholme *Te Waimate* (1954) 23 The brown Teal were very numerous [at the Bluff]. **1869** *TrNZI* I. (rev. edn.) 125 Of aquatic birds I saw the Grey Duck, Brown Teal. **1876** PEACHE *Journal* in Gray *Quiet with Hills* (1970) 43 Our bag was 4 brace of swamp hens, 1½ brace of Red teal, 1 brace of Blue duck. **c1899** DOUGLAS in *Mr Explorer Douglas* (1957) 239 There are two varieties of this duck [*sc.* teal and widgeon]; the brown teal and the black teal or widgeon. **1957** WILLIAMS *Dict. Maori Lang.* 409 *Tete... Anas chlorotis*, brown teal. **1966** [see DUCK 2 (3)]. **1979** [see PATEKE]. **1985** *Reader's Digest Book NZ Birds* 146 *Brown Teal. Anas aucklandica... Pateke, brown duck, teal duck*... Brown teal are birds of heavily vegetated wetlands, preferably but not necessarily with some still or slow-flowing open water. **1990** *Dominion Sunday Times* (Wellington) 9 Dec. 30 [The zoo] is also developing expertise in the breeding management of natives such as the..brown teal duck..and giant weta.

(4) **Campbell Island teal**. *Anas aucklandica nesiotis*, a flightless species.

1955 BAILEY *Birds NZ* 55 The Auckland Island..and the Campbell Island Teal..are local forms. **1986** FRASER *Beyond the Roaring Forties* 182 Attempts were made to capture three female Campbell Island teal on Dent Island. **1990** *Checklist Birds NZ* 104 *Anas aucklandica nesiotis..Campbell Island Teal*... Now only on a closely adjacent islet..where it was rediscovered in 1975. **1994** *Evening Post* (Wellington) 29 Oct. 9 Conservationists watching anxiously over one of the world's rarest ducks and her new clutch of eggs didn't want anything to go wrong, so they asked for a temporary halt to roadwork... So sensitive is the Campbell Island teal that the high-pitched noises of concrete cutters..could have put the birds right off the job.

(5) **grey teal**. [AND 1900.] *Anas gracilis*. See also *little teal* (6) below, TETE.

1849 TORLESSE *Papers* (1958) 79 Returned up the Avon in canoe having shot a bittern and grey teal which J. Deans stuffed. **1904** TREGEAR *Maori Race* 105 The paradise duck..a bird of beautiful plumage, but not of such flavour as the grey duck or teal, was considered a prize. **1917** WILLIAMS *Dict. Maori Lang.* 479 *Tete... Nettion castaneum*, grey teal. **1952** WILKINSON *Kapiti Bird Sanctuary* 98 We have not been able to learn very much about the little grey teal. **1966** FALLA et al. *Birds NZ* 88 Grey Teal *Anas gibberifrons*... Tete... Like the Grey Duck has pale throat, but noticeably smaller. **1985** *Reader's Digest Book NZ Birds* 145 Grey teal are remarkably mobile. **1990** *Checklist Birds NZ* 103 *Anas gracilis*... Grey Teal (Tete).

(6) **little teal**. See *grey teal* (5) above.

1871 HUTTON *Catalogue Birds NZ* 36 *Querquedula gibberifrons*... Little Teal *Anas gracilis*. **1886** [see TETE].

TEAL /til/, *n.*² *Obs*. Occas. early **T.E.A.**, the acronym of Tasman Empire Airways Ltd., now Air New Zealand.

1948 *Evening Post* (Wellington) 4 Feb. 8 T.E.A. as a State undertaking, is subject to political pressure. **1952** *Evening Post* (Wellington) 28 Apr. 8 The only major airline operating flying-boats today is TEAL. **1965** CAMERON *NZ* 35 New Zealand's ties with Fiji have been strengthened by air services (such as TEAL's Coral Route). **1981** GEE *Meg* 138 But for all the flying you did for TEAL. I think an M.B.E. would have fitted the bill. **1992** *Evening Post* (Wellington) 18 Dec. 1 Don..also spent eight years at Teal (now Air NZ).

team. *Mustering*. [Spec. use of *team* a set of players working towards a common goal under a leader.] A musterer's or shepherd's pack of specialist sheep-dogs.

1933 *Press* (Christchurch) (Acland Gloss.) 23 Dec. 15 *Team*.—Each shepherd's dogs. He may have anything from two to eight. Usually in large *t[eam]s* only three are much use. The rest are for sale or being broken in. The distinction between *t[eam]* and *pack*..was general in Canterbury until a few years ago [from 1933]; but several North Canterbury correspondents have told me that many of the younger shepherds now speak of their sheepdogs as a *p[ack]*. **1947** NEWTON *Wayleggo* 23 I loosened my 'team' of two dogs. **1966** NEWTON *Boss's Story* 190 *Team*: A shepherd refers to his dogs as his team. An ideal high country team would be one heading dog, two handy dogs and two huntaways. Or alternatively, two heading dogs, one handy dog and two huntaways.

tear, *v*. In the phr. **tear** (someone) **up for arsepaper** (occas. **dunny paper**), to reprimand, or scold severely; to attack and demolish (in argument); occas. as an exclam. of surprise or disbelief, **Well, I'll be torn up for arsepaper**.

1937 PARTRIDGE *Dict. Slang* 869 *tear up for arsepaper*. To reprimand severely: New Zealand soldiers': in the G.W. **1947** DAVIN *For Rest of Our Lives* 300 'Livingstone, I believe,' said Frank. 'Well, I'll be torn up for arsepaper,' said Pat Murphy. **1982** SHADBOLT *Once on Chunuk Bair* (1990) 38 I should tear you up for arse paper. Harkness: I was expecting to stop a blast, sir. **1989** RICHARDS *Pioneer's Life* 86 The irate gardener was bad enough but when his spouse appeared..she nearly tore me up for dunny paper.

tear /tiə/, *n*. *Obs*. [f. a fancied resemblance to a *tear* i.e., a translucent droplet.] An exudation of clear gum from a living kauri tree.

1881 *TrNZI* XIII. 138 The greater part of the *kauri-gum*..is found in a fossil condition, a very small portion being the produce of living trees, although occasionally it occurs in recent masses or 'tears' of several pounds weight, at the junction of a large branch with the stem. **1889** KIRK *Forest Flora* 154 [Resin] may exude on the underside of a branch, especially at its junction with the trunk, forming rounded masses usually termed 'tears'.

tea-shower: see SHOWER.

tea-tree. Also regularly **ti-tree**, occas. **ti-tri**, **titri**, variants which may occas. have been affected by confusion with TI *n.*¹ (cabbage-tree). [Transf. use of *tea-tree*, the plant *Camellia sinensis* (fam. Theaceae): AND 1790.]

[*Note*] Cook first noticed the superficial similarity between *Leptospermum* and the true tea-plant (*Camellia*), gave it the name *tea plant, tea shrub* or *tea-tree* (see TEA 1 b), brewed a drink from its leaves, and during a subsequent voyage, used it to temper the astringency of spruce beer. The Australasian form *tea-tree* was taken up by early whalers, bushmen and settlers.

1. a. MANUKA (*Leptospermum scoparium*) and KANUKA (*Kunzea ericoides*), the plants and their wood, valued esp. in later times as firewood. Also *attrib*. (a) **tea-tree** forms.

1773 BAYLY *Journal* 12 Apr. in McNab *Hist. Records* (1914) II. 206 There is..great quantities of a shrub which is called the Tea tree from our peoples using it instead of Tea, & tho' it was not so good as common Tea from the East, it made very good holesome drink for breckfast. **1793** *Raven to Lieut-Gov. King* 19 Nov. in McNab *Hist. Records* (1908) I. 179 [Of a sealing party left in Dusky Bay, 1792–1793.] Tea they made from the spruce and tea-trees. **1826** SHEPHERD *Journal* 22 Mar. in Howard *Rakiura* (1940) 362 The low grounds are full of brush wood from 6 to 20 feet high principally of the Tea tree or Diocema. **1841** *NZ Jrnl.* II. 35 There is a tree called the Tea tree, very hard and prolific. **1856** FITTON *NZ* 74 [Grass can be grown] upon grounds partly cleared of the tea-tree—*manuka*. **1872** *TrNZI* IV. 249 The rawiri (*Leptospermum ericoides*) or tea-tree, with spray-like branches laden with myriads of white flowers. **1889** KIRK *Forest Flora* 236 An infusion of the leaves is often used by bushmen as a substitute for tea: in all probability it owes its common name 'tea-tree' to its having been used for this purpose by the early voyagers. **1902** *Bulletin Reciter* (Satchell 'Ballad of Stuttering Jim') 98 And pale as the tea-tree flower that blows at the end of the winter rain. **1919** *Quick March* 11 Aug. 7 At old Puketu where the tea-tree grew, and I was a little kid, They didn't think much of the things you said—but a lot of the things you did. **1939** CRESSWELL *Present Without Leave* 262 The

New Zealand 'tea'-tree, or manuka, is an affable shrub. **1962** *Listener* 19 Apr. 5 They took this [pig] down and he got them in a very thick patch of teatree. **1984** WILSON *S. Pacific Street* 7 In my spare time I went continually down to our muddy creek among..high teatree.

(b) **ti-tree, ti-tri, titri** forms.
  1843 SELWYN *Journal* (ATLTS) 55 Ti Trees **1859** THOMSON *Story NZ* (1974) I. 19 Out of..Totara and Kauri pines canoes were scooped, and tough Ti tree furnished paddles and spears. **1866** HUNT *Chatham Is.* 11 I..interlaced the whole with branches of *ti-tree*. **1879** FEATON *Waikato War* 73 They..plunged into the high fern and ti-tree and rushed on the natives. **1885** *Wairarapa Daily* 24 Jan. 2 Settlers and others visited the ground..to see the trial of Mr. Henry Reynolds' new Triumph ti-tree cutter. **1895** *Otago Witness* (Dunedin) 19 Dec. 23 Our way lay across two or three cultivations into a grove of handsome titri. **1910** COCKAYNE *NZ Plants & Their Story* 146 Through corrupt spelling the spurious Maori 'ti-tree' has followed, a term beloved of journalists. Worse than this is the usage in South Otago, where, 'plain for all eyes to see', is the legend 'Ti-Tri' on a certain wayside station. **1918** *NZ at the Front* 77 They've turned the sheep on the long fern hill... Stringing far out to their camping ground in the ti-tree on the ridge. **1936** HYDE *Passport to Hell* 70 [He] handled the slim grey stems of ti-tree like an artist with his paint-brushes. **1962** *Landfall Country* 151 The road unwound slowly, a thin strip of clay and bluish metal edged with ti-tree and gorse. **1981** GEE *Meg* 116 I boiled napkins..and pegged them up to dry on a line held clear..by a ti-tree prop.

b. Esp. as **ti-tree, titri,** manuka or kanuka as a firewood valued for its fierce heat.
  1913 *NZ Observer* 23 Aug. 3 Auckland people are glad to get stumpy little bagfuls of ti-tree at half a crown a bag. **1925** MANDER *Allen Adair* (1971) 138 Allen lingered by the fire..., hesitating to put out the glow of the fine titree coals. **1942** ANDERSEN *Maori Place Names* 397 The wood is a favourite for firewood and logs..are advertised as ti-tree. **1986** OWEN & PERKINS *Speaking for Ourselves* 132 Before there was a ready supply of electricity the demand was for tea-tree firewood, and so we built up a constant trade.

2. With a modifier: **red, white.**

(1) **red tea-tree.** *red manuka* (MANUKA 2 (2)).
  1882 HAY *Brighter Britain* I. 190 Red, black, and white birch are used [for stakes], also red and white ti-tree, the last variety being most esteemed, as it is more durable. **1910** COCKAYNE *NZ Plants & Their Story* 149 The colour of the wood differs in the two species. This has led to *L. scoparium* being called 'red' and *L. ericoides* 'white' tea-tree. **1969** *Standard Common Names Weeds* 63 red tea-tree [=] manuka.

(2) **white tea-tree.** KANUKA.
  1882 [see (1) above]. **1889** KIRK *Forest Flora* 124 Young trees [of *Leptospermum ericoides*] are sometimes termed 'white tea-tree', as they are supposed to belong to a different plant, owing..to the wood being whiter and more elastic than in old specimens. **1910** [see (1) above]. **1930** *NZJST* XI. 152 [Three Kings] is clothed principally with white tea-tree—manuka rauriki. **1969** *Standard Common Names Weeds* 85 white tea-tree [=] kanuka.

3. a. In Comb. **tea-tree brush, bush** [AND 1820], **scrub, shrub.**
  1946 SARGESON *That Summer* 13 There was a sandy bit of garden close by the bach. It was ringed round with **tea-tree brush** to keep out the wind. **c1826–27** BOULTBEE *Journal* (1986) 110 **Tea tree bush**—mannook. **1834** MARKHAM *NZ* (1963) 33 Ettay [= he ti] is a Tea tree [*sc. a Cordyline*], quite different to the Tea tree bush, a sort of myrtle. **1872** in Meredith *Adventuring in Maoriland* (1935) 25 My attention was drawn to the tea-tree bushes growing alongside the [Rimutaka] road. **1964** TUWHARE *No Ordinary Sun* (1977) 21 No one comes..through straggly tea tree bush and gorse, past the hidden spring and bitter cress. **1863** LUSH *Auckland Jrnls.* 26 Sept. (1971) 250 I skirted round and struck into the **ti tree scrub**. **1873** TINNE *Wonderland of Antipodes* 5 My horse..pitched heavily..sending me head first among the manuka or ti-tree scrub. **1978** MCARA *Gold Mining Waihi* 46 The country was mostly covered with heavy bush, except for the Waihi Plains which were clothed in fern and stunted tea-tree scrub. **1847** ANGAS *Savage Life* II. 4 The **tea-tree shrub** (*leptospermum*) was in full bloom amongst the fern.

b. Special Comb. **tea tree broom**, a broom made from tea-tree twigs; **teatree (ti-tree) jack, tea-tree straw insect**, a native stick insect of the family Phasmatidae; **tea-tree ranges**, hills or ranges with a predominantly tea-tree cover.
  1986 RICHARDS *Off the Sheep's Back* 44 The earthen floor [of the nikau whare] would be kept clean with a **tea tree broom**. **1970** *Te Reo* 13 25 (Smithyman) A third name [for stick-insect] survives, derived from the frequent association of this insect with *Leptospermum* shrubs, the teatree which gave the insect its name **teatree jack**... *Teatree jack* is recollected mainly by older informants as a word from childhood or as a word acquired from people who were old in the informants' childhood. Otherwise *teatree jack* survives apparently as a current name only in pocket areas. **1972** GEE *My Father's Den* 16 I launched..pink and blue [paper] ships manned by spiders, caterpillars, beetles and small ti-tree jacks. **1987** GEE *Prowlers* 138 All this for insects, I thought, and..considered him an insect himself, tea-tree jack. **1874** BAINES *Edward Crewe* 206 I got out of the forest and on the bare fern and **tea-tree ranges**. I sat down to take a spell and think. **1908** *TrNZI* XL. 170 Gum-digging may be roughly divided into..that on..the high tea-tree ranges where the ground is too hard to work in dry weather, and that on the 'summer fields'. **1971** SMITHYMAN (ed.) in Satchell *Land of the Lost* 215 'Animated straws'. Sometimes the Straw or **Teatree Straw Insect**, usually the New Zealand Stick Insect or (formerly) Walking Stick Insect also known as the Teatree Jack.

4. In various phr. a. **brush the tea-tree out of your hair**, said to a person who has made a foolish remark; wake up!
  1954 Kaingaroa State Forest ranger to a worker. (Ed.) 'Come on Joe, brush the tea-tree out of your hair.'

b. **(away, up) in the tea-tree**, in the remote country areas, the 'sticks'.
  1904 *NZ Observer* 5 Mar. 4 The present writer was asked..to go and see the hot water away in the ti-tree somewhere. **1966** TURNER *Eng. Lang. Austral. & NZ* 122 I know the word [*sc.* woop-woops] but think of it as *wook wooks*.., *the sticks, the tea tree* and *the cactus*, some semantic differentiation is not impossible.

technicolour yawn. [AND 1964.] An act of vomiting.
  1976 GIFFORD *Loosehead Len's Bumper Thump Book* 31 About an hour from home he leaps to the slidin' window [of the bus] and does a technicolour yawn that MGM would have been proud to produce. **1978** TUCKER *Thoroughbreds Are My Life* 21 Jerry suddenly lurched to the side of the vessel and produced what is now commonly referred to as 'the technicolour yawn'. **1980** LELAND *Kiwi-Yankee Dict.* 102 *technicolour yawn*: To empty the contents of one's stomach through the oral orifice; often done as a response to an excess of alcohol in the system.

Teddy Woodbine: see WOODBINE 3.

tee, var. TI *n.*[1]

teegoomme, var. TIKUMU.

teetee, var. TITI.

teetotum /ˌtiːˈtʌutəm/. *Obs.* [Transf. use of Sc. and Irish dial. *teetotum* a diminutive person: see OED 1 b.] grey warbler (WARBLER 2 (3)), a tiny bird.
  1856 [see BUCKJUMP v.]. **1870** *TrNZI* II. 58 Gerygone assimilis.., Piripiri. Warbler, Teetotum. **1884** [see WARBLER 2 (3)]. **1985** *Reader's Digest Book NZ Birds* 278 Grey Warbler. *Gerygone igata*... Riroriro, teetotum.

tee-tree, var. TI-TREE.

tehori, var. TAIORE.

tekoteko. [Ma. /ˈtekoteko/: Williams 411 *tekoteko*..Carved figure on the gable of a house, figurehead of a canoe.] A carved figure on the gable-end of a Maori (meeting-)house.
  1848 TAYLOR *Leaf from Nat. Hist.* 76 Tekoteko, figure placed at the top of the gable end of a native house. **1876** *TrNZI* VIII. 175 Where the barge-boards meet is a carved face, surrounded with feathers, and surmounted with a small figure called a tekoteko. **1895** *Ibid.* XXVII. 674 The *tekoteko* on the roof above is Takenga, one of the descendants of Tama te Kapua. **1904** TREGEAR *Maori Race* 273 A carved face (*koruru*) was placed at the junction of the barge-boards, and above this was an image (*tekoteko*) which, especially on state occasions, was decked with feathers and ornaments. **1930** ANDERSEN in *NZ Short Stories* 32 Her eyes like *paua*-eyes of the gable-*tekoteko*. **1946** *JPS* LV. 159 *tekoteko*, grotesque carved human figure standing on the gable of a Maori house, above the koruru covering the join of the barge-boards at the gable. **1953** *Here & Now* Aug. 21 Beneath the carven counterparts of their ancestors and the fierce *teko teko* on guard high above..the Maoris lament on their mats. **1979** TAYLOR *Eyes of Ruru* 15 Above me the tekoteko raged. He ripped his tongue from his mouth and threw it at my feet. **1986** *Listener* 12 Apr. 36 I am nervous as I look towards the powerful tekoteko created by Murupaenga.

te-matau kauri, var. TUMATAKURU.

tenakoe /təˈnakwæi/. Also with much variety of early form as **jenokoi, tenago, te nakohi, tenaqui, tinaque,** etc.; also occas. in a variant Ma. form **tena ra ko koe**. [Ma. /ˈteːna ˈkoe/: Williams 411 *Tēnā. 1*... That, this, near or connected with the person addressed... *Tēnā* enters into the common forms of greeting *Tēnā koe! Tēnā korua!* and *Tēnā koutou! Tēnā ra ko koe!* is also found: *koe* is the personal pronoun second person singular. The form *tenakoe!* literally means 'There' or 'Here you are.'] A common form of mainly Maori greeting (to one person), more formal (and less used by non-Maori) than the frequent KIA ORA. Compare TENA KOUTOU.
  [**1820** LEE & KENDALL *NZ Gram. & Vocab.* 211 Téna ra ko koe; Be thou healthy! or Good morning (day, or night) to thee! **c1826–27** BOULTBEE *Journal* (1986) 112 how do you do?—tànna ràkkoo kòee [?tena ra ko koe]] **1840** MATHEW *Journal* 16 Feb. in *Founding of NZ* (1940) 48 They flocked out..to welcome us, with their usual salutation of 'Tanerakakoi' or 'How do you do'. **1842** BARNICOAT *Journal* (ATLTS) 18 Aug. 66 We were everywhere saluted with the usual Tenago or Howdyedo and..the shake of the hand. **1849** POWER *Sketches in NZ* 160 [The wahines] can only afford to

greet the visitor with a whining 'tena koe pakeha'. **1853** ADAMS *Spring Canterbury Settlement* 77 They are both harmless and friendly; they never meet you without a passing 'tenaqui' (how d'ye do). **1856** TANCRED *Nat. Hist. Canterbury* 32 The salutation 'Tina-koe', which being pronounced rapidly has the sound of a single word 'tinaque'. **1869** THATCHER *Local Songs* 33 Ropata's whare soon they spied, 'Tenakoe!' the deputation cried. **1881** CAMPBELL *Poenamo* 162 But inasmuch as we only knew Maori enough to the extent of being able to say, 'Tena koe?' ('How do you do?'). **1897** SCOTT *How I Stole 10,000 Sheep* 38 We had so far met..one man who took no notice whatever of us except to say 'Jenokoi' (good day to one person) and if we had been three or four he would have said 'Jenokuru'. **1898** MORRIS *Austral-English* 466 *Tena koe*... a Maori salutation used in North Island of New Zealand. **1907** MANSFIELD *Urewera Notebook* (1978) 70 They meet a Maori again—barefooted and strong—she shouted Te nakohi? **1918** *Hawkes Bay Herald* 29 Aug. 6 [On the completion of the Otira tunnel.] Tenakoe, Sister Province, 'Neath Otira's snowy crest A hundred thousand welcomes I extend you to the West. **1938** *Press* (Christchurch) (McNab Slang) 2 Apr. 18 Now that our political leaders are less lavish with Maori greetings, spoken and cabled, 'tenakoe' and 'kia ora' are less assured of a long life. **1960** SCRYMGEOUR *Memories of Maoriland* 176 Jim gave the salutation 'Tenaqua'. 'Tenaqua Ehoa'. **1969** BAXTER *Collected Poems* (1980) 460 At the church I murmured, 'Tena koe', To the oldest [Maori] woman and she replied, 'Tena koe.' **1980** LELAND *Kiwi-Yankee Dict.* 102 *tena koe*: pronounced tenáqway means Aloha or hello and goodbye.

Hence **tenakoe** *v.*, to greet with *tenakoe*.
  1841 WEEKES *Progress of Colony* in Rutherford & Skinner *Establish. New Plymouth* (1940) 92 Half a dozen lean dogs..commenced a yelping chorus which they kept up lustily during the period of *teneàko*-ing, handshaking, etc. **1856** ABRAHAM *Walk with Bishop NZ* in Taylor *Early Travellers* (1959) 110 Two natives put their heads in at the tent-door, and *tena koe'd* the Bishop.

te nakohi, var. TENA-KOE.

tena koutou. Also **tena koutou katoa**. [See etymological note to TENA-KOE: Ma. /ˈteːnaˈkoutou/.] A greeting to more than one person which has become more frequent in general non-Maori use since the 1980s. Cf. TENA-KOE.
  1842 HEAPHY *NZ* 94 Canoes..meet you..with the everlasting greeting of 'Naumai', or 'tena-koit-ou', 'welcome' or 'hail to you', and exchange, as they pass, news up and down the river. **1863** MANING *Old NZ* iii 58 I stepped into the circle formed by my new friends, and had just commenced a *tena koutou*, when a breeze of wind came. **1946** *JPS* LV. 159 *tēnākoe, tenakorua, tenakoutou*, greeting to one, two, or more. Really two words in all three—Tena koe! (That you! or There you are! Fancy!) I have heard it Tenaaqui! **1967** BRATHWAITE *Evil Day* 382 Tena koutou Good morning! (To several people.) **1988** FRAME *The Carpathians* 30 These days you even say *tena koutou* or *haere mai* without saying *Hairy My* and looking nervous.

tenaqui, tena ra ko koe, varr. TENA-KOE.

ten bob: see BOB, POUND, SHILLING.

tender, *a.* Of wool, having a tensile weakness.
  1915 MACDONALD *NZ Sheepfarming* 88 *Tender Wool*—Wool that will not resist reasonable strain without breaking. **1973** FERNANDEZ *Tussock Fever* 5 'How's this hogget wool going, Bill?' 'First class wool, just first class but it's tender—fleece after fleece...' He plucked a specimen of the fine wool from the tender bin..and gave a sharp tug. The wool parted along a line of weakness in its growth. **1982** *Agric. Gloss.* (MAF) 60 *Tender*: Wool with a tensile weakness. A less severe form of break.

tent.
  1. *Obs.* Part of the paraphenalia of a 'backyard' abortion.
  1907 *Truth* 13 July 5 A 'tent', if used, would cause a miscarriage within twenty-four hours, but it was absurd to say that one used in January would take effect in May. *Ibid.* 28 Sept. 4 She did not know what a 'seaweed pencil' was, nor what a 'tent' was. She had informed no girl that she had used a crochet needle for a certain purpose, and she had, as a matter of fact, never used the needle.
  2. In the phr. **to be born in a tent**, said of, or addressed as a rhetorical question to, a person who leaves a door or window open.
  1925 Used in Auckland p.c. R. Mason. 'Were you born in a tent?' to a person not shutting a door. **1965** ANDERSON & AITKEN *Speech and Idiom of Maori Children* (TS) 96 When we leave the door open they say, 'Hey were you born in a tent'. **1988** McGILL *Dict. Kiwi Slang* 122 *were you born in a tent?* sarcastic question of somebody who has left the door open and let draughts in.

tenth. Also as **native tenths**, or *spec.* **Wellington, Nelson** (etc.) **tenths**. Usu. *pl.* One tenth by area of the land purchases made by the New Zealand Company reserved for the use of local iwi.
  [**1840** *NZ Jrnl.* I. 14 You will take care to mention in every *booka-booka*, or contract for land, that a proportion of the territory ceded, equal to one-tenth of the whole, will be reserved by the Company, and held in trust by them for the future benefit of the chief families of the tribe. **1922** COWAN *NZ Wars* (1955) I. 443 [Quoting the Land Claims Court, Wellington, in 1842.] Barrett was afterwards asked, 'Did you tell the natives who signed the deed that one-tenth of the land described should be reserved for the use of themselves and their families?'] **1941** SUTHERLAND *Numismatic Hist. NZ* 40 In addition to the trade goods, certain lands [in Wellington] known as 'Native Tenths' were set aside as reserves for the natives who signed the deed. [1941 Note] At Wanganui, Brooke, an interpreter, explained similar reservations by marking out a chequer board and informing the natives 'that nine portions would be occupied by the Europeans, and the tenth would be for themselves.' **1955** *NZPD* CCCVII. 2947 [The Maori reserves] comprise, for example, the Wellington, Nelson, and Motueka 'tenths', being a tenth part of the land reserved for the Maoris by the New Zealand Company. **1981** *Evening Post* (Wellington) 2 Jan. 16 Athletic Park, and two other Wellington sites, is owned by the Wellington Tenths (the name refers to the one-tenth share allocated to the Maori owners by the New Zealand Company last century) who lease the ground to the Wellington Rugby Football Union. **1985** *Evening Post* (Wellington) 12 Apr. 1 The North Island Tenths, also known as the Wellington Tenths because of the location of the land, are the beneficial owners of one-tenth of the land ceded by Maori chiefs and reserved from sale to the New Zealand Company in 1839. **1986** *New Outlook* July–Aug. 28 The Whakarewa Grant was part of what was called the 'tenth', a term coined by the New Zealand Company for land it reserved for Maori people. The principle of the tenths was conveyed in the instructions from the New Zealand Company in 1839 to its principal agent, Colonel William Wakefield, before he set out for New Zealand... To Alexander MacKay, commissioner of Native Lands, writing in 1872, the [Otago] tenths 'guarded the natives from..want of foresight, and it secured them from the dangers to which colonisation exposed them'... In Nelson the 'tenth' comprised a total of 15,000 acres... Most of that land remains in Maori ownership. **1992** *North & South* (Auckland) Nov. 60 Attempts to place a contemporary value on the nearly four million acres Ngai Tahu should have owned had the Crown set aside the promised 'tenth' of all land sold is extraordinarily difficult.

teo, var. TIO.

tepau, var. TIPAU.

terakee, terakihi, varr. TARAKIHI.

Te Reinga: see REINGA.

terekehi, var. TARAKIHI.

Te Reo. Also **reo** (Maori). [Ma. *te* def. art. + /reo/: Williams 336 *reo*... 4. Language, dialect.] The Maori language.
  [**1837** *Ko te Pukapuka Tuatahi o te Reo Maori* [Title] in Williams *A Bibliography of Printed Maori* (1975) 8] **1878** BULLER *Forty Yrs. NZ* 174 It is easy to make a serious mistake in the New Zealand tongue, or *reo Maori*. **1993** *National Education Weekly* 28 June 10 Tolaga Bay Area School... Second teacher for Te Reo, total immersion unit. **1995** *Mana* 10 (Spring issue) 9 So that puts to rest the theory that here was another young sportsman (like Adam Parore) with a Maori name and a tendency to mispronounce the reo.

terms, *n.*[1] *pl. Hist.* Esp. in the phr. **to have (keep, run)** (sheep, stock etc.) **on terms**, see quot. 1860. See also EVEN TERMS, THIRDS 1.
  1855 *Canterbury Papers* II. 250 Russell is giving up his sheep on terms at the Upper Station. **1856** FITTON *NZ* 229 I may here explain the..custom of placing out capital under the care of an experienced manager, to be invested in sheep, or occasionally in cattle also. This is a well-known arrangement in the colonies, under the name of 'keeping stock on terms'. **1860** BUTLER *First Year* 10 Feb. (1863) iv 36 One says buy sheep and put them out on terms. I will explain to you what this means. I can buy a thousand ewes.., these I should place in charge of a squatter whose run is not fully stocked... This person would take my sheep for either three..or more years..and would allow me yearly 2*s.* 6*d.* per head in lieu of wool. This would give me 2*s.* 6*d.* as the yearly interest on 25*s.* Besides this he would allow me 40 per cent. per annum of increase,.. moreover, the increase would return me 2*s.* 6*d.* per head wool money as soon as they became sheep. At the end of the term, my sheep would be returned to me as per agreement. **1888** DUNCAN *Wakatipians* 64 [In 1862] Mr. Switzer bought some few hundred sheep..which were 'running on terms' with Mr. Rees. **1933** *Press* (Christchurch) (Acland Gloss.) 25 Nov. 15 *Sheep on terms.*—A favourite investment in the fifties and sixties... The practice was so much in vogue that in 1863 C.M. Ollivier published a pamphlet computing the interest and profit of *s[heep] o[n] t[erms]* at the various lengths of time. The last of such agreements at Horsley Down ran out in 1870 (H. D. letter book) and these are the latest I have found any record of. **1952** RICHARDS *Chatham Is.* 146 Jim..evidently must have had some money for he owned sheep which Ritchie kept for him 'on terms', that is, Ritchie fed and looked after Jim's sheep, keeping half the wool and natural increase in return. **1972** McLEOD *Mountain World* 310 *Terms*: Sheep grazed on behalf of another owner under the terms of an agreement by which profits are shared.

TERMS

terms, *n.*² *pl.* [Transf. use of *term* a division of the academic year.] The requirement of attendance and satisfactory completion of set work as a pre-requisite to sitting final degree examinations; usu. in the phr. **to keep terms** (also familiarly **to get (miss, fail) terms**), to fulfil (or not) such requirements.

1874 *Calendar Univ. NZ* 22 Any person matriculated to the University, and whose name shall be upon the books of an affiliated college, and who shall have passed the yearly College examination, shall be deemed to have kept the three Terms of that year. **1879** *Calendar Univ. NZ* 54 No person shall be admitted to the final examination for the B.A. degree who has not kept three years terms at an institution affiliated to the University of New Zealand. **1916–17** *VUW Calendar* 312 To keep first year terms, a student must pass in two subjects. **1934** MULGAN *Spur of Morning* 56 To take a degree you had to pass matriculation and keep terms, but the college also welcomed anybody who cared to come to lectures. **1959** SLATTER *Gun in my Hand* 37 [The old Prof] gave me 'terms' out of the kindness of his heart, but it was no use. **1962** JOSEPH *Pound of Saffron* ii 38 You know the way he barks at you like a sergeant-major and then sees you don't miss terms. **1990** *VUW Calendar* 86 An internal student shall keep terms by complying with the University regulations regarding enrolment and payment of fees, attending the classes in that subject..and performing..such written, oral, practical and other work as the Professorial Board may require.

tern.

1. Transf. use of the northern hemisphere name *tern* for any of numerous slim, graceful, coastal and marine birds of fam. Laridae with pointed wings and forked tails. See also KAHAWAI BIRD, *sea-swallow* (SEA 1 b), TARA.

1773 FORSTER *Resolution Jrnl.* 25 Mar. (1982) II. 237 Saw common Albatrosses,.. & some affirmed to have seen Eggbirds or Terns. *Ibid.* 289 *Capt Furneaux* dined with us & I described a new *Owl* & a new *Tern*. **1838** POLACK *NZ* I. 306 *Blue herons, auks, sand larks, sand plovers, terns.* **1853** ADAMS *Canterbury Settlement* 8 Among these may be noticed the albatross..and several varieties of tern and petrel. **1870** [see *fish-hawk* (FISH *n.* 3)]. **1882** POTTS *Out in Open* 199 The popokatea, that defends his home with almost the courage of the falcon or tern. **1936** GUTHRIE-SMITH *NZ Naturalist* 110 We were informed that the eggs of Tern and Seagull colonies were appropriated by the local pastrycook industry.

2. With a modifier: **Antarctic (New Zealand Antarctic), black-fronted** (formerly **common**), **caspian, fairy, inland** (or **riverbed**), **little, sooty, swallow-tailed, white (little white), white-fronted.**

(1) **Antarctic (New Zealand Antarctic) tern**. *Sterna vittata bethunei*, a red-billed tern of southern waters. See also *swallow-tailed tern* (8) below.

1948 *NZ Bird Notes* III. 74 *Antarctic Tern (Sterna vittata bollonsi)* nested in considerable numbers around [Snares] Island. **1955** OLIVER *NZ Birds* 336 The Antarctic Tern in its various subspecies ranges from the coast of the Antarctic Continent to S. lat. 36°. **1966** FALLA et al. *Birds NZ* 160 Antarctic Tern *Sterna vittata..*Circumpolar, represented in New Zealand by the subspecies *bethunei*. **1985** *Reader's Digest Book NZ Birds* 228 The Antarctic tern is virtually non-migratory, with some birds remaining close to the breeding islands, even in winter. **1990** *Checklist Birds NZ* 166 *Sterna vittata bethunei...* New Zealand Antarctic Tern.

(2) **black-fronted** (formerly **common**) **tern**. *Sterna albostriata* (formerly *antarctica*), a grey white-rumped tern of inland South Island waterways. See also *inland tern* (5) below, PLOUGH BIRD, TARA 1.

1870 *TrNZI* II. 77 Sterna antarctica... The Common Tern, very often termed the Whale-bird, seems even more gregarious than its congener *S. longipennis*. **1882** POTTS *Out in Open* 215 The common tern..was once exceedingly abundant in the Canterbury district. **1904** HUTTON & DRUMMOND *Animals NZ* 224 *The Black-fronted Tern.—Tara. Sterna albostriata*. **1949** *NZ Bird Notes* III. 193 An odd black-fronted tern... Keeps close behind the plough, landing for an instant to snatch a worm, and then off again. **1955** OLIVER *NZ Birds* 329 The Black-fronted Tern..has decreased in numbers with the progress of European settlement, the occupation of its breeding grounds being the main cause. **1973** MARSHALL et al. *Common Birds of NZ* (1978) 59 Black-fronted Tern..(Tara)..only breeding South Island, inland on shingle riverbeds east of main ranges. **1985** *Reader's Digest Book NZ Birds* 227 Black-fronted terns rarely venture far from water.

(3) **caspian tern**. *Sterna caspia*, a large, red-billed cosmopolitan tern. See also *fish-hawk* (FISH 3), *taranui* (TARA 3).

1871 HUTTON *Catalogue Birds NZ* 42 Sterna caspia... Caspian Tern. **1891** *TrNZI* XXIII. 221 Caspian Tern (*Sterna caspia*). **1901** *Ibid.* XXXIII. 218 The big Caspian tern is a bird of much dignity, and somewhat shier than his lesser relative the common tern. **1917** WILLIAMS *Dict. Maori Lang.* 97 *Kahawai... Caspian tern*; a bird. **1936** GUTHRIE-SMITH *NZ Naturalist* 51 The birds breeding on [Bird Island, Nelson] were Caspian Tern.., Sea Swallows..and Blackbilled Gulls. **1955** OLIVER *NZ Birds* 330 *Caspian Tern. Tara-nui...* The Caspian Tern crept rather unostentatiously into the lists of New Zealand birds. **1981** JOHNSTON *Fish Factory* 53 They'd left the Cove in his boat to troll for kahawai amidst the white cloud of swirling and darting Caspian terns that had appeared the previous afternoon. **1990** *Checklist Birds NZ* 167 *Sterna caspia...* Caspian Tern (Taranui).

(4) **fairy tern**. *Sterna nereis*, a very small, rare, black-crowned tern. See also *little tern* (6) below, *tara-iti* (TARA 2).

1946 *JPS* LV. 158 Several other birds are known as tern with suffix, as..fairy tern, tara-iti. **1955** OLIVER *NZ Birds* 337 *Fairy Tern. Tara-iti. Ibid.* 338 The Fairy Tern frequents the coasts usually in pairs. **1966** FALLA et al. *Birds NZ* 163 Fairy Terns reappear at breeding grounds in September and begin to make trial nest scrapes in the sand. **1985** *Reader's Digest Book NZ Birds* 230 At the turn of the century the fairy tern was a common bird along the coasts of both main islands... Today it is rare.

(5) **inland** (or **riverbed**) **tern**. See *black-fronted tern* (2) above.

1936 GUTHRIE-SMITH *NZ Naturalist* 121 The Inland Tern..seems specially plentiful throughout the provinces of Otago and Southland. **1966** FALLA et al. *Birds NZ* 157 Black-fronted Tern... Tara, Sea Martin, Ploughboy, Inland Tern, Riverbed Tern... The common inland tern of the South Island.

(6) **little tern**. An occas. early name for *fairy tern* (4) above.

1871 HUTTON *Catalogue Birds NZ* 42 Sterna nereis... Little Tern. **1886** *TrNZI* XVIII. 128 Sterna nereis... Little Tern. **1904** HUTTON & DRUMMOND *Animals NZ* 227 *The Little Tern. Sterna nereis*. **1936** GUTHRIE-SMITH *NZ Naturalist* 46 The Little Tern..which I thought we might have come across never blessed our vision.

(7) **sooty tern**. *Sterna fuscata serrata*, a striking black and white tropical and subtropical tern, called by sailors from its cry the 'wideawake'.

TERRACE

1904 HUTTON & DRUMMOND *Animals NZ* 227 *The Sooty Tern. Sterna fuliginosa.* **1955** OLIVER *NZ Birds* 342 A denizen of all tropical and subtropical seas, the Sooty Tern or Wideawake touches the New Zealand region at the Kermadecs. **1966** FALLA et al. *Birds NZ* 165 Sooty Tern... Wideawake... Sooty Terns are sometimes blown inland. **1985** *Reader's Digest Book NZ Birds* 233 The sooty tern is the most oceanic of all terns; it ranges over most tropical and sub-tropical seas and comes to land only to breed. **1990** *Checklist Birds NZ* 165 *Sterna fuscata serrata..*Sooty Tern... Breeds abundantly in the southwest Pacific, especially at Norfolk and Kermadec Islands.

(8) **swallow-tailed tern**. See *Antarctic tern* (1) above.

1904 HUTTON & DRUMMOND *Animals NZ* 225 The Swallow-tailed Terns are noted for their skill in diving, and are characterised by great courage. **1909** CHILTON *Subantarctic Islands NZ* II. 559 Swallow-tailed tern... Small black-headed, white-tailed terns were frequently seen at the Snares and in Carnley Harbour. **1936** GUTHRIE-SMITH *NZ Naturalist* 120 The Swallow-tailed Tern..breeds..on the Snares Group.

(9) **white** (occas. **little white**) **tern**. *Gygis alba* (formerly *candida*) *royana*, a small tern, completely white except for black ringed eyes.

1891 *TrNZI* XXIII. 222 Little White Tern (*Gygis candida*). **1904** HUTTON & DRUMMOND *Animals NZ* 228 *The White Tern. Gygis candida*. **1955** OLIVER *NZ Birds* 346 The White Tern is one of the tropical noddies that, within the New Zealand region, breeds only at the Kermadecs. **1966** FALLA et al. *Birds NZ* 166 White Tern... White Noddy, Love Tern, Fairy Tern... The most ethereal of seabirds. **1985** *Reader's Digest Book NZ Birds* 236 The white tern does not build a nest, but balances its egg in a depression on the branch or trunk of a tree. **1990** *Checklist Birds NZ* 171 *Gygis alba royana..White Tern...* Breeds at Norfolk and Kermadec Islands.

(10) **white-fronted tern**. *Sterna striata* (formerly *frontalis*), the commonest New Zealand coastal tern, having a black crown and white underparts, a long forked tail, and dark bill. See also *barracouta bird* (barracouta 2), *black cap* (BLACK *a.*² 2), GRENADIER *n.*¹, KAHAWAI BIRD, NODDY, *sea-swallow* (SEA 1 b), TARA 1, TIKKITAK.

1873 BULLER *Birds NZ* 281 Sterna frontalis. (White-fronted Tern.) **1904** HUTTON & DRUMMOND *Animals NZ* 227 *The White-fronted Tern.—Tara. Sterna frontalis.* **1932** STEAD *Life Histories NZ Birds* 36 White-fronted Terns are very fond of bathing, in either fresh or salt water, but they prefer fresh. **1949** *NZ Bird Notes* III. 123 White-fronted Tern... Large parties are frequently seen skimming gracefully over the open sea coast, or resting in stormy weather on shores and rocks. **1955** OLIVER *NZ Birds* 341 The White-fronted Tern breeds in large colonies on shingly river beds and also on rocks on the sea coast. **1966** FALLA et al. *Birds NZ* 164 White-fronted Tern *Sterna striata*... Sea-swallow, Kahawai Bird, Tara..Noddy (Chathams). **1985** *Reader's Digest Book NZ Birds* 232 The white-fronted tern eats fish, such as yellow-eyed mullet. **1990** *NZ Geographic* VII. 45 Two hundred pairs of white-fronted terns fledged only 30 young in the 1987–88 season.

terrace. [Spec. use of *terrace* 'a natural terrace formation', and *geol.* 'a horizontal shelf on the side of a hill, or sloping ground': see OED *terrace* 2 (a) and (b): used elsewhere but freq. in New Zealand land-use and SI gold-mining applications, esp. for *river-terrace*.]

1. a. A horizontal shelf in a river valley, or on sloping ground, often as part of a series of such shelves at different levels. Compare FLAT *n.*¹ 1.

1773 Forster *Resolution Jrnl.* 27 Apr. (1982) II. 267 The Scenery of the country was bold & worthy of the Pencil of a *Salvator Rosa*, all the Sides of hills were steep, rocky, & on all the little slopes & small terrasses or Settlements covered with fine shrubs, of various kinds. **1860** in Butler *First Year* (1863) vii 96 The terraces, which are so abundant all over the back country, and which rise, one behind another, to the number, it may be, of twenty or thirty, with the most unpicturesque regularity (on my run there are fully twenty), are supposed to be elevated sea-beaches. **1874** Caird *Sheepfarming NZ* 26 The words 'terrace' and 'flat', so often used, rather aptly describe the general nature of the country. A flat means a plain, but it is a rare thing to gallop along a flat for more than a mile without coming across a terrace, which terrace may be only six feet high, or it may be a hundred..[and] is certain to be as regular as if it formed part of some ornamental ground. **1885** *NZJSc.* II. 511 One of the most remarkable features in the scenery of the South Island..is the series of river terraces which flank the broad shingle-filled vallies [*sic*] on either side. **1892** Douglas in *Mr Explorer Douglas* (1957) 175 At the Forks [on the West Coast] the terrace flats taking in both sides of the river, are about a mile wide. **1917** *TrNZI* XLIX. 4 This 'river-bed' is bounded on either side by a broad expanse of flat land, chiefly tussock-covered, termed colloquially 'river-flat', but in this paper 'terrace'. **1930** Dobson *Reminiscences* 141 A number of gold-diggers were working in the neighbourhood, some on the beaches and some on the adjoining terraces. **1963** Pearson *Coal Flat* 53 [She] saw in the shadow of a mountain range a forlorn cluster of roofs..perched on a terrace.

b. Contoured sheep-tracks (or 'benches') formed on hillsides grazed by sheep.
1951 Levy *Grasslands NZ* (1970) 254 On steep hillsides stock will tend to track and contour the land, and the ultimate surface formation of well-stocked country will be a series of broad or narrow terraces with steep slopes between them upon which stock seldom tread.

c. Comb. with alluvial goldmining reference: **terrace bottom**, **terrace workings**.
1863 *AJHR* D-6 18 Terrace workings are in many places proving highly remunerative. **1906** Galvin *NZ Mining Handbook* 124 South of Hokitika, there are no marine deposits on higher levels beyond the existing run of the beaches; the 'terrace bottom' (i.e. gravel wash) abuts on the lagoons.

Hence **terrace** *v*., to work a terrace claim.
1867 *Trip to Thames Gold-fields* (1978) 27 A few yards further on, a party were 'terracing'.

2. Applied to natural features formed by geothermal mineral action, *spec.* the 'Pink and White Terraces', a scenic attraction at Rotomahana near Rotorua, destroyed by the eruption of Mount Tarawera on 10 June 1886.
1873 *Weekly News* (Auckland) 10 May 20 At Rotomahana we saw the terraces of enamelled baths of pink and white. **1882** Potts *Out in Open* 54 Soon we gaze on the white terrace, the boiling geysers, and the other wonderful phenomena. **1883** Domett *Ranolf and Amohia* II. 58 Each terrace a wide basin brimmed With water, brilliant yet in hue.

terraki, var. TARAKIHI.

terror. [See OED 1889, 'a holy terror'.] Ellipt. for *holy terror*, used jocularly for anything surprisingly distinctive or outstanding, either good or bad; esp. in the phr. **to be a terror for**, to be 'a great one' for, to be 'terribly' keen on.
1886 Kershaw *Col. Facts & Fictions* 266 The roads were terrors, the lake was a terror, some of the women were terrors... Terror is a New Zealand adjective. Shilling knives are advertised as 'perfect terrors'. You can't go far wrong if you call a thing a terror. **1892** *Auckland Weekly News* 26 Mar. 31 The botanical name of rat-tail or Chilian grass is..*Sporobolus elongatus*... Land full of rat-tail is a terror to plough, as too many settlers know. **1947** Davin *For Rest of Our Lives* 24 Your uncle was a terror for the drink after you went away. **1963** *Weekly News* (Auckland) 30 Oct. [The plough] would quite often overturn. Having done so, it was a terror of a thing to get upright again. **1988** *Heinemann Dictionary of NZ Quotations* 42 I don't know about that [*sc.* boiled elephant's foot], but I'm a terror for me veges.

tete. [Ma. /'te:te:/: Williams 409 *Tē* (iii)... *tētē* [applied to various duck species, shoveller, brown, grey, and black teal].] Any of various native ducks. DUCK 2 (7), TEAL *n.*[1] 2 (2), (3), (5).
1858 Smith *Notes of a Journey* in Taylor *Early Travellers* (1959) 354 [We] saw very few ducks. We shot at some Tetes, but could not hit them, because they dived so frequently. **1871** Hutton *Catalogue Birds NZ* 37 Rhynchaspis variegata... Shoveller. Tete. **1886** *TrNZI* XVIII. 117 *Querquedula gibberifrons.*—Tete, Little Teal. **1888** Buller *Birds NZ* II. 269 (New-Zealand Shoveller)... *Native name*. Tete, Pateke..'Spoon-bill Duck' of the colonists. **1955** Oliver *NZ Birds* 410 *Grey Teal. Tete. Anas gibberifrons gracilis*... *Ibid.* 415 *Shoveller. Tete. Kuruwhengi Spatula rhynchotis variegata*. **1966** [see TEAL *n.*[1] 2 (5)]. **1985** *Reader's Digest Book NZ Birds* 145 *Grey Teal. Anas gibberifrons gracilis... Tete.*

teteawaka. Occas. **teteaweka**, **titi-a-weka**. [Ma. /'te'te:awaka/: Williams 413 *Tetēawaka..Olearia angustifolia*.] *Olearia oporina* (now including *O. angustifolia* and *O. chathamica*) (fam. Asteraceae or Compositae), a coastal shrub or tree daisy of the southern South Island, Stewart and Chatham Islands, distinguished by showy flowers having yellow or purple centres. Cf. MUTTONBIRD SCRUB, TREE DAISY.
1889 Kirk *Forest Flora* 287 *Olearia angustifolia*... The Tete-a-weka... The plant is extremely rare. **1890** *PWD Catalogue Timbers* (NZ & South Seas Exhib.) 15 Tete-a-waka..Olearia angustifolia..Timber small and of little use. **1906** Cheeseman *Manual NZ Flora* 281 *O[learia] angustifolia*... South Island..near Bluff Hill..Stewart Island: sea-coast south of Paterson's Inlet..*Titi-a-weka*. **1910** Cockayne *NZ Plants & Their Story* 76 The teteawaka..which has flower-heads 2 inches or so in diameter, with violet centres, occurs in Stewart Island. **1940** Howard *Rakiura* xvii A characteristic scrub [of Stewart Island] known locally as 'Mutton-bird scrub', the principal constituents..being Puheretaiko..Tete-a-weka..and Daisy Tree. **1952** in Sansom *In Grip of Island* (1982) 154 In the house, big fire of dead tete-a-weka wood going. **1979** Wilson *Titi Heritage* 83 On one visit we were thrilled to find a Titiaweka in flower. It had a large daisylike flower, the centre of which is ringed with clusters of tiny yellow flowers.

tetoki, var. TITOKI.

tewai, var. TIWAI.

Te Waipounamu. Also occas. **Te Wahi** [Ma. ='place'] **Pounamu**, with much variety of early form and initial capitalization. [Ma. /te'wai'pounamu/ *te waipounamu* (*wai* ='water'): cf. Williams 476 *Waipounamu*..Greenstone, jade.] The South Island of New Zealand, or an early name for a locality on its west coast. See also POUNAMU 2.
1770 Cook *Journals* 31 Jan. (1955) I. 243 This man spoke of three lands, the two above mentioned which he call'd *Tovy-poenammu* which signifies green Talk or stone such as the[y] Make their tools on. **1777** Cook *Journals* 25 Feb. (1967) III. 73 This Water [from which the greenstone 'fish' is taken] is called by them Tovy poenammoo that is the Water of green talc, and the land about it *Poenammo*, which is all of the Southern island of New Zealand they know by that name. **1838** Polack *NZ* I. 275 Singular to relate, the centrical island, has existed hitherto unnamed [Polack suggests *Victoria* as a name]. As a distinguishing mark, it has been called *Te Wai Poenámu*, or the waters of green talc (*rather* an anomalous name for *terra firma*), from the time of Cook's survey: but that navigator repeatedly observes, this name is appropriated to a very small proportion of the country, on the south-west, where the lake of green stone is situated. **1840** *Thomas Bunbury's Report* in *GBPP House of Commons 1841 (No.311)* 17 June 112 This island, called Tavai Poenammoo or Middle Island of New Zealand..was accordingly taken possession of. **1848** Wakefield *Handbook NZ* 314 It is called by them 'Ponamu', whence the name once assigned to the Middle Island—'Te Wahi Ponamu' or, 'The Place of Green Stone'. **1851** Shortland *S. Dist. NZ* 154 The name Tovy Poenammoo, or, as it would now be written, Te Wai-pounamu, meaning the Pounamu-water, by many still imagined to be that of the Middle Island, is, as Captain Cook suspected, 'only the name of a particular place, where the natives got the green talc, or stone, of which they made their ornaments and tools, and not a general name of the whole southern district.' **1905** Baucke *White Man Treads* 40 'Pounamu' (greenstone) was only to be found in the creeks of the inland ranges of the Middle Island, and hence called 'Te wai pounamu'. **1926** Cowan *Travel in NZ* II. i This volume..is descriptive of the varied landscapes of the South Island, more particularly the alpine, lake and fiord scenery for which the Wai-Pounamu is famous. **1933** in *Na To Hoa Aroha* (1988) III. 72 Dissatisfied younger sons, ambitious women or slighted elders sought redress by force of arms or went into the open spaces of Aotearoa or Tewaipounamu. Our Courts recognised the arikiship in the award of shares in land. **1952** Taylor *Lore and History of the South Island Maori* 186 The Maoris of the South Island in their poetic references to their country invariably refer to it as Te Waipounamu, the island of greenstone.

tewhatewha. Also **tewa-tewa**. [Ma. /'tefatefa/: Williams 413 *tewhatewha..1*. A weapon carved from a single piece of wood, or sometimes bone, shaped something like an axe, with the handle straight and pointed, the blade serving as a fly [i.e. something (as a flag) attached by the edge] when a blow was struck.] See Williams's definition above and quot. 1946 below. See also BATTLE-AXE.
1856 Shortland *Traditions & Superstitions* 244 The *tewhatewha*, a wooden battle-axe, having a sharp-pointed handle to enable it also to answer the purpose of a spear. **1882** Potts *Out in Open* 13 In the..armament might be seen the broad-edged tewa-tewa with its dangling tuft of feathers. **1894** *TrNZI* XXVI. 441 The *tewhatewha*, or *paiaka*, was used in somewhat similar fashion to the *taiaha*. **1904** Tregear *Maori Race* 312 Another weapon of authority or direction was the battle-axe (*tewha-tewha* or *paiaka*) made of bone or hard wood. **1930** Reischek *Yesterdays in Maoriland* (1933) 152 Others carried wooden lances or long, hatchet-like weapons called tewhatewha. **1946** *JPS* LV. 159 *tewhatewha*, a weapon with a terminal broad semi-crescent of one side, the other end sharpened for thrusting, the lower side of the crescent pierced with a

Te Whiti. [Ma. /te 'fiti/.]

1. The name of Erueti *Te Whiti*-o-Rongomai (?-1907), Maori leader and prophet, used *attrib.* of the spiritual movement he founded, and of its followers.

1885 CHUDLEIGH *Diary* 12 Feb. (1950) 332 I think there will be quite 20,000 eels in all for Te Whiti. Piripiri and Pene took a large contract from me [for] fencing. They gave their word as Te Whiti men but would not sign an agreement. *Ibid.* 3 Sept. 367 In Wellington. It is settled that Major Gudgeon, a sargeant and six A.C. go to the Chathams..to run in the Te Whiti Maoris. [See also quot. 1950 below.]

2. In composition: **Te Whiti-ism (Te Whitism)**, the spiritual teachings and doctrine promulgated by Te Whiti; **Te-Whitiite**, a follower of Te Whiti's teachings.

1930 COWAN *The Maori* 66 In Taranaki the adherents of **Te Whiti-ism**—quite a different brand of old-time religion from the Ringatu—have their monthly meetings for prayer and exhortation at Manu-korihi, on the Waitara. **1952** RICHARDS *Chatham Is.* 121 Rev. Croasdaile Bowen came in '76 but was unable to do much as Te Whiti-ism had such a grip of the Islanders. **1986** SORRENSON in *Na To Hoa Aroha* (1986) I. 14 Buck, going to Te Aute from a boyhood in Taranaki, where the missions had given way to Pai Marire and Te Whitism, was pleasantly surprised at the strength of Anglicanism among the East Coast Maoris. **1925** *Patea & Waverley Press* 26 Jan. 2 Many Ratanaites were present at the customary meeting held at Waitara on a recent Sunday by the **Te Whitiites**. **1950** RICHARDS in Chudleigh *Diary* (1950) 14 The most ardent Te Whitiites were the Chatham Island Maoris who used to send their prophet much money and many tons of food each year.

that, *adv.* The sense 'so' is frequent in New Zealand speech, and possibly more widespread or usual than implied by OED *that* III: 'now only *dial.* and *Sc.*'

1897 WRIGHT *Station Ballads* 41 I'm that glad I think I'll go cranky. **1937** MARSH *Vintage Murder* 158 That young bleeder's run orf behind this shed and it's that narrer I can't foller. **1946** SARGESON *That Summer* 32 We got on that well together.

that, *pronoun.* As **that'll (that will)** prefixed to various phrases indicating disbelief on the part of the speaker, or the improbability of stated predictions, etc.

1. As **that'll be the day!** [see OED *day n.* 20 b 'app. orig. *N.Z.*': now widespread in many varieties of English (cf. Partridge *A Dictionary of Catchphrases*, 1985 ed. Beale 296f.)], used ironically of something most unlikely to happen, or beyond belief. Compare 1867 Barker *Station Life* (1874) 113 Ah but it'll be a far day first [before I'll believe that].

1941 BAKER *NZ Slang* 50 *That'll be the day!*..a cant phrase expressing mild doubt following some boast or claim by a person. **1942** *NZEF Times* 7 Sept. 8 Tokyo will get worse punishment than London ever got. 'That will be the day.' **1951** MARSH *Opening Night* (1968) xi 186 'If I've bungled,' Alleyn muttered, 'I've..bungled in a big way.'.. Bailey astonished everyone by saying... 'That'll be the day.' 'Don't talk Australian,' Mr Fox chided. **1964** HARVEY *Any Old Dollars Mister?* 35 I asked some Wellington people if they'd like a shine, and all they said was, 'You've got a bloody nerve,' or 'That'll be the day,' or something mean like that. **1963** MORRIESON *Scarecrow* 142 'I don't want ole Charlie trying to kiss you or something.' 'Tha'll be the day,' said Prudence. **1983** HENDERSON *Down from Marble Mountain* 239 'That'll be the Day,' we say. 'The Day' is getting closer.

2. In various elaborations: **that'll be the frosty Friday (the frozen fortnight, the Saturday afternoon, the Sunday afternoon, the sunny Sunday)**.

1942 *NZEF Times* 12 July 6 That *will* be the Sunday afternoon. **1944** HOBBS in *Listener* 28 Jan. 20 There are [from the 2NZEF], of course, the eternal variations on the old theme which nearly wrecked New Zealand's slang two or three years ago—'That'll be the day', 'That'll be the sunny afternoon', and so on. **1945** HENDERSON *Gunner Inglorious* 131 Work? In a Quartermaster's store? That will be the Frosty Friday. **c1949** p.c. R. Mason, heard in Dunedin. That'll be the Saturday afternoon; or That'll be the sunny Sunday afternoon. **1966** TURNER *Eng. Lang. Austral. & NZ* 177 *That'll be the day*, a way of expressing a strong disinclination to do something, was unknown to visiting Americans during the war, one of whom thought it expressed gay anticipation and answered 'That'll be the day' when asked to visit a New Zealand family. The expression was worked to death and in its dying agonies produced some contortions as *That'll be the frosty Friday* etc. **1970** SLATTER *On the Ball* 137 'That'll be the Sunday afternoon,' says Spandau Craig. **1988** McGILL *Dict. Kiwi Slang* 112 *that'll be the frosty Friday/frozen fortnight* Kiwi variants of 'that'll be the day', which Partridge thinks derives from WW1 officer usage.

there's an old boot for every sock: see BOOT *n.* 5.

thermal, *a.* [A shortened form of *geothermal* produced by the internal heat of the earth.]

1. *Ellipt.* for **thermal spring, thermal pool**, a spring or pool heated geothermally.

1952 6 May A member of a VUC first-year English class responding to an assignment on NZ vocabulary: I would include among New Zealand English words: *thermal*, a thermal pool. **1989** TE AWEKOTUKU *Tahuri* 66 But still, the steam. Ngawha. 'They call it thermal here, dear,' wise Jessie informed her sister. *Ibid.* 102 ngawha: boiling water, thermal.

2. Special Comb. **thermal area (district, region, wonderland)**, a geothermally active region, esp. that of the central North Island. Cf. *hot lake* (HOT *a.* 2).

1918 *Evening Post* (Wellington) 20 Jan. 6 There were fewer visitors to the thermal district during the recent holidays. **1920** BOLITHO *With the Prince in NZ* 43 From the rolling Wairarapa plains and the steam breathing towns of the thermal region eight thousand Maoris had come to welcome the son of King Hori. **1955** *Evening Post* (Wellington) 7 Sept. 10 After all, argued Mr. Fox, a good many holes had been bored in the thermal areas of the North Island. **1974** AVERY *The Ken Avery Songbook* [Title 'Paekakariki'] It's south of the Thermal Region,—Only six hundred miles from the Bluff. **1977** STAFFORD *Romantic Past of Rotorua* 10 All of this fuelled the desire..to travel into what was now being described as 'The Thermal Wonderland'. **1993** *Evening Post* (Wellington) 5 Apr. 13 She decided to go to Waiotapu, a witch's brew of blasting steam..and giddy smells, a storm of the senses in a Thermal Wonderland.

Thermette. Also occas. **Thermet**. [f. a proprietary name.] A patent outdoor water-boiler (see esp. quot. 1963). Cf. BENGHAZI BURNER.

1937 *NZ Patent Office Jrnl.* [no number given] 3 June Thermette B35119 [filed] 23rd July, 1936. John Ashley Hart..An improved quick-boiling picnic kettle. **1945** Thermet [see BENGHAZI BURNER]. **1952** *Evening Post* (Wellington) 4 Sept. 14 [Advt] For a stop on the road there's little to beat the efficiency of the 'Thermette'. This wonderful little kettle burns twigs, paper, rubbish, etc., creating its own forced draft. **1963** BACON *In the Sticks* 184 Thermette—An ingenious portable water-heater-fireplace, consisting of a short metal chimney surrounded by a water jacket. Extremely popular on picnic excursions, they will burn anything combustible, and provide a considerable quantity of boiling water in a very short time. **1971** ARMFELT *Catching Up* 59 But first Ray had to set up the thermette—a sort of tall cylindrical kettle, with a hollow up the middle in which Ray stuffed some paper and kindling for a fire. The fire was lit and the water in the walls around it boiled in next to no time. 'She's a New Zealand invention, the thermette: the servicemen brought it back from the war.' **1983** *Listener* 5 Nov. 67 Other families had 'Thermettes', which I coveted as they involved lighting a real fire. **1991** *Ibid.* 10 June 34 But it hadn't been called a Thermette [in WW2]. They knew it as the Benghazi Boiler or chip heater. Every small unit had one as standard equipment... John Ashley Hart, a New Zealander, had first patented the Thermette. John Hart began making the Thermette in 1931.

they're off, Mr Cutts. *Obs.* [Orig. uncertain: poss. an elaboration of the 19–20c. Brit. slang *they're off, said the monkey* (see Partridge 8; also heard in NZ c1940, Ed.), with a play on the name of a horse-racing trainer *E. Cutts*, poss. (see quot. 1943) a horse-racing starter, with an allusion to castration. Cf. 1960 SCRYMGEOUR *Memories Maoriland* 60 One student [of Canterbury Agricultural College]..the son of a sporting and well-known racing baronet of North Canterbury, would take Jim into the stables at 'Cutts' to see the horses in training. 1966 *Encycl. NZ* III. 58 In 1875 G.G. Stead (1841–1908), the famous racehorse owner, bought a half-share in Redwood's racing stud. Under the partnership agreement Stead managed the business side while the training was put in the hands of E. Cutts... This arrangement..lasted into the 1890s and was terminated when Stead bought out Redwood's share of the stud.]

1911 *Truth* 4 Nov. 6 'They're off, Mr Cutts!' At least, they will be about three o'clock today (Saturday), and in less than four minutes afterwards, you will all know whether you have lost your money or not. **1941** BAKER *NZ Slang* 50 *They're off Mr Cutts!*, meaning 'things have started!' or 'now we're getting down to business!' **1943** BENNETT *English in NZ* in *Amer. Speech* XVIII. 90 Horse-racing, another popular pastime (including trotting races, or *the trots*) provides two colloquialisms which need explanation. The exclamation 'They're off, Mr Cutts!', announcing that any contest or affair has begun, contains the name of a one-time popular starter at the Auckland races. **1966** *Encycl. NZ* II. 680 Examples of slang and colloquial expressions of local origin are..*they're off Mr Cutts* for 'the performance is about to start'.

thick. [An elaboration of *thick* stupid.] In the phr. **thick as pigshit**, very stupid.

1990 KIDMAN *True Stars* 40 'Thick as pigshit, if you ask me,' said Gary... He picked up one of the attendant's limp wrists. **1993** O'SULLIVAN *Let the River Stand* 11 Others confidently said the boy was thick as pig-shit. **1995** *Evening Post* (Wellington) 21 July 4 The apt expression to describe that kind of closed-mindedness is 'Thick as pigshit and twice as nasty'.

thieve out. To sneak out.
   1922 MANSFIELD *Stories* (1984) 503 Isabel and Lottie, who liked visitors, went upstairs to change their pinafores. But Kezia thieved out at the back. Nobody was about.

thin. In phr. of comparison, indicating extreme thinness of farm animals: **so thin you could cut your fingers on its spine**, **as thin as the back of a chair**.
   1960 MASTERS *Back-Country Tales* 25 The sheep were half wild Merino wethers, as thin as the back of a chair, and as fast and scattery as a sou-westerly gale. **1980** MCLEOD *Tussock Ranges* 168 Some years ago I was riding round one of the blocks when I saw a young steer so thin that you could have 'cut your fingers on his spine'.

thing.
1. In the phr. **like one thing** [see OED *thing* 14 k 'Austral. colloq. and U.S. dial.', 1946], 'like anything'.
   1948 BALLANTYNE *Cunninghams* (1963) 67 He saw Phil..and some other Standard Four jokers skiting like one thing.
2. See *hard thing* (HARD *a*. 1 d).

think, *v*.
1. In the phr. **to think no small beans of**, see BEAN.
2. think big. [Spec. and transf. uses of *to think big* to be ambitious.] **a.** Used nominally or attributively of the capital-intensive policies for the development of natural resources associated with the Muldoon administration of the early 1980s; often collocated with **policy** and **project**.
   1981 KENNEDY *Straight from Shoulder* 133 The present [Muldoon] Government of New Zealand is in danger of being mesmerised by its 'think big' policies. **1982** LAMBERT & PALENSKI *NZ Almanac* 280 Thinking big. The National Government plans a range of energy-related projects under what it terms its 'growth strategy', colloquially known as 'think big'. **1987** MOORE *Hard Labour* 92 On 29 September 1986, Cabinet invited me to prepare a report on the previous Government's decision-making on the Think Big projects. **1992** *Dominion Sunday Times* (Wellington) 9 Aug. 9 Little changed behind the Think Big facade.
b. In verbal use.
   1981 KENNEDY *Straight from Shoulder* 73 At the moment the [Muldoon] Government is firmly committed to 'thinking big'; Labour seems equally firmly against it. **1985** SHERWOOD *Botanist at Bay* 27 He [*sc*. a politician] tried to add something about the need to 'think big' and plan for industrial development, but the youngsters set up a massive shout of 'hypocrite'.
c. *transf*. Applied to grandiose non-political ventures which fail.
   1991 *North & South* (Auckland) June 74 Anthony Morris is a potter who decided to think big, too big he would now say. A natural expansionist who 'wants to see things happen', Morris is hardly your backyard potter... Morris and James went into receivership. Something was happening all right but it wasn't what the think-big potter had intended.

thirds. *Hist*.
1. [AND 1823] Esp. in the phr. (**sheep**) **on thirds**, a system of flock-sharing whereby an owner put his sheep into the care of a station owner who received a third of the wool and lambs in lieu of rent for grazing. Cf. TERMS *n*.[1]
   1849 TORLESSE *Papers* (1958) 99 Stafford renewed his offer to me of looking after his sheep on thirds. **1850** GODLEY *Letter* 8 July in *Speeches & Documents* (1971) 28 It is customary here, & sometimes very profitable, to have sheep 'on thirds'; which means to send them to a station, & allow the owner of it half the wool, & $^1/_3$d. of the increase for the trouble & expense of looking after them—the owner receives half the wool, & $^2/_3$ds. of the increase, as profit on his capital. **1878** JOLLIE *Reminiscences* (ATLTS) 17 Watt, who was starting a sheep-farm in the Wairau Valley [before 1850 was] on 'Thirds' for three years. This meant one third of the wool and lambs each year to Watt and I have two thirds. **1939** BEATTIE *First White Boy Born Otago* 100 Johnny Jones saw that Trotter was a reliable man and gave him a start [in the 1850s] with a flock of 1000 sheep on thirds—that is to say, Jones got the wool and two-thirds of the lambs while Trotter got one-third for his work.
2. *Local Bodies*. See quot.
   1902 *Settler's Handbook NZ* 188 'Thirds.'—All endowment lands leased under the [Land] Act are subject to the 'thirds' clause, which gives one-third of the rent to the local bodies for roads for access.

thirty-niner. WW2 (North Africa). [Poss. influenced by *forty-niner*, one who joined the 1849 Californian gold-rush, as celebrated in the well-known song 'Clementine'.] Often init. cap. A soldier who volunteered for war service in 1939; a First Echelon man. Cf. *four-figure man* (FOUR).
   1942 *NZEF Times* 19 Oct. 12 That's not a Wog, son—that's a Thirty-Niner, my oath. **1945** WEBBER *Johnny Enzed in Middle East* 3 With the exception of the 'thirty-niners' and other pioneers, most members of the 2NZEF left New Zealand with a reasonably fitting battledress. **1959** BRUNO *Hellbuster* [back dust-jacket] Frank Bruno left New Zealand as a machine-gunner with the 'Thirty-Niners' (First Echelon) of the N.Z. Division. **1964** *Evening Post* (Wellington) 18 Apr. 1 First Echelon reunion, Dunedin, Labour Weekend. 'Thirty-Niners' and their wives who intend travelling to Dunedin. **1982** *Evening Post* (Wellington) 18 Sept. 12 The forgotten legion, the thirty-niners, the four-figure man..all sound like mysterious titles.

thistle, *n*.
1. Of the forty or more 'thistles' given common names in New Zealand, only a few have a distinctive local application and are dealt with in 2 below (in alphabetical order of modifiers) as transf. or spec. uses of international English *thistle* 'any of various spiny herbs of the daisy family Asteraceae'.
2. With a modifier: **Californian (California, Canadian, Canada), Chatham Island, French, Scotch (bastard Scotch), sowthistle, wind, winged (wind, wing, slender winged)**.
   (1) **Californian** (occas. **California**) **thistle** (and *ellipt*. **Californian**) or **Canadian (Canada) thistle.** *Cirsium arvense*, a creeping thistle, orig. from Eurasia, now a common weed of esp. farm land. See also CALI. (Known elsewhere also as *Canada thistle*, *corn thistle*, *creeping thistle*, *field thistle*.)
      1890 *Otago Witness* (Dunedin) 20 Feb. 7 There are two varieties of the thistle which are very stubborn to eradicate... They have been called respectively the American and the Californian thistles... Both plants are natives of Britain. **1891** WALLACE *Rural Econ. Austral. & NZ* 310 'Canadian' or 'Californian' thistle... said to have been introduced about 1886 in Californian barley. **1902** *Settler's Handbook NZ* 241 This plant is termed the Californian or Canada thistle in Australia and New Zealand; the corn thistle or green thistle in England; and Canada thistle in Canada and United States. **1913** *NZJAg.* Aug. VII. 250 The settler writes as follows:—'I spent the whole of last summer fighting Californians.' **1921** GUTHRIE-SMITH *Tutira* (1926) 254 Corn thistle.., in New Zealand rechristened Californian or Canadian thistle, was first detected by me on Putorino. **1948** BALLANTYNE *Cunninghams* (1976) 17 Last time he wrote he said it's been awful with the Californian thistle up there this year. **1959** DAVIN *No Remittance* 100 What was down in grass..was eaten up by ragwort and Canadian thistle. **1970** DAVIN *Not Here Not Now* 125 Goldfinches swung on the tall Canadian thistles. **1980** TAYLOR *Weeds of Crops* 24 Californian Thistle..is known as creeping thistle in England. It is native to Europe but known as Canadian thistle in many countries.
   (2) **Chatham Island thistle.** *Embergeria grandifolia* (fam. Asteraceae), a robust endemic herb of Chatham Island sand dunes.
      1952 RICHARDS *Chatham Is*. 49 *Sonchus.. grandifolius*... Chatham Island Thistle. **1984** HOLMES *Chatham Is*. 93 *Embergeria grandifolia* (Chatham Island Thistle, Sonchus)... It is a large waxy-green soft-prickled plant which dies down in Autumn.
   (3) **French thistle.** A local Banks Peninsula name for the variegated thistle, *Silybum marianum*.
      1926 HILGENDORF *Weeds* 192 Milk Thistle (*Silybum marianum*), sometimes called St. Mary's thistle, variegated or spotted thistle, and, near Akaroa, French thistle... It is abundant in scattered localities in both islands, sometimes forming dense masses. It is an annual or biennial, grows up to 6 ft. in height, and has large leaves without wings. **1969** *Standard Common Names Weeds* 78 thistle, French [=] *variegated thistle*.
   (4) **Scotch thistle.** [Transf. use of Brit. *Scotch thistle* (also called *heraldic thistle*) usu. *Onopordum acanthium*.] **a.** Applied (as occas. in Britain) to *Cirsium vulgare* (formerly *C. lanceolatum*), the spear thistle.
      1856 *Scotch Thistle Ordinance* 1856 in *Ordinances of Taranaki* (1867) 60 An Ordinance to prevent the spread of Scotch Thistle. **1861** WELLS *Diary* 9 Nov. (1970) 23 Went to Mangorei cutting in Scotch thistles. **1890** WALLACE *Rural Econ. Austral. & NZ* 310 The species commonly called the 'Scotch' thistle is the spear thistle. **1926** HILGENDORF *Weeds* 186 Scotch Thistle..is also called Spear thistle. This exceedingly common weed is a biennial. [1967 edn. makes *spear thistle* the preferred name.] **1951** LEVY *Grasslands NZ* (1970) 302 Weeds that are neglected by all classes of stock..Scotch thistle, Californian thistle, winged thistle, variegated thistle. **1984** *Standard Common Names Weeds* 93 Scotch thistle [=] *cardoon: cotton thistle... Scotch thistle Cirsium vulgare*.
   b. As **bastard Scotch thistle**, occas. applied to *Carduus nutans*, the nodding thistle.
      1926 HILGENDORF *Weeds* 192 Nodding Thistle (*Carduus nutans*), also called bastard Scotch thistle, is found in Auckland, South Canterbury and Otago. **1984** *Standard Common Names Weeds* 94 *bastard scotch thistle* [=] *nodding thistle*.
   (5) **sowthistle.** [Spec. use of *sowthistle Sonchus* spp.: see OED.] **a.** Also occas. **sour-thistle**. Any of various native and introduced species of *Sonchus* (fam. Asteraceae), used as green vegetables by the Maori and by European explorers and settlers; PUHA 1. See also *bush thistle* (BUSH B 4), *Maori cabbage* (CABBAGE 2), RAURIKI.
      1770 BANKS *Journal* (1962) Mar. II. 8 Sow thistle, garden nightshade were exactly the same as in England. **1777** FORSTER *Voyage Round World* I. 200 We also

found [at Queen Charlotte Sound] a species of sow-thistle (*sonchus oleraceus,*)..which we frequently used as sallads. **1815, 1820** [see PUHA 1 a]. **1844** MONRO *Notes of a Journey* in Hocken *Contributions* (1898) 235 We descended towards the [Canterbury] plain by gentle slopes beautifully grassed, and well stocked with anise and sowthistle. **1868, 1873** [see PUHA 1 a]. **1882** POTTS *Out in Open* 17 Amongst the edibles..boiled sow-thistle often appeared in the same basket. **1894** *TrNZI* XXVI. 263 In all probability there are no common New Zealand plants about which the ideas of local botanists and agriculturalists are so confused as the sow-thistle. **1906** CHEESEMAN *Manual NZ Flora* 388 *S[onchus] oleraceus*... Sow-thistle; Pororua; Rauriki... Perhaps not truly native... [*Sonchus asper*...] *Sowthistle*; *Rauroroa*; *Tawheke*; *Puwha*... As this was collected by Banks and Solander it must be regarded as indigenous. **1926** HILGENDORF *Weeds* 209 Sour Thistle [1967 edn. *Sowthistle*]..is frequently called milk thistle, from its milky juice, and in the north is quite commonly given its Maori name of Rauriki. **1958** WALL *Queen's English* 48 *Sowthistle*. Here I note a case of what is called 'folk etymology'. I hear this native plant (and introduced weed) as 'sour thistle'. The speaker mistakenly supposes the plant to be named from its taste. It is actually edible and much used by the Maoris as *rauriki*, corruptly 'radicky'. **1965** [see RAURIKI].

b. With a modifier: **coastal** (occas. **shore**) **sow-thistle**, *Sonchus kirkii* (formerly *littoralis*), a native herb with blue-green leaves growing on wet coastal cliffs; **prickly sowthistle, wild sow-thistle** *Sonchus asper*, (PUHA 1 b).

1909 *AJHR C-12* 64 *Sonchus littoralis*. **Coastal sow-thistle.** Dunes. **1911** *AJHR C-13* 41 *Sonchus littoralis*. Coastal sowthistle. Stewart Island dunes. **1926** HILGENDORF *Weeds* 210 **Prickly Sour Thistle** (*Sonchus asper*) is also called rough sour thistle and also by its Maori name of Puwha. This is very similar to the former [*S. oleraceus*] in all respects, except that the margins of the leaves are much more prickly... This form seems scarcely as common as the former, though it was found in New Zealand when Cook arrived here. **1969** *Standard Common Names Weeds* 61 *prickly sow thistle. Sonchus asper*. **1980** TAYLOR *Weeds of Crops* 90 Prickly Sow Thistle (*Sonchus asper*). Annual, like sow thistle, growing in similar places and almost as common. It grows a little taller than sow thistle and has leaves more prickly with a saw-tooth edge. **1975** *Tane* 21 8 Compositae *Sonchus littoralis* **shore sowthistle**. **1951** PARK *Witch's Thorn* 152 Mrs Hush..preferred to cook the **wild sow-thistle** that was called puha in those parts, a prickly dark green weed.

(6) **wind thistle**, var. *winged thistle* (7) below (quot. 1926).

(7) **winged (wind, wing) thistle.** *Carduus tenuiflorus* or *C. pycnocephalus* (**slender winged thistle**) (fam. Asteraceae), an introduced annual thistle having wing-like protuberances on the stem, common throughout New Zealand esp. on tracks and sheep camps.

1895 *Leaflets for Farmers* (NZ Dept. Agric.) No.18 7 Winged Thistle (*Carduus pycnocephalus*)... Leaves with deeply-cut spiny margins, which are developed downwards, so as to form spiny wings down the angles of the stem, hence the name—winged thistle. **1915** *NZJAg.* June X. 550 Winged thistle [seed]..about the same size as spear-thistle seed. **1926** HILGENDORF *Weeds* 192 Winged Thistle (*Carduus* [*tenuiflorus*]), sometimes has the name softened to wind thistle; it is abundant in scattered localities, two of the best known being the Marlborough Sounds and Central Otago. It is an annual. **1944** *NZEF Times* 4 Dec. 7 A noxious weed, new to Auckland province, wing thistle, had made its appearance in the Waikato. **1951** LEVY *Grasslands NZ* (1970) 302 Scotch thistle, Californian thistle, winged thistle, variegated thistle, and the like are all weeds which, when properly established, are unpalatable to stock. **1969** *Standard Common Names Weeds* 70 *slender winged thistle. Carduus pycnocephalus*. **1981** TAYLOR *Weeds of Lawns* 125 Winged thistle (*Carduus tenuiflorus*). The name winged thistle is often applied collectively to both winged and slender winged thistles, but is correctly used for one species only.

thistle, *v.*

a. To grub out or eradicate thistles.

1890 CHUDLEIGH *Diary* 6 Feb. (1950) 370 Little wife walked all the afternoon thistleing and gardened till dark.

b. In transf. use as **go thistling**, a euphemism in the New Zealand Wars for 'go scouting for or shooting Maoris'.

1864 *Richmond-Atkinson Papers* (1960) II. 83 Went up to Harry's, at 7 expecting to go thistling (indeed No 1 had marched off)..[*sic*] Before long we got the order to march for Bell Block, the Col. & troops following.

thorn. Usu. as **native (New Zealand) thorn** *obs.*, MATAGOURI.

1867 HOOKER *Handbook* 768 Thorn, native. *Discaria Toumatou*. **1869** *TrNZI* I. (rev. edn.) 267 The spines of the tumatukuru, or New Zealand thorn..were sometime used for tattooing. **1889** FEATON *Art Album NZ Flora* 93 *Discaria toumatou*... The 'Toumatou'... In the Middle Island, more particularly towards Otago, it is called 'Native Thorn'.

thornfish. *Bovichthys variegatus* (fam. Bovichthyidae), a fish of coastal southern New Zealand and south-east Australian waters. See also HORNY.

1938 *TrRSNZ* LXVIII. 414 *Bovichthys variegatus*... Thornfish (horny). **1956** GRAHAM *Treasury NZ Fishes* 300 On handling this fish I knew at once why it had been called Horny or Thornfish, as my hand began to bleed from the effect of its spines. **1967** NATUSCH *Animals NZ* 224 The thornfish..is a rock-pool fish, up to ten inches long, of Stewart Island and the islands further south. **1982** AYLING *Collins Guide* (1984) 274 The thornfish is a small, cylindrical fish with scaleless body... There is a distinctive strong spine directed upward and backward on each gill cover behind the eyes.

thousand-jacket. Also **thousand-jackets.** [f. the many-layered inner bark.] LACEBARK, esp. 1 a.

1886 BUTLER *Glimpses Maoriland* 130 Hohai or Thousand Jacket. **1889** [see LACEBARK 1 a]. **1898** MORRIS *Austral-English* 467 *Thousand-Jacket*, n. a North Island name for *Ribbon-wood*..a New Zealand tree. Layer after layer of the inner bark can be stripped off. **1905** WHITE *My NZ Garden* 90 [Lacebark] has yet another name of 'Thousand Jackets', owing to the number of lace-like layers of bark. **1933** SCANLAN *Tides of Youth* 59 Clematis, bush lawyer, manuka, thousand-jacket twined and wreathed both trunk and branch. **1946** *JPS* LV. 149 *houhere*, a tree..ribbonwood, lacebark, thousand-jacket. **1958** *Whitcombe's Mod. Jun. Dict.* (8edn.) 411 *thousand-jacket* One of the names used for the New Zealand 'lace-bark' or 'ribbon-wood' tree.

thousand-leaves. *Hypolepis millefolium* (fam. Dennstaedtiaceae), a native fern with finely dissected fronds.

1882 POTTS *Out in Open* 256 Thousand Leaves *H[ypolepis] millefolium*... Root wide and creeping; frond eight to sixteen inches long, broadly oval..three times divided... Found..on the outskirts of gullies, in spreading masses. **1909** *AJHR C-12* 14 All the ferns are evergreen, excepting the thousand-leaves (*Hypolepis millefolium*).

thrash, *v.* [Transf. use of *thrash* to beat or handle severely.] *trans.* To overwork (anything mechanical, esp. an engine or vehicle); to work or drive at an excessive pace; hence, to overexploit.

1960 CRUMP *Good Keen Man* 24 I found that deer don't hang about in the open once you start thrashing [*sc.* overshooting] a place, and it became necessary to go farther and farther along the range. **1989** Heinemann *NZ Dict.* 1204 *thrash*... 2. to overwork a machine, land, a topic or argument etc.

thrash, *n.* In the phr. **(to be) on the thrash** [var. of *on the bash* (BASH *n.*[1] a)], (to be) on a drinking spree, 'on the booze'.

1959 DAVIN *No Remittance* 169 It depended entirely on Dan himself how long the spells of work lasted and how long the periods when he was on the thrash.

thray. *Obs.* [An alteration of Brit. *trey, tray* influenced by *thr*eepence.] A threepenny bit.

1943 BENNETT *English in NZ* in *Amer. Speech* XVIII. 91 In New Zealand slang a penny is a *brown*, a threepenny piece is a *thray* (cf. English *tray*). **1972** HARGREAVES *Beads to Banknotes* 151 Threepence [:] thray.

three(-). Used in various combinations and collocations where the number (of) *three* is of significance: **three As** [f. the initials A.A.A.], the Amateur Athletic Association; **three-ball foundry** *obs.* [f. three brass balls, a pawnshop sign], a pawn-shop; **three corner(s)**, FLOUNDER *n.* 2 (9); **three-finger**, *Pseudopanax colensoi* (fam. Araliaceae), a small forest tree or subalpine shrub with 3–7 foliate leaves (see also FIVE-FINGER 1, IVY-TREE); **three-o** /ˈθri ˌʌu/, in full *three-o-three*, a .303 calibre Lee-Enfield rifle; **three o'clock**, a centaury; **three-spot** *prison*, a three-year prison sentence; **three-titter**, a disabled milking cow; **three-wire**, *ellipt.* for three-wire fence, one having only three strands of wire between ground and the top of the fence posts.

1974 *Dominion* (Wellington) 24 Oct. 30 I am bitterly disappointed the **three As** have taken this attitude. Here you have a young go-ahead promoter and he is squashed. **1911** *Truth* 23 Sept. 5 On Friday, September 8, last, a well-known, popular pawnbroker, called Walter Gabriel Rossiter, who runs a **three-ball 'foundry'** in George-Street, Dunedin, was aroused at the early hour of 3 a.m. by Constable Johnston. **1911** WAITE *Rec. Canterbury Museum* I. 197 Sand Flounder New Zealand Flounder, Patiki, **Three corner**, Tinplate *Rhombosolea plebeia*. **c1920** BEATTIE *Trad. Lifeways Southern Maori* (1994) The raututu is here [at Ellesmere] called 'Three Corners' by the Pakeha from its shape. **1956** GRAHAM *Treasury NZ Fishes* 191 New Zealand Sand-flounder (Patiki)... Some refer to it as Tinplate or Three Corner; the latter name is derived from its fancied triangular shape. **1970** three corners [see PLAICE]. **1961** MARTIN *Flora NZ* 183 Next we have the Five-finger, the **Three-finger**, the Haumakaroa, and the Raukawa, all species of *Nothopanax*..the three-finger or Mountain Ivy-tree has as a rule three sessile leaflets. **1982** [see ORIHOU]. **1984** *Hanmer Forest Park* 33 Where the canopy is tight the ground cover is sparse, except for occasional specimens of coprosma..three finger (*Pseudopanax colensoi*)..and lancewood. **1971** *Listener* 19 Apr. 56 Just as he reached the burn he spotted a spiker. He grabbed his **three-O**, rammed one up the spout and bowled it. **1926** Hilgendorf *Weeds* 134 Centaury ([*Centaurium umbellatum*]), also called **three o'clock** and red centaury, is common in grass lands throughout the islands. It is an annual, hairless, up to 18 inches high, with square erect green stems much branched at the top. **1982** Newbold *Big Huey* 62 He was just old junkie, he said, doing a **three-spot** for trying to make a buck. **1963** Casey *As Short a Spring* 159 Arh, some of them cows you were keeping on there just weren't earning their keep—**three-titters** and two-titters and some hardly turning out a cupful of milk—I gave them the bullet smartly. **1980** Neave *Land of Munros* 91 At 'Hillside'..there were few fences, and any, were sod walls with gorse planted on top with a **three-wire** and a barb.

Three Kings. [f. the name *Three Kings Islands*, to the north of NZ, so called from Abel Tasman's leaving their vicinity on the 6th January 1643, the Feast of the *Three Kings*, now more usu. known as the Feast of the Epiphany.]

1. In the names of plants and animals, see: BELLBIRD 2 (3), MILK-TREE.

2. In the occas. phr. **from the Three Kings to the Snares** [formed on *North Cape to the Bluff* (NORTH CAPE b) using far northern and far southern island groups as reference points], from one end of New Zealand to the other.

1924 Anthony *Follow the Call* (1975) 112 If you searched the outback district, from the Three Kings to the Snares, I doubt if a worse built whare than that could have been found.

threepenny. [f. an alteration of the early specific name *tripenne*, now *tripennis*, influenced by *threepenny* pronounced /ˈθrɪpəni/.] *Gilloblennius tripennis* (fam. Tripterygiidae), a blenny.

1938 *TrRSNZ* LXVIII. 416 *Tripterygion tripenne* (Forster). Threepenny. **1956** Graham *Treasury NZ Fishes* 326 Threepenny *Gilloblennius tripennis*... Threepenny is a small fish and a close relative to the well known Cockabully but is less abundant though often taken for the latter fish. **1967** Moreland *Marine Fishes* 18 Threepenny [*Gilloblennius tripennis*]. Threepenny is the only name in use. **1967** Natusch *Animals NZ* 229 *Gilloblennius tripennis*..is exceptional [among cockabully] in being evenly coloured. Its popular name—'threepenny'—looks like a broken-down version of 'tripennis', i.e. three-winged, a reference to the dorsal fin. **1981** Wilson *Fisherman's Bible* 28 In his various forms [the Blenny] is the Cockabully, Threepenny, Twister, and Topknot. All are slightly different in looks but come under the collective name of Blenny for easy grouping.

threepenny bit. [f. the shape of the leaf, rounded, small and silvery, resembling the former threepenny piece.] A willowherb, *Epilobium* spp. Cf. COINLEAF.

1952 Richards *Chatham Islands* 35 The coinleaf or threepenny bit [*Epilobium* sp., a willowherb] has dull green fleshy round leaves.

three-quarter bred. [Spec. use of *three-quarter bred* having three-quarters of a pure breed: see OED *three-quarter* D.] Of sheep, see quot. 1936.

1892 *NZ Official Handbook* 122 The average clips for the various breeds of sheep are approximately as follow: Merino, from 4lb. to 7lb.; quarter-breds, about 6½lb.; half-breds, 7½lb.; three-quarter breds, 8½lb. **1936** Belshaw et al. *Agric. Organiz. NZ* 415 In the South Island particularly, there is a further breakup of 'cross-breds' into 'three-quarter-bred', this term being applied to the progeny of any long-woolled ram with 'half-bred' ewes, or by mating 'half-bred' rams with any long-woolled ewe.

thresher shark: see SHARK 2 (18).

throw, *v.*

1. [f. Brit. dial. *throw* (a tree), to cause to fall: see OED *throw* 20 a; EDD 8.] *trans.* To fell (a tree); to direct the fall of (a tree).

1854 *Richmond-Atkinson Papers* 10 Nov. (1960) I. 158 The pines should be thrown last because then they do not cover up the other stuff until it is dry. **1857** Hursthouse *NZ* II. 331 The trees are thrown with the x [*sic*] cut saw and American axe. **1905** Thomson *Bush Boys* 138 They could swing an axe and fell a tree in real bushwhackers' style, and could judge how best to 'throw' the tree too.

2. [AND 1847.] *trans.* To cast (an animal) to the ground.

1856 Roberts *Diary* 18 Dec. in Beattie *Early Runholding* (1947) 43 We had to head rope those [cattle] requiring branding, and after hauling them up to the corner post, leg-roped and threw them on their side.

3. *Shearing. trans.* To cast (a newly-shorn fleece) on to the wool-table.

1965 Macnicol *Skippers Road* 94 George had to be shown how to pick up a fleece and how to throw it. **1981** Sutherland & Taylor *Sunrise* 46 Bill hadn't learned to pick up and throw a fleece... The aim was to stand by as the shearer made his last blow, gather the fleece into a compact armful, and throw it like a tablecloth on the wooltable, weather side up.

4. To put on (as of a performance); to pretend (to be ill, injured): see (*throw a*) HOLLYWOOD, SICKIE, WOBBLY.

throwdown. [AND 1890.] A mild banger or modified firework composed of small shot or pebbles and an explosive mixture in a paper casing, to be set off by throwing down on a hard surface. (Occas. called a *sand cracker*, see quot. 1975.)

1935 Guthrie *Little Country* (1937) 114 It was a fireworks thing, called a 'throw-down'. **1948** Ballantyne *Cunninghams* (1976) 67 All along Stout Road kids were exploding throwdowns on the footpaths, making women and girls squeak. **1975** Davin *Breathing Spaces* 13 After they had spent Joe's sixpences on some sand crackers and a bomb each and had had some fun throwing the crackers at people's feet in Post Office Square [in Southland, c1920s].

throw open. To officially open up (a block of virgin land) for settlement.

1899 Bell *In Shadow of Bush* 84 By Jove! I mean to have a buck at some of those sections in the Whakatangi Block that'll be thrown open shortly. **1959** Sinclair *Hist. NZ* 155 The system of 'free selection' enabled a would-be 'cockatoo' to choose land in localities 'thrown open' to selectors (under certain conditions regarding residence, improvement, and area) and to buy the freehold.

throwover. SHOWER.

1980 Woollaston *Sage Tea* 10 They grew like a pretty throwover, all embroidered, that you put over the food [c1915] to keep flies off when afternoon tea is waiting for visitors.

thrum. *Obs.* Also **thrummer.** [f. Brit. slang *thrum(s)*: see OED.] A threepenny piece. See also SCRUM *n.*[1] **a.** As **thrum.**

1899 *Bulletin* (Sydney) 14 Jan. (Red Page) [Letter from *Loafer*, Tauranga.] Following are other local money-names... 3d. thrum, half-tiz, tray or tray-piece. **1904** *NZ Observer* 19 Mar. 16 There was ten bob in pennies..four bob in thrums. **1905** *Truth* 30 Sept. 1 A large number of casuals have dropped in [to the pub] to spend a thrum. **1928** Devanny *Dawn Beloved* 28 The knife would strike [in the duff] a 'thrum', a sixpence, or, joy unspeakable, perhaps a shilling! **1945** *NZ Dairy Exporter* 2 Apr. 71 'Got a duff?'.. 'Oh, yes, I made two, filled ours with thrums.' **1977** *NZ Numismatic Jrnl.* Oct. 15 A *tray-bit*, or *trey*, *thrum*, or *half-tiz* are recorded for the threepence.

b. As **thrummer** [AND 1898].

1918 *Chron. NZEF* 24 May 183 The humble 'thrummer' is a big item on a shilling and two bob a day stunt. **a1950** Whitworth *Otago Interval* 52 Mother..what about a thrummer? **1988** Smith *Southlanders at Heart* 120 How I hoarded every 'thrummer' that would get me to the 'flicks'. *Ibid.* 122 A term commonly used for a threepenny-bit—a silver coin about the same size as a cent.

thrummer: see THRUM b.

thrush. [Transf. use of *thrush* for any of various small bush-birds fancifully or superficially resembling the European song-thrush.]

1. Usu. and mainly (often with the modifiers: **native, New Zealand**), the extinct *Turnagra capensis* (fam. Paradiseidae). See also PIOPIO (the name now preferred by ornithologists).

1773 Forster *Resolution Jrnl.* 3 May (1982) II. 269 The male & female of a small Thrush was shot, which we hitherto had taken for a variety of the small yellow legged Thrush, commonly called *Robin* by our Ship's-crew. **1777** Forster *Voyage Round World* I. 148 The birds seemed to retire from it to a little distance, where the shrill notes of thrushes..resounded on all sides. **1846** Heaphy *Exped. Kawatiri* in Taylor *Early Travellers* (1959) 243 Our breakfast..had consisted of three small potatoes each, and a thrush amongst the party. **1863** Butler *First Year* ix 137 We have a thrush, but it is rather rare. **1888** Buller *Birds NZ* I. 27 This bird was the Piopio, or New-Zealand Thrush..the best of the native songsters. **c1899** Douglas in *Mr Explorer Douglas* (1957) 264 [Heading] The New Zealand Thrush. This is..a sort of parody on the Mavis. It has no song and its cry is only a harsh twitter, a note the bird is evidently ashamed off [*sic*], as it seldom uses it... They are a good deal larger than the home thrush. **1904** *TrNZI* XXXVI. 124 The Piopio, or Native Thrush..and the Long-tailed Cuckoo..are somewhat [similar] in appearance. **1935** Jackson *Annals NZ Family* 129 In one [of Buller's aviary cages], there were parrakeets..and a pio pio (New Zealand thrush) one of our best songsters. **1957** Williams *Dict. Maori Lang.* 145 Koropio..Turnagra capensis and Turnagra tanagra, N.Z. thrushes. **1966** Falla et al. *Birds NZ* 238 New Zealand Thrush... Piopio... The early settlers found the native Thrush a common bird of the forest, yet, like the Wattlebirds, it was reported to be fast disappearing by 1880. **1985** *Reader's Digest Book NZ Birds* 308 Extinct birds..New Zealand Thrush *Turnagra capensis*... Piopio, korohea.

2. With a modifier localizing the two subspecies, the white-throated **North Island thrush,** *Turnagra capensis tanagra*, and the ventrally speckled **South Island thrush** *T. c. capensis*.

1873 Buller *Birds NZ* 135 Turnagra hectori. (North Island Thrush)... Piopio, Korohea, and Tiutiukata. *Ibid.* 139 Turnagra crassirostris. (South-Island Thrush.) **1886** *TrNZI* XVIII. 112 *T. hectori*.—Piopio, Northern Thrush. Southern part of North Island... *Turnagra crassirostris*.—Piopio, Southern Thrush. South Island.

Now rare, and in many parts extinct. **1904** HUTTON & DRUMMOND *Animals NZ* 61 *The South Island Thrush.—Piopio. Turnagra crassirostris. Ibid.* 62 *The North Island Thrush.—Piopio. Turnagra tanagra.* **1936** GUTHRIE-SMITH *NZ Naturalist* 175 The species we hoped to make friends with [on Stewart Island] were the Snipe..and the South Island Thrush. **1967** NATUSCH *Animals NZ* 286 Any thrushes most of us see today are likely..to be imported ones... The last North Island one definitely recorded was encountered in 1887. **1985** *Reader's Digest Book NZ Birds* 308 The North Island thrush, described as 'unquestionably the best of our native songsters', was not common in European times... The first specimen of the South Island thrush collected by Europeans was a bird shot at Cascade Cove, Dusky Sound, on 2 April 1773, during Cook's second voyage.

thud. [Cf. Partridge *thud* a figurative fall: Austral. since ca1930.] In the phr. **to come a thud (over)** *fig.*, to make a bad mistake; to 'come a cropper' over (something or someone).

1946 SARGESON *That Summer* 94 I'd nearly come a thud over Maggie. **1960** 16C F B5 Wellington Girls C. 16 Thud, come a thud. **1964** PEARSON *Glossary* to Sargeson *Collected Stories 1935–63* (1964) 304 thud: *came a thud*, fallen in, made a mistake.

thumb bird. Also **thumbie.** [f. (Tom) *Thumb*, the proverbial 'little person' applied to the smallest of NZ birds.] RIFLEMAN. Cf. TOM THUMB BIRD.

1936 GUTHRIE-SMITH *NZ Naturalist* 62 From two localities [Nelson province] came the silvery 'tic-tic' of a squad of Thumb Birds—Rifleman—the males most desperate fellows for all their littleness. **1953** SUTHERLAND *Golden Bush* (1963) 109 We came to think that the novelty of having calico under their feet was chief attraction to the 'thumbies'—a local name given to New Zealand's smallest bird. **1966** FALLA et al. *Birds NZ* 191 Rifleman... Titipounamu, Thumbie (Nelson).

thumbie: see THUMB BIRD.

thunder-dirt. [A euphemised translation of Ma. *paru-* or *tūtae-whatitiri* 'thunder excrement': the reference is perhaps to the often sudden appearance above ground of the latticed 'basket'.] *basket fungus* (FUNGUS 2 (1)). See also PARUWHATITIRI.

1883 TURNER in *Good Words* Sept. 590 The gelatinous [fungus] which the New Zealand natives know as 'thunder-dirt'. **1898** MORRIS *Austral-English* 469 *Thunder-dirt, n.* In New Zealand, a gelatinous covering of a fungus (*Ileodictyon cibarium*) formerly eaten by the Maoris. **1961** [see FUNGUS 2 (1)].

thunderplump. [f. Sc. dial.: see OED 'chiefly Scots.' 1821.] A heavy downpour.

1977 *Otago Daily Times* (Dunedin) 18 Nov. (Griffiths Collect.) I am beginning to think that I must be the only ignoramus in Dunedin who has never heard of a thunderplump. Everyone else has known the word since childhood and, as a Buccleuch Street reader neatly put it, I was fairly deluged with thunderplumps yesterday... A colleague who came from Winton certainly knew of it; and it was even noised abroad by the Canterbury English.

thyme. [Transf. use of *thyme Thymus* spp. for often unrelated New Zealand plants.]

1. Also **native** (or **wild**) **thyme.** A native shrub of the genus *Pimelea* (fam. Thymelaeaceae).

1851 WELD *Letter* 21 Feb. in *NZGG* (1851) 34 Several veronicas of great beauty, wild thyme..harebell, a lily, and several varieties of ranunculus. **1921** GUTHRIE-SMITH *Tutira* (1926) 169 Other species like native Thyme (*Pimelea laevigata*)..selected small holdings about the camps.

2. *Samolus repens* (fam. Primulaceae), a small native herb of saltmarshes superficially resembling the creeping thyme, *Thymus vulgaris.*

1867 HOOKER *Handbook* 768 Thyme, wild of Otago. *Samolus* [sp.].

ti /tī/, *n.*[1] Occas. early **ettay** (=he *te* or *ti*), **T**, **te(e)**, **tii**, **titi**. [Ma. /ˈtiː/: Williams 413 *Tī* (i) *Cordyline* of several species: particular species are indicated in Maori by special suffixes (see Williams 413): PPN **tī* Walsh & Biggs 113: see also OED *Ti.*] [*Note*] *ti*(-) 'cordyline', can be confused with *ti-* as a variant of *tea-*(*tree*) 'manuka' (see esp. quot. 1834 below).

1. a. Species of *Cordyline* (fam. Asphodelaceae), esp. *Cordyline australis*. CABBAGE-TREE 1. See also TI-PALM, TI-TREE. Often *attrib.*

1834 MARKHAM *NZ* (1963) 33 Hattay [crossed out by Markham, =he ti] or Ettay is a Tea tree, quite different to the Tea tree bush [sc. manuka], a sort of myrtle. *Ibid.* 34 Tay [sc. *cordyline*], it is useless, it only grows eight to twelve feet and the bark rough, and does not change. It seems very often Solitary. Away from every other Tree. **1838** [see CABBAGE-PALM a]. **1842** BEST *Journal* 9 Apr. (1966) 344 This last [sc. Mauku] the root of a shrub called by the Mauries T is of extraordinary sweetness when dressed. **1848** WAKEFIELD *Handbook NZ* 462 An unmixed growth of stunted *manuka* is a bad sign [for the quality of the soil], a quantity of ti-shrubs, commonly called the cabbage-tree, a very good one. **1851** SHORTLAND *S. Dist. NZ* 314 Ti, in North Island commonly called Whanake (*cordyline ti*), a liliaceous plant. **1869** *TrNZI* I. (rev. edn.) 261 The young inner blanched leaves and heart of the ti, or 'cabbage-tree'..were eaten both raw and cooked. **1905** BAUCKE *White Man Treads* 16 For in their season he could supplement his dry fare with..the tender bulbous shoots of the tii (cabbage tree), at heart white and delicate, baked in a haangi. **1922** COWAN *NZ Wars* (1955) II. 399 The Kapenga tableland..is covered with a thick growth of..fern with many ti or cabbage trees. **1946** *JPS* LV. 146 *tī*, a tree (*Cordyline* spp.), cabbage-tree, palm-lily, the various species... ti is the only term in common use, and it has been wonderfully maltreated. **1983** HULME *Bone People* 304 A greasy little fellow with buck teeth and hair styled like ti was still the rocking fifties.

b. As **titi** an occas. early (?SI) reduplicated form. Also **titi-tree.**

1844 MONRO *Notes of a Journey* in Hocken *Contributions* (1898) 236 The part of the [Canterbury] plain which we crossed..is..in some places, thickly dotted over with the ti-ti. *Ibid.* 249 Looking up at [sc. Molyneux River] we could trace its course..by the thick fringe of ti-ti trees upon its banks,... producing a most picturesque effect.

2. The root of the ti prepared by the Maori as food.

1820 LEE & KENDALL *NZ Gram. & Vocab.* 212 *Tí, s.* The root called Tee, which, when baked is very sweet. **1843** DIEFFENBACH *Travels in NZ* II. 387 Ti—sweet root of the dragon-tree. **1847** BRUNNER *Exped. Middle Is.* 19 Jan. in Taylor *Early Travellers* (1959) 265 The natives prepare a very palatable dish of ti and fern root. **1860** *Richmond-Atkinson Papers* 20 Dec. (1960) I. 670 Eat kumara, ti & kuharu. [1860*Note*] The root of the ti—rather like licorice root.

3. With suffixed Maori modifiers distinguishing various species: **ti-kapu, ti-kauka (ti-kouka), ti-koraha, ti-ngahere(here), ti-pore, ti-rauriki.** See also WHANAKE.

(1) [Ma. /ˈtiːˈkapu/.] **ti-kapu,** the broad-leaved cabbage tree, *Cordyline indivisa*; TOI *n.*[1]

1853 HOOKER II *Flora Novae-Zelandiae* I *Flowering Plants* 258 *Cordyline indivisa*... Nat. name, 'Tikapu'. **1867** HOCHSTETTER *NZ* 157 A little coarser than the Ti fibre is the fibre of a second species of Cordyline (perhaps *C. indivisa*) with larger, broader leaves, which the natives call Kapu or Ti Kapu.

(2) ti-kauka, ti-kouka, also as **kauka (kouka).** [Ma. /ˈtiːˈkaːuka/, /-ˈkoːuka/: Williams 151 *Kōuka, kāuka..Cordyline australis*.] CABBAGE-TREE, occas. *spec.* the edible crown.

1867 HOOKER *Handbook* 766 Kouka, Lindsay. *Cordyline australis*. **1889** KIRK *Forest Flora* 295 This grand palm-lily is commonly termed 'ti', or..properly ti-kouka, 'ti' being a kind of generic name applied to the different species of *Cordyline*: it is sometimes simply termed 'kouka'... W.L. Williams informs me that it is termed 'kauka' or 'whanaka' by the East Cape natives. **1906** CHEESEMAN *Manual NZ Flora* 707 *Ti; Ti-kauka..Palm-lily*... Universally known to New Zealand residents by the inappropriate name of 'cabbage-tree'. **1907** LAING & BLACKWELL *Plants NZ* 93 *Cordyline australis*. (*Ti-kouka*. The Cabbage-Tree or Palm Lily). **1910** GROSSMAN *Heart of Bush* 147 Kauka Tree..known to New Zealanders generally under the term of 'cabbage tree'. **1978** FULLER *Maori Food & Cook.* 34 The bushy crowns (kouka) of *Cordyline australis*, the Maori ti tree, were relished..also by early European settlers, who found the kouka tasted like cabbage and named the tree accordingly. **1982** BURTON *Two Hundred Yrs. NZ Food* 7 The sweetish, sago-like fecula (kouka) [of the cabbage tree] was eaten and the fibres spat out. **1991** TV1 News leadup 5.55 p.m. 3 Dec. The race to save ti kouka the cabbage tree. Scientists now know what's killing them.

(3) ti-koraha. [Ma. /ˈtiːˈkoraha/.] *Cordyline pumilio*, a small cabbage-tree of northern New Zealand.

1867 HOOKER *Handbook* 768 Tikoraha, Geolog. Surv. *Cordyline pumilio*. **1869** *TrNZI* I. (rev. edn.) 265 The roots of the tikoraha..were tied separately for baking.

(4) ti-ngahere(here). [Ma. /ˈtiːˈŋahere/.] *Cordyline banksii*, a small cabbage tree of forest margins, having drooping leaves.

1867 HOOKER *Handbook* 768 Tingahere, Geolog. Surv. *Cordyline stricta*. **1874** *TrNZI* VI. 56 Ti ngaherehere, *Cordyline banksii*.—A much smaller plant than the [ti]. **1882** HAY *Brighter Britain* II. 192 The Tingahere..is another species of the same family. **1906** CHEESEMAN *Manual NZ Flora* 706 *C[ordyline] Banksii*... *Ti-ngahere*.

(5) ti-pore. [Ma. /ˈtiːˈpore/.] *Cordyline terminalis*, a shrub cabbage tree introduced from the Pacific Islands and cultivated by the Maori.

1906 CHEESEMAN *Manual NZ Flora* 705 *C[ordyline] terminalis*... Kermadec Islands... North Island: Formerly cultivated by the Maoris in the Bay of Islands.., now nearly extinct. *Ti-pore*. **1907** MANSFIELD *Urewera Notebook* (1978) 48 Walking breast high through the manuka—Lily of the valley—the ti pore we approach Galatea.

(6) ti-rauriki. [Ma. /ˈtiːˈrauriki/.] See *ti-koraha* (3) above.

1867 HOOKER *Handbook* 768 Tirauriki, Geolog. Surv. *Cordyline pumilio*. **1870** *TrNZI* II. 126 Cordyline Pumilio. Tirauriki. **1901** *TrNZI* XXXIII. 303 The old settlers generally remembered that in the early days a certain species of ti..had been cultivated by the Maoris, but most of them confused it with the ti rauriki (*C. pumilio*), a wild species which was commonly

TI 834 TIGER

eaten but never cultivated. **1906** CHEESEMAN *Manual NZ Flora* 708 *C[ordyline] pumilio*... North Island:..*Ti-rauriki*. **1910** COCKAYNE *NZ Plants & Their Story* 53 The dwarf cabbage-tree (ti-rauriki), (*Cordyline pumilio*), not looking a little bit like its tall relative, is abundant.

ti /ti/, *n*.² *Obs. Ellipt.* for *ti-tree* a var. of TEA-TREE 1 a, MANUKA; also as **ti-bush**. See also TEA 1 a.
1838 POLACK *NZ* II. 397 The *ti* is a useful close grained wood, well adapted for handspikes. It grows to forty feet with crooked branches. **1851** *Richmond-Atkinson Papers* 7 Feb. (1960) I. 77 At first the old hands predicted that when cleared of fern, ti and bush it would blow away. **1886** FROUDE *Oceana* 280 We walked afterwards around the farm..saw the young men cutting Ti-bush, and carting it to the sea to be shipped for Auckland.

tiaka, tiaki, varr. TIEKE.

ti-bush: see TI *n*.²

tick: see FULL *a*. 1.

ticket, *n*.¹ [f. a fig. use of *have tickets on* (a raffle), to have taken more than one chance of winning, thus, be keen and well-placed to win; poss. influenced by *ticket* a label or mark of ownership: see OED *n*.¹ 5 c.] **a.** Usu. *pl.*, in the phr. **to have tickets on** (someone), to be keen on (a person); esp. to set one's cap at a man or woman, to have a special interest in, to be courting.
1908 KOEBEL *Anchorage* 140 I don't know whether she's got any tickets on me. **1916** INGLIS in Boyack *Behind Lines* (1989) 114 Harding to use his words, says she 'has tickets' on me, so for heaven's sake tell her you're my fiancee or something. **1938** NOR *Years Condemn* 179 'She's a nice girl, that Sister Collins.' 'You must have tickets on her, Starkie.' **1950** CHERRILL *Story NZ Sheep Farm* 99 But although you had tickets and no mistake on Ju at the *time*, you didn't forget to put the acid on him proper afterwards. *Ibid.* 139 'She had tickets on Ju once'. 'Had what?' The term was new to her [as a recently arrived English wife]. **1980** LELAND *Kiwi-Yankee Dict.* 48 *got tickets on*: I've got tickets on that bird (car, job. etc.) Means, I've got my eye on, (I desire) that. **1985** SHERWOOD *Botanist at Bay* 135 Got tickets on you, has he? Pity, he's too old for you.

b. In the phr. **to have tickets on oneself** [AND 1918], to have a high regard for oneself, to be full or too fond of oneself.
1988 MCGILL *Dict. Kiwi Slang* 113 *tickets on oneself, have* to be conceited; eg 'That stuck-up bastard, he's got tickets on himself.' **1995** *Dominion* (Wellington) 9 Oct. 10 But my latest boyfriend told me he thought I had tickets on myself, because whenever he says I'm looking good I just beam and say thank you.

ticket, *n*.² [AND 1899.] A Union membership card.
1910 *Awards, etc.* 113 When a shearer applies for a shed, and his application is granted, he shall forward his union ticket (if a unionist) to the employer... [He] shall..collect his ticket and forward it to the second employer with whom he has engaged. **1953** HAMILTON *Till Human Voices Wake Us* 127 Bluey had lost his seaman's ticket over his jail blues, and I don't suppose he'll ever get it back. **1983** *Press* (Christchurch) 7 Dec. 4 He was told that Campbell and Liggett had said that if he was not going to pay the levy they [*sc.* the Union] were going to have his 'ticket' and they would have him down the road. **1990** MARTIN *Forgotten Worker* 48 As Bob Tutaki reported, another shearer..'came back again not as a shearer but as an organiser of the union... From him I received my first union ticket.'

ticket boy. *Freezing works.* See quot. 1951.
1949 STRONACH 'The End Of It All' in Woodhouse *Farm and Station Verse* (1950) 188 Past the meat-inspector and ticket-boy In a line that never fails, Goes your dear wee lamb to the cooling room From the grader and his scales. **1951** May 17 Feilding Freezing Works terms p.c. Colin Gordon. A *ticket-boy* puts a grade ticket on them [*sc.* carcasses] out at the scales after the *grader* has graded them for weight and size. **1981** *Evening Post* (Wellington) 24 Jan. 7 Just by the slaughterhouse office [of the Gear Meat Co.] was a place called the Ticket Room, and not surprisingly perhaps, the boys who worked there were called Ticket Boys.

tickle: see PETER *n*.¹ 1 (*tickle the peter*).

tidal creek: see CREEK 1 b.

tide. In New Zealand, as in Sc. dial. (see SND *tide* 4; EDD 4), a synonym for 'sea', without reference to ebbing or flowing (OED 7) or to poetic use (OED 12), and poss. mainly used in localities where tidal ebb and flow is significant (e.g. in estuaries, Marlborough Sounds).
1918 MACGILL *An Anzac's Bride* 19 They sat silent on the grey stone wall listening to the eternal wash of the waves as the tide rolled in. **1940** In Havelock (Marlborough) *tide* was a frequent use for *sea*. (Ed.) **1951** p.c. Barry Mitcalfe. In Whangaroa, Maunganui, in Northland, one always speaks of going for a swim in the tide. These places are silted up with mudflats: one cannot swim etc. when the tide is out, so 'tide' and 'sea' are identified. **1977** SARGESON *Never Enough* 11 And a great Christmas tree in flower reached out far enough to colour the tide. **1992** SMITHYMAN *Auto/Biographies* 62 At the edge of the tide one..native blue reef heron picks for what can be had.

tieke. Also **tiaka, tiaki.** [Echoic from its cry: Ma. /ˈtiːeke/: Williams 415 *Tīeke* (i)..saddleback, a bird.] SADDLEBACK.
1835 YATE *NZ* (1970) 56 *Tiaki*, or *Purourou*—This elegant bird is about the size of the sky-lark; and its plumage..is of glossy black. **1842** GRAY *Fauna* in Dieffenbach *Travels in NZ* (1843) II. 192 Tieke of the natives of Tasman Bay... Tiaka or Purourou... Tira-oua-ké.. Tierawaki, Cook's Straits. **1869** *TrNZI* I. (rev. edn.) 104 Tieke. Saddle-back. Not uncommon. **1873** BULLER *Birds NZ* 149 (The Saddle-back). Tieke, Tiraweke, and Purourou. [*Ibid.* 151 It [*sc.* tieke] is naturally a noisy bird, and when excited or alarmed becomes very clamorous, hurrying through the woods with cries of 'tiaki-rere', quickly repeated.] **1882** POTTS *Out in Open* 201 Watch the tieke perched for a few moments..its glossy black plumage is relieved from sameness by the quaint saddle-mark of deep ferruginous that crosses his back and wings. **1898** MORRIS *Austral-English* 469 Tiaki (spelt also *Tieke*), *n*. Maori name for the *Saddle-back* or *Jack-bird*. **1930** REISCHEK *Yesterdays in Maoriland* (1933) 107 I shot a tieke, and was pleased to notice that this starling had increased in numbers since my earlier visit in 1880. **1946** *JPS* LV. 159 *Tieke*, a bird.., saddleback, now a rare bird: its saddle is the mark of the hot hand of Maui. **1955** OLIVER *NZ Birds* 514 According to Buller, the Tieke was not wilfully killed by the Maori, it being regarded with a degree of superstitious reverence and as a bird of omen. **1988** MORRIS & SMITH *Wild South* 113 The [saddleback's] shrill voice was echoed in its Maori name 'tieke' and the cries were said to be good or bad omens, depending on the direction in which the bird flew. **1990** *Dominion* (Wellington) 7 July 10 The birds..would provide a safeguard in case the saddleback, or tieke, was wiped out in the wild.

tie the knot. [from fastening the tie-string of a swag before shouldering it.] To become a swagger; to be on the swag.
1974 AGNEW *Loner* 66 During the four years I was to tie the knot I became known as simply The Kid... It was an unspoken rule never to question a fellow-swagger about his past. *Ibid.* 68 He's a miserable bastard who claims we're [*sc.* swaggers] lazy buggers who'd rather tie the knot than work.

tie up fence: see TAIEPA.

tiger.
1. [See OED *tiger* 3 d 'chiefly *Austral.* and *N.Z.*'; AND 1896.] Esp. in the phr. **a tiger for work**, an energetic, enthusiastic, persevering person such as a fast, vigorous tramper.
1958 *Tararua* Sept. 39 With the following dawn two tigers stood by for a quick trip back to Maruia Springs while each pack was searched and emptied. **1968** SLATTER *Pagan Game* 162 Doesn't know if he's punched, bored, or countersunk—A tiger for punishment. **1989** *NZ Eng. Newsletter* III. 28 *tiger:* A shearer who works very hard.

2. In the phr. **to toss the tiger**, see TOSS *v*.

3. Special Comb. **tiger country** [AND 'remote and inaccessible country', 1945]. **a.** Country difficult to tame or bring into farming use; also *fig.*, a situation or environment difficult to deal with.
1971 LETHBRIDGE *Sunrise on Hills* 126 It had been pretty hard 'tiger' country in the first place, but when the land had been cleared..the subsequent pasture was good enough..to run a dairy herd. **1984** DAVIES *Bread & Roses* 177 Come down to Wellington if you feel that your batteries need to be recharged. I think it's going to be tiger country up there for a permanent union official, but we trust you to do your best. **1987** *Dominion* (Wellington) 9 May 11 They come from a mostly fatherless family settling on the Pori Hill's legendary 'tiger country'. **1993** *Evening Post* (Wellington) 27 Sept. 21 South Westland is wild, rugged 'tiger country'.

b. WW2. With init. cap. [Transf. use, with a play on the name of the German Army's 'Tiger' tank.] Country where one is likely to meet German armour.
1959 SLATTER *Gun in My Hand* 158 We pushed on over the Sillaro into the Tiger country..waiting desperately anxious for..the Bailey bridges..so our tanks could rejoin us.

4. In the names of plants and animals **tiger**, in full *tiger shark*, see SHARK 2 (19); **tiger shell**, the strikingly patterned top shell *Calliostoma* (formerly *Maurea*) *tigris* (fam. Trochidae).
1964 RUHEN *Lively Ghosts* 38 He was so old a **tiger** that his stripes had faded, and his colour was a even as a porbeagle's. **1947** POWELL *Native Animals NZ* 25 **Tiger Shell** (*Maurea tigris*). Grows to 3 inches in diameter and is at once recognised by its delicately tapered spire and conspicuous pattern of zig-zag reddish-brown radiating bands. **1957** WILLIAMS *Dict. Maori Lang.* 197 *Maurea*. *Maurea tigris*, a univalve mollusc, the tiger shell. **1966** *Encycl. NZ* III. 710 Tiger shell .. matangongore, maurea.. *Maurea tigris*. **1970** PENNIKET *NZ Seashells in Colour* 18 Tiger Shell... Greatly prized by collectors for both appearance and rarity, it lives among seaweed on rocky open coasts and down to moderate depths. **1983** GUNSON *Collins Guide to Seashore* 89 The Maurea top shells include..the very

striking tiger shell *M. tigris*, at 75mm our largest topshell.

tigger: see TIGGY.

tiggy. Also **tigger**, **tiggie**. [f. n. Brit. dial. *tiggy* (*touch-wood*), a children's game of 'touch last' or 'touch wood' (f. *tig* or *tick v*. to touch), once popular in NZ as elsewhere.]
1. A children's game of *tig*, where some players have to 'tig' or touch others to make them also 'he'.
    1953 14 M A5 Thames DHS 21 Tiggy [2] **1982** KEENE *Myrtle & Sophia* 6 Because most of us were too small to be of any use in team games, we played hide-and-seek, 'tigger', marbles or whipped tops [c1877]. **1984** 16 F E5 Pakuranga Coll. 21 Tiggie. **1984** 16 F E7 Pakuranga Coll. 21 Tiggy.
2. Special Comb. **tiggy (tiggy-tiggy) touchwood.** A children's game in which the 'prey' could not be caught (or 'tigged') by the 'he' if they were touching wood of any kind.
    1953 in *Growing Up at the Diggings* in Heinz *Bright Fine Gold* (1974) 38 Some of the simple games played by the [West Coast] children [c1870s] were rounders, shinty, duckstone, tiggy touchwood, kiss in the ring. **1992** CONDON *Hurleyville* 25 Other games played by the whole school from time to time included rounders, bedlam, tick-tack, tiggy tiggy touchwood..and cock fights—a form of piggy back.

tight, *a*. In the phr. **tight as a duck's** (occas. **bull's**) **arse,** very mean (esp. with money), often further elaborated by adding 'and that's watertight'.
    1969 HILLIARD *Green River* 38 Yet in spite of it all he was as tight as a bull's arse going uphill in the fly season. **1988** MCGILL *Dict. Kiwi Slang* 113 *tight as a duck's arse*, also *bull's*/*gnat's*/*fish's* mean with money; often carrying the response: *and that's water tight*.

tight five. The nucleus of the rugby scrum, the three front-row forwards and two locks. Contrast *loosie* (LOOSE *a*. 2).
    1992 *Evening Post* (Wellington) 6 July 28 The scrum was stronger than the World Cuppers' and should stay intact in the tight five. **1992** *Dominion* (Wellington) 6 Aug. 36 Our tight five laid the platform and that made it easier for the rest of us.

tigi, var. TIKI.

tihore. Also early occas. **tihori**. [Ma. /'tiːhore/: Williams 416 *Tīhore*..6. n. The best varieties of *Phormium tenax*, of which the fibre can be stripped from the refuse without the use of a shell.] A variety of FLAX I (*Phormium tenax*), cultivated by the Maori for use in fine work.
    1845 WAKEFIELD *Adventure NZ* II. 286 The species of *Phormium tenax* thus cultivated is the tihore, literally the 'skinning' flax. This name describes the ease with which it submits to the scraping process. **1867** HOCHSTETTER *NZ* 152 We may distinguish..principal varieties: 1) *Tuhara*, swamp flax, with a coarse, yellowish-white fibre; used especially for ropes, lines, etc. 2) *Tihore*, a cultivated variety..used for mats and garments. **1868** LINDSAY *Contribs. NZ Bot*. 79 [They use the fibre] of that variety or species [of flax] known to the natives as 'Tihori', or 'Tihore',—all other forms yield a coarser fibre. **1898** MORRIS *Austral-English* 470 *Tihore, n.* Maori name for a species of New Zealand flax. Name used specially in the North Island for the best variety of *Phormium*. **c1930** *Whitcombe's Etym. Dict. Aust.-NZ Suppl*. 12 *tihore n*. New Zealand flax.

tii, var. TI *n*.¹

tii-tree, var. TI-TREE.

tika, *a*. [Ma. /'tika/: Williams 416 *Tika*..4. Right, correct.] Correct; straight; proper.
    [**1820** LEE & KENDALL *NZ Gram. & Vocab*. 213 *Tíka, a.* Straight, even.] **1843** DIEFFENBACH *Travels in NZ* II. 387 Tika—just, straight, even. **1851** SHORTLAND *S. Dist. NZ* 135 Only get him to assent that your proposition is 'tika' or straight, and you will soon obtain his consent to it. **1863** MANING *Old NZ* xii 178 Maoris seldom act against the law, and always try to be able to say what they do is 'correct'—(*tika*). **1879** FENTON in Best *Journal* (1966) The object of this attack was to balance an 'utu' account... Ngati Paoa say this account had been previously squared, and the killings which took place at this attack were murders. The other side deny this and say that..the deaths of the three men who fell wound up the account and the whole proceeding was 'tika' (correct). **1904** TREGEAR *Maori Race* 33 A High Chief's conduct had to be 'straight' (*tika*) and justified by their ideas as to the behaviour of a great noble. **1912** *NZ Free Lance Christmas Annual* (Wellington) 35 It's all tino tika, quite correct. **1921** GUTHRIE-SMITH *Tutira* (1926) 388 The writer can see that he himself was in part responsible for what had occurred, that his conduct had not been *tika*, not been correct. **1952** LYON *Faring South* 118 Notable among the neighbours was one that even a Maori would have classed as not tika or correct. **1963** CAMPBELL *Collected Poems* (1981) 45 All that he did was *tika*, strictly correct, and would have raised grim smiles of approbation. **1978** HILLIARD *Glory & Dream* 191 Tika, she had said. That was their word to justify doing what you like. Behaving according to character, she had said. Doing what you feel the urge to do. If that's the way you are, you do it. **1983** HULME *Bone People* 151 It's [*sc*. a cup's] the right size, tika size, fitting his hand. **1990** *Te Karanga* Nov. 3 In the Maori view the action [*sc*. fighting] was tika, a proper thing to do.

tikanga. [Ma. /'tikaŋa/: Williams 416 *tikanga*..2. Custom, habit.] Also **tikanga Maori.** (Maori) customary values and practices.
    1858 *Richmond-Atkinson Papers* (1960) I. 367 The greatest reception the Governor has had from natives, the most loyal reverence for the Queen's name and 'mana', the most intelligent acquaintance with the English tikanga [**1858** *Note* Policy.]..are to be found in the Ngapuhi. **1881** *Auckland Weekly News* 4 June 19 If any man attempts to adopt some other tikanga, he will be wrong (punished), no matter who he is. **1985** HOWE *Towards 'Taha Maori'* in *English* (NZATE) 23 Tikanga—see 'kawa'. This term refers to the customs, rules, habits and accepted ways of behaving in each tribal area, and as such may differ from marae to marae. **1988** *Dominion* (Wellington) 24 Dec. 7 John Clarke is a highly respected professional who enjoys wide support from the Maori community and who has a great depth of knowledge of tikanga (things) Maori. **1993** *National Education Weekly* 28 June 10 Long-term relieving teacher... Knowledge and interest in tikanga Maori an advantage. **1995** *Mana* 10 (Spring issue) 1 The preparations for..the [Maori-Samoan] wedding were my first experience of grappling with Samoan tikanga... Because of..their struggles in a society where Pakeha tikanga rules, it's a story of special interest.

ti-kapu: see TI *n*.¹ 3 (1).

tikati. [Ma. /'tiːkati/: Williams 417 *Tīkati*..1... frost-fish. 2..hake.] Either of the unrelated sea-fish *Rexea* (formerly *Jordanidia*) *solandri* (GEMFISH), or (locally) *Lepidotus caudatus* (FROSTFISH).
    1927 PHILLIPPS *Bibliogr. NZ Fishes* (1971) 48 *Jordanidia solandri*... Hake or Southern Kingfish; Tikati. **1929** BEST *Fishing Methods* 48 Karihi might as well have added the *tikati*, to his family, it being a sea-fish resembling the barracouta in form and colour, but is thicker. [**1929** *Note*] Tikati said to be *Jordanidia solandri*. **1932** *NZJST* XIII. 232 *Frost-fish*... This is the para of most New Zealand Natives, and the tikati of Taranaki. **1956** GRAHAM *Treasury NZ Fishes* 315 Southern Kingfish or Hake (Tikati) *Rexea solandri*. **1981** WILSON *Fisherman's Bible* 201 Tasmanian kingfish, barraconda and 'tikati' (Maori) are other names [for the southern kingfish or hake].

ti-kauka, see TI *n*.¹ 3 (2).

tike. Also **tyke**. [Prob. an alteration of *Teague, Tighe* (ad. Gaelic *Taidgh*), a nickname for an Irishman: AND *tyke*, 1902.] An Irish Catholic.
    1948 in Pearson *Six Stories* (1991) 43 When dad came in I got another hiding. 'I suppose you've been playing with the Mickie kids... That's the kind of talk you'd learn from the tikes.' **1968** *NZ Contemp. Dict. Suppl*. (Collins) 21 *tyke n*. (*Sl*.) anyone professing the Roman Catholic faith. **1981** GEE *Meg* 189 Once it fell to me to..explain to a pair of Jehovah's Witnesses that we were all good Catholics in this house... 'At least the tikes have got some style... Shall I nail a crucifix on the door?' **1984** BEARDSLEY *Blackball 08* 245 tyke Roman Catholic.

tiki, var. TARAKIHI.

tiki. Also early **Tigi.** [Ma. /'tiki/: Williams 417 *Tiki* (ii)..*1.* A personification of primeval man... *4.* A flat grotesque figure of greenstone worn on a string round the neck.]
1. a. A small, flat carving, often in greenstone, worn as a neck pendant, and in shape a grotesque foetal figure representing the first man in embryo form. See also HEI-TIKI.
[*Note*] *Tiki* was the name of the Maori Creator of Man, and thence taken to represent an ancestor, often in the form of large wooden images made by Maori to represent their *Tiki*, and thus called 'Tiki', the name being later transferred to a miniature flat carving in greenstone worn as a neck pendant. English speakers often use *tiki* where poss. *heitiki* would be more correct; and occas. use the word in a weakened sense of 'a lucky charm worn from the neck'.
    1777 SAMWELL *Account* in Cook *Journals* (1967) III. 1001 They had brought many Articles of Trade such as Ahoos, green Images called Tigis, Stone Adzes etc. **1839** TAYLOR *Journal* (ATLTS) II. 120 Their Tikis or green jade ornaments are becoming so scarce that I could not procure one without paying an exorbitant price. **1847** ANGAS *Savage Life* I. 267 She was dressed in the European fashion..but..wore suspended round her neck the *tiki*, or household god of green jade, which passes as an heir-loom amongst families. *Ibid*. I. 308 We can trace in the carvings of the New Zealanders—in their huge *tikis* or *wakapokokos*..a strong analogy to the architectural ornaments of the Mexicans. **1882** POTTS *Out in Open* 27 A few bore much more interesting bosom friends in the shape of the tiki. **1910** *Truth* 9 July 7 Gladys Wood..said that between 9 and 10 p.m. on February 18 a[n]..enamelled bracelet, gold neck chain, two tiki curios and a peggy bag were stolen from her bedroom. **1924** LYSNAR *NZ* 62 The eyes of the tiki were filled with rings cut from the parva [*sic*], or mother-of-pearl, but recently this has been quite superseded by the charm of red sealing-wax. **1930** GUTHRIE *NZ Memories* 115 They filled an old canoe with treasures from the pa..greenstone implements, tikis and carvings. **1946** *JPS* LV. 150 *tiki*, flat carved greenstone image worn on

a cord round the neck, particularly by women: a charm for fertility, being a rough representation of the human embryo. The name in full is heitiki, hei signifying anything worn round the neck; and the tiki being the chief object so worn the hei has been dropped. The tiki is highly valued, and genuine ones can rarely be obtained; fakes are plentiful. **1959** SLATTER *Gun in My Hand* 224 The Maoris must smile at the pakeha going all Maori when he's overseas. People on the ship to England wearing tikis and saying good kai this morning. **1970** JENKIN *NZ Mysteries* 101 On another occasion she found a beautiful greenstone *tiki*.

b. In Maori mythology, the first man.

1925 *Evening Post* (Wellington) 1 Aug. 13 In his recent book of the Maori, Elsdon Best states that Tiki, the man, realising that it was the eel which had led him astray, slew it and cut it into six pieces, from which sprang the six kinds of eels.

2. a. Used as symbolic of New Zealand in trade names, etc.: e.g. **Tiki Tour**, the name of a tourist transport organization. Also *transf.* (see quot.).

1989 McGILL *Dinkum Kiwi Dict.* 101 *tiki-tour* unlicensed driving;.. [quoting *New Zealand Herald*, 22 February 1989] 'When I was 12 I had an old BSA Bantam motorbike hidden on the farm, and used to tiki-tour all round the back of Cambridge.'..—a look or nosy around. **1991–92** The Telephone Directory, Wellington 469 Tiki Dairy... Tiki-Tape NZ Ltd.

b. As **plastic tiki** [the literal reference is to imitation greenstone necklets often made outside New Zealand], an emblem of a debased or false cultural interest.

1996 *Education Review* 24 July 1 The 'culture and heritage' [curriculum] strand had been reduced to 'plastic tiki' by removing the principle of teaching social studies within contexts.

tikkitak. *Stewart Island.* [Poss. imitative of the cry; poss. ad. Ma. *Te-akiaki* (Williams 7) the *red-billed gull.*] *white-fronted tern* (TERN 2 (10)).

1966 FALLA et al. *Birds NZ* 164 White-fronted Tern *Sterna striata* Other names: Sea-swallow, Kahawai Bird, Tara, Blackcap, Grenadier, Swallowtail, Noddy (Chathams), Tikkitak (Stewart Is.).

ti-koraha, ti-kouka: see TI *n.*¹ 3 (3), (2).

tikumu. Also early **teegoomme**. [Ma. /ˈtikumu/: Williams 418 *Tikumu*. 1. n. *Celmisia* [and similar] species of plants; the silky pellicle or skin of *tikumu* leaves, used for plaited fillets.] COTTON PLANT (*Celmisia* spp.).

1770 PARKINSON *Journal* (1773) 15 Jan. 115 At one particular place we met with a substance that appeared like a kid's skin..and were afterwards informed, by the natives, that it was gathered from some plant called Teegoomme: one of them had a garment made of it, which looked like their rug cloaks. **1869** *TrNZI* I. (rev. edn.) 266 Sometimes..the thin transparent epidermis from the leaves of the mountain Tikumu (*Celmisia coriacea*), were also used..to ornament..the head. **c1920** BEATTIE *Trad. Lifeways Southern Maori* (1994) 233 [Caption] Hori Kerei Taiaroa is wearing a cloak made with tikumu leaves. **1945** BEATTIE *Maori Place-names Canterbury* 65 Tikumu, the mountain celmisia... The white fibrous down was scraped from its under side and manufactured in taupa (leggings). **1946** *JPS* LV. 159 *Tikumu*, an alpine plant (Celmisia spectabilis, C. coriacea). **1981** BROOKER et al. *NZ Medicinal Plants* 41 *Celmisia coriacea*..and allied spp... Maori name: *Tikumu*. **1989** PARKINSON *Travelling Naturalist* 139 Among these are the large mountain daisy, or tikumu..the New Zealand eyebright, or tutumako.

tilter. *Farming. Obs.* BACK DELIVERY.

1940 STUDHOLME *Te Waimate* (1954) 170 When cutting crop with the old tilters (back deliveries) [c1880s], it was advisable to start when the straw was on the green side. *Ibid.* 174 It took a lot of men to work the old back-delivery [harvesting] machines or 'tilters', which looked rather like grass-mowers. **1990** MARTIN *Forgotten Worker* 123 The 'tilter'—also known as the 'back-delivery' because it dropped the sheaves from the back of a tilting hinged platform—was drawn by two horses and was first used in the early 1860s.

Timaruvian. *Occas.* **Timarusian.** [f. *Timaru* + *-vian.*] One born, or residing in, Timaru. (Also heard *joc.* **Timarooster.**)

1889 McKAY *Spirit of Rangatira* 32 Loud are the shouts that the far echoes fill, As the brave Timaruvians answer 'We will!' **1906** *Truth* 20 Oct. 1 A thirsty Timarusian, fined for entering a pub on Sunday, [said] that he hadn't had a drink. **1916** *Chron. NZEF* 15 Nov. 134 Timaruvians rise and bite like trout. **1972** MITCHELL *Pavlova Paradise* 34 To be a Timaruvian means as much as to be a New Zealander. **1980** LAWRY *Good Luck & Lavender* 50 No Lawry and no Timaruvian can tell me who won that contest. **1990** *Evening Post* (Wellington) 3 Apr. 1 But local Timaruvians are not so happy about the article.

timber, *n.*¹ [Spec. use of *timber* standing trees or their wood.] Special Comb. **timber-drag**, an apparatus for hauling logs from the bush; **timber-jack**, usu. a rack and pinion jack (see quot. 1874); **timber-jacking** *vbl. n.*, the moving of logs with a timber-jack; **timber-line** [cf. OED 'Chiefly *U.S.*'], BUSHLINE; **timber-man** (*mining*), see quot. 1978; **timber rearing** (*mining*), see quot.; **timber-wheel**, a kind of CATAMARAN 1, or JANKER (q.v.) for hauling logs from the bush; **timber-worrier**, a jocular name for a carpenter.

1848 WAKEFIELD *Handbook NZ* 447 The Colonist's attention should be directed to the following articles, with which he must provide himself according to his means and his intentions. For clearing and cultivating *timbered land*:- Waggons, bullock-drays, and **timber-drags**. [**1854** *Richmond-Atkinson Papers* (1960) I. 150 Broadmore says a screw jack is no use with logs. If a rack and pinion jack can be procured that is the right thing.] **1874** BAINES *Edward Crewe* 171 The principal tools required [by the kauri bushman] were Yankee axes, cross-cut saws, and **timber** (not screw) **jacks**. *Ibid.* 173 The timber-jacks consist of a toothed spear, two pinions, a cogged wheel, all of wrought iron, and properly arranged in a strong piece of wood. A double handle puts in motion the gear, and the spear can be ground out about two feet with power, one man being able to lift at the handle a ton easily. **1889** KIRK *Forest Flora* 150 The logs are propelled along these roads by 'timber-jacks' until they reach the water. **1894** *NZ Official Year-book* 331 The logs are forced along this [rolling] road by timber-jacks, which the bushmen use with remarkable skill. **1923** MALFROY *Small Sawmills* 21 [Caption] Timber-jack made in New Zealand... This is a..well-tried-out jack which is extensively used in logging operations from North Cape to the Bluff. **1969** MOORE *Forest to Farm* 38 The bushmen..performed amazing feats with a few quite primitive tools. These were axes..and the versatile New Zealand-made timber jack. These jacks weighed about 80 pounds and by geared cogs multiplied the man power applied to the revolving handles so that the 'spear' with its two chisel points, when applied to a log, could exert a lifting pressure of 5 tons. **1985** HAWKE & SCOTT *Early Farm Machinery in NZ* 129 First timber jacks were used [*sc.* for stumping] and later a Trewella stumping machine which had a thirteen ton pull on it. **1904** *NZ Illustr. Mag.* Dec. 177 Booreedy Jack was a specimen of the old-time bushman..kauri-cutting, **timber-jacking**, pit-sawing, rafting and mill-work, etc. **1935** ODELL *Handbook Arthur's Pass National Park* 23 Probably the best camping site is on the edge of the **timber line**, for the bush stops abruptly to give place to tussock and snow grass. **1952** Dec. Busdriver, Routeburn, Otago. The timber-line as you North Islanders call it—the snow-line as we call it down here. **1978** MOORE & IRWIN *Oxford Book NZ Plants* 80 A hardy tree, growing from sea level to timber line. **1963** PEARSON *Coal Flat* 28 There was soon a crowd of miners, truckers and **timbermen**. **1978** McARA *Gold Mining Waihi* 335 *Timberman*: A man specially skilled in the repair and installation of mine timbers. **1978** McARA *Gold Mining Waihi* 335 **Timber rearing**: Usually a wall at the end of a stope partitioning off the ladderway and consisting of 5 ft slabs nailed vertically to stulls wedged between the walls. Also used to make the central 'box' in a three-compartment rise. Sometimes cribbing was used instead of building a rearing. **1894** *NZ Official Year-book* 332 In portions of the Taranaki District, where milling timber is somewhat sparse, **timber-wheels** are commonly used. **1910** *Truth* 9 Apr. 5 Frederick William Tapling, a youthful Linwood carpenter... Tapling is a dark-complexioned **timber-worrier** of highly-strung disposition.

timber, *n.*² [Transf. use of *timber* a structural beam.] The main frame of deer antlers which carry the tines.

1921 *Quick March* 10 May 13 These antlers had four points and were well developed, carrying good solid timber. **1953** SUTHERLAND *Golden Bush* (1963) 171 The top tines were badly finished and without much symmetry. The timber was light in weight for all its size pointing to an abnormal amount of pith at the heart and the stag was past his best by several years. **1984** HOLDEN *Razorback* 13 He avoided stepping in the cast antler of a red stag, but noted from habit the number of the points—five well-shaped ones, good timber, a decent length.

tin, *n.*¹ [f. *tin* tinned or galvanized iron.]

1. Used *attrib.* in special Comb. to designate an article made of tinplate or galvanized iron, or the contents of a tin receptacle: **tin billy**, see BILLY *n.*¹ 1 a; **tin (tinned) cow**, tinned (usu. condensed) milk, see COW 5; **tin dish**, a gold-pan (PAN *n.*¹, DISH *n.*¹); **tin (tinned) dog**, (a) [AND 1895], mainly in cookhouse, boarding-school, etc. cuisine, bully beef or other tinned preserved meat; (b) *transf.* [with allusion to a sled dog-team], a term used by Antarctic personnel for a motor toboggan; **tin hare**, a nickname for an early railcar; **tin mill** [f. the 'tinned iron' from which they were constructed], a threshing mill (see esp. quot. 1944); **tin of fish**, in the phr. **not worth a tin of fish**, worthless; **tinplate** [transf. use of *tin-plate* a metal dinner-plate, or perh. referring to the metallic colour], FLOUNDER *n.* 2 (9); **tin-pot** *a.* [spec. use of *tin-pot* cheap, inferior], of a place or town, small, insignificant; **Tin Shed** *obs.*, a nickname (c1912) for the Wellington Fever Hospital at Newtown, constructed of galvanized iron; **tin-tippy** *obs.*, a tin canoe made of bent corrugated iron fastened at both ends and made watertight with tar.

1860 in Butler *First Year* (1863) iv 56 We did not wash any of the gravel, for we had no **tin dish**, neither did we know how to wash. **1862** *Otago Witness* (Dunedin) 23 Aug. 7 We bought a little flour, and borrowed a tin dish from one of the stations..and panned out forty ounces [of gold] in about a week. **1873**

TIN 837 **TIN-KETTLE**

Pyke *Wild Will Enderby* (1889, 1974) I. iv 17 Borrowing a pan (*Anglice* : tin-dish) from some neighbourly miners, he progressed up the Gorge trying 'prospects'. **1896** O'Regan *Poems* 33 Life's claim is almost duffered..Swag, billy, and tin-dish I'll need no more In the new field that I'm off to. **1914** Pfaff *Diggers' Story* 94 Some few of them had done a little desultory gold getting with shovel and tin dish. **1939** Beattie *First White Boy Born Otago* 166 The shops supplied..mostly diggers, and all I saw of their goods were tin dishes and diggers' tools hanging outside. **1943** Hislop *Pure Gold* 69 All we got for our trouble with the tin dish were a few colours and black sand. **1918** *Quick March* 25 Apr. 3 He [*sc.* a soldier on Gallipoli] loathed plum-and-apple jam, **tinned dog** and granite-like biscuit. **1921** Foston *At the Front* 116 The living..consisted chiefly in some camps [for labourers on the Main Trunk construction]..of 'tin dog' (meat) or 'tin cat' (fish). **1992** *North & South* (Auckland) Feb. 23 In recent years the '**tin dog**' or motor toboggan had become the main mode of transport [in the Antarctic]. **1972** Leitch *Railways of NZ* 194 The Wairarapa cars..were designed to negotiate the Rimutaka Incline under their own power... Of special lightweight construction, these forty-nine-seaters, which soon earned the affectionate nickname of 'the **tin hares**', proved to be fast and reliable machines. **1990** Churchman & Hurst *Railways of NZ* 158 Railcars (nicknamed 'tin hares') were placed on the run in 1936. **1944** *Korero* (AEWS Background Bulletin) 10 Apr. 10 The **tin mill** is smaller, slower but more portable [*sc.* than the threshing mill]. **1971** Ogilvie *Moonshine Country* 158 Next to the header harvester, the 'tin' mill did the mill men most disservice. This smaller style of mill came in with the tractor by which it was drawn and driven. The 'tin' mill only needed seven or eight men to operate it, and its output was no more than half that of the 'big' mill. But within a short time these small mills became so popular that many farmers bought their own and could thresh their grain exactly when it suited them and their crops. The 'tin' mill and the 'Sunshine' header thus put an effective end to the era of the [threshing] mill men [in South Canterbury c1910]. **1980** Neave *Land of Munros* 90 Then the tin mill and tractor came in,.. and [threshing] work was reduced to a few days only. **1990** Martin *Forgotten Worker* 134 Some eleven to twelve men were required to operate a mill, and between 1,800 and 2,000 bushels could be threshed in a day. This organisation of labour continued until the advent of the smaller local farmer-owned 'tin' mills in the early twentieth century. (Their name derives from the fact that they were made of metal rather than the wood of the older mills.) **1959** Slatter *Gun in My Hand* 44 He tried to skedaddle the very first night in the line... He **wasn't worth a tinna fish** over there. And now he skites about when he was at the war. **1911** Waite *Rec. Canterbury Museum* I. 197 Sand Flounder New Zealand Flounder, Patiki, Three corner, **Tinplate**. **1956** [see **three-corner** (three-)]. **1967** [see flounder *n.* 2 (9)]. **1970** [see plaice]. **1981** Wilson *Fisherman's Bible* 71 Flounder Sand... Other names are 'dab', tinplate, square flounder. **1959** Slatter *Gun in My Hand* 75 I'm a cosmopolitan now. I don't stick up for any **tin-pot** place any more. *Ibid.* 167 I've never been in the tin-pot place. Never heard of it. **1986** Watson *Address to a King* 59 Erin Carter born in March 1932, brought up on his father's farm in Northland, near a tin pot village where there's only the store with the red benzine bowsers in front of it. **1938** Hyde *Godwits Fly* (1970) 26 When they [*sc.* a Newtown slum family] took the scarlet fever..and were sent off in the ambulance to be isolated at the **Tin Shed**—the fever hospital—Augusta sent them custards. **1962** Glover *Hot Water Sailor* (1981) 29 We [*sc.* schoolboys, c1920] discovered that once a **tin-tippy** was capsized or rammed it was difficult to get it up again.

2. *Cookery. Ellipt.* for *cake-tin*, or *biscuit tin*, a receptacle in which home-baked cake, biscuits etc. are stored, esp. in the (now old-fashioned) phr. **to have** (something) **in the tins**, **to fill the tins**, **to keep one's tins full**, to have a good supply of home-baking on hand.

1983 Henderson *Down from Marble Mountain* 79 I don't know how she coped. I never knew of her ever having been caught with empty cake tins. **1986** *Beyond Expectations* 131 We..had a mother who stayed home..cut our lunches..filled the tins with cakes and biscuits every Thursday. **1989** Daish *Good Food* 94 Not long ago it would have been embarrassing, if not shameful, to be caught with your tins empty. **1991** Keith *Lovely Day Tomorrow* 42 'Keeping the tins full' was a housewifely virtue for which school girls were trained at an early age. **1993** *Dominion* (Wellington) 12 Jan. 6 These were the staple of her everyday cooking— the delicacies always to be found in the 'tins' when we came home from school.

tin, *n.*² [f. *tinny* lucky.] Used *attrib.* connoting 'unexpected good luck' in special Comb. **tin-arse** [AND 1941] *n.*, **tin-arsed** *a.*, lucky; **tin-arsing** *quasi-vbl. n.*, being on a lucky streak; **tin-bum** [AND 1955], a lucky fellow.

1984 Beaton *Outside In* 20 Kate: Good ol' Ginny [for escaping the consequences]! Sandy: Yeah! Kate: **Tin arse**! *Ibid.* Glossary 110 *tin arse.* lucky; a lucky person (used ironically). **1984** 16–17 M E90 Pakuranga Coll. 32 Tin-arse [luckiness] [M13 F4] **1988** McGill *Dict. Kiwi Slang* 113 *tin arse* lucky person; also *tinbum*; eg 'First time he's ever swung a golf club and he scores a hole in one. What a tin arse!' **1937** Partridge *Dict. Slang* 888 *tinny...* lucky: Australia and New Zealand: C. 20. Occ. **tin-arsed**. **1991** Duff *One Night Out Stealing* 51 These fullas still winning. Tin-arsing, more like it. **1954** Baxter *Collected Poems* (1980) 137 [Title] *Song of* **Tinbum** *Kelly*. **1968** Slatter *Pagan Game* 158 The luckiest player that ever pulled on a jersey, said Old Bert. He's been a bit of a tin-bum. Not like me. I'm always shit out of luck. **1975** Anderson *Men of Milford Road* 57 The result had appeared in the Invercargill paper and the nom-de-plume published was 'Tinburn'. Dan of course wanted to know what prompted him to use such a curious nom-de-plume, and the proud winner said that he hadn't used that nom-de-plume at all. 'Well what did you use?' asked Dan. 'Tinbum.' Obviously the press in those days was a little more prudish than it is today. **1992** *Sunday Times* (Wellington) 22 Nov. 1 It's [*sc.* winning Lotto] a bizarre and miraculous thing to happen. It's a real tin-bum thing.

tin-can, *n.*

1. As an instrument of tin-kettling.

1890 *NZ Observer* 22 Nov. 17 It is rumoured that several couples are going to run in double harness soon, so get your tin-cans ready, boys.

2. Used *attrib.* alluding to tin-kettling in special Comb. **tin-can army**, **tin-can party**, a group engaged in or intent on tin-kettling newlyweds; **tin-canner**, *tin-kettler* (tin-kettle *v.*).

1893 *NZ Observer* 9 Sept. 22 There will be a job for the **tin-can army** in the good time coming. **1904** *NZ Observer* 13 Aug. 21 Why wouldn't E.W. join the **tin-canners**? **1925** Webb *Miss Peters' Special* 64 'I forgot to warn you. It's the tin-canners, the first lot—youngsters you know.' He dashed out..and was greeted by shrieks, cheers, and a deafening banging on benzine and kerosene tins. After a brief parley..the giggling boys departed, and the bridegroom returned to explain to his wife that 'It was just a custom—you know. They always do it in this part of the country. The men will be here a bit later, and I'll have to give them something to go and drink our health.' **1967** McLatchie *Tang of Bush* 55 Now he was on hand early to ensure that the tin canners did not overstep the mark in decorum. **1925** Webb *Miss Peters' Special* 62 He..recalled how he had himself described a man as 'a stingy blackguard' who only offered the **tin-can party**..twenty-five shillings to be spent on beer.

tin-can, *v.* [See note at tin-kettling.] *trans.* tin-kettle *v.*

1891 [see tin-canning]. **1918** *Wairarapa Daily Times* 15 June 4 Little boys 'tincan' the happy pair. **1957** Frame *Owls Do Cry* (1967) 67 And there's Bill Trout and Mary. How funny. We tin-canned them and threw rice at them and they gave us a cream bun. **1959** Davin *No Remittance* 96 At that moment the very devil of a noise started up outside, as if a thousand mongrel dogs with two thousand tin cans tied to their tails had been suddenly let loose on a corrugated-iron roof. 'What on earth is that?' I gave a jump that nearly sent Norah sprawling. 'They must be tin-canning us.' 'And what, I'd like to know, is tin-canning?' 'Oh, it's a thing they always do round here when a newly married couple comes home.' **1982** Frame *To the Is-land* (1984) 81 Florrie married. We tin-canned her and her new husband and had a feast of fizzy drinks and cakes. **1988** *Letter from Napier* in Stone *Folder* (ATLMS) My mother was born and lived in Invercargill up to 1915, and has told me of the custom there to go 'tin-canning' newly-weds.

tin-canning, *vbl. n.* and *ppl. a.* [See tin-kettling.] tin-kettling.

1891 *Waikato Times* in Norris *Settlers in Depression* (1964) 197 Eight young men were convicted of disturbing an inhabitant [of Hamilton] and fined 5s. and costs each. The magistrate gave them a lecture on the absurdity of the barbarous custom of tin-canning. **1911** *Truth* 11 Feb. 5 They say they are going to give me an awful tincanning when I get married. Hope you won't mind, Dora. **1925** Webb *Miss Peters' Special* 62 He..had taken his full share in the New Year's Eve pranks and mischief in which colonial youth delights, as well as being a promoter of most of the tin-canning parties when anyone got married. **1944** *Franklin Times* 20 Dec. 2 [Caption] 'Tin Canning'. Bride and groom surprised. **1959** Davin *No Remittance* 96 'There was bound to be a tin-canning. We'd hardly be married without it. Don't they have them everywhere?' 'No, indeed they don't.' **1964** Howe *Stamper Battery* 116 I suppose our [children's wedding] celebrations [c1880] were rather childish... We called them 'tin-canning'. We usually started rather late because by then the guests were fairly drunk and their reactions more amusing. Our drums were empty kerosene tins beaten with copper-sticks and the din could be heard for miles... Tradition decreed that red-hot pennies be thrown to us when the tin-canning started. **1988** *Letter from Wellington* in Stone *Folder* (ATLMS) I was growing up in Central Southland in the 1920ies when tincanning was very common.

ti-ngahere(here): see ti 3 (4).

tinker grass, tinker-tailor: see grass 2 (39).

tin-kettle, *v.* [See note at tin-kettling.] *trans.* To noisily serenade newly-weds; rarely (orig. Brit. dial., now obsolete in NZ use) to show dislike or opposition (to a person) by performing a 'rough music' (see quot. 1888). See also tin-can *v.*

1875 Wood & Lapham *Waiting for Mail* 110 Presently we heard an awful uproar in the ball-room. 'Oh! Glory,' said Bridget, 'they're tin-kettling them [*sc.* the newly-weds]; come on,' and she seized an empty kerosene tin and was off... There stood Ned and

Maggie in the centre, while round marched the rest of the people armed with kerosine tins, billies half filled with stones, and tin dishes, shouting, yelling, and singing. **1881** BATHGATE *Waitaruna* 234 I was wakened by the din caused by a lot of the diggers tin-kettling the newly-married pair. **1888** BRADSHAW *NZ of Today* 323 The members of the school committee hostile to our popular and excellent teacher were hooted and tin-kettled to their houses. **1981** ANDERSON *Both Sides of River* 103 One night, when I had been on the station [newly-married] about a month, Ron..announced, 'We'll be having visitors tomorrow night. They're coming for miles around to tin-kettle us.'

Hence **tin-kettler**; also *transf*., a supporter (see quot. 1910).
1904 *NZ Observer* 23 Apr. 7 At a recent wedding, the next-door neighbours of the bridal party provided cakes for the tin-kettlers. **1905** [see TIN-KETTLING]. **1910** *Truth* 1 Jan. 1 I'm a stout tin-kettler For the small, but honest settler. **1934** MARKS *Memories* 18 But it was to the uninvited guests [to the wedding] that we boys paid most attention—the tin-kettlers. **1988** *Letter from Rotorua* in Stone *Folder* (ATLMS) Six months ago, here in Rotorua, my young neighbour remarried and I was surprised and delighted to see and hear the 'tin-kettlers' arrive when the young couple returned from their honeymoon.

tin-kettling, *vbl. n.* and *ppl. a.* (Formerly) a house-warming custom whereby a newly-wed couple, usu. on return from the honeymoon, were welcomed by friends and neighbours circling the marriage home banging on kerosene (etc.) tins until provided with refreshments. Also *attrib*.
[*Note*] The word *kettle* is poss. used in its older, more inclusive sense 'pot, cauldron for boiling over a fire' (as in *camp-kettle*, *gipsy-kettle*, and presumably as in 'kettle of fish'), and not in its more confined modern sense of '(tea-)kettle'. The custom was almost obsolete in New Zealand by 1960, and always probably more popular in the country than in the towns. The New Zealand custom seems always to have been friendly-disposed (but see TIN-KETTLE *v*. quot. 1888), that is, of *welcoming* newly-weds into the community, in contradistinction to the English 'rough music' customs which seem to be a form of moral and social punishment or pressure, of excluding newly-weds or others: cf. OED *tin-kettle*, 'to punish a notorious offender by rough music', *tin-pan;* EDD *tin* 1 (7), *tinkettle* Hampshire; (10) *tin-pan* Notts. Later N. American customs of *shivaree* seem often to include these light-hearted '(?bride-)ransoming' practices.
1874 *Otago Guardian* 13 Nov. 2 (Griffiths Collect.) The practice of tin-kettling and levying blackmail on people after a wedding was of frequent occurrence, especially in St Alban's District... Serenaded a newly wedded happy couple with a tintinnabulation of tin kettles. **1905** *Truth* 23 Sept. 8 *A Tin-kettling Episode*: The detestable practice of tin-kettling a newly-married couple [with kerosene tins] doesn't seem to die out like other barbarities in this country; it is a relic of by-gone days... The tin-kettlers expect the happy bridegroom to stop the din by handing them cakes and ale... It is only the idiotic low-class class of people who would go banging tin-cans opposite a man's house after dark. **1934** MARKS *Memories* 18 There were about fifty boys in the tin-kettling party. **1943** *NZ Farmer Weekly* 25 Mar. 16 This was called 'tin-canning' or 'tin-kettling', and newly married couples were those who suffered. **1956** SUTHERLAND *Green Kiwi* (1960) 204 After it [*sc*. the house] had weathered two traditional 'tin kettlings' we knew we had nothing to fear. **1959** HOBBS *Wild West Coast* 139 Tin-kettling parties for newlyweds are solemn rites and noisy ones, especially in the country districts. **1979** MARSHALL *Supper Waltz Wilson* 47 'Used to be real live-wires when we were first married,' said Mrs Foden philosophically. 'Never missed a tin-kettling or first-footing.' **1981** HUNT *Speaking a Silence* 30 [On the Chatham Islands] another thing they've dropped now is tin-kettling after a wedding..thirty or forty of you, all with kerosine tins, you'd make a hell of a din. Then you'd all be called in for drink and tucker. **1988** *Letter from Nelson* in Stone *Folder* (ATLMS) I was present at both the tin-kettling and the presentation [to the new bride of a chamber-pot filled with salt and tied about with a wideish ribbon..with a large bow tied in it..with the advice that if they used up all of the salt in the chamber-pot they would have Good Luck] which probably took place between 1925 and 1930.

tinny, *a.*[1] [Poss. fig. and extended use of *tin money*; not related to 'des)*tiny*' as occas. suggested: AND 1919.] Lucky. See also TIN *n.*[2]
1918 *Chron. NZEF* 7 June 205 Remarks are heard on the 'tinny' luck or otherwise of the [poker-]players, while the 'stiffs' bemoan their luck. **1935** MITCHELL & STRONG in Partridge *Slang Today* 286 [The] following [was] employed by those who served in the [Great] War..*tinny*, lucky; *Ibid*. 287 When I said 'Hooray' he called me back and gave me a few francs; I reckon I was very tinny. **1960** KEINZLY *Tangahano* 151 I won two houseys. Ten quid.... Tinny, eh? **1968** SLATTER *Pagan Game* 164 The tinniest player that ever wore the jersey. **1978** HENDERSON *Soldier Country* 126 Flukes? Destiny? Fate? Or just: How Tinny Can You Be? **1988** *Sunday News* (Auckland) 3 Apr. 11 Soon there'll be something worse than reading about some tinny person who's just won Lotto. **1996** PERKINS *Not Her Real Name* 92 He's got away with it, the tinny bastard.

Hence **tinniness**, luckiness.
1938 *Tararua Tramper* Mar. 4 We congratulated ourselves on our good fortune or just plain 'tinniness'.

tinny, *a.*[2] [f. *tinny* (appearing to be) made of tin-plate.] Unsubstantial; jerry-built, badly-made (though often, superficially, appearing well-made).
1951 *2YA Wellington Women's Session* 12 Apr. The shaving cabinets you buy always seem a bit tinny to me. **1988** MCGILL *Dict. Kiwi Slang* 113 *tinny*... not very impressive; from its being regarded as of inferior metal to iron or steel; eg 'I tell you that horse is tinny, it'll never amount to anything.'

tinny, *n.*[1] [f. TIN *n.*[1]]
1. *tin-tippy* (TIN *n.*[1] 1).
1991 *Metro* (Auckland) Sept. 30 Another popular occupation was building 'tinnies', canoes made from old corrugated iron, pointed to a bow at one end and with a wooden stern nailed in at the other... Before the days of television and 'spacies' this was one of the ways Devonport kids amused themselves, scooting in their trusty tinnies in among Ngataringa Bay's scrubby mangroves.

2. A depreciatory name for a dinghy constructed of aluminium.
1993 *Evening Post* (Wellington) 4 Sept. 38 More than 30 years ago Parkercraft introduced the first aluminium dinghy to New Zealand boaties. The ubiquitous 'tinnies' have since come of age.

tinny. *n.*[2] *Drug-users.* [f. *tin*foil.] A BULLET q.v. Also **tinny house**, see quot.
1995 *Dominion* (Wellington) 24 Nov. 1 She later suspected that drug deals were taking place at her former home... Judge Bouchier said large numbers of people from all over Auckland went to the house between 1990 and 1995 to buy 'tinnies' (cannabis bullets) for $20. **1995** National Radio 'Morning Report' 4 Apr. [Auckland detective explains:] Drug distributors organize young people to run drug houses, with the locations continually changing, and deal drugs to customers from them. The drug is usually cannabis in the form of 'bullets', that is enough cannabis for about 3 cigarettes wrapped in aluminium foil. Hence they get their names 'bullet houses' or 'tinny houses'. **1995** *Dominion* (Wellington) 6 Dec. 1 They could buy a 'tinny' (cannabis leaf wrapped in tin foil and enough for two or three joints), for about $20.

tio. Also early **teo**. [Ma. Williams 420 *Tio* (i)... *4. Saxostrea glomerata*, rock-oyster. *Tio-para, Ostrea sinuata*, mud-oyster.] OYSTER 1.
[**1815** KENDALL *New Zealanders' First Book* 8 Teo Oyster.] **c1846** WEEKES *My Island* in Rutherford *Establishment of New Plymouth* (1940) 119 Whilst it was being prepared I strayed along the beach knocking off rock oysters (native name *tio*). **1913** SUTER *Manual NZ Mollusca* 889 Mud-oyster; commonly known as Stewart Island oyster... Tio. **1945** BEATTIE *Maori Place-names Canterbury* 62 Notable omissions from this list [of food sources compiled by Maori hands [c1920] are..tio-kohatu (rock-oysters), tio-pati (oysters), and various kinds of shellfish. **1987** POWELL *Native Animals* 18 Auckland Rock Oyster (Tio) *Crassostrea glomerata*... Stewart Island Oyster (Tio Para). *Ostrea lutaria*.

Tip, *n.*[1] *Goldfields. Hist*. [Abbrev. of *Tipperary*, a county in Eire, used (occas. as *Tipperary Boys*) as an emblem of rowdy violence: AND 1862 (Thatcher quot.), 1888.] Usu. *pl*. as (the) **Tips**, 'Tipperary boys', Irish rowdies, larrikins.
[**1862** CHUDLEIGH *Diary* 16 Oct. (1950) 63 It was a good sale. Lots of fellows got drunk and we had a regular Tiperairy riot. They stuck to the rule where ever you see a head, hit it.] **1862** THATCHER *Canterbury Songster* 19 To rescue him this rowdie Tip unto his mates he hollered. **1863** GOLDIE in Beattie *Pioneers Explore Otago* (1947) 149 Some of these distant and retired mountain gorges are often the scene of many a wild encounter between the Tipperary or Tips as they are generally termed and the Galway Boys. **1871** MONEY *Knocking About NZ* 73 *En passant*, no class of men..are less generally known and appreciated than the digger. In saying this, I do not for one moment refer to those curses of a gold-field, the low Irish 'tips', for a more cowardly, ruffianly, or brutal character I have never met with than that lively specimen from the green isle, who seems to flourish with rank luxuriance in the neighbourhood of gold. **1873** PYKE *Wild Will Enderby* (1889, 1974) I. v 19 In those days the diggings were infested by gangs of rowdies, who (whether rightly or wrongly I know not) were designated by the generic name of 'Tips'. **1888** PRESHAW *Banking Under Difficulties* 59 I do not for one moment refer to those curses of a goldfield, the low Irish 'Tips'.

tip, *n.*[2] *Farming*. In full **tip-pen**. A pen constructed to tip its occupants out (into a dip, etc.).
1949 NEWTON *High Country Days* 102 The tip, a small pen capable of holding ten or a dozen sheep, was situated a foot or so above and partly overhanging the dip. Constructed on a large axle..with the aid of a lever it could be tipped and the sheep sent slithering into the dip below.

tip, *n.*[3] *Farming*. A fine point on the staple of wool.
1966 NEWTON *Boss's Story* 29 Unshorn hoggets, having more 'tip' to their wool, are particularly prone to entanglement.

Hence **tippy** *a*., wool with a very pointed tip to the staple.
1938 *NZJST* XX. 250B In a study of 'tippy' or unlevel dyeing of loose wool..he found that..samples

ti-palm. *Obs.* Mainly *SI*. Also **ti-ti palm**. CABBAGE-TREE 1. See also CABBAGE-PALM 1, TI *n.*¹ a.

1838 POLACK *NZ* I. 229 The provisions consisted of about three thousand baskets of potatoes, kumeras..the baked roots of the Ti palm, &c. graced the festal scene. **1844** SELWYN *Journal* 18 Jan. in *NZ Part III* (Church in the Colonies VIII) (1851) 14 Walked over a beautiful grass plain [south Canterbury]..after twelve miles covered with the Ti palm. **1851** *Lyttelton Times* 12 Apr. 5 The appearance of Ti palms on the Canterbury plains is very remarkable. They rise amidst the short rich grass with their thick stalks and graceful crew... One of our wags remarked of these plants, that they looked 'like men as trees walking'. **1856** Ti-ti palm [see CABBAGE-TREE 1]. **1863** BUTLER *First Year* ix 132 The cabbage-tree or ti palm is not a true palm, though it looks like one. **1866** BARKER *Station Life* (1870) 52 Ti-ti palms are dotted here and there. **1870** *TrNZI* II. 49 The constantly recurring bush fires have cleared off the stately Ti palms (so fragrant in early spring). **1882** POTTS *Out in Open* 48 The stem of a dead ti-palm or cabbage tree..just meets its requirement in this particular. **1890** *Richmond-Atkinson Papers* (1960) II. 558 The banks are bare with the exception of a few small patches of kahikatea and ti palm. **1933** *Press* (Christchurch) (Acland Gloss.) 23 Dec. 15 *Ti-palm, Ti-tree.—Cabbage-tree*.

tipau. Also early **tepau**, **tipow**. [Ma. /'ti:pau/: Williams 421 *Tīpau..Myrsine australis...* (Ng[apuh]i) = *māpau, māpou*.]

1. A small forest tree of the genus *Myrsine* (fam. Myrsiniaceae), especially MAPAU 1 a (*M. australis*), less commonly TORO 2 (*M. salicina*).

[**1820** LEE & KENDALL *NZ Gram. & Vocab.* 213 *Tīpau, s.* A shrub so called.] **1838** POLACK *NZ* I. 109 Many other trees abounded..such as the..tipow..and various kinds of akkas. *Ibid.* II. 399 The *Tepau* is a similar wood to Towai. **1844** WILLIAMS *NZ Jrnl.* (1956) 106 The Tipau, although not remarkable yet a stately tree. *Ibid.* 120 *Tipau..Suttonia australis* or the larger *S. salicina*. **1853** HOOKER *II Flora Novae-Zelandiae I Flowering Plants* 173 *Suttonia australis...* 'Mapau'..Middle Island... 'Tipau', north of the Thames river. **1869** *TrNZI* I. (rev. edn.) 276 The tipau, or mapau, (*Myrsine australis*,) is a small leafy tree..more plentiful at the north. **1889** KIRK *Forest Flora* 24 This species [*sc. Myrsine salicina*] is sometimes erroneously called 'tipau', but, Mr. Colenso informs me, the name is rightly applied to *M. Urvillei* alone. **1906** CHEESEMAN *Manual NZ Flora* 432 *M[yrsine] Urvillei... Mapau; Tipau*.

2. A small forest tree *Pittosporum tenuifolium*, KOHUHU.

1869 *TrNZI* I. (rev. edn.) 194 Black mapau, or tipau (*Pittosporum Colensoi*). A shrub tree, very ornamental in contrast with the last [*sc.* white mapau], the whole tree very dark coloured... black mapau, tipau (*Pittosporum tenuifolium*).

ti-pore: see TI *n.*¹ 3 (5).

tipow, var. TIPAU.

tipuna. [Ma. /'tipuna/: Williams 458 *Tupuna, tipuna* (pl. *tūpuna, tīpuna*). Ancestor, grandparent.] Ancestor; grandparent.

1983 HULME *Bone People* 383 The old man moans, his fingers twitching helplessly by his sides... 'E pou, tipuna, we all die like this, do not worry.' *Ibid.* 469 Tipuna = grandfather/mother. **1986** *Landfall* 160 492 Only his 'tipuna' had had the gift of communication, and now he was dead, while Danny's 'kuia' thought of nothing but Pakeha mores. **1991** *Dominion* (Wellington) 30 Mar. 12 We maintain the practice of our ancestors, our tipuna, which is that you never write or sing a waiata unless you had a good reason to... It was considered bad taste to sing anything for nothing.

ti-rauriki: see TI *n.*¹ 3 (6).

Tiriti: see TREATY.

tishy: see TISSUE.

tissue. Also **tishy**. [AND 'chiefly Tasmanian', 1966.] A cigarette paper.

1952 *Here & Now* Jan. 32 Might just as well settle down to rolling your own. Better go and see if the parole-jumper in Number 8 has got any tissues left. **1982** WOODHOUSE *Blue Cliffs* 226 A customary test [for wet wool] was to rub a cigarette tishy along the wool next to the skin. **1987** GEE *Prowlers* 165 Her papers—tishies, she called them—were inside with the tobacco.

tit, *n.*¹ [Transf. use of the northern hemisphere bird-name *tit*.]

[*Note*] In the *Checklist of Birds of NZ* (1990) 209f. TOMTIT, the name now preferred by ornithologists, replaces the TIT of the 1970 edition in the names of the subspecies included in **a.** and **b.** below.

a. Often as **New Zealand tit**, *Petroica macrocephala* (fam. Eopsaltriidae), a small insectivorous forest bird of mainland New Zealand. Often with a modifier indicating the provenance of subspecies, and occas. defining their colour characteristics: **North Island (pied, white-breasted) tit** *P. m. toitoi*; **South Island (southern, yellow-breasted, yellow-headed) tit** *P. m. macrocephala*. See also TITMOUSE.

1870 *TrNZI* II. 47 Perhaps the Tit (Petroica) darted to the ground from the tall [flax] flower-stalk, to snatch the larva of the grasshopper. **1872** *Appendix Proc. Otago Prov. Council* 39 The following is a list of the birds shot... *Anthornis melanura*, bell bird or mocker..*Petroica macrocephala*, yellow-breasted tit. **1873** pied tit [see MIROMIRO]. **1882** POTTS *Out in Open* 130 The tit or yellow-breasted robin (*Petroica macrocephala*)..in some parts..is called a robin. **1884** *NZJSc.* II. 286 *Petro[i]ca toi-toi*..Pied Tit, Miro-miro... *Petro[i]ca macrocephala...* Yellow-breasted Tit or Robin, miro-miro. **1904** HUTTON & DRUMMOND *Animals NZ* 7 The New Zealand Tits, like those of the Old Country, are bold to the extent of impudence, but they are also very friendly and sociable... The Southern, or Yellow-breasted, Tits are sprightly and graceful little birds. *Ibid.* 72 The White-breasted Tit.—Miro-miro... The North Island species is one of the birds that will probably become extinct. **1914** GUTHRIE-SMITH *Mutton Birds & Other Birds* 187 Neither in plumage nor in habits does the Yellow-breasted Tit of the South, differ greatly from the Pied Tit of the North Island. **1938** *Auckland Weekly News* 27 Apr. 38 Another bird with pert and pretty ways is the North Island or white-breasted tit. **1946** *JPS* LV. 154 *Miromiro*, a bird.., North Island tomtit; white-breasted tit it differs from the South Island..yellow-breasted tit in the colouration of the breast. **1955** OLIVER *NZ Birds* 478 Among the discoveries made on this occasion [*sc.* the visit of the *Coquille* in 1824] was the White-breasted Tit, specimens of which were first described by Lesson who based his specific name on one of the Maori names. **1964** HINTZ *Trout at Taupo* 124 The little miromiro..the tomtit that abounds in the upper river valley, his sooty plumage relieved by the dazzling white of his breast. **1983** *Whakarewarewa Forest Park* 59 Along the tracks among the older stands of trees the native tomtit (sometimes called a pied tit) is likely to be seen.

b. Subspecies from offshore islands: **Auckland Island tit** *Petroica macrocephala marrineri*; **black (or Snares) tit** *P. m. dannefaerdi*; **Chatham Island tit** *P. m. chathamensis*.

1970 *Annot. Checklist Birds NZ* 68 *P. macrocephala chathamensis..Chatham Island tit* Chatham Islands..*P. macrocephala dannefaerdi..Black Tit* Snares Island..*P. macrocephala marrineri...* Auckland Island Tit. **1985** *Reader's Digest Book NZ Birds* 284 Chatham Island Tit *P.m. chathamensis...* Black Tit *P.m. dannefaerdi...* Auckland Island Tit *P.m. marrineri...* Snares tit, Snares Island robin. **1986** *Listener* 12 Apr. 49 Cross-fostering techniques..on..Chatham Island tits on South East Island are experiments that have excited the conservation world.

tit, *n.*²

1. In various phrases. **a. to pull (someone's) tit** [Partridge 8 regards it as Austral. and NZ], to have (someone) on.

1947 DAVIN *For Rest of Our Lives* 331 Don't get knotted, Franky boy. I'm just pulling your tit. **1988** McGILL *Dict. Kiwi Slang* 88 *pull someone's tit* to make a fool of or tease; eg 'Take it easy, Moss. Can't you see he's just pulling your tit?'

b. to pull the other tit, usu. *imp.* expressing disbelief in a claim made.

1968 SLATTER *Pagan Game* 163 Didn't know him from a bottle of detergent—Pull the other tit, boy.

2. (as) useful as tits on a bull, useless.

1964 DAVIS *Watersiders* 124 Blooming disgraceful. Some of these fancy-pants young stevedore are about as useful as tits on a bull.

3. to get one's tits in a tangle, used mainly in neg., to become very upset or frustrated, to 'get one's knickers in a twist'.

1984 BEATON *Outside In* 36 Di: Don't get your tits in a tangle, Ma, No harm meant and none taken.

4. Special Comb. **tit-proud**, said of a woman vain about her breasts.

1956 *Numbers five* May 16 This no question to obsess his heart while juke box melodies can graph a tit-proud blonde to tickle up desire.

5. In the phr. **tits on toast** [belly-pork often has nipples attached], see quot.

1985 HUNT *I'm Ninety-five* 29 We'd make dumplings, too, fried up in the camp oven. Buggers afloat we called them [c1916]... And what did we call the poached eggs? A pair of bastards on a raft, and we'd have tits on toast—belly pickled pork on toast. I still use those old names; everyone laughs at me.

titi.

1. Also **teetee**. [Ma. /'ti:ti:/: Williams 414 *Tī* (iv), *tītī, v. intr. 1.* Squeak, make a sharp inarticulate sound..*tītī, n. Puffinus griseus*, and perhaps other species, mutton-bird; also *Pterodroma cooki*, a petrel.] MUTTONBIRD *n* 1. See also *Cook's petrel* (PETREL 2 (6)), HAKOAKOA 1, *mottled petrel* (PETREL 2 (16)), SHEARWATER 2 (4), (6).

[**c1826–27** BOULTBEE *Journal* (1986) 113 Mutton bird,—tèe tèe] **1842** GRAY *Fauna* in Dieffenbach *Travels in NZ* (1843) II. 199 *Pelecanoides urinatrix...* Procellaria... Teetee of the natives of Queen Charlotte's Sound... *Procellaria Cookii. Ibid.* 200 Titi. **1859** THOMSON *Story NZ* I. 28 Six species of the *Procellaridae* are found on the sea-coasts. The *Titi*, or mutton bird, and the Toroa, or albatross, are the most celebrated birds of this family. **1879** *Auckland Weekly News* 5

Apr. 16 The *titi* (mutton bird) seeks the land, and flies direct to the one bright object of its desire. **1888** BULLER *Birds NZ* II. 217 Oestrelata cookii. (Cook's Petrel)... Titi. *Ibid.* 232 Puffinus griseus... Titi, Hakoakoa, and Totore: 'Mutton-bird' of the colonists. **1904** HUTTON & DRUMMOND *Animals NZ* 249 Cook's Petrel.—Titi. Oestrelata cooki. *Ibid.* 250 Mr. Reischek says... 'After sunset', to use his own words, 'they begin to call, like "ti, ti, ti", repeated rapidly.' **1922** [see MUTTONBIRD *n*. 1]. **1937** *NZ Railways Mag.* Mar. 23 The taking of Titi seems to the white man like one big picnic for the Maoris. **1946** ZIMMERMAN *Where People Sing* 68 We sat down at last, and then it was told me that the *titi* is a traditional Maori dish, a bird that is known among the Pakeha as mutton bird, because of the richness of its flesh. **1952** in Sansom *In Grip of Island* (1982) 154 Titis sizzling in their own kato fat (fat from insides). **1980** LOCKLEY *House Above Sea* 188 In the 'good old days', each Maori village had its own taiko colony, which was visited in the autumn to collect the fat 'titi' (young birds).

2. Special Comb. **titi islands**, MUTTONBIRD ISLANDS; **titi time**, the season for taking muttonbird young.
 1864 *Deed of Sale* in Howard *Rakiura* (1940) 394 The **Titi Islands** following:—Horomamae, Wharepuaitaka, Kaihuka. **c1920** BEATTIE *Trad. Lifeways Southern Maori* (1994) 177 The hakuai is another mystery of the titi islands. **1944** BEATTIE *Maori Place-names Otago* 83 [Heading] Titi islands... I was about the only old person on the titi islands this year, and do not know whether I will go again. **1935** LAWLOR *Confessions of a Journalist* 113 When **titi time's** at hand There come from far and near The Maori folk.

titi, var. TI *n*.[1]

titi-a-weka, var. TETEAWAKA.

titihimi, var. TIKIHEMI.

ti-ti palm, var. TI-PALM.

titipounamu. Also **teetee tee pomou**. [*Pounamu* (usu. 'greenstone') indicates the green plumage: Ma. /ti:titi'pounamu/: Williams 425 *Tītitipounamu*... rifleman.] RIFLEMAN.
 [*Note*] Williams does not record the shortened form *titipounamu*; the 1842 quot. may refer to the *bush wren* (WREN 2 (1)).
 1842 GRAY *Fauna* in Dieffenbach *Travels in NZ* (1843) II. 188 *Acanthisitta longipes*... É teetee [*sic*] tee pomou of the natives of Dusky Bay. **1873** [see RIFLEMAN]. **1884** [see PIWAUWAU b]. **1898** MORRIS *Austral-English* 471 Titipounamu... Maori name for the bird..the *Rifleman*. **1904** HUTTON & DRUMMOND *Animals NZ* 115 *Acanthidositta chloris*. The Bush Wren, or Rifleman, inhabits the sub-alpine forests. **1990** [see RIFLEMAN]. **1995** *Tablet* (Dunedin) 5 Feb. 7 It's a titipounamu, and you often find him in the ti-tree scrub... It is the rifleman, very shy and a friend of the scrub-cutter.

titi-wainui. [Ma. /'ti:ti:wainui/: Williams 414 *Tītī wainui*, *Pachyptila turtur*, southern fairy prion.] *fairy prion* (PRION 3 *Pachyptila turtur*). See also TITI.
 1914 GUTHRIE-SMITH *Mutton Birds & Other Birds* 16 We also got four kinds of Petrel in their burrows,— the Mutton Bird, Parara, Titi Wainui, and the Kuaka. **1940** HOWARD *Rakiura* 205 These are the names used by the southern Maori... Titi Wainui: *Prion Turtur* or Dove Petrel. **1947** [see PRION 3]. **1955** OLIVER *NZ Birds* 117 *Southern Fairy Prion. Titi Wainui Pachyptila turtur turtur*. **1967** [see PRION 3]. **1982** SANSOM *In Grip of Island* 91 With [the titi] were scatterings of the smaller titi-wainui, the Fairy Prions. **1990** [see PRION 3].

title: see MAORI TITLE.

titmouse. *Obs*. Also **New Zealand titmouse**. A fanciful or erron. use of Brit. *titmouse* for either the TIT *n*.[1] (*Petroica macrocephala*) or the YELLOWHEAD (*Mohoua ochrocephala*).
 1838 POLACK *NZ* I. 298 The n[g]irungiru..or great-headed titmouse, is very common in the country. **1869** *TrNZI* I. (rev. edn.) 109 The other birds..were..the Fantail..the New Zealand Titmouse (*Certhiparus Novae Zelandiae*). **1887** *TrNZI* XIX. 183 The high slopes would be a..resort for..New Zealand titmouse (*Orthonyx ochrocephala*).

tito. [Ma. /'tito/: Williams 426 *Tito* (i) v. trans. Compose, invent impromptu... *He kōrero tito*, a fabrication.] A fib or lie, esp. in the phr. **to tell titos**, to tell fibs or lies.
 1845 WAKEFIELD *Adventure NZ* II. 43 [The natives] were sure we were telling them tito, 'lies'. **1883** DOMETT *Ranolf & Amohia* I. 190 A *tito* this—a fib, I know. **1930** GUTHRIE *NZ Memories* 80 Dr. Logan told them they could no longer consider him a romancer, or one who had told 'tito' where New Zealand was concerned. **c1938** In Marlborough use by older people to children. 'None of your titos /'titʌuz/, now.' (Ed.)

titoki. [Ma. /'ti:toki/: Williams 426 *tītoki* (i).]
 1. Also early **pitoku**, **tetoki**, **ti-toke**; **titongi**. *Alectryon excelsus* (fam. Sapindaceae), a tree bearing in a scarlet aril a lustrous black seed used by the Maori as a source of oil; the fruit of the tree. See also ALECTRYON, *New Zealand ash* (ASH). Often *attrib*.
 1842 HEAPHY *NZ* 43 One of these [natural productions] is the oil of the *Pitoku* berry, which is of very fine quality, and much used by the natives in anointing their hair. **1843** DIEFFENBACH *Travels in NZ* II. 54 The hair is often greased with..an oil pressed from the seeds of the titoki. **1849** ALLOM *Letter* in Earp *Handbook* (1852) 130 The *tetoki* berry is a fruit resembling a raspberry, but somewhat lighter. **1869** *TrNZI* I. (rev. edn.) 261 The curious red fruit of the titoki, or titongi. **1872** DOMETT *Ranolf & Amohia* 253 The youth, with hands beneath his head, Against a great titoki's base. **1889** KIRK *Forest Flora* 183 Mr. Colenso informs me that the titoki is often called 'titongi' by the Maoris, the former being a northern, the latter a southern name. **1890** *PWD Catalogue Timbers* (NZ & South Seas Exhib.) 15 Titoki..Timber strong and very tough..bark suitable for tanning. **1900** [see ASH]. **1921** *Quick March* 10 Feb. 13 This reminiscence reminds me, too, of the variety of bush berries which we children would eat [in Carterton in the 1860s]— the white pine berries..and ti-toke, these last very much resembling a raspberry, with a black seed on the head of it. **1946** *JPS* LV. 146 The [titoki] fruit yields a scent used with the oil with which chiefs anoint themselves, apparently plentifully once every three years or so, whence the proverb applied to an upstart: 'Chief of the titoki year,' since anyone can use the scent that year. **1978** MOORE & IRWIN *Oxford Book NZ Plants* 92 The growing seed is often destroyed by the titoki fruit borer, a caterpillar that feeds only on this species. **1981** HUNT *Speaking a Silence* 29 We ate lots of nikau too, and lawyer berries—they were like raspberries—and miro and titoki berries.

2. *Obs*. [In transferred use, from the red raspberry cordial in or under the darker beer or stout suggesting the colour and appearance of the titoki berry (see 1 above quot. 1921).] Beer, stout, shandy or shandy gaff with raspberry cordial added.
 1937 PARTRIDGE *Dict. Slang* 881 *ti-toki*. A mixed drink of beer, lemonade and raspberry: New Zealanders': C. 20. Ex Maori. **1941** BAKER *NZ Slang* 56 When we call a shandygaff *titoki* we are giving an authentic native word a meaning it has never had before. **1952** 6 Nov. 2ZB 'Taylor's Quiz' 'Titoki is the New Zealand ash.' 'I always thought it was something else' [laughter]. **1968** *NZ Contemp. Dict. Suppl.* (Collins) 20 *Titoki..n.* N.Z. tree..; mixed drink, usually lemonade or raspberry essence, and beer. **1981** HUNT *Speaking a Silence* 29 Very often you'd get a Maori ask for a 'titoki' at the pub and that was a stout with a drop of raspberry in it.

titongi, var. TITOKI.

ti-tree, var. TEA-TREE.

ti-tree. Also **tee-tree**, **te tree**, **tii-tree**, occas. **ti-tri**. CABBAGE-TREE 1. See also TI *n*.[1]
 1820 LEE & KENDALL *NZ Gram. & Vocab.* 181 Me Tí; Sleeping on the Tee-tree. **1840** *NZ Jrnl.* I. 202 Land, partly covered with..a jungle of flax, fern, and the native ti-tree, a sort of cabbage tree. **1844** TUCKETT *Diary* 7 May in Hocken *Contributions* (1898) 217 I observed a continued line of dry land, indicated by the number of Te trees. **1850** ANGAS *Savage Life* 4 An occasional *ti-tree* (dracoena) gives a foreign and palm like aspect to the swampy ground. **1861** HAAST *Rep. Topogr. Explor. Nelson* 150 Here I also observed several species of Cordyline (ti tree). **1881** *TrNZI* XIII. 26 [A] coarse sieve, made of the long..mid-ribs obtained from the linear leaves of the tii-tree (*Cordyline australis*). **1898** HUDSON *NZ Moths & Butterflies* 138 Ti-tri, or Cabbage tree, as it is usually called. **1926** *TrNZI* LVI. 661 To one section of the public it will always be cabbage-tree; to the other section, let it be lily-palm. 'Ti-tree' and 'ti-palm' should certainly be banned, because of the hopeless confusion with tea-tree. **1969** HILLIARD *Green River* 55 There was always something in the big black pot, even if it was only the sour core of the titree to eat with karawakas from the creek. **1982** CURNOW *You Will Know When You Get There* 13 Watch for it [*sc*. wind] animate the bunched long-bladed heads of the *ti* tree.

ti-tree Jack, var. *tea-tree Jack* (TEA-TREE 3 b).

titri, var. TEA-TREE.

titter. *Obs*. [f. Brit. slang *titter* a young woman or girl: see OED *n*.[3],1812.] In early whalers' or traders' parlance, a girl. Cf. HEIFER 1.
 1845 WAKEFIELD *Adventure NZ* I. 319 A chief was called a '*nob*'; a slave, a '*doctor*'; a woman, a '*heifer*'; a girl, a '*titter*'; and a child, a '*squeaker*'. **1953** *Landfall* 27 179 Portugee Jow was dishing out the liquor, Boasting, 'Boys, she's a larky little titter'.

tiver: see TAEWA.

tiwai. Also **tewai**. [Ma. /'ti:wai/: Williams 427 *Tīwai*... 3. Hull, main body of a canoe. 4. Canoe without attached sides, and, in poetry, canoe.] A 'dugout' canoe without top strakes. Contrast WAKA.
 1838 POLACK *NZ* I. 158 The canoe he sat in, which was a very large tewai of the red pine. **1841** BIDWILL *Rambles in NZ* (1952) 61 We embarked on Towpo..in a very large Ti-wai (Tee-why) or canoe, hollowed out of a single log of wood, without top sides. **1846** HEAPHY *Exped. Kawatiri* in Taylor *Early Travellers* (1959) 236 At low water crossed the river..in a *tiwai*, or canoe without top sides. **1859** *Richmond-Atkinson Papers* (1960) I. 450 Today is Auckland regatta... The Maori canoe race was not in one respect as good as usual. A

tiwai ran with the waka tauas and *ran away* from them. [1960 *Note*] A canoe made out of a single log.

tiwaikawaka, tiwai waka, varr. TIWAKAWAKA.

tiwakawaka. With many variants esp. **tiwaikawaka, tiwai waka, towákáwáká.** [Ma. /tiːˈwakawaka/: Williams 427 *Tīwaikawaka, tīwakawaka*... fantail... Each species is generally or locally known by one or more of the names [there follows a series of names].] FANTAIL 1. Cf. PIWAKAWAKA.

[**1820** LEE & KENDALL *NZ Gram. & Vocab.* 214 Tí waka waka; A bird so called.] **1838** POLACK *NZ* I. 113 From their ears were appended the dried feathered skin of the towákáwáká-bird [*sic*] whose body, when living, is scarcely larger than a walnut. **1871** [see FANTAIL 2 (1)]. **1873** [see PIWAKAWAKA]. **1882** HAY *Brighter Britain* II. 226 The Waka-waka (*Rhipidura flabellifera*) is the robin of our Brighter Britain. It is a fantail, or flycatcher. **1882** POTTS *Out in Open* 158 Usually the black fantail, *Rhipidura fuliginosa*, called by the Natives tiwaikawaka, breeds under conditions so very similar to the [flycatcher], that one description will serve for both. **1885** *NZJSc.* II. 375 [*Rhipidura flabellifera*] Pied Fantail, Pied Flycatcher, Ti-waka-waka... Ibid. 375 *Rhipidura fuliginosa*... Black Fantail, Black Flycatcher, Ti-waka-waka. **1904** [see FANTAIL 2 (1), 2 (3)]. **1929** DUGGAN *NZ Bird Songs* 44 O little Tiwai Waka, O kind little wing! I've seen a woman hunt you, With haste and muttering. **1946** *JPS* LV. 159 *Tīwakawaka*, a bird, the black fantail, *see* piwakawaka. **1965** HILLIARD *Power of Joy* 179 A fantail flickered across the glade, tiwakawaka, tiwakawaka.

tizzie. *Obs.* Also **tizzey, tizzy.** [f. Brit. slang *tizzy* (of obscure origin) a sixpenny piece, current in 19th century NZ: the 1873 and 1984 quots. contain a play on the name Tanner, a local notable: see OED *n.*¹, 1804.] A sixpence. See also *half-tiz* (HALF- 1).

1868 DILKE *Greater Britain* I. 332 [The Hokitika newsboy] put [a newspaper] into my hand. 'How much?' I asked. 'A snapper.' 'A snapper?' 'Ay—a tizzy.' Understanding this more familiar term, I gave him a shilling. [Dilke is either mistaken or generous. (Ed.)] **1869** *Auckland Punch* I. 140 [Caption] That 'ere eye is a veeping to think that there aint a tizzy in the house to vet the other. **1873** *Richmond-Atkinson Papers* (1960) II. 347 We are now in the thick of the cross examinatn [*sic*]..by Sheehan of the chiefest of the apostles—Tizzey the Tanner (Ko Tanera). **1899** *Bulletin* (Sydney) 14 Jan. (Red Page) [Letter from Loafer, Tauranga.] Following are other local money-names... 6d.—*tizzie, sprat* or *tanner*. **1958** WALL *Queen's English* 97 A sixpence was a 'tizzy', a term not yet quite extinct. **1966** TURNER *Eng. Lang. in Australia and NZ* 133 *Tizzie*, perhaps from *tester*, is said to have been current in New Zealand, but again I do not know it. **1977** *NZ Numismatic Jrnl.* Oct. 15 The sixpence attracted many slang terms—*tizzy, tanner, sprat, bender*, and a *kick*. **1984** BOYD *City of the Plains* 6 The chief lessee and purchaser was Thomas Tanner, sometimes called [from the 1860s] Tizzy the Tanner or Tommy Tickles, and by Maori, Ko Tanera.

tizzy, var. TIZZIE.

toa. [Ma. /ˈtoa/: Williams 429 *Toa..4*...Brave man, warrior.] A brave man, a warrior.

1860 *Richmond-Atkinson Papers* (1960) I. 671 A remark of Manuka's was rather good—Maori chiefs (leaders) were toas & went out at the head of their men, Pakeha chiefs stayed in Town and ate biscuit. **1881** *Richmond-Atkinson Papers* (1960) II. 486 Tuninia was a celebrated toa. **1901** GRACE in *NZ Short Stories* (1953) 19 You can imagine what joy it is to become the wife of such a brave *toa*. **1949** BUCK *Coming of Maori* III. 362 Those who had distinguished themselves in battle were named *toa* and were usually of the *rangatira* class, for ruling chiefs had to lead in war as well as in peace. **1959** BRUNO *Hellbuster* 99 In a far corner, the few Maoris watched the pakehas making a cruel game of one of their own whiteskins. And was this the *toa* who had stood up to..'Bully' Krausen with his bare hands? **1971** *New Zealand's Heritage* I. 277 But the *Daedalus* succeeded in taking two Maoris on board, a warrior and a tohunga [to teach flax-dressing]—rather unfortunate choices when it is considered that flax-dressing was neither toa nor tohunga work but wahine work.

toadfish. [Named from its toad-like appearance or habits: AND 1801.] Any of several squat-bodied fishes of the cosmopolitan family Psychrolutidae (tadpole scupins), esp. *Neophrynichthys latus*, or the Australasian globefish family Tetraodontidae. See also GLOBEFISH, TOADO.

[*Note*] The mainly New Zealand application of the name to Psychrolutids derives from the similarity, esp. of *Neophrynichthys latus*, to the northern hemisphere true toadfishes (fam. Batrachoididae), mostly broadheaded and mottled fishes, some of which produce grunting or whistling sounds. The mainly Australasian application (often abbreviated to TOADO) to the Tetraodontids derives presumably from the toad-like habits of pufferfishes of inflating when caught or alarmed.

1885 *TrNZI* XVII. 166 *Neophrynichthys latus*... The Toad Fish... A specimen of this fish said..to be very rare, was got in the trawl of the cutter *Dauntless*, off Otago Heads, in 1884. **1898** MORRIS *Austral-English* 471 *Toad-fish, n.* In New Zealand, a scarce marine fish of the family *Psychrolutidae, Neophrynichthys latus*. **1906** *TrNZI* XXXVIII. 549 *Neophrynichthys latus*... Sometimes called 'toad-fish'. **1927** SPEIGHT et al. *Nat. Hist. Canterbury* 201 The Pig-fish..and the Toad-fish..whose names appropriately suggest something out of the run of ordinary fish shapes [are members of the same order]. **1939** *TrRSNZ* LXIX. 370 *Neophrynichthys latus*... Toadfish... Spawning occurs in July. **1956** GRAHAM *Treasury NZ Fishes* 357 The head of the Toadfish is wide and flat with an extraordinarily wide mouth... All Toadfish have..a loose flabby naked slimy skin which is repulsive to the touch. **1967** NATUSCH *Animals NZ* 231 The spotted toadfish..burrows and hides (with only eyes and mouth exposed) in ambush for prey. **1982** AYLING *Collins Guide* (1984) 201 Dark Toadfish *Neophrynichthys latus*... The dark toadfish is very similar in size and appearance to the pale toadfish but..has the colour pattern reversed; numerous whitish splotches and spots on a dark background... Pale Toadfish *Neophrynichthys angustus*... A rather repulsive toadlike fish... Pale toadfish have a smooth loose skin that is a pale olive green on the head, back and flanks with a dense scattering of dark brown spots. **1986** PAUL *NZ Fishes* 147 *Pufferfish. Contusus richei*. Alternatively globefish, or toadfish.

toado /ˈtʌudʌu/. [f. TOAD(FISH + -O: AND 1906.] Usu. with a modifier as **clown toado, common toado, sand toado, starry toado,** TOADFISH (fam. Tetraodontidae).

1966 DOOGUE & MORELAND *Sea Anglers' Guide* 296 Globefish... *Spheroides richei*; puffer, common toado, sand toado. **1967** MORELAND *Marine Fishes* 24 Globefish... Puffer, toado, common toado, are alternative names sometimes heard here. **1982** AYLING *Collins Guide* (1984) 316 Clown Toado (Sharpnosed pufferfish) *Canthigaster callisternus*... The clown toado is a small puffer. *Ibid.* 318 Starry Toado *Arothron firmamentum*... The starry toado is a large puffer... In life the body is dark purple-brown above..with a regular pattern of close-set bright blue oval spots. **1986** PAUL *NZ Fishes* 147 *Clown toado. Canthigaster callisternus*. Alternatively sharpnosed pufferfish... *Starry toado. Arothron firmamentum*. Alternatively starry toadfish.

toak: see TOKO.

toanui. [Ma. /ˈtoanui/: Williams 429 *Toanui..Procellaria parkinsoni*, black petrel. =..*tāiko*.] Any of several large dark seabirds, esp. *Procellaria parkinsoni*, the black petrel (PETREL 2 (1)).

1869 *TrNZI* I. (rev. edn.) 105 Procellaria Parkinsoni. Toanui. Very common. **1871** HUTTON *Catalogue Birds NZ* 46 Procellaria parkinsoni... Toa-nui. **1904** HUTTON & DRUMMOND *Animals NZ* 243 The Black Petrel.—*Toanui. Majaqueus parkinsoni*. **1922** *Quick March* 11 Sept. 15 The tuatara lives in the same burrows as are used by the oii, the titi and the toanui. All three of the petrels are included in the term mutton-birds. **1952** RICHARDS *Chatham Is.* 85 *Majaqueus..Parkinsoni*... Black Petrel. Toa-nui. **1985** *Reader's Digest Book NZ Birds* 95 *Pale-footed shearwater, toanui*.

toatoa. [Ma. /ˈtoatoa/: Williams 429 *toatoa..1. Phyllocladus* [spp.] 2. *Haloragis erecta*, a small plant.]

1. Any of various coniferous trees of the genus *Phyllocladus* (fam. Podocarpaceae), having flattened stems ('phyllocladdes') that act as leaves.
a. Esp. *P. trichomanoides*, TANEKAHA. See also *celery pine* (PINE 2 (4)), *pitch pine* (PINE 2 (11)).

1831 BENNETT in *London Med. Gaz.* 12 Nov. 184 Toatoa, of the natives of New Zealand, is an unpublished species of Phyllocladus. **1834** toá toá [see TANEKAHA]. **1844** MONRO *Notes of Journey* in Hocken *Contributions* (1898) 249 I may mention also another dye with which I saw flax stained of a rich reddish brown colour at Molyneux. It is obtained from a shrub or small tree named toa-toa, which is said to be rather scarce. **1853** [see TANEKAHA]. **1869** *TrNZI* I. (rev. edn.) 158 From 1000 feet upwards..in addition to the common kinds [of Pine], the toatoa or celery pine (*Phyllocladus alpinus*) becomes abundant. **1883** HECTOR *Handbook NZ* 125 *Phyllocladus alpinus*... Toatoa. A small ornamental and densely-branched tree sometimes 2 feet in diameter. Bark used for dyeing and making tar. **1898** MORRIS *Austral-English* 472 *Toatoa, n.* Maori name of New Zealand tree, *Phyllocladus glauca*... The Mountain Toatoa is *P. alpinus*. **1940** LAING & BLACKWELL *Plants NZ* 81 *Phyllocladus glauca* (the toatoa) is found chiefly in Northern Auckland, and was considered by Hooker to be the 'most charming of all the New Zealand pines.' **1968** *NZ Contemp. Dict. Suppl.* (Collins) 20 *toatoa..n.* small N.Z. tree with bright red wood, prized for walking sticks.

b. As **mountain** (occas. **alpine**) **toatoa,** *Phyllocladus aspleniifolius* var. *alpinus* (formerly *P. alpinus*), a small aromatic tree of subalpine forest and scrub.

1889 KIRK *Forest Flora* 199 *Phyllocladus alpinus*... The Mountain Toatoa... This species is most plentiful in mountain districts, and is most generally known in the South Island as 'toatoa', but is frequently termed 'tanekaha'; by settlers and bushmen it is called 'celery-pine' or 'celery-topped pine', and in Southland 'New Zealand hickory'. **1890** *PWD Catalogue Timbers* (NZ & South Seas Exhib.) 15 Toatoa, mountain..Timber white, straight grained, and tough. **1906** CHEESEMAN *Manual NZ Flora* 659 *P*[*hyllocladus*] *alpinus*... A shrub or small tree, usually from 8 ft. to 25 ft. high,...

Mountain Toatoa. **1940** LAING & BLACKWELL *Plants NZ* 79 *Phyllocladus alpinus* (The Mountain Celery Pine or Alpine Toa-toa). **1973** MARK & ADAMS *Alpine Plants* (1979) 18 These shrubs, often no higher than the tussocks, vary somewhat from place to place but snow totara..[and] mountain toatoa..are widespread. **1989** PARKINSON *Travelling Naturalist* 104 Trees that would seem more at home on the..West Coast..mountain toatoa, sweet hutu, and southern rata.

2. *Haloragis erecta* (formerly *alata*) (fam. Haloragaceae), a small bushy herb of coastal dunes and forest margins.

1853 HOOKER *II Flora Novae-Zelandiae I Flowering Plants* 62 *Haloragis alata*... Nat. name, 'Toa-Toa'. **1870** *TrNZI* II. 122 *Haloragis alata*. Toa toa. **1889** FEATON *Art Album NZ Flora* 178 Toatoa [Maori name]..Toatoa [Settlers' name]..*Haloragis alata*..Herb. **1926** HILGENDORF *Weeds* 129 Toa Toa (*Haloragis alata*). This is a native to which no English name has become attached, though it is abundant in lowland country from Auckland to Stewart Island. **1952** RICHARDS *Chatham Is.* 35 *Haloragis..erecta*... It was used as greens by the Maoris... Toa-toa (greens). **1982** WILSON *Stewart Is. Plants* 144 *Haloragis erecta* Toatoa... Perennial bushy herb with 4-angled stems, tough near the base.

tobacco. Also **tobacco plant**, usu. **Maori (native, wild) tobacco**. [Transf. use of *tobacco Nicotiana tabacum* (fam. Solanaceae) for various introduced herbs and shrubs with leaf rosettes and leaves resembling the tobacco plant.] *Verbascum thapsus* (fam. Scrophulariaceae), mullein, occas. applied to other plants having a tall flower stem rising from a rosette of soft leaves. See also FLANNEL-LEAF.

1908 DON *Chinese Mission Work* 22 Some slopes are golden with the 'Maori Onion', others bright with the 'Maori Tobacco'. **1926** tobacco plant, native tobacco [see FLANNEL-LEAF]. **1969** *Standard Common Names Weeds* 87 *wild tobacco* [=] *woolly mullein: woolly nightshade*. **1974** [see FLANNEL-LEAF]. **1986** JOHNSON *Wildflowers Central Otago* 87 Before even knowing its [*sc.* woolly mullein's] name I thought of it as 'the tobacco plant', figuring (mistakenly) that it might be some sort of tobacco. **1993** MARSHALL *Ace of Diamonds Gang* 128 On the dry terraces were plenty of those low plants with furry, white-grey leaves that you could wipe your bum with. Tobacco plants wasn't their real name.

Tobacco Country. *Chatham Islands*. [Origin uncertain: see quot. 1920.] The name of a block of tableland in the southern part of Chatham Island.

1920 *Otago Witness* (Dunedin) 28 Dec. 55 We had three glorious days pig-shooting in the 'Tobacco Country', a wild waste of bog and bush land lying across the south of the [Chatham] island so called because it was bought by a speculative white in the early days from the Maori conquerors for a box or barrel of tobacco. **1923** SKINNER *Morioris Chatham Is.* 12 The first part of the track from Waitangi to Owenga lies through well-grassed, hilly country..a region which the settlers have given the name 'Tobacco Country'. **1952** RICHARDS *Chatham Is.* 3 Whatever the cause, the further and more steeply you rise, the deeper and wetter the bogs become.., till they reach the foot of the Tobacco Country as the tableland block is locally called.

tobacco pouch. As **red tobacco pouch** *Weraroa erythrocephala*, and **violet tobacco pouch** *Thaxterogaster porphyrea*, brightly coloured toadstools with fertile tissue resembling flakes of tobacco.

1978 MOORE & IRWIN *Oxford Book NZ Plants* 12 *Thaxterogaster porphyrea*, *violet tobacco pouch*... Like the red tobacco pouch, this was once placed in *Secotium*. **1978** MOORE & IRWIN *Oxford Book NZ Plants* 12 *Weraroa (clavogaster) erythrocephala*, *red tobacco pouch*. **1983** *Land of Mist* 64 [Caption] (1) Honey mushroom (2) Red tobacco pouch fungus (3) Violet tobacco pouch fungi..(5) Basket..fungus.

tobacco weed. Occas. **tobacco tree**. *Solanum mauritanium* (fam. Solanaceae), the woolly nightshade, a naturalized South American small tree with large woolly leaves and hairy fruits.

1964 DAVIS *Watersiders* 39 A billygoat. Doing a great job on the danthonia, tobacco weed, thistles and blackberry. **1969** *Standard Common Names Weeds* 79 *tobacco weed* [=] *woolly mullein: woolly nightshade*. **1979** SARGESON review of *Tidal Creek* in *Islands* 27 550 [At the end of my Auckland street is] a wilderness of giant solanum (which children called 'the tobacco tree'), fern and teatree, grass in patches. **1992** *Listener* 3 Feb. 25 Woolly nightshade, also known as the kerosene plant or tobacco weed, is more common in the North Island.

toby /'tʌubi/, *n.*[1] Also **toby-box** (see quot. 1989). [f. Sc. dial. *toby* or *toby-cock* a stopcock in a water- or gas-main, usu. in a public roadway; prob. orig. from slang *toby* street, highway ed. Irish Shelta *tōbar* road: see SND *toby*, also applied to the covering, lid, or box protecting the cock (Aberdeen 1896).] The water-supply tap (often with its protective casing) between the mains and a consumer's property.

1954 *Toby* first heard by Ed. in Upper Hutt; the term previously heard and used was '(mains) stopcock'. **1979** *Gloss. Bldg. Terminol.* 119 *Toby*—Surface box generally set flush with paving or other surface to cover the stop-cock or control valve of a water or gas supply. [Also glossed in the 1956 (TS) edition: not sighted by Ed.] **1980** LELAND *Kiwi-Yankee Dict.* 104 *toby*: (A) the master water valve for a building, ordinarily located under a metal cover in the sidewalk outside. **1982** *Evening Post* (Wellington) 28 Apr. 15 A temporary worker had been engaged to detect unauthorised connections to council tobies (mains taps), and he had found the connections were mostly a normal hose connection to the toby. **1985** MARSHALL *Nest of Cuckoos* 107 I'll change the washer on that tap... Go out and turn off the toby, will you dear. **1989** 6 Nov. p.c. James M. Dermody, Warkworth. My parents, and I as a four-year-old, came out from Ireland in 1921. My father became involved in a new water-supply scheme for Blenheim. In the later 1920s the 'toby-box' was an item of daily reference: my father had a small supply in his shed at home. They were a cast-iron cylinder of about four inches diameter and not much greater length.

toby /'tʌubi/, *n.*[2] *Farming*. [Transf. use of *Toby* a familiar form of the name Tobias: AND 1957.] A raddle stick used by the owner to mark any of his sheep badly shorn.

1989 *NZ Eng. Newsletter* III. 26 Any sheep considered unsatisfactorily shorn was marked with red or blue raddle and such a sheep would not be counted in the shearer's tally. The raddle stick was also called a 'Toby'.

tochee, var. TOKI.

tod, *v*. [Poss. f. *Tod* Sloan (occas. used in full), the name of a US jockey (1874–1933), used as rhyming slang for 'own' in the phr. *on one's tod*.] To ride (a horse) in a race.

1911 *Truth* 3 June 2 E. Murtagh was offered the ride on Ribstone Pippin in the Great Northern Hurdles, but he was unable to accept it, as he had been engaged to 'tod' a couple of prads at Otaki.

todea /'tʌudiə/. [Named for H.J. Tode (1733–97), a German mycologist.] A genus of southern hemisphere ferns *Todea* (fam. Osmundaceae), represented in New Zealand by the rare *T. barbara* of northern New Zealand and once including PRINCE OF WALES' FEATHER, now *Leptopteris* (formerly *Todea*) *superba*.

1883 GREEN *High Alps* 83 Though ferns are not absolutely peculiar..from the great arborescent species..the lovely todea (*Leptopteris superba*), down to the exquisite little *Hymenophyllum*—a most characteristic feature of the forest scenery. **1905** WHITE *My NZ Garden* 51 The Todeas are very beautiful, especially *Todea superba*, which is commonly called Prince of Wales' Feather.

toebiter. [Applied fancifully to water animals having a gaping mouth, and hence often a folk reputation for biting toes.]

1. CREEPER *n.*[2], the Dobson fly larva.

1921 *NZJST* III. 273 This larva is called the 'black creeper', or sometimes the 'toe-biter'. **1967** [see CREEPER *n.*[2]].

2. STARGAZER 1.

1970 SORENSEN *Nomenclature NZ Fish* 37 *Monkfish*..Churchills, Toebiters, Bulldogs.

toenail. Also **mermaid's toenail, toenail shell**. *Waltonia inconspicua* (Phylum Brachiopoda), a small red lampshell.

1967 NATUSCH *Animals NZ* 65 Probably the best known [brachiopods are] the small, smooth *Waltonia* (formerly *Terebratella*) *inconspicua*..which is scarlet or pink or white. Some people call them toenails. **1970** SANSOM *Stewart Islanders* 146 At low tide this is a good place [on Stewart Island] to find the pretty toenail shells, the small pink and red brachiopods which are cast up on the firm white sand of Bathing Beach. **1982** GUBBINS et al. *Statistics at work* 12 Mermaid's toenails on display... We look here at a particular species of lampshell, often called 'mermaids toenail'. **1990** FOORD *NZ Descr. Animal Dict.* 222 Lamp Shells. The Brachiopoda... Other names: Toe-nails, Roman Lamps.., Rose Petals.

toe-rag. *Obs*. [Transf. fanciful use of *toe-rag* a strip of cloth used instead of socks.] A handkerchief.

c1938 *Toe rag* used at Havelock (Marlborough) school for 'handkerchief'. (Ed.) **1943** HISLOP *Pure Gold* 78 Out came my toe rag, as we called our handkerchiefs [in the 1880s in Central Otago], and up went my other hand.

toetoe /'tʌui,tʌui/, /'tʌuwi,tʌuwi/, /'toi,toi/. Also with much variety of form reflecting the modes **toe** or **toi**, or reduplicated **toetoe** or **toitoi** (the latter a freq. erron. spelling) or (following non-Maori perceptions of glide-consonants) with internal -*h*- (**tohe, tohi**), or -*w*- (**towi, towy**). *Pl.* often with -*s*. [Ma. /'toetoe/: Williams 429 *Toe* (ii)..*1... toetoe*..*2*...Grass, sedge, etc., of various species.]

1. a. *Cortaderia* spp. (fam. Poaceae), a robust native grass with tall, plumed flower-heads, forming large tussocks, esp. *C. toetoe* (formerly *Arundo conspicua*) common in swamps and coastal sandhills of the North Island; often applied to the flower-head. Also *attrib.* See also CUTTY-GRASS, *feathery grass* (GRASS 2 (16)), FLAG *n.* 2, KAKAHO, PAMPAS GRASS, *plume(d) tussock* (TUSSOCK 3 (7)), SWORD GRASS, TOETOE GRASS. (a) **toetoe** forms.

[**1820** LEE & KENDALL *NZ Gram. & Vocab.* 215 Toé toé; A long rushy grass so called.] **1832** WILLIAMS *Early Jrnls.* 4 Jan. (1961) 212 They cut a few sticks..and thus form the frame of their shed, and cover it with *toetoe*, a kind of long grass, four to five feet long. **1853** MACKIE *Traveller under Concern* (1973) 88 This day's journey was over a level grassy plain diversified with patches of flax and toetoe. **1883** DOMETT *Ranolf & Amohia* I. 303 Toe-toe... (See Sword-grass). **1908** BAUGHAN *Shingle-Short* 191 *Toe-toe* (*toy-toy*): A tall plumed grass, very much like the Pampas. **1940** COWAN *Sir Donald Maclean* 146 And along the river bank the *kakaho*, the *toetoe* or pampas grass, once waved its plumes abundantly. **1946** *JPS* LV. 146 *toetoe*, giant ornamental grass.., the flower-culms used for reed-work between the carved slabs of house-walls. **1964** MIDDLETON *Walk on Beach* 47 It seemed impossible that this..estuary, with its toe toe and flax-covered banks, was only half-an-hour's fast drive from the city. **1982** WILSON *Stewart Is. Plants* 372 *Cortaderia richardii* Toetoe... Native to: S[outh and] St[ewart Islands].

(b) **tohe** and **tohi** forms.

1847 ANGAS *Savage Life* I. 235 Close to Pipitea is a whare karakia, or chapel..which is built of *raupo* and *tohi-tohi* grass, according to the native fashion. **1851** *Lyttelton Times* 18 Jan. 6 This is a rich tract of land..portions of it more or less swampy, with a vegetation of flax, *tohe-tohe*, (a long riband-grass with graceful feathery seed-tufts). **1866** BARKER *Station Life* (1870) 47 The banks of the..Avon..are thickly fringed with weeping willows, interspersed with..clumps of tohi, which is exactly like the Pampas grass you know so well in English shrubberies. **1870** *TrNZI* II. 47 Then..amongst the..tohe tohe reeds, and saw-edged grass, a pair of Harriers had built their rough, flat-topped home. **1911** *Piraki Log* 155 All the open ground surrounding the settlement [at Piraki]..being covered with tussac-grass, raupo, or tohitohi (N.Z. pampas-grass).

(c) **toitoi** forms.

1834 MARKHAM *NZ* (1963) 35 The Thatch is the Toie Toie a kind of Flags that is used for the Huts. **1838** POLACK *NZ* I. 320 The most disgusting insects in nature exist among the spear-grass, called toi toi, of the swamps and plains. **1851** *Lyttelton Times* 7 June 1 [Request for tenders for the supply of bedding to the Colonial Hospital]..10 Mattresses, 10 Bolsters—Raupo or Toitoi. **1861** BOWEN *Poems* 57 High o'er them all the toi waved, To grace that savage ground. **1895** *Otago Witness* (Dunedin) 19 Dec. 6 Where Christmas lillies [*sic*] wave and blow, Where fan-tails tumbling glance, And plumed toi-toi heads the dance. **1907** MANSFIELD *Urewera Notebook* (1978) 34 Below us lay a shivering mass of white native blossom..a clump of toi-toi waving in the wind—and looking for all the world like a family of little girls drying their hair. **1934** HYDE *Journalese* 109 But here, a little stream meandered under cream-plumed shimmer of huge toi-toi bushes. **1957** FRAME *Owls Do Cry* (1967) 11 The place was like a shell with gold tickle of toi-toi around its edges and grass and weeds growing in green fur over the mounds of rubbish. **1990** *Landfall 174* 205 One is a pale strained woman of her own age in a pale blue raincoat whose smile is slim and supple like toi toi in the wind.

(d) **towi** forms.

1846 JOHNSON *Notes from Jrnl.* 25 Dec. in Taylor *Early Travellers* (1959) 128 Islands now began to appear, generally covered with flax and *towi towi*, a species of reed with long drooping leaves.

b. In *attrib.* use.

1843 *NZ Jrnl.* IV. 216 I had a fine view of the Toi-toi flat..at present it is quite dry, and not of a swampy nature, as the generality of the *Toi-toi* land about this part of the country. **1853** ROCHFORT *Adventures of Surveyor* 22 The house is what is called a toi-toi whare; the toi-toi is a reed which the natives use for the walls and roofs of their huts. **1917** *Chron. NZEF* 17 Jan. 235 My father has a large 'toi-toi' estate in the north. **1952** in Baxter *Collected Poems* (1980) 122 Like a toi-toi arrow shot in the air *Never no more never no more*. **1983** HENDERSON *Down from Marble Mountain* 122 Never forget the toitoi plumes of the dogs' tails leading on.

Hence **toe-toe** *v. obs.*, to thatch with toetoe.

1842 *NZ Jrnl.* III. 55 That [house] in which I am is solid mud, the roof new-thatched, or *toey-toed* by a native for ten herring, that is 10s.

2. With a modifier: **mountain**, **South Island**.

(1) **mountain toetoe**. *Chionochloa* (formerly *Danthonia*) *conspicua*, a snowgrass. Cf. *snowgrass*, *snow tussock* (GRASS 2 (36)).

1961 MARTIN *Flora NZ* 130 Beside the tall snow grass and the larger Mountain Toetoe..other smaller species of *Danthonia* occupy extensive areas of the subalpine grasslands of South Island.

(2) **South Island toetoe**. *Cortaderia richardii*, a widespread South Island grass.

1978 MOORE & IRWIN *Oxford Book NZ Plants* 206 *Cortaderia richardii*. South Island toetoe... The old-time Maori probably used the name 'toetoe' for all big tufted grasses and children today call them all 'cutty grasses' because the edges of the leaves are razor-sharp. **1984** *Hanmer Forest Park* 36 Toe toe (*Cortaderia richardii*, South Island toe toe) is the only toe toe native to the South Island.

3. Also applied to the sedge *Cyperus ustulatus*. See also CUTTING-GRASS 2.

1867 HOOKER *Handbook* 768 Toe-toe, Col[enso]. *Cyperus ustulatus*. **1869** *TrNZI* I. (rev. edn.) 264 The outer thatch [was] toetoe, (*Cyperus ustulatus*)..or of two kinds of wiwi, or rushes. **1874** *Ibid.* VI. 52 *Cyperus ustulatus*, prickly toe-toe.—Abundant throughout the Colony, and of great value. **1888** [see CUTTING-GRASS 2]. **1891** WALLACE *Rural Econ. Austral. & NZ* 243 The two most objectionable Weeds..on [reclaimed Hawkes Bay swamp] land are..the Sedge Toi-toi (*Cyperus ustulatus*), a tufty or tussocky plant with very sharp leaves. **1969** *Standard Common Names Weeds* 79 toetoe, giant [=] *Cyperus ustulatus*. **1981** BROOKER et al. *NZ Medicinal Plants* 49 *Cyperus ustulatus*... Common name: *Cutty grass* Maori names: *Toetoe, upokotangata*... The name 'toetoe' was applied to various grasses and sedges... Cheeseman's name for it was *Mariscus ustulatus*.

toetoe grass. Also **tohi grass, toi (toitoi) grass, towai grass, tui grass** (prob. a perception of *toe* infl. by *tui*), etc. TOETOE 1.

1838 POLACK *NZ* II. 29 Small sticks are made to intersect the hut fastened with flax, and the whole is covered with raupo flags, over which the toitoi grass is plentifully sprinkled, which ensures the place being water-proof. **1842** HEAPHY *NZ* 92 The land on its banks is..principally covered with fern, towai grass, and flax. **1857** HARPER *Lett. from NZ* 1 Sept. (1914) 19 Thickets also of cabbage trees, toi-toi grass, and flax. **1864** MUELLER *Vegetation of Chatham Is.* 6 The toi-grass..is employed for thatching. **1866** BARKER *Station Life* (1870) 85 The open fireplace [was] filled with ferns and tufts of the white feathery Tohi grass in front of the green background. **1874** CAIRD *Sheepfarming* 30 Tui grass..a very graceful plant, closely resembling a grass that is grown in the gardens, called, I think, Spanish grass. **1889** DAVIDSON *Stories of NZ Life* 55 A cluster of tui-grass. **1898** HOCKEN *Contributions* 79 A widespread level lies below, covered with flax and cabbage trees, toe-toe grass, and Maori-heads. **1902** WALKER *Zealandia's Guerdon* 80 Silver plumes of 'tui' grass. **1984** MILLER *Common Insects NZ* 60 The Flax Notcher Moth..[attacks] the foliage of toetoe grass.

toey, *a.*

1. [AND 1930.] On edge; edgily angry; touchy.

1966 NEWTON *Boss's Story* 86 This was our third child so I wasn't as 'toey' as John had been. **1972** *Dominion* (Wellington) 30 Oct. 4 West Coasters sometimes get toey. In fact they probably coined the phrase. But the toey-ist people in the South Island at present are the voters of Otago Central. **1982** NEWBOLD *Big Huey* 145 By about the third day cooped up in that little box I began feeling really toey. **1986** O'SULLIVAN *Pilate Tapes* 38 Yet Rat gets toey As the veil rends, Mr P. edgy as a knife-drawer When the sky burls up. **1992** *Dominion* (Wellington) 17 Aug. (IT suppl.) 3 The Australians are getting toey about a lack of Gosip development funds from New Zealand.

2. Of racehorses, rugby footballers, sports people, 'on one's toes', ready or able to move quickly.

1983 *National Bus. Rev.* 4 July 32 Don't let them down. You've got to be toey and eager to get after them; tough but not dirty. **1986** HAITANA *Fine Cotton & Me* 90 'He's [*sc.* a horse] a bit of a bastard to handle..' 'Well, if he was toey before, he won't be now. He'll be stiff as a board.' **1988** *Dominion* (Wellington) 19 Mar. 38 A toey field which included Olympic Games aspirant Richard Lockart lined up for the men's 100 metres breaststroke final.

toey-toey, var. TUI.

togho-togho, var. TOKOTOKO.

togie, var. TOKI.

togs, *n. pl.*

1. [AND 1918.] Also as **bathing togs, swimming togs,** a swimming costume.

1927 *NZ Dairy Produce Exporter* 28 Jan. 33 At least one of the teachers..should be in their swimming togs and stay with the children. **1935** GUTHRIE *Little Country* (1937) 216 We tore down to a quiet beach, stripped off our clothes, and plunged in... We didn't bother about togs. **1944** TEXIDOR in *In Fifteen Minutes* (1987) 162 Mum's bag..was bulging with bathing togs and things to change. **1956** WILSON *Sweet White Wine* 92 You want to see her in swimming togs. **1964** HARVEY *Any Old Dollars Mister?* 64 Old Pimply Face was starting to take off her bathing togs. **1979** FRAME *Living in Maniototo* 95 Our bathing suits, rolled in their towels (there was a special way of parceling up your 'togs'), were forever wet. **1986** MCCAULEY *Then Again* 57 Minute white creatures that lodge themselves in your swimming togs and cause a rash. **1992** *North & South* (Auckland) Apr. 40 We haunted the Marton baths..lining up..with our bundles of togs and towel.

2. Often also **football togs**. A (rugby) football jersey and shorts; also the 'strip' or playing uniform of other sports teams.

1918 *Chron. NZEF* 25 Oct. 158 Our great trouble is the 'togs' question, as with Rugby, Soccer, and Hockey on the go we have a large family to fit out. **1968** SLATTER *Pagan Game* 88 He knew very well what [the coach] would say when his boys were changed out of their cadet uniforms into their football togs ready to practice. **1971** GLOVER *Diary to a Woman* 1 Once you have your

tohe, var. TOETOE.

toheroa. Also early **tairoa**, **toi-roa**. [Ma. /'toheroa/: Williams 430 *Toheroa*..a bivalve mollusc.]

1. a. *Paphies* (formerly *Amphidesma*) *ventricosa* (fam. Mesodesmatidae), a large edible bivalve prized both for its meat and the delectable greenish soup made from it.

1838 POLACK *NZ* I. 71 These [carved monuments] had been erected here to prevent native travellers or strangers from grubbing in the sand for a favourite large cockle, called *toi-roa*, which are steamed and dried by the natives, and taken as portable food for a journey. 1873 TINNE *Wonderland of Antipodes* 66 She sent us a present of a basket of tairoas, a large white shell-fish from the coast, which is considered a delicacy. 1913 SUTER *Manual NZ Mollusca* 959 The animal of this species is considered a great delicacy by many people, and is sometimes exhibited for sale in Auckland fish shops... In the North generally known under the name toheroa. 1924 BUCKNILL *Sea Shells NZ* 101 The Toheroa is a favourite dish with some people, and makes a remarkably good soup. It is found buried in the sand between tide marks. 1934 HYDE *Journalese* 124 The toheroa taste has spread among members of the Royal Family. 1946 BEAGLEHOLE *Some Modern Maoris* 99 From the sea, the principal foods obtained are the toheroa shellfish (local [Otaki] variety, tohemanga) and flounders. 1986 PAUL *NZ Fishes* 161 *Toheroa. Paphies ventricosa*... The flesh (foot and viscera) can be minced and prepared as fritters, but toheroa are best known and most delicious as a thick, pale green soup. 1990 *Dominion Sunday Times* (Wellington) 16 Sept. The Toheroa has become as stitched into Southland's cultural fabric as white gumboots, bush shirts, and..the Bluff oyster.

b. In *attrib*. use.

1924 *AJHR* H-15 13 *Toheroa-beds*... From No. 2 area 980 cases were canned at Meredith's factory at Tikinui. 1928 *NZ Free Lance* (Wellington) 15 Feb. 34 We hear strange reports of spectators who preferred toheroa-hunting on the Muriwai sands to watching the speed-kings. 1931 *AJHR* H-15 18 The output of the two toheroa-canneries in the North Auckland district for the 1930 season was 2,336 cases... These toheroa beaches are somewhat isolated..and are therefore scarcely ever patrolled by an Inspector of Fisheries. 1971 POWNALL *NZ Shells & Shell Fish* 66 There was a time when toheroa hunters quite legally could, after locating a heavily populated toheroa bed, dig along the beach with a garden fork turning up toheroa as if digging potatoes.

2. Special Comb. **a.** In cookery: **toheroa fritter**, **toheroa soup**.

1928 BLACKMORE *Cooking of NZ Fish* 34 **Toheroa fritters** and bacon..Egg..Butter..Milk and Water..Flour..Salt and Pepper..Toheroas or other shellfish. 1936 *Recipe Book* 21 *Toheroa fritters*..toheroas.. [etc.]..flour..pepper and salt..cook tablespoonful in smoking fat..garnish with lemon. 1976 FINLAYSON *Other Lovers* 85 We were lucky to be in on toheroa fritters, the [hotel] proprietor's son having just come back from the coast with a bag of toheroas. 1928 BLACKMORE *Cooking of NZ Fish* 8 **Toheroa Soup**... Cover the shelled and well-washed toheroa with the milk and water and boil 20 minutes. 1934 *Bulletin* (Sydney) 18 Apr. 20 It is only quite recently that toheroa soup has had any standing in culinary circles. 1956 WILSON *Sweet White Wine* 54 We could look over half the restaurant and watch the waitresses..hurrying between the tables with wooden trays filled with plates of sausages-and-mash, baked beans on toast, or toheroa soup. 1970 THOMAS *Way Up North* 61 None of us dreamed that the day was coming when toheroa soup and toheroa fritters would be featured on menus at home and abroad; that they would be popularly recognised as being the most distinctive of our national delicacies. 1982 BURTON *Two Hundred Yrs. NZ Food* 40 It is in the area of soups that we find New Zealand's greatest contribution to international cuisine—the legendary toheroa soup. 1986 LATHAM *The WAAC Story* 20 The lisle stockings were a ghastly greenish-khaki colour that the girls called 'toheroa soup'.

b. toheroa stakes, a gambling game.

1970 THOMAS *Way Up North* 100 But my friends in the far north tell tales of parties going to the beach to fish, and spending their time engrossed in a game known as the Toheroa Stakes. The game is based on the shellfish's remarkable ability to bury itself and disappear in the solid sand of the wet beach... The game is, or was, played by drawing a circle on the beach. Each player selects a toheroa. The bets are made. On the word go each toheroa is placed on its side within the circle. The first to disappear is the winner.

Hence **toheroa** *v. intr.*, to dig for toheroas.

1967 MCLEOD *Dorinda* 64 The four of them had been toheroa-ing, hunting the large, slithery-tongued shell-fish delicacy with wooden spades, and a sack.

tohetohe, **tohi(tohi)**, varr. TOETOE.

tohi, var. TOI.

tohi grass, var. TOETOE GRASS.

tohora. Also early **Eto-ho-ro-hā** (=he tohora). [Ma. /toho'ra:/: Williams 431 *Tohorā*..southern right whale.] Any of various species of whale, but esp. the *southern right whale* (WHALE 2 (14)).

[1804 COLLINS *English Colony in NSW* 561 Eto-ho-ro-hā, A whale. 1820 LEE & KENDALL *NZ Grammar & Vocab.* 215 Tohóra, *s.* A sperm-whale.] 1838 POLACK *NZ* I. 323 Among the leviathans, who sport in shoals around these shores..[is] the tohora, or *right-whale* (Balaena mysticoetus). 1842 GRAY *Fauna* in Dieffenbach *Travels in NZ* (1843) II. 183 Tohora, or Right Whale. 1855 TAYLOR *Te Ika a Maui* 136 Fable of the Kauri (pine-tree) and Tohora (whale). 1878 *TrNZI* X. 90 Looking at it as it lay extended, it resembled a very large whale (nui tohora). 1883 HECTOR *Handbook NZ* 21 In the open sea, and to the south, the most prized whale next to the sperm is the black whale, or tohora (*Eubalaena Australis*), which is like the right whale of the North Sea, but with baleen of less value. 1898 *Morris Austral-English* 473 *Tohora*... Maori name for a whale. 1947 [see WHALE 2 (14)]. 1952 RICHARDS *Chatham Islands* 94 *Balaena australis*... Southern Right Whale. Tohora.

tohunga. Also early **E-ta-hon-ga** [=he tohunga]. [Ma. /'tohuŋa/: Williams 431 *tohunga* 1... Skilled person..2. Wizard, priest.]

1. A Maori wizard; priest; gifted or learned person; teacher. By English speakers, esp. c1900-50, it is often used dismissively as 'medicine man' (see quot. 1910). See also PRIEST *n.*[1], WIZARD.

[1804 COLLINS *Eng. Colony in NSW* 344 Etanga-roa, or E-ta-hon-ga, is a priest; whose authority in many cases is equal, and in some superior to the Etiketica [or chief].] 1817 NICHOLAS *NZ* II. 174 He was told by the *tohunga*, or priest, that if he presumed to put one finger to his mouth before he had completed the work..the Etua would certainly punish his impious contempt. 1838 POLACK *NZ* I. 130 He informed me that both fire and water was tapued by the tohunga, or priest. 1843 DIEFFENBACH *Travels in NZ* I. 141 An old Tohunga, or priest, was therefore persuaded to show me the way. 1857 *Lyttelton Times* 15 Aug. 3 The Tohunga (priest) predicts in doleful accents the ultimate extinction of the Maori race. 1863 MANING *Old NZ* viii 141 I sat in the doorway, and soon perceived that my visitor was a famous *tohunga*, or priest, and who also had the reputation of being a witch of no ordinary dimensions. 1872 DOMETT *Ranolf & Amohia* 102 But he whose grief was most sincere..was Kangapo the Tóhunga—a Priest And fell Magician famous far and near. 1891 *Richmond-Atkinson Papers* (1960) II. 583 All the witnesses on one side declare the testatrix was 'porangi' (mad). The other side say she was a 'tohunga' and a prophet and had gifts of healing. 1904 TREGEAR *Maori Race* 124 After these [*sc.* the chiefs] ranked the ordinary 'professional' (*tohunga*) who though generally a priest or wizard needed not always to be a priest, but must be a 'skilled person'. 1907 *NZ Statutes* No.13 26 *Title*. An Act to suppress Tohungas. *Preamble*. Whereas designing persons, commonly known as *tohungas*, practise on the superstition and credulity of the Maori people by pretending to possess supernatural powers in the treatment and cure of disease, the foretelling of future events, and otherwise, and thereby induce the Maoris to neglect their proper occupations and gather into meetings where their substance is consumed and their minds unsettled, to the injury of themselves and to the evil example of the Maori people generally. 1910 *Kai Tiaki* July 103 Educated Maoris favour the new order, and impute the national decay [in health] to modern tohungas, who are but imposters. 1920 *Quick March* 10 May 38 When a party goes out eel-fishing at night, the old man of the band, the kaumatua or tohunga, divests himself of his clothes and goes first to the river-bank. 1933 BAUME *Half-caste* 52 Dear Paul, you are a great tohunga [=teacher]..your very, very loving Ngaire, so aroha nui, Paul. 1946 BEAGLEHOLE *Some Modern Maoris* 236 These [Otaki Maori] people tend to make a distinction along these lines between the semi-respectable curing-tohunga and the completely unrespectable sorcerer-tohunga. 1959 SINCLAIR *Hist. NZ* 22 The ministers of religion were the *tohunga*, who were usually chiefs, though they did not form a hereditary or distinct caste. 1973 FINLAYSON *Brown Man's Burden* 142 tohunga: traditionally an expert, learned man or priest; in recent time a faith-healer. 1983 *Dominion* (Wellington) 6 July 4 Mr Manihera held one of the most prestigious positions in Maoridom as tohunga (high priest of knowledge) in the Mataatua canoe tribes. 1991 *Victoria News* (Victoria University) 16 Dec. 2 Mr Pou Temara, tohunga at the Te Herenga Waka [University] Marae, said the regional win [in a haka competition] had brought mana to Victoria [University].

Hence **tohungaess**, a female tohunga.

1905 BAUCKE *White Man Treads* 262 Some years ago a famous tohunga makutu..opposed his craft to that of an equally famous tohungaess of the Maniapoto.

2. *transf.* A reputedly wise person or intellectual leader.

1905 *Truth* 30 Dec. 5 The Rival Tohungas. [A poem.] Tohungas white, Tohungas brown. 1907 *NZPD* 19 July CXXXIX. 518 It was not so very long ago that I heard these two gentlemen characterized in this Chamber as political tohungas. That term was applied to them by the late Premier.

tohungaess: see TOHUNGA 1.

tohungaism. *Obs*. The practice of (often merely reputed) sorcery or faith healing by a tohunga. Cf. *Jimmy-work* (JIMMY *n.*[2]).

1904 *NZ Observer* 1 Oct. 3 Tohungaism is not a lawful means of subsistence. 1905 BAUCKE *White man*

TOI

Treads 262 In my recent outback explorations I have met with scenes which horrified..and brought home to me..the imperative necessity..that it be a criminal offence, punishable with hard labour imprisonment, to practise tohungaism, boast of tohungaistic reputation, apply to a tohunga for illegal operations, and learning the incantations. **1911** *Kai Tiaki* Jan. 38 Our readers will remember a most interesting article from her pen on 'Maori Customs and Tohungaism'. **1922** *Auckland Weekly News* 5 Jan. 42 One of Ratana's ambitions is to stamp out the tohungaism prevalent among the native people. **1936** LAMBERT *Pioneering Reminisc. Old Wairoa* 77 Tohungaism, and the practice of *makutu*..are all practically dead. **1955** *Truth* 9 Nov. 13 A man who said he was a Roman Catholic..claimed that he had been instantly cured of chest trouble..by [the accused], charged..with practising the cult of tohungaism. **1962** Nov. 1 NZBS News (9.00 a.m.) The Tohunga Suppression Act of 1908 is now to be repealed although some Maoris say that tohungaism still exists. **1979** WEBSTER *Rua* 225 At [the Anglican Synod, Napier, 1907] the Rev. F.W. Chatterton moved 'That this Synod views with satisfaction the recent action of the Government in the direction of the suppression of *Tohungaism*.'

toi, var. TOETOE, TUI.

toi, *n.*[1] Also **toii**. [Ma. /'toːiː/: Williams 431 *Tōī* (i) *n.* *1. Cordyline indivisa*... = *tī tōī*.] Also occas. as **toi-palm**, *Cordyline indivisa* (fam. Asphodelaceae), the broad-leaved *mountain* or *Waimarino cabbage tree* (CABBAGE-TREE 2), a stout plant of wet mountains, distinguished by its tuft of sword-shaped leaves at the top of an unbranched stem. See also *ti-kapu* (TI *n.*[1] 3 (1)).
   1851 *Lyttelton Times* 8 Mar. 7 We had travelled on till dark, and there was neither *toi*, flax, nor sticks to build a shelter. **1871** *AJHR F-1* 44 The Maungapouhatu Natives are a wild, restless set, with large shaggy heads of hair, and clad in mats made from the coarse fibres of the *toi* (*cordyline indivisa*). **1903** *TrNZI* XXXV. 110 The tap-root of the *toi*..was eaten formerly, as also the young undeveloped leaves. **1930** REISCHEK *Yesterdays in Maoriland* (1933) 177 The leaves of these *Dracaenae*—called by the Maoris tohi-palms—possess flexible fibres out of which the natives weave their waterproof rain-mats. **1966** [see CABBAGE-TREE 2]. **1979** WEBSTER *Rua* 81 A feature of the high ranges of the Huiarau is the toii (*Cordyline indivisa*), a variety of cabbage tree which grows at a much higher altitude than the well known *Cordyline australis*.

toi, *n.*[2] Also **toii**. [Ma. /'toˈiː/: not recorded in Williams.] *Barbarea intermedia* (formerly *australis*) and *B. vulgaris* (fam. Brassicaceae), 'winter cress', introduced European herbs of damp soils.
   1853 HOOKER *II Flora Novae-Zelandiae I Flowering Plants* 14 Barbarea *australis*... Nat. name, 'Toi'. **1869** *TrNZI* I. (rev. edn.) 261 The cooked leaves and herbaceous tops of the toi (*Barbarea Australis*). **1882** HAY *Brighter Britain* II. 192 The name of Toi likewise belongs to a herb (*Barbarea vulgaris*), the leaves of which are eaten like cabbage or spinach. **1889** FEATON *Art Album NZ Flora* 17 Barbarea vulgaris... The Common Herb of St. Barbara... This herb is indigenous to the Northern Island, and was formerly used by the natives as food. Upon the authority of Mr. Colenso, the native name of this plant is 'Toii'.

toii, var. TOI.

toiler. [Spec. use of *toiler* one who toils.] Often used with the intensifying adjectives **great**, **real**, a hard, persevering, or conscientious worker whose attitude or work is praiseworthy. Cf. BATTLER 2, *grafter* (GRAFT *v.* b).
   1906 *Truth* 6 Jan. 5 'Truth' is the toilers' paper. **1908** *Ibid.* 25 July 4 His irreverance [*sic*] opened by smooging to the toiler with the remark: 'Whatever is said of the labah [*sic*] and Socialistic movements, there is in the heart of them a d[i]vine fire.' **1924** ANTHONY *Follow the Call* (1975) 12 The only reason they do it is because Peter is a toiler, and puts in solid permanent improvements in the way of stumping and draining. **1947** NEWTON *Wayleggo* 120 A great toiler, he was as tough as leather. **1969** MASON *Awatea* (1978) Appendix II 110 He was a great toiler, strong as an ox, heaving huge carcases around as if they were bags of paper. **1970** THOMAS *Way Up North* 39 As a toiler Jack Hutley could be classed with Scut Cheeseman. **1986** OWEN & PERKINS *Speaking for Ourselves* 64 I heard of one helluva tough bushman, Charlie Moore—he and his brother Bill were the two of greatest toilers I have ever seen.
   b. *Rugby union.* A hard 'grafting' forward.
   1968 SLATTER *Pagan Game* 114 You'll beat Tuarau without him... Besides MacFarlane is a real toiler. He'll be a good substitute. **1986** *Dominion* (Wellington) 12 Aug. 5 'He was as hard as anyone,' he said, 'but was a very fair player. Certainly not vicious. He was a good honest toiler.'

toi-palm: see TOI *n.*[1]

toi-roa, var. TOHEROA.

to-i-toe, var. TOITOI *n.*[1]

toitoi, var. TOETOE.

toitoi, *n.*[1] Also early **toe toe**, **to-i-toe**. [Ma. /'toitoi/: Williams 431-432 *toitoi*..pied tit =..miromiro... 6..brown creeper.] Either of the *brown creeper* (CREEPER *n.*[1]) (*Finschia novaeseelandiae*) or the TOMTIT (*Petroica macrocephala*).
   [**1820** LEE & KENDALL *NZ Gram. & Vocab.* 215 Tóí tói; A bird so called; also a spattle [=pied tit].] **1842** GRAY *Fauna* in Dieffenbach *Travels in NZ* (1843) II. 189 *Certhiparus Novae Seelandiae*... Toe Toe of the natives of Dusky Bay... Miro toitoi... To-i-toe. **1871**, **1888** [see CREEPER *n.*[1]]. **1924** *Otago Witness* (Dunedin) 11 Mar. 6 The brown creeper, or toi-toi..was seen..on Otago Peninsula.

toitoi, *n.*[2] [Ma. /'toitoi/: Williams 431 *Toi* (i)..*toitoi*..3..a small fish [of]..fresh-water lakes.] BULLY *n.*[1] 1.
   1880 *TrNZI* XII. 316 *Toitoi* are a small blue fish similar to those caught in lakes, but larger. They are fair eating, but rather full of bones. **1921** *Ibid.* LIII. 450 The kokopu and toitoi were eaten locally [Lake Rotorua] and not preserved. **1929** BEST *Fishing Methods* 191 The *toitoi..Gobiomorphus gobioides*..has been *tapu* to the Tuhoe folk since the days of Uhia, medium of the famed war-god Te Rehu-o-tainui, and hence has not been eaten by them during that time. **1934** *Press* (Christchurch) (Acland Gloss.) 27 Jan. 15 Toi toi means a cockabully. **1978** MCDOWALL *NZ Freshwater Fishes* 175 Toitoi is a name that was applied to one of the bullies, probably either the Common Bully or the Redfinned Bully as these are the commonest species.

tojo crab: see CRAB 2 (4).

tokee, var. TOKI.

TOKO

token.
   1. [Spec. use of *token* something serving as proof of an action: see OED *n.* 3 a.] Also as **opossum (possum) token**, the ears of a possum attached to a strip of skin taken to the tail as a proof of capture for payment of a bounty. Also similarly **rabbit token**.
   1952 *Tararua Tramper* Dec. 7 The Government last year introduced a bounty of 2s. 6d. for every token representing an opossum killed. **1965** GILLHAM *Naturalist in NZ* 171 The Government bounty at the time was half a crown a token, the token consisting of two ears and a strip of fur ten inches by two passing down the back... Today the bounty has been abolished. **1978** *Manawatu Tramping Club Jubilee* 84 Hundreds of opossum tokens—the ears and a strip of the back—were hanging on the washing lines in front of a wharepuni. **1981** PINNEY *Early N. Otago Runs* 29 From June to the end of 1892, 87,696 rabbit tokens were counted at the [Benmore] station.
   2. See *milk token* (MILK).

toki. Also early **tochee**, **togie**, **tokee**. [Ma. /'toki/: Williams 433 *Toki* (i).. Adze or axe generally made of stone.]
   1. ADZE, an early Maori stone implement. Cf. AXE 1.
   1773 PARKINSON *Journal* (1773) 127 Tochee *A hatchet, or adze*. **1773** BAYLY *Journal* 4 June in McNab *Hist. Records* (1914) II. 209 The Indians are fond of green stone they have among them which they call Poanamo... With this they make their Togie, or ads of. **1838** POLACK *NZ* II. 25 The name for the [stone] axe was toki, which is another name for rock or stone. **1860** *Richmond-Atkinson Papers* (1960) I. 530 We are much more likely to die of despair in Town at not being taken to Waitara than by bullet or 'toki' if we are taken. **1878** BULLER *Forty Yrs. NZ* 249 They used a variety of manual weapons, such as the mere, the hani, the hoeroa, the patu, the taiaha, the toki, etc. **1904** TREGEAR *Maori Race* 319 The most valuable of Maori tools was the stone axe (*toki*) in some shape or dimension, for with its aid trees were felled. **1928** *NZ Free Lance* (Wellington) 15 Feb. 7 Pigeon spears and Hau's famous long-handled 'toki' or axe..were again brought into use. **1943** MARSH *Colour Scheme* 38 When your friend..speaks of my grandfather's *toki*, relate this story to him. **1962** JOSEPH *Pound of Saffron* 113 'And these,'—he ran his fingers along a row of..nephrite adzes—'toki.'
   2. *Hist.* In early use an iron 'trade' tomahawk, or axe or tomahawk head, often transferred to other objects of iron or steel such as a nail or fishhook. In later use, an axe.
   1807 SAVAGE *Some Acc. of NZ* 77 Tokee..Iron. **1817** NICHOLAS *NZ* I. 82 He [*sc.* Marsden] observed..that if he [*sc.* the NZ chief] would order his people to supply him with pigs and flax, they should be regularly paid either in axes or tokees. *Ibid.* I. 243 The chief, in allusion to our having no tokees to purchase his pigs with, cried out after me, 'no tokee, no tokee, no porkee, no porkee,' laughing heartily at his own wit. **1823** CRUISE *Journal* (1957) 101 Having got from one of the officers a small bit of iron, called by the natives a *tokee*, he threw it into his canoe. **1836** in Bailey & Roth *Shanties* (1967) 19 For toki, pigs, and murphies we exchange our traps, you know. **1955** BJ CAMERON *Collection* (TS July) toki (n) An axe.

toko /'tʌukʌu/. Also **toak**. [Prob. a local use of *toco* Royal Navy and Public School slang for punishment (orig. Hindi, a whip, a thrashing) recorded in NZ in 1887; poss. reinforced by Ma. *toko* a staff.] The cane, the strap. (*Toak* in quot. 1960 is prob. a verb 'to hit'.)

TOKOEKA

1939 Combs *Harrowed Toad* 27 [The children] take what I gather they call 'toko' with a stoicism bordering upon effrontery. **1960** 18C M B11 Nelson Boys C. 30A Toak, sock ['to hit'] or toak.

tokoeka. The form **tokoweka** has equal standing. [Ma. /toˈkoeka/, /ˈtokoweka/: Williams 435 *Tokoweka, tokoeka*..S.I. kiwi.]

1. Either of the *South Island brown kiwi* or the *Stewart Island kiwi* KIWI 2 (1).

1873 Buller *Birds NZ* 365 Apteryx australis. (South-Island Kiwi.)... Kiwi and Tokoeka. **1906** *TrNZI* XXXVIII. 338 Another remarkable flightless bird..is the member of the *Apteryx* family commonly called by naturalists the '*roa*'. The Maoris say that the proper name of this bird is the '*tokoweka*'. **1947, 1955** [see KIWI 2 (1)]. **1985** Hunt *I'm Ninety-five* 260 The tokoeka, the Stewart Island kiwi, is an unusual case. **1990** *Checklist Birds NZ* 8 *Apteryx australis australis*..*South Island Brown Kiwi (Tokoeka)*... *Apteryx australis lawryi*..*Stewart Island Brown Kiwi (Tokoeka).*

2. A newly discovered southern species of kiwi.

1993 *Dominion* (Wellington) 23 Apr. 3 The Conservation department..proposed to adopt the [Ngai Tahu] tribe's traditional name of 'tokoeka' for the [new] southern species... Tokoeka, literally translated as weka with a rod or walking stick, will be the name of the Haast, Stewart Island and Fiordland varieties of brown kiwi and the other [*sic*] will be the North Island and Okarito.

tokotoko. Also early **togho-togho, tóko tóko.** [Ma. /ˈtokotoko/: Williams 434 *tokotoko 1*. n. Staff..2. Walking-stick.] A staff or walking-stick.

1773 Forster *Resolution Jrnl.* 8 June (1982) II. 300 They have short Darts about 5 or 6 feet long called *Togho-togho*. [**1820** Lee & Kendall *NZ Gram. & Vocab.* 216 Tóko tóko; A walking-stick.] **1847** Angas *Savage Life* II. 3 Clad in our 'bush' costume, but without weapons, and each with a *toko toko* or long walking-staff in our hands, my fellow traveller and myself set off in excellent spirits. **1861** *Richmond-Atkinson Papers* 18 Sept. (1960) I. 719 Ahipene came into the office with a tokotoko in his hand. **1935** Cowan *Hero Stories NZ* 238 They, like Wiremu Kingi.., were not armed with guns; each carried a *tokotoko* or walking-staff and directed his men. **1986** Ihimaera *Matriarch* 75 The elder walked slowly out in front of the meeting house. He had a tokotoko in his hand, a walking stick, which he raised suddenly.

tokoweka, var. TOKOEKA.

toll. [Formerly the standard term in freq. (though not exclusive) NZ use: see OED *toll n.*³] Often *ellipt.* for **toll-call,** a 'trunk' or 'long distance' telephone call, one made to an area outside a local exchange for which a special charge is made. Also used in combination (often as **tolls**) with reference to the servicing of toll-calls: **toll-bar,** an arrangement for institutional telephones where toll-calls cannot be made without contacting an operator; **toll(s) operator, toll(s) service.**

1918 *NZJST* I. 339 For toll service the subscriber calls a certain number, which connects him to one of a group of lines running to the toll operator, who then handles his call as in manual equipment. **1939** Grieve *Sketches from Maoriland* (1961) 30 Fingers which handled the telephone with an airy nonchalance.. delivering the..strictly unofficial back-chat which invariably opened and closed this toll-call. **1944** Scott *Life with Barbara* 88 As for toll calls... I'll leave you the little forms you fill in. **1955** *BJ Cameron Collection* (TS July) toll call (n) A long-distance telephone call. **1987** *National Bus. Rev.* 23 Jan. 10 Handing over a large sum of cash to pay for what the teller announced was a 15-minute toll call, he seemed sheepish on discovering he had been observed.

tolly, *v.* Otago children. *Obs.* [f. northern Brit. and Sc. dial. *tollie* excrement: see EDD *tollie 2*.] To defecate. Also as a noun, excrement.

c1934 p.c. Alistair Campbell, quoting a Dunedin schoolchildren's parody of 'Mary Had a Little Lamb': She took it up to school one day It tollied on the floor. Mary had to lick it up And hoick it out the door.

tom, *n.*¹ Goldmining. [Orig. US: AND 1852.] A trough for washing gold; occas. applied to a goldminer's cradle with a trough attached. See also CRADLE *n.* 1, LONG TOM 1. Cf. TOMMING *vbl. n.*

1852 *NZGG* 10 Dec. V. 30:187 Wednesday, Nov. 3. How employed Down to bar at junction of path and stream,.. setting 'Tom', &c. Digging and washing. Remarks. The earth passed through the 'Tom' was top stuff. **1865** *AJHR* C-4A 14 Sluice Boxes and Toms. **1906** Galvin *NZ Mining Handbook* 8 When sufficient water was not available, the use of a tom (or rocker) had to be resorted to. **1966** Turner *Eng. Lang. Austral. & NZ* 152 A year earlier a report in the *Press*, 28 April 1864, included such technicalities as 'though only four "toms" are at work, all others are "dashing" without exception, getting extraordinary results.' The tom was a sort of cradle with an extended sluice.

tom, *n.*² [Also US (Webster (1961) 3): AND 1932.] A timber prop or brace, esp. that used by sawmillers, miners, builders.

1887 *Auckland Weekly News* 7 May 19 In tapping under the rafter, the tom slipped, lifted the catch, and opened the dam. **1906** *Red Funnel* II. 16 In a timber dam..the thirty-foot sluice is closed by a lever which is held back by a wedge of wood called a 'tom'. When the dam is 'tripped' the 'tom' is pulled out by a rope, and the sluice flies open. **1943** Bennett *English in NZ* in *Amer. Speech* XVIII. 86 Some who came for gold remained to dig for coal. Two words still in use in coal-mining districts—*tom*, an artificial support, and *gad*, a sharp iron instrument—are said to have been introduced by Cornish miners who were among such early immigrants. **1953** Reed *Story of Kauri* 163 As a safety measure, strong pieces of timber called 'toms' were placed in position on the lower side of the log. A niche was cut in the side of the log, and the 'tom', immovably grounded, was driven into the niche by blows from a maul. *Ibid.* 208 If the gate [of the timber dam] were made plumb there would be too much strain on the trips and 'tom'—a stout squared log, the purpose of which was to hold the gate planks until 'tripped'. **1956** *Weekly News* (Auckland) 1 Feb. 44 Billet was up the range with a gang of men erecting stout bush 'toms' under the stringers of each bridge. **1961** Crump *Hang On a Minute Mate* 42 During the next few weeks Jack learned about scarfing, backing, limbing..jiggerboards, platforms, toms, strops..and axe sharpening. **1979** *SANZ Gloss. Bldg. Terminol.* 119 Tom (post, prop)- A length of timber erected for the temporary support of part of a structure of formwork usually firmed up by driven folding wedges. **1991** *Historic Places* Sept. 29 The trips [of the driving dam] were held in place by a tom... The knocker tripped the trigger which in turn released the tom.

tomahawk, *n.* Also **tommyhawk, tomyhawk.**

1. [Transf. use of *tomahawk* the axe of the native North American.] A hatchet or small axe, in early times used as trade with the Maori (and hence often romantically associated with savage

TOMAHAWK

violence), and as a useful tool of the settler; occas. also a Maori stone implement. See also TOMMY *n.*¹, *tommy-axe* (TOMMY *attrib.*). Cf. TOKI.

a. As **tomahawk.**

1820 McCrae *Journal* (1928) 23 In return [for her gift] I gave her a small Tomahawk. **1830** Craik *New Zealanders* 92 First, the chief threw off the mat which he wore as a cloak, and, brandishing a tomahawk in his hand, began a war-song. **1842** *Bay of Islands Observer* in Cowan *NZ Wars* (1955) I. 12 [Thomas Spicer, 'Korareka Beach', announced that he had for sale such articles as] duck frocks and trousers..tomahawks..and crockery. **1851** *Richmond-Atkinson Papers* (1960) I. 79 After tiring of [singing] they set off with burning brand & tomahawk to catch crawfish & tuna. **1861** *Otago Witness* (Dunedin) 26 Jan. 6 One man..discovered..a pah of which till then we knew nothing... He returned in less than two minutes with a long-handled tomahawk. **1873** Tinne *Wonderland of Antipodes* 34 The father took down his tomahawk, and creeping up cautiously, lest he himself should be makutu-ed by a look, brained his parent. **1890** *Otago Witness* (Dunedin) 28 Aug. 36 The spear might be long, his 'mere' heavy, and his tomahawk of the best polished greenstone [etc.]. **1893** *TrNZI* XXV. 198 An old axe or tomahawk answers the purpose. **1933** [see TOMMY *n.*¹]. **1941** Sutherland *Numismatic Hist. NZ* 37 Clad in a shoulder mat, native fashion, or when stripped to the waist with the haft of a tomahawk in his flax-cord belt.

b. As **tommyhawk.**

1815 Marsden *Lett. & Jrnls.* (1932) 138 (Griffiths Collect.) [Heading] A List of Articles Wanted for the Use of the *Active* and the Settlement in New Zealand, 1815... Twenty dozen tommy hawkes, twenty dozen of sickles. **1834** Markham *NZ* (1963) 59 Two Sawyers present saying don't strike him, for your life Sir; he also drew his tomy hawk which I caught hold of. **1845** Taylor *Journal* (ATLTS) III. 187 He mangled his body with a tomahawk. **1962** Hori *Half-gallon Jar* 17 I would rather cut up a three-ply tea chest for kindling with a blunt tommyhawk. **1963** Morrieson *Scarecrow* 86 Nice little tommyhawk you've got there, Mrs Poindexter.

2. *transf.* [f. its habit of excavating rotten wood for grubs.] KAKA.

c1899 Douglas in *Mr Explorer Douglas* (1957) 251 The Ka Ka. [Heading] Or as it used to be called in parts of Otago, the tomahawk, from its habit of digging into rotton [*sic*] trees for the large white grub.

tomahawk, *v.* Also **tommyhawk.**

1. *Hist. trans.* To strike or kill (someone) with a tomahawk.

1851 *Richmond-Atkinson Papers* (1960) I. 100 The danger of being shot by wild Irishmen may be set off against that of being tomahawked by the Maoris. **1853** in Cutten *Cutten Lett.* (1979) 46 But here again the back of my neck resting upon the sharp edge of the..furniture I arose in the morning with the faint conception that I had been tommy hawked in the night. **1854** Taylor *Journal* 8 May (ATLTS) VIII. 179 Anyone who shd. try to sell within these boundaries shd. be tomyhawked. **1864** Nicholl *Journal* (ATLMS) 30 Apr. 216 None of them [the dead officers in the pa] or the men were tommyhawked [by the Maori fighters] which is a great wonder. **1879** Featon *Waikato War* 55 (Griffiths Collect.) Tomahawked a boy... Dreadfully tomahawked. **1890** *Otago Witness* (Dunedin) 7 Aug. 36 The first man was tomahawked from behind. **1938** Finlayson *Brown man's Burden* (1973) 36 He remembered well how he himself had once tomahawked a Pakeha who broke the tapu of a burial ground.

2. *transf.* and *fig. Shearing. trans.* and *intr.* To cut a sheep while shearing it. Also as a *vbl. n.*

TOMATAGOR(R)A

1875 *Otago Witness* (Dunedin) 18 Sept. 18 Every sheep to be shorn closely and cleanly, and the fleece taken off whole. 'Tomahawking' will in no case be allowed. **c1930** *Whitcombe's Etym. Dict. Aust.-NZ Suppl.* 12 *Tommy-hawk. v.t.* to cut a sheep when shearing. **1989** *NZ Eng. Newsletter* III. 28 *tomahawk*: To shear very roughly and cut sheep about.

tomatagor(r)a, tomataguru, tomatakuru, varr. MATAGOURI, TUMATAKURU.

tomato.

1. As **black tomato**, *black nightshade* (NIGHTSHADE).
  1926 HILGENDORF *Weeds* 152 Black Nightshade (*Solanum nigrum*), is called also white nightshade, mother-of-thousands, black tomato, black potato, wonder berry, and by a serious confusion deadly nightshade and bittersweet.

2. See TREE TOMATO.

3. In *transf.* uses as special Comb. **tomato blonde** WW2, an Egyptian with European blood; **tomato house** *obs.* (usu. with **the**) [f. a resemblance to a glass-house used for tomato-growing], a nickname for former prefabricated temporary buildings within the Government Buildings grounds in Wellington; **tomato sauce** [AND 1905], rhyming slang for 'horse'.
  1986 *Islands* 37 35 The dark girl..appeared to be Nubian, though with mix of European blood to leaven swart African, so giving to velvet skin a rich midnight bronze matching densely crimped black curls tinged with deepest red. In soldier dialect **tomato blondes** were tuppence a dozen in the Cairo melting pot. Here in startling relief Port Said offered all-over tomato brunette. **c1930** at least p.c. 1957 J. Winchester (Wellington). The 'temporary' buildings erected as offices during WW1 in the vicinity of the wooden Government Buildings, Wellington, were (and still are in 1957) called **the tomato house** from their shape and appearance, which resembles a glass house. **1947** SMITH *N to Z* 24 In an endeavour to sidetrack the innocent, a big new building called the Kremlin or Tomato House was erected in the middle of one side of the triangle [of Government buildings in Wellington]. **1963** *Truth* 21 May 19 We wander over to the bar for a pen and ink, where the talk gets round to **tomato sauces**. tomato sauces... horses.

tom-bobbler. A kind of marble.
  1972 SUTTON-SMITH *Folkgames Children* 174 Then there were the terms referring to particular kinds of marbles: for example, agates, aggies..tom-bobblers. **1984** KEITH & MAIN *NZ Yesterdays* 288 Marbles were the currency of childhood and there were an astonishing number of names for them..stinkies, stonies, stripies, tom-bobblers and whities.

tomming, *vbl. n.* Goldmining. *Obs.* [AND *tom v.*[1] *Obs.* 1855.] Using a tom to wash paydirt for gold. Cf. TOM *n*[1].
  1857 *Lyttelton Times* 4 July 5 There is every reason to believe that many other gullies that have not paid for tomming, will yield well to sluicing parties, especially for a ground sluice. **1858** HODGKINSON *Description Canterbury* 19 A claim for the purposes of sinking, surface digging, tomming or cradling.

tommy: see SPOTTED TOMMY.

tommy, *n.*[1] [Ellipt. for TOMMYHAWK.] TOMAHAWK *n.* 1. See also *tommy-axe* (TOMMY *attrib.*).
  1872 in Meredith *Adventuring in Maoriland* (1935) 32 There was nothing else for it [*sc.* a hard loaf] but the tomahawk. With this I managed to hack a hunk off one side; but I had to 'mellow it' with the back of the tommy before it was soft enough to bite. **1873** BARKER *Station Amusements* 148 I had to get the tommy (*anglicé—* tomahawk), and *chop* his boots off. **1933** *Press* (Christchurch) (Acland Gloss.) 23 Dec. 15 *Tommy.-* A tomahawk, hatchet. A much-used tool on stations.

Tommy, *n.*[2] [For a suggested origin see quot. 1911 which implies rhyming slang for 'rook' (an early name for 'bookmaker') or 'book'.] A bookmaker.
  1907 *Truth* 23 Mar. 2 The Tommies got 'rats' over the Napier Park meeting. The Hutt trained Moata's successes depleting the ring of a lot of money. **1911** *Ibid.* 6 May 2 Wonder how bookmakers came to be known as 'Tommies'? 'Tommy [*sic*] is short for Tommy Rook, and probably it was owing to 'rook' sounding something like 'book' that caused some wag to term him as such. A rook would apply to some bookmakers, but where does the 'Tommy' come in? The bookmakers were never named Tommies after soldiers, who are so dubbed. **1978** TUCKER *Thoroughbreds Are My Life* 167 By the same token some of the bookmakers that I have known have been fearless fielders. There is a fascinating story of one of New Zealand's 'tommies' who went through a very bad patch.

tommy, *n.*[3] Prison. [See Partridge *tommy v.* to decamp: Australian low: C.20.] In the phr. **to go and see tommy**, to escape (from prison).
  1938 HYDE *Nor Yrs. Condemn* 254 After that, I got warned, because a warder heard me say I was going to see Tommy. That's what a man says in prison when he's going to try and escape.

tommy, *attrib.* In various uses in special Comb. **tommy-axe** [f. TOMMY *n.*[1] + *axe*; also Brit. dial: see EDD], usu. a tomahawk, also occas. applied to any small axe (occas. as a *v. trans.* to chop (something) with a tommy-axe); **tommy cod** Northland [spec. use of *tom-cod* a name for several small fishes: see OED], any of various unidentified small fish, usu. fam. Tripterygiidae; **Tommy Dodd** [origin unknown], see quots.; **Tommy hat** WW1, a British-army type of headgear issued to NZ troops at the start of WW1 (later replaced by slouch hats, then by 'lemon-squeezers'); **tommy stick**, PIT SPIDER.
  1898 MORRIS *Austral-English* 474 **Tommy-axe**..a popular corruption of the word *Tomahawk..*; it is an instance of the law of Hobson-Jobson. **1955** BJ Cameron Collection (TS July) tommyaxe (n) A small short-handled axe. **1968** *NZ Contemp. Dict. Suppl.* (Collins) 20 *tommy axe n.* literally, half-axe, in size between axe and tomahawk; any axe-type implement. **1968** DALLAS *Collected Poems* (1987) 96 I could show you my tommy-axed finger Bound together without stitches. **1914** SATCHELL *Greenstone Door* 47 Then to pause in mid-stream to chase **Tommy cod** among the rocks. **1987** *Listener* 8 Aug. 61 But it [*sc.* a reef in Auckland harbour] was also alive, with mussels, oysters, crabs, pools full of shrimp and tommy-cod. **1991** BRADSTOCK *Fishing* 17 *Cockabully*. This is a general name for a lot of different kinds of small fish called triplefins. Other names are bully, blenny, twister, topknot, tommy cod. (Family Tripterygiidae.) **1941** BAKER *NZ Slang* 46 The following New Zealand terms, recorded in the closing twenty years of the last century, are also worthy of comment:.. **Tommy Dodd**, an alcoholic drink. **1949** PARTRIDGE *Dict. Slang Addenda* 1205 *Tommy Dodd*... A small glass of beer: New Zealand and Australian: late C. 19–20. **1935** BURTON *Silent Division* 81 The '**Tommy hats**' in which the New Zealanders were landed were soon thrown away and replaced by Australian felts. **1984** *Evening Post* (Wellington) 13 Oct. 48 'The consensus seems to be that the object is a pit-candle holder. There are different names for them in Australia and New Zealand where they're known as pit spiders or in New Zealand only as **tommy sticks**,' Mrs Hall said. She said many old miners or children of miners had rung her to identify the object. Pit-candle holders were used with carbide lamps in mines. The pointed part was put into the pit prop with the hook hanging down. The candle was put through the hoop.

tommyhawk, var. TOMAHAWK.

tomo /ˈtʌumʌu/. [Ma. /ˈtomo/: cf. Williams 435 *Tomo* (ii) 1. v. intr. Pass in, enter; Williams 435 *Tomoau,* n. Abyss: as it seems orig. a King Country word, it is poss. a back-formation from *Waitomo*, with *tomo* being understood as 'cave' in local Maori dial.; Hochstetter (1867) uses a Maori plural *tomo*.] **a.** A chute-like hole made by water in especially volcanic material; a sink-hole in limestone (or pumice) country. Cf. UNDER-RUNNER.
  1859 *Auckland Provincial Gazette* 8 July 94 The plateau..would form an excellent cattle run but for the deep funnel-shaped holes which everywhere abound. The Natives call them *tomo*. **1867** HOCHSTETTER *NZ* 340 The limestone formation..forms a plateau..remarkable for subterraneous water-courses, caves and deep funnel-shaped holes, called by the natives Tomo... Tomo signifies crumbling, sinking down, and is therefore very appropriate. **1920** *Quick March* 10 May 39 The biggest paddock in my [King Country] section is chock-full of 'tomos'. A 'tomo'..is a deep natural well in the limestone formation, formed in the course of centuries, maybe by surface drainage. **1946** *NZ Geol.SB (NS)* No.41 20 The drainage of this limestone dip-slope area is mostly underground by means of sink-holes or 'tomos', which are so common as to give the name 'Tomo Country' to the district. **1965** WATSON *Stand in Rain* 122 A lot of new things came into our life when we were at Taupo... And there weren't any fears in our life then, either; except for tomos that might be there covered with bracken and you wouldn't see them and you might fall in. **1972** NEWTON *Wake of Axe* 155 A characteristic of this limestone country [near Te Kuiti] are its caves and underground tunnels or holes— 'tomos'. One of the Puketi tomos has been measured to run for two miles. **1982** HOLDEN *Wild Pig* 168 He seemed to think that the dog was stuck down a tomo (deep chute-like hole) somewhere [in the Waione-Galaxy area of Rotorua]. **1992** PARK *Fence around the Cuckoo* 14 Occasionally [at Te Kuiti] the ground fell in, creating an oubliette of raw earth out of which rose frightening plinks and gurgles and squishing sighs. These pits were called tomo, an abstruse word used sometimes of caves, such as the celebrated Waitomo Caves. But the race from whose language it comes had no doors, so tomo could well mean entrance or exit or both.

b. Special Comb. **tomo group**, a cavers' or speleological group.
  1972 *Affairs* July 23 There are now quite a number of Tomo Groups in New Zealand. In what places do they practise their rather chilly sport?

tom thumb. [f. its small size.] A small (approx. 15 mm) fire-cracker, smaller than the 'standard' double-happy.
  c1960 *tom thumb* used by Wellington children. (Ed.) **1977** JOSEPH *Time of Achamoth* 40 Exhausted as he was, he began to see..a whole city burning for Guy Fawkes' night (children shouting in the garden for rocket and roman candle, mount vesuvius, jumping jack, bridal veil and bengal light, hellzapoppin, flying

Tom Thumb bird. [f. the small size of the bird.] WREN. Cf. THUMB BIRD.
1966 FALLA et al. *Birds NZ* 192 Bush Wren *Xenicus longipes*..Matuhi, Tom Thumb Bird (Stewart Is.). **1985** *Reader's Digest Book NZ Birds* 265 *Bush Wren. Xenicus longipes... Matuhituhi, green wren, Tom Thumb bird.*

tomtit. [Transf. use of the northern hemisphere bird-name *tomtit.*] Now the standard name preferred by ornithologists (to *miromiro* or *tit*) for the small insectivorous forest bird *Petroica* (formerly *Myiomoira*) *macrocephala* (fam. Eopsaltriidae), with modifiers indicating the provenance of subspecies: **North Island** *P. m. toitoi* (see also MIROMIRO), **South Island** (or **yellow-breasted**) *P. m. macrocephala* (see also NGIRUNGIRU), **Chatham Island** *P. m. chathamensis*, **Snares Island** *P. m. dannefaerdi*, and **Auckland Island** *P. m. marrineri*. See further TIT *n.*¹ and note there. See also *butcher-bird* (BUTCHER *n.* 2), MIRO *n.*², NGIRUNGIRU, TOITOI *n.*¹, WHEEDLER. Contrast ROBIN.
1860 BUTLER *Forest Creek* (MS) (1960) 44 The wren and the tomtit and the thrush all are represented quite as nearly or even more so than the robin save that the tomtit is black headed with a yellow breast. **1878** *TrNZI* X. 203 Pied Tit. This familiar little bird, the 'Tomtit' of the Colonists, is far less plentiful than it formerly was. **1888** BULLER *Birds NZ* I. 39 Pied Tit North Island Tomtit. *Ibid.* 42 Myiomoira macrocephala. (South-Island Tomtit). **1898** MORRIS *Austral-English* 474 *Tomtit*..name applied in New Zealand to two New Zealand birds of the genus *Myiomoira*.. *M. toitoi*..in North Island; *M. macrocephala*..in South Island. **1904** *TrNZI* XXXVI. 119 I have paid special attention to the nests of three birds—the Native Canary..the Robin..and the Tomtit. **1914** GUTHRIE-SMITH *Mutton Birds & Other Birds* 203 *Petro[i]ca macrocephala*—Southern Tit—South Island Tom-tit. **1922** *Auckland Weekly News* 8 June 15 North Island tomtits, males particularly were much in evidence. **1930** *Evening Post* (Wellington) 6 Dec. 17 The pert little tomtit popped into view now and again, and at other times the male bird of the species announced his presence in his usual style of 'te-oly-oly-oly-o'. **1948** RICHDALE *Wild Life on Is. Outpost* 113 The Snares Island Tomtit (*Petroica dannefaerdi*) is evenly distributed all over the island. **1955** yellow-breasted tomtit [SEE NGIRUNGIRU]. **1968** JOHNSON *Turn of Tide* 69 Tiny birds began to appear: perky tomtits in immaculate suits of black and white. **1985** HUNT *I'm Ninety-five* 261 No, my father didn't mind us shanghaiing thrushes [on Stewart Island] and that, but he always said don't touch the natives. We did, though—pigeons and tomtits and tuis. **1990** *Checklist Birds NZ* 209 *Chatham Island Tomtit. Ibid.* 210 *Auckland Island Tomtit.*

tomyhawk, var. TOMAHAWK.

tonga, var. TAONGA.

Tonga granite. *Hist.* A granite from Nelson province.
1912 *NZ Free Lance Christmas Annual* (Wellington) 29 [Advt] This Tonga granite, so-called from its abiding place at Tonga Bay, between Motueka and Takaka..is an asset of considerable value to the Dominion.

tongs, *n. pl.* [Transf. use of *tongs* to instruments of similar shape or action.]
1. *Shearing.* [AND 1895.] Hand shears, esp. as **a pair of tongs.**
1934 *Press* (Christchurch) (Acland Gloss.) 27 Jan. 15 *Tongs.*—Nickname for blade shears. **1941** BAKER *NZ Slang* 39 We find shears called *jingling johnnies* and *tongs.* **1960** MILLS *Sheep-O* 41 For the benefit of the non-farming reader, blade shearing is done by twin-bladed sheep shears (called 'tongs'). **1973** NEWTON *Big Country SI* (1977) 20 A top blade-man in his day... He's past using a pair of tongs now but I noticed that he's still got a dog tied up in his backyard. **1984** *Country GP* 29 Oct. TV1 soap opera: I can handle a pair of tongs. **1989** [see HAND SHEARS].
2. *Forestry.* See quot.
1958 *NZ Timber Jrnl.* Dec. 73 *Tongs*: Mechanism with a scissors action used in logging for lifting and dragging timber. Syn. Skidding tongs.

tonguer.
1. *Whaling. Obs.* **a.** [For etym. see quot. 1836.] One who for the work of cutting in whales, abandoned whale carcasses, or parts of them, receives the oil of the tongue (also of other parts) in payment.
1836 *Log 'Mary Mitchell'* 28 Apr. in McNab *Old Whaling Days* (1913) 435 Came on board and despatched the boat the other side for a linguist our tounger. (The Ships all employ Toungers and it is a general custom I have acceded on the same terms as others)... I must not omit here Some mention of what are called toungers. they [*sic*] are here 2 and 3 white people who have a boat and some natives[. O]n a ship arriving they repair on board to solicit the Job for the ship. The terms are that they occasionally furnish a crew to help tow whales they furnish a boats crew to help cut the whale in and do any talking for the captain whose ignorance of the language requires their aid in any matters with the natives. When the whale is cut in they are entitled to the carcass and the tongue which in plentiful Whaling is always left on the carcass and they contrive to get 6 to 8 barrels of oil from each carcass but they are in general Blackguards and no dependence can be put in them—Runaways from Ships Mostly. [1913 Note] The Americans had..to rely to a great extent upon Maori labour and to be indebted to the services of interpreters. These men were locally [?at Cloudy Bay] called 'tonguers'... In 'The Piraki Log' [1911] the word 'tonguer' is suggested as a corruption of the Maori 'tonga'. This is quite wrong. The tonguer was a man who interpreted and assisted in cutting up and who was paid with the tongue of the whale. **1839** *Piraki Log* 10 Apr. (1911) 82 [He] found it to be James Robinson, the *Tonguer* from Wongooloa. **1845** WAKEFIELD *Adventure NZ* I. 323 The ['tonguer'] takes his name from having an exclusive right to the oil obtained from the tongue and other interior parts of the whale in payment for his duty of 'cutting in', or dissecting the whale. **1913** MCNAB *Old Whaling Days* 323 The Robinsons, so their names were given to the Doctor [Thiercelin in January 1840 at Akaroa], acted as 'carcassiers', as the French called them, collecting stray floating whales, or the intestines of whales..blown into the Bay, and melting them down to produce an inferior class of oil which they sold to the whalers. Among the English-speaking whalers these men were called 'tonguers'.
b. As **tonguer's oil**, an inferior whale-oil.
1838 WRIGHT *Let.* 20 Nov. McNab *Old Whaling Days* (1913) 232 Also you must be more particular in keeping your dark or tonguers oil separate and branded as such, as I have been obliged to allow a deduction of £3 per tun. **1843** DIEFFENBACH *Travels in NZ* I. 109 To this quantity must be added the tonguer's oil, so called from the man who 'cuts-in the whale', for which he is allowed the oil of the tongue, of the heart, and of the intestines, for his own benefit.
2. *Freezing works.* The worker who takes out the tongue and weasands.
1951 May 17 p.c. Colin Gordon (Feilding Freezing works). *Tonguer:* one who cuts out tongue and who also 'pulls the weasands'.

tonk. [Origin unknown.]
1. [AND 1964.] An effeminate person, a male homosexual.
1946 SARGESON *That Summer* 84 The cook got my goat when he started trying to do the same thing [*sc.* pinch my backside]. He was a tonk all right, just a real old auntie. **1964** PEARSON *Glossary* to Sargeson *Collected Stories 1935–63* (1964) 304 tonk: homosexual.
2. [AND 1941.] Esp. among schoolboys, a fool or simpleton; an unlikeable person.
c1941 St Patrick's College, Silverstream (Ed.) e.g. Come here you silly tonk. **1951** 14 M 10 Wellington H.S. 1 Tonk. **1955** *BJ Cameron Collection* (TS July) tonk (n) A fool, clot.

tonky, *a.* Applied to something or someone fashionable, 'swanky', trendy; or to one who 'puts on airs'.
1943 BENNETT *English in NZ* in *Amer. Speech* XVIII. 89 *Tonky* suggests superior social standing or 'tone'. **1984** PARTRIDGE *Dict. Slang* 1248 tonky, adj. Fashionable: NZ: since ca. 1935. Slatter, 'She's probably been to a tonky school.' Perhaps a blend of *tony* + swa*nky*. **1988** MCGILL *Dict. Kiwi Slang* 114 *tonky* fashionable..eg 'My, my, doesn't she look tonky.'

toodle-em-buck. *Obs.* Also with much variety of form **doodle-em (doodlum) buck, toodleumbucks,** often with init. caps. [Prob. f. Brit. *tootle* to walk, wander + th)*em* + *buck* a gambling marker (cf. 'pass the buck'): AND 1959.] A pitching or marble game (see quots. for various forms of the game), played either for purposes of gambling or as a test of skill.
1885 *Wairarapa Daily* 6 Nov. 2 [Gambling] which disgraces horse-racing, is benignly smiled upon by grandmotherly legislators who know as much of betting and turf gambling as they do of three card monte, or the ways of doodlum-buck. **1916** *Stratford Evening Post* 13 Apr. 3 Soldiers' Day Attractions... Coconut shys... Doodle-em Buck. **1932** BRUCE *Early Days Canterbury* 152 Peter Poski..with his crown and anchor game and his confrere with his game of 'Doodlum Buck'. **1953** SUTTON-SMITH *Unorganized Games NZ Primary School Children* (VUWTS) II. 741 Pitching games were Pitch and Toss, Quoits, Ninepins, Egg Cap and Toodle-em-buck. In the game of Toodle-em-buck (Richmond [Nelson] ([19]19)) a piece of broom a foot in length with a button on top of it stood upright in a circle of about two feet in diameter. Players pitched another piece of broom at this upright stick from a set distance in an endeavour to knock it over and send the button out of the circle. The game was played to the cry of 'Roll up, Tumble up, come and play the game of Toodle-em-Buck.' **1959** LAWLOR *Old Wellington Days* 37 Also, there was [c1900] the big gamble of 'toodleumbucks'... 'Toodleumbucks' were little wooden stands containing apertures of various sizes. The owner of one of these contraptions had to pay out in kind for any marble that was propelled through one of the apertures. If it was a very small opening he paid out three marbles and for the larger openings one marble. If a player were unsuccessful..he forfeited the marble he was playing with.

tooee, tooi, varr. TUI.

tookytooky, var. KOTUKUTUKU.

Tooley Street. Formerly used allusively and (usu.) unkindly for the British wholesale butter interest and buyers with headquarters in Tooley Street, London.
   1912 *NZ Free Lance* (Wellington) 4 May 8 We have the three tailors of Tooley Street with us still. **1922** *Auckland Weekly News* 24 Aug. 23 [Caption] Tooley Street Control...The Prime Minister stated.. that..the butter market in London was controlled by a committee of Tooley Street merchants who met daily and fixed a price. **1926** *NZ Observer* 10 Nov. 2 Who are we to think we make Tooley Street toe the mark? **1936** *NZPD* CCXLIV. 682 Our officers in London have been asked to work with Tooley Street for the purposes of implementing the new policy.

too right: see RIGHT.

toot, tooted, varr. TUTU, TUTUED.

tooth-leaved beech: see BEECH 2 (12).

top, *n.*¹ [Spec. use of *top* or *tops* mountain tops, high moorland: see OED *n.*¹ 3 a.]

1. Usu *pl.* as **the tops**, mountain or ridge tops, esp. (often as **high** (or **open**) **tops**) the highest parts of a high country farm or station.
   [**1862** CHUDLEIGH *Diary* 13 Dec. (1950) 70 It is a fine sight..the lofty back ranges looking blue and the tops covered with snow. *Ibid.* 202 Abner and I took the top of the range and had a great run after the sheep. **1868** BARKER *Station Life* (1870) 217 We lost very few sheep; they were all up at the tops of the high hills, their favourite summer pasture.] **1893** ROBERTS in *Mr Explorer Douglas* (1957) 28 We were so late in the season we could not tackle the high tops. **1902** *Settler's Handbook NZ* 31 The tops, however, often carry tussock and other herbage, affording admirable pasture for sheep in summer. **1917** *Triad* 10 Apr. 66 Dawn finds the leader [of the musterers] on the tops, six thousand feet up. **1933** *Press* (Christchurch) (Acland Gloss.) 23 Dec. 15 *Tops.*—Often called *high tops.* (1) High summer country... (2) In North Canterbury, country above the bush. **1946** ACLAND *Early Canterbury Runs* 210 There was a wedge-shaped block of ninety thousand acres of high tops, mostly bush-bound, in the middle. **1952** THOMSON *Deer Hunter* 44 On the high open tops shooting was also at reasonably close range. **1968** SLATTER *Pagan Game* 174 On the sheep station they called me Cloudburst... I was on the tops while you were still on the titty. **1988** PICKERING *Hills* 46 Basic tops travel involves little more than following a track out of the bushline and onto the crest of a tussock ridge.

2. *Mustering.* As a noun, the highest high-country mustering beat, i.e. one closest to the 'tops'. In the phr. **under the top,** alluding to the second highest beat; or in *attrib.* use in special Comb. **top beat,** see BEAT *n.* 2 b; **top man,** musterer working a higher (or the highest) beat.
   1952 BLAKISTON *My Yesteryears* 18 Starting at dawn, we climbed up the Clayton side of the range, leaving men at intervals to muster along the side, and the top man waited while others went through the saddle. **1953** STRONACH *Musterer on Molesworth* 46 Most of them end up, day after day, 'under the top'; that is, on the second beat from the top one, usually the least responsible.

top, *n.*² *Watersiders.* The deck (of a ship) or wharf (distinct from the hold 'down below'). Also used *attrib.* 'on deck' in Comb. **top hand, job, man.**
   1911 *Maoriland Worker* 9 June 12 Before preference to unionists was passed the pay [for coal workers in the Wellington Branch of the Waterside Workers' Federation] was per hour for shovellers 1s 6d and for top hands (i.e. winchmen, bullrope-men, trimmers, and tippers), is 3d... A gang of men consists of eight—four shovellers—and four top men—with an aggregate of 11s per hour, before preference. **c1926** THE MIXER *Transport Workers' Song Book* 65 And I never strike a top-job That the other fellows get... For there's things I won't come at: I never shout for bosses—I'm a lumper, I'm a rat.

top, *v. Criminals.* Also **top off, top on.** [AND *top off* to tip off, 1939.] To inform on (someone).
   1953 *Here & Now* Nov.–Dec. 44 He wasn't exactly a topper, but you couldn't trust him not to top you off if the occasion was right. **1964** DAVIS *Watersiders* 31 'That flaming tally-clerk must have topped me,' I heard Gaint groan. **1973** *Truth* 9 Oct. 51 Detective Denis O'Rourke said Spence denied knowledge of the alleged rapes, and said he would 'do time rather than top on his mates'. **1980** MACKENZIE *While We Have Prisons* (Lag's Lexicon) 99 *top, to* to inform on someone. To hang. **1982** NEWBOLD *Big Huey* 255 Top off (v) Inform against.

Hence **topper** *n.*, an informer; **topping** *vbl. n.*, informing.
   1950 *Here & Now* Nov. 14 Glossary of technical terms: A boobhead is a prisoner..a **topper** is a toady or an informer. **1953** HAMILTON *Till Human Voices Wake Us* 53 Toppers are what used to be called copper's narks in England. **1965** WATSON *Stand in Rain* 109 He wanted a statement about Jerry... 'I'm not a topper,' he said after Detective Crome had gone. **1973** JUSTIN *Prisoner* 23 So, a slot was a cell. A topper was a kind of pimp. I was learning. **1987** KEOGH in *Metro Fiction* 10 The phone rang twenty times a day, with accusations of topper, pakeha topper. **1973** *Truth* 24 Dec. 3 The complainant's fiance said '**topping**' was a term the gang used to describe reporting a matter to the police.

topdressing, *vbl. n.*

1. See AERIAL TOPDRESSING.

2. See *Taranaki topdressing* (TARANAKI B 2).

3. *transf.* or *fig.* Deceiving (customers, clients, etc.) by presenting a polished or rich surface appearance not supported by evidence (or analysis) in depth.
   1954 *Standard* (Wellington) 31 Mar. 2 The claims of the National Party are similar to an offence in the fruit industry which is termed 'top-dressing'. This consists of deceiving a buyer by placing high-quality fruit on the top layer of the case and inferior quality fruit underneath it.

tope /'tʌupi/. [Local use of British *tope* of uncertain etymology, a small shark.] *school shark* (SHARK 2 (15), *Galeorhinus galeus*).
   1872 HUTTON & HECTOR *Fishes NZ* 81 Galeus canis... Tope. **1880** *Senior Travel & Trout* 298 [The Maori] have a sweet tooth for sharks, especially the smooth-hound dog-fish and tope. **1898** MORRIS *Austral-English* 475 *Tope, n.* an Australasian Shark, *Galeus australis*... It differs somewhat from..the *Tope* of Britain. **1913** *TrNZI* XLV. 235 *Galeus australis*... The tope is common along the east coast of Otago. **1924** *NZJST* VI. 259 The southern tope, or school shark, *Galeorhinus australis*, is one of the small so-called dogfish commonly taken by trawlers around New Zealand. **1938** *TrRSNZ* LXVIII. 400 *Galeorhinus australis*... Southern tope. **1947** POWELL *Native Animals NZ* 61 School Shark or Tope (*Notogaleus australis*). This is very similar in shape to the Dog-fish... but it..is much larger. **1956** GRAHAM *Treasury NZ Fishes* 63 Tope or School Shark... The origin of the vernacular name Tope is not certain, but local fishermen who followed this occupation in Britain, said this name is a corruption of 'top'... Other New Zealand common names are Southern Tope and School Shark. **1979** *Catch* May 16 School Shark..Tope, Sand shark. Family Triakidae (Smooth dogfishes). **1986** *Evening Post* (Wellington) 11 July 12 Mrs Heather Morgan, of New Plymouth, caught a 21.77kg tope on an 8kg line in Northland's Parengarenga Harbour. **1992** *Evening Post* (Wellington) 16 Sept. 42 Some anglers have been catching good sized ling and tope sharks out at Nicholson's Trench.

top-hamper. [Transf. use of *top-hamper* an encumbrance on top of something: see OED.] The top layer, growth, etc., overlaid on a base of different material.
   1969 MCCASKILL *Molesworth* 210 Superphosphate was hand-sown on top of areas where good cocksfoot and clover had been established..but with the first heavy frosts..the top-hamper was killed and there was no extra feed remaining for the winter.

top-knot.

1. *Whaling.* A protuberance near the spout-hole of a whale.
   1843 DIEFFENBACH *Travels in NZ* I. 54 The whalers can distinguish..a bull from a cow;—the elevation near the spout-holes, called the top-knot, being much higher in the bulls, and this part is always above the water.

2. *Farming.* A tuft of wool on the top of a sheep's head; the wool shorn from such a tuft. See also WIG *v.*
   1922 PERRY *Sheep Farming* 37 A top-knot of true wool, not down, should cover the forehead [of the Leicester]. **c1927** SMITH *Sheep & Wool Industry* 77 He..removes the top-knot—a small cap of fuzzy oily wool which grows on the top of the sheeps's [*sic*] head. **1950** *NZJAg.* Oct. LXXXI. 313 Pick out stained wool, face pieces..and top-knots, as these wools make the buyer suspicious. **1973** FERNANDEZ *Tussock Fever* 166 'What about Lbs Wigs?' 'Lamb top-knots—off the head.' **1982** *Agric. Gloss.* (MAF) 60 *Topknot*: Wool shorn from the top of a sheep's head.

3. The name for a small marine fish of family Tripterygiidae; COCKABULLY 1.
   1991 BRADSTOCK *Fishing* 17 *Cockabully.* This is a general name for a lot of different kinds of small fish called triplefins. Other names are bully, blenny, twister, topknot, tommy cod.

top shelf. *fig.* [f. the custom of fixing inverted spirit bottles above the bar-level.] Spirits as an alcoholic drink.
   1959 SLATTER *Gun in My Hand* 14 So we did our drinking in the town. Hard stuff from the top shelf in the hotels. **1981** JOHNSTON *Fish Factory* 32 'Moody bugger when he's had a session on the top shelf,' Jamie put to Pop. **1989** BIOLETTI *The Yanks Are Coming* 130 Of course there was no top shelf stuff in the war years, so it was all beer.

topuni. *Hist.* [Ma. /ˈtoːpuni/: Williams 437 *Tōpuni* 4.... Black dogskin mat.] A fine Maori flax cloak interwoven with native dog's hair and used as a war-mat. Cf. WAR-MAT.
   1840 in Wilkes *US Exploring Exped.* (1852) I. 303 In his hand [Pomare] usually carries a short cloak of dog-skin, called *topuni, shupuni* [= ihupuni], or *patutu*. **1847** ANGAS *Savage Life* I. 297 These two distinguished chiefs sat to me..wearing the *topuni*, or war-mat of

tora, var. TORO.

torairi, var. TARAIRE.

torch, v. [See OED 3, 1887.] To seek out and take muttonbirds by torchlight from either burning or electric torches (occas. also to take flatfish with spear and torchlight). Usu. as a *vbl. n.* or *ppl. a.* Cf. *spotlighting* (SPOTLIGHT v.).

c1920 BEATTIE *Trad. Lifeways Southern Maori* (1994) 178 Mutton-birding is downright hard work... A Southland representative footballer says a night's torching is far more arduous than ninety minutes of strenuous football. *Ibid.* 506 [The kuaka muttonbird] was the only bird he knew that was 'torched' [in Nelson]. c1940 in Bailey & Roth *Shanties* (1967) 136 We catch all our birds in the torching, And after the cleaning we're scorching. **1952** in Sansom *In Grip of Island* (1982) 153 First part of the work over except for scrapings. Coming up to torching time. Birds excellent in quality and quantity. **1964** DEMPSEY *Little World Stewart Is.* 60 It is during this period that mutton-birders go out at night, 'torching', catching the young birds. **1966** *Dominion* (Wellington) 5 Mar. 6 The hunting system [for muttonbirds] known as 'torching'..takes place right at the end of the season. **1970** JENKIN *NZ Mysteries* 156 It is heard only at torching time..when muttonbirders search out the young birds by torchlight. *Ibid.* 157 He and his companions were on one of the hills of Poutama Island, torching, when they heard an unusual sound. **1979** WILSON *Titi Heritage* 68 The 'torching' season became known as such because the birders used flaming torches thick enough to be held aloft comfortably grasped in the hand. They were about three feet long and well soaked in muttonbird fat, before being set alight and were made from dry tree branches. Piles of these 'torches' were prepared and set aside awaiting the start of the 'torching' and each family had their torch bearers. **1995** *Evening Post* (Wellington) 15 July 15 In the second half of the [muttonbird] season, called 'torching', they [*sc.* chicks] come out at night in the wind and rain to lose the grey fluffy down.

torea. Also **torea-pango**; occas. early **toria**. [Ma. /'toːrea/: Williams 438 *Tōrea..1*... pied oystercatchers..black oystercatcher. Called also *tōrea tai* and *tōrea pango*... 2... pied stilt... =*poaka. Tōrea pango* (Ar[awa])..black stilt. = *kakī* (ii).]

1. Either of the *black* and *pied oystercatcher* (OYSTERCATCHER 2 (1) and (3)), or (usu. as **torea-pango**) the *variable oystercatcher* (OYSTERCATCHER 2 (4)). See also *mussel-picker* (MUSSEL 4).

[**1820** LEE & KENDALL *NZ Gram. & Vocab.* 216 Toréa; A bird with a long red bill.] **1842** GRAY *Fauna* in Dieffenbach *Travels in NZ* (1843) II. 196 *Haematopus picatus*... Toria of the natives. **1849** TORLESSE *Papers* (1958) 110 Shot 9½ couple of ducks besides 2 torias and 2 quail. **1861** HAAST *Rep. Topogr. Explor. Nelson* 50 We continued our route along this beach..endeavouring in the meantime to shoot some toreas (redbills)..to add a little to our small stock of provisions. **1873** BULLER *Birds NZ* 225 Haematopus unicolor. (Black Oyster-catcher)... Torea-pango. **1882** HAY *Brighter Britain* II. 225 The Torea, or oyster-catcher..is one of the sea-coast birds, and is often to be seen about our tidal rivers. **1898** MORRIS *Austral-English* 475 *Torea..*Maori name for all the New Zealand species of the *Oyster-catchers*. **1904** TREGEAR *Maori Race* 180 The large sea-gull..and another gull, the Oyster-catcher (*torea*: Haematopus sp.), were domesticated, but merely as pets. **1945** BEATTIE *Maori Place-names Canterbury* 18 An island further up the river is known as Torea (redbill) because these birds nest there. **1955** OLIVER *NZ Birds* 250 *Black Oystercatcher. Torea-pango. Haematopus unicolor unicolor.* **1970** [see OYSTERCATCHER 2 (3)]. **1985** [see OYSTERCATCHER 2 (4)].

2. *Obs.* Poss. the *pied stilt* (STILT 2 (2)).

1855 DRURY *Sailing Directions* 66 Birds met with in Pelorus... Oysterpickers—two kinds, called Toria by the natives... Stilts—two kinds, called Toria by natives. **1873** [see STILT 2 (3)]. **1966** [see BARKER].

torea-pango: see TOREA 1.

toria, var. TOREA.

toro. [Ma. /'toro/ /'toru/: Williams 438 *Toro* (i)..*1. Persoonia toru*... 2. *Myrsine salicina*... *Ibid.* 441 *Toru* (ii) = *toro* (i) 1.]

[*Note*] English usage appears to follow the Maori, in which (so Williams) *toro* applies to both *Toronia* and *Myrsine* spp.; *toru* (on Colenso's authority) only to a *Toronia* sp.

1. As **toro** or **toru** (also early **tora**), *Toronia* (formerly *Persoonia*) *toru* (fam. Proteaceae), a small, highly branched tree of northern New Zealand having fragrant flowers and long narrow leaves arranged in whorls. **a.** As **toro**.

1843 DIEFFENBACH *Travels in NZ* I. 430 Of the *Proteaceae*, the Tora (Persoonia tora) and Rewa-rewa..are the only known species. **1844** WILLIAMS *NZ Jrnl.* (1956) 105 The Toro, this tree grows naturally into a perfect oval, and the leafs [*sic*] at the extremity of each branch are pink... It seldom grows larger than 40 feet and its flower has a pleasing and odoriferous smell. **1853** HOOKER *II Flora Novae-Zelandiae I Flowering Plants* 219 Persoonia *toro*... Hab. Northern Island. Woods, from Auckland northward,.. Nat. name, 'Toro'. **1875** KIRK *Durability NZ Timbers* 23 Toro.-(*Persoonia toro.*) A small tree, 20 to 30 feet high, confined to the Province of Auckland. **1889** KIRK *Forest Flora* 135 This handsome tree [*Persoonia toro*] is commonly termed toro by northern Natives; but Mr. Colenso informs me that it should be toru... The present species..is often confused with *Myrsine salicina*..'toro' being commonly applied to both plants. **1907** LAING & BLACKWELL *Plants NZ* 148 *Persoonia toru* (*The Toru or Toro*). A small tree. **1951** LEVY *Grasslands NZ* (1970) 3 The development of the kauri to dominance was preceded by scrub and low-forest phases, the chief species being mingimingi..toro [etc.]. **1980** BRASCH *Indirections* 53 He had collected too a number of North Island trees and shrubs, at that time rareties in Dunedin..a toro, a tawa and others.

b. As **toru**.

1889 [see a above]. **1906** CHEESEMAN *Manual NZ Flora* 605 *P[ersoonia] Toru*... North Cape to Rotorua and East Cape... *Toru; Toro*... The specific name was given as 'Toru' in Cunningham's original description..and according to Mr Colenso this is the proper spelling of the Maori name. It was, however, changed to 'Tora'.. and was again altered to 'Toro' by Sir J.D. Hooker. **1961** MARTIN *Flora NZ* 164 Toru leaves (Persoonia toru) 4–8 in., narrow. **1978** MOORE & IRWIN *Oxford Book NZ Plants* 22 *Persoonia (toronia) toru*. Toru is common in the north and extends to the Volcanic Plateau where it can be seen..on Rainbow Mountain... 'The name is derived from the epithet *toru*, of Maori origin, and the ending *-onia* to suggest the affinity with *Persoonia*'. (Johnson and Briggs 1975).

2. As **toro**, *Myrsine* (formerly *Suttonia*) *salicina* (fam. Myrsinaceae), a small tree of lowland to montane forest with long smooth leaves and clusters of flowers arising from branchlets. See also TIPAU 1.

1880 CRAWFORD *Recoll. of Travel* 185 [Near Wellington there are] red, black, white birch—hinau..toro, rata, tawa. **1906** CHEESEMAN *Manual NZ Flora* 432 M[yrsine] *salicina*... A small tree 15–30 ft. high... *Toro*. **1940** LAING & BLACKWELL *Plants NZ* 353 *Suttonia salicina* (*The Toro*). A small tree, sometimes 40 ft. in height... Maori name, *Toro*. **1978** MOORE & IRWIN *Oxford Book NZ Plants* 116 *Myrsine salicina, toro.* A small, narrow-headed tree of forest margins and second growth in the North Island and warmer parts of the South Island. **1982** *Field Guide Common NZ Trees & Shrubs* 26 *Toro Myrsine salicina.* Tree reaching 10m. **1988** DAWSON *Forest Vines to Snow Tussocks* 102 Other species which tend to be more wide ranging are mahoe.., pigeonwood.., toro (*Myrsine salicina*).

toroa. [Ma. /'toroa/: Williams 439 *Toroa..1. Diomedea exulans.*] Any of various species of albatross, but usu. the *royal albatross* and the *wandering albatross* (ALBATROSS); occas. MOLLYMAWK 2 (1).

[**1815** KENDALL *New Zealanders' First Book* 14 Toroa. An albatross.] **1842** GRAY *Fauna* in Dieffenbach *Travels in NZ* (1843) II. 200 In the New Zealand seas, exist several kinds of albatrosses, which the natives call Toroa. **1859** THOMSON *Story NZ* I. 28 Six species of the *Procellaridae* are found on the sea-coasts. The Titi, or mutton bird, and the Toroa, or albatross, are the most celebrated birds of this family. **1904** HUTTON & DRUMMOND *Animals NZ* 258 *The Wandering Albatross.—Toroa. Diomedea exulans.* **1928** BAUCKE *White Man Treads* 61 And truly it was even so! Like a toroa (albatross) swimming with wings extended, rising for flight! **1946** *JPS* LV. 159 *Toroa*, a sea-bird (Diomedea exulans), albatross: tuft of down much valued as an ear-ornament. **1963** KEENE *O te Raki* 195 A few [*waka*] might even be decorated..with the white feathers of the..*toroa* (albatross). **1979** FALLA *New Guide Birds NZ* 29 Wandering Albatross *Diomedea exulans...* Wanderer, Toroa. **1983** [see MOLLYMAWK 1].

toropapa. [Ma. /'toropapa/: Williams 440 *Toropapa* (ii)..*Alseuosmia* [spp.].] Any of several native shrub species of *Alseuosmia* (fam. Caprifoliaceae), distinguished by their highly fragrant flowers and crimson berries.

1940 LAING & BLACKWELL *Plants NZ* 428 *Alseuosmia macrophylla* (*The Large-leaved Alseuosmia*). A shrub, 4 ft.–10 ft. in height... Maori name, *Toropapa*. **1978** MOORE & IRWIN *Oxford Book NZ Plants* 120 *Alseuosmia macrophylla. Toropapa..*is common in the northern half of the North Island, less so at its southern limit about Nelson. **1982** SALE *Four Seasons* 33 The Maoris call it toropapa, and the botanists alseuosmia—perfume of the grove.

torori. *Hist.* Also **torore**. [Ma. /'toːrori/: Williams 440 *Tōrori..*Native-grown tobacco. (mod.)] A tobacco grown and cured by Maori. Cf. RAURAU.

1851 TAYLOR *Journal* 28 Apr. (ATLTS) VII. 198 That [tobacco] which they grow universally obtains the name of Torore which signifies intoxicating. **1868** TAYLOR *Past & Present NZ* 134 The native, unable to purchase tobacco to the extent he formerly did, began to grow it himself, and from instructions he has contrived

torotoro

to pick up, he now manufactures it; this he calls *torore*. **1905** BAUCKE *White Man Treads* 144 She inquired if I objected to the smell of 'torori' (native tobacco). **1917** *Chron. NZEF* 16 May 126 Torori—Tobacco of Maori manufacture; smokes like Boer tobacco but has an odour peculiarly its own. **1938** FINLAYSON *Brown Man's Burden* (1973) 34 Taranga just sat up there smoking her pipe of evil-smelling torori. **1992** PARK *Fence around the Cuckoo* 37 It had..an interior atmosphere thick with the woeful fumes of torori, the black native pigtail tobacco.

torotoro. [Ma. /'torotoro/: Williams 439 *torotoro*..5. Hawser, cable for securing a canoe... 6. *Metrosideros perforata*, a climbing plant, the vines which were used for lashing various things.] *rata-vine* (RATA II).

[**1820** LEE & KENDALL *NZ Gram. & Vocab.* 217 Tóro tóro;.. the root of a shrub so called.] **1834** MARKHAM *NZ* (1963) 35 In tying the Rafters to the Ridge Pole, and in making their Parrs, the same Creeper is used, but I forget its name Toro Toro. **1863** MANING *Old NZ* iii 41 I..worked all day lashing the fence; the fence being of course not nailed, but lashed with *toro-toro*, a kind of tough creeping plant, like a small rope, which was very strong and well adapted for the purpose. **1874** BAINES *Edward Crewe* 85 Stout pieces of timber were securely fastened horizontally, by a good lashing of 'Toro-Toro' vine. **1888** BULLER *Birds NZ* I. 12 The spot fixed upon was..sheltered all round by close-growing porokaiwiria, torotoro, and other shrubby trees. **1952** HYDE *Houses by Sea* 63 Soak the lithe toro-toro, and best yarn Was not so strong for tying up stockades.

torpedo ray: see RAY 2 (4).

torrentfish. [Named from its preferred habitat of fast-running water.] *Cheimarrichthys fosteri* (fam. Pinguipedidae (formerly Mugiloididae)), a small, but robust, somewhat shark-like freshwater fish found amongst boulders in rapids. See also PANOKO, PAPANOKO, SHARK-BULLY.

1910 *TrNZI* XLII. 389 The original specimens were taken in the Otira River, on the Western slopes of the dividing-range, 'where the alpine torrent leaves its picturesque Gorge'; hence the generic name signifying 'torrent-fish'. **1929** [see PAPANOKO]. **1936** [see SHARK-BULLY]. **1967** NATUSCH *Animals NZ* 222 The torrent fish..spends part of its life in salt or brackish water, and part in rapids of lower stretches of shingly rivers. **1978** MCDOWALL *NZ Freshwater Fishes* 143 In appearance, the Torrentfish looks superficially rather like a lightly pigmented Blue Cod with a depressed, flattened head and receding lower jaw. **1981** DENNIS *Paparoas Guide* 189 The curious-looking torrentfish..also comes out of the sea in spring. **1990** [see PAPANOKO].

toru, var. TORO.

toss, *v.* In various phrasal elaborations of *toss up* to vomit, 'throw up': **to toss the tiger, toss a reverse lunch, toss one's lollies.**

c**1960** p.c. Vincent O'Sullivan: *toss the tiger* used among Auckland University students and others. **1979** GIFFORD *Loosehead Len's Gluepot Greats* 154 He claimed incident in Eastern Moon had arisen when local person had 'tossed a reverse lunch' of prawns, sweetcorn, and tomato skins over his person. **1986** *Metro* (Auckland) Mar. 27 They were seen..tossing back Tequila Slammers and then heard together in the *pissoir* on their knees tossing their lollies long and loud.

Totalisator Agency Board: see TAB.

totalla, var. TOTARA *n*.¹

totara /'tʌutrə/, /'tʌutərə/, /to'tærə/, *n*.¹ Also with much variety of early form as **tatare, tatatarra, tòtalla, totarra, totora.** [Ma. /'to:tara/: Williams 441 *Tōtara*.]

1. a. *Podocarpus totara* (fam. Podocarpaceae), a large coniferous tree prized for its durable timber and its wood; occas. as **golden totara** a horticultural var. Aureus, having golden-yellow foliage (see quot. 1993). Also *attrib.* See also *mahogany-pine* (PINE 2 (7)), YEW.

1817 NICHOLAS *NZ* I. 329 A species of pine, called by the natives *totarra*, excited our astonishment, from the bulk and height to which it grew. [**1820** LEE & KENDALL *NZ Gram. & Vocab.* 217 Tòtara, *s.* A species of pine.] c**1826-27** BOULTBEE *Journal* (1986) 109 The wood with which they make a light—cōwatti [=kauati] and tòtalla. **1835** YATE *NZ* (1970) 56 It lays seven purely white eggs, in a compact nest, in the lower branches of the Totara-tree. **1841** HODGSKIN *Narr. Eight Months Sojourn NZ* 27 Tatatarra, growing between 60 and 70 feet in high[t]. **1844** WILLIAMS *NZ Jrnl.* (1956) 49 Bark of Tatare Tree. **1851** *Lyttelton Times* 1 Feb. 4 For Sale, a few 2-inch Totara Counter Tops, 2 feet wide. **1854** GOLDER *Pigeons' Parliament* 16 [A pigeon muses.] Upon Te Aro tot'ra Line (Which natives from its trees define), Reflecting on my lonely state, I mourned the loss of my dear mate. **1866** BARKER *Station Life* (1870) 95 There are traces..of vast forests..chiefly of totara, a sort of red pine. **1872** DOMETT *Ranolf & Amohia* 107 One lone totara-tree that grew Beneath the hill-side rising high. **1890** *PWD Catalogue Timbers* (NZ & South Seas Exhib.) 15 Totara..Podocarpus totara..Timber of a reddish colour, soft, easily worked, and of great durability. **1911** *Truth* 3 June 5 When they got to a fence overlooking a deep gully, prisoner and Sergeant Moore dismounted, and the former said: 'You see that totara tree and a fern. The body is there.' **1937** AYSON *Thomas* 64 Totara posts were put in at intervals, leaving spaces for doors and windows according to the plan. **1951** HUNT *Confessions* 38 It appeared as a small inverted totara canoe. **1974** SARGESON *I Saw in My Dream* 99 Behind the house totaras grew on the bank of the creek. **1993** *Dominion* (Wellington) 26 May 5 [Caption] Mr Falloon wearing a possum-skin hat with a golden totara.

b. *Obs.* As **totara-pine.**

1841 *NZ Jrnl.* II. 51 The dark green foliage and reddish bark of the totarra pine give a variety to the appearance of the vegetation. **1879** HAAST *Geol. Canterbury & Westland* 81 Along the rather wet track appeared, besides the Totara pine, white pines..and black pines. **1900** *Canterbury Old & New* 184 Broadleaf, five-fingered Jack..and the totara pine jostle one another in the dense dry bush.

2. With a modifier: **alpine (mountain, snow), Hall's (mountain, thin-bark(ed)).**

(1) **alpine (mountain, snow) totara.** *P. nivalis* a prostrate sub-alpine shrub.

1889 KIRK *Forest Flora* 66 The alpine totara is restricted to alpine and sub-alpine localities..but has not been observed on Stewart Island. **1908** *AJHR* C-11 35 *[Podocarpus] nivalis*. Mountain totara..shrub steppe. **1916** *TrNZI* XLVIII. 169 *Podocarpus nivalis*, the mountain-totara, is extremely abundant [on coarse stony debris], its shoots far-spreading and closely hugging the ground in espalier fashion. **1940** LAING & BLACKWELL *Plants NZ* 68 *Podocarpus nivalis* (The Alpine Totara). **1958** *Tararua* Sept. 49 We followed deer tracks zigzagging up through snow totara and *Dracophyllum*. **1961** *Merriam-Webster Third Internat. Dict.* 62 *alpine totara* n: a dense New Zealand shrub..often low and widely spreading with leaves closely and irregularly arranged. **1973** MARK & ADAMS *Alpine Plants* 18 These shrubs, often no higher than the tussocks, vary somewhat from place to place but snow totara (*Podocarpus nivalis*)..and *Coprosma*..are widespread. **1981** DENNIS *Paparoas Guide* 164 Snow totara..is found here and there in the west [of Westland].

(2) **Hall's** (occas. **mountain, thin-barked) totara.** *P. hallii*, a tall forest tree with thin flaking bark and sharp-tipped leaves.

1890 *PWD Gen. Catalogue* (NZ & South Seas Exhib.) 16 Lithograph of 'Hall's totara' foliage. **1894** *NZ Official Year-book* 330 The miro, matai, totara, Hall's totara, are generally distributed. **1908** *AJHR* C-11 35 *Podocarpus Hallii*... Thin-barked totara... Forest, sub-alpine scrub. **1909** *AJHR* C-11 11 *[Podocarpus Hallii]*... Mountain-totara. Higher forests. **1940** HOWARD *Rakiura* xviii In the northern and eastern portions of the Island, the predominant trees are..thin-barked Totara (*Podocarpus Hallii*) and southern Rata. **1954** *Bull. Wellington Bot. Soc. No.27* 10 Traces of burnt forest with mountain totara [*P. hallii*] were seen above the Spray River. **1966** *Encycl. NZ* III. 409 [Totara] is closely related to another species *P. hallii*, or Hall's totara, which is a somewhat smaller species growing at higher altitudes. **1981** DENNIS *Paparoas Guide* 159 Hall's totara..is now uncommon in the west [of Westland].

3. The wood of the totara, esp. when its grain takes prized or preferred decorative forms: **bird's eye totara,** see BIRD *n.* 4; **totara burr, totara knot,** configurations of grain due to knots in the wood of the trunk. See also BURR *n.*²

1887 *Auckland Weekly News* 23 Apr. 18 The woods used are **totara burr,** wairangi, kauri..piriri and kohutuhutu. **1879** *Ibid.* 4 Oct. 7 Over the back of the principal mirrors..are six panels of **totara knot,** moki, pukaki, and figwood, studded with moki buttons. **1890** *PWD Catalogue Timbers* (NZ & South Seas Exhib.) 20 Totara knot slab.

4. Special Comb. **totara bark,** the thick bark of the totara shed from the tree in long strips, and used by the Maori and early European settlers esp. for thatching, and for the construction or protection of storage vessels.

1844 TUCKETT *Diary* 2 May in Hocken *Contributions* (1898) 214 We arrived at a Maori settlement [at Henley], two or three decent huts made of totara bark. **1858** SMITH *Notes of Journey* in Taylor *Early Travellers* (1959) 362 Most of the houses are built of slabs of totara bark which is taken from the tree in sheets, often 20 feet long by 10 broad. *Ibid.* 385 It was still raining fast..but we continued on till two, when we halted, and commenced building a totara bark hut. **1864** *Richmond-Atkinson Papers* 12 Feb. (1960) II. 87 [At the abandoned Maori camp was] a pannikin of native manufacture made of totara-bark. **1876** *TrNZI* VIII. 166 We may divide colonial architecture into periods or ages. First, the wattle-and-dab period, with its contemporaneous, but more advanced, varieties of fern tree and totara bark. **1903** *Ibid.* XXXV. 22 The roof was..covered with raupo—sometimes with an inner sheeting of totara-bark. **1922** COWAN *NZ Wars* (1955) II. 282 The camp..contained thirty thatched houses roofed with totara-bark. **1940** HOWARD *Rakiura* 208 The tightly packed [kelp bags of mutton-birds] are then cased in longitudinal strips of totara bark and placed in flax bags.

5. Totara as an emblem of something fine, tall, and outstanding of its kind.

1987 *Landfall* 162 208 N.Z. Rail is the totara in the rain forest of inter-island communication.

totara, *n.*² Also **totaratara.** [Ma. 'to:tara/: Williams 441 *Tōtara*..2. *Leucopogon fraseri*, a plant.] PATOTARA 1 (*Leucopogon fraseri*).

1843 TAYLOR *Journal* Aug. (ATLTS) 51 [Word list] totaratara a small shrub like a heath. **1867** HOOKER *Handbook* 768 Totara..*Leucopogon Frazeri* [sic]. **1869** *TrNZI* I. (rev. edn.) 262 The small berries..of the heath-like totara (*Leucopogon Fraseri*)..were eagerly sought after. **1906** CHEESEMAN *Manual NZ Flora* 415 *L[eucopogon] Fraseri*... A small shrubby plant 2–6 in. high,.. branching from the base... *Totara*... The drupe is juicy, sweetish, and edible.

totarra, var. TOTARA *n.*[1]

tote, var. TUTU.

tothersider: see SIDE 1 b.

totokipio. Also **totokepio**. [Ma. /to'tokipio/: Williams 434 *Tokitokipia..totokipio..*little grebe.] DABCHICK.
1870 *TrNZI* II. 73 *Podiceps rufipectus*... Totokipio. Dab-chick, Little Grebe. **1873** [see DABCHICK]. **1904** HUTTON & DRUMMOND *Animals NZ* 305 *The Little Grebe.—Totokipio. Podicipes rufipectus.* c**1920** BEATTIE *Trad. Lifeways Southern Maori* (1994) 164 The bird known to the Maori as the totokipio and to the settler as the diver is apparently the dabchick. **1945** BEATTIE *Maori Place-names Canterbury* 64 Totokepio is the 'little diver' of the settler to distinguish it from the 'big diver' (the crested grebe). The Canterbury compiler spells it as given, but in Southland the name is Totokipio, and if taken in sections To-toki-pio it is easy to pronounce. **1945** [see DIVER].

totora, var. TOTARA *n.*[1]

totowai, var. TOUTOUWAI.

toubouna, var. TUPUNA.

touch, *v.* In various phrases.
1. to touch noses, see NOSE *n.*[1] f.
2. to touch (one's) kick (pants, strides, tweeds), to produce money and pay for (a treat, liquor, etc.).
1955 BJ *Cameron Collection* (TS July) touch one's strides (v) To pay for a round. **1962** HORI *Half-gallon Jar* 23 This side-of-the-mouth coot says for me to touch the pants first, so I say, 'O.K. Five beers please.' *Ibid*. 75 There is all sorts of plonk, and the little joker tells me to touch my kick [to shout]... I think all the others have death adders in their pockets, 'cause not one of them touches his tweeds. **1971** NEWTON *Ten Thousand Dogs* 169 *Touch the kick*: To pay out money—put your hand in your pocket.
Hence **touch** *n.*, a turn to treat.
1988 McGILL *Dict. Kiwi Slang* 114 *touch* somebody's turn to buy a round of drinks; eg 'Hey, Sid, isn't it your touch?'
3. wouldn't touch it with a red-hot poker, expressing extreme aversion.
1988 McGILL *Dict. Kiwi Slang* 125 *wouldn't touch it with a red-hot poker* extreme aversion; eg 'If I was you I wouldn't touch those shares with a red-hot poker.'
4. to touch (one) **up,** to remind (someone), to give (someone) a 'hurry up'.
1908 *Truth* 20 June 4 Messrs Littlejohn and Sons are the parties you should make reference to, as I sub-lease from them that portion of the building, but not the clock so you had better touch them up about it.

toughie, var. TUI.

tourist. [Ironic use of *tourist* a holidaymaker: AND 1916.]
1. *WW1.* **a.** Often as **Bill Massey's Tourists** (cf. BILL MASSEY), an ironic nickname for the First (volunteer) Contingent of the Main Body of the NZEF which landed in Egypt in Dec. 1914.
1915 *Let.* 4 Mar. in Malthus *ANZAC* (1965) 29 Cyprus would be nice to see, just the thing for 'Bill Massey's tourists', but I would rather be going to France. **1935** BURTON *Silent Division* 25 Great days [in Egypt] for 'Bill Massey's Tourists'—the most glorious picnic they ever had. **1984** PUGSLEY *Gallipoli* 85 All the action was in France and 'Bill Massey's Tourists' were stuck among the desert sands.
Hence **Bill Masseying** *WW1*, enlisting for overseas service.
1917 *NZ Free Lance* (Wellington) 27 Apr. 5 'Bill Masseyin'' we called it, on the way to Egypt. On five sweet bob a day.
b. As **The Tourists**.
1916 Ross *Light & Shade* 177 The men from the Antipodes have brought with them a humour and a slang of their own. Their definition of the various batches of volunteers that have come out to fight is worth quoting. The first contingent became known as 'The Tourists'. They were out to see a bit of the world. Incidentally they would do any fighting that came along... Then came 'The Dinkums'—the true fighting men as they called themselves... There followed 'The Super-Dinkums', 'The War Babies', and 'The Hard Thinkers', the latter having thought a great deal before they came.
2. *WW2.* As an ironic nickname for the Second Echelon, 2NZEF, see COOK'S TOURISTS.

toutouwai. Also **totowai**. [Ma. /'toutou'wai/: Williams 442 *Toutouwai, tōtōwai*, n..robin.] ROBIN 1.
[**1820** LEE & KENDALL *NZ Gram. & Vocab.* 217 *Tóu tou wai*; A bird so called.] **1835** YATE *NZ* (1970) 56 *Toutouwai*—This bird is nearly the size of the sparrow..its feathers are dark, tinged with white about the breast and tail. **1844** WILLIAMS *NZ Jrnl.* (1956) 113 The Toutouwai is a smaller slate coloured bird, has a shrill whistling note and is particularly fond of gazing (if I may so express it) at strangers. **1869** *TrNZI* I. (rev. edn.) 104 *Petroica longipes*. Totowai. Robin. Common. **1873** [see ROBIN 1 a]. **1885** *TrNZI* XVII. 419 I noticed the following:—Pigeon, tui..toutouwai..and various sea birds. **1904** HUTTON & DRUMMOND *Animals NZ* 74 *The South Island Wood Robin.—Toutouwai. Miro albifrons*. *Ibid*. 75 *The North Island Wood Robin.—Toutouwai. Miro australis*. **1946** *JPS* LV. 159 *Toutouwai*, a bird..the North Island form; the South Island form..bears the same name. **1952** RICHARDS *Chatham Is.* 71 Found now only on Little Mangere Island... Black Wood Robin. Tou-tou-wai, Miro. **1985** *Reader's Digest Book NZ Birds* 282 Robin. *Petroica australis*... Bush robin, toutouwai.

tovy-poenammu, var. TE WAIPOUNAMU.

tow. In the phr. **to get in tow with** (someone), to go steadily with.
1949 SARGESON *I Saw in My Dream* (1974) 117 No, I don't know, but there's a yarn his father was a whaler that stayed out here and got in tow with some maori tart. He's part maori for sure though, because once he got me to witness a paper and it was about maori land.

towa, var. TAWA, TOWAI.

towai /'tʌuwai/. Also **towhai,** early **towha, towa;** occas. erron. **tawai**. [Ma. /'to:wai/: Williams 442 *Tōwai*..*1. Weinmannia* [spp.]... *2. Paratrophis banksii*, a tree.]

1. A native forest tree of the genus *Weinmannia* (fam. Cunoniaceae). **a.** *Weinmannia silvicola*, TAWHERO 2.
[**1820** LEE & KENDALL *NZ Gram. & Vocab.* 217 *Tówai*; A shrub so called.] **1834** McDONNELL *Extracts Jrnl.* (1979) 19 A great variety of hard-wood grows at New Zealand, admirably adapted for the timbering of any sized ships; among them is the..to wá..and many others. **1844** WILLIAMS *NZ Jrnl.* (1956) 106 The towai is not remarkable for a tree, makes fair fencing. **1869** *TrNZI* I. (rev. edn.) 89 The bark of the towai, *Weinmannia silvicola*, does not appear to have been collected for tanning purposes. **1875** KIRK *Durability NZ Timbers* 20 The towai (*W. silvicola*), a closely allied tree, which is abundant in the north,.. would probably prove more durable [than tawhero]. **1883** *Auckland Weekly News* 24 Feb. 22 The bark used for tanning..is not the bark of the tawa..but it is the bark of the towai—a tree that grows to the height of about twenty feet. **1958** *NZ Timber Jrnl.* Dec. 73 *Towai: Weinmannia silvicola*... Moderate size tree of N.Z. forest of northern half of North Island. **1988** DAWSON *Forest Vines to Snow Tussocks* 38 In towai (*Weinmannia silvicola*) the trend is from one to five pairs of leaflets.
b. *Weinmannia racemosa*, KAMAHI **a.** (a) **towai** forms.
1843 DIEFFENBACH *Travels in NZ* II. 389 Towai—a timber tree. **1867** HOOKER *Handbook* 768 Towai, *Col[enso]. Weinmannia racemosa*. **1883** HECTOR *Handbook NZ* 132 *Weinmannia racemosa*... Towhai, Kamahi. A large tree; trunk 2–4 feet in diameter, and 50 feet high. **1889** KIRK *Forest Flora* 133 Mr. Colenso informs me that..[*Weinmannia racemosa*] is the towai of the Maoris; and I learn from..W.L. Williams that it is termed 'tawhero' by the East Cape Natives—the name commonly applied to..*W. silvicola*. **1906** CHEESEMAN *Manual NZ Flora* 139 *W[einmannia] racemosa*... Towai; Kamahi. Very closely allied to *W. sylvicola* [*Tawhero*]. **1910** COCKAYNE *NZ Plants & Their Story* 41 The towai or kamahi (*Weinmannia racemosa*), yielding an excellent bark for tanning, and a wood both ornamental and strong. **1966** *Encycl. NZ* III. 712 Towai . . towai . . *Weinmannia* spp.
(b) Erron. and obsolete **tawai** form, poss. influenced by the form **tawhero**.
1843 DIEFFENBACH *Travels in NZ* I. 27 Intermixed with these are the tawai [1843 *Note* Leiospermum racemosum.] and hinau. **1848** WAKEFIELD *Handbook NZ* 142 Tawai. (*Leiospermum racemosum*.) This tree has a rough, dark-brown bark, and a small round leaf, in shape like that of an elm. **1853** HOOKER *II Flora Novae-Zelandiae I Flowering Plants* 80 *Weinmannia racemosa*... Nat. names, 'Tawai', Cunn.; 'Tawhere', Southern Island, Lyall. **1867** HOOKER *Handbook* 768 Tawai, Cunn. *Weinmannia racemosa*.
2. MILK-TREE (*Streblus* (formerly *Paratrophis*) *heterophyllus*).
1853 [see MILK-TREE]. **1867** HOOKER *Handbook* 768 Towai... *Epicarpurus microphylla* [=*Streblus*]. **1870** *TrNZI* II. 122 *Epicarpurus microphyllus*. Towai.
3. Uncertain or erron. attributions. **a.** Also **towa, towha**. Poss. TAWA 1; or a conifer species, poss. MIRO *n.*[1] a.
1817 NICHOLAS *NZ* I. 330 The *towha*, another species of pine, though not so large as the *totarra*, grew here [Waimate, Northland] at the same time to a considerable size, and the forest abounded with it. This tree has likewise a small and narrow leaf, but its bark is thin and quite smooth; it bears a berry which is eaten by the natives. **1835** YATE *NZ* (1970) 46 Towai—a tree of the *Podocarpus* species, with a dark-brown bark, and a leaf similar to, and about the size of, the moss-rose.

1838 POLACK *NZ* II. 396 The *Towai*, (a podocarpus) is but a small tree compared with those preceding. Its wood..has a handsome deep red colour when polished. It grows to the heighth [*sic*] of twenty-five feet, and then is richly furnished with virent leaves. The wood is heavy and but little used hitherto. **1842** HEAPHY *NZ* 42 The red pines are the *Totara*, *Towa*, *Mahi*, and *Rata*, all of which are close-grained, and moderately hard... The *Towa* spars are considered the best for this purpose. *Ibid*. 43 The *Towa* and the *Kraka* berries also yield an useful oil, but not in such quantity as that first mentioned.

b. Poss. TAWAI (cf. SI use of *red birch* for *kamahi*).
1845 WAKEFIELD *Adventure NZ* II. 95 Its banks..are covered wholly with the towai... It is used for ship building and is called by Englishmen 'black birch'. **1890** 28 Feb. in Wilson *Land of Tui* (1894) 78 [Near Castle Hill] there is but one patch of forest, the dull, sad green of the Towai (black birch). [1894 *Note*] *Weinmannia racemosa*.

towai grass, var. TOETOE GRASS.

towakawaka, var. TIWAKAWAKA.

tower, var. TAWA.

towha, towhai, varr. TOWAI.

towi, var. TOETOE.

towie. Also **tow truckie.** [f. *tow*(-truck driver + -IE: AND 1975.] A tow-truck driver or operator.
1983 *Salient* (Wellington) 28 Feb. 3 If the general confusion worsens, and anarchy prevails, he said that towies would simply 'sit back and let Rafferty's Rules take over'. **1983** *Dominion* (Wellington) 7 Apr. 7 The tow truckies say it's common for car owners to storm into the yard exploding with unrepeatable criticism of the qualities of the towies. **1990** *Sunday Magazine* 22 Apr. 46 Hunt looks like a towie—black tee-shirt, black jeans, black shoes, long hair, tattoos, stud earrings. **1991** *AA Motoring Today* Sept.–Oct. 19 In 1989, after widespread reports of thuggery and extortion by 'towies'..new laws were passed designed to exclude criminals and tighten controls.

towitowi: see TOETOE.

town. Various spec. uses and combinations in early and later settlement.
1. *Obs.* A Maori village.
1814 MARSDEN *Lett. & Jrnls.* (1932) 91 The next day (24th) we landed the horses and cattle, and fixed upon a place for the present residence of the settlers, and began to clear away the rubbish and prepare for erecting the houses for their reception on a piece of ground adjoining to the native town pitched upon by Duaterra and the chiefs of the place. **1814** KENDALL 6 Sept. in Elder *Marsden's Lieutenants* (1934) 59 I and Mr. Hall accompanied him to his principal hipwah or town, called Ranghee Hoo (Rangihoua). **1815** CAPT. HOVELL 31 Aug. quoted in Elder *Marsden's Lieutenants* (1934) 89 At 10 a.m. sent a party of men on shore to destroy the town and the canoes. At noon the people returned with two pigs, having destroyed the principal part of the town and canoes with fire. At 2 p.m. the people went on shore again and set fire to the remainder part of the town, canoes, huts, and all their food, and returned with one large pig and two small ones.
2. In various special Comb. in contexts of early settlement or land-sales: **town acre** *hist.* (occas. init. cap.) [AND 1838], an allotment of land in a prospective town to a New Zealand Company settler, usu. an acre-section for every twenty (or hundred) acres of uncleared rural land purchased (cf. ACRE *n.*¹ 1, COUNTRY-ACRE); **town allotment**, a *town section*; **town board**, the elected local authority formerly in control of a town or township; **town lot**, a *town section* sold by auction; **town reserve** [AND 1836], land set aside for the site of a town; **town section**, in early land sales, ballots, or auctions, a section of land (often an acre, see *town acre* above) within a planned town, as distinct from a rural section; in modern use an urban residential section (see quot. 1992).

1839 *Terms of Sale of NZ Land Co. G.B.P.P.* in *Speeches & Documents* (1971) 19 These doubly-selected lands will be divided into 1100 sections, each section comprising one **town-acre**, and 100 country-acres. 110 sections will be reserved by the Company. **1840** DEANS in *Pioneers* (1964) 4 The land, I am sorry to say, will be a long time of being surveyed, and we are now located on patches of about an acre till such time as the Town Acres are surveyed. **1842** Mary F. Swainson letter in *William Swainson* 21 Aug. (1992) 90 I will now explain to you about the quantity of the land: each section is one hundred acres, and Papa rents three... Each section had a town acre attached to it at the first sale the Land Company held. The house that we are in is on one acre... We are on the Thorndon Flat. **1851** HEAPHY in *Lyttelton Times* 11 Jan. 5 The immediate choosing of a town acre section has been a most important and useful measure. **1853** SEWELL *Journal* (1980) I. 188 He is jealous of Clifford and the Squatters,—is addicted to Landscrip, Town Acres and Rural Sections. **1964** NORRIS *Settlers in Depression* 6 Because most of his men [of the Number 1 Company of the Fourth Waikato Militia Regiment] received their town acre grants in what is now the suburb of Whitiora, that locality was once called Number One. **1995** ARVIDSON in *Source of the Song* 49 The family took up their town acre on the east side of the river in Grey Street [Hamilton]. c**1863–64** *NZ Gaz.* in Featon *Waikato War* (1879) 52 On the expiration of three years.., each settler [in the Waikato]..will be entitled to a Crown Grant of the **town allotment**, and farm section allotted to him. **1864** THATCHER *Invercargill Minstrel* 6 And the booth they visited for prog, And sometimes took a nip of grog; There was Grieve, one of your famed **Town Board**, McIvor too his orders roared. **1945** SARGESON in *Listener Short Stories* (1977) 20 He worked for the town board and in the dry weather he'd have to drive about the streets on the water-cart. **1841** VILLIERS & LEFEVRE *Col. Land & Emigration Office* in *GBPP 1842 (No.569)* 130 The memorial [from Mr.Sinclair, Wellington] states that certain **town lots**..had been advertised for sale by auction, but that several allotments, comprising some of the most valuable lands in the township..had been reserved from such sale..; that these sections were to be paid for at the average price of half the town sections. **1881** CAMPBELL *Poenamo* 342 It was at a very early stage of the existence of the embryo capital, when we were all squatters, and the survey lines of the town were only half cut, and when we were all helping each other to do nothing until the first sale of town lots should come off. **1853** SEWELL *Journal* 12 Feb. (1980) I. 139 A large space has been set apart as what is called a **Town Reserve** near Lyttelton. **1840** *Port Nicholson Deputies to Gipps* 24 Sept. in *GBPP House of Commons 1841 (No.311)* 123 In June 1839, the New Zealand Land Company, issued proposals for the sale of nine-tenths of a township of 110,000 acres, in lots of 101 acres, each comprising 100 acres of country land and one **town section**. **1841** [see *town lot* above]. **1848** in *Lett. from Otago* 2 May (1978) 10 We have had a selection of town sections of land, by the different proprietors... The town section measures a quarter of an acre, and costs in London 10s. **1853** SEWELL *Journal* 1 July (1980) I. 336 He wants to take some of the Church Lands at Kaiapoi, a rural section and a Town Section. **1898** HOCKEN *Contributions* 99 The 21st of April [1848] was fixed for the formal selection of their own town sections by the land purchasers... Mr.David Garrick..was the first private individual to select in Dunedin. **1992** SMITHYMAN *Auto/Biographies* 52 Outside his house is a tower uplifted from a town section, which topped a home but grew too much for it.

3. In various special Comb. in modern contexts: **town district**, see quot.; **town milk** or **town supply**, the supplying, or a contract for supplying, urban milk treatment stations with milk.

1955 *BJ Cameron Collection* (TS July) **town district** (n) A former smaller unit of town government (usually an intermediate stage between rural and borough status) having a council elected by the residents and a Chairman elected by the council. **1950** *NZJAg.* Oct. LXXXI. 303 The **town-milk** industry is composed of three fairly clearly defined sections, production, treatment, and distribution, all of which seek to serve the interests of the housewife. *Ibid*. 306 In New Zealand about 85 per cent. of all town milk sold in urban areas is pasteurised... Too much 'billy' milk is still sold. **1959** *NZ Dairy Exporter* 10 Aug. 41 Town Milk Supply is..a question of Quotas. *Ibid*. 10 Sept. 19 [Heading] Price-Determining Formula for Town Milk—New Approach sought at Annual Conference. **1966** FALLA et al. *Birds NZ* 79 A single bird spent the cold winter of 1963..near Christchurch alternating between two herds of Friesian-Holsteins 'on **town supply**'. **1974** *NZ Agric.* 93 [Caption] Tanker collecting milk from a town-supply farm at Te Awamutu... A town-supply farmer undertakes to supply a fixed quota of milk all year round.

town belt. Also init. cap(s). [Spec. use of *belt* a strip of land or trees.] A belt of reserved land (a 'green belt') around or in a town or city, kept mainly in parkland and trees, vested in the town authority and reserved for public, (usu.) scenic or recreational, purposes. See also BELT *n.*¹ 1.

1848 WAKEFIELD *Handbook NZ* 97 [Karori] district begins immediately outside the boundary of the Town-belt. **1853** SEWELL *Journal* 27 Apr. (1980) I. 256 What, cut up the Town Belt which we..were legally bound to keep open? **1874** BATHGATE *Col. Experiences* 23 This town-belt, as it is called, is pretty much in a state of nature. **1889** DAVIDSON *Stories NZ Life* 61 The native bush which covers a large portion of the [Dunedin] 'town belt' is in itself a heritage to be highly prized. **1902** *Settler's Handbook NZ* 55 The whole is admirably set off by Hagley Park.., the Domain and Botanical Gardens..., Lancaster Park, the Town Belts, and other public and private gardens and plantations. **1938** HYDE *Nor Yrs. Condemn* 40 The best houses [in Dunedin] stood up on the hills, set back in the dark native green of the Town Belt. **1959** DAVIN *No Remittance* 84 Every night I took her out I used to see her safely home [to Maori Hill]..and come down through the Town Belt. **1961–62** BAXTER *Collected Poems* (1980) 256 Lying awake on a bench in the town belt, Alone. **1974** SARGESON in *Islands* 7 92 He was off this high summer evening along the road that led to the Town Belt—that was to say a back-to-nature acre or so with a name that derived from many decades previously. **1988** *Dominion* (Wellington) 7 Oct. 6 A hall is to be extended on Wellington's town belt land so a Cook Islands language nest can be established.

town bike. [Supposedly because 'ridden' by every person in the town: AND 1945.] A local small-town prostitute, or a person free with sexual favours.

1964 MORRIESON *Came a Hot Friday* (1981) 164 Why don't you tell the old tit you're the town bike.

1972 GEE *My Father's Den* 55 I was having my first real affair with a girl of fifteen called Melva Butter. Charlie said she was the town bike (he was sour at missing his turn) but she had her own sort of morality:.. she took on only one boy at a time. **1986** BROWN *Weaver's Apprentice* 126 Hey, Fleming... Going to have a wee ride on the town bike, are ya? **1993** *Dominion* (Wellington) 1 Jan. 20 Howard is the archetypal beaten-down ghost of a bloke and Marina literally is the town bike.

townhouse. A high-quality urban house, semi-detached or free-standing on a minimal section. (Also in Australian use; quot. 1959 illustrates the usual British sense.)

[**1959** MIDDLETON *The Stone* 50 Mr Silva [the owner] went back to his town house and..there were only Charlie and his wife and I on the station.] **1977** ELDRED-GRIGG *Of Ivory Accents* 8 So a moving van was eventually sent from..Dick's townhouse. **1980** MANTELL *Murder Or Three* 79 She's moved into one of those town houses next door. **1983** BAUER *English Word-formation* 58 In New Zealand a *town house* is a semi-detached house with a very small garden, and not just any house in a town—this can be contrasted with the traditional British English sense of *town house* with its implications of secondary residence. **1987** *Te Reo 30* 132 'My town house is a townhouse', correctly distinguishes, on the page, and will be distinguished in speech; two stresses for the one, and one stress (TOWNhouse) for the other. There is as well a question of nuance to be noticed. A *townhouse* is emphatically upmarket from a *home unit*.

town Maori: see MAORI A 7.

township.

1. *Hist.* [AND 1789.] A tract of surveyed land as a proposed site for a town; a 'paper' (or proposed) town.

1840 [see *town section* (TOWN 2)]. **1840** *Gipps to Russell* 6 Oct. in *GBPP House of Commons 1841 (No.311)* 122 A township can, I apprehend, have no meaning other than a continuous block of land. **1842** *Capt. Smith's Rep.* Nov. in Wakefield *Handbook NZ* (1848) 329 Port Ashley..is quite unfit for settlement..as there is no fit place for a Township. **1851** SHORTLAND *S. Dist. NZ* 174 This is now the site of a township, called Dunedin, founded by a Scotch company. **1853** SEWELL *Journal* 4 Feb. (1980) I. 424 The fact is that when the Gladstone scheme was abandoned, Simeon and I agreed that the opportunity should not be lost of realising a Township Scheme upon the same site for the benefit of the Church.

2. a. A village or small town. (Quots. 1842, 1846 poss. belong at 1 above.)

1842 HEAPHY *NZ* 21 The additional circumstance of Auckland possessing a tolerable harbour, would also have always caused its pre-eminence over the adjoining township [at Thames]. **1846** MARJORIBANKS *Travels in NZ* 62 It is fortunate that it [*sc.* the Hutt] was abandoned as a township. **1852** *NZGG* 19 Nov. V. 28:169 (Governor Grey's Proclamation) Ordinance to abate the Dog nuisance, the boundaries of the township of Akaroa in the Middle Island of New Zealand, shall be hereafter known as follows. **1871** MONEY *Knocking About NZ* 17 About this time, though almost a 'new chum' myself, I was much amused by a trio who arrived in the township. **1881** BATHGATE *Waitaruna* 181 The village, or township as they call it in this part of the world, has an unpronounceable Maori name. **1890** *Otago Witness* (Dunedin) 23 Dec. 17 He was a digger, living..seven or eight miles from the township (school, store, and ever present 'pub') of Cockabully burn. **1894** ARTHUR *Kangaroo & Kauri* 89 Townships are the smaller colonial towns, and vary in size from the dimension of a moderate English village to about a fifth-rate English country town. **1907** HULL *College Songs* 46 Generally speaking, a township [in North Auckland] consists of a 'pub', a store, half-a-dozen scattered homesteads, and about thirty-nine million Maori bugs. **1913** MANSFIELD *Stories* (1984) 134 He had ridden over to the township with four of the boys. **1920** MANDER *Story NZ River* (1974) 198 The bay was now a township. It had its own post office, its little public school, its town hall, its football field. **1954** MACFARLANE *Te Raka* 19 These many widely-scattered urban oases in the rural desert have been known for all their short lives as 'townships'. A very ugly name coming down to us from the old digging days. 'Village' or just 'town' are now gaining ground over the ugly old name, and rightly so. **1964** MIDDLETON *Walk on Beach* 161 I remember I was jiving with a girl..who worked in a milkbar in the township. **1971** ARMFELT *Catching Up* 20 Down to Elgin: sprawling, squat, bungaloid: not even large enough to be a 'township'.

b. *Spec.* **Maori** (earlier **Native**) **township**, an area of Maori reserve laid off or gazetted as a township for the exclusive use of the Maori owners with the intention of encouraging closer settlement of Maori land.

1895 *NZ Statutes* No.12 30 [Native Townships Act] In every native township there shall be reserved and laid off for the use of the native owners such allotments, hereinafter called 'native allotments', not exceeding in the whole an area of twenty per centum of the total area of the township... It shall be the duty of the Surveyor-General to include in such reservations every native burying-ground, and every building actually occupied by a Native at the date of the gazetting of the Proclamation. **1903** *NZPD* CLI. 275 It is only by purchasing land from the Natives, and giving the lessees or their successors a freehold title, that you will get these Native townships lifted out of the ruck they are in at the present moment. **1919** *NZ Statutes* No.22 67 [Native Townships Amendment Act] Any land acquired by the Crown in any Native Township..may be disposed of by way of sale, lease, or otherwise in accordance with the regulations. **1955** *NZPD* CCCVII. 2947 There are Maori townships at Tokaanu, Te Kuiti, and Otorohanga... The Maori township lands comprise areas which, mainly at the opening of the present century, were carved out of tracts of Maori land with the idea that they would be likely centres of population.

3. The shopping centre of a suburb. See also VILLAGE 2.

1955 BJ Cameron Collection (TS July) township (n) 1. A block of land newly surveyed for small settlement in holdings of 100 acres or so. (Historical.) 2. A village or small settlement. 3. The centre of a suburb where most of the shops and amenities are.

towra cracca, towrikka, varr. TAUREKAREKA.

tow truckie: see TOWIE.

trace high: see KILT *v*.

track, *n*.

1. a. *Spec.* uses of *track* 'a way made by the feet of people or animals; a path; a rough unmade road' (see OED *n.* 3) are esp. frequent in New Zealand English, as in **sheep track, goat track, pig track, walking track**. See also *bush track* (BUSH C 3 a), *Maori track* (MAORI B 5 a).

[*Note*] *Trail* is comparatively seldom used; *path* usu. refers to a formed pathway.

1853 ROCHFORT *Adventures of Surveyor* 27 We did not stay at Whanganui, and returning made a slight diversion from the usual track to visit Otaki. **1866** BARKER *Station Life* (1870) 76 After we had passed our own boundary fence we came upon a very bad *track*—this is the name by which all the roads are called, and they do not deserve a better. **1933** *Press* (Christchurch) (Acland Gloss.) 23 Dec. 15 Track.—Pack t[rack], etc. Originally an unformed, unfenced way, but Leach's T[rack], Shand's T[rack], etc., perpetuate the name. The county councils will probably alter these in time. **1958** *Tararua* Sept. 24 In the bush or in the open do you tramp on a *track*, a *trail*, or a *path*? Not on a path one may be sure, seldom if ever on a trail, almost always on a track, like a proper New Zealander... *Track* is undoubtedly the established word in New Zealand. It is the only one occurring on maps or applied to named routes, such as *Hongi's track*, the *Milford track*, the *Pahiatua Bush Track Road*. Ibid. 25 *Deer track* still seems to be used far more than *deer trail*. **1963** BACON *In the Sticks* 62 There's nothing but a few pig tracks through the scrub. **1964** DEMPSEY *Little World Stewart Is.* 47 Most mornings found Dad and Arthur out with slashers, opening up tracks.

b. Special Comb. **track-cutter, track-maker,** one employed to cut or form tracks in the back-country; hence, **track-cutting; track-making.**

1976 BROWN *Difficult Country* 48 G. Snow, who had been..a **track-cutter** on the Mangles, undertook..to cut the track from Walkers to the Grey. **1984** HOLDEN *Razorback* 76 A short distance below them he came to a gametrail so pronounced and so well defined that a party of Forest Service trackcutters, using grubber, slasher and spade, might have fashioned it out of a steep hillface. **1995** CRUMP *Bushwoman* 71 Their [*sc.*deercullers'] rifles were confiscated. That's why they're track cutters now. **1889** PRINCE *Diary of Trip* 5 The writer started from Quinten McKinnon's (**track cutting**) camp, now called Trackton. **1967** MAY *West Coast Gold Rushes* 75 Besides..track-cutting on the West Coast, the Nelson Provincial Government endeavoured to shorten the inland route. **1995** CRUMP *Bushwoman* 136 Bill had some track-cutting to do in a lot of the Golden Bay valleys. **1976** BROWN *Difficult Country* 34 Then in April 1864 a note was brought by a **track-maker** and left at the store for Moffat. **1981** HENDERSON *Exiles Asbestos Cottage* 7 Roy Mytton, trackmaker, musterer, Mount Arthur and Cobb Valley, Motueka, August 1979. Ibid. 117 On **trackmaking** over the hills and far away..with payment being made by the distance covered, usually so much per chain.

2. In the phr. **to take the track, to be put down the track,** to be dismissed from a job. Cf. *sent down the road* (ROAD 3).

1911 *Maoriland Worker* 7 July 14 And a 'drummer' is the man with the lowest tally—perhaps because he is likeliest to take and keep the track with his 'load'. **1986** RICHARDS *Off the Sheep's Back* 98 The lamb would have to be killed. I felt embarrassed and upset because I was sure I would be 'put down the track'.

3. *Obs.* In the phr. **on the track** [AND 1869], of a swagger or itinerant, to be on the move carrying a swag. See also WALLABY.

1906 PICARD *Ups & Downs* 8 Picard has a great big spot for the man on the track. **1968** *NZ Contemp. Dict. Suppl.* (Collins) 20 track, on the (*Phr.*) on the road, carrying one's swag. **1986** OWEN & PERKINS *Speaking for Ourselves* 68 Well, I took to the track. I came up north [from Southland] and swagged with a character that was well known on the track at that time [*sc.* the mid 1920s]... They were fellows that were on the track permanently, and they all had their beats.

tract and treacle. *Hist.* Applied to an early colonial government policy towards Maori activists consisting of exhortation followed by a material reward. Cf. SUGAR AND BLANKET.

1865 HURSTHOUSE *England's NZ War* 52 A mere bit of [Gore-Browne's] old 'Tract and Treacle' Policy. *Ibid.* 63 He [*sc.* Grey] is a Governor who in his former reign in New Zealand was an administrator of that 'Tract and Treacle' Policy toward the Maori.

trade. *Hist.* [Used elsewhere but recorded earliest in NZ: see OED 12, 1859.] Trade goods.
1816 HALL in Elder *Marsden's Lieutenants* (1934) 123 If I had a little trade to pay the natives with. **1844** BURNS *A Brief Narrative* 7 The only plan that he [*sc.* the Maori chief] advised was for me to get a large war canoe, and take the best part of my trade along with me, and proceed to Poverty Bay.

trail. [See OED 'chiefly *U.S.* and *Canada*; also *N.Z.* and *Austral.*', 1807.] TRACK 1 a (see note there).
1860 BURNETT *Let.* 15 Mar. in Haast *Life & Times Sir Julius von Haast* (1948) 85 Crossed the Alexander stream and struck Mackay's last year's trail. **1908** *NZGeol.SB (NS)* No.6 21 A foot-track, which branching off near Frew Creek from the Whitcombe Pass trail, leads to Frew Saddle. **1938** HYDE *Godwits Fly* (1970) 126 There was a dark trail..and a stream came with edgings of fine malachite ferns. **1958** *Tararua* Sept. 24 I [*sc.* Miss R. Mason] well remember the shock of astonishment when in 1937 I first saw *trail* used in New Zealand. The word was on a rough signpost pointing out the beginning of White's Track at Piha. I am afraid I thought somewhat scornfully, 'Hm, some townie who has never been out of the city or set foot off a pavement has got all his ideas of New Zealand outdoor life from reading books about North America.' *Ibid.* 25 It is interesting to compare the use of *track* and *trail* in *The Tramper*. Through the first volumes *track* is always used when referring to an actual track, and *trail* occurs rarely and then only in the expression *blazed trail* or more or less figuratively—'to fare forth on the trail'. In 1935 there is the first definite use of *trail* as a synonym for *track* in a reference to the 'Handbook of Arthur's Pass National Park'. It is significant that it occurs in reference to Arthur's Pass for trail seems to have come into use in Canterbury in this sense before it reached Wellington. **1966** TURNER *Eng. Lang. Austral. & NZ* 161 *Track, trail* and *path* compete in a semantic field in which *track* is the general word, *trail* a more recent word differentiated as a track that is narrow and hard to follow, especially one made by animals, as a *deer trail*, and *path* is hardly used at all.

trailer sailer. [Also Aust.: OEDAS, 1981.] A sailing boat (usu. under 8 m in length and with a centreboard or retractable keel) which can be transported on a trailer.
1962 *Sea Spray* Oct. 41 [Heading] Trailer-Sailer Sloop. **1964–65** *Ibid.* Dec.–Jan. 116 [Advt] Trailer Sailers (Plywood)... Trailer Sailer 21´: 21´x 7´11. Four Bunks, Centreboard or Fixed Keel. £18... People interested in forming a New Zealand Trailer Sailer Association write direct to Secretary..Takapuna North. **1970** *NZ Boating World* Sept. 82 All the attributes of a small keeler are crammed into a Dick-Hartley designed trailer sailer. **1975** *Evening Post* (Wellington) 17 Jan. 9 [Advt] 15´ Hartley trailer sailer... Yours for only $600. *Ibid.* 21 Wanted, plans for trailer sailer, 16 to 18 feet.

train. [See OED *pull v.* 11 g: AND 1976.] In the phr. **to pull a train**, of a woman, to be forced to submit to serial copulation or gang rape.
1971 *Truth* 20 July 14 An 11-man and one woman jury had found Jones guilty of the rape of a girl picked up from a city bus terminal on the night of Friday, April 23, and taken to a house on the Ellerslie Main Highway where she was forced to 'pull a train' of Hell's Angels and Storm Troopers gangsters.

training college: cf. COLLEGE c.

tram. [Spec. use of *tram* a continuous line or track of timber beams or 'rails' orig. in or from a mine: see OED *tram n.*² 4 and 5.]
1. a. In New Zealand often *bush tram* (BUSH C 3 a), a rake of trucks or bogies running usu. on wooden rails, hauled by a locomotive (see LOCI) or occas. by bullocks or horses, and used to carry logs from the bush to the mill; less frequently of similar coal-mining or goldmining arrangements, often without locomotive power.
1869 WILBY *Diary* in Pfaff *Diggers' Story* (1914) 116 1869—occupation, driving tram from Marsden to Paeroa with passengers and luggage, in conjunction with the Greymouth train. **1885** *Wairarapa Daily* 17 Mar. 2 He will be able to fetch the logs right in to the mill by means of a tram without using junkers at all. **1986** OWEN & PERKINS *Speaking for Ourselves* 161 In some cases steam engines were employed [to get logs out of bush], or locomotives running on a bush railway, or 'tram'.

Hence **tram** *v.*, to convey logs by tram.
1953 REED *Story of Kauri* 259 It had been the intention of the k[auri] T[imber] C[ompany] to tram the Kauri in from No Gum Camp.

b. Comb. **tram-car, -cart, -laying, -road, truck**.
1894 WILSON *Land of Tui* 234 We had grand weather for our return journey from Greymouth, and began it..by a drive..through the Bush in a **tram-car** that went on wooden lines. **1891** *TrNZI* XXIII. 488 These logs are then rolled on to a kind of sleigh or **tram-cart** by the help of screw-jacks, and conveyed by horses to the mill. **1961** HENDERSON *Friends in Chains* 71 The guv'nor offered them a good **tram-laying** job at the Waitahu mill. **1842** HEAPHY *NZ* 131 A few short **tram-roads** formed [in the Chathams]. **1852** *Coromandel Gold Field. Provisional Regs.* in Swainson *Auckland* (1853) 162 Persons desirous of constructing Tram Roads..on the gold field..must make application to the Commissioner for permission so to do. **1955** WILSON *Land of My Children* 28 Frank..went to the mill and, selecting the best boards, loaded them onto the **tram trucks**.

2. Special Comb. **tramline, tramway,** a carriageway with usu. wooden rails, most often used to convey logs from the bush to the mill (see also *bush tramway* (BUSH C 3 a)); **tramwayman,** one who works on a bush tramway, or, occas., drives a bush tram.
1894 *NZ Official Year-book* 331 The trees are felled..the logs being conveyed to the mill by flotation, by **tramline**, or..by oxen or horses. **1923** MALFROY *Small Sawmills* 15 When setting out to put in a tramline be careful to select..an easy hauling grade. **1946** SARGESON *That Summer* 174 It was really what was left of the tramline that had been used for bringing out logs. **1955** WILSON *Land of My Children* 23 He led the way along the mill tramline—wooden rails laid on sleepers and ballasted with red sawdust. **1986** DEVANNY *Point of Departure* 45 [The coal] was conveyed from the mines to the wharf [c1900] in trucks, drawn by..a miniature steam engine, along rails which led through hill cuttings. The tramline, this railway was called. **1867** HOCHSTETTER *NZ* 147 A broad clearing leads from the interior of the forest..and forms a kind of road along which the logs are rolled down to the head of a regular **tramway**. **1879** HINGSTON *Australian Abroad* 293 [Hokitika] has a wooden road also, in the shape of a tramway..on which cars go to the diggings fourteen miles away. **1889** KIRK *Forest Flora* 32 The tramway forms an important part of the sawmiller's plant. It is constructed of split or sawn sleepers placed from 24in. to 30in. apart from centre to centre, sawn rails 3in. by 4in., which are laid in notches cut in the ends of the sleepers, and secured by wooden wedges driven home. **1892** *NZ Official Handbook* 158 In the south, rough tramways are laid down in the bush, and the logs hauled on low carriages to the mills by horse- or bullock-teams. **1913** *NZGeol.SB (NS)* No.16 19 The logs were transported to the mill in the case of the Waitanui by a wooden-railed tramway. **1948** JEWELL *Accounting in Timber Industry* 130 Tramway: A light railway built for the transportation of logs and/or sawn timber. **1966** *Encycl. NZ* III. 444 The term 'tramway' could be applied in New Zealand from 1860 onwards to lines constructed to carry timber from bush to sawmill. **1923** *Awards, etc.* 112 [Westland Timber Yards and Sawmill Employees] [Rates of wages] Winchman [£]0 14[s.] 0[d.] Leading **tramwayman** 0 14 0 Other tram workers 0 13 0. **1951** *Awards, etc.* 452 [Westland Timber-Workers Award] In the case of all tramwaymen and bush workers of all descriptions, the hours of work shall be the same as mill men.

trammie. *Obs.*

1. Also **trammy**. [f. *tram* urban tram-car + -IE: AND 1919.] One who works on (esp. drives for) a municipal electric tramway system; a tram-driver or tram-conductor.
1906 *Truth* 7 Apr. 5 In fact, the [Christchurch] trammies, justly wild, made up their minds to strike. **1912** *Ibid.* 3 Feb. 5 Many there were who refused to believe that the 'Trammies' would do such a thing [i.e. stop work], but it was perceptible that..the conductors and the motormen meant it, and the street cars were gradually deserted. **c1926** THE MIXER *Transport Workers' Song Book* 23 Then he slathers up the 'trammies' As the conductor goes through. **1947** COLE in *Landfall* 3 162 Two trammies..waiting with ticket-boxes under their arms. **1955** *BJ Cameron Collection* (TS July) trammie (n) A conductor or motorman on the trams. **1975** ANDERSON *Men of Milford Road* 131 Little did that trammie realise that I had just reached the point where one more *Ding-ding* would have precipitated a tribal war in Conon Street, Invercargill. **1991** *Sunday Star* (Auckland) 1 Sept. A2 Three of Auckland's oldest former trammies got back on track yesterday at a reunion to mark 35 years since the last four trams rattled up town to Epsom.

2. [f. TRAM 1 a + -IE.] One who drives or operates a bush tram.
1967 HENDERSON *Return to Open Country* 236 The trammie was at the skids with his tandem-yoked horses ready to load the logs on the tram.

trammy, var. TRAMMIE.

tramp, *n.* [Spec. use of *tramp* a walking excursion: see OED 3 a and b, senses which are also recorded in NZ from the 1860s.] A walking expedition (often extensive) into rough country undertaken as a sport or for recreation, food and necessary equipment being (usu.) carried on the back; occas. a tramping-route (see 1936 quot.). (Non-New Zealand usage might prefer *hike* or *bush-walk(ing)* for similar activities: see esp. TRAMPER 1 quot. 1933.)
1928 *Tararua Tramper* Nov. 2 Tramps tramped. **1936** *Hills & Valleys* II. 4 The [Hutt Valley] Tramping Club—always seeking new 'tramps'—made an official trip there. **1966** *Weekly News* (Auckland) 3 Aug. 7 Two-day tramps from the Milford Hotel up to the Sutherland Falls. **1984** *NZ Woman's Weekly* 30 Apr. 121 Day tramps are popular. **1993** *Dominion* (Wellington) 14 Sept. 3 We..would highlight areas she needs to improve on in the preparation and execution of her tramps.

TRAMP

tramp, v.¹ intr. To walk for long distances in rough country as a sport or for recreation. Also quasi-trans. (see quot. 1988), to undertake a tramping expedition in (a district, area).

1928 *Tararua Tramper* Nov. 2 Tramps tramped. Ibid. 3 Coming trips... Boat to Rona Bay and tramp thence to McIntosh's camp. **1940** GILKISON *Peaks, Packs & Mountain Tracks* 80 Along the road you can 'hike', but over the winding trails and trackless hills you can really tramp. **1984** *Listener* 28 Apr. 62 One of my correspondents tramping with her husband, referred to the 'benched out' track they were following up the hillside. **1985** McGILL *G'day Country* 170 Peter was tramping Te Anau, having tramped Britain and Borneo. **1995** ANDERSON *House Guest* 98 Rob had absorbed bush lore at primary... You never tramped alone. Not unless you were extremely experienced and well-equipped.

tramp, v.² To speed, to go fast, to 'hike'. (Ed. recalls this use from the late 1930s.)

1969 *Listener* 23 May 12 It was a souped-up Ford. They were tramping, in anybody's language. 'Better leave it for the zambucs,' Payne said.

tramper. [f. TRAMP v.¹ + -er.]

1. One who travels on foot over rough country for sport or recreation. Also as **tramperess** joc., a female tramper (see quot. 1929).

1928 *Tararua Tramper* Nov. 1 Trampers all! Greetings! **1929** Ibid. Aug. 2 [Heading] A Word of Encouragement to New Tramperesses. **1930** Ibid. May 2 Trampers pant crazily over the hills, ruthlessly crashing their heavy boots through old records and pridefully claiming new ones. **1933** Ibid. Apr. 2 Undoubtedly many trampers—and others dislike the word 'hike'. Trampers have been known to bite viciously when called 'hikers'. **1953** STRONACH *Musterer on Molesworth* 55 The homestead was full of people: two parties of deerstalkers, one party of trampers—the word 'hiker' had not then arrived. **1960** *Over the Whitcombe Pass* 14 Today fit trampers can journey from the pass to the farmland in Koiterangi in two days. **1988** PICKERING *Hills* 5 Who were the first trampers? The first person who carried a swag and did it for pleasure and not for its own sake? **1995** ANDERSON *House Guest* 71 The limpid call of the bellbird delighted her as did the tramper-friendly fantails.

2. In special collocations: **trampers' biscuit**, orig. hikers' biscuit, a hard nutritious biscuit; **trampers' hut**, a back-country whare or shelter for members of tramping clubs and others.

1939 *Tararua Tramper* Oct. 4 [Advt] The Star Stores..Specialises in concentrated foods, **trampers biscuits**, etc. **1951** DUFF *Shepherd's Calendar* (1961) 25 It is true that this is primarily a **trampers' hut**.

tramperess: see TRAMPER 1.

tramping, vbl. n.

1. Extensive recreational walking in rough country, carrying food and necessary equipment on one's back.

1919 [see tramping club 2 b below]. **1928** *Tararua Tramper* Nov. 2 They felt that they had been out tramping. **1959** McLINTOCK *Descr. Atlas* 74 New Zealanders are a people who take full advantage of these open spaces for all manner of recreational activity, including..shooting and fishing, and tramping and mountaineering. **1966** TURNER *Eng. Lang. Austral. & NZ* 160 *Tramping* (called *bushwalking* in Australia). **1976** McDERMOTT *Lost & Found NZ* 15 There are simply sensational hikes in NZ of every description. New Zealanders say 'tramping'. **1985** McGILL *G'day*

Country 170 'Best country in the world.' 'Eh?' 'For tramping. Beautiful walks and always a hut.'

2. a. In *attrib*. use.

1928 *Tararua Tramper* Nov. 3 To help our members in the selection of really serviceable..tramping gear, a special sub-committee has been appointed. **1934** MARKS *Memories* 192 This was brought home to me very bitterly once in a tramping expedition. **1949** *Tararua Tramper* July 7 A small amount of work remains to be done on this track..to make available to all a large block of tramping country. **1980** MANTELL *Murder or Three* 155 Tramping gear instead of business clothes... Had a tramping pack ready just in case... He was always going off on tramping trips.

b. Special Comb. **tramping boots**, stout boots specially prepared for tramping over rough country; **tramping club**, an organization or sports club whose members engage in extensive recreational back-country expeditions on foot.

1935 *Tararua Tramper* Nov. 3 All-wool first grade blankets..**Tramping Boots** 24/6, Khaki Shirts. [The first use of the term in these long-running advts from Army Stores.] **1952** *Tararua Tramper* Dec. 7 [Advt] Tramping Boots All the *Best Boots* by the following makers:- *Trojan—Sargoods—King Leo—Obrien*. **1985** McGILL *G'day Country* 169 Smoked lens glasses, bush shirt, shorts, tramping boots. **1919** *Evening Post* (Wellington) 5 Aug. 10 The Tararua **Tramping Club** held its adjourned meeting last week when a draft constitution and set of rules were submitted and adopted. **1931** *Tararua Tramper* Nov. 3 Events are open to all members of tramping clubs. **1935** GUTHRIE *Little Country* (1937) 319 After the band came the Tem Boy Scouts..and the members of the Tem Tramping Club. **1946** GREIG *Tararua Story* 13 The public meeting held on July 3, 1919..resulted in the foundation of the Tararua Tramping Club. **1951** *Tararua Tramper* Aug. 2 The word 'tramping' is not included in the names of Australian clubs, where the term 'bush walkers' is used. Nor is it used in Britain, where 'hikers' is the popular term. **1958** *Tararua* Sept. 28 First there is the word *tramp* itself... The Club in 1919 was the first in New Zealand and probably the first in the world to take the name of *tramping club*, and by its usage and activities has played a considerable part in establishing the term. **1965** GILLHAM *Naturalist in NZ* 187 Eventually I was persuaded..that 'gentle stroll of ten miles..' was as typical a tramping club day as any. **1988** PICKERING *Hills* 6 The first tramping club was formed in 1919 and many more followed in the twenties.

tramp metal. [Cf. OED *tramp* (in) v.² Sc. *Obs*. rare trans. to steep, to soak.] A metal whose salts are soluble and able to invade porous rock.

1957 *NZ Geogr. Soc. Rec.* 24 15 Uranium is soluble, even more so than copper, which is commonly known as 'tramp metal', and consequently uranium salts have the ability to move through rocks provided they are porous. **1958** *Weekly News* (Auckland) 10 Sept. 4 Uranium is what the old miners used to call 'tramp metal'... What they meant was that it reacts readily with the weak acids in the ground water and the salts of uranium resulting from this reaction are very soluble moving through the space in porous rocks, or the cracks in denser rocks for miles from where they originated.

trannie. [f. *tran*(ssexual + -IE.] A transsexual.

1996 *Evening Post* (Wellington) 14 Aug. 1 Once she had started to live the life of a woman, she encountered opposition because she was a 'trannie'.

transtasman, *a*. Also **trans-Tasman**. Travelling or extending across the Tasman Sea; of a pact, agreement, accord, etc., held or holding between New Zealand and Australia.

TREATY

1938 *The Times* (London) 17 Feb. 13 The flying-boat Centaurus showed her unsuitability for Trans-Tasman traffic. **1966** MARSH *Black Beech and Honeydew* 175 In..1928 the Trans-Tasman steamer sailed..into Cook Strait. **1970** *Te Reo 16* 9 Some of the coastal ships or trans-Tasman vessels were scarcely less regarded. **1987** *Evening Post* (Wellington) 8 Sept. 40 Transtasman rationalisation. Union Shipping has joined forces with the New Zealand Line and the Australian National Line in a rationalisation of transtasman shipping. **1990** *Dominion* (Wellington) 8 May 3 Australian author Thomas Keneally believes closer transtasman economic ties will inevitably lead to political union.

trap. *Obs.* [AND n.¹ 'A survival of Brit. sl. *trap* one whose business it is to 'trap' offenders.' 1812-1978.] A policeman, esp. in *pl*. as **the traps**, the police. (In frequent New Zealand use on the 19th century goldfields, and in early *Truth*: occas. still heard.)

1853 ROCHFORT *Adventures Surveyor in NZ* 72 If he is taken by the 'traps', he will be sent to prison handcuffed to a common felon. **1864** THATCHER *Invercargill Minstrel* 3 The traps I twigged, all got up very nobby, By Mr Weldon their commanding bobby. And Sergeant Chapman, too, I noticed there, Togged up just like a trooper I declare. c**1875** *Trap, Trap in NZ Songster No.3* 62 I'm a Dunedin peeler,... Trap, trap, trap, trap! they calls me trap, But that I never mind. **1905** *Truth* 12 Aug. 1 The imagination can't conceive what would make an average trap blush. **1986** OWEN & PERKINS *Speaking for Ourselves* 65 Apparently Black pulled a doublecross on McRae, and when the traps came through—'traps' being what the police were called at the time—Black did nothing about it.

tray.

1. [AND 1960.] The flat open part of a truck or similar vehicle on which the load is carried.

1940 *Tales Pioneer Women* 290 We had what I think was called a 'station waggon' [on our Otago station], or four-wheeled buggy; the back seat of this was taken off, leaving the front seat unaltered, and behind it the open tray, like a lorry. **1986** BROWN *Weaver's Apprentice* 17 Leaping Lena's [sc. an old truck's] back tray contained only a kerosene tin and a broken fishing grapnel.

2. A utility (truck).

1975 ANDERSON *Men of Milford Road* 190 Beryl Sutherland refers in her story to a trip across The Wilderness with the bridge overseer..in his Ford Utility or 'tray' as it was referred to those in days.

treatment station: see *milk-treatment station* (MILK).

Treaty. Also **tiriti, Tiriti.** [Ma./'tiriti/: Williams Appendix *Tiriti*, treaty; Duval III. 436, 1857.]

1. a. In modern use usu. with init. cap. Ellipt. for the *Treaty of Waitangi*, an understanding, signed and marked on (and after) 6 February 1840, between a representative of the British Crown and certain Maori chiefs. Often *attrib*. Compare DECLARATION OF INDEPENDENCE.

1840 TAYLOR *Journal* 5 Feb. (ATLTS) II. 189 The rough copy of the treaty was sent to me to get copied... I sat up late copying the treaty on parchment and I kept the original draft for my pains. **1840** MATHEW *Journal* 4 Mar. in *Founding of NZ* (1940) 70 Accordingly, [we] sailed down to the place of Rendezvous where the ceremony of signing the Treaty (as it was called) was soon performed. **1840** *Stack to Shortland, Acting Col. Secretary* 23 May in *GBPP House of Commons 1841*

(No.311) 104 I beg to apologize for the very soiled state of the treaty, but the native habits are so filthy it could hardly be avoided. **1868** Taylor *Past & Present NZ* 111 [Maori] fears afterwards were abundantly confirmed by Earl Grey's celebrated despatch to Governor Grey, ordering him to seize the waste lands of the natives, contrary to the express provision of the treaty, which guaranteed all their territorial rights to them. **1891** A Tramp *Casual Ramblings* 31 That famous treaty is as dead as the jumbuck that supplied the parchment for it. The native children rattle the old bones of the dead treaty occasionally. It amuses them, and does us no harm. **1936** Lambert *Pioneering Reminisc. Old Wairoa* 138 The wealth of its carving..will compare favourably with those of the Waitangi meeting-house, contemplated to memorialize the..Treaty centenary celebrations. **1975** *Treaty of Waitangi Act* [preamble] An Act to provide for the observance, and confirmation, of the principles of the Treaty of Waitangi by establishing a Tribunal to make recommendations on claims relating to the practical application of the Treaty and to determine whether certain matters are inconsistent with the principles of the Treaty. **1985** Sherwood *Botanist at Bay* 49 Don't let the *pakehas* brainwash you... All the time we're here I feel guilty because I'm not up north campaigning against the Treaty. **1986** *Listener* 9 Aug. 11 Mr Chapman also raised the interesting question of whether or not the tiriti was abrogated by the 1845–72 Anglo-Maori wars. If these wars were a case of foreign invasion, then the members of those tribes which resisted did lose the rights conferred by the tiriti. **1990** *Dominion Sunday Times* (Wellington) 30 Dec. 8 Liberals of the type generally known as 'bone people'..would have us believe that they alone can interpret the treaty's meaning.

Hence **treatyism** *derog.*, the state or attitude of indiscriminate asserting or claiming rights under the Treaty of Waitangi.

1990 *Dominion Sunday Times* (Wellington) 2 Dec. 12 Under the Lockwood Smith regime school boards will retain the right to push feminism and treatyism if they want to. **1992** *Dominion* (Wellington) 26 Sept. 10 In America during the fifties people who dared stand up and question McCarthyism were vilified... We now have a similar situation emerging called 'treatyism'.

b. *Obs.* Also applied in the 1840s to the various copies of the Treaty circulated for further signatures.

1840 17 Feb. in *TrNZI* (1901) XXXIII. 423 It will be found of interest to give in regular order the printing that was done after the treaty was signed:—Feb. 17 Captain Hobson, R.N.: Compositing and printing 200 copies of treaty, foolscap folio, £1 10s. 6d.; 4½ quires of foolscap paper for above, at 2s., 9s. [from Colenso 'The Signing [etc.]']. **1840** *Hobson to Bunbury* 25 Apr. in *GBPP House of Commons 1841* (No.311) 17 The treaty which forms the base of all my proceedings was signed at Waitangi on the 6th February 1840, by 52 chiefs. This instrument [*sc.* a copy of treaty] I consider to be *de facto* the treaty, and all signatures that are subsequently obtained are merely testimonials of adherence to the original document.

2. Special Comb. **treaty trout** *joc.*, trout taken by Maori, illegally in the eyes of New Zealand law, but allegedly justified by fishing rights given under the Treaty.

1938 Finlayson *Brown Man's Burden* (1973) 22 The sport turned out to be spearing trout... Seeing Henry's wonderment, Moses gave him a sly dig in the ribs. 'These the treaty trout,' he grinned. 'Waitangi, you know, the Maori own all the fish for ever. God bless the Queen!'

tree. In the names of plants having a tree form, see: Fern 2 (20), Flax 8, Fuchsia 2, Grass 2 (40), Karamu 2, Manuka 2 (3), Nettle 2 b, Tussock 3 (12), Tutu 2 (3), and see also Tree daisy, Tree tomato; in the names of animals associated with trees, see: Creeper *n.*¹, Frog *n.*¹ 3, Weta 2 (5), and see also Tree-cricket.

tree-cricket. *Obs.* Weta.
1888 Buller *Birds NZ* I. 12 Rahui informed us that this [manuka grove] was a favourite resort of the Huia when feeding on the weta or tree-cricket. *Ibid.* I. 195 Judge Munro informs me that..he found in [a morepork's] stomach a specimen of the weta-punga, or tree-cricket (*Deinacrida heteracantha*), with a body as large as a magnum-bonum plum. **1896** *TrNZI* XXVIII. 323 [Heading] On a new Species of *Deinacrida* or *Forest-cricket from Nelson*... I have the pleasure of exhibiting..a perfectly new species of..orthopterous insects known as Wetas or Tree-crickets.

tree daisy. Daisy tree.
1929 *Tararua Tramper* Oct. 2 On the outskirts of the forest multitudes of tree-daisy, *Olearia rani*, promise a wonderful display of bloom. **1951** Levy *Grasslands of NZ* (1970) 87 Such species as..five finger, patete, toru, tree daisies, broadleaf. **1966** *Encyclopedia NZ* III. 712 Olearia, tree daisy—akepiro *Olearia furfuracea*... Senecio, tree daisy—puheretaiko *Celmisia* spp., *Senecio* spp. **1988** Dawson *Forest Vines to Snow Tussocks* 103 Accompanying species may be..the 'tree daisies' heketara (*Olearia rani*). **1991** *NZ Gardener* Aug. 29 I expected to find both of the Chatham Island tree daisies, *Olearia chathamica* and *O. semidentata*, growing in homestead gardens.

tree-gum: see Gum 2.

tree tomato. Also occas. early **Queensland tomato** (see quot 1894). *Cyphomandra betacea* (fam. Solanaceae), a small Andean tree with (usu.) a dark red and also in recent cultivars, yellowish, edible fruit, cultivated in frost-free regions of New Zealand; its edible fruit, since 1967 called Tamarillo q.v.

1887 *Auckland Weekly News* 21 May 28 It appears that from Kew, during the last three years, hundreds of packets of seed of the tree tomato have been distributed to various people in the colonies, very favourable accounts having been received of the introduction of the fruit into Southern India, Ceylon and other places. **1894** *Ann. Rep. Dept. Agric.* II. 79 Tree-tomato (*Cyphomandra betacea*). This plant is a native of tropical America, but has been introduced into Jamaica..and other countries, including the Australasian Colonies. A quantity of fruit was this summer sold by Wellington fruiterers under the name of 'Queensland tomato', and quite took the fancy of buyers. **1922** *Auckland Weekly News* 30 Mar. 46 Tree tomatoes sold at 3s 6d to 6s per case. **1936** *Cookery Book of NZ Women's Institutes* 168 Tree Tomato Chutney. Put 2 dozen tree tomatoes in boiling water to remove skins. **1948** *Our Own Country* 10 Other fruits [grown at Kerikeri], of which there are fairly extensive plantings, are Chinese gooseberries and tree tomatoes. **1959** *Listener* 8 May 22 Tree Tomato Sauce. Eight pounds tree tomatoes, [etc.]. **1967** *Orchardist* Feb. 23 On February 1, 1967, the name tamarillo officially replaced tree tomato. **1972** Gee *MY Father's Den* 83 For household use we had..a small grove of tree tomatoes (tamarillos today). **1982** Burton *Two Hundred Years of NZ Food* 141 New Zealanders always used to know the tamarillo by the rather uninspired name of 'tree tomato'. **1991** *NZ Geographic* Apr.–June 58 The former name [*sc.* of tamarillo] 'tree tomato', was considered inappropriate for use overseas where people buying the fruits for the first time might expect them to taste like tomatoes.

trembling Bob. [See OED *trembling* c, *trembling beef. Obs.*, 1806: *bob* perh. from *bob(by) veal*.] A kind of jellied or potted beef.
1917 Miller *Econ. Tech. Cook. Book* 67 Trembling Bob 1 Shin of Beef..1 Pig's Cheek..Salt and Pepper.. Boil slowly until tender..fill moulds and basins. Turn out when cold.

Trents, *n. pl.* WW1. See quot. 1918. See also Dink *n.* 1.
1915 Gray, Norman *MS Papers 4134* (ATLMS) 19 Nov. The NZ Rifle Brigade, alias the 'Trents' is now known as the Keystone Brigade. **1918** *Quick March* 1 July 26 Sir,—'The Gosling'..warbles a satirical ditty on the Dinkums. (Applause.) Now listen. As an 'Extra Unit' we hit Trentham like any mudlarks in the early winter of 1915. We were dubbed, inter alia:—The Trentham Battalion, Trentham Regiment, 'Trents,' Lord Liverpool's Own..The Dinkums, and The Dinks. **1933** Scanlan *Tides of Youth* 267 With the formation of the Rifle Brigade, or the Trents, as they were affectionately called, for they were trained at Trentham [Military Camp], the shortage of men became acute.

trevalli, var. Trevally.

trevally. Also **trevalli**. [OED 1825; AND 1871.]
1. a. *Pseudocaranx dentex* (fam. Carangidae), a marine fish, often common in coastal waters of central and northern New Zealand, and occurring elsewhere. See also Araara, Yellowtail 2 (4). [*Note*] *Cavalli*, an older synonymous form, is found in occas. early New Zealand references.
1872 Hutton & Hector *Fishes NZ* 110 The Arara of the Maoris, or the Trevally or Cavalli of the fishermen (*Caranx georgianus*), is a highly esteemed fish. **1892** *NZ Official Handbook* 167 Of the sea-fishes that are used as food in New Zealand, we have..the hapuku, tarakihi, trevally. **1902** Drummond & Hutton *Nature in NZ* 71 The snapper, the mullet, and the trevally are essentially northern. **1918** *NZJST* I. 271 Small quantities of trevally appear for sale on several days during each of the summer months. **1938** Hyde *Nor Yrs Condemn* 141 If you take home a string of trevalli to your old lady, she's going to fall on your neck. **1947** [see Araara]. **1959** Middleton *The Stone* 13 Around the wharf piles where barnacles and mussels clung..flitted the little pakirikiri..and down in the..shadows swam the trevalli. **1972** Doak *Fishes* 37 In summer the trevally is most conspicuous in huge, close-packed schools, hundreds of backs humping above the water as euphausiid shrimps and other plankton are snapped up. **1981** Wilson *Fisherman's Bible* 261 Trevally. Abundant inhabitant of our warmer waters.

b. *s. South Island.* Warehou 2 (1), esp. a small warehou.
1886 Sherrin *Handbook Fishes* 99 The fish known as trevalli in the Dunedin market is a different fish, allied to the warehou. **1913** [see Warehou 1]. **1921** *NZJST* IV. 120 Seriolella brama... *Warehou*. Commonly sold as 'trevally' in Christchurch and Dunedin. **1956** Graham *Treasury NZ Fishes* 234 For some unknown reason small Warehou sold on the Dunedin Fish Market and in the shops of Dunedin were called Trevally and the same fish with the same markings when grown to eighteen or twenty-four inches in length were known as Warehou. *Ibid.* 235 The mistake of calling the young Warehou by the name of Trevally is not made in the North Island, as both species are caught there; only odd Trevally are caught south of Cook Strait. **1967** Moreland *Marine Fishes* 44 Warehou [*Seriolella brama*]... In southern waters the name trevally is sometimes used.

2. With a modifier: **Archey's trevally** [f. the name of Sir Gilbert *Archey* (1890–1974) former director, Auckland War Memorial Museum], and **school trevally**, names for forms of *Pseudocaranx dentex* in its surface schooling phase.

1938 *TrRSNZ* LXVIII. 410 Trevally (school trevally). **1947** POWELL *Native Animals of New Zealand* 67 School Trevally is a common school fish in North Auckland waters. **1957** PARROTT *Sea Angler's Fishes* 79 Archey's Trevally *Usacaranx archeyi*. **1981** WILSON *Fisherman's Bible* 265 Trevally, Archey's. A rare trevally distinguished by bands down the side of its body. Discovered in the Hauraki Gulf... It possesses smaller, and more numerous scutes along the end of the lateral line than the school trevally.

Triangle Dinks: see DINK *n.* 1 b.

tribe. [Spec. use of *tribe*, a community formed from an aggregate of families.] IWI. (Also **sub-tribe,** HAPU.)

1822 MARSDEN 17 Jan. in Elder *Marsden's Lieutenants* (1934) 183 I approve of your itinerating amongst the natives. Nothing will tend more to increase your influence amongst them than your visiting them from tribe to tribe. **1839** SIR GEORGE GIPPS *Proclamation* 14 Aug. in Rutherford *Sel. Documents* (1949) 3c I do further proclaim..that all purchases of land in any part of New Zealand which may be made..from any of the native chiefs or tribes of these islands..will be considered null and void. **1840** Mar. in Wilkes *US Exploring Exped.* (1852) I. 306 It is remarkable that every tribe has a name peculiar to itself, and distinct from the district which it inhabits. **1856** [see IWI a]. **1863** MANING *Old NZ* 52 And then my tribe, (I find I am already beginning to get Maorified.) **1875** HOGG *Lays & Rhymes* 315 They've saved the fame of the British name, In this queer war with the Maori tribes. **1904** [see IWI a]. **1949** BUCK *Coming of Maori* 333 The smallest sociological unit is the biological family, which the Maoris termed *whanau*, derived from *whanau*, to give birth... The term *hapu* (pregnancy) was used to denote this expanded family group for it expressed the idea of birth from common ancestors... The term *iwi* (bone) was brought into current use to include all the *hapu* descended from common ancestors and thus related to each other by a blood tie. To denote the groupings in English, the *iwi* has been termed tribe and the *hapu* a sub-tribe. **1958, 1979,** [see IWI a]. **1989** *Gisborne Herald* 1 Feb. 1 Mr Ngata was from the Whanau-a-Karuwai, Whanau-a-Rakairoa and Te Aitanga-a-Materoa hapu (sub-tribe) of Ngati Porou. **1996** *Dominion* (Wellington) 22 June 9 Tribes name forest partner. Maori tribal consortium Te Ama Ltd and Carter Holt Harvey said..they had formed a partnership to bid for Forestry Corporation... The tribes are considered vital partners.

Hence **tribespeople**.

1906 *TrNZI* XXXVIII. 1 For, as far as the Native Land Court records run, the Natives always proved the title of their tribe to the mana over certain land by matters relating to the feeding of the tribespeople. **1988** *Press* (Christchurch) 30 Aug. 6 He failed to fulfil the terms of the agreement reached between a previous agent, H.T. Kemp, and Ngai Tahu tribespeople at Akaroa in 1848.

tribute. Mining. [f. *tribute* orig. used in Cornish tin-mining: see OED *n.* 3.] See quot. 1892.

1886 *NZ Herald* (Auckland) 1 June 6 Tributes were let to several parties, whose contributions to the company during the year amounted to £153 19s. 6d. The receipts showed calls to be £1573 4s., tributers £153 19s. 6d., sundries (such as crushing, interest, and overdraft) £47 9s. 6d.; total, £1774 13s. **1892** PYKE *Gold-Miners' Guide* 10 'Tribute' means payment of a portion or percentage of the proceeds of a mine to the owner by the persons working the same. **1952** LYON *Faring South* 168 As the quartz mines began to decline in output and could no longer pay a large wage sheet, it became the custom to let them on tribute, by which parties of men were given the right to mine and raise quartz from the resultant crushing, of which a proportionate share of the gold went to the company. **1972** *Press* (Christchurch) 2 Nov. 5 Their [sc. mineowners'] offer [in 1928] to allow the mine to be worked under tribute (which it was for several years) was bitterly opposed by the unions which claimed that the co-operative system meant the speeding of production at the expense of conditions. **1986** DEVANNY *Point of Departure* 11 Dad..had used to dolly the stolen gold for the men on tribute, amassing by this means a large collection of nuggets.

Hence **tributer**, see quot. 1892.

1886 [see above]. **1892** PYKE *Gold-Miners' Guide* 10 A tributer has a lien or first claim equal to half the current rate of wages in the district, but not exceeding *twenty shillings* per week, upon the earnings of the mine, the result of the labours of the said tributer. **1909** *TrNZI* XLI. 92 Mining at Boatman's has declined very much, and work is now limited to intermittent tributers and occasional prospectors. **1967** MAY *West Coast Gold Rushes* 528 Tributer: one who contracts to work a claim for nominal wages and a fixed share of the profits, or for a percentage of the profits only.

trig.

1. [Used elsewhere but recorded earliest in NZ.] *Ellipt.* for *trig station* (see 2 below).

1862 CHUDLEIGH *Diary* 19 Aug. (1950) 54 Made a plant of some 60 yds. of rope near 22 trig pole. **1901** *TrNZI* XXXIII. 492 In these colonies especially the proportion of land occupiers and owners is so large that most of us are directly or indirectly interested in 'section pegs', 'trigs', and such-like, while at Home the expression of this interest is practically limited to the impersonal 'beating the bounds of the parish.' **1955** WILSON *Land of My Children* 71 A flying survey of the hill country was taking place and the 'Eldest Brother' [a hill] had been selected as a trig station. The trig twinkled and aroused curiosity. **1960** MASTERS *Back-Country Tales* 136 I believe the trig rotted away at ground level and has now disappeared altogether.

Hence **trig** *v. trans.*, to survey and erect trig stations in (country).

1861 *McLean Papers* (ATLTS) XX. 87 A Trig Station erected by Captain Smith when he was trigging the valley.

2. Special Comb. **trig (trig.) station** (also occas. in full **trigonometrical station**, see quot. 1849 below) [abbrev. of *trigonometrical station*: used elsewhere but recorded earliest in NZ], a survey reference point on high ground used in triangulation, usu. in the form of a pyramidal wooden structure.

[**1849** *Torlesse Papers* (1958) 102 I walked with Cass over the plains fixing on trigonometrical stations, at Courtenay..&c.] **1849** *Ibid.* (1958) 103 I and Cass attempted to observe angles to trig. stations from the base line. **1861** *McLean Papers* (ATLTS) XX. 87 Mr Swainson informs me that the Trig Station pulled down was not the one erected by him. **1874** WILSON *Diary* 20 Apr. in Wierzbicka *Wilson Family* (1973) 178 A stranger immediately upon coming to New Zealand spots the 'Trig' stations and asks what they are. **1885** *TrNZI* XVII. 425 The cliffs in this bay..extend to the end of the range below the Taupiri trig. station (585 feet). **1897** *Ibid.* XXIX. 346 From the trig.-station on the summit we struck southwards to the coast towards Herekino. **1904** *NZ Illustr. Mag.* Sept. 410 The sight of a trig station effectually dispelled the illusion. **1925** BEST *Tuhoe* 98 They..ascended Puke-nui-o-raro (a hill, a Trig. station one) and made a plant of some 60 yds. of rope near 22 trig pole. **1955** *BJ Cameron Collection* (TS July) trig-station (n) A wooden erection in the form of an open pyramid on prominent hilltops to serve as a survey mark. **1964** DEMPSEY *Little World Stewart Is.* 53 I'm leaning against a trig station.

triggerfish. [Spec. use of a general name for fishes having a trigger-like spine on the back which can be locked into a vertical position at will.] In New Zealand, usu. LEATHERJACKET 1 (*Parika scaber*). See also KOKIRI *n.*[1]

1927 SPEIGHT et al. *Natural History of Canterbury* 202 In the Leather jackets or Trigger fish..the anterior dorsal fin is reduced to a couple of spines, the first of which is very large and is the characteristic 'trigger'. **1938** *TrRSNZ* LXVIII. 418 Leather-jacket (trigger-fish, file-fish). **1956** [see LEATHERJACKET 1]. **1967** MORELAND *Marine Fishes* 24 Leatherjacket... The names filefish and triggerfish are sometimes used, but more properly belong to a related group of tropical fishes. The Maori name kokiri is still in use. **1970, 1982** [see LEATHERJACKET 1].

trim, *v. Kauri logging.* To clear stranded (kauri) logs and debris from a creek after a drive. Also as *vbl. n.*, and **trimmer** *n.*, one who clears such logs.

1953 REED *Story of Kauri* 151 Trimming creeks after drives. *Ibid.* 214 After that came the 'trimming'—jacking stranded logs into the bed of the creek, and clearing away debris which might impede the next drive. *Ibid.* 248 When a drive goes down it always leaves numerous logs behind on the banks, and the 'trimmers' have to jack and roll these into the creek bed again, ready to catch the next drive. **1969** MOORE *Forest to Farm* 41 The operation of jacking the logs stranded on the banks back into the stream-bed was known as 'trimming'.

trimmer, *n.*[1] [f. Brit. dial. *trimmer* anything of superior quality: see EDD (4); AND 1878.] Anything or anyone of note; also used ironically.

1937 *Tomorrow* III. 310 A trimmer, wasn't it. **1943** MARSH *Colour Scheme* 92 'Running well, isn't she?' asked Dikon. 'She's a trimmer,' said Simon. **1953** 14–16 M A2 Thames DHS 8 Trimmer [M10]. **1965** WILSON *Outcasts* 105 Jess, I'm proud of you. You're a trimmer. **1970** *Listener* 12 Oct. 13 Dave, you're a trimmer. You'll go places. Take a top seat. **1988** MCGILL *Dict. Kiwi Slang* 128 *you're a trimmer!* a compliment or a curse... 'What did you move that for? I had them in the right order. Gawd, you're a trimmer.'

trimmer, *n.*[2] *Freezing works.* One who cuts 'points' off brisket, and trims skin from carcasses.

1951 May 17 Feilding Freezing Works, p.c. Colin Gordon. After *plucking*, a *trimmer* cuts *points* off the top of the brisket. **1976** MORRIESON *Pallet on Floor* 95 The trimmers who lined the table, even the foreman who supervised the spraying of the skins, were gone.

trimmings, *pl. Farming.* The inferior parts of a fleece removed during skirting. Cf. PIECE 1.

1897 WRIGHT *Station Ballads* 34 What's the blooming use of talking!—Ain't that sheep as good as most? Trimmings! What's the good of trimmings? Mighty lot of wool you've lost! **1938** BURDON *High Country* 84 The sheep they shore were not so well woolled on the belly and carried less wool on the points than they do now, so that fewer short blows were required to take off the trimmings. **1949** NEWTON *High Country Days* 51 Broom in hand, the fleecie would dash back down the board to sweep up the 'locks' and 'trimmings'. **1955** BOWEN *Wool Away* 3 Wrinkles, dense wool, trimmings all have a bearing on shearing.

trog. *Tramping.* [Abbrev. and transf. use of *troglodyte* cave-dweller.] A natural rock shelter.

1958 *Tararua* Sept. 28 For shelter, hillmen may seek a *trog*, a large overhanging boulder or bluff giving shelter like a cave. These are most likely to be found in the south-west of the South Island, so presumably the term originated with those who frequent those parts. *Troglodyte*, a race or tribe dwelling in caves, suggests the origin. The word has been known to trampers for eight or nine years. **1971** *Listener* 19 Apr. 56 They cooeed out, and while he skinned the spiker they found a possie in a bit of a trog and boiled-up.

troll. Also occas. **trol**, **trull**, perh. indicating an uncertainty of derivation as well as of pronunciation. [Abbrev. of *trollop*: AND 1963; cf. OED *trull*.] A trollop, often used in a weakened sense as a mildly derogatory or dismissive term for a woman. Cf. TART.

1947 DAVIN *For Rest of Our Lives* 344 The room at the pub, the whisky.., the terrible hangovers.., the terrible trulls. **1952** WILSON *Julien Ware* 222 'You're a swine, Julien Ware,' he heard her say... 'For Christ's sake, Stella, shut up!' he shouted. 'You sound like a bloody troll.' **1959** SLATTER *Gun in My Hand* 205 Say, have you seen that trol in the blue mocker. The dark one with the long ear-rings. **1964** FRANCES *Johnny Rapana* 67 A pro. A troll. A prostitute. **1984** WILSON *S. Pacific Street* 55 'You alone?' she asked. 'Who did you think I'd be with?' 'Don't know. Some trull.'

trolley, *n.* Also **trolly.**

1. a. A flat truck for carrying logs on a bush tramline. Also *attrib.*

c1900–20 in Henderson *Friends In Chains* (1961) 189 Trolley: Bush or mine flat truck. **1923** MALFROY *Small Sawmills* 39 Trollies..Usually four-wheeled vehicles with a single bolster; run in pairs on tramlines—one at each end of the log to be hauled.

b. Special Comb. **trolly-line**, *tramline* (TRAM 2); **trollyman**, see quot.

1955 WILSON *Land of My Children* 23 He led the way along the mill tramline—wooden rails laid on sleepers and ballasted with red sawdust. The bush had been hacked and smashed to build the **trolly-line**. **1923** MALFROY *Small Sawmills* 28 The **trollyman** will have charge of the [mill] trollies.

2. A go-cart, often elaborately made. Also *attrib.*

1920 p.c. R. Mason. Auckland & Pukekohe. R. Mason notes that when the *soap-box derby* was introduced from the US after WW2, the name quickly changed to *trolley derby*. **1934** LEE *Children of Poor* (1949) 146 I stole a box. Soon I had a trolley. I stole boards from the timber yard and built a wooden hut for my gang in the backyard. **1959** SHADBOLT *New Zealanders* (1986) 119 Then he slowed, seeing suddenly the neat homes.., two boys racketing a trolley. **1968** SLATTER *Pagan Game* 231 He liked to be called Tank, a name which derived from a trolley he had made, shaped like a racing car, in which he pelted down Reservoir Hill. **1987** *Metro* (Auckland) May 50 Stockcars on Saturday nights at the Epsom Showgrounds and trolley racing down the steep hill on Otahuri Crescent. My left hand still has an ugly scar sustained from a spectacular trolley-racing pile-up.

trooper. *Hist.* [Transf. use of *trooper* a cavalry soldier: AND 1840.] An armed, mounted constable. Cf. ARMED CONSTABULARY.

1864 [see TRAP]. **1864** *Gold Digger's Notes* (1950) 51 My mate..then heard of a job at the camp at the Arrow.., putting up quarters for the commissioner, troopers, etc. **1873** PYKE *Wild Will Enderby* (1889, 1974) III. viii 98 The divil a one, sir, barrin' the folk going up and down the road, and the trooper..that brought the ordhers. **1882** POTTS *Out in Open* 10 Here lounges a tall dapper trooper..in his quiet-looking uniform, wearing his small forage cap cocked so much aside. **1914** PFAFF *Diggers' Story* 134 I once went to Charleston..in company with the Gold Escort, and it was a picture to see those fine troopers turn out, 'armed to the teeth', as the saying is. **1924** *Otago Witness* (Dunedin) 10 June 68 A mounted trooper in glittering uniform was espied riding down the bridle-track from the saddle of Mount Pisa. **1937** AYSON *Thomas* 36 Armed troopers were guarding the coach and its load of gold. **1947-48** BEATTIE *Pioneer Recolls.* (1956) 18 The gold escort..usually consisted of a banker with the gold and two armed troopers or mounted police. **1976** VEITCH *Clyde on Dunstan* 19 The first Gold Escort left Clyde for Dunedin on 3 October 1862..under the supervision of Major Bracken and three troopers.

tropic bird. In New Zealand usu. **red-tailed tropic bird**; AMOKURA.

1891 *TrNZI* XXIII. 223 Tropic bird (*Phaeton rubricauda*, Bod.). **1904, 1927** [see AMOKURA]. **1917** WILLIAMS *Dict. Maori Lang.* 10 *Amokura*, n. *Phaet[h]on rubricauda*, red-tailed tropic bird. **1941** [see AMOKURA]. **1946** *JPS* LV. 159 *tawake*, a bird, the red-tailed tropic bird, see amokura. **1955, 1966** Western Pacific Red-tailed Tropic Bird [see AMOKURA]. **1985** [see AMOKURA]. **1990** *Checklist Birds NZ* 76 *Phaethon rubricauda*..Red-tailed Tropicbird.

troppo. *Orig. WW2* (Pacific theatre). [f. *trop*(ic + -o: AND 1941.] Mentally disturbed (as, fancifully, from 'sun-stroke'), esp. in the phr. **to go troppo.**

1944 *Korero* (AEWS Background Bulletin) 17 July 24 'Sand-happy', with its suggestion of 'slap-happy', may be compared with the Pacific 'troppo', both pithily indicating the impact of alien climes on some New Zealand temperaments. **1964** DAVIS *Watersiders* 133 But you know what Blue's like, goes a bit troppo when he sights game. **1976** WILSON *Pacific Star* 184 These jokers were victims of what you might call despair, a wartime tropical malaise. We said they'd gone troppo. **1986** *Sunday Star* (Auckland) 17 Aug. C2 He seemed happy enough with Garnier's explanation that he wanted to see more of Fiji and was going on a drive. As it was pitch black outside, Harman concluded Garnier had gone troppo and didn't pursue the matter. **1991** *Dominion Sunday Times* (Wellington) 1 Dec. 24 Going troppo can drive others mad.

trot.

1. [AND 1911.] A succession of heads in the game of two-up, esp. in the phr. **to throw (do) a trot.**

1917 do a trot [see SPIN *n.* 1 b]. **1937** LEE *Civilian into Soldier* 99 Sometimes a man would succeed daringly, doubling up and breaking the ring with a long run of heads, 'throwing a trot'. **1944** BRUNO *Desert Daze* 20 Some..who had..struck a trot of 'heads' at two-up.

2. Any run of luck.

1988 McGILL *Dict. Kiwi Slang* 115 *trot* luck, usually in 'bad trot' or 'good trot', mostly sport use; probably from two-up game, where a trot is a sequence of heads; eg 'It's ages since I had a decent trot.'

trots, *n. pl.* [Spec. use of the *pl.* of *trot* a trotting race: AND 'used elsewhere but recorded earliest in Aust.', 1890.] As **the trots**, a race meeting for trotters and pacers harness racing. Cf. GALLOPS.

1900 *Otago Witness* (Dunedin) 10 May 38 [Heading] Tahuna Trots. **1909** *Truth* 9 Feb 2 The Club's trots are held on a picturesque course at Sockburn. **1928** *NZ Free Lance* (Wellington) 4 Jan. 18 We chatted brightly about the weather, the 'trots' and what not. **1942** WHIM-WHAM *Verses* 30 Some People I have met find Lots Of Entertainment at the Trots. **1959** SLATTER *Gun In My Hand* 51 If you're a friend of his ya oughta know he would be goin to the trots. **1963** CASEY *As Short a Spring* 99 I can't stand races either. Call it a sport?..Stick to the trots, that's what I say. **1987** VIRTUE *Redemption of Elsdon Bird* (1988) 54 He was a boozer and loved the trots, went every Saturday. **1992** *Dominion Sunday Times* (Wellington) 8 Nov. 22 Those who want the reality of racing should try the night trots.

trout. [Transf. use of *trout* a fish of the genus *Salmo*: AND 1833.]

1. Any of several native fish (esp. freshwater fish of fam. Galaxiidae) resembling in some way the European trout.

[1777 FORSTER *Voyage Round the World* I. 159 He came to a fine lake of fresh water..he observed no other inhabitant in it than a small species of fish (*esox*), without scales, resembling a little trout; its colour was brown, and mottled with yellowish spots.] **1845** in Deans *Pioneers of Canterbury* 28 Sept. (1937) 93 There is a sort of fish called trout in some of the rivers, but they are the worst fish ever I ate; they are never almost seen in the daytime. **1857** HURSTHOUSE *NZ* I. 122 The spotted Kokopu, called trout..abounds in every brook. **1873** *TrNZI* V. 278 Kokopu or Para... This is the 'trout' of the first New Zealand settlers in the early gold rushes. **1890** *Otago Witness* (Dunedin) 27 Feb. 18 The kokopu of the Maoris is the well known fish found in streams and from its appearance often called the New Zealand trout. **1903** *TrNZI* XXXV. 314 Large fish locally called 'trout'..were sometimes cast up on the beaches of the great inland lakes of Otago in the early days before trout were introduced. **1922** THOMSON *Naturalisation of Animals and Plants* 187 The kokopu..was sometimes popularly called trout.

2. With a modifier: **barred, bull, Maori, mountain, native, rock, sea.** See also *treaty trout* (TREATY 2).

(1) **barred trout.** *Galaxias postvectis.*

1899 *TrNZI* XXXI. 89 *Galaxias postvectis*... This species is not in full roe until December, and is generally called in Westland 'barred trout'. **1939** *TrRSNZ* LXIX. 230 The correct name of the Mountain Trout or Black Kokopu is *Galaxias argenteus*..and the Barred Trout or Kokopu is apparently the young, with conspicuous markings. **1990** McDOWALL *NZ Freshwater Fishes* 100 *Galaxias postvectis*..Shortjawed kokopu..Clarke (1899) said it was called barred trout in Westland.

(2) **bull trout**, see BULL TROUT.

(3) **Maori trout**. Either of *Galaxias fasciatus* or *G. argenteus*, KOKOPU.

1956 GRAHAM *Treasury NZ Fishes* 118 Minnow or Whitebait (Inanga)... The early settlers called it Maori Trout, Native Trout, Rock Trout and Minnow. But it is not a Trout... While the name Trout is not correct, it is and will always be known as such by farmers and naturalists. **1978** Maori Trout [see KOKOPU 2 (1)]. **1984** McDOWALL *NZ Whitebait Book* 13 Much less common is the banded kokopu (*Galaxias fasciatus*) sometimes known as the Maori trout or native trout. *Ibid.* 14 The fourth species..is the giant kokopu (*Galaxias argenteus*), again commonly known as the Maori trout or native trout. **1990** McDOWALL *NZ Freshwater Fishes* 89 The giant kokopu..was the first galaxiid discovered, being collected by naturalists visiting New Zealand with Captain Cook in 1773... Common names..include Maori trout, bull trout and native trout.

(4) **mountain trout**. [AND *Galaxias* spp., 1882.] *Galaxias* spp. usu. *G. brevipinnis*. See also KOARO, KOKOPU.

1840 *NZ Journal* Aug. 29 I. 205 We also have some mountain trout..; the surveyors..discovered a stream..which..was stocked with trout, on which they made a hearty meal. **1842** Gillingham *Letter* 2 Mar. in Rutherford *Establishment of New Plymouth* (1940) 203 The town [of New Plymouth] is situated between two small rivers, both of which abound with mountain trout and eels. **1899** *TrNZI* XXXI. 87 *Galaxias kokopu*..The Westland people generally call this species the 'mountain trout'. **1929** BEST *Fishing Methods* 183 The *kokopu* seems to be found in all districts..It is sometimes called the mountain trout. **1939** *TrRSNZ* LXIX. 230 The correct name of the Mountain Trout or Black Kokopu is *Galaxias argenteus*. **1956** GRAHAM *Treasury NZ Fishes* 114 Kokopu *Galaxias fasciatus*... It is often called Mountain Trout but it is also found practically at sea level, just above high-tide mark. **1965** GILLHAM *Naturalist in NZ* 147 The tiny fish..were the young of the inanga—'mountain trout', one of the fishers called them. **1990** MCDOWALL *NZ Freshwater Fishes* 104 *Galaxias brevipinnis*..Koaro..Mostly it is called the mountain trout, but it has also been called lowland galaxias, so obviously there is some conflict in perspective.

(5) **native trout**. Freshwater *Galaxias* spp., esp. *G. argenteus* or *G. fasciatus*, KOKOPU.

1927 SPEIGHT et al. *Natural History of Canterbury* 196 The species of *Galaxias* may broadly be divided into the small, sea-running whitebait minnows.., the larger native 'trout' (*G. fasciatus* and allied species), which probably breed inland. **1939** *TrRSNZ* LXIX. 215 Among fishes, the 'native trout' (*Galaxias fasciatus*). **1940** native trout [see KOKOPARA]. **1952** LYON *Faring South* 79 To wade up the clear gully stream in pursuit of the small koura, or crayfish, and any native trout or kokopu we could spear. **1966** *Encycl. NZ* II. 235 Sometimes the banded and giant galaxias are called 'native trout', but they are not related to the trout. **1990** MCDOWALL *NZ Freshwater Fishes* 89 *Galaxias argenteus*... Common names for this fish include Maori trout, bull trout, and native trout. *Ibid.* 94 *Galaxias fasciatus*... Like the giant kokopu, the banded kokopu is sometimes known as Maori trout or native trout.

(6) **rock trout**. *Galaxias argenteus*. Poss. also applied to TORRENTFISH. See also PARA *n.*[1]

1842 GRAY *Fauna* in Dieffenbach *NZ* (1843) II. 219 *Galaxias alepidotus*... Named by the natives of Dusky Bay 'He-para,' and by Cook's sailors 'Rock-trout'. **1867** GUNTHER *Ann. and Mag. of Natural History* Nov. in Hutton & Hector *Fishes NZ* (1872) 128 The settlers of at least some parts of New Zealand have dignified the larger kinds [of *Galaxias*] with the name of 'Trout', or 'Rock Trout'. **1945** BEATTIE *Maori Place-names Canterbury* 63 The panako is the rock trout, and is nearly extinct. It looks like the kokopara in shape, but it is black in colour. **1956** GRAHAM *Treasury NZ Fishes* 118 Minnow or Whitebait (Inanga) *Austrocobitus attenuatus*... The early settlers called it Maori Trout, Native Trout, Rock Trout and Minnow.

(7) **sea trout**. KAHAWAI 1.

1877 *TrNZI* IX. 488 On the 30th, a fine Sea Trout, weighing 10 ½lbs., was caught in the Lower Harbour. **1956** GRAHAM *Treasury NZ Fishes* 241 This fish [sc. kahawai] has a variety of popular names, the most common being that of sea trout. It is sold in the fish retailers' shops as such. **1986** PAUL *NZ Fishes* 92 Known principally by its Maori name, kahawai, in New Zealand and only occasionally (and erroneously, despite its scientific name) as sea trout or salmon. **1990** MCDOWALL *NZ Freshwater Fishes* 275 Kahawai... The Australian common name is sea salmon, while the name sea trout is unfortunately, gaining a small foothold in New Zealand.

3. *fig.* or *transf.* **a.** As **brown trout**, *chocolate fish* (CHOCOLATE 1).

1987 p.c. George Griffiths, Dunedin. 6 Feb. Used by a storekeeper at Portobello on February 6, 1987 for the sweet, 'chocolate fish'.

b. As **trout of blade (steak)** [f. its resemblance in shape to a trout], a roasting piece of blade steak.

1984 17 *National Radio* 11.25 a.m. [Alison Holst, Cookery Host speaks:] Trout of steak or a trout of blade, as we used to call it in Dunedin—a lovely name as it looks rather like a trout.

c. See *fit as a trout* (FIT *a*. 1 b).

truant officer. *Obs.* Occas. **truancy officer**. [US 1872: contrast Brit. *truant inspector*.] An officer (later *attendance officer*) formerly employed by Education Boards to enforce the attendance at school of those children required to attend by law.

1901 *School Attendance Act S* 9 It shall be lawful for Education Boards to appoint Truant Officers; and any Truant Officer..may lay informations, make complaints, conduct prosecutions, and take all other proceedings under this act. **1920** *Educ. Amendment Act* 64/515 All persons holding office..as truant officers shall be deemed to have been appointed as Attendance Officers. **1938** HYDE *Godwits Fly* (1970) 26 Augusta, the Truant Officer, Mr Forrest and John were all getting weary of the change of schools war. **1991** *Dominion* (Wellington) 3 Jan. 2 Truancy officers no longer exist. Jim Taia, a former Auckland truancy officer, cannot put a figure on the numbers these days but says many pupils are avoiding school.

trucker. *Coalmining.* [Spec. use of *trucker* a labourer who uses a truck or trolley: AND 1882.] An underground mineworker who shifts trucks of coal.

1901 *NZ Illustr. Mag.* IV. 613 Then there is the wheeler or trucker. Some wheelers push the trucks with their hands, others with their heads. **1963** PEARSON *Coal Flat* 27 'Why do you think we pay you truckers threepence a box?' the other asked. **1984** BEARDSLEY *Blackball 08* 128 As you dug your way in the rails followed, enabling the truckers to push empty tubs right up to where you were working.

truckie. [f. *truck*(driver + -IE: AND 1958.] One who drives heavy trucks for a living; a truckdriver.

1960 KEINZLY *Tangahano* 23 I hope our truckie hasn't any ideas about sitting down to lunch. **1970** *Listener* 21 Dec. 8 Another time you'll thumb a truck—truckies will generally stop for you. **1984** *Sunday News* (Auckland) 19 Aug. 2 While travelling north on the Desert Road, a reader was interested in the stencilled sign on the back of a large truck: If Dolly Parton were taxed like a Kiwi truckie, she would be flat-busted. **1991** *Dominion* (Wellington) 9 Nov. 14 The days of goods depots up and down the country have gone and their work is now being carried out by, in most cases, the truckies.

true dink(s): see DINK *complement*.

trull, var. TROLL.

trump. [f. *trump* a playing-card ranking above others.] **a.** WW1. In the phr. **the trump of the dump**, anyone in authority.

1935 STRONG in Partridge *Slang Today* 287 He said he had to be careful because the other fellow was the trump of the dump... Although, he said, he was the white-haired boy with the trump he was due for a shake-up... He winked at me when the trump of the dump asked him if he had barbered the spuds for tomorrow's breakfast. **1938** *Press* (Christchurch) (McNab Slang) 2 Apr. 18 [Slang of the N.Z.E.F.] There is a touch of irreverence in 'the trump of the dump,' for O.C., and in 'one-star artist'.

b. [AND 1925.] The boss; one in authority.

1950 *Landfall 14* 7 The trump comes in and calls us gentlemen. *Ibid.* 126 The hoops are on the last cask by 11.45, and the trump calls out all hands to load the last railway wagon.

trumpeter, *n.*[1] [f. the sounds made by the fish when taken out of the water: AND esp. *Latris* spp., 1827.]

1. Any of several large food fish, but esp. *Latris lineata* (fam. Latrididae). See also KOHIKOHI, YELLOWTAIL 2 (2).

c1826–27 BOULTBEE *Journal* (1986) 113 trumpeter fish, gooee gooee. **1858** SHAW *Gallop to Antipodes* 135 Besides cod, there are seals, trumpeter, moki, barracouta, flounders, skate and warihou. **1884** REID *Rambles Golden Coast* 29 Blue-cod, trumpeter and crayfish came up from the depths, and in over the side. **1892** *NZ Official Handbook* 167 The trumpeter, butterfish, and red-cod are confined to the south. **1906** BULLEN *Cruise 'Cachalot'* 328 That [southern] part of New Zealand is famous for a fish something like a bream, but with a longer snout, and striped longitudinally with black and yellow... I..only [know] it by its trivial and local appellation of the 'trumpeter', from the peculiar sound it makes when out of water. **1922** *Auckland Weekly News* 15 June 14 Here, too, are trumpeters striped like a zebra, black and white and blue. **1945** BEATTIE *Maori Place-names Canterbury* 62 Others omitted are the tarakihi, or terakihi, the moki,.. and the ko[h]ekohe (trumpeter). **1953** *Landfall 27* 175 Hapuka hooked like a rock on his line, Trumpeter barked like a sea-dog for his bone, When Antonio fished. **1967** NATUSCH *Animals NZ* 222 [The] trumpeter..is dark olive-green to brown striped with light yellow-lime; its silvery sides gleam with yellow. **1978** *Catch '78* Sept. 15 Trumpeter..Occurs from the Bay of Plenty southwards, most common around South Island.

2. With a modifier: **bastard**, **silver**.

(1) **bastard trumpeter**. *copper moki* (MOKI *n.*[1] 2 (2), *Latridopsis forsteri*).

1898 MORRIS *Austral-English* 21 *Bastard Trumpeter, n.* a fish. In Sydney it is *Latris ciliaris*..which is called *Moki* in New Zealand. **1938** *TrRSNZ* LXVIII. 412 *Latris forsteri*... Bastard trumpeter. **1956** GRAHAM *Treasury NZ Fishes* 259 Bastard Trumpeter *Latridopsis forsteri*... It can be distinguished from the New Zealand Trumpeter by the absence of the three wide longitudinal bands on the upper half of the Bastard Trumpeter. **1972** [see MOKI *n.*[1] 2 (2)]. **1982** AYLING *Collins Guide* (1984) 246 Five species [of trumpeter] are recorded from New Zealand but there appears to be some confusion regarding..the bastard trumpeter *Latridopsis forsteri*.

(2) **silver trumpeter**. *Obs.* A trade name for either of *Congiopodus leucopaecilus* (PIGFISH 2 (2)) or *Callorhinchus milii* (ELEPHANT FISH).

1921 *NZJST* IV. 121 *Congiopodus leucopaecilus*... *Pigfish*; *Puramorua*. Large numbers commonly sold throughout the year in Christchurch under the name of 'silver trumpeter.' *Ibid.* 123 *Callorhynchus milii*... *Elephant-fish*; *Reperepe*. In Christchurch large numbers are sold under the name of 'silver trumpeter.' **1956** GRAHAM *Treasury NZ Fishes* 355 It is said that at one time [the pigfish] was sold on the Christchurch Fish Market as Silver Trumpeter.

trumpeter, *n.*[2] [Compare Partridge *Your trumpeter is dead*: applied to a confirmed

TRUMPET SHELL

braggart: C18: obsolescent.] In the phr. **your trumpeter is not dead**, said of a boaster, i.e., still 'blowing one's own trumpet'.
    1911 *Triad* 10 July 16 'Your trumpeter is not dead' said to a person who has a great deal to say about his own merits.

trumpet shell. Any of several large univalves of the family Cymatiidae but esp. the **large trumpet**, *Charonia lampas capax*, a 24 cm shell used by the Maori as the basis of a war trumpet.
    [**1904** TREGEAR *The Maori Race* 65 Shell-trumpets (*pu-moana* or *potipoti*) were made from the shell of the Triton australis, the apex being cut off, and a carved wooden mouthpiece fixed on.] **1947** POWELL *Native Animals* 27 Large Trumpet (*Charonia capax eucloides*). Grows to about 8 inches in length and is found adjacent to rocks near the entrance to harbours in many localities from Tauranga northwards. **1955** DELL *Native Shells* 23 Large Trumpet... *Charonia capax*... Although similar to the large tropical Trumpet Shells, our New Zealand Large Trumpet is neither as large nor as beautifully marked. The shell was used by the Maoris as a trumpet. **1971** POWNALL *NZ Shells & Shell Fish* 42 Trumpet Shell... Marked with various shades of brown. **1983** GUNSON *Collins Guide to Seashore* 93 The large trumpet *Charonia lampas capax* (240mm) is seen mostly in the north... Early Maoris made good use of our own species, the finished product being called a putarara. **1990** FOORD *NZ Descriptive Animal Dictionary* 439 Trumpet Shell. *Charonia lampas capax*. A large gastropod, 25cm tall.

trundler. A two-wheeled receptacle holding golf-clubs, shopping etc. and dragged behind its owner.
    1976 MCDERMOTT *Lost & Found NZ* 9 [Golf] Carts are called *trundlers* and spikes are called *sprigs*. **1980** LELAND *Kiwi-Yankee Dict.* 106 *trundler*: A two-wheeled shopping basket used by those who would rather roll their purchases home than carry them there. **1983** *Listener* 20 Aug. 100 [Such] can be virtually restricted to the Antipodes..or even to New Zealand—*dairy* (the shop), *trundler*.

trust.

1. In full **licensing trust** (often init. cap.). An elective local body set up by statute to sell liquor, establish and manage hotels, etc. in its district through an elected board of directors, with profits going to local community improvement.
    1944 *Korero* (AEWS Background Bulletin) 28 Aug. 4 Back from Parliament came the Invercargill Licensing Trust Act constituting the Invercargill Licensing Trust—a body corporate to run the hotels of Invercargill on distinctly different lines. **1944** *NZ Statutes* No.4 23 [Invercargill Licensing Trust Act] The functions of the Trust shall be to provide accommodation and other facilities for the travelling public within the Invercargill Licensing District, to establish and maintain hotels and suitable places within the district for the sale or supply of refreshments, to sell and supply intoxicating liquor within the district and establish and maintain premises for that purpose. **1963** *Truth* 26 Mar. 12 Seek election to one of New Zealand's licensing trusts..all members of all trusts seem to get to the annual conference. **1988** *Karori News* 11 Oct. 1 A petition to force a by-election for two new trustees for the Terawhiti Licensing Trust never got off the ground. **1990** *NZPD* DV. 682 Members were welling up with tears, worrying about licensing trusts.

2. Special Comb. **Trust control**, of a tavern, hotel, etc. under the control of a Licensing Trust.
    1955 FAIRBURN in *Woman Problem* (1967) 53 The extension of Trust control might be beneficial in New Zealand, provided it did not conceal a crypto-wowser motive.

trustee: see *Maori Trustee* (MAORI B 5 a); *Public Trustee* (PUBLIC TRUST 1); *school trustee* (SCHOOL 2).

trying, *vbl. n. Whaling. Hist.* [f. *try, try out* to render blubber.] In special Comb. **trying-house** [OED 1891], the building on a shore whaling station where blubber is tried out; **trying-pan**, **trying-pot**, TRYPOT.
    1843 DIEFFENBACH *Travels in NZ* I. 37 There was much stench from whale-oil... After I had inspected the **trying-houses**..I went through the village. **1857** THOMSON *S. Dists. Otago* 316 The monster is towed in..to be cut up for the '**trying pans**'. **1843** DIEFFENBACH *Travels in NZ* I. 51 The blubber is cut off in square pieces by means of a sharp spade; it is then carried to the shore, and immediately put into the **trying-pots**.

try out, *v. Whaling.* [See OED *try v.* 4.] **a.** Also **try down** (see quot. 1952). To extract oil from (usu. whale or seal) blubber by applying heat; occas. to similarly extract oil from muttonbirds (see quot. 1965) or other birds (see quot. 1952).
    1831 BELL *Let.* Nov. in McNab *Old Whaling Days* (1913) 9 The blubber is boiled out in try pots erected on deck as in a sperm whaler. From its being tried out immediately after the fish is caught the oil is much purer and is free from the rancid smell of Greenland oil. **1843** TAYLOR *Journal* (ATLTS) Apr. 15 There is a large building containing about 6 large coppers with furnaces beneath which the blubber is boiled or technically speaking tryed out. **1878** JOLLIE *Reminiscences* (ATLTS) 12 The last whale caught was nearly 'tryed out', as it was called, or in other words, melted down into oil. **1895** CHUDLEIGH *Diary* 10 July (1950) 391 Bob McLurg tryed out blackfish oil, a nice job for a cold day. **1915** HAY *Reminiscences Early Canterbury* 56 When they got a whale they landed the blubber also and left men to try out the oil on shore. **1952** RICHARDS *Chatham Is.* 88 Then the [mollymawk] meat was tried down over a very hot fire in whalers [*sic*] trypots, the brown cooked meat drained of oil, trimmed, packed in casks covered with oil and headed. **1965** GILLHAM *Naturalist in NZ* 35 [Maori experts] will fillet certain [mutton]birds..then 'try them out' (cook them in their own fat)..in iron cauldrons.

b. *intr.* Of a whale, to yield oil.
    1845 WAKEFIELD *Adventure NZ* I. 330 So passes the season; except that while a whale is trying out, the operation goes on night and day.

Hence **trying out** *vbl. n.* and *ppl. a.*, the action or process of extracting oil from blubber by applying heat.
    1843 DIEFFENBACH *Travels in NZ* I. 36 Large fires glared through the darkness from the neighbouring beach, lighted for the *trying out* of the blubber of a large whale. **1905** [see TRY-POT]. **1917** HOWES *Marlborough Sounds* 8 A trying-out plant smokes across the water on our left, with the humped, red flesh of a freshly-caught whale showing plainly on the little beach. **1921** *Quick March* 11 Apr. 29 There were lashings of rum..and for a few days the trying-out fires and the whale-boats had a rest. **1982** GRADY *Perano Whalers* 228 Trying-out— The cooking or boiling out of the oil from the blubber.

try-pot. *Whaling.* A (usu. legged) iron pot for trying out oil from whale or seal blubber.
    1795 MURRY *Journal* Oct. in McNab *Hist. Records* (1914) II. 523 The Try pot and steam were as they were left [by the sealers]. [Murry's note.] An Iron Boiler of 84 gallons. **1831** BELL *Let.* Nov. in McNab *Old Whaling Days* (1913) 9 If the fishing is to be carried on by a shore party, the try pots and huts are erected on the beach. **1844** MONRO *Notes of a Journey* in Hocken

TUANGI

Contributions (1898) 250 Waikawa is totally uninhabited, but the traces of its former occupation by a whaling party are to be seen in old try-pots and oil-casks and bones of whales. **1887** CHUDLEIGH *Diary* 11 Apr. (1950) 353 We brought home a 5 cwt. trypot and a load of manure. **1890** *Otago Witness* (Dunedin) 9 Oct. 31 At that remote period..(1856) the fair city of Timaru consisted of two houses, some sheds and half a dozen abandoned whalers' 'try pots' on the beach. **1905** BAUCKE *White Man Treads* 75 The shore equipment [of a whaling station] consisted principally of 'trying out' gear—two large try-pots of about 200 gallons capacity, in which the blubber was rendered down. **1915** HAY *Reminiscences Early Canterbury* 56 I can remember seeing the bricks on which the try-pots had been supported. **1932** *Tararua Tramper* Jan. 2 Near the old trypot sites, facing the bushy slope, are old rubbish heaps. **1952** *Diary* 20 Apr. in Sansom *In Grip of an Island* (1982) 154 Two witch's pots (small edition of whaler's try-pot) and a camp oven swinging above fire.

tryworks. *Whaling.* [Used elsewhere but of historical significance for NZ: OED 1792 '*U.S.*'] The apparatus used for trying out oil from blubber, on board ship, or (usu. in early New Zealand) on shore.
    1836 *Piraki Log* 25 Apr. (1911) 33 All hands employed preparing for the tryworks on shore, &c. &c. **1838** POLACK *NZ* II. 417 These vessels are fitted with tryworks or fire-places above which is a battery containing two, and sometimes three iron pots, sufficiently capacious to contain from one hundred and fifty to two hundred gallons each; the fire-place is built of bricks, so laid below as to form channels for water to preserve the floor or main deck from injury. The water is kept confined by a square, formed with a two-inch plank, around the sides, negligence in leaving this pen (as it is termed) dry, has caused many accidents... These fire-works are taken down when the cargo is completed. **1840** *NZ Jrnl.* I. 41 Another settler and whaler..owns a little bay and tryworks. **1845** WAKEFIELD *Adventure NZ* I. 45 A large gang were busy at the *try-works*, boiling out the oil from the blubber of a whale lately caught. **1851** SHORTLAND *S. Dist. NZ* 109 It is also necessary to build try-works, as they are called, where are the furnaces for melting the blubber.

tuakura. [Ma. /ˈtuːaːkura/: Williams 446 *Tūākura. 1...Dicksonia [spp.] = tūōkura*.] WHEKI.
    1867 HOOKER *Handbook* (List of Names) 768 Tuakura... *Dicksonia squarrosa*. **1882** HAY *Brighter Britain* II. 203 The Tuakura (*Dicksonia squarrosa*) and the Ponga..are the two principal varieties of fern-tree. **1920** *Quick March* 10 Mar. 38 Different again is the more common fern-tree, the tuakura (dicksonia squarrosa).

tuangi. Also Sl **tòakki** (early), **tuaki**. [Ma. /ˈtuaŋi/: Williams 446 *Tuangi..1...cockle*.] COCKLE 1 b (*Austrovenus stutchburyi*). See also *Venus's shell* (VENUS 3).
    [**c1826–27** BOULTBEE *Journal* (1986) 110 cockles—tòakki.] **c1920** BEATTIE *Trad. Lifeways Southern Maori* (1994) 503 The tuaki or tuangi (a sort of cockle)..appears to be one of the few shells with identical names all over New Zealand. **1947** POWELL *Native Animals NZ* 21 Tuangi (*Chione* (*Austrovenus*) *stutchburyi*). Well known as the New Zealand 'cockle', but is not a true cockle. Venus shell, or the Maori name, Tuangi, are preferable. **1955, 1968** [see COCKLE 1 b]. **1977** *Glenfield College Maori Cookbook* 41 The *Tuangi* is a round and plump shellfish, light grey in colour on the outside, which is often confused with the pipi... Tuangi can be picked all the year round. **1987** POWELL *Native Animals* (3edn.) 20 The Tuangi grows to 50mm wide, and is

tuatara. /ˈtuəˈtarə/. Also **tuatera**. [Ma. /ˈtuatara/: Williams 447 *Tuatara..1*.]

1. Either of *Sphenodon* (formerly *Hatteria*) *punctatus* or *S. guntheri* (fam. Sphenodontidae), large (60 cm) lizard-like reptiles now found only on New Zealand offshore islands, the only living members of the Order Rhynchocephalia otherwise best known from Upper Jurassic-Lower Triassic fossils. Also *attrib*. See also RUATARA. Cf. NGARARA 2.

[**1820** LEE AND KENDALL *NZ Grammar and Vocabulary* 218 Túa tára; A species of lizard.] **1838** POLACK *NZ* I. 221 On the edge of the bank I caught a small lizard, or tuátárá beautifully striated with bright green lines... The Ruatárá or lizard, is accounted a very virulent deity. **1856** SHORTLAND *Traditions & Superstitions* 75 The creature spoken of in the traditions of the New Zealanders is frequently called *Tuatara*, a name also common to the iguana of the country, derived from the circumstance of its back being armed with a row of spines. **1866** ANGAS *Polynesia* 73 Captain Cook mentions a gigantic lizard in New Zealand, which the natives call 'tuatera'. It is..now nearly extinct. **1870** *TrNZI* II. 17 A daughter of Mr. Houghton missed a favourite rabbit, and commencing a thorough search, put her hand into one of the numerous sand holes, and grasped what she joyfully supposed to be her rabbit, but found it was a live specimen of the *Tuatara*. **1880** *Ibid*. XII. 64 It was called a Moa... It was attended and guarded by two immense *Tuataras*, who, Argus-like kept incessant watch while the *Moa* slept. **1899** *Ibid*. XXXI. 253 In the adult Tuatara the parietal eye, although quite invisible externally, exhibits a higher degree of perfection in structure than in perhaps any other known type. **1904** HUTTON & DRUMMOND *Animals of NZ* 355 Formerly, the Tuatara lived on both the main islands of New Zealand, but it is now confined to a few islets lying off the coast. **1913** *NZ Gazette* 4 Aug. 620 I..do hereby declare that, from and after the date hereof, the lizard known as tuatara..shall come within the operation of the..'Animals Protection Act, 1880'. **1922** *Auckland Weekly News* 4 May 18 A tuatara lizard..was discovered the other day on the rocks close to the water at Plimmerton. **1949** *Tuatara* II. 91 During a walk at Stephens Island in daylight there may be few signs of tuataras unless it is sunny enough for them to bask in the warmth at the entrance of their burrows. **1959** LAWLOR *Old Wellington Days* 129 We found 'the hermit' as uncommunicative as a tuatara. **1963** GLOVER *Bedside Book* 148 We were mildly astonished when a new comer to the shores told us she was simply dying to taste our famous tuatara soup. **1974** *NZ Nature Heritage* I. 32 During daylight hours there is little remarkable about a tuatara island, except that the ground is riddled with the entrances of burrows. **1980** ROBB *NZ Amphibians & Reptiles* 32 The Maori word *tuatara* means 'peaks on the back', and refers to the triangular folds of skin which form a conspicuous crest along the middle of the back and tail of the male, and a rudimentary crest on the female. **1990** *Nature: Internat. Weekly Jrnl. of Science* 13 Sept. 179 The present study [by C.H. Daugherty et al.] shows that neglect of described taxonomic diversity may unwittingly have consigned one subspecies of tuatara *S. p. reischeki*, to extinction. A second species *S. guntheri*, has survived on one small island only by good fortune.

2. *fig. derog*. A derogatory epithet or nickname.

1863 MOSER *Mahoe Leaves* 47 He had a nephew, a small boy of a most precocious nature, who was termed 'Tua Tara', from a horrid sort of lizard that the natives abhor. **1943** BENNETT *English in NZ* in *Amer. Speech* XVIII. 93 *Tuatara*, a species of lizard, had a similar but ephemeral use in a limited circle some years ago, when it was applied to anyone toadying to a superior.

3. In composition **tuataran** *a. rare*., somnolent, somewhat grim and withdrawn; **tuatarium**, (a construction or enclosed area housing) an artificial habitat for displaying tuataras.

1948 IRVINE-SMITH *Streets of my City* 105 Rather somnolent in appearance, with a grim, somewhat **tuataran** aloofness. **1955** *BJ Cameron Collection* (TS July) tuataran (adj) Extremely remote and withdrawn. **1991** *National Radio* 30 Oct. (12.00 p.m. news) [On the theft of tuataras at Invercargill.] Because of the pyramid shape it is thought that it would have taken two people to break into the **tuatarium**. **1996** *Newsvuw* 19 Feb. 16 A permanent live display of tuatara will be opened in the next few weeks... The area enclosed by glass has been made to resemble closely the habitat on Stephens Island... Ratproof netting and other security measures have been incorporated to protect the four or five tuatara that will be resident in the 'tuatarium'... Much of the cost of the tuatarium project has been met by two generous donations.

tuatera, var. TUATARA.

tuatini. [Ma. /ˈtuatini/: Williams 447 *Tuatini..1. Carcharinus brachyurus,* whaler shark... 2... *Notorynchus* [spp.] seven-gilled sharks.] Any of various large sharks, esp. *seven-gilled shark* (SHARK 2 (16)).

1844 TAYLOR *Journal* (ATLTS) 28 Nov. III. 41 I went to see the fish which is called the Tatera its skin is rough like the shark..8 feet long..6 gills [sketch with caption]. The Tatera or ururoa or Tuatini. 8 ft. long. **1855** TAYLOR *Te Ika a Maui* 412 *Tuatini* is a species of shark, often taken ten feet long, it is very savage. The teeth were set in rows, and formerly used as knives for cutting up human bodies for the oven. **1904** TREGEAR *Maori Race* 313 The chief cutting tool was a knife... It was made of wood and had inserted..the teeth of the Blue-shark (*Tuatini*: Carcharias brachyurus). **1956** GRAHAM *Treasury NZ Fishes* 62 Seven-gilled Shark (Tuatini) *Notorynchus cepedianus*... The teeth differ in each jaw. **1981** WILSON *Fisherman's Bible* 220 Seven-gilled Shark *Notorynchus cepedianus*: Not regarded as harmful to man in New Zealand, but any shark of ten feet (3.04m) could well be. Its Maori name, 'Tuatini', comes from the strangely shaped teeth, with which weapons were made.

tuatua. [Ma. /ˈtuatua/: Williams 444 *tuatua..3*...a bivalve mollusc.] **a.** Either of the edible bivalves *Paphies* (formerly *Amphidesma*) *subtriangulata* or *P. donacina* (fam. Mesodesmatidae), living on open sandy beaches throughout New Zealand. See also PIPI 1 d.

1913 SUTER *Manual NZ Mollusca* 958 This mollusc [*Mesodesma subtriangulatum*] is much used as food by the Maoris and white people. *Maori*—Tua-tua (*teste* Hutton); kahitua (*teste* Captain Bollons). **1924** BUCKNILL *Sea shells NZ* 100 The native name for the M. subtriangulatum is Tuatua and Kahitua. **1937** POWELL *Shellfish of NZ* 23 Allied to the toheroa is a heavier and more triangular species, the tuatua. **1955** DELL *Native Shells* 43 Tuatua... The foot is long and very muscular which enables the animal to crawl quickly through the sand but also renders the animal considerably tougher than the Pipi. **1973** WILSON *NZ Jack* 71 We used to call them pipis, but I think that at this place they were really called tua-tuas. **1986** PAUL *NZ Fishes* 160 There are two New Zealand species commonly known as tuatua (sometimes less accurately as pipi). In general, *P. subtriangulata* occurs around the North Island and *P. donacina* around the South Island and southern North Island. **1993** *Evening Post* (Wellington) 7 Jan. 6 And mid-40, dreadlockless and with clothes as cool as a scorched tuatua.

b. *attrib. transf.* Of the shape of a tuatua.

1986 *Landfall* 158 191 Knocked himself unconscious (Jesus leans over him—slides out the fat, tuatua wallet—'For the poor'—he smiles).

tub-oarsman. *Whaling*. [Occas. used elsewhere but recorded earliest in NZ: OED 1845, 1891.] The oarsman in a whaleboat who ensures the free-running of the whale-line from the tub in which it is coiled.

1845 WAKEFIELD *Adventure NZ* I. 318 The common men have nothing to do but ply their oars according to orders, except one, called the *tub-oarsman* who sits next to the tub containing the whale-line, and has to see that no entanglement takes place.

tucker, *n*. [f. Brit. slang *tuck* food, or as a *v*., to consume (food and drink): see OED *tucker n.*[1] 6 or *v.*[1] 10; AND a meal *Obs*. 1833, food 1850.]

1. a. Orig. in goldfields and rural use, thence in general use, a (daily) supply of food or provisions; rations; food for humans and animals; occas. a meal (see quot. 1930). Often *attrib*.

1862 THATCHER *Dunedin Songster* 1 5 But if out of his tucker you cheat him, Blow me if I think he will stay. **1871** MONEY *Knocking About NZ* 77 Our mates had visited the township..for supplies of tucker. **1888** D'AVIGDOR *Antipodean Notes* 170 Tucker is colonial for food—no doubt derived from the schoolboy expression: 'to tuck in, to have a good tuck in.' 'He works for bare tucker' is very often heard in New Zealand. **1888** BARLOW *Kaipara* 145 He..has no particular use for the surplus money after his 'tucker' bill is paid. **1914** PFAFF *Diggers' Story* 10 Over this steep hill..the diggers carried their tucker in loads up to more than 100lbs. **1930** REISCHEK *Yesterdays in Maoriland* (1933) 70 But the crowd of bushmen soon followed, and asked me to have tucker with them. **1933** *Press* (Christchurch) (Acland Gloss.) 30 Dec. 13 *Tucker*... Food; meals; rations. In the earliest days the only t[*ucker*] was mutton, damper, tea, and sugar. **1943** HISLOP *Pure Gold* 16 [Stanley's Hotel at Macraes Flat, Central Otago] was one of the best tucker houses on the road, and with bacon and eggs for breakfast. **1958** *Tararua* Sept. 26 It is rather surprising that *tucker*, that title for food so commonly used in Australia and New Zealand, particularly by country and outdoor people, is so little used by mountain club members. **1986** *Contact* (Wellington) 28 Nov. 2 A letter from Sam Pikimaui... He chides me for using in a recent column the Australian slang word for food—tucker. **1991** *NZ Geographic* Apr.–June 22 People would turn up on the steamer with no money and no idea. He'd kit them out with gear and tucker on the condition they'd sell the gum to him.

b. Special Comb. **tuckertime**, mealtime.

1908 *Auckland Weekly News* 13 Aug. 53 [Caption] Tucker-time: Specials at Dinner at Mount Cook Barracks, Wellington. **1947** BEATTIE *Early Runholding* 12 Another pioneer [said that]..a meal was often alluded to as 'tucker-time', and there would sound forth what the hungry men regarded as the welcome call of 'tucker's ready'. **1955** *BJ Cameron Collection* (TS July) tuckertime (n) Mealtime. **1992** FARRELL *Skinny Louie Book* 270 They're back in a minute..waiting for tuckertime.

2. In mainly goldfields use, but occas. elsewhere. [AND 1858.] **a.** Esp. in the phr. **to make (earn, get, work for) (bare, one's) tucker,** the means of subsistence. Cf. WAGES 1.

1862 *Otago Witness* (Dunedin) 23 Aug. 7 A shepherd hailed them one day as they were working on a river, but they got rid of him by the old tale—'just making tucker'. **1863** CHUDLEIGH *Diary* 20 Aug. (1950) 99 He has been diging [*sic*] for 7 months more for amusement than aught else. He got his 'tucker' and enough to make some rings and broaches beside but nothing more. **1875** WOOD & LAPHAM *Waiting for Mail* 33 We..heard of big nuggets.., but only made tucker. **1888** D'AVIGDOR *Antipodean Notes* 128 The majority of the washings..now only yield what the Colonials call 'bare tucker'—i.e. just a day's wage, which may be estimated at nine or ten shillings. **1888** COX *Diaries 1888–1925* (ATLMS) 27 Nov. I was cutting flax all day but did not earn tucker, my hands are so bad I could not work. **1896** HARPER *Pioneer Work* 30 True, there are still many working the alluvial ground [on the West Coast], but those making more than 'tucker' are few. **1933** *Press* (Christchurch) (Acland Gloss.) 30 Dec. 13 *To make t[ucker]* is frequent, or rather, *could not m[ake] t[ucker]*. **1937** AYSON *Thomas* 29 Thirty shillings a day was regarded as 'tucker' and sixty shillings as wages. **1946** REED *Farthest North* 15 I stuck..out [gumdigging] for a week... and was rejoiced to find that, although we had considered the gumfield nearly worked out.., I was still able to make 'tucker'. **1964** ANDERSON *Doctor in Mountains* (1974) 26 Therefore I signed on to go to the Kenway brothers' station to work for the first year in return for my board and lodgings, and to be taught the art of sheepfarming— what is in common parlance called 'working for one's tucker'.

b. Special Comb. **tucker claim** [AND 1859], **tucker diggings** [AND 1874], **tucker ground** [AND 1869], a claim, etc. returning the bare means of subsistence (cf. WAGES 1).

1953 SUTHERLAND *Golden Bush* (1963) 97 'The Jeweller's Shop' supported its owner generously and allowed him leisure and relaxation which his hard work entitled him to and exciting week-ends in the city that no '**tucker**' **claim** would have given him. **1974** HEINZ *Bright Fine Gold* 200 *Claims*... Those yielding up to £3 per week per man were known as 'tucker' claims; up to £8 per week were known as 'wages' claims. **1967** MAY *West Coast Gold Rushes* 107 'The field,' wrote a Waimea digger, 'is what is usually termed "**tucker**" **diggings**..there is gold everywhere, but it has been scattered with a sparing hand.' **1865** *Otago Daily Times* (Dunedin) 27 Mar. 4 The whole country has been prospected..and ascertained to afford only very ordinary '**tucker ground**'. **1870** *AJHR* D-40 4 Tucker Flat, which for a long time has been looked upon as containing worse than 'tucker' ground, will ere long be able to boast of four or five large water-wheels. **1887** *Handbook NZ Mines* 125 [In c1865] the diggings were only considered 'tucker-ground'. **1914** PFAFF *Diggers' Story* 80 [The Scandinavian field] was called in those days 'Flash Tucker Ground,' and paid over £20 per week. **1952** HEINZ *Prospecting for Gold* 56 *Tucker ground*: Poor ground, just rich enough to allow the miner to buy the necessities of life. **1967** MAY *West Coast Gold Rushes* 244 The digger recognized four classes of payable ground: 'tucker ground' kept him in food with nothing to spare.

3. In combination **tuckerless**, *a*. [AND 1910.] Without food.

1946 HARPER *Memories Mountains & Men* 162 We were left almost 'tuckerless' on Christmas day.

tucker, *v*. [f. TUCKER *n*.: AND to eat food 1870, to supply food 1891.]

1. *intr*. To eat food, to feed.

1903 KING *Bill's Philosophy* 24 I'm sick of starving, when a cove can tucker free. **1912** *Maoriland Worker* 19 Jan. 14 The bosses like them[,]..they tucker themselves and they put the men to sleep in any sort of a stable or pig stye. **c1920** verse in Harper *Eight Daughters* (1975) 78 We've tuckered on the roughest joints We've seen the whisky freeze. **1966** NEWTON *Boss's Story* 25 When they were out at camp the cowboy tuckered at the house.

2. *trans*. or *reflexive*. To supply (someone) with 'tucker' (provisions, food).

1892 COX *Diaries 1888–1925* (ATLMS) 1 Mar. Newman and his two sons are tuckering themselves. **1910** *Truth* 12 Feb. 6 He had been getting 9s a day on sewers and tuckered himself. **1913** CARR *Country Work* 15 All shearing work in New Zealand..is so much and found. In..some sheds, the Maoris tucker themselves. **1933** *Press* (Christchurch) (Acland Gloss.) 30 Dec. 13 *To t[ucker]* a man is to find him in *t[ucker]*... Hence *t[ucker] box* and *t[ucker] bag*. **1940** LORD *Old Westland* 137 He 'tuckered' many a down and out digger. *Ibid*. 159 The expedition was tuckered by Messrs Hudson and Price.

tucker bag. [AND 1885.] A bag holding usu. the (midday) meal of an outdoors worker, esp. a farm worker. See also *hill-bag* (HILL 1 c).

1899 BELL *In Shadow of Bush* 51 It was midday when he roused himself, opened his tucker-bag, and made a fair meal of what he found there. **1900** AYTON *Diary* 18 Apr. (1982) 27 Cooking meat and vegetables. Making new tucker bag. Destroyed one tom kitten. **1933** [see TUCKER *v*. 2]. **1949** SARGESON *I Saw in My Dream* (1974) 119 Mr Anderson took off the tucker-bag he had carried on his back—and there were sandwiches, wholemeal scones, slices of cold mutton, bananas and fancy cakes. **1952** NEWTON *High Country Journey* 180 Bundling the bird up in his tucker bag he finished his meal and..gave it to the packie. **1968** JOHNSON *Turn of Tide* 69 A tucker bag with a bottle of oatmeal water was soon prepared and the two set off. **1974** AGNEW *Loner* 103 I handed [the swagger] a couple of thick-sliced mutton sandwiches from the tucker bag. **1986** RICHARDS *Off the Sheep's Back* 38 [To our British teacher] our tucker or crib bags (made out of sugar bags) became satchels or lunch bags and our oilskin coats became macs.

tucker box.

a. [AND 1897.] The box holding musterers' or other outdoor workers' tucker (and occas. eating utensils) when camped away from the homestead or base.

1890 *Otago Witness* (Dunedin) 30 Jan. 13 The carrier hospitably produced the proverbial tucker box. **1900** [see BROWNIE]. **1933** [see TUCKER *v*. 2]. **1969** HAMILTON *Wild Irishman* 107 In the [mustering] hut were two bunks, a tucker box, an old frying pan, various billies and a teapot. **1971** LETHBRIDGE *Sunrise on Hills* 42 Ivan [the cook] had his 'tucker boxes' packed, the horses loaded with all our gear. **1987** HARTLEY *Swagger on Doorstep* 113 Sometimes we came across one [swagger] boiling his billy in a roadman's clearing..and eating cold meat and bread from his tucker box.

b. *Boarding-school*. A tuck-box.

1960 SCRYMGEOUR *Memories Maoriland* 35 Tucker boxes from home were a source of gratification.

tue(e), varr. TUI.

tuere. Also erron. **turi.** [Ma. /ˈtuere/: Williams 448 *Tuere, tuare*..blind eel.] HAGFISH.

1855 TAYLOR *Te Ika a Maui* 627 Fam. *Cyclostomi* has the *Tuere*... Found in Dusky Bay, and also in Cook's Straits, it is about two feet long, has several small feelers attached to the head, and a broad flat tail, the color [*sic*] is dark brown, and the body of uniform thickness; it is known as the mud eel and is remarkable for its power of emitting slime to such an extent as completely to envelop it. **1929** BEST *Fishing Methods* 72 They are Para (frostfish), Ngoiro (conger-eel), Tuna (river-eel), and Tuere (blind eel); these were the offspring of Te Ihorangi who came down to this world. **1938** [see HAGFISH]. **1945, 1967** [see EEL 2 (1)]. **1982** turi [see HAGFISH]. **1992** EDWARDS *Mihipeka* 39 Blind eels like tuere and piharau—very unusual taste.

tuft-grass: see GRASS 2 (41).

tuggewai, var. TANGIWAI.

Tuhoeland. [Prob. formed on analogy of MAORILAND 3.] A name given orig. by Elsdon Best to the Urewera and other neighbouring areas of ancestral lands of the Tuhoe Maori.

1925 BEST *Tuhoe* 9 The bush which still covers the greater part of Tuhoeland is what an European bushman would term 'light bush'. **1929** FIRTH *Primitive Econ. NZ Maori* 43 He [a Tuhoe elder] knew the old Native names of every tree, shrub, plant, or fern in the forests of Tuhoeland. **1936** LAMBERT *Pioneering Reminisc. Old Wairoa* 58 But while it may not be possible to claim for Tuhoeland a monopoly of fairy-folk, it is true that nowhere in Maoriland are there such varieties of legends.

tui. Also with much variety of early form as **toey toey, toi, tooee, toohee, tooi, toughie, tue(e), tui-tui, tuuii, zooe**; and occas. **pi-tui, ptui** (prob. a hearing of *Pī tūī* 'young tui'). *Pl*. **tuis,** occas. **tui.** [Ma. /ˈtuːiː/: Williams 449 *Tūī*..parson bird.]

1. a. *Prosthemadera novaeseelandiae* (fam. Meliphagidae), the familiar, glossy black honey-eater of bush and wooded urban areas, a mimic and songbird with a distinctive tuft of white throat feathers; having two subspecies: *P. n. novaeseelandiae* of mainland New Zealand, and *P. n. chathamensis* of the Chatham Islands. See also BELLBIRD 1 b, *New Zealand blackbird* (BLACKBIRD 2), KOKO, MOCKER *n*.[1], MOCKIE *n*.[1], MOCKING-BIRD, PARSON 2, PARSON-BIRD, POE.

[**1815** KENDALL *New Zealanders' First Book* 14 Toohee A bird. **1820** LEE AND KENDALL *NZ Grammar and Vocabulary* 218 Túi, *s*. A bird so called.] **1823** CRUISE *Journal* 21 May (1957) 196 [The dawn chorus ceased] with the exception of the tooi, and some other birds whose songs are almost uninterrupted. **1834** Toi bird [see PARSON-BIRD]. **1834** MCDONNELL *Extracts from Journal* (1979) 34 The Pigeon and *Zooe* are perhaps the handsomest. **1835** YATE *NZ* (1970) 52 *Tui*—This remarkable bird, from the versatility of its talents for imitation, has, by some, been called 'the Mocking Bird'. **1838** [see MOCKING-BIRD]. **1840** BEST *Journal* May (1966) 248 Just as I had shot the 2nd Toughie (or Toey Toey as it is also spelt) spied a Barque beating in. **1840** *NZ Jrnl*. I. 221 Picture a most enchanting serpentine river, overshadowed by trees of richest verdure..enlivened by the deep mellow and quaint notes of the ptui or mocking bird. **1843** *Ibid*. IV. 216 We made a meal of some *tuées* roasted in the leaf of a tree called *heraurekau*. **1844** *Piraki Log* 27 Feb. (1911) 150 Henry went in the bush: shot two Birds and two toes. **1866** [see PARSON-BIRD]. **1870** *TrNZI* II. 55 However much the white-tufted Tui may add to the interest of our forest scenery by the beauty of its glossy plumage..in the eyes of the omnivorous settler, it possesses the higher merit of furnishing a savoury article of food, and no weak sentimental feeling saves it from the camp-oven. **1873** Pi-tui [see KOKO]. **1875** WHITWORTH *Cobb's Box* 5 The tui-tui in his coat of metallic black. **1892** *TrNZI* XXIV. 456 [The] true pet [of the Ancient Maori]..was the *tuuii*... This bird was taken great care of and kept in a decent rustic cage.

1920 Mansfield *Stories* (1984) 233 A *tui* sang his three notes and laughed and sang them again. **1934** Hyde *Journalese* 12 Sit about singing to tuis and babbling of bellbirds for the term of your natural life. **1940** McCormick *Letters and Art in NZ* 161 The tui was sometimes no more than a nightingale in New Zealand garb. **1982** Tuwhare *Year of the Dog* 21 That day in the streets, batons whistled just like a tui strangling. **1990** *Evening Post* (Wellington) 14 Nov. 27 The tui sing their welcome and the fat woodpigeons just sit and get fatter.

b. As an occasional gauge of musical accomplishment.

1904 Lancaster *Sons o' Men* 136 Whistles like a tui, Harry does.

2. *WW1*. Usu. *pl.* as **the Tuis**, a New Zealand services entertainment (or pierrot) troupe or concert party.

1918 let. June in *Boots, Belts* (1992) 105 We were at a performance given by the Tuis, the N.Z. Concert party [*sic*]... The Tuis run a real decent show. **1918** *Chron. NZEF* 5 July 248 A few evenings ago we were treated to a..musical entertainment by 'The Tuis' Pierrots (mobile). *Ibid.* 2 Aug. 10 The existing pierrot troupes 'The Kiwis', 'Tuis' and others have reached..a high standard of excellence. **1979** Downes *Top of the Bill* 54 The concert party was enlarged by members of the small free-lance entertainment troupe of the 4th Brigade, the Tuis. **1991** Wolfe *Kiwi* 34 Another bunch of theatrical New Zealanders who sometimes swelled the ranks of the Kiwis were the Tuis, whose costume was ornithologically correct with white frothy ruffles and pompoms.

3. *WW2*. Often *pl.* as **the Tuis**, a familiar nickname for the NZ Women's Auxiliary Army Corps (formerly the NZ Women's Royal Army Corps or NZ Women's War Service Auxiliary).

1941 *NZEF Times* 20 Oct. 17 'Tuis' is the name by which the girls are likely to become known. **1942** *Ibid.* 29 June 5 [Heading] A 'Tui' wedding... A very quiet wedding took place between Corporal Joyce Gilmour, N.Z.W.W.S.A..and Lieutenant Kenneth Webb, R.N. **1972** *Press* (Christchurch) 24 Oct. 6 Lady Freyberg was 'mother' to the New Zealand girls, a special relationship she maintains, Miss Neeley said. It was her idea, she said, to settle on 'Tuis' as a nickname for the women. 'The New Zealand men were always known as Kiwis, so they wanted a slang term for us.' **1986** Latham *The WAAC Story* 21 On October 29th the unit was welcomed at Tewfik by Brigadier Falconer and Mrs B.C. Freyberg (who christened them the 'Tuis'). *Ibid.* 37 [Caption] First draft of 30 WWSA (called 'Tuis') on steps of Parliament House, September 1941.

4. A rejected name for the unit of decimal currency, now dollar 4 q.v.

1974 Muldoon *Rise & Fall of a Young Turk* 76 We [on the Decimal Currency Board] had had trouble with the name of the major unit... Other names [than dollar] flooded in: zealer, crown, royal, zeal, tui, fern, doubloon.

tui-grass, var. toetoe grass.

tukutuku. [Ma. /'tukutuku/: Williams 451 *Tuku* (ii)..*tukutuku* 3... Ornamental lattice-work between the upright slabs of the walls in a native house.] The ornamental lattice-work panels in the walls of a Maori meeting house. Also *attrib*.

1904 Tregear *Maori Race* 272 The panels of this lattice-work (*tukutuku*) had elaborate patterns, and the horizontal laths were gaily painted. **1933** 11 June *Na To Hoa Aroha* (1988) III. 88 It is nearly time now to devote some attention at the school to tukutuku. The idea is to reintroduce the kakaho reeds at the back, instead of milled laths. **1946** *JPS* LV. 160 *tukutuku*, ornamental lattice-work of toetoe-reeds (kakaho) cross-laced in various patterns with narrow strips of flax and pingao: a panel of tukutuku was placed between every pair of poupou on the whare walls. **1950** *NZJAg.* Aug. LXXXI. 187 The tuhu tuhu or kowhaiwhai (coloured scroll work) and the tukutuku (decorative reed panels) are admirable examples of Maori art. **1966** Baxter *Collected Poems* (1980) 374 An old church Where the tukutuku work Plaited by women's fingers, has split and dried. **1980** Mantell *Murder & Chips* 66 It [*sc.* a banner] was about two foot square... An edging of *tukutuku*..pattern enclosed trade symbols of motorcycles. **1988** *Listener* 5 Mar. 16 The whare nui is boarded up... None of its carvings and tukutuku are in place.

tulip: see *Cape tulip* (cape A c).

tumatagowry, tumatakura, tumata-kuri, varr. tumatakuru.

tumatakuru. Also with much variety of form deriving from reflexes of (a) **tūmatakuru** and (b) **tūmataguru** poss. a SI Maori dialectal variant. Thus (a) **te-matau Kauri**; tomatakuru; **toumatukuru, tumatakura, tumata-kuri**; **tumatikura, tumatikuru**; (b) **tomatagora, tomatagorra; tomataguru; toumatu gowrie**, **tumatagora, tumatagowry:** see matagouri for further variants. [Ma. /'tu:mata'kuru/: Williams 453 *Tūmatakuru*..1...*Discaria toumatou*, a thorny shrub.] matagouri.

1844 Selwyn *Journal* Jan. (ATLTS) 70 Slow walk over the plain from the Tumatakuru Bush which made the men feel their way very cautiously. **1845** Taylor *Journal* (ATLTS) 13 Mar. III. 93 We passed over a grassy plain filled with the Tumatikura. **1858** Thomson *Reconn. Survey S. Dist. Otago* in Taylor *Early Travellers* (1959) 333 The country here bears fine grass, but much overrun with a scrub called Tomataguru by the natives, or *Wild Irishman* by the colonists. **1860** *Puketoi Station Diary* 2 Aug. (Hocken MS) Snow. Tom and J.F. collecting Tomatagora up the Gully. **1868** Taylor *Past and Present of NZ* 202 In the Middle Island..a great proportion of the land..is one grand plain of shingle..filled also with spiny bushes of the Tumatakura. **1873** Pyke *Wild Will Enderby* (1889, 1974) III. iii 81 Amidst these the native flax flourishes.., and even the cantankerous Tumatukuru attains considerable magnitude. **1887** Pyke *History of the Early Gold Discoveries in Otago* (1962) 61 The only 'trees' to be found on the Tuapeka goldfields were Te-matau Kauri (better known as 'Wild Irishmen'). **1888** Duncan *Wakatipians* 82 A shovelful of earth from under a tomatagorra bush. **1898** *TrNZI* XXX. 268 I remember, in 1867, visiting a runholder who had a small lawn of English grass..which..was covered with toumatukuru bushes, which had been collected from the run. **1898** Morris *Austral-English* 482 *Tumata-kuri, n*... *Tumatagowry*, or *Matagory*..is the Southern corruption of contractors, labourers, and others. **1906** [see wild irishman]. **1920** *Otago Witness* (Dunedin) 2 Nov. 54 The so-called roads were generally bridle tracks through the ordinary tussock and toumatou gowrie. **1952** Richards *Chatham Is.* 54 *Discaria..Toumatu*... Wild Irishman. Matagowri, Tumata-kuri. **1957** Park *One-a-pecker, Two-a-pecker* 45 Between the long deltas of screes the thickets of tumatagora grew, a shrub as grey as old bones. **1966** Mead *Richard Taylor* 69 Crossing first a grassy plain filled with tumatikuru..taramea..and a pretty cream-coloured star flower. **1978** tumatu-kuri [see matagouri].

tumatikura, tumatikuru, varr. tumatakuru.

tumble. [See OED 1 d, apparently orig. U.S. (1877), Brit. dial. and NZ.] In the phr. **to take a tumble (to)**, to suddenly understand the facts of a situation; to 'wake up to'.

1935 Strong in Partridge *Slang Today* 287 Although, he said, he was the white-haired boy with the trump he was due for a shake-up and he had to take a tumble to himself as to how he gave the company-rations away. **1949** Cole *It Was So Late* (1978) 19 The woman, taking a tumble to our set up, gave me the come on. **1959** *NZ Short Stories* (1966, 1976 repr.) 267 After a while I give up, and I take a tumble to what's happening. I'm getting the bum's rush.

tumble grass: see grass 2 (42).

tumble-weed. The dried seed or flower-heads of *silvery sand grass* (grass 2 (35) b *Spinifex sericeus*); or of *nassella tussock* (tussock 3 (5)).

1942 Andersen *Maori Place Names* 274 The globular, spiked flower-head drops when the seed is mature and trundles along the beach in the wind... The Pakeha name of such spherical flower-heads is 'tumble-weed'. **1948** Hilgendorf & Calder *Pasture Plants* 48 Nassella Tussock's..seed heads break off when mature and are blown along the ground by strong winds. It is sometimes referred to as 'tumble-weed' on this account.

tumuaki. [Ma. /'tumuaki/: Williams 454 *Tumuaki*... 2. Head, president.] The head, chairperson, leader, etc. of a council or organisation.

[*Note*] From the late 1980s freq. in advertisements and other public use for 'head', 'principal' (of a school, polytechnic, etc.), 'chief executive officer', 'chairperson' (of a university department).

1922 Cowan *NZ Wars* (1955) I. 184 This *runanga* consisted of Rewi Maniapoto (the *tumuaki*, or head of the council), his..cousins..and several other chiefs. **1993** *Sunday Times* (Wellington) 4 Apr. 11 [Advt] Director/Tumuaki (Chief Executive)..Christchurch Polytechnic.

tuna /'tunə/, *n.*[1] Also occas. early **toòna**. [Ma. /'tuna/: Williams 454 *Tuna*.] Any of various species of eel, esp. the common freshwater *Anguilla* spp.; eel 1.

[**1820** Lee and Kendall *NZ Grammar and Vocabulary* 219 *Túna*; An eel. **c1826–27** in Boultbee *Journal* (1986) 113 Large eels—toòna.] **1844** Taylor *Journal* 2 Oct. (ATLTS) III. 26 My boys are feasting on a large tuna they caught [at Otaki] as they came along. **1851** *Richmond-Atkinson Papers* (1960) I. 79 They set off with burning brand & tomahawk to catch..tuna, the eels of the country, in a little brook near our encampment. **1885** Chudleigh *Diary* 12 Feb. (1950) 332 Mabel and I called on Wi Te Tahuhu..and saw some 2000 tuna drying. **1892** *NZ Official Handbook* 167 The following is a list of the fishes which are chiefly met with in the market: hapuku, kahawai..eel (tuna). **1903** *TrNZI* XXXV. 66 The fisher trudges off, sans clothing, and prowls along in the stream, feeling under the banks with his hands for the wily *tuna* (eel, Generic term). **1918** *Ibid.* L. 296 The eel, or tuna as it is called by the Maoris, has ever been conspicuous upon the native bill of fare. **1938** *TrRSNZ* LXVIII. 403 *Anguilla aucklandii*... Long-finned eel. *Tuna*. **1946** *JPS* LV. 147 *Tuna*, a fish (Anguilla sp.), eel, of which there are only two species in New Zealand, though there are about 110 supposed varieties named by the Maori, and even Pakehas think there are several varieties going by size, shape, and colour, but these variations are due to age and sex. **1951** Park *Witch's Thorn* 138 Old grandfather eel, old king tuna, you are dead meat now! **1967** [see eel 2 (5)]. **1990** McDowall *NZ Freshwater Fishes* 411

Best listed more than 150 Maori names for various types of eels... About the only name that still has wide usage is tuna, a generic name that is not even exclusive to freshwater eels.

tuna /ˈtunə/, /ˈtjunə/, *n.*² With a modifier: **bluefin (southern bluefin) tuna** (also *ellipt.* **bluefin**), *Thunnus maccoyii* (fam. Scombridae), bluish-black above and silvery below, widely distributed in the southern hemisphere; **skipjack tuna**, *Katsuwonus pelamis* (fam. Scombridae) (see also SKIPJACK *n.*¹ 1); **yellowfin tuna** (and *ellipt.* **yellowfin**), *Thunnus albacares* (fam. Scombridae), a large tuna widespread in tropical and subtropical seas, having metallic blue back, silvery-white belly and yellow fins. See also *butterfly fish* (BUTTERFLY B 1 b).
[Note] *Tuna, tunny,* and *albacore* are names in international English for cosmopolitan fish species. *Tunny* was until fairly recently the preferred common name. Of their many quasi-common names, the preceding general names only are admitted (with minimal citation) as being used of fish taken frequently in New Zealand waters.
    1956 GRAHAM *Treasury NZ Fishes* 409 Bluefin Tuna *Thunnus maccoyii*..Yellowfin Tuna *Neothunnus macropterus.* **1966** DOOGUE & MORELAND *Sea Anglers' Guide* 269 Southern Tuna. *Ibid.* 270 Other names: *Thunnus maccoyii;* southern bluefin tunny or tuna. **1970** SORENSEN *Nomenclature of NZ Fish* 50 *Thunnus maccoyii...* Other common names: Bluefin Tuna; Southern Bluefin; Southern Tuna. **1981** WILSON *Fisherman's Bible* 266 Tuna were generally known as 'tunny' until the discovery of a potentially big export market to America, where tuna is rated a luxury fish. The name was then changed to conform with that used in America. Since then Southern Bluefin tuna, Yellowfin tuna and Striped, or Skipjack, tuna have been developed into important export fishes. **1982** AYLING *Collins Guide* (1984) 291 Yellowfin Tuna *Thunnus albacares...* The yellowfin has a long pectoral fin, and very long scythe-like second dorsal and anal fins that, along with the small finlets, are bright yellow. **1986** PAUL *NZ Fishes* 127 *Southern bluefin tuna Thunnus maccoyii...* Widely distributed through the Southern Hemisphere... Off the South Island's west coast..bluefin are caught by trolling and handlines from small vessels in coastal waters. *Ibid.* 128 Skipjack Tuna *Katsuwonus pelamis..*Skipjack are also splendid light-tackle gamefish and will take a variety of lines or small baits. **1991** *Evening Post* (Wellington) 3 Jan. 22 The yellowfin tuna have started to run in the Bay of Islands.

tuniwa, var. TANIWHA.

tunny. For **scaled tunny (scaly tuna)**, see *butterfly fish* (BUTTERFLY B 1 b) and quots. 1913, 1956 there. See also note at TUNA *n.*²

tupake, tupaki, varr. TUPAKIHI.

tupakihi. Also **tupake, tupaki, tu pákii. a.** [Ma. /ˈtu:paˌkihi/: Williams 456 *Tūpākihi..* = *tāweka, tutu.*] TUTU 1.
    [**1820** LEE AND KENDALL *NZ Gram. & Vocab.* 219 Tu pákii; A fruit-tree resembling the alder.] **1835** YATE *NZ* (1970) 111 The juice of the Tupakihi..a berry similar in taste to that of the elder, whose leaves, branches and seed, are highly poisonous. **1838** POLACK *NZ* I. 288 The *tu pakihi..,* or elder-berry, is a very pleasing fruit. **1842** BEST *Journal* (1966) 16 Apr. 351 Tupake that bane of New Zealand may be found here. **1851** SHORTLAND *S. Dist. NZ* 195 'Tupakihi', the name by which the 'tutu' is there [*sc.* in the North Island] known, appears to be a contraction of 'tutupakihi', or 'tutu' of the plains. **1868** LINDSAY *Contributions to NZ Botany* 85 The too-well-known 'Toot' of the Otago farmer;.. the 'Tutu', 'Tupakihi', and 'Puhou' of the North Island Maoris; the 'Taweku' of the Waikatos; the 'Tupāké' of Coromandel district. **1883** DOMETT *Ranolf and Amohia* I. 184 Then a store Of jellies.. pressed..[from] Rich clusters of *tupaki,* luscious sweet. **1904** TREGEAR *Maori Race* 18 In case..of poisoning by having swallowed the seeds of the *tutu* or *tupakihi* plant..the smoke remedy was resorted to. **1935** COWAN *Hero Stories of NZ* 163 Its carved slopes..are softened with fern and flax and *tupakihi* bushes.
b. The expressed juice of the tupakihi berry; *tutu wine* (TUTU 3 b).
    1861 *Richmond-Atkinson Papers* 21 Jan. (1960) I. 680 Went on to Kapoai..had dinner—well supplied with pipis but alas no tupakihi.

tu pakii, var. TUPAKIHI.

tupara. *Hist.* Also early **tupera, two Purra.** [Ma. /ˈtu:para/: a Maori adaptation of *two-barrel,* not recorded in Williams.] A double-barrelled gun.
    1834 MARKHAM *NZ* (1963) 42 On arriving I was requested to fire my two Purra as the Natives call a double barreled Gun. **1845** WAKEFIELD *Adventure in NZ* II. 109 He had previously despatched a messenger to me, begging me to bring some tupara, or 'two-barrel'. **1863** MANING *Old NZ* 236 *Tupara*—A double gun; an article, in the old times, valued by the natives above all other earthly riches. **1881** CAMPBELL *Poenamo* 115 Little wonder that Waipeha declared 'pigeons we should have', but a little hitch did crop up nevertheless, for all the *tuperas,* double-barrel guns, were at Mangare. **1905** BAUCKE *White Man Treads* 152 He cleaned his 'tupara' (double-barrelled gun), but never a word to me! **1920** *Quick March* 10 Apr. 13 Led by a chainman..with his slasher, and Wirihana with his tupara—a bushmanlike figure was the Boss. **1938** *Auckland Weekly News* 7 Sept. 94 He was an unborn participant in the siege of Orakau, his mother..fighting in the earthworks alongside her husband, beating off the pakeha line regiments and colonial riflemen with rifle and tupara. **1940** COWAN *Sir Donald Maclean* 117 He..only surrendered..when his last home-made cartridge for his *tupara* had gone. **1986** BELICH *NZ Wars* 169 Men with *tupara* were ordered to reserve their second barrel.

tupare. Also **tupari**. [Ma. /ˈtupare/: Williams 456 *Tūpare..*2. *Olearia colensoi* and other species, shrubs.] Any of various native tree daisies possessing leathery leaves, usu. *Olearia* spp., esp. LEATHERWOOD (*Olearia colensoi*). See also MUTTONWOOD. Cf. DAISY TREE.
    1867 HOOKER *Handbook* (List of Names) 768 Tupari... *Olearia operina* and *O. Lyallii.* **1870** *TrNZI* II. 176 [The Snares are] almost entirely covered with scrub and trees of stunted growth, the Tupari, Akeake, and Kokomuka. **1885** *Ibid.* XVII. 216 The deep green leaves of the puheretaiko and the tupari. **1889** [see MUTTONWOOD]. **1906** CHEESEMAN *Manual NZ Flora* 282 *O[learia] Colensoi...* [mainly on mountains] Stewart Island: Abundant from sea-level... Tupari. **1950** *Bull. Wellington Bot. Soc. No. 23* 17 At 3300 feet [on Mt Stokes, Pelorus Sound] the forest..gives way to a scrub of tupari (*Olearia colensoi*). **1961** MARTIN *Flora NZ* 208 The Tupari..is an allied plant forming extensive areas of subalpine and coastal scrub. **1964** [see MUTTONBIRD SCRUB]. **1979** WEBSTER *Rua* 192 The Maori call this shrub tupare, and for Tuhoe its significance is that it grows on the sacred mountain. **1982** WILSON *Stewart Is. Plants* 98 *Olearia colensoi* Leatherwood... Tūpare... Stiffly branching shrub or small tree. Leaves leathery.

tupari, var. TUPARE.

tupera, var. TUPARA.

tupuna. Also early **tepuna, toubouna.** [Ma. /ˈtupuna/ /ˈtu:puna/: Williams 458 *Tupuna, tipuna...* Ancestor, grandparent.] Grandparent, ancestor.
    [**1770** COOK *Journals* 31 Mar. (1955) I. 287 English Grand Father *New Zealand* Toubouna *South-sea Islands* Toubouna.] **1845** WAKEFIELD *Adventure in NZ* II. 113 I asked his permission to ascend Tonga Riro... But he steadily refused, saying, 'I would do anything else to show you my love and friendship, but you must not ascend my tepuna, or ancestor.' **1855** TAYLOR *Te Ika a Maui* 202 Tupuna, to stand, to spring; an ancestor; hence Tu-pu, to grow. **1860** BUDDLE *Maori King Movement* 15 [Ngaruawahia] has been surveyed..the streets being named after Maori tupunas (ancestors) and living chiefs. **1887** *Auckland Weekly News* 19 Mar. 8 This stream is called Rangoriri, after an old native tupuna, who fell in and was scalded to death. **1968** *NZ Contemp. Dict. Suppl.* (Collins) 20 *tupuna..n.* Maori word for ancestor, progenitor [Maori].

turangawaewae. [Ma. /ˈtu:raŋa ˈwaewae/: Williams 443 *Tū* (iii)..*tūranga..*2. Site, foundation.: 472 *waewae..*foot..footmark.] The ability, conferred by belonging to a home-turf, to realize a strong independence; a strong homeland-based identity.
    1969 HILLIARD *Green River* 13 These acres were his [a Maori farmer's] turangawaewae; the only heirloom of consequence his family ever had. **1984** *Te Maori* 31 Although economic factors have helped to scatter the Maori people from their homelands, the majority of them see themselves as belonging to a tribe whose turangawaewae (place for the feet to stand) and whose ahi-ka (burning fire) are located at specific regions. **1985** HOWE *Towards 'Taha Maori'* in *English* (NZATE) 23 Turangawaewae—this term refers to the ability to stand on one's own two feet because one belongs (see papakainga) to a piece of land which reflects one's history—one's identity. It combines therefore, the feeling of belonging and the idea of the place itself. If one loses one's papakainga, one has no turangawaewae. **1987** *Metro* (Auckland) May 70 I put my $16,000 into a 36-perch piece of land behind Hekerua Bay... It is my *turangawaewae* and I'll pass it on to my successors. **1990** *Listener* 9 July 100 In our own time, land as the tuurangawaewae [*sic*] of tribal identity was reduced to the 700 or so marae reserves around the country.

turban shell: see COOK'S TURBAN SHELL.

turbot. Also **New Zealand turbot**, occas. **turbot sole**. [Transf. use of the English fish-name *turbot*.] *Colistium nudipinnis* (fam. Pleuronectidae), a large, mottled flatfish; formerly occas. applied to BRILL (*Colistium* (formerly *Ammotretis*) *guntheri*).
    1872 HUTTON & HECTOR *Fishes NZ* 117 Occasionally a large flat fish, said to resemble the Patiki, has been brought to market and sold as Turbot. **1898** MORRIS *Austral-English* 482 Turbot, n. The name is given to a New Zealand fish, called also *Lemon-Sole..*or *Yellow-belly,.. Ammotretis guntheri.* **1901** *TrNZI* XXXIII. 558 [Flatfish submitted for opinion included] The turbot sole, wrongly named 'brill', about one-fortieth its adult size. **1911** WAITE *Rec. Cant. Mus.* I. 197 Turbot... *Ammotretis rostratus. Ammotretis nudipinnis;.*. Brill— Turbot—*Ammotretis guntheri.* **1913** *TrNZI* XLV. 232 *Ammotretis nudipinnis...* This fine fish is named 'New Zealand turbot' by Waite. **1927** SPEIGHT et al. *Natural History of Canterbury* 202 These two are the Turbot (*Colistium nudipinnis*) with broadly blotched upper

surface, and the Brill (*C. guntheri*). **1947** POWELL *Native Animals of New Zealand* 67 Thirteen species of flat-fishes are known from New Zealand waters, including a large Turbot, *Colistium nudipinnis*, which is comparatively rare. **1956** GRAHAM *Treasury NZ Fishes* 404 New Zealand Turbot *Colistium nudipinnis*... My experience was that it was best to keep Turbot a day or two before cooking, as the flavour improved. **1982** *Evening Post* (Wellington) 8 Dec. 37 Closely related to the brill is the turbot, the largest New Zealand flatfish. It has a reddish-brown back with darker brown splotches and is found mainly on the west coasts of both the North and South Islands, although only about 20 tonnes is trawled annually.

turehu. [Ma. /'tu:rehu/: Williams 459 *Tūrehu*..6. Ghost, fairy. 7. Apparently a supposed light-skinned race who came early to New Zealand.] A light-skinned fairy people. Cf. PATUPAIAREHE.
  1889 *TrNZI* XXI. 32 In those good old times the interior was occupied, they say, by Turehu or Patupaiarehe, a race short in stature and of fair skin. **1922** *Auckland Weekly News* 15 June 15 Intelligent Maoris..believe..that on its upper slopes there lived a race of little red men, Turehu, parties of whom went down at night to fish in some of the bays near Port Jackson. **1947** REED *Dict. Suppl.* 176 *turehu:* fairy people. **1978** HILLIARD *Glory & Dream* 116 'Then the fairy won't forget to come.' 'The turehu won't take to sugar,'.. 'It's not turehu,'.. 'It's patupaiarehe where we come from. And they take to sugar.'

turepo. Also early **turipa**. [Ma. /'tu:repo/: Williams 459 *Tūrepo..Paratrophis banksii*.] MILK-TREE (*Streblus* (formerly *Paratrophis*) spp.).
  1886 KIRK in *Settler's Handbook of NZ* (1902) 122 [Native name] Turepo..[Settlers' name] Milk-tree..[Family] Articeae. **1898** MEREDITH *Reminiscences and Experiences* 21 We lived on the tender bleached ends of cabbage tree leaves, and the inner bark of the turipa tree, which is sweet and not unpalatable but not very satisfying. **1906** CHEESEMAN *Manual NZ Flora* 632 Turepo; Milk-tree... Abounding in milky sap, which is said to be palatable. **1924** *NZJST* VII. 186 In *Paratrophis Banksii* there is an example of a large-leaf form of the turepo, or 'milkwood' of the bushman. **1959** TAYLOR *Early Travellers* 37 [On cutting its bark, a profusion of thick, viscid milky juice gushed out.] [1959 *Note*] Presumably..Turepo, Milk-tree. **1961** ALLAN *Flora NZ* I. 402 Lowland forests and forest margins throughout. *Turepo, Milk tree*. **1978** FULLER *Maori Food and Cookery* 84 The turepo..trunk will slowly exude a creamy sap if it is cut or bruised. The sap was used as a substitute for milk by early colonists. **1982** BURTON *Two Hundred Years of NZ Food* 20 Those pioneers who were without dairy cattle made a kind of 'milk' from the creamy sap of the turepo or milk tree.

turi, var. TUERE.

turipa, var. TUREPO.

turiwata, turiw(h)ati: see TUTURIWHATU.

turkey, *n.*[1]

1. *South Island. Obs.* [Transf. use of *turkey*.] Usu. as **swamp-turkey**, occas. **New Zealand turkey**, PUKEKO.
  1874 BATHGATE *Colonial Experiences* 85 The following day [in 1879] the station manager..visited the camp and was shown a rather curious 'swamp turkey'... The latter duly pronounced it as the rare takahe. **c1899** DOUGLAS in *Mr Explorer Douglas* (1957) 234 Besides being a jack of all trades, this bird [*sc.* pukeko] has a variety of names, no two people being agreed as to which is correct... I have heard it also called bald pate and New Zealand Turkey. **1920** *TrNZI* LII. 64 The common name of the swamp-turkey in the South was pakura. **c1920** BEATTIE *Trad. Lifeways Southern Maori* (1994) 387 The pakura or the swampturkey of settlers; pukeko in North Island.

2. See *head over turkey* (HEAD *n.*[2] 4 a).

Turkey, *n.*[2] *WW1*. With init. cap. [A play on *Turk* and *turkey*: AND 1916.] A Turk(ish soldier). Cf. ABDUL.
  [**c1915–1918**] in Bailey & Roth *Shanties* (1967) 115 Old Abdul under cover was as cunning as a rat; As yet we'd done no shootin'—saw nothin' to shoot at, Till a Turkey popped his head up; that head he ne'er withdrew, For a rifle pinged.

turkey off, *v.* To depart quickly, to decamp.
  1935 MITCHELL & STRONG in Partridge *Slang Today* 286 [The] following [was] employed by those who served in the [Great] War..*turkey off,* to go away without permission. *Ibid.* 287 Well, I was so stiff I nearly turkeyed off from the line, but I decided to wait. **1938** RAWLINSON *Music* in *The Listening Place* 15 Everyone thought he'd just turkeyed off.

turn, *v.*

1. In the phr. **to turn a seven** [?f. throwing the impossible at single dice], to turn a somersault; **to turn tail** (also *vbl. n.*), see quot. 1982.
  1947 BEATTIE *Early Runholding* 157 Even the best horsemen were not proof against their horses putting a foot in a grass-hidden hole and 'turning a seven'. **1982** *Agric. Gloss.* (MAF) 25 Turning tail: Fault in a dog whereby it turns away from the sheep in a complete circle. It fails to 'face up' to the sheep all the time.

2. As **to turn in**, to give up, esp. in the phr. **turn it in**, to give up a job.
  1938 HYDE *Godwits Fly* (1970) 129 Timothy..began to scribble. Birkett called, 'Hey, what're you making, Sonny Boy?' 'Writing to my girl.' 'Christ. Fancy turning in a smoke for a bint. What's her name?' **1964** PEARSON *Glossary* to Sargeson *Collected Stories 1935–63* (1964) 304 turning it in: giving up the job.

3. As **to turn on** [AND 1941], esp. in the phr. **to turn it on**, to provide liquor (for a party or a group).
  1988 McGILL *Dict. Kiwi Slang* 115 *turn it on* give a party or buy drinks; eg 'What do you say we turn it on for the boys tonight?'

4. As **to turn it up**, of a woman, to offer or allow sexual intercourse.
  1973 *Truth* 16 Oct. 18 She said he tried to rape her behind the hedge and then in her flat. He said she told him sometimes 'turns it up' and he thought she was an easy mark. **1988** McGILL *Dict. Kiwi Slang* 115 *turn it up* make oneself, usually a female, available for sex; eg 'Hey, Mort, reckon that sheila over there'd turn it up?'

turnip.

1. Also **Maori (native, wild) turnip**. A variety of *Brassica rapa* (fam. Brassicaceae), an introduced turnip as a garden escape. See also *yellow-weed* (YELLOW 2).
  1838 POLACK *NZ* II. 134 Not a spot on the earth lay waste; many parts teeming with the kéhá or wild turnip whose yellow flower on stalks of six feet in height, covered the distance, as far as the eye could discern, and emitted a pleasing fragrance. **1842** HEAPHY *NZ* 31 The native turnip has increased in size, but degenerated in quality, since its introduction, in consequence of neglect of culture. **1851** SHORTLAND *S. Dist. NZ* 170 These fish [*sc.* eels], 'korau' or wild turnip tops, and fern root, were just now the natives' only food. **1866** HUNT *Chatham Islands* 9 We found ourselves in Evans' Bay; and here, to our great surprise, we discovered wild oats and turnips growing luxuriantly. By whom the seed was first sown God only knows; but as the Maori designates the turnip Captain Cook's cabbage, I presume that great circumnavigator had something to do with it. **1898** HOCKEN *Contributions* 37 At the kaik they remained two days, supplementing their old fare of salt beef and biscuit with the delicious addition of fernroot and wild turnip tops. **1940** *Tales of Pioneer Women* (1988) 207 For vegetables [in early Banks Peninsula] there was plenty of pora, the Maori turnip, and puwha (rauriki) or sowthistle. **1967** HILGENDORF & CALDER *Weeds* 98 *Brassica campestris* (Wild Turnip) with one faint line on the sides of the pods. **1982** WILSON *Stewart Is. Plants* 140 *Brassica rapa* subsp. *sylvestris*. Wild Turnip... Erect herb up to a metre or more tall... Native to Europe.

2. In the phr. (**hot**, or **straight**) **off the turnips**, applied to an exceedingly countrified, raw or naive person.
  1937 PARTRIDGE *Dict. Slang* 918 *turnips, straight off the.* Applied to one who is a country bumpkin or very green: New Zealanders' (–1932). **1983** HENDERSON *Down from Marble Mountain* 83 My first steamrollered week at Riwaka School, hot off the turnips, included: 'Wanna try an electric shock?'

3. As a *v. trans.*, to feed (stock) on turnips.
  1922 [see TUSSOCK 2]. **1975** NEWTON *Sixty Thousand on the Hoof* 35 Alan recalls one trainload of 5,000 [*sc.* sheep]..arriving from Fairlie to be 'turnipped' on their place.

turnip beetle, turnip flea: see TURNIP FLY.

turnip fly. *Obs.* Also occas. **turnip beetle, turnip flea**. [Transf. use of Brit. *turnip-fly*.] The adult flying beetle of the native grass-grub *Costelytra zealandica*. See also *grass-grub beetle* (GRASS GRUB 1 b), *brown beetle* (BEETLE 2).
  1878 *NZ Country Jrnl.* II. 85 No sooner has the turnip seed vegetated in the ground and protruded its seedling leaves above the surface, than these leaves..become the prey of a voracious little insect—the turnip flea..also called the turnip fly, it is however, no farther related to the flea than being endowed with a like power of jumping, nor is it a fly properly so called: it is a *coleopterous* insect, that is, it is furnished with cases under which its wings are folded when not required, is of a dark colour with yellowish stripe down each wing case. **1883** *Brett's Colonists' Guide* 217 There are the ravages of the turnip-fly..to be taken into consideration. **1883** *NZ Country Jrnl.* VII. 390 It will then be safe from the attack of the turnip beetle (or fly). **1895** *Ibid.* XIX. 179 Turnip, Cabbage, and Mustard—We had presence of turnip flea beetle, diamond-back moths, turnip and cabbage gall weevil, turnip seed weevil, smynthurus or spring tails. **1934** MILLER *Garden Pests* 57 The commonest and most destructive..is the so-called brown beetle (*Odontria zealandica*), misnamed the 'turnip fly', which is on the wing for about six weeks each year, during November and early December as a rule. **1943** [see GRASS GRUB 1 b].

turpentine. Often as a modifier denoting any of various native plants with aromatic (or flammable) leaves or resin.

1. a. turpentine tree. Any of various trees of the *Pittosporum* genus (fam. Pittosporaceae) that are rich in resins, esp. KARO, TARATA, MAPAU.
  1842 HEAPHY *NZ* 43 The turpentine tree is likewise

very common in the neighbourhood of Port Nicholson. A considerable quantity of the gum which I obtained by tapping the trees, was very strong in flavour, and beautifully transparent. **1848** TAYLOR *Leaf from Nat. Hist.* 19 *Kaikaro*, [=karo] turpentine tree. **1872** *TrNZI* IV. 262 *Pittosporum tenuifolium* is the 'turpentine tree' of the Otago settlers, who plant it for hedges, as it bears clipping freely. **1889** FEATON *Art Album* 34 The 'Karo'... In common with some of the other Pittosporads, it is known to the settlers as one of the 'Turpentine' trees; which are probably so called on account of the gluten, in which the seeds in the capsule are immersed, emitting a peculiar odour, when expressed. **1898** MORRIS *Austral-English* 484 *Turpentine-Tree*... In New Zealand, it is also applied to the *Tarata*.

b. Ellipt. for *turpentine tree*.
1877 *TrNZI* IX. 143 *Turpentine—Pittosporum eugenioides*. This is the largest of the mapau family... The bark exudes a thick gum, and the juice of the leaves, which is somewhat similar, was formerly used by the Maoris as a perfume, but I fear it is too resinous for European tastes. **1889** =tarata [see MAPAU 2 (3) a]. **1890** *PWD Catalogue of Timbers* (NZ and South Seas Exhibition) 15 Turpentine (tarata)... Timber white and elastic. *Ibid.* 16 Tarata (turpentine) slab. **1967** McLATCHIE *Tang of Bush* 34 Hina hina abounded [near Owaka, Otago], also turpentine with its light foliage and sweetly scented flowers of palest green.

2. Applied to various *Dracophyllum* spp. **a. turpentine bush (plant, scrub, wood)**, INANGA *n.*² Also *ellipt*.
1899 *TrNZI* XXXI. 400 Such scrub occurs more or less on all the high mountains. Its tendency to burn is well exemplified by the local name 'turpentine scrub'. **1926** COWAN *Travel in NZ* II. 66 The flowering *koromiko*..and the turpentine plant—the latter invaluable to the camper-out because it burns well even when green—are two of the most plentiful shrubs. **1940** *Tararua Tramper* Mar. 13 The Tableland.. harboured..many other sub-alpine plants such as whipcord Hebes..and Dracophyllum or perhaps as you would have it, turpentine wood. **1947** NEWTON *Wayleggo* 40 The fourth man took his turn in keeping a small fire of turpentine twigs alight. **1953** SUTHERLAND *The Golden Bush* (1963) 167 The verdure was eighteen inches high all over it broken here and there by rock outcrops and turpentine scrub. **1958** turpentine wood [see GRASS-TREE 2]. **1978** MOORE & IRWIN *Oxford Book of NZ Plants* 114 *Dracophyllum filifolium* is..known [as]..'turpentine bush' to those who use the twigs to make a quick fire. **1982** WILSON *Stewart Is. Plants* 80 *Dracophyllum longifolium* Inaka. Turpentine scrub. **1984** *Hanmer Forest Park* 36 *Low alpine*—comprises vegetation dominated by snow tussocks in association with species such as turpentine bush (*Dracophyllum uniflorum*). **1995** CRUMP *Bushwoman* 15 I boiled the billy with the aid of alpine scrub, some of which is called turpentine wood. It burns wet, burns dry, burns green.

b. turpentine shrub. *Dracophyllum uniflorum* (fam. Epacridaceae), a widespread subalpine shrub distinguished by its single flowers at the tips of branches.
1924 COCKAYNE *Cultivation of NZ Plants* 48 *D[racophyllum] uniflorum* (turpentine-shrub vh.)..is brownish, with wide-spreading branches. *Hab.*, stony ground of drier mountains. **1969** *Standard Common Names Weeds* 81 turpentine shrub. *Dracophyllum uniflorum*. **1973** MARK & ADAMS *Alpine Plants* (1979) 114 *Dracophyllum uniflorum*... Turpentine Shrub.

turps. [Transf. use of *turps* abbrev. of *turpentine*: AND 1865, then 1944–80.] Also as **the turps**. Alcoholic liquor, esp. beer. In the phr. **on the turps**, 'on the booze'.

c1945 'Turps' commonly used as a general word for 'booze' by members of the Weir House University Hostel (Wellington) (Ed.). **1974** GIFFORD *Loosehead Len's Big Brown Book* 8 They can get a bit snooty at football grounds about carrying in jars of turps. **1982** SHADBOLT *Once on Chunuk Bair* (1990) 24 It means our Brigadier General Johnston's slurping the turps again and calling us cowards. **1990** *Sunday Star* (Auckland) 20 May B3 There was a good chance we'd see the biggest all-in brawl since the Taihape pub ran out of turps with half a shearin' gang's cheque still on the bar! **1991** *Examiner* (Auckland) 22 Aug. 6 He went on the turps with some colleagues, all of whom left the business lunch for some recreation at a house. **1995** COCHRANE *Tin Nimbus* 173 'Now what can I get you?' Sean was asked to choose between two bottled beers sold at twice their usual price... 'More of the turps you was drinking last time?'

turret shell. Any of various species of univalve mollusc of the family Turritellidae, but esp. the common *Maoricolpus roseus*.
1947 POWELL *Native Animals* 26 Turret Shell (*Maoricolpus roseus*)... Beds off Devonport, Auckland Harbour, are so prolific that there are several hundreds of these shells to each square yard. **1955** DELL *Native Shells* 22 There are some eight kinds of Turret shell in New Zealand, all of which are very similar in general plan and the family is found in most parts of the world. **1971** POWNALL *NZ Shells & Shell Fish* 39 Turret Shell... Low tide, in sandy, muddy or rocky areas, and in deeper water. **1983** GUNSON *Collins Guide to Seashore* 90 Inhabiting the quiet waters of our harbour channels are several turret shells, the most common being *Maoricolpus roseus* (80mm).

turutu. [Ma. /'tu:rutu/: Williams 461 *tūrutu*, 1. *Dianella intermedia* and *Libertia ixioides*, plants.]

1. BLUEBERRY (*Dianella nigra*).
1867 HOOKER *Handbook* (List of Names) 768 Turutu... *Dianella intermedia*. **1910** COCKAYNE *NZ Plants* 53 The iridaceous plant, turutu (*Dianella intermedia*), a plant with bright-blue berries, is very common. **1946** *JPS* LV. 160 *tūrutu*, a plant..sedge-like blades and very small flowers followed by surprisingly large beautiful blue berries which fall at once if picked. **1978** [see WHISTLES]. **1984** *Standard Common Names Weeds* 111 turutu. *Dianella nigra*. **1990** WEBB et al. *Flowering Plants NZ* 124 Our only native is *D[ianella] nigra*, inkberry or turutu, found under dry forest or scrub, but sometimes in swampy ground.

2. *Obs.* MIKOIKOI (*Libertia ixioides*).
1853 HOOKER *II Flora Novae-Zelandiae I Flowering Plants* 252 Libertia ixioides... Nat. name, 'Turutu'. **1869** *TrNZI* I. (rev. edn.) 209 Turutu. Libertia ixioides. **1870** *TrNZI* II. 126 Libertia ixioides. Turutu.

tusked weta: see WETA 2 (6).

tussac, var. TUSSOCK.

tussock, *n.* Also freq. early **tussac**, **tussuck**. [Ellipt. for *tussock-grass* itself from *tussock* a tuft, clump: see OED 2, 4; AND *tussock grass*, 1870.] Cf. *snowgrass* (GRASS 2 (36)).

1. a. (With *pl. tussocks*.) A clump or tuft of grass.
c1856 THOMSON *Report* in Beattie *Early Runholding* (1947) 19 The natural grasses are always found to grow in bunches known by the name of tussocks and these tussocks vary in colour and dimensions with the quality of the soil and the nature of climate. **1860** 27 Jan. in Butler *First Year* (1863) iii 28 How shall I describe everything..the scattered wooden boxes of houses, with ragged roods of scrubby ground between them—tussocks of brown grass. **1873** PYKE *Wild Will Enderby* (1889, 1974) I. i 9 The American..chewed away at it [*sc*. the tobacco]..aimed a well-directed shot at an unoffending tussac. **1886** HART *Stray Leaves* 31 Armed with tussocks, having a fairly good quantity of earth attached, the..warriors [*sc*. boys] would open fire on the enemy. **1898** HOCKEN *Contributions* 160 The town sadly need improvement too;.. swamp and tussac demanded cat-like agility in traversing many a street. **1943** HISLOP *Pure Gold* 116–117 A good layer of chopped-up tussocks was then evenly spread over the top. **1962** *Landfall Country* 164 Sheep grazed among the tussocks.

b. Applied to a clump of ASTELIA (*Astelia banksii*). See also *tree-tussock* 3 (12) below.
1988 DAWSON *Forest Vines to Snow Tussocks* 120 *Neomyrtus pedunculata* may be prominent in the subcanopy and large tussocks of *Astelia fragrans* may be abundant on the forest floor.

2. (With *pl*. often *tussocks*.) Any of various (esp. high-country) grasses or sedges which grow in clumps ('tussocks') as distinct from mats, esp. *Chionochloa* and *Poa* spp; *tussock-grass* (5 b below).
1866 MURRAY *Description Southland* 8 Short and succulent grass is found to be growing in greater or less profusion between the tufts of coarser and more conspicuous 'tussac'. **1915** *TrNZI* XLVII. 127 The presence of either of these 'tussocks' [*sc. Chionochloa* spp.] is evidence of relative dryness. **1922** PERRY *Sheep Farming* 93 If [the hoggets] are turniped, then the shepherd must watch them carefully when they are once more put back on the tussocks, for they will usually fret for a time. **1933** *Press* (Christchurch) (Acland Gloss.) 30 Dec. 13 Tussock.—Up-country people only recognise..the small blue t[ussock] (Poa colensoi) and the common yellow. **1951** LEVY *Grasslands of NZ Glossary* (1970) 363 Tussock.—Tufted, harsh grasses that characterise the montane belt. **1961** MARTIN *Flora NZ* 129 The name 'tussock' is applied to those tufted grasses which hold water in the decaying leaves at the base. Tall tussock is dominant in subalpine regions and low tussock in montane and lowland country.

3. With a modifier: **blue, bristle, fescue (brown, alpine fescue), hard, nassella, oat, plume(d), poa, red, silver, snow, tree, white, yellow**.

(1) blue-tussock. a. *Poa colensoi*, a tufted grass of variable form, common in subalpine and alpine habitats. Cf. *blue-grass* (GRASS 2 (5)).
1908 *AJHR* C-11 36 *[Poa] Colensoi*..Blue tussock..Grass-steppe, shrub-steppe. **1910** COCKAYNE *NZ Plants* 87 The blue-tussock (*Poa colensoi*) forms much smaller tussocks than either of the above, and is a most valuable economic grass. **1923** *NZJST* V. 146 *Poa Colensoi*... (blue-tussock). Abundant from about 1,500 ft. upwards [on Banks Peninsula] on the sunny faces and level spurs. **1933** [see 2 above]. **1940** STUDHOLME *Te Waimate* (1954) 246 Blue tussock was not plentiful except on some of the spurs running down to the Waihao. **1973** MARK & ADAMS *Alpine Plants* (1979) 258 *Poa colensoi*... Blue Tussock... One of the most common grasses throughout the alpine zone.

b. *Elymus rectisetus*, formerly called *Agropyron* (or *Triticum*) *scabrum*. See also *blue wheat grass* (GRASS 2 (44)).
1891 WALLACE *Rural Economy* 296 The Blue-tussock (*Triticum scabrum*..), a grass of superior quality, has been mostly eaten out of the South Island of New Zealand.

(2) bristle tussock. DANTHONIA (*Rytidosperma setifolium*).
1973 MARK & ADAMS *Alpine Plants* (1979) 22 Some of the smaller tussock (*Poa colensoi*), alpine

fescue tussock (*Festuca matthewsii*) and bristle tussock (*Notodanthonia setifolia*), have become aggressive in this way. Bristle tussock now dominates in parts of Marlborough and North Canterbury while the other two are more important in inland areas of South Canterbury and Otago.

(3) **a. fescue** (occas. **brown**) **tussock**. See *hard tussock* (4) below.
1856 ROBERTS *Diary* in Beattie *Early Runholding* (1947) 18 Some persons have an idea that snowgrass and brown tussock were the only native grasses then, but that is a great mistake. **1916** *TrNZI* XLVIII. 157 The two leading grasses of the montane tussock grassland are the fescue tussock (*Festuca novae-zealandiae*) and the blue tussock (*Poa Colensoi*). **1926** CROOKES *Plant Life in Maoriland* 160 In the montane tussock country the dominant plant is the Fescue tussock (*Festuca Novae Zealandiae*) which is golden brown in colour and admirably suited to withstand the rigour of life on those wind swept altitudes. **1988** DAWSON *Forest Vines to Snow Tussocks* 148 [Caption] Short tussock grassland dominated by fescue-tussock (*Festuca novae-zelandiae*). Central South Island.

b. alpine fescue tussock. *Festuca matthewsii*, a small blue-green tufted grass of the South Island mountains.
1973 [see (2) above].

(4) **hard tussock**. *Festuca novae-zelandiae*, an erect fine-leaved tussock that dominates low tussock grasslands. See also *fescue tussock* (3) a above.
1919 COCKAYNE *NZ Plants and Their Story* 86 Where the climate is drier..one or the other of two tussocks—the silver-tussock (*Poa caespitosa*) or the hard-tussock (*Festuca novae-zelandiae*)—is the physiognomic plant. **1973** MARK & ADAMS *Alpine Plants* (1979) 11 Most of the conspicuous grassland species cross this [ancient tree] line today, but one of them, the common hard tussock, *Festuca novae-zelandiae*, reaches its upper altitudinal limit in many areas close to the natural tree line. **1988** DAWSON *Forest Vines to Snow Tussocks* 149 Short tussock grassland..is characterised by the light brown tufts..of hard tussock (*Festuca novae-zelandiae*).

(5) **nassella tussock**. Also *ellipt*. **nassella**. [Cf. OED mod. L. (E. Desvaux in C. Gay *Historia Física y Política de Chile, Botánica* (1853) VI. 263), f. L. *nassa* net + *-ella*, fem. of *-ellus*, diminutive suffix.] *Stipa* (formerly *Nassella*) *trichotoma*, an unpalatable South American tussock, a troublesome noxious weed of eastern South Island grasslands. See also TUMBLE-WEED.
[**1936** ALLAN *Introduction to Grasses NZ* 118 *Nassella trichotoma*, a rather graceful tussocky species, somewhat resembling *Festuca novae-zelandiae* in habit, but with very different spikelets. Recently collected by Professor A. Wall on the Waipara River bed, and in the Omihi Valley, where it appears to be thoroughly established.] c**1944** *Whitcombe's Mod. Jun. Dict.* 220 *nassella*. A South American tussock grass introduced into New Zealand and rapidly becoming a serious pest. **1946** *NZ Statutes* No.2 7 An Act [the Nassella Tussock Act] to make Provision for the Control and Eradication of the Plant known as Nassella Tussock, and for the Constitution of the North Canterbury and Marlborough Nassella Tussock Boards. *Ibid.* 8 'Nassella tussock' means the plant *Nassella trichotoma*. **1950** *NZJAg.* June LXXX. 515 Nassella tussock... This insidious pest crept almost unawares on to some of our good pastoral country. **1981** TAYLOR *Weeds of Lawns, Pasture* 74 Nassella Tussock..is native to Argentina... Since about 1930 it has been regarded as a serious weed in New Zealand.

Hence **Nassella Tussock Board**, any one of various local statutory boards set up to eradicate nassella tussock.
1946 *NZ Statutes* No.2 32 There shall be for the North Canterbury nassella tussock district a Board to be known as the North Canterbury Nassella Tussock Board... The principal function of the Board shall be to do all such acts and things as appear necessary or expedient for eradicating nassella tussock within its district or for preventing the spread thereof. **1966** TURNER *English Language in Australia and NZ* 172 The recently troublesome *Nassella tussock* has no more popular name. It is controlled by the Nassella Tussock Act of 1946 by Nassella Tussock Boards. **1981** TAYLOR *Weeds of Lawns, Pasture* 74 Nassella tussock boards were established in Marlborough and North Canterbury to control and possibly eradicate this weed.

(6) **oat tussock (oat tussock grass)**. A native, tall tussock grass of the genus *Chionochloa* (formerly *Danthonia*). See also *oatgrass* (GRASS 2 (27) a).
1898 MORRIS *Austral-English* 171 Tussock G[rass]—Broad-leaved Oat—*Danthonia flavescens*..(N.Z.). *Ibid.* 172 Tussock G[rass]—Narrow-leaved Oat—*Danthonia raoulii*..(N.Z.)... Tussock G[rass]—Small-flowered Oat—*Danthonia cunninghamii*..(N.Z.).

(7) **plume (plumed) tussock**. TOETOE.
1898 MORRIS *Austral-English* 172 Tussock G[rass]—Erect Plumed... (N.Z.) Maori name, *Toitoi*... Tussock G[rass]—Plumed—*Arundo conspicua*..Maori name, *Toitoi*. **1934** LEE *Children of the Poor* (1949) 28 In those days the rolling hill-tops were still native grass and virgin plume tussock, good natural pasturage long since ploughed under and replaced with imported grasses.

(8) **poa tussock**. Any of various native *Poa* spp., esp. *silver tussock P. cita* (10) below. See also *poa* (GRASS 2 (30)).
1951 LEVY *Grasslands of NZ* (1970) 10 Poa tussock, danthonia tussock, stunted bracken, stunted manuka, monoao, mingimingi, tauhinu, patotara, and *Pimeleas* were the more dominant plants of the poorer areas. **1969** *Standard Common Names Weeds* 65 *rough poa tussock Poa australis*. *Ibid.* 81 *tussock, poa* [=] *silver tussock*.

(9) **red tussock**. *Chionochloa rubra* (formerly *Danthonia raoulii*). HAUMATA; *snowgrass* (GRASS 2 (36)).
1908 *AJHR* C-11 21 At between 3,000ft. and 3,500ft., plains with an even brown covering of the red tussock *Danthonia Raoulii* extend for miles. **1919** COCKAYNE *NZ Plants and Their Story* 86 Where the soil is specially 'sour', the rainfall fairly heavy, and cloudy skies frequent, the red-tussock..dominates. **1939** BEATTIE *First White Boy Born Otago* 119 The red tussock was seldom seen on the plains, but around the creeks it grew to a big size. **1958** *Tararua* Sept. 12 So..we tramped up and down through the red tussock..[in the Ruahine Range]. **1982** WHEELER *Historic Sheep Stations of NZ* 80 Jack has seen photos of the Gentle Annie area in the 1890s, all in native red tussock with odd stands of bush. **1993** [see BURN-OFF *n.*].

(10) **silver tussock**. *Poa cita* (formerly *caespitosa*), a silvery native tussock-forming grass of coastal banks and tussock grasslands. See also *tussock poa* (GRASS 2 (30) c).
1881 *TrNZI* XIII. 326 *Poa australis* (silver or white tussock) is by no means plentiful [on Stewart Island]. **1919** [see (4) above]. **1937** AYSON *Thomas* 74 They breasted the top of a ridge and saw a beautiful stretch of sloping ridges covered with silver tussock and almond grass, facing the sun. **1946** *NZJST* XXVII. 139 The native vegetation on the Wither Hills was low tussock grassland in which the silver tussock..was probably the dominant species. **1970** MCNAUGHTON *Tat* 59 For several days they travelled over miles of silver tussock country. **1982** WILSON *Stewart Is. Plants* 380 Silver tussock... Bushy, rather shiny tussock..fawn-green from mixture of pale dead leaves and fresh green ones.

(11) **snow tussock**. [Poss. ellipt. for *snowgrass tussock*: cf. 1868 *TrNZI* 47 (Potts) Amidst the snow-grass tussock.] Any of various stiff tussock grasses with tough leaves found in the eastern SI, esp. *Chionochloa rigida*, and various tall tussocks of subalpine grasslands, esp. **broad-leaved snow tussock** *Chionochloa flavescens*, and **narrow-leaved snow tussock** *C. rigida*. See also *snowgrass* (GRASS 2 (36) a).
1864 CHUDLEIGH *Diary* 13 Feb. (1950) 121 The soil about here is lime and consequently you sink ankle deep in mud and the grass, snow tussock, up to your waste [*sic*]. **1908** DON *Mission Work in Otago* 22 Can any words describe the snow-tussock in its full-seeded glory. **1933** [see GRASS 2 (36) a]. **1952** BLAKISTON *My Yesteryears* 20 After about an hour the fog cleared, and we had a wet muster through scrub and snow tussock coated with globules of water. **1969** *Standard Common Names Weeds* 8 *broad-leaved snow tussock Chionochloa flavescens*. *Ibid.* 32 *grass, narrow-leaved snow* [=] *narrow-leaved snow tussock*. *Ibid.* 48 *mid-ribbed snow tussock Chionochloa pallens*. *Ibid.* 52 *narrow-leaved snow tussock Chionochloa rigida*. *Ibid.* 81 *tussock, snow Chionochloa*. *Ibid.* 81 *tussock, curly snow Chionochloa crassiuscula*. **1973** MARK & ADAMS *Alpine Plants* (1979) 250 Genus Chionochloa Snow Tussock; Snowgrass... An Australasian genus of some 20 species formerly included in *Danthonia*. **1988** DAWSON *Forest Vines to Snow Tussocks* 148 [In Canterbury] the higher altitude forests..were replaced by shrubland and narrow-leaved snow tussock (*Chionochloa rigida*)..and red tussock (*C. rubra*) which moved out from the poorly drained sites on to sometimes quite well-drained hillsides.

(12) **tree-tussock**. ASTELIA 1 (*Astelia banksii*).
1955 BOSWELL *Dim Horizons* 150 There were to be had for the climbing the honey-sweet berries of the wharawhara, the tree-tussock, beautiful long scarlet fingers of gelatinous black-seeded berries which were our favourite of all.

(13) **white tussock**. *Obs.* A former name for *silver tussock* (10) above, and *hard tussock* (4) above.
1881 *TrNZI* XIII. 326 *Poa australis* (silver or white tussock) is by no means plentiful [on Stewart Island]. **1933** *Press* (Christchurch) (Acland Gloss.) 30 Dec. 13 White t[ussock] includes at least two varieties, a poa and a fescue (Festuca [novae-zealandiae]). **1940** STUDHOLME *Te Waimate* (1954) 100 The land towards the hills was covered with tussock and scrub—white tussock chiefly, but with some blue. **1962** EVANS *Waikaka Saga* 239 The whole [Waikaka] valley and the..ridges were covered [in 1876] with luxurious white tussocks (Poa caespitosa).

(14) **yellow tussock**. See *silver tussock* (10) above.
1865 BARKER *Station Life* (1870) 25 For miles and miles you see nothing but..undulating downs of yellow tussocks, the tall native grass. **1891** *TrNZI* XXIII. 195 Burnt Hill, standing alone like an island surrounded by an endless sea of yellow tussock. **1940** STUDHOLME *Te Waimate* (1954) 246 There was a fair area of yellow tussock on the northern end of the run.

4. As **the tussock**, in occas. use for *tussock country*.
1946 *NZ Geogr.* Apr. 234 So let the steppes remain in U.S.S.R., the pusstas in Hungary, the veld in South Africa... Let New Zealand stick to its tussock grassland, colloquially known as 'the tussock'.

5. In *attrib.* use. **a.** Pertaining to, or characteristic of, tussock, tussocks, or tussock grassland; composed of tussock; covered with tussock; bred or fed on tussock land.

1868 LINDSAY *Contribs NZ Botany* 80 Like the 'Tussock-swamps', [flax-swamps] are frequently very 'tussocky'. **1873** BARKER *Station Amusements* 68 The frost sparkled on every broad flax-blade or slender tussock-spine. **1924** *Otago Witness* (Dunedin) 9 Sept. 15 Lister's lambs were about as good a quality of tussock lambs as he had seen. *Ibid.* 7 Oct. 33 If the original tussock-burners could revisit this area they would be terribly shocked to see the change. **1937** *Tararua Tramper* Feb. 11 Crossing the divide, a high tussock tableland, we passed over tussock plains. **1952** BLAKISTON *My Yesteryears* 14 John Grigg told me that..he..saw a peculiar object, not far from the tussock track between Ashburton and Rakaia. **1968** TOMLINSON *Remembered Trails* 40 The lambs stopped about halfway down the spur on a big tussock face.

b. Special Comb. **tussock butterfly** (also **tussock ringlet** and *ellipt.* **Tussock**), a large, common, straw-coloured butterfly of *Argyrophenga* spp. (fam. Nymphalidae) restricted to the tussock grasslands of the South Island; **tussock country**, land, usu. high-country, whose predominant natural growth is tussock (see also *tussock grassland* below); **tussock grass**, *tussock* 2 above; also occas. TOETOE (*Cortaderia* spp.); **tussock grassland**, also collective *pl.* **tussock grasslands**, land, esp. high-country, naturally covered by tussock-grass; **tussock jumper**, a term for a musterer (poss. later or loosely generalized to 'station hand'), from an alleged habitual jumping over tussocks following recalcitrant sheep; **tussock knot** *obs.*, a knot used to tie a horse or dog to a tussock; **tussock land**, occas. **tussock lands**, see *tussock grassland* above; **tussock madness**, an excitement supposedly induced by the loneliness of tussock country. **tussock-tether**, **tussock tie** *v. trans.*, to tether (horses) to twisted tussock grass.

1929 *Otago Daily Times* (Dunedin) 26 Nov. [J. Drummond] A **Tussock Butterfly**... When the Dominion's butterflys [*sic*] are known to others than entomologists, Argyrophenga antipodum doubtless will receive a popular and easier name. **1965** MANSON *Nature in NZ* 26 The Tussock Butterfly—*Argyrophenga antipodum*. This species is found only in the South Island and as its common name suggests is associated with the tussock grass..., which is the food plant of the larva. **1971** *Tussock Grasslands Institute Review* No. 21 May 87 One is the orange and brown 'Tussock Butterfly'..featured on our current 2c stamp, which is often very common on tussock areas. **1980** GIBBS *NZ Butterflies* 82 This endemic genus contains three similar species of orange and brown 'tussock butterflies' restricted to the grasslands of the South Island. **1995** Tussock [see *southern blue* (SOUTHERN *a.* 3)]. **1885** MRS VINCENT *40,000 Miles* 227 The same bleak..weather made the '**tussock country**' look drearier than ever. **1907** LAING & BLACKWELL *Plants NZ* 4 The tussock country is dearly loved by every New Zealander. **1925** *NZ Dairy Produce Exporter* 31 Oct. 35 I never did think anythin' o' those Maori ponies that yer drive into the sale from the tussock country 'yond Rotorua. **1938** *Tararua Tramper* Dec. 4 To our surprise it was seen that the tussock-country was white with snow. **1951** DUFF *Shepherd's Calendar* (1961) 25 July 41 I should no doubt have seen them [*sc.* rabbits] emerge now and again for the titbits that tussock country provides even in the coldest weather. **1965** MCLAGLAN *Stethoscope and Saddlebags* 163 The Canterbury side was tussock country but the West Coast was rain-forest. **1973** FERNANDEZ *Tussock Fever* 37 He intended enjoying to the full his first season up in the tussock country. **1838** POLACK *NZ* I. 111 This swamp was covered with a wiry kind of **tussuck grass**, almost the consistence of small reeds and sharp-pointed. **1848** *White Journal* (ATLMS) Feb. 217 The top [of the house] is of nikau leaf and tussock grass. **1851** LEE in Paul *Letters from Canterbury* (1857) 110 Where the fire has passed over the country the tussock-grass has nearly disappeared. **1863** BUTLER *First Year* ix 132 The flax and the cabbage-tree and the tussock-grass are the great botanical features of the country. **1876** *TrNZI* VIII. 497 All this species [*sc.* Danthonia] are large 'tussock' grasses the leaves being from three to five feet in length. **1912** MANSFIELD *Stories* (1984) 109 The wind blew close to the ground—rooted among the tussock grass—slithered along the road. **1977** TUWHARE *No Ordinary Sun* 23 standing sentinel to your bleak loneliness the tussock grass. **1867** THOMSON *Rambles with a Philosopher* 25 [Our horses] were also trained, by use, to traverse the natural **tussock-grass lands** that stretched beyond the narrow precincts of incipient colonization. **1916** tussock grassland [see 3 (3) above]. **1951** LEVY *Grasslands of NZ* (1970) 95 The tussock grasslands, originally some 14,000,000 acres, mainly in the South Island, have pioneered the clothing of new country. **1986** ASHDOWN & LUCAS *Tussock Grasslands—Landscape Values and Vulnerability* ii [Caption] The Lindis Pass, Otago, our most famous tussock grassland landscape, showing depleted snow tussock in the foreground. **1966** *NZ Farmer* 28 Apr. 37 Even the hardiest, most seasonal tussock-jumper is reduced to 'tenderfoot' status by the end of the day. **1988** MCGILL *Dict. of Kiwi Slang* 116 **tussock jumper** station hand. **1989** *NZ English Newsletter* III. 29 *tussock jumper:* Musterer. [**1860** BUTLER *Forest Creek MS* (1960) June 48 We kept one [horse] on the tether—tethered to a tussock of grass by a peculiar kind of New Zealand knot—and let the others loose.] **1934** *Press* (Christchurch) (Acland Gloss.) 27 Jan. 15 *Tussock knot.*—The knot by which the leaves of a t[ussock] are doubled over so that it will hold a tether rope or dogchain safely. **1941** tussock knot [see *tussock tether* below]. **1881** BATEMAN *The Colonist* 186 The **tussock land** abounds in the Middle Island, although the richest land was originally what are termed 'flax swamps'. **1967** RICKARD *Strangers in Wilderness* 52 In any study of farming in early New Zealand the men who operated the big sheep runs of the tussock lands must occupy a prominent..place. **1982** WHEELER *Hist. Sheep Stations of NZ* 5 George drove us up into the foothills, which open out into unexpectedly wide rolling tussocklands, with good stands of native bush in the gullies. **1991** *Dominion* (Wellington) 5 Sept. 8 I wish to draw attention to the Department of Conservation case to catch or shoot hundreds of wild horses roaming the Kaimanawa Range and tussock land. **1989** RICHARDS *Pioneer's Life* 74 Like me, he had the '**tussock madness**' and we competed against each other in Veterans [*sic*] shearing competitions around the country. **1929** MARTIN *NZ Nature Book 1* 146 **Tussock Ringlet** (*Argyrophenga antipodum*).—This South Island butterfly is commonly seen flitting somewhat heavily and leisurely among the tussocks of the hill country. **1902** WALKER *Zealandia's Guerdon* 30 We'll ride to the end of that spur, '**tussock-tether**' our horses on the plain and walk up till we get to the good pig gullies. **1968** *NZ Contemp. Dict. Supp.* (Collins) 21 *tussock n...* hence *v. tussock tether*, tie horse to a clump of *tussock.* **1941** BAKER *NZ Slang* 41 *Tussock tether* or *tie*, to tie a horse to a clump of tussock in such country, and *tussock knot*, the method of tying to prevent the horse breaking away.

6. With *ppl. a.* in adjectival combinations in senses 'covered with tussock(s)', **tussock-clad**, **tussock-clothed**, **tussock-covered**; or 'living in or on tussock (grasses)', **tussock-dwelling**; 'affected by too long living or working in tussock country', **tussock-happy**.

1885 *NZJSc.* II. 507 Dottrel [*sic*].—One of the earlier breeders, whether on the **tussock-clad** plains or on river-bed spits and flats. **1940** LAING & BLACKWELL *Plants of NZ* 5 The edges of streams on the tussock-clad plains are often fringed with flax and bulrush. **1951** LEVY *Grasslands of NZ* (1970) 272 The original tussock-clad country of the lower levels in the South Island has either been turned under by the plough or so burnt and grazed..almost beyond recognition. **1960** MASTERS *Back-Country Tales* 185 Beneath me, stretching back into the legend haunted ranges of the Urewera country, was a **tussock clothed** valley. **1870** *TrNZI* II. 45 When the Lark is flushed from her nest on the wide expanse of the **tussock-covered** plains..what rare instinct.. enables her to find her nest. **1909** THOMPSON *Ballads About Business* 46 Sendin' all the sheep a-pantin' to the shady-sided slopes Of the tussock-covered foothills. **1936** *Agricultural Organization in NZ* 77 The typical, originally tussock-covered plains land, the soils of which vary from light and stony..to heavy silts. **1968** TOMLINSON *Remembered Trails* 40 Long tussock-covered spurs about a mile long, reached to the top on both sides. **1958** *Tararua* Sept. 13 As we returned across the plateau to our camp we disturbed some **tussock-dwelling** birds, probably pipits. **1966** *NZ Farmer* 23 June 37 Some leisure activity is a must if [the high-country farmer] is to avoid becoming what is jocularly referred to as '**tussock happy**'.

tussock, *v.* [AND 1888.] *trans.* To remove tussocks, tussock, or coarse herbage from (land, etc.).

1866 MURRAY *Description Southland* 28 [The intending farmer] will do well to 'tussac' a few acres;—that is chip off with an adze the flax and coarse grass growing on the land.

Hence **tussocking** *vbl.n.*, removing tussocks or tussock from land.

1971 WATT *Centenary of Invercargill* 8f. [Caption] Early view of the south portion of the town... The tussocks are noticeable. Their removal from street lines and sections provided work for contractors, who charged so much an acre for what was known as tussocking. *Ibid.* 64 On February 26, 1874, the council called tenders for tussacing the remainder of the untussocked streets south of the Puni.

tussocked, *a.* Covered with tussock. Also as **untussocked**, lacking tussock.

1934 LEE *Children of the Poor* (1949) 173 There was a tussocked hill I examined every morning about sunrise. **1971** untussocked [see TUSSOCK *v.*].

tussocker. *Obs.* SUNDOWNER 1.

1873 [see SUNDOWNER 1]. **1898** MORRIS *Austral-English* 485 *Tussocker, n.* a New Zealand name for a *Sundowner*. **1946** SOLJAK *NZ* 118 New Zealanders have coined or adapted many expressions to meet local requirements, as illustrated by the following:... *tussocker:* hobo.

tussocky. [OED 1805.] Of grass, in tussock form; of land, (partially) covered with tussock or tussocks.

1868 LINDSAY *Contribs NZ Botany* 80 Like the 'Tussock-swamps', [flax-swamps] are frequently very 'tussocky'—causing walking thereon to be extremely..fatiguing. **1877** *TrNZI* IX. 497 This species [of grass] is somewhat tussocky in habit when not closely cropped. **1878** *Ibid.* X. 323 We came across four wild dogs baiting a sow..in a dry tussocky lagoon. **1909** THOMPSON *Ballads About Business* 84 On those tussocky valleys and tussocky hills. **1920** *Quick March*

TUSSUCK

10 Jan. 13 The lonely little settlement..was more than two thousand feet above the sea, squatting on the tussocky banks of a cold clear stream. **1943** HISLOP *Pure Gold* 57 I went back to bed..leaving them..to mount their 'neddies' for a long day's mustering in those lovely tussocky hills and gullies. **1952** THOMSON *Deer Hunter* 42 Most of my previous shooting had been done on more open tussocky country. **1969** SARGESON *Joy of the Worm* 33 Jeremy upon their first [motorbike] excursion tumbled his beloved young woman upon a tussocky verge. **1980** MARSH *Photo-Finish* 33 The air up here [in the Southern Alps]..smelt aromatically of manuka scrub patching warm tussocky earth.

tussuck, var. TUSSOCK.

tutae. Also early **toòtai**, erron. **tutai**. [Ma. /'tu:tae/: Williams 461 *Tūtae*..Dung.]
1. Dung, excrement (lit. and *fig.*); a defecation.
 [c**1826–27** BOULTBEE *Journal* (1986) 111 dung—toòtai.] **1974** *Salient* (Wellington) 3 Apr. 13 In my next reincarnation I'm coming back as a full blooded maori, that'll scare the tutai out of all those pakeha statisticians. **1981** *Climate* Oct.–Nov. 34 Black tutai... It was left by Archy, the scrubcutter. **1985** *Women's Work* 223 [Maori girl speaks] 'Howzat you fullas?'... Charlotte was enraged..she was going to throw that Macky in the tutae for sure.
 Hence **tutae** *v.*
 1990 *Listener* 1 Oct. 109 His tarau's in a real mess... He's tutaed himself.
2. tutae kehua, tutae whetu. [Ma. /'tu:tae 'ke:hua//'tu:tae fe'tu:/: Williams 461 *Tūtae kēhua, Clathrus cibarium*: f. *Tūtae* dung, *kēhua* ghost, spirit; *whetū*, star: the delicate, white latticework globe seems to appear quite suddenly as though dropped by sky spirits, often apparently after thunder(-farting).] *basket fungus* (FUNGUS 2 (1)). Cf. FAIRIES' CLOSET.
 1922 *NZJST* V. 247 *Clathrus cibarius*... This fungus..[is] known variously as 'basket fungus'..'*tutae whetu*', '*tutae kehua*'.

tute, var. TUTU.

tuted, var. TUTUED.

tutin. [f. TUTU + *-in* formative.] A toxic glucoside $C_{17}H_{20}O_7$ found in TUTU (*Coriaria* spp.).
 1901 *TrNZI* XXXIII. 348 All the New Zealand species of *Coriaria* contain a highly poisonous crystalline glucoside of the formula C17H20O7, to which the authors [*sc.* Easterfield and Aston] give the name 'tutin'. **1906** CHEESEMAN *Manual NZ Flora* 106 *Tutu; Tupakihi*... The poisonous principle appears to be a glucoside, to which the name 'tutin' has been applied. **1950** *NZJAg.* Dec. LXXXI. 552 The toxin in tutu is tutin, which is allied to the picrotoxin group of poisonous substances. **1981** BROOKER et al. *NZ Medicinal Plants* 11 A new chapter was begun when T.H. Easterfield..and B.C. Aston..collaborated (1900-1) in isolating..tutin, the poisonous principle of tutu.

tutu /'tutu/, /tut/. Also commonly **toot**; early **etootoo** (=he tutu), also occas. **tote, tute**.
1. a. [Ma. /'tutu/: Williams 462 *Tutu* (i)..*Coriaria arborea*.] A native shrub or small tree of *Coriaria* spp. (fam. Coriariaceae) having pulpy black fruits which contain potable juice but also poisonous seeds, and leaves which, when ingested, can poison stock. In early use the name is also applied to the tutu berry. See also ELDERBERRY, TUPAKIHI a.

(a) **tutu** forms.
 [**1820** LEE AND KENDALL *NZ Grammar and Vocabulary* 220 Tútu, *s.* Fruit from the Tu pákii.] c**1835** BOULTBEE *Journal* (1986) 68 His face and hands were stained with the juice of Etootoo, a berry which when squeezed, affords a nutritious beverage... This is a berry that grows in clusters like currants, on a plant about three feet high, in colour they are like the elderberry; they are full of seeds, which are of a pernicious nature. **1843** DIEFFENBACH *Travels in NZ* I. 26 Near the beach appear..solanum, the karaka tree, tutu and flax. **1851** *Lyttelton Times* 11 Jan. [5] Three [cows] have died..by eating tutu... To beasts just out of a ship, the tutu, of which there is abundance here, is certainly fatal. **1860** in Butler *First Year* (1863) vii 97 The tutu not having yet begun to spring I yarded my bullocks at Main's. **1879** *Auckland Weekly News* 19 Apr. 14 The tutu grows upon the plain, but what living thing can rear its head within its deadly shade? **1904** [see TUPAKIHI a]. **1912** *NZJAg* 15 Jan. 78 I mention this cure because I have actually seen it done when droving cattle through tutu-areas. **1926** *NZ Dairy Produce Exporter* 30 Sept. 40 This has been a day of sorrow..one of our best cows died of tutu and curiosity. **1933** *Press* (Christchurch) (Acland Gloss.) 30 Dec. 13 *Tutu.*- Pronounced 'toot'. Various species of Coriaria. A poisonous plant. There are three sizes and the smaller (like a fern) is the most dangerous. **1977** CONNOR *Poisonous Plants NZ* 13 Early in the recorded history of New Zealand, tutu caused some fatalities and much sublethal poisoning. **1982** BURTON *Two Hundred Years of NZ Food* 5 A more flavoursome delicacy was prepared by soaking the [fernroot] cakes in the juice of tutu..petals.

(b) **toot** (or **tute**) forms.
 1844 TUCKETT *Diary* May in Hocken *Contributions* (1898) 215 The prevailing growth [at Taieri mouth] is flax, fern, toot, and grass. **1861** BARR *Poems & Songs* 149 Grub away, tug away, toil till you're weary, Haul oot the toot roots, and everything near ye. **1870** *TrNZI* II. 174 I find the opinion that there are three 'kinds' of 'toot' unanimous among the more observant settlers alike of Otago and Auckland. **1891** *NZ Country Journal* 201 His hearty salutation [in Maori] in its faultiness proved to be about on a par with 'rummy rum', 'triddy', and 'toot'. **1908** BAUGHAN *Shingle-Short* 14 *Tute*, correctly *tutu* (toot): A poisonous native shrub. **1915** *Saunders Diary* 27 Apr. in Pugsley *Gallipoli* (1984) 160 [The scrub at Anzac Cove] 'was very thick and stood about 5ft high and was of a laurel leaf type very like "Tote" that is found in New Zealand.' **1949** SARGESON *I Saw in My Dream* (1974) 166 And your toes, with a bit of toot to hang on to. But say it pulled out? Divide your holds then between rock and toot. **1966** *Encycl. NZ* III. 712 Tutu, toot, tute .. tupakihi, tutu .. *Coriaria* spp. **1985** MCGILL *G'day Country* 154 There was a shrub like a peach tree, with red flowers. Doug called it 'tute'.

b. *Ellipt.* for *tutu wine* 3 b below.
 1842 WADE *Journey in Nthn Is.* 57 The Tupakihi..produces..berries, the expressed unfermented juice of which is called tutu. **1843** DIEFFENBACH *Travels in NZ* II. 390 Tutu—a wine made from the berries of the tupakihi.

2. With a modifier: **alpine, feathery** (or **mountain), tree**.

(1) **alpine tutu.** *Coriaria angustissima*, a small subalpine spreading shrub with feathery leaves.
 1869 *TrNZI* I. (rev. edn.) 196 Alpine Tutu (*Coriaria angustissima*). A very distinct species, found only in Sub-alpine localities.

(2) **feathery** (or **mountain**) **tutu.** *Coriaria plumosa*, a small subalpine shrub with feathery leaves.
 1950 WODZICKI *Introduced Mammals* 223 On the tops they feed on *Hebe* sp., mountain tutu..and snowgrass. **1973** MARK & ADAMS *Alpine Plants* (1979) 70 *Coriaria plumosa* W.R.B Oliver. Mountain Tutu. **1982** WILSON *Stewart Is. Plants* 112 *Coriaria plumosa* Feathery Tutu... Summer-green prostrate to ascending shoots in colonies.

(3) **tree tutu.** *Coriaria arborea*, a stout shrub or small tree of fertile gullies and riverbanks.
 1868 LINDSAY *Contributions to NZ Botany* 84 *C[oriaria] arborea*... The 'Tree Tutu'; which Dr. Hector asserts is quite distinct from the common 'Herbaceous Tutu', or 'Tutu' proper... Tree Toot also occurs in the forests of the Te Anau and Manipori [*sic*] Lakes. **1883** HECTOR *NZ Handbook* 131 Tupakihi, Tree Tutu.— A perennial shrub 10-18 feet high; trunk 6–8 inches in diameter. The seeds and leaves contain a poisonous alkaloid. **1901** *TrNZI* XXXIII. 347 *Coriaria ruscifolia*..is commonly known as the tree-toot. **1939** COCKAYNE & TURNER *Trees NZ* 40 *Coriaria arborea* (Coriariaceae). Tupakahi, [*sic*] Tree-tutu. **1940** LAING & BLACKWELL *Plants of NZ* 241 The other New Zealand species [of *Coriaria*] are *C. lurida*, *C. angustissima*, and *C. arborea*, the tree tutu. There are many hybrids. **1961** MARTIN *Flora NZ* 183 [On] the forest margin the Tree Tutu (toot)..is a common small tree. **1978** MOORE & IRWIN *Oxford Book of NZ Plants* 64 *Coriaria arborea*. Tree tutu is found throughout [New Zealand]. **1982** WILSON *Stewart Is. Plants* 112 *Coriaria arborea*. Tree Tutu... Shrub with stout, arching, perennial branches.

3. a. Used *attrib*. in Comb. **tutu-berry, -plant, -tree** (see also *tree-tutu* 2 (3) above).
 1859 THOMSON *Story of NZ* (1974) I. 19 From the poisonous **Tutu berries**..a grateful and not intoxicating drink was expressed. **1864** BARRINGTON *Diary* 16 Mar. in Taylor *Early Travellers* (1959) 402 Simonin gathered a handful of tutu berries..and got a pint of wine. **1880** *TrNZI* XII. 434 Imagine an old Maori chief suffering from *rich gout*..his favourite tipple being a mild infusion of tutu-berries. **1909** *Ibid.* XLI. 290 In another case two young men partook of some tutu-berries, about 4 p.m. **1940** *Tales Pioneer Women* (1988) 39 Quick, come here; Ella has been eating tutu berries and I think she is dying. **1971** LETHBRIDGE *Sunrise on the Hills* 140 One died as a small boy—eating 'toot' berries on his way home from school. **1867** HOCHSTETTER *NZ* 139 The **Toot-plant**, Tutu or Tupakihi of the Maoris..is a small bush. **1868** LINDSAY *Contributions to NZ Botany* 83 By reason of its including the too-familiar and fatal '*Toot*' plant, [*Coriaria*] is..of no secondary importance to the New Zealand colonist. **1883** DOMETT *Ranolf and Amohia* I. 152 So men compared him to the **tutu-tree**. **1960** HILLIARD *Maori Girl* 215 And there's the lights on the leaves of the *taupata*, and on the *tutu* trees over the creek where the cows can't get at them.

b. Special Comb. **tutu beer**, see *tutu wine* below; **tutu-poison, tutu-poisoning**, poison(ing) from the berry seeds (or the young shoots) of the tutu; **tutu wine**, occas. **tutu beer**, a beverage made from juice expressed from the flesh of tutu-berries.

 1977 CONNOR *Poisonous Plants NZ* 56 **Tutu beer** and tutu pie made with fruits including the seeds caused death or serious illness in Europeans early in New Zealand history. **1851** WARD *Journal* 6 Jan. (1951) 101 Saw his cow lying dying of '**toot**' **poison**. **1862** LINDSAY *Place and Power of Natural Hist.* 9 The nature of the Tuta [*sic*] poison. **1901** *TrNZI* XXXIII. 346 Birds are said to be unaffected by the seeds, but..domestic fowls have been poisoned by eating the berries, the symptoms being typical of **tutu-poisoning**. **1912** *NZJAg.* Jan. IV. 78 Treatment of a beast suffering from tutu poisoning by pulling its tongue as far as possible out of the mouth towards the ear would be of very little avail. **1926** *NZ Dairy Produce Exporter* 30 Sept. 4 Do any readers know a remedy for tutu poisoning? **1937** AYSON *Thomas* 115 The danger of tutu poisoning and the pleuro scare made constant observation of the cattle necessary, but all went well in this corner of the south. **1977** CONNOR *Poisonous Plants NZ* 56 A more remarkable case of tutu poisoning is reported in dogs that ate the rumen contents of a sheep poisoned by tutu. **1868** LINDSAY *Contribs. NZ Bot.* 57 In the New Zealand Exhibition of 1865, there was shown an 'Unintoxicating Wine, made from the juice of the "Wild Bramble" growing in Hawke's Bay'. This is probably a mere expressed juice, sweetened or not; and analogous to **Toot Wine. a1906** STACK *Through Canterbury* (1972) 50 But what a ridiculous ending that would be to my praise of tutu wine? **1907** LAING & BLACKWELL *Plants NZ* 229 [Heading] Tutu Wine. Though the green berries and seeds are intensely poisonous, the Maoris prepared from the juice of the berries a beverage, of which, according to Colenso, they drank large quantities. In the early days of the Colony the settlers also used to make a wine from the fruit, after removing the seeds. However, this wine was not above suspicion. Canon Stack relates how he drank the wine upon one occasion when travelling in company with Bishop Harper. Fortunately, neither of them did more than taste it. Shortly after swallowing it, the Canon lost all feeling in his extremities, and could scarcely retain his seat, but felt that he must fall forward on his face. A mist appeared to come over the room, and he perceived that he was being poisoned, and must ask for an emetic. Soon, however, his feet began to tingle, and the strange sensation passed. The good Bishop was similarly affected, so, judging from this case, the beverage can scarcely be recommended for general use. **1915** HAY *Reminisc. Early Canterbury* 19 With the advent of 'waipiro' it no longer became necessary to make tu-tu wine. **1939** BEATTIE *First White Boy Born Otago* 13 I have tasted tutu wine made by the Maoris, and I thought it all right—nice and sweet—but I was a boy then and perhaps I would not care for it now.

4. Mainly *early Canterbury*. In various phrases.
a. *Obs.* **to eat** (one's) **tutu** (**toot**), of stock, to eat tutu shoots and leaves and become poisoned; in transferred use, of people, to go through the first (often painful) steps of gaining colonial experience.
1851 *Lyttelton Times* 11 Jan. in Turner *English Language in Australia and NZ* (1966) 165 Of the five cows landed from the ships, three have died, Mr Brittan's by falling over the cliff, Mr Fitzgerald's and Mr Phillips's by eating tutu. **1857** PAUL *Letters from Canterbury* 26 [The newly-arrived settlers] passed with unprecedented rapidity through the crisis of unreasonableness, false pride and grumbling, which old settlers call 'eating their tutu'. [1857 *Note*] 'Toot' as it generally pronounced, the leaves of which may be eaten safely by cattle gradually accustomed to its use, is often fatal to newly-landed animals. **1889** WILLIAMS & REEVES *Colonial Couplets* 20 You will gather from this I am not 'broken in', And the troublesome process has yet to begin, Which old settlers are wont to call 'eating your tutu'; (This they always pronounce as if rhyming with boot) 'Tis that 'experencia docet' they mean. **1891** *NZ Country Journal* XV. 103 The Cockney new chum soon learned to 'eat his toot', and he quickly acquired a good position in the district. **1894** WILSON *Land of the Tui* 9 Feb. 291 I am only riding my hobby again, which is not the slightest use, for, as the saying is here, I shall have to 'eat my Tutu', and be very glad if it does not poison me, for to utter a protest is to beat the air. **1933** *Press* (Christchurch) (Acland Gloss.) 14 Oct. 15 *Eat Tutu.*—An old expression in Canterbury... Newly arrived immigrants took a certain time to settle down to New Zealand conditions... It was a very expressive saying, but had died out before my time.

b. to get the toot, of stock, to be poisoned by eating tutu.

1864 *Richmond-Atkinson Papers* 19 Apr. (1960) II. 107 When we got back to camp we found 13 or 14 bullocks had got the 'toot'—i.e. had eaten tutu & so poisoned themselves.

tutued /ˈtutɪd/. Also **tooted, tuted**. Of stock, poisoned or affected by eating tutu shoots.
1863 tooted [see BLEED v]. **1890** *Otago Witness* (Dunedin) 10 Apr. 20 It appears that a station manager in going his rounds..found a good fat bullock tutued, of which he could not save the life. **1898** *Merriam-Webster International Dict.* 2032 *Toot´ed..a.* Poisoned by tutu;—said of *tu´tued* cattle.

tutukiwi. [Ma. /ˈtutuˌkiwi/: Williams 463 *Tutukiwi..1.* an orchidaceous plant.] *Pterostylis banksii* (fam. Orchidaceae), a native green-hood orchid distinguished by the long curved tip to its hood which resembles the beak of a kiwi. See also ORCHID 2.
1940 LAING & BLACKWELL *Plants NZ* 129 *Pterostylis Banksii...* Maori name, *Tutu Kiwi*. **1952** RICHARDS *Chatham Islands* 24 The hood is upright at the bottom and then curves forward, the upper sepal often forming a long tail... Elf's Hood. Tutu-kiwi. **1961** MARTIN *Flora NZ* 309 Much the largest and commonest [helmet orchid] is the tutukiwi. **1982** WILSON *Stewart Is. Plants* 290 *Pterostylis* Greenhood Orchids... Tutukiwi... Greenhood are familiar Australasian orchids, but the individual species are not yet fully understood.

tuturiwata, tuturiwatu, tuturiwhati, varr. TUTURIWHATU.

tuturiwhatu. Also with much variety of form in the Maori originals and their various adaptations as **tchūriwat** (Chatham Is.), **turiwata, turiwhati, tuturiwata, tuturiwatu, tuturiwhati.** [Ma. /ˈturifati/ /ˈtuːturifati/ /ˈtuːturifatɪ/: Williams 460 *Turiwhati, tūturiwhati, turiwhatu, tūturiwhatu, turuwhatu, tuturuwhatu, turuturuwhatu, turuatu, tuturuatu,* n. *1. Pluvialis obscurus, New Zealand red-breasted dotterel.*] *Tuturiwhatu* and the variants (and also TUTURUATU) are mainly applied to a dotterel (or plover) (fam. Charadriidae), and occur in the various forms frequently in the literature being prob. fairly common in early New Zealand spoken English but now confined to mainly Maori use. DOTTEREL esp. 2 (1) and (3). Cf. POHOWERA, TUTURUATU.
1835 YATE *NZ* (1970) 65 *Tuturiwatu-* This is a small delicate bird, not much larger than the thrush; with short black legs; and a pigeon-beak, with the nostrils very far down and widely extended. **1838** POLACK *NZ* I. 298 *Tuturi wátu* (hirundo) is a swallow, of a small size. **1842** GRAY *Fauna* in Dieffenbach *Travels in NZ* (1843) II. 195 *Charadrius xanthocheilus...* Tuturiwhatu of the natives. *Miss Stone.* Takahikahi of the natives. *Yate. Tuturuata* Of the natives of Cook's Straits. **1869** *TrNZI* I. (rev. edn.) 105 *Charadrius obscurus.* Tuturiwata. East Coast. Common. **1871** HUTTON *Catalogue Birds NZ* 24 *Charadrius obscurus...* Red-breasted Plover. Tuturiwata. **1885** *NZJSc.* II. 506 Tuturiwatu, Paturiwhata, Tituriwhatu-pukunui.—This excellent gamebird formerly bred on the Canterbury Plains. **1888** BULLER *Birds NZ* II. 1 (New-Zealand Dottrel)...*Native names.-* Tuturiwhati and Tuturiwhatu. *Ibid.* II. 3 *Charadrius bicinctus.* (Banded Dottrel.).. *Native names.-* Tuturiwhata, Tuturiwhatu, and Pohowera. **1904, 1928** Tuturiwatu, turiwati, tchūriwat [see DOTTEREL 1]. **1947** Tuturiwhatu [see DOTTEREL 2 (1)]. **1955** [see DOTTEREL 2 (3)]. **1966, 1970, 1985** [see DOTTEREL 2 (1)]. **1990** *Checklist Birds NZ* 132 *Chadrius obscurus... New Zealand Dotterel (Tuturiwhatu).*

tuturuatu. Also early **doodooroo-attoo, tuturuata.** [Ma. /tutuˈruatu/: Williams 463 *Tuturuatu..Pluvialis obscurus, New Zealand red-breasted dotterel,* and *Thinornis novaeseelandiae, the shore plover.* [=] *turiwhati.*] DOTTEREL 2 (3) (or PLOVER 2 (6)); see TUTURIWHATU for discussion of variants.
1842 GRAY *Fauna* in Dieffenbach *Travels in NZ* (1843) II. 196 *Charadrius obscurus...* Doodooroo-attoo of the natives of Queen Charlotte's Sound. **1874** *TrNZI* VI. 151 *Tuturuatu,* the name given to [the Masked Plover] by the natives is expressive of the call-note. **1888** BULLER *Birds NZ* II. 11 Thinornis novae zealandiae. (New-Zealand Sand-Plover.).. *Native names.—*Kohutapu and Tuturuatu. **1955** OLIVER *NZ Birds* 265 Shore Plover. Tuturuatu *Thinornis novaeseelandiae.* Forster, during Cook's second voyage, met with this endemic species both at Dusky and Queen Charlotte Sounds. **1966, 1970, 1985** [see PLOVER 2 (6)].

tuturuwhatu, var. TUTURIWHATU.

tuuii, var. TUI.

twacking. *Mangaroa Prison.* The beating or violent illegal punishment of prisoners.
1993 *Dominion* (Wellington) 30 Mar. 1 Violence used against inmates by staff at Napier's Mangaroa Prison was common practice, according to a sociology lecturer... Staff concerned about the practice—called 'twacking' by inmates and staff—had told him of it about the middle of last year.

twang. Also as **colonial twang,** a non-New Zealander's term for features of a native-born New Zealander's accent as distinguished from those of a speaker of southern British 'educated' English; often noted in respect of pronunciation of the diphthongs /æu/, /æi/, /ai/, or of a reputedly 'nasal' mode of delivery.
1903 BARNICOAT *Life in NZ As It Is* in *Empire Review* Nov. 394 Everyone, of course, is prepared for the 'colonial twang'—an evil worse in some parts of New Zealand than in others, but increasing everywhere. **1905** *Patea County Press* (Patea) 20 Jan. 3 [Quoting Dr Herz of Christchurch writing in the Berlin *Tageblatt.*] The New Zealander speaks bad English, and with a 'twang' which to the ear is horrible. He pronounces paper 'paiper', home 'heome'... The whole pronunciation has a greater similarity to cat music than to King's English. **1912** HERZ *NZ* 352 The disregard of the external evidences of culture, is shown in the speech of the people. Sad to relate, one far too often hears the younger generation talk with a twang that horrifies the ear of anyone used to good English... A mother will request her daughter '*Kyte*' to ask the '*lydy*' whether she will '*tyke*' another piece of '*cyke*'. The vowels and diphthongs are so drawn and twisted that it is often difficult to recognise the King's English... This twang is worse in Australia than in New Zealand but is gaining ground here and ought to be strenuously eradicated by school-teachers, for it really does not sound nice, and robs sweet girlish lips of all their poetry. **1924** REES *Heather of South* 17 She spoke without the faintest 'twang' which Creed had grown accustomed to expect, in a greater or lesser degree, amongst the back-block girls of New Zealand. *Ibid.* 29 Billy [a back-country farm-boy] always said 'didjer' [did you], and..no one had ever taught him..that well-known and useful little formula 'How now, brown cow!' in order to correct his colonial twang and get his vowel sounds rounded correctly. **1985** MARSHALL *Nest of Cuckoos* 24 Although he was ex-Hutt High, he now had an Oxford accent. He said his antipodean twang

undermined his credibility with his patients. **1991** *Dominion* (Wellington) 23 Aug. 1 A Victoria University project is trying to define the idiosyncrasies of the Kiwi twang and drawl.

tweeds, *n. pl.* [AND 1954.] Men's (sports) trousers or 'strides' in New Zealand are rarely made of tweed.
1917 INGRAM *Anzac Diary* 4 Jan. (1987) 9 Some in navy serge suits, some in grey tweeds, some even in knickerbockers. **c1946** University students, Victoria University catch-cry. 'Down with the tweeds.' **1951** *Moa on Lambton Quay* 21 Some drongo's beer spills on your tweeds As you're drinking, as you're drinking in the pubs. **1962** HORI *Half-gallon Jar* 75 I think all the others have death adders in their pockets, cause not one of them touches his tweeds.

Twelve Apostles. *Hawke's Bay. Hist.* Occas. init. cap. Also as **the apostles**, a nickname for a group of Hawke's Bay land speculators of the 19th century (quot. 1985 makes speculation into legend). Cf. FORTY THIEVES b, SIGNS OF THE ZODIAC.
1873 *Richmond-Atkinson Papers* (1960) II. 347 We are now in the thick of the cross examinatn. by Sheehan of the chiefest of the apostles—Tizzey the Tanner (Ko Tanera)... have not found anything that can be called a rat. **1877** *NZPD* XXV. 316 They were retained for £300 to do all that the Heretaunga people required—I mean the 'twelve apostles'. **1885** *Wairarapa Daily* 21 Aug. 2 Owing to the action taken by those 'Apostles', the land has been largely increased in value. **1887** *Auckland Weekly News* 8 Oct. 8 The Heret[au]nga Plain, some forty square miles in extent—a block of the fattest land in the colony—was parcelled out amongst a syndicate of twelve gentlemen, notoriously known as the twelve apostles. **1890** *NZ Observer* 15 Nov. 1 The Napier *Telegraph* has treated the Twelve Apostles of Hawke's Bay to some healthy reading for once. **1895** *NZPD* LXXXIV. 182 There is a Tory Party—or, in other words, what they call the land-grabbers, or 'Twelve Apostles' in Hawke's Bay. **1958** REED *Story of Hawke's Bay* 171 The names of twelve owners of these properties were so much in the news at the time that they came to be known as 'The Twelve Apostles'. **1984** BOYD *City of the Plains* 10 A rival of *The Hawke's Bay Herald*, *The Times* had increased its circulation prodigiously by publishing articles headed *Acts of the Apostles* and *Apostolic Creed*. Though there were 7 lessees and 12 shares, not 12 apostles, the name stuck. **1985** SHERWOOD *Botanist at Bay* 129 It was a Hastings lawyer did the fixing, to keep it out of the papers. He acts for a lot of those awesome Hawkes Bay families who came over with the Twelve Apostles. [**1985** *Note*] A nickname for the Founding Fathers of the town of of Hastings.

twinkie. Also **twinkle** (poss. erron. for **twinkie**). [Prob. from sudden star-like 'twinkling' showings of the white eye-circle, caused by the rapid, darting movements of a bird whose body tends to be indistinguishable from its preferred backgrounds.] SILVEREYE.
1922 *Auckland Weekly News* 10 Aug. 17 Among their [*sc.* white-eyes'] familiar English names are, wax-eyes, blighties, winter migrants, pennyweights, and twinkles. **1946** *JPS* LV. 159 *tauhou*, a wandering bird..blight-bird; twinkie; button-eye; wax-eye.

twister.
1. [For origin, see quot. 1956.] *Helcogramma medium* (fam. Trypterygiidae), a small marine fish; COCKABULLY 2.
1956 GRAHAM *Treasury NZ Fishes* 334 The name Twister was given..(1) from the characteristics twisted or wavy markings on each side of the body, (2) from its amazing habit in captivity of eluding other fish, 'twisting' and escaping capture when a larger fish was chasing it. **1972** DOAK *Fishes* 103 The estuarine blenny..and the twister, *Helcogramma medium*, of the splash zone, have gay signal hues; the first dorsal fin when erected is patterned with red, blue or orange. **1982** AYLING *Collins Guide* (1984) 283 Like all small blenny-like fishes twisters do not live very long; most die before they are two years old. This species is common on rocky coasts. **1991** BRADSTOCK *Fishing* 17 *Cockabully*. This is a general name for a lot of different kinds of small fish called triplefins. Other names are bully, blenny, twister, topknot, tommy cod.

2. A tool to make a twitch in fencewire.
1982 *Agric. Gloss.* (MAF) 30 *Twister*: Tool to make a twitch.

twitch. [f. spec. use of *twitch* a loop which can be tightened by twisting: see OED *n.*¹ 3 b.]
1. *Northland logging.* The bight of a loop in a logging chain. Also *vbl. n.*, the action of tightening a chain holding logs to a truck by using a twitch as a levering loop.
1950 p.c. R. Gilberd Okaihau. The old method of tightening the chain securing the logs to trucks is called 'twitching', or 'taking a twitch'. First the chain is fastened leaving it quite slack. A lever is passed through the bight and used to twist the slack up on itself. When the chain is tight enough the end of the lever is tied to the chain. A 'chain-rack' is now used—a giant Hayes wire-strainer. It is sometimes, but improperly, called a 'twitch'. 'Twitch' is probably an amalgamation of 'twist' and 'hitch'.

2. Special Comb. **twitch-chain** *obs.*; **twitch-stick, twitching-stick**, a rod used to twist chains tight; **twitchwire** (also **twitch**), terms used in fencing.
1961 HENDERSON *Friends In Chains* 189 Twitch Chain: Chains holding load and tightened by short iron rod. *Ibid.* 190 *Twitch up.* Tighten twitches; finish. **1924** *Otago Witness* (Dunedin) 11 Mar. 65 Twitching sticks were put on the chains to make them tight. **1982** *Agric. Gloss.* (MAF) 30 Twitch, [twitchwire]: A twisted tie-wire of two or more strands. Twitch stick: Twister made of wood or steel.

twitch elder. WHISTLEWOOD (*Leycesteria formosa*).
1946 *Bull. Wellington Bot. Soc. No.14* 8 Here are some [vernacular names]... *Leycesteria formosa*.. Japanese spiderwort, twitch elder.

two. Used in various combinations and collocations where the number (of) *two* is of significance: **two-and-a-buck, two-and-a-kick,** see BUCK *n.*³ 1 and KICK *n.*; **two bastards** (or **B's**) **on bikes** *two up*, see quot. 1988; **two bob**, see *two bob in the quid* (QUID 1), also *crazy as a two-bob watch* (SILLY A b); **two-cut** *shearing*, SECOND CUT; **two draws and a spit**, a smoke; **two ladies on bicycles** *two up*, see quots.; **two-one-eight** (also **218**), see SECTION 218; **two ones** *two-up*, 'head' and a 'tail' turning up after the spin of two coins; **twopence** *obs.*, a two-shilling piece; **twos-and-threes**, a group game; **two-spot**, 200 dollars; **two-tooth** [f. the number of permanent teeth a sheep has at a particular time: see OED *two* IV 1 a, 1742], a sheep aged from 18 to 22 months, as an absolute age; also a name for a two-toothed sheep; **two-year artist**, see quot.
1937 two bastards on bikes [see *two ladies on bicycles* below]. **1956** CODY *28 (Maori) Battalion* 13 Of an evening throughout the [troop] ship many strange and illegal cults could be heard reciting a formula which included 'Heads a pair' and '**Two B's on bikes**, presided over by a tohunga. **1955** BOWEN *Wool Away* 3 My advice to all is to concentrate on shearing to a pattern, keeping the comb on the sheep, watching yourself for '**two-cut**' and keeping it to a minimum. *Ibid.* 158 Two-cut. This happens where the staple of wool is cut above its base on the sheep, making it necessary for the handpiece to come back and trim off a short piece of wool that has been cut before. Such short pieces are of little value. **1953** STRONACH *Musterer on Molesworth* 10 Everyone managed a cigarette—'**two draws and a spit**', as the musterers called it. **1937** PARTRIDGE *Dict. Slang* 921 **two ladies on bikes.** The figure of Britannia on the obverse of the two pennies: two-up players', esp. New Zealanders': C. 20. I.e. when both turned up tails; the 'heads' betters call them the *two bastards on bikes*. **1938** *Press* (Christchurch) (McNab Slang) 2 Apr. 18 A 'boxer' is a gratuity to the 'ringie' at two-up, a game supplying the phrase 'two ladies on bicycles', two pennies showing Britannia. **1912** *Truth* 20 Jan. 7 Even the metallic ring of the coins could be heard, followed by the suppressed sighs of 'heads' bettors as 'tails' were cried while '**two ones**', 'barred', 'heads a dollar'..and other equally quaint and even classic chants, were wafted on the midnight breezes. **1899** *Bulletin* (Sydney) 14 Jan. (Red Page) [Letter from *Loafer*, Tauranga.] We have here three slang words for 'florin'—*zweideener* (from *zwei*=two, *deener* a shilling); **twopence**..and *a brace of pegs*. **1868** *Marlborough Express* (Blenheim) 7 Nov. 4 Steeple-chasing, cricket..were varied by a game known as 'tig', or '**twos and threes**', rounders, &c., in some of which the ladies assisted. **1982** NEWBOLD *Big Huey* 19 he asked if he could have an ounce of skag on credit... I said ok, they could have it for twelve hundred. I was still scoring for a grand so it seemed like an easy **two-spot** for the morning. **1855** *Nelson Examiner* 7 Feb. 2 The sheep were **two**, four, and six-**tooth** ewes. **1860** *Puketoi Station Diary* (Hocken TS) 14 Mar. Ewe lambs 32 two tooth ewes 402 four & six tooth 638, full mouthed 1322 broken mouthed 11, wedders 290 total 2695. **1892** *NZ Official Handbook* 124 The weight of these half-bred sheep at two-tooth varies..from 56lb. to 65lb. **1962** SHARPE *Country Occasions* 51 A hill-country flockowner keeps all his ewe lambs, turning a percentage of eighteen-month-old ewes—two-tooths, as they are called—into his main flock every year. **1973** FERNANDEZ *Tussock Fever* 1 The boss was there working the drafting gate—two-tooths to the left-hand gate, six-tooths to the right. **1987** [see FULL-MOUTHED]. **1992** ANDERSON *Portrait Artist's Wife* 29 They spoke of falling prices at the yards. Frank's two-tooths had been a disaster. **1955** BJ Cameron Collection (TS July) **two-year artist** (n) A man or girl who comes out from England under the assisted immigration scheme with an already formed intention of going back as soon as the two-year contract is up.

two purra, var. TUPARA.

two up. [AND 1884.]
1. A gambling game where two coins are tossed in the air usu. from a flat piece of wood (see KIP), and players bet on whether the coins on landing will show two 'heads' or two 'tails'. See also SWI(-UP). (For terms used in two-up, see: GREY *n.*¹ 1, HEADING 'EM, KIP, SPIN *n.* and *v.*, SPINNER 2, *two bastards on bikes, two ladies on bicycles, two ones* (TWO).)
1900 SCOTT *Colonial Turf* 96 You belong to a gang of..robbers of widows,—spielers is the term—who play 'two up' with pennies. **1904** *NZ Observer* 23 Apr. 7 The money to be made at the game of 'two-up' is not worth the risk. **1913** CARR *Country Work* 47 In some

camps a school of poker, nap or 'two up' is sometimes started. **1936** [see SPIN *n.* 1 a]. **1953** 13–17 M A1 Thames DHS 20 Two up [M5]

Hence **two-upper** [AND 1905], a two-up player.

1914 *Evening Post* (Wellington) 22 Mar. 2 Two-uppers Fined.

2. Special Comb. **two-up ring** [AND 1913], the 'ring' within which a two-up game is played; **two-up school** [AND 1897], a group of two-up gamblers.

1918 WESTON *Three Yrs. with New Zealanders* 252 The 'two up' ring is their billiard room or bridge parlour. **1938** HYDE *Nor Yrs. Condemn* 125 He hadn't been lucky at the two-up ring lately. **1906 two-up school** [see KIP 3]. **1917** *NZ At the Front* 10 Roll of men proceeding to Crown and Anchor and Two Up schools. **1938** HYDE *Nor Yrs. Condemn* 71 Starkie drew £84..and at two the same day was broke, the two-up school taking the proceeds. **1945** HENDERSON *Gunner Inglorious* 121 During play in a two-up school in Tripoli, one of the coins was sent spinning high in the air. **1987** KEOGH in *Metro Fiction* 8 The two-up school goes on in the small bedroom.

tyke, var. TIKE.

typo, var. TAIPO.

tyre kicker. *Car-salesmen.* A person who merely examines used cars, tests the tyres, but does not buy; hence a politician who talks round but does not take up difficult choices.

1986 *NZ Herald* (Auckland) 22 Jan. 2 Car dealers have a collection of jargon they use on the yard, so if you are thinking of taking up selling cars as a career, there are a few terms you should know... 'Sandwich munchers' and 'tyre kickers' are not very popular in car yards. **1991** *Dominion* (Wellington) 13 May 1 Mr Peters yesterday hit out at 'political tyre-kickers', populist prejudice and shallow analysis, after Mr Bolger slammed the idea of a Maori super-ministry.

U

U.E. /juːˈwiː/: see UNIVERSITY ENTRANCE.

uhunga, var. HAHUNGA.

umbrella-tree. [f. the long, downward-pointed leaves resembling the spines of an umbrella.] The juvenile form of LANCEWOOD.
1856 TANCRED *Nat. Hist. Canterbury* 21 The singular umbrella-tree of the colonists..grows also in the woods near the sea. The native name is 'horoeka'. **1952** RICHARDS *Chatham Is.* 65 *Pseudopanax..chathamicum*... Of the young unbranched plants the leaves are horizontal or erect not hanging straight down as in the New Zealand species (and therefore known as the umbrella tree).

umu. Also occas. early **humu**, **oòhmoo**; **uma**. [Ma. /ˈumu/: Williams 467 *umu*, *imu*. n. *1*. Earth oven... =*hangi*.] HANGI 1.
[*Note*] In recent times *umu* can connote Pacific Island cooking (methods) which do not necessarily involve steaming in a subterranean oven (see quot. 1995).
[**1820** LEE & KENDALL *NZ Gram. & Vocab.* 147 U'mu, *s.* An oven. **c1826–27** in Boultbee *Journal* (1986) 111 oven—oòhmoo] **1845** WAKEFIELD *Adventures in NZ* I. 75 The tangi had terminated; the *umu* or 'cooking holes' were smoking away for the feast. **1849** TORLESSE *Papers* (1958) 68 We knocked up a warre..and made a humu to cook our pork. **1864** *Richmond-Atkinson Papers* 12 Feb. (1960) II. 87 There were eight large *umus* (ovens) some of them not yet opened. **1873** *TrNZI* V. 96 Being all in and around the *umus* (or native ovens) in which they had been cooked. **1905** [see HANGI 1]. **1937** *Tararua Tramper* May 4 That evening we dined on roast lamb cooked in the Club 'umus'. **1948** COWAN *Down the Years in the Maniototo* 4 When the Murisons came first to Puketoi..several uma or Maori cooking places were observed. **1950** *Landfall 13* 85 The passage describes in detail the well-remembered lighting of the *umu* fires. **1963** [see HANGI 2]. **1972** SHADBOLT *Strangers and Journeys* 474 Mother, grandmother and children scattered around in vague blue smoke for their *umu*, or earth oven. **1982** BURTON *Two Hundred Yrs. NZ Food* 1 There are countless ways of preparing food Maori style, but basically there were only three ways of cooking it. The first, which involves steaming in a subterranean oven called an *umu* or *hangi*, is known as *tao* cooking. It was the preferred method of cooking for groups of people. **1995** *Evening Post* (Wellington) 6 Feb. 1 Waitangi Day hangi and umu meals for lunch and dinner [at Porirua's multicultural Polynesian festival] were well in preparation around the lagoon, with the smell of pork wafting in the air.

unco. *a.* [f. *unco*(ordinated.] Applied contemptuously, mainly by adolescents, to one physically or intellectually clumsy or inept.
1984 14–16 F E29 E127 Pakuranga Coll. 10 unco (unco–ordinated) [F4 useless person or thing] **1994** *Dominion* (Wellington) 19 July 22 Being selected for Brazil as the goalkeeper is probably some sort of national joke. He's the unco one. That's the way it was at school—you're unco, you go goalie... Us co-ordinated guys will head up and do the scoring.

under below!, *int.* [f. a nautical call.] A call warning of a timber drive; or, by watersiders, a warning when working cargo in slings.
1955 BOSWELL *Dim Horizons* 24 All day long across the valleys and hills came the long-drawn cry of 'Jah-ho-o-o', and the still longer sing-song call of 'Under—below—in the vall-ee-eee!' as bushman warned bushman of a dangerous fall or a 'drive'. **1957** *Star-Sun* (Christchurch) 19 Oct. 9 The watersider witnesses gave evidence that the customary 'under below' warning was given as the strain was taken on the sling and it began to swing. **1969** MOORE *Forest to Farm* 49 All preparations [for the drive] having been made, and everyone cleared out of the area below, the big tree was felled, with a bellow of 'under below' as he started to tip over.

underbush. *Obs.* UNDERSCRUB *n.*
1848 BRUNNER *Exped. Middle Island* 8 Feb. in Taylor *Early Travellers* (1959) 301 With some difficulty [I] pushed my way through the low underbush, and ascended to the grass terrace. **1849** BREES *Panorama NZ* 27 Crawling along the ground among the underbush and trees. **1850** TORLESSE *Papers* (1958) 169 Fine Totara Forest with underbush cleared. **1854** *Richmond-Atkinson Papers* (1960) I. 157 You commence a clearing by cutting what is called the under bush—that is the supple jacks, small trees and all the ferns; this is done with a bill hook. **1874** KENNAWAY *Crusts* 154 The pigs escaped ino the dense underbush, and got away into the interior.

underdungers, *n. pl.* Also **underdungas**. [f. *under*(pants + *dunga*(ree)s, with a possible play on *dung*.] A jocular name for underpants.
1981 JOHNSTON *Fish Factory* 88 'I hope he hasn't changed, but I suppose he could have...' 'Yeah. Underdungers once a week and socks every fortnight,' Jamie retorted. **1988** MCGILL *Dict. Kiwi Slang* 117 *underdungas* underpants, possibly from dungas as short for dungarees.

underground mutton. [AND 1919.] A euphemistic name for rabbit(-flesh) as meat.
1960 SCRYMGEOUR *Memories Maoriland* 39 This 'underground mutton' was taken to a depot, frozen, then carted to railhead, then to the wharves, and exported to Britain, where..a ready market was always assured for New Zealand rabbit. **1975** ANDERSON *Men of Milford Road* 33 With the millions of rabbits running round Southland there was no shortage of meat as long as you liked 'underground mutton'. **1986** OWEN & PERKINS *Speaking for Ourselves* 76 What was known in those days [of the Great Depression] as 'underground mutton', that was the average struggler's meat, and the average family depended on it. **1990** *Listener* 23 July 103 Morioris, rastas, the ones who feed off unnergroun' mutton, puha, eels in ditches, you try and find an unsprayed ditch!

under-run: see UNDER-RUNNER.

under-runner. Also **under-run**. [Poss. f. *under* + an adaptation of *runnel*.] An underground stream or stream channel. Cf. TOMO.
1904 CAMPBELL *Reminiscences* 47 Dobbin was a little tired, and the doctor (a fearless rider), going at a hard pace..toppled with poor old Dobbin into a hole, known as an 'under-runner'. **1921** GUTHRIE-SMITH *Tutira* 34 The..grit [is] carried off particle by particle between the floor of marl and the ceiling of humus. In process of time the sharp pumice grit chisels out of the former a minute irregular bed. It deepens into a tiny hidden runnel; at last there is created a subterranean stream, or, in shepherd's phrase, an 'under-runner'. Its course is at first unseen, then, as through process of time its channel is gouged out, and as the carpet of humus fibre gives way at irregular intervals, great rents and holes betray its presence. The bed continues to deepen, the carpet of turf falls in more and more, until finally the under-runner becomes an open rivulet. **1937** AYSON *Thomas* 66 It went head foremost into a big under-runner hole, dashing Thomas against the bank. **1953** DUFF *Shepherd's Calendar* (1961) 140 Then a faint sound came from almost under my feet, and I realized that the lamb had slipped into an under-runner 15 or 20 feet higher up, and had worked downhill to the point where I was standing. **1973** FERNANDEZ *Tussock Fever* 105 They came to a little gut where water drained from the swampy flats... 'This is an under-run,' warned Rusty. 'It's hollow underneath. You'll have to jump.' **1976** FISHER *Divers of Arakam* 55 I had fallen into a fifteen foot boulder-and-sand-lined hole known as an 'under-run'.

underscrub, *n.* [f. *under*(growth + SCRUB: AND 1861.] Forest undergrowth. See also SCRUB *n.* 1 a, UNDERBUSH.
1870 PRENTICE *A Tale of NZ* (GALMS) 56 To force a passage through lighter underscrub [in the forest]. **1885** *Wairarapa Daily* 15 Jan. 2 Went up the river about three and a half miles..underscrub light, timber not heavy. **1892** KELLY *Journey Upper Waitara Valley* 5 The underscrub was not so dense, but the cattle feed still existed. **1903** *NZ Illustr. Mag.* Oct. 19 Steel went ahead..slashing supplejack and underscrub with a huge straight-bladed knife. **1937** BUICK *Moa-Hunters NZ* 132 Today..the camp site [is] overgrown with trees and tangled underscrub. **1959** *Tararua 13* 45 *Underscrub* to denote undergrowth has been in occasional use whereas *underbrush* I have found so far only in Brunner. **1988** WARR *Bush-burn to Butter* 42 Work [*sc.* clearing] began by cutting down the underscrub.

underscrub, *v. trans.* To remove undergrowth from (bush or bush land).
1883 *Brett's Colonists' Guide* 18 A good bushman will underscrub and fall an acre of average bush in a week. **1902** *Settler's Handbook NZ* 285 Here experience has shown that good results are obtained by letting the felled bush lie for an extra season, then underscrubbing any fresh growth, together with close lopping. **1913** CARR *Country Work* 31 The bulk of this is cut with a slasher in the same manner as underscrubbing heavy bush.

Hence **underscrubber**, one who clears undergrowth; **underscrubbing**, *vbl. n.* [OED 1935], the clearing of undergrowth.
1913 CARR *Country Work* 31 **Underscrubbers** vary from 30s a week... Grass seeders 1s to 1s 6d an

hour and tucker themselves. **1892** *NZ Official Handbook* 156 So, also, the handling of axe and bill-hook so as to avoid danger in **under-scrubbing**, felling, and clearing, is not learnt in a day. **1913** CARR *Country Work* 30 The work of clearing [lawyer] ready for the axemen is called underscrubbing. **1935** MCKENZIE *Gael Fares Forth* 79 To the small boys was assigned the task of 'underscrubbing' or cutting the small trees, shrubs, vines..and other plants which grow so luxuriantly on the forest floor. **1948** MUNDY *There's Gold* 83 The under-scrubbing in New Zealand would be done for about four to five shillings. **1951** LEVY *Grasslands NZ* (1970) (Gloss.) 363 *Underscrubbing*—The removal of undergrowth from standing forest. **1969** MOORE *Forest to Farm* 48 The underscrubbing was done first.

unimproved, *ppl. a.* Of land, having no 'improvements' made in the form of clearing, laying down pasture, fencing, buildings, etc. Cf. *improved* (IMPROVE *v.*), IMPROVEMENT.

1892 *NZ Official Handbook* 121 The percentage of increase [in lambing]..is very high, particularly so in the paddocks..while on the hill or unimproved country it varies from 45 to 80 per cent. **1914** CHUDLEIGH *Diary* 1 Nov. (1950) 464 An Estate agent came over to see the land. He valued the unimproved at £15 p.a...and some sections higher. **1936** BELSHAW et al. *Agric. Organiz. NZ* 30 It has been indicated that, of the 43 million acres of occupied land, about 24 million acres are 'unimproved,' and are under native grasses..scrub and virgin bush. **1953** *Evening Post* (Wellington) 24 Mar. 4 [Advt] Unimproved Land for Selection: Applications..are invited for the undermentioned unimproved farm. **1966** TURNER *Eng. Lang. Austral. & NZ* 171 [The European New Zealander] still talks of unspoilt nature but in town a section without buildings is called *unimproved*. **1986** RICHARDS *Off the Sheep's Back* 100 A large block of unimproved Maori land..proved a stumbling block to the progress of the valley.

unit, *n.*[1] Also **electric unit**, **multiple-unit**. [Abbrev. of *electric multiple-unit*.] A suburban electric train composed of a motorized coach attached to one or several trailer-coaches (see esp. quot. 1969).

[**1951** *NZ Geogr.* Oct. 160 Meanwhile multiple-unit train sets meet suburban demands on the electrified sections between Wellington and Paekakariki and between Wellington and Johnsonville.] **1953** *Weekly News* (Auckland) 14 Oct. 26 [Caption] A multiple-unit electric train proceeding to Wellington. Ibid. 27 [Caption] An electric train unit in Taita station. **1959** in Holcroft *Voice in Village* (1989) 18 New Zealand railway carriages, except the electric units of Wellington..have 'toilets'. **1969** p.c. E.H. Hitchcock, formerly NZ Railways electrical engineer. The full official title is *Electric Multiple Unit*, often shortened to *Multiple Unit*, or to *Electric Unit* (the latter also obtains in general popular usage). The 'unit' is actually a motor-coach with one or two trailer-coaches attached. Depending on traffic, gradients, etc., up to three of these 'units' can be put together under one driver to form, say, a nine-car train. *Units* were introduced to the Wellington–Johnsonville line in 1938; then to the Wellington–Paekakariki line in 1946; and a few years later to the heavily-used Hutt Valley line. The word came into popular usage (e.g. 'I'm off to catch the unit.') probably c1939–40. **1976** O'SULLIVAN *Miracle* 15 Each morning he would take the unit into town, take it back each evening at five-thirty. **1988** LAY *Fools on Hill* 218 You'd have a nice little house in Newlands, be travelling into town every day on the unit, be hiring a telly from the PSIS [*sc.* Public Service Investment Society].

unit, *n.*[2]

1. [Abbrev. of *home* or *housing unit*: AND 1949.]
a. An accommodation 'unit' as part of a larger building or block or cluster of buildings (as a (semi-detached) flat or house or one of a block or cluster built around central facilities; or detached accommodation at a motel, etc.). See also *home unit* (HOME *n.*[2] 3).

1974 *Dominion* (Wellington) 9 Mar. 27 [Advt] In principal tourist area... 11 [motel] units plus two separate flats as well as owner's house. **1976** SARGESON *Sunset Village* [dustcover] Sunset Village is a 'pensioner housing settlement' containing uniform living units into which society via local government has cornered a number of pensioners. **1980** *Islands* 29 131 Bit of a stir tonight in my unit, end of conference party sort of thing. **1983** BUCKLEY *Of Toffs & Toilers* 143 The little fencible cottages built for the men and their families were at first double units of kauri weatherboards. **1985** FRAME *Envoy from Mirror City* 165 Arriving at Oamaru, I went at once to the motor camp where I had rented a unit for the night. **1986** *Evening Post* (Wellington) 9 Oct. 32 The..Housing Corporation will start hiring small relocatable units to elderly or disabled people wanting to live near family or close friends. **1988** *New Women's Fiction* 54 At Makarora, they took a motel unit.

b. Special Comb. **unit title**, a title to one of a group of flats or other premises separate from the land on which it is built. Cf. STRATUM TITLE.

1987 *Evening Post* (Wellington) 7 Jan. 20 *Kelburn*: OYO. $79,500 ono. Architect designed 2 dbr unit in block of 2, sep amenities, parking, unit title.

2. a. A block of farmland; esp. as **economic unit**, a farm (or occas. a number of farm animals) of sufficient size to be a viable business proposition.

1916 *TrNZI* XLVIII. 12 It's all economic units. When it's sheep, that means about a thousand acres of this sort of land. **1953** *Evening Post* (Wellington) 24 Mar. 4 [Advt] Nukumaru Farm Settlement..; 2 dairy units estimated to carry about 53 and 55 dairy cows and replacements respectively... [Advt] Santoft: 5 dairy units estimated to carry 45–55 dairy cows and replacements, and 1 fat lamb unit estimated to carry about 700–900 ewes and 50–70 cattle. **1982** WHEELER *Hist. Sheep Stations NZ* 25 'Why halfbreds?' He replied: 'They are good economic units—strong, free-mustering sheep that suit our country.' **1985** LANGDALE-HUNT *Last Entail Male* 47 Frederick Hunt leased three blocks of land at the back of his farm to three tenants... None of these units was economic and the only way these tenants could exist was by taking outside work. **1994** *Dominion* (Wellington) 27 May 18 Hill country grazing unit up for sale... It is described as a very efficient farming unit.

b. A person farming a 'unit'.

1934 in KING *Whina* (1983) 262 You told Mr Findlay that it would be alright to put a Maori unit off his land, and elect another man to take his place, so long as the natives were consulted.

unit, *n.*[3] [Compare the wider US application, OED 1 g, 1894 (Chicago).] Formerly, a full year's work in a subject or course to be credited (if passed) towards a university degree. (Now usu. replaced by systems in which the standard module is a 'credit' or 'paper', each being of less than a full year's work in a subject.)

1927 *NZ Univ. Calendar* 65 Every course for the degree of Bachelor of Arts shall consist of nine units, a unit being defined as one year's work in a subject. **1958** *Victoria Univ. of Wellington Calendar* 74 A candidate who has been credited with passes in units (or subjects) common to two or more courses may transfer not more than three units (or subjects). **1965** *Salient* (Wellington) 1 Mar. 1 The average number of units taken by a student in New Zealand is 2.5. **1979** PARTON *University of NZ* 80 The BA degree of six pass subjects had..failed to survive the Reichel-Tate Commission. However, the degree involving nine 'units' with two taken to stage III, did not meet all needs. **1988** *New Women's Fiction* 68 I was going to be a librarian and take some extra-mural units. **1991** *Metro* (Auckland) Nov. 76 But the second year I did really well and passed all my units.

United. *Hist.* The name of the political party formed in 1927, comprising remnants of the former Liberal Party.

1948 LIPSON *Politics of Equality* 222 In desperation at their successive defeats [from 1922] the Liberals had sought an elixir of political life under new slogans and labels, calling themselves first Liberal, then Liberal-Labor, then National, and eventually rising as the United party. **1959** SINCLAIR *Hist. NZ* 246 Droves of them [*sc.* voters], believing the newspapers' figure, returned to the Liberal (now called 'United') fold, hoping nostalgically that the pastures would be as lush as when Seddon had been the shepherd. **1966** *Encycl. NZ* II. 813 The United Party, the successor to the Liberal Party, was formed in 1927 and, after a surprising success in the general election in the following year, it formed a Government under the veteran Sir Joseph Ward.

University Entrance. Usu. as the acronym **U.E.** (with an occas. joc. form **yew-ee**), and in full **University Entrance Examination.** Formerly, an award allowing entry to a university gained by public examinations or accrediting in the last years of secondary schooling.

1926 *NZ Statutes* No.70 742 [NZ Universities Amendment Act] There is hereby established a University Entrance Board..whose duty shall be to consider the curricula and courses of study at secondary schools in relation to the..requirements for matriculation at any constituent college. **1929** *AJHR* E-6 2 The present lower leaving-certificate is granted to a pupil who has..in general reached a standard of attainment comparable to that required in the University Entrance or Class D examination. **1937** BEAGLEHOLE *University of NZ* 378 This result had been remedied in 1907..by the extension of the bursary system in 1912 to all secondary school pupils who qualified for a Higher Leaving Certificate, that is, had had at least one year's secondary education after passing the University Entrance Examination. **1952** WILSON *Julien Ware* 73 At the end of 1926 Julien Ware passed the University Entrance examination. **1963** *Evening Post* (Wellington) 3 Mar. 17 His [*sc.* Burchfield's] nieces and nephews here were talking about taking 'U.E.'—it was 'matric' when he left [in 1949]. **1971** SHADBOLT *Bullshit & Jellybeans* 30 You know these days Shadbolt School Cert doesn't mean very much... What you need in life is UE. **1986** *Listener* 26 Apr. 46 The inclusion of *University Entrance* reminds us how subject to change such words are. **1988** LAY *Fools on Hill* 47 'Got to get yew-wee first,' said Helen.

unreal. [OEDAS II. 283 'Chiefly N. Amer. and Austral.', *US 1965*.] As an exclamation of approval or delight, mainly in adolescents' use; as an adjective, pleasant, delightful, pleasantly surprising.

1984 14 F E131 Wgton Girls C. 18 Unreal [F3] **1984** 16–17 E14 Pakuranga Coll. 35A Unreal! [MF3] **1992** *Dominion* (Wellington) 20 Jan. 1 [Sergeant Wall said] 'It's unreal the amount of information the public has fed through to us.'

untold. Mainly *adolescents*.

1. As a quantifier, indicating a limitless quantity.

1981 *Auckland Secondary Teachers College* (Goldie Brown Collect.) *untold*: endless quantity; also used alone, e.g., *I have untold* [object understood]. **1985** BENTLEY & FRASER *Grand Limerick Tour* [No.] 56 It's Fair Day at Mangatainoka, What's the guts for your average joker? Pitching possums is big, There's calf roping, greased pig, And a yahoo, with untold strip poker. **1985** MITCALFE *Hey Hey Hey* 103 'How many [free games] you got?' 'Countless. Untold!' said that hardened space hero.

2. Among children and adolescents, an exclamation or expression of delight; often an intensifier.

1984 15–16 F E1 Pakuranga Coll. 8 Untold [F3] **1984** 14 F E135 Wgton Girls C. 8 Untold [F5] **1987** *Chosen Place* 38 'That's untold gross man! How could you go to something like that?' Sally, our fourteen year old looked at us in disgust.

unveiling, *vbl. n.* and *ppl. a.* The English name of a post-European Maori custom (called *hurahanga kōhatu* or *pōhatu*) comprising a ceremonial unveiling of a memorial gravestone a certain time after an interment.

[*Note.*] See note at HAHUNGA, the ancient ceremony modified by that of 'unveiling', the latter also having ritual exemplars in European formal ceremonies of unveiling foundation stones, etc.

1911 *King's Collegian* X(1) May 73 A large gathering of Maoris took place here last month, on the occasion of the unveiling of two monuments in honour of the late Hone Heke... The ceremony of the unveiling of the large stone on Kaikohe Hill, erected by the Government, was most imposing. **1918** *Hawera Star* 9 Apr. 4 On Monday, in the presence of a large gathering of Natives at the Taiporohenui pa, the unveiling of the memorial stone to the memory of the late Mrs Alex Campbell, who died just a year ago, took place. **1928** *Na To Hoa Aroha* (1986) I. 89 I should personally like to have the unveiling ceremony the same week as the Ngaruawahia meeting. **1935** 17 Aug. in *Na To Hoa Aroha* (1988) III. 145 Rima Wakarua..was moved to suggest to his people a visit to the Tai-rawhiti district, ostensibly to attend the unveiling of the monument to young Jack Raru, who died in Rotorua last year. **1964** METGE *New Maori Migration* 49 At unveilings, the ties attaching the cover to the gravestone were loosed and the cover removed by someone generally close to and beloved by the deceased. **1969** MEAD *Traditional Maori Clothing* 205 *Unveilings.* Unveiling ceremonies, especially those known as hura koowhatu ['to remove a covering', 'stone'], the unveiling of memorial headstones, are a common practice, particularly in the northern districts of the North Island. In 1958, 1,000 people attended an unveiling ceremony, at Taheke, Northland, during which the headstones of six Taheke people were unveiled. **1985** *Dominion* (Wellington) 10 Jan. 1 Her family said yesterday they feared she was dead because she failed to arrive for the unveiling of a family memorial stone. **1995** *Dominion* (Wellington) 29 Oct. 10 An unveiling ceremony of her husband's headstone was due to be held in mid October.

Hence **unveil** *v. trans.*, the loosening and removal of a cover ('veil') from a headstone during an unveiling ceremony.

1969 [see above]. **1983** OLIVER *James K. Baxter* 155 Some of these people gathered, a year later, to unveil his gravestone. **1987** *Undiscovered Country, Customs of Death and Dying* 9 The final event in the [Maori] grieving process is the Hurahanga Pohatu (unveiling of the memorial stone). This takes place some time after the deceased has been buried—usually one to five years later. **1992** *Landfall 183* 335 Nanny Bella's unveiling is today... The priest unveils the stone with a simple hymn and ceremony... Nanny's photo looks up at me.

up, *adv.* [Local uses of various senses of *up adv.*]

1. [AND *up adv.* away from a centre of population, 1805.] In the adverbial phr. **up the country**, away from the coast or a centre of settlement. Cf. UP-COUNTRY B.

1816 HALL in Elder *Marsden's Lieutenants* (1934) 124 My friendly natives being up the country in search of potatoes, a strange party came over from the other side of the Bay. **1843** *NZ Jrnl.* IV. 200 I have been twenty miles up the country. **1854** PAUL *Canterbury Settlement* 37 Those who go 'up the country' must provide accommodation for themselves. **1856** FITTON *NZ* 271 There are now..many ladies, living, not only in the towns..but also..on sheep or cattle stations, 'up the country'. **1874** BATHGATE *Col. Experiences* 67 Nothing can be vaguer than the phrase 'up the country' especially as when used in Dunedin it means anywhere out of town... The phrase is, however, susceptible of a little narrower interpretation than that indicated, as it is mostly limited to the gold fields districts of the interior.

2. *Chatham Islands.* In the phr. **to go up**, to travel to mainland New Zealand.

1934 *Press* (Christchurch) (Acland Gloss.) 20 Jan. 15 *Go up, to.*—Chatham Island term for 'going over to New Zealand'. **1951** *NZ Geogr.* Apr. 97 The Chatham Islands are legally part of New Zealand but are not of it. Islanders speak in their soft dialect of 'going up to New Zealand'.

up, *prep.* [Local uses of various senses of *up prep.*]

1. [OED *up prep.*[2] 6 c =up at '*colloq.* and *dial.*', 1960.] With ellipsis of a following modified **at**, **in**, **to**, etc., esp. **up the** 'up at'. Cf. DOWN *prep.*

1840 *NZ Jrnl.* I. 301 A good back country up the Hutt. **1843** in *William Swainson* June (1992) 98 You will see that we are at last 'up the Hutt', after all the talking of removing up here [from Wellington]. **1866** *Puketoi Station Diary* (Hocken TS) 6 Aug. Jamie getting gravel from 'up the gully'. **c1875** MEREDITH *Adventuring in Maoriland* (1935) 155 Presently, I bade them adieu, mounted my horse, and started for 'up the district.' **1942** GASKELL in *All Part of the Game* (1978) 7 Well, pretty soon old Rangi die and we have the big tangi up the pa. **1959** SLATTER *Gun in My Hand* 170 Picking fruit up the Bay and forking peas into the cannery. **1974** MASON *Hand on Rail* (TS 1987) 39 He'll be sittin' in that bach up Huia [*sc.* up Huia way]. **1978** WATSON *World Is an Orange* 118 It is just after lunch; Dale and Terry have been getting wood up the back. **1985** BENTLEY & FRASER *Grand Limerick Tour* [No.] 8 A cow cocky up Tokoroa Rang his agent to order a moa.

2. Of places, north of the speaker. Contrast DOWN *prep.*

1850 GODLEY *Letters* 16 Nov. (1951) 129 [Mr Hadfield] and his wife did not return from 'up the coast' [from Wellington]. **1966** TURNER *Eng. Lang. Austral. & NZ* 198 Generally *up* is used in New Zealand for places north and *down* for south.

3. [Prob. a shortened form of *be stuck up (oneself).*] In the phr. **to be up oneself**, to be very conceited.

1980 LELAND *Kiwi-Yankee Dict.* 107 *up himself*: In practice this refers to someone who has a severely exaggerated idea of his own importance (and/or qualifications, intelligence, etc. etc.). It derives from the suggestions that someone with such strong narcissistic tendencies could find only himself worthy of his own concupiscent attentions. **1984** 15–17 F E1 Pakuranga Coll. 17 Up him/herself [MF31] **1984** 14 F E135 Wgton Girls C. 17 Up himself [F8]

up-country, *a., adv.,* and *n.* [Used elsewhere, but now rare in Britain: see OED.]

A. *adj.* [AND 1816.] Situated in, pertaining or belonging to, localities away from the coast or centres of population.

1834 McDONNELL *Observations NZ* 14 Nearly all the up-country settlers have been ruined. **1859** FULLER *Five Years' Residence* 162 Up-country life. **1860** in Butler *First Year* (1863) iv 50 Every now and then he leaves his up-country avocations and becomes a great gun at the college in Christ Church. **1874** KENNAWAY *Crusts* 106 Now the grand up-country rule when you have lost your horse is..'*Hump your saddle and look for him.*' **1887** HOPEFUL *Taken In* 144 The bushmen and up-country men work *very hard* as agricultural labourers, or sawyers. **1897** WRIGHT *Station Ballads* 27 They used to keep the Sabbath in their own up-country way. **1933** SCANLAN *Tides of Youth* 17 I'll get on some up-country place, and later I may be able to pick up a bit of new country cheap. **1948** SCOTTER *Run Estate & Farm* 18 The runholders..did attempt something better than the rough housing common on the upcountry runs.

B. *adv.* In or to country or a district which is away from the coast or from a centre of settlement. See also *up the country* (UP *adv.* 1).

1863 WALKER *Jrnl. & Lett.* (ATLTS) 9 Jan. Going up country tomorrow prospecting as everything here is taken up. **1866** BARKER *Station Life* (1870) 37 Early in the evening I had danced with a young gentleman whose station was a long way 'up country,' and who..seldom found time for even the mild dissipations of Christchurch. **1889** DAVIDSON *Stories NZ Life* 40 My brother Jim had to do the roughest of the 'grafting';.. he had to push his way up-country. **1891** CHAMIER *Philosopher Dick* 43 Here, up country, we have mostly a roving population of tramps, topers and outcasts. **1905** *Truth* 9 Sept. 8 We should make it a condition that [assisted immigrants] be strong and willing to go up-country and bullock hard. **1914** in *Hist. N. Otago from 1853* (1978) 173 One night a young married woman arrived from Dunedin by the up coach. She had a young baby in her arms and was going to join her husband up country. **1922** MANSFIELD *Stories* (1984) 465 I could cut off to sea, or get a job up-country. **1930** MANSFIELD *Novels & Novelists* 140 [16 Jan. 1920] Mr. James Agate's new novel..put us in mind of a conjurer whose performance we witnessed many years ago at a little tin theatre up country. **1983** MANTELL *Murder to Burn* 166 He wanted me to go up country to set another fire.

C. *n.* Land, or a district, remote from town, the coast, or the lowland plain.

1874 KENNAWAY *Crusts* 173 I do give scores of the men who had the hard lines of first finding tracks over the roadless New Zealand up-country very complete credit for the way in which they worked through it. **1875** COCKBURN-HOOD *Chowbokiana* 90 'Wild spaniard' or spear grass..renders walking in the up-country of the Middle Island anything but pleasant. **1926** DEVANNY *Butcher Shop* (1981) 44 What they..thought of..was the pure air of the up-country. **1982** *Oxford Bk. of Contemporary NZ Poetry* 27 Sweating mangrove swamps, cabbage tree prairies inland, an oceanic upcountry of pig fern.

upland bully: see BULLY *n.*[1] 2 (6).

up north, *adv.* Also occas. with init. cap. **N**. Used as a nominal or adverbial phrase referring or relating to any district north of the speaker, the specific meaning often depending on the location of the speaker: e.g. '(to) the North Island' (by South Islanders), '(to) Auckland' (by (southern) North Island speakers), or '(to) North Auckland' (by Auckland speakers). See also UP *prep.* Contrast DOWN SOUTH.

1869 Thatcher *Local Songs* 6 Says he, Plummer's bound to go up North, And call upon his brother. 'Go up,' says he, 'towards Albertland' [*sc*. North Auckland]. **1874** Trollope *NZ* 117 'A railway for you gentlemen down South!' says a northern member [of Parliament]. 'Certainly,—but on condition that we have one here, up North.' **1898** *Tom Bracken's Annual* 39 He came from somewhere in the bush up north. **1901** *NZ Illustr. Mag.* IV. 538 There is fighting up North. **1946** Sargeson *That Summer* 34 It was a long road [from Auckland], that road up North. **1957** Frame *Owls Do Cry* (1967) 19 Up north in the winter-time or midsummer the rain drips in sheets of silver paper, my mother said, who lived there a long time ago. **1968** Baxter *Collected Plays* (1982) 39 We'll go up North and start a boarding house. **1975** Anderson *Men of Milford Road* 134 This bit of news may not convey much to people 'up North', which often meant the rest of the world, but to Invercargill residents it was a message loud and clear. **1985** Sherwood *Botanist at Bay* 49 All the time we're here I feel guilty because I'm not up north campaigning against the Treaty.

upokororo. Also **upokoro.** [Ma. /ˈupokororo/: Williams 468 *Upokororo*..grayling.] GRAYLING.
1847 Brunner *Exped. Middle Is.* in Taylor *Early Travellers* (1959) 265 *18th.* [Jan.].. In the evening took a draught of about fifty good-sized fish with it [*sc*. a net], called the *upokororo*, or fresh-water herring. **1855** Taylor *Te Ika A Maui* 383 The *upokororo* is a fish about eight inches long, with scales; it is caught in the autumn; it bites at the hair of the legs, and is thus caught by the natives going into the water. **1872** Hutton & Hector *Fishes NZ* 123 Upokororo. The above is the native name of the Grayling..a fish that has been long familiar to settlers in certain districts, but..remained undescribed till last year. **1892** *AJHR* H-45 3 In the earlier days there were no edible fish of any size in the streams of the colony if we except the bright little upokororo..and the wretched kokopu. **1901** *TrNZI* XXXIII. 243 The graceful upokororo..or native grayling..is found in many of our streams... The upokororo used to be plentiful in our rivers. **1926** *TrNZI* LVI. 638 The general name is *upokororo* ('head full of brains'), derived from the fatness which characterizes it. **1934** Best *Maori As He Was* 265 The upokororo, or grayling, was taken by means of a hoop-net. **1955** Stokell *Freshwater Fishes* 41 The upokororo is New Zealand's mystery fish. Although it was abundant in many localities during the early days of colonisation and was sold in the fish shops as a food fish its life history has remained almost unknown. **1990** McDowall *NZ Freshwater Fishes* 413 Known as upokororo, it was a fast-moving, rather shy fish and required care in its capture.

upokotea. [Ma. /ˈupokotea/ *upokotea*: *upoko* head + *tea* white: Williams 468 *Upokotea*..whitehead... = *pōpokotea*.] WHITEHEAD. Cf. POPOKOTEA.
1873 [see POPOKOTEA]. **1884** *NZJSc.* II. 282 *Orthonyx albicilla*... Hihipopokera, Upokotea. **1946** *JPS* LV. 160 *Upokotea*, a bird... the North Island form of the bush-canary, often contracted to pokotea.

Upper House. A name for the former LEGISLATIVE COUNCIL.
1859 Swainson *New Zealand* 289 The Legislative Council, or Upper House. **1941** *NZEF Times* 21 Dec. 2 A firm handshake..from the Prime Minister..followed by a seat in the Upper House and a pension. **1959** Sinclair *Hist. NZ* 87 The 1852 constitution was extremely democratic, more so than those then in force in the Australian colonies. The six Provincial Councils, the House of Representatives, and the Superintendents of the Provinces were all elective, though the members of the Legislative Council (the Upper House) were nominated for life by the Governor.

up you /ˌʌpˈju/, or /ˈʌpjə/, *exclam.* [AND 1941.] A euphemistic abbrev., variously pronounced, of **up your arse**, etc., an expression of contempt or rude dismissal (of a person, proposition, attitude, etc.), often elaborated as (e.g.) **up you for the rhubarb season!**, **up you for the winter!** In speech usu. represented by **upya!**, and used with other personal pronouns. Cf. BOOHAI 3 (quot. 1930).
1959 Slatter *Gun in My Hand* 233 Him and his cup of tea. **Up him for the rhubarb season**. Pommie bastard. **1964** Morrieson *Came a Hot Friday* (1981) 127 'Up you for the rhubarb season,' he muttered. **1968** Slatter *Pagan Game* 168 Bert..took it as a slight upon his family but Erik said it was of infinitesticle importance to him how he took it and up him for the rhubarb season. **1978** Tucker *Thoroughbreds Are My Life* 27 Well we did the only thing possible by rushing back to the bookies..and seeking a refund of our hard-earned brass. This in the main was greeted with 'get lost' or 'rhubarb season' or several other epithets which are unprintable here. **1960** Muir *Word for Word* 255 **Up you for the winter**, mate. I got some booze to get stuck into now.

ureure. [Ma. /ˈureure/: Williams 468 *Ure..1. Membrum virile... ureure...* Fruit of *kiekie*.] The penis-shaped fruit of the KIEKIE 1.
1867 Hooker *Handbook* 768 Ureure... Fruit of *Freycinetia Banksii*. **1906** Cheeseman *Manual NZ Flora* 742 *Kiekie*; *Tawhara* (the edible bracts); *Ureure* (the fruit)... ripe fruit in May... The white fleshy bracts surrounding the spadices are often eaten; the fruit less commonly so. **1938** *Auckland Weekly News* 21 Aug. 31 The fruit, called 'ureure' is an oblong mass of fleshy berries which are developed on the spadices. **1946** *JPS* LV. 144 *kiekie*, a scrambling plant..; flower-bracts (tāwhara) eaten as a sweetmeat; also banana-like fruit (ureure).

urupa. [Ma. /uruˈpaː/: Williams 470 *Urupā*... 4. Fence around a grave, burying place.] A cemetery.
1992 Grace *Cousins* 54 'We'll go there tomorrow... To the urupa, to the cemetery, where your mother's buried.' **1995** *Listener* 27 May 21 They carried the coffin up the slopes to the urupa.

ute /ut/, var. UTU.

ute /jut/. [AND 1943.] A freq. abbrev. of UTILITY.
1971 *Listener* 8 Nov. 15 Wind whipped at the ute and rocked it on the road's sharp corners. **1985** Sherwood *Botanist at Bay* 94 'There was a ute parked outside the locked gate over the cattle stop, did you go anywhere near it?' 'I'm sorry. A what?..Would you please explain the meaning of the word "ute"?'.. 'A ute is a farmer's utility vehicle with seats for three persons in front and a load space behind, don't you have them in the UK?' **1992** *Evening Post* (Wellington) (TV Week) 9 June 3 You won't hear a utility vehicle called a 'ute' because the word is unique to New Zealand. Truck or pick-up will be substituted.

utick /ʊˈtɪk/. *Obs.* [Imitative from the call.] FERNBIRD 1.
[*Note*] In his 1888 edn. Buller replaced the 1873 edn. name *utick* with *fernbird*.
1870 *TrNZI* II. 57 Mata. Grass-bird, Grass-pheasant, Utick. *Ibid.* 58 From its call, it is in some places named the Utick. **1873** Buller *Birds NZ* 128 *Sphenoeacus punctatus*. (Common Utick.). *Ibid.* 131 *Sphenoeacus rufescens*. (Chatham-Island Utick.)... This well-marked species is confined to the Chatham Islands. **1884** *NZJSc.* II. 284 Thirty years ago it [*sc*. fernbird] was one of the most common species that affected the open country about Rockwood in the Malvern district; the lads called it 'utick' from its note. **1896** [see FERNBIRD 1]. **1908** *TrNZI* XL. 491 Our utick, or fern-bird, heard everywhere in swampy ground..has become very rare. **1927** Guthrie-Smith *Birds* 163 Like a young bird swung in the air, the Utick seems to use his tail for balancing.

utility. [AND 1935.] Commonly **ute**. A small truck with a tray and a cab used for carrying light loads; a pick-up truck.
1957 Rooke *NZ Twins* 48 They heard the rattle of the utility as it crossed the cattle-guard at the gate. **1964** Tullett *Red Abbott* 76 We'd better take my utility, hadn't we? No use driving two vehicles where one is sufficient. **1971** *Listener* 8 Nov. 15 He got in the utility by Honi, who waited with the motor running. **1985** Sherwood *Botanist at Bay* 74 A utility was standing in the yard behind the farm house.

utiwai, var. HUTIWAI.

utu. Also HOOT: usu. **utu** in Maori contexts, **hoot** in non-Maori. Also with much variety of form **hootoo**, **hout**, **hute**, **hutu**, **ootu**, **ute**. [Ma. /ˈutu/: Williams 471 *Utu* (i) *1*. n. Return for anything; satisfaction, ransom, reward, price, reply: contrast *uto*, ibid. 471 *Uto 1*. Revenge... *2*. Object of one's revenge, sworn enemy.]
[*Note*] In esp. European perceptions Ma. *utu* 'compensation' is occas. not clearly distinguished from Ma. *uto* 'revenge' (see quot. 1904 below). *Utu* was widely used by participants in early Maori-European contacts in all its Maori senses, as well as developing in English a concrete colloquial sense 'money, cash'. *Hutu* (*hoot*) forms are possibly from those with the Ma. particle *he utu* 'an utu, some utu'; or from the 'error' noted by Robert Maunsell in the second edn. of his *Grammar of the New Zealand Language* (1862, p.4) 'In pronouncing *u*, the speaker will have to guard against the error of those who prefix the aspirate when no aspirate is admissible. According to them *u*, *utu*, etc., are pronounced as if spelt *hu*, *hutu*... U [final]..is sometimes, by careless speakers, confounded with *o*.' The devoicing of -*u* final is not unusual: cf. *toot* (see TUTU).

I. utu in Maori contexts: forms transliterated with (mainly early), and without, initial *h*-. **1.** Satisfaction (occas. understood as 'revenge'); material compensation, payment; price.
1820 Butler *Jrnl. & Corr.* (1977) 66 He and his people went and robbed Boyle for the (hutu) payment. **1827** *Church Missionary Register* in Marsden *Lett. & Jrnls.* (1932) 433 They had particular reason to entertain such apprehensions as to the Rarawa tribe, who would seek hutu or satisfaction for their hostility towards the Ngate-po. **1830** Craik *New Zealanders* 242 What he now wanted..was *hootoo*, or payment, for a hurt. **1834** Markham *NZ* (1963) 30 The Cabin boy counted 8 Teeth marks [in the Chief's buttocks] and the Hout or Compensation money was 8 Figs of Tobacco. **1841** Best *Journal* 14 Jan. (1966) 275 Our Messenger returned bringing in a quantity of goods stolen at various times and also two pigs as a 'Hootoo' or compensation. **1841** *Revans to Chapman* (ATLTS) 8 Aug. 154 A native was found dead the other day. It is the opinion of the medical men that he died in a fit but some of the natives for purpose of seeking 'hoot'— payment declare he has been bewitched by white men. **1843** Barnicoat *Journal* (ATLTS) 4 June 111 There was also a little table top that I saw lying in the canoe and which a Maori informed me was kept for ute for bringing us down. **1846** Marjoribanks *Travels in NZ* 88 Nothing is done, however slight, without demanding the *ootu* or payment, and, if instead of higgling, you at once give what is asked, they [*sc*. Maori disputants]

become uneasy. **1863** Maning *Old NZ* ii 31 'What *can* he mean?' said I. 'He is challenging you to wrestle..he wants *utu*' 'What is *utu*?' said I. 'Payment.' 'I won't pay him.' 'Oh, that's not it, he wants to take it out of you wrestling.' **1874** Baines *Edward Crewe* 139 I have known a native, a lucky finder of a new..Hapuku ground, to receive from his tribe a considerable 'utu'. **1884** Martin *Our Maoris* 37 Only a few months, however, before our visit to the Waimate, a 'taua', *i.e.*, a fighting-party, had come to the Bishop's house to demand 'utu' (payment) for a trespass. **1894** Tua-o-Rangi *Utu* [preface] Most born New Zealanders, whether fair or dark, have some conception of the meaning of the word utu, albeit, to pakeha ears it too frequently conveys nothing more than a hazy idea of money compensation... Practically, utu meant payment. The ancient Maori did nothing for nothing... No man could accept service or gifts without requital and retain the esteem of his fellows; still less could he allow injuries to pass unavenged. Utu (value) he expected for the presents he made; utu (payment) he required for goods or produce; utu (satisfaction) he exacted from hereditary foes and all whom he conceived [had] injured him. A vendor [in] the early days of settlement, would request utu for his produce; a settler desiring to purchase would enquire in his pidgin Maori, 'How muchee te utu?' From this milder meaning, expressive of compensation and commodities exchanged, comes the pakeha use of the word signifying money. In settler's parlance 'Kahore ti utu' means 'I have no money', for to their ears utu is synonymous with 'tin', 'sugar', and other slang terms used to denote our medium of exchange. **1904** Tregear *Maori Race* 360 Ordinary revenge or payment (*utu*) for a wrong was less intense than *uto*. If a vendetta had been going on for generations, then when a victim was secured his eyes were eaten by the *ariki* as *uto*. **1930** Guthrie *NZ Memories* 115 The Maoris..strongly objected when my grandfather's cattle strolled into their maize, and for *utu* would unblushingly help themselves to one of his cows. **1989** *Evening Post* (Wellington) 10 July 3 Francis Shaw..said he wanted utu (revenge) after being thrown out of a party so he shot a man in the leg. **1993** *Dominion* (Wellington) 20 Feb. 3 Utu, or revenge, had led to a convicted rapist's daughter being sexually abused at the instigation of his victim's mother. **1996** *Sunday Star-Times* (Auckland) 25 Aug. F13 Flora [a politician's wronged wife] waited for her utu in last Sunday's episode on TV1.

2. In concrete or material senses, money, cash-payment.

[*Note*] Often as **the utu** when referring to money requested or received, or an actual price to be established.

1841 in *NZ Jrnl.* (1842) III. 117 Ask [the Maori] what is the *hute* or price. **1869** Thatcher *Local Songs* 9 There's Bobby Graham, who has got the Maories well in hand, And for a bottle or two of rum from the natives bought the land; Though with Whitaker and Lundon he's having a dispute, Old Bobby chuckles to himself and says kanui te utu. **1877** Pratt *Col. Experiences* 51 [The chiefs] had..a critical knowledge of the value of the 'utu' (money). **1894** [see 1 above]. **1905** Satchell *Toll of Bush* 215 How much the utu?

II. 3. hoot as an English word in non-Maori contexts. [AND 1881–1977.] Money, cash.

1864 *Saturday Review* (Dunedin) 30 Apr. XI. 62 Picton opens up a glorious harvest for the Dunedin harlots whose trade here is, from the want of hoot, decidedly on the wane. **1879** Barr *Old Identities* 333 The land that's waste they'll parcel oot..and sell't to all that's got the hoot. [1879 *Note*] *Hutu*, Maori for money. **1894** [see 1 above]. [**1896** *Truth* (Sydney) 12 Jan. 4 There are several specimens of bush slang transplanted from the Maori language. 'Hoot' is a very frequent synonym for money or wage [in Australia]. I have heard a shearer at the Pastoralist Union office in Sydney when he sought to ascertain the scale of remuneration, enquire of the gilt-edged clerk beyond the barrier, 'What's the hoot, mate?' The Maori equivalent for money is *utu*, pronounced by the Ngapuhi and other Northern tribes with the last syllable clipped, and the word is very largely used by the kauri-gum diggers and station-hands in the North Island... *Utu*..eventually became recognised as the Maori word for money.] **1917** *Chron. NZEF* 5 Sept. 28 Pig Island n.c.o.'s only go for the extra couple of bob a day..the hoot is all they're chasing. **1921** *Quick March* 11 July 13 Everybody..must think every day of money, but although one may think 'money' he may call it 'gonce', 'oof', 'hoot', 'stuff', 'brass', 'ooftish', 'boodle', 'cash', 'gilt', 'kale', or a dozen other..things. **1938** *Katipo* 20 Aug. 331 Then pand'ring to the powers that be: 'I'll wreck a radio' said he, And smiled with hope of extra hoot Until those powers got the boot. He wrecked the radio alright And his patrons overnight. **1948** Finlayson *Tidal Creek* (1979) 144 'Wonder just how much hoot does go with it,' says Uncle Ted, scratching his chin. **1960** Muir *Word for Word* 143 We could do with some chips at the moment... We need all the hoot we can muster. **1970** *Listener* 30 Jan. 12 'Hoot?' I said. I hadn't heard that word for money in years. I suppose in an isolated cut-off place..slang would ossify. **1986** *Contact* (Wellington) 28 Nov. 2 For some reason this paper had deployed an investigative team to find out how much hoot the lads had received for their capers on the veldt.

V

V /viː/, *n.*

1. *pl. Obs.* Men's brief swimming trunks.
1938 HYDE *Godwits Fly* (1970) 114 Boys with dark gold bodies, wearing only V's, jump on the stanchions..then plunge down like gannets.

2. *WW2.* See VEEFER.

vag /væg/, *n.*

1. *Obs.* [AND 1888.] A vagrant, *spec.* one charged under the provisions of the Vagrancy Act (1866).
1905 *Truth* 9 Sept. 1 Was dealt with as a 'vag.' 1906 *Truth* 21 July 2 Stoney-broke and friendless, he was, with a number of others, nabbed at Napier as a 'vag', and pleaded guilty. 1920 *NZ Free Lance* (Wellington) 22 Dec. 2 The auditorium glows in anticipation of a good morning's fun, especially if the drunks and 'vags' list is fairly long.

2. *Obs.* **a.** [AND 1877.] The Vagrancy Act (1866), esp. to be charged **under the vag**.
1906 *Truth* 21 July 3 A by no means unprepossessing damsel named Winnie Hepburn, charged 'under the vag' was given a chance by Dr. McArthur, S.M., at the Magistrate's Court last Monday. *Ibid.* 6 Under the Vag... Cassidy was carpeted by the 'demons' under the..Vagrancy Act.

b. [AND 1896.] A charge of vagrancy under the Vagrancy Act. See also CRUST *n.*²
1912 *Truth* 13 Jan. 7 As a consequence Albert, the mendicant, was charged with 'vag,' otherwise known as 'the crust,' and Magistrate Bartholomew let him off.

3. In the phr. **on the vag** [AND 1877], on the road, on the swag (seeking work).
1961 CRUMP *Hang On a Minute Mate* 61 I'd been on the vag for a few months because there was about two dozen blokes for every job that was going.

vag, *v. Obs.* [Also US: AND 1903.] *trans.* To charge (someone) with vagrancy.
1862 THATCHER *Dunedin Songster 1* 9 Bracelets I've got in my pocket for thee, And then in Court I'll jolly soon 'vag' you, Months then in quod you'll get two or three. 1907 *Truth* 27 Apr. 5 A little time ago the police successfully vagged a couple of very unvirtuous, frowsy, filthy females named Annie Evans and Jessie Hay.

Vandemonian, *a.* and *n. Obs.* [Transf. use of *Vandemonian* (f. *Van Diem*en's land) a convict: AND 1847.]

A. *adj.* Applied in 19th century New Zealand in a sense pertaining to (orig. ex-convict) immigrants from Tasmania having a reputation for violent or ruffianly behaviour; also occas. **Vandemonish,** violent, ruffianly.
1864 THATCHER *Invercargill Minstrel* 10 Now in the dock the prisoner's there, Such a horrid looking creature!.. Hobart Town in every feature;.. And now this Vandemonian gent [on a theft charge] Tries hard to save his bacon, And says that he is innocent. 1873 PYKE *Wild Will Enderby* (1889, 1974) I. xi 40 'That's the smooth-faced Vandemonian cuss,' quoth the Senior Partner... He 'spotted' his man..and with him two others, not quite as greasy, but fully as Vandemonish in appearance. 1899 BELL *In Shadow of Bush* 235 But when Davie called him an old Vandemonian, a demoniacal gleam overspread his grim features.., and shone from his evil eyes.

B. *n.* A Tasmanian ex-convict.
1886 HART *Stray Leaves* 30 In later years, we [in Christchurch] had an infusion of Vandemonians, *i.e.*, convicts from Van Dieman's Land, who caused our then existing police force some trouble. 1900 *Canterbury Old & New* 33 In those early years the whaling vessels often brought doubtful characters from Australia, most of them ticket-of-leave men or ex-convicts, commonly called 'T'othersiders', or 'Van Demonians', etc.

varsity. Also **'varsity, 'Varsity.** [See OED 1846.] **a.** [OED 1863 'Now (in the UK) somewhat *joc.*'.] A usual local New Zealand abbrev. of *University.*
1890 *Otago Witness* (Dunedin) 26 June 28 The Kaikorai forwards rushed the ball to the 'Varsity quarters. 1905 *Weekly Press* (Christchurch) 8 Feb. 70 Two of the Professors at the 'Varsity have New Zealand men for assistants. 1916 IVORY in *Anzac Book* 130 He and I had been friends at the same New Zealand 'varsity. 1929 *Evening Post* (Wellington) 2 Sept. 6 [Heading] Senior A 'Varsity A beats Wesley. 1944 *NZ New Writing* III. 5 Keep on as you're going and we'll soon have you back at the 'varsity. 1959 SLATTER *Gun in My Hand* 26 Roger in his cricket whites and maroon blazer carrying his own bat on the way to play for varsity. 1963 DUCKWORTH *Barbarous Tongue* 22 I wanted to pass my two subjects at 'varsity. 1972 MITCHELL *Pavlova Paradise* 184 *varsity:* University where *Salad Days* has been performed. Much of the language and folklore of Edwardian Oxford survives in New Zealand. 1986 *Listener* 26 Apr. 46 *Varsity*..is a very common word in the mouths both of students and the public, much more so than *uni*, which the NZPOD implies is preferred.

b. *attrib.* or *adj.*
1908 BARR *Brit. Rugby Team in Maoriland* 39 Before taking up classes [at Otago University] he delivers a lecture on the previous Saturday's play of the 'Varsity team. 1915 21 Feb. in Pilling *Anzac Memory* (1933) 12 We ''Varsity Blokes' collected. 1927 FAIRBURN *Letters* 5 May (1981) 20 R.A.K. and I are going to try to write the next Varsity play. 1939 BEATTIE *First White Boy Born Otago* 28 Bill Haberfield, a varsity man, and an early whaler, published a good account of the thirties. 1958 *Tararua* Sept. 44 Somewhere along the way we spied the Wellington 'varsity party making some progress up-river on the other bank. 1985 STEWART *Gumboots & Goalposts* 14 And they're just a bunch of pen-pushing clerks and Varsity students.

Vasey grass: see GRASS 2 (43).

V.D.L. *Hist.* An acronym of Van Diemen's Land, formerly used esp. to identify by mark or stamp hardwood timber imported from Tasmania. Cf. VANDEMONIAN.
1840 BEST *Journal* Apr. (1966) 217 The Members are mostly speculators in Land from England, N.S.W. and V.D.L. 1853 MACKIE *Traveller under Concern* (1973) 109 V.D.L. timber is in high repute here for fencing, shingles etc., it is so much more durable than the N.Z. wood. [1866 *Marlborough Express* (Blenheim) 21 Apr. 1 [Advt] Blenheim Timber Yard... Stone and Wood Piles. Van Diemen's Land Palings.] 1933 *Press* (Christchurch) (Acland Gloss.) 30 Dec. 13 *V.D.L.*— Hard timber of several kinds which comes from Australia and is used for making gates, etc. The letters stand for Van Dieman's Land, and prove, which I suppose everyone knows, that this trade began before Tasmania changed its name.

Veefer. *WW2* (N. Africa). Also **V.** [f. the title 'V for (Victory)' on the packet.] Often *pl.* An inferior, issue cigarette.
1944 *NZEF Times* 13 Mar. 7 Give me the fragrant, yet much despised 'V', Standing for Victory and issued out free. *Ibid.* 20 Mar. 4 No one could smoke Veefers and be a mother—or a father of six. 1945 WEBBER *Johnny Enzed in Middle East* 45 Save them to swap for V's. 1945 *NZEF Times* 10 Sept. 2 More and more people agree that V's were so much better.

vege, var. VEGIE.

vegetable caterpillar. Also occas. formerly **vegetating (vegetative) caterpillar.** The porina caterpillar (*Wiseana* spp.) when invaded by the fungus *Cordyceps robertsii* while pupating underground. See also AWHATO 1 (and note), BULRUSH CATERPILLAR, HOTETE a, PLANT-CATERPILLAR, *rata grub* (RATA 5). **a.** As **vegetable caterpillar.**
1843 DIEFFENBACH *Travels in NZ* II. 363 Hotete— a caterpillar, the so-called vegetable caterpillar. 1847 ANGAS *Savage Life* I. 292 The most remarkable characteristic of the vegetable caterpillar is, that every one has a very curious plant, belonging to the fungi tribe, growing from the *anus*; this fungi varies from three to six inches in length, and bears at its extremity a blossom-like appendage, somewhat resembling a miniature bulrush, and evidently derives its nourishment from the body of the insect. This caterpillar, when recently found, is of the substance of cork; and it is discovered by the natives seeing the tips of the fungi, which grow upwards. Specimens of these vegetable caterpillars have been transmitted to naturalists in England, by whom they have been named *Sphaeria Robertsii*. 1886 *TrNZI* XVIII. 209 Notes on the so-called 'Vegetable Caterpillar' of New Zealand. 1892 HUDSON *Elementary Manual of NZ Entomology* 72 The curious 'vegetable caterpillar', which is usually referred to this species, probably belongs to one of the larger subterranean larvae of the family. 1905 WHITE *My NZ Garden* 56 It is called the Vegetable Caterpillar. The specimens that I have seen were large, dead Caterpillars, with apparently the root of a shrub protruding from the region of the tail. 1929 MARTIN *NZ Nature Book I* 153 The subterranean [*Porina*] larvae thus attacked have long been known as *Vegetable Caterpillars*. 1930 GUTHRIE *NZ Memories* 170 Close to the root of these scarlet myrtles..the little vegetable caterpillar is found.

vegetable sheep (cont.)

1947 POWELL *Native Animals of New Zealand* 56 Vegetable Caterpillar Moth (*Porina*). There are some 19 New Zealand species of these reddish-brown moths. **1964** BACON *Along the Road* 129 You've heard of vegetable caterpillars?.. Well, we've found a few of those. **1971** SHARELL *NZ Insects* 55 The story of the subterranean caterpillars of these moths would not be complete without mentioning a very strange creature known as the Vegetable Caterpillar. The name has been taken over from an English scientist, who in a paper, published in 1763 described a species of Cordyceps as Vegetable fly. He states, what at that time was commonly believed, that Cordyceps, which is really a fungus, is an insect which can change into a plant. **1984** MILLER *Common Insects* 7 Porina caterpillars are also destroyed by diseases, the most notable of which are various species of *Cordyceps* fungus which convert their victims into the so-called 'vegetable caterpillars'.

b. As **vegetating caterpillar**. *Obs*.
1848 [see AWHATO 1]. **1855** TAYLOR *Te Ika A Maui* 424 A small vegetating caterpillar is also found in Britain. **1867** [see AWHATO 1]. **1873** BULLER *Birds of NZ* 67 We..had halted to dig specimens of the curious vegetating caterpillar (*Sphaeria robertsii*), which was abundant there. **1884** KERRY-NICHOLLS *King Country* 365 Pepeaweto.—The grub which begets the *hotete*, or vegetating caterpillar. **1896** *TrNZI* XXVIII. 623 The term 'vegetable caterpillar' is a corruption of the old name of 'vegetating caterpillar', by which Sphoeria was called forty or fifty years ago by those colonists who then took interest in scientific matters.

c. As **vegetative caterpillar**. *Obs*.
1914 SATCHELL *Greenstone Door* 208 If the bearer picked up a vegetative caterpillar..he would keep the party waiting till more were discovered.

vegetable sheep. Any of various subalpine and alpine plants with a cushion-like growth form which from a distance resembles a reposing sheep, esp. *Raoulia* and *Haastia* spp. (fam. Asteraceae).
c1861–62 HAAST in *Julius Von Haast* (1948) 188 There are similar plants on the ranges near Nelson, called by the shepherds 'vegetable sheep' as they often have taken them for so many sheep lying on the side of the mountains. **1866** *Treas. Bot.* 959 [OED] The name of Vegetable Sheep (!) is given by the settlers in New Zealand to *R. eximia*, because, from its growing in large white tufts on elevated sheep-runs, it may be readily mistaken for the sheep. **1872** *TrNZI* IV. 255 Perhaps the most singular forms..are the species of *Raoulia* and *Gnaphalium*, known to the shepherds as 'vegetable sheep'. **1895** *TrNZI* XXVII. 276 Mr. Wallace asks me, did the kea mistake the live sheep for the vegetable sheep. **1907** LAING & BLACKWELL *Plants NZ* 428 When species of these genera [*Haastia* and *Raoulia*] are covered with woolly hairs, they may, from a short distance, so resemble a sheep, as to deceive the unwary. Hence has arisen the name 'vegetable sheep'. **1924** *Otago Witness* (Dunedin) 15 Jan. 6 Some members of the [Raoulia] group which form large cushions, are known as vegetable sheep, because, resting on hillsides, they look, from a fair distance, very like sheep. **1988** FRAME *Carpathians* 114 Others have named it as the flower known to bloom from the plant, *vegetable sheep*, used lately for its contraceptive properties. **1992** *Dominion Sunday Times* (Wellington) 26 July 21 Vegetable sheep dot the most inhospitable faces.

vegetable silk. *Obs*. An early, poetic name for New Zealand flax (*Phormium*).
1780 SEWARD *Elegy on Capt. Cook* 12 First gentle Flora... Thin folds of vegetable silk, behind, Shade her white neck, and wanton in the wind; Strange sweets, where'er she turns, perfume the glades, And fruits unnam'd adorn the bending shades. [1780 *Note*] *Vegetable silk.*—In New Zealand is a flax of which the natives make their nets and cordage.

vegetable wool. *Sphaerophorus tener*, a very common woolly white or pale pink epiphytic lichen forming densely-branched cushions up to 25 cm in diameter on tree trunks and branches in both moist humid shaded areas and exposed alpine or subalpine grasslands.
1982 WILSON *Stewart Is. Plants* 486 *Sphaerophorus tener* Vegetable wool... Woolly clumps of intricately branching, fine white stems, sometimes stained pale pink... It can look similar to Old Man's Beard Lichens, *Usnea* spp., which drape dead branches, shrubs and rocks.

vegetating, vegetative caterpillar, varr. VEGETABLE CATERPILLAR.

vegetation. *Flaxmilling*. The green tissue in the flax (*Phormium*) leaf 'stripped' out to isolate the fibre.
1889 COX *Diaries 1888–1925* (ATLMS) 1 Feb. We were stripping at the mill two hours this morning, and I have been moving vegetation since. **1929** *NZJST* X. 236 The fibre bundles, which are white in the leaf, are, to a greater or lesser extent, coloured green in stripping by the chlorophyll and tannin of the vegetation. **1952** *NZ Farmer* 23 Oct. 9 The green flax is fed into the stripping machine. This removes all of the green vegetation... The strippings of green vegetation are readily eaten by dairy cattle.

vegie /ˈvedʒi/. Also **vege, veggie, vegy**. *Pl. veges* as the popular familiar use, also *veg(g)ies*. [Used elsewhere, but recorded earliest in NZ, and preferred to *veg*: see OED.] An abbreviation of vegetable, esp. as food at the table. Often *attrib*.
1942 TEXIDOR in *In Fifteen Minutes* (1987) 184 Our neighbours don't bother to grow veges. **1966** TURNER *Eng. Lang. Austral. & NZ* 173 If a child eats his *vegies* as he should, he is soon ready for *kindy*. **1969** HASCOMBE *Down & Almost Under* 80 We passed what was described to us as the 'vegy' garden. **1981** HUNT *Speaking a Silence* 7 We were always great people for growing our own food; everyone had a vege garden those days. **1982** MACKENZIE *WAAF Book* 77 Early days at Rongotai saw her..with a period of 'doing the veggies', while her later work included the running of the large airmen's mess..at Mount Eden. **1993** *Metro* (Auckland) Feb. 132 The vast fruit and vege auction rooms are to be relocated.

vegy, var. VEGIE.

velvet fern: see FERN 2 (22).

Venus. In the names of plants and animals:

1. Venus's ear. *Obs*. PAUA.
1864 NICHOLL *Journal* 2 Dec. (ATLMS) 356 I went down to the beach to look for crabs... I also found lots of..live Venus's ears and I saw a few sea anemones. **1898** *Merriam-Webster Internat. Dict.* (Australasian Suppl.) 2033 Venus's ear (Zoöl.), the shell of the mutton fish (*Haliotis*); the ear-shell.

2. Venus'(s) necklace. A necklace seaweed. See also NEPTUNE'S NECKLACE.
1961 MARTIN *Flora NZ* 3 Flattish rock surfaces near mid-tide levels are the usual station for such well-known seaweeds as the Sea Bomb, Sea Cactus, Venus' Necklace, or Purple Laver. *Ibid.* 9 To this end [*sc.* to prevent desiccation] Venus' Necklace has water-filled, swollen internodes; and the sea bomb is also filled with water. **1968** MORTON & MILLER *NZ Sea Shore* 66 The most familiar associate of *Corallina* is the Venus' necklace, *Hormosira banksii*.., which often overshadows the lower half of the turf with its braided carpet of olive to golden brown. **1982** WILSON *Stewart Is. Plants* 318 *Hormosira banksii* Neptune's Necklace..Venus' necklace..Necklace seaweed... Brown or yellow-brown strings of thick-walled bladders, flopped over rocks..at low tide.

3. Venus('s) shell. COCKLE 1 b, TUANGI.
1947 [see TUANGI]. **1966** [see COCKLE 1 b]. **1970** *NZ Boating World* July 71 What about when we collect a half bucket of Venus shell, and mix them with a half-bucketful of tuangi? **1982** BURTON *Two Hundred Yrs. NZ Food* 58 The New Zealand [cockle] species belongs to a completely different family from that of the English cockle. Venus' shell or the Maori tuangi are better names.

verandah. [See AND 'important because of its frequency in Australia', 1805; OED 1, 1711.]

1. As 'an opensided roofed structure attached to a house', not exclusively of New Zealand, but a common local architectural feature (recorded from 1834); also occas. transferred to the porch-like over-hang in the front of a Maori meeting or other house.
1834 MARKHAM *NZ* (1963) 36 I have seen Fern tied up in the Verandahs of the Missionaries huts, from eleven to fifteen Feet in Height. *Ibid.* 48 We employed ourselves for four or five days in making a Verandah to our House. It was as good as an other room to it. **1835** YATE *NZ* (1970) 81 As soon as a child is born, it is wrapped up, and laid to sleep in the verandah, which most of the New-Zealand houses possess.

2. a. [See OED 1 c 'Austral. and NZ.'; AND 1842.] A street or 'shop' verandah, a continuous roof-like structure or canopy projecting from business premises over public pavements as shelter for pedestrians.
1876 KENNEDY *Colonial Travel* 199 The asphalte [*sic*] pavements [in Christchurch] are sheltered with glass-roofed verandahs—some painted green, some white, but most left transparent. **1913** *NZ Observer* 12 July 16 Most people are heartily sick of the shop verandah poles, rubbed shiny by the innumerable backs of loafers. **1959** DAVIN *No Remittance* 24 I think the thing that struck me most [about New Zealand] was the way the shopping streets had continuous first-floor verandas, corrugated iron as a rule, apparently to keep off the rain or sun according to season. **1964** SUMMERS *Smoke & the Fire* 12 I expect that's why all the shops have verandahs on them—I'd not thought of that. To stop the sun fading the goods through the glass. I thought it was to keep shoppers from getting wet in the rain. It was the first difference I noticed. **1979** *Gloss. Bldg. Terminol.* 126 Veranda—A roofed space extending from a building.

b. Hence, in verbal use, **verandah'd** *ppl. a*.
1874 KENNAWAY *Crusts* 225 The streets of the town [Christchurch] are all wide and open, with broad pavements; and the shops are verandah'd along nearly the whole line.

3. *transf.* In the phr. **on the verandah**, on the outer or periphery of interest, etc.
1984 *Landfall 150* 134 But she wasn't on the verandah on this journey.

veronica. [f. medieval Latin *Veronica*, app. named from *St. Veronica*.] Until 1921 the generic name and until the 1940s a general popular name for (members of) the genus *Hebe* (fam. Scrophulariaceae); KOROMIKO a. Cf. HEBE.

VERTICAL DRINKING

1843 DIEFFENBACH *Travels in NZ* I. 26 Near the beach appear shrublike veronicas, myrtles..and flax. **1856** HARPER *Lett. from NZ* 25 Dec. (1914) 2 There are shrubs and plants..besides various kinds of Veronica, white and purple. **1868** *Puketoi Station Diary* (Hocken TS) 7 Oct. Walked up the gully & transplanted some veronicas in the afternoon. **1883** GREEN *High Alps* 172 More than sixty species of veronicas have been described as indigenous to New Zealand. **1889** NEIL *Family Herb Doctor* (1980) 28 Koramika (Native Veronica)... It is found growing in almost every native bush. **1939** *Silhouettes of Past* 206 We used to wander up [the Southland trout streams] into the hills, gathering veronicas and other native flowers. **1940** *Tararua Tramper* Feb. 4 Smashing through the veronica..we put up a performance which would have made Tarzan green with envy. **1951** HUNT *Confessions* 136 It has..speedwells or veronicas which in England are modest little blue flowers..but which here in New Zealand are not only an enormous family of numerous species with a range of colours varying from white to dark purple, but, in the form of shrubs and trees (known as Hebes), reach a height of forty feet. **1966** *Encycl. NZ* I. 710 For many years this genus [*sc*. Hebe] was known as Veronica, with the Maori name koromiko applied to many species.

vertical drinking. Occas. **vertical swill.** Drinking while standing in a public bar, esp. during the former rush hours of 5 to 6.15 p.m. Cf. SWILL.

1955 *BJ Cameron Collection* (TS July) vertical drinking (n) Drinking standing up. **1959** BOLLINGER *Grog's Own Country* 97 First target [*sc*. of the campaign against six o'clock closing] was the 'vertical swill' type bar. **1966** TURNER *Eng. Lang. Austral. & NZ* 131 This [*sc*. six o-clock closing] gives in New Zealand the terms *vertical drinking* (in crowded bars with standing room only). **1988** MCGILL *Dict. Kiwi Slang* 119 *vertical drinking* standing room only drinking in some pubs in the good old, bad old days.

V house: see V-HUT.

V-hut. *Hist.* Mainly *Canterbury*. Also **V house**, **V roof**. A hut or house shaped like an inverted V, built as a shelter by the first settlers in Canterbury.

1851 *Lyttelton Times* 5 Apr. 1 Substantial V house to be sold by auction..a strong and well-built V house situate on Section 55, in the town of Lyttelton. **1851** GODLEY *Letter* 27 Feb. in Carrington *Godley* (1950) 125 You would laugh if you saw the place from which I am writing. It is a little 'plank tent' or 'V. hut', as a thing made of long boards leaning against each other is indiscriminately called. **1851** *Lyttelton Times* 29 Nov. 1 A V roof for sale. **1857** PAUL *Lett. from Canterbury* 57 [A Canterbury woman avers] 'Not long ago..I was born in a V-hut, and christened in a pie-dish.' **1860** BUTLER *Forest Creek MS* (1960) 47 A V hut is a roof, in shape of course like the letter V, set down without any walls upon the ground—mine is 12 foot long by 8 foot broad. It is not customary to have a fireplace in a hut of this description. **1874** KENNAWAY *Crusts* 89 We found we had steered within a quarter of a mile of a low slab V hut, which we had knocked up there a short time before. **1886** HART *Stray Leaves* 9 The most popular [architecture, built from free Association timber for temporary residence] was what is known as the V hut, from being in the shape of a letter V inverted. **1890** *Otago Witness* (Dunedin) 16 Oct. 30 The 'V' hut was the most popular style of building in Canterbury in the early days. It was so called after the letter V inverted. **1949** REED *Story Canterbury* 156 On the plain, tents and 'V' huts began to give place to little weatherboard houses. **1958** GILLESPIE *S. Canterbury* 208 [Caption] V huts, Hagley Park, Christchurch. The V huts built on the South Canterbury runs were probably of a more primitive type. **1981** HUNT *Speaking a Silence* 120 At first they lived in a V-hut, two poles put in the ground like a V, poles lashed right along them and the whole outfit thatched with rushes.

villa. [Spec. use of *villa* a house of some architectural pretension: see OED *villa* 1 d.]

1. a. Also occas. **colonial villa.** A detached house built c1870–1914 commonly of wood and usu. with a high stud, central passage, verandah, fretwork, and a bay window.

1874 *Hawke's Bay Herald* 27 Nov. in Boyd *City of the Plains* (1984) 28 'A better site for villa residences cannot be found in the vicinity of Napier', read the sale notice. **1881** CAMPBELL *Poenamo* 99 The white gleam of the farmer's homestead dots the landscape, there are villas on the height, and cottages on the shore. **1902** IRVINE & ALPERS *Progress of NZ* 363 The average New Zealand villa or cottage is a square box, with a four to six foot passage, pretentiously called a 'hall', running through it from front to back. On either side of this, arranged with all a Scotch gardener's love of symmetry, are sitting-room, dining-room, bedrooms and kitchen..the evolutionary starting point of the New Zealand villa must have been the tin-lined packing case in which the pioneer settler imported his goods and chattels. **1973** MCELDOWNEY *Arguing with My Grandmother* 20 Ours was the oldest house, and had been built about 1910 in a style of villa, with bay window and veranda, that was even then beginning to go out in more fashionable areas. **1988** *Back Then— Volume Two* (Oral History Birkenhead) 77 We got a house [in 1920]... An old villa house... It was just the time when bungalows were coming in and it was not 'quite, quite', you know. And here we had a villa house. Nowdays some people want a villa house. **1988** *Through the Looking Glass* 154 They shifted..to a large old colonial villa..overlooking Glenfield. **1991** SHAW *NZ Architecture* 56 The villa and its derivatives dominated domestic housing in New Zealand from 1860 to 1910.

b. As **bay villa**, a villa type having a 'bay' window (hence the epithet) on the front facade and, in larger versions, also on a side facade.

1978 SINCLAIR & HARREX *Looking Back* 118 By the later decades of the [19th] century the most popular house was the villa or 'bay villa'. **1991** SHAW *NZ Architecture* 45 By the 1870s the basic forms of the simple symmetrical cottage had been elaborated. Successful European settlers were no longer satisfied with a cramped life inside small, four-roomed, passageless houses, architects and builders began to think of ways to satisfy clients' needs for more space. A central hall giving access to more generously proportioned rooms became common; the lean-to verandah became almost an obligatory feature. When one of the front rooms was pushed out under a gable to form a bay window, the *bay villa* was born. The *bay villa* caught the imagination of home owners and examples sprang up all over New Zealand. They are still to be seen in great profusion today. **1992** *Dominion* (Wellington) 11 Nov. 9 It was a lot cheaper when factories mass-produced the components and clients could simply point out which finial, balustrade, plaster ceiling, verandah trim, [etc.]..they liked from a catalogue. So the bay villa flowered rampantly, a prolific colonial expression of Victorian style.

2. A detached ward or patient accommodation unit at a psychiatric hospital. [Poss. from the name given to Sir Truby King's detached units at Seacliff Hospital.]

1927 BOTHAMLEY in Williams *Out of Sight* (1987) 93 The new villas on the hill... The patients could not have a more ideal home. **1938** *AJHR H-7* 8 Wherever possible patients have been encouraged to interest themselves..in domestic tasks about the villas and wards. **1941** *NZEF Times* 17 May 6 The complete demolition of the Porirua mental hospital..is in progress. It will make way for 11 new villas, each with accommodation for 50 patients. **1975** MCFARLANE *Mixed Media* 41 We're working at Cherry Farm just now. What if we let out *a whole villa of patients*? **1987** WILLIAMS *Out of Sight* 92 In 1926 the five new villas were completed... The remaining villa was for helpless male patients. **1992** *Evening Post* (Wellington) 17 July 3 The hospital had a number of villas (wards) which were not full. **1993** *Contact* (Wellington) 25 Feb. 1 The closing of villas at Porirua Hospital could mean at least 150 patients entering the community early... The villas are living areas in the hospital that include accommodation, cafeterias, and meeting places.

village. [Spec. uses of *village* a small rural settlement: see OED 1 a.]

1. Often with a modifier **Maori**, **native**, a Maori settlement; KAINGA a. Cf. MARAE, PA *n*.[1] 2 a.

1769 [see PA *n*.[1] 1]. **1807** SAVAGE *Some Acc. of NZ* 7 There are several villages in the neighbourhood, and a great number of straggling huts. **1815** MARSDEN *Lett. & Jrnls.* (1932) 105 This information determined me to visit the village in the morning... After this Mr. Nicholas accompanied me to Houpa's fortified village. **1820** [see NATIVE B 1 a]. **1835** YATE *NZ* (1970) 154 The villages of the New Zealanders are generally scattered over a large plot of ground. **1843** WOOD *Twelve Months in Wellington* 12 The inhabitants of the Pah or native village would not ferry us across the stream. **1859** THOMSON *Story NZ* I. 209 [Caption] Native village with swing and pa in the distance. **1861** SIR GEORGE GREY 2 Nov. *Memorandum* in Rutherford *Sel. Documents* (1949) 112b For providing for the health..of the inhabitants of any native village, pa, or assemblage of houses. **1879** HAAST *Geol. Canterbury & Westland* 98 I use the habitual expression Maori pah, but a description of this settlement would give a very poor idea of such a Maori village, consisting as it did of three miserable low huts, in which a very old couple..were living. **1900** *NZ Statutes* No. 48 258 [Maori Councils Act] To appoint from among the Maoris of any Maori kainga, village, or pa a Committee..who shall be called the Village Committee (Komiti Marae). **1910** [see KAINGA a]. **1943** MARSH *Colour Scheme* 33 Old Rua Te Kahu sat on the crest of a hill that rose..above his native village. **1959** [see PA *n*.[1] 1]. **1964** HINTZ *Trout at Taupo* 30 At the little Maori village of Waihi nearby hot springs bubble away at boiling point.

2. In familiar (often humorous) use, the shopping centre of a settlement, small town, or suburb, or as 'the Village' with reference to the suburb or settlement itself; also in modern use, a name preferred by developers for a specially designed shopping complex. See also TOWNSHIP 3.

[*Note*] The British use of *village* as 'small rural settlement' has been mainly replaced in New Zealand by TOWNSHIP 2 a.

1920 *NZ Free Lance* (Wellington) 26 May 25 Nobody..anticipated that the lads from the village [*sc*. Petone] would have been beaten both back and forward so soundly. **1938** HYDE *Nor Yrs. Condemn* 13 Murphy and Leask and me are going to the village [*sc*. Trentham or Upper Hutt picture] show tonight. **1949** *Southern Cross* (Wellington) 13 Aug. 10 The people from the go-ahead town [Petone], which is proud to be known as 'The Village', have a real interest in sport. **1953** p.c. R. Mason. In Wellington, 'village' is used of the shopping area(s) in Karori, and occasionally in Ngaio, but there I think it means the whole suburb. Until c1933 I had never heard *village* used in New Zealand—always town, township, or settlement. **1966** *Encycl. NZ* II. 679 Under the heading of Vocabulary may be included the preferences shown for certain English words in ordinary use such as *village* for the shopping centre in suburbs. **1980** MANTELL *Murder & Chips* 18 The only access road snaked up the eastern hills, dropped down the other side,.. passing through..the original [Wainuiomata] settlement affectionately called 'the Village'. **1986** HOLCROFT *Sea of Words* 73 Every afternoon a neighbourhood bus—diverted briefly from the Paraparaumu run, carried housewives to the village for shopping. **1992** *Independent Herald* (Johnsonville) 18 Nov. 10 The dairy was just one of a host of buildings that has disappeared from the Johnsonville village over the last 20 years.

3. Special Comb. **village settlement** *hist.*, a State-sponsored small-farming scheme.

1894 *NZ Official Year-book* 202 The 'village settlement system' of New Zealand has become widely known in the Australian Colonies, and has excited much inquiry with a view to its adoption in other parts... The system was initiated in 1886 by the late Hon. John Ballance, with the intention of assisting the poorer classes to settle on the land... The features of the system were, originally, the possession of a small farm, not exceeding 50 acres in extent, held under a perpetual lease for terms of thirty years, with recurring valuations at the end of each terms... Residence and improvement of the soil were compulsory. *Ibid.* 203 The present law admits of similar village settlements, but the area which a selector may hold has been increased to 100 acres. **1898** MORRIS *Austral-English* 490 *Village Settlement*, the system, first adopted in New Zealand, whence it spread to the other colonies, of settling families on the land in combination. The Government usually helps at first with a grant of money as well as granting the land. **1959** SINCLAIR *Hist. NZ* 163 Ballance also tried to establish 'village settlements'. Some two thousand people were settled on plots of twenty to fifty acres, but the land was often as poor as the tenants and the scheme was not a success.

villain. WW1. Usu. *pl.*, the military police.

1936 HYDE *Passport to Hell* 98 Mounted on Arabs rode through the streets the Gippo 'Villains', military police who wore white uniforms and carried rifle, sword, revolver, and a knife on each hip. *Ibid.* 205 The Villains picked him up and he spent a night in the lock-up.

vine. With a modifier, as **Maori vine**, *Muehlenbeckia* spp., esp. POHUE b. See also *wire vine* (WIRE *n.* 1 a).

1923 COCKAYNE *Cultivation NZ Plants* 117 Certain climbing-plants are suitable for draping some of the trees, or hiding ugly objects. For the latter purpose the most effective, and rapid, is the Maori-vine (*Muehlenbeckia australis*). **1952** Maori Vine [see POHUE b].

Vinnie. [St V*in*cent de Paul Society + -IE.] Usu. collective *pl.* as **the Vinnies**. (A member of) the St Vincent de Paul Society, a Catholic charitable organization (see quot.).

1995 *Tablet* (Dunedin) 8 Jan. 6 Over 20 percent of the St Vincent de Paul Society belong to the youth section or young 'Vinnies'... The 'Vinnies' visit people in hospitals, assist in soup kitchens, and with clothing and food drives for the society's shops and foodbanks.

violet. Also **native** (or **New Zealand**) **violet**, occas. **mountain violet**. [Spec. use of European *violet*, *Viola* spp.] Any of various native *Viola* spp. (fam. Violaceae), small herbs of damp sites.

1855 TAYLOR *Te Ika A Maui* 447 *Haka*... A small white violet; another with purple stripes, and a purple one are found, but all without scent. **1869** *TrNZI* I. (rev. edn.) 200 English..name..violet..Viola cunninghamii. **1889** FEATON *Art Album NZ Flora* 26 Viola filicaulis... The 'Native Violet'. This little plant is common to both..Islands as far south as Otago. **1909** THOMSON *NZ Naturalist's Calendar* 49 In moist ground are still to be met with numerous small delicately scented violets, white with blue or purple stripes on the lower petals, and yellow throats. **1926** CROOKES *Plant Life Maoriland* 155 All those who have carefully observed our dainty little native violet will have noticed that, in the late summer, when the ordinary white flowers are beginning to wither, a number of curious little green buds will appear on the plant. **1952** RICHARDS *Chatham Is.* 34 *Viola Cunninghamii*... New Zealand Violet. **1973** MARK & ADAMS *Alpine Plants* (1979) 48 *Viola cunninghamii*..Mountain violet.

virgin bush: see BUSH A 1 c.

virgin's bower. *Obs.* Also **virgins bower**. [Transf. use of Brit. dial. *virgin's bower, Clematis vitalba*, traveller's joy: cf. EDD *virgin* 1 (1).] Native *Clematis* spp.

1777 ANDERSON *Journal* Feb. in Cook *Journals* (1967) III. 805 Amongst the known kinds of plants are..Sow thistles, Virgins Bower, Vanelloe. **1838** POLACK *NZ* I. 295 *Speedwell, sow,* and *melon thistles* (coetus), *virgin's bower, vanilloe.* **1857** HURSTHOUSE *NZ* II. 365 The perfumed manouka, the scarlet myrtle and giant fuchsia, the red and yellow parrot's bill, the splendid clematis or virgin's bower.

visiting teacher. A trained teacher-social-worker who deals with 'problem' children by contact 'visits' to their homes.

1943 *AJHR E-1* 4 I have given approval for the appointment..of 'visiting teachers'. These teachers will be attached to schools..without responsibility for class-teaching but with the special function..of maintaining contact between the school and the home. **1949** *Education* II. iii 19 But there are always a few children whose personal problems seem insurmountable... These are the children with whom the Visiting Teacher deals. **1974** *Let. from NZEI to Minister of Educ.* 3 Dec. (NZ Educational Institute archives) [We should not underestimate] the value of the visiting teacher service and the importance of these support services to the work of the schools by relating the school to the home.

volcanic, *a*. In special collocations: **volcanic land**, see quot.; **volcanic plateau**, the central North Island area which was affected by the Taupo eruption.

[*Note*] There was a long series of ash-showers in the Central North Island going back as far as 750,000 years: the ignimbrite plateau was formed in such a shower about 140,000 years ago; the present fertile plateau by the Taupo eruption of about 1800 years ago.

1922 *NZJST* V. 191 In the Whangarei and Bay of Islands basic lava-flows cover 163 square miles of country and form what is locally called '**volcanic**' **land**. *Ibid.* V. 194 *Basalt soils*:—These are the soils which form the 'volcanic land' of the farmer. **1963** POOLE & ADAMS *Trees & Shrubs* 160 Shrub land; especially on so-called 'frost flats' of the **volcanic plateau**.

Volunteer. *Hist.* Also **Volunteer Company**. A member of a volunteer section of the settler-militia formed as a defensive force in the New Zealand Wars.

1861 *Taranaki Punch* 27 Mar. 1 'Methinks I'm all there,' quoth the fat Volunteer. **1868** *Richmond-Atkinson Papers* (1960) II. 278 Whitmore has only gone as a Volunteer to the front. I need hardly say that he is Commandant of the Armed Constabulary. **1879** *Auckland Weekly News* 20 Sept. 17 The question of clothing the Volunteers of the colony in a proper uniform has been taken up by the government who have applied to the Volunteer companies and officers to decide on some fixed uniform. **1981** CAMPBELL et al. *Years Between* 132 'Drill instruction' was extended in 1883 by the formation of a cadet corps under a master..who had been a captain in one of the old Volunteer Companies.

vow, var. WHAU.

V roof: see V-HUT.

vug /vʌg/. *Geol.* or *Mining*. [f. Cornish dial. or mining *vug*: see OED, EDD (also *vugh*).] A natural cavity in rock.

1907 *NZGeol.SB* (NS) No.4 105 Although these vugs are in the main small, they occasionally attain large dimensions. In the Tokatea and Tribute veins of the Royal Oak Mine, these cavities sometimes exceeded 10ft. in length and a foot in width. *Ibid.* 123 Vugs or cavities occurring within the actual veins..are a not uncommon feature in these mines. **1922** *NZJST* V. 174 Incoherent, finely crystalline cinnabar filled interstices and vugs. **1978** MCARA *Gold Mining* (Glossary of Waihi Mining Terms) 337 *Vugs*: Occasional voids which occurred in the reefs; they were usually lined with quartz or calcite crystals. They might be tiny pockets or could be several yards in length and depth.

Hence **vuggy** *a.* (occas. **vughy**), of rock, etc., having natural cavities.

1890 *TrNZI* XXII. 405 I believe that nuggets have grown as defined above, but think it has been in the hollow vughy water-channels or lodes in the rock, not in the drift-gravel. **1912** *NZGeol.SB* (NS) No.15 61 These present the vuggy, conky, massive, and occasionally crustified structures usually associated with fissure filling of crystalline quartz.

W

W. [Used elsewhere, but recorded earliest in NZ: OED *W.* 3, 1953.] A WC, or (often outdoor) DUNNY.

1916 MANSFIELD *Aloe* 31 'You've only got one w. at your place,' said Miriam scornfully. 'We've got two at ours. One for men and one for ladies. The one for men hasn't got a seat.' **c1940** and prob. much earlier, in a children's variant of *Old King Cole*: Old King Cole was a merry old soul And a merry old soul was he; He called for a light in the middle of the night To go to the W.C. The wind blew round the W. [later occas. 'dunny'] door The candle had a fit; Old King Cole fell down the hole And came up covered in shit.

waddy. Also **waddie**. [AAW ad. Aboriginal Dharuk (Sydney) dial. *wadi* 'tree, stick, club': AND *wady* an Aboriginal war-club, 1790; in non-Aborig. use 'stick, club', 1809.]

1. *Obs.* A Maori club; PATU *n.*

1807 SAVAGE *Some Acc. of NZ* 52 The men, whether dressed or in their ordinary clothing, carry a waddy, suspended by a thong from the wrist. The waddy is in figure somewhat resembling a large battledore, and is usually formed of hard black stone. **1837** BURFORD *Description of a View* 10 The waddy, or patoo patoo. **1868** *Punch in Wellington* 58 The Hau Hau Chief has sent into Napier, demanding..the right thigh bone of Mr. Colenso, for a waddy.

2. a. A heavy stick; a small club; a baton.

c1875 MEREDITH *Adventuring in Maoriland* (1935) 138 [The horse] was given a mile, at full speed..with a Maori boy on his back armed with a stout supple-jack waddy, which was vigorously applied from the jump. **1914** PFAFF *Diggers' Story* 113 We saw where they buried [the murdered man], so we got good waddies, and every man we met that day we took to be Burgess or Sullivan [*sc.* the murderers]. **c1924** ANTHONY *Me & Gus* (1977 Gus Tomlins) 53 Take that waddy, Mark, and if they don't start off together fetch the slowest [horse] a good clip. **1939** VAILE *Pioneering Pumice* 299 *Waddy* Short, heavy stick: a small club. **1964** DAVIS *Watersiders* 112 Possums drop down in hundreds..and me running along with a bit of a manuku [*sic*] waddy clobbering anything that moved. **1983** HENDERSON *Down from Marble Mountain* 152 Calling the faithful to prep or parades, he'd belt [the iron strip] with a huge nut-and-bolt waddie two feet long.

b. A club for killing birds (esp. muttonbirds), or for stunning or killing eels. Cf. PRIEST *n.*[2]

1928 BAUCKE *Manuscript* (Bishop Museum Memoirs Vol. X No. 5 pp. 343–382) in Skinner & Baucke *Morioris* 364 The [Moriori] men to do the [bird] killing, killing waddy — a short club 18 inches long and 2 inches in diameter — strapped to the waist. **1943** HISLOP *Pure Gold* 139 Sure enough, there was his old waddy [*sc.* a sharpened willow-stick] growing out of the back of his Loch Ness eel. **1962** SHARPE *Country Occasions* 185 Full equipment for this sort of fishing [*sc.* for eels] includes a strong waddy, a butcher's knife, a small sharp axe, and a sack. **1978** SUTHERLAND *Elver* 62 You have to stun [the eels] with the waddy and put them in the bag.

c. A long heavy stick for protection against stock or other animals.

1949 NEWTON *High Country Days* 93 Each man selected and cut a long [manuka] pole and armed with these 'waddies' they trooped..across the yards. **1960** MASTERS *Back-Country Tales* 38 I picked up a good stout waddy, and sailed in with the idea of stunning the animal... The dogs, seeing me with the waddy..let the pig go. **1969** MOORE *Forest to Farm* 106 To protect himself against a beast that charged..he carried what he called his 'dream tablet' a large heavy 'waddie' which he did not hesitate to use on the head of a dangerous beast. **1978** JARDINE *Shadows on Hill* 66 The others armed themselves with good solid waddies..to ward the bull off.

wae, var. WHAI.

waerenga. Also early **wairenga**. [Ma. /ˈwaereŋa/: Williams 473 *waerenga*.] A clearing for cultivation.

[**1820** LEE & KENDALL *NZ Gram. & Vocab.* 222 Wai énga, or Wai rénga: A place cleared of wood and rubbish for a farm.] **1888** BULLER *Birds NZ* I. 143 A new growth has covered the long-abandoned 'wairengas'. **1905** BAUCKE *White Man Treads* 222 The nervous advance of men..showed that those away in their 'waerengas' (plantations) had also heard the commotion. **1953** GUTHRIE-SMITH *Tutira* (3edn.) 100 An arrangement [was] reached by which four parties of Tutira men show four parties of the Urewera the *Waerenga* or crop lands where the latter could gather their own food.

waeroa. Also early **waiwai-roa**. [Ma. /ˈwaeroa/: Williams 473 *Waeroa*, n. Mosquito.] A mosquito (fam. Culicidae). Compare MOZZIE.

1840 POLACK *Manners and Customs* I. 126 It is the scourge of sand-flies (*namu*) and mosquitoes. (*waiwairoa*). **1848** TAYLOR *Leaf from Nat. Hist.* xii The only noxious insects are the *namu*, a small black sand-fly, the *waeroa* or mosquito, and the small black spider. **1860** *Richmond-Atkinson Papers* (1960) I. 670 Turned out by waeroas about 4 a.m. **1971** MILLER *Common Insects in New Zealand* 52 So it was that *namu*, the sandfly, and *waeroa* the mosquito, veterans in the art of war, claimed the right of feud. **1986** ANDREWS *The Southern Ark* 1 Insects were ever-present — the shrill, summer chirping of Kihikihi the cicada, Namu the sandfly, Waeroa the mosquito and Kutu the louse.

waewaekaka. [Ma. f. *waewae* foot + *kākā* parrot /ˈwaewaeˈkaːkaː/: Williams 472 *Waewaekākā..waewae-matuku, Gleichenia microphylla,* a fern.] *Gleichenia microphylla* (fam. Gleicheniaceae), a tangle fern the frond of which divides in a manner fancifully resembling a kaka's foot. Cf. *tangle fern* (FERN 2 (19)).

1867 HOOKER *Handbook* 769 Wae-wae-kaka, *Col[enso]. Gleichenia semi-vestita*. **1882** [see FERN 2 (19)]. **1906** CHEESEMAN *Manual NZ Flora* 1018 [*Gleichenia circinata, Swartz.*] *Waewaekaka*; *Waewaematuku*. **1982** WILSON *Stewart Is. Plants* 432 *Gleichenia microphylla* Parasol Fern... Waewaekākā... Very similar to [tangle fern]. **1989** BROWNSEY & SMITH-DODSWORTH *NZ Ferns* 56 *Gleichenia microphylla*.. Carrier tangle, Waewaekaka.

waewaekoukou. Also **waiwaikoko**. [Ma. f. *waewae* foot + *koukou* owl: /ˈwaewaeˈkoukou/: Williams 272 *Waewae-koukou, Lycopodium* [spp.].] *Lycopodium volubile* (fam. Lycopodiaceae), OWL'S-FOOT MOSS, a clubmoss with leaves set on a stem in a fashion fancifully resembling an owl's foot.

1867 HOOKER *Handbook* 769 Wae-wae-koukou... *Lycopodium volubile*. **1869** *TrNZI* I. (rev. edn.) 266 Elegant female head-dresses were formed of..the graceful Waewaekoukou. **1903** *Ibid.* XXXV. 21 The kumara..were piled radially around the sides on a bed of soft fern or *Lycopodium* (waewaekoukou). **1905** SATCHELL *Toll of Bush* 236 The boys on the [Northland] station were getting the big shed ready for a dance... Another young man..was engaged in looping up garlands of 'waiwaikoko' or owl's-foot moss, together with branches of Christmas tree. **1915** *TrNZI* XLVII. 88 *L[ycopodium] volubile..*the 'waewaekoukou' of the Maori, is probably the most widespread species we have, and the most beautiful. **1989** BROWNSEY & SMITH-DODSWORTH *NZ Ferns* 23 Waewaekoukou... Main stems scrambling or climbing... Sterile leaves flattened into one plane..the larger lateral slightly sickle-shaped... Common throughout in scrub, on bush margins, banks, and on road cuttings.

wage round. A former recurrent period of industrial bargaining over the renewal of wages and salary awards.

1981 *Evening Post* (Wellington) 2 June 4 The two issues — tax reform in an election year and the need for a low wage round — have now become inextricably linked. **1984** BOSTON *Incomes Policy in NZ* 197 The 1977–78 wage round settled at a moderate level.

wages, *n. pl. Goldmining.*

1. [AND 1853.] An amount of gold recovered roughly equivalent in value to the ruling rate of labourers' hire, esp. in the phr. **to make wages**. Cf. TUCKER *n.* 2 a.

1861 *NZ Goldfields 1861* 20 Sept. (1976) 15 Well, they were first comers, and they are on Gabriel's Gully, and making wages. **1862** HODDER *Memories NZ Life* 223 The claim may not yield sufficient 'wages' to pay for lost time. The term 'making wages' is employed to indicate that the proceeds of a day's labour is equal to the amount paid in the labour market [*sc.* eight to ten shillings a day]. **1873** WILSON *Diary* 30 Jan. in Wierzbicka *Wilson Family* (1973) 158 At last we see the gold in the bottom of the sluicing box and they tell us after about a month's work they have only got three ounces..not wages, as they express it. **1937** [see TUCKER *n.* 2 a].

2. Special Comb. **wages claim** [AND 1871] (**wages ground**), a claim or diggings where the gold recovered returns 'wages' to the miner (cf. *tucker ground* (TUCKER 2 b)); **wages man**, a miner who makes 'wages'; also a labourer who works for wages at an occupation other than mining.

1884 REID *Rambles on Golden Coast* 68 At this rush a '**wages**' **claim** usually bore the interpretation of £8 to

£10 per man per week. **1967** May *West Coast Gold Rushes* 244 The digger recognized four classes of payable ground: 'tucker ground' kept him in food with nothing to spare; a 'wages claim' gave him a pound or two above living expenses [etc.]. **1974** Heinz *Bright Fine Gold* 200 Those yielding up to £3 per week per man were known as 'tucker' claims; up to £8 per week were known as 'wages' claims. **1870** *AJHR* D-40 6 Shamrock Terrace..is a locality where what is termed '**wages ground**' is always to be found. **1883** Scandrett *Southland & Its Resources* 7 Each of these [mining] localities contains what is known as 'wages ground'; men can always earn on an average fifteen shillings or more a day. **1880** in Cowan *Down the Years in the Maniototo* (1948) 39 One claim was still [*sc*. in 1880] so rich that 'a **wages man** would be quite satisfied if he was allowed a shovelful and a half of wash dirt for his day's work'. **1899** Bell *In Shadow of Bush* 12 'You would be the right man for the bush country,' McKeown said, '..Flash Harry, who has a contract..was saying only this morning that he would take on a couple of wages men at bushfalling—so there's a job at hand.'

wagga /ˈwɒgə/. Also **wogga**. [AND f. *Wagga Wagga* a town in N.S.W, 1900.] In full **wagga rug**. A covering made of split sacks.

1913 Carr *Country Work* 6 Sheets are not fashionable, while three sacks sewn together make what is termed a 'New Zealand Possum Rug' or 'Wogga'. **1978** Jardine *Shadows on Hill* 103 On a cross strut [in the musterers' hut] were hung the eight big rough blankets covered by a rag rug, or wagga. **1986** Owen & Perkins *Speaking for Ourselves* 72 Another important part of the swaggy's equipment was his bedroll. Generally it was called a 'wagga'. Now the old wagga was popular in the wintertime—a bit heavy to carry, but it came into its own in the winter. The wagga rug was made out of the old one-striper sacks... The old heavy one-striper made a wonderful wagga. The wagga originated over on the Aussie side, and generally to improve it you opened up two sacks, and this made a wonderful rug.

waheine(e), varr. WAHINE.

wahhe taboo, var. WAHI-TAPU.

wahine /waˈhini/, *n.*[1] Also with much variety of early form as **waheine(e)**, **wahini**, **waihina**, **whaheen**, **wha-hei-né**, **whiena**, **whihiene**, **whinie**, **whye(e)nee**, **wiena**, **wyeena**, etc. [Ma. /ˈwahine/, /ˈwaːhine/: Williams 474 *wahine* (pl. *wāhine*). Woman; female; wife.]

1. A Maori woman or wife. Contrast SQUAW.

1770 Banks *Journal* Mar. (1962) II. 35 a Woman (Northern) Wahine (Southern) Wahine (Otahite) Wahine. **1773** Bayly in McNab *Hist. Records* 12 Apr. (1914) II. 204 Their Whinies (or women) are not regular featured in general as the men, tho' some of them were fine jolly girls. [**1804** *Collins Eng. Colony in NSW* (NZ Vocab.) 562 Wha-hei-né, *A woman*.] **1834** Markham *NZ* (1963) 41 [The Chief] asked me if I had a Waheinee? No. Would I like one? Certainly. Then take my daughter. **1842** *Piraki Log* 14 July (1911) 139 Give to Richards Whaheen 10 regatta shirts. **1849** McKillop *Reminiscences* 252 The men do not shew the same desire to intermarry with white women, as the white men do with the maori wihihenes (women), who make the working classes far better wives..than any Europeans. **1852** Mundy *Our Antipodes* (1855) 289 A group of whyenees and piccaninnies. **1874** Baines *Edward Crewe* 19 The New Zealand 'Wahini' has a pattern of her own. **1881** Campbell *Poenamo* 48 I was often afterwards navigated across it on the back of a Maori *wahine*. **1890** *Otago Witness* (Dunedin) 28 Aug.

38 'You goin' Wanganui 'long o' us?' bawled an old waihena as I passed her. **1907** Mansfield *Urewera Notebook* (1978) 44 Met a most fascinating Maori..he took Mrs Webber and me to see his 'wahine'—and child. **1930** Guthrie *NZ Memories* 49 This Maori boy's *wahine* called upon the wife of her husband's pakeha to beg..European clothes. **1960** Scrymgeour *Memories Maoriland* 110 Wahines..did the sorting, and Maori girls did the sweeping on the shearing board. **1974** Mason *Hand on Rail* (TS 1987) 20 *Hingawaru*... When Rangi chooses his wahine, someone else pays, ne? *Rangi*: When I choose, Dad, I'll choose a *girl*, not a wahine! Hate that word! Makes me see fat slobbery old tarts waddling along the beach. **1988** Somerset *Sunshine & Shadow* 13 Her father's brother..had a Maori wife or 'wahine'.

2. A Pakeha woman or wife.

c**1846** Weekes *My Island* in Rutherford & Skinner *Establish. New Plymouth* (1940) 119 They inquired for the *waihina* and I led the party up to the house to introduce them to my wife. **1856** Hammet in May *West Coast Gold Rushes* (1967) 71 There was a grand Ball given on the opening of a fine large Billiard room where you might have seen whienas both Maori and Pakeha in crinolines and satin boots. **1893** *Otago Witness* (Dunedin) 21 Dec. 11 It is not fit that the daughter of the great tribe..should be the slave-wife of the pakeha and the slave of the white wahine. **1937** Partridge *Dict. Slang* 935 *wahine*. A woman: New Zealand coll.: late C. 19–20. **1941** Baker *NZ Slang* 56 We have long since adopted *wahine*. **1984** Wilson *S. Pacific Street* 48 Skiting to everyone about his groovy wahine, then won't speak to me when we get home. *Ibid.* 51 I want you to meet a friend of mine, Cynthia Black. Meet Joff Smith, and my wahine, Martha Whitwell.

Wahine /waˈhini/, *n.*[2] [With reference to the southerly gale during which the interisland ferry *Wahine* was sunk in Wellington Harbour, 10 April 1968.] **Wahine Day**, 10 April 1968; **Wahine storm**, a violent storm (as *attrib*., very stormy).

1993 *Tablet* (Dunedin) 9 May 17 The phrase 'Iron Curtain' caught on after Winston Churchill used it... In New Zealand, '**Wahine Day**' emerged spontaneously, just like that, on April 10, 1968. **1981** *St Patrick's College, Silverstream 1931–80* 40 [Caption] In 1968 disaster struck the college in the shape of the **Wahine storm**, and many of the fine old trees in the grounds were blown down. **1987** *Alfredton* 220 The front verandah was blown off during the Wahine storm. **1987** Knox *After Z-Hour* 66 'It would have to be *Wahine*-storm weather for them not to clear the slip off in the morning,' Hannah said. **1993** *Sunday Times* (Wellington) 10 Apr. 8 Gales in Wellington are met by comments such as 'It's not as bad as the Wahine storm' or 'We haven't had a day like this since the Wahine'.

wahini, var. WAHINE *n.*[1]

wahi tapu. Also **wahhe taboo**, **wai-tápu**. [Ma. /ˈwaːhi ˈtapu/: Williams 474 *wāhi*..2. Place, locality.] A sacred place or burial ground.

1817 Kendall 25 July in Elder *Marsden's Lieutenants* (1934) 140 In selecting a portion of land for a settlement, it would be advisable to take care that it be as clear as possible of what the natives call the wahhe tabboo. Wherever a person has breathed his last, or his bones have been laid for a time, there is always a piece of timber set up, if there is no tree already growing, to perpetuate his memory. **1828** Williams *Early Jrnls.* 22 June (1961) 136 Upon enquiring it appeared that they were on a *Wahitapu* and consequently could not be driven home. **1838** Polack *NZ* I. 137 We passed an extensive grove containing a Wai-tápu. In this place was deposited the bones of a male and female chief. **1843** Dieffenbach *Travels in NZ* II. 65 All these places, wahi-tapu (sacred places), as they are called generally..are strictly sacred. **1851** Shortland *S. Dist. NZ* 293 A slave or other person not sacred would not enter a 'wahi tapu' or sacred place, without having first stripped off his clothes. **1874** Baines *Edward Crewe* 27 The particular spot of ground where the canoe was beached has been a Wahi Tapu (sacred place) ever since. **1904** Tregear *Maori Race* 283 The sacred portion (*wahi-tapu*) of a village was a place set apart from common uses, generally just outside the *pa* and usually fenced off... In more modern times the *wahitapu* has become a cemetery. **1924** Lysnar *NZ* 88 The remains of the dead and all connected therewith, were, and are, extremely tapu, and certain places, such as wahi tapu (burial grounds) are similarly sacred. **1988** Mikaere *Te Maiharoa* 39 A god called Karutahi (One Eye) had revealed to Te Ito that the reason why so many Maori were dying was that the people no longer knew where the wahi tapu (sacred places) were.

wai, var. WHAI.

waiariki. Also **waireka**. [Ma. /ˈwaiariki/: Williams 475 *Waiariki*..Hot spring.] A warm thermal spring or pool.

1867 Hochstetter *NZ* 392 Finally the springs suited to bathing-purposes, the water of which never reaches the boiling-point, and all naturally warm baths are called Waiariki, corresponding to the Laugar of Iceland. **1873** Tinne *Wonderland of Antipodes* 12 We were soon luxuriating in the delights of a 'waireka' (hot tank). **1878** Buller *Forty Yrs. NZ* 11 Hochstetter divides the steam jets into three kinds:.. 3. *Waiarikis*, which mean any sort of cistern of hot water suitable for bathing. **1989** Te Awekotuku *Tahuri* 16 They relaxed enjoying the soak, enjoying the big risk..because the waiariki here was no longer theirs.

waiata. Also early **wyata**. [Ma. /ˈwaiata/: Williams 475 *waiata*.] A (Maori) song. Also *fig*.

[**1807** Savage *Some Acc. of NZ* 75 Wyata..Singing.] **1839** *Report* 30 July in Wily & Maunsell *Robert Maunsell* (1938) 54 For so accommodating are their tunes and metres that they now set the Catechism to them and thus, when they join us, still find a substitute for their ancient *waiata*. **1843** Dieffenbach *Travels in NZ* II. 57 E' Waiata is a song of a joyful nature; E' Haka, one accompanied by gestures or mimics. **1853** Power *Recollections* 356 One or two little Anacreontic anecdotes, preserved in the 'Waiatas', or love-songs, are recorded of the [Polynesian] immigrants. **1878** Buller *Forty Yrs. NZ* 85 He did so by..using a well-known waiata, or poem, which wrought them into a frenzy. **1893** *TrNZI* XXV. 426 The following Maori *waiata*, or song, has a somewhat interesting history. **1905** Baucke *White Man Treads* 88 Then Puke, leaping up like a geyser, howled a last despairing howl, sang a waiata. **1936** Hyde *Passport to Hell* 140 A New Zealand captain, marching at the head of the Maori Pioneer Corps, started them off singing the Maori *waiatas*—the very sweet, very plaintive tribal songs that from one generation to another have been handed down among the people of the Maori race. **1962** Baxter *Collected Poems* (1980) 251 Treading with polished shoes on the face of the dead, The willow, the evergreen waiata. **1974** Mason *Hand on Rail* (TS 1987) 18 But I remember my grandfather. Spoke not a word of English, never, till he died. Full of waiata and karakia. **1991** *Dominion* (Wellington) 30 Mar. 12 We maintain the practice of our ancestors, our tipuna, which is that you never write or sing a waiata unless you had a good reason to.

wai enga, var. WAERENGA.

Waihi disease. *Obs.* [f. the name of a NI town and locality in the Bay of Plenty.] A disease of cattle caused by phosphate deficiency.

1929–30 *TrNZI* LX. 43 'Waihi disease', or bone mal-nutrition trouble, so called because it first appeared in cattle at Waihi... is often very prevalent in many parts of the North Island. **1930** *NZJST* XII. 304 There are, however, certain areas in which a decided malnutrition disease develops in stock, mostly in dairy cattle, in which the deficiency is phosphoric acid, since the symptoms are those of 'Waihi disease', a bone-malnutrition trouble manifested by lameness, swollen joints, and curable by dosing the subjects with phosphates as a lick or medicinal drench. **1936** BELSHAW et al. *Agric. Organiz. NZ* 82 'Waihi disease' in cattle gives as its most prominent symptom extreme lameness in milking cows. Epidemics of 'Waihi disease' occur in exceedingly droughty seasons in many parts of the North Island indicating a shortage of phosphoric acid in the herbage.

waihina, var. WAHINE *n.*[1]

waika, var. WEKA.

Waikikamukau /ˈwaiˌkɪkəˈmukæu/. *Joc.* Also variously **Kikamukau, Waikikamookau, Whykickamoocow.** An imaginary New Zealand rural place-name, or town, parodying the form of Maori place names.

1928 MINHINNICK in *Acid Test* (1981) 17 A special meeting of the Waikikamookau rate payers was called today..on the subject of Evolution. **1936** *NZ Railways Mag.* June 13 No, the 7.30 from Waikikamukau is running an hour late. **1946** BRUNO *Maleesh George* 58 A stringy private, as long as a wet weekend in the suburbs of Waikikamookau, snarled. **1955** *BJ Cameron Collection* (TS July) Waikikamukau (n) A mythical township used to symbolise the remote and parish-pump minded settlement. More or less the equivalent of the English Little-Toad-in-the-Hole. **1969** HENDERSON *Open Country Calling* 179 By the Powers, there's nothing beats, A night in Kikamukau, when the School Committee meets! **1980** LELAND *Kiwi-Yankee Dict.* 112 *Whykickamoocow:* An imaginary town located in the back of beyond; Hicksville, New Zealand. **1994** *Sunday Star-Times* 26 June C3 'Whykickamoocow Land', and head to Queenstown.

Waimarino cabbage tree: see CABBAGE TREE 2.

waipera, waipero, waipira(u), varr. WAIPIRO.

waipiro. Also with much variety of early form as **waipera, waipero, waipira, waipirau, why pirah, wypiero.** [Ma. /ˈwaiˈpiro/: f. Ma. *wai* water, *piro* stinking, putrid.]

1. In Maori contexts, alcoholic liquor, esp. spirits.

1834 MARKHAM *NZ* (1963) 45 I would give the Natives, a dram of Rum to wash it down. It used to be called Why Pirah or Stinking Water. Now they call it Why Pie or good Water. **1840** BEST *Journal* July (1966) 230 He went down to the Pah and drank Wypiero (Spirits) until he was beastly drunk. **1863** MANING *Old NZ* xi 166 He *would* go on shore, in spite of every warning, to get some water to mix with his *waipiro.* **1873** TINNE *Wonderland of Antipodes* 25 A crowd of drunken natives..ready to sponge..for another glass of their beloved waipero (stinking water), the curse of their race here as in America. **1881** CAMPBELL *Poenamo* 341 We had the inevitable percentage of indulgers in '*waipirau*'. **1890** ROBERTS *Hist. Oamaru and N. Otago* 63 Beer, or as the Maoris called it, Waipero. **1905** BAUCKE *White Man Treads* 272 When it [*sc.* Government] asked for permission to take a road through..it covenanted that it would..[not] bring waipiro within its boundaries. **1917** *Chron. NZEF* 17 Jan. 227 How much better, we say, would have been that glad day If we only had got more 'waipira'. **1938** FINLAYSON *Brown Man's Burden* (1973) 25 You strike the money there, boy! Some good waipiro too perhaps if we're lucky. **1947** BEATTIE *Early Runholding* 54 The Maori shearer of the early 'sixties..unfortunately..proved a ready convert to the custom of drinking waipiro and 'doing-in' his cheque at the nearest grog shanty. **1964** HORI *Fill It Up Again* 23 I don't believe in anyone, Maori or pakeha, drinking the waipiro to knock themselves stupid. **1992** *Dominion Sunday Times* (Wellington) 15 Mar. 2 It is a blot on the character of the white man that the Maori was introduced to waipiro —fire water or stinking water—which facilitated orgies of drunkeness and debauchery ever since.

2. In non-Maori contexts, any alcoholic liquor.

1869 *Auckland Punch* 147 Waipera 'liquor'. **1887** *Auckland Weekly News* 26 Mar. 7 Very often at the close of the performance, many were greatly under the influence of waipiro. **1909** OWEN *Philip Loveluck* 85 Try the rum..very good *waipiro.* [**1909** *Note*] Strong drink; almost slang, and in common use among Colonials. **1910** *NZ Free Lance* (Wellington) 29 Jan. 13 He had previously been known as a great consumer of waipirau, a wife-hitter, loafer, and general ne'er-do-well. **1921** *Quick March* 11 July 25 The slumbering form of the..[King Country] policeman who set out to keep night-watch in the fern for a motor-load of illicit grog, and who was found..with a 'dead marine' tied to his foot bearing a joyful note from the waipiro-laden gauntlet-runners. **1935** MITCHELL & STRONG in Partridge *Slang Today* 286 [The] following [was] employed by those who served in the [Great] War... *waipiro,* intoxicating liquor, from the Maori. **1957** *Racing in Rangitikei* 7 Many of the early race meetings were run on a free-and-easy style, with much squabbling and fighting, and not a little 'waipiro' or other strong drinks. **1967** ELLIOT & ADSHEAD *Cowshed to Dog Collar* 119 These men [barmen] toiled like galley slaves, pushing out the 'waipiro' (Maori for stinking water).

waipounamu: see TE WAIPOUNAMU.

Wairarapa death. *Obs.* New Zealand death (NEW ZEALAND B 4 b), death by drowning.

[**c1860**] MANSON *Widow of Thorndon Quay* (1981) 127 Mrs Vallance's first husband, Donald Drummond, had suffered [c1860] what was called the 'Wairarapa Death'—drowning.

Wairau. In special collocations: **Wairau Massacre, Wairau Affray, Wairau Affair,** names for an armed conflict over land purchase between Maori and Pakeha at Tuamarina, Marlborough on 17 June 1843.

[*Note*] The main 19th century name, current until fairly recently, was *Wairau Massacre,* reflecting the perceptions of white settlers; modern usage prefers *Wairau Affray* or *Affair,* or occas. *Wairau Incident.*

a. As **Wairau Massacre.**

1844 WILLIAMS *NZ Jrnl.* (1956) 81 A second Wairoo Massacre is staring them in the face [in Kororareka]. **1896** HODGSON *Poems* ii Besides the dire effects of the Wairau Massacre..the suspension of the New Zealand Company..had caused widespread distress amongst the Nelson settlers. **1911** *Piraki Log* (Gloss.-Index) 155 Scene, also, of the so-called 'Wairau Massacre' of the 'pakehas' by [Rauparaha]. **1930** GUTHRIE *NZ Memories* 92 But a little later news of the Wairau Massacre filtered through from the north, brought down by a whaler. **1945** HALL-JONES *Hist. Southland* 78 The date of his arrival is not fixed, but he returned north on hearing of the Wairau massacre. **1959** SINCLAIR *Hist. NZ* 75 Two years after the second Company settlement, Nelson, was established in 1841, there was a serious incident (termed by the settlers the 'Wairau massacre') when Captain Arthur Wakefield and several other Europeans were killed while attempting to arrest two turbulent chiefs, Te Rauparaha and Te Rangihaeata, ostensibly for burning surveyors' huts, but in reality for resisting the survey of land which the Maoris denied having sold. **1981** KING *New Zealanders at War* 29 Settlers were horrified by the incident, which quickly came to be called 'the Wairau Massacre'.

b. As **Wairau affair, Wairau affray.**

1985 MCGILL *G'day Country* 120 It was known to the Wellington settlers as the Wairau Massacre. Later it was called the Wairau Affray. Today it is simply the **Wairau Affair.** [**1848** SELWYN 30 Aug. in *NZ Part V* (Church in the Colonies XX) (1849) 74 On the other side of the [Tuamarina] river, along which the path to the Wairau lies, the ground itself explained the circumstances of the **affray.**] **1971** WRIGHT-ST CLAIR *Man of the World* 58 In June 1843 the settlement had suffered its first major disaster in the **Wairau affray. 1982** CHAMBERS *Samuel Ironside* 148 When news of the Wairau affray reached Wellington the passions of the settlers were so inflamed that eighty settlers..embarked for the Wairau. **1986** BELICH *NZ Wars* 73 One cause of trouble was the hasty New Zealand Company land purchasing which had also contributed to the Wairau Affray.

waireka, var. WAIARIKI.

wairenga, var. WAERENGA.

wairepo, var. WHAI-REPO.

wairua. Also early **whidooa, whydua.** [Ma. /ˈwairua/: Williams 477 *Wairua*... Spirit..] The spirit or soul.

[**1815** KENDALL *New Zealanders' First Book* 14 Whidooa: A spirit.] **1819** MARSDEN *Lett. & Jrnls.* (1932) 183 I answered in the affirmative; he replied, 'That is the whydua or spirit of Shunghee's father.' **1838** POLACK *NZ* I. 202 On my advancing near the Wai-tápu, the natives, in a piteous tone, begged me not to go near, as the spirits (wairua) of the place would kill them. **1843** DIEFFENBACH *Travels in NZ* II. 129 The dead bodies are 'tapu' until the tohunga has taken a part of the flesh, and..has hanged it up on a tree..as an offering to the Atuas, or to the wairua of him to revenge whom the war was undertaken. **1869** *TrNZI* I. (rev. edn.) 383 All were alike firmly believed to be remembrances of what they had seen in the *reinga,* or unseen world (or place of the departed,) whither the spirit (*Wairua*) was supposed to have been during the sleep of the body. **1883** DOMETT *Ranolf & Amohia* I. 150 The '*Wairua*', Spirits of the myriad dead. **1948** HENDERSON *Taina* 181 The fellowship of friends and relations is most necessary to a Maori at such times when the *wairua* of the dead is still not far away and perhaps present in the house. **1970** JENKIN *NZ Mysteries* 96 To the Maori..the soul or *wairua* of a man was believed to depart to the spirit world on the death of the body..sometimes the spirit did return, and these ghosts or *kehua* were greatly loved. **1986** IHIMAERA *Matriarch* 69 What I'm trying to say..is that the conflict was not only over the land, the tinana, but also over the spirit, the wairua.

wait, *v.*

1. *Shearing. Obs.* [AND 1898.] In the phr. **to wait for a death,** to wait for a man to be sacked in the hope of getting his job.

1911 *Maoriland Worker* 6 Oct. 17 In many cases

good honest shearers are cast off to make room for these 'guns.' Of course, the 'gun' shearer who comes along does not know that this has happened, as the 'gun' shearers are as a rule good unionists, and would not demean themselves by 'waiting for a death.' **1989** *NZ Eng. Newsletter* III. 22 The old custom of unemployed shearers waiting round in case someone got 'the bullet' was called 'waiting for a death'.

2. As **wait on**, wait!, hang on!

1943 BENNETT *English in NZ* in *Amer. Speech* XVIII. 91 The verb *to wait* has acquired an obtuse preposition in ordinary use; one is told to 'wait on' rather than to 'wait', but if any prepositional sense was ever felt in *on*—as in the American 'wait on me'—it has now been lost. **1957** p.c. Winfield Petch 1 Dec. My father came from..Dorset in 1880, one thing we used to say always amused him, and that was 'Wait on' for 'Wait for me'. I suppose I picked it up at school, as we certainly did not hear it at home.

wait-a-bit, wait-a-while.

1. Also **wait-a-minute.** BUSH LAWYER *n.*[1] Cf. STOP-A-BIT CREEPER.

1861 *NZ Goldfields 1861* (1976) 21 Scrubby higher ground, covered with a bright green-leaved thick-growing bramble, called 'wait-a-bit', entirely removed the sameness of colour. **1890** *Zealandia* I. 441 The bush..was composed principally of 'bush-lawyer' or 'wait-a-bit'. **1898** *Merriam-Webster Internat. Dict.* 2033 *Wait´-a-bit´*..the bush lawyer of New Zealand;—called also *wait-awhile.* c**1930** *Whitcombe's Etym. Dict. Aust.-NZ Suppl.* 12 *wait-a-bit, -a-minute, -awhile n.* the bush-lawyer. **1940** wait-a-bit [see BUSH LAWYER *n.*[1]].

2. As **wait-a-while**, TAIHOA B 2 (*Cassytha paniculata*).

1946 REED *Farthest North* 28 Closer inspection disclosed a curious creeper, common hereabouts [in Northland], its favourite habitat a clump of scrub, amongst which it contrives to involve itself in an inextricable tangle... This creeper bears the appropriate name of Taihoa (wait-a-while). **1948** REED *Gumdigger* 53 The stringy tendrils of the aptly named *taihoa*, or 'wait-awhile' native creeper, tough enough to trap and hold a horse.

Waitangi Day. [Ma. /ˈwaiˈtaŋi/: f. the name *Waitangi*, a locality in the Bay of Islands.] The sixth of February as a national summer holiday to commemorate the signing of the Treaty of Waitangi (see TREATY) on and after that date in 1840. Cf. *New Zealand Day* (NEW ZEALAND B 4 b).

1960 *NZ Statutes* No.46 343 An Act [Waitangi Day Act] to provide for the commemoration of the signing of the Treaty of Waitangi... 2. Waitangi Day—The sixth day of February in every year shall be known as Waitangi Day and shall be observed throughout New Zealand as a national day of thanksgiving in commemoration of the signing of the Treaty of Waitangi. **1966** *Encycl. NZ* III. 529 By the Waitangi Day Act of 1960, the 6th day of February in each year is known as Waitangi Day, to be observed throughout New Zealand as a national day of thanksgiving in commemoration of the signing of the Treaty of Waitangi. **1973** HAYWARD *Diary Kirk Years* 13 Feb. (1981) 112 Mr K. announced at the Waitangi Day celebrations that henceforth it would be called New Zealand Day and become a public holiday, 'though I think that this will still often be called Waitangi Day rather than New Zealand Day.' [1981 *Note*] On 6 February 1976 the day again became officially known as Waitangi Day. **1980** LELAND *Kiwi-Yankee Dict.* 109 *Waitangi Day*... Despite the controversy and the fact that the Treaty will never be ratified, Waitangi Day is New Zealand's national day. **1990** *Salient* (Wellington) 5 June 2 One minute it [*sc.* 1990] was here and we were getting all excited..about Sesqui and Waitangi Day and the Commonwealth Games.

wai-tapu, var. WAHI-TAPU.

waitoreke. [Not recorded in Williams: poss. from Ma. *wai* water + *toreke ptc.* left behind.] Also ?erron. **waitoteke**, and also called the **New Zealand** or **South Island 'otter'**, poss. from a misidentification of any of various small introduced mammals, or, more probably, from a Maori mythical creature later elevated to a dubious reality. Cf. KAUREHE.

[**1844** BARNICOAT *Journal* (ATLTS) 1 June 178 On the Banks of the Wanuk [*sc.* Lake Wanaka] shore are animals that from Rakiraki's account must be beavers. He describes them as building waries like the mouries and as making a screaming noise.] **1848** TAYLOR *Leaf from Nat. Hist.* 4 *Waitoreke*, otter. (Uncertain, perhaps the seal.) **1867** HOCHSTETTER *New Zealand* 161 We find the word Waitoreke, which has been only lately clearly defined, having been hitherto applied to an otter-like, and sometimes to a seal-like animal. According to..Haast, the existence of the animal has been recently established beyond a doubt; it lives in the rivers and lakes in the mountain ranges of the South Island, and is of the size of a large cony with a glossy brown fur, and is probably to be classed with the otters. [**1926** *Press* (Christchurch) 28 Aug. 13 The rumour of the 'beaver or otter' is mentioned by Butler in his 'First Year in the Canterbury Settlement'.] **1949** BEATTIE *Maoris & Fiordland* 79 About 70 years ago two Southland residents visited Lake Hauroko and 'while there shot an animal very like in size and appearance to the English otter'... On being appealed to the Maoris said the animal described was very rare and was a Waitoteke. **1954** BEATTIE *Our Southernmost Maoris* 76 The Maori account of a small animal known traditionally to them as the waitoteke, was brought forward as a proof of the existence of an 'otter' in New Zealand, but is more likely to have been the remembrance of some animal they knew in one of the Hawaikis... Asking after the waitoteke I was informed by an old man that he could not say if it was an otter or a water-rat as he knew neither, but it had been described to him in his youth as like a small rabbit (introduced by the whalers) but with a different shaped head. It was like an eel in the water—quite at home. **1960** *Rec. Canterbury Mus.* VII. 180 The word *waitoreke* appeared in a little Maori dictionary published in 1848 (Taylor) and is there translated 'otter [but see quot. 1848 above] (uncertain, perhaps seal)'... Sir Peter Buck considered the word *waitoreke* to be quite ungrammatical. [**1965** WALL *Long and Happy* 107 [Sir Dudley Dobson] told me how a waggish member of that party [*sc.* Haast's exploring party] hoaxed von Haast by making imitative animal footprints in the sand with a stick supplying the 'evidence' of the existence in New Zealand of some mammal, believed in by many and supposed to be 'an otter'.] **1966** *Encycl. NZ* I. 49 Of a slightly higher degree of probability were stories told to the early explorers of the South Island of an aquatic, otter or beaver-like animal, the *kaurehe* or *waitoreke*, supposedly a denizen of Fiordland and the Southern Lakes. **1970** *Proc. NZ Ecol. Soc.* XVII. 129 The waitoreke, or supposed South Island otter, has remained a mystery for over a century; for, despite the authoritative evidence of Haast..zoologists generally have been only too happy to dismiss the animal as a myth. **1986** *Daniel & Baker Collins Guide Mammals NZ* 120 In the early 1800s, South Island Maori tradition among the Ngatimamoe and Ngaitahu tribes apparently included ancestral knowledge of the existence of an animal kept as a pet by the old Maori. This animal was variously called waitoreke, kaurehe or kaureke, and was believed to live in certain South Island lakes and rivers. *Ibid.* 122 Unfortunately for the waitoreke theory, no convincing and unequivocal reports or specimens were documented before the flood of mammal introductions from about 1850 onwards. **1990** *Handbook NZ Mammals* 287 There are reports, in both popular and technical publications, that there is or once was a New Zealand 'otter', known to the Maori as 'waitoreke'... Most of these stories can be traced to sightings of unidentified animals in dubious circumstances... Pollock's theory, that it is one of the small species of Asian otters, brought to New Zealand by shipwrecked fishermen hundreds of years ago and still present in the South Island, is attractive but wholly unsupported. Daniel and Baker's suggestion, that it is a mythical Maori creature unwittingly elevated into a real animal, seems much more likely.

waitoteke, var. WAITOREKE.

waiu-atua. [Ma. *waiu* milk + *atua* god: /ˈwaiˈuːˈatua/: Williams 478 *Waiū..1.* Milk... *Waiū-atua, Rhabdothamnus solandri, Euphorbia glauca,* and *Gaultheria oppositifolia*.] Any of various plants having a milky sap, or milky appearance, esp. *Euphorbia* spp., milkweeds, and *Rhabdothamnus* spp.

1853 HOOKER *II Flora Novae-Zelandiae I Flowering Plants* 227 *Euphorbia glauca*... Nat. name 'Waiuatua' (*Demon's milk*). **1867** HOOKER *Handbook* 769 *Waiuatua... Euphorbia glauca... Waiuatua Rhabdothamnus Solandri.* **1906** CHEESEMAN *Manual NZ Flora* 628 *E[uphorbia] glauca*... A tall stout perfectly glabrous and glaucous herb 1–3 ft. high... *Waiuatua.* **1910** COCKAYNE *NZ Plants & Their Story* 39 Birds also fertilise New Zealand plants, amongst others..the waiuatua (*Rhabdothamnus Solandri*). **1911, 1952** [see SPURGE]. **1975** *Tane 21* 8 Gesneriaceae *Rhabdothamnus solandri* waiuatua. **1981** *Euphorbia* spp. [see SPURGE].

waiwaikoko, var. WAEWAEKOUKOU.

waiwai-roa, var. WAEROA.

waka /ˈwɒkə/. Also with much variety of early form as **hewaca, e-waka, e'wakka** (=he waka), **wa-kaw, walker, wauka** (?/wokʌ/), **whacka, whaka.** [Ma. /ˈwaka/: Williams 478 *Waka*.]

1. a. A Maori ocean-going canoe with straked sides; often used loosely as a name for any canoe, including the Chatham Island 'raft-canoe'. Also *transf.* See also CANOE *n.*[1] Contrast TIWAI.

[*Note*] *waka* and *waka maori* were fairly frequent in English use during the 19th century, becoming infrequent in the 20th century until the approach of 1990, the sesquicentenary of the signing of the Treaty of Waitangi and the building of a waka fleet as part of the celebration.

[**1770** PARKINSON *Journal* (1773) 127 A Vocabulary of the Language of New Zealand. Egooree, *A dog*... Hewaca, *A canoe.* **1777** ANDERSON *Journal* 25 Feb. in Cook *Journal* (1967) III. 817 E'wakka..A boat or Canoe. **1807** SAVAGE *Some Acc. of NZ* 77 Wauka..A canoe.] **1814** NICHOLAS *NZ* (1817) I. 52 The constellation forming the Belt of Orion, they call the *Whacka* or the *Canoe.* **1834** MARKHAM *NZ* (1963) 29 When the Bar was crossed Canoes or in the Native Mourie Tongue, Walker Mouries, or Native Boats, boarded us. **1841** BIDWILL *Rambles in NZ* (1952) 61 Those [canoes] with top sides..are called Wa-kaw, or in common pronunciation 'Walkers'. **1867** HOCHSTETTER *NZ* 292 Generally those wakas are wrought from the much more durable red Totara-wood. **1873** *Weekly News* (Auckland) 8 Mar. 14 A couple of 'Kai wheros' rushed down to the beach; the 'waka' was brought alongside;

out jumped the crew. **1905** TrNZI XXXVII. 146 With regard to the term '*waka*', or canoe as we call it, the term, having in view the present-day build of such, is certainly a misnomer, and the word 'vessel' would be more appropriate, for no canoe of the present type could..ever have crossed the long stretch of ocean between Rarotonga and New Zealand. **1923** SKINNER *Morioris Chatham Is.* 13 These beaches were probably the point of departure for the *waka* (the wash-through canoe of the Morioris) in making the passage to Pitt Island. **1937** *NZ Railways Mag.* Nov. 18 He..set off up the river, alongside Bates' *waka*. **1988** *Dominion* (Wellington) 22 Nov. 10 Skills were developed for selecting, felling, transporting and hollowing totara trunks to make waka (canoes). **1992** *Ibid.* 2 May 13 The book culminates in the year of the waka, when 19 waka were built by tribes around New Zealand for 1990 as a statement of identity and mana.

b. As a symbol of ancestry, a group of Maori tribes with descent from one of the traditional 'landing' canoes.

1843 SHORTLAND *Letter* 15 Aug. in Shortland *Traditions & Superstitions* (1856) 305 And it seems probable that the term *Waka* (canoe), which is used to denote these primary divisions, has reference to its origin of the tribes. At the present day, these *Waka* are divided into many distinct *Iwi*; each of which is subdivided again into *Hapu*, or smaller communities. **1863** MOSER *Mahoe Leaves* 38 He commenced a long rigmarole about the 'waka', the canoe of his ancestors.

c. *Fig.*
1996 *Evening Post* (Wellington) 9 Mar. 14 At the beginning I said to the facilitators, 'Don't get on this waka if you can't last the distance'.

2. With a Maori suffix indicating a specific kind of canoe. (See also quot. 1949 1 a above.) **a. waka korari**, the Moriori canoe of the Chatham Islands, often constructed from KORARI (flax sticks).

1866 HUNT *Chatham Is.* 35 Some noted fisherman [on dying]..would be secured, lashed in a *waka korari*, or flax-stem canoe, in a sitting position, as if in the attitude of fishing.

b. waka taua, WAR-CANOE.
1859 *Richmond-Atkinson Papers* 31 Jan. (1960) I. 451 The Maori canoe race [at the Auckland regatta] was not in one respect as good as usual. A tiwai ran with the waka tauas and *ran away* from them. **1874** whaka taua [see WAR-CANOE]. **1882** POTTS *Out in Open* 10 At a favourite landing-place near the town were moored three of these quaint-looking vessels of the olden days, each abundantly decorated with the plumed ornamentation proper for the waka tawa. **1991** *Dominion* (Wellington) 9 Nov. 1 A Marlborough waka taua (war canoe) was due to arrive at Clyde Quay wharf this morning after an overnight crossing of Cook Strait.

waka waka, var. WEKA.

waka blonde, var. WHAKA BLONDE.

waka huia. [Ma. /'waka 'huia/: Williams 478 *Waka. n.* 2. Any long narrow receptacle, as..a box for feathers.] A canoe-shaped receptacle for treasured (orig. huia) feathers. See also FEATHER-BOX .

1898 MORRIS *Austral-English* 493 *Waka, n... Waka huia* is a box for keeping feathers, originally the feathers of the *huia*. **1904** TREGEAR *Maori Race* 244 Feather plumes were kept by their owners in small boxes (*waka-huia*) often beautifully carved. **1946** *JPS* LV. 143 A small, long, narrow, carved box (equivalent of our jewel-box) called waka-huia (waka here means container), a receptacle for feathers; but only huia-feathers. **1955** PHILLIPPS *Maori Carving* (1961) 7 [Caption] Enlarged waka huia end, Norwich Castle Museum. **1966** *Encycl. NZ* II. 122 Beautifully carved boxes, waka-huia, were made and used solely for the storage of feathers. **1984** *Te Maori* 21 An art object such as a wakahuia (treasure box) is an enriched creation. **1993** *Evening Post* (Wellington) 8 Jan. 3 The [feather] boxes (waka huia) were slung from the rafters so people in the house were not endangered, possibly by spiritual beings.

wa-kaw, var. WAKA.

Wakefield. *Hist.*

1. [f. the name of Edward Gibbon *Wakefield* (1796–1862), author and colonist.] Used *attrib.* to designate Wakefield's doctrines on colonization and their application, esp. **Wakefield colony**, **plan**, **settlement**, **theory**.

1858 *Fox to Godley* in *Speeches & Documents* 31 Dec. (1971) 34 There is no doubt..that the original intention was to carry out the Wakefield theory, and there is no doubt at all that the basis of that theory is a high price laid on for the avowed purpose of preventing the labouring man from acquiring land too quickly. **1936** BELSHAW et al. *Agric. Organiz. NZ* 4 Failure of the Wakefield Plan. **1938** BURDON *High Country* 3 His views, known as the 'Wakefield Theory', were not formed at once but evolved over a period of years. **1949** REED *Story Canterbury* [Subtitle] Last Wakefield Settlement. **1959** MCLINTOCK *Descr. Atlas* 38 From the stagnation they faced in the early 1840s, the Wakefield settlements were rescued by the energy of the young 'squatters'. **1989** BURNS *Fatal Success* 14 The Wakefield Plan was based on the assumption that vast areas..of New Zealand would be bought for a trifle, the real payment to the people of the land being their 'civilising' through colonisation. **1990** in Majourum *Sergeant. Sinner* 6 This conflict [over land sale] was threatening to spill over into the Wakefield settlement of New Plymouth.

Hence **Wakefieldian**, *n.* [AND 1843], one following the colonizing theories of E.G. Wakefield; a settler sponsored by the companies subscribing to Wakefield's theories.

1959 SINCLAIR *Hist. NZ* 92 All of the districts where the Wakefieldians had established their settlements, with the exception of Taranaki, were pre-eminently suitable for sheep.

2. Spec. Comb. **Wakefield** (occas. **Wakefield's**) **system** [AND 1839], the establishment outside Britain of a complete English (or British) community based on assisted emigration to a colony where cheaply acquired land would be sold at a 'sufficient' price to would-be colonists to defray the costs of settlement.

1839 *Glasgow Constitutional* 26 Oct. [New Zealand Colonization Dinner] The learned Professor concluded by drinking, 'Mr. Wakefield—the author of the Wakefield system of Emigration'. **1842** HEAPHY *NZ* 68 The happy effect of the 'Wakefield system', has been to cause the supply of labour and the demand to be at all times equal. **1843** WOOD *Twelve Months in Wellington* 50 The '*sufficient*' price of the Wakefield system is a fallacy... Waste land is often dear at a gift. **1931** COAD *Such Is Life* 36 You see, Wellington was colonised under the Wakefield system. **1948** COWAN *Down the Years in the Maniototo* 8 The few farmers did not have enough capital to buy sheep runs..for land under the Wakefield System was £2 an acre. **1959** SINCLAIR *Hist. NZ* 91 In these important respects Wakefield's system offered useful, practical hints for colonizers. On the whole, however, it failed to work. The experiments in New Zealand produced colonies—but not 'Wakefield' colonies. It proved impossible to regulate either the expansion of the frontier or the form of class structure by means of a price upon land. **1961** *Distance Looks Our Way* 31 A book could be written about the consequences of wool. For one thing Wakefield's 'system', which required smallish farms and numerous farm employees, would not work. **1989** BURNS *Fatal Success* 100 The Wakefield System attached great importance to the concept of the colony being established as a complete community, and this meant that all the landowners and their servants would arrive simultaneously.

wake up, *a.* Aware; esp. in the phr. **to be (a) wake-up (awake up) (to)** [AND 1930], **to be wake-ups**, to be aware (of), to be awake (to).

1936 SARGESON *Letter to Press* 26 Sept. in *Islands 21* (1978) 222 So it looks as if your reviewer can't be too much of a wake up to New Zealand life. **1946** SARGESON *That Summer* 91 Now I was a wake-up to what was in Maggie's mind. *Ibid.* 92 The pair of us were wake-ups when we heard somebody coming up the stairs. **1955** *BJ Cameron Collection* (TS July) awake to be awake-up to (v) To see through someone's game. **1960** HILLIARD *Maori Girl* 248 Well, I'm a wake-up! **1968** SLATTER *Pagan Game* 164 Tried to put me in crook with the missus—I'm awake up to that one. **1987** GEE *Prowlers* 126 He was wake-up to that sort of trick.

walker: see WAKA.

Walker's weed. *West Coast.* [Orig. unknown.] See quot.

1926 HILGENDORF *Weeds* 59 Perhaps also it is this weed [*sc.* Redshank (*Polygonum persicaria*)] that on the west coast of the South Island is called water pepper or Walker's weed. It is an annual weed of gardens, crops, and wet pastures.

walking country. *Mustering.* Country that is too steep to be traversed on horseback.

1947 NEWTON *Wayleggo* 35 It was all walking country..the musterers travelling either per 'Harry Pannell' (walking) or riding on the pack dray. **1966** NEWTON *Boss's Story* 191 *Walking Country*: Most South Island high country is too steep and rugged to be traversed on horseback. This is termed 'walking country' as apart from easier and rideable country.

walk off, *v.*

1. [Used elsewhere but recorded earliest in NZ if the quot. is more than merely punning: see OED *walk v.*[1] 8 b, 1898.] Said of objects presumed borrowed or stolen.

1846 PHARAZYN *Journal* (ATLMS) 34 The only serviceable pair of boots had walked off.

2. *absol.* as **walk off** and also in the stock phr. **to walk off (one's farm, land)**, said of a farmer whose holding is so uneconomic or mortgaged as to be not worth the attempt to recover any of the investment in it.

[*Note*] The phr. was used esp. during the rural 'downturns' of the early 1930s and later 1980s.

1930 in Grant *Unauthorised Version* (1980) 124 [Caption] 'Walking off: Processes of Rural Development' [with cartoon pictures captioned:] 'The profits walk off', 'The men walk off', 'The farmer walks off' [in an expensive car], 'The farm walks off'. **1963** BACON *In the Sticks* 62 The Government partly developed the land, then put returned soldier farmers on it. One by one they went broke and walked off. **1977** BRUCE *Life in Hinterland* 62 Block 3: Taken up in 1919 and abandoned 15 years late... Held for 10 years by the second occupier, who also walked off. **1981** HUNT

Speaking a Silence 46 Men'd just walked off that land in the slump but those cattle were breaking it all in again. **1989** CAMPBELL *Frigate Bird* 112 Some have chucked up everything and walked off their farms. **1992** PARK *Fence around the Cuckoo* 26 'It's them banks!' said people, commiserating with dazed families who had walked off their land [in the Depression].

Hence **walk-off** *n.*, the abandonment of an uneconomic farm.

1990 *Pacific Way* May 51 As a farm it proved untenable..and there was the heartbreak of a walk-off.

walk shorts. *pl.* Comfortable dress shorts for business and casual wear.

1968 *Evening Post* (Wellington) 5 Jan. 8 More and more city offices and shops are making concessions to the warmer weather by allowing their male staff members to wear neat walk shorts and knee-high socks to work during the summer months. **1969** *NZ Herald* (Auckland) 10 Apr. sect. i. 4 [Advt] Men's Walk Shorts. **1988** [see WALK SOCKS]. **1995** *Sunday Star-Times* (Auckland) 23 Apr. sect. D 1 He has worked with government departments where walkshorts and sandals are still the most favoured uniform.

walk socks. *pl.* Thick socks worn nearly knee-high with (walk-)shorts.

1988 *Evening Post* (Wellington) 11 Jan. 14 30% off all walk socks. **1988** *Listener* 27 Feb. 65 First there are those New Zealand words [in *Collins English Dictionary*, 2edn.]..for example..*solo mother, walk socks* (but not *walk shorts*).

walk-through cow-shed: see SHED 4 b.

wallaby. *Obs.* **a.** Usu. in the phr. **on the wallaby track** [AND 1849], on the tramp, on the road, 'on the swag'; occas. (as in quot. 1881) to move on from one job to another. See also *on the track* (TRACK *n.* 3).

1871 CLARKE in Money *Knocking About NZ* (1871) vi It is lamentable to witness the discomfiture of your after-dinner Colonist, when he meets with some unpretending fellow (who does not even swear), but who has 'humped his swag' into strange lands, and traversed the 'wallaby-track' under the direst conditions. **1881** BATHGATE *Waitaruna* 167 You ought to have gone up yourself, and not left it to such a born fool as Mike. He'll have to take the Wallabi [*sic*] track tomorrow morning. I wonder how I came to keep such an idiot on the place. **1904** *NZ Illustr. Mag.* Dec. 178 I can see him now as he came on the 'Wallaby track'.

b. In shortened form **on the wallaby.**

c**1890** BODELL *Soldier's View Empire* (1982) 141 He had the appearance of a fighting man or a dog fancier a brutish countenance and he had often been on the Wallaby (or tramp) about the various Gold Fields and Squatters Stations. **1897** WRIGHT *Station Ballads* 26 I used to read the Bible once, and thought it pretty clear That Christ was on the wallaby that time that He was here. **1909** *Truth* 6 Nov. 1 Therefore, Woollcombe, get thee hence; go home thou wowser on the wallaby; hump bluey. **1990** MARTIN *Forgotten Worker* 33 The swaggers who moved around on the roads and tracks in search of work were not described as being 'on the wallaby'.

wallop. *v. Obs. trans.* To fork straw into a stack usu. as part of the work of a thrashing-mill team. See also STRAW-WALLOPER.

1917 *Otago Witness* (Dunedin) 11 Apr. 23 Where there is a man short the straw has to be 'walloped'—that is, pitched into a heap anyhow.

wampo. Also **wompo.** [Origin unknown: see Partridge *wampo* intoxicating liquor: RAF: from ca.1930; see also AND *wompy a.* Ill (1920).] Beer slops or the leakage from beer taps or overflowed glasses, served again to unsuspecting customers. See also SLOP 1 a.

1946 MANDERSON *Beer Slops* 10 The resulting concoction..is commonly called 'Wampo'. This name was well known throughout Auckland among barmen. *Ibid.* 14 I refused to sell the slop beer ('wampo' as it is commonly known by barmen). **1946** *AJHR H-38* 113 When these dregs are mixed with beer for sale, the resultant liquid is colloquially known as 'Wompo'. The term has been in use among barmen for as long as one experienced licensee could recollect—from twenty to thirty years.., and it is known to the man in the street. *Ibid.* 115 The resultant 'Wompo' was then served to the public. **1957** *Truth* 18 June 24 Wampo was beer slops from overflowing glasses. In the old days some publicans kept these slops in a bucket, then strained them through a bar cloth back into a keg... The plastic beer-hose sounded the death-knell of potential wampo...It gave the wampo-pushers what-ho.

wampy, *a.* [See etym. note at WAMPO.] Queer, mad.

1950 BEATTIE *Far Famed Fiordland* 85 Old 'Arawata Bill', like so many men who spend many years in solitude, went quite 'wampy' in the end. **1975** p.c. Kendrick Smithyman 11 Jan. He must have been *wampy* (or *wampo*) [i.e. mad].

wanaki, var. WHANAKE.

wandering albatross: see ALBATROSS.

Wanganella weather /wɒŋɡəˈnelə/. Unexpectedly fine calm weather such as the long spell in Wellington from 19 January 1947 allowing the stranded *Wanganella* to be extricated safely from Barrett's Reef. Cf. *cockatoo's weather* (COCKATOO *n.* 2), *earthquake weather* (EARTHQUAKE 2).

1948 p.c. R. Mason. *Wanganella weather* heard in Wellington for a spell of unexpectedly fine, calm weather, but with uncertainty of when it is going to break. **1953** *Evening Post* (Wellington) 29 Aug. 10 Wellington, having had the experience of 'Wanganella weather,' may soon be persuaded that there is also such a thing as 'Ranfurly Shield weather'. **1962** LAWLOR *More Wellington Days* 190 We have only to remember that wonderful episode of the stranding of the *Wanganella*, (January 19, 1947) when for eighteen days wind and weather showed a compassion we must never forget. Indeed, this happening brought into the Wellington dictionary the words '*Wanganella* weather'. **1978** *Evening Post* (Wellington) 18 Mar. 19 A new phrase entered the Wellington vocabulary in early 1947—'Wanganella weather'... The transtasman passenger liner Wanganella..was wrecked on Barrett's Reef at the entrance to Wellington Harbour on January 19, 1947 and was not freed from the reef until February 6. For these 19 days the sun shone and there was hardly a breath of wind and the ship was saved. **1988** *Those Were the Days* 28 There was the grounding of the passenger steamer *Wanganella* off Wellington Heads.., and her refloating after 18 fine days of 'Wanganella weather'.

wannuae, var. WHENUA.

waoriki. Also prob. erron. **wha(u)riki.** [Ma. Williams 479 *Waoriki*... *Ranunculus* [spp.]..= *raoriki*.] *Ranunculus rivularis* (fam. Ranunculaceae), a native buttercup of swamps and still waters. Cf. BUTTERCUP 1.

1905 *NZ Medical Jrnl.* IV. 13 22 The responsibility [for poisoning wild honey] rests with the yellow flowers of a cress-like plant called 'whauriki,' which grows in swamps. **1905** *TrNZI* XXXVII. 113 *Ranunculus rivularis. (Waoriki.)* The expressed juice, which has blistering qualities, is used for rheumatic..joint-diseases. **1913** *NZJAg.* Jan. VI. 559 Would waoriki..or any other species of Ranunculus produce the symptoms described? **1952** LYON *Faring South* 105 A peculiar fatality in wild honey was a poisonous quality in the honey itself... The natives blame a small yellow flower growing on the banks of streams in the King Country, which they call whariki, but whether this is so I cannot say. **1969** *Standard Common Names Weeds* 83 *waoriki Ranunculus rivularis.* **1981** TAYLOR *Weeds of Lawns* 25 Waoriki (*Ranunculus rivularis*)... This native is our most poisonous buttercup. It grows in both Islands but its occurrence is localised.

wapuku, var. HAPUKU.

war. War has long been of historical significance to New Zealand and New Zealanders as both an expression of and an opportunity for (often well-intentioned) violence. Combinations and phrases including the word *war* (often with init. cap.) apply to three main areas of use.

1. Fighting between Maori tribes or inter-iwi conflict. **a.** See GIRLS' WAR, MUSKET WAR, and *native war* (NATIVE B 3 b).

b. Special Comb. with reference to Maori martial arts: **war-cloak,** a strongly-woven defensive cloak; **war-club,** MERE or PATU; **war-path** *obs.*, one of many usual tracks in various localities taken by Maori proceeding on raids on enemy tribes. See also WAR-CANOE, WAR-DANCE, WAR-MAT, WAR-PARTY.

1885 TREGEAR *Aryan Maori* 94 The old Maori dogs, nevermore to be seen by mortal eyes (they have all perished, but their hides are on the **war-cloaks**). **1830** CRAIK *New Zealanders* 47 While thus employed, and with numbers of the islanders mixed with them, in one moment each was fallen upon by..barbarians, who..instantly overpowered..resistance..beating out their brains with..their short stone **war-clubs**. **1848** WAKEFIELD *Handbook NZ* 314 The natives procure.. quantities of a green jade, or serpentine, much prized by them for the purpose of making war-clubs. **1885** W.J. Swainson let. in *William Swainson* (1992) 106 Their route was up the Valley of the Hutt..ascending the ranges and descending to the Tauherenikau Plain, by an old native track and **warpath** almost untraceable except by marked trees. **1888** BULLER *Birds NZ* I. 162 At the time..this place could be only reached by a canoe journey..from Foxton, or by a rude bush-track—one of the Maori war-paths of former times.

2. Fighting between Maori and Pakeha troops, usu. now called the NEW ZEALAND WAR(S) q.v., and occas. (formerly) referred to as **colonial wars** (see quot. 1930 below), or **war of races** (see quot. 1908 below). **a.** See also *Anglo-Maori war* (ANGLO-MAORI B 2), FLAGSTAFF WAR, HEKE WAR, *Land War* (LAND 1), MAORI WAR, *Native war(s)* (NATIVE B 3 b), TARANAKI WAR(S).

1908 GORST *NZ Revisited* 1 My public life had begun..in the interval between the local insignificant Taranaki War of 1860 and the outbreak of the terrible war of races in 1863. **1930** REISCHEK *Yesterdays in Maoriland* (1933) 7 Perhaps, also, he will help to remind them how good, how strenuous life was 'in the good old days', when their Dominion was still half-savage, still unsettled after the toughest of colonial wars, and before the fire and axe of succeeding generations of peaceful settlers had robbed her of so much of her incomparable possession, the native bush. **1934** MULGAN *Spur of Morning* 42 'Pillar of the Church and sweats his work girls.' 'Made money in the war selling stores to the troops and ammunition to the natives.'

b. In the phr. **War in the North**, a name for the HEKE (or FLAGSTAFF) WAR. (Belich *The New Zealand Wars* (1986) prefers 'The Northern War'.)
1862 MANING *History of the War in the North of New Zealand against the Chief Heke. In the Year 1845.* [Title] **1886** BURROWS *Extracts from a diary kept..during Heke's war in the North in 1845.* [Title] **1922** COWAN *NZ Wars* (1955) I. xvii The principal campaigns and expeditions dealt with in the History are as follows: (1) Hone Heke's War in the North, 1845–46.

c. Special Comb. **war-flag** *obs.*, see quot.; **war-news** *obs.*, news from the Taranaki War.
1861 *Otago Witness* (Dunedin) 6 Apr. 5 The Maories observed [the advance of the Royal Artillery] at first with apparent indifference, and continued to fly the flag of truce in the pah..until eleven o'clock when the white flag was lowered from the Maori staff, and replaced by a blood-red **war flag**. **1862** HODDER *Memories NZ Life* 204 Proclamations and **war-news** from Taranaki.

3. Fighting overseas: special Comb. *WW1*: **War Babies**, a late batch of reinforcements arriving among battle-experienced men; **war cake**, a plain cake, having no eggs; **war-time toffee**, a recipe requiring no butter at a time when butter was rationed.
1916 ROSS *Light & Shade* 177 The men from the Antipodes have brought with them a humour and a slang of their own. Their definition of the various batches of volunteers that have come out to fight is worth quoting. The first contingent became known as 'The Tourists'... There followed [later] 'The Super-Dinkums', 'The **War Babies**', and 'The Hard Thinkers'. **1915** *Celebrated Amuri Cook. Book* (1927) 76 **War Cake**. Two cups flour..[no eggs but mixed spice, fruit]. **1915** MCCREDIE *Patriotic Fete... Bungalow Recipe Book* 84 **War time toffee**..sugar..water..vinegar..boil.

warangai, warangi, varr. WHARANGI.

wara wara, var. WHARAWHARA.

waratah. [f. a proprietary name *waratah* transferred from that of the Austral. shrub (fam. Proteaceae), the floral emblem of N.S.W., orig. ad. Aborig. *warata*.] A slim iron fence standard or stake, whose cross-section comprises 3 ribs each at 120° to the other.
[**1923** *NZ Patent Office Jrnl.* [no number given] 22 Feb. Waratah 19698 [filed] 19th December, 1922. Rylands Bros. (Australia), Ltd..Metal goods not included in other classes.] **1980** GLEN *Bush in Our Yard* 129 There were concrete posts and heavy gauge wire and netting of various sizes strung on to waratahs—for the life of me I could not see what this distinctly Australian name had to do with a 2-metre hunk of mild steel. **1988** PICKERING *Hills* 26 Routes became, as the maps put it, 'poled', which meant that metal standards were studded along the tops. These can also be called snow-poles or sometimes waratahs.

warbler.

1. [Transf. use of *warbler* a species of small bird.] Either of the New Zealand species of small insectivorous birds of the genus *Gerygone* (fam. Acanthizidae), usu. and commonly *grey warbler* (see 2 (3) below).
1870 *TrNZI* II. 58 Gerygone assimilis... Piripiri. Warbler, Teetotum. **1927** GUTHRIE-SMITH *Birds* 158 Then comes a day at last when the Warblers begin to think of their second nest. **1984** SOPER *Birds NZ* 139 Warblers... A large and complex family of insectivorous birds... Five of the New Zealand species are contained in the sub-family Malurinae, the Australian warblers.

2. With a modifier: **bush** (occas. **wood**), **Chatham Island, grey**.

(1) **bush** (occas. **wood**) **warbler**. See *grey warbler* (3) below.
1884 *NZJSc.* II. 286 Gerygone sylvestris... Wood Warbler.—Nothing has yet been ascertained of the breeding habits of this little warbler, whose cheerful notes enliven the fern gullies of the dense forests between Okarito and Lake Mapourika. **1888** BULLER *Birds NZ* I. 50 (Bush-warbler)... The above Warbler..was first made known by Mr. T.H. Potts [in]..'The Ibis' in 1872 (p. 325). **1898** MORRIS *Austral-English* 498 Warbler... In New Zealand,.. now only specifically applied to the—Bush Warbler—*Gerygone silvestris*... Chatham Island W[arbler]—*G. albofrontata*... Grey W[arbler]—*G. flaviventris*.

(2) **Chatham Island warbler**. *Gerygone albofrontata*. See also *woodpecker* (WOOD *n.*¹ 2 b).
1884 *NZJSc.* II. 285 Gerygone albofrontata... Chatham Island warbler. Larger than the preceding species [*G. flaviventris*, grey warbler]. **1888** BULLER *Birds NZ* I. 49 Gerygone albofrontata. (Chatham-Island Warbler.) **1898** [see (1) above]. **1904** HUTTON & DRUMMOND *Animals NZ* 69 The Chatham Island Warbler is slightly larger than the New Zealand species. **1966** FALLA et al. *Birds of NZ* 213 Chatham Island Warbler... *Local name*: Woodpecker.— The Chatham Island Warbler has a much bigger bill than the Grey Warbler. **1976** SOPER *NZ Birds* 216 All these birds are common, as is the Chatham Warbler—a larger bird than the Grey Warbler, browner and with a lemon flush on the breast. **1986** *Listener* 12 Apr. 49 Cross-fostering techniques using Chatham Island warblers on Mangere and Chatham Island tits on South East Island are experiments that have excited the conservation world.

(3) **grey warbler**. *Gerygone igata*, a diminutive songbird known as a chief host for the eggs and young of the shining cuckoo. See also PIRIPIRI *n.*², RIRORIRO, TEETOTUM, WARCHIE.
1870 *TrNZI* II. 48 Then we might note where..the grey warbler (Piripiri) with quivering notes flustered near its cosy, dome-shaped nest. **1873** BULLER *Birds NZ* 107 Gerygone flaviventris. (Grey Warbler)... Riroriro and Koriroriro. **1884** [see PIRIPIRI *n.*²]. **1905** THOMSON *Bush Boys* 174 Pity, Peace and Purity—these are the notes sounded forth by our tiny grey warbler, so modest unpretentious, contented, sweet. **1919** *TrNZI* LI. 217 The Grey warbler is a bird which I think will adapt itself to the new conditions attendant upon the settlement of the country. **1930** *Evening Post* (Wellington) 6 Dec. 17 In the bush the grey warbler is..quite at home. **1946** [see RIRORIRO]. **1967** NATUSCH *Animals NZ* 277 The grey warbler.., a small common species, is the inconspicuous owner of the clear shrilling, abruptly cut off, that we hear in suburban gardens as well as in the bush. **1976** SOPER *NZ Birds* 72 The widely distributed Grey Warbler, so characteristically found in scrub lands and open clearings in and around the forest edge, is a small slender greenish-grey bird with an undulating, floating, feather-like flight. **1985** *Reader's Digest Book NZ Birds* 278 According to Maori folklore, the melodic, rambling song of the grey warbler heralded spring, the time of planting.

war canoe. [Spec. use of *war-canoe* for a Maori *waka taua*: see OED *war* 8 b.] A large, often decorated ocean-going Maori canoe, orig. used for the transport of tribal war parties. See also CANOE *n.*¹, *waka taua* (WAKA 2 b).
1773 FORSTER *Resolution Jrnl.* 25 Nov. (1982) III. 428 We saw on their war-canoe the head ornamented with bunches of brown Feathers, & there stuck the heart of the unhappy boy. **1807** SAVAGE *Some Acc. of NZ* 28 The chieftains of the coast are..no less formidable when commanding a fleet of war canoes. **1817** NICHOLAS *NZ* I. 89 These [cargo] canoes had scarcely left us, when we were visited by two others of a different description, the war canoes. **1830** CRAIK *New Zealanders* 131 The war-canoes of the New Zealanders..have their heads..elaborately carved. **1841** HODGSKIN *Narr. Eight Months Sojourn NZ* 13 A great deal of time..is required to finish a large war-canoe. **1869** *TrNZI* I. (rev. edn.) 350 Their fishing and voyaging canoes, also with raised sides. [**1869** *Note*] Commonly called 'War Canoes' by the Colonists. **1874** BAINES *Edward Crewe* 82 The large war-canoes, whaka taua, are constructed out of five..pieces, the first the main part which has been 'dug out' of a huge tree. **1906** GAMBIER *Links in My Life* (1907) 161 After a day or two of Corroborries..more war-dancing and races..between the huge war canoes. **1922** COWAN *NZ Wars* (1955) I. 417 The large flotilla of war-canoes was drawn up on the beach at the mouth of the Waitahanui Stream. **1991** *Evening Post* (Wellington) 4 Nov. 2 A Maori war canoe carrying up to 70 people including 64 paddlers is due in Wellington... [The] 30m waka is to leave Waikawa..on Friday evening.

warchie ?/ˈwɒtʃi/. *grey warbler* (WARBLER 2 (3)).
1959 MIDDLETON *The Stone* 27 There was a flutter of feathers..and a Grey Warbler flew out... 'Look!' I said. 'I've found a warchie's nest.'

war-dance. [Spec. use of *war-dance* a dance before a warlike excursion.] HAKA.
[*Note*] Many *haka*, for example those part of a welcoming ceremony, were often misinterpreted by non-Maori observers as war-dances.
1769 COOK *Journals* 9 Oct. (1955) I. 169 But they answered us by flo[u]rishing their weapons over their heads and danceing, as we supposed the war dance. **1823** CRUISE *Journal* 26 Apr. (1957) 87 As soon as [the Maori party] reached the shore, they..ran up to the village, close to which they halted, and immediately commenced their war-dance. **1841** BIDWILL *Rambles in NZ* (1952) 111 I saw this evening a grand war-dance, and certainly think it would be sufficient to strike terror into the heart of any man. **1851** *Lyttelton Times* 17 May 6 The war dance was danced at an early hour. **1863** MANING *Old NZ* iii 52 At last the war-dance ended; and then my tribe..endeavoured to out-do even their amiable friends' exhibition. **1873** *Weekly News* (Auckland) 8 Mar. 14 A war dance, properly performed, is not a sight any father of a family would care about his daughter witnessing. **1878** BULLER *Forty Yrs. NZ* 91 The war-dance was performed by sixteen hundred. **c1920** [see HAKA 1 a]. **c1937** HYDE *Selected Poems* (1984) 37 The lost war-dance thudded through the North. **1946** SOLJAK *NZ* 28 The thunderous haka, or war dance, later adopted by New Zealand Rugby football teams, is performed solely by men.

warden.

1. *Goldfields.* **a.** Also **goldfields warden**. [AND 1855.] A government official with magisterial powers placed in charge of a goldfield (see esp. quot. 1892).
1858 *Gold Fields Act* in *Speeches & Documents* (1971) 42 XV. It shall be lawful for the Governor, by

Order in Council, from time to time to constitute for any Gold Field, or for any part thereof, Wardens' Courts for the administration of Justice therein, and to appoint Wardens as Judges of such Courts, with power to act alone or with Assessors or Juries, and in such manner, and to exercise all or any of the powers hereinafter mentioned as the Governor shall think fit to direct. **1863** PYKE *Report* in *Handbook NZ Mines* (1887) 8 In one day they obtained 2oz. of rough gold..and immediately reported the circumstance to the Warden at Dunstan. **1892** PYKE *Gold-Miners' Guide* 64 [s.270] The Governor may constitute and abolish Wardens' Courts and appoint Wardens. [s.278] Every Warden's Court has jurisdiction to hear and determine all complaints concerning—(1) Forfeitures for non-compliance with this or any previous Act and regulations; (2) The area of claims; (3) Encroachments or injuries to any claim; (4) Water-rights, and encroachments thereon or injuries thereto; (5) Roads, tramways, and fences held or occupied under the Act; (6) Partnerships relating to mining, and dissolutions thereof; (7) Breaches of mining laws, rules, and regulations; (8) And generally concerning debts, contracts, torts, and disputes of any kind relating to mining. **1914** PFAFF *Diggers' Story* 6 The Goldfields Warden..for the Canterbury Government was kept busily employed marking off sections [in Hokitika]. **1940** HOWARD *Rakiura* 234 The Gold Fields Warden hastened once more to the area, and the rumour stole abroad that the whole Island was to be declared a gold field. **1971** GRIFFITHS *King Wakatip* 116 Holidays could only be taken by decree of the goldfields warden.

b. Special Comb. **Warden's Court**, see quot. 1858 a above.

1858 [see 1 above]. **1866** MUELLER *My Dear Bannie* (1958) 185 I could not well refuse, understanding that some of the diggers were stopped from working until the case was settled at the Warden's Court. **1892** [see 1 above]. **1902** *Brett's Colonists' Guide* 1167 The Warden's Court has jurisdiction to determine all suits and complaints cognisable by Courts of civil or criminal jurisdiction. **1914** PFAFF *Diggers' Story* 121 Price was told off to open the Warden's Court. **1959** MILLAR *Westland's Golden 'Sixties* 146 Selfishness and carelessness were to lead to endless appeals to the Warden's Courts in years to come. **1984** BEARDSLEY *Blackball 08* 131 ''Ickey. Oi 'ave 'ere a bluey for you to appear in the Warden's Court at Greymouth on the fourteenth inst.' 'Much obliged, constable. Oi'll be there.'

2. See *Maori Warden* (MAORI B 5 a).

3. In early colonial times applied to various local officials.

1991 LA ROCHE *Hist. of Howick & Pakuranga* 213 The Hundred of Howick [in Auckland] also included..1055 acres of 'Waste Land'... Wardens were elected to control the grazing rights. These Wardens were the first recognisable local administrators. They used the revenue from 'depasturing' leases..to provide a common fund for the provision of roads, bridges, and other essential community needs.

Ward's weed. [Origin unknown.] A member of the fam. Brassicaceae, see quot. 1988.

1969 *Standard Common Names Weeds* 83 *Ward's weed Carrichtera annua* (L.) Asch. **1988** WEBB et al. *Flora of NZ* IV. 418 Carrichtera DC. [Fam. Brassicaceae] C[*arrichtera*] *annua*... Ward's Weed. Def. Taprooted annual herb... Christchurch, a casual occurrence in several city railway yards in 1959 but apparently not establishing. (*Mediterranean, S.W. Asia*, 1959.) The sp. was introduced as an impurity in Australian wheat.

ware, var. WHARE.

wareho, var. WAREHOU.

warehou. Also **wareho**, **wharehou**, **whario**. [Ma. /'warehou/: Williams 480 *Warehou*.]

1. Any of several snub-nosed midwater fishes of the family Centrolophidae, but esp. the common commercial food fish *Seriolella brama* (see esp. *blue warehou* 2 (1) below). See also BREAM 1 a and c, TREVALLY 1 b, a name given to esp. young warehou in southern markets (see quot. 1913 below).

1848 WAKEFIELD *Handbook NZ* 161 The *Wareho* is a fish somewhat resembling the *kawai*, but of much better flavour. This is an excellent fish when cured and smoked. **1855** TAYLOR *Te Ika A Maui* 624 Fam. *Gadioideae* contains the *Warehou* and the *Hapuku*, two of the best of the New Zealand fish. **1857** HURSTHOUSE *NZ* I. 122 The best [sea fish] are the Hapuka..the Moki, the Wharehou. **1872** HUTTON & HECTOR *Fishes NZ* 112 Warehou. The Sea Bream (*Neptonemus Brama*) is a fish deservedly prized by the natives. **1902** DRUMMOND & HUTTON *Nature in NZ* The warehou, tarakihi, and gurnet are common in the north. **1913** *TrNZI* XLV. 230 The warehou is commonly sold in Dunedin as 'trevally', but the latter name belongs to *Caranx platessa*. **1929** BEST *Fishing Methods* 41 A rod secured to the side of a canoe..[was] used in fishing for warehou. **1946** *JPS* LV. 160 *Warehou*, a sea-fish.., vulg. the 'h' is not sounded; a good market fish. **1952** LYON *Faring South* 131 In the vicinity of Wellington a fish large enough for a family meal, the whario, was, at certain seasons, very plentiful. **1967** NATUSCH *Animals NZ* 217 Sub-order Stromateoidae... includes..the warehou..of Wellington, the South Island and Bay of Plenty waters. **1979** *Commercial Fishing* Mar. 29 Wesermunde has been fishing in southern deep waters and has been catching quite a range of species including hoki, southern blue whiting, warehou and ling. **1986** PAUL *NZ Fishes* 136 The warehou family (Centrolophidae) contains about twenty species of oceanic midwater fishes.

2. With a modifier: **blue** (or **common**), **blue-nose**, **silver** (**bastard**, **spotted**), **white**.

(1) **blue** (or **common**) **warehou**. *Seriolella brama*, a food fish bluish green above, silvery to white below with a blackish blotch by the pectoral fin. See also TREVALLI 1 b.

1978 *Catch '78* Mar. 13 Common Warehou *Seriolella brama* Blue warehou... The shallowest occurring warehou, often taken in coastal set-nets. **1982** AYLING *Collins Guide* (1984) 300 The common warehou is superficially similar in shape to the trevally and grows to a similar size. **1986** PAUL *NZ Fishes* 136 Blue warehou *Seriolella brama*... Often just warehou or common warehou. Also occurs off southern Australia.

(2) **blue-nose warehou**, see BLUENOSE.

(3) **silver** (**bastard**, **spotted**) **warehou**. *Seriolella punctata* (or *porosa*), a pale-bluish to silver fish, slightly iridescent and metallic with a dark head and finely pitted skin. See also SILVERFISH.

1938 *TrRSNZ* LXVIII. 409 *Seriolella porosa* Guichenot. Silver warehou. **1956** GRAHAM *Treasury NZ Fishes* 221 *Seriolella porosa*. [Two] fisherman after examining the above specimen said they had seen this fish and knew it as Silver Warehou. **1970** SORENSEN *Nomenclature NZ Fish* 50 The Spotted Warehou, *Seriolella punctata*, taken in very small quantities, is usually counted in with the warehou catch. **1978** *Catch '78* Mar. 13 Silver Warehou *Seriolella punctata* = *S. porosa*. Spotted warehou. **1980** *Catch '80* Aug. 5 The control area for silver warehou is east of Stewart Island... The area is not a spawning area or nursery, but a feeding area for silver warehou. **1986** PAUL *NZ Fishes* 137 Silver warehou... Also called spotted warehou, and the smallest fish were once known as bastard warehou.

(4) **white warehou**. *Seriolella caerulea*, a deepwater fish, silvery grey to creamy white with a dark brownish head and no pectoral blotch.

1977 *Catch '77* Apr. 3 Silver and White warehou (*Seriolella punctata* and *S. tinro*). These were caught only in the Snares region. **1980** *Catch '80* Aug. 6 Until discovered on the Chatham Rise by The Russians in the early 1970's and described by them as *Seriolella tinro*, white warehou were not known from New Zealand waters. Since then they have been taken in thousands of tonnes. **1986** PAUL *NZ Fishes* 138 *White warehou Seriolella caerulea*. A deepwater warehou that also occurs off southern Australia and southern South America. **1990** *Dominion* (Wellington) 13 Feb. 8 Fisheries officers suspected that the four trawlers had caught the quota species of silver warehou and mislabelled it white warehou, a non-quota species.

wari, var. WHARE.

wariki, see WHARIKI.

war-mat. *Obs*. A protective cloak (or 'mat') worn in battle. See also *war-cloak* (WAR 1 b), TOPUNI.

1807 SAVAGE *Some Acc. of NZ* 53 The war-mat [so tightly woven, that when hanging loose a spear will not penetrate it] is generally ornamented with a border, which frequently displays a great degree of taste. **1817** NICHOLAS *NZ* I. 101 Having brought off with him from the North Cape a handsome war-mat. **1823** MARSDEN *Lett. & Jrnls.* (1932) 357 Shunghee said, 'I have seen King George, as you may see by my war mat, or coat of mail...' The men threw off their common mats, put on their war mats, and prepared for action. **1847** ANGAS *Savage Life* I. 237 Amongst them were several fine old chiefs, most elaborately tattoed, and adorned with the *topuni*, or war-mat; which is made of dog's hair, assorted, and interwoven with a garment of fine flax, so as to resemble a cloak of rich fur. **1922** COWAN *NZ Wars* (1955) II. 399 In olden days the Kapenga Plain was celebrated for its special quality of *harakeke* (flax), much used in making strong, tough..war-mats, which were worn as a kind of armour in hand-to-hand battles.

war-party. *Hist*. A body of Maori warriors dedicated to fighting or raiding away from the home territory. See also FIGHT *n*., TAUA.

1840 in Wilkes *US Exploring Exped.* (1852) I. 305 This ceremony was supposed to represent that used on the return of a war-party. **1856** SHORTLAND *Traditions & Superstitions* 7 The New Zealanders' favourite number for a war-party is always *hokowhitu*, or one hundred and forty. **1864** CAMPBELL *Martin Tobin* I. 64 She told him the war party had gone across the river, meaning the Pelorus. **1883** *TrNZI* XV. 440 The other division of the war-party had gone by the plains..without meeting anyone. **1936** LAMBERT *Pioneering Reminisc. Old Wairoa* 149 A strong taua (war-party) was being organized. **1940** MATTHEWS *Matthews of Kaitaia* 40 The war party set out for Tauranga and Maketu about the middle of the month.

warrant of fitness. A certificate of roadworthiness (strengthened in 1994 by the addition of a 'vehicle inspection certificate') valid for a fixed period and required to be displayed on most classes of light motor vehicle.

1936 *NZ Statutory Regs. 1936–37* (1938) 331 Save as provided in clause (3) hereof, the driver of every motor-vehicle used on a road after the 31st day of March, 1937, shall carry in the vehicle a warrant of fitness... The warrant of fitness shall be issued only by a city authority or a person or firm appointed or approved for the purpose by the Minister. **1948** *NZ Law Rep.* 1229 I am convinced that a warrant of fitness does not extend to the drag link or steering assembly of a car. **1953** *Road Code* 1 Jan. 39 There must be carried on a motor vehicle a Warrant of Fitness issued within the past six months. **1969** HASCOMBE *Down & Almost Under* 137 Eventually it had to happen—one of us bought a 'bomb'. It was a game little car; although its..blue paint invited confidence, as did its 'warrant of fitness', it seemed to possess everything but reliability. **1986** RICHARDS *Off the Sheep's Back* 80 Road code, drivers' licences and warrants of fitness were unheard of in those days.

warre(e), warri, war(r)y, varr. WHARE.

Wasa, Waser, varr. WAZZA.

wash, *v.*[1] *Farming. Obs.* [Used elsewhere but of significance in NZ farming history: AND 1847.]

1. a. *trans.* To wash (sheep) before shearing.

1850 TORLESSE *Papers* (1958) 177 Gebbie washing sheep—very ill. **1862** *Puketoi Station Diary* (Hocken TS) 27 Jan. McMaster washed sheep. **1862** CHUDLEIGH *Diary* 19 Nov. (1950) 67 Washing sheep in the afternoon. The washing is all over. They have washed some 14000 sheep and lambs this week.

b. *intr.* or *absol.* use.

1860 in Butler *First Year* (1863) 32 I was rather startled at hearing one gentleman ask another whether he meant to wash this year and receive the answer 'No'. I soon discovered that a person's sheep are himself. If his sheep are clean, he is clean. He does not wash his *sheep* before shearing, but *he* washes. **1861** *Puketoi Station Diary* (Hocken TS) 29 Nov. Found that they were not ready and they will wash now in some Lagoon on their own side. **1864** CHUDLEIGH *Diary* 20 Oct. (1950) 149 Mr Acland and I went to the wash pen in the morning. They have been washing since Monday and will be at it all next week.

2. a. washing *vbl. n.* [AND 1847.] The washing of sheep before shearing.

1857 *Richmond-Atkinson Papers* (1960) I. 319 Looking at the woolshed and contrivances for washing, during which Boyse and I nearly tilted ourselves off a marvellous platform contrived for w[h]isking the sheep into a tank of water five feet deep. **1938** BURDON *High Country* 83 Washing consisted of two separate operations, the first of which was called 'soaking'. The soak was a sort of bath..let into the ground beside a creek... It was filled and kept full by water flowing in through a two-inch pipe and a supply of boiling water was kept handy... Soap and sometimes ammonia were added to it. After the sheep were let out of the soak they were driven..[to] the creek..tipped in..and washed clean by men standing in the water.

b. In *attrib.* use in special Comb. **washing pen** [AND 1847], *wash-pen* (WASH *n.*[1] 2); **washing-place, washing pond,** *washpool* (WASH *n.*[1] 2).

1846 PHARAZYN *Journal* 11 Dec. (ATLMS) 67 George finished **washing pen** at river with Robin and Teddy and self to wool shed at Watarangi and finished the same. **1857** PAUL *Lett. from Canterbury* 90 A horse-paddock, ram-paddock,.. oats or wheat paddock, and a good, permanent **washing-place**. **1882** WILLIAMS *Diary* 9 July in Stevens *John Grigg* (1952) 64 We saw also the sheep dip, the **washing pond** &c., the manager's house &c.

wash, *v.*[2] *Goldmining.*

1. a. *trans.* WASH UP *v.* (a) To remove non-auriferous matter from (paydirt) by manipulating it with water in a dish or similar receptacle, or by passing it through a special contrivance.

1852 *NZGG* 9 Nov. V. 26:165 (Rep. Gold Discovery in Coromandel) A hole was dug..and a quantity of the soil washed, but without any visible satisfactory result... A panful was taken from about two feet below the surface and washed, it produced a number of scales of gold. **1863** LAUPER in Pascoe ed. *Over Whitcombe Pass* (1960) 42 I took the lid of the billy and washed about two handsful, and found some fine specks of gold. **1871** MONEY *Knocking About NZ* 79 I was one day washing a dish of stuff in the creek below the claim. **1935** BLYTH ed. *Gold Mining Year Book* 11 *Cradle*: The apparatus, made of wood used for washing gold-bearing wash or dirt.

(b) Similarly, to wash (gold) from paydirt. See also *wash off* (2 b below).

1852 *Coromandel Gold Field. Provisional Regs.* in Swainson *Auckland* (1853) 162 Persons desirous of..forming Reservoirs or Dams on the gold field, for the purpose of washing gold, must make application to the Commissioner. **1853** *NZGG* 12 Jan. VI. 1:2 (Heaphy's Rep.) On the resumed diggings, the parties..washed [$^1/_4$oz of dust].

b. *intr.*

1852 *NZGG* 10 Dec. V. 30:187 Wednesday, Nov. 3. How employed Down to bar at junction of path and stream..setting 'Tom', &c. Digging and washing. **1861** HAAST *Rep. Topogr. Explor. Nelson* 18 I gave orders again to wash for gold, and every dishful of dirt yielded some specks. **1863** *Diary Unsuccessful Digger* 22 May in *Star* (Christchurch) 27 Aug. (1931) in Heinz *Bright Fine Gold* (1974) 96 Sunk paddock..*Saturday 24th*. Washed hard from very early to very late and brought home the blacksand. **1873** ST. JOHN *Pakeha Rambles* in Taylor *Early Travellers* (1959) 555 In the days of bush fighting it used to be a common occurrence at the end of a day's march, when the *maemaes* had been knocked up by the side of a stream, to see..men..set to work with pannikin..and 'wash' for a prospect.

Hence **washing** *ppl. a.*

1862 *Otago Goldfields & Resources* 19 The gullies, from being shallow, are easily worked, requiring only the cradle for washing operations.

2. As **to wash (down)**, to erode by sluicing.

1862 *Otago Goldfields & Resources* 20 Washing down these hills.

b. As **wash off** [AND 1862], to wash (dirt, etc.) for gold (in a pan, cradle, sluice-box, etc.).

1873 PYKE *Wild Will Enderby* (1889, 1974) I. xi 40 When the Senior Partner first sighted them, one..was washing off a pan of earth; whilst the others..eagerly awaited the result.

wash, *n.*[1] *Farming. Hist.*

1. A washpool and its ancillary plant (see quot. 1873).

1873 WILSON *Diary* 3 Feb. in Wierzbicka *Wilson Family* (1973) 166 We came to McLeans [*sic*] wash and I went down to see how it was worked... They have only to divert a small stream and bring it down to the wash in a small race... First, to take the rough off the sheep, they were swum through a creek in a basin built up each side and deep, at the end they were thrown in at... A yard carried them on to the hot water soak..and from there they are pushed down to the spouts, six in number. **1951** ACLAND *Early Canterbury Runs* 391 *Wash.*- Place and plant for washing sheep. Until the 1870s washing sheep before shearing was a fairly common practice... The remains of these *sheep washes* were not uncommon twenty years ago. **1978** PRESTON *Woolgatherers* 43 There was a 'wash' [for washing wool] and a drying paddock at both Longlands and Haldon; the pool was fed by a race which had to be cleaned out before each shearing and kept in repair.

2. Special Comb. **wash-pen** [AND 1847], an enclosure holding sheep about to be washed, or after washing; **washpool** [also in Brit. use: AND 1830], a pool, often in a creek, in which sheep are washed before shearing, or, occas., where wool is scoured.

1855 PHILLIPS *Rockwood Jrnl.* (Canterbury Pub. Lib. TS) 20 John went with him to wash-pen in afternoon... H.P. Seal Richards..went eeling down to **Wash-pen** Creek. *Ibid.* 28 Dec. 26 John Richards & Seal mending Washpen. **1864** CHUDLEIGH *Diary* 20 Oct. (1950) 149 Mr Acland and I went to the wash pen in the morning... On Tuesday a large bird flew over the pen. **1859** *Puketoi Station Diary* (Hocken TS) 15 Nov. Packed bale of greasy wool..put up **washpool** in Wedderburn. **1861** BUTLER in Jones *Samuel Butler* (1919) I. 93 Yet without good wash pools and a good woolshed the wool can never be well got up. **1878** ELWELL *Boy Colonists* 32 His work at [the station] was to be..the formation of a wash-pool..for the sheep. **1978** PRESTON *Woolgatherers* 43 Much of the wool was scoured on the farm [in the early days], especially the merino... But scoured wool took a good deal of time— the bales were carted to the washpool, the wool washed, dried and turned in the open.

wash, *n.*[2] *Goldmining.* [Used elsewhere but recorded earliest in NZ: see Mathews *wash n.* 2; OED 13 b.]

1. The finer alluvial material (sand, gravel, etc.) from which gold may be recovered.

1864 BARRINGTON *Diary* 29 Mar. in Taylor *Early Travellers* (1959) 404 The creeks look very well for gold; splendid quartz boulders, and a fine wash. **1875** HECTOR *Handbook NZ* 171 Gold was obtained on terraces..and in the river bed, the wash everywhere resting on water-worn bars and ledges of greenstone. **1887** *Handbook NZ Mines* 130 The party bottomed on a bluish-grey wash. *Ibid.* 358 Sand, gravel and stones..together are called in mining parlance 'wash'. **1896** *AJHR* D-4 210 Then you have what we call the 'river-wash'. **1897** McKAY *Older Auriferous Drifts of Central Otago* 28 At higher levels, under and surrounding the upper township, there is what is called the 'mountain-wash', a thick deposit of coarse gravels evidently derived from the eastern slopes of..the Carrick Range. **1914** PFAFF *Diggers' Story* 79 This lead was about 600 yards long, and the wash varied from 1 foot to 4 feet. **1937** *NZ Railways Mag.* Nov. 37 Gold deposited usually sinks to a 'wash,' that is some conglomerate that will hold it. **1943** HISLOP *Pure Gold* 69 All we got for our trouble..were a few colours and black sand, which is always an indication that you are in gold-bearing wash. **1967** [see *washdirt* 2 below].

2. Special Comb. **washdirt** (occas. **washing-dirt**) [see Mathews *wash n.* 2, 1852], the alluvial deposit from which gold can be extracted by washing (see also DIRT, WASH *v.*[2] 1); **wash-dish**, a gold pan (PAN *n.*[1]), see also *tin dish* (TIN *n.*[1] 1); **wash gold**, alluvial gold found in wash.

1861 *NZ Goldfields 1861* (1976) 30 In some places the **wash-dirt** contains little or nothing. **1866** SMALL *NZ & Austral. Songster* (1970) 21 A thumping pile of **washing dirt** he happen'd just to see; He let a mighty howl then, And says he, 'Upon my soul, then, I'm thinking that's the pile of stuff yez stole away from me.' **1867** HOCHSTETTER *NZ* 101 The gold is obtained partly as alluvial gold from deposits of gold drift ('wash-dirt') of the miner. **1873** PYKE *Wild Will Enderby* (1889, 1974) I. xi 39 To render themselves more secure from [flooding], they removed the 'washdirt' to a spot above flood-mark, where they could afterwards sift the golden grains from the soil at leisure. **1892** PYKE *Gold-Miners' Guide* 8 Holders of *prospecting areas* must report the discovery of *payable wash-dirt* to the Warden within three days from the date of such discovery. **1906** *NZGeol.SB (NS)* No.1 2 It was not until the end of 1864, however, that the discovery of rich 'wash-dirt' in the Greenstone district..called public attention to the golden possibilities of Westland. **1940** HOWARD *Rakiura* 233 Other seekers..moved down..to Codfish Bay, where payable gold was found in company with black sand occurring in wash-dirt three feet deep. **1953** [see PADDOCK *v.*² 2]. **1967** MAY *West Coast Gold Rushes* 528 Wash-dirt: the auriferous gravel, sand, clay or cement in which the greater proportion of gold is found. Synonyms were 'wash', 'pay-dirt', or just 'dirt'. **1898** BROWN *Lay of Bantry Bay* (1917) 12 His **wash-dish** serves as a pillow. **1915** *Canterbury Times* 3 Mar. (VUW Fildes Clippings 421/58) A tin wash-dish for testing the creek gravels, and his old black billy, made [the prospector's] 'pikau'. **1926** COWAN *Travel in NZ* II. ix The men of wash-dish and pick and sluice-box had their rugged prototypes in the pioneers of 'Forty-nine'. **1931** COAD *Such Is Life* 53 In no time he had his wash dish ready and was sluicing for gold. **1879** HAAST *Geol. Canterbury & Westland* 85 The **wash gold** is fine, scaly, and very much rolled, so that there is no doubt it has come some distance in the great river-bed.

washing-stuff. *Goldmining. Obs.* [AND 1852.] *washdirt* (WASH *n.*² 2).

1861 *NZ Goldfields 1861* 23 Sept. (1976) 16 This morning a man..showed me a prospect which he had obtained from several dishes of washing-stuff. **1863** LAUPER in Pascoe ed. *Over Whitcombe Pass* (1960) 42 Looking towards the bank of the stream I observed some splendid looking washing stuff—fine gravel mixed with quartz and ironstone. **1866** [see WASH UP *v.*].

washing-up bill. *Parliament.* A Bill presented to the House of Representatives near the end of a session containing those odds and ends of legislation which need to be passed but often cannot be fitted formally into other Bills (e.g. the alienation of particular pieces of Crown land or State Forest).

1917 *Press* (Christchurch) 25 Oct. 7 There are no fewer than 126 clauses in the Reserves and Other Lands Empowering Bill, commonly known as the 'Washing Up Bill'. **1919** *Otago Daily Times* (Dunedin) 1 Nov. 8 By the Native 'Washing Up' Bill..the provision..for granting areas of Crown lands to landless South Island natives..is revived. **1928** *Evening Post* (Wellington) 6 Oct. 10 The Native 'Washing-up' Bill introduced into the House of Representatives contains several matters of general interest affecting the Native race. **1935** *Star Sun* (Christchurch) 26 Oct. 12 Then we see the abuse of the Washing-Up Bill for the incorporation without adequate consideration of many contentious matters which normally require separate Bills. **1986** in *Na To Hoa Aroha* I. 27 But Ngata replied, as he did to numerous such invitations... He had to prepare legislation for the forthcoming session. 'You wouldn't have the heart to entice me away from a prospect so alluring! Compare washing up bills with banana groves, Maori Councils with your lotus-eaters!'

wash up, *v. Goldmining.* [AND 1859.] *trans.*, also *absol.* To recover (gold), often from accumulated washdirt, by washing in a pan, sluice-box, cradle, etc.; *intr.* of claims, to produce gold by washing.

1866 SMALL *NZ & Austral. Songster* (1970) 21 Paddy..went out to wash up his little heap; But on coming to his claim—By my conscience, what a shame!—Some thieves had stolen his washing stuff while he was fast asleep. **1866** HARPER *Lett. from Canterbury* Oct. (1914) 104 They turned the hose off... 'We don't wash up till Saturday, but if you look here you can see some gold in the boxes.' **1874** BATHGATE *Col. Experiences* 142 After some months' work, we would wash up, and my mate would go off to sell the gold. **1911** BREMNER in *Mt. Ida Goldfields* (1988) 26 He and his mates left suddenly after washing up. **1943** HISLOP *Pure Gold* 69 An old Victorian miner washed up 200 ozs. in one day. **1952** HEINZ *Prospecting for Gold* 32 The length of the sluicing run depended on the richness of the ground, some claims washing up monthly others after several months.

Hence **washing-up** *vbl. n.*, the process or act of extracting gold by washing auriferous material; also *fig.*, death, or the Day of Judgement (see quot. 1896).

1870 *AJHR D-40* 4 But now the best of the ground having been worked..the old rough ways of washing-up must be abandoned. **1887** [see DIRT]. **1892** PYKE *Gold-Miners' Guide* 10 [s.39] A tributer may deduct such amount from the earnings of the mine after each washing-up or retorting. **1896** O'REGAN *Poems* 33 Life's claim is almost duffered, the washing-up is near, Swag, billy, and tin-dish I'll need no more In the new field that I'm off to. **1925** BATHGATE *Random Recolls.* 27 We [bank officers] had to go to Hyde and Sowburn when we heard there was to be a washing up in any of the claims. **1952** HEINZ *Prospecting for Gold* 32 Washing up on these large claims was complicated and interesting to watch, particularly the final phases when one might see a billy of gold recovered. **1967** MAY *West Coast Gold Rushes* 528 Washing-up. The whole operation of saving gold from the wash-dirt. 'Cleaning up' had the same meaning.

wash-up, *n. washing-up* (WASH UP *v.*); also the gold recovered from a washing-up.

1863 in Heinz *Bright Fine Gold* (1974) 95 Finished wash-up of first paddock. **1903** *NZ Illustr. Mag.* VIII. 333 I stole his wash-up. **1903** *TrNZI* XXXV. 403 This explanation seemed to me insufficient to account for the large quantities of lead obtained at the periodical 'wash-up'. **1934** *Press* (Christchurch) 23 Jan. 11 The Okarito wash-up for the week ended Jan. 20 was 48ozs 15dwt for 117 hours' dredging. **1946** MILLER *There Was Gold* 76 At this rate of working, thought I, I would have a wash-up in a very short time, and I began to speculate on the amount of gold the ever-widening paddock contained. **1953** SUTHERLAND *Golden Bush* (1963) 99 At the end of a predetermined period comes the 'wash-up' when the floor of the newly worked area is washed clear of all debris and possibly dried off and scraped, such scrapings being fed into the sluice-box. **1964** ANDERSON *Doctor in Mountains* (1974) 125 This is called the 'wash-up' and is a great and exciting occasion on a gold claim, but always conducted in secrecy.

Wassa, Wasser, varr. WAZZA.

waste land. *Hist.* [Spec. use of *waste* uninhabited or uncultivated: AND 1804.] Usu. *pl.* Unoccupied and unimproved Crown land(s) (or Maori land claimed by the Crown), often leased out, sold, or otherwise disposed of by central or provincial government authorities.

1839 *Instructions from Sec. of State to Hobson* 14 Aug. 209 in *Speeches & Documents* (1971) 13 It will be your duty to obtain, by fair and equal contracts with the Natives, the Cession to the Crown of such Waste Lands as may be progressively required for the occupation of Settlers resorting to New Zealand. **1840** DEANS in *Pioneers* (1964) 8 There are plenty of waste lands for this purpose where you may squat without purchasing from anyone. **1843** WOOD *Twelve Months in Wellington* 50 The '*sufficient*' price of the Wakefield system is a fallacy... Waste land is often dear at a gift. **1858** *The Waste Lands Act 21 & 22 Vict.* s16 The Acts passed by the General Assembly of New Zealand intituled respectively 'The Waste Lands Act, 1854' and 'The Provincial Waste Lands Act, 1854' are hereby repealed. **1860** in Butler *First Year* (1863) iv 42 Most of the waste lands in the province are now paying three farthings per acre. **1875** *Official Handbook NZ* 103 Public—or as they are called 'waste'—lands are sold on several principles. **1883** *Brett's Colonists' Guide* 761 The Waste Lands of the Colony are administered in each Provincial District by a Board of Commissioners appointed by the Governor. **1949** REED *Story Canterbury* 106 These 'first purchasers' were to be accorded a special privilege;.. unsold rural areas, termed 'waste lands', might be leased for pasturage. **1976** VEITCH *Clyde on Dunstan* 43 'Waste lands' or runs, which lay outside the 'Hundreds', were leased by the Government to pastoralists. **1991** LA ROCHE *Hist. of Howick & Pakuranga* 213 The Hundred of Howick [in Auckland] also included..1055 acres of 'Waste Land'. This misleading description applied to land purchased from Maori tribes, that was surveyed, and offered at auction, but not taken up by prospective settlers.

Hence **Waste Lands Board**, a local board appointed to administer the lease or sale of waste lands.

1869 *Letter* 20 May in Evans *Waikaka Saga* (1962) 16 As these runs are likely to be wanted for settlement, I should not recommend their being thrown into a gold field till after they have been thrown into Hundreds when the Waste Lands Board could refuse to sell any portion..considered highly auriferous.

wata: see WHATA.

water.

1. In the phr. **across the water**, across the Tasman Sea, (in) Australia. Cf. *other side* (SIDE 1 b).

1933 *Press* (Christchurch) (Acland Gloss.) 23 Dec. 15 These brass boxes to hold tinder [on early sheep stations] were said to have been made originally for keeping the licenses of ticket-of-leave men across the water.

2. Used *attrib.* **a.** In the names of plants and animals, see: FERN 2 (23), LILY 2 (18); see also WATER-HEN. As **water-milfoil** [spec. use of *milfoil* a water plant], a native milfoil *Myriophyllum* spp. (fam. Haloragaceae), an aquatic plant with finely divided or linear leaves, often in whorls.

1869 *TrNZI* I. (rev. edn.) 202 Water Milfoil. *Myriophyllum elatinoides.* **1899** KIRK *Students' Flora of NZ* 151 *M[yriophyllum] elatinoides*... Stems 6 in.–30 in. long. Leaves 4 in a whorl, rarely more. [1899 *Note*] Water-milfoil. **1907** *AJHR* C-8 20 *Myriophyllum elatinoides.* Common water-milfoil. Pond. **1926** HILGENDORF *Weeds NZ* 129 Water Milfoil... These plants are also called mare's tail. They have very finely divided leaves, giving the name milfoil [orig. =thousand-leaf], and live submerged in ponds and slow-running streams. **1982** WILSON *Stewart Is. Plants* 306 *Myriophyllum triphyllum.* Water Milfoil. Soft feathery herb rooted in mud and forming dark green underwater masses, or emergent on water's edge.

b. Special Comb. **water burner**, see quot.; **water joey** [AND 1916] (occas. init. cap.), the workman responsible for the water-supply of a traction engine running a threshing mill; also as **wood and water joey**, the general hand, often the youngest in a gang of workmen, assigned to 'boiling up' for his gang's smokos, meal breaks, etc. (see quot. 1995); **water pot** *shearing*, see quots. 1934, 1989; **water-tight** *n. obs.* [used elsewhere but recorded earliest in NZ: see OED], a watertight boot.

1989 *NZ Eng. Newsletter* III. 29 **water burner**: Shearer's cook. **1939-45** *Expressions & Sayings 2NZEF (TS N.A. WAII DA 420/1)* **Water Joey** .. Water cart man. **1944** *Korero* (AEWS Background Bulletin) 10 Apr. 9 A steam-mill needs a 'water-joey'. **1976** ANDERSON *Water Joey* 1 Occasionally the older joey was a man who had been..an embarrassment to his family. *Ibid.* 2 The water-joey's first job in the morning was to catch the draught-horse, yoke it to a dray which carried a 200-gallon square water-truck, then..fill the tank by hand-pump. **1978** SINCLAIR & HARREX *Looking Back* 86 The 'water-joey' who drove it [*sc.* the threshing mill]..had to maintain the water supply for the traction engine, and for cooking and washing. **1980** NEAVE *Land of Munros* 90 Later, traction engines [for threshing]..had their own galley and cook, and it was a great sight to see engine, mill, water-cart and dog box—a two wheeled hut. The boss and Water Joey slept near the machinery to be handy to get up steam in the morning, and then get the cookshop going. **1984** *Knapdale Run* 147 In many areas, the most difficult job was to organise a water supply for the [traction] engines... As these often had very difficult access the life of a 'water joey' was no bed of roses. **1990** MARTIN *Forgotten Worker* 133 The water-joey's..position was usually filled by a lad or older man no longer fit enough to work on the mill itself. The water-joey had to fill the water-cart with hundreds of gallons of water fetched from the nearest stream, well or other source of water. **1995** WINTER *All Ways Up Hill* 121 Sharp, skinny and vigorous, he was noticeable among a gang of heavy Scandinavian navvies, where he was employed as a 'wood and water Joey'. **1934** *Press* (Christchurch) (Acland Gloss.) 27 Jan. 15 The **water pot** is a tin of water (usually disinfected) which a shearer has tied by him to wet his shears in. **1949** NEWTON *High Country Days* 50 As each man finished his sheep he gave his blades a brief touch with the oilstone and placed them in the 'water-pot' nailed to the wall beside his porthole. As he caught his next sheep, the water would free the grease which would otherwise clog the blades. **1952** MEEK *Station Days* 111 Water Cup or Pot: A receptacle holding water, in which the shearers dip their shears in to free them from stickiness. Usually a tin of some sort. **1989** *NZ Eng. Newsletter* III. 29 *water pot*: Old paint tin, plastic bucket or similar item with water in it for a shearer to leave his/her shears in while catching a sheep. Contains disinfectant to stop the transfer of disease from one sheep to another. Also contains wool to stop shedhands from drinking out of it. **1867** THOMSON *Rambles with Philosopher* 14 A shoemaker [singing]..beat time with his mallet on the hob-nails of an old **water-tight** he was mending.

water-hen. *Obs.* [Spec. use of Brit. *water-hen* for ralline birds or for genus *Porphyrio*.] Either of two rails. **a.** WEKA (prob. from being found by early explorers near beaches).

1773 COOK *Journals* 16 Apr. (1961) II. 121 I found a vast number of Water or Wood Hens a score of them I shott. **1817** NICHOLAS *Voyage NZ* II. 256 Towards the southward there are also water hens of a large species, rails in vast numbers. **1838** POLACK *NZ* I. 307 The small *noddies*..abound in large flocks, as also the *oyster-catchers* and *water-hens*, whose excessive tameness has nearly annihilated them.

b. PUKEKO.

1843 DIEFFENBACH *Travels in NZ* I. 276 Flights of the common brown duck..and of the blue-breasted red-billed water-hen..people these swamps. **1871** WILLIAMS *Dict. NZ Lang.* (3edn.) 106 *Paakura..water-hen*; *porphyrio melanotus*. **1936** GUTHRIE-SMITH *NZ Naturalist* 229 The Pukeko's—the New Zealand big blue Water Hen's—stretch of claw.

Waterlooing, *vbl. n. Obs.* [Origin unknown.] See quot.

1946 MILLER *There Was Gold* 129 Another time-honoured practice [in Central Otago] is 'Waterlooing'. That is done by getting up a little earlier in the morning, figuratively and literally, than the legitimate rabbiter and going over the poison lines where the carcases lie, not yet cold, and skinning them.

water-race. [Spec. use of *race* artificial channel for water: OED 1869.]

1. Goldmining. a. An artificial channel to carry water to a mine or claim.

1869 *Letter* in Evans *Waikaka Saga* (1962) 16 I have the honour to enclose herewith application..for water races from Waikaka..and Shepherds Hut Creek. **1888** D'AVIGDOR *Antipodean Notes* 124 A vast clearing..is filled with a perfect network of 'water-races', as these wooden channels are termed. **1909** THOMPSON *Ballads About Business* 67 [A miner] Digs a ditch with sloping base, Which he terms a water race. **1947–48** BEATTIE *Pioneer Recolls.* (1956) 2 Many creeks were dammed and water-races were everywhere. If a miner asked for so many heads, the water was measured out to him by a gauge.

b. Special Comb. **water-race company**, a company selling raced water to miners.

c**1870s** in *Otago Daily Times* (Dunedin) 25 July (1932) in Cowan *Down the Years in the Maniototo* (1948) 43 Water-race companies often made their fortunes more easily than the miners. **1911** BREMNER in *Mt. Ida Goldfields* (1988) 16 The Extended Water race Co. had secured the right to all waste water running in Main Gully. **1914** PFAFF *Diggers' Story* 142 I came down in 1872 to the Auckland Beach, where I bought..a water-race company and opened up a claim. **1967** MAY *West Coast Gold Rushes* 242 In a separate category were the water-race companies, specializing in the sale of water to mining parties and common to all fields. Although only two or three registered, the amount of capital invested in this branch of the industry was probably considerable.

2. A water-table; a stormwater ditch or drain (esp. at the sides of a road).

1879 BARRY *Up & Down* 284 They were very 'cheeky' and I knocked one of them into a water-race. **1925** WEBB *Miss Peters' Special* 47 The dog paddled slowly up and down in the water-race on the opposite side of the road. **1948** SUMPTER *In Search of Central Otago* 7 Cleaning out a water-race with a flame-thrower. **1974** SIMPSON *Sugarbag Years* 90 My first job on relief was cleaning out the water races in Paparua County.

waterside.

1. As **the waterside**, the wharves, the waterfront.

1914 PFAFF *Diggers' Story* 118 A well-known figure along Wellington's waterside a few years ago was Bob, the Shipwright. **1964** DAVIS *Watersiders* 108 I came down to the waterside. The old union. Never been off it since, except for the six months during the 'fifty-one bust up.

Hence **watersider** [AND 1937], one employed to load and unload a ship's cargo; a docker (see also WHARFIE).

1914 *Evening Post* (Wellington) 4 Feb. 10 [Letter from] 'Watersider' [about] 'work on the wharves'. **1921** *Auckland Univ. College Carnival Souvenir* 19 [Cast of Carnival play includes] Watersiders, Factory Girls, cabinet Ministers..and Femmes savantes from Symonds Street. **1938** *Auckland Weekly News* 9 Feb. 11 The watersiders refused to handle passengers' luggage on the Awatea because it was raining. **1949** SARGESON *I Saw in My Dream* (1974) 187 Now, about those water-siders. **1959** SHADBOLT *New Zealanders* (1986) 29 I would stay with my uncle, the watersider. **1984** *Listener* 10–16 Mar. 22 There, tattooed watersiders drink away the profits of a crown and anchor session down at the wharves.

2. Special Comb. **waterside worker** [AND 1903], a watersider.

1910 *Awards, etc.* 496 [Auckland Waterside Workers Award] The defendant was charged with a breach of the Auckland Waterside Workers' award. **1944** *Short Guide NZ* 39 Waterside worker—longshoreman. **1952** *Evening Post* (Wellington) 4 Sept. 8 The use of waterside workers as tally clerks should be discontinued. **1967** MILLER *Ink on My Fingers* 86 The shipping reporter put in a claim for expenses following an interview with a waterside worker. **1987** *Dominion* (Wellington) 16 July 2 Reform of the ports industry, including waterside worker numbers, was Labour's first transport priority for the next three years.

watta, wattie, varr. WHATA.

wattle-and-dab. *Hist.* Also **wattle-and-daub.** [Used elsewhere but of significance in early European settlement: see OED *wattle*[1] 1 b with mainly rural and provincial quots., 1808–1913.] A common building material in early colonial New Zealand consisting of slender branches, vines, etc., interwoven among uprights, and holding a mud plaster. Often *attrib.* esp. as **wattle-and-dab house (hut)**. **a.** As **wattle-and-dab**.

1827 WILLIAMS *Early Jrnls.* 17 Dec. (1961) 91 The circumstance of the burning of Capn. Duke's house has made us somewhat thoughtful relative to *raupo* buildings... This question will require some consideration but wattle and dab is exceedingly expeditious and very durable. **1840** BEST *Journal* 5 June (1966) 226 Govt. House is a Mauri built dwelling of Wattle and dab and Wattle and dab is this. A number of stakes are driven into the ground and a species of [v]ine worked in between them so as to form a wall of basketwork exactly like a Gabion. This big basket is then pelted with soft clay untill [*sic*] all the interstices are completely filled up both inside and out and then the ragged bits are carefully smo[o]thed off when dry it makes a tolerably good wall. **1857** PAUL *Lett. from Canterbury* 27 As soon as maybe after his arrival, [the new settler] engages himself as a shepherd..at a station..makes a hut of sod or wattle and dab. **1876** *TrNZI* VIII. 166 We may divide colonial architecture into periods or ages. First, the wattle-and-dab period, with its contemporaneous, but more advanced, varieties of fern tree and totara bark. **1898** HOCKEN *Contributions* 101 By degrees little houses sprang up in every direction, the usual order of architecture being that of 'wattle and dab'; saplings were fixed side by side, and the interstices filled with clay. **1937** AYSON *Pioneering Otago* 26 After breakfast..we continued..through Lovell's Flat, named after John Lovell who built a wattle-and-dab hut there for his shepherd. **1952** LYON *Faring South* 140 Even back in these gale-rifted solitudes [of Cape Terawhiti], one came on the remains of 'wattle and dab' homesteads which marked the abortive attempt of some early settler.

b. As **wattle-and-daub**.

1867 THOMSON *Rambles with Philosopher* 30 The accommodation-house..consisted of a small wattle-and-daub hut containing two apartments. **1939** BEATTIE *First White Boy Born Otago* 41 These huts were of the old-time 'wattle-and-daub' construction—that is, posts were driven into the ground and 'wattles' (round sticks) were nailed across them 4 or 5 inches apart, and then clay was 'daubed' in between and around them and smoothed over. **1957** PARK *One-a-pecker* 124 A wattle-and-daub house is tight and snug. **1986** SALMOND

Gloss. Bldg. Terminol. 233 Wattle and daub. Walls made of wickerwork or woven *wattles* (thin branches) and plastered by hand with mud or clay thrown on both sides.

wattle bird. Any of three species of native birds of the family Callaeidae with fleshy pendulous growths on either side of the base of the bill, HUIA, KOKAKO (most freq.), or SADDLEBACK.
   1773 WALES *Journal* 10 May in Cook *Journals* (1961) II. 786 First the Wattle-Bird, so called because of its having two Wattles under its beak as large as those of a small dunghill Cock, is considerably larger..than an English Blackbird. Its Bill is short & thick..the colour of its Wattles is a dull yellow; almost an Orange-colour. 1773 FORSTER *Resolution Jrnl.* 11 Apr. (1982) II. 253 The great noise caused by the Cascade is now & then conquered by the shriller note of a small bird, & by the graver pipe of wattle birds. 1777 ANDERSON *Journal* Feb. in Cook *Journals* (1967) III. 806 Another sort..is black with a brown back & wings and two small gills under the root of the Bill which we call'd the small wattle Bird..to distinguish it from another which we call'd the large one [*sc.* kokako]. 1839 DIEFFENBACH *Report to the NZ Company* in *Documents Appended to the Twelfth Report of the Directors of the NZ Company* (1844) 81F The bird called Kokako, and Wattle Bird by the Europeans, from its two gold-coloured and indigo maxillary flaps, I found only at Ship Cove. 1869 *TrNZI* II. 45 The Crow or Wattle Bird. 1871 BRACKEN *Behind the Tomb* 79 The wattle-bird sings in the leafy plantation. 1885 *NZJSc.* II. 376 *Glaucopis cinerea*... Wattlebird or Crow, Kokako.—I first became acquainted with this bird on the flats of the Wilberforce river.

wauka, var. WAKA.

wauwaupaku, wawapaka, wawapaku, varr. WHAUWHAUPAKU.

waxeye. [Poss. f. the white eye-ring's suggesting the colour of wax as in the circular base of a beeswax candle.] SILVEREYE.
   1871 HUTTON *Catalogue Birds NZ* 6 Zosterops lateralis... White-eye. Wax-eye. Blight-bird. Tauhou. 1888 [see RINGEYE]. 1898 MORRIS *Austral-English* 506 *Wax-eye*... One of the many names for the bird called Silver-Eye, White-Eye, Blight-Bird, etc. 1900 *Canterbury Old & New* 195 The honey-eaters are represented by the musical tui..the bell-bird, and the wax-eye. 1914 in *Hist. N. Otago from 1853* (1978) 43 Of all these creatures..the grey duck and waxeye seem to be the only survivors, and that in greatly reduced numbers. 1927 GUTHRIE-SMITH *Birds* 152 These little Waxeyes, when paired, show great affection for each other, stroking and preening one another's feathers, and cuddling together on the bough. 1946 [see BLIGHT-BIRD]. 1957 FRAME *Owls Do Cry* (1967) 32 If it is near winter the wax-eyes hungry for honey, will make their green and yellow cloud to follow her. 1984 BRASCH *Collected Poems* 53 And rifled quickly by fantail, wax-eye, tui, In the shade of indifferent leaves.

wayback, *adv., a.,* and *n.* Also **away back,** **'wayback.** [U.S. *way back*: see OED.]
A. *adv.* [AND 1899.] In the (remote) hinterland or backblocks. See also BACK C.
   1904 LANCASTER *Sons o' Men* 30 He had saved his craven life at the undercut bluff when it parted the mob wayback in the dry creek. 1905 THOMSON *Bush Boys* 183 Bristled faces, unshaven for weeks, and hair unkempt told they had come from a spell away back. 1916 THORNTON *Wowser* 85 The condition of those living 'wayback'. 1932 BLAIR *By Pacific Waters* 12 I'm sure they're getting a storm wayback. 1937 AYSON *Pioneering Otago* 94 One day I got notice to..put my flock of 3,000 sheep away back on the hill country of 'Lochindorb'.
B. *adj.* [AND 1899.] BACKBLOCK B.
   1905 *Red Funnel* II. 491 The 'way-back' settler. 1906 *Truth* 6 Jan. 8 At the wayback township of Mataroa. 1913 BEATTIE *Trade Hunting* [16] My great friend..was 'a white man'. His way back hotel was a home. 1920 *Quick March* 10 Mar. 39 There is a piquancy in the 'wayback race-meeting that one..misses in the..gatherings at Trentham. 1934 HYDE *Journalese* 26 I liked the 'wayback articles signed 'C.J.M.' every bit as much as the most highly-paid overseas 'whimsicalities'. 1943 HISLOP *Pure Gold* 35 To use the expression of a wayback shed hand, it is real dinkum. 1952 NEWTON *High Country Journey* 50 Lilybank is one of the real way-back stations... Fifty odd miles from Fairlie and often cut off by flooding rivers, it is one of Canterbury's most isolated stations. 1973 WALLACE *Generation Gap* 155 I and two other interpreters had been engaged by the [Provincial] Council to accompany some of them into a wayback pa.
C. *n.* [AND 1899.]
1. Usu. as **the wayback** (occas. **waybacks**), BACKBLOCK A 2 a.
   1906 *Truth* 15 Sept. 3 When woolly whiskers of the Wayback goes into the township and is fined a quid for being drunk his boss never thinks of parting up for him. 1910 *Triad* 10 Aug. 47 [Heading] 'Wayback likes it'. 1921 FOSTON *At the Front* 70 Loans for opening up the away-back. 1926 COOK *Far Flung* 39 Some fifty miles in the 'wayback'. 1926 *NZ Dairy Produce Exporter* 31 Oct. 41 I can't claim to be a female pioneer from the waybacks, or a fern fighter from Te Kuiti.
2. A person (or occas. animal) from the wayback; a BACKBLOCKER.
   1927 *NZ Dairy Produce Exporter* 29 Oct. 40 She noticed a real 'old wayback' [*sc.* man] eyeing her very interestingly.
   Hence **waybacker** *n.*, a person from the wayback.
   1926 *NZ Dairy Produce Exporter* 31 June 34 [Nom-de-plume] Mrs. Waybacker... Polly Waybacker.

wayleggo! *Mustering.* Also **awaileggo, Wareleggo, 'Way're le' go, Where-a-go.** [Origin uncertain: supposedly from the cry *away here, let go,* or a similar cry, variously re-formed as a musterer's cry.] A musterer's cry to recall a dog.
   1945 *NZ Geogr.* 38 It is music in the chill mountain dawn to hear the musterer start his dogs on their long, hard day's work with a lusty cry that sounds 'Awailago', with all the cadence on the second 'a'. One man told me this was Gaelic, but when I asked a Scot he said it was more likely to be a corruption of an original exhortation such as 'Away and let her go.' 1947 NEWTON *Wayleggo* 11 'Wayleggo'! A strange word, its origin is somewhat obscure. It is a command a shepherd gives to call his dog off sheep, and is presumably an abbreviation of 'come away and let them go'. 1950 in Woodhouse *Farm & Station Verse* (1950) 195 I love the clean brown tussock And the hills where the cool winds blow. It is my prayer I may still be there When the Lord calls 'Way're le' go. [1950 *Note*] The shepherds' command to a dog who has completed the job: 'Away here. Let go.' Wareleggo is the musterers' call to a dog to come back and I believe it's supposed to be a sort of portmanteaux [*sic*] word made up of 'Way-here-let-go,' meaning let go the sheep and come away here. 1951 McLEOD *NZ High Country* 20 Every now and then [he] will shout 'get in behind, Dark', 'come out o' that, Ben' or 'Wareleggo Maid'. 1964 DICK *High Country Family* 64 Life had been tame for the dogs for many miles, so, heedless of their master's cries to 'Wayleggo there, Tip', 'Get in behind, Jock'..they rushed madly hither and thither. 1981 CHARLES *Black Billy Tea* 35 There's my mate just down below, I can hear his 'Where-a-go!' I can hear his kelpie bark... [1981 *Note*] Musterer's command to his dog—'Away here, let go!'

Wazir, var. WAZZA.

Wazza /ˈwɒzə/, /ˈwazə/, /-s-/. *WW1.* Also **Was(s)a, Was(s)er, Wazir, Wozzer.** [f. a Cairo street name *Haret el Wazza*: see 1925 quot.] As **the Wazza**, a name given by soldiers to a Cairo street in the red-light district, scene of riots (now legendary) on 3 April 1915. Cf. BERKA, BULL RING 2.
   c1914–18 TRONSON in Boyack *Behind the Lines* (1989) 26 Some trouble arose..in that disreputable quarter known as 'The Bullring' and 'The Waser'. 1919 *Quick March* 10 May 23 Last month saw the fourth anniversary of the 'Wassa' Riot... Troops took charge of that part of Cairo known as the 'Wassa' and the 'Bull Ring'. [1925 FRASER & GIBBONS *Soldier & Sailor Words* 310 *Wozzer, the*: The name among the Australians in Egypt for the street 'Haret el Wazza' in Cairo, a low neighbourhood. Two encounters there in 1915 between police and native mobs were given the name of the 'Battle of the Wozzer'.] 1936 TREADWELL *Recolls. Amateur Soldier* 47 At last the [VD] situation became so bad that the men took into their own hands the task of cleaning up the [Cairo] brothel area, which consisted of one principal street and some minor ones, comprehensively called the Wasser. *Ibid.* 48 The two raids, popularly known as the 'Battles of the Wasser', were conducted with the object of preventing the continued misuse of the premises attacked. 1943 JACKSON *Passage to Tobruk* 97 Doubtless any old soldier who fought in Egypt in the last war will remember the 'Wasser', with the streets the same, the houses..; but the soldiers of this war call this unsavoury portion of Cairo the 'Berker'. 1981 KING *New Zealanders at War* 94 This was the so-called 'Battle of the Wazza', named for the street in which the attack took place: the Haret el Wasser near Shepheards Hotel. 1989 BOYACK *Behind the Lines* 131 Likewise, although the Battle of the Wazir has been alluded to..the riot has usually been referred to in a jocular manner. 1990 DAWBER *Floods, Slips, and Washouts* 51 The night before there had been a riot in Cairo. What was afterwards known as the Battle of the Wasa? The Wasa was a street called the Wak-El-Birket... I believe [the red-light area] was known to the chaps of the 2nd. World War as the Birk[a], but we knew it as the Wasa.

weaner. [Used elsewhere but recorded earliest in NZ: AND 1865.] A farm animal not long weaned.
   1861 *Puketoi Station Diary* (Hocken TS) 2 May Looked for lambs... He has been told..that a small mob of weaners are just to the right of the dray spur on the rough ridge. 1878 CHUDLEIGH *Diary* 14 Mar. (1950) 267 Drafted our Ewes and E. weaners..turned about 1100 Ewe weaners back on the run. 1891 *Ibid.* 14 May 375 Mustered lamb weaners. 1934 *Press* (Christchurch) (Acland Gloss.) 27 Jan. 15 *Weaner*.—Lambs, calves, and pigs are sometimes so called when they are lately weaned. 1950 *NZJAg.* Jan. LXXX. 63 Pigs sold as weaners through saleyards. 1966 TURNER *Eng. Lang. in Aust. & NZ* 150 When the calves are no longer fed..they are called weaners till the next batch comes along. 1975 NEWTON *Sixty Thousand on the Hoof* 101 At the 1973 sale their top pen of weaners..realised $113... It takes good country to produce calves like that. 1981–82 *Deer*

Farmer X. 3 The trial of disbudding of 80 to 100 weaner bucks will start in March next year.

wear the Silver fern: see *silver fern* (FERN 2 (18) b).

weasel.
1. Also **weasel shit**. A sly or devious person.
1968 SLATTER *Pagan Game* 155 He's a streak of weasel shit. Too fast for the rest of them, that's the trouble. 1982 NEWBOLD *Big Huey* 255 Weasel (n) Sly or devious person. In the sense of an informer, British, since the early 1930s.
2. *Univ. students.* Applied to left-wing student politicians.
1985 *Salient* (Wellington) 22 Apr. 7 She said that she 'cannot put it down to anything other than NZUSA's being full of weasels'. (Student politico slang for members of the Workers Communist League.)

weatherboard, *a.* [Attrib. use of *weatherboard* a series of boards nailed horizontally with overlapping edges as an outside covering for walls; used elsewhere but very freq. in a context of the predominant local tradition of building in wood: AND 1827.] Of a building, having external walls of weatherboard; weather-boarded. Usu. in collocations: **weatherboard building**, **cottage**, **house**, **hut**, **residence**.
1835 YATE *NZ* (1970) 173 A two-story weatherboard house. 1840 BUNBURY *Report* 28 June in *GBPP House of Commons 1841 (No.311)* 107 The chief took us to his cottage, a weather-board hut, and offered us rum. 1840 PUCKEY *Letter* 12 June in Matthews *Matthews of Kaitaia* (1940) 135 [Our chief, Noble,] has a neat little weatherboard cottage, which is furnished with tables and chairs like our own. 1844 MONRO *Notes of a Journey* in Hocken *Contributions* (1898) 236 We found them [*sc.* the Deans family] living in an excellent weather-board verandah house. 1861 *Otago Witness* (Dunedin) 2 Feb. 4 There is a substantial weatherboard house, stockyard, etc. c1875 MEREDITH *Adventuring in Maoriland* (1935) 48 Being a weatherboard house, the walls are not sound-proof. 1899 BELL *In Shadow of Bush* 2 The slab wharé will have given place to the weatherboard cottage. 1903 *NZ Illustr. Mag.* Nov. 108 He had seen weatherboard shanties and slab huts replace gumdiggers' tents and Maori whares. 1922 COWAN *NZ Wars* (1955) I. 10 Follow the stores-buying captain..into one of the weatherboard trading-houses..thick with the tang of tarred rope. 1939 BEATTIE *First White Boy Born Otago* 69 It was a weatherboard residence with two rooms below and two above. 1955 *Dominion* (Wellington) 26 May 9 The red tin roofs topping the weather board walls..did not seem to have acquired either roots or character.

wecka, var. WEKA.

wedgie, var. WIDGIE.

wee, *a.* [In Britain, chiefly northern or Sc. dial.] In freq. general use in New Zealand replacing *little*, esp. in collocations such as **wee beaut**, **wee bit**, **wee corker** (or **beaut wee**, **corker wee**).
1866 LUSH *Waikato Jrnls.* 8 July (1982) 88 I went back and found a very thin and very delicate but interesting looking young woman with a wee little baby in her arms. 1920 BOLITHO *With the Prince in NZ* 202 There were hundreds of neat wee children in spotless white frocks and with shining ruddy faces. 1929 DEVANNY *Riven* 127 They stared at..the Chinese..the Indians and negroes..; the fewer brown skins of the Maori race and here and there a wee half-caste. 1933 SCANLAN *Tides of Youth* 91 Perhaps it's a wee bit exaggerated. 1943 MARSH *Colour Scheme* 62 The railroad twists..round the shoulder of the hill and then comes through a wee tunnel. 1959 SLATTER *Gun in My Hand* 134 Not that he was a hangman all the time. You should've seen him nursing the wee Ite babies. 1966 TURNER *Eng. Lang. Austral. & NZ* 126 In the South of New Zealand *a wee bit* would be added, a phrase extending north of the isoglosses for most Scotticisms into Canterbury. 1971 ARMFELT *Catching Up* 238 They drove to Ray's wee home in Elgin. *Ibid.* 242 Melva gave birth to a lovely wee daughter named Dawn. 1982 SANDYS *Love & War* 179 'She's a wee beaut, my Humber,' he declared proudly. 'Purrs like a kitten.' 1988 *Back Then—Volume Two* (Oral History) 13 To supplement it we had a little small wee creek up the back of the farm [at Birkenhead]. 1995 ANDERSON *House Guest* 98 We'll just have a wee bit of a look round then.

weed, *n.*[1] As a suffix in the names of plants, see: CAPE WEED, *horse's mane weed* (HORSE *n.*[1] 5), MERCURY BAY WEED, *missionary weed* (MISSIONARY *n.* 2 b), *noxious weed* (NOXIOUS *a.* a), SILVERWEED, STRATHMORE WEED, WALKER'S WEED, WARD'S WEED, WESTPORT WEED, WIREWEED, *yellow-weed* (YELLOW 2).

weed, *n.*[2] [Transf. use of *weed* a poor, leggy horse: see OED *n.*[1] 5 a.] A stunted or ill-thrifty farm animal. See also *Maori weed* (MAORI B 5 b).
1892 SWANTON *Notes on NZ* 99 After the shearing is over, all old 'weeds', badly wooled, and otherwise defective sheep are culled out. 1922 PERRY *Sheep Farming* 94 Any undue disturbance of the [Merino] ewes at this time will result in much mis-mothering of lambs, many of which will subsequently die or survive as 'poddies' and 'weeds'.

weedfish. Any of various small tidepool fishes esp. of fam. Clinidae, and esp. **crested weedfish** (see quot. 1986).
1927 PHILLIPPS *Bibliogr. NZ Fishes* (1971) 50 *Cristiceps australis...* Weed-fish... *Cristiceps auriantiacus...* Crested Weed-fish. 1956 GRAHAM *Treasury NZ Fishes* 411 Crested Weedfish *Cristiceps aurantiacus.* 1966 DOOGUE & MORELAND *Sea Anglers' Guide* 284 Threefin Blenny... *Tripterygion sp.*; cockabully, twister, weedfish. 1975 *NZ Nature Heritage* LV. 1539 One of the few families of bony fishes which bear their young alive instead of laying eggs are the weedfishes, of which there are two species commonly found in New Zealand... The Crested Weedfish is confined to the waters from Hawke Bay northwards, and lives on coarse brown seaweed at and below low tide mark. 1986 PAUL *NZ Fishes* 135 *Weedfishes* Family Clinidae. The crested weedfish, *Cristiceps aurantiacus*, is a blunt-headed, thin and tapering blenny-like fish.

week-ender. [Extended use of *week-ender* one who spends weekends away from home.] A person who is not a permanent resident of (esp.) a beach or holiday resort.
1987 SLIGO *Final Things* 186 The lagoon was sunken farmland and took the sewage that leaked from the dry lavatories of the weekenders.

weeping matipo: see MATIPO 2 (4).

weetau, var. WHITAU.

Weetbix rock. [Transf. use of *weetbix* the proprietary name of a flaked grain breakfast cereal moulded into oblong pieces easily fragmented.] Breccia, rock composed of angular fragments.
1981 DENNIS *Paparoas Guide* 136 *Hawkes Crag Breccia.* Sometimes popularly called 'Weetbix rock', breccias..consist of angular fragments cemented together in a parent material or matrix. 1992 *NZ Geographic* Jan.–Mar. 9 The loose shattered rock he saw was what mountaineers call 'Weet-Bix'.

wee-wee, var. WIWI (Frenchman).

weight. [Poss. transf. or fig. use of *weight* the amount a jockey is expected to carry (see OED *n.*[1] 12), with an allusion to causing a hindrance by raising (perhaps, publishing) these.] **a.** In the phr. **to put** (occas. **blow**) **one's weights up**, to inform on, to 'put one's pot on'.
1939–45 *Expressions & Sayings 2NZEF (TS N.A. WAII DA 420/1)* Put weights up—put in bad—inform on. 1968 SLATTER *Pagan Game* 163 Got the pricker with me because I put his weights up. 1988 10 Nov. *National Radio* 'Spectrum Documentary' 10 Nov. You couldn't get away with it [*sc.* insurance fraud] today. Somebody would blow your weights up.
b. In the phr. **to get** (**have**) (a person's) **weights up**, to have (a person's) measure.
1978 TAYLOR *Twilight Hour* 38 'I'm always asking you something, and you always reply you don't know.' I laughed. 'Well, Dicky, you have got my weights up, haven't you?'

wek, var. WEKA.

weka /ˈwɛkə/; early SI /ˈwæikə/, occas. /ˈwikə/. Also with much variety of early form as **waika** (prob. /ˈwæikə/), **waka waka**, **wecka**, **wek**, **weka-weka**, **wika**, **woka**. [Prob. onomatopoeic in origin from the cry: Ma. /ˈwɛka/: Williams 481 *weka*.]

1. Also **weka rail**. *Gallirallus australis* (fam. Rallidae), a large flightless and omnivorous brown rail with a jackdaw-like larcenous attraction to small and shiny objects. See also *bush hen* (BUSH C 4), *Maori chicken* (MAORI B 4 b), MAORI HEN, *ground pheasant* (PHEASANT), WATER-HEN a, WOODHEN 1 a, *woodrail* (WOOD 2 a). Also *attrib.*
[1820 LEE & KENDALL *NZ Gram. & Vocab.* 227 Wéka, *s.* A large bird so called. c1826–27 BOULTBEE *Journal* (1986) 109 Woodhen—wek.] 1840 BEST *Journal* 30 Oct. (1966) 257 One [purchase] was a pair of Waka Wakas or Wood Hens. 1842 GRAY *Fauna* in Dieffenbach *Travels in NZ* (1843) II. 197 *Ocydromus Australis...* Weka or Weka-weka of the natives of Cook's Strait. 1843 DIEFFENBACH *Travels in NZ* II. 197 Weka or Weka-weka of the natives of Cook's Strait, Wood-hen of the Settlers. 1850 ACHERON *Journal* May in Howard *Rakiura* (1940) 391 One of the wekas brought on board. 1870 *TrNZI* II. 70 Weka, Wood-hen. This bird is so mischievous to the fruit garden and poultry-yard of the up-country settler, that an unrelenting war is usually waged against it. 1873 BULLER *Birds NZ* 166 The Weka Rail or Woodhen is one of the few New-Zealand birds that already possess a literature. 1884 DAVIES *Poems & Literary Remains* 263 Wood-hens or waikas [*sic*] are a great stand-by in the bush... A man knowing their language and character can catch them easily. 1889 [see MAORI HEN]. 1896 HODGSON *Poems* 6 The weka brown, with its zig-zag run. 1905 THOMSON *Bush Boys* 170 A shrill whistle sounded in his ears, long drawn with a double staccato note, and then..the plaintiff [*sic*] cry of the Maori-hen (Woka) with its peculiar turn and break at the end. 1908 BAUGHAN *Shingle-Short* 46 *Weka* (wek-kah): The New Zealand wood-hen. 1918 *NZJAg.* July XVII. 5 A Raglan

correspondent states that he is troubled with wekas, and wishes to know the best way to get rid of them. **1929** DUGGAN *NZ Bird Songs* 26 Weka, O Weka, O little brown Weka, Why do they hate you, and cry on your name? They tell me you're sly and you swoop without warning, Your wings have no flight and your beak has no shame. **1936** HYDE *Check to your King* (1960) 208 That was the work of the *wekas*, incorrigible thieves, with their beady bright eyes and their long-billed heads cocked on one side. **1946** *JPS* LV. 147 *Weka*, a ground-bird.., wood-hen, Maori hen; it has wings, but too small for flight, but it can dodge and run well; and whilst its long toes are unwebbed it swims well. **1953** *Landfall* 27 175 Suddenly she darted in the scrub like a weka. **1959** CURNOW *Best of Whim-wham* 51 I don't have much Trouble with Kiwi or Tui, But a Bird I call Weaker (or do I say Wecker?) Is as bad as that Place, Motchu-eeka (or -ecka?). **1970** BAXTER *Collected Poems* (1980) 340 'Have the young no brains at all?' Chirped the fat brown weka. **1990** *Listener* 16 July 14 An introduced avian virus may have caused..[the bellbird's] demise (just as the weka once succumbed to a chicken illness).

2. With a modifier: **black**, **buff**, **North Island**, **South Island**, **Stewart Island**, **western**.

(1) **black weka**. The dark colour phase of the *western weka* (6) below. See also WEKA-PANGO.
   1886 *TrNZI* XVIII. 113 *O[cydromus] fuscus.*—Black Weka. West Coast of South Island. **1919** *TrNZI* LI. 222 The black weka is undoubtedly becoming more plentiful in the Fiord County forest. **1955** OLIVER *NZ Birds* 366 The Black Weka inhabits the dense forests of the western portion of Otago from sea level to about 3000 feet altitude. **1979** FALLA et al. *New Guide Birds NZ* 96 'Black' wekas are not uncommon along the Milford Track and range to the top of the Mackinnon Pass.

(2) **buff weka**. *Gallirallus australis hectori*, having yellowish-buff plumage.
   1955 OLIVER *NZ Birds* 370 The Buff Weka is a characteristic species of the open tussock country of the eastern side of the dividing range of the South Island. **1966** *Encycl. NZ* I. 207 The weka extended both into alpine and into lowland tussock country, especially the sub-species (the 'buff weka') occupying the eastern South Island. **1979** FALLA et al. *New Guide Birds NZ* 96 The Buff Weka (*hectori*) was found in low rainfall districts east of the main range in the South Island. **1984** SOPER *Birds NZ* 82 East of the [South Island] divide there was once a race known as the Buff Weka. It is now extinct over its original range but in 1905 was introduced to the Chatham Islands where it is now plentiful. **1993** *Evening Post* (Wellington) 9 July 15 The buff weka became extinct in Canterbury during the 1950s, but a small population survive liberation on Pitt and Chatham islands earlier in the century.

(3) **North Island weka**. *Gallirallus australis greyi*, now mainly found in the Northland and Poverty Bay regions.
   1947 POWELL *Native Animals NZ* 82 The North Island weka, once abundant everywhere, has now disappeared from most districts. **1955** OLIVER *NZ Birds* 363 The North Island Weka is not likely to trouble us for long judging by the rapidity with which the species has disappeared during the last fifty years. **1990** *Checklist Birds NZ* 120 *Gallirallus australis greyi*... North Island Weka... Now confined mainly to the Poverty Bay area.

(4) **South Island weka**. See *western weka* (6) below.
   1875 *TrNZI* VII. 205 Ocydromus australis... South Island Weka. **1889** *TrNZI* XXI. 219 *Ocydromus australis* (South Island Weka)... When a number collect near the camp it is almost impossible to sleep, owing to their loud calls through the night. **1926** *NZJST* 331 South Island Weka... It is quite without fear of man, coming out in the open and looking for food within a few feet of him. **1955** OLIVER *NZ Birds* 364 *South Island Weka..Chestnut Phase*. Though the name South Island Woodhen or Weka is adopted for this subspecies, it is absent from a large area of the eastern side of the island, where it is replaced by the Buff Woodhen. **1957** MONCRIEFF *Birds NZ* (5edn.) 59 South Island Weka or Woodhen... Differs in red legs and large size and brighter colouring from the North Island Weka.

(5) **Stewart Island weka**. *Gallirallus australis scotti*, a species confined to Stewart Island.
   1914 GUTHRIE-SMITH *Mutton Birds & Other Birds* 160 The plumage of the Stewart Island Weka is chestnut in hue, his legs are reddish, his bill also reddish at its base, in fact he is altogether a much more handsome species than our North Island species. **1948** *NZ Bird Notes* III. 55 The usual reddish form of the Stewart Island weka, of which no plumage variant was noted, is abundant and bold on Big Solander. **1955** OLIVER *NZ Birds* 368 The Stewart Island Weka hides its nest so well that no one has yet placed on record a description of it or of the measurements of the eggs. **1979** FALLA et al. *New Guide Birds NZ* 96 The Stewart Island Weka (*scotti*) is slightly smaller [than the South Island Weka].

(6) **western weka**. *Gallirallus australis australis*, the preferred name of the principal South Island subspecies. See also *black weka* (1) and *South Island weka* (4) above. See also KELP-HEN.
   1955 BAILEY *Birds NZ* 65 The Western Weka. The race is dimorphic in Fiordland, the dark form being known as the Black Weka. **1984** SOPER *Birds NZ* 82 In the South Island, the principal subspecies, the Western Weka, occurs west of the divide and in South Westland and Fiordland and has a black phase. **1990** *Checklist Birds NZ* 120 *Gallirallus australis australis* (Sparrman) Western Weka... South Island.

3. The cry of the weka.
   1873 PYKE *Wild Will Enderby* (1889, 1974) III. iii 82 'Wé-ká! Wé-ká! Wé-ká!' Three times the plaintive cry of the 'wood-hen' was heard. **1884** DAVIES *Poems & Literary Remains* 263 They call each other by name, pronounced 'Weeka', latter syllable being shrill and prolonged, an octave higher than the first note. **1902** LANCASTER in *Happy Endings* (1987) 104 Wait till I call him. We-ka-a! **1964** DEMPSEY *Little World of Stewart Island* 74 We all heard the moreporks calling in the dark, 'More *pork*! More *pork*!' and once the shrill 'Wee-ka, *wee*-ka,' of our camp followers. **1967** NATUSCH *Animals NZ* 268 Besides their 'a-wek! a-wek! a-wek!' call, [wekas]..make curious bumping noises.

4. A Chatham Islander.
   1988 McGILL *Dict. Kiwi Slang* 121 *weka* a Chatham Islander; used by Islanders themselves, being proud of their weka population.

5. Special Comb. **weka-berry** *Gaultheria* spp., SNOWBERRY; **weka-hunting**, the hunting of the weka for food, now confined mainly to the Chatham Islands; **weka-oil**, oil or fat extracted from weka and having various real and supposed healing and other properties (also **woodhen oil** q.v.); **weka stew**, a stew made from wekas.
   1947 HUTCHINSON *At Omatua's Fireside* 13 [In the Ruahine range] shrubby Gaultherias (**weka-berry** and snow-berry). **1888** BULLER *Birds NZ* II. 109 When proving, in the Native Land Court, the tribal title to this country,.. I was always glad to fall back upon evidence of **Weka-hunting** within the disputed boundaries, as affording proof of ancient title. **1867** BARKER *Station Life* (1870) 166 [I] equipped myself in a huge pair of..riding-boots made of kangaroo-skin, well greased with **weka-oil** to keep the wet out. **1964** DEMPSEY *Little World of Stewart Island* 49 Could I obtain, from a mutton-bird island, some weka oil for an old lady who was a great believer in this oil for rheumatism? **1989** *NZ Eng. Newsletter* III. 29 *weka oil:* A very special oil used only by the best of shearers. The weka or woodhen is to be caught on a full moon, prior to a month with four letters in it, under the Hurunui Bridge. To be hung for four days and the oil collected in a bottle. **1985** HUNT *I'm Ninety-five* 261 A lot of old weka-eaters [on Stewart Island] would still like to cook up a few... I could live on **weka stew** myself, just like it says in one of our old songs: *What would a Maori do For a good old weka stew*.

weka-pango. [Ma. /ˈwekaˈpaŋo/: Williams 481 *Weka pango*, black weka.] *black weka* (WEKA 2 (1)).
   1873 BULLER *Birds NZ* 174 Ocydromus fuscus. (Black Woodhen)... *Weka-pango*... It is the bird referred to by Captain Cook. They are a sort of Rail, about the size and a good deal like a common dunghill hen. **1955** OLIVER *NZ Birds* 366 *Black Weka. Weka-pango Gallirallus australis australis*... The Black Weka differs from the ordinary South Island Weka in the greater amount of black in its plumage.

weka rail: see WEKA.

wekau, var. WHEKAU.

weka-weka, var. WEKA.

weki, var. WHEKI.

weki-ponga, var. WHEKI-PONGA.

well-gone, *a*. Much in love; (*WW1*) severely wounded.
   1937 PARTRIDGE *Dict. Slang* 944 *well-gone*. Much in love; fatally or very severely wounded: New Zealand coll.: resp. from ca. 1913 and from ca. 1915. **1938** *Press* (Christchurch) (McNab Slang) 2 Apr. 18 'Blinded with science' comes from boxing, as does 'well gone.'

well in. In the phr. **to be well in**, to be well-informed.
   1945 SARGESON in *Listener Short Stories* (1977) 21 A cow-cocky who was reckoned to be pretty well in said he'd killed and eaten a lot of meat in his time, and he knew for a fact that no man..could eat a whole calf.

Wellington, *n*.

1. *WW1*. Usu. as **the Wellingtons**, until the formation of the New Zealand Division in 1916, the Wellington Battalion of the Infantry Brigade; thence, either the 1st or 2nd Wellington Battalions of variously organized Infantry Brigades. Occas. early in WW1, the Wellington Regiment of the Mounted Rifles.
   1917 *Chron. NZEF* 27 June 223 The Wellingtons then went out in front of their trench and waited for the barrage to lift. **1919** [see AUCKLAND 1]. **1922** POWLES *New Zealanders in Sinai & Palestine* 148 About this time the Wellingtons captured the enemy's third position. **1966** [see OTAGO A]. **1982** SHADBOLT *Once on Chunuk Bair* (1990) 79 You're not even a Wellington.

2. *attrib*. in special collocations: **Wellington swell** *obs.*, see quot.; **Wellington tenths**, see TENTHS.
   1859 THOMSON *Story NZ* II. 188 It is worthy of notice, that the colonists, soon after the formation of all the settlements, acquired distinguishing epithets; thus there was an Auckland cove, a Wellington swell, a Nelson snob, a Taranaki exquisite... These epithets, almost already forgotten, are too characteristic to be buried in oblivion.

Wellingtonian. [f. *Wellington* + *-ian.*] A person born or resident in Wellington city or (occas.) Wellington province. Also *attrib.*, of or pertaining to Wellington.

1840 WAKEFIELD *Letter* 8 Jan. in Fawcett *Sir William Molesworth* (1901) 173 But I am satisfied..that the more and greater settlements there are in New Zealand..the better for the Wellingtonians. 1851 *Austral. & NZ Gaz.* 29 Nov. 483 She [*sc.* the Government schooner] was bought by an old Wellingtonian for the sum of 125*l*. 1868 *Punch in Wellington* 30 These sickening, nauseous Wellingtonian smells. 1880 SENIOR *Travel & Trout* 209 I..was admitted into the party of four—two Wellingtonians..one Londoner, one Queenslander. 1901 *TrNZI* XXXIII. 500 The geography of some prominent Wellingtonians on board was rather at fault. 1918 *NZ at the Front* 14 We adjust the barbed wire gate to block the path down the dere, incidentally shutting in two belated Wellingtonians. 1948 LIPSON *Politics of Equality* 45 Up to 1876 political sentiment was regionalized... Provincial loyalties were paramount; people considered themselves Aucklanders or Wellingtonians rather than New Zealanders. 1956 WILSON *Sweet White Wine* 53 In Palmerston North we are sensitive about Wellingtonians calling us 'country'. 1987 *Metro* (Auckland) May 61 In those days..I had started to become a Wellingtonian, one of the most horrible things that can happen to a New Zealander.

wentletrap. [Transf. use of *wentletrap*, *Scalaria* spp.] *Cirsotrema zelebori* (fam. Epitoniidae), a small delicately ribbed univalve shellfish.

1924 BUCKNILL *Sea Shells NZ* 58 Epitonium zelebori... Although this Wentletrap, popularly known as the Curly, is the commonest of the five species found in New Zealand, it is by far the most beautiful of these charming little shells. 1947 POWELL *Native Animals* 28 Curly or Wentle-trap... A charming little white shell up to an inch in length with a long tapered spire sculptured with regular vertical ridges crossed by finer spirals. 1966 *Encycl. NZ* I. 425 Curly or Wentle-trap (*Cirsotrema zelebori*). A pure white shell up to 1 in. in height, beautifully ornamented in ladderlike patterns. 1983 GUNSON *Collins Guide to Seashore* 96 Its name derived from the Dutch word for a spiral staircase, the wentletrap *Cirsotrema zelebori* (30 mm) is a delicately ribbed shell found in the sand of northern beaches.

wenua, var. WHENUA.

werri, var. WHARE.

west coast, *n.* and *a.*

A. *n.* Usu. as **the West Coast**, with or without initial caps. Orig. applied (a) mainly by whalers, sealers, Australian and other traders, etc. to the west coast of usu. the South Island (often by sealers and whalers called **the west side**, see quot. 1844[2]), rarely to that of the North Island; thence, with eastern and northern SI settlement, the area beyond the Southern Alps; and later (b) the last-mentioned area looked upon as an extension of the Canterbury (occas. of Nelson) provincial district; thence (c) after the discovery of gold, to the provincial district or province, later named Westland. In modern use, often that part of Westland south (approx.) of Westport. See also COAST 2, GOLD COAST a. **a.** As a general term.

c1835 BOULTBEE *Journal* (1986) 90 The schooner was from Sydney, bound to the West Coast of New Zealand, on a sealing voyage. 1844 TUCKETT *Letter* 16 Aug. in Hocken *Contributions* (1898) 228 I reluctantly abandoned exploration of the west coast, convinced by the unanimous representation of the sealers who alone frequent that coast, that there was only one extensive tract of available land about 40 miles north of Milford Haven. 1844 MONRO *Notes of a Journey* in Hocken *Contributions* (1898) 260 On the west coast of the Middle Island, commonly called by the whalers the 'West Side', we heard a good deal both from the whites and the natives. All accounts agreed that it is of a most rugged and inaccessible character. *Ibid.* 261 The kivi, called by the sealers the emu, is met with in great abundance on the west side. 1860 in Butler *First Year* (1863) v 72 The few Maories that inhabit this settlement travel to the west coast by way of this river.

b. As an extension of Canterbury or other provinces.

1847 BRUNNER *Exped. Middle Is.* 8 Apr. in Taylor *Early Travellers* (1959) 273 We espied the mountain range that bounds the West Coast. 1861 HAAST *Rep. Topogr. Explor. Nelson* 40 The climate of the West Coast [is] most horrid, and I could not but concur with one of my party, who proposed to change its name to *Wet Coast.* 1891 *NZJSc.* (NS) I. 31 Past experiences have satisfied me that rabbits never will do much mischief on the West Coast.

c. With init. caps. As a province or sub-provincial district; hence as a general term for the coast and country roughly from south of Westport (or 'the Buller') to the Haast highway.

1865 CHUDLEIGH *Diary* 4 July (1950) 192 The first Overland Mail to the West Coast went through today. 1866 SMALL *NZ & Austral. Songster* (1970) 23 It [the letter] came from the West Coast, a wonderful quarter, Where men made their fortunes by digging. 1876 KENNEDY *Colonial Travel* 202 A telegram was published in Christchurch from a man on the West Coast. 1887 *Auckland Weekly News* 24 Sept. 28 On the West Coast we were in a new world. 1896 HARPER *Pioneer Work* 30 Westland, or 'West Coast', as it is more commonly called, was rushed by gold-diggers in the early sixties. 1912 MANSFIELD *Stories* (1984) 113 The husband was a pal of mine once, down the West Coast. 1967 MAY *West Coast Gold Rushes* 15 'West Coast' continued to be used in the 1860's, but after 1864 the official names, 'West Canterbury' and 'Nelson South West', had some popular currency. Then a further complication was introduced. In 1859 John Rochfort had coined the name 'Westland', a shortened form of 'Westmoreland', the name he used on a map showing his West Coast explorations. After August 1865 the form 'Westland' was resurrected and was used both for electoral and judicial districts which covered part or whole of the West Coast... 'West Coast' remains the popular term for the strip of country on the wrong side of the Southern Alps, though recently New Zealand geographers have adopted 'Westland' for the whole West Coast. Whatever its merits, this term is unsatisfactory. It has some popular currency south of Greymouth, and it may acquire popularity through its teaching in the schools; but at an indefinable point north of Greymouth one is likely to be told, 'This isn't Westland, this is the Buller'.

B. *adj.*

1. Also occas. **west-coast.** Characteristic of or pertaining to the West Coast of the South Island, or to West-Coasters.

1865 MUELLER *My Dear Bannie* (1958) 75 [Camp at the Manakaiau] I found Kerei, the Chief of all the West Coast natives, at my camp. This West Coast seems to be the abode of husbands. 1879 HAAST *Geol. Canterbury & Westland* 99 Above the forest plains rose low hillocks, also clothed with the same intensely green West Coast vegetation. 1881 NESFIELD *Chequered Career* 76 We travelled to..the Buller, calling at Charleston..familiar diggings to any west-coast digger. 1936 HYDE *Passport to Hell* 31 In a week's time he was taken down and put aboard the *Kittawa*, which was..the bloodiest little coal-boat on the West Coast run. 1957 FRAME *Owls Do Cry* (1967) 54 Now Toby, what will you be..in freezing works west-coast mine or foundry.

2. With connotations of 'generous, open-hearted'.

1913 SEDDON 10 Dec. in Pfaff *Diggers' Story* (1914) 40 The miners and other friends were waiting to give us a reception, which was a real West Coast one, and everybody knows what that means. 1963 PEARSON *Coal Flat* 56 I suppose you've heard about West Coast hospitality. Well, we've just take people how we find them and we expect them to do the same. 1965 MCLAGLAN *Stethoscope & Saddlebags* 179 Near her was an old girl, also whitebait-fishing, who, in true West Coast style, told the story of her ups and downs.

3. In special collocations: **West Coast lantern,** a 'bottle' lantern made from a candle placed in the neck of an inverted bottle the bottom of which has been knocked or cut off (see LANTERN for synonyms).

1913 SEDDON 10 Dec. in Pfaff *Diggers' Story* (1914) 39 We then walked up the creek, lighted by the West Coast lantern (a candle in a bottle). 1992 LATHAM *Golden Reefs* 134 Rushes by candlelight were quite the vogue..and West Coast lanterns (a candle stuck in a bottle) were much in evidence.

West Coaster. One born or resident on the WEST COAST, a member of a community having reputed qualities of pioneering independence, hospitality, and conviviality, and a history of exploitation of natural resources. See also COASTER 1.

1887 RAE in Heinz *Bright Fine Gold* (1974) 125 I saw a ghastly array of departed and altogether forgotten West Coasters on this stormy night off Paringa. In the morning I found that the Something which conjured up these ghastly visions, taking the shape of many Westlanders in spirit land, was the steward's towel hanging on the cabin door. 1890 [see ASPHALT]. 1904 MCMURRAN *New York to NZ* 81 The West-Coasters are proud of their parliamentary product. 1916 *Chron. NZEF* 15 Nov. 134 Billie's a We't Coaster. 1936 HYDE *Passport to Hell* 54 He washed shirts for the brawny West Coasters, who decked themselves out for dancing after nightfall. 1941 DUFF *NZ Now* 71 The people are never 'Southlanders' (except once a year at football) as the people of the West Coast are 'West Coasters'. 1966 *Encycl. NZ* III. 635 The widely accepted image of the 'West Coaster' depicts a product of a close-knit community, generous, friendly, and self-reliant, yet distrustful of authority. 1986 *Listener* 11 Jan. 1 Health status data has indicated that West Coasters have significantly high rates of death and hospitalisation. 1991 *North & South* (Auckland) June 80 His credo is classic simple West Coaster.

westie. *Auckland local.* Also **westy**, and with init. cap. [f. *west*(ern suburbs+ *-IE*; cf. AND 1977, applied similarly to a resident of the western suburbs of Sydney.] A resident of the middle-class (north)western suburbs of Auckland, often used with a derogatory 'poor white' connotation.

1992 *Listener* 3 Oct. 44 Songwriter Jan Hellriegel sashays out of the Western Auckland suburbs blot with 'Westy Gals'... The song is a slow, strong-tempered memory of rage..which Hellriegel..went through while growing up in Henderson, the great metropolis of 'westies'—hoons, yobs, chicks and party animals of numerous vivid subcultures—who charge into the New Zealand night. 1993 *Metro* (Auckland) Dec. 104 Boag describes herself as a 'westie'. She was born in Glen Eden where her father was an earthmoving contractor, educated at local primary and intermediate schools, then out-of-zone at Auckland Girls' Grammar. 1994 *Ibid.* Apr. 26 Cortinaloads of screaming young Westies were ecstatic to see a *Shortland Street* 'star'.

Westland. In the names of plants and animals, see: PETREL 2 (20), PINE 2 (18), SHOEMAKER.

Westport weed. [f. *Westport*, a port on the SI west coast serving the Buller district.] *Leptinella* (or *Cotula*) *dioica* (fam. Asteraceae), a small native creeping daisy of salt marsh and bog margins.
 1946 *Jrnl. NZ Inst. Hort.* Jan. XV. No. 2 11 This little creeping weed [*Cotula dioica*] grows in our bowling green, and..with the regular mowing it forms a smooth, ever-green carpet. It bears many very small groundsel-like flower heads, and is sometimes referred to as Westport weed. **1969** *Standard Common Names Weeds* 85 Westport weed [=] *Cotula dioica*.

west side: see WEST COAST A a.

wet, *a.*

1. *Farming.* [AND 1894.] Of sheep, with fleeces too wet to shear, esp. in the phr. **to declare (sheep) wet**, see quot. 1989.
 1890 *Otago Witness* (Dunedin) 27 Feb. 19 After the dinner hour the pens were refilled with sheep which were wet... He had had 12 years' experience, and had never been asked to shear wet sheep. **1952** MEEK *Station Days* 111 Wet Sheep. When it has been decided that the sheep are too wet to shear. **1960** SCRYMGEOUR *Memories Maoriland* 49 Conferences would be held, a slight glistening on the fibre of the fleece, when sunlight decreed 'wet sheep' and then the shearers would declare a break. **1989** *NZ Eng. Newsletter* III. 23 *declare them wet:* When there is the question of whether the sheep are too wet to shear, a vote is taken after each man shears two sheep. If more vote wet than dry they 'declare them wet', and no-one shears. If the vote is even or in favour of the dry the shearing continues.

2. In the phr. **to get** (someone) **wet**, to have a person beaten, to gain the upper hand over.
 c1926 THE MIXER *Transport Workers' Song Book* 29 He skites about in-fighting. Stick to him, Mick; you've got him wet. **1945** SARGESON *When Wind Blows* 40 Now we've got 'em wet [in a tennis game].

3. In special collocations: **wetback**, of a wood or coal stove, incorporating water-heating capability; **wet-bird**, see SHEARWATER; **wet claim** *goldmining*, a claim liable to flooding; **wet diggings** *goldmining*, see quot. 1948 (see also *river-workings* (RIVER 2 b)); **wet or dry**, an early workers' expression indicating that wages should be paid whether the weather is wet (and no work can be done) or dry; **wet-timer**, see quot. 1990.
 1980 LELAND *Kiwi-Yankee Dict.* 111 A wetback is a set of pipes or a hot water drum attached to the back or bottom of a fireplace or solid fuel stove. **1986** McCAULEY *Then Again* 78 In case the wet-back explodes, being empty of water and the fire still hot with embers, she gets the kids to carry out the water-catching pots. **1986** OWEN & PERKINS *Speaking for Ourselves* 130 The stove had a wetback and a hot water system. **1995** [see DOVER STOVE]. **1862** WEKEY *Otago As It Is* 61 Claims shall be classified thus;.. Wet Claims, *i.e.*, alluvial claims in flooded ground. **1892** PYKE *Gold-Miners' Guide* 45 [s.175] The owners of a 'wet claim' must, whenever practicable, cut a drain to carry their water to a main channel, which shall be cut and kept clear at the joint expense of all parties interested. **1862** RICHARDSON *Sketch of Otago* 48 In the winter, the same has been said concerning the summer,—'See how the **wet diggings** will pay in the summer time.' **1867** HOCHSTETTER *NZ* 104 The conglomerates accumulated on the slopes of the mountains are the proper field for the '*dry diggings*', while from the gravel and sand of the beds of the rivers and smaller streams the gold is obtained by '*wet diggings*'. [**1948** HAAST *Sir Julius von Haast* 35 [translating from the German of *Wiener Zeitung* (1860) Nos 57–65.] He explained to his readers that there were two kinds of diggings, the 'wet' and the 'dry'. The first were in the bed of the river, the water of which had often to be diverted in order that the diggers might wash the gold taken out. If these diggings offer a larger profit to those who strike the right spot, they have the disadvantage, that the necessary labour is hard and unhealthy, for the diggers must often stand breast-high in the cold water from the mountains.] **1865** *Evening Post* (Wellington) 40 The price is now lower [in a wage claim] and may be called a pound a day **wet or dry**. **1871** MONEY *Knocking About NZ* 69 We received 10s. per day, 'wet or dry,' *i.e.*, whether we were working or not, and provisions at Government prices. **1888** D'AVIGDOR *Antipodean Notes* 226 Surveying work for two guineas a week, wet or dry, which is an important qualification. **1990** CHURCHMAN & HURST *Railways of NZ* 196 The early afternoon train back to Greymouth was known as the '**wet-timer**', as miners working in wet parts of the mine worked a shorter shift.

weta /ˈwetə/, occas. /ˈwæitə/. Also occas. **weita**. [Ma. /ˈweːtaː/: Williams 482 *Wētā*.]

1. A flightless, often large, cricket-like insect of either of the families Stenopelmatidae or Rhaphidophoridae, having spiny hind-legs. The arrangement in 2 below follows modern (1991) entomological practice.
 [*Note*] In some of the Stenopelmatidae (*Hemideina* spp.), a mask-like face has often given rise among both Maori and non-Maori to the weta's reputation of being frightening, fearsome, or harmful, hence the common names *bush devil* (BUSH C 4), JIMMY NIPPER, *Maori devil* (MAORI B 4 b), SAWYER, SCORPION, TAIPO 5, *wood-devil* (WOOD *n.*¹ 2 a). Some *Deinacrida* spp. are very large and heavy-bodied, hence *giant weta*, WETAPUNGA. Some of the fam. Rhaphidophoridae (esp. *Pharmacus montanus*) are long-legged and active jumpers, hence MOUNT COOK FLEA, *jumping spider* (JUMPING 1), TREE-CRICKET; some are cave-dwelling, hence *cave weta*; some have 'tusks', hence *tusked weta*.
 [**1820** LEE AND KENDALL *NZ Gram. and Vocab.* 227 Wéta, *s.* An insect so called. Wéta punga; ditto.] **1844** WILLIAMS *NZ Journal* (1956) 112 The notable Weta about the size of a Cockroach when full grown. **1857** HURSTHOUSE *NZ* I. 123 The weta, a suspicious-looking, scorpion-like creature, apparently replete with 'high concocted venom', but perfectly harmless. **1863** BUTLER *First Year* ix 141 We have, too, one of the ugliest-looking creatures that I have ever seen. It is called 'weta', and is of tawny scorpion-like colour, with long antennae and great eyes, and nasty squashy-looking body. **1878** BULLER *Forty Yrs. NZ* 499 The *Weta* is a forest cricket, three inches long. **1887** *Auckland Weekly News* 24 Dec. 15 Would [X] be good enough to tell me..whether the 'weta,' the brown scorpion-like insect found in the Auckland province is poisonous or not? **1885** weita [see SAWYER]. **1895** *TrNZI* XXVII. 174 Captain Fairchild collected..[on Bounty Island] specimens of one of those wingless locusts called weta by the Maoris—by which name they are known to all New-Zealanders. **1930** DOBSON *Reminiscences* 150 The wetas made a loud creaking sound, as they called to each other from time to time. **1942** ANDERSEN *Maori Place Names* 452 There are four kinds [of wetas]: the *bush-weta*, the *cave-weta*, smaller in body with very long legs and feelers—the *rock-weta* found under rocks on mountain sides, *ground-weta*, as small as a cricket and found buried under the soil. **1947** POWELL *Native Animals of New Zealand* 47 Large-headed Weta (*Hemideina megacephala*). The common weta found throughout New Zealand in rotten logs, old trees, and under loose bark. **1954** BEATTIE *Our Southernmost Maoris* 68 The weta (wayt-ta) was a grasshopper on a big scale and was the same shape. It was once plentiful but is now gone. **1968** BAXTER *Collected Poems* (1980) 429 And if in Paremata you Should find a weta in your shoe, Ugly, hard-shelled, with snapping jaws..Don't hit it with a shovel. **1971** MILLER *Common Insects in NZ* 136 Weta are often incorrectly called locusts, and even the Maori word *weta* requires some comment, I think, since perhaps its explicit application has been lost. There are two kinds of these usually nocturnal insects— the most robust and heavily-armoured species found on trees and ground,—and the fragile Cave Weta with their long and slender legs and small bodies. From a study of ancient Maori lore, it appears possible that the word *weta* was originally restricted to the former kind, while the Cave Weta were his *tokoriro*..probably because of their progression on delicate stiltlike legs [*toko* 'stilt']. **1983** *Whakarewarewa Forest Park* 70 A close relative of the katydid and cricket is the tokoriro weta. **1984** *Hanmer Forest Park* 67 *Hemideina femorata* (the Canterbury weta), is moderately common but seldom seen. **1990** *Evening Post* (Wellington) 28 July 4 The alpine weta, or hemideina maori, is believed to be able to survive the lowest temperatures of any sizeable, internally well-organised, land animal. **1992** *Evening Post* (Wellington) 24 Aug. 18 The tyrannical father..devours everyone and everything 'like a weta sucking fruit from the inside'.

2. With a modifier: **cave, giant, ground** (occas. **bush**), **tree (bush), tusked** (or **elephant**).

(1) **cave weta**. Any of various long-legged, active ground- and cave-living species of the fam. Rhaphidophoridae. See also *jumping spider* (JUMPING 1), MOUNT COOK FLEA.
 1897 *TrNZI* XXIX. 208 The wetas are nocturnal insects... Most of them are solitary, but the cave-wetas live together in considerable numbers. **1929** MARTIN *NZ Nature Book* I 106 Three or more species of *Cave Weta* occur in New Zealand, belonging to genera distinct from cave-dwelling forms in other parts of the earth... Cave Wetas are colonial in habit, in strong contrast to the solitary habits of the true wetas. **1935** DIXON *Nature Study Notes* 35 The two species most frequently seen are the Cave Weta and the Tree Weta. **1947** POWELL *Native Animals* 47 Cave Weta (*Pachyrhamma acanthocera*). A large insect, remarkable for the extreme length of its antennae and hind legs. **1955** MILLER *Nature in NZ* 50 The Cave Weta are spider-like, frail, and agile leapers; the body is small, and the legs and antennae long and delicate, the largest species measuring 12 to 14 inches from the tips of the extended antennae to the hind feet. They shelter in caves, under stones and bark, or in cavities in logs. **1971** BALE *Maratoto Gold* 22 He handed us each a candle and as we entered the tunnel warned us not to disturb the cave wetas. **1986** *Sunday Star* (Auckland) 28 Dec. B1 She moved the packs behind a rocky outcrop jutting into the cave's centre;.. and not at the back, where the ghostly cave wetas waved anaemic limbs. **1990** MEADS *The Weta Book* 34 Cave wetas are long-legged, jumping, spider-like wetas often associated with caves.

(2) **elephant weta**, see *tusked weta* (6) below.

(3) **giant weta**. Any of various ground- or tree-dwelling species, esp. *Deinacrida* (fam. Stenopelmatidae), having large, heavy bodies. See also WETAPUNGA.
 1947 POWELL *Native Animals of New Zealand* 47 Giant Weta (*Deinacrida heteracantha*). A large, fearsome-looking insect with a body up to four inches in length. It is now very rare on the mainland. **1966** *Encycl. NZ* III. 636 Giant wetas are now rare and appear to be restricted to several off-shore islands. **1971** SHARELL *NZ Insects* 138 Nearly extinct is the giant weta, *Deinacrida heteracantha*...This magnificent looking insect was once common in the northern part

of the North Island, but is confined now to some islands in the Hauraki Gulf and north of Auckland. **1989** PARKINSON *Travelling Naturalist* 136 [The Mackenzie Country] has a few claims to fame: a giant weta, the scree weta, and an endemic butterfly, the southern blue. **1990** MEADS *Weta Book* 33 The 'Mahoenui weta' is a new species of giant weta, first discovered during 1963 in scattered forest remnants on farmland near Mahoenui, in the King Country.

(4) **ground weta**. Any of various ground-dwelling species of *Hemiandrus* and *Zealandosandrus* (fam. Stenopelmatidae). See also *jumping jack* (JUMPING 1).

1947 MARTIN *NZ Nature Study* 204 The Jumping Jack is a ground weta commonly disturbed while turning over garden soil. The body is about an inch long and the legs *are* used for jumping, though this is not so with the [tree weta]. **1955** MILLER *Nature in NZ* 50 The Ground Weta shelter under stones and logs. **1974** CHILD *NZ Insects* 36 They are the Bush Wetas and Ground Wetas, which live under logs, leaf litter or in burrows in the ground. **1987** *NZ Entomologist* X. 57 Ground wetas (*Hemiandrus similis*) were present on all 4 islands in the Queen Charlotte Sound. **1990** MEADS *Weta Book* 23 Ground wetas resemble small tree wetas, but they lack the heavy spines on their back legs, and the males do not develop such large heads or massive jaws.

(5) **tree** (or **bush**) **weta**. A tree-dweller of *Hemideina* spp. (fam. Stenopelmatidae), the weta most commonly met with; often large-headed, with spiny hind legs producing a rasping sound when rubbed against the abdomen. See also *bush devil* (BUSH C 4), JIMMY NIPPER, *Maori devil* (MAORI B 4 b), SAWYER, TAIPO 5, *wood-devil* (WOOD *n.*¹ 2 a).

1935 [see (1) above]. **1947** MARTIN *NZ Nature Study* 203 The Tree Weta..found throughout New Zealand inhabits beech, matai, mahoe and other timbers. It is a large insect of which the males have a grotesquely large head due to greatly developed mandibles. **1955** MILLER *Nature in NZ* 52 The Tree Weta shelter under bark and in the abandoned burrows made by wood-boring beetles in trees. **1966** [see TAIPO 5]. **1971** MILLER *Common Insects in NZ* 136 Another species is the Mountain Tree-weta (*Hemideina broughi*) which forms burrows in southern beech. **1989** *DSIR Ecology Notes* 17 1 This defensive action is probably why the most commonly encountered weta is the tree or 'bush' weta, which is widespread in all parts of New Zealand except Southland. **1990** MEADS *Weta Book* 5 A giant weta and a tree weta from forests in Northland were described by Adam White in 1842 during voyages of HMS Erebus and HMS Terror.

(6) **tusked** (or **elephant**) **weta**. *Hemiandrus monstrosus*, a weta with tusks.

1990 MEADS *Weta Book* 26 Two species of tusked weta are found in the north of the North Island... The tusks of the male tusked weta are rubbed together to make a loud, shrill noise, and they are also used for fighting and for defence against predators. **1990** *Victoria University Review* 18 The tusked weta was discovered about 20 years ago when one small male was found on the island, but no more had been seen until recently and they have not yet been thoroughly studied. **1991** *Australian Natural History* XXIII. No.8 602 The spectacular 'Elephant Weta' or 'Tusked Weta' of Middle Mercury Island..is a giant 'ground' weta (flightless cricket-like insect) found only on one small..island... The popular names refer to large size (males can reach nine to ten centimetres..) combined with an enlarged head and elephant-like 'tusks' in males... A scientific name awaits publication. **1991** *The Weta* Aug. 30 Field Observations on Two Species of Tusked Weta... 1. *Hemiandrus monstrosus* Salmon 1950...The Hokianga weta known as *Hemiandrus monstrosus* is a species of the far north of New Zealand.

wetapunga. [Ma. /ˈweːtaːˈpuŋa/: Williams 483 *Wētāpunga*.] *Deinacrida heteracantha* (fam. Stenopelmatidae), a large, tree-dwelling weta of Northland, and reputedly the heaviest known insect in the world. See also *giant weta* (WETA 2 (3)).

[**1820** LEE AND KENDALL *NZ Grammar and Vocabulary* 227 *Wéta, s.* An insect so called. Wéta punga; ditto.] **1843** DIEFFENBACH *Travels in NZ* II. 396 Weta punga— a spider. Weta— an insect so called. **1871** *TrNZI* III. 35 In another case, a large Weta-punga which he had immersed in water almost boiling, and then laid aside in his insect-box as killed, revived in the course of a few hours. **1888** BULLER *Birds of NZ* I. 195 Judge Munro informs me that..he found in [a morepork's] stomach a specimen of the weta-punga, or tree-cricket.., with a body as large as a magnum-bonum plum. **1895** *TrNZI* XXVII. 145 The Maoris attribute its disappearance to the introduced Norway rat. They distinguish it [*sc.* Deinacrida heteracantha] as the Wetapunga. **1897** *TrNZI* XXIX. 213 This species [*sc.* Deinacrida heteracantha] is the weta-punga of the Maoris. **1925–26** *NZJST* VIII. 16 The first evidences of that..insect, *Deinacrida heteracantha* (*weta punga* of the Maori), were seen [at poor Knights island] on a rock used by the harrier as a table. **1955** MILLER *Nature in NZ* 52 A large northern species (*Deinacrida heteracantha*) he [*sc.* the Maori] called *wetapunga*, Punga being the deity presiding over ugly things. **1971** SHARELL *NZ Insects and their Story* 139 The giant weta of the north was called wetapunga. **1985** ORBELL *The Natural World of the Maori* 176 Insects and similar creatures are usually said to be the children of Tane and of Punga, whose children are all ugly... Weta were proverbially ugly, above all the giant weta, which was known for this reason as *te wētā Punga*, 'Punga's weta'. **1990** MEADS *Weta Book* 30 Wetapunga..is the biggest species at 82 mm in length, and is now found only on Little Barrier Island in the Hauraki Gulf.

wet hen. In various phrases indicating silliness or moodiness: **a. silly (mad) as a wet hen**, very silly or stupid; also, very angry (see quot. 1992). See also SILLY A.

1956 SUTHERLAND *Green Kiwi* (1960) 123 I gathered that Baily approved of Barrit because he described him a little later as being 'as silly as a wet hen'. **1957** CROSS *God Boy* 63 I really felt as mad as a wet hen, although I didn't quite know why. **1966** TURNER *Eng. Lang. Austral. & NZ* 177 New Zealand seems to be able to claim some similes, e.g. 'as silly as a wet hen'. **1973** WILSON *NZ Jack* 145 Dad's just a stupy [*sic*] old coot... Ouu! He's as silly as a wet hen. **1976** WILSON *Pacific Star* 8 'What a lot of twaddle!' I said... 'Mad as a wet hen in a thunderstorm. Poor people, Dick,' said Ted. **1992** PARK *Fence around the Cuckoo* 213 When.. someone else has put the boot in..you can read it [*sc.* a discouraging message] again, and get as mad as a wet hen.

b. mopey as a wet hen.

1941 BAKER *NZ Slang* 53 *Mopey as a wet hen, rough as a bag*. **1955** *BJ Cameron Collection* (TS July) mopey as a wet hen. Very glum.

wettie. [f. *wet* (suit + -IE.] A wet suit.

1995 *Dominion* (Wellington) 3 Feb. 7 They [*sc.* surfers] donned their 'wetties' and ran into the water.

we-we, wewi, varr. WIWI (Frenchman).

weweia. [Ma. /ˈweweia/: Williams 481 *weiweia*, *weweia*..dabchick (little grebe).] DABCHICK.

1873 BULLER *Birds NZ* 350 Podiceps rufipectus. (New-Zealand Dabchick)... Weweia, Totokipio. **1955** [see DABCHICK]. **1966** [see DIVER]. **1989**, **1990** [see DABCHICK].

whaariki, var. WHARIKI.

whack, *v.*

1. *trans*. To fell (trees). See also BUSHWHACK 1.

1922 TURNER *Happy Wanderer* 7 Only eighteen months ago I was whacking some bush on a siding.

Hence **whacker**, BUSHFALLER. See also BUSHWHACKER 1.

1930 DEVANNY *Bushman Burke* 288 She flashed Taipo a glance of temper and went over to the other whackers.

2. As **whack into**, to attack (esp. food) vigorously.

1964 PEARSON *Glossary* to Sargeson *Collected Stories 1935–63* (1964) 304 whack into (food): attack vigorously.

3. As **whack up**, to make and bake (at short notice) (scones, a loaf, etc.), to prepare, to 'knock up'; to build.

1961 CRUMP *Hang On a Minute Mate* 51 Now pass me pants and I'll whack up a loaf that your mother'd be proud of. **1995** *Dominion* (Wellington) 11 Jan. 13 He's whacked up a shed as well. A neat little corrugated iron job.

whaheen, wha-hei-ne, whaiheine, varr. WAHINE *n.*¹

whai. Also early **hewhài** (=he whai), **wae, wai**. [Ma. /ˈfai/: Williams 484 *Whai* (i) *1. n.*..sting ray, and *Raja nasuta*, skate.] Any of various skates and rays. See also RAY, SKATE, WHAI-REPO.

1770 PARKINSON *Journal* (1773) 127 Hewhài, A skate. **1844** COLENSO *Excurs. Northern Is.* in Taylor *Early Travellers* (1959) 50 One pretty little species, I once saw, had a very long filiform cylindrical and smooth tail. These fish are called 'Wai [*sic*], by the natives. **1855** TAYLOR *Te Ika A Maui* 627 (*Whai*,) the rays attain a very large size, feet in diameter. **1886** SHERRIN *Handbook Fishes NZ* 90 The skate is not often brought to market, but is not scarce, and as a food fish has few superiors. It is called by the Maoris wae. **1921** *NZJST* IV. 123 Raja nasuta... *Skate*; *Whai*. **1929** BEST *Fishing Methods* 43 The *whai*, or sting-ray, was taken by means of a hardwood spear. **1946** *JPS* LV. 160 *Whai*, a fish (*Trygon thalassia* and other spp.), sting-ray. **1966** DOOGUE & MORELAND *Sea Anglers' Guide* 192 Stingray, stingaree; whai, pakaurua, oru, roha (Maori)... Rough Skate...*Raja australis;* whai (Maori). **1987** POWELL *Native Animals NZ* 56 Rough Skate (Whai) *Raja nasuta*. The Rough Skate is common at all depths around the New Zealand coast.

whai-repo. Also **wairepo**. [Ma. /ˈfai ˈrepo/: Williams 484 *Whai repo*..electric ray.] Either the *stingray* (RAY 2 (3)) (STINGAREE), or (less frequently) *electric ray* (RAY 2 (2)).

1872 HUTTON & HECTOR *Fishes NZ* 121 To this family of fishes also belongs the formidable Stingaree, or Wairepo of the Maoris (*Trigon thalassia*), which is greatly prized as food among the natives. **1898** MORRIS *Austral-English* 493 *Wairepo, n.* Maori name for the fish called *Sting-ray*. **1927** PHILLIPPS *Bibliogr. NZ Fishes* (1971) 10 *Narcobatus fairchildi*... Electric Ray; Whai Repo. **1929** BEST *Fishing Methods* 48 The smaller brown sting-ray is called whai kuku in the Otaki district, and the larger black one whai repo. **1930** *NZJST* XI. 98 *Narcobatus fairchildi*... Southern Numbfish, or Whai Repo. *Ibid.* 105 *Dasyatis* *brevicaudatus*... Whai Repo; Sting-ray, or Stingaree. **1947** POWELL *Native Animals NZ* 63 Electric Ray... Whai repo of the Maoris, has a shark-like tail, but the front of the body is expanded as a large flat disc. **1956** GRAHAM *Treasury NZ Fishes* 100 Sting Ray or Stingaree (Whai Repo) *Bathytoshia brevicaudata*. **1968** *NZ Contemp. Dict. Suppl.* (Collins) 21 *Wairepo... n.* in N.Z., sting-ray.

whaka blonde /ˈwɒkəˈblɒnd/. *Derog*. Also **waka blonde**. [f. ironical application to the Maori guides at the *Whaka*(rewarewa) tourist attraction at Rotorua.] A Maori woman.
1950 p.c. Robert Barraclough. *whaka blonde*, a North Island term for Maori women. **1953** 14 M A17 Thames DHS 28 Waka blonde (wocka blonde) **1981** *Avondale College Slang Words* (Auckland) (Goldie Brown Collect.) Feb. *whaka blonde*: bleached/dyed hair on a Maori. **1988** MCGILL *Dict. Kiwi Slang* 121 *waka blonde* a Maori woman; offensive.

whakahuia, var. WAKA HUIA.

whakapapa. [Ma. /ˈfakapapa/: Williams 259 *Whakapapa*... 6. n. Genealogical table.] A genealogical table, family tree. **a.** Of Maori.
1904 TREGEAR *Maori Race* 384 The recital of genealogies (*whaka papa*) was sometimes assisted by the use of a notched or carved piece of wood (*rakau whakapapa*). **1933** *Na To Hoa Aroha* (1988) III. 73 The whakapapas preserved are those of rangatira lines, which practically obliterated existing genealogies... You must deny the latter any whakapapa system. **1940** WAITE *Port Molyneux* 35 To check the foregoing, here is Tuhawaiki's own Whakapapa (family tree) as dictated by him to Shortland in 1844. **1963** HILLIARD *Piece of Land* 18 You don't know them yourself! You don't even know your own *whakapapa*! **1977** REED *Treasury Maori Exploration* 21 A study of various whakapapa casts a great deal of doubt on such an assumption, for there may have been as many as three Kupes. **1982** *Dominion* (Wellington) 17 Feb. 9 He nods toward the dark interior of the meeting house. 'I couldn't get up in there and recite my whakapapa.' **1994** *Marist Messenger* Nov. 45 Many early societies lay..stress on descent and kinships, and we are all familiar in New Zealand with the term 'Whakapapa'.
b. Of Pakeha.
1992 *Metro* (Auckland) Feb. 118 White people too need a sense of whakapapa and a place to stand. **1992** *Listener* 17 Oct. 37 The Brierley tribe has a proud whakapapa. **1992** *Dominion* (Wellington) 28 Dec. 6 The *whakapapa* of the House of Windsor and its extended family is stored in Ken's mind.
Hence **whakapapa** *v*., to recite or recall a whakapapa; to trace a lineage.
1992 *Evening Post* (Wellington) 5 Nov. 6 He fails to mention..the fact that all the tribes can whakapapa back to the first landing of the canoes more than 1000 years ago. **1995** *Mana* 9 (Winter issue) 7 Mawhera's shareholders are people who can whakapapa back to the original owners of the Arahura land.

Whakatane harrow(s). *Obs*. [A proprietary name f. the town of *Whakatane* in the Bay of Plenty where the harrows were manufactured.] A set of patent harrows, often familiarly called (p.c. Dr Des Hurley, Taranaki) 'Whakatanes'.
1928 *NZ Dairy Produce Exporter* 26 May 29 [Advt] Get to grips with the sod bound grass... The strong tines of the harrows break up the unproductive root-mats and destroy moss, therefore, treat your pastures with— The Whakatane Harrows... Pulled one way these harrows give a 5-inch tine cultivation; reversed and pulled the other way, a 3-inch tripod effect. **1931** *Exporter and Home Jrnl.* Feb. [front cover] [Advt] Superior to all Imitations. The Whakatane Harrow. Three Harrows in One.

whakou, var. WHAWHAKOU.

whale.
1. Whales, whalers, and whaling were of special significance in early New Zealand. The names of only those whales most freq. found or previously hunted in New Zealand waters are represented in 2 below with a few select (mainly early) quotations. See also *bay whale* (BAY 2), FIN FISH.
2. With a modifier: **beaked, black, blue, Bryde's, finback (finner, fin,** occas. **razorback), goose-beak(ed), humpback (New Zealand humpback,** also **humpy), killer, pike (piked, pike-headed, minke, stickleback), pilot, porpoise (Arnoux's beaked), pygmy right, pygmy (pigmy) sperm, right (southern right), scamperdown (Gray's beaked), sei, sperm** (early **spermaceti), strap-toothed, sulphur-bottom.**

(1) **beaked whale.** [Cf. OED *whale* 1 b (a).] See *scamperdown whale* (15) below. See also *Arnoux's beaked whale* (11) below.
1922 *NZJST* V. 136 The southern beaked whale..has been frequently cast ashore at the Chatham Islands, less commonly on the New Zealand coast.

(2) **a. black whale.** See *right whale* (14) below. Also *attrib*.
1831 BELL *Let.* Nov. in McNab *Old Whaling Days* (1913) 3 The black whale fishery was tried in New Zealand some years ago, but it was abandoned until last year, when it was renewed. **1835** YATE *New Zealand* (1970) 27 In Cloudy Bay are several large whaling establishments; as, in calving time, that large sheet of water is visited by immense numbers of the black whale. **1873** *TrNZI* V. 156 The Black Whale is the largest and best known of all the whales on the New Zealand coast, reaching a length of 60 feet. Its huge bones may be seen strewn on the beach in great profusion at any of the Whaling Stations. **1887** *Auckland Weekly News* 28 May 8 The baleen from our Southern 'right whale,' commonly known as the 'black whale,' is not so valuable as that procured from the northern animal. **1972** GASKIN *Whales Dolphin & Seals* 85 In the days of bay whaling in the southern hemisphere, and particularly New Zealand, this species was called the 'common whale' or 'black whale'. To the pelagic whalers it was the 'right' whale to catch since it floated after being killed and had a very high oil yield compared with rorquals or the humpback. **1982** MORTON *Whale's Wake* 23 The Southern right whale—usually called the black whale by the British—migrated to calve in New Zealand..bays.
b. In composition: **black whaler,** a whaling ship (or person) that fishes for the black whale; **black-whaling** *n*. and *attrib*., the hunting and capture of the black whale.
1832 HAY *Notices of NZ* 136 The Middle Island is frequented by the **black whalers** belonging to Van Diemen's Land..fisheries. **1836** RHODES *Jrnl. Barque 'Australian'* 7 Aug. (1954) 10 He plainly saw..[the crew] were too lazy for **black whaling**, and advised me to go after sperm. **1836** WELLER *Lett.* 29 Feb. in McLintock *Hist. of Otago* (1949) 70 People are Black Whaling mad, since the news of [failure of the] Davis Straits Fishery has arrived. **1954** STRAUBEL in Rhodes *Jrnl. Barque 'Australian'* (1954) xv He was authorised, should the prospects of black whaling not prove to be good, to..engage in sperm whaling.

(3) **blue whale.** *Balaenoptera musculus* (fam. Balaenopteridae), a giant (25–30 m) whale, once a mainstay of the Antarctic whaling industry and occasionally taken in New Zealand waters. See also *sulphur-bottom* (19) below.
1912 WAITE *Guide to Whales & Dolphins of NZ* 5 The Canterbury Museum possesses..the skeleton of an enormous Blue Whale, 87 feet in length. **1922** *NZJST* V. 133 The blue whale..is the first of the four species of rorquals, or finners, to be mentioned. It is the largest species of whale, and, indeed, of all animals, living and extinct. **1990** BAKER *Whales & Dolphins* 66 There have been 9 strandings of Blue Whales on the New Zealand coast, the most celebrated of which was the 26.5m specimen which came ashore at Okarito, South Westland, in 1908.

(4) **Bryde's whale** /ˈbrudəz/. [Origin unknown.] *Balaenoptera edeni* (fam. Balaenopteridae), a small (14 m), slender baleen whale taken at Great Barrier Island Whaling Station in the 1950s.
1965 *NZSc. Review* XXIII. 19 For a time Bryde's Whales..figured in the catches at Great Barrier Island. **1990** BAKER *Whales & Dolphins* 72 At close quarters at sea, Bryde's (pronounced broodahs) whales can be distinguished by the presence of three ridges on the head anterior to the blowhole, rather than the single ridge characteristic of other rorquals.

(5) **finback (finner, fin,** occas. **razorback).** [Cf. OED *finner* esp. the Rorqual from the fact of having a dorsal fin, 1793.] *Balaenoptera physalus* (fam. Balaenopteridae), once an important species in the Antarctic whaling industry, occasionally seen in New Zealand waters.
1837 BEST *Journal* 2 July (1966) 89 [On the voyage out] There was a cry of 'a fish, a fish' how very odd thought I but..there *was* a fish..this creature which was a Finner and consequently not near the size of a Whale proper. **1838** POLACK *NZ* I. 323 Among the leviathans, who sport in shoals around these shores *fin-back. Ibid.* II. 407 The Razorback is so termed from that part being remarkably serrated; its snout is very much pointed, like to the Porpoise. **1848** WAKEFIELD *Handbook for NZ* 180 Shingles, N.Z. [per] 1000, 6s. to 8s..whalebone [per] ton, 135*l*. to 140*l*.—finners, 40*l*. **1875** *TrNZI* VII. 252 Finners (or Fin-backs) [1875 *Note*] Whalers often speak of right whales as finners or fin-fish, from their yielding baleen or 'fin' as they term it. **1922** *NZJST* V. 133 The common finner (*Balaenoptera physal[u]s*) may be thus defined: Dorsal fin triangular, low, at commencement of last fourth of body. **1972** GASKIN *Whales, Dolphins & Seals* 70 The fin whale, also known as the finner, finback or common rorqual by whalers, is somewhat sleeker in build than the blue whale, with a less blunt snout and a more streamlined head. **1985** DAWSON *NZ Whales & Dolphin Digest* 53 In size, Fin Whales are second only to Blue Whales... The species is also known as Finback or Finner, and Razorback.

(6) **goose-beak(ed) whale.** *Ziphius cavirostris* (fam. Ziphiidae), a toothed whale of up to 5–7 m in length, often stranded on New Zealand beaches.
1880 *TrNZI* XII. 241 [Title] Notes on *Ziphius (Edpidon) novae-zealandia*..Goose-beaked whale. **1922** *NZJST* V. 136 The goose-beak whale (*Ziphius cavirostris*) has a short beak with the lower jaw slightly longer than the upper and turned up a little at the tip. **1944** *NZEF Times* 24 Jan. 2 It was identified by museum authorities..as a goose-beaked whale. **1985** DAWSON *NZ Whale & Dolphin Digest* 101 Cuvier's Beaked Whale... The species is also known as Goosebeak Whale.

(7) **a. humpback (New Zealand humpback) whale** (also *ellipt*. **humpback, humpy,** occas. **hunchback).** *Megaptera novaeangliae* (fam.

Balaenopteridae), a long-finned, hump-backed, commercially depleted baleen whale.

1836 Log 'Mary Mitchell' 7 Aug. in McNab Old Whaling Days (1913) 453 5 boats in chased a humpback. **1848** WAKEFIELD Handbook NZ 129 They [sc. shore-stations] are fitted out for the capture of the black or 'right' whale, but occasionally sperm or hump-back [Balaena Gibbosa] also near the land sufficiently to be taken by the shore-parties. **1904** HUTTON & DRUMMOND Animals NZ 44 The Hump-back is known by its long flippers, which are indented along the margins. **1874** TrNZI VI. 255 Megaptera novae-zealandiae... The New Zealand Humpback. **1922** [see whaling-station (WHALING)]. **1947** POWELL Native Animals NZ 89 The Humpback is taken commercially in Cook Strait, the whaling station being situated just within the entrance to Tory Channel. **1956** TrRSNZ LXXXIV. 149 Humpback oil is listed in an account of progress at Cloudy Bay in 1841. **1982** GRADY Perano Whalers 19 [The Perano whalers] used to 'round up' humpback whales much as a sheepdog rounds up sheep and drives them into a pen. Ibid. 227 Humpies—Humpback whales. **1982** MORTON Whale's Wake 26 Humpback whales are so named because of the curved shape of their backs when diving and not because of a real hump. English whalemen usually referred to them..more correctly as 'hunchbacks', and 'four hunchbacks' were reported as being taken at Kapiti Island in 1841.

b. Special Comb. **humpback hook**, see quot.

1982 MORTON Whale's Wake 26 Humpbacks..very often sank after being killed... A special harpoon was developed which, if plunged into a sinking whale, would hold well enough to enable the whale to be raised from the bottom by the ship's winch. It was called a 'humpback hook'.

(8) **killer whale**. Also ellipt. **killer**. Orcinus orca (fam. Delphinidae), a strikingly coloured black and white toothed whale commonly seen in New Zealand waters.

1836 Log 'Mary Mitchell' in McNab Old Whaling Days (1913) 435 4 boats returned without Seeing anything except a Killer. **1838** POLACK NZ II. 407 A more destructive and wholesale species of enemy is found in a species of Grampus, called by the South seamen the 'Killer,' which is said to be (man excepted)..[the Razorback whale's] greatest scourge. **1982** GRADY Perano Whalers 227 Killer whales—Grampus, or Orcinus orca. Attacks other whales and marine animals.

(9) **minke** /'mɪŋki/)(or **pike, piked, pikeheaded**) **whale**, occas. **stickleback** (see quot. 1982). Balaenoptera acutorostrata (fam. Balaenoptridae), a small (9 m) streamlined baleen whale occas. commercially fished.

1848 WAKEFIELD Handbook for NZ 153 Of Whales, there are the Sperm.., the Pike-headed.., and the Black or Right whale. **1878** TrNZI X. 27 Balaenoptera huttoni... This is the pike whale of the southern seas. **1968** Fish Res Bull I. 29 Balaenoptera acutorostrata..the Piked or Minke Whale. **1949** Southern Cross (Wellington) 23 June 2 The whale was a little fellow, a bull of the variety known as the piked whale. **1982** GRADY Perano Whalers 228 Stickleback—A minke whale. Balaenoptera acutorostrata... The stickleback was also sometimes called the pike whale by the Perano whalers. **1985** DAWSON NZ Whale & Dolphin Digest 46 Minkes are also known as Piked Whales, Little Finners and Lesser Rorquals. The name Minke is most common, and is pronounced 'minkie'.

(10) **pilot whale**. Globicephala melaena (fam. Delphinidae), a toothed whale up to 6 m in length, blue or dark grey with often a light saddle-patch behind the dorsal fin, frequently involved in mass strandings on New Zealand beaches. See also BLACKFISH n.[1] 1.

1877 TrNZI IX. 481 Globicephalus macrorhynchus... Large-beaked Pilot Whale, or South Sea Blackfish. **1965** NZ Sc. Review XXIII. 23 Also numbered in this group is the common blackfish or pilot whale, which sometimes strands itself on the coast. **1985** DAWSON NZ Whale & Dolphin Digest 80 Pilot whales are also known as Pothead Whales or Blackfish, from the shape of the head and the colour of the fin and back.

(11) **porpoise whale**. Obs. (Now known as **Arnoux's beaked whale**.) Berardius arnouxi (fam. Ziphiidae), a heavy, robust, beaked, toothed whale of up to 9 m in length occasionally stranded on New Zealand beaches.

1878 TrNZI X. 338 Berardius arnuxii.. [sic] An adult male of the porpoise whale was captured in the entrance to Wellington Harbour on 12th July 1877. **1993** Dominion (Wellington) 5 Jan. 8 The rare arnoux's beaked whale towed out of the Marlborough Sounds..had not been seen since it was set free... The nine-metre whale became stranded near Havelock.

(12) **pygmy right whale**. Caperea marginata (fam. Balaenidae), the smallest (6 m) of the baleen whales, distinguished by a dorsal fin and strongly arched mouth.

1922 NZJST V. 132 The pygmy right whale..differs from the right whale in having a dorsal fin and in its much smaller size, 20 ft. being about its maximum length. **1990** BAKER Whales & Dolphins 77 Pygmy Right Whales live in the southern hemisphere between about 31° and 52° S, and are mostly known from strandings.

(13) **pygmy (pigmy) sperm whale**. Kogia breviceps (fam. Physeteridae), a small (3–4 m) toothed whale occasionally stranded on New Zealand beaches.

1922 NZJST V. 135 The pygmy sperm whale (Kogia breviceps) agrees with its huge cousin in having teeth in the lower jaw only, and in the asymmetrical skull. **1972** GASKIN Whales Dolphins & Seals 102 The head of the pigmy sperm whale is bluntly pointed and the lower jaw is small and set back beneath the head, so that to the layman it has a strong superficial resemblance to a shark. **1985** DAWSON NZ Whale & Dolphin Digest 92 Pygmy sperm whales seldom jump.

(14) **right (southern right) whale**. Balaena glacialis (fam. Balaenopteridae), a large (18 m) robust baleen whale most sought after by 19th century whalers in New Zealand waters. Hence also **right whaling**, the capture and processing of right whales (see quot. 1956). See also bay whale (BAY 2), black whale (2) a above, FIN FISH, TOHORA.

1836 Piraki Log 18 Apr. (1911) 33 Saw and was in chase of a Right Whale but could not come up. **1839** WALTON Twelve Months' Residence 20 From May to December, the bays of New Zealand are frequented by what is called the Black or Right Whale. **1848** WAKEFIELD Handbook for NZ 129 They [sc. shore-stations] are fitted out for the capture of the black or 'right' whale. **1887** southern 'right whale' [see (2) a above]. **1947** POWELL Native Animals NZ 88 Southern Right Whale (Balaena australis), or Tohora of the Maoris... The advent of flexible steel rendered whalebone obsolete and valueless, but not before the Right Whale was harassed to near extinction. **1956** TrRSNZ LXXXIV. 155 In the 1830's and 1840's extensive right whaling was carried on from vessels anchored in Cloudy Bay. **1972** [see (2) a above].

(15) **scamperdown (Gray's beaked) whale**. [Origin uncertain: poss. from a local place-name (unidentified); poss. from the name of an early sailing vessel; perhaps an alteration or adaptation of Camperdown used, e.g., as the name of the A. Thomson's west Otago station near Kelso.] Mesoplodon grayi (fam. Ziphiidae), a small, slender, beaked and toothed whale regularly stranded on New Zealand beaches. See also (1) above.

1864 THATCHER Songs of the War 10 The harpoon skilfully they threw, And fastened on the Scamperdown. **1873** TRNZI V. 166 Dolichodon layardi Scamperdown Whale. **1917** WILLIAMS Dict. Maori Lang. 39 Hakura,.. Mesoplodon species, Scamperdown whale. **1969** KNOX Natural History Canterbury 523 Several specimens of goose-beaked whales, porpoise whales, and straptooth and scamperdown whales have been recorded [off Canterbury]. **1972** GASKIN Whales, Dolphins & Seals 109 The Scamperdown Whale or Gray's Beaked Whale... This whale, which appears on the basis of known strandings..to be the commonest member of the genus in New Zealand waters, reaches a maximum length of about 18ft. **1985** DAWSON NZ Whale & Dolphin Digest 95 The name Scamperdown is commonly used in New Zealand, and is derived from the location of an early New Zealand stranding of this species. Elsewhere it is usually known as Gray's Beaked Whale. **1996** Sunday Star-Times (Auckland) 14 Jan. A3 A fisherman spotted the dead whales—thought to be scamperdowns, a type of beaked whale—on the beach 24km north of Muriwai.

(16) **sei whale**. Balaenoptera borealis (fam. Balaenopteridae), a surface-feeding baleen whale up to 18 m in length which replaced blue and fin whales in commercial catches in the 1960s.

1922 NZJST V. 133 The Sei whale (Balaenoptera borealis) has a falcate dorsal fin situated at the commencement of the last third of the body. **1985** DAWSON NZ Whale & Dolphin Digest 51 Sei Whales are most likely to be confused with Bryde's Whales, and possibly Fin Whales and Minke Whales—these are all species which never show the flukes on sounding.

(17) **sperm** (early **spermaceti**) **whale**. Physeter macrocephalus (fam. Physeteridae), the largest of toothed whales (20 m), and from 1792 commercially exploited in New Zealand waters for sperm oil. See also PARAOA n.[1]

1797 Minute of Board of Trade 26 Dec. in McNab Hist. Records (1908) I. 216 A memorial of the merchant-adventurers in the southern whale-fishery..representing..that they have strong reason to suppose that the spermaceti whale and seal fishery might be carried on to great advantage..off the coasts of New Holland, the New Hebrides..New Zealand. **1802** KING Queries to Whalers 21 May in McNab Hist. Records (1908) I. 234 We have always observed the spermaceti whales going in large scholes [sic] to the northward. **1838** POLACK NZ I. 323 Among the leviathans, who sport in shoals around these shores, the párá párúá, or sperm-whale. **1956** TrRSNZ LXXXIV. 149 Whaling in New Zealand waters commenced with the arrival of the 'William and Anne' in 1792, but sperm whales were then the main objective and remained so until right whaling commenced in the 1820's. **1982** GRADY Perano Whalers 228 Sperm whale—Also called Cachalot... This species was hunted by the Peranos off the N.Z. coast in their Antarctic pattern chaser, s.s. Orca in their last two years of whaling, 1963–64. **1990** BAKER Whales & Dolphins 76 Sperm whales in southern Cook Strait are now the subject of popular whale-watching cruises from Kaikoura.

(18) **strap-toothed whale** (or ellipt. **straptooth**). Mesoplodon layardi (fam. Ziphiidae), a magpie-coloured, toothed whale, distinguished by a striking tusk-like tooth on each jaw.

1922 NZJST V. 136 The strap-toothed whale (Mesoplodon layardi) is, at least when adult, at once recognized by the two long strap-shaped teeth which, originating from the mandible in front of the hinder end of the symphysis, grow upwards and backwards, eventually curving round the upper jaw and preventing the mouth from being opened beyond a certain distance. **1985** DAWSON *NZ Whale & Dolphin Digest* 99 The bizarre teeth of the lower jaw give rise to the name strap-tooth.

(19) **sulphur-bottom (whale)**. The *blue whale* (3) above, the belly of which is often covered with a yellowish film of diatoms, hence 'sulphur (=yellow) bottom'.

1871 *TrNZI* III. 124 The *Physalus antarcticus*, also established on finner-fins or baleen imported from New Zealand, has been proved to be a distinct species of that genus, named Sulphur-bottoms by the whalers. **c1913** *Marlborough Express* (Blenheim) in Johnson *Life's Vagaries* (1970) 59 The sighted whale was a sulphur-bottom, rather a difficult whale to catch. **1968** *Fish Res. Bull. (NS)* I. 20 After blue whales have been in the polar seas for some months a film of diatoms begins to accumulate thickly on the skin, mainly on the ventral surface. When it becomes thick this film is yellow or orange, and this has led to the well known term 'sulphur bottom'. **1982** GRADY *Perano Whalers* 167 A red-letter day that caused considerable excitement was Saturday 2 July 1938 when the Peranos caught a sulphur bottom blue whale over 27 metres long.

3. *Special Comb*. **whaleback (whale's back)** [see OED *whaleback* (Geol.) a large mound shaped like the back of a whale, 1893], a whale-shaped ridge of land or hill-ridge; **whaleboat** *hist*. [used elsewhere but of special significance in NZ coastal waters: see OED 1756], a usu. double-ended rowing or sailing boat, built for speed and the ability to work in open water, equipped orig. to pursue and kill whales, but often used as a means of local travel (see esp. 1874 quot.); **whale chaser** *obs*. (also *ellipt*. **chaser**), a fast motor-boat, equipped with a harpoon gun, and built for pursuing and killing whales; **whale-chasing** *vbl. n*., the pursuit and capture of whales by the use of whale chasers; **whale-food** (also **whale's food**) [used elsewhere but recorded earliest in NZ: see OED 1865], WHALEFEED 1; **whale gun** (also **harpoon-gun**), a gun designed for firing harpoons at whales; **whale station**, *whaling-station* (WHALING); **whale-watching**, an organized tourist activity in an area frequented by whales, *spec*. one off the north-east coast of the SI centred on the town of Kaikoura.

1889 WILLIAMS & REEVES *Colonial Couplets* 3 Only think how much more graceful all the landscape will appear. No more pigroots, **whalebacks**, hogbacks— these names that shall not last. **1900** *Canterbury Old & New* 106 A low saddle (now known as Whale's back). **1933** *Press* (Christchurch) (Acland Gloss.) 30 Dec. 13 *Whale's back*.—A hill that rises steeply and slopes gradually down suggests a whale, and so there are hills and blocks of country in various parts of Canterbury called the W[hale]'s B[ack]. **1810** CHACE *Declaration* 12 Mar. in McNab *Hist. Records* (1908) I. 299 Being afraid of the consequences, he gave the natives who came on board the ship in a canoe off the East Cape a **whaleboat** to go on shore with another New Zealander. **1815** ELDER *Marsden's Lieutenants* (1934) 120 The next day I accompanied Mr. Kendall to Rangheehoo in the *Jefferson's* whaleboat. **1823** KENT *Log 'Mermaid'* 1 June in Howard *Rakiura* (1940) 343 James Caddell informed me of his having picked up part of a wreck together with most part of a whale boat upon a beach directly opposite this reef. **1838** *Piraki Log* 1 Mar. (1911) 67 Two men repairing the Whale Boat. **1843** SELWYN in *NZ Part II* (Church in the Colonies VII) 17 Aug. (1845) 11 [We] came to the house of a respectable English settler..who lent us his whale-boat, in which we rowed..across Wangaroa Harbour. **1850** TORLESSE *Papers* (1958) 126 Bought whale boat and paid John Hay for it..£20. **1863** MOSER *Mahoe Leaves* 18 We landed through the breakers..while a whaleboat that was out with us..had a very narrow chance of being capsized. **1874** BAINES *Edward Crewe* 127 I built her whale-boat fashion, twenty-nine feet over all, five feet eight inches beam, and two feet deep midships, sharp at both ends, the stem more bluff above the water-line than the bow. **1898** HOCKEN *Contributions* 54 According to instructions the whaleboat met the weary travellers at the head of the Otago. **1926** COWAN *Travel in NZ* II. 169 Three of us once cruised about [Stewart Island's] secret coves..in a whaleboat carrying mainsail and jib. **1948** HENDERSON *Taina* vii He also trained his crews and steered, winning altogether thirty-two first-class prizes for yachts, whale-boats, and other types. *Ibid.* 4 Whaleboat men..are not easily put out of action. **1951** CRESSWELL *Canterbury Tales* 144 Captain Cain lived in a cob house on the hill and superintended the whaleboat service. **1985** LANGDALE-HUNT *Last Entail Male* 127 We made it safely back to Pitt after a fairly long tow because the whaleboat was thirty feet long and it was a fairly stiff head wind. **1948** *Our Own Country* 166 Two chocolate-coloured **whale-chasers** were lying still..at the entrance to the [Queen Charlotte] Sound. **1965** GILLHAM *Naturalist in NZ* 133 Bearing down on it at 40 miles an hour went the two tiny speedboat whale chasers, each with the harpoon gunner poised in the bow. **1973** NEWTON *Big Country* (1977) 39 Originally a 'chaser' in the Perano whaling fleet she was purchased by the Moletas when the Peranos discontinued their whaling operations... These boats have a maximum speed of well over 30 knots. **1993** *North & South* (Auckland) July 107 I showed her the old whale chaser that had, inexplicably, ended up inland. **1965** GILLHAM *Naturalist in NZ* 132 The Cook Strait islands must be one of the few places in the world where one could watch **whale-chasing** from the shore. *Ibid*. 133 The Cook Strait method of whale-chasing, which was first used in 1911, has been described as the most exciting. **1836** GREENE in McNab *Old Whaling Days* (1913) 154 Scarcity of **Whale Food**. **1867** THOMSON *Twelve Yrs. Canterbury* 29 The surface of the sea..was literally crowded for miles together with swarms of small bright-red fish, rather larger than good sized shrimps. I was told..that no use is ever made of them, nor could I find that they had any name assigned to them but that of 'whale's food', as the whales are said to live on them. **1904** LANCASTER *Sons o' Men* 112 The water ran rust-brown with the whale food. **1920** *Quick March* 10 Feb. 37 [Heading] A **Whale Gun**. Down at the whaling station at Kaikoura some time ago I saw the first breechloader..manufactured in this country. This was a whaling gun used for harpooning 'right' and humpback whales by the Johnson party... The sight of this harpoon-gun..set me thinking. **1849** McKILLOP *Reminiscences* 41 Frequent attempts have been made at the **whale stations** (at which places he was even more dreaded than elsewhere) to poison him. **1990** BAKER *Whales & Dolphins* 76 Sperm whales in southern Cook Strait are now the subject of popular **whale-watching** cruises from Kaikoura. **1993** *Dominion* (Wellington) 27 Mar. 20 Apparently whale-watching was a favourite Maori activity... This rubbish is on a par with Maori claims to special rights to commercial whale-watching activities. **1995** *Ibid*. 27 Nov. 5 [Heading] Whale-watching Diana gets a show. Endangered whales off Patagonia put on a show..for Princess Diana on..her debut..in Argentina.

whalebird. *Obs*. [Spec. use of *whalebird*: see OED 1768.] Any of various seabirds thought to indicate the presence of plankton-feeding whales by following the same food, esp. *Prion* spp., and esp. the *fairy prion Pachyptila turtur* (PRION 3), and the *broad-billed prion P. vittata* (PRION 2) also known as the *dove petrel* (PETREL 2 (8)).

1849 POWER *Sketches in NZ* 72 A few curlews, whale-birds, sand-pipers, and wild ducks frequent the coast and river swamps, but are generally fishy, and unfit for the table. **1862** CHUDLEIGH *Diary* 12 Nov. (1950) 65 I roade [*sic*] into a fligh[t] of whalebirds on the coast. There must have been near a million. **1870** *TrNZI* II. 76 Sterna longipennis... The black-billed, swallow-tailed Whale-bird seems constantly to frequent our coasts and harbours. **1888** BULLER *Birds NZ* II. 210 The presence of large flocks at sea is regarded by whalers as a favourable sign..and among sailors the Dove Petrel is generally known as the 'Whale bird'. **1904** HUTTON & DRUMMOND *Animals NZ* 253 The Whale Birds generally fly in flocks, with a zig-zag movement and a sharp motion of the wings, like a Snipe, and are rarely seen to sit on the water. **1917** WILLIAMS *Dict. Maori Lang.* 518 *Totorore*,.. *Prion banksii*, whale-bird. **1957** MONCRIEFF *NZ Birds* 43 Dove Petrel or Whale Bird (*Prion* spp)... Cut through the air with the swiftness of a meteor. **1966** FALLA et al. *Birds of NZ* 38 On superficial view, all prions, or whale-birds as they are sometimes known in sealers' usage, look very much alike. **1985** [see PRION 2].

whale-feed.

1. *Munida gregaria* (fam. Galatheidae), a small (4 cm) red lobster-like animal, the swimming juveniles of which congregate in dense surface shoals esp. in southern New Zealand waters, and are also known as **grit**, **koura rangi**, **lobster krill**, and (from a component of the shoal) **squat lobster**; occas. applied loosely and colloquially to other small marine shoaling organisms. See also *whale-food* (WHALE 3).

1880 SENIOR *Travel & Trout* 292 In the autumn..they follow the 'grit', or whale-feed, which is chiefly a small shrimp. **1898** *TrNZI* XXX. 580 It is closely allied to the red crustacean or 'whale-feed' (*Grimothea gregaria*), which is so abundant in Dunedin Harbour in the summer months. **1907** *Ibid*. XXXIX. 485 We are not yet able to establish the identity of this species with the free-swimming form known as 'whale-feed'. **1917** WILLIAMS *Dict. Maori Lang.* 176 *Koura rangi*, *Grimothea gregaria*, whale-feed. **1923** *NZJST* VI. 111 Every summer large shoals of a bright-red shrimp are met with in the sea round the coast of New Zealand. This animal, popularly known as 'whale-feed,' is a swimming stage in the life-history of a crustacea technically known as *Munida gregaria*. **1929** BEST *Fishing Methods* 64 The *pehipehi* [porpoise] acts as a guide to whales, conducting them to places where *terehua* (whale-feed) abounds. **1956** GRAHAM *Treasury NZ Fishes* 252 Many Tarakihi..were found crammed to capacity with Whalefeed..in both stages, namely, bottom and swimming forms. **1967** NATUSCH *Animals NZ* 113 Known in the south as whale-feed, shoals of pinkish red *Munida*..swarm near the surface at times. **1974** *NZ Nature Heritage* XLIII. 1195 The Euphausiacea are shrimp-like and include species known as krill or whalefeed. **1981** PROBERT *Seas Around NZ* 129 [Caption] Adult lobster krill, or red whale feed. **1987** POWELL *Native Animals NZ* 33 In Cook Strait and off the east coast of the South Island 'whale-feed' commonly occurs in such vast concentrations that pinkish or bluish patches on the surface of the sea are visible from a distance. The Squat Lobster *Munida gregaria* can be one of the principal species occurring in these swarms.

2. *transf. West Coast*. The young of *Gobiomorphus* spp. caught by whitebaiters.

1981 DENNIS *Paparoas Guide* 189 Tiny, largely transparent bullies [*Gobiomorphus* spp.] are also amongst the migrants... These are sometimes caught in large quantities by whitebaiters. The [whitebait] fishermen call them 'Dan Doolin Spawn' or 'Whalefeed'.

whaler: see SHARK 2 (6).

whaler.

1. [Used elsewhere but recorded earliest in NZ: see OED 2 a, 1806.] A ship fitted to catch and process whales usu. for their oil. See also *black whaler* (WHALE 2 (2) b).

1801 Lieut.-Gov. *King* 31 Dec. in McNab *Hist. Records* (1908) I. 224 The objection on the part of the masters of the whalers is the frequent gales of wind that happen on this coast. **1815** KENDALL 25 Nov. in Elder *Marsden's Lieutenants* (1934) 90 Saturday, 25th.— Went on board the whalers, and also paid a visit to some natives. **1825** MARSDEN *Lett. & Jrnls.* 17 Mar. (1932) 415 He was so far lost to all religious feelings when I was in New Zealand that he would contend that the civilization of the young women was promoted by their living as prostitutes on board the whalers. **1830** CRAIK *New Zealanders* 175 [Timber] had been brought to England by the Catherine whaler. **1840** BUNBURY *Report* 28 June in *GBPP House of Commons 1841 (No.311)* 108 Disputes also among the English residents on shore and the crews of the whalers, are by no means unfrequent. **1978** JARDINE *Shadows on Hill* 15 The whaler was taken in tow then drawn stern first to the shallow water.

2. [f. *whaler* a person engaged in whaling: see OED 1, 1684.] **a.** In special collocations: **whalers' Maori**, a kind of pidgin Maori; **whalers' tea**, an infusion of manuka ('tea-tree') leaves.

c1840-41 IRONSIDES *Journal* in MacDonald *Pages from Past* (1933) 130 The language was a piebald mixture, generally known as '**Whalers' Maori**'. **1859** THOMSON *Story NZ* I. 294 Whalers, in their intercourse with each other, were guided by well-defined laws and customs; and intercourse between the races was conducted in a piebald language called Whaler's Maori, which was English embroidered with native words. **1880** SENIOR *Travel & Trout* 236 In this bay [*sc.* Poverty] the whalers—the rollicking, hard-drinking, Maori-marrying fellows from Botany Bay, who..invented a mixed language known as whalers' Maori—had important stations. **1843** 4 Nov. in Shortland *S. Dist. NZ* (1851) 127 As Mr Hughes and his [companion whalers at Onekakara] had long since drained their last can of grog, a capacious kettle of **whalers' tea** stood on the hearth, ready for use of those who liked it. This tea, an infusion of 'manuka' boughs, is a beverage much drunk by the whalers; it is very wholesome, and, although not palatable at first, appears to be agreeable to those who have become accustomed to it.

b. *transf.* Also **Murrumbidgee whaler**. [Orig. Austral.: see AND *n.*[1] b, 1878 'A swagman whose route follows the course of a river.'] SWAGGER 1; also transf. to an itinerant Australian preacher (see quot. 1909).

1899 BELL *In Shadow of Bush* 17 Get up, Davie [a Sundowner]..Get up, you Murrumbidgee whaler, and clear the deck. **1905** *Truth* 11 Nov. 1 What then is Woolley [who has admitted enjoying free hospitality]— He's a murrumbidgee whaler or sundowner. **1909** *Ibid.* 6 Nov. 1 Therefore, Woollcombe, get thee hence; go home thou wowser on the wallaby; hump bluey, carry Matilda, pad the hoof, thou parsonical howler, thou Wowseristic whaler Woollcombe.

whaling. *Hist.* Used *attrib.* in special Comb. **whaling-ground**, an area of ocean wherein whales, being abundant, may be profitably taken (see quot. 1843); **whaling party**, a gang of men engaged on a shore whaling-station; **whaling season**, the time of the year when whales may be profitably taken, usu. April to October for right whales; **whaling station** [recorded earliest in Australia: see AND 1833] (also *ellipt.* **station**), *shore-station* (STATION 1).

1843 DIEFFENBACH *Travels in NZ* I. 46 During the six remaining months of the year the ships cruising in the '**whaling-ground**' fall in with many whales. This whaling-ground extends from the Chatham Islands to the eastward of the northern island of New Zealand, and from thence to Norfolk Island. **1921** *Quick March* 11 Apr. 29 When the **whaling parties** [on Kapiti] were paid for their greasy work—so much a 'lay'—there were lashings of rum. **1837** 20 Jan. in McNab *Old Whaling Days* (1913) 178 The **whaling season** commences at Otago the latter end of March, during which whales are in abundance throughout the bay, and often caught within the harbour. **1839** *Piraki Log* 1 Oct. (1911) 99 This day the Whaling Season ends, when the Boats were clear'd out, wash'd, oil'd, and taken on the Flat; likewise the Whaling Gear put up, Falls coiled away, &c. **1892** Osborn in RICHARDS *Foveaux Whaling Yarns* (1995) 40 But it was coming on the whaling season [*i.e. winter*] and so we left for the west coast of New Zealand for a three months hunt for bay whales. **1840** *NZ Jrnl.* I. 113 The settlement is abreast of our anchorage, at the foot of the slope, and consists of the owner's house and small **whaling station**. **1851** SHORTLAND *S. Dist. NZ* 176 At several of the stations, I had been able to obtain information from sources equally trustworthy. **1863** MOSER *Mahoe Leaves* 11 Our work was but begun, and considering the examples that the whaling stations exhibited..we dreaded the introduction of more. **1898** HOCKEN *Contributions* 38 One night..Dr. Shortland took up his quarters in a cask, probably an old whale oil barrel which had been washed ashore from some whaling station. **1922** *NZJST* V. 132 Whaling-stations for hunting humpbacks are now established at Whangamumu, near the Bay of Islands; Tory Channel, in the Marlborough Sounds district; and Kaikoura. **1930** GUTHRIE *NZ Memories* 11 Later, whaling stations were established all along the coast. **1959** SLATTER *Gun in My Hand* 171 The *Tamahine* rounding Dieffenbach Point and out past the whaling station at Te Awaiti. **1968** JOHNSON *Turn of Tide* 12 At the beginning of the year I was appointed to Te Awaiti, the whaling station.

whanake. Also early **wanaki**, **whanaka**, **whanako**. [Ma. /ˈfanake/: Williams 487 *Whanake*.] CABBAGE-TREE 1. See also TI *n.*[1] 1 a.

1844 in Shortland *S. Dist. NZ* (1851) 230 This was also the season for digging the 'ti' or 'whanake', which grows in great plenty and vigour near the base of the mountains. **1867** HOOKER *Handbook* 769 Whanako. *Cordyline australis*. **1874** BAINES *Edward Crewe* 45 The natives often snare these birds [*sc.* pigeons], particularly when they are feeding on the 'Wanaki', a kind of cabbage-tree palm. **1889** KIRK *Forest Flora* 295 W.L. Williams informs me that it [*sc.* cabbage tree] is termed 'kauka' or 'whanaka' by the East Cape natives. **1922** COWAN *NZ Wars* (1955) I. 353 In the rear of the church surrounded by lines of *whanake* or cabbage-trees (these *whanake*, now grown to enormous trees, still adorn the old village-site), was the *kainga* Te Reinga. **1978** FULLER *Maori Food & Cook.* 6 Ti-kouka and whanake are varieties of the ti and there are many others.

whanako, var. WHANAKE.

whanau. [Ma. /ˈfaːnau/: Williams 487 *Whānau... 3. n.* Offspring, family group... *4.* Family. (mod.).] The extended family group. Often *attrib.* Cf. HAPU.

1938 MAKERETI *Old-Time Maori* 34 These families began with a man and his wife and children. When their children got married and had children, they would call themselves a whanau, or family group. **1949** [see TRIBE]. **1959** SINCLAIR *Hist. NZ* 20 The tribe was an extended kinship organisation made up of sub-tribes and whanau, family groups larger than the European family. **1972** IHIMAERA in *Some Other Country* (1984) 159 Anyway, she used to say, what with all my haddit kids and their haddit kids and all this haddit whanau being broke all the time..how can I afford to buy a new house? **1983** *Dominion* (Wellington) 12 Dec. 5 Two types of shares [in the Maori International company] will be available. The 'Whanau' or group package shares, resaleable only to the company to ensure it retains control, will be available to Maori groups with a small percentage offered to members of the public. **1986** *Metro* (Auckland) Sept. 68 Open plan schools..are able to put into practice many of the family values of taha Maori in what is sometimes termed a whanau grouping. **1991** *Dominion Sunday Times* (Wellington) 8 Dec. 9 Eddie had never really associated with the Glover Park whanau [*sc.* of the 'tribe' of street-people], preferring to find other places to sleep.

Hence **whanau-based**, founded on elements from within an extended family group; **whanauistic**, of or relating to the (communal) nature of a whanau.

1988 *Press* (Christchurch) 24 Aug. 3 The board cancelled a contract with the Rev. Harvey Ruru to run a **whanau-based** skills programme for young, disadvantaged people. **1994** *Dominion* (Wellington) 16 Sept. 9 Boarding house operator Billy White told Auckland District Court..a 'whanauistic' concept prevailed at his premises.

whapuka, whapuku, varr. HAPUKU.

wharangi. Mainly *NI*. Also early **warangai**, **warangi**. [Ma. /ˈfaraŋi/: Williams 489 *Wharangi...Melicope ternata*.] *Melicope ternata* (fam. Rutaceae), a spreading shrub or small tree. See also WHARANGIPIRO.

[**1820** LEE & KENDALL *NZ Gram. & Vocab.* 225 Wárangi; A tree so called.] **1838** POLACK *NZ* II. 400 There are many other woods of much service to Europeans, differing in quality, among others: the *Warangai*. **1853** HOOKER *II Flora Novae-Zelandiae I Flowering Plants* 43 Melicope *ternata*... 'Wharangi'. **1869** *TrNZI* I. (rev. edn.) 276 The Wharangi, or Wharangi-pirou..is a small tree, 12–25 feet high. **1878** BULLER *Forty Yrs. NZ* 502 The *Ririwa..Warangi..*and many more, are all flowering shrubs. **1905** *TrNZI* XXXVII. 114 *Melicope ternata..(Wharangi)*. The gum of this tree is chewed by the Maoris for foul breath. **1961** MARTIN *Flora NZ* 229 Amongst the shrubs that do not grow naturally in the southern part of the South Island we may note the Wharangi..and others less common. **1978** MOORE & IRWIN *Oxford Book NZ Plants* 90 *Melicope ternata*, wharangi. A small, much-branched tree of wooded cliffs facing the sea. **1995** CROWE *Which Native Plant?* 37 Māori traditionally used wharangi branchlets for head wreaths at tangi and the resin as a form of chewing gum... The white wood of wharangi turns pale brown as it dries..and was used by early cabinetmakers for inlaying. It also made good firewood.

wharangipiro. [Ma. /ˈfaraŋiˈpiro/ (*piro* =?'scented'): Williams 489 *Wharangi... Wharangi-piro, Olearia rani, O. furfuracea,* and *Melicope ternata*.] Any of the small trees AKEPIRO, HEKETARA, WHARANGI.

1853 HOOKER *II Flora Novae-Zelandiae I Flowering Plants* 117 Eurybia *Cunninghamii*... 'Wharangi-piro',

WHARARIKI

Middle Island. **1867** HOOKER *Handbook* 769 Wharangi-pirou... *Melicope ternata*. **1869** [see WHARANGI]. **1906** CHEESEMAN *Manual NZ Flora* 284 *O[learia] furfuracea*... A much branched shrub or small tree 8–20 ft. high; North Island... *Wharangipiro*; *Akepiro*. **1940** LAING & BLACKWELL *Plants NZ* 444 *Olearia furfuracea* (*The Akepiro*)... A bush plant. Maori names, *Wharangipiro, Akepiro*.

wharariki. [Ma. /ˈfarariki/: Williams 489 *Wharariki... 1. Phormium cookianum*, an inferior kind of New Zealand flax.] *Phormium cookianum* (formerly *colensoi*), *mountain flax* (FLAX 2 (1)).

1867 HOCHSTETTER *NZ* 152 We may distinguish about three principal varieties: 1) *Tuhara*..2) *Tihore*..3) *Wharariki*, mountain flax, with coarse fibres; little used. **1906** CHEESEMAN *Manual NZ Flora* 717 *Wharariki*... The small size, pale colour, yellowish flowers, and long twisted capsules distinguish this [*P. cookianum*] from *P. tenax*. **1946** *JPS* LV. 160 *Wharariki*..an inferior Maori flax. **1982** WILSON *Stewart Is. Plants* 300 *Phormium cookianum* Mountain Flax... Wharariki.

wharawhara. Also **Wara Wara**. [Ma. /ˈfarafara/: Williams 488 *Whara* (i)..*wharawhara* ..*Astelia banksii*.] ASTELIA 1. See also KOWHARAWHARA.

1844 Wara Wara [see KAHAKAHA]. **1874** BAINES *Edward Crewe* 154 [It was] greatly overgrown with whara-whara (aste[l]ia Banksii), a sword-leaved orchid. **1911** *TrNZI* XLIII. 198 Of epiphytes..the commonest and most noticeable are forms of wharawhara. **1922** [see ASTELIA 1]. **1946** *JPS* LV. 160 *Wharawhara*..has densely-growing tufts of ensiform leaves, and scrambles by long vines in the trees as does the kiekie; and among the leaves of these two plants was the home of the wood-fairies Nukumaitore. **1955** BOSWELL *Dim Horizons* 150 There were to be had for the climbing of the honey-sweet berries of the wharawhara, the tree-tussock, beautiful long scarlet fingers of gelatinous black-seeded berries which were our favourite of all. **1981** CROWE *Field Guide Native Edible Plants NZ* 74 Wharawhara has bright green berries which turn a deep red as they ripen, and are about 8 mm long.

whare. Also with much variety of form as **ware, wari, warree, warré, warri, warry, war-y** [?= /ˈwɒri/]; **wèrri, wharé, whari, wharre(y), wharry; wurrie** etc.; also occas. **fārre, forra, forry**, reflecting the main anglicized pronunciations /ˈwɒri/, /ˈwʌri/, /ˈfʌri/, /ˈfɒri/, and possibly with some type of initial aspirate ?/hwɒri/. [Ma. /ˈfare/: Williams 489 *whare 1*. n. House, hut, shed, habitation.: PPN **fale*.]

I. In Maori contexts. 1. A Maori house, building, or hut used for domestic or communal purposes.

[**1778** FORSTER *Observations* 284 A Comparative Table of the Various Languages in the Isles of the South-Sea... [English] *A House*... [New-Zeeland] te-fārre. **1807** SAVAGE *Some Acc. of NZ* 77 Wurrie..A house, or hut.] **1814** KENDALL 6 Sept. in Elder *Marsden's Lieutenants* (1934) 59 [The pa] consists of several warrees or small huts about five feet in height, seven in breadth, and eight or ten feet in length. **c1826–27** BOULTBEE *Journal* (1986) 111 house—wèrri. **1834** MARKHAM *NZ* (1963) 38 The House or as the Natives call it (Wurrie puppar) or Wooden House. **1841** BRIGHT *Handbook Emigrants* 46 These [potatoes] they store in *war-ys*. **1853** *NZGG* 13 June I. 9/57 The native population of Witiangi is very small. There are no wharres on the south shore. **1866** LUSH *Waikato Jrnls.* 13 Mar. (1982) 69 The chief gave up..his own *whare*, a comparatively new one. **1874** BAINES *Edward Crewe* 141 Enter a deserted native 'whari' or bushman's hut, see! the fern is alive with fleas. **1882** POTTS *Out in Open* 12 The visitors..joined the escort which stood grouped about some native warris. **1902** IRVINE & ALPERS *Progress of NZ* 429 A few expressive terms have been adopted into daily speech from Maori—*whare* (a hut), *pa* (a village)..are examples. **1908** BAUGHAN *Shingle-Short* 11 *Whare* (pronounce *Wharray*): A hut. **1921** [see OHU 1]. **1938** HYDE *Nor Yrs. Condemn* 131 He was in a comparatively big *whare*, with two rooms. **1965** BAXTER *Collected Poems* (1980) 323 And if I [a Maori gunner] could fly like a bird To my old granny's whare. **1986** OWEN & PERKINS *Speaking for Ourselves* 111 The Maoris at that time lived in whares, and they were just like the meetinghouse scaled down, with raupo walls and thatch, and an earthen floor covered with beautiful flax mats on which they used to sit or sleep.

2. Special Comb. with a Maori suffix defining the use or characteristics of a particular building including the occas. jocular or twee 'Pakeha' uses of *whare* (see *whare-iti, whare-tutae* below), and the occas. observed use of *Te Whare, Whareiti, Wharenui* as house-names in middle-class residential suburbs; or the parodic name *Waiwhare* ('why worry'). **whare hauhau** *Chatham Island hist.* [Ma. /ˈfare ˈhauhau/: cf. Williams 46 *Whare herehere, prison*: prob. a play on the Chatham Island *whare herehere* and its Hauhau occupants in the late 1860s], a lockup; **whare-iti** *tramping* [Ma. /ˈfare ˈiti/, lit. 'little house'], an outdoor toilet; **whare kai** [Ma. /ˈfare ˈkai/], the building on a marae in which food is served and eaten, the dining-hall; **whare karakia** [Ma. /ˈfare ˈkarakia/, *karakia* prayer], a house of prayer, a church or chapel; **whare-kura** [Ma. /ˈfare ˈkura/: Williams 490 *Wharekura*... The building in which the *tohunga* imparted esoteric lore to his pupils. Applied sometimes simply to the common meeting house of the *kāinga*: *kura* here (see Williams 157 *kura 11*) is 'Knowledge of *karakia* and other valuable lore'], a Maori house of knowledge or learning; **wharenui** (occas. init. cap.) [Ma. /ˈfare ˈnui/ 'big house'], MEETING-HOUSE; **wharepuni** (also **wharepuna, wharepune**) [Ma. /ˈfare ˈpuni/ from *puni* 'stopped up, covered up': Williams 490 *Wharepuni*... A closely built house with three layers of raupo in the walls, such as those generally used for sleeping in. Sometimes the term is applied to the principal house of the *kainga*], a Maori house specially built for warmth, used esp. as a sleeping house; occas. in *transf*. use, a European house-name; **whare runanga** [Ma. /ˈfare ˈruːnaŋa/: Williams 352 *Whare-rūnanga, public meeting house*: from *runanga* 'assembly, council'], a Maori MEETING HOUSE q.v.; **whare-tutae** [Ma. /ˈfare ˈtuːtae/: from *tūtae* 'excrement'], a nickname (see quot. 1968), a tramper's term (see also *whare-iti* above) for the outdoor toilet of a tramping hut; **whare-wananga** [Ma. /ˈfare ˈwaːnaŋa/: Williams 479 *Whare wānanga, house for instruction in occult lore*: from *wananga*, 'lore of the tohunga'], a Maori house of learning; also in modern use, a university.

1868 CHUDLEIGH *Diary* 4 July (1950) 224 They [*sc.* the Hauhaus] laughed and put on a smaller pair [of handcuffs] and said you can go to the lockup now (**whare hau hau**). No one guarded me and I walked to the whare hau hau through crowds of them and took in all I could see in the time. **1958** *Tararua* Sept. 15 Round the corner we found a permanent camp [in the Ruahine ranges]—two sleeping tents and a large living tent with carpets, table, deck chairs..a radio, and a really swept-up **whare-iti** with chromium trimmings. **1899** *Auckland Weekly News* (Suppl.) 23 June 1 Photographs were taken of..a curious long building called a **whare kai**, or dining room. **1933** *Tararua Tramper* Jan. 3 After lunch we went up to the Pa, where we were conducted to the Wharekai for a farewell concert. **1989** HOGG *Angel Gear* 26 Kai in the whare kai and chat to Keith, the headmaster and Rotarian. **1833** WILLIAMS *Early Jrnls.* 28 Apr. (1961) 309 Flags of various colours displayed [by Kororarika grog shops], bidding welcome to all who would enter therein; the natives referred to them as the *ware karakia* of Satan, where his followers assembled to do him honour. **1847** ANGAS *Savage Life* I. 235 Close to Pipitea is a *ware karakia*, or chapel, belonging to the Christian natives, which is built of *raupo* and *tohi-tohi* grass, according to the native fashion. **1850** LUSH *Auckland Jrnls*. 22 Oct. (1971) 29 Adjoining the *whare Karakia*—'prayer house'—as all chapels and churches are called, was the residence of the native *Kaiwhakaako* (Teacher). **1871** MEADE *Ride through Disturbed Dist*. in Taylor *Early Travellers* (1959) 436 Meanwhile the evening-bell was rung at the *whare-karakia*, and prayers were read by the native deacon. **1940** *Tales Pioneer Women* (1988) 250 The missionaries came and built their own meeting houses (whare karakia). **1879** FEATON *Waikato War* 10 A site was chosen.., and a pa was built, and, at the request of the **Whare Kura**, I drew up laws and regulations for them. **1900** *Canterbury Old & New* 156 The sons of chiefs were taught the history of their ancestors, and the legends of their gods, by the tohungas, in schoolhouses known as wharekura. **1904** TREGEAR *Maori Race* 376 The name Whare-kura..was transferred on the arrival of the Maori in New Zealand to tribal buildings with something of the old [Polynesian] attributes. **1946** *JPS* LV. 160 *whare-kura*, school of learning; building where esoteric law was imparted to fit pupils: knowledge of karakia and other valuable lore was called kura, and kura also means treasure. **1947** STEVENSON *Maori & Pakeha* 84 The last session of a Whare-kura in the South Island was held at Moeraki in 1868. The Whare-kura was a school in which selected students were instructed in religion, ritual, tribal lore, agriculture, and the art of warfare etc. **1967** BRATHWAITE *Evil Day* 382 Wharekura House of Knowledge. **1928** *Na To Hoa Aroha* 9 Feb. (1986) I. 67 Te Puea is re-establishing a marae at Ngaruawahia... Her present mission was to raise funds for a **whare nui**. [1986 *Note*] Meeting house. **1985** GRACE in *Landfall* 156 455 Waimarie moved to greet the men at the front of the Wharenui. **1986** [see PANUI]. **1987** *Karori News* 12 May 13 On Saturday 2 May I had the privilege of being present at the dawn ceremony to lift the tapu at the new Wharenui at Wellington Teachers' College. [**1820** LEE & KENDALL *NZ Gram. & Vocab.* 225 Wáre púne; A close house, or bed-room.] **1846** TAYLOR *Journal* 2 July (ATLTS) IV. 68 I walked along the beach to a little kainga and entered a **warepuni** which may be likened to a kind of oven for sleeping in. **1847** ANGAS *Savage Life* II. 123 The night being exceedingly cold, I slept in the *ware pune*, or 'close house': after a fire had been lighted inside, and the little den heated to at least 90° of Farenheit, I entered it and lay down upon my blanket. **1863** MOSER *Mahoe Leaves* 22 We will look at another sort of house called a whare-puni... In these horrid places they sleep huddled up together, with a roaring fire. **1873** TINNE *Wonderland of Antipodes* 9 Enjoying dry..quarters at the great 'whare-puna', or meeting-house, of the tribe. **1905** THOMSON *Bush Boys* 45 It was a merry party which gathered that Saturday..in the big kitchen of 'Te Wharepuni', the name Mr. MacLean had given to his homestead. In every Maori 'pah' or village, there is one specially large 'whare', or house, used as a meeting place for all important tribal gatherings, and known to them as 'te wharepuni'. **1911** BOREHAM *Selwyn* 54 Here and there several [Maori] families had established their domestic economy upon socialistic or cooperative principles, all living together in a *whare-puni* or larger *whare*. **1920** *Quick March* 10 Jan. 13 Not an evening falls without these prayers..in the gargoyled wharepuni. **1933** *Tararua Tramper* Jan. 3 Nearer the camp was a disused wharepuni, which we..decorated with manuka and ragwort. **1949** REED *Story Canterbury* 28 At the close of day he would take his precious greenstone with him to the *wharepuni* or sleeping house, rub it till he fell asleep, and pick it up again at wakeful moments. **1972** BAXTER *Collected Poems* (1980) 541 Don and Francie, here with me at home In the wharepuni. **1873** BULLER *Birds NZ* 89 I had been addressing a large meeting of natives in the **Whare-runanga**, or Council-house [at Rangitikei], on a matter of considerable political importance. **1891** WALLACE *Rural Econ. Austral. & NZ* 218 A special house of assembly, the *whare runanga* or *whare pani*. **1905** BAUCKE *White Man Treads* 7 The monstrosities which decorated his whare runanga (meeting-house) posts. **1924** *Otago Witness* (Dunedin) 22 July 4 The whare runanga, or meeting house, still formed a fairly large part in Maori life. **1946** ZIMMERMAN *Where People Sing* 108 These buildings were usually brick red and chocolate brown, the old Maori colors, and they were the communal meeting houses, the *whare runanga*, centers and focal points of the communal spirit of the people. **1950** *NZJAg.* Aug. LXXXI. 187 [Caption] The whare-runanga, carved house, with war canoe house in the background. **1976** FINLAYSON *Other Lovers* 100 'You're our visitor and you sleep tonight in the whare runanga—you know, the meeting–house...' Johnny took Jim over the paddock to the carved house. **1968** GRUNDY *Who'd Marry a Doctor?* 62 I heard there was a [person called] **Whare-tutae** on the island—his rather undignified venture into the world was made in the toilet. **1971** *VUWTC' 71* 41 And there was now no Harold Gretton to celebrate the re-building of the whare-tutae. **1984** GRETTON in Knox *Thousand Mountains Shining* (1984) 42 At Tauwharenikau there's a fine whare-tutae: The seat gives a view of unusual beautae. **1947** STEVENSON *Maori & Pakeha* 84 The higher branches of learning, known as the **Whare-wananga**, included all knowledge and ceremonial for the spiritual enlightenment of mankind. **1959** SINCLAIR *Hist. NZ* 22 The superior kind of priest received an arduous training in a *whare wananga*, a house of learning. **1964** FRANCES *Johnny Rapana* 167 'Whare wananga, house of learning,' the reporter said. 'A place where the tohungas teach history and mythology, things like that.' **1971** MASON *Hongi* (TS) 9 Hongi: Did I not offer my tongue to your whare wananga—Kendall: University! **1986** IHIMAERA *Matriarch* 26 You really have to know your stuff, the stuff that is usually taught only to the men in the whare wananga.

II. In non-Maori contexts as an English word. **3. a.** A hut or cottage (often rough or makeshift) for human occupation esp. as a first, often primitive shelter, on a newly occupied run or bush farm; in earliest use often with a modifier **raupo**, etc. denoting one built by a Maori or in Maori style (see 5 below), and in later common use replaced by BACH (or CRIB), HUT.

1840 BEST *Journal* 13 Nov. (1966) 258 My *Wharrey* is the best general rendezvous in the forenoon. **1843** *Lett. from Settlers* (1843) 103 We had built our houses, or as they are more generally called by the native name (warries). **1854** GOLDER *Pigeons' Parliament* 76 My warré or bush cottage. **1857** PAUL *Lett. from Canterbury* 88 Pitch your tent and run up a couple of grass warrés. The next point will be to make a sheep-yard. **1860** SCOTT *Rough Notes on Travels* 32 Warries is the name given to dwelling places either for man or beast. **1869** THATCHER *Local Songs* 8 It looks just like a rabbit-warren, as you're coming down, And you'll see the diggers' whares perched high above the town. **1899** BELL *In Shadow of Bush* 8 A little way back from the road-line stood a slab hut—or wharé, as it is generally called in New Zealand. **1909** OWEN *Philip Loveluck* 156 *Wharé*—The Maori for dwelling. Often used by Colonials to signify a hut or makeshift living room. **1912** MANSFIELD *Stories* (1984) 110 We were on the brow of the hill, and below us there was a whare roofed in with corrugated iron. **1933** SCANLAN *Tides of Youth* 42 And look here, Kelly, when you've got a whare built [as first accommodation on a bush farm], I'll [*sc.* his prospective bride] come up and keep house. **1939** [see PAMPAS GRASS]. **1946** *JPS* LV. 147 *whare*, house, dwelling; if a Pakeha house it is usually a small inferior one: the Maori added qualifying words to describe its use. **1950** *Listener* 3 Mar. 8 I left Dawson shouting the odds in the office and ran over to the whare to change and push some things into a suitcase. **1965** SHADBOLT *Among Cinders* 140 Night coming in, stars in the sky, manuka smoke drifting out of the tin chimney of our whare. **1980** MARSH *Photo-Finish* 127 That's right [it is a small station]. With about three *whares* and a pub.

b. A temporary, often hastily constructed, hut or shelter; a MAIMAI 1 a.

1849 TORLESSE *Papers* (1958) 68 We partook of their repast and then walked.., when being very tired, we knocked up a warre for the night and made a humu to cook our pork. **1854** 10 Feb. in Studholme *Te Waimate* (1954) 23 We..supped on it [*sc.* a duck] in a whare by the estuary, which McDonald had constructed when bringing north McCoy's cattle. **1871** MONEY *Knocking About NZ* 28 At the [river] junction..we found a diminutive wharry or grass hut, just big enough for four persons to crawl into and pack close. **1896** wharé [see MAIMAI 1 a].

4. a. A workman's or farm labourer's (or shepherd's) hut on a station, farm, forestry or public works camp, etc.; a gumdigger's hut.

1855 PHILLIPS *Rockwood Jrnl.* 5 Dec. (Canterbury Pub. Lib. TS) 22 John helping Seal [a stationhand] thatch his whare in afternoon. **1871** *TrNZI* III. 64 A shepherd's whare. **1888** BARLOW *Kaipara* 152 In most of the gumdiggers' huts (or whares, as they are called)..are to be found specimens of amateur gum-carving. **1891** CHAMIER *Philosopher Dick* 192 My abode, a thatched 'wàrrie'. **1906** *Truth* 10 Mar. 5 Single men [at Cross Creek railway camp] had either to bachelorise in their whares or board with one..of the married men. **1926** DEVANNY *Butcher Shop* (1981) 60 The rabbiters' whare was a two-roomed shanty occupied by two old cronies who were rabbitting for Messenger. **1975** DAVIES *Outback* 7 Buck came out of his whare rubbing the sleep from his eyes..and peered across at the homestead to see if the chimney was smoking. **1980** WOOLLASTON *Sage Tea* 164 The whare where I would live [at a Riwaka orchard, Jan. 1928] was built recently, of pale grey asbestos sheets on a timber frame. It was by far the best workers' accommodation in the district.

b. A communal living and sleeping quarters on a rural property; MEN'S HUT, *swaggers' hut* (SWAGGER 2).

1875 RIVES *Jottings on the Spot* (Canterbury Pub. Lib. TS) 23 Mar. 15 I lunched in the men's whare [at Chaters' Station] and resumed my road. **1889** *Collinson's Col. Mag.* 24 He prefers to sit in the 'wharé' (men's hut). **1894** WILSON *Land of Tui* 21 Dec. 249 Sundowners..walk from station to station during the day, and, sleeping under a haystack until sunset, make their appearance at that hour before the 'whares' or huts provided for them. **1911** *Maoriland Worker* 23 June 4 In addition to the wages, 'sleeping accommodation' has to be provided; in Taranaki this has been interpreted to mean 'whares' but no stretchers or bunks. **1936** ESCOTT *Show Down* (1973) 124 He didn't keep his dogs close to the bungalow but further out over the other side of the men's whare. *Ibid.* 134 Whare:.. Commonly used in New Zealand for a cottage or shack housing unmarried farm workers. **1952** RHODES *Fly Away Peter* 120 They're taking it easy over in the whare—that's the men's sleeping quarters, Mr Poyndestre. **1964** MIDDLETON *Walk on Beach* 166 At the station, the shepherd showed me the shearers' whare. **1977** [see SWAGGER 2]. **1984** *Knapdale Run* 147 The approach of the [threshing] mill and [traction] engine [c1900]..trundling the big wooden mill and the 'whare', the sleeping quarters, all on steel wheels. **1994** *Dominion* (Wellington) 27 May 18 The buildings include a four-bedroom farmhouse..a three-bedroom cottage and a three-bedroom whare, a modern six-stand woolshed.

c. A men's hut or crib-room on a work site.

1952 *Here & Now* Sept. 31 [Title] Smoke-o. The siren blows: time to breathe, tea In the grim whare... In this context, combined lunch and locker room. Pakeha pronunciation, 'warrie'.

5. As the second part of a compound: see also *raupo whare* (RAUPO 3), *slab-whare* (SLAB *n.*[1] 2 b), *sod whare* (SOD).

1890 *Otago Witness* (Dunedin) 7 Aug. 36 In those days we lived on in all the glory of our ti-tree whares. *Ibid.* 21 Aug. 32 We went up to the Hutt, and purchased a tois-tois whare, where we took up temporary abode. **1891** WALLACE *Rural Econ. Austral. & NZ* 225 Pioneering, or cutting a place out of the bush and building a log 'whare', is extremely rough and lonely work.

6. In jocular or ironic use for a substantial residence.

1911 *Truth* 8 July 4 Cabs and motor cars were tangled up, and general sad havoc was played with the shrubs and lawns gracing the vice-regal whare. **1968** SEDDON *The Seddons* 54 A large brake was ordered and my family and..Mr. Harold Beauchamp and Mrs. Beauchamp..and the Beauchamp children, Aunt Belle Dyer and Kitty Dyer..all had a happy day at the old whare.

7. Used *attrib.* **a.** Comb. **whare door, fire, step**.

1871 MONEY *Knocking About NZ* 138 Our little farrier-major..firing off all the barrels of his revolver..round the corner of a '**wharry**' door. **1881** CAMPBELL *Poenamo* 314 So one fine calm morning, locking up our *whare* door by tying it with a piece of flax, and leaving Tartar in charge we got into our canoe and paddled up to town. **1879** FEATON *Waikato War* 35 (Griffiths Collect.) The Maori braves..no doubt round the **whare fire** recounted..the glorious deeds that they had done. **1964** FRANCES *Johnny Rapana* 3 Lowering himself to sit on the **whare step**, hollowed with the passage of many years and passing feet, the old man let his mind wander.

b. Special Comb. **whare bug**, *black-beetle* (BEETLE 1 a).

1867 COOPER *Digger's Diary* (1978) 6 Nov. 9 The annoyances [on Thames Goldfield] are, armies of mosquitoes, showers of sand flies, frequent visitations of the stinking or whare bug..and a deficiency..of all vegetable food.

wharehou, var. WAREHOU.

wharf. *Pl.* usu. *wharves*.

1. In *pl.* the standard New Zealand term for *docks*.

1840 MATHEW *Journal* 19 Mar. in *Founding of NZ* (1940) 94 Immediately on the beach [at the Bay of Islands] stands an extensive well-built store, with wharfs and such buildings as boat houses, etc. **1848** WAKEFIELD *Handbook NZ* 317 In laying out the Chief Town..to be named 'Dunedin', —due provision to be made for..Baths, Wharfs, Quays, Cemeteries. **1875** KIRK *Durability NZ Timbers* 1 Some of the oldest totara piles in our wharves and piers are equally good. **1889** KNOX *Boy Travellers* 248 We [in Wellington] have several clubs, half a dozen banks, wharves and dry docks for shipping. **1913** MANSFIELD *Stories* (1984) 133 He walked on to the wharves, past the wool-bales, past the loungers and the loafers to the extreme end of the wharves. **1936** HYDE *Passport to Hell* 15 A one-armed man solemnly proffers a large and gleaming mackerel, caught off the edge of the Auckland wharves. **1960** SCRYMGEOUR *Memories Maoriland* 39 This 'underground mutton' was taken to a depot, frozen, then carted to railhead, then to the wharves.

2. Used *attrib.* in special Comb. **wharf-labourer**, WATERSIDER; **wharf police**, a police section stationed on the wharves; **wharf-shed**, the building on or near a wharf for the storage of cargo; **wharfside**, (in) the vicinity of the wharves; **wharf truck**, a truck for moving cargo.

1891 *Evening Post* (Wellington) 11 July 2 A **wharf-labourer**..stands charged with the theft of an oil skin coat... The accused was at work discharging coal on the Mawhera. **1897** *Royal Commission* in *Here & Now* July (1952) 11 Is not this a fact: that the Canterbury Stevedoring Association wholly controls the Lyttelton Lumpers' and Wharf-labourers' Association? **1904** *Awards, etc.* 180 [Heading] Napier Wharf-Labourers— Recommendations. **1905** *NZ Observer* 14 Jan. 16 The coat was discovered in the hold of the vessel on which a party of wharf labourers were working. a**1948** ACLAND *Early Canterbury Runs* (1951) 321 Trouble with wharf labourers..kept them six weeks in Auckland. **1952** *Here & Now* July 11 After the defeat of the 1890 strike the Lyttelton port employers sponsored a Lumpers and Wharf-Labourers Association. **1925** *Evening Post* (Wellington) 5 Oct. 6 Sergeant Melville and Constables..of the **wharf police** were quickly on the scene. **1904** *Awards, etc.* 180 [Napier Wharf-Labourers Award] **Wharf-sheds** wages to be at the rate of 1s. 6d. per hour for ordinary time. **1905** *NZ Observer* 14 Jan. 16 That the coat was found in the hold, and not in the wharf shed..appears to be beyond question. **1913** MANSFIELD *Stories* (1984) 133 He crossed the railway line, he crept behind the wharf-sheds and along a little cinder path that threaded through a patch of rank fennel. **1948** FINLAYSON *Tidal Creek* 19 As they scurry round the end of the wharf-shed they see the steamer, the oldest..of the small steamers tied up to this old wharf. **1973** *Evening Post* (Wellington) 21 June 8 The Jervois Quay wharf sheds are vital symbols of our beginnings as a trading nation. **1959** SHADBOLT *The New Zealanders* (1986) 130 And there was the shabby **wharfside** milk-bar where, from a rainbow juke-box, a thin masculine voice wheedled for the return of lost love. **1936** HYDE *Passport to Hell* 50 Alf was a ganger on the wharf at Lyttelton; and his son..worked down among the cranes and **wharf-trucks**.

wharfie. Also **wharfy**. [f. *wharf*(-labourer + -IE: AND 1911.]

1. *watersider* (WATERSIDE 1).

1913 *NZ Observer* 10 May 21 The two Frontiersmen did not 'go through' the 'wharfies'. **1918** THE MIXER *N.Z. Watersider* Oct. in Bailey & Roth *Shanties* (1967) 116 The Milit'ry Service Board Sat in state... The first case was a wharfie Who'd a wooden leg from birth. **1926** DEVANNY *Lenore Divine* 47 Imagine Holly haranguing the wharfies from the soap-box. **1938** HYDE *Godwits Fly* (1970) 69 The wharfies sit with backs against the tin sheds. **1950** *Southern Cross* (Wellington) 27 May 7 [Heading] Wharfies want mass protest. **1969** MASON *Awatea* (1978) 115 Timi and his eighty-one wharfie friends stacked away trestles, loaded up the trucks. **1976** SINCLAIR *Nash* 282 The tactics of Barnes and Hill, in fighting for better pay and conditions for 'wharfies', seemed to be non-stop aggression. **1984** MARSHALL *Day Hemingway Died* 38 The wharfies kept jobs like tally-clerk and winchman to themselves. **1995** *Independent* (Auckland) 24 Mar. 7 [Heading] Wharfies v Seagulls. Scene set for big stoush on the Auckland waterfront.

2. In the special collocation **wharfies' sunshine**, wet weather.

1963 *Comment* 17 Oct. 11 The Golden Coast has been dulled by leaden skies and as I write is in a sodden state. Month after month of what the Wellington watersiders call 'wharfies' sunshine' have checked its growth.

wharfy, var. WHARFIE.

whariki, var. WAORIKI.

whariki. Also **wáriki, whaariki**. [Ma. /'faːriki/: Williams 490 *Whāriki. 1....* Anything spread on the ground or on a floor; floor mat, etc.] A foundation for a bed on the ground or floor, often a mat.

[**1820** LEE & KENDALL *Gram. & Vocab.* 226 Wáriki, *s.* A covering, as a blanket.] **1874** BAINES *Edward Crewe* 140 My companion set about..cutting fern for a 'whariki', a foundation to cover the ground and on which to spread our blankets. **1888** BULLER *Birds NZ* I. 12 Our Maori attendant (Rahui) had barely time to fix up our tent and collect 'whariki' for bedding before thick darkness had set in. **1975** KNIGHT *Poyntzfield* 45 Father drove four stakes into the ground and Mother took out sheets with which to make a kind of a roofless tent with two floor mats (whariki) on the ground. **1985** *Listener* 7 Sept. 12 Then, I'd roll out my threadbare Whaariki—to help you remember to take your boots off—spread an old newspaper on the floor and on it place a steaming pot of puha.

Hence **whariki** (also **wariki**) *v.* [Ma. Williams 490 *Whāriki... 2. v.* trans. Carpet, cover over with mats, etc.] *trans.*, see quot.

1842 SELWYN in *NZ Part I* (Church in the Colonies) 23 Dec. (1844) 90 We found water, which the natives drew for us with the least possible admixture of mud, by 'wariki'ing the bottom of the hole; that is, spreading the branches of trees over the mud, and letting the water filter up through the leaves.

whario, var. WAREHOU.

wharrey, wharri, wharry, varr. WHARE.

whata. Also with much variety of form reflecting English speakers' perceptions of the Maori initial bilabial fricative as /w/ (**wata, watá, watta, wáttá, watti(e)** (?/'wɒti/), **wutter**) or /f/ (**futta(h), futter**); *pl.* often with *-s*. [Ma. /'fata/: Williams 490 *Whata. 1....* Elevated stage for storing food and for other purposes.]

1. In Maori contexts (usu. North Island and with *wh-* or *w-* forms), an elevated platform or stand, occas. roofed, for storing foodstuffs and for other purposes. See also PATAKA.

[**1820** LEE & KENDALL *NZ Gram. & Vocab.* 226 Wáta; A platform, or scaffold for stores.] **1832** WILLIAMS *Early Jrnls.* 16 May (1961) 244 The boys preparing a *Wata*, a high stand for native food, about 16ft. long and 10 wide, 16ft. from the ground, to preserve it from the English rats. **1834** MARKHAM *NZ* (1963) 43 I saw the Potatoes on (Wutters) for the first time; there are two sorts, one is four upright Posts, 20 to 30 feet high. **1838** POLACK *NZ* I. 65 The many *watás*, or platforms raised on trees. **1844** BARNICOAT *Journal* (ATLTS) 29 Aug. 186 The absence of futtas or provision stores seemed to indicate poverty [among the local South Island Maori].

1847 ANGAS *Savage Life* I. 331 The bones, after being well scraped and cleaned, are then deposited in a *whata*, or elevated box, somewhat resembling a provision store. **1850** TAYLOR *Journal* 26 May (ATLTS) VII. 103 The sacred food which in former days they placed on their watas as an offering to their gods. **1904** TREGEAR *Maori Race* 282 Rough *whata* for holding firewood were also to be seen in a *pa*. **1930** DOBSON *Reminiscences* 68 This good *whata* belonged to Purua, a rangatira wahine, who lived here with her servants. **1945** BEATTIE *Maori Place-names Canterbury* 33 Besides the whare (houses), there were whata (futtahs) standing there when I was a boy.

2. In non-Maori (esp. early SI sheep-station) contexts (often with *futta(h)* forms), a storehouse raised off the ground used to protect farm and station stores, explorers' provision caches, etc. from rodents and other animals.

1850 TORLESSE *Papers* (1958) 144 Spittal..making a watta for preserving the flour on. **1857** PAUL *Lett. from Canterbury* 90 You are fairly entitled to something better than a..large, strong wata, or store raised on posts to keep your provisions safe from rats. **1861** HAAST *Rep. Topogr. Explor. Nelson* 32 A very nice and well covered whata (provision store) erected by Mr. Rochfort's native labourers. **1863** HAMMET *Journal* 11 June in *Examiner* (1863) in Heinz *Bright Fine Gold* (1974) 98 The Darkie..who they had found camped at the Watti..had eaten about 40lbs of flour. **1878** ELWELL *Boy Colonists* 100 Walker..afterwards gave him another pair of trousers from the futtah. **1888** DUNCAN *Wakatipians* 22 The buildings of the home-station were represented by a 'futter' and a long narrow hut. **1896** HARPER *Pioneer Work* 181 A 'futtah' is a small shelter of bark and canvas, raised off the ground, in which to leave provisions and stores sheltered from the weather, wekas, and rats. **1913** BEATTIE *Trade Hunting* [16] Every station had a 'futtah', a small wooden building on stilts, a rat-proof store for provisions. **1921** GUTHRIE-SMITH *Tutira* (1926) 150 The other buildings of the primitive homestead were..a *whata* or store-house on piles, empty now in the station's dire extremity. **1933** *Press* (Christchurch) (Acland Gloss.) 21 Oct. 15 *Futtah.*—A station store, built on high posts to keep rats and mice out... Some people used to call them *watties*. **1940** *Tales of Pioneer Women* (1988) 299 Several..have recorded details of their daily lives..rats that necessitated the erection of futtahs (whatas). **1970** MCNEISH *Mackenzie* 55 He walked right under the whata. A rat scurried down. The tinfoil was peeling, Droo would have to sheathe the legs again against the rats. **1982** SANSOM *In Grip of Island* 55 A few sheep, pigs and geese supplied food for the whatas, the long legged rat-proof food safes.

whau. Also early **vow** (poss. reflecting Ma. initial bilabial fricative /ɸ/), **wau, wou**. [Ma. /'fau/: Williams 492 *Whau* (i) n. *Entelea arborescens.*] *Entelea arborescens* (fam. Tiliaceae), a small native tree of coastal and lowland forest with large broad-ovate leaves, hairy fruit capsules and remarkable for its light wood. See also CORK TREE, CORKWOOD, HAUAMA, MULBERRY 2.

1817 NICHOLAS *Voyage NZ* II. 245 The trees which the natives chiefly make subservient to their purposes, are [besides the pines]..a species of cork-tree, called by these people vow. **1830** CRAIK *New Zealanders* 175 Among those which the natives principally make use of, are the *henow*..and the *vow*, a species of cork tree. **1838** POLACK *NZ* II. 399 The *Pongo*, and *Wou*..are varieties of the corktree. **1853** [see HAUAMA]. **1869** *TrNZI* I. (rev. edn.) 264 For floats, the light wood of the small tree Whau, or Hauama, (*Entelea arborescens,*) was used. **1878** BULLER *Forty Yrs. NZ* 502 The *Wau*

whaupaku, var. WHAUWHAUPAKU.

whauriki, var. WAORIKI.

whauwhau. [Ma. /ˈfaufau/: Williams 492 *whauwhau... Nothopanax arboreum = houhou*; also *Hoheria glabrata* and *Pseudopanax lessoni.*]
a. FIVE-FINGER 1 a (*Pseudopanax arboreus*). See also OHAU, WHAUWHAUPAKU a.

[**1820** LEE & KENDALL *NZ Gram. & Vocab.* 226 Wauwau, *s.* A shrub so called.] **1907** LAING & BLACKWELL *Plants NZ* 324 *Nothopanax arboreum* (The Tree Nothopanax)... Maori name *Whauwhau*, often corrupted to *Ohau*. **1982** *Field Guide Common NZ Trees & Shrubs* 22 Five Finger (Whauwhau) *Neopanax a[r]boreum*... Leaves palmate with 3–7 leaflets.

b. *Pseudopanax lessoni* (fam. Araliaceae).
1853 HOOKER *II Flora Novae-Zelandiae I Flowering Plants* 96 *Aralia Lessoni...* Nat. name, 'Whau whau'. **1867** HOOKER *Handbook* 769 Whau-whau, *R.Cunn. Panax Lessoni.*

c. *Plagianthus* spp. RIBBONWOOD.
1867 HOOKER *Handbook* 769 Whau-whau, *Lindsay. Plagianthus Lyallii.*

whauwhaupaku. Also with some variety of Ma. and transliterated forms as **wau taku, wauwaupaku, wawa-paku, whaupaku, whawhaupuku,** etc. [Ma. /ˈfaufaupaku/: Williams 492 *Whaupaku, whauwhaupaku.*] Either a small forest tree FIVE-FINGER 1 a (*Pseudopanax arboreus*), or a related forest understory shrub *P. anomalus* (fam. Araliaceae).
a. FIVE-FINGER 1. See also WHAUWHAU a.

1839 TAYLOR *Journal* 13 Apr. (ATLTS) II. 100 The tree called the wau taku [=Whaupaku] bears a bunch of seeds in color and appearance very much like the English Elder tree. **1853** HOOKER *II Flora Novae-Zelandiae I Flowering Plants* 94 *Panax arborea...* 'Wawa-Paku'.. 'Whau-Whau Paku'. **1869** *TrNZI* I. (rev. edn.) 203 Wha[u]whaupuku. *Panax arboreum,* Forst. **1882** HAY *Brighter Britain* II. 196 The Whau-whau-paku..is similarly to be noticed for its elegant glossy leaf. **1939** COCKAYNE & TURNER *Trees NZ* 88 *Nothopanax arboreum* (Araliaceae). Whauwhaupaku. **1966** FALLA et al. *Birds of NZ* 234 On Hen Island pate..and whauwhaupaku (*Neopanax arboreum*) are an important berry source [for the saddleback]. **1978** [see FIVE-FINGER 1 a].

b. *Pseudopanax anomalus.*
1853 HOOKER *II Flora Novae-Zelandiae I Flowering Plants* 93 *Panax anomala...* Nat. name, 'Wawa paku'. **1906** CHEESEMAN *Manual NZ Flora* 230 *P[anax] anomalum,* Hook. *Wauwaupaku.* **1919** COCKAYNE *NZ Plants & Their Story* 77 Very conspicuous in this scrub [on the Kaukau Range] are the supra-divaricating whauwhaupuku (*Nothopanax anomalum*), and the three myrtles. **1940** LAING & BLACKWELL *Plants NZ* 322 *Nothopanax anomalum* (The Anomalous Notho-panax)... Maori name *Whaupaku.* A curious plant, with a habit quite unlike that of the ordinary *Nothopanax,* but like that of a *Coprosma.*

whauwhi. [Ma. /ˈfaufi/: Williams 492 *Whauwhi = houhi..Hoheria* [spp.] and *Plagianthus betulinus.*] HOUHERE, LACEBARK (*Hoheria* and *Plagianthus* spp.).

1853 HOOKER *II Flora Novae-Zelandiae I Flowering Plants* 31 *Hoheria Lyallii...* Hab. Middle Island... Nat. name, 'Whau-whi'. **1869** [see HOUHERE]. **1877, 1889** [see LACEBARK 1 b]. **1889** FEATON *Art Album NZ Flora* 54 The tree [*Plagianthus betulinus*] is known by the native name of 'Houi' or 'Whau-whi'. **1907** [see HOUI].

whawhakou. Also **whakou** (referring to the blooms). [Ma. /ˈfa:fa:kou/: Williams 486 *Whākou, whāwhākou... Ixerba brexioides,* a tree; particularly when in flower. = *tāwari. whāwhākou... Eugenia maire...* = *maire tawake.*] Either of two trees, TAWARI or *maire-tawake* (MAIRE 1 c).

1849 MCKILLOP *Reminiscences* 162 The whakou also yields a handsome blue [dye]. **1867** HOOKER *Handbook* 769 Whawhako, *Geolog. Surv. Eugenia Maire.* **1889** FEATON *Art Album* (Plant Names) 178 Whawhako [Maori name]..Maire Tawhake [Settlers' name]..Eugenia maire..Small tree. **1892** *NZ Official Handbook* 150 Whawhako (see also Maire) (*Eugenia maire*). **1910** whakou [see TAWARI]. **1981** BROOKER et al. *NZ Medicinal Plants* 70 *Eugenia maire...* Common name: *Black maire* Maori names: *Whawhakou, maire tawake.*

whawhaupuku, var. WHAUWHAUPAKU.

wheat grass: see GRASS 2 (44).

wheedler. [f. the tone of its call.] TOMTIT.
1966 FALLA et al. *Birds NZ* 200 Tomtit *Petroica macrocephala* Other names: Miromiro (North Island), Ngirungiru (South Island), Wheedler, Butcher-bird (Taranaki).

wheelbarrow.

1. In the phrases **as drunk as a wheelbarrow** [see OED *wheelbarrow* c, 1675], so drunk as to be unable to move without help; **like smoke in a wheelbarrow,** an exclamation indicating strong disbelief.

1982 SANSOM *In Grip of Island* 41 Adam's ale is the only tipple on tap there today. No one will get as **drunk as a wheelbarrow** on that. **1972** SUTTON-SMITH *Folkgames Children* 138 [c1920–50] there are vigorous Slanging Contests in which the contestants try to outdo each other by using phrases like the following: 'You're up the shoot'. 'Oh, bullswool'. 'Go jump in the lake'... 'Shiver me timbers'... '**Like smoke in a wheelbarrow**'.

whekau. Also **wekau.** [Ma. /ˈfe:kau/: Williams 493 *Whēkau* (ii)... laughing owl.] *Sceloglaux albifacies* (fam. Strigidae), a distinctively noisy but now extinct owl, commonly called laughing owl. See also LAUGHING JACKASS 1, *laughing owl* (OWL 2 (1)).

1866 ANGAS *Polynesia* 62 Amongst the strange ornithological forms that occur in New Zealand is a very remarkable bird of the owl tribe, called the 'wekau' by the natives. **1873** BULLER *Birds NZ* 24 A Whekau entered a shepherd's abode at the foot of Mount Hutt, and remained for several days perching in the roof. **1882, 1898** [see LAUGHING JACKASS 1]. **1904, 1947, 1966** [see OWL 2 (1)]. **1972** *Notornis* XIX. 8 [The Laughing Owl] apparently hunted for its food over open ground..and roosted and nested in fissures in rocks (having an alternative name of rock owl as well as its common Maori name of whekau). **1985** *Reader's Digest Book NZ Birds* 308 Whekau, hakoke (North Island), rock owl. The 'doleful shrieks' of the laughing owl, which varied seasonally, were heard incessantly on rainy nights... Reports say that it cooeyed in the evening, yelped like a young dog and mewed and chuckled... The most recent record of sighting was at Manapouri in 1950. **1990** *Checklist Birds NZ* 185 *Sceloglaux albifacies albifacies... South Island Laughing Owl* (*Whekau*)... Declined rapidly after about 1880; almost certainly now extinct.

wheke. Also **feggie, weki.** [Ma. /ˈfeke/: Williams 493 *Wheke...* Squid, octopus.] *Octopus maorum* (fam. Octopodidae), a common octopus.

1855 TAYLOR *Te Ika A Maui* 415 *Weki,* is one with a very small body and five long rays. **1880** *TrNZI* XII. 311 They also say that the large '*whekes*' are very apt to seize a man and tear his inside out. No more sea-bathing for me! **1929** BEST *Fishing Methods* 43 Small wheke (octopus) were taken by hand and utilized as food. **1946** *JPS* LV. 160 *Wheke,* squid, octopus; different species distinguished by suffix, but wheke only in Pakeha use. **1956** HALL-JONES *Early Timaru* 61 Wheke m[e]ans octopus, and the Foveaux Strait oystermen speak of the feggies. **1977** ALPERS *Maori Myths* 135 In a large cave there a wheke, or giant octopus, had its home and Kupe surprised this wheke. **1982** SANSOM *In Grip of Island* 101 'I don't want the wheke to get at me, that's all.' 'Wheke' is the Maori name for the octopus and the squid.

whekeponga, var. WHEKI-PONGA.

wheki. Also early **weki.** [Ma. /feˈki:/: Williams 493 *Whekī... Dicksonia squarrosa.*] *Dicksonia squarrosa* (fam. Dicksoniaceae), a very common slender tree-fern. See also *rough tree-fern, slender tree-fern* (FERN 2 (20) b (b) and (d)), TUAKURA. Cf. WHEKI-PONGA.

1855 HOOKER *II Flora Novae-Zelandiae II Flowerless Plants* 9 *Dicksonia squarrosa,* Sw... Nat. name, 'Weki'. **1870** *TrNZI* II. 90 A remarkable feature..is the social character of the arborescent ferns, more especially the Mamaku..and the Weki. **1890** [see FERN 2 (20) b (b)]. **1906** CHEESEMAN *Manual NZ Flora* 953 *D[icksonia] squarrosa,* Swartz,... Trunk 6–20 ft. high.. *Weki* or *Whekī*. **1915** [see FERN 2 (20) b (d)]. **1922** COWAN *NZ Wars* (1955) I. 130 The slopes are black-pencilled with the stumps of the *wheki,* a fern-tree whose butt is as hard as ironbark and almost indestructible. **1952** [see FERN 2 (20) b (b)]. **1965** GILLHAM *Naturalist in NZ* 24 Another [tree fern] is the wheki; a tree with harsher leaves, which reaches only about 18 feet from the ground. **1988** DAWSON *Forest Vines to Snow Tussocks* 86 Wheki..has a trunk surface similar to that of the ponga.

wheki-ponga. Also **wekiponga, whekeponga.** [Ma. /feˈki:ˈpoŋa/: Williams 493 *whekī-ponga, Dicksonia fibrosa.*] *Dicksonia fibrosa* (fam. Dicksoniaceae), a tall tree-fern having a thick fibrous trunk and a heavy skirt of dead fronds. See also PUNUI 2.

1867 HOOKER *Handbook* 769 Wekiponga... *Dicksonia antarctica.* **1869** *TrNZI* I. (rev. edn.) 264 Sometimes..the outside was formed of hard fibrous slabs cut from the stout red-brown fern-tree, Wekiponga. **1876** *TrNZI* VIII. 412 *Cyathea medullaris,* black fern..*Dicksonia antartica* [sic], wekiponga. **1922** *Auckland Weekly News* 11 May 15 The two Dicksonias—wheke and whekeponga to the Maoris—are medium tree ferns, confined to New Zealand. **1952** RICHARDS *Chatham Is.* 7 *Dicksonia fibrosa.* This is the

whelk.

1. Transf. use of *whelk* for any of various univalve molluscs resembling northern hemisphere whelks in shape.

1773 Wales *Journal* in Cook *Journals* (1961) II. 787 Amongst the crustaceous Tribe we found Crawfish, Muscles, Cockles, Scollops, Whelks. **1917** Williams *Dict. Maori Lang.* 115 *Kakara, Thais haustrum, whelk.* **1937** Powell *Shellfish NZ* 34 Our Local Whelks. The nearest local relatives to the English whelks are our several species of *Cominella*. **1950** Beattie *Far Famed Fiordland* 83 [Black woodhens] came down to the shore to pick whelks when the tide was out. **1971** Pownall *NZ Shells & Shell Fish* 70 Toss the whelks into a pot of boiling water, wait until it reaches boiling point again and count to twenty-five (slowly). **1983** Gunson *Collins Guide to Seashore* 94 The common grouping of whelks is made up of several families including the Penion, Cominella and Neptune Shells.

2. With a modifier: **knobbed**, **speckled** (or **spotted mud**).

(1) **knobbed whelk**. *Austrofusus glans* (fam. Buccinidae), a wavy-banded univalve.

1947 Powell *Native Animals* 28 Knobbed Whelk... This..has a thin shell gaily painted with vertical wavy bands of reddish-brown on a white base. **1955** Dell *Native Shells* 25 Knobbed Whelks... A carnivore of sandy shores. **1970** Penniket *NZ Seashells in Colour* 62 Knobbed whelk... A thin shell patterned with wavy bands of red to brown lines on a paler base. **1983** Gunson *Collins Guide to Seashore* 94 The knobbed whelk *Austrofusus glans* (50 mm) resembles the ostrich foot but lacks the calcareous lip.

(2) **speckled** (occas. **spotted mud**) **whelk**. *Cominella adspersa* (fam. Buccinidae), a small (5–6 mm) carnivorous univalve.

1947 Powell *Native Animals NZ* 28 Speckled Whelk... Kawari... Abundant in the North Island, particularly on rocky ground, near mud, in harbours. **1955** Dell *Native Shells* 25 Speckled Whelk... A common shell of the mud flats in the vicinity of rock. **1966** *Encycl. NZ* III. 646 Whelk, Speckled (*Cominella adspersa*)... These fish are carnivorous scavengers and may be seen clustered around a cockle on mud flats, one doing the job of boring into the shell of the cockle, the others hanging on to share in the feast. **1974** Child *NZ Shells* 78 Large Spotted Mud Whelk (*Cominella adspersa*).

whenua. Also early **fènwa**, **wannuae**, **wénua**, **whennoòā**. [Ma. /ˈfenua/: Williams 494 *Whenua*. *1.* Land, country: PPN **fanua* 'land' (Walsh & Biggs 8).] A native country, land; perh. best known in the collocation TANGATA WHENUA q.v.

1770 Cook *Journals* 31 Jan. (1955) I. 243 We questioned the old man..who said that it consisted of two *Wannuaes*, that is, two lands or Islands. **1778** Forster *Observations* 284 A Comparative Table of the Various Languages in the Isles of the South-Sea..[English] *Land*... [Friendly-Isles] *Fannoã*,.. [New-Zeeland] *Whennoòā*. [**1820** Lee & Kendall *NZ Gram. & Vocab.* 227 *Wénua, s.* The earth; the placenta. **c1826–27** Boultbee *Journal* (1986) 112 land—fènwa] **1851** Shortland *S. Dist. NZ* 155 It was he [*sc.* Maui] who is supposed to have hauled up 'Whenua' or the Earth from the depths of the ocean. **1969** Mason *Awatea* (1978) 60 [Our people] move from the whenua to the city: from wood to brick, from old quiet to new clamour. **1972** Baxter *Collected Poems* (1980) 580 [The little flies] regard me as their whenua.

whennooa, var. WHENUA.

where the whips are cracking: see WHIP *n.* 2.

whey: see WAI.

whi, var. WI.

whihiene, whinie, varr. WAHINE.

whio.

1. Also early **he-weego** (=he whio); **whio-whio, wiho, wihu, wio.** [Echoic from the cry; cf. Brit. *whew-duck* OED *whew n.*¹ 4: Ma. /ˈfio/: Williams 496 *whio 1.* v. intr. whistle *2*... blue duck; sometimes called whistling duck.] blue duck (DUCK 2 (2) a). See also *whistling duck* (DUCK 2 (8)).

[**1820** Lee & Kendall *NZ Gram. & Vocab.* 227 *Wío, a.* Whistling.] **1842** Gray *Fauna* in Dieffenbach *Travels in NZ* (1843) II. 198 *Malacorynchus Forsterorum*... He-weego of the natives of Dusky Bay. **1845** Taylor *Journal* 8 Nov. (ATLTS) III. 166 Mr Maclean here shot a *wihu*, or blue duck, which, being divided among the five of us, served for a meal until morning. **1848** Wakefield *Handbook NZ* 164 High up among the mountains, the rapid streams are inhabited by the *Wiho*..a black duck with a white bill, whose cry is a shrill whistle. **1847** Brunner *Exped. Middle Is.* 2 Apr. in Taylor *Early Travellers* (1959) 272 Shot a *wihu*, or blue duck. **1849, 1855,** [see DUCK 2 (2) a]. **1861** Haast *Rep. Topogr. Explor. Nelson* 11 Our provisions here began to fail, but catching some eels and whios (blue ducks), they made a good addition to our scanty commissariat. **1882** Potts *Out in Open* 94 At this wild spot, that nought frequents, save the wailing paradise duck, or the soft-billed whio, this fern grows in abundance. **1906, 1916** [see DUCK 2 (2) a]. **1946** *JPS* LV. 160 *Whio*, a water-bird (Hymenolaimus malacorhynch[o]s), blue-duck, mountain-duck, whistling duck; name echoic, like English whew-duck having a similar name for the same reason. **1955** Oliver *NZ Birds* 421 Both the European name of Whistling Duck and the Maori name Whio are derived from the call of this bird. **1976** Soper *NZ Birds* 26 In addition to the whistle, from which is derived the bird's Maori name Whio-whio, Blue Ducks have a guttural rattling call, difficult to describe, but resembling the noise made by running a stick along a board fence. **1989** Parkinson *Travelling Naturalist* 97 A lover of fast-flowing waters, the whio has a fairly restricted habitat.

2. The call of the whio.

[**1893** *TrNZI* XXV. 83 The ordinary note of the species is a sibilant whistle, whence it derives its native name, 'Wio'.] **1927** Guthrie-Smith *Birds* 43 Every now and again from the parents would come the rattling note or the sibilant 'whio', 'whio', one of the most delightful sounds of wild nature in New Zealand. **1957** Moncrieff *NZ Birds* 60 Blue or Mountain Duck... Peculiar whistle 'Whio'. **1985** *Reader's Digest Book NZ Birds* 149 Male gives a high-pitched, wheezy whistle as territorial or advertisement call—Maori *Whio* is good representation. Also short *Whi* whistle.

whip, *n.*

1. *pl.* As **whips (of)** [f. Brit. dial. *whips* an abundance: see OED *n.* 3 c '*dial, Austral. & N.Z.*'; AND 1890], 'lashings (of)', an abundance (of).

1897 Scott *How I Stole 10,000 Sheep* 29 I was glad to hear Jim come cantering up with 'whips' of bread, cheese, beer and horse-feed. **1902** Satchell *Land of Lost* (1971) iv 18 There was whips of money in it. It couldn't last, you know, but while it held out it would be a fair pour. **1948** Finlayson *Tidal Creek* (1979) 50 'Didn't think old Podder would ever bother about that bit of land,' says Uncle Ted. 'Got whips of land.' **1988** McGill *Dict. Kiwi Slang* 122 *whips* plenty of.

2. WW1. In the phr. **to be where (when) the whips are** (occas. **whip is**) **cracking** [AND 1906], to be in the firing line, to be where the action is.

1937 Partridge *Dict. Slang* 952 *whips are cracking, where the*. The front line: New Zealanders': in G.W. Ex the activity of cattle-mustering. **1938** *Press* (Christchurch) (McNab Slang) 2 Apr. 18 [Slang of the N.Z.E.F.] 'To be smacked up', 'to take one's hook', 'to be where the whips are cracking' are clear. **1939–45** *Expressions & Sayings 2NZEF* (TS N.A. WAII DA 420/1) Whips cracking—action. **a1974** Syder & Hodgetts *Austral. & NZ English* (TS) 1092 *Where the whips are cracking*. In the thick of the action, where the challenge to the endeavour is at its most severe. 'Take no notice of their casual attitude. Those chaps are as game as they come. They'll be there where the whips are cracking.' **1978** Taylor *Twilight Hour* 46 Big Snowy Tate kept jumping about yelling and waving his bayonet... 'I'll be there when the whip is cracking,' he kept shouting.

whip, *v.* In the phr. **to whip the cat** [transf. use of Brit. dial. and colloq. *whip the cat* used in various senses: see OED *v.* 16 a; AND 1847], to complain; to express useless regret, to 'cry over spilt milk'.

1909 Thompson *Ballads About Business* 12 You could make tenners den like vinkin', Dough now you are vipping der cat. **1910** *Truth* 11 June 1 But 'Critic' asks the said gentleman to submit the following sentence to any school boy or a semi-intelligent adult: 'The Opposition are whipping the cat because they've got Buckley's chance of pulling the leg of the farmer with an onkus freehold lurk.' **1911** *Triad* 10 June 18 Tell him [*sc.* a misled person] he has leave to go and whip the cat. **1952** p.c. Peter Newton (Southland). Musterers use 'whip the cat' in the sense of expressing regret at some act or decision. **1988** McGill *Dict. Kiwi Slang* 122 *whip the cat* to moan or reproach yourself; make a fuss.

whip behind. *Obs.* Orig. with reference to a boys' game of taking a swinging ride on the back of a moving horse-drawn vehicle. Also to play such a game or take such a ride, thence a cry of various meanings (see esp. quot. 1961).

1905 in Lawlor *More Wellington Days* (1962) 80 June 17 Had a fight with a boy because he called out whip behind. **1935** Guthrie *Little Country* (1937) 102 And him one of the boys you used to whip behind when hanging on to the back of the coach on his way to school. **1961** p.c. A.S. Wickens (Wellington). A 'whip-behind' was used by children for a swinging ride behind a cart or wagon—perhaps from the driver having to turn around and try to slash them off behind with his whip; perhaps from using the momentum of the cart to get a whip-like release; perhaps from 'whipping' (that is, dashing quickly there and away again) in behind the cart for a ride. It was said, e.g.,: 'I'll give you a hiding if you whip behind the baker's cart again!' My father remembered this word from when he was a boy in Dunedin in the 1870s to 1880s. **1962** Lawlor *More Wellington Days* 80 The hitch-hiker of the days of horse vehicles was the one who surreptitiously jumped on the back of a dray, an express or a lorry as it ambled slowly down the street... It was known as a 'whip behind'... It was this action with the whip that brought into being the well known cry of 'Whip behind!' which, if shouted by an enemy from the sidewalk, warned the driver of his extra load... My favourite 'whip behind' was a cab. **1982** SUTTON-SMITH *Hist. Children's Play* 89 The coach to Dunedin used to stop at Fagerty's Hotel for watering the horses..and then we got ready to hang on behind. The boys who could not get hold of a strap or something would call out, 'Whip behind,' and one ill-natured driver did it, too, as the coach went on.

whipping side. *Shearing.* [f. *whip, v.* to move (something) vigorously or quickly, with reference to the stroke of the shears: AND 1899.] The last side of a sheep to be shorn. See also MONEY SIDE.
    1955 BOWEN *Wool Away* 40 [Heading] Last or Whipping Side. **1981** SUTHERLAND & TAYLOR *Sunrise* 45 He started on the whipping side, shearing with those long full easy blows. **1989** *NZ Eng. Newsletter* III. 29 *whipping side:* The last side of the sheep to be shorn and also known as the 'money-making' side.

whiptail. Any of various unrelated fishes with tapering or whip-like tails but esp. HOKI *n.*[1] (*Macruronus novaezelandiae*), and *whiptail ray* (RAY 2 (1)).
    1927 PHILLIPPS *Bibliogr. NZ Fishes* (1971) 23 *Macruronus novae-zelandiae* (Hector). Whiptail; Hoki. **1938** [see HOKI]. **1956** GRAHAM *Treasury NZ Fishes* 163 Whiptail (Hoki) *Macruronus novae-zelandiae*. Ibid. 403 Whiptail *Oxygadus kermadecus*.. Whiptail *Coryphaenoides serrulatus*.. Whiptail *Coryphaenoides rudis*.. Whiptail *Coelorinchus aspercephalus*.. Whiptail *Fuyangia murrayi*.. Whiptail *Trachyrincus longirostris*.. Whiptail *Lepidorhynchus denticulatus*.. Whiptail *Nematonurus armatus*.. Whiptail *Bathygadus cottoides*. **1960** PARROTT *Queer & Rare Fishes* 80 *Paramacrurus australis*..whiptail..Hoki..The body of the Whip tail is compressed and tapers towards the tail. **1967** MORELAND *Marine Fishes* 14 Eagleray [*Myliobatis tenuicaudatus*]... Whiptail, stingray and cowfish are among other names in use. **1983** *NZ Clubman* May 24 Hoki—alias whiting or whiptail—is ideally suited to the catering and restaurant trade. **1986** PAUL *NZ Fishes* 36 Long-tailed stingray *Dasyatis thetidis* Alternatively black ray, or whiptail.

whistle-boy, whistleman. *Logging.* A (junior) bush-hand who gives signals to the hauler-driver by means of a *whistle-line* (see quot 1904) to begin hauling.
    [**1904** LANCASTER *Sons o' Men* 166 He had laid his fingers to the line that connected with the engine-whistle... 'Richt she is, Hond us the whustle-line.'] **1923** *Awards, etc.* 112 [Westland Timber Yards and Sawmill Employees] [Rates of wages] Other tram workers [£]0 13[s.] 0[d.] Whistle-boy under eighteen years 0 9 0. **1951** *Awards, etc.* 454 [Westland Timber-Workers Award] [Rates of wages] Bush-winch driver, other than steam 4[s.] 1³/₄[d.] Whistleman 3 11¹/₄ Leading tramwayman 4 0³/₄. **1983** BREMER *Port Craig* 5 The man accompanying the logs to the hauler was known as a shoeman and he generally had a whistle boy who stopped the hauler by means of a whistle when the log reached one of the snatch blocks. **1992** *NZ Geographic* 13 Jan.-Mar. 119 Monty's older brother worked as a whistle boy,... signalling the hauler driver to slacken or tighten the wire ropes which ran off the winch drums.

whistler, *n.*[1] *Obs.* [f. Brit. dial. *whistler:* see EDD 8 anything exceptionally large, 1895.] Something exceptional of its kind.
    1862 GOLDIE *Journal* 18 May in Beattie *Pioneers Explore Otago* (1947) 99 Monday night was a 'whistler', with a fall of six inches of snow, and a keen frost.

whistler, *n.*[2]
    1. *shining cuckoo* (CUCKOO 2 (3)).
    1870 *TrNZI* II. 65 Pipiwharaupa, Bronze-winged Cuckoo... This little bird, in some districts, is most commonly known by the name of Whistler. It is so called from its peculiarly clear note, which exactly resembles the sound made by a man whistling his dog. **1885** [see CUCKOO 2 (1)]. **1948** MONCRIEFF *NZ Birds* 47 Shining Cuckoo... Sometimes known as Whistler. **1966** FALLA et al. *Birds of NZ* 180 Shining Cuckoo *Chalcites lucidus*... Pipiwharauroa, Whistler. **1985** [see CUCKOO 2 (3)].
    2. *blue* (or *whistling*) *duck* (DUCK 2 (2) and (8)).
    1924 *Otago Witness* (Dunedin) 1 Apr. 71 One bird that has not been noticed much by writers is the blue mountain duck... They are sometimes called the whistler.

whistles, *n. pl.* [f. its hollow stem.] BLUEBERRY.
    1978 MOORE & IRWIN *Oxford Book NZ Plants* 182 *Dianella nigra*. Turutu, blueberry, inkberry, or whistles thrives in lowland scrub, on clay banks, and along bush tracks... The reddish leaf-base leaves a yellow scar when broken..; often it is folded into a tube so that skilful blowing can force air out in an ear-splitting whistle.

whistlewood. [Spec. use of Brit. dial. *whistlewood*: see OED 4 a name for various trees having easily-peeled bark, whose stems are used by boys to make whistles, as the alder, basswood, mountain ash.] *Leycesteria formosa*, the Himalaya(n) honeysuckle, or Japanese spiderwort, having a hollow stem which can be used for whistles and pea-shooters. See also PAGODA PLANT, TWITCH ELDER.
    1920 p.c. M. Rason: Hutt Valley, *fide* A.G. Hutson and I.E. Ashforth: must be from 1920 at least. From the hollow stems used for whistles. **1935** Marlborough boys (Ed.). The plant was called *whistlewood* or *(wild) alder*, not *Himalayan honeysuckle*. The stems were hollow and also used also for peashooters. **1946** *Bull. Wellington Bot. Soc. No.14* 8 Here are some [vernacular names]... *Leycestria formosa*, whistlewood, pagoda plant (both in the Hutt Valley), Japanese spiderwort, twitch elder.

whistling duck: see DUCK 2 (8).

whitau. Also early **feetou, feetow, weetau, whiitau, witau.** [Ma. /'fi:tau/: Williams 497 *Whītau*.] The prepared fibre of *Phormium tenax*.
    [**c1826-27** BOULTBEE *Journal* (1986) 113 flax—feětou] **1856** ROBERTS *Diary* 19 Sept. in Beattie *Early Runholding* (1947) 42 The whip was rawhide..finishing off with a twisted 'cracker' made of 'weetau' or dressed flax in place of whipcord. **1868** LINDSAY *Contrib. NZ Bot.* 83 The flax, dressed or not, or scraped fibre, manufactured from the leaf, [was called] 'Whitau,' or 'Muka.' **1897** *TrNZI* XXIX. 174 Several bundles of dressed flax *(whitau),* in hanks *(whenu).* **c1920** *South Is. Maori Lists 'Wahi Mahika Kai'* in Beattie *Maori Place-names Canterbury* (1945) 65 The dressed flax fibre is called whitau, also witau, and at one place it is erroneously written 'wituu'. **1939** BEATTIE *First White Boy Born Otago* 11 The Maori mats were made of feetow (whitau or dressed flax)... They were hung over one shoulder and fastened under the other. **1974** HENDERSON *Open Country Muster* 178 The boss had cut a blade of flax, and, having stripped it into *whiitau*, was making a cracker for his stockwhip.

white, *n.* [Spec. use of *white* a person of a race distinguished by a light complexion.] A light-skinned non-Maori, usu. of European descent. See also PAKEHA 1, WHITE MAN 1.
    1838 *Journal 'Eliza Scott'* 10 Dec. in McNab *Old Whaling Days* (1913) 464 We have seen some marks of visitors [at Chalky Inlet] but whether natives or whites for the bay fishery (I should suppose the latter) I do not know. **1853** MACKIE *Traveller under Concern* (1973) 77 The settlers are now busily engaged in the harvest, a few employ Maoris—these earn 3/- per day, the whites 6/-. The whites through the island bear but a small proportion to the aborigines. **1875** COCKBURN-HOOD *Chowbokiana* 12 The rising generation of 'mean whites' in both islands, but especially in the northern one are fearfully profane, and most offensive in their conversation. **1939** BEATTIE *First White Boy Born Otago* 12 The whites would copy the native way of scraping flax for various purposes [c1840].

white, *a.*
    1. In the names of plants and animals, see: BIRCH 3 (11), CLEMATIS a, CRANE b, EGRET, HERON 2 (3), MAIRE 2 (2), MANGROVE 1, MANUKA 2 (4), MAPAU 2 (3), MATIPO 2 (5), PINE 2 (19), SHARK 2 (20), TEA-TREE 2 (2), WAREHOU 2 (4). See also WHITEBAIT, WHITEHEAD, WHITEWOOD. See below **white-eye** [AND 1843], SILVEREYE; **white fingers,** see quot.; **white grub,** GRASS GRUB 1 a; **white-throat,** ROBIN.
    1869 *TrNZI* I. (rev. edn.) 104 *Zosterops dorsalis*. White eye. I did not see this bird, but Mr. Allon informed me that it had been on the island [Great Barrier] for the last four years. **1871** [see WAXEYE]. **1882** POTTS *Out in Open* 130 The white eye or blight bird..with cheerful note, in crowded flocks, sweeps over the face of the country. **1891** *TrNZI* XXIII. 218 White-eye... I met with this species several times in the bush on Sunday Island. **1906** CHEESEMAN *Manual NZ Flora* 575 The fruits [of *Pisonia brunoniana*] are so excessively viscid that small birds, such as the white-eye..are often caught and glued down by the feathers. **1919** *TrNZI* LI. 220 The White-eye appears to build about the end of October in [South-western Otago]. **1930** [see SILVEREYE]. **1940** STUDHOLME *Te Waimate* (1954) 230 The White-eye has a pretty little song, but so faint that one has to be close alongside to appreciate it properly. **1952** RICHARDS *Chatham Is.* 73 The white-eye feeds on insects and fruit besides honey. **1966** *Notornis* XIII. 182 White-eyes at this time of year tended to move through the forest canopy in flocks of fifteen or more individuals. **1985** *Reader's Digest Book NZ Birds* 288 Silvereye *Zosterops lateralis lateralis*... White-eye, waxeye, blightbird, tauhou. **1982** WILSON *Stewart Is. Plants* 284 *Caladenia lyallii* White orchid... **White fingers**... With a single, sparsely hairy leaf at base of each erect, hairy flower stem... Flowers 1–2,.. white or flushed with pink. **1943** *NZJST* XXIII. 306A There are twenty-eight native species belonging to the genus *Odontria*, but all observers agree that the principal grass grub is *Odontria zealandica*. In the larval stage this is known as 'grass grub,' '**white grub**,' or 'curl grub', and the adult stage is known as 'grass grub beetle', 'brown beetle' or 'turnip fly.' **1930** REISCHEK *Yesterdays in Maoriland* (1933) 250 I was able, while in Chalky Sound, to watch the delightful **white-throat** (*Miro albifrons*), which jealously and obstinately guards its own piece of territory against all comers.

    2. In special collocations: **white alley,** a valued white marble; **whitecomber** *goldmining obs.* [an adaptation of *Whitecoomb* a creek and peak in remote Central Otago rather than the reverse as the quot. implies], a large boulder; **white Continent,** Antarctica; **white fillet,** a trade-name for processed elephant fish flesh; **white lady** [see

OED *white* 11 e (b), 1935 (*Austral.*)], methylated spirits as a drink; **white lake**, see quot.; **white light** [prob. a short form of *white lightning*], methylated spirits as a drink; **white lightning** [see OED *white* 11 e (a), 1921], raw (occas. illicit) spirituous liquor; **white Maori**, see MAORI 6 a; **white-pointer**, see SHARK 2 (20); **white rag**, a white (Sunday) shirt; **white spirit**, see quot.; **White-Stone City**, Oamaru from the extensive use in building of OAMARU STONE q.v.

   1972 SUTTON-SMITH *Folkgames Children* 174 Then there were the terms referring to particular kinds of marbles: for example, agates..tom-bobblers, **white alleys**, and in more recent years ball-bearings. **1975** HARPER *Eight Daughters* 21 Mail was taken every two weeks from Waikaia to the miners in the bush as far as Whitecoombe, at the foot of the Whitecoombe Range. This name was derived from the enormous boulders lodged in the creek flats, as large as the rooms of a house, which the miners called whitecombers. **1938** HYDE *Nor Yrs. Condemn* 160 You get the feeling that Antarctica begins there... the **white Continent**, the last of the clean places in the world. Starkie thought it sounded like a lot of Anzac Day dinner. He was getting sullen under the mixture of beer and Scotch. **1970** SORENSEN *Nomenclature NZ Fish* 22 *Elephant Fish* (a) Scientific name: *Callorhynchus millii*... **White fillet** (a trade name for the processed product)... This fish rarely appears in commerce in other than fillet form and trade name of White Fillets is applied. **1976** BAXTER *Collected Poems* (1980) 241 Their ghosts at daybreak in my room..Ask me for a bottle of **White Lady**. **1988** *Dominion Sunday Times* (Wellington) 14 Feb. 19 Meths is blue or white lady, and steam is a mixture of meths and sherry. **1906** *TrNZI* XXXVIII. 29 The gas escaping through the water of the [Ohaewai] pools..is partially oxidized, liberating sulphur, which imparts a milky-white colour to the pools, locally known as '**white lakes**'. **1938** HYDE *Nor Yrs. Condemn* 190 They drink a lot of metha, don't they. Great names they've got for it—Phar Lap, and Johnny Gee, and **White Light**. There's one old Maori down here who went blind, drinking the metha. **1984** WILSON *S. Pacific Street* 9 I imagine he provided them with little money, unless he paid the grocery bill when he'd made a horse trade or sold some **white lightning**. **1916** THORNTON *Wowser* 89 I rigged up the sack [shirt] to save my only remaining '**white rag**', as men here call them, for Sunday. **1979** *SANZ Gloss. Bldg. Terminol.* 130 **white spirit**. Colourless petroleum distillate with a boiling range between 150° C and 100° C, and containing approximately 20 percent aromatic hydrocarbons. **1926** COWAN *Travel in NZ* II. 104 Oamaru has been called the '**White-Stone City**'; the good white limestone of which much of it is built is quarried in the neighbourhood and is largely used in other parts of the Dominion.

3. In special collocations usu. referring to skin colour, often in a sense 'exclusive of non-whites': **white flight** [transf. use of orig. US *white flight* the movement of white people from urban mainly black areas: see OED 11 e], the movement or moving of Pakeha children from schools with a predominantly Maori roll; **white Gurkha**, usu. *pl.*, from their fierce reputation as fighters, a name given to New Zealand soldiers on Gallipoli Peninsula; **white joker**, an 'ordinary' New Zealander of exemplary character, WHITE MAN 2; **white New Zealand policy** [on analogy of the *White Australia Policy*: cf. the Immigration Restriction Act of 1920], the covert selection of mainly northern European people as immigrants.

   1986 *National Bus. Rev.* 23 May 19 A clear frontrunner for each and any marketing, public relations or packaging award in the 'best socio-intellectual catch-phrase of '86' category: '**White flight**'. Think about it, talk it out, see and hear how it rolls off your tongue. Doesn't matter what it means or involves or entails—the two-word phrase is the attention-grabbing winner of the year... So what the hell is 'white flight' anyway? According to race relations conciliator Wally Hirsch, it's that startling new phenomenon of honky parents taking their kids away from schools whose rolls have significant numbers of different-tinted folk. **1986** *Metro* (Auckland) Sept. 68 The parents caught up in the 'white flight' phenomenon have been taken unawares by the quiet revolution among a significant group of Pakeha who have steadily embraced the concept of biculturalism. **1990** *Evening Post* (Wellington) 1 Oct. 2 He is critical of the 'white flight' phenomenon that has hit schools in areas like Porirua. **1915** MALONE *Diary* 12 May in *Great Adventure* (1988) 47 The Tommies have christened my men [on Gallipoli] the '**White Gurkhas**'. We are very proud of the soubriquet and mean to live up to it. **1915** let. 14 May in *Wanganui Herald* 17 July 5 The Essex and Inniskillings (British regulars) have dubbed us the 'White Gurkhas'. **1988** SHADBOLT *Voices of Gallipoli* 38 It was somewhere around then [May 1915 after the Daisy Patch] that New Zealanders got the name of 'the white Gurkhas'. **1952** *Landfall* 23 Sept. 220 Men are in two classes, the '**white jokers**' and the 'bastards'. **1917** GLOVER *Cartoon in Truth* in Grant *Unauthorised Version* (1980) 128 A door closing on an Indian has a notice '**White New Zealand Policy**'. **1987** *NZJH* Apr. 142 In the 1920s New Zealanders' fears that the superior white races would be swamped by inferior coloured races led to the White New Zealand policy and anti-Chinese feeling.

whitebait. [Spec. use of English *whitebait* the fry of small fishes.]

1. The tiny (40–55 mm) juveniles of esp. the freshwater inanga *Galaxias attenuatus* and also of four other species of *Galaxias*; once an important food for Maori and settler, now an expensive national delicacy. Occas. applied to smelt *Retropinna retropinna*, the so-called *second-class whitebait* of 2 a below. See also BAIT, GALAXIAS, HIWI, INANGA *n.*[1] Also *attrib.* and *transf.*

   1840 BEST *Journal* 24 Oct. (1966) 254 The Natives were employed catching White Bait which the[y] took in nets in great numbers [at Waikanae]. **1858** SMITH *Notes of Journey* in Taylor *Early Travellers* (1959) 365 This morning, we breakfasted off the whitebait or *inanga*, which is so common in Taupo; and it is very nice fried. **1867** HOCHSTETTER *NZ* 165 In the smaller brooks I gathered the Inangas of the natives, the whitebait of the colonists. **1870** *TrNZI* II. 84 I venture to settle..the vexed question, 'What is Whitebait?'... English Whitebait..has been looked upon as the young of the Sprat, the Shad, and the Herring... The New Zealand Whitebait has no affinity with the English fish, whose name it bears. **1883** DOMETT *Ranolf & Amohia* I. 183 That he the first might touch and taste, In flax-wov'n basket for a dish, A dainty pile of delicate fish... Like *whitebait* some. **c1899** DOUGLAS in McDowall *JRSNZ* (1980) X. 320 I dont think many people on the Coast purchase many tins of whitebait... The Westland tinned whitebait is at least genuine. **1899** *Auckland Weekly News* (Suppl.) 23 June 3 This lure he finds quite as killing as the deadly whitebait minnow. **1904** TREGEAR *Maori Race* 108 A small fish (*inanga*), resembling the minnow, swarmed in tidal streams... They were eaten and pressed into a solid mass, and are now called whitebait by the settlers. **1916** *Chron. NZEF* 29 Nov. 158 We can get her a job in N.Z., filleting 'whitebait'. **1922** *NZJST* V. 94 Retropinna retropinna. Smelt. The larval smelt, which has a strong cucumber-smell, is rarely sold as 'whitebait.' Canning-factories at Hokitika do not purchase any fish under the term 'whitebait' other than the larval *Galaxias attenuatus*. **1940** PHILLIPPS *Fishes NZ* 30 He had seen cart-loads of whitebait brought to Wellington from the Hutt River and..this was not an uncommon sight in 1880. **1986** *NZ Woman's Weekly* 14 July 12 We've always lived on the road up to now. In vans or whitebait camps. **1990** *Evening Post* (Wellington) 10 Nov. 58 [Caption: Footrot Flats] 'The-one-that-got-away-' stories about whitebait lack a bit of drama.

2. a. second-class whitebait. SMELT (*Retropinna retropinna*).

   1978 McDOWALL *NZ Freshwater Fishes* 190 The Common Smelt fishery has no regulations applied to it, but it is effectively a part of the whitebait fishery, the fish caught being sold on the Auckland fish market as 'second class whitebait'. **1981** WILSON *Fisherman's Bible* 288 Second-class Whitebait. These are the young of the smelt (*Retropinna retropinna*) which are caught from wharves mainly—especially Auckland's Devonport Wharf—and sold as whitebait. There are no regulations governing them as they are not regarded as being 'true' whitebait. **1986** PAUL *NZ Fishes* 49 Smelt..are taken with whitebait in some harbours and rivers, particularly the Waikato; although sold as 'second class whitebait' they are good eating. **1990** McDOWALL *NZ Freshwater Fishes* 433 As the abundance of *Galaxias* whitebait has declined, the..catch of these juvenile common smelt..possibly ranks as equally important to the whitebait. It is not as highly regarded, being sold as 'second class whitebait' but..finds ready acceptance on the markets in Auckland.

b. mock whitebait. See quot. Cf. MOCK *a*.

   1928 *Everybody's Cookery Book of Tested Recipes* 67 *Mock Whitebait* One egg..potatoes..Pepper and salt... Drop in spoonfuls onto boiling fat.

c. mother whitebait. The adult INANGA *n.*[1]

   1989 *Pacific Way* Nov. 94 Many people refer to the inanga as 'mother whitebait'.

3. *fig.* **a.** A puny or diminutive person.

   1938 HYDE *Nor Yrs. Condemn* 185 That Dickie, do you think I listen to him? That little whitebait.

b. In the phr. **not to have the guts of a whitebait**, to be very cowardly.

   1984 *Listener* 28 July 32 He hasn't got the guts of a whitebait or If his brain were gunpowder the blast wouldn't raise his hat.

4. Special Comb. **whitebait-fishing**, netting whitebait; **whitebait fritter**, see quot.; **whitebait net**, a fine-mesh, usu. funnel-shaped scoop or set net (see also 1980 quot. WHITEBAITER); **whitebait season**, the times when whitebait may be taken, now from 1 September to 15 November each year though the dates are under review (see also quot. 1980); **whitebait stand**, see STAND *n.*[2] 2; **whitebait tax**, **whitebait tribute**, see quot. 1990.

   1965 McLAGLAN *Stethoscope & Saddlebags* 179 Near her was an old girl, also **whitebait-fishing**, who, in true West Coast style, told the story of her ups and downs. **1906** *Teteka Kai Book Well Tried Recipes* 8 **Whitebait fritters**..flour..egg..milk... Drop a small quantity at a time into plenty of boiling fat, and fry. **1947** DAVIN *For the Rest of Our Lives* 101 Len had a dixieful of whitebait fritters for his passport. **1991** VIRTUE *Always the Islands of Memory* 134 Parnell cooked whitebait fritters. **1897** *TrNZI* XXIX. 175 Fragment of a **whitebait-net** made of flax. **1968** SEDDON *The Seddons* 20 The equipment for the expedition in the form of large whitebait nets..are found and the family goes fishing. **1982** *Listener* 6 Nov. 131 The whitebait net was made of coarse cotton, with a frame of supplejack tied with flax. **1889** *TrNZI* XXI. 215 In the Grey during the **whitebait season** (September and October) the birds are very numerous. **1903** *Ibid.* XXXV. 310 During the last whitebait season, Mr.

WHITEBAITER

James King, secretary of the Westland Acclimatisation Society, obtained a quantity of whitebait. **1965** GILLHAM *Naturalist NZ* 147 It was September, soon after the start of the whitebait season and we had not gone far from our cars when we saw what the equinoctial spring gales can do on this part of the coast. **1980** *Freshwater Catch* VIII. 15 The whitebait season is from 1 September to 30 November each year and fishing is permitted between 5 a.m. and 8 p.m. **1990** McDOWALL *NZ Freshwater Fishes* 420 A **whitebait tax** was levied against whitebait bought from Maori on the Waikato to help cover the expenses of the movement... The money, referred to as moni ika (fish money), was voluntarily paid. **1977** KING *Te Puea* 38 [The Mercer and Ngati Tipa people] initiated the '**whitebait tribute**' by which commercial buyers from Maori fishermen paid a tax that went towards expenses for King Movement Practices.

Hence **whitebait** v., **whitebaiting** vbl. n.
1959 SLATTER *Gun in My Hand* 145 Mick..casually talked about whitebaiting on the Coast. **1963** PEARSON *Coal Flat* 42 In a few months..he was going whitebaiting in one of the rivers of South Westland... He would make big money there. **1978** McDOWALL *NZ Freshwater Fishes* 189 Reid..wrote that 'whitebait was sold from August to November by the pint, peck or bushel', and that whitebaiting was a livelihood for the Chinese on the West Coast. **1980** *Freshwater Catch* VIII. 15 Whitebaiting is generally most successful on an incoming tide. **1980** McGILL *Ghost Towns NZ* 238 Once a whale was washed up on the beach, down by The Cut, where Dad whitebaited, successfully. **1990** McDOWALL *NZ Freshwater Fishes* 436 [Caption] Whitebaiting in South Westland is carried out from rickety stands built out into the river from the banks.

whitebaiter. One who nets whitebait for pleasure or profit.
1920 *Weekly News* 21 Oct. [Caption] 4. A buyer in his launch meeting the whitebaiters. **1955** STOKELL *Fresh Water Fishes* 44 These are thus two influences that..contributed directly to the disappearance of the upokororo—unrestricted commercial exploitation of the adult fish, and in the inadvertent destruction of the young by whitebaiters. **1965** GILLHAM *Naturalist NZ* 147 The Whitebaiters righted themselves, retrieved their long funnel-shaped nets, and moved upshore to start operations again in safer quarters. **1980** *Freshwater Catch* VIII. 15 Most whitebaiters use hand-held scoop nets and fish in the surf at the river outlet while others prefer set nets on the river margins. **1990** McDOWALL *NZ Freshwater Fishes* 433 At times the common smelt is regarded as a nuisance by the commercial whitebaiters of the West Coast.

white-chinned petrel: see PETREL 2 (21).

white-eyed duck: see DUCK 2 (9).

white-faced heron, storm petrel: see HERON 2 (2), PETREL 2 (19) b (c) and (e).

white-fronted tern: see TERN 2 (10).

whitehead. *Mohoua albicilla* (fam. Pachycephalidae), a noisy small North Island bush canary, having a brown back and pale or whitish head and underparts. See also CANARY n.[1] 1, POPOKOTEA, UPOKOTEA.
1871 HUTTON *Catalogue Birds NZ* 9 Orthonyx albicilla... White-head. Popokatea. **1898** MORRIS *Austral-English* 511 *White-head*..a bird of New Zealand... Found in North Island, but becoming very rare. **1907** *Ibis* I. 531 The Whiteheads keep more forward in the lower tops, hunting methodically and with a few harsh notes. **1923** *NZJST* VI. 92 In the early days of settlement..the numbers of the Whitehead began to decrease even in the absolutely untouched forests of the interior. **1930** *Evening Post* (Wellington) 6 Dec. 17 The bush canary, or whitehead, a bird which seems to enjoy a fairly wide range in the North Island, was heard on many occasions. **1955** OLIVER *NZ Birds* 470 Proceeding continuously from a flock of Whiteheads is a short single note which may be vocalised 'cheet'. **1981** *Dominion* (Wellington) 13 Feb. 11 Whiteheads (the North Island bush canary), the most common birds on the island, are also high in the trees.

white-headed petrel, stilt: see PETREL 2 (22), STILT 2 (3).

white man.

1. [Spec. use of *white man* a man belonging to a race having naturally light-coloured skin or complexion.] A light-skinned non-Maori usu. of European descent; often used to translate Maori uses of *Pakeha*. See also WHITE n.
c**1826–27** BOULTBEE *Journal* (1986) 109 white man—tongata bulla (Bay of Islands—tongata pàkihow) [tangata pora, tangata pakeha]. **1832** EARLE *NZ* 146 The white taboo'd day [sc. Sunday], when the packeahs (or white men) put on clean clothes and leave off work. **1840** MATHEW *Journal* 29 Apr. in *Founding of NZ* (1940) 132 As it came alongside we perceived that it contained several white men and a number of natives. **1853** ROCHFORT *Adventures of Surveyor* 14 On going down to the beach, some Maories came ashore in a canoe. They were about building a market-place to trade with the white man. **1898** HOCKEN *Contributions* 57 They [sc. the South Island Maori] consented to the terms, and on the 31st of July the deed was read to them..that they must respect the white man's land, and that the white man would not touch the land reserved for them. **1936** BEASLEY *Pioneering Days* 27 The chief 'tapued' (or to use the white man's pronunciation of the word 'tabooed'). **1940** HOWARD *Rakiura* 210 Muttonbirding is..the only phase of primitive economic development which has withstood the destructive competition..introduced by the white man.

2. [Used elsewhere but recorded early in NZ: see OED 2 b 'orig. U.S.', 1883; AND 1891.] A good bloke, a 'dinkum joker', a thoroughly acceptable fellow. Cf. ORDINARY BLOKE.
1888 BARLOW *Kaipara* 192 With a couple of good dogs and a 'white man' (as a good fellow is called out here) for a companion, what more enjoyable than a day after the long tails [sc. Chinese pheasants]. **1897** WRIGHT *Station Ballads* 44 He was a whiteman through and through. **1914** PFAFF *Diggers' Story* 66 On our way down we met a man in rags... He went back with us... He said we were 'white men' for feeding him so well. **1916** THORNTON *Wowser* 45 He was—to use a colonialism—'a white man'. **1921** *Quick March* 11 Apr. 23 'White man—First to Last' is evidently a suitable epitaph for the late Corporal A.C. Sumner.

white man's grass: see GRASS 2 (45).

white-naped petrel: see PETREL 2 (23).

white shroud: see LAND OF THE LONG WHITE CLOUD 2.

white-throated shag: see SHAG 2 (18).

whitewashing, vbl. n. *Shearing.* [AND v. 1905.] The result of shearing young lambs which have little wool.
1955 BOWEN *Wool Away* 158 White-washing. Shearing of young lambs, from whom little wool is taken. **1982** *Agric. Gloss.* (MAF) 61 *Whitewashing*: Shearing of young lambs, from which little wool is shorn.

WHITING

white-winged duck: see DUCK 2 (9).

whitewood. Also **whiteywood.** [From the colour of the wood and bark.]

1. a. MAHOE (*Melicytus ramiflorus*). Also *attrib.*
1889 FEATON *Art Album* (Plant Names) 177 Hinahina [Maori name]..Whitewood [Settlers' name]..Melicytus ramiflorus... Small tree. **1890** [see MAHOE]. **1904** TREGEAR *Maori Race* 94 Only two sorts of wood being used, viz the supplejack..and the White-wood (*mahoe*..) to kindle the fire. **1915** HAY *Reminisc. Earliest Canterbury* 105 Whitewood is a small tree bearing branches of beautiful blue berries. **1926** COWAN *Travel in NZ* II. 32 Here and there a little watercourse..arboured over by a matted roofing of *kotukutuku*..and *mahoe* or whitewood and glossy-green *karaka*. **1927** GUTHRIE-SMITH *Birds* 2 The limestone range east of the lake [Tutira] at one time grew..a considerable area of 'whitey-wood' bush. **1947** white wood [see TARANAKI WOOL]. **1952** THOMSON *Deer Hunter* 161 Most of the greener type of shrubs, such as Whitewood and Five-finger, had almost disappeared, leaving nothing but bare, barked trunks and branches. **1980** WOOLLASTON *Sage Tea* 43 Two were whiteywoods..if I had known their Maori name.. *mahoe*.

b. As **twiggy whiteywood.** *Melicytus micranthus.*
1982 *Field Guide Common NZ Trees & Shrubs* 7 Manakura (Swamp mahoe or twiggy whitey wood). *Melicytus micranthus.*

2. *Obs.* PATE (*Schefflera digitata*).
1870 *TrNZI* II. 122 Schefflera digitata. White wood.

whiteywood: see WHITEWOOD.

whiting. [Transf. use of *whiting* a northern hemisphere gadoid fish *Merlangus vulgaris*: AND 1792.]

1. Any of various fishes resembling the northern hemisphere whiting. **a.** Unidentified species.
1835 YATE *NZ* (1970) 71 Those saltwater fish most plentiful, and of greatest note, are, soles, mackarel.. whiting. **1841** HODGSKIN *Narr. Eight Months Sojourn NZ* 34 Whiting, bream, and snappers are abundant, with several kinds of skate. **1855** DRURY *Sailing Directions* 68 Fish [met with in Pelorus]. Whiting (or resembling the European Whiting).

b. HAKE 1 b (*Merluccius australis*).
1911 WAITE *Rec. Canterbury Mus.* I. 175 *Merluccius Gayi*... Hake, Whiting. **1927, 1938** [see HAKE 1 b]. **1956** GRAHAM *Treasury NZ Fishes* 164 Hake or whiting *Merlangius australis*. *Ibid.* 166 Hake is known in Christchurch, and by some in Otago, as Whiting, but it is not a true Whiting. **1966** [see HAKE 1 b]. **1970** [see HAKE 1 b].

c. (*erron.*) HOKI (*Macruronus novaezelandiae*).
1983 *NZ Clubman* May 24 Hoki—alias whiting or whiptail—is ideally suited to the catering and restaurant trade. **1986** [see HOKI].

d. *bastard red cod* (COD 2 (1), *Pseudophycis breviuscula*).
1879 *TrNZI* XI. 381 The Whiting, *Pseudophycis breviusculus*, is got occasionally. **1886** SHERRIN *Handbook Fishes NZ* 17 Whiting (*Pseudophycis breviusculus*). Another fish of the cod kind, which has a deeper body than the *Lotella rhacinus*, and more delicate flesh, resembling that of the whiting. **1898** MORRIS *Austral-English* 511 *Whiting*, n. The New Zealand Whiting is *Pseudophycis breviusculus*. **1906** *TrNZI* XXXVIII. 551 *Pseudophycis breviusculus*... Occasionally taken, and locally known as 'whiting'.

2. blue (southern blue) whiting. *Micromesistius australis* (fam. Gadidae).
1978 *Catch '78* Mar. 12 Southern Blue Whiting

Micromesistius australis Southern poutassou... Abundant on the Campbell Plateau. **1979** *Catch '79* July 23 The development of a European market for southern blue whiting appears a likely spin-off from research and commercial fishing by the joint vessel *Wesermunde* in New Zealand's southern waters. **1982** AYLING *Collins Guide* (1984) 149 The southern blue whiting is very similar to the blue whiting from the North Atlantic and grows to a similar size. **1991** *Contact* (Wellington) 21 Feb. 1 New Zealanders may not at present find blue whiting in the shops, but the Japanese, who catch most of it, add value to the fish by turning it into surimi.

whole box and dice: see BOX *n.*² 7.

whoop, *v.* [Orig. uncertain: poss. f. *hoop* to bowl a hoop; or f. *whoop*, an extended sense of *whoop it up.*] Often constr. with preps., esp. as **to whoop along**, to speed, to go fast.

c**1938** popular among Marlborough boys, for speeding (on a bike, etc.): to whoop up or along the road. **1944** COOZE *Kiwis in Pacific* 29 A car whooped along in a cloud of dust. **1946** COOZE *My Little State Home* 62 A bus which whoops along.

whooa-whaa: see HOOER.

whopcacker: var. WOPCACKER.

whore: see HOOER.

whydua, var. WAIRUA.

whye(e)nee, varr. WAHINE.

whykickamoocow, whykikamookau, varr. WAIKIKAMUKAU.

why pirau, var. WAIPIRO.

wi: see WIWI *n.*¹

wideawake, *n.* and *attrib.*

1. With init. cap., the nickname given by the Maori to Colonel William Wakefield, the New Zealand Company's Wellington-based agent: a play on *Wake*field, with reference to his freq. wearing of a 'wideawake' hat, and possibly to the fact that he was an alert businessman.

1840 *NZ Jrnl.* I. 298 This is Wide Awake's ship [*sc. Tory*] come to watch his son. **1852** MUNDY *Our Antipodes* II. 390 In the same year [*sc.* 1848] E Puni attended as a pall-bearer the funeral of..'Wideawake'—as the Maoris styled the gallant and lamented Colonel Wakefield. **1890** *Otago Witness* (Dunedin) 21 Aug. 32 Colonel Wakefield..was not idle; 'Wideawake' the Maoris called him and wideawake they found him.

2. [Used elsewhere (see OED 1837, and poss. so named from a play on its material not having a 'nap' or raised pile) but of special significance as part of the 'bush-costume' of colonial New Zealand.] In full **wideawake cap**, or **wideawake hat**. A soft felt hat with a broad brim and a low flat crown, the common headgear of early settlers and pioneers.

1851 LUSH *Auckland Jrnls.* 29 Mar. (1971) 70 The Lady looking remarkably well in her [riding] habit and wideawake cap. **1854** [see BUSH COSTUME]. **1867** [see DIGGER *n.*¹ 3 c]. **1871** MONEY *Knocking About NZ* 18 In a place [*sc.* the diggings] where open shirts, moleskin trousers tucked into long boots, crimson sashes tied round the waist, and tall American wide-awakes, were the prevailing attire. **1883** GREEN *High Alps* 279 In walked an elderly gentleman in a wideawake hat, black coat, neat spring-side boots, and, for luggage, an umbrella. **1898** REEVES *Long White Cloud* 242 [In Canterbury c1850] the Australian coo-ee, the Australian buck-jumping horse, the Australian stockwhip and wideawake hat came into New Zealand pastoral life. **1912** MANSFIELD *Stories* (1984) 109 Wisps of white hair straggled from under his wideawake. **1924** *Otago Witness* (Dunedin) 11 Mar. 60 Those were the early..goldfield days when the pioneer miner appeared in his..wide awake hat and nugget boots.

wide comb: see COMB.

widgeon. *Obs.* Also **wigeon**. [Spec. use of *widgeon* a wild duck: AND 1840.] Occas. as **black widgeon**, any of various wild ducks (see esp. SCAUP and TEAL *n.*¹); and also rarely (see quot. 1966) *banded rail* (RAIL 2 (2)).

1842 [see TEAL *n.*¹ 1]. **1856** PHILLIPS *Rockwood Jrnl.* (Canterbury Pub. Lib. TS) 29 Dec. 61 Got to 'Widgeon Lake' (a good sized Lagoon at the head of Lake Coleridge)... Seal then went and killed 6 more widgeon. **1868** PYKE *Province Otago* 31 Grey ducks, Paradise ducks,.. teal, and widgeon frequent the streams. **1870** *TrNZI* II. 48 Amongst them [*sc.* visitors to the water], the Black Widgeon and variegated Shoveller were rarely to be seen. **1873** [see SCAUP]. **1882** POTTS *Out in Open* 288 At a turn is seen a goodly flock of black widgeon; as they rise a couple are tumbled over. **1953** GUTHRIE-SMITH *Tutira* (3edn.) 210 The future of the Widgeon or Scaup (*Aythya novaeseelandiae*) is less easy to forecast. **1966** FALLA et al. *Birds of NZ* 104 Banded Rail *Rallus philippensis*... Landrail, Striped Rail... (The old sealers' name for the Macquarie Island race was Wigeon!)

widgie /ˈwɪdʒi/. *Hist.* Also **wedgie**. [Of unknown origin: AND 1950.] A female member of a street group of the 1950s distinguished by peculiarities of dress or behaviour; the female counterpart of BODGIE q.v.

1955 *Truth* 2 Nov. 1 The island was overrun with hundreds of boozing, cursing, bottle-smashing bodgies and widgies... The bodgies favour blue jeans, the widgies black sweaters and tight black skirts. **1956** *Street Society Christchurch* 1 At various times these young people were referred to as 'Teddy Boys', 'Milk Bar Cowboys' and 'Bodgies and Widgies'. *Ibid.* 5 Very few girls in Widgie clothes (tight black skirts, white, high-collared shirts) were seen, but there were large numbers of girls of 'Widgie-type'. **1963** DUCKWORTH *Barbarous Tongue* 43 The Rosemarie [milk-bar]? That ghastly place. You'll get all the cowboys and widgies on Saturday. **1966** *Encycl. NZ* II. 680 Australian importations include..*bodgies* and *widgies* for young male and female delinquents. **1986** *Manukau Courier* 1 May in *Listener* 9 Aug. (1986) 4 [Life in NZ] Attention Sth Auckland Rock'n'Roll club presents Budgie & Wedgie Nite.

widow-maker. A workmen's name for an implement or feature of a workplace considered very dangerous.

1952–53 *NZ Forest Service Gloss.* (TS) *Sailer.* A falling branch. syn. Widowmaker. **1978** MCARA *Gold Mining Waihi* 185 It was not until considerably later that the 'swing type' stoper..known as the 'popper', came into use... At first the miners did not like it, as they considered it 'shook up' the roof too much, causing falls of ground... At one stage the popper was given the rather undeserved name of the 'widow-maker'.

wiena, var. WAHINE *n.*¹

wife beater, wife-dodger: see DEBT-DODGER.

wig, *n. Sealing.* [Used elsewhere but recorded earliest from the NZ coast: see OED *n.* 5 a.] An old male seal. Cf. CLAPMATCH.

1821 *McDonald's Evidence to Commissioner Bigge's Inquiry* May in McNab *Hist. Records* (1908) I. 559 Q. Is any oil obtained from the seals..? A. There is. A pup seal will give about 2 gallons more or less. A wig, that is an old male seal, will yield 5 or 6 gallons. **1870** *TrNZI* II. 30 The Maoris speak of them [*sc.* seals] as much larger than the *wigs*, as they call the full-grown Brown Seal of our coasts. **1888** DOUGALL *Far South* 10 When full grown..each male [sea lion], or 'old wig' as the sailors call him, will weigh about seven.. hundredweight. **c1920** [see KEKENO]. **1940** HOWARD *Rakiura* 40 Incoming skins are sorted to arbitrary standards—wigs (old males), clap-matches (females), bulls, yearlings, grey or silver pups (under one year), black pups. **1945** HALL-JONES *Hist. Southland* 28 The bull seals (sea-lions, or wigs) come ashore in spring and take up their stance on the rocks. **1950** BEATTIE *Far-Famed Fiordland* 24 The sealers called the old male seals wigs, the female seals clapmatches, and the young were pups. **1982** SANSOM *In Grip of Island* 92 Stretched out on the rocks, relaxed or asleep, only one watchful old wig had his head raised and on the alert.

wig, *v. Farming.* Also **wink**. [AND 1913.] *trans.* To clip wool from the head of a sheep, esp. from over the eyes. Often as a *vbl. n.* See also EYE-WIG.

1933 *Press* (Christchurch) (Acland Gloss.) 30 Dec. 13 *Wink* or *Wig.*- Other names for *eyeclip.* **1950** *NZJAg.* Oct. LXXXI. 349 Lambs..while ewes are being shorn..are being wigged or eye-clipped. **1982** *Agric. Gloss.* (MAF) 61 *Wigging:* Shearing wool from the head of sheep. Normally carried out at crutching. The trade term for this wool is eye clips. Also known as topknots or wigs.

Hence **wig** *n.* (often *pl.*) [AND 1964], TOPKNOT.

1973 FERNANDEZ *Tussock Fever* 166 'What's 2nd Pcs H?' 'Grade 2, pieces—that's skirtings'... 'What about Lbs Wigs?' 'Lamb top-knots—off the head.' **1982** [see above].

wigeon, var. WIDGEON.

wiggle-stick. *Whitebaiting.* See quot.

1995 *Dominion* (Wellington) 11 Jan. 13 The whitebait are supposed to go round the screens and into the net. If they don't then they are herded in the right direction with a wiggle-stick—a pole with the flag on the end.

wiggy. Also **wiggybush**. [f. its habit resembling a rough wig.] Any of several highly-branched shrubs. **a.** *Muehlenbeckia* spp., esp. *M. complexa*.

1927 *TrNZI* LVII. 969 wiggybush *Muehlenbeckia* sp. Ver. [= Vernacular names, supplied [to Johannes Andersen] by B.C. Aston, Chief Chemist, Department of Agriculture, collected in various parts of New Zealand.] **1940** LAING & BLACKWELL *Plants NZ* 160 It is the straggling unattractive *Mūhlenbeckia complexa*... 'wiggy-bush'..describes its habit very well. **1969** *Standard Common Names Weeds* 86 *wiggy* [=] *wire vine*... *wiggy bush* [=] *wire vine*.

b. *Coprosma* spp.

1961 MARTIN *Flora NZ* 215 A majority of small bushy shrubs with twiggy branches and small opposite leaves are Coprosmas, colloquially known as 'wiggy bushes' or 'miki-miks'.

wiggybush: see WIGGY.

wigwam /ˈwɪɡˌwɒm/. *Obs.* [Transf. use of N. Amer. *wigwam* a Native American dwelling.]

1. *rare.* WHARE 1.

1867 THOMSON *Rambles with Philosopher* 47 He brought us to the front of a small wigwam or *whare*.

2. *transf.* In the phr. **a wigwam for a goose's bridle**. [Prob. an alteration of Brit. dial. *a whim-wham for a goose's bridle*, 'something that April fools are sent in search of': see EDD *whim-wham* 4 (3) Northern Ireland, among other 'evasive answers given to a child or other unauthorized questioner'; also 2 a trifle; a fanciful invention; AND 1960.] An evasive reply to an inquisitive child, or a gauge of fancifulness or usefulness.

c1938 Used by W.H. Orsman (b. Nelson, 1863), usu. as *wigwam for a goose's bridle*, as a reply to an inquisitive child (Ed.). **1980** LELAND *Kiwi-Yankee Dict.* 112 *wigwam for a goose's bridle*: an old unusual and uncommon Southland term for something that is totally useless. 'That's about as much use as a wigwam for a goose's bridle'. **1982** FRAME *To the Is-land* (1984) 80 Those answers were as meaningless as the teasing answer people gave when you asked them what they were making: 'A wigwam for a goose's bridle.' **1988** *Through the Looking Glass* 94 The people at 195 were full of sayings... 'What's that?' I would enquire. 'A wigwam for a goose's bridle,' he would reply. **1989** *Evening Post* (Wellington) 14 Nov. 6 Mum was an old Scot and had a great deal of homespun philosophy. If I asked what something was she would often tell me 'It's a wigwam for a goose's bridle.'

wiho, wihu, varr. WHIO.

wika, var. WEKA.

Wilbur. *WW2* (Italy). [f. a common US first-name.] An American soldier, a GI.

c1945 *Sixes & Sevens* (Troopship pub.) 7 'Then you've got to remember the Wilburs,' I said. 'All hands to the PX for an extra ration of coca-cola.' **1946** WEBBER *Johnny Enzed in Italy* (gloss.) *Wilbur*: New Zealand for American.

wild, *a.* In the names of plants and animals, see: CABBAGE 1, CARROT 1 a, CATTLE 1, CELERY 2 (2), CONVOLVULUS, CRESS, DOG 2, DUCK 2 (10), MINT, ONION 1, PARSLEY 1, PIG *n.*¹ 1 b, PIGEON 2 (4), PORTULACA a, RADISH, SPANIARD, SPINACH, THYME 1, TOBACCO, TURNIP 1. See also WILD IRISHMAN.

wild Irishman. Also in shortened form **Irishman**, with or without init. cap., *pl.* occas. *Irishmen*. [Origin uncertain, but compare *Scotsman* (thistle), *wild Spaniard*, and the plant's thorny intractability perh. inviting comparison with the *Wild Irish* (OED *Irish* B 1 a).] MATAGOURI, TUMATAKURU.

1851 WELD *Letter* Jan. in *NZGG* 21 Feb. (1851) 32 We had remarked little or no wood [near the Awatere] but gigantic 'wild Irishmen' here as large as hawthorns. **1860** in Butler *First Year* 27 Jan. (1863) iii 29 There was a great deal..of a very uncomfortable prickly shrub, which they call Irishman, and which I do not like at all. *Ibid.* vii 106 On either side is a long flat..with fine feed for sheep or cattle among the burnt Irishman thickets. **1873** PYKE *Wild Will Enderby* (1889, 1974) I. iii 17 *Tumata-kuru*—Better known as 'Wild Irishman'—a thorny plant, very difficult to handle. **1883** HECTOR *NZ Handbook* 131 *Discaria toumatou*... Tumatakuru, Wild Irishman.—A bush or small tree with spreading branches; if properly trained would form a handsome hedge. **1897** *Otago Witness* (Dunedin) 25 Nov. 47 The scrub was of the thorny kind That some dead wag who often ran Against it, cursing, left behind His name for it—'Wild Irishman.' **1906** ROBERTS in *Hist. N. Otago from 1853* (1978) 4 Tumatakuru, a small thorny scrub, one of the few deciduous plants of New Zealand, which Europeans nick-named 'Wild Irishman'. c1919 [see MATAGOURI]. **1922** *NZJST* IV. 282 The wild-irishman..attained a greater stature and was more abundant than now. **1926** *TrNZI* LVI. 663 [Fantastic plant-names] seem appropriate though often it is impossible to give any definite reason for the name. No trace has been found of any reason for the name 'wild-irishman' as applied to *Discaria toumatou*. Many old settlers have been questioned without result, or with such barren result as the following: One being asked, 'Why was the wild-irishman called the wild-irishman?' answered 'I suppose because it is *like* a wild Irishman.' 'What characteristics have they in common?' 'Well, I-I-I really can't say.'.. Whilst it is often written with a capital, it is now as often written with a small letter, 'irishman'. **1933** *Press* (Christchurch) (Acland Gloss.) 28 Oct. 17 *Irishman scrub*.- Discaria. Also called *wild I[rishman]*, or *matagouri*. A hard prickly scrub, almost leafless, which grows on almost any land and stands any amount of drought or frost. The early settlers always called it by its English names: but since the [1914–18] war it is as often as not called by its Maori one. **1953** STRONACH *Musterer on Molesworth* 38 Our camp was in a small bay surrounded by..very big matagouris or Irishman, some more than a foot through. **1987** OGONOWSKA-COATES *Boards, Blades & Barebellies* 98 *Wild Irishman*. Matagouri; native, spikey, very hardy.

wild Spaniard: see SPANIARD.

willey waugh, var. WILLIWAW.

william: see BILLY *n.*¹ 1 a.

Willie away. *Rugby union.* Also **Willy Away**. [f. *Wil*(son + -IE, after Wilson ('Willie') James Whineray (1935–), All Black captain (1958–65), and exponent of the move.] A forward play in which the front-of-lineout forwards follow the throw-in, receive the tapped ball, and drive it out round the back of the lineout into the opponents' mid-field. Also *attrib*.

1964 MCLEAN *Willie Away* 7 Willie away, they called it... As the ball left the threequarter's arm..the Number 4 began running along the back of the lineout. The halfback of the day kept pace with him. Other forwards, 2, 3 and 5, tailed after him. Number 6 or number 7 tensed and poised and made ready to spring into the air to touch, tap or grab and pass the ball down into the arms of the first runner. And within seconds, the whole pack was shambling in his wake into the open field. This was 'Willie Away', a favourite ploy of the 1963–64 All Black Rugby Union team... The name came from the captain, Wilson James Whineray, who was the principal instrument in it. **1975** HOWITT *NZ Rugby Greats* 291 In 1961 the 'Willie Away' move was born. It was inspired by the French touring team... The French kept peeling off the rear of the lineout and driving up the middle of the field... We thought if we could create a blindside by driving up midfield from a lineout..we could extend the move where it kept dying out with France. **1986** KNIGHT *Shield Fever* 132 He scored a crucial try. It came from a 'Willie Away' movement in a lineout nearly 30 metres out. **1992** *Dominion* (Wellington) 6 Aug. 35 McDowell showed up, leading the willy-aways from the line-out.

williwaw /ˈwɪliˌwɔ/. Mainly *Marlborough Sounds*. Also **willey waugh**, **willie-wa**, **willy waugh**. [Origin uncertain.]

[*Note*] It is noticed as 'a sudden, strong, cold wind from land usually along mountainous coasts in northernmost and southernmost latitudes' and as a whalers' term from the Straits of Magellan in *Ocean and Marine Dictionary* 1979 (Cornell Maritime Press) p. 349; and recorded also from the Straits of Magellan 1842, 1863 by authors with a NZ connection, J.D. Hooker and Robert Fitzroy, and later used by Kipling in *Kim* (see OED *williwaw*). The first element (perh. a var. of *whirly*) is poss. the *willy* 'a violent coastal whirlwind or squall from or near cliff faces' recorded (1832, 1941) from the Atlantic (Tristan da Cunha: see OED *n.*³) in 1832 by Augustus Earle, Robert Fitzroy's draughtsman during the voyage of the *Beagle*, who had resided in Tristan da Cunha as well as in early New Zealand writing an account of both places; and also from Wellington in 1840. This *willy* is prob. represented by the Falkland Islands *woo(l)ly* recorded by Bernadette Hince (DANTE) from H.A. Baker *Final report on geological investigations in the Falkland Islands* (1924) 3 'Violent winds (termed locally 'woolies') were a real menace when proceeding by sea in a small boat'. (Austral. *willy-willy* is not relevant, being from a north-western Aborig. dial. and unrecorded before 1894.) The *-waw* element is perh. a variant of Brit. dial. *waft*, *waff* (cf. *waft*, *whiff*, a whalers' signal flag, recorded on the NZ coast from the 1830s) 'a puff of air, a blast', used as an alliterative suffix and poss. altered under the influence of a rhyme with the nautical *cat's paw* 'a light variable breeze' (see Bowen's definition of *willi-waw*); or with *flaw* 'a squall' recorded from NZ in 1857 (see OED *flaw n.*² 1 and quot. 1857 below). See also the introductory quots. below which describe a 'willie-waw' phenomenon under different names. The evidence strongly indicates a nautical provenance; the Marlborough Sounds and Cook Strait have since early times been heavily involved with whaling; there is a 'Williwa Point' on the southern end of Oyster Bay on the westernmost head of Port Underwood, in Cloudy Bay, Marlborough, an early haunt of shore-whalers (1979 *Wises NZ Guide*, 514).

A sudden violent coastal squall or powerful whirling gust of wind which comes off land, esp. from steep coastal faces or cliffs. See also WILLY.

a. Non-New Zealand and related evidence.

1827 in King *Narrative of HMS Adventure and Beagle* (1839) I. 50 [and 3 further occurrences] On the north shore [of Gabriel Channel, Straits of Magellan] we noticed some extraordinary effects to the whirlwinds which so frequently occur in Tierra del Fuego. The crews of sealing vessels call them 'williwaws' or 'hurricane-squalls', and they are most violent. **1836** *Log 'Mary Mitchell'* 4 May in McNab *Old Whaling Days* (1913) 439 Heavy wind at SE and Whirlwinds [at Cloudy Bay]. *Ibid.* 440 8 May Latter [SE] heavy wind and Gusts real Whirlwinds taking the water up in eddies. **1857** HURSTHOUSE *NZ* I. 246 [In Dusky Bay] it will generally be necessary to secure to the trees also, to prevent being drifted off from the steep bank by a flaw of wind. These flaws, or squalls, frequently blow with great violence off the high land, or down the gullies, during heavy gales outside. **1900** *Sailing Alone around the World* 106 By this time [off Patagonia] the wind had gone down and cat's-paws took the place of williwaws.

b. New Zealand evidence.

1849 ARNOLD *Letters* 22 Nov. (1966) 157 The skipper..was a French Canadian. There were three men besides, one an old whaler, another a native of Nova Scotia, the third..[from] the Azores... [We] entered Queen Charlotte's Sound. By this time the wind had increased to a gale from the North West, and blowing over the low ridge which divides the Sound from Port Gore, it came to us in 'williwaws', that is, violent puffs, succeeded by temporary calms. You can see the Williwaw coming from a long distance; the sea is blown up in a cloud of spray; curling and whirling it sweeps down upon you, and immediately before it comes, 'Let go,' shouts the skipper, and the fore and main sheets are let go, blocks rattle, masts strain, canvas flaps violently, and the weight of wind forces the vessel nearly on her beam ends. Then in half a minute it is nearly a dead calm. **1897** BRACKEN *Second Annual* 49 The next thing we saw was the boat upside down... Fisher said it must have been a 'Willey Waugh', whatever that might be. **1901** *TrNZI* XXXIII. 504 [E.E. Morris, ed. *Austral-English* writes:] A special inconvenience [in Queen Charlotte Sound] introduced me to a new word—viz., the 'willy waughs', [**1901** *Note* Thus was I instructed to spell.] brief gusts of wind that blew across the sound, carrying spindrift with them. Sometimes, crossing the mouth of a bay, we caught these gusts full and were well-nigh drenched... I found the word in the Standard [Dictionary] as Patagonian. 'Willi-wa, a violent wind from mountains in the fiords of Patagonia'. **1902** WALKER *Zealandia's Guerdon* 108 'Willie-wa reach' and 'Doldrum Point' [in the Marlborough Sounds]. **1933** EADDY *Hull Down* 58 With a north-easter and easterly gale the 'willie waws' which come down over the high peaks are very sudden and severe. **1970** JOHNSON *Life's Vagaries* 46 During one southerly gale when the bay [in the Marlborough Sounds] was white with willie-waws our tin *whare* was demolished. **1979** in Cutten *Cutten Lett.* (1979) 13 The *John Wickliffe* arrived within the Heads on 22 March 1848..and the next day she was at Port Chalmers, much buffeted by 'williwaws' as the local whalers call the sudden gusts of wind. **1984** *2YA Wellington Local News* 15 June Boats sailing to east of Kapiti Island should beware of willie-waws coming down the valley.

willow.

1. *Obs.* As **native willow**, WINEBERRY 1.
 1939 BEATTIE *First White Boy Born Otago* 13 The mako or native willow has a little blue-black berry full of seeds which you spit out when eating.

2. *Obs.* As **New Zealand willow**, KOROMIKO.
 1865 MUELLER *My Dear Bannie* (1958) 61 It is in the midst of what was..an old Mauri plantation or garden, with small scrub, especially New Zealand willow, as far as the plantation went and heavy timber encircling that again. **1868** LINDSAY *Contribs. NZ Bot.* 68 V[*eronica*] *Salicifolia*... In allusion to its frequent habit and habitat—on the banks of streams—it is locally known as the New Zealand 'Willow'.

willy. *Obs. Wellington.* [Perh. a var. of *whirly*: see OED *willy n.*³, first recorded from Tristan da Cunha; see discussion at WILLIWAW.] A whirling wind-squall.
 1840 *NZ Jrnl.* I. 203 A strong north-west gale in squalls and willies.

Willy away, var. WILLIE AWAY.

willy waugh, var. WILLIWAW.

wilsonite. *Obs.* [*Wilson* identity unknown: poss. from a local quarry-name in the Waihi-Hauraki district, used locally by mining men: the term seems unrelated to other geol. uses of *wilsonite*.] IGNIMBRITE.
 1905 SOLLAS & MCKAY *Rocks of Cape Colville Peninsula* I. 123 A very important problem is presented by the rock named 'wilsonite' which I am quite prepared to accept as having once been in a state of flow. **1912** *NZGeol.SB (NS)* No.15 19 Two special types of flow rhyolites form the plain of the Waihi Basin. The older is the peculiar rock locally termed 'wilsonite', which is fairly regularly jointed, and is extensively quarried for road metal. *Ibid.* 125 Brecciated flow rhyolite, containing much pumice, pitchstone, andesitic lapilli, etc. (locally known as 'wilsonite'). **1922** *NZJST* V. 113 The Waihi Plain, is for the most part covered by a remarkable rhyolitic tuff, to which the special name of 'wilsonite' was given by the late Alexander McKay. **1934** *Ibid.* XVI. 58 The name 'wilsonite' is applied to the rhyolites used by mining men in Waihi and Karangahake districts, and Sollas used it in describing the rock..from Owharoa [near Waikino] and from Waihi. Other writers have used it, and have placed it in inverted commas, as wilsonite is a [different] mineral that was named in 1853. It seems advisable to find a new name for the rock; the writer proposes to call the rock owharoaite, after one of the places where it occurs. **1946** *NZGeol.SB (NS)* No.41 64 The term 'owharoite' [was proposed] to replace the local miners' name 'wilsonite', which is the name of a mineral with prior rights. **1978** MCARA *Gold Mining at Waihi* 20 These rocks [*sc.* quartz andesite lavas] were succeeded [at Waihi]..by what are known as the more recent, non-productive, younger andesites—tridymite rhyolite and rhyolitic tuffs, the latter sometimes referred to locally as Wilsonite.

wind. *Special Comb.* **wind-berry** [OED *obs.* Brit. dial. for *whim-berry*, a bilberry or whortleberry], an edible berry of the SI tussock country; **wind grass**, see GRASS 2 (46); **windpipe of the Pacific** *obs.*, Cook Strait; **wind thistle**, see *winged-thistle* (THISTLE *n.* 2 (6) and (7)).
 1947–48 BEATTIE *Pioneer Recolls.* (1956) 5 On the tussocky sides of gullies the pleasant-tasting snowberries grew in profusion, while a berry known as the **wind-berry** grew on a little plant similar to the snowberries and both kinds were eaten and enjoyed. **1898** REEVES *Long White Cloud* 77 The Strait, it may be mentioned, is still playfully termed, 'the **windpipe of the Pacific**'.

windie. [f. *wind*(-surfer + -IE.] A wind-surfer.
 1985 *Metro* (Auckland) Jan. 101 The launchies [were] now confronting 'yachties' (of a miniature variety)..the eventual result being the setting up of a windsurfing association. Not only that; the windies charged an entrance fee for the next race.

window. A bald patch in the fur of possum pelts.
 1982 *Listener* 6 Feb. 17 The possum has a well-founded reputation for ferocious if not vicious mating which leaves pelts with..gaps in fur, called 'windows'.

windy, *a.*

1. a. In special collocations with reference to the strong winds associated with the city, **Windy Wellington**, later **Windy City**.
 1870 *Evening Post* (Wellington) 14 Dec. 2 Windy Wellington. **1887** *Auckland Weekly News* 18 June 21 [Heading] Windy Wellington. **1890** *NZ Observer* 8 Feb. 1 Weeping Wellington! This phrase is for the nonce more appropriate than the usual descriptive one of 'windy Wellington'. **1907** *Free Lance* (Wellington) 8 June 1 I spent a day or two in the Capital of the Colony, which might now well change the name of 'Windy Wellington' to the 'City of Noises!' **1913** *NZ Observer* 12 Apr. 4 It is freely stated in the Windy City that Willy can read two proofs at one time in his sleep. **1938** HYDE *Nor Yrs. Condemn* 89 Blowy old place, isn't it? Windy Wellington... But I like the wind. **1962** LAWLOR *More Wellington Days* 184 Windy Wellington: Whisper this, if you dare, to any true Wellingtonian. **1982** O'BISO *First Light* (1987) 40 We are now in Wellington, called the Windy City, and they are not kidding around. **1986** *Listener* 20 Sept. 38 'Hello, Basil,' I said, 'what are you doing back in the Windy City?'

b. Hence, *ellipt.* as a noun, Wellington City.
 1907 MACLENNAN *Neptune's Toll* 38 And hold a famous parliament of woe... Just the same as folk in 'Windy' do, you know. **1942** *Wall Newspaper 13th Field Ambulance* 7 July As 'Windy's' bleak and wintry blast Tore off our tottering hood at last. **1972** *Evening Post* (Wellington) 31 Oct. 1 [Heading] No Chance of Losing 'Windy' Title.

2. As **windy buoy**, an air-filled buoy used by fishermen to mark the position of set long-lines.
 c1949 *Windy buoy*, used by Marlborough Sounds fishermen to mark set longlines. (Ed.) **1970** SORENSEN *Nomenclature NZ Fish* 27 Methods [groper] fished: Motor trawl, longline and handlines; 'Windy Buoys'... Cook Strait area is..where the principal catches are made in the winter months on 'Windy Buoy' set lines.

wineberry. [f. the clusters of dark reddish-purple currant-like berries, from which a wine-like juice can be expressed.]

1. *Aristotelia serrata* (formerly *racemosa*) (fam. *Elaeocarpaceae*), a small tree or shrub notable for its clusters of berries; also the berry. See also CURRANT, MAKOMAKO *n.*², MOCKIE *n.*², WILLOW 1.
 1870 *TrNZI* II. 122 Aristotelia racemosa. Wine berry. **1889** FEATON *Art Album NZ Flora* 62 In some districts the tree is known as the 'Wine-berry', and wine has been prepared from its abundant and juicy fruit. **1890** [see CURRANT]. **1907** LAING & BLACKWELL *Plants NZ* 246 [*Aristotelia serrata*] goes by different names in different districts... In Canterbury, it is called the Wine-berry. **1920** *Quick March* 10 Jan. 41 The construction..was that of most bush bunks; the main supports consisting of a section of 'bungi'... These supported wine-berry poles. **1935** *Tararua Tramper* July 2 Many fruits can be eaten raw. Amongst these are the wine-berry, the konini,.. astelia berries. **1951** LEVY *Grasslands NZ* (1970) 13 These gave protection to many secondary growths, including wineberry, lacebark, konini..and later, blackberry. **1971** *Listener* 6 Sept. 17 There were wineberry trees in the bit of bush. **1982** BURTON *Two Hundred Yrs. NZ Food* 7 Other berries popular as delicacies were the..ripe, black berries of the..wineberry.

2. Also **wineberry shrub**, TUTU 1, or its berry used to make tutu wine.
 1860 BENNETT *Gatherings of Naturalist* 411 Tutu, the Wine-berry shrubs of Europeans. **1868** LINDSAY *Contribs. NZ Botany* 85 The too-well-known 'Toot' of the Otago farmer; the 'Wine-berry Shrub' of the early settlers about the Bay of Islands. **1898** MORRIS *Austral-English* 513 *Wine-berry, n.* See *tutu*. **1909** *TrNZI* XLI. 292 Indeed, in the very early days the tutu was known as the wine-berry shrub. This wine, however, has not always proved to be above suspicion. **1958** *Whitcombe's Modern Jun. Dict.* (8edn.) 445 *wineberry*. See *tutu*, for which it is another name. **1985** MCGILL *G'day Country* 154 The township was now under tute, which Bill identified as a wild brambleberry with clusters of wineberries.

3. mountain wineberry. *Aristotelia fruticosa.* See also *mountain currant* (CURRANT).
 1908 *AJHR* C-11 38 [*Aristotelia fruticosa*]. Mountain wineberry. Forest, sub. scrub. **1923** COCKAYNE *Cultivation NZ Plants* 26 A[*ristotelia*] *fruticosa* (mountain wineberry, vh.), is a shrub with reddish bark, interlacing branches..and abundant red, rose or white berries. **1961** MARTIN *Flora NZ* 232 [Subalpine shrubs worthy of note include] the Mountain Wineberry (*Aristotelia fruticosa*). **1982** WILSON *Stewart Is. Plants* 61 *Aristotelia fruticosa* Mountain Wineberry... Shrubby wineberry... Shrub up to 1 m.

winebox, *n.* and *attrib.* Occas. with init. cap. [A name given allusively to a set of documents indicating an international scheme of questionable legality, domiciled in the Cook Islands, which was designed to minimize NZ corporate tax, the documents being orig. presented to the Serious Fraud Office in a cardboard carton intended to hold 12 bottles of Montana Cabernet Sauvignon, and tabled in Parliament in March 1994 by Winston Peters M.P.] Often *attrib.*, also *transf.* or *fig.*

1. a. In a literal sense, the original cardboard wine carton holding documents of interest to various parties.

1994 *Independent* (Auckland) 18 Mar. 1 [Heading] Tax dodgers 'wine box' goes to Parliament. **1994** *NZPD* 22 Mar. DXXXIX. 587 I [Paul East, Attorney-General] am also advised that this wine box of documents was made available to the Serious Fraud Office some 18 months ago. **1994** *Independent* (Auckland) 31 Mar. 1 Both men..told the House that the documents were part of the so-called 'wine box' of papers.

b. By metonomy, in a transferred or extended sense (a) alluding to the import or implications of the documents contained in the 'winebox'; thence to the resultant public interest, debate and inquiry.

1994 *Dominion* (Wellington) 5 July 7 The Winebox records transactions or proposed schemes. **1995** *Ibid.* 14 Oct. 21 Mr Scott had been making disparaging remarks about the department's role in the Winebox. **1996** *Tablet* (Dunedin) 28 Jan. 24 The subsidising of previous [America's] cup challenges appears to have been too close to the wine box [*sc.* to parties interested in tax avoidance schemes] for comfort.

(b) As an exemplar of the need for exposure of inefficiencies or lapses in organizations' dealings with the public.

1996 *Dominion* (Wellington) 2 Jan. 6 Or is it another example of a winebox [*sc.* a 'whistle- blowing' or public exposure exercise] being needed to ensure an agency of the state is diligent in its duties?

c. In various *attrib.* uses.

1994 *Independent* (Auckland) 3 June 3 It is unlikely Cook Islanders will see last Sunday's TVNZ *Frontline* programme which outline two of the wine box deals. **1995** *Independent* (Auckland) 13 Oct. 8 It has been that crazy with the first 'wine-box' book to hit the market.

2. a. Used attrib. in Special combinations such as **winebox Commission** or **Commissioner**, the 'Commission of Inquiry into Certain Matters relating to Taxation in the Cook Islands' set up in late 1994 to examine the implications of the winebox documents, or its chairman, Sir Ronald Davison; **winebox industry**, a large, corporate industry which would benefit greatly from workable tax avoidance schemes; **winebox inquiry**, orig. referring to the inquiry by the Parliamentary Select Comittee on Finance and Expenditure (quot. 1994), then to the *winebox Commission* above (quots. 1995, 1996).

1995 *Independent* (Auckland) 13 Oct. 8 The long-expected showdown between the **wine-box Commissioner** Sir Ron Davison and Cook Islands tax dodge designer European Pacific is scheduled for Monday. **1995** *Evening Post* (Wellington) 23 Nov. 4 This will primarily be to suit the profits of the shareholders of the big food chains—people who are in the **winebox industries**, I guess. **1994** *Dominion* (Wellington) 5 July 7 [Heading] **Winebox inquiry** committee faces limits. *Ibid.* 25 July 2 [Heading] Dissension is fermenting nicely in the winebox inquiry. **1994** *Sunday Star-Times* (Auckland) 6 Nov. C8 With the Winebox inquiry starting tomorrow, Winston Peters should be preparing to take his place in the sun. He's gone from the winebox to the dogbox in the space of a week. **1996** *North & South* (Auckland) Mar. 66 So What's the Winebox Inquiry? [Heading] A commission of inquiry conducted by the former chief justice Sir Ronald Davison to examine whether former Inland Revenue Department chief David Henry and Serious Fraud Office director Chas Sturt acted properly and lawfully when investigating the transactions set out in the Winebox.

b. In composition (often *joc.*): **wineboxer**, any party interested in 'winebox' matters; **wineboxful**, *fig.* a great number of 'wineboxers'.

1996 *Sunday Star-Times* (Auckland) 18 Feb. A8 Happiest **wineboxer** of the week was the New Zealand First leader, Winston Peters. **1996** *Listener* 17 Feb. 46 [He] also makes a convincing case for the true perpetrators being a veritable **wineboxful** of those in big business, who corrupt a largely unaccountable government.

wing. [Transf. or spec. use of *wing* a lateral part or appendage.]

1. a. One of the walls or barriers built out on either side of the central release gate of a timber dam.

1874 BAINES *Edward Crewe* 174 I first cut a trench in the rock right across the bed of the creek, into which I placed a squared spar. I did the same up the good or rock side of the stream. On the other bank I made a 'wing' by driving piles [for a flood-dam]. **1953** REED *Story of Kauri* 206 After the bottom had been secured, a start was made on the wings, as the walls on either side of the gate were called.

b. Also **wing fence**. [AND 1891.] A fence, or pair of fences, built out from a stockyard and serving to channel stock into the entrance.

1953 STRONACH *Musterer on Molesworth* 45 They [*sc.* sheep for killing] have to be run into a small pen, sometimes with one 'wing' fence, sometimes with two, and quite often with none... The killing pen is difficult there. The wing was broken down.

2. Special Comb. **wing dam** goldmining [orig. US: see OED *wing* 24, 1809], a dam or barrier built out into a stream to deflect the current.

1863 *AJHR* D-6 18 Many..who held river claims worked very successfully by wing-dams, consisting of bags of sand laid into the stream, so as to cut off a portion of its bed, which, being drained by pumping, was paddocked out and passed through the cradle. **1874** BATHGATE *Col. Experiences* 133 They built a wing-dam..them stakes is the remains of it—and they did get splendid gold. **1888** PRESHAW *Banking Under Difficulties* 176 Groins and wing dams were constructed at considerable expense. **1976** VEITCH *Clyde on Dunstan* 30 Many favoured a 'wing dam' when working in very shallow beaches. Bags filled with earth formed a 12 feet by 20 feet square. The water enclosed in this square was then baled or pumped out and the area worked dry. **1988** STAFFORD *New Century in Rotorua* 31 The wing-dam was completed during the 1907–08 year.

winged thistle: see THISTLE *n.* 2 (7).

winger: see WING–FORWARD.

winger. [AND 1951.] The stockman controlling the 'wing' or flank of a travelling mob of sheep.

1940 STUDHOLME *Te Waimate* (1954) 123 In driving a big mob of scary sheep across country it was usual to flank it with a man on each wing who would guide the leaders in the right direction, the rest following... There were considerable beds of tutu in many places and the 'winger's' job included steering the mob clear of these.

wingfish. *Pteraclis velifera* (fam. Bramidae), a spectacular midwater pelagic fish having large symmetrical sail-like fins dorsally and ventrally. See also BATFISH.

1956 GRAHAM *Treasury NZ Fishes* 407 Wingfish *Pteraclis* [sp.]. **1982** AYLING *Collins Guide* (1984) 222 The wingfish is one of the most unusual of the larger midwater pelagic fishes... The most unusual features..are the huge sail-like dorsal and anal fins that run the entire length of the body from the snout to the tail. **1986** PAUL *NZ Fishes* 94 *Wingfish Pteraclis velifera* A spectacularly different and unmistakable fish..anal fins very large and sail-like.

wing-forward, *n.* and *attrib. Rugby union.* Also early **winging-forward**. [OED soccer only; but see *winger* 2, =rugby wing-forward.] Each of the two players positioned off the flanks of the former 2-3-2 scrum. Also occas. called **winger**.

1900 *NZ Illustr. Mag.* III. 237 The practice of playing winging-forwards is almost universal. **1908** BARR *Brit. Rugby Team in Maoriland* 165 At this stage it might not be out of place to mention that wing-forwards were played for the first time in 1876 [the year Canterbury sent a touring team as far as Auckland]. Thus early the 'winger', who was to cause a great deal of controversy in later years, was much in evidence. **1910** FANNING *Players & Slayers* 1 Anyone who has watched two dogs fighting over a bone has observed that the animals have a very fair notion of the old wing-forward work.

wingwam, var. WIGWAM 2.

wink: see WIG *v.*

winter. Used *attrib.* in special Comb. often in a sense 'able to be negotiated, worked or used in winter conditions': **winter block**, **winter** (occas. **wintering**) **country** *SI farming*, a farm block or area of a high-country farm suitable for wintering stock (see also COLD COUNTRY, contrast *summer country* (SUMMER)); **winter field** gumdigging, an area of a gumfield able to be excavated in the winter; **winter migrant** *obs.*, an occasional early name for the SILVER-EYE.

1978 JARDINE *Shadows on Hill* 45 The basic requirements in the selection of a **winter block** are: that it should have sufficient scope of country below the settled winter snowline to carry the necessary number of sheep for the required period. **c1895–96** HOPE *Letter* in Harper *Kettle on Fuchsia* (1967) 145 I began the winter with 20,000 sheep..on a block of **wintering country**, near Fairlie Creek. **1898** MORRIS *Austral-English* 513 **Winter Country**, in New Zealand (South Island), land so far unaffected by snow that stock is wintered on it. **1912** WALL *Century of NZ's Praise* 80 Good winter-country, where sweet grasses grow. **1916** *TrNZI* XLVIII. 156 The lower montane belt is usually called 'winter country', as it is the only ground on which stock can be carried during the winter months. **1922** PERRY *Sheep Farming* 88 The lower [high] country, which can be used all the year round without serious risk of loss from snow, and which usually consists of low safe hills or steep country with a sunny aspect, is termed 'winter country'. **1938** BURDON *High Country* 156 The safety of winter country depends not so much on its low altitude as on whether its slopes steeply and brokenly towards the north, so that it receives what heat there may be in the weak winter sun. **1945** *Korero* (AEWS Background Bulletin) 18 June 9 Now the cold season is approaching, so most of the sheep go on to 'winter country' and 'the farm'. **1969** MOORE *Forest to Farm* 21 All these stations in the mountain tussock lands would be divided by fencing into what was known as 'summer' and 'winter' country... Sheep were..brought down to the lower country—the winter country—in the late autumn. This consisted of rolling downs, the lower hills, and faces lying to the sun where snow did not lie. **1908** *TrNZI* XL. 170 Gum-digging may be roughly divided into two classes—viz., that on the '**Winter-fields**', or the high tea-tree ranges where the ground is too hard to work in dry weather, and that on the 'summer-fields', or low swampy situations, where digging would be impossible during the wet season. **1888** BULLER *Birds NZ* I. 82 By the settlers it [*sc. Zosterops*] has been variously designated as Ring-eye, Wax-eye, White-eye, or Silver-eye, in allusion to the beautiful circlet of satiny-white feathers which surrounds the eyes; and quite as commonly as the 'Blight-bird', or '**Winter Migrant**'.

winterless north. With and without init. cap. The North Auckland peninsula as a sub-tropical region; NORTHLAND 1.
   1917 *Wanganui Herald* 5 Feb. 4 Girls mature very quickly in the 'Winterless north', but this rapid approach to womanhood generally brings with it a loss of complexion and good looks. **1921** *Quick March* 10 May 19 Up in the Winterless North I am learning how good the month may be. **1950** *Truth* 29 Mar. 19 No one has seen the 'winterless north' until they have crossed the..Maunganuka range. **1968** SLATTER *Pagan Game* 23 He knew the winterless north was a tourist gimmick, the Hibiscus Coast hallucinatory, winter was winter anywhere in the land. **1970** JOHNSON *Life's Vagaries* 74 And a blazing log fire even in the winterless north brings a feeling of deep content. **1989** PARKINSON *Travelling Naturalist* 23 The long narrow peninsula extending some 800 kilometres north of Auckland is known as Northland—occasionally, in flights of fancy, as the 'winterless north'. **1993** *Dominion* (Wellington) 15 June 6 News has reached us..of a strange new ritual from the winterless, jobless north.

Winton disease. [f. *Winton* a town in Southland.] A chronic hepatic disease of stock due to poisoning from eating ragwort.
   1894 *Ann. Rep. Dept. Agric.* II. 43 I regret to say that the disease known in this district as the Winton Disease has increased very much, and there have been a number of reported cases of horses dying through it. **1896** *Ibid.* IV. 41 'Winton Disease'. This disease seems to be prevalent in a certain part of the colony called Winton, from whence the name is derived. It appears to have carried off many horses and cattle during the last ten or twelve years... Some have an opinion that ragwort is the cause of the disease, while others are opposed to this view. **1903** *Otago Daily Times* (Dunedin) 9 Dec. 17 [The report] deals..with a disease in New Zealand known as the 'Winton disease', and in Canada as the Picton disease. **1912** *NZJAg.* Jan. IV. 416 The animals which seem most susceptible to its ill effects are horses and cattle, and it has been practically proved that ragwort is the cause of the so-called 'Winton' disease. **1935** *NZJST* XVII. 638 J.A. Gilruth was the first to show that the hepatic cirrhosis occurring in horses and cattle, the so-called 'Winton' disease, in certain districts of New Zealand could be reproduced by feeding these animals on fresh or dried ragwort. **1977** CONNOR *Poisonous Plants* 11 The livestock problem it [*sc.* ragwort] caused came to be known as 'Winton disease'.

wio, var. WHIO.

wipe, *v.*

1. [AND 1941.] *trans.* To dismiss or disown (a person, idea, etc.); to dispense with.
   1939–45 *Expressions & Sayings 2NZEF* (TS N.A. WAII DA 420/1) Wipe it—Cancel it or do away with it. **1946** WEBBER *Johnny Enzed in Italy* 54 Any question of slapping us on a 252 can be wiped here and now.

2. *trans.* To bankrupt.
   1953 *Evening Post* (Wellington) 21 Jan. 8 An Auckland [pre-cut house importing] firm..says it has been 'completely wiped' by the cutting of overseas exchange funds.

wiper kick. *Rugby union.* Also **wipers kick**. [An allusion to *windscreen wipers* which sweep from approx. 45° from the vertical.] A (usu. long low) kick across the field at an angle of approximately 45° aimed at finding the openside wing, or touch.
   1968 SLATTER *Pagan Game* 44 The wet weather first five-eighths..with sure hands and a practised wiper kick to the corner flag that presented his wings with tries. *Ibid.* 141 The Coach had the halfback and the first five working up the sideline with short kicks and..he had the backs exhibit their varied roles, the wiper kick to the wings, the scissors move. **1970** ALLEN & MCCLEAN *Fred Allen on Rugby* 82 Whatever kick he was making—the hook back..or the long one we used to call 'Wipers' pitching ahead of the openside wing. **1994** *Dominion* (Wellington) 15 June 40 You can't see..if a wing or fullback is in position for a wipers kick.

wire, *n.*

1. Special Comb. in the names of plants in a sense 'with stems having characteristics of wire': **wirebush**, POHUE b (*Muehlenbeckia complexa*); **wire-netting bush**, *Corokia cotoneaster*, KOROKIO 1 a; and also occas. *Plagianthus divaricatus, saltmarsh ribbonwood* (RIBBONWOOD 2 (3)); **wire plant** *obs. local*, *Olearia* spp. esp. *O. virgata*, a slender divaricate shrub of boggy ground; **wire rush**, see RUSH 2 (8); **wire vine**, *Muehlenbeckia* spp., esp. *M. complexa*, POHUE.
   1947 HUTCHINSON *At Omatua's Fireside* 127 The vernacular [name] varies in different districts... Muehlenbeckia australis..grape weed..Muehlenbeckia complexa..**wirebush**. **1969** *Standard Common Names Weeds* 88 wire bush [=] wire vine... **wire-netting bush** [=] korokio. **1995** *Dominion* (Wellington) 18 Mar. 19 There are also many natives..which should be considered [for hedge plants including] the wire-netting bush *Corokia cotoneaster*. **1995** *Plagianthus divaricatus* [see RIBBONWOOD 2 (3)]. **1856** ROBERTS *Diary* in Beattie *Early Runholding* (1947) 18 Writing of the Waimea Plain in 1856:.. There was a good deal of scrub in the bends of the Mataura known as '**wire plant**' (*Olearia virgata*). **1969** [see POHUE b]. **1981** TAYLOR *Weeds of Roadsides* 101 **Wire Vine** (*Muehlenbeckia complexa*) Native perennial climber... Wire vine grows in many hedges, where it may entwine the shafts of rotary hedgecutters. **1995** wire vine [see POHUE b].

2. Special Comb. in fencing use: **wire spinner**, JENNY 1; **wire-stretcher** *obs.* [used elsewhere but recorded earliest in NZ: see OED *wire* 16 a 'Chiefly *N. Amer.*' 1877], a wire-strainer, a device for straining or tightening fence-wires.
   1982 wire spinner [see JENNY 1]. **1876** *Saturday Advertiser* 8 July 10 [Ironmongery advt includes] Fencing Wire, Nos. 6, 7, 8, 9, and 10; Fencing Staples and **Wire Stretchers**.

wire, *v. Flaxmilling. Obs. trans.* To hang (dressed flax) on a wire line or fence to bleach and dry.
   1928 *NZJST* X. 236 It is probably slightly erroneous to apply the term 'bleaching' to the usual process of grassing and wiring the fibre. *Ibid.* X. 246 Hank No 6 was given a second mill-wash, grassed and wired along with No 3.

Hence **wiring** *vbl. n.*, the hanging of dressed flax on wires.
   1928 *NZJST* X. 239 By the use of thorough hot-water washing, grassing can be eliminated and wiring cut down to a two-days' process, thus saving land and time.

wireweed.

1. [AND 1875.] Any of several plants having wiry stems, usu. *Polygonum* spp. (fam. Polygonaceae), a weed of cultivated land, so-called from its tough, trailing stem. See also *pigweed* (PIG *n.*[1] 4).
   1904 *TrNZI* XXXVI. 213 *Polygonum aviculare*, the so-called wire-weed, and the var. *Driandri*, are abundant everywhere. **1910** COCKAYNE *NZ Plants & Their Story* 126 Even experts cannot agree on the nativity of certain species..as in the case of the wireweed (*Polygonum aviculare*). **1926** HILGENDORF *Weeds* 61 Wireweed (*Polygonum aviculare*), also called road weed, mat weed, knot grass, and hog weed, is common in cultivated land all over the country. It is an annual, with stems up to 2ft. in length trailing over the ground. The stems have swollen nodes ('knot grass') and are very tough ('wireweed'). **1950** WILSON *My First Eighty Yrs.* 15 [In the McKenzie Country, 1870–80s there was]..a harsh brown weed that dried in autumn and blew away in balls hanging on to fences. We called it wire weed. **1969** *Standard Common Names Weeds* 88 wireweed *Polygonum aviculare* agg. **1980** TAYLOR *Weeds of Crops* 122 Wireweed (*Polygonum aviculare*)... This European weed is widespread in New Zealand in gateways, driveways, and other places where its tolerance to treading enables survival.

2. *Melanthalia abscissa*, an abundant North Island seaweed esp. of surge channels, easily recognized by its bushy habit and wiry leafless stems almost black when dry.
   1961 MARTIN *Flora NZ* 5 A little lower down where the seaweeds are permanently submerged we have such plants as the Grapelet, the Wire-Weed, and Ox-tongue; the Flap-jack and Girdle Weeds.

wiring diagram. [A transf. use of the name of the electrical or electronic diagram.] A diagram showing the relationship of connections and components of complex financial or administrative transactions.
   1994 *NZPD* DXXXIX. 745 Hon. Winston Peters... Both are handwritten wiring diagrams. One is labelled 'JAP Bank'..and another is labelled 'Telecom NZ'. **1996** *Dominion* (Wellington) 7 June 5 The wiring diagram of the $100 million redeemable preference share transaction, involving Bank of New Zealand, Capital Markets Ltd and shelf companies..was displayed..on the computer screen.

wiro(o), varr. WHIRO.

witau, var. WHITAU.

witch. [f. Brit. dial. *witch* applied to the lemon sole and similar fishes, poss. (so OED) from an uncanny appearance, paralleled by the similar use as a fish-name of Latin *saga*, French *sorcière*: see EDD *n.*[1] 6 the lemon sole (Grimsby and Sussex).] *Arnoglossus scapha* (fam. Bothidae), a widely distributed but commercially unattractive flounder of little value as a food fish. See also *bludger's fish* (BLUDGER 5 b), CADGER'S FISH, LANTERN FISH 2, MAHUE, MEGRIM.
   1911 WAITE *Rec. Canterbury Museum* I. 197 Megrim..Brill, Mahoa, Witch. **1913** *TrNZI* XLV. 232

Caulopsetta scapha... This specific name belongs to the megrim, or witch, a common form, not sold as a food fish on account of its lean, bony character. **1927** SPEIGHT et al. *Nat. Hist. Canterbury* 201 The 'commonest and most widely distributed of the flat fishes of New Zealand, and yet, unfortunately, the least valuable,' is the Megrim or Witch... It is our only left sided flat fish, and is a very thin species full of long bones. **1938** *TrRSNZ* LXVIII. 407 *Caulopsetta scapha*... Witch (megrim). **1956** GRAHAM *Treasury NZ Fishes* 187 Some fishermen, more especially those who were fishing in Britain and are now fishing in this country, will insist on using the name Witch instead of Megrim. This fish has no claim to such a name, as the Witch in Britain has the eyes on the right side of the head. **1967** NATUSCH *Animals NZ* 218 [Caption] Megrim or witch, *Caulopsetta* (eyes left!). **1978** *Catch '78* Dec. 17 Witch *Arnoglossus scapha* Family Bothidae (left-eye flounders), NZ only. **1986** PAUL *NZ Fishes* 145 Witch *Arnoglossus scapha* Also called megrim, both names derived from similar European flatfishes. Found only in New Zealand.

wiwi, *n.*¹ Also **wi**. [Ma. /'wi:wi:/: Williams 483 *Wī.* n. 1. *Poa caespitosa*, tussock grass... 3. *Juncus* [spp.]... *Wīwī.* 1. Rushes, *Juncus polyanthemos* and *P. maritimus*.]

1. Any of a group of common native rushes or rush-like plants, the name being applied esp. by early writers to various rushes (*Juncus* spp.), or tussock grasses (*Poa* spp.), and occas. locally later to *Cladium* spp.; RUSH *n.*¹ 1. **a.** *Juncus* spp., a rush; also a rush-clump.

[**1820** LEE & KENDALL *NZ Gram. & Vocab.* 228 Wíwi; Rushes.] **1843** *Ordinance for imposing a tax on Raupo Houses* Session II. No. xvii. of the former Legislative Council of New Zealand (From A. Domett's collection of Ordinances, 1850.) Section 2..there shall be levied in respect of every building constructed wholly or in part of *raupo, nikau, toitoi, wiwi, kakaho,* straw or thatch of any description [£20]. **1867** HOOKER *Handbook* 769 Wiwi... *Juncus maritimus* and *effusus.* Wiwi... *Isolepis nodosa.* **1898** MORRIS *Austral-English* 513 *Wiwi, n.* Maori name for a jointed rush. **1908** [see RUSH *n.*¹ 2 (1)]. **1911** *TrNZI* XLIII. 201 Low-lying grass lands will, if neglected, be smothered in wiwi (*Juncus effusus*) in a few years. **1918** HILGENDORF *Weeds* 54 Rushes (*Juncus* [spp.]), often called by their Maori name of Wiwi, are well known in all damp pastures. **1960** HILLIARD *Maori Girl* 14 Ivan Brown! I see you hiding there behind the wiwis. **1986** CARR *Diary of a Pig Hunter* 124 There were wiwis scattered in clumps above me while just below was another stand of totara trees.

b. A tussock grass.

1840 POLACK *Manners & Customs* II. 285 Wiwi, a kind of wiry grass that is pulled up by tufts, found in marshes. **1887** *Auckland Weekly News* 9 Apr. 7 There is very little growth in the grass all this distance, except the wi, which has found its way through, and is quite green... The plains are quite level, nothing growing on them except stunted tea-tree and wi-grass. **1946** ZIMMERMAN *Where People Sing* 73 In the bottom land, tufts of *wiwi*, a coarse, tough-stemmed swamp grass. **1964** NORRIS *Settlers in Depression* 76 They crossed the great Tokoroa Plains [in 1883], thickly covered with 'wi' and white grass, offering good feed for sheep and cattle, and travelled over the partly formed road leading to the Maori settlement of Maungaiti. **1981** BROOKER et al. *NZ Medicinal Plants* 59 *Poa caespitosa*... Common name: *Tussock grass* Maori name: *Wi.*

2. Used *attrib.* or in Comb. **wiwi-covered, wiwi-swamp**; or special Comb. **wiwi rattling** *fig.,* upsetting Maori with a hollow show of strength.

1888 BULLER *Birds NZ* I. 59 Intersecting these fern-ridges are narrow belts of wiwi-swamp, of a dark green colour from the character of the vegetation. **1922** COWAN *NZ Wars* (1955) II. 391 From here they..traversed a long level *wiwi*-covered valley. **1990** *Contact* (Wellington) 22 Nov. 8 Northern Maori MP, Bruce Gregory, accused National's headmaster, Lockwood Smith, in a recent press statement of 'wiwi-rattling' over Maori education.

wi-wi, *n.*² *Hist.* Also **we(e)-we(e), Wewi**. [Ma. /'wi:wi:/: Williams Appendix *Wīwī* a (nick)name for a Frenchman; in plural, the French.: f. early Maori imitation of French *oui oui*.] Usu. *pl.* as **wiwi** or **wiwis**, the French. Cf. MARION.

1841 JAMESON *NZ, S. Austral. & NSW* 196 The name *wee-wee* (so the French were called from frequently making use of the words 'Oui Oui'). **1841** WAKEFIELD *Journal* 20 Feb. in Heaphy *NZ* (1842) 59 I told him [*sc.* Te Heu Heu]..the white people of my country would do the same, should the *Wi-wis*, or French, kill any of our chiefs. **1859** THOMSON *Story NZ* I. 236 Before the Wewis, as the French are now called, departed, they violated sacred places. **1905** BAUCKE *White Man Treads* 221 'May be they are of that to be dreaded people the "wi wi"' (oui oui, their name for the French). **1941** BAKER *NZ Slang* 23 Herein the version *we-we* is used of French and American sailors. **1952** RICHARDS *Chatham Is.* 104 The Maoris call the French 'Wi-wis' to this day.

wizard. *Obs.* In Maori contexts, applied to a tohunga, or to tohunga lore. See also TOHUNGA 1.

1835 YATE *NZ* (1970) 95 There is but small chance of the wizard escaping punishment. **1846** WHITE *Journal* (ATLMS) 2 Heard a wizard story wrote it down.

wobbly. [Used elsewhere but recorded earliest in NZ: see OED *n.*² 1977.] A tantrum, a fit of anger or nerves, etc., esp. in the phr. **to throw a wobbly**, to lose control of oneself.

1964 DAVIS *Watersiders* 29 What's the matter with you? You look queer. Ain't going to throw a wobbly, are you? *Ibid.* 147 Somebody could get hurt if one of these days he went berkers or threw a wobbly in the middle of a job. **1985** STEWART *Gumboots & Goalposts* 40 I did this once and the other bloke really threw a wobbly. All I could say was, 'Sorry!..', while he made nasty remarks. **1993** *Dominion* (Wellington) 24 Mar. 3 But it was hard to ensure violent incidents never happened [among intellectually handicapped clients]. People were expected to 'throw a wobbly' sometimes.

wogga, var. WAGGA.

women, *n. pl.* Often pronounced /'wʊmən/ in New Zealand.

wonder berry. *Solanum nigrum* (fam. Solanaceae), the introduced black nightshade.

1926 HILGENDORF *Weeds* 152 Black Nightshade (*Solanum nigrum*), is called also white nightshade, mother-of-thousands, black tomato, black potato, wonder berry, and by a serious confusion deadly nightshade and bittersweet. **1950** *Here & Now* Nov. 16 The thing [*sc.* a flogging] leaves a broad weal..soft, pulpy and the colour of one of those wonderberries.

wood, *n.*¹

1. New Zealand usage has traditionally preferred BUSH to the Brit. *wood*, or *woods* for 'an area of naturally wooded country', *woods* being mainly confined to the usage of early writers on (and in) New Zealand, and often, from the mid-19th century, to that of natural historians (esp. botanists). In combination it has been generally superseded by *bush* in popular use (except for the items in 2 a below), and by *forest* in technical use. See also the note at BUSH A *n.*

1773 FORSTER *Resolution Jrnl.* 24 Apr. (1982) II. 266 The brow on the larboard side of the Ship, which a few days ago was an inpenetrable forest, is now clear & airy..and more than an acre of ground is cleared of the woods. **1814** KENDALL 13 June in Elder *Marsden's Lieutenants* (1934) 61 We observed no woods near us of any magnitude. **1834** MARKHAM *NZ* (1963) 56 When in the Woods she looked out for the (Coo Coupers) or Pigeons. **1840** POLACK *Manners & Customs* I. 126 The bushes are literally filled with them [*sc.* fantailed flycatchers], their varied note resounding through the woods until sunrise. **1888** BULLER *Birds NZ* I. xliii The compass and variety of their notes [add] greatly to the charm of the New-Zealand woods. **1912** *TrNZI* XLIV. 213 The oldest material supports pure woods of *Corynocarpus* (karaka). **1981** BROOKER et al. *NZ Medicinal Plants* 28 *Gully fern...* This common fern is found in woods throughout New Zealand.

2. Used *attrib.* in special Comb.: **a.** in a sense 'forest' mainly in the names of animals: **wood-devil**, WETA 2 (5) (cf. *bush devil* (BUSH C 4), *Maori devil* (MAORI B 4 b)); **wood mouse**, a feral house mouse, see FIELD MOUSE; **wood pigeon**, see PIGEON 2 (4); **wood quest** *obs.,* an occasional early name for *wood pigeon* (PIGEON 2 (4)); **woodrail** [poss. f. WOOD(HEN + RAIL], a bookname for WEKA; **wood robin**, see ROBIN 1.

1942 wood-devil [see SCORPION]. **1840 Wood Quest** [see PIGEON 1]. **1966** FALLA et al. *Birds of NZ* 102 Weka *Gallirallus australis...* Woodhen, **Woodrail**. **1985** *Reader's Digest Book NZ Birds* 169 [*Weka Gallirallus australis.*] Woodhen, woodrail. **1986** TV1 *University Challenge* Massey/Canterbury 14 Oct. What is the *rail*? Weka is also called wood-rail or woodhen.

b. In a sense 'associated with the material, wood': **wood-beetle**, HUHU; **wood block**, a chopping-block or wooden block used for a base for chopping or splitting short lengths of firewood; **wood-bug** (also **black wood-bug**), *black-beetle* (BEETLE 1 a); **wood-chop, wood chopping**, an axe-man's chopping contest (or carnival) (see also CHOP *n.*²); **wood duck**, see quot.; **wood-grub**, HUHU; **wood-heap** [AND 1918], **wood-pile**, a stack or store of firewood lengths; **woodpecker** Chatham Island [transf. use of northern hemisphere *woodpecker*], WARBLER 2 (2), see quot.; **wood range (stove)**, a wood-burning (rather than a coal-burning) domestic range or stove; **wood rash** *joc.,* injury inflicted by a police truncheon; **wood rose (wooden rose, wood flower)** [from its resemblance to a rose bloom], the fluted end of a plant root that has been parasitized by the native plant *Dactylanthus taylorii* (fam. Balanophoraceae), see also DACTYLANTHUS.

1873 BULLER *Birds NZ* 20 In the stomachs of some [moreporks] I have found the remains of the large **wood-beetle** (*Prionoplus reticularis*). **1920** MANSFIELD *Stories* (1984) 249 He simply threw it [*sc.* the newly beheaded duck] away from him..and jumped round the **wood block**. **1960** CRUMP *Good Keen man* 14 The stack of firewood stood waist-high beside the chopping block. There was little enough to see... I'd sat on the wood block, dredged out the letter..and worked the flap open with a knife. **1848** TAYLOR *Leaf from Natural Hist.* 15 Kekeriru, *large* **black wood-bug**. **1867** HOCHSTETTER *NZ* 171 Blatta (vulgo 'cock-roach') [which squirts strong and evil-smelling liquid]. Because of this property which is especially characteristic of wood-bugs, the colonists call it wood-bug. **1871** WILLIAMS *Dictionary of the New Zealand Language* (3edn.) 51 Keekereru, n. black wood-bug. **1884** KERRY-NICHOLLS *The King Country* 365 Kekeriru.—*Cimex nemoralis*. A large black wood-bug. **1939** BEATTIE *First White Boy Born in Otago* 189 Up in Auckland he noticed that wood bugs in furniture made a nasty smell. **1977** REED *Treasury of Maori Exploration* 267 kekerengu: black wood-bug (*Platyzosteria novaeseelandiae*). **1951** PARK *Witch's Thorn* 139 It was all very well showing excitement at a football match, or the **wood-chops** at the Sports. **1959** SLATTER *Gun in My Hand* 227 [The tourists] never see the **wood-chopping** at the bush-bordered showgrounds at Tuatapere. **1986** *NZ Herald* (Auckland) 22 Jan. sect. ii 1 Car dealers have a collection of jargon words they use on the yard, so if you are thinking of taking up selling cars as a career, there are a few terms you should know... A '**wood duck**' is a person who walks onto the yard and says he will buy a car—without even so much as a struggle. **1922** COWAN *NZ Wars* (1955) II. 294 [The Hauhaus were reduced to existing upon] the *hakeke* or *wood-fungus*, and the *huhu*, or large white **wood-grub**. **1956** *Numbers 1* May 8 He drove the axe savagely into the rotten wood. It split lengthwise and fell apart, baring the wet sawdust tunnels of woodgrubs. He put the inch-long grubs on top of the chopping stump, their white wrinkled bodies curling blindly in the foreign sunlight. **1967** GROVER *Another Man's Role* 13 I gratefully followed him out to the **woodheap**. He chopped and I talked. **1981** HENDERSON *Exiles Asbestos Cottage* 60 Slinging the burden of today so casually up on the wood-heap. **1966** FALLA et al. *Birds NZ* 212 Chatham Island Warbler *Gerygone albofrontata* Local name: **Woodpecker**. **1958** ASHTON-WARNER *Spinster* 145 I set out down the back garden to the **wood-pile**. **1949** *Here & Now* Oct. 17 We can still number by thousands the homes (not all of them R.D.) where meals are cooked on the **wood range**. **1964** HOWE *Stamper Battery* 7 Mum sweated over a wood range..preparing hash, stews, roasts and vegetables for the ever-hungry bushmen. **1987** HARTLEY *Swagger on Our Doorstep* 40 The wood range was the only article salvaged from the cottage. **1982** NEWBOLD *Big Huey* 255 **Wood rash** (n) Injury inflicted by a truncheon. Increasingly common from Auckland southward to Otago. **1961** MARTIN *Flora NZ* 26 Many [endemic genera] bear no close relationship to any other known plant. Such, for instance are..the root parasite (*Dactylanthus*) responsible for the **wood roses** often sold as curios. **1978** MOORE & IRWIN *Oxford Book NZ Plants* 86 About 1850 Rev. Richard Taylor discovered this strange plant [sc. *Dactylanthus*] near Hikurangi... A common practice is to remove the whole rhizome by boiling and scraping, so displaying the fluted end of the root, the so-called 'wooden rose'. **1986** *Press* (Christchurch) 7 Feb. 18 Although the Canterbury Museum no longer houses a botanical collection, it still has a box of those rather bizarre botanical specimens known as 'wood flowers' or 'wooden roses' retained for their curiosity rather than their scientific value. Wooden roses are the deformed roots of trees or shrubs, the deformation being caused by the attack of another plant, the root-parasite, *Dactylanthus taylori*. It is found most abundantly on the volcanic plateau in the centre of the North Island, but also in other parts of the same island. **1988** DAWSON *Forest Vines to Snow Tussocks* 93 These 'wooden roses', as they are called, are prized as curios. *Dactylanthus* is restricted to New Zealand. **1992** *North & South* (Auckland) June 18 It has neither roots nor green leaves, and is found only in New Zealand. Maori named it Pua o te reinga, Europeans call it the Flower of Hades, or Wood Rose. **1938** *Auckland Weekly News* 1 June 95 These old **wood-stoves** are rather out of date, aren't they?

wood, *n.*[2] In the phr. **to have (get, hold) the wood on** (a person) [orig. uncertain: AND 1949 derives from WOODEN *v.* to knock out], to have an advantage over (someone).

c1926 THE MIXER *Transport Workers' Song Book* 7 I hold the 'wood' on those who work. **1943** FULLARTON *Troop Target* 168 Then we've taken another hiding. And I thought we had the wood on Jerry to-day. **1951** 14 M 10 Wellington H.S. 9 Wood, got the wood on **1964** PEARSON *Glossary* to Sargeson *Collected Stories 1935–63* (1964) 304 wood: *had got the wood on*, had the advantage over. **1976** MORRIESON *Pallet on Floor* 118 Got the wood on Jamieson. He's coming across with the section. **1988** MCGILL *Dict. Kiwi Slang* 124 *wood* have the advantage, often to *have the wood on*; as in woodchopping contests, at least from 1941; eg 'Long as his first serve is not working, you've got the wood on him.'

Woodbine. WW1. [Transf. use of (*Wild*) *Woodbine* the proprietary name of an English cigarette: AND 1919.]

1. An English soldier.
1918 *Chron. NZEF* 2 Aug. 18 We also visited Hitchin R.E. Depot last Saturday, to show the 'Woodbines' what we 'foreigners' could do. **1919** *Great Adventure* (1988) 248 I'm afraid that our cooks are Woodbines, which being interpreted is English. **1935** STRONG in Partridge *Slang Today* 288 I think he is a Woodbine, but he will do me for a tin plate.

2. *attrib.* passing into Comb. English; esp. as **woodbine bride**, a New Zealand soldier's English war-bride.
1922 TURNER *Happy Wanderer* 55 Their 'woodbine brides' were laughing. **1919** in *Great Adventure* (1988) 255 I wandered off to town travelling..first class on a third ticket, to the annoyance of certain Woodbine officers in the carriage. **1921** *Quick March* 10 Mar. 21 It is the hiding of unemployment which makes New Zealand a snare for Woodbine immigrants.

3. As **Teddy Woodbine**, a New Zealand soldiers' nickname for Edward, Prince of Wales, later Edward VIII.
1935 STRONG in Partridge *Slang Today* 287 There is Church Parade tomorrow and Teddy Woodbine with all the heads of the Army is going to review the troops. **1937** PARTRIDGE *Dict. Slang* 963 *Woodbine, Teddy*. Edward, Prince of Wales Australian and N.Z. soldiers': GW.

wooden, *a.* In special collocations: **wooden aspro** prison, a blow on the head with a police truncheon (cf. *wood rash* (WOOD *n.*[1] 2 b)); **wooden god**, see DRY *a.* 2; **wooden rose**, see *wood rose* (WOOD *n.*[1] 2 b); **wooden spoon** [spec. or local use of *wooden spoon*, orig. Cambridge University (1803) for a student lowest in the class, thence a consolation prize for a competitor scoring lowest: see OED *wooden a.* 7], in modern New Zealand use esp. with reference to university students' contests for the 'booby-prize' of a wooden spoon awarded to the university scoring the least points in inter-universities sports tournaments; also occas. awarded to an individual low-performing competitor (cf. SPOON *n.*[2]); hence **wooden spooner**, a competitor or team unsuccessful in a set of competitive fixtures.
1980 LELAND *Kiwi-Yankee Dict.* 114 (a) **wooden aspro**: Prison argot for a clout on the head with a truncheon. **1988** MCGILL *Dict. Kiwi Slang* 124 *wooden aspro* a truncheon across the head, as encountered most often in prisons. **1868** *Marlborough Express* (Blenheim) 7 Nov. 4 10th prize—Two Shillings and Sixpence..; '**Wooden Spoon**', Private Buchanan. **1912** *Auckland Univ. Carnival Programme* 6 June 46 And we laboured in vain, the reward of our pain [in the Inter-Varsity Tournament] Being only a wooden spoon. **1912** *Auckland Capping Book* 14 Shall Auckland hold the old Wooden Spoon Whenever the Tournament comes round? **1941** *Salient* (Wellington) 24 Apr. 3 Canterbury souvenired the Tournament and Athletics wooden spoons. **1958** *Ibid.* 1 Apr. 4 This year at tournament Victoria has every hope of disassociating itself from the wooden spoon. **1981** *Ibid.* 6 Apr. 12 It was really a case of bad luck that Varsity ended up with the wooden spoon [in cricket]. **1993** *Evening Post* (Wellington) 13 Apr. 24 Canterbury [netball] side Hearts..has what should be two comfortable matches against table **wooden spooners** Gisborne Old Girls..next week.

wooden, *v.* [Orig. uncertain: AND 1905.] *trans.* Often as **wooden out**, to knock up; to 'flatten'.
1904 LANCASTER *Sons o' Men* 252 He'll wooden more of you if you scare him. **1911** *Truth* 23 Dec. 5 Battye picked up a piece of timber that had once done duty as a handle to a domestic article, and literally 'woodened' Gibbons out. **1920** *Quick March* 10 Apr. 31 A twig no bigger'n yer big finger flew back and woodened him out. **c1926** THE MIXER *Transport Workers' Song Book* 126 [The block of ice] 'woodened' him out, and he lay there quite flat. **1959** SLATTER *Gun in My Hand* 43 'I gotta get away.' 'Ya bloody piker!' A man oughta wooden ya out.' **1968** SLATTER *Pagan Game* 172 Woodened out the five-eighths with a straight arm tackle. **1978** JARDINE *Shadows on Hill* 28 I..told this bloke that if he didn't control them [sc. sheep-dogs] I'd wooden them out next time. **1986** HULME *Te Kaihau* 35 And some cunt woodens me.

Hence **woodener** [AND 1899], a knockout blow.
c1875 MEREDITH *Adventuring in Maoriland* (1935) 39 I was in a tight corner, so I just 'landed' him another woodener between the eyes, and while he was counting the stars I dodged under his arm.

woodhen.

1. a. [Transf. use of Brit. *wood-hen* a female woodcock.] WEKA 1.
1773 COOK *Journals* 11 May (1961) II. 135 The Wild fowl are Ducks, Shaggs..Water or wood Hens, which are something like our English Rails, these inhabet [sic] the Skirts of the Woods and feed upon the Sea beach they are very like a Common Hen and eat very well in a Pye or Fricasee. **1791** BELL *Jrnl. Voyage H.M.S. 'Chatham'* Nov. (Vancouver exped.) (ATLMS) 45 Some of the Officers who had been away shooting return'd with some Birds, that proved acceptable—though they were only Wood Hens. *Ibid.* 50 The Wood Hen very much resembles the Common Barn door Fowl in England. **c1826–27** [see WEKA 1]. **c1835** BOULTBEE *Journal* (1986) 37 Milford Haven is a wild romantic looking place..the woods are abundantly supplied with game, as woodhens, green birds, emus etc. **1842** GRAY *Fauna* in Dieffenbach *Travels in NZ* (1843) II. 197 Weka or Weka-weka of the natives of Cook's Strait, Wood-hen of the Settlers. **1851** *Lyttelton Times* 8 Mar. 7 Woodhens..formed our chief food in the latter part of our expedition. **1860** in Butler *First Year* 24 Mar. (1863) iv 54 The night was warm and quiet, the silence only interrupted by the occasional cry of a wood-hen and the rushing of the river. **1879** HAAST *Geol. Canterbury & Westland* 98 The children..were often covered with sores and ulcers, living, as they did, upon anything they could obtain and greedily sucking the fat of the woodhens they were able to catch. **1882** POTTS *Out in Open* 131 The woodhen or weka..a valuable destroyer of vermin and insects, usually displays very destructive properties when it visits poultry yards. **1904** HUTTON & DRUMMOND *Animals NZ* 173 Our Wood Hens, the Wekas, have been branded as rogues and vagabonds. **c1926** THE MIXER *Transport Workers'*

Song Book 59 He's like a woodhen, quick to dodge when a list is put about. **1933** *Press* (Christchurch) (Acland Gloss.) 30 Dec. 13 *Wood hen.*—Still in use but more frequently called *weka*. W[ood]h[en], however, may survive, as it is often used figuratively. 'Running like a w[ood]h[en]' (being very busy), 'sheep no bigger than w[ood]h[en]s', etc. Their feathers make the best pipe cleaners in the world, and w[ood]h[en] oil was excellent for anything, metal or leather. **1945** BEATTIE *Maori Place-names Canterbury* 64 Weka—the familiar 'woodhen' of Captain Cook, and 'Maori hen' of the settlers. **1981** HENDERSON *Exiles Asbestos Cottage* 70 The Chaffeys recommended woodhen fat to everyone with great enthusiasm.

b. In *fig.* use, a fussy or hyperactive person; see also quot. 1933 above.
1914 GRACE *Tale of Timber Town* 113 An' that fussy old wood-hen'll be in, first thing tomorrow, asking for 'the memento of my poor dear 'usband'.

c. Special Comb. **woodhen oil**, *weka oil* (WEKA 5).
c**1920** BEATTIE *Trad. Lifeways Southern Maori* (1994) 63 This juice or gum [from the taramea plant] was mixed with woodhen oil (hinu-weka) and was used to dress the hair and to rub on the body.

2. With a modifier: **black, brown, North Island (northern), South Island (southern,** occas. **hill), Stewart Island**.

(1) black woodhen. *black weka* (WEKA 2 (1)). See also WEKA-PANGO.
1871 HUTTON *Catalogue Birds NZ* 32 *Ocydromus fuscus...* Black Wood Hen. **1873** [see WEKA-PANGO]. **1886** *TrNZI* XVIII. 105 *Ocydromus fuscus...* Black Wood-hen (*Weka*). **1890** *Otago Witness* (Dunedin) 3 Apr. 18 The black woodhen..is found in the secluded forests of the west coast of Otago. **1904** HUTTON & DRUMMOND *Animals NZ* 178 *The Black Wood Hen. Ocydromus brachypterus*. **1923** *NZJST* VI. 80 Black Woodhen... In the mining days 'many were killed for food, and many more were destroyed needlessly by the miners' dogs.' **1950** BEATTIE *Far Famed Fiordland* 83 Later in Dusky he found you would see three black woodhens to every grey (or brown) one. They came down to the shore to pick whelks when the tide was out.

(2) brown woodhen. *buff weka* (WEKA 2 (2)).
1888 BULLER *Birds NZ* II. 115 (Brown Woodhen)... This bird..belongs really to the South Island, [and] had been, for many years, confounded with the North-Island Woodhen under the above name. **1897** *TrNZI* XXIX. 193 *Ocydromus earli...* (Brown Woodhen.) **1923** *NZJST* VI. 80 *Gallirallus australis...* Brown Woodhen or Weka.

(3) North Island (northern) woodhen. *North Island weka* (WEKA 2 (3)).
1873 BULLER *Birds NZ* 165 *Ocydromus earli*. (North-Island Woodhen)... Weka. **1886** *TrNZI* XVIII. 113 *Ocydromus earli.*—Weka, Northern Wood-hen. **1895** *TrNZI* XXVII. 118 North Island Woodhen... This species of Woodhen is still numerous on the wooded hill-sides and mountain gullies in the Murimotu-Taupo country. **1904** HUTTON & DRUMMOND *Animals NZ* 178 *The North Island Wood Hen.*—*Weka. Ocydromus earli*.

(4) South Island (southern, occas. **hill) woodhen**. *South Island weka* (WEKA 2 (4)).
1873 BULLER *Birds NZ* 170 *Ocydromus australis*. (South-Island Woodhen.)... Weka. **1886** *TrNZI* XVIII. 113 *O. australis.*—Weka, Southern Wood-hen. **1890** *Otago Witness* (Dunedin) 3 Apr. 18 The southern woodhen..is a well-known bird... I have known it carry off a meerschaum pipe, spoons, pannikins. **1904** HUTTON & DRUMMOND *Animals NZ* 180 *The Hill Wood Hen. Ocydromus hectori*. **1923** *NZJST* VI. 80 *Gallirallus hectori...* South Island Woodhen. **1955** [see WEKA 2 (4)].

(5) Stewart Island woodhen. *Stewart Island weka* (WEKA 2 (5)).
1967 NATUSCH *Animals NZ* 267 My father says Stewart Island woodhens have two young in early spring, two more in midsummer, and two or three more in late summer.

3. In the phr. **to run like a woodhen**, to be very busy.
1933 [see 1 a above].

woofterish. [f. *woolly) woofter* + *-ish*.] Of argument, thin, airy, and unconvincing.
1988 *Dominion* (Wellington) 30 Dec. 8 [Heading] *Woofterish on Aids*. Of all your editorial comments..surely the effort on Aids and the Bishop of Christchurch takes the biscuit for wooly [*sic*] woofterism. **1993** *Evening Post* (Wellington) 22 May 5 By banning the woofterish gloves-on scrapping..the Minister may well inspire a resurgence of the bare-knuckle classicism New Zealanders once held dear.

wool. See also DEAD WOOL, TARANAKI WOOL.

1. wool away! [AND 1879.] The shearers' call to the fleece-picker to clear the shorn fleeces from the board.
1878 *Otago Witness* (Dunedin) 28 Sept. 3 Very little conversation goes on among the men in the two hours' work before breakfast. Only the cry of 'wool away'. **1897** WRIGHT *Station Ballads* in *Woodhouse Farm & Station Verse* (1950) 33 'All aboard! All aboard!' is the cry. They're a ripping lot of shearers in the shed;.. 'Wool away! Wool away!' is the cry... [1950 Note] In old-time sheds these calls indicated the beginning and end of a run. **1934** *Press* (Christchurch) (Acland Gloss.) 27 Jan. 15 *Wool away!*- The shearer's call to the fleece picker to take the fleece off the board. **1949** STRONACH in *Woodhouse Farm & Station Verse* (1950) 185 Is the ringer all set for [a] two-fifty day—'Wool away, and a bag for guts!' **1955** BOWEN *Wool Away* 158 'Wool away.' When the fleece has not been cleared off the board by the 'fleeco' and is in the shearer's way, a shearer will make this call. **1978** JARDINE *Shadows on Hill* 127 The gang is here, The shed's alive, It's 'Wool-away' As the shearers strive. **1988** *More* (Auckland) Mar. 32 Even more excited hooting and hollering can be heard from the shearers when one of their number gets ahead of the rousie and has to yell 'woolaway'.

2. In the phr. **to get one's wool combed (to comb** (someone's) **wool)**, to receive or give a scolding or thrashing; **by the wool**, by the 'short hairs', at one's mercy.
1881 NESFIELD *Chequered Career* 109 I expect he got his '**wool combed**' that evening, when he summoned up pluck to go home. **1909** *Truth* 31 July 1 The people are not at their back as the English masses were at the back of the Grey government, when it sought to pass the Reform Bill of 1832. The English middle classes then had all sections of the people, except the Lords, '**by the wool**'.

3. Special Comb. **wool-baron**, see *wool-king* below; **wool bin** [AND 1879], BIN *n.* 1 a; **wool-blind** *a*. [AND 1914], of a sheep, with sight obscured by wool growing over the eyes, hence **wool-blindness**; **woolboard**, BOARD 1 a; **wool book** [AND 1961], the official detailed record of all bales pressed in a woolshed; **woolbox**, either of the upper or (esp.) the lower 'boxes' forming the two sections of an hydraulic wool-press (see also BOX *n.*² 4); **wool brand**, see quot. 1987; **wool-bug**, a nickname for a shearer; **wool cheque** [AND 1930], the amount a sheep-farmer receives for a season's wool-clip, or the amount sheep-farmers collectively receive on a national or district level; **wool-classer** (a) [AND 1879], one trained to grade fleeces according to their type of wool (see also CLASSER); (b) *transf.*, a dog which bites sheep; **wool-classing** *vbl. n.* [AND 1847], the grading of fleeces; **wool clip** [AND 1844], the annual yield of wool from a farm or mob, or from the whole of New Zealand (see also CLIP *n.*¹); **wool count**, see quot. 1982; **wool dray** *obs*. [AND 1835], a bullock dray in which wool was carried from station to town (see also DRAY); **wool dumper**, one who 'dumps' or compresses wool-bales (see also DUMP *v.*); **wool dumping** *vbl. n.* and *attrib.*, the compressing of two bales of wool into the volume of one; **woolfaller** *obs.*, a (?non-union) shearer (also **woolfall** *v. intr.*, to shear sheep (?as a non-union shearer)); **woolhandler**, FLEECE-PICKER, ROUSEABOUT, hence **woolhandling**; **wool-hook** [AND 1908], see *bale-hook* (BALE b); **wool-jamming** *vbl. n.*, see quot.; **wool king** *obs.* [AND 1839], a large-scale sheep-farmer; **wool-pack** [?rare now in Brit. use: cf. OED *wool-pack* 1 (1297–1866)], the large bag, now of standard dimensions, made of jute or artificial fibre into which fleeces or wool are packed to form a bale; **wool-picker**, usu. FLEECE-PICKER, occas. SKIRTER (see quot. 1894 below); **woolpocket**, POCKET; **wool-press** [AND 1829] (see also PRESS *n.* 1), the device in which wool is compacted into bales; **wool-presser** [AND 1846], one who operates a wool-press (see also PRESSER a, *pressman* (PRESS *n.* 2); **wool-pressing** *vbl. n.* [AND 1848], the compressing and baling of wool in a wool press (see also *pressing* (PRESS *v.*)); **wool puller**, a person (usu. a freezing works employee) or machine which removes the (often chemically loosened) wool from a sheepskin or carcase (see also PULLER); **wool roller** [AND 1879] (see also ROLLER 1), a shed-hand who trims off the skirtings and rolls up a newly-shorn (classed) fleece; **wool rolling** [AND 1882] *vbl. n.*, see ROLL *v.* 1; **wool room** [AND 1836], an area or room in a woolshed where fleeces and wool are processed, pressed and (often) stored; **wool-rope**, see quot.; **wool scour**, see SCOUR; **wool season** [AND 1841], the annual period of shearing and marketing wool; **wool ship** *hist.* [revival of *woolship obs.* (1481): see OED *wool n.* 5 a], a ship dedicated to the wool-trade with Britain; **wool sorter** *obs.* [AND 1805], see *wool-classer* (a) above; **wool store** [AND 1840], a warehouse where wool is stored; **wool table** [AND 1879], a bench or table in a woolshed on which a newly-shorn fleece is classed (see also CLASSING TABLE); **wool truck**, *obs.* ?a wheeled vehicle towed behind a wool wagon; **wool wagon** *obs.*, a bullock-wagon used to transport wool from the station to town; **wool-walking**, a sheep-dog's manoeuvre of walking across the backs of massed sheep; **wool wash** [AND 1900], a commercial firm which washes and scours wool, a wool-scour; **woolwashing** *vbl. n.* and *attrib.*, the washing of farm wool.

1916 *Lyttelton Times* 14 Dec. (VUW Fildes Clippings 621/34) We are in the Cheviot country, the land of a famous '**wool-baron**' of his day, now beneficially divided among..small farmers. **1922** PERRY *Sheep Farming* 20 The **wool bins** are hinged, and can thus be swung against the wall when shearing is finished. The pieces bins are collapsible, and therefore able to be removed when not in use. **1933** *Press* (Christchurch) (Acland Gloss.) 30 Dec. 13 *Wool bins.*—Open compartments like stalls in a stable, where wool is stacked by classes until it is pressed. **1978** Jardine *Shadows on Hill* 129 The long shearing board, the wooltable, woolbins and woolroom floor lay unsullied..tally and wool books, all were ready. **1987** Ogonowska-Coates *Boards, Blades & Barebellies* 98 *Wool bin.* Open compartments in the woolshed where the classed wool is held until pressed. **1933** *Press* (Christchurch) (Acland Gloss.) 14 Oct. 15 The wool, especially on merinos is apt to grow over the eyes and make the sheep ***wool-blind***. **1940** Studholme *Te Waimate* (1954) 108 We got a few of the [Steiger sheep] breed.., but they were not a success, being..'buffalo headed' and very wool blind. **1955** [see eye-wig]. **1969** Moore *Forest to Farm* 18 These [hermit sheep]..often had two or three years' growth of wool, and because of this were nearly wool blind. **1989** [see crutching 1 a]. **1940** Studholme *Te Waimate* (1954) 119 One of the difficulties of mustering was **wool-blindness**, many of the sheep being as blind as the proverbial bat. **1950** [see eye-clip]. **1986** Richards *Off the Sheep's Back* 113 A steam whistle..blew for the commencement and finish of each run. The wool tables for rolling and skirting were in the centre of the **woolboard**. **1933** *Press* (Christchurch) (Acland Gloss.) 30 Dec. 13 ***Wool book.***—The pressers write down in it the number, description, and weight of each bale as they press it. **1940** Studholme *Te Waimate* (1954) 130 In addition to filling up the catching pens, [the sheep-o] weighed the bales and recorded them, with their descriptions, in the wool book. **1978** [see *wool bin* above]. **1973** Wheeler *Hist. Sheep Stations NI* 71 [Caption] The mobility of the two sections of this hydraulic woolpress enable a bale to be sewn while the **woolboxes** are being refilled. **1933** *Press* (Christchurch) (Acland Gloss.) 30 Dec. 13 ***Wool brand.***—Usually the name of the station now, but in old days frequently the owner's name or intials, e.g. *Acland* is the Mount Peel brand and *C.O.T.* (Charles Obins Torlesse, the first owner) the Birch Hill brand. The brand and number are put on with a *stencil*. **1987** Ogonowska-Coates *Boards, Blades & Barebellies* 98 *Wool brand.* The name of each station, branded on the full bale. **1926** Devanny *Butcher Shop* (1981) 57 He pictured the shearers, the '**wool-bugs**', in their dirt and grease. **1927** Devanny *Old Savage* 30 Look here, you wool-bugs! All them yarns I told yer was lies. **1938** Scanlan *Guest of Life* 397 Daddy was quite pleased with his **wool cheque** this year. **1946** Miller *There Was Gold* 15 In the old days..he was willing to wait for the farmer's wool cheque before he was paid. **1953** Scott *Breakfast at Six* 180 Our interest and repayment of principal came easily out of the wool cheque. **1988** Smith *Southlanders at Heart* 133 Their wool cheque is down, and their lambing percent. **1876** *William Shirres Copybook* in Neave *Land of Munros* (1980) 55 One [grave] is that..of a **woolclasser** who was drowned in the Otematata River. **1883** *Brett's Colonists' Guide* 215 There are many so-called wool-classers whose experience is limited to a few years at the rolling table. **1892** [see roller]. **c1927** Smith *Sheep & Wool Industry* 80 On all large stations..a wool-classer is employed at shearing-time to 'get-up' the clip. **1933** [see roller]. **1988** *More* (Auckland) Mar. 31 In sheds shearing fine wool (from Merino, Halfbred or Corriedale sheep) a woolclasser is employed to make lines of wool; that is, to define the differences between wool from each sheep after it has been shorn and skirted..and to group similar wools together in baled lines for ease of sale and subsequent processing. **1966** Turner *Eng. Lang. Austral. & NZ* 146 There is the *Sunday dog* who declines to work in a difficulty, the **woolclasser** who bites at the sheep, and the *sooner* who would sooner rest than work. **c1875** Meredith *Adventuring in Maoriland* (1935) 86 I want to go in for **wool-classing**. **1912** *Sheepowners' Handbook* 11 Satisfactory arrangements were made for..classes in both Machine-Shearing and Wool-Classing. **1922** Perry *Sheep Farming* 119 The farmer should be careful to distinguish between 'wool classing' and 'wool sorting'. Wool sorting is a process employed in manufacture. In wool classing groups of qualities are dealt with, generally representing the fine and coarse wools of a flock, and lines are made according to condition (*i.e.* amount of grease), soundness, and length of staple. *Wool classing* is the placing of *whole* fleeces, after skirting, into different classes or grades according to the condition, quality, and strength and length of fibre. **1968** *NZ Contemp. Dict. Suppl.* (Collins) 22 *woolclasser n.* a grader of wool; whence *woolclassing*, art of grading wool. **1976** Vance *Bush, Bullocks & Boulders* 25 For years he did the wool classing at Buccleugh station. **1855** *Nelson Examiner* 22 Nov. 2 I am led to believe that the **wool clip** this season will be a very good one..in the Wairau. **1887** *Auckland Weekly News* 12 Nov. 19 An application has just been made to permit the wool clip of the district to pass over the line... Today they are applying to have the clip of 30,000 sheep, or something like 1000 bales of wool passed over the Marton-Hunterville Railway. **1892** *NZ Official Handbook* 124 Growers..very often obtain at their doors more for their wool-clip than they would realise in London. **1928** *Free Lance* (Wellington) 18 Apr. 28 New Zealand's wool clip still remains her most important single staple. **1936** Belshaw et al. *Agric. Organiz. NZ* 710 Moreover, in every wool clip, wherever it is classed, there are always some fleeces which cannot be placed in any of the set lines without spoiling its evenness. **1973** Fernandez *Tussock Fever* 160 At the dinner table..Andrew brought up the subject of his wool-clip. **1986** Richards *Off the Sheep's Back* 68 John was busy drinking to the success of his woolclip. **1951** Duff *Shepherd's Calendar* (1961) 35 I wish I could remember the standard **wool counts**, or even the meaning of a count in the first place. [**1982** *Agric. Gloss.* (MAF) 54 *Count*: Shortened form of yarn count. Commonly misused to mean a subjective assessment of fineness of greasy wool [based on the Bradford worsted yarn count system for wools spun to their limit].] **1866** Barker *Station Life* (1870) 40 The **wool drays** are all going back empty, and we can get them to take the loads at reduced prices. **1874** Kennaway *Crusts* 166 [He] was now driving wool-drays in New Zealand. **1892** Kipling *One Lady at Wairakei* (1983) 37 He shall lie under wool-drays in summer. **1893** Mackenzie *Overland Auckland to Wellington* 37 I am told [c1853] that the **wool dumpers** in Wellington are taking to iron hoops instead of flax lashings. **1991** *Ann. Rep. Farmers' Co-op. Org. Soc. NZ* 5 The Wanganui Wool Dumpers Partnership had concluded its first financial year of operations... The stockpile of unsold wools in store will contribute to the dumping trade as it is sold. **1885** **wool-dumping** [see dump *v.*]. **1902** *Settler's Handbook NZ* 42 The Harbour Board has an up-to-date wool-dumping press and hydraulic pumps. **1948** Bowman *Port Chalmers* 43 Working [i.e. handling] wool today..is made easier..by what became known as 'wool dumping'. *Ibid.* 49 It was [at the woolstore of John Mill and Co.] that the practice of what has been called wool dumping originated in New Zealand. **1911** *Maoriland Worker* 8 Dec. 14 I have unearthed five more of the **woolfallers** who see their way clear to engage at 19s 6d. All are small farmers and gun shearers. **1912** *Maoriland Worker* 26 Jan. 14 On Sunday morning I visited Westoe, and found six local chaps **woolfalling** but found it utterly useless tarying [*sic*] to arm them with a green ticket. **1988** *More* (Auckland) Mar. 31 A rouseabout—also variously known as a rousie, **woolhandler**, shedhand, fleeco, the person 'picking up' or a blue tongue—is responsible for the passage of wool after being shorn from the sheeps' back to the wool press where it is baled. **1995** *Mana 9* (Winter issue) 73 The work of woolhandlers may not look all that tough. We once knew them as rouseabouts, rousies or shedhands, before thay adopted the modern upmarket label. Their job is to clear the wool away from the action on the shearing board—and sort it into different bins. **1988** *More* (Auckland) Mar. 28 I've even had the thrill of climbing onto the revered boards of the Golden Shears stage to collect a prize; second in the junior **woolhandling**. **1995** *Mana 9* (Winter issue) 73 Despite the hard-case reputation of rousies, woolhandling is a job for professionals. **1964** Davis *Watersiders* 23 The very latest thing in steel **wool-hooks**, so the counterjumper had informed me. **1948** Bowman *Port Chalmers* 43 Captain Shortland personally supervised the stowing [of the wool cargo 1880–90s], 'screwing' the bales into the hold to the singing of sea-shanties. The bales were stowed by hand until the last in each row when 'screw-jacks' were used, based on 'samson posts', to screw the last bale of the tier into position... This method of stowing wool was sometimes referred to as '**wool-jamming**' or 'screwing'. **1886** Hart *Stray Leaves* 19 [Shagroons] ultimately became the founders of the present race of **wool kings** in many parts of Canterbury. **1891** A Tramp, Esq. *Casual Ramblings* 59 The wool-king reposes on rosebuds and down, while his men are downed in 'quarters' that a Chinaman would turn his nose up at. **1905** *Truth* 23 Sept. 5 The swindling wool-kings of the Canterbury Plains who make up cronk bales of wool and palm them off..as the best. **1912** *Free Lance* (Wellington) 21 Dec. 4 Concerning the late Mr. Richard Beetham..of the big 'wool-king' family of that name—Mr. M. Donnelly has a tiny anecdote to tell. **1926** *NZ Observer* 9 June 6 Hawke's Bay had lost the shield and that after getting..half the All Blacks to go and live in the capital of the province of the wool kings. **1938** *Ibid.* 18 Aug. 14 The death..of A.L. Allan..recalls the heyday of the New Zealand wool-kings. **1980** Eldred-Grigg *Southern Gentry* 102 [Caption] Otekaike. 'This palatial residence..enables one to understand the term "Wool Kings"', wrote one journalist. **1851** *Lyttelton Times* 9 Aug. 3 Table of Duties of Customs... **Woolpacks**, each—6d. **1860** *Puketoi Station Diary* (Hocken TS) 7 Nov Harry went over to Eweburn with woolpacks. **c1875** [see *wool-pressing* below]. **1892** woolpack [see *woolpocket* below]. **1902** [see *wool-pressing* below]. **1939** Beattie *First White Boy Born Otago* 86 It appeared to be sacking and may have been a woolpack lightly stuffed with straw. **1950** *NZJAg* 16 Oct 311 Frames hinged to a wall can be very useful to support a wool pack for bellies, necks, etc. **1982** *Agric. Gloss.* (MAF) 61 *Woolpack*: Jute or polypropylene bag of regulated dimensions for packing wool in a shearing shed or wool store. **1894** Wilson *Land of Tui* 244 Meanwhile the shorn fleeces are carried to a large table in the wool-shed by a man appropriately named 'Fleecy', and are spread out by four **wool-pickers**, who tear away the bad parts and fold the fleeces square, passing them to the classer. **1892** *NZ Official Handbook* 297 [Table of Duties of Customs] Woolpacks of the kind known as '**woolpockets**', and not exceeding the measurement of 18 by 21 by 30 inches, 6d. the dozen. **1846** Pharazyn *Journal* (ATLMS) 67 Employed all day at Watarangi assisting in packing fleeces. George making **wool press**. **1861** Harper *Lett. from NZ* 20 July (1914) 62 A wool press..bins for fleeces. **1876** Chudleigh *Diary* Mar. (1950) 249 Anderson [foundry] is making a Speedy wool press for the station. **1881** [see woolshed 1]. **1894** [see bin *n.* 1]. **1936** Belshaw et al. *Agric. Organiz. NZ* 433 Machinery peculiar to sheep farms is confined to shearing-shed plant, and consists of shearing machines and wool-presses. **1947** *NZ Observer* 15 Oct. 21 I considered the wool-press, a marvellous invention. **1986** Richards *Off the Sheep's Back* 82 The woolpress could not be used because the roof of the shed was too low to permit the top box to be filled. **c1875** Meredith *Adventuring in Maoriland* (1935) 103 I had a remarkable **woolpresser**—a Maori who had had both eyes blinded by an explosion of gunpowder. **1892** SWANTON *Notes on NZ* 96 There is the wool-presser and his mate to bale up the wool. **1908** *Normanvale Wages Book* in Hayes *Toss Of a Coin* (1978) 155 A. Niall (wool-classer), R. Finn (wool-presser). **1940** STUDHOLME *Te Waimate* (1954) 130 The wool-pressers in a big shed had a most strenuous time, especially in the days of the old screw press. **1953** STRONACH *Musterer on Molesworth* 31 The wool pressers, on the wool room among the bins, had a strenuous job, and were generally two very strong men. **c1875** MEREDITH *Adventuring in Maoriland* (1935) 96 **Wool-pressing** is done by means of a tall square box, in which the woolpack is placed and fastened to the top by means of a few spikes fixed around the outside top of the box. **1902** *Brett's Colonists' Guide* 320 Wool-pressing.—The rolled fleeces should be placed in even tiers in the wool pack. **1913** CARR *Country Work* 7 A young London clerk, who found work on a sheep station, where I was wool-pressing two seasons ago, told me that he..passed..without difficulty. **1913** CARR *Country Work* 19 There is only one [freezing-works] job that the most fastidious could refuse, and that is 'picking pie'. This consists in pulling the wool off the trimmings that have been taken off by the '**wool pullers**' at the beam. **1976** MORRIESON *Pallet on Floor* 95 No one around the washers; no one at the paint table; no one on the 'bull-wagons' which transported the treated skins to the wool-pullers. **1982** *Agric. Gloss.* (MAF) 63 *Wool puller*: Person or machine who removes the wool from a lamb/sheep skin after it has been chemically loosened. **1910** *Maoriland Worker* 15 Dec. 3 Evidence was given for the [shearers'] Union by Messrs. J. Ormiston (picker-up and **woolroller**). **1911** [see *wool-table* below]. **c1927** SMITH *Sheep & Wool Industry* 84 Two wool-rollers should be at each skirting table. **1933** *Press* (Christchurch) (Acland Gloss.) 30 Dec. 13 *Wool roller*.—Assistant to the *classer*. He *skirts* the fleece and *rolls* it. **1940** STUDHOLME *Te Waimate* (1954) 130 Fleece-pickers received 15s. a week, wool-rollers 25s. to 30s. [in 1882]. **1953** STRONACH *Musterer on Molesworth* 30 The wool rollers at the table whereon the fleecies had thrown the wool took what was necessary off each fleece and then rolled it, ready for the classer's inspection. **1987** OGONOWSKA-COATES *Boards, Blades & Barebellies* 98 *Wool roller*. The assistant to the classer; usually skirts the fleece and rolls it. **c1875** MEREDITH *Adventuring in Maoriland* (1935) 41 We have just started shearing, and I am kept pretty busy mustering sheep, **wool-rolling**, pressing, and dipping. **1913** CARR *Country Work* 15 Wool Rolling.—When the fleece is thrown on the table by the fleece-picker, the wool rollers (generally there are two) skirt—i.e., take off the dirty wool—the neck (in some sheds) and legs,.. turn in the sides and roll up, from each end. The Classer, by feel, sight, and general knowledge, decides what class it belongs to. **1982** WOODHOUSE *Blue Cliffs* 89 Fred Stuthridge came as a wool-classer in 1904 and was paid £1 for each 1000 fleeces with 25/- a week extra for wool-rolling. **c1875** MEREDITH *Adventuring in Maoriland* (1935) 145 I returned to the shed. I then said. 'I'll give you five minutes to make up your mind,' and went into the **wool-room**. **1913** CARR *Country Work* 17 In sheds where Maori girls are employed, it is the custom to have dances in the wool room every Saturday night. **1922** PERRY *Sheep Farming* 123 *Pressing*.—It is in the wool room that the greatest care must be exercised to ensure that nothing is done to mar otherwise careful treatment. **1933** [see WOOLSHED 1]. **1949** NEWTON *High Country Days* 48 Round in the woolroom the pressers were already at work. **1951** McLEOD *NZ High Country* 10 Along the front [of the woolshed] is the shearing board..and the wool room usually forms a large projection on the front of this again. **1978** JARDINE *Shadows on Hill* 129 The long shearing board, the wooltable, woolbins and woolroom floor lay unsullied. **1986** wool room [see WOOLSHED 1]. **1952** MEEK *Station Days* 111 **Wool-rope**: A rope twisted from the fleece where fleeces are tied for throwing up to top bins. **1857** *Lyttelton Times* 1 July Contracts have been let for the completion of the works on the Weka pass, which will be open for the next **wool season**. **1914** in *Hist. N. Otago from 1853* (1978) 45 This spot presented a busy scene in the wool season, January and February, when wool wagons with their spans of..bullocks were arriving. **1861** *Otago Witness* (Dunedin) 19 Jan. 4 First **Wool Ship** for London Direct. **1866** BARKER *Station Life* (1870) 40 The expense of carriage [of furniture], though moderate enough by sea (in a wool ship), is enormous as soon as it reaches Lyttelton. **1874** BAINES *Edward Crewe* 103 I quickly made it fast to..my raft, and with many a helping hand I gained the deck of the *Charles Martel*..wool ship from Sydney—Homeward bound. **1899** *NZ Times* (Wellington) 28 Dec. 2 Wool wagons are daily to be seen..bringing down wool..to the dumping sheds..and from thence to the wool ships which roll at anchor in the Bay. **1861** HARPER *Lett. from NZ* 20 July (1914) 54 Shearing..is in full swing, so there are a number of extra men..shearers, fleece-pickers, **wool sorters**, and 'rouse-abouts'. **1865** [see *wool table* below]. **1894** *NZ Official Year-book* 268 Table showing the occupations of persons who insured in the Government Insurance Department in 1893... flaxmillers..wool-buyer, wool-scourer, wool-sorter. **1901** [see WOOLSHED 1]. **1878** *Press* (Christchurch) in Deans *Pioneers Port Cooper Plains* (1964) 21 To sell, on Tuesday, August 13, at the Canterbury **wool stores**, At 12 o'clock sharp in sections, As per plan. **1912** RUTHERFORD *Impressions NZ Pastoralist on Tour* 86 These London stores are not..to be compared with the wool stores of Australasia. **1936** HYDE *Passport to Hell* 41 Dave arrived with news of a job for Starkie in Dalgety's wool-store. **1947** *Landfall 1* 70 [Gaskell] is quite at home with the Maori, or the wool-store worker. **1959** SHADBOLT *The New Zealanders* (1986) 113 [They met] in the dust and dag-stink of a woolstore. **1968** SLATTER *Pagan Game* 94 She had been the office typist at the wool store where he worked in the vacation. **1973** FERNANDEZ *Tussock Fever* 149 Bill was away every day at the woolstore. **1982** *Agric. Gloss.* (MAF) 61 *Woolstore*: Place where wool is prepared and offered for sale. **1865** BARKER *Station Life* (1870) 1 Dec. 33 We next inspected the **wool tables**, to which two boys were incessantly bringing armfuls of rolled-up fleeces; these were laid out on the tables before the wool-sorters. **1874** CAIRD *Sheepfarming NZ* 23 In the perpendicular part of the T [of the woolshed] are the wool tables where the fleeces are rolled up and classed. **1901** *TrNZI* XXXIII. 196 White wool divides, when skirted by the roller at the wool-table, thus: Belly pieces, say, 6d. per pound [etc.]. **1911** *Maoriland Worker* 20 Mar. 15 Why shouldn't the 'picker up' get as much as the wool-roller? Surely running up and down the board all day is as hard work as standing at a wool table. **1915** [see SECOND-CUT 2]. **1922** PERRY *Sheep Farming* 17 There should be good large windows in the roof over the classing or wool tables. **1978** [see *wool-bin* above]. **1982** *Agric. Gloss.* (MAF) 61 *Wool table*: Slatted table on which fleece wool is skirted and classed. **c1885** ACTON-ADAMS in McCaskill *Molesworth* (1969) 57 I'll provide the yokes and chains [for the bullocks]; you would have to get two **wool trucks** and covers. **1899** *NZ Times* (Wellington) 28 Dec. 2 **Wool wagons** are daily to be seen..bringing down wool from the various farms. **1914** in *Hist. N. Otago from 1853* (1978) 45 This spot presented a busy scene in the wool season, January and February, when wool wagons with their spans of 5 to 9 yoke (two abreast) of bullocks were arriving. **1935** *Tararua Tramper* Jan. 2 The crossing of the Wilberforce [was] made possible by the Mt. Algides [*sic*] wool-waggon. **1953** SUTHERLAND *Golden Bush* (1963) 112 I..got a passage out to Taumarunui station on a wool waggon where I bought a ticket to Masterton. **1982** WHEELER *Hist. Sheep Stations NZ* 41 [Caption] The old wool wagon, veteran of many river crossings [at Mt Algidus]. **1980** MOMATIUK & EASTCOTT *High Country* 74 When a frightened mob clusters into one solid mass, a good collie jumps on their backs to break the congestion and get them moving again—a manoeuvre called '**wool-walking**'. **c1880s** in Masters *Tales of the Mails* (1959) 45 Crossing the Rangitikei river we were soon inside the cookhouse at Messrs. Birch's **woolwash**, and were regaled with mugs of tea and plenty of good bread. **1959** MASTERS *Tales of Mails* 157 A bullocky named Bob Anderson..could not get his team to cross the bridge over the Erewhon woolwash creek. However, I worked on Erewhon years ago. In fact, I camped with Jerry O'Brien in the old woolwash buildings. There is a small creek, not far from the woolshed, called Woolwash Creek, wherein Pringle scoured his clip. **1984** BOYD *City of the Plains* 64 He grew up in Howick and served in the Anglo-Maori wars of the sixties before..marrying Jane Tucker, whose uncle had a wool wash at Clive. **1868** *Marlborough Express* (Blenheim) 4 Jan. 1 **Wool Washing** Establishment, Nelson Street, Blenheim **1985** BREMNER *Woolscours NZ* 14 Woolwashing was done on the stations before commercial firms were established.

woolling-up, *vbl. n. Shearing.* The accumulating of fleeces on the shearing board or wool table.

1957 *NZJAg.* Oct. XCV. 325 He holds up clearing of the shearing board, picking-up, and skirting, and eventually causes 'woolling-up' of the wool room.

Hence **woolled-up** *ppl. a.*, of a shearing board or wool table, encumbered with accumulated fleeces thus hampering the shearing operation. See also SNOWED IN.

1982 *Agric. Gloss.* (MAF) 61 *Woolled-up*: When the shearers are ahead of the wool table, so that wool is lying around the floor waiting to go on the wool table. Also described as snowed-in. **1986** RICHARDS *Off the Sheep's Back* 83 Throughout the day we were never held up for sheep, nor was the board ever 'woolled up'.

woolly, *a.* and *n.*

A. *adj.* [Spec. and transf. uses of *woolly* wool-bearing.]

1. Of a sheep, in full fleece, unshorn.

1879 KIERNAN *Diary* 26 Feb. in Guthrie-Smith *Tutira* (1921) 127 Would have done more but for the number of previously shorn sheep being mixed up with the woolly... [27 Feb.] Drafted out all the woolly sheep and took them to the shed... C.H.S..drafting and putting shorn sheep out to the paddocks. **1936** BELSHAW et al. *Agric. Organiz. NZ* 425 In addition to the well-defined periods of risk enumerated above, a small percentage of deaths is incurred through woolly sheep getting entangled in second growth. **1973** WHEELER *Hist. Sheep Stations NI* 70 Huiarua's big fourteen-stand shed..holds 3,000 woolly sheep, and has a shearing board seventy feet long.

2. In special collocations: **woolly hog** *farming*, see quot. 1982; **woolly-pointed** *ppl. a.*, of a sheep, having wool on the points, as distinct from a 'bare-point'; **woolly woofter** (a) [poss. from an original **willy-woofter**] rhyming slang for 'poofter' a (passive) male homosexual, or transvestite; (b) a 'woolly' or unconvincing thinker or arguer (see quot. 1981) hence, **woolly woofterism** (see also WOOFTERISH); (c) a soft-natured foolish person, a 'wimp'.

1982 *Agric. Gloss.* (MAF) 61 ***Woolly hog***: a fleece from a hogget unshorn as a lamb. **1955** BOWEN *Wool Away* 26 On an average **woolly-pointed** sheep the first blow of the off leg is out the top of the leg to part the wool over for the next blow. **1982** NEWBOLD *Big Huey* 128 I was inclined to think that getting it off with a woolly woofter might be a go for me. *Ibid.* 255 Woolly woofer (n) Passive homosexual. Rhyming slang for Poofter. **1981** *Staff Officer NZ Police Nat. Headquarters* (Goldie Brown Collect.) *woolly woofter*: term used to describe a person who has woolly thinking and is a bit dense; e.g., 'Nice guy, but a real woolly woofter.' **1987** *Evening Post* (Wellington) 7 Dec. 6 [Norman Jones] would have despised his unwanted defenders..the wimps or woolly woofters as he called them, whom he spent a life-time fighting. **1989** *NZPD* 20 Sept. DI. 12757 Wellington Government back-benchers—a pack of woolly-woofters if ever there was one—are utterly terrified of criticising the Minister of the House. **1992** *Listener* 29 June 34 It's the war-cry of the woolly woofters and they're on the march again. **1993** *North & South* (Auckland) June 60 I'm sure their first reaction was, 'Who's this willy-woofter in a thousand-dollar Italian suit showing us pictures of champagne and french perfume?'

B. *n.*

1. [Used elsewhere but recorded earliest in New Zealand: AND 1897.] An unshorn sheep; a sheep before shearing.

1888 Chudleigh *Diary* 6 Dec. (1950) 365 Found rails shaken out by sheep and 1200 woolies [*sic*] got into shorn Ewes and lamb mob. **1909** Meek in Woodhouse *Farm & Station Verse* (1950) 59 Woollies shorn in nineteen-eight will be fit to shear again. **1918** *Otago Witness* (Dunedin) 31 July 27 It tries one's powers of endurance to look out and see the..long-suffering 'woollies' trying hard to find a nibble. **1947** Newton *High Country Days* 56 Two of the musterers arrived at the [wool] shed with another 'cut' of woollies. **1952** Lyon *Faring South* 198 The shearing, with fresh lots of woollies every day and drovers taking a return lot of shorn sheep, was put through in a week. **1966** *NZ Short Stories* (1976) 126 See him coming in..at mustering-time with a mob..and his dogs handling each woolly as though its fleece was worth its weight in gold.

2. *double-fleecer* (double *a.*), a sheep which has missed a shearing.

1945 *NZ Geogr.* I. 39 'Woollies' are sheep which have escaped the shearing and as a result carry more than one year's wool on their backs. **1947** Newton *Wayleggo* 94 It is, of course, unfenced and affords plenty of opportunities for cunning woollies to dodge the musterers.

woolly-bear. [Spec. use of *woolly bear*, the larva of the tiger moth: cf. OED *woolly a.* 3 c.] In New Zealand, the larva of the magpie moth *Nyctemera annulata* (fam. Nymphalidae).

1929 Martin *NZ Nature Book I* 152 Indeed it is rare during the warmer months of the year to find any area of these plants free from the 'woolly-bear' caterpillars of this [magpie] moth. **1934** Miller *Garden Pests in NZ* 24 Most easily obtained in all stages and commonest in any part of the country from spring to autumn, is the magpie moth..and its caterpillar, the 'woolly bear'. **1947** Powell *Native Animals of New Zealand* 55 The caterpillar [of the magpie moth] is black and red, covered with numerous tufts of black hair, it is the well-known 'woolly-bear' commonly found feeding on the leaves of many plants of the daisy family. **1950** *NZJ Ag.* Nov. LXXXI. 478 The most common enemy of cinerarias in New Zealand is the 'woolly-bear' caterpillar, the larva of the magpie moth. **1972** *Press* (Christchurch) 16 Sept. 11 When full grown, the caterpillars are almost 1¼ inches long; black and ornamented with narrow brick red lines along the body and are covered with tufts of long black hairs. Because of this hairy covering the caterpillars of the Magpie Moth are known as 'woolly bears'. **1984** Miller *Common Insects* 112 The most conspicuous..is the

Magpie Moth..and its hairy caterpillars, the so-called Woolly Bears.

woollyhead. *Craspedia* spp. (fam. Compositae), a mainly alpine genus having a rounded flower-head, usu. yellow or white, having white hairs on the fringes of leaves and often in shaggy masses on the flower stalks.

1952 Richards *Chatham Is.* 47 *Craspedia.. uniflora...* A perennial plant with flannelly leaves bordered with a fringe of white hairs... Woolly Head. Putea (white flower). **1981** Dennis *Paparoas Guide* 150 Bare rock and salt air make life tough but not impossible for the yellow-flowering woollyhead (*Craspedia uniflora* var. *maritima*). **1993** Gabites *Wellington's Living Cloak* 24 Woollyhead, for example [*sc.* of a variation in Wellington rocky shore plants], has a variety which is larger-leaved, and its pompom-like flowers are a sulphur yellow instead of the usual white.

wool money.

1. *Obs.* The payment by the grazier to the owner of sheep 'on terms' for the wool they produce.

1860 [see terms *n.*¹]. **1864** Muter *Travels* II. 263 The squatter [offers] to take sheep 'on terms', whereby he guarantees an increase of forty per cent, and a rent, called 'wool money', of half-a-crown per head.

2. The money received for a (year's) wool-clip; *wool-cheque* (wool 3).

1861 Butler *Letter* 31 May in Jones *Samuel Butler* (1919) I. 93 It is true I can wash well enough and can manage to stave over next shearing..when my wool money will be something considerable. **1868** Chudleigh *Diary* 23 Mar. (1950) 219 All the wool in the sea somewhere... We do not expect to realise one farthing on this years wool money. **1872** Barker *Christmas Cake* ch. iii I shall be three hundred pounds short in my wool-money this year.

woolshed.

1. [AND 1835.] A farm building in which sheep are shorn and fleeces processed and packed. See also *shearing-shed* (shearing B 3), shed 2.

1846 *Pharazyn Journal* (ATLMS) 67 Teddy and self to wool shed at Watarangi and finished the same. **1856** Fitton *NZ* 221 Wool sheds must also be erected for shearing and storing away the wool. **1871** Money *Knocking About NZ* 6 There was the usual..woolshed, where the sheep were shorn and the wool packed in bales for transmission home. **1881** Bathgate *Waitaruna* 171 The shed, a large building of corrugated iron, was surrounded outside by innumerable sheep, most of them crowded with sheep packed as close as they could stand. Inside, the woolshed was also filled with penned sheep, except at the end where the wool-press stood, and along each side, where space was left for the shearers. **1901** Butler *Erewhon* (1932) ii 24 A wool-shed is a roomy place, built somewhat on the same plan as a cathedral, with aisles on either side full of pens for the sheep, a great nave, at the upper end of which the shearers work, and a further space for wool sorters and packers. **1933** *Press* (Christchurch) (Acland Gloss.) 30 Dec. 13 *Woolshed.*—Often *shed* for short. Building in which sheep are shorn. All w[ool]s[ed]s have three parts, the *pens* (formerly skillions) where the sheep are held, the *board* where they are shorn, and the *wool room* where the wool is classed, pressed, and stored. **1951** McLeod *NZ High Country* 10 The most important outbuilding on the place is the wool-shed. This is usually a corrugated iron building with holding space for anything up to 1500 sheep. **1986** Richards *Off the Sheep's Back* 72 The woolshed was..enormous with its four-stand shearing plant, large wool room and storage space for about 200 bales.

2. Special Comb. **woolshed dance** [AND 1965], a dance held in a woolshed, esp. a dance formerly held to celebrate the end of the shearing season. See also *shearers' dance* (shearer 2).

1960 Rogers *Long White Cloud* 13 'After the woolshed dance,' said Jill. **1973** Fernandez *Tussock Fever* 29 'Mum, I've nothing to wear to the shearers' dance..' 'I haven't time to sew for you now, dear. You don't need a new dress for a woolshed dance.' **1986** Richards *Off the Sheep's Back* 143 The Red Cross socials, woolshed dances, stock drives and many other functions that I remembered as a boy, appeared to be only half-heartedly supported.

woopcacker, woopkacker, varr. wopcacker.

woop-woops /ˈwʊpˌwʊps/. Also occas. **woop-woop.** [f. the Austral. *woop-woops*: AND 'Jocular formation, prob. infl. by the use of reduplication in Aboriginal languages', 1918.] woop-wops.

1968 *NZ Contemp. Dict. Suppl.* (Collins) 22 *woop woop.. n.* (*Phr.*) name jocularly applied to small remote or outback districts. **1970** *Listener* 21 Dec. 51 While you're out in the woop-woops next time, spare a thought for the local farmer. **1976** Hilliard *Send Somebody Nice* 119 'Me for the woop-woops smartly,' Trevor said. 'That'd be the stone cold end of it for me.'

wop. [Orig. unknown.] In phr. **up the wop. a.** askew, awry; broken.

1960 Muir *Word for Word* 212 Fair go. The whole idea's up the wop. I can think of a hundred explanations straight off. **1988** McGill *Dict. of Kiwi Slang* 118 *up the wop* pregnant.—broken, not functioning; eg 'That doll's house you've built is totally up the wop.'

b. Of a woman, pregnant.

1981 Hooper *Goat Paddock* 13 There's always something happening, like..some sheila you know getting put up the wop. **1988** [see **a** preceding].

wopcacker /ˈwɒpˌkækə/. Also **whopcacker, woopcacker, woopkacker, wop-kacker.** [Poss. a portmanteau of or a play on *whop*(per + *cracker*(jack.] Anything large, superior or occas. surprising of its class. Often *attrib.*

1941 Baker *NZ Slang* 51 Of children's terms..we may note *snitcher, snitch, whopcacker*..descriptive of something superlative or excellent, both as nouns and adjectives. **1959** Slatter *Gun in My Hand* 91 He's a hard shot. Yeah, he's a woopkacker all right. **1964** Hori *Fill It Up Again* 63 At last [I] bring in a whopcacker stingray. **1966** Turner *Eng. Lang. Austral. & NZ* 121 *Woopcacker* seems to apply to things as well as people. The word illustrates the lack of standardization in these seldom written words: I would have spelt it *wopcacker*. Baker records the word as *whopcacker* but gives a slightly variant meaning, as 'very good'. **1969** Mason *Awatea* (1978) 37 Will you just look at this dirty big wop-kacker! *Ibid.* 98 *wop-kacker*: New Zealand slang for 'thingummy', implying size, proportion, remarkable qualities. Etymology dubious. Now slightly archaic: Miss Gilhooly's stock of *argot* is behind the times, nor does she always know the full meaning of her blunt and scabrous expressions. **1972** *Dominion* (Wellington) 17 June 26 I've been trying to find space for my notes on a 'Glossy' subtitled 'This Will Really Kill You'. It's a wopcacker if ever there was, so here goes. **1982** Shadbolt *Once on Chunuk Bair* (1990) 66 You wop-cacker, Scruf. Scruffy: I told you I could. **1991** Virtue *Always the Islands of Memory* 151 It had been a woopkacker day. **1993** Marshall *Ace of Diamonds Gang* 122 Yea, well remember the size of some of them. Bloody wopcackers.

wop-kacker, var. wopcacker.

wops: see WOP-WOPS.

wop-wops /ˈwɒp ˌwɒps/. [Origin uncertain: poss. a variation of (Austral.) *woop-woops*.]

1. The remote or primitive rural districts, the BACKBLOCKS; the remote hinterland. See also WOOP-WOOPS, WOPS. **a.** As **the wop-wops**.

1959 SLATTER *Gun in My Hand* 205 You kidding? Where you been? Out in the wop-wops? Sonny's dead for ages. 1965 WATSON *Stand in Rain* 102 What on earth would a shy bushman like Fergus do with a woman away out in the wop-wops. 1971 ARMFELT *Catching Up* 243 For to them Waitapa was an Endsville in the wop-wops. 1986 HULME *Te Kaihau* 122 Where you been this time? Commune? Nga Tama Toa? The wopwops? 1991 *Dominion Sunday Times* (Wellington) 24 Feb. 15 Even by New Zealand standards Otekaieke is in the wop wops and many New Zealanders would be hard put to find the place on a map. 1995 *Dominion* (Wellington) 29 Apr. 20 I grew up in Rangiwahia which is in the wopwops of Manawatu.

b. As **the wops** (an occas. use).

1980 LELAND *Kiwi-Yankee Dict.* 114 *wops or wop-wops*:... The wop-wops are the boondocks or backblocks. 1981 *Avondale College Slang Words* (Auckland) (Goldie Brown Collect.) Feb. *out in the wops*: far from town. 1986 *Listener* 4 Oct. 28 '[Hawke's Bay's] got the best wop-wops in the world. I do love the wop-wops'... He should know—he's seen European, African and 'lots of Aussie wop-wops'... Since then..he has just received an ICI writer's bursary for a novel set in (of course) the wops.

2. In *attrib.* use **wop-wop**, backblock, countrified.

1986 *National Bus. Rev.* 19 Sept. 22 [Heading to a Warren Mayne review of a book of paintings of NZ scenery.] Wop-wop scenery for coffee tables. 1995 *Sunday Star-Times* (Auckland) 16 Apr. sect. D 18 Miranda Harcourt, who's always struck me as a..cosmopolitan citygirl [*sic*], emerged..warm towards these wop wop oddities.

work, *v.* Used in various phrases and applications.

1. [Spec. use of *work* to employ or use in a specific activity: see OED *v.* 19 a.] *trans.* To use (a dog) to control farm stock; *intr.* of a farm dog, to respond to commands to work farm stock. Also as **work wide**, see quot. 1891.

1872 BARKER *Christmas Cake* ch. iii His dogs were new and wouldn't work properly for him. 1878 ELWELL *Boy Colonists* 48 Fricker..[was] delighted to shew the 'new chum'..how to work a cattle dog. 1891 CHAMIER *Philosopher Dick* II. 338 The greatest difficulty lies in teaching dogs to *work wide*, that is, to keep well away from the sheep. 1928 KENWAY *Pioneering in Poverty Bay* 56 It was said of the Highland shepherd in New Zealand, that he would..work his dogs, getting in stray sheep, every day for a month. 1930 ACLAND *Early Canterbury Runs* 5 The practice was for a shepherd to go round the boundary once or twice a day, and at night work the sheep below one of the river terraces to camp. 1950 CHERRILL *NZ Sheep Farm* 160 [The sheep-dog] was never allowed to be worked by anyone but her own master. 1968 JOHNSON *Turn of Tide* 63 Mr Parkins and Stan were to leave at 3 a.m. for the range, the former working his two dogs and the latter his faithful Pat.

2. [Spec. use of *work* to drive on a particular course: see OED *v.* 16 b; AND 1880.] *trans.* To herd (stock). Also as a *vbl. n.*

1878 ELWELL *Boy Colonists* 183 The two mobs now took opposite directions and it was a long time before Ernest and 'Maidie' by careful working could bring them together. 1891 CHAMIER *Philosopher Dick* II. 335 What do you want a dog for? You need not be driving the sheep about... Work them in circles, my man; work them in circles.

3. *Goldmining.* In the phr. **to work away from home**, to sluice up a slope away from the tail-race; **to work home**, to sluice down a slope towards a tail-race already constructed.

1908 *NZ Geol. SB (NS)* No.5 47 In ordinary sluicing.. the practice is to begin operations at the lowest part of the ground, and to work forward on the rising bottom, the main tail-race being extended as the working face recedes. This is *working away from home*. 1908 *Loc. cit.* Two strips of ground about 3 yards wide, one on each side, are now sluiced into the gutter, beginning at the top of the slope. This is *working home*.

4. In the phr. **to work the nails off** (someone), to work (someone) excessively hard.

1910 *Truth* 2 July 6 In Auckland there are countless numbers of these ex-slavies who have married some successful beef-canner or other high sassiety person, and they would work the nails off any poor girl as long as she could stand up to it.

5. In the phr. **to work a dead horse**, see DEAD HORSE.

6. to work a slinter, see SLINTER.

7. In the phr. **to work (a place) out**, to reconnoitre with criminal intent.

1982 *Evening Post* (Wellington) 22 Dec. 17 While working as a driver he had delivered goods frequently to the warehouse and had plenty of opportunity to work the place out.

8. In the phr. **to work the smorgs** [f. *smorg*(asbord in transf. use], see quot.

1985 *Listener* 7 Sept. 14 The few who will talk about some of the truly wondrous perks available, do so with extreme care... Those really 'working the smorgs', as the jargon has it, are positively purse-lipped. (Working the smorgs is where the employer offers, over and above a salary, a 'smorgasbord' of perks.)

workers' compensation. *Hist.* [AND 1902.] **a.** Formerly used *attrib.* to designate legislation which provided (as does 1990s 'Accident Compensation' legislation) for monetary compensation for an injury sustained in the course of employment.

[1897 *Evening Post* (Wellington) 25 Oct. [The questions] are as follows—'(1) If the Premier has seen a copy of a Bill recently passed in the Imperial parliament intituled "The Workingmen's Compensation for Accidents Act"?'] 1900 *NZ Statutes* No.43 227 The Short Title of this Act is 'The Workers' Compensation for Accidents Act, 1900'. 1908 *NZPD* CXLV. 1072 The Workers' Compensation Act was largely a tentative measure of which..Mr. Joseph Chamberlain was either the father, or..he had a good deal to do with advocating its main provisions. 1936 *Ibid.* CCXLVII. 1001 It was the intention of the Government to make a complete overhaul of the Workers' Compensation Act. 1956 *Ibid.* CCCX. 2089 The first Workers' Compensation Act was passed in 1900, the Bill having been largely fashioned on the English legislation... In 1939, the Workers' Compensation Court was established... In 1950..a Workers' Compensation Board was set up.

b. A payment or series of payments made under the legislation, or the system, facilitating such payments (also *attrib.*).

1922 *NZPD* CXCVIII. 660 A little advance had been made in the question of workers' compensation under the present Minister of Labour. 1956 *Ibid.* CCCX. 2089 In the same year [1947] workers' compensation was made a State monopoly.

working? In the phr. **(are you) working?**, a query to someone who may be using a party or extension telephone line.

1982 MCNEISH *Joy* 72 'Hang up, sir. I'll call you back.' 'Working?' a voice said in the magistrate's ear. 'Are you *working*?'.. Some instinct told him to stay on the line. 1987 HARTLEY *Swagger on Our Doorstep* 127 She stopped only to abuse a woman listening in on the party line. 'Working? Working? Get off the line!'

working bee. [AND 1908.] An unpaid working party, often for social or charitable purposes; a group of volunteers formed to carry out a specific task. Compare OHU 1.

[1882 HAY *Brighter Britain* I. 214 Nearly all the men in the district had been asked to come and assist at the mustering..of the herd. It was a gathering of the kind known in America as a 'bee'.] 1883 A LADY *Facts* 68 The ladies of the community..meet for a common cause... Working bees are then got up. 1899 *Hawera & Normanby Star* 1 Nov. 2 From the president (who was at the head of the working bee nearly all last week) to the ordinary member there was a general effort towards maintaining smartness. 1933 *NZ Tablet* (Dunedin) 31 May 37 'Working bees' are still being held every Thursday and Saturday. 1941 *Tararua Tramper* Aug. 7 On 18th August a working bee is scheduled to pack the next lot of parcels for our pals overseas. 1965 MCLAGLAN *Stethoscope & Saddlebags* 154 We formed a working bee with volunteers..and all proceeded to 'Ilfracombe' where we camped for nearly a week, sweeping, cleaning, and touching up the paintwork. 1974 MULDOON *Rise and Fall of a Young Turk* 22 Most of the work was done by working bees and most of the money raised by flower shows. 1983 KING *Whina* 99 [Caption] One of Whina's working bees prepares to plant seed potatoes.

working bullock. *Obs.* **a.** [AND 1805.] A draught bullock as distinct from a beef bullock or milking cow.

1848 WAKEFIELD *Handbook NZ* 169 Some poley Devons, and a few long-horned Devon and Hereford working bullocks have also been received. 1851 *Lyttelton Times* 1 July 1 For sale. One pair of working bullocks.

b. *transf.* [AND 1874.] A hard-working person.

1911 *Truth* 12 Aug. 4 To tell the truth, he was a working bullock in the movement, and it is owing to his efforts that lots of things were accomplished.

workings, *vbl. n. pl.*

1. *Goldmining.* [Restricted use of *working* a mining excavation: see OED *vbl. n.*] An area of ground on which alluvial or quartz mining operations are being carried out.

1852 *NZ Gov. Gaz.* (New Munster) 10 Dec. V. 30:183 The party..are rather 'prospecting'..than digging continuously, and thence the fluctuation in the daily yield of our workings. 1853 *NZ Gov. Gaz.* (New Munster) 12 Jan. VI. 1:2 On the resumed diggings, the parties..are continuing their work with every prospect of finding eventually the matrix Gold, which the nuggets now obtained indicate to be in the vicinity of the workings. 1862 *Otago Goldfields & Resources* 23 The principal workings here are blind gullies and streams.

2. *Logging.* Bush which is being or has been logged. See also *bush-workings* (BUSH 3 a).

1893 *TrNZI* XXV. 439 The fires..originate among..the old kauri-workings. 1911 *Ibid.* XLIII. 445 The same thing is taking place in the old kauri-workings on the Coromandel peninsula. 1961 CRUMP *Hang On a Minute Mate* 37 The [logging] boss told them he'd be down in the morning to take them up to the workings and get them started on the job.

works, *n. pl.* [Spec. use of *works* an establishment where some industrial labour, esp. manufacture, is carried on: see OED *n.* 18 a.] Also as **the works**, in New Zealand usu. FREEZING WORKS.

1888 D'AVIGDOR *Antipodean Notes* 84 These gentlemen [Messrs Nelson Brothers] have under their own control the many manufactures subsidiary to the slaughter and freezing-houses, and their works [at Napier] have increased enormously since they were first started a few years ago. **1892** *NZ Official Handbook* 140 The number of works and hands employed..were as follows. **1901** *TrNZI* XXXIII. 197 Messrs. Nelson Brothers, of the meat-freezing works at Tomoana, kindly proposed to receive and paddock any black lambs forwarded..to their works. **1918** *NZJST* I. 342 In addition, there would be stock which would be fit to slaughter at a local works. **1928** REES *Wild Wild Heart* 17 Fat lambs from the Works. **1952** DUFF *Shepherd's Calendar* (1961) 106 I felt like following him to the 'works' and driving a bargain with the butcher. **1960** MASTERS *Back-Country Tales* 221 Strange to say that domestic beast was the only one out of the whole mob to be condemned by the works inspector. **1971** TAYLOR *Plekhov Place* 11 The drafting and picking of lambs for despatch to the works..was in progress. **1986** *Landfall* 160 491 The Works closed at four, which meant at least two hours before Danny could expect them.

wou, var. WHAU.

would. As a colloquial replacement for simple present or past. **a.** See *how would you be* (HOW 2).

b. As **that would be**, a form of words replacing *that is*, when the speaker is hinting for polite agreement from the person(s) addressed.

1978 BALLANTYNE *Talkback Man* 193 'I dare say he was pissed and confused.' 'That would be the strong of it,' said Sid. **1985** MCGILL *G'day Country* 68 'Nah,' said Fred. '... Now that'd be maize over there. Not for Watties. More for meal.'

wouldn't. In various phrases.

1. As **you wouldn't read about it**, see READ. *v.* 3.

2. As **wouldn't call the king (queen) my uncle (aunt)**, see CALL *v.* 3.

3. Various expressions apparently orginating during WW2. **a.** [AND 1940.] As **wouldn't it** (occas. **wouldn't that**), *ellipt.* for one of the fuller phrases below, often used with a suffixed verbal element to express surprise, exasperation, disgust, etc.

1941 *NZEF Times* 19 Nov. 6 Well, *wouldn't it*. **1950** 2ZB Wellington (Advt for Columbus Radio). And your radio gives out. Wouldn't it! **1968** *NZ Contemp. Dict. Suppl.* (Collins) 22 *wouldn't it*? (*Army sl. phr.*) shortened form of *Wouldn't it make you sick?* **1988** MCGILL *Dict. Kiwi Slang* 125 *wouldn't it!* exclamation of disgust or exasperation; eg 'Wouldn't it make you spit tacks!'

b. As **wouldn't it liberate you**, using the catchword *liberate*, often a euphemism for 'steal'.

1945 *Johnny Enzed* in *NZEF Times* 29 Jan. 4 Wouldn't it liberate you?

c. As **wouldn't it rock you**.

1944 *NZEF Times* 22 May 2 'Wouldn't it rock you,' says Snow. 'Here's a bloke in a magazine nattering about what a well-dressed man will wear... Wouldn't it!' **1944** *Korero* (AEWS Background Bulletin) 17 July 24 'Wouldn't it rock you?' is also popular, this indicating astonished reaction, usually to the 'Army way'. It has been fairly recently shortened to 'Wouldn't it?'... 'Wouldn't it rotate you?' is..also common... Several soldiers have solemnly explained that when the flanges of a tank become loaded with sand, it tends to spin the vehicle to one side, causing a 'rotation' and confusion to its occupants. **1945** HENDERSON *Gunner Inglorious* 120 'The poor cow,' say his cobbers. 'What rotten luck. Wouldn't it rock you.'

d. As **wouldn't it (that) rotate you** [AND 1961].

1942 *NZEF Times* 21 Dec. 17 Wouldn't it rotate you! Have to waste another half mug of water to get clean again. **1944** [see c above]. **1944** FULLARTON *Troop Target* 18 Wouldn't that rotate you! *Ibid.* 55 Wouldn't that bloody well rotate you.

4. As **wouldn't touch it with a red-hot poker**, see TOUCH *v.* 3.

wow, var. WHAU.

wow. Also **Wau**. Mainly *Auckland*. [Prob. f. 'the Whau' (pronounced /wæu/), the local familiar name of a district in Avondale, Auckland, bounded on one side by the Whau Creek and including Oakley Creek, long associated (from 1867) with psychiatric hospitals, the latest being Oakley and the former Carrington. Kendrick Smithyman (p.c. 26 Oct. 1993, Auckland) quotes a report in the *NZ Herald* (Jan. 1879) on the blasting of local quarry-stone to rebuild the asylum, with a sub-heading 'Miniature Earthquake at the Whau', the reference being to the district not to the gutted asylum, and confirms more recent general use of 'the Whau' as applying to the district rather than specifically to the creek of that name.] As **the wow**, a psychiatric hospital.

1948 BALLANTYNE *Cunninghams* (1976) 21 They took John back to the wow because one night at tea he grabbed a knife and reckoned he was going to chop the head off the first one to look up from his plate. **1952** let. Sargeson to Davin 16 Apr. in King *Frank Sargeson* (1995) 330 The poor girl is out of the Wow at last. **1982** NEWBOLD *Big Huey* 30 But when he said 'gidday mate' to the magistrate..they..just remanded him straight out to the wow. *Ibid.* 255 Wow (n) Mental asylum. Originates from Maori 'Whau', the name of the Auckland river next to which Oakley Mental Hospital is situated. **1987** PFAHLERT & WATSON *Some Must Die* 30 Mr Hasty would usually open the batting with 'Well, how are things at the "wow"?' It was some time before I discovered that the Wau was, in fact, the stream which flowed through the Mental Hospital grounds. **1991** MACDONALD *Book of NZ Women* 472 [caption] The *Whau* Asylum (later the Auckland Lunatic Asylum at Avondale). **1993** SINCLAIR *Halfway Round the Harbour* 38 To get there a boy had to cycle up..Gladstone Road (as Carrington Road was then called) past the mental hospital, which everyone called the Wow. I believed that this term meant 'the loony bin', another local name. In fact it was so called because of the nearby Whau Creek.

wowse, *v. Obs.* [f. WOWSER.] To preach or advocate temperance or teetotalism.

1909 *Truth* 29 Feb. 4 He has our full forgiveness for being angry, but he shouldn't wowse about it and talk of 'Christian restraints'. **1913** *NZ Observer* 12 July 2 So much of the self-denial so many people 'wowse' about is pure meanness. **1916** THORNTON *Wowser* 170 No doubt as you gets a good fat screw for wowsin'.

wowser. *Derog.* [Of obscure origin: AND 'Prob. f. Brit. dial. *wow* to howl or bark as a dog; to whine, grumble, make complaint (see EDD *v.*¹); claimed by John Norton (c1858–1916), editor of the Sydney *Truth* (1891–1916), as his coinage.' 1 *Obs.* an obnoxious person, 1899 2 a censorious person, 1900.]

1. a. [AND 1899.] A prudish person, often religious, censorious of the habits or pleasures of others, esp. of drinking alcoholic liquor.

1903 in Lawlor *Old Wellington Days* (1959) 50 1903 May 9... Fought a bloke because he called me a wowser. **1905** *Truth* 12 Aug. 1 The moderate drinker, the fellow who makes the water wowser so blanketty wild. *Ibid.* 26 Aug. 1 Weary Wesleyan Wowsers. **1910** *Ibid.* 2 Apr. 4 To call a man a wowser is to indicate him as being a hypocritical, shuffling, double-lived person, who preys when not praying; who is eternally canting and ranting, while remaining inwardly a whited sepulchre... A wowser is a crepuscular-minded person of religious proclivities, having one eye on Paradise and the other on the main chance. He generally—but not always—belongs to one of the Non-conformist churches. **1916** THORNTON *Wowser* 8 Wowser is a term somewhat indefinite in its application and meaning. The following definitions given to the author by bushmen themselves may help the reader to understand what a Colonial means when he uses the word. It may mean:— 1) 'A man who tries to rob a bloke of his beer and pleasure'—therefore especially applicable to the temperance reformer. 2) 'A bloke who wears out the knees of his pants on Sundays praying, and another part of his pants all the week backsliding'—i.e. a hypocrite. 3) 'Any sky-pilot, priest, or local preacher who makes a bloke uncomfortable, and pretends to be religious.' **1921** FOSTON *At the Front* 123 *Wowser*: The word, it is understood, was derived from a Chinese term, meaning a man of probity and character; but he had seen it stated that the word was a corruption of 'rouser'. However, neither definition worried him, because it was the sneer now implied that he proposed to deal with. According to opponents, the 'wowser' was the most objectionable person in the world. **1933** SCANLAN *Tides of Youth* 124 I'm no wowser... I like me glass of beer and five bob on a horse. **1949** SARGESON *I Saw in My Dream* (1974) 98 You like a spot Johnny don't you? Don't tell me you're a wowser. **1952** *Dominion* (Wellington) 19 Mar. 6 Regarding the origin of the term 'Wowser'... During the latter part of the last century a crusade was launched by the Women's Christian Temperance Union against the social evils in Australia. One woman who spoke always had a ready answer to the jeers and jibes of her audience. On one occasion when she and her party were accused of being 'kill-joys' she retorted 'We only want social evils removed'. The initial letters of those words were taken up by her opponents, and 'wowser' became a term of opprobrium which has continued to the present time. **1968** SLATTER *Pagan Game* 171 [They] were out in the alley, leaning on each other..and vowing eternal friendship in the face of all drongos, no-hopers, wowsers and bush carpenters. **1980** LELAND *Kiwi-Yankee Dict.* 114 A wowser started off to be a teetotaller, but has expanded in meaning to cover any sort of puritan attitudes.

b. *attrib.* Repressively puritanical, 'spoil-sport'; occas. merely a generally abusive term.

1912 *Triad* 10 July 22 New Wowser parson. **1916** THORNTON *Wowser* 87 The blessed wowser dodge. **1972** GEE *My Father's Den* 146 That cretin, I thought, that half-man, that self-castrated, mother-worshipping, obscurantist, priestly, wowser prick. **1991** *Evening Post* (Wellington) 26 Nov. 22 Mr Corrigan said the decorated nikau palms outside the new library would no doubt get the 'wowsers barking'.

2. a. Special Comb. (all *obs.*): **wowser-bird**, a derogatory term for a minister of religion; **Wowserland**, an ironic name for New Zealand; **wowser-ridden** *a.*, severely troubled by wowsers.

1918 *Quick March* 2 Sept. 1 A **wowser-bird** of the harp-and-halo variety (i.e., fire-escape, devil-dodger, hell-buster,—really a *Bookie* disguised as a *Curate*) happened along. **1913** *NZ Observer* 15 Feb. 2 It is perhaps the rather arrogant insistence of various sectarian bodies on pushing their particular wares at every opportunity that has made outsiders refer contemptuously to New Zealand as **Wowserland**. **1917** *Free Lance* (Wellington) 9 Mar. 21 Otherwise I might succeed in naming the winner which is against the laws of this **wowser-ridden** land.

b. In composition: **anti-wowser** *n.* and *attrib.*, one who opposes wowsers and wowserism; **wowserdom**, wowsers collectively and the body of their beliefs; **wowserishness**, the behaviour pattern of a wowser; **wowsery** *obs.* [AND 1912], a church or chapel.

1913 *NZ Observer* 29 Nov. 4 To ride a buckjumping horse—why, it's almost **anti-wowser**! **1921** anti-wowser [see WOWSERISM]. **1910** *Truth* 2 July 6 [Heading of letter to editor] Immigration, Sweating and **Wowserdom**. **1993** *Listener* 9 Jan. 5 In the frenzy of corporatising Aotearoa, a tsunami of **wowserishness** has swept the land. **1909** *Truth* 31 July 4 In connection with the 'anniversary of a suburban **wowsery**' a choir of 300 mixed voices was announced.

wowserism. [f. WOWSER + *-ism*: AND 1906.] The behaviour or ideology of a wowser.

1908 *Truth* 9 May 1 It is that latter-day form of Puritanism that we in Australasia call Wowserism that is now the chief cause of the weakness of the British Government. **1919** *Quick March* Apr. 71 [Advt] Kaiserism was defeated in Europe. Help to Defeat Wowserism in New Zealand... I Vote for National Continuance. **1921** FOSTON *At the Front* 123 What is wowserism?.. In short, to support [moral] reform was wowserism. The cry of the anti-wowser was Liberty. **1952** *Landfall* 23 215 It isn't only wowserism that keeps women out of bars. **1962** LAWLOR *More Wellington Days* 25 Except for the playing of hymns it was forbidden in many homes to open the piano on a Sunday. 'Wowserism', as it was called, was rife in Wellington in the early part of the century. **1976** SINCLAIR *Nash* 267 This observation, the fruit of his [*sc.* Sir Walter Nash's] own experience (for he used to smoke, and to sell acid drops) caused much hilarity. It was also wrongly interpreted—by smokers—as an example of wowserism.

Hence **wowseristic** *a.* [AND 1907], puritanical, excessively prudish.

1909 *Truth* 24 July 1 To such a wowseristic whopper the right word is bosh! **1943** BENNETT *English in NZ* in *Amer. Speech* XVIII. 89 The adjective *wowseristic* has been formed from [wowser].

Wozzer, var. WAZZA.

wrasse. [Spec. use of *wrasse* a marine fish of fam. Labridae.]

1. Any of various elongated, compressed, usu. brilliantly coloured, spiny-finned fishes of the family Labridae, including (in warm seas) some important food fishes, as well as some believed poisonous. See esp. PARROTFISH. The wrasse family includes the following: BUTTERFISH 2, KELPFISH, PIGFISH 2 (1), PODDLY, SOLDIER *n.*², SPOTTY 1.

1773 FORSTER *Resolution Jrnl.* 27 Mar. (1982) II. 240 The *Sea-Pearch* is a fine hard fish; the red *Wrasse* is likewise good, and the striped *Sciaena* is commonly fat. **1872** HUTTON & HECTOR *Fishes NZ* 43 Labrichthys bothryocosmus... Wrasse. **1879** [see SPOTTY 1]. **1880** SENIOR *Travel & Trout* 288 Amongst the sea-fishes fit for food there are..aua, rock cod, wrasse, and patiki. **1892** [see SPOTTY 1]. **1921** [see PARROTFISH 2 (4)]. **1967** [see KELPFISH 2]. **1974** *NZ Nature Heritage* XLV. 1256 The labrid family, or wrasses, are brilliantly coloured reef fishes. **1982** [see PARROTFISH 1].

2. With a modifier: **banded, girdled, green, orange, Sandagers, scarlet**.

(1) **banded wrasse**. *Notolabrus* (formerly *Pseudolabrus*) *fucicola*, *banded parrotfish* (PARROTFISH 2 (1)).

1982 AYLING *Collins Guide* (1984) 255 *Banded Wrasse* (Banded parrotfish)... The banded wrasse is the largest species of labrid found in New Zealand waters. *Ibid.* 256 Banded wrasses..change sex at any time after they first move permanently out of the plankton as small juveniles. **1986** PAUL *NZ Fishes* 108 *Banded wrasse Pseudolabrus fucicola*. Also occurs off south-eastern Australia. **1988** FRANCIS *Coastal Fishes NZ* 43 Banded wrasse (Taangahangaha) *Notolabrus fucicola*... Banded wrasse are also unusual in that a high proportion of fish in the initial colour phase (about 40 per cent) are males.

(2) **girdled wrasse**. *Notolabrus* (formerly *Pseudolabrus*) *cinctus*, *girdled parrotfish* (PARROTFISH 2 (2)).

1982 AYLING *Collins Guide* (1984) 259 *Girdled Wrasse* (Girdled parrotfish) *Pseudolabrus cinctus*... The girdled wrasse is similar in shape and appearance to the spotty but grows to a larger size. **1988** FRANCIS *Coastal Fishes NZ* 43 Girdled wrasse *Notolabrus cinctus*... Girdled wrasse are very active by day.

(3) **green wrasse**. *Notolabrus inscriptus*.

1982 AYLING *Collins Guide* (1984) 258 *Green Wrasse* (Green parrotfish)... The green wrasse is a large deep-bodied species similar in shape and size to the banded wrasse. **1986** PAUL *NZ Fishes* 108 *Green wrasse*... Also occurs off south-eastern Australia, and appears to be increasing along our rocky coastline and islands from Bay of Plenty northwards. **1988** FRANCIS *Coastal Fishes NZ* 43 Green wrasse *Notolabrus inscriptus*... Males green with yellow dots on each scale.

(4) **orange wrasse**. *Pseudolabrus luculentus*. See quot. 1982.

1982 AYLING *Collins Guide* (1984) 257 *Orange Wrasse* (Orange parrotfish)... The orange wrasse is a small fish... Young fish and females are similar in shape and colour, with a pointed snout, a plump belly, and a bright red-orange body colour. **1986** PAUL *NZ Fishes* 109 *Orange wrasse*... In New Zealand it is not uncommon around our offshore islands from Bay of Plenty north.

(5) **Sandager's wrasse**. [After A.F.S. Sandager (1851–1904) Asst. Lighthouse Keeper at Moko Hinau Island and elsewhere, amateur naturalist.] *Coris sandageri*, *Sandager's parrotfish* (PARROTFISH 2 (3)).

1982 AYLING *Collins Guide* (1984) 261 *Sandagers Wrasse*..(Sandagers parrotfish, king wrasse)... The sandagers wrasse is an elongate labrid... Like the green wrasse this species has these completely different colour phases. **1986** PAUL *NZ Fishes* 108 *Sandagers wrasse*... In the natural state males hold large harems, but in some areas feeding by divers has disrupted this territorial behaviour. **1988** FRANCIS *Coastal Fishes NZ* 42 Sandager's wrasse are very active during the day and are strongly attracted to divers.

(6) **scarlet wrasse**. *Pseudolabrus miles*, *scarlet parrotfish* (PARROTFISH 2 (4)).

1982 AYLING *Collins Guide* (1984) 256 *Scarlet Wrasse*..(Scarlet parrotfish, pawaiwhakarua)... Scarlet wrasses frequent rock reefs in deeper water than that preferred by most other members of this family. **1986** PAUL *NZ Fishes* 107 Alternatively soldierfish... Scarlet wrasse feed on a variety of bottom invertebrates. **1988** FRANCIS *Coastal Fishes NZ* 44 Scarlet wrasse (Puuwai whakarua) *Pseudolabrus miles*... All phases have prominent triangular black wedge in front of tail, and scarlet head with a white lower jaw and throat.

wren.

1. Transf. use of *wren* a European bird of the family Troglodytidae for any of various small wren-like, short-tailed birds with short tails of the endemic family Acanthisittidae. See also MATUHI, RIFLEMAN, TITIPOUNAMU.

1847 ANGAS *Savage Life* II. 106 Among the smaller varieties, I observed the white-headed manakin, a black and yellow fly-catcher, and an extremely diminutive wren. **1864** BARRINGTON *Diary* 13 Apr. in Taylor *Early Travellers* (1959) 406 Killed a robin and three wrens; roasted them: the smallest joints I ever saw. **1884** [see PIWAUWAU b (=RIFLEMAN)]. **1898** MORRIS *Austral-English* 519 *Wren*... In New Zealand, the name is applied to the Bush-Wren, *Xenicus longipes*..and the Rock (or Mountain) Wren, X. *gilviventris*. **1930**, **1965** [see RIFLEMAN].

2. With a modifier: **bush** (also with prefixes defining provenance), **green, mountain, rock, Stephen(s) Island** (or **Island**).

(1) **bush wren**. Either the RIFLEMAN (*Acanthisitta chloris*) or (usu.) the probably now extinct *Xenicus longipes*; occas. with prefixed modifiers indicating the provenance of subspecies: **North Island bush wren**, *Xenicus longipes stokesii*; **South Island bush wren**, *Xenicus longipes longipes*; **Stewart Island** (or **Stead's**) **bush wren**, *Xenicus longipes variabilis*. See also MATUHI, PIWAUWAU a and b.

1873 [see MATUHI]. **1888** BULLER *Birds NZ* I. 108 Xenicus longipes. (Bush-wren)... It is generally met with singly or in pairs. **1904** HUTTON & DRUMMOND *Animals NZ* 115 The Bush Wren, or Rifleman, inhabits the sub-alpine forests of both Islands, as well as the Great Barrier Island. **1905** WHITE *My NZ Garden* 70 Another tiny bird is the Bush Wren; this, on the contrary, has hardly any tail at all. **1917** WILLIAMS *Dict. Maori Lang.* 75 Houtuutu... *Acanthidositta chloris*, bush wren. **1923** *NZJST* VI. 87 Fulton..states that the 'rifleman and bush wrens abound wherever are our native trees'. **1936** GUTHRIE-SMITH *NZ Naturalist* 74 As in the case of the..Bush Wren (*Xenicus longipes*).. restriction of food..may have reduced an originally large clutch. **1947** REED *Dict. Suppl.* 174 matuhi: bush wren. **1955** OLIVER *NZ Birds* 452 *North Island Bush Wren Xenicus longipes stokesi*. About 1850 two specimens of a Bush Wren were collected in the Rimutaka Range... No further specimens of the North Island Bush Wren have since been taken. *Ibid.* 453 *South Island Bush Wren. Matuhi Xenicus longipes longipes*. The South Island Bush Wren is found sparingly in the damp beech and rimu forests of the Southern Alps. *Ibid.* 454 *Stewart Island Bush Wren Xenicus longipes variabilis*. **1966** *Encycl. NZ* III. 689 There is another species, *Xenicus longi[pes]*, the bush wren or matuhi. This bird is also very small, of darker green colouring and with a white throat. **1966** FALLA et al. *New Guide Birds NZ* 179 Bush Wren *Xenicus longipes*... Matuhi, Tom Thumb Bird (Stewart Is.). *Ibid.* 180 The Bush Wren shares with..the Rock Wren, the habit of bobbing the whole body, a vigorous action repeated frequently on alighting. **1985** *Reader's Digest Book NZ Birds* 265 Bush Wren *Xenicus longipes*... On the main islands bush wrens were found mostly in dense mountain forest, usually beech forest at high altitude but as far as the subalpine scrub zone... *Stead's bush wren* has been observed feeding moths, flies, daddy-long-legs spiders to its chicks... *North Island bush wren*: once widespread, but now rare... *South Island bush wren*: once common, but by 1950s rare, with most records from Fiordland. **1991** GILL & MARTINSON *NZ's Extinct Birds* 82 The loss of the Bush Wren (*Xenicus longipes*) is the saddest story in this book because it is the latest New Zealand bird to die out, and because its demise was realised in retrospect and attracted no public attention.

(2) **green wren**. See *bush wren* (1) above.

1904 Hutton & Drummond *Animals NZ* 111 *The Green Wren. Xenicus longipes.* **1917** Williams *Dict. Maori Lang.* 227 *Matuhituhi..Xenicus longipes, green wren.* **1923** *NZJST* VI. 87 *Xenicus longipes...* The green wren seems never to have been very plentiful in any North Island locality.

(3) **mountain wren**. An occas. name for *rock wren* (4) below.

1896 Harper *Pioneer Work* 39 The canaries..and the little mountain wrens (*Xenicus gilviventris*) are useful as foretellers of the weather.

(4) **rock wren**. *Xenicus gilviventris*, a small bird found among the rocky subalpine areas of the Southern Alps.

1871 Hutton *Catalogue Birds NZ* 7 *Xenicus gilviventris...* Rock Wren. **1879** Haast *Geol. Canterbury & Westland* 146 The remarkable small rock wren..was also found to enhabit [sic] the large taluses of debris..on the sides of the high mountains. **1893** *TrNZI* XXV. 59 I have..seen only one Bush Wren, two Rifle Wrens, two Saddlebacks, and no Rock Wrens [in Nelson]. **1904** Hutton & Drummond *Animals NZ* 113 *The Rock Wren...* This little bird is found only in the mountain regions of the South Island among stunted vegetation, and is rarely seen. **1924** *Otago Witness* (Dunedin) 11 Mar. 6 The rock-wren and the bush-wren resemble each other generally in the colours of their plumage, but the rock-wren is much rarer. **1939** Beattie *First White Boy Born Otago* 121 In the Central [Otago, c1860s]..I saw the sparrow-hawk, the rock wren, and plenty of hawks. **1955** Oliver *NZ Birds* 455 In the Homer cirque from 3,000 to 4,000 feet the Rock Wren is found among the large angular blocks that make up the talus slopes below the precipitous sides of the valley. **1966** *Encycl. NZ* III. 689 The rock wren is slightly larger than the rifleman..and, like it, has a high-pitched call. **1985** *Reader's Digest Book NZ Birds* 266 The rock wren spends most of its time hopping and flitting through boulders in search of food.

(5) **Stephen(s) Island** (or **Island**) **wren**. The extinct *Traversia lyalli* of Stephens Island, Cook Strait.

1897 *TrNZI* XXIX. 188 Island Wren. Very diligent search has been made on Stephen Island for further specimens of the Island Wren, but without success. **1904** Hutton & Drummond *Animals NZ* 114 *The Stephen's Island Wren...* This bird is now extinct, having been killed off by the cats. **1923** *NZJST* VI. 87 No reports of the Stephen Island wren have been recorded since its supposed extinction by lighthouse-keepers' cats soon after its discovery. **1936** Guthrie-Smith *NZ Naturalist* 93 There might yet lurk furtive in the scrub the Stephen Island Wren. **1955** Oliver *NZ Birds* 457 *Stephen Island Wren...* The history of this species, so far as human contact is concerned, begins and ends with the exploits of a domestic cat... The cat which discovered the species also inevitably exterminated it. **1990** *Checklist Birds NZ* 194 *Traversia lyalli... Stephens Island Wren...* Formerly Stephens Island, Cook Strait..; discovered 1894, but..became extinct almost immediately.

wrybill: see PLOVER 2 (8).

wurrie, var. WHARE.

wutter, var. WHATA.

wyata, var. WAIATA.

wyeena, var. WAHINE *n.*[1]

wypiero, var. WAIPIRO.

Y

-y: see -IE suffix.

yacca, var. YACKER.

yachtie /ˈjɒti/. Also **yachty**. [f. *yacht*(sman + -IE: AND 1951.] A yachtsman. Contrast BOATIE.
1943 BENNETT *English in NZ* in *Amer. Speech* XVIII. 88 The same method of word-formation gives, in both [Australia and New Zealand] *yachtie* (yachtsman), *bullocky*. **1962** GLOVER *Hot Water Sailor* (1981) 183 This was an occasion for much merriment on the part of yachties around us. **1983** MANTELL *Murder to Burn* 153 The two yachties were not so knowledgeable about Nolan.

yacker /ˈjækə/, *n.*[1] Also **yacca, yakka, yakker**. [AND f. *yakker v*. ad. Aboriginal Yagara *yaga* 'work', 1847; *n. yakka* 1888.]
1. Work, esp. as **hard yacker**, hard or strenuous work, toil, but not necessarily physical.
1905 *Truth* 26 Aug. 4 Salvarmy's 'ome of 'ope soap, and hard yacker. **1909** THOMPSON *Ballads About Business* 91 'Come along with me to Southland,' said my old mate then to me, 'You'll be sure to get some yacker.' **1920** *Quick March* 10 Apr. 31 We knocks off 'yakker' for the day about sundown. **1959** SLATTER *Gun in My Hand* 91 You'll haveta shake ya shirt and get down to some hard yakker. **1960** MASTERS *Back-Country Tales* 109 A tough job: Or as one member, Reg. Petrowski put it, 'Hard yacca'. **1971** *Listener* 19 Apr. 56 He..had to bash through the lawyers and windfalls. It was hard yakka. **1980** *Dominion* (Wellington) 7 June 24 Devising methods to counter cervical injuries in rugby was yesterday described as 'hard yakker'. 'Trying to get messages across to all concerned is hard yakker.' **1992** *Contact* (Wellington) 3 Dec. 6 It would seem to be hard yacker standing for parliamentary seats if you're in there with a chance.
2. Shearing. *Obs*. See quot.
1934 *Press* (Christchurch) (Acland Gloss.) 27 Jan. 15 *Yacca*.—The pull-back of the shears.

yacker /ˈjækə/, *n.*[2] Also **yakker** and occas. **yak**. [Poss. a var. of *yatter* chatter (see OED), or imitative of *chatter, natter*: AND 1882, 1941, 1973.] Idle noisy talk, chatter.
1955 Heard in Wellington (Ed.). This K-force yacker is damned hard to understand. **1981** JOHNSTON *Fish Factory* 65 'Yeah, yeah! All bloody yak and no do,' Danny flung contemptuously at his long suffering pater. **1991** *Listener* 10 June 69 Talk-back is humble, it's for the little person... I don't give a damn how exalted that sounds. It's good basic yacker, that's all, and I can't imagine a world without it.

Hence *v*., to chatter (away).
1964 HARVEY *Any Old Dollars Mister?* 114 We all yakkered away about the Yanks for some time. **1981** HOOPER *Goat Paddock* 7 I was feeling good..so Noeline and me thought we'd go round to Day's Bay and swim..[and] yacker all the day. **1986** TAYLOR *Shooting Through* 16 She'd like another Maori around the place to yakker away to.

yahoo /ˌjaˈhuː/, *v*. [Poss. a development from *yahoo* a hooligan (orig. from the name of Swift's subhumans), influenced by (or from) *yahoo* an echoic representation of a raucous cry.] Also **yahoo about (around)**. *intr*. To behave in a rowdy 'larrikin' fashion; to barrack rowdily.
[**1975** HOWITT *NZ Rugby Greats* 110 The [Canterbury] crowd yahoo-ed when I put the ball down on halfway.] **1980** LELAND *Kiwi-Yankee Dict*. 115 *yahoo*:.. Well, a yahoo is a lout, and to 'yahoo around' is to do nothing constructive noisily. **1985** SHERWOOD *Botanist at Bay* 27 Thornhill replied by calling them yobbos and warning them that they would be chucked out of the meeting unless they stopped yahooing about. **1986** O'SULLIVAN *Pilate Tapes* 29 The crowd back into town was yahoo-ing with deliverance. **1992** *Dominion* (Wellington) 10 Jan. 3 There was a call saying there was a fire engine yahooing in Lyttelton with nude women on it.

Hence **yahooing** *vbl. n*., behaving in a crude and rowdy fashion; rowdy behaviour; also by back-formation, **yahoo** *n*., a rowdy (see quot. 1980 above); a spree, a 'rage'.
1984 *Listener* 19 May 16 There is a great deal of yahooing and complaining; obscenities fall as thickly as the rain. **1986** *NZ Woman's Weekly* 14 July 12 Barry Crump squats by the fire... We used to do a lot of huntin' and yahooin' about the place. **1995** *Dominion* (Wellington) 2 Feb. 24 [Heading] Fleming ready for yahooing. Stephen Fleming expects there will be some hostile reaction when he returns to the New Zealand [cricket] team... 'If the public want to take it upon themselves to make something of it and yahoo or whatever, then that's up to them. **1985** BENTLEY & FRASER *Grand Limerick Tour* [No.] 56 It's Fair Day at Mangatainoka, What's the guts for your average joker? Pitching possums is big, There's calf roping, greased pig, And a **yahoo**, with untold strip poker.

yak, yakka, yakker, varr. YACKER *n.*[1] and *n.*[2]

yam.
1. *Hist*. [Spec. use of *yam* Dioscorea spp., for the Pacific Island yam, of historical significance during early European contact.] *Dioscorea alata* (fam. Dioscoreaceae), with a large cordate leaf and a large edible tuber, introduced and formerly cultivated by Maori as *uwhi*, and now imported from the Pacific Islands as a vegetable.
1769 MONKHOUSE 21 Oct. in Cook *Journals* (1955) I. 583 The Yams are planted in like manner with the sweet potatoes. [**1955** *Note*] The *yam* or *uwhi* disappeared after the introduction of the easily-grown potato. **1777** LEDYARD *Journal* (1963) 14 They also have some yams upon the northern Island, but not in plenty. **1815** MARSDEN *Lett. & Jrnls*. (1932) 125 We here found some pretty little cottages and their gardens..neatly fenced and laid out, and the potatoes, yams, etc., all planted in separate beds. **1834** MCDONNELL *Extracts Jrnl*. (1979) 15 There is no lack of cabbages..a particularly fine species of yam, with other esculent roots. **1917** WILLIAMS *Dict. Maori Lang*. 553 *Uwhi, uhi*, (i) n. 1. *Discorea* sp., *yam*, which was formerly cultivated. **1982** BURTON *Two Hundred Yrs*. *NZ Food* 3 These plants [brought by the Maori colonists] were the island yam (Dioscorea esculenta), the bottle gourd, the taro..and the kumara.
2. The New Zealand name for the *oca*, *Oxalis tuberosa* (formerly *crenata*) (fam. Oxalidaceae), an orig. South American plant widely cultivated for its edible, (usu.) reddish-purple or golden tubers.
[**1889** FEATON *Art Album NZ Flora* 77 Oxalis crenata..is well known as the [Oxalis] which, some years ago, was introduced into Europe as a substitute for the potato.] **c1920** p.c. W.H.B. Orsman, Marlborough. *Yam* is the usual name for the tubers of this plant [indicating the *oca*] whose leaves look like oxalis. **1950** *NZJAg*. May LXXX. 471 The oka plant (*Oxalis crenata*), a native of Peru..produces tubers which can be used as vegetables. The tubers are sometimes called yams, but do not resemble those tropical vegetables either botanically or in appearance. **1983** *Press* (Christchurch) 13 May 2 The yams available locally are of the small pink variety with white flesh. **1988** WEBB, SYKES & GARNOCK-JONES *Flora NZ* IV. 923 Oca is very commonly cultivated for its edible tubers in most parts of the country. Most plants in N.Z. belong to 1 of 2 forms. One has purple stems and petioles: the other has green... Oca is erroneously called yam in N.Z., but is very dissimilar to the true yams, a name applied to various species of the monocotyledonous genus *Dioscorea*. **1991–92** *Cuisine* Dec.–Jan. 51 [He] grows for export the little pink New Zealand yam (actually a South American tuber favoured by the Incas).

Yank.
1. See CUBA STREET YANK, *Queen Street Yank* (QUEEN STREET 2).
2. As **Yank tank**, any large American car.
1980 LELAND *Kiwi-Yankee Dict*. 115 *Yank tank:* This device does not bear General Sherman's name or that of any other general. It's your everyday V8 family car. **1990** *Evening Post* (Wellington) 9 Oct. 12 A gastronomic treat that's worth gassing up the Yank tank to reach.

Yankee, *a*. In special collocations: **Yankee axe**, AMERICAN AXE; **Yankee clock**, a cheap American-made clock; **Yankee coach**, usu. a coach swung on leather thongs; **Yankee grab** [AND 1879], a gambling game played with dice (cf. *The Official World Encyclopedia of Sports and Games* Paddington Press (1979) 120 *Going to Boston*. Also known as Newmarket or Yankee Grab... Each player in turn rolls..three dice together. After the first roll..leaves the highest number on the table, then rolls the other two again. [The highest is again left, the third then rolled again, completing the player's throw, and his score is the total of his three dice: the player with highest score wins.]); **Yankee Hustle**, ?a shop or warehouse in early Wellington; **Yankee shout** [AND 1945], a treat where each person pays a share, a 'Dutch treat' (cf. PARNELL 1); **Yankee**

start, an unfairly advantageous start, an unfair advantage over; **Yankee tournament**, a tournament in which each entrant plays everyone else.

1874 BAINES *Edward Crewe* 152 Good stands of kauri..still untouched by the **Yankee axe** of the bushmen. *Ibid.* 172 One day, since my return to this worn-out old country, I happened to meet a friend who some time previous having heard of the superiority of the Yankee axe, had bought one of these British imitations, and finding the tool a poor one, had jumped to the conclusion that, 'after all,' there was no axe equal to the old-fashioned one in use in England, and was considerably 'riled' at my intense derision and scorn of that conservative weapon. **1874** KENNAWAY *Crusts* 92 We started as the moon rose, and got home as the **Yankee clock**, on our rough-hewn mantel-piece, pointed with both hands to midnight. **1880** GRANT & FOSTER *Rep. on Agriculture* 54 The vehicle is what is known as a '**Yankee coach**'. **c1870–71** *Grey River Argus* in Latham *Golden Reefs* (1992) 85 It was suggested by a correspondent [of the 'Argus'] that a great saving of money could have been achieved if the parties had 'thrown a "**Yankee grab**" for the ground before they went to the law about it'. **1875** WOOD & LAPHAM *Waiting for Mail* 106 There [at the bar] we did Yankee grab for half-crowns till Bill lost a note and cleared out. **1889** MITCHELL *Rhymes & Rambles* 19 One night, at the hotel where I put up, several of us had a go in at Yankee grab. I was unlucky. Next morning..I had but one pound left. **1891** CHAMIER *Philosopher Dick* 363 A game of Yankee Grab. **1962** LAWLOR *More Wellington Days* 41 In my case I know the cry was insulting for I must have been wearing one of the red tam-o'-shanters bought by my father for a song at the **Yankee Hustle**. *Ibid.* 114 We read you had bought a watch at the 'Yankee Hustle'. **1980** LELAND *Kiwi-Yankee Dict.* 115 **Yankee shout**: go Dutch. **1887** *Auckland Weekly News* 27 Aug. 15 The exorbitant charges are easily accounted for—I mean what every digger knows as '**Yankee starts**'. **1935** MACKENZIE *Gael Fares Forth* 174 Whereas British gum-diggers of the disreputable kind were not ashamed to give the storekeeper what they called a 'Yankee start'—that is, to defraud him by secretly leaving the district without settling their accounts for goods supplied—such an action was unknown among the Yugoslavs. **c1938** Used by Jane Morison, Havelock, Marlborough (b 1868). 'Yankee start' used in the sense of getting in slyly ahead of a competitor (for a bargain, etc.) by underhand means, or for cheating at cards at euchre parties. **1934** *Daily Telegraph* (Napier) 23 July 2 The **Yankee tournament** in the second grade section of the Napier basketball teams was replayed on Saturday. **1982** MACKENZIE *WAAF Book* 76 Apparently, chocolate was doled out for prizes in the all ranks and both sexes Yankee tennis tournament held at Woodbourne.

yard, *n.* [Spec. use of *yard* an enclosure for poultry or cattle adjacent to a farm building: see OED *n.*¹ 2.]

1. Usu. *pl.*, often collective as **the yards**. An enclosure, sometimes makeshift and often subdivided into various pens, in which farm stock are confined for various purposes. See also *cattle-yard* (CATTLE 2), *drafting yard* (DRAFTING 2), FORWARDING YARD, HOLDING-YARD, RECEIVING YARD, SALEYARD 1, *sheep-yard* (SHEEP 2), STOCKYARD.

1856 ROBERTS *Diary* 18 Dec. in Beattie *Early Runholding* (1947) 43 At Macfarlane's the men saddled fresh horses and rode in some cattle which we had a great bother to yard, as everything was new... The yard was divided into three—one large and two small. **1863** BUTLER *First Year* x 154 Without good yards it is impossible to do this [sheep-work] well—they are an essential of the highest importance. **1871** MONEY *Knocking About NZ* 7 A mile or so distant was the pool where the sheep were washed, approached by yards (*i.e.*, passages and squares composed of hurdles or fences) leading to the dip. **1881** NESFIELD *Chequered Career* 37 In a few months' time I had learnt all the most important items of a bush education: how to..make bread or damper,.. work in the yards. **1899** BELL *In Shadow of Bush* 8 Farther back from the road were yards and a larger building evidently used as a wool-shed. **1910** [see MEN'S HUT c]. **1926** [see BOOK *n.*²]. **1933** *Press* (Christchurch) (Acland Gloss.) 30 Dec. 13 *Yard*.—For sheep, usually in the plural, for stock, usually singular, probably because the oldest s[*tock*]y[*ard*]*s* only had one pen. **1949** SARGESON *I Saw in My Dream* (1974) 9 They were going through the big open gateway into the yards. **1992** ANDERSON *Portrait Artist's Wife* They spoke of falling prices at the yards. Frank's two-tooths had been a disaster.

2. Special Comb. **yard book**, one used to record details of stock processed in the yards; **yard dog**, one specially trained to control sheep confined in yards; **yard-man**, one who works stock in the yards.

1978 JARDINE *Shadows on Hill* 129 Branding paint had to be mixed..and **yard books** made ready at the branding-race shed. **1913** CARR *Country Work* 33 He can practice [*sic*] on..a good noisy **yard dog**, as all station hands are liable to be called upon to assist in drafting, etc. **1966** *Encycl. NZ* I. 493 *Backing and Yard Dog*: Usually this is a 'huntaway' or 'handy dog' trained to run over the backs of tightly packed sheep and to walk back through a mob in the yards to keep them moving ahead. It is a useful dog for loading and unloading sheep. **1970** MCNAUGHTON *Tat* 101 He could hunt a mob away, as well as pull, and he was also a champion yard dog, barking when commanded. **1949** SARGESON *I Saw in My Dream* (1974) 249 Over that way a **yard-man** with his dog was opening up a pen for them [*sc.* the sheep] and signalling them on. **1982** PEAT *Detours* 176 He said he was the yardman and explained the system of [auction] whistling [codes at the saleyards].

yard, *v.*

1. [AND 1845.] *trans.* To confine (farm stock) temporarily in the yard(s) for a particular purpose.

1856 [see YARD *n.* 1]. **1867** *Richmond-Atkinson Papers* (1960) II. 236 His master took the slip-panel down and the dog then rounded the sheep in and yarded them without any orders. **1881** NESFIELD *Chequered Career* 36 In Australia, sheep are either in large paddocks which are boundary-ridden, or else they are shepherded and yarded every night. **1924** *Otago Witness* (Dunedin) 23 Sept 20 Very few wethers were yarded.

Hence **yarding** *vbl. n.* [AND 1889], the rounding up and confining of farm stock (esp. sheep) in yards; the number of animals so confined regarded as a group or series of lots to be sold, shorn, etc.

1865 CHUDLEIGH *Diary* 25 Oct. (1950) 202 The sheep broke repeatedly before we could get them in. I..rode home after the yarding and had a plunge bath. **1924** *Otago Witness* (Dunedin) 5 Aug. 15 Sheep were more numerous in the store pens that at any sale since the autumn yardings. **1937** *King Country Chronicle* 12 Jan. 3 The yarding of store sheep was comprised principally of lambs of all classes. **1982** *Agric. Gloss.* (MAF) 25 *Yarding*: Putting sheep into yards or woolshed with a dog or team of dogs. **1988** *Press* (Christchurch) 11 Feb. 27 The first sizable yarding of adult breeding ewes this year was a feature of yesterday's Addington sale. **1993** *Dominion* (Wellington) 26 Mar. 12 The quality of the yarding and its reputation have built up over the last five or six years.

2. As **yard up** [see OED *v.*¹ 1 a, 1885], to round up and direct (farm stock) into yards. Also as a *vbl. n.*

1902 *Brett's Colonists' Guide* 315 A piece of sacking or a handfull of flax leaves tied together are quite sufficient for yarding-up. *Ibid.* 318 The sheep being yarded up into the drafting pens, the operator stands outside. **1904** CHUDLEIGH *Diary* 11 May (1950) 422 I..yarded up, cut and branded and help [*sic*] to catch.

Hence **yarder-up** [AND *yarder* 1883], one who yards up livestock.

[**1881**] BREMNER *Woolscours NZ* (1985) 15 A description of an unidentified sheepstation in 1881 recorded that a twenty-two man gang..put through [the sheep-wash] 1250 sheep in a..day. The 'yarder-up' kept the pen nearest the wash full of sheep.

yarn, *v.* [Transf. use of *yarn* to spin a tale: of freq. use in NZ: AND 'Used elsewhere but earliest in Aust.', 1847; see OED *v. a.*] *intr.* To pass the time in amicable chat; to gossip.

1857 *St Leonard's Station Diary* 14 May in MacFarlane *Amuri* (1946) 125 Hanging round the station, yarning and sleeping. **1873** TINNE *Wonderland of Antipodes* 31 The korero might have been indefinitely prolonged, for, like all colonials, they [*sc.* the Maori] are much given to 'yarning'. **1925** MANDER *Allen Adair* (1971) 137 They had a comfortable evening, smoking and yarning about impersonal matters. **1938** HYDE *Nor Yrs. Condemn* 165 If you can get some of the older Maoris yarning, you might hear a few ghost stories connected with that tree. **1965** SHADBOLT *Among Cinders* 102 She liked yarning with me. There weren't too many people she could yarn with any more. **1972** SHADBOLT *Strangers & Journeys* 195 In the town, where men gathered to yarn on street corners.

yarn, *n.* [f. YARN *v.*: AND 1852.] A chat, a talk.

1857 HARPER *Lett. from NZ* (1914) 49 This has been a long yarn. **1862** CHUDLEIGH *Diary* 23 July (1950) 49 We had a long yarn on things in general. **1864** *Ibid.* 2 Dec. 155 We always have great yarns when we get together. **1876** PEACHE *Journal* in Gray *Quiet with Hills* 14 June (1970) 46 I enjoyed my trip to town and it certainly is jolly to have a yarn with friends after being 'up country' for some time. **1943** BENNETT *English in NZ* in *Amer. Speech* XVIII. 91 A yarn is simply a talk or a chat, not a sailor's story, not even a tall story. **1952** *Listener* 4 Apr. 7 You never speak with a man; you have a 'yarn' to him. **1965** SHADBOLT *Among Cinders* 108 He'd be delighted to have a quick little yarn with you. He'd be awfully sorry to miss you.

yellow.

1. In the names of plants and animals, see: BIRCH 3 (12), BOARFISH, KOWHAI 2 (2), MISTLETOE 2 (2), PINE 2 (20), SCRUB *n.* 2 (2), TUSSOCK *n.* 3 (14). See also YELLOWHEAD, YELLOWTAIL.

2. In special collocations: **yellow admiral**, a large, dark butterfly *Bassaris* (formerly *Pyrameis* or *Vanessa*) *itea* (fam. Nymphalidae), having yellow patches on the upper surfaces of the forewings; **yellow-belly,** (a) see FLOUNDER 2 (11); (b) see quot. 1961 below; **yellow-button**, BACHELOR'S BUTTON (*Cotula coronopifolia*); **yellow-eye**, see PENGUIN 2 (9); **yellow fever** [AND 1849], *gold fever* (GOLD 3); **yellowfin**, see TUNA; **yellow-hammer** *farming* [f. its coloration, a transf. use of *yellow hammer*, a bunting], see quot. 1971; **yellow-leaf**, a mosaic virus disease of flax (*Phormium tenax*); **yellow weed**, TURNIP; **yellow wood**, any of several *Coprosma* spp.

(fam. Rubiaceae), native shrubs or small trees with yellowish wood, including COPROSMA, KARAMU, MIKI-MIKI 2, MINGIMINGI 2 qq.v.

1929 MARTIN *NZ Nature Book 1* [Frontispiece] **Yellow Admiral** (*Pyrameis itea*). **1947** POWELL *Native Animals of NZ* 54 Yellow Admiral (*Vanessa itea*). A common butterfly with a wing expansion of up to 2¹/₂ inches, seen from November till May. The fore-wings are black and reddish-brown, divided by a broad diagonal patch of yellow. **1955** MILLER *Nature in NZ* 10 The Yellow Admiral..has black and brown wings, the fore pair with a large yellow diagonal patch and white spots towards the apex, while the hind pair have four black spots with blue centres. **1965** MANSON *Nature in NZ* 24 The Yellow Admiral can perhaps best be described as a 'twin' of the Red Admiral. **1975** *NZ's Nature Heritage* LII. 1455 Two [butterflies], the Yellow Admiral..and the Common Grass Blue..are also found in Australia and on Norfolk Island. **1989** LESSITER *Butterflies and Moths* 11 The Yellow Admiral can be found from November to May throughout the North Island and the north of the South Island, and hibernates for the winter. **1961** MARTIN *Flora NZ* 74 On the stems of forest trees few mosses are more common than the **Yellow-belly** (*Hypnum cupressiforme* var. *chrysogaster*). **1899** KIRK *Students' Flora* 322 *C[otula] coronopifolia*... Glabrous. Stems succulent, creeping, rooting at the nodes... [**1899** *Note*] **Yellow-button**. **1907** LAING & BLACKWELL *Plants NZ* 434 *Cotula coronopifolia* (*The Coronopus-leaved Cotula*)... English name *Yellow-button*. (The English Coronopus is the Wart-Cress. The name is originally from the Greek, meaning *raven-footed*.) **1952** RICHARDS *Chatham Is.* 47 *Cotula..coronopifolia*..Yellow Buttons. **1966** *Encycl. NZ* III. 479 A few of the more widespread plants [*sc.* on rocky shores in the south] are the true flax.., some hardferns..., and the yellow-button. **1865** *West Coast Times* 12 Aug. in May *West Coast Gold Rushes* (1967) 280 Truly the Kanieri..presents but a rueful appearance, suffering..from the worst of all maladies incidental to a young goldfield, viz. **yellow fever** introduced from a distance. **1868** LUSH *Waikato Jrnls.* 6 Sept. (1982) 152 There again..the congregation was chiefly women: the male population having been stricken with yellow fever and gone to the diggings. **1914** PFAFF *Diggers' Story* 149 Here..he used to burn the quicksilver out of the amalgam brought to the bank, and contracted a certain amount of 'yellow fever'. **1971** NEWTON *Ten Thousand Dogs* 169 **Yellowhammer**: A dog with a black back but a yellow (or tan) head, neck, and legs. **1921** *NZJST* IV. 34 Compared with the difficulties confronting other types of fibre, New Zealand flax was in a favourable position, but it was necessary to obtain immunity from the **yellow-leaf** disease. **1923** *NZJST* VI. 7 [The New Zealand flax industry] is depressed at present, and a disease, known as 'yellow leaf', for which no effective remedy has yet been found, threatens it with extinction. **1988** BROOKER et al. *Economic Native Plants NZ* 40 Yellow-leaf disease, which caused the death of considerable areas of flax in the Manawatu, was traced to a virus carried by a leaf hopper. **1926** HILGENDORF *Weeds* 90 Wild Turnip..is also commonly called charlock and **yellow weed**, and even wild mustard. It is exceedingly common on rich agricultural lands, at any rate in Canterbury and Otago, where masses of it often rival gorse in brilliancy. **1969** *Standard Common Names Weeds* 89 *yellow weed* [=] *galinsoga*: *wild turnip*. **1868** LINDSAY *Contribs. NZ Bot.* 72 [*Coprosma linariifolia*..] The 'Mikimik' or '**Yellow Wood**' of the Otago settler. A tall shrub. **1889** [see MINGIMINGI 2]. **1890** *PWD Catalogue Timbers* (NZ & South Seas Exhib.) 15 Yellow-wood..Coprosma linariifolia..Wood of a deep yellow colour, close and straight grained. **1909** *AJHR C-11* 8 [*Coprosma*] *lucida*. *Karamu*. Yellow-wood. Forest and scrub. **1918** *NZJST* I. 265 *C[oprosma] linariifolia* (the mikimiki, or yellow-wood), which, although rare in Wellington, is commoner in the South Island, where it attains a good size and is remarkable for the yellow colour of the wood. **1939** COCKAYNE & TURNER *Trees NZ* 36 *Coprosma linariifolia* (Rubiaceae). Yellow-wood. **1982** *Field Guide Common NZ Trees & Shrubs* 29 Yellow Wood *Coprosma linariifolia*.

yellow-breasted tit: see TIT *n.*¹ a.

yellow-eye(d) mullet: see MULLET 2 (3).

yellowhead. [f. the colour of its head.] *Mohoua ochrocephala* (fam. Pachycephalidae), a small bird of the South Island bush with a brown back and canary-yellow head and breast. See also *bush canary*, (CANARY *n.*¹ 1), MOHUA, POPOKOTEA, TITMOUSE.

1773 FORSTER *Resolution Jrnl.* 13 May (1982) II. 278 Pohebirds, Fantails..Yellowheads & various other birds inhabit these impenetrable Forests. **1871** HUTTON *Catalogue Birds NZ* 8 Canary. Yellow-head. Popokatea. **1873** BULLER *Birds NZ* 103 Orthonyx ochrocephala. (The Yellow-head)... 'Canary' of the colonists. **1898** MORRIS *Austral-English* 523 Yellow-head..or Native Canary..common in South Island. **1914** PFAFF *Diggers' Story* 11 Flocks of Yellow Heads would be seen every hour [in the West Coast bush]. **1923** *NZJST* VI. 92 Philpott (1919) states that 'the yellowhead disappeared from the neighbourhood of Invercargill about ten years ago'. **1948** MONCRIEFF *NZ Birds* 45 Yellowhead or Bush Canary: South Island only; differs from Whitehead in superior size, richer colouring, call-note of 'sweet'. Canary-like song including a trill like a coin spinning. **1955** OLIVER *NZ Birds* 472 The Yellowhead is characteristic of the gloomy beech forests of the South Island. **1976** SOPER *NZ Birds* 52 The stoat eventually retreated down the limb and thence to the ground, being followed all the way by the Yellowheads. The birds continued to mob the animal even on the ground. **1985** *Readers' Digest Book NZ Birds* 277 While searching for food in the forest canopy, yellowheads pass quickly through the branches, thoroughly inspecting each leaf and twig from all angles, including upside down, and prying into small cracks and crevices.

yellow-headed tit (tomtit): see TIT *n.*¹ a, TOMTIT.

yellowtail. [Prob. named from a yellow coloration of the tail, though this is not always prominent; AND esp. *Trachurus novaeseelandiae*, 1839.]

1. Any of various marine fishes, esp. of fam. Carangidae: *Seriola lalandi* (KINGFISH or HAKU), *Pseudocaranx dentex* (formerly *trevally*), *Trachurus novaezelandiae* (*horse* or *jack* MACKEREL), *Decapterus koheru* (KOHERU); but also, in obsolete and erroneous or confusing application, fam. Latrididae: *Latris lineata* (TRUMPETER); and fam. Moridae: *Pseudophycis bachus* (*red cod* (COD 2 (6)). (The species entries in 2 below are presented in chronological order.)

2. (1) *Trachurus novaezelandiae* (fam. Carangidae), *horse* or *jack mackerel* (MACKEREL 2 (2) and (3)).

1769 *An 'Endeavour' Log* 12 Nov. in McNab *Hist. Records* (1914) II. 147 The Indians [of Mercury Bay] brought us some large fish, calld Yellow tails. **1841** in Ross *Voyage of Discovery* (1847) II. 117 The largest [fish caught at Kawa Kawa], a kind of mackarel called yellow tail, and sometimes cavallo, though coarse, was found to be very good eating. **1967** MORELAND *Marine Fishes* 48 Horse Mackerel [*Trachurus declivis*]... Mackerel and yellowtail are alternative names. **1981** WILSON *Fisherman's Bible* 162 The Horse Mackerel is also known as the Yellowtail.

(2) *Latris lineata* (fam. Latrididae), TRUMPETER 1.

1842 GRAY *Fauna* in Dieffenbach *Travels in NZ* (1843) II. 209 *Latris lineata*... This fish was taken by Cook's crew in Dusky Bay, and named by them 'Yellow Tail.' **1887** *Auckland Weekly News* 5 Nov. 7 One of the most pleasant sights..was a vast shoal of fish, known as yellow tails (latris lineata) which came along joyfully, so close as to touch each other, their heads slightly projecting above the water, and their mouths wide open, skimming the surface. **1898** [see (4) below].

(3) *Seriola lalandi* (fam. Carangidae), KINGFISH a.

1849, 1872, 1892 [see HAKU]. **1926** [see KINGFISH a]. **1938** *TrRSNZ* LXVIII. 410 *Regificola grandis*... Yellowtail (Otago), kingfish (Auckland). **1945** DUGGAN in *Coll. Stories* (1981) 35 One of them caught a small yellow-tail and threw it on to the wharf. **1956** GRAHAM *Treasury NZ Fishes* 238 Yellow Tail or Kingfish (Auckland) (Haku) *Regificola grandis* (Castelnau)... This fish has always been the Yellowtail of Otago, but in Auckland it is known as Kingfish. **1967** NATUSCH *Animals NZ* 221 Family Carangidae. This family contains..the yellowtail or kingfish. **1979, 1986** [see KINGFISH a].

(4) *Pseudocaranx dentex* (fam. Carangidae), TREVALLY 1 a.

1872 HUTTON & HECTOR *Fishes NZ* 111 In Auckland [Trevally] is sometimes called the Yellow Tail. **1898** MORRIS *Austral-English* 523 *Yellow-tail*... In New Zealand, the word is used for the fish *Latris lineata*..and is also a name for the *King-fish*.., and for the *Trevally*. **1958** *Whitcombe's Modern Jun. Dict.* (8edn.) 449 *Yellow-tail*. A name used for various Australian fishes, and in New Zealand for 'trevalli' and 'king-fish'.

(5) *Pseudophycis* (formerly *Lotella*) *bachus* (fam. Moridae), *red cod* (COD 2 (6)).

1872 HUTTON & HECTOR *Fishes NZ* 115 Red Cod. Also called the Yellow Tail and the Haddock, (*Lotella bacchus*) is a well known fish on some parts of the coast. **1957** PARROTT *Sea Angler's Fishes* 169 Red Cod *Physiculus bachus*. Yellow-tail; Haddock.

(6) *Decapterus koheru* (fam. Carangidae), KOHERU.

1921 *NZJST* IV. 117 Decapterus koheru (Hector). *Yellowtail*; *Koheru*. Common around North Auckland Peninsula during the early summer months. **1981** WILSON *Fisherman's Bible* 140 Koheru. Commonly-caught inhabitant of our northern coastal waters who is also known as Yellowtail or Horse Mackerel.

yellowtail kingfish: see KINGFISH a, YELLOWTAIL 2 (3).

yew. *Obs.* Also **New Zealand yew.** [Transf. use of English *Yew Taxus baccata* (fam. Taxodiaceae) for a New Zealand tree with similar foliage.] TOTARA *n.*¹ 1 a.

1850 COLLINSON *Timber Trees of NZ* in *Papers Royal Soc. Van Diemen's Land* 10 July 51 *Totara*.— (New Zealand Yew, *Podocarpus Totara*). **1883** DOMETT *Ranolf & Amohia* I. 157 Made..Fast to a single lightsome yew, One lone *totára*-tree that grew Beneath the hillside rising high.

yoke up, *v*. *Hist.* [AND 1848 'Elsewhere constructed without *up*.': see OED *v.* 1.] To attach the yoke and its accessories to a draught bullock.

1856 ROBERTS *Diary* 19 Sept. in Beattie *Early Runholding* (1947) 42 I yoked up the bullocks. The bullock yoke was a square piece of white pine smoothed and hollowed out to fit the necks of the two bullocks. **1933** *Press* (Christchurch) (Acland Gloss.) 30 Dec. 13 *Yoke*.—Bullocks are *yoked up* and *unyoked*—not *harnessed* or *in* and *out spanned*. **1947** [see BOW 1].

you. As **you can('t)**, **you wouldn't**, introducing various phrases often used as exclamations: **you can't fatten thoroughbreds**, see FATTEN *v.*; **you wouldn't read about it**, see READ *v.*; **you can put a ring around that**, see RING *n.*²; **you can say that again**, certainly.

1962 HORI *Half-gallon Jar* 37 This pakeha coot says, 'Boy, you can say that again'. So I say, 'It's a corker day, pakeha...' 'Yes, I heard you the first time, so don't repeat yourself.' But I say, 'You told me to say that again'... 'Yes, but I did not mean for you to say it again.'

young, *a.* In special collocations: **young colonial**, the colonial youth; **Young Gun** [?after a 'Western' film title *The Young Guns*], a promotional nickname for a member (often an aging member) of the New Zealand national cricket eleven in the 1991 and following seasons; in *pl.*, a promotional name for the team itself; **Young Maori Party** *hist.*, orig. in the 1890s an informal group of influential Maori men mainly educated at Te Aute College, hoping to revitalize the Maori race through policies of land-ownership and education: formally established as a political party in 1909 but disbanded before WW1 (the leading members included Te Rangi Hiroa (Peter Buck), Apirana Ngata, Maui Pomare and Tutere Wi Repa); **Young New Zealand**, the youth of New Zealand collectively; **Young Turk**, usu. *pl.* [a transf. use of *Young Turk* one of a band of Turkish reformers c1908], a name given to a member of a group of junior National Party activist MPs during the Holyoake administration of the 1960s; **Young Turkism**, the mood and philosophy of the 'Young Turks'; **young'un**, YOUNKER.

1905 THOMSON *Bush Boys* 23 They were as good types of the **young Colonial** as one would find, sturdy of frame, brown as a berry, and the picture of health and strength. 1991 *Sunday Star* (Auckland) 3 Mar. A1 **Young Gun** ace bowler Danny Morrison left Eden Park on a very special surprise mission yesterday just after the New Zealanders had dismissed Sri Lanka for 380 and gone in to bat. 1992 *Evening Post* (Wellington) 4 Feb. 4 The Young Guns carry only pop guns. 1992 *Capital Times* 10–17 Mar. 11 The Young Guns will be wanting to get the Poms well and truly in their sights in this World Cup qualifier. 1993 *Dominion* (Wellington) 17 Mar. 12 A couple of not so young guns made short work of the last 33 runs yesterday to dent New Zealand's reputation as the easy beat of test cricket. 1899 *NZ Times* (Wellington) 18 Dec. 5 If the Government is persuaded that the work of the '**Young Maori Party**' is likely to benefit the Maori people, a financial grant should be made to enable it to carry on the good work. 1928 KEESING *Changing Maori* 169 The rise of the Young Maori Party in the 'nineties, was the first practical demonstration of the fact that the result of a truly liberal education among the best of the Maori youth seems to be a freeing of energy which immediately asserts itself in race-pride and individuality. 1930 Ngata in *Na To Hoa Aroha* (1987) II. 17 [Carroll] left his blessing on the Young Maori Party and went out in the confidence that the welfare of the Race was in good hands. 1963 HENDERSON *Ratana* (1972) 15 With Apirana Ngata as organizing secretary, the Young Maori Party worked for efficient..farming..on the East Coast. 1988 *Na To Hoa Aroha* (1988) III. 233 The knighthood was very important to Buck because it enabled him to stand alongside Carroll and the other giants of the Young Maori Party. 1863 MANING *Old New Zealand* 105 Right down to the present time talking of '**Young New Zealand**', and within a hair's-breadth of settling 'the Maori difficulty' without having been paid for it, which would have been a great oversight, and contrary to the customs of New Zealand. 1919 WAITE *New Zealanders at Gallipoli* 17 Young Australia was welcoming Young New Zealand in no uncertain manner in the first meeting of those brothers-in-arms soon to be known by a glorious name as yet undreamed of. 1974 MULDOON *Rise & Fall of a Young Turk* 44 MacIntyre, Gordon and I soon found [c1961] we were on the same wavelength and thus were born the '**Young Turks**'. *Ibid.* 45 The term Young Turks was coined some time later by a newspaper columnist, Ian Templeton, I think, but Gordon, MacIntyre, and Muldoon acted in concert from the beginning of the 1961 session. 1984 *Listener* 26 May 13 The man..the *Dom's* Richard Long tellingly dubbed the leader of the new 'Young Turks' [*sc.* Derek Quigley] clashed with his leader over the introduction of further regulations. 1991 *Dominion* (Wellington) 22 Nov. 22 With his National-blue, go-thither eyes, Muldoon was one of the 'young Turks' (meaning a handful of Kiwi MPs aged fortysomething) who in the spirit of the times, were busting to wear their hair short and get down to some funky Vera Lynn. 1974 MULDOON *Rise & Fall of a Young Turk* 53 My first bit of '**Young Turkism**' was a solo effort. 1905 THOMSON *Bush Boys* 64 'There are some eggs there, too,' he said, 'but it is no use taking them, as they are sure to have **young uns** in them.'

youngker, var. YOUNKER.

younker /ˈjʌŋkə/. Also **youngker**. [f. Brit. dial. *younker* occas. used of the young of animals: see OED 3 b (ad. Middle Dutch *jonckher*).] **a.** A schoolboys' term for esp. young of birds, but also for baby rabbits, rarely mice.

1920 p.c. R. Mason. I remember hearing younkers used of rabbits in Pukekohe in the early 1920s. 1949 DAVIN *Roads from Home* 165 It wasn't too early for younkers then... Their eyes closed, they would be down there, a half-dozen or so of them [*sc.* rabbits]. 1968 SLATTER *Pagan Game* 230 Tank was renowned for his mighty deeds..for wringing younkers' necks and blowing up frogs. 1982 FRAME *To the Is-land* (1984) 198 Mother, like the mother bird of the world, sprang always to defend all races and creeds..as if they were her own 'youngkers' (our word for baby birds). 1987 *Listener* 29 Aug. 45 Once I stood on an empty blue egg with freckles..and I hope that the younker had got out of it safely.

b. *transf.* A new pupil.

1951 14–18 M 59 Wellington H.S. 25 Younker [new kid] [M2]

youse, yous /juːz/. [Also in Brit. and US dial., a var. of *you*: cf. Anglo-Irish *yez*; AND 1902.] **a.** Used mainly with a plural noun (esp. *fulla, joker*) as a term of familiar (often jocular) address to more than one person.

1908 *Truth* 22 Apr. 2 'Orl rite,' I sez, 'yewse blokes take ther blades [=razors].' 1918 *Quick March* 2 Sept. 27 [N.C.O. speaks to recruits] Youse 'roughies' 'ave really ter get ter know me better, or we won't be friends. 1928 SMYTH *Jean of Tussock Country* 47 [A station-hand speaks] Hold still youse awkward cow. 1946 SARGESON *That Summer* 55 Well, a knock-back from one of yous isn't going to make me lose any sleep. 1964 HARVEY *Any Old Dollars Mister?* 86 The fat Yank yelled out, 'Hey, youse guys. Chow!' 1968 JOHNSON *Turn of Tide* 12 [A whaler speaks] 'Is youse the teacher for the Parkins?' 1970 MASON *Golden Weather* in *Solo* (1981) 15 'Now I've told yas before an' I'll say it again. The first a yous jokers start anything lands in gaol.'.. 'Keep law n'order, n youse fullas outa mischief.' 1970 BALL *People Makers* 170 'Hey, yous kids,' I screamed, dropping naturally into the local idiom. 1984 BEATON *Outside In* 21 et passim Ma: Stuff it, yous... If yous're not careful. 1986 *Listener* 27 Sept. 32 [Cartoon: after-match function] Hey—youse jokers—watch this—Brownie's going to do a down-trou. 1987 GEE *Prowlers* 124 Shane read the page. 'Yous jokers know what you're doing?' 1993 *North & South* (Auckland) Feb. 86 Some of yous is going to get pregnant, some of yous are going to start fighting.

b. Esp. freq. in representations of the language of Maori speakers of English.

1965 SHADBOLT *Among Cinders* 202 I'll give the pair of yous ten minutes to make yourselves scarce. 1969 MASON *Awatea* (1978) 20 Irapeta, *approaching*: Hi, yous. 1974 HILLIARD *Maori Woman* 171 He [*sc.* a Pakeha] said,... 'Can I buy yous all a beer?' 'Why did you say *yous* all?'.. 'Is it because you think that's a Maori way of talking? Are we supposed to fall in love with you because you suddenly start talking Maori English like we do—or like you suppose we do?' 1985 ROSIER-JONES *Cast Two Shadows* 15 'Hi youse guys.' Tui is at home. 'I didn't expect to see you so early.' 1989 VIRTUE *Upon Evil Season* 82 [A Maori speaks.] She knows who yous are.

Z

zack. *Obs.* Also **zac**, **zak**. [Prob. an alteration of Sc. dial. *sax*(pence: AND 1898.] Sixpence or a sixpenny piece. See also SAX.
1941 BAKER *NZ Slang* 62 Sixpence is termed a *zack*. **1944** BRUNO *Desert Daze* 48 The day's seven-and-a-zac's worth for King and Country. **1954** *Truth* 14 Apr. 12 This broad hint that his 'zac's worth' has yet a way to climb, is taken according to the humour of the serving tapster. **1964** DAVIS *Watersiders* 93 He held out his hand to Whiskey Bill. 'Give us the zack.' **1970** DUGGAN *O'Leary's Orchard* 130 Obol and diobol, the two in the one like a symbol of something... Two zacs to the deener, too. Nonsense. **1986** OWEN & PERKINS *Speaking for Ourselves* 68 And when everything was sorted out, the Old Man came out of that contract without a zak to show for it. *Ibid.* 76 Winter [rabbit] hides might bring in as much as a zak each; sixpence a skin at that time [the early 1930s].

zambuk /ˈzæmˌbʌk/. Also **zambuc(k)**. Often init. cap. [f. *Zam-buk* the proprietary name of a former popular brand of all-purpose ointment.]

1. *Hist.* The name of the ointment as recorded in New Zealand.
1903 *Supplement to the N.Z. Gazette* 12 Nov. Zambuk 4439 [filed] 4th November, 1903..The Bile Bean Manufacturing Co..of Leeds, England..vendors of Proprietary Medicines. Chemical substances prepared for use in medicine and pharmacy. **1984** TRAIL *Child of the Arrow* 5 My first memories of Bullendale are..of chilblains carefully dressed with Zambuck.

2. *transf.* **a.** Orig. among sportspeople, a member of the Order of St John trained in first aid, or other uniformed first-aider, in attendance at a sports meeting; thence, an ambulance officer attending accidents. Also *attrib.*
1911 MCKENZIE *Rugby Football in Wellington & Wairarapa* 105 There was no Zambuk or ambulance man in those days. **1938** *NZ Observer* 26 May 21 What do the Zambuks carry in their cases besides bandages? **1943** BENNETT *English in NZ* in *Amer. Speech* XVIII. 95 A few trade names have caught the public fancy, and become generalised. Thus *Zambuk*, a brand of ointment, is regularly used for 'first aid man' (usually a member of the St. John's Ambulance Corps), or even as an appeal for first aid. **1968** SLATTER *Pagan Game* 172 Call on the zambucks to cart him off [the football field]. **1966** *Arena* 65 June 23 Then the Zambuks ran up with a stretcher. **1969** *Listener* 23 May 12 The driver was dead... There was a girl in a bad way mixed up with him. 'Better leave it for the zambucs,' Payne said. **1973** MCCARTHY *Listen..!* 53 The 'Zambuks' pulled it back into place and then bandaged it. **1983** HUTCHINS *Rugby Rabbits* 62 Taking things a step further,.. the coach also questioned Ralph about the zambuck incident of the previous Saturday. **1988** SMITH *Southlanders at Heart* 82 Two 'Zambucks' and a linesman chased them yelping from the ground. [**1988** *Note*] Rugby parlance for St. John Ambulance men. 'Zambuck' was a well known brand of ointment salve. **1995** *Hutt News* (Lower Hutt) 7 Nov. 5 Mary was also involved as a Zambuk on duty at basketball, hockey and especially rugby games, where most Saturdays she would be on duty at the St Johns Ambulance rooms.

b. *WW1*. A medical (or first-aid) orderly.
1918 *Chron. NZEF* 27 Feb. 39 Right here on the Ewshott Front is the place to take a calm..view of the situation, where..the voice of the 'Zambuck' is heard loudly in the land. *Ibid.* 21 June 221 Believe ye..that the tenderfoot and Zambuk, Working madly in the trenches.

3. A crowd-cry (often joc.) for first-aid attention for an injured player; earlier in Dunedin (see quot. 1991) a rhyme associated with a children's street-game.
1943 [see 2 a above]. **1950** SUTTON-SMITH *Our Street* 50 Everybody would shout, 'Zambuk! Zambuk!' until the first-aid man came to the rescue. **1959** SLATTER *Gun in My Hand* 80 The ambulance men run for the prone body on the field. The game is in a serious state because there is not the usual fatuous cry of zambuck from some oaf in the crowd who has never known the shock and pain of a [rugby] football injury. **1991** *Dominion Sunday Times* (Wellington) 17 Feb. 15 Another one of her quotes is about street games; 'and we'd play on the [Dunedin] street [c1910–20] with these hoops and say "Zambuk"—Zambuk was an ointment just coming on the market—we'd sing—"Zambuk, Zambuk, Zammazammazam"—please give Jamelee a smack on the hand' or something like that.

zamzoid /ˈzæmˌzoid/. [A pronunciation spelling of Brit. dial. *samsaw(der)ed*: see EDD *sam*, *zam adj.* sw. dial. 'half-heated, half-done' used of food with *-sawed*, *-zawed*, a truncated form of *-sawdered*, *-zoddered*, a dial. form related to *sodden* 'boiled'; damp, wet.] Damp, greasy.
1938 HYDE *Godwits Fly* (1970) 42 Eliza, don't recite while you're washing up the dishes. Don't leave those forks to the last, they'll get all cold and zamzoid. How often have I got to tell you? **1985** I.A. GORDON in *Listener* 21 Dec. 102 *Zamzoid*... A further scan [of EDD] produced (in various phonetic spellings *samsawed*, *samsawdered*, *samzawed*, *sam-zawey*) a clutch of examples of past-participle[–]adjectival forms all with the sense of 'lukewarm'—used of food that has been cooked and then laid aside until it has begun to coagulate into a sticky mess.

Zealand. *Hist.* [Poss. meant as an abbrev., or poetic use, of *New Zealand*, occas. shortened for reasons of metre as in quots. 1780, 1839.] NEW ZEALAND A 1.
1773 BAYLY *Journal* 17 Apr. in McNab *Hist. Records* (1914) II. 208 When they [*sc.* Capt. Cook's ship] came near the Longd. [*sic*] of Zealand they hawled [*sic*] up northerly & went into Dusky Bay. **1780** SEWARD *Elegy on Capt. Cook* 8 And now antarctic Zealand's drear domain Frowns. **1821** *Sugden to Earl of Bathurst* 18 Jan. in McNab *Hist. Records* (1908) I. 516 A party about emigrating to New Zealand begs most respectfully to solicit the assistance of Government in their undertaking... One thing I must beg Your Lordship's most serious attention to—that is, the heavy duty (1/- per foot) on timber imported into N.S. Wales from Zealand. **1839** *Glasgow Constitutional* 26 Oct. [leader page] [A parody or alteration of Thomas Campbell's *The Pleasures of Hope*, orig. 'On Eyrie's banks.'] On *Zealand's Hills*, where Tigers steal along, And the dread Indian chaunts a dismal song. **1883** FERGUSON *Castle Gay* 3 From Zealand's hoary mountains to India's burning plains. *Ibid.* 101 When 'neath the swagman's weary load..Zealand's rugged hills I trod.

Zealander. *Hist.* Also **Zeelander**. [Poss. ad. French *zélandais*: OED 1773.] NEW ZEALANDER 1, a Maori. (Contrast quot 1948.)
1773 BAYLY *Journal* 12 Apr. in McNab *Hist. Records* (1914) II. 207 The Zeelanders never eat greens of any kind, nor do they seem to be the least affected with scurvey. **1777** EDGAR *Log 'Discovery'* 24 Feb. in McNab *Hist. Records* (1914) II. 228 The Zealander often appear'd to have a great deal of Friendship For us—speaking sometimes in the most tender compassionate tone of Voice imaginable. **1780** SEWARD *Elegy on Capt. Cook* 9 The Zealander had hitherto subsisted upon fish, and such coarse vegetables as their climate produced. **1821** EDGEWORTH *Letters from England* 7 Dec. (1971) 288 Captain Thompson..went some years ago to New Zealand and when he was taking leave of the Zealanders one of their chiefs consented to accompany him to England. **1941** BAKER *NZ Slang* 18 Doubtless because of this French influence we find the natives frequently described as *Zealanders* in early documents. [**1948** EZRA POUND *Pisan Cantos* canto lxxx And persuaded an Aussie or Zealander or S. African To kneel with him in prayer.]

Zealandia. [f. New) *Zealand* + Britann)*ia*: usu. represented as a buxom young white woman with long hair, often bareheaded and dressed in a loose-fitting white robe.]

1. As an old-fashioned (usu. poetic) name for New Zealand, often ironically applied and not now seriously used.
1857 *New Zealand, or Zealandia, the Britain of the South*... By Charles Hursthouse, a New Zealand colonist. [Title: *NZ Nat. Bibliography* (1980) I. i 506: 'Zealandia' is omitted in the tile of the 2edn. of 1861: but see quot. 1861.] **1861** HURSTHOUSE *NZ* 260 Drowsy matrimonial four-posters give place, in Zealandia, to elastic iron bedsteads and hair mattresses. **1867** HOCHSTETTER *NZ* 33 The Dutch named it *New Zealand*. [1867 *Note*] English writers..protest strongly against this name... Taylor says..New Zealand ought to be re-christened. To this end he proposes names such as '*Austral Britain*', or '*Austral Albion*'. *Zealandia* was likewise proposed. **1876** *Saturday Advertiser* 8 July 5 When the Day King... With genial ray, did greet Zealandia's Isles. **1889** MITCHELL *Rhymes & Rambles* 64 Thirteen knots I'm sure she's doing, Soon we'll hail Zealandia's shore. **1896** O'REGAN *Poems* 21 While song-birds greet Zealandia's natal morn, And seem to say 'Rejoice, a Nation great is born.' **1906** *Truth* 25 Aug. 5 Hats off! I say, throughout Zealandia, to the right sort of Justice that we want! **1910** *Ibid.* 24 Dec. 1 It is reported from across the Tasman that when a sheep was being shorn at a station near Penhurst, a starling's nest with one egg in it was found in the wool. To hold the belt, Zealandia will require to produce a duck that has hatched a sitting of eggs in a collection plate. **1922** [see MAORILAND 3 a]. **1952** *Here & Now* Jan. 14 And from Zealandia's stormy seas Huge whales are almost absentees. **1966**

Encycl. NZ III. 703 [Denis Glover 'Zealandia A National Symbol?'] And so rose up Zealandia, full-armed, from the head first of one artist, then another, Britannia's daughter, more than ocean-girt.. she became the mother-mistress symbol of young nationhood... Depending on the skill of the artist, her expression ranged from vacuous insipidity to a crystal-gazing trance. **1988** Dix *Stranded in Paradise* 39 Peter Lewis recorded..'You've Got Love'..and arguably the best local recording of 1961, a slice of Zealandia called 'Four City Rock'.

Hence **Zealandian**, NEW ZEALAND B 2 a.
1889 SKEY *The Pirate Chief and the Mummy's Complaint with Various Zealandian Poems* by William Skey. [Title]

2. As an element in a trade or proprietary name, now archaic but extant as the name of a Catholic weekly newspaper 'The (New) Zealandia'.
1890 *Otago Witness* (Dunedin) 18 Sept. 43 [Advt] Zealandia Knife Polish...Zealandia Sheep Dip. The Cheapest, Safest, and Most Popular. **1892** *The NZ Wheelman* 5 Nov. 15 [Advt] Oates' Zealandia Bicycles.

zebra bird. [Prob. from the banded appearance of its breast: cf. CHECKSHIRT BIRD.] *shining cuckoo* (CUCKOO 2 (3)).
1887 *Auckland Weekly News* 19 Mar. 36 We refer to the Pipiwharauroa or Zebra bird, a native of New Zealand, which during the present season had developed a remarkable appetite for the black leech.

zebra moth: see MOTH 9.

zeddy. A familiar name for a Z-class sailing boat; see TAKAPUNA 2.
1970 SMITHYMAN in *Te Reo 16* 9 Local [Auckland] variations on yacht-design abounded, and local namings (*patiki, mulley, fourteen-footer, zeddy*) were coinages. **1971** HOLMES *Century of Sail* [dust-jacket] Noel Holmes, Auckland journalist, began his yachting conventionally in zeddies. **1989** [see TAKAPUNA 2.]

Zeelander, var. ZEALANDER.

ziff. [Of unknown orig.: AND 1917.] A beard.
1940 *Tararua Tramper* Jan. 9 [The women] must have expected nothing short of a six-inch ziff on men worthy of the name. **1968** *NZ Contemp. Dict. Suppl.* (Collins) 22 *ziff..n.* (*Sl.*) a beard. **1971** *Listener* 19 Apr. 56 So up he goes and finds he knows one of them, the one with the ziff, a bloke they call Slalom Sam.

Zip, *n.* Also usu. init. cap. [f. the proprietary name *Zip* (Industries, see quot. 1933] Usu. applied to a small water-heater often installed over sinks to provide boiling water for tea-making, washing-up, etc.
1933 *Patent Office Jrnl* 19 Oct. 313 [Registration] No. 32323 Zip [of] 14th September, 1933. H.N. Maunder, Ltd., of 45 Lower Cuba Street, Wellington.. Electrical Engineers... Class 18. Water-heaters and all other goods included in Class 18. **1946** *Blue & White* xvi [Advt] There's nothing like a handy 'Zip' Rapid Kitchen Unit for fast, economical and safe water-heating. **1966** *Cappicade* (Wellington) 16 [Advt] I was suffering from an advanced case of Zippomania. I could touch nothing unless it carried the Zip name-plate. **1971** ARMFELT *Catching Up* 43 'Why so late with the tea, Wayne?' 'I don't know, sir. The Zip didn't boil.' **1987** MARSHALL *Lynx Hunter and Other Stories* 66 An outline of a hand in felt pen and a list of instructions concerning the Zip were the only decorations on the cream walls of the tea-room: points about not leaving the Zip unattended when filling and so on. **1991** *Listener* 14 Jan. 69 He did not even stop for a pot of tea from the Zip in the clubhouse.

zip, *v. Schoolboys. Obs.* To unzip quickly or rip open another's fly. Also as *vbl. n.*
1953 SUTTON-SMITH *Unorganized Games NZ Primary School Children* (VUWTS) II. 665 Another indirect sexual play is the universal practice of 'zipping' amongst boys. In my experience, this is practiced [*sic*] more by boys in the 12 to 15 year age group than by primary school boys. In this play, boys attempt to rip open each others [*sic*] trouser flys [*sic*]. **1968** SLATTER *Pagan Game* 230 Tank was renowned for his mighty deeds..for putting razor blades in his fly to stop other kids zipping him. **1982** SUTTON-SMITH *Hist. Children's Play* 96 Among boys, especially secondary-school boys, 'zipping' that is, the ripping open of another's pants, was universal, although New Zealand boys did not make a habit of collecting the buttons as did English boys.

zone, *v.* Usu. as *vbl. n.* **zoning.** [An extended or spec. use of the town planning term *zoning* (see OED 2), the regulation of land use by particular planning restrictions in designated areas.] *trans.* To restrict to a defined catchment area or zone as defined in an enrolment scheme the enrolment of pupils at any particular (secondary) school which operates such an enrolment scheme.
1953 *Evening Post* (Wellington) 24 Mar. 14 [Heading] School Zoning Decision Arouses Protests... 'If one school is zoned, then all others must be also,' said Mr Matthew. **1955** *PPTA Jrnl.* Nov. 1 The main objection to zoning is that it limits freedom of choice. **1977** DRYLAND *Curious Conscience* 88 'I wanted to go to Auckland Grammar, but I can't because of the zoning.' 'Zoning?' 'Where you live.'..'If you live in this area you have to go to Mount Vincent.' **1985** *Dominion* (Wellington) 12 Sept. 4 The present method of zoning enrolments at the seven Wellington secondary schools will continue. **1987** *Evening Post* (Wellington) 22 Dec. 13 The school has been zoned to prevent it growing much bigger. **1989** *Education Act* S 12 'Zoned School' means a school that has an enrolment scheme.

Hence **zone** *n.*, a defined catchment area from which pupils may be enrolled in (usu.) a secondary school in accordance with its enrolment scheme; also as **no zone, out-of-zone**, describing students from outside their school's official zone.
1953 *Evening Post* (Wellington) 24 Mar. 14 At last week's meeting of the Wellington Education Board, in reference to the board's refusal to admit two out-of-zone children to Kelburn School. **1993** *Metro* (Auckland) Dec. 104 She was..educated at local [Glen Eden] primary and intermediate schools, then out-of-zone at Auckland Girls' Grammar. **1995** *Dominion* (Wellington) 20 Feb. 3 [Heading] Schools won't enrol 'no zone' child. An Auckland family had to enrol their five-year-old..in a private school after four state schools refused to take her because she did not live within their zones.

zooe, var. TUI.

zwei, var. SWY.

zweideener. *Obs.* [f. Germ. *zwei* two + DEENER shilling.] A two-shilling piece.
1899 *Bulletin* (Sydney) 14 Jan. (Red Page) [Letter from *Loafer*, Tauranga.] We have here three slang words for 'florin'—*zweideener* (from *zwei*=two, *deener* a shilling). **1977** *NZ Numismatic Jrnl.* Oct. 16 Along with the Australians, New Zealanders used *zweideener* for the florin (*zwei* meaning two), and *zack* for sixpence.

LIST OF WRITTEN SOURCES

I. BOOKS

This is essentially a 'finding list'. Not all the sources given below have been quoted in the text of the dictionary. A full list has been included, first, because it would have been an expensive and tedious task to eliminate all reference to material now discarded (only about a quarter to a third of the original collections remain); and second, it indicates to any well-wishers who may like to enrich the present collections those sources which have **not** been examined by the editor and readers.

A *'quotation edition'* (usually a first or early edition) provides a date at the head of a dateline and the text of the quotation. However, in the interests of both users and compilers, a quotation is sometimes sourced to the page number of a more accessible *'reference edition'*, usually a later facsimile or reprint, or an edition of an important historical manuscript. The texts of quotation and reference editions have been compared and matched. The reference edition date is given in the dateline in parentheses. In the list below 1938, (1960) indicates that page-references in the dateline are to a 1960 reprint of a work originally published in 1938. Similarly, an item from a short story collection is often given the publication date of the individual story when this can be accurately and conveniently established, the collection date appearing in parentheses.

When two or more *quotation* editions with different texts have been used, the date of each is shown unbracketed, and only one date will appear in the dateline of any particular quotation (see for example LAING & BLACKWELL *Plants of NZ* of which both the 1907 and 1940 editions are quoted on occasion).

Small roman numerals ('i, ii' etc.) in the dateline indicate for ease of reference either the chapter number (for frequently cited books which are available in many editions), or a section of a book, newspaper, etc. which may have a separate or individualized pagination.

Pseudonyms in the form of proper names are usually treated as such and appear in datelines without quotation marks. The index treats pseudonyms of known principals thus:

BATTEN, I.M. pseud. of I.M. COOK
COOK, I.M., see BATTEN, I.M. (pseud.)
'A TRAMP, ESQ.' pseud. of J.D. WICKHAM.

Note: MAC and MC comprise a single section before MA. Definite and indefinite articles have been ignored alphabetically in titles, but not in pseudonyms.

AA guide to New Zealand 1981
ABBERLEY, A. *Chase me a kiwi* 1946
ABBOTT, E. *The English and Australian cookery book* 1864
ABERCROMBY, R. *Seas and skies in many latitudes* 1888
ABRAHAM, C.J.H. *An account of the institution and present condition of Nelson College* 1860
— *Journal of a walk with the Bishop of New Zealand..in August 1855*, 1856 in *Early travellers in New Zealand*; N.M. Taylor (ed.) 1959
ACHESON, F.O.V. *Plume of the Arawas* 1930
The acid test; an anthology of New Zealand humorous writing; G. McLauchlan (ed.) 1981
ACKER, A. (pseud.) *Newzild and how to speak it* 1966
ACLAND, J.B. *Notes on sheep-farming in New Zealand* 1858
ACLAND, L.G.D. *The early Canterbury runs* 1930 First Series; 1940 Second Series; 1946 1st with 2nd, 3rd Series; 1951 (3edn.), (1975)
— *A sheep station glossary* (reprinted *Early Canterbury Runs* 1951, 1975, pp. 351 ff.) in *The Press* (Christchurch) 9 Sept.–2 Dec. 1933, 13 Jan.–27 Jan. 1934
Acts of the Provincial Legislature of the Province of Wellington 1873
ADAIR, H. *Mistress Mary* 1936
— *Red bunting* 1937
— *A torch is lit* 1936
— *Wanted a son* 1935
ADAM, J. *Emigration to New Zealand; description of the province of Otago, New Zealand* 1867
— *Twenty-five years of emigrant life in the south of New Zealand* 1876 (2edn.)
ADAMS, A.H. *Collected verses* 1913
— *Galahad Jones* 1909
— *Grocer greatheart* 1915
— *In London streets* 1906
— *Kowhai blossom; a New Zealand love story* 1903
— *A man's life* 1929
— *Maoriland and other verses* 1899
— *My friend, remember!* 1914
— *A touch of fantasy* 1912
— *Tussock land* 1904
ADAMS, C.W. *A spring in the Canterbury settlement* 1853
ADAMS, E.C. *The law of death and gift duties in New Zealand* 1940
ADAMS, J.G.E. *Kauri; a king among kings* 1973
ADAMS, L.S. *Thomas Dagger Adams* 1954
ADAMS, N.M. *The Fiat book of New Zealand trees* 1967, (1980, as *New Zealand native trees*)
— *Wild flowers* 1980
ADAMS, R.N. *The counterfeit seal* 1897
ADAMSON, G.E. *Twelve sonnets* 1918
ADCOCK, F. *High tide in the garden* 1971
— *Selected poems* 1983
ADCOCK, I. *Butter in a lordly dish* 1979
Address to the native inhabitants of New Zealand; Aborigines' Protection Society 1864
ADKIN, G.L. *The great harbour of Tara; traditional Maori place-names..of Wellington harbour* 1959
— *Horowhenua; its Maori place-names & their topographic & historical background* 1948, (1986)
ADLAM, A., see LOWTH, A.
ADSETT, D. *A magpie sings* 1963
Affairs of New Zealand; extracted from *Westminster Review* [London] 1846
'A GERMAN LADY' pseud. of M. MULLER *Notes of a tour through various parts of New Zealand* 1877
AGNEW, I. *The loner* 1974
Agricultural glossary; Ministry of Agriculture and Fisheries 1982
Agricultural organization in New Zealand: see BELSHAW, H. et al. (eds.)
AHL, F.N. *New Zealand through American eyes* 1948
AIREY, W.T.G. *New Zealand, a nation* c1925
AITKEN, A. *Gallipoli to the Somme* 1963
'AJOR' pseud. of JOHN PETRIE *The secret of Mount Cook* 1894
ALACK, F. *Share my joys* 1974
'A LADY' pseud. of MRS. WILLIAM *Facts; or the experiences of a recent colonist in New Zealand* 1883
ALDERTON, G.E. *Treatise and handbook of orange-culture in Auckland, New Zealand* 1884
ALDIS, M. *Thoughts on Anzac day* 1930
ALEXANDER, J.E. *Bush fighting* 1873
— *Incidents of the Maori war* 1863
— *Notes on the Maoris of New Zealand, with suggestions for their pacification and preservation.* 1865
ALEXANDER, W.F. (comp.) *A treasury of New Zealand verse* 1926
ALEXANDER, W.F. & CURRIE, A.E. (comp.) *New Zealand verse* 1906
Alfredton, the school and the people; J. Edmonds (comp.) 1987
ALGAR, F. *Handbook to Canterbury, 1863* 1863
— *A hand-book to the province of Wellington, New Zealand* 1858
— *New Zealand; a handbook for emigrants* 1860
— *New Zealand, its emigration and goldfields* 1853
ALINGTON, M.H. *Unquiet earth; a history of the Bolton Street cemetery* 1978
ALISON, E.W. *A New Zealander looks back* 1946
— *A New Zealander looks on* 1939
All about New Zealand being a complete record of colonial life 1873
ALLAN, A. *City of the plains* 1894
ALLAN, ANN *See our island* 1981
ALLAN, H.H. *Flora of New Zealand; vol. I. indigenous Tracheophyta* 1961 (1982 facs.)
ALLEN, C.R. *Brown smock* 1926
— *The child in the sun* 1912
— *The hedge-sparrow* 1937
— *A poor scholar* 1936
— *The ship beautiful* 1925
— *Sonnets and studies* 1933

— *Tales by New Zealanders* (ed.) 1938
— *Tarry, knight!* 1927
— *The young pretender* 1939
ALLEN, F. & MCLEAN, T. *Fred Allen on rugby* 1970
ALLEY, G.T. & HALL, D.O.W. *The farmer in New Zealand* 1941
ALLOM, A Letter 'Stock Farming in the Wairarapa': see EARP, G.B. *Handbook* (1852 edn.) [Also included in *Notes on New Zealand II* 1849.]
ALPERS, A.F.G. *A book of dolphins* 1960
— *The life of Katherine Mansfield* 1982
— *Maori myths and tribal legends retold* 1977
ALPERS, O.T.J. *Cheerful yesterdays* 1928
— (ed.) *College rhymes; an anthology of verse written by members of Canterbury College 1873–1923* 1923
— *Jubilee book of Canterbury rhymes* 1900
— *Three in a coach* 1891
'ALPHA' (pseud.) *Reminiscences of the goldfields* 1924
'AMNEMA' pseud. of A. MALCOLM
Amuri cookery book: see *The celebrated Amuri* [etc.]
ANDERSEN, J.C. *Jubilee history of South Canterbury* 1918
— *The lamp of psyche* 1908
— *Maori life in Ao-tea* 1922
— *Maori place names* 1942
— *Maori tales* 1924
— *New Zealand tales* 1927
— *Place-names in New Zealand* 1934
— *Popular names of New Zealand plants* Part 1 *TrNZI* LVI. pp.659–714 1926
— *Popular names of New Zealand plants* Part 2 *TrNZI* LVII. pp.905–977 1927
— *Songs unsung* 1903
ANDERSON, A. *Prodigious birds* 1989
ANDERSON, BARBARA *All the nice girls* 1993
— *Girls High* 1990
— *The house guest* 1995
— *Portrait of the artist's wife* 1992
ANDERSON, H. *The colonial minstrel* 1960
ANDERSON, H.J. *Men of the Milford Road* 1975
ANDERSON, L. & AITKEN, R. *A study of the speech and idiom of Maori children in the western Bay of Plenty* 1965
ANDERSON, M. *Both sides of the river* 1981
— *A letter from James* 1972
— *Mary-Lou; the story of a high-country lamb* 1975
— *A river rules my life* 1983
— *The water joey; a nostalgic look at the old wheat mills* 1976
ANDERSON, P.C. *The Chatham Islands* 1882
ANDERSON, W.A. *Doctor in the mountains* 1964, (1974)
ANDREWS, I. *Something to tell* 1944
ANDREWS, J.R.H. *The southern ark; zoological discovery in New Zealand 1769–1900* 1986
ANGAS, G.F. *Polynesia* 1866
— *The New Zealanders* 1847
— *Savage life and scenes in Australia and New Zealand* 1847, (1850)
ANGUS, J.H. *Donald Reid Otago Farmers Limited; a history of service to the farming community of Otago* 1978
ANNABELL, N. *Official history of the New Zealand Engineers 1914–1919* 1927
Annotated checklist of the birds of New Zealand 1970 (see also *Checklist* [etc.] 1990)
Annual review [of New Zealand Loan and Mercantile Coy] 1902
'AN OLD ACQUAINTANCE' pseud. of R. HENRY *The New Zealand rabbit and its prey* 1887
'AN OLD COLONIST' (pseud.) *Report of proceedings of the Legislative Council* 1849
ANSON, G.E. *Chats for the times* 1899
— *Jingo jingles* 1901
Antarctica; great stories from the frozen continent 1985
ANTHONY, F.S. *Follow the call; together with an unfinished novel..'Dave Baird'*; T.L. Sturm (ed.) 1924, (Dave Baird, a1927), (1975)
ANTHONY, F.S. *Gus Tomlins; together with the original stories of 'Me and Gus'*; T.L. Sturm. (ed.) various dates c1924, a1927, 1938, (1977)
ANZAAS Congress 1937: see *Handbook for New Zealand*
The Anzac book 1916
'ANZAC' (pseud.) *On the Anzac trail; being extracts from the diary of a New Zealand sapper* 1916
'A PROVINCIALIST' (pseud.) *Politics; a contribution to the question of the day* 1875
ARCHEY, G. *The native fishes of Canterbury* in SPEIGHT, R. et al. *Natural history of Canterbury* 1927
'A RESIDENT' (pseud.) *New Zealand; its history, institutions and industries* 1884
ARMFELT, N. *Catching up* 1971
ARMSTRONG, C.N. *Life without ladies* 1947
ARNOLD, R. *New Zealand's burning; the settlers' world in the mid 1880s* 1994
ARNOLD, T. *New Zealand letters of Thomas Arnold the younger*; J. Bertram (ed.) 1966
ARTHUR, J.K. *Kangaroo and Kauri* 1894

ARVIDSON, K.O. *Riding the pendulum; poems 1961–69* 1973
ASHBY, E. *Phantom fleet; the scows and scowmen of Auckland* 1975
ASHBY, W. *New Zealand* 1889
ASHCROFT, J. *Auriferous resources of Otago and Southland* 1889
— *Public morals* 1900
ASHDOWN, M. & LUCAS, D.J. *Tussock grasslands; landscape values and vulnerability* 1986
ASHTON-WARNER, S. *Bell call* 1964
— *Greenstone* 1967 (NZ edn.)
— *Incense to idols* 1960
— *I passed this way* 1979, (1980)
— *Teacher* 1963
— *Spinster* 1958
ASHWELL, B.Y. *Journal of a visit to the Loyalty, New Hebrides and Banks' Islands* 1860
ASHWORTH, H. *The fairies' secret wishing well* 1928
ASKEW, J. *A voyage to Australia and New Zealand* 1857
ASPDEN, ROB *A new life, 1865* 1981 (or 1982, privately printed)
Aspects of the apostolates of the Society of Mary in New Zealand since 1838; P. Ewart (ed.) 1989
'A SUFFOLK LADY' pseud. of E.L.M. WHITE
Atea, Nireaha, Putara, 1887–1987 centennial 1987
Atlas cookery book 1949, c1964
'A TRAMP, ESQ.' pseud. of J.D. WICKHAM *Casual ramblings in gumland and squatterdom* 1897
— *Casual ramblings. Up and down New Zealand* 1891
— *Ramblings* 1888
A trip to the Thames gold-fields, 1867
Auckland at full stretch; G.W.A. Bush & C.D. Scott (eds.) 1977
Auckland University College souvenir 1921
AUDLEY, E.H. *No boots for Mr. Moehau* 1963
AUGUST, S.G. *The Oreti anthology* 1933
— *Pictures and dreams* 1906
— *Princes Street and other Otago rhymes* 1917
— *Song of the children of Leda and other poems* 1935
— *Stewart Island verses* 1923
— *A trinket of rhyme* 1913
AUSTIN, W.S. *The official history of the New Zealand Rifle Brigade* 1924
The Australasian cookery book 1913
Australasian universal dictionary A.H. Irvine (ed.) ['New Zealand words and terms' pp.1266ff.] 1962
Australian and New Zealand Association for the Advancement of Science: see *Handbook for New Zealand*
AVERILL, A.W. *Fifty years in New Zealand* 1945
AVERY, K. *The Ken Avery songbook* 1974 (unpaged)
AWEKOTUKU, see TE AWEKOTUKU
AYLING, T. *Collins guide to the sea fishes of New Zealand* 1982, (1984 repr.)
AYLMER, I.E. *Distant homes; the Graham family in New Zealand* 1862
AYSON, W. *Pioneering in Otago; the recollections of William Ayson* 1937
— *Thomas; a pioneering story of adventures..in the life of the late Thomas Ayson* 1937
AYTON, C.J. *Diary 1899–1904* 1982

BABBAGE, S.B. *Hauhauism; an episode in the Maori wars 1863–1866* 1937
'BABBIE THE EGYPTIAN' (pseud.) *Gleams and glooms* 1905
Back then — (vol. 2) oral history interviews from the Birkenhead Public Library collection; C. Christie (comp.) c1988–89
BACON, R.L. *Along the road* 1964
— *In the sticks* 1963
BAGNALL, A.G. & PETERSEN, G.C. *William Colenso* 1948
BAILEY, A.M. *Birds of New Zealand*; (Museum Pictorial No.11) 1955
BAILEY, A.M. & SORENSEN, J.H. *Subantarctic Campbell Island*; (Denver Museum of Natural History Proceedings No.10) 1962
BAINES, W.M. *The narrative of Edward Crewe* 1874
BAIRD, J. *Tasmania and New Zealand; an emigrant's guide to Australasia* 1871
BAKER, A.N. *Whales & dolphins of New Zealand & Australia; an identification guide* 1983, 1990 (2edn.)
BAKER, L.A. *A daughter of the King* 1884
— *The devil's half-acre* 1900
— *In golden shackles* 1896
— *The majesty of man* 1895
— *Not in fellowship* 1902
— *A slum heroine* 1904
— *The untold half* 1899
— *Wheat in the ear* 1898
BAKER, M. *Never the faint hearted; Charles Baker, pioneer missionary, 1803–1875* 1986
BAKER, N. (ed.) *A surveyor in New Zealand (1857–1896)* 1932
BAKER, S.J. *New Zealand slang; a dictionary of colloquialisms* 1941
BAKEWELL, R.H. *The loyalty of the colonies*; extracted from *19th Century Magazine* Aug 16, 1890

BAKEWELL, R.J. *A coaster's freight* 1915
— *The lost tribute* 1926
BALDWIN, BEE *The home vegetable garden* 1984
BALDWIN, O. *New Zealand's French Pass and D'Urville Island; book two* 1981
BALE, A. *Maratoto gold* 1971
BALL, M. *The people makers* 1970
BALLANTYNE, D. *The Cunninghams* 1948, (1976 repr.)
— *A friend of the family* 1966
— *The last pioneer* 1963
— *The penfriend* 1980
— *Sydney Bridge upside down* 1968
— *The talkback man* 1978
BALLIS, P.H. *In and out of the world; Seventh-day Adventists in New Zealand* 1985
BALLOU, M.M. *Under the Southern Cross* 1888
BANKS, J. *The Endeavour journal of Joseph Banks 1768–1771*; J.C. Beaglehole (ed.) 1962
BANNERMAN, J.W.H. *Milestones; or wrecks of southern New Zealand* 1913
BARBER, L. *New Zealand; a short history* 1989
— *Red coat to jungle green* 1984
BARCLAY, P. *Notes on New Zealand* 1872
BARKER, H. *Todays and yesterdays* 1978
BARKER, M.A. *A Christmas cake in four quarters* 1872
— *Colonial memories* 1904
— *Station amusements in New Zealand* 1873
— *Station life in New Zealand* 1870 (reference edn. the 1973 repr. of the 1874 edn., the text and pagination of which, but not details of layout, are identical with those of the 1870 edn.)
— *Travelling about over new and old ground* 1883
BARLOW, P.W. *Kaipara* 1888
BARNETT, A.A. *Information for emigrants proceeding to New Zealand* 1874
BARNETT, S. & WOLFE, R. *At the beach; the great New Zealand holiday* 1993
— *New Zealand! New Zealand! In praise of kiwiana* 1989
BARNS-GRAHAM, J.W. *Sheep-station, New Zealand* 1950, 1959
BARR, JAMES *The old identities* 1879
BARR, JOHN *Poems and songs* 1861
— *Mihawhenua* 1888
BARR, R.A. *British rugby team in Maoriland; true story of the tour* 1908
BARRATT, G. *Bellinghausen; a visit to New Zealand, 1820* 1979
BARRETT, A. *Life of the Rev. J.H. Bumby* 1852
BARRINGTON, A.J. *Diary of a West Coast prospecting party* [1863–64], in *Early travellers in New Zealand*; N.M. Taylor (ed.) 1959
BARROW, N. *The smokers of hashish* 1934
BARROW, T. *Maori wood sculpture of New Zealand* 1969
— *The decorative arts of the New Zealand Maori* 1964 (1edn.)
BARRY, L.S. *In the lee of the Hokonuis*; L.C. Brown (ed.) 1966
BARRY, W.J. *Glimpses of the Australian colonies and New Zealand* 1903
— *Past and present* 1897
— *Up and down; or fifty years colonial experience* 1879
BARSTOW, R.C. *Our earliest settlers* 1882
BARTHORP, M. *To face the daring Maoris* 1979
BARTLETT, H.R. *A day with the oysterman* 1947
BARTLETT, J. *The emigrants; the story of John and Sarah Bell* 1974
BARTON, I.C. (ed.) *Kauri; its place in forest management.* 1972
BARTON, L.L. *Australians in the Waikato war 1863–1864* 1979
BASHAM, M.R. *The Aunt Daisy cookbook with household hints* 1968
— *Aunt Daisy's book of selected recipes* c1939
— *Aunt Daisy's cookery book of approved recipes* 1934
BASSETT, J. *Sir Harry Atkinson* 1969
— *Sir Harry Atkinson 1831–1892* 1975
BATEMAN, W. *The colonist* 1881
BATHGATE, A. *Colonial experiences* 1874
— *Far south fancies* 1890
— *Picturesque Dunedin* 1890
— *A plea for the establishment of Arbor Day* 1891
— *Random recollections* 1925
— *Sodger Sandy's bairn* 1913
— *Waitaruna* 1881
BATHGATE, J.A. *An illustrated guide to Dunedin* 1883
— *New Zealand, its resources and prospects* 1880
BATISTICH A.E. *Another mountain another song* 1981
— *Olive tree in Dalmatia* 1963
— *Sing Vila in the mountain* 1987
BATTEN, I.M. pseud. of I.M. COOK *Maori love legends* 1920
— *Silver nights* 1920
— *Star dust and sea foam* 1915
BATTEN, MADELEINE, see D. QUENTIN (pseud.)
BATTYE, S. & EAKIN, T. *The shadow of the valley; a play about the Brunner mine disaster* 1980

BAUCKE, W. *Where the white man treads* 1905, 1928 (2edn.)
— see also Skinner, H.D.
BAUER, L. *English word-formation* 1983
BAUGHAN, B.E. *Arthur's Pass and the Otira Gorge* 1925
— *Brown bread from a colonial oven* 1912
— also T.I.S. (pseud.) *People in prison* 1936
— *Reuben and other poems* 1903
— *Shingle-short and other verses* 1908
— *Verses* 1898
BAUME, F.E. *Burnt sugar* 1938
— *Half-caste* 1933
— *Tragedy track* 1933
BAXTER, A. *We will not cease* 1939
BAXTER, J.K. *Autumn testament* 1972
— *Beyond the palisade* 1944
— *Blow, wind of fruitfulness* 1948
— *Collected Plays*; H. McNaughton (ed.) 1982
— *Collected Poems*; J.E. Weir (ed.) 1980 [1979 is the copyright date]
— *The fire and the anvil* 1955
— *Horse* 1985 (composed 1962)
— *Selected poems* 1982
BAXTER, M. *The memoirs of Millicent Baxter* 1981
BAYLISS, DANIEL *A glimpse of shepherd life in New Zealand*; extracted from *Good Words* VII. 620 Sept. 1866
BAYLY, E.B. *A New Zealand courtship* 1896
BAYLY, G. *Sea life 60 years ago* 1885
BEADON, G. *Piako* 1876
BEAGLEHOLE, E. & P. *Some modern Maoris* 1946
BEAGLEHOLE, J.C. *New Zealand; a short history* 1936
— *The University of New Zealand* 1937
— *Victoria University College; an essay towards a history* 1949
— *Words for music* 1938
BEALE, G.C. *70 years in and around Auckland* 1937
BEARDSLEY, E.T. *Blackball 08* 1984
BEASLEY, A. *Pioneering days* 1936
BEATON, H. *Outside in* 1984
BEATON, J. *The universal cookery book* c1910
BEATTIE, J.H. *Early runholding in Otago* 1947
— *Far famed Fiordland, historic and descriptive* 1950
— *The first white boy born in Otago; story of T.B. Kennard* 1939
— *Mackenzie the sheep stealer* 1959
— *Maori place-names of Canterbury* 1945
— *Maori place-names of Otago* 1944
— *The Maoris and Fiordland* 1949
— *Otago place names* 1948
— *Our southernmost Maoris* 1954
— *Pioneer recollections*; fourth series, mainly of the Gore district 1956
— *The pioneers explore Otago* 1947
— *Trade hunting in the backblocks in the early seventies* 1913
— *Traditional lifeways of the southern Maori* c1920, (ed. Atholl Anderson 1994)
BEAUCHAMP, KATHLEEN, see MANSFIELD, K. (pseud.)
BEDFORD, L.H. *Under one standard* 1916
BEECHAM, J. *Remarks upon the latest official documents relating to New Zealand* 1838
BEGG, A.C. *Early voyages to Otago; diaries of Mr and Mrs A.C. Begg* 1960
BEGG, A.C. & N.C. *The world of John Boultbee* 1979
— *Port preservation* (Includes Appendix B *The journal of John Rodolphus Kent of the cutter 'Mermaid' 1823*; Appx. D *George Valintine Biggar and his diary of a trip to Preservation Inlet and the surrounding goldfields 1896*.) 1973
BEGG, J. *A visit to New Zealand* 1874
BEGGS, D. *Nature study; a handbook for teachers* 1954, (with freq. re-issues to 1965)
BELICH, J. *The New Zealand wars and the Victorian interpretation of racial conflict* 1986
BELL, G. *Sarabande* 1915
BELL, JAMES M. *The wilds of Maoriland* 1914
BELL, J.E. *Ballads of a racegoer* 1974
BELL, JOHN *In the shadow of the bush* 1899
BELLAIRS, E.H.W. *Thirty years ago* 1884
BELSHAW, H. (ed.) *New Zealand* 1947
BELSHAW, H. et al. (eds.) *Agricultural organization in New Zealand* 1936
BELSHAW, S.M. *Man of integrity; a biography of Sir Clifton Webb* 1979
BELTON, C. *Outside the law in New Zealand* 1939
BENNETT, F.O. *A Canterbury tale* c1980
BENNETT, G. *Gatherings of a naturalist in Australasia* 1860
— *Wanderings in New South Wales, [etc.] during 1832, 1833, and 1834* 1834
BENSEMANN, E.C. *Apple Culture* 1939
BENTLEY, J.H. & FRASER, M. *A grand limerick tour* 1985
BERENS, L.H. & SINGER, I. *The story of my dictatorship* 1894

BERROW, N. *Fingers for ransom* 1939
— *It howls at night* 1937
— *Oil under the window* 1936
— *One thrilling night* 1938
— *The secret dancer* 1936
BERRY, J. *Farming in north New Zealand* 1880
— *New Zealand at the beginning of the century* 1901
BERRY, KEN *First offender* 1980
BERTRAM, J.M. *Capes of China slide away* 1993
— *Occasional verses* 1971
— *Return to China* 1957
— *The shadow of a war; a New Zealander in the Far East, 1939–1946* 1947
BEST, A.D.W. *The journal of Ensign Best 1837–1843*; N.M. Taylor (ed.) 1966
BEST, E. *Fishing methods and devices of the Maori*; Dom. Museum Bull. No.12 1929
— *The lore of the whare-wananga* 1913
— *The Maori as he was* 1924 (reissued 1934)
— *Maori religion and mythology* 1924, (1976) pt. 1; c1930, (1982) pt. 2
— *Maori storehouses and kindred structures* 1916
— *Tuhoe; the children of the mist* 1925
BETHELL, M.U. *Collected poems* 1950
— *Day and night; poems 1924–34* 1939
— *From a garden in the Antipodes* 1929
— *Time and place* 1936
BEVERIDGE, J.C.B. *Antipodes notebook* 1949
Beyond expectations; fourteen New Zealand women write about their lives; Margaret Clark (ed.) 1986
BEZAR, E. *Some reminiscences of the 'Die Hards'*; (57th West Middlesex Battalion) 1891
BIDWILL, J.C. *Rambles in New Zealand* 1841, (1952)
BIDWILL, W.E. & WOODHOUSE, A.E. *Bidwill of Pihautea* 1927
BIERNACKI, C.C. *Poems, verse & rhymes* 1949
BILLING, G. *The alpha trip* 1969
— *Forbush and the penguins* 1965
— *The primal therapy of Tom Purslane* 1980
— *Statues; a novel* 1971
BINNEY, D.H. *Long lives the king* 1985
BINNEY, J. et al. *Mihaia — the prophet Rua and his community at Maungapohatu* 1979
BINSWANGER, O. *And how do you like this country?* 1945
BIOLETTI, H. *The Yanks are coming* 1989
BISHOP, C. *Home and abroad* 1985
BISHOP, W.K. (publisher) *Guide to Wellington and district* 1882, (1883)
BLACKE, S.E.M. *Flights from the land of the bellbird and rata* 1900
BLACKIE, I.D. & M. *A brief history of the Blackie family* 1981
BLACKMORE, A.A. *The cooking of New Zealand fish and other seafoods* ?1928
— *Vegetable cookery and meatless dishes* 1927
BLAIR, I.D. *Life and work at Canterbury Agricultural College* 1956
BLAIR, J. *Lays of the old identities* 1889
BLAIR, M.R.E. *At Fort Turanga* 1932
— *By Pacific waters* 1932
— *Kowhai blossoms* 1929
— *The stained glass-window* 1934
BLAIR, W.N. *The industries of New Zealand* 1884
BLAKE, A.H. *Sixty years in New Zealand* 1909
BLAKE, L. *In the rough* 1894
— *Supper flies and other pieces* 1895
BLAKISTON, A.J. *My yesteryears* 1952
BLANC, A.D.G. *Money, medicine and the masses* 1949
BLAND, P. *Primitives* 1979
BLAND, W.B. *Slums of Auckland* 1942
BLOUET, P.L. *John Bull and Co.* 1894
BLOXHAM, A. & L. *The jet boat; the making of a New Zealand legend* 1983
The blue and the white; Merivale-Papanui Rugby Football Club 1982
BLYTH, J.A. ed. *New Zealand gold mining yearbook* 1935
BODELL, J. *A soldier's view of empire; the reminiscences 1831–1892*; K. Sinclair (ed.) 1982
BOLITHO, H.H. *The glorious oyster* 1929, (1960)
— *Book of the C1 camp; Tauherenikau MC* 1918
— *Judith Silver* 1929
— *The New Zealanders* 1928
— *Solemn boy* 1927
— *Thirty years* 1947
— *With the prince in New Zealand* 1920
BOLLARD, E.G. *Prospects for horticulture; a research viewpoint*; DSIR discussion paper No.6 1981
BOLLINGER, C. *Against the wind; the story of the New Zealand Seamen's Union* 1968
— *Grog's own country; the story of liquor licensing in New Zealand* 1959
BONWICK, J. *Geography of Australia and New Zealand* 1855, (1856)
The book of Canterbury rhymes 1866, 1883 (2edn.)

A book of New Zealand; J.C. Reid (ed.) 1964
The book of Waimate 1929
BOOTH, G.T. *Anzac Day; Rakaia* 1917
BOOTH, P. *Footsteps in the sea* 1964
— *Long night among the stars* 1961
BOOTH, R.B. *Five years in New Zealand (1859–1864)* 1912
Boots, belts, rifle & pack; a New Zealand soldier at war 1917–1919; Dorothy McKenzie & L. Malcolm (eds.) 1992
BOREHAM, F.W. *The bachelors of Mosgiel* 1933
— *Empty pitchers* c1932
— *George Augustus Selwyn D.D.; pioneer bishop of New Zealand* 1911
— *My manse in Maoriland* 1929
— *A vagabond of the bush* 1937
BOSTON, J. *Incomes policy in New Zealand* 1984
BOSTON, J., MARTIN, J, PALLOT, J, & WALSH, P. *Public management; the New Zealand model* 1996
BOSWELL, JAMES *Life of Johnson*; R.W. Chapman. (ed.) 1953, (1960)
— *The ominous years 1774–1776*; C. Ryskamp & F.A. Pottle (eds.) 1963
BOSWELL, JEAN *Dim horizons* 1955
— *Ernie and the rest of us* 1960
BOSWORTH, I. *A trip to New Zealand* 1930
Botany Division (New Zealand DSIR); triennial report 1982–1984 1987
BOULTBEE, J. *Journal of a rambler; the journal of John Boultbee*; June Starke (ed.) 1986
Note: c1835 is used as the date of composition for the body of the journal; c1826–27 is used for the vocabulary as the terminal date of its compilation.
BOWDEN, G.W.B. *Roads and fairies* 1918
— *Wellington verses* 1917
BOWDEN, T.A. *Manual of New Zealand geography* 1869
— *A memorial upon colonial education* 1868
BOWEN, C.C. *Poems* 1861
BOWEN, W.G. *Wool away! the technique and art of shearing* 1955
BOWERBANK, F.T. *A doctor's story* 1958
BOWMAN, HILDEBRAND, see *The travels of Hildebrand Bowman*
BOWMAN, H.O. *Port Chalmers, gateway to Otago* 1948
BOWRON, W. *The manufacture of cheese, butter and bacon in New Zealand* 1883
BOYACK, N. *Behind the lines; the lives of New Zealand soldiers in the First World War* 1989
BOYD, J. *Pumice & pines; the story of Kaingaroa Forest* 1992
BOYD, J.P. *Moonlight* 1971
BOYD, M. *Reminiscences of fifty years* 1871
BOYD, M.C. *City of the plains; a history of Hastings* 1984
BOYD, M.S. *Our stolen summer* 1900
BRACKEN, T. *Behind the tomb and other poems* 1871
— *Flowers of the free lands* 1877
— *Lays and lyrics* 1893
— *The lays of the land of the Maori and moa* 1884
— *Musings in Maoriland* 1890
— *The New Zealand tourist* 1879
— *Paddy Murphy's annual* 1886
— *Paddy Murphy's budget* 1880
— *Tom Bracken's Annual* 1896 [No.1], 1897 [No.2]
BRADBURY E.E. (ed.) *Settlement and development of the King Country* 1923
BRADLEY, E.K. *The great Northern Wairoa* (1972), 1982 4edn. (repr.)
BRADSHAW, J. *New Zealand as it is* 1883
— *New Zealand of to-day* 1888
BRADSTOCK, M.A. *Fishing; a guide for Kiwi kids* 1991
BRAIM, T.H. *New homes* 1870
BRAMBLEY, M. *The Sea-cockies of Manukau* 1966
BRANDENBURG, W. *Outdoor vegetable growing* 1980
BRANDON, L.E. *'Ukneadit'; Home for Incurables bazaar* 1905
BRASCH, C. *Ambulando* 1964
— *Collected poems* 1984
— *Indirections; a memoir 1909–1947* 1980
— *The land and the people* 1939
BRATHWAITE, E. *The evil day* 1967
BRAYSHAW, N.H. *Canvas and gold; a history of the Wakamarina goldfields and Lower Pelorus Valley* 1964
Bread Making in New Zealand; Bycroft Ltd. (publisher) 1934
Bread; the basic food; facts & recipes issued by New Zealand's leading bakers c1936
BREAM, F. *I'm sorry Amanda* 1974
— *Island of fear* 1982
BREES, S.C. *Guide and description of the panorama of New Zealand* 1849
BREMER, J.E. *Port Craig and the Waitutu forest 1925 and 1983* 1983
BREMNER, J. *Woolscours of New Zealand* 1985
BREMNER, J.G. *The Mt. Ida goldfields, a merchant's memories*; (Rutherford, J. (ed.) from the *Mt. Ida Chronicle*, 1911) 1988
BRENCHLEY, H.F. *Little gardens* 1929

BRERETON, C.B. *No roll of drums* 1947
BRETON, W.H. *Excursions in New South Wales* [etc.] 1833
BRETT, H. *White wings* 1924
BRETT, H. & HOOK, H. *The Albertlanders* 1927
Brett's colonists guide 1883 (1902)
Brett's gardening guide for New Zealand gardeners 1921 (2edn.), 1949 (rev. edn.)
Brett's New Zealand and South Sea Pacific pilot; T.C. Tilly (ed.) 1886
BRIDGFORD, S.H. *Dunedin and other poems* 1936
BRIGHT, A.D. *By bush and sea* 1931
— *The fortunate princeling* 1909
— *Three Xmas gifts* 1901
BRIGHT, J. *A handbook for emigrants and others* 1841
BRIGHT, W. *From southern climes* 1881
BRINSDEN, J.B. *Dame Mugford's cat* 1938
British overseas settlement delegation report 1923
BRITTAIN, P.J. *Report on New Zealand* 1883
BRITTENDEN, R.T. *Red leather and silver fern* 1965
BROAD, I.L.M. *The New Zealand exhibition cookery book* 1889
BRODIE, J., see GUTHRIE, J. (pseud.)
BRODIE, J.W. *A history of Government Life postage stamps* 1988
BRODIE, W. *Remarks on the past and present state of New Zealand* 1845
BROMBY, R. *An eyewitness history of New Zealand* 1985
BROOKER, S.G. et al. *New Zealand medicinal plants* 1981
BROOKER, S.G., CAMBIE, R.C., & COOPER, R.C. *Economic native plants of New Zealand* 1988
BROOKES, E.S. *Frontier life* 1892
BROOKFIELD, H. *The fugitives* 1939
BROOKING, T.W.H. *Massey; its early years* 1977
BROOME, F.N. *The crisis in New Zealand*; extracted from *Macmillan's Magazine* 1869
— *Poems from New Zealand* 1868
BROOMHALL, J. *Fragments from the journal of J. Broomhall..during..a sojourn [1876–77]..in the colony of New Zealand* 1877
BROWN, A.E. *The farmer's wife* 1939
BROWN, G.P. *Lay of the Bantry Bay* 1917
BROWN, J.C. *Plain and practical letters to working people* 1889
BROWN, J. MACMILLAN *Modern education* 1908
BROWN, JOHN *Ashburton, New Zealand* 1940
BROWN, JOHN JNR. *Hours of leisure* 1884
BROWN, M. *The weaver's apprentice* 1986
BROWN, M.C. *Difficult country; an informal history of Murchison* 1976
BROWN, W. *New Zealand and its aborigines* 1845
BROWN, W.E. *A short history of Belfast, Canterbury, New Zealand* 1949
BROWNING, R.K. *Watch your language* 1978
BROWNSEY, P.J. & SMITH-DODSWORTH, J.C. *New Zealand ferns and allied plants* 1989
BRUCE, A.S. *The early days of Canterbury* 1932
BRUCE, G. *Life in the hinterland of the South Island* 1977
BRUCHER, H. *Useful plants of neotropical origin and their wild relatives* 1989
BRUNNER, T. *Journal of an expedition to explore the interior of the Middle Island, New Zealand, 1846–48*; in *Early travellers in New Zealand*; N.M. Taylor (ed.) 1959
BRUNO, F. pseud. of A.F. ST BRUNO *Desert daze* 1944
— *The hellbuster* 1959
— *Maleesh George* ?1946
— *Sa-eeda wog!* 1944
BRUNTON, A. *Messengers in blackface* 1973
BRYANT, J.C. *Woodland echoes* 1906
BRYCE, J.J. *Modern democracies* 1921, (1929)
BRYSON, E. *Look back in wonder* 1965
BUCHANAN, E.M. *The song of the Christmas tree* 1908
BUCHANAN, J. *Manual of the indigenous grasses of New Zealand* 1880
BUCK, P.H. *The coming of the Maori* (Cawthron lecture 1922), 1925, (1929)
— *The coming of the Maori* 1949
— *Vikings of the sunrise* 1938, 1954 (NZ edn.)
BUCK, P.H., see also *Na to hoa aroha*
BUCKLAND, W.F. *Morning rays* 1870
BUCKLEY, G.C. *Of toffs and toilers from Cornwall to New Zealand* 1983
BUCKNILL, C.E.R. *Sea shells of New Zealand* 1924
BUDDLE, T. *The aborigines of New Zealand* 1851
— *The Maori King movement in New Zealand* 1860
BUICK, T.L. *The moa-hunters of New Zealand* 1937
— *The Treaty of Waitangi* 1936 (3edn.)
BULL, F. *Dominion ditties, patriotic and pungent* 1911
BULLEN, F.T. *The cruise of the 'Cachalot'* 1897, (1906)
BULLER, JAMES *Forty years in New Zealand* 1878
— *The Maori war; a lecture* 1869
— *New Zealand; the future England of the southern hemisphere* 1857
— *New Zealand past and present* 1880
BULLER, W.L. *A history of the birds of New Zealand* 1873, 1888 (2edn.)

The Bulletin reciter; A.G. Stephens (ed.) 1901, (1902 repr.)
BULLOCK, M., see also 'TUA-O-RANGI' (pseud.)
— *Wonderland* 1899
Bull's Wellington almanack and mercantile directory 1866
BUNBURY, T. *Reminiscences of a veteran* 1861
BURDON, R.M. *High country* 1938
— *Outlaw's progress* 1943
BURFORD, R. *A description of a view of the Bay of Islands* c1838
BURGESS, R. *Confessions of Richard Burgess*; D. Burton (ed.) 1983
— *Life of Richard Burgess the notorious highwayman and murderer* 1866
BURLEIGH, C.J. *The Burleigh family* 1984
BURN, D.W.M. *Advent hymn* 1911
— *Cantilenosae nugae* 1891
— *Eggs and olives* 1930
— *Flax and fernseed* 1933
— *Ode for peace day* 1904
— *Pedlar's pack* 1932
— *Soundings* 1931
BURNS, B. *A brief narrative of the remarkable history of Barnet Burns* 1835, 1844
BURNS, D. *Scottish echoes from New Zealand* 1883
BURNS, P. *Fatal success; a history of the New Zealand Company* 1989
BURNS, T. *A brief account of origin and history..of the Presbyterian Church of Otago* 1865
BURR, B. *The better way* 1918
BURR, VAL A. *Mosquitoes and sawdust; a history of Scandinavians in early Palmerston North and surrounding districts* 1995
BURROWS, R. *Extracts from a diary kept..during Heke's war in the North in 1845* 1886
BURTON, A.H. *The Maori at home* 1885
BURTON, D. *Delectable fruits; cookery for New Zealanders* 1985
— *Two hundred years of New Zealand food and cookery* 1982
BURTON, M. *South Wairarapa Workingmen's Club centennial book* 1977
BURTON, O.E. *The Auckland regiment* 1922
— *In prison* 1945
— *The silent division* 1935
— *Youth versus the liquor traffic* 1925
BUSBY, J. *Our colonial empire and the case of New Zealand* 1866
'BUSH LAWYER' pseud. of F.W. SHORTLAND *Police court tales of Maoriland* 1916
BUTCHERS, A.G. *The education system* 1932
— *Young New Zealand* 1929
BUTLER, A.R. *Glimpses of Maoriland* 1886
BUTLER, F.B. *Early days; Taranaki* 1942
BUTLER, J.G. *Earliest New Zealand; the journals and correspondence of the Rev. John Butler*; R.J. Barton (comp.) 1977
BUTLER, P. *Opium and gold* 1977
BUTLER, R. *Trial of Butler for the Dunedin tragedy* 1880
BUTLER, S. *Erewhon* 1872 (1873), 1901 (the reference edn. is the rev. edn. of Everyman Library 1932, 1960 repr.)
— *Erewhon Revisited* 1872 (the reference edn. is the 1873 edn. of Everyman Library 1932, 1960 repr.)
— *The family letters of Samuel Butler*; A. Silver (ed.) 1962
— *A first year in Canterbury settlement* 1863 (chapter numbers given)
— *The 'Forest Creek' Manuscript* 1860 (Canterbury Museum), see MALING, P.B. *Samuel Butler in Mesopotamia* 1960
BUTLER, W.E. *Poems* 1930
BYRNE, A.E. *Official history of the Otago Regiment, N.Z.E.F.* 1921
BYRNE, J.C. *Twelve years' wanderings in the British colonies* 1848

CADEY: see PRUDENCE CADEY (pseud.)
CAIRD, J.A.H. *Notes on sheep-farming in New Zealand* 1874
CALLAGHAN, F.R. (ed.) *Science in New Zealand* 1957
Cambridge history of the British Empire vol. VII, pt. II 1933
CAMERON, B. *In fair New Zealand* 1899
CAMERON, D.J. *Caribbean crusade* 1972
CAMERON, E.M. (comp.), see *The ideal cookery book*
CAMERON, W.J. *New Zealand* 1965
A campaign on the West Coast of New Zealand 1866
CAMPBELL, ALISTAIR *Blue rain* 1967
— *Collected Poems 1947–1981* 1981
— *The dark lord of Savaiki* 1980
— *The frigate bird* 1989
— *Island to island* 1984
— *Mine eyes dazzle* 1950
— *Sanctuary of spirits* 1963
— *Wild honey* 1964
CAMPBELL, E. *The present state, resources and prospects of New Zealand* 1840
CAMPBELL, G. *The golden north* 1963
CAMPBELL, J.F. *The postcripts of Crowbar (J. Finlay Campbell)* 1943
CAMPBELL, J.L. *Poenamo; sketches of the early days of New Zealand* 1881

CAMPBELL, LADY *Martin Tobin* 1864
CAMPBELL, R. *Reminiscences of a long life in Scotland, New Zealand, &c.* 1894, 1904 (These are separate publications for private circulation.)
CAMPBELL, R.W. *The kangaroo marines* 1915
CAMPBELL, W.M. *By reef and range; weird tales and wildlife stories of Maoriland* 1955
CANNON, F.E. *Irene O'Neal* 1911
The Canterbury almanac 1853–4
The Canterbury colony; its sites and prospects 1976
Canterbury (New Zealand); its resources and progress 1889
Canterbury old and new 1850–1900 1900
Canterbury Provincial Council; the Lyttelton & Christchurch railway proposals 1860
Canterbury Rhymes: see *The Book of Canterbury Rhymes*
CAREY, R. *Narrative of the late war in New Zealand* 1863
CARGILL, J. *Otago, New Zealand* 1860
CARKEEK, W.C. *The Kapiti Coast* 1966
CARLETON, H. *The life of Henry Williams* 1874
— *A page from the history of New Zealand* 1854
CARLYON, C.C., see JENKYNS, C.C. (pseud.)
CARMAN, DULCE pseud. of E.M. DULCE DRUMMOND *The broad stairway* 1924
— *Dream of the dark* 1955
— *Golden windows* 1951
— *Neath the Maori moon* 1948
— *The riddle of the ranges* 1950
CARPENTER, W. *Relief for the unemployed; emigration and colonization considered* 1841
CARR, A.I. *Country work and life in New Zealand* 1913
CARR, C. *Poems* 1944
CARR, R. *Diary of a pig hunter* 1986
CARRICK, R.O. *Historical records of New Zealand South prior to 1840* 1903
— *New Zealand's lone lands* 1892
— *A romance of Lake Wakatipu* 1892
CARRINGTON, C.E. *John Robert Godley of Canterbury* 1950
CARRINGTON, MARY *Memories of Mary Carrington by H.V.L.*; H.V. Langford (ed.) 1914
CARRINGTON, MOLLY *Home to the mountains* 1932
CARTER, C.R. *Life and recollections of an early colonist* 1866 (vol. I & II), 1875 (vol. III)
— *Round the world leisurely* 1878
CARTER, REV. ROBERT *From the black rocks, on Friday*; extracted from *All the Year Round* 17 May 1862, 1862, (1950)
CARTER, RONALD *Little ships; New Zealand's yachting fleet* (1944), 1948 (rev. edn.)
CARTER, S.D. *Life in New Zealand*; extracted from *Hours at Home*, II. 426ff. (New York) 1865
CARTER, U.I. *The national cookery book* 1922
Carterton District School Centennial Celebration 1961
CASEY, R. (pseud.) *As short a spring* 1963
— *Spoke in the wheel* 1987
CASTLE, R.B. *Arcadian grove* 1939
— *Fleeting music* 1937
— *Psaltery and trumpet* 1948
Catalogue of New Zealand stamps; Campbell Paterson Ltd, loose-leaf handbook 1984
CAWKWELL, W.J. *Local industry and the New Zealand government* 1874
The celebrated Amuri cookery book; J. Thomson (Waiau Plunket Branch) (comp.) 1916, (1927)
A centennial treasury of Otago verse; A.E. Currie (ed.) 1949
CHALMERS, A. *The wintering house* 1989
CHAMBERLIN, T.C. *Songs from the forests of Tane* 1912
CHAMBERS, W. *A word about Otago*; extracted from *Chambers Journal* 6 Sept. 1873
CHAMBERS, W.A. *Samuel Ironside in New Zealand 1839–1858* 1982
CHAMBERS, W.F. *The new chum and other verses* 1903
CHAMIER, G. *Philosopher Dick* 1891
— *A south sea siren* 1895
CHAPMAN, A.B. & LOVE, V. *Menus, recipes and why?* 1939
CHAPMAN, B. & PENMAN, D.R. *The garden pest book* 1982
CHAPMAN, F. *The interest and value of New Zealand history* 1928
CHAPMAN, F.R. *Notes on the depletion of the fur seal in the southern seas* 1893
CHAPMAN, H.S. *The New Zealand portfolio* 1843
CHAPMAN, M.A. & LEWIS, M.H. *An introduction to the freshwater crustacea of New Zealand* 1976
CHAPMAN, R. & SINCLAIR, K. *Studies of a small democracy* 1963
CHAPMAN-COHEN, J. *Woodland poems* 1936
Chapman's handbook to the farm and garden 1862
CHAPPELL, A.B. *Souvenir of Hamilton's diamond jubilee 1864–1924; early Hamilton* 1924
CHAPPLE, G. *South* 1986
— *The tour* 1981
CHARLES, J. *Black billy tea; New Zealand ballads* 1981
CHAVASSE, G. *Integrity* 1990
Checklist of the birds of New Zealand and the Ross Dependency, Antarctica 1990 (3edn.)

CHEESEMAN, C.E. *A rolling stone* 1886
CHEESEMAN, T.F. *Manual of the New Zealand flora* 1906
CHEPMELL, F.D. *Songs of the unseen* 1933
CHERRILL, A.L. *Story of a New Zealand sheep farm* 1950
CHESNEY, CAPT. C. *New Zealand considered as a field for the emigration of military men* 1859
CHILD, J. *New Zealand insects* 1974
— *New Zealand shells* 1974
CHILTON, C., see *The subantarctic islands of New Zealand* 1909
CHINNOCK, R.J. *Common ferns and fern allies in New Zealand* 1987
— *Ferns and fern allies in New Zealand* 1974
CHISHOLM, D. *From the heart; a biography of Sir Brian Barratt-Boyes* 1987
CHISHOLM, J. *Brind of the Bay of Islands* 1979
CHOLMONDELEY, T. *A letter to John Robert Godley Esq.* 1852
— *Ultima thule; thoughts suggested by residence in New Zealand* 1854
The chosen place and other stories, poems and reflections; Mairangi writers 1987
CHRISTIE, J. *About poets and poetry* 1903
— *A letter from New Zealand Atlantic Monthly* 1900
— *Offerings* 1909
— *Poems and prose* 1892
— *A prophet of the people* 1898
— *The spell of Alpin* 1915
CHRISTIE, P.L. *Candles and canvas; a Danish family in New Zealand* 1987
CHRISTMAS-HARVEY, M.S. *The strawberry patch and leaves from life* 1948
CHUDLEIGH, E.R. *Diary of E.R. Chudleigh 1862–1921, Chathams Islands*; E.C. Richards (ed.) 1950
CHURCH, H. *Poems* 1904
— *Poems* 1912
— *Tonks* 1916
CHURCHMAN, G.B. *The route of the coastal Pacific Express* 1989
CHURCHMAN, G.B. & HURST, A.W. *Railways of New Zealand; a journey through history* 1990
CLAPPERTON, A.A. *The Lauder brothers, New Zealand* 1936
CLARK, A. *My erratic pal* 1918
CLARKE, B. *His imported wife* 1932
CLARKE, D.B. & BOOTH, PAT *The boot* 1966
CLARKE, G. *Notes on early life in New Zealand* 1903
CLARKE, J. *The thoughts of chairman Fred* 1976
CLARKE, K. *Diary 1864 in* BEGG, A.C. *Early voyages to Otago* 1960
CLARK, K.M. *A Southern Cross fairy tale* 1891
CLARKSON, R.E. *Brick dust* 1934
CLARKSON, B.D., SMALE, M.C., ECROYD, C.E. *Botany of Rotorua* 1991
CLAYDEN, A. *The England of the Pacific* 1879
— *New Zealand in 1884*; extracted from the proceedings of the Royal Colonial Institute 1885
— *A popular handbook to New Zealand, its resources and industries* 1886
CLEARY, F. *A pocketful of years* 1975
CLEARY, H. (ed.) *God or no-God in schools* 1911
CLEVELAND, L. *Dark laughter; war in song and popular culture* 1994
— *The great New Zealand songbook* 1991
— *The iron hand; New Zealand soldiers' poems from WWII* 1979
CLIFFORD, G. *Notes from a Skipper's log book; an account of New Zealand's Bay of Islands* 1985, (1986 repr.)
CLOKE, F. *Songs of New Zealand and various verses* 1931 (3edn.)
CLOUGH, A.H. *The poems* 1974
CLYDE, A. *Te Kooti and other poems* 1872
CLYDE, CONSTANCE pseud. of CONSTANCE (CLYDE) MCADAM *New Zealand; country and people* 1925
— *A pagan's love* 1905
COAD, N.E. *Such is life and other New Zealand stories* 1931
COATES, D. *The principles, objects, and plan of the New Zealand Association examined* 1837, (1838)
COCHRANE, G. *Images of midnight city* 1976
— *The sea the landsman knows; poems* 1980
— *Tin nimbus* 1995
COCHRANE, G. et al. *Solstice* 1979
COCKAYNE, L. *The cultivation of New Zealand plants* 1923
— *New Zealand plants and their story* 1910, 1919 (2edn.)
— *The vegetation of New Zealand* 1921, 1928 (2edn.)
COCKAYNE, L. & TURNER, E.P. *The trees of New Zealand* 1939 (2edn.)
COCKBURN-HOOD, T.H. *Chowbokiana, or notes about the antipodes and antipodeans* 1875
— *Notes of a cruise in HMS 'Faun' in the western Pacific in the year 1862* 1863
COCKER, J. *Blossomby idylls* 1903
— *Winning from scratch* 1926
COCKERTON, J.S. *'Merely a moke'—a summary in light verse of Apuleius' metamorphoses* 1916

CODY, J.F. *21 Battalion*; (New Zealand in the Second World War: official history) 1953
— *28 (Maori) Battalion*; (New Zealand in the Second World War: official history) 1956
— *Man of two worlds; Sir Maui Pomare* 1953
COLE, J.R. *It was so late* 1949, (1978)
COLENSO, W. *The authentic and genuine history of the signing of the Treaty of Waitangi, New Zealand, February 5 and 6, 1840* 1890
— *A classification and description of some newly discovered ferns* 1845
— *Excursion in the Northern Island of New Zealand in the summer of 1841–2*; in *Early travellers in New Zealand*; N.M. Taylor (ed.) [The publication date was Jan. 1844 in the London Journal of Botany: Taylor replaces this text with one from TrNZI 1894 for pp.17–34.] 1959
— *Fiat justitia; being a few thoughts respecting..Kereopa* 1871
— *Fifty years ago in New Zealand* 1888
— *In memoriam; an account of visits to and crossing over the Ruahine mountain range* 1884
— *Journal of a naturalist in some little known parts of New Zealand*; extracted from London Journal of Botany 3 1844
— *Three literary papers* 1883
College rhymes: see ALPERS, O.T.J.
COLLIER, J. *The literature relating to New Zealand* 1889
COLLINS, D. *An account of the English colony in New South Wales 1798, 1804* (2edn.)
COLLINS, J.C. *Bugle notes* 1914
COLLINSON, T.B. *Remarks on the military operations in New Zealand* in *Papers connected with the duties of the Corps of Royal Engineers vol. III new series* 1853
Colonial everyday cookery c1897, rev. edn. 1908 [This eventually became *Whitcombe's everyday cookery* c1942, and various dates thereafter.]
The colonial songster (Nos. 1–5) (also in some copies and editions called *The New Zealand Songster*) c1875
The colonization of New Zealand from the counties of Devon and Cornwall 1839, (1840)
COMBS, F.L. *Half lengths of pupils & people* 1944
— *The harrowed toad* 1939
Comic guide to Dunedin: see WHITWORTH, R.P.
The mutual relations between the Canterbury Association and the purchasers of land in the Canterbury settlement; Committee of Land Purchasers, Canterbury Association 1853
COMPTON, A.G. *Through the open door* 1951
CONDLIFFE, J.B. *New Zealand in the making* 1930
CONDON, M.P. *Hurleyville* 1992
CONEY, J. *The playing mantis* 1986
CONEY, S. *Out ot the frying pan; inflammatory writings 1972–89* 1990
CONNELL, R.P. & HADFIELD, J.W. *Agriculture; a textbook* 1940 (5edn.)
CONNELLY, M.H. *Twelve poems* 1948
CONNOR, H.E. *The poisonous plants in New Zealand* 1951, 1977 (2edn.)
CONSTABLE, L.M.B. *Poems up to sixteen* 1937
— *Poet in khaki* 1940
— *Song of youth* 1942
— *Stories in embryo* 1938
Consultation on observance of Anzac Day; Church and Society Commission 1972
Contemporary New Zealand; (New Zealand Institute of International Affairs) 1938
Contemporary New Zealand poetry; F. Adcock (ed.) 1982
COOK, E. *The small world of the roadside* 1986
COOK, H. CALDWELL *The play way; an essay in educational method* 1917
COOK, H.H. *The cave of Endor* 1927
— *Far flung* 1925
COOK, I.M., see BATTEN, I.M. (pseud.)
COOK, J. *The journals of Captain James Cook on his voyages of discovery*; J.C. Beaglehole (ed.) I(1955), II(1961), III(1967), IV(1974)
COOKE, G.S. *Phantom gold* 1925
COOKE, M.C. *Vegetable wasps and plant worms* 1892
The cookery book of the New Zealand Women's Institutes 1936 (4edn.), 1957 & various edns.
Cookery calendar, 200 recipes; special Maori section; Poverty Bay Federation of Women's Institutes (comp.) 1935
The Cook's Bread Book; M. Browne, H. Leach, & N. Tichborne (eds.) 1989
COOP, I.E. *Shearing ewes before lambing* 1950
COOPER, A.F. *Wag's Tales* 1983
COOPER, G.S. *Journal of an expedition overland from Auckland to Taranaki (1849–50)* 1851
COOPER, I.R. *A handbook to the province of Nelson, New Zealand* 1858
— *The New Zealand settler's guide* 1857
COOPER, L. & R. *New Zealand gemstones* 1966
COOPER, T. *A digger's diary at the Thames* 1867; in *Victorian New Zealand*; [Hocken Library] reprint series No.5 1978
COOPER, W. *His wedding-day wish* 1913
— *Majority memento* 1914
COOTE, W. *Wanderings south and east* 1882, (1883)

COOZE, F.I. *Kiwis in the Pacific* 1944
— *My little state home in suburbia* 1946
— *Ten bob each way* 1946
CORBALLIS, R. & GARRETT, S. *Introducing Witi Ihimaera* 1984
CORK, A.G. *Green wood — white wood* 1938
CORLETT, MRS *Claribel and other poems* 1874
— *Parliamentary skits and sketches* 1871
Correspondence between the Wesleyan Missionary Committee and the Rt. Honourable Earl Grey 1848
COSTELLO, J. *Howard; the life and times of Sir Howard Morrison* 1992
COSTELLO, JOHN & FINNEGAN, P. *Tapestry of turf; the history of New Zealand racing* 1988
COTTLE, T. *Frank Melton's luck* 1891
COTTRELL, V.M. *The lost cave of Pukerangi* 1942
The Countess of Liverpool's gift book 1915
Country Calendar 1987
County of Westland, New Zealand 1880
COURAGE, J. *Desire without content* 1950
— *The fifth child* 1948
COURAGE, S.A. *Lights and shadows of colonial life* 1897
COURY, R.E. *The steep place* 1936
COUTTS, J. *Vacation tours in New Zealand & Tasmania* 1880
COWAN, F. *The terraces of Rotomahana; fact and fancy in New Zealand; a poem* 1885
COWAN, J. *The bush explorers; a memory of the King Country*; extracted from *Canterbury Times* 5 Apr 1916 (Also as VUWTS, with attachment 'More Reminiscences')
— *Hero stories of New Zealand* 1935
— *The Maoris of New Zealand* 1910
— *The Maori yesterday and to-day* 1930
— *New Zealand or Ao-Tea-Roa* 1907
— *The New Zealand wars; a history of the Maori campaigns and the pioneering period* 2 vols 1922, (1955, 1983 reprints)
— *Pakeha and Maori* 1937
— *Sir Donald Maclean* 1940
— *Travel in New Zealand (vol. II The South Island)* 1926
COWAN, JANET C. *Down the years in the Maniototo* 1948
COWIE, D. *New Zealand from within* 1939
COWIE, D. & MOUNTAIN, J. *Prose and verse* 1946
COWIE, W.G. *Our last year in New Zealand* 1888
COWLEY, J. *Bow down Shadrach* 1991
— *The growing season* 1978
— *Heart attack and other stories* 1985
— *Man of straw* 1970
COWLEY, J. & MELSER, JUNE *The hungry giant* 1980
COX, A. *Recollections* 1884
COX, G.S. *The road to Trieste* 1947
COX, N. *Dirty Work* 1987
— *Waiting for Einstein* 1984
CRADOCK, M. *Sport in New Zealand* 1904
CRAIG, J.J. (ed.) *Historical record of jubilee re-union of old colonists* 1893
CRAIK, G.L. *The New Zealanders* 1830
CRANE, E. *I can do no other; a biography of the Reverend Ormond Burton* 1986
CRANNA, J. *Visitors* 1989
The crash on Mount Erebus, Antarctica of a DC10 aircraft; report of the Royal Commission of Inquiry 1981
CRAWFORD, J. *Killing time* 1980
CRAWFORD, J.C. *Recollections of travel in New Zealand and Australia* 1880
CRAWFORD, N. *The station years* 1981
CRAWFORD, S.S. *Sheep & sheepmen of Canterbury* 1949
CRAY, G.S. *National welfare* 1933
CRESSWELL, D. *Canterbury tales* 1951
— *The case for the South Island* 1957
— *Early New Zealand families* 1949
— *Early New Zealand families; second series* 1956
CRESSWELL, J. *MOTAT; Museum of Transport and Technology of New Zealand (Inc.)* 1976
CRESSWELL, W. D'A. *The letters of D'Arcy Cresswell*; selected by H. Shaw 1971
— *Lyttelton harbour* 1936
— *Poems 1921–27* 1928
— *The poet's progress* 1930
— *Present without leave* 1939
CRICHTON, D.A. *The Australasian fruit culturalist* 1893
CRICHTON, E.L. & C.E. *Songs and ballads of the Transvaal war* 1900
Crime in New Zealand; (Department of Justice pub.) 1968
'CRITIC' (pseud.) *Our state system of primary instruction and its shortcomings, 1881* 1881
CROOKES, M. *Plant life in Maoriland; a botanist's notebook* 1926
CROSS, I.R. *After Anzac Day* 1961
— *The backward sex* 1960
— *The God Boy* 1957
— *The unlikely bureaucrat; my years in broadcasting* 1988

CROSS, P. (ed.) *New Zealand agriculture; a story of the past 150 years* 1990
CROWE, A. *A field guide to the native edible plants of New Zealand* 1981
    — *Native edible plants of New Zealand* 1990
CROWE, A.S. *Selected poems* 1938
CROWE, D. & A. *The Crowe style; Martin & Jeff's world of cricket* 1987
CROZIER, A., see GRAVE, W.G.
CRUICKSHANK, G. *Robert Graham 1820–1885, an Auckland pioneer* 1940
CRUISE, R.A. *Journal of ten months' residence in New Zealand* 1823, (1957)
CRUMP, B. *Barry Crump's bedtime yarns* 1988
    — *Bastards I have met* 1971
    — *A good keen man* 1960
    — *Hang on a minute mate* 1961
    — *One of us* 1962
CRUMPTON, E.W. *Spencer; the gold seeker* 1979
CULE, W.E. *Two little New Zealanders* 1909
CUMMING, C.G. *New Zealand in blooming December* 1884
CUNNINGHAM, W.H., TREADWELL, C.A.L., & HANNA, J.S. *The Wellington Regiment NZEF* 1928
CURNOW, T. ALLEN M. (also as pseud. 'WHIM-WHAM') *At dead low water* 1948
    — *The axe; a verse tragedy* 1949
    — *The best of Whim-Wham* 1959
    — *A book of New Zealand verse 1923–45* (ed.) 1945
    — *Collected poems 1933–1973* 1974
    — *Enemies; Poems 1934–36* 1937
    — *Four plays* 1972
    — *An incorrigible music* 1979
    — *Island and time* 1941
    — *Jack without magic* 1946
    — *Not in the narrow seas* 1939
    — *A present for Hitler* 1940
    — *Sailing or drowning* 1944
    — *A small room with large windows* 1962
    — *Valley of decision* 1933
    — *Verses by Whim-wham 1941–1942* 1942
    — *You will know when you get there; poems 1979–81* 1982
    — et al. *Another Argo* 1935
    — et al. *Recent poems* 1941
CURNOW, TREMAYNE M. *Bad King Wenceslas* 1945
CURR, E.M. *The waste lands of the Province of Wellington* 1856
CURRAN, M.M.S. *Sanctuary* 1944
CURRIE A.E. (ed.) *A centennial treasury of Otago verse* 1949
CURRIE A.E. (ed.), see also ALEXANDER, W.F.
CUTTEN, W.H. *Cutten; letters revealing the life and times of William Henry Cutten the forgotten pioneer*; presented by Stewart W. Greif and Hardwicke Knight 1979
The cyclopedia of New Zealand 6 vols. I(1897), II(1902), III(1903), IV(1905), V(1906), VI (1908)

Dairy farming in New Zealand 1921
DAISH, LOIS *Good food* 1989
DAKIN, J.C. *Education in New Zealand* 1973
DALDY, Y. *John New Zealand* 1937
DALLAS, R. *Collected poems* 1987
    — *Curved horizon; an autobiography* 1991
DALZIEL, R. *Julius Vogel; business politician* 1986
    — *Sir Julius Vogel* 1968
DANIEL, M.J. *New Zealand mammals* 1972
DANIEL, M.J. & BAKER, A. *Collins guide to the mammals of New Zealand* 1986
DARE, J. *Rouseabout Jane* 1956
DARWIN, C. *A calendar of the correspondence of Charles Darwin 1821–1882*; F. Burkhardt & S. Smith (eds.) 1985
    — *Journal of Researches into the natural history and geology of the countries visited during the voyage of HMS Beagle around the world* 1845 (2edn. rev., as found in 1959 Dent 'Everyman' edn.)
DASH, G. *No-license handbook* 1908
    — *Te pono; temperance dialogues* 1904
    — *Waimate verse* 1935
DASHFIELD, H. *To the stars* 1989
DAVIDSON, JANET *The prehistory of New Zealand* 1984, 1987
DAVIDSON, J.W. *Samoa mo Samoa* 1967
DAVIDSON, W.O. *Stories of New Zealand life* 1889
DAVIDSON, W.S. *A sketch of his life..1864–1916 in the employment of the New Zealand and Australian Land Company* 1930
DAVIES, G.P. *Outback* 1975
DAVIES, J.M. *Warriors in mufti* 1939
DAVIES, R.L.A. *Poems and other literary remains* 1884
DAVIES, S. *Bread and roses* 1984
DAVIES, W.C. *New Zealand native plant studies* 1956

D'AVIGDOR, E.H. *Antipodean notes* 1888
DAVIN, D.M. *Breathing spaces* 1975
    — *Brides of price* 1972
    — *Closing times* 1975
    — *For the rest of our lives* 1947
    — *The gorse blooms pale* 1947
    — *No remittance* 1959
    — *Not here, not now* 1970
    — *Psychological warfare*; in *Meanjin Quarterly* June 1973
    — *Roads from home* 1949
    — *The salamander and the fire; collected war stories* 1986
    — *The sullen bell* 1956
Davis dainty dishes; Davis Gelatine Organisation (pub.), in various edns referred to as: 1922, 1923, 1924, 1925, 1926, 1927, 1928, 1937, (1943)
DAVIS, F. *Kohimarama; a collection of fragments* 1989
DAVIS, M. *The watersiders* 1964
DAVIS, W.M. *Nimrod of the sea or, the American whale-man* 1874
DAWBER, R.R. *Floods, slips and washouts*; 1990 (2edn.)
DAWSON, J. *Forest vines to snow tussocks* 1988
DAWSON, J. & LUCAS, R. *Lifestyles of New Zealand forest plants* 1993
DAWSON, S. *The New Zealand whale & dolphin digest; the official Project Jonah guidebook* 1985
Day—and night; a collection of short stories and poems; C. Hewison (ed.) 1986
DEAMER, D. *In the beginning* 1909
DEANS, J. *Pioneers of Canterbury; letters 1840–54* 1937
    — *Pioneers on Port Cooper plains; the Deans family of Riccarton and Homebush* 1964
Debate in House of Representatives 28 Sept. 1899 on a proposal to send a contingent of mounted rifles to fight against the Transvaal in MCINTYRE, W.D. *Speeches and documents on New Zealand history* 1971 pp.260–264
DE COURTE, L.M.J. *La Nouvelle-Zélande* 1904
Defiance cookery recipes; Defiance Dried Milk Factory (pub.) 1905
DELL, R.K. *Native crabs* 1963
    — *Native shells* 1955, (1957)
DE MAUNY, E.C.L. *The huntsman in his career* 1949
DEMPSEY, G. *The little world of Stewart Island* 1964
    — *A wind from the sea* 1950
DENNAN, R. *Guide Rangi of Rotorua* 1968
DENNIS, A. *The Paparoas guide* 1981
DEMSEM, A. *The playcentre way* 1980
DEROLES, V. *A kowhai fairy; a New Zealand nature study story* ?1924
D'ESTERRE, E. *Central Otago; its prospects and resources* 1902
    — *The Molyneux valley* 1905
DEVANNY, J. *Bushman Burke* 1930
    — *The butcher shop* 1926, (1981)
    — *Dawn, beloved* 1928
    — *Devil made saint* 1930
    — *The ghost wife* 1935
    — *Lenore Divine* 1926
    — *Old savage* 1927
    — *Point of departure* 1986
    — *Riven* 1929
    — *Sugar heaven* 1936
DEVENISH, L.H. *The tiki of greenstone* 1934
DEVERELL, E. *Eve Stanley of New Zealand* 1909
DEVON, J.M. *1940 and after, 1 & 2* 1940
DEWAR, D.L. *Marlborough in verse* 1962
DEWAR, G.E. *Chaslands; pioneering days in southern New Zealand* 1953
D'EWES, J. *China, Australia and the Pacific Islands in the years 1853–56* 1857
DICK, B. *High country family* 1964
DICKENS, I.E. *Out of the mountains* 1938
DICKSON, J. *History of the Presbyterian Church of New Zealand* 1899
DIEFFENBACH, J.K.E. *New Zealand and its native population* 1841
    — *Travels in New Zealand* 1843
DILKE, C.W. *Greater Britain* 1868
DILLON, C.A. *The Dillon letters 1842–1853*; C.A. Sharp (ed.) 1954
DILLON, J.H. *Echoes of the war and other poems* 1897
DINGLE, G. & HILLARY, P. *First across the Roof of the World; the first-ever traverse of the Himalayas* 1984
Diploma day— songs to be sung; Canterbury College Students' Association 1893
Distance looks our way; the effects of remoteness on New Zealand; K. Sinclair (ed.) 1961
DIX, J. *Stranded in paradise* 1988
DIXON, G.H. *The triumphant tour of the New Zealand footballers, 1905* 1906
DIXON, M.H. *Nature study notes* 1935
DOAK, W. *Encounters with whales* 1988
    — *Fishes of the New Zealand region* 1972
DOBBIE, H.B. *NZ ferns* 1921 (2edn.)

Dobson, A.D. *Reminiscences of Arthur Dudley Dobson, engineer* 1930
Documents relating to the Second World War; (War Histories) 1951
Domestic scenes in New Zealand 1845, see S.P.C.K.
Domett, A. *The diary of Alfred Domett, 1872–1885*; E.A Horsman (ed.) 1953
— *Flotsam and jetsam* 1877
— *Ranolf and Amohia; a dream of two lives* 1872, 1883 (2edn.)
Don, A. *Chinese mission work in Otago* (Variously titled 'Annual up country tour' or 'Annual inland tour' and issued approx. annually on various dates from 1891–1911.) 1891, 1908
Donaldson, R. *Bush lays and rhymes* 1860
Donne, T.E. *The Maori, past and present* 1927
— (as pseud. 'Spindrift') *Yankee slang* 1932
Donnelly, F. *One priest's life* 1982
Donnelly, W.I.M. *The crazed philosopher* 1928
— *Joyous pilgrims* 1935
Doogue, R.B. & Moreland, J.M. *New Zealand sea anglers' guide* 1960, 1966 (2edn.)
Dougall, W. *Far south* 1888
Doughty, R.A. *The Holyoake years* 1977
Douglas, A.P. *The Dominion of New Zealand* 1909
Douglas, Charles E., see *Mr Explorer Douglas*
Dovedale's History; Dovedale Agricultural and Craft Centre Committee (comp.) 1990
Dowling, B. *Bedlam, a mid-century satire* 1972 (composed 1958)
— *Canterbury, and other poems* 1949
— *A day's journey* 1941
— *Hatherley; recollective lyrics* 1968
— *A little gallery of characters* 1971
— *Signs and wonders* 1944
— *The unreturning native and other poems* 1973
Downes, P. *Top of the bill; entertainers through the years* 1979
Downes, P. & Harcourt, P. *Voices in the air* 1976
Dowsing, St.G.A. *He* 1894
Doyle, C. *A splinter of glass (poems 1951–1955)* 1956
Dreschfelt, Mrs, see Prudence Cadey (pseud.)
Drug dependency and drug abuse in New Zealand; first report of the Board of Health Committee 1970
Drummond, Alison & L.R. *At home in New Zealand* 1967
Drummond, E.M.D., see Carman, Dulce (pseud.)
Drummond, G. *A holiday on horseback* 1947
Drummond, J. *The life and work of Richard John Seddon* 1907
Drummond, J. & Hutton, F.W. *Nature in New Zealand* 1902
Drury, B. (Capt.) *Revised sailing directions* 1854, (1855)
Dryden, G. *Out of the red* 1978
Dryland, G. *Curious conscience* 1977
— *A multiple texture* 1973
Duchess of Buckingham (Egerton, A.A.) *Glimpses of four continents* 1897
Duckworth, M. *A barbarous tongue* 1963
— *Disorderly conduct* 1984
— *Married alive* 1985
— *The matchbox house* 1960
— *Pulling faces* 1987
— *Rest for the wicked* 1986
Duder, T. *Alex* 1987
— *Alex in winter* 1989
Duff, A. *Once were warriors* 1990
— *One night out stealing* 1991
Duff, O. *New Zealand now* 1941
— *A shepherd's calendar* 1961
Duff, R. *The moa-hunter period of Maori culture* (1950), 1977
— *Moas and moa-hunters* 1951
— *Pyramid Valley, Waikari, North Canterbury* 1949
Du Fresne, Y. *The book of Ester* 1982
Duggan, E.M. *More poems* 1951
— *New Zealand bird songs* 1929
— *New Zealand poems* 1940
Duggan, M. *Collected stories* 1981
— *O'Leary's orchard and other stories* 1970
Duncan, A.H. *The Wakatipians* 1888
Duncan and Davies' complete catalogue and cultural guide 1964
Dunedin Field Club catalogues of the indigenous and introduced flowering plants 1916
Duperrey's visit to New Zealand in 1824; A. Sharp (ed.) 1971
Durrell, G. *Two in the bush* 1966
Dutton, W.H. *The bird of paradise* 1896
Dyne, D.G. *Famous New Zealand murders* 1969, (1974)
Dyson, J. *Yachting the New Zealand way* 1966

Eaddy, P.A. *Hull down* 1933
— *'Neath swaying spars* 1939
— *Sails beneath the Southern Cross* 1954
Earle, A.A. *Narrative of a nine months residence in New Zealand*; E.H. McCormick (ed.) 1832, (1966 repr.)
Earp, G.B. *The emigrant's guide to New Zealand* 1848
— *Hand-book for intending emigrants to the southern settlements of New Zealand* 1849, 1852 (3edn. including A. Allom's letter 'Notes on NZ')
— *New Zealand; its emigration and goldfields* 1853
Ebbett, E. *In true colonial fashion; a lively look at what New Zealanders wore* 1977
— *When the boys were away* 1984
Eccles, A. *The old identities* 1931
Eccles, A. & Reed, A.H. *John Jones of Otago* 1949
Economic cooking lessons tested and given by different ladies; W.C.T.U (pub.) 1889
Eden, A.W. *Islands of despair* 1955
Eden, Dorothy *An important family* 1982
— *Sleep in the woods* 1960
Edgeworth, Maria *Letters from England, 1813–1844*; C. Colvin (ed.) 1971
Edmond, L. *Bonfires in the rain* 1991
— *High country weather* 1984
— *Hot October; an autobiographical story* 1989
— *Selected poems* 1984
Edmonds cookery book or '*Sure to rise*': see *The 'Sure to rise' cookery book*
Edmonds microwave cookery book 1989
Education development conference [working party] report; organization and administration 1974
Edwards, B. *The public eye* 1972 (2edn.)
Edwards, J. *AWOL: the true story of a reluctant New Zealand soldier* 1990
— *Riot 1932* 1974
Edwards, L. *Scrim; radio rebel in retrospect* 1971
Edwards, M. *Mihipeka; time of turmoil* 1992
Egerton, A.A. *Glimpses of four continents* 1894
Eggleton, D. *After Tokyo* 1987
When there's an egg in the house there's a meal in the house; NZ Egg Marketing Authority (pub.) a1967
Elder, J.R. (ed.) *Glimpses of old New Zealand* 1924
— *Goldseekers and bushrangers in New Zealand* 1930
— *Marsden's lieutenants* 1934
Eldred-Grigg, S.T. *Of ivory accents* 1977
— *Oracles & miracles; a novel* 1987
— *The shining city* 1991
— *A southern gentry; New Zealanders who inherited the earth* 1980
Electric cookery; hints instructions and recipes c1930
Elias, M.D. *The boy from New Zealand* 1940
Elkington, E.W. *Adrift in New Zealand* 1906
— *The lucky shot* 1902
Ell, G. *The children's guide to wildflowers and weeds of New Zealand* 1983
Elley, W.B. *External examinations and internal assessments; alternative plans for reform* 1972
Elliott, J.H. *Odes & episodes* 1950
— *Poetic pot-pourri* 1946
Elliott, J.S. *Firth of Wellington* 1937
— *The hundred years* 1939
— *Scalpel and sword* 1936
Elliott, K. & Adshead, R. *From cowshed to dog collar* 1967
Elliot, W.S. *Service* 1924
Ellis, W. *Polynesian researches..in the South Sea Islands* 1829
Ellison, O.E. *The road of life* 1926
Ellison, R. *Sandy & Co.* 1927
Ellison, T.R. *The art of rugby football* 1902
Elmslie, J.G. *John Elmslie 1831–1907; he came from Bennachie* 1961, (1963)
Elvey, W.J. *Kaikoura coast; the history, traditions and Maori place-names of Kaikoura* 1949
Elwell, E.S. *The boy colonists* 1878
Elworthy, S. *Ritual song of defiance; a social history of students at the University of Otago* 1990
Emigrants' letters from the British colonies (emigrants school fund) 1850
Emigrant voices from New Zealand; extracted from *Chambers Edinburgh Journal* 1848
Emigration to Van Diemen's land and New Zealand; Chamber's Information for the People, new series No.20 1841
An encyclopaedia of New Zealand; A.H. McLintock (ed.) 3 vols. 1966
Enderby, C. *The Auckland Islands* 1849
England, W. *A pamphlet that all should read before emigrating* 1877
Escott, M. *Showdown* 1936 (1973)
Escott-Inman, H. *The castaways of Disappointment Island* 1911, (1980)
The establishment of the New Plymouth Settlement [etc.]: see Rutherford, J. (ed.)
Evans, A. *New Zealand in flower* 1987
Evans, B.L. *A history of farm implements and implement firms in New Zealand* 1956, 1984
Evans, C. *Over the hills and far away* 1874

— *A strange friendship; a story of New Zealand* 1874
EVANS, M.S. *The Britain of the south* 1904
EVANS, N. *The change agent* 1986
EVANS, P. *Making it* 1989
EVANS, R.A. *Waikaka saga* 1962
EVERSLEY, A. *New Zealand voices and other poems* 1889
Everybody's cookery book of tested recipes; collected by the ladies of Trinity Congregational Church, Christchurch 1928
EVISON, H.C. *Te Wai Pounamu, the greenstone island* 1993
EVISON, J.S. *Murder will out!* 1889
— *Political portraits* 1892
EWING, J.L. *Development of the New Zealand primary school curriculum 1877–1970* 1970
Exotic fruit forum; the New Zealand Fruitgrowers' Federation (comp.) 1990
Extracts of letters from New Zealand on the war question 1861
EYTON, T. *Rugby football (past and present) and the tour of the native team..in 1888–89* 1896

'FABRICIUS' pseud. of C.D. WRIGHT *The maid of Avon* 1882
Facsimiles of the Declaration of Independence and the Treaty of Waitangi 1877, (1976)
FAIRBURN, A.R.D. *Dominion* 1938
— *He shall not rise; poems* 1930
— *How to ride a bicycle* 1947
— *The letters of A.R.D. Fairburn*; L. Edmond (ed.) 1981
— *The rakehelly man* 1946
— *Three Poems* 1952
— *Woman Problem* 1967
FAIRBURN, A.R.D. & GLOVER, D. *Poetry harbinger* 1958
FAIRBURN, M. *Nearly out of heart and hope; the puzzle of a colonial labourer's diary* 1995
FALLA, R.A. *The holiday naturalist in New Zealand* 1971
FALLA, R.A. et al. *A field guide to the birds of New Zealand* 1966
— *The new guide to the Birds of New Zealand* 1979
Family history at National Archives 1990, (1991)
FANNING, L.S. *Players and slayers* 1910
— *Politics and the public* 1919
FARJEON, B.L. *Grif; a story of colonial life* 1866
— *Shadows on the snow* 1865
FARMER, LIEUT. pseud. of J.M. VERRALL *The stockwhip* 1886
Far off; or, Africa and America described, with anecdotes and numerous illustrations 1856 (part 2)
FARRELL, B.H. *Power in New Zealand* 1962
FARRELL, FIONA *The Skinny Louie book* 1992
Favourite recipes; Milton Home and School cookery book 1979
FAWCETT, M.G. *Life of the Rt. Honourable Sir William Molesworth Bart* 1901
Featherston military training camp 1917
FEATON, E.H. (ed.) *The art album of New Zealand flora* 1889
FEATON, J. *The Waikato war 1863–1864* 1879
FELL, H.B. *Native sea-stars* 1962
FENTON, F.D. *Observations on the state of the aboriginal inhabitants of New Zealand* 1859
FENWICK, (SIR) G. *I Romance of the flora of New Zealand. II Farthest north in New Zealand; a memorable tour* 1922
FENWICK, N.A. *Rhyme or reason* c1949
FERGUSON, C. *Marie Levant* 1913
FERGUSON, DAVID *The history of the Canterbury regiment N.Z.E.F., 1914–1919* 1921
FERGUSON, DUGALD *Bush life in Australia and New Zealand* 1893
— *Castle Gay and other poems* 1883, 1912
— *The king's friend* 1907
— *Mates* 1912
— *Poems and sketches, grave and humorous by a New Zealander* 1905
— *Poems of the heart* 1897
— (as pseud. 'DANIEL FROBISHER') *Sketches of Gossiptown* 1893
— *Vicissitudes of bush life* 1891
FERNANDEZ, N. *Tussock fever* 1973
FIAT, J. (pseud.) *The prisoner escaped; the true story of Dick Humphreys* 1949
FIELD, A.N. *The money spider* 1933
FIELD, H.C. *The ferns of New Zealand and its immediate dependencies* 1890
FINDLAY, J.G. *Humbugs and homilies* 1908
— *Our man in the street* 1909
FINLAY, I. *Cookery* 1930, 1933
— *Dunedin City Gas Department cookery book* 1948 (11edn.)
FINLAYSON, R.D. *Brown man's burden and later stories*; B. Pearson (ed.) 1938, (1973) (Orig. pub. 1938: first publication dates of individual stories used; text that of the 1938 edn.)
— *Other lovers* 1976
— *Our life in this land* 1941
— *The schooner came to Atia* 1952
— *Sweet Beulah land* 1942
— *Tidal creek*; D. McEldowney (ed.) 1948, (1979) (Orig. pub. 1948: first publication dates of individual stories used; text that of the 1948 edn.)
FINNEMORE, J. *The little Maories* 1912
FINN, G. *Datus* 1931, (1932)
FIRTH, J.C. *Lectures on lions in the way and luck* 1877
— *Nation making* 1890
— *Weighed in the balance* 1882
FIRTH, R. *Primitive economics of the New Zealand Maori* 1929
— *Primitive Polynesian economy* 1939
FISHER, B. *Angels wear black* 1977
— *Divers of Arakam* 1976
— *Dolphins and killer whales* 1978
FITTON, E.B. *New Zealand; its present condition, prospects, and resources* 1856
FITZGERALD, J.E. *The native policy of New Zealand* 1862
— *The present government of New Zealand; a letter to the electors of Lyttelton* 1856
— *Religious teaching* 1864
— *The self-reliant policy in New Zealand* 1870
— *Speech delivered at the breakfast by the early colonists of Canterbury* 1868
FITZROY, R. *Remarks on New Zealand* 1846
FLETCHER, T.A. *School football* 1925
Flora of New Zealand: see Allan, H.H. (Vol.I), Moore, L.B. (Vol.II), Healy, A.J. (Vol.III), Webb, C.J. (Vol.IV)
FLOWER, TUI *The New Zealand Woman's Weekly cookbook* 1971
A flying start; commemorating fifty years of the Ornithological Society of New Zealand 1940–1990; B.J. Gill & B.D. Heather (comp.) 1990
FOLJAMBE C.G.S. *Three years on the Australian station* 1868
FOORD, M. *The New Zealand descriptive animal dictionary* 1990
FORBES, JACK *New Zealand deer heads* 1924
FORSAITH, J.S. (printer) *The Rev. Thomas Spencer Forsaith [1814–98]; three pamphlets reprinted from originals in the possession of J.W. Forsaith, London* 1942
FORSAITH, T.S. *A handbook for emigrants to New Zealand* 1856
FORSTER, G. *A voyage round the world* 1777
FORSTER, J.R. *Observations made during a voyage round the world* 1778
— *The Resolution journal of Johann Reinhold Forster 1772–1775*; M.E. Hoare (ed.) 1982
FOSTON, H. *At the front* 1921
— *In the bell bird's lair* 1911
The founding of New Zealand: see MATHEW, F.
The Fowlds papers, index of correspondence and subjects 1878–1934; F. Rogers (comp.) 1980
FOWLER, F. *Southern lights and shadows* 1859, (1975 facs.)
FOX, W. *Colonization and New Zealand* 1842
— *Report on the settlement of Nelson* 1849
— *The revolt in New Zealand* 1865
— *The war in New Zealand* 1860
FRAME, J. *The adaptable man* 1965
— *An angel at my table* 1984
— *The Carpathians* 1988
— *Daughter buffalo* 1972
— *The edge of the alphabet* 1962
— *The envoy from Mirror City* 1985
— *Faces in the water* 1961
— *The lagoon (and other) stories* 1951, (1961)
— *Living in the Maniototo* 1979
— *Owls do cry* 1957, (1967 'Sun' edn. quoted)
— *The rainbirds* 1968
— *The reservoir; stories and sketches* 1963, (1966)
— *Snowman snowman* 1963
— *To the is-land* 1982, (1984)
FRANCE, H.R. *Ice cold river* 1961
— *The race* 1958
FRANCES, C. *Johnny Rapana* 1964
FRANCIS, K. *Wildlife ranger* 1983
FRANCIS, M. *Coastal fishes of New Zealand; a diver's identification guide* 1988
FRANCIS, R. *A New Zealand harp* 1926
FRANKS, L. *All the stamps of New Zealand* 1977
FRASER, C. *Beyond the roaring forties; New Zealand's subantarctic islands* 1986
FRASER, E. & GIBBONS, J. *Soldier and sailor words and phrases* 1925
FRASER, K.G. *Ungrateful people* 1952, 1985 (2edn.)
FREEMAN, W. *He who digged a pit* 1889
FRERE, A.M. *Antipodes and round the world* 1870
FREYBERG, B.C. *A study of unit administration* 1933, (1940)
FROBISHER, DANIEL pseud. of DUGALD FERGUSON
From the black rocks, on Friday: see CARTER, REV. ROBERT
FROST, E.T. *By Maori trail and Pakeha road* 1947
FROUDE, J.A. *Oceana* 1886
FRY, P.S. *Brushed words and poems personal* 1977

FULLARTON, J.H. *Troop target* 1944
— *We walked alone* 1946
FULLER, D. *Maori food and cookery* 1978
FULLER, F. *Five years' residence in New Zealand* 1859
FULLER, M. (ed.) *The story of a tramping and skiing club; Manawatu 50th Jubilee 1928–1978* 1978
FURNISS, C. *Servants of the north* 1977
FUSSELL, J.C. *Corporal Tikitanu, V.C.* 1918
— *Letters from Private Henare Tikitanu* 1917
FUTTER, E. *Home cookery for New Zealand* ?1926

GABITES, I. *Wellington's Living Cloak* 1993
GALBREATH, R.A. *Walter Buller; the reluctant conservationist* c1989
GALLAHER, D & STEAD, W.J. *The complete rugby footballer on the New Zealand system* 1906
GALVIN, P. *The New Zealand mining handbook* 1906
GAMBIER, J.W. *Links in my life on land and sea* 1906, (1907)
GANT, P. *The fifth season* 1976
GARDINER, H. *Skyways of Maoriland* 1934
GARLAND, T.T. *Judy carries on* 1936
GARNIER, T. et al. *The hunter and the hill* 1978
GASCOYNE, F.J.W. *Soldiering in New Zealand being reminiscences of a veteran* 1916
GASKELL, A.P. pseud. of A.G. PICKARD *All part of the game; the stories of A.P. Gaskell* 1978
— *The big game* 1947
GASKIN, C. *Remote the land's heart; wildlife and landscape in Southern New Zealand* 1985
GASKIN, D.E. *The butterflies and common moths of New Zealand* 1966
— *Whales, dolphins and seals* 1972
GAZE, H. *The china cat* 1921
— *The enchanted fish* 1921
GEACH, E.C. *From the soul of the ti-tree* 1909
GEBBIE, F. & MCGREGOR, J. *The incredible 8-ounce dream* 1979
GEE, M.G. *The fire-raiser* 1986
— *The halfmen of O* 1982
— *In my father's den* 1972
— *Meg* 1981
— *Plumb* 1979
— *Prowlers* 1987
— *Sole survivor* 1983
— *A special flower* 1965
GEORGE, M. *Ohakune; opening to a new world* 1990
Geraldine County jubilee 1927
GERARD, J.D. *Unwilling guests* 1945
GIBBONS, W.H. *Recollections of a childhood in the twenties* 1988
GIBBS, G.W. *New Zealand butterflies; identification and natural history* 1980
GIBSON, H.T. *That Gibbie Galoot; the tale of a teacher* 1924
GIFFORD, P. (also as 'LOOSEHEAD LEN', pseud.) *Loosehead Len's big brown book* 1974
— *Loosehead Len's bumper thump book* 1974, (1976)
— *Loosehead Len's Gluepot greats* 1979
GIFFORD, W.H. & WILLIAMS, H.B. *A centennial history of Rotorua* 1940
GIFKINS, M. *Through the looking glass* 1988
GILBERT, G.R. *Free to laugh and dance* 1942
GILBERT, F.R. *Lazarus & other poems* 1949
GILBERT, T. *New Zealand settlers and soldiers* 1861
GILDERDALE, B. *A sea change; 145 years of New Zealand junior fiction* 1982
GILES, J. *Poems* 1908
GILFILLAN, S. *Mary and her friend, Aggie* 1891
GILKISON, R. *Early days in Central Otago* 1930
— *Early days in Dunedin* 1938
GILKISON, W.S. *Aspiring, New Zealand* 1951
— *Peaks, packs & mountain tracks* 1940
GILL, B. *Collins handguide to the frogs and reptiles of New Zealand* 1986
GILL, B. & MARTINSON, P. *New Zealand's extinct birds* 1991
GILL, P. *The New Zealand international exhibition cookery book* 1907
GILLESPIE, O.A. (ed.) *Base wallahs (2NZEF in the Pacific No.3)* 1946
— (ed.) *The gunners (2NZEF in the Pacific No.11)* 1948
— (ed.) *Headquarters (2NZEF in the Pacific No.4)* 1947
— (ed.) *Pacific kiwis (2NZEF in the Pacific No.9)* 1947
— (ed.) *Pacific pioneers (2NZEF in the Pacific No.2)* 1946
— (ed.) *Pacific saga (2NZEF in the Pacific No.10)* 1947
— (ed.) *Pacific service (2NZEF in the Pacific No.8)* 1948
— (ed.) *Shovel sword and scalpel (2NZEF in the Pacific No.1)* 1946
— (ed.) *South Canterbury; a record of settlement* 1958, (1971)
— (ed.) *Stepping stones to the Solomons (2NZEF in the Pacific No.6)* 1947
— (ed.) *The story of the 34th (2NZEF in the Pacific No.7)* 1947
— (ed.) *The tanks (2NZEF in the Pacific No.12)* 1947
— (ed.) *The 35th battalion (2NZEF in the Pacific No.5)* 1947
— (ed.) *The 36th battalion (2NZEF in the Pacific No.13)* 1948
GILLESPIE, O.N.: see *New Zealand short stories* 1930
GILLHAM, M. *A naturalist in New Zealand* 1965
GILLIES, T.B. *Our system of government* 1871
GILRUTH, J.A. *The sheep-maggot (New Zealand D.S.I.R. Bulletin, No.12)* 1907
GINDERS, A. *The thermal springs district of New Zealand* 1890
GIPPS, H.S. *Outward bound* 1907
GISBORNE, W. *The colony of New Zealand* 1888
A glance at Dunedin; extracted from Chambers Journal vol. XLI. 344 1864
GLEN, E. *Robin of Maoriland* 1929
— *Six little New Zealanders* 1917, (1983)
— *Uncles three at Kamahi* 1926
GLEN, F. *Bush in our yard* 1980
— *Holy Joe's people; a parson in Fiordland* 1968
Glenfield College Maori cookbook 1977
GLENN, REWA, see JOHNSON, MARGUERITE M. (pseud.)
Glossary of building terminology; Standards Association of New Zealand (comp.) 1979
GLOVER, D.J.M. *The arraignment of Paris* 1937
— *Denis Glover's bedside book* 1963
— *Diary to a woman* 1971
— *Enter without knocking; selected poems* 1964
— *Hot water sailor* 1982
— *Hot water sailor and landlubber ho* 1962, (1981)
— *Men of God* 1978
— *Short reflection on the present state of literature in this country* 1935
— *Sings Harry* 1951, (1957)
— *Six easy ways of dodging debt collectors* 1936
— *Summer flowers* 1946
— *Thirteen poems* 1939
— *To a particular woman* 1970
— *Towards Banks Peninsula* 1979
— *Wellington harbour* 1974
— *The wind & the sand; poems 1934–44* 1945
GOALEN, L. *Olla podrida* 1891
GODLEY, C. *Letters from early New Zealand (1850–53)* 1951
GODLEY, J.R. *A selection from the writings and speeches;* J.E. Fitzgerald (ed.) 1863
GOLDBLATT, D. *Democracy at ease* 1957
A gold digger's notes; extracted from *All the Year Round* 2 Apr. 1864 pub. with *From the black rocks, on Friday* 1864, (1950)
Gold dredging in Otago 1899
GOLDER, W. *New Zealand minstrelsy* 1852
— *The New Zealand survey* 1867
— *Pigeons' parliament* 1854
GOLDMAN, L.M. *The history of the Jews in New Zealand* 1958
GOODING, B. *KZ7; inside stories of fear and loathing* 1987
GOODING, P. *Picturesque New Zealand* 1913
GORDON, D.C. & BENNETT, F. *Gentlemen of the jury* 1937
GORDON, E.M. & DEVERSON, TONY *Finding a New Zealand voice; attitudes towards English used in New Zealand* 1989
— *New Zealand English; an introduction to New Zealand speech* 1985
GORDON, H.A. *A miners' guide* 1889
— *Mining and engineering* 1894, (1906)
GORDON, MONA C. *The children of Tane; bird life in New Zealand* 1938
— *Torn tapestry* 1929
— *Vintage; people & things in old New Zealand* 1948
GORDON, T. *Hot lakes, volcanoes and geysers of New Zealand* 1888
GORE, R. *Levins 1841–1941* 1956
GORMACK, R.S., see also 'J.A.K. HAY' (pseud.) *Diary of a hundred days* 1975
GORST, J.E. *The Maori king* 1864
— *New Zealand revisited; recollections of the days of my youth* 1908
GOULAND, H.G. *Plan of a proposed new colony, to be called Britannia* 1851
GOWANS, E. *Heart of the high country; a New Zealand saga* 1985
'G. R.' (pseud.) *Poems by G.R.* 1891
GRACE, A.A. *Hone Tiki dialogues* 1910
— *Maoriland stories* 1895
— *The tale of a timber town* 1914
— *Tales of a dying race* 1901
GRACE, M.S. *A sketch of the New Zealand war* 1899
GRACE, PATRICIA *Cousins* 1992
— *Mutuwhenua* 1978
GRACE, T.S. *A pioneer missionary among the Maoris, 1850–1879* 1928
GRADY, D. *The Perano whalers of Cook Strait (1911–1964)* 1982
— *Sealers and whalers in New Zealand waters* 1986
GRAEME-HOLDER, W. *Restless earth* 1933
GRAHAM, D.H. *A treasury of New Zealand fishes* 1956 (2edn.)
GRAHAM, J. *Breaking the habit; life in a New Zealand Dominican convent* 1992

GRAHAM, SUSAN *Susan in springtime* 1960
GRANT, A.K. *I rode with the epigrams* 1979
— *Land uprooted high* 1971
— *Unauthorised version* 1980
GRANT, A.K. & SCOTT, T. *The paua and the glory* 1982
GRANT, D. *On a roll; a history of gambling and lotteries in New Zealand* 1994
GRANT, J.G.S. *The delphic oracle* 1866
GRANT, S. & FOSTER, J.S. *New Zealand; a report on its agricultural conditions and prospects* ?1880
GRAVE, W.G. *Beyond the southern lakes; the explorations of W.G. Grave*; A. Crozier (ed.) 1950
GRAY, ALISON *The marriage maze* 1979
— *Stepping out* 1987
GRAY, ARTHUR J. *An Ulster plantation* 1938
GRAY, C.A. (comp.), see PEACHE, A.E.
GRAY, J. E. *Notes on the materials at present existing towards a fauna of New Zealand, by John Edward Gray, F.R.S* in DIEFFENBACH, J.K.E. *Travels in New Zealand* vol. 2 1842
GRAY, R. & BECHT, R. *The All Whites; their World Cup road to Spain* 1982
GRAYLING, W.I. *Taranaki and its resources* 1886
— *The war in Taranaki* 1862
The great adventure; New Zealand soldiers describe the First World War; J. Phillips, N. Boyack & E.P. Malone (eds.) 1988
GREENWOOD, H. *Gloaming, the wonder horse* 1927
GREENWOOD, J. *Journey to Taupo from Auckland* 1850
GREEN, W.S. *The high alps of New Zealand* 1883
GREIF & KNIGHT, see CUTTEN, W.H.
GREVILLE, A.T. *Bush baby songs* 1926
GREY, G. *Address on the principles which should guide the citizens in founding a free public library* 1883
— *Ko nga moteatea, me nga hakirara o nga Maori* 1853
— *Polynesian mythology and ancient traditional history of the New Zealanders, as furnished by their priests and chiefs* 1855
GREY, J. *His island home* 1879
GREY, POWINA (or GRAY) pseud. of RONALD E. MACDONALD
GREY, Z. *Tales of the angler's Eldorado* 1926
GRIEVE, H. *It's nothing serious; a novel* 1950
— *Sketches from Maoriland* 1939, (1961)
— *Something in the country air* 1947
— *Spring manoeuvres* 1944
GRIFFIN, G.W. *New Zealand; her commerce and resources* 1884
GRIFFITHS, G.J. *King Wakatip* 1971
GRIGG, J.R. *Murchison, New Zealand* 1947
GRIMSTONE, S.E. *The southern settlements of New Zealand* 1847
GROSSMAN, E.H. *Angela* 1890
— *The heart of the bush* 1910
— *In revolt* 1893
— *A knight of the holy ghost* 1907
GROVER, R. *Another man's role* 1967
— *Cork of war; Ngati Toa and the British mission* 1982
GROWDEN, O.H. *Matthew Redmayne* 1892
The growth and development of social security in New Zealand; (a survey of social security in New Zealand from 1898 to 1949) 1950
GRUNDY, E. *Who'd marry a doctor? A Chatham Islands casebook* 1968
GUBBINS, S. et al. *Statistics at work* 1982
GUDGEON, T.W. *The defenders of New Zealand* 1887
— *Reminiscences of the war in New Zealand* 1879
GUNSON, D. *Collins guide to the New Zealand seashore* 1983
GURNEY, E. M. *A pageant from the foothills* 1943
GUSTAFSON, B. *From the cradle to the grave; a biography of Michael Joseph Savage* 1986
GUTHRIE, B. pseud. of A.B.B. NORTHCROFT *New Zealand memories* 1930
GUTHRIE, J. pseud. of J. BRODIE *The little country* 1935
— *So they began* 1936
GUTHRIE-SMITH, W.H. *Bird life on island and shore* 1925
— *Birds of the water, wood and waste* 1910, 1927 (2edn.)
— *Mutton birds and other birds* 1914
— *Sorrows and joys of a New Zealand naturalist* 1936
— *Tutira; the story of a New Zealand sheep station* 1921 (often referenced to the 1926 reprint, a so-called '2edn.'), 1953 (3edn.)
GWYNN, R.D. *Collecting New Zealand stamps* 1988

'H' (pseud.) *The grain of gold* 1898
HAAST, H.F. VON *The life and times of Sir Julius von Haast* 1948
— *New Zealand Privy Council Cases, 1840–1932* 1938
HAAST, J. VON *Geology of the provinces of Canterbury and Westland, New Zealand* 1879
— *Report of a topographical and geological exploration of the western districts of the Nelson Province* 1861

HADEN, A. *Lock, stock 'n barrel* 1988
HADLEE, R. *Hadlee on cricket* 1982
HAITANA, H. *Fine Cotton & me; the Kiwi trainer's inside story on racing's famous ring-in.* 1986
HALCOMBE, A.F. *New Zealand*; extracted from the *Proceedings of the Royal Colonial Institute* 1880
HALEY, R. *The settlement* 1986
— *The transfer station* 1989
HALKETT, J & SALE, E.V. *The world of the kauri* 1986
HALL, D.O.W. *The New Zealanders in South Africa* 1950
HALL, J. as J.H.L. (pseud.) *Potona; or unknown New Zealand* 1885, (1892)
HALL, JOHN *Experience of 30 years in..Wellington* 1884, (1885)
HALL, M. *A woman in the Antipodes* 1914
HALL, P. & WRIGHT, V. *A Shepherd's year* 1987
HALL, ROGER *Glide time* 1977
— *Hot water* 1983
— *Middle-age spread* 1978
— *Prisoners of Mother England* 1980
HALL-JONES, F.G. *Early Timaru; some historical records of the pre-settlement period* 1956
— *Historical Southland* 1945
HALL-JONES, J. *Early Fiordland* 1968
— *Mr. Surveyor Thomson* 1971
HAMILTON, ARCHIBALD *On the economic progress of New Zealand* 1869
HAMILTON, AUGUSTUS *Fishing and sea-foods of the ancient Maori*; Dom. Mus. Bull. No.2 1908
— *Maori art*; first issued in 5 parts; pt. 1 (1896), 2 (1897), 3 (1898), 4 (1899), 5 (1900)
HAMILTON, G.D. *Trout-fishing and sport in Maoriland* 1904
HAMILTON, I. *Till human voices wake us* 1953
HAMILTON, J. *The lay of the bogle stone* 1892
HAMILTON, P. *Wild Irishman* 1969
HAMILTON-BROWNE, G. *Camp fire yarns of the lost legion* 1913
HAMMOND, R.T. *Under the shadow of dread* 1908
HANCOCK, T. *A short sketch of some incidents in the colonial life of Mr Thos. Hancock* 1885
Handbook for NZ; prepared for the 1937 ANZAAS meeting, Auckland 1936
The handbook of New Zealand mammals; C.M. King (ed.) 1990
The handbook of New Zealand mines; P. Galvin (ed.) 1887
Handbook on the Dominion of New Zealand; Great Britain Colonial Office, Overseas Settlement Office 1925
The handbook to the suburban and rural districts of the Otago settlement 1849
HANGER, P. *Three fronts of war* 1943
HANLON, A.C. *Random recollections* 1939
Hanmer Forest Park 1984
HANSEN, R.E. *Vital themes and varied topics* 1945
HANSON, ELIZABETH *The politics of social security* 1980
Happy endings; stories by Australian and New Zealand women, 1850s–1930s; E. Webby & L. Wevers (eds.) 1987
HARCOURT, M. *A parson in prison; a biography of the Rev. George Edgar Moreton* 1942
HARCOURT, PETER *A dramatic appearance; New Zealand theatre 1920–1970* 1971
HARDIE, N.D. *In highest Nepal; our life among the Sherpas* 1957
HARGREAVES, R.P. *From beads to banknotes; the story of money in New Zealand* 1972
HARMAN, A.S. *The New Zealand domestic cookery book* 1903, 1905 (3edn.); 1921 (7edn. as 'Domestic Cookery')
HARPER, A.P. *Camping and bushcraft in New Zealand for beginners* 1945
— *Memories of mountains & men* 1946
— *Pioneer work in the Alps of New Zealand* 1896
HARPER, B. *Eight daughters, three sons* 1975
— *The kettle on the fuchsia; the story of Orari Gorge* 1967
HARPER, H.T.A. *Windy island* 1934
HARPER, H.W. *Letters from New Zealand (1857–1911)* 1914
HARPER, P.C. & KINSKY, F.C. *Southern albatrosses and petrels; an identification guide* 1978
HARRIS, G. *Field guide to common New Zealand trees and shrubs* 1982
HARRIS, J.C. *The southern guide to the hot lake district of the North Island of New Zealand* 1878
HARRIS, L. *The New Zealand firearms handbook* 1985
HARRIS, N. *The fly away people* 1971
HARRIS, R. *The poetry of Dick Harris*; P. Lawlor (ed.) 1927
HARRISON, C. *Broken October* 1976
— *Days of starlight* 1988
— *The quiet earth* 1981
HARRISON, R.J. *Ebb and flow; a centennial history of the Christchurch Yacht Club* 1991
HARROP, A.J. *My New Zealand* 1939
— *New Zealand after five wars* 1947
— *The romance of Westland* 1923
— *Touring in New Zealand* 1935

HARROW, E. *New Zealand as I have found it; or The harrowing experiences of a settler* 1890
HART, G.R. *Stray leaves from the early history of Canterbury* 1886
HARTLEY, C.W.G. *The shepherd's dogs* 1949
HARTLEY, N. *Swagger on our doorstep* 1987
HARVEY, N.B. *Any old dollars mister?* 1964
HARVEY, N.B & GODLEY, E.J. *New Zealand botanical paintings* 1969
HARWOOD, V. *Heritage trail* 1982
HASCOMBE, J. *Down and almost under* 1969
HASELDEN, J. *A winter's night in a settler's home* 1900
HASTINGS, A. *Bright conversations* 1942
HASTINGS, J.R. (ed.) *A digger's diary* 1941
— *Uncle Scrim and the waterside workers* 1942
— *The 'Uncle Scrim' mystery* 1942
HATTAWAY, R. *Reminiscences of the northern war* 1889
HAUGHEY, T.E. *Railway reminiscences* 1946
HAWDON, S.E. *New Zealanders and the Boer war* 1907
HAWKE, V. & SCOTT, T. *Early farm machinery in New Zealand* 1985
HAWKINS, C.W. *Out of Auckland; a survey of the commercial sailing craft built in the Auckland province* 1960
'HAWKSWOOD' (pseud.) *Reminiscences of New Zealand* 1880
HAWTHORNE, J. *A dark chapter from New Zealand history* 1869
HAY, E.S. *Some characteristics of Wordsworth's poetry* 1881
HAY, J. *Reminiscences of earliest Canterbury* 1915
'HAY, J.A.K.' pseud. of R.S. GORMACK *Swagger Jack; a station tale*; in *Bookie 3* 1951
HAY, R.W. *Notices of New Zealand, from documents in the colonial office*; extracted from the Journal of the Royal Geographical Society 1832
HAY, W.D. *Brighter Britain! or settler and Maori in northern New Zealand* 1882
HAYDON, W.D. *New Zealand soldiers in England* 1941
HAYES, M.A. *From the toss of a coin; the story of Alpheus Hayes and Normanvale, South Canterbury* 1978
HAYNES, S.I. *A ramble in the New Zealand bush* 1865
HAYNES, W. *My log; a journal of the proceedings of the flying squadron* 1871
HAYTER, H.H. *Notes of a tour in New Zealand* 1874
HAYWARD, B.W. *Trilobites, dinosaurs and moa bones; the story of New Zealand fossils* 1990
HAYWARD, M. *Diary of the Kirk years* 1981
HEALE, T. *New Zealand and the New Zealand Company* 1842
HEALY, A.J. & EDGAR, E. *Flora of New Zealand Vol. III, adventive..monocotyledons* 1980
HEAPHY, C. *Account of an exploring expedition to the south-west of Nelson, 1846* in *Early travellers in New Zealand*; N.M. Taylor (ed.) 1959
— *Narrative of a residence in various parts of New Zealand* 1842
— *Notes of an expedition to Kawatiri and Araura..1846* in *Early travellers in New Zealand*; N.M. Taylor (ed.) 1959
HEARN, T.J. *Nenthorn; gold and the gullible* 1988
HEBER, D. *Netta, or a plea for an old age pension* 1894
HECTOR, J. *Geological expedition to the west coast of Otago* 1863
— *Handbook of New Zealand* 1879, 1880, 1883
— *Notes on the edible fishes of New Zealand* in HUTTON, F. W. and HECTOR, J. *Fishes of New Zealand* 1872
Heinemann dictionary of New Zealand quotations; H.W. Orsman & J. Moore (eds.) 1988
Heinemann New Zealand dictionary; H.W. Orsman (ed.) 1979, 1989 (2edn.)
HEINZ, W.F. *Bright fine gold; stories of the New Zealand goldfields* 1974
— *Prospecting for gold* 1952
HELLIER, F. *Colonials in khaki* 1916
HELM, A.S. *Fights & furloughs in the Middle East* 1944
— *Kiwis on tour in Egypt and Italy* 1946
HELMER, R.M. *Stag party* 1964, (1990 Canadian paperback edn.)
The help the babies cookery book; Royal Society for the Health of Women and Children, Picton branch (comp.) 1924
HELSON, G.A.H. *Insect pests* 1974
HEMPLEMAN, G., see *Piraki log*
HENDERSON, CAPT. *Otago, and the Middle Island of New Zealand; a warning to emigrants* 1866
HENDERSON, G.M. *The antecedents and early life of Valentine Savage, known as Taina* 1948
HENDERSON, J.A. *Poultry and eggs for the market and export* 1896
HENDERSON, J.H. *Down from marble mountain* 1983
— *The exiles of Asbestos Cottage* 1981
— *Gunner inglorious* 1945
— *Jim Henderson's home country* 1990
— *Jim Henderson's people* 1986
— *Open country calling; people and places out of town* 1969
— *Open country muster; people and places out of town* 1974
— *Open country; people and places out of town* 1965
— *Our open country; people and places out of town* 1971
— *Return to open country* 1967
— *Soldier country* 1978
— *Tales of the Coast* 1984
HENDERSON, J.M. *Ratana; the origins and the story of the movement* 1963, (1972)
HENDERSON, M. *The log of a superfluous son* 1975
HENDERSON, R. *Friends in chains* 1961
HENDRY, C. *Boots of the Bamas* 1984
Henry Ancrum: see 'J.H.K.' (pseud.)
HENRY, R. (see also 'AN OLD ACQUAINTANCE', pseud.) *The habits of flightless birds of New Zealand with notes on other New Zealand birds* 1903
HENTY, G.A. *Maori and settler* 1890, (1891)
HEPBURN, G. *The journal of George Hepburn*; W.D. Stewart (ed.) 1934
HERMANS, R.T. *Capital coppers* 1985
HERON, H.A. *Early Wairarapa* 1929
HERVEY, J.R. *Man on a raft* 1949
— *New poems* 1942
— *Selected poems* 1940
HERZ, M. *New Zealand; the country and the people* 1912
HETHERINGTON, J. *Air-borne invasion* 1944
HETLEY, G.B. *The native flowers of New Zealand* 1888
HETTERLEY, K. *Nursing nomad* 1944
HEYWOOD, B.A. *A vacation tour at the antipodes* 1863
HICKEY, P.H. *Red Fed. memoirs* 1925
HICKSON, R. *Flight 901 to Erebus* 1980
HIGHAM, T. (ed.) *New Zealand's subantarctic islands; a guidebook* 1991
The Highlander economical cookery book 1922, 1923 (3edn.)
HILGENDORF, F.W. *Weeds of New Zealand* 1926
HILGENDORF, F.W. & CALDER, J.W. *Pasture plants and pastures of New Zealand* 1918, (1948)
— *Weeds of New Zealand*; (2edn. rev. by J.W. Calder) 1967
HILL, D. *Moaville magic* 1985
— *More from Moaville* 1988
HILL, L.B. *The model ombudsman; institutionalizing New Zealand's democratic experience* 1976
HILL, R.S. *The colonial frontier tamed; New Zealand policing in transition 1867–1886* 1986
HILL, S. & J. *Richard Henry of Resolution Island* 1987
HILLARY, L.M. *Keep calm if you can* 1964
HILLIARD, N. *The glory and the dream* 1978
— *Maori girl* 1960
— *Maori woman* 1974
— *A night at Green River* 1969, (1975)
— *A piece of land* 1963
— *Power of joy* 1965
— *Send somebody nice* 1976
Hills and Valleys; B.E. Mabin (ed.) 1936
HILTON, T. *The Wellington Racing Club; a centennial history* 1979
HINDE, G.W., see *Mozley and Whiteley's law dictionary*
HINDE, G.W. & M.S. *New Zealand Law Dictionary* 1986 (3edn.)
HINDE, G.W., MCMORLAND, D.W., & SIM, P.B.A. *Land Law* 1978
— *Introduction to land law* 1986
HINDLEY, D. *Rotorua, Bay of Plenty* 1989
HINDMARSH, W.H.S., see 'WARATAH' (pseud.)
HINDS, S. *The latest official documents relating to New Zealand* 1838
'HINEMOA' (pseud.) *The travels of a New Zealand feather* 1892
HINGSTON, J. *Among the Maoris*; extracted from *Victorian Review* (Melbourne) 1 Oct 1883
— *The Australian abroad* 1879
HINTZ, O.S. *Trout at Taupo* 1955, 1964
HISLOP, J.B. *Pure gold and rough diamonds* 1943
The historical records of New South Wales 7 vols. 1893–1901; 1 pt. 1(1893), pt. 2(1892), 2(1893), 3(1895), 4(1896), 5(1897), 6(1898), 7(1901)
Historic Trentham, 1914–1917; W. Lawson (ed.) 1918
History and natural history of the Boulder Bank, Nelson haven, Nelson, New Zealand 1976
History of Drummond and Gladfield; Drummond Historical Committee c1978
History of North Otago from 1853; (personal reminiscences, etc. of various dates from *Oamaru Mail*) 1937, (1978 repr.)
HOARE, B. *Figures of fancy including the Maori; a new Australian poem* 1869
HOBBS, L.R. *The wild West Coast* 1959
HOBHOUSE, MARY *The selected letters of Mary Hobhouse*; S. Tunnicliff (ed.) 1992
HOCHSTETTER, F. VON *New Zealand* 1867
HOCHSTETTER, F. VON & PETERMAN, A. *The geology of New Zealand in explanation of the Geographical and Topographical atlas of New Zealand* 1864
HOCKEN, T.M. *Contributions to the early history of New Zealand* 1898
HOCKEN, T.M. & FENWICK, G. *A holiday trip to the Catlins district* 1892
HODDER, E. *Memories of New Zealand life* 1862
HODDER, W.R. *The daughter of the dawn* 1903, (1923)
HODGE, H.E.M. *The wind and rain* 1936

HODGKINSON, E. *A handful of New Zealand verse* 1935
HODGKINSON, S. *Emigration to New Zealand; a description of the province of Canterbury* 1856, (1858 2edn.)
HODGSKIN, R. *A narrative of eight months sojourn in New Zealand* 1841
HODGSON, C.W.D. *Tales of a town clerk* 1972
HODGSON, W.C. *Poems*; Alfred A. Grace (ed.) 1896
HOGAN, D. *Billy-can ballads* 1962
— *The roads that go up and down* 1946
HOGAN, H.M. (ed.) *Nowhere far from the sea* 1971
HOGG, C. *Angel gear; on the road with Sam Hunt* 1989
HOGG, J.W. *Snow man* 1934
HOGG, M. *Tints of turquoise* 1934
HOGG, W. *Lays and rhymes; descriptive, legendary, historical* 1875
HOGGARD, N.F. *Adventure tales of Maoriland* 1932
— (ed.) *Centennial miscellany* 1939
— *Who's who in New Zealand authorship* 1941
HOGGINS, A.C. *An essay on prison reform* 1901
HOHMAN, E.P. *The American whaleman* 1928
HOLCROFT, M.H. *Beyond the breakers* 1928
— *Brazilian daughter* 1931
— *Dance of the seasons; an autobiograhical essay* 1952
— *Encircling seas* 1946
— *The flameless fire* 1929
— *Graceless islanders* 1970
— *The line of the road; a history of Manawatu County* 1977
— *Old Invercargill* 1976
— *A sea of words* 1986
— *Timeless world* 1945
— *A voice in the village; the Listener editorials of M.H. Holcroft* 1989
— *The way of a writer* 1984
HOLDEN, ANNE J. *The empty hills* 1967
HOLDEN, P. *A guide to hunting in New Zealand* 1987
— *Pack and rifle* 1971
— *Razorback* 1984
— *Stag* 1980
— *The wild pig in New Zealand* 1982
HOLDER, W.G. *Restless earth* 1933
HOLE, T.R.C.P. *Anzacs into battle* 1942
HOLGATE, C.W. *An account of the chief libraries of New Zealand* 1886
HOLLAND, H.E. *Armageddon or Calvary* 1919
— *Red roses on the highways* 1924
HOLLAND, M.K. *History of the Manawatu River and the Manawatu Catchment Board* 1982
HOLLAND, W.L. & LILIENTHAL, P.E. *Meet the Anzacs* 1942
HOLLISS, R. *Killer on the coast; the true story of Stan Graham* 1959
HOLMES, F. *Chatham Islands Rekohu* 1984
HOLMES, N. *The best of homespun* 1977
— (ed.) *Century of sail* 1971
Home of Compassion book of recipes 1936
The Hon. John Bryce and the colonial office; preface by J. Duthie 1914
HOOD, A. *Dickey Barrett* 1890
HOOD, L. *Sylvia; the biography of Sylvia Ashton Warner* 1988
HOOKER, J. *Jacob's season* 1971
HOOKER, J.D. *The botany of the Antarctic voyage of HM discovery ships Erebus and Terror vol. II flora Novae-Zealandiae, pt. I flowering plants* 1853
— *The botany of the Antarctic voyage of HM discovery ships Erebus and Terror vol. II flora Novae-Zealandiae, pt. II flowerless plants* 1855
— *Handbook of the New Zealand flora* 1864, (1867)
— *Introductory essay to [the flora of New Zealand]* 1853
HOOPER, P. *The goat paddock and other stories* 1981
HOPE, CAPT. *30 years policy in New Zealand*; extracted from *Blackwood's Mag.* June 1865
'HOPEFUL' (pseud.) *Taken in* 1887
'HORI' pseud. of W.N. MCCALLUM *Fill it up gain* 1964
— *Flagon fun* 1966
— *The half-gallon jar* 1962
HORNBY, J. *Mystery in Maori land* 1958
HORNE, A. *New Zealand; a special place* 1986
HORN, W.A. *Notes by a nomad; an olla-podrida* 1906
Horse racing, trotting and dog racing in New Zealand; report of the Royal Commission of Inquiry 1970
HORTON, S. *Memoirs of a colonial goose* 1984
HORTON, W. *New Zealand* 1828
HOSKEN, E. *Life on a five pound note* 1964
— *Turn back the clock* 1968
HOSKINS, R. *Goldfield balladeer; the life and times of..Charles R. Thatcher* 1977
HOUGHTON, J. *Rural New Zealand, the Britain of the south* 1893
HOUGHTON, P. *The shadow of the land* 1966
Housing in New Zealand; report of the Commission of Inquiry 1971

HOWARD, B.H. *Rakiura* 1940
HOWE, A. *Stamper battery; reminiscences of a goldfield's childhood* 1964
HOWE, E.W. *Travel letters from New Zealand, Australia and South Africa* 1913
HOWE, P. *Towards 'taha Maori' in English* 1985
HOWES, B.M. *Marlborough Sounds; the waters of restfulness* 1919
HOWES, E.A. *The great experiment* 1932
— *Mrs Kind Bush* 1933
— *Safe going* 1931
— *Stewart Island* 1913
— *The sun's babies* 1910
— *Tales out of school* 1919
— *Where bell-birds chime* 1912
— *Young pioneer* 1934
HOWITT, R.J. *New Zealand rugby greats* 1975
HOWITT, W. *The history of discovery in Australia, Tasmania and New Zealand* 1865
HOWITT, W.K. *A pioneer looks back* 1945
— *A pioneer looks back again* 1947
HOY, D.G. *West of the Tararuas* 1972
HOYLE, F.W. *Fragments of a journal saved from shipwreck* 1868
HUBNER, J.A. *Through the British Empire* 1886
HUDSON, F. *The song of the manly man* 1908
HUDSON, G.V. *An elementary manual of New Zealand entomology* 1892
— *New Zealand beetles and their larvae* 1934
— *New Zealand moths and butterflies* 1898
HUDSON, R.L. *Organic gardening in New Zealand* 1982
HUIE, E.C. *A plain talk about the slump* 1934
HULL, T.P. *College songs and other verses* 1907
HULME, K. *The bone people* 1983
— *The silences between (Moeraki conversations)* 1982
— *The windeater; te kaihau* 1986
HULME, K. & MORRISON, R. *Homeplaces; three coasts of the South Island of New Zealand* 1989
'HUMANIST' pseud. of S. WIGNALL *C.O's and the community* 1940
HUNN, J.K. *Not only affairs of state* 1982
HUNT, A. L. *Confessions of A. Leigh Hunt* 1951
HUNT, A.N. *Foxton 1888–1898; the first hundred years* 1987
HUNT, C. *I'm ninety-five. Any objection?* 1985
— *Speaking a silence* 1981
HUNT, FRANCES, see 'F. KEINZLY' (pseud.)
HUNT, FREDERICK *Twenty-five years' experience in New Zealand and the Chatham Islands*; J. Amery (ed.) 1866 (2edn.); also 1990 a new edn. with additional matter ed. Rhys Richards *Frederick Hunt of Pitt Island*
HUNT, L. *Defence until dawn* 1949
HUNT, S. *Drunkard's garden* 1977
HUNT, S. et al. *Poems for the eighties* 1979
HUNTER, G.E. *Round and about* 1937
HUNTER, O. *Country life in New Zealand* 1945
Hurleyville School 65th anniversary 1892–1957; P.M. Barry (ed.) 1957
HURST, M. *Music and the stage in New Zealand; a century of entertainment 1840–1943* 1944
HURSTHOUSE, C.F. *An account of the settlement of New Plymouth* 1849
— *Emigration; where to go and who should go; New Zealand and Australia as emigration fields* 1852
— *England's New Zealand war* 1865 (2edn.)
— *A lecture on New Zealand* 1849
— *Letters on New Zealand subjects* 1865
— *A letter to the Hon. E.W. Stafford* 1866
— *The New Zealand handbook* 1832, 1864 (10edn.)
— *New Zealand, or Zealandia, the Britain of the south* 1857, 1861 (2edn.)
— *New Zealand wars; a letter to the Times* 1869 (2edn.)
— *Remarks on 'New Zealand immigration'* 1871
HUTCHESON, G.R. *H.B. & J.'s handbook for the guidance of buyers of letterpress printing in New Zealand* (Parts I and II) 1938
HUTCHINS, G. *The Howarth years* 1985
— *Rugby rabbits* 1983
— *Tall half-backs; a ticket to ride to yesterday* 1987
HUTCHINSON, F. *At Omatua's fireside* 1947
HUTCHINSON, I. *Forbidden marriage* 1971
Hutchinson's Australasian encyclopaedia 1890
HUTT, M. *New Zealand; your future* 1948
HUTTON, F.W. *Catalogue of the birds of New Zealand* 1871
— *Catalogue of the marine mollusca of New Zealand* 1873
— *Echinodermata of New Zealand* 1872
— *Geological report on the geology of the Thames gold fields* 1867
— *Notes on some of the birds inhabiting the southern ocean* 1865
HUTTON, F.W. & DRUMMOND, J. *The animals of New Zealand* 1904

HUTTON, F.W. & HECTOR, J. *Fishes of New Zealand; catalogue with diagnoses of the species* 1872
HUXLEY, L. *Life and letters of Thomas Henry Huxley* (vol. I) 1903
Hyacinths and biscuits; the diamond jubilee of the Penwomen's Club 1985
HYDE, N. *Earthly delights* 1989
HYDE, ROBIN pseud. of I.G. WILKINSON *Check to your king* 1936
— *The desolate stars* 1930
— *The godwits fly* 1938, (1970 facs.)
— *A home in this world* written 1937, pub. 1984
— *Houses by the sea & the later poems of Robin Hyde* 1952
— *Journalese* 1934
— *Nor the years condemn* 1938
— *Passport to hell* 1936
— *Persephone in winter* 1937
— *Selected poems*; selected & edited by Lydia Wevers 1984
— *Wednesday's children* 1937
'HYGROLOGY' (pseud.) *The reign of pain and plaguy drain* 1876

The ideal cookery book; E.M. Cameron (comp.) 1929
IHIMAERA, W. *The matriarch* 1986
— *The new net goes fishing* 1977
— *Pounamu, pounamu* 1972
— *Tangi* 1973
The illustrated encyclopedia of New Zealand; G. McLauchlan (ed.) 1986, 1989
Illustrations of the New Zealand flora; T.F. Cheeseman (ed.) 1914
In and out of the world; Seventh-day Adventists in New Zealand; P.J. Ballis (ed.) 1985
Information respecting the settlement of New Plymouth 1841
INGLESON, A. *The battle of life; or reminiscences of a working man* 1881
INGLEWOOD, K. pseud. of K.E. ISITT *Patmos* 1905
INGLIS, J. *Our New Zealand cousins* 1887
INGRAM, N.M. *Anzac diary* 1987
INGRAM, W. *Legends in their lifetime* 1962
INNES, C.L. *Canterbury sketches* 1879
In their own words; from the sound archives of Radio New Zealand 1988
In the matter of Dr. Buller's petition before the House of Representatives 1877 1878
Introducing New Zealand 1950
Invercargill Middle School jubilee souvenir 1923
INWOOD, F.R. *The christian year beneath the Southern Cross* 1906
IRVINE R.F. & ALPERS O.T.J. *The progress of New Zealand in the century* 1902
IRVINE-SMITH, F.L. *The streets of my city* 1948
ISDALE, A.M. *The hotels of old Thames* 1950
— *Several things* 1937
ISITT, F.W. (pseud.) *New Zealand; as it was in 1870; as it is in 1880* 1880
ISITT, K.E., see INGLEWOOD, K. (pseud.)
IZETT, J. *The blood that makes the Empire* 1901
— *Maori lore; the traditions of the Maori people* 1904

JACKSON, A.F. *Passage to Tobruk* 1943
JACKSON, L.L. *Annals of a New Zealand family* 1935
JACKSON, M. *Rainshadow; a novel* 1988
JACKSON, R.M. *Wildlife New Zealand; an artist's impression* 1982
JACKSON, W.K. *The New Zealand legislative council* 1972
JACOBS, H. *A lay of the Southern Cross* 1893
— *Shadows of the old church* 1870
JACOBSON, H.C. *Tales of Banks Peninsula* 1893 (2edn.)
JAEGER, E.C. *A source-book of biological names and terms* 1944
JAMES, C. *The quiet revolution* 1986
James K. Baxter 1926–1972; a memorial volume 1972
JAMESON, R.G. *New Zealand, South Australia and New South Wales* 1841
JARDINE, D.G. *Shadows on the hill; The Remarkables station, Queenstown* 1978
JARVEY, W.A. *Trial of Captain Jarvey* 1865
JELLYMAN, D.J. & TODD, P.R. *MAF Fisheries Research Division information leaflet XI. 1* 1982
JEFFERY, M. *Mairangi* 1964
JEFFREYS, F.J. *Immanuel and other poems* 1898
JENKIN, R. *New Zealand mysteries* 1970
JENKINSON, S.H. *New Zealanders and science* 1940
JENKYNS, C.C. (pseud. of C.C. CARLYON) *Hard life in the colonies* 1892
JEWELL, A.T. *Accounting in the timber industry*; (glossary pp. 128–130) 1948
Jewlius Rex and men of his time 1876
'J.H.K.' (pseud.) *Henry Ancrum* 1872
JILLETT, D. *Malvina; a biography of Dame Malvina Major* 1995
'J.K.M.' pseud. of J.K. MOILLET
Johnny Morton's Mastodon Minstrel song book 1882
'JOHN O'DREAMS' pseud. of H.E. LONGFORD
JOHNSON, C. *Snow flakes from Egmont* 1889
JOHNSON, DAVID *Summer cruise; behind the grand pleasure trip of the S.S. Ngapuhi along the northern coast of New Zealand* 1983

JOHNSON, J. *Notes from a journal [1846–1847]* in *Early travellers in New Zealand*; N.M. Taylor (ed.) 1959
JOHNSON, J. P. *Plain truths told by a traveller* 1840
JOHNSON, LOUIS *Coming and going; poems* 1982
— *Onion* 1972
— *Roughshod among the lilies* 1951
— *The sun among the ruins* 1951
JOHNSON, MARGUERITE M., also as 'REWA GLENN' (pseud.) *Life's vagaries* 1970
— *The turn of the tide* 1968
JOHNSON, MIKE *Anti body positive* 1988
— *Foreigners* 1991
JOHNSON, P. *Wildflowers of Central Otago* 1986
JOHNSON, S. *The glass whittler* 1988
JOHNSTON, A. ST. *A distant sketching ground*; extracted from *The Argosy* (Dec.) 1883
JOHNSTON, CHRISTINE *Blessed art thou among women* 1991
JOHNSTON, C.M. & MORTON, H. *Dunedin Teachers College; the first hundred years* 1976
JOHNSTON, G. *The fish factory* 1981
JOHNSTON, L. F. *Twenty-one years with boots and pack* 1947
JOHNSTON, R.J. *New Zealanders* 1976
JOHNSTONE, J.C. *Maoria* 1874
— *The Maories and the causes of the present anarchy in New Zealand* 1861
JOLLIFFE, W. *A history of New Zealand stamps* 1913
JONES, E. *Autobiography of an early settler* 1933
JONES, H.F. *Samuel Butler; author of Erewhon; a memoir vol. I* 1919
JONES, K.L. (comp.) *Goldfields seminar 1980; Cromwell, New Zealand; selected papers from the proceedings* 1981
JONES, L. *Gilmore's dairy* 1985
— *Splinter* 1985
JONES, N.P.H. *Jonesy* 1981
JONES, PEI TE H. *King Potatau; an account of the life of Potatau Te Whirowhiro the first Maori king* 1960
— *Puhiwahine Maori poetess* 1961
JONES, R.E. *Letters* 1982
— *New Zealand the way I want it* 1978
— *Wimp walloping* 1987
— *'80s letters* 1990
JOSEPH, G.I. *Distorted torts; leaves from a lawyer's memory* 1972
— *The horse with the delicate air and other stories* 1945
JOSEPH, M.K. *The hole in the zero* 1967
— *Imaginary islands* 1950
— *Inscription on a paper dart; selected poems 1945–72* 1974
— *The living countries* 1959
— *A pound of saffron* 1962
— *A soldier's tale* 1976
— *The time of Achamoth* 1977
Journal of Agriculture cookery book 1955
JOURNET, T. *Take my tip* 1954
JOYCE, A. *Land ho!* 1881
Jubilee of the civic government, borough of Gisborne and county of Cook..1877–1927 1927
JUSTIN, J. *Prisoner* 1973

'K.' pseud. of A. KENNEDY *A visit to Lake Rotoaira* 1885
Kahikatea, cabbage trees and koromiko; a history of the pioneering and early days in the Waerenga Valley; C. Sherson (ed.) 1981
KAYE, E.B. *Haromi* 1900
KEENE, F. *Myrtle and Sophia* 1982
— *O te rake; Maori legends of the north* 1963
KEENE, K., see MCLATCHIE, R.L.
KEESING, F.M. *The changing Maori* 1928
'KEINZLY, F.' pseud. of HUNT, FRANCES *Tangahano* 1960
— *A time to prey* 1969
KEITH, H. *A lovely day tomorrow; New Zealand in the 1940s* 1991
KELLIHER, H.J. *New Zealand at the crossroads* 1935, (1937)
KELLY, G. *Gun in the hills* 1968
KELLY, J.L. *Heather and fern* 1902
— *Zealandia's jubilee* 1890
KELLY, T. *Narrative of a journey through upper Waitara Valley* 1892
KEMP, H.T. *Revised narrative of incidents and events in the early colonizing history of New Zealand* 1901
KENDALL, T. *A korao no New Zealand; or, the New Zealander's first book* 1815, (1957 facs.)
KENNAWAY, L.T. *Crusts; a settler's fare due south* 1874
KENNAWAY, W. & L.T. *Biscuit and butter; a colonist's shipboard fare; the journal kept by William and Laurence Kennaway on board the emigrant ship Canterbury*; R.C. Lamb & R.S. Gormack (eds.) 1973
KENNEALLY, J. & B. *Johnsonville Yesterday* ?1981

KENNEDY, ALEXANDER (of Auckland) *New Zealand* 1873
— *Notes of a short tour into the interior of the northern colony* 1852
KENNEDY, ALEXANDER (of Napier) (as 'K.' pseud.) *A visit to Lake Rotoaira* 1885
KENNEDY, D. *Kennedy's colonial travel; a narrative of a four years' tour through Australia, New Zealand, Canada &c.* 1876
KENNEDY, J. *Straight from the shoulder* 1981
KENNELLY, A.G. *The home vegetable garden* 1951
KENNY, A.A. *The Elmslie mystery* 1934
— *The rebel* 1934
KENWAY, P.T. *Pioneering in Poverty Bay* 1928
— *Quondam quaker* 1947
KERNOHAN, D. *Wellington's new buildings; a photographic guide to new buildings in central Wellington* 1989
KERR, I.S. *Campbell Island; a history* 1976
KERR, W. *Our home in the roaring forties* 1926
KERRY-NICHOLLS, J.H. *The King Country* 1884
KERSHAW, M. *Colonial facts and fictions* 1886
KIDMAN, F. *The book of secrets* 1987, (1988)
— *Mandarin summer* 1981
— *Mrs Dixon and friend* 1982
— *Paddy's puzzle* 1983
— *True stars* 1990
KING, C.M. (ed.), see *The handbook of New Zealand mammals*
— *Seals of the world* 1983
KING, D. *Seen but not heard* 1982
KING, F. TRUBY *The evils of cram* 1906
— *Feeding and care of baby* 1913 edn.
KING, H.B. *Bill's philosophy and other verses* 1903
KING, MARY TRUBY *Truby King the man; a biography* 1948
KING, MICHAEL *Apirana Ngata* 1988
— *Being Pakeha; an encounter with New Zealand and the Maori renaissance* 1985
— *The collector; a biography of Andreas Reischek* 1981
— *Frank Sargeson; a life* 1995
— *A land apart; the Chatham Islands* 1990
— *Moriori; a people rediscovered* 1989
— *New Zealanders at war* 1981
— *Pakeha; the quest for identity in New Zealand* 1991
— *Te Puea* 1977
— *Whina; a biography of Whina Cooper* 1983
KING, P.P. *Narrative of the surveying voyages of His Majesty's ships Adventure and Beagle between the years 1826 and 1836* 1839
KINGMA, J.T. *The geological structure of New Zealand* 1974
KINGSTON, W.H.G. *Holmwood; or, the New Zealand settler* 1868
— *Waihoura; or the New Zealand girl* 1872
KINGTON, J. (ed.) *Pataka* 1936
KINROSS, A. *My life and lays* 1899
KINROSS, S. *Please to remember* 1963
KINSKY, F.C. & ROBERTSON, C.J.R. *Handbook of common New Zealand birds* 1987
KIPLING, R. *One lady at Wairakei* 1892, (1983)
KIPPENBERGER, H.K. *Infantry brigadier* 1949
KIRK, HENRY, see 'THE MIXER' (pseud.)
KIRK, T. *The forest flora of New Zealand* 1889
— *Report on the durability of New Zealand timber* in *New Zealand Government reports on the durability of New Zealand timber* 1875
— *The students' flora of New Zealand and the outlying islands* 1899
KITTO, J.F. *The practical dredgeman's manual* 1900
'KIWI' pseud. of B. MAITLAND *On the swag; sketches of station life in Hawkes Bay* 1911
The Knapdale run; E. Kerse (ed.) 1984
KNELL, B. (pseud.) *As the story goes* 1929
KNIGHT, JIM *Greville* 1977
KNIGHT, LINDSAY *Gary Knight, Andy Dalton, John Ashworth; the geriatrics* 1986
— *Shield fever* 1986
— *They led the All Blacks* 1991
KNIGHT, H. & WALES, N. *Buildings of Dunedin* 1988
KNIGHT, R. *Poyntzfield; the McKenzies of lower Rangitikei* 1975
KNOX, E. *After Z-hour* 1987
KNOX, G.A. (ed.) *The natural history of Canterbury* 1969
KNOX, T.W. *The boy travellers in Australasia* 1889
KOEA, S. *The grandiflora tree* 1989
— *Staying home and being rotten* 1992
KOEBEL, W.H. *The anchorage* 1908
— *In the Maoriland bush* 1911
— *The return of Joe* 1907
KOHERE, R.T. *The autobiography of a Maori* 1951
— *The story of a Maori chief* 1949

LACEY, LEN pseud. of P. GIFFORD
LAIDLAW, C. *Mud in your eye* 1973

LAING, R.M. & BLACKWELL, E.W. *Plants of New Zealand* 1907 (2edn.), 1940 (4edn.)
Lake Taupo (DSIR Information Series No.158) 1983
LAMB, K.A.S. *Sons of the south and other verses* 1927
LAMBERT, G. & R. *An illustrated history of Taranaki* 1983
LAMBERT, M.G. *Diary written while on a fortnight's tour* 1873
LAMBERT, M. & PALENSKI R. *The New Zealand almanac* 1982
LAMBERT, T. *Pioneering reminiscences of Old Wairoa* 1936
LAMBRECHTSEN, N.C. *What grass is that?* 1992 (4edn.)
LANCASTER, G.B. pseud. of EDITH J. LYTTLETON *The altar stairs* 1908
— *Fool divine* 1917
— *The honourable Peggy* 1911
— *Jim of the ranges* 1910
— *The law bringers* 1913
— *Pageant* 1933
— *Promenade* 1938
— *Sons o' men* 1904
— *A spur to smite* 1905
— *The tracks we tread* 1907
Landfall country; work from Landfall, 1947–61; C. Brasch (comp.) 1962
Land of the mist; the story of Urewera National Park 1983
LANG, J.D. *An historical and statistical account of New South Wales* 1834, (1837)
— *New Zealand in 1839* 1839, (1873)
LANGDALE-HUNT, E. *The last entail male* 1985
LANGE, D. *The wit of David Lange*; D. Barber (comp.) 1987
LANGFORD, G. *Newlands* 1990
LANGTON, W. *Mark Anderson* 1889
LAPHAM, H. *We four, and the stories we told* 1880
LAPHAM, H., see also WOOD, SUSAN
LARKWORTHY, F. *New Zealand revisited* 1881
LA ROCHE, A. (ed.) *The history of Howick & Pakuranga* 1991
LASENBY, J. *The conjuror* 1992
LASLETT, T. *Timber and timber trees* 1875
LATHAM, D. *The golden reefs* 1992 (2edn.)
LATHAM, I. *WAAC story* 1986
LAUPER, J., see *Over the Whitcombe Pass* 1863
LAURIDSEN, W.J. *Linton, 1889–1989* 1989
LAWLOR, P. *Confessions of a journalist* 1935
— *The house of Templemore* 1938
— *Maori tales* 1926
— *More Wellington days* 1962
— *Murphy's moa* 1936
— *Old Wellington days* 1959
LAWRENCE, W.R.C. (ed.) *Yours and mine* 1936
— *Three mile bush* 1934
LAWRY, M. *Good luck and lavender* 1980
LAWSON, J. *Jenny Lawson cook book* 1986
LAWSON, R. *Fragmenta animi* 1942
LAWSON, W. *Between the lights* 1906
— *Gold in their hearts* 1951
— *Historic Trentham 1914–1917* 1917
— *The laughing buccaneer* 1935
— *Mary Smith's hotel*; (a reissue of *Gold in their hearts* 1951) 1957
— *The Red West Road and other verses* 1903
— *Stokin' and other verses* 1908
LAY, G. *The fools on the hill* 1988
Leases & lands; a handbook for residential leaseholders; St John's College Trust Board 1978
LEATHES, E. *An actor abroad* 1880
LECOY, A. *New Zealand state forests* 1878
LEDYARD, J. *John Ledyard's [1783] journal of Captain Cook's last voyage*; J.K. Mumford (ed.) 1963
LEE, G.R., COLLINS, R.J.G., & WATTS, C.V. *The penny universal of New Zealand* 1953
LEE, I. *The bush fire and other verses* 1897
LEE, J.A. *Children of the poor* 1934, (1949)
— *Civilian into soldier* 1937
— *The hunted* 1936
— *The John A. Lee diaries 1936–1940* 1981
— *Mussolini's millions* 1970
— *Political notebooks* 1973
— *The politician* 1987
— *Rhetoric at the red dawn* 1965
— *Shiner Slattery* 1964
— *Shining with the shiner* 1944
— *Soldier* 1976
— *The yanks are coming* 1943
LEE, MARY I. *The not so poor; an autobiography* 1992 (written 1936)
LEE, S. & KENDALL, T. *Grammar and vocabulary of the language of New Zealand* 1820

LEITCH, D.B. *Railways of New Zealand* 1972
LELAND, L.S. *A personal Kiwi-Yankee dictionary* 1980
LENNOX, C. *A guilty innocence* 1895
LENTLE, R. & SAXTON, F. *Red deer in New Zealand; a complete hunting manual* 1991
LE PROU, C. *Waters back* 1989
LESSITER, M. *Butterflies and moths* 1989
LETHBRIDGE, C. *Sunrise on the hills; a musterer's year on Ngamatea New Zealand's biggest sheep station* 1971
Letters from Gunner 7/516 and Gunner 7/517; B. Harper (ed.) 1978
Letters from Otago 1848–1849; Victorian New Zealand; a [Hocken Library] reprint series No.4 1978
Letters from settlers and labouring emigrants in the New Zealand company's settlements..Feb. 1842 to Jan. 1843 1843
Letters from New Plymouth [A selection from *Letters from settlers 1843*] 1843, (1968 facs.)
LEVIEN, J.M. *The woods of New Zealand* 1861
LEVY, E. B. *Grasslands of New Zealand* 1951 1edn., 1970 (3edn.)
Lexicographical and linguistic studies; essays in honour of G.W. Turner 1988
Liberal and Labour Federation; report of proceedings of the conference..1903 1903
LILICO, J. *Sheep dog memoirs* 1934
LIND, C.A. *A cut above; early history of the Alliance Freezing Company (Southland) Ltd.* 1985
LINDSAY, W.L. *Contributions to New Zealand botany* 1868
— *The place and power of natural history in colonization* 1862
LINDSAY-BUCKNALL, H. *A search for fortune* 1878
LINGARD, F. *Prison labour in New Zealand* 1936
LINKLATER, E. *A year of space* 1953, (1954)
LIPSON, L. *The politics of equality* 1948
Listener: see also *New Zealand Listener*
Listener short stories 3; M. Gifkins (ed.) 1984
LLEWELLYN, S.P. *Journey towards Christmas; official history of the 1st Ammunition Company* 1949
— *Troopships* 1949
LLOYD, H.D. *Newest England* 1900
LLOYD, V.S. *Son of Peter* 1930
'L.M.B.' (pseud.) *The present position of education in New Zealand* 1903
LOCHORE, R.A. *From Europe to New Zealand* 1951
LOCKE, E. *The gaoler* 1978
— *The kauri and the willow* 1984
— *Student at the gates* 1981
LOCKLEY, R. *The house above the sea* 1980
LOGAN, H.F. *Ferns* 1875
LONGFORD, H.E. as 'JOHN O'DREAMS' (pseud.) (comp.) *Gift book of New Zealand verse* 1931
LORD, E.I. *Old Westland* 1940
— *Revised ballads of Bung* 1921, (1976 facs.) [unpaged]
LORETZ, G. *Moments of life* 1976
LOUGHNAN, R.A. *The first gold discoveries in New Zealand* 1906
— *New Zealand at home* 1908
— *Royalty in New Zealand* 1902
LOVELL-SMITH, E.M. *Old coaching days in Otago and Southland* 1931, (1976)
LOW, D.C. *Salute to the scalpel* 1972
Lower Hutt past and present 1941
LOWTH, A. *Emerald hours in New Zealand* 1907
LUCETT, E. *Rovings in the Pacific, from 1837 to 1849* 1851
LUSH, V. *The Auckland journals of Vicesimus Lush 1850–63*; A. Drummond (ed.) 1971
— *The Thames journals of Vicesimus Lush 1868–82*; A. Drummond (ed.) 1975
— *The Waikato journals of Vicesimus Lush 1864–8*; A. Drummond (ed.) 1982
LUSK, E., see MILTON, E. (pseud.)
LUXFORD, J.H. *The liquor laws of New Zealand* 1964 edn.
LYNN, R. *Under the Lynnwood tree 1840–1940* 1982
LYON, J.H. *Faring south; memoirs of a pioneer family* 1952
LYSNAR, F.B. *New Zealand; the dear old Maori land* 1915, (1924 2edn.)
LYTTLETON, G.W. *New Zealand and the Canterbury colony* 1859
— *Two lectures on a visit to the Canterbury colony in 1867–8* 1868
LYTTLETON, EDITH J., see LANCASTER, G.B. (pseud.)

MCADAM, C., see CLYDE, CONSTANCE (pseud.)
MACAIRE, R. *To prohibit or not to prohibit! That is the question; the disease and the remedy* 1911
MCALLISTER, C. *Old Taranaki and its mountain* 1976
MACANDREW, J. *Address to the people of Otago* 1875
MCARA, J.B. *Gold mining at Waihi 1878–1952* 1978
MCCALLUM, A. *A meeting of gentlemen on matters agricultural; the Masterton show 1871–1986* 1986
MCCALLUM, R.M. *Report on Dairy Factories in New Zealand* 1888
MCCALLUM, W.N., see 'HORI' (pseud.)

MCCARROLL, H.S. *The days of the kauri bushmen*; (Radio talks 1–4; TS) [a1914], (1951)
MCCARROLL, R. *Life is so complicated* c1992
MCCARTEN, A. *A modest apocalypse and other stories* 1991
MCCARTHY, B. *Castles in the soil* 1939
MCCARTHY, W.J. *Broadcasting with the kiwis* 1947
— *Listen ...! it's a goal* 1973
MCCASKILL, L.W. *Hold this land; a history of soil conservation in New Zealand* 1973
— *Molesworth* 1969
MCCAULEY, S. *Other halves* 1982
— *Then again* 1986
MCCLENAGHAN, J. *Fiordland* 1966
— *Travelling man* 1976
MCCLUNIE, A. *The adventures of Toby and Sphinx in Flowerland* c1922
— *The enchanted packman* 1919
MCCLYMONT, W.G. *The exploration of New Zealand* 1940, 1959 (2edn.)
MCCONNELL, C.L. *Challenge and change; a history of the South Canterbury Catchment Board* 1989
MCCONNELL, L. *Something to crow about; centennial history of the Southland RFU* 1986
MCCORMICK, E.H. *The inland eye* 1959
— *Letters and Art in New Zealand* 1940
— *New Zealand literature; a survey* 1959
MCCRAE, A. *Journal kept in New Zealand in 1820*; F.R. Chapman (ed.) 1928
MCCREDIE, N. *The bungalow recipe book; tried recipes* 1915
MCCULLOUGH, W. *Jubilee of Thames goldfield; souvenir* 1917
MCDERMOTT, J. *How to get lost and found in New Zealand* 1976
MACDONALD, C.A. *Pages from the past* 1933
MACDONALD, CHARLOTTE *The vote, the pill and the demon drink; a history of feminist writing in New Zealand 1869–1993* 1993
MACDONALD, CHARLOTTE, PENFOLD, M. & WILLIAMS, B. (eds.) *The book of New Zealand women; ko kui ma te kaupapa* 1991
MCDONALD, G. *Grand hills for sheep* 1949
— *Stinson's bush* 1954
MACDONALD, G.R. *The Canterbury Frozen Meat Company Ltd* 1957
MACDONALD, J. *Away from home* 1945
MACDONALD, J.R. *New Zealand sheepfarming* 1915, 1920 (as *Australian and New Zealand sheep farming*)
MCDONALD, K.C. *History of Waitaki Boys' High School 1883–1958* 1958
MACDONALD, RONALD E. as 'POWINA GRAY' (or GREY) (pseud.) *Demos; reflections; morning* 1935
— *A reasonable survey* 1901
MACDONALD, W.M. *Fair morning* 1949
MCDONNELL, G. *Grow your own fruit and vegetables* 1991
MCDONNELL, T. (1788–1864) *Extracts from a journal containing observations on New Zealand* 1834
MCDONNELL, T. (1832–99) *An explanation of the principal causes which led to the war on the west coast of New Zealand* 1869
MCDOWALL, R.M. *New Zealand freshwater fishes, a natural history and guide* 1978, 1990 (2edn.)
— *The New Zealand whitebait book* 1984
MCELDOWNEY, R.D. *Arguing with my grandmother* 1973
— *Full of the warm south* 1983
— *Shaking the bee tree* 1992
— *The world regained* 1957
MCELDOWNEY, W.J. *The New Zealand Library Association 1910–1960* 1962
MACFARLANE, J.S. *Craig's troubles* 1871
MACFARLANE, L.R.C. *Amuri* 1946
— *Te Raka; land of happy sunshine* 1954
— *This New Zealand* 1948
MCFARLANE, SHONA *Mixed media* 1975
MCGEE, G. *Foreskin's lament* 1981
MCGILL, D. *The baby boomers* 1989
— *A dictionary of Kiwi slang* 1988
— *The dinkum Kiwi dictionary* 1989
— *The g'day country; a rail journey back into New Zealand* 1985
— *Ghost towns of New Zealand* 1980
— (ed.) *My brilliant suburb* 1985
— *The other New Zealanders* 1982
MCGILL, D. & TILLY, G. *In praise of older buildings* 1988
MACGILL, MARGARET *An Anzac's Bride* 1918
MACGILLIVRAY, J. *Narrative of the voyage of H.M.S. Rattlesnake* 1852
MCHUTCHESON, W. *Camp-life in Fiordland, New Zealand* 1892
— *The New Zealander abroad in England, America* 1888
MCINDOE, J. *A sketch of Otago* 1878
MCINNES, G. *Castle on the run* 1969
MCINTOSH, A.D. (ed.) *Marlborough; a provincial history* 1940
MACINTOSH, J. *A history of Fortrose* 1972
MCINTYRE, W. D. & FIELD, M. *Cook's wild Strait; the interisland story* 1983

MACKAY, A. (1833–1909) *A compendium of official documents relative to native affairs in the South Island* 1873
MCKAY, A. (1842–1917) *The Canterbury Gilpin* 1880
— *Lines written on a scene from Lake Harris Saddle* 1880
— *Preliminary report on the earthquakes in the Amuri and Marlborough district* in *Geological Reports* 1888
— *Report on the geology of the south-west part of Nelson* [orig. pub. 1895 *AJHR* C-13] 1897 (2edn.)
— *Report on the older auriferous drifts of central Otago* 1897
MACKAY, D. *Working the kauri* 1991
MCKAY, F.M. *The life of James K. Baxter* 1990
MACKAY, I. *Puborama* 1961
MACKAY, JAMES *Narrative of the opening of the Hauraki District for gold mining* 1896
— *Our dealings with Maori lands* 1887
MACKAY, JESSIE *The sitter on the rail* 1891
— *The spirit of the Rangatira* 1889
MCKAY, K.J. *Practical home cookery chats and recipes* 1929
MCKEARNEY, S. *Just me; the life story of a nobody* 1938
MACKENZIE, A. *Splash of red* 1949
MACKENZIE, B. *The WAAF book; a scrapbook of wartime memories* 1982
MACKENZIE, COMPTON *Gallipoli memories* 1929
MCKENZIE, DANIEL *Rugby football in Wellington and Wairarapa, 1868–1910* 1911
MACKENZIE, D.F. *While we have prisons* 1980
MCKENZIE, DONALD FRANCIS *Oral culture literacy and print in early New Zealand; the treaty of Waitangi* 1985
MACKENZIE, F.W. *Overland from Auckland to Wellington in 1853* 1893
MACKENZIE, M.S. *Doctor Fram* 1933
— *Three dead, one hurt* 1934
MCKENZIE, N.R. *The Gael fares forth* 1935, 1942 (heavily revised edn.)
MCKENZIE, ROY *The Roydon heritage; 50 years of breeding and harness racing* 1978
MCKEON, W.J. *The fruitful years; a cavalcade of memories* 1971
MACKIE, F. *Traveller under concern; the Quaker journals of Frederick Mackie on his tour of the Australasian colonies 1852–55* 1973
MCKILLOP, H.F. *Reminiscences of twelve months service in New Zealand* 1849
MCKINLEY, E. *Ways and by-ways of a singing kiwi; with the N.Z. divisional entertainers in France* 1939
MCLACHLAN, P. *New Zealand rhymes and parody unbeautiful* 1967
MCLAGLAN, E.S.B. *Stethoscope and saddlebags* 1965
MCLAREN, D. *The back-to-front runner poems* 1974
MCLAREN, I.A. *Education in a small democracy; New Zealand* 1974
MCLATCHIE, R.L. *The tang of the bush; the story of Robert McLatchie 1875–1963 as told to his daughter Kathleen Keene* 1967 (2edn.)
MCLAUCHLAN, G.W. *The farming of New Zealand* 1981
— *The passionless people* 1976, 1989
— *The story of beer* 1994
MACLEAN, C. & PHILLIPS, J.O.C. *The sorrow and the pride; New Zealand war memorials* 1990
MCLEAN, D. *The long pathway; te ara rua* 1986
MCLEAN, F. *Otago Boys High School* 1990
MACLEAN, H. *Nursing in New Zealand* 1932
MACLEAN, N. *A lifetime at school* 1982
MCLEAN, P.S. *History and policy of the native land laws* 1886
MCLEAN, T.P. *Kings of rugby; the British Lions' 1959 tour of New Zealand* 1960
— *Willie away* 1964
— *Winter of discontent; the 1977 Lions in NZ* 1977
MACLENNAN, J. *Neptune's toll* 1907
MCLEOD, C. *Dorinda* 1967
MCLEOD, D. (ed.) *Alone in a mountain world; a high country anthology* 1972
— *Down from the tussock ranges* 1980
— *Many a glorious morning* 1970
— *New Zealand high country* 1951
— *The tall tussock; stories of the high country* 1959
MCLEOD, JANET *Rhyming roads to good speech* 1940
MACLEOD, N.F.H. *A voice on the wind; the story of Jessie Mackay* 1955
MCLINTOCK A.H. *Crown colony government in New Zealand* 1958
— *A descriptive atlas of New Zealand* 1959
— *The history of Otago* 1949
MCLINTOCK, A.H. & WOOD, G.A. *The Upper House in colonial New Zealand* 1987
MCMEEKAN, C.P. *Grass to milk* 1960
MCMENAMIN, K. *Glory days; Alex Wyllie and the Canterbury Ranfurly Shield team, 1982–85* 1986
MACMILLAN, D. *By-ways of the history of medicine* 1946
MACMORRAN, B. *In view of Kapiti* 1977
— *Octavius Hadfield* 1969
MACMORRAN, G. *Some schools and schoolmasters of early Wellington* 1900
MACMURRAN, C.W. *From New York to New Zealand* 1904
MCNAB, R. *Historical records of New Zealand* (2 vols.) 1(1908), 2(1914)

— *Murihiku and the southern islands* 1907
— *Murihiku; a history of the South Island of New Zealand* 1909
— *The old whaling days* 1913
MCNAB, R.G.C. *New Zealand slang*; extracted from *The Press* (Christchurch) p.18, 2 Apr. 1938
MCNAUGHTON, N. *Tat; the story of a New Zealand sheep dog* 1970
MCNEILL, M. *The legend of the everlasting* 1884
MCNEISH, J.H.P. *Joy* 1982
— *Lovelock* 1986
— *Mackenzie; a novel* 1970
— *A tavern in the town* 1957, (1984)
MACNICOL, T.M. *Beyond the Skippers road* 1965
— *Echoes from Skippers canyon* 1967
MCPHERSON, J.A. *Whitcombe's complete New Zealand gardener* c1943 (2nd wartime printing)
MACPHERSON, R.V. *The mystery of the forecastle* 1889
MACRAE, A. *Awful childhoods; a novel* 1988
MCRAE, S. *By the braes of Balquether* 1963
— *Gone for good* 1985
MABIN, B.E. (ed.), see *Hills and valleys*
MACTIER, S. *The hills of Hauraki* 1908
— *Miranda Stanhope* 1911
MADDOCK, S. *These antipodes; a New Zealand album 1814 to 1854* 1979
MAGURK, S. & JOURNET, T. *Hysteric New Zealand* 1949
MAHY, M. *The catalogue of the universe* 1985
— *Underrunners* 1992
MAINWARING, R., see 'A RESIDENT' (pseud.)
MAIR, G. *The story of Gate Pa* 1926
MAITLAND, B., see KNELL, B. (pseud.)
MAJOURAM, W. *Sergeant, sinner, saint and spy; the Taranaki war diary of Sergeant William Majouram, R.A.*; Barber, L. et al. (eds.) 1990
'MAKERETI' Maori by-name of MAGGIE PAPAKURA *The old-time Maori* 1938, (1986 repr.)
MALCOLM, A. as 'AMNEMA' (pseud.) *Rudolph* 1906
— *Trials and travels of a dominie* 1874
MALCOLM, M. *Where it all began; the story of Whangaruru* 1982
MALFROY, C.M. *Small sawmills* 1923
MALING, P.B. *Samuel Butler at Mesopotamia together with Butler's 'Forest Creek' manuscript* 1960
MALLOCH, D.W. *Early Waikouaiti* 1940
MALONE, R.E. *Three years' cruise in the Australasian colonies* 1854
MALTHUS, C. *ANZAC; a retrospect* 1965
Manawatu County cookery book 1913
Manawatu Tramping Club jubilee 1978
MANDER, M.J. *Allen Adair* 1925, (1971)
— *The besieging city* 1926
— *The passionate puritan* 1922
— *Pins and pinnacles* 1928
— *The story of a New Zealand river* 1920, (1974 repr.)
— *The strange attraction* 1923
MANDER, P. & O'NEILL, B. *Give a man a boat* 1964
MANDERSON, J.A. *Beer slops* 1946
Mangamaire School Jubilee (1897–1967) 1967 [unpaged]
MANHIRE, B. *The brain of Katherine Mansfield* 1988
— *The elaboration* 1972
— *Good looks* 1982
— *My sunshine* 1996
— *Zoetropes; Poems 1972–82* 1981
MANING, F.E. *A history of the war in the north of New Zealand* 1862
— *Old New Zealand; a tale of the good old times* 1863
MANNERING, G.E. *Eighty years in New Zealand* 1943
— *With axe and rope in the New Zealand Alps* 1891
MANNING, A.E. *The bodgie; a study in abnormal psychology* 1958
MANNING, W. *Below and above the waterline* 1909
— *Interned* 1915
MANN, P. *The eye of the queen* 1982
MANSFIELD, KATHERINE pseud. of KATHLEEN BEAUCHAMP *The aloe*; V. O'Sullivan (ed.) 1982
— *The collected letters of Katherine Mansfield* vol. 1 1903–1917, vol. 2 1918–1919, vol. 3 1919–1920; V. O'Sullivan & M. Scott (eds.) 1(1984), 2(1987), 3(1993)
— *The journal of Katherine Mansfield*; J.M. Murry (ed.) 1927, 1954
— *Katherine Mansfield's letters to John Middleton Murry 1913–1922*; J.M. Murry (ed.) 1951
— *Novels and Novelists* 1930
— *Poems* 1923
— *The poems of Katherine Mansfield*; V. O'Sullivan (ed.) 1988
— *The scrapbook of Katherine Mansfield*; J.M. Murry (ed.) 1974
— *The stories of Katherine Mansfield*; A. Alpers (ed.) 1984

— *Undiscovered country; the New Zealand stories of Katherine Mansfield*; I.A. Gordon (ed.) 1974
— *The Urewera note book*; I.A. Gordon (ed.) 1978
MANSON, CECIL M. *Doctor Agnes Bennett* 1960
— *I take up my pen* 1971
MANSON, CECILIA E. *The story of a New Zealand family; the beginnings* 1974
— *Widow of Thorndon Quay* 1981
— *Willow's point; a New Zealand adventure story* 1948
MANSON, D.C.M. *Native and introduced butterflies and moths* 1965
— *Native beetles.* 1960
— *Nature in New Zealand* 1965
MANTELL, G.A. *Petrifactions* 1851
MANTELL, L. *Murder and chips* 1980
— *Murder in fancydress* 1978
— *Murder in vain* 1984
— *A murder or three* 1980
— *Murder to burn* 1983
Manuka blossoms; an anthology by New Zealand authors 1936
Maori cookbook; Glenfield College home and school association (comp.) 1977
Maoriland; an illustrated handbook to New Zealand (USS Company) 1884
The Maori Land Courts; report of the Royal Commission of Inquiry 1980
Maori mementos; being a series of addresses, presented by the native people, to his Excellency Sir George Grey; C.O.B. Davies (comp.) 1855
Maori poetry; an introductory anthology; M. Orbell (ed.) 1978
MARAIS, J.S. *The colonisation of New Zealand* 1927
The marigold book of recipes; Greymouth Women's Institute (comp.) 1934
MARJORIBANKS, A. *Travels in New Zealand* 1846, (1973 facs.)
MARK, A.F. & ADAMS, N. *New Zealand alpine plants* 1973, (1979 repr.)
MARKHAM, E. *New Zealand or recollections of it, 1834*; E.H. McCormick (ed.) 1963
MARKS, M. *Memories (mainly merry)* 1934
MARKS, R. *Hammer and tap; shaping Tuapeka County* 1977
Marlborough Art & Industrial Society; a selection of competitive stories 1884
The Marlborough Sounds; a recreational guide to the Marlborough and Kaikoura areas; (Marlborough Harbour Board/Marlborough Sounds Maritime Park Board pub.) c1981
MARMON, J. *The life and adventures of John Marmon; the Hokianga Pakeha Maori*; reprinted from Auckland *Evening Star* (Auckland) Nov 19 1881
MARRIOT, J.H. *The constitutional budget..; songs intended to be sung by lovers of constitutional principles* 1858
MARRIOTT, L. *Life in the gorge* 1981
MARRIOTT-WATSON, H.B. *The web of the spider; a tale of adventure* 1891
MARRYAT, E. *Amongst the Maoris* 1874
MARSDEN, J.B. *Life and work of Samuel Marsden*; J. Drummond (ed.) 1913
— *Memoirs of the life and labours of the Rev. Samuel Marsden* 1857
MARSDEN, S. *Letters and journals of Samuel Marsden 1765–1838*; J.R. Elder (ed.) 1932
MARSH, E.G. *An inquiry into the equity..of the proposal for colonizing New Zealand* 1838
— *Enquiry into the equity..of colonizing New Zealand* 1838
MARSH, N. *Black beech and honeydew* 1965, 1981 (2edn.)
— *Colour scheme* 1943
— *Died in the wool* 1944
— *Light thickens* 1982
— *Opening night* 1951, (1968)
— *Photo-finish* 1980
— *Surfeit of lampreys* 1941
— *Vintage murder* 1937
MARSH, N. & BURDON, R.M. *New Zealand* 1942
MARSHALL, B.J. & STARTUP, R.M. *From the bay to the bush* 1984
MARSHALL, HEATHER *A nest of cuckoos* 1985
— *The secret diary of a telephonist* 1985
MARSHALL, (SIR) JOHN *Memoirs* 1983 (vol. 1)
MARSHALL, J., KINSKY, F.C. & ROBERTSON, C.J.R. *The Fiat book of common birds in New Zealand; vol. 1 Town, pasture and freshwater birds* 1972, (1973)
— *The Fiat book of common birds in New Zealand vol. 2 Mountain, bush and shore birds* 1973, (1978 repr.)
MARSHALL, O. *The ace of diamonds gang* 1993
—— *The day Hemingway died and other stories* 1984
— *The divided world* 1989
— *The lynx hunter and other stories* 1987
— *The master of big jingles and other stories* 1982
— *Supper Waltz Wilson and other New Zealand stories* 1979
MARSHALL, W.B. *A personal narrative of two visits to New Zealand..A.D. 1834* 1836
MARSHMAN, J. *Canterbury, New Zealand, in 1862* 1862, (1864 corrected and amended)
MARTENS, E.V. *Critical list of the mollusca of New Zealand contained in New Zealand collections with references to description and synonyms* 1873
MARTIN, J.E. *The forgotten worker; the rural wage earner in nineteenth-century New Zealand* 1990
MARTIN, M.A. *Our Maoris* 1884

MARTIN, S.M. *New Zealand in 1842* 1845
MARTIN, W. *The flora of New Zealand* 1961 (4edn.)
— *The New Zealand nature book* 1929
— *New Zealand nature study* 1948
MARTIN, (SIR) WILLIAM *Remarks on notes published for the New Zealand government on Sir William Martin's pamphlet entitled 'The Taranaki question'* 1861
— *The Taranaki question* 1860
MARTYN, F. *Tripoli and beyond* 1943
MASKELL, W.M. *The lay of a lost spec* 1882
MASON, B.E.G. *Awatea* 1969, (1978)
— *Bruce Mason solo* 1981
— *The hand on the rail* 1974, (1987)
— *Hongi or the noble savage* 1971, (1987)
— *The pohutukawa tree* 1963, (1978, 1987)
— *Swan song* 1974, (1987)
MASON, H.G.R. *Education today and tomorrow* 1945
MASON, M.J. *The way out; a Kiwi escapes in Italy* 1946
MASON, R.A.K. *Collected poems* 1962, (1963, 1971)
— *This dark will lighten* 1941
MASSEY, B. *Woodturning in New Zealand; the complete guide to timbers, materials and processes* 1987
MASTERS, L. *Back-Country tales* 1960
— *Tales of the mails* 1959
MASTERTON, T. *Mountain enginemen* 1973
MATHEW, F. & S.L. *The founding of New Zealand; the journals of Felton Mathew..and his wife, 1840–1847*; J. Rutherford (ed.) 1940
Matriarchs; a generation of New Zealand women talk to Judith Fyfe 1990
MATTHEWS, B. *A New Zealand gardener's notebook* 1983
MATTHEWS, JAMES W. *The New Zealand Gardening Dictionary* 1943 (3edn.)
MATTHEWS, JULIAN AA *trees in New Zealand* 1983
— *The New Zealand garden book* 1986
MATTHEWS, L. HARRISON *Wandering albatross* 1951
MATTHEWS, S.C. *Matthews of Kaitaia; the story of Joseph Matthews and the Kaitaia Mission* 1940
MAUDSLAY, A.P. *Life in the Pacific fifty years ago* 1930
MAUGHAN, C.W. *Good and faithful servants* 1974
MAWSON, D. *The home of the blizzard* 1938
MAXWELL, E. *Days with the old force* 1936
— *Pioneering at Tauranga* 1936
— *Recollections and reflections of an old New Zealander* 1935
MAY, J. *Journal of a Voyage to the South Seas* 1838
— *May's guide to farming in New Zealand* 1869
MAY, J.A.S. *A bone to pick for freetraders* 1872
MAY, P.R. *The West Coast gold rushes* 1962, 1967 (2edn.)
MAYHEW, W.R. *Tuapeka* 1949
MEAD, ARTHUR D. *Native flora of the Waitakere Range, Auckland* 1969
— *Richard Taylor; missionary tramper* 1966
MEAD, DAVID *Taranaki tales; a light-hearted look at Taranaki history* 1990
MEAD, S.M. *The art of Maori carving* 1961
— *Traditional Maori clothing* 1969
MEADE, E.H. *A ride through the disturbed districts of New Zealand*; [1870 (1edn.)] 1871 (2edn.) in *Early travellers in New Zealand*; N.M. Taylor *(ed.)* 1959
MEADS, M. *The weta book* 1990
MEEK, G. *Station days in Maoriland and other verse* 1952
Memoirs of pioneers 1943
A memorandum on New Zealand affairs; Church Missionary Society 1861
The Mercury dictionary of textile terms; compiled by the staff of Textile Mercury Ltd. (Manchester) c1930
MEREDITH, E. *Biographical sketch; reminiscences and experiences of an early colonist* 1898
MEREDITH, G.L. *Adventuring in Maoriland in the 70's* 1935
MEREDITH, V.R.S. *A long brief; recollections of a Crown solicitor* 1966
MEREWEATHER, H.A. *By sea and by land* 1874
MERGENDAHL, C.H. *This spring of love* 1948
Merriam-Webster international dictionary (Australasian supplement) 1898
Merriam-Webster third international dictionary 1961
MERRINGTON, E.N. *A great coloniser; the Rev. Dr. Thomas Burns* 1929
The merry meal maker cookery book 1936
MESSENGER, E. *Dine with Elizabeth* 1981
METGE, A.J. *The Maoris of New Zealand* 1967
— *A new Maori migration* 1964
MÉTIN, A. *Le socialisme sans doctrines* 1901
MEYER, O.P. *The four of us* 1935
MICHAELIS, HALLENSTEIN, & FARQUHAR *On the cultivation of the wattle or mimosa in New Zealand* 1882
MIDDLETON, O.E. *The stone* 1959
— *A walk on the beach* 1964

Mihaka, D.Te R. *Whakapohane* 1984
Mikaere, B. *Te Maiharoa and the promised land* 1988
Milk in cookery; Wellington City Corporation (pub.) 1937
Milkmade cook book 1938
Millar, J.H. *Beyond the marble mountain* 1949
— *High noon for coaches* 1953, (1965)
— *Westland's golden sixties* 1959
Millen, J. *Panama hats and pony tails* 1987
Miller, D. *Blow-flies (calliphoridae) and their associates in New Zealand* 1939
— *Common insects in New Zealand* 1971, 1984 (rev. A.K. Walker)
— *Forest and timber insects in New Zealand* 1925
— *Garden pests in New Zealand* 1934, 1945 (2edn.)
— *Native insects*; (Nature in New Zealand) 1955, 1970
Miller, E. *Camps, tramps and trenches; diary of a New Zealand sapper, 1917* 1939
Miller, E.B. *Economic technical cookery book* 1917
Miller, E.B. & J.A. *Elementary cookery book* 1903
Miller, F.W.G. *Beyond the Blue Mountains; a history of the West Otago district* 1954, (1978 repr.)
— *Golden days of Lake County* 1949
— *Ink on my fingers* 1967
— *There was gold in the river* 1946
Miller, H.G. *New Zealand* 1950
Miller, I.J. *Gemina* 1986
Miller, J.O. *Early Victorian New Zealand; a study of racial tension and social attitudes* 1958
Miller, M & Batt, G. *Reef and beach life in New Zealand; an introduction* 1973
Miller, R.S. *Captain Robert Strang* 1964
Mills, A.R. *Sheep-o* 1960
Mills, T.L. *Verse by New Zealand children* 1943
Milne, C.D.A. (ed.) *Handbook of environmental law* 1992
Milne, R.S. *Political parties in New Zealand* 1966
Milner, I.F.G. *Intersecting lines; the memoirs of Ian Milner* 1993
Milner, I.F.G. & Glover, D.G.M. *New poems* 1934
Milton, E. pseud. of E. Lusk *Desert quest* 1931
— *Love and chiffon* 1929
— *Stange horizon* 1930
— *They called her faith* 1932
— *Waimana* 1934
— *Wand'ring wood* 1930
Mining handbook: see Galvin, P.
Mitcalfe, B. *Hey hey hey* 1985
— *Look to the land* 1986
— *Maori poetry; the singing word* 1974
— *Pighunter* 1979
Mitchell, A. *The half-gallon quarter-acre pavlova paradise* 1972
— *Waitaki votes* 1962
Mitchell, B. *Rhymes and rambles* 1889
Moa Flat Estate; past and present 1909
Moa on Lambton Quay; animal, vegetable and funereal verse 1951
A modern junior dictionary 1949, 1958
Moeller, M.A. *An appeal to the men of New Zealand* 1869
Moffatt, H.L. *Adventures by sea and land; an autobiography (1839–1913)* 1979
Moillet, J.K. as 'J.K.M.' (pseud.) *The Mary Ira* 1867
Moir, G.M. *Guide book to the tourist routes of the great southern lakes..and the fiords of Western Otago, New Zealand* 1925, (1948 as *Moir's guide book to the tramping tracks..of Western Otago and Southland*)
Molineaux, A. & Randall, J.E. *The nurse's cookery book* 1930
Momatiuk, Y. & Eastcott, J. *High Country* 1980
Moncrieff, P. *New Zealand birds and how to identify them* 1925, 1957 (5edn.)
Money, C.L. *Knocking about in New Zealand* 1871
Monigatti, R. *New Zealand headlines* 1963
'Monowai' (pseud.) *Lady Karine* 1904
— *The waif* 1904
Monro, D. *Notes of a journey through a part of the Middle Island* in Hocken *Contributions* (Appendix C) 1844
Montgomery, E.E.M. *The land of the moa* 1896
— *Songs of the singing shepherd* 1885
Monypenny, K. *From whaling station to sheep run* 1938
Moody, W. *The dynamic doctor; Arthur Moody of Otago* 1978
Moon, H. *An account of the wreck of the H.M. sloop 'Osprey'* 1858
Moore, A. B. *From forest to farm* 1969
Moore, J.G.H. *With the fourth New Zealand rough riders* 1906
Moore, J.M. *New Zealand for the emigrant, invalid, and tourist* 1890
Moore, L.B. & Edgar, E. *Flora of New Zealand; vol. II, indigenous Tracheophyta* 1970
Moore, L.B. & Irwin, J.B. *The Oxford book of New Zealand plants* 1978
Moore, M.K. *Hard labour* 1987
Moore, S.R. *Fairy land in New Zealand* 1919

More earlier days on the coast; more local folk stories by more local folk; Egmont Pub. Lib., Opunake (comp.) 1991
Moreland, John M. (see also Doogue, R.B. & Moreland, Paul, L.J. & Moreland) *Marine fishes of New Zealand* 1967
Moreland, M.A. *Through south Westland* 1911
Moreton, H.S., see 'The Gadfly' (pseud.)
Moreton, Samuel H. *A scramble over the mountains* 1885
Morgan, W. *The journal of William Morgan; pioneer settler and Maori war correspondent*; N. Morris (ed.) 1963
Morison, J. *Australia as it is* 1867
Morrell, W.P. *Memoirs* 1979
— *New Zealand* 1935
Morrell W.P. & Hall, D.O.W. *A history of New Zealand life* 1957
Morrieson, R.H. *Came a hot Friday* 1964, (1981)
— *Pallet on the floor* 1976, (1983)
— *Predicament* 1974, (1981)
— *The scarecrow* 1963, (1976)
Morris, E.E. *Austral-English; a dictionary of Australasian words, phrases and usages* 1898
Morris, J.G. *The Westland minstrel* 1893
Morris, R. & Smith, H.W. *Wild south; saving New Zealand's endangered birds* 1988
Morrison, C. *The junior naturalist* [1966]
Morrison, R. *Auckland city and sea* 1989
Morrison, S.S. *Poems* 1934
Mortimer, J. & B. *Trees for the NZ countryside; a planter's guide* 1984
Morton, F. *The angel of the earthquake* 1909
— *Laughter and tears* 1908
— *The yacht of dreams* 1911
Morton, Harry *The whale's wake* 1982
Morton, H.B. *From Auckland to Preservation Sound* 1877
— *Notes of a New Zealand tour* 1873
— *Recollections of early New Zealand* 1925
Morton, J. et al. *To save a forest; Whirinaki* 1984
Morton, J. & Miller, M. *The New Zealand sea shore* 1968
Morton, K.E. *Along the road* 1928
— *The joy of the road* 1929
Moser, T. *Mahoe leaves; being a selection of sketches of New Zealand and its inhabitants* 1863
Mosley, M. *Illustrated guide to Christchurch* 1885
Mountain, J. *Love is vanity* 1947
— *The pioneers* 1946
Mourie, G.N.K. & Palenski, R.A. *Graham Mourie captain* 1982
Mousley, E.O. *The secrets of a Kuttite* 1922 (2edn.)
Mozley & Whiteley's Law Dictionary New Zealand Edition; G.W. Hinde (ed.) 1964
Mr Explorer Douglas; J. Pascoe (ed.) 1957
MsCellany; Women writers' prose and poetry; B. Bremner et al. (comp.) 1987
Mueller, F.J.H. von *Extra-tropical plants* 1888 (2edn.)
— *The vegetation of the Chatham Islands* 1864
Mueller, G. *My dear Bannie; Gerhard Mueller's letters from the West Coast 1865–6*; M.V. Mueller (ed.) 1958
Muir, D.C.W. (ed.) *Long time passing*; (Mataura Rugby Football Club) 1986
Muir, M.R. *Word for word* 1960
Muldoon, R.D. *The rise and fall of a young Turk* 1974
Mulgan, A.E. *The city of the strait; Wellington and its province* 1939
— *First with the sun* 1939
— *From track to highway* 1944
— *Golden wedding* 1932
— *Home; a New Zealander's adventure* (reprinted 1934 as *Home; a colonial's adventure*) 1927
— *Literature and authorship in New Zealand* 1943
— *Literature and landscape in New Zealand* 1946
— *The making of a New Zealander* 1958
— *Pastoral New Zealand* 1946
— *A pilgrim's way in New Zealand* 1935
— *Spur of morning* 1934
— *Three plays of New Zealand* 1922
Mulgan, E.K. & A.E. *The New Zealand citizen* 1914
Mulgan, J. *Man alone* 1939
— *Report on experience* 1947
Mulgrew, P. *The Gentleman's Magellan* 1974
Mulhall, M.G. *England's new sheep-farm* 1882
Mulinder, O.C.A. (comp.) *A pioneer family* 1977
Muller, M., see 'A German Lady' (pseud.)
Mundy, D.L.G. *The bodysnatcher and the seagull*; (unpaged pamphlet) 1954
— *The days that are no more* 1953
— *There's gold in them hills* 1948
Mundy, G.C. *Our antipodes* 1852, also 4edn. in one vol. 1857

Mune, Ian *The mad dog gang meets Rotten Fred and Ratsguts* 1979
The murder of the Rev. C.S. Volkner in New Zealand 1865
Murdoch, H.H. *Dainties, or how to please our lords and masters* 1887
Murdoch, J.H. *The high schools of New Zealand; a critical survey* 1943
Murgatroyd, A. *Poems* 1900
Murphy, R.C. *Oceanic birds of South America*; (American Museum of Natural Hist. New York) 1936
Murphy, W.E. *The relief of Tobruk*; (New Zealand in the second world war 1939–45; official history) 1961
Murray, D.C. *The antipodeans*; extracted from *Contemporary Review* 1890
Murray, J. *A description of the province of Southland* 1866
Murray, J.M. *The New Zealand Alliance handbook* 1925
— *The temperance problem in New Zealand* 1936
Murray, J.S. & R.W. *Costly gold* 1977
Murray-Oliver, A.St.C.M. (comp.) *An anthology of high school verse* 1936
Musgrave, H. *Myola* 1917
Musgrave, T. *Castaway on the Auckland Isle* 1865
Muter, E. *Travels and adventures of an officer's wife* 1864
Myers, M.W. *Valiant love* 1941
My home town; a selection from *North & South* magazine 1991

Nalder, M. as 'Pakeha' (pseud.) *Battle-smoke ballads or rhymes of the Transvaal war* 1902
Napier, W.J. *Letters to the people on the political situation* 1891
Narrative of the Maungatapu murders 1866
Nash, W. *New Zealand, a working democracy* 1943
Na to hoa aroha, from your dear friend; the correspondence between Sir Apirana Ngata and Sir Peter Buck, 1925–50; Sorrenson, M.P.K. (ed.) 3 vols., 1(1986), 2(1987), 3(1988)
Natusch, S.E. *Animals of New Zealand* 1967
— *The cruise of the Acheron; 1848–51* 1978
— *Hell and high water* 1977
— *Wild fare for wilderness foragers* 1979
Neal, P.E. *From London to lonely Rai* 1969 (2edn.)
Neave, E. & M. *The land of Munros, merinos and matagouri; its kirk, pioneers and descendants* 1980
Nees, E. & D. *This is our story* 1982
Neil, J.F. *The New Zealand family herb doctor* 1889, (1980)
Neill, J.C. *The New Zealand tunnelling company* 1922
Nelson College Old Boys register 1856–1956 1956
The Nelson cookery book; Nelson Plunket Society (comp.) c1929
Nelson, E.M. *A Song of Southland* 1949
Nesfield, H.W. *A chequered career* 1881
Newbold, G. *The big huey; an inmate's candid account of five years inside New Zealand's prisons* 1982
— *Punishment and politics; the maximum security prison in New Zealand* 1989
The new Collins concise dictionary of the English language; New Zealand edition; I.A. Gordon (ed.) 1982
The new cookery book for 1909 1909
The new home cookery book; New Zealand Country Women's Institutes (comp.) 1955 edn.
Newman, A.K. *Who are the Maoris?* 1912
Newnham, T.O. *25 years of C.A.R.E.* 1989
— *1840–1990. A long white cloud?* 1989
The new Oxford book of light verse 1978
Newport, J.N.W. *Collingwood; a history of the area from earliest days to 1912* 1971
— *Footprints* 1962
— *Footprints too; further glimpses into the history of the Nelson province* 1978
Newton, A. *Dictionary of birds* (Britain) 1896
Newton, J. *Successful recipes* 1907
Newton, N.E.B. *The New Zealand prison system* 1946
Newton, P. *Big country of the North Island* 1969
— *Big country of the South Island (north of the Rangitata)* 1973 (1977)
— *The boss's story* 1966
— *High country days* 1949
— *High country journey* 1952
— *In the wake of the axe; big country of the west and north* 1972
— *Sheep thief* 1972
— *Sixty thousand on the hoof; big country south of the Rangitata* 1975
— *Ten thousand dogs* 1971
— *Wayleggo* 1947
New Women's fiction; A. McLeod (ed.) 1988
New Zealand agriculture; (MAF) 1974
New Zealand and its six colonies historically and geographically described 1853
New Zealand and south seas exhibition; papers read at the mining conference 1890
New Zealand at the front 1917 (first series), 1918 (second series)
New Zealand best poems; C.A. Marris (ed.) 1932

New Zealand Company; latest information from the settlement of New Plymouth 1842
The New Zealanders; extracted from *Blackwood's Magazine* Oct 1851
New Zealand for the Britisher; (Dominion Settlement Association) 1925
New Zealand, a glance at the first history of its colonization; extracted from *The Monthly Chronicle* 1841
The New Zealand goldfields 1861; a series of letters reprinted from the *Melbourne Argus* in *Victorian New Zealand*; a [Hocken Library] reprint series No.1 1861, (1976)
The New Zealand Government and the Maori War of 1863–4; (Aborgines Protection Society) 1864
New Zealand in the 1830's; a reprint from *The Independent* (Launceston) 9 Aug 1834 in *Victorian New Zealand*; a [Hocken Library] reprint series No.6 1834, (1979)
New Zealand; its progress and resources; extracted from the *Quarterly Review*, London No.212 Oct. 1859 1859
The New Zealand junior encyclopaedia 1960
New Zealand Listener: see also *Listener short stories 3* 1984
New Zealand Listener short stories [volume 1] B. Manhire (ed.) 1977
New Zealand Listener short stories volume 2; B. Manhire (ed.) 1978
New Zealand mining handbook: see Galvin, P.
The New Zealand official handbook 1892
The New Zealand pocket Oxford dictionary; R.W. Burchfield (ed.) 1986
New Zealand; Port Nicholson, Nelson; extracted from *The Journal of Civilisation* 1841
A New Zealand prayer book; (The Church of the Province of New Zealand) 1989
The New Zealand reader; prepared for use in the fifth and sixth standard classes 1895
New Zealand rules of racing; New Zealand Racing Conference 1986
New Zealand's best apple recipes; Apple & Pear Marketing Board (pub.) 1991
New Zealand Shearers' and Woolshed Employees' Industrial Association of Workers; report of the third annual conference, Wellington April 9th to 12th, 1912 1912
New Zealand short stories; O.N. Gillespie (ed.) 1930
New Zealand short stories (first series); D.M. Davin (ed.) 1953
New Zealand short stories (second series); C.K. Stead (ed.) 1966
New Zealand short stories (third series); V. O'Sullivan (ed.) 1975
New Zealand short stories (fourth series); L. Wevers (ed.) 1984
New Zealand's jubilee; (pub. *Evening Post*, Wellington) 1890
New Zealand's jubilee, 1840–1890; the first fifty years of our history; reprinted from the *New Zealand Herald* 1890
The New Zealand songster number 3: see *The colonial songster* c1875
A New Zealand station; extracted from *Chamber's Journal* Feb. 4 1871
New Zealand women's household guide 1936
New Zealand Yesterdays; H. Keith & W. Main (comp.) 1984
Ngata, A.T., see *Na to hoa aroha*
Nicholas, J.L. *Narrative of a voyage to New Zealand, performed in the years 1814 and 1815* 1817
Nicholls, M.F. *With the All Blacks in Springbokland* 1928
Nicol, C.G. *The story of two campaigns* 1921
Nilson, B. *Penguin cookery book* 1972
Nisbet, H. *The rebel chief* 1896
Nolan, P.E. *Rewi Maniapoto..and other poems* 1894
Nolan, T. *The bad old days; a century in the young colony of New Zealand* 1979
— *The gold fossicker's handbook* 1983
— *Historic gold trails of Nelson and Marlborough* 1976
Noonan, R. *By design* 1975
Nordmeyer, A. *Waitaki; the river and its lakes, the land and its people* 1981
Norgrove, R. *The shoestring sailors* 1987
Norman, W.H. & Musgrave, T. *Journals of the voyage and proceedings of H.M.C.S. 'Victoria', 1866* 1866
Norris, E. *Amongst the Maoris* 1874
Norris, H.C.M. *Armed settlers; the story of the founding of Hamilton..1864–1874* 1963
— *Settlers in depression; a history of Hamilton, New Zealand* 1964
Northcote-Bade, S. *Colonial Furniture in New Zealand* 1971
Northcroft, A.B.B., see Guthrie, B. (pseud.)
Notes on New Zealand; N.Z. company pub. of 6 series of extracts from letters 1849 (let.1–4), 1850 (5 & 6)
Nott, Jean *Sound living; memoirs of a resident of Kenepuru Sound* 1994

O'Biso, C. *First light* 1987
O'Brien, C. *AA book of New Zealand wildlife* 1981
Odell, R.S. *Handbook of the Arthur Pass National Park* 1935
The official handbook of New Zealand 1875 and 1883
Of pavlovas, poetry and paradigms; essays in honour of Harry Orsman; L. Bauer & C. Franzen (eds.) 1993
Ogilvie, G. *Moonshine country; the story of Waitohi, South Canterbury* 1971
Ogonowska-Coates, H. *Boards, blades & barebellies* 1987
O'Hara, J. *The history of New South Wales* 1817
The old clay patch 1910 (1edn.), 1920 (2edn.), 1949 (3edn.)
Olds, P. *After looking for Broadway* 1985
— *Beethoven's guitar* 1973
— *Doctor's rock* 1976

OLIPHANT, P. *Bill the namer* 1905
OLIVER, G. *Homes for the people in the provincial district of Otago* 1879
OLIVER, S. *Chance to laugh* 1972
OLIVER, W.H. *James K. Baxter; a portrait* 1983
— *Poor Richard* 1982
— *The story of New Zealand* 1960, (1963)
OLIVER, W.R.B. *New Zealand birds* 1930, 1955 (2edn.)
OLLIVANT, J.E. *Hine Moa; the Maori maiden* 1879
OLLIVIER, J. *The system of provincial government* 1856
OLLIVIER, S. *Petticoat farm* 1965
'OMEGA' (pseud.) *The sheep, long-woolled as well as short-woolled for Victoria, Tasmania, and New Zealand* 1865
OPPENHEIM, R.S. *Maori death customs* 1973
ORBELL, G.B. *Comfort and common sense in the bush* 1952
ORBELL, M. *Maori poetry; an introductory anthology* 1978
— *The natural world of the Maori* 1985
O'REGAN, C.J. *Poems* 1896
— *Voices of wave and tree* 1894
O'REGAN, P. *Aunts and windmills* 1991
— *A changing order* 1986
ORSMAN, CHRIS *Ornamental gorse* 1994
O'SULLIVAN, K. *The loves of Dretta Gray* 1948
O'SULLIVAN, V.G. *The boy, the bridge, the river* 1978
— *Butcher and Co.* 1977
— *The Butcher papers* 1982
— *Let the river stand* 1993
— *Miracle; a romance* 1976
— *The Pilate tapes* 1986
— *The rose ballroom and other poems* 1982
— *Shuriken* 1985
— *The snow in Spain* 1990
Otago; its goldfields and resources 1862
Otago mining conference, Clyde, 1874. Report of proceedings 1874
The Otago settlement; extracted from *Chambers' Edin. Journal* 1848
Otago University capping book 1934
Our boys cookery book 1915
Our own country; being reports on various New Zealand towns; as described in *Korero*, magazine of the Army Education Welfare Service 1948
OVENDEN, K. *O.E.* 1986
— *Ratatui* 1984
Overland journey of the Governor of New Zealand 1872
Over the Whitcombe Pass; the narrative of Jakob Lauper, reprinted from the Canterbury Gazette, July 1863; J. Pascoe (ed.) 1960
OWEN, A. & PERKINS, J. *Speaking for ourselves; echoes from New Zealand's past from the award-winning 'Spectrum' radio series* 1986
OWEN, C. *Captain Sheen* 1905
— *Philip Loveluck* 1909
The Oxford book of contemporary New Zealand poetry; F. Adcock (ed.) 1982
Oxford New Zealand encyclopedia; J. Pascoe (ed.) 1965

Pacific index of abbreviations and acronyms in common use in the Pacific Basin area; A.E.E. Ivory (ed.) 1982
PACKER, R. *Being out of order* 1972
— *Prince of the plague country* 1964
PAGE, J. *Among the Maoris or daybreak in New Zealand* ?1894
'PAKEHA' pseud. of M. NALDER
PALENSKI, R. *Loveridge master halfback* 1985
— *Our national game; a celebration of 100 years of NZ rugby* 1992
PALMER, G.W.R. *Unbridled power* 1979
PAPAKURA, MAGGIE, see 'MAKERETI' (pseud.)
PARHAM, B.E.V. & HEALY, A.J. *Common weeds in New Zealand* 1985
PARK, G.M. *The unemployed and the remedy* 1886
PARK, J.B. *A school primer of the geography and history of Oceania* 1866
PARK, R. RUTH L. *A fence around the cuckoo* 1992
— *One-a-pecker, two-a-pecker* 1957, (1959)
— *Poor man's orange* 1949
— *The witch's thorn* 1951
PARKER, T. *And not to yield; the story of a New Zealand family, 1840–1940* 1987
PARKINSON, B. *The travelling naturalist around New Zealand* 1989
PARKINSON, S. *A journal of a voyage to the south seas in His Majesty's ship, the Endeavour* 1773
PARNWELL, E.C., see *Stories of the South Seas*
PARROTT, A.W. *Big game fishes and sharks of New Zealand* 1958
— *The queer and the rare fishes of New Zealand* 1960
— *Sea angler's fishes of New Zealand* 1957
PARSONS, F. *The story of New Zealand* 1904
PARTINGTON, J.E. *Random rot* 1883

PARTON, H. *The University of New Zealand* 1979
PARTRIDGE, C. *Calumny refuted, the colonists vindicated* 1864
PARTRIDGE, E.H. *A dictionary of catch phrases* 1977; 2edn. P. Beale (ed.) 1985 (pback 1986)
— *A dictionary of slang and unconventional English*; 1edn. to 8edn. 1937, 1949, 1951, 1961 Suppl., 1984 (8edn.)
— *A dictionary of the underworld* 1941, 1961
— *Slang today and yesterday* 1935 (2edn.)
PASCOE, J.D. *Explorers and travellers* 1971, (1983)
— *Great days in New Zealand mountaineering* 1958
— *Land uplifted high* 1952
— *Unclimbed New Zealand* 1939
PASH, J.B. *Mr. J. Brittain Pash's report on New Zealand..for 'The Essex Chamber of Agriculture'* 1883
PATRICK, M.G. *From bush to jubliee; Karori 1840–1880* 1990
PATTERSON, G.W.S. *Kauri-Gum; an important New Zealand industry* 1904
PAUL, J. & ROBERTS, N. *Evelyn Page; seven decades* 1986
PAUL, L.J. *Handbook of New Zealand marine fishes* 1993
— *New Zealand fishes; an identification guide* 1986
PAUL, R.B. *Letters from Canterbury, New Zealand* 1857
— *New Zealand, as it was and as it is* 1861
— *Some account of the Canterbury settlement* 1854
PAULIN, C. et al. *New Zealand fish a complete guide* 1989
PAULIN, R. *The wild West Coast of New Zealand* 1889
PAYNE, BILL *Staunch; inside the gangs* 1991
PAYTON, E.W. *Round about New Zealand* 1888
'P.C.B.' (pseud.) *Two years experience of the Maoris* 1866
PEACHE, A.E. *Quiet with the hills; the life of Alfred Edward Peache of Mount Somers*; Constance Gray (comp.) 1970
PEACOCKE, G. *Rays from the southern cross* 1876
PEACOCKE I.M. *Butter fingers* 1946
— *His kid brother* 1926
— *Misdoings of Micky and Mac* 1919
— *My friend Phil* 1915
— *When I was seven* 1927
PEARSON, WALTER H. *Review of the position of Southland* 1866
PEARSON, WILLIAM H. *Coal flat* 1963
— *Six Stories* 1991
PEART, J.D. *Old Tasman Bay* 1937
PEAT, N.D. *Cascade on the run; a season with the whitebaiters of South Westland* 1979
— *Detours; a journey through small-town New Zealand* 1982
PEDDIE, B. *Christchurch Girls' High School* 1977
PEGLER, E.S. *Dominion bowler's book* 1926
PEMBERTON, P. *The happy colony* 1854
The Penguin book of New Zealand verse; Allen Curnow (ed.) 1960
The Penguin book of New Zealand verse; I. Wedde & H. McQueen (eds.) 1985
The Penguin Tasman dictionary; an international dictionary for all New Zealanders 1986
PENNIKET, J.R. *Common seashells* 1982
— *New Zealand seashells in colour* 1970
PERCEVAL, W.B. *New Zealand; a paper read before the Royal Colonial Institute, May 10, 1892* 1892
PERHAM, F. *The Kimberley flying column; Boer War reminiscences* ?1958
PERKINS, EMILY *not[sic] her real name; and other stories* 1996
PERRIAM, T. *Where it all began* 1989
PERRY, C.S. *The New Zealand whisky book* 1980
PERRY, W. *Sheep farming in New Zealand* 1922
PETERSON, H. *Glasshouses but no haughty culture* 1981
PETRE, H.W. *An account of the settlements of the New Zealand Company* 1841
PETRIE, J., see 'AJOR' (pseud.)
PFAFF, C.J. *The diggers' story* 1914
PFAHLERT, J. & WATSON, L. *Some must die* 1987
PHILIPS, P.A. *Memories of the past (first series)* 1897
— *More reminiscences of early days* 1897
— *Reminiscences of early days* 1890
PHILLIPPS, W.J. *Bibliography of New Zealand fishes* 1927, (1971)
— *Carved Maori houses* 1955
— *The fishes of New Zealand* 1940
— *Maori carving* 1938, (1941), 1950
— *Maori carving illustrated* 1955, 1961
— *Maori life and custom* 1966
— *Sharks of New Zealand*; Dom. Museum records in zoology vol. I. No.2 1946
PHILLIPS, H. *Survey of fellmongering in New Zealand and Australia* 1957
PHILLIPS, N.C. *Italy vol. I; the Sangro to Cassino*; (New Zealand in the Second World War; official history) 1957
Phormium tenax as a fibrous plant; being selections from reports of Commissioners; J. Hector (ed.) 1870–72
PICARD, A. *Some ups and downs in New Zealand and Australia* 1906

PICKARD, A.G. , see GASKELL, A.P. (pseud.)
PICKERING, M. *The hills* 1988
Pictorial New Zealand; Cassell and Co. pub. 1895
PIERRE, B. *North Island main trunk; an illustrated history* 1981
PIKE, B. *A guide to Auckland* 1987
PILLING, E.G. *An Anzac memory* 1933
PINFOLD, J.T. *Fifty years in Maoriland* 1930
PINNEY, R. *Early northern Otago runs* 1981
The Piraki Log; or diary of George Hempleman; F.A. Anson (ed.) 1911
PITTAR, A. *The last voyage of the Wairarapa* 1895
'PLACEBO ASPEN' (pseud.) *Experiences of a medical man in New Zealand* 1883
PLIMMER, J. *A trip through fairyland* 1884
POATA, T.R. *The Maori as a fisherman* 1919
Poetry yearbook 1971
POLACK, J.S. *Manners and customs of the New Zealanders* 1840 (2 vol.)
— *New Zealand; being a narrative of travels and adventures..between the years 1831 and 1837* (2 vol.) 1838
POLASCHEK, R.J. *Government administration in New Zealand* 1958
'POLICEMAN X' (pseud.) *The great medicine man of Dancoyle* [Sir George Grey] 1879
Political and other ballads, compiled from the Auckland Free Lance 1879
The poo-bah of the Pacific and the misrule of the Cook Islands 1911
POOLE, A.L. & ADAMS, N.M. *Trees and shrubs of NZ* 1963
POOLE, Fiona FARRELL, see also FARRELL, FIONA
POPE, C.Q. (ed.) *Kowhai gold* 1930
POPE, J. *Mobil N.Z. tour guide (South Island)* 1978
POPE, R.J. *A New Zealander's fancies in verse* 1945
— *Some New Zealand lyrics* 1928
PORTER, G. & T. *Under the Nor'West arch; a high country story* 1970
POSPISIL, B. *Wandering on the islands of wonders* 1935
Postage stamps of New Zealand 1983
POTTON, C. *The Story of the Nelson Lakes National Park* 1984
POTTS, T.H. *National domains*; (reprinted from the *NZ Country Journal*) 1878
— *On recent changes in the fauna of New Zealand* 1874
— *Out in the open; a budget of scraps of natural history* 1882
POUND, J.N. *From oak to kowhai* 1979
POWDRELL, W.D. *Dairy farming in New Zealand* 1920
POWELL, A.W.B. *Native animals of New Zealand* 1947, 1987 (3edn.)
— *The shellfish of New Zealand; an illustrated handbook* 1937
— *Shells of New Zealand; an illustrated handbook* 1937, 1976 (5edn.)
POWER, E. *New Zealand Water Birds* 1973
— *Waders in New Zealand* 1971
POWER, P.J. *New Zealand islands of the blest* 1908
POWER, W.J.T. *Recollections of a three years' residence in China; including peregrinations in..India, Australia and New Zealand* 1853
— *Sketches in New Zealand* 1849
POWINA GREY (or GRAY) pseud. of R.E. MACDONALD
POWLES, C.G. *The New Zealanders in Sinai and Palestine* 1922
POWNALL, G. *New Zealand shells and shell fish* 1971
POWNALL, R.W. *Illustrated guide to the west coast of the North Island, New Zealand* 1885
Practical household recipes..adapted to colonial requirements c1890
'PRACTICAL SHOT' (pseud.) *The rifleman's handbook* 1863
PRAIN, M. *Seized* 1982
PRATT, W. *Colonial experiences* 1877
PREBBLE, G.K. *Horses, courses and men; early New Zealand racing* 1972
PRESHAW, G.O. *Banking under difficulties* 1888
PRESTON, F.I. *A family of woolgatherers* 1978
—— *From rocks to roses* 1978
—— *Lady doctor vintage model* 1974
PRICE, HUGH *School books published in New Zealand to 1960* 1992
PRICE, R. *Through the Uriwera* [sic] *country* 1891
PRINCE, W. *Diary of a trip from Lake Te Anau to the Sutherland Falls* 1889
Principles for crown action on the Treaty of Waitangi; NZ Dept. of Justice pub. 1989
PROBERT, K. *The seas around New Zealand* 1981
Progressive Youth Movement; the bush-lawyer's handbook 1976 (pamphlet)
'PROPHETES' pseud. of C.M. THOMPSON *Primary education in New Zealand; bible in schools* 1880
The prospects of New Zealand; extracted from *The Monthly Chronicle* 1841
Province; new Nelson writing; R. Bush and C. Markwell (ed.) 1987
Province of Otago; see also PYKE, V.
Province of Otago, New Zealand; correspondence between..the Premier..and the Superintendent of Otago on the subject of the proposed abolition of the provinces 1876
PRUDENCE CADEY pseud. of MRS DRESCHFELT *Broken Pattern* 1933
PUGSLEY, C. *Gallipoli; the New Zealand story* 1984
PURNELL, C.W. *An agrarian law for New Zealand* 1874
— *The modern Arthur and other poems* 1912
— *The New Zealand confederation* 1877

— *Poems* 1868
PUSELEY, D. *Number one, or the way of the world* vol. 1 (1862), vol. 2 (1866)
— *The rise and progress of Australia, Tasmania and New Zealand* 1857
PWD [Public Works Department] *general catalogue of the New Zealand and South Seas Exhibition* 1890
PYKE, V. *The adventures of George Washington Pratt* 1874
— *The gold-miners' guide; a handy book of mining law* 1892
— *History of the early gold discoveries in Otago* 1887, (1962)
— *The province of Otago in New Zealand; its progress, present condition, resources and prospects* 1868
— *The story of wild Will Enderby* (quots. referenced to pages of the 1974 facsimile of the 1889 edn. checked against the text of the 1873 edn. whose internal Part and Book numbers are indicated in the dateline) 1873, (1889, 1974)
PYKE, V. & TALBOT, T. *White hood and blue cap* 1881

QUENTIN, D. pseud. of MADELEINE BATTEN *Sparkling waters* 1945

Racing in Rangitikei 1857–1957 1957
Radio NZ sporting annual 1991
RAFTER, PAT *Never let go! the remarkable story of Mother Aubert* 1972
RAIMONDO, H. *Our company before* 1987
RANDLE, R. *Lilts and lyrics of New Zealand* 1893
'RAVENSWORTH' (pseud.) *A freethought ramble in verse* 1886
RAWLINSON, G. *Music in the listening place* 1938
— *Of clouds and pebbles* 1963
RAY, J. *The scene is changed* 1932
Reach out; Toro mai; (Family Violence Prevention Co-ordinating Committee pub.) 1994
Reader's Digest complete book of New Zealand birds 1985
Recipe book featuring special diet section and savouries; (St. Mary's) 1936
Records of the Gore; (Early Settlers' Assoc. comp.) 1927
Red Cross cookery book 1916
REDMAN, F.T. *Martyrdom of Jacob Rush* 1899
REDWOOD, M.M. *Proud silk* 1979
REDWOOD, R. pseud. of M.C. THOMAS *Mocking Shadows* 1940
REECE, W. *Canterbury old and new 1850–1900* 1900
REED, A.H. *Annals of early Dunedin* 1973
— *Coromandel holiday* 1952
— *Farthest east* 1946
— *Farthest north* 1946
— *From North Cape to Bluff* 1961
— *The gumdigger; the story of kauri gum* 1948
— *The gumdiggers; the story of kauri gum* 1972
— *The story of Canterbury* 1949
— *The story of Hawke's Bay* 1958
— *The story of the kauri* 1953
REED, A.H. & A.W. *Farthest west* 1950
— *First New Zealand Christmases* 1937
REED, A.W. *Myths and legends of the Maori* 1961 (3edn.)
— *Treasury of Maori exploration* 1977
REED, G.M. *The angel Isafrel* 1896
— *Hunted* 1889
Reeds' school dictionary; New Zealand supplement 1947
REES, A.J. *The merry marauders* 1913
REES, R.F. *April's sowing* 1924
— *Concealed turning* 1932
— *Dear acquaintance* 1929
— *Heather of the south* 1924
— *Home's where the heart is* 1935
— *Lake of enchantment* 1925
— *Life's what you make it* 1927
— *Local colour* 1933
— *Miss Tiverton's shipwreck* 1936
— *New Zealand holiday* 1933
— *Sane Jane* 1931
— *Wild, wild heart* 1928
— *You'll never fail me* 1939
REES, W.L. *The coming crisis* 1874
REEVES, A. *The reward of virtue* 1911
REEVES, E. *Homeward bound after thirty years* 1892
REEVES, H.J. *In the years that are gone* 1947
REEVES, W.P. *The long white cloud* 1898, 1924 (3edn.)
— *New Zealand* 1908
— *New Zealand and other poems* 1898
— *State experiments in Australia & New Zealand* 1902
Reflections; voices from Paremoremo 1973
REID, A. & REID, D. *Paddle wheels on the Wanganui* 1967
REID, H.M. *The turning point* 1944

REID, J.C. *A book of New Zealand* 1964
— *Creative writing in New Zealand* 1946
— (ed.) *The Kiwi laughs* 1961
REID, R.C. *Rambles on the golden coast of the South Island of New Zealand* 1884
REIDY, S. *Modettes and other Stories* 1988
REILLY, C. *The deputy head* 1986
— *Jim's Elvis* 1992
REISCHEK, A. *The story of a wonderful dog* 1889
— *Yesterdays in Maoriland* 1930, (1933 repr.)
Remarks on the credit of New Zealand and the honour of Great Britain 1865
RENÉE *Wednesday to come* 1985
RENNIE, N. *Working dogs* 1984
RENNIE, N.W. *The super man* 1988
RENWICK, F.E. (possibly the pseud. of V. PYKE) *Craigielinn* 1884
Report of the Commission of Inquiry into vocational training 1965
Report of the Commission on Education in New Zealand 1962
Report of the ministerial conference on education 1944
Report of the Royal Commission on monetary, banking, and credit systems 1956
Report of the Royal Commission into the sheep–farming industry in New Zealand 1949
RHODES, D. *Fly away Peter* 1952
RHODES, H.W. *Frederick Sinclaire* 1984
RHODES, W.B. *The whaling journal of Captain W.B. Rhodes, Barque 'Australian' of Sydney 1836–1838*; C.R. Straubel (ed.) 1954
RIBBANDS, H.S.B. *An original romantic comedy opera, Marama* 1921
RICHARDS, BILL *A pioneer's life* 1989
— *Off the sheep's back* 1986
RICHARDS, E.C. *The Chatham Islands; their plants, birds and people* 1952
RICHARDS, R. *American whaling on the Chatham grounds* 1971
— *Frederick Hunt of Pitt Island* 1990
— *Whaling and sealing at the Chatham Islands* 1982
RICHARDSON, C.H. *Gabrielle; and other poems* 1875
RICHARDSON, J. & GRAY, J.E. (eds.) *The zoology of the voyage of HMS Erebus and Terror 1839–1843* 1844–75
RICHARDSON, J.L.C. *The first Christian martyr of the New Zealand church* 1854
— *Sketch of Otago, New Zealand as a field of British emigration* 1862
— *A summer's excursion in New Zealand* 1854
RICHARDSON, J.R. (comp.) *Recent Brachiopods from New Zealand*; (Collected offprints of a suite of eleven papers published in NZ *Journal of Zoology* Vol.8 No.2) 1981
RICHARDSON, M.R. *Cornish headlands and other lyrics* 1920
RICHARDSON, P. *Choices* 1986
RICHDALE, L.R. *Wildlife on an island outpost; expedition to the Snares Islands (1947–48)* 1948
The Richmond-Atkinson papers; G.H. Scholefield (ed.) (2 vols.) 1960
RICHMOND, H.R. *The supposed luminiferous ether is matter and matter is force* 1866
RICHMOND, J.C. *Reminiscences of a Minister for Native Affairs in New Zealand* 1888
RICHMOND, M.E. *Poems* 1903
— *Roundels, sonnets and other verses* 1898
RICKARD, L.S. *Strangers in the wilderness* 1967
— *The whaling trade in New Zealand* 1965
RIDDLE, J. (ed.) *Violet; Marian Campbell Riddle, 1852–1922* 1990
RILEY, M. *New Zealand wildlife* 1983
RINGLAND, W.R. *In southern seas* 1888
RITCHIE, K.W. *From the south* 1972
RITTER, C. *The colonisation of New Zealand* 1842
ROBACK, A. *A dictionary of international slurs* 1944, (1979 repr., Maledicta Press)
ROBB, J. *New Zealand amphibians and reptiles* 1980, (1986)
ROBERTS, EDWARD *A personal history* 1990
ROBERTS, ELLEN *New Zealand, land of my choice* 1935
ROBERTS, F.A. *By forest ways in New Zealand* 1916
ROBERTS, J. *The diary of Jonathan Roberts* 1895
ROBERTS, J.L. *Politicians, public servants and public enterprise* 1987
ROBERTS, W.H.S. *The history of Oamaru and North Otago* 1890
— *Place names and the early history of Otago and Southland* 1913
— *Southland in 1856–1857* 1895
ROBERTSON, A.C. *Advance New Zealand!* 1933, (1948)
ROBERTSON, J. *With the cameliers in Palestine* 1938
ROBIN, J. *A trip to Maoriland* 1907
ROBINSON, R. *Heroes and sparrows* 1986
ROBJOHNS, H.C. *Bluff oyster industry* 1979
ROBLEY, H.G. *Pounamu; notes on New Zealand greenstone* 1915
ROCHE, S. *Foreigner; the story of Grace Morton* 1979
ROCHFORT, J. *The Adventures of a Surveyor in New Zealand and the Australian gold diggings* 1853
— *Journal of two expeditions to the west coast of the Middle Island in the year 1859*; extracted from the *Journal of the Royal Geographic Society* (London) 1862
ROCK, G. *By passion driven* 1888
RODGER, R.O. *Blue mountain rhymes; grave and gay* 1914

Rogernomics; reshaping New Zealand's economy; S. Walker (ed.) c1989
ROGERS, R.M. *The long white cloud* 1960
ROLLESTON, R. *The master; J.D. Ormond of Wallingford* 1980
ROMANOS, J. *Famous fullbacks* 1989
ROOKE, D. *The New Zeland twins* 1957
ROSE, R. *New Zealand green; about marijuana in New Zealand* 1976
ROSE, RICHARD *The New Zealand guide* 1879
ROSE, W.E. *Old Puhoi*; Raupo Reader No.18 1937
ROSIER-JONES, J. *Cast two shadows* 1985
ROSS, A.S.C. & MOVERLEY, A.W. *The Pitcairnese language* 1964
ROSS, C.S. *Early Otago and some of its notable men* 1907
ROSS, D.M. *The afterglow* 1904
ROSS, F.E. & N. *Mixed Grill* 1934
ROSS, J.C. *A Voyage of discovery and research in the southern and Antarctic regions* 1847
ROSS, J.O. *Capt. F.G. Moore, mariner and pioneer* 1982
ROSS, M. *Aorangi; or the heart of the Southern Alps* 1892
— *A climber in New Zealand* 1914
— *A complete guide to the lakes of Central Otago* 1889
ROSS, M. & N. *Light and shade in war* 1916
ROSS, N. *Noel Ross and his work* 1919
ROUGH, D. *Narrative of a journey through part of the north of New Zealand* 1852
ROUT, E.A. *Native diet, with numerous practical recipes* 1926
ROWAN, M.E. *A flower hunter in Queensland and New Zealand* 1898
Royal N.Z. Institute of Horticulture; official judging rules and guide to exhibitors 1950
RUHEN, O. *Lively ghosts* 1964
Rules and regulations of the constabulary force of New Zealand (New Zealand Police) 1852
RUSDEN, G.W. *History of New Zealand* 1883
— *Notes on the history of New Zealand* 1885
RUSSELL, G.W. *A new heaven* 1919
— *New Zealand today* 1919
RUSSELL, JOHN [of Ihumatao] *Some account of a singular expedient employed by Providence to throw light upon the present complications of the Government of New Zealand* 1862
RUSSELL, M. *Polynesia* 1842
RUST, A.M. *Whangarei and districts, early reminiscences* 1936
RUTHERFORD, A.W. *The impressions of a New Zealand pastoralist on tour* 1912
RUTHERFORD, J. & SKINNER, W.H. *The establishment of the New Plymouth settlement in New Zealand 1841–1843* 1940
RYAN, P.M. *The Reed dictionary of modern Māori* 1995
— *Revised dictionary of modern Māori* 1989

SADD, N. *Beaten by graft; a novel* 1939
SADLER, W.E. *Roving diggers to become colonial settlers; how?* 1869
SAINSBURY, A.G. *Misery mansion* 1946
St. Andrew's Cookery Book 1932
ST. JOHN, J.H.H. *Pakeha rambles through Maori lands* 1873 in *Early travellers in New Zealand*; N.M. Taylor (ed.) 1959
St Mary's recipe book 1936
St Patrick's College 1883–1935, the first fifty years; J.P. Kavanagh (ed.) 1935
St Patrick's College, Silverstream 1931–1956 1956
St Patrick's College, Silverstream 1931–1980 1981
St Patrick's College, Silverstream 1931–1991; a diamond jubilee magazine 1991
SALE, E.V. *Four seasons of country diary* 1982
Sale of liquor; A.Dormer, A.G. Sherriff, J.C. Crookson (eds.) 1990
SALMON, J.T. *A field guide to alpine plants of New Zealand* 1968 (1edn.)
— *Field guide to the native trees of New Zealand* 1986
— *Heritage destroyed* 1960
SALMOND, JEREMY *Old New Zealand houses 1800–1940* 1986
SALMOND, (SIR) JOHN W. *'My son,' said the philosopher. Being the meditations of the late Epaphroditus McTavish* 1920
SALMOND, R. *Prohibition; a blunder* 1911
SANDYS, E. *Love and war* 1982, (1989)
SANGSTER, A. *Pathway to establishment; the history of Wanganui Collegiate School* 1985
SANSOM, O.R. *In the grip of an island* 1982
— *The Stewart Islanders* 1970
SANZ glossary: see *Glossary of building terminology*
SARGENT, W. *The palms bend down* 1944
SARGESON, F. *The collected stories*; W.H. Pearson (ed.) 1964
— *Conversation in a train and other critical writing*; K. Cunningham (ed.) 1983
— *Conversation with my uncle* 1936
— *The hangover* 1967, (1984)
— *I saw in my dream*; H. Winston Rhodes (ed.) 1949, (1974)
— *Joy of the worm* 1969
— *A man & his wife* 1940, 1944 (rev. edn.)
— *Man of England now* 1972
— *Memoirs of a peon* 1965
— *More than enough* 1975

— *Never enough* 1977
— *Once is enough* 1973
— (ed.) *Speaking for ourselves* 1945
— *Sunset village* 1976
— *That summer & other stories* 1946
— *When the wind blows* 1945
— *Wrestling with the angel; two plays* 1964
SATCHELL, W. *The elixir of life* 1907
— *The greenstone door* 1914
— *Land of the lost; a tale of the New Zealand gum country* 1902, (1971)
— *Patriotic and other poems* 1900
— *The toll of the bush* 1905
SAUNDERS, A. *History of New Zealand 1642–1861* 1896
— *New Zealand; its climate, soil, natural and artifical productions* 1868
SAVAGE, J. *Some account of New Zealand; particularly the Bay of Islands* 1807
SCANDRETT, W.B. *Southland and its resources* 1883
SCANLAN, N.M. *Ambition's harvest* 1935
— *Confidence corner* 1950
— *A guest of life* 1938
— *Kit Carmichael* 1946
— *Leisure for living* 1937
— *March moon* 1944
— *The marriage of Nicholas Cotter* 1936
— *Pencarrow* 1932
— *Primrose hill* 1931
— *Road to Pencarrow* 1963
— *The rusty road* 1948, (1949)
— *Tides of youth* 1933
— *The top step* 1931
— *Winds of heaven* 1934
SCANLON, H. *Bon jour digger* 1920, (1924)
— *Bon sonte* 1932
— *Forgotten men* 1926
— *Great short stories* 1932
— *Humoresque* 1922
— *In a nutshell* 1921
— *In a soldier's life* 1927
— *Memories of a soldier* 1929
— *Much in little* 1922, (1925)
— *Old memories* 1929
— *Remembrance* 1929
— *Triolette* 1931
— *Veterans of the war* 1928
SCARROW, E. *New Zealand vegetable garden guide* 1976
SCARROW, E. & GOODING, B. *Scarrow's guide to gardening in New Zealand* 1983
SCHAFFER, E.C. *Absent without leave* 1943
SCHOLEFIELD, G.H. *Epic year 1893* 1946
— *Historical sources and archives in New Zealand* 1929
— *New Zealand in evolution* 1909
School Football; a rugby handbook; T. Fletcher (ed.) 1939
SCHOUTEN, H. *Tasman's legacy* 1992
SCHRODER, J.H.E. *Remembering things and other essays* 1938
The Scotch colony of Otago; extracted from *Chambers Edinburgh Journal* 1847
SCOTT, C.D. & BUSH, G. *Auckland at full stretch; issues of the seventies* 1977
SCOTT, I. *How I stole over 10,000 sheep in Australia and New Zealand* 1897
SCOTT, J. *Tales of the colonial turf* 1900
SCOTT, K.J. *The New Zealand constitution* 1962
SCOTT, M.E. *And shadows flee* 1935
— *Barbara and the New Zealand black-blocks* 1936
— *Barbara prospers* 1937
— *Breakfast at six* 1953
— *Days that have been; an autobiography* 1966
— *Life with Barbara* 1944
— *Where the apple reddens* 1934
SCOTT, R.G. (DICK) *Ask that mountain* 1975
— *Inheritors of a dream* 1969
— *The Parihaka story* 1954
— *Seven lives on Salt River* 1987
— *151 days; history of the great waterfront lockout1951* 1952
SCOTT, R.H. *Ngamihi; or the Maori chief's daughter* 1895
SCOTT, ROBERT *Rough notes of travels from Liverpool to Southhampton by way of Australia and New Zealand and South America* 1860
SCOTT, ROSIE *Glory days* 1988
SCOTT, R.R. (ed.) *New Zealand pest and beneficial insects* 1984
SCOTT, S.C. *Imported timbers in New Zealand* 1987
SCOTT, T. *Snakes and leaders* 1981
— *Tom Scott's life & times* 1977

SCOTT, W.J. *Reading, film & radio tastes of high school boys & girls* 1947
SCOTTER, W.H. *Run, estate and farm; a history of the Kakanui and Waiareka Valleys, North Otago* 1948
SCOULLAR, J.G. *The Dorrington mystery* 1896
SCRIMGEOUR, C.G. *Chats; talks on the 'Friendly Road'* 1937
The Scrim-Lee Papers; C.G. Scrimgeour and John A. Lee remember the crisis years 1930–40 1976
SCRYMGEOUR, J.T.S. *Memories of Maoriland* 1960
SEALY, H.J. *Are we to stay here?* 1881
SEAMAN, S. *Thoughts by the way* 1884
The secret history of the Auckland electric train swindle 1907
SEDDON, L.R. *Whims of a W.A.A.F.* 1945
SEDDON, T.E.Y. *The Seddons; an autobiography* 1968
SEFFERN, W.H.J. *Chronicles of the garden of New Zealand* 1896
— *The early settlement of New Zealand*; extracted from the 'Household Supplement' of the *European Mail 1888–1890*
SELFE, H.S. *The accounts of the Canterbury Association* 1854
SELWYN, G.A. *Letters from Bishop Selwyn October 1842 to January 1843* in *Early travellers in New Zealand*; N.M. Taylor (ed.) 1959
— *New Zealand pt. I (The Church in the Colonies); letters from the Bishop to the Society for the Propagation of the Gospel together with extracts from his visitation journal..July 1842 to January 1843* 1844 (1edn.)
— *New Zealand pt. II (The Church in the Colonies No.VII); journal of the Bishop's visitation tour from August to December 1843* 1845 (1edn.)
— *New Zealand pt. III (The Church in the Colonies No.VIII); journal of the Bishop's visitation tour from December 1843 to March 1844* 1851 (3edn.)
— *New Zealand pt. IV (The Church in the Colonies No.XII); a letter from the Bishop of New Zealand* 1847 (2edn.)
— *New Zealand pt. V (The Church in the Colonies No.XX); a journal of the Bishop's visitation tour..including a visit to the Chatham Islands in the Year 1848* 1849
SENIOR, W. *Travel and trout in the antipodes* 1880
The settler's handbook of New Zealand 1902
Seven one act plays; (British Drama League, Wellington Branch) 1934
The severed hand or the Howard mystery 1886
SEVERINSEN, K. *Hunter climb high* 1962
— *Hunt the far mountain* 1970
SEWARD, A. *Elegy on Captain Cook* 1780 (2edn.)
SEWELL, H. *The case of New Zealand and our colonial policy* 1869
— *The journal of Henry Sewell 1853–7*; W.D. McIntyre (ed.) 1980
— *A lecture on New Zealand* 1870
— *The New Zealand native rebellion* 1864
SHADBOLT, M. *Among the cinders* 1965
— *Love and legend; some 20th century New Zealanders* 1976
— *Monday's warriors* 1990
— *The New Zealanders* 1959
— *Once on Chunuk Bair* 1982, 1990 (2edn.)
— *Strangers and journeys* 1972
— *This summer's dolphin* 1969
— *A touch of clay* 1974
— *Voices of Gallipoli* 1988
SHADBOLT, T. *Bullshit & jellybeans* 1971
— *Concrete reality* 1981
SHAND, A. *The Moriori people of the Chatham Islands* 1911
Shanties by the way; a selection of New Zealand popular songs and ballads; Bailey, R. & Roth, H. (eds.) 1967
SHARELL, R. *New Zealand insects and their Story* 1971, (1982 2edn.)
— *The Tuatara, lizards and frogs of New Zealand* 1966
SHARPE, R. *Fiordland muster* 1966
SHARPE, R.J.D. *Country occasions; episodes and occasions in New Zealand farm life* 1962
SHAW, D. *North-west Nelson tramping guide* 1991
SHAW, G.B. *What I said in New Zealand* 1934
SHAW, J.A. *A gallop to the antipodes* 1858
— *A tramp to the diggings* 1852
SHAW, MISS, see *Camp cooking, recipes and useful information*
SHAW, M.S. & FARRANT E.D. *The Taieri plain* 1949
SHAW, P. *New Zealand architecture; from Polynesian beginnings to 1990* 1991
SHAW, T. *Longfin* 1983
SHEEHAN, J.R. *Famous murders in New Zealand* 1933
— *The Lora Gorge mystery and other famous trials* 1934
The sheepowners' handbook 1912
SHELFORD, W. *Buck; the Wayne Shelford story*; as told to Wynne Gray 1990
Shell-shocks by the New Zealanders in France 1916
SHEPHERD, M. *Some of my yesterdays* 1989
SHERRIN, R.A.A. *Handbook of the fishes of New Zealand* 1886
SHERSON, C., see *Kahikatea, cabbage trees and koromiko*
SHERWOOD, J. *A botanist at bay* 1985
SHIRLEY, H. *Just a bloody piano player* 1971

A short guide to New Zealand; United States Army Special Services Division 1944
A short history of Newlands 1991
SHORTLAND, E. *The southern districts of New Zealand* 1851
— *Traditions and superstitions of the New Zealanders* 1854, 1856 (2edn.)
SHORTLAND, F.W., see 'BUSH LAWYER' (pseud.)
Shortland town by night in *Victorian New Zealand*; (a [Hocken Library] reprint series No.5 1978) 1868
Short stories from New Zealand; A. Paterson (ed.) 1988
SHRIMPTON, A.W. & MULGAN, A.E. *Maori and Pakeha* 1922
Silhouettes of the past 1939
SILVERSTONE, H. *We can stop the Japs* 1942
SIMMONS, A. *Old England and old New Zealand; the government, laws* [etc.] 1879
SIMMONS, E.R. *Pompallier, prince of bishops* 1984
SIMMS, N. *Intersecting worlds* 1979
SIMONS, W. *Harper's mother* 1979
SIMPSON, F.A. *Chatham exiles* 1950
SIMPSON, H.P.L.J. *If you'd care to know* 1946
SIMPSON, THOMAS E. *Kauri to radiata* 1973
SIMPSON, TONY *The Sugarbag years* 1974, 1984 (2edn.)
SINCLAIR, K. *Halfway round the harbour* 1993
— *A history of New Zealand* 1959
— *A history of the University of Auckland 1883–1983* 1983
— *The origins of the Maori wars* 1957
— *Walter Nash* 1976
— *William Pember Reeves; New Zealand Fabian* 1965
SINCLAIR, K. & HARREX, W. *Looking back; a photographic history of New Zealand* 1978
SINCLAIR, MARGARET A. as 'ROSLYN' (pseud.) *Echoing oars* 1904
— *The huia's homeland* 1897
SINCLAIR, MARY *Tena koe* 1903
SINCLAIR, PETER *The frontman; a telethon* 1992
SINCLAIR, R. *Rail, the great New Zealand adventure* 1987
SINCLAIRE, F. *Ballads and poems from the Pacific* 1885
SINGLETON-GATES, P. *General Lord Freyberg VC; an unofficial biography* 1963
Sir Ernest Marsden, 80th birthday book; a tribute from his friends and colleagues 1969
SKETCHLEY, A. *Mrs Brown in New Zealand* 1880
SKEY, W. *Patriotic rhymes* 1900
— *The pirate chief and the mummy's complaint with various Zealandian poems* 1889
SKINNER, E. *Waitahuna memories* 1947
SKINNER, H.D. *The Morioris of the Chatham Islands* 1923
SKINNER, H.D. & BAUCKE, W. *The Moriois*; Bernice C. Bishop Museum Memoirs vol. 9 No.5 1928
SLADEN, D.B.W. *Australian ballads and rhymes; poems inspired by life and scenery in Australia and New Zealand* 1888
SLATTER, G.C. *Great days at Lancaster Park* 1974
— *A gun in my hand* 1959
— *One more river* 1995
— *On the ball; the centennial book of New Zealand rugby* 1970
— *The pagan game* 1968
SLIGO, J. *Final things* 1987
SLOCUM, J. *Sailing alone around the world* 1900, (1986)
SMALL, J. *The New Zealand and Australia songster* 1866, (1970)
SMART, P. *Introducing Alistair Campbell* 1982
SMEATON, W.H.O. *District high schools in New Zealand*; extracted from the *Victorian Review*, Melbourne July 2 1883
SMEDLEY, B. *Homewood and its families; a story of Wellington* 1980
SMITH C.V. *From N to Z* 1947, 1949 (2edn.)
SMITH, E. *Early adventures in Otago*; W.D. Stewart (ed.) 1940
SMITH, E.M. *A history of New Zealand fiction* 1939
SMITH, G. *Will the real Mr New Zealand please stand up?* 1990
SMITH, G.M. *Medical advice from a backblock hospital* 1942
— *More notes from a back-block hospital* 1941
— *Notes from a backblock hospital* 1938
SMITH, H. *Poetical works* 1946
SMITH, H.B. *The sheep and wool industry of Australasia* 1914
— *The sheep and wool industry of Australia and New Zealand* 1929 (3edn.)
SMITH, H.G. *New Zealand calling* 1936
SMITH, J.M. *Southlanders at heart* c1988
SMITH, L. *Poems by a New Zealander* 1897
SMITH, P. *Twist and shout; New Zealand in the 1960s* 1991
SMITH, SIDNEY *The settler's new home; or whether to go and whither?* 1852 (reissue)
SMITH, S.PERCY *The lore of the whare-wananga; or teachings of the Maori College on religion, cosmogony, and history*. Written down by H.T. Whatahore, *Polynesian Society Memoirs vol. III (1913)* 1913
— *Notes of a journey from Taranaki to Mokau, Taupo, Rotomahana, Tarawera, and Rangitikei, 1858* in *Early travellers in New Zealand*; N.M. Taylor (ed.) 1959
SMITHER, E. *Brother-love sister-love* 1986
— *First blood* 1983

SMITHYMAN, W.K. *Auto/Biographies; poems* 1992
— *The blind mountain and other poems* 1990
SMYTH, W. *Bonzer Jones* 1929
— *The girl from Mason Creek* 1929
— *Jean of the tussock country* 1928
— *Wooden rails* 1930
SMYTHE, S.M. *Ten months in the Fiji islands* 1864
SMYTHIES, H. *Report of the case of Henry Smythies* 1872
SNOOK, B. *Snookered* 1988
SNOWDEN, R.F. *Through open windows* 1933, (1937)
Social progress at the antipodes; extracted from *Chambers Journal* 1857
Social security in New Zealand; report of the Royal Commission of Inquiry 1972
SOLJAK, J.P. *New Zealand; Pacific pioneer* 1946
SOLLAS, W.J. & MCKAY, A. *The rocks of Cape Colville Peninsula, Auckland, New Zealand (vol. 1)* 1905
Some other country; New Zealand's best short stories; M. McLeod & B. Manhire (eds.) 1984
SOMERSET, G. *Sunshine and shadow* 1988
SOMERSET, H.C.D. *Littledene* 1938
SOPER, E.L. *The leaves turn* 1973
— *The Otago of our mothers* 1948
SOPER, M.F. *Birds of New Zealand and outlying islands* 1984
— *New Zealand Birds* 1976
SORENSEN, J.H. *Nomenclature of New Zealand fish of commercial importance*; Fisheries Technical Report No.56 1970
— *The royal albatross*; DSIR Cape Expedition Series Bull. No.2 1950
— *Wild life in the subantarctic* 1951
SORRENSON, M.P.K. *Maori origins and migrations* 1979
The source of the song; New Zealand writers on Catholicism; Mark Williams (ed.) 1995
SOUTHAN, W.M. *The two lawyers* 1881
South Auckland queen cookery book; H.T. Gillies et al. (ed.) 1915
SOUTHEY, T. *The rise, progress and present state of colonial sheep and wools* 1852
SOUTHGATE, B. *Participants and others* 1973
Souvenir book of cookery recipes 1938 (4edn.)
Souvenir of All Nations fair: see Williams, B.L.G.
SPACKMAN, W.H. *Trout in New Zealand; where to go and how to catch them* 1892
SPARKS, J. *Memoirs of the life and travels of John Ledyard* 1828
SPARKS, J. & SOPER, TONY *Penguins* 1987
S.P.C.K. *Domestic scenes in New Zealand*; (Society for Promoting Christian Knowledge) 1845
Speeches and documents on New Zealand history; W.D. MCINTYRE & W.J. GARDNER (eds.) 1971
SPEIGHT, R. et. al. *Natural history of Canterbury* 1927
SPENCER, M.K. *Let us not falter* 1979
'SPINDRIFT' pseud. of T.E. DONNE
SPIVEY, A. *Relations* 1973
SPURDLE, E.G. *New Zealand community* 1946
SQUIRE, JILLIAN pseud. of JOYCE THOM *Family daze* 1954
STACK, J.W. *Early Maoriland adventures*; A.H. Reed (ed.) 1935
— *South Island Maoris* 1898
— *Through Canterbury and Otago with Bishop Harper in 1859–60* 1906, (1972)
— *A white boy among the Maoris in the forties* 1934
STAFFORD, D.R. *The founding years in Rotorua* 1986
— *The new century in Rotorua; a history of events from 1900* 1988
— *The romantic past of Rotorua* 1977
STALLWORTHY, J. *Early northern Wairoa* 1916
Standard common names for weeds in New Zealand; J. Healy (comp., for the Weed and Pest Control Society) 1969, 1984 2edn.
STANNAGE, J.S.W. *High adventure* 1944
STAPLEDON, R.G. *A tour in Australia and New Zealand* 1928
STAPYLTON–SMITH, M. *The other end of the Harbour* 1990
The Star garden book 1990
STARK, R. *Maori herbal remedies* 1979
STARTUP, R.M. *Travelling mails* 1960
STEAD, C.K. *All visitors ashore* 1984
— *The death of the body* 1986
— *Smith's dream* 1971, (1973)
— *Voices* 1990
STEAD, E.F. *The life histories of New Zealand birds* 1932
STELIN, E. *A New Zealand pearl* 1896
STENHOUSE, D. *Crisis in abundance* 1966
STEPHENSON, G.K. *Wetlands; discovering New Zealand's shy places* 1986
STEVENS, F.A. *Children first* 1941
STEVENS, G.R. et al. *Prehistoric New Zealand* 1988
STEVENS, P.G. *John Grigg of Longbeach* 1952
STEVENS, T.B. *An anthology of Australian verse* 1906
STEVENS, W.G. *Major General Freyberg, V.C.; the man 1939–45* 1965

STEVENSON, G.B. *Maori and Pakeha in North Otago* 1947
STEWARD, W.J. *Carmina varia being miscellaneous poems by Justin Aubrey* 1867
— *The vision of Aorangi* 1906
STEWART, A.B. *My simple life in New Zealand* 1908
STEWART, BRUCE *Broken arse* 1991
— *The hot and copper sky* 1981
STEWART, D.A. *Green lions; poems* 1937
— *Springtime in Taranaki* 1983, (1991)
STEWART, G. *The end of the penny section; a history of urban transport* 1973
STEWART, G.V. *New Zealand, Te Puke, Bay of Plenty* 1880
STEWART, H. *The New Zealand division 1916–1919* 1921
STEWART, J.J. *Gumboots and goalposts* 1985
STIRLING, J. *On four legs and two* 1989
STOCK, A. *The evidence against and for Walter Tricker* 1867
STOCK, E. *The history of the Church Missionary Society in New Zealand* 1935
— *The history of the Church Missionary Society; its environment, its men and its work* (3 vols) 1899
— *The story of the New Zealand mission* 1913
STOCKMAN, G.E. *Poems* 1936
STOKELL, G. *Freshwater fishes of New Zealand* 1955
STOKES, J.L. *Survey of the southern part of the Middle Island* 1851
STONE, D. *Verdict on New Zealand* 1959
STONE, R.A. *Rugby players who have made New Zealand famous* 1938
STONES, W. *New Zealand (the land of promise) and its resources* 1858, (1862)
STONEY, B. *Taranaki; a tale of the war* 1861
STORER, H.C. *The body settler* 1907
Storey's tourist guide to Picton, the Sounds district and Northern Marlborough generally 1903
Stories of the South Seas; E.C. Parnwell (comp.) 1928 (4edn.)
STORY, E.M. *The tired angel* 1924
The story of the kiwi; Kiwi Polish Co. Pty Ltd (pub.) c1950
STOUT, R. *Address on education; delivered..at the meeting of the [Otago Educational] Institute* 1879
— *Notes on the progress of New Zealand* 1886
— *Public education in New Zealand* 1886
STOWELL, H.M. *Maori–English tutor* 1913
STRACHAN, A. *The life of Rev. Samuel Leigh* 1863
— *Remarkable incidents in the life of the Rev. S. Leigh* 1853
STRACHAN, W.N. *A century of philately* 1988
STRATTON, H.W. & ROBB, F.S. *Variety of dishes which can be produced from the government ration* 1917
Strawberry fields; R. Glover (ed.) 1967
Street society in Christchurch; Canterbury University College psychological report No.3, D.M. Crowther (ed.) 1956
STRICKLAND, R.R. *Nga tini a Tangaroa; a Maori–English, English–Maori dictionary of fish names* (NZ Fisheries Occas. Pub. No.5) 1990
STRONACH, B. *Musterer on Molesworth* 1953
STRONGMAN, T. *The gardens of Canterbury* 1984
STUART, A. *Sir G. Grey; his friends and foes* 1882
STUART, W.D. *The satyrs of Southland* 1982
STUDHOLME, E.C. *Te Waimate; early station life in New Zealand* 1940, (1954)
STUDHOLME, E.J. *Coldstream* 1985
The subantarctic islands of New Zealand, Vols. I & II; Chas. Chilton (ed.) 1909
SUMMERS, E. *Anna of Strathallan* 1975
— *Moon over the alps* 1960, (1974)
— *The smoke and the fire* 1964
SUMPTER, D.J. & LEWIS, J.J. *Faith & toil* 1949
SUMPTER, G.H., see also 'THE SARGE' (pseud.) *In search of Central Otago* 1948
Supreme Court Procedure Commission 1852
The 'Sure to rise' cookery book; T.J. Edmonds Ltd (pub.) 1909 (and numerous later edns.)
A Surveyor in New Zealand (1857–1896); N. Baker (ed.) 1932
SUTER, H. *Manual of the New Zealand Mollusca* 1913
SUTHERLAND, ALEX *Sutherlands of Ngaipu* 1947
SUTHERLAND, ALLAN *Numismatic history of New Zealand* 1941
SUTHERLAND, E.G. (comp.) *The New Zealand turf historical review; racing, trotting and breeding as an industry* 1945
SUTHERLAND, G. *Tales of the goldfields* 1880
SUTHERLAND, J.H. *The Elver* 1978
SUTHERLAND, J.H. & TAYLOR, W. *Sunrise on Hikurangi* 1981
SUTHERLAND, W.T. *The golden bush* 1953 (1963)
— *Green kiwi* 1956 (1960)
SUTTON-SMITH, B. *The folkgames of children* 1972
— *The games of New Zealand children* 1959
— *The historical and psychological significance of the unorganized games of New Zealand primary school children* Typescript, Victoria University of Wellington Library; 2vol. 1953
— *A history of children's play; New Zealand 1840–1950* 1982

— *Our street* 1950
SWAINSON, W. *Auckland and its neighbourhood* 1852
— *Auckland, the capital of New Zealand* 1853
— *New Zealand and its colonization* 1859
— *New Zealand and the war* 1862
— *William Swainson F.R.S. F.L.S, naturalist and artist, family letters and diaries 1809–55*; G.M. Swainson (ed.) 1992
SWAN, A.C. *History of New Zealand rugby football vol. I. 1870–1945* 1948
SWANTON, W.E. *Notes on New Zealand* 1892
SYKES, J. *The song of the Mariposa* 1893
SYMES, D. *Whitcombe's speech training the phonetic way* 1942
SYMMS, S. *Chronicles of Gotham* 1865
SYMONDS, W.C. *Notes on Cloudy Bay*; extracted from *Journal of the Royal Geog. Society* [London], v.8 p.416 1838

TAIT, C.W. *Short sketches of life in New Zealand* 1948
Tales of pioneer women; A.E. Woodhouse (ed.) 1940, (1988)
Talking about ourselves; twelve New Zealand poets in conversation with Harry Ricketts 1986
Tall and short stories; (Bardac Group, Remuera) 1976
TANCRED, T. *New Zealand, the colonists and natives* 1869
— *Notes on the natural history of the province of Canterbury* 1856
TANNOCK, D. *Manual of gardening in New Zealand* 1921
— *Practical gardening in New Zealand* 1934
Taranaki Provincial Council, Ordinances; Session I 1853–4 to Session XIV 1865–6 1867
Tararua story; Greig, B.D.A. (ed.) 1946
TATE, R.D. *The doughman* 1933
TAYLOR, A. *Eyes of the ruru* 1979
TAYLOR, E. *A thousand pities* 1901
TAYLOR, J.E. *To all New Zealand voters, a warning; beware of the New Zealand Alliance proposal to rob voters of their right to vote* 1918
TAYLOR, N.M. (ed.) *Early travellers in New Zealand* 1959
— *The New Zealand people at war; the home front* (2 vols.) 1986
TAYLOR, R. *The age of New Zealand* 1866
— *A leaf from the natural history of New Zealand* 1848
— *The past and present of New Zealand with its prospects for the future* 1868
— *Te Ika a Maui; or, New Zealand and its inhabitants* 1855, 1870 2edn.
— *Wanganui, its past present and future* 1867
TAYLOR, R.L. *Weeds of crops and gardens in New Zealand* 1980
— *Weeds of lawns, pasture & lucerne in New Zealand* 1981
— *Weeds of roadsides and waste ground in New Zealand* 1981
TAYLOR, T. *The shadow of Tammany* 1898
TAYLOR, W.A. *Lore and history of the South Island Maori* 1952
TAYLOR, W.C. *Jottings in Australia and New Zealand* 1872
TAYLOR, WILLIAM *The education of the people* 1870
TAYLOR, WILLIAM (1940–) *Fast times at Greenhill High* 1992
— *The Plekhov place* 1971
— *Shooting through* 1986
— *The twilight hour* 1978
TE AWEKOTUKU, NG. *Tahuri* 1989
'TE MANUWIRI' (pseud.) *Sketches of early colonization in New Zealand* 1907
Te Maori; Maori art from New Zealand collections; S.M. Mead (ed.) 1984
TEMPLE, N.G. *A tragedy in black and white* 1888
TEMPLE, P. *Stations; a high country novel* 1979
TEMPLE, P. & APSE, ANDRIS *New Zealand from the air* 1986
TENDALL, M. *The Kirkcaldie and Stains' cookery book* 1911
TERRY, C. *New Zealand, its advantages and prospects, as a British colony* 1842
TERRY, L. *The shadow* 1904
Tetaka kai; a book of well tried recipes Napier Rowing Club (comp.) 1906
TEXIDOR, G. *In fifteen minutes you can say a lot; selected fiction Greville Texidor*; W.K. Smithyman (ed.) 1987
— *These dark glasses* 1949
The Thames miner's guide 1868
THATCHER, C.R. *The Auckland songster* 1864
— *Songs of the war* 1864
— *Thatcher's Auckland vocalist* 1862
— *Thatcher's Canterbury songster* 1862
— *Thatcher's Dunedin songster* nos. 1, 2, & 3 1862
— *Thatcher's Invercargill minstrel* 1864
— *Thatcher's Lake Wakatipu songster* 1863
— *Thatcher's Otago songster* 1865
— *Wit and humour; local songs written and sung by him at Auckland and the Thames* 1869
'THE GADFLY' pseud. of H.S. MORETON *Semple Iscariot* 1948
'THE MIXER' pseud. of HENRY KIRK *The transport workers' song book* c1926
'THE SARGE' pseud. of G.H. SUMPTER *Excuse my feet* 1949
They came by ship; centenary of Bombay, Auckland, 1865–1965 1965

THIERCELIN, L. *Journal d'un baleinier; voyages en Oceanie* 1866
THOM, JOYCE, see SQUIRE, JILLIAN (pseud.)
THOMAS, H.T. *Way up north* 1970
THOMAS, M.C., see REDWOOD, R. (pseud.)
THOMPSON, C.M., see 'PROPHETES' (pseud.)
THOMPSON, E.H. *Light diet; a collection of caricatures and sketches* 1918
THOMPSON, H. pseud. of T.H. THOMPSON *Ballads about business and backblock life* 1909
THOMPSON, H.M. *East of the rock and pillar; a history of the Strath Taieri and Macraes districts* 1949
THOMPSON, ISAAC M. *The Lyalldale waltz* 1975
THOMPSON, M. *All my lives* 1980
THOMPSON, R. *Retreat from apartheid; New Zealand's sporting contacts with South Africa* 1975
THOMPSON, T.H., see THOMPSON, H. (pseud.)
THOMSON, A.S. *The story of New Zealand; past and present, savage and civilized;* 2 vols. 1859, (1974 facs.)
THOMSON, B. & NEILSON, R. *Sharing the challenge; a social and pictorial history of the Christchurch police district* 1989
THOMSON, C. *Twelve years in Canterbury* 1867
THOMSON, G.M. *Introductory class-book of botany* 1906 (2edn.)
— *The naturalisation of animals & plants in New Zealand* 1922
— *A New Zealand naturalist's calendar* 1909
THOMSON, G.M. & ANDERTON, T. *History of the Portobello Marine Fish-hatchery and Biological Station* 1921
THOMSON, J.A. *Deer hunter; the experiences of a New Zealand stalker* 1952
THOMSON, J.B. *My early recollections Kuriwao Gorge and Clinton districts* 1948
THOMSON, J.M. *The bush boys of New Zealand* 1905
THOMSON, J.T. *Extracts from a journal kept during the performance of a reconnoissance survey of the southern districts of the province of Otago [in 1857]* in *Early travellers in New Zealand;* N.M. Taylor (ed.) [Occas. reference, as *S. Dists. Otago,* to the original 1858 publication for material omitted by Taylor.] 1959
— *Rambles with a philosopher* 1867
THORNTON, E. *Guy D. Thornton, athlete, author, pastor* ?1936
— *Soul secrets* c1919
THORNTON, G. *With the ANZACS in Cairo; the tale of a great fight* 1917
— *The wowser* 1916
THORPY, F. *Wine in New Zealand* 1971
Those were the days (1930s) 1987
A thousand mountains shining; stories from New Zealand's mountain world; R. Knox (ed.) 1984
Three Poets (P. Bland, J. Boyd, V. O'Leary) 1958
Through the looking glass; recollections of childhood; M. Gifkins (ed.) 1988
TICHBORNE, H. *Noqu Talanoa; stories from the south seas* 1896
TILLY, O. *The battle angel* 1901
TILLYARD, R.J. *Insects in relation to the New Zealand food supply;* repr. from *Mid-Pacific magazine,* Vol XXIX. 665–680 1925
— *The insects of Australia and New Zealand* 1926
TINNE, J.E. *The wonderland of the antipodes* 1873
'T.I.S.' a pseud. of B.E. BAUGHAN
TITCHENER, P. *Little ships of New Zealand* 1978
TOLEMAN, E. *Growing vegetables* 1976
TOMLINSON, H. *A farm labourer's report of New Zealand* 1876
TOMLINSON, J.E. *Remembered trails* 1968
TONKIN, L.C. *Dunedin gaol in the 1870's* 1980
TOOGOOD, S. *Out of the bag* 1979
TORLESSE, C.O. *The Torlesse papers; the journals and papers of Charles Obins Torlesse;* P.B. Maling (ed.) 1958
TORRENS, J.M. *A song of Auckland* 1900
— *A trip to Mars* 1901
TOWNS, D.R. *A field guide to the lizards of New Zealand* 1985
TRACY, M. *Lawless days* 1928
— *Piriki's princess* 1925
— *Rifle and tomahawk* 1927
TRAIL, J. *Child of the arrow* 1984
Transport workers' song book: see 'THE MIXER' (pseud.)
TRASK, L.J. *Elizabeth of Lavington* 1976
The travels of Hildebrand Bowman into..Carnovirria..in New Zealand [etc., etc.] 1778
TREADWELL, C.A.L. *Recollections of an amateur soldier* 1936
Treaty of Waitangi: see *Facsimiles* [etc.]
TREGEAR, E. *The Aryan Maori* 1885
— *The Maori–Polynesian comparative dictionary* 1891
— *The Maori race* 1904
— *'Shadows' and other verses* 1919
— *Southern parables* 1884
TRENT, M.A. *The up-to-date cook's book* 1931
A trip to the Thames gold-fields, 1867; (by 'A Traveller') in *Victorian New Zealand;* (a [Hocken Library] reprint series 1978) 1867

TROLLOPE, A. *New Zealand; being a portion of the work entitled 'Australia and New Zealand'* [one of the 4 separate parts of the 1874 edn.] 1874
TROTTER, M.M. (comp.) *Marlborough Sounds archeological survey* 1974
TROTTER, M.M. & MCCULLOCH, B. *Unearthing New Zealand* 1989
TROUP, G. (ed.) *Steel roads of New Zealand; an illustrated survey* 1973
'TUA-O-RANGI' (pseud.) *Utu; a story of love, hate and revenge* 1894
TUCKER, G. *Thoroughbreds are my life* 1978
TUCKER, H.B. *Letters from abroad, or scraps from New Zealand* 1884
TUCKER, S. *The Southern Cross and the Southern Crown* 1855
TUCKETT, F. *Diary 1844* in HOCKEN, C.M. *Contributions* 1898 (Appendix B) 1844
— *Letter to Dr. Hodgkins Aug 16 1844* in HOCKEN, C.M. *Contributions* 1898 (Appendix A) 1844
Tui's commonsense cookery c1945
TULLETT, J.S. *Red Abbott* 1964
TURNBULL, E.L. *Happy voyage* 1935
TURNER, C.G. *The happy wanderer* 1922
TURNER, G. *Brand book for Canterbury* 1861
TURNER, G. & B. *Opening up* 1987
TURNER, G.W. *The English language in Australia and New Zealand* 1966
TURNER, J.G. *The pioneer missionary* 1872
TURNOVSKY, F. *Turnovsky; fifty years in New Zealand* 1990
TURTON, A. *The rare justice of woman* 1896
Tussock Grasslands and Mountain Lands Institute review May No.21 1971
TUWHARE, H. *Come rain hail* 1970
— *No ordinary sun* 1977
— *Sap-wood and milk* 1979
— *Selected poems* 1980
— *Year of the dog* 1982
TWISLETON, H.L. *Poems* 1895

Ukneadit [cookery book]: see BRANDON, L.E.
'UNCLE JOHN' (pseud.) *Hints to Colonists; a series of letters* 1859
Undiscovered country; customs..concerning death and dying; Dept. of Health (pub.) 1987
United Stores syndicate cookery book; a collection of tested recipes 1932
UREN, M. *Diamond trails of Italy* 1945
— *They will arise* 1945

VAILE, E.E. *Pioneering the pumice* 1939
VAILE, S. *The present position and future prospects of the New Zealand railways* 1886
VANCE, W. *Bush, bullocks and boulders; the story of upper Ashburton* 1976
VEITCH, BETTY *Clyde on the Dunstan* 1976
VENIMORE, C.W. *Last port Lyttelton* 1982
VERRALL, J. M., see FARMER, LIEUT. (pseud.)
VERSCHUUR, G. *At the antipodes* 1891
Views of English 2; D. Norton & R. Robinson (eds.) 1980
VINCENT, E.G. *Forty thousand miles over land and water* 1885
A vindication of the character of the missionaries and native Christians; Church Missionary Society (pub.) 1861
VIRTUE, N. *Always the islands of memory* 1991
— *In the country of salvation* 1990
— *The redemption of Elsdon Bird* 1987, (1988 repr.)
— *Then upon the evil season* 1988, (1989 repr.)
VOGEL, H.B. *Gentleman garnet* 1902
— *A Maori maid* 1898
— *My dear sir* 1899
— *The tragedy of flirtation* 1909
— *Two million* 1925
VOGEL, J. *Anno Domini 2000* 1889
— *The colonies generally and New Zealand in particular;* extracted from *Social Notes* [London] June 15 1878
— *Land and farming in New Zealand* 1879
— *New Zealand and the South Sea Islands and their relation to the empire* 1877
VOGT, A. *Anti — all that* 1940
— *Poems for a war* 1943
— (ed.) *Verse 1950* 1950
Voices from Auckland, New Zealand 1860; Alex F. Ridgway & Sons (pub.) 1860, (also 1861)
Voices I; a quarterly of poetry; A.R.D. Fairburn (ed.) 1948
VOLLER, L.C. *Sentinel at the gates* 1982
VON HAAST, VON HOCHSTETTER, VON TEMPSKY, see HAAST, HOCHSTETTER, TEMPSKY
VUWTC '71 a publication to mark the 50th jubilee [of the] Victoria University Tramping Club; B.A. Sissons (ed.) 1971

WADDELL, R. *Old Christmas* 1914
WADDINGTON, R. *Notes of a tour in the England of the Antipodes and Brighter Britain* 1887
WADE, W.R. *A journey in the Northern Island of New Zealand* 1842
WADIA, A.S. *The call of the Southern Cross* 1932

WADMAN, H.D. *Life sentence* 1949
WAGENER, W.E. *A Kiwi's soliloquy* 1943
Waikaka Valley jubilee 1924
Waimate County jubilee 1926
WAITE, E.R. *Guide to the Maori tomb in the Canterbury Museum* 1912
— *Guide to the whales and dolphins of New Zealand* 1912
— *Records of the Canterbury Museum I* 1911
— *Scientific results of the New Zealand government trawling expedition 1907* 1909
WAITE, F. *The New Zealanders at Gallipoli* 1919
— *Pioneering in South Otago* 1948
— *Port Molyneux* 1940
WAITE, REUBEN *A narrative of the discovery of the West Coast gold-fields* 1869
WAITT, ROBERT *The progress of Canterbury, New Zealand; a letter* 1856
WAKEFIELD, EDWARD *New Zealand* extracted from the *Cosmopolitan Magazine* June 1892
— *New Zealand after 50 years* 1889
WAKEFIELD, E.GIBBON *The British colonization of New Zealand* 1837
— *The founders of Canterbury; being letters..to the late John Robert Godley* 1868
WAKEFIELD, E.J. *Adventure in New Zealand, from 1839 to 1844* (2vols) 1845
— *The handbook for New Zealand* 1848
— *A letter to His Excellency Sir George Grey* 1851
— *New Zealand half a century ago*; repr. from *Chambers Journal* 1845 by *Canterbury Times* 19 May 1892 1892
— *Reasons for not voting in favor of Mr. Moorhouse* 1866
— *What will they do in the General Assembly?* 1863
WAKEFIELD, F. *The gardener's chronicle for New Zealand* 1870
— *Colonial surveying with a view to the disposal of waste land* 1849
WAKELIN, R. *History and politics* 1877
WALDRON, F.H. *Parson, drat him!* 1947
The Wales test 1905; match reports and commentary on the first Wales v. New Zealand rugby test..16 December 1905 1983
WALKER, A.K. *Common insects 1; insects in the field and garden* 1983
— *Common insects 2; insects in the bush and fresh water* 1984
WALKER, J.R. *New Zealand; the Great Barrier Island 1898-99 pigeon post stamps* (Handbook No.22, Collectors Club, New York) 1968
WALKER, W.S. *Zealandia's guerdon* 1902
WALL, A. *Blank verse, lyrics, and other poems by a colonial professor* 1900
— *A century of New Zealand's praise* 1912, 1950 (2edn.)
— *The flora of Mount Cook* 1925
— *The jeweller's window* 1964
— *Long and happy; an autobiography* 1965
— *The mother tongue in New Zealand* 1936
— *New Zealand English* 1938 [1939?], 1941 (2edn.), 1959 (3edn.)
— *The pioneers & other poems* 1948
— *The Queen's English* 1958
WALL, A. & ALLAN, H.H. *The botanical names of the flora of New Zealand* 1950
WALL, A. & CRANWELL, L.M. *The botany of Auckland* 1943 (2edn.)
WALLACE, DORIS *The generation gap; unimportant people and the Parapara* 1973
WALLACE, J.H. *Manual of New Zealand history* 1886
WALLACE, R. *The rural economy and agriculture of Australia and New Zealand* 1891
WALLIS, R. *Point of origin* 1963
WALSH, H. *The fourth point of the star* 1947
WALTON, J. *Twelve months' residence in New Zealand* 1839
The Wanganui cookery book 1928
'W.A.Q.' (pseud.) *The story of Hawera* 1904
'WARATAH' (pseud.) *Under Aorangi, New Zealand* 1906
WARBRICK, A. *Adventures in Geyserland* 1934
WARD, C. *Letter to the Rt. Honourable the Lord Lyttelton on the relations of Great Britain with the colonists and aborigines of New Zealand* 1863
WARD, E.R. *The Journal of Edward Ward 1850-51* 1951, (1956)
WARD, G. *Hail Otago!* 1948
— *The hermit at the hermitage* 1943
WARD, J. *Information relative to New Zealand* 1839, (1840), (1842)
— *New Zealand; Nelson the latest settlement of the New Zealand Company* 1842
WARD, J.P. *Wanderings with the Maori prophets Te Whiti and Tohu* 1883
WARD, R. *Lectures from New Zealand* 1862
— *Life Among the Maories* [sic] *of New Zealand* 1872
WARDLE, J. *The New Zealand beeches* 1984
WARDON, R. *MacPherson's Gully* 1892
WARR, E. *From bush-burn to butter* 1988
WARWICK, W. *Surfriding in New Zealand* 1968
WASHBOURN, E. *Courage and camp ovens; five generations at Golden Bay* 1970
WASHBOURN, H.P. *Reminiscences of early days* 1933
WATERWORTH, G.E. *One man in his time* 1960
WATSON, H.B.M. *Alarums and excursions* 1904
— *Couch fires and primrose ways* 1912
— *The web of the spider* 1891
WATSON, J. *Address to a king* 1986

— *Flowers from Happyever; a prose lyric* 1980
— *Stand in the rain* 1965
— *The world is an orange and the sun* 1978
WATSON, T. *The rose of the elkhorn* 1907
WATT, J.O.P *Centenary of Invercargill municipality 1871-1971* 1971
WATT, T. *Wild horses and me* 1990
WATT, W.M. *Fire down below* 1935
— *Home from Callao in a hoodoo ship* 1933
WATTS, G. *A husband in the house* 1969
WAYTE G.H. *Prospecting; or, eighteen months in Australia and New Zealand* 1879
WEBB, A.F. *Miss Peters' special and other stories* 1925
WEBB, C.J., JOHNSON, P.N., & SYKES, W.R. *Flowering Plants of New Zealand* 1990
WEBB, C.J., SYKES, W.R., & GARNOCK-JONES, P.J. *Flora of New Zealand IV, naturalised pteridophytes, gymnosperms, dicotyledons* 1988
WEBB, L. *Government in New Zealand* 1940
WEBBER, E.G. *Johnny Enzed in Italy* 1946
— *Johnny Enzed in the Middle East* 1945
— *Look no hands!* 1962
— *Try again Friday* 1965
WEBSTER, A.H.H. *Teviot tapestry* 1948
WEBSTER, J. *Reminiscences of an old settler in Australia and New Zealand* 1908
WEBSTER, L.D. (ed.) *Greys war dictionary* 1942
WEBSTER, P. *Rua and the Maori millenium* 1979
WEDDE, I. *Georgicon* 1984
— *Made over* 1974
— *Symmes Hole* 1986
WEIR, J.H. *A New Zealand ambassador's letters from Moscow* 1988
WEKEY, S. *Otago as it is, its goldmines and natural resources* 1862
WELD, F.A. *Hints to intending sheep-farmers in New Zealand* 1851
— *Notes on New Zealand affairs* 1869
The Wellington and Canterbury almanack 1855
Wellington election songs: see J.H. MARRIOTT
WELLS, B. *The history of Taranaki* 1878
WELLS, Z.W. *Diary 1st Jan. 1861 to 31st Dec. 1864* 1970
WENDT, A. *Sons for the return home* 1973
WESTERSKOV K. & PROBERT K. *The seas around New Zealand* 1981
WEST, J.T. *Drovers road* 1953
— *Sheep kings* 1936
Westland today; E.I. Lord (ed.) 1940
WESTON, C.H. *Three years with the New Zealanders* 1918
WESTON, J. *Ko meri; or a cycle of Cathay* 1890
Whakarewarewa Forest Park; a guide to its recreation facilities; J. Boyd (ed.) 1983
Whaling and fishing; the sequel to a boy's voyages on board a man-o-war and in the merchant service, 1821-1843 1857
WHEELER, C. *Historic sheep stations of New Zealand* 1982
— *Historic sheep stations of the North Island* 1973
WHEELER, C.E. *The pastoral industry in New Zealand* 1922
WHEELER, E.R. *A cabinet secret and other stories* 1926
'WHIM-WHAM' pseud. of T.A.M. CURNOW
WHITAKER A.H. & THOMAS, B. *New Zealand lizards; an annotated bibliography* 1989
Whitcombe's everyday cookery: see *Colonial everyday cookery*
Whitcombe's modern junior dictionary (1949), 1958 (8edn.)
Whitcombe's school etymological dictionary with a supplement of Australian and New Zealand words; D.K. Parr (comp.) c1930
WHITE, A.G. *Nashi; Asian pear in New Zealand* 1990
WHITE, E.L.M. as 'A SUFFOLK LADY' (pseud.) *My New Zealand garden* (1902), 1905
WHITE, J. *Te rou; or the Maori at home* 1874
WHITE, J.H & BURTON, W.M. *Emigration to New Zealand* 1876
WHITE, P. *Mystery Island* 1930
WHITE, W. *Important information relative to New Zealand* 1839
WHITECAR, W.B. JNR *Four years aboard the whaleship* 1860
WHITTAKER, A. *The practical cookery book* 1912
WHITWORTH, J. *Otago interval* 1950
WHITWORTH, R.P. *Cobb's box* 1875
— *Grimshaw, Bagshaw and Bradshaw's comic guide to Dunedin* 1869
— *Hine-Ra, or the Maori scout* 1887
— *Martin's Bay settlement* 1870
— *Spangles and sawdust* c1872
Who's who in New Zealand; (11edn. J.E. Traue (ed.)) 1978
Who's who in New Zealand and the western Pacific 1908
WHYTE, A.D. *Change your sky* 1935
— *Lights are bright* 1936
Why the 'All Blacks' triumphed; 'Secret of our success' by the New Zealand captain; 'Daily Mail' story of the tour 1906
WICKHAM, J.D., see 'A TRAMP, ESQ.' (pseud.)
WIERZBICKA, C. *The story of the Wilson family* 1973
WIGLEY, M. *Some southern songs and other poems* 1934

WIGNALL, S., see 'HUMANIST' (pseud.)
WILCOX, D. *Verses from Maoriland* 1905
WILKES, C. *Narrative of the United States exploring expedition (1838–1842) vol. 1* 1852
WILKINS, D. *The veteran perils* 1990
WILKINS, W. *Australasia* 1888
WILKINSON, A.K. *Kapiti diary*; R.D.H. Stidholph (ed.) 1957
WILKINSON, A.S. & A. *Kapiti bird sanctuary; a natural history of the island* 1952
WILKINSON, I.G., see HYDE, R. (pseud.)
WILKINSON, V.F. *The New Zealand way* 1981
WILLIAM, MRS, see 'A LADY' (pseud.)
WILLIAMS, B.L.G. *Souvenir of All Nations fair, Gisborne 1908; 300 choice cookery recipes* 1908
WILLIAMS, E.P. *A New Zealander's diary; Gallipoli and France 1915–1917* c1922
WILLIAMS, F.W. *Through ninety years; 1826–1916* ?1939
WILLIAMS, G.J. *The economic geology of New Zealand* 1965, 1974 rev. edn.
WILLIAMS, G.P. *A new chum's letter home* 1904
WILLIAMS, G.P. & REEVES, W.P. *Colonial couplets* 1889
— *In double harness* 1891
WILLIAMS, G.R. *A natural history of New Zealand* 1973
WILLIAMS, H. *The early journals of Henry Williams, senior missionary 1826–40*; L.M. Rogers (ed.) 1961
WILLIAMS, HERBERT W. *A bibliography of printed Maori to 1900 and supplement* 1924, (1928, 1975)
— *A dictionary of the Maori language; edited under the auspices of the Polynesian Society and based upon the dictionaries of William Williams and W.L. Williams* 1917 (5edn.); 1957 (6edn.), 1971 (7edn.) reprinted 1975
WILLIAMS, J.B. *The New Zealand Journal 1842–1844 of John B. Williams of Salem*; Robert W. Kenny (ed.) 1956
WILLIAMS, JOHNNY *Racing for gold; Thames and the goldfields with the history of the Thames Jockey Club* 1987
WILLIAMS, MONA *Bishops; my turbulent colonial youth* 1995
WILLIAMS, R.J. *Skin deep* 1979
WILLIAMS, T.C. *New Zealand, the Manawatu purchase completed; or, the Treaty of Waitangi broken* 1867
— *A page from the history of a record reign* 1899
— *Religion and the law* 1897
WILLIAMS, W. *Christianity among the New Zealanders* 1867
— *A dictionary of the New Zealand language* 1844, 1852 (2edn.), 1871 (3edn.), 1892 (4edn.)
WILLIAMS, W. & JANE *The Turanga journals 1840–1850; letters and journals of William and Jane Williams, missionaries to Poverty Bay*; Frances Porter (ed.) 1974
WILLIAMS, WENDY H. *Out of sight; out of mind [Porirua Hospital]* 1987
WILLIAMS, W.L. *East Coast (N.Z.) historical records; compiled and left typed by the late Bishop W.H. Williams*; reprinted from the *Poverty Bay Herald* 1932
WILLIS, A. D. *Geysers and gazers* 1888
WILLIS, H.A. *Manhunt; the story of Stanley Graham* 1979
WILLMER, G. *Courts of archery* 1874
— *The lowing herd and Zealandia* 1869
— *Zealandia's hope* 1874
WILLOX, J. *Willox's New Zealand handbook; or practical hints for emigrants to New Zealand* 1860
WILLS, T.J. *The church and the liquor traffic* 1894
WILLS, W.R. *A bunch of wild pansies* 1885
— *God's splendid son and other poems* 1891
WILLSON, R.J. *Home building; a practical guide* 1987
WILSON, A. *Education of girls*; [Presidential address to the Otago Educational Institute] 1905
WILSON, CHARLES. *More rambles in bookland* 1923
— *New Zealand cities* 1919
— *Rambles in bookland* 1922
WILSON, CHARLES A. *The Empire's junior partner* 1927
WILSON, D. *Rutherford; simple genius* 1983
WILSON, D.M. *A hundred years of healing; Wellington Hospital 1847–1947* 1948
WILSON, ELIZA *New Zealand and other poems* 1851
WILSON, E.S. *Rambles at the antipodes* 1859
WILSON, EVA *Titi heritage; the story of the Muttonbird Islands* 1979
WILSON, G.E.M. *Brave Company* 1951
— *Dear Miranda* 1959
— *The feared and the fearless* 1954
— *Julien Ware* 1952
— *Strip Jack naked* 1957
— *Sweet white wine* 1956
WILSON, GEOFFREY *Linkwater* 1962
WILSON, G.H. *Ena, or the ancient Maori* 1874
WILSON, H.D. *Field guide; Stewart Island plants* 1982
WILSON, H.M. *Land of my children* 1955
— *Moonshine* 1944
— *My first eighty years* 1950

WILSON, J. (ed.) *Reminiscences of the early settlement of Dunedin and South Otago* 1912
WILSON, J.A. *Missionary life and work in New Zealand, 1833 to 1862* 1889
— *The modus operandi of judgement without trial* 1884
— *The story of Te Waharoa* 1866
WILSON, J.C. *The New Zealand fisherman's bible* 1981
WILSON, JOHN (ed.) *The past today; historic places in New Zealand* 1987
WILSON, (MRS) MINGHA *In the land of the tui; my journal in New Zealand* 1894
WILSON, O. *From Hongi Hika to Hone Heke* 1985
— *An outsider looks back* 1982
WILSON, P. *The Maorilander; a study of William Satchell* 1961
— *New Zealand jack* 1973
— *The outcasts* 1965
— *Pacific star* 1976
— *South Pacific Street* 1984
WILSON, R.A. *Bird islands of New Zealand* 1959
WILY, H.E.R.L.. & MAUNSELL, H. *Robert Maunsell, LLD, a New Zealand pioneer; his life and times* 1938
WIN, J.W. *The history and experiences of the Win family* 1929
— *Some facts concerning the early history of the Dovedale Valley* 1929
WINKS, R.W. *These New Zealanders* 1954, (1956)
WINTER, G.W. *All ways up hill* 1995
WINTER, N.A. *The King Country; recollections of an old timer* 1938
— *Northern King Country; random sketches* 1938
WISE, H.L. *Tobacco growing and manufacture in New Zealand* 1945
WITHEFORD, H. *Shadow of the flame* 1950
With rod and gun in New Zealand; New Zealand Tourist and Health Resorts Department (pub.) 1946
WITTY, J.W. *Colonial songs* 1912
WODZICKI, K.A. *Introduced mammals of New Zealand*; N.Z. DSIR Bulletin No.98 1950
WOLFE, R. *Kiwi; more than a bird* 1991
Women of Westland 1959 (2edn.)
Women's work; contemporary short stories by New Zealand women chosen by Marion McLeod and Lydia Wevers 1985
WOOD, F.L.W. *New Zealand in the world* 1940
— *This New Zealand* 1958 (3edn.)
— *Understanding New Zealand* 1944
WOOD, J. *New Zealand and its claimants with some suggestions for the preservation of the aborigines* 1845
— *Twelve months in Wellington, Port Nicholson* 1843
WOOD, J.A. *Gold trails of Otago* 1970
— *Victorian New Zealanders* 1974
WOOD, SUSAN & LAPHAM, H. *Waiting for the mail* 1875
WOODHOUSE, A.E. *Blue cliffs* 1982
— *George Rhodes of the levels* 1937
— (ed.) *New Zealand farm and station verse* 1950
WOODS, C.S. *Native and introduced freshwater fishes* 1963
WOOLLASTON, T. *Sage tea; an autobiography* 1980
WORTHY, T.H. *An illustrated key to the main leg bones of moas*; National Museum of NZ, Misc. Series no.17 1988
WRIGHT, A. *Te Aroha, New Zealand; a guide* 1887
WRIGHT, C.D., see 'FABRICIUS' (pseud.)
WRIGHT, D.McK. *Aorangi and other verses* 1896
— *An Irish heart* 1918
— *New Zealand chimes* 1900
— *Station ballads and other verses* 1897
— *The station ballads and other verses*; selected and arranged by Robert Solway 1945
— *Wisps of Tussock; New Zealand rhymes* 1900
WRIGHT, S. *Clifton; a centennial history of Clifton County* 1989
WRIGHT-ST CLAIR, R.E. *Thoroughly a man of the world; a biography of Sir David Munro, M.D.* 1971
WYLIE, A.H. *Chatty letter from east and west* 1879

YATE, W. *An account of New Zealand* 1835, (1970)
Yates garden guide 1920 (14edn.), 1987
YEREX, D. *The best of both worlds* 1988
— *The farming of deer* 1982
YORKE, A.T. *The animals came first* 1980
YONGE, C.M. *Life of John Coleridge Patteson* 1874
YOUNG, F. *New Zealand, in past, present, and future* 1874
YOUNG, G. *Life and voyages of Captain James Cook* 1836
YOUNG, J. (ed.) *The life of John Plimmer* 1901
YOUNG, P. *Penguin summer; or a rare bird in Antarctica* 1971
YOUNG, R. *The southern world* 1854, (1858)
YSKA, R. *All shook up* 1993

ZAVOS, S. *After the final whistle* 1979
ZEAGLER, J.W. *A trip through New Zealand* 1910
ZIMMERMAN, J.L. *Where the people sing* 1946

II. PERIODICALS

This is a select list of the main periodicals cited, with the dates of first publication. Newspapers, ephemeral publications such as broadsheets, advertising and other 'fliers', and periodicals yielding one or two only quotations are excluded, being identified as they occur in the text rather than by a separate listing.

As far as possible periodical references are to date and page, or to vol. (in roman numerals) and page (in Arabic: e.g. I. 1), occasionally with issue number added (e.g. I. No.4 1). Articles extracted from (esp. 19th century) periodicals have been regarded as separate publications and placed in I ('Books') above.

Abbreviations are used for some sessional publications of parliament, annual or regular official or government publications and gazettes such as the Appendices to the Journals of the House of Representatives (AJHR), or the Irish University Press series of British Parliamentary Papers *Great Britain, Parliamentary Papers* (Colonies. New Zealand) (GBPP), New Zealand Parliamentary Debates or 'Hansard' (NZPD), and for regularly quoted periodicals such as *Transactions and Proceedings of the NZ Institute* (TrNZI) (see further *List of Abbreviations* p. xii).

For **AJHR**, spine-dates on bound volumes have been cited in the datelines: these are consistent with the publication (or 'tabling') dates of the various documents to 1931; from then until 1984 (the last cited) these differ by no more than a year.

For **TrNZI**, printed publication dates have been cited, usually the year following the delivery of any paper. For vol. I, the 1869 text has been cited but with the less confusing pagination of the more accessible 1875 reprint.

For **Statutes and Regulations**, the consolidated *New Zealand Statutes* have been cited either by year, short title, section (etc.); or by year, statute number, and page, often with the short title of the relevant act indicated within the quotation. Volume numbers are given only for those years generating more than one volume; reference to the regnal year was dropped from official citation after Geo. VI 3 (1938).

For **Industrial Awards, Agreements**, etc. of the Court of Arbitration and other authorities, the consecutively paged annual consolidations variously titled *Awards, Recommendations, Agreements, etc.* have been cited by year of publication and page under an abbreviated title *Awards, etc.*

Archaeology in New Zealand; (continued from the *Newsletter (New Zealand Archaeological Association)* 1988–
Architecture in New Zealand; (continued from *New Zealand Architect* 1977–87) 1987–
Arena, a quarterly of New Zealand writing 1943–
Art(s) in New Zealand; (superseded by the *Yearbook of Arts in New Zealand*) 1928–46
The Arts Times 1986–91 (1–20); then as *Arts Times* Apr. 1992– (No.1–) (QEII Arts Council, now 'Creative New Zealand' publication)
Auckland University carnival (or *capping*) books various dates
Aussie; the cheerful monthly; (Sydney) 1918–
Australian and New Zealand Gazette; (London) 1850 (No.1) (see also *NZ Journal* below) 1850
Awards, etc. the consolidated *Awards, Recommendations, Agreements, etc.* pub. annually by the Department of Labour 1900–

Better Business 1938–
Blue and White; the annual magazine of St Patrick's Colleges 1906– (Wellington), 1931– (Silverstream)
Book, a Miscellany; (Christchurch) 1941 (No.1)–1949 (No.9)
Bookie; (partly a parody of *Book*) 1948 (No.1), 1950 (2), 1951 (3)
Bottle News; a magazine for 'antique bottle' enthusiasts (TS unpaged) 1971–72
Broadsheet 1972–
The Bulletin; (Sydney) 1880–
Bulletin of the Wellington Botanical Society 1941–

Campus News; (a University news–sheet) 1986
The Canterbury Mountaineer; 1932– (identified by year and page) [From No.1 pub. annually each Aug., each issue individually numbered and paged to No.16 which is also tagged vol. 4; henceforth annual numbers (e.g. No. 17, 1948 pp.119–247, 18, 1949 p.248–) consecutively paged by volume.]
Canterbury Papers; (Canterbury Association, London) 1850–52 (No.12); new series 1859
The Capital Letter, a weekly review of administration, legislation and law 1978–
Captain COQK; (Christchurch Philatelic Society) 1972–
Catch; (MAF Fisheries Division) 1974–
Chambers' Papers for the People; (Edinburgh) 1850 (No.1)–1851 (No.12)
Chapman's New Zealand Monthly Magazine 1862 (nos.1–5)
Chronicles of the N.Z.E.F.; records of matters concerning the troops and gazette of patriotic effort 1916–19
Church Missionary Intelligencer 1849–1906
Church Missionary Record 1830–76
The Citizen; the journal of the forward movement 1895–96

Climate, see *Mate*
Colonia; the Colonial College magazine 1889–1902
The Colonial Church Chronicle and Missionary Journal 1847–74
The Colonial Gazette 1838–47
Commercial Fishing 1972–
Coral Dust; (WW2 (Pacific) RNZAF publication) 1944
Cuisine 1987–

Defence Quarterly 1993–
Directions; (NZ Automobile Assoc. publication) 1991–
Dive; South Pacific underwater magazine 1968 (vols.8–9)
Dunedin Punch 1865–66

Education; School Publications Branch, Department of Education 1948–

Fildes, see *VUW Fildes*
Forest and Bird; (Forest & Bird Protection Society of New Zealand publication) 1923–

The Gramophone 1923–

Here & Now; (Auckland) 1949–1957
Historic Places in New Zealand; (Historic Places Trust publication) 1983–
The Huia; a New Zealand annual (No.1) 1903

In Touch; pop music monthly (Wellington) 1980–
Islands; a literary quarterly (referenced by issue number) 1972–

Journal of the Polynesian Society; (JPS) 1892–
Journal of Public Administration (1938–49), then *New Zealand Journal of Public Administration* (1949–77), then *Public Administration* (1978); superseded by *Public Sector*; (NZ Institute of Public Administration)
Journeys; (a South Island publicity magazine) 1949

Kai Moana; Food of the Waters (New Zealand Marine Department publication) 1964–
Kai Tiaki; the New Zealand Nursing Journal (I.1–V.86) 1909–93
Kia-ora Coo-ee, the Magazine for the Anzacs in the Middle East, 1918; First series No.1– 4 Mar. 15–June 15, second series No.1–6 July 15–Dec. 15 1918, (facsimile reissue 1981)
Korero; AEWS background bulletin 1943–45

The Landscape; (New Zealand Institute of Architects publication) 1976–
Landfall; a New Zealand quarterly (referenced by issue number) 1947–
The Lantern; (Adelaide) 1870 (No.1–No.12)
Listener: see *New Zealand Listener*.

Mana, the Maori News Magazine for All New Zealanders 1993–
Marist Messenger 1930–
Mate 1957–77 (thence renamed *Climate* 1979–)
(Auckland) Metro; (Auckland) 1981–
More; (Auckland) 1983–
Motoring Today; (Automobile Assoc. Central publication, replaced by *Directions*) 1988–91

National Museum: see *Records*
NewsVUW; a fortnightly newspaper (Victoria University of Wellington) 1992–
New Zealand Bird Notes; (to vol.I–III No.9, thence renamed *Notornis*)
New Zealand Books 1991–
New Zealand Bulletin 1913 issue
New Zealand Company Reports 1840 (No.1)–1858 (No.35)
New Zealand Country Journal; (Christchurch) 1877–98
New Zealand Dairy [Produce] Exporter 1925–
New Zealand Educational and Literary Monthly; (Dunedin) 1883–85
New Zealand Education Gazette; (official gazette of the Department (Ministry) of Education) 1921–
New Zealand English Newsletter; (Canterbury University) 1987–
New Zealand Entomologist 1951–
The New Zealander; a weekly magazine of politics and literature 1896 (nos.1–3)
New Zealand Farmer; (with various early titles) 1882–
New Zealand Farmer's Weekly (and Land Agent's Record) 1905–
The New Zealand Fishing and Shooting Gazette 1930 (vol.3 No.4)
New Zealand Free Lance; (Wellington) 1900–60
New Zealand Gardener 1944–
New Zealand Geographer (NZ Geogr.) 1945–
New Zealand Geographic 1989–
New Zealand Geological Survey Bulletin; New Series (*NZGeol.SB (NS)*; intermittent: referenced by issue-number and page) 1906–
New Zealand Government Gazette; (NZGG; referenced by date and(or) vol., sheet, and page (I. 1.1))

New Zealand Illustrated Magazine; (Auckland) 1899–1905
New Zealand Institute, Transactions; (*TrNZI*; referenced by vol. pub. date: I, 1869 (see introductory note p. 000 above)–LXIII, 1934; thence re–named *Transactions of the Royal Society of New Zealand* (*TrRSNZ*) 1935–70; thence *Journal of the Royal Society of New Zealand* (*JRSNZ*) 1971–
New Zealand Journal; (London) (with No.283 of 5 Oct. 1850 amalgamated with the *Australian Gazette* to become *The Australian and New Zealand Gazette* (q.v.), resuming as *New Zealand Journal* with No.281 (1851) to 331 (1852) (Referenced by month, vol. and page.) 1840–
New Zealand Journal of Agriculture; (*NZJAg.*; referenced by month and page) 1910–
New Zealand Journal of Archaeology 1979–
New Zealand Journal of Ecology;(*NZJEcol.*) 1978–
New Zealand Journal of Educational Studies 1966–
New Zealand Journal of History; (*NZJH*) 1967–
New Zealand Journal of Marine and Freshwater Research (*NZJMFR*) 1967–
New Zealand Journal of Science; (Dunedin) (*NZJSc.*) 1882–85, 1891
New Zealand Journal of Science and Technology; (*NZJST*; referenced by vol. and page) 1918–50
New Zealand Journal of Zoology; (*NZJZ*) 1974–
New Zealand Law Journal 1925–
New Zealand Listener; (earlier *NZ Radio Record*) 1939–
The New Zealand Magazine; (Wellington) 1850 Jan.–Apr.
New Zealand Magazine; a quarterly journal of general literature (Dunedin) 1876–77
New Zealand Meat Producer 1956–
New Zealand Medical Journal 1887–
New Zealand Mercury; (Wellington) 1933–36
The New Zealand Mines Record; (referenced by month & page) vol. I no.1 Aug. 1897–
New Zealand National Bibliography; (*NZNB*) ed. A.G. Bagnall (6 vol. 1980–85, and continuations on fiche and disk)
New Zealand's Nature Heritage; (consecutively paged; referenced by vol. and page.) 1974–76
New Zealand New Writing; I.A. Gordon (ed.) 1942–45
New Zealand Orchardist, see *Orchardist*
New Zealand Outdoor 1984–
New Zealand Parliamentary Debates; (*NZPD*) 'Hansard' 1854–66, 1867–
New Zealand PC World; (earlier *Info World New Zealand* 1988–89) 1989–
New Zealand P(ost) P(rimary) T(eachers) A(ssociation) Journal 1952–90
New Zealand Radio Record 1927–39 (then merged with *(NZ) Listener*)
New Zealand Railways Magazine 1926–
New Zealand Skeptic 1986–
New Zealand Stamp Collector 1919–
New Zealand Timber Journal 1954–
New Zealand Truth [weekly] 1905–
New Zealand Valuer 1943–
New Zealand Woman's Weekly 1934–
New Zealand Yachtsman; (Auckland) 1909–c1918
North & South; (Auckland) 1986–
Notornis; (vol.I–III No.9 as *NZ Bird Notes*) 1943–
Numbers (nos. 1–10) July 1954–Oct. 1959
NZEF Times; (the newspaper of the 2NZEF) 1941–45

Orchardist; (NZ Fruitgrowers Federation publication) 1928–
Otago Journal; (Otago Association, Edinburgh (nos.1–8; referenced by number, month, page.) 1848–52
Otago Provincial Government Gazette (various numbers)

Pacific Way; (the in-flight magazine of Air New Zealand)
The Patler; (the monthly newspaper of St Patrick's College, Wellington) (TS) 1950–
The Penguin New Writing; ed. J. Lehmann (nos. 27–29) 1946–47
People's Voice; (a Communist party of NZ publication) 1940–
The Phoenix; (Auckland) 1932–33
Political Science; (Victoria University School of Political Science) 1948–
Postage Stamps of New Zealand; (Royal Philatelic Society of New Zealand, intermittent publication) Vol.I 1938, II 1950, III 1955, IV 1964 (and continuation)
P.S.A. Journal; (Public Service Association publication) 1912–
Punch in Canterbury; (nos.1–20) 1865
Punch or the Auckland Charivari 1868–69
Punch or the Wellington Charivari (nos.1–8) 1868

Quick March; (RSA magazine) 1918–23 (1924– renamed 'RSA Review')
Quote Unquote 1993–

Records of the Auckland Institute and Museum 1930–
Records of the Canterbury Museum 1907–
Records of the Dominion Museum; 1942–75; thence *National Museum of New Zealand Records* 1975–92; thence *Tuhinga: Records of the Museum of New Zealand* 1995–
The Red Funnel; (Dunedin) 1905–09

Rip it up; (pop music monthly, Auckland) 1977–
Royal Society of New Zealand, Transactions (and Proceedings) (TrRSNZ) 1935–70; *Journal* (JRSNZ) 1971– (see note at *New Zealand Institute* above)
RSA Review; (RSA magazine replacing *Quick March*) 1924–

Salient; (the student newspaper of Victoria University) 1938–
The Saturday Review; (ed. J.G.S. Grant, Dunedin) 1864–71
School Journal 1907–
Sea Spray 1945–
Sixes & Sevens; (a troopship publication, WW2)
The Southern Mercury; (Dunedin) 1874–77
The Southern Monthly Magazine; (Auckland) 1863–66
The Spike; (a former Victoria University College annual) 1902–61
Sport; (a literary magazine) 1989–
Sports Post; (a weekly magazine of the Wellington *Evening Post*) 1936–78
Sterling monthly; (Sterling Stamp Co., Nelson, publication) June–Dec. 1903
Straight Furrow; (the journal of Federated Farmers of NZ Inc.) 1941–
Sunday Magazine; (a free supplement to some issues of Sunday newspapers) early 1990s

The (New Zealand) Tablet; (a Catholic weekly, Dunedin) 1873–1996
Taranaki Punch 1860–61
Tararua; (the annual magazine of the Tararua Tramping Club) 1947–
Tararua Tramper; (Tararua Tramping Club periodical pub.) 1928–
Te Karanga; (Canterbury Maori Studies Association publication) 1985–
Tiki Talk; (a troopship publication) 1917
Tom Bracken's Annual; (Dunedin) 1896 (No.1), 1897 (No.2)
Tomorrow; (Christchurch) 1934–40
Tramping & Mountaineering; (the journal of the Wellington Tramping and Mountaineering Club) June 1948–
The Triad; (Dunedin, Wellington, Sydney) 1893–1927
Truth see *New Zealand Truth*
Tuatara; (Victoria University Biological Society) 1948–
The Tui; (Te Aute College magazine) 1899

VUW Fildes Newsclippings; volumes of miscellaneous newsclippings collected by Horace Fildes and housed in the Fildes Collection, Victoria University of Wellington Library (Indexed and referenced by Fildes vol. and number.)

Weekly News (Auckland); (the official titles of, familiarly, 'the Auckland Weekly' were: 1861–62 *Aucklander*; 1863 *Auckland Weekly News*; 1863–77 *Weekly News*; 1877–1934 *Auckland Weekly News*; 1934–64 *Weekly News*)
Wesleyan Missionary Notices; (London) 1816–38

Zealandia, a monthly magazine of New Zealand literature; (Dunedin) No.1 (July 1889)–No.12 (Jan. 1990)
Zealandia; (later *New Zealandia*, a Catholic weekly, Auckland) 1934–

III. MANUSCRIPT AND TYPESCRIPT MATERIAL

The following abbreviations are used:

ATL   Alexander Turnbull Library
GAL   General Assembly Library
Hocken   Hocken Library, Dunedin
NLNZ   National Library of New Zealand
MS   manuscript copy read
TS   typescript copy read
VUW   Victoria University of Wellington Library

ALDRED, J. *Journal 1832–64* (ATLTS)
ALGIE, COLVIN *MS papers 1374* (ATLMS)
ASHWELL, B.Y. *Letters and journals vol. 1 1834–48* (ATLTS)
ASHWORTH, E. *Journal of Edward Ashworth* (ATLMS) 1843 Dec.
AUTC (Auckland University Tramping Club) *song book (TS)* 1969 (3edn.)
BARNICOAT, J.W. *Journal (1841–44)* (ATLTS; references are to pencilled page numbers in this copy)
BELL, E. *Journal of a voyage in the H.M.S. Chatham to the Pacific Ocean 1791–94* (ATLTS)
Bradey papers (1843–53) (ATLTS)
BUTLER, J. *Correspondence (1819–24, 1840)* (ATLTS)
CAMERON, W. (comp.) *Post Office English course (revised) (TS)* 1950
CARBERRY, A.T. *Journal 1863–65* (ATLTS)
CARRINGTON, F.A. *Papers 1840–45* (ATLTS)
CHAPMAN, F. *The illustrated diary of life in the bush* (ATLMS) 1854
CHAPMAN, T. *Letters and journals 1830–69* (ATLTS)
CHEVALIER, C. *Reminiscences of a journey across the South Island in 1866* (ATLTS)

COLENSO, W. *Papers (journals 1833–35, letters 1834–35)* (ATLMS)
— *Letters to A. Luff (1875–93)* (ATLTS)
COOK, J. *Extract from the log or journal of John Cook kept on MacQuarie Island 1852* (ATLTS)
COOTE, R. *Extracts from diary (1853–67)* (ATLMS)
COTTERELL, J.S. *Extracts from the letters to his mother 1842* (ATLTS)
COX, JAMES *Diaries 1888–1925* (ATLMS)
DAVIS, C. *Journal 1827–8 (vol. 3 Colenso papers)* (ATLTS)
FAIRBURN, E. *Maharatanga* ATLTS 1947
GEORGE, J. *A few odds and ends of remembrances (1823–1876)* (GATS) 1875–76
GIBSON, A.H. *Autobiography* (ATLTS) 1931
GRAY, NORMAN *MS papers 4134* (ATLMS)
HAMLEY, ROBIN *MS papers 2499* (ATLMS)
HEALEY, C.A. *MS papers 2244* (ATLMS)
HEBERLEY, JAMES *Autobiography Jan. 1809–June 1843* (ATLTS) 1878
Hokitika Signal Station diary 21 Oct 1865 to 31 Dec 1868 West Coast Hist. Museum MS
HOLLOWAY, C. *Journal of a visit to New Zealand 1873–75* (ATLTS)
HURSTHOUSE, J. *Journal 1843* (ATLMS)
JOLLIE, E. *Extracts taken by A.J. Allom from Edward Jollie's reminiscences 1841–1865* (ATLTS) 1878
KENNEDY, W.L. *A few early recollections [c1900]* (ATLMS) 1941
LANGFORD, E.H. *MS papers 2242* (ATLMS)
MCCARROLL, H.S. *The days of the kauri bushmen* (Radio Talks TS) 1951
MACDONALD, A. *Reminiscences 1840–c1910* c1910 (VUWTS)
MCKILLOP, W. *The topsail schooner 'Lark';* MS in W.L. Crowther Library of the Tasmanian State Library. [See J. Starke ed. *Journal of a Rambler* 38] n.d.
MCLEAN, DONALD *Journal* (4 vols.), *Papers* (42 vols.), *Miscellaneous Papers* 1839–c1877 (ATLTS)
MASTERS, J. *Autobiography* (ATLMS) c1871
MATHEW, F. *Reports and essays 1840–1847* (ATLTS)
MATHEW F. & S. *Journals 1840* (ATLTS)
MEURANT, E. *Diary from 17 Apr 1845 to 24 Dec 1845* (ATLTS)
The Missionaries Journale [sic] *in the Royal Admiral* (ATLTS) 13 March–28 July 1801
MOORE, F.G. *Journal and correspondence 1840–1906* (ATLTS)
MOORE, T.R. *Reminiscences of Thomas R. Moore of Waimarama 1845–* (ATLTS) c1937
New Zealand forest glossary (TS) 1952–53
NICHOLL, S.P.T. *Journal 1863–64* (ATLMS)
NUTTALL, G.W. *MS papers 2192* (ATLMS)
O'BRIEN, S.E. & STEPHENS, A.G. *Materials for an Austrazealand slang dictionary* (ATLTS) c1910
PARNELL, S.D. *Farm diary and notebook 1844–63* (ATLMS)
PHARAZYN, C.J. *Journal of the voyage from London to New Zealand 1840–50* (ATLMS)
PHILLIPS, H. *Journal kept at Rockwood and the Point from July 1855 to May 1871* (Canterbury Public Library TS) 1855–
PRENTICE, S.F. *A tale of New Zealand..a narrative of experiences in New Zealand 1855–70* (GALMS) 1870
Puketoi Station Diary 1858– (Hocken Lib. MS)
REVANS, S. *Letters principally to [H.S.] Chapman 1839–1865* (ATLMS)
Family letters of the Richmonds and Atkinsons 1824–1862 ed. E. Richmond (ATLTS)
RIVES, F.R. *Jottings on the spot; a diary 11 Feb–26 Mar 1875* (Canterbury Public Lib. MS)
RUTHERFORD, J. (comp.) *Select documents relative to the development of responsible government in New Zealand 1839–1865* (TS copy in VUW library) 1949
SELWYN, G.A. *Papers 1839–65* (ATLMS)
— *Letters 1842–67* (ATLTS)
— *Journal..from 1 Jan. 1843 to 23 Mar. 1844* (ATLTS)
SELWYN, SARAH H. *Reminiscences 1809–1867;* with notes by E.A. Evans (1961) (Auckland War Memorial Museum TS)
STAFFORD, E.W. *Papers 1846–92* (ATLMS)
STEPHENS, A.G. & O'BRIEN, S.E., see O'BRIEN, S.E & STEPHENS, A.G.
STEPHENS, S. *Letters and journals 1842–55* (ATLTS)
St Leonard's Station Journal 1855–61 (ATLTS)
SUTTON, E.R. *MS papers 1917–18* (ATLMS)
SUTTON-SMITH, B. *The historical and psychological significance of the unorganized games of New Zealand primary school children* (VUW TS 2 vols.) 1953
TAYLOR, R. *Journals 1833–65 (12 vols.)* (ATLTS)
— *Journals 1833–1873 (15 vols)* (ATLTS)
— *Journal 1842 and 1843 [etc.]* (ATLTS)
— *Journal 1825–1836 (2 vols)* (ATLMS)
TEMPSKY, G.F. VON *Memoranda of the New Zealand campaign, 1863–64* (ATLTS)
TWIDLE, J.V. *War diaries (12th Nelson Co.) 1916–1917* (MS)
WADE, J. *Letters 1842–..transcribed from original in possession of the Early Settlers Historical Association Wellington* (ATLTS) 1950
WAKEFIELD, A. *Diary 1841–42 (3 vols.)* (ATLMS)
WAKEFIELD, E.J. *Diary* (ATLMS) 1839
WAKEFIELD, W. *Diary 1839* (ATLTS)
WAKEFIELD et al. *Letters to Chapman 1839–64* (ATLTS)
WALKER, J.G. *Journal of a voyage to New Zealand, 1862 and letters from New Zealand and Australia to his mother (mostly) continuing from log of voyage from England (July to Oct 1862)* (ATLTS)
WEEKES, H. *Journal 1840–42* (ATLTS)
WHISKER, A. *Memorandum book 1844–52* (ATLMS)
WHITE, J. *Repository of rough material 1845–46* (ATLMS)
— *Notebook in English and Maori (1846–48)* (ATLMS)
— *Poetry 1846* (ATLTS) 1846
— *Private journal, written at Mata recording his farming activities 1846* (ATLTS)
WHITELEY, J. *Journal 1832–63* (ATLTS)
YOUNG, W. *The first crossing of the Whitcome Pass 1863* (ATLMS)
— *West Coast notes 1863–64* (ATLMS)

IV. PRIVATE COLLECTIONS

The following people kindly allowed use of their collections of New Zealand lexical items, copies of which are now deposited in the Dictionary Room, Department of English, Victoria University of Wellington:
Miss Ruth Mason
Mr George Griffiths (Dunedin)
Mr Goldie Brown (Auckland)
Mr B.J. Cameron: compiled July 1955 (Greytown)
F.H. Syder & G.A. Hodgetts *Australian and New Zealand English; a selection of 1116 expressions from the spoken language* TS copy a1974 (compiled 1962–63, revised 1974)

V. QUESTIONNAIRE

The following questionnaire was completed by secondary school pupils in various years between 1951 and 1984. The results are deposited in the Dictionary Room, Department of English, Victoria University of Wellington. Datelines cited in the text list: *Date, Age-group, Gender (M/F), Batch Identification Number, School, Quest. No., No. of occurrences among M/F participants* (e.g. M6F13), *Peculiarities noted by participants, Brief indication of reference of the question.*

Please write down the colloquial or slang words or phrases you would use for or about the following people and things.
[YEAR AGE & FORM SCHOOL M/F]
1. A silly person: (e.g. nitwit (noun); dotty (adjective))
2. A mad person: (e.g. looney (noun and adjective))
3. Someone or something you dislike: (e.g. swine; rotten)
4. Someone or something you like (e.g. corker)
5. Annoyance: (e.g. dash it!)
6. Impatience: (e.g. get cracking)
7. Something that's not good: (e.g. a bummer; shitty)
8. Something that's good: (e.g. the best; beaut)
9. For beating or being better than somebody: (e.g. have the wood on)
10. Uselessness: (person or thing — e.g. a mucker)
11. Addressing an equal: (e.g. mate; or, hiya!)
12. It doesn't matter: (e.g. she's right)
13. When you can get no further with anything: (e.g. no go; beggared)
14. Waste time: (e.g. muck about)
15. A short time: (e.g. in a mo; half a shake)
16. Have a fall: (come a cropper)
17. Boasting: (e.g. skite (noun and verb))
18. Delight: (e.g. boy oh boy!)
19. Make a mess of something: (e.g. muck up)
20. Sport, organised: (e.g. footy etc.)
21. Games: [out of school]
22. Food: A) Sweets in general: (e.g. lollies) B) Meal-foods: (e.g. hash)
23. School discipline: (e.g. smack-up; lashes; detentions, etc.)
24. Names for authorities: (Not personal nicknames but general names e.g. 'cops' for policemen; 'bosses' for teachers, etc.)
    A) Parents: B) Teachers: C) Police: D) Clergy: E) Others
25. New kids: (e.g. tinies)
26. Swot and exams:
27. Courting: (e.g. woo)
28. Boy Friends/Girl Friends:
29. Friendship terms: (e.g. pal, mate, etc.)
30. Fighting: A) Verbs: (e.g. to hit, to smash) B) Nouns and adjectives: (e.g. scrap; row)
31. Sickness: (e.g. the flu; 'spotties' for measles, etc.)
32. Luckiness: (e.g. tinny)
33. Illegal activities: (e.g. names for smoking, etc.)
34. Something amusing: (e.g. a laugh)
35. Exclamations: A) of approval (e.g. beaut-ee) B) of disapproval (e.g. no way) C) of surprise (e.g. hell!)